ISBN 978-1-5285-3634-9
PIBN 10915337

FB &c Ltd, Dalton House, 60 Windsor Avenue, London, SW19 2RR.
Company number 08720141. Registered in England and Wales.

For support please visit www.forgottenbooks.com

THE

LOCAL GOVERNMENT ACT,

1888,

WITH THE INCORPORATED PROVISIONS OF THE

MUNICIPAL CORPORATIONS ACT, 1882,

AND OTHER ACTS.

AND THE WHOLE OF THE

STATUTES, RULES AND ORDERS PASSED OR ISSUED SINCE 1888,

RELATING TO THE

POWERS AND DUTIES OF COUNTY COUNCILS,

WITH

NOTES AND INDEX.

Third Edition.

BY

ALEXANDER MACMORRAN, M.A.,

One of Her Majesty's Counsel,

AND

T. R. COLQUHOUN DILL, B.A.,

Of the Inner Temple; Barrister-at-Law,

JOINT AUTHORS OF A WORK ON "THE LOCAL GOVERNMENT ACT, 1894."

LONDON:

SHAW & SONS, 6, 7 & 8, FETTER LANE, AND CRANE COURT;

BUTTERWORTH & CO., 7, FLEET STREET;

Law Printers and Publishers.

1898.

LONDON:

PRINTED BY SHAW AND SONS, FETTER LANE AND CRANE COURT, E.C.

PREFACE TO THE THIRD EDITION.

THE Second Edition of this work has long been out of print, and since it appeared there have been large additions to the statute law affecting county councils. The increase in size of this Edition will sufficiently indicate the extent of such legislation.

It has been thought convenient to divide the work into Four Parts. The First deals with the Local Government Act, 1888; and the notes to the several sections of that Act have been carefully revised and in many cases re-written. The Second Part contains the incorporated provisions of the Municipal Corporations Act, 1882, the Ballot Act, 1872, the Municipal Elections (Corrupt and Illegal Practices) Act, 1884, and other statutes. The notes to these have also been carefully revised and brought down to date. The Third Part contains the statutes passed since the Local Government Act, 1888, in so far as these relate to the powers and duties of county councils. The Fourth Part contains the existing Statutory Rules and Orders affecting county councils, arranged in alphabetical order of the subjects to which they relate, with the explanatory circulars issued with them. The Third and Fourth Parts, and the notes to them, are of course an addition to the original work.

It was at one time in the contemplation of the Authors to include in the Third Part all the statutes relating to county councils other than those set out in the First and Second Parts. It was found, however, that this would add greatly to the bulk of the volume, and the Authors have therefore, for the present, limited the Third Part as above stated.

Care has been taken to note every decided case down to the date of publication, and no pains have been spared to render the Index and Tables of Statutes and Cases complete and reliable.

A. M.

T. R. C. D.

CONTENTS.

PART I.

Local Government (England and Wales) Act, 1888.

(51 & 52 Vict. Cap. 41.)

Part I. — County Councils.

Constitution of County Council.

Powers of County Council.

Financial Relations between Exchequer and County, and Contributions by County for Costs of Union Officers.

General Provisions as to Transfer.

PART II.—APPLICATION OF ACT TO BOROUGHS, THE METROPOLIS, AND CERTAIN SPECIAL COUNTIES.

Application of Act to Boroughs.

Application of Act to Metropolis.

Application of Act to Special Counties and to Liberties.

PART III.—BOUNDARIES.

PART IV.—FINANCE.

Property Funds and Costs of County Council.

Local Financial Year and Annual Budget.

PART V.—SUPPLEMENTAL.

Application of Acts.

Proceedings of Councils and Committees.

Officers.

Regulations for Bicycles, etc.

Adaptation of Acts.

Savings.

Definitions.

PART VI. — TRANSITORY PROVISIONS.

First Election of County Councillors.

General Provision as to First Elections.

Appointed Day.

Transitional Proceedings.

Transitory Provisions as to Metropolis.

Existing Officers.

Temporary Provision as to Grant from Exchequer.

Savings.

Repeals.

PART II.

Statutes incorporated with the Local Government Act, 1888.

BALLOT ACT, 1872 (35 & 36 VICT. CAP. 33.)

PART I.—PARLIAMENTARY ELECTIONS.

Procedure at Elections.

Duties of Returning and Election Officers.

PART III.—PERSONATION.

PART IV.—MISCELLANEOUS.

SCHEDULES.

FIRST SCHEDULE.

SECOND SCHEDULE.

PARLIAMENTARY ELECTIONS (RETURNING OFFICERS) ACT, 1875.

(38 & 39 VICT. CAP. 84.)

SCHEDULES.

FIRST SCHEDULE.

SECOND SCHEDULE.

PARLIAMENTARY ELECTIONS (RETURNING OFFICERS) ACT, 1875, AMENDMENT ACT, 1886.

(49 & 50 VICT. CAP. 57.)

MUNICIPAL CORPORATIONS ACT, 1882 (45 & 46 VICT. CAP. 50.)

PART II.—CONSTITUTION AND GOVERNMENT OF BOROUGHS.

Corporate Name.

Council; Mayor, Aldermen, and Councillors.

Officers of Council.

Meetings and Proceedings of Council; Committees.

Bye-laws.

Accounts and Audit.

Revising Assessors.

Division of Borough into Wards, or Alteration of Wards.

Supplemental and Exceptional Provisions.

Supplemental and Exceptional Provisions—continued.

PART III.—PREPARATIONS FOR AND PROCEDURE AT ELECTIONS.

Parish Burgess Lists; Burgess Rolls; Ward Rolls.

Election of Councillors.

Election of Aldermen.

Election of Mayor.

Election of Auditors and Assessors.

Supplemental and Exceptional Provisions.

Supplemental and Exceptional Provisions—continued.

PART IV.—CORRUPT PRACTICES AND ELECTION PETITIONS.

Corrupt Practices.

Election Petitions.

PART V.—CORPORATE PROPERTY AND LIABILITIES.

Misapplication of Corporate Property.

PART XII.—LEGAL PROCEEDINGS.

PART XIII.—GENERAL.

Boundaries.

Time.

Distance.

Notices.

Inspection and Copies.

Fees.

Seals and Signatures.

Applications to Treasury.

Deputy.

Overseers.

Declarations and Oaths.

Forms.

Misnomer or Inaccurate Description.

Substitution in Former Acts.

Returning Officers at Parliamentary Elections.

Disfranchised Parliamentary Boroughs.

Licensing.

Freedom of Trading.

Cinque Ports.

Cambridge.

Savings.

SCHEDULES.

THE SECOND SCHEDULE.

THE THIRD SCHEDULE.

ELECTIONS.

THE EIGHTH SCHEDULE.

FORMS.

MUNICIPAL ELECTIONS (CORRUPT AND ILLEGAL PRACTICES) ACT, 1884.

(47 & 48 VICT. CAP. 70.)

Disqualification of Electors.

Proceedings on Election Petitions.

Miscellaneous.

Application of Act to other Elections.

Repeal.

Extent of Act.

COUNTY ELECTORS ACT, 1888.

(51 VICT. CAP. 10.)

PART III.

Statutes subsequent to the Local Government Act, 1888, affecting County Councils.

PART IV.

Orders, Circulars, and other Official Documents relating to the Powers and Duties of County Councils.

Adjustment.

Borrowing.

County Stock.

Land, Compulsory Hiring and Purchase of.

Light Railway.

Local Inquiries.

Locomotives on Highways.

TABLE OF STATUTES.

PAGE

TABLE OF CASES.

I.

J.

K.

L.

T.

U.

ADDENDA.

Page 125, after the reference to "*Worcestershire County Council* v. *Worcester Union*," add :—"As to the rating of the official residence of the chief constable of a county, see *Leicestershire County Council* v. *Leicester Assessment Committee*, Times, April 23rd, 1898."

Page 263, after the reference to "*Burnett* v. *Berry*," add :—"This case was followed in *Jones* v. *Walters*, 78 L. T. (N.S) 167; 14 T. L. R. 265."

Page 531, at end of note (*u*) add :—"This view of the commissioners was upheld by the court in *Cumberland County Council* v. *Commissioners of Inland Revenue*, Times, May 14th, 1898."

Page 619, add note to s. 22 of Local Government Act, 1894 :—"Where a person, who held the office of clerk to the justices for a division of a county, accepted the office of mayor, which, under this section, carried with it the position of justice, it was held that by his acceptance of the latter office he vacated the office of clerk to the justices. (*Reg.* v. *Douglas*, [1898] 1 Q. B. 560; 67 L. J. Q. B. 406; 78 L. T. (N.S.) 198; 62 J. P. 277.)"

PART I.

THE LOCAL GOVERNMENT (ENGLAND AND WALES) ACT, 1888.

(51 & 52 Vict. Cap. 41.)

An Act to amend the Laws relating to Local Government in England and Wales, and for other purposes connected therewith. [13th August, 1888.]

Be it enacted by the Queen's most Excellent Majesty, by and with the advice and consent of the Lords Spiritual and Temporal, and Commons, in this present Parliament assembled, and by the authority of the same, as follows :—

Part I.—County Councils.

Constitution of County Council.

Establishment of county council.

1. A council shall be established in every administrative county as defined by this Act, and be entrusted with the management of the administrative and financial business of that county, and shall consist of the chairman, aldermen, and councillors.

This section contains in brief a statement of the effect of the Act. Its object is to create in every county a council elected by the persons registered as county electors. Such a council is to be elected in every administrative county as defined by s. 100, for some counties are divided and have a council for each division (see s. 46). To this council is transferred the whole of the administrative and financial business formerly exercised by courts of quarter sessions, together with some other powers and duties mentioned in the Act itself. The Act also contemplates the transfer at some future day to the county councils, by means of provisional orders, of many of the powers now exercised by departments of state. See s. 10, *post*. The council is to consist of a chairman, aldermen, and councillors, and its constitution is prescribed by the next section.

Composition and election of council and position of chairman.

2.—(1.) The council of a county and the members thereof shall be constituted and elected and conduct their proceedings in like manner, and be in the like position in all respects, as the council of a borough divided into wards, subject nevertheless to the provisions of this Act, and in particular to the following provisions, that is to say:—

This provision is more fully carried out by s. 75, *post*, which incorporates with this Act the provisions of the Municipal Corporations Act, 1882, as to the constitution and election of the council. These provisions are hereafter

Sect. 2 (1).

NOTE.

set out, and the modifications of them which are contained in this section and in s. 75 and elsewhere throughout this Act have been noticed under each section.

(2.) As respects the aldermen or councillors—

(*a.*) Clerks in holy orders and other ministers of religion shall not be disqualified for being elected and being aldermen or councillors;

This provision prevents the application to county councillors of s. 12, sub-s. (1) (*b*), of the Municipal Corporations Act, 1882, *post*. It may be mentioned here that a woman cannot be elected a member of a county council. *Beresford-Hope* v. *Lady Sandhurst*, 23 Q. B. D. 79; 58 L. J. Q. B. 316; 61 L. T. (N.S.) 150; 37 W. R. 548; 53 J. P. 805; *De Souza* v. *Cobden*, [1891] 1 Q.B. 687; 60 L.J.Q.B. 533; 65 L.T.(N.S.) 130; 39 W.R. 454; 55 J.P. 375, 565; 7 T. L. R. 441.

45 & 46 Vict c. 50.

(*b.*) A person shall be qualified to be an alderman or councillor who, though not qualified in manner provided by the Municipal Corporations Act, 1882, as applied by this Act, is a peer owning property in the county, or is registered as a parliamentary voter in respect of the ownership of property of whatsoever tenure situate in the county;

The qualification of a councillor is that prescribed by s. 11 of the Municipal Corporations Act, 1882, *post*. An alderman must by s. 14 of the same Act be a councillor or a person qualified to be a councillor.

This provision qualifies two classes of persons to be aldermen or councillors besides those qualified under the Municipal Corporations Act as applied by this Act. These are (1) peers owning property (presumably land, notwithstanding the definition in s. 100, *post*), and (2) ownership voters.

(*c.*) The aldermen shall be called county aldermen, and the councillors shall be called county councillors; and a county alderman shall not, as such, vote in the election of a county alderman;

This prevents the application to county aldermen of the Municipal Corporations Act, 1882, s. 60, *post*, which enables aldermen other than outgoing aldermen to vote as members of the council at the election of aldermen. The meaning of the words "as such" is not clear. It has been suggested that they are inserted to provide for the case where an outgoing alderman has been elected a councillor, and ought therefore to be permitted to vote as a councillor. But in such a case by being elected councillor he would have ceased to be an alderman. See *Reg.* v. *Bangor* (*Mayor, etc., of*), 18 Q. B. D. 349; 56 L. J. Q. B. 326; 56 L. T. (N.S.) 434; 35 W. R. 158; 51 J. P. 51. It has also been suggested that it was intended to enable a councillor, who had himself been elected alderman, to vote for the other aldermen, but this is very doubtful.

(*d.*) The county councillors shall be elected for a term of three years, and shall then retire together, and their places shall be filled by a new election; and

In this respect the election of county councillors differs from that of borough councillors, of whom one-third go out of office in each year. See the Municipal Corporations Act, 1882, s. 13, *post*. The date of the triennial election was originally under this Act November 1st, but the date is now altered to the beginning of March by the 54 & 55 Vict. c. 68, *post*. Sect. 2 (2). NOTE.

(*e*.) The divisions of the county for the purpose of the election of county councillors, shall be called electoral divisions and not wards, and one county councillor only shall be elected for each electoral division:

When a borough is divided into wards, the number of councillors assigned to each ward must be three or a multiple of three, so as to admit of the retirement of one-third in each year. In a county one councillor only is to be returned for each electoral division.

(3.) As respects the number of the county councillors, and the boundaries of the electoral divisions in every county—

(*a*.) The number of the county councillors and their apportionment between each of the boroughs which have sufficient population to return one councillor and the rest of the county, shall be such as the Local Government Board may determine ; and

The Local Government Board determined in the first instance the number of the councillors for each county, and apportioned them between boroughs having sufficient population to return one or more members and the rest of the county. Alterations in the number of county councillors and electoral divisions are made under s. 44, *post*.

(*b*.) Any borough returning one councillor only shall be an electoral division ; and

(*c*.) In the rest of the county the electoral divisions shall be such as in the case of a borough returning more than one councillor the council of the borough, and in the rest of the county the quarter sessions for the county, may determine, subject in either case to the directions enacted by this Act ; and in the case of elections after the first, to any alterations made, in accordance with the said directions, in manner in this Act mentioned :

Where the Local Government Board assign one councillor to a borough that borough is to be an electoral division ; where they assign more than one, the council of the borough must divide the borough into electoral divisions. The directions for the constitution of electoral divisions are contained in s. 51, *post*, and the future alteration of the boundaries of electoral divisions is provided for by s. 54, *post*.

(4.) As respects the electors of the county councillors—

The persons entitled to vote at their election shall be, in a borough, the burgesses enrolled in pursuance of the Municipal Corporations Act, 1882, and the Acts amending the same, and elsewhere the persons registered as county electors under the County Electors Act, 1888 : 45 & 46 Vict. c. 50. 51 & 52 Vict. c. 10.

In a borough the electors will be the persons whose names are on the burgess roll ; in a county the electors will be the persons whose names are on

Sect. 2 (4). NOTE.

the roll of county electors. The persons who are qualified to be so enrolled are described in the notes to s. 9 of the Municipal Corporations Act, 1882, *post*.

Notwithstanding the provision in the text, a person whose name is on the register of county electors may not be entitled to vote. Thus it has been held that an elector, though registered in more than one division of the same county, is not entitled to vote in more than one division of the same county. *Knill* v. *Towse*, 24 Q. B. D. 186, 697; 59 L. J. Q. B. 455; 63 L. T. (N.S.) 47; 38 W. R. 521; 54 J. P. 789.

(5.) As respects the chairman of the county council—

(*a*.) He shall be called chairman, instead of mayor; and

As to the election of mayor, see the Municipal Corporations Act, 1882, s. 61, *post*. The chairman will not have such precedence in the county as the mayor has in a borough, for s. 15, sub-s. (5), of the Municipal Corporations Act, 1882, is not to apply to him. See s. 75, sub-s. (16) (*b*), *post*.

(*b*.) He shall, by virtue of his office, be a justice of the peace for the county; but before acting as such justice he shall, if he has not already done so, take the oaths required by law to be taken by a justice of the peace other than the oath respecting the qualification by estate.

The oaths required by law to be taken by a justice, other than the oath of qualification, are the oath of allegiance and the judicial oath. See 31 & 32 Vict. c. 72, s. 6; 34 & 35 Vict. c. 48. The chairman is to be selected from among the aldermen or councillors or persons qualified to be such, and it will be seen from the notes to s. 9 of the Municipal Corporations Act, 1882, *post*, that a person may be qualified to be a councillor without possessing any property qualification.

(6.) The county council may from time to time appoint a member of the council to be vice-chairman, to hold office during the term of office of the chairman, and subject to any rules made from time to time by the county council, anything authorized or required to be done by, to, or before the chairman may be done by, to, or before such vice-chairman.

The term of office of the chairman is one year. See s. 15 of the Municipal Corporations Act, 1882, *post*.

This provision presumably supersedes s. 16 of the Municipal Corporations Act, 1882, which enables the mayor to appoint a deputy.

The London County Council have power to appoint a paid deputy chairman under s. 88, *post*.

Powers of County Council.

Transfer to county council of administrative business of quarter sessions.

3. There shall be transferred to the council of each county on and after the appointed day, the administrative business of the justices of the county in quarter sessions assembled, that is to say, all business done by the quarter sessions or any committee appointed by the quarter sessions, in respect of the several matters following, namely,—

The appointed day is defined by s. 109, *post*.

Section 28, *post*, provides that the council shall have, as respects business transferred to them from quarter sessions, the same powers, etc., as the quarter sessions or any committee thereof had or were subject to. The same section

Section 3.

NOTE.

enables the county council to delegate their powers and duties to committees or district councils, and in some cases to justices in petty sessions, but this is not to include the power to make a rate or loan.

Section 78, *post*, provides for the construction of Acts relating to business transferred to the county council, and enacts that the transfer of powers and duties under this Act shall not authorize the county council to exercise the powers of a court of record, administer an oath, or perform any judicial business.

(i.) The making, assessing, and levying of county, police, hundred, and all rates, and the application and expenditure thereof, and the making of orders for the payment of sums payable out of any such rate or out of the county stock or county fund, and the preparation and revision of the basis or standard for the county rate ;

The Acts relating to the county rate are the County Rate Act, 1852 (15 & 16 Vict. c. 81), and the County Rate Act, 1866 (29 & 30 Vict. c. 78) ; and see the Agricultural Rates Act, 1896 (59 & 60 Vict. c. 16), *post*.

County rate.—By the County Rate Act, 1852, s. 2, it is provided that the justices in quarter sessions in every county shall from time to time appoint any number of justices not exceeding eleven, nor less than five, to be a committee for preparing a basis or standard for fair and equal county rates to be founded and prepared rateably and equally according to the full and fair annual value of the property rateable to the relief of the poor in every parish, township, borough, or place, whether parochial or extra-parochial, within the respective limits of the said justices' commissions, or which in any place within such limits not maintaining its own poor, would be liable to be rated if such last-mentioned place were a parish, or of altering or amending such basis or standard from time to time as circumstances may require : provided that in counties containing more than eleven petty sessional divisions the committee may be extended to the actual number of divisions, so that one justice from each division may be selected to act on the committee. A county rate committee is now appointed by the county council under the above section. The committee must not be less than five in number, and it may number eleven, or, if there are more than eleven petty sessional divisions, as many as there are divisions. In the latter case it is apparently still necessary to see that each division is represented on the committee. On the section just quoted it has been decided that tenants in ancient demesne are liable to pay county rates, as they are liable for poor rates, though they are exempt from taxes and tollages granted by Parliament to the Crown. *Reg.* v. *Aylesford* (*Inhabitants of*), 2 E. & E. 538 ; 29 L. J. M. C. 83 ; 25 J. P. 534. It has also been held that in a valuation under the section all property, whether occupied or not, must be included. *Reg.* v. *Hammersmith*, 7 W. R. 524 ; 33 L. T. 183 ; 24 J. P. 387 (followed in *Reg.* v. *Malden*, L. R. 4 Q. B. 326 ; 38 L. J. M. C. 125 ; 33 J. P. 645). The county council must also make the county rate upon all parishes and places liable to contribute to it, the proportion payable by each place being regulated by the basis or standard prepared and revised from time to time by the committee and confirmed by the council. The rate is levied by precepts addressed to the guardians requiring them to pay to the county treasurer the sums due from each parish in their union, and the guardians obtain these sums from the overseers in the same manner as money for the relief of the poor. See 7 & 8 Vict. c. 33.

Police rate.—This rate is made pursuant to 3 & 4 Vict. c. 88, s. 3, for the purpose of defraying the expenses of the county police. It is made on the same

Sect. 3 (i)

NOTE.

basis as the county rate, and is levied with it. The same Act provides for the raising of the proportion of the county rate payable by detached parts of other counties and by liberties. Such detached portions are by 7 & 8 Vict. c. 61, s. 1, to be deemed to form part of the county of which they form parts for the purposes of parliamentary elections; and justices had power under 3 & 4 Vict. c. 88, s. 2, and 21 & 22 Vict. c. 68, s. 1, to transfer detached portions from one county to another for the purposes of police. Section 50, sub-s. (1), *post*, contains a saving for transfers made before this Act; such transfers can now be effected by county councils. Liberties are now merged in the administrative county. See s. 48, *post*, which contains provisions as to the police in such liberties.

It should be observed that though the control and management of the police (including the control over the division of the county into police districts: *Ex parte Leicestershire County Council*, [1891] 1 Q. B. 53; 60 L. J. M. C. 45; 64 L. T. (N.S.) 25; 39 W. R. 160; 55 J. P. 87; 7 T. L. R. 61) is entrusted to the standing joint committee under s. 9, *post*, the police rates are made by the council.

Hundred rate.—The hundred rate used to be levied for the purpose of making good compensation for damage by riot pursuant to 7 & 8 Geo. 4, c. 31, and 2 & 3 Will. 4, c. 72. These Acts are now repealed, and such compensation is payable out of the police rate of the district in which the damage was done. See the Riot (Damages) Act, 1886, *infra*, clause (xiv.). A hundred rate may be levied for the purposes of certain main roads and bridges under s. 20 of the Highway Act, 1878, the text of which is set out in the notes to s. 11, sub-s. (13), *post*.

The application and expenditure of these rates will devolve upon the county council. As to the making of orders for the payment of sums out of the county fund (to which all receipts of the county council are to be carried), see s. 68, which also contains provisions for the raising of county contributions. The powers to make a rate cannot be delegated. See s. 28, sub-s. (3), *post*.

(ii.) The borrowing of money;

The borrowing of money by the county council is regulated by s. 69, *post*. In the notes to that section will be found a list of the principal purposes for which money may be borrowed.

The power of borrowing must be exercised by the council and cannot be delegated. See s. 28, sub-s. (3), *post*.

(iii.) The passing of the accounts of and the discharge of the county treasurer;

The duty of the county treasurer to account for sums received and paid by him is regulated by 12 Geo. 2, c. 29, and 15 & 16 Vict. c. 81, s. 50. By the first of these Acts the treasurer must deliver accounts upon oath with vouchers, and when these have been passed by the county council they must be deposited with the clerk of the council and by him kept among the records of the county. The Act also provides for the discharge of the treasurer.

(iv.) Shire halls, county halls, assize courts, judges lodgings, lock-up houses, court houses, justices rooms, police stations, and county buildings, works, and property, subject as to the use of buildings by the quarter sessions and the justices to the provisions of this Act respecting the joint committee of quarter sessions and the county council;

NOTE.

A shire hall, county hall, or other building, lodgings for Her Majesty's judges, may be purchased, built, or repaired under 7 Geo. 4, c. 63. The provisions of that Act are extended by 7 Will. 4 & 1 Vict. c. 24, to the building, altering, and repairing of any shire hall or county hall, or any building used partially as a town hall, in cases where assizes and sessions have been held in a town hall not belonging exclusively to the county. The same Act enables shire halls, etc., to be purchased when the assize town is changed, or to be hired. These Acts are amended by 10 & 11 Vict. c. 28, and by 40 & 41 Vict. c. 21, s. 49. The provisions of 7 Geo. 4, c. 63, are also extended by 2 & 3 Vict. c. 69, in respect of the purchase, etc., of judges' lodgings.

Lock-up houses are provided for counties under 5 & 6 Vict. c. 109, s. 22, and for two or more counties or boroughs jointly under 11 & 12 Vict. c. 101, and 31 & 32 Vict. c. 22, s. 10. The Act last referred to enables counties and boroughs to contract for the reception in lock-up houses of persons belonging to another jurisdiction. Under 28 & 29 Vict. c. 126, s. 71, certain discontinued prisons may be used as lock-up houses.

Petty sessional court-houses are provided in counties and boroughs under 12 & 13 Vict. c. 18; 31 & 32 Vict. c. 22; 42 & 43 Vict. c. 49, s. 30; 47 & 48 Vict. c. 43, s. 8.

Police stations are provided under 3 & 4 Vict. c. 88, and if unnecessary, may be disposed of under 19 & 20 Vict. c. 69, s. 24, which extends to them the provisions of 7 Geo. 4, c. 18, under which unnecessary prisons might be disposed of.

As to the use of county buildings by sessions and justices, see s. 30, *post*, which relates to the powers of the standing joint committee: s. 64, which vests existing county buildings in the county council: and s. 55, which enables the council to acquire, etc., such halls, buildings, or offices as they may from time to time require, whether within or without their county.

As to the rating of county buildings, see *Middlesex County Council* v. *St. George's Union Assessment Committee*, [1896] 2 Q. B. 143; 65 L. J. M. C. 141; 75 L. T. (N.S.) 153; 44 W. R. 666; 60 J. P. 518; *Worcestershire County Council* v. *Worcester Uuion*, [1897] 1 Q. B. 480; 66 L. J. Q. B. 323; 76 L. T. (N.S.) 138; 45 W. R. 309; 61 J. P. 244.

(v.) The licensing under any general Act of houses and other places for music or for dancing, and the granting of licences under the Racecourses Licensing Act, 1879; 42 & 43 Vict. c. 18.

There is only one general Act under which quarter sessions had powers relating to music and dancing licences, and that is local in its operation. The Act in question is the Disorderly Houses Act, 1751 (25 Geo. 2, c. 36), s. 2, which provides that any house, room, garden, or other place kept for public dancing, music, or other public entertainment of the like kind, in the cities of London and Westminster, or within twenty miles thereof, without a licence had for that purpose from the quarter sessions, (who are thereby authorized and empowered to grant such licence as they in their discretion shall think proper), shall be deemed a disorderly house or place.

This Act no longer applies to Middlesex, the granting of music and dancing licences by the county council of that county being regulated by 57 & 58 Vict. c. 15, *post*.

Although the county council have no power to administer an oath (see s. 78 (2), *post*), yet in determining applications for music and dancing licences they act judicially, and are bound by the same principles as are binding on justices in determining questions which come before them for judicial decision;

Sect. 3 (v)

NOTE.

hence it was held that the presence at the hearing of such an application of certain members of a county council, who had themselves instructed counsel to oppose the application, vitiated the proceedings. *Reg.* v. *London County Council, ex parte Akkersdyk*, [1892] 1 Q. B. 190; 61 L. J. M. C. 75; 66 L. T. (N.S.) 168; 40 W. R. 285; 56 J. P. 8; 8 T. L. R. 175. At the same time, the county council is not a court so as to give to the councillors the immunity of judges in respect of statements made at the licensing meeting. *Royal Aquarium, etc., Society* v. *Parkinson*, [1892] 1 Q. B. 431; 61 L. J. Q. B. 409; 66 L. T. (N.S.) 513; 40 W. R. 450; 56 J. P. 404; 8 T. L. R. 352. And it has been doubted whether the rule as to disqualification from interest, applicable to purely judicial bodies, applies to the proceedings at such a meeting merely by reason of the fact that the council, which is an administrative body, exercises functions involving something of a judicial character. *Reg.* v. *London County Council, ex parte Edwardes*, 71 L. T. (N.S.) 638.

The Racecourses Licensing Act, 1879 (42 & 43 Vict. c. 18), provides that it shall not be lawful that any horse race be held or take place within a radius of ten miles from Charing Cross, unless within a place for which a licence for horse racing has been obtained. The power and duty of granting licences under this Act devolve on the county councils in the metropolitan area.

Applications under the above Acts had to be made at the Michaelmas quarter sessions; as to the time at which they should be made to a county council, see s. 78 (2), *post*.

(vi.) The provision, enlargement, maintenance, management, and visitation of and other dealing with asylums for pauper lunatics;

Lunatic asylums are provided for counties and boroughs under the Lunacy Act, 1890 (53 & 54 Vict. c. 5), which repeals the earlier statutes, and is itself amended by the Lunacy Act, 1891 (54 & 55 Vict. c. 65). The parts of these Acts particularly affecting county councils are set out *post*; for the Acts in full, with notes, the reader is referred to *Archbold's Law of Lunacy* (4th ed.). Visiting committees are appointed under the Act of 1890.

It should be observed that the text deals only with pauper lunatics. As to the appointment by the justices of visitors of licensed houses, see the Lunacy Act, 1890, ss. 177—182.

(vii.) The establishment and maintenance of and the contribution to reformatory and industrial schools;

The Acts relating to reformatories and industrial schools, so far as here material, are the 29 & 30 Vict. cc. 117, 118. Under these Acts a prison authority (viz., as respects county prisons the justices in quarter sessions) may contract with the managers of a certified reformatory school, or of an industrial school, for the reception and maintenance therein of offenders whose detention is ordered by quarter sessions or justices. Such an authority may contribute towards the alteration, enlargement, or rebuilding of such a school, or towards the support of the inmates, or towards its management, or towards its building, etc., with the approval of a Secretary of State. By 35 & 36 Vict. c. 21, a prison authority are empowered themselves to undertake anything towards which they may contribute under the Act first mentioned. Under 37 & 38 Vict. c. 47, a prison authority are enabled to borrow money for the purposes of industrial and reformatory schools. The county council now have the powers of a prison authority.

There are other Acts relating to reformatory and industrial schools, but these do not affect the powers hereby transferred to county councils. See 54 & 55 Vict. c. 23 ; 56 & 57 Vict. c. 48 ; 57 & 58 Vict. c. 33. **Sect. 3 (vii).** NOTE.

(viii.) Bridges and roads repairable with bridges, and any powers vested by the Highways and Locomotives (Amendment) Act, 1878, in the county authority ; 41 & 42 Vict. c. 77.

By the Statute of Bridges, 22 Hen. 8, c. 5, it was provided that all public bridges, with the highway for a distance of 300 feet from each end of the bridge, should be repaired by the quarter sessions. This applied to every public bridge in the county, the power and duties of the justices being regulated by the Act already mentioned, and by 1 Anne, stat. 1, c. 18, and 12 Geo. 2, c. 29. Power to widen, improve, and alter the situation of county bridges is given by 14 Geo. 2, c. 33 ; 43 Geo. 3, c. 59 ; 52 Geo. 3, c. 110 ; 54 Geo. 3, c. 90 ; 55 Geo. 3, c. 143 ; 5 & 6 Will. 4, c. 50, ss. 21, 22 ; 4 & 5 Vict. c. 49, etc. By the 43 Geo. 3, c. 59, it is provided that no bridge thereafter to be erected by any private person or body corporate should be deemed to be a county bridge repairable by the county unless it were erected under the direction or to the satisfaction of the county surveyor. By 5 & 6 Will. 4, c. 50, s. 21, if any bridge be built after 1836, which is or shall be repairable by the county, all highways leading to, passing over, and next adjoining to such bridge, are to be repaired by the parish, etc., previously bound to repair them. By 33 & 34 Vict. c. 73, s. 12, where a turnpike road shall have become an ordinary highway, all bridges previously repaired by the turnpike trustees are to become county bridges, and be kept in repair accordingly ; but such bridges are to be deemed to have been erected subsequently to the 5 & 6 Will. 4, c. 50. By the 41 & 42 Vict. c. 77, s. 21, any bridge erected before 1878, in any county, without such superintendence as is required by 43 Geo. 3, c. 59, and which is certified by the county surveyor or other person appointed in that behalf by the county authority to be in good repair and condition, shall, if the county authority think fit so to order, become and be deemed to be a bridge which the inhabitants of the county shall be liable to maintain and repair. By s. 22 of the same Act the county authority may make such contributions towards the cost of any bridge to be thereafter erected, after the same has been certified in accordance with the provisions of 43 Geo. 3, c. 59, as a proper bridge to be maintained by the inhabitants of the county ; so always that such contribution shall not exceed one-half of the cost of erecting such bridge. By 43 & 44 Vict. c. 5, the county authority may borrow on mortgage of the county rate for the purpose of contributing towards the cost of a bridge under s. 22 of the 41 & 42 Vict. c. 77. By 44 & 45 Vict. c. 14, county authorities in South Wales were enabled to take over and contribute towards certain bridges. The 54 & 55 Vict. c. 63 (*post*), enables county councils to make agreements with one another or with highway authorities for the construction, reconstruction, alteration, or improvement or the freeing from tolls of any bridge, including the approaches thereto, wholly or partly within the jurisdiction of any one or more of the agreeing authorities. By s. 6 of this Act, *post*, p. 17, the county council have power to purchase or take over existing bridges, not being at present county bridges, and to erect new bridges.

The 41 & 42 Vict. c. 77, conferred the following powers upon a county authority, and these powers, so far as they are now exercisable, are transferred to the county council :—Enforcing performance of duty by defaulting highway authority, s. 10 ; declaring highway to be a main road, s. 15 ; reducing main road to status of ordinary highway, s. 16 ; directing form of accounts for maintenance of main roads, s. 18 ; power to declare main roads repairable by

Sect. 3 (viii).

NOTE.

the hundred in certain cases, s. 20; accepting bridges as county bridges, s. 21; contributing towards the cost of erecting county bridges, s. 22; reviving liability to repair highways discontinued as unnecessary, s. 24; making bye-laws, s. 26; authorizing use of locomotives of certain sizes and weights, s. 28; making bye-laws as to hours for use of locomotives, s. 31; licensing locomotives, s. 32. The provisions as to locomotives have been amended by the Locomotives on Highways Act, 1896 (59 & 60 Vict. c. 36), which is set out *post.*

(ix.) The tables of fees to be taken by and the costs to be allowed to any inspector, analyst, or person holding any office in the county other than the clerk of the peace and the clerks of the justices;

By the Weights and Measures Act, 1878 (41 & 42 Vict. c. 49), s. 47, inspectors of weights and measures were to take the fees fixed by the county authority, not exceeding the fees mentioned in the schedule to that Act, and to account for them to the county authority. That section is now repealed by 52 & 53 Vict. c. 21, s. 13, *post,* under which inspectors are to take the fees therein mentioned and no others, and to account for the same to the county council.

Subsequent Acts relating to weights and measures (55 & 56 Vict. c. 18, and 56 & 57 Vict. c. 19) impose upon county councils duties other than those mentioned in the text. These Acts, and also the Weights and Measures (Metric System) Act, 1897 (60 & 61 Vict. c. 46), are set out *post.*

The analyst is appointed under the Sale of Food and Drugs Act, 1875 (38 & 39 Vict. c. 63), s. 10, but the Act is silent as to any table of fees or costs, as the cost of analysis of any article of food or drug is fixed by s. 12. Under the Fertilizers and Feeding Stuffs Act, 1893 (56 & 57 Vict. c. 56), s. 4, *post,* county councils are required to appoint analysts for the purposes of that Act.

It is doubtful whether a parish constable is an officer holding office in the county, but it is submitted that he is, and that the county council must fix the fees and allowances payable to such constables under 5 & 6 Vict. c. 109, s. 17; 13 & 14 Vict. c. 20, s. 2; 35 & 36 Vict. c. 92, s. 11.

For the fees payable to inspectors of gas meters, see 22 & 23 Vict. c. 66, s. 4.

(x.) The appointment, removal, and determination of salaries, of the county treasurer, the county surveyor, the public analysts, any officer under the Explosives Act, 1875, and any officers whose remuneration is paid out of the county rate other than the clerk of the peace and the clerks of the justices;

38 & 38 Vict. c. 17.

The county treasurer is appointed pursuant to 12 Geo. 2, c. 29, s. 6. He must give security under that Act to be accountable for the moneys paid to him. He is removable at pleasure (*ib.* s. 11). His remuneration is in the discretion of the council. 55 Geo. 3, c. 51, s. 17.

The county surveyor is not appointed pursuant to any statute, though by the Statute of Bridges, 22 Hen. 8, c. 5, s. 3, justices are empowered to appoint surveyors for the repair of bridges. The county surveyor is referred to in other statutes, such as those relating to highways, but none of those Acts refer to his appointment or remuneration.

The public analysts are appointed under 38 & 39 Vict. c. 63, s. 10, at such rates of remuneration as may be agreed upon. See s. 39, *post,* as to analysts in the smaller boroughs.

NOTE.

The county council is the local authority for the administration of the Explosives Act, 1875 (38 & 39 Vict. c. 17) (see s. 7 (*b*), p. 18, *post*), and it is necessary for them to appoint officers under that Act. But the provision in the text relates to the powers of quarter sessions, and the officer here referred to as being appointed by quarter sessions is a person whose duty it is to inspect any wharf, carriage, boat, etc., having explosives *in transitu*. See s. 75 of the Act.

The other officers referred to in the section include clerks and servants necessarily employed with reference to county business and in county offices.

It has been held that the provision in the text does not apply to coroners: *Ex parte London County Council*, [1892] 1 Q. B. 33; 61 L. J. Q. B. 27; 65 L. T. (N.S.) 614; 56 J. P. 279; 8 T. L. R. 24. See further as to coroners the notes to s. 5, *post*.

(xi.) The salary of any coroner whose salary is payable out of the county rate, the fees, allowances, and disbursements allowed to be paid by any such coroner, and the division of the county into coroners' districts, and the assignment of such districts;

All county coroners are paid out of the county rate. 23 & 24 Vict. c. 116, s. 4, provides for the payment of the coroner's salary, and its revision from time to time, having regard to the number of inquests held. By the Coroners Act, 1887 (50 & 51 Vict. c. 71), s. 25, as applied by this Act, the county council may from time to time make, vary, and alter a schedule of fees, allowances, and disbursements, which, on the holding of an inquest, may lawfully be paid and made by the coroner holding such inquest (other than the fees payable to medical witnesses in pursuance of that Act). By s. 27 of the same Act every coroner is required within four months after holding an inquest to lay his accounts of all sums paid by him before the county council. The Coroners Act, 1892 (55 & 56 Vict. c. 56), *post*, enables a coroner to appoint a deputy with the approval of the chairman of the county council.

Districts are assigned to coroners under 7 & 8 Vict. c. 92, s. 5, as amended by this Act. See ss. 5, 38, 39, **114**, *post*.

For the purposes of the Coroners Acts the ridings of Yorkshire are (from April 1st, 1898) separate counties, and the county council of each riding is, exclusively, the county authority: Yorkshire Coroners Act, 1897 (60 & 61 Vict. c. 39), *post*.

As to the right of a coroner to the payment of his salary after the division of his district, see *Baxter* v. *London County Council*, 63 L. T. (N.S.) 767; 55 J. P. 391.

The provisions in the text do not apply to county boroughs. See s. 34, *post*.

(xii.) The division of the county into polling districts for the purposes of parliamentary elections, the appointment of places of election, the places of holding courts for the revision of the lists of voters, and the costs of and other matters to be done for the registration of parliamentary voters;

It will be the duty of a county council, under 30 & 31 Vict. c. 102, s. 34, to divide their county into polling districts, and assign to each district a polling place in such manner, as far as practicable, as to enable each voter to have a polling place within a convenient distance of his residence . . . and to name the polling places at which the revising barristers are to hold their courts. This power may be exercised from time to time as may be found ct. 3 (xii.) necessary, 31 & 32 Vict. c. 58, s. 18. See also 35 & 36 Vict. c. 33, s. 5; 46 & 47 Vict. c. 51, ss. 47, 68 (2), 69 (9); 48 & 49 Vict. c. 15, ss. 4, 13. And see as to county boroughs, s. 34, sub-s. (6), *post*.

NOTE.

As to the expenses and remuneration of clerks of the peace, town clerks, returning officers, overseers, relieving officers, etc., in connection with the registration of voters, see 6 & 7 Vict. c. 18, ss. 54, 55, 57; 30 & 31 Vict. c. 102, s. 31; 31 & 32 Vict. c. 58, ss. 23, 31, 32; 41 & 42 Vict. c. 26, s. 30; 48 & 49 Vict. c. 15, ss. 8, 14; 51 Vict. c. 10, ss. 8, 9, 11.

It is impossible in the space at disposal in a work of this kind to do more than enumerate the statutory provisions, for full details respecting which the reader is referred to the recent edition of Messrs. Mackenzie and Lushington's work on the Registration of Voters.

(xiii.) The execution as local authority of the Acts relating to contagious diseases of animals, to destructive insects, to fish conservancy, to wild birds, to weights and measures, and to gas meters, and of the Local Stamp Act, 1869;

& 33 Vict. 9.

The Contagious Diseases (Animals) Acts were repealed and consolidated by the Diseases of Animals Act, 1894 (57 & 58 Vict. c. 57), except as to 41 & 42 Vict. c. 74, s. 34, and 49 & 50 Vict. c. 32, s. 9. It is provided by s. 39, *post*, that nothing in that section shall transfer to the county council any powers, duties, or liabilities under s. 34 of the 41 & 42 Vict. c. 74, as amended by s. 9 of the 49 & 50 Vict. c. 32. This provision is explained in the note to s. 39, *post*. The Act of 1894 has been amended by the Diseases of Animals Act, 1896 (59 & 60 Vict. c. 15). These Acts are set out *post*.

The Destructive Insects Act is the 40 & 41 Vict. c. 68. Under it the county council as local authority might be ordered by the Privy Council to make compensation for any crops removed or destroyed for the purpose of preventing the spreading of the Colorado beetle.

The county council have the power of appointing conservators of rivers and of applying to the Board of Trade to form fishery districts under 24 & 25 Vict. c. 109, s. 33; 28 & 29 Vict. c. 121, ss. 4 to 19; 36 & 37 Vict. c. 71, ss. 9, 10, 26 to 33; 41 & 42 Vict. c. 39, s. 6; 47 & 48 Vict. c. 11, s. 2; 49 & 50 Vict. c. 39.

By the Wild Birds Protection Act, 1880 (43 & 44 Vict. c. 35), s. 8, a Secretary of State may upon application by the county justices (now the county council) extend or vary the time during which the killing and taking of wild birds or any of them is prohibited by that Act. The Act is amended by 44 & 45 Vict. c. 51, but that Act does not confer any additional power on the county council. It is further provided by 57 & 58 Vict. c. 24, *post*, that a Secretary of State may, upon application of a county council, by order prohibit the taking or destroying of wild birds' eggs in any year or years in any place or places within a county, or the taking or destroying of the eggs of any specified kind of wild birds within the county or part thereof as recommended by the county council. Under the same Act an order may also be made applying the principal Act within any county to any species of wild bird not included in the schedule to the principal Act. By the 59 & 60 Vict. c. 56, *post*, an order may also be made extending the close time for particular birds to the whole or any part of the year and enabling the council of a county borough to exercise the same powers as a county council under 57 & 58 Vict. c. 24.

Under the Weights and Measures Act, 1878 (41 & 42 Vict. c. 49), s. 40, it is the duty of the county council, as local authority, to provide local standards of weights and measures, and fix the place at which the standards are to be deposited. They must also provide proper means for verifying weights and measures by comparison with the local standards, and for stamping the weights and measures so verified. The expenses of executing the Act are payable out of the county rate. Two or more county councils may combine as regards either the whole or any part of the areas within their jurisdiction for all or any of the purposes of the Act upon such terms and in such manner as may be from time to time mutually agreed upon. The county council may under s. 53 make bye-laws as to the local verification of weights and measures. The county council also appoint an inspector under s. 43, and fix the times and places at which he is to attend. By s. 39, *post*, in the boroughs having a population of less than 10,000, such boroughs are, for the purposes of the Weights and Measures Acts, to form part of the county. The Act of 1878 has been amended by 52 & 53 Vict. c. 21 ; 55 & 56 Vict. c. 18 ; 56 & 57 Vict. c. 19 ; and 60 & 61 Vict. c. 46 ; some of these Acts impose important duties on county councils ; they are set out *post*. **Sect. 3 (xiii)**

NOTE.

The Acts relating to gas meters are 22 & 23 Vict. c. 66, and 23 & 24 Vict. c. 146. By these Acts models of gas holders measuring the cubic foot are to be deposited with the (county council) at such places as they shall direct. The council are also to appoint inspectors. The expenses are to be paid out of the county rates. By s. 39, *post*, smaller boroughs are to form part of the county for the purposes of these Acts. The verification of local and working standards used by a county council in testing meters is regulated by the Weights and Measures Acts, 1878 and 1889 ; see s. 15 of the latter Act.

The Local Stamp Act is the 32 & 33 Vict. c. 49. It provides that when all the clerks of petty and special sessions and justices within a county are paid by salary, the justices in quarter sessions may order that all fees and penalties payable to the treasurer be paid and received by stamps. Questions as to the application of the Act are to be referred to and determined by the Standing Joint Committee under s. 30 (3), *post*, p. 66. The expenses of the Act are to be defrayed out of the county rate.

(xiv.) Any matters arising under the Riot (Damages) Act, 1886 ; 49 & 50 Vict. c. 38.

The county council thus succeed to the powers and duties of the quarter sessions under the Riot (Damages) Act, 1886 (49 & 50 Vict. c. 38). Compensation payable under that Act to any person whose property has been injured, stolen, or destroyed by rioters will be paid by the council out of the police rate.

These matters are not transferred to the council of the county of London. See s. 93, sub-s. (2), *post*.

(xv.) The registration of rules of scientific societies under the Act of the session of the sixth and seventh years of the reign of Her present Majesty, chapter thirty-six ; the registration of charitable gifts under the Act of the session of the fifty-second year of the reign of George the Third, chapter one hundred and two ; the certifying and recording of places of religious worship under the Act of the session of the fifty-second year of the reign of George the Third, chapter one hundred and fifty-five ; the confirmation and record of the rules of loan societies under the Act of the session of the third and fourth years of the reign of Her present Majesty, chapter one hundred and ten ; and

The 6 & 7 Vict. c. 36, is the Act under which scientific and literary societies are entitled to exemption from payment of rates. In order to entitle any

Sect. 3 (xv).

NOTE.

society to exemption under the Act a copy of its rules must be submitted to the barrister appointed to certify the rules of friendly societies, who inquires and certifies whether the society is within the Act. His certificate, given upon the copy of the rules, is afterwards affirmed and allowed by the (county council) and filed by the clerk of the (council). The central office under the Friendly Societies Act, 1896 (59 & 60 Vict. c. 25), is now substituted for the barrister above mentioned. See s. 2 of that Act.

The 52 Geo. 3, c. 102, provides that a memorial or statement of the real and personal estate, and of the income, investment, and objects of all charities and charitable donations for the benefit of the poor or other persons in England and Wales, together with the names of the founders, the names of the persons possessing the deeds, wills, or other instruments by which the charities were founded, and the names of the trustees shall, within twelve months after execution of such deeds, wills, etc., be registered in the office of the clerk of the (county council).

The 52 Geo. 3, c. 155, s. 2, provides that no congregation or assembly for religious worship of protestants (at which there shall be present more than twenty persons besides the immediate family and servants of the person in whose house or upon whose premises such meeting, assembly, or congregation shall be held) shall be permitted or allowed, if the same shall not have been duly certified to the bishop of the diocese, or to the archdeacon, or to the (county council). The provisions of the Act were extended to places of worship of Roman Catholics by the 2 & 3 Will. 4, c. 115, and of Jews by the 9 & 10 Vict. c. 59, s. 2. The 18 & 19 Vict. c. 81, s. 1, exempts certain congregations or assemblies from its provisions. It should be observed also that these places may now be registered and recorded by the Registrar-General, and in these cases they need not be registered under the 52 Geo. 3, c. 155 (see 18 & 19 Vict. c. 81).

By the 3 & 4 Vict. c. 110, s. 4, it is provided that copies of the rules of every loan society are to be submitted to the barrister appointed to certify the rules of savings banks, who is to certify whether such rules are in conformity with law, and a transcript as certified is to be sent to the clerk of the peace and allowed and confirmed by the (county council). The central office under the Friendly Societies Act, 1896, is now substituted for the barrister. See s. 2 of that Act.

(xvi.) Any other business transferred by this Act.

See Part II. of this Act, *post*.

For the general provisions as to powers transfered to county councils, see ss. 28, 29, *post*.

Transfer of certain powers under local Acts.

4. Where it appears to the Local Government Board that any powers, duties, or liabilities of any quarter sessions or justices, or any committee thereof, under any local Act are similar in character to the powers, duties, and liabilities transferred to county councils by this Act, or relate to property transferred to a county council by this Act, the Board may, if they think fit, make a provisional order for transferring such powers, duties, and liabilities to the county council.

This section provides for the transfer to county councils of powers, duties, and liabilities similar to those transferred by the last section where these depend on local Acts, or relate to property transferred to a county council by this Act. A transfer under this section is to be effected by Provisional

Order of the Local Government Board. As to the making of a Provisional Order, see s. 87, *post*.

Section 4.

NOTE.

Appointment of coroners by county council.

5.—(1.) After the appointed day a coroner for a county shall not be elected by the freeholders of the county, and on any vacancy occurring in the office of a coroner for a county, who is elected to that office in pursuance of a writ *de coronatore eligendo*, a like writ for the election of a successor shall be directed to the county council of the county instead of to the sheriff, and the county council shall thereupon appoint a fit person, not being a county alderman or county councillor, to fill such office, and in the case of a county divided into coroners' districts shall assign him a district; and any person so appointed shall have like powers and duties, and be entitled to like remuneration, as if he had been elected coroner for the county by the freeholders thereof.

For the meaning of the phrase "appointed day," see s. 109, *post*.

Formerly the county coroner was elected by the freeholders of the county. A writ *de coronatore eligendo* was issued to the sheriff, who thereupon held an election. See the sections of the Coroners Act, 1887 (50 & 51 Vict. c. 71), repealed by sub-s. (6), *infra*. The writ is now directed to the county council. It should be observed that this section only applies to such a coroner as would previously have been elected by the freeholders, not to the coroner for a liberty or other franchise. *Ex parte London County Council*, [1892] 1 Q. B. 33; 61 L. J. Q. B. 27; 64 L. T. (N.S.) 614; 56 J. P. 279; 8 T. L. R. 24.

As an alderman or councillor may not be appointed, a member of the council must resign if he desires to become a candidate for the coronership. This will involve payment of the usual fine under the Municipal Corporations Act, 1882, s. 36, *post*.

The duty of assigning coroners' districts devolves upon the county councils under s. 3 (xi.), *ante*. See further as to coroners' districts sub-s. (3), *infra*, and s. 114 as to coroners' districts situate in the county of London. The area of a borough with a population under 10,000 is to be subject to the authority of the county coroner, and may be annexed by the county council to a coroner's district of the county. See s. 38, *post*.

As to the effect of the divisions of a district on a coroner's right to receive his salary fixed at the last revision, see *Baxter* v. *London County Council*, 63 L. T. (N.S.) 767; 55 J. P. 391. As to the appointment of a deputy coroner, see the Coroners Act, 1892 (55 & 56 Vict. c. 56), *post*.

(2.) Where the district of any such coroner is situate wholly within any administrative county, the council of that county shall, subject as hereinafter mentioned, appoint the coroner.

For the definition of "administrative county," see s. 100, *post*.

The case of a district extending into two administrative counties is provided for by the next sub-section.

(3.) Where the district of any such coroner is situate partly in one and partly in another administrative county forming part of an entire county, the joint committee for the entire county may arrange for the alteration in manner provided by law of the district,

Sect. 5 (3). so that, on the next avoidance of the office of coroner of that district, or at any earlier time fixed by the joint committee when the alteration is made, the coroners' district shall not be situate in more than one administrative county.

The joint committee here referred to is the committee of the two or more county councils appointed under s. 46, *post*.

The manner provided by law is by petition to Her Majesty praying that an alteration be made in the division of the county into coroners' districts. Notice of the petition is given to the coroners of the county. If the divisions are altered to the prejudice of any of the coroners, compensation must be paid to him (7 & 8 Vict. c. 92). The alteration may take effect on the next avoidance of the office of coroner of the district, or at an earlier period fixed by the joint committee.

As to the application of this sub-section to the ridings of Yorkshire, see the Yorkshire Coroners Act, 1897 (60 & 61 Vict. c. 39), *post*.

(4.) Until such arrangement is made, the joint committee for the entire county shall appoint the coroner for the said district, and the amount payable in respect of the salary, fees, and expenses of such coroner shall be defrayed in like manner as costs of the joint committee are directed by this Act to be defrayed.

As to the joint committee and their expenses, see s. 46, *post*. As to the salary, fees, and expenses of the coroner, see the note to s. 3 (xi.), *ante*.

(5.) Nothing in this Act respecting the appointment of a coroner shall alter the jurisdiction of a coroner for the entire county, or any power of removing such coroner, whether by writ *de coronatore exonerando* or otherwise, and all writs for the election or removal of a coroner shall be altered so as to give effect to this section.

Though a coroner has a district assigned to him, he is nevertheless coroner for the entire county. See 7 & 8 Vict. c. 92, s. 19.

A coroner is chosen for life, but he may be removed either by being made sheriff or chosen verderer, which are offices incompatible with that of coroner, or by the writ *de coronatore exonerando* for a cause to be therein assigned, as that he is engaged in other business, is incapacitated by years or sickness, hath not a sufficient estate in the county, or lives in an inconvenient part of it. Fitz. N. B. 163, 184; 2 Inst. 132. By the Coroners Act, 1887 (50 & 51 Vict. c. 71, s. 8), the Lord Chancellor may remove any coroner for inability or misbehaviour in the discharge of his duty. An instance of an application to remove a coroner on the ground of misbehaviour is *In re the Coroner for West Surrey*, 47 J. P. 166. By the same section a coroner who is guilty of extortion, or of corruption, or of wilful neglect of his duty, or of misbehaviour in the discharge of his duty, shall be guilty of a misdemeanor, and, in addition to any other punishment, may, unless his office of coroner is annexed to any other office, be adjudged by the court before whom he is so convicted to be removed from his office. By s. 10 a coroner shall not by himself or his partner, directly or indirectly, act as solicitor in the prosecution or defence of a person for an offence for which such person is charged by an inquisition taken before him as coroner, whether such person is tried on that inquisition or on any bill of indictment found by a grand jury. If a coroner acts in contravention of this section he shall be deemed guilty of misbehaviour in the discharge of his duty. Sect. 5 (5).

NOTE.

(6.) Sections eleven and fourteen and the First Schedule of the Coroners Act, 1887, and any other enactment relating to the election of a coroner for a county by the freeholders of such county or any district thereof, are hereby repealed as from the appointed day, without prejudice to anything done or suffered, or any legal proceeding commenced or penalty incurred before such repeal takes effect. 50 & 51 Vict. c. 71.

For the meaning of the phrase "appointed day," see s. 109, *post*.

The repealed sections of the Coroners Act, 1887, are those which regulate the election of a coroner by the freeholders.

(7.) A person who holds the office of coroner shall not be qualified to be elected as a county alderman or county councillor for the county for which he is a coroner.

By sub-s. (1) a person who is an alderman or councillor may not be elected coroner for the county. This sub-section provides that a county coroner shall not be qualified to be elected an alderman or councillor.

6. The county council shall have power to purchase, or take over on terms to be agreed on, existing bridges not being at present county bridges, and to erect new bridges, and to maintain, repair, and improve any bridges so purchased, taken over, or erected. Power of council as to bridges.

In the note to s. 3 (viii.) the public bridges which are not county bridges have been mentioned. These are for the most part bridges which have been built since the passing of the 43 Geo. 3, c. 59, s. 5, and without such superintendence as is provided by that section, and which have not been taken over by the county under 41 & 42 Vict. c. 77, s. 21. Such bridges may now be taken over on such terms as may be agreed upon, though it is not quite clear who are to be the other parties to the agreement, unless it is some person or local authority now liable to repair the bridges. In addition to these bridges there are bridges built by private persons or bodies which have never been dedicated to public use, though the public may have used them by permission or on payment of toll. The county council may purchase or take over such bridges on terms to be agreed on.

It is further provided by the Highways and Bridges Act, 1891 (54 & 55 Vict. c. 63), that county councils and highway authorities may enter into agreements in relation to the construction, etc., of bridges. This Act is set out, *post*.

7. There shall be transferred to the county council on and after the appointed day the business of the justices of the county out of session— Transfer to county council of certain powers of justices out of session.

(*a.*) in respect of the licensing of houses or places for the public performance of stage plays, and

(*b.*) in respect of the execution as local authority of the Explosives Act, 1875. 38 & 39 Vict. c. 17.

As to the transfer to the county council of similar powers formerly vested in borough justices, see s. 36, *post*, p. 82.

Houses or places for the performance of stage plays are licensed under

Sect. 7.

NOTE.

6 & 7 Vict. c. 68. The licences were formerly granted by the justices of a division in special sessions, the sessions being convened by the clerk. It is difficult to apply such a provision to the county council, for it can hardly be contemplated that a special meeting of the county council must be called to hear an application for a theatre licence. The difficulty is frequently avoided by delegating this duty under s. 28, *post.*

The Explosives Act, 1875, is the 38 & 39 Vict. c. 17. Under that Act the local authority were the justices in petty sessions (except in the city of London, the metropolis, boroughs, and harbours within the jurisdiction of harbour authorities). In the metropolis the local authority was the Metropolitan Board of Works, whose powers and duties are now transferred to the London County Council. The duties of local authorities under the Act cannot here be stated in detail. They relate to (1) the manufacture, (2) keeping, (3) sale, (4) transport, and (5) importation of explosives; and they include the granting of licences and the registration of premises for the manufacture, keeping, etc., of explosives.

It is provided by s. 28, *post,* that the county council may delegate their powers under the Act to any committee or district council, and may delegate their powers under the above-mentioned Acts to justices in petty sessions.

Reservation of business to quarter sessions.

8.—(1.) Nothing in this Act shall transfer to a county council any business of the quarter sessions or justices in relation to appeals by any overseers or persons against the basis or standard for the county rate or against that or any other rate.

This sub-section reserves to quarter sessions their powers and duties of hearing appeals against rates generally, and also appeals against the county rate basis. It will be remembered that by s. 3 (i.), *ante,* the duty of preparing the basis is transferred to the county council.

As to appeals against the county rate basis, and against the county rate, see 15 & 16 Vict. c. 81, ss. 17 and 22, and Local Government Act, 1894, s. 6 (1) (*c*) (i), *post.*

(2.) All business of the quarter sessions or any committee thereof not transferred by or in pursuance of this Act to the county council shall be reserved to and transacted by the quarter sessions or committee thereof in the same manner, as far as circumstances admit, as if this Act had not passed.

This is a general reservation in respect of business not transferred to the county council. It was really unnecessary, and was probably inserted *ex cautelâ.*

Powers as to police.

9.—(1.) The powers, duties, and liabilities of quarter sessions and of justices out of session with respect to the county police shall, on and after the appointed day, vest in and attach to the quarter sessions and the county council jointly, and be exercised and discharged through the standing joint committee of the quarter sessions and county council appointed as herein-after mentioned:

The Acts relating to county police are 2 & 3 Vict. c. 93; 3 & 4 Vict. c. 88; 19 & 20 Vict. c. 69; 20 & 21 Vict. c. 2; 22 & 23 Vict. c. 32; 28 & 29 Vict.

c. 35; 53 & 54 Vict. c. 45; and 56 & 57 Vict. c. 10. The duty of appointing the chief constable, and the general control of the police in counties, which has formerly been exercised by the county justices, is now exercised by the standing joint committee appointed under s. 30, *post*. Sect. 9 (2). NOTE.

It has been held that the control over the division of a county into police districts is by this section vested in the standing joint committee. *Ex parte Leicestershire County Council*, [1891] 1 Q. B. 53; 60 L. J. M. C. 45; 64 L. T. (N. S.) 25; 39 W. R. 160; 55 J. P. 87; 7 T. L. R. 61.

It should be observed that s. 33, *post*, provides for the continuance of one police force for any county borough or other borough and any county where these have been united for the purposes of a police force. In the smaller boroughs the existing police forces are abolished by s. 39, *post*, which provides that for the purposes of the Acts relating to county police such boroughs are to form part of the counties in which they are situated.

(2.) Provided that the powers conferred by section seven of the County and Borough Police Act, 1856, which requires constables to perform, in addition to their ordinary duties, such duties connected with the police as the quarter sessions may direct or require, shall continue to be exercised by the quarter sessions as well as by the said standing joint committee, and may also be exercised by the county council; and the said section shall be construed as if the county council and the said standing joint committee were therein mentioned as well as the quarter sessions. 19 & 20 Vict. c. 69.

The 19 & 20 Vict. c. 69, s. 7, provides that constables shall, in addition to their ordinary duties, perform all such duties connected with the police in their respective counties or boroughs as the justices in general or quarter sessions assembled, or the watch committees of such respective counties or boroughs, from time to time direct and require. Justices in general or quarter sessions are still to retain their powers under this section, and the same powers are extended to the standing joint committee appointed under s. 30, *post*, and to the county council.

(3.) Nothing in this Act shall affect the powers, duties, and liabilities of justices of the peace as conservators of the peace, or the obligation of the chief constable or other constables to obey their lawful orders given in that behalf.

This provision was inserted for the purpose of continuing the existing powers of justices as conservators of the peace to issue such orders as they may think necessary to the police for the preservation of the peace, the prevention of offences, and the apprehension of offenders.

10.—(1.) After the passing of this Act it shall be lawful for the Local Government Board to make from time to time a Provisional Order for transferring to county councils— Transfer to county council of powers of certain government departments and other authorities.

(*a*.) Any such powers, duties, and liabilities of Her Majesty's Privy Council, a Secretary of State, the Board of Trade, the Local Government Board, or the Education Department, or any other Government Department, as are

Sect. 10 (1).

conferred by or in pursuance of any statute and appear to relate to matters arising within the county, and to be of an administrative character : also

(*b.*) Any such powers, duties, and liabilities arising within the county, of any commissioners of sewers, conservators, or other public body, corporate or unincorporate (not being the corporation of a municipal borough or an urban or rural authority, or a school board, and not being a board of guardians), as are conferred by or in pursuance of any statute ;

and such Order shall make such exceptions and modifications as appear to be expedient, and also such provisions as appear necessary or proper for carrying into effect such transfer, and for that purpose may transfer any power vested in Her Majesty in Council :

As to the making of Provisional Orders, see s. 87, *post*.

Without attempting to give an exhaustive list of the powers of Government Departments which might be transferred, the following are the principal of such powers and duties :—

Privy Council.—Powers (now transferred to the *Board of Agriculture*) under the Diseases of Animals Act, the Destructive Insects Act, etc.

Secretary of State.—Powers under the Artizans Dwellings Acts, Burial Acts, etc.

Board of Trade.—Powers under the Pier and Harbour Acts, the Fishery Acts, Electric Lighting Act, Gas and Waterworks Acts, Merchant Shipping Acts, Tramway Acts, etc.

Local Government Board.—Powers under the Public Health Acts, Baths and Washhouses Acts, Artizans Dwellings Acts, Highway Acts, Rivers Pollution Act, etc.

Education Department.—Powers under the Education Acts.

The powers transferred must be such as are conferred by or in pursuance of a statute, and must be of an administrative (*i.e.* as distinguished from a judicial) character.

The statutory powers of public bodies, other than those expressly excepted, may also be transferred by Provisional Order. The most important of these are the powers of commissioners of sewers or drainage boards under the Acts relating to the drainage of land.

(2.) Provided that before any such Order is made the draft thereof shall be approved, if it relates to the powers, duties, or liabilities of a Secretary of State, or the Board of Trade, or any other Government Department, by such Secretary of State, Board, or department, and approved, if it affects the powers, duties, or liabilities of any commissioners, conservators, or body, corporate or unincorporate, by such commissioners, conservators, or body ; and every such Provisional Order shall be of no effect until it is confirmed by Parliament.

This provision renders it necessary that the draft of the Order should be perused and approved by the department or body whose powers are to be transferred, and it makes such approval in effect a condition precedent to the Order.

(3.) If any such powers, duties, or liabilities as are referred to in any Provisional Order under this section arise within two or more counties, they may be transferred to the county councils of such two or more counties jointly, and may be exercised and discharged by a joint committee of such councils.

As to the appointment and powers of joint committees, see s. 81, *post*.

(4.) The Act of Parliament confirming any Provisional Order made under this section shall be a public general Act.

This provision enables an Order to be made altering the general law in the district to which it relates. It has also the effect of preventing its being treated for purposes of construction as a private or local Act.

Entire maintenance of main roads by county council.

41 & 42 Vict c. 77.

11.—(1.) Every road in a county, which is for the time being a main road within the meaning of the Highways and Locomotives (Amendment) Act, 1878, inclusive of every bridge carrying such road if repairable by the highway authority shall, after the appointed day, be wholly maintained and repaired by the council of the county in which the road is situate, and such council, for the purpose of the maintenance, repair, improvement, and enlargement of, and other dealing with such road, shall have the same powers and be subject to the same duties as a highway board, and may further exercise any powers vested in the council for the purpose of the maintenance and repair of bridges, and the enactments relating to highways and bridges shall apply accordingly; and the county council shall have the same powers as a highway board for preventing and removing obstructions, and for asserting the right of the public to the use and enjoyment of the roadside wastes; and the execution of this section shall be a general county purpose, and the costs thereof shall be charged to the general county account.

Highways, etc., Act, 1878: Main Roads.—The chief provisions of the Highway Act, 1878 (41 & 42 Vict. c. 77), relating to main roads are ss. 13—17. These so far as they are unrepealed are here set out in full.

Section 13. "For the purposes of this Act and subject to its provisions, any road which has, within the period between the thirty-first day of December, one thousand eight hundred and seventy, and the date of the passing of this Act, ceased to be a turnpike road, and any road which, being at the time of the passing of this Act a turnpike road, may afterwards cease to be such, shall be deemed to be a main road."

[The remainder of this section is repealed by the Statute Law Revision Act, 1894, having been rendered obsolete by the provisions in the text.]

Section 14. "The following areas shall be deemed to be highway areas for the purpose of this Act; (that is to say,)

"(1) Urban sanitary districts;

"(2) Highway districts;

"(3) Highway parishes not included within any highway district or any urban sanitary district.

Sect. 11 (1).

NOTE.

[The expression "urban sanitary districts" as defined by the Act of 1878, did not include quarter sessions boroughs; but these are now included by virtue of ss. 35 (4) and 38 (3), *post*].

Section 15. "Where it appears to any highway authority that any highway within their district ought to become a main road by reason of its being a medium of communication between great towns, or a thoroughfare to a railway station or otherwise, such highway authority may apply to the county authority for an order declaring such road, as to such parts as aforesaid, to be a main road; and the county authority, if of opinion that there is probable cause for the application, shall cause the road to be inspected, and if satisfied that it ought to be a main road shall make an order accordingly.

"A copy of the order so made shall be deposited at the office of the clerk of the peace of the county, and shall be open to the inspection of persons interested at all reasonable hours; and the order so made shall not be of any validity unless and until it is confirmed by a further order of the county authority made within a period of not more than six months after the making of the first-mentioned order."

Section 16. ". . . . where it appears to a county authority that any road within their county which has become a main road in pursuance of this Act ought to cease to be a main road and become an ordinary highway, such authority may apply to the Local Government Board for a provisional order declaring that such road has ceased to be a main road and become an ordinary highway.

"The Local Government Board, if of opinion that there is probable cause for an application under this section, shall cause the road to be inspected, and if satisfied that it . . . . ought to cease to be a main road, and become an ordinary highway, shall make a [*provisional*] order accordingly [*to be confirmed as hereinafter mentioned*].

"All expenses incurred in or incidental to the making or confirmation of any order under this section shall be defrayed by the county authority applying for such order."

[Parts of the above section were repealed by the Statute Law Revision Act, 1894 (57 & 58 Vict. c. 56), and are here omitted. The remainder of the section is amended by s. 4 of the Highways and Bridges Act, 1891 (54 & 55 Vict. c. 63), *post*, whereby it is provided that s. 16 of the Highways and Locomotives (Amendment) Act, 1878, shall apply to any part of a main road in any county, and so much of that section as requires that any order made thereunder shall be provisional, and shall be confirmed as in the said Act mentioned, is hereby repealed, but no such order shall be made in respect of any main road within a municipal borough without the assent of the council of the said borough having been first obtained].

Section 17. "Where a turnpike road subject to one trust extends into divers counties, such road, for the purposes of this Act, shall be treated as a separate turnpike road in each county through which it passes."

The following cases have been decided on the foregoing sections of the Highways and Locomotives (Amendment) Act, 1878:—

A provision in Turnpike Acts coming into operation before December 31st, 1870, that turnpike trustees shall not spend money or levy toll upon certain portions of turnpike roads does not prevent such portions of the roads from being still turnpike roads on December 31st, 1870, within the meaning of s. 13 of the Highways and Locomotives (Amendment) Act, 1878. So as to an agreement under the Local Government Act, 1858 (21 & 22 Vict. c. 98), s. 41, made before December 31st, 1870, between turnpike trustees and a corporation, under which the turnpikes upon certain portions of turnpike roads were removed, and the repair of such portions was undertaken by the corporation. *West Riding JJ.* v. *Reg.*, 8 App. Cas. 781 ; 53 L. J. M. C. 41 ; 49 L. T. (N.S.) 786; 32 W. R. 253 ; 48 J. P. 228.

The corporation of the borough of Rochdale was the highway authority of the Rochdale highway area. Under ss. 47—50 of the Towns Improvement Clauses Act, 1847 (10 & 11 Vict. c. 34), the obligation to repair all public highways within the area of the "town" was imposed upon the corporation, and the turnpike trustees were forbidden to collect any toll or lay out any money on any road within that area. By a local Act of 1872 the boundaries of the borough were enlarged, and all the provisions of the Acts relating to the "town" were made applicable to the enlarged area of the borough. The effect was that further portions of turnpike roads were for the first time brought within the area of the borough, and within the operations of the Towns Improvement Clauses Act, 1847 :—*Held*, reversing the decision of the Court of Appeal, that these further portions, being only parts of turnpike roads, had not "ceased to be turnpike roads," and were not to be deemed to be "main roads" within s. 13 of the Highways and Locomotives (Amendment) Act, 1878, and that the county authority were not liable to pay half the expenses of their maintenance. *Lancashire JJ.* v. *Rochdale* (*Mayor of*), 8 App. Cas. 494 ; 53 L. J. M. C. 5 ; 49 L. T. (N.S.) 368 ; 32 W. R. 65 ; 48 J. P. 20.

In 1855 a portion of a turnpike road was included in an improvement district under a local Act incorporating the Towns Improvement Clauses Act, 1847. Thereupon, by virtue of ss. 47—51 of the latter Act, the maintenance of this portion of the road became vested in the Improvement Commissioners, and the turnpike trustees ceased to have power to collect toll or lay out money upon it. In 1877 the turnpike trust expired. The Commissioners were the highway authority for the district, and the district was a highway area within the meaning of s. 13 of the Highways and Locomotives (Amendment) Act, 1878. It was held that notwithstanding the operation of ss. 47—51 of the Towns Improvement Clauses Act, 1847, the road only ceased to be a turnpike road and became a main road within s. 13 upon the expiration of the turnpike trust ; and that as that event happened after 1870, the county authority was liable to pay to the Commissioners one half the expenses incurred by them in the maintenance of the portion of the road within their district. *Lancashire JJ.* v. *Newton-in-Makerfield Improvement Commissioners*, 11 App. Cas. 416 ; 55 L. T. (N.S.) 615 ; 35 W. R. 185 ; 56 L. J. M. C. 17 ; 51 J. P. 68.

By a local Act passed in 1874 the limits of the borough of M. were extended. By s. 20 of that Act it was enacted that the extended area "shall be exempt from all county rates save only in respect of the purposes for which any county rates are now leviable within the existing borough." At the time of the passing of that Act general county rates were leviable within the existing borough for all purposes for which such rates could be levied in any part of the riding. It was held that the saving of such liability rendered the exemption in s. 20 inoperative ; and therefore the inhabitants of the extended area of the borough were not exempt from liability to pay county rates for the maintenance of main roads under s. 13 of the Highways, etc. Act, 1878. *Middlesborough Overseers* v. *North Riding JJ.*, 12 Q. B. D. 239 ; 32 W. R. 671.

The word "situate" in s. 13 means geographically situate. *Over Darwen* (*Mayor of*) v. *Lancashire JJ.*, 15 Q. B. D. 20 ; 54 L. J. Q. B. 51 ; 52 L. T. (N.S.) 739 ; 48 J. P. 437.

Inasmuch as by ss. 35 (4) and 38 (3) of the Local Government Act, 1888, *post*, quarter sessions boroughs are urban sanitary districts within the meaning of s. 14 of the Highways, etc. Act, 1878, a question such as arose in *Kent JJ.* v.

s. 11 (1). NOTE. *Sandgate Local Board*, 7 T. L. R. 571, can hardly occur again; it was there held that where the quarter sessions had for many years paid half the expenses of maintaining a road under the belief that it was a main road for which they were liable, and it was afterwards discovered that they were not liable by reason of the road being within a borough, an action would not lie in the name of the justices to recover the sum so paid to the highway authority.

And as rural district councils have now (under s. 25 of the Local Government Act, 1894, *post*), in almost all cases superseded all other highway authorities in their district, questions are not likely to arise as to what is a highway area or a highway authority within the meaning of s. 14 and other sections of the Highways, etc., Act, 1878, in a rural district, such as the question which arose in *R.* v. *Norfolk County Council*, 60 L. J. Q. B. 379; 65 L. T. (N.S.) 222; 56 J. P. 7. With that case can now be compared *Isle of Wight Highway Commissioners* v. *Isle of Wight County Council*, 72 L. T. (N.S.) 569; 59 J. P. 438; *Marshland Smeeth and Fen District Commissioners* v. *Marshland Rural District Council*, 73 L. T. (N.S.) 563; 59 J. P. 824.

A road which had ceased to be a turnpike road within the period between December 31st, 1870, and August 16th, 1878 (the date of the passing of the Highways, etc. Act, 1878), and had become a main road, there being no application for a provisional order before February 1st, 1879 (the now repealed part of s. 16 of the Act, of 1878), is not excluded from the operation of the provisions of s. 16 above set out, and the Local Government Board has, therefore, jurisdiction to make a provisional order declaring such road an ordinary highway upon an application made subsequently to February 1st, 1879. *R.* v. *Local Government Board*, 15 Q. B. D. 70; 54 L. J. M. C. 104; 54 L. T. (N.S.) 194; 49 J. P. 580.

The changes effected by the text are very important. A main road is not, except in the case provided for by the succeeding sub-sections, repairable by the highway authority at all. The duty of repairing it belongs to the county council, who, for all purposes of repairing, etc., have the powers of a highway board.

Maintenance, Repair, Improvement, etc.—They may not merely maintain the road, but they may improve and enlarge it. The questions often raised as to the meaning of maintenance are to a great extent avoided by the language of the text. See *Amesbury Guardians* v. *Wiltshire JJ.*, 10 Q. B. D. 480; 52 L. J. M. C. 64; 31 W. R. 521; 47 J. P. 184; *Leek Improvement Commissioners* v. *Staffordshire JJ.*, 20 Q. B. D. 794: *R.* v. *Essex JJ.*, 4 T. L. R. 676; *Burnley (Mayor, etc., of)* v. *Lancaster County Council*, 54 J. P. 279; *Lancashire Road Trustees* v. *Fleaning*, W. N. 1886, p. 180; 14 Ct. of Sess. Cas. (H. L.) 18; *Warminster Local Board* v. *Wiltshire County Council*, 25 Q. B. D. 450; 59 L. J. Q. B. 434; 62 L. T. (N.S.) 902; 38 W. R. 670; 54 J. P. 375; *London (Mayor, etc., of)* v. *Barnes*, 12 T. L. R. 135. The improvements which a highway board may make in a highway are enumerated in 27 & 28 Vict. c. 101, ss. 47, 48. They include the conversion of any main that has not been stoned into a stoned road, the widening of any road, the cutting off the corners in any road where land is required to be purchased for that purpose, the levelling roads, the making any new road, and the building or enlarging bridges, and the doing of any work in respect of highways beyond ordinary repairs essential to placing any existing highway in a proper state of repair.

For the purpose of repairing main roads the county council have the same right under this section of taking gravel for repairs from a pit as a surveyor of highways. *Norfolk County Council* v. *Bittering Highway Surveyor*, 58 J. P. 497.

As to repairs where a main road is broken up for sewerage or otherwise, see sub-s. (12), *post*.

As to the liability of the county council to repair footpaths by the side of main roads, paved or pitched crossings, etc., see *Warminster Local Board* v. *Wiltshire County Council*, and other cases, the effect of which is stated in the notes to the next sub-section.

It was held in *R.* v. *Poole (Mayor, etc. of)*, 19 Q. B. D. 602; 56 L. J. M. C. 131; 57 L. T. (N.S.) 485; 36 W. R. 239; 52 J. P. 84, that an urban sanitary authority is not liable to be indicted at common law for non-repair of a highway. But they may be indicted under s. 10 of the Highways, etc. Act, 1878. *R.* v. *Wakefield (Mayor, etc. of)*, 20 Q. B. D. 810; 57 L. J. M. C. 52; 36 W. R. 911; 52 J. P. 422.

Bridges.—The county council have now all the powers formerly exercised by justices in quarter sessions as to the repair of county bridges. See s. 3 (viii.) of this Act. If the county council make any alteration in the road such as to cause a nuisance, they will be liable in damages to any person injured thereby. See *Shill* v. *Gloucestershire County Council*, "Times," October 30th, 1893; 15 M. C. C. 454. But where a road forming part of the approach to a county bridge had subsided and the county council proposed to raise it to its original height, it was held that they could not be restrained from so doing at the instance of a frontager who alleged injury to his property. *Atherton* v. *Cheshire County Council*, 60 J. P. 6. As to the liability of a canal company under the Canal Act to repair the approaches to bridges carrying main roads over a canal, see *Nottingham County Council* v. *Manchester, Sheffield, and Lincolnshire Railway Co.*, 71 L. T. (N.S.) 430.

Where a bridge at B. was partly within Staffordshire and partly within Derbyshire, and by a local Act the expenses of repairing it were to be borne equally out of the two county rates, and by virtue of s. 50 (1) (*b*), *post*, the whole of the bridges became included in the county of Stafford, it was held that the local Act remained in force and that both counties were still liable to pay equally for repairs. *In re Staffordshire and Derbyshire County Councils*, 54 J. P. 566.

Obstructions.—County councils have the powers of highway boards for preventing and removing obstructions. It has been held that the costs of prosecuting by indictment for obstructing a highway are properly chargeable as part of the cost of maintaining a highway. *R.* v. *Heath*, 29 J. P. 452. JESSEL, M.R., expressed an opinion that the Crown or the conservators of a road had by their agents a right to remove an obstruction, though a private person had no such right if he could pass without doing so, and that in any case a body or person who represented the public would have such a right after judicial determination that there was an obstruction. *Bagshaw* v. *Buxton Local Board*, 1 Ch. D. 224; 45 L. J. Ch. 260; 34 L. T. (N.S.) 112; 24 W. R. 231; 40 J. P. 197.

But in *Reynolds* v. *Presteign Urban District Council*, [1896] 1 Q. B. 604; 65 L. J. Q. B. 400; 74 L. T. (N.S.) 422; 44 W. R. 479; 12 T. L. R. 327, it was held by Lord RUSSELL OF KILLOWEN, C.J., and WRIGHT, J., that an urban district council has power to remove encroachments on highways within their district without first taking proceedings against the person alleged to have encroached. The ground of this decision was that the highway was a street vested in the district council under s. 149 of the Public Health Act, 1875: the decision will therefore, it seems, apply in favour of county councils in whom main roads are vested by sub-s. (6) of this section, *infra*; and in *Harris* v. *Northamptonshire County Council*, 61 J. P. 599, it was held by BYRNE, J., that a county council had this power as a highway authority apart from any vesting in them of the soil of the main road. See also *Louth District Council* v. *West*, 65 L. J. Q. B. 535; 12 T. L. R. 477, in which it was held by CAVE and WILLS, JJ., that a rural district council in exercising the

Sect. 11 (1).

NOTE.

duties imposed upon it by s. 26 of the Local Government Act, 1894, *post*, is entitled to remove an obstruction, and may recover the expenses incurred in so doing in an action against the obstructor. See further as to the position of highway authorities as to the removal of obstructions, *Murray* v. *Epsom Local Board*, [1897] 1 Ch. 35; 66 L. J. Ch. 107; 75 L. T. (N.S.) 579; 45 W. R. 185; 61 J. P. 71.

Roadside wastes.—The highway is presumably the entire space between the fences which has been dedicated to the public and is capable of being used for passage. *R.* v. *United Kingdom Telegraph Co.*, 3 F. & F. 73; 9 Cox C. C. 114, 174; 31 L. J. M. C. 166; 2 B. & S. 647; 6 L. T. (N.S.) 378; *Turner* v. *Ringwood Highway Board*, L. R. 9 Eq. 418; *Nicol* v. *Beaumont*, 63 L. J. Ch. 853; 50 L. T. (N.S.) 112; *Harris* v. *Northamptonshire County Council*, 61 J. P. 699; *Locke-King* v. *Woking Urban District Council*, *Times*, November 12th, 1897. But the highway does not include an open and uninclosed ditch by the side of it: *Field* v. *Thorne*, 20 L. T. (N.S.) 563; 33 J. P. 727; nor any part of the uninclosed land adjoining a highway which had never been dedicated as part of the highway though within fifteen feet from the centre of the road: *Easton* v. *Richmond Highway Board*, L. R. 7 Q. B. 69; 41 L. J. M. C. 25; 25 L. T. (N.S.) 586; 36 J. P. 485. And see *Robinson* v. *Cowpen Local Board*, 63 L. J. Q. B. 235; 9 R. 858.

The rights of a county council in respect of roadside wastes over which it was admitted that the public had a right of passage were considered in *Curtis* v. *Kesteven County Council*, 45 Ch. D. 504; 60 L. J. Ch. 103; 63 L. T. (N.S.) 543; 39 W. R. 199. In that case the facts were as follows:—A main road was 3,746 yards long; the metalled part of the road was of a uniform width of 22 feet; the total width of the road between hedge and hedge varied from 65 to 95 feet. The unmetalled portion of the road was covered with grass, timber, and other growths. C., the plaintiff, was tenant for life of the whole of the inclosed land on each side of the road. The uninclosed strips of waste land at the sides of the road were let annually by the plaintiff, C., to cottagers, two of whom were also plaintiffs. The defendants, the county council, contended that the strips were vested in them by the provisions of sub-s. (6), *infra*, and they let the herbage to L., a co-defendant. The plaintiff claimed a declaration that C. was seised of the strips, and entitled to the herbage, trees, and other growths thereon, and for an injunction restraining the defendants from cutting or removing the grass, trees, or other growths. It was held by NORTH, J., that the strips in question were "roadside wastes" within the meaning of sub-s. (1), but were not vested in the county council by sub-s. (6) of this section, and he gave the judgment claimed "without prejudice to the rights of the county council under the Local Government Act." The view taken by the learned judge was that "what the county council have given to them is a power of asserting the right of the public to the use and enjoyment of these roadside wastes"; and that seemed to him inconsistent with the idea that the waste was the property of the county council itself.

It does not appear that a highway board has any express power to assert the right of the public to the use and enjoyment of roadside wastes. But it is now the duty of every district council to prevent any unlawful encroachment on any roadside waste within their district (see the Local Government Act, 1894, s. 26 (1), *post*); and if the district council fail upon a representation being made to them by a parish council to take proper proceedings for preventing the encroachment, the county council may, upon the petition of the parish council, resolve to take over the powers and duties of the defaulting district council in that respect (*ib.* sub-s. (4)); but nothing in s. 26 of the Act of 1894 is to affect the powers of a county council in relation to roadside wastes (*ib.* sub-s. (6)). **Sect. 11 (1).**

NOTE.

For the definition of the phrase "general county purpose," see s. 68, *post*, and as to the effect of the concluding words of sub-s. (1), where main roads were partially repairable out of rates levied in the hundreds into which a county was divided, see *R.* v. *Dolby*, cited in the note to sub-s. (13), *post*.

It should be mentioned that, by s. 35, *post*, the provisions of this section are to apply to the larger quarter sessions boroughs, and these boroughs are, for the purposes of main roads, to be deemed part of the county. As to main roads in the smaller boroughs, see s. 38, *post*.

(2.) Provided that any urban authority may, within twelve months after the appointed day, or in case of a road in the district of such authority becoming a main road at any subsequent date then within twelve months after that date, claim to retain the powers and duties of maintaining and repairing a main road within the district of such authority, and thereupon they shall be entitled to retain the same, and for the purpose of the maintenance, repair, improvement, and enlargement of, and other dealing with such road, shall have the same powers and be subject to the same duties as if such road were an ordinary road vested in them, and the council shall make to such authority an annual payment towards the costs of the maintenance and repair, and reasonable improvement connected with the maintenance and repair of such road.

For the definition of the phrase "appointed day," see s. 109, *post*.

An urban authority is the council of a borough, or the district council of an urban district (Local Government Act, 1894, s. 21, *post*).

Under the Highway Act, 1878, a borough having a separate court of quarter sessions was not a highway area for the purposes of the Act, and consequently the provisions of that Act as to main roads did not apply. By ss. 35, 38, of this Act, *post*, such boroughs are to be deemed urban sanitary districts, and therefore highway areas.

If an urban authority claim to retain their right of repair, the county council will be free from liability to repair, etc.

It seems clear that a newly created urban authority cannot claim under this sub-section to take over a road within their district which has been a main road for twelve months prior to the creation of their district; nor could such a claim be made where an existing district was extended so as to include such a road. It may even be doubted whether this sub-section can be acted upon by any urban authority which was not in existence when this Act came into operation.

Considerable doubt was for some time felt as to whether upon the construction of this sub-section a county council is liable to make a payment to an urban authority which have retained the duty of maintaining and repairing a main road, for the costs of the maintenance and repair of the paved footways at the sides of the road and of the paved or pitched crossings over the main roads. This question has now been set at rest by a series of decisions in which it has been held that the county council is so liable. *In re Warminster Local Board and Wilts County Council* (GRANTHAM and CHARLES, *JJ.*) 25 Q. B. D. 450; 59 L. J. Q. B. 434; 62 L. T. (N.S.) 902;

Sect. 11 (2).

Note.

38 W. R. 671; 54 J. P. 375. *In re Burslem (Mayor, etc. of)* v. *Staffordshire County Council* (Court of Appeal), [1896] 1 Q. B. 24; 65 L. J. Q. B. 1; 73 L. T. (N.S.) 651; 59 J. P. 772; *Derby County Council* v. *Matlock Bath and Scarthin Nick Urban District Council* (House of Lords), [1896] A. C. 315. The order in the *Warminster Case* (the decision in which case was approved by the House of Lords in the *Matlock Case*) was settled by CHARLES, J., in Chambers, and is to the following effect: (1.) The county council is liable to make an annual payment towards the cost of the maintenance and repair and reasonable improvement connected with the maintenance and repair of all footpaths by the sides of main roads whether these are gravelled, paved, asphalted, etc., and whether such footpaths are or are not footpaths which the turnpike trustees were exempted from repairing under 3 Geo. 4, c. 126, s. 112. (2.) The county council are under the like liability as to paved or pitched crossings over main roads. (3.) The county council are liable to contribute an annual sum towards the cost of scavenging, cleansing, and watering main roads, in so far as such scavenging and cleansing are necessary for maintenance and repair as distinguished from purposes of public health. (4.) The county council are under no liability with respect to the lighting of main roads (see sub-s. (11), *post*). (5.) If the local authority alter the paving or flagging of the footways, as, for instance, by substituting flagging, pavement, wood, or asphalte for gravel or other substance, the county council are bound to make an annual payment in respect of such alteration, in so far as it is a reasonable improvement connected with maintenance and repair, the question whether it is reasonable in any particular case being, in case of dispute, settled by arbitration under sub-s. (3). (6.) The county council are not liable to make any payment in respect of the principal or interest of any money borrowed before the passing of this Act; but the court expressed no opinion as to moneys borrowed after that date. See further on this subject *In re Wiltshire County Council and Mayor, etc., of Marlborough*, 58 J. P. 213. In that case the court held that although the whole burden might be cast upon the county council, that council were only bound to discharge their liability in the same way as the urban authority, so that if money was borrowed or capital expenditure incurred by the urban authority, the county council were only bound to pay the instalments or were entitled to spread the expenditure over a number of years. And it was further held that this sub-section did not forbid the recovery from the county council of expenses defrayed out of borrowed money.

It has been contended that notwithstanding the use of the word "towards" in this sub-section, a county council is liable to pay the entire cost properly incurred of the maintenance, repair, and reasonable improvement of a main road retained by an urban authority; that in fact, their liability is no less than it would have been if the road had not been retained, but was maintainable and repairable by the county council under sub-s. (1). The *Marlborough Case* above cited gives some support to this view; but in *In re Bedfordshire County Council and Bedford Urban Sanitary Authority*, [1894] 2 Q. B. 786; 64 L. J. Q. B. 26; 71 L. T. (N.S.) 433; 58 J. P. 786, MATTHEW, J., said: "The legislature plainly contemplated the case ordinarily arising in which it would not be fair that the whole amount incurred in respect of repair and maintenance should be paid by the county council, although it would certainly be just that some part should be cast upon the county council. The Act does not, however, exclude cases where the whole amount of costs incurred might be paid by the county council." See also on this point *Middlesex County Council* v. *Willesden District Council*, cited *infra*.

As to the liability of a county council in respect of the cost of re-building a sea-wall and esplanade supporting a main road, see *Sandgate Local Board* v. *Kent County Council*, 13 T. L. R. 333 ; 61 J. P. 517. **Sect. 11 (2).**

NOTE.

The words "maintenance, repair, and reasonable improvement" meet the decision in *Leek Improvement Commissioners* v. *Staffordshire JJ.*, cited in the notes to the last sub-section.

As to how the amount of the annual payment is to be determined, see the next sub-section.

Where trust funds arising under various settlements were applicable for the maintenance, repair, lighting, watching, and watering of certain main roads to which this sub-section applied, the court (without dealing with any question of amount) declared that in settling the payment to be made by the county council to the urban authorities who claimed to retain the roads the existence of the trust funds ought not to be excluded from consideration, but that as the funds ought according to the trusts to be applied not only to maintenance and repair but also to lighting, watching, and watering, the amount usually required to be expended out of the trust funds on these last-mentioned purposes should not be treated as money to be brought into account in assessing the payment to be made by the county council towards maintenance, repair, and improvement. *Middlesex County Council* v. *Willesden District Council*, 60 J. P. 630 ; 12 T. L. R. 437.

(3.) The amount of such payment shall be such annual sum as may be from time to time agreed on, or in the absence of agreement may *be determined by arbitration of the Local Government Board.*

This sub-section is to have effect as if for the words printed in italics were substituted the words "be determined by the Local Government Board either as arbitrators or otherwise at the option of the Board" (Local Government (Determination of Differences) Act, 1896 (59 Vict. c. 9), s. 1, *post*). And s. 2 of the same Act provides that an order of the Board made before the passing of that Act (May 21st, 1896) and purporting to have been made for the determination of any matter under s. 11 of the Local Government Act, 1888, shall not be invalid by reason only of the Board having determined the matter as arbitrators or otherwise instead of appointing an arbitrator to determine it.

This Act seems to have been passed to meet the decision in *In re Kent County Council and Sandgate Local Board*, [1895] 2 Q. B. 43; 64 L. J. Q. B. 502 ; 72 L. T. (N.S.) 725 ; 43 W. R. 652 ; 59 J. P. 456 ; 11 T. L. R. 421, in which it was decided that where under this Act the Local Government Board are to determine differences "by arbitration" (as in the unaltered text) they must proceed under s. 63, *post*, with the consequence that an arbitrator appointed by them under that section may be compelled under s. 24 of the Arbitration Act, 1889 (52 & 53 Vict. c. 49) to state a case for the opinion of the court. In that case the Board in determining a difference under this sub-section had proceeded under s. 87, *post*, by holding a local inquiry, and the court held that this method of procedure was inapplicable. The effect of the Act of 1896 is that when the Board are called upon to determine a difference under this section they may at their option proceed under s. 63 (in which case the arbitrator appointed by them must state a case if called upon to do so) or under s. 87 (in which case the Board do not act as arbitrators and cannot be compelled to state a case).

The High Court has no jurisdiction to determine a question of amount under this sub-section. *In re Bedfordshire County Council and Bedford Urban*

Sect. 11 (3). *Sanitary Authority*, [1894] 2 Q. B. 786 ; 64 L. J. Q. B. 26 ; 71 L. T. (N.S.) 433 ; 58 J. P. 786.

NOTE.

(4.) The county council and any district council may from time to time contract for the undertaking by the district council of the maintenance, repair, improvement, and enlargement of, and other dealing with any main road, and, if the county council so require, the district council shall undertake the same, and such undertaking shall be in consideration of such annual payment by the county council for the costs of the undertaking as may from time to time be agreed upon, or, in case of difference, *be determined by arbitration of the Local Government Board;* and for the purposes of such undertaking the district council shall have the same powers and be subject to the same duties and liabilities as if the road were an ordinary road vested in them.

In this sub-section for the words printed in italics are to be substituted the words "be determined by the Local Government Board either as arbitrators or otherwise at the option of the Board" (Local Government (Determination of Differences), Act, 1896, *post.*) For the effect of this substitution, see the note to the last sub-section.

As to the meaning of the term "district council," see s. 100, *post*, and Local Government Act, 1894 (56 & 57 Vict. c. 73), ss. 21, 25.

The provisions of this sub-section apply to all main roads save those which an urban authority have elected to maintain under sub-s. (2), *ante.* The county council and district council may contract, but in the absence of contract the county council may require the district council to undertake the repair of all or any main roads in their district.

The contract may apparently be for a term of years or for any less period. An agreement under this sub-section between a county council and a highway authority does not take away from the former their rights and liabilities as the road authority under the Tramways Act, 1870. *Stockport and Hyde Highway Board* v. *Cheshire County Council*, 61 L. J. Q. B. 22 ; 65 L. T. (N.S.) 85 ; 39 W. R. 696 ; 55 J. P. 808.

The Highways and Bridges Act, 1891 (54 & 55 Vict. c. 63), *post*, contains further provisions enabling county councils and highway authorities to make agreements for the improvement, etc., of main roads, highways, and bridges.

The highway authority have no option if required by virtue of the provision in the text to undertake the maintenance, etc., of main roads. They must in that case provide the necessary cost out of the funds in their hands for the repair of the highways in their district, and the payments made to them by the county council will be paid into the same fund.

On the concluding words of this sub-section it may be observed that ordinary roads are not vested in a district council, unless such council is an urban authority, in which case the highways repairable by the inhabitants at large are vested in the authority by virtue of s. 149 of the Public Health Act, 1875. The words "vested in them" must not, therefore, be read literally, but *as equivalent to* "subject to their control," or some similar expression.

(5.) Provided that in no case shall a county council make any payment to a district council towards the costs of such undertaking as respects any road, or towards the costs of the maintenance, repair, or improvement of any road by an urban authority, until the county council are satisfied by the report of their surveyor, or such other person as the county council may appoint for the purpose, that the road has been properly maintained and repaired, or that the improvement or enlargement of or other dealing with the road, as the case may be, has been properly executed. **Sect. 11 (5).**

This sub-section has reference both to an undertaking under sub-s. (4), and to maintenance by an urban authority under sub-s. (2). As to the procedure in case of refusal to make a payment under this section, see sub-s. (9), *infra.*

(6.) A main road and the materials thereof, and all drains belonging thereto, shall, except where the urban authority retain the powers and duties of maintaining and repairing such road, vest in the county council, and where any sewer or other drain is used for any purpose in connexion with the drainage of any main road, the county council shall continue to have the right of using such sewer or drain for such purpose, and if any difference arises between a county council and any highway or sanitary authority as respects the authority in whom the drain is vested, or as to the use of any sewer or other drain, the council or the highway or sanitary authority may require such difference to be referred to arbitration, and the same shall be referred to arbitration in manner provided by this Act.

The main road, the materials thereof, and the drains belonging thereto, are to *vest* in the county council, except where the urban authority retain the right of repairing under sub-s. (2). When the urban authority does not retain this right, the road which had hitherto been vested in the urban authority by s. 149 of the Public Health Act, 1875, will cease to be vested in them, and will *vest* in the county council. The meaning of the word *vest* will appear from the following decisions on the Public Health Act, 1875, s. 149:—

In *Hinde* v. *Chorlton*, L. R. 2 C. P., at p. 116, WILLES, J., referring to the words *vest in* as used in a local Act, said, "There is a whole series of authorities in which words which in terms vested the freehold in persons appointed to perform some public duties, such as canal companies and boards of health, have been held satisfied by giving to such persons the control over the soil which was necessary to the carrying out of the objects of the Act without giving them the freehold. In *Stracey* v. *Nelson*, 12 M. & W. 535; 13 L. J. Ex. 97, it was provided by an Act that certain lands should be *vested* in the Commissioners of Sewers, and the court held, notwithstanding, that only the control over the land, and not the freehold, passed to them." In *Bagshaw* v. *Buxton Local Board* (*ante*, p. 25), 1 Ch. D., at p. 222, JESSEL, M.R., said that by the term *vested* he meant vested *sub modo*, as far as a highway can be, not necessarily giving to the local authority the right to the soil. The words *vest in* do not give the property in the street, but merely the property in the surface of the street, and in such part of the soil as is or can be used for the ordinary purposes of a street. *Coverdale* v. *Charlton*, 4 Q. B. D. 104; 48 L. J. Q. B. 128; 40 L. T. (N.S.) 88; 26 W. R. 687; 43 J. P. 268. In that case, by an award

Sect. 11 (6).

NOTE.

made under an Inclosure Act passed in 1766, two private roads, E. and H., were set out. About 1818 the road E. became a public highway. Down to 1863 the surveyors of highways for the parish of C., within which E. and H. were situate, had from time to time let the pasturage upon E. and H. to various persons. A local board was formed in 1863 for the parish of C., who in 1876 let the pasturage on E. and H. to the plaintiff. He thereupon commenced to depasture the herbage with his cattle on the roads. The defendant interfered with the plaintiff's enjoyment of the pasturage. It was held that the property in the soil of E., being a street, so far vested in the local board that they could demise the right of pasturage thereon to the plaintiff, who was entitled to maintain an action. It was held also that the local board having no power to demise H., being a private way, the plaintiff had not sufficient exclusive possession as occupier to enable him to maintain an action. In a subsequent case, JAMES, L.J., explained this decision as to the meaning of the words *vest in* as follows :—"What that case decided, and all that it was necessary to decide in that case, was that something more than an easement passed to the local board, and that they had some right of property in and on and in respect of the soil, which would enable them as owners to bring a possessory action against trespassers. Now what was that something more? It is impossible to read any of the three judgments delivered on that occasion without seeing that in the view of the learned judges the soil and freehold, in the ordinary sense of the words 'soil and freehold,' that is to say, the soil from the centre of the earth up to an unlimited extent in space, did not pass, and that no *stratum* or portion of the soil, defined or ascertainable like a vein of coal, or stratum of ironstone, or anything of that kind, passed, but that the board had only the surface, and with the surface such right below the surface as was essential to the maintenance and occupation and exclusive possession of the street, and the making and maintaining of the street for the use of the public." *Rolls* v. *St. George the Martyr, Southwark* (*Vestry of*), 14 Ch. D. 785 ; 49 L. J. Ch. 691 ; 43 L. T. (N.S.) 140 ; 28 W. R. 867 ; 44 J. P. 680. In that case the plaintiff having, with the sanction of the Metropolitan Board of Works, made a new street over his land, upon which land were two old streets, N. and A., an order was made at quarter sessions for stopping up part of N. street as unnecessary, and an order was also made for diverting a part of A. street, and opening the new street in lieu thereof. The vestry of the parish gave notice to the plaintiff that he must not convert to his own use the stopped-up part of N. nor stop up A., or convert any part of the soil of it to his own use until he had purchased the same from the vestry. It was held by the Court of Appeal, reversing the decision of the Master of the Rolls, that under 18 & 19 Vict. c. 120, s. 96, all streets being for the time being highways, are vested in the vestry, but only so long as they are highways, and that when they cease to be highways by being legally stopped up or diverted, the interest of the vestry determines. And it was therefore held that the plaintiff was entitled to convert to his own use the stopped-up part of N. and the diverted part of A., subject, as to A., to his first obtaining a certificate under 5 & 6 Vict. c. 50, s. 91, that the substituted street had been completed and put into good condition and repair. Where a street was carried across a railway situate in a deep cutting, the bridge being erected pursuant to the Railways Clauses Act, 1845 (8 & 9 Vict. c. 20, ss. 46—51), it was held that the vesting of the street in the vestry under 18 & 19 Vict. c. 120, s. 105, did not give the vestry any property in the bridges or its fences, but merely vested in them the carriageway and foothpaths and the materials of which these were made. *Great Eastern Rail. Co.* v. *Hackney Board of Works*, 8 App. Cas. 687 ; 52 L. J. M. C. 105 ; 49 L. T. (N.S.) 509 ; 48 J. P. 52. The vesting of the streets in the urban authority does not confer upon them such a property in the streets as to entitle them to maintain an action for an injunction against the erection of a telephone wire across a street, the telephone wire being erected at a great height, and causing no appreciable danger to the public or to the traffic in the street. *Wandsworth District Board of Works* v. *United Telephone Co*, 13 Q. B. D. 904 ; 53 L. J. Q. B. 449 ; 51 L. T. (N.S.) 148 ; 32 W. R. 776 ; 48 J. P. 676. The earlier cases were discussed and explained by the House of Lords in *Tunbridge Wells (Mayor, etc., of)* v. *Baird*, [1896] A. C. 434 ; 65 L. J. Q. B. 451 ; 74 L. T. (N.S.) 385 ; 60 J. P. 788. There it was held that the vesting of the street vests in the urban authority such property and such property only as is necessary for the control, protection, and maintenance of the street as a highway for public use. It has since been held that a local authority in whom a street is vested under s. 149 of the Public Health Act, 1875, have no greater right of property in the materials, etc., of such street than they have in the street itself. See *Salt Union* v. *Harvey*, 61 J. P. 212 ; 13 T. L. R. 297.

The right of the public to use a highway *primâ facie* extends not only to the *via trita*, but includes the entire space between the fences dedicated to the use of the public, and capable of being used by them. See on this subject *R.* v. *United Kingdom Telegraph Co.*, and other cases cited *ante*, p. 26. But NORTH, J., has held that the waste land at the side of the metalled portion of a main road was not vested in the county council by the text. *Curtis* v. *Kesteven County Council*, 45 Ch. D. 504; 60 L. J. Ch. 103; 63 L. T. (N.S.) 543 ; 39 W. R. 199, *ante*, p. 26.

As to the effect of the vesting of a road in a highway authority in relation to their right to remove obstructions, see *Reynolds* v. *Presteign Urban District Council*, and *Harris* v. *Northampton County Council*, referred to *ante*, p. 25.

Ordinary highway drains will vest with the main road in the county council. But where the drainage of the road flows into a drain or sewer belonging to a sanitary authority the right of user is to continue.

The mode of arbitration referred to in this sub-section is that prescribed by s. 62, sub-ss. (2), (3), *post*.

(7.) Where a county council declare a road to be a main road, such declaration shall not take effect until the road has been placed in proper repair and condition to the satisfaction of the county council.

This provision is in effect an amendment or proviso to the Highway Act, 1878, s. 15, which has been quoted in the note to sub-s. (1), *ante*. As to the method of determining any dispute arising as to the condition of the road, see sub-s. (9), *infra*.

(8.) If at any time the county council are satisfied, on the report of their surveyor or other person appointed by them for the purpose, that any portion of a main road, the maintenance and repair of which are undertaken by any district council, is not in proper repair and condition, the county council may cause notice to be given to such district council, requiring them to place the road in proper repair and condition ; and, if such notice is not complied with within a reasonable time, the county council may do everything that seems to them necessary to place the road in proper

Sect. 11 (8). repair and condition, and the expenses of so doing shall be a debt of the said district council to the county council.

This provision applies only to main roads of which the repair has been undertaken under sub-s. (4). It does not apply to main roads repaired by an urban authority under sub-s. (2). As to the method of determining cases of dispute under this sub-section, see sub-s. (9), *infra.*

The expenses incurred being hereby made a debt, will be recoverable by action in the High Court, or in the county court if less than 50*l.*

(9.) If any difference arises under this section between a county council and a district council as to the refusal of the county council to make a payment under this section to the district council in respect of any undertaking or road, or as to a road having been placed in proper repair and condition previously to its becoming a main road, or as to any notice given to the district council by the county council to place a road in proper repair and condition, such difference shall, if either council so require, *be referred to the arbitration of the Local Government Board.*

In this sub-section for the words printed in italics are to be substituted the words "be determined by the Local Government Board, either as arbitrators or otherwise, at the option of the Board" (Local Government (Determination of Differences) Act, 1896, *post*). For the effect of this sub-section, see the note to sub-s. (3), *ante.*

The differences here referred to are such as may arise under sub-ss. (5), (7), and (8).

(10.) The county council may, if they think fit, contribute towards the cost of the maintenance, repair, enlargement, and improvement of any highway or public footpath in the county, although the same is not a main road.

For the meaning of the term "improvement," see the note to sub-s. (1).

A contribution towards the cost of a highway under this sub-section may be made subject to any such conditions for the proper maintenance and repair of such highways (*sic*) as may be agreed on between the county council and the highway authority: Local Government Act, 1894, s. 25 (3), *post.*

See further as to agreements between county councils and highway authorities in relation to the construction, improvement, etc., of highways, s. 3 of the Highways and Bridges Act, 1891 (54 & 55 Vict. c. 63), *post.*

The text uses the words "highway or public footpath," but a public footpath is to all intents and purposes a highway, and is repairable like any other highway. See *per* Lord Ellenborough in *R.* v. *Salop*, 13 East, at p. 97.

(11.) Every authority having any power or duty to light the roads in their district shall have the same power and duty to light any main road in their district.

The county council are not liable to light the main roads in any case. In urban districts the power and duty devolves on the urban authority under ss. 161, 162, of the Public Health Act, 1875. They may under these sections contract for the supply of gas or other means of lighting the streets, and if there is no company having statutory powers in their district they may themselves provide a supply of gas for public or private purposes. In the latter case they may obtain a provisional order under the Gas and Waterworks Facilities Acts. They may also purchase the undertaking of any gas company in their district. Sect. 11 (11). NOTE.

In rural districts urban lighting powers may be obtained by order of the Local Government Board under s. 276 of the Public Health Act, 1875. In rural parishes powers of lighting may be obtained under the Lighting and Watching Act (3 & 4 Will. 4, c. 90), and the Local Government Act, 1894, s. 7, the lighting authority being the parish council, or where there is no parish council, inspectors appointed by the parish meeting.

An urban or rural sanitary authority may obtain a licence or provisional order for the supply of electricity for public or private purposes. See the Electric Lighting Act, 1882 (45 & 46 Vict. c. 56).

(12.) Anything authorized or required by law to be done by or to a highway or road authority shall, as respects a main road maintained by a county council, be authorized or required to be done by or to that council; and every authority having any power to break up any road in their district for the purpose of sewerage or otherwise shall have the like power of breaking up any main road in their district, but if the road is broken up the authority shall repair it to the satisfaction of the county council maintaining such road, and if it is not repaired to the satisfaction of the county council, that council may cause the necessary repairs to be done and may charge the costs against the authority, and the same shall be a debt due from the authority to the council.

This provision apparently confers upon a county council, with respect to main roads, all the powers and liabilities of a highway surveyor or a highway board.

A sanitary authority may lay sewers and water mains in any road, and may break up roads for that purpose (Public Health Act, 1875, ss. 16, 54).

Among other authorities who may break up roads may be mentioned water companies under the Waterworks Clauses Act, 1847, ss. 28—34; gas companies under the Gasworks Clauses Act, 1847, ss. 6—12; tramway companies under the Tramways Act, 1870, ss. 26, 27, 30; electric lighting companies under the Electric Lighting Act, 1882, ss. 12, 13.

The provisions of the text as to the reinstating of the road are in addition to those contained in the above Acts.

(13.) Section twenty of the Highways and Locomotives (Amendment) Act, 1878, shall apply as if it were herein re-enacted and in terms made applicable to this section. 41 & 42 Vict. c. 77.

The 41 & 42 Vict. c. 77, s. 20, is as follows:—

"Notwithstanding the provisions of this Act, in the case of any county in which certain of the bridges within the county are repairable by the county at large, and others are repairable by the several hundreds within the county

Sect. 11 (13).

NOTE.

in which they are situate, it shall be lawful for the county authority from time to time, by order, to declare any main road or part of a main road within their county to be repairable to the extent only and in manner provided by section thirteen of this Act, either by the county or by the hundred in which such main road or part is situate, as they think fit; and where a main road or part thereof is declared to be repairable by a hundred, the expense of repairing the same shall, to the extent to which but for this section the expense or any contribution towards the expense of repairing the same would be repayable out of the county rate, be repayable out of a separate rate which shall be raised and charged in the like manner as the expenses of repairing the hundred bridges in the same hundred would have been raised and charged."

The following is an extract from a letter dated September 18th, 1878, from the Local Government Board with reference to this section :—

"The wording of this section, which was introduced at a very late stage of the Bill, and is limited in its application to the county of Lancaster chiefly, is somewhat obscure ; and it may be assumed that the effect of declaring a main road repairable by the hundred is simply intended to be that the hundred rate shall be substituted for the county rate as the fund from which a moiety of the cost is to be repaid to the highway authorities. The justices will not fail to observe that where the alternative given by the section is adopted, it is desirable that all the main roads in the county should be declared to be repairable by the several hundreds through which they pass, otherwise the ratepayers of those hundreds will not only have to contribute towards the roads within their own hundreds, but also towards any roads within the county in respect of which a contribution is payable from the county rate."

The provisions of the above section remain in force where it is applicable. The hundred rate is made and levied by the county council under s. 3 (1), *ante.*

The county authority of a county (Lancaster), the whole of which was divided into hundreds, made an order under s. 20 of the Highways and Locomotives (Amendment) Act, 1878, declaring every main road in each hundred to be repairable by that hundred, and one-half the expense of repairing the same to be repayable out of a separate rate levied on the hundred.

Held, that the maintenance and repair of main roads in the hundreds were "general county purposes" within the meaning of ss. 11, 23, and 68 of the Local Government Act, 1888, so that the county council were entitled to apply moneys taken from the Exchequer contribution account in recouping the general county fund so much of the costs of such maintenance and repair as was not provided for by the special rates on the hundreds. *R.* v. *Dolby*, [1892] 2 Q. B. 736 ; 61 L. J. Q. B. 826 ; 67 L. T. (N.S.) 619.

Roads and tolls in Isle of Wight.

12.—(1.) After the appointed day, tolls shall cease to be taken on any road maintained and repaired by the Isle of Wight Highway Commissioners, under the Isle of Wight Highway Acts, 1813 and 1883, and after such day the Highways and Locomotives (Amendment) Act, 1878, as amended by this Act, shall apply to the Isle of Wight, and to every such road above mentioned, in like manner as if it were ceasing within the meaning of the said Act to be a turnpike road, and the Act of the session of the forty-fourth and forty-fifth years of the reign of Her present Majesty, chapter seventy-two, shall be repealed.

44 & 45 Vict c. 72.

Sect. 12 (1).

NOTE.

The Isle of Wight Highway Acts are 53 Geo. 3, c. xcii. and 46 & 47 Vict. c. ccxxvi.

The Isle of Wight was formerly exempt from the operation of the Highway Acts. See 5 & 6 Will. 4, c. 50, s. 113 ; 25 & 26 Vict. c. 61, s. 7 ; 41 & 42 Vict. c. 77, ss. 2, 27 ; 44 & 45 Vict. c. 72. The text repeals the last-mentioned Act, which exempted the Isle of Wight from liability to contribute to the county rate for the expenses of main roads ; this exemption is now taken away and the roads in the island are now repairable as main roads.

(2.) Until provision is otherwise made by Parliament, or by a provisional order confirmed by Parliament, the repair and maintenance of the said roads shall continue to be undertaken by the said commissioners, and the county council for the county of Southampton shall pay such commissioners, in respect of the said repairs and maintenance, and of the expenses of the commissioners, such sums as may be agreed upon, or, in case of difference, be settled by arbitration under this Act, and the provisions of this Act with respect to main roads shall apply as if the commissioners were a district council who had undertaken the maintenance and repair of such road.

In the year 1889 the Isle of Wight was made a separate administrative county by provisional order confirmed by 52 & 53 Vict. cc. lxxvii. Article 21 of the Order provides for the substitution of the county council of the Isle of Wight for that of the County of Southampton in the text.

The commissioners above referred to were the Isle of Wight Highway Commissioners mentioned in the preceding sub-section, appointed under 46 & 47 Vict. c. ccxxvi., ss. 5—15. These commissioners were abolished by the Local Government Act, 1894, s. 25, *post*, and their duties under this section were transferred to the rural district councils. *In re the Isle of Wight Highway Commissioners* 78 L. T. (N.S.) 569 ; 59 J. P. 438.

It should be observed that the text provides only for the cost of repair and maintenance ; the words "improvement and enlargement of and otherwise dealing with" used in s. 11 *ante*, are here omitted ; the arbitration, moreover, is under s. 62, and not by the Local Government Board as under s. 11.

Adaptation of Act to South Wales roads.

13.—(1.) After the appointed day no county road rate shall be levied, and tolls shall cease to be taken on any road maintained and repaired by a county roads board in South Wales, in pursuance of the South Wales Turnpike Trusts Act, 1844, and the Acts amending the same, and after such day the Highways and Locomotives (Amendment) Act, 1878, as amended by this Act, shall apply to every county in South Wales as if the highway districts in that county had been constituted under the Highway Act, 1862, and the Highway Act, 1864, or one of those Acts, and shall apply to every such road as above-mentioned, in like manner as if it were ceasing, within the meaning of the said Act, to be a turnpike road.

7 & 8 Vict. c. 91.

25 & 26 Vict. c. 61.

27 & 28 Vict. c. 101.

By 7 & 8 Vict. c. 91, in each of the six counties of South Wales—namely, Glamorgan, Brecknock, Radnor, Carmarthen, Pembroke, and Cardigan—a

Sect. 13 (1)

NOTE.

county roads board was appointed, consisting of from six to twelve justices appointed by quarter sessions and certain *ex officio* members, to have the superintendence, control, and management of all turnpike roads in the county. They had power to continue existing toll gates and to erect others and to take tolls. They might discontinue tolls on any road, and thereupon such road became an ordinary highway. By the same Act the commissioners who were appointed by the Act "for consolidating and adjusting the turnpike trusts of South Wales" might mark out and define in each county districts, which, subject to the superintendence and authority of the county roads board, should be placed under the care and management of district roads boards. The members of these district boards were originally nominated by the commissioners out of persons possessing a prescribed qualification, all justices residing within the district being *ex officio* members; vacancies were from time to time filled up by the board, the elective members retiring by rotation. The officers of the district boards were appointed by the county roads board. The duties of a district board were to direct and superintend all matters and things relating to the maintaining, repairing, and draining of the turnpike roads in the district, and the execution of any work or improvement placed under their direction and superintendence by the county roads board. Each district board annually elected two members to serve on the county road board. The tolls received were paid into the county roads fund, and if that were insufficient for the expenses payable out of it, the quarter sessions had to make a county road rate to supply the deficiency.

By 14 & 15 Vict. c. 16, the county roads board of each county was required to divide the county into highway districts for the separate management of the ordinary highways therein. For each district a highway board was to be appointed, consisting of the guardians elected for each parish in the district and the resident justices. The Act was repealed by 23 & 24 Vict. c. 68, but the repeal did not affect existing districts. The county roads board were empowered to alter districts and appoint surveyors for each district. All land or property which would otherwise have become vested in the surveyor of any parish under 5 & 6 Will. 4, c. 50, was transferred to the highway board, which took over the care and management of the ordinary highways.

The expenses of maintenance, etc., are chargeable to each parish and levied by a highway rate. Subject to the provisions of the Act and later amending Acts, the 5 & 6 Will. 4, c. 50, applies to ordinary highways in South Wales.

The text abolishes these county roads boards and makes the roads formerly repairable by them main roads. Consequently they are now repairable by the county councils under the provisions of s. 11, *ante*, and that section applies in all respects as if these roads had been main roads under the Highways, etc., Act, 1878.

(2.) On the appointed day every county roads board and district roads board in each county shall cease to exist, and the property, debts, and liabilities of any such board shall be transferred to the county council, and that council shall be the successors of the county and district roads boards, and the provisions of this Act, with respect to the transfer of the property, debts, and liabilities of quarter sessions to county councils, and with respect to the officers and servants of quarter sessions, shall apply as if they were herein re-enacted and made applicable to the property, debts, liabilities, and officers of the said county and district roads boards.

As to these county roads boards and district roads boards, see note to sub-s. (1) *supra*. These bodies are now abolished, and their property, debts, etc., are transferred to the county councils in like manner as if it were property, etc., under s. 64, *post*. The provisions as to officers are contained in ss. 118 -120, *post*.

(3.) For the following purposes (that is to say):

(*a*.) For giving effect to the said transfer of the property, debts, and liabilities, and for controlling the officers and servants transferred by this section to the county council, and otherwise winding up the affairs of the county and district roads boards; and

(*b*.) For the purpose of the appointment of the surveyor of a highway board, the alteration of a highway district, and other purposes relating to highway boards;

the county council of every county in South Wales shall have all the powers of a county roads board in a county under the South Wales Turnpike Trusts Act, 1844, and the Acts amending the same, so, however, that nothing shall confer on the county council any power to levy any toll or county road rate.

This provision simply provides that the county councils shall have all the powers of a county roads board for the purposes specified.

The surveyor of a highway board is appointed under 23 & 24 Vict. c. 68, s. 3; highway districts are altered under s. 2.

Power to county council to enforce provisions of 39 & 40 Vict. c. 75.

14.—(1.) On and after the appointed day a county council shall have power, in addition to any other authority, to enforce the provisions of the Rivers Pollution Prevention Act, 1876 (subject to the restrictions in that Act contained), in relation to so much of any stream as is situate within, or passes through or by, any part of their county, and for that purpose they shall have the same powers and duties as if they were a sanitary authority within the meaning of that Act, or any other authority having power to enforce the provisions of that Act, and the county were their district.

Parts I. and II. of the Rivers Pollution Prevention Act, 1876, relate to pollution of streams by solid matters and sewage. Section 6 provides that proceedings shall not be taken under Part III. of the Act (which deals with manufacturing and mining pollution), save by a sanitary authority and with the consent of the Local Government Board. If the sanitary authority, on the application of a person interested, refuses to take proceedings, such person may apply to the Local Government Board, who, after inquiry, may direct the sanitary authority to take proceedings. The Local Government Board are not to give their consent to proceedings by the sanitary authority of any district which is the seat of any manufacturing industry, unless they are satisfied, after due inquiry, that means for rendering harmless the poisonous, noxious, or polluting

Sect. 14 (1).

NOTE.

liquids proceeding from the processes of such manufactures, are reasonably practicable and available under all the circumstances of the case, and that no material injury will be inflicted by such proceedings on the interests of such industry. Any person against whom proceedings are proposed to be taken under Part III. of the Act, notwithstanding any consent of the Local Government Board, may object before the sanitary authority to such proceedings being taken, and the authority must, if required in writing by such person, afford him an opportunity of being heard against such proceedings being taken, so far as the same relate to his works or manufacturing processes. The authority must thereupon allow such person to be heard by himself, agents, and witnesses, and after inquiry such authority must determine, having regard to all the considerations to which the Local Government Board are by the section directed to have regard, whether such proceedings shall be taken or not. When any authority has taken proceedings under the Act, no other sanitary authority may take proceedings under this Act, until the party against whom the proceedings are intended has failed in reasonable time to carry out the order of any competent court under the Act. By s. 8, every sanitary authority, subject to the restrictions in the Act, have power to enforce the provisions of the Act in relation to any stream being within or passing through or by any part of their district, and for that purpose to institute proceedings in respect of any offence against the Act which causes interference with the due flow within their district of any stream, or the pollution within their district of any stream, against any other sanitary authority or person, whether such offence is committed within or without the district of the first-named sanitary authority. Proceedings under the Act may be taken in the county court (s. 10). By s. 13, two months' notice of proceedings under the Act must be given.

The provision in the text enables a county council to institute proceedings under the Rivers Pollution Prevention Act, in all cases in which that could be done by a sanitary authority, and, of course they will be able to institute proceedings against any sanitary authority in respect of sewage pollution.

Proceedings against a sanitary authority are facilitated by the 56 & 57 Vict. c. 31 (1893), which provides that where any sewage matter falls or flows or is carried into any stream after passing through or along a channel which is vested in a sanitary authority, the sanitary authority shall for the purposes of s. 3 of the Act of 1876, be deemed to knowingly permit the sewage matter so to fall, flow, or be carried.

This Act may be said to embody the decisions in *Yorkshire West Riding County Council* v. *Holmfirth Urban Sanitary Authority*, [1894] 2 Q. B. 842; 63 L. J. Q. B. 485; 71 L. T. (N.S.) 217; 59 J. P. 213. See also s. 17 of the Public Health Act, 1875, and the notes thereto in Lumley's Public Health. The Acts of 1876 and 1893 are set out in the last mentioned work pp. 1058, 1336.

(2.) Any county council shall have power to contribute towards the costs of any prosecution under the said Act instituted by any other county council or by any urban or rural authority.

The prosecution here referred to is a proceeding in the county court under the Act.

(3.) The Local Government Board, by Provisional Order made on the application of the council of any of the counties concerned, may constitute a joint committee or other body representing all the administrative counties through or by which a river, or any specified portion of a river, or any tributary thereof, passes, and may confer on such committee or body all of the powers of a sanitary authority under the Rivers Pollution Prevention Act, 1876, or such of them as may be specified in the Order; and the Order may contain such provisions respecting the constitution and proceedings of the said committee or body as may seem proper, and may provide for the payment of the expenses of such committee or body by the administrative counties represented by it, and for the audit of the accounts of such committee or body, and their officers. Sect. 14 (3).

As to the making of a Provisional Order, see s. 87, *post*.

As to the definition of an "administrative county," see s. 100, *post*.

The joint committee may be invested under this sub-section with all necessary powers to prevent the pollution of a stream at any point of its course. Under sub-s. (1) the control of a county council is limited to so much of the stream as is within or adjoins the county.

Council to have power to oppose Bills in Parliament.

15. The county council of an administrative county shall have the same powers of opposing Bills in Parliament, and of prosecuting or defending any legal proceedings necessary for the promotion or protection of the interests of the inhabitants of the county, as are conferred on the council of a municipal borough by the Act of the thirty-fifth and thirty-sixth years of Victoria, chapter ninety-one; and subject as hereinafter provided the provisions of that Act shall extend to a county council as if such council were included in the expression "governing body," and the administrative county were the district in the said Act mentioned.

Provided that—

(*a*.) No consent of owners and ratepayers shall be required for any proceedings under this section;

(*b*.) This section shall not empower a county council to promote any Bill in Parliament, or to incur or charge any expense in relation thereto.

The Municipal Corporations (Borough Funds) Act, 1872 (35 & 36 Vict. c. 91), s. 2, enables a governing body to promote or oppose any local and personal Bill in Parliament, or to prosecute or defend any legal proceedings necessary for the promotion or protection of the interest of the inhabitants of the district, and to apply the public funds or rates under their control to the payment of the costs and expenses attending the same. This power is now extended to county councils, except that they have no power to promote a Bill in Parliament. The Act further provides that no parliamentary costs shall be incurred except in pursuance of a resolution of an absolute majority of the whole number of the governing body, after ten clear days' notice by public advertisement of such meeting and of the purpose thereof in some local newspaper published or circulating in the district, such notice to be in addition to the ordinary notices required for summoning such meeting. Further, the resolution must be published twice in a local newspaper, and must receive the approval of the Local Government Board in respect of matters within the jurisdiction of that Board, and in respect of other matters of a Secretary of State. The text dispenses with the consent of the owners and

Sect. 15.

NOTE.

ratepayers of the district, which must be given in the case of other governing bodies.

It does not follow, however, from the Borough Funds Act as applied by the text, that the county council will have no power to institute or defend legal proceedings, or to oppose Bills in Parliament, except pursuant to the provisions of that Act. A body like a county council may have power independently of any statute to devote the funds in their hands for the protection of the rates or of their powers and privileges. See on this subject *Bright* v. *North*, 2 Ph. 216; *Att.-Gen.* v. *Wigan (Corporation of)*, Kay, 268; 5 D. M. & G. 52; *R.* v. *Sheffield (Mayor, etc., of)*, L. R. 6 Q. B. 652; *R.* v. *Kingsbridge Highway Board*, 32 J. P. 562; *Att.-Gen.* v. *Brecon (Mayor, etc. of)*, 10 Ch. D. 204; *R.* v. *White*, 14 Q. B. D. 358; 54 L. J. M. C. 23; 52 L. T. (N.S.) 116; 23 W. R. 248; 49 L. P. 294; *Cleverton* v. *St. Germains Rural Sanitary Authority*, 56 L. J. Q. B. 83.

The 54 Vict. c. 12 provides that a county council shall be entitled to be a petitioner and to appear and oppose any Bill to confirm a Provisional Order made under s. 24 of the Railway and Canal Traffic Act, 1888, and to provide or contribute towards providing the expenses of the appearance or opposition of a petitioner out of the funds or rates under their control, as if the Bill was a local or personal Bill within the meaning of s. 2 of the Borough Funds Act, and the provisions of that Act are to apply to any such appearance or opposition, and to any expenses incurred or to be incurred in relation thereto. It is further provided that no consent of owners or ratepayers shall be required.

Power of county council to make bye-laws.

45 & 46 Vict. c. 50.

38 & 39 Vict. c. 55.

16.—(1.) A county council shall have the same power of making bye-laws in relation to their county, or to any specified part or parts thereof, as the council of a borough have of making bye-laws in relation to their borough under section twenty-three of the Municipal Corporations Act, 1882, and section one hundred and eighty-seven of the Public Health Act, 1875, shall apply to such bye-laws:

(2.) Provided that bye-laws made under the powers of this section shall not be of any force or effect within any borough.

The provisions of s. 23 of the Municipal Corporations Act, 1882, are set out, *post*. See the notes to that section, where the cases are collected.

Section 187 of the Public Health Act, 1875, is as follows:—

"Bye-laws made by the council of any borough under the provisions of section ninety of the Act of the sixth year of King William the Fourth chapter seventy-six, for the prevention and suppression of certain nuisances, shall not be required to be sent to a Secretary of State, nor shall they be subject to the disallowance in that section mentioned; but all the provisions of this Act relating to bye-laws shall apply to the bye-laws so made as if they were made under this Act."

It would appear at first sight that all bye-laws made by a county council under the provisions in the text (whether for good rule and government, or for the prevention and suppression of nuisances), require to be confirmed by the Local Government Board under ss. 187 and 184 of the Public Health Act, 1875. But reading s. 23 of the Municipal Corporations Act, 1882 (which is incorporated by s. 75, *post*), with the present section, the true view seems to be that in the case of a county council, as well as of a borough council, bye-laws for good rule and government come into force on the expiration of forty days after a copy has been sent to the Secretary of State, if not disallowed in the interval, and do not require confirmation by the Local Government Board under the Public Health Act. This view has been acted on by that Board, and was upheld by LINDLEY and KAY, L.JJ. (sitting as a Divisional Court), in *Strickland* v. *Hayes*, 65 L. J. M. C. 55; 74 L. T. (N.S.) 137; 44 W. R. 398; 60 J. P. 164; the decision on this point is omitted from the report of the same case, [1896] 1 Q. B. 290. And in *Mantle* v. *Jordan*, [1897] 1 Q. B. 248; 66 L. J. Q. B. 224; 75 L. T. (N.S.) 552; 61 J. P. 119, although the point was not argued, a bye-law of a county council for good rule and government, approved only by the Secretary of State, was held to be valid by WILLS and WRIGHT, JJ. Bye-laws for the prevention and suppression of nuisances must be made and confirmed pursuant to ss. 182—186 of the Public Health Act, which are as follows :—

"182. All bye-laws made by a local authority under and for the purposes of this Act shall be under their common seal; and any such bye-law may be altered or repealed by a subsequent bye-law made pursuant to the provisions of this Act: Provided that no bye-law made under this Act by a local authority shall be of any effect if repugnant to the laws of England or to the provisions of this Act.

"183. Any local authority may, by any bye-laws made by them under this Act, impose on offenders against the same such reasonable penalties as they think fit, not exceeding the sum of five pounds for each offence, and in the case of continuing offence a further penalty not exceeding forty shillings for each day after written notice of the offence from the local authority: but all such bye-laws imposing any penalty shall be so framed as to allow of the recovery of any sum less than the full amount of the penalty.

"Nothing in the provisions of any Act incorporated herewith shall authorize the imposition or recovery under any bye-laws made in pursuance of such provisions of any greater penalty than the penalties in this section specified.

"184. Bye-laws made by a local authority under this Act shall not take effect unless and until they have been submitted to and confirmed by the Local Government Board, which Board is hereby empowered to allow or disallow the same as it may think proper; nor shall any such bye-laws be confirmed—

"Unless notice of intention to apply for confirmation of the same has been given in one or more of the local newspapers circulated within the district to which such bye-laws relate, one month at least before the making of such application; and

"Unless for one month at least before any such application a copy of the proposed bye-laws has been kept at the office of the local authority, and has been open during office hours thereat to the inspection of the ratepayers of the district to which such bye-laws relate, without fee or reward.

"The clerk of the local authority shall, on the application of any such ratepayer, furnish him with a copy of such proposed bye-laws or any part thereof, on payment of sixpence for every hundred words contained in such copy.

"A bye-law required to be confirmed by the Local Government Board shall not require confirmation, allowance, or approval by any other authority.

"185. All bye-laws made by a local authority under this Act, or for purposes the same as or similar to those of this Act under any local Act, shall be printed and hung up in the office of such authority; and a copy thereof shall be delivered to any ratepayer of the district to which such bye-laws relate, on his application for the same; a copy of any bye-laws made by a rural authority shall also be transmitted to the overseers of every parish to which

Sect. 16 (2).

NOTE.

such bye-laws relate, to be deposited with the public documents of the parish, and to be open to the inspection of any ratepayer of the parish at all reasonable hours.

"186. A copy of any bye-law made under this Act by a local authority (not being the council of a borough), signed and certified by the clerk of such authority to be a true copy and to have been duly confirmed, shall be evidence until the contrary is proved in all legal proceedings of the due making, confirmation and existence of such bye-laws without further or other proof."

The provisions of the last of the above-quoted sections should be noticed, as they supersede apparently s. 24 of the Municipal Corporations Act, 1882, so far as regards bye-laws made by a county council for the suppression of nuisances.

Power of county councils to appoint medical officer of health.

17.—(1.) The council of any county may, if they see fit, appoint and pay a medical officer of health, or medical officers of health, who shall not hold any other appointment or engage in private practice without express written consent of the council.

For the qualification of these medical officers of health, see the next section.

(2.) The county council and any district council may from time to time make and carry into effect arrangements for rendering the services of such officer or officers regularly available in the district of the district council, on such terms as to the contribution by the district council to the salary of the medical officer, or otherwise, as may be agreed, and the medical officer shall have within such district all the powers and duties of a medical officer appointed by a district council.

The powers and duties of a medical officer of health appointed by a district council (*i.e.*, by a sanitary authority; see s. 100, *post*) are contained in the Public Health Act, 1875, but are too numerous to be stated here in detail.

(3.) So long as such an arrangement is in force, the obligation of the district council under the Public Health Act, 1875, to appoint a medical officer of health shall be deemed to be satisfied without the appointment of a separate medical officer.

The obligation of a district council here referred to is that arising under ss. 189, 190, of the Public Health Act, 1875. If the district council enter into an arrangement with the county council under sub-s. (2), they need not appoint a medical officer for their own district.

Qualification of medical officers of health.

18. Except where the Local Government Board, for reasons brought to their notice, may see fit in particular cases specially to allow, no person shall hereafter be appointed the medical officer of health of any county or county district, or combination of county districts, or the deputy of any such officer, unless he be legally qualified for the practice of medicine, surgery, and midwifery.

For definition of "county district," see s. 100, *post*.

A county district is an urban or rural district. See s. 100, *post*, and s. 21 (3) of the Local Government Act, 1894, *post*.

The Public Health Act, 1875, s. 191, simply required that a medical officer of health should be a legally qualified medical practitioner, *i.e.*, simply a

Sect. 18.

NOTE.

person registered under 21 & 22 Vict. c. 90. A person might, before June 1st, 1887, when the 49 & 50 Vict. c. 48 came into operation, have been registered though qualified for the practice of medicine only, or of surgery only. A medical officer of health must now possess the triple qualification, unless the Local Government Board grants a special dispensation, and this cannot be done in cases falling within the next sub-section.

The same medical officer may be appointed for two or more districts under s. 191 of the Public Health Act, 1875, with the sanction of the Local Government Board. And by s. 286 the Local Government Board may, by order, unite two or more districts in the same county for the purpose of appointing a medical officer of health. The same section provides that in case of illness or incapacity of the medical officer of health, a local authority may appoint and pay a deputy medical officer, subject to the approval of the Local Government Board.

(2.) No person shall after the first day of January, one thousand eight hundred and ninety-two, be appointed the medical officer of health of any county or of any such district or combination of districts, as contained, according to the last published census for the time being, a population of fifty thousand or more inhabitants, unless he is qualified as above-mentioned, and also either is registered in the medical register as the holder of a diploma in sanitary science, public health, or State medicine under section twenty-one of the Medical Act, 1886, or has been during three consecutive years preceding the year one thousand eight hundred and ninety-two a medical officer of a district or combination of districts, with a population according to the last published census of not less than twenty thousand, or has before the passing of this Act been for not less than three years a medical officer or inspector of the Local Government Board.

49 & 50 Vict. c. 48.

Since January 1st, 1892, it has not been lawful to appoint a medical officer of health for any county, district, or combination of districts containing a population of over 50,000, unless he possesses the triple qualification already mentioned, and has, in addition, either (1) been registered as the holder of a diploma in sanitary science under 49 & 50 Vict. c. 48, s. 21; or (2) during 1889, 1890, and 1891 been a medical officer for a district or combination of districts having a population of over 20,000; or (3) been for three years previous to August 13th, 1888, a medical officer or inspector of the Local Government Board.

The 49 & 50 Vict. c. 48, s. 21, provides that every registered medical practitioner to whom a diploma for proficiency in sanitary science, public health, or State Medicine has, after special examination, been granted by any college or faculty of physicians or surgeons, or university, in the United Kingdom, or by any such bodies acting in combination, shall, if such diploma appears to the Privy Council, or to the General Council, to deserve recognition in the medical register, be entitled, on payment of such fee as the General Council may appoint, to have such diploma entered in the said register, in addition to any other diploma or diplomas in respect of which he is registered.

The medical officer of health of the Local Government Board is appointed under 21 & 22 Vict. c. 97, s. 4; 34 & 35 Vict. c. 70. Inspectors are appointed under 10 & 11 Vict. c. 109, s. 19, and 34 & 35 Vict. c. 70.

Sect. 19.

Power of county council as to report of medical officer of health.

19.—(1.) Every medical officer of health for a district in any county shall send to the county council a copy of every periodical report of which a copy is for the time being required by the regulations of the Local Government Board to be sent to the Board, and if a medical officer fails to send such copy the county council may refuse to pay any contribution, which otherwise the council would in pursuance of this Act pay, towards the salary of such medical officer.

The periodical reports here referred to are those prescribed by the Local Government Orders, which are set out in the Appendix to Lumley's Public Health, at p. 1497. They include the periodical reports as to sickness and mortality and the annual report made in the month of December in every year.

The contribution of the county council towards the salary of the medical officer is payable under s. 24, sub-s. (2), *post.*

(2.) If it appears to the county council from any such report that the Public Health Act, 1875, has not been properly put in force within the district to which the report relates, or that any other matter affecting the public health of the district requires to be remedied, the council may cause a representation to be made to the Local Government Board on the matter.

This representation will probably amount to a complaint under s. 299 of the Public Health Act, 1875. If so, the Local Government Board, if satisfied of the alleged default after due inquiry, may make an order on the local authority for the performance of their duty, and may enforce this order by *mandamus*, or they may appoint a person for the performance of the duty and recover the expenses from the authority.

A further remedy in a case where a district council have failed to enforce the Public Health Acts may be put in force by the county council on the complaint of a parish council or parish meeting: Local Government Act, 1894, ss. 16, 19 (8), *post.*

Financial Relations between Exchequer and County, and Contributions by County for Costs of Union Officers.

Payment to county council of proceeds of duties on local taxation licences.

20.—(1.) After the financial year ending on the thirty-first day of March next after the passing of this Act, the Commissioners of Inland Revenue shall from time to time, in such manner and under such regulations as the Treasury from time to time prescribe, pay into the Bank of England to such account (in this Act referred to as the Local Taxation Account) as may be fixed by the regulations, such sums as may be ascertained in manner provided by the regulations, to be the proceeds of the duties collected by those Commissioners in each administrative county in England and Wales on the licences (in this Act referred to as local taxation licences) specified in the First Schedule to this Act, and for the purposes of this section all penalties and forfeitures recovered in respect of the said duties shall be considered as part of the proceeds of the duties. Sect. 20 (1)

As to the financial year, see s. 73, *post*.

For the definition of "administrative county," see s. 100, *post*.

See Schedule I., *post*, as to the licences here referred to.

In addition to these licences however, the excise duty and the duty on the licence for a light locomotive are to be dealt with in manner directed with respect to duties on local taxation licences, within the meaning of this Act. See Locomotives on Highways Act, 1896 (59 & 60 Vict. c. 36), s. 8, Appendix, *post*.

There has also to be paid into the Local Taxation Account the annual grant under the Agricultural Rates Act, 1896 (59 & 60 Vict. c. 16); that grant has to be issued from the account half-yearly to each spending authority in manner provided by the Act, which is set out in the Appendix, *post*.

(2.) The amount ascertained as aforesaid to have been collected in each county in respect of duties on local taxation licences shall, from time to time, be certified by the Commissioners of Inland Revenue, and paid under the direction of the Local Government Board out of the Local Taxation Account to the council of such county. The Commissioners may, if they think fit, vary such certificate, but unless so varied, their certificate shall be conclusive.

The amount is to be ascertained in manner provided by the regulations of the Treasury, under sub-s. (1).

(3.) It shall be lawful for Her Majesty the Queen from time to time, by Order in Council made on the recommendation of the Treasury, to transfer to county councils as from the date specified in the Order the power to levy the duties on all or any of the local taxation licences, and after such date every county council and their officers shall (subject nevertheless to any exceptions and modifications contained in the Order) have within their county, for the purpose of levying the duties transferred, the same powers, duties, and liabilities as the Commissioners of Inland Revenue and their officers have with respect to the duties transferred, and to the issue and cancellation of licences on which the duties are imposed, and other matters under the Acts relating to those duties and licences, and all enactments relating to those duties and licences, and to punishments and penalties connected therewith, shall apply accordingly.

The duties are still collected, and the Acts relating to the licences enforced, by the officers of Inland Revenue as heretofore, the amount levied being paid in to the Local Taxation Account under sub-s. (1). The text enables all the powers, etc., as to the levying and enforcing of these duties, to be transferred to the county council and their officers, subject to the provisions of the next sub-section, but no Order in Council making such transfer has yet been made.

Sect. 20 (4).

(4.) Provided as follows:—

(i.) All penalties and forfeitures recovered by a county council in pursuance of this section shall, instead of being paid to the Exchequer, be paid to the county fund, and carried to the same account as the duties.

(ii.) The county council shall have, as respects the said duties and licences, the power given by the said Acts to the Treasury for the restoration of any forfeiture, and the mitigation or remission of any penalty or any part thereof.

(iii.) Nothing in this section shall confer on the county council any special privileges of the Crown as respects legal proceedings.

As to the county fund and accounts, see s. 68. The duties and penalties will be paid to the Exchequer Contribution Account, under s. 23, *post*.

As to the powers of the Treasury to restore forfeitures, etc., see now 53 & 54 Vict. c. 21, s. 35.

See also s. 98, which contains a saving for the powers of Commissioners of Inland Revenue and Customs.

(5.) On a transfer under this section of the power to levy the duties on any licence—

(*a.*) The county council shall provide for issuing, in different parts of their county, their licence for the same purpose, so as to enable persons to obtain it near their residences; and

(*b.*) If such licence has operation in any place in the United Kingdom outside the county in which it is issued, the licence of a county council for the same purpose shall continue to have the like operation outside the county in such place.

Many licences, such as gun and dog licences, are available throughout the country. Such licences would have the same operation notwithstanding any transfer made under this section.

Grant to county council of portion of probate duty.

21. After the financial year ending the 31st day ot March next after the passing of this Act, the Commissioners of Inland Revenue shall, from time to time, in such manner and under such regulations as the Treasury may from time to time prescribe, pay into the Bank of England to the Local Taxation Account, such sums as may be ascertained in manner provided by the regulations to be four-fifths parts of one half of the proceeds of the sums collected by them in respect of the probate duties, and for the purpose of this section "probate duties" means the stamp duties charged on the affidavit required from persons applying for probate or letters of administration in England, Wales, or Ireland, and on the

Sect. 21.

inventory exhibited and recorded in Scotland, and also the stamp duties charged on such accounts of personal and movable property as are specified in section thirty-eight of the Customs and Inland Revenue Act, 1881, and also includes the proceeds of all penalties and forfeitures recovered in relation to such stamp duties.

44 & 45 Vict. c. 12.

The Finance Act, 1894 (57 & 58 Vict. c. 30), s. 19, provides that in substitution for the grant out of the probate duties under this Act, there shall be paid out of the proceeds of the estate duty derived from personal property such sum as the Commissioners in accordance with regulations made by the Treasury under this Act may determine to be an amount equal to one and a-half per cent. on the net value of such of the property in respect of which estate duty is leviable as would formerly have been chargeable with the duty imposed by s. 27 of the Customs and Inland Revenue Act, 1881, on inland revenue affidavits.

The accounts specified in 44 & 45 Vict. c. 12, s. 38, as amended by 52 & 53 Vict. c. 7, s. 11, include accounts of property taken under a *donatio mortis causa*, or under certain other dispositions, etc., made by a deceased person.

The Finance Act, 1894, s. 1, provides that where property is chargeable with estate duty under that Act, the duties mentioned in 44 & 45 Vict. c. 12, s. 38, as so amended, shall not be levied in respect of such property.

In addition to the share of the estate duty payable under this section to the Local Taxation Account, certain additional duties on spirits and beer are also to be paid into that account under 53 Vict. c. 8, s. 7, *post*. A portion of the sum so paid in is applicable to police superannuation, and the residue is to be distributed between county and county borough funds, and carried to the Exchequer Contribution Accounts of those funds, under s. 23, *post*. The sums so received may be applied for purposes of technical education. See 53 & 54 Vict. c. 60 ; 54 & 55 Vict. c. 4, s. 2. Both these Acts are set out *post*.

Distribution of probate duty grant.

22.—(1.) The sums paid in pursuance of this Act to the Local Taxation Account, in respect of the proceeds of the probate duties (in this Act referred to as the "probate duty grant"), shall, until Parliament otherwise determine, be distributed among the several counties in England and Wales in proportion to the share which the Local Government Board certify to have been received by each county during the financial year ending the thirty-first day of March next before the passing of this Act out of the grants heretofore made out of the Exchequer in aid of local rates, which will cease to be granted after the passing of this Act, and the share to be so certified shall be estimated in such manner as the Local Government Board direct.

The share to which each county is entitled thus depends on the amount received by it during the year ending March 31st, 1888, out of the Exchequer in aid of local rates, and (subject to any variation, made under sub-s. (3) of this section, of the certificate of the Local Government Board) the proportion so determined will remain fixed until Parliament otherwise provides.

Sect. 22 (2).

(2.) In the case of the six counties of South Wales and the Isle of Wight there shall be added to the amount actually received out of such grants as aforesaid such additional sum as the Local Government Board certify to be the amount which each of the said counties and the Isle of Wight would have received, if the roads maintained by the county roads boards or the highway commissioners had been main roads.

As already stated (see the notes to ss. 12 and 13, *ante*), the Isle of Wight and the counties in South Wales were not subject to the Highway Acts, and consequently no sum was ever granted out of the Exchequer in respect of main roads in these places. The sections referred to having made them subject to the Highway Acts, it was necessary to make provision for them as stated in the text.

(3.) The proportion to be paid to each county shall, from time to time, be paid under the direction of the Local Government Board to the county council out of the Local Taxation Account. The Board may, if they think proper, vary their certificate, but unless it is so varied, their certificate shall be conclusive.

As to the Local Taxation Account, see s. 20, *ante*.

Application of duties on local taxation licences and probate duty grant.

23.—(1.) All sums from time to time received by a county council in respect of—

(*a*.) The duties on the local taxation licences, whether collected by the Commissioners of Inland Revenue or by the county council; and

(*b*.) The probate duty grant,

shall be paid to the county fund and carried to a separate account, in this Act referred to as the Exchequer Contribution Account.

As to the duties on local taxation licences, see s. 20, *ante*.
As to the probate duty grant, see ss. 21, 22, *ante*.
As to the county fund, see s. 68, *post*.

(2.) All sums for the time being standing to the Exchequer Contribution Account shall be applied—

(i.) In paying the costs incurred in respect thereof, or otherwise chargeable thereon ; and

(ii.) In payment of the sums required by this Act to be paid by the county council in substitution for local grants ; and

(iii.) In payment of the grant required by this Act to be made by the county council in respect of costs of union officers ; and

(iv.) In repaying to the general county account of the county fund the costs on account of general county purposes for which the whole of the area of the county is liable to be **Sect. 23 (2).** assessed to county contributions;

and shall be so applied in the order above mentioned.

This and the following sub-sections will not apply to moneys received from the beer and spirit duties under 53 & 54 Vict. c. 60, and directed to be appropriated for technical or manual instruction. Such moneys, although not wholly expended during the financial year, are to remain applicable for the purposes of such instruction, and are not to be applied in manner provided by the text without a special order of the county council. See 54 Vict. c. 4, s. 2, *post.*

It is not quite clear what costs are incurred in respect of the Exchequer Contribution Account or are chargeable thereon.

The payment in substitution for local grants is made under s. 24, *post.*

The payment in respect of union officers is made under s. 26, *post.*

General county purposes are defined by s. 68, *post.*

(3.) If any surplus remains after paying the above costs and sums, such proportion of the surplus, as the total rateable value of the area of each quarter sessions borough exempt from contributing to any special county purpose, bears to the rateable value of the whole county, shall be paid to the council of that borough, and the remainder shall be applied as follows:

For the definition of a quarter sessions borough, see s. 100, *post.*

As to the determination of the rateable value, see sub-s. (10) and s. 100, *post.*

Special county purposes are defined by s. 68, *post.*

(4.) It shall first be applied towards repaying to the proper special accounts of the county fund, the costs on account of which the area of the county, exclusive of such quarter sessions boroughs, is liable to be assessed to county contributions;

As to the special accounts of the county fund, see s. 68, *post.*

(5.) Provided that where any of the said quarter sessions boroughs to which a payment of a proportion of the surplus is made as aforesaid is liable to be assessed to county contributions for any of such last-mentioned costs, there shall be deducted from the amount payable to the council of that borough in respect of the said surplus, such sum as would have been raised within the area of the borough if the amount of such costs had been raised by county contributions.

A proportion of the surplus is payable to a quarter sessions borough under sub-s. (3). The deduction to be made is to be the sum which would have been raised within the borough in respect of the costs mentioned in sub-s. (4).

(6.) If there remains any sum after repaying the said costs to the said accounts of the county fund, such residue shall be divided

Sect. 23 (6). as follows, that is to say, such proportion thereof as the total rateable value of the area of each borough maintaining a separate police force under the County and Borough Police Acts, and not being a quarter sessions borough above-mentioned, bears to the rateable value of the whole county, after deduction of the rateable value of every quarter sessions borough above-mentioned, shall be paid to the council of the borough, and the rest shall be applied towards repaying to the proper special accounts of the county fund the costs of the police, and other costs on account of which the area of the county, exclusive of all the said boroughs, is liable to be assessed to county contributions. Where, a town, not being a borough, maintains its own police and receives any payment from the county council in pursuance of this Act towards the pay and clothing of such police, this enactment shall apply to such town as if it were a borough, and as if the sanitary authority therein were the council of the borough.

In applying this sub-section it is necessary first to ascertain the rateable value of the county, exclusive of the quarter sessions boroughs mentioned in sub-s. (3). The proportion payable to the boroughs maintaining a separate police force is the proportion which the rateable value of such borough bears to that ascertained as above stated.

As to rateable value, see sub-s. (10) and s. 100, *post.*

As to the special county accounts, see s. 68, *post.*

The latter part of the sub-section applies only to a few towns which are boroughs in everything but name, and are governed under a local Act. See s. 24, sub-s. (4) and note, *post.*

(7.) If any balance remains after all the above payments are made, and is in excess of what the county council consider necessary to carry forward to the next account, such excess shall be divided among the district councils other than the councils of quarter sessions or other boroughs to whom portions of the surplus have been paid under the foregoing provisions of this section, and shall be so divided in proportion to the rateable value of the area of each district.

The county council have therefore a discretion to carry over the entire balance to the next account.

The district councils are the urban and rural district councils other than borough councils receiving any payment under the preceding sub-sections. As to rateable value, see sub-s. (10) and s. 100, *post.*

(8.) Where any part of a county is situate within the Metropolitan Police District, this section shall apply as if that part were the area of a borough maintaining a separate police force, save that the sum which would be payable to such borough shall be paid to the district councils of the county districts wholly or partly situate in such part, and shall be divided among such district councils in proportion to the rateable value of the area of each district, or of so much thereof as is within the Metropolitan Police District. Sect. 23 (8)

The Metropolitan Police District comprises an area which may be roughl described as within a radius of 15 miles from Charing Cross. Its boundaries are fixed by 10 Geo. 4, c. 44, and by Orders in Council made under 2 & 3 Vict. c. 47, s. 2. The area is to be treated as if it were a borough within sub-s. (6), but the sum ascertained as provided by that sub-section is to be distributed among the district councils.

(9.) All sums paid in pursuance of this section shall be carried, if paid to the council of a borough, to the borough fund, and if paid to a district council other than the council of a borough, to the district fund, and shall be applied to purposes for which the whole of the borough or district is liable to be rated.

The district fund is, in urban districts, the general district fund under the Public Health Act, 1875, s. 209. In a rural district, the sum paid must be applied like a sum raised for general expenses under ss. 229, 230, of that Act.

(10.) The rateable value, for the purpose of this section, shall be determined according to the standard or basis for county contributions for the time being.

As to the rateable value when there is no such standard or basis, see s. 100; and as to the mode of calculating the rateable value of both a county and a county borough, see s. 33, *post*.

24. Whereas certain grants heretofore made out of the Exchequer in aid of local rates (in this Act referred to as local grants) will by reason of the duties on the local taxation licences and the probate duty grant being by this Act made payable to local authorities, cease, it is therefore hereby enacted as follows:—

Payments by county council in substitution for annual local grants out of Exchequer in aid of local rates.

(1.) So much of any enactment as requires or authorizes payment out of the Exchequer of any local grant in substitution for which the county council is required by this Act to make any payment is hereby repealed as from the thirty-first day of March next after the passing of this Act without prejudice to any right accrued before that day.

As to the local taxation licences, see s. 20, *ante*.

As to the probate duty grant, see ss. 21, 22, *ante*.

Under this and the subsequent provisions of this section it was held that the county council in substitution for the Exchequer were bound to pay out of the county fund local grants in respect of the period between September 24th, 1888, and April 1st, 1889, though the county council did not come into existence until the latter date. *Re West Riding County Council*, 54 J. P. 533.

(2.) In substitution for local grants, the council of each county shall from time to time as from the said day pay out of the county

(2) fund and charge to the Exchequer Contribution Account the following sums, that is to say—

(*a.*) They shall pay to the guardians for every poor law union or officer for any other area wholly or partly in the county (as the case may be) such sums as the Local Government Board from time to time certify to be due from the said council in substitution for the local grants towards the remuneration of teachers in poor law schools, and for payments to public vaccinators under section five of the
Vict. Vaccination Act, 1867 ; and

As to the Exchequer Contribution Account, see s. 23, *ante.*

The sums formerly paid were the whole of the salaries of teachers in poor law schools ; their salaries are therefore payable by the county council.

By 30 & 31 Vict. c. 84, s. 5, on reports made to the Lords of the Privy Council with regard to the number and quality of the vaccinations performed in the several vaccination districts in England, or any of them, the said Lords might from time to time, out of moneys provided by Parliament, and under regulations to be approved by the Treasury, authorize to be paid to any public vaccinators, in addition to the payments received by them from guardians or overseers, further payments not exceeding in any case the rate of one shilling for each child whom the vaccinator had successfully vaccinated during the time to which the award of the said Lords related.

In both of these cases the sums to be paid to the guardians of unions or officers of other poor law areas will be ascertained and certified by the Local Government Board.

(*b.*) They shall pay to the guardians of every poor law union the school fees paid for pauper children sent from a workhouse to a public elementary school outside the workhouse ; and

This provision meets the case of children not educated in the workhouse but sent to a public elementary school.

(*c.*) They shall pay to every local authority, for any area wholly or partly in the county, by whom a medical officer of health or inspector of nuisances is paid, one-half of the salary of such officer, where his qualification, appointment, salary, and tenure of office are in accordance with the regulations made by order under the Public
Vict. Health Act, 1875, or any Act repealed by that Act, but if the Local Government Board certify to the council that such medical officer has failed to send to the Local Government Board such report and returns as are for the time being required by the regulations respecting the duties of such officer made by order of the Board under any of the said Acts, a sum equal to such half of the salary shall be forfeited to the Crown, and the council

shall pay the same into Her Majesty's Exchequer and not to the said local authority ; and Sect. 24 (2).

The reference in the text to the Public Health Act, 1875, is to be construed to include a reference to the Public Health (London) Act, 1891 (54 & 55 Vict. c. 76). See s. 108 of that Act.

Every urban and rural district council are required by ss. 189 and 190 of the Public Health Act, 1875, to appoint one or more medical officers of health and inspectors of nuisances, but if any authority avail themselves of the services of a county medical officer under s. 17, *ante*, p. 44, they are to be deemed to have made the necessary appointment of a medical officer. (See sub-s. (3), *post.*)

The qualification of medical officers of health, save in so far as it is expressly provided by this Act (see s. 18, *ante*), and the appointment, salary, etc., of these officers and the inspectors of nuisances, are prescribed by ss. 189—191 of the Public Health Act, 1875, and various orders of the Local Government Board, which are referred to in the notes to those sections in Lumley's Public Health.

As to the reports of the medical officer, see the note to s. 19, sub-s. (1), *ante*, p. 46. The medical officer must send copies of these reports to the county council, otherwise they may refuse to pay the contribution towards his salary, but it is only in case of his failure to send the reports to the Board that the amount of the contribution is to be paid into the Exchequer.

(*d.*) They shall pay to the guardians paying the registrars of births and deaths for any district wholly or partly in the county a sum equal to the amount paid out of local grants towards the remuneration of the registrars paid by those guardians during the financial year ending on the thirty-first day of March next after the passing of this Act ; and

This will be a fixed amount determined by the sum paid in the year ending March 31st, 1889.

The Acts relating to registrars of births and deaths are 6 & 7 Will. 4, c. 86 ; 1 Vict. c. 22 ; 29 & 30 Vict. c. 113, s. 1 ; 31 & 32 Vict. c. 122, s. 26 ; 37 & 38 Vict. c. 88. Registrars are paid by the guardians under 6 & 7 Will. 4, c. 86, s. 29.

(*e.*) They shall transfer to that account of the county fund to which the maintenance of any pauper lunatic chargeable to the county is charged, a sum equal to four shillings a week for each such pauper lunatic, for whom the net charge upon the county council, after deducting any amount received by the county council for the maintenance of such lunatic from any source other than local rates, is equal to or exceeds four shillings a week throughout the period of maintenance for which the sum is so transferred ; and

Pauper lunatics may be chargeable to the county by virtue of justices' orders under the Lunacy Act, 1890 (53 Vict. c. 5), s. 290, *post*. They become so chargeable only when they have no known union of settlement. The amounts referred

Sect. 24 (2).

NOTE.

to which may be received by the county council may consist of property of the lunatic ordered to be applied towards his maintenance under s. 299 of that Act, *post.*

(*f.*) They shall pay to the guardians of every poor law union wholly or partly in the county a sum equal to four shillings a week for each pauper lunatic chargeable to that union, and maintained in an asylum, registered hospital, or licensed house, for whom the net charge upon the guardians, after deducting any amount received by them for the maintenance of such lunatic from any source other than local rates, is equal to or exceeds four shillings a week throughout the period of maintenance for which the sum is so paid; and

A pauper lunatic is chargeable to the union from which he is sent unless it be established that he is settled in some other union, or that it cannot be ascertained in what union he was settled. See Lunacy Act, 1890, ss. 286, 290, *post.*

(*g.*) They shall pay to the council of each borough to which the maintenance of any pauper lunatic is chargeable, a sum equal to four shillings a week for each such pauper lunatic for whom the net charge upon the council of the borough, after deducting any amount received by them for the maintenance of such lunatic from any source other than local rates, is equal to or exceeds four shillings a week throughout the period of maintenance for which the sum is so paid; and

A pauper lunatic may be made chargeable to the council of a borough if his settlement cannot be ascertained, and if he was sent to the asylum from a quarter sessions borough which is free from contributing to the payment of the expenses of pauper lunatics chargeable to the county in which the borough is situate. See Lunacy Act, 1890, s. 290, *post.*

(*h.*) They shall transfer to that account of the county fund to which the compensation payable to the clerk of the peace of a county, or any other officer of quarter sessions for the county, under section eighteen of the Act of the session of the eighteenth and nineteenth years of the reign of Her present Majesty, chapter one hundred and twenty-six, is charged, the amount of such compensation; and

The 18 & 19 Vict. c. 126, s. 18, provides as follows:—"Immediately after the passing of this Act, the Commissioners of Her Majesty's Treasury shall, upon the application of any clerk of the peace or other officer of quarter sessions, by such means and in such manner as they may think proper, inquire into and ascertain the annual amount to be computed upon an average of five years immediately preceding the passing of this Act or of such shorter period

NOTE.

as such clerk of the peace or other officer shall have been in office, of the fees and emoluments in criminal prosecutions received by the clerk of the peace or such other officer, and the said commissioners shall on the like application also ascertain, in such manner as they may think proper, the total amount of fees and emoluments in criminal prosecutions received by such clerk of the peace or other officer during any year after the passing of this Act, and the said Commissioners are hereby authorized and empowered by warrant under their hands to award to such clerk of the peace or other officer the deficiency when and so often as the same shall occur between the last-mentioned amount and the annual average amount so ascertained as aforesaid, and the sum so awarded shall be paid out of any moneys which may be provided by Parliament for that purpose: Provided that in all cases where any such clerk of the peace, by reason of his being paid by salary under an order made by virtue of 14 & 15 Vict. c. 55, shall pay such fees and emoluments as aforesaid to the treasurer of the county or borough for which he is clerk of the peace in aid of the county or borough rate, as the case may be, such deficiency when so ascertained as aforesaid shall be paid to the treasurer of such county or borough respectively."

(*i.*) They shall, subject to the provisions of this Act, transfer to the police account of the county fund a sum equal to one-half of the costs of the pay and clothing of the police of the county during the preceding year; and

One half the cost of the pay and clothing of the county police will be paid out of this fund.

(*j.*) They shall, subject to the provisions of this Act, pay to the council of each borough maintaining a separate police force under the County and Borough Police Acts, one-half of the costs of the pay and clothing of the police of that borough during the preceding year; and

The County and Borough Police Acts are the 19 & 20 Vict. c. 69, and the 22 & 23 Vict. c. 32; see sub-s. (4), *post*. The reference to the provisions of this Act is to s. 39, by which the separate police force in the smaller boroughs is abolished.

It was held in *R.* v. *West Riding County Council*, [1895] 1 Q. B. 805; 64 L. J. M. C. 145; 72 L. T. (N.S.) 520; 43 W. R. 386; 59 J. P. 340, that a borough which maintains a separate police force is entitled to be paid by the county council under the provision in the text one half of the costs of the pay and clothing of extra police temporarily added from another police force under s. 25 of the Police Act, 1890 (53 & 54 Vict. c. 45), and paid for by agreement under that Act.

(*k.*) They shall, if within their county sums are raised by rates for the purpose of the metropolitan police, pay to the receiver for the Metropolitan Police District in each year, a sum bearing such proportion to the sum actually raised in the same year by rates from the parishes in that county for the said purpose as a Secretary of State certifies to be the proportion which would have been

Sect. 24 (2).

contributed out of the Exchequer under the arrangement in force during the financial year next before the passing of this Act.

The Metropolitan Police Rate Act, 1868 (31 & 32 Vict. c. 67), s. 2, provides that the annual sum to be provided in pursuance of the Acts relating to the metropolitan police force shall not exceed ninepence in the pound, calculated on the full annual value of all property rateable to the relief of the poor within the parishes and places comprised in the Metropolitan Police Districts, and of such annual sum to be so provided, one-fourth part shall be contributed by the Treasury out of moneys for that purpose provided by Parliament and three-fourth parts shall be raised by a rate in manner provided by the said Acts. The payment provided for by the text takes the place of the Treasury grant, and is limited to the amount certified by the Secretary of State.

The Acts relating to the expenses of the metropolitan police are 10 Geo. 4, c. 44, ss. 23—33 ; 2 & 3 Vict. c. 47, ss. 2, 6 ; 19 & 20 Vict. c. 2 ; 20 & 21 Vict. c. 64, ss. 11—14 ; 24 & 25 Vict. c. 124, ss. 1, 7 ; 31 & 32 Vict. c. 67, s. 2 ; 32 & 33 Vict. c. 67, ss. 45, 77 ; and 53 & 54 Vict. c. 45, s. 27.

The boundaries of the Metropolitan Police District are fixed by the 10 Geo. 4, c. 44, and by Orders in Council made under 2 & 3 Vict. c. 47. The district now comprises an area within about fifteen miles from Charing Cross.

(3.) A reference in sections one hundred and eighty-nine and one hundred and ninety-one of the Public Health Act, 1875, to officers any portion of whose salary is paid out of moneys provided by Parliament shall be construed to refer to those officers in respect of whose salaries payment is made by a county council in pursuance of this section.

The Public Health Act, 1875, ss. 189 and 191, are as follows :—

"189. Every urban authority shall from time to time appoint fit and proper persons to be medical officer of health, surveyor, inspector of nuisances, clerk and treasurer : Provided that if any such authority is empowered by any other Act in force within their district to appoint any such officer, this enactment shall be deemed to be satisfied by the employment under this Act of the officer so appointed, with such additional remuneration as they think fit, and no second appointment shall be made under this Act. Every urban authority shall also appoint or employ such assistants, collectors, and other officers and servants as may be necessary and proper for the efficient execution of this Act, and may make regulations with respect to the duties and conduct of the officers and servants so appointed or employed.

"Subject in the case of officers any portion of whose salary is paid out of moneys voted by Parliament, to the powers of the Local Government Board under this Act, the urban authority may pay to the officers and servants so appointed or employed such reasonable salaries, wages, or allowances as the urban authority may think proper ; and, subject as aforesaid, every such officer and servant appointed under this Act shall be removable by the urban authority at their pleasure."

"191. A person shall not be appointed medical officer of health under this Act unless he is a legally qualified medical practitioner ; and the Local Government Board shall have the same powers as it has in the case of a district medical officer of a union with regard to the qualification, appointment, duties, salary and tenure of office of a medical officer of health or other officer of a local authority any portion of whose salary is paid out of moneys voted by Parliament, and may by order prescribe the qualification and duties of other medical officers of health appointed under this Act. Sect. 24 (3).

NOTE.

"The same person may, with the sanction of the Local Government Board, be appointed medical officer of health or inspector of nuisances for two or more districts, by the local authorities of such districts; and the Local Government Board shall by order prescribe the mode of such appointment, and the proportions in which the expenses of such appointment, and the salary and charges of such officer, shall be borne by such authorities.

"Any district medical officer of a union may, with the sanction of the Local Government Board, and subject to such conditions as the said board may prescribe, be appointed a medical officer of health; and a medical officer of health may exercise any of the powers with which an inspector of nuisances is invested by this Act.

"In case of illness or incapacity of the medical officer of health a local authority may appoint and pay a deputy medical officer, subject to the approval of the Local Government Board."

(4.) Where any payment towards the pay and clothing of the police of any town has been made in pursuance of section eighteen of the County and Borough Police Act, 1856, which authorizes such payment to be made until the discontinuance of the police, the like payment shall, notwithstanding anything in this section, be made by the county council to the authority of such town until such discontinuance. 19 & 20 Vict. c. 69.

The 19 & 20 Vict. c. 69, s. 18, provides that "until the constables or watchmen appointed in and for any parish, town, or place under the 3 & 4 Will. 4, c. 90, or under any local Act authorizing the appointment of constables or watchmen, and authorizing rates to be made and levied for the purpose of defraying the expenses of such constables or watchmen, are discontinued as a separate force in manner provided by s. 20 of the 3 & 4 Vict. c. 88, and by this Act, all the provisions of this Act applicable to the constables of any borough acting under the 5 & 6 Will. 4, c. 76, shall be applicable to the constables or watchmen appointed under the 3 & 4 Will. 4, c. 96, or under such local Act as aforesaid, in and for such parish, town, or place, and until such discontinuance, all the provisions of this Act applicable to the watch committee of a borough shall be applicable to the inspectors, commissioners, or other persons having the appointment of constables or watchmen in and for such parish, town, or place; and the police of such parish, town, or place shall be visited and inquired into by the inspectors under this Act; and the provision in this Act enabling the Commissioners of Her Majesty's Treasury to make payment towards the expenses of the police of a borough having a population exceeding 5,000, shall, until such discontinuance, extend to the police of such parish, town, or place as aforesaid having the like population."

(5.) Where a sum is payable under this section to the guardians, authority, or officer of a union or other area, and such union or area is situate in more administrative counties than one, a proportionate part only of the sum otherwise payable shall be paid by the council of each of such counties to the guardians, authority, or

Sect. 24 (5).

officer, and the Local Government Board shall certify the proportionate part due from the council of each such county.

For the definition of "administrative county," see s. 100, *post*. This provides for the cases of unions and similar areas which extend into more than one county; since the passing of the Local Government Act, 1894, these are far fewer than formerly.

(6.) The guardians, authority, or officer to whom a sum is payable under this section on the certificate of the Local Government Board, shall submit to the Board their claim to the payment in such manner, and produce such evidence and comply with such rules as the Board from time to time require or make, and the Board shall fix the amount due on the like principles, and may impose the like conditions for the payment thereof as before the passing of this Act.

(7.) The Local Government Board may, if they think fit, vary a certificate granted for the purposes of this section, but, unless so varied, it shall be conclusive.

As to Secretary of State's power respecting efficiency of police.

25.—(1.) If a Secretary of State withholds, as respects the police of any county, his certificate under the County and Borough Police Act, 1856, that the police of the county has been maintained in a state of efficiency in point of numbers and discipline during the year ending on the twenty-ninth day of September, then last past, the council of that county, in lieu of transferring any sum under the foregoing provisions of this Act to the police account of the county fund, shall forfeit to the Crown, and shall pay into Her Majesty's Exchequer out of the county fund, and shall charge to the Exchequer Contribution Account of that fund, such sum as the Secretary of State certifies to be in his opinion equivalent to one half of the cost of the pay and clothing of the police of the county during the said year.

By the 19 & 20 Vict. c. 69, s. 15, Her Majesty is empowered to appoint inspectors whose duty it is to visit and inquire into the state and efficiency of the police appointed for every county and borough, and whether the provisions of the Acts under which the police are appointed are duly observed and carried into effect, and also into the state of the police stations, charge rooms, cells, or lock-ups, or other premises occupied for the use of the police; and each of such inspectors is to report to a Secretary of State, who is to cause the report to be laid before Parliament, and the inspectors are to be paid out of moneys provided by Parliament. By s. 16, on the certificate of a Secretary of State that the police of any county or borough has been maintained in a state of efficiency in point of number and discipline for the year ending on September 29th then last past, the Treasury may pay out of moneys provided by Parliament such sum towards the expenses of the police as shall not exceed one-fourth of the charge for their pay and clothing (but such payment is not to extend to additional constables appointed under 3 & 4 Vict. c. 88, s. 19): Provided that before any certificate shall be finally withheld in respect of the police of any county or borough, the report of the inspector shall be sent to the justices or the watch committee, as the case may be, and in every case in which the certificate is withheld a statement of the grounds on which the Secretary of State has withheld such certificate, together with any such statement of the justices or watch committee, shall be laid before Parliament. The grant by the Treasury will cease after this Act comes into operation and will be replaced by the grant out of the Exchequer Contribution Account under s. 24, sub-s. (2), *ante*. In future, if the certificate is withheld, the grant is to be paid into the Exchequer (see s. 27, *post*), instead of being placed to the credit of the police account. **Sect. 25 (1).** NOTE.

(2.) If a Secretary of State withholds, as respects the police of any borough, his certificate under the County and Borough Police Act, 1856, that the police of the borough has been maintained in a state of efficiency in point of numbers and discipline for the year ending on the twenty-ninth day of September then last past, no payment shall be made by the county council to the council of the borough in respect of one-half of the costs of the pay and clothing of the police of that borough during the said year, and such amount as a Secretary of State certifies to be in his opinion the equivalent of such one-half shall be transferred by the county council from the Exchequer Contribution Account to the general county account and applied to the general purposes of the county. 19 & 20 Vict. c. 96.

See the note to the preceding sub-section.

In this case if the certificate is withheld the grant is to be paid to the general county account, as to which see s. 68, *post*.

26.—(1.) After the thirty-first day of March next after the passing of this Act, every county council, other than the London County Council, shall grant to the guardians of every poor law union wholly or partly in their county, an annual sum for the costs of the officers of the union and of district schools to which the union contributes; and, until Parliament otherwise determine, the said annual sum shall be such sum as the Local Government Board certify to have been expended by the guardians of each poor law union during the financial year ending the twenty-fifth day of March next before the passing of this Act, on the salaries, remuneration, and superannuation allowances of the said officers (other than teachers in poor law schools), and on drugs and medical appliances. Grant by county council towards costs of officers of union.

The grant by the London County Council to the poor law unions is regulated by s. 43, *post*.

In a Circular Letter dated January 10th, 1889, and issued by the Local Government Board to boards of guardians throughout the country, the following opinion as to the meaning of the expression "officers of the union" is given :—

"The Act contains no definition of the expression 'officers of the union'; but the words clearly do not include parochial officers or officers appointed for

Sect. 26 (1). NOTE.

areas such as rural sanitary districts in which the jurisdiction of the guardians is not in all cases co-extensive with the union. In the opinion of the board, the following officers cannot be regarded as officers of the union for the purposes of the grant ; and care should be taken to exclude any expenditure of the guardians in respect of them :—

Collectors of poor rates.
Assistant overseers.
Officers of rural sanitary authorities.
Officers of school attendance committees.
Superintendent registrars, and
Registrars of births, deaths, and marriages.

"On reference to section 100 of the Act, it will be seen that the expression 'officer' is to be construed according to the definition of 'office,' which is to include any 'place, situation, or employment.' (And see note to that definition, *post.*)

"In some instances officers, in respect of whose services in certain capacities no claim can properly be made against the grant, will have acted also in other capacities, and their salaries, remuneration, or superannuation allowances in the latter capacities will properly be chargeable on the grant. In these cases care should be taken to include only so much of the expenditure of the guardians as has been incurred on account of the services of these officers in the latter capacities.

"The board consider that the cost of the rations of officers may be included. The expenditure of the guardians for this purpose should be taken from the 'Rations Account' in the Union Ledger, with the necessary deduction in respect of teachers and assistant teachers."

Unions, or parishes not in unions, may be combined into school districts for the management of any class or classes of infant poor under the age of sixteen years chargeable to any such union or parish, who are orphans or deserted by their parents, or whose parents or surviving parent or guardians consent to the placing of such children in the school of the district. The Acts containing provisions relating to district schools are 7 & 8 Vict. c. 101 ; 11 & 12 Vict. c. 82 ; 14 & 15 Vict. c. 105 ; 29 & 30 Vict. c. 113 ; 30 & 31 Vict. c. 106 ; 31 & 32 Vict. c. 122 ; 42 & 43 Vict. c. 54.

The amount of the grant will, until Parliament otherwise determine, be the sum certified to have been expended during the year ending March 25th, 1889.

The salaries, etc., of teachers in poor law schools are provided for by the grant out of the Exchequer Contribution Account under s. 24, sub-s. (2) (*a*), *ante.*

The grant under this section will be paid out of the Exchequer Contribution Account as provided by s. 23, sub-s. (2), *ante.*

(2.) Where a poor law union is situate in more counties than one, the payment under this section to the guardians of the union shall be borne by the counties in which each portion of such union is situate, in proportion to the rateable value of that portion, ascertained on such day as the Local Government Board may fix.

The rateable value is to be ascertained by the standard or basis of the county rate, or if there is no such standard then by the valuation lists ; see s. 100, *post.*

Sect. 27 (1).

Supplemental provisions as to Local Taxation Account and Exchequer Contribution Account.

27.—(1.) When a county council are required under the provisions of this or any other Act to pay any sum into Her Majesty's Exchequer, or to the Treasury, or to the Receiver for the Metropolitan Police District, such sum shall be deducted from the amount payable under the provisions of this Act out of the Local Taxation Account to such county council, and instead of being paid to the county council shall be paid into Her Majesty's Exchequer, or to the Receiver for the Metropolitan Police District, as the case requires.

Sums are payable into the Exchequer under s. 24, sub-s. (2) (*c*), s. 25, sub-s. (1).

The Treasury means the Commissioners of Her Majesty's Treasury. See s. 100, *post*.

Sums are payable to the Receiver for the Metropolitan Police District under s. 24, sub-s. (2), (*k*).

The text provides in effect that the total sum shall not be paid out of the Local Taxation Account and then partly repaid, but deducted in the first instance and paid directly to the Exchequer by the Commissioners of Inland Revenue.

(2.) The account of the receipts and expenditure of the Local Taxation Account shall be audited as a public account by the Comptroller and Auditor-General in accordance with such regulations as the Treasury may from time to time make.

(3.) If at any time in any financial year the moneys standing to the Local Taxation Account are insufficient to meet such sums as the Local Government Board consider proper for the time being to pay thereout, the Local Government Board may borrow temporarily on the security of the said account and of moneys becoming payable thereto such sums as they require for the purpose of meeting such deficiency, and the Bank of England may lend such sums, but all sums so borrowed shall be repaid with the interest thereon during the same financial year out of moneys payable to the said account.

The Bank of England means the Governor and Company of the Bank of England. See s. 100, *post*.

As to the financial year, see s. 73, *post*.

General Provisions as to Transfer.

General provisions as to powers transferred to county council.

28.—(1.) The county council shall, as respects the business by this Act transferred to them from quarter sessions or the justices out of sessions, be subject to the provisions and limitations in this Act specified, but, save as aforesaid, shall have and be subject to all the powers, duties, and liabilities which the quarter sessions, or

Sect. 28 (1). any committee thereof, or any justice or justices had or were subject to in respect of the business so transferred,

As to the transfer of business from quarter sessions, see in particular ss. 3, 4, 7, and 9, *ante*. As to the limitations in this Act specified, see s. 78, *post*. And as to the settlement of disputes as to transfer see the next section.

(2.) The county council shall, with the exceptions hereinafter mentioned, have power to delegate, with or without any restrictions or conditions as they may think fit, any powers or duties transferred to them by or in pursuance of this Act, either to any committee of the county council appointed in pursuance of this Act, or to any district council in this Act mentioned; the county council may also, without prejudice to any other power whether to appoint committees or otherwise, delegate to the justices of the county sitting in petty sessions any power or duty transferred by this Act to the county council in respect of the licensing of houses or places for the public performance of stage plays, and in respect of the execution as local authority of the Explosives Act, 1875, or of the Act relating to contagious diseases of animals.

38 & 39 Vict. c. 17.

Committees of the county council are appointed in pursuance of the Municipal Corporations Act, 1882, s. 22, *post*, which is applied to connty councils by s. 75 of this Act. The proceedings of committees are regulated by s. 82. Joint committees are appointed under s. 81.

District councils are urban and rural district councils: see s. 100, *post*, and s. 21 of the Local Government Act, 1894, *post*.

In addition to the power of delegation to committees conferred upon county councils by the text there are provisions in several recent Acts requiring or authorizing county councils to appoint committees for the purposes mentioned in such Acts; see for instance, the Allotments Act, 1890 (53 & 54 Vict. c. 65), s. 3; the Small Holdings Act, 1892 (55 & 56 Vict. c. 31), ss. 5, 16; the Local Government Act, 1894 (56 & 57 Vict. c. 73), s. 83; the Local Government (Elections) Act, 1896 (58 & 59 Vict. c. 1), s. 1. These provisions are set out, *post*.

The Act relating to contagious diseases of animals under which a county council now has powers and duties, is the Diseases of Animals Act, 1894 (57 & 58 Vict. c. 57), *post*. That Act contains provisions enabling county councils to form committees, but it is expressly provided by s. 31 that nothing therein contained shall prejudice or affect the power of a county council to delegate their powers to any committee or body under the provisions in the text.

As to the powers of an executive committee appointed under the Diseases of Animals Act, see *Huth* v. *Clarke*, 25 Q. B. D. 391; 59 L. J. M. C 120; 63 L. T. (N.S.) 348; 38 W. R. 655; 6 T. L. R. 373. It appears from that decision that the delegation of powers to a committee will not deprive the county council of the right to exercise any power which the committee might exercise under the delegation.

The duties which may be delegated to justices are those transferred by s. 7, *ante*, and the execution of the Diseases of Animals Act, 1894. It is presumed that the committees appointed under this section must be composed only of members of the council, but the council may under the Diseases of Animals Act, 1894, appoint committees consisting partly of persons not members of the council.

Sect. 28 (3)

(3.) Provided that the county council shall not under this section delegate any power of raising money by rate or loan.

As to the rates to be made by the county council, see s. 3 (i.), *ante*.
As to borrowing by county councils, see s. 69, *post*.

Summary proceeding for determination of questions as to transfer of powers.

29. If any question arises, or is about to arise, as to whether any business, power, duty, or liability is or is not transferred to any county council or joint committee under this Act, that question, without prejudice to any other mode of trying it, may, on the application of a chairman of quarter sessions, or of the county council, committee, or other local authority concerned, be submitted for decision to the High Court of Justice in such summary manner as, subject to any rules of court, may be directed by the court; and the court, after hearing such parties and taking such evidence (if any) as it thinks just, shall decide the question.

As to joint committees, see ss. 46, 81, 82, *post*.

The local authority here referred to is probably the local authority whose powers and duties are alleged to be or not to be transferred to the county council.

This is a useful provision, and has been put in operation in a considerable number of cases where questions have arisen as to the respective liabilities of county councils and other authorities. By a rule of the High Court dated August 10th, 1892, which came into operation on October 1st of that year, the procedure is by special case to be agreed on by the parties, or in default of such agreement to be settled by an arbitrator agreed on by the parties or (if necessary) appointed by a judge at chambers, or to be settled by a judge at chambers. The special case when settled is to be filed at the Crown Office Department at the Central Office of the Supreme Court, by the chairman of quarter sessions, the county council, or the local authority concerned, within eight days from the settlement thereof, and is to be put into the Crown Paper for argument as if it were a case stated by justices under 20 & 21 Vict. c. 43. Without attempting to give an exhaustive list of the reported cases decided under this section, the following may be mentioned :—*Ex parte Somerset County Council*, 58 L. J. Q. B. 513 ; 61 L. T. (N.S.) 512 ; 54 J. P. 182 ; 5 T. L. R. 712 ; *Ex parte Staffordshire Quarter Sessions*, 54 J. P. 72 ; 6 T. L. R. 45 ; *Ex parte West Riding County Council*, 54 J. P. 533 ; 6 T. L. R. 265 ; *Warminster Local Board* v. *Wilts County Council*, 25 Q. B. D. 450 ; 59 L. J. Q. B. 434 ; 62 L. T. (N.S.) 902 ; 38 W. R. 671 ; 54 J. P. 375 ; *Re Cardigan County Council*, 54 J. P. 468 ; *Re Staffordshire and Derbyshire County Councils*, 54 J. P. 566 ; *Ex parte Kent County Council and Dover*, [1891] 1 Q. B. 389 ; 60 L. J. Q. B. 314 ; 60 L. T. (N.S.) 421; 55 J. P. 248 ; 7 T. L. R. 250: *Ex parte Leicestershire County Council*, [1891] 1 Q. B. 53 ; 60 L. J. M. C. 45 ; 64 L. T. (N.S.) 25 ; 39 W.R. 160; 55 J. P. 87 ; 7 T. L. R. 61 ; *Re Salop County Council*, 65 L. T. (N.S.) 416 ; 56 J. P. 213; *Montgomeryshire County Council* v. *Pryce-Jones*, 57 J. P. 308 ; *Marlborough Town Council* v. *Wilts County Council*, 58 J. P. 213 ; *Cornwall County Council* v. *Truro Town Council*, 63 L. J. M. C. 60; 70 L. T. (N.S.) 354; 58 J. P. 299; 10 R. 595 ; *In re Bedford Urban Sanitary Authority* [1894] 2 Q. B. 786; 64 L. J. Q. B. 26; 71 L. T. (N.S.) 433 ; 58 J. P. 786 ; *Norfolk County Council* v. *Bittering Highway Surveyor*, 58 J. P. 497 ; *Notts County Council* v. *Manchester, Sheffield, etc. Rail. Co.*, 71 L. T. (N.S.) 430

Sect. 29.

NOTE.

Herefordshire County Council v. *Leominster Town Council*, [1895] 1 Q. B. 43; 64 L. J. M. C. 26; 71 L. T. (N.S.) 576; 59 J. P. 38. But the court will not under the above section answer abstract questions on the construction of the Act. *Re Cardigan County Council, supra.*

Standing joint committee of quarter sessions and county council for the purpose of police, clerk of the peace, officers, etc.

30.—(1.) For the purposes of the police, and the clerk of the peace, and of the clerks of the justices, and joint officers, and of matters required to be determined jointly by the quarter sessions and the council of a county, there shall be a standing joint committee of the quarter sessions and the county council, consisting of such equal number of justices appointed by the quarter sessions and of members of the county council appointed by that council as may from time to time be arranged between the quarter sessions and the council, and in default of arrangement such number taken equally from the quarter sessions and the council as may be directed by a Secretary of State.

As to the appointment of the standing joint committee and their tenure of office, see s. 81, *post.* A committee may be appointed under that section for two or more counties or county boroughs. The proceedings of the committee will be regulated by s. 82, *post.*

The control of the county police is transferred to the standing joint committee by s. 9, *ante.*

Clerks of the peace will in future be appointed by this committee under s. 83, *post.*

This committee will fix and pay the salaries of justices' clerks under s. 84, *post.*

As to joint officers, see s. 118, *post.*

The committee will consist of an equal number of justices and members of the county council. If the number cannot be agreed upon it is to be determined by the Secretary of State.

(2.) The joint committee shall elect a chairman, and, in the case of an equality of votes for two or more persons as chairman, one of those persons shall be elected by lot.

There will be no casting vote in the election of the chairman. But it seems to follow from ss. 81, 82, *post,* that the chairman, when elected, will have a casting vote.

(3.) Any matter arising under this Act with respect to the police, or to the clerk of the peace, or to clerks of the justices, or to officers who serve both the quarter sessions or justices and the county council, or to the provision of accommodation for the quarter sessions or justices out of session or to the use by them or the police or the said clerks of any buildings, rooms, or premises, or to the application of the Local Stamp Act, 1869, to any sums received by clerks to justices, or with respect to anything incidental to the above-mentioned matters, and any other matter requiring to be

32 & 33 Vict. c. 49.

determined jointly by the quarter sessions and county council, shall be referred to and determined by the joint committee under this section; and all such expenditure as the said joint committee determine to be required for the purposes of the matters above in this section mentioned shall be paid out of the county fund, and the council of the county shall provide for such payment accordingly. Sect. 30 (3).

As to the police, clerk of the peace, justices' clerk, and joint officers, see the sections of this Act referred to in note to sub-section (1), *ante*.

The Acts under which shire and county halls, assize courts, and judges' lodgings are provided and maintained are 7 Geo. 4, c. 63; 7 Will. 4 & 1 Vict. c. 24; 2 & 3 Vict. c. 69; and 10 & 11 Vict. c. 28. Buildings for petty sessions are provided under 12 & 13 Vict. c. 18, ss. 2, 3; 31 & 32 Vict. c. 22; and 42 & 43 Vict. c. 49, ss. 20, 30.

The County Courts Act, 1888 (51 & 52 Vict. c. 43), s. 179, provides that in every town or place where there is a court-house or other public building belonging to a county, it may be used for the holding of the county court without charge save for lighting, warming, and cleaning, but so, however, as not to interfere with the ordinary use of the building.

See also s. 54, *post*, as to the providing of accommodation for quarter sessions and justices.

As between the county council on the one hand and the standing joint committee on the other, the latter has exclusive control of buildings and premises within the purview of the above sub-section for the accommodation of quarter sessions or justices out of sessions, or for the use of the police or clerks to justices. All questions as to the maintenance, repair, alteration, or improvement of such buildings and premises are to be determined by the standing joint committee. The county council has no power to place its veto upon the requirements of the committee under this sub-section: it is the duty of the county council to raise and pay such sums as the committee shall in their discretion deem it necessary to expend in and about such buildings and premises. *Ex parte Somerset County Council*, 58 L. J. Q. B. 513; 61 L. T. (N.S.) 512; 54 J. P. 183; 5 T. L. R. 712.

As to the Local Stamp Act, 1869, see the note to s. 3 (xiii.), *ante*, p. 13.

The fees and costs payable to justices' clerks are to be paid into the county fund, and the standing joint committee take the place of the quarter sessions and local authority in the enactments relating to the salaries and fees of justices' clerks. See s. 84, *post*.

As to the county fund, see s. 68, *post*.

PART II.

APPLICATION OF ACT TO BOROUGHS, THE METROPOLIS, AND CERTAIN SPECIAL COUNTIES.

Application of Act to Boroughs.

31. Each of the boroughs named in the Third Schedule to this Act being a borough which on the first day of June, one thousand eight hundred and eighty-eight, either had a population of not less Certain large boroughs named in the schedule to

Sect. 31.

be county boroughs.

than fifty thousand, or was a county of itself shall, from and after the appointed day, be for the purposes of this Act an administrative county of itself, and is in this Act referred to as a county borough.

Provided that for all other purposes a county borough shall continue to be part of the county (if any) in which it is situate at the passing of this Act, and if a separate commission of assize, oyer and terminer, or gaol delivery is not directed to be executed within the borough, the borough shall, for the purposes of any such commission, and of the service of jurors, and the making of jury lists, be part of the county in which it is specified in the said schedule to be deemed for the purposes of this Act to be situate.

See the third schedule, *post*. In addition to the boroughs mentioned in this schedule, other county boroughs have been created under the provisions of s. 54 (1) (*d*), *post*, viz.: Grimsby, Oxford, and Newport (Mon.).

As to the appointed day, see s. 109, *post*.

For the definition of the phrase "administrative county," see s. 100, *post*.

"The purposes of this Act" as applied to county boroughs appear from s. 34, *post*.

The principal Acts relating to the service of jurors and the jury lists are 6 Geo. 4, c. 50; 25 & 26 Vict. c. 107; 33 & 34 Vict. c. 77.

Adjustment of financial relations between counties and county boroughs.

32.—(1.) An equitable adjustment respecting the distribution of the proceeds of the local taxation licences, and probate duty grant, and respecting all other financial relations, if any, between each county, and each county borough specified in the said schedule as being deemed for the purposes of this Act to be situate in that county, shall be made by agreement, within twelve months after the appointed day, between the councils of each county and each borough, and in default of any such agreement, by the Commissioners appointed under this Act; and such adjustment shall provide, in the case of any expenses which may in future be incurred by the county wholly or partly on behalf of the borough for the liability of such borough to contribute, and save as provided by this Act, any existing liability to contribute or to incur expense shall, after the appointed day, cease, and an equitable provision for such cessation shall be made in the adjustment.

By s. 33, *post*, county boroughs are entitled to receive a share from the local taxation account like other administrative counties. But as the amounts payable are to depend to some extent (see s. 22, *ante*) upon the grants made to each county before the county boroughs were separated from it, this section provides for an equitable adjustment of the share of each county between that county, exclusive of the county boroughs within it, and the county boroughs.

The Commissioners appointed under s. 61, *post*, made this adjustment, and their report stating the principles on which the adjustment provided is set out, *post*.

(2.) Where a county borough is specified in the said schedule as being deemed for the purposes of this Act to be situate in more than one county, the necessary adjustment shall be made between the counties. Sect. 32 (2).

(3.) In such adjustment regard shall be had to the existing property, debts, and liabilities (if any) connected with the financial relations of the county and borough, and to the consideration that the county is not to be placed in any worse financial position by reason of the boroughs therein being constituted county boroughs, and that a county borough is not to be placed in a worse financial position than it would have been if it had remained part of the county and had shared in the division of the sums received by a county in respect of the licence duties and the probate duty grant, as provided by this Act, and to the amount of benefit and value of the services which the borough receives in return for existing contributions, if any, and to all the circumstances of each case which it appears equitable to consider, subject nevertheless to the following provisions :—

(*a.*) Where separate commissions of assize, oyer and terminer, and gaol delivery are not directed to be executed in a county borough, the borough council shall contribute a proper share of the costs of and incidental to the assizes of the county :

(*b.*) If the borough is not at the passing of this Act a quarter sessions borough, the borough council shall contribute a proper share of the costs of and incidental to the quarter sessions and petty sessions of the county, and of and incidental to the coroners of the county or any franchise therein, and if a grant of a court of quarter sessions is hereafter made to the borough, the borough shall redeem the liability to such contribution, on such terms as may be agreed upon, or, in default of agreement, may be determined by arbitration under this Act :

(*d.*) Each county borough shall be liable for the maintenance of pauper lunatics in like manner as any other county.

The report of the Commissioners relating to equitable adjustments under this sub-section is set out, *post.*

Where a local Act created a stipendiary justice's district and enabled the quarter sessions to levy rates on that district in the same manner as county rates, it was held that after the passing of this Act, which created two county boroughs within the district, that the power to levy rates was transferred to the county council as to that part of the district not within either of the

Sect. 32 (3)

NOTE.

boroughs, and that the liability of the county boroughs should be redeemed by adjustment under this section. *Ex parte Staffordshire*, 54 J. P. 72; 6 T. L. R. 45.

The expression "costs of assizes" is defined by s. 100, *post*. The same section provides that the term "assizes" shall include the Central Criminal Court.

If the borough is not a quarter sessions borough it will, for the purpose of the appointment and jurisdiction of the coroner, form part of the county, subject, however, to the provisions of s. 34, sub-ss. (4), (5), *post*.

Arbitration under the Act is regulated by s. 62, *post*, which also provides for the method by which a liability is to be redeemed.

Clause (*c*) of this sub-section is wholly repealed by the Lunacy Act, 1890 (53 & 54 Vict. c. 5), and re-enacted substantially by s. 244 of that Act. That section contains provisions for cases where a county borough has contributed to the cost of a county asylum: substantially it provides for a continuance of the existing state of things, but it enables the councils concerned to make a new arrangement, and to adjust property, debts, and liabilities; if one council refuses to make a new arrangement, the matter must be referred to arbitration under this Act.

The county boroughs will be liable for the maintenance of pauper lunatics adjudged chargeable to them under 53 & 54 Vict. c. 5, s. 290, as to which see the note to s. 24, sub-s. (2) (*g*), *ante*, p. 56.

(4.) In the adjustment of any financial relations other than the distribution of the proceeds of the licences and probate duty grant, no borough wholly or partially exempt from contributing to any object shall be rendered liable so to contribute or to contribute in greater proportion than at present.

This sub-section has reference only to such contributions as are to continue under the preceding sub-section. All other liabilities are, by sub-s. (1), to cease.

(5.) The provisions of Part III. of this Act, with respect to the adjustment of property, income, debts, liabilities, and expenses, and to borrowing for the purpose, shall apply as if the Commissioners under this Act were the arbitrator in that Part mentioned.

This has the effect of applying to the Commissioners the powers of an arbitrator under s. 62, *post*.

(6.) Provided that at any time after the end of five years from the date of an agreement or award adjusting the financial relations of any county and borough, if the council of either the county or borough satisfy the Local Government Board that the adjustment has become inequitable, and that the councils are unable to agree on a new adjustment, the board shall appoint an arbitrator; and such arbitrator shall proceed to make a new equitable adjustment as if he were the Commissioners under this Act, and the provisions of this Act shall apply accordingly. Any new adjustment made by agreement, or by the award of an arbitrator under this section, may, after the expiration of five years from the date of such agreement or award, be altered either by agreement or by arbitration as above-mentioned. Sect. 32 (6).

As to the powers of the arbitrator appointed under the sub-section, see s. 62, *post.* The councils may agree on a new adjustment without appointing an arbitrator.

(7.) Until the adjustment in pursuance of this section has come into operation, the county or borough council shall pay out of the county or borough fund to the borough or county council, as the case may be, the average annual amount which, during the three years next before the appointed day, has been expended by the county for the benefit of the borough, or contributed by the borough to the county, as the case may be, but any sum so paid shall be taken into account in the making of the adjustment, and the adjustment shall be made so as to take effect as from the appointed day.

This provision was temporary only : for an illustration of its operation, see *Ex parte Staffordshire,* cited in the note to sub-s. (3) of this section.

(8.) Any contribution by a county borough to the county in pursuance of this section shall be required and made in accordance with section one hundred and fifty-three of the Municipal Corporations Act, 1882, and that section, except so far as relates to the appointment of an arbitrator, shall apply in like manner as if every such borough were a quarter sessions borough situate in the county.

Section 153 of the Municipal Corporations Act, 1882, omitting sub-s. (4), which relates to the appointment of an arbitrator, is as follows :—

"(1.) The treasurer of each county shall, not more than twice in every year, send to the council of each borough situate in the county, and having a separate court of quarter sessions, an account showing separately—

(*a.*) The sums, if any, expended out of the county rate in respect of the costs arising out of the prosecution, maintenance, conveyance, transport, or punishment of offenders committed for trial from the borough to the assizes for the county ; and

(*b.*) If the borough is liable to contribute to the county rate for general county purposes, all sums expended out of the county rate for general county purposes, and all sums received in aid or on account of the county rate, and the proportion chargeable on the borough of the sums so expended after deduction of the sums so received ;

and shall make an order on the council for the payment of the sum appearing by this account to be due from the municipal corporation of the borough.

"(2.) The council shall thereupon forthwith order the sum so appearing to be due, with all reasonable charges of making and sending the account, to be paid to the treasurer of the county out of the borough fund.

"(3.) If the order is not complied with, two justices for the county may, on the complaint of the treasurer of the county, made within one month after the issue of the order, issue and send to the treasurer of the borough a warrant requiring him to pay to the treasurer of the county, besides the sum mentioned in the order, the additional sum mentioned in the warrant, the same being calculated in the proportion of one shilling to every ten on the sum mentioned

Sect. 32 (8)

NOTE.

in the order; and until payment thereof the treasurer of the county shall have, in respect of the warrant, all the powers for the recovery thereof which are given against a guardian or overseer for the recovery of county rates and surcharges."

(9.) Expressions in this section relating to contributions by a borough to a county shall be construed to include any sum raised by the assessment of the parishes or hereditaments in the borough to the county rate.

Provisions as to police and rateable value in county boroughs.

33.—(1.) Nothing in this Act with respect to county boroughs shall prevent the continuance of one police force for any county borough and any county, or the consolidation of the police forces of any county borough and any county in like manner as heretofore, but where the provisions of this Act affect the arrangement with respect to the consolidated police force for a county and borough, an adjustment shall be made between the council of the borough and county in accordance with the provisions of this Act. The foregoing provisions of this section shall apply to boroughs which are not county boroughs in like manner as if they were re-enacted and in terms made applicable to those boroughs.

The 3 & 4 Vict. c. 88, s. 14, enables boroughs to agree to consolidate their police with the county police, and by 19 & 20 Vict. c. 69, s. 5, the Queen in Council may arrange terms of consolidation on representations made by boroughs. The chief constable of the county has the general disposition and government of the consolidated police. An agreement for the consolidation of county and borough police cannot be terminated without the sanction of a Secretary of State; 19 & 20 Vict. c. 69, s. 20. As to the superannuation of the consolidated police, see the Police Act, 1890 (53 & 54 Vict. c. 45), s. 19 (3), *post*.

The provisions of the Act may affect an arrangement between a county and borough with reference to the sums to be contributed by each to the cost of the police under s. 24, sub-s. (2) (*i.*).

As to adjustment, see s. 62, *post*.

(2.) Where, for the purpose of calculating any contribution or payment to be made under this Act, it is necessary to ascertain the rateable value of both a county and a county borough, such rateable value shall be ascertained and fixed by a joint committee composed of representatives of all the councils concerned, and such committee shall for that purpose, have all the powers and jurisdiction of quarter sessions and of a committee of justices appointed under the County Rate Act, 1852, and the Acts amending the same, and the number of representatives for the county and each county borough respectively shall be settled by agreement, or, in default of agreement, by the Local Government Board.

15 & 16 Vict. c. 81.

Contributions and payments will have to be calculated under the preceding section and under s. 62, *post*. The rateable value will be determined by a joint committee, who will have the same power as a committee have under

15 & 16 Vict. c. 81, for the purpose of preparing a standard or basis for the county rate, see s. 3 (i.), *ante*, p. 5. It will be necessary, in fact, to prepare such standard or basis specially for the purposes of this sub-section.

Sect. 33 (2).

NOTE.

Application of Act with modifications to county boroughs.

34.—(1.) The mayor, aldermen, and burgesses of each county borough acting by the council shall, subject as in this Act mentioned, have and be subject to all the powers, duties, and liabilities of a county council under this Act (in so far as they are not already in possession of or subject to the same), and in particular shall, subject to the provisions of this Act as to adjustment between counties and county boroughs, be entitled to receive the like sums out of the Local Taxation Account, and be bound to make the like payments in substitution for local grants and the like grants in respect of the costs of the officers of unions and of district schools as in the case of a county council, so far as the circumstances make such payments applicable, and all the provisions of this Act (including those with respect to the forfeiture on the withholding by a Secretary of State of his certificate as respects the police of the county) shall accordingly, so far as circumstances admit, apply in the case of every such borough, with the necessary modifications, and in particular with the following modifications:—

(*a.*) The county borough shall be substituted for the county, and borough fund shall be substituted for county fund, and town clerk shall be substituted for clerk of the peace and clerk of the council:

(*b.*) A reference to two or more counties shall include a reference to county boroughs as well as counties:

(*c.*) Such powers, duties, and liabilities of the court of quarter sessions or justices as in the case of a county are transferred to the county council shall be transferred to the council of the county borough, whether the same are vested in or attached to the court of quarter sessions or justices of the borough or of the county in which the borough is situate:

(*d.*) In the case of the duties collected by the Commissioners of Inland Revenue in respect of the licences for trade carts, locomotives, horses, mules, and horse dealers under any Act of the present session, those Commissioners shall certify the amount collected in each county in like manner as if the county included each county borough specified in the Third Schedule to this Act as deemed to be situate in that county, and the amount as so ascertained shall be divided between the said boroughs and the residue of the said county in proportion to rateable value as fixed by the joint committee in pursuance of this Act, and until such value is fixed in proportion to

Sect. 34 (1)

rateable value according to the standard or basis for county contributions for the time being, and the share so ascertained shall be paid in like manner as if it had been collected in the county borough or in the residue of the county, as the case may be :

(*e.*) Any sum standing to the Exchequer Contribution Account of a county borough which remains after payment of the grant required to be made in respect of the costs of union officers shall be carried to the borough fund, or be applied in aid of such rate leviable over the whole of the borough as the council may determine, and the provisions respecting the payment of the same to the general county account of the county fund, and the subsequent application and division thereof, shall not apply.

In many cases the business formerly administered by justices in or out of sessions, and transferred to county councils by this Act, was already administered by the council of a borough as local authority. In such cases no transfer was necessary under this Act.

The provisions as to adjustment are contained in s. 32, *ante.*

The sums to be received out of the Local Taxation Account are described in ss. 20—22. The payments in substitution for local grants, etc., are contained in ss. 24—26.

A forfeiture of the police grant is provided for by s. 25, *ante.*

A reference to two or more counties is contained in s. 24, sub-s. (5), and s. 26, sub-s. (1).

The council of the borough, as county council, will have transferred to them all powers and duties, transferred by Part I. of this Act, whether these have been exercised hitherto by the county or borough quarter sessions, or the county or borough justices.

The Act referred to in paragraph (*d*) was never passed.

The Locomotives on Highways Act, 1896, *post* (59 & 60 Vict. c. 36), s. 8, does, however, provide for the payment of excise and licence duties on light locomotives, and these duties are to be dealt with in manner directed by this Act with respect to duties on Local Taxation Licences, *i.e.*, under s. 20, *ante*, p. 46.

Paragraph (*e*) substitutes, so far as relates to county boroughs, a provision in lieu of s. 23, sub-s. (2) (iv.), *ante*, p. 50. The surplus is to be paid to the borough fund, or in aid of some rate leviable over the whole of the borough.

(2.) On the appointed day there shall be transferred to the mayor, aldermen, and burgesses of each county borough all such bridges and approaches thereto, or parts thereof, situate within the borough as were previously repairable by the county or any hundred therein, and the costs of the council in repairing such bridges and approaches, or parts thereof, and in repairing any roads in the borough which by virtue of this Act or any Act applied by this Act are main roads, shall be payable out of the borough fund.

This sub-section transfers to a county borough the liability to repair all bridges within its boundaries which were previously repairable as county or hundred bridges. As to county bridges, see the note to s. 3 (viii.), p. 9, *ante*. Sect. 34 (2)

NOTE.

As to the liability of a borough to repair bridges within the borough other than those repairable by the county, see the Municipal Corporations Act, 1882, s. 119; also *R.* v. *Dorset (Inhabitants of)*, 45 L. T. (N.S.) 308; *R.* v. *Southampton*, (No. 1), 17 Q. B. D. 424; 55 L. J. M. C. 158; 55 L. T. (N.S.) 322; 35 W. R. 10; 50 J. P. 773; *R.* v. *Southampton*, (No. 2), 19 Q. B. D. 590; 56 L. J. M. C. 112; 57 L. T. (N.S.) 261.

(3.) The provisions of this Act with respect to—

(*a.*) The constitution, election, proceedings, or position of the county council or the chairman thereof,

(*b.*) The county treasurer, county surveyor, and other county officers,

(*c.*) The standing joint committee of the justices and the council, or

(*d.*) Coroners, or

(*e.*) Gas meters, or

(*f.*) The transfer to the council of powers relating to county and other rates, and the preparation or revision of the basis or standard for the county rate;

shall not apply to county boroughs, nor shall Part IV. of this Act relating to finance apply, save so far as is expressly provided in that Part.

The constitution, etc., of the council is provided for by the Municipal Corporations Act, 1882, the borough council in a county borough being also the county council.

The provisions of this Act as to county officers are inapplicable for the like reason, the appointment and duties of the borough officers being regulated by the Municipal Corporations Act, 1882.

The purposes for which a standing joint committee are appointed are in a borough administered by the borough council as such, or by the watch committee.

In a borough which has a separate quarter sessions the coroner is appointed by the council under the Municipal Corporations Act, 1882, s. 171. In other boroughs the county coroner has jurisdiction, but the election of a coroner in a county borough which has not separate quarter sessions is specially provided for by sub-s. (4) and (5), *post*. Section 5 of this Act is therefore inapplicable to county boroughs.

The Acts relating to gas meters (as to which, see note to s. 3 (xiii.), *ante*, p. 13) are in boroughs administered by the town councils, if they have adopted the Acts; but if they have not adopted the Acts, or if they are manufacturers or sellers of gas, the powers and duties under the Acts are exercised by the borough justices. If these powers and duties are not at present vested in the borough councils they are to remain in the borough justices.

As to the county and other rates, see s. 3 (i.), *ante*, p. 5; there cannot of course be county rates in a county borough.

(4.) Provided that where the district of any county coroner is wholly situate within a county borough, the coroner for that district shall be appointed by the council of that borough, and the

Sect. 34 (4). writ for his election may be issued to that council instead of to the county council, and where the district of any county coroner is situate partly within and partly without a county borough, the writ for the election of such coroner shall be issued to the county council, but if there is a joint committee of the county and borough councils for the purpose, the question of the person to be elected shall be referred to that joint committee, and the county council shall appoint the person recommended by the majority of such committee.

This sub-section provides for the case where a county borough has not separate quarter sessions and has not, therefore, a coroner of its own under s. 171 of the Municipal Corporations Act, 1882. Where the district assigned to a county coroner is wholly within the borough, the writ, instead of being directed to the county council, under s. 5, sub-s. (1), *ante*, is to be directed to the borough council. When it is partly within the borough the writ is to be directed to the county council, who are to appoint the person recommended by a joint committee appointed under the next sub-section.

(5.) If the council of a county borough so require, a joint committee shall from time to time be appointed for the purposes of coroners, consisting of such number of members of the county and borough councils as may be agreed upon, or in default of agreement may be determined by a Secretary of State.

See the note to the preceding sub-section.

(6.) Nothing in this Act shall transfer to the council of any borough any power in relation to the division of the county into polling districts for the purpose of a parliamentary election for the county, the appointment of places of election for the county, the places of holding courts for the revision of the list of voters, and the costs of, and other matters to be done for, the registration of parliamentary voters for the county.

For purposes of county elections, etc., the powers above referred to are exercisable by county councils in succession to quarter sessions under s. 3 (xii.) *ante*, p. 11.

The same powers as to dividing a municipal borough for purposes of borough elections are vested in the borough council by 30 & 31 Vict. c. 102, s. 34; 31 & 32 Vict. c. 58, s. 18; 46 & 47 Vict. c. 51, s. 47, sub-s. (3).

(7.) The powers and duties of the county authority under the Allotments Act, 1887, shall, as respects the borough, continue to be exercised and performed by the Local Government Board.

50 & 51 Vict. c. 48.

It is provided by the Allotments Act, 1887 (50 & 51 Vict. c. 48), s. 16, that for the purposes of that Act the county authority should be any representative body elected by the inhabitants of the county which might be established

Sect. 34 (7).

NOTE.

under any future Act, and until such representative body should be established the powers and duties of the county authority should be exercised and performed by the Local Government Board. The county councils, therefore, are the county authorities under the Act, but this will not apply to county boroughs, in which the Local Government Board will continue to exercise jurisdiction as county authority.

It may be added that in applying s. 9 of the Local Government Act, 1894, to county boroughs, sub-s. (18) of that section provides that an order for compulsory purchase of land for allotments shall, in the case of a county borough, be both made and confirmed by the Local Government Board.

(8.) This Act and the Municipal Corporations Act, 1882, shall be construed so as to give effect to the provisions of this section. 45 & 46 Vict. c. 50.

The provisions of the Municipal Corporations Act, 1882, bearing on this section have been noticed in the notes.

Application of Act to larger quarter sessions boroughs, not counties.

35. In the case of a quarter sessions borough, not being one of the boroughs named in the Third Schedule to this Act, but containing, according to the census of one thousand eight hundred and eighty-one, a population of ten thousand or upwards, the following provisions shall, on and after the appointed day, apply:

(1.) Nothing in this Act shall transfer to the county council any power of the council of the borough as local authority under any Act, or (save as in this Act expressly mentioned) alter the powers, duties, and liabilities of the council of the borough under the Municipal Corporations Act, 1882, but subject to the above provisions and to the savings hereinafter contained, the borough shall form part of the county for the purposes of this Act, and the parishes in the borough shall, subject to the exemptions hereinafter mentioned, be liable to be assessed to county contributions in like manner as the rest of the county.

It has already been pointed out in the note to s. 34, sub-s. (3), that in many cases where the local authorities for the execution of Acts were in counties the quarter sessions, in boroughs the local authorities under the same Acts were the borough councils. In these cases, while the powers of the quarter sessions are transferred to the county councils by this Act, the councils of the larger boroughs to which this section relates will, under the provision in the text, retain their powers as local authorities. These will include powers under the Explosives Act, 1875; the Weights and Measures Act, 1878 to 1893; the Petroleum Acts, 1871 to 1881, and the Reformatory and Industrial Schools Acts.

In so far as the powers of the councils under the Municipal Corporations Act, 1882, are altered by this Act, the alterations are indicated in the notes to the incorporated sections of that Act, *post*. Subject, however, to the provisions of this section, the boroughs in question are, for the purposes of this Act, to form part of the county.

(2.) Where such borough is at the passing of this Act exempt, in whole or in part, from contributing towards costs

Sect. 35 (2).

incurred for any purpose for which the quarter sessions of the county in which the borough is situate are authorised to incur cost the parishes in the borough shall not, save as in this Act expressly mentioned, be assessed by the county council to county contributions in respect of costs incurred for any such purpose, nor in the case of a partial exemption, be so assessed for any larger sum than such as will give effect to that exemption, but this exemption shall not extend to any costs incurred for the purpose of any powers, duties, or liabilities of the justices of the borough, which will by virtue of this Act be exercised or discharged by the county council nor to any costs of or incidental to the assizes of the county.

This sub-section preserves existing exemptions from contributions to the county rate. The exemption extends to contributions to the costs of new county bridges taken over by a county council under s. 6, *ante*, p. 17. *Bury St. Edmunds (Mayor, etc. of)* v. *West Suffolk County Council*, Times, May 21st, 1898.

The powers, duties, and liabilities of the justices of the borough which are by this Act transferred to the county council are those transferred by s. 36, *post.*

As to the costs of the assizes, see sub-s. (5), and s. 100, *post.*

As to the mode of assessment, see s. 100, *post.*

(3.) Notwithstanding the last enactment the borough shall, for the purposes of the provisions of the Highways and 41 & 42 Vict c. 77. Locomotives (Amendment) Act, 1878, respecting main roads, form part of the county, and the costs of maintaining, repairing, improving, enlarging, or otherwise dealing with any main road in the borough shall be paid out of the county fund, and the payment of the costs incurred in the execution of the provisions of this Act with respect to main roads shall be a general county purpose for which the parishes of the borough may be assessed to county contributions :

A borough having separate quarter sessions was not included in the definition of an urban authority under the Highway Act, 1878, and therefore the provisions of that Act as to main roads did not apply to such a borough. The boroughs mentioned in this section are now declared to be within the definition of urban sanitary authorities (see the next sub-section), and for the purposes of main roads they are to be deemed to be part of the county, and liable to be assessed like the rest of the county to county contributions.

For the definition of general county purposes, see s. 68, *post.*

(4.) Provided that—

(*a.*) The borough shall be deemed to be an urban sanitary district within the meaning of the 41 & 42 Vict. c. 77. Highways and Locomotives (Amendment) Act, 1878 ; and the council of the borough shall have the power under the Highways and Locomotives (Amendment) Act, 1878, of making bye-laws respecting locomotives, and authorizing locomotives to be used on any road within the borough, save that if any difference is made by such bye-laws or authority between any main road maintained by the county council and the other roads in the borough, such authority and bye-laws shall require the approval of the county council; and Sect. 35 (4)

(*b.*) The council of the borough shall have power as an urban authority to claim, in accordance with this Act, to retain the powers and duties of maintaining and repairing any main road in the borough; and

(*c.*) The council of the borough may within two years after the passing of this Act apply to the county council to declare such roads in the borough as are mentioned in the application to be main roads within the meaning of the Highways and Locomotives (Amendment) Act, 1878, and the county council shall consider such application and inquire whether such roads are or ought to be main roads within the meaning of the said Act, and shall make or refuse the declaration accordingly, and if the county council refuse to make the declaration, the council of the borough may within a reasonable time after such refusal apply to the Local Government Board, and that Board shall have power, if after a local inquiry they think it just so to do, to make the said declaration, which shall have the same effect as if made by the county council.

See the note to the preceding sub-section.

The power to make bye-laws respecting locomotives, and authorizing locomotives to be used on any road within the borough, is conferred by s. 31 of the Highway Act as amended by this section. The saving in case of differences between the county bye-laws applicable to main roads maintained by the county council within the borough and the borough bye-laws, is obviously necessary to avoid an inconvenient or even absurd result. It is to be feared, however, that inconvenience will result from the differences in bye-laws of the county council and those of the borough council, when by reason of the borough itself maintaining its main roads the approval of the county council is not necessary.

It should be mentioned that these bye-laws as to locomotives will not apply to "light locomotives" as defined by the Locomotives on Highways Act, 1896. See s. 1 of that Act, *post*.

Sect. 35 (4).

NOTE.

The power of an urban authority to claim to retain the maintenance of its main roads is conferred by s. 11, sub-s. (2), *ante*, p. 27.

As already stated, the provisions of the Act of 1878 as to main roads did not previously apply to these boroughs, and hence it was necessary to allow a period within which roads in the borough may be declared main roads under the Act.

(5.) The payment of the costs of assizes and sessions shall be a general county purpose for which the parishes in the borough may be assessed to county contributions, and all costs of prosecutions mentioned in section one hundred and sixty-nine of the Municipal Corporations Acts, 1882, shall be paid out of the county fund.

45 & 46 Vict. c. 50.

As to what is included in "the costs of assizes and sessions," see s. 100, *post*.

The general scheme of the Act with reference to the costs of assizes and sessions was thus stated by STEPHEN and VAUGHAN WILLIAMS, JJ., in *Ex parte The County Council of Kent and the Councils of Dover and Sandwich*, [1891] 1 Q. B. 389 ; 60 L. J. Q. B. 314 ; 60 L. T. (N.S.) 421 ; 55 J. P. 248 ; 7 T. L. R. 250 :— "Boroughs with populations over 10,000 having a separate court of quarter sessions are made part and parcel of the county, and are thus subject generally to county rates, but retain the power and duty to raise by rates the expenses of the borough quarter sessions and of petty sessional divisions within the area of the jurisdiction of the borough quarter sessions, and *pro tanto* are exempted from proportionate contribution to the expenses of county sessions. Quarter sessions boroughs with a population of less than 10,000, though retaining their judicial functions, have neither the duty nor the power to raise the expenses of sessions by rates, such expenses being a general county purpose . . . . We are not unaware that there are provisions in the Act, particularly in section 35, sub-section (5), which are difficult to reconcile with this view, but it seems to us that a construction must be put upon them consistent with the Act as a whole." It was held, therefore, in the case of Dover, which had a population exceeding 10,000, that the borough quarter sessions had still the power of making a rate in the nature of a county rate in the liberties of the borough, but that such power was limited to expenses of borough quarter sessions, that the liability for costs of quarter sessions was not transferred to the county council, and that, on the other hand, the borough was not subject to county rates in respect of the costs of county quarter sessions. It was held further that the salaries of the recorder and justices' clerk were payable as formerly out of the borough fund into which the fees and fines were paid, and that the costs for prosecution for indictable offences incurred in the borough were payable by the county council, as the text repealed s. 169 of the Municipal Corporations Act, 1882, and made those costs payable out of the county funds. In the case of Sandwich, which depended upon s. 38 (5), *post* (that borough having a population of less than 10,000), it was held that for all such purposes the borough was part of the county and liable to be assessed accordingly, and that the costs of the borough quarter sessions, salaries of recorder, etc., were payable by the county council. But in *Thetford (Mayor of)* v. *Norfolk County Council*, 14 T. L. R. 35, WILLS, J., differed from the latter part of this decision, and held that in the case of a smaller quarter sessions borough the salaries of the recorder and clerk of the peace are payable by the borough, that of the justices' clerk being payable by the county under s. 84, *post*.

Section 169 of the Municipal Corporations Act, 1882, is as follows :—"A municipal corporation of a borough having a separate court of quarter sessions shall be liable to pay the costs and expenses attending the prosecution of any felony committed or supposed to have been committed in the borough, and of any other offence committed or supposed to have been committed in the borough, and costs and expenses attending the prosecution whereof are by law payable as in the case of a felony. The amount of those costs and expenses shall be ascertained as directed by law, and the order of the court for the payment thereof shall be directed to the treasurer of the borough."

As to the offences to which this section applies, see the notes to s. 67, *post*.

(6.) The county councillors elected for an electoral division consisting wholly of such borough, or of some part of such borough, shall not act or vote in respect of any question arising before the county council as regards matters involving expenditure on account of which the parishes in the borough are not, for the time being, liable to be assessed equally with the rest of the county to county contributions.

The councillors hereby disqualified from voting are those who represent a division consisting wholly of the borough, or wholly of part of the borough. The sub-section will not apply to councillors who represent a division consisting partly of the borough and partly of a county district exterior to the borough.

(7.) The county council and the council of any such borough may agree for the cessation in whole or in part of any exemption under this section of the parishes in the borough from assessment to county contributions, in consideration either of payment by the county council of a capital sum, or of an annual payment, or of a transfer of property or liabilities, or of the county council undertaking in substitution for the council of the borough any powers or duties, or partly for one consideration and partly for another, or in any other manner, according as may be determined.

The consideration for the agreement may be all or any of the matters herein stated, or any other consideration which the councils in their discretion may deem adequate. On the cessation of the exemption the parishes in the borough will become liable to be assessed to county contributions in respect of the costs incurred for the purposes, from contributing to which they were previously exempt.

(8.) A borough which is a county of a city or a county of a town shall, for the purposes of this section, be deemed to be situate in and form part of the county which it adjoins, or if it adjoins more than one county, then in and of the county of which it forms part for the purposes of parliamentary elections.

A borough which is not a county of a city or county of a town will, of

Sect. 35 (8). course, for the purposes of this section be deemed to form part of the county in which it is geographically situate.

NOTE.

General application of Act to boroughs with separate commission of the peace.

36.—(1.) Where a borough has a separate commission of the peace, whether a quarter sessions borough or not (and is not a borough named in the Third Schedule to this Act), then, subject to the provisions of this Act, all such powers, duties, and liabilities of the court of quarter sessions or justices of the borough, as in the case of the county are by this Act transferred to the county council, shall cease, and the county council shall have those powers, duties, and liabilities within the area of the borough in like manner as in the rest of the county;

This section applies to all boroughs which have a separate commission of the peace, other than county boroughs, whether they have separate quarter sessions or not, and without regard to their population.

This section provides that such powers of the borough quarter sessions or justices as would, in a county, be transferred to the county council, shall in these boroughs be transferred to the county councils, so that for these purposes the county council will supersede the borough sessions or justices within the area of the borough. As to the costs incurred for these purposes, see s. 35, sub-s. (2), *ante*, p. 77.

(2.) Provided that such powers, duties, or liabilities, so far as they are under the Acts relating to pauper lunatics, shall, save as otherwise provided by this Act, be transferred to the council of the borough and not to the county council, and the provisions of this Act with respect to the transfer to a county council shall apply with the necessary modifications to such transfer to the council of the borough.

This sub-section contains an exception to the preceding one. The transfer of the powers of the borough sessions or justices under the Acts relating to pauper lunatics is to the borough council, not to the county council.

This Act contained a clause (s. 86, *post*) adapting the Acts relating to lunatic asylums to the provisions of this Act: that clause has been repealed (but is in substance re-enacted) by the Lunacy Act, 1890.

Observe that this clause relates only to *pauper* lunatics. This Act does not in any way interfere with the powers and duties of justices in relation to private lunatic asylums.

The expression "save as otherwise provided by this Act," has reference to the provisions in s. 38, sub-s. (1), *post*, whereby in the smaller quarter sessions boroughs the powers, etc., of the borough justices relating to pauper lunatic asylums are transferred to the county councils.

Application of Act to quarter sessions boroughs hereafter created.

37. The grant after the passing of this Act of a court of quarter sessions to any borough not being a county borough, shall not affect the powers, duties, or liabilities of the county council as respects the area of that borough, nor exempt the parishes in the borough from being assessed to county contributions for any purpose to which such parishes were previously liable to be assessed, and shall not confer or impose on the mayor, aldermen, and burgesses, or the council of such borough, any powers, duties, or liabilities further than such as are necessary for establishing and maintaining the court of quarter sessions in the borough.

The effect of this section is that the grant of separate quarter sessions will not in future affect the position of a borough under this Act, so far as relates to county councils and county contributions.

In the case of a grant of quarter sessions to a county borough which had not separate quarter sessions at the passing of this Act, the borough is to redeem its liability to contribute a share of the costs of quarter sessions and coroners. See s. 32, sub-s. (3), *ante*, p. 69.

Application of Act to smaller quarter sessions boroughs with population under 10,000.

38. Where a borough having a separate court of quarter sessions contained according to the census of one thousand eight hundred and eighty-one a population of less than ten thousand, the following provisions shall after the appointed day apply :—

(1.) There shall be transferred to the county council the powers, duties, and liabilities of the council and justices of the borough as regards the provision, enlargement, maintenance, management, and visitation of and other dealing with asylums for pauper lunatics ;

These powers, duties, and liabilities are similar to those transferred from the quarter sessions in counties under s. 3, sub-s. (vi.), *ante*, p. 8. As to the larger quarter sessions boroughs, see s. 35 (1), *ante*, p. 77.

The justices of the county of Salop and the borough of Wenlock, in the year 1884, agreed to provide a common lunatic asylum and to bear the costs of its provision and maintenance in agreed proportions, and shortly afterwards an agreement was entered into between the justices of Montgomery and the committee of visitors appointed by Salop and Wenlock under the above arrangement whereby Montgomery became united with Salop and Wenlock for the purposes of the Lunacy Acts. A visiting committee was appointed by the two counties and the borough of Wenlock jointly. Under agreements with this visiting committee three boroughs in the county of Salop joined the union on the terms of paying certain annual rents to the treasurer of the asylum. Each of these three boroughs was a quarter sessions borough with a population of less than 10,000 when the Local Government Act, 1888, came into operation. *Held* (by CAVE and CHARLES, JJ.) on a case stated under s. 29, *ante*, that the liability of the three boroughs under their agreements with the visiting committee was transferred under this section to the county council of Salop, and that that council was bound to pay to the treasurer of the asylum the rents reserved by those agreements. *In re County Council of Salop*, 65 L. T. (N.S.) 416.

(2.) There shall be transferred to the county council the powers, duties, and liabilities of the council of the borough—

(*a*) as regards coroners ; and

(*b*) as regards the appointment of analysts under the Acts relating to the sale of food and drugs ; and

Sect. 38 (2).

(c) under the Acts relating to—
(i.) reformatory and industrial schools; and
(ii.) fish conservancy; and
(iii.) explosives; and

(d) under the Highways and Locomotives (Amendment) Act, 1878;

Provided that the transfer by this section—

(a) shall be subject to the provisions in this Act for the protection of existing officers and the continuance of existing contracts; and

(b) shall not, save as respects the coroners, affect the powers, duties, and liabilities of the council of the borough under the Municipal Corporations Act, 1882;

In all quarter sessions boroughs the coroner was formerly appointed by the council of the borough, under s. 171 of the Municipal Corporations Act, 1882. In the boroughs to which this section relates that council no longer has this power, and it would appear from sub-s. (5) that the offices of existing coroners were determined. The area of these boroughs has now, for the purposes of the coroners, become part of the counties. (See sub-s. (5), *post.*)

Analysts were formerly appointed in boroughs having separate courts of quarter sessions by the councils of such boroughs (38 & 39 Vict. c. 63, s. 10). This power of appointment remains with the town councils of the larger quarter sessions boroughs, under s. 35, *ante*. In the smaller quarter sessions boroughs the power passes to the county councils, subject to the proviso in this sub-section.

Under the Reformatory and Industrial Schools Acts the councils of boroughs had certain powers as prison authorities similar to those of justices in quarter sessions in counties, as to which see s. 3. sub-s. (vii.), *ante*, p. 8.

As to the Acts relating to fish conservancy, see s. 3, sub-s. (xiii.), *ante*, p. 12.

Under the Explosives Act, 1875, the local authority in a borough not assessed to the county rate were the council of the borough (s. 67), and in boroughs so assessed the council might become a local authority by order of a Secretary of State (s. 68). The powers and duties of the town councils in the smaller quarter sessions boroughs passed under the text to the county councils.

As to the Highway Act, 1878, compare the provisions of s. 35, sub-s. (4), *ante*, p. 78, and see the notes to that section. See also sub-ss. (3) and (4), *infra*.

The provisions of this Act as to existing officers and as to the continuance of existing contracts are contained in ss. 118, 120, and ss. 122, 125, *post*.

41 & 42 Vict. c. 77.

(3.) The borough shall be an urban sanitary district within the meaning of the Highways and Locomotives (Amendment) Act, 1878:

See the notes to s. 35, sub-ss. (3) and (4), *ante*, pp. 78, 79.

(4.) The council of the borough may, within two years after the passing of this Act, apply to the county council to declare such roads in the borough as are mentioned in the application to be main roads within the meaning of the Highways and Locomotives (Amendment) Act, 1878, and the county council shall consider such application, and inquire whether such roads are, or ought to be main roads within the meaning of the said Act, and shall make or refuse the declaration accordingly, and if the county council refuse the declaration, the council of the borough may, within a reasonable time after such refusal, apply to the Local Government Board, and that Board, after a local inquiry, shall have power, if they think it just so to do, to make the said declaration, which shall have the same effect as if it had been made by the county council: Sect. 38 (4).

This sub-section is identical with s. 35, sub-s. (4) (*c*), *ante*, p. 79.

(5.) The area of the borough shall for the purposes of the above-mentioned Acts and all other administrative purposes of the county council be included in the county, as if the borough had not a separate court of quarter sessions, and accordingly shall be subject to the authority of the county council and the county coroners, and may be annexed by the county council to a coroner's district of the county, and the parishes in the borough shall be liable to be assessed to all county contributions:

See *Ex parte The County Council of Kent and The Councils of Dover and Sandwich*, and *Thetford (Mayor of)* v. *Norfolk County Council*, *ante*, p. 80.

See the note to sub-s. (2) as to coroners, *supra*. The borough is to be liable to be assessed to all county contributions.

(6.) Any property, debts, or liabilities of the county, or of any borough affected by this or the next succeeding section (including the charge to be made for lunatics which but for this Act would have been maintainable by the borough), may be adjusted in manner provided by Part Three of this Act:

The provisions of this Act as to adjustment are contained in s. 62, *post*.

As to lunatics maintainable by the borough, see the note to s. 24, sub-s. (2) (*g*), *ante*, p. 56. The lunatics in question are now chargeable to the county.

(7.) It shall be lawful for Her Majesty the Queen, on petition from the council of any borough to which this or the next succeeding section applies, by Order in Council, to revoke the grant of a court of quarter sessions to the borough, and by letters patent to revoke the grant of a commission of the peace for the borough, and to make

8 (7). such provision as to Her Majesty seems proper for the protection of interests existing at the date of the revocation, and after the date of the revocation all enactments and laws relating to courts of quarter sessions and justices and their jurisdiction shall apply as if such court of quarter sessions or commission of the peace, as the case may be, did not exist:

This is a novel provision. If it is put into effect the offices of the recorder of the borough, clerk of the peace, etc., will be abolished, but they will be entitled to compensation under s. 120, *post*.

(8.) A borough which is a county of a city or a county of a town shall, for the purposes of this and the next succeeding section, and if Her Majesty revokes the grant of a Court of quarter sessions or a commission of the peace to such borough, then also for all purposes of quarter sessions and justices, be deemed to be situate in and form part of the county of which it forms part for the purpose of parliamentary elections:

Compare the somewhat similar provisions of s. 35, sub-s. (8), *ante*, and see the notes to that sub-section. In the case of a revocation of a grant of quarter sessions to the borough, the county justices would exercise concurrent jurisdiction with the borough justices. See the Municipal Corporations Act, 1882, s. 154, and *Reigate* (*Mayor of*) v. *Hart*, L. R. 3 Q. B. 244; 37 L. J. M. C. 70; 18 L. T. (N.S.) 237; 16 W. R. 896; 32 J. P. 342.

(9.) Where this section applies to a cinque port it shall apply also to all the members thereof, and those members when not situate in a quarter sessions borough shall form part of the county for all purposes.

As to the cinque ports, see the note to s. 48, *post*.

ation to all hs with tion 10,000.

39.—(1.) Where a borough, whether with or without a separate court of quarter sessions, contained according to the census of one thousand eight hundred and eighty-one a population of less than ten thousand, then after the appointed day all powers, duties, and liabilities of the mayor, aldermen, and burgesses, or council of the borough, or the watch committee of the borough in relation—

(*a*) to the police force of the borough, or

(*b*) to the appointment of analysts under the Acts relating to the sale of foods and drugs, or

Vict. (*c*) to the execution of the Contagious Diseases (Animals) Acts, 1878 to 1886, or the Destructive Insects Act, 1877, or

Vict. 47. (*d*) to gas meters, or

Sect. 39 (1).

(e) to weights and measures, if the council exercise any jurisdiction in relation thereto,

shall cease, and, subject to the provisions of this Act as to the members of the police force holding office on the said day, the area of the borough shall for all purposes of the Acts relating to the county police force, or other matters above in this section mentioned, form part of the county in like manner as if it were not a borough.

49 & 50 Vict. c. 32.
40 & 41 Vict. c. 68.

This section applies to all boroughs having a population of less than 10,000, whether they have separate quarter sessions or not. To these boroughs sub-ss. (6) and (8) of the preceding section are made expressly applicable.

The police force of the borough will cease to exist as a separate force, and the existing borough constables will become county constables as provided by ss. 118, 119, *post*. This provision as to police repeals that part of the Municipal Corporations Act, 1882, relating to borough police, so far as relates to these smaller boroughs.

It has been shown in the notes to the last section that analysts were appointed in quarter sessions boroughs under 38 & 39 Vict. c. 63, s. 10, by the borough councils. In boroughs which had no separate quarter sessions, but had a separate police force, those councils had a similar power of appointment. As the separate police force will cease to exist in these smaller boroughs, the power to appoint analysts is to cease also.

The Contagious Diseases (Animals) Acts referred to in the text (except the two sections mentioned in sub-s. (2), *infra*), have been repealed and consolidated by the Diseases of Animals Act, 1894. By s. 3 of that Act, the local authorities in England and Wales are (1) for each borough not being a borough to which s. 39 of the Local Government Act, 1888, applies, the borough council; (2) for the residue of each administrative county the county council.

As to the Destructive Insects Act, see the note to s. 3 (xiii.), *ante*, p. 12.

As to the jurisdiction of a borough council under the Acts relating to gas meters, see the note to s. 34, sub-s. (3), *ante*, p. 75.

Under the Weights and Measures Act, 1878, the borough councils were the local authorities in boroughs which had separate quarter sesssions. In boroughs not having separate quarter sessions they were the local authorities only if they so resolved, or if in 1878 they possessed separate local standards (41 & 42 Vict. c. 49, s. 50). All powers of borough councils ceased under this Act in the smaller boroughs.

The provisions of this Act, as to members of the police force holding office on the appointed day, are contained in ss. 118, 119, *post*.

(2.) Provided that nothing in this section shall transfer to the county council any powers, duties, or liabilities under section thirty-four of the Contagious Diseases (Animals) Act, 1878, as amended by section nine of the Contagious Diseases (Animals) Act, 1886.

41 & 42 Vict. c. 74.
49 & 50 Vict. c. 32.

The sections above referred to are not repealed by the Diseases of Animals Act, 1894; they are set out in Lumley's Public Health, p. 486. By s. 9 of the Act of 1886, the powers of local authorities under s. 34 of the Act of 1878, and the Orders made under that section applying to dairies and milkshops,

Sect. 39 (2). are vested in sanitary authorities. The powers of a borough council, as urban authority under that Act, are preserved by this sub-section.

NOTE.

(3.) The urban authority for any borough or town with such population as above in this section mentioned shall cease to be the local authority under the Acts relating to explosives, and the county council shall have the like authority under the said Acts in the said borough or town as they have in the rest of their county.

The word "town" is not defined by this Act. It refers probably to improvement districts in which, by s. 68 of the Explosives Act, 1875, the commissioners might, by order of the Secretary of State, have become the local authority in like manner as the council of a borough assessed to the county rate, as to which see the note to s. 38, sub-s. (2), *ante*, p. 84. This sub-section puts an end to the powers of such commissioners.

Application of Act to Metropolis.

Application of Act to metropolis as county of London.

40. In the application of this Act to the Metropolis, the following provisions shall have effect :—

(1.) The Metropolis shall, on and after the appointed day, be an administrative county for the purposes of this Act by the name of the administrative county of London.

For the definition of "the Metropolis," see s. 100, *post.* The term "administrative county" is defined by the same section. It will be seen by the next sub-section that the county of London exclusive of the city of London is a separate county for all non-adminstrative purposes.

The appointed day is defined by s. 109, *post.*

It was held that by virtue of this section the London County Council was the proper authority to certify under 6 Vict. c. 18, s. 55, for the costs of the returning officer preparing the register of parliamentary voters in the borough of Deptford, notwithstanding s. 92, *post*, which retains that borough in the county of Kent for county parliamentary purposes. *Weller* v. *Collins*, 54 J. P. 441 ; 6 T. L. R. 342.

(2.) Such portion of the administrative county of London as forms part of the counties of Middlesex, Surrey, and Kent, shall on and after the appointed day be severed from those counties, and form a separate county for all non-administrative purposes by the name of the county of London ; and it shall be lawful for Her Majesty the Queen to appoint a sheriff of that county, and to grant a commission of the peace and court of quarter sessions to that county ; and, subject to the provisions of this Act, all enactments, laws, and usages with respect to counties in England and Wales, and to sheriffs, justices, and quarter sessions shall, so far as circumstances admit, apply to the county of London : Sect. 40 (2)

The county of London as here limited is a separate county for all non-administrative purposes, with a sheriff, quarter sessions, and commission of peace for itself.

(3.) Provided that, for the purpose of the jurisdiction of the justices under such commission, and of such court, as well as other non-administrative purposes, the county of the city of London shall continue a separate county, but if and when the mayor, commonalty, and citizens of the city assent to jurisdiction being conferred therein on such justices and court, may by commission under the Great Seal be made subject to the jurisdiction thereof.

The city of London is part of the administrative county of London for the purposes of this Act. For non-administrative purposes it will continue to be a separate county until the event mentioned in the text.

(4.) The number of the county councillors for the administrative county of London shall be double the number of members which, at the passing of this Act, the parliamentary boroughs in the metropolis are authorized by law to return to serve in Parliament ; and each such borough, or, if it is divided into divisions, each division thereof shall be an electoral division for the purposes of this Act, and the number of county councillors elected for each such electoral division shall be double the number of members of Parliament which such borough or division is, at the passing of this Act, entitled to return to serve in Parliament :

The number of councillors in the county of London is thus fixed by the Act itself, and not by the Local Government Board, under s. 2, sub-s. (3), *ante*. In like manner the electoral divisions are fixed, and consist of the parliamentary divisions. The result is that the city of London returns four county councillors, and the rest of the metropolis one hundred and fourteen; this, of course, is in addition to the aldermen elected under the next sub-section, who are nineteen in number.

(5.) Provided that the number of county aldermen in the administrative county of London shall not exceed one-sixth of the whole number of county councillors.

In other counties the number of aldermen is one-third of the council. See s. 14 of the Municipal Corporations Act, 1882, *post*.

(6.) The provisions of this Act with respect to the powers, duties, and liabilities of county councils, and the transfer

(6). of property, debts, and liabilities of counties to county councils, shall apply to the administrative county of London in like manner, so nearly as circumstances admit, as if the quarter sessions, justices, and clerks of the peace of the counties of Middlesex, Surrey, and Kent had been, so far as regards the Metropolis, the quarter sessions, justices, and clerk of the peace for the administrative county of London.

This provision applies in effect to the first part of this Act so far as regards the transfer to the county councils from quarter sessions and justices, and the transfer of property under Part IV.

(7.) Provided that any property, debts, or liabilities of the county of Kent shall not, by reason only of this enactment, be vested in the county council of London, but such property, debts, and liabilities, and also the property, debts, and liabilities of the counties of Middlesex and Surrey, shall be apportioned between the portions of those counties situate within the metropolis and the portions situate outside the metropolis in such manner as may be determined by agreement between the respective county councils, or in default of agreement by the Commissioners under this Act, and the property, debts, and liabilities apportioned to the portions within the metropolis shall be the property, debts, and liabilities of the whole of the administrative county of London.

As to the Commissioners under this Act, see s. 61, *post.*

(8.) There shall also be transferred to the London County Council the powers, duties, and liabilities of the Metropolitan Board of Works, and after the appointed day that board shall cease to exist, and the property, debts, and liabilities thereof shall be transferred to the London County Council, and that council shall be in law the successors of the Metropolitan Board of Works.

The Metropolitan Board of Works had not only extensive powers in the metropolis as to drainage, streets, open spaces, bridges, etc., but were the local authority for the execution of numerous Acts in the metropolis, such as the Artizans Dwellings Acts, the Contagious Diseases (Animals) Acts, etc. The provisions of the several statutes relating to the powers, duties, and liabilities hereby transferred are too numerous for insertion here.

(9.) If the London County Council borrow for the purposes of this Act they shall borrow in accordance with the provisions of the Acts relating to the Metropolitan Board of Works, but save as aforesaid Part Four of this

Act shall apply to the London County Council when acting as successors of the Metropolitan Board of Works, and the costs incurred when so acting shall be paid out of the county fund, and the payment thereof shall be a general county purpose. Sect. 40 (9).

The effect of this sub-section is that the provisions of this Act as to borrowing (*post*, ss. 69, 70) do not apply to the London County Council, whose borrowing powers are regulated by special legislation. See the note to s. 70 (2), *post*, p. 136.

Position of city of London, and application of Highway Acts.

41.—(1.) Of the powers, duties, and liabilities of the court of quarter sessions and justices of the city of London—

(*a.*) such of them as would, if the city were a quarter sessions borough, with a population exceeding ten thousand, be exercised by virtue of this or any other Act by the council of the borough, shall be transferred to the mayor, commonalty, and citizens of the city acting by the council (in this Act referred to as the common council); and

(*b.*) such of them as would, in the said case, be by virtue of this Act exercised and discharged by the county council shall cease, and the county council shall, subject to the provisions of this Act, have those powers, duties and liabilities within the city of London in like manner as within the rest of the administrative county of London.

As to the definition of the quarter sessions of the city of London, see s. 100, *post*.

Under this sub-section such powers as would, if the city were a quarter sessions borough under ss. 35, 36, be exercised by the council, will be exercised by the common council. These include the powers, duties, and liabilities of a local authority under the Explosives Acts, 1875, the Petroleum Acts, 1871 to 1881, the Weights and Measures Acts, 1878 to 1893, the Reformatory and Industrial Schools Acts, (see *ante*, p. 77). The common council are expressly created a "local authority" under the Lunacy Act, 1890, s. 240. Such other powers of the quarter sessions and justices as would, under ss. 35, 36, be transferred to a county council, will be transferred to the London County Council. This includes the licensing of places for music and dancing under 25 Geo. 2, c. 36.

(2.) The provisions of this Act with respect to the transfer to a county council shall apply with the necessary modifications to such transfer to the common council, and the common council shall be entitled to receive from the London County Council in respect of each pauper lunatic, the same amount as is required by this Act to be paid by any other county council to the council of a borough.

The amount required to be paid for each pauper lunatic is that provided by s. 24, sub-s. (2) (*g*), *ante*, p. 56.

(3.) Where at the passing of this Act the Metropolitan Board of Works or the quarter sessions of Middlesex are authorized to incur

Sect. 41 (3). costs for any purpose, and the common council of the city are not liable to contribute to such costs, the parishes in the city of London shall not, save as in this Act expressly mentioned, be liable to be assessed to county contributions in respect of costs incurred by the county council for such purpose, but this exemption shall not extend to any costs incurred for the purpose of any powers, duties, or liabilities of the quarter sessions or justices of the city of London, which will be exercised and discharged by the London County Council.

This continues exemptions of the city and forms an exception to the provisions in s. 40 (9), *ante*, which makes all costs of the London County Council as successors to the Metropolitan Board of Works payable as for general county purposes. As to the costs of quarter sessions, see sub-s. (5), *infra*.

41 & 42 Vict. c. 77. (4.) The provisions of the Highways and Locomotives (Amendment) Act, 1878, with respect to main roads, as amended by this Act, shall extend to the Metropolis in like manner as if the expression "urban sanitary district" in that Act included, as respects the Metropolis, the city of London, and a parish in Schedule A., and a district in Schedule B., of the Metropolis Management Act, 1855, as amended by subsequent Acts, and as if the Commissioners of Sewers, or vestry, or district board (as the case may be) were the urban sanitary authority: Provided that—

18 & 19 Vict c. 120.

(*a.*) in the city of London the common council shall have the power under the Highways and Locomotives (Amendment) Act, 1878, of making bye-laws respecting locomotives, and authorizing locomotives to be used on any road within the city, save that if any difference is made by such bye-laws or authority between any main road maintained by the county council and the other roads in the city, such authority and bye-laws shall require the approval of the county council; and

(*b.*) the common council in the city of London, and in any other part of the Metropolis, the vestry, or district board, shall be deemed to be a district council and an urban authority within the meaning of the provisions of this Act with respect to main roads, and may accordingly claim to retain the power of maintaining and repairing a main road, and in such case shall have all such powers and duties of maintaining, repairing, improving and enlarging, and otherwise dealing with the main road as they would have if it were an ordinary highway repairable by them, and such powers and duties shall in the city of London be discharged by the Commissioners of Sewers. **Sect. 41 (4).**

The commissioners of sewers no longer exist, their powers having been transferred to the common council of the city of London by 60 & 61 Vict. c. cxxxiii.

This sub-section down to the end of the first paragraph is similar to that contained in s. 35, which provides for the larger quarter sessions boroughs. The county council for London exercise the general powers of a county authority in the metropolis. See s. 3 (viii.), *ante*, p. 9.

In the city the common council make bye-laws as to locomotives. The saving to this provision is similar to that contained in s. 35, sub-s. (4).

The provisions of this Act as to main roads are contained in s. 11, *ante*, pp. 21 *et seq.*

(5.) The payment of the costs of assizes and sessions shall be a general county purpose for which the parishes in the city may be assessed to county contributions, and all such costs of prosecutions in the city as are by law payable out of the county rate shall be paid out of the county fund.

As to what is included in the "costs of assizes and sessions," see s. 100, *post*.

The expression "assizes" includes the Central Criminal Court.

As to the prosecutions the costs of which are payable out of the county rate, see the statutes mentioned in the note to s. 67, *post*.

(6.) The county councillors elected for the city, shall not act or vote in respect of any question arising before the county council as regards matters involving expenditure on account of which the parishes in the city are not for the time being liable to be assessed equally with the rest of the administrative county to county contributions.

Compare the similar provisions of s. 35, sub-s. (6), *ante*, p. 81.

(7.) The London county council, and the common council of the city of London may agree for the cessation in whole or in part of any exemption under this section from assessment, in consideration either of payment by the county council of a capital sum, or of an annual payment, or of a transfer of property or liabilities, or of the county council undertaking, in substitution for the common council, any powers or duties, or partly for one consideration and partly for another, or in any other manner, according as may be determined.

This sub-section is identical with s. 35, sub-s. (7), *ante*, p. 81.

(8.) The sheriffs of the city of London shall not have any authority except in the city.

As to the sheriff of Middlesex, see s. 46, sub-s. (6), *post*.

42.—(1.) If the London county council petitions Her Majesty the Queen in that behalf, it shall be lawful for Her Majesty from **Arrangements for paid chairman**

Sect. 42 (1).

and sitting of quarter sessions for London.

time to time to appoint a barrister of not less than ten years' standing to be paid chairman or deputy chairman, or one of the paid deputy chairmen, as the case may be, of the quarter sessions for the county of London.

As to the appointment of a substitute for the chairman or deputy chairman in case of sickness or absence, and as to the pensions payable to the chairman and deputy chairman, see the Quarter Sessions (London) Act, 1896 (59 & 60 Vict. c. 55).

(2.) Any person so appointed shall hold office during good behaviour, and shall by virtue of his office be a justice of the peace for the county of London.

(3.) There shall be paid to him out of the county fund as a general county purpose such yearly salary not exceeding that stated in the petition in consequence of which the appointment was made, as Her Majesty directs.

As to general county purposes, see s. 68, *post.*

(4.) Such chairman or deputy chairman shall not, during his office, be eligible to serve in Parliament, and shall not, during his continuance in office practise as a barrister.

(5.) Where there is any such paid chairman or deputy chairman of the quarter sessions, the court may be held before such chairman or deputy chairman alone.

(6.) Separate courts of quarter sessions may be held at different parts of the county of London at the same time if so directed by the county council with the approval of a Secretary of State, and every court of general sessions of the peace for the county of London and every adjournment thereof shall have the same jurisdiction in all respects, including the power of hearing and determining appeals, as if such court were quarter sessions.

(7.) The London county council may from time to time submit to a Secretary of State a scheme for regulating the holding of courts of quarter sessions in London either at any one place or at different places, and in the latter case either at the same time or at different times, and for determining the legal character of each sessions so held, that is to say, whether quarter, general, original, or adjourned sessions, or otherwise, and for making such regulations respecting committals for trial, recognisances, depositions, and other matters as are necessary or proper for giving effect to the scheme, and such scheme, when approved by a Secretary of State, shall be published in the London Gazette, and thereupon shall have effect as if it were enacted in this Act.

A scheme under this sub-section was approved by the Secretary of State on March 24th, 1892, and is published in the Statutory Rules and Orders, 1892, p. 587.

(8.) Until the quarter sessions for the county of London constitute special sessional divisions, every petty sessional division of the counties of Middlesex, Surrey, and Kent existing at the appointed day, or so much of such division as is situate in the county of London, shall form a special or petty sessional division of the county of London. Sect. 42 (8).

Counties are divided into petty sessional districts under 9 Geo. 4, c. 43 ; 6 & 7 Will. 4, c. 12 ; 22 & 23 Vict. c. 65.

(9.) Where any special or petty sessional division of the counties of Middlesex, Surrey and Kent, existing at the appointed day, is situate partly within and partly without the county of London, so much thereof as is situate without the said county shall, until any alteration is made by the quarter sessions for the county of Middlesex, Surrey, or Kent, as the case may be, be a special or petty sessional division of that county.

As to the salaries of existing clerks of these divisions, see s. 119, (11), *post*.

(10.) The quarter sessions for the county of London shall be substituted for the general assessment sessions under the Valuation (Metropolis) Act, 1869, and have all the jurisdiction vested in those sessions, and shall exercise the same within the same area. Upon the hearing of any appeals in relation to property in the city of London, such two members of the court of quarter sessions of the city of London as may be appointed by that court for the purpose, shall be entitled to attend and sit as members of the quarter sessions for the county of London. 32 & 33 Vict. c. 67.

Under this sub-section the general assessment sessions ceased to exist. The London quarter sessions exercise the jurisdiction of that court within the same area, *i.e.*, in all unions or parishes not in unions wholly or for the greater part in value situate within the jurisdiction of the Metropolitan Board of Works under the 18 & 19 Vict. c. 120. The jurisdiction transferred by this sub-section is exercised by the quarter sessions under the same conditions as those under which it was formerly exercised by the general assessment sessions : *R.* v. *London JJ. and London County Council*, [1893] 2 Q. B. 476 ; 69 L. T. (N.S.) 682 ; 41 W. R. 668 ; 58 J. P. 8 ; 9 T. L. R. 652.

The concluding part of this sub-section provides for the representation of the city of London, having regard to the fact that the city may not be within the jurisdiction of the London quarter sessions. See s. 40, sub-s. (3), *ante*, p. 89.

(11.) The enactments respecting the times for holding sessions of the peace for the county of Middlesex, and the appointment and payment of any assistant judge or deputy assistant judge, or of a person to preside in a second court at any sessions in the county of Middlesex, shall cease to apply to the county of Middlesex. 7 & 8 Vict. c. 71. 22 & 23 Vict. c. 4. 37 & 38 Vict. c. 7.

The effect of this clause is that in the county of Middlesex sessions are now

Sect. 42 (11)

NOTE.

held at the same times as in other counties not regulated by local Acts. See 11 Geo. 4, and 1 Will. 4, c. 70, s. 35.

(12.) Quarter sessions for the counties of Middlesex, Surrey, and Kent respectively may be held, and the justices of each of those counties may hold special and petty sessions for any division of such county, and appoint a petty sessional or occasional court house, at any place in the county of London, and for all purposes relating to such sessions or any business transacted at such court house, such place shall be deemed to be within the county and division for which the justices holding the same are justices, but no jurors shall be summoned for such sessions from within the county of London.

As to the appointment of petty sessional and occasional court houses, see 42 & 43 Vict. c. 49, s. 20; 47 & 48 Vict. c. 43, s. 8.

As to the summoning of jurors for quarter sessions, see 6 Geo. 4, c. 50, s. 13; 1 Vict. c. 4.

(13.) Nothing in this Act shall alter the powers or duties of the justices, quarter sessions, recorder, or common serjeant of the city of London, further or otherwise than is expressly provided or than the powers and duties of the justices or quarter sessions of any county are altered.

See s. 40, sub-s. (3), and s. 41, *ante*.

(14.) Provided that from and after the appointed day the rights claimed by the court of common council to appoint to the offices of common serjeant and judge of the City of London Court, shall cease, and in any future vacancy in each of the said offices it shall be lawful for Her Majesty the Queen to appoint a duly qualified barrister to be such common serjeant or judge; and from and after the next vacancy no recorder shall exercise any judicial functions unless he is appointed by Her Majesty to exercise such functions.

As to the definition of the appointed day, see s. 109, *post*.

These officers were formerly appointed by the common council. Under the provisions in the text only the recorder can be appointed by that body, and he will not be able to exercise any judicial functions unless so appointed by the Crown.

Grant by London County Council to poor law unions.

43.—(1.) In the administrative county of London the county council:—

(*a*.) Shall pay to the guardians for every poor law union wholly in the county such sums as the Local Government Board from time to time certify to be due from the said council in substitution for the local grants towards the remuneration of poor law medical officers, and towards the cost of drugs and medical appliances; and **Sect. 43 (1.)**

(*b*.) Shall grant to the guardians of every poor law union wholly in their county an amount equal to fourpence a day per head for every indoor pauper maintained in that union, and such grant, during the five local financial years beginning on the appointed day, shall be reckoned according to the average number of indoor paupers so maintained during the five financial years ending on the twenty-fifth day of March next before the passing of this Act, and shall, after the end of the said five local financial years, unless Parliament otherwise determine, continue to be reckoned in accordance with the same average number; and

(*c*.) Shall pay to the guardians of every poor law union, a portion of which only is situate in their county, such proportion of the annual sum which is, under the other provisions of this Act, payable by the county council of a county to the guardians of that union, as the rateable value of the portion within the administrative county of London bears to the rest of the union.

As to what is the administrative county of London, see s. 40, sub-s. (1), *ante*, p. 88, and notes.

The payment under (*a*) is similar to that made by other county councils under ss. 24 and 26, *ante*.

The grant in respect of indoor paupers is to be in addition to any payment made out of the Metropolitan Common Poor Fund. See s. 94, *post*.

For the definition of "indoor paupers," see the next sub-section.

As to the estimate of the average number, see sub-s. (3), *infra*.

Payments are made by county councils to guardians under ss. 24 and 26, *ante*.

(2.) For the purposes of this section the expression "indoor pauper" includes all paupers maintained in a workhouse, and all paupers maintained in any district school, separate school, separate infirmary, sick asylum, hospital for infectious diseases, or institution for the deaf, dumb, blind, or idiots, or in any certified school under the Act of the session of the twenty-fifth and twenty-sixth years of the reign of Her Majesty, chapter forty-three, and includes any children boarded out, whether within or without the limits of the union, and in the metropolitan asylum district includes all inmates of any asylum for imbeciles provided by the managers of that district, but excludes paupers relieved in casual wards, and such number of indoor paupers in a workhouse or in a district or separate school or in a separate infirmary or asylum, as exceeded the number prescribed by the Local Government Board for that

Sect. 43 (2) workhouse, school, infirmary, or asylum, and also excludes paupers maintained for part only of a day: Provided always, that any paupers maintained under any contract or agreement in a workhouse other than that of the union to which they are chargeable, shall be included only in the number of indoor paupers of the union to which they are so chargeable.

The text contains a very elaborate definition of indoor paupers, but its importance is limited to the Local Government Board, whose duty it will be to consider it with a view to making the estimate under the next subsection.

(3.) The average number of paupers shall be estimated in such manner as the Local Government Board direct, and shall be certified by the Board. The Board may, if they think proper, vary their certificate, but unless it is so varied, their certificate shall be conclusive.

Transfer of duties under 32 & 33 Vict. c. 67, of clerk of metropolitan asylum managers.

44. On and after the appointed day all powers and duties of the clerk to the managers of the metropolitan asylums district under the Valuation (Metropolis) Act, 1869, shall be transferred to the clerk of the county council of London, and the said Act shall be construed as if the county council were substituted therein for the managers of the metropolitan asylums districts.

By the Valuation (Metropolis) Act, 1869 (32 & 33 Vict. c. 67), s. 14, a duplicate of the revised valuation list is to be sent to the clerk of the managers of the metropolitan asylums district; and by s. 16 the list so sent is to be deposited at the office of such managers. The clerk is by s. 17 to cause the totals of the gross and rateable values of all the lists to be printed, and a copy to be sent to every assessment committee and to the clerks of the peace for every county in which any parish to which such totals relate is situate.

By s. 41 notice of every alteration in the total of the gross and rateable value of any valuation list, made in consequence of any decision on appeal, is to be sent by the clerk of the assessment committee to the clerk of the managers, and by him sent to every person and body who have power to make any rate, or require any contribution based on such total.

By s. 42, sub-s. (8), the assessment committee are to approve and send the lists to the clerk before November 1st in each year, and by sub-s. (11) the clerk is to send out the printed totals before December 1st, and is to return the valuation list to the committee not sooner than fourteen, nor later than twenty-one, days after the totals are sent out.

These duties devolve under this section on the clerk of the London County Council.

45. [*Adjustment of law as to slaughter-houses in the metropolis.*]

This section is repealed by the Public Health (London) Act, 1891 (54 & 55 Vict. c. 76), and substantially re-enacted by s. 20 of that Act.

46. For the purposes of this Act there shall be enacted the provisions following; that is to say, Application of Act to certain special counties.

(1.)—(*a.*) The ridings of Yorkshire and the divisions of Lincolnshire shall respectively be separate administrative counties.

(*b.*) The eastern and western divisions of Sussex, under the County of Sussex Act, 1865, and the eastern and western divisions of Suffolk, shall respectively be separate administrative counties for the purposes of this Act. 28 & 29 Vict. c. 37.

(*c.*) The Isle of Ely, and the residue of the county of Cambridge, shall be respectively separate administrative counties for the purposes of this Act, and are in this Act referred to as divisions of the county of Cambridge.

(*d.*) The soke of Peterborough and the residue of the county of Northampton shall be respectively separate administrative counties for the purposes of this Act, and are in this Act referred to as divisions of the county of Northampton.

These divisions of counties, which for the purposes of this Act are treated as separate counties, necessitated the introduction of the phrase "administrative counties," defined in s. 100, *post.*

The divisions of Lincolnshire are the parts of Holland, Kesteven, and Lindsey. See s. 100, *post.*

(2.)—(*a.*) In the case of the county of York and the county of Lincoln respectively, the administrative business which would, if this Act had not passed, have been transacted by the justices of all the ridings and divisions at their gaol sessions, or by any joint committee of the justices of such ridings or divisions, or by any commissioners appointed by the justices, or otherwise jointly by such justices, shall be transacted by a joint committee of the county councils of the three ridings or three divisions, as the case may be, appointed in manner provided by this Act with respect to joint committees of county councils.

(*b.*) The administrative business which would, if this Act had not passed, have been transacted by any general sessions of the peace for the county of Sussex or Suffolk, or by any joint action of the quarter sessions of the divisions of the county of Cambridge, or the county of Northampton, and all matters under this Act which concern the two

Sect. 46 (2).

divisions of Sussex, Suffolk, Cambridge or Northampton jointly, shall be transacted by a joint committee of the respective county councils concerned, appointed in manner provided by this Act with respect to joint committees of county councils.

(c.) A joint committee formed in pursuance of this section shall, if the business transacted by them so require, comprise a joint committee of the quarter sessions of the several ridings and divisions.

(d.) If any difference arises as to the number of members, or the mode or time of appointing a joint committee under this section, the difference shall be determined by a Secretary of State.

As to gaol sessions in Yorkshire and Lincolnshire, see 5 Geo. 4, c. 12, and 28 & 29 Vict. c. 126, ss. 5, 6.
As to the formation of joint committees, see sub-s. (3), *infra*.

(3.) A joint committee formed in pursuance of this section shall, in respect of the business to be transacted by them, stand in the same position as if the entire county were not divided for the purposes of county councils, and as if the committee were the county council of the entire county, and the provisions of this Act shall, so nearly as circumstances admit, apply accordingly, and all costs or sums payable by the joint committee shall be apportioned by the joint committee between the several administrative counties in such manner as is provided by law, or by the practice heretofore adopted, or in such other manner as may be from time to time agreed upon by the councils of the several administrative counties, or in default of agreement may, upon the application of any of such councils, be determined by arbitration in manner provided by this Act; and each county council shall pay the sum so apportioned to the treasurer of the joint committee, and the sum so paid shall be deemed to be paid for general county purposes.

The "entire county" is defined by s. 100, *post*.
As to "arbitration in manner provided by this Act," see s. 62, *post*.

(4.) The powers, duties, and liabilities of the county authority, under the Yorkshire Registries Act, 1884, and the Acts amending the same, shall, after the appointed day, be transferred to the county council, and the expression "county authority" in those Acts shall mean, as respects each riding, the county council of that riding. Sect. 46 (4).

The Yorkshire Registries Act, 1884, is the 47 & 48 Vict. c. 54, and it is amended by 48 & 49 Vict. c. 26. See also the Land Transfer Act, 1897 (60 & 61 Vict. c. 65), s. 23, *post*, under which agreements may be made for the transfer of the business of three local registries to the office of land registry.

Before this Act the "county authority" under these Acts was, as regards each riding, the justices in quarter sessions. There is an office for registration of deeds in each riding.

(5.) In the application of this Act to Lancashire, the provisions of this Act with respect to county rates shall apply to the special rates levied in Lancashire for the purposes of the salary or pension of any chairman of quarter sessions or stipendiary justice, or for any assize courts, and such rates shall continue to be levied within the respective areas within which they would have been levied if this Act had not passed, and, subject as aforesaid, the position and salary of any such chairman or justice shall not be affected by any provision of this Act.

(6.) From and after the appointed day the right of the mayor, commonalty, and citizens of the city of London to elect the sheriff of Middlesex shall cease, and it shall be lawful for Her Majesty the Queen to appoint a sheriff of the county of Middlesex, and the law relating to sheriffs shall apply in the case of the county of Middlesex in like manner as in the case of any other county.

As to the sheriff of the county of London, see s. 40, sub-s. (2), *ante*, p. 88. By s. 41, sub-s. (8), the sheriffs of the city of London are not to have authority beyond the city.

(7.) In this section "administrative business" means such business as is by this Act transferred from quarter sessions or justices, or any committee thereof, to county councils.

See ss. 3, 4, 7, 9, *ante*.

Saving for Manchester Assize Courts Act, 1858, 21 & 22 Vict c. xxiv.

47.—(1.) Notwithstanding anything in this Act, the courts of assize at Manchester, with the lodgings for Her Majesty's judges, offices, lock-ups, and all other property vested in the justices of the peace of the county palatine of Lancaster by the Manchester Assize Courts Act, 1858, shall be vested in the county council of the said county palatine, and shall be under the control and management of a joint committee of members of the said county council, and of the council of every county borough locally situate in the hundred of Salford; and that joint committee shall have and exercise all such powers and rights (except the power of

Sect. 47 (1) levying, imposing, or assessing a rate or of borrowing money) as are conferred on the said justices by the said Act; and the hundred of Salford (including every borough locally situate therein) shall continue liable to contribute towards expenses incurred under the authority of the said Act.

(2.) The number of members of a joint committee appointed for the purposes of this section shall not exceed twelve, and the quorum requisite for the transaction of business shall be three.

(3.) Any disagreement as to the number of members of the committee or as to the proportions in which the several councils are to be represented thereon, shall be settled by a Secretary of State.

Merger of liberties in county.

48.—(1.) For all purposes of this Act, every liberty and franchise of a county, wholly or partly exempt from contribution to the county rate, shall, save as may be otherwise provided by or in pursuance of this Act, form part of the county of which it forms part for the purposes of parliamentary elections.

This provision practically abolishes liberties and franchises for all purposes of the Act. If it is desired to abolish any liberty for all purposes whatever, it may be done by Her Majesty in Council under 13 & 14 Vict. c. 105.

It may be observed that this Act does not transfer to the county council the powers of the freeholders of a liberty to elect a coroner for that liberty. See s. 5 (1), *ante*, p. 15, and the case of *Ex parte London County Council*, cited in the notes thereto.

(2.) The provisions of this Act with respect to the transfer to the county council of the powers, duties, and liabilities of the quarter sessions and justices of a county, and of their property, debts, and liabilities, whether vested in or attaching to the clerk of the peace or any justice or justices or otherwise on behalf of the county, shall apply to every such liberty and franchise as above-mentioned in like manner in all respects as if they were herein re-enacted and in terms made applicable to such liberty and franchise; and the county council shall have and exercise in every such liberty and franchise the powers and duties transferred to them by this Act from the quarter sessions and justices of the county;

This transfers to the county council all such powers, duties, etc., of the quarter sessions or justices of a liberty as are transferred to them from the quarter sessions of the county at large.

(3.) Provided that where at the passing of this Act the police force in such liberty or franchise is under the control of the quarter sessions for such liberty or franchise, there shall be one police force for the whole administrative county under the county council, and the quarter sessions of such liberty or franchise shall appoint such number of the members of the standing joint committee under this Act as may be agreed upon by the county council, the quarter sessions of the county, and the quarter sessions of the liberty or franchise, or in default of agreement may be determined by a Secretary of State.

As to the standing joint committee, see s. 30, *ante*, p. 66. The separate police force for the liberty will thus be abolished, and the police of the liberty will become county police.

(4.) The Cinque Ports and two ancient towns and their members shall for all purposes of the county council and of the powers and duties of quarter sessions and justices out of sessions under this Act form part of the county in which they are respectively situate, without prejudice nevertheless to the position of any such port, town, or member as a quarter sessions borough under the Municipal Corporations Act, 1882, as amended by this Act, and without prejudice to the existing privileges of such ports, towns, and members as respects matters which are not affected by this Act.

45 & 46 Vict. c. 50.

The Cinque Ports were originally Sandwich, Dover, Hythe, Romney, and Hastings, but to these were added the two "ancient towns" of Winchelsea and Rye. To each of these municipal towns, except Hythe and Winchelsea, were attached subordinate ports or towns, called corporate members of the principal port. Besides these there were a number of towns, villages, and hamlets, which formed the unincorporated members of the Cinque Ports, all exclusively under the jurisdiction of their respective ports, from which they were in some cases a long distance off. See Archbold's Quarter Sessions, p. 50, where an account of the jurisdiction of the justices and the quarter sessions of the Cinque Ports is shortly stated. For the purposes of the powers and duties transferred to the county council, the Cinque Ports are to be merged in the counties of Kent, Sussex, or Essex, as the case may be. Hastings is a county borough; Sandwich, Dover, and Hythe are quarter sessions boroughs. Of these last mentioned Dover only has a population exceeding 10,000. The effect of the Act upon the Cinque Ports was to some extent considered in the case of *Ex parte The Kent County Council and the Councils of Dover and Sandwich*, cited in the notes to s. 35 (5), *ante*, p. 80.

Power to make Provisional Order for Scilly Islands

49.—(1.) It shall be lawful for the Local Government Board to make a Provisional Order for regulating the application of this Act to the Scilly Islands, and for providing for the exercise and performance in those islands of the powers and duties both of county councils and also of authorities under the Acts relating to highways and the Public Health Act, 1875, and the Acts amending the same, and for the application to the islands of any provisions of any Act touching local government, and any such order may provide for the establishment of councils and other local authorities separate from those in the county of Cornwall, and for the contribution by

Sect. 49 (1). the Scilly Islands to the county council of Cornwall in respect of costs incurred by the county council for matters specified in the said order as benefiting the Scilly Islands, and such order may also provide for all matters which appear to the Local Government Board necessary or proper for carrying the order into full effect.

(2.) Any such order shall not be in force until it is confirmed by Parliament.

(3.) Subject to the provisions of a Provisional Order under this Act, the county council of Cornwall shall have no greater powers or duties in the Scilly Islands than the quarter sessions of Cornwall have hitherto in fact exercised or performed therein, and the Scilly Islands shall not be included for the purposes of this Act in any electoral division of the county of Cornwall.

A provisional order under this section was made by the Local Government Board on May 19th, 1890, and was confirmed by the Local Government Board's Provisional Order Confirmation (No. 6) Act, 1890 (53 & 54 Vict. c. clxxvi.). It establishes the "council of the Isles of Scilly," and applies certain of the provisions of this Act to the Scilly Islands.

PART III.

Boundaries.

Boundary of county for first election.

50.—(1.) The first council elected under this Act for any administrative county shall, subject as hereinafter mentioned, be elected for the county at large as bounded at the passing of this Act for the purpose of the election of members to serve in Parliament for the county: Provided always, that—

(*a.*) This enactment shall not apply to the boundary between two administrative counties which are portions of one entire county, and in case of those administrative counties, the boundary between the portions, as existing for the purposes of county rate, shall, subject to any change made by or in pursuance of this Act, be the boundary of the administrative county for which the council is elected; and,

(*b.*) Where any urban sanitary district is situate partly within and partly without the boundary of such county, the district shall be deemed to be within that county which contains the largest portion of the population of the district, according to the census of one thousand eight hundred and eighty-one.

(*c.*) Where any portion of an administrative county has before the passing of this Act been transferred to another administrative county for the purposes of the Acts relating to the police or Contagious Diseases (Animals) or otherwise, nothing in this Act shall affect such transfer. Sect. 50 (1).

(*d.*) The wapentake of the ainsty of York (except so much as is included in the municipal borough of York as extended by the York Extension and Improvement Act, 1884) shall for all purposes of this Act be deemed to be part of the west riding of the county of York. 47 & 48 Vict. c. ccxxxii.

As to the definition of "administrative county," see s. 100, *post.* The boundary of an entire county is that which exists for the purposes of parliamentary elections, but where an entire county is divided into administrative counties, the boundary between these is to be that existing for the purposes of the county rate.

As to future changes of county boundaries, see s. 54, *post.*

The provision as to urban sanitary districts in two or more counties deserves attention.

Notwithstanding this provision, however, it was held that a county might continue liable for a share of the expenses of repairing a bridge which by virtue of this provision became wholly situate within another county, the repairs being payable under a local Act and therefore within the saving in s. 125, *post. Re Staffordshire and Derbyshire County Councils*, 54 J. P. 566.

A portion of a county may have been transferred to another for purposes of police under 2 & 3 Vict. c. 93, s. 27; 3 & 4 Vict. c. 88, s. 2, and 21 & 22 Vict. c. 68, s. 2, and for purposes of the Contagious Diseases (Animals) Acts by 47 & 48 Vict. c. 47. Such transfers are now effected under the Diseases of Animals Act, 1894, s. 39, which repeals the last mentioned Act. And by the Lunatic Asylums Act, 1853 (16 & 17 Vict. c. 97), s. 131, every city, town, liberty, parish, place or district, not being a borough within the meaning of that Act, but being situate partly in one county and partly in another, might be annexed for asylum purposes to one of such counties in the manner therein provided.

(2.) The county council elected under this Act shall have for the purposes of this Act authority throughout the administrative county for which it is elected, and the administrative county as bounded for the purpose of the election shall, subject to alterations made in manner hereinafter mentioned, be for all the purposes of this Act the county of such county council.

(3.) If any difference arises as to the county which contains the largest portion of the population of any such district as above in this section mentioned, such difference shall be referred to the Local Government Board, whose decision shall be final.

(4.) This section applies to an administrative county within the meaning of this Act, save that it shall not apply to the administrative county of London, nor to any county borough, and any place which, though forming part of any such borough for the purposes of the election of members to serve in Parliament, is not within the municipal boundary of such borough shall, notwithstanding anything in the foregoing provisions of this section, form for

Sect. 50 (4). the purposes of this section part of the county in which such place is situate.

An administrative county within the meaning of this Act is defined by s. 100, *post*.

Directions for constitution of electoral divisions.

51. In the constitution of electoral divisions of a county, whether for the first election or for subsequent elections, the following directions shall be observed—

(1.) The divisions shall be arranged with a view to the population of each division being, so nearly as conveniently may be, equal, regard being had to a proper representation both of the rural and of the urban population, and to the distribution and pursuits of such population, and to area, and to the last published census for the time being, and to evidence of any considerable change of population since such census ;

Electoral divisions were formed in the first instance in counties by the quarter sessions, and in boroughs returning more than one councillor by the councils of such boroughs. See s. 2, sub-s. (3), *ante*, p. 3. The boundaries of electoral divisions can be altered by order of the Local Government Board, under s. 54, *post*.

This section lays down the lines on which these divisions should be formed and maintained.

The divisions are to contain, as nearly as possible, the same population, but this principle is not to apply universally. Regard is to be had to area, so that one division shall not be too extensive through containing a smaller population while another containing a larger population is unduly limited in area. The relative distribution of the urban and rural population and their pursuits is also to be taken into account. Regard must also be had to the areas for which separate lists or parts of lists of voters have been made, so that the electoral divisions may be formed in such a way that there will be no difficulty in ascertaining who are the voters entitled to vote in each division.

As to the electoral divisions in the metropolis, see s. 40, sub-s. (4), *ante*, p. 89.

(2.) Electoral divisions shall, so far as may be reasonably practicable, be framed so that every division shall be a county district or ward, or a combination of county districts or wards, or be comprised in one county district or ward, but where an electoral division is a portion of a county district, or ward, and such portion has not a defined area for which a separate list or part of a list of voters is made under the Acts relating to the registration of electors, such portion shall, until a new register of electors is made, continue to be part of the district or ward of which it has been treated as being part in the then current register of electors ;

(3.) Whenever under the provisions of this section a county district is divided into two or more portions, every such portion shall, as far as possible, consist of an entire parish or of a combination of entire parishes ; Sect. 51 (3).

The general principle of these directions is that the electoral divisions are to be formed so as not to overlap an urban sanitary district, ward, or rural sanitary district, except in so far as it may be necessary to give effect to sub-s. (1). Regard is also to be had to the boundaries of parishes. Where a parish is partly within and partly without a borough or urban district, each parish is to be considered a separate parish for this purpose (see s. 100, *post*), but since the passing of the Local Government Act, 1894 (*post*), such a case can hardly occur.

The word "ward" is not defined in the Act, but it evidently means a ward of an urban district.

For the definition of "parish," see s. 100, *post*.

(4.) In determining the electoral divisions for the first election, the foregoing provisions shall apply as if, where a rural sanitary district is situate in more than one county, each portion of the district which is situate in the same county were a county district, and any such portion may be combined with a county district, or portion of a county district, although not adjoining ;

(5.) The electoral divisions for the first election shall be fixed on or before the eighth day of November next after the passing of this Act.

As to the future alteration of electoral divisions, see s. 54, *post*.

Provisional Order as respects boroughs and urban sanitary districts in same area

52.—(1.) The Local Government Board shall make provisional orders for dealing with every case where the council of a borough is not the urban sanitary authority for the whole of the area of such borough, and the area of the borough is either co-extensive with or is wholly or partly comprised in any urban sanitary district, and such order shall determine whether the area of the borough or of the sanitary district, or an area comprising both the borough and the urban sanitary district, or a portion of such united area, shall, whether with or without any adjoining area, be the area of the county district for the purposes of this Act, so, however, that in either case the order shall provide for the council of the borough becoming the district council, and the order may for that purpose alter the boundaries of the borough, and may, if need be, alter the boundaries of the county ; and if the population exceeds fifty thousand, the order may constitute the borough into a county borough, and make such provision as may be necessary for carrying this Act into effect as respects such county borough ; and

Sect. 52 (1) the provisions of this Act respecting county boroughs shall, subject to the provisions of the order, apply.

The foregoing provision applied only to fourteen exceptional cases:—Banbury, Blandford Forum, Colne, Cambridge, Chippenham, Faversham, Folkestone, Launceston, Lyme Regis, Lymington, Morpeth, Oxford, St. Ives, and Wenlock. Provisional Orders have been issued dealing with all these districts, and Oxford has been created a county borough.

(2.) Where certain members of the sanitary authority for any such urban sanitary district are appointed by a university or any colleges therein, the order may provide for the appointment by such university, or colleges, of members on the district council.

(3.) A provisional order under this section shall not be of any effect until it is confirmed by Parliament.

Consideration of alterations of boundaries by county councils.

53.—(1.) Every report made by the Boundary Commissioners under the Local Government (Boundaries) Act, 1887, shall be laid before the council of any administrative county or county borough affected by that report.

These reports were made by the Boundary Commissioners appointed under 50 & 51 Vict. c. 61. A similar provision is contained in the Local Government Act, 1894, s. 36 (12), *post*.

(2.) It shall be the duty of the council to take into consideration such report, and to make such representations to the Local Government Board as they think expedient for adjusting the boundaries of their county, and of other areas of local government partly situate in their county, with a view of securing that no such area shall be situate in more than one county.

There is no definition in the Act of "areas of local government," but it appears to be wide enough to include all areas which exist for such purposes as lighting, burials, highways, sanitary purposes, and possibly education, etc.

The representations made by the county councils will be dealt with under the next section.

With regard to unions situate in more than one county, see s. 58, *post*.

Since the passing of the Local Government Act, 1894, orders have been made by county councils, which have in most cases secured that the areas mentioned shall not be in more than one county. See s. 36 of that Act, *post*.

Future alterations of boundaries.

54.—(1.) Whenever it is represented by the council of any county or borough to the Local Government Board—

(*a*.) That the alteration of the boundary of any county or borough is desirable; or

(*b*.) That the union, for all or any of the purposes of this Act, of a county borough with a county is desirable; or (*c*.) That the union, for all or any of the purposes of this Act, of any counties or boroughs or the division of any county is desirable; or Sect. 54 (1)

(*d*.) That it is desirable to constitute any borough having a population of not less than fifty thousand into a county borough; or

(*e*.) That the alteration of the boundary of any electoral division of a county, or of the number of county councillors and electoral divisions in a county, is desirable; or

(*f*.) That the alteration of any area of local government partly situate in their county or borough is desirable;

the Local Government Board shall, unless for special reasons they think that the representation ought not to be entertained, cause to be made a local inquiry, and may make an order for the proposal contained in such representation, or for such other proposal as they may deem expedient, or may refuse such order, and if they make the order may by such order divide or alter any electoral division.

This sub-section enumerates the several kinds of representation which may be made by county councils under the last section.

It is difficult to suggest what special reasons may exist to induce the Local Government Board not to entertain a representation. This provision seems to give that Board an absolute discretion as to whether they will entertain a representation or not.

As to local inquiries, see s. 87, *post*.

In the cases (*a*), (*b*), (*c*), and (*d*), the order of the Board is to be provisional. (As to Provisional Orders, see s. 87, *post*.) In other cases the order will be final.

(2.) Provided, that in default of such representation by the council of any county or borough before the first day of November, one thousand eight hundred and eighty-nine, the Local Government Board may cause such local inquiry to be made, and thereupon may make such order as they may deem expedient.

(3.) Provided, that if the order alters the boundary of a county or borough, or provides for the union of a county borough with a county, or for the union of any counties or boroughs, or for the division of any county, or for constituting a borough into a county borough, it shall be provisional only, and shall not have effect unless confirmed by Parliament.

See the note to sub-s. (1), *supra*.

(4.) Where such order alters the boundary of a borough, it may, as consequential upon such alteration, do all or any of the following things, increase or decrease the number of the wards in the borough, and alter the boundaries of such wards, and alter the

Sect. 54 (4).

apportionment of the number of councillors among the wards, and alter the total number of councillors, and in such case make the proportionate alteration in the number of aldermen.

This provision is obviously necessary when a borough is divided into wards.

(5.) At any time before the appointed day the Local Government Board may make an order in pursuance of this section without any such representation as in this section mentioned.

Contents of Provisional Order amalgamating two county boroughs.

55.—(1.) Where the Local Government Board make a provisional order for uniting two county boroughs, such order may make them one borough and one county for the purposes of this Act.

Such a Provisional Order may be made under s. 54, sub-ss. (1) and (3), *ante*.

(2.) Such order and also any other order under this Act for uniting boroughs, whether county boroughs or not, may also contain such provisions as may seem necessary or proper for regulating the division of the combined borough into wards, the number of councillors to be elected for each ward, and the first election of the council of the combined borough, and for providing for the clerks of the peace, coroners, town clerks, and officers of the boroughs, and the application to them of the provisions of this Act as to existing officers, and for providing for all matters incidental to or consequential on the union of the boroughs.

An order for uniting boroughs may be made under s. 54, sub-ss. (1) and (3), *ante*.

The provisions of this Act as to existing officers are contained in ss. 118—120, *post*.

(3.) When any such provisional order is confirmed, it shall be lawful for Her Majesty to grant a commission of the peace and court of quarter sessions to the combined borough in like manner as to any other borough under the Municipal Corporations Act, 1882, and the Provisional Order may contain such provisions as appear necessary or proper for regulating all matters incidental to such grant, and to the changes caused by the union of the boroughs in matters connected with such commission or court or otherwise with the administration of justice.

A Provisional Order must be confirmed by Parliament. See s. 54, sub-s. (3), *ante*.

A commission of the peace is granted to a borough under s. 156 of the Municipal Corporations Act, 1882. A separate court of quarter sessions is granted under s. 162 of the same Act. See s. 37 of this Act as to the effect of such a grant.

Sect. 56.

Procedure for charter of new borough.

56. Where a petition is presented to Her Majesty the Queen by the inhabitant householders of any town or towns or district, in pursuance of the Municipal Corporations Act, 1882, for the grant of a charter of incorporation, notice of such petition shall be given to the county council of the county in which such town, towns, or district is or are situate, and shall also be sent to the Local Government Board, and the Privy Council shall consider any representations made by such county council or the Local Government Board, together with the petition for such charter.

A charter is granted to a new borough under Part XI. of the Municipal Corporations Act, 1882, on petition to the Queen by the inhabitant householders of the district for which the charter is desired. The petition is referred to a committee of the Privy Council, and considered by them after notices have been duly published of their intention to do so. The notice of petition must now be sent to the county council and the Local Government Board, whose representations (if any) must be considered by the committee of the Privy Council along with the petition for the charter.

Future alteration of county districts and parishes and wards and future establishment of urban districts.

57.—(1.) Whenever a county council is satisfied that a *primâ facie* case is made out as respects any county district not a borough, or as respects any parish, for a proposal for all or any of the following things; that is to say—

(*a.*) The alteration or definition of the boundary thereof;

(*b.*) The division thereof or the union thereof with any other such district or districts, parish or parishes, or the transfer of part of a parish to another parish;

(*c.*) The conversion of any such district or part thereof, if it is a rural district, into an urban district, and if it is an urban district, into a rural district, or the transfer of the whole or any part of any such district from one district to another, and the formation of new urban or rural districts;

(*d.*) The division of an urban district into wards; and

(*e.*) The alteration of the number of wards, or of the boundaries of any ward, or of the number of members of any district council, or of the apportionment of such members among the wards,

the county council may cause such inquiry to be made in the locality, and such notice to be given, both in the locality and to the Local Government Board, Education Department, or other Government Department as may be prescribed, and such other inquiry and notices (if any) as they think fit, and if satisfied that such proposal is desirable, may make an order for the same accordingly.

For the definition of a county district, see s. 100, *post*. The effect of the creation of a district under this section is the same as if it had been created

Sect. 57 (1) under the Public Health Act, 1875. See *R.* v. *Overseers of Barnes*, 13 T. L. R. 25.

NOTE.

This section applies to the alteration of boundaries of urban districts (other than boroughs), rural districts, and parishes, the establishment of urban districts, and the creation or alteration of wards in urban districts.

The existing powers for the alteration, etc., of parishes are those of the Local Government Board under the Acts mentioned in the note to sub-s. (7), *infra.*

Urban districts were formerly created by the Local Government Board under the provisions of the Public Health Act, 1875, s. 270. The board have also power to divide urban districts into wards under s. 271, and to define boundaries under s. 272 of the same Act. The powers of the Local Government Board under that Act are not taken away, but they are not now exercised, and probably may be regarded as superseded by the text.

As to the effect of the extension of an urban district in reference to the rights of supplying water in the added area, see *Huddersfield Corporation* v. *Ravensthorpe Urban District Council*, referred to in the note to s. 59 (4), *infra.*

The "prescribed" notices to Government Departments are those prescribed by the Local Government Board under s. 87, sub-s. (4), *post.*

The Order of the Local Government Board dated September 14th, 1889, which is set out, *post*, contains the regulations at present in force as to the notices to be given under this section.

The order under this sub-section is made by the county council, subject, however, to the provisions contained in the following sub-sections. See also as to these orders, ss. 59 and 60, *infra.*

Further powers of making orders under this section have been conferred on county councils by the Local Government Act, 1894; see in particular Part III. of that Act, *post.* That Act also gives power to the county council as to the establishment and dissolution of parish councils, the grouping of rural parishes under a common parish council, and other matters.

(2.) Notice of the provisions of the order shall be given, and copies thereof shall be supplied in the prescribed manner, and otherwise as the county council think fit, and if it relates to the division of a district into wards, or the alteration of the number of wards or of the boundaries of a ward, or of the number of the members of a district council, or of the apportionment of the members among the wards, shall come into operation upon being finally approved by the county council.

The "prescribed manner" means as the Local Government Board may prescribe. See s. 87, sub-s. (4), *post.*

After the notices here referred to have been given, the order, if it relates to the matters above specified, must be again approved by the county council, and it will then come into operation at once. The cases mentioned are those specified in sub-s. (1) (*d*) and (*e*). The order of the Local Government Board of September 14th, 1889, *post*, provides for the manner in which the final approval is to be given.

(3.) In any other case the order shall be submitted to the Local Government Board; and if within three months after such notice of the provisions of the order as the Local Government Board determine to be the first notice, the council of any district affected by the order, or any number of county electors registered in that

Sect. 57 (3).

district or in any ward of that district, not being less than one-sixth of the total number of electors in that district or ward, or if the order relates only to a parish, any number of county electors registered in that parish, not being less than one-sixth of the total number of electors in that parish, petition the Local Government Board to disallow the order, the Local Government Board shall cause to be made a local inquiry, and determine whether the order is to be confirmed or not.

"In any other case" means in any of the cases mentioned in sub-s. (1) (*a*) (*b*) and (*c*). The order of the Local Government Board already referred to provides that the first advertisement in pursuance thereof shall be deemed to be the first notice for the purposes of this sub-section.

The period of three months limited by this sub-section for petitioning is reduced to six weeks by s. 41 of the Local Government Act, 1894. During that period the order will be of no effect. If petitioned against as here provided, the Local Government Board must hold a local inquiry under s. 87. After such inquiry the Board may refuse to confirm the order, or they may confirm it with modifications. See sub-s. (5), *infra*.

The expression "district" in this sub-section appears to mean "county district," as defined by s. 100, *post*.

It may be mentioned that in all cases in which it is necessary that boundaries should be defined in an order to be confirmed by them, the Local Government Board prefer that the definition should be by reference to a map only, without verbal description.

(4.) If any such petition is not presented, or being presented is withdrawn, the Local Government Board shall confirm the order.

Observe that this provision is imperative. The Local Government Board have no discretion in the matter. Where an order has been confirmed, it will, at the expiration of six months from such confirmation, be presumed to have been duly made and to be within the powers of this section, and no objection to its legality can be entertained in any legal proceeding. Local Government Act, 1894, s. 42, *post*.

(5.) The Local Government Board, on confirming an order, may make such modifications therein as they consider necessary for carrying into effect the objects of the order.

See the note to sub-s. (3), *supra*.

The Local Government Board may presumably insert in an order by way of modification, any provision which the county council might have inserted in the first instance.

(6.) An order under this section, when confirmed by the Local Government Board, shall be forthwith laid upon the table of both Houses of Parliament, if Parliament be then sitting, and, if not, forthwith after the then next meeting of Parliament.

(7.) This section shall be in addition to, and not in derogation of, any power of the Local Government Board in respect of the union or division or alteration of parishes.

The powers of the Local Government Board as to the adjustment of parishes

Sect. 57 (7).

NOTE.

are conferred by 30 & 31 Vict. c. 106, s. 3 ; 34 & 35 Vict. c. 70; 39 & 40 Vict s. 61, ss. 1—9 ; 42 & 43 Vict. c. 54 ; 45 & 46 Vict. c. 58.

Additional power of Local Government Board as to unions.

58. The Local Government Board, where it appears expedient so to do with reference to any poor law union which is situate in more than one county, instead of dissolving the union may by order provide that the same shall continue to be one union for the purposes of indoor paupers or any of those purposes, and shall be divided into two or more poor law unions for the purpose of outdoor relief, and may by the order make such provisions as seem expedient for determining all other matters in relation to which such union is to be one union or two or more unions.

The Local Government Board has power to alter or dissolve a union under 4 & 5 Will. 4, c. 76, s. 32 ; 7 & 8 Vict. c. 101, s. 66 ; 31 & 32 Vict. c. 122, s. 4 ; 39 & 40 Vict. c. 61, s. 11.

The text enables the Board to divide a union for the purpose of outdoor relief while continuing it as one union for other purposes, such as the workhouse.

The Local Government Act, 1894, s. 36 (6), *post*, provides that where the alteration of a poor law union seems expedient by reason of any of the provisions of that Act, a county council may by their order (under that Act) provide for such alteration in accordance with the provision in the text "or otherwise."

Supplemental provisions as to alteration of areas.

59.—(1.) A scheme or order under this Act may make such administrative and judicial arrangements incidental to or consequential on any alteration of boundaries, authorities, or other matters made by the scheme or order as may seem expedient.

This provision applies apparently to any scheme or order under the Act. A scheme for regulating quarter sessions in London may be made under s. 42, sub-s. (7), *ante*, p. 94. Orders may be made under many sections, but see especially ss. 52—57, *ante*.

Provisional orders may be made under ss. 4, 10, 12, 14, 49, 52, 54, 55, and 69.

(2.) A place which is part of an administrative county for the purposes of this Act shall, subject as in this Act mentioned, form part of that county for all purposes, whether sheriff, lieutenant, *custos rotulorum*, justices, militia, coroner, or other. Provided that—

(*a.*) Notwithstanding this enactment, each of the entire counties of York, Lincoln, Sussex, Suffolk, Northampton and Cambridge shall continue to be one county for the said purposes so far as it is one county at the passing of this Act ; and

(*b.*) This enactment shall not affect the existing powers or privileges of any city or borough as respects the sheriff, lieutenant, militia, justices, or coroner ; but, if any county borough is, at the passing of this Act, a part of any county for any of the above purposes, nothing in this Act shall prevent the same from continuing to be part of that county for that purpose; and Sect. 59 (2)

(c.) This enactment shall not affect parliamentary elections nor the right to vote at the election of a member to serve in Parliament, nor land tax, tithes, or tithe rentcharge, nor the area within which any bishop, parson, or other ecclesiastical person has any cure of souls or jurisdiction.

As to the definition of "administrative county," see s. 100, *post.*

The opening words of the sub-section merely mean that a place "shall form part of such county for the exercise therein of their respective offices by the officers there named; the section cannot be treated as intended to affect the question of the coroner's appointment," in a liberty which by this Act forms part of the county. *Ex parte London County Council,* [1892] 1 Q. B. 33; 61 L. J. Q. B. 27; 65 L. T. (N.S.) 614; 56 J. P. 279; 8 T. L. R. 24.

As to coroners whose district is in two administrative districts, see s. 5, sub-ss. (3), (4), *ante*, p. 16.

(3.) For the purposes of parliamentary elections, and of the registration of voters for such elections, the sheriff, clerk of the peace, and council of the county in which any place is comprised at the passing of this Act, for the purpose of parliamentary elections shall, save as otherwise provided by the scheme or order, or by the County Electors Act, 1888, or this Act, continue to have the same powers, duties, and liabilities as they would have had if no alteration of boundary had taken place. 51 & 52 Vict. c. 10.

(4.) Any scheme or order made in pursuance of this Act may, so far as may seem necessary or proper for the purposes of the scheme or order, provide for all or any of the following matters, that is to say,—

(a.) May provide for the abolition, restriction, or establishment, or extension of the jurisdiction of any local authority in or over any part of the area affected by the scheme or order, and for the adjustment or alteration of the boundaries of such area, and for the constitution of the local authorities therein, and may deal with the powers and duties of any council, local authorities, quarter sessions, justices of the peace, coroners, sheriff, lieutenant, *custos rotulorum*, clerk of the peace, and other officer therein, and with the costs of any such authorities, sessions, persons, or officers as aforesaid, and may determine the status of any such area as a component part of any larger area, and provide for the election of representatives in such area, and may extend to any altered area the provisions of any local Act which were previously in force in a portion of the area; and

Sect. 59 (4).

(*b.*) May make temporary provision for meeting the debts and liabilities of the various authorities affected by the scheme or order, for the management of their property, and for regulating the duties, position, and remuneration of officers affected by the scheme or order, and applying to them the provisions of this Act as to existing officers; and

(*c.*) May provide for the transfer of any writs, process, records, and documents relating to or to be executed in any part of the area affected by the scheme or order, and for determining questions arising from such transfer; and

(*d.*) May provide for all matters which appear necessary or proper for bringing into operation and giving full effect to the scheme or order; and

(*e.*) May adjust any property, debts, and liabilities affected by the scheme or order.

It is necessary before any order altering areas or boundaries is made to make careful inquiry for the purpose of ascertaining what authorities have jurisdiction within the area affected, in order that overlapping of areas of local government may be avoided: see s. 60, *post.*

The expression "local authority" as used in paragraph (*a*) of this sub-section seems to have a very wide application, and to include not only urban and rural district councils, but parish councils, burial boards, school boards, joint hospital boards, and, in fact, any body which exercises jurisdiction in the area dealt with by the orders. It has been held that the expression includes a burial board, and that a county council may in exercise of its powers under this section alter an area formed under the Burial Acts. *R.* v. *Durham County Council* (WRIGHT and BRUCE, JJ.), January 13th, 1897, reported only in *Local Government Chronicle*, 1897, p. 70. If an order dividing a parish, in the whole of which the Burial Acts were in force, does not expressly provide for the alteration of the Burial Acts area, that area will, it seems, remain unaltered, and to meet the expenses under those Acts, precepts may be issued to the overseers of the new parishes (formed by the division) under 18 & 19 Vict. c. 128, s. 13. *R.* v. *Keighley* (*Overseers of*) (WRIGHT and BRUCE, JJ.), January 11th, 1897, *Local Government Chronicle*, 1897, p. 47.

It is submitted, however, that in such a case the order itself should definitely provide either for the continuance of the old authority, or some substitute for it, over both parts with all proper powers of raising money for expenses and the like, or for the abolition of the jurisdiction of the authority in one of the parts, and its continuance in the other. For instance, where a parish divided by the order has a school board, that board might be kept alive as the school board of a united district comprising the new parishes formed by the division, see Elementary Education Act, 1870, ss. 40 *et seq*; where the old parish has adopted the Burial Acts, recourse may be had to some such expedient as was adopted in s. 53 of the Local Government Act, 1894, *post*, and supplemented by the 60 & 61 Vict. c. 40, *post.*

In *Huddersfield Corporation* v. *Ravensthorpe Urban District Council*, [1897] 2 Ch. 121; 66 L. J. Ch. 581; 76 L. T. (N.S.) 817; 45 W. R. 642; 61 J. P. 596; it was held by the Court of Appeal that the mere extension of their district by an order under s. 57, *ante*, does not give power to an urban district council to supply water in the added area except subject to s. 52 of the Public Health Act, 1875, and LINDLEY, L.J., there

Sect. 59 (4).

NOTE.

expresses a doubt whether a county council can (by an order under s. 57, *ante*, and this section) interfere with the rights of the existing water authority in the added area under s. 52 of the Public Health Act, 1875.

The division of a district or parish may also involve making provision for the status of each part as a component part of the union or county district.

In every case, any necessary provision should be made for the continuance in office of existing representatives and for the election of future members.

It will be necessary to extend the provisions of a local Act in the case of the extension of an urban district in which the local Act is in force.

The provisions of this Act as to existing officers are contained in s. 120, *post*. The Local Government Board generally require some provision as to existing officers to be made in every order. This provision should clearly specify the fund out of which compensation to existing officers should be paid, otherwise a difficulty may arise as in *West* v. *Wilts County Council*, 10 T. L. R. 19.

As to adjustment, the county council appear to have power by their order to provide for everything to which the parties to the order may agree under s. 62, *post*. In so far as the order does not so provide, it seems that the provisions of s. 62 will apply. See *Sowerby Urban District Council* v. *Mytholmroyd District Council*, 74 L. T. (N.S.) 313; 12 T. L. R. 300.

(5.) Where an alteration of boundaries of a county is made by this Act an order for any of the above-mentioned matters may, if it appears to the Local Government Board desirable, be made by that Board, but such order, if petitioned against by any council, sessions, or local authority affected thereby, within three months after notice of such order is given in accordance with this Act, shall be provisional only, unless the petition is withdrawn or the order is confirmed by Parliament.

An alteration of boundaries of a county is made by the Act under ss. 40, 48, 49, 50.

As to provisional orders, see s. 87, *post*.

(6.) A scheme or order may be made for amending any scheme or order previously made in pursuance of this Act, and may be made by the same authority and after the same procedure as the original scheme or order. Where a provision of this Act respecting a scheme or order requires the scheme or order to be laid before Parliament, or to be confirmed by Parliament, either in every case or if it is petitioned against, such scheme or order may amend any local and personal Act.

Orders must be laid before Parliament under s. 57, sub-s. (6). Provisional orders must in every case be confirmed by Parliament. See s. 87, *post*.

As to what is a local and personal Act within the meaning of this subsection, see *R.* v. *London County Council*, [1893] 2 Q. B. 455; 63 L. J. Q. B. 4; 69 L. T. (N.S.) 580; 42 W. R. 1; 58 J. P. 21.

General provision as to alteration of boundaries.

60. In every alteration of boundaries effected under the authority of this Act, care shall be taken that, so far as practicable, the boundaries of an area of local government shall not intersect the boundaries of any other area of local government.

Areas of local government include unions, urban and rural districts, parishes, and similar areas.

Sect. 60.

NOTE.

The Local Government Act, 1894, s. 36, *post*, contains more explicit directions as to the avoidance of the overlapping of boundaries of areas of local government.

Appointment of commissioners.

61.—(1.) For the purposes of this Act the Right Honourable Edward Henry, Earl of Derby, the Right Honourable George John Shaw-Lefevre, John Lloyd Wharton, Esquire, Francis Mowatt, Esquire, C.B., and Joseph J. Henley, Esquire, shall be appointed Commissioners.

(2.) If a vacancy occurs in the office of any of the Commissioners by reason of death, resignation, incapacity, or otherwise, it shall be lawful for Her Majesty the Queen, under Her Royal Sign Manual, to appoint some other person to fill the vacancy, and so from time to time as often as occasion requires.

(3.) The Commissioners may from time to time, with the assent of the Treasury as to number, appoint or employ such number of officers and persons as they may think necessary for the purpose of the execution of their duties under this Act, and may remove any officer or person so appointed or employed.

(4.) There shall be paid to any officer or person appointed or employed under this section, such salaries or other remuneration as the Treasury may assign, and that remuneration and all expenses of the Commissioners, incurred with the sanction of the Treasury in the execution of this Act, shall be paid out of moneys provided by Parliament.

(5.) On holding any inquiry for the purposes of this Act, any Commissioner or officer of the Commissioners shall have the same powers as an inspector of the Local Government Board has on holding a local inquiry under the Public Health Act, 1875.

38 & 39 Vict. c. 55.

(6.) There shall be paid to the Commissioners by the councils of the counties and county boroughs whose financial relations are adjusted by the Commissioners in pursuance of this Act, such amounts as the Treasury may fix as necessary for the payment of the costs of such adjustment, including a proper share of the salaries and remuneration of the officers and persons appointed or employed by such Commissioners, and such amounts shall be paid into the Exchequer, and the amount so paid shall be included as part of the adjustment.

(7.) The authority of the Commissioners shall extend to the settlement and the determination by them, on such terms and in such manner as they, in their absolute discretion, think most just and fit, of the matters referred to them, and also of all such matters and questions as are, in their judgment, incident thereto or consequent thereon, to the end that their award or awards may effect a final settlement, and until a final settlement is made the authority of the Commissioners shall extend to determine the proportions in which payments are to be made to the councils of counties and county boroughs out of the Local Taxation Account, and all payments so made shall be taken into account in the making of the adjustment. Sect. 61 (7).

(8.) Every award, order, and other instrument made by or proceeding from the Commissioners, shall be binding and conclusive to and for all intents and purposes, and shall have the like effect as if it had been made by a judge of the High Court of Justice in England, and shall be acted on, obeyed, executed, and enforced by all sheriffs and other officers and persons accordingly. No such award, order, or other instrument shall be removable by any writ or process into any of Her Majesty's Courts, and the Commissioners proceedings or acts shall not be liable to be interfered with or questioned by or in any court, or elsewhere, by way of mandamus, prohibition, injunction, or otherwise.

(9.) The costs of and attending the inquiry and award shall be borne and paid by the parties out of the fund or rate applicable to their general expenses, in such proportions as the Commissioners may direct, and the Commissioners may order the taxation of any costs in such manner as they may see fit.

(10.) The powers of the Commissioners shall, unless continued by Parliament, cease on the last day of December, one thousand eight hundred and ninety.

The powers of the Commissioners were kept in force by the Expiring Laws Continuance Acts, 1890 and 1891, but finally expired on June 30th, 1892. The final report of the Commissioners as to their proceedings is set out, *post*.

Adjustment of property and liabilities

62.—(1.) Any councils and other authorities affected by this Act or by any scheme, order, or other thing made or done in pursuance of this Act, may from time to time make agreements for the purpose of adjusting any property, income, debts, liabilities, and expenses, so far as affected by this Act or such scheme, order, or thing, of the parties to the agreement, and the agreement and any other agreement authorised by this Act to be made for the purpose of the adjustment of any property, debts, liabilities, or financial relations, may provide for the transfer or retention of any property, debts, and liabilities, with or without any conditions, and for the joint use of any property, and for the transfer of any duties, and for payment by either party to the agreement in respect of property, debts, duties, and liabilities so transferred and retained, or of such joint user, and in respect of the salary, remuneration, or compensation payable to any officer or person, and that either by way of a capital sum, or of a terminable annuity for a period not exceeding that allowed by the commissioners under this Act or the Local Government Board.

This provision gives to councils and other authorities very wide powers as

Sect. 62 (1). to agreements for the adjustment of property, etc., when that is necessary under this Act.

NOTE.

It is not quite clear that a mere transfer of rateable value from one authority to another renders an adjustment necessary. The Act contains no provision applicable to such a transfer similar to that contained in s. 32 (3), *ante*, p. 69.

But as what matters require adjustment where local areas have been altered under this Act or the Local Government Act, 1894, see *Re Rochdale Union and Haslingden Union*, Times, May 21st, 1898.

In a case stated under s. 29, *ante*, the court has no jurisdiction to decide questions of adjustment of liabilities under this section. *Re Salop County Council*, 65 L. T. (N.S.) 416.

(2.) In default of an agreement as to any matter requiring adjustment for the purpose of this Act, or any matter which, in case of difference, is to be referred to arbitration, then, if no other mode of making such adjustment or determining such difference is provided by this Act, such adjustment or difference may be made or determined by an arbitrator appointed by the parties, or in case of difference as to the appointment, appointed by the Local Government Board.

Where an order of a county council has not in fact provided for adjustment, although such order might have done so under s. 59 (4) (*e*), *ante*, an arbitrator may be appointed under this sub-section to make the adjustment. *Sowerby Urban District Council* v. *Mytholmroyd Urban District Council*, 74 L. T. (N.S.) 313 ; 12 T. L. R. 300.

8 & 9 Vict. c. 18.

(3.) An arbitrator appointed under this Act shall be deemed to be an arbitrator within the meaning of the Lands Clauses Consolidation Act, 1845, and the Acts amending the same, and the provisions of those Acts with respect to an arbitration shall apply accordingly ; and, further, the arbitrator may state a special case, and notwithstanding anything in the said Acts, shall determine the amount of the costs, and shall have power to disallow as costs in the arbitration the costs of any witness whom he considers to have been called unnecessarily, and any other costs which he considers to have been incurred unnecessarily.

The Lands Clauses Acts, in so far as they relate to arbitration, are 8 Vict. c. 18, ss. 23, 25—37 ; 32 & 33 Vict. c. 18 ; 46 Vict. c. 15. These Acts will be found in the Appendix to Lumley's Public Health. An arbitrator under this Act will, however, have the further powers above mentioned, viz., to state a case, to determine and disallow costs. By the text he is required, and not merely empowered, to decide as to the costs.

(4.) Any award or order made by the Commissioners or any arbitrator under this Act may provide for any matter for which an agreement might have provided.

As to what might have been provided for by agreement, see sub-s. (1), *supra*.

(5.) Any sum required to be paid for the purpose of adjustment, or of any award or order made by the Commissioners, or an arbitrator under this Act, may be paid out of the county or borough fund or out of such other special fund as the council, with the approval of the Commissioners under this Act or of the Local Government Board, may direct. Sect. 62 (5).

(6.) The payment of any capital sum required to be paid for the purposes of the adjustment, or of an agreement under this Act, or of any award or order made upon any arbitration under this Act, shall be a purpose for which a council may borrow under this Act, or in the case of a borough council, under the Municipal Corporations Act, 1882, or any local Act, and such sum may be borrowed on the security of all or any of the funds, rates, and revenues of the council, and either by the creation of stock or in any other manner in which they are for the time being authorized to borrow, and such sum may be borrowed without the consent of the Treasury, or any other authority, so that it be repaid within such period as the Local Government Board may sanction, by such method as is mentioned in Part Four of this Act for paying off a loan, or, if the sum is raised by stock under a local Act, by such method as is directed by that Act.

The reference in the text to borrowing "under this Act," raises a doubt whether this borrowing power extends to district councils as well as to county councils, but having regard to the section as a whole it is probable that district councils are empowered by this clause to borrow for the purpose of settling claims for adjustment. The borrowing will be in accordance with the provisions of the Public Health Act, 1875, as to borrowing by sanitary authorities; the repayment of the loan must be made in accordance with the provisions of s. 69, *post*, as to repayment.

The power of a county council to borrow under this Act depends upon s. 69, *post*.

As to borrowing by a borough council under the Municipal Corporations Act, 1882, see s. 72, *post*, which substitutes the Local Government Board for the Treasury. No consent will be required for borrowing for the purpose above mentioned if the loan is made repayable within a period prescribed by the Local Government Board, by a method mentioned in s. 69, *post*, or in manner prescribed by a local Act.

(7.) Any capital sum paid to any council for the purpose of any adjustment, or in pursuance of any order or award of an arbitrator under this Act, shall be treated as capital, and applied, with the sanction of the Local Government Board, either in the repayment of debt, or for any other purpose for which capital money may be applied.

The sanction of the Local Government Board will be necessary for any application of this capital sum. See s. 69, sub-s. (3), *post*.

Arbitration by Local Government Board.

31 & 32 Vict. c. 119.

63. Where the local Government Board *are required in pursuance of this Act to decide* any difference or other matter referred to arbitration in pursuance of this Act, the provisions of the Regulation of Railways Act, 1868, respecting arbitrations by the Board of Trade, and the enactments amending those provisions,

Sect. 63.

shall apply as if they were herein re-enacted, and in terms made applicable to the Local Government Board and the decision of differences and matters under this Act.

It is provided by the Local Government (Determination of Differences) Act, 1896 (59 Vict. c. 9), s. 1, *post*, that the Local Government Act, 1888, shall have effect as if in s. 63 of that Act for the words "are required in pursuance of this Act to decide" were inserted the words "determine as arbitrators."

This enactment appears to have been rendered necessary by the decision in *Kent County Council* v. *Sandgate Local Board*, [1895] 2 Q. B. 43 ; 64 L. J. Q. B. 502 ; 72 L. T. (N.S.) 725 ; 43 W. R. 601 ; 59 J. P. 456 ; 11 T. L. R. 421. See the note to s. 11, sub-s. (3), *ante*.

The provisions of the Regulation of Railways Act, 1868 (31 & 32 Vict. c. 119), here referred to are contained in ss. 30—32 of that Act. Under these, as applied by the above section, the Local Government Board may appoint an arbitrator, whose award or decision shall be that of the Board. The Board may fix the remuneration of the arbitrator.

Section 32 of the Act of 1868 incorporates the Railway Companies Arbitration Act, 1859, ss. 18—29, the effect of which is shortly as follows :—

Section 18 empowers the arbitrator to call for books and documents and administer oaths ; s. 19 gives him discretion as to the manner of proceeding with the arbitration ; s. 20 enables him to proceed in the absence of parties ; s. 21 enables him to make several awards each on part of the matters referred ; s. 22 makes the award conclusive ; s. 23 gives the arbitrator power to extend the time for making an award ; s. 24 prevents the setting aside of an award for irregularity ; s. 25 provides that parties shall obey awards ; s. 26 that all courts shall give effect to awards ; s. 27, that costs shall be in the discretion of the arbitrator ; and s. 28, that in absence of order costs are to be borne by parties equally ; s. 29, that submission may be made a rule of court.

PART IV.

FINANCE.

Property Funds and Costs of County Council.

Transfer of county property and liabilities.

64.—(1.) On and after the appointed day all property of the quarter sessions of a county, or held by the clerk of the peace, or any justice or justices of a county, or treasurer, or commissioners, or otherwise for any public uses and purposes of a county, or any division thereof, shall pass to and vest in and be held in trust for the council of the county, subject to all debts and liabilities affecting it, and shall be held by the county council for the same estate, interest, and purposes, and subject to the same covenants, conditions, and restrictions, for and subject to which that property is or would have been held if this Act had not passed so far as those purposes are not modified by this Act. Provided that—

(*a.*) The existing records of or in the custody of the court of quarter sessions shall, subject to any order of that court, remain in the same custody in which they would have been if this Act had not passed ; and (*b.*) Where any property belongs to a charity, nothing in this Act shall affect the trust of such charity, and until otherwise directed by the Charity Commissioners for England and Wales, the trustees or managers of the charity shall be appointed in like manner as if this Act had not passed; and **Sect. 64 (1).**

(*c.*) The justices of any county may retain any pictures, chattels, or property on the ground that the same have been presented to them or purchased out of their own funds or otherwise belong to them, and are not held for public purposes of the county, and any difference arising between the county council and the justices with respect to any such retention shall be referred to and determined by the Commissioners under this Act.

For the definition of the expressions "property," "liabilities," "division," etc., see s. 100, *post.*

As to the "appointed day," see s. 109, *post.*

The records of the county are in the custody of the *custos rotulorum* or of the clerk of the peace, who was formerly appointed by him. See now as to the appointment of the clerk of the peace and his duties as to the custody of documents, s. 83, *post.*

The saving as to pictures, chattels, etc., is intended to preserve to the justices property which may have been presented to them or are not held for public purposes.

The justices of a county, as the local authority for the county, neglected between the years 1869 and 1878 to recoup to the plaintiffs, as the local authority for a borough within the county, the proportionate amount contributed by the borough to the expenses incurred by the local authority of the county, in carrying out the provisions of the Contagious Diseases (Animals) Act, 1869, which they were bound to repay under s. 97 of that Act. After the passing of the Local Government Act, 1888, the plaintiffs sued the defendants, as successors of the local authority for the county, to recover the sums which should have been recouped. Held, that the only remedy against the justices would have been by *mandamus* to them to pay the amounts claimed out of moneys in their hands, or to levy a rate for the purpose; and that, as the Local Government Act, 1888, vests in the county council the property of the justices for the county subject to the same conditions and restrictions as if the Act had not been passed, the defendants were not liable in the action. Held, also, that if any action would lie it would be an action on the case and not an action for debt on a statute, and therefore the Statute of Limitations was a bar to the claim. *Salford (Mayor, etc., of)* v. *Lancashire County Council*, 25 Q. B. D. 384; 59 L. J. Q. B. 576; 63 L. T. (N.S.) 409; 38 W. R. 661; 54 J. P. 328; 6 T. L. R. 362.

In pursuance of a resolution passed by the watch committee of a borough incorporated under the Municipal Corporations Act, 1835, the justices of the county provided police for the borough from 1869 to 1887. The expenses of such police for each half year were provided for in advance by a rate levied on the borough, and the sum so raised was, together with the sums collected from the other townships of the union in which the borough was situate, paid to the county treasurer by the guardians of the union in obedience to a precept addressed to them by the county justices. By the Municipal Corporations

ect. 64 (1).
NOTE.

Act, 1835, the watch committee were required to appoint police for the borough, and on June 30th, 1887, they withdrew the county police and appointed borough constables. At this date the county justices had in their hands a sum arising from a rate levied on the borough applicable for the future expenses of the police in the division in which the borough was situate, but there was no ascertained sum applicable exclusively to the police provided for the borough. In an action by the mayor and corporation (suing on behalf of all the ratepayers of the borough) and the guardians of the union against the council of the county, as successors of the county justices, to recover the amount overpaid by the borough :—Held, first, that the plaintiffs were not entitled to represent the ratepayers of the borough; secondly, that the remedy against the defendants (if any) was by *mandamus*; thirdly, on the merits that the money was not recoverable on the ground of extortion *colore officii*, as it was paid under a voluntary arrangement; nor on the ground of a partial failure of consideration, as the proportion overpaid was not properly ascertainable. *Bootle (Mayor, etc., of)* v. *Lancashire County Council*, 60 L. J. Q. B. 323; 7 T. L. R. 179.

The committee of visitors of a lunatic asylum which was built and managed under the provisions of the Lunatic Asylums Act, 1853 (now repealed), had in their hands a sum of money, being the excess of receipts over the cost incurred in maintaining lunatics committed to them. Three classes of lunatics were committed to the asylum, namely, lunatics from unions within the county, lunatics from unions in other counties, and private patients. The questions to be decided were, whether the committee of visitors (the plaintiffs), or the county council (the defendants), who, under the Local Government Act, represented the interests of the quarter sessions, should have the control of the above-mentioned sum of money, and whether any part of this sum should be credited to the unions, the other defendants in the action, from whose payments it had partly arisen :—Held, that the guardians of several unions had no claim to the funds, but that as between the committee of visitors and the county council, whose predecessors had provided the money to build the asylum, the county council were entitled. *Proctor* v. *Cheshire County Council*, 56 J. P. 532.

By an agreement between a private owner of certain rooms and the clerk of the peace, as trustee for the justices in quarter sessions, the justices in quarter sessions were permitted to use the rooms for the purpose of transacting their duties in quarter sessions free of charge :—Held, that the use of the rooms by the county council, free of charge, was not transferred by s. 64 of the Local Government Act, 1888, to the county council. *Montgomeryshire County Council* v. *Pryce-Jones*, 57 J. P. 308; 8 T. L. R. 754.

(2.) On and after the appointed day all debts and liabilities of the quarter sessions, or of the clerk of the peace, or any justice or justices, or treasurer, or commissioners, incurred for county purposes, shall become debts and liabilities of the county council, and shall, subject to the provisions of this Act, be defrayed by them out of the like property and funds out of which they would have been defrayed if this Act had not passed.

(3.) The county council shall have full power to manage, alter, and enlarge, and, with the consent of the Local Government Board, to alienate any land or buildings transferred by this section, or otherwise vested in the council, but shall provide such accommodation and rooms, and such furniture, books, and other things as may from time to time be determined by the standing joint committee of quarter sessions and the county council, to be necessary or proper for the due transaction of the business, and convenient keeping of the records and documents, of the quarter sessions and justices out of sessions, or of any committee of such quarter sessions or justices. Sect. 64 (3).

This clause applies to any land or buildings vested in a county council, not only to those transferred from the quarter sessions.

Notwithstanding the provision in the text, the standing joint committee have under s. 30 (3), *ante*, exclusive control of buildings and premises for the accommodation of quarter sessions or justices out of session or for the use of the police or clerks to justices. See *Ex parte Somersetshire County Council*, 58 L. J. Q. B. 513 ; 68 L. T. (N.S.) 512 ; 54 J. P. 183 ; 5 T. L. R. 712.

The consent of the Local Government Board is necessary for the alienation of the lands of a county council. As to the proceeds of any sale, see s. 65, sub-s. (3), *post*. It will be observed that no distinct leasing power is given ; but perhaps the power to "alienate" may be said to include such a power. The leasing power given by s. 65, *post*, does not appear to apply to land transferred under this section from the quarter sessions.

As to the rating of a sessions house used by a county council and quarter sessions jointly, see *Middlesex County Council* v. *St. George's, Hanover Square*, [1897] 1 Q. B. 64 ; 66 L. J. Q. B. 101 ; 75 L. T. (N.S.) 464 ; 45 W. R. 215 ; 61 J. P. 38 ; *Worcestershire County Council* v. *Worcester Union*, [1897] 1 Q. B. 480 ; 66 L. J. Q. B. 323 ; 76 L. T. (N.S.) 138 ; 45 W. R. 309 ; 61 J. P. 244.

(4.) This section shall apply, with the necessary modifications, to the administrative counties of Sussex and Suffolk.

As to these administrative counties, see s. 46, *ante*, p. 99.

(5.) This section shall apply in the case of the property, debts, and liabilities of the justices of all the ridings and divisions of the counties of York or Lincoln at their gaol sessions, or of commissioners appointed by the justices, in like manner as if it were herein re-enacted with the substitution of gaol sessions or commissioners for quarter sessions, and of clerk of gaol sessions for clerk of the peace, and as if the joint committee of the councils of the three ridings or divisions were the council of the county ; and the said joint committee shall, for the purposes of the said property, debts and liabilities, and for the transaction of the administrative business and execution of their duties under this Act, be a body corporate, with perpetual succession and a common seal, by the name of the county committee, with the prefix of the name of the county, and with power to acquire and hold land for the purposes of their constitution without licence in mortmain.

As to the gaol sessions in these counties, see note to s. 46, sub-s. (2), *ante*, p. 100.

The joint committees are the corporate bodies known as the Yorkshire County Committee and the Lincolnshire County Committee.

(6.) The county council of the soke of Peterborough shall be liable to repair the county bridges in the soke, and if any costs are

Sect. 64 (6).

incurred by the county council of the county of Northampton for the benefit of the soke, an adjustment thereof shall be made by agreement, or by arbitration in manner provided by this Act.

As to the soke of Peterborough and the residue of the county of Northampton, see s. 46, *ante*, p. 99.

As to arbitration under this Act, see s. 62, *ante*, p. 119.

Power to acquire lands.

65.—(1.) A county council may, from time to time, for the purpose of any of their powers and duties, including those which are to be executed through the standing joint committee, acquire, purchase, or take on lease, or exchange any lands or any easements or rights over or in land, whether situate within or without the county, and may acquire, hire, erect, and furnish such halls, buildings, and offices as they may from time to time require, whether within or without their county.

Existing county buildings passed to county councils under the last section, subject, however, to the right of the quarter sessions or justices to use them for the holding of courts. See s. 30, sub-s. (3), *ante*, p. 66.

As to the standing joint committee, see s. 30, *ante* p. 66.

It should be mentioned that the county council have, by s. 3 (iv.), all the powers formerly possessed by the quarter sessions of providing shire halls, county halls, etc., subject as to the use of buildings by the quarter sessions and justices to the provisions of the Act respecting the standing joint committee.

Observe that the lands, etc., acquired may be within or without the county.

Express powers of acquiring land for various purposes are conferred upon county councils by several of the Acts set out in Part III. of this work.

(2.) For the purpose of the purchase, taking on lease, or exchange of such lands, sections one hundred and seventy-six, one hundred and seventy-seven, and one hundred and seventy-eight of the Public Health Act, 1875, shall apply as if they were herein re-enacted, and in terms made applicable to the county council.

"Such lands" must, it seems, mean lands acquired under sub-s. (1): the powers here given are not expressed to extend to lands transferred from the quarter sessions under s. 65, *ante*. It will be observed that a power of leasing is given by the incorporation of s. 177 of the Public Health Act, 1875, though it does not appear how such a power can be exercised "for the purpose of the purchase, etc., of such lands." The incorporated sections of the Public Health Act are as follows :—

"176. With respect to the purchase of lands by a local authority for the purposes of this Act, the following regulations shall be observed ; (that is to say,)

"(1.) The Lands Clauses Consolidation Acts, 1845, 1860, and 1869, shall be incorporated with this Act, except the provisions relating to access to the special Act, and except section one hundred and twenty-seven of the Lands Clauses Consolidation Act, 1845 :

"(2.) The local authority, before putting in force any of the powers of the said Lands Clauses Consolidation Acts with respect to the purchase and taking of lands otherwise than by agreement, shall

Publish once at the least in each of three consecutive weeks in the month of November, in some local newspaper circulated in their district, an advertisement describing shortly the nature of the undertaking in respect of which the lands are proposed to be taken, naming a place where a plan of the proposed undertaking may be seen at all reasonable hours, and stating the quantity of lands that they require; and shall further

Serve a notice in the month of December on every owner or reputed owner, lessee or reputed lessee, and occupier of such lands, defining in each case the particular lands intended to be taken, and requiring an answer stating whether the person so served assents, dissents, or is neuter in respect of taking such lands:

"(3.) On compliance with the provisions of this section with respect to advertisements and notices, the local authority may, if they think fit, present a petition under their seal to the Local Government Board. The petition shall state the lands intended to be taken, and the purposes for which they are required, and the names of the owners, lessees, and occupiers of lands who have assented, dissented, or are neuter in respect of the taking such lands, or who have returned no answer to the notice; it shall pray that the local authority may, with reference to such lands, be allowed to put in force the powers of the said Lands Clauses Consolidation Acts with respect to the purchase and taking of lands otherwise than by agreement, and such prayer shall be supported by such evidence as the Local Government Board requires:

"(4.) On the receipt of such petition, and on due proof of the proper advertisements having been published and notices served, the Local Government Board shall take such petition into consideration, and may either dismiss the same, or direct a local inquiry as to the propriety of assenting to the prayer of such petition; but until such inquiry has been made no provisional order shall be made affecting any lands without the consent of the owners, lessees, and occupiers thereof:

"(5.) After the completion of such inquiry the Local Government Board may, by provisional order, empower the local authority to put in force, with reference to the lands referred to in such order, the powers of the said Lands Clauses Consolidation Acts with respect to the purchase and taking of lands otherwise than by agreement, or any of them, and either absolutely or with such conditions and modifications as the Board may think fit, and it shall be the duty of the local authority to serve a copy of any order so made in the manner and on the person in which and on whom notices in respect of such lands are required to be served:

Provided that the notices by this section required to be given in the months of November and December may be given in the months of September and October or of October and November, but in either of such last-mentioned cases an inquiry preliminary to the provisional order to which such notices refer shall not be held until the expiration of one month from the last day of the second of the two months in which the notices are given; and any notices or orders by this section required to be served on a number of persons having any right in, over, or on lands in common may be served on any three or more of such persons on behalf of all such persons.

"177. Any local authority may, with the consent of the Local Government Board, let for any term any lands which they may possess, as and when they can conveniently spare the same.

Sect. 65 (2).
—
NOTE.

"178. The Chancellor and Council of the Duchy of Lancaster for the time being may, if they think fit (but subject and without prejudice to the rights of any lessee, tenant, or occupier), from time to time contract with any local authority for the sale of, and may (subject as aforesaid) absolutely sell and dispose of, for such sum as to the said Chancellor and Council may appear sufficient consideration, the whole or any part of any lands belonging to Her Majesty, her heirs or successors in right of the said duchy, or any right, interest, or easement in, through, over, or on any such lands which, for the purposes of this Act, such local authority from time to time deem it expedient to purchase; and on payment of the purchase money, as provided by the Duchy of Lancaster Lands Act, 1855, the said Chancellor and Council may grant and assure to the said authority, under the seal of the said duchy, in the name of Her Majesty, her heirs or successors, the subject of such contract or sale, and such money shall be dealt with as if such subject had been sold under the authority of the Duchy of Lancaster Lands Act, 1855."

(3.) Where the county council, with the consent of the Local Government Board, sell any land, the proceeds of such sale shall be applied in such manner as the said Board sanction towards the discharge of any loan of the council, or otherwise for any purpose for which capital may be applied by the council.

The consent of the Local Government Board to the sale of any land of a county council is required by s. 64, sub-s. (3), *ante*, p. 124.

The sanction of the Board will be necessary for any appropriation of the proceeds of sale.

Costs of justices to be payable out of county fund.

66. All costs incurred by the quarter sessions or the justices out of session of a county, and all costs incurred by any justice, police officer, or constable, in defending any legal proceedings taken against him in respect of any order made, or act done, in the execution of his duty as such justice, police officer, or constable shall, to such amount as may be sanctioned by the standing joint committee of the county council and quarter sessions, and, so far as they are not otherwise provided for, be paid out of the county fund of the county, and the council of the county shall provide for such payment accordingly.

This section was probably inserted in the Act having regard to the case of *Stops* v. *Northamptonshire JJ.*, 4 T. L. R. 78, where it was held that the justices of a county cannot lawfully pay out of the county funds the costs and damages incurred by the chief constable of the county in an action brought against him in respect of acts done in the execution of his duty.

The Municipal Corporations Act, 1882, contains a somewhat similar provision enabling a borough council to pay costs or damages in any action against one of their officers, agents, or servants. This provision is contained in s. 226, sub-s. (3), of that Act, which is incorporated with this Act, and therefore applies to county councils. See the section and the notes thereto, *post*.

Adjustment of law as respects costs ordered by

67. Any order of a court of quarter sessions, or of any justices or justice out of session, for the payment by the county treasurer of costs in criminal proceedings or of costs under the Act of the forty-eighth year of the reign of King George the Third, chapter seventy-five, shall be obeyed by the county treasurer in like manner as heretofore, and the county council shall cause the treasurer, or some other person on his behalf, to attend at every court of quarter sessions for the purpose of paying such sums as may be ordered by the court to be so paid.

Sect. 67.

quarter sessions or justices to be paid.

By 7 Geo. 4, c. 64, s. 22, the court before which any person is tried for any felony is empowered to order payments to the prosecutor of his costs and expenses in preferring the indictment, and to the prosecutor and the witnesses for the prosecution of such sums as shall seem sufficient and reasonable to reimburse them for the expenses they may have incurred in attending before the examining magistrates and the grand jury, and in otherwise carrying on the prosecution, and also to compensate them for their trouble and loss of time therein; and such order may be made where any person shall have *bonâ fide* attended in obedience to recognizance or subpœna, though no indictment is preferred. The amount of the expenses of attending before the magistrates is to be ascertained by the certificate of the magistrates, and the other expenses by the proper officer of the court. By s. 23, the court is empowered to make a similar order in certain specified cases of misdemeanor. By s. 24 the order for payment is to be made upon the county treasurer, who is authorized and required to pay the amount and is to be allowed the same in his accounts. By s. 25 all sums ordered to be paid under the Act in respect of felonies or misdemeanors committed in liberties, franchises, cities, towns and places, which do not contribute to the county rate, are to be paid out of the rate in the nature of a county rate, or out of any fund applicable to similar purposes where there is such a fund, by the treasurer or other officer having the collection or disbursement of such rate or fund, and where there is no such rate or fund, out of the poor rate by the overseers, and the order of the court is to be directed to the treasurer, officer or overseers, and not to the county treasurer. By 14 & 15 Vict. c. 55, s. 2, the provisions of the former statute were extended to certain other specified misdemeanors. By s. 5 the Secretary of State is to make regulations as to the scale of costs to be granted to prosecutors and witnesses. By 29 & 30 Vict. c. 52, s. 1, magistrates were empowered to grant a certificate for costs and expenses of prosecutors and witnesses in any case of felony or of one of the specified misdemeanors mentioned in 7 Geo. 4, c. 64, s. 23, or 14 & 15 Vict. c. 55, s. 2, though there might be no committal for trial; by s. 3 such certificates are to be forwarded by the clerks of the peace, and laid before quarter sessions, who may allow the amount wholly or partially and make orders on the treasurer, etc., for payment as under 7 Geo. 4, c. 64. By 30 & 31 Vict. c. 35, the provisions of the preceding Acts were extended to the expenses of witnesses for the defence who were bound over to appear at the trial. In addition to the misdemeanors specified in 7 Geo. 4, c. 64, and 14 & 15 Vict. c. 55, the costs of the prosecution are to be allowed as in cases of felony in misdemeanors under 14 & 15 Vict. c. 19, s. 14; 24 & 25 Vict. c. 96, s. 121; 24 & 25 Vict. c. 97, s. 77; 24 & 25 Vict. c. 98, s. 54; 24 & 25 Vict. c. 99, s. 42; 24 & 25 Vict. c. 100, ss. 74, 77; 32 & 33 Vict. c. 62, s. 17; 35 & 36 Vict. c. 33, s. 24; 48 & 49 Vict. c. 69, s. 18; 52 & 53 Vict. c. 52, s. 4; 52 & 53 Vict. c. 69, s. 5; 57 & 58 Vict. c. 41, s. 20; also in cases of indictable offences dealt with summarily under the Summary Jurisdiction Act, 1879 (42 & 43 Vict. c. 49), ss. 17, 28, 50.

The 48 Geo. 3, c. 75, provides that the overseers shall bury any dead bodies cast up by the sea, and that their expenses shall be reimbursed by the county

Sect. 67.

NOTE.

treasurer on the order of a justice. The provisions of that Act are extended by 49 Vict. c. 20, to the burial of any dead human bodies found in or cast on shore from any tidal or navigable waters, and to any such body found floating or sunken in any such waters and brought on to the shore or bank thereof. The last-mentioned Act was passed in consequence of the decision in *Woolwich* (*Overseers of*) v. *Robertson*, 6 Q. B. D. 654; 50 L. J. M. C. 87.

As to the form of the order under 48 Geo. 3, c. 75, see *R.* v. *Treasurer of the County of Kent*, 22 Q. B. D. 603; 58 L. J. M. C. 71; 60 L. T. (N.S.) 426; 37 W. R. 619; 53 J. P. 279.

Funds of county council.

68.—(1.) All receipts of the county council, whether for general or special county purposes, shall be carried to the county fund, and all payments for general or special county purposes shall be made in the first instance out of that fund.

General and special county purposes are defined in the subsequent sub-sections of this section.

(2.) In this Act the expression "general county purposes" means all purposes declared by this or any other Act to be general county purposes, and all purposes for contributions to which the county council are for the time being authorized by law to assess the whole area of their administrative county, and the expression "general county account" means the account of the county fund to which the contributions so raised are carried, and any costs incurred for a general county purpose shall be general expenses, and all costs incurred by the county council in the execution of their duties which are not by law made special expenses shall be general expenses.

Purposes declared by this Act to be general county purposes are found in s. 11, sub-s. (2), s. 23, sub-s. (2), s. 25, sub-s. (2), s. 35, sub-ss. (3), (5), s. 41, sub-s. (5), s. 42, sub-s. (3), s. 75, sub-s. (17), s. 76, sub-s. (4).

Where main roads are repairable by hundreds under s. 11 (13), *ante*, the expenses of maintenance are general county purposes under this section. See *R.* v. *Dolby*, [1892] 2 Q. B. 736; 61 L. J. Q. B. 826; 67 L. T. (N.S.) 619.

Other Acts declare various expenses to be expenses incurred for general county purposes. See, for instance, the Allotments Act, 1890 (53 & 54 Vict. c. 65), s. 6, *post*; the County Councils Association Expenses Act, 1890 (53 Vict. c. 3), *post*.

(3.) In this Act the expression "special county purposes" means any purposes from contribution to which any portion of the county is for the time being exempt, and also includes any purposes where the expenditure involved is by law restricted to a hundred, division, or other limited part of the county, and the expression "special county account" means any account of the county fund to which contributions for special county purposes are carried, and any costs incurred for a special county purpose shall be special expenses.

(4.) If the moneys standing to the general county account of the county fund are insufficient to meet the expenditure for general county purposes, county contributions may be levied to meet the deficiency on the whole administrative county, and shall be assessed on all the parishes in the county. Sect. 68 (4).

(5.) If the moneys standing to any special county account of the county fund are insufficient to meet the expenditure for the special county purposes chargeable to that account, county contributions may be levied to meet the deficiency on any parishes in the county liable to be assessed to county contributions for those purposes.

(6.) Any precept for county contributions may include as separate items a contribution for general county purposes, and a contribution for any special county purpose or purposes, and subject as in this or any other Act mentioned, county contributions, whether for general or special county purposes, which are liable to be assessed on the parishes, shall be assessed on such parishes in proportion to the annual value thereof, as determined by the standard or basis for the county rate, and all enactments applying to such standard or basis or to county rate shall (save as altered by this Act) apply so far as may be consistently with the tenor thereof, to county contributions, and those enactments shall extend to all parishes within any borough which are liable under this Act to be assessed to county contributions.

As to the preparation of the standard or basis for the county rate, see s. 3 (i.), *ante*, p. 5. See also s. 33, *ante*, p. 72.

(7.) The county council shall keep such accounts as will prevent the whole administrative county from being charged with expenditure properly payable by a portion only of the county, and will prevent any sums raised in a portion only of the county being applied in reduction of expenditure properly payable by the whole or a larger part of the county, and will further secure any such exemption as above in this section mentioned, and will prevent any sums by law specifically applicable to any particular purpose from being applied to any other purpose.

(8.) In determining the amount of expenditure for any particular county purpose, general or special, a proper proportion of the cost of the officers and buildings and establishment of the county council may be added to the expenditure directly expended for that purpose.

The establishment charges are to be apportioned between the general and special county accounts.

(9.) County contributions may be made retrospective in order to raise money for the payment of costs incurred, or having become

Sect. 68 (9). payable at any time within six months before the demand of the contributions.

This provision is similar to that contained in the Public Health Act, 1875, s. 210, as to general district rates. It is intended to prevent the raising of legal objections to county rates on the ground that they are retrospective. It will be remembered that retrospective rates are illegal. See *R.* v. *Read*, 18 L. J. M. C. 164; *R.* v. *Bedlington* (*Overseers of*), 48 J. P. 486.

Borrowing by county council.

69.—(1.) The county council may from time to time, with the consent of the Local Government Board, borrow, on the security of the county fund, and of any revenues of the council, or on either such fund or revenues, or any part of the revenues, such sums as may be required for the following purposes, or any of them, that is to say:

(*a.*) For consolidating the debts of the county; and

(*b.*) For purchasing any land or building any building, which the council are authorized by any Act to purchase or build; and

(*c.*) For any permanent work or other thing which the county council are authorized to execute or do, and the cost of which ought, in the opinion of the Local Government Board, to be spread over a term of years; and

(*d.*) For making advances (which they are hereby authorized to make) to any persons or bodies of persons, corporate or unincorporate, in aid of the emigration or colonisation of inhabitants of the county, with a guarantee for repayment of such advances from any local authority in the county, or the government of any colony; and

(*e.*) For any purpose for which quarter sessions or the county council are authorized by any Act to borrow,

but neither the transfer of powers by this Act nor anything else in this Act shall confer on the county council any power to borrow without the consent above mentioned, and that consent shall dispense with the necessity of obtaining any other consent which may be required by the Acts relating to such borrowing, and the Local Government Board, before giving their consent, shall take into consideration any representation made by any ratepayer or owner of property rated to the county fund.

As to borrowing by the London County Council, see s. 40, sub-s. (9), *ante*, p. 90, and the note to s. 70 (2), *post*, p. 136.

The power of borrowing in aid of emigration can only be exercised if a guarantee for repayment is given as provided by the text.

Section 3 (ii.) transfers to the county council the powers of the quarter sessions in respect of the borrowing of money.

The chief purposes for which a county council as successor to quarter sessions may borrow are as follows: Shire halls, county halls, sessions houses, and judges' lodgings, 7 Geo. 4, c. 63; 35 & 36 Vict. c. 7; station houses and strong rooms, 3 & 4 Vict. c. 88, s. 12; 38 & 39 Vict. c. 89, s, 40; county bridges, 4 & 5 Vict. c. 49; 8 & 9 Vict. c. 32; 43 & 44 Vict. c. 5; 44 & 45 Vict. c. 14; reformatory and industrial schools, 37 & 38 Vict. c. 47; militia store-houses, 17 & 18 Vict. c. 105.

County councils are also specially empowered to borrow under the Lunacy Act, 1890 (53 & 54 Vict. c. 5), s. 274; the Highways and Bridges Act, 1891 (54 & 55 Vict. c. 63), s. 1; the Small Holdings Act, 1892 (55 & 56 Vict. c. 31), s. 19; the Isolation Hospitals Act, 1893 (56 & 57 Vict. c. 68), s. 22; the Diseases of Animals Act, 1894 (57 & 58 Vict. c. 57), s. 42; the Local Government Act, 1894 (56 & 57 Vict. c. 73), s. 12 (2); the Light Railways Act, 1896 (59 & 60 Vict. c. 48), s. 16. See these Acts, *post*.

A county council may also borrow for the purposes of the Allotments Act, 1890 (53 & 54 Vict. c. 65), *post*, on the credit of the sanitary rates of the authority in whose default they act. See s. 4 of that Act.

As to borrowing for the purposes of adjusting property, debts, and liabilities, see *ante*, s. 62 (6).

The consent of the Local Government Board is necessary in all cases where money is borrowed under this section, except in the case of re-borrowing under sub-s. (3), *infra*. The provision as to representations by owners and ratepayers is worthy of attention.

It should be borne in mind that a statutory corporation have no power to borrow except such as is given to them by statute, and that the overdrawing of a banking account may amount to an unauthorized borrowing, in respect of which the auditor may surcharge. See *R.* v. *Reed*, 5 Q. B. D. 483; 49 L. J. Q. B. 600; 42 L. T. (N.S.) 835; 28 W. R. 787.

(2.) Provided that where the total debt of the county council, after deducting the amount of any sinking fund, exceeds, or if the proposed loan is borrowed will exceed, the amount of one-tenth of the annual rateable value of the rateable property in the county, ascertained according to the standard or basis for the county rate, the amount shall not be borrowed, except in pursuance of a provisional order made by the Local Government Board and confirmed by Parliament.

As to provisional orders, see s. 87, *post*.

(3.) A county council may also from time to time, without any consent of the Local Government Board, during the period which was fixed for the discharge of any loan raised by them under this Act or transferred to them by this Act, borrow on the like security such amount as may be required for the purpose of paying off the whole or any part of such loan, or if any part of such loan has been repaid otherwise than by capital money for re-borrowing the amount so repaid, and for the purpose of this section, "capital money" includes any instalments, annual appropriations, and sinking fund and the proceeds of the sale of land or other property,

Sect. 69 (3). but does not include money previously borrowed for the purpose of repaying a loan.

As to discharging loans out of the proceeds of the sale of land, see s. 65, sub-s. (3), *ante*.

(4.) All money re-borrowed shall be repaid within the period fixed for the discharge of the original loan, and every loan for re-borrowing shall for the purpose of the ultimate discharge be deemed to form part of the same loan as the original loan, and the obligations of the council with respect to the discharge of the original loan shall not be in any way affected by means of the reborrowing.

(5.) A loan under this section shall be repaid within such period, not exceeding thirty years, as the county council, with the consent of the Local Government Board, determine in each case.

(6.) The county council shall pay off every loan either by equal yearly or half-yearly instalments of principal, or of principal and interest combined, or by means of a sinking fund set apart, invested, and applied in accordance with the Local Loans Act, 1875, and the Acts amending the same.

38 & 39 Vict. c. 83.

The Local Loans Act, 1875, is the 38 & 39 Vict. c. 83. The provisions of that Act as to a sinking fund are contained in ss. 13—16, amended by 48 & 49 Vict. c. 30. These Acts will be found set out in Lumley's Public Health, pp. 1018, 1201.

See further, as to the investment of sinking funds, the Trust Investment Act, 1889 (52 & 53 Vict. c. 32), s. 7.

(7.) Where a loan is raised for any special county purpose, the council shall take care that the sums payable in respect of the loan are charged to the special account to which the expenditure for that purpose is chargeable.

As to special county purposes, see s. 68, sub-s. (3), *ante*, p. 130.

(8.) Where the county council are authorized to borrow any money on loan they may raise such money either as one loan or several loans, and either by stock issued under this Act or by debentures or annuity certificates under the Local Loans Act, 1875, and the Acts amending the same, or, if special reasons exist for so borrowing, by mortgage, in accordance with sections two hundred and thirty-six and two hundred and thirty-seven of the Public Health Act, 1875.

38 & 39 Vict. c. 55.

As to the Local Loans Act, see the note to sub-s. (6), *supra*.

As to the issue of county stock, see s. 70, *post*.

Sections 236 and 237 of the Public Health Act, 1875, are as follows :—

" 236. Every mortgage authorized to be made under this Act shall be by deed, truly stating the date, consideration, and the time and place of payment, and shall be sealed with the common seal of the local authority, and may be made according to the form contained in Schedule IV. to this Act, or to the like effect. Sect. 69 (8).

NOTE.

"237. There shall be kept at the office of the local authority a register of the mortgages on each rate, and within fourteen days after the date of any mortgage an entry shall be made in the register of the number and date thereof, and of the names and description of the parties thereto, as stated in the deed. Every such register shall be open to public inspection during office hours at the said office, without fee or reward; and any clerk or other person having the custody of the same, refusing to allow such inspection, shall be liable to a penalty not exceeding five pounds."

(9.) Provided that where a county council have borrowed by means of stock they shall not borrow by way of mortgage except for a period not exceeding five years.

As to borrowing by mortgage, see the last sub-section.

The Local Government Board have expressed the opinion that the above sub-section does not preclude a county council who have issued stock from borrowing temporarily on mortgage any sums which they may have power to raise, and from subsequently issuing stock in respect of the balances of the loans after making provision for the repayment of the loans during the time they are secured by mortgages, such repayment being calculated on the full period sanctioned for the loan.

(10.) Where the county council borrow by debentures such debentures may be for any amount not less than five pounds.

Under the Local Loans Act, 1875, s. 5, a debenture under that Act shall not be issued for a sum less than the sum prescribed by a local Act, or where no sum is prescribed for a sum less than 20*l.*

(11.) The provisions of this section which authorize advances in aid of the emigration or colonization of inhabitants of the county, and borrowing for those advances, except the provisions respecting the total debt, shall extend to the councils of boroughs mentioned in the Third Schedule to this Act.

These are the county boroughs to which ss. 31—34, *ante*, apply.

(12.) Nothing in this section shall be taken to empower the Cheshire County Council to borrow on the security of any revenue estimated to accrue from the surplus funds of the River Weaver Navigation.

70.—(1.) County stock may be created, issued, transferred, dealt with, and redeemed in such manner and in accordance with such regulations as the Local Government Board may from time to time prescribe. Issue of county stock.

These regulations were prescribed by the Local Government Board and

Sect. 70 (1).

NOTE.

confirmed under sub-s. (4), *post*, by an Order of the Privy Council of September 26th, 1891. They have been amended by a similar order confirmed August 3rd, 1897. Both orders are set out, *post*.

It may be mentioned that county stock is a trustee investment under the Trustee Act, 1893 (56 & 57 Vict. c. 53), s. 1 (*m*).

(2.) Without prejudice to the generality of the above power, such regulations may provide for the discharge of any loan raised by such stock, and in the case of consolidation of debt for extending or varying the times within which loans may be discharged, and may provide for the consent of limited owners and for the application of the Acts relating to stamp duties and to cheques, and for the disposal of unclaimed dividends, and may apply for the purposes of this section, with or without modifications, any enactments of the Local Loans Act, 1875, and the Acts amending the same, and of any Act relating to stock issued by the Metropolitan Board of Works, or by the corporation of any municipal borough.

The Local Loans Acts are 38 & 39 Vict. c. 83, and 48 & 49 Vict. c. 30.

As to the issue of metropolitan consolidated stock, see 32 & 33 Vict. c. 102; 33 & 34 Vict. c. 24; 34 & 35 Vict. c. 47; 38 & 39 Vict. cc. 36, 65; 43 & 44 Vict. c. 20; 48 & 49 Vict. c. 50; 50 & 51 Vict. c. 31; 51 & 52 Vict. c. 40.

These Acts, however, have been amended from time to time by the Annual Money Acts of the London County Council, a list of which to the end of the year 1895 will be found in the Index to the Statutes, Appendix VI.

(3.) Such regulations shall be laid before each House of Parliament for not less than thirty days during which such House sits, and if either House during such thirty days resolves that such regulations ought not to be proceeded with the same shall be of no effect, without prejudice nevertheless to the making of further regulations.

(4.) If no such resolution is passed, it shall be lawful for Her Majesty by Order in Council to confirm such regulations, and the same, when so confirmed, shall be deemed to have been duly made and to be within the powers of this Act, and shall be of the same force as if they were enacted in this Act.

Audit of accounts of county council.

71.—(1.) The accounts of the receipts and expenditure of county councils shall be made up to the end of each local financial year as defined by this Act, and be in the form for the time being prescribed by the Local Government Board.

As to the local financial year, see s. 73, *post*. As to the form, see note to sub-s. (3) of this section.

(2.) The provisions of the Municipal Corporations Act, 1882, with respect to the return to the Local Government Board of the accounts of a council of a borough and to the accounts of the treasurer of the borough, and to the inspection and abstract thereof, shall apply to the accounts of a county council, and of the treasurer and officers of such council, and the said provisions respecting the return to the Local Government Board shall extend to the return to that Board of a printed copy of the abstract of the said accounts. Sect. 71 (2).

The provisions of the Municipal Corporations Act, 1882, here referred to are ss. 26—28 and s. 233. They are set out *post*.

As to the accounts of a joint committee and its officers, see s. 81, sub-s. (6), *post*.

(3.) The accounts of a county council, and of the county treasurer and officers of such council, shall be audited by the district auditors appointed by the Local Government Board in like manner as accounts of an urban authority and their officers under sections two hundred and forty-seven and two hundred and fifty of the Public Health Act, 1875, and those sections and all enactments amending them or applying to audit by district auditors, including the enactments imposing penalties and providing for the recovery of sums, shall apply in like manner as if, so far as they relate to an audit of the accounts of an urban authority and the officers of such authority, they were herein re-enacted with the necessary modifications, and accordingly all ratepayers and owners of property in the county shall have the like rights, and there shall be the same appeal as in the case of such audit. Provided that the First Schedule to the District Auditors Act, 1879, shall be modified in manner described in the Second Schedule to this Act. 38 & 39 Vict. c. 55. 42 & 43 Vict. c. 6.

By an Order of the Local Government Board, dated March 16th, 1892, that Board has prescribed the form of financial statement to be submitted to the district auditor by the council of each administrative county, except London. The Order is too long for insertion in this work. It will be found in the Statutory Rules and Orders, 1892, p. 195. A further order as to the form of the financial statement relating to the police pension fund was made by the Board on September 19th, 1892, and will be found in the same volume.

Sections 247 and 250 of the Public Health Act, 1875, are as follows :—

"247. Where an urban authority are not the council of a borough, the following regulations with respect to audit shall be observed, namely,

"(1.) The accounts of the receipts and expenditure under this Act of such authority shall be audited and examined once in every year, as soon as can be after the twenty-fifth day of March, by the auditor of accounts relating to the relief of the poor for the union in which the district of such authority or the greater part thereof is situate, unless such auditor is a member of the authority whose accounts he is appointed to audit, in which case such accounts shall be audited by such auditor of any adjoining union as may from time to time be appointed by the Local Government Board :

"(2.) There shall be paid to such auditor in respect of each audit under this Act such reasonable remuneration, not being less than two guineas for every day in which he is employed in such audit, as

Sect. 71 (3).

NOTE.

such authority from time to time appoint, together with his expenses of travelling to and from the place of audit:

"(3.) Before each audit such authority shall, after receiving from the auditor the requisite appointment, give at least fourteen days' notice of the time and place at which the same will be made, and of the deposit of accounts required by this section, by advertisement in some one or more of the local newspapers circulated in the district; and the production of the newspaper containing such notice shall be deemed to be sufficient proof of such notice on any proceeding whatsoever:

"(4.) A copy of the accounts duly made up and balanced, together with all rate books, account books, deeds, contracts, accounts, vouchers, and receipts, mentioned or referred to in such accounts, shall be deposited in the office of such authority, and be open, during office hours thereat, to the inspection of all persons interested for seven clear days before the audit, and all such persons shall be at liberty to take copies of or extracts from the same, without fee or reward; and any officer of such authority duly appointed in that behalf neglecting to make up such accounts and books, or altering such accounts and books, or allowing them to be altered when so made up, or refusing to allow inspection thereof, shall be liable to a penalty not exceeding five pounds:

"(5.) For the purpose of any audit under this Act, every auditor may, by summons in writing, require the production before him of all books, deeds, contracts, accounts, vouchers, receipts, and other documents and papers which he may deem necessary; and may require any person holding or accountable for any such books, deeds, contracts, accounts, vouchers, receipts, documents, or papers to appear before him at any such audit, or any adjournment thereof, and to make and sign a declaration as to the correctness of the same; and if any such person neglects or refuses so to do, or to produce any such books, deeds, contracts, accounts, vouchers, receipts, documents, or papers, or to make or sign such declaration, he shall incur for every neglect or refusal a penalty not exceeding forty shillings; and if he falsely or corruptly makes or signs any such declaration, knowing the same to be untrue in any material particular, he shall be liable to the penalties inflicted on persons guilty of wilful and corrupt perjury:

"(6.) Any ratepayer or owner of property in the district may be present at the audit, and may make any objection to such accounts before the auditor; and such ratepayers and owners shall have the same right of appeal against allowances by an auditor as they have by law against disallowances:

"(7.) Any auditor acting in pursuance of this section shall disallow every item of account contrary to law, and surcharge the same on the person making or authorizing the making of the illegal payment, and shall charge against any person accounting the amount of any deficiency or loss incurred by the negligence or misconduct of that person, or of any sum which ought to have been but is not brought into account by that person, and shall in every such case certify the amount due from such person, and on application by any party aggrieved shall state in writing the reasons for his decision in respect of such disallowance or surcharge, and also of any allowance which he may have made:

"(8.) Any person aggrieved by disallowance made may apply to the Court of Queen's Bench for a writ of *certiorari* to remove the disallowance into the said court, in the same manner and subject to the same conditions as are provided in the case of disallowances by auditors under the laws for the time being in force with regard to the relief of the poor; and the said court shall have the same powers with respect to allowances, disallowances, and surcharges under this Act as it has with respect to disallowances or allowances by the said auditors; or in lieu of such application any person so aggrieved may appeal to the Local Government Board, which Board shall have the same powers in the case of the appeal as it possesses in the case of appeals against allowances, disallowances, and surcharges by the said poor law auditors:

"(9.) Every sum certified to be due from any person by an auditor under this Act shall be paid by such person to the treasurer of such authority within fourteen days after the same has been so certified, unless there is an appeal against the decision; and if such sum is not so paid, and there is no such appeal, the auditor shall recover the same from the person against whom the same has been certified to be due by the like process and with the like powers as in the case of sums certified on the audit of the poor rate accounts, and shall be paid by such authority all such costs and expenses, including a reasonable compensation for loss of time incurred by him in such proceedings, as are not recovered by him from such person:

"(10.) Within fourteen days after the completion of the audit, the auditor shall report on the accounts audited and examined, and shall deliver such report to the clerk of such authority, who shall cause the same to be deposited in their office, and shall publish an abstract of such accounts in some one or more of the local newspapers circulated in the district.

"Where the provisions as to audit of any local Act constituting a board of improvement commissioners are repugnant to or inconsistent with those of this Act, the audit of the accounts of such improvement commissioners shall be conducted in all respects in accordance with the provisions of this Act."

"250. The accounts under this Act of officers or assistants of any local authority who are required to receive moneys or goods on behalf of such authority, shall be audited by the auditors or auditor of the accounts of such authority, with the same powers, incidents and consequences as in the case of such last-mentioned accounts."

The Acts relating to audit by district auditors are the 7 & 8 Vict. c. 101, ss. 32—36; 11 & 12 Vict. c. 91, ss. 4—9; 12 & 13 Vict. c. 103, ss. 9, 11; 29 & 30 Vict. c. 113, ss. 5—7; 42 Vict. c. 6. All these Acts will be found in the Appendix to Lumley's Public Health.

The county accounts are not audited, as formerly, by the county auditors, and the provisions of the Municipal Corporations Act, 1882, relating to borough auditors, do not apply to county councils. See s. 75, sub-s. (16), *post*.

As to the modification of the schedule to the District Auditors Act, 1879, see the second schedule to this Act and the notes thereto, *post*.

It may be mentioned that by the Local Authorities (Expenses) Act, 1887 (50 & 51 Vict. c. 72), "expenses paid by any local authority whose accounts are subject to audit by a district auditor shall not be disallowed by that auditor if they have been sanctioned by the Local Government Board."

Sect. 72.

Adaptation of Part V. of 45 & 46 Vict. c. 50, as to corporate property and liabilities.

72. After the appointed day the Local Government Board shall exercise, as regards any county borough, or other borough, the powers conferred by Part V. of the Municipal Corporations Act, 1882, relating to corporate property and liabilities, as respects the approval of loans and of the alienation of property and other matters therein mentioned, and that part shall, as respects any transactions commenced after the appointed day, be construed as if "Local Government Board" were throughout that part substituted for "Treasury."

This is an amendment of Part V. of the Municipal Corporations Act, 1882. That part is not (save as to one section) incorporated with this Act, and the provision in the text has no real connection with the purposes of this Act.

Local Financial Year and Annual Budget.

Fixing of local financial year and consequent adjustments.

73.—(1.) After the appointed day, not being more than three years after the passing of this Act, the local financial year shall be the twelve months ending the thirty-first day of March, and the accounts of the receipts and expenditure of every county council shall be made up for that year, but until the appointed day the local financial year shall be the twelve months ending the twenty-fifth day of March, and the said accounts shall be made up for that year.

As to the "appointed day," see s. 109, *post.*

Before this section came into operation the local financial year ended on March 25th.

As to making up of the accounts of county councils, see s. 71, *ante.*

(2.) All enactments relating to accounts of local authorities or the audit thereof, or to returns touching their receipts and expenditure, or to meetings, or other matters, shall be modified so far as is necessary for adapting them to the provisions of this section, and the Local Government Board shall from time to time give such orders and make such arrangements as appear to the Board to be necessary or proper for effecting such adaptation, and giving effect to the provisions of this section.

Annual budget of county councils.

74.—(1.) At the beginning of every local financial year, every county council shall cause to be submitted to them an estimate of the receipts and expenses of such council during that financial year, whether on account of property, contributions, rates, loans, or otherwise.

(2.) The council shall estimate the amount which will require to be raised in the first six months and in the second six months of the said financial year by means of contributions.

This sub-section contemplates the making of two county rates, one at the beginning of each half-year.

(3.) If at the expiration of the first six months of such financial year it appears to the council that the amount of the contribution or rate estimated at the commencement of the year will be larger than is necessary, or will be insufficient, the council may revise the estimate and alter accordingly the amount of the contribution or rate. Sect. 74 (3).

PART V.

Supplemental.

Application of Acts.

Application of 45 & 46 Vict c. 50, to county councils and this Act. 47 & 48 Vict. c. 70.

75. For the purpose of the provisions of this Act with respect to county councils, and to the chairmen, members, committees, and officers of such councils, and otherwise for the purpose of carrying this Act into effect, the following portions of the Municipal Corporations Act, 1882, namely, Part Two, Part Three, Part Four (as amended by the Municipal Elections (Corrupt Practices) Act, 1884), section one hundred and twenty-four, in Part Five, Part Twelve, Part Thirteen, the Second Schedule, Part Two, and Part Three of the Third Schedule, and Part One of the Eighth Schedule shall, so far as the same are unrepealed and are consistent with the provisions of this Act, apply as if they were herein re-enacted with the enactments amending the same, in such terms and with such modifications as are necessary to make them applicable to the said councils, and their chairmen, members, committees, and officers, and to the other provisions of this Act.

The provisions of these incorporated Acts are set out *post*, and in the notes to each section it has been attempted to indicate its application to county councils as modified by the provisions of this Act.

As to the effect of this section in incorporating the provisions of the Municipal Elections (Corrupt Practices) Act, 1884, see *Ex parte Walker*, 22 Q. B. D. 384; 58 L. J. Q. B. 190; 60 L. T. (N.S.) 581; 37 W. R. 293; 53 J. P. 260; 5 T. L. R. 217.

This whole section has been materially altered by the County Councils (Elections) Act, 1891 (54 & 55 Vict. c. 68), *post*.

Provided as follows:—

(1.) * * * *

This sub-section, which provided for the election of county councillors (in years in which they are elected) and borough councillors being conducted together, was repealed by the County Councils (Elections) Act, 1891 (54 & 55 Vict. c. 68). Under that Act the elections of county councillors are held in March; the ordinary day of election of councillors of a borough is November 1st: Municipal Corporations Act, 1882, s. 52, *post*.

(2.) Such person as the county council may appoint shall be the returning officer for the election of county

(2). councillors of the county council, in substitution for the mayor, and for the aldermen assigned for that purpose by the council.

The returning officer will be returning officer for the entire administrative county. The council will not appoint a returning officer for each division corresponding to the alderman appointed for each ward of a borough.

(3.) The returning officer, without prejudice to any other power, may by writing under his hand appoint a fit person to be his deputy for all or any of the purposes relating to the election of any such councillor, and may by himself or such deputy exercise any powers and do any things which a returning officer is authorized or required to exercise or do in relation to such election, and shall, for the purposes of the election, have all the powers of the sheriff.

Under this sub-section a deputy may be appointed for a division or group of divisions. Divisions may be grouped so as to have only one place for nominations, etc. See sub-s. (7), *post.* It is difficult to understand the reference to the sheriff. The election of county councillors resembles a municipal election, with which the sheriff as such has nothing to do. The sheriff was, however, the returning officer at the first election, and this may afford the explanation of this reference. See s. 103, *post.*

(4.) A reference in this Act, or in the enactments applied by this Act, to the returning officer or to the mayor or to the alderman shall, so far as relates to the election of any such councillor, be construed to refer to the returning officer, and any such deputy as above mentioned.

These references have been noticed under the several sections.

(5.) A reference in the said enactments to the town clerk, so far as respects the election of any such councillor, shall be construed to refer to the returning officer or his deputy, and as respects matters subsequent to the election, shall be construed to refer to the clerk of the county council.

These references have been noticed under the several sections. Nothing in this clause substituting the returning officer or his deputy for the town clerk is to extend to any election of county councillors for an electoral division co-extensive with or wholly comprised in a municipal borough; at such an election the town clerk will perform all the duties imposed upon the town clerk by the enactments referred to in the text. See the County Councils (Elections) Act, 1891, s. 3, *post.* After the election the duties of the town clerk are to be performed by the clerk of the county council. Thus in a division not comprised within a borough the returning officer must provide nomination papers under the Municipal Corporations Act, 1882, Sched. 3, Part II., rule 6; but a copy of an election petition must be sent to the clerk of the council under s. 88 of that Act. Sect. 75 (5).

NOTE.

As to the clerk of county council, see s. 83, 106, *post*.

(6.)

This clause related to the person to act as returning officer at an election of county councillors in an electoral division of a county co-extensive with or wholly comprised in a borough. It is now repealed by the County Councils (Elections) Act, 1891, which provides by s. 3 for the person to act as returning officer in such a case. See that Act, *post*.

(7.) Some place fixed by the returning officer shall, except where the election is in a borough, be substituted for the town clerk's office, and, as respects the hearing of objections to nomination papers, for the town hall, but such place shall, if the electoral division is the whole or part of an urban district, be in that district, and in any other case shall be in the electoral division or in an adjoining electoral division.

In a borough nomination papers will be delivered to the town clerk, at his office, as at an election of town councillors.

In a division of a county not wholly within a borough, the nomination papers will be delivered to the returning officer (see sub-s. (5), *supra*), at some place fixed by him.

As to the application of s. 232 of the Municipal Corporations Act, 1882, which deals with the fixing of notices on the town hall, see the note to that section, *post*.

If any part of the division is within an urban district the place for receiving nomination papers and for hearing objections must be within that district. But if it is wholly rural, the place may be in an adjoining division. It is therefore possible to group several rural divisions adjoining an urban division so that the same place may be fixed for all, and so as to enable one person to perform the duties of returning officer for all. But see the note to sub-s. (3), *ante*.

(8.) The returning officer shall forthwith, after the election of county councillors for the county, return the names of the persons elected to the clerk of the county council.

(9.) *

This clause is repealed by the County Councils (Elections) Act, 1891.

(10.) An outgoing alderman shall not, as alderman, vote in the election of a chairman.

This is an amendment of s. 60 (3) of the Municipal Corporations Act, 1882. The meaning of the words "as alderman" are obscure. Perhaps they are intended to meet a case where an outgoing alderman has in the meantime been

Sect. 75 (10). — NOTE.

elected a councillor, and therefore votes as councillor. Compare the provisions of s. 2 (2) (*c*), *ante*, p. 2.

48 & 49 Vict. c. 10.

(11.) The hours of the poll shall be those fixed by the Elections (Hours of Poll) Act, 1885.

The hours fixed by the Act are from 8 a.m. to 8 p.m. See the note to the Municipal Corporations Act, 1882, s. 58, *post*.

(12.) Section eleven of the Municipal Corporations Act, 1882, with respect to the qualification of a county councillor by reason of his being entered in the separate non-resident list, shall include, for the purposes of this Act, all persons entered in such separate list in any municipal borough by reason of occupation of property in the borough, and all persons entered in such separate list for any part of a county not in a municipal borough by reason of the occupation of property in that part.

See the section referred to, *post*.

By the provision in the text a person will be entitled to be elected a councillor if he is entered in the county separate non-resident list, or in the corresponding list for any borough under s. 49 of the Municipal Corporations Act, 1882.

(13.) * * *

This clause was repealed by the County Councils (Elections) Act, 1891, which provides (s. 1) that the ordinary day of election of the chairman and county aldermen, etc., shall be the 16th day of March or such other day within ten days after the ordinary day of retirement of county councillors as the county council may from time to time fix.

(14.) Ten days shall be substituted for five days in section thirty-four of the Municipal Corporations Act, 1882, as the time within which a person elected to a corporate office is to accept that office, and twelve months shall be substituted for six months in section thirty-nine of the said Act, as the period of absence which disqualifies an alderman or councillor.

See the sections referred to, *post*. The period of ten days above mentioned has been extended to three months after notice of election by the County Councils (Elections) Act, 1891, s. 5, *post*. Absence will not disqualify the chairman or deputy chairman. See sub-s. (16) (*c*), *post*.

(15.) The quorum of the council shall be one-fourth of the whole number of the council, and one-fourth shall, for the purposes of this section, be substituted for one-third in paragraph ten of the second schedule to the Municipal Corporations Act, 1882.

See the paragraph referred to, *post*.

(16.) Nothing in the Municipal Corporations Act, 1882, as applied by this section— Sect. 75 (16).

(a.) Shall alter the application of any fine, penalty, or forfeiture recoverable in a summary manner ; or

This prevents the application to counties of the Municipal Corporations Act, 1882, s. 221, *post*.

(b.) Shall apply any of the provisions of the Municipal Corporations Act, 1882, with reference to boundaries or the alteration of wards or borough auditors, nor any of the following provisions, namely, sub-section five of section fifteen, section sixteen, section two hundred and fifty-one, or section two hundred and fifty-seven ; or

The provisions of the Municipal Corporations Act, 1882, as to boundaries, are contained in ss. 228, 229 ; as to alteration of wards, in s. 30 ; as to borough auditors, in ss. 25, 27, 37, 41, 42, 62. Section 15, sub-s. (5), provides that the mayor shall have precedence in all places in the borough ; s. 16 relates to the appointment of deputy mayor ; s. 251 contains a saving for local Acts ; and s. 257 contains a saving for the universities.

(c.) Shall render any person elected to a corporate office without his consent to his nomination being previously obtained liable to pay a fine on non-acceptance of office, or render a chairman or deputy-chairman disqualified as such by reason of absence ; or

This provision modifies the Municipal Corporations Act, 1882, ss. 34 and 39, *post*.

The deputy chairman is an officer appointed by the London County Council only. See s. 88, *post*, p. 166. He must not be confounded with the vice-chairman appointed under s. 2 (6), *ante*, p. 4, who may apparently become disqualified by absence.

(d.) * . . .

This clause is repealed by the County Councils (Elections) Act, 1891, but it is substantially re-enacted by s. 1 (4) of that Act, *post*. The effect is that a casual vacancy which occurs within six months before a triennial election shall not be filled up.

(e.) Shall apply to a county council section seventeen of the said Act with respect to the town clerk, nor, unless the county council so resolve, section eighteen respecting the treasurer, but, if the county council so resolve, section eighteen shall supersede the existing enactments with respect to the county treasurer ; or

See the sections referred to, *post*.

As to the appointment of county treasurers, see s. 3 (x), *ante*, p. 10.

Sect. 75 (16)

(*f.*) Shall require the acts and proceedings of the standing joint committee of the county council and quarter sessions to be submitted to the county council for their approval; or

Under s. 22 (2) of the Municipal Corporations Act, 1882, the acts of committees must be submitted to the council for their approval. The text provides that such approval shall not be necessary in the case of the acts and proceedings of the standing joint committee, as to which, see s. 30, *ante*, p. 66.

As to the approval of the acts and proceedings of other committees, see s. 82, *post.*

(*g.*) Shall prevent the use of schools and public rooms for the purpose of taking the poll at elections under this Act, but section six of the Ballot Act, 1872, shall apply in the case of elections under this Act, and the returning officer may, in addition to using such rooms free of charge for taking the poll, use the same free of charge for hearing objections to nomination papers and for counting votes.

35 & 36 Vict. c. 33.

Section 6 of the Ballot Act, 1872, provides that a returning officer may use, free of charge, for the purpose of taking the poll at an election, any room in a school receiving a grant out of moneys provided by Parliament, and any room the expense of maintaining which is payable out of any local rate, but he shall make good any damage done to such room, and defray any expense incurred by the person or body of persons, corporate or unincorporate, having control over the same, on account of its being used for the purpose of taking the poll as aforesaid. This section does not apply to municipal elections (see the Municipal Corporations Act, 1882, Sched. 3, Part III., r. 1, *post*). It will, however, apply to elections of county councillors, for the purposes of taking the poll, hearing objections, and counting votes.

(17.) All costs properly incurred in relation to the holding of elections of councillors of county councils, so far as not otherwise provided for by law, shall be paid out of the county fund as general expenses.

As to what are general expenses, see s. 68, sub-s. (2), *ante*, p. 130.

(18.) The said costs shall not exceed those allowed by Part I. of the First Schedule to the Parliamentary Elections (Returning Officers) Act, 1875, as amended by the Parliamentary Elections (Returning Officers) Act, 1885, or by such scale as the county council may from time to time frame.

38 & 39 Vict. c. 84.
48 & 49 Vict. c. 62.

The enactments referred to in the text are set out in Part II. of this work, *post.*

(19.) Sections four, five, six, and seven of the Parliamentary Elections (Returning Officers) Act, 1875, as amended by the Parliamentary Elections (Returning Officers) Act (1875) Amendment Act, 1886, shall apply as if they were herein re-enacted with the necessary modifications, and in particular with the substitution of the county council for the person from whom payment is claimed, and of one month for the period of fourteen days within which application may be made for taxation. Sect. 75 (19). 49 & 50 Vict. c. 57.

The incorporated sections are set out in Part II. of this work, *post*.

The expenses of the returning officers are payable by the county council under sub-s. (17), *supra*, not by the candidate.

(20.) A county council shall, on the request of the returning officer, prior to a poll being taken at any election of a councillor of such council, advance to him such sum not exceeding ten pounds for every thousand electors at the election as he may require.

This is a useful and necessary provision, for the expenses of holding a number of elections simultaneously throughout a county must necessarily be heavy.

(21.) The meeting of a county council, or of any committee thereof, may be held at such place, either within or without their county, as the council from time to time direct.

76.—(1.) The provisions of section four of the County Electors Act, 1888, with respect to the framing of the lists and register of voters in parts, shall extend to parishes situate within a parliamentary borough. Amendment of 51 & 52 Vict. c. 10.

The County Electors Act, 1888, is set out *in extenso* in Part II. of this work *post*.

The County Electors Act, 1888, s. 4, sub-s. (2), provides that in the construction of the Registration of Electors Acts for the purposes of their application to a parish not situate in a municipal borough, there shall be made the variations following, and such other variations as may be necessary for carrying into effect the application, that is to say :—

"(*e*) Where such parish is not within a parliamentary borough, section 21 of the Parliamentary and Municipal Registration Act, 1878, shall not apply, and the lists and register of voters shall be made out alphabetically, but shall be framed in parts for polling districts and electoral divisions and for urban districts, and for wards of urban and rural districts in such a manner that the parts may be conveniently compiled or put together to serve as lists for

Sect. 76 (1). polling districts and elections in urban districts, and as electoral division or ward lists."

NOTE.

This provision will now apply to parishes within as well as without a parliamentary borough. But it is to be observed that the sub-section only relates to parishes not situate within a *municipal* borough.

As to the framing of the lists of parochial electors in parts for wards, see the Locol Government Act, 1894, s. 44, *post*.

(2.) In the provisions of section four of the said Act with respect to making out the lists of voters according to the order in which the qualifying premises appear in the rate book, the county authority shall mean the county council.

The following is the provision in s. 4 above referred to :—

"(3.) Notwithstanding anything in this Act contained, where a municipal borough or an urban district is co-extensive with any electoral division or divisions of a parliamentary county, the lists of voters may be directed by the county authority to be made out according to the order in which the qualifying premises appear in the rate book, and section twenty-one of the Parliamentary and Municipal Registration Act, 1878, shall apply to such borough or urban district, and where lists of voters are so made out nothing in this Act shall require such part of the county register as consists of these lists to be arranged alphabetically."

(3.) The names of the parliamentary electors and county electors in the lists in each polling district may be numbered consecutively, and such portion of those lists as consists of the names of parliamentary electors may be taken to form the register for the purpose of parliamentary elections, and such portion of those lists as contains the names of county electors may be taken to form the register of county electors.

In the lists of occupation voters divisions 1 and 3 will contain the names of the county electors, and divisions 1 and 2 will contain the names of the parliamentary voters.

See also s. 44 (6) of the Local Government Act, 1894, *post*.

(4.) For the purpose of the provisions of the Acts relating to the appointment of revising barristers, and of section nine of the County Electors Act, 1888, the county of Surrey and such portion of the county of London as is situate south of the Thames shall be deemed to be separate counties forming part of the south-eastern circuit; and such portion of the administrative county of London as is situate north of the Thames shall be deemed to form part of the county of Middlesex; and the county of Middlesex, inclusive of that portion, shall be deemed to be a separate county on a circuit; but any sum payable by the London County Council in respect of either of the said portions of the county shall be paid as for a general county purpose.

Sect. 76 (4).

NOTE.

Section 9 of the County Electors Act is as follows :—

"Every barrister appointed to revise any list of voters under the Parliamentary Voters Registration Act, 1843, shall be paid the sum of two hundred and fifty guineas by way of remuneration to him, and in satisfaction of his travelling and other expenses, and every such barrister, after the termination of his last sitting, shall forward his appointment to the Commissioners of Her Majesty' Treasury, who shall make an order for the payment of the above sum to every such barrister.

"The maximum amount to be paid to an additional barrister in pursuance of the Revising Barristers Act, 1886, shall not exceed the amount authorized by this section to be paid to a revising barrister.

"The sums so paid to a revising barrister or an assistant barrister shall be payable partly out of moneys provided by Parliament and partly by the county authorities as hereinafter mentioned.

"(1.) There shall be annually paid by the county authority of every county out of the county fund into Her Majesty's Exchequer such sum as the Treasury certify to be one-half of the cost incurred for the payment of revising barristers at the then last revision of the lists of parliamentary electors, burgesses, and county electors in that county.

"(2.) The Treasury shall yearly ascertain the total cost of the revising barristers appointed for all the counties and boroughs on any circuit, and shall divide one-half of such cost among the counties comprised in such circuit in proportion to the number of burgesses and county electors in each county, and certify the amount which under such apportionment is due under this section from each county. The Treasury may vary such certificate if they think fit, but unless it is so varied the certificate shall be final.

"(3.) So much of any Act as requires a payment out of the borough fund of any borough to a revising barrister, in respect of the revision of the burgess lists, shall be repealed, without prejudice to any payment or liability previously made or incurred."

The text amends the provision as to the revising barristers for Middlesex and Surrey.

As to general county purposes, see s. 68, *ante*, p. 130.

In the county of Middlesex, the city of London, the city of Westminster, and the several parliamentary boroughs in London north of the Thames, the revising barristers are appointed by the Lord Chief Justice. In other counties, cities, and boroughs they are appointed by the senior judge in the commission of assize for the county actually travelling the summer circuit. The Acts relating to the appointment of revising barristers are 6 & 7 Vict. c. 18, ss. 28, 29 ; 31 & 32 Vict. c. 58, s. 25 ; 36 & 37 Vict. c. 70, s. 3 ; 37 & 38 Vict. c. 53 ; 49 & 50 Vict. c. 42 ; and the County Electors Act, 1888 (51 Vict. c. 10), ss. 9, 10.

(5.) The provisions of section eleven of the County Electors Act, 1888, with respect to the payment of the sums therein mentioned shall apply to the payment of the said sums in the year one thousand eight hundred and eighty-eight in like manner as if a county authority had not been established under this Act.

Section 11 of the County Electors Act is as follows :—

"(1.) In the event of a county authority being established under any Act of the present session, the provisions of this Act with respect to county authority,

Sect. 76 (5).

NOTE.

county, and county fund shall refer to the said county authority and to the county and county fund of such authority, and in case of any borough which, for the purposes of the said Act, is a county of itself, to the council of the borough and to the borough and borough fund.

"(2.) In the event of a county authority not being established under any Act during the present session, the sums directed by this Act to be paid out of and into the county fund shall be paid by or under the direction of the local authority of every county quarter sessional area within the meaning of the Registration Act, 1885, in like manner as expenses or receipts of the clerk of the peace for such area under the Registration of Electors Acts, and by and under the direction of the council of every municipal borough which is also a parliamentary borough out of and into the borough fund, and the amount to be paid for revising barristers shall be apportioned between such quarter sessional areas and boroughs upon the principles above mentioned in this Act."

As to the county fund, see s. 68, *ante*, p. 130.

51 & 52 Vict. c. 10.

(6.) It is hereby declared that nothing in section twelve of the County Electors Act, 1888, applies to any person occupying property within a borough.

Section 12 of the County Electors Act is as follows :—

"A list of persons occupying property in a county, and residing within fifteen miles but more than seven miles from the county, shall be made out in accordance with section forty-nine of the Municipal Corporations Act, 1882, and that section shall apply as if it were herein re-enacted, with the substitution of 'county for 'borough,' and of 'county elector' for 'burgess,' and of 'clerk of the peace' for 'town clerk.'"

The effect of this amendment is stated in the notes to s. 49 of the Municipal Corporations Act, 1882, *post*.

(7.) It shall be lawful for Her Majesty the Queen, by Order in Council, from time to time to alter the instructions, precepts, notices, and forms under the Registration of Electors Acts, in such manner as appears to Her Majesty necessary for carrying into effect this Act and the County Electors Act, 1888, and any other Act for the time being in force amending or affecting the Acts mentioned in this sub-section, and the instructions, precepts, notices, and forms specified in any such Order in Council shall be observed and be valid in law, and clerks of the peace, and town clerks, and other officers shall act accordingly.

This provision is supplemental to that contained in s. 13 of the County Electors Act, which is as follows :—

"All precepts, notices, and forms required for the purposes of the Registration of Electors Act, shall be altered in such manner as may be declared by Her Majesty in Council to be necessary for carrying into effect this Act, and clerks of the peace and town clerks shall alter their precepts and forms accordingly, and if clerks of the peace or town clerks have sent out precepts to the overseers before the passing of this Act, they shall send to them such supplemental precepts as are necessary or desirable for instructing them to carry into effect this Act."

Sect. 76 (7).

NOTE.

The last Registration Order issued under this provision is published in the *London Gazette* of March 19th, 1895. It is set out in Mackenzie and Lushington's Registration Manual.

(8.) The provisions of section six of the said County Electors Act, 1888, requiring the statement of the barrister for the purpose of an appeal to be made not less than four days before the first day of the Michaelmas sittings, shall not apply in the year one thousand eight hundred and eighty-eight.

The provisions of s. 6 of the County Electors Act, above referred to, are as follows :—

"(2.) In sections sixty-two and sixty-three of the Parliamentary Voters Registration Act, 1843 (relating to appeals from revising barristers in England), 'the Michaelmas sittings of the High Court of Justice' shall be substituted for 'the Michaelmas term,' and forthwith after the fourth day of the Michaelmas sittings a court or courts shall sit for the purpose of hearing such appeals, and those appeals shall be heard and determined continuously and without delay, and any statement by the barrister for the purpose of any such appeal made in pursuance of section forty-two of the said Act may be made at any time within ten days after the conclusion of the revision, so that it be made not less than four days before the first day of the said Michaelmas sittings, and the statement need not be read in open court, but shall be submitted to the appellant, who, if he approves the same, shall sign the same as directed by the said section, and return the same to the barrister."

Residential qualification of county electors in administrative county of London.

77. A person who is entitled to be registered as a county elector in respect of any qualification in the administrative county of London, in all respects except that of residence, and is resident beyond seven miles but within fifteen miles of the county, shall be entitled to be registered as a county elector.

This provision is in effect that the persons whose names would in the ordinary way be placed in the separate non-resident list shall in London be qualified not only to be elected county councillors, but to be registered as county electors. There will not, therefore, be any need for a separate non-resident list in the county of London. See the notes to ss. 9 and 49 of the Municipal Corporations Act, 1882, *post.*

As to the "administrative county of London, see s. 40, *ante,* p 88.

Construction of Acts referring to business transferred.

78.—(1.) All enactments in any Act, whether general or local and personal, relating to any business, powers, duties, or liabilities transferred by or in pursuance of this Act from any authority to a county council, either alone or jointly with the quarter sessions, or to any joint committee, shall, subject to the provisions of this Act, and so far as circumstances admit, be construed as if—

(*a*) any reference therein to the said authority or to any committee or member thereof or to any meeting thereof (so far as it relates to the business, powers, duties, or liabilities transferred) referred to the county council or to a

Sect. 78 (1).

committee or member thereof or to a meeting thereof, as the case requires, and as if—

(*b*) a reference to any clerk or officer of such authority referred to the clerk or officer of a county council or committee thereof, as the case requires,

and all the said enactments shall be construed with such modifications as may be necessary for carrying this Act into effect.

This is a general provision making all Acts relating to business transferred applicable to the county council as the authority for the execution of these Acts and to the committees, members, and officers of the county council.

As to the standing joint committee, see s. 30, *ante*, p. 66.

As to other joint committees under this Act, see ss. 5 (3), 10, 14, 33 (2), 34 (5), 46, 47, 81, 82, and 111.

(2.) Provided that the transfer of powers and duties enacted by this Act shall not authorize any county council or any committee or member thereof—

(*a*) to exercise any of the powers of a court of record; or

(*b*) to administer an oath; or

(*c*) to exercise any jurisdiction under the Summary Jurisdiction Acts, or perform any judicial business, or otherwise act as justices or a justice of the peace;

but this enactment shall be without prejudice to the position of the chairman of the county council as justice of the peace during his term of office.

This proviso preserves to justices all their judicial powers and authority. See also ss. 8, 9, *ante*, p. 18.

As to the authority of the chairman as a justice, see s. 2, sub-s. (5), *ante*, p. 4.

Although this section prohibits the administration of an oath by the county council, it was held that in considering applications for music and dancing licences the London County Council act judicially. See the cases cited in the note to s. 3 (v.), *ante*, p. 7.

(3.) Where under any such enactment as in this section mentioned, any powers, duties, or liabilities are to be exercised or discharged after any presentment or in any particular manner, or at any particular meeting, or subject to any other conditions, the county council may, by the standing orders for the regulation of their proceedings, provide for the exercise and discharge of those powers, duties, and liabilities without any such prior presentment or in a different manner, or at any meeting of the council fixed by the standing orders, or without such other conditions; and until such standing orders take effect shall exercise and discharge them in the like manner, and at the like time, and subject to the like conditions, so nearly as circumstances admit; and a presentment by a grand jury in relation to any such powers, duties, or liabilities shall cease to be made otherwise than by way of indictment. Sect. 78 (3).

It will be the duty of the county council to make standing orders for the regulation of their business and for the purposes of the foregoing provisions. Their power to make standing orders is derived from the Municipal Corporations Act, 1882, Sched. 2, 13, *post*, which is incorporated by s. 75, *ante*.

At common law the grand jury or any twelve of them may make presentments for offences, etc., within their own knowledge. Such presentments are delivered into court to the clerk of the peace, who put them into the form of indictments on which process may issue as in the case of indictments found; Archbold's Quarter Sessions, p. 202. A common presentment was that a county bridge is out of repair. By reason of the provision in the text, presentments by a grand jury cannot now be made as to any powers, etc., transferred to the county council, except by way of indictment.

(4.) For the purposes of this section the expression "authority" means a Secretary of State, the Board of Trade, the Local Government Board, and any Government Department, also any commissioners, conservators, or public body, corporate or incorporate, specified in a provisional order transferring any powers, duties, or liabilities to the county council, also any quarter sessions and any justices, also the Metropolitan Board of Works, or other local authority mentioned in this Act; and the expression "member of an authority" includes, where the authority are quarter sessions or justices, any justice, and the expression "meeting of an authority" includes a court of quarter sessions and the assembly of justices in special or petty sessions; and the expression "clerk of an authority" includes in relation to any quarter sessions or justices, the clerk of the peace or the clerk to a justice, as the case requires.

This section shall apply as if a joint committee were a committee of the county council.

As to the provisional orders here referred to, see s. 10, *ante*, p. 19.

As to the Metropolitan Board of Works, see s. 40, sub-s. (8), *ante*, p. 90.

As to joint committee. see the note to sub-s. (1), *supra*.

Proceedings of Councils and Committees.

79.—(1.) The council of each county shall be a body corporate by the name of the county council with the addition of the name of the administrative county, and shall have perpetual succession and a common seal and power to acquire and hold land for the purposes of their constitution without licence in mortmain.

Incorporation of county council.

(2.) All duties and liabilities of the inhabitants of a county shall become and be duties and liabilities of the council of such county.

One result of this sub-section appears to be that the county council will be liable to be indicted for non-repair of a county bridge. See also as to the

Sect. 79 (2). — NOTE.

effect of this sub-section, *Salford (Mayor, etc., of)* v. *Lancashire County Council*, cited *ante*, p. 123, and the note to this section in Pratt's Law of Highways, 14th ed., p. 488.

(3.) Where any enactment (whether relating to lunatic asylums or bridges, or other county purposes, or to quarter sessions) requires or authorizes land to be conveyed or granted to, or any contract or agreement to be made in the name of the clerk of the peace or any justice or justices, or other person, on behalf of the county or quarter sessions, or justices of the county, such land shall be conveyed or granted to, and such contract and agreement shall be made with, the council of the administrative county concerned.

The conveyance or contract, as the case may be, is to be made directly to or with the council, which is a corporate body; see sub-s. (1), *supra*.

Payments out of fund and finance committee of county council.

80.—(1.) All payments to and out of the county fund shall be made to and by the county treasurer, and all payments out of the fund shall, unless made in pursuance of the specific requirement of an Act of Parliament or of an order of a competent court, be made in pursuance of an order of the council signed by three members of the finance committee present at the meeting of the council and countersigned by the clerk of the council, and the same order may include several payments. Moreover, all cheques for payment of moneys issued in pursuance of such order shall be countersigned by the clerk of the council or by a deputy approved by the council.

As to the county treasurer, see s. 3 (iii.), *ante*, p. 6, and s. 118, sub-s. (13), *post*.

The finance committee is appointed under sub-s. (3), *infra*.

As an illustration of the reference to payments in pursuance of an order of a competent court, reference may be made to 9 Geo. 4. c. 61, s. 29, under which on a licensing appeal the quarter sessions may order the treasurer to pay the costs of the respondent justices.

An order for the payment of money is to be made pursuant to an order of the council directed to the treasurer. It must be signed by three members of the finance committee present at the meeting at which the order is made, and it must be countersigned by the clerk.

The treasurer's cheques issued in pursuance of this order must also be countersigned by the clerk or a deputy approved by the council.

(2.) Any such order may be removed into the High Court of Justice by writ of *certiorari*, and may be wholly or partly disallowed or confirmed on motion and hearing, with or without costs, according to the judgment and discretion of the court.

This provision is similar to that contained in the Municipal Corporations Act, 1882, s. 141, as to which see *R.* v. *Lichfield*, 4 Q. B. 893; *R.* v. *Greene*, *ib.* 646; *R.* v. *Dunn*, 5 Q. B. 959; *R.* v. *Prest*, 16 Q. B. 32; 20 L. J. Q. B. 17; 14 J. P. 750; *Att.-Gen.* v. *Wigan*, 1 Kay, 268; *R.* v. *Sheffield*,

NOTE.

L. R. 6 Q. B. 652 ; 40 L. J. Q. B. 247 ; 24 L. T. (N.S.) 659 ; 19 W. R. 1159; *R.* v. *Norwich*, 30 W. R. 752 ; *Att.-Gen.* v. *Blackburn*, 57 L. T (N.S.) 385 ; *R.* v. *Ramsgate (Mayor, etc., of)*, 23 Q. B. D. 66 ; 58 L. J. Q. B. 352 ; 61 L. T. (N.S.) 333 ; 37 W. R. 781 ; 53 J. P. 740. And as to the liability to pay the costs of the proceedings, see *R.* v. *Vaile or Whiteley*, 23 Q. B. D. 483 ; 58 L. J. M. C. 164 ; 61 L. T. (N.S.) 253 ; 54 J. P. 134.

A writ of *certiorari* under this sub-section need not be applied for within six months, for the 13 Geo. 2, c. 18, s. 2, applies only to orders, etc., of justices. *R.* v. *Sheffield*, *supra.*

(3.) Every county council shall from time to time appoint a finance committee for regulating and controlling the finance of their county ; and an order for the payment of a sum out of the county fund, whether on account of capital or income, shall not be made by a county council, except in pursuance of a resolution of the council passed on the recommendation of the finance committee, and (subject to the provisions of this Act respecting the standing joint committee) any costs, debt, or liability exceeding fifty pounds shall not be incurred except upon a resolution of the council passed on an estimate submitted by the finance committee.

As to the form of the order, see sub-s. (1), *supra.*

As to the joint committee, see s. 30, *ante*, p. 66.

The provision in the text that costs not exceeding 50*l.* shall only be incurred on an estimate submitted by the finance committee may be inconvenient in practice. An emergency may require the immediate expenditure of money ; for example, a county bridge may be washed away or injured by a flood.

(4.) The notice of the meeting at which any resolution for the payment of a sum out of the county fund (otherwise than for ordinary periodical payments), or any resolution for incurring any costs, debt, or liability exceeding fifty pounds will be proposed, shall state the amount of the said sum, costs, debt, or liability, and the purpose for which they are to be paid or incurred.

The notice of the meeting here referred to is that which must be given pursuant to the Municipal Corporations Act, 1882, Sched. 2, rr. 5 and 6.

(5.) This section shall not apply to county boroughs.

As to county boroughs, see ss. 31—34, *ante*, and Sched. 3, *post.*

81.—(1.) Any county council or councils, and any court or courts of quarter sessions, may from time to time join in appointing out of their respective bodies a joint committee for any purpose in respect of which they are jointly interested.

Appointment of joint committees.

This joint committee is distinct from the standing joint committee appointed under s. 30, *ante*, p. 66. It is difficult to suggest any matter in which county councils and quarter sessions can be jointly interested which is not within the jurisdiction of the standing joint committee. The section, however, relates not merely to joint committees of councils and sessions, but of two

Sect. 81 (1). or more county councils for purposes in which such councils are jointly interested.

NOTE.

As to joint committees particularly referred to in the Act, see note to s. 78, *ante*, p. 152.

(2.) Any council or court taking part in the appointment of any joint committee under this section, may from time to time delegate to the committee any power which such council or court might exercise for the purpose for which the committee is appointed.

(3.) Provided that nothing in this section shall authorize a council to delegate to a committee any power of making a rate or borrowing any money.

Compare the provisions of s. 28 (3), *ante*, p. 65.

(4.) Subject to the terms of delegation, any such joint committee shall, in respect of any matter delegated to it, have the same power in all respects as the councils and courts appointing it, or any of them, as the case may be.

(5.) The members of a joint committee appointed under this Act shall be appointed at such times and in such manner as may be from time to time fixed by the council or court who appointed them, and shall hold office for such time as may be fixed by the council or court who appointed them, so that where any members of the committee were appointed by the county council, such committee do not continue for more than three months after any triennial election of councillors of such county council.

It is presumed that notwithstanding the concluding words of this sub-section, any member of the committee who has not been re-elected at a triennial election will cease to act as a member of the committee. The committee as a body will, however, continue to act for three months after the election, or until they are re-appointed.

(6.) The costs of a joint committee shall be defrayed by the council by whom any of its members were appointed, or if appointed by more than one council in the proportion agreed to by them ; and the accounts of such joint committee and their officers shall, for the purposes of the provisions of this Act, be deemed to be accounts of the county council and their officers.

As to the accounts of the county council and their officers, see s. 71, *ante*, p. 136.

(7.) This section shall apply to the councils of county boroughs in like manner as to councils of administrative counties, and a standing joint committee may be appointed for two or more administrative counties, inclusive of county boroughs, and the members of such joint committee shall be appointed by the several quarter sessions and councils in such proportion and manner as they respectively may arrange, and in default of arrangement as may be directed by a Secretary of State. **Sect. 81 (7).**

The effect of this provision is that a single standing joint committee may be appointed for two or more counties, or counties and county boroughs.

(8.) This section shall apply to the standing joint committees.

82.—(1.) A county council appointing under this Act any committee may from time to time make, vary, and revoke regulations respecting the quorum and proceedings of such committee, and as to the area (if any) within which it is to exercise its authority; and subject to such regulations the proceedings and quorum and the place of meeting, whether within or without the county, shall be such as the committee may from time to time direct, and the chairman at any meeting of the committee shall have a second or casting vote. **Proceedings of committees.**

The duly appointed executive committee of a county council made an order delegating to local sub-committees its powers under the Contagious Diseases (Animals) Acts and under certain Orders in Council, including the Rabies Order, 1887. Subsequently to such delegation the executive committee, without expressly revoking the delegation, issued certain regulations under the Rabies Order, 1887, as to the muzzling of dogs and keeping them under control. No regulations under that order had been issued by the local sub-committees. It was held that the delegation was not equivalent to a resignation by the executive committee of its own powers, that the delegated authority was subject to resumption at any time, and that the regulations were therefore valid. *Huth* v. *Clarke*, 25 Q. B. D. 391 ; 59 L. J. M. C. 120 ; 63 L. T. (N.S.) 348 ; 38 W. R. 655 ; 6 T. L. R. 373.

It would appear that separate regulations must be made for each committee unless general regulations are made, which may, with or without modification, be applied to each committee when appointed.

Observe that the text provides for the casting vote of the chairman.

As to the general appointment of committees, see s. 28, *ante*, p. 63.

(2.) Every committee shall report its proceedings to the council by whom it was appointed, but to the extent to which the council so direct, the acts and proceedings of the committee shall not be required by the provisions of the Municipal Corporations Act, 1882, to be submitted to the council for their approval.

The council may dispense with the necessity of submitting the acts of the committee for their approval. This provision modifies the Municipal Corporations Act, 1882, s. 22 (*post*). Compare s. 75, sub-s. (16) (*f*), *ante*, p. 146.

(3.) In the case of a joint committee the councils and courts appointing the joint committee shall jointly have the powers given

Sect. 82 (3). by this section, and the provisions of this section shall apply accordingly.

As to joint committees, see s. 81, *ante*.

Officers.

Clerk of the peace and of county council.

83. Subject to the provisions of this Act for the protection of clerks of the peace holding office at the passing of this Act, the following provisions shall have effect :—

The provisions of this Act here referred to are contained in s. 118, *post*.

(1.) The clerk of the peace of a county, besides acting as clerk of the peace of that county, shall also (subject to the provisions of this Act as respects particular counties) be the clerk of the county council, and in that capacity is referred to in this Act as the clerk of the county council.

The provisions of this Act as to particular counties are contained in the subsequent sub-sections of this section, and in s. 118, *post*.

(2.) He shall be from time to time appointed by the standing joint committee of the county council and the quarter sessions, and may be removed by that joint committee.

As to the standing joint committee, see s. 30, *ante*, p. 66.
As to the removal of the clerk of the peace under the law which is still in force so far as regards a clerk of the peace holding office on the appointed day, see 1 Will. & M. c. 21, ss. 5, 6 ; 27 & 28 Vict. c. 65.

(3.) He shall, subject to the directions of the custos rotulorum or the quarter sessions or the county council, as the case may require, have charge of and be responsible for the records and documents of the county.

The records of the county are to remain in the same custody as heretofore. See s. 64, sub-s. (1), *ante*, p. 122. Anything necessary for the convenient keeping of records and documents is to be provided by the standing joint committee, s. 64, sub-s. (3), *ante*, p. 124.

(4.) The joint committee may appoint a deputy clerk to hold office during their pleasure, and to act in lieu of such clerk in case of his death, illness, or absence, or in such other cases as may be determined by the joint committee, and wherever the deputy so acts, all things authorized or required to be done by, to, or before the clerk of the peace, or clerk of the county council, may be done by, to, or before any such deputy without prejudice to the appointment of a deputy clerk for the purpose of a second court on the division of the court of quarter sessions for judicial business.

But see s. 118, *post*, as to the power of existing clerks of the peace to appoint and act by deputy. The power to appoint a deputy clerk for a second court is given by 21 & 22 Vict. c. 73, s. 9. **Sect. 83 (4).** NOTE.

(5.) The council shall pay to the clerk of the peace in respect of his services as clerk of the peace and as clerk of the county council such salary as may be from time to time fixed under the enactments relating thereto, and all fees and costs payable to the clerk of the peace which are not excluded when the salary of the clerk of the peace is fixed shall be paid to the county fund, and for the purpose of the enactments relating to such salary and fees, the standing joint committee of the county council and the quarter sessions shall be substituted for the quarter sessions and the local authority respectively.

The enactments relating to the salary and fees of the clerk of the peace are the 57 Geo. 3, c. 91; 11 & 12 Vict. c. 43, s. 30; 14 & 15 Vict. c. 55, ss. 9, 12; 18 & 19 Vict. c. 126, s. 18 (set out, *ante*, p. 56); 32 & 33 Vict. c. 89, s. 11; 45 & 46 Vict. c. 50, s. 164.

For the provisions of these Acts the reader is referred to Archbold's Quarter Sessions.

As to the county fund, see s. 68, *post*.

(6.) The clerk of the peace, when acting in relation to any business of the county council, and when acting under the Acts relating to the registration of parliamentary voters, or to the deposit of plans or documents, or to jury lists, or to any registration matters, shall act under the direction of the county council, and all enactments relating to such business, registration, or deposit, shall be construed as if clerk of the county council were therein substituted for clerk of the peace.

The duties of the clerk of the peace under the Acts relating to the registration of voters are very numerous and cannot here be stated in detail. The reader is referred to the recent edition of Messrs. Mackenzie and Lushington's work on these Acts.

As to the deposit of plans and documents, see the Cemeteries Clauses Act (10 & 11 Vict. c. 65), s. 60; the Commissioners Clauses Act (10 & 11 Vict. c. 16), ss. 109—111; the Gas Works Clauses Act (10 & 11 Vict. c. 15), ss. 45, 46; the Harbours, &c., Clauses Act (10 & 11 Vict. c. 27), ss. 97, 98; the Lands Clauses Act (8 Vict. c. 18), ss. 151, 152; the Markets and Fairs Clauses Act (10 & 11 Vict. c. 14), ss. 58, 59; the Railways Clauses Act (8 Vict. c. 20), ss. 8—10, 59, 130, etc. By the 7 Will. 4 & 1 Vict. c. 83, clerks of the peace are required to take the custody of all such documents as shall be directed to be deposited with them under the standing orders of either House of Parliament, and to permit all persons interested to inspect them and make copies and extracts on payment by each person of the sum of 1*s.* for each such inspection, and the further sum of 1*s.* for every hour during which such inspection shall continue

Sect. 83 (6). after the first hour, and after the rate of 6*d.* for every 100 words copied therefrom.

NOTE.

As to the duties of the clerk of the peace with reference to the jury lists, see 6 Geo. 4, c. 50, s. 6, and 25 & 26 Vict. c. 107, s. 4.

All these duties are now to be performed under the direction of the county council by the clerk of the county council as such.

(7.) The office of clerk of the peace of each of the administrative counties of Sussex and Suffolk shall be a separate office; but nothing in this Act shall prevent the same person from being appointed to both such offices, and the justices in general sessions assembled for the entire county of Sussex or Suffolk may from time to time appoint the person who is clerk of the peace for either administrative county to be clerk of the peace of such general sessions, and may remove such clerk, and the remuneration to be paid to such clerk shall be determined jointly by the standing joint committees for the administrative counties.

As to the divisions of Sussex and Suffolk, see s. 46, sub-s. (1) *ante*, p. 99.

(8.) The existing records of the county of Sussex and of the county of Suffolk shall, subject to the order of quarter sessions, continue to be kept by the clerk of the peace of East Sussex and by the clerk of the peace for East Suffolk respectively.

(9.) This section shall apply to the clerks of the peace and deputy clerks of the peace of the county of Lancaster, in like manner as it applies to clerks of the peace of any other county, but the appointment of any such deputy clerk of the peace may be discontinued if the standing joint committee think fit.

(10.) The joint committee of the councils of the three ridings or divisions of Yorkshire and Lincolnshire may from time to time appoint a clerk of such joint committee, and may from time to time remove such clerk.

As to this joint committee, see s. 46, sub-s. (2), *ante*, p. 99.

(11.) The clerk of the peace for the county of London shall be a separate officer from the clerk of the county council for the administrative county of London, and

(*a.*) The clerk of the peace shall, subject to the directions of the quarter sessions, have charge of and be responsible for the records and documents of those sessions and of the justices out of session, and the clerk of the county council shall, subject to the directions of the council, have charge of and be responsible for all other documents of the county; and (*b.*) The council may from time to time appoint a deputy clerk of the council, and the foregoing provisions of this section with respect to the deputy clerk shall apply; and

Sect. 83 (11).

(*c.*) The council shall pay to the clerk of the council such salary as may be fixed from time to time fixed by them.

(12.) The county council shall cause their clerk or other officer from time to time to send to a Secretary of State or the Local Government Board such returns and information as may from time to time be required by either House of Parliament.

(13.) Provided always, that no paid clerk or other paid official in the permanent employment of a county council who is required to devote his whole time to such employment shall be eligible to serve in Parliament.

Appointment of the justices' clerks and clerks of committees.

84.—(1.) The salaried clerk of every petty sessional division shall be from time to time appointed and removed as heretofore.

Clerks to justices are appointed in counties by the justices of the petty sessional division under 40 & 41 Vict. c. 43, s. 5, and in boroughs by the borough justices under 45 & 46 Vict. c. 50, s. 159.

(2.) The county council shall pay to the salaried clerks of petty sessional divisions such salaries as may be fixed under the enactments relating to those clerks, and all fees and costs payable to such clerks which are not excluded in the fixing of their salaries shall be paid into the county fund, and in the enactments relating to such salaries and fees the standing joint committee shall be substituted for the quarter sessions justices and the local authority respectively.

The enactments relating to the salaries and fees of justices' clerks are 11 & 12 Vict. c. 43, s. 31; 14 & 15 Vict. c. 55, ss. 9—12; 40 & 41 Vict. c. 43. See also the Local Stamp Act, 1869 (32 & 33 Vict. c. 49), referred to in s. 3 (xiii.) *ante*, p. 12, and s. 30, *ante*, p. 66.

The duties of the quarter sessions justices and local authority under these Acts will henceforth be fulfilled by the standing joint committee appointed under s. 30.

As justices' clerks are not appointed by the county councils nor removable by them, it is submitted that they are not disqualified by s. 12 of the Municipal Corporations Act, 1882, to be county councillors.

The enactment in the text imposes on a county council the duty of paying the salary of the justices' clerk in a borough within the county; and all fees and costs payable to such clerk, which are not excluded in the fixing of his salary, should be paid into the county fund. *Cornwall County Council* v. *Truro Town Council*, 63 L. J. M. C. 60; 70 L. T. (N.S.) 354; 58 J. P. 299; *Herefordshire County Council and Leominster Town Council*, *in re*, [1895] 1

Sect. 84 (2). Q. B. 43 ; 64 L. J. M. C. 26 ; 71 L. T. (N.S.) 576 ; 59 J. P. 348 ; *Thetford* (*Mayor*

NOTE. *of, etc.* v. *Norfolk County Council*, 67 L. J. Q. B. 55 ; 14 T. L. R. 35.

Regulations for Bicycles, etc.

Regulations for bicycles, etc.

85.—(1.) The provisions of section twenty-six, sub-section five, of the Highways and Locomotives (Amendment) Act, 1878, and section twenty-three, sub-section one, of the Municipal Corporations Act, 1882, in so far as it gives power to the council to make bye-laws regulating the use of carriages herein referred to, and all other provisions of any public or private Acts, in so far as they give power to any local authority to make bye-laws for regulating the use of bicycles, tricycles, velocipedes, and other similar machines, are hereby repealed, and bicycles, tricycles, velocipedes, and other similar machines are hereby declared to be carriages within the meaning of the Highway Acts; and the following additional regulations shall be observed by any person or persons riding or being upon such carriage:—

(*a*.) During the period between one hour after sunset and one hour before sunrise, every person riding or being upon such carriage shall carry attached to the carriage a lamp, which shall be so constructed and placed as to exhibit a light in the direction in which he is proceeding, and so lighted and kept lighted, as to afford adequate means of signalling the approach or position of the carriage ;

(*b*.) Upon overtaking any cart or carriage, or any horse, mule, or other beast of burden, or any foot passenger, being on or proceeding along the carriage way, every such person shall within a reasonable distance from and before passing such cart or carriage, horse, mule, or other beast of burden, or such foot passenger, by sounding a bell or whistle, or otherwise, give audible and sufficient warning of the approach of the carriage.

Section 26, sub-s. (5), of the Highway Act, 1878, enabled a county authority to make bye-laws for regulating the use of bicycles. These bye-laws differed considerably in the different counties, and from bye-laws regulating the use of bicycles and tricycles in boroughs made under s. 23 of the Municipal Corporations Act, 1882, *post*. The power to make bye-laws for these purposes is now repealed, as also are the provisions of any public or private Acts giving power to make such bye-laws. The additional regulations under this sub-section are of universal application, and superseded all previously existing local regulations.

The declaration that bicycles, etc., are carriages within the meaning of the Highway Acts was, perhaps, unnecessary, for it was held in *Taylor* v. *Goodwin*, 4 Q. B. D. 228 ; 43 J. P. 653, that a bicycle is a carriage within the meaning of s. 78 of the Highway Act, 1835, and that a person might be convicted under

Sect. 85 (1). — NOTE.

it of furious driving, and see *McKee* v. *McGrath*, 30 L. R. Ir. 41. But possibly there was some doubt on the point, having regard to *Williams* v. *Ellis*, 5 Q. B. D. 175; 42 L. T. (N.S.) 249; 44 J. P. 394, where it was held that a bicycle was not a carriage liable to toll under a Turnpike Act. At all events, the text makes an express provision, the effect of which is to apply to bicycles, etc., the provisions of the Highway Acts as to driving on footpaths, keeping to the near side of the road, furious driving, etc. See, in particular, ss. 72 and 78 of the Highway Act, 1835.

At the Sussex Assizes before HAWKINS, J., a defendant was convicted and sentenced to four months hard labour under 24 & 25 Vict. c. 100, s. 35, for riding a bicycle in a furious manner, thereby causing bodily harm. *R.* v. *Parker*, 59 J. P. 793. A bicycle was held to be a vehicle within a local Act, which prohibited the use of vehicles for advertisement. *Ellis* v. *Nott Bower*, 13 T. L. R. 35.

An offence against the regulations made by the text is not, of course, an offence against the Highway Acts; it follows that the powers given by ss. 78 and 79 of the Highway Act, 1835, to apprehend offenders without warrant, do not apply to an offence against these regulations, and that a constable cannot arrest a bicyclist who is riding at night without a lamp. *Hatton* v. *Treeby*, [1897] 2 Q. B. 452; 66 L. J. Q. B. 712; 61 J. P. 567.

(2.) Any person summarily convicted of offending against the regulations made by this section, shall for each and every such offence, forfeit and pay any sum not exceeding forty shillings.

This penalty will be recovered summarily, *i.e.*, on summons before two justices.

Adaptation of Acts.

Adaptation of Lunatic Asylum Acts.

86. For the purpose of adapting the Acts relating to pauper lunatic asylums to the provisions of this Act, the following provisions shall have effect:—

The whole of this section except sub-s. (5) is repealed by the Lunacy Act, 1890 (53 & 54 Vict. c. 5).

(5.) Any asylum provided in whole or in part at the cost of a county shall for the purposes of this Act be included in the expression "county lunatic asylum."

Application of provisions of 38 & 39 Vict. c. 55, as to local inquiries and provisional orders

87.—(1.) Where the Local Government Board are authorized by this Act to make an inquiry, to determine any difference, to make or confirm any order, to frame any scheme, or to give any consent, sanction, or approval to any matter, or otherwise to act under this Act, they may cause to be made a local inquiry, and in that case, and also in a case where they are required by this Act to cause to be made a local inquiry, sections two hundred

Sect. 87 (1). and ninety-three to two hundred and ninety-six, both inclusive, of the Public Health Act, 1875, shall apply as if they were herein re-enacted, and in terms made applicable to this Act.

This section is confined to cases of difference which are to be determined by the Local Government Board otherwise than by arbitration: see *per* CAVE, J., *In re Kent County Council and Sandgate Local Board*, [1895] 2 Q. B. 43; 64 L. J. Q. B. 502; 72 L. T. (N.S.), 725; 43 W. R. 601; 59 J. P. 456.

See further as to determination of differences by the Local Government Board, 59 & 60 Vict. c. 9, *post*, and ss. 11 (3) (4) and 63, *ante*, pp. 29, 30, 121.

Sections 293—296 of the Public Health Act, 1875, are as follows:—

"293. The Local Government Board may from time to time cause to be made such inquiries as are directed by this Act, and such inquiries as they see fit in relation to any matters concerning the public health in any place, or any matters with respect to which their sanction, approval, or consent is required by this Act.

"294. The Local Government Board may make orders as to the cost of inquiries or proceedings instituted by, or of appeals to the said Board under this Act, and as to the parties by whom or the rates out of which such costs shall be borne; and every such order may be made a rule of one of the superior courts of law on the application of any person named therein.

"295. All orders made by the Local Government Board in pursuance of this Act shall be binding and conclusive in respect of the matters to which they refer, and shall be published in such manner as that Board may direct.

"296. Inspectors of the Local Government Board shall, for the purposes of any inquiry directed by the Board, have in relation to witnesses and their examination, the production of papers and accounts, and the inspection of places and matters required to be inspected, similar powers to those which poor law inspectors have under the Acts relating to the relief of the poor for the purposes of those Acts."

The notes to these sections in Lumley's Public Health, p. 389, may be referred to.

(2.) Sections two hundred and ninety-seven and two hundred and ninety-eight of the Public Health Act, 1875 (which relate to the making of provisional orders by the Local Government Board), shall apply for the purposes of this Act as if they were herein re-enacted, and in terms made applicable thereto.

Sections 297 and 298 of the Public Health Act, 1875, are as follows:—

"297. With respect to provisional orders authorized to be made by the Local Government Board under this Act, the following enactments shall be made:—

"(1.) The Local Government Board shall not make any provisional order under this Act unless public notice of the purport of the proposed order has been previously given by advertisement in two successive weeks in some local newspaper circulating in the district to which such provisional order relates:

"(2.) Before making any such provisional order, the Local Government Board shall consider any objections which may be made thereto by any persons affected thereby, and in cases where the subject-matter is one to which a local inquiry is applicable, shall cause to be made a local inquiry, of which public notice shall be given in manner aforesaid, and at which all persons interested shall be permitted to attend and make objections: Sect. 87 (2).

NOTE.

(3.) The Local Government Board may subject to Parliament for confirmation any provisional order made by it in pursuance of this Act, but any such order shall be of no force whatever unless and until it is confirmed by Parliament:

' (4.) If while the Bill confirming any such order is pending in either House of Parliament, a petition is presented against any order comprised therein, the Bill, so far as it relates to such order, may be referred to a Select Committee, and the petitioner shall be allowed to appear and oppose as in the case of private Bills:

"(5.) An Act confirming any provisional order made in pursuance of any of the Sanitary Acts or of this Act, and any order in council made in pursuance of any of the Sanitary Acts, may be repealed, altered, or amended by any provisional order made by the Local Government Board and confirmed by Parliament;

"(6.) The Local Government Board may revoke, either wholly or partially, any provisional order made by them before the same is confirmed by Parliament, but such revocation shall not be made whilst the Bill confirming the order is pending in either House of Parliament;

"(7.) The making of a provisional order shall be *primâ facie* evidence that all the requirements of this Act in respect of proceedings required to be taken previously to the making of such provisional order have been complied with:

"(8.) Every Act confirming any such provisional order shall be deemed to be a public general Act.

"298. The reasonable costs of any local authority in respect of provisional orders made in pursuance of this Act, and of the inquiry preliminary thereto, as sanctioned by the Local Government Board, whether in promoting or opposing the same, shall be deemed to be expenses properly incurred for purposes of this Act by the local authority interested in or affected by such provisional orders, and such costs shall be paid accordingly; and if thought expedient by the Local Government Board, the local authority may contract a loan for the purpose of defraying such costs."

See the notes to these sections in Lumley's Public Health, p. 392.

(3.) Provided that, where a provisional order transfers to county councils generally any powers, duties, or liabilities of Her Majesty's Privy Council, a Secretary of State, the Local Government Board, or other Government Department, it shall not be necessary to hold a local inquiry, nor to advertise in any local newspaper.

In the cases mentioned in the text, the advertisements and notices required by s. 297 of the Public Health Act (see the note to sub-s. (2)) are dispensed with.

The provisional order here referred to is that which may be made under s. 10, *ante*, p. 19.

(4.) Where any matter is authorized or required by this Act to be prescribed, and no other provision is made declaring how the

Sect. 87 (4). same is to be prescribed, the same shall be prescribed from time to time by the Local Government Board.

See, for example, s. 57, *ante*, p. 111.

(5.) Where the Board cause any local inquiry to be held under this Act, the costs incurred in relation to such inquiry, including the salary of any inspector or officer of the Board engaged in such inquiry, not exceeding three guineas a day, shall be paid by the councils and other authorities concerned in such inquiry, or by such of them and in such proportions as the Board may direct, and the Board may certify the amount of the costs incurred, and any sum so certified and directed by the Board to be paid by any council or authority shall be a debt to the Crown from such council or authority.

Adaptation of Act to Metropolis.

88. In the administrative county of London the following provisions shall have effect:

(*a.*) The county council may from time to time appoint any fit person to be deputy chairman, and to hold office during the term of office of the chairman, and may pay to such deputy chairman such remuneration as the county council may from time to time think fit;

As to the administrative county of London, see s. 40, *ante*, p. 88.
The chairman may himself receive remuneration under s. 15 (4) of the Municipal Corporations Act, 1882, *post*: but the vice-chairman appointed under section 2 (6), *ante*, p. 4, is not a paid officer.

(*b.*) Subject to any rules from time to time made by the county council, anything authorized or required to be done by, to, or before the chairman, may be done by, to, or before such deputy chairman;

See the last preceding note, and compare the provisions of s. 2 (6), *ante*, p. 4.

(*c.*)

This sub-section related to the appointment, qualification, and duties of medical officers of health and sanitary inspectors in the metropolis. It is repealed by the Public Health (London) Act, 1891 (54 & 55 Vict. c. 76), which substantially re-enacts it: see s. 108 of that Act and the Order of the Local Government Board made under it, dated December 8th, 1891.

Adjustment of law as regards courts, juries,

89.—(1.) The Central Criminal Court Act, 1834, shall be construed as if the county of London were throughout mentioned therein as well as the county of Middlesex.

Sect. 89 (2).

(2.) The County Juries Act, 1825, and the Acts amending the same, shall apply to the county of London in like manner as they apply to the county of Middlesex, and persons shall be qualified to serve as jurors, and lists of jurors shall be made out in like manner, so nearly as circumstances admit, as in that county; and the present exemption of inhabitants of the liberty and city of Westminster from serving on juries at quarter sessions for the county of Middlesex shall cease; but nothing in this section shall alter the qualification of persons to serve as jurors within the city of London.

Sittings, and legal proceedings in Middlesex and London. 4 & 5 Will. 4, c. 36. 6 Geo. 4, c. 50.

(3.) Subject to rules of court made by the authority having power to make rules for the Supreme Court of Judicature, the county of London and the county of Middlesex shall be deemed to be one county for the purpose of all legal proceedings, civil or criminal, in the Supreme Court or Central Criminal Court, or any other court except the court of quarter sessions, and also for the purpose of the sittings of the Supreme Court, Central Criminal Court, or such other court as aforesaid, or of any judge of any of such courts, and also for the purpose of any jury, and of any court of assize, oyer and terminer, and gaol delivery; and all enactments, rules, orders, and documents referring to Middlesex shall be construed so as to give effect to this section; and rules of court may be from time to time made for the purpose of carrying this section into effect, and for regulating the issue of precepts to the sheriffs of the counties of London and Middlesex for the return of jurors, and the jurors so returned shall have the same powers, duties, and liabilities as if the two counties were one county.

The authority having power to make rules for the Supreme Court consists of any five or more of the following persons, of whom the Lord Chancellor shall be one, viz., the Lord Chancellor, the Lord Chief Justice, the Master of the Rolls, the President of the Probate Division, four other judges of the Supreme Court appointed by the Lord Chancellor, the President of the Incorporated Law Society, and two persons (one of whom must be a practising barrister), also appointed by the Lord Chancellor. 44 & 45 Vict. c. 68, s. 19; 57 & 58 Vict. c. 16, s. 4.

For the purposes of all legal proceedings in any court, save that of quarter sessions, London and Middlesex are to be deemed one county.

90. In the adjustment of the property, debts, and liabilities between the counties of Surrey and Middlesex respectively and the county of London, the annual sums payable by the counties of Surrey and Middlesex respectively in respect of certain bridges in pursuance of the Metropolis Toll Bridges Act, 1877, shall be

Special provisions as to adjustment in the metropolis. 40 & 41 Vict. c. 99.

Sect. 90. deemed to be liabilities which shall be taken into consideration upon such adjustment.

The adjustment here referred to is that made under s. 40, sub-s. (7), *ante*, p. 90. The Metropolis Toll Bridges Act, 1877, is a local Act, and should be described as 40 & 41 Vict. c. xcix., not as in the margin.

Adjustment as regards the Militia Acts.

91. The Acts relating to the general and local militia of the rest of England and Wales shall apply to the whole of the county of London in like manner as they apply to any county at large; and accordingly Her Majesty shall from time to time appoint a lieutenant of the county of London, provided that nothing in this section shall affect section fifty of the Militia Act, 1882.

45 & 46 Vict. c. 49.

By the 45 & 46 Vict. c. 49, s. 50, the city of London is a separate county for the purposes of the militia.

Savings.

Saving for votes at any parliamentary elections.

92.—(1.) Nothing in this Act, nor anything done in pursuance of this Act, shall alter the limits of any parliamentary borough or parliamentary county, or the right of any person to be registered as a voter at any parliamentary election.

For the definition of a parliamentary voter or parliamentary county, see s. 100, *post*.

(2.) Where by virtue of the provisions of this Act with respect to the county of London, or to urban sanitary districts situate partly within and partly without the boundary of a county, a place situate in a parliamentary county becomes part of the county of a council other than the council having authority over the largest part of the parliamentary county, that is to say, the part which contains the largest number of occupation voters, then, for the purpose of making out and revising the lists of voters, of conducting any parliamentary election, of polling districts, and assigning polling places, and for all purposes of and incidental to such matters, including the payment of expenses, such place shall be deemed to be part of the same county as the said largest part of the said parliamentary county, and the sheriff, council, clerk of the peace, authorities, and officers of that county shall have authority accordingly in the said place, and the provisions of the Registration Act, 1885, with respect to parliamentary counties extending into more county quarter sessional areas than one, shall apply with the necessary modifications.

48 & 49 Vict. c. 15.

The London County Council is the proper authority to certify under 6 Vict. c. 18, s. 55, for the costs of the returning officer in preparing the register of Parliamentary voters for the Parliamentary borough of Deptford, which was transferred by s. 40, *ante*, from Kent to London, notwithstanding the provisions of this and the preceding sub-section, which retain it in the county of Kent for county Parliamentary purposes; the expression "occupation voters" in the text means "county occupation voters." *Weller* v. *Collins*, 54 J. P. 441; 6 T. L. R. 342. **Sect. 92 (2).** NOTE.

The provisions of this Act as to the county of London are contained in s. 40, *ante*, p. 88. As to urban districts situate partly within and partly without the boundary of an administrative county, see s. 50, *ante*, p. 104.

(3.) Provided that the clerk of the peace who receives from the revising barrister the lists of voters in any such place shall supply to any other clerk of the peace or other officer such number of revised lists as he may require for the purpose of making up a register of county electors.

93.—(1.) Nothing in this Act shall alter the metropolitan police district, nor (save as is expressly provided with respect to contributions in substitution for local grants) affect the metropolitan police force, or the raising of money for the same, and nothing in this Act shall affect the police of the city of London. Saving for metropolitan and city police.

As to the metropolitan police district, see note to s. 24 (2) (*k.*) *ante* p. 57, which provides also for contributions in substitution for local grants in that district.

(2.) Nothing in this Act shall authorize any county council to raise any sum for the purposes of any police force by any contribution or rate levied within the metropolitan police district; and nothing in this Act shall alter the authority under the Riot (Damages) Act, 1886, within the metropolitan police district or the city of London. 49 & 50 Vict. c. 38.

As to the rates for the police in the metropolis, see 30 & 31 Vict. c. 67, s. 2, set out *ante*, p. 58.

As to the Riot (Damages) Act, see s. 3 (xiv.), *ante*, p. 13. The authority under that Act is, in the city of London, the common council; in the metropolitan police district, the receiver for the metropolitan police district. The London County Council will not, therefore, exercise jurisdiction under that Act; and the county councils of Middlesex, Surrey, Kent, Essex, and Hertford will only act as local authority in places beyond the metropolitan police district.

94. The grant made by the county council of London in respect of indoor paupers shall be in addition to any payment made out of the metropolitan common poor fund, and nothing in this Act shall affect the enactments relating to the fund. Saving for metropolitan common poor fund.

The grant made by the London County Council in respect of indoor paupers is made under s. 43, *ante*, p. 96.

The metropolitan poor fund was established by the 30 Vict. c. 6. It is a fund raised by contributions from the several unions, parishes, and places in

Sect. 94.

NOTE.

the metropolis. These contributions are paid to a receiver appointed by the Local Government Board. The fund is applied in payment of the expenses of lunatic asylums, fever or smallpox hospitals, medicine and medical and surgical appliances supplied by guardians by way of relief, salaries of officers of guardians, district school managers and asylum managers, and officers of dispensaries, registration of births and deaths, vaccination, maintenance of pauper children in schools, etc.; also in payment of the expenses of the maintenance of paupers above the age of sixteen years in any workhouse in the metropolis, the amount to be repaid being at the rate of fivepence per day for each pauper. The Acts which contain provisions relating to the fund are 30 Vict. c. 6; 31 & 32 Vict. c. 122; 32 & 33 Vict. c. 63; 33 & 34 Vict. c. 18; 34 & 35 Vict. c. 15; 39 & 40 Vict. c. 61; 39 & 40 Vict. c. 79, ss. 10, 16, 40, and 43; 42 & 43 Vict. c. 54; 54 & 55 Vict. c. 76, s. 104 (1).

Saving as to Middlesex, Surrey, and Kent.

95.—(1.) Any enactment providing that any magistrate, commissioner, or other officer shall be a justice of the peace for Middlesex, shall be construed to refer to the county of London as well as the county of Middlesex.

See, for example, 2 & 3 Vict. c. 71, ss. 1, 3, which provides that metropolitan stipendiary magistrates shall be justices of the county of Middlesex; and 10 Geo. 4, c. 44, s. 1; 2 & 3 Vict. c. 47, s. 4; 19 & 20 Vict. c. 2, s. 2, which provide that the commissioner and assistant commissioners of police shall be justices for the home counties.

(2.) Where any enactment, deed, instrument, or document refers to the county of Middlesex, Surrey, or Kent, such enactment, deed, instrument, or document shall be construed to apply to the same area to which it would have applied if this Act had not passed, except where such application is inconsistent with this Act, or where the object of such enactment, deed, instrument, or document requires that it shall be construed to apply to the county of London.

Saving for Middlesex Land Registry.

96. Nothing in this Act shall alter the area to which the enactments relating to the registration of land in the county of Middlesex apply, and any reference in those enactments or in any deed, instrument, or document made or issued under or for the purpose of those enactments, to the county of Middlesex, shall be construed to apply to the same area to which it would have applied if this Act had not passed.

The enactments relating to land registry in Middlesex are 7 Anne, c. 20; 25 & 26 Vict. c. 53, s. 104; 37 & 38 Vict. c. 78, s. 8; 38 & 39 Vict. c. 87, ss. 127, 128; 44 & 45 Vict. c. 41, s. 34; 54 & 55 Vict. c. 64.

Saving as to liability for main roads.

97. Nothing in this Act with respect to main roads shall alter the liability of any person or body of persons, corporate or unincorporate, not being a highway authority, to maintain and repair any road or part of a road. Sect. 97.

This section was inserted to preserve the liability of persons or corporations to repair roads which have or may become main roads, when such roads were previously repairable by them *ratione tenuræ*, or by prescription, or under an Act of Parliament, such as the Railways Clauses Act, which imposes on railway companies the duty of repairing roads in some cases.

Saving for powers of Commissioners of Inland Revenue and Customs.

98. Notwithstanding anything in the foregoing sections of this Act, the Commissioners of Inland Revenue and the Commissioners of Customs, and the officers of those Commissioners respectively, shall have the same powers in relation to any articles subject to any duty of customs or excise, manufactured, imported, kept for sale or sold, and any premises where the same may be, and to any machinery, apparatus, vessels, utensils, or conveyances used in connection therewith or the removal thereof, and in relation to the person manufacturing, importing, keeping for sale, or having the custody of the same, as they would have had if this Act had not passed, and any licences transferred in pursuance of this Act had continued to be granted by the Commissioners of Inland Revenue.

Definitions.

Definition of "written."

99. All notices and documents required by this Act to be in writing may be in writing or print, or partly in writing and partly in print, and for the purposes of this section "print" includes any mechanical mode of reproduction.

Interpretation of certain terms in the Act.

100. In this Act, if not inconsistent with the context, the following terms have the meanings hereinafter respectively assigned to them; that is to say:

The definitions contained in this section are incorporated with some exceptions in the Local Government Act, 1894; see s. 75 of that Act, *post*.

The expression "county" does not include a county of a city or county of a town:

The expression "entire county" means, in the case of a county divided into administrative counties, the whole of the county formed by those administrative counties:

The expression "division of a county," in the provisions of this Act respecting the property of quarter sessions, includes any hundred, lathe, wapentake, or other like division:

The reference here is to s. 64, *ante*, p. 122, which transfers to county councils property held for a division of a county.

The expression "administrative county," means the area for which a county council is elected in pursuance of this Act,

Sect. 100.

but does not (except where expressly mentioned) include a county borough:

The administrative counties which were not entire counties at the passing of this Act are those enumerated in s. 46, *ante*, p. 99.

Since the passing of the Act the boundaries of administrative counties have in many cases been altered under s. 54, *ante*, p. 108, without interference with the boundaries of the parliamentary counties.

18 & 19 Vict. c. 120.

The expression "metropolis" means the city of London and the parishes and places mentioned in Schedules A., B., and C. to the Metropolis Management Act, 1855, as amended by subsequent Acts:

45 & 46 Vict. c. 50.

The expression "borough" means any place for the time being subject to the Municipal Corporations Act, 1882, and any reference to the mayor, aldermen, and burgesses of a borough shall include a reference to the mayor, aldermen, and citizens of a city:

The expression "quarter sessions borough" means a borough having a separate court of quarter sessions and includes a county of a city and a county of a town, subject to the Municipal Corporations Act, 1882:

The expression "quarter sessions" as respects any county, riding, division, or liberty, means the justices in quarter or general sessions assembled, and includes justices assembled in gaol sessions, annual general sessions, and adjourned sessions, and as respects any borough, means any court of quarter or general sessions held for the borough or for any county of a city or town consisting of the borough, whether held by the recorder or by justices, and as respects the city of London, means the court of the mayor and aldermen in the inner chamber:

The expression "parish" means a place for which a separate overseer is or can be appointed, and where part of a parish is situate within, and part of it without, any county, borough, urban sanitary district, or other area, means each such part:

The definition of "parish" appears to exclude the definition contained in the Interpretation Act, 1889 (52 & 53 Vict. c. 63), s. 5, which applies only where a contrary intention does not appear. The definition in the text is not incorporated in the Local Government Act, 1894. See s. 75 of that Act, *post*. It should also be pointed out that since the Act last mentioned there are few, if any, instances of parishes situate partly within and partly without a county district. See ss. 1 (3) and 36 (1), (2), of that Act, *post*.

The expressions "parliamentary county," and "parliamentary election," and "parliamentary voters," have the same meaning as in the Registration Act, 1885, and the Acts therein referred to. Sect. 100. 48 & 49 Vict. c. 15.

By 48 Vict. c. 15, s. 19, the expression "parliamentary county" means a county returning a member or members to serve in Parliament, and where a county is divided for the purpose of such return means a division of such county.

By 41 & 42 Vict. c. 77, s. 4, amended by 48 Vict. c. 15, s. 1 (3), the term "parliamentary voter" means a person entitled to be registered as a voter, and when registered to vote at the election of a member or members to serve in Parliament for a parliamentary borough or county.

The expression "Secretary of State" means one of Her Majesty's Principal Secretaries of State :

The expression "Treasury" means the Commissioners of Her Majesty's Treasury :

The expression "Bank of England" means the Governor and Company of the Bank of England :

The expression "existing" means existing at the time specified in the enactment in which the expression is used, and if no such time is expressed, then at the day appointed to be for the purpose of such enactment the appointed day :

For the appointed day, see s. 109, *post*

The expression "guardians" means guardians elected under the Poor Law Amendment Act, 1834, and the Acts amending the same, and includes guardians or other bodies of persons performing under any local Act the like functions to guardians under the Poor Law Amendment Act, 1834 : 4 & 5 Will. 4, c. 76.

Guardians are now elected under the Local Government Act, 1894. See s. 20 of that Act, *post*.

The expression "poor law union" means any parish or union of parishes for which there is a separate board of guardians :

The expressions "district council" and "county district" mean respectively any district council established for purposes of local government under an Act of any future session of Parliament, and the district under the management of such council, and until such council is established, mean respectively—

(*a*) as regards the provisions of this Act relating to highways and main roads, a highway authority and highway area ; and

(*b*) save as aforesaid, an urban or rural sanitary authority within the meaning of the Public Health Act, 1875, and the district of such authority : 38 & 39 Vict. c. 55.

This definition became necessary when it was resolved to omit from this Act the clauses relating to district councils.

Sect. 100.

NOTE.

District councils have now been established by the Local Government Act, 1894. See s. 21 of that Act, *post*.

The expression "highway area," means, as the case may require, an urban sanitary district, a highway district, or a highway parish not included within any highway or urban sanitary district:

The expression "highway authority" means, as respects an urban sanitary district, the urban sanitary authority, and as respects a highway district, the highway board, or authority having the powers of a highway board, and as respects a highway parish, the surveyor or surveyors of highways or other officers performing similar duties:

It should be borne in mind that by virtue of ss. 35 (4) and 38 (3), *ante*, boroughs are included in the definition of an urban sanitary district in the Highway Act, 1878, and the council of the borough is therefore the highway authority.

Under the Local Government Act, 1894, rural district councils have, with few exceptions, become the highway authorities for their respective districts. See s. 25 of that Act, *post*.

The expression "urban authority" means, until the establishment of district councils as aforesaid, an urban sanitary authority; and after their establishment, the district council of an urban county district:

By the Public Health Act, 1875, s. 6, urban authorities were in a borough, the town council; in a local government district, the local board; and in an Improvement Act district, the Improvement Commissioners.

By the Local Government Act, 1894, s. 21 (3), *post*, it is provided that urban sanitary authorities, other than borough councils, shall be called urban district councils and their districts urban districts.

The expression "rural authority" means, until the establishment of district councils as aforesaid, a rural sanitary authority; and after their establishment, the district council of a rural county district:

By the Public Health Act, 1875, s. 9, the area of a union outside an urban district was a rural sanitary district in which the guardians were the rural sanitary authority.

Under the Local Government Act, 1894, the rural sanitary authority is the rural district council, which is a distinct body from the guardians. See ss. 21 and 24 of that Act, *post*.

The expression "person" includes any body of persons, whether corporate or unincorporate:

Sect. 100.

Any expression referring to the value of any parish, borough, or area as ascertained by the standard or basis for the county rate or contributions shall, where any rateable value has been fixed by agreement between the councils of any county and county boroughs, be that value, and subject thereto, shall, in the case of any parish, borough, or area for which there is no such standard or basis, refer to the total rateable value as determined by the last valuation lists, or if there is no valuation list, by the last poor rates for such parish or the parishes comprised in such borough or area ; and where an area is authorized or directed by this Act to be assessed to any contributions or rates, the same shall, unless otherwise provided by law, be assessed according to the standard or basis for the county rate :

See as to this definition, s. 33, *ante*, p. 72. See also s. 26 (2).

The expression "property" includes all property, real and personal, and all estates, interests, easements, and rights, whether equitable or legal, in, to, and out of property real and personal, including things in action, and registers, books, and documents ; and when used in relation to any quarter sessions, clerk of the peace, justices, board, sanitary authority, or other authority, includes any property which on the appointed day belongs to, or is vested in, or held in trust for, or would but for this Act have, on or after that day, belonged to, or been vested in, or held in trust for, such quarter sessions, clerk of the peace, justices, board, sanitary authority, or other authority ; and the expression "property" shall further include, in the case of the county of Chester, any surplus revenue of the River Weaver Trust, which is or would but for this Act be payable to the quarter sessions :

As to the appointed day, see s. 109, *post*.
As to the transfer of property, see s. 64, *ante*, p. 122.
As to the River Weaver Trust, see s. 69 (12), *ante*, p. 135.

The expression "powers" includes rights, jurisdiction, capacities, privileges, and immunities :

The expression "duties" includes responsibilities and obligations :

The expression "liabilities" includes liability to any proceeding for enforcing any duty or for punishing the breach of any duty, and includes all debts and liabilities to which any authority are or would but for this Act be liable or subject to, whether accrued due at the date of the transfer or

Sect. 100

subsequently accruing, and includes any obligation to carry or apply any money to any sinking fund or to any particular purpose :

The expression "powers, duties, and liabilities," includes all powers, duties, and liabilities conferred or imposed by or arising under any local and personal Act :

The expression "expenses" includes costs and charges :

The expression "costs" includes charges and expenses :

The costs of assizes and of quarter and petty sessions include such of the following costs as are applicable, that is to say, the costs of maintaining and providing the courts and offices and the judges' lodgings, the salaries and remuneration of a chairman of quarter sessions, clerks of assize, clerks of the peace, clerks of the justices, and other officers, the costs of the jury lists, the costs of rewards ordered to be paid by the court, the costs of prosecutions, including the costs of the defendants' witnesses, and all other costs incidental to the assizes, quarter sessions, petty sessions, or the judges, but nothing shall require a quarter sessions borough to contribute towards the costs of prosecutions at assizes, except in the case of prisoners committed for trial from the borough :

A quarter sessions borough may be a county borough ; see the definition, *supra*. Quarter sessions boroughs are to contribute towards the cost of assizes, etc., under ss. 32 (3) (*a*), 35 (5), 38 (5), and 39 (1), *ante*.

The expression "assizes" includes the Central Criminal Court :

The expression "pension" includes any superannuation allowance, gratuity, or other payment made on the retirement of any officer :

The expression "office" includes any place, situation, or employment, and the expression "officer" shall be construed accordingly :

The expression "the divisions of Lincolnshire" means the parts of Holland, the parts of Kesteven, and the parts of Lindsey :

19 & 20 Vict. c. 69.

The expression "County and Borough Police Act, 1856," means the Act of the session of the nineteenth and twentieth years of the reign of Her present Majesty, chapter sixty-nine, intituled "An Act to render more effectual the Police in Counties and Boroughs in England and Wales," and the expression "County and Borough Police Acts" means the County and Borough Police Act, 1856, and the Acts therein recited :

Sect. 100

The expression "main road" when used in relation to the district of any highway or road authority, means so much of the main road as is situate within the district of such authority.

In relation to the election of county councillors, the day of nomination shall be deemed to be the day on which the names of the persons nominated are fixed on the town hall or other conspicuous place.

As to the meaning of this provision, see the note to the Municipal Corporations Act, 1882, Sched. 3, Part II., r. 15, *post*.

101. This Act shall not extend to Scotland or Ireland. Extent of Act.

102. This Act may be cited as the Local Government Act, 1888. Short title.

PART VI.

Transitory Provisions.

Except where it otherwise appears by the notes to the several sections of this Part of the Act, these transitory provisions, though unrepealed, are spent.

First Election of County Councillors.

103.—(1.) The first election of county councillors under this Act shall be held in the month of January next after the passing of this Act on such day in each county not earlier than the fourteenth day of January as the returning officer for that county may fix, and the returning officer shall publish notice of such day in the preceding month of December, and the day so fixed shall be deemed for the purposes of the first election to be the ordinary day of election of county councillors. First election of county councillors.

(2.) The sheriff of each county shall be the returning officer for such first election, but if the sheriff desires to be a candidate at such election the county quarter sessions on his application may appoint another person to be the returning officer, and the person so appointed shall, for the purpose of such election, have the powers and duties of the sheriff.

(3.) At the first election the returning officer may, if it appears to him necessary, divide an electoral division into polling districts, so however that every polling district shall be an area or a combination of areas for which separate parts of the register of electors are made out, and he shall settle and give proper notice of the places at which the poll for each electoral division, or district of a division, shall be taken.

Sect. 103 (4).

(4.) The clerk of the peace, who will by virtue of this Act become the clerk of the county council when elected, shall make up the county register and division registers of the county electors for the purposes of the first election, and shall deliver the same to the returning officer, and every clerk of the peace who has in his custody any revised lists of electors required for making up such registers, shall supply to the above-mentioned clerk of the peace such number of copies of those lists as he may require for the purpose of making up the said registers.

(5.) The returning officer shall send to the clerk of the peace, who will, by virtue of this Act, become the clerk of the county council, the names of the persons elected, and shall send to each person elected a county councillor notice of his election, accompanied by a summons to attend the first meeting of the provisional council fixed by this Act at such time and place as the returning officer may fix.

(6.) The costs properly incurred by the returning officer in reference to the first election, and in reference to such first meeting of the provisional council, shall be defrayed as expenses of the county council, and may be taxed on an application made by or by direction of the provisional council.

(7.) In the administrative county of London, the returning officer for the first election shall be such fit person as the Local Government Board may appoint, and such returning officer shall, for the purposes of such election, have the powers and duties of the sheriff, and any sheriff, under-sheriff, officer of the London School Board, or other public officer having authority in the metropolis, and being in possession of any ballot boxes or other fittings or arrangements for an election, shall permit such returning officer to use the same for the purposes of such first election.

(8.) Such returning officer shall make up the county register and division registers of the county electors for the purposes of the first elections, and shall make them up out of the lists of voters made out in the year one thousand eight hundred and eighty-eight for the City of London, and for such portions of the counties of Middlesex, Surrey, and Kent, as are comprised in the metropolis, and shall make the necessary alteration in the forms of those lists, and the secondary of the City of London, and the town clerks within the meaning of the Registration Acts for the parliamentary boroughs in the administrative county of London, and the clerks of the peace of Middlesex, Surrey, and Kent, shall deliver to the said returning officer such number of copies of the revised lists of electors as he may require. The returning officer for the administrative county of London shall send the names of the persons elected to the clerk of the Metropolitan Board of Works.

(9.) The court of quarter sessions in any county, and the Metropolitan Board of Works in the Metropolis, shall advance to the returning officer such sum as is authorized by this Act to be advanced by county councils to returning officers for the purposes of an election. **Sect. 103 (9).**

(10.) The sheriff having authority in any administrative county, or the largest part thereof, shall for the purposes of this Act be deemed to be the sheriff of that county.

104.—(1.) The county councillors of a county council elected at the first election shall retire from office on the ordinary day of election in the third year after the passing of this Act, and their places shall be filled by election. **Retirement of first county councillors.**

The ordinary day of election in the third year after the passing of this Act was November 1st, 1891. This date was subsequently altered to March 8th, 1892. See the County Councils (Elections) Act, 1891 (54 & 55 Vict. c. 68), s. 1.

(2.) Of the first county aldermen one-half shall retire on the ordinary day of election of county aldermen in the third year next after the passing of this Act, and the one-half who are so to retire shall be determined by ballot by the provisional councillors at the time of the election of the county aldermen: Provided that where the total number of aldermen is not divisible by two the larger half shall first retire.

The county aldermen number one-third of the number of councillors (see s. 14, sub-s. (2), of the Municipal Corporations Act, 1882, *post*), except in London, where the number is one-sixth. See s. 40, sub-s. (5), *ante*, p. 89.

The one-half who were first to retire were determined by ballot, and they retired on March 16th, 1892. See the County Councils (Elections) Act, 1891, *post*.

(3.) The remaining half of the county aldermen shall retire on the ordinary day of election of county aldermen in the sixth year next after the passing of this Act.

This took place on March 16th, 1895.

(4.) In this section the word "year" shall be construed to mean calendar year.

105.—(1.) The members of a county council first elected under this Act shall not enter on their ordinary duties or become the county council until the first day of April next after their election, or such other day as on the application of the provisional council the Local Government Board may appoint. **Preliminary action of county councillors as provisional council.**

Sect. 105 (2).

(2.) Such members shall, on the second Thursday next after the day fixed for the first election, and thenceforward from time to time until the day above mentioned in this section, meet and act as a provisional council for arranging to bring this Act into operation.

(3.) The provisional councillors shall at their first meeting elect one of their number to be chairman of that meeting and of the second meeting, and shall then at that meeting, or some adjournment thereof, proceed to elect the county aldermen in like manner as if they were a fully constituted county council, and such county aldermen shall be summoned to attend at the second meeting of the provisional council, and shall form part of the provisional council both for the election of chairman and all other purposes.

(4.) The provisional council shall, at their second meeting, or some adjournment thereof, proceed to elect as their chairman a person qualified to be chairman of the county council, and may from time to time fill any vacancy in the office of such chairman, and the person elected chairman shall be chairman of the provisional council, and also on and after the appointed day of the county council, and the term of office of such chairman shall end on the next ordinary day of election of chairman.

(5.) This enactment shall extend to the vice-chairman and deputy-chairman.

First proceedings of provisional council.

106.—(1.) The provisional council after disposing of the preliminary business shall proceed to provide for bringing the various provisions of this Act into full operation on the appointed day or days, and to make the necessary arrangements with the quarter sessions, and with reference to the distribution of duties among the different officers, and to provide for all matters which appear necessary or proper for enabling the county council as constituted under this Act to execute their duties, and for giving full effect to this Act.

(2.) The provisions of this Act, and the enactments applied by this Act with respect to the proceedings of the county council, shall apply to the proceedings of the provisional council, and any act of the provisional council may be signified under the hand of the chairman and any two members of the council present at the meeting, and countersigned by the officer acting as their clerk.

(3.) The provisional council of a county shall be entitled to use the buildings belonging to the quarter sessions of that county, so that they do not interfere with the holding of any court, and the clerk of the peace and his officers, and the officers of the quarter sessions shall, if required, act as the officers of such provisional council, and, further, the provisional council may from time to time hire such buildings and appoint such interim officers as appear to them necessary for the performance of their duties, and the costs incurred in the hiring of such buildings and payment of such officers or otherwise in the performance of their duties shall be defrayed as costs properly incurred by the county council. Sect. 106 (3).

(4.) There shall be paid out of the county rate to the clerk of the peace of the county, such reasonable remuneration as the court of quarter sessions may award for extra services rendered by him in bringing this Act into operation, and in acting as clerk of the county council, until his salary for acting as such clerk is fixed in manner provided by this Act.

(5.) In the metropolis the foregoing provisions with respect to the use of buildings and the action of officers shall apply as if the Metropolitan Board of Works were the quarter sessions of the county, and as if any quarter sessions for the counties of Middlesex and Surrey were the quarter sessions of the county of London, but the provisional council for the administrative county of London shall make arrangements with the provisional councils of Middlesex and Surrey as respects the use of buildings and the employment of the clerk of the peace and his officers and the officers of the quarter sessions.

(6.) The provisional council shall have the same power of levying contributions for the purpose of their costs and for the future costs of the county council as they would have if they were constituted a county council under this Act.

(7.) The quarter sessions of every county and liberty, and in the metropolis the Metropolitan Board of Works, shall, by the appointment of committees, or the holding of sessions and meetings, and otherwise, make such provisions as are necessary or proper for making arrangements with the provisional council for carrying this Act into effect; and the quarter sessions may, after the appointed day, meet in like manner as if this Act had not passed, for the purpose of receiving reports from the committees and county officers for the period subsequent to the last quarter sessions and prior to the appointed day, and for making the ordinary quarterly payments, the usual sessional orders, and otherwise concluding and winding up the business of the county.

General Provision as to First Elections.

Casual vacancies at first elections.

107.—(1.) If at the first election a person is elected a county councillor for more than one electoral division of a county, his choice as to the division for which he will serve shall be made by writing addressed to the returning officer, and if not so made, the returning officer shall, on or before the day for the first meeting

Sect. 107 (1). of the provisional council, determine the division for which such person shall sit.

(2.) Any casual vacancy arising at the first election from a person being elected for more than one electoral division, or being elected a county alderman, or from a failure of election or otherwise, may be filled in like manner as a casual vacancy in the county council may be filled, and the sheriff or other officer authorized to act as returning officer at the first election shall be the returning officer at any election held to fill a casual vacancy before the appointed day.

(3.) Such number of members as have been elected for a county council at the first election shall, subject to any order of the Local Government Board to the contrary under this Act proceed to act as a provisional council under this Act, notwithstanding any vacancy or vacancies arising from failure of election or otherwise.

(4.) In case of equality of votes at the first or second meeting of a provisional county council, the chairman of the meeting shall have a second or casting vote, and where on the selection of the chairman of the meeting an equal number of votes is given to two or more persons, the meeting shall determine by lot which of those persons shall be the chairman.

(5.) The first meeting of the county council shall be held on the day appointed for the council coming into office, and shall be convened by the chairman of the provisional county council.

(6.) Such first meeting, and also the first meeting of the provisional county council, shall be convened in like manner as meetings of the county council are required by this Act, and the enactments applied by this Act, to be convened, and as if the person convening the same were the chairman.

Power of Local Government Board to remedy defects.

108.—(1.) If from any cause there is no returning officer able to act in any county at the first election of a county council, or no register of electors properly made up, or no proper election takes place, or an election of an insufficient number of persons takes place, or any difficulty arises as respects the holding of the first election of county councillors, or as to the first meeting of a provisional council, the Local Government Board may by order appoint a returning officer or other officer, and do any matter or thing which appears to them necessary for the proper holding of the first election, and for the proper holding of the first meeting of the provisional council, and may, if it appears to them necessary, direct a new election to be held, and fix the dates requisite for such new election; any such order may modify the provisions of this Act and the enactments applied by this Act so far as may appear to the Board necessary for the proper holding of the first election and first meeting of the provisional council. Sect. 108 (1).

(2.) The Local Government Board in the case of the first election may also authorize an electoral division to return two or more members, in any case where the difficulties arising out of the registers of voters and the population of any area appear to render it necessary, and may also authorize portions of two or more county districts, or wards for which a separate register can be made, to be united for the purpose of an electoral division.

(3.) The Local Government Board, on the application of a county council or provisional council, may, within six months after the day fixed for the first election of the councillors of such council, from time to time, make such orders as appear to them necessary for bringing this Act into full operation as respects the council so applying, and such orders may modify any enactment in this or any other Act, whether general or local and personal, so far as may appear to the Board necessary for the said purpose.

The provisions of this sub-section were continued in force by the Expiring Laws Continuance Acts, 1889 and 1890, but finally expired on December 31st, 1891.

(4.) The Local Government Board may also, if satisfied that an election cannot properly be held for any county council by reason of the electoral divisions not having been duly made, cause such steps to be taken as they consider necessary for constituting such electoral divisions and making up the registers of electors.

Appointed Day.

109.—(1.) Subject as in this Act mentioned, the appointed day for the purposes of this Act shall in each county be the first day of April next after the passing thereof, or such other day, earlier or later, as the Local Government Board (but after the election of county councillors for such county on the application of the provisional council or county council) may appoint, either generally or with reference to any particular provision of this Act, and different days may be appointed for different purposes and different provisions of this Act, whether contained in the same section or in different sections, or for different counties. Appointed day.

(2.) Any enactment of this Act authorizing anything to be done by the Commissioners of Inland Revenue or the Local Government Board, or relating to the registration of electors, or to the elections, or to any matter required to be done for the purpose of bringing this Act into operation on the appointed day, shall

Sect. 109 (2). come into effect on the passing of this Act; but save as aforesaid and save so far as there may be anything in the context inconsistent therewith, any enactment of this Act shall come into operation on the appointed day.

Transitional Proceedings.

Current rates, jury lists, etc.

110.—(1.) Every rate and precept for contributions made before the appointed day may be levied and collected, and proceedings for the enforcement thereof taken in like manner as nearly as may be as if this Act had not passed.

(2.) The accounts of all receipts and expenditure before the appointed day shall be audited, and disallowances, surcharges, and penalties recovered and enforced, and other consequential proceedings had in like manner as nearly as may be as if this Act had not passed, and every officer whose duty it is to make up any accounts, or to account for any portion of the receipts or expenditure in any account, shall, until the audit is completed, be deemed for the purpose of such audit to continue in office and be bound to perform the same duties and render the same accounts, and be subject to the same liabilities, as before the appointed day.

(3.) In the counties of Middlesex, Kent, and Surrey, the lists of jurors in force on the appointed day shall continue in force until the lists which are next made come into force, and all jurors summoned before the appointed day shall attend that day as if summoned in accordance with this Act.

(4.) All proceedings, legal and other, commenced before the appointed day, may be carried on in like manner, as nearly as may be, as if this Act had not passed, and may be so carried on by the county council in substitution for the authorities by whom such proceedings were commenced. Every legal proceeding commenced before the appointed day may be amended in such manner as may appear necessary or proper in order to bring the same into conformity with the provisions of this Act.

(5.) Every militiaman enlisted before the appointed day shall continue liable to serve in the same corps as if this Act had not passed.

Transitory provisions as to lunatic asylums.

111.—(1.) Any committee for providing an asylum for pauper lunatics, or any committee of visitors of an asylum for pauper lunatics holding office on the day fixed for the first election of county councillors under this Act, shall continue to hold office until the expiration of one week after the county council have elected a committee for the like purposes and no longer.

(2.) Any committee elected by the county council shall come into office at the expiration of the said week, and shall be deemed to be a continuance of the old committee of visitors elected by the quarter sessions. Sect. 111 (2).

(3.) All visitors of an asylum appointed on behalf of a borough, or subscribers who are visitors at the date of the first election of the county council under this Act, shall continue to be such visitors until the annual election of visitors which happens next after such election.

(4.) Anything done in pursuance of the enactments relating to pauper lunatics by the quarter sessions or any committee thereof before the appointment of any committee by the county council shall have effect as if it had been done by the county council or by a committee elected by the county council.

(5.) Where there is a joint committee of visitors for two or more counties or boroughs, this section shall apply to each portion of the committee appointed by the justices of any such county, or by the justices or council of any such borough, in like manner as if it were a separate committee.

Transitory provisions as to Contagious Diseases (Animals) Acts.

112.—(1.) Every executive committee appointed by the quarter sessions under the Contagious Diseases (Animals) Acts, and holding office on the appointed day, shall continue to hold office until the expiration of one week after the county council shall have appointed a committee for the like purpose, and no longer.

(2.) An executive committee appointed by the county council shall come into office at the expiration of the said week, and shall be deemed to be a continuance of the outgoing executive committee.

(3.) Every sub-committee of an executive committee under the said Acts holding office on the appointed day shall continue in office until a sub-committee for the like purposes shall be appointed by the county council, or by the executive committee appointed by the county council.

(4.) Every committee and sub-committee continued in office by virtue of this section shall, during such continuance, have all such powers as it would have had if this Act had not been passed.

Transitory Provisions as to Metropolis.

Transitory provisions as to sheriffs of London and Middlesex.

113.—(1.) The first sheriffs appointed by Her Majesty for the county of Middlesex and for the county of London may be nominated and appointed at the same time as the sheriff of any other county in England, and each of such sheriffs when appointed may make the declaration, and shall enter upon office, in like manner and at the like time as any other sheriff.

Sect. 113 (2). (2.) Upon the first sheriff of Middlesex so entering into office, the sheriffs of London shall cease to have jurisdiction in the county of Middlesex.

(3.) Upon the first sheriff of the county of London so entering into office, the area which will become that county shall, for the purpose of the sheriff, be considered to be the county of London, and the sheriffs of the city of London shall cease to have any jurisdiction in the said area, and the sheriffs of Surrey and Kent shall cease to have any jurisdiction within the said area.

(4.) Provided that for the purpose of any sessions of the peace held by the justices of the counties of Middlesex, Surrey, and Kent, after the sheriff has so entered into office but prior to the date at which the justices of the county of London will come into office, the sheriffs of Middlesex, Surrey, and Kent, shall continue to act and have jurisdiction as such sheriffs throughout those portions of the metropolis which originally formed part of those counties.

(5.) Lists of prisoners, writs, process, and particulars, and all records, jury lists, books, and matters appertaining to the county of Middlesex, and to such part of the counties of Surrey and Kent as are included in the metropolis, shall be delivered, turned over, transferred, and signed in like manner in all respects, so nearly as circumstances admit, as is required to be done upon a new sheriff coming into office, in like manner as if the sheriff of Middlesex appointed by Her Majesty were, as respects such part of the county as will, after the appointed day, be the county of Middlesex, the new sheriff in succession to the sheriffs of London, and as if the sheriff of the county of London appointed by Her Majesty were, as respects the area of the metropolis exclusive of the city, the successor to the sheriffs of London, Surrey, and Kent.

(6.) If any question arises as to the delivery, turning over, transfer, or signature under this section, or any other matter relating to the change in the office of sheriff in the metropolis, such question shall be referred to the Lord High Chancellor, whose decision shall be final.

As to existing coroners for Middlesex, Surrey, and Kent.

114.—(1.) The persons who, at the passing of this Act, are coroners for any districts which become wholly or partly, by virtue of this Act, part of the county of London, shall continue to act for such districts until otherwise directed as hereinafter mentioned, and while so continuing to act shall, as respects such part of their districts as is within the county of London, be deemed to be coroners for the county of London, and the amount payable in respect of the salaries, fees, and expenses of any such coroner, where the district is partly within and partly without the county of London, shall be apportioned between the counties in which such district is situate. Sect. 114 (1).

(2.) In the case of any coroner's district being situate partly within and partly without the county of London, the county councils of the counties in which such district is situate shall arrange for the alteration in manner provided by law of the district, so that on the next avoidance of the office of coroner, or any earlier date fixed when the alteration is made, the coroner's districts shall not be situate in more than one county.

(3.) For the purposes of this Act respecting compensation, the coroners shall be deemed to be officers of the quarter sessions of the county for which they are coroners.

As to commission of the peace for London.

115.—(1.) A commission of the peace for the county of London may be issued at any time after the passing of this Act, which shall be provisional until the appointed day, and the justices acting under such commission shall, until the appointed day, act provisionally for the purpose of bringing this Act into operation, and may from time to time be convened and meet and conduct their proceedings in like manner in all respects as if they were the justices of a county, and they shall proceed to make such arrangements as appear necessary or proper for bringing this Act into operation, and may for that purpose appoint any committee or committees, either alone or jointly with any quarter sessions or provisional council.

(2.) Nothing in this section shall confer on such justices any power to act as justices or as quarter sessions, nor any judicial jurisdiction, nor constitute any part of the metropolis a county for the purposes of justices and quarter sessions until the appointed day.

(3.) Any sessions of the peace held after the appointed day may be convened by the said justices acting provisionally before the said day, and the first sessions of the peace held after the appointed day shall be deemed to be legally held, although no justice there present has taken the oaths required by law to be taken by justices of the peace, and any justice may nevertheless take the oaths at such sessions.

(4.) The clerk of the peace for Middlesex holding office at the passing of this Act shall act as the clerk to the said justices for the county of London when acting provisionally in pursuance of this Act.

(5.) The fees payable to the clerk of the peace and clerks of the justices, and other officers and authorities in Middlesex, at the passing of this Act, shall be the first fees which may be taken in the county of London by the clerk of the peace, the clerks to the justices, and other officers and authorities in the county of London,

Sect. 115 (5). and may continue to be taken until they are abolished or altered in manner provided by law with respect to the abolition and alteration of such fees.

As to places for holding quarter sessions.

116. Until a scheme respecting the holding of courts of quarter sessions in the county of London comes into force, the following regulations shall be observed :—

As to this scheme, see the note to s. 42 (7), *ante*, p. 94.

(*a.*) Courts of quarter sessions for the trial of persons charged with offences shall be held at Clerkenwell and Newington, and courts of quarter sessions for appeals and other business shall be held at the places in London at which sessions are usually held at present, or at such of the said places as the county council may from time to time appoint; and courts of quarter sessions for the said purposes shall be respectively held at the same times, as nearly as may be, at each such place as heretofore;

(*b.*) Cases triable at quarter sessions for the county of London shall (save as otherwise directed by the court of quarter sessions) be heard and determined, if they arose on the north side of the River Thames, at Clerkenwell, and if they arose on the south side of the River Thames, at Newington; and persons shall be committed for trial, and bail and recognizances shall be taken, and depositions, recognizances, documents, and things transmitted in such manner as appears necessary for carrying into effect this section, but a committal for trial or recognizance shall not be invalidated, nor shall the powers of the quarter sessions be affected by any disregard of this enactment, and every court of quarter sessions held in and for the county of London at whatever place such court is held shall have complete power to hear and determine any case arising in the county of London, notwithstanding an objection that the case ought to be heard and determined at the sessions held at another place in the county of London.

(*c.*) Every sessions shall, as the circumstances require, be deemed to be quarter or general sessions, and if held at different places to be original sessions or adjourned sessions, and if held simultaneously at two or more places to be divided courts of the same sessions;

(*d.*) Every matter, civil or criminal, arising before the appointed day which would have been heard, tried, determined, or otherwise dealt with by any court of quarter sessions or assessment sessions, or any justices or otherwise, may be heard, tried, determined, and dealt with in like manner as if this Act had come into operation before the said matter arose, and recognizances existing at the appointed day shall have effect and be enforced in like manner, so nearly as circumstances admit, as they would have been if this Act had not passed; and where any trial, motion, or other matter has been adjourned from any previous court of quarter sessions, assessment sessions, special sessions, or petty sessions, and would if this Act had previously come into operation have been heard, determined, or otherwise dealt with at sessions held under this Act, the same shall be heard and determined and otherwise dealt with at the sessions held under this Act in like manner as if the same were held by the same justices by whom the same would have been held if this Act had not passed. **Sect. 116** (*d*).

117.—(1.) Nothing in this Act shall prevent a person who is an existing justice of the peace for any of the counties of Middlesex, Surrey, or Kent, from continuing to be a justice of the peace for that county, and every such person and also every person who at the appointed day is a justice of the peace for the liberty and city of Westminster, the liberty of the Tower of London, or any liberty which by virtue of this Act becomes part of the county of London, shall, if and so long as he is resident or occupies property in the county of London, be a justice of the peace for that county in like manner as if he were assigned by a commission of the peace, but a person shall not after the passing of this Act be named in any commission as a justice of the peace for any liberty which by virtue of this Act becomes part of the county of London. As to existing justices in Metropolis.

A justice for Middlesex appointed before the passing of this Act will continue to be such justice, and as long as he is resident or occupies property in the county of London, he will also be a justice for that county; so also as to justices of Surrey and Kent. Justices are not to be appointed for liberties in London.

As to the merger of liberties in the county, see s. 48, *ante*, p. 102.

(2.) Provided always, that the provisions of this section shall not apply to any justice of the peace of the counties of Surrey, Kent, or Middlesex, or either of them, so long as he shall hold any office connected with any court of quarter sessions of the county of London.

(3.) The persons who at the passing of this Act are members of

Sect. 117 (3). a visiting committee of any prison situate in the county of London shall continue to form such visiting committee until a new visiting committee has been appointed in accordance with a rule of the Secretary of State.

The Prison Act, 1877 (39 & 40 Vict. c. 21), s. 13, provides that a visiting committee shall be annually appointed for every prison under that Act, consisting of such number of persons, being justices of the peace, to be appointed at such time and by such court of quarter sessions, or such bench or benches of magistrates, as the Secretary of State, having regard to the locality of the prison, to the justices theretofore having jurisdiction over such prison, and to the class of prisoners to be confined in such prison, may from time to time by any general or special rule prescribe.

See the rules made by the Secretary of State, dated March 10th, 1890, S. R. O. 1890, p. 930.

(4.) Where a person is a justice of the peace in and for the county of London by reason of his being personally declared by this Act to be a justice of the peace in and for the county of London, the Lord High Chancellor shall have the same power of removing such person from being a justice of the peace as if he were named in a commission of the peace.

A justice is personally declared by this Act to be a justice of the county of London by s. 95 (1), *ante*, p. 170, and by sub-s. (1) of this section.

Any justice may be discharged from the commission by writ under the Great Seal; 3 Burn's Justice, 123.

(5.) The existing assistant judge of the court of the sessions of the peace for the county of Middlesex shall cease to be chairman of that court, and shall be the first chairman of the court of quarter sessions of the county of London, and while he holds his office he shall receive such salary, not less than what he has hitherto received, as Her Majesty, on the petition of the county council, may assign, and the enactments respecting the appointment and payment of a deputy assistant judge or of a person to preside at a second court at any sessions in the county of Middlesex shall apply to the county of London, and upon the said assistant judge ceasing to hold office shall be repealed.

The enactments hereby repealed as to the appointment and payment of a deputy assistant judge, etc., in Middlesex are the 22 & 23 Vict. c. 4, s. 3; 37 & 38 Vict. c. 7, ss. 2—4. As to future appointments of chairman and deputy chairmen of quarter sessions in London, see s. 42, *ante*, p. 93.

(6.) Nothing in this Act shall affect existing deputy lieutenants appointed by the Constable of the Tower of London as Lord Lieutenant of the Tower Hamlets.

Existing Officers.

Existing clerks of the peace and other officers.

118.—(1.) A person holding office at the appointed day as clerk of the peace of a county, besides continuing to be such clerk of the peace shall, subject to the provisions respecting certain counties in this Act mentioned, become the clerk of the county council, and if appointed before the passing of this Act shall, notwithstanding anything in this Act, hold his offices by the same tenure and have the same power of appointing and acting by a deputy as heretofore in his capacity of clerk of the peace.

An "existing" clerk of the peace became clerk of the council, except in the cases specially mentioned in this section.

Appointments of the clerk of the peace and deputy clerk made after the passing of this Act are made under s. 83, *ante*, p. 158, by the standing joint committee.

An "existing" clerk of the peace will appoint his own deputy as hitherto. See 37 Hen. 8, c. 1; 1 Will. & M. c. 21, s. 4.

(2.) A person holding office at the passing of this Act as clerk of the peace, clerk of the general assessment sessions, or salaried clerk of a petty sessional division, shall be deemed to be an existing officer within the meaning of the provisions of this Act relating to compensation to existing officers who suffer pecuniary loss.

The provisions as to compensation are contained in s. 120, *post*.

It will be remembered that the quarter sessions for the county of London supersede the general assessment sessions. See s. 42 (10), *ante*, p. 95.

As to petty sessional divisions and clerks, see s. 84, *ante*, p. 161; in London, s. 42 (8), *ante*, p. 95, and sub-s. (11), *infra*.

(3.) The person who at the appointed day is clerk of the peace for Sussex, if he held office at the passing of this Act, shall be clerk of the peace for East Sussex and clerk of the peace for West Sussex, and clerk of the peace for the justices of Sussex in general sessions assembled.

(4.) Such person shall also be clerk of the county council for East Sussex and clerk of the county council for West Sussex, and shall, notwithstanding anything in this Act, hold his offices by the same tenure, and have the same power of appointing and acting by a deputy as heretofore in his capacity of clerk of the peace.

(5.) The person who, at the appointed day, is clerk of the peace for Suffolk, if he held office at the passing of this Act, shall be clerk of the peace for East Suffolk and clerk of the peace for West Suffolk, and clerk of the peace for the justices of Suffolk in general sessions assembled.

Sect. 118 (6).

(6.) Such person shall also be clerk of the county council for East Suffolk and clerk of the county council for West Suffolk; and shall, notwithstanding anything in this Act, hold his offices by the same tenure and have the same power of appointing and acting by a deputy as heretofore.

As to future clerks of the peace in Sussex and Suffolk, see s. 83, sub-ss. (7), (8), *ante*, p. 160.

(7.) This section shall apply to the persons holding office at the appointed day as clerk of the peace and deputy clerks of the peace for the county of Lancaster, in like manner as it applies to clerks of the peace of other counties.

See s. 83 (9), *ante*, p. 160.

(8.) The person who, at the appointed day, is clerk of the peace for Middlesex, if he held office at the passing of this Act, shall continue to be that clerk, and, subject to the provisions of this Act, shall also be the first clerk of the peace for the county of London, and shall, notwithstanding anything in this Act, hold the office of clerk of the peace for each of the said counties by the same tenure and have the same power of appointing and acting by a deputy as heretofore.

(9.) The person who, at the appointed day, is the clerk of the gaol sessions in Yorkshire or Lincolnshire shall, if he holds office at the passing of this Act, continue to be that clerk, and shall also be the first clerk of the joint committee for the county councils of the three ridings or divisions of those counties, and shall hold that office by the same tenure and have the same power (if any) of acting by a deputy as heretofore.

As to the gaol sessions and the joint committee in Yorkshire and Lincolnshire, see s. 46 (2), *ante*, p. 99.

(10.) If the person who at the appointed day is clerk of the peace for Surrey held office at the passing of this Act, then so long as he holds that office,—

(*a.*) He shall, besides continuing to be that clerk, continue to be clerk of the peace at any quarter sessions held for the county of London at Newington, and be, for the purpose of all business transacted at those quarter sessions, deemed to be the clerk of the peace for the county of London, and as such shall have the same power of appointing and acting by a deputy as heretofore in his capacity of clerk of the peace for Surrey; and (*b*.) Such of the records of the county of Surrey as at the passing of this Act are in his custody at Newington, and, if this Act had not passed, would have remained in that custody, shall, subject to any order of the court of quarter sessions, continue to be kept in his custody at Newington. **Sect. 118 (10).**

(11.) The persons who at the appointed day are salaried clerks for the petty sessional divisions, wholly or in part in the county of London shall, if appointed before the passing of this Act, be as to so much of such divisions as are in the county of London, the first salaried clerks of the petty sessional divisions of the county of London, and as to much of such divisions as are not in the county of London, such persons shall also be the first salaried clerks of the petty sessional divisions of the counties in which such parts are situate.

Each portion of the existing division became a separate petty sessional division. See s. 42 (8), (9), *ante*, p. 95.

(12.) In the case of any of the following persons who, by virtue of this Act, become clerk of the peace for the county of London or salaried clerks of petty sessional divisions for the county of London, or who, for the purpose of all business transacted at the quarter sessions, held for the county of London at Newington, is to be deemed to be the clerk of the peace for the county of London, or who become clerk of the peace for East Sussex and clerk of the peace for West Sussex, or clerk of the peace for East Suffolk, and clerk of the peace for West Suffolk, their services as such clerks after the appointed day in the county of London, or in the administrative counties of East Sussex and West Sussex, or East Suffolk and West Suffolk, respectively, shall be deemed to be a continuous service with their service as clerks of the peace and clerks of petty sessional divisions in the counties of Middlesex, Surrey, and Kent respectively, and clerk of the peace for Sussex and Suffolk respectively.

This may be important in reckoning the duration of service for the purposes of s. 120, *post*.

(13.) All persons who at the appointed day hold office as county treasurer, county auditor, county solicitor, or county surveyor, or are officers (whether inspectors of weights and measures, public analysts, inspectors of petroleum or explosives, or other) of the quarter sessions or justices of the county, or of the assessment sessions in the metropolis, or any committee of such justices or any committee of visitors for lunatic asylums, or are servants under such sessions or justices and perform any duties in respect of the business

Sect. 118 (13). transferred by or in pursuance of this Act to the county council, shall become the officers and servants of the county council.

(14.) All persons who at the appointed day are officers and servants of the Metropolitan Board of Works shall become the officers and servants of the London County Council.

The Metropolitan Board of Works was superseded by the London County Council; see s. 40, sub-s. (8), *ante*, p. 90.

(15.) Every person who, on the appointed day, is the chief or other constable of the police force of any county, or is an officer or servant employed in connection with that force, shall, after the said day, be chief or other constable of the police force of the same county under the standing joint committee appointed in pursuance of this Act, or be an officer or servant of a county council appointing a portion of such joint committee, as the case may be.

This transfers the chief and other constables to the control of the standing joint committee under s. 30, *ante*, p. 66. See s. 119 (4), *post*.

(16.) Where any constable at the appointed day belongs to the police force of any borough the council of which will by virtue of this Act cease to maintain a separate police force, such constable shall, after the said day, become a constable of the county police force, and the provisions of this Act with respect to officers of any authority who become officers of the county council shall apply to such constable, with the substitution of the standing joint committee for the county council.

The boroughs which by virtue of this Act ceased to have a separate police force are the smaller boroughs under s. 39, *ante*, p. 86. See also s. 119, sub-s. (4), *post*.

As to officers transferred to county councils.

119.—(1.) The officers and servants of the quarter sessions or general asssessment sessions, or justices, or any committee of such sessions, or justices, or of any committee of visitors for lunatic asylums, or of the Metropolitan Board of Works, or other authority, who held office at the passing of this Act, and who by virtue of this Act become officers and servants of a county council (in this Act referred to as existing officers), shall hold their offices by the same tenure and upon the same terms and conditions as if this Act had not passed, and while performing the same duties, shall receive not less salaries or remuneration, and be entitled to not less pensions (if any), than they would have if this Act had not passed, and where any such officer can only be removed with the consent of a Secretary of State or the Local Government Board, such consent shall be part of the tenure of his office.

The officers and servants here referred to are those mentioned in s. 118.

Sect. 119 (2)

(2.) The county council may distribute the business to be performed by existing officers in such manner as the council may think just, and every existing officer shall perform such duties in relation to that business as may be directed by the council.

This gives the county councils power to require officers to perform duties different from those they have previously had to perform.

(3.) The county council may abolish the office of any existing officer whose office they may deem unnecessary, but such officer shall be entitled to compensation under this Act.

As to compensation, see s. 120, *post*.

(4.) The provisions of this section shall apply to the chief and other constables of any police force, and to any officers employed in connection with such force, in like manner as if they were herein re-enacted with the substitution of the standing joint committee under this Act for the county council.

See s. 118, sub-ss. (15), (16), *ante*.

Compensation to existing officers.

120.—(1.) Every existing officer declared by this Act to be entitled to compensation, and every other existing officer, whether before mentioned in this Act or not, who by virtue of this Act, or anything done in pursuance of or in consequence of this Act, suffers any direct pecuniary loss by abolition of office or by diminution or loss of fees or salary, shall be entitled to have compensation paid to him for such pecuniary loss by the county council, to whom the powers of the authority whose officer he was, are transferred under this Act, regard being had to the conditions on which his appointment was made, to the nature of his office or employment, to the duration of his service, to any additional emoluments which he acquires by virtue of this Act or of anything done in pursuance of or in consequence of this Act, and to the emoluments which he might have acquired if he had not refused to accept any office offered by any council or other body acting under this Act, and to all the other circumstances of the case, and the compensation shall not exceed the amount which, under the Acts and Rules relating to Her Majesty's Civil Service, is paid to a person on abolition of office.

This section is applied by s. 81 of the Local Government Act, 1894, to existing officers affected by that Act.

Regard is to be had to the following considerations in fixing the amount of compensation :

1. The loss must be a direct pecuniary loss.

2. The conditions of appointment must be considered, *e.g.*, whether the appointment is at pleasure, or for life, as in the case of a coroner. The fact that an office is held at pleasure does not *per se* disentitle the holder to compensation : *R.* v. *Norwich (Mayor, etc., of)*, 8 A. & E. 633.

Sect. 120 (1).

NOTE.

3. The nature of the office or employment, *e.g.*, the office may be an important public office, or it may be that merely of a clerk.

4. The duration of his service. For this purpose his service under the quarter sessions, etc., and under the county, is to be deemed to be continuous ; see s. 118, sub-s. (12), *ante*, p. 193.

5. Additional emoluments under or in consequence of the Act.

6. Emoluments which might have been acquired but for the refusal to accept an office under the Act.

7. The circumstances of the case.

The Civil Service scale is regulated by 22 Vict. c. 66, and 47 & 48 Vict. c. 57. It is, for a person who has served ten years or upwards, ten-sixtieths of his salary, and a further addition of one sixtieth for every year's service over ten up to forty years.

In case of abolition of office a special allowance may be made by adding a number of years, not exceeding ten, to the number of years of actual service. See s. 7 of 22 Vict. c. 66. Under 47 & 48 Vict. c. 57, a number of years may be added to those of actual service in the case of an office which requires professional or other peculiar qualification. Reference should be made to the Treasury minutes relating to superannuation.

(2.) Every person who is entitled to compensation, as above mentioned, shall deliver to the county council a claim under his hand setting forth the whole amount received and expended by him or his predecessors in office, in every year during the period of five years next before the passing of this Act, on account of the emoluments for which he claims compensation, distinguishing the offices in respect of which the same have been received, and accompanied by a statutory declaration under the Statutory Declaration Act, 1835, that the same is a true statement according to the best of his knowledge, information, and belief.

5 & 6 Will. 4 c. 62.

It appears from this that a claimant is entitled to compensation though he may have been in office for a period less than five years.

(3.) Such statement shall be submitted to the county council, who shall forthwith take the same into consideration, and assess the just amount of compensation (if any), and shall forthwith inform the claimant of their decision.

(4.) If a claimant is aggrieved by the refusal of the county council to grant any compensation, or by the amount of compensation assessed, or if not less than one-third of the members of such council subscribe a protest against the amount of the compensation as being excessive, the claimant or any subscriber to such protest (as the case may be) may, within three months after the decision of the council, appeal to the Treasury, who shall consider the case and determine whether any compensation, and if so what amount, ought to be granted to the claimant, and such determination shall be final.

The Treasury means the Commissioners of the Treasury. See s. 100, *ante*, p. 173.

(5.) Any claimant under this section, if so required by any member of the county council, shall attend at a meeting of the council and answer upon oath, which any justice present may administer, all questions asked by any member of the council touching the matters set forth in his claim, and shall further produce all books, papers, and documents in his possession or under his control relating to such claim. **Sect. 120 (5).**

Any member of the council may require the claimant to attend, but he cannot be examined on oath unless a justice is there to administer it. The chairman is, however, a justice *ex officio*; see s. 2, sub-s. (5), *ante*, p. 4. Once sworn, the claimant may be interrogated by any members.

(6.) The sum payable as compensation to any person in pursuance of this section shall commence to be payable at the date fixed by the council on granting the compensation, or, in case of appeal, by the Treasury, and shall be a specialty debt due to him from the county council, and may be enforced accordingly in like manner as if the council had entered into a bond to pay the same.

It is difficult to suggest why this debt should be deemed to be a specialty debt or what advantage is derived from this provision. A specialty debt, like any other, is enforceable by action, and its only advantage over simple contract debts is that the statutory period of limitation is twenty years, as compared with six years.

A county council were held (by CHARLES and WRIGHT, JJ.) liable under this sub-section for payment of compensation awarded to the clerk to a school board, part of whose parish had been transferred to another parish by order under s. 57 of this Act, although the order provided that such compensation should be payable out of such fund as the county council might direct: WRIGHT, J., intimated that under s. 68 a special county rate might be levied on the parishes concerned for the amount required. See, however, sub-s. (8), *infra*; *West* v. *Wilts County Council*, 10 T. L. R. 19.

(7.) If a person receiving compensation in pursuance of this section is appointed to any office under the same or any other county council, or by virtue of this Act, or anything done in pursuance of or in consequence of this Act, receives any increase of emoluments of the office held by him, he shall not, while receiving the emoluments of that office, receive any greater amount of his compensation, if any, than, with the emoluments of the said office, is equal to the emoluments for which compensation was granted to him, and if the emoluments of the office he holds are equal to or greater than the emoluments for which compensation was granted, his compensation shall be suspended while he holds such office.

This provision prevents an officer from obtaining compensation and then getting appointed to another office, thus drawing, as it were, two salaries.

Sect. 120 (8).

(8.) All expenses incurred by a county council in pursuance of this section shall be paid out of the county fund, as a payment for general county purposes.

As to general county purposes, see s. 68, *ante*, p. 130.

Temporary Provision as to Grant from Exchequer.

Grant and application of part of probate duty and of horse and wheel tax during the year ending March 31st, 1889.

121.—(1.) In the financial year ending the thirty-first day of March, one thousand eight hundred and eighty-nine, the Commissioners of Inland Revenue shall from time to time, in such manner and under such regulations as the Treasury from time to time make, pay into the Bank of England to the Local Taxation Account—

(*a.*) Such sum as may be ascertained in manner provided by the said regulations to be four-fifth parts of one-third of the proceeds of the sums collected by them in the said year in respect of the probate duties, and for the purpose of this section, the expression "probate duties" means the stamp duties charged on the affidavit required from persons applying for probate or letters of administration in England, Wales, or Ireland, and on the inventory exhibited and recorded in Scotland, and the stamp duties charged on such accounts of personal and movable property as are specified in section thirty-eight of the Customs and Inland Revenue Act, 1881, and includes the proceeds of all penalties and forfeitures recovered in relation to such stamp duties; and

45 & 46 Vict. c. 12.

(*b.*) Such sum as may be ascertained in manner provided by the regulations to be the proceeds of the sums collected by them in the said year in respect of the duties on licences for trade carts, locomotives, horses, mules, and horse dealers under any Act of the present session.

(2.) The sums so paid shall be distributed by the Local Government Board as follows; that is to say,

(i.) In paying to every county, highway, and other local authority who have heretofore received out of moneys provided by Parliament a contribution to the costs of roads, or to the successors of such authority, sums calculated in like manner and according to the like scale and regulations as in the financial year ending on the thirty-first day of March, one thousand eight hundred and eighty-eight;

(ii.) If the amount received by the local taxation account from the duties on licences for trade carts, locomotives, horses, mules, and horse dealers under any Act of the present session exceeds the sum so payable to county and highway or other local authorities, the excess shall be divided between the metropolis and quarter sessions boroughs, in proportion to their rateable value, as ascertained by the valuation lists, or where there is no valuation list by the last poor rate ; Sect. 121 (2).

(iii.) The share of the excess distributed to the metropolis shall be divided between the Commissioners of Sewers in the city of London and the vestries and district boards in the parishes in Schedule A. and the districts in Schedule B. in the Metropolis Management Act, 1855, as amended by subsequent Acts, according to rateable value as ascertained by the last valuation lists, and the share distributed to quarter sessions boroughs shall be paid to the councils of such boroughs ; 18 & 19 Vict. c. 120.

(iv.) If any payment is made under the foregoing provisions of this section respecting roads to the council of any quarter sessions borough, or to any authority for a highway area wholly or partly situate in such borough, or to the highway authority of any parish or district in the metropolis, the share of such quarter sessions borough, parish, or district in the distribution of the balance shall be reduced by the amount of the said payment, and, if less than that amount, shall not be paid, and any sum arising from such reduction or non-payment shall be added to the balance and distributed accordingly ;

(v.) Any sum payable in pursuance of this section to a county authority or the council of any borough, not being a highway authority, shall be paid to the county or borough fund as the case may be, but any other sum payable under the provisions of this section respecting roads, or respecting the division of the excess to any highway authority, commissioners of sewers, vestry, or district board, shall be applied in aid of the costs of the roads maintained by such authority, commissioners, vestry, or board ;

(vi.) Any balance remaining after the above payments shall be divided among the counties in England and Wales, in accordance with the provisions of this Act with respect to the division of the probate duty grant, and for the purpose of such division the metropolis shall be deemed to be a county, and the share assigned to each county on such division shall be applied towards paying to the guardians of each poor law union wholly or partly situate in the county such sum as is directed by this Act to be annually

Sect. 121 (2).

paid by the county council of such county to such guardians;

(vii.) Any balance remaining after the payment to the guardians of such union shall be paid to the county council of the county upon its coming into office, and, if there is any county borough in the county, the sum so paid shall be included in the adjustment under this Act between the councils of the county and borough.

(3.) Every local authority shall produce to the Local Government Board such evidence and comply with such rules as the Board may require or make for the purpose of effecting the distribution under this section.

(4.) A certificate of the Local Government Board of the sum due to any authority under this section may be varied by that Board, but unless so varied shall be final.

(5.) The Treasury may, from time to time during the financial year ending on the thirty-first day of March next after the passing of this Act, issue out of the Consolidated Fund or the growing produce thereof and pay to the Local Taxation Account such sums as appear to them to be required for the purpose of paying the highway authorities and county authorities such sums in respect of main roads as have been paid to them in previous years out of moneys provided by Parliament; and the sums so issued shall be treated as an advance, and shall be repaid to the Consolidated Fund out of the Local Taxation Account before any balance is distributed in manner provided by this section.

Savings.

Saving for existing securities and discharge of debts.

122.—(1.) Nothing in this Act shall prejudicially affect any securities granted before the passing of this Act on the credit of any rate or of any property by this Act transferred to a county council; and all such securities, as well as all unsecured debts, liabilities, and obligations incurred by any authority in the exercise of any powers or in relation to any property transferred from them to the county council under this Act shall be discharged, paid, and satisfied by such council.

(2.) Where for the purpose of satisfying any such security or any debt or liability, it is necessary to continue the levy of any rate or the exercise of any power which would have existed but for the provisions of this Act, such rate may continue to be levied and power to be exercised either by the authority who otherwise would have levied or exercised the same or by the county council as the case may require.

(3.) It shall be the duty of every authority whose powers, duties, and liabilities are transferred to any council by this Act to liquidate so far as practicable before the appointed day all current debts and liabilities incurred by such authority. Sect. 122 (3).

123. All such bye-laws, orders, and regulations of the Privy Council, Secretary of State, Board of Trade, Local Government Board, or Government Department, or of any quarter sessions, council of a borough, the Metropolitan Board of Works, or other authority, whose powers and duties are transferred by or in pursuance of this Act to any county council, as are in force at the time of the transfer, shall, so far as they relate to or are in pursuance of the powers and duties transferred, continue in force as if they had been made by such council, subject, nevertheless, to revocation or alteration by such council in the manner in which bye-laws can be made by such council, and also to any exceptions or modifications which may be made at the time of the transfer. Saving for existing bye-laws.

124.—(1.) If at the date of the transfer in this section mentioned any action or proceeding, or any cause of action or proceeding, is pending or existing by or against any authority in relation to any powers, duties, liabilities, or property by this Act transferred to the county council, the same shall not be in anywise prejudicially affected by reason of the passing of this Act, but may be continued, prosecuted, and enforced by or against such council as successors of the said authority in like manner as if this Act had not been passed. Saving for pending actions, contracts, etc.

(2.) All contracts, deeds, bonds, agreements, and other instruments entered into or made and subsisting at the time of the transfer in this section mentioned, and affecting any such powers, duties, liabilities, or property of any authority as are by this Act transferred to a county council, shall be as of full force and effect against or in favour of the council, and may be enforced as fully and effectually as if, instead of the authority, the said council had been a party thereto.

For an illustration of the effect of this provision on existing contracts, see *Re Salop County Council*, 65 L. T. (N.S.) 416 ; 56 J. P. 213, the facts of which are set out in the note to s. 38 (1), *ante*, p. 83.

(3.) All contracts or agreements which, prior to the appointed day, have been made by the clerk of the peace or any justice or justices or otherwise on behalf of a county, or any division or part of a county, shall have effect as if the council of that county had been named therein instead of the clerk of the peace or such justice or justices, and may be enforced by or against the county council accordingly.

(4.) This section shall apply in the case of a committee of any authority in like manner as if the committee were such authority

Sect. 124 (4).

and the committee of a county council were that council, and as if contracts and agreements by any such committee appointed by quarter sessions were contracts and agreements on behalf of a county.

Saving for charters, local Acts, etc.

125. Save so far as may be necessary to give effect to this Act or any scheme or order or other thing made or done thereunder, nothing in this Act shall prejudicially alter or affect the powers, rights, privileges, or immunities of any municipal corporation, or the operation of any municipal charter, local Act of Parliament, or order confirmed by Parliament, which immediately before the passing of this Act was in force.

For an illustration of the effect of this section in keeping alive the provisions of a local Act, notwithstanding the provisions of this Act, see *Re Staffordshire and Derbyshire County Councils*, 54 J. P. 566, cited *ante*, p. 105.

As to the power of a county council to amend local Acts by order, see s. 59 (6), *ante*, p. 117.

Repeals.

Repeal of Acts.

126. All enactments inconsistent with this Act are hereby repealed; Provided that—

(1.) Any enactment or document referring to any Act or enactment hereby repealed shall be construed to refer to this Act, or to the corresponding enactment in this Act:

(2.) This repeal shall not affect—

(*a.*) The past operation of any enactment hereby repealed, nor anything duly done or suffered under any enactment hereby repealed; or

(*b.*) Any right, privilege, obligation, or liability acquired, accrued, or incurred under or in accordance with any enactment hereby repealed; or

(*c.*) Any penalty, forfeiture, or punishment incurred in respect of any offence committed against any enactment hereby repealed; or

(*d.*) Any power, investigation, legal proceeding, or remedy in respect of any such right, privilege, obligation, liability, penalty, forfeiture, or punishment as aforesaid; and any such power, investigation, legal proceeding, and remedy may be exercised and carried on as if this Act had not passed.

See also ss. 11 and 38 of the Interpretation Act, 1889 (52 & 53 Vict. c. 63).

SCHEDULES.

Schedule 1.

Section 20.

FIRST SCHEDULE.

Local Taxation Licences.

Licences for the sale of intoxicating liquor for consumption on the premises :

Retailers of spirits (publicans).
Retailers of spirits, occasional licences.
Retailers of beer.
Retailers of beer, occasional licences.
Retailers of beer and wine.
Retailers of cider.
Retailers of wine.
Retailers of wine, occasional licences.
Retailers of sweets.

Licences for the sale of intoxicating liquor by retail, by persons not licensed to deal therein, for consumption off the premises :

Retailers of beer.
Retailers of beer and wine.
Retailers of cider.
Retailers of wine.
Retailers of sweets.
Retailers of table beer.

Licences to deal in game.

Licences for

Beer dealers.
Spirit dealers.
Sweets dealers.
Wine dealers.
Refreshment house keepers.
Dogs.
Killing game.
Guns.
Appraisers.
Auctioneers.
Tobacco dealers.
Carriages.
Trade carts.
Locomotives.
Horses and mules.
Horse dealers.
Armorial bearings.
Male servants.
Hawkers.
House agents.
Pawnbrokers.
Plate dealers.

Note.—These are the licences the duties payable on which are transferred to the county council under s. 20, *ante*, p. 46. As to the duties on trade carts, locomotives, horses and mules, and horse dealers, see the note to s. 34 (1) (*d*), *ante*, p. 74.

To the list of licences above-mentioned must now be added those for light locomotives under the Locomotives on Highways Act, 1896 (59 & 60 Vict. c. 36), s. 8, *post*.

Schedule 2

Section 71.

SECOND SCHEDULE.

Alteration of Schedule to District Auditors Act, 1879.
(42 *&* 43 *Vict. c.* 6).

The following scale shall, unless otherwise determined by Parliament, be substituted for so much of the scale set forth in the First Schedule to the District Auditors Act, 1879, as relates to expenditure amounting to 100,000*l.* and upwards :—

Where the total of the expenditure comprised in the financial statement is	The sum shall be
100,000*l.* and under 150,000*l.* - - - - - - -	50*l.*
150,000*l.* and under 200,000*l.* - - - - - - -	60*l.*
200,000*l.* and upwards - - - - - - - -	15*l.* in addition for every 50,000*l.*, or part thereof.

NOTE.—The District Auditors Act, 1879, s. 2, provides as follows :—

"After the twenty-fifth day of March, one thousand eight hundred and seventy-nine, all payments to district auditors out of any local rate shall cease, and the whole of the salaries or remuneration and of the expenses of district auditors, to such amount as may be sanctioned by the Treasury, shall be paid out of moneys provided by Parliament; and for the purpose of contributing to the amount required for the payment of such salaries, remuneration, and expenses, there shall be charged on every local authority whose accounts are audited by a district auditor a stamp duty for the use of Her Majesty, according to the scale contained in the First Schedule to this Act, and such duty shall be levied by a stamp on the certificate of the auditor hereinafter mentioned."

The First Schedule to the Act is as follows :—

Scale of Stamp Duties payable by Local Authorities.

Where the total of the expenditure comprised in the financial statement is	The sum shall be
Under 20*l.* - - - - - - - - - - - -	5*s.*
20*l.* and under 50*l.* - - - - - - - -	10*s.*
50*l.* and under 100*l.* - - - - - - - -	1*l.*
100*l.* and under 500*l.* - - - - - - - -	2*l.*
500*l.* and under 1,000*l.* - - - - - - - -	3*l.*
1,000*l.* and under 2,500*l.* - - - - - - - -	4*l.*
2,500*l.* and under 5,000*l.* - - - - - - - -	5*l.*
5,000*l.* and under 10,000*l.* - - - - - - - -	10*l.*
10,000*l.* and under 20,000*l.* - - - - - - - -	15*l.*
20,000*l.* and under 50,000*l.* - - - - - - - -	20*l.*
50,000*l.* and under 100,000*l.* - - - - - - -	30*l.*
100,000*l.* and upwards - - - - - - - -	50*l.*

Schedule 2.

NOTE.

"For the purpose of this schedule the expenditure comprised in the financial statement shall be exclusive of any sum paid to another local authority in pursuance of a precept."

Section 71 (3), *ante*, p. 137, modifies the above schedule to the extent mentioned in the text.

THIRD SCHEDULE.

Sections 31, 34, 35, 36, 69.

County Boroughs.

Name of Borough.	Name of County in which, for the purpose of this Act, the Borough is deemed to be situate.
Barrow - - - - - - -	Lancaster.
Bath - - - - - - - -	Somerset.
Birkenhead - - - - - - -	Chester.
Birmingham - - - . - -	Warwick.
Blackburn - - - - - - -	Lancaster.
Bolton - - - - - - - .	Lancaster.
Bootle-cum-Linacre - - - - -	Lancaster.
Bradford - - - - - - -	York, West Riding.
Brighton - - - - - - -	Sussex.
Bristol - - - - - - - -	Gloucester and Somerset.
Burnley - - - - - - -	Lancaster.
Bury - - - - - - - -	Lancaster.
Canterbury - - - - - - -	Kent.
Cardiff - - - - - - - -	Glamorgan.
Chester - - - - - - -	Chester.
Coventry - - - - - - -	Warwick.
Croydon - - - - - - -	Surrey.
Derby - - - - - - - -	Derby.
Devonport - - - - - - -	Devon.
Dudley - - . - - - - -	Worcester.
Exeter - - - - - - - -	Devon.
Gateshead - - - - - - -	Durham.
Gloucester - - - - - - -	Gloucester.
Great Yarmouth - - - - - -	Norfolk and Suffolk.
Halifax - - - - - - -	York, West Riding.
Hanley - - - - - - - -	Stafford.
Hastings - - - - - - -	Sussex.
Huddersfield - - - - - -	York, West Riding.
Ipswich - - - - - - -	Suffolk.
Kingston-upon-Hull - - - - -	York, East Riding.
Leeds - - - - - - - -	York, West Riding.
Leicester - - - - - - -	Leicester.
Lincoln - - - - - - -	Lincoln (parts of Lindsey).
Liverpool - - - - - - -	Lancaster.
Manchester - - - - - - -	Lancaster.
Middlesborough - - - - - -	York, North Riding.
Newcastle-upon-Tyne - - - - -	Northumberland.
Northampton - - - - - -	Northampton.
Norwich - - - - - - -	Norfolk.
Nottingham - - - - - - -	Nottingham.
Oldham - - - - - - -	Lancaster.
Plymouth - - - - - - -	Devon.
Portsmouth - - - - - - -	Hants.
Preston - - - - - - -	Lancaster.
Reading - - - - - - -	Berks.
Rochdale - - - - - - -	Lancaster.
Saint Helen's - - - - - -	Lancaster.

Schedule 3.

Name of Borough.	Name of County in which for the purpose of this Act, the Borough is deemed to be situate.
Salford - - - - - - -	Lancaster.
Sheffield - - - - - - -	York, West Riding.
Southampton - - - - - -	Hants.
South Shields - - - - - -	Durham.
Stockport - - - - - - -	Chester and Lancaster.
Sunderland - - - - - - -	Durham.
Swansea - - - - - - -	Glamorgan.
Walsall - - - - - - -	Stafford.
West Bromwich - - - - - -	Stafford.
West Ham - - - - - - -	Essex.
Wigan - - - - - - - -	Lancaster.
Wolverhampton - - - - - -	Stafford.
Worcester - - - - - - -	Worcester.
York - - - - - - - -	York, North, East, and West Ridings

NOTE.—The provisions of the Act relating to county boroughs are contained in ss. 31—34, *ante*, p. 67.

In addition to the boroughs above-mentioned the following have been created county boroughs under s. 54 (1) (*d*), *ante*, viz., Grimsby, Oxford, and Newport (Mon.).

PART II.

Statutes Incorporated with the Local Government Act, 1888.

THE BALLOT ACT, 1872 (35 & 36 VICT. CAP. 33.)

An Act to amend the Law relating to Procedure at Parliamentary and Municipal Elections. [18th July 1872.]

WHEREAS it is expedient to amend the law relating to procedure at parliamentary and municipal elections: Be it enacted, etc.:

This Act is applied to municipal elections, and therefore to elections of county councillors, by the Municipal Corporations Act, 1882, s. 58, and Sched. 3, Part III., *post.* See also the provisions of the Act itself as to its application to municipal elections.

Only those portions of the Act which apply to elections of county councillors are set out in the following pages.

PART I.—PARLIAMENTARY ELECTIONS.

Procedure at Elections.

1. * * * * *

If after the adjournment of an election by the returning officer for the purpose of taking a poll one of the candidates nominated shall die before the poll has commenced, the returning officer shall, upon being satisfied of the fact of such death, countermand notice of the poll, and all the proceedings with reference to the election shall be commenced afresh in all respects as if the writ had been received by the returning officer on the day on which proof was given to him of such death; provided that no fresh nomination shall be necessary in the case of a candidate who stood nominated at the time of the countermand of the poll.

Nomination of candidates for parliamentary elections.

The earlier part of this section applies only to parliamentary elections, but it was held in a recent case that the paragraph above set out is applied to a county council election by s. 58 of the Municipal Corporations Act, 1882, *post*, and the court by *mandamus* ordered a returning officer to countermand the poll, a candidate having died after nomination: *Westacott* v. *Stewart*, 14 T. L. R. 261: W. N. 1898, p. 23. The court afterwards granted a *mandamus* to hold the election on a specified day under s. 70 of the Municipal Corporations Act, 1882, *post.* Times, March 4th, 1898.

2. In the case of a poll at an election the votes shall be given by ballot. The ballot of each voter shall consist of a paper (in this Act called a ballot paper) showing the names and description of the candidates. Each ballot paper shall have a number printed on the back, and shall have attached a counterfoil with the same number printed on the face. At the time of voting, the ballot paper shall be marked on both sides with an official mark, and delivered to the voter within the polling station, and the number of such voter on the register of voters shall be marked on the counterfoil, and the voter having secretly marked his vote on the paper, and folded it up so as to conceal his vote, shall place it in a closed box in the presence of the officer

Poll at elections.

Sect. 2.

presiding at the polling station (in this Act called "the presiding officer") after having shown to him the official mark at the back.

Any ballot paper which has not on its back the official mark, or on which votes are given to more candidates than the voter is entitled to vote for, or on which anything, except the said number on the back, is written or marked by which the voter can be identified, shall be void and not counted.

After the close of the poll the ballot boxes shall be sealed up, so as to prevent the introduction of additional ballot papers, and shall be taken charge of by the returning officer, and that officer shall, in the presence of such agents, if any, of the candidates as may be in attendance, open the ballot boxes, and ascertain the result of the poll by counting the votes given to each candidate, and shall forthwith declare to be elected the candidates or candidate to whom the majority of votes have been given, and return their names to the Clerk of the Crown in Chancery. The decision of the returning officer as to any question arising in respect of any ballot paper shall be final, subject to reversal on petition questioning the election or return.

Where any equality of votes is found to exist between any candidates at an election for a county or borough, and the addition of a vote would entitle any of such candidates to be declared elected, the returning officer, if a registered elector of such county or borough, may give such additional vote, but shall not in any other case be entitled to vote at an election for which he is returning officer.

It must be borne in mind that it is no part of the duty of the returning officer to determine questions as to the qualification or disqualification of a candidate; that is a matter to be decided on an election petition. The returning officer must count the valid papers and "forthwith" declare the candidate or candidates receiving the majority of votes to be elected. *Pritchard* v. *Bangor* (*Mayor of*), 13 App. Cas. 241; 57 L. J. Q. B. 313; 58 L. T. (N.S.) 502; 37 W. R. 103; 52 J. P. 564.

At an election of county councillors no return is made to the Clerk of the Crown in Chancery. See Municipal Corporations Act, 1882, Sched. 3, Part III. (6), *post*.

As to the return to be made to the county returning officer by the returning officer for an electoral division wholly within a borough, see the County Councils (Elections) Act, 1891 (54 & 55 Vict. c. 68), s. 3, *post*.

The concluding paragraph of this section does not apply to elections of county councillors. See the Municipal Corporations Act, 1882, Sched. 3, Part III. r. 1, *post*.

Provision is, however, made for a casting vote being given by the returning officer at a municipal election by s. 58 (5) of that Act, *post*.

As to the validity of votes irregularly marked, etc., see the note to r. 36 in the schedule, *post*.

Offences at Elections.

Offences in respect of nomination papers, ballot papers and ballot boxes.

3. Every person who,—

(1.) Forges or fraudulently defaces or fraudulently destroys any nomination paper, or delivers to the returning officer any nomination paper, knowing the same to be forged; or

Sect. 3 (2).

(2.) Forges or counterfeits or fraudulently defaces or fraudulently destroys any ballot paper, or the official mark on any ballot paper ; or

(3.) Without due authority supplies any ballot paper to any person ; or

(4.) Fraudulently puts into any ballot box any paper other than the ballot paper which he is authorized by law to put in ; or

(5.) Fraudulently takes out of the polling station any ballot paper ; or

(6.) Without due authority destroys, takes, opens, or otherwise interferes with any ballot box or packet of ballot papers then in use for the purposes of the election ;

shall be guilty of a misdemeanor, and be liable, if he is a returning officer or an officer or clerk in attendance at a polling station, to imprisonment for any term not exceeding two years, with or without hard labour, and if he is any other person, to imprisonment for any term not exceeding six months, with or without hard labour.

Any attempt to commit any offence specified in this section shall be punishable in the manner in which the offence itself is punishable.

In any indictment or other prosecution for an offence in relation to the nomination papers, ballot boxes, ballot papers, and marking instruments at an election, the property in such papers, boxes, and instruments may be stated to be in the returning officer at such election, as well as the property in the counterfoils.

Sub-section (1) does not apply to an election of county councillors; the Municipal Corporations Act, 1882, s. 74, *post*, contains the corresponding provision applicable to such an election.

Infringement of secrecy.

4. Every officer, clerk, and agent in attendance at a polling station shall maintain and aid in maintaining the secrecy of the voting in such station, and shall not communicate, except for some purpose authorized by law, before the poll is closed, to any person any information as to the name or number on the register of voters of any elector who has or has not applied for a ballot paper or voted at that station, or as to the official mark, and no such officer, clerk, or agent, and no person whomsoever, shall interfere with or attempt to interfere with a voter, when marking his vote, or otherwise attempt to obtain in the polling station information as to the candidate for whom any voter in such station is about to vote or has voted, or communicate at any time to any person any information obtained in a polling station as to the candidate for whom any voter in such station is about to vote or has voted, or as

Sect. 4.

to the number on the back of the ballot paper given to any voter at such station. Every officer, clerk, and agent in attendance at the counting of the votes shall maintain and aid in maintaining the secrecy of the voting, and shall not attempt to ascertain at such counting the number on the back of any ballot paper, or communicate any information obtained at such counting as to the candidate for whom any vote is given in any particular ballot paper. No person shall directly or indirectly induce any voter to display his ballot paper after he shall have marked the same, so as to make known to any person the name of the candidate for or against whom he has so marked his vote.

Every person who acts in contravention of the provisions of this section shall be liable, on summary conviction before two justices of the peace, to imprisonment for any term not exceeding six months, with or without hard labour.

Every officer, etc., is required by Sched. 1, r. 54, *post*, to make a declaration of secrecy in the form contained in Sched. 2.

An information was laid against the respondent under the above section, charging that he, being a personating agent duly appointed and in attendance at a certain polling station in connection with a municipal election, did not then and there maintain the secrecy of the voting in such station, but did then and there communicate before the poll was closed to a certain person or persons certain information as to the names and numbers on the register of voters of certain electors who had and had not applied for ballot papers or voted at that election. It appeared that the respondent having been appointed personating agent, as stated in the information, attended at the polling booth with a copy of the burgess-roll, and remained there some hours, placing a mark against the name of each voter who obtained a ballot paper, and then before the close of the poll left the station, taking with him his copy of the burgess-roll, which he left in the committee room of the candidate by whom he was employed. There was no proof that the copy of the burgess-roll was seen by any person while in the room. *Held*, that there was not sufficient evidence to warrant a conviction under the above section, as there was no proof that the information as to the voters was actually communicated to any person, and it was not enough that the means of acquiring such information were afforded to any one. *Stannanought* v. *Hazeldine*, 4 C. P. D. 191; 48 L. J. M. C. 89; 40 L. T. (N.S.) 589; 27 W. R. 620; 43 J. P. 352.

* * * * *

Use of school and public room for poll.

6. The returning officer at a parliamentary election may use, free of charge, for the purpose of taking the poll at such election, any room in a school receiving a grant out of moneys provided by Parliament, and any room the expense of maintaining which is payable out of any local rate, but he shall make good any damage done to such room, and defray any expense incurred by the person or body of persons, corporate or unincorporate, having control over the same on account of its being used for the purpose of taking the poll as aforesaid.

Sect. 6.

The use of any room in an unoccupied house for the purpose of taking the poll shall not render any person liable to be rated or to pay any rate for such house.

This section does not apply to municipal elections. See the Municipal Corporations Act, 1882, Sched. 3, Part III. r. 1, *post*. It does, however, apply to elections of county councillors, and the schools and rooms above mentioned may be used at such elections for the purpose of taking the poll and hearing objections to nomination papers, and counting votes. See the Local Government Act, 1888, s. 75, sub-s. (16) (*g*), *ante*, p. 146.

* * * * *

Duties of Returning and Election Officers.

8. Subject to the provisions of this Act, every returning officer shall provide such nomination papers, polling stations, ballot boxes, ballot papers, stamping instruments, copies of register of voters, and other things, appoint and pay such officers, and do such other acts and things as may be necessary for effectually conducting an election in manner provided by this Act.

General powers and duties of returning officer.

* * * * *

It is the duty of the returning officer at an election of county councillors to provide polling stations, etc., under this section. See the Municipal Corporations Act, 1882, Sched. 3, Part III. r. 3, *post*. As to the providing of nomination papers, see the same Act, Sched. 3, Part II. r. 6.

As to the liability of a returning officer for mistakes in the printing of the names on the ballot papers, see *Wilson* v. *Ingham*, noted under s. 13, *infra*.

The remainder of this section is not applicable to elections of county councillors.

9. If any person misconducts himself in the polling station, or fails to obey the lawful orders of the presiding officer, he may immediately, by order of the presiding officer, be removed from the polling station by any constable in or near the station, or any other person authorized in writing by the returning officer to remove him ; and the person so removed shall not, unless with the permission of the presiding officer, again be allowed to enter the polling station during the day.

Keeping of order in station.

Any person so removed as aforesaid, if charged with the commission in such station of any offence, may be kept in custody until he can be brought before a justice of the peace.

Provided that the powers conferred by this section shall not be exercised so as to prevent any elector who is otherwise entitled to vote at any polling station from having an opportunity of voting at such station.

A candidate has a general right to be present in a polling station, and he cannot be excluded under this section, though he has not undertaken the duties of an agent, unless he misconducts himself. *Clementson* v. *Mason*, L. R. 10 C. P. 209 ; 44 L. J. C. P. 171 ; 32 L. T. (N.S.) 325 ; 39 J. P. 360.

Sect. 10.

Powers of presiding officer and administration of oaths, etc.

10. For the purpose of the adjournment of the poll, and of every other enactment relating to the poll, a presiding officer shall have the power by law belonging to a deputy returning officer; and any presiding officer and any clerk appointed by the returning officer to attend at a polling station shall have the power of asking the questions and administering the oath authorized by law to be asked of and administered to voters, and any justice of the peace and any returning officer may take and receive any declaration authorized by this Act to be taken before him.

As to the adjournment of the poll it is provided by the 5 & 6 Will. 4, c. 36, s. 8, that when the proceedings at an election are interrupted or obstructed by any riot or open violence the lawful deputy of any returning officer shall not finally close the poll but shall adjourn the taking the poll at the particular polling place or places at which such interruption or obstruction shall have happened until the following day, etc.

As to the questions which may be put to voters, see the Municipal Corporations Act, 1882, s. 59, *post*.

As to the declaration of secrecy, see Sched. 1, r. 54, *post*.

Liability of officers for misconduct.

11. Every returning officer, presiding officer, and clerk who is guilty of any wilful misfeasance, or any wilful act or omission in contravention of this Act shall, in addition to any other penalty or liability to which he may be subject, forfeit to any person aggrieved by such misfeasance, act, or omission a penal sum not exceeding one hundred pounds,

30 & 31 Vict. c. 102.

Section 50 of the Representation of the People Act, 1867 (which relates to the acting of any returning officer, or his partner or clerk, as agent for a candidate), shall apply to any returning officer or officer appointed by him in pursuance of this Act, and to his partner or clerk.

This Act imposes a duty on the presiding officer at a polling station during an election to deliver to the voters voting papers bearing the official mark appointed under the Act for the election, and to be present during such election at the polling station, so that the voters, before depositing their voting papers in the ballot box, can show to him the official mark on the back of such papers, in accordance with the statute. For breach of these duties, being merely ministerial, an action will lie by a party aggrieved, *e.g.*, who has thereby lost the election through votes given to him being void for the official mark without malice or want of reasonable care on the part of the defendant. If a clerk be appointed by the returning officer to assist at the polling station, the presiding officer may, by the Act, depute to such clerk so much of his duties as he thinks fit, with certain specified exceptions. For the Acts of commission or omission of the clerk in the performance of the duties so delegated, the presiding officer will not be responsible, inasmuch as he does not appoint the clerk, and the relation of master and servant does not exist between them. *Per* BOVILL, C.J., and GROVE, J. :—The Act does not impose on the presiding officer the duty of ascertaining, before the voter deposits a voting paper in the ballot box, whether the official mark is on such paper. *Per* KEATING and BRETT, JJ. :—The statute does impose such duty on the presiding officer.

Sect. 11.

NOTE.

Pickering v. *James*, L. R. 8 C. P. 489 ; 42 L. J. C. P. 217 ; 29 L. T. (N.S.) 211 ; 21 W. R. 786 ; 37 J. P. 679.

The view taken by the last-mentioned judges was followed by Lord COLERIDGE, C.J., HAWKINS and MATHEW, JJ., in *Ackers* v. *Howard*, 16 Q. B. D. 739 ; 55 L. J. Q. B. 273 ; 54 L. T. (N.S.) 651 ; 54 W. R. 609 ; 50 J. P. 519.

The 30 & 31 Vict. c. 102, s. 50, provides that no returning officer nor his deputy, nor any partner or clerk of either of them, shall act as agent for any candidate in the management and conduct of his election . . . . and if he so act he shall be guilty of a misdemeanor.

Prohibition of disclosure of vote.

12. No person who has voted at an election shall, in any legal proceeding to question the election or return, be required to state for whom he has voted.

A similar provision is contained in the Municipal Corporations Act, 1882, s. 104, *ante*.

Non-compliance with rules.

13. No election shall be declared invalid by reason of a non-compliance with the rules contained in the First Schedule to this Act, or any mistake in the use of the forms in the Second Schedule to this Act, if it appears to the tribunal having cognizance of the question that the election was conducted in accordance with the principles laid down in the body of this Act, and that such non-compliance or mistake did not affect the result of the election.

At a municipal election for three councillors six burgesses were nominated and one of them twice. In the ballot paper the name of each burgess nominated was printed, and that of the petitioner, who was twice nominated, was twice printed, his description as given by the nominators somewhat differing, so that there appeared to be seven candidates on the ballot paper in which the petitioner's name appeared, as No. 5 and No. 6, and there was nothing to indicate on the ballot paper that Nos. 5 and 6 were the same person but the similarity of the name. Of the voters who voted for petitioner some put their crosses against both names, Nos. 5 and 6. By adding the numbers together, after rejecting the eight who put their crosses to both Nos. 5 and 6, the petitioner had a majority over the respondent *Pulsford*, who was declared to be elected. *Held*, that although the ballot paper was wrong in form, as the petitioner's name ought not to have appeared twice in it, the mistake did not affect the result of the election, and was therefore cured by s. 13 of the Ballot Act, 1872 (35 & 36 Vict. c. 33), and that the votes against the petitioner's names, Nos. 5 and 6, might be counted together, there being nothing to prevent it but the irregular form of the ballot paper. *Northcote* v. *Pulsford*, L. R. 10 C. P. 476 ; 44 L. J. C. P. 217 ; 32 L. T. (N.S.) 102 ; 23 W. R. 700 ; 39 J. P. 487.

But where a ballot paper contained by mistake the name of a candidate who had withdrawn and a number of votes were given for that candidate which might have affected the result, the election was declared void ; and the court held that under such circumstances the returning officer might be liable to pay the costs of the election petition. *Wilson* v. *Ingham*, 64 L. J. Q. B. 775 ; 72 L. T. (N.S.) 796 ; 43 W. R. 621 ; 59 J. P. 614.

And see generally as to the effect of this section, *Woodward* v. *Sarsons*, L. R. 10 C. P. 733 ; 44 L. J. C. P. 293 ; 32 L. T. (N.S.) 867 ; 39 J. P. 776, and the other cases cited in the notes to r. 36 of Sched. 1, *post*.

Sect. 14.

Use of municipal ballot boxes, etc., for parliamentary election and *vice versâ.*

14. Where a parliamentary borough and municipal borough occupy the whole or any part of the same area, any ballot boxes or fittings for polling stations and compartments provided for such parliamentary borough or such municipal borough may be used in any municipal or parliamentary election in such borough free of charge, and any damage other than reasonable wear and tear caused to the same shall be paid as part of the expenses of the election at which they are so used.

This section is applied to elections of county councillors by s. 75 (19) of the Local Government Act, 1888, incorporating 38 & 39 Vict. c. 84, s. 6, *post.* It is there provided that in any case to which s. 14 of the Ballot Act, 1872, is applicable, it shall be the duty of the returning officer, so far as is practicable, to make use of ballot boxes, fittings, and compartments provided for municipal or school board elections, and the court, upon taxation of his accounts, shall have regard to this provision.

Construction of Act.

15. This part of this Act shall, so far as is consistent with the tenor thereof, be construed as one with the enactments for the time being in force relating to the representation of the people and to the registration of persons entitled to vote at the election of members to serve in Parliament, and with any enactments otherwise relating to the subject matter of this part of this Act, and terms used in this part of this Act shall have the same meaning as in the said enactments; and in construing the said enactments relating to an election or to the poll or taking the votes by poll, the mode of election and of taking the poll established by this Act shall, for the purposes of the said enactments, be deemed to be substituted for the mode of election or poll, or taking the votes by poll, referred to in the said enactments; and any person applying for a ballot paper under this Act shall be deemed "to tender his vote," or "to assume to vote," within the meaning of the said enactments; and any application for a ballot paper under this Act, or expressions relative thereto, shall be equivalent to "voting" in the said enactments and any expressions relative thereto; and the term "polling booth," as used in the said enactments, shall be deemed to include a polling station; and the term "proclamation," as used in the said enactments, shall be deemed to include a public notice given in pursuance of this Act.

* * * * *

PART III.

PERSONATION.

Definition and punishment of personation.

24. The following enactments shall be made with respect to personation at parliamentary and municipal elections :—

A person shall for all purposes of the laws relating to parliamentary and municipal elections be deemed to be guilty of the offence of personation who, at an election for a county or borough, or at a municipal election, applies for a ballot paper in the name of some other person, whether that name be that of a person living or dead or of a fictitious person, or who, having voted once at any such election, applies at the same election for a ballot paper in his own name. Sect. 24

* * * * *

It shall be the duty of the returning officer to institute a prosecution against any person whom he may believe to have been guilty of personation, or of aiding, abetting, counselling, or procuring the commission of the offence of personation by any person, at the election for which he is returning officer, and the costs and expenses of the prosecutor and the witnesses in such case, together with compensation for their trouble and loss of time, shall be allowed by the court in the same manner in which courts are empowered to allow the same in cases of felony.

The provisions of the Registration Acts, specified in the Third Schedule to this Act, shall in England and Ireland respectively apply to personation under this Act in the same manner as they apply to a person who knowingly personates and falsely assumes to vote in the name of another person as mentioned in the said Acts.

* * * * *

As to personation at municipal elections and at elections of county councillors, see the Municipal Elections (Corrupt Practices) Act, 1884, s. 2, and Sched. 3, Part I., *post.*

The punishment for personation is now prescribed by the Corrupt and Illegal Practices Prevention Act, 1883 (46 & 47 Vict. c. 51), s. 6, which is applied to municipal elections by the Act of 1884, s. 2, above referred to.

If a man applies for a ballot paper in a name which is not his own name but is the name under which he is registered and which was intended to designate him and no other person, he does not commit the offence of personation. *R.* v. *Fox*, 16 Cox C. C. 166. Nor does a man who applies for a ballot paper honestly believing that he is entitled to vote. *Gloucester Election Petition*, 2 O'M. & H. 62; *Athlone Election Petition*, 3 O'M. & H. 57; *Isaacson* v. *Durant*, 54 L. T. (N.S.) 684; 4 O'M. & H. 34.

"Procuring" is complete if the person procured actually applies for a ballot paper though he never gets it, and "counselling" is complete though the person counselled never even applies for a ballot paper. *R.* v. *Hayne*, 9 Cox C. C. 412; *S.C. sub. nom. Hayne* v. *Brown*, 22 J. P. 231.

It is not necessary to allege in an indictment under this section or to prove at the trial that the presiding officer at the polling station where the offence was committed was duly appointed. *R.* v. *Garvey*, 16 Cox C. C. 252.

The duty of the returning officer to prosecute is not one which the court can enforce by *mandamus*. *R.* v. *Preston* (*Mayor, etc. of*). 46 J. P. 324.

The provisions of the Registration Acts above referred to are the 6 & 7 Vict. c. 18, ss. 85--89. They are also referred to in the Municipal Corporations Act, 1882, s. 86, *post*, and they are as follows:—

"85. It shall be lawful for any candidate, at any election of a member or members to serve in Parliament for any county, city, or borough, previous to

Sect. 24.

Note.

the time fixed for taking the poll at such election, to nominate and appoint an agent or agents on his behalf to attend at each or any of the booths appointed for taking the poll at such election, for the purpose of detecting personation; and such candidate shall give notice in writing to the returning officer, or his respective deputy, of the name and address of the person or persons so appointed by him to act as agent for such purpose; and thereupon it shall be lawful for every such agent to attend during the time of polling at the booth or booths for which he shall have been so appointed.

"86. If at the time any person tenders his vote at such election, or after he has voted, and before he leaves the polling booth, any such agent so appointed as aforesaid shall declare to the returning officer, or his respective deputy, presiding therein, that he verily believes, and undertakes to prove, that the said person so voting is not in fact the person in whose name he assumes to vote, or to the like effect, then and in every such case it shall be lawful for the said returning officer or his said deputy, and he is hereby required, immediately after such person shall have voted, by word of mouth to order any constable or other peace officer to take the said person so voting into his custody, which said order shall be a sufficient warrant and authority to the said constable or peace officer for so doing: Provided always, that nothing herein contained shall be construed or taken to authorize any returning officer, or his deputy, to reject the vote of any person who shall answer in the affirmative the questions authorized by this Act to be put to him at the time of polling, and shall take the oaths or make the affirmations authorized and required of him; but the said returning officer, or his deputy, shall cause the words, 'protested against for personation,' to be placed against the vote of the person so charged with personation when entered in the poll book.

"87. Every such constable or peace officer shall take the person so in his custody, at the earliest convenient time, before some two justices of the peace acting in and for the county, city, or borough within which the said person shall have so voted as aforesaid: Provided always, that in case the attendance of two such justices as aforesaid cannot be procured within the space of three hours after the close of the poll on the same day on which such person shall have been so taken into custody, it shall be lawful for the said constable or peace officer, and he is hereby required, at the request of such person so in his custody, to take him before any one justice of the peace acting as aforesaid, and such justice is hereby authorized and required to liberate such person on his entering into a recognizance, with one sufficient surety, conditioned to appear before any two such justices as aforesaid, at a time and place to be specified in such recognizance, to answer the said charge; and if no such justice shall be found within four hours after the closing of the said poll then such person shall forthwith be discharged from custody: Provided also, that if in consequence of the absence of such justices as aforesaid, or for any other cause, the said charge cannot be inquired into within the time aforesaid, it shall be lawful nevertheless for any two such justices as aforesaid to inquire into the same on the next or on some other subsequent day, and, if necessary, to issue their warrant for the apprehension of the person so charged.

"88. If on the hearing of the said charge the said two justices shall be satisfied, upon the evidence on oath of not less than two credible witnesses, that the said person so brought before them has knowingly personated and falsely assumed to vote in the name of some other person within the meaning of this Act, and is not in fact the person in whose name he voted, then it shall be lawful for the said two justices to commit the said offender to the gaol of the county, city, or borough within which the offence was committed, to take his trial according to law, and to bind over the witnesses in their respective

Sect. 24.

NOTE.

recognizances to appear and give evidence on such trial as in the case of other misdemeanors.

"89. If the said justices shall, on the hearing of the said charge, be satisfied that the said person so charged with personation is really and in truth the person in whose name he voted, and that the charge of personation has been made against him without reasonable or just cause, or if the agent so declaring as aforesaid, or some one on his behalf, shall not appear to support such charge before the said justices, then it shall be lawful for the said justices, and they are hereby required, to make an order in writing under their hands, on the said agent so declaring as aforesaid, to pay to the said person so falsely charged, if he shall consent to accept the same, any sum not exceeding the sum of ten pounds nor less than five pounds, by way of damages and costs; and if the said sum shall not be paid within twenty-four hours after such order shall have been made, then the same shall be levied, by warrant under the hand and seal of any justice of the peace acting as aforesaid, by distress and sale of the goods and chattels of the said agent; and in case no sufficient goods or chattels of the said agent can be found on which such levy can be made, then the same shall be levied in like manner on the goods and chattels of the candidate by whom such agent was so appointed to act; and in case the said sum shall not be paid or levied in the manner aforesaid, then it shall be lawful for the said person to whom the said sum of money was so ordered to be paid to recover the same from the said agent or candidate, with full costs of suit, in an action of debt to be brought in any one of Her Majesty's Superior Courts of Record at Westminster: Provided always, that if the person so falsely charged shall have declared to the said justices his consent to accept such sum as aforesaid by way of damages and costs, and if the whole amount of the sum so ordered to be paid shall have been paid or tendered to such person, in every such case, but not otherwise, the said agent, candidate, and every other person shall be released from all actions or other proceedings, civil or criminal, for or in respect of the said charge and apprehension."

* * *

PART IV.

MISCELLANEOUS.

Effect of schedules.

28. The schedules to this Act, and the notes thereto, and directions therein, shall be construed and have effect as part of this Act.

29. In this Act—

Definitions. "Municipal borough."

The expression "municipal borough" means any place for the time being subject to the Municipal Corporation Acts, or any of them:

"Municipal Corporation Acts."

The expression "Municipal Corporation Acts" means—

(*a.*) As regards England, the Act of the session of the fifth and sixth years of the reign of King William the Fourth, chapter seventy-six, intituled "An Act to provide for the regulation of Municipal Corporations in England and Wales," and the Acts amending the same:

* * * *

Sect. 29.

"Municipal election."

The expression "municipal election" means—

(a.) As regards England, an election of any person to serve the office of councillor, auditor, or assessor of any municipal borough, or of councillor for a ward of a municipal borough; and

* * * * *

Those portions of the above section which relate to Scotland and Ireland only have been omitted.

The reference to the 5 & 6 Will. 4, c. 76, must be read as a reference to the Municipal Corporations Act, 1882; see s. 242 of the latter Act, *post*.

The expression "municipal election," as used in this Act, includes the election of a county councillor.

Application of Act.

30. This Act shall apply to any parliamentary or municipal election which may be held after the passing thereof.

* * * * *

Short title.

33. This Act may be cited as the Ballot Act, 1872, and shall continue in force till the thirty-first day of December one thousand eight hundred and eighty, and no longer, unless Parliament shall otherwise determine; and on the said day the Acts in the fourth, fifth, and sixth schedules shall be thereupon revived; provided that such revival shall not affect any act done, any rights acquired, any liability or penalty incurred, or any proceeding pending under this Act, but such proceeding shall be carried on as if this Act had continued in force.

The Ballot Act is continued in force from year to year, and is now in force by virtue of the Expiring Laws Continuance Act, 1897.

SCHEDULES.

FIRST SCHEDULE.

Part I.

Rules for Parliamentary Elections.

The Poll.

* * * * *

15. At every polling place the returning officer shall provide a sufficient number of polling stations for the accommodation of the electors entitled to vote at such polling place, and shall distribute the polling stations amongst those electors in such manner as he thinks most convenient, provided that in a district borough there shall be at least one polling station at each contributory place of such borough.

At an election of county councillors this duty will devolve on the returning officer. See the Local Government Act, 1888, s. 75, sub-s. (4), *ante*, and the Municipal Corporations Act, 1882, Sched. 3, Part III. r. 3, *post*.

Rule 16 does not apply to municipal elections or elections of county councillors. See the Municipal Corporations Act, 1882, Sched. 3, Part III. r. 1, *ante*.

* * * * *

17. A separate room or separate booth may contain a separate polling station, or several polling stations may be constructed in the same room or booth.

18. No person shall be admitted to vote at any polling station except the one allotted to him.

As to the duty of the returning officer to give notice of the description of persons entitled to vote at each polling station, see the Municipal Corporations Act, 1882, Sched. 3, Part III. r. 2.

Rule 19 does not apply to municipal elections or to elections of county councillors. See the Municipal Corporations Act, 1882, Sched. 3, Part III. r. 1, *post.*

* * * * *

20. The returning officer shall provide each polling station with materials for voters to mark the ballot papers, with instruments for stamping thereon the official mark, and with copies of the register of voters, or such part thereof as contains the names of the voters allotted to vote at such station. He shall keep the official mark secret, and an interval of not less than seven years shall intervene between the use of the same official mark at elections for the same county or borough.

As to the duty of the returning officer at an election of county councillors to provide the things mentioned in the above rule, see the Municipal Corporations Act, 1882, Sched. 3, Part III. r. 1, *ante.*

21. The returning officer shall appoint a presiding officer to preside at each station, and the officer so appointed shall keep order at his station, shall regulate the number of electors to be admitted at a time, and shall exclude all other persons except the clerks, the agents of the candidates, and the constables on duty.

The candidates cannot be excluded. See *Clementson* v. *Mason*, cited in the note to s. 9, *ante.*

22. Every ballot paper shall contain a list of the candidates described as in their respective nomination papers, and arranged alphabetically in the order of their surnames, and (if there are two or more candidates with the same surname) of their other names: it shall be in the form set forth in the Second Schedule to this Act or as near thereto as circumstances admit, and shall be capable of being folded up.

See the form in the Second Schedule, *post.*

23. Every ballot box shall be so constructed that the ballot papers can be introduced therein, but cannot be withdrawn therefrom, without the box being unlocked. The presiding officer at any polling station, just before the commencement of the poll, shall show the ballot box empty to such persons, if any, as may be present in such station, so that they may see that it is empty, and shall then lock it up, and place his seal upon it in such manner as to prevent its being opened without breaking such seal, and shall place it in his view for the receipt of ballot papers, and keep it so locked and sealed.

24. Immediately before a ballot paper is delivered to an elector, it shall be marked on both sides with the official mark, either stamped or perforated, and the number, name, and description of the elector as stated in the copy of the register shall be called out, and the number of such elector shall be marked on the counterfoil, and a mark shall be placed in the register against the number of the elector, to denote that he has received a ballot paper, but without showing the particular ballot paper which he has received.

A ballot paper not marked with the official mark is void. See r. 36, *post*, and the notes thereto.

It is the duty of the presiding officer to see that the official mark is put on the paper. See *Pickering* v. *James*, and *Ackers* v. *Howard*, *ante*, p. 213.

Schedule 1.

RULE 25.

25. The elector, on receiving the ballot paper, shall forthwith proceed into one of the compartments in the polling station, and there mark his paper, and fold it up so as to conceal his vote, and shall then put his ballot paper, so folded up, into the ballot box; he shall vote without undue delay, and shall quit the polling station as soon as he has put his ballot paper into the ballot box.

26. The presiding officer, on the application of any voter who is incapacitated by blindness or other physical cause from voting in manner prescribed by this Act, or (if the poll be taken on Saturday) of any voter who declares that he is of the Jewish persuasion, and objects on religious grounds to vote in manner prescribed by this Act, or of any voter who makes such a declaration as hereinafter mentioned that he is unable to read, shall, in the presence of the agents of the candidates, cause the vote of such voter to be marked on a ballot paper in manner directed by such voter, and the ballot paper to be placed in the ballot box, and the name and number on the register of voters of every voter whose vote is marked in pursuance of this rule, and the reason why it is so marked, shall be entered on a list, in this Act called "the list of votes marked by the presiding officer."

The said declaration, in this Act referred to as "the declaration of inability to read," shall be made by the voter at the time of polling, before the presiding officer, who shall attest it in the form hereinafter mentioned, and no fee, stamp, or other payment shall be charged in respect of such declaration, and the said declaration shall be given to the presiding officer at the time of voting.

The form of declaration of inability to read is contained in the Second Schedule, *post*.

27. If a person, representing himself to be a particular elector named on the register, applies for a ballot paper after another person has voted as such elector, the applicant shall, upon duly answering the questions and taking the oath permitted by law to be asked of and to be administered to voters at the time of polling, be entitled to mark a ballot paper in the same manner as any other voter, but the ballot paper (in this Act called a tendered ballot paper) shall be of a colour differing from the other ballot papers, and, instead of being put into the ballot box, shall be given to the presiding officer and endorsed by him with the name of the voter and his number in the register of voters, and set aside in a separate packet, and shall not be counted by the returning officer. And the name of the voter and his number on the register shall be entered on a list, in this Act called the tendered votes list.

28. A voter who has inadvertently dealt with his ballot paper in such manner that it cannot be conveniently used as a ballot paper, may, on delivering to the presiding officer the ballot paper so inadvertently dealt with, and proving the fact of the inadvertence to the satisfaction of the presiding officer, obtain another ballot paper in the place of the ballot paper so delivered up (in this Act called a spoilt ballot paper), and the spoilt ballot paper shall be immediately cancelled.

29. The presiding officer of each station, as soon as practicable after the close of the poll, shall, in the presence of the agents of the candidates, make up into separate packets, sealed with his own seal and the seals of such agents of the candidates as desire to affix their seals,—

(1) each ballot box in use at his station, unopened but with the key attached; and

Schedule 1.

RULE 29.

(2) the unused and spoilt ballot papers, placed together ; and
(3) the tendered ballot papers ; and
(4) the marked copies of the register of voters, and the counterfoils of the ballot papers ; and
(5) the tendered votes list, and the list of votes marked by the presiding officer, and a statement of the number of the voters whose votes are so marked by the presiding officer under the heads "physical incapacity," "Jews," and "unable to read," and the declarations of inability to read ;

and shall deliver such packets to the returning officer.

It would appear that the marked copies of the register and the counterfoils should be sealed up separately. See *per* BRETT, J., in *Stowe* v. *Jolliffe*, L. R. 9 C. P. 446 ; 43 L. J. C. P. 173 ; 30 L. T. (N.S.) 299 ; 22 W. R. 946 ; 38 J. P. 617.

30. The packets shall be accompanied by a statement made by such presiding officer, showing the number of ballot papers entrusted to him, and accounting for them under the heads of ballot papers in the ballot box, unused, spoilt, and tendered ballot papers, which statement is in this Act referred to as the ballot paper account.

Counting Votes.

31. The candidates may respectively appoint agents to attend the counting of the votes.

As to the appointment of agents at a municipal election or an election of county councillors, see the Municipal Corporations Act, 1882, s. 58 (6) *ante*.

32. The returning officer shall make arrangements for counting the votes in the presence of the agents of the candidates as soon as practicable after the close of the poll, and shall give to the agents of the candidates appointed to attend at the counting of the votes notice in writing of the time and place at which he will begin to count the same.

The non-attendance of the agents will not invalidate the counting ; see r. 55, *post*.

33. The returning officer, his assistants and clerks, and the agents of the candidates, and no other person, except with the sanction of the returning officer, may be present at the counting of the votes.

The candidates are entitled to be present. See *Clementson* v. *Mason*, cited in the note to s. 9, *ante*, p. 211.

34. Before the returning officer proceeds to count the votes, he shall, in the presence of the agents of the candidates, open each ballot box, and, taking out the papers therein, shall count and record the number thereof, and then mix together the whole of the ballot papers contained in the ballot boxes. The returning officer, while counting and recording the number of ballot papers, and counting the votes, shall keep the ballot papers with their faces upwards, and take all proper precautions for preventing any person from seeing the numbers printed on the backs of such papers.

35. The returning officer shall, so far as practicable, proceed continuously with counting the votes, allowing only time for refreshment, and excluding (except so far as he and the agents otherwise agree) the hours between seven o'clock at night and nine o'clock on the succeeding morning. During the excluded time the returning officer shall place the ballot papers and other documents relating to the election under his own seal, and the seals of such

Schedule 1. —— Rule 35.

of the candidates as desire to affix their seals, and shall otherwise take proper precautions for the security of such papers and documents.

36. The returning officer shall endorse "rejected" on any ballot paper which he may reject as invalid, and shall add to the endorsement " rejection objected to," if an objection be in fact made by any agent to his decision. The returning officer shall report to the Clerk of the Crown in Chancery the number of ballot papers rejected and not counted by him under the several heads of—

(1.) Want of official mark ;

(2.) Voting for more candidates than entitled to ;

(3.) Writing or mark by which voter could be identified ;

(4.) Unmarked or void for uncertainty ;

and shall on request allow any agents of the candidates, before such report is sent, to copy it.

The decision of the returning officer as to any question arising in respect of any ballot paper is final, subject to reversal on petition questioning the election on return. See s. 2, *ante*.

To render an election void under the Ballot Act by reason of a non-observance of, or non-compliance with, the rules or forms given therein, such non-observance or non-compliance must be so great as to satisfy the tribunal before which the validity of the election is contested that the election has been conducted in a manner contrary to the principle of an election by ballot, and that the irregularities complained of did affect or might have affected the result of the election. The ballot paper must not be marked so as to show that the voter intended to vote for more candidates than he is entitled to vote for, nor so as to leave it uncertain whether he intended to vote at all, or for which candidate he intended to vote, nor so as to make it possible by seeing the paper itself or by reference to other available facts to identify the way in which he has voted. If these requirements are not substantially fulfilled the ballot paper is void, and should not be counted, and if it is counted it should be struck out on a scrutiny. Ballot papers with the name of the voter or of the candidate voted for written opposite to the name of the latter and not marked with a cross, or with the addition of a "*cw*" to the cross, were held to be void. But the placing of two crosses or three crosses, or a single stroke in lieu of a cross, or a straight line, or a mark like an imperfect letter P in addition to the cross, or a star instead of a cross, or a cross blurred or marked with a tremulous hand, or a cross placed on the left-hand side of the ballot paper, or a pencil line drawn through the name of the candidate not voted for, or a ballot paper torn longitudinally through the centre, were held not to avoid the vote in the absence of evidence of connivance or pre-arrangement. Twenty ballot papers were marked by the presiding officer by the direction of voters who were unable to read. Each of these ballot papers was placed by the presiding officer in the ballot box wrapped up in the declaration of inability to read made by the voter. The declarations of inability to read of the votes so marked by the presiding officer were not made up into a separate packet and sealed as required by rr. 26, 29, *ante*, but were delivered to the returning officer in the ballot box with the ballot papers as above mentioned. These votes could have been, but were not, in fact, identified by the returning officer at the counting of the votes. It was held that, notwithstanding this breach by the presiding officer of the directions in the rules, the votes in question were properly counted. At one of the polling stations the presiding officer before delivering the ballot papers to the electors attending to vote, marked upon each (to the extent of 294) the number of the voter appearing on the burgess roll, which would enable any of the persons present to identify the way in which the party had voted. Of the electors who received these ballot papers, 234 voted for the petitioner and 60 for the respondent. These votes were not counted by the returning officer. It was held that this admitted error of the presiding officer which did not affect the result, did not render the election void either at common law or under the Ballot Act. Where there have been irregularities in the conduct of an election by the presiding officer at a particular polling station, but there has been no personal default on the part of the returning officer, and the result of the election has not been affected by the mistake of the presiding officer, the returning officer will not be visited with costs. *Woodward* v. *Sarsons*, L. R. 10 C. P. 733 ; 44 L. J. C. P. 293 ; 32 L. T. (N.S.) 867 ; 39 J. P. 776.

In another case, where the presiding officer marked the number of the elector n the register of electors on about one-third of the total number of ballot

Schedule 1.

NOTE to RULE 36.

papers issued, as well as on the counterfoils, but the result of the election was not affected by the irregularity, it was held that the election was not void under the statute nor at common law. *Deans* v. *Haddington Magistrates*, 9 Ct. of Sess. Cas. 1077.

In the *Wigtown Election Petition* (Ct. of Sess. Cas. 4th series, vol. i. p. 925, 2 O'M. & H. 215), it was held (1) that it is essential to a valid vote that the ballot paper be marked with a cross, and not a mere line (see, however, *The Cirencester case, post*, as to this), but that a badly formed cross, or a cross with the addition of small strokes so as to resemble the letter X, will not render the vote null; (2) (diss. Lord BENHOLME), that a ballot paper with a cross decidedly to the left of the candidate's name must be rejected; (3) that any mark on the back of the ballot paper, other than the printed number, renders the vote null; (4) (diss. Lord BENHOLME), that any substantive and separate mark on the face of the ballot paper in addition to the cross, such as a superfluous cross, will render the vote null; (5) that it is not essential that the cross be made with the pencil provided in the compartment, but that it may be made with any pencil or any ink not peculiar.

Where the cross was partly in the space opposite one candidate's name and partly in that opposite another's, the vote was held good for the candidate opposite whose name the two limbs of the cross intersected. *M'Laren* v. *Milne Home*, 7 Q. B. D. 477. In the same case it was held that though the mark did not discolour the ballot paper, it might be well marked, as if done by a thumb-nail or blunt instrument.

A ballot paper which conforms in other respects to the requirements of the Act is not void because it has not on its face the official mark directed by s. 2 to be marked on both sides. *Ackers* v. *Howard*, 16 Q. B. D. 739; 55 L. J. Q. B. 273; 54 L. T. (N.S.) 651; 54 W. R. 609; 50 J. P. 519.

A ballot paper ought not to be rejected because the voter's mark, placed on the right-hand side, after the candidate's name, is placed on the left of the vertical line delineated on the ballot paper. *Sheil* v. *Ennis*, 8 Ir. R. C. L. 240; 2 O'M. & H. 186.

Schedule 2 of this Act, *post*, p. 231, which applies to municipal elections, directs that a voter shall vote by placing a cross on the right-hand side of the ballot paper opposite the name of each candidate for whom he votes. A general order of the Education Department, made under the Elementary Education Acts, provided that the poll at elections of school boards in boroughs shall be conducted in like manner as the poll at a contested municipal election is directed by the Ballot Act, 1872, to be conducted, and the provisions of that Act shall, subject to the provisions of this Order, apply to the elections of school boards, provided that "every voter shall be entitled to a number of votes equal to the number of the members of the school board to be elected, and may give all such votes to one candidate, or may distribute among the candidates as he thinks fit. The voter may place against the name of any candidate for whom he votes the number of votes he gives to such candidate in lieu of a cross, and the form of directions for the guidance of the voter in voting contained in the Ballot Act, 1872, shall be altered accordingly:" *Held*, applying the principle of *Woodward* v. *Sarsons*, L. R. 10 C. P. 733; 44 L. J. C. P. 293, that the provisions of the general order, and of the Ballot Act, 1872, were sufficiently complied with where ballot papers at the election of a school board in a borough were marked otherwise than in the mode prescribed by the order if it could be ascertained with reasonable certainty for whom the voter in each case intended to vote, and how many votes he intended to give, and if it appeared that he had not intended to give a greater number of votes than there were members of the school board to be elected. Applying the above principles the court held that ballot papers marked by placing crosses instead of figures, or crosses and figures, or single strokes, opposite the names of candidates, were valid. *Phillips* v. *Goff*, 17 Q. B. D. 805; 55 L. J. Q. B. 512; 35 W. R. 197; 50 J. P. 614; and see *Morris* v. *Beves*, [1897] 1 Q. B. 449; 66 L. J. Q. B. 299; 76 L. T. (N.S.) 120; 45 W. R. 430; 61 J. P. 263.

Where the cross was put, not opposite to any of the candidates' names, but at the top of the paper or in the right-hand top corner, just above the line, it was held that the vote was void for uncertainty: *The Stepney case*, 4 O'M. & H. 37; *The Buckrose Division case*, *ib.* 111.

In the latter case, again, a paper with a cross on the back which could be seen through the paper, and appeared there opposite a candidate's name, was rejected, the court holding that the mark must be on the face of the paper. Where there was a mark on the face and another on the back, the vote given by the mark on the face was allowed. A paper with a cross on the left-hand side of one candidate's name, and a straight line on the right-hand side of another candidate's name, was held void for uncertainty.

Schedule 1.

NOTE TO RULE 36.

A mark like a circle instead of a cross has been held good in *The Buckrose Division case*, 4 O'M. & H. 112, and bad in *The Stepney case*, *ib.* 37. Probably the former is the better view.

In *The Buckrose Division case*, again, a paper in which a cross was made immediately *upon* a candidate's name was rejected, apparently upon the ground that it was possible that the voter intended to strike the name out (4 O'M. & H. 112).

In *The Cirencester case* (1893), 4 O'M & H. 194, HAWKINS, J., in delivering the judgment of the court (HAWKINS and VAUGHAN WILLIAMS, JJ.), said: "A good many objections were raised to the ballot papers before us upon which votes were recorded on the ground that although the official mark was stamped upon the inside or face, there was no official mark upon the outside or back of the papers. Upon the backs of several of the papers no trace of an official mark was discernible; these were clearly void according to the express provisions of s. 2 of the statute. In several of the remaining papers (all of which had the official mark stamped with ink upon the face), the stamp so marked on the face had been so imprinted thereon with the official stamp that the ink had been forced through the paper, and had left a distinct mark upon the back sufficient to indicate that it had been caused by the application of the stamp to the front. Nobody acquainted with the official stamp could doubt this. Although such mark was not all that could be desired, it seemed to us to be sufficient; but for the act of the presiding officer the mark could not have been there, and, viewed from the back only, the presiding officer could not fail to recognize it as a ballot paper which had been given out by him to a voter, and thus the object of the statute in requiring the paper to be marked on the back was fulfilled. It will be observed that the statute does not require that the stamp shall be applied to the back; it merely requires that the back shall bear the official mark. In several others of the ballot papers, the official stamp itself had, beyond doubt, been applied to the back, but there seems to have been a deficiency of ink upon the stamp, and the impression was not by any means so clear as it would have been if greater care had been taken by the stamper. It was obvious, however, to us, and would be equally obvious to the presiding officer; and we think it is not necessary that there should be in every respect a clear and distinct impression of every part of the stamp, but that it is quite sufficient if the evidence afforded by that which appears on the back of the paper leads us to the conclusion that the stamp was applied there with the intention of making the required mark; and we cannot help remembering that which we constantly see—official stamps upon law proceedings imperfectly impressed, and yet not open to objection nor even questioned. We think, therefore, that all the objections to the ballot papers upon the ground that the official marks were defectively marked upon the backs of them fail, and that it is quite sufficient if there is such evidence of the official mark, whether it is perforated through the paper, whether the ink is caused to run through the paper so as to indicate the official mark, or whether the stamp is applied but fails to make a perfect mark; in all such cases, if there be evidence that the presiding officer has intended to make, and has in fact made, what, fairly looked at, indicates that a recognizable official mark is upon the back of the ballot paper, votes marked on such papers ought to be held good votes in the absence of any other substantial objection."

In dealing with ballot papers alleged to be improperly marked by the voters, HAWKINS, J., continued: "With regard to those votes as to which objections have been raised to the mode in which they were marked by the voters, we have proceeded upon what we think was the true intention of the legislature in framing the Act of Parliament. We have, first of all, asked ourselves whether the voter received his paper with the intention to vote. The mere fact that he has applied for and received a voting paper affords abundant evidence that such was his intention. Then we have looked at the face of the paper itself with a view to see whether or not the voter has by any mark clearly indicated the person for whom he wished and intended to vote; and if we have found such a mark we have upheld the vote, regardless of the very technical, and, as we think, unsubstantial objections which have been allowed in some of the earlier cases to be found in the reports of election cases, our view being that we ought to interpret the Ballot Act liberally, and, subject to other objections, to give effect to any mark on the face of the paper which, in our opinion, clearly indicated the intention of the voter, whether such mark was in the shape of a cross, or a straight line, or in any other form, and whether made with pen and ink, pencil, or even an indentation made on the paper, and whether on the right or the left hand of the candidate's name or elsewhere within his compartment on the voting paper. Of course, every deviation from the course pointed out in the rules tends to create difficulties which may be avoided by a rigid observance of it. It is highly prudent, therefore, to adhere to it, though we do not think it essential.

Schedule 1.

NOTE TO RULE 36.

"There are some marks, however, which undoubtedly gave us much trouble to discover what was the real meaning of them. Upon each one we have come to the best conclusion we could with the materials before us. There were some marks and blotches of a very irregular character which might be well mistaken as indications of temporary unsteadiness in the voters, who by their unsteadiness imperilled their votes. In such cases we have done our best to discover whether although obscured by the blots, blurs, and other marks, there existed positive indications on the part of the voter of an intention to vote, without a thought of leaving behind a trace to enable him to be identified. We have not been astute to give way to objections of an unsubstantial character, but we have endeavoured to interpret the language of the statute in the liberal spirit in which it is conceived, and to carry out the intentions of the legislature in the spirit in which the enactments were passed, supporting every vote which we have found to be clearly indicated, except in a few cases in which the language of the Act expressly declared them void.

"There is a class of cases in which it was said that doubt was apparent on the paper for which candidate the voter intended to give his vote. Of course, if it is on the face of the ballot paper left in doubt whether the man intended to vote for one candidate or the other, the weight of the objection that the vote is uncertain is obvious, for the simple reason that one candidate has just as much right to claim the vote as the other, and so it ought not to be counted for either, and the statute so enacts."

In the same case, the court was called upon to decide as to the validity of ballot papers containing marks, which, it was asserted, might lead to the identification of the voters. On this point, HAWKINS, J., said: "That would be a serious objection if it were maintained—indeed the statute enacts that it shall render the vote void. It was argued before us that if the marks were such as *might* lead to the indentification of the voter that would be quite sufficient to vitiate and render void the vote. That is not our opinion. It is not a question whether by some accident or other a challenged mark *might* possibly lead to the identification of the voter. If that were so, it would be necessary to fix some simple, well-defined cross, or other mark by which alone every ballot paper should be marked to indicate the vote; but this would render strict compliance with the requirement of the law extremely difficult and practically impossible. Very few persons, none with unsteady hands, would be capable of making a definite mark with strict accuracy, and yet any deviation from it might lead to the identification of the voter. But that in our opinion, is not the way in which these objections ought to be dealt with. We think we ought to adhere to the language of the statute itself, which says that the mark must be a mark by which the voter *can* (not *might* possibly) be identified; whether the mark is such, is a matter of fact.

"In the cases before us, altough one or two of the papers bore marks other than that necessary to indicate the vote, we have been unable to come to the conclusion that such marks standing alone could lead to the identification of the voter, and we think we ougnt not to give way to objections which were supported only by the mere suggestion that the marks referred to *might* possibly afford a clue to the identification of the voter."

37. Upon the completion of the counting, the returning officer shall seal up in separate packets the counted and rejected ballot papers. He shall not open the sealed packet of tendered ballot papers or marked copy of the register of voters and counterfoils, but shall proceed, in the presence of the agents of the candidates, to verify the ballot paper account given by each presiding officer by comparing it with the number of ballot papers recorded by him as aforesaid, and the unused and spoilt ballot papers in his possession and the tendered votes list, and shall re-seal each sealed packet after examination. The returning officer shall report to the Clerk of the Crown in Chancery the result of such verification, and shall, on request, allow any agents of the candidates, before such report is sent, to copy it.

In the case of a municipal election or an election of county councillors, no return is to be made to the Clerk of the Crown in Chancery. See the Municipal Corporations Act, 1882, Sched. 3, Part III. r. 6, *post*.

38. Lastly, the returning officer shall forward to the Clerk of the Crown in Chancery (in manner in which the poll books are by any existing enactment required to be forwarded to such clerk, or as near thereto as

Schedule 1. — Rule 38.

circumstances admit) all the packets of ballot papers in his possession, together with the said reports, the ballot paper accounts, tendered votes list, lists of votes marked by the presiding officer, statements relating thereto, declarations of inability to read, and packets of counterfoils, and marked copies of registers, sent by each presiding officer, endorsing on each packet a description of its contents and the date of the election to which they relate, and the name of the county or borough for which such election was held; and the term poll book in any such enactment shall be construed to include any document forwarded in pursuance of this rule.

In municipal elections the packets, etc., are to be forwarded to the town clerk. See r. 64, *post*. In an election of county councillors they will be forwarded to the clerk of the council. See the Local Government Act, s. 75, sub-s. (5), *ante*, p. 142.

39. The Clerk of the Crown shall retain for a year all documents relating to an election forwarded to him in pursuance of this Act by a returning officer, and then, unless otherwise directed by an order of the House of Commons, or of one of Her Majesty's Superior Courts shall cause them to be destroyed.

In a municipal election the documents are retained by the town clerk and destroyed by him, subject to the directions of the borough council. In an election of county councillors the clerk of the council will perform the like duties. See the note to the preceding rule.

40. No person shall be allowed to inspect any rejected ballot papers in the custody of the Clerk of the Crown in Chancery, except under the order of the House of Commons or under the order of one of Her Majesty's Superior Courts, to be granted by such court on being satisfied by evidence on oath that the inspection or production of such ballot papers is required for the purpose of instituting or maintaining a prosecution for an offence in relation to ballot papers, or for the purpose of a petition questioning an election or return; and any such order for the inspection or production of ballot papers may be made subject to such conditions as to persons, time, place and mode of inspection or production as the House or court making the same may think expedient, and shall be obeyed by the Clerk of the Crown in Chancery. Any power given to a court by this rule may be exercised by any judge of such court at chambers.

In the case of a municipal election, or an election of county councillors, the order for inspection will be made by the county court. See r. 64, *post*.

A prosecution having been instituted against the deputy-returning officer, who had presided at a booth during a municipal election, for offences under the Ballot Act, 1872 (35 & 36 Vict. c. 33), a county court judge, in the exercise of jurisdiction given by Sched. 1, Part II. r. 64 of the Act, made an order directing the town clerk of the borough to produce and show, for the purpose of the prosecution, certain rejected ballot papers, counterfoils, counted ballot papers, and spoilt ballot papers relating to the same polling station, and to open the sealed packets containing those documents, and the marked copy of the register, and to take all such proper means as he should deem necessary in order that the mode in which any particular elector had voted should not be discovered; and further ordered that no person should be allowed to see the face of the counted ballot papers. At the trial of the indictment against the prisoner, charging him with having fraudulently placed papers purporting to be, but to his knowledge not being, ballot papers in the ballot box, BLACKBURN, J., allowed the counterfoils and marked register produced under the aforesaid order to be given in evidence, and the face of the voting papers to be inspected so as to show how the votes appeared to have been given. *Held*, that this was rightly done. *R.* v. *Beardsall*, 1 Q. B. D. 452; 45 L. J. M. C. 157; 34 L. T. (N.S.) 660; 40 J. P. 583.

Liberty was given to the Clerk of the Crown to open the packet of rejected ballot papers, and to permit a petitioner and his agents to inspect certain ballot papers which had been rejected by the returning officer on the ground that there were upon them writings or marks by which the voters could be identified, but

Schedule 1.

NOTE TO RULE 40.

so as not to permit any inspection of the numbers on the backs of the ballot papers corresponding with the number on the counterfoils. *Tyrone Election Petition*, 7 Ir. R. C. L. 190; 21 W. R. 627. Where at a parliamentary election there was a bare majority on a large number of votes and an affidavit was filed that it was impossible that the return could be correct and that there must have been a miscounting, the court would not allow an inspection of the ballot papers in the absence of a petition, and doubted whether they hadj urisdiction to make such an order unless a petition had been presented. *Darwen case*, 2 T. L. R. 220. Generally as to when inspection will be granted, see *Stowe* v. *Jolliffe*, *ante*, p. 221.

41. No person shall, except by order of the House of Commons or any tribunal having cognizance of petitions complaining of undue returns or undue elections, open the sealed packet of counterfoils after the same has been once sealed upon, or be allowed to inspect any counted ballot papers in the custody of the Clerk of the Crown in Chancery; such order may be made subject to such conditions as to persons, time, place, and mode of opening or inspection as the House or tribunal making the order may think expedient; provided that on making and carrying into effect any such order, care shall be taken that the mode in which any particular elector has voted shall not be discovered until he has been proved to have voted, and his vote has been declared by a competent court to be invalid.

In the case of municipal elections, or elections of county councillors, an order may be made under this rule by the county court. See r. 64, *post*.

42. All documents forwarded by a returning officer in pursuance of this Act to the Clerk of the Crown in Chancery, other than ballot papers and counterfoils, shall be open to public inspection at such time and under such regulations as may be prescribed by the Clerk of the Crown in Chancery, with the consent of the Speaker of the House of Commons, and the Clerk of the Crown shall supply copies of or extracts from the said documents to any person demanding the same, on payment of such fees and subject to such regulations as may be sanctioned by the Treasury.

In the case of a municipal election, or an election of county councillors, the regulations for the inspection of documents and the fees for the supply of copies of documents of which copies are directed to be supplied are to be prescribed by the borough council (or county council as the case may be), with the consent of a Secretary of State. See r. 64, *post*.

Leave to inspect the marked register of voters, returned by the presiding officer to the Clerk of the Crown in Chancery under the Ballot Act, 1872, will be granted where the petition against the return of a candidate at a parliamentary election charges bribery and treating although it does not pray a scrutiny. *James* v. *Henderson*, 43 L. J. P. C. 238; 30 L. T. (N.S.) 527; 38 J. P. 663.

43. Where an order is made for the production by the Clerk of the Crown in Chancery of any document in his possession relating to any specified election, the production by such clerk or his agent of the document ordered, in such manner as may be directed by such order, or by a rule of the court having power to make such order, shall be conclusive evidence that such document relates to the specified election; and any endorsement appearing on any packet of ballot papers produced by such Clerk of the Crown or his agent shall be evidence of such papers being what they are stated to be by the endorsement. The production from proper custody of a ballot paper purporting to have been used at any election, and of a counterfoil marked with the same printed number and having a number marked thereon in writing, shall be *primâ facie* evidence that the person who voted by such ballot paper was the person who at the time of such election had affixed to his name in the register of voters at such election the same number as the number written on such counterfoil.

*

Schedule 1.

RULE 45.

45. The returning officer shall, as soon as possible, give public notice of the names of the candidates elected, and, in the case of a contested election, of the total number of votes given for each candidate, whether elected or not.

By stating at the close of the poll the number of votes given to each candidate at a municipal election, the returning officer makes a sufficient declaration under s. 2 of this Act, and the effect of that declaration is not altered by reason of a public notice given on the following day under this rule and the next. *R.* v. *Bangor* (*Mayor, etc., of*), 18 Q. B. D. 349; 56 L. J. Q. B. 326; 56 L. T. (N.S.) 434; 35 W. R. 158; 51 J. P. 51.

46. Where the returning officer is required or authorized by this Act to give any public notice, he shall carry such requirement into effect by advertisements, placards, handbills, or such other means as he thinks best calculated to afford information to the electors.

47. The returning officer may, if he think fit, preside at any polling station, and the provisions of this Act relating to a presiding officer shall apply to such returning officer with the necessary modifications as to things to be done by the returning officer to the presiding officer, or the presiding officer to the returning officer.

48. In the case of a contested election for any county or borough, the returning officer may, in addition to any clerks, appoint competent persons to assist him in counting the votes.

49. No person shall be appointed by a returning officer for the purposes of an election who has been employed by any other person in or about the election.

50. The presiding officer may do, by the clerks appointed to assist him, any act which he is required or authorized to do by this Act at a polling station except ordering the arrest, exclusion, or ejection from the polling station of any person.

As to the power to order arrest, see 6 & 7 Vict. c. 18, s. 86, *ante*, p. 216. As to the power to order the exclusion or ejection of any person, see s. 9 of this Act, *ante*, p. 211.

51. A candidate may himself undertake the duties which any agent of his if appointed might have undertaken, or may assist his agent in the performance of such duties, and may be present at any place at which his agent may, in pursuance of this Act, attend.

But though a candidate does not himself undertake the duties of an agent and does not assist his agent, he is nevertheless entitled to be present at polling stations. *Clementson* v. *Mason*, cited in the notes to s. 9, *ante*.

52. The name and address of every agent of a candidate appointed to attend the counting of the votes shall be transmitted to the returning officer one clear day at the least before the opening of the poll; and the returning officer may refuse to admit to the place where the votes are counted any agent whose name and address has not been so transmitted, notwithstanding that his appointment may be otherwise valid, and any notice required to be given to an agent by the returning officer may be delivered at or sent by post to such address.

As to agents at municipal elections and elections of county councillors, see the Municipal Corporations Act, 1882, s. 58, sub-s. (6), *post*.

53. If any person appointed an agent by a candidate for the purposes of attending at the polling station or at the counting of the votes dies, or becomes incapable of acting during the time of the election, the candidate may appoint another agent in his place, and shall forthwith give to the returning officer notice in writing of the name and address of the agent so appointed.

54. Every returning officer, and every officer, clerk, or agent authorized to attend at a polling station, or at the counting of the votes, shall before the

opening of the poll make a statutory declaration of secrecy, in the presence, if he is the returning officer, of a justice of the peace, and if he is any other officer or an agent, of a justice of the peace or of the returning officer; but no such returning officer, officer, clerk, or agent as aforesaid shall, save as aforesaid, be required, as such, to make any declaration or take any oath on the occasion of any election.

As to the penalties for infringement of secrecy, see s. 4.
As to the form of declaration, see Sched. 2, *post*.

55. Where in this Act any expressions are used requiring or authorizing or inferring that any act or thing is to be done in the presence of the agents of the candidates, such expressions shall be deemed to refer to the presence of such agents of the candidates as may be authorized to attend, and as have in fact attended, at the time and place where such act or thing is being done, and the non-attendance of any agents or agent at such time and place shall not, if such act or thing be otherwise duly done, in anywise invalidate the act or thing done.

56. In reckoning time for the purposes of this Act, Sunday, Christmas Day, Good Friday, and any day set apart for a public fast or public thanksgiving, shall be excluded; and where anything is required by this Act to be done on any day which falls on the above-mentioned days such thing may be done on the next day, unless it is one of the days excluded as above mentioned.

57. In this Act—

* * * * *

The expression "agents of the candidates," used in relation to a polling station, means agents appointed in pursuance of section eighty-five of the Act of the session of the sixth and seventh years of the reign of Her present Majesty, chapter eighteen.

See s. 85, of 6 & 7 Vict, c. 18, in the notes to s. 24, *ante*, p. 215, and as to agents at a municipal election or an election of county councillors, see the Municipal Corporations Act, 1882, s. 58, sub-s. (6), *post*.

* * * *

PART II.

Rules for Municipal Elections.

64. In the application of the provisions of this schedule to muncipal elections the following modifications shall be made:—

(*a*.) The expression "register of voters" means the burgess roll of the burgesses of the borough, or, in the case of an election for the ward of a borough, the ward list; and the mayor shall provide true copies of such register for each polling station:

(*b*.) All ballot papers and other documents which, in the case of a parliamentary election, are forwarded to the Clerk of the Crown in Chancery shall be delivered to the town clerk of the municipal borough in which the election is held, and shall be kept by him among the records of the borough; and the provisions of Part One of this schedule with respect to the inspection, production, and destruction of such ballot papers and documents, and to the copies of such documents, shall apply respectively to the ballot papers and documents so in the custody of the town clerk, with these modifications; namely,

(*a*.) An order of the county court having jurisdiction in the borough, or any part thereof, or of any tribunal in which a municipal election

Schedule 1.

RULE 64.

is questioned, shall be substituted for an order of the House of Commons, or of one of Her Majesty's Superior Courts; but an appeal from such county court may be had in like manner as in other cases in such county court;

(*b.*) The regulations for the inspection of documents and the fees for the supply of copies of documents of which copies are directed to be supplied, shall be prescribed by the council of the borough with the consent of one of Her Majesty's Principal Secretaries of State; and, subject as aforesaid, the town clerk, in respect of the custody and destruction of the ballot papers and other documents coming into his possession in pursuance of this Act, shall be subject to the directions of the council of the borough:

(*c.*) Nothing in this schedule with respect to the day of the poll shall apply to a municipal election.

Municipal election includes an election of county councillors. Register of voters at the latter election means the division register, *i.e.*, that part of the roll of county electors which relates to the electoral division.

The other modifications above-mentioned have been noticed in the notes to the several rules.

SECOND SCHEDULE.

Note.—The forms contained in this schedule, or forms as nearly resembling the same as circumstances will admit, shall be used in all cases to which they refer and are applicable, and when so used shall be sufficient in law.

Form of Ballot Paper.

Form of Front of Ballot Paper.

Counterfoil No.

NOTE: *The counterfoil is to have a number to correspond with that on the back of the Ballot Paper.*

1	**BROWN** (John Brown, of 52, George St., Bristol, Merchant.)	
2	**JONES** (William David Jones, of High Elms, Wilts, Esq.)	
3	**MERTON** (Hon. George Travis, commonly called Viscount Merton, of Swanworth, Berks.)	
4	**SMITH** (Henry Sydney Smith, of 72, High Street, Bath, Attorney.)	

Form of Back of Ballot Paper.

No.

Election for county [*or* borough, *or* ward].
18

Note.—The number on the ballot paper is to correspond with that in the counterfoil.

Directions as to Printing Ballot Paper.

Nothing is to be printed on the ballot paper except in accordance with this schedule.

The surname of each candidate, and if there are two or more candidates of the same surname, also the other names of such candidates, shall be printed in large characters, as shown in the form, and the names, addresses, and descriptions, and the number on the back of the paper, shall be printed in small characters.

Form of Directions for the Guidance of the Voter in voting, which shall be printed in conspicuous Characters, and placarded outside every Polling Station, and in every Compartment of every Polling Station.

The voter may vote for candidate .

The voter will go into one of the compartments, and, with the pencil provided in the compartment, place a cross on the right-hand side, opposite the name of each candidate for whom he votes, thus **X**

The voter will then fold up the ballot paper so as to show the official mark on the back, and leaving the compartment will, without showing the front of the paper to any person, show the official mark on the back to the presiding officer, and then, in the presence of the presiding officer, put the paper into the ballot box, and forthwith quit the polling station.

If the voter inadvertently spoils a ballot paper, he can return it to the officer, who will, if satisfied of such inadvertence, give him another paper.

If the voter votes for more than candidate , or places any mark on the paper by which he may be afterwards identified, his ballot paper will be void, and will not be counted.

If the voter takes a ballot paper out of the polling station, or deposits in the ballot box any other paper than the one given him by the officer, he will be guilty of a misdemeanor, and be subject to imprisonment for any term not exceeding six months, with or without hard labour.

Note.—These directions shall be illustrated by examples of the ballot paper.

Form of Statutory Declaration of Secrecy.

I solemnly promise and declare, That I will not at this election for do anything forbidden by section four of the Ballot Act, 1872, which has been read to me.

Note.—The section must be read to the declarant by the person taking the declaration.

Form of Declaration of Inability to Read.

I, *A.B.*, of , being numbered on the register of voters for the county [*or* borough] of , do hereby declare that I am unable to read.

A.B., his mark.

day of .

I, the undersigned, being the presiding officer for the polling station for the county [*or* borough] of , do hereby certify, that the above declaration, having been first read to the above-named *A.B.*, was signed by him in my presence with his mark.

Signed, *C.D.*,
Presiding officer for polling station
for the county [*or* borough of .

day of

PARLIAMENTARY ELECTIONS (RETURNING OFFICERS) ACT, 1875.

(38 & 39 Vict. Cap. 84.)

An Act to regulate the Expenses and to control the Charges of Returning Officers at Parliamentary Elections.

[13th August, 1875.]

Whereas it is expedient to amend the law relating to the expenses and charges of returning officers at parliamentary elections:

Be it enacted by the Queen's most Excellent Majesty, by and with the advice and consent of the Lords Spiritual and Temporal, and Commons, in this present Parliament assembled, and by the authority of the same, as follows:

This Act is set out so far as it is incorporated by the Local Government Act, 1888, s. 75 (18) (19), *ante*, p. 147. It is amended by the 48 & 49 Vict. c. 62, in a small particular mentioned in a note to Sched. 1, Part I., of this Act, *post*, and by the 49 & 50 Vict. c. 57, which is set out *post*.

* * * *

The accounts of a returning officer may be taxed.

4. Within twenty-one days after the day on which the return is made of the persons elected at the election, the returning officer shall transmit to every candidate or other person from whom he claims payment either out of any deposit or otherwise of any charges in respect of the election, or to the agent for election expenses of any such candidate, a detailed account showing the amounts of all the charges claimed by the returning officer in respect of the election, and the share thereof which he claims from the person to whom the account is transmitted. He shall annex to the account a notice of the place where the vouchers relating to the account may be seen, and he shall at all reasonable times and without charge allow the person from whom payment is claimed, or any agent of such person, to inspect and take copies of the vouchers.

The returning officer shall not be entitled to any charges which are not duly included in his account.

If the person from whom payment is claimed objects to any part of the claim, he may, at any time within fourteen days from the time when the account is transmitted to him, apply to the court as defined in this section for a taxation of the account, and the court shall have jurisdiction to tax the account in such manner and at such time and place as the court thinks fit, and finally to determine the amount payable to the returning officer and to give and enforce judgment for the same as if such judgment were a judgment in an action in such court, and with or without costs at the discretion of the court. Sect. 4.

The court for the purposes of this Act shall be in the city of London the Lord Mayor's Court, and elsewhere in England the county court, and in Ireland the Civil Bill Court, having jurisdiction at the place of nomination for the election to which the proceedings relate.

The court may depute any of its powers or duties under this Act to the registrar or other principal officer of the court.

Nothing in this section shall apply to the charge of the returning officer for publication of accounts of election expenses.

The expenses of the returning officer are payable by the county council out of the county fund as general expenses, and not by the candidate, and claims must be made accordingly. See s. 75 (17) (19) of the Local Government Act, 1888, *ante*, p. 147, 148.

The period within which application for taxations may be made in the case of a county council election is one calendar month instead of fourteen days as provided by the above section. See s. 75 (19) of the Local Government Act, 1888.

It was held that where the accounts of a returning officer had been taxed by the registrar of a county court, under the above section, the county court judge had no discretion to review the registrar's taxation. *R.* v. *Lambeth (County Court, Judge of)*, 17 Q. B. D. 96. But see now 49 & 50 Vict. c. 57, *post.*

An application made within the specified time to the registrar of the county court when the judge is not sitting is properly made within the above section. *R.* v. *Bloomsbury (County Court, Judge of)*, 17 Q. B. D. 788; 55 L. J. Q. B. 443; 56 L. T. (N.S.) 321; 51 J. P. 212.

A returning officer at a parliamentary election is not entitled to remuneration for personal services rendered by him in the conduct of the election, under the heading of professional or other assistance, which he has not, as a matter of fact, employed. *Ex parte Walker, re Shoreditch (Hoxton Division) Parliamentary Election* (1886), 56 L. T. (N.S.) 529.

At a parliamentary election the high sheriff was the returning officer, the duties being performed on his behalf by a firm of solicitors, one of whom was under-sheriff. The returning officer's charges included a charge for professional assistance rendered to him by the under-sheriff's firm, which was disallowed on taxation, on the ground that no detailed account was sent in to the returning officer within fourteen days of the return, as required by s. 5 of the Returning Officers Act, 1875. *Held*, that the charge was wrongly disallowed on the above ground, the section not being applicable as between the returning officer and the candidates to charges made for work done for the returning officer by his own agents. The right of a returning officer under s. 2 of the same Act to be paid his reasonable charges and expenses is not limited to such charges only as have been vouched under ss. 4 and 5 of the Act, nor is a charge made by him to be disallowed merely because in the account sent in by him to candidates it appears under a wrong heading. A returning officer is not limited to charging for such services and expenses as come *verbatim et literatim* within the descriptions of the schedule to the Act, if they are services and expenses of one of the kinds mentioned in the schedule. A charge for storing ballot boxes from one election to another, in order to

Sect. 4.

NOTE.

avoid the expense of procuring fresh ones, was therefore allowed, although no such charge is expressly provided for in the schedule to the Act. *In re Election for South-Eastern Division of Essex,* 19 Q. B. D. 252; 56 L. J. Q. B. 365; 57 L. T. (N.S.) 104; 36 W. R. 44.

Claims against a a returning officer.

5. Every person having any claim against a returning officer for work, labour, materials, services, or expenses in respect of any contract made with him by or on behalf of the returning officer for the purposes of an election, except for publication of accounts of election expenses, shall, within fourteen days after the day on which the return is made of the person or persons elected at the election, transmit to the returning officer the detailed particulars of such claim in writing, and the returning officer shall not be liable in respect of anything which is not duly stated in such particulars.

Where application is made for taxation of the accounts of a returning officer, he may apply to the court as defined in this Act to examine any claim transmitted to him by any person in pursuance of this section, and the court after notice given to such person, and after hearing him, and any evidence tendered by him, may allow or disallow, or reduce the claim objected to, with or without costs, and the determination of the court shall be final for all purposes, and as against all persons.

Use of ballot boxes, etc. provided for municipal elections.

6. In any case to which the fourteenth section of the Ballot Act, 1872, is applicable, it shall be the duty of the returning officer, so far as is practicable, to make use of ballot boxes, fittings, and compartments provided for municipal or school board elections, and the court, upon taxation of his accounts, shall have regard to the provisions of this section.

Notices to be given by returning officers.

7. There shall be added to every notice of election to be published under the provisions of the Ballot Act, 1872, the notification contained in the second schedule to this Act with respect to claims against returning officers.

SCHEDULES.

Schedule 1.

FIRST SCHEDULE.

Charges of Returning Officers.

The following are the maximum charges to be made by the returning officer, but the charges are in no case to exceed the sums actually and necessarily paid or payable.

Part I.—Counties and District or Contributory Boroughs.

This Part of this Schedule applies to an election for a county, or for either of the boroughs of Aylesbury, Cricklade, Monmouth, East Retford, Stroud, and New Shoreham, or for any borough or burgh consisting of a combination of separate boroughs, burghs, or towns.

	£ s. d.
For preparing and publishing the notice of election	2 2 0
For preparing and supplying the nomination papers	1 1 0
For travelling to and from the place of nomination, or of declaring the poll at a contested election, per mile.	0 1 0
For hire or necessary fitting up of rooms or buildings for polling, or damage or expenses by or for use of such rooms or buildings.	The necessary expenses, not exceeding at any one polling station the charge for constructing and fitting a polling station.
For constructing a polling station, with its fittings and compartments, in England.	7 7 0
And in Ireland the sum or sums payable under the provisions of the 13th and 14th Victoria, chap. 68, and 35th and 36th Victoria, chap. 33.	
In Ireland the returning officer shall use a court house where one is available as a polling station, and his maximum charge for using and fitting the same shall in no case exceed three pounds three shillings.	
For each ballot box required to be purchased	1 1 0
For the use of each ballot box, when hired	0 5 0
For stationery at each polling station	0 10 0
For printing and providing ballot papers, per thousand	1 10 0
For each stamping instrument	0 10 0
For copies of the register	The sums payable by statute for the necessary copies.
For each presiding officer	3 3 0
For one clerk at each polling station where not more than 500 voters are assigned to such station.	1 1 0
For an additional clerk at a polling station for every number of 500 voters, or fraction thereof beyond the the first 500 assigned to such polling station.	1 0 0
For every person employed in counting votes, not exceeding six such persons where the number of registered electors does not exceed 3,000, and one for every additional 2,000 electors.	1 1 0
For making the return to the clerk of the Crown	1 1 0
For the preparation and publication of notices (other than the notice of election).	Not exceeding for the whole of such notices 20*l.*, and 1*l.* for every additional 1,000 electors above 3,000.

Schedule 1.

	£ s. d.
For conveyance of ballot boxes from the polling stations to the place where the ballot papers are to be counted, per mile.	0 1 0
For professional and other assistance in and about the conduct of the election.	In a contested election not exceeding 25*l.*, and an additional 3*l.* for every 1,000 registered electors or fraction thereof above 3,000 and up to 10,000, and 2*l.* for every 1,000 or fraction thereof above 10,000. In an uncontested election, one fifth of the above sums.
For travelling expenses of presiding officers and clerks, per mile.	0 1 0
For services and expenses in relation to receiving and publishing accounts of election expenses, in respect of each candidate.	2 2 0
For all other expenses - - - - - - -	In a contested election not exceeding 10*l.*, and an additional 1*l.* for every 1,000 electors or fraction thereof above 1,000. In an uncontested election, nil.

NOTE.—*Travelling expenses are not to be allowed in the case of any person unless for distances exceeding two miles from the place at which he resides.*

The provisions of the above Schedule are modified by s. 4 of the Parliamentary Elections (Returning Officers) Act, 1885 (48 & 49 Vict. c. 62), which provides that notwithstanding the above scale of charges it shall be lawful in any county constituency in England for the returning officer to charge four guineas for each presiding officer, and thirty shillings for each clerk at a polling station.

* * * * *

SECOND SCHEDULE.

1. NOTIFICATION to be added to the NOTICE of ELECTION.

Take notice, that by the Parliamentary Elections (Returning Officers) Act, 1875, it is provided that every person having any claim against a returning officer for work, labour, materials, services, or expenses in respect of any contract made with him by or on behalf of the returning officer, for the purposes of an election (except for publications of account of election expenses), shall, within fourteen days after the day on which the return is made of the person or persons elected at the election, transmit to the returning officer the detailed particulars of such claim in writing, and the returning officer shall not be liable in respect of anything which is not duly stated in such particulars.

PARLIAMENTARY ELECTIONS (RETURNING OFFICERS) ACT (1875) AMENDMENT ACT, 1886.

(49 & 50 VICT. CAP. 57.)

An Act to amend the provisions of the Parliamentary Elections (Returning Officers) Act, 1875. [25th June, 1886.]

BE it enacted by the Queen's most Excellent Majesty, by and with the advice and consent of the Lords Spiritual and Temporal, and Commons, in this present Parliament assembled, and by the authority of the same as follows :

This Act amends the 38 & 39 Vict. c. 84, *ante* p. 232, and with that Act is incorporated by the Local Government Act, 1888, s. 75 (19), *ante*, p. 147.

1. The judge or officer by whom any account or claim is taxed or examined under the Parliamentary Elections (Returning Officers) Act, 1875 (herein called the "principal Act"), shall deliver to the returning officer, and to the other party to the taxation or examination, a certificate showing the items and amounts allowed or disallowed, with a copy of any order or judgment made thereon. Review of taxation.

Either party may, within seven days of the delivery to him of such certificate, give notice in writing to the said judge or officer of intention to appeal, specifying in the notice the items and amounts in respect of which he intends to appeal.

The said judge or officer shall thereupon forthwith transmit to the prescribed taxing officer of the superior court the said account or claim, with any vouchers relating thereto, the certificate and the notice of appeal, and such taxing officer shall forthwith proceed to review the taxation or examination in the usual manner, or in such manner as may be prescribed, and shall, if required, receive evidence in relation to the matters in dispute, and may confirm or vary the certificate, and direct by whom all or any part of the costs of review are to be paid, and shall return the certificate as confirmed or varied to the said judge or officer with any such direction, and effect shall be given to a certificate as so confirmed or varied, and to any such direction, as if the same had been a judgment of the court as defined in the principal Act.

Any taxation or review of taxation under this Act shall be subject to appeal to the superior court in like manner as any ordinary taxation of costs is now subject.

Sect. 1. In this Act "superior court" means in England the Queen's Bench Division of the High Court of Justice in England, and in Ireland the Common Pleas Division of the High Court of Justice in Ireland. "Prescribed" means prescribed by rules of the superior court in England or Ireland as the case may be.

Short title. **2.** This Act may be cited as the Parliamentary Elections (Returning Officers) Act (1875) Amendment Act, 1886, and shall be read as one with the principal Act.

MUNICIPAL CORPORATIONS ACT, 1882.

(45 & 46 Vict. Cap. 50.)

The following sections and schedules of this Act are incorporated with the Local Government Act, s. 75, *ante*, p. 141. Some other sections of this Act are referred to in the Local Government Act, but these are set out in the notes to the sections of that Act containing such references.

The notes to the following sections have been for the most part limited to their application to county councils.

PART II.

Constitution and Government of Borough.

Corporate Name.

8. The municipal corporation of a borough shall bear the name of the mayor, aldermen, and burgesses of the borough, or, in the case of a city, the mayor, aldermen, and citizens of the city. Name of municipal corporation.

This section does not really apply to county councils, for by s. 79 of the Local Government Act, *ante*, p. 153, the council of each county are incorporated by the name of the county council, with the prefix of the name of the administrative county. By s. 34, sub-s. (1), of the same Act, *ante*, p. 73, the mayor, aldermen, and burgesses of each borough mentioned in the Third Schedule, that is, of the county boroughs acting by the council, have all the powers and duties of the county council within the borough ; but this involves no change of the name of the borough or city.

Burgesses (a).

9.—(1.) A person shall not be deemed a burgess for any purpose of this Act unless he is enrolled as a burgess (*b*). Qualification of burgess.

(2.) A person shall not be entitled to be enrolled as a burgess unless he is qualified as follows (*c*) :

(a.) Is of full age ; and

(b.) Is on the fifteenth of July in any year, and has been during the whole of the then last preceding twelve months, in occupation (*d*), joint or several (*e*), of any house, warehouse, counting-house, shop or other building (*f*) (in this Act referred to as qualifying property) in the borough (*g*); and

(c.) Has during the whole of those twelve months resided in the borough, or within seven miles thereof (*h*) ; and

Sect. 9 (2).

(d.) Has been rated in respect of the qualifying property to all poor rates made during those twelve months for the parish wherein the property is situate (*i*); and

(e.) Has on or before the twentieth of the same July paid all such rates, including borough rates (if any), as have become payable by him in respect of the qualifying property up to the then last preceding fifth of January (*k*).

(3.) Every person so qualified shall be entitled to be enrolled as a burgess, unless he—

(a.) Is an alien (*l*); or

(b.) Has within the twelve months aforesaid received union or parochial relief or other alms (*m*); or

(c.) Is disentitled under any Act of Parliament (*n*).

(*a*) It is provided by the County Electors Act, 1888 (51 Vict. c. 10), s. 2, *post*, that "for the purpose of the election of county authorities in England the burgess qualification, that is to say, the qualification enacted by s. 9 of the Municipal Corporations Act, 1882, shall extend to every part of a county not within the limits of a borough, and a person possessing in any part of a county outside the limits of a borough such burgess qualification shall be entitled to be registered under the Act as a county elector in the parish in which the qualifying property is situate. Sections 9, 31, 33, and 63 of the Municipal Corporations Act, 1882, and any enactments of that or any other Act affecting the same, shall extend to so much of every county as is not comprised within the limits of a municipal borough, in like manner as if they were herein re-enacted, with the substitution of 'county' for 'borough,' and of 'county elector' for 'burgess,' and with the other necessary modifications."

(*b*) By s. 45, sub-s. (8), *post*, every person enrolled in the burgess roll shall be deemed to be enrolled as a burgess, and every person not enrolled in the burgess roll shall be deemed to be not enrolled as a burgess.

By s. 63, *post*, women may be enrolled as burgesses, and by that section, as applied by the County Electors Act, 1888 (51 Vict. c. 10), s. 2, sub-s. (2), women may also be enrolled as county electors.

(*c*) This is no longer the only qualification of a burgess or county elector. It is provided by the County Electors Act, 1888 (51 Vict. c. 10), s. 3, that every person who is entitled to be registered as a voter in respect of a 10*l*. occupation qualification within the meaning of the provisions of the Registration Act, 1885, which are set out in the schedule to that Act, shall be entitled to be registered as a county elector, and to be enrolled as a burgess, in respect of such qualification, in like manner in all respects as if the section of the Municipal Corporations Act, 1882, relating to a burgess qualification included the said 10*l*. occupation qualification. The schedule to the 51 Vict. c. 10, above referred to, is as follows :—

"DEFINITION OF TEN POUNDS OCCUPATION QUALIFICATION.

"A person entitled to be registered as a voter in respect of a ten pounds occupation qualification in a borough, municipal or parliamentary—

(a.) Must during the whole twelve months immediately preceding the fifteenth day of July have been an occupier as owner or tenant of some land or tenement in a parish [or township] of the clear yearly value of not less than ten pounds; and

Sect. 9 (3).

NOTE.

(b.) Must have resided in or within seven miles of the borough during six months immediately preceding the fifteenth day of July; and

(c.) Such person, or someone else, must during the said twelve months have been rated to all poor rates made in respect of such land or tenement; and

(d.) All sums due in respect of the said land or tenement on account of any poor rate made and allowed during the twelve months immediately preceding the fifth day of January next before the registration, or on account of any assessed taxes due before the said fifth day of January, must have been paid on or before the twentieth day of July.

"If two or more persons jointly are such occupiers as above mentioned, and the value of the land or tenement is such as to give ten pounds or more for each occupier, each of such occupiers is entitled to be registered as a voter.

"If a person has occupied in the borough different lands or tenements of the requisite value in immediate succession during the said twelve months, he is entitled in respect of the occupation thereof to be registered as a voter in the parish [or township] in which the last occupied land or tenement is situate."

(*d*) **Occupation.**—It is provided by s. 257, sub-s. (3), *post*, that nothing in this Act shall entitle any person to be enrolled as a citizen of the city of Oxford or burgess of the borough of Cambridge by reason of his occupation of any rooms, chambers, or premises in any college or hall of either of these universities.

By s. 33, sub-s. (2), *post*, the qualifying property need not be throughout the twelve months constituting the period of qualification the same property, or in the same parish.

For the distinction between an occupier and a lodger the following cases may be referred to:—*Bradley* v. *Baylis*, 8 Q. B. D. 194; 51 L. J. Q. B. 183; 46 L. T. (N.S.) 253; 30 W. R. 823; 45 J. P. 847; *Morton* v. *Palmer*, 9 Q. B. D. 89; 51 L. J. Q. B. 307; 46 L. T. (N.S.) 285; 30 W. R. 115; 46 J. P. 150; *Ness* v. *Stevenson*, 9 Q. B. D. 245; 47 J. P. 134; *Anckctill* v. *Baylis*, 10 Q. B. D. 577; 52 L. J. Q. B. 104; 48 L. T. (N.S.) 343; 31 W.R. 233; 47 J. P. 356; *Heawood* v. *Bone*, 13 Q. B. D. 179; 51 L. T. (N.S.) 125; 48 J. P. 710; *M'Laughlin* v. *Chambers*, [1896] 2 Ir. Rep. 497.

Occupation of a dwelling-house by virtue of an office, service or employment within the meaning of 48 Vict. c. 3, s. 3, is no qualification for the municipal franchise. *McClean* v. *Pritchard*, 20 Q. B. D. 285; 58 L. T. (N.S.) 337; 36 W. R. 508; 52 J. P. 519. This decision will also apply to county electors. The distinction between occupation such as gives the occupier the service franchise and occupation within the meaning of this section, is pointed out in *Marsh* v. *Estcourt*, 24 Q. B. D. 147; 59 L. J. Q. B. 100; 38 W. R. 495: 54 J. P. 294.

Spaces in a market place the precise position of each of which was known and determined, were held to entitle the occupiers to the borough franchise. *Hall* v. *Metcalfe*, [1892] 1 Q. B. 208; 61 L. J. Q. B. 53; 66 L. T. (N.S.) 496; 8 T. L. R. 46.

Where a tenant became bankrupt, but continued in occupation and paid rent during the whole of the qualifying period, the trustee in bankruptcy not interfering, it was held that he must be regarded as having been in occupation during the whole of the qualifying period for the purposes of the parliamentary franchise. *Mackay* v. *McGuire*, [1891] 1 Q. B. 250; 60 L. J. Q. B. 24; 64 L. T. (N.S.) 83; 39 W. R. 109; 55 J. P. 214; 7 T. L. R. 55.

Where the occupier of premises transferred them to a company, and on the same day took from the company a demise of part of the premises which he

Sect. 9 (3).

NOTE.

continued to occupy as an office, it was held that there had been a continuous occupation of the office during the whole of the qualifying period: *Timmins* v. *Albiston*, [1895] 2 Q. B. 58; 64 L. J. Q. B. 564; 59 J. P. 663.

A husband residing with his wife, who carried on business in her own name, and was the rated occupier of the premises, was held not to be entitled to be registered as the occupier. *Prentice* v. *Markham*, 9 T. L. R. 58.

Weekly tenants of stalls in a market building which was closed and locked during the night, were held not to be occupiers within the meaning of s. 30 of the Municipal Corporations (Ireland) Act, 1840. *Lovell* v. *Callaghan*, [1894] 2 Ir. R. 346.

As to occupation on succession by descent, marriage, etc., see s. 33, *post*.

(*e*) The words "joint or several" were inserted with reference to the decision in *R.* v. *The Mayor, etc. of Exeter*, L. R. 4 Q. B. 114, *post*. Where several persons entitled to occupy a house jointly by agreement between themselves, arranged to occupy separately in turn during the year, it was held that they were not entitled to be registered as having been in joint occupation during the qualifying year. *Rowland* v. *Pritchard*, 62 L. J. Q. B. 319; 68 L. T. (N.S.) 586; 57 J. P. 759; 9 T. L. R. 279. For a case where several persons had separate rooms in a house, using the rest of the rooms in common, see *Hollands* v. *Chambers*, 32 L. R. Ir. 156.

It is provided by s. 31, *post*, that where an occupier is entitled to the sole and exclusive use of any part of a house, that part shall not be deemed to be occupied otherwise than separately by reason only that the occupier is entitled to the joint use of some other part. See the note to that section.

(*f* **House, warehouse, etc.**—By s. 31, *post*, the terms house, warehouse, counting-house, shop, or other building, include any part of a house, where that part is separately occupied for the purposes of any trade, business, or profession; and any such part may, for the purpose of describing the qualification, be described as office, chambers, studio, or by any like term applicable to the case. See the notes to that section, *post*.

It will be observed that the text requires occupation of some building. The alternative qualification under s. 3 of the County Electors Act, 1888, already mentioned (see note (*c*) *supra*), requires occupation only of some land or tenement.

Upon the meaning of these terms reference may be made to the following cases:—

The word "house" means *primâ facie* a dwelling-house. *Surnam* v. *Darley*, 14 M. & W. 181; *Nunn* v. *Denton*, 8 Scott N. R. 794; *Daniel* v. *Coulsting*, *ib.* 949. It probably means a dwelling-house in the above section, contrasted as it is with places of business. It should be observed that the meaning of a word may vary considerably according to the purposes and objects of the Act in which it is used. Consequently, the decisions on the meaning of the word "house" as used in the Metropolis Management and Public Health Acts must not be taken to apply generally. Under these Acts a church has been held not to be a house, while a dissenting chapel is a house. *Angell* v. *Paddington Vestry*, L. R. 3 Q. B. 714; 37 L. J. M. C. 171; 32 J. P. 742; *Caiger* v. *St. Mary, Islington (Vestry of)*, 50 L. J. M. C. 59; 45 J. P. 570; *Wright* v. *Ingle*, 16 Q. B. D. 379; 55 L. J. M. C. 17; 34 W. R. 221. On the other hand, a church has been held to be a house within the meaning of a bye-law prescribing a building-line. *Folkestone (Mayor, etc. of)* v. *Woodward*, L. R. 15 Eq. 159; 42 L. J. Ch. 782. It may be doubted whether these decisions throw any light on the meaning of the word "house" as used in the text.

"Counting-house" includes a solicitor's office. *Re Creek*, 3 B. & S. 459.

Sect. 9 (3)

NOTE.

"Shop." In an Irish case stalls in a market building which were open in front, and fitted with moveable benches, and let to weekly tenants, were held not to be shops. *Lovell* v. *Callaghan*, [1894] 2 Ir. R. 346.

The words "or other building" must be read as signifying other buildings *ejusdem generis*, according to the well-known rule for the construction of statutes. The words are almost precisely similar to those in the Reform Act, 2 Will. 4, c. 45, s. 27. Under that Act a stable built of stone and having a tiled roof was held to be a building. *Whitmore* v. *Bedford*, 5 M. & G. 9; 13 L. J. C. P. 55. Rooms in a factory were let to cotton spinners separately, the rents varying according to the size of the room. The approach to the room was either by a common staircase leading from the entrance to the factory (to which there was a door which was never fastened), or by separate outside staircases, or by doors opening into the yard. Each tenant had his own spinning machine (which was worked by a steam-engine belonging to the landlord), it being part of each contract that the landlord should supply steam power), and also the exclusive use of his room, and the key to the door thereof. It was held that the occupier of each room was the exclusive occupier of a building within the meaning of 2 Will. 4, c. 45, s. 27. *Wright* v. *Stockport (Town Clerk of)*, 5 M. & G. 33; 13 L. J. M. C. 50. A shed stood against a wooden paling, but was not fastened to it. Six posts put into the ground supported a tarpaulin or a tar cloth which formed the roof. One of the sides of the shed was boarded up with boards fastened to the posts by nails. It was held that the shed was a building. *Watson* v. *Cotton*, 5 C. B. 51; 17 L. J. C. P. 68. The tenant of land in a borough erected thereon at his own expense a wooden structure with boarded sides and a thatched roof, and supported by wooden posts let into the ground, and used the same for storing potatoes and other things connected with his business of a market gardener. It was held that the shed was a building. The tenant had erected in like manner on the land a pigstye with a slated roof; but in other respects similar to the structure before mentioned. *Semble*, that this was not a building. But where an electioneering agent, for the purpose of creating a vote, erected a shed made of wood having four boarded sides and a boarded roof and being supported by four posts let into the ground, the court, acting on *Cook* v. *Humber*, 11 C. B (N.S.) 33, held that this was not a building. ERLE, C.J., said that an erection to be a building within the Act ought to be in some degree adapted to be used by man either for residence or for the industry to which the statute relates, and also to have the degree of durability which is included in the idea of a building. *Powell* v. *Farnie*, *Powell* v. *Boraston*, 18 C. B. (N.S.) 168, 175; 34 L. J. C. P. 73: 11 L. T. (N.S.) 736; 11 Jur. (N.S.) 162. A stone building having four walls and a door, used by the tenant for keeping guano and other manures used upon the adjoining land, was held to be a building. So also a stone building roofed, having three sides, and being open in front, with a loft over, used only for milking a cow and keeping a pig, was held a building; and similar erections used only for keeping hay or affording shelter to cattle were held to be buildings. *Morrish* v. *Harris*, L. R. 1 C. P. 156; 35 L. J. C. P. 101.

These cases indicate with tolerable clearness what is a building within the meaning of the text. The decisions on the meaning of the word in other Acts, such as the Public Health Acts, can hardly be cited as authorities upon the construction of the text, having regard to the different objects of the statutes. Some of the more important of these may, however, be enumerated. *Tunstall Turnpike Trustees* v. *Lowndes*, 20 J. P. 374; *R.* v. *Gregory*, 5 B. & Ad. 555; 3 L. J. M. C. 25; *Stevens* v. *Gourlay*, 7 C. B. (N.S.) 99; 1 F. & F. 498; 29 L. J. C. P. 1; 1 L. T. (N.S.) 33; *Poplar Board of Works* v. *Knight*, 13

Sect. 9 (3). E. & E. 408; 28 L. J. M. C. 37; 5 Jur. (N.S.) 196; *Bowes* v. *Lowe*, L. R. 9 Eq. 636; *Thompson* v. *Sunderland Gas Co.*, 2 Ex. D. 429; *Fielding* v. *Rhyl Improvement Commissioners*, 3 C. P. D. 272; *Richardson* v. *Brown*, 49 J. P. 661.

NOTE.

(*g*) The qualifying property need not during the whole qualifying year be the same property or in the same parish. See s. 33, *post*.

(*h*) **Residence.**—It is provided by the 48 Vict. c. 9, that from and after the passing of that Act (1885) a man shall not be disqualified from being enrolled or voting as a burgess at any municipal election in a borough, in respect of the occupation of any house, by reason only that during a part of the qualifying period, not exceeding four months in the whole, he has, by letting or otherwise, permitted such house to be occupied as a furnished dwelling-house by some other person, and during such occupation by another person has not resided in or within seven miles of the borough.

It is also provided by 54 Vict. c. 11, *post*, that a person shall not be disqualified from being registered in the local government register of electors for a county or borough in respect of his occupation of any house, warehouse, counting-house, shop, building, land or tenement, by reason only that during part of the qualifying period not exceeding four months at any one time, he has in the performance of any duty arising from or incidental to any office, service, or employment held or undertaken by him, not resided in or within the required distance from such county or borough.

These enactments must be borne in mind as qualifying some of the cases hereafter cited with reference to continuity of residence.

The term "residence" has always to be interpreted with reference to the purpose of the statute in which it is used. See *Blackwell* v. *England*, 27 L. J. Q. B. 124. As used in the text it has evidently the same meaning as it has in the Parliamentary Registration Acts, and the following cases decided with reference to these Acts and to the corresponding provisions of the Municipal Corporations Act, 1835, will serve to explain the text. A., a freeman of the borough of T., resided with his wife and family and carried on his business of a wine merchant at G., more than seven miles from T. He paid ninepence a week for the use of a bedroom and a dark closet in the house of a friend at T., A. keeping the key of the closet in which he deposited wine samples. He slept in the bedroom twelve times in six months. It was held that he had not resided in T. during the twelve months. *Whithorn* v. *Thomas*, 7 M. & G. 1. It was held in *Powell* v. *Guest*, 18 C. B. (N.S.) 72; 34 L. J. C. P. 69; 11 L. T. (N.S.) 599, that a man had not resided in a borough when he had for a portion of the qualifying period been detained in a gaol situate more than seven miles distant therefrom under a sentence of imprisonment for an assault without the option of paying a fine. A., after carrying on business and residing at Exeter for many years, went to live in London. He continued his business, which compelled him often to visit Exeter, and he kept some offices and rooms there. He was in Exeter about twenty times during the period from Michaelmas to July, staying each time from four to ten days. On these occasions he always transacted his business, slept, and took some of his meals in his own rooms. It was held that the question was one of fact, and depended upon whether there had been such a degree of inhabitance as to be in substance and in common sense a residence, and that there was sufficient evidence to show that A. had a residence in Exeter as well as in London. *R.* v. *Exeter* (*Mayor of*), *Wescomb's case*, L. R. 4 Q. B. 110; 19 L. T. (N.S.) 397. A. occupied a house in Exeter jointly with his partner, and carried on his business there. He had the exclusive use of a furnished bedroom and sitting-room. He lived more than seven miles from Exeter. He visited Exeter every day, except Sundays, to attend to his business, which he always transacted at this house, and sometimes he took his meals and slept there. It was held that this did not make him an inhabitant householder within the meaning of 5 & 6 Will. 4, c. 76, s. 9. *R.* v. *Mayor of Exeter, Dipstale's case*, L. R. 4 Q. B. 114; 19 L. T. (N.S.) 432. Under the corresponding Irish Act it was held that where a man had within the city of Cork a store to which was attached a room in which he had a bed, and occasionally slept and took his meals, he did not reside so as to be an inhabitant householder. *M'Dougal* v. *Creedon*, 7 Ir. Rep. C. L. 165. But it was held that to qualify under 5 & 6 Will. 4, c. 76, s. 9, it was sufficient for a municipal officer to have a *bonâ fide* place of residence, although from fortuitous circumstances he did not sleep there. *R.* v. *Boycott*, 14 L. T. (N.S.) 599. A clergyman claimed to be qualified to vote for a borough in respect of the occupation of a dwelling-house in which he usually resided. He entered into an arrangement with another clergyman by which they agreed to exchange duties and residences for a certain period for the purpose of obtaining relaxation and change of scene. In pursuance of this arrangement the claimant left his house and resided for two months, which included the last month of the qualifying year, at a distance of more than seven miles from the borough, in the house of the other clergyman, who came and resided during the same period in the claimant's house. It was held that there was a break of residence which prevented the claimant from being duly qualified. *Ford* v. *Pye*, L. R. 9 C. P. 269; 43 L. J. C. P. 21. The claimant, a freeman of a borough, was an officer in the army serving with his regiment. When he obtained leave of absence, which he usually did for three months in the year, he used to reside at the house of his mother, within seven miles of the borough, occupying apartments there which were always reserved for his use. He was unmarried, and had no other home than his mother's house. It was held that in the case of an officer subject to the will and pleasure of the Queen, and who was not therefore *sui juris*, there could not be such an intention of returning as to constitute a constructive residence, and consequently that the claimant was not qualified. *Ford* v. *Hart*, L. R. 9 C. P. 273; 43 L. J. C. P. 24; 29 L. T. (N.S.) 685. The incumbent of a benefice was absent from October to June, having obtained a license for non-residence. He arranged with a curate to take his duties and live in the rectory-house. He could not have returned without providing another residence for the curate. It was held that the incumbent had not resided in the house. *Durant* v. *Carter*, L. R. 9 C. P. 261. A. occupied lodgings in a borough in London separately and as sole tenant for the qualifying period. He had also a house in the country where he kept an establishment of servants all the year round. When in London he resided at his lodgings, and had done so at intervals for two months out of the twelve. This was held a sufficient residence to entitle him to the lodger franchise. *Bond* v. *St. George, Hanover Square (Overseers of)*, L. R. 6 C. P. 312. A. being employed to attend upon a gentleman, lodgings were taken for him in the same house as the gentleman, in which he might and did usually sleep, but he was not bound by his agreement to do so. A. had also lodgings in the borough of C., where his wife and children resided, and in which he could sleep at any time, and did in fact sleep at least once a week. It was held that A. resided in C. BOVILL, C.J., said he could not distinguish the case from that of a man who has two houses and lives at each when he pleases. In such a case he would reside at both houses. *Taylor* v. *St. Mary Abbots, Kensington*, L. R. 6 C. P. 311. (The last two of the preceding cases are important as showing that a person may reside in more than one place, and it

Sect. 9 (3). may be anticipated that many cases of this kind will arise in the application of this section to county electors.) For a portion of the qualifying period A. lived and slept with his wife and child in a room in a cottage allotted to the wife's mother by the trustees of a charity, the rules of which prohibited the inmates from allowing any stranger to reside with them. It was held that this was a sufficient residence to satisfy 2 Will. 4, c. 45, s. 33, and that the continuity of residence was not broken by A.'s absenting himself for one night when sent to London upon his employer's business. *Beal* v. *Ford*, 3 C. P. D. 73; 47 L. J. C. P. 56; 37 L. T. (N.S.) 468. During part of the qualifying period a freeholder who had a bedroom kept for his exclusive use in his father's house in Exeter was absent, serving under articles to a solicitor in London. It was held that, being bound by the articles, he could not be deemed to have had either the liberty or intention to return to the room whenever he liked, and therefore had not resided within the city during the required time. *Ford* v. *Drew*, 5 C. P. D. 59; 49 L. J. C. P. 172: 41 L. T. (N.S.) 478. And see on a similar point, *Ford* v. *Barnes*, 16 Q. B. D. 254; 55 L. J. Q. B. 24; 53 L. T. (N.S.) 675; 34 W. R. 75; 50 J. P. 23; *Spittal* v. *Brook*, 18 Q. B. D. 426; 56 L. J. Q. B. 48; 56 L. T. (N.S.) 364; 35 W. R. 520. The appellant had a bedroom kept for his exclusive use in his father's house in Exeter. During the qualifying year he went to London in quest of employment, and having obtained a temporary situation in London remained there, and then returned to his father's house in Exeter. He remained in Exeter three weeks, and then went back to London, and, obtaining employment there, did not return to Exeter during the rest of the qualifying period. It was held that the facts did not show a constructive residence in Exeter during the qualifying period. *Beal* v. *Exeter* (*Town Clerk of*), 20 Q. B. D. 300; 57 L. J. Q. B. 128; 58 L. T. (N.S.) 407; 36 W. R. 507; 52 J. P. 501; and see *Ward* v. *Mackonochie*, 7 T. L. R. 536; *Sim* v. *Palt*, 20 Ct. of Sess. Cas. 84; *Barlow* v. *Smith*, 9 T. L. R. 57; *Rowland* v. *Pritchard*, 62 L. J. Q. B. 319; 68 L. T. (N.S.) 586; 57 J. P. 759; 9 T. L. R. 279.

NOTE.

As to the effect of imprisonment as constituting a break in the residence necessary to qualify under this section, see *Donnelly* v. *Graham*, 24 L. R. Ir. 127; *McCurran* v. *Chambers*, 28 L. R. Ir. 294; *Charlton* v. *Morris* [1895] 2 Ir. R. 541; *Holland* v. *Hogan*, *ibid*, 551; *Criglington* v. *Gallagher*, 26 L. R. Ir. 134; as to militiamen required to be in camp, *Donoghue* v. *Brook*, 57 L. J. Q. B. 122; 38 L. T. (N.S.) 411; as to sailors under contract of service, see *Hasson* v. *Chambers*, 24 L. R. Ir. 139; *Dutty* v. *Chambers*, 26 L. R. Ir. 100.

As to residence in cases of succession by marriage, descent, etc., see s. 33, *post*.

The seven miles must be measured in a straight line in a horizontal plane, and may be determined by the Ordnance survey map. See s. 231, *post*. It should be mentioned that by s. 77 of the Local Government Act, 1888, *ante*, p. 151, a person who is entitled to be registered as a county elector in respect of any qualification in the administrative county in London in all respects except that of residence, and is resident beyond seven miles but within fifteen miles of the county, shall be entitled to be registered as a county elector.

(*i*) **Rated.**—It is sufficient if it can be shown that a person was intended to be rated, though there may be a mistake in his name as entered in the rate. *R.* v. *Gregory*, 17 Jur. 439.

The 32 & 33 Vict. c. 41, s. 19, provides that the overseers in making out the poor rate shall in every case, whether the rate is collected from the owner or occupier, or the owner is liable to the payment of the rate instead of the occupier, enter in the occupiers' column of the rate book the name of every occupier of every rateable hereditament, and such occupier shall be deemed to be duly rated for any qualification or franchise depending upon rating; and it is further provided that any occupier whose name has been omitted, shall, notwithstanding such omission, and that no claim to be rated has been made by him, be entitled to every qualification and franchise depending upon rating, in the same manner as if his name had not been so omitted. This section applies generally to every case in which the owner is rated and not the occupier, without regard to the value of the premises. See *Smith* v. *Seghill (Overseers of)*, L. R. 10 Q. B. 422; 44 L. J. M. C. 114; 32 L. T. (N.S.) 859; 23 W. R. 745; 40 J. P. 228; *Barton* v. *Birmingham (Town Clerk of)*, 48 L. J. C. P. 87; 39 L. T. (N.S.) 352; 43 J. P. 24. As to the claim of an occupier to be rated in other cases, see s. 32, *post.*

Observe that this clause refers only to the poor rate, while the next refers to poor rates and borough rates, or, as applied to county electors, county rates.

As to rating in cases of succession by descent, marriage, etc., see s. 33, *post.*

In an Irish case where the qualifying premises had not been rated at all during a part of the qualifying period, the occupier was, nevertheless, held entitled to the franchise. *Bell* v. *Black*, 22 L. R. Ir. 591; and see *Criglington* v. *Anderson*, 26 L. R. Ir. 131; see, however, *Wade* v. *Perkins*, 1 Fox 338, and *Palmer* v. *Wade*, [1894] 1 Q. B. 268; 70 L. T. (N.S.) 407; 58 J. P. 511; from which it would appear that if the premises though rateable have been omitted from the rate the occupier is not entitled to the franchise.

(*k*) **Payment of rates.**—The 32 & 33 Vict. c. 41, s. 7, provides that every payment of a rate by the occupier, notwithstanding the amount thereof may be deducted from his rent as therein provided, and every payment of a rate by the owner, whether he is himself rated instead of the occupier or has agreed with the occupier or with the overseers to pay such rate, and notwithstanding any allowance or deduction which the overseers are empowered to make from the rate, shall be deemed a payment of the full rate by the occupier for the purpose of every qualification or franchise which, as regards rating, depends upon the payment of the poor rate. It is probable, though it has not as yet been expressly decided, that this section applies to every case when the rates are paid by the owner. See *Moger* v. *Escott*, L. R. 7 C. P. 163; 41 L. J. C. P. 86; 26 L. T. (N.S.) 99; 20 W. R. 368; 36 J. P. 247; *Abel* v. *Lee*, L. R. 6 C. P. 365; 40 L. J. C. P. 154; 23 L. T. (N.S.) 844; 19 W. R. 625; *Cross* v. *Alsop*, L. R. 6 C. P. 315; 40 L. J. C. P. 154; 23 L. T. (N.S.) 844; 19 W. R. 625; *Cross* v. *Alsop*, L. R. 6 C. P. 315; 40 L. J. C. P. 53; 23 L. T. (N.S.) 589; 19 W. R. 131; 35 J. P. 153; the judgment of LUSH, J., in *Smith* v. *Seghill (Overseers of)*, *ante.*

On the subject of the payment of rates by a person other than the owner, the following cases may be referred to:—The payment must be by the party's own act; it is not sufficient that another person without his authority pays them for him. *R.* v. *Bridgnorth*, 10 A. & E. 66. Where one building in which there were several occupiers was rated as a whole, and it was part of the agreement with the landlord that he should pay the rates, the rent being higher in consideration of such payment, the landlord and the tenants were jointly rated, and it was held that a payment by any of the persons so jointly rated would be a payment by each of them. *Wright* v. *Stockport (Town Clerk of)*, 5 M. & G. 33; 13 L. J. C. P. 50; 7 Jur. 1112. An officer in a royal dockyard had the exclusive use of a house in the dockyard in part remuneration for his services. The rates were paid by the Paymaster-General. It was held that this was a sufficient payment by A., as he was rated and liable to pay the rates, and the payment was on his account in part remuneration for his

Sect. 9 (3). services. *Hughes* v. *Chatham (Overseers of)*, 5 M. & G. 54; 13 L. J. C. P. 14; 7 Jur. 1136.

NOTE.

The words "borough rates" will, in a county, mean "county rates." In a borough they mean only borough rates under the Act, not a rate under a local Act for paving and lighting the borough. *R.* v. *Lichfield (Mayor of)*, 2 Q. B. 693. A. came into the occupation of the qualifying property in August. A poor rate had been made in the preceding April, and another was made in the September following. A. had paid the last-mentioned rate; but no demand had been made upon him for, nor had he paid or tendered, his proportion of the April rate, though it had not been paid by the outgoing tenant whose name appeared upon that rate. It was held that A. had paid all poor rates which had become payable from him, the liability to pay the proportion of the April rate being subject to the contingency of the outgoing tenant having made default, and of the overseers demanding his proportion from A. *Flatcher* v. *Boodle*, 18 C. B. (N.S.) 152. But an occupier is not entitled to be enrolled if the rates are payable by the owner and have not been paid, though no demand has been made on him as required by the statute. See *Clarke* v. *Buchanan*, 20 L. R. Ir. 244.

As to the payment of rates payable by instalments, see s. 33, *post*.

(*l*) **Alien.**—Persons born in Hanover before the Queen's accession and not naturalised are, though resident in the United Kingdom, aliens. *Stepney Election Petition*, 17 Q. B. D. 54; 55 L. J. Q. B. 331; 54 L. T. (N.S.) 684; 34 W. R. 547.

(*m*) **Alms.** –The word "alms" applies only to such as are parochial. It does not apply to moneys distributed annually from the income of a public charitable institution established by an individual for the use and benefit of the poor housekeepers of a borough not receiving parochial relief from any parish therein. *R.* v. *Lichfield (Mayor of)*, 2 Q. B. 693. Parochial relief given to a man's her is not relief to the man himself within the meaning of the above section. *R.* v. *Ireland*, L. R. 3 Q. B. 130; 37 L. J. Q. B. 73; 17 L. T. (N.S.) 466; 6 W. R. 358; 32 J. P. 726; and see *Doherty* v. *Chambers*, 22 L. R. Ir. 434. But relief to a man's wife or to any of his children under sixteen is relief to himself by virtue of 4 & 5 Will. 4, c. 76, s. 56. The Medical Relief Disqualification Removal Act, 1885 (48 & 49 Vict. c. 46), provides that when a person has received for himself or for any member of his family any "medical or surgical assistance or any medicine at the expense of any poor rate, such person shall not by reason thereof be deprived of any right to be registered, or to vote as a voter, at any election to certain offices, including the office of member of a local board." The term "medical and surgical assistance" is defined to mean all medical and surgical attendance, and all matters and things supplied by or on the recommendation of the medical officer having authority to give such attendance and recommendation at the expense of any poor rate. Several cases have been decided upon the provisions of 2 Will. 4, c. 45, s. 36. The appellant having applied to the guardians for work, was employed by them, by way of relief, in breaking stones, and paid out of the parochial funds, the amount paid to him being much greater than the value of his work to the guardians. It was held that he had received "parochial relief or other alms" within 2 Will. 4, c. 26, so as to disqualify him from voting. *Magarrill* v. *Whitehaven (Overseers of)*, 16 Q. B. D. 242; 55 L. J. Q. B. 38; 53 L T. (N.S.) 667; 34 W. R. 279; 40 J. P. 743. By the provisions of a charity, regulated by a scheme of the Charity Commissioners, a certain number of the poor inhabitants of a borough, who had not been for two years in receipt of parish relief, were received into an almshouse where certain weekly payments and other benefits were bestowed on them. They were liable to be removed for misconduct and other causes. It was held (following *Harrison* v. *Carter*, 2 C. P. D. 26; 46 L. J. C. P. 27; 35 L. T. (N.S.) 511; 25 W. R. 182) that they were disqualified from voting, having received alms within 2 Will. 4, c. 45, s. 36. *Baker* v. *Monmouth (Town Clerk of)*, 53 L. T. (N.S.) 668; 34 W. R. 64; 49 J. P. 776. The wife of the appellant, being near her confinement, applied to the relieving officer of the union for an order for the attendance of a medical man. The guardians authorized the relieving officer to give her an order for such attendance, but she was, in fact, attended during her confinement by an uncertificated midwife, who was sent to her and paid by the relieving officer. It was held that the relief afforded to his wife was "medical assistance" within 48 & 49 Vict. c. 46, s. 2, and that the appellant was not disqualified from being registered as a voter. *Honeybone* v. *Hambridge*, 18 Q. B. D. 418; 56 L. J. Q. B. 46; 51 J. P. 103.

The claimants during the qualifying period occupied almshouses in a borough, and received out of a charitable fund for the sustenance of the inmates allowances of 6*s.* a week. The charity was regulated by an Act of Parliament, which provided that the inmates of the almshouses were to be persons who from age, ill-health, accident, or infirmity, should be unable to maintain themselves. It was held that the facts showed a receipt of alms, which by the law of Parliament disqualified from voting under 2 & 3 Will. 4, c. 45, s. 36. *Edwards* v. *Lloyd*, 20 Q. B. D. 302; 57 L. J. Q. B. 121; 58 L. T. (N.S.) 409; 52 J. P. 519; and see *Dix* v. *Kent*, 63 L. T. (N.S.) 641; 39 W. R. 173; 55 J. P. 213; 7 T. L. R. 46.

On the other hand, the inmates of a licensed victuallers, asylum who were only eligible as inmates by reason of their having contributed to the funds of the institution were held not to be disqualified on being in receipt of alms though the institution was largely supported by private benevolence. *Daniels* v. *Allard*, 1 Fox, 70; W. N. (1887), 222.

It is provided by s. 33, *post*, that a person shall not be disentitled to be enrolled as a burgess by reason only (a) that he has received medical or surgical assistance from the trustees of the municipal charities, or has been removed, by order of a justice, to a hospital or place for reception of the sick, at the cost of any local authority, or (b) that his child has been admitted to and taught in any public or endowed school.

(*n*) Constables were formerly disentitled under various Acts of Parliament from voting at elections; their disabilities have now been removed by 50 & 51 Vict. c. 9 and 56 Vict. c. 6.

Persons may be "disentitled" within the meaning of the text under the Corrupt Practices Acts (46 & 47 Vict. c. 51), ss. 6, 10; 47 & 48 Vict. c. 70, ss. 2, 7; the Felony Act (33 & 34 Vict. c. 23), s. 2; the Public Bodies Corrupt Practices Act, 1889 (52 & 53 Vict. c. 69), s. 3, and perhaps under some other statutes.

Council: Mayor, Aldermen, and Councillors.

Constitution of council.

10.—(1.) The municipal corporation of a borough shall be capable of acting by the council of the borough, and the council shall exercise all powers vested in the corporation by this Act or otherwise.

(2.) The council shall consist of the mayor, aldermen, and councillors.

It is provided by the Local Government Act, s. 1, *ante*, p. 1, that a council shall be established in every county, and shall consist of the chairman, aldermen, and councillors. And, by s. 2, the council of a county and the

Sect. 10 (2)

NOTE.

members thereof shall be constituted and elected and conduct their proceedings in like manner, and be in the like position in all respects, as the council of a borough divided into wards, subject to various modifications which are indicated throughout this volume. The county council is incorporated by s. 79 of the Local Government Act, *ante*, p. 153.

Qualification of councillors

11.—(1.) The councillors shall be fit persons elected by the burgesses.

(2.) (*a*) A person shall not be qualified to be elected or to be a councillor, unless he—

(a) is enrolled and entitled to be enrolled as a burgess (*b*) ; or

(b) being entitled to be so enrolled in all respects except that of residence, is resident beyond seven miles, but within fifteen miles of the borough, and is entered in the separate non-resident list directed by this Act to be made (*c*) ; and

(c) in either of those cases, is seised or possessed of real or personal property, or both, to the value or amount, in the case of a borough having four or more wards (*d*), of one thousand pounds, and in the case of any other borough, of five hundred pounds, or is rated to the poor rate in the borough, in the case of a borough having four or more wards, on the annual value (*e*) of thirty pounds, and in the case of any other borough of fifteen pounds.

(3.) Provided, that every person shall be qualified to be elected and to be a councillor, who is, at the time of election, qualified to elect to the office of councillor ; which last mentioned qualification for being elected shall be alternative for and shall not repeal or take away any other qualification (*f*).

(4.) But if a person qualified under the last foregoing proviso ceases for six months to reside in the borough, he shall cease to be qualified under that proviso, and his office shall become vacant, unless he was at the time of his election and continues to be qualified in some other manner.

(*a*) This section contains three qualifications of a councillor. These are :—

(1.) Enrolment as a burgess and possession of the property qualification.

(2.) Enrolment in the non-resident list and possession of the property qualification.

(3.) The right to elect to the office of councillor without property qualification, but subject to this modification, that the office shall become vacant after six months' non-residence.

To these qualifications must be added certain others provided by the Local Government Act, s. 2, *ante*, p. 2.

(4.) Being a peer owning property in the county.

(5.) Registration as a parliamentary voter in respect of the ownership of property.

(*b*) The right of a person to be enrolled as a burgess depends upon s. 9, as amended by the County Electors Act, 1888. See the notes to that section, *ante*.

The mere fact of enrolment on the burgess roll is not sufficient. The candidate must also be entitled to be enrolled. If a person is on the roll but not entitled to be enrolled, he is not qualified to be a councillor, but in that case he is not liable to penalties under s. 41 (2), *post*. See *Middleton* v. *Simpson*, 5 C. P. D. 183 ; 49 L. J. C. P. 312 ; 28 W. R. 629 ; 44 J. P. 251.

On the trial of a petition against the election of the respondent to the office of town councillor, it was proved that two years before the election the respondent, with his wife, family, and furniture, moved into an inn kept by his mother, and a verbal agreement was entered into, by which the mother was to retire from the business, the respondent was to take it over, and the mother was to continue to reside in the house and have her board, lodging, and clothing free of charge. The respondent took over the entire management of the inn, but there was no assignment of the lease or transfer of the licence to the respondent, and the excise licences were still taken out in the mother's name, which remained alone over the door. The respondent requested that his name might be inserted in the rate book as joint occupier, but this was not done. The demand notes and receipts for rates during the twelve months preceding July 15th next before the election were made out in the mother's name, but the respondent paid the rates out of the profits of the inn. Before the publication of the lists next preceding the election, the respondent's name was inserted upon the burgess roll as joint occupier, his mother's name still remaining on the roll as joint occupier. Held, that the respondent was qualified by occupation and payment of rates, and was, therefore, "entitled to be enrolled as a burgess" within the meaning of the Municipal Corporations Act, 1882, s. 11, sub-s. (2) (a), and was duly elected. *Unwin* v. *McMullen*, [1891] 1 Q. B. 694 ; 60 L. J. Q. B. 400 ; 39 W. R. 712 ; 55 J. P. 582 ; 7 T. L. R. 450.

It is sufficient to entitle a person to be nominated for the office of councillor that, if otherwise duly qualified, he is enrolled in the burgess roll at the time of the election, though his name may not be upon the burgess roll which was in force at the time of his nomination. *Budge* v. *Andrews*, 3 C. P. D. 510 ; 47 L. J. C. P. 586 ; 39 L. T. (N.S.) 166.

(*c*) The separate non-resident list is made out under s. 49, *post*. In a borough, in order that a person may be entitled to be placed on that list, he must be duly qualified to be a burgess in all respects save that of residence, and he must reside within fifteen miles of the borough.

A similar list is to be made for a county. It is provided by the Local Government Act, s. 76, sub-s. (12), *ante*, that the above section shall include, for the purposes of that Act, all persons entered in such separate list for any municipal borough by reason of occupation of property in the borough, and all persons entered in such separate list for any part of a county not in a municipal borough by reason of the occupation of property in that part.

By the County Electors Act, 1888, s. 12, a list of persons occupying property in a county and residing within fifteen miles, but more than seven miles from the county, shall be made out in accordance with s. 49 of the Municipal Corporations Act, 1882. But by the Local Government Act, 1888, s. 76, sub-s. (6), it is provided that nothing in that section shall apply to any person occupying property within a borough. See the several sections and the notes to them in this work.

(*d*) In applying this section to county electors this phrase must be read, "in the case of a county having four or more electoral divisions." See the Local Government Act, s. 2, *ante*, p. 3.

(*e*) This means rateable value. *Baker* v. *Marsh*, 4 E. & B. 144 ; 24 L. J. Q. B. 1 ; 1 Jur. (N.S.) 44 ; 3 W. R. 13 ; 19 J. P. 117. The poor rate in the

Sect. 11 (4). case of county electors may, apparently, be the poor rate of any parish in the county. But the real or personal estate need not be within the county.

NOTE.

(*f*) The words "qualified to elect" in this proviso are not equivalent to "entitled to vote." Therefore a person who, though not qualified to be a burgess, had been enrolled on the burgess roll, and was, therefore, entitled to vote under s. 51, *post*, was not qualified to be a councillor under this proviso. *Flintham* v. *Roxburgh*, 17 Q. B. D. 44; 55 L. J. Q. B. 472; 54 L. T. (N.S.) 797; 34 W. R. 543; 50 J. P. 311. So also it was held that a woman was not qualified to be a county councillor under this sub-section. *Beresford-Hope* v. *Sandhurst*, 23 Q. B. D. 79; 58 L. J. Q. B. 316; 61 L. T. (N.S.) 150; 37 W. R. 548; 53 J. P. 805; *De Souza* v. *Cobden*, [1891] 1 Q. B. 687; 60 L. J. Q. B. 533; 65 L. T. (N.S.) 130; 39 W. R. 454; 55 J. P. 565; 7 T. L. R. 441.

Note that this qualification need only exist at the time of election. The subsequent loss of the qualification to elect will not affect the right to sit and act as councillor so long as the councillor resides in the county as required by the next sub-section.

Disqualifications for being councillor.

12.—(1.) A person shall be disqualified (*a*) for being elected and for being a councillor, if and while he—

(a.) Is an elective auditor (*b*) or a revising assessor (*c*), or holds any office or place of profit, other than that of mayor or sheriff, in the gift or disposal of the council (*d*); or

(b.) Is in holy orders, or the regular minister of a dissenting congregation (*e*); or

(c.) Has directly or indirectly, by himself or his partner, any share or interest in any contract or employment with, by, or on behalf of the council (*f*):

(2.) But a person shall not be so disqualified, or be deemed to have any share or interest in such a contract or employment, by reason only of his having any share or interest in—

(a.) Any lease, sale, or purchase of land, or any agreement for the same (*g*); or

(b.) Any agreement for the loan of money, or any security for the payment of money only (*h*); or

(c.) Any newspaper in which any advertisement relating to the affairs of the borough or council is inserted; or

(d.) Any company which contracts with the council for lighting or supplying with water or insuring against fire any part of the borough (*i*); or

(e.) Any railway company, or any company incorporated by Act of Parliament or Royal Charter, or under the Companies Act, 1862.

25 & 26 Vict. c. 89.

(*a*) These are not the only disqualifications for being councillor. Other disqualifications arise under the Corrupt Practices Acts (46 & 47 Vict. c. 51), ss. 6, 10; 47 & 48 Vict. c. 70, ss. 2, 7; the Felony Act (33 & 34 Vict. c. 23), s. 2; the Bankruptcy Act (46 & 47 Vict. c. 52), s. 32, as amended by the Bankruptcy Act, 1890 (53 & 54 Vict. c. 71), s. 9; the Public Bodies (Corrupt Practices) Act, 1889 (52 & 53 Vict. c. 69), s. 2. A woman cannot be elected.

See s. 63, *post*, and the notes thereto. A county coroner may not be a member of the council of his county. See the Local Government Act, s. 5, *ante*, p. 15.

By the Army Act, 1881 (44 & 45 Vict. c. 58), s. 146, officers of the regular forces were disqualified for holding office in any municipal corporation; but that section is to be read as containing the proviso "that nothing in this section shall disqualify any officer for election to or being a member of a county council." Army (Annual) Act, 1891 (54 Vict. c. 5), s. 8.

(*b*) See s. 25, *post*.

(*c*) Revising assessors will no longer be elected. See s. 29, *post*, and the County Electors Act, 1888, s. 4.

(*d*) This provision disqualifies the clerk, treasurer, and other officers of the council. But it is submitted that it does not disqualify the mayor's auditor, who must, under s. 25, be a member of the council, though he may receive remuneration for his services under this Act, or under the Public Health Act, 1875, s. 246.

By the County Councils (Elections) Act, 1891 (54 & 55 Vict. c. 68), s. 6, *post*, it is declared that a person shall not be disqualified nor be deemed ever to have been disqualified under s. 12 of the Municipal Corporations Act for being a member of a county council by reason only of his being appointed returning officer by that council, except where he has directly or indirectly by himself or his partner received any profit or remuneration in respect of such appointment.

(*e*) This will not apply to county councillors. See the Local Government Act, s. 2, *ante*, p. 2. It will still apply to borough councillors. It has been held that a person appointed to officiate occasionally or temporarily to a dissenting congregation is not disqualified. *R.* v. *Oldham*, L. R. 4 Q. B. 290; 38 L. J. Q. B. 125.

(*f*) The following cases decided with reference to the Act of 1835, and to similar provisions in other Acts, may be referred to as illustrating the meaning of the text:—

A trustee of a turnpike road let his horse and cart at a certain sum to a contractor for works on a road, to be used in the performance of the works. It was held that he was liable to a penalty as being interested in a contract with the turnpike trustees. *Towsey* v. *White*, 5 B. & C. 125.

A contract entered into with a person as trustee for a councillor is within the provision in the text. *Simpson* v. *Ready*, 12 M. & W. 736; 13 L. J. Ex. 193.

The text applies to a contract with the council under which a councillor has been employed and has acted, though the contract is one which should be sealed, and it is not sealed. Where such a contract arises, the disqualification arises *de die in diem*. *R.* v. *Francis*, 18 Q. B. 526; 21 L. J. Q. B. 304; 16 Jur. 1046.

An alderman of a borough sold some iron to a party who had contracted to supply the corporation with iron railings, and who purchased the iron for the purpose of performing his contract. It was held that the alderman had not an interest in a contract with the council. *Le Feuvre* v. *Lankester*, 3 E. & B. 530; 23 L. J. Q. B. 254; 18 Jur. 894; 18 J. P. 198; but see *Tomkins* v. *Joliffe*, *infra*.

A single bargain—as if the council bought a brush in a shop—would not disqualify the seller, though the price had not been paid. *Per* ALDERSON and BRAMWELL, BB., in *Woolley* v. *Kay*, 1 H. R. 307; 25 L. J. Ex. 351; 20 J. P. 776; but see *Lewis* v. *Carr*, *infra*.

An invoice addressed to town commissioners for several separate quantities of lime supplied at different times during four months was held to be sufficient

Sect. 12 (2).

NOTE.

evidence of interest in a contract with the commissioners. *Nicholson* v. *Field*, 7 H. & N. 810; 31 L. J. Ex. 233; 10 W. R. 304.

A person who had entered into a contract with the Corporation of Dublin was held disqualified to be elected a member of that corporation, though he had before the election, but without the privity of the corporation, assigned his contract to a third person. *R.* v. *Franklin*, 6 Ir. Rep. C. L. 239.

The disqualification applies only during the continuance of the contract, so that a councillor does not, by becoming interested in a contract, cease to be qualified or become disqualified within the meaning of s. 41, so as to incur penalties for acting after the termination of the contract. *Lewis* v. *Carr*, 1 Ex. D. 484; 46 L. J. Ex. 314; 36 L. T. (N.S.) 44; 24 W. R. 940.

Where a member of a local board received payments from the board for work done for the surveyor of the board, the work consisting of the use of men and horses at intervals during two years, it was held that he was interested in a contract with the board. *Fletcher* v. *Hudson*, 7 Q. B. D. 611; 51 L. J. Q. B. 48; 46 L. T. (N.S.) 125; 30 W. R. 349; 46 J. P. 372.

The brother of the defendant entered into a contract with a metropolitan vestry, and in order to enable him to carry it out borrowed money of the defendant, who by way of security took an assignment of the contract. Afterwards the defendant was elected a member of the vestry. It was held that he was interested in a contract with the vestry. *Hunnings* v. *Williamson*, 11 Q. B. D. 533; 52 L. J. Q. B. 416; 49 L. T. (N.S.) 361; 32 W. R. 267; 48 J. P. 132.

C. contracted with a local board to make certain alterations to gas fittings in a town hall. C. employed the defendant, who was a member of the board and a builder, to erect scaffolding for the purpose of enabling him to effect the alterations. It was held by FIELD, J., that the defendant was interested in a contract with the board. *Tomkins* v. *Joliffe*, 51 J. P. 247.

By the terms of contracts entered into with a local authority, the surveyor was to receive from the contractors, in respect of bills of quantities to be prepared by him, percentages on the amounts he should certify to be due to such contractors by the local authority: it was held that the surveyor was interested or concerned in the contracts. And where he was employed, apart from his ordinary duties, to superintend the construction of certain drainage works as engineer of the local authority, who were to remunerate him by a percentage on the outlay, it was held that he was interested in the contract for the work. *Whiteley* v. *Barley*, 21 Q. B. D. 154; 54 L. J. Q. B. 643; 36 W. R. 823; 52 J. P. 595.

The defendant, a member of a local board, was employed by persons with whom the board had contracted for the performance of certain works on the premises and the board to do portions of the works so contracted for. It was held that the defendant had been concerned in contracts entered into by the board within the meaning of the above rule. LOPES, L.J., said: "I express no opinion with regard to such very trifling matters as were suggested in the argument, *e.g.*, the purchase of a paint brush or a few nails from a member of the board. It may be that the maxim *de minimis non curat lex* would be applicable in such cases." *Nutton* v. *Wilson*, 22 Q. B. D. 744; 58 L. J. Q. B. 443; 37 W. R. 522; 53 J. P. 644; 5 T. L. R. 439. But see as to similar trifling matters, *Nell* v. *Longbottom*, *infra*. A. and his partner, S., were under contract and bound to repair roads and do other works for a borough council. In October, A. dissolved the partnership and made over the contracts to S. In November, A. was elected councillor. It was held that A. was disqualified on the ground that he remained liable under his contracts. The petitioner had published a notice before the election to the effect that A.

Sect. 12 (2).

NOTE.

was disqualified by reason of the contracts with the council, and the question was publicly discussed in the ward. *Held*, that votes given for A., whose disqualification was notorious, were thrown away, and that the petitioner who had the next highest number of votes must be declared elected. *Cox* v. *Ambrose*, 55 J. P. 23; 60 L. J. Q. B. 114; 7 T. L. R. 59.

The interest in the contract continues so long as the contract itself exists. This may be important in considering whether an action for penalties has been brought in time. See *Todd* v. *Robinson*, 14 Q. B. D. 739; 54 L. J. Q. B. 47; 52 L. T. (N.S.) 120; 49 J. P. 278. As to the liability of a member for contracts entered into without his knowledge or against his orders, see *Miles* v. *McIlwraith*, 8 App. Cas. 120; 31 W. R. 591; 48 L. T. (N.S.) 689; 52 L. J. M. C. 17.

It appears from the decision in *Mellis* v. *Shirley Local Board*, 16 Q. B. D. 446; 55 L. J. Q. B. 143; 53 L. T. (N.S.) 810; 34 W. R. 187; 50 J. P. 214, that a contract between a local board and a member is altogether void and cannot be enforced. But the case does not decide whether the contract would be void if the member became interested in it after it had been made. COTTON, L.J., seemed to be of opinion that it would not, though the member would be prohibited from taking any benefit under it.

(*g*) Under the Public Health Act, 1875, it has been held that a member of a local board is not disqualified by the lease to him of a sewage farm containing covenants on the part of the board to supply, and on his part to use, the sewage of the district. *R.* v. *Gaskarth*, 5 Q. B. D. 321; 49 L. J. Q. B. 409; 42 L. T. (N.S.) 688; 28 W. R. 596; 44 J. P. 507. The letting of a building for the purposes of a polling station for one day is within the exception in the text. *Nell* v. *Longbottom*, [1894] 1 Q. B. 767; 63 L. J. Q. B. 490; 70 L. T. (N.S.) 499.

The text would probably cover such cases as the letting of rooms or offices to the council. See *Burgess* v. *Clark*, 14 Q. B. D. 735; 33 W. R. 269; 59 J. P. 388.

(*h*) L. contracted with certain commissioners to supply a town with water. This contract not having been fully carried out, he gave it up by deed to the commissioners, they agreeing to pay him a certain balance if they abandoned the works or completed them, and obtained a specific quantity of water. The deed contained releases by L., and covenants by L., not to molest the commissioners, etc. The works remained incomplete, but not abandoned. It was held that the deed was only a security for a sum of money. *Le Feuvre* v. *Lankester*, *supra*.

(*i*) But for this provision a councillor could not have held shares in a gas or water company contracting with the council. See *Todd* v. *Robinson*, 14 Q. B. D. 739; 54 L. J. Q. B. 47; 52 L. T. (N.S.) 120; 49 J. P. 278.

Another exception to the disqualification by interest in a contract is created by the Highways and Bridges Act, 1891 (54 & 55 Vict. c. 63), s. 5, *post*, which provides that no person shall be disqualified for being elected or for being a member of a county council by reason only of his having any share or interest in any contract with such county council for the supply from land of which he is owner or occupier of stone, gravel, or other material for making or repairing highways or bridges. Provided always that no such share or interest in any contract shall exceed the amount of 50*l.* in any one year.

Term of office and rotation of councillors.

13.—(1.) The term of office of a councillor shall be three years.

(2.) On the ordinary day of election of councillors in every year one-third of the whole number of councillors for the borough or

Sect. 13 (2). NOTE.

for the ward, as the case may be, shall go out of office, and their places shall be filled by election.

(3.) The third to go out shall be the councillors who have been longest in office without re-election.

It is provided by the Local Government Act, s. 2, *ante*, p. 3, that county councillors shall be elected for a term of three years, and shall then retire together, and their places shall be filled by a new election. The above section does not, therefore, apply to county councillors.

Number, term of office, and rotation of aldermen.

14.—(1.) The aldermen shall be fit persons elected by the council (*a*).

(2.) The number of aldermen shall be one-third of the number of councillors (*b*).

(3.) A person shall not be qualified to be elected or to be an alderman unless he is a councillor or qualified to be a councillor.

(4.) If a councillor is elected to, and accepts, the office of alderman he vacates his office of councillor.

(5.) The term of office of an alderman shall be six years.

(6.) On the ordinary day of election of aldermen in every third year one-half of the whole number of aldermen, shall go out of office, and their places shall be filled by election (*c*).

(7.) The half to go out shall be those who have been aldermen for the longest time without re-election.

(*a*) In a county council the aldermen are to be called county aldermen.

(*b*) In London the number is to be one-sixth. See the Local Government Act, s. 40, sub-s. (5), *ante*, p. 89.

(*c*) As to the election of aldermen, see s. 60, *post*. As to the election of an alderman to fill a casual vacancy, see s. 40, *post*. The ordinary day of election of aldermen in a borough is November 9th; but in a county it is March 16th, or such other day within ten days after the ordinary day of retirement of county councillors (*viz.* March 8th), as the county council may from time to time fix for their county. Local Government (Election) Act (54 & 55 Vict. c. 68), s. 1 (3), *post*.

It was decided in *R.* v. *Cooks*, 3 E. & B. 251; 23 L. J. Q. B. 134, that an alderman was not qualified to be elected councillor; some doubt was thrown upon this by the Court of Appeal in *R.* v. *Bangor* (*Mayor, etc., of*), 18 Q. B. D. 349, but no opinion was expressed on the point by the House of Lords in the same case. *Pritchard* v. *Bangor* (*Mayor, etc., of*), 13 App. Cas. 241; 57 L. J. Q. B. 313; 58 L. T. (N.S.) 502; 37 W. R. 103; 52 J. P. 564.

Qualification, term of office, salary, procedure and powers of mayor.

15.—(1.) The mayor shall be a fit person elected by the council from among the aldermen or councillors or persons qualified to be such.

(2.) An outgoing alderman is eligible.

(3.) The term of office of the mayor shall be one year, but he shall continue in office until his successor has accepted office and made and subscribed the required declaration.

(4.) He may receive such remuneration as the council think reasonable.

(5.) He shall, subject to the provisions of this Act respecting justices, have precedence in all places in the borough. Sect. 15 (5).

(6.) The mayor of a borough named in the schedules to the Municipal Corporations Act, 1835, shall be capable in law to do and suffer all acts which the chief officer of the borough might at the passing of that Act lawfully do or suffer, as far as the same were not altered or annulled by that Act, or have not been altered or annulled by any subsequent Act.

In a county council the chairman may be elected from within or without the council. His term of office is one year, and apparently the text requires him to remain in office until his successor has made the declaration. (See Sched. 8, *post.*) He is a justice by virtue of his office. See the Local Government Act, s. 2 (5), *ante*, p. 4.

As to the remuneration of the mayor or the chairman of a county council, see *Att.-Gen.* v. *Blackburn* (*Corporation of*), 57 L. T. (N.S.) 385. In that case a corporation voted a sum of money to the mayor by way of remuneration, at the same time resolving that the mayor should be requested to take such steps as he might deem proper for the due celebration of Her Majesty's Jubilee. Some of the burgesses moved to restrain the corporation from applying any part of the borough fund for this purpose, but it was held that the provisions of the Act had not been contravened, and an interlocutory injunction was refused.

But it was held that a corporation were not entitled to make a colourable addition to the remuneration of the mayor merely that the addition might be applied in indirectly making payments such as subsidies to a college which would not be justified if made directly. *Att.-Gen.* v. *Cardiff* (*Mayor, etc., of*), [1894] 2 Ch. 337 ; 63 L. J. Ch. 557 ; 70 L. T. (N.S.) 591 ; 10 T. L. R. 420.

Sub-section (5) is not to apply to the chairman of a county council. See the Local Government Act, s. 75, sub-s. (16) (*b*), *ante*, p. 145.

Sub-section (6) of the above section has no application to the chairman of a county council.

Power of mayor to appoint deputy.

16.—(1.) The mayor may from time to time appoint an alderman or councillor to act as deputy mayor during the illness or absence of the mayor.

(2.) The appointment shall be signified to the council in writing and be recorded in their minutes.

(3.) A deputy mayor may, while acting as such, do all acts which the mayor as such might do, except that he shall not take the chair at a meeting of the council unless specially appointed by the meeting to do so, and shall not, unless he is a justice, act as a justice, or in any judicial capacity.

This section does not apply to county councils, having regard to the Local Government Act, s. 75, sub-s. (16) (*b*). Section 2 (6) of that Act, *ante*, p. 4, enables the council to appoint a vice-chairman. See also s. 88 of that Act as to the deputy chairman in London.

Sect. 17 (1).

Officers of Council.

The town clerk and deputy.

17.—(1.) The council shall from time to time appoint a fit person, not a member of the council, to be the town clerk of the borough.

(2.) The town clerk shall hold office during the pleasure of the council.

(3.) He shall have the charge and custody of, and be responsible for, the charters, deeds, records, and documents of the borough, and they shall be kept as the council direct.

(4.) A vacancy in the office shall be filled within twenty-one days after its occurrence.

(5.) In case of the illness or absence of the town clerk, the council may appoint a deputy town clerk, to hold office during their pleasure.

(6.) All things required or authorized by law to be done by or to the town clerk may be done by or to the deputy town clerk.

The officer of a county council corresponding to the town clerk is the clerk of the council, who in all counties, except London, will also be the clerk of the peace. The appointment of the clerk of the council and the deputy clerk, and their duties, are regulated by the Local Government Act, 1888, s. 83, *ante*, p. 158.

By the Local Government Act, s. 75 (16) (*e*), *ante*, p. 145, it is provided that nothing in the above section shall apply to the county council.

The treasurer

18.—(1.) The council shall from time to time appoint a fit person, not a member of the council, to be the treasurer of the borough.

(2.) The treasurer shall hold office during the pleasure of the council.

(3.) A vacancy in the office shall be filled within twenty-one days after its occurrence,

(4.) The offices of town clerk and treasurer shall not be held by the same person.

The Local Government Act, s. 75, *ante*, p. 145, provides that this section shall not apply to a county council unless that council so resolve; but if the county council so resolve, the above section is to supersede the existing enactments with respect to the county treasurer.

Other borough officers.

19. The council shall from time to time appoint such other officers as have been usually appointed in the borough, or as the council think necessary, and may at any time discontinue the appointment of any officer appearing to them not necessary to be re-appointed.

In applying this section to a county council, the provisions of the Local Government Act, ss. 118, 119, *ante*, pp. 190—195, as to existing officers and compensation, must be borne in mind. By s. 120, if the county council abolish the office of any existing officer, they must pay him compensation.

Sect. 20.

Security by and remuneration of officers.

20. The council shall require every officer appointed by them to give such security as they think proper for the due execution of his office, and shall allow him such remuneration as they think reasonable.

It is provided by the Local Government Act, s. 119, *ante*, p. 194, that existing officers, *i.e.*, officers transferred to the county councils under that Act, shall hold their offices by the same tenure, and upon the same terms and conditions, as if that Act had not passed. The above section, in so far as it applies to security, will not apply to an existing officer who has not hitherto given security. But upon new appointments to any offices security must be taken, the amount and nature of the security being in the discretion of the county council.

Accountability of officers.

21.—(1.) Every officer appointed by the council shall at such times during the continuance of his office, or within three months after his ceasing to hold it, and in such manner as the council direct, deliver to the council, or as they direct, a true account in writing of all matters committed to his charge, and of his receipts and payments, with vouchers, and a list of persons from whom money is due for purposes of this Act in connection with his office, showing the amount due from each.

(2.) Every such officer shall pay all money due from him to the treasurer, or as the council direct.

(3.) If any such officer—

(a.) Refuses or wilfully neglects to deliver any account or list which he ought to deliver, or any voucher relating thereto, or to make any payment which he ought to make; or

(b.) After three days' notice in writing, signed by the town clerk or by three members of the council, given or left at his usual or last known place of abode, refuses or wilfully neglects to deliver to the council, or as they direct, any book or document which he ought so to deliver, or to give satisfaction respecting it to the council, or as they direct;

a court of summary jurisdiction having jurisdiction where the officer is or resides may, by summary order, require him to make such delivery or payment, or to give such satisfaction.

(4.) But nothing in this section shall affect any remedy by action against any such officer or his surety, except that the officer shall not be both sued by action and proceeded against summarily for the same cause.

This section will apply to officers of the county council.

The expression "court of summary jurisdiction" is defined by the Interpretation Act, 1889 (52 & 53 Vict. c. 63), s. 13 to mean any justice or justices of the peace or other magistrate by whatever name called, to whom jurisdiction is given by or who is authorized to act under the Summary Jurisdiction Acts, and whether acting under those Acts or under any other Act or by virtue of his commission or under the common law.

Sect. 22.

Meetings and Proceedings of Council; Committees.

Quarterly and other meetings of council, appointment of committees, minutes, etc.

22.—(1.) The rules in the Second Schedule shall be observed (*a*).

(2.) The council may from time to time appoint out of their own body such and so many committees, either of a general or special nature, and consisting of such number of persons, as they think fit, for any purposes which, in the opinion of the council, would be better regulated and managed by means of such committees (*b*); but the acts of every such committee shall be submitted to the council for their approval (*c*).

(3.) A member of the council shall not vote or take part in the discussion of any matter before the council, or a committee, in which he has, directly or indirectly, by himself or by his partner, any pecuniary interest (*d*).

(4.) No act or proceeding of the council, or of a committee, shall be questioned on account of any vacancy in their body.

(5.) A minute of proceedings at a meeting of the council, or of a committee, signed at the same or the next ensuing meeting by the mayor, or by a member of the council, or of the committee, describing himself as, or appearing to be, chairman of the meeting at which the minute is signed, shall be received in evidence without further proof (*e*).

(6.) Until the contrary is proved, every meeting of the council, or of a committee, in respect of the proceedings whereof a minute has been so made, shall be deemed to have been duly convened and held, and all the members of the meeting shall be deemed to have been duly qualified; and where the proceedings are proceedings of a committee, the committee shall be deemed to have been duly constituted, and to have had power to deal with the matters referred to in the minutes.

(*a*) See this schedule, *post*.

(*b*) This provision will apply to county councils. As to the appointment of joint committees by county councils or quarter sessions, see the Local Government Act, s. 81, *ante*, p. 155, and as to the proceedings of such committee, see s. 82. As to the standing joint committee, see s. 30, *ante*, p. 66.

By the Local Government Act, s. 28, *ante*, p. 64, the county council shall have power to delegate, with or without any restrictions or conditions, as they may think fit, any powers or duties transferred to them by that Act, to any committee, except the power of raising money by rate or loan.

The delegation of powers to a committee will not deprive a county council of the right to exercise any power which the committee might have exercised under the delegation. *Huth* v. *Clarke*, 25 Q. B. D. 391; 59 L. J. M. C. 120; 63 L. T. (N.S.) 348; 38 W. R. 655; 6 T. L. R. 373.

(*c*) The acts and proceedings of the standing joint committee need not be submitted to the county council for their approval. (Local Government Act, s. 75 (16) (*f*), *ante*, p. 146.) Every committee of a county council is required

Sect. 22.

NOTE.

to report its proceedings to the council, but to the extent to which the council so direct the acts and proceedings of the committee shall not be required by the provisions of the Municipal Corporations Act, 1882, to be submitted to the council for their approval. (Local Government Act, s. 82, *ante*, p. 157). It seems that the act of the committee will not be invalid merely because the approval of the council (where necessary) is not given until after the act has been done. *Firth* v. *Staines*, 13 T. L. R. 394.

(*d*) Where, by a resolution of a town council under s. 15 (4), *ante*, a salary is attached to the office of mayor, a candidate for that office is disqualified under the provision in the text from voting for himself, as he has a pecuniary interest in the matter. *Nell* v. *Longbottom*, [1894] 1 Q. B. 767; 63 L. J. Q. B. 490; 70 L. T. (N.S.) 499. It has already been pointed out that a member of the council is disqualified by any interest in a contract with the council. (See s. 12, *ante*, p. 252.) But there are certain excepted interests which do not disqualify, and the provisions in the text will apply to these.

(*e*) As to the taking and signing of the minutes, see Sched. 2, r. 12, *post*.

Bye-laws (a).

Power of council to make bye-laws.

23.—(1.) The council may, from time to time, make such bye-laws as to them seem meet for the good rule and government of the borough, and for prevention and suppression of nuisances (*b*) not already punishable in a summary manner by virtue of any Act in force throughout the borough, and may thereby appoint such fines, not exceeding in any case five pounds, as they deem necessary for the prevention and suppression of offences against the same.

(2.) Such a bye-law shall not be made unless at least two-thirds of the whole number of the council are present.

(3.) Such a bye-law shall not come into force until the expiration of forty days after a copy thereof has been fixed on the town hall.

(4.) Such a bye-law shall not come into force until the expiration of forty days after a copy thereof, sealed with the corporate seal, has been sent to the Secretary of State; and if within those forty days the Queen, with the advice of Her Privy Council, disallows the bye-law or part thereof, the bye-law or part disallowed shall not come into force; but it shall be lawful for the Queen, at any time within those forty days, to enlarge the time within which the bye-law shall not come into force, and in that case the bye-law shall not come into force until after the expiration of that enlarged time.

(5.) Any offence against such a bye-law may be prosecuted summarily (*c*).

(6.) Nothing in this section shall interfere with the operation of section one hundred and eighty-seven of the Public Health Act, 1875; and that section shall have effect as if this section were therein referred to, instead of section ninety of the Municipal Corporations Act, 1835; but nothing in the Public Health Act, 1875, shall be construed as having restricted the meaning or scope of the Municipal

38 & 39 Vict. c. 55.

Sect. 23 (6). Corporations Act, 1835, or as restricting the meaning or scope of this section, with respect to prevention or suppression of nuisances(*d*).

(*a*) As to the application of this section to county councils, see the Local Government Act, 1888, s. 16, and notes, *ante*, p. 42.

By s. 85 of the same Act, *ante*, p. 162, the provisions of sub-s. (1) of this section, in so far as it gives power to a council (whether town council or county council) to make bye-laws regulating the use of bicycles and tricycles, are repealed.

(*b*) It will be observed that the bye-laws are of two kinds, one for the good rule and government of the borough, and one for the suppression of nuisances. The distinction is important, for, as noted below, the two kinds are differently confirmed.

The leading case on the subject of the reasonableness of these bye-laws, is *Kruse* v. *Johnson*, 14 T. L. R. 416 ; 42 Sol. J. 509, W. N. (1898), 48, in which it was held by Lord RUSSELL OF KILLOWEN, C.J., Sir FRANCIS JEUNE, P., and WRIGHT, DARLING and CHANNELL, JJ. (MATHEW, J., dissenting), that the bye-law of a county council that "no person shall sound or play upon any musical or noisy instrument or sing in any public place or highway within 50 yards of any dwelling-house after being requested by any constable or by an inmate of such house personally, or by his or her servant, to desist," was reasonable, and general principles were laid down as to the validity of bye-laws made by a local representative body. The cases noted below must be considered in the light of this decision.

A bye-law made under this section provided that "every person who shall sound, or play upon any musical instrument, or sing or make any noise in any street, or near any house after having been required by any householder resident in such street or by any police constable to desist, either on account of any illness of any inmate of such house or for any reasonable cause." A captain in the Salvation Army was convicted under this bye-law for playing a concertina on a Sunday morning, surrounded by a large crowd, after a constable had required him to desist, telling him that he had reasonable cause for so doing, as several complaints had been made by the inhabitants. *Held*, that the bye-law was reasonable, and that it was for the justices to decide whether there was reasonable cause. *R.* v. *Powell*, 51 L. T. (N.S.) 92 ; 48 J. P. 740.

A bye-law that no person, not being a member of Her Majesty's army or auxiliary forces, acting under the orders of his commanding officer, shall sound or play upon any musical instrument in any of the streets of the borough on Sunday, was held unreasonable and *ultra vires*. *Johnson* v. *Croydon (Mayor of)*, 16 Q. B. D. 708; 55 L. J. M. C. 117; 54 L. T. (N.S.) 295; 50 J. P. 487 ; so also a bye-law that every person who in any street should sound or play upon any musical or noisy instrument, or should sing, recite, or preach in any street without having previously obtained a licence in writing from the mayor, and every person who having obtained such licence should fail to observe, or should act contrary to any of the conditions of such licence, should forfeit a sum not exceeding 20*s*. *Munro* v. *Watson*, 57 L. T. (N.S.) 366 ; 51 J. P. 660.

A bye-law which forbade the keeping of swine within a borough was held bad. *Everett* v. *Grapes*, 3 L. T. (N.S.) 669 ; 25 J. P. 644. So also a bye-law that parents should be liable to a penalty if they suffered a child to sell articles in the street after a certain hour. *Macdonald* v. *Lochrane*, 51 J. P. 629.

A bye-law that no person should erect any booth for the purpose of any show or public entertainment in any place within a borough without licence from the mayor, which licence should only be given during the annual fair time, if any three inhabitants objected, was held void. *Elwood* v. *Bullock*, 6 Q. B. 383 ; 13 L. J. Q. B. 330 ; 8 Jur. 1044.

The following borough bye-law was held valid: "If any butcher or dealer in meat, or any fishmonger, poulterer, or other person, shall expose or offer for sale on his premises, or have in his possession with intent to sell or to expose for sale, any meat, fish, poultry, or other victuals or provisions unfit for the food of man, he shall be subject to a penalty, to be recovered before two justices, who shall decide on the unfitness." *Shillito* v. *Thompson*, 1 Q. B. D. 12; 45 L. J. Q. B. 18; 33 L. T. (N.S.) 506; 24 W. R. 57.

One of the Salvation Army used a concertina in a street of a borough, a bye-law of which, made under 5 & 6 Will. 4, c. 74, prohibited the use of any noisy instrument to the annoyance of any of the inhabitants. The justices found it was a noisy instrument, and some inhabitants proved being annoyed. *Held*, there was evidence to support a conviction; that it was not necessary to prove that the instrument was a public nuisance to all the inhabitants, and that the bye-law was not *ultra vires*. *Booth* v. *Howell*, 53 J. P. 678; 5 T. L. R. 449.

In a prosecution under a bye-law of a town providing that any person making a violent noise in the streets to the annoyance of the inhabitants shall be guilty of an offence, it is sufficient to prove that one inhabitant has been annoyed. *Innes* v. *Newman*, [1894] 2 Q. B. 292; 63 L. J. M. C. 198; 70 L. T. (N.S.) 689; 42 W. R. 573; 58 J. P. 543.

A Local Improvement Act authorized conservators of a common to make bye-laws and regulations for the prevention of, and protection from, nuisances, and for keeping order. The appellant was charged for placing on the common a boat-van for pleasure without licence and without payment of the prescribed fee, contrary to a bye-law made. *Held*, that the bye-law was not *ultra vires* merely because it prohibited vans without leave, and because it did not confine this to such as were nuisances. *Nash* v. *Manning*, 58 J. P. 718.

A bye-law made by a county council under s. 16 of the Local Government Act, 1888, was in the following terms: "No person shall in any street or public place, or on land adjacent thereto, sing or recite any profane or obscene song or ballad, or use any profane or obscene language." *Held*, that the bye-law was invalid, since even if the words "or on land adjacent thereto," which were clearly too wide, were struck out, it was still unreasonable, because it did not contain any words importing that the acts must be done so as to cause annoyance. *Strickland* v. *Hayes*, [1896] 1 Q. B. 290; 65 L. J. M. C. 55; 74 L. T. (N.S.) 137; 44 W. R. 398; 60 J. P. 164. In a later case, however, a defendant was charged with using indecent and obscene language in a dwelling-house, in a room abutting on and then open to the public street, to the annoyance of persons in the street, contrary to a bye-law of the county council. It was held that the bye-law was valid. *Mantle* v. *Jordan*, [1897] 1 Q. B. 248; 66 L. J. Q. B. 224; 75 L. T. (N.S.) 552; 61 J. P. 119; 13 T. L. R. 121.

A bye-law made under this section prohibited, under a penalty, any person from frequenting and using any street or other public place within the borough, for the purpose of bookmaking or betting. *Held*, that the bye-law was one which could properly be made for the good rule and government of the borough, and was therefore valid. *Burnett* v. *Berry*, [1896] 1 Q. B. 641; 65 L. J. M. C. 118; 74 L. T. (N.S.) 494; 44 W. R. 512; 60 J. P. 375; 12 T. L. R. 362. As to the evidence in a charge under such a bye-law, see *Whickham* v. *Ashe*, *Times*, January 16th, 1897.

A bye-law of a county council provided as follows: "A person shall not, together with any other person or persons, assemble in any street or public place for the purpose of betting." This bye-law was held valid. *Godwin* v. *Walker*, 60 J. P. 308; 12 T. L. R. 367.

Sect. 23.

NOTE.

A bye-law made by the county council of Warwickshire, under s. 16 of the Local Government Act, 1888, was as follows: "Lights on vehicles. A person driving or having charge of any vehicle . . . shall from the end of the first hour after sunset to two o'clock a.m., except during such part (if any) of that period as shall be between the rising and the setting of the moon, carry attached to such vehicle a lighted lamp or lighted lamps, which shall be so constructed or placed as to exhibit a light in the direction in which he is proceeding, and so as to prove adequate means of signalling the approach or position of the vehicle . . . Provided also that where such vehicle is carrying timber, such person shall also carry attached at the end thereof a lamp or lamps so constructed as to exhibit a light or lights visible to persons overtaking such vehicle." The respondent, a carter, was summoned for driving a waggon laden with timber during the prohibited hours without proper lights, contrary to the bye-law. The charge was dismissed, on the ground that the bye-law was invalid as being unreasonable. *Held*, that the bye-law was valid. *Walker* v. *Stretton*, 44 W. R. 425; 60 J. P. 313; 12 T. L. R. 363.

A bye-law made by a county council provided that "no person shall drive, or cause to be driven, any timber carriage over any main road or other highway in the county between sunset and sunrise, unless it has lamps showing a bright and adequate light both to the front and rear of the carriage. *Held*, that the bye-law was reasonable, and therefore valid. *Williams* v. *Groves*, 12 T. L. R. 450.

By a bye-law made by the council of a municipal borough, purporting to act under s. 23 of the Municipal Corporations Act, 1882, it was provided that "no person shall, to the annoyance or disturbance of residents or passengers, keep or manage a shooting gallery, swing-boat, roundabout, or other like thing, in any street or public place, or on land adjoining or near to such street or public place, provided always that this bye-law shall not apply to any fair lawfully held." The respondent erected and kept two sets of swing-boats and roundabouts, worked by steam power, with organs attached, on private land near a public street, and not on the day of any lawful fair, to the annoyance of certain residents who lived near by, and were disturbed by the noise of the organs and the crowds attracted, as well by the respondent's erections as by other shows held at the same place and time. The borough justices dismissed an information against the respondents for a breach of the above bye-law, on the ground that it was *ultra vires*, and bad for extending to land adjoining or near to a street or public place. *Held*, that the bye-law was valid, and case remitted to the justices for conviction. *Teale* v. *Harris*, 61 J. P. 744.

A bye-law of the borough of C. provided: "No person shall in the following streets (certain streets were named), post, paste, or affix any bill, notice, or placard on any building, wall, fence, gate, door, pillar, tree or post in or abutting on any street, between nine a.m. and six p.m., provided that notices of the effect of the foregoing bye-law shall be affixed and kept affixed in each of the above-mentioned streets. *Held*, that the bye-law was repugnant to the general law, and, therefore, *ultra vires* and bad. *R.* v. *Richards*, 61 J. P. 40.

A bye-law may be good in part. *R.* v. *Faversham*, 8 T. R. 352; *R.* v. *Lundie*, 31 L. J. M. C. 157; 8 Jur. (N.S.) 640; 5 L. T. (N.S.) 830; 10 W. R. 267.

A bye-law in restraint of trade is bad. *Hesketh* v. *Braddock*, 3 Burr. 1847; *Bodwick* v. *Fennell*, 1 Wils. 233; *Clark* v. *Le Cren*, 9 B. & C. 52; *Shaw* v. *Poynter*, 2 A. & E. 312. But a mere regulation not in restraint of trade, as that no person should slaughter animals within a city, is valid. *Pierce* v. *Bartrum*, Cowp. 269. And a bye-law prohibiting the sale of articles in a public recreation ground, except in places to be specified, was held valid in *Gray* v. *Sylvester*, 46 W. R. 63; 14 T. L. R. 12.

Sect. 23.

Note.

As to the general doctrine that bye-laws must be reasonable, see *Slattery* v. *Naylor*, 13 App. Cas. 446; 57 L. J. P. C. 79; 59 L. T. (N.S.) 41; 36 W. R. 897; *Toronto Municipal Corporation* v. *Virgo*, [1896] A. C. 88; 65 L. J. P. C. 4; 73 L. T. (N.S.) 449.

(*c*) That is, in manner provided by the Summary Jurisdiction Acts. See s. 219, *post*. The council cannot summon offenders before them to answer complaints for offences against the bye-laws. *In re Wiseman*, 3 T. L. R. 12; and see the Local Government Act, s. 78, *ante*, p.

(*d*) Section 187 of the Public Health Act, 1875, is as follows:—

"Bye-laws made by the council of any borough under the provisions of s. 90 of the Act of the 6th year of King William the 4th, c. 76, for the prevention and suppression of certain nuisances, shall not be required to be sent to a Secretary of State, nor shall they be subject to the disallowance in that section mentioned; but all the provisions of this Act relating to bye-laws shall apply to the bye-laws so made as if they were made under this Act." The meaning of this provision, read with the text, is that while bye-laws relating to the good government of a borough are confirmed by a Secretary of State, and may be disallowed by the Queen in Council as provided by sub-s. (4), *supra*, bye-laws for the prevention and suppression of the nuisances mentioned in sub-s. (1) must be made in manner provided by the Public Health Act, 1875, and must be confirmed by the Local Government Board under s. 184 of that Act. The Local Government Act, s. 16, *ante*, p. 42, which enables a county council to make bye-laws under the above section, provides that s. 187 of the Public Health Act, 1875, shall apply to such bye-laws. Consequently, any bye-laws made by a county council for the suppression and prevention of nuisances within the county must be made and confirmed in manner provided by the Public Health Act. But bye-laws for the good government of the county other than those relating to nuisances do not require the confirmation of the Local Government Board; the approval of a Secretary of State is sufficient. See the note, *ante*, pp. 42—43.

Evidence of bye-laws.

24. The production of a written copy of a bye-law made by the council under this Act, or under any former or present or future general or local Act of Parliament, if authenticated by the corporate seal shall, until the contrary is proved, be sufficient evidence of the due making and existence of the bye-law, and, if it is so stated in the copy, of the bye-law having been approved and confirmed by the authority whose approval or confirmation is required to the making or before the enforcing of the bye-law.

In the case of bye-laws for the prevention of nuisances, a copy certified by the clerk under s. 186 of the Public Health Act, 1875, will be sufficient evidence; see *ante*, pp. 42—44. But having regard to the provisions in the text it seems desirable that a copy of any bye-laws to be tendered as evidence should be authenticated by the seal of the county council.

The word "written" includes "printed." See s. 20 of the Interpretation Act, 1889 (52 & 53 Vict. c. 63).

Accounts and Audit.

The borough auditors.

25.—(1.) There shall be three borough auditors, two elected by the burgesses, called elective auditors, and one appointed by the mayor, called mayor's auditor(*a*).

Sect. 25 (2).

(2.) An elective auditor must be qualified to be a councillor, but may not be a member of the council or the town clerk or the treasurer.

(3.) The mayor's auditor must be a member of the council.

(4.) The term of office of each auditor shall be one year.

(5.) The appointment of the mayor's auditor shall be made on the ordinary day of election of the elective auditors (*b*).

(6.) On a casual vacancy in his office an appointment to fill it shall be made within ten days after the occurrence of the vacancy (*c*).

(*a*) The above section will have no application to a county council, for by the Local Government Act, s. 71, *ante*, p. 136, the accounts of county councils are to be audited by the district auditors appointed by the Local Government Board. But in county boroughs the above section will still apply, for by the Local Government Act, s. 34, *ante*, p. 75, Part IV. of that Act relating to finance is not to apply to county boroughs.

There is no provision in the Municipal Corporations Act, 1882, relating to the remuneration of the borough auditors. But by the Public Health Act, 1885, s. 246, the borough auditors may be paid at a rate not exceeding three guineas a day for auditing the accounts of the borough as urban sanitary authority.

(*b*) The ordinary day for the election of borough auditors is March 1st, or such other day as the council, with the approval of the Local Government Board, from time to time appoint. See s. 62, *post*.

(*c*) As to the filling of casual vacancies, see ss. 40 and 66, *post*.

Half-yearly accounts of treasurer.

26. The treasurer shall make up his accounts half-yearly to such dates as the council, with the approval of the Local Government Board, from time to time appoint; and, subject to any such appointment, to the dates in use at the commencement of this Act.

The Local Government Act, s. 71, *ante*, p. 136, provides that the provisions of the Municipal Corporations Act, 1882, with respect to the accounts of the treasurer of a borough shall apply to the accounts of a county council.

The same section provides that the accounts of the receipts and expenditure of county councils shall be made up to the end of each local financial year as defined by that Act, and shall be in the form for the time being prescribed by the Local Government Board. The local financial year is defined by s. 73, *ante*, p. 140. It will be observed that the accounts of county councils are to be made out yearly, not half-yearly.

The above section will, however, continue to apply to county boroughs without alteration.

By s. 233, *post*, the treasurer's accounts may be inspected by any member of the council.

Audit and publication of treasurer's accounts.

27.—(1.) The treasurer shall within one month from the date to which he is required to make up his accounts in each half year, submit them, with the necessary vouchers and papers, to the borough auditors, and they shall audit them.

(2.) After the audit of the accounts for the second half of each financial year the treasurer shall print a full abstract of his accounts for that year. Sect. 27 (2).

This section will apply to county boroughs without alteration. With regard to other county councils, the accounts are to be made out to the end of each financial year, and are to be audited by the district auditors. Save to this extent the section will apply to county councils, for by the Local Government Act, s. 71, *ante*, p. 136, the provisions of the Municipal Corporations Act, with respect to the accounts of the treasurer of a borough and the abstract thereof, are to apply to the accounts of the county council.

By s. 233, *post*, all the ratepayers are entitled to inspect the abstract and to obtain a copy on payment of a reasonable sum.

28.—(1.) The town clerk shall make a return to the Local Government Board of the receipts and expenditure of the municipal corporation for each financial year. Returns to Local Government Board.

(2.) The return shall be made for the financial year ending on the twenty-fifth of March, or on such other day as the Local Government Board, on the application of the council, from time to time prescribe.

(3.) The return shall be in such form and contain such particulars as the Local Government Board from time to time direct.

(4.) The return shall be sent to the Local Government Board within one month after the completion of the audit for the second half of each financial year.

(5.) If the town clerk fails to make any return required under this section, he shall for each offence be liable to a fine not exceeding twenty pounds, to be recovered by action on behalf of the Crown in the High Court.

(6.) The Local Government Board shall in each year prepare an abstract of the returns made in pursuance of this section, under general heads, and it shall be laid before both Houses of Parliament.

The section will also apply to county councils with certain modifications. See s. 71 (2) of the Local Government Act, *ante*, p. 136. The clerk of the council must perform the duties of the town clerk ; see s. 75 (5) of that Act, *ante*, p. 142. The financial year ends on the 31st, not March 25th, *ib.* s. 73, *ante*, p. 140.

Revising Assessors.

29.—(1.) In every borough whereof no part of the area is co-extensive with or included in the area of a parliamentary borough, there shall be two revising assessors elected by the burgesses. Revising assessors in non-parliamentary boroughs.

(2.) Every person shall be eligible who is qualified to be a councillor and is not a member of the council or the town clerk or treasurer.

Sect. 29 (3).

(3.) The term of office of each revising assessor shall be one year.

(4.) Every revising assessor shall, as soon as conveniently may be after his election, and from time to time as occasion requires, appoint, by writing signed by him, a person eligible to the office of revising assessor, to be his deputy, to act for him in case of his illness or incapacity to act.

(5.) The appointment shall be signified to the council in writing, signed by the assessor, and be recorded in their minutes.

This section is practically repealed. The function of the revising assessors was to assist the mayor in revising the burgess lists in boroughs to which the 41 & 42 Vict. c. 26, did not apply. But by the County Electors Act, 1888 (51 Vict. c. 10), the 41 & 42 Vict. c. 26, is now applied to every municipal borough, and by s. 4, it is provided that revising assessors for such borough shall not be elected.

Division of Borough into Wards, or alteration of Wards.

Proceedings for division of borough into wards, or alteration of wards.

30.—(1.) If two-thirds of the council of a borough agree to petition, and the council thereupon petition, the Queen for the division of the borough into wards, or for the alteration of the number and boundaries of its wards, it shall be lawful for Her Majesty from time to time, by Order in Council, to fix the number of wards into which the borough shall be divided; and the borough shall be divided into that number of wards.

(2.) Notice of the petition, and of the time when it pleases Her Majesty to order that the same be taken into consideration by Her Privy Council, shall be published in the London Gazette one month at least before the petition is so considered.

(3.) Where an Order in Council has been so made, the Secretary of State shall appoint a commissioner to prepare a scheme for determining the boundaries of the wards and apportioning the councillors among them.

(4.) In case of division into wards, the commissioner shall apportion all the councillors among the wards.

(5.) In case of alteration of wards, he shall so apportion among the altered wards the councillors for those wards as to provide for their continuing to represent as large a number as possible of their former constituents.

(6.) In either case, each councillor shall hold his office in the ward to which he is assigned for the same time that he would have held it had the borough remained undivided or the wards unaltered.

(7.) In case of division into wards the returning officer at the first election for each ward held after the division shall, notwithstanding anything in this Act, be the mayor or a person appointed by the mayor.

(8.) If by reason of any division or alteration under this section any doubt arises as to which councillor should go out of office, the doubt may be determined by the council. Sect. 30 (8).

(9.) The division of a borough into a greater number of wards shall not affect the qualification of aldermen or councillors.

(10.) The number of councillors assigned to each ward shall be a number divisible by three; and in fixing their number the commissioner shall, as far as he deems it practicable, have regard as well to the number of persons rated in the ward as to the aggregate rating of the ward.

(11.) The commissioner shall make the scheme in duplicate, and shall deliver one of the duplicates to the town clerk, and shall send the other to the Secretary of State, to be submitted by him to Her Majesty in Council for approval.

(12.) The scheme shall be published in the London Gazette, and shall come into operation at the date of that publication, and thenceforth the boundaries of wards and apportionment of councillors determined and made by the scheme shall be observed and be in force.

(13.) If Her Majesty in Council does not approve the scheme as originally prepared by the commissioner, it shall nevertheless be published in the London Gazette, and shall be in force for the purposes of any municipal election until Her Majesty in Council, on further information and report from the commissioner, definitively approves a scheme in that behalf.

(14.) The commissioner may administer oaths, and may require any person having the custody of any book containing a poor rate made for a parish to produce the book for his inspection; and every person required by the commissioner to answer any question put to him for the purposes of this section shall answer it.

(15.) The commissioner shall have remuneration as appearing by the Fourth and Fifth Schedules.

A petition under this section may be presented upon a resolution passed by a majority of the whole council, and may pray for the alteration of the boundaries of the wards of a borough without any alteration of their number; and where any such petition prays for the alteration of boundaries only, the provisions of the said section shall apply so far as applicable. Where the powers conferred by this section have been exercised in pursuance of a petition by the council of any borough, a further petition from the council of the same borough shall not be presented before the expiration of seven years from the date of the previous Order in Council under this section, 56 Vict. c. 9, ss. 2, 3.

It is provided by the Local Government Act, s. 2, *ante*, p. 3, that the divisions of the county for the purpose of the election of county councillors shall be called electoral divisions, and not wards, and one county councillor only shall be elected for each electoral division. The same section further

Sect. 30.

NOTE.

provides that as respects the number of the county councillors, and the boundaries of the electoral divisions in every county—

(a) the number of the county councillors, and their apportionment between each of the boroughs which have sufficient population to return one councillor and the rest of the county, shall be such as the Local Government Board may determine ; and

(b) any borough returning one councillor only shall be an electoral division ; and

(c) in the rest of the county the electoral divisions shall be such as in the case of a borough returning more than one councillor the council of the borough, and in the rest of the county the quarter sessions for the county, may determine ;

subject in either case to the directions enacted by that Act ; and in the case of elections after the first, to any alterations made, in accordance with the said directions, in manner in this Act mentioned.

The directions here referred to are contained in s. 51, *ante*, p. 106, and future alterations of electoral divisions are to be effected in manner provided by s. 54, *ante*, p. 108.

It appears, therefore, that the above section will not apply to electoral divisions. It will, of course, continue to apply to the division of boroughs into wards.

Supplemental and Exceptional Provisions.

Occupation of part of house.

31. In and for the purposes of this Act—

(a.) The terms house, warehouse, counting-house, shop, or other building include any part of a house, where that part is separately occupied for the purposes of any trade, business, or profession ; and any such part may, for the purpose of describing the qualification, be described as office, chambers, studio, or by any like term applicable to the case.

(b.) Where an occupier is entitled to the sole and exclusive use of any part of a house, that part shall not be deemed to be occupied otherwise than separately by reason only that the occupier is entitled to the joint use of some other part.

See s. 9, *ante*, and the notes thereto.

It is provided by the County Electors Act, 1888 (51 Vict. c. 10), s. 2, sub-s. (2), that the above section shall extend to so much of every county as is not comprised within the limits of any municipal borough, for the purpose of the qualification of county electors.

But for the provision in the text, the tenant of offices or chambers might be in law only a lodger, and not an occupier within the meaning of s. 9. See note (*d*) to s. 9, *ante*, p. 241.

A. occupied two rooms in a house in which there were four other residents. The landlord did not live on the premises, but paid the rates. It was held that A. was entitled to the municipal franchise by reason of the provision in the text. *Greenway* v. *Batchelor*, 47 J. P. 792.

A house not structurally severed was let partly to one tenant and partly to another, and each had the exclusive occupation of the part let to him ; there

Sect. 31.

NOTE.

was a staircase leading from the front door to the upper rooms and a joint use of the front garden and the backyard, in which was a closet. It was held that each was the occupier of a separate tenement capable of being rated. *Allchurch* v. *Hendon Union*, [1891] 2 Q B. 436 ; 61 L. J. M. C. 27 ; 65 L. T. (N.S.) 450 ; 40 W. R. 84 ; 56 J. P. 117 ; 7 T. L. R. 634.

A cubicle in a dormitory in a police station, of which a policeman had the exclusive use, was held not to be "part of a house separately occupied as a dwelling," so as to confer the parliamentary franchise. *Clutterbuck* v. *Taylor*, [1896] 1 Q. B. 395 ; 65 L. J. Q. B. 314 ; 74 L. T. (N.S.) 177; 44 W. R. 531 ; 60 J. P. 273, following *Burnett* v. *Hickmott*, [1895] 1 Q. B. 691 ; 64 L. J. Q. B. 407 ; 72 L. T. (N.S.) 236 ; 43 W. R. 284 ; 59 J. P. 230.

Claim by occupier to be rated.

32.—(1.) If an occupier of any qualifying property, whether the landlord is or is not liable to be rated to the poor rate in respect thereof, claims to be rated to the poor rate in respect thereof, and pays or tenders to the overseers of the parish where the property is situate the full amount of the poor rate last made in respect of the property, the overseers shall put the occupier's name on the rate book in respect of that rate.

(2.) If they fail to do so, he shall nevertheless, for the purposes of this Act, be deemed rated to that rate.

The 32 & 33 Vict. c. 41, s. 19, provides that the overseers in making out the poor rate shall in every case, whether the rate is collected from the owner or occupier, or the owner is liable to the payment of the rate instead of the occupier, enter in the occupiers' column of the rate book the name of the occupier of every rateable hereditament, and such occupier shall be deemed to be duly rated for every qualification or franchise as aforesaid ; and if any overseer negligently or wilfully and without reasonable cause omits the name of the occupier of any rateable hereditament from the rate, or negligently or wilfully misstates any name therein, such overseer shall for every such omission or misstatement be liable on summary conviction to a penalty not exceeding 2*l.* : Provided that any occupier whose name has been omitted shall, notwithstanding such omission and that no claim to be rated has been made by him, be entitled to every qualification and franchise depending upon rating in the same manner as if his name had not been so omitted. This provision applies only in cases where the owner pays the rate, but in such cases it is of wider application than the text in that no claim to be rated is necessary. The text provides for all other cases of omission to be rated. See *Marsh* v. *Estcourt*, 24 Q. B. D. 147 ; 59 L. J. Q. B. 100 ; 38 W. R. 495 ; 54 J. P. 294 ; 1 Fox, 157. As an illustration of the effect of sub-s. (2) of the text, see *Unwin* v. *McMullen*, [1891] 1 Q. B. 694 ; 60 L. J. Q. B. 400 ; 39 W. R. 712 ; 55 J. P. 582 ; 7 T. L. R. 450.

Rules as to qualification of burgess on succession, etc.

33.(*a*)—(1.) Where a person succeeds to qualifying property by descent, marriage, marriage settlement, devise, or promotion to a benefice or office, then, for the purposes of qualification, the occupancy of the property by a predecessor in title, and the rating of the predecessor in respect thereof, shall be equivalent to the occupancy and rating of the successor ; and rating in the name of the predecessor shall, until a new rate is made after the date of

Sect. 33 (1). succession, be equivalent to rating in the name of the successor; and the successor shall not be required to prove his own residence, occupancy, or rating before the succession.

(2.) The qualifying property need not be throughout the twelve months constituting the period of qualification the same property or in the same parish (*b*).

(3.) Where by law a borough rate is payable by instalments, payment by any person of any such instalment shall, as regards his qualification to be enrolled as a burgess, be deemed a payment of the borough rate in respect of the period to which the instalment applies.

(4.) A person shall not be disentitled to be enrolled as a burgess by reason only—

(a.) That he has received medical or surgical assistance from the trustees of the municipal charities, or has been removed, by order of a justice, to a hospital or place for reception of the sick, at the cost of any local authority; or

(b.) That his child has been admitted to and taught in any public or endowed school (*c*).

(*a*) The County Electors Act, 1888, s. 2, applies this section to county electors.

(*b*) But the property must be in the same county and outside the limits of a borough in order to qualify a county elector, just as in order to qualify a burgess it must be within the borough. See s. 2 of the County Electors Act.

(*c*) This forms an exception to s. 9, sub-s. (3), which disqualifies a person to be enrolled as a burgess if he has within the qualifying period received parochial relief or other alms. See note (*m*) to that section.

It is provided by the Elementary Education Act, 1876, s. 10, that the parent of a child whose fees are paid under that section shall not be deprived of any franchise, right, or privilege, and shall not be subject to any disability or disqualification.

Obligation to accept office or pay fine.

34.—(1.) Every qualified (*a*) person elected to a corporate office (*b*), unless exempt under this section or otherwise by law (*c*), either shall accept the office by making and subscribing the declaration required by this Act, within five days after notice of election (*d*), or shall in lieu thereof be liable to pay to the council a fine of such amount not exceeding, in case of an alderman, councillor, elective auditor, or revising assessor, fifty pounds, and in case of a mayor one hundred pounds, as the council by bye-law determine.

(2.) If there is no bye-law determining fines, the fine, in case of an alderman, councillor, elective auditor, or revising assessor shall be twenty-five pounds, and in case of a mayor fifty pounds.

(3.) The persons exempt under this section are— Sect. 34 (3).

(a.) Any person disabled by lunacy or imbecility of mind, or by deafness, blindness, or other permanent infirmity of body; and

(b.) Any person who, being above the age of sixty-five years, or having within five years before the day of his election either served the office or paid the fine for non-acceptance thereof, claims exemption within five days after notice of his election (*e*).

(4.) A fine payable under this section shall be recoverable summarily (*f*).

(*a*) In proceedings under this section there need not be express or actual evidence, but there must be some evidence of qualification, and if in fact the party was not qualified he is not liable to the penalty, and a conviction is invalid. *R.* v. *Stockton JJ.*, 11 W. R. 65; 26 J. P. 771.

(*b*) In a borough the term "corporate office" includes the office of mayor, alderman, councillor, and elective auditor. In a county it will include the chairman, county alderman, and councillors.

(*c*) There are exemptions under many statutes from the liability to serve in a corporate office. Thus officers of customs are exempt under 39 & 40 Vict. c. 36, s. 9; persons registered as dentists under 41 & 42 Vict. c. 33, s. 30; commissioners and officers of excise under 7 & 8 Geo. 4, c. 53, s. 11; inspectors of factories under 41 & 42 Vict. c. 16, s. 67; officers of inland revenue under 53 & 54 Vict. c. 21, s. 8; registered medical practitioners under 21 & 22 Vict. c. 90, s. 35; officers of the post office under 7 Will. 4 & 1 Vict. c. 33, s. 12; registrars of births under 7 Will. 4 & 1 Vict. c. 22, s. 18; men belonging to the army reserve under 45 & 46 Vict. c. 48, s. 7; officers in the army under s. 253, *post*; resident members of the university, see s. 257, *post*. To these must be added persons disqualified under the Corrupt Practices Acts, the Bankruptcy Acts, the Felony Act, etc., as to which see s. 12, note (*a*), *ante*, p. 252.

(*d*) The form of declaration is set out in Sched. 8. As to persons not accepting office by reason of refusal on conscientious grounds to make the declaration, see s. 36, *post*.

The declaration required by this section to be made by a person appointed to a corporate office in a county may be made at any time within three months after notice of the election, and may be made either in the manner prescribed by the Local Government Act, 1888, or before any justice of the peace or commissioners to administer oaths in the supreme court of judicature, 54 & 55 Vict. c. 68, s. 5, *post*.

(*e*) A further ground of exemption is that the person elected was nominated without his consent. See the Local Government Act, s. 75, 16 (*c*), *ante*, p. 145.

(*f*) That is to say, before a court of summary jurisdiction consisting of two or more justices sitting in open court. See the Summary Jurisdiction Act, 1879, ss. 20, 51.

35. A person elected to a corporate office shall not, until he has made and subscribed before two members of the council, or the Declaration on acceptance of office.

Sect. 35.

town clerk, a declaration as in the Eighth Schedule, act in the office except in administering that declaration.

It has been held that a councillor before whom this declaration is taken cannot be the relator in proceedings by way of *quo warranto* to avoid the office on the ground of disqualification. *R.* v. *Greene*, 2 Q. B. 460. The ground of this decision was that as a councillor need not act unless he chooses in taking the declaration, by acting he must be taken to concur in the irregularity. *Quære*, if this would prevent his presenting an election petition under s. 87, *post.*

In applying this section to county councillors, the clerk of the council must be substituted for the town clerk. As to the time and manner of making the declaration, see note (*d*) to s. 34, *supra.*

As to the penalty for acting without making this declaration, see s. 41, *post.*

Fine on resignation, etc.

36.—(1.) A person elected to a corporate office may at any time, by writing signed by him and delivered to the town clerk, resign the office, on payment of the fine provided for non-acceptance thereof (*a*).

(2.) In any such case the council shall forthwith declare the office to be vacant, and signify the same by notice in writing, signed by three members of the council and countersigned by the town clerk, and fixed on the town hall, and the office shall thereupon become vacant (*b*).

(3.) No person enabled by law to make an affirmation instead of taking an oath shall be liable to any fine for non-acceptance of office by reason of his refusal on conscientious grounds to take any oath or make any declaration required by this Act or to take on himself the duties of the office (*c*).

(*a*) But a person who has become disqualified, *e.g.*, by compounding with his creditors, under s. 39, cannot resign. *Hardwick* v. *Brown*, L. R. 8 C. P. 406 ; 28 L. T. (N.S.) 502 : 21 W. R. 639 : 37 J. P. 407 ; *R.* v. *Blizard*, *infra.*

If a person who is an alderman is elected a councillor, he vacates his office of alderman, but *quære*, whether he is liable to a fine under this section. See *R.* v. *Bangor* (*Mayor, etc., of*), 18 Q. B. D. 362, 366.

This point was not dealt with by the House of Lords in the same case *sub nom. Pritchard* v. *Bangor* (*Mayor, etc., of*), 13 App. Cas. 241.

If a man elected and admitted to an office discovers that for want of qualification or for any other sufficient reason he is not entitled to hold the office, and resigns it, a proceeding by *quo warranto* would not be necessary in order to vacate his office and so make way for a fresh election. But when the relator not only denies the validity of the election, but claims to be elected himself, he is entitled to the judgment of the court accordingly. *R.* v. *Blizard*, L. R. 2 Q. B. 55 ; 36 L. J. Q. B. 18 ; 15 L. T. (N.S.) 242 ; 15 W. R. 105 ; 31 J. P. 200 ; 7. B. & S. 922. This principle would be equally applicable to proceedings by way of election petition under s. 87, *post.*

As to the fine, see s. 34, *ante*, p. 272. The resignation is completed by the delivery of the writing and payment of the fine, and cannot afterwards be withdrawn. *R.* v. *Wigan* (*Mayor of*), 14 Q. B. D. 908 ; 54 L. J. Q. B. 338 ; 52 L. T. (N.S.) 435 ; 33 W. R. 547 ; 49 J. P. 327. The council are thereupon bound to declare the office vacant. As to the necessity for this declaration in order to create a vacancy, see note to s. 39 (2), *post*.

(*b*) In a county the notice must be countersigned by the clerk of the council. As to the affixing of the notice, see s. 232, *post*. It would appear from that section that the notice may be posted in a conspicuous place in the electoral division to which the notice relates.

(*c*) No oath is required to be taken as a condition of holding a municipal office. See 31 & 32 Vict. c. 72.

37. A person ceasing to hold a corporate office shall, unless disqualified to hold the office, be re-eligible. Re-eligibility of office holders.

See *Futcher* v. *Saunders*, cited in the note to s. 39, *post*.

38. The mayor and aldermen shall, during their respective offices, continue to be members of the council, notwithstanding anything in this Act as to councillors going out of office at the end of three years. Mayor and aldermen to continue members of council.

In applying this section to county councils the chairman must be substituted for the mayor. By the Local Government Act, s. 2, the term of office of the chairman is one year.

39. (1.) If the mayor, or an alderman or councillor— Avoidance of office by bankruptcy or absence.

(a.) Is declared bankrupt, or compounds by deed with his creditors, or makes an arrangement or composition with his creditors, under the Bankruptcy Act, 1869, by deed or otherwise (*a*) ; or

(b.) Is (except in case of illness) continuously absent from the borough, being mayor, for more than two months, or, being alderman or councillor, for more than six months (*b*) :

he shall thereupon immediately become disqualified and shall cease to hold the office.

(2.) In any such event the council shall forthwith declare the office to be vacant, and signify the same by notice, signed by three members of the council and countersigned by the town clerk, and fixed on the town hall, and the office shall thereupon become vacant (*c*).

(3.) Where a person becomes so disqualified by being declared bankrupt, or compounding, or making an arrangement or composition, as aforesaid, the disqualification, as regards subsequent elections, shall, in case of bankruptcy, cease on his obtaining his order of discharge, and shall, in case of a compounding or composition as aforesaid, cease on payment of his debts in full, and shall, in case of an arrangement as aforesaid, cease on his obtaining his certificate of discharge (*d*).

(4.) Where a person becomes so disqualified by absence, he shall be liable to the same fine as for non-acceptance of office,

Sect. 39 (4). recoverable summarily, but the disqualification shall, as regards subsequent elections, cease on his return (*e*).

(*a*) Where an alderman made a composition with his creditors, but not by deed, it was held that as the proceedings were not under the Bankruptcy Act, he was not disqualified, and the court granted an injunction restraining the council from holding a meeting declaring the office void. *Aslatt* v. *Southampton* (*Corporation of*), 16 Ch. D. 243; 50 L. J. Ch. 31; 43 L. T. (N.S.) 464.

S. served as councillor for the St. T. Ward from 1877 to July 21st, 1880, when he left at the office of the town clerk a notice of resignation addressed to the mayor and council. No action was taken thereon by the council, and no fine paid or tendered by S. S. did not sit in council or vote after the date of the notice. On the following day S. filed a petition for liquidation. In August a composition was accepted by the creditors of S. S. did not pay his debts in full. At an election of town councillors for the St. T. Ward in November, 1884, S. was returned. The objection was then taken that S. was disqualified, he having been in liquidation when he was a member of the council, and not having paid twenty shillings in the pound. *Held*, that the objection was valid. *Held also*, that where a statute provides that in a given event persons shall be re-eligible for election, that is tantamount to saying that they shall be disqualified until they comply with the conditions of re-qualification. *Futcher* v. *Saunders*, 49 J. P. 424.

An assignment of a man's entire property for the benefit of his creditors is not a composition. *R.* v. *Cooban*, 18 Q. B. D. 269; 56 L. J. M. C. 33; 51 J. P. 500.

Where a firm of partners made an arrangement with the creditors of the firm, it was held that every member of the firm had made an arrangement with his creditors within the meaning of s. 46 of the Local Government Act, 1894. *Ward* v. *Radford*, 10 T. L. R. 349. See also as to partnership affairs in bankruptcy, *Ex parte Atherton*, 2 T. L. R. 631.

(*b*) In the case of county councillors this period is extended to twelve months. See the Local Government Act, s. 75 (14), *ante*, p. 144. The same section (sub-s. (16) (c)) provides that nothing in this section shall disqualify the chairman or vice-chairman of a council by reason of absence.

It has been held in a case arising under Sched. 2, Part I. (14) of the Elementary Education Act, 1870, disqualifying a member by absence, "except from temporary illness, or other cause to be approved by the board," that a school board are not entitled to proceed to the election of a new member without first giving the defaulting member an opportunity of explaining or excusing his absence. *Richardson* v. *Methley School Board*, [1893] 3 Ch. 510; 62 L. J. Ch. 943; 69 L. T. (N.S.) 308; 42 W. R. 27; 9 T. L. R. 603. It will be noticed, however, that the language of the statutes in that case differs from that of the text.

Turnbull v. *West Riding Athletic Club* (1894), W. N. 4, a case arising under a disqualifying provision as to directors in the articles of association of a company, may also be referred to on this point.

(*c*) Until this notice has been given the office is not vacant. See *R.* v. *Leeds* (*Mayor, etc., of*), 7 A. & E. 963; *Hardwick* v. *Brown*, *ante*, p. 274; *R.* v. *Welshpool* (*Mayor, etc., of*), 35 L. T. (N.S.) 598.

As to the publication of the notice, see s. 232, *post*. It would probably be sufficient to post it in a conspicuous place in the electoral division for which a county councillor was elected.

(*d*) The provisions of the text as to bankruptcy are to some extent superseded by the Bankruptcy Act, 1883 (46 & 47 Vict. c. 52). By s. 32 of that

Act, where a debtor is adjudged a bankrupt, he shall be disqualified for being elected to, or holding or exercising, the office of mayor, alderman, or councillor; and this disqualification is to be removed and cease if and when (a) the adjudication in bankruptcy is annulled, or (b) he obtains from the court his discharge with a certificate to the effect that his bankruptcy was caused by misfortune without any misconduct on his part. The court may grant or withhold such certificate as it thinks fit, but any refusal of such certificate shall be subject to appeal. By the Bankruptcy Act, 1890 (53 & 54 Vict. c. 71), s. 9, it is provided that no disqualification arising under the Act of 1883 shall exceed a period of five years from the date of any discharge granted to the debtor. Sect. 39. NOTE.

(*e*) As to the fine for non-acceptance of office, see s. 34, *ante*, p. 272.

As to the effect of the above section in the common law power of amotion from a corporate office in cases of corrupt or dishonest conduct, see *per* LOPES, L.J., in *Booth* v. *Arnold*, [1895] 1 Q. B. 571; 64 L. J. Q. B. 443; 72 L. T. (N.S.) 310; 43 W. R. 360.

40.—(1.) On a casual vacancy in a corporate office, an election shall be held by the same persons and in the same manner as an election to fill an ordinary vacancy; and the person elected shall hold the office until the time when the person in whose place he is elected would regularly have gone out of office, and he shall then go out of office (*a*). Filling of casual vacancies.

(2.) In case of more than one casual vacancy in the office of councillor being filled at the same election, the councillor elected by the smallest number of votes shall be deemed to be elected in the place of him who would have regularly have first gone out of office, and the councillor elected by the next smallest number of votes shall be deemed to be elected in the place of him who would regularly have next gone out of office, and so with respect to the others; and if there has not been a contested election, or if any doubt arises, the order of rotation shall be determined by the council (*b*).

(3.) Non-acceptance of office by a person elected creates a casual vacancy.

(*a*) As to the returning officer in elections of county councillors, see the Local Government Act, s. 75, *ante*, p. 141, and the County Councils (Elections) Act, 1891, *post*. The latter Act provides (s. 1) that nothing shall authorize or require a returning officer to hold an election of a county councillor to fill a casual vacancy which occurs within six months before the ordinary day of retirement of county councillors—viz., March 8th in every third year.

As to the time within which casual elections should be filled, see s. 66, *post*.

(*b*) It is necessary to distinguish the ordinary from the extraordinary vacancies where these are filled up at the ordinary annual election, otherwise the election may be avoided. *R.* v. *Rowley*, 6 Q. B. 668; 14 L. J. Q. B. 62; 8 Jur. 1170; *R.* v. *Rippon*, 1 Q. B. D. 217; 45 L. J. Q. B. 188; 34 L. T. (N.S.) 444; 24 W. R. 633; 40 J. P. 536. The provision in the text applies where two or more casual vacancies are filled at the same time, but the cases referred to cannot apply to county councillors, all of whom go out of office at the same time.

Sect. 41 (1)

Penalty on unqualified person acting in office.

41.—(1.) If any person acts in a corporate office without having made the delaration by this Act required (*a*), or without being qualified at the time of making the declaration, or after ceasing to be qualified (*b*), or after becoming disqualified (*c*), he shall for each offence be liable to a fine not exceeding fifty pounds, recoverable by action (*d*).

(2.) A person being in fact enrolled in the burgess roll shall not be liable to a fine for acting in a corporate office on the ground only that he was not entitled to be enrolled therein (*e*).

(*a*) See s. 35, *ante*, p. 273.

(*b*) See s. 11 and the notes to that section, *ante*, p. 250.

(*c*) As to the disqualification of a councillor, see ss. 12, 39, *ante*, and the notes to those sections.

(*d*) This action must be brought in a borough by a burgess, in a county by a county elector. See s. 224, *post*, which deals with the procedure in such an action.

(*e*) But for this provision a person whose name was on the burgess roll might be liable to a penalty under this section if he were not qualified. But this provision will not in any way prevent the removal of a disqualified person by *quo warranto* or election petition. See *Flintham* v. *Roxburgh*, *ante*, p. 252.

Nor does it protect a person who acts, although disqualified, *e.g.* a woman. *De Souza* v. *Cobden*, [1891] 1 Q. B. 687 ; 60 L. J. Q. B. 533 ; 65 L. T. (N.S.) 130 ; 39 W. R. 454 ; 55 J. P. 565.

Validity of acts done notwithstanding disqualification, etc.

42.—(1.) The acts and proceedings of a person in possession of a corporate office, and acting therein, shall, notwithstanding his disqualification or want of qualification, be as valid and effectual as if he had been qualified (*a*).

(2.) An election of a person to a corporate office shall not be liable to be questioned by reason of a defect in the title, or want of title, of the person before whom the election was had, if that person was then in actual possession of, or acting in, the office giving the right to preside at the election.

(3.) A burgess roll shall not be liable to be questioned by reason of a defect in the title, or want of title, of the mayor or any revising authority (*b*) by whom it is revised, if he was then in actual possession and exercise of the office of mayor or revising authority.

(*a*) See s. 102, *post*. Sub-section (1) does not prevent an inquiry on an election petition into the validity of a vote given by a disqualified person in virtue of the corporate office. *Nell* v. *Longbottom*, [1894] 1 Q. B. 767 ; 63 L. J. Q. B. 490 ; 70 L. T. (N.S.) 499.

(*b*) The revising authority is now the revising barrister. See note to s. 29, *ante*.

Duties of town clerk, deputy, and treasurer, during vacancy or incapacity.

43. If there is no town clerk, and no deputy town clerk, or there is no treasurer, or the town clerk, deputy town clerk, or treasurer (as the case may be) is incapable of acting, all acts by law authorized or required to be done by or with respect to the town clerk or the treasurer (as the case may be) may, subject to the provisions of any other Act, be done by or with respect to a person appointed in that behalf by the mayor. Sect. 43.

It is presumed that this section would enable the chairman of a county council to make an appointment in the cases mentioned in the section.

PART III.

PREPARATIONS FOR AND PROCEDURE AT ELECTIONS.

Parish Burgess Lists ; Burgess Rolls ; Ward Rolls.

44.—(1.) Where the whole or part of the area of a borough is co-extensive with or included in the area of a parliamentary borough, the lists of burgesses are to be made out and revised, and claims and objections relating thereto are to be made, in accordance with the provisions of the Parliamentary and Municipal Registration Act, 1878. Preparation and revision of parish burgess list.

(2.) Where no part of the area of a borough is co-extensive with or included in the area of a parliamentary borough, the lists of burgesses shall be made out and revised, and claims and objections relating thereto may be made in accordance, as nearly as may be, with the provisions of Part I. of the Third Schedule.

(3.) In either case the lists shall be styled the parish burgess lists.

It is provided by the County Electors Act, 1888, s. 4, *post*, that in all boroughs the lists of burgesses shall be revised by the revising barrister in manner provided by the 41 & 42 Vict. c. 26, and that revising assessors shall no longer be appointed. Sub-section (2) of the above section is therefore practically repealed. The same section also provides that the lists of county electors in parishes outside boroughs shall be made out and revised in like manner as burgess lists in boroughs, with certain qualifications for which reference may be made to the section itself, *post*.

45. (*a*)—(1.) When the parish burgess lists have been revised and signed, the revising authority (*b*) shall deliver them to the town clerk (*c*), and a printed copy thereof (*d*), examined by him and signed by him, shall be the burgess roll of the borough. The burgess roll and ward rolls.

(2.) The burgess roll shall be completed on or before the twentieth of October in each year, and shall come into operation on the first of November in that year, and shall continue in operation for the twelve months beginning on that day (*e*).

(3.) The names in the burgess roll shall be numbered by wards or by polling districts, unless in any case the council direct that the same be numbered consecutively without reference to wards or polling districts (*f*).

(4.) Where the borough has no wards, the burgess roll shall be made in one general roll for the whole borough.

Sect. 45 (5).

(5.) Where the borough has wards, the burgess roll shall be made in separate rolls called ward rolls, one for each ward, containing the names of the persons entitled to vote in that ward, and the ward rolls collectively shall constitute the burgess roll (*g*).

(6.) A burgess shall not be enrolled in more than one ward roll (*h*).

(7.) Where a duplicate of a burgess list is made under section thirty-one of the Parliamentary and Municipal Registration Act, 1878, it shall have the same effect as the original, and may be delivered instead thereof (*i*).

(8.) Every person enrolled in the burgess roll shall be deemed to be enrolled as a burgess, and every person not enrolled in the burgess roll shall be deemed to be not enrolled as a burgess.

(9.) No stamp duty shall be payable in respect of the enrolment of a burgess.

(*a*) It is provided by the County Electors Act, 1888, s. 7, that the clerk of the peace of every county shall make up a register of all persons registered as burgesses or county electors in the county, both for the county and for each electoral division into which the county is divided for the purpose of election of the county authority, and such number of copies as the clerk of the peace may require of the list of burgesses as revised shall be delivered by the town clerk to such clerk of the peace for the purpose of making up such register. Consequently in all boroughs the revised list of burgesses will be delivered to the town clerk as provided by the above section, and it will be his duty to print and sign the burgess roll, and to send copies of it to the clerk of the peace to enable the latter to make up the roll of county electors. Section 7 of the County Electors Act contains a further provision applying the above section to the roll of county electors. It provides that "the Registration of Electors Acts, and ss. 45, 48 and 71 of the Municipal Corporations Act, 1882, shall apply for the purposes of this section, with the substitution of clerk of the peace for town clerk, and of county register and division register for burgess roll and ward roll respectively, and of electoral division for ward, and of county fund for borough fund."

(*b*) The revising authority is now in every case the revising barrister.

(*c*) In making out the burgess roll of a municipal borough the names of eighty-two persons were put in the wrong wards, and the mistake was not discovered till after the revising barrister had settled the list. *Held*, that the proper remedy was not a *mandamus* to the town clerk to correct the roll. *Quære* whether the remedy was not a *mandamus* to the revising barrister. *Ex parte Keay*, 56 J. P. 470 ; 65 L. T. (N.S.) 323.

(*d*) The town clerk of a borough must print the burgess list (s. 48, *post*). The clerk of the peace must print the list of county electors in places not in boroughs. See note (*a*), *supra*.

(*e*) The County Councils (Elections) Act, 1891 (54 & 55 Vict. c. 68), s. 2, *post*, provides that the county register shall be completed before December 20th, in every year, and come into operation on the next January 1st, and that the burgess lists forming the burgess roll which comes into operation on November 1st in every year, shall on and after that day until the next January 1st, form part of the county register in substitution for the former burgess lists.

(*f*) The County Electors Act, 1888, s. 4, amended by the Local Government Act, s. 76, *ante*, p. 147, provides as follows : (2) In the construction of the

NOTE.

Registration of Electors Acts for the purpose of their application to a parish *not situate within a municipal borough*, there shall be made the variations following, and such other variations as may be necessary for carrying into effect the application, that is to say :—(*e*) Section 21 of the Parliamentary and Municipal Registration Act, 1878, shall not apply, and the list and register of voters shall be made out alphabetically, but shall be framed in parts for polling districts and electoral divisions . . . in such a manner that the parts may be conveniently compiled, or put together to serve as lists for polling districts . . . and as electoral division lists. (3) Notwithstanding anything in this Act contained, where a municipal borough or an urban district is co-extensive with any electoral division or divisions of a parliamentary county, the list of voters may be directed by the county council to be made out according to the order in which the qualifying premises appear in the rate book, and s. 21 of the Parliamentary and Municipal Registration Act, 1878, shall apply to such borough or urban district, and where lists of voters are so made out, nothing in this Act shall require such part of the county register as consists of these lists to be arranged alphabetically. The names of the parliamentary electors and of the county electors in the lists may be numbered consecutively, and such portion of these lists as consist of the names of parliamentary electors may be taken to form the register for the purpose of parliamentary elections, and such portion of these lists as contains the names of county electors may be taken to form the register of county electors.

(*g*) See s. 7 of the County Electors Act, 1888, set out in note (*a*), *supra*.

(*h*) This will not apply to county electors, for by s. 7 of the County Electors Act, 1888, it is expressly provided that nothing in that section shall prevent a county elector from being registered in more than one division register. But though he may be registered in more than one, he can only vote in one division at the same election. *Knill* v. *Towse*, 24 Q. B. D. 697 ; 59 L. J. Q. B. 455 ; 63 L. T. (N.S.) 47 ; 38 W. R. 521 ; 54 J. P. 789 ; 6 T. L. R. 310.

(*i*) It is provided by 41 & 42 Vict. c. 26, s. 31, that the revising barrister shall, as part of the business of the revision, at the request of the town clerk of any municipal borough sign and deliver to him a duplicate of the whole or part of any revised list made out in divisions and relating to that municipal borough. Every such duplicate shall be prepared by the town clerk at whose request it is so signed and shall be kept by him for use for municipal purposes. This section now applies to all boroughs, and also to parishes in new boroughs. See note (*a*), *supra*.

Arrangement of lists and rolls.

46.—(1.) If and as far as the council so direct, the parish burgess lists, and the burgess roll, and the ward rolls (if any), and the lists of claimants and respondents, or any of those documents, shall be arranged in the same order in which the qualifying properties appear in the rate-book for the parish in which they are situate, or otherwise in such order as will cause those lists and rolls to record the qualifying properties in successive order in the street or other place in which they are situate.

(2.) Subject to any such direction, and to the provisions of this Act as to polling districts, the arrangement of the lists and rolls shall be alphabetical.

This section will not apply to parishes not situate in a municipal borough, and even in boroughs it may be superseded by the County Electors Act, 1888, s. 4 (3), set out in note (*f*) to the last section. It is there provided that, where

Sect. 46.

NOTE.

a municipal borough or urban district is co-extensive with an electoral division or divisions of a parliamentary county, the list of voters may be directed by the county council to be made out according to the order in which the qualifying premises appear in the rate book, and s. 21 of the 41 & 42 Vict. c. 26, shall apply to such borough or district. The 41 & 42 Vict. c. 26, s. 21, is substantially to the same effect as the text so far as regards the burgess lists and rolls. Therefore, if the county council make no order under s. 7 of the County Electors Act, it will be open to the borough council to make an order under the provisions in the text.

Correction of burgess roll.

47.—(1.) Where the parish burgess lists are revised under the Parliamentary and Municipal Registration Act, 1878, the burgess roll is subject to alteration or correction in manner provided by section thirty-five of that Act (*a*).

(2.) Where the parish burgess lists are revised under this Act, any person whose claim has been rejected or name expunged at the revision of the lists may apply, within two months after the last sitting of the revision court, to the High Court in the Queen's Bench Division for a mandamus to the mayor to insert his name in the burgess roll; and thereupon the court shall inquire into the title of the applicant to be enrolled (*b*).

(3.) If the court grants a mandamus, the mayor shall insert the name in the burgess roll, and shall add thereto the words "by order of Her Majesty's High Court of Justice," and shall subscribe his name to those words (*b*).

(*a*) The parish burgess lists and the lists of county electors must now be revised in every case under the Act of 1878. By s. 35 of that Act, "the provisions of the Parliamentary Registration Acts as to appeal from the decision of the revising barrister shall apply to a decision on a revision of the burgess lists, and the provisions of the said Acts as to the alteration or correction of the register, in pursuance of any judgment or order of the Court of Appeal, shall apply to the alteration or correction of the burgess roll made up from the burgess lists as if it were a register of parliamentary voters, except that the notice of the judgment or order shall be given to the town clerk having the custody of the burgess roll, and the alteration or correction shall be made and signed by him." This provision will apply to the lists and roll of county electors with the necessary modifications.

(*b*) As no lists will henceforth be made out "under this Act," sub-ss. (2) and (3) are practically repealed.

Printing and sale of burgess roll and other documents.

48.—The town clerk shall cause the parish burgess lists, the lists of claimants and respondents, and the burgess roll to be printed, and shall deliver printed copies to any person on payment of a reasonable price for each copy.

(2.) Subject to section thirty of the Parliamentary and Municipal Registration Act, 1878, the proceeds of sale shall go to the borough fund.

For the provisions of the County Electors Act, 1888, applying this section to the roll of county electors, see note (*a*) to s. 45, *ante*, p. 280.

Sect. 48.

NOTE.

The 41 & 42 Vict. c. 26, s. 30, sub-s. (1) of which now applies to all boroughs, provides that one-half of the moneys received in respect of the burgess lists shall be applied in the manner directed by the Parliamentary Registration Acts, and the other half shall be paid to the borough fund.

Separate list of persons qualified to be councillors but not to be burgesses.

49.—(1.) The overseers of each parish shall, at the same time that they make the parish burgess list, make a list of the persons entitled in respect of the occupation of property in that parish to be elected councillors, as being resident within fifteen miles although beyond seven miles from the borough.

(2.) The provisions of this Act as to the parish burgess lists, and claims and objections relating thereto, and the revision of those lists shall, as nearly as circumstances admit, apply to the lists made under this section.

(3.) The town clerk shall arrange the names entered in these lists, when revised, in alphabetical order as a separate list (in this Act called the separate non-resident list), with an appropriate heading, at the end of the burgess roll.

The separate non-resident list will continue to be made out in boroughs as heretofore. The list so made out in boroughs will contain the names of persons who are entitled to be enrolled as burgesses in all respects save that of residence within seven miles of the borough, but who, by reason of residence within the fifteen mile limit, are qualified to be elected councillors under s. 11, sub-s. (2), *ante*, p. 250. If a person is enrolled on a borough non-resident list, he will also be qualified to be elected a county councillor for the county of which the borough forms a part. See the Local Government Act, s. 75 (12), *ante*, p 144.

A precisely similar list is to be made out for each county. The County Electors Act, 1888, s. 12, provides that "a list of persons occupying property in a county, and residing within fifteen miles, but more than seven miles, from the county, shall be made out in accordance with s. 49 of the Municipal Corporations Act, 1882, and that section shall apply as if it were herein re-enacted, with the substitution of 'county' for 'borough,' and of 'county elector' for 'burgess,' and of 'clerk of the peace' for 'town clerk.'" It is provided by the Local Government Act, s. 76 (6), *ante*, p. 150, that nothing in s. 12 of the County Electors Act applies to any person occupying property in a borough. The reason of this provision is obvious; it avoids the necessity of including in the county non-resident list the names of persons who are enrolled in the corresponding list in the borough. But the result is that a person who occupies property in a borough, and who resides more than fifteen miles from the borough, will not be qualified to be elected a councillor, though his residence may be in the county, or within fifteen miles of its boundary. This hardship is more apparent than real, for such a person will generally be qualified as a county elector in respect of his residence.

In counties outside boroughs the overseers must make a separate non-resident list for their parishes. These lists will be revised by the revising barrister and arranged by the clerk of the peace, as provided by the above section.

As to the mode of measuring the distance, see s. 231, *post*.

In the county of London there will be no separate non-resident list, for by s. 77 of the Local Government Act, *ante*, p. 151, the persons whose names would appear upon it in London are to be registered as county electors.

Sect. 50 (1).

Election of Councillors.

Borough and ward elections.

50.—(1.) Where a borough has no wards, there shall be one election of councillors for the whole borough.

(2.) Where a borough has wards, there shall be a separate election of councillors for each ward.

The Local Government Act, s. 2, *ante*, p. 1, provides that the members of a county council shall be elected in like manner as the council of a borough divided into wards. The divisions of a county are to be called electoral divisions, and not wards. There will therefore be a separate election of councillors for each electoral division.

Title to vote.

51.—(1.) At an election of councillors a person shall be entitled to subscribe a nomination paper (*a*), and to demand and receive a voting paper, and to vote (*b*), if he is enrolled in the burgess roll, or in the case of a ward election, the ward roll, and not otherwise.

(2.) No person shall subscribe a nomination paper in or for more than one ward, or vote in more than one ward (*c*).

(3.) Nothing in this section shall entitle any person to do any act therein mentioned who is prohibited by law from doing it, or relieve him from any penalty to which he may be liable for doing it (*d*).

(*a*) As to nomination papers and nominations, see Sched. 3, Part II., *post.*

(*b*) But observe, that though a person whose name is on the burgess roll (or roll of county electors, as the case may be) is entitled to vote, yet unless he is entitled to be so enrolled, he is not qualified to be elected a councillor. See *Flintham* v. *Roxburgh*, *ante*, p. 252.

(*c*) It is provided by s. 45, sub-s. (6), *ante*, p. 280, that a burgess shall not be enrolled in more than one ward roll. By the County Electors Act, 1888, s. 7, sub-s. (4), a county elector may be registered in more than one division register. But though he may be registered in more than one he cannot vote in more than one division of the county at the same election. *Knill* v. *Towse*, *ante*, p. 281.

(*d*) Persons found guilty of corrupt or illegal practices, or of illegal payment, employment, or hiring at a municipal election, are prohibited from voting by 47 & 48 Vict. c. 70, ss. 2, 22, 23 and Sched. 3, Part II., *post.*

Day of election.

52. The ordinary day of election of councillors shall be the first of November.

The ordinary day of election of county councillors is now a day to be fixed by the county council not less than six weeks before the ordinary day of retirement of county councillors. 54 & 55 Vict. c. 68, s. 1, *post.*

Returning officer at election.

53.—(1.) At an election of councillors for a whole borough the returning officer shall be the mayor.

(2.) At an election for a ward the returning officer shall be an alderman assigned for that purpose by the council at the meeting of the ninth of November. Sect. 53 (2).

It is provided by the Local Government Act, s. 75 (2), *ante*, p. 141, that such a person as the county council may appoint shall be the returning officer for the election of county councillors of the county council, in substitution for the mayor, and for the aldermen assigned for that purpose by the council. It has been pointed out in the note to s. 50, *ante*, p. 284, that there must be a separate election for each electoral division. It will be necessary to appoint a returning officer for the entire county, corresponding to the mayor, who has special duties to perform in connection with the hearing of objections to nomination papers under Sched. 3, Part II., r. 9, *post*. This official will be the county returning officer, and he will in all divisions of the county be returning officer in the place of the mayor and aldermen. He will have to appoint a deputy returning officer for all divisions in which he does not himself undertake the duties of his office. See the notes to the Local Government Act, s. 75, sub-ss. (2) (3), *ante*, p. 142.

It is now provided by 54 & 55 Vict. c. 68, s. 3, that for the purpose of the election of county councillors for any electoral division which is co-extensive with or wholly comprised in a municipal borough the following provisions shall have effect :—(a) The mayor of the borough, or some person appointed by him, or, if the mayor is dead or absent or otherwise incapable of acting, an alderman appointed by the council of the borough, shall be the returning officer, and so far as respects such election shall follow the instructions of and return the names of the persons elected to the county returning officer. (b) Nothing in s. 75 of the Local Government Act, 1888, substituting the returning officer or his deputy for the town clerk, shall extend to any such election. It may be mentioned here that a returning officer cannot act as such at an election at which he is a candidate, and that if he returned himself his election would be void. *R.* v. *Owens*, 2 E. & E. 86; 28 L. J. Q. B. 316; 23 J. P. 741; *R.* v. *Blizard*, L. R. 2 Q. B. 55; 36 L. J. Q. B. 18; 15 L. T. (N.S.) 242; 15 W. R. 105; 31 J. P. 200; *R.* v. *White*, L. R. 2 Q. B. 557; 36 L. J. Q. B. 267; 16 L. T. (N.S.) 828; 15 W. R. 988; 32 J. P. 595; *R.* v. *Ward*, L. R. 8 Q. B. 210; 42 L. J. Q. B. 126; 28 L. T. (N.S.) 118; 21 W. R. 632; 37 J. P. 453; *R.* v. *Morton*, [1892] 1 Q. B. 39; 61 L. J. Q. B. 39; 65 L. T. 611; 40 W. R. 109; 56 J. P. 105; 8 T. L. R. 50; *Fanagan* v. *Kernan*, 8 L. R. Ir. 44; *Tralee Election Petition*, 28 Ir. C. L. 10.

54. Nine days at least before the day for the election of a councillor, the town clerk shall prepare and sign a notice thereof, and publish it by fixing it on the town hall, and, in the case of a ward election, in some conspicuous place in the ward. Notice of election.

The ordinary day of election of borough councillors is November 1st. In general the last day for giving notice under this section will be October 22nd. But if November 1st happens to be a Sunday, the day of election will be November 2nd (see s. 230, *post*), and the period of nine days must be reckoned with reference to that date. See 49 J. P. 675. The ordinary day of election of county councillors is now fixed by the county council not less than six weeks before March 8th (54 & 55 Vict. c. 68, s. 1, *post*) but the mode of computation of time for purposes of the notice of election is as above stated.

In elections of county councillors the returning officer must give this notice, which must be fixed in some conspicuous place in the electoral division. See s. 232, *post*, and the Local Government Act, s. 75, *ante*, p. 141.

Care must be taken to calculate the last day for delivery of nomination

Sect. 54.

papers, for a mistake may avoid the election. *Howes* v. *Turner*, 1 C. P. D. 670; 45 L. J. C. P. 550; 35 L. T. (N.S.) 58.

NOTE.

It is provided by the Parliamentary Elections (Returning Officers) Act, 1875 (38 & 39 Vict. c. 84), s. 7, *ante*, p. 234, that there should be added to every notice of election published under the Ballot Act, 1872, the notification with respect to claims against returning officers which is set out in Sched. 2 to the first-mentioned Act.

Nomination of candidates.

55. The nomination of candidates for the office of councillor shall be conducted in accordance with the rules in Part II. of the Third Schedule.

See the schedule, *post*.

Relation of nomination to election.

56.—(1.) If the number of valid nominations exceeds that of vacancies, the councillors shall be elected from among the persons nominated.

(2.) If the number of valid nominations is the same as that of the vacancies, the persons nominated shall be deemed to be elected.

(3.) If the number of valid nominations is less than that of the vacancies, the persons nominated shall be deemed to be elected, and such of the retiring councillors for the borough or ward as were highest on the poll at their election, or, if the poll was equal, or there was no poll, as are selected for that purpose by the mayor, shall be deemed to be re-elected to make up the required number.

(4.) If there is no valid nomination the retiring councillors shall be deemed to be re-elected.

In county council elections the selection referred to in sub-s. (3), will be made by the returning officer. See the Local Government Act, s. 75 (4), *ante*, p. 142.

Where on a casual vacancy no valid nomination is made, a *mandamus* will be granted under s. 70, *post*, on the application of a burgess, to hold the election, and the court will order the costs of the application to be paid by the corporation. *R.* v. *Stratford-upon-Avon (Mayor of)*, 2 T. L. R. 431. This case was followed as to a county council election in *R.* v. *West Sussex County Council*, 65 L. J. Q. B. 184; 59 J. P. 808; 73 L. T. (N.S.) 566; 12 T. L. R. 99; *Reg.* v. *Surrey County Council*, *Times*, August 5th, 1896.

By a "valid nomination" is to be understood a nomination to which no objection has been made before the mayor or returning officer, or a nomination to which the objections made before the mayor or returning officer have been disallowed by him. But it does not mean a nomination which is absolutely valid for all purposes so as not to be questionable on a petition questioning the election or return. *Pritchard* v. *Bangor (Mayor of)* 13 App. Cas. 241; 57 L. J. Q. B. 313: 58 L. T. (N.S.) 502; 37 W. R. 103; 52 J. P. 564.

Publication of uncontested election.

57.—(1.) If an election of councillors is not contested, the returning officer shall publish a list of the persons elected not later than eleven o'clock in the morning on the day of election.

The hour must be determined by Greenwich time, as provided by 43 & 44 Vict. c. 9. As to the day of election, see the note to s. 52, *ante*, p. 284. The day of election to fill a casual vacancy is the day fixed by the mayor, or in elections of county councillors by the returning officer under s. 66, *post*. Sect. 57. NOTE.

Mode of conducting poll at contested election. 35 & 36 Vict. c. 33.

58.—(1.) If an election of councillors is contested, the poll shall, as far as circumstances admit, be conducted as the poll at a contested parliamentary election is by the Ballot Act, 1872, directed to be conducted, and subject to the modifications expressed in Part III. of the Third Schedule (*a*), and to the other provisions of this Act, the provisions of the Ballot Act, 1872, relating to a poll at a parliamentary election (including the provisions relating to the duties of the returning officer after the close of the poll), shall apply to a poll at an election of councillors.

(2.) Every person entitled to vote may vote for any number of candidates not exceeding the number of vacancies (*b*).

(3.) The poll shall commence at nine o'clock in the forenoon and close at four in the afternoon of the same day (*c*).

(4.) But if one hour elapses during which no vote is tendered, and the returning officer has not received notice that any person has within that hour been prevented from coming to the poll by any riot, violence, or other unlawful means, the returning officer may, if he thinks fit, close the poll at any time before four o'clock (*d*).

(5.) Where an equality of votes is found to exist between any candidates, and the addition of a vote would entitle any of those candidates to be declared elected, the returning officer, whether entitled or not to vote in the first instance (*e*), may give such additional vote by word of mouth or in writing.

(6.) Nothing in the Ballot Act, 1872, as applied by this Act, shall be deemed to authorize the appointment of any agents of a candidate at a municipal election; but if, in the case of a municipal election, an agent of a candidate is appointed, and notice in writing of the appointment is given to the returning officer, one clear day before the polling day, then the provisions of the Ballot Act, 1872, with respect to agents of candidates, shall, as far as regards that agent, apply in the case of that election.

(*a*) See the schedule, *post*.

(*b*) See the note to s. 40, *ante*, p. 277, as to a case where ordinary and casual vacancies are filled at the same election.

(*c*) This provision is superseded by the 48 Vict. c. 10, which provides that at every municipal election the poll (if any) shall commence at eight o'clock in the forenoon, and be kept open until eight o'clock in the afternoon of the same day, and no longer. The Local Government Act, s. 75, (11), *ante*, p. 144, expressly provides that at an election of county councillors the hours of the poll shall be those fixed by the 48 Vict. c. 10.

(*d*) This provision also seems to be superseded by the 48 Vict. c. 10.

(*e*) This means that the returning officer may give this vote whether or not he is enrolled as a burgess or as an elector for the division, as the case may be.

Sect. 58.

NOTE.

Where no casting vote was given, and the proceedings were therefore abortive, *mandamus* was granted to the returning officer to hold a fresh election. *Croone* v. *Waugh*, *Times*, June 3rd, 1892. But in a subsequent case where the application was made by a candidate and not by electors, and a year had elapsed since the election, the court in the exercise of their discretion refused to grant a *mandamus*. *Ex parte Barnes*, *Times*, February 7th, 1893. And see *Richmond* (*Borough of*), *In re*, *Times*, March 24th, 1893.

Questions which may be put to voters.

59.—(1.) At an election of councillors, the presiding officer shall, if required by two burgesses, or by a candidate or his agent, put to any person offering to vote, at the time of his presenting himself to vote, but not afterwards, the following questions, or either of them :—

(a.) Are you the person enrolled in the burgess [*or* ward] roll now in force for this borough [*or* ward] as follows [*read the whole entry from the roll*] ?

(b.) Have you already voted at the present election [*add in case of an election for several wards*, in this or any other ward] ?

(2.) The vote of a person required to answer either of these questions shall not be received until he has answered it.

(3.) If any person wilfully makes a false answer thereto he shall be guilty of a misdemeanor.

(4.) Save as by this Act authorized, no inquiry shall be permitted at an election as to the right of any person to vote.

This section will apply to an election of county councillors with certain modifications. "County electors" must be substituted for "burgesses," "division register" for "ward roll," "county" for "borough," and "electoral division" for "ward."

Election of Aldermen (*a*).

Time and mode of election of aldermen.

60.—(1.) The ordinary day of election of aldermen shall be the ninth of November, and the election shall be held at the quarterly meeting of the council (*b*).

(2.) The election shall be held immediately after the election of the mayor (*c*), or, if there is a sheriff, the appointment of the sheriff.

(3.) An outgoing alderman, although mayor elect, shall not vote (*d*).

(4.) Every person entitled to vote may vote for any number of persons not exceeding the number of vacancies, by signing and personally delivering (*e*) at the meeting to the chairman a voting paper containing the surnames and other names (*f*), and places of abode and descriptions of the persons for whom he votes.

(5.) The chairman, as soon as all the voting papers have been delivered to him, shall openly produce and read them, or cause them to be read, and then deliver them to the town clerk to be kept for twelve months (*g*). Sect. 60 (5).

(6.) In case of equality of votes the chairman, although as an outgoing alderman or otherwise not entitled to vote in the first instance (*h*), shall have the casting vote.

(7.) The persons, not exceeding the number of vacancies, who have the greatest number of votes, shall be declared by the chairman to be, and thereupon shall be, elected.

(*a*) In county councils, the aldermen are to be called county aldermen. See the Local Government Act, s. 2, *ante*, p. 2.

(*b*) The ordinary day of election of chairman and aldermen of a county council and the day for holding a quarterly meeting of a county council is March 16th, or such other day within ten days after the ordinary day of retirement of county councillors as the county council may fix. See County Councils (Elections) Act, 1891, *post*.

(*c*) See the next section. If the election of aldermen precedes that of the mayor, it will be void. *R.* v. *McGowan*, 11 A. & E. 869.

(*d*) It is provided by the Local Government Act, s. 2, *ante*, p. 2, that a county alderman shall not, as such, vote in the election of a county alderman. The meaning of the words "as such" is obscure. In a borough council the aldermen may vote with the exception mentioned in the text. Where an alderman was elected mayor, and thereupon made and subscribed the declaration, and then voted in the election of aldermen, it was held that his vote was invalid, for at the time when he voted he had not ceased to be an outgoing alderman within the meaning of the text. *Bridport Election Petition*, *Hounsell* v. *Suttill*, 19 Q. B. D. 498 ; 56 L. J. Q. B. 502 ; 57 L. T. (N.S.) 102 ; 36 W. R. 157 ; 51 J. P. 440.

(*e*) The collection of the voting papers by the town clerk in the presence and view of the chairman, who received them immediately from the town clerk, was held to be a sufficient compliance with this sub-section. *Baxter* v. *Spencer*, 64 L. J. Q. B. 644 ; 72 L. T. (N.S.) 838 ; 59 J. P. 376.

(*f*) The other names may probably be denoted by initials. See *R.* v. *Plenty*, L. R. 4 Q. B. 346, and the cases cited in the notes to s. 241, *post*.

(*g*) In counties, the clerk of the council must keep the voting papers.

(*h*) These words appear to be inserted to make it clear that his right of a casting vote was not intended to confer a right to a first vote where none such existed in fact. *Nell* v. *Longbottom*, [1894] 1 Q. B. 767 ; 63 L. J. Q. B. 490 ; 70 L. T. (N.S.) 499.

Election of Mayor.

61.—(1.) The ordinary day of election of mayor shall be the ninth of November (*a*). Time and mode of election of mayor.

(2.) The election of mayor shall be the first business transacted at the quarterly meeting of the council on the day of election.

(3.) An outgoing alderman may vote although the person for whom he votes is an alderman (*b*).

(4.) In case of equality of votes, the chairman, although not entitled to vote in the first instance, shall have the casting vote (*c*).

(*a*) In counties, the chairman of the county council is called chairman, instead of mayor. See the Local Government Act, s. 2, *ante*, p. 4. As to the

Sect. 61.

NOTE.

ordinary day of election of chairman of a county council and the date of the quarterly meeting, see note (*b*) to s. 60, *ante*.

(*b*) An outgoing alderman is eligible. See s. 15, sub-s. (2), *ante*, p. 256. But this sub-section will not apply to a county council. See the Local Government Act, 1888, s. 75 (10), *ante*, p. 143.

(*c*) This sub-section does not prevent the chairman from voting in the first instance unless he is otherwise disqualified. See *Nell* v. *Longbottom*, cited in the note to the preceding section.

Election of Auditors and Assessors.

Time and mode of election of auditors and assessors.

62.—(1.) The ordinary day of election of elective auditors shall be the first of March, or such other day as the council, with the approval of the Local Government Board, from time to time appoint.

(2.) The ordinary day of election of revising assessors shall be the first of March.

(3.) If the election of elective auditors and that of revising assessors are held at the same time, then at the poll one voting paper only shall be used by any person voting. The names of the candidates for the respective offices shall be therein separate, and distinguished so as to show the office for which each is a candidate, and the provisions of the Ballot Act, 1872, shall be varied accordingly; but in the counting of the votes every voting paper shall be deemed to be a separate voting paper in respect of each office, and any objections thereto shall be considered and dealt with accordingly.

(4.) An elector shall not vote for more than one person to be elective auditor or revising assessor.

(5.) Elections of elective auditors and of revising assessors shall be held at the town hall or some one other convenient place appointed by the mayor.

(6.) Save as in this section provided, all the provisions of this Act with respect to the nomination and election of councillors for a borough not having wards shall apply to the nomination and election of elective auditors and revising assessors.

It is provided by the Local Government Act, s. 75 (16) (b), *ante*, p. 145, that the provisions of this Act as to borough auditors shall not apply to county councils.

Revising assessors are no longer to be elected in any borough. See the note to s. 29, *ante*, p. 268.

Supplemental and Exceptional Provisions.

Right of women to vote.

63. For all purposes connected with and having reference to the right to vote at municipal elections words in this Act importing the masculine gender include women.

The County Electors Act, 1888, s. 2, extends the provisions of this section to so much of every county as is not comprised within the limits of a municipal borough. Women are therefore qualified to be enrolled and to vote as burgesses or county electors. But it is to be inferred from this section that women may not be elected. Had no express provision been made, a woman might have been deemed a "person" within the meaning of ss. 9 and 11, having regard to the provisions of 13 & 14 Vict. c. 21. But this section by providing in effect that a woman shall be a "person" within s. 9, implies that she is not a person within s. 11. See the judgments in *Flintham* v. *Roxburgh*, and *Beresford Hope* v. *Sandhurst*, *ante*, p. 252. The right of women to vote under this section does not extend to married women. See *R.* v. *Harrald*, L. R. 7 Q. B. 361; 41 L. J. Q. B. 173; 26 L. T. (N.S.) 616; 20 W. R. 328; 36 J. P. 438. Sect. 63. NOTE.

64. The council may divide the borough or any ward into polling districts, and thereupon the overseers shall, so far as practicable, make out the parish burgess lists so as to divide the names in conformity with the polling districts. Polling districts.

This section enables a county council to divide any electoral division into polling districts.

In a parish which is not within a municipal borough, the lists of voters are to be framed in parts for polling districts and electoral divisions, and for urban districts and for wards in such a manner that the parts may be conveniently compiled or put together to serve as lists for polling districts and elections in urban districts and as electoral division or ward lists. See the County Electors Act, 1888, s. 4, sub-s. (2), amended by the Local Government Act, s. 76, *ante*, p. 147.

65. Any notice required to be given in connection with a municipal election may, as to elective auditors and revising assessors, be comprised in one notice, and may, as to ward elections, comprise matter necessary for several wards. Notices as to elections.

The provisions as to elective auditors do not apply to elections of county councillors, and revising assessors are no longer to be elected. See the note to s. 62, *ante*. The provision as to notices will, however, apply to elections of county councillors, and will enable one notice to be given comprising matter necessary for several electoral divisions.

66.—(1.) On a casual vacancy in a corporate office, the election shall be held within fourteen days after notice in writing of the vacancy has been given to the mayor or town clerk by two burgesses. Time for filling casual vacancies.

(2.) Where the office vacant is that of mayor, the notice of the meeting for the election shall be signed by the town clerk.

(3.) In other cases the day of election shall be fixed by the mayor.

As to the holding of elections to fill casual vacancies, see s. 40, *ante*, p. 277.

For a case where there was no valid nomination to fill a casual vacancy, see *R.* v. *Stratford-upon-Avon*, *ante*, p. 286.

The notice of a casual vacancy may be given by any two burgesses or county electors. It may be given in county councils to the chairman or clerk of the council. Where a person has been elected and has resigned, the new election

Sect. 66.

may be within fourteen days after notice under this section. *R.* v. *Bester*, 3 L. T. (N.S.) 667; 9 W. R. 277; 7 Jur. (N.S.) 262.

NOTE.

It seems that the word "mayor" in sub-s. (1) must be read as "chairman of the county council," but whether this be so or not the word must be read as standing for "returning officer" in sub-s. (3). See the Local Government Act, s. 75, *ante*, p. 142.

Illness, etc. of mayor or returning officer.

67.—(1.) If the mayor is dead, or is absent, or otherwise incapable of acting in the execution of his powers and duties as to elections under this Act, the council shall forthwith choose an alderman to execute those powers and duties in the place of the mayor.

(2.) In case of the illness, absence, or incapacity to act of the alderman assigned to be returning officer at a ward election, the mayor may appoint to act in his stead another alderman, or, if the number of aldermen does not exceed the number of wards, a councillor, not being a councillor for that ward, and not being enrolled in the ward roll for that ward.

This section does not apply to county councils, unless it is read as an express provision that in case of the death, etc., of the county returning officer the county council may appoint another person in his stead. The county council appoint the county returning officer under s. 75 (2) of the Local Government Act, *ante*, p. 141, and there seems to be no reason why they should not, without the aid of this section, appoint another person in case of his death, etc. Sub-s. (2) cannot apply, for the county returning officer is to be substituted for the alderman as well as for the mayor. See the note to s. 53, *ante*, p. 284.

Election of councillor in more than one ward.

68. If a person is elected councillor in more than one ward, he shall, within three days after notice thereof, choose, by writing signed by him and delivered to the town clerk, or in his default the mayor shall, within three days after the time for choice has expired, declare for which of those wards he shall serve, and the choice or declaration shall be conclusive.

The reference to the mayor and town clerk must be read as a reference to the returning officer, having regard to the Local Government Act, s. 75, sub-ss. (4) and (5), *ante*, p. 142.

Upon the declaration being made a casual vacancy will be created in the division or ward for which the councillor has elected not to serve. As to the filling up of such casual vacancies, see s. 40, *ante*, p. 277; s. 66, *ante*, p. 291.

Elections not in churches.

69. A municipal election shall not be held in any church, chapel, or other place of public worship.

Omission to hold election or election void.

70.—(1.) If a municipal election is not held on the appointed day, or within the appointed time, it may be held on the day next after that day or the expiration of that time.

(2.) If a municipal election is not held on the appointed day, or within the appointed time, or on the day next after that day or the expiration of that time, or becomes void, the municipal corporation shall not thereby be dissolved or be disabled from electing, but the High Court may, on motion, grant a mandamus for the election to be held on a day appointed by the court (*a*). Sect. 70 (2).

(3.) Thereupon public notice of the election shall, by such person as the court directs, be fixed on the town hall (*b*), and shall be kept so fixed for at least six days before the day appointed for the election; and in all other respects the election shall be conducted as directed by this Act respecting ordinary elections.

(*a*) For cases where *mandamus* was granted, see the notes to s. 56, *ante*, p. 286; s. 58, pp. 287—288.

(*b*) See s. 231, *post*. In the election of county councillors the notice may be fixed in a conspicuous place in the division.

Burgess roll to be in operation until revision of new burgess roll.

71.—(1.) If a parish burgess list is not made or revised in due time, the corresponding part of the burgess roll in operation before the time appointed for the revision shall be the parish burgess list until a burgess list for the parish has been revised and become part of the burgess roll.

(2.) If a burgess roll is not made in due time, the burgess roll in force before the time appointed for the revision shall continue in force until the new burgess roll is made.

The above section is expressly applied to elections of county councillors by s. 7 of the County Electors Act, 1888. See that section, *post*. As to the dates on which the burgess roll and the county register come into operation, see s. 45, sub-s. (2), and note (*e*) *ante*, p. 280.

Non-compliance with rules.

72. An election shall not be invalidated by non-compliance with the rules in the Third Schedule, or mistake in the use of the forms in the Eighth Schedule, if it appears to the court having cognizance of the question that the election was conducted in accordance with the principles laid down in the body of this Act.

See Sched. 3, *post*.

Schedule 8 is not incorporated by the Local Government Act except as to the Forms of Declaration in Part I.

The deputy returning officer for an electoral division of a county supplied for use at an election of a county councillor printed nomination forms in which the name of the division did not appear, but space was left for it. A candidate was nominated by one of such forms, which was signed by the nominators and delivered to the officers without the name of the division having been inserted. It was held that the omission was a mistake in the use of the form within the above section. *Marton* v. *Gorrill*, 23 Q. B. D. 139; 58 L. J. Q. B. 329; 60 L. T. (N.S.) 867; 54 J. P. 181; 5 T. L. R. 443. And see the cases cited in the note to s. 241, *post*.

Election valid unless questioned within twelve months.

73. Every municipal election not called in question within twelve months after the election, either by election petition or by information in the nature of a *quo warranto*, shall be deemed to have been to all intents a good and valid election.

Although an election may not have been questioned within the twelve months above mentioned, yet an unqualified person who has been elected will

Sect. 73.

NOTE.

not be able to take his seat, and will be liable to penalties under s. 41, *ante*, p. 278, if he acts in the office. See *De Souza* v. *Cobden*, [1891] 1 Q. B. 687; 60 L. J. Q. B. 533; 65 L. T. (N.S.) 130; 39 W. R. 454; 55 J. P. 565; 7 T. L. R. 441.

A municipal election must be questioned by means of an election petition, and cannot be questioned by *quo warranto* on any of the grounds mentioned in s. 87, *post*. That section does not, however, apply to prevent proceedings in the nature of *quo warranto* against a person who has been duly elected and subsequently becomes disqualified. As to the time within which and the manner in which proceedings by way of *quo warranto* must be taken, see s. 225, *post*.

Offences in relation to nomination papers.

74.—(1.) If any person forges or fraudulently defaces or fraudulently destroys any nomination paper, or delivers to the town clerk any forged nomination paper, knowing it to be forged, he shall be guilty of a misdemeanor, and shall be liable to imprisonment for any term not exceeding six months, with or without hard labour.

(2.) An attempt to commit any such offence shall be punishable as the offence is punishable.

Where a person signed the name of a voter to a paper with the consent of the voter's wife, but without his knowledge and believing that he might do so, it was held that he could not be convicted of *fabricating* the voting paper within the meaning of 21 & 22 Vict. c. 98, s. 13. *Aberdare Local Board* v. *Hammett*, L. R. 10 Q. B. 162; 44 L. J. M. C. 49; 32 L. T. (N.S.) 20; 39 J. P. 69.

The respondent, a candidate at a local board election, called at the house of a voter to whom a voting paper had been sent, and asked her how she intended to vote, and to hand him the voting paper, which she did. He then inquired if she knew how to fill it up, and she replied in the affirmative. The respondent thereupon, without any authority, express or implied, from the voter, wrote in pencil the initials of the voter against his own name. The voter objected to his doing so. The respondent left the voting paper with the voter with her initials so written by him against his own name, but with no other mark upon it. The voter subsequently struck out the initials so written by the respondent and placed his initials against the names of three other candidates, and signed her own name to the voting paper. It was found that the respondent so pencilled the initials of the voter with the intent of indicating on her behalf that she intended to vote for him, and of inducing and procuring her to vote for him. The respondent was successful at the poll. A petition was presented against his return, on the ground of illegal practices, *inter alia*, of fabricating in whole or in part a voting paper, and of falsely assuming to act in the name or on behalf of a voter. It was held that the act of the respondent did not amount to a fabrication in whole or in part of the voting paper, nor to falsely assuming to act in the name or on behalf of the voter. *Gough* v. *Murdoch*, 57 L. T. (N.S.) 308; 35 W. R. 836; 51 J. P. 471. See also *Bell* v. *Morsar*, 40 L. T. (N.S.) 128; 43 J. P. 174.

Offences in relation to lists and elections.

75.—(1.) If a mayor or revising assessor neglects or refuses to revise a parish burgess list (*a*), or a mayor or alderman (*b*) neglects or refuses to conduct or declare an election, as required by this Act, he shall for every such offence be liable to a fine not exceeding one hundred pounds, recoverable by action (*c*).

(2.) If— Sect. 75 (2).

(a.) An overseer neglects or refuses to make, sign (*d*), or deliver a parish burgess list, as required by this Act; or

(b.) A town clerk (*e*) neglects or refuses to receive, print, and publish a parish burgess list or list of claimants or respondents, as required by this Act; or

(c.) An overseer or town clerk (*e*) refuses to allow any such list to be inspected by a person having a right thereto;

he shall for every such neglect or refusal be liable to a fine not exceeding fifty pounds, recoverable by action (*c*).

(3.) An action under this section shall not lie after three months from the neglect or refusal. A moiety of any fine recovered therein shall, after payment of the costs of action, be paid to the plaintiff.

(*a*) It has already been pointed out that in future no parish burgess list will be revised by the mayor and revising assessors. See s. 44, *ante*, p. 279, and the notes thereto.

(*b*) In applying this section to county councils the returning officer must be substituted for the mayor or alderman. See the Local Government Act, s. 75, *ante*, p. 142.

A mere omission, though not wilful, is an offence against this section. *King* v. *Burrell*, 12 A. & E. 460; *King* v. *Share*, 3 Q. B. 31; *Clarke* v. *Gant*, 8 Ex. 252; *Hunt* v. *Hibbs*, 5 H. & N. 123; 29 L. J. Ex. 122; 6 Jur. (N.S.) 78; 2 L. T. (N.S.) 379; 8 W. R. 238; 24 J. P. 118; *Harwich* (*Mayor, etc., of*) v. *Grant*, 5 E. & B. 182.

(*c*) See s. 226, *post*. But observe that by sub-s. (3) the action must be brought within three months. Notice of action is not necessary. *King* v. *Burrell*, *supra*.

(*d*) The delivery of a printed copy, corrected by an overseer in his own handwriting, is not a sufficient signature. *King* v. *Burrell*, *supra*.

(*e*) This will apply to the clerk of a county council with regard to the county electors' lists. Where liability is incurred for neglecting to make out a list, a second penalty is not incurred under this sub-section. *Gregory* v. *Fell*, 6 Jur. 422.

Revival of former law on expiration of Ballot Act.

76.—(1.) If the Ballot Act, 1872, ceases to be in force, so much of this Act as directs that the poll at a contested election of councillors shall be conducted as the poll at a contested parliamentary election is by the Ballot Act, 1872, directed to be conducted, and as applies provisions of the Ballot Act, 1872, to a poll at a contested election of councillors, shall forthwith cease to be in force, and thereupon the enactments in Part IV. of the Third Schedule shall revive and be in force.

(2.) But this cesser and revivor shall not affect any act done, right acquired, or liability or fine incurred, or the institution

Sect. 76 (2). or prosecution to its termination of any proceeding in respect of any such right, liability, or fine.

The Ballot Act, 1872, is continued in force until December 31st, 1898, by the Expiring Laws Continuance Act, 1897.

PART IV.

Corrupt Practices and Election Petitions.

Corrupt Practices.

Definitions. **77.** In this Part—

"Bribery," "treating," "undue influence," and "personation" (*a*), include respectively anything done before, at, after, or with respect to a municipal election, which if done before, at, after, or with respect to a parliamentary election would make the person doing the same liable to any penalty, punishment, or disqualification for bribery, treating, undue influence, or personation, as the case may be, under any Act for the time being in force with respect to parliamentary elections (*b*) :

"Candidate" means a person elected, or having been nominated, or having declared himself a candidate for election, to a corporate office (*c*) :

"Voter" means a burgess or a person who votes or claims to vote at a municipal election :

"Election court" means a court constituted under this Part for the trial of an election petition :

"Municipal election petition" or "election petition" means a petition under this Part complaining of an undue municipal election :

"Parliamentary election petition" means a petition under the Parliamentary Elections Act, 1868 :

"Prescribed" means prescribed by general rules made under this Part :

"Borough" and "election" when used with reference to a petition mean the borough and election to which the petition relates.

(*a*) The definition of these offences will be found in the Municipal Elections (Corrupt Practices) Act, 1884 (47 & 48 Vict. c. 70), Sched. 3, *post*, which amends this part of the Municipal Corporations Act, 1882, and is incorporated with the Local Government Act by s. 75, *ante*, p. 141.

(*b*) The definition of "corrupt practice" and "canvasser" are repealed by 47 & 48 Vict. c. 70, *post*.

(*c*) See the note to s. 4 of the Municipal Elections (Corrupt Practices) Act, 1884, *post*.

78. * * * **79.** * * * **80.** * * *

These sections were repealed by the 47 & 48 Vict. c. 70, *post*.

81. A municipal election shall be wholly avoided by such general corruption, bribery, treating, or intimidation at the election as would by the common law of Parliament avoid a parliamentary election.

Sect. 81.

Avoidance of election for general corruption.

An election might be avoided under this section, although the candidates and their agents had nothing to do with the general corruption, etc. See *The Lichfield case*, 1 O'M. & H. 26; 20 L. T. (N.S.) 14; *The Bradford case*, 1 O'M. & H. 40; 19 L. T. (N.S.) 725; *The Cheltenham case*, 19 L. T. 818; *The Salford case*, 1 O'M. & H. 140; *The Nottingham case*, 1 O'M. & H. 246; *The Galway case*, 2 O'M. & H. 56; *The Drogheda case*, 1 O'M. & H. 255; *The Dudley case*, 2 O'M. & H. 121.

82. * * * **83.** * * * **84.** * * *

These sections were repealed by 47 & 48 Vict. c. 70, *post*.

85. The votes of persons in respect of whom any corrupt practice is proved to have been committed at a municipal election shall be struck off on a scrutiny.

Striking off votes.

The 47 & 48 Vict. c. 70, s. 22, *post*, provides that every person guilty of a corrupt or illegal practice, or of illegal employment, payment, or hiring at a municipal election, is prohibited from voting at such election, and if any such person votes his vote shall be void, and shall be struck off on a scrutiny. This provision is of wider application than the above section, and practically supersedes it.

86. The enactments for the time being in force for the detection of personation and for the apprehension of persons charged with personation at a parliamentary election shall apply in the case of a municipal election.

Personation.

These enactments are contained in 6 Vict. c. 18, ss. 85—89, which are incorporated with the Ballot Act, 1872 (35 & 36 Vict. c. 33), s. 24, and are set out, *ante*, p. 215. They provide for the appointment of agents to detect personation at the time of polling, for the giving of persons charged with personation into custody, and for the proceedings before justices on the charge.

Election Petitions.

87.—(1.) A municipal election may be questioned by an election petition on the ground—

Power to question municipal election by petition.

(a.) That the election was as to the borough or ward wholly avoided by general bribery, treating, undue influence, or personation (*a*); or

(b.) That the election was avoided by corrupt practices or offences against this Part committed at the election (*b*); or

(c.) That the person whose election is questioned was at the time of the election disqualified (*c*); or

(d.) That he was not duly elected by a majority of lawful votes (*d*).

Sect. 87 (2).

(2.) A municipal election shall not be questioned on any of those grounds except by an election petition (*e*).

(*a*) For the definition of these offences, see Part I. of Sched. 3 of the 47 & 48 Vict. c. 70, *post*, and the notes to that schedule; and see s. 81 and notes *ante*.

(*b*) An election may also be questioned for illegal practices. See 47 & 48 Vict. c. 70, ss. 8, 25, *post*.

(*c*) This applies only to disqualifications existing at the time of the election. If a councillor becomes disqualified after he has been elected, the proper remedy is by *quo warranto*. Where the mayor disallowed an objection to a nomination paper, relating not to its form, but to the time of its delivery, it was held that this decision might be questioned on petition under the provision in the text. *Howes* v. *Turner*, 1 C. P. D. 670; 45 L. J. C. P. 550; 35 L. T. (N.S.) 58. BRETT, J., pointed out that the word *disqualified* was not limited to personal disqualification only.

Two candidates, R. and P., were nominated for the office of councillor of a ward of a borough. P. objected to R.'s nomination on the ground that he was disqualified, but the mayor disallowed the objection. P. insisted on the objection throughout the election. At the poll R. received a majority of votes. The day after the poll the returning officer issued a public notice, stating the number of votes given for each candidate and the objections, and declaring P. to be duly elected. Both P. and R. subscribed the declaration of acceptance of office under ss. 34, 35, *ante*. It was held by the House of Lords (affirming the Court of Appeal) that the returning officer had no jurisdiction to determine the question of disqualification, the proper method for determining that question being an election petition under this section. *Pritchard* v. *Bangor (Mayor, etc., of)*, 13 App. Cas. 241; 57 L. J. Q. B. 313; 58 L. T. (N.S.) 502; 37 W. R. 158; 52 J. P. 564.

If an elector having knowledge or notice of the disqualification of a candidate wilfully votes for him, his vote is thrown away. But knowledge of the fact which creates a legal disqualification does not involve knowledge that the candidate is legally disqualified, unless the fact that the disqualification exists is notorious. *Gosling* v. *Veley*, 7 Q. B. 406; *Drinkwater* v. *Deakin*, L. R. 9 C. P. 626; *R.* v. *Tewkesbury (Mayor, etc., of)*, L. R. 3 Q. B. 629; 37 L. J. Q. B. 288; 18 L. T. (N.S.) 851; 16 W. R. 1200; *Beresford-Hope* v. *Sandhurst*, 23 Q. B. D. 79. See, further, as to votes thrown away, *R.* v. *Hiorns*, 7 A. & E. 960; *R.* v. *Leeds (Mayor, etc., of)*, *ib.* 963.

Under Sched. 3, Part II. r. 7, *post*, a nomination paper must be delivered by the candidate, or his proposer or seconder, personally, and not by an agent. A nomination objected to on this ground is cognizable by the mayor, whose decision allowing it may be questioned on petition. *Monks* v. *Jackson*, 1 C. P. D. 683; 46 L. J. C. P. 162; 35 L. T. (N.S.) 95.

(*d*) In this case the petition will, in most cases, involve a scrutiny. But where a returning officer has improperly allowed an objection to a nomination paper, a petition lies under this head, for if the paper had not been rejected the votes might have been differently given. *Budge* v. *Andrews*, 3 C. P. D. 510; 47 L. J. C. P. 586; 39 L. T. (N.S.) 166.

(*e*) It follows from this provision that *quo warranto* will not lie on any of the grounds mentioned in this section.

At a municipal election A. and B. were candidates for the office of councillor. A. obtained a majority of votes over B., and was declared elected, but, being disqualified, refused to serve. B. thereupon claimed to have been elected, and having made the necessary declaration, acted on several occasions as councillor.

NOTE.

A petition under 35 & 36 Vict. c. 60, was presented against both A. and B., and both of them gave notice of their intention not to oppose the petition. No notice of A.'s disqualification was given to the electors. On an application by B. to the court that his name might be struck out of the petition, the court refused the application on the ground that he was properly made a respondent. *Yates* v. *Leach*, L. R. 9 C. P. 605 ; 43 L. J. C. P. 377 ; 30 L. T. (N.S.) 790.

Where a councillor became disqualified through having made a composition with his creditors, but his office was never declared vacant under s. 39, *ante*, p. 275, and he was afterwards re-elected, it was held that if there was any remedy in such a case it was by petition, and not by *mandamus*, to declare the office void. *R.* v. *Welshpool* (*Mayor of*), 35 L. T. (N.S.) 594.

At an election of an alderman for a borough there were two candidates, one of whom was the mayor. The mayor presided and voted for himself, which carried an equality of votes. He then gave a casting vote in his own favour, and declared himself elected. On application for a *quo warranto* to question his right to act as alderman, it was held that, assuming that he was improperly elected, the case fell within either (c) or (d) of sub-s. (1) of this section, and that the election could not be questioned except by election petition, and *quo warranto* would not lie. *R.* v. *Morton*, [1892] 1 Q. B. 39 ; 61 L. J. Q. B. 39 ; 65 L. T. 611 ; 40 W. R. 109 ; 56 J. P. 105 ; 8 T. L. R. 50 ; and see *R.* v. *Miles, Ex parte Cole*, 64 L. J. Q. B. 420 ; 72 L. T. (N.S.) 502 ; 43 W. R. 445 ; 59 J. P. 407.

Presentation of petition.

88.—(1.) An election petition may be presented either by four or more persons who voted or had a right to vote at the election or by a person alleging himself to have been a candidate at the election.

(2.) Any person whose election is questioned by the petition, and any returning officer of whose conduct a petition complains, may be made a respondent to the petition (*a*).

(3.) The petition shall be in the prescribed form and shall be signed by the petitioner, and shall be presented in the prescribed manner to the High Court in the Queen's Bench Division, and the prescribed officer shall send a copy thereof to the town clerk, who shall forthwith publish it in the borough (*b*).

(4.) It shall be presented within twenty-one days after the day on which the election was held, except that if it complains of the election on the ground of corrupt practices, and specifically alleges that a payment of money or other reward has been made or promised since the election by a person elected at the election, or on his account or with his privity, in pursuance or furtherance of such corrupt practices, it may be presented at any time within twenty-eight days after the date of the alleged payment or promise, whether or not any other petition against that person has been previously presented or tried (*c*).

(*a*) A petition may be presented against some only of the persons returned, though the ground of the petition is one affecting the validity of the election as a whole ; and the court can in such a case declare the person so petitioned against not to have been duly elected. *Line* v. *Warren*, 14 Q. B. D. 548 ; 54 L. J. Q. B. 291 ; 49 J. P. 516.

Sect. 88.

NOTE.

An unsuccessful candidate at an election cannot be made a respondent to a petition, although he coalesced for the purposes of the election with two successful candidates, so as to be responsible equally with them for any acts done by any of the three in furtherance of the common purpose. *Lovering* v. *Dawson*, L. R. 10 C. P. 726 ; 44 L. J. C. P. 321 ; 32 L. T. (N.S.) 819.

Where a mayor *bonâ fide* decides on an objection to a nomination paper, a complaint of such decision as erroneous is not a complaint of the conduct of the mayor within the meaning of this section, and he ought not to be made a respondent. If an election is avoided through the negligence of the returning officer, the court may order him to pay the costs of the petition. *Wilson* v. *Ingham*, 64 L. J. Q. B. 775 ; 72 L. T. (N.S.) 796 ; 43 W. R. 621 ; 59 J. P. 614 ; *Harmon* v. *Park*, 6 Q. B. D. 323 ; 50 L. J. Q. B. 227 ; 44 L. T. (N.S.) 81 ; 29 W. R. 750 ; 45 J. P. 436.

(*b*) The word "prescribed" here means prescribed by general rules. See s. 77, *ante*, p. 296 ; see also s. 100, *post*, and the general rules made thereunder, which are set out, *post*.

In applying this sub-section to county council elections, the term "town clerk must be read "clerk of the council," and "borough" as "county." The publication should evidently be made in the electoral division to which it relates.

(*c*) If the petition is founded on an illegal practice it must be presented within fourteen days after the date when the town clerk or clerk of the council receives the return and declaration respecting election expenses ; and in the event of an illegal practice after the election within twenty-eight days thereafter : 47 & 48 Vict. c. 70, s. 25, *post*. By the same section it is provided that any election petition presented within the time limited by the Municipal Corporations Act, 1882, may, for the purpose of complaining of the election upon an allegation of an illegal practice, be amended, with the leave of the High Court, within the time within which a petition complaining of the election on the ground of that illegal practice can, under that section, be presented.

The court cannot after the period of twenty-one days here mentioned allow an amendment which would practically amount to a new petition, as by adding a charge of treating. *Maude* v. *Lowley*, L. R. 9 C. P. 165 ; 43 L. J. C. P. 105 ; *Clark* v. *Wallond*, 52 L. J. Q. B. 321 ; 48 L. T. (N.S.) 762 ; 31 W. R. 551 ; 47 J. P. 551.

As to an order for particulars of the charges, see r. 6 of the General Rules, and the notes thereto, *post*.

Security for costs.

89.—(1.) At the time of presenting an election petition, or within three days afterwards, the petitioner shall give security for all costs, charges, and expenses which may become payable by him to any witness summoned on his behalf, or to any respondent.

(2.) The security shall be to such amount, not exceeding five hundred pounds, as the High Court, or a judge thereof, on summons directs, and shall be given in the prescribed manner (*a*), either by a deposit in money, or by recognizance entered into by not more than four sureties, or partly in one way and partly in the other.

(3.) Within five days after the presentation of the petition the petitioner shall in the prescribed manner (*b*) serve on the respondent a notice of the presentation of the petition, and of the nature of the proposed security, and a copy of the petition.

(4.) Within five days after service of the notice the respondent may object in writing to any recognizance on the ground that any surety is insufficient or is dead, or cannot be found or ascertained for want of a sufficient description in the recognizance, or that a person named in the recognizance has not duly acknowledged the same.

(5.) An objection to a recognizance shall be decided in the prescribed manner (*c*).

(6.) If the objection is allowed, the petitioner may, within a further prescribed time not exceeding five days, remove it by a deposit in the prescribed manner of such sum of money as will, in the opinion of the court or officer having cognizance of the matter, make the security sufficient.

(7.) If no security is given, as prescribed, or any objection is allowed and is not removed, as aforesaid, no further proceedings shall be had on the petition.

(*a*) See rr. 16 to 38, *post*. As to the amount of the security, see r. 26, *post*.

(*b*) See rr. 14, 15, *post*. By r. 36, the petitioner or his agent must file an affidavit of the time and manner of the service immediately after such service. The observance of these provisions as to service of the petition is a condition precedent to the trial of the petition. *Williams* v. *Tenby* (*Mayor of*), 5 C. P. D. 135; 49 L. J. C. P. 325; 42 L. T. (N.S.) 187; 28 W. R. 616; 44 J. P. 348.

(*c*) See rr. 27—34, *post*.

90. On the expiration of the time limited for making objections, or, after objection made, on the objection being disallowed or removed, whichever last happens, the petition shall be at issue. Petition at issue.

The objections here referred to are the objections to recognizances under the preceding section. See r. 37, *post*.

91.—(1.) The prescribed officer (*a*) shall as soon as may be make a list, in this Act referred to as the municipal election list, of all election petitions at issue, placing them in the order in which they were presented, and shall keep at his office a copy of this list, open to inspection in the prescribed manner (*b*). Municipal election list.

(2.) The petitions shall, as far as conveniently may be, be tried in the order in which they stand in the list.

(3.) Two or more candidates may be made respondents to the same petition, and their cases may be tried at the same time, but for the purposes of this Part the petition shall be deemed to be a separate petition against each respondent (*c*).

(4.) Where more petitions than one are presented relating to the same election, or to elections held at the same time for different

Sect. 91 (4). wards of the same borough (*d*), they shall be bracketed together in the list as one petition, but shall, unless the High Court otherwise directs, stand in the list in the place where the last of them would have stood if it had been the only petition relating to that election.

(*a*) That is, the master for the time being nominated as prescribed officer. See r. 1, *post.*

(*b*) As to the making out of the lists and the inspection of such lists, see r. 39, *post.*

(*c*) See *Line* v. *Warren*, *ante*, p. 299.

(*d*) This must, in relation to county council elections, be read as "different electoral divisions of the same county."

Constitution of election court.

92.—(1). An election petition shall be tried by an election court, consisting of a barrister, qualified and appointed as in this section provided, without a jury.

(2.) A barrister shall not be qualified to constitute an election court if he is of less than fifteen years' standing, or is a member of the Commons House of Parliament, or holds any office or place of profit under the Crown, other than that of recorder.

(3.) A barrister shall not be qualified to constitute an election court for trial of an election petition relating to any borough for which he is recorder, or in which he resides, or which is included in a circuit of Her Majesty's judges on which he practises as a barrister.

(4.) As soon as may be after a municipal election list is made out the prescribed officer shall send a copy thereof to each of the judges for the time being on the rota for the trial of parliamentary election petitions * * * (*a*).

(5.) If a commissioner to whom the trial of a petition is assigned dies, or declines or becomes incapable to act, the said judges or two of them may assign the trial to be conducted or continued by any other of the commissioners appointed under this section.

(6.) The election court shall for the purposes of the trial have the same powers and privileges as a judge on the trial of a parliamentary election petition, except that any fine or order of committal by the court may on motion by the person aggrieved be discharged or varied by the High Court, or in vacation by a judge thereof, on such terms, if any, as the High Court or judge thinks fit (*b*).

(*a*) The remainder of this sub-section was repealed by 47 & 48 Vict. c. 70, Sched. 2, *post.* Section 36, sub-s. (2) of that Act, *post*, contains the substituted provision. It provides that the judges may annually appoint a number of barristers, not exceeding five, to be commissioners for the trial of election petitions, under Part IV. of the Municipal Corporations Act and that Act, and shall from time to time assign the petitions to be tried by each commissioner.

Sect. 92.

NOTE.

(b) The High Court has no appellate jurisdiction over the commissioner, and cannot review his decisions except upon a question of law reserved by him under s. 93 (8), *post*. *Preece* v. *Harding*, 24 Q. B. D. 110 ; 59 L. J. Q. B. 82. *Ex parte Ayres*, 54 L. T. (N.S.) 296. *Marsland* v. *Hickman*, 2 T. L. R. 398.

Trial of election petition.

93.—(1.) An election petition shall be tried in open court, and notice of the time and place of trial shall be given in the prescribed manner not less than seven days before the day of trial (*a*).

(2.) The place of trial shall be within the borough (*b*), except that the High Court may, on being satisfied that special circumstances exist rendering it desirable that the petition should be tried elsewhere, appoint some other convenient place for the trial (*c*).

(3.) The election court may in its discretion adjourn the trial from time to time (*d*), and from any one place to any other place within the borough (*b*) or place where it is held.

(4.) At the conclusion of the trial the election court shall determine whether the person whose election is complained of, or any and what other person, was duly elected, or whether the election was void, and shall forthwith certify in writing the determination to the High Court, and the determination so certified shall be final to all intents as to the matters at issue on the petition.

(5.) Where a charge is made in a petition of any corrupt practice or offence against this Part having been committed at the election, the court shall, in addition to the certificate, and at the same time, report in writing to the High Court as follows :

(a.) Whether any corrupt practice or offence against this Part has or has not been proved to have been committed by or with the knowledge and consent of any candidate at the election, and the nature of the corrupt practice or offence ;

(b.) The names of all persons (if any) proved at the trial to have been guilty of any corrupt practice or offence against this Part ;

(c.) Whether any corrupt practices have, or whether there is reason to believe that any corrupt practices have, extensively prevailed at the election in the borough or in any ward thereof (*e*).

(6.) The election court may at the same time make a special report to the High Court as to any matters arising in the course of the trial, an account of which ought, in the judgment of the election court, to be submitted to the High Court.

(7.) If, on the application of any party to a petition made in the prescribed manner to the High Court, it appears to the High Court that the case raised by the petition can be conveniently stated as a

Sect. 93 (7). special case, the High Court may direct the same to be stated accordingly, and any such special case shall be heard before the High Court, and the decision of the High Court shall be final (*f*).

(8.) If it appears to the election court on the trial of a petition that any question of law as to the admissibility of evidence, or otherwise, requires further consideration by the High Court, the election court may postpone the granting of a certificate until the question has been determined by the High Court, and for this purpose may reserve any such question, as questions may be reserved by a judge on a trial at *nisi prius*.

(9.) On the trial of a petition, unless the election court otherwise directs, any charge of a corrupt practice or offence against this Part may be gone into, and evidence in relation thereto received before any proof has been given of agency on behalf of any candidate in respect of the corrupt practice or offence.

(10.) On the trial of a petition complaining of an undue election, and claiming the office for some person, the respondent may give evidence to prove that that person was not duly elected, in the same manner as if he had presented a petition against the election of that person (*g*).

(11.) The trial of a petition shall be proceeded with, notwithstanding that the respondent has ceased to hold the office his election to which is questioned by the petition (*h*).

(12.) A copy of any certificate or report made to the High Court on the trial of a petition, and, in the case of a decision by the High Court on a special case, a statement of the decision, shall be sent by the High Court to the Secretary of State.

(13.) A copy of any such certificate and a statement of any such decision shall also be certified by the High Court, under the hands of two or more judges thereof, to the town clerk of the borough (*i*).

(*a*) See rr. 40, 42, *post*. See also rr. 43 as to the postponement of the trial if the barrister does not arrive in time.

(*b*) Or county, in case of a petition against the election of a county councillor.

(*c*) Where the allegations of fact in a petition are not in dispute, but are specifically admitted by the respondent, so as to render it unnecessary at the trial to call witnesses from the district in which the election took place, the court may order the petition to be tried in London, on the ground that special circumstances exist which render it desirable that the petition should be tried elsewhere than in the county or division where the election took place. *Arch* v. *Bentinck*, 18 Q. B. D. 548; 56 L. J. Q. B. 458; 56 L. T. (N.S.) 360; 35 W. R. 476. Mere questions of expense or convenience do not constitute special circumstances enabling the High Court to order that the petition shall be tried elsewhere than in the borough or county. *Lawson* v. *Chester-Master*, [1893] 1 Q. B. 245; 62 L. J. Q. B. 231; 68 L. T. (N.S.) 60; 41 W. R. 221; 57 J. P. 806; 9 T. L. R. 168. Nor the absence of local accommodation for the persons engaged in the petition. *Collins* v. *Price*, 5 C. P. D. 544.

The existence of intimidation in the locality would constitute "special circumstances." *Sligo case*, 1 O'M. & H. 309. Sect. 93.

NOTE.

(*d*) A formal adjournment is not necessary. See r. 45, *post*. See also 47 & 48 Vict. c. 70, s. 27, *post*, p. 362.

(*e*) The court must further report as to illegal practices in manner prescribed by 47 & 48 Vict. c. 70, s. 8, sub-s. (2), *post*. Before a report is made affecting any person, opportunity must be given to such person to be heard. See s. 38 of the Corrupt Practices Act, 1883, which is set out in Schedule I., Part 2, of the Municipal Elections (Corrupt Practices) Act, 1884, *post*.

(*f*) Notwithstanding this sub-section, if leave be given, appeal lies from a judgment of the Queen's Bench Division to the Court of Appeal. See s. 242, *post*, which incorporates s. 14 of the Judicature Act, 1881 (44 & 45 Vict. c. 68); and see *Line* v. *Warren*, 14 Q. B. D. 548; 54 L. J. Q. B. 291; 49 J. P. 516; and *Beresford-Hope* v. *Sandhurst*, 23 Q. B. D. 79; 58 L. J. Q. B. 316; 61 L. T. (N.S.) 150; 37 W. R. 548; 53 J. P. 805; 5 T. L. R. 472. Without leave no appeal lies. *Unwin* v. *McMullen*, [1891] 1 Q. B. 694; 60 L. J. Q. B. 400; 39 W. R. 712; 55 J. P. 582; 7 T. L. R. 450.

(*g*) In this case the respondent must deliver to the master, six days before the day appointed for trial, a list of the objections to the election upon which he intends to rely, and the master is to allow inspection and office copies of such list to all parties concerned; and no evidence is to be given by the respondent of any objection not specified in the list, except by leave of the High Court. See r. 8, *post*.

(*h*) The respondent may have ceased to hold office by having resigned or become disqualified.

(*i*) The clerk of the county council must, in relation to county council elections, be substituted for the town clerk.

94.—(1.) Witnesses at the trial of an election petition shall be summoned and sworn in the same manner, as nearly as circumstances admit, as witnesses at a trial at nisi prius, and shall be liable to the same penalties for perjury (*a*). Witnesses.

(2.) On the trial the election court may, by order in writing, require any person who appears to the court to have been concerned in the election to attend as a witness, and any person refusing to obey the order shall be guilty of contempt of court (*b*).

(3.) The court may examine any person so required to attend, or being in court, although he is not called and examined by any party to the petition.

(4.) A witness may, after his examination by the court, be cross-examined by or on behalf of the petitioner and respondent, or either of them (*c*).

* * * *

(9.) The reasonable expenses incurred by any person in appearing to give evidence at the trial of an election petition, according to the scale allowed to witnesses on the trial of civil actions at the assizes, may be allowed to him by a certificate of the election court or of the prescribed officer, and if the witness was called and examined by the court, shall be deemed part of the

Sect. 94 (9). expenses of providing a court, but otherwise shall be deemed costs of the petition (*d*).

(*a*) As to the order of the court to compel the attendance of a witness, see r. 54, *post*.

(*b*) As to the procedure in a committal for contempt of court, see rr. 55, 56, *post*.

(*c*) Sub-ss. (5)—(8), are repealed by the 47 & 48 Vict. c. 70, *post*.

(*d*) The prescribed officer is the registrar appointed under r. 50, *post*. Under r. 53 it is his duty to ascertain and certify the amount of the allowance to a witness whose expenses are allowed by the commissioner. As to the costs of providing a court, see s. 101, *post*; as to the costs of the petition, see s. 98, *post*.

Withdrawal of petition.

95.—(1.) A petitioner shall not withdraw an election petition without the leave of the election court or High Court on special application made in the prescribed manner, and at the prescribed time and place (*a*).

(2.) The application shall not be made until the prescribed notice of the intention to make it has been given in the borough (*b*).

(3.) On the hearing of the application any person who might have been a petitioner in respect of the election may apply to the court to be substituted as a petitioner, and the court may, if it thinks fit, substitute him accordingly (*c*).

(4.) If the proposed withdrawal is, in the opinion of the court, induced by any corrupt bargain or consideration, the court may by order direct that the security given on behalf of the original petitioner shall remain as security for any costs that may be incurred by the substituted petitioner, and that, to the extent of the sum named in the security, the original petitioner and his sureties shall be liable to pay the costs of the substituted petitioner.

(5.) If the court does not so direct, then security to the same amount as would be required in the case of a new petition (*d*), and subject to the like conditions, shall be given on behalf of the substituted petitioner before he proceeds with his petition and within the prescribed time after the order of substitution.

(6.) Subject as aforesaid, a substituted petitioner shall, as nearly as may be, stand in the same position and be subject to the same liabilities as the original petitioner.

(7.) If a petition is withdrawn, the petitioner shall be liable to pay the costs of the respondent (*e*).

(8.) Where there are more petitioners than one, an application to withdraw a petition shall not be made except with the consent of all the petitioners.

(*a*) The form of notice of application to withdraw a petition is prescribed by r. 58, *post*. The notice of application is to be left at the master's office, and copies are to be served on the respondent and on the town clerk or clerk of the county council, as the case may be, and published in the borough or county to which the petition relates. See rr. 59, 60, *post*. As to the effect of the notice, see r. 46, *post*.

The petitioners, who had presented a petition and subsequently found out

Sect. 95.

NOTE.

that their agent's report, upon which the petition was based, was untrustworthy, were allowed by the court to withdraw the petition, the Public Prosecutor having ascertained by special inquiry that there was no reliable evidence to support it, and having received from the petitioners copies of the report and details of the subsequent inquiries. On a motion for leave to withdraw a petition, the court has a discretion as to the costs of the parties, and may order them to be paid by the petitioners on the higher scale and taxed as between solicitor and client. They cannot give costs to the Public Prosecutor. *Pascoe* v. *Puleston*, 54 L. T. (N.S.) 733; 50 J. P. 135; *cf. The Lichfield Election Petition*, 9 T. L. R. 92.

Where, after a recount, in which the majority of the sitting member was found to be the same as it was when announced by the returning officer, the petitioner applied for leave to withdraw, but there was no affidavit of notice to the Public Prosecutor and no affidavit of the election agent, but only of the London solicitors on each side and of the petitioner, whose affidavits showed that the parties making them did not know of any agreement nor of any terms having been entered into respecting the withdrawal, but did not state on what grounds the petition was to be withdrawn, the court refused the application. *Halifax Election Petition*, 9 T. L. R. 563. And see s. 26 of the Corrupt Practices Act, 1884, p. 361, *post*.

After a municipal election a petition was presented by an unsuccessful candidate, claiming that he was returned by a majority of lawful votes. The mayor, to save expense, induced the petitioner and the returned candidate to submit the question to the arbitration of the town clerk, who was to recount the votes. On the award being against the petitioner, he asked leave to withdraw the petition, and the court allowed him to do so on payment of the costs, the Public Prosecutor not opposing. *Mallam* v. *Bean*, 51 J. P. 230.

(*b*) See rr. 59, 60, *post*.

(*c*) See r. 61, *post*.

(*d*) See s. 89 and note, *ante*, p. 300, and r. 26, *post*.

(*e*) See *Pascoe* v. *Puleston*; *Mallam* v. *Bean*; *Lichfield case, supra*; and *Devonport case*, 2 T. L. R. 345; *Penton* v. *Naoroji*, 4 O'M. & H. 171; *George* v. *Price-Jones*, 4 O'M. & H. 166; and as to the scale of costs, s. 29 (3) of the 47 & 48 Vict. c. 70, *post*.

Abatement of petition.

96.—(1.) An election petition shall be abated by the death of a sole petitioner or of the survivor of several petitioners.

(2.) The abatement of a petition shall not affect the liability of the petitioner or of any other person to the payment of costs previously incurred.

(3.) On the abatement of a petition the prescribed notice thereof shall be given in the borough, and, within the prescribed time after the notice is given, any person who might have been a petitioner in respect of the election may apply to the election court or High Court in the prescribed manner and at the prescribed time and place to be substituted as a petitioner; and the court may, if it thinks fit, substitute him accordingly.

(4.) Security shall be given on behalf of a petitioner so substituted, as in the case of a new petition.

As to notice of abatement of a petition, and the procedure on the application to be substituted as a petitioner, see r. 63, *post*.

As to security for costs, see s. 89, *ante*, p. 300.

Sect. 97 (1).

Withdrawal and substitution of respondents.

97.—(1.) If before the trial of an election petition a respondent other than a returning officer (*a*)—

(a.) Dies, resigns, or otherwise ceases to hold the office to which the petition relates (*b*) ; or

(b.) Gives the prescribed notice that he does not intend to oppose the petition (*c*) ;

the prescribed notice thereof shall be given in the borough (*d*), and within the prescribed time (*e*) after the notice is given any person who might have been a petitioner in respect of the election may apply to the election court or High Court to be admitted as a respondent to oppose the petition, and shall be admitted accordingly, except that the number of persons so admitted shall not exceed three.

(2.) A respondent who has given the prescribed notice that he does not intend to oppose the petition shall not be allowed to appear or act as a party against the petition in any proceedings thereon.

(*a*) The returning officer may be a respondent if the petition complains of his conduct. See s. 88, sub-s. (2), *ante*, p. 299. See also r. 64, *post*. As to the procedure after the master has received notice of the happening of any of these events, see rr. 46, 47, *post*.

(*b*) The petition does not abate merely because the respondent ceases to hold office.

(*c*) The notice is prescribed by r. 65, *post*. The name of a respondent will not be struck out of a petition merely because he has given this notice. See *Yates* v. *Leach*, *ante*, p. 299.

(*d*) See r. 66, *post*.

(*e*) The prescribed time is ten days. See r. 67, *post*.

Costs on election petitions.

98.—(1.) All costs, charges, and expenses of and incidental to the presentation of an election petition, and the proceedings consequent thereon, except such as are by this Act otherwise provided for, shall be defrayed by the parties to the petition in such manner and proportions as the election court determines ; and in particular any costs, charges, or expenses which, in the opinion of the court, have been caused by vexatious conduct, unfounded allegations, or unfounded objections on the part either of the petitioner or of the respondent, and any needless expense incurred or caused on the part of petitioner or respondent, may be ordered to be defrayed by the parties by whom it has been incurred or caused, whether they are or not on the whole successful (*a*).

(2.) The costs may be taxed in the prescribed manner, but according to the same principles as costs between solicitor and client in an action in the High Court, and may be recovered as the costs of such an action, or as otherwise prescribed (*b*).

(3.) If a petitioner neglects or refuses for three months after demand to pay to any person summoned as a witness on his behalf, or to the respondent, any sum certified to be due to him for his costs, charges, and expenses, and the neglect or refusal is, within one year after the demand, proved to the satisfaction of the High Court, every person who has under this Act entered into a recognizance relating to the petition shall be held to have made default in the recognizance, and the prescribed officer (*c*) shall thereon certify the recognizance to be forfeited, and it shall be dealt with as a forfeited recognizance relating to a parliamentary election petition (*d*). Sect. 98 (3).

(*a*) An overloaded petition will be visited with costs, even if it is successful. *Birkbeck* v. *Bullard*, 54 L. T. (N.S.) 625. When a petition is wholly unfounded the court may order the petitioner to pay the costs of the Public Prosecutor. *Crossman* v. *Gent-Davis*, 54 L. T. (N.S.) 628. In certain cases the parties may be ordered to pay the expenses of the election court. See s. 101, *post*.

The barrister appointed to try the petition has an absolute discretion over the costs. In a case where the petitioners had improperly made an unsuccessful candidate a respondent, it was held that they could not object that he was not a party to the petition so as to deprive the barrister of jurisdiction to make an order upon them for his costs. *Lovering* v. *Dawson*, L. R. 10 C. P. 726; 44 L. J. C. P. 321; 32 L. T. (N.S.), 823.

(*b*) So much of this sub-section as relates to the principle of taxation is repealed by 47 & 48 Vict. c. 70, *post*. As to the mode of taxation and recovery of the costs, see ss. 29 and 32 of that Act, and r. 68, *post*, and *Pare* v. *Hartshorn*, 31 L. T. (N.S.) 486; 23 W. R. 138.

(*c*) That is, the Master. See r. 1, *post*.

(*d*) That is, in manner provided by 30 & 31 Vict. c. 125, s. 42.

Reception of and attendance on the election court.

99.—(1.) The town clerk shall provide proper accommodation for holding the election court; and any expenses incurred by him for the purposes of this section shall be paid out of the borough fund or borough rate (*a*).

(2.) All chief and head constables, superintendents of police, head-boroughs, gaolers, constables, and bailiffs shall give their assistance to the election court in the execution of its duties, and if any gaoler or officer of a prison makes default in receiving or detaining a prisoner committed thereto in pursuance of this Part, he shall be liable to a fine not exceeding five pounds for every day during which the default continues.

(3.) The election court may employ officers and clerks as prescribed (*b*).

(4.) A shorthand writer shall attend at the trial of an election petition, and shall be sworn by the election court faithfully and truly to take down the evidence given at the trial. He shall take down the evidence at length. A transcript of the notes of the evidence taken by him shall, if the election court so directs, accompany the certificate of the election court. His expenses, according to a prescribed scale, shall be treated as part of the expenses incurred in receiving the court (*c*).

(*a*) This duty will, in county council elections, devolve upon the clerk to the council (see the Local Government Act, s. 75, sub-s. (5), *ante*, p. 142. The expenses will be payable out of the county fund.

Sect. 99.

NOTE.

(b) See rr. 50, 51, *post*.

(c) The shorthand writer is to be the shorthand writer to the House of Commons or his deputy. See r. 52, *post*.

Rules of procedure and jurisdiction.

100.—(1.) The judges for the time being on the rota for the trial of parliamentary election petitions may from time to time make, revoke, and alter General Rules for the effectual execution of this part, and of the intention and object thereof, and the regulation of the practice, procedure, and costs of municipal election petitions, and the trial thereof, and the certifying and reporting thereon (*a*).

(2.) All such rules shall be laid before both Houses of Parliament within three weeks after they are made, if Parliament is then sitting, and if not, within three weeks after the beginning of the then next session of Parliament, and shall, while in force, have effect as if enacted in this Act.

(3.) Subject to the provisions of this Act (*b*), and of the rules under it, the principles, practice, and rules for the time being observed in the case of parliamentary election petitions, and in particular the principles and rules with regard to agency and evidence, and to a scrutiny, and to the declaring any person elected in the room of any other person declared to have been not duly elected, shall be observed, as far as may be, in the case of a municipal election petition.

(4.) The High Court shall, subject to this Act, have the same powers, jurisdiction, and authority with respect to a municipal election petition and the proceedings thereon as if the petition were an ordinary action within its jurisdiction (*c*).

(5.) The duties to be performed by the prescribed officer under this Part shall be performed by the prescribed officer of the High Court (*d*).

(6.) The general rules in force at the commencement of this Act with respect to matters within this Part shall, until superseded by rules made under this section, and subject to any amendment thereof by rules so made, have effect, with the necessary modifications, as if made under this section.

(*a*) See also 47 & 48 Vict. c. 70, s. 30, *post*. The rules now in force are set out *post*.

(*b*) See *Clarke* v. *Wallond*, *ante*, p. 300; *Lovering* v. *Dawson*, *ante*, p. 309.

(*c*) The High Court has no power to entertain an appeal against the decision of a commissioner appointed to inquire into alleged corrupt or illegal practices at an election, except on points of law reserved for its decision by way of a case stated by the commissioners. *Ex parte Ayres*, 54 L. T. (N.S.) 296. A petition against the election of members of a local board alleged undue influence by the respondents and their agents, and that corrupt and illegal practices extensively prevailed. The commissioner reported to the High Court that no corrupt practice had been proved against the respondents or otherwise, that illegal practices extensively prevailed, and that the respondents had been guilty of illegal practices; and he certified that the respondents had not been

Sect. 100.

NOTE.

duly elected. On a motion for a new trial or a prohibition, on the ground that the petitioner had exceeded his jurisdiction, it was held that the report was not in excess of the jurisdiction. *Quære*, whether the Court has jurisdiction to entertain an appeal from a commissioner. *Per* STEPHEN, J. The jurisdiction, if any, ought only to be exercised under extraordinary circumstances, and when necessary in order that justice should be done. *Marshland* v. *Hickman* (*Goole Election Petition*), 2 T. L. R. 398.

(*d*) That is, by the Master. See r. 1, *post*.

Expenses of election court.

101.—(1.) The remuneration and allowances to be paid to a commissioner for his services in respect of the trial of an election petition, and to any officers, clerks, or shorthand writers employed under this Part, shall be fixed by a scale made and varied by the election judges on the rota for the trial of parliamentary election petitions with the approval of the Treasury. The remuneration and allowances shall be paid in the first instance by the Treasury, and shall be repaid to the treasury, on their certificate, out of the borough fund or borough rate (*a*).

(2.) But the election court may in its discretion order that such remuneration and allowances, or the expenses incurred by a town clerk for receiving the election court (*b*), shall be repaid, wholly or in part, to the Treasury or the town clerk, as the case may be, in the cases, by the persons, and in the manner following (namely):

(a.) When in the opinion of the election court a petition is frivolous and vexatious, by the petitioner;

(b.) When in the opinion of the election court a respondent has been personally guilty of corrupt practices at the election, by that respondent.

(3) An order so made for the repayment of any sum by a petitioner or respondent may be enforced as an order for payment of costs (*c*); but a deposit made or security given under this Part shall not be applied for any such repayment until all costs and expenses payable by the petitioner or respondent to any party to the petition have been satisfied.

(*a*) In the case of a county council these expenses will be payable out of the county fund.

(*b*) See s. 99, *ante*, p. 309. The reference to the town clerk includes a reference to the clerk to the county council. See the Local Government Act, s. 75, sub-s. (5), *ante*, p. 142.

(*c*) See s. 98, *ante*, p. 308.

Upon the trial of a petition against the return of a borough councillor under the Municipal Elections (Corrupt Practices) Act, 1872, the barrister in delivering judgment said that he found the councillor guilty of personal bribery, and that all the costs of the inquiry were to be borne by him, and made an order in writing for the payment by the councillor of certain costs under s. 19 of that Act. The written order made no provision for the remuneration and allowances to the barrister and other persons under s. 22

Sect. 101

NOTE.

(corresponding to the text). The Treasury paid the amount of such remuneration and allowances, and certified the payment to the borough treasurer, and required him to repay them the amount out of the borough fund. A rate was accordingly made and levied. The Treasury afterwards, on receiving from the barrister a letter stating that he had always intended to visit all the costs upon the councillor, and had said so in giving judgment, cancelled their certificate, and the borough corporation abandoned the rate and returned the sums levied to the ratepayers. Afterwards, the Treasury, finding that the barrister had made no written order for the payment of the remuneration and allowances, issued a fresh certificate requiring the borough treasurer to repay them the amount out of the borough fund or rates. These facts being found upon a return to a *mandamus* commanding the treasurer to repay the Treasury, it was held that no valid order had been made by the barrister for the payment of the remuneration and allowances by the councillor; that the election court was a court of record, and that neither the High Court nor the Court of Appeal on the return could amend the order so as to make it include such payment; that the act of the Treasury in certifying was not a judicial act, and that they had the power to make a second certificate, and were entitled to a peremptory *mandamus* compelling the treasurer to repay to them the amount of such remuneration and allowances out of the borough fund or rates, and compelling the corporation to order such amount to be levied by a borough rate. *R.* v. *Maidenhead (Mayor of)*, 9 Q. B. D. 494; 51 L. J. Q. B. 444; 46 J. P. 724.

Acts done pending a petition not invalidated.

102. Where a candidate who has been elected to a corporate office is, by a certificate of an election court or a decision of the High Court, declared not to have been duly elected, acts done by him in execution of the office, before the time when the certificate or decision is certified to the town clerk, shall not be invalidated by reason of that declaration.

See also s. 42 (1), *ante*, p. 278.

Provisions as to elections in the room of persons unseated on petition

103. Where on an election petition the election of any person to a corporate office has been declared void, and no other person has been declared elected in his room, a new election shall be held to supply the vacancy in the same manner as on a casual vacancy (*a*); and for the purposes of the election any duties to be performed by a mayor, alderman, or other officer, shall, if he has been declared not elected, be performed by a deputy, or other person who might have acted for him if he had been incapacitated by illness (*b*).

(*a*) As to the manner in which casual vacancies are to be filled up, see s. 40, *ante*, p. 277, and s. 66, *ante*, p. 291, and the notes to those sections.

(*b*) The reference to the mayor and aldermen must, with regard to elections of county councils, be read as a reference to the returning officer (see the Local Government Act, s. 75, sub-s. (4), *ante*, p. 142).

Prohibition of disclosure of vote

104. A person who has voted at a municipal election by ballot shall not in any proceeding to question the election be required to state for whom he has voted.

See also s. 12 of the Ballot Act, 1872, *ante*, p. 213.

PART V.

Corporate Property and Liabilities (a).

*   *   *   *   *

Misapplication of Corporate Property.

Prohibition of expenditure of corporate funds on parliamentary elections.

124.—(1.) It shall not be lawful for a municipal corporation, or the council of a borough, or a corporate officer, or a trustee, or other person acting for a municipal corporation, to pay or apply any money, stocks, funds, securities, or personal property, of or held in trust for the corporation, in payment of any expenses occasioned by a parliamentary election or incurred by any person offering himself as a candidate at or before a parliamentary election.

(2.) Any bond, covenant, recognizance, or judgment given by a corporation, council, officer, trustee, or person as aforesaid, for securing payment of such expenses, shall be void.

(3.) Any payment, application, bond, covenant, recognizance, or judgment made or given by a corporation, council, officer, trustee, or person as aforesaid, for inducing any person to labour in a parliamentary election at a future time, or to pay or incur expenses as aforesaid at a future time, shall be deemed to be forbidden and declared void by this section, although colourably made or given for any other cause or consideration.

(4.) Any mortgage or other disposition of corporate land for securing or satisfying any expenses or engagements incurred or to be incurred as aforesaid, and any estate or charge thereby created, shall be void.

(5.) Any resolution, bye-law, or other proceeding of a council, purporting to direct or authorize any payment or thing forbidden by this section, or made or adopted for evading the provisions thereof, shall be void.

(6.) If any member of a municipal corporation authorizes or directs any payment or application forbidden by this section, or assents to, or concurs or participates in, any affirmative vote or proceeding relating thereto, or signs or seals in his individual capacity, or affixes the corporate seal to, any instrument by this section declared void, he shall be guilty of a misdemeanor, and, on conviction thereof in the High Court, shall, in addition to such punishment as the court awards, be for ever disabled to take, hold, or exercise any office in the same corporation.

(7.) If any corporate officer, trustee, or other person as aforesaid makes, or concurs in making, any payment or application of money or property as aforesaid, he shall be deemed to have done so in his own wrong, and he shall be individually liable to repay and make good the amount or value thereof to the corporation, notwithstanding any release or pretended indemnity given to him in the name or on behalf of the corporation.

Sect. 124 (8).

(8.) Any two or more burgesses may bring and prosecute any action in the name of the corporation against any officer, trustee, or person making any illegal payment or application as aforesaid, as if they, their executors and administrators were jointly and severally appointed the irrevocable attorneys of the corporation for that purpose; but the plaintiffs shall, on the application of the defendant, give reasonable security, as the court directs, for costs, as between solicitor and client.

(9.) Nothing in this section shall affect the provisions of the Ballot Act, 1872, or of any other Act for the time being in force regulating the payment by the returning officer or otherwise of expenses relating to parliamentary elections.

(*a*) This is the only section of Part V. which is applied to county councils. See the Local Government Act, s. 75, *ante*, p. 141.

* * * *

PART XII.

Legal Proceedings.

Prosecution of offences and recovery of fines.

219.—(1.) In summary proceedings for offences and fines under this Act the information shall be laid within six months after the commission of the offence (*a*).

(2.) Any person aggrieved by a conviction of a court of summary jurisdiction under this Act may appeal therefrom to a court of quarter sessions (*b*).

(3.) Any fine incurred under this Act and not recoverable summarily may be recovered by action in the High Court (*c*).

(*a*) This provision was unnecessary, having regard to 11 & 12 Vict. c. 43, s. 11, and 42 & 43 Vict. c. 49. s. 31.

(*b*) The procedure on such appeals is regulated by 42 & 43 Vict. c. 49, s. 31.

(*c*) As to the procedure in actions against corporate officers, see s. 224, *post*.

Exclusion of *certiorari*.

220. A conviction, order, warrant, or other matter made or done, or purporting to be made or done, by virtue of this Act shall not be quashed for want of form, and shall not, unless it is an order of the council for payment of money out of the borough fund, be removed by *certiorari* or otherwise into the High Court.

Notwithstanding this provision, a writ of *certiorari* will be granted where the proceedings show on the face of them a want of jurisdiction. *R.* v. *Gosse*, 3 E. & E. 277; 30 L. J. M. C. 41; 3 L. T. (N.S.) 404; *Broughton Local Board, Re*, 12 L. T. (N.S.) 310; *R.* v. *Staffordshire* (*Justices of*), 16 L. T. (N.S.) 430; *R.* v. *Rose*, or *Wood*, 5 E. & B. 49; *Colonial Bank of Australasia* v. *Willan*, L. R. 5 P. C. 417; 43 L. J. P. C. 39; 30 L. T. (N.S.) 237; 22 W. R. 516. In the case last mentioned it was laid down that when

Sect. 220.

NOTE.

a *certiorari* is said to be taken away by statute, the superior court is not absolutely deprived of the power to issue the writ; but its action as to the writ is controlled and limited, and it cannot quash the order removed by *certiorari* except upon the ground either of a manifest defect of jurisdiction in the tribunal that made the order, or of manifest fraud in the party procuring it. Matters on which the defect of jurisdiction depends may be apparent on the face of the proceedings, or may be brought before the superior court by affidavit, but they must be intrinsic to the adjudication impeached. Objections on the ground of defect of jurisdiction may be founded on the character and constitution of an inferior court, the natue of the subject-matter of the inquiry, or the absence of some preliminary proceeding which was necessary to give jurisdiction to the inferior court. The objection of defect of jurisdiction cannot be entertained if it rests solely on the ground that the judge has erroneously found a fact which was essential to the validity of his order, but which he was competent to try. *Ibid.* And see *Bradlaugh, Ex parte*, 3 Q. B. D. 509; 43 J. P. 125, and the cases cited in Paley on Convictions, 7th edition, at p. 354, Short and Mellor's Crown Office Practice, p. 116.

Where both parties agreed to waive this provision, and stated a case for the opinion of the court, the fact that the corresponding section in 11 & 12 Vict. c. 63, had taken away the *certiorari*, was held not to prevent the court from determining the question. *R.* v. *Dickenson*, 7 E. & B. 831; 26 L. J. M. C. 204; 3 Jur. (N.S.) 1076; 22 J. P. 243.

As to the practice relating to the removal of convictions, etc., by *certiorari*, see Paley on Convictions, p. 348. See also the Crown Office Rules, Nos. 28—42. It was held that the six days' notice to the justices, under No. 33 of these rules, as a preliminary to the grant of a writ of *certiorari*, must precede the motion for a rule *nisi*, and not merely the motion for the rule absolute. *Ex parte Roberts*, 50 J. P. 567. An application for *certiorari* to the Queen's Bench Division does not lie after conviction and judgment in the superior court. *Nally* v. *The Queen*, 16 L. R. Ir. 1; 15 Cox C. C. 638.

The reference in the section to an order for payment of money out of the borough fund has no application to county councils, a provision corresponding to that referred to being expressly made in the Local Government Act, s. 80, sub-s. (2), *ante*, p. 154.

Application of penalties in quarter sessions boroughs.

221.—(1.). Where by any Act passed or to be passed, any fine, penalty, or forfeiture is made recoverable in a summary manner before any justice or justices and payable to the Crown or to any body corporate, or to any person whomsoever, the same if recovered and adjudged before any justice of a borough having a separate court of quarter sessions shall, notwithstanding anything in the Act under which it is recovered, be recovered for and adjudged to be paid to the treasurer of the borough.

(2.) But this section shall not apply to a fine, penalty, or forfeiture, or part thereof, where the Act under which it is recovered—

(a.) Directs payment thereof to the informer or to any person aggrieved; or

(b.) If passed since the Municipal Corporations Act, 1835, directs that the same shall go in any other manner and not to the borough fund; or

Sect. 221 (2)

(c.) Relates to the customs, excise, or post office, or to trade or navigation, or to any branch of the revenue of the Crown.

The above section will not apply to county councils, for by the Local Government Act, s. 75 (16) (*a*), *ante*, p. 145, it is provided that nothing in the Municipal Corporations Act, 1882, as applied by that section, shall alter the application of any fine, penalty, or forfeiture recoverable in a summary manner.

In a borough which has not a separate court of quarter sessions, though it has a separate commission, unappropriated penalties are payable in manner provided by 11 & 12 Vict. c. 43, s. 31, to the county treasurer. *Reigate (Mayor, etc. of)* v. *Hart*, L. R. 3 Q. B. 244; 37 L. J. M. C. 70; 18 L. T. (N.S.) 237; 16 W. R. 896; *Winn* v. *Mossman*, L. R. 4 Ex. 492; 38 L. J. Ex. 203; 20 L. T. (N.S.) 672; 33 J. P. 743.

It has been held that penalties recovered under the Regulation of Railways Act (3 & 4 Vict. c. 97), are payable to the borough fund, and not to the Crown. *Att.-Gen.* v. *Moore*, 3 Ex. D. 276; 47 L. J. M. C. 103; 38 L. T. (N.S.) 251; 26 W. R. 366; 42 J. P. 7.

As to the appropriation of penalties under local Acts applying to boroughs, see *Alison* v. *Charlesworth*, 49 J. P. 294; *Alison* v. *Hall*, 4 T. L. R. 524.

Duties of clerk of peace as to fines and forfeitures.

222. Where the offices of town clerk and clerk of the peace for a borough are not held by the same person, the clerk of the peace shall perform all duties imposed on the town clerk by the Act of the third year of King George the Fourth, chapter forty-six, "for the more speedy return and levying of fines, penalties, and forfeitures, and recognizances estreated": and the clerk of the peace shall make all returns, issue all processes, and do all other acts required by that Act to be made, issued, and done by the town clerk.

This section cannot apply to county councils, for in all counties, except London, the clerk of the council and the clerk of the peace will be the same person. See the Local Government Act, s. 83, *ante*, p. 158.

Service of summons or warrant.

223. Any summons for appearance, warrant to enforce appearance, warrant for apprehension, or search warrant, may, if issued by a justice for a borough, be served or executed in any county wherein the borough or any part thereof is situate, or within any distance not exceeding seven miles from the borough, and, within those limits, shall have the same effect as if it had been issued or indorsed by a justice having jurisdiction in the place where it is served or executed, and may be served or executed by the constable or special constable to whom it is directed.

It is not clear whether the incorporation of this section with the Local Government Act (if it is incorporated) will have the effect of enabling the process of county justices to be executed within seven miles of the county without being backed. The Local Government Act, s. 75, *ante*, p. 141, provides that "for the purpose of the provisions of this Act with respect to county councils, and to the chairman, etc., of such councils, and otherwise for the purpose of carrying this Act into effect," the several parts of the Municipal

Sect. 223.

NOTE.

Corporations Act, 1882, shall apply as if therein re-enacted with such modifications as are necessary to make them applicable to the said councils and their chairmen, etc. It cannot be said that the application of the above section to the process of county justices fulfils the purpose thus stated in any way, and if the statement of the purpose limits the extent of the incorporation of the Municipal Corporations Act, the above section will not apply to the process of county justices. It will be prudent to refrain from acting on the above section in counties until the point has been judicially determined.

Procedure in penal actions against corporate officers.

224.—(1.) An action to recover a fine from any person for acting in a corporate office without having made the requisite declaration, or without being qualified, or after ceasing to be qualified, or after becoming disqualified, may not be brought except by a burgess of the borough, and shall not lie unless the plaintiff has, within fourteen days after the cause of action arose, served a notice in writing personally on the person liable to the fine of his intention to bring the action, nor unless the action is commenced within three months after the cause of action arose (*a*).

(2.) The court or a judge shall, on the application of the defendant within fourteen days after he has been served with writ of summons in the action, require the plaintiff to give security for costs (*b*).

(3.) Unless judgment is given for the plaintiff, the defendant shall be entitled to costs, to be taxed as between solicitor and client.

(4.) Where any such action is brought against a person on the ground of his not being qualified in respect of estate, it shall lie on him to prove that he was so qualified.

(5.) A moiety of the fine recovered shall, after payment of the costs of action, be paid to the plaintiff.

(*a*) See ss. 41 and 219, and the notes thereto, *ante*, pp. 278, 314. An action under this section to recover a fine from any person for acting in a corporate office without being qualified is not a "proceeding" to which the Public Authorities Protection Act, 1893, applies, and this section is not therefore repealed by that Act. *Humphries* v. *Wormwood*, 64 L. J. Q. B. 437.

(*b*) Security must be given, if demanded.

Quo warranto and mandamus.

225.—(1.) An application for an information in the nature of a quo warranto against any person claiming to hold a corporate office shall not be made after the expiration of twelve months from the time when he became disqualified after election (*a*).

(2.) In the case of such an application, or of an application for a mandamus to proceed to an election of a corporate officer (*b*), the applicant shall give notice in writing of the application to the person to be affected thereby (in this section called the respondent) at any time not less than ten days before the day in the notice specified for making the application.

(3.) The notice shall set forth the name and description of the applicant, and a statement of the grounds of the application.

Sect. 225 (4).

(4.) The applicant shall deliver with the notice a copy of the affidavit whereby the application will be supported.

(5.) The respondent may show cause in the first instance against the application.

(6.) If sufficient cause is not shown, the court, on proof of due service of the notice, statement, and copy of affidavits used in support of the application, may, if it thinks fit, make the rule for the information or mandamus absolute.

(7.) The court may, if it thinks fit, direct that any issue of fact on an information be tried by a jury in London or at Westminster.

(8.) The court may, if it thinks fit, direct that any writ of mandamus issued shall be peremptory in the first instance.

(*a*) See the Crown Office Rules, 51—59, some of which are identical with the provisions of this section. It is provided by s. 73, *ante*, p. 293, that every municipal election not called in question within twelve months after the election, either by election petition or by *quo warranto*, shall be deemed to have been to all intents a good and valid election. In respect of all or nearly all the grounds upon which an election can be questioned the only remedy, as we have seen by s. 87, is election petition. The text deals with disqualification after election, and for this the proper mode of questioning the right to sit and act is by *quo warranto*. The proceedings must be taken within twelve months from the date of the disqualification, though the disqualification may continue to the time of the proceedings ; but after the twelve months the person disqualified may be liable to penalties under s. 41, *ante*, p. 278. See *Ex parte Birkbeck*, L. R. 9 Q. B. 256 ; *De Souza* v. *Cobden*, *ante*, p. 278. Where an office is full *de facto* the court will not grant a *mandamus* for a new election until the vacancy has been judicially determined by *quo warranto*. *R.* v. *Phippen*, 7 A. & E. 966.

(*b*) See *R.* v. *Phippen*, *supra*.

Provisions for protection of persons acting under Act.

226.—(1.) An action, prosecution, or proceeding against any person for any act done in pursuance or execution or intended execution of this Act, or in respect of any alleged neglect or default in the execution of this Act, shall not lie or be instituted unless it is commenced within six months next after the act or thing is done or omitted, or, in case of a continuance of injury or damage, within six months next after the ceasing thereof.

(2.) Where the action is for damages, tender of amends before the action was commenced may, in lieu of or in addition to any other plea, be pleaded. If the action was commenced after the tender, or is proceeded with after payment into court of any money in satisfaction of the plaintiff's claim, and the plaintiff does not recover more than the sum tendered or paid, he shall not recover any costs incurred after the tender or payment, and the defendant shall be entitled to costs, to be taxed as between solicitor and client, as from the time of the tender or payment; but this provision shall not affect costs on any injunction in the action (*a*).

(3.) Subject and without prejudice to any other powers, the council, where the defendant in any such action, prosecution, or other proceeding is their officer, agent, or servant, may, if they think fit, except so far as the court before which the action, prosecution, or other proceeding is heard and determined otherwise directs, pay out of the borough fund or borough rate all or any part of any sums payable by the defendant in or in consequence of the action, prosecution, or proceeding, whether in respect of costs, charges, expenses, damages, fine or otherwise (*b*). **Sect. 226 (3).**

(*a*) Sub-sections (1) and (2) appear to be superseded, though not expressly repealed, by the similar provisions contained in the Public Authorities Protection Act, 1893 (56 & 57 Vict. c. 61), *post*. As to actions for penalties in relation to lists and elections, see s. 75, *ante*, p. 294. As to actions for fines incurred by corporate officers, see s. 224, *ante*, p. 317. The provision in the text is evidently applicable to proceedings other than those under these sections. Under the text, notice of action is not necessary, though it is required under s. 224.

(*b*) A similar provision is contained in the Local Government Act, s. 66, *ante*, p. 128. The text is, however, wider in its operation, as it applies to all officers.

Power for borough constables to take bail.

227.—(1.) Where a person charged with a petty misdemeanor is brought without the warrant of a justice into the custody of a borough constable during his attendance at a watch-house in the borough, at any time (by day or night) at which a justice is not actually sitting for the public administration of justice at the justices' room or town hall, or other place used for that purpose in the borough, the constable may, if he thinks fit, take bail without fee from that person, by recognizance conditioned for his appearance for examination within two days before a justice in the borough at some time and place therein specified (*a*).

(2.) A recognizance so taken shall be of equal obligation on the parties entering into the same, and liable to the same proceedings for the estreating thereof as if taken before a justice (*b*).

(3.) The constable shall enter in a book, kept for that purpose in every watch-house, the name, residence, and occupation of the person entering into the recognizance, and of his surety or sureties, if any, with the condition of the recognizance, and the sums acknowledged (*c*).

(4.) The constable shall lay the book before the justice present at the time when and place where the recognisor is required to appear (*d*).

* * * * *

(7.) If the recognisor applies by any person on his behalf to postpone the hearing of the charge against him, and the justice thinks fit to consent thereto, the justice may enlarge the recognizance to such further time as he appoints.

Sect. 227 (8).

(8.) When the matter is heard and determined, either by the dismissal of the charge, or by binding over the recognisor to answer the matter of the complaint at quarter sessions, or otherwise, the recognizance for his appearance before a justice shall be discharged without fee.

(*a*) For the reason stated in the note to s. 223, *ante*, p. 316, it is doubtful whether this provision is now extended to counties by the Local Government Act, s. 75, *ante*, p. 141. It is more extensive in its operation than s. 38 of the Summary Jurisdiction Act, 1879, but it does not repeal that section. See 47 & 48 Vict. c. 43, s. 9.

(*b*) The recognizance may be enforced under s. 9 of the Summary Jurisdiction Act, 1879.

(*c*) It will now be necessary for county constables to have this book if the section applies to counties.

(*d*) Sub-sections (5) and (6) are repealed by the Summary Jurisdiction Act, 1884, which substitutes the corresponding provisions of the Summary Jurisdiction Acts. The repealed sub-sections related to the forfeiture and enforcing of the recognizance, as to which see note (*b*), *supra*.

PART XIII.—General.

Boundaries.

Boundaries of boroughs and transfer of parts to counties.

228.—(1.) Every place at the commencement of this Act included within each borough then existing, and no other place, shall be part of the borough, and in each borough then existing which is a county of itself shall be part of that county and of no other, as if this Act had not been passed.

(2.) Where under the Municipal Corporations Act, 1835, or any Act amending it, any such county or borough does not, at the commencement of this Act, include a place which, before the passing of the Municipal Corporations Act, 1835, was part thereof, that place shall continue to be part of the county wherein it is situate, or with which it has the longest common boundary, as if this Act had not been passed.

(3.) But nothing in this Act shall prevent any gaol, house of correction, lunatic asylum, court of justice, or judges' lodgings, which at the passing of the Municipal Corporations Act, 1835, was, and at the commencement of this Act is, taken to be, for any purpose in any county, from being still, for that purpose, taken to be in that county, as if this Act had not been passed.

(4.) Any gaol, court, depôt for arms, and any land thereto belonging, which at the commencement of this Act is parcel of a county shall continue to be parcel of the county, and under the exclusive jurisdiction of the authorities of the county, as if this Act had not been passed.

(5.) Nothing in this Act shall be construed to affect the assessments of the land tax or assessed taxes, as those assessments exist

Sect. 228 (5).

at the commencement of this Act, or to extend or diminish the jurisdiction of any commissioners of those taxes, as such commissioners then exist; but all lands, and all parishes, parts of parishes, and places shall continue to be charged as at the commencement of this Act towards the land tax charged on the county or other district whereof at the commencement of this Act they are part, and to be subject in that behalf to the jurisdiction of the commissioners of the same county or other district, as if this Act had not been passed.

It is provided by the Local Government Act, s. 75, sub-s. (16), *ante*, p. 145, that nothing in the Municipal Corporations Act, as applied by that section, shall apply any of the provisions of the Municipal Corporations Act, 1882, with reference to boundaries. Consequently the above section will not apply to counties. For the provisions of the Local Government Act, 1888, as to boundaries, see Part III. of that Act, *ante*, p. 104; and see also Part III. of the Local Government Act, 1894, *post*.

Adjustment between boroughs and counties on change of boundaries.

229. If any place, which under the Municipal Corporations Act, 1835, or any Act amending it, ceased to be included in a borough or county of a town or city, was before the passing of the Municipal Corporations Act, 1835, liable to contribute to any rate for satisfying any lawful debt to which the ratepayers of that borough or county were then liable, and if after the commencement of this Act any difference arises concerning the proportion of that debt to be contributed in respect of that place, the Secretary of State, on the application of the council, or of the chairman of a public meeting of the ratepayers of the place, may appoint by writing under his hand a barrister not having any interest in the question to arbitrate between the parties, and by his award under his hand and seal to assess the proportion aforesaid, if any; and the arbitrator shall assess the costs of the arbitration, and direct by whom and in what proportion and out of what fund they shall be paid; and the rate aforesaid shall continue to be levied by warrant of the council and to be paid by the place aforesaid to the treasurer of the borough, as if the Municipal Corporations Act, 1835, or any Act amending it, or this Act, had not been passed, until the proportion aforesaid is satisfied, and no longer.

The above section does not apply to counties. See the note to last section.

The Local Government Act, s. 54, *ante*, p. 108, deals with future alterations of the boundaries of counties and boroughs, and s. 62, *ante*, p. 119, provides for the due adjustment of property and liabilities upon any such alteration.

Time.

Computation of time.

230.—(1.) Where by this Act any limited time from or after any date or event is appointed or allowed for the doing of any act or the taking of any proceeding, then in the computation of

Sect. 230 (1).

that limited time the same shall be taken as exclusive of the day of that date or of the happening of that event, and as commencing at the beginning of the next following day; and the act or proceeding shall be done or taken at the latest on the last day of the limited time as so computed, unless the last day is a Sunday, Christmas Day, Good Friday, or Monday or Tuesday in Easter week, or a day appointed for public fast, humiliation, or thanksgiving, in which case any act or proceeding shall be considered as done or taken in due time if it is done or taken on the next day afterwards, not being one of the days in this section specified (*a*).

(2.) Where by this Act any act or proceeding is directed or allowed to be done or taken on a certain day, then if that day happens to be one of the days in this section specified, the act or proceeding shall be considered as done or taken in due time if it is done or taken on the next day afterwards, not being one of the days in this section specified (*a*).

(3.) Where by this Act any act or proceeding is directed or allowed to be done or taken within any time not exceeding seven days, the days in this section specified shall not be reckoned in the computation of such time (*b*).

(*a*) Thus, if something is to be done within ten days after the 1st of a month, the last day for doing it would be the 11th, unless that were Sunday, or one of the days specified, in which case the act would be done on the 12th.

(*b*) This provision will not apply to the nine days' notice of election under s. 54, *ante*, p. 285, nor to the seven days mentioned in Sched. 3, Part. II., r. 7, *post*.

Distance.

Measurement of distances.

231. The distances mentioned in this Act shall be measured in a straight line on a horizontal plane, and may be determined by the map made under the survey commonly known as the Ordnance Survey.

This is a useful provision, otherwise the Ordnance map could not have been used.

Notices.

Notices on town hall.

232. Any notice or other document required by this Act to be fixed on the town hall shall be fixed in some conspicuous place on or near the outer door of the town hall, or if there is no town hall, in some conspicuous place in the borough or ward to which the notice or document relates.

In applying this section to counties and electoral divisions of counties some modification must be made. No doubt, if there were public offices in the division, the notice might be published there, as by so doing the above section would be satisfied, whether such offices were a town hall within the meaning or this section as applied, or a conspicuous place in the division.

See the Local Government Act, s. 75 (7), *ante*, p. 143, as to the substitution of a place for the town hall for hearing objections to nomination papers.

Inspection and Copies.

Sect. 233 (1).

Inspection of documents.

233.—(1.) The minutes of proceedings of the council shall be open to the inspection of a burgess on payment of a fee of one shilling, and a burgess may make a copy thereof or take an extract therefrom (*a*).

(2.) A burgess may make a copy of or take an extract from an order of the council for the payment of money (*b*).

(3.) The treasurer's accounts shall be open to the inspection of the council, and a member of the council may make a copy thereof or take an extract therefrom.

(4.) The abstract of the treasurer's accounts shall be open to the inspection of all the ratepayers of the borough, and copies thereof shall be delivered to a ratepayer on payment of a reasonable price for each copy (*c*).

(5.) The Freemen's Roll shall be open to public inspection, and the town clerk shall deliver copies thereof to any person on payment of a reasonable price for each copy.

(6.) A document directed by this Act to be open to inspection shall be so open at any reasonable time during the ordinary hours of business, and without payment, unless it is otherwise expressed.

(7.) If a person having the custody of any document in this section mentioned—

(a.) Obstructs any person authorized to inspect the same in making such inspection thereof as in this section mentioned ; or

(b.) Refuses to give copies or extracts to any person entitled to obtain the same under this section ;

he shall, on summary conviction, be liable to a fine not exceeding five pounds.

(*a*) It would seem that while a burgess is not entitled to inspect minutes of a committee, he is entitled to inspect the epitome of such minutes as presented to the council for their approval under s. 22 (2). *Williams* v. *Manchester* (*Mayor, etc., of*), 45 W. R. 412 ; 13 T. L. R. 299. As to the right of inspection by the solicitor of a burgess, see *R.* v. *Wimbledon Urban District Council*, 14 T. L. R. 146.

(*b*) Sub-sections (1) and (2) will apply to county councils with the substitution of "county elector" for "burgess."

As to the minutes of the council, see s. 22, *ante*, p. 260, and Sched. 2, r. 12, *post*, p. 337.

As to orders for the payment of money, see the Local Government Act, s. 80, *ante*, p. 154.

(*c*) It is provided by the Local Government Act, s. 71, *ante*, p. 136, that the provisions of the Municipal Corporations Act, 1882, as to the accounts of the treasurer of a borough and to the inspection and abstract thereof shall apply to the accounts of a county council.

Fees.

Tables of fees to be posted.

234. The town clerk of every borough shall cause a true copy of the tables of fees for the time being authorized to be taken by

Sect. 234.

the clerk of the peace (if any) for the borough, by the clerk to the justices (if any) for the borough, and by the registrar and officers of the borough civil court (if any), to be posted conspicuously in the following places :

(a.) The room where the business of the town clerk's office is transacted ;

(b.) The room (if any) where the justices of the borough sit for transacting their business ;

(c.) The room (if any) where the court of quarter sessions of the borough is held ; and

(d.) The room (if any) where the borough civil court is held.

As to the tables of fees to be taken by justices' clerks generally, see 14 & 15 Vict. c. 55, and 40 & 41 Vict. c. 43.

It would appear that this section will apply in counties except in so far as it refers to the borough civil court. See s. 75 of the Local Government Act, *ante*, p. 141.

Seals and Signatures.

Forgery.

235. If any person forges the seal or signature affixed or subscribed to a bye-law made under this Act, or the signature subscribed to any minute of proceedings of the council, or tenders in evidence any such document with a false or counterfeit seal or signature, knowing it to be false or counterfeit, he shall be liable to imprisonment with hard labour for any term not exceeding two years.

As to the authentication of bye-laws, see s. 24, *ante*, p. 265. As to the signature of minutes, see s. 22, sub-s. (5), *ante*, p. 260.

Applications to Treasury.

Notice of application to and correspondence with Treasury.

236.—(1.) Where the council intend to apply to the Treasury for their approval of any sale, loan, or other financial arrangement under this Act, notice of the intention to make the application shall be fixed on the town hall one month at least before the application, and a copy of the intended application shall during that month be kept in the town clerk's office, and be open to public inspection.

(2.) If the Treasury either refuse their approval or grant it conditionally or under qualifications, notice of the correspondence between the Treasury and the council shall forthwith and during one month be fixed on the town hall, and a copy of the correspondence shall during that month be kept in the town clerk's office, and be open to public inspection.

It is provided by the Local Government Act, s. 72, *ante*, p. 140, that after the appointed day the Local Government Board shall exercise, as regards any county borough, or other borough, the powers conferred by Part V. of the Municipal Corporations Act, 1882, relating to corporate property and liabilities, as respects the approval of loans and the alienation of property and other matters therein mentioned, and that part shall, as respects any transactions commenced after the appointed day, be construed as if "Local Government Board" were throughout that part substituted for "Treasury." Sect. 236. NOTE.

The above section will apparently apply to all applications to the Local Government Board, whether by a borough council under this Act, or by a county council under the provisions of the Local Government Act as to property, borrowing, etc.

As to fixing the notice on the town hall, see s. 232, *ante*, p. 322.

The town clerk's office will, in counties, be the office of the clerk of the council.

Deputy.

237. No defect in the appointment of a deputy under this Act shall invalidate his acts. Acts of deputy not to be invalidated by defect in appointment.

This section will apply to a deputy clerk of the peace appointed under the Local Government Act, ss. 83 or 118; a deputy chairman of the London County Council (*ib.* s. 88); a deputy returning officer (*ib.* s. 75).

Overseers.

238.—(1.) Every matter by the Municipal Corporations Acts directed to be done by overseers may be lawfully done by the major part of them. Notices to and acting of overseers.

(2.) Any notice by the Municipal Corporations Acts required to be given to overseers may be delivered to any one of them, or left at his place of abode, or at his office for transacting parochial business.

The expression "Municipal Corporations Acts" is defined by s. 7 (1) of this Act to mean "this Act and any Act to be passed amending this Act."

The chief duties of the overseers under this Act as applied by the Local Government Act, 1888, consist in the preparation of the burgess lists and lists of voters, etc., under Part III., as amended by the County Electors Act.

An assistant overseer may also be counted as one of the majority. See *Baker* v. *Locke*, 11 Jur. (N.S.) 65; 34 L. J. C. P. 49; 18 C. B. (N.S.) 52.

Declarations and Oaths.

239.—(1.) Where by or under this Act a declaration or oath is required to be made or taken by the holder of a corporate office or other person before the council or any members thereof, or any other persons, they shall have authority to receive and administer the same without any commission or authority other than this Act. Power to administer oaths, etc.

(2.) Nothing in this Act in any case shall require or authorize the taking or making of any oath or declaration that would not have been required or authorized under the Promissory Oaths Act, 1868, or otherwise by law, if this Act had not been 31 & 32 Vict. c. 72.

Sect. 239 (2).

passed, or interfere with the operation of the Promissory Oaths Act, 1868.

As to the declaration on acceptance of office, see s. 35, *ante*, p. 273, and Sched. 8, *post*. This declaration may be made before two members of the council or the town clerk.

As to the oaths to be taken by the chairman of the county council before acting as a justice of the peace, see the Local Government Act, s. 2, *ante*, p. 4.

Forms.

Forms in schedule.

240. The forms in the Eighth Schedule, or forms to the like effect, varied as circumstances require, may be used, and shall be sufficient in law.

The only part of the Eighth Schedule which is incorporated with the Local Government Act is Part I., which is set out, *post*.

Misnomer or Inaccurate Description.

Misnomer or inaccurate description not to hinder.

241. No misnomer or inaccurate description of any person, body corporate, or place named in any schedule to the Municipal Corporations Act, 1835, or in any roll, list, notice, or voting paper required by this Act, shall hinder the full operation of this Act with respect to that person, body corporate, or place, provided the description of that person, body corporate, or place be such as to be commonly understood.

Where in a voting paper *Gonville Place* was stated as the address of a voter, whereas his real address was *Newmarket Road*, it was held that this inaccuracy was not cured by the corresponding provisions of 5 & 6 Will. 4, c. 76, s. 142. *R.* v. *Coward*, 16 Q. B. 819; and see *R.* v. *Deighton*, 5 Q. B. 896; 13 L. J. Q. B. 241; 8 Jur. 686; *R.* v. *Hammond*, 17 Q. B. 772; 21 L. J. Q. B. 153; 16 Jur. 194; *R.* v. *Avery*, 18 Q. B. 576; 21 L. J. Q. B. 153; 17 Jur. 194.

Joseph C., a person entitled to vote at a municipal election, was by mistake entered on the burgess roll as James C. He voted by the name of James C. On motion for a *quo warranto*, the vote was objected to on the ground that C. was not entitled to vote, and had fraudulently personated a person entitled to vote. It was held that neither objection was sustained. And, *semble*, that if the objection had been that C. had voted in a wrong name, and was not rightly entered on the burgess roll, this objection could not have been sustained, but that the misnomer would have been cured under 5 & 6 Will. 4, c. 76, s. 142. *R.* v. *Thwaites*, 1 E. & B. 704; 22 L. J. Q. B. 238; 17 Jur. 712.

A voting paper signed W. J., of K. street, was rejected on the ground that the qualification of W. J. on the burgess roll was described as "house in M. street." It was shown by affidavits that K. and M. streets intersected; that the house in question was the corner house; that it was one house, with a street door in each street, consisting of what had formerly been two distinct houses, one in each street, and one of them being the house in M. street. It was held that having regard to 5 & 6 Will. 4, c. 76, s. 142, the description was such as to be commonly understood, and that the vote was improperly rejected. *R.* v. *Gregory*, 1 E. & B. 600; 22 L. J. Q. B. 120; 17 Jur. 272.

Sect. 241.

NOTE.

Voting papers were tendered signed "A. B., voting for property situate in the parish of C." They were rejected, and the rejection altered the majority. In proceedings by *quo warranto*, it was admitted that the borough consisted of two parishes, of which C. was one; that though there were streets and lanes in the borough, the description in the voting papers was such as to be commonly understood, and that the boundaries of the parish were well known and defined. It was held that the fault, if there was one, was cured by 5 & 6 Will. 4, c. 76, s. 142. *R.* v. *Spratley*, 6 E. & B. 363; 25 L. J. Q. B. 257; 2 Jur. (N.S.) 735.

A voting paper contained the christian name and surname of the candidate and his place of abode, but no description (such as is required by Sched. 3, Part II. r. 5, *post*). It was held that this was not an inaccurate description, but a total omission of the description of the candidate, and was not cured by 5 & 6 Will. 4, c. 76, s. 142. *R.* v. *Tugwell*, L.R. 3 Q. B. 704; 37 L. J. Q. B. 275; 16 W. R. 1039.

At an election of councillors voting papers designated the person voted for by the initial of his christian name. It was held that this was a misnomer and cured by 5 & 6 Will. 4, c. 76, s. 142. *R.* v. *Plenty*, L. R. 4 Q. B. 346; 38 L. J. Q. B. 205; 20 L. T. (N.S.) 521; 17 W. R. 792. But in a later case it was held that a similar use of initials in a nomination paper was not cured, for s. 142 did not extend to a nomination paper, which was unknown when 5 & 6 Will. 4, c. 76, was passed. *Mather* v. *Brown*, 1 C. P. D. 596; 45 L. J. C. P. 547; 34 L. T. (N.S.) 869; 24 W. R. 736.

A mistake in the number on the burgess roll as stated in a nomination paper was held not cured by 35 & 36 Vict. c. 33, s. 13, and 41 & 42 Vict. c. 26, s. 41; *Gothard* v. *Clark*, 5 C. P. D. 253; 49 L. J. C. P. 474; 42 L. T. (N.S.) 776; 29 W. R. 102; 44 J. P. 587.

A nomination paper at the election of a town councillor pursuant to the Municipal Elections Act, 1875, was held sufficiently to state the Christian name (William) of the person nominated by the abbreviation "Wm." *Henry* v. *Armitage*, 12 Q. B. D. 257; 33 L. J. Q. B. 111; 50 L. T. (N.S.) 4; 32 W. R. 192; 48 J. P. 424.

A nomination paper was subscribed with the full and correct name of Charles Arthur Burman as an assenting burgess; but his name was erroneously entered on the burgess roll as Charles Burman only. It was held that the defect was not cured by the text, the words "commonly understood" meaning commonly understood by any person comparing the nomination paper and the burgess roll. *Moorhouse* v. *Linney*, 15 Q. B. D. 273; 53 L. T. (N.S.) 343; 33 W. R. 704; 49 J. P. 471.

But in a case where a nomination paper was subscribed by three of the assenting burgesses, "Edwin J. Hooper," "W. E. Waller," and "R. Turner," whose names appeared on the burgess roll as "Edwin John Hooper," "William E. Waller," and "Robert Turner" respectively, it was held that the nomination paper had been duly subscribed by those persons. *Bowden* v. *Besley*, 21 Q. B. D. 309; 57 L. J. Q. B. 473; 59 L. T. (N.S.) 219; 36 W. R. 839. In this case it will be observed that the signatures and surnames on the burgess roll, though not identical, were not inconsistent with each other.

A nomination paper at a county council election was signed by a nominator "James Sykes, junr." The name James Sykes appeared on the register of county electors, but without the addition of "junior." It appeared that the nominator was generally known as James Sykes, junior, and that was his usual signature. It was held that the nomination paper, being signed with the ordinary signature of the nominator, was valid. *Gledhill* v. *Crowther*, 23 Q. B. D. 136; 58 L. J. Q. B. 327; 60 L. T. (N.S.) 866; 53 J. P. 677.

Sect. 241.

NOTE.

A nomination paper was subscribed with the correct name of Henry D. Davenport, as an assenting burgess, but his name was erroneously stated on the burgess roll as Davenport, Henry D. Evereux. *Held*, that the nomination paper was not invalid. *Harding* v. *Cornwall*, 60 L. T. (N.S.) 959.

See also s. 72, *ante* p. 293, s. 13 of the Ballot Act, 1872, *ante*, p. 213, and notes.

Substitution in Former Acts.

Provision for references in unrepealed enactments to 5 & 6 Will. 4, c. 76, etc.

242.—(1.) In the several enactments described in Part I. of the Ninth Schedule, a reference to this Act shall be deemed to be substituted for a reference to the Municipal Corporations Act, 1835, and any Act amending it.

(2.) In each of the enactments described in Part II. of the Ninth Schedule, there shall be substituted for the respective provision of the Municipal Corporations Act, 1835, in that part mentioned in connection therewith, such provision of this Act as is also mentioned in connection therewith.

(3.) Where any Act passed before this Act, and not specified in the First or in the Ninth Schedule, refers to the Municipal Corporations Act, 1835, or any Act amending it, or to boroughs or corporations subject to that Act or any Act amending it, the reference shall be deemed to be to this Act, or to the corresponding provision of this Act, or to boroughs or corporations subject to this Act (as the case may require).

(4.) All enactments to which this section relates shall, except as in this section provided, continue to operate as if this Act had not been passed.

The effect of this section in incorporating s. 14 of the Judicature Act, 1881 (44 & 45 Vict. c. 68), as to appeals to the Court of Appeal from the decision of a divisional court upon a question of law in a municipal election petition, has been stated in the note (*f*) to s. 93 (7), *ante*, p 305.

Short titles of Acts partly repealed.

243. Such of the Acts specified in the First Schedule as will remain in force to any extent after the commencement of this Act may continue to be cited by the short titles in that schedule mentioned.

Returning Officers at Parliamentary Elections.

Mayor of certain boroughs to be returning officer in parliamentary elections.

244.—(1.) In boroughs, other than cities and towns being counties of themselves, the mayor shall be the returning officer at parliamentary elections; but this provision shall not extend to the borough of Berwick-upon-Tweed.

(2.) If there are more mayors than one within the boundaries of a parliamentary borough, the mayor of that borough to which the writ of election is directed shall be the returning officer.

(3.) If when a mayor is required to act as returning officer the mayor is absent, or incapable of acting, or there is no mayor, the council shall forthwith choose an alderman to be returning officer. Sect. 244 (3).

This section does not apply to counties.

Disfranchised Parliamentary Boroughs.

245. Where a borough has, in pursuance of the Representation of the People Act, 1867, or of any Act passed in the session of the thirty-first and thirty-second years of the reign of Her Majesty, ceased to return a member to serve in Parliament, and the persons entitled to vote for the member or members formerly returned by the borough were by law electors for any other purpose, the burgesses of the borough shall be electors for that purpose, and shall in all respects, as regards that purpose, be substituted for the persons so entitled to vote.

Electors in disfranchised boroughs. 30 & 31 Vict. c. 102.

This section cannot apply to a county.

Licensing.

246. In the Act of the ninth year of the reign of King George the Fourth, chapter sixty-one, "to regulate the granting of licenses to keepers of inns, alehouses, and victualling houses in England," the expressions "town corporate," "county or place," and "division or place," include every borough having a separate commission of the peace, and the expression "high constable" includes any constable of any such borough to whom the justices of the borough direct their precept under that Act.

Explanation of terms "town corporate," etc., in Licensing Act.

This section applies only to boroughs.

Freedom of Trading.

247. Notwithstanding any custom or bye-law, every person in any borough may keep any shop for the sale of all lawful wares and merchandises by wholesale or retail, and use every lawful trade, occupation, mystery, and handicraft for hire, gain, sale, or otherwise within any borough.

Right of free trading in boroughs.

Bye-laws cannot be made in restraint of trade. See the cases cited in the notes to s. 23, *ante*, p. 264.

This section is in fact a proviso to s. 23, and will apply to county bye-laws as well as to those of boroughs. See s. 16 of the Local Government Act, *ante*, p. 42.

Cinque Ports.

248.—(1.) The boroughs of Hastings, Sandwich, Dover, Hythe, being four of the Cinque Ports, and the borough of Rye, are in this section referred to as the five boroughs.

Special provisions as to certain of the Cinque Ports.

(2.) The jurisdiction, powers, and authorities of the court of quarter sessions, recorder, coroner, and clerk of the peace for each

Sect. 248 (2). of the five boroughs shall extend to the non-corporate members and liberties thereof, and to such corporate members thereof as have not a separate court of quarter sessions.

(3.) The jurisdiction, powers, and authorities of the persons constituted justices within and throughout the liberties of the Cinque Ports by virtue of their commission, shall extend to all places being within the limits of the five boroughs or of their members or liberties, corporate or non-corporate, and not being within the limits of a borough having a separate commission of the peace.

(4.) The justices for the five boroughs respectively shall have all the jurisdiction, powers, and authorities of justices for a county relating to the granting of licenses or authorities to persons to keep inns, ale-houses, or victualling houses, or to sell exciseable liquors by retail within any of the corporate or non-corporate members or liberties of the five boroughs respectively, not being within the limits of a borough having a separate commission of the peace.

(5.) The non-corporate members and liberties of the five boroughs and such corporate members thereof as have not a separate court of quarter sessions shall be charged by the respective courts of quarter sessions of the five boroughs with a due proportion of all those expenses of the five boroughs, to the payment whereof rates in the nature of county rates are applicable; and such rates may be assessed and levied in the manner in which rates of that description were assessed and levied before the passing of the Municipal Corporations Act, 1835, under any enactment then in force, but subject to the operation of any subsequent enactment affecting the same.

(6.) A due proportion of inhabitant householders to serve as grand jurors and jurors at the respective courts of quarter sessions of the five boroughs shall be summoned by the clerks of the peace thereof from the non-corporate members and liberties thereof, and such corporate members thereof as have not a separate court of quarter sessions; and the attendance of such jurors shall be enforced, and their defaults punished, in the manner by this Act directed with respect to jurors in boroughs.

32 & 33 Vict. c. 53. (7.) Nothing in this section shall effect the Cinque Ports Act, 1869, or the Acts therein recited.

The Local Government Act, 1888, s. 48, sub-s. (4), *ante*, p. 103, provides that "the Cinque Ports and two ancient towns and their members shall for all purposes of the county council and of the powers and duties of quarter sessions and justices out of sessions under this Act form part of the county in which they are respectively situate, without prejudice nevertheless to the position of any such port, town, or member as a quarter sessions borough under the Municipal Corporations Act, 1882, as amended by this Act, and without prejudice to the existing privileges of such ports, towns, and members as respects matters which are not affected by this Act." Sect. 248.

NOTE.

Cambridge.

249.—(1.) It shall be lawful for the Queen, from time to time, by her commission of the peace for the borough of Cambridge, to constitute the Vice-Chancellor for the time being of the University of Cambridge a justice for that borough. Vice-Chancellor of Cambridge.

(2.) He shall not, by reason of being so constituted, have any greater authority as to the grant of licences to alehouses than any other justice named in the commission.

(3.) But nothing in this section shall affect the rights and privileges which the Vice-Chancellor lawfully has or enjoys, or might have lawfully had or enjoyed if he were not so constituted a justice.

Savings.

250.—(1.) Nothing in this Act shall prejudicially affect any charter granted before the commencement of this Act, or take away, abridge, or prejudicially affect any of the rights, powers, privileges, estates, property, duties, liabilities, or obligations vested in or imposed on any municipal corporation existing at the commencement of this Act, or in or on the mayor, or the council of a borough then existing, or any members or committee of the council, by the incorporation of the inhabitants of the borough, or by transfer from any other authority, or otherwise; but every such charter shall continue to operate, and every such corporation shall continue to have perpetual succession and a common seal, and to be capable in law by the council to do and suffer all acts which at the commencement of this Act they and their successors respectively may lawfully do or suffer, and the corporation and all members and officers thereof and their sureties, and every such mayor and every such council and committee, and every such officer, shall continue to have, enjoy, and be subject to the like rights, powers, offices, privileges, estates, property, duties, liabilities, and obligations as if this Act had not been passed, without prejudice, nevertheless, to the operation of the repeal of enactments by this Act, and to the other express provisions of this Act. Saving for existing corporations.

(2.) Nothing in this Act shall alter the boundaries of any borough existing at the commencement of this Act, or the number, apportionment, or qualification of the aldermen or councillors thereof, or the division thereof into wards.

(3.) Nothing in this Act shall affect the right of the council of a borough to collect by their own officers the borough rate and watch rate, or either of them, where, at the commencement of this

Sect. 250 (3).

Act, they are authorized by law to so collect, and are so collecting, the same.

(4.) Nothing in this Act shall alter the respective jurisdiction of county and borough justices.

(5.) Nothing in this Act shall affect the right of any borough named in Schedule (A.) to the Municipal Corporations Act, 1835, to have a separate commission of the peace.

Compare the provisions of the Local Government Act, s. 125, *ante*, p. 202.

Saving for local Acts.

251. Nothing in this Act shall alter the effect of any local Act of Parliament.

The Local Government Act, s. 75, sub-s. (16), *ante*, p. 145, provides that nothing in the Municipal Corporations Act, 1882, as applied by that section, shall apply the provisions of s. 251, *supra*. Section 125 of that Act, *ante*, p. 202, contains a saving for local Acts.

Saving for Prison Acts. 28 & 29 Vict. c. 126. 40 & 41 Vict. c. 21. 13 & 14 Vict. c. 91.

252. Nothing in this Act, except the provision referring to the Ninth Schedule, shall affect the Prison Act, 1865, or the Prison Act, 1877, and nothing in this Act shall affect the Act of the session of the fifth and sixth years of Her Majesty, chapter ninety-eight, "to amend the laws concerning prisons," or revive or restore any enactment which, being contained in that Act, or in the Municipal Corporation (Justices) Act, 1850, or in any other Act, is virtually repealed or superseded by the Prison Act, 1865, or the Prison Act, 1877.

Saving for military and naval officers, etc.

253. Nothing in this Act shall compel the acceptance of any office or duty whatever in any borough by any military, naval, or marine officer in Her Majesty's service on full pay or half pay, or by any officer or other person employed and residing in any of Her Majesty's dockyards, victualling establishments, arsenals, barracks, or other naval or military establishments.

See the note to s. 34, *ante*, p. 273.

Saving for dockyards, barracks, etc.

254. Nothing in this Act shall affect the watching, paving, or lighting, or the internal regulations for the government of any of Her Majesty's dockyards, victualling establishments, arsenals, barracks, or other naval or military establishments, or make the tenements therein or the inhabitants thereof liable to any rate for watching, paving, or lighting.

Saving as to Admiralty.

255. Nothing in this Act shall affect the authority of justices vested in the Commissioners for executing the office of Lord High Admiral of the United Kingdom, or any authority to appoint coroners to act within the jurisdiction of the Admiralty.

Saving for Lord Warden.

256. Nothing in this Act shall affect the jurisdiction and office of the Lord Warden in his office of Admiral of the Cinque Ports.

257. Nothing in this Act shall— Sect. 257 (1).

Saving for universities.

(1.) Affect the rights, privileges, duties, or liabilities of the chancellor, masters, and scholars of the Universities of Oxford and Cambridge respectively, as by law possessed under the respective charters of those universities or otherwise ; or

(2.) Entitle the mayors of Oxford and Cambridge respectively to any precedence over the vice-chancellors of those universities respectively ; or

(3.) Entitle any person to be enrolled a citizen of the city of Oxford or burgess of the borough of Cambridge by reason of his occupation of any rooms, chambers, or premises in any college or hall of either of those universities ; or

(4.) Compel any resident member of either of those universities to accept any office in or under the municipal corporation of Oxford or of Cambridge ; or

(5.) Authorize the levy of any rate within the precincts of those universities, or of any of the colleges or halls thereof, which now by law cannot be levied therein, or make either of those universities, or the members thereof, liable to any rate to which they are not liable to contribute at the commencement of this Act ; or

(6.) Authorize the transfer of any rights or liabilities by a local authority to the municipal corporation of the borough of Cambridge without the consent of the chancellor, master, and scholars of the University of Cambridge ; or

(7.) Affect the rights or privileges granted by charter or Act of Parliament to the University of Durham.

This section does not apply to counties. See the Local Government Act, s. 75, sub-s. (16), *ante*, p. 145.

Saving for jurisdiction over cathedral precincts.

258. Nothing in this Act shall prevent any jurisdiction or authority exercised in or over the precinct or close of any cathedral from being continued concurrently with the jurisdiction and authority of the justices of the borough in which the precinct or close is situate.

Saving for royal prerogative.

259. Nothing in this Act shall prejudicially affect Her Majesty's royal prerogative ; and the enabling provisions of this Act shall be deemed to be in addition to, and not in derogation of, the powers exerciseable by Her Majesty by virtue of her royal prerogative.

Saving as to repealed enactments.

260.—(1.) The repeal effected by this Act shall not affect—

(a.) Anything done or suffered before the commencement of this Act under any enactment repealed by this Act ; or

Sect. 260 (1).

(b.) Any proceeding or thing pending or in course of being done at the commencement of this Act under any enactment repealed by this Act; or

(c.) Any jurisdiction or practice established, confirmed, or transferred, or right or privilege acquired or confirmed, or duty or liability imposed or incurred, or compensation secured by or under any enactment repealed by this Act; or

(d.) Any disability or disqualification existing at the commencement of this Act under any enactment repealed by this Act; or

(e.) Any fine, forfeiture, punishment, or other consequence incurred or to be incurred in respect of any offence committed before the commencement of this Act against any enactment repealed by this Act; or

(f.) The institution or the prosecution to its termination of any legal proceeding or other remedy for ascertaining, enforcing, or recovering any such jurisdiction, practice, right, privilege, duty, liability, compensation, disability, disqualification, fine, forfeiture, punishment, or consequence as aforesaid; or

(g.) The terms on which any money has been borrowed before the commencement of this Act under any enactment repealed by this Act.

(2.) The repeal effected by this Act shall not extend to Scotland or Ireland, and shall not, as regards the enactments described in Part II. of the First Schedule, operate in respect of any place other than a borough to which this Act applies, and shall not revive or restore any statute, law, usage, custom, royal or other charter, grant, letters patent, bye-law, jurisdiction, office, right, title, claim, privilege, liability, disqualification, exemption, restriction, practice, procedure, or other matter or thing abolished by the Municipal Corporations Act, 1835, or not in force or existing at the commencement of this Act, or otherwise affect the past operation of any enactment repealed by this Act.

(3.) All elections, declarations, appointments, bye-laws, rates, tables of fees, and regulations made, or pending, or in the course of being made, and all other things done, or pending, or in the course of being done, under the Municipal Corporations Act, 1835, or any other enactment repealed by this Act, before or at the commencement of this Act, shall for the purposes of this Act be of the like effect as if they had been made or done, or were pending, or in the course of being made or done, under this Act, and shall, as far as may be requisite for the continuance, validity, and effect thereof, be deemed to have been made or done, or may be carried on and be made or done, as the case may require, under this Act.

SECOND SCHEDULE.

Schedule 2.

MEETINGS AND PROCEEDINGS OF COUNCIL.

1. The council shall hold four quarterly meetings in every year for the transaction of general business.

This schedule is incorporated by s. 75 of the Local Government Act, 1888, *ante*, p. 141.

General business is presumably business prescribed by the Act itself or some other Act relating to the council. Any other business must be specified in the summons to attend the meeting. See r. 8, *post*.

County councils must hold quarterly meetings as herein provided.

It may be added that, by the Local Government Act, s. 2, *ante*, p. 1, county councils are to conduct their proceedings in like manner as the council of a borough, and that by s. 22 (1) *ante*, p. 260, the rules in this schedule "shall be observed."

2. The quarterly meetings shall be held at noon on each ninth of November, and at such hour on such other three days before the first of November then next following as the council at the quarterly meeting in November decide or afterwards from time to time by standing order determine.

This provision is superseded by s. 1 of the County Councils (Elections) Act, 1891 (54 & 55 Vict. c. 68), *post*, which enacts that "the sixteenth day of March or such other day within ten days after the ordinary day of retirement of councillors" (viz., March 8th) "as the council of any county may from time to time fix for that county shall, in substitution for the ninth day of November, be the ordinary day of election of the chairman and of the aldermen, and the day for holding a quarterly meeting, and if the county council fix any hour for the quarterly meeting that hour shall be substituted for the hour specified in the Municipal Corporations Act, 1882."

Noon means 12 o'clock by Greenwich time. 43 & 44 Vict. c. 9.

At the quarterly meeting in March the first business to be done will be the election of the chairman (s. 61, *ante*, p, 289); then the election of the aldermen, (s. 60, *ante*, p. 288).

As to the standing orders, see r. 13, *post*.

3. The mayor may at any time call a meeting of the council.

The chairman of a county council will have this power.

4. If the mayor refuses to call a meeting after a requisition for that purpose, signed by five members of the council, has been presented to him, any five members of the council may forthwith, on that refusal, call a meeting. If the mayor (without so refusing) does not within seven days after such presentation call a meeting, any five members of the council may, on the expiration of those seven days, call a meeting.

This rule provides for two cases :—(1.) if the mayor (or chairman) signifies his refusal to call a meeting; (2) if he does not refuse, but does not in fact call a meeting within seven days. The seven days are to be reckoned exclusive of Sunday, Christmas Day, Good Friday, Easter Monday or Tuesday, or public fast, humiliation, or thanksgiving days. See s. 230, *ante*, p. 321.

5. Three clear days at least (*a*) before any meeting of the council, notice of the time and place of the intended meeting, signed by the mayor, or if the meeting is called by members of the council, by those members, shall be fixed on the town hall (*b*). Where the meeting is called by members of the council, the notice shall specify the business proposed to be transacted thereat (*c*).

(*a*) This means that three clear days must intervene, not counting either the day of giving the notice or the day of the meeting. [*R.* v. *Shropshire JJ.*, 8 A. & E. 173; *Young* v. *Higgon*, 6 M. & W. 49.

(*b*) See s. 232, *ante*, p. 322. It will probably be a sufficient compliance with this provision if the notice is affixed to the building at which meetings of the county council are usually held.

(*c*) When the meeting is summoned by the mayor (or chairman) the business need not be specified in this notice.

Schedule 2.

6. Three clear days at least (*a*) before any meeting of the council, a summons to attend the meeting, specifying the business proposed to be transacted thereat (*b*), and signed by the town clerk (*c*), shall be left or delivered by post in a registered letter at the usual place of abode of every member of the council, three clear days at least before the meeting.

(*a*) See r. 5, note (*a*), *supra*.

(*b*) This notice must in every case specify the business.

(*c*) The clerk of the council must sign the summons calling a meeting of the county council.

7. Want of service of the summons on any member of the council shall not affect the validity of a meeting.

This rule is evidently intended to obviate any difficulty which might arise in case of the accidental omission of notice to any member. But it may be doubted whether the failure to send notices to a considerable number of members might not affect the validity of the meeting.

8. No business shall be transacted at a meeting other than that specified in the summons relating thereto, except, in case of a quarterly meeting, business prescribed by this Act to be transacted thereat.

A quarterly meeting may be adjourned to complete unfinished business, and in such cases no summons may be necessary; but no fresh business which may casually arise can be transacted at this adjourned meeting unless notice and summons have been issued as required by the preceding rules. *R.* v. *Grimshaw*, 10 Q. B. 747; 16 L. J. Q. B. 385; 11 Jur. 965.

As to the quarterly meetings, see the note to r. 1, *ante*, p. 335.

9. At every meeting of the council, the mayor, if present, shall be chairman. If the mayor is absent, then the deputy mayor, if chosen for that purpose by the members of the council then present, shall be chairman. If both the mayor and the deputy mayor are absent, or the deputy mayor. being present, is not chosen, then such alderman, or in the absence of all the aldermen, such councillor, as the members of the council then present choose, shall be chairman.

In county councils the chairman or vice-chairman will preside. In the event of their absence the councillors present must elect an alderman, or if there is no alderman present, a councillor, to preside.

See the note to s. 16, *ante*, p. 257, as to the vice-chairman.

In the absence of the chairman of the London County Council it is presumed that the deputy chairman appointed under s. 88 of the Local Government Act, *ante*, p. 166, will preside.

10. All acts of the council, and all questions coming or arising before the council, may be done and decided by the majority of such members of the council as are present and vote at a meeting held in pursuance of this Act, the whole number present at the meeting, whether voting or not, not being less than one-third of the number of the whole council.

The majority will be determined by the members voting, though others may be present and do not vote.

The quorum of a county council is one-fourth, instead of one-third. See the Local Government Act, s. 75, sub-s. (15), *ante*, p. 144.

A quorum of two-thirds is required for making bye-laws under s. 23, *ante*, p. 261.

Before parliamentary costs are incurred by a county council in opposing a Bill an absolute majority of the whole number of the council is required. See Local Government Act, s. 15 and note, *ante*, p. 41.

11. In case of equality of votes, the chairman of the meeting shall have a second or casting vote.

A difficulty might arise if the chairman were disqualified from voting by reason of his having a pecuniary interest in the subject of discussion. See s. 22, sub-s. (3), *ante*, p. 260. In such a case he could not, apparently, give an original or a casting vote.

12. Minutes of the proceedings of every meeting shall be drawn up and fairly entered in a book kept for that purpose, and shall be signed in manner authorized by this Act. **Schedule 2.**

As to the signature and authentication of the minutes, see s. 22, sub-s. (5), *ante*, p. 260.
As to forging the signature to any minutes, see s. 235, *ante*, p. 324.

13. Subject to the foregoing provisions of this schedule, the council may from time to time make standing orders for the regulation of their proceedings and business, and vary or revoke the same.

THIRD SCHEDULE.

* * *

PART II.

Rules as to Nomination in Elections of Councillors.

1. Every candidate for the office of councillor must be nominated in writing.

2. The writing must be subscribed by two burgesses of the borough or, in the case of a ward election, of the ward, as proposer and seconder, and by eight other burgesses of the borough or ward, as assenting to the nomination.

The burgesses must be enrolled in the burgess roll or ward roll, as the case may be. See s. 51, *ante*, p. 284.
This will apply to an election of county councillors, so as to render it necessary that the proposer, seconder, and persons assenting should be county electors for the electoral division.
A burgess was nominated in a paper signed by B. and H. as proposer and seconder, and by eight other assenting burgesses. After the nomination paper had been delivered to the town clerk it was altered in the absence of the seconder and assenting burgesses by striking out the name of B. as proposer and substituting that of G. another burgess. It was held that the nomination was invalid. *Harmon* v. *Park*, 7 Q. B. D. 369; 50 L. J. Q. B. 775; 45 L. T. (N.S.) 174; 45 J. P. 714.
The form of the nomination paper prescribed by this Act is contained in Sched. 8, Part II., which is not incorporated with the Local Government Act. Whether, having regard to s. 240, *ante*, p. 326, the form prescribed will apply to county councillors is not quite clear, but it will be advisable to follow it. Assuming that the form is to be followed with the necessary modifications the following points must be attended to :—1. The full christian names and surnames of the candidates must be stated. Initials for the christian names or any of them will render the nomination paper void (*Mather* v. *Brown*, *ante*, p. 327); though such abbreviations as Wm. for William, Fredk. for Frederick, or the like, are sufficient. *Henry* v. *Armitage*, *ante*, p. 327. 2. The abode and description of the candidate must be stated in the columns for these purposes. The omission of either is fatal. *R.* v. *Tugwell*, *ante*, p. 327. 3. The proposer and seconder and the assenting burgesses are merely required to sign or subscribe the paper; therefore they may sign using initials for their christian names. *Bowden* v. *Besley*, *ante*, p. 327. 4. But the names of the proposer, seconder, and assenting burgesses as signed by them must correspond to their names as entered on the burgess roll or division register. *Moorhouse* v. *Linney*, *ante*, p. 327. 5. The numbers on the burgess roll or division register of the proposer, seconder, and assenting burgesses must be stated accurately. *Gothard* v. *Clarke*, 5 C. P. D. 253; 49 L. J. Q. B. 474; 42 L. T. (N.S.) 776; 29 W. R. 402.
And see the other cases cited in the notes to ss. 72, 241, *ante*, and to r. 5, *infra*.

3. Each candidate must be nominated by a separate nomination paper, but the same burgesses, or any of them, may subscribe as many nomination papers as there are vacancies to be filled, but no more.

Where there were four vacancies, and a burgess subscribed four nomination papers which were delivered in time, and afterwards a fifth, which was also

Schedule 3. delivered in time, it was held that the first four were valid. *Burgoyne* v. *Collins*, 51 L. J. Q. B. 335; 30 W. R. 923; 46 J. P. 390.

This rule will not apply to elections of county councillors, as there can never be more than one vacancy in an electoral division. See the Local Government Act, s. 2 (2) (*e*), *ante*, p. 3.

4. Each person nominated must be enrolled in the burgess roll or entered in the separate non-resident list required by this Act to be made.

As to the non-resident list, see the notes to s. 49, *ante*, p. 283.

The candidate must be enrolled and entitled to be enrolled. See *Flintham* v. *Roxburgh*, *ante*, p. 252.

5. The nomination paper must state the surname and other names of the candidate, with his abode and description.

The initials of the christian names of the candidates are not sufficient. *Mather* v. *Brown*, *ante*, p. 327.

But an abbreviation, such as Wm. for William, is sufficient. *Henry* v. *Armitage*, 12 Q. B. D. 257; 53 L. J. Q. B. 111; 50 L. T. (N.S.) 4; 32 W. R. 192; 48 J. P. 424. And see *R.* v. *Hammond*, *ante*, p. 326.

See the cases cited in the notes to r. 2, *ante*, and to s. 241, *ante*, p. 326.

Where the surname of a candidate called Miller was inserted in a nomination paper as Millar in accordance with the entry in the burgess roll it was held that that was a sufficient surname of the candidate. *Miller* v. *Everton*, 64 L. J. Q. B. 692; 72 L. T. (N.S.) 838; 59 J. P. 358.

6. The town clerk shall provide nomination papers, and shall supply any burgess with as many nomination papers as may be required, and shall, at the request of any burgess, fill up a nomination paper.

This duty will, in counties, devolve upon the returning officers. See the Local Government Act, s. 75, sub-s. (5), *ante*, p. 142.

7. Every nomination paper subscribed as aforesaid must be delivered by the candidate, or his proposer or seconder, at the town clerk's office, seven days at least before the day of election, and before five o'clock in the afternoon of the last day for delivery of nomination papers.

It is provided by the Local Government Act, s. 75, sub-s. (7), *ante*, p. 143, that some place fixed by the returning officer shall, except where the election is in a borough, be substituted for the town clerk's office, but such place shall, if the electoral division is the whole or part of an urban district, be in that district, and in any other case shall be in the electoral division or in an adjoining electoral division.

The nomination paper must be delivered to the town clerk (or returning officer) by the candidate himself, or by his proposer or sender personally, and not by an agent. And the objection is one which is cognizable by the mayor, (or returning officer) under r. 9, *post*, whose decision allowing it may be questioned on a petition against the return of the successful candidate. *Monks* v. *Jackson*, 1 C. P. D. 683; 46 L. J. Q. B. 162; 35 L. T. (N.S.) 95; 41 J. P. 231.

8. The town clerk shall forthwith send notice of every such nomination to each candidate.

This duty will, in elections of county councillors, devolve upon the returning officer. See the Local Government Act, s. 75, sub-s. (5), *ante*, p. 142. The meaning of the rule is not very clear. The word "forthwith" appears to have reference to the time of receipt of the nomination papers mentioned in the last rule. If so it will be the duty of the returning officer at once to send to each candidate a notice of the nomination of himself and of all the other candidates.

9. The mayor shall attend at the town hall on the day next after the last day for delivery of nomination papers for a sufficient time, between the hours of two and four in the afternoon, and shall decide on the validity of every objection made in writing to a nomination paper.

This duty will devolve upon the returning officer in elections of county councillors. See the Local Government Act, s. 75, sub-s. (4), *ante*, p. 142. By the same section, sub-s. (7), some place fixed by the returning officer shall,

Schedule 3.

except where the election is in a borough, be substituted for the town hall, but such place shall, if the electoral division is the whole or part of an urban district, be in that district, and in any other case shall be in the electoral division or in an adjoining electoral division. By sub-s. (16) (*g*) of the same section, *ante*, p. 146, schools and public rooms, may be used free of charge for hearing objections to nomination papers.

As the returning officer will hardly be able himself to perform the above duty in every electoral division, he must in many cases entrust it to his deputies, as he may under the Local Government Act, s. 75, sub-s. (3), *ante*, p. 142.

As to his power to revise the decisions of his deputies, see sub-s. (6) of the same section, and the note to s. 53 of this Act, *ante*, p. 285.

"It is not the duty of the returning officer to look out for objections in fact to nomination papers when handed in, much less to call the attention of a rival candidate to them." *Per* Lord RUSSELL OF KILLOWEN, C.J., in *R.* v. *Taylor*, 59 J. P. 393.

10. Where a person subscribes more nomination papers than one, his subscription shall be inoperative in all but the one which is first delivered.

This rule does not apply to a case where there are several vacancies, and no burgess signs more than one nomination paper for any one candidate or more nomination papers than there are vacancies. *Line* v. *Warren*, 14 Q. B. D. 73, 548; 54 L. J. Q. B. 146; 52 L. T. (N.S.) 258, and see the note to r. 3, *supra*.

11. Each candidate may, by writing signed by him, or, if he is absent from the United Kingdom, then his proposer or seconder may, by writing signed by him, appoint a person (in this schedule referred to as the candidate's representative) to attend the proceedings before the mayor on behalf of the candidate, and this appointment must be delivered to the town clerk before five o'clock in the afternoon of the last day for delivery of nomination papers.

12. Each candidate and his representative, but no other person, except for the purpose of assisting the mayor, shall be entitled to attend the proceedings before the mayor.

13. Each candidate and his represesentative may, during the time apppointed for the attendance of the mayor for the purposes of this schedule, object to the nomination paper of any other candidate for the borough or ward.

The time appointed is between two and four in the afternoon. See r. 9, *supra*.

14. The decision of the mayor shall be given in writing, and shall, if disallowing an objection, be final, but, if allowing an objection, shall be subject to reversal on petition questioning the election or return.

The mayor (or returning officer) has no power to deal with an objection as to the time of delivering the nomination papers, and if he does so his decision may be questioned on petition. *Howes* v. *Turner*, 1 C. P. D. 670; 45 L. J. Q. B. 550; 35 L. T. (N.S.) 58; 40 J. P. 680. Nor can he entertain an objection relating to the qualification of a candidate. *Pritchard* v. *Bangor* (*Mayor, etc., of*), *supra*, p. 286.

The mayor may properly deal with an objection that a nomination paper has not been delivered by the candidate or his proposer or seconder personally, as required by r. 7, *ante*, p. 338. *Monks* v. *Jackson*, 1 C. P. D. 683; 46 L. J. Q. B. 162; 35 L. T. (N.S.) 95; 41 J. P. 231.

If an objection to a nomination paper is improperly allowed, an election petition will lie on the ground that the candidates elected were not duly elected by a majority of lawful votes (s. 87 (1) (*d*), *ante*, p. 297). For if the nomination paper had not been held bad, the votes might have been differently given. *Budge* v. *Andrews*, 3 C. P. D. 510; 47 L. J. C. P. 586; 39 L. T. (N.S.) 166.

Where the mayor *bonâ fide* decides an objection, he cannot be made respondent to an election petition questioning the election on the ground of such decision. *Harmon* v. *Park*, 6 Q. B. D. 323; 45 J. P. 436.

An objection that the nominations of four persons were bad on the ground that one of the assenting burgesses had subscribed five nomination papers ought not to be entertained by the mayor. *Burgoyne* v. *Collins*, 30 W. R. 923; 46 J. P. 390.

Schedule 3.

15. The town clerk shall, at least four days before the date of election, cause the surnames and other names of all persons validly nominated, with their respective abodes and descriptions, and the names of the persons subscribing their nomination papers as proposers and seconders, to be printed and fixed on the town hall, and, in the case of a ward election, in some conspicuous place in the ward.

This duty, in elections of county councillors, will devolve upon the returning officer. See the Local Government Act, s. 75, sub-s. (5). *ante*, p. 142. As to the substitution of a place for the town hall, see the same Act, s. 75, sub-s. (7), *ante*, p. 143.

The day of publishing the names under this rule is to be deemed the day of nomination (see the Local Government Act, s. 100, *ante*, p. 177); and the period between this day and the day of election is to be such period, not exceeding six days, as the returning officer may fix (*ib.*, s. 75, sub-s. (9), *ante*, p. 143).

16. The nomination of a person absent from the United Kingdom shall be void, unless his written consent given within one month before the day of his nomination in the presence of two witnesses is produced at the time of his nomination.

As to the nomination of a person without his consent, see the Local Government Act, s. 75, sub-s. (16) (*c*), *ante*, p. 145.

For a case where an election was avoided on petition for want of the written consent hereby required, see *Brown* v. *Benn*, 53 J. P. 167; 5 T. L. R. 247.

17. Where the number of valid nominations exceeds that of the vacancies, any candidate may withdraw from his candidature by notice signed by him, and delivered at the town clerk's office not later than two o'clock in the afternoon of the day next after the last day for delivery of nomination papers: Provided that such notices shall take effect in the order in which they are delivered, and that no such notice shall have effect so as to reduce the number of candidates ultimately standing nominated below the number of vacancies.

18. In and for the purposes of the provisions of this Act relating to proceedings preliminary to election, the burgess roll or ward roll which will be in force on the day of election shall be deemed to be the burgess roll or ward roll, and a person whose name is inserted in one of the lists from which the burgess roll or ward roll will be made up, shall be deemed to be enrolled in that roll, although that roll is not yet completed.

The provisions of this Act relating to proceedings preliminary to elections are contained in Part III., *ante*, pp. 279 *et seq.*

Burgess roll and ward roll must be read as including roll of county electors and division register for the purposes of county elections.

PART III.

Modifications of the Ballot Act in its Application to Municipal Elections.

1. The provisions of the Ballot Act, 1872, with respect to the voting of a returning officer, the use of a room for taking a poll, and the right to vote of persons whose names are on the register of voters, and Rules 16 and 19 in the schedule to that Act, shall not apply in the case of a municipal election.

The provisions of the Ballot Act, 1872, as to the use of a room for taking the poll are contained in s. 6, *ante*, p. 210. By the Local Government Act, s. 75, sub-s. (16) (*g*), *ante*, p. 146, the above provision is not to prevent the use of schools and public rooms for taking the poll and hearing objections to nomination papers at elections of county councillors.

The power of the returning officer to vote, in case of an equality of votes, is given by s. 58, sub-s. (5), *ante*, p. 287.

The title to vote is regulated by s. 51, *ante*, p. 284.

2. The mayor shall, at least four days before the day of election, give public notice of the situation, division, and allotment of polling places for taking the poll at the election, and of the description of the persons entitled to vote thereat, and at the several polling stations. **Schedule 3.**

This duty will devolve on the returning officer at elections of county councillors. See the Local Government Act, s. 75, sub-s. (4), *ante*, p. 142.

3. The mayor shall provide everything which, in the case of a parliamentary election, is required to be provided by the returning officer for the purpose of a poll, and shall appoint officers for taking the poll and counting the votes.

This duty will devolve on the returning officer at elections of county councillors. See the Local Government Act, s. 75, sub-s. (4), *ante*, p. 142.
As to what is required to be provided, see s. 8 of the Ballot Act, *ante*, p. 211.

4. The mayor shall furnish every polling station with such number of compartments in which the voters can mark their votes screened from observation, and furnish each presiding officer with such number of ballot papers as, in the judgment of the mayor, may be necessary for effectually taking the poll at the election.

See the note to the preceding rule.

5. All expenses of the election shall be defrayed in manner by this Act provided.

As to the expenses of the elections of county councillors, see the Local Government Act, s. 75, sub-ss. (17) to (19), *ante*, p. 146.

6. No return shall be made to the Clerk of the Crown in Chancery.

* * * * *

EIGHTH SCHEDULE.

FORMS.

Part I.—Declarations on Accepting Office.

FORM A.

FORM OF DECLARATION ON ACCEPTANCE OF CORPORATE OFFICE.

I, *A. B.*, having been elected mayor, [*or* alderman, councillor, elective auditor, *or* revising assessor] for the borough of , hereby declare that I take the said office upon myself, and will duly and faithfully fulfil the duties thereof according to the best of my judgment and ability [*and in the case of the person being qualified by estate say,* And I hereby declare that I am seised or possessed of real or personal estate, or both [*as the case may be*], to the value or amount of one thousand pounds, or five hundred pounds [*as the case may require*], over and above what will satisfy my just debts].

FORM B.

DECLARATION BY RECORDER OR BOROUGH JUSTICE.

I, *A. B.*, hereby declare that I will faithfully and impartially execute the office of recorder [*or* justice of the peace] for the borough of according to the best of my judgment and ability.

Form A. is the form of declaration which must be made by county councillors under ss. 35, 41, *ante*.
Form B. does not appear to have any application to counties.

MUNICIPAL ELECTIONS (CORRUPT AND ILLEGAL PRACTICES) ACT, 1884.

(47 & 48 VICT. CAP. 70.)

An Act for the better Prevention of Corrupt and Illegal Practices at Municipal and other Elections. [14th August, 1884.]

BE it enacted by the Queen's most Excellent Majesty, by and with the advice and consent of the Lords Spiritual and Temporal, and Commons, in this present Parliament assembled, and by the authority of the same, as follows (that is to say,) :

Short title.

1. This Act may be cited as the Municipal Elections (Corrupt and Illegal Practices) Act, 1884.

This Act is incorporated with the Local Government Act, 1888. See s. 75 of that Act, *ante*, p. 141. It is, in so far as relates to election petitions, supplemental to Part IV. of the Municipal Corporations Act, 1882, which has been already set out.

Corrupt Practices.

Definition and punishment of corrupt practice at municipal election.

2.—(1.) The expression "corrupt practice" in this Act means any of the following offences, namely, treating, undue influence, bribery, and personation as defined by the enactments set forth in Part One of the Third Schedule to this Act, and aiding, abetting, counselling, and procuring the commission of the offence of personation (*a*).

(2.) A person who commits any corrupt practice in reference to a municipal election shall be guilty of the like offence, and shall on conviction be liable to the like punishment, and subject to the like incapacities, as if the corrupt practice had been committed in reference to a parliamentary election (*b*).

(*a*) See Sched. 3, Part I., *post*.

(*b*) By the Corrupt Practices Act, 1883 (46 & 47 Vict. c. 51), s. 6, corrupt practices other than personation or aiding, etc., in the commission of personation, are declared to be misdemeanors, and any person convicted of any of them is liable to be imprisoned, with or without hard labour, for a term not exceeding two years, or to be fined any sum not exceeding 200*l*. A person who commits the offence of personation or of aiding, etc., the commission of that offence is guilty of felony, and liable on conviction to be imprisoned, with or without hard labour, for a period not exceeding two years. In addition to these punishments, a person who is convicted on indictment of any corrupt practice shall not be capable for a period of seven years from the date of his conviction of being registered as an elector, or voting at any election in the United Kingdom, whether it be a parliamentary election or an election for any public office (see *infra*); or of holding any public or judicial office (see *infra*), and if he holds any such office the office shall be vacated. Any person

Section 2.

NOTE.

so convicted of a corrupt practice in reference to any election shall also be incapable of being elected to and of sitting in the House of Commons during the seven years next after the date of his conviction, and if at that date he has been elected to the House of Commons, his election shall be vacated from the time of such conviction. By s. 64, the expression "public office" means any office under the Crown or under the charter of a city or municipal borough, or under the Acts relating to municipal corporations, or to the poor law or under the Elementary Education Act, 1870 (33 & 34 Vict. c. 75), or under the Public Health Act, 1875 (38 & 39 Vict. c. 55), or under any Acts amending the above-mentioned Acts, or under any other Acts for the time being in force (whether passed before or after the commencement of this Act) relating to local Government, whether the office is that of mayor, chairman, alderman, councillor, guardian, member of a board, commission, or other local authority in any county, city, borough, union, sanitary district, or other area, or is the office of clerk of the peace, town clerk, clerk, or other officer under a council, board, commission, or other authority, or is any other office to which a person is elected and appointed under any such charter or Act as above mentioned, and includes any other municipal or parochial office; and the expressions "election," "election petition," "election court," and "register of electors," shall, where expressed to refer to an election for any such public office, be construed accordingly.

The expression "judicial office" includes the office of justice of the peace and revising barrister.

As to the form of indictment for corrupt practices, see *R.* v. *Stroulger*, 17 Q. B. D. 327; 55 L. J. M. C. 137; 55 L. T. (N.S.) 122; 34 W. R. 719; *R.* v. *Norton*, 16 Cox C. C. 59.

Each act of bribery is a distinct offence, for which separate penalties are incurred. *Milnes* v. *Bale*, L. R. 10 C. P. 591; 44 L. J. C. P. 336; 33 L. T. (N.S.) 174; 23 W. R. 660; 39 J. P. 743.

Incapacity of candidate reported guilty of corrupt practice. 45 & 46 Vict. c. 50.

3.—(1.) Where upon the trial of an election petition respecting a municipal election for a borough or ward of a borough (*a*), it is found by the report of an election court made in pursuance of section ninety-three of the Municipal Corporations Act, 1882 (*b*), that any corrupt practice other than treating and undue influence has been proved to have been committed in reference to such election by or with the knowledge and consent of any candidate at such election, or that the offence of treating or undue influence has been proved to have been committed in reference to such election by any candidate at such election, that candidate shall not be capable of ever holding a corporate office in the said borough (*c*), and if he has been elected his election shall be void; and he shall further be subject to the same incapacities as if at the date of the said report he had been convicted of a corrupt practice (*d*).

(2.) Upon the trial of an election petition respecting a municipal election for a borough or ward of a borough in which a charge is made of any corrupt practice having been committed in reference to such election, the election court shall report in writing to the High Court whether any of the candidates at such election has

Sect. 3 (2).

been guilty by his agents of any corrupt practice in reference to such election, and if the report is that any candidate at such election has been guilty by his agents of a corrupt practice in reference to such election, that candidate shall not be capable of being elected to or holding any corporate office in the said borough (c), during a period of three years from the date of the report, and if he has been elected, his election shall be void.

(a) This includes an election of a county councillor.

(b) See this section, *ante*, p. 303.

(c) This will apply so as to disqualify a candidate from being elected as county councillor for his county.

(d) For these incapacities see the note to the last section.

Illegal Practices.

Certain expenditure to be illegal practice.

4.—(1.) No payment or contract for payment shall, for the purpose of promoting or procuring the election of a candidate (a) at a municipal election, be made—

(a.) On account of the conveyance of electors to or from the poll, whether for the hiring of horses or carriages, or for railway fares, or otherwise; or

(b.) To an elector, on account of the use of any house, land, building, or premises for the exhibition of any address, bill, or notice, or on account of the exhibition of any address, bill, or notice; or

(c.) On account of any committee room in excess of the number allowed by this Act (that is to say), if the election is for a borough, one committee room for the borough, and if the election is for a ward, one committee room for the ward, and if the number of electors in such borough or ward exceeds two thousand, one additional committee room for every two thousand electors and incomplete part of two thousand electors over and above the said two thousand (b).

(2.) Subject to such exception as may be allowed in pursuance of this Act (c), if any payment or contract for payment is knowingly made in contravention of this section either before, during, or after a municipal election, the person making such payment or contract shall be guilty of an illegal practice, and any person (d) receiving such payment or being a party to any such contract, knowing the same to be in contravention of this Act, shall also be guilty of an illegal practice.

(3.) Provided that where it is the ordinary business of an elector as an advertising agent to exhibit for payment bills and advertisements, a payment to or contract with such elector, if made in the ordinary course of business, shall not be deemed to be an illegal practice within the meaning of this section.

Section 4.

NOTE.

(*a*) The Municipal Corporations Act, 1882, s. 77, *ante*, p. 296, defines candidate as "a person elected or having been nominated or having declared himself a candidate for election." The date of such a declaration must, therefore, be the earliest date at which it can be said to have commenced so as to make him liable as a candidate for acts which, if committed by a candidate or his agents, would clearly be election offences. Difficult questions might, however, arise as to when a person had declared himself to be a candidate, for this might be inferred from his acts without a formal declaration. The question of when a candidature commences has often been discussed in parliamentary election cases (see, in particular, *The Kennington case*, 4 O'M. & H. 93; *The Rochester case*, 4 O'M. & H. 156; *Elgin and Nairn*, 5 O'M. & H. 1; *Lancaster*, 5 O'M. & H. 39). Although the cases are not strictly in *pari materia* (the Municipal Corporations Act, 1882, having no application to parliamentary elections), the views of HAWKINS, J., as stated in *The Walsall case*, 4 O'M. & H. 123, are quoted as bearing on the question of the commencement of a candidature. In that case the learned judge said: "I cannot help thinking that the period during which a candidate can be held responsible for the illegal and injudicious acts of his recognized supporters must be confined within reasonable limits. It would not be reasonable to say that a man who contemplates in the year 1892 becoming a candidate in the year 1896, could not illegally employ a person to do for him a variety of acts to ingratiate him with those whose votes and suffrages he intends to seek in some future year. Upon the present occasion, I think the limit of time to which we ought fairly to apply our minds is a period commencing from the time when it was first known that the respondent announced his intention to present himself as a candidate for election at the next ensuing election. . . . I cannot think that the period of candidature or the period of agency is to be limited either by the date of the issuing of the writ or by the day of nomination; but I think that when an election is contemplated as probable in the course of a few months, and it is well recognized that to secure the election of a particular candidate active steps must be taken, and every exertion made at once to secure that object, it cannot be reasonably said that there can be no agency to take such steps or to make such exertions until the immediate approach of the election by the issuing of the writ."

(*b*) This provision will apply to an election of a county councillor as if the division in which the election takes place were the ward of a borough.

(*c*) See ss. 19—21, *post*.

(*d*) The word *person* is here presumed to mean *elector* in cases falling within sub-s. (1) (*b*), as it does not appear to be illegal to make payments such as those mentioned in that clause to a person other than an elector. And see sub-s. (3).

Expense in excess of maximum to be illegal practice.

5.—(1.) Subject to such exception as may be allowed in pursuance of this Act (*a*), no sum shall be paid and no expense shall be incurred by or on behalf of a candidate at an election, whether before, during, or after an election, on account of or in respect of the conduct or management of such election, save that in the case of an election of a councillor a sum may be paid and expense incurred not in excess of the maximum amount following; (that is to say,)

The sum of twenty-five pounds, and, if the number of electors in the borough or ward exceeds five hundred, an additional amount of threepence for each elector above the first five hundred electors (*b*).

Sect. 5 (2).

(2.) Any candidate or agent of a candidate or person who knowingly acts in contravention of this section shall be guilty of an illegal practice.

(3.) Where there are two or more joint candidates at an election the maximum amount of expenses shall, for each of such joint candidates, be reduced by one-fourth, or if there are more than two joint candidates by one-third (*c*).

(4.) Where two or more candidates at the election, by themselves or any agent or agents, hire or use the same committee rooms for such election, or employ or use the services of the same clerks, messengers, or polling agent at such election, or publish a joint address or joint circular or notice at such election, those candidates shall be deemed, for the purposes of this enactment, to be joint candidates at such election : Provided that—

(a.) The employment and use of the same committee room, clerk, messenger, or polling agent, if accidental or casual, or of a trivial and unimportant character, shall not be deemed of itself to constitute persons joint candidates :

(b.) Nothing in this enactment shall prevent candidates from ceasing to be joint candidates :

(c.) Where any excess of expenses above the maximum allowed for one of two or more joint candidates has arisen owing to his having ceased to be a joint candidate, or to his having become a joint candidate after having begun to conduct his election as a separate candidate, and such ceasing or beginning was in good faith, and such excess is not more than under the circumstances is reasonable, and the total expenses of such candidate do not exceed the maximum amount allowed for a separate candidate, such excess shall be deemed to have arisen from a reasonable cause within the meaning of the enactments respecting the allowance by the High Court or election court of an exception from the provisions of this Act, which would otherwise make an act an illegal practice, and the candidate may be relieved accordingly from the consequences of having incurred such excess of expenses (*d*).

(*a*) See ss. 19—21, *post*.

(*b*) This will apply to an election of a county councillor, as if the word *ward* meant an electoral division.

(*c*) As only one county councillor is to be elected for each division, the provisions of this section as to joint candidates are inapplicable to elections of county councillors.

(*d*) See ss. 19—21, *post*.

Voting by prohibited persons and

6.—(1.) If any person votes or induces or procures any person to vote at a municipal election, knowing that he or such person is prohibited, whether by this or any other Act, from voting at such election, he shall be guilty of an illegal practice (*a*). Sect. 6 (1).

Publishing of false statements of withdrawal to be illegal.

(2.) Any person who before or during a municipal election knowingly publishes a false statement of the withdrawal of a candidate at such election for the purpose of promoting or procuring the election of another candidate shall be guilty of an illegal practice.

(3.) Provided that a candidate shall not be liable, nor shall his election be avoided, for any illegal practice under this section committed without his knowledge and consent (*b*).

(*a*) As to persons prohibited from voting by this Act, see ss. 22, 23, and Sched. 3, Part II., *post*.

While it is incumbent on an agent to warn persons disqualified not to vote, his failure to do so does not amount to procuring within this section. *Stepney Case*, 4 O'M. & H. 178.

(*b*) But *quære* whether the election would not be avoided by the commission of such an offence by an agent. See s. 8 (2), *post*.

Punishment on conviction of illegal practice.

7. A person guilty of an illegal practice in reference to a municipal election (*a*), shall on summary conviction be liable to a fine not exceeding one hundred pounds, and be incapable during a period of five years from the date of his conviction of being registered as an elector or voting at any election (whether it be a parliamentary election or an election for a public office (*b*) within the meaning of this Act) held for or within the borough (*c*) in which the illegal practice has been committed.

(*a*) This will include an election of a county councillor.

(*b*) As to what is a public office, see s. 34, *post*, and the notes to s. 2, *ante*.

(*c*) This word includes county in the application of the section to elections of county councillors.

Incapacity of candidate reported guilty of illegal practice.

8.—(1.) An illegal practice within the meaning of this Act shall be deemed to be an offence against Part Four of the Municipal Corporations Act, 1882 (*a*), and a petition alleging such illegal practice may be presented and tried accordingly.

45 & 46 Vict. c. 50.

(2.) Upon the trial of an election petition respecting a municipal election for a borough or ward of a borough (*b*) in which a charge is made of any illegal practice having been committed in reference to such election, the election court (*c*) shall report in writing to the High Court whether any of the candidates at such election has been guilty by himself or his agents of an illegal practice in reference to such election, and if the report is that a candidate at such election has been guilty by himself or his agents of an illegal practice in reference to such election, the candidate shall not be capable of being elected to or of holding any corporate office in the said borough (*d*) during the period for which he was elected to serve, or for which if elected he might have served, and if he was elected,

Sect. 8 (2). his election shall be void; and, if the report is that such candidate has himself been guilty of such illegal practice, he shall also be subject to the same incapacities as if at the date of the report he had been convicted of such illegal practice (*e*).

(*a*) See this Part, *ante*, p. 296.

(*b*) This includes an election for an electoral division of a county.

(*c*) As to the election court, see s. 92 of the Municipal Corporations Act, 1882, *ante*, p. 302.

(*d*) See s. 3, note (*c*), *ante*, p. 344.

(*e*) See s. 7, *ante*.

Illegal Payment, Employment, and Hiring.

Providing of money for illegal practice or payment to be illegal payment.

9. Where a person knowingly provides money for any payment which is contrary to the provisions of this Act, or for any expenses incurred in excess of any maximum amount allowed by this Act (*a*), or for replacing any money expended in any such payment, except where the same may have been previously allowed in pursuance of this Act to be an exception (*b*), such person shall be guilty of illegal payment (*c*).

(*a*) See s. 5, *ante*, p. 345.

(*b*) See ss. 19—21, *post*.

(*c*) Money paid for the employment of persons to keep order at meetings is an illegal employment. *Packard* v. *Collings*, 54 L. T. (N.S.) 619.

Gratuitous refreshments to workers renders their employment illegal within the meaning of this section. *Barrow Election Petition*, *ib.* 618.

A payment to a voter for damage done to a banner or for loss of his hat at a meeting is not an illegal payment. *Stepney Case*, 4 O'M. & H. 39.

Employment of hackney carriages, or of carriages and horses kept for hire.

10.—(1.) A person shall not let, lend, or employ for the purpose of the conveyance of electors to or from the poll at a municipal election (*a*), any public stage or hackney carriage, or any horse or other animal kept or used for drawing the same, or any carriage, horse, or other animal which he keeps or uses for the purpose of letting out for hire, and if he lets, lends, or employs such carriage, horse, or other animal, knowing that it is intended to be used for the purpose of the conveyance of electors to or from the poll, he shall be guilty of illegal hiring.

(2.) A person shall not hire, borrow, or use for the purpose of the conveyance of electors to or from the poll any carriage, horse, or other animal which he knows the owner thereof is prohibited by this section to let, lend, or employ for that purpose, and if he does so he shall be guilty of illegal hiring.

(3.) Nothing in this Act shall prevent a carriage, horse or other animal being let to or hired, employed, or used by an elector, or several electors at their joint cost, for the purpose of conveying him or them to or from the poll.

(4.) No person shall be liable to pay any duty or to take out a licence for any carriage by reason only of such carriage being used without payment or promise of payment for the conveyance of electors to or from the poll at an election. Sect. 10 (4).

(a) This includes the election of a county councillor.

11. Any person who corruptly induces or procures any other person to withdraw from being a candidate at a municipal election (a), in consideration of any payment or promise of payment, shall be guilty of illegal payment, and any person withdrawing in pursuance of such inducement or procurement shall also be guilty of illegal payment. Corrupt withdrawal from a candidature.

(a) This includes an election of a county councillor.

12.—(1.) No payment or contract for payment shall, for the purpose of promoting or procuring the election of a candidate at a municipal election (a), be made on account of bands of music, torches, flags, banners, cockades, ribbons or other marks of distinction (b). Certain expenditure to be illegal payment.

(2.) Subject to such exception as may be allowed in pursuance of this Act, if any payment or contract for payment is made in contravention of this section, either before, during, or after an election, the person making such payment shall be guilty of illegal payment, and any person being a party to any such contract, or receiving such payment, shall also be guilty of illegal payment if he knew that the same was made contrary to law.

(a) This includes an election of a county councillor.

(b) As to the meaning of "marks of distinction," see *The Walsall case*, 4 O'M. & H. 126, in which a parliamentary election was held to be void on the ground that the use of certain cards distributed by the respondent and intended to be worn by voters in their hats was an illegal practice. As to these cards, POLLOCK, B., said: "The cards which were printed were not merely the card of invitation as of old, but bore the photographic likeness of the candidate and words of invitation and encouragement to fight for him. In themselves they cannot be found fault with as being within the Act of Parliament under the words 'marks of distinction,' and so long as cards alone are used there can be no objection. I may even go further and say that sometimes the cards may be put in a man's coat or fixed to the outside of his hat and yet not necessarily be 'marks of distinction.' But if the card is made specially adaptable to place in the hat as these cards were in fact, and if they were used for that purpose, then, after being ordered, having been used, and having been so described in the account, the person who pays that account pays it knowing what it is. . . . The legislature have decided to prohibit any mark of distinction and any party badge from being supplied and paid for by candidates their agents."

But compare *Clare*, 4 O'M. & H. 162; *Pontefract*, *ib.* 200. Broad strips of canvas with words printed on them and stretched across streets were held to be banners in the *Stepney case*, 4 O'M. & H. 178.

Sect. 13 (1).

Certain employment to be illegal.

13.—(1.) No person shall, for the purpose of promoting or procuring the election of a candidate at a municipal election (*a*), be engaged or employed for payment or promise of payment for any purpose or in any capacity whatever, except as follows (that is to say),—

(a.) A number of persons may be employed, not exceeding two for a borough or ward (*b*), and if the number of electors in such borough or ward exceeds two thousand one additional person may be employed for every thousand electors and incomplete part of a thousand electors over and above the said two thousand, and such persons may be employed as clerks and messengers, or in either capacity; and

(b.) One polling agent may be employed in each polling station:

Provided that this section shall not apply to any engagement or employment for carrying into effect a contract bonâ fide made with any person in the ordinary course of business (*c*).

(2.) Subject to such exceptions as may be allowed in pursuance of this Act, if any person is engaged or employed in contravention of this section, either before, during, or after an election, the person engaging or employing him shall be guilty of illegal employment, and the person so engaged or employed shall also be guilty of illegal employment if he knew that he was engaged or employed in contravention of this Act.

(3.) A person legally employed for payment under this section may or may not be an elector, but may not vote.

(*a*) This includes an election of a county councillor.

(*b*) In applying this section to the election of a county councillor, "electoral division" must be substituted for "ward."

(*c*) This appears to be intended to meet the case of a person who contracts for the purposes of the election, *e.g.*, for printing. The employés of such persons are not to be deemed to be employed within the meaning of this section. This section makes illegal the employment of a paid election agent (other than a polling agent under sub-s. (1) (b). *Ex parte Walker*, 22 Q. B. D. 384; 58 L. J. Q. B. 190; 60 L. T. (N.S.) 581; 37 W. R. 293; 53 J. P. 260.

Name and address of printer on placards.

14. Every bill, placard, or poster having reference to a municipal election (*a*) shall bear upon the face thereof the name and address of the printer and publisher thereof; and any person printing, publishing, or posting, or causing to be printed, published, or posted any such bill, placard, or poster as aforesaid, which fails to bear upon the face thereof the name and address of the printer and publisher, shall, if he is a candidate, be guilty of an illegal practice (*b*), and if he is not the candidate, shall be liable on summary conviction to a fine not exceeding one hundred pounds (*c*)

(*a*) This includes an election of a county councillor.

(*b*) As to the punishment of an illegal practice, see s. 7, *ante*, p. 347.

NOTE.

(c) The appellant was a candidate for a seat on a local board. The respondent received from his own servant at his residence a printed address and letter having reference to the election, and purporting to be signed by the appellant, but having no printer's name thereon. This document was printed for publication by instructions conveyed to the printer in a letter from the appellant's brother, who resided with him. The printer debited the appellant with the cost of printing, but was not paid. It was held on these facts that there was no evidence that the appellant had " printed or caused to be printed " the document in question. Placards or posters, also without the printer's name and address, printed by the instructions of one E., who was advertised in a local newspaper as chairman of a committee for promoting the election of the appellant, and who sent the copy to the printer, were proved to have been posted about the district at E.'s expense. The court doubted whether this was evidence of the printing and posting by an agent of the appellant; but the justices having convicted the appellant in one penalty for both offences, and the conviction being bad as to the first, *held*, that it was bad altogether. *Bettesworth* v. *Allingham*, 16 Q. B. D. 44; 34 W. R. 296; 50 J. P. 55. It should be observed, with reference to this case, that the court seemed to assume that an election address was a bill, etc., within the meaning of this section.

It has, however, been held in some cases that an election address printed on note paper to be sent by post is not a " bill " within this section. See the cases noted 5 T. L. R. 159, 160, 170.

Notice that if the address is published by a person other than the printer, his name and address, as well as those of the printer, must be stated.

Saving for creditors.

15. The provisions of this Act prohibiting certain payments and contracts for payments, and the payment of any sum, and the incurring of any expense, in excess of a certain maximum, shall not affect the right of any creditor who, when the contract was made or the expense was incurred, was ignorant of the same being in contravention of this Act.

See ss. 9—13, *ante*.

In the case of an expense incurred in contravention of the Act, the illegality of the expense will be no defence to an action by a creditor who, when the expense was incurred, was ignorant of its being in contravention of the Act. This provision is necessary for the protection of creditors who have no means of knowing what other expenses have been incurred by a candidate.

Use of certain premises for committee rooms or meetings to be illegal hiring.

16.—(1.) (a.) Any premises which are licensed for the sale of any intoxicating liquor for consumption on or off the premises, or on which refreshment of any kind (whether food or drink) is ordinarily sold for consumption on the premises, or

(b.) Any premises where any intoxicating liquor is supplied to members of a club, society, or association, or any part of any such premises,

shall not, for the purpose of promoting or procuring the election of a candidate at a municipal election (*a*), be used either as a committee room or for holding a meeting, and if any person hires or uses any such premises or any part thereof, in contravention of this section he shall be guilty of illegal hiring, and the person letting or permitting the use of such premises or part thereof, if he

Sect. 16 (1).

knew it was intended to use the same in contravention of this section, shall also be guilty of illegal hiring.

(2.) Provided that nothing in this section shall apply to any part of such premises which is ordinarily let for the purpose of chambers or offices or the holding of public meetings or of arbitrations, if such part has a separate entrance and no direct communication with any part of the premises on which any intoxicating liquor or refreshment is sold or supplied as aforesaid (*b*).

(*a*) This includes an election of a county councillor.

(*b*) The use of a room in a coffee tavern having a separate entrance from that into the portion of the house where refreshments were sold, and no direct communication therewith, was held not to be illegal. *Pascoe* v. *Puleston,* 45 L. T. (N.S.) 732 ; 50 J. P. 134. But where there was a door between the part used for the election and a public house, though the door was kept locked, the section was held to apply. *Ex parte Payne, Times*, November 2nd, 1894.

Punishment of illegal payment, employment, or hiring.

17.—(1.) A person guilty of an offence of illegal payment, employment, or hiring shall, on summary conviction, be liable to a fine not exceeding one hundred pounds.

(2.) Where an offence of illegal payment, employment, or hiring is committed by a candidate, or with his knowledge and consent, such candidate shall be guilty of an illegal practice (*a*).

(*a*) The offence will, therefore, be punishable under s. 7, *ante*, p. 347.

Avoidance of election for extensive illegal practices, etc.

18. Where upon the trial of an election petition respecting a municipal election for a borough or ward of a borough (*a*) it is found by the election court that illegal practices or offences of illegal payment, employment, or hiring, committed in reference to such election for the purpose of promoting the election of a candidate at that election, have so extensively prevailed that they may be reasonably supposed to have affected the result of that election, the election court shall report such finding to the High Court, and the election of such candidate, if he has been elected, shall be void, and he shall not, during the period for which he was elected to serve, or for which if elected he might have served, be capable of being elected to or holding any corporate office in the said borough (*b*).

(*a*) This includes an election of a county councillor for an electoral division of a county.

(*b*) This phrase includes the office of county councillor in the said county.

Excuse and Exception for Corrupt or Illegal Practice or Illegal Payment, Employment, or Hiring.

Report exonerating candidate in

19. Where upon the trial of an election petition respecting a municipal election (*a*), the election court (*b*) reports that a candidate at such election has been guilty by his agents of the offence of treating and undue influence, and illegal practice, or of any of such offences (*c*), in reference to such election, and the election court further report that the candidate has proved to the court—

Sect. 19.

certain cases of corrupt and illegal practice by agents.

(a.) That no corrupt or illegal practice was committed at such election by the candidate or with his knowledge or consent, and the offences mentioned in the said report were committed without the sanction or connivance of such candidate ; and

(b.) That all reasonable means for preventing the commission of corrupt and illegal practices at such election were taken by and on behalf of the candidate; and

(c.) That the offences mentioned in the said report were of a trivial, unimportant, and limited character ; and

(d.) That in all other respects the election was free from any corrupt or illegal practice on the part of such candidate and of his agents;

then the election of such candidate shall not, by reason of the offences mentioned in such report, be void, nor shall the candidate be subject to any incapacity under this Act.

(*a*) This includes the election of a county councillor.

(*b*) As to the election court, see s. 92 of the Municipal Corporations Act, 1882, *ante*, p. 302.

(*c*) Observe that this does not include corrupt practices.

Power of High Court and election court to except innocent act from being illegal practice, etc.

20. Where, on application made, it is shown to the High Court or to a municipal election court (*a*), by such evidence as seems to the court sufficient—

(a.) That any act or omission of a candidate at a municipal election for a borough or ward of a borough (*b*), or of any agent or other person, would, by reason of being in contravention of any of the provisions of this Act, be but for this section an illegal practice, payment, employment, or hiring (*c*) ; and

(b.) That such act or omission arose from inadvertence or from accidental miscalculation or from some other reasonable cause of a like nature, and in any case did not arise from any want of good faith ; and

(c.) That such notice of the application has been given in the said borough as to the court seems fit ;

and under the circumstances it seems to the court to be just that the said candidate, agent, and person, or any of them, should not be subject to any of the consequences under this Act of the said act or omission, the court may make an order allowing such act or omission to be an exception from the provisions of this Act which would otherwise make the same an illegal practice, payment,

Sect. 20.

employment, or hiring, and thereupon such candidate, agent, or person shall not be subject to any of the consequences under this Act of the said act or omission (*d*).

(*a*) As to this court, see s. 92 of the Municipal Corporations Act, 1882, *ante*, p. 302.

(*b*) This will apply to a candidate at an election of county councillors.

(*c*) Observe that corrupt practices are not mentioned here.

(*d*) In order to support an application under this section, it will not be sufficient that notice of intention to make the application has been advertised in the local papers, but such notice should be published in such a manner as will ensure a reasonable certainty that persons interested had notice; and it will also be insufficient, in the affidavits upon which the application is made, merely to state that the act in respect of which relief is sought arose from inadvertence, and not from any want of good faith, without showing some reasonable excuse for such inadvertence. *Ex parte Perry*, 48 J. P. 824; *Ex parte Haseldine*, 59 J. P. 71.

The court requires that the notice should be given to the opposing candidate or candidates, and to the returning officer, and should be posted about in the borough or district, besides being advertised in the local newspapers. *Ex parte Levanton*, *Ex parte Pierce*, 53 J. P. 263; 5 T. L. R. 173; and see *Ludlow*, 54 L. T. (N.S.) 129; 34 W. R. 352. In that case, HUDDLESTONE, B., interpreted "inadvertence" as used in this section to mean "negligence or carelessness where the circumstances show an absence of bad faith."

In the year 1889, relief was granted in many cases arising out of the first election of county councillors, but in several of these the court acted on the ground that the penal provisions of this Act being made applicable to county council elections by incorporation only, it was difficult for candidates to be aware of the illegality of certain acts. "The court was disposed to treat the excuses with greater leniency than would be done hereafter when the knowledge of the Act had been promulgated throughout the country." *Per* HUDDLESTONE, B., in *Ex parte Levanton*, *supra*, and see also *Ex parte Walker*, *infra*. Each case must depend upon its own circumstances, and it would be unsafe to rely upon the reported decisions as governing future cases.

Relief was granted in the following cases: employment of too many messengers; *Ex parte Darlington* (1889), 53 J. P. 71; 5 T. L. R. 183; holding meeting at public-house: *Ex parte Hutchinson* (1889), 5 T. L. R. 136; compare *Ex parte Montefiore*, 5 T. L. R. 78, a case relating to a school board election, and *Ex parte Terry*, 1 T. L. R. 183, a case relating to a municipal election where meetings had been held in clubs in which liquors were supplied to members; issue of election address or placard without the printer's name: *Ex parte Clark*, 52 L. T. (N.S.) 260; *Ex parte Ives* (1889), 5 T. L. R. 136; and see *ib*, p. 195. There is no power to grant relief to the printer in such a case. *Ex parte Levanton*, *supra*. As to paid canvassers and agents, relief was granted in *Ex parte Birley* and *Ex parte Measom*, 5 T. L. R. 220, 221, and refused in *Ex parte Thomas*, 60 L. T. (N.S.) 728; 5 T. L. R. 198; and *Ex parte Hobbs*, *ib*. 272.

An appeal lies to the Court of Appeal against the refusal of a Divisional Court to make an order under this section exempting a candidate from penalties inadvertently incurred under s. 17, *ante*, by reason of practices declared to be illegal by s. 13, *ante*, such a matter not being a criminal matter within the meaning of s. 47 of the Judicature Act, 1883. *Ex parte Walker*, 22 Q. B. D. 384; 58 L. J. Q. B. 190; 60 L. T. (N.S.) 581; 37 W. R. 293; 53 J. P. 260. In that case, Lord COLERIDGE, C.J., and HAWKINS, J., had refused to grant to a candidate at the first election of county councillors exemption from penalties

Sect. 20.

NOTE.

for the employment of an election agent for promise of payment, the candidate being ignorant of the provisions of s. 13, *ante*; relief had been granted by Divisional Courts differently constituted in similar cases, and upon the ground of ignorance. The Court of Appeal with the full assent of Lord COLERIDGE, C.J., and HAWKINS, J., granted the relief asked on the terms of the applicant paying the costs in both courts. Lord ESHER, M.R., expressed a strong opinion that at any future election it would be very difficult to excuse anyone from penalties on the ground of ignorance of the provisions of the Act; and see *Walsall*, 4 O'M. & H. 128; *Southampton*, 12 T. L. R. 237. See also as to this right of appeal, *Ex parte Thomas*, 60 L. T. (N.S.) 728; 5 T. L. R. 234. *Ex parte Birtwhistle*, 5 T. L. R. 321.

If the application is made by a person against whom a petition is pending, the court will order the application to stand over till after the trial of the petition. *Ex parte Wilks*, 16 Q. B. D. 114; 55 L. J. Q. B. 576; 34 W. R. 273; 50 J. P. 487. *Ex parte Evans*, 5 T. L. R. 206. *Secus*, where a petition is merely threatened. *Ex parte Stephens*, 5 T. L. R. 203.

Relief if given does away with the illegal practice relieved against, and prevents the election from being avoided. *Hexham*, 4 O'M. & H. 144.

Sending in claims and making payments for election expenses.

21.—(1.) Every claim against any person in respect of any expenses incurred by or on behalf of a candidate at an election of a councillor (*a*) on account of or in respect of the conduct or management of such election (*b*) shall be sent in within fourteen days after the day of election, and if not so sent in shall be barred and not paid, and all expenses incurred as aforesaid shall be paid within twenty-one days after the day of election, and not otherwise, and any person who makes a payment in contravention of this section, except where such payment is allowed as provided by this section, shall be guilty of an illegal practice (*c*), but if such payment was made without the sanction or connivance of the candidate, the election of such candidate shall not be void, nor shall he be subject to any incapacity under this Act by reason only of such payment having been made in contravention of this section.

(2.) Every agent of a candidate at an election of a councillor shall, within twenty-three days after the day of election, make a return to the candidate in writing of all expenses incurred by such agent on account of or in respect of the conduct or management of such election, and if he fails so to do shall be liable, on summary conviction, to a fine not exceeding fifty pounds.

(3.) Within twenty-eight days after the day of election of a councillor (*a*) every candidate at such election shall send to the town clerk (*d*) a return of all expenses incurred by such candidate or his agents on account of or in respect of the conduct or management of such election, vouched (except in the case of sums under twenty shillings) by bills stating the particulars and receipts, and accompanied by a declaration by the candidate made before a justice in the form set forth in the Fourth Schedule to this Act, or to the like effect (*e*).

Sect. 21 (4).

(4.) After the expiration of the time for making such return and declaration the candidate, if elected, shall not, until he has made the return and declaration (in this Act referred to as the return and declaration respecting election expenses) or until the date of the allowance of such authorised excuse, as is mentioned in this Act, sit or vote in the council, and if he does so shall forfeit fifty pounds for every day on which he so sits or votes to any person who sues for the same (*f*).

(5.) If the candidate without such authorised excuse as is mentioned in this Act fails to make the said return and declaration he shall be guilty of an illegal practice (*c*), and if he knowingly makes the said declaration falsely he shall be guilty of an offence, and on conviction thereof on indictment shall be liable to the punishment for wilful and corrupt perjury, and such offence shall also be deemed to be a corrupt practice within the meaning of this Act (*g*).

(6.) The county court for the district in which the election was held, or the High Court, or an election court, may, on application either of the candidate or a creditor, allow any claim to be sent in and any expense to be paid after the time limited by this section, and a return of any sum so paid shall forthwith after payment be sent to the town clerk.

(7.) If the candidate applies to the High Court or an election court, and shows that the failure to make the said return and declaration, or either of them, or any error or false statement therein, has arisen by reason of his illness or absence, or of the absence, death, illness, or misconduct of any agent, clerk, or officer, or by reason of inadvertence, or of any reasonable cause of a like nature, and not by reason of any want of good faith on the part of the applicant, the court may, after such notice of the application and on production of such evidence of the grounds stated in the application, and of the good faith of the applicant, and otherwise as to the court seems fit, make such order for allowing the authorised excuse for the failure to make such return and declaration, or for an error or false statement in such return or declaration, as to the court seems fit (*h*).

(8.) The order may make the allowance conditional upon compliance with such terms as to the court seems calculated for carrying into effect the objects of this Act, and the order shall relieve the applicant from any liability or consequences under this Act in respect of the matters excused by the order.

(9.) The date of the order, or if conditions and terms are to be complied with, the date at which the applicant fully complies with them, is referred to in this Act as the date of the allowance of the excuse.

(10.) The return and declaration sent in pursuance of this Act to the town clerk (*d*) shall be kept at his office, and shall at all reasonable times during the twelve months next after they are received by him be open to inspection by any person on payment of the fee of one shilling, and the town clerk shall on demand furnish copies thereof or of any part thereof at the price of twopence for every seventy-two words. Sect. 21 (10).

(11.) After the expiration of the said twelve months the town clerk (*d*) may cause the return and declaration to be destroyed, or if the candidate so require shall return the same to him.

(*a*) This will include the election of a county councillor.

(*b*) Money paid by an agent of a candidate for the employment of persons to keep order at meetings is within this provision. *Packard* v. *Collings*, 54 L. T. (N.S.) 619.

(*c*) And therefore punishable under s. 7, *ante*.

(*d*) In elections of county councillors this return must be sent to the clerk of the county council. See the Local Government Act, s. 75, sub-s. (5), *ante*, p. 142.

(*e*) This return and declaration must be made, although no expenses have actually been incurred by the candidate. But the court will, on satisfactory proof that the omission happened under such circumstances as to amount to an authorized excuse under the Act, make an order that the return and declaration be made notwithstanding the lapse of the prescribed period for making them. *Ex parte Robson*, 18 Q. B. D. 336; 55 L. T. (N.S.) 813; 35 W. R. 290; 51 J. P. 199.

For a case where a candidate was allowed to make payments after the expiration of the proper time, see *South Shropshire Election*, 2 T. L. R. 347; *Ipswich Election*, 3 T. L. R. 397. For a case where a candidate was allowed to make the return and declaration prescribed by the next section after the prescribed time, see *Ex parte Robson*, *supra*.

Where a person voted and afterwards accepted payment for services rendered as an agent the court refused to relieve him from the consequences. *Re Essex (South West Division) Election*, 2 T. L. R. 388.

In *Ex parte Matthews*, 2 T. L. R. 548, the court granted relief to a candidate who had acted as his own agent and had through ignorance omitted to make a return of his expenses, but the court intimated that in future candidates must make themselves better acquainted with the law.

Where a person had obtained a certificate of indemnity for a late return of his expenses, and subsequently on the same day (but after the order had been drawn up) a voter appeared to oppose the granting of such certificate, it was held that the application of the voter must be dismissed in the absence of any sufficient explanation of his delay. *Wigan Election*, 2 T. L. R. 159.

(*f*) Observe that any person may sue. The Crown cannot remit the penalties. See *Todd* v. *Robinson*, 12 Q. B. D. 530; 53 L. J. Q. B. 251; 50 L. T. (N.S.) 298; 32 W. R. 858; 48 J. P. 692.

(*g*) See s. 2, *ante*.

(*h*) See the cases cited in the notes to the last section; also *Ex parte Robson*, *supra*. Where a claim was disputed, and afterwards decided against the candidate, leave was given to pay it in. *Re Lowestoft Election*, 4 T. L. R. 38.

Notice of application to the court must be given to the other candidates, to

Sect. 21.

NOTE.

the returning officer, and to the public by advertisements. *Re Ludlow Election*, 54 L. T. (N.S.) 129; 34 W. R. 352.

An application for leave to pay the hire of a brougham used without authority by the clerk of a candidate was refused in *Re Chelsea Election*, 2 T. L. R. 374.

Disqualification of Electors.

Prohibition of persons guilty of offences from voting.

22. Every person guilty of a corrupt or illegal practice or of illegal employment, payment, or hiring at a municipal election is prohibited from voting at such election, and if any such person votes his vote shall be void, and shall be struck off on a scrutiny.

This will apply to election of county councillors.

Application of ss. 37 and 38 of 46 & 47 Vict. c. 51.

23. So much of sections thirty-seven and thirty-eight of the Corrupt and Illegal Practices Prevention Act, 1883, as is set forth in Part II. of the Third Schedule to this Act shall apply as part of this Act.

See the schedule, *post.* The sections referred to relate mainly to the incapacities of persons convicted or reported by an election court for corrupt or illegal practices, and s. 38 (1) gives a person an opportunity of being heard before he is reported.

List in burgess roll of persons incapacitated for voting by corrupt or illegal practices.

24.—(1.) The town clerk in every municipal borough (*a*) shall annually in July make out a list containing the names and description of all persons who, though otherwise qualified to be enrolled as burgesses of such borough, have under this Act, or under the Corrupt and Illegal Practices Prevention Act, 1883, or under any other Act for the time being in force relating to a parliamentary election, or an election to any public office, become after the commencement of this Act, by reason of conviction of a corrupt or illegal practice, or of the report of any election court or election commissioners, incapable of voting at a municipal election in such borough or any ward thereof, and the town clerk shall state in the list (in this Act referred to as the corrupt and illegal practices list), the offence of which each person has been found guilty (*b*).

(2.) For the purpose of making out such list he shall examine the report of any election court or election commissioners who have respectively tried an election petition or inquired into an election where the election (whether a parliamentary election or an election to any public office) (*c*) was held in the said borough or in the county in which such borough is situate.

(3.) The town clerk of any municipal borough (*a*) shall, not less than fourteen days before the first day appointed by law for the publication of the parish burgess lists in such borough (*d*), send the corrupt and illegal practices list to the overseers of every parish wholly or partly within the borough, and the overseers shall publish that list together with the parish burgess lists, and shall also, in the case of every person in the corrupt and illegal practices list, omit his name from the list of persons entitled to be enrolled as burgesses or to be elected councillors, or, as circumstances require, add " objected " before his name in the list of claimants published by them, in like manner as is required by law in any other cases of disqualification. Sect. 24 (3).

(4.) Any person named in the corrupt and illegal practices list may claim to have his name omitted therefrom, and any person entitled to object to any parish burgess list may object to the omission of the name of any person from such first-mentioned list. Such claims and objections shall be sent in within the same time and be dealt with in like manner, and any such objection shall be served on the person referred to therein in like manner, as nearly as circumstances admit, as other claims and objections under the enactments relating to the enrolment of burgesses.

(5.) The revising authority (*e*) shall determine such claims and objections, and shall revise such list in like manner, as nearly as circumstances admit, as in the case of other claims and objections and of any parish burgess list and list of persons entitled to be elected councillors.

(6.) Where it appears to the revising authority (*e*) that a person not named in the list is subject to have his name inserted in the corrupt and illegal practices list, he shall (whether an objection to the omission of such name from the list has or has not been made, but) after giving such person an opportunity of making a statement to show cause to the contrary, insert his name in that list and expunge his name from any list of burgesses or of persons entitled to be elected councillors.

(7.) A revising authority (*e*) in acting under this section shall determine only whether a person is incapacitated by conviction or by the report of any election court or election commissioners, and shall not determine whether a person has or has not been guilty of any corrupt or illegal practice.

(8.) The corrupt and illegal practices list shall be appended to the burgess roll (*f*), and shall be printed and published therewith wherever the same is printed or published.

(9.) Any town clerk or overseer who fails to comply with the provisions of this section shall be liable to the like fine as he is liable to under section seventy-five of the Municipal Corporations Act, 1882, for any neglect or refusal in relation to a parish burgess list as therein mentioned (*g*). 45 & 46 Vict. c. 50.

(*a*) In counties this duty will devolve on the clerk of the county council.

(*b*) The terms used in this section must be modified to make them applicable

Sect. 24

NOTE.

to elections of county councillors. Thus county electors must be substituted for burgesses, electoral division for ward, etc.

(c) See the note (b) to s. 2, *ante*, p. 342.

(d) The day here referred to is August 1st. The term parish burgess lists will include lists of county electors. See note (b), *supra*.

(e) That is, the revising barrister. See the County Electors Act, 1888 (51 Vict. c. 10), s. 4, *post*.

(f) The term burgess roll includes roll of county electors.

(g) See the section here referred to, *ante*, p. 294.

Proceedings on Election Petitions.

Petition for illegal practice.

25.—(1.) A municipal election petition (a) complaining of the election on the ground of an illegal practice may be presented at any time before the expiration of fourteen days after the day on which the town clerk receives the return and declaration respecting election expenses by the candidate to whose election the petition relates, or where there is an authorized excuse for failing to make the return and declaration then within the like time after the date of the allowance of the excuse (b).

Time for presentation of petition alleging illegal practices.

(2.) A municipal election petition, complaining of the election on the ground of an illegal practice, and specifically alleging a payment of money or other act made or done since the election by the candidate elected at such election, or by an agent of the candidate, or with the privity of the candidate, in pursuance or in furtherance of such illegal practice, may be presented at any time within twenty-eight days after the date of such payment or act, whether or not any other petition against that person has been previously presented or tried.

45 & 46 Vict. c. 50.

(3.) Any election petition presented within the time limited by the Municipal Corporations Act, 1882 (c), may, for the purpose of complaining of the election upon an allegation of an illegal practice, be amended with the leave of the High Court within the time within which a petition complaining of the election on the ground of that illegal practice can, under this section, be presented.

(4.) This section shall apply notwithstanding the illegal practice is also a corrupt practice.

(a) This includes a petition against the return of a county councillor.

(b) As to this return and declaration and authorized excuse, see s. 21, *ante*.

(c) As to the time for presentation of a petition alleging corrupt practices, see s. 88, sub-s. (4), of the Municipal Corporations Act, 1882, *ante*, p. 299.

Where a petition has not been amended in time the petitioner cannot include in his particulars or give evidence of offences alleged to have been committed after the date of the petition. *Cremer* v. *Lowles*, [1896] 1 Q. B. 504 ; 65 L. J. Q. B. 289 ; 74 L. T. (N.S.) 42 ; 44 W. R. 629 ; 60 J. P. 100.

26—(1.) Before leave for the withdrawal (*a*) of a municipal election petition is granted, there shall be produced affidavits by all the parties to the petition and their solicitors, but the High Court may on cause shown dispense with the affidavit of any particular person if it seems to the court on special grounds to be just so to do. Sect. 26 (1). Withdrawal of election petition.

(2.) Each affidavit shall state that, to the best of the deponent's knowledge and belief, no agreement or terms of any kind whatsoever has or have been made, and no undertaking has been entered into, in relation to the withdrawal of the petition; but if any lawful agreement has been made with respect to the withdrawal of the petition, the affidavit shall set forth that agreement, and shall make the foregoing statement subject to what appears from the affidavit.

(3.) The affidavits of the applicant and his solicitor shall further state the ground on which the petition is sought to be withdrawn.

(4.) If any person makes any agreement or terms, or enters into any undertaking, in relation to the withdrawal of an election petition, and such agreement, terms, or undertaking is or are for the withdrawal of the election petition in consideration of any payment, or in consideration that the seat shall at any time be vacated, or in consideration of the withdrawal of any other election petition, or is or are (whether lawful or unlawful) not mentioned in the aforesaid affidavits, he shall be guilty of a misdemeanor, and shall be liable on conviction on indictment to imprisonment for a term not exceeding twelve months, and to a fine not exceeding two hundred pounds.

(5.) Copies of the said affidavits shall be delivered to the Director of Public Prosecutions (*b*) a reasonable time before the application for the withdrawal is heard, and the court may hear the Director of Public Prosecutions or his assistant or other representative (appointed with the approval of the Attorney-General), in opposition to the allowance of the withdrawal of the petition, and shall have power to receive the evidence on oath of any person or persons whose evidence the Director of Public Prosecutions or his assistant, or other representative, may consider material.

(6.) Where in the opinion of the court the proposed withdrawal of a petition was the result of any agreement, terms, or undertaking prohibited by this section, the court shall have the same power with respect to the security as under section ninety-five of the Municipal Corporations Act, 1882 (*c*), where the withdrawal is induced by a corrupt consideration. 45 & 46 Vict. c. 50.

(7.) In every case of the withdrawal of an election petition by leave of the election court (*d*), such court shall report in writing to

Sect. 26 (7). the High Court whether, in the opinion of such election court, the withdrawal of such petition was the result of any agreement, terms, or undertaking, or was in consideration of any payment, or in consideration that the seat should at any time be vacated, or in consideration of the withdrawal of any other election petition, or for any other consideration, and if so, shall state the circumstances attending the withdrawal.

(8.) Where more than one solicitor is concerned for the petitioner or respondent, whether as agent for another solicitor or otherwise, the affidavit shall be made by all such solicitors.

(*a*) As to the procedure for withdrawal of a petition, see s. 95 of the Municipal Corporations Act, 1882, *ante*, p. 306, and rr. 58—62, *post*.

(*b*) The Solicitor to the Treasury is now the Director of Public Prosecutions. 47 & 48 Vict. c. 58.

(*c*) See sub-s. (4) of the section referred to, *ante*.

(*d*) See s. 92 of the Municipal Corporation Act, 1882, *ante*, p. 302.

Continuation of trial of election petition.

27.—The trial of every municipal election petition shall, so far as is practicable consistently with the interests of justice in respect of such trial, be continued *de die in diem* on every lawful day until its conclusion.

As to the adjournment of the trial, see s. 93, sub-s. (3), of the Municipal Corporations Act, 1882, *ante*, p. 303.

Attendance of Director of Public Prosecutions on trial of election petition, and prosecution by him of offenders.

28.—(1.) On every trial of a municipal election petition (*a*) the Director of Public Prosecutions (*b*) shall by himself or by his assistant, or by such representative as hereinafter mentioned, attend at the trial, and it shall be the duty of such Director to obey any directions given to him by the election court (*c*) with respect to the summoning and examination of any witness to give evidence on such trial, and with respect to the prosecution by him of offenders, and with respect to any person to whom notice is given to attend with a view to report him as guilty of any corrupt or illegal practice.

(2.) It shall also be the duty of such Director, without any direction from the election court, if it appears to him that any person is able to give material evidence as to the subject of the trial, to cause such person to attend the trial, and with the leave of the court to examine such person as a witness.

(3.) It shall also be the duty of the said Director, without any direction from the election court, if he thinks it expedient in the interests of justice so to do, to prosecute, either before the said court or before any other competent court, any person who has not received a certificate of indemnity (*d*) and who appears to him to have been guilty of a corrupt or illegal practice at a municipal election.

(4.) Where a person is prosecuted before an election court for any corrupt or illegal practice, and such person appears before the court, the court shall proceed to try him summarily for the said offence, and such person, if convicted thereof upon such trial, shall be subject to the same incapacities as he is subject to under this or any other Act (*e*), upon conviction, whether on indictment or in any other proceeding for the said offence; and further, may be adjudged by the court, if the offence is a corrupt practice, to be imprisoned, with or without hard labour, for a term not exceeding six months, or to pay a fine not exceeding two hundred pounds, and if the offence is an illegal practice, to pay such fine as is fixed by this Act for the offence (*f*). Sect. 28 (4).

Provided that in the case of a corrupt practice, the court, before proceeding to try summarily any person, shall give such person the option of being tried by a jury.

(5.) Where a person is so prosecuted for any such offence, and either he elects to be tried by a jury or he does not appear before the court, or the court thinks it in the interests of justice expedient that he should be tried before some other court, the court, if of opinion that the evidence is sufficient to put the said person upon his trial for the offence, shall order such person to be prosecuted on indictment or before a court of summary jurisdiction, as the case may require, for the said offence (*g*); and in either case may order him to be prosecuted before such court as may be named in the order; and for all purposes preliminary and of and incidental to such prosecution the offence shall be deemed to have been committed within the jurisdiction of the court so named (*h*).

(6.) Upon such order being made,

(a.) If the accused person is present before the court, and the offence is an indictable offence, the court shall commit him to take his trial, or cause him to give bail to appear and take his trial for the said offence; and

(b.) If the accused person is present before the court, and the offence is not an indictable offence, the court shall order him to be brought before the court of summary jurisdiction before whom he is to be prosecuted, or cause him to give bail to appear before that court; and

(c.) If the accused person is not present before the court, the court shall as circumstances require issue a summons for his attendance, or a warrant to apprehend him and bring him before a court of summary jurisdiction, and that court, if the offence is an indictable offence, shall, on proof only of the summons or warrant and the identity of the accused, commit him to take his trial, or cause him to give bail to appear and take his trial

Sect. 28 (6).

for the said offence, or if the offence is punishable on summary conviction, shall proceed to hear the case, or if such court be not the court before whom he is directed to be prosecuted shall order him to be brought before that court.

(7.) Any order or act of an election court under this section shall not be subject to be discharged or varied under sub-section six of section ninety-two of the Municipal Corporations Act, 1882 (*i*).

45 & 46 Vict. c. 50.

(8.) The Director of Public Prosecutions may nominate, with the approval of the Attorney-General, any barristers or solicitors of not less than ten years' standing, one of whom shall, when required, act as the representative for the purposes of this section of such Director, and when so acting shall receive such remuneration as the Treasury may approve. There shall be allowed to the Director and his assistant or representative, for the purposes of this section, such allowance for expenses as the Treasury may approve.

(9.) The costs incurred in defraying the expenses of the Director of Public Prosecutions under this section (including the remuneration of his representatives) shall, in the first instance, be paid by the Treasury, and so far as they are not in the case of any prosecution paid by the defendant, shall be deemed to be expenses of the election court, and shall be paid as the expenses of that court are directed by section one hundred and one of the Municipal Corporations Act, 1882, to be paid; but if for any reasonable cause it seems just to the court so to do, the court shall order all or part of the said costs to be repaid to the Treasury by the parties to the petition, or such of them as the court may direct (*k*).

45 & 46 Vict. c. 50.

(*a*) This includes an election of county councillors.

(*b*) The Solicitor to the Treasury is now the Director of Public Prosecutions.

(*c*) As to the court, see s. 92 of the Municipal Corporations Act, 1882, *ante*.

(*d*) See as to this certificate, s. 30, *post*.

(*e*) See ss. 2, 7, *ante*.

(*f*) See s. 7, *ante*.

(*g*) The "evidence" which is to satisfy the court before it makes an order for a prosecution means the evidence given during the trial of the petition. A commissioner was, therefore, held to have acted within his jurisdiction in ordering the prosecution of a person to whom he had refused a certificate of indemnity, and who did not appear, without rehearing the evidence affecting him, and also in issuing a summons under sub-s. (6) (*c*) of this section for his attendance before a court of summary jurisdiction for the purpose of being formally committed for trial. *R.* v. *Shellard*, 23 Q. B. D. 273; 58 L. J. M. C. 142; 61 L. T. (N.S.) 120; 53 J. P. 821; 5 T. L. R. 519.

(*h*) A commissioner ordered persons to be prosecuted in the next county. The order was held valid, although it did not specify the particular nature of the corrupt practice, and although the grand jury of the county where the

Sect. 28.

NOTE.

offence was committed had not found a true bill; and although the indictment did not state the fact that the corrupt practice was committed in another county; and although the indictment specified several distinct acts of bribery and the prosecutor elected to proceed on one or more of them. *R.* v. *Riley*; *R.* v. *Campion*, 59 L. J. M. C. 122; 63 L. T. (N.S.) 119; 55 J. P. 21; 17 Cox C. C. 120.

(*i*) See this sub-section, *ante*.

(*k*) If a petition is utterly unfounded the petitioner may be ordered to pay the costs of the Director of Public Prosecutions. *Crossman* v. *Gent-Davis*, 54 L. T. (N.S.) 628; *Worcester*, 4 O'M. & H. 153. This section applies only to the trial of a petition. The costs of the Public Prosecutor cannot be ordered where the petition is withdrawn. *Pascoe* v. *Puleston*, 54 L. T. (N.S.) 733; 50 J. P. 135.

Power to election court to order payment by borough or individual of costs of election petition.

29.—(1.) Where upon the trial of a municipal election petition (*a*) it appears to the election court (*b*) that a corrupt practice has not been proved to have been committed in reference to the election by or with the knowledge and consent of the respondent to the petition, and that such respondent took all reasonable means to prevent corrupt practices being committed on his behalf, the court may make one or more orders with respect to the payment either of the whole or such part of the costs of the petition as the court may think right, as follows:

(a.) If it appears to the court that corrupt practices extensively prevailed in reference to the said election, the court may order the whole or part of the costs to be paid by the borough (*c*); and

(b.) If it appears to the court that any person or persons is or are proved, whether by providing money or otherwise, to have been extensively engaged in corrupt practices, or to have encouraged or promoted extensive corrupt practices in reference to such election, the court may, after giving such person or persons an opportunity of being heard by counsel or solicitor and of examining and cross-examining witnesses to show cause why the order should not be made, order the whole or part of the costs to be paid by that person, or those persons or any of them, and may order that if the costs cannot be recovered from one or more of such persons they shall be paid by some other of such persons or by either of the parties to the petition.

(2.) Where any person appears to the court to have been guilty of the offence of a corrupt or illegal practice, the court may, after giving such person an opportunity of making a statement to show why the order should not be made, order the whole or any part of the costs of or incidental to any proceeding before the court in relation to the said offence or to the said person to be paid by the said person to such person or persons as the court may direct.

Sect. 29 (3).

(3.) The rules and regulations of the Supreme Court of Judicature with respect to costs to be allowed in actions, causes, and matters in the High Court shall in principle and so far as practicable apply to the costs of petitions and other proceedings under Part Four of the Municipal Corporations Act, 1882, and this Act, and the taxing officer shall not allow any costs, charges, or expenses on a higher scale than would be allowed in any action, cause, or matter in the High Court on the higher scale, as between solicitor and client (*d*).

45 & 46 Vict. c. 50.

(*a*) This includes a petition against the return of a county councillor.

(*b*) See s. 92 of the Municipal Corporations Act, 1882, *ante*.

(*c*) The word *borough* will include *county* when this section is applied to an election of county councillors. See *R.* v. *Maidenhead (Mayor of)*, cited in the notes to the Municipal Corporations Act, 1882, s. 101, *ante*, p. 311. As to the fund out of which this payment is to be made, see s. 32, *post*. Where the respondents on the second day of the inquiry abandoned their defence, but the proceedings were prolonged at the instance of the representative of the public prosecutor, it was held that the costs of the petitioner in attending the prolongation of the inquiry were costs of the petition and payable by the borough under this section. *Preece* v. *Harding*, W. N. (1889), p. 217.

(*d*) As to the taxation of costs, see r. 68, *post*.

Miscellaneous.

General provisions as to prosecution of offences under this Act.

30. Subject to the other provisions of this Act, the procedure for the prosecution of a corrupt or illegal practice or any illegal payment, employment, or hiring committed in reference to a municipal election, and the removal of any incapacity incurred by reason of a conviction or report relating to any such offence, and the duties of the Director of Public Prosecutions in relation to any such offence, and all other proceedings in relation thereto (including the grant to a witness of a certificate of indemnity), shall be the same as if such offence had been committed in reference to a parliamentary election; and sections forty-five and forty-six and sections fifty to fifty-seven (both inclusive), and sections fifty-nine and sixty of the Corrupt and Illegal Practices Prevention Act, 1883, shall apply accordingly as if they were re-enacted in this Act with the necessary modifications, and with the following additions (*a*):

46 & 47 Vict. c. 51.

(a.) Where the Director of Public Prosecutions (*b*) considers that the circumstances of any case require him to institute a prosecution before any court other than an election court for any offence other than a corrupt practice committed in reference to a municipal election in any borough (*c*), he may, by himself or his assistant, institute such prosecution before any court of summary jurisdiction in the county in which the said borough is situate or to which it adjoins, and the offence shall be deemed for all purposes to have been committed within the jurisdiction of such court; and Sect. 30.

(b.) General rules for the purposes of Part Four of the Municipal Corporations Act, 1882, shall be made by the same authority as rules of court under the said sections (*d*); 45 & 46 Vict. c. 50.

(c.) The giving or refusal to give a certificate of indemnity to a witness by the election court shall be final and conclusive.

(*a*) Section 45 requires the Director of Public Prosecutions (now the solicitor to the Treasury) to inquire into alleged corrupt or illegal practices; s. 46 provides for the removal of incapacity on the ground that it was procured by perjury; ss. 50—57 relate to legal proceedings; s. 59 relates to the obligation of a witness to answer and the giving of a certificate of indemnity to a witness who answers truly all questions which he is required by the election court to answer; and s. 60 provides for the submission of the report of an election court to the Attorney-General.

(*b*) See the preceding note.

(*c*) This will include an election of a county councillor.

(*d*) That is, by the same authority by whom rules of court for procedure and practice in the Supreme Court of Judicature can be made. 46 & 47 Vict. c. 51, s. 56.

31. If any person, in consequence of conviction or of the report of an election court under this Act, becomes not capable of being elected to or sitting in the House of Commons, or of being elected to or holding any public or judicial office (*a*), and such person, at the date of the said conviction or report, has been so elected or holds any such office, then his seat or office, as the case may be, shall be vacated as from that date. Person incapacitated by conviction or report to vacate seat or office.

(*a*) See the note to s. 2, *ante*, p. 342.

32.—(1.) Where any costs of a petition are, under an order of a municipal election court, to be paid by a borough (*a*), such costs shall be paid out of the borough fund or borough rate (*b*). Payment and recovery of costs.

(2.) Where any costs or other sums are, under the order of an election court or otherwise under this Act, to be paid by any person, those costs shall be a simple contract debt due from such person to the person or persons to whom they are to be paid, and if payable to the Treasury shall be a debt to Her Majesty, and in either case may be recovered accordingly.

(*a*) See s. 29, *ante*, p. 365.

(*b*) With reference to elections of county councillors, this must be read as county fund or county rate.

33. Where any summons, notice or document is required to be served on any person with reference to any proceeding respecting Service of notices.

Sect. 33.

a municipal election in any borough or ward of a borough (*a*), whether for the purpose of causing him to appear before the High Court or any election court, or otherwise, or for the purpose of giving him an opportunity of making a statement, or showing cause, or being heard by himself, before any such court, for any purpose of this Act, such summons, notice, or document may be served either by delivering the same to such person, or by leaving the same at, or sending the same by post by a registered letter to, his last known place of abode in the said borough (*b*), or, if the proceeding is before any court, in such other manner as the court may direct, and in proving such service by post it shall be sufficient to prove that the letter was prepaid, properly addressed, and registered with the post office.

(*a*) This will apply to an election of a county councillor in an electoral division.

(*b*) *Borough* must be read as *county* with reference to an election of a county councillor.

Definitions. 45 & 46 Vict. c. 50. 46 & 47 Vict. c. 51.

34. In this Act expressions have the same meaning as in the Municipal Corporations Act, 1882, and in the Corrupt and Illegal Practices Prevention Act, 1883 (*a*); except that the words "borough," "election petition," "election court," and "candidate," shall, unless the context otherwise requires, have the meaning given by the Municipal Corporations Act, 1882, and not the meaning given by the Corrupt and Illegal Practices Prevention Act, 1883; and except that "election" shall, unless the context otherwise requires, mean a municipal election (*b*).

For the purposes of this Act the number of electors shall be taken according to the enumeration of the electors in the burgess roll (*c*).

(*a*) For the definitions of expressions used in these Acts, see s. 7 of the Municipal Corporations Act, 1882, and s. 64 of the Corrupt, etc., Practices Act, 1883.

(*b*) As applied to elections of county councillors, the word election will include an election for electoral division.

(*c*) The division register corresponds to the burgess roll in boroughs.

Application to city of London of Act and of Part IV. of 45 & 46 Vict. c. 50.

35. This Act and Part IV. of the Muncipal Corporations Act, 1882, shall apply to a municipal election in the city of London, subject as follows:—

(1.) For the purpose of such application "municipal election" means an election to the office of mayor, alderman, common councilman, or sheriff, and includes the election of any officer elected by the mayor, aldermen, and liverymen in common hall, and the expression "corporate office" includes each of the aforesaid offices, and the expression "borough" shall be deemed to apply to the said city : Sect. 35 (1).

(2.) The expression "burgess," means in relation to each municipal election, any person entitled to vote at such election :

(3.) Any costs or expenses directed to be paid out of the borough fund or borough rate shall, if incurred in respect of the election of an alderman or common councilman for any ward, be paid out of the ward rate of that ward, and in any other case shall be paid by the chamberlain of the said city out of the city's cash :

(4.) * * * * *

(5.) A vacancy in any office created by the decision of an election court shall be filled by a new election, and every summoning officer is hereby authorized and required to summon the electors for such election :

(6.) In the case of an election of an alderman and common councilman a sum may be paid and expense incurred not in excess of the maximum fixed by this Act for the election of a councillor :

(7.) In the cáse of an election by liverymen in common hall a sum may be paid and expenses incurred, if a poll be not demanded, not exceeding forty pounds, and, if a poll be demanded, then not exceeding two hundred and fifty pounds, and, in the event of a poll being demanded, such poll shall take place on the third day after the demand for a poll be made, unless such third day be a Sunday, in which case the poll shall take place on the fourth day, and the poll shall last for one day only, and commence at the hour of eight in the morning and close at six in the evening :

(8.) The town clerk shall send the corrupt and illegal practices list, when made out by him, to the ward clerk of each ward, not less than fourteen days before the day on which the list of persons entitled to vote in such ward is required to be made out, and the aldermen and common councilmen of each ward shall omit from such last-mentioned list the names of all persons mentioned in the corrupt and illegal practices list, and the corrupt and illegal practices list shall be printed and appended to every copy of the list of persons entitled to vote in such ward.

This section applies to municipal elections in the city of London, and has no bearing on the election of county councillors.

Sub-section (4) was repealed by 50 & 51 Vict. c. xiii.

Sect. 36 (1).

Application of Act to other Elections.

Application of this Act and Part IV. of 45 & 46 Vict. c. 50, to other elections.

36.—(1.) Subject as hereinafter mentioned, the provisions of this Act and of Part IV. of the Municipal Corporations Act, 1882, as amended by this Act, shall extend to elections for the offices mentioned in the first column of the First Schedule to this Act as if re-enacted herein, and in terms made applicable thereto, and petitions may be presented and tried, and offences prosecuted and punished, and incapacities incurred in reference to each such election accordingly.

Provided that in the application of the said provisions to any such election :

(a.) The area, officer, and rate mentioned opposite to the office in the second, third and fourth columns of the said schedule, shall be deemed to be substituted for the borough or ward, town clerk, and borough fund or rate respectively.

(b.) The expression "corporate office" in the said provisions shall mean an office mentioned in the said schedule, and in relation to the election of a guardian of a union includes any such office in the union, and "a municipal election" shall mean an election to such office, and the expressions "municipal election court," "municipal election list," and "municipal election petition" shall be construed accordingly.

(c.) No corrupt and illegal practices list shall be made for any such election.

(d.) Vacancies created by the decision of an election court shall be filled by a new election.

(e.) A petition relating to the election of a guardian of the union may be tried at any place within the union.

(f.) Nothing in the said provisions shall render it unlawful to hold a meeting for the purpose of promoting or procuring the election of a candidate to any office mentioned in the said schedule on any licensed or other premises not situate in an urban sanitary district or in the metropolis ;

(g.) Where the poll at any election to an office in the said schedule is taken by means of voting papers, such of the said provisions as relate to personation, polling agents, disclosure of votes and conveyance of voters, shall not apply ; but any offence in relation to voting papers or to personation or to voting at such election, which is punishable on summary conviction (that is to say), the offences mentioned in section three of the Poor Law Amendment Act, 1851, and in rule sixty-nine of

14 & 15 Vict. c. 105.

Schedule Two to the Public Health Act, 1875, shall, without prejudice to the punishment under such section and rule of a person guilty of such offence, be deemed to be an illegal practice within the meaning of the said provisions.

Sect. 36 (1).

38 & 39 Vict. c. 55.

* * * * *

(2.) The judges for the time being on the rota for the trial of parliamentary election petitions, or any two of those judges, may annually appoint as many barristers, not exceeding five, as they may think necessary to be commissioners for the trial of election petitions under Part Four of the Municipal Corporations Act, 1882, and this Act, and shall from time to time assign the petitions (whether relating to a municipal election or to any other election to which this Act extends) to be tried by each commissioner.

This section has no application to elections of county councillors, with the exception of sub-s. (2), which is substituted for a repealed provision in s. 92 of the Municipal Corporations Act, 1882, *ante*.

Clause (g) is not expressly repealed, but since the passing of the Local Government Act, 1894, it has no longer any application, as no election to an office now takes place by means of voting papers.

Clause (h) of sub-s. (1), which related to the powers of the Local Government Board to determine questions as to the right of a person to act as guardian, was repealed by the Local Government Act, 1894 (56 & 57 Vict. c. 73) s. 89.

Exemption from provisions as to maximum expenses.

37. The provisions of this Act, which prohibit the payment of any sum, and the incurring of any expense by or on behalf of a candidate at an election, on account of, or in respect of, the conduct or management of the election, and those which relate to the time for sending in and paying claims, and those which relate to the maximum amount of election expenses, or the return or declaration respecting election expenses, shall not apply to any of the elections mentioned in the First Schedule to this Act.

This section does not apply to elections of county councillors.

Repeal.

Repeal of Acts.

38. The Acts specified in the Second Schedule to this Act are hereby repealed as from the commencement of this Act to the extent in the third column of that schedule mentioned, but such repeal shall not affect anything duly done or suffered, or any right acquired or accrued, or any incapacity incurred, before the commencement of this Act; and any person subject to any incapacity under any enactment hereby repealed, or under any enactment for which such repealed enactment was substituted, shall continue subject thereto, and this Act shall apply to him as if he had become so subject in pursuance of the provisions of this Act.

Sect. 39.

Commencement of Act.

39. This Act shall come into operation on the first day of October, one thousand eight hundred and eighty-four, which day is in this Act referred to as the commencement of this Act.

Act not to extend to Scotland or Ireland.

Extent of Act.

40. This Act shall not extend to Scotland or Ireland.

Duration of Act.

41. This Act shall continue in force to the end of the year one thousand eight hundred and eighty-six, and no longer.

This Act has been continued from time to time, and is now in force until December 31st, 1898, by virtue of the Expiring Laws Continuance Act, 1897 (60 & 61 Vict. c. 54).

SCHEDULES.

FIRST SCHEDULE.

ELECTIONS to which this Act Extends.

In England.

Office.	Area.	Officer.	Rate.
Member of local board as defined by the Public Health Act, 1875.	Local Government district or ward of such district.	Clerk to the local board or person performing like duties.	The general district rate.
Member of Improvement Commissioners, as defined by the Public Health Act, 1875.	Improvement Act district or ward of such district.	Clerk to the Improvement Commissioners, or person performing like duties.	The general district rate or other rate out of which the expenses of the Improvement Commissioners are payable.
Guardian elected under the Poor Law Amendment Act, 1834.	Parish or ward of a parish or united parishes.	Clerk to the guardians, or person performing like duties.	The poor rate of the parish or united parishes.
Member of school board.	School district or division of the metropolis.	Returning officer of school board.	The school fund.

Section 38.

SECOND SCHEDULE.

ENACTMENTS REPEALED.

A description or citation of a portion of an Act is inclusive of the words, section, or other part first and last mentioned, or otherwise referred to as forming the beginning or as forming the end of the portion comprised in the description or citation.

As in England.

33 & 34 Vict. c. 75. -	The Elementary Education Act, 1870.	Section thirty-three.
45 & 46 Vict. c. 50. -	The Municipal Corporations Act, 1882.	Section seventy-seven from "corrupt practice" down to "or personation," and from "canvasser" down to "candidate at a municipal election." Section seventy-eight. Section seventy-nine. Section eighty. Section eighty-two. Section eighty-three. Section eighty-four. Section ninety-two, sub-section four, from "and those judges" down to the end of the sub-section. Section ninety-four, sub-sections five, six, seven, and eight. So much of section ninety-eight, sub-section two, as relates to the principles of taxation.

THIRD SCHEDULE.

Schedule 3.

Part I.

Enactments defining Corrupt Practices—Enactments defining the Offence of Bribery.

The Corrupt Practices Prevention Act, 1854 (17 & 18 Vict. c. 102), ss. 2 and 3.

2. The following persons shall be deemed guilty of bribery, and shall be punishable accordingly;— Bribery defined.

(1.) Every person who shall, directly or indirectly, by himself or by any other person on his behalf, give, lend, or agree to give or lend, or shall offer, promise, or promise to procure or endeavour to procure, any money or valuable consideration to or for any voter, or to or for any person on behalf of any voter, or to or for any other person, in order to induce any voter to vote or refrain from voting, or shall corruptly do any such act as aforesaid on account of such voter having voted or refrained from voting at any election.

(2.) Every person who shall, directly or indirectly, by himself or by any other person on his behalf, give or procure, or agree to give or procure, or offer, promise, or promise to procure, or endeavour to procure, any office, place, or employment to or for any voter, or to or for any person on behalf of any voter, or to or for any other person, in order to induce such voter to vote or refrain from voting, or shall corruptly do any such act as aforesaid on account of any voter having voted or refrained from voting at any election.

(3.) Every person who shall directly, or indirectly, by himself, or by any other person on his behalf, make any such gift, loan, offer, promise, procurement, or agreement as aforesaid, to or for any person, in order to induce such person to procure or endeavour to procure the return of any person to serve in Parliament, or the vote of any voter at any election.

(4.) Every person who shall, upon or in consequence of any such gift, loan, offer, promise, procurement, or agreement, procure, or engage, promise, or endeavour to procure the return of any person to serve in Parliament, or the vote of any voter at any election.

(5.) Every person who shall advance or pay, or cause to be paid, any money to or to the use of any other person with the intent that such money, or any part thereof, shall be expended in bribery at any election, or who shall knowingly pay or cause to be paid any money to any person in discharge or repayment of any money wholly or in part expended in bribery at any election: Provided always, that the aforesaid enactment shall not extend or be construed to extend to any money paid or agreed to be paid for on account of any legal expenses bonâ fide incurred at or concerning any election.

3. The following persons shall also be deemed guilty of bribery, and shall be punishable accordingly:—

(1.) Every voter who shall, before or during any election, directly or indirectly, by himself or by any other person on his behalf, receive, agree, or contract for any money, gift, loan, or valuable consideration, office, place, or employment, for himself or for any other Bribery further defined.

Schedule 3.

person, for voting or agreeing to vote, or from refraining or agreeing to refrain from voting at any election.

(2.) Every person who shall, after any election, directly or indirectly, by himself or by any other person on his behalf, receive any money or valuable consideration on account of any person having voted or refrained from voting, or having induced any other person to vote or refrain from voting at any election.

The Representation of the People Act, 1867 (30 & 31 Vict. c. 102), s. 49.

Corrupt payment of rates to be punishable as bribery.

49. Any person, either directly or indirectly, corruptly paying any rate on behalf of any ratepayer for the purpose of enabling him to be registered as a voter, thereby to influence his vote at the future election, and any candidate or other person, either directly or indirectly, paying any rate on behalf of any voter for the purpose of inducing him to vote or refrain from voting, shall be guilty of bribery, and be punishable accordingly; and any person on whose behalf and with whose privity any such payment as in this section is mentioned is made, shall also be guilty of bribery, and punishable accordingly.

It is beyond the scope of the present work to enter into a detailed discussion of the law relating to bribery and other corrupt practices. For information on this subject the reader is referred to works on the law of election. A few modern decisions may, however, be mentioned.

As to corrupt employment, see *Harding* v. *Stokes*, 1 M. & W. 354; 2 M. & W. 233; giving money after election, *R.* v. *Thwaites*, 1 E. & B. 704; 22 L. J. Q. B. 238.

Bribery includes not merely giving, but any promise or agreement to give, money or valuable consideration to a voter to influence his vote. The following acts have been held to come within the definition of this offence: the promise of a dinner (*Bodmin case*, 1 O'M. & H. 124); the gift of a pair of boots (*Tewkesbury case*, 3 O'M. & H. 97); distribution of coals (*Boston case*, 2 O'M. & H. 161); allowing a voter to shoot rabbits (*Launceston case*, 2 O'M. & H. 129); a promise to remunerate a voter for any loss of time (*Simpson* v. *Yeend*, L. R. 4 Q. B. 626; 38 L. J. Q. B. 313; 33 J.P. 677); a gift of money made under pretence of payment for work done (*Penryn case*, 1 O'M. & H. 130; *Truscott* v. *Bevan*, 44 L. T. (N.S) 64). A person guilty of several acts of bribery is liable to a penalty for each such act (*Milnes* v. *Bale*, L. R. 10 C. P. 591). A single case of bribery avoids an election (*Norwich case*, 54 L. T. (N.S) 625).

"In order to make the payment of a rate for the purpose of enabling voters to be registered affect the election, you must prove that it was done corruptly; that it was done thereby to influence their votes, which in my judgment means to induce them to vote for the person on whose behalf the payment was made." *Per* MARTIN, B., *Cheltenham Election*, 1 O'M. & H. 63. In order to make a third person responsible for the payment of a rate, it must be proved that he gave authority to the person to do the act. The common law rules of agency, therefore, and not those of election law, apply to this case. *Wigan Election*, 1 O'M. & H. 190.

To offer a voter his travelling expenses if he will come and vote for a particular candidate is bribery. *Packard* v. *Collings*, 54 L. T. (N.S.) 619.

Enactment defining the Offence of Personation.

The Ballot Act, 1872 (35 & 36 Vict. c. 33), s. 24.

Personation defined.

24. A person shall, for all purposes of the laws relating to parliamentary and municipal elections, be deemed to be guilty of the offence of personation who, at an election for a county or borough, or at a municipal election, applies for a ballot paper in the name of some other person, whether that name be that of a person living or dead, or of a fictitious person, or who, having voted once at any such election, applies at the same election for a ballot paper in his own name.

See the notes to this section, *ante*, p. 214.

Enactments defining the Offences of Treating and Undue Influence. **Schedule 3.**

The Corrupt and Illegal Practices Prevention Act, 1883 (46 & 47 Vict. c. 51), ss. 1 and 2.

1. Any person who corruptly, by himself or by any other person, either before, during, or after an election, directly or indirectly gives or provides, or pays wholly or in part the expense of giving or providing any meat, drink, entertainment, or provision to or for any person for the purpose of corruptly influencing that person or any other person to give or refrain from giving his vote at the election, or on account of such person or any other person having voted or refrained from voting, or being about to vote or refrain from voting at such election, shall be guilty of treating. What is treating.

And every elector who corruptly accepts or takes any such meat, drink, entertainment, or provision, shall also be guilty of treating.

2. Every person who shall directly or indirectly, by himself or by any other person on his behalf, make use of or threaten to make use of any force, violence, or restraint, or inflict or threaten to inflict, by himself or by any other person, any temporal or spiritual injury, damage, harm, or loss upon or against any person in order to induce or compel such person to vote or refrain from voting, or on account of such person having voted or refrained from voting at any election, or who shall by abduction, duress, or any fraudulent device or contrivance impede or prevent the free exercise of the franchise of any elector, or shall thereby compel, induce, or prevail upon any elector, either to give or refrain from giving his vote at any election, shall be guilty of undue influence. What is undue influence.

Treating is not the entertainment of equals by equals, but of an inferior by a superior with the object of securing the goodwill of the inferior. *Norwich Election Petition*, 54 L. T. (N.S.) 625.

The offence of treating is *corrupt* treating, viz., treating intended to affect the election (*Bewdley case*, 1 O'M. & H. 16; *Wallingford case*, *ib.* 59); charity will not avail as a cloak for corrupt treating (*Wigan case*, 4 O'M. & H. 13). And see as to charitable gifts, the *Haggerston case*, 5 O'M. & H. 68 (in which the judges differed as to the motive with which relief was distributed to the poor); *Lichfield*, *ib.* 27; *St. George's*, *ib.* 91.

Undue influence includes (besides force, either actual or threatened) threats of loss of employment, or of eviction by a landlord (*North Norfolk case*, 1 O'M. & H. 240; *Westbury case*, *ib.* 50; *Oldham case*, *ib.* 161; *Blackburn case*, *ib.* 204), and threats of spiritual damage exercised by ministers of religion or other persons having spiritual influence (*South and North Meath cases*, 4 O'M. & H. 130, 185).

Enactment defining the Offences of Bribery, Treating, Undue Influence, and Personation.

The Municipal Corporations Act, 1882 (45 & 46 Vict. c. 50), s. 77.

77. "Bribery," "treating," "undue influence," and "personation" include respectively anything done before, at, after, or with respect to a municipal election, which, if done before, at, after, or with respect to a parliamentary election, would make the person doing the same liable to any penalty, punishment, or disqualification for bribery, treating, undue influence, or personation, as the case may be, under any Act for the time being in force with respect to parliamentary elections. Definitions.

PART II.

Enactments relating to Disqualification of Electors. Section 23.

The Corrupt and Illegal Practices Prevention Act, 1883 (46 & 47 Vict. c. 51), ss. 37 and 38.

37. Every person who, in consequence of conviction or of the report of any election court or election commissioners under this Act or under the Prohibition of disqualified persons from voting.

Schedule 3.

35 & 36 Vict. c. 60.
45 & 46 Vict. c. 50.

Corrupt Practices (Municipal Elections) Act, 1872, or under Part IV. of the Municipal Corporations Act, 1882, or under any other Act for the time being in force relating to corrupt practices at an election for any public office, has become incapable of voting at any election, whether a parliamentary election or an election to any public office, is prohibited from voting at any such election, and his vote shall be void.

Hearing of person before he is reported guilty of corrupt or illegal practice, and incapacity of person reported guilty.

38.—(1.) Before a person, not being a party to an election petition nor a candidate on behalf of whom the seat is claimed by an election petition, is reported by an election court (*a*) . . . to have been guilty, at an election, of any corrupt or illegal practice, the court . . . shall cause notice to be given to such person (*b*), and if he appears in pursuance of the notice, shall give him an opportunity of being heard by himself (*c*), and of calling evidence in his defence to show why he should not be so reported.

* * * * *

(5.) Every person who, after the commencement of this Act, is reported by any election court . . . to have been guilty of any corrupt or illegal practice at an election, shall, whether he obtained a certificate of indemnity or not, be subject to the same incapacity as he would be subject to if he had at the date of such election been convicted of the offence of which he is reported to have been guilty . . .

(6.) Where a person who is a justice of the peace is reported by any election court . . . to have been guilty of any corrupt practice in reference to an election, whether he has obtained a certificate of indemnity or not, it shall be the duty of the Director of Public Prosecutions to report the case to the Lord High Chancellor of Great Britain, with such evidence as may have been given of such corrupt practice, and where any such person acts as a justice of the peace by virtue of his being or having been mayor of a borough, the Lord High Chancellor shall have the same power to remove such person from being a justice of the peace as if he was named in a commission of the peace.

(7.) Where a person who is a barrister or solicitor, or who belongs to any profession the admission to which is regulated by law, is reported by any election court . . . to have been guilty of any corrupt practice in reference to an election, whether such person has obtained a certificate of indemnity or not, it shall be the duty of the Director of Public Prosecutions to bring the matter before the Inn of Court, High Court, or tribunal having power to take cognizance of any misconduct of such person in his profession, and such Inn of Court, High Court, or tribunal may deal with such person in like manner as if such corrupt practice were misconduct by such person in his profession.

(8.) With respect to a person holding a license or certificate under the Licensing Acts (in this section referred to as a licensed person) the following provisions shall have effect:—

(*a*.) If it appear to the court by which any licensed person is convicted of the offence of bribery or treating that such offence was committed on his licensed premises, the court shall direct such conviction to be entered in the proper register of licenses:

(*b*.) If it appears to an election court . . . that a licensed person has knowingly suffered any bribery or treating in reference to any election to take place upon his licensed premises, such court . . (subject to the provisions of this Act as to a person having an opportunity of being heard by himself and producing evidence before being reported) shall report the same; and, whether such person obtained a certificate of indemnity or not, it shall be the duty of the

Director of Public Prosecutions to bring such report before the licensing justices from whom or on whose certificate the licensed person obtained his license, and such licensing justices shall cause such report to be entered in the proper register of licenses : Schedule 3.

(c.) Where an entry is made in the register of licenses of any such conviction of or report respecting any licensed person as above in this section mentioned, it shall be taken into consideration by the licensing justices in determining whether they will or will not grant to such person the renewal of his licence or certificate, and may be a ground, if the justices think fit, for refusing such renewal.

* * * * *

(a) As to this report, see the Municipal Corporations Act, 1882, s. 93, *ante*, p. 303, and the Corrupt Practices Act, 1884, s. 8, *ante*, p. 347.

(b) Where after the trial of a municipal election petition, the commissioner has reported persons as having been guilty of corrupt practices, the High Court has no jurisdiction to set aside or amend his report upon the ground that the notice prescribed by the text had not been given to the persons reported. *Preece* v. *Harding*, 24 Q. B. D. 110 ; 54 L. J. Q. B. 82 ; 61 L. T. (N.S.) 837 ; 38 W. R. 350; 6 T. L. R. 65.

(c) The words "by himself" in the above section exclude the person charged from being heard either by counsel or solicitor. *R.* v. *Mansel Jones*, 23 Q. B. D. 29 ; 60 L. T (N.S.) 860 ; 37 W. R. 408 ; 53 J. P. 739.

FOURTH SCHEDULE.

Section 21.

Form of Declaration by Candidate as to Expenses.

I , having been a candidate at the election of councillor for the borough [or ward] of , on the day of [and my agents] do hereby solemnly and sincerely declare that I have paid for my expenses at the said election, and that, except as aforesaid, I have not, and to the best of my knowledge and belief, no person, nor any club, society, or association, has on my behalf, made any payment, or given, promised, or offered any reward, office, employment, or valuable consideration, or incurred any liability on account of or in respect of the conduct or management of the said election.

And I further solemnly and sincerely declare that, except as aforesaid, no money, security, or equivalent for money, has to my knowledge or belief been paid, advanced, given or deposited by anyone to or in the hands of myself, or any other person, for the purpose of defraying any expenses incurred on my behalf on account of or in respect of the conduct or management of the said election.

And I further solemnly and sincerely declare that I will not at any future time make or be a party to the making or giving of any payment, reward, office, employment, or valuable consideration for the purpose of defraying any such expenses as last mentioned, or provide or be a party to the providing of any money, security, or equivalent for money for the purpose of defraying any such expenses.

(Signature of declarant) *C.D.*

Signed and declared by the above-named declarant on the day of , before me.

(Signed) *E.F.*

Justice of the Peace for .

GENERAL RULES.

The following are the general rules made pursuant to the Municipal Corporations Act, 1882, s. 100, and the Municipal Elections (Corrupt Practices) Act, 1884, s. 30, *ante*.

I. The presentation of a Municipal Election Petition shall be made by leaving it at the office of the Master for the time being nominated as prescribed officer, under the Parliamentary Elections Act, 1868, and such Master or his clerk shall (if required) give a receipt, which may be in the following form :—

Received on the day of at the Master's office a petition touching the election of *A.B.*, alderman, councillor, [etc., *as the case may be*] for the borough of purporting to be signed by [*insert the names of petitioners*].

C.D., Master's Clerk.

With the petition shall also be left a copy thereof for the Master to send to the town clerk, pursuant to section 88, sub-section (3), of the Act.

II. A municipal election petition shall contain the following statements :—

(1.) It shall state the right of the petitioner or petitioners to petition within section 88, sub-section (1), of the Act.

(2.) It shall state the holding and result of the election, and shall briefly state the facts and grounds relied on to sustain the prayer.

III. The petition shall be divided into paragraphs, each of which, as nearly as may be, shall be confined to a distinct portion of the subject, and every paragraph shall be numbered consecutively, and no costs shall be allowed of drawing or copying any petition not substantially in compliance with this rule, unless otherwise ordered by the High Court or a judge thereof.

IV. The petition shall conclude with a prayer, as, for instance, that some specified person should be declared duly returned or elected, or that the election should be declared void, or that a return may be enforced, (as the case may be,) and shall be signed by all the petitioners.

V. The following form, or one to the like effect shall be sufficient :—

In the High Court of Justice,
"The Municipal Corporations Act, 1882."

Election for [*state the place and office for which election held*], holden on the day of A.D.

The petition of *A.* of [*or* of *A.* of , and *B.* of *as the case may be*] whose names are subscribed.

(1) Your petitioner *A.* is a person who voted [*or* had a right to vote, *as the case may be,*] at the above election [*or* was a candidate at the above election]; and your petitioner *B.* [*here state in like manner the right of each petitioner*].

(2.) And your petitioners state that the election was holden on the day of A.D. , when *A.B.*, *C.D.*, and *E. F.* were candidates, and that *A.B.* and *C.D.* have been in the usual manner declared to be duly elected.

(3.) And your petitioners say that [*here state the facts and grounds on which the petitioners rely*].

Wherefore your petitioners pray that it may be determined that the said *A.B.* and not duly elected, and that the election was void [*or* that the said *E.F.* was duly elected and ought to have been returned, *or as the case may be*].

(Signed)
A.
B.

VI. Evidence need not be stated in the petition, but the High Court or a judge thereof may order such particulars as may be necessary to prevent surprise and unnecessary expense, and to insure a fair and effectual trial in the same way as in ordinary proceedings in the said High Court, and upon such terms as to costs and otherwise as may be ordered. **Rule 6.**

An order for particulars of the corrupt practices alleged in a municipal election petition was made at chambers in the following form :—That the petitioners do within a week deliver to the respondents particulars of all the persons alleged to have been bribed or treated, by whom, and when and where; and of all the persons alleged to have been retained or employed as canvassers and by whom, and when and where; and of all persons to whom money was paid or agreed to be paid, on account of the conveyance of voters to the poll, and by whom, and when, and where such moneys were paid or agreed to be paid. On appeal to the court, the order was varied by inserting the words "as far as known" at the end of each item of the particulars. *Maude* v. *Lowley*, L. R. 9 C. P. 165; 43 L. J. C. P. 103; 30 L. T. (N.S.) 168; 22 W. R. 649; 38 J. P. 280.

There is no inflexible rule of practice as to the period before the trial at which particulars must be delivered; the time fixed for delivery must depend on the circumstances of each case, such as the character of the division, its area and population, and the number of witnesses it is proposed to call. In the case of a small borough, seven days before trial is the time usually ordered. *Lenham* v. *Barber* (Hereford), 10 Q. B. D. 293; 48 J. P. 23. In populous places, ten days has frequently been the period. *Munro* v. *Balfour* (Manchester), [1893] 1 Q. B. 113; 67 L. T. (N.S.) 526; 41 W. R. 143; 57 J. P. 789; 9 T. L. R. 2; *Rushmore* v. *Isaacson* (Stepney), [1893] 1 Q. B. 118; 41 W. R. 124; 57 J. P. 790; 9 T. L. R. 47; *Barrow-in-Furness*, 2 T. L. R. 356; *Cremer* v. *Lowles* (Haggerston), [1896] 1 Q. B. 504; 65 L. J. Q. B. 289; 74 L. T. (N.S.) 42; 44 W. R. 629; 60 J. P. 100.

A petitioner cannot include in his particulars or give evidence of offences alleged to have been committed after the date of the petition, the petition not having been amended within the time limited for amendment. *Cremer* v. *Lowles*, *supra*.

Where a petition alleged that "the respondent by himself and other persons on his behalf was guilty of bribery, etc.," and the judge ordered particulars to be given of all persons alleged to have been bribed, etc., but refused to order particulars of the "other persons" alleged to have bribed, etc., the Exchequer Chamber held that the judge had exercised a right discretion and declined to interfere. *Beal* v. *Smith*, L. R. 4 C. P. 145; 38 L. J. C. P. 145; 17 W. R. 317.

VII. When a petitioner claims the office for an unsuccessful candidate, alleging that he had a majority of lawful votes, the party complaining of or defending the election shall, six days before the day appointed for trial deliver to the Master and also at the address, if any, given by the petitioners and respondent, as the case may be, a list of the votes intended to be objected to, and the heads of objection to each such vote, and the Master shall allow inspection and office copies of such lists to all parties concerned; and no evidence shall be given against the validity of any vote, nor upon any head of objection not specified in the list, except by leave of the High Court or a judge thereof, upon such terms as to amendment of the list, postponement of the inquiry, and payment of costs, as may be ordered.

This rule deals with cases where the petitioner demands a scrutiny and claims the seat. Particulars under r. 6 cannot be ordered as to matters to which r. 7 applies. *Munro* v. *Balfour*, *supra*.

As to the calculation of the six days in this and the next rule, see r. 37, *post*.

The trial of a municipal election petition was appointed for January 20th. A list of objections was tendered at the Rule Office of the Common Pleas on January 13th, and refused on the ground that it was too late, and it was taken away by the person tendering it. On the 14th a list of objections was left at the Rule Office, and one was also delivered to the respondent. It was held that the list was not delivered in due time according to the rule, and that the court had no jurisdiction to order delivery *nunc pro tunc* under the last clause of the rule. *Nield* v. *Batty*, 38 J. P. 264.

VIII. When the respondent in a petition under the Act complaining of an undue election, and claiming the office for some person, intends to give evidence to prove that the election of such person was undue, pursuant to the 93rd section of the Act, sub-section (10), such respondent shall, six days

Rule 9. before the day appointed for trial, deliver to the Master, and also at the address, if any, given by the petitioner, a list of the objections to the election upon which he intends to rely, and the Master shall allow inspection and office copies of such list to all parties concerned ; and no evidence shall be given by a respondent of any objection to the election not specified in the list, except by leave of the High Court or a judge thereof, upon such terms as to amendment of the list, postponement of the inquiry, and payment of costs as may be ordered.

This rule relates to recriminatory charges. See the Municipal Corporations Act, 1882, s. 93 (10) *ante*, and see note to last rule.

IX. With the petition the petitioner or petitioners shall leave at the office of the Master a writing, signed by him or them or on his or their behalf, giving the name of some person entitled to practise as a solicitor in the High Court of Justice, whom he or they authorize to act as his or their agent, or stating that he or they act for himself or themselves, as the case may be, and in either case giving an address, within three miles from the General Post Office, at which notices addressed to him or them may be left ; and if no such writing be left or address given, then notice of objection to the recognizances, and all other notices and proceedings may be given by sticking up the same at the Master's office.

X. Any person elected to any municipal office may at any time after he is elected send to or leave at the office of the Master a writing, signed by him or on his behalf, appointing a person entitled to practise as a solicitor in the High Court of Justice, to act as his agent in case there should be a petition against him, or stating that he intends to act for himself, and in either case giving an address within three miles from the General Post Office at which notices may be left, and in default of such writing being left in a week after service of the petition, notices and proceedings may be given and served respectively by sticking up the same at the Master's office.

XI. The Master shall keep a book or books at his office, in which he shall enter all addresses and the names of agents given under either of the preceding rules, which book shall be open to inspection by any person during office hours.

XII. The Master shall, upon the presentation of the petition, forthwith send a copy of the petition to the town clerk, pursuant to section 88 of the Act, sub-section (3), and shall therewith send the name of the petitioner's agent, if any, and the address, if any, given as prescribed, and also the name of the respondent's agent, and the address, if any, given as prescribed, and the town clerk shall forthwith publish those particulars along with the petition.

The cost of publication of this and any other matter required to be published by the town clerk shall be paid by the petitioner or person moving in the matter, and shall form part of the general cost of the petition.

XIII. The time for giving notice of the presentation of a petition and of the nature of the proposed security shall be five days, exclusive of the day of presentation.

XIV. Where the respondent has named an agent or given an address, the service of a municipal election petition may be by delivery of it to the agent or by posting it in a registered letter to the address given at such time, that in the ordinary course of post, it would be delivered within the prescribed time.

Rule 14.

In other cases the service must be personal on the respondent, unless a judge of the High Court, on an application made to him not later than five days after the petition is presented on affidavit, showing what has been done, shall be satisfied that all reasonable effort has been made to effect personal service and cause the matter to come to the knowledge of the respondent, in which case the judge may order that what has been done shall be considered sufficient service, subject to such conditions as he may think reasonable. An agent employed for the petitioner or respondent shall forthwith leave written notice at the office of the Master of his appointment to act as such agent, and service of notices and proceedings upon such agent shall be sufficient for all purposes.

XV. In case of evasion of service the sticking up a notice in the office of the Master of the petition having been presented, stating the petitioner, the prayer, and the nature of the proposed security, shall be deemed equivalent to personal service if so ordered by a judge.

XVI. The deposit of money by way of security for payment of costs, charges, and expenses payable by the petitioner, shall be made by payment into the Bank of England to an account to be opened there by the description of "The Municipal Corporations Act, 1882, Security Fund," which shall be vested in and drawn upon from time to time by the Lord Chief Justice of England for the time being, for the purposes for which security is required by the said Act, and a bank receipt or certificate for the same shall be forthwith left at the Master's Office.

As to the security for costs, see the subsequent rules and s. 89 of the Municipal Corporations Act, 1882, *ante*, p. 300.

XVII. The Master shall file such receipt or certificate, and keep a book open to inspection of all parties concerned, in which shall be entered from time to time the amount and the petition to which it is applicable.

XVIII. All claims at law or in equity to money so deposited or to be deposited in the Bank of England shall be disposed of by the High Court of Justice or a judge thereof.

XIX. Money so deposited shall, if and when the same is no longer needed for securing payment of such costs, charges, and expenses, be returned or otherwise disposed of as justice may require, by rule of the High Court or order of a judge thereof.

XX. Such rule or order may be made after such notice of intention to apply, and proof that all just claims have been satisfied or otherwise sufficiently provided for, as the Court or judge may require.

XXI. The rule or order may direct payment either to the party in whose name the same is deposited, or to any person entitled to receive the same.

XXII. Upon such rule or order being made, the amount may be drawn for by the Lord Chief Justice of England for the time being.

XXIII. The draft of the Lord Chief Justice of England for the time being shall in all cases be a sufficient warrant to the Bank of England for all payments made thereunder.

XXIV. The recognizance as security for costs may be acknowledged before a judge of the High Court or the Master in town, or a justice of the peace in the country.

There may be one recognizance acknowledged by all the sureties, or separate recognizances by one or more, as may be convenient.

Rule 25.

XXV. The recognizance shall contain the name and usual place of abode of each surety, with such sufficient description as shall enable him to be found or ascertained, and may be as follows :—

Be it remembered that on the day of , in the year of our Lord 18 , before me [*name and description*] came *A.B.*, of [*name and description as above prescribed*] and acknowledged himself [*or* severally acknowledged themselves] to owe to our Sovereign Lady the Queen the sum of five hundred pounds [*or* the following sums], (that is to say) the said *C.D.* the sum of £ , the said *E.F.* the sum of £ , the said *G.H.* the sum of £ , and the said *J.K.* the sum of £ , to be levied on his [*or* their respective] goods and chattels, lands and tenements, to the use of our said Sovereign Lady the Queen, her heirs and successors.

The condition of this recognizance is that if [*here insert the names of all the petitioners, and if more than one, add*, or any of them] shall well and truly pay all costs, charges and expenses in respect of the election petition signed by him [*or* them] relating to the [*here insert the name of the borough*] which shall become payable by the petitioner [*or* petitioners or any of them] under the Municipal Corporations Act, 1882, to any person or persons, then this recognizance to be void, otherwise to stand in full force.

Signed,

[*Signature of Sureties.*]

Taken and acknowledged by the above name [*name of sureties*] on the at , before me,

C.D.

A Justice of the Peace [*or as the case may be*].

XXVI. The recognizance or recognizances shall be left at the Master's office, by or on behalf of the petitioner, in like manner as before prescribed for the leaving of a petition forthwith after being acknowledged.

The security may (unless the High Court or a judge thereof shall otherwise order on summons) be given to any amount not less than 300*l.* ; but the High Court or a judge thereof may, on summons taken out within five days from the service of the notice of the nature and amount of the security, order that the same shall be increased within a time to be fixed in the order by further security to be given in the manner directed by the Act, for a further amount not exceeding with the amount for which security shall have been already given, 500*l.* And in default of compliance with such order, no further proceedings shall be had on the petition.

XXVII. The time for giving notice of any objection to a recognizance under the 89th section of the Act, sub-section (4), shall be within five days from the date of service of the notice of the petition and of the nature of the security, exclusive of the day of service, or in case of further security within five days after service of notice of the nature thereof, exclusive of the day of such service.

XXVIII. An objection to the recognizance must state the ground or grounds thereof, as that the sureties, or any and which of them, are insufficient, or that a surety is dead, or that he cannot be found, or that a person named in the recognizance has not duly acknowledged the same.

XXIX. Any objection made to the security shall be heard and decided by the Master, subject to appeal within five days to a judge, upon summons taken out by either party to declare the security sufficient or insufficient.

XXX. Such hearing and decision may be either upon affidavit or personal examination of witnesses, or both, as the Master or judge may think fit.

XXXI. If an objection be allowed and the security be declared insufficient, the Master or judge shall in his order state what amount he deems requisite to make the security sufficient, and the further prescribed time to remove the objection by deposit shall be within five days from the date of the order, not including the day of the date, and such deposit shall be made in the manner already prescribed. Rule 31.

XXXII. The costs of hearing and deciding the objections made to the security given shall be paid as ordered by the Master or judge, and in default of such order shall form part of the general costs of the petition.

XXXIII. The costs of hearing and deciding an objection upon the ground of insufficiency of a surety or sureties, shall be paid by the petitioner, and a clause to that effect shall be inserted in the order declaring its sufficiency or insufficiency, unless at the time of leaving the recognizance with the Master there be also left with the Master an affidavit of the sufficiency of the surety or sureties sworn by each surety before a justice of the peace, which affidavit any justice of the peace is hereby authorized to take, or before some person authorized to take affidavits in the High Court of Justice that he is seised or possessed of real or personal estate, or both, above what will satisfy his debts, of the clear value of the sum for which he is bound by his recognizance, which affidavit may be as follows :

In the High Court of Justice,
Municipal Corporations Act, 1882.

I *A.B.* of [*as in recognizance*] make oath and say that I am seised or possessed of real [*or* personal] estate above what will satisfy my debts, of the clear value of £ .

Sworn, *etc.*

XXXIV. The order of the Master for payment of costs shall have the same force as an order made by a judge, and may be enforced in like manner as a judge's order in an ordinary proceeding in the High Court of Justice.

XXXV. A copy of every order (other than an order giving further time for delivering particulars, or for costs only), or, if the Master shall so direct, the order itself, or a duplicate thereof, also a copy of every particular delivered, shall be forthwith filed with the Master, and the same shall be produced at the trial by the Registrar, stamped with the official seal. Such order shall be filed by the party obtaining the same, and such particular by the party delivering the same.

XXXVI. The petitioner or his agent shall, immediately after notice of the presentation of a petition and of the nature of the proposed security shall have been served, file with the Master an affidavit of the time and manner of service thereof.

XXXVII. The days mentioned in Rules VII. and VIII., and in any rule of court or judge's order, whereby particulars are ordered to be delivered, or any act is directed to be done, so many days before the day appointed for trial, shall be reckoned exclusively of the day of delivery, or of doing the act ordered and the day appointed for trial, and exclusively also of Sunday, Christmas Day, Good Friday, and any day set apart for a public fast or public thanksgiving.

XXXVIII. When the last day for presenting petitions, or filing lists of votes or objections, under Rules VII. and VIII., or recognizances, or any other matter required to be filed within a given time, shall happen to fall on a holiday, the petition or other matter shall be deemed duly filed if put into the letter box at the Master's office at any time during such day; but an affidavit, stating with reasonable precision the time when such delivery was made, shall be filed on the first day after the expiration of the holidays.

XXXIX. The Master shall make out the municipal election list. In it he shall insert the names of the agents of the petitioners and respondents, and

Rule 39. the addresses to which notices may be sent, if any. The list may be inspected at the Master's office at any time during office hours, and shall be put up for that purpose upon a notice board appropriated to proceedings under the said Act, and headed "Municipal Election List."

XL. The time of the trial of each municipal election petition shall be fixed by the election judges on the rota or any one of them, who shall signify the same to the Master, and notice thereof shall be given in writing by the Master by sticking notice up in his office, sending one copy by post to the address given by the petitioner, another to the address given by the respondent, if any, and a copy by the post to the town clerk of the borough to which the petition relates, fifteen days before the day appointed for the trial.

The town clerk shall forthwith publish the same in the borough.

In a county council election petition "clerk of the county council" must be substituted for "town clerk," and "electoral division" for "borough," in this and subsequent rules as to notices. See Municipal Corporations Act, 1882, s. 88 (3), *ante*, p. 299.

XLI. The sticking up of the notice of trial at the office of the Master shall be deemed and taken to be notice in the prescribed manner within the meaning of the Act, and such notice shall not be vitiated by any miscarriage of or relating to the copy or copies thereof to be sent as already directed.

XLII. The notice of trial may be in the following form :—

Municipal Corporations Act, 1882.

Election petition of

Borough of

Take notice that the above petition [*or* petitions] will be tried at on the day of and on such other subsequent days as may be needful.

Dated the

Signed, by order
A.B.,
The Master appointed under the above Act.

XLIII. A judge may from time to time, by order made upon the application of a party to the petition, or by notice in such form as the judge may direct to be sent to the town clerk, postpone the beginning of the trial to such day as he may name, and such notice when received shall be forthwith made public by the town clerk.

XLIV. In the event of the barrister to whom the trial of the petition is assigned not having arrived at the time appointed for the trial, or to which the trial is postponed, the commencement of the trial shall *ipso facto* stand adjourned to the ensuing day, and so from day to day.

XLV. No formal adjournment of the court for the trial of a municipal election petition shall be necessary, but the trial is to be deemed adjourned, and may be continued from day to day until the inquiry is concluded.

XLVI. After receiving notice of the petitioner's intention to apply for leave to withdraw, or of the respondent's intention not to oppose, or of the abatement of the petition by death, or of the happening of any of the events mentioned in the 97th section of the Act, if such notice be received after notice of trial shall have been given, and before the trial has commenced, the Master shall forthwith countermand the notice of trial. The countermand shall be given in the same manner, as near as may be, as the notice of trial.

See s. 97 of the Municipal Corporations Act, 1882, *ante*, p. 308.

XLVII. If all the respondents shall give notice of their intention not to oppose the petition, and no other person shall be admitted as a respondent, the High Court of Justice, or a judge, may either declare the election void or direct the trial to proceed. Notice of such order shall be forthwith given by the Master to the town clerk, and if the election be declared void the office shall be deemed to be vacant from the first day (not being a *dies non*) after the date of such order. Rule 47.

The court or judge may also make such order as to costs as may be just.

XLVIII. The application to state a special case may be made by motion in the High Court of Justice, or by a summons before a judge thereof.

XLIX. The title of the court held for the trial of a municipal election petition may be as follows :—

"Court for the trial of a municipal election petition for the borough of [*or* as may be] between petitioner and respondent,"

and it shall be sufficient so to entitle all proceedings in that court.

L. An officer shall be appointed for each court for the trial of a municipal election petition by the election judges, at the time that they assign the petition to the barrister; such officer shall attend at the trial in like manner as the clerks of assize and of arraigns attend at the assizes.

Such officer may be called the registrar of that court. He, by himself, or in case of need, his sufficient deputy, shall perform all the functions incident to the officer of a court of record, and also such duties as may be prescribed to him.

LI. The Commissioner may appoint a proper person to act as crier and officer of the court.

LII. The shorthand writer to attend at the trial of a petition shall be the shorthand writer to the House of Commons for the time being or his deputy, and the Master shall send a copy of the notice of trial to the said shorthand writer to the House of Commons.

LIII. The amount to be paid to any witness whose expenses shall be allowed by the Commissioner trying the petition shall be ascertained and certified by the registrar; or in the event of his becoming incapacitated from giving such certificate, by the Commissioner.

LIV. The order of the court to compel the attendance of a person as a witness may be in the following form :—

Court for the trial of a municipal election petition for [*complete the title of the court*] the day of .

To *A.B.* [*describe the person*]. You are hereby required to attend before the above court at [*place*] on day of at the hour of [*or* forthwith, *as the case may be*], to be examined as a witness in the matter of the said petition, and to attend the said court until your examination shall have been completed.

As witness my hand, *A. B.*,
The Commissioner to whom the trial of the said petition is assigned.

LV. In the event of its being necessary to commit any person for contempt, the warrant may be as follows :—

At a court holden on at for the trial of a municipal election petition for the borough of before *A. B.*, one of the barristers appointed for the trial of municipal election petitions, pursuant to "The Municipal Corporations Act, 1882."

Whereas *C. D.* has this day been guilty, and is by the said court adjudged to be guilty, of a contempt thereof. The said court does therefore sentence the said *C. D.* for his said contempt to be imprisoned in the gaol for calendar months [*or as may be*], and to pay to our Lady the Queen a fine of £

Rule 55.

and to be further imprisoned in the said gaol until the said fine be paid, and the court further orders that the sheriff of the borough [*if any, or as the case may be*], and all constables and officers of the peace of any county, borough, or place where the said *C. D.* may be found, shall take the said *C. D.* into custody and convey him to the said gaol, and there deliver him into the custody of the gaoler thereof, to undergo his said sentence; and the court further orders the said gaoler to receive the said *C. D.* into his custody, and that he shall be detained in the said gaol in pursuance of the said sentence.

A. B.

Signed the day of

A. B.

LVI. Such warrant may be made out and directed to the sheriff or other person having the execution of process of the High Court, as the case may be, and to all constables and officers of the peace of the county, borough, or place where the person adjudged guilty of contempt may be found, and such warrant shall be sufficient without further particularity, and shall and may be executed by the person to whom it is directed or any or either of them.

LVII. All interlocutory questions and matters, except as to the sufficiency of the security shall be heard and disposed of before a judge, who shall have the same control over the proceedings under the Municipal Corporations Act, 1882, as a judge in the ordinary proceedings of the High Court, and such questions and matters shall be heard and disposed of by any judge of the High Court.

LVIII. Notice of an application for leave to withdraw a petition shall be in writing, and signed by the petitioners or their agent.

It shall state the ground on which the application is intended to be supported.

The following form shall be sufficient:—

Municipal Corporations Act, 1882.

Borough of . Petition of [*state petitioners*] presented day of .

The petitioner proposes to apply to withdraw his petition upon the following ground [*here state the ground*], and prays that a day may be appointed for hearing his application.

Dated this day of

(Signed)

As to the withdrawal of a petition, see Municipal Corporations Act, 1882, s. 95, *ante*, p. 306. As to the statement of the parties negativing any corrupt arrangement, see *Johnson* v. *Rankin*, 5 C. P. D. 553; *Arnold* v. *Shaw*, 4 O'M. & H. 203; 9 T. L. R. 563; *Lichfield case*, 9 T. L. R. 92.

LIX. The notice of application for leave to withdraw shall be left at the Master's office.

LX. A copy of such notice of the intention of the petitioner to apply for leave to withdraw his petition shall be given by the petitioner to the respondent, and to the town clerk, who shall cause the same to be published in the borough to which it relates.

The following may be the form of such notice:—

Municipal Corporations Act, 1882.

In the election petition for in which is petitioner and respondent.

Notice is hereby given, that the above petitioner has on the day of lodged at the Master's office notice of an application to withdraw the petition, of which notice the following is a copy [*set it out*].

And take notice, that by the rule made by the judges, any person who might have been a petitioner in respect of the said election may, within five days after publication by the town clerk of this notice, give notice in writing of his intention on the hearing to apply for leave to be substituted as a petitioner. Rule 60.

(Signed)

LXI. Any person who might have been a petitioner in respect of the election to which the petition relates, may, within five days after such notice is published by the returning officer, give notice in writing, signed by him or on his behalf, to the Master of his intention to apply at the hearing to be snbstituted for the petitioner, but the want of such notice shall not defeat such application if in fact made at the hearing.

LXII. The time and place for hearing the application shall be fixed by a judge, and whether before the High Court, or before a judge, as he may deem advisable, but shall not be less than a week after the notice of the intention to apply has been given to the Master as hereinbefore provided, and notice of the time and place appointed for the hearing shall be given to such person or persons, if any, as shall have given notice to the Master of an intention to apply to be substituted as petitioners, and otherwise in such manner and at such time as the court or judge directs.

LXIII. Notice of abatement of a petition, by death of the petitioner or surviving petitioner, under section 96, sub-section (1), of the said Act, shall be given by the party or person interested in the same manner as a notice of an application to withdraw a petition, and the time within which application may be made to the High Court, or a judge thereof, by motion or summons at chambers, to be sustituted as a petitioner, shall be one calendar month, or such further time as upon consideration of any special circumstances the High Court or a judge thereof may allow.

LXIV. If the respondent dies, any person entitled to be a petitioner under the Act in respect of the election to which the petition relates, may give notice of the fact in the borough by causing such notice to be published in at least one newspaper circulating therein, if any, and by leaving a copy of such notice signed by him or on his behalf with the town clerk, and a like copy with the Master.

LXV. The manner of the respondent's giving notice that he does not intend to oppose the petition shall be by leaving notice thereof in writing at the office of the Master signed by the respondent.

LXVI. Upon such notice being left at the Master's office, the Master shall forthwith send a copy thereof by the post to the petitioner or his agent, and to the town clerk, who shall cause the same to be published in the borough.

LXVII. The time for applying to be admitted as a respondent in either of the events mentioned in the 97th section of the Act shall be within ten days after such notice is given as hereinbefore directed, or such further time as the High Court or a judge thereof may allow.

LXVIII. Costs shall be taxed by the Master, or at his request by any Master of the superior court upon the rule of court or judge's order by which the costs are payable, and costs when taxed may be recovered in like manner as if payable under a rule of court, judgment, or order of a judge in the ordinary proceedings in the High Court of Justice, or in case there be money

Rule 68. in the bank available for the purpose, then to the extent of such money by order of the Lord Chief Justice of England for the time being.

The office fees payable for inspection, office copies, enrolment, and other proceedings under the Act and these rules, shall be the same as those payable, if any, for like proceedings according to the present practice of the High Court of Justice.

LXIX. No proceedings under the Municipal Corporations Act, 1882, shall be defeated by any formal objection.

LXX. Any rule made or to be made in pursuance of the Act shall be published by a copy thereof being put up at the Master's office.

Dated the 17th day of April, 1883.

C. E. POLLOCK,
H. MANISTY,
HENRY C. LOPES,
The Judges for the time being on the rota for the trial of Parliamentary Election Petitions.

COUNTY ELECTORS ACT, 1888.

(51 Vict. Cap. 10.)

An Act to provide for the Qualification and Registration of Electors for the purposes of Local Government in England and Wales.

[16th May, 1888.]

Whereas it is expedient to make provision with respect to the qualification and registration of electors of any representative bodies (in this Act referred to as "county authorities") which may be established under any Act of the present session of Parliament for the purposes of local government in counties in England:

Be it therefore enacted by the Queen's most Excellent Majesty, by and with the advice and consent of the Lords Spiritual and Temporal, and Commons, in this present Parliament assembled, and by the authority of the same, as follows:

Short title and construction. 48 & 49 Vict. c. 15.

1. This Act may be cited as the County Electors Act, 1888.

The Registration Act, 1885, and the Parliamentary Registration Acts within the meaning of that Act, are in this Act referred to as the Registration of Electors Acts, and, together with this Act, may be cited as the Registration of Electors Acts, 1843 to 1888.

This Act shall be construed as one with the Registration of Electors Acts.

This Act deals with the registration of county electors, and was passed with a view to the establishment of county councils under the Local Government Act, 1888. It is amended in several points (noticed *infra*) by that Act.

Extension of burgess franchise to county electors outside municipal boroughs. 45 & 46 Vict. c. 50.

2.—(1.) For the purpose of the election of county authorities in England, the burgess qualification, that is to say, the qualification enacted by section nine of the Municipal Corporations Act, 1882, shall extend to every part of a county not within the limits of a borough, and a person possessing in any part of a county outside the limits of a borough such burgess qualification, shall be entitled to be registered under this Act as a county elector in the parish in which the qualifying property is situate.

See s. 9 of the Municipal Corporations Act, 1882, and the notes to that section, *ante*, p. 239.

(2.) Sections nine, thirty-one, thirty-three, and sixty-three of the Municipal Corporations Act, 1882, and any enactments of that or any other Act affecting the same, shall extend to so much

Sect. 2 (2).

of every county as is not comprised within the limits of a municipal borough in like manner as if they were herein re-enacted, with the substitution of "county" for "borough," and of "county elector" for "burgess," and with the other necessary modifications.

Section 9 of the Municipal Corporations Act, 1882, *ante*, deals with the qualification of burgesses and county electors; s. 31, *ante*, p. 270, and s. 33, *ante*, p. 271, contain some supplemental provisions relating to the same matter; and s. 63, *ante*, p. 290, provides that women shall have the right to vote.

Occupation of land of the value of 10*l*. to qualify.

3. Every person who is entitled to be registered as a voter in respect of a ten pounds occupation qualification within the meaning of the provisions of the Registration Act, 1885, which are set out in the schedule to this Act, shall be entitled to be registered as a county elector, and to be enrolled as a burgess in respect of such qualification, in like manner in all respects as if the sections of the Municipal Corporations Act, 1882, relating to a burgess qualification included the said ten pounds occupation qualification.

See the description of this qualification in the schedule, *post*. It has already been pointed out that this section creates an alternative qualification for a burgess or county elector. See notes (*c*) (*f*), *ante*, pp. 240, 242, as to the difference between the two qualifications.

Registration of county electors.

41 & 42 Vict. c. 26.

4.—(1.) The Registration of Electors Acts shall, so far as circumstances admit, apply to the enrolment of burgesses in a municipal borough to which the Parliamentary and Municipal Registration Act, 1878, does not apply, and to the registration of county electors within the meaning of this Act; and the lists of burgesses, and of county electors, and of occupation voters for parliamentary elections, shall, so far as practicable, be made out and revised together; and the Registration of Electors Acts shall accordingly—

(a.) Apply to every such municipal borough in like manner as if it were a borough to which sub-section two of section six of the Registration Act, 1885, applied (sub-section one of which section is hereby repealed), and revising assessors of such borough shall not be elected; and

(b.) Apply to every parish not situate in a municipal borough, in like manner as if such parish were a municipal borough to which the Parliamentary and Municipal Registration Act, 1878, applies, and the said lists of county electors and of occupation voters for parliamentary elections in such parish shall be made out in divisions, as provided in the said Act: Provided that a person whose name appears in any list of county electors or burgesses in a county may object to the name of any other person on a list of county electors or burgesses for a parish in a county, and may oppose the claim of a person to have his name inscribed in any such list. **Sect. 4 (1).**

Before the passing of this Act, in boroughs to which the 41 & 42 Vict. c. 26, did not apply, the lists of burgesses were revised by the mayor and the revising assessors in manner provided by the Municipal Corporations Act, 1882. See s. 29 of that Act, *ante*, p. 267. The effect of the above provision is that in every parish, whether in a borough or not, and in every borough, the lists of county electors and burgesses will be made out in manner provided by the 41 & 42 Vict. c. 26, and revised by the revising barrister together with the lists of parliamentary voters. The occupation voters lists will always be made out in the three divisions prescribed by that Act. Divisions 1 and 2 will form the list of parliamentary voters, and 1 and 3 the register of county electors. See the Local Government Act, 1888, s. 76, sub-s. (3), *ante*, p. 148.

(2.) In the construction of the Registration of Electors Acts for the purpose of their application to a parish not situate in a municipal borough, there shall be made the variations following, and such other variations as may be necessary for carrying into effect the application, that is to say :—

(a.) Where such parish is not within a parliamentary borough, "parliamentary county" shall be substituted for "parliamentary borough ;"

(b.) Where such parish is not within a parliamentary borough, the clerk of the peace shall perform the duties of and be substituted for the town clerk ; but any notice required to be given to the town clerk by section twenty-seven of the Parliamentary and Municipal Registration Act, 1878, relating to the withdrawal and revival of objections, shall be given to the overseers and not to the clerk of the peace ;

(c.) County elector shall be substituted for burgess ;

(d.) Section nine of the Parliamentary and Municipal Registration Act, 1878, shall not apply to any parish which is not wholly situate in an urban district ;

(e.) Where such parish is not within a parliamentary borough section twenty-one of the Parliamentary and Municipal Registration Act, 1878, shall not apply, and the lists and register of voters shall be made out alphabetically, but shall be framed in parts for polling districts and electoral divisions and for urban districts and for wards of urban and rural districts in such a manner that the parts may be conveniently compiled or put together to serve as lists for polling districts, and elections in urban districts and as electoral division or ward lists ;

The above provision is amended by the Local Government Act, s. 76, sub-s. (1), *ante*, p. 147. It is there provided that the provisions of the above

Sect. 4 (2).

NOTE.

section with respect to the framing of the lists and register of voters in parts shall extend to parishes situate within a parliamentary borough.

(f.) Where such parish is within a parliamentary borough—

This provision applies to a parish within a parliamentary borough, but it must not be forgotten that the whole section deals only with parishes not situate in municipal boroughs.

(i.) The overseers shall send to the clerk of the peace for the county two copies of the lists of voters at the same time at which they send copies to the town clerk; and

(ii.) The town clerk shall cause to be printed such number of copies of the revised lists as the clerk of the peace may require, and shall transmit the same to the clerk of the peace, who shall deal with the same as with other lists of county electors in his county; but

(iii.) Save as aforesaid, the clerk of the peace shall not act in relation to the registration of county electors in the said parish, and the town clerk of the parliamentary borough shall be the town clerk within the meaning of the Registration of Electors Acts and this Act in relation to such parish, and shall include in his precept to the overseers proper directions respecting the registration of the county electors within the meaning of this Act.

(g.) The lists of occupation voters and county electors shall be revised by the revising barrister for the parliamentary borough or county in which such parish is situate, and the revising barrister for revising the county electors lists for the whole or any part of an electoral division of any county shall, if so required by the county council, hold a court in that electoral division or at some convenient place in a division adjoining thereto.

(h.) The guardians of a union which is not wholly comprised in an urban district may, with the consent of the overseers of any parish or parishes within their union for which an assistant overseer has not been appointed, annually appoint a fit person to act as registration officer for such parish or parishes, and may remove any such person, and fill up any vacancy caused by death, resignation, or otherwise. Such registration officer shall perform all the duties of overseers of the parish or parishes for which he is appointed in respect of the registration of county electors and parliamentary voters, and the provisions of the Registration of Electors Acts relating to overseers, including those providing for penalties, shall apply to him accordingly: Sect. 4 (2).

Provided that his remuneration shall be fixed and paid by the guardians of the union, and charged on the poor rates of the parish or parishes for which he is appointed, and (if he acts for more than one parish) in proportion to the number of persons on the registers made during the year of his appointment of county electors and parliamentary voters for each parish.

(3.) Notwithstanding anything in this Act contained, where a municipal borough or an urban district is co-extensive with any electoral division or divisions of a parliamentary county, the lists of voters may be directed by the county authority to be made out according to the order in which the qualifying premises appear in the rate book, and section twenty-one of the Parliamentary and Municipal Registration Act, 1878, shall apply to such borough or urban district, and where lists of voters are so made out nothing in this Act shall require such part of the county register as consists of these lists to be arranged alphabetically.

The term "county authority" here means the county council. See the Local Government Act, s. 76, sub-s. (2), *ante*, p. 148.

Making out of lists and registers in the metropolis.

5. After the year one thousand eight hundred and eighty-eight, in every part of the metropolis, and in every part of a parliamentary borough, the whole or greater part of which is situate in the metropolis, the lists and registers of parliamentary voters, and of county electors, shall, unless the local authority otherwise direct, be arranged in the same order in which the qualifying premises appear in the rate book for the parish in which those premises are situate, or as nearly thereto as will cause those lists and registers to record the qualifying premises in successive order in the street or other place in which they are situate.

For the purpose of this section "metropolis" means the city of London and the parishes and places mentioned in Schedule (A), (B), and (C) of the Metropolis Management Act, 1855. 18 & 19 Vict. c. 120.

The local authority here referred to is the London County Council. See the Local Government Act, 1888, s. 3 (xii.), *ante*, p. 11.

Revision of electoral lists.

6.—(1.) The lists of parliamentary voters, and of burgesses, and of county electors, shall be revised between the eighth day of September and the twelfth day of October, both inclusive, and shall be revised as soon as possible after the seventh day of September, and the eighth day of September shall be substituted in the Acts relating to the registration of parliamentary voters for the fifteenth day of September; and the declarations under

Sect. 6 (1).

28 & 29 Vict. c. 36.
41 & 42 Vict. c. 26.

section ten of the County Voters Registration Act, 1865, and section twenty-four of the Parliamentary and Municipal Registration Act, 1878, shall be sent to the clerk of the peace or town clerk on or before the fifth day of September.

This provision alters and makes uniform in counties and boroughs the dates for holding revision courts.

The declarations under 28 & 29 Vict. c. 36, s. 10, are declarations by county voters relating to change of abode or to objections founded on the second column of the list: those under 41 & 42 Vict. c. 26, s. 24, are declarations by borough voters as to misdescription.

6 & 7 Vict. c. 18.

(2.) In sections sixty-two and sixty-three of the Parliamentary Voters Registration Act, 1843 (relating to appeals from revising barristers in England), the "Michaelmas sittings of the High Court of Justice" shall be substituted for "the Michaelmas term," and forthwith after the fourth day of the Michaelmas sittings a court or courts shall sit for the purpose of hearing such appeals, and those appeals shall be heard and determined continuously and without delay, and any statement by the barrister for the purpose of any such appeal made in pursuance of section forty-two of the said Act may be made at any time within ten days after the conclusion of the revision, so that it be made not less than four days before the first day of the said Michaelmas sittings, and the statement need not be read in open court, but shall be submitted to the appellant, who, if he approves the same, shall sign the same as directed by the said section, and return the same to the barrister.

Roll of county electors.

7.—(1.) The clerk of the peace of every county shall make up a register of all persons registered as burgesses or county electors in the county, both for the county and for each electoral division into which the county is divided for the purpose of election of the county authority, and such number of copies as the clerk of the peace may require of the list of burgesses as revised shall be delivered by the town clerk to such clerk of the peace for the purpose of making up such register.

It will be the duty of the clerk of the peace to prepare the division registers, and when the lists as revised do not correspond with the electoral divisions he must, presumably, do what is necessary to divide and arrange them.

45 & 46 Vict. c. 50.

(2.) The Registration of Electors Acts, and sections forty-five, forty-eight, and seventy-one of the Municipal Corporations Act, 1882, shall apply for the purposes of this section, with the substitution of the clerk of the peace for town clerk, and of county register and division register for burgess roll and ward roll respectively, and of electoral division for ward, and of county fund for borough fund. Sect. 7 (2)

See s. 45 of the Municipal Corporations Act, *ante*, p. 279; s. 48, *ante*, p. 283; and s. 71, *ante*, p. 293.

(3.) If district councils are established under any Act of the present session of Parliament, the clerk of every such council, not being the council of a borough, shall make up a register of all persons registered as county electors in his district, and where there are wards in a district, of all county electors in each ward, and he shall obtain from the clerk of the peace a sufficient number of copies of the list of the county electors so registered as may be required for the purpose of making up such register and supplying the same to the public, and the above-mentioned Acts and sections shall apply for that purpose, with the substitution of "clerk of the district council" for "town clerk," and of "district register" for "burgess roll" respectively.

This sub-section never came into force, district councils not being established in the session of 1888. They were, however, established by the Local Government Act, 1894, *post*.

(4.) Provided that nothing in this section shall prevent a county elector from being registered in more than one division register.

This prevents the application to county electors of the Municipal Corporations Act, 1882, s. 45, sub-s. (6), *ante*, p. 280. As to the effect of this sub-section, see note (*h*) on p. 281, *ante*, and the case of *Knill* v. *Towse* there referred to.

(5.) Where in pursuance of section four of the Registration Act, 1885, the revising barrister has power to erase the name of any person as a parliamentary voter from division one of the occupiers' list, such barrister, in lieu of erasing the name, shall place an asterisk or other mark against the name, and, in printing such list, the name shall be numbered consecutively with the other names, but an asterisk or other mark shall be printed against the name, and a person against whose name such asterisk or other mark is placed shall not be entitled to vote in respect of such entry at a parliamentary election, but shall have the same right of voting at an election of a county authority as he would have if no such mark were placed against his name. 48 & 49 Vict. c. 15.

See the alterations made in the above provisions with the object of distinguishing persons entitled to vote as parochial electors only, s. 44 of the Local Government Act, 1894, *post*.

(6.) If under any Act of the present session of Parliament establishing a council for a county any portion of another county

ect. 7 (6).

is added to that county for the purpose of such election, such portion of the county register as relates to the electors having qualifying property in the said part so added shall be deemed to be part of the county register of the county for which such council is elected, and the clerk of the peace and other officers shall take such steps as may be necessary for giving effect to these enactments.

The reference in the text is explained by s. 92, sub-s. (2), of the Local Government Act, *ante*, p. 168.

xpenses.

8.—(1.) All expenses properly incurred and all sums received in carrying into effect the provisions of this Act and the Registration of Electors Acts with respect to county electors,—

(a.) If incurred or received by overseers, shall be respectively paid and applied as expenses and receipts of overseers under the Registration of Electors Acts in the case of the lists of parliamentary voters ; and

(b.) If incurred or received by the clerk of the peace or town clerk, shall be paid out of or into the county or borough fund ; and such expenses shall include all proper and reasonable fees and charges made and charged by him for the trouble, care, and attention of such clerk in the performance of the services and duties imposed on him by the said provisions.

The 54 Vict. c. 18, provides that where a parish is situate in a parliamentary but not in a municipal borough, one half of the expense and receipts under the Registration Acts in respect of such parish shall, as from the passing of the County Electors Act, 1888, be defrayed out of and paid to the county fund, and the other half defrayed out of and paid to the poor rate.

emuneration revising rristers and ntribution y county ithorities.

9. Every barrister appointed to revise any list of voters under the Parliamentary Voters Registration Act, 1843, shall be paid the sum of two hundred and fifty guineas by way of remuneration to him, and in satisfaction of his travelling and other expenses, and every such barrister, after the termination of his last sitting, shall forward his appointment to the Commissioners of Her Majesty's Treasury, who shall make an order for the payment of the above sum to every such barrister.

& 50 Vict. 42.

The maximum amount to be paid to an additional barrister in pursuance of the Revising Barristers Act, 1886, shall not exceed the amount authorised by this section to be paid to a revising barrister.

The sums so paid to a revising barrister or an assistant barrister shall be payable partly out of moneys provided by Parliament and partly by the county authorities, as hereinafter mentioned.

(1.) There shall be annually paid by the county authority of every county out of the county fund into Her Majesty's Exchequer such sum as the Treasury certify to be one-half of the costs incurred for the payment of revising barristers at the then last revision of the list of parliamentary electors, burgesses, and county electors in that county. Sect. 9 (1).

(2.) The Treasury shall yearly ascertain the total costs of the revising barristers appointed for all the counties and boroughs on any circuit, and shall divide one-half of such cost among the counties comprised in such circuit in proportion to the number of burgesses and county electors in each county, and certify the amount which under such apportionment is due under this section from each county. The Treasury may vary such certificate if they think fit, but unless it is so varied the certificate shall be final.

(3.) So much of any Act as requires a payment out of the borough fund of any borough to a revising barrister, in respect of the revision of the burgess lists, shall be repealed, without prejudice to any payment or liability previously made or incurred.

It is provided by the Local Government Act, 1888, s. 76, sub-s. (4), *ante*, p. 148, that for the purposes of this section the county of Surrey and such portion of the county of London as is situated south of the Thames shall be deemed to be separate counties forming part of the south-eastern circuit; and such portion of the administrative county of London as is situate north of the Thames shall be deemed to form part of the county of Middlesex: and the county of Middlesex inclusive of that portion shall be a separate county on a circuit; but any sum payable by the London County Council in respect of either of the said portions of the county shall be paid for as a general county purpose.

10.—(1.) Section four of the Revising Barristers Act, 1886, is hereby repealed, and that Act, as amended by this Act, shall be perpetual. Perpetuation of 49 & 50 Vict. c. 42. Repeal of 6 & 7 Vict. c. 18, s. 59.

(2.) So long as a separate commission of assize is issued for the county of Surrey, that county shall be deemed to be a circuit within the meaning of section two, as well as of section one of the Revising Barristers Act, 1886.

(3.) An application to appoint an additional barrister under the said Act may be made at any time after the first day of September.

(4.) Section fifty-nine of the Parliamentary Voters Registration Act, 1843, is hereby repealed.

Sect. 11 (1).

Application of provisions of Act respecting county fund.

11.—(1.) In the event of a county authority being established under any Act of the present session, the provisions of this Act with respect to county authority, county, and county fund shall refer to the said county authority and to the county and county fund of such authority, and in case of any borough which, for the purposes of the said Act, is a county of itself, to the council of the borough and to the borough and borough fund.

48 & 49 Vict. c. 15.

(2.) In the event of a county authority not being established under any Act during the present session, the sums directed by this Act to be paid out of and into the county fund shall be paid by or under the direction of the local authority of every county quarter sessional area within the meaning of the Registration Act, 1885, in like manner as expenses or receipts of the clerk of the peace for such area under the Registration of Electors Acts, and by and under the direction of the council of every municipal borough which is also a parliamentary borough out of and into the borough fund, and the amount to be paid for revising barristers shall be apportioned between such quarter sessional areas and boroughs upon the principles above mentioned in this Act.

Separate list of persons residing within fifteen miles of county.

12. A list of persons occupying property in a county, and residing within fifteen miles, but more than seven miles from the county, shall be made out in accordance with section forty-nine of the Municipal Corporations Act, 1882, and that section shall apply as if it were herein re-enacted, with the substitution of "county" for "borough," and of "county elector" for "burgess," and of "clerk of the peace" for "town clerk."

The Local Government Act, s. 76, sub-s. (6), *ante*, p. 150, provides that nothing in the above section applies to any person occupying property in a borough. The meaning of these provisions is stated in the note to s. 49 of the Municipal Corporations Act, 1882, *ante*, p. 283.

Precepts by clerk of the peace.

13. All precepts, notices, and forms required for the purposes of the Registration of Electors Acts shall be altered in such manner as may be declared by Her Majesty in Council to be necessary for carrying into effect this Act, and clerks of the peace and town clerks shall alter their precepts and forms accordingly, and if clerks of the peace or town clerks have sent out precepts to the overseers before the passing of this Act, they shall send to them such supplemental precepts as are necessary or desirable for instructing them to carry into effect this Act.

The Local Government Act, s. 76, sub-s. (7), *ante*, p. 150, contains a similar provision giving power to the Queen in Council from time to time to alter the instructions, precepts, etc.

See now the Registration Order, 1895, which was published in the *London Gazette* of March 19th, 1895, and will be found in the S. R. O., 1895, p. 274.

Definitions.

14. In this Act, unless the context otherwise requires,—

The expressions "urban district" and "rural district" respectively mean an urban or rural sanitary district, also any urban or rural district under any Act of the present session of Parliament;

The expression "clerk of the peace" means, in the event of the establishment of a county authority, the person acting as clerk of that authority, and such person shall act as clerk of the peace throughout the whole county of such authority, both for the purposes of this Act and of the Registration of Electors Acts; subject nevertheless—

(a.) To the provisions of the Registration Act, 1885, respecting the case of any parliamentary county extending into more county quarter sessional areas than one, and

(b.) To the proviso that where at the passing of this Act any clerk of the peace acts as clerk of the peace under the Registration of Electors Acts he shall continue so to act, but shall act as deputy of the person acting as clerk of the peace by virtue of this Act.

Transitory provisions as to the year 1888.

15. In the year one thousand eight hundred and eighty-eight, notwithstanding anything in this Act or the enactments applied by this Act, the revision of the lists of parliamentary voters and county electors may be later than the twelfth day of October, so that it be not later than the thirty-first day of October, and the register of county electors shall be completed on or before the thirty-first day of December in the said year, and shall come into operation on the first day of January, one thousand eight hundred and eighty-nine, and shall continue in operation until the next register of county electors comes into operation.

In the year one thousand eight hundred and eighty-eight, notwithstanding anything in this Act or the enactments thereby applied, the clerk of the peace in a county may, if he thinks fit, instead of directing the occupiers' list to be made out in three divisions as provided by the Registration of Electors Acts, direct the overseers to make supplemental lists containing the names which would otherwise be contained in division two and division three of the occupiers' list respectively, and the names so contained in the supplemental list corresponding to division two shall be struck by the revising barrister out of division one of the list, and the supplemental list corresponding to division two or division three shall be treated as if it were division two or three of the said list, as the case may be.

Schedule.

SCHEDULE.

Registration Act, 1885.

Definition of Ten Pounds Occupation Qualification.

Ten pounds occupation qualification.

A person entitled to be registered as a voter in respect of a ten pounds occupation qualification in a borough, municipal or parliamentary—

(a.) Must during the whole twelve months immediately preceding the fifteenth day of July have been an occupier as owner or tenant of some land or tenement in a parish [or township] of the clear yearly value of not less than ten pounds; and

(b.) Must have resided in or within seven miles of the borough during six months immediately preceding the fifteenth day of July; and

(c.) Such person, or some one else, must during the said twelve months have been rated to all poor rates made in respect of such land or tenement; and

(d.) All sums due in respect of the said land or tenement on account of any poor rate made and allowed during the twelve months immediately preceding the fifth day of January next before the registration, or on account of any assessed taxes due before the said fifth day of January, must have been paid on or before the twentieth day of July.

If two or more persons jointly are such occupiers as above mentioned, and the value of the land or tenement is such as to give ten pounds or more for each occupier, each of such occupiers is entitled to be registered as a voter.

If a person has occupied in the borough different lands or tenements of the requisite value in immediate succession during the said twelve months, he is entitled in respect of the occupation thereof to be registered as a voter in the parish [or township] in which the last occupied land or tenement is situate.

PART III.

Statutes subsequent to the Local Government Act, 1888, affecting County Councils.

SEA FISHERIES REGULATION ACT, 1888.

(51 & 52 VICT. CAP. 54) (*a*).

An Act for the Regulation of the Sea Fisheries of England and Wales.
[24th December, 1888.]

* * * * *

1.—(1.) The Board of Trade may from time to time on the application of a county council or borough council, by order,

Establishment of sea fisheries districts and local fisheries committees.

(a) create a sea fisheries district comprising any part of the sea within which Her Majesty's subjects have by international law the exclusive right of fishing, either with or without any part of the adjoining coast of England and Wales; and

(b) define the limits of the district, and the area chargeable with any expenses under this Act; and

(c) provide for the constitution of a local fisheries committee for the regulation of the sea fisheries carried on within the district;

and may from time to time on like application by subsequent order vary any order made under this section, or unite two or more districts or parts of districts into a separate district, or dissolve any district that may have been formed.

(2.) The local fisheries committee for a sea fisheries district shall be a committee of a county council or borough council, or, if two or more councils appear to be interested, a joint committee of those councils, with the addition in each case of such members representing the fishing interests of the district, including members representing any board of salmon conservators having jurisdiction within the district, as may be directed by the order creating the district, such number of fishery members not being in the aggregate less than the number of members of the county or borough councils provided by the order creating the district. The fishery members shall hold office for the same time as the members appointed by the county or borough council or councils, and any vacancy amongst the fishery members which may arise in the interval shall be filled up

(*a*) Under this Act a county council may be empowered to appoint or join in appointing a local fisheries committee for the regulation of sea fisheries within a fisheries district created by Order of the Board of Trade. This Act is amended by Part II. of 54 & 55 Vict. c. 37, and by 57 & 58 Vict. c. 26, which enactments, together with this Act, are comprised in the title "The Sea Fisheries Regulation Acts, 1888 to 1894." The amending Acts are set out *post*.

Sect. 1 (2).

by a representative of the fishing interest in respect of which it occurs. The members representing a board of salmon conservators shall be appointed by that board.

(3.) The law relating to committees and joint committees of county councils (*b*) shall, subject to the provisions of the order constituting a local fisheries committee, apply to the local fisheries committee in like manner as if the powers and duties of that committee were powers and duties transferred by the Local Government Act, 1888, to the council or councils represented on the committee and delegated to the committee by the said council or councils, and as if any borough council represented on the committee were a county council.

51 & 52 Vict. c. 41.

(4.) Every order made by the Board of Trade under this section shall be laid for thirty days before both Houses of Parliament while in session, and if either House within that period resolves that the whole or any part of the order ought not to be in force the same shall not have any force, without prejudice nevertheless to the making of any other order in its place. Subject to any such resolution every order so made shall come into force at the expiration of the thirty days aforesaid.

(5.) In case a county council or borough council to whom application has been made by not less than twenty inhabitant ratepayers interested in sea fisheries, refuse or neglect to apply to the Board of Trade to create a sea fisheries district for the space of six months from the date of the application, the persons making such application shall, within twelve months from the date thereof, be entitled to apply to the Board of Trade for an order establishing such sea fisheries district, and the Board of Trade shall, unless the council can show to their satisfaction that such order should not be made, proceed as if an application had been made by the council.

(6.) Before making any order creating a sea fisheries district the Board of Trade shall cause the draft of such order to be locally published in such manner as they direct, and shall, if any objections are made to such orders, or any of the provisions thereof, cause such local inquiry to be held as may in their opinion be required. Due notice of such inquiry shall be given by advertisement or otherwise, and the report of the person holding such inquiry shall, if the order is made, be laid with the order before both Houses of Parliament.

Byelaws for regulation of sea fisheries.

2.—(1.) A local fisheries committee for a sea fisheries district may from time to time, subject to such regulations as may be made in that behalf by the Board of Trade, make bye-laws (*c*) to be

(*b*) As to committees and joint committee of county councils, see ss. 28 (2), 81, and 82 of the Local Government Act, 1888, and s. 22 of the Municipal Corporations Act, 1882, *ante*, pp. 64, 155—158, and 260. The form of financial statement to be submitted by fisheries committees is prescribed by an order of the Local Government Board, January 26th, 1893; S. R. O., 1893, p. 67.

(*c*) As to the necessity for confirmation of these bye-laws, see s. 4, *infra*. The purposes for which the bye-laws may be made are extended by 54 & 55 Vict. c. 37, s. 7, and 57 & 58 Vict. c. 26, *post*.

observed within their district, for all or any of the following purposes, namely,— Sect. 2 (1).

(a.) For restricting or prohibiting, either absolutely or subject to such regulations as may be provided by the bye-laws, any method of fishing for sea fish or the use of any instrument of fishing for sea fish, and for determining the size of mesh, form, and dimensions of any instrument of fishing for sea fish;

(b.) For constituting within their district any district of oyster cultivation for the purposes of section four of the Fisheries (Oyster, Crab, and Lobster) Act, 1877 (*d*); 40 & 41 Vict. c. 42.

(c.) For directing that the proviso to section eight of the Fisheries (Oyster, Crab, and Lobster) Act, 1877, which permits edible crabs in certain conditions or under a certain size to be taken by or be in the possession of any person if those crabs are intended for bait for fishing, shall not apply (*e*);

(d.) For repealing or amending any order made under section ten of the Fisheries (Oyster, Crab, and Lobster) Act, 1877, or under the Fisheries (Oyster, Crab, and Lobster) Act (1877) Amendment Act, 1884 (*f*); 47 & 48 Vict. c. 26.

(*d*) Section 4 of 40 & 41 Vict. c. 42, makes it an offence to sell, expose, consign, or buy for sale, oysters during certain seasons of the year; but a person is not to be guilty of an offence under that section if he satisfies the Court that the oysters alleged to have been sold, etc., in contravention of the section: "(1) Were taken within the waters of some foreign state; or (2) were preserved in tins or otherwise cured; or (3) were intended for the purpose of oyster cultivation within the same district in which the oysters were taken, or were taken from any place for cultivation with the sanction of the Board of Trade; and for this purpose the Thames estuary, bounded by a line drawn from Oxford Ness to the North Foreland, shall be deemed to be a district, and also any other area for the time being constituted a district for the purposes of this section by an Order of the Board of Trade; and also where the place at which the oysters are taken is not within any such district as aforesaid, so much of the area within ten miles of the said place where the oysters are taken as is not included in any other such district as aforesaid, and the Board of Trade may from time to time make, and when made, revoke or vary an order for the purposes of this section." A local fisheries committee may, under the provision in the text, constitute within their district a district of oyster cultivation for the purposes of paragraph (3), above set out.

A local fisheries committee may enforce within their district the provisions of the 40 & 41 Vict. c. 42, and of any other Act relating to sea fisheries; see 54 & 55 Vict. c. 37, s. 9. *post.*

(*e*) Section 8 of the Act referred to, makes it an offence to take, have in possession, sell, or expose, consign, or buy for sale, edible crabs under certain dimensions and in certain conditions; the nature of the exceptions contained in the proviso is sufficiently stated in the text. The local fisheries committee may by their bye-laws abolish the exception in their district. A similar power was given to the Board of Trade as to any area named in their Order under 47 & 48 Vict. c. 26; but this Act is repealed by s. 16, *infra.*

(*f*) Section 10 of 40 & 41 Vict. c. 42, empowers the Board of Trade by order to restrict or prohibit, either entirely or subject to any exceptions and regulations, the fishing for and taking of edible crabs and lobsters, or either of them, or any description of them or either of them, within the area named in the Order during such period of years, or during such period either in every year, or in such number of years as may be limited by the Order, and may by the order provide for enforcing the order, and any prohibition, restriction, or

Sect. 2 (1).

(e.) For prohibiting or regulating the deposit or discharge of any solid or liquid substance detrimental to sea fish or sea fishing; and

(f.) For repealing or amending any bye-law made in pursuance of this Act.

(2.) A bye-law made in pursuance of this Act may provide for its application either to the whole or any specified part or parts of the district for which it is made, and either during the whole or any specified part or parts of the year.

Penalties for breach of bye-laws.

3. A local fisheries committee may, by their bye-laws, impose as penalties for the breach of any bye-law fines not exceeding for any one offence the sum of 20*l.*, and in the case of a continuing offence the additional sum of 10*l.* for every day during which the offence continues, and in any case forfeiture of any fishing instrument used or sea fish taken in contravention of, or found in the possession of a person contravening, any bye-law; and any such penalties may be recovered and enforced on summary conviction (*g*).

Confirmation of bye-laws.

4.—(1.) A bye-law made in pursuance of this Act shall not be of any validity until it has been confirmed by the Board of Trade.

(2.) The Board of Trade may, if they think fit, before confirming a bye-law made in pursuance of this Act, cause such local inquiry as they think fit to be held with respect to the byelaw, and may, in any case, confirm any such byelaw, either without modifications, or with such modifications as may be assented to by the local fisheries committee.

Copies and evidence of bye-laws.

5.—(1.) The local fisheries committee shall cause copies of all bye-laws made by them under this Act, and for the time being in force, to be kept posted up in some conspicuous place or places within their district, and shall supply copies of all such byelaws to any applicant, on payment of a sum not exceeding one penny for each copy.

(2.) The production of a copy of any bye-law made in pursuance of this Act, purporting to be signed by a secretary or assistant secretary of the Board of Trade, shall be conclusive evidence of the bye-law and of the due making and confirmation thereof.

Appointment and powers of fishery officers.

6.—(1.) Subject to any restrictions or conditions as to expenditure made by the council or councils by whom a local fisheries committee

---

regulation contained therein by fines not exceeding twenty pounds for each offence. Such an order may from time to time be varied or revoked by a subsequent order, and nothing in such order shall apply to a several right of fishery. Such an order may be repealed or amended by bye-laws under the provisions in the text, and such bye-laws may also repeal or amend an order under the repealed Act, 47 & 48 Vict. c. 26, as to which, see note (*e*), *ante*.

(*g*) As to offences committed on the coast or at sea beyond the ordinary jurisdiction of a court of summary jurisdiction, see 54 & 55 Vict. c. 37, s. 8, *post*.

is appointed (*h*) the committee may appoint such fishery officers as they deem expedient for the purpose of enforcing the observance within their district of bye-laws made by the committee: Provided that nothing in this section shall exempt the coastguard and Admiralty officers from their statutory duty in enforcing the laws and regulations affecting vessels engaged in sea fishing. **Sect. 6 (1).**

(2.) For the purpose of enforcing those bye-laws every such fishery officer may within the limits of the district, or of any adjoining sea fisheries district or district under the jurisdiction of salmon conservators, or of a harbour authority,—

(a.) Stop and search any vessel or vehicle used within the district in fishing or in conveying either fish or any substance the deposit or discharge of which is prohibited or regulated by any such bye-laws; and

(b.) Search and examine all instruments used in catching or carrying fish; and

(c.) Seize any sea fish or instrument liable to be forfeited in pursuance of any such bye-laws.

(3.) If any person without reasonable excuse (proof whereof shall lie on him) refuses to allow any such officer to exercise the powers conferred upon him by this Act, or resists or obstructs any such officer in the performance of his duty, he shall for every such offence be liable on summary conviction to a fine not exceeding five pounds.

(4.) For the enforcement of the provisions of any such bye-laws every such officer shall be deemed to be a constable, and to have the same powers and privileges and be subject to the same liabilities as a constable duly appointed has and is subject to in his constablewick at common law or by statute.

(5.) A local fisheries committee may, with the consent of any board of salmon conservators, appoint as an officer of the committee any officer of the board; and a board of salmon conservators may, with the consent of a local fisheries committee, appoint as an officer of the board any officer of the committee.

Power to enter suspected places.

7. It shall be lawful for any justice of the peace upon information on oath that there is probable cause to suspect any breach of any bye-law made under this Act to have been committed on any premises, or that any sea fish or instrument liable to be forfeited in pursuance of any such bye-law is concealed on any premises, by warrant under his hand and seal to authorize and empower any fishery officer appointed under this Act, or any police officer, to

(*h*) Restrictions and conditions as to expenditure in connection with the appointment of a particular officer cannot be made after the officer has been appointed. *Semble*, that when a local fisheries committee has been appointed by more councils than one, it is open to any one of such councils to make restrictions or conditions as to expenditure under this section, without the assent of the other councils. *R.* v. *Plymouth* (*Mayor*, *etc.*, *cf*), [1896] 1 Q. B. 158; 65 L. J. Q. B. 258; 44 W. R. 620.

Sect. 7.

enter the premises for the purpose of detecting the offence or the concealed fish or instrument at such time or times in the day or night as in the warrant may be mentioned, and to seize any such fish or instruments which may be found on the premises: Provided that the warrant shall not continue in force for more than one week from the date thereof.

Returns by local fisheries committees.

8. Every local fisheries committee shall collect such statistics relating to the sea fisheries within the district of the committee and make such returns to the Board of Trade as to the proceedings of the committee under this Act, and as to the sea fisheries aforesaid as the Board of Trade may reasonably require: Provided that any expenses which the local fisheries committee may be required by the Board of Trade to incur in the collection of statistics shall be borne by moneys to be provided by Parliament.

Annual meeting of representatives of local committees.

9. The Board of Trade shall convene a meeting composed of not less than one representative selected by each of the local fisheries committees at least once in each year, to confer with the heads of the Fishery Department of the Board of Trade, and for consultative purposes on matters relating to this Act.

Expenses of committee.

10. The expenses of a local fisheries committee, so far as payable by a county council, shall, according as is provided by the order providing for the constitution of the local fisheries committee, be general or special expenses within the meaning of the Local Government Act, 1888 (*i*), and if special expenses shall be charged in manner directed by the order, and the expenses of the committee, so far as payable by the council of a borough, shall be paid out of the borough rate or borough fund.

51 & 52 Vict. c. 41.

Contents of order for constitution of committee.

11. An order providing for the constitution of a local fisheries committee may contain such regulations consistent with this Act with respect to the number and mode of appointment of the members of the committee, and with respect to other matters relating to the constitution of the committee, as may seem expedient to the Board of Trade.

Relations of local fisheries committees to conservators under Salmon Acts and harbour authorities.

12.—(1.) Where a proposed sea fisheries district will adjoin or overlap the district of a board of salmon conservators, the Board of Trade shall, by the order defining the limits of the sea fisheries district, draw a line at or near the mouth of every river or stream flowing into the sea, or into any estuary within those limits, or at the option of the Board of Trade at or near the mouth of any estuary within those limits, and the sea fisheries district shall not extend into any such river, stream, or estuary above that line; but the order may provide that with respect to any such river, stream, or

(*i*) As to general and special expenses of a county council, see s. 68 of the Local Government Act, 1888, *ante*, p. 130. As to contributions to expenses of salmon conservators under this Act, see note to s. 12 (1), *infra*.

estuary, or any area subject to a bye-law made under section thirty-nine, sub-section eight, of the Salmon Fishery Act, 1873, the conservators shall have the powers of a local fisheries committee (*k*). Sect. 12 (1).

(2.) Where an area is under the jurisdiction of salmon conservators, or of a harbour authority, and an application for the creation of a sea fisheries district comprising that area or any part thereof has not been made or has been refused, the Board of Trade may, if they think fit, by order, confer on the conservators or harbour authority the powers of a local fisheries committee with respect to that area, and may vary or rescind any such order if the area, or any part thereof, is subsequently comprised in a sea fisheries district.

(3.) A local fisheries committee shall not have jurisdiction within any area for the time being subject to a bye-law made under section thirty-nine, sub-section eight, of the Salmon Fishery Act, 1873 (*l*).

(4.) Where salmon conservators or a harbour authority have the powers of a local fisheries committee in pursuance of this section, those powers shall be exercised subject to the same conditions as if exercised by a local fisheries committee, and the provisions of this Act shall apply in the case of bye-laws made or officers appointed in exercise of any such powers as if the byelaws were made or the officers appointed by a local fisheries committee.

Saving for several fisheries, etc.

13. Nothing in this Act shall authorize a local fisheries committee to make any bye-law

(a) prejudicially affecting any right of several fishery, or any right on, to, or over any portion of the seashore, where any such right is enjoyed by any person under any local or special Act of Parliament, or any Royal charter, letters patent, prescription, or immemorial usage, without the consent of that person ; or

(b) affecting any bye-law made, or to be made, by a board of salmon conservators, and for the time being in force within the district of the committee, or restricting the power of a board of salmon conservators to make any such bye-law; or

(c) affecting any power of a sanitary or other local authority to discharge sewage in pursuance of any power given by a general or local Act of Parliament, or by a Provisional Order confirmed by Parliament.

(*k*) Under s. 39 (8) of the Salmon Fishery Act, 1873 (36 & 37 Vict. c. 71), a board of conservators may make bye-laws (subject to confirmation), "to prohibit the use of nets within a certain distance of the mouth of any river, and of the point of confluence of rivers in any part of the district (not being a several fishery), and to erect and fix posts, buoys, and landmarks to indicate such distances respectively."

The 54 & 55 Vict. c. 37, s. 10, *post*, empowers a county or borough council to pay or contribute to any expenses incurred by salmon conservators under this Act.

(*l*) See the preceding note.

Sect. 14.

Definitions.

14. For the purposes of this Act—

The expression "county council" shall mean a county council established under the Local Government Act, 1888.

The expression "borough council" shall mean the council of any municipal borough containing, according to the census of one thousand eight hundred and eighty-one, a population of not less than twenty thousand.

The expression "sea fish" shall not include salmon as defined by any Act relating to salmon, but, save as aforesaid, shall mean fish of all kinds found in the sea, and shall also include lobsters, crabs, shrimps, prawns, oysters, mussels, cockles and other kinds of crustaceans and shell fish.

The expression "sea" includes the coast up to high-water mark.

The expression "vessel" includes ship, boat, lighter, and craft of every kind, whether stationary or navigated by steam or otherwise.

The expression "person" includes any body of persons corporate or unincorporate.

The expression "fishing interests" includes all persons interested in fisheries, either as owners of fisheries or interests therein, fishermen, fishing-boat owners, smack owners, fish curers, fish merchants, or otherwise, and any board of salmon conservators.

The expression "salmon conservators" means conservators under the Salmon and Freshwater Fisheries Acts, 1861 to 1886, or any of them.

The expression "harbour authority" means any body corporate, persons, or person being or claiming to be proprietors or proprietor of, or entrusted with the duty of improving, managing, maintaining, or regulating any harbour.

Extent of Act.

15. This Act shall not extend to Scotland or Ireland.

Repeal.

16. The Acts described in the schedule to this Act are hereby repealed, without prejudice to any order made or thing done under any such Act before the passing of this Act.

Short title.

17. This Act may be cited as the Sea Fisheries Regulation Act, 1888.

SCHEDULE.

Acts Repealed.

Session and Chapter.	Short Title.
44 & 45 Vict. c. 11. -	The Sea Fisheries (Clam and Bait Beds) Act, 1881.
47 & 48 Vict. c. 26. -	The Fisheries (Oyster, Crab, and Lobster) Act (1877) Amendment Act, 1884.

WEIGHTS AND MEASURES ACT, 1889.

(52 & 53 VICT. CAP. 21) (*m*).

An Act for amending the Law relating to Weights and Measures, and for other purposes connected therewith [26th July, 1889.]

WHEREAS it is expedient to amend the Weights and Measures Act, 1878 (herein-after referred to as the principal Act), and the law relating to the sale of coal: 41 & 42 Vict. c. 49.

* * *

PART I.

Weights and Measures.

1.—(1.) Every weighing instrument used for trade (*n*) shall be verified and stamped by an inspector of weights and measures with a stamp of verification under this Act. Verification of weighing instruments.

(2.) Every person who, after the expiration of twelve months from the commencement of this Act, uses, or has in his possession for use, for trade (*n*) any weighing instrument not stamped as required by this Act, shall be liable to a fine not exceeding two pounds, or in the case of a second offence five pounds.

(3.) The power of making bye-laws conferred by section fifty-three of the principal Act shall extend to the making of bye-laws for giving effect to this section (*o*).

(*m*) The county council is the local authority for the execution of the Acts relating to weights and measures in their county. Local Government Act, 1888, s. 3 (xiii.), and notes, *ante*, p. 12. This Act is an amendment of the principal Act, the Weights and Measures Act, 1878 (41 & 42 Vict. c. 49), and is to be construed as one with that Act; see s. 34, *infra*. The subject is also dealt with by three subsequent Acts, the 55 & 56 Vict. c. 18, which authorizes county and borough councils to purchase franchises of weights and measures, the 56 & 57 Vict. c. 19, which deals with the contributions of certain boroughs towards the expenses of executing the Weights and Measures Acts, and the 60 & 61 Vict. c. 46, which legalizes the use of weights and measures of the metric system. These Acts are set out *post*.

(*n*) Trade is defined by s. 19 of the Weights and Measures Act, 1878, as follows:—"Every contract, bargain, sale, or dealing made or had in the United Kingdom for any work, goods, wares, or merchandise, or other thing which has been or is to be done, sold, delivered, carried, or agreed for by weight or measure, shall be deemed to be made and had according to one of the imperial weights or measures ascertained by this Act, or to some multiple or part thereof, and if not so made or had shall be void; and all tolls and duties charged or collected according to weight or measure shall be charged and collected according to one of the imperial weights or measures ascertained by this Act, or to some multiple or part thereof. Such contract, bargain, sale, dealing, and collection of tolls and duties as is in this section mentioned, is in this Act referred to under the term 'trade.'"

A lead manufacturer and smelter had upon her works a beam scale used for the purpose of checking the weight of the produce of the works. Invoices bearing the weights so obtained were sent to the purchasers of the lead and the railway company who carried it. *Held*, that the scale was used for trade, and must be stamped under the provision in the text. *Crick* v. *Theobald*, 64 L. J. M. C. 216; 72 L. T. (N.S.), 807; 59 J. P. 502; 11 T. L. R. 445. And see the cases cited in the note to s. 3, *infra*.

(*o*) Section 53 of the Weights and Measures Act, 1878, provides that a local authority, from time to time, with the approval of the Board of Trade, may

Sect. 1 (4).

(4.) Section thirty-two of the principal Act shall apply to weighing instruments in like manner as it applies to weights and measures (*p*).

Local verification of metric weights and measures.

2. The Board of Trade may, if they think fit, at the expense of the local authority, deposit with any inspector of weights and measures copies of any of the metric standards in their custody, and cause to be verified with any copy so deposited any metric weights and measures which can under section thirty-eight of the principal Act be compared with the metric standards in their custody (*q*).

Amendment of 41 & 42 Vict. c. 49, ss. 25 and 26.

3. The fine for a second or subsequent offence under section twenty-five or section twenty-six of the principal Act shall be a sum not exceeding twenty pounds, and the provisions of the said section twenty-six with respect to forfeiture shall apply to weighing instruments in like manner as they apply to weights, measures, scales, balances, and steelyards (*r*).

---

make, revoke, alter, and add to bye-laws for regulating the comparison with the local standards of such authority, and the verification and stamping of weights and measures in use in their county or borough, and for regulating the local comparison of the local standards of such authority, and generally for regulating the duties under that Act of the inspectors appointed by the local authority, or of any of those inspectors. Such bye-laws may impose fines not exceeding twenty shillings for the breach of any bye-law, to be recovered on summary conviction. The Board of Trade, before approving any such bye-laws, shall cause them to be published in such manner as they think sufficient for giving notice thereof to all persons interested.

(*p*) Section 32 of the Act of 1878 imposes penalties upon persons forging or counterfeiting stamps used for stamping under the Act any measure or weight, or wilfully increasing or diminishing a weight so stamped, or knowingly using, selling, etc., a measure or weight with a forged or counterfeit stamp thereon, or a weight so increased or diminished.

(*q*) Section 38 of the Act of 1878 enables the Board of Trade, if they think fit, to cause to be compared with the metric standards in their custody and verified all metric weights and measures which are submitted to them for the purpose, and are of such shape and construction as may be from time to time in that behalf directed by the Board, and which the Board are satisfied are intended to be used for the purpose of science or of manufacture, or for any lawful purpose not being for the purpose of trade within the meaning of that Act. But see as to this section 60 & 61 Vict. c. 46, s. 2, sub-s. (2), *post*.

(*r*) Section 25 of the Act of 1878 imposes a penalty (not exceeding 5*l*., or in case of a second offence, 10*l*.) upon any person using or having in his possession for use for trade any false or unjust weight, measure, scale, balance, steelyard, or weighing machine. Section 26 imposes the like penalties upon every person wilfully committing or party to a fraud in the use of any of the instruments above mentioned. In either case, the weight, measure, scale, balance or steelyard is liable to be forfeited, but there is no such provision as to weighing machines. By the text, the maximum fine for a second or subsequent offence is raised from 10*l*. to 20*l*., and the provisions of s. 26 as to forfeiture are extended to weighing instruments, and see the next section of this Act.

Where an information under s. 25 was laid against a postmaster, who traded as a baker on the same premises, for having an unjust scale in his possession for use for trade, the scale being the property of the Crown and belonging to the Post Office, a prohibition was granted on the ground that the Act did not apply to scales the property of the Crown. *R.* v. *Kent* (*Justices of*), 24 Q. B. D. 181; 59 L. J. M. C. 51; 62 L. T. (N.S.) 114; 38 W. R. 253; 54 J. P. 453; 17 Cox C. C. 61. Where a seller of milk sent it by train in his

Sect. 4.

4. Where a person is convicted under any section of the principal Act or this Act of a second or subsequent offence, and the court by which he is convicted is of opinion that such offence was committed with intend to defraud, he shall be liable, in addition to or in lieu of any fine, to be imprisoned with or without hard labour for a term not exceeding two months.

Liability to imprisonment in cases of fraud.

5. The following sections of the principal Act are hereby repealed:

Repeal of 41 & 42 Vict. c. 49, ss. 16, 46.

(a.) Section sixteen, relating to the measure of capacity for goods formerly sold by heaped measure;

(b.) Section forty-six, giving power to stamp measures made partly of metal and partly of glass.

6. The Board of Trade shall from time to time cause such new denominations of standards for the measurement of electricity, temperature, pressure, or gravities as appear to them to be required for use for trade to be made and duly verified, and those new denominations of standards when approved by Her Majesty in Council shall, whether derived from imperial or from other standards, be Board of Trade standards, in like manner as if they were mentioned in the Second Schedule to the principal Act.

New denominations of standards.

7. Any local authority may provide for the use of their officers working standards of measure and weight, and scale-beams of such material and in such form as the Board of Trade may approve, and those standards may, if verified in such manner as the Board of Trade from time to time direct, be used for the inspection and verification of weights and measures as if they were local standards.

Working standards.

8.—(1.) The Board of Trade may, on the comparison and verification of weights and measures, not being standards for the use of a local authority or their officers, and not being coin weights, and on the examination or testing of weighing or measuring instruments, charge and take such fees as may from time to time be approved by the Treasury.

Power for Board of Trade to take fees.

(2.) The fees taken under this section may be applied in such manner and to such extent as the Treasury may from time to time direct in aid of money provided by Parliament for expenses of the Board of Trade under this Act, and if and as far as not so applied shall be paid into the Exchequer.

9.—(1.) Every local authority within the meaning of this Act, and every other person or authority having power to appoint inspectors of weights and measures, shall, with the approval of the Board of

General regulations.

---

own churns, which were, by agreement with the railway company, fitted with gauges to indicate the number of gallons they contained, and the purchaser was entitled to have the churns regauged when he deemed it necessary, it was held that the churns were measures which the seller had in his possession for use for trade, and that he was properly convicted under s. 25, two of the churns having been proved to contain less than the quantity they purported to contain: *Harris* v. *London County Council*, [1895] 1 Q. B. 240; 64 L. J. M. C. 81; 71 L. T. (N.S.) 844; 11 T. L. R. 113; 18 Cox C. C. 65.

Sect. 9 (1). Trade, make for the guidance of the inspectors appointed or employed by that authority or person, and may from time to time with the like approval amend or rescind general regulations with respect to—

(a.) The procedure to be observed in the verification and stamping of weights, measures, and weighing and measuring instruments, including the prohibition of stamping in cases where the material or mode of construction appears likely to facilitate the commission of fraud; and

(b.) The inspection of weights, measures, and weighing and measuring instruments.

(2.) If any such authority or person, on being required by the Board of Trade to make, amend, or rescind any general regulations in pursuance of this section fails to comply with the requirement, the Board of Trade may make, amend, or rescind such regulations, and any regulations so made or amended shall have effect as if made by that authority or person.

(3.) All regulations made under this section shall be duly observed and kept published in such manner as the Board of Trade from time to time shall direct.

Provision as to local inquiries.

10.—(1.) The Board of Trade may from time to time appoint an officer to hold a local inquiry with respect to the administration of the law relating to weights and measures within the jurisdiction of any local authority.

(2.) The appointment may be made either on the application of the local authority or without such application, but with the concurrence of the Treasury.

(3.) The officer so appointed shall visit the office of the local inspector of weights and measures, and shall, among other things, inquire into the procedure observed in the verification and inspection of weights, measures, and weighing instruments within that jurisdiction; and, on the completion of the local inquiry, shall report to the Board of Trade and to the local authority on the condition and equipment of the office visited, and on the mode in which the law relating to weights and measures is being carried out within the jurisdiction of that authority.

(4.) Where the appointment is made on the application of a local authority, the costs incurred in relation to the inquiry, including the remuneration of any officer engaged in the inquiry, not exceeding three guineas a day, shall be paid by the local authority applying for or assenting to the inquiry (*s*), and the Board of Trade may certify the amount of the costs incurred, and any sum so certified and directed by the Board to be paid by any local authority shall be a debt to the Crown from that authority.

(*s*) These costs will, it is presumed, be payable as expenses incurred by the local authority under the Act of 1878, viz., in the case of a county council, out of the county rate; see the Act of 1878, s. 51, and Sched. 4.

Sect. 10 (5).

(5.) Where the appointment is made otherwise than on the application of a local authority, the costs incurred in relation to the inquiry, including the remuneration aforesaid, shall be paid out of moneys provided by Parliament.

Qualification of inspectors of weights and measures

11.—(1.) The Board of Trade shall provide for the holding of examinations for the purpose of ascertaining whether persons acting or appointed to act as inspectors of weights and measures possess sufficient practical knowledge for the proper performance of their duties as such, and for the grant of certificates to persons who satisfactorily pass such examinations.

(2.) In the case of persons who have been appointed inspectors before the commencement of this Act, the passing of an examination under this section shall be permissive, but not obligatory; but a person who, after the commencement of this Act, is for the first time appointed to be an inspector of weights and measures shall not act as such unless and until he has obtained such a certificate as aforesaid (*t*).

(3.) There shall be charged in respect of the examinations under this section such fees as the Board of Trade, with the concurrence of the Treasury, from time to time direct, and all such fees shall be applied in such manner and to such extent as the Treasury from time to time direct, in aid of money provided by Parliament for expenses of the Board of Trade under this Act, and if and as far as not so applied shall be paid into the exchequer.

Inspector not to be maker, seller, or adjuster of weights, measures, or weighing instruments.

12.—(1.) An inspector of weights and measures shall not, during the time he holds office, be a person deriving any profit from or employed in the making, adjusting, or selling of weights, measures, or measuring or weighing instruments:

(2.) Provided that in any district where, on the representation of the local authority, it appears to be desirable for an inspector of weights and measures to be allowed to adjust weights and measures, the Board of Trade may, if they think fit, authorize an inspector appointed by that local authority to act as an adjuster of weights and measures.

(3.) An inspector so authorized may for any such adjustment make such charges as the local authority approve, and shall account for and pay any money received by him in respect of such charges in such manner as the local authority direct.

Fees for verification and stamping by inspectors.

13.—(1.) An inspector of weights and measures may take in respect of the verification and stamping of weights, measures, and weighing instruments the fees specified in the first Schedule to this Act, and no others, and no discount shall be allowed, and such

(*t*) This provision does not prevent a person who has been appointed an inspector, but has not yet obtained a certificate from laying an information for a breach of bye-laws under this Act; for the Act contains no provision that only an inspector can lay such an information. *Crabtree* v. *Bulman*, 60 J. P. 489; 12 T. L. R. 469.

Sect. 13 (1). inspector shall at such times, not less often than once a quarter, as the local authority direct, account for and pay over to the local authority, or as they direct, all fees so taken.

(2.) If the Board of Trade represent to Her Majesty that it would be expedient to fix fees to be paid on the verification and stamping of weights, measures, or weighing instruments, in cases other than those specified in the said schedule, it shall be lawful for Her Majesty, by Order in Council, from time to time to direct such fees to be paid.

Publication of convictions.

14. Where a person is convicted before any court of any offence under the principal Act or this Act, the court may, if it thinks fit, cause the conviction to be published in such manner as it thinks desirable.

Application of 41 & 42 Vict. c. 49, s. 66 to gas standards.

15. The provisions of the principal Act and of this Act as to the verification and re-verification of local and working standards shall apply to the standards used by any local authority in testing meters under the Act of the Session held in the twenty-second and twenty-third years of the reign of Her present Majesty, chapter sixty-six, intituled "An Act for regulating measures used in sales of gas," and the Acts amending the same (*u*).

Powers to London County Council to exercise jurisdiction throughout the county.

16. Notwithstanding anything in section fifty-four of the principal Act, and any other provision in that or any other Act, the inspectors of weights and measures appointed by the London County Council shall alone within the whole of the county of London, exclusive of the city of London, have the powers and discharge the duties of inspectors of weights and measures appointed under the principal Act; provided that any inspector of weights and measures who, at the passing of this Act, though not an officer of the county council, holds office in any parish or place in the county of London, exclusive of the city of London, shall become an officer of that council, and if removed from such appointment by the London County Council he shall be entitled to be regarded as an existing officer under the Local Government Act, 1888, and to receive such compensation as existing officers whose offices are affected are under that Act entitled to receive (*x*).

51 & 52 Vict. c. 41.

Provision as to city of London.

17. Notwithstanding anything in section sixty-seven or sixty-eight of the principal Act, a person using weights or measures in the city of London shall not be required to have his weights or measures verified or stamped by more than one authority (*y*).

18. * * **19.** * * (*z*).

(*u*) As to the Sale of Gas Act, 1859 (22 & 23 Vict. c. 66), see the note to s. 3 (xiii) of the Local Government Act, 1888, *ante*, p. 12.

(*x*) This section practically repeals s. 54 of the Act of 1878 so far as the county of London is concerned; that section enabled local inspectors of weights and measures to be appointed by the same authority as formerly. As to compensation to existing officers under the Local Government Act, 1888, see s. 120 of that Act, and notes, *ante*, p. 195.

(*y*) Sections 67 and 68 contain savings as to the rights of the Founders Company and of the Corporation of London.

(*z*) Sections 18 and 19 relate to Ireland only.

PART II.—*Sale of Coal.*

Coal to be sold by weight.

20.—(1.) All coal shall be sold by weight only, except where by the written consent of the purchaser it is sold by boat load or by waggons or tubs delivered from the colliery into the works of the purchaser.

(2.) If any person sells coal otherwise than is required by this section he shall be liable to a fine not exceeding five pounds for every such sale.

Weight ticket or note on delivery of coal over two hundred-weight.

21.—(1.) Where any quantity of coal exceeding two hundred-weight is delivered by means of any vehicle to a purchaser, the seller of the coal shall therewith deliver, or cause to be delivered, or to be sent by post or otherwise, to the purchaser or to his servant, before any part of the coal is unloaded, a ticket or note according to the form in the Third Schedule to this Act, or according to a form to the like effect (*a*).

(2.) If default is made in complying with the requirements of this section with respect to the delivery or sending of a ticket or note, or if the quantity of coal delivered is less than the quantity expressed in the ticket or note (*b*), the seller of the coal shall be liable to a fine not exceeding five pounds.

(3.) If any person attending on any such vehicle, having received any such ticket or note for delivery to the purchaser, refuses or neglects to deliver it as required by this section, or, on being requested so to do, to exhibit it to any inspector of weights and measures, or other officer appointed for the purpose by the local authority, he shall be liable to a fine not exceeding five pounds.

Tare weight of vehicle where coal sold in bulk.

22.—(1.) Where any quantity of coal exceeding two hundred-weight is conveyed for delivery on sale in a vehicle in bulk, the seller of the coal shall, unless the vehicle is provided by the purchaser, cause the weight of the vehicle, as well as of the coal contained therein, to be previously ascertained by a weighing instrument, stamped by the inspector of weights and measures, and being on or near to the place from which the coal is brought, and shall from

---

(*a*) A truck load of coal was bought for delivery at the premises of the purchaser, and was delivered by means of three carts, each taking two journeys, and each carrying more than 2 cwt. of coal; no ticket or note under this section was delivered at the end of the first journey of any cart, but at the end of the second journey a ticket was delivered showing only the weight of the entire truckload, but not the weight delivered by any of the carts on either journey, nor the tare weight of any cart. *Held*, that the seller ought to be convicted under this section. *Stangoe* v. *Slatter*, 60 J. P. 342 ; 12 T. L. R. 335.

(*b*) When the ticket stated that the purchaser was to receive two tons of coal in twenty sacks, each containing 2 cwt., and some of the sacks contained less than 2 cwt., but the total amount delivered was not less than two tons, it was held that no offence was committed under this section. *Godfrey* v. *Radford*, 75 L. T. (N.S.) 224 ; 60 J. P. 615.

Sect. 22 (1). time to time cause the tare weight of the vehicle to be marked thereon in such manner as the local authority approve.

(2.) In any such case the seller of the coal shall insert or cause to be inserted in the ticket required by this Act to be given by him a statement of the correct weight of the vehicle, or of the vehicle and of the animal drawing it where both are weighed together with the load, as well as of the correct weight of the coal contained in the vehicle (*c*).

(3.) If any person fails to comply with the requirements of this section, he shall be liable to a fine not exceeding five pounds.

Frauds by drivers of coal carts.

23. If the person in charge of any vehicle in which coal is being carried wilfully makes any false statement as to the tare weight of the vehicle, or wilfully does any act by which either the seller or the purchaser of the coal is defrauded, he shall be liable to a fine not exceeding five pounds.

Penalty on deficiency in weight of coal on small sales.

24. If any person on the sale of coal in any quantity not exceeding two hundredweight fraudulently delivers to the purchaser a less quantity of coal than is agreed to be sold, he shall be liable to a fine not exceeding five pounds.

Weighing instrument to be kept in place where coal sold by retail.

25.—(1.) Where coal is sold by retail for delivery at the place where it is kept for sale and there is not at or near such place any weighing instrument stamped by an inspector of weights and measures at which the coal can be weighed, the seller shall keep at that place a weighing instrument stamped as aforesaid, and shall, if so required by any purchaser, or by any inspector of weights and measures, or by any other officer appointed for the purpose by the local authority, weigh any coal before the sale or delivery thereof.

(2.) If any person fails to comply with the requirements of this section he shall be liable to a fine not exceeding for a first offence two pounds, and for any subsequent offence five pounds.

Erection and maintenance of weighing instruments.

26.—(1.) The local authority may erect and maintain fixed weighing instruments at convenient places for the purpose of weighing coal, and may provide, furnish, and maintain portable weighing instruments for the same purpose, and may appoint proper persons to keep and attend any such instruments.

(2.) If the keeper of any such fixed weighing instrument refuses, without reasonable excuse, to weigh or re-weigh any vehicle or coal, or so weighs any vehicle or coal as wilfully to defraud either the seller or the purchaser of coal, he shall be liable to a fine not exceeding five pounds.

Power to require weighment of coal or vehicle.

27.—(1.) Any seller or purchaser of coal, person in charge of a vehicle in which coal is carried, inspector of weights and measures,

(*c*) Where coal exceeding 2 cwt. is conveyed for delivery on sale in a vehicle not belonging to the purchaser, the correct weight to be inserted in the ticket is the weight as ascertained at the place from which the coal is brought and not the weight at the time of delivery. *Knowles* v. *Sinclair*, W. N. (1897) p. 176. See also *Stangoe* v. *Slatter*, *supra*.

or other officer appointed for the purpose by the local authority (*d*), may require that any coal or any vehicle used for the carriage of coal in bulk be weighed or re-weighed by any weighing instrument stamped by an inspector of weights and measures. Sect. 27 (1).

Provided as follows:

(a.) No seller of coal or person in charge of a vehicle in which coal is carried shall be required under this section to carry coal beyond such distance, not exceeding half a mile as may be prescribed in that behalf by the local authority:

(b.) Where any such coal or vehicle has at the instance of the purchaser been weighed or re-weighed in pursuance of this section, and found to be of the weight stated in that behalf by the seller of the coal or the person in charge of the vehicle, the purchaser shall be liable to the payment of all reasonable costs actually incurred of and incidental to the weighing or re-weighing.

(2.) If any person obstructs any weighing or re-weighing authorized by this section he shall be liable to a fine not exceeding five pounds.

Power to make bye-laws with respect to the sale of coal.

28.—(1.) Any local authority may from time to time make, revoke, and alter byelaws (*e*),

(a) regulating for the purposes of this Act the sale of coal in quantities not exceeding two hundredweight; and,

(b) requiring either generally or in specified classes of cases, a weighing instrument, of a form approved by the local authority, to be carried with any vehicle in which coal is carried for sale or delivery to a purchaser; and

---

(*d*) "The Act contemplated the selection of special persons for this purpose, and not the general delegation of the power to all constables," *per* Lord RUSSELL of KILLOWEN, C.J. *Alty* v. *Farrell*, *infra*.

(*e*) A bye-law under this section, that "every coal dealer shall provide, and every person employed by him who shall convey or carry coal for sale or delivery to a purchaser from or out of any vehicle, shall carry therewith a correct and stamped weighing machine of the form approved by the county council," was held to be warranted by clause (b) of this section, and valid; *Kent County Council* v. *Humphrey*, [1895] 1 Q. B. 903; 64 L. J. M. C. 190: 72 L. T. (N.S.) 563; 43 W. R. 506; 59 J. P. 520. See also *Martin* v. *Clarke*, 62 L. J. M. C. 178; 9 T. L. R. 656.

But where a bye-law, after containing a provision to the same effect as in the above cases, went on to require that the person in charge of a vehicle carrying coal for sale in quantities not exceeding 2 cwt. "shall re-weigh the coal upon being requested to do so by any purchaser, or by any one on behalf of the purchaser, or by an inspector of weights and measures, or by any constable," the latter part of the bye-law was held to be unreasonable, on the grounds that it contained no limitation that the request to re-weigh must be reasonable, and that it made it possible that the man might have to weigh the coal again and again on different requests, and that the Act did not intend that a power to require re-weighing should be conferred on all the constables of a borough. And WRIGHT, J., doubted whether the Act authorized a bye-law requiring the person in charge of the vehicle to re-weigh the coal himself. *Alty* v. *Farrell*, [1896] 1 Q. B. 636; 65 L. J. M. C. 115; 74 L. T. (N.S.) 492; 60 J. P. 373.

Sect. 28 (1).

(c) prescribing the distance beyond which coal is not to be required to be carried for the purpose of being weighed or re-weighed in pursuance of this Act; and

(d) fixing the fees to be paid for the use of any weighing instrument maintained by the local authority;

and may by such bye-laws impose fines, recoverable summarily, and not exceeding in each case five pounds, for the breach of any such byelaw.

(2.) Every bye-law made under this section shall, before being brought into operation, be approved by the Board of Trade and be published in such manner as the local authority think sufficient for giving notice thereof to all persons interested, and a copy of every such bye-law shall be sent by the local authority to the Board of Trade.

Power to weigh coal in shop or vehicle.

29.—(1.) Any inspector of weights and measures or officer appointed for the purpose by the local authority may, at all reasonable times enter any building or part of a building or other place in which coal is sold or kept or exposed for sale, and may stop any vehicle carrying coal for sale or for delivery to a purchaser, and may test any weights and weighing instruments found in any such place or vehicle, and may weigh any load, sack, or other less quantity of coal, found in any such place or vehicle, or which is in course of delivery to any purchaser.

(2.) If it appears to a court of summary jurisdiction that any load, sack, or less quantity so weighed is of less weight than that represented by the seller, the person selling or keeping or exposing the coal for sale, or the person in charge of the vehicle, as the case may be, shall be liable to a fine not exceeding five pounds (*f*).

(3.) Any person who obstructs or hinders any inspector acting under this section shall be liable to a fine not exceeding five, or, in the case of a second or subsequent offence ten, pounds.

Power to make local exemptions.

30. Her Majesty the Queen may from time to time, on the application of the local authority for any area, and on being satisfied

(*f*) In order to convict the seller of an offence under this section, there must be an actual representation by him as to the weight of the coal sold, and a representation made to an inspector by a servant in charge of a vehicle carrying coal for delivery to a purchaser is not of itself the representation of the master so as to make him liable. *Roberts* v. *Woodward*, 25 Q. B. D. 412; 59 L. J. M. C. 129; 63 L. T. (N.S.) 200; 38 W. R. 770; 55 J. P. 116; 17 Cox C. C. 139.

But where a seller sent out coals in sacks, to each of which was attached a metal label bearing the inscription "½ cwt." and the inspector weighed a sack, when in course of delivery by the seller's carman, and found that it contained 7 lbs. less than half a cwt., it was held that the label constituted a representation by the seller, and that he was properly convicted under this section. *Franklin* v. *Godfrey*, 63 L. J. M. C. 239; 43 W. R. 46. And where the delivery ticket, made out in the seller's office and delivered to the inspector by a carman who was not the seller's servant, but the servant of a contractor employed by the seller to deliver the coals, represented coals sold to be of a certain weight, and they were found on weighing by the inspector to be of a less weight, the conviction of the seller under this section was upheld. *Baker* v. *Herd*, 58 J. P. 413; 10 T. L. R. 181.

that the provisions made by or under any local Act in force at the commencement of this Act, with respect to the sale of coal in that area are more stringent than the corresponding provisions of this Act, by Order in Council exempt that area from the provisions of this Part of this Act to such extent, and under such conditions, as may appear to Her Majesty in Council expedient. Sect. 30.

Extent.

31. This Part of this Act, except the provision requiring coal to be sold by weight only, shall not extend to Scotland.

PART III.

Bread.

Explanation of law as to bakers.

32. Nothing in the enactments referred to in the Fourth Schedule to this Act shall render any baker or seller of bread, or the journeyman, servant, or other person employed by such baker or seller of bread, liable to any forfeiture or penalty for refusing to weigh in the presence of the purchaser any bread conveyed or carried out in any cart or other carriage, unless he is requested so to do by or on behalf of the purchaser (*g*).

PART IV.

Supplemental.

Saving for liabilities otherwise than under Act.

33.—(1.) No proceeding or conviction for any offence punishable under this Act shall affect any civil remedy to which any person aggrieved by the offence may be entitled.

(2.) This Act shall not exempt any person from any indictment or other proceeding for an offence which is punishable at common law or under some Act of Parliament other than this Act, so that no person be punished twice for the same offence.

(3.) Where proceedings are taken before any court against any person in respect of any offence punishable under this Act, and the offence is also punishable at common law or under some Act of Parliament other than this Act, the court may direct that, instead of those proceedings being continued, proceedings shall be taken against that person at common law or under some Act of Parliament other than this Act.

(*g*) The enactments referred to are the 3 Geo. 4, c. cvi., s. 9 (relating to the city of London), and 6 & 7 Will. 4, c. 37, s. 7 (relating to areas outside the city). These enactments require bakers and their servants selling bread from a cart to carry proper scales for weighing the bread so sold, and impose a penalty on any such person who refuses to weigh the bread so sold in the presence of the purchaser. The text only applies to such parts of those sections as relate to a refusal to weigh; there is to be no penalty unless there is a refusal after the purchaser, or someone on his behalf, has requested that the bread shall be weighed. See *Copeland* v. *Walker*, 65 L. T. (N.S.) 262; 55 J. P. 809; 17 Cox C. C. 331. The enactments in the two statutes as to the sale of bread by weight (including the sections above referred to) apply to all bread except bread usually sold under the denomination of "French or fancy bread or rolls;" as to what falls under this denomination, see *The V. V. Bread Co.* v. *Stubbs*, 74 L. T. (N.S.) 704; 60 J. P. 424, and the cases there cited.

Sect. 34.

Construction of Act.

34. This Act and the principal Act shall be construed together as one Act.

Definitions.

35. In this Act, unless the context otherwise requires,—

"Weighing instrument" includes scales, with the weights belonging thereto, scale-beams, balances, spring-balances, steelyards, weighing machines, and other instruments for weighing:

"Measuring instrument" includes any instrument for the measurement of length, capacity, volume, temperature, pressure, or gravity, or for the measurement and determination of electrical quantities:

"Vehicle" means any carriage, cart, waggon, truck, barrow, or other means of carrying coal by land, in whatever manner the same may be drawn or propelled, but does not include a railway truck or waggon:

"Inspector" means an inspector under the principal Act:

Other expressions have the same meaning as in the principal Act (*h*): Provided that the expression "local authority" shall, in its application to England, be construed subject to the provisions of the Local Government Act, 1888 (*i*), and the expression "weighing machine" in the principal Act shall include any weighing instrument as defined by this Act.

51 & 52 Vict. c. 41.

Repeal.

36.—(1.) The enactments specified in the Fifth Schedule to this Act are hereby repealed to the extent mentioned in the third column of that schedule.

(2.) The repeal of any enactment by this Act shall not affect—

(a) the past operation of any enactment so repealed, or anything duly done or suffered under any enactment so repealed; or

(b) any right or liability acquired or incurred under any enactment so repealed: or

(c) any penalty, forfeiture, or punishment incurred in respect of any offence committed against any enactment so repealed; or

(d) any power, legal proceeding, or remedy in respect of any such right, liability, penalty, forfeiture, or punishment as aforesaid; and any such power, legal proceeding, and remedy may be exercised and carried on as if this Act had not passed.

Commencement.

37. This Act shall come into operation on the first day of January one thousand eight hundred and ninety, which date is in this Act referred to as the commencement of this Act:

Provided as follows:

(a.) At any time after the passing of this Act any appointment, bye-law, or regulation may be made, and any other thing

(*h*) See the definitions in s. 70 of the Act of 1878.

(*i*) See the Local Government Act, 1888, s. 3 (xiii.), *ante*, p. 12.

may be done, which appears to a local authority to be necessary or proper for the purpose of bringing this Act into operation at the commencement thereof; Sect. 37.

* * * * * * (k)

39. This Act may be cited as the Weights and Measures Act, 1889; and the principal Act and this Act may be cited together as the Weights and Measures Acts, 1878 and 1889 (l). Short titles.

SCHEDULES.

FIRST SCHEDULE.

Section 13.

Fees to be taken on the verification and stamping of Weights, Measures, and Weighing Instruments by Inspectors of Local Authorities.

Weights.

	s.	d.
Avoirdupois:		
Each weight of 100 lb. (cental)	0	4
" " 56 lb. and 28 lb.	0	3
" " 14 lb. and 7 lb.	0	2
" " from 4 lb. to 1 lb., inclusive	0	1
" " " 8 oz. to ½ dram, inclusive	0	0½
" " " 4,000 grains to $\frac{1}{100}$th of a grain, inclusive	0	0½
" " " 240 to 24 grains, inclusive, commonly called pennyweights	0	0½
Troy:		
Each weight from 500 oz. to 100 oz., inclusive	0	4
" " " 50 oz. to 10 oz., inclusive	0	2
" " " 5 oz. to $\frac{1}{1000}$th of an oz., inclusive	0	1
Apothecaries:		
Each weight from 10 oz. to 1 oz. inclusive	0	2
" " " 4 drachms to ½ grain, inclusive	0	1

Measures.

Length:		
Each measure from 100 feet to 7 feet inclusive	0	3
" " " 6 feet to 4 feet inclusive	0	2
" " of a yard, 2 feet, foot and inch respectively, including their sub-divisions	0	1
Measures from 0·500 to 0·001 inch, in the form of wire-gauge plates:		
For each notch, or for each internal gauge or separate size, from half an inch to $\frac{1}{1000}$th of an inch	0	0¼
Capacity:		
Dry and liquid measures:		
Each measure of 4 bushels (32 gallons) and 1 bushel (8 gallons)	0	6
" " from 5 gallons to 2 gallons (peck), inclusive	0	3
" " " 1 gallon to a ¼ gill, inclusive	0	1
Apothecaries:		
Each subdivided measure containing not more than twelve sub-divisions	0	1
" " " containing more than twelve sub-divisions but not more than fifteen	0	1¼
" " " containing more than fifteen sub-divisions but not more than eighteen	0	1½

(k) Clause (b) of s. 37 and s. 38 relate exclusively to Ireland.

(l) The Act of 1878, this Act, and the Acts of 1892 and 1893 (see note (m) *ante*, p. 409), are now comprised in the collective title, "The Weights and Measures Acts, 1878 to 1893;" Short Titles Act, 1896 (59 & 60 Vict. c. 14).

Schedule 1. Apothecaries—*continued.*

	s.	d.
Each subdivided measure containing more than eighteen subdivisions but not more than twenty-one	0	1¾
" " " containing more than twenty-one subdivisions but not more than twenty-four	0	2
" " " containing more than twenty-four subdivisions but not more than thirty	0	2½
" " " containing more than thirty subdivisions but not more than thirty-six	0	3
" " " containing more than thirty-six subdivisions but not more than forty-two	0	3½
" " " containing more than forty-two subdivisions but not more than fifty	0	4
" " " containing more than fifty subdivisions but not more than one hundred	0	6
" " " containing more than one hundred subdivisions but not more than one hundred and fifty	0	9
" " " containing more than one hundred and fifty	1	0
Each separate measure from 40 fluid oz. to 10 fluid oz. inclusive	0	2
" " " " 10 fluid oz.	0	0½

Weighing Instruments.

	s.	d.
For 10 tons and above	10	0
For under 10 tons and above 1 ton	5	0
For 1 ton and above 5 cwt.	2	0
For 5 cwt. and above 1 cwt.	1	6
For 1 cwt. and above 56 lbs.	1	0
exclusive of cost of cartage and lifting of standards in each of the above cases.		
For 56 lb. and above 14 lb.	0	6
For 14 lbs. and above 1 lb.	0	3
For 1 lb. or under	0	2

Section 19.

SECOND SCHEDULE (m).

Section 21.

THIRD SCHEDULE.

Weight Ticket or Consignment Note on delivery of Coal over Two Hundredweight.

Mr. *A.B.* [*here insert the name of the buyer*].

Take notice that you are to receive herewith tons cwt. lbs. of coal.

[*When sold in sacks, add*]

in sacks, each containing cwt.

[*When sold in bulk, add*]

	tons.	cwts.	lbs.
Weight of coal and vehicle			
Tare weight of vehicle			
Net weight of coal herewith delivered to purchaser			

C.D. [*here insert the name of the seller*].

E.F. [*here insert the name of the person in charge of the vehicle*].

(*m*) This Schedule relates to Ireland only.

Where coal is delivered by means of a vehicle the seller must deliver or send by post or otherwise to the purchaser or his servant, before any part of the coal is unloaded, a ticket or note in this form. Schedule 3.

Any seller of coal who delivers a less quantity than is stated in this ticket or note is liable to a fine.

Any person attending on a vehicle used for the delivery of coal who, having received a ticket or note for delivery to the purchaser, refuses or neglects to deliver it to the purchaser or his servant, is liable to a fine.

FOURTH SCHEDULE.

Section 32.

Session and Chapter.	Title.	Enactments referred to.
3 Geo. 4, c. cvi.	An Act to repeal the Acts now in force relating to bread to be sold in the city of London and the liberties thereof, and within the weekly bills of mortality, and ten miles of the Royal Exchange; and to provide other regulations for the making and sale of bread, and preventing the adulteration of meal, flour, and bread, within the limits aforesaid.	Section nine.
6 & 7 Will. 4, c. 37	An Act to repeal the several Acts now in force relating to bread to be sold out of the city of London and the liberties thereof, and beyond the weekly bills of mortality, and ten miles of the Royal Exchange; and to provide other regulations for the making and sale of bread, and for preventing the adulteration of meal, flour, and bread, beyond the limits aforesaid.	Section seven.

FIFTH SCHEDULE.

Section 36.

ENACTMENTS REPEALED.

Session and Chapter.	Short title.	Extent of Repeal.
41 & 42 Vict. c, 49.	The Weights and Measures Act, 1878.	Section sixteen. Section forty three, from "A maker or seller of weights" to "measures under this Act." Section forty-six. Section forty-seven. Section eighty-six, so far as it re-enacts section nine of the Weights and Measures Act, 1835. The Fifth Schedule.

WELSH INTERMEDIATE EDUCATION ACT, 1889.

(52 & 53 VICT. CAP. 40) (*n*).

An Act to promote Intermediate Education in Wales.

[12th August, 1889.]

* *

Preliminary.

1. This Act may be cited for all purposes as the Welsh Intermediate Education Act, 1889, and shall, so far as is consistent with

Short title and construction.

(*n*) This Act constitutes a "joint education committee" for every county in Wales and for Monmouthshire for the purpose of submitting to the Charity Commissioners a scheme or proposal for a scheme for the intermediate and

Sect. 1.

the tenour thereof, be construed as one with the Endowed Schools Acts (*o*), and may be cited together with those Acts, as the Endowed Schools Acts, 1869 to 1889. This Act shall come into operation on the first day of November next after the passing thereof, which day is in this Act referred to as the commencement of this Act.

Purpose of Act.

2. The purpose of this Act is to make further provision for the intermediate and technical education of the inhabitants of Wales and the county of Monmouth.

Schemes for Intermediate Education.

Schemes by joint education committee.

3.—(1.) It shall be the duty of the joint education committee as hereinafter mentioned (*p*) of every county in Wales and of the county of Monmouth to submit to the Charity Commissioners a scheme or schemes for the intermediate and technical education of the inhabitants of their county, either alone or in conjunction with the inhabitants of any adjoining county or counties, specifying in each scheme the educational endowments within their county which in their opinion ought to be used for the purpose of such scheme.

(2.) A county council may recommend their committee to insert in such scheme a provision for a payment out of the county rate to an amount not exceeding that in this Act mentioned (*q*), of the expenses of carrying into effect the scheme, or any particular part thereof, and such provision may accordingly, if it is thought fit, be inserted in the scheme.

(3.) Such scheme, if the Commissioners (after such examination or inquiry as mentioned in section thirty-two of the Endowed Schools Act, 1869 (*r*)) approve it, either without modification, or with

32 & 33 Vict, c. 56.

technical education (as defined by s. 17, *infra*) of the inhabitants of the county. The county council appoints some of the members of the joint committee and exercises a certain control over their proceedings. The powers of a joint education committee are temporary (see s. 11, *infra*), but are now in force until December 31st, 1898, by virtue of the Expiring Laws Continuance Act, 1897 (60 & 61 Vict. c. 54).

(*o*) The Endowed Schools Acts comprise the 32 & 33 Vict. c. 56 (1869), the 36 & 37 Vict. c. 87 (1873), the 37 & 38 Vict. c. 87 (1874), and this Act.

(*p*) The constitution of the joint education committee is provided for by s. 5, *infra*.

(*q*) The addition to the county rate for contributions under this Act is not to exceed in any year one halfpenny in the pound on the rateable value of the property as ascertained for the purpose of levying county contributions, s. 8 (3), *infra*.

(*r*) Section 32 of the Endowed Schools Act, 1869, empowered the Charity Commissioners, after such examination or public inquiry as they think necessary, to prepare drafts or schemes for the purposes of that Act subject to certain conditions, one of which was that any governing body of any such endowment might within a certain period after the commencement of the Act, and upon giving certain notices to the Commissioners, prepare and submit to the Commissioners in writing a scheme relating to such endowment, and the Commissioners shall consider such scheme before they themselves prepare any such modifications as may be assented to by the joint education committee, shall be adopted and proceeded on by the Commissioners in the same manner as if it were a draft scheme originally prepared by themselves. Sect. 3 (3).

(4.) If the scheme is not so adopted by the Commissioners, it shall be deemed to be a scheme prepared and submitted by a governing body to the Commissioners within the meaning of section thirty-two of the Endowed Schools Act, 1869, and shall be dealt with accordingly (*r*).

(5.) Where a county council recommend a payment out of the county rate a scheme may be made in pursuance of this Act, although there is no other endowment.

(6.) The Charity Commissioners may, if they think fit, accept a joint scheme from two or more joint education committees.

(7.) A joint education committee may, instead of submitting a scheme, submit to the Charity Commissioners proposals for a scheme, and such proposals may include, if so recommended by the county council, a payment out of the county rate; and the Commissioners shall prepare a scheme for carrying into effect such proposals, either with or without modifications, but any modification to which the joint education committee do not assent shall be struck out of the scheme, and the scheme as so prepared, with the omission of any modification to which the joint education committee do not assent, shall be deemed for the purposes of this section to be a scheme submitted by a joint education committee to the Charity Commissioners, and the Commissioners shall proceed accordingly.

Restrictions on powers of joint education committee.

4.—(1.) A joint education committee shall not without the assent of the county council direct by their scheme any contribution to be made out of the county rate exceeding the amount recommended by the county council.

(2.) Where any part of the expenses of the establishment or maintenance of a school or of scholarships attached thereto is to be defrayed out of the county rate a scheme relating to such school shall provide that the county council shall be adequately represented on the governing body of such school.

(3.) Where a scheme under this Act does not relate to a school maintained out of the endowment, or forming part of the foundation, of any cathedral or collegiate church, or where a scheme under this Act does not relate to any other educational endowment which by section nineteen of the Endowed Schools Act, 1869, is excepted from the foregoing provisions of that Act therein mentioned, such scheme shall, in addition to the provisions of section fifteen of

---

draft of a scheme relating to the same endowment; and any scheme so prepared by the governing body and submitted to the commissioners shall, if approved by them, be adopted and proceeded with by them in the same manner as if it were a draft scheme originally prepared by themselves.

Sect. 4 (3). the said Act, provide that no religious catechism or religious formulary which is distinctive of any particular denomination shall be taught to a scholar attending as a day scholar at the school established or regulated by the scheme, and that the times for prayer or religious worship or for any lesson or series of lessons on a religious subject shall be conveniently arranged for the purpose of allowing the withdrawal of a day scholar therefrom in accordance with the said section fifteen (*s*).

(4.) Where any power of appeal to the Queen in Council, or power to present a petition praying that a scheme may be laid before Parliament, is given by the Endowed Schools Acts to any persons or body of persons in relation to any endowment, a like power may be exercised by a county council required by the scheme to contribute a sum out of the county rate, or by a joint education committee in relation to any matter which has been introduced into the scheme against the wishes of the county council or committee, as the case may be, as expressed in objections sent in writing to the Charity Commissioners before the scheme was submitted by those Commissioners for the approval of the Education Department (*t*).

(*s*) Section 15 of the Act of 1869 provides for the exemption of day scholars from attendance at religious worship and lessons on religious subjects in certain cases. Section 16 deals with similar exemptions in the case of boarders. Sections 17 and 18 prevent religious tests being required in the case of the governing body and masters. Section 19 provides that a scheme relating to—

(1) any school which is maintained out of the endowment of any cathedral or collegiate church, or forms part of the foundation of any cathedral or collegiate church; or

(2) any educational endowment, the scholars educated by which are, in the opinion of the Commissioners (subject to appeal to Her Majesty in Council as mentioned in this Act) required by the express terms of the original instruments of foundation or of the statutes or regulations made by the founder or under his authority, in his lifetime or within fifty years after his death (which terms have been observed down to the commencement of this Act) to learn or to be instructed according to the doctrines or formularies of any particular church, sect, or denomination,

is excepted from the foregoing provisions respecting religious instruction and attendance at religious worship (other than the provisions for the exemption of day scholars from attending prayer or religious worship, or lessons on a religious subject, when such exemption has been claimed on their behalf), and respecting the qualification of the governing body and masters (unless the governing body, constituted, as it would have been if no scheme under this Act had been made, assents to such scheme); and a scheme relating to any such school or endowment shall not without the consent of the governing body thereof make any provision respecting the religious instruction or attendance at religious worship of the scholars (except for securing such exemption as aforesaid) or respecting the religious opinions of the governing body or masters.

The above exceptions are extended by s. 7 of the Endowed Schools Act, 1873.

(*t*) As to appeals to the Queen in Council and laying schemes before Parliament, see ss. 39 *et seq* of the Act of 1869 and ss. 14 and 15 of the Act of 1873. As to the approval of the Education Department, see ss. 37 and 38 of the Act of 1869 and s. 13 of the Act of 1873.

Constitution and Powers of Joint Education Committee. **Sect. 5.**

Establishment of joint education committee.

5. For the purposes of this Act there shall be appointed in every county in Wales and in the county of Monmouth a joint education committee of the county council of such county consisting of three persons nominated by the county council, and two persons, being persons well acquainted with the conditions of Wales and the wants of the people, preference being given to residents within the county for which such joint committee is to be appointed, nominated by the Lord President of Her Majesty's Privy Council. Any vacancy in the joint education committee among the persons appointed by the county council may be filled up by the county council, and any vacancy among the persons nominated by the Lord President may be filled up by the Lord President.

Transaction of business by and proceedings of joint education committee.

6.—(1.) Sub-sections one and two of section eighty-two of the Local Government Act, 1888 (*u*), respecting the proceedings of committees of county councils, shall apply to proceedings of the joint education committee of a county council under this Act, but the acts and proceedings of the committee shall not be required to be submitted to the county council for their approval.

(2.) The county council shall make proper provision for enabling the committee to transact its business, and the clerk of the county council shall act as the clerk of the joint education committee. Any act of the committee may be signified under the hands of any three members thereof or under the hand of the clerk.

(3.) Any of the assistant commissioners of the Charity Commissioners shall be at liberty to attend any meeting of a joint education committee, and to take part in the proceedings, but shall not have a right to vote.

Contributions from county rate.

7.—(1.) Where a county council has recommended that any scholarship should be paid out of the county rate a scheme under this Act may contain provisions to that effect.

(2.) Where a county council has recommended that any annual contribution should be made out of the county rate a scheme under this Act may direct the contribution so recommended or any less contribution to be made accordingly, and shall specify the persons to whom the contribution so directed to be made is from time to time to be paid.

(3.) The recommendation of a county council in respect of a contribution out of the county rate, and a scheme giving effect to such recommendation, may provide that such contribution shall be either a fixed annual sum, or an annual sum not exceeding a certain amount, such amount to be determined annually in manner specified in the scheme.

(4.) The annual contribution to be paid to any school out of the county rate in pursuance of any scheme shall not exceed the amount

---

(*u*) *Ante*, p. 157.

Sect. 7 (4).

stated in such scheme, but may be reduced by an amending scheme made on the application of the county council or of the governing body of such school.

Finance.

Expenses of county council.

8.—(1.) Where a scheme under this Act providing for a contribution out of a county rate comes into operation, the amount from time to time payable out of the county rate in pursuance of such scheme shall be paid by the county council out of the county fund.

(2.) That amount and any expenses otherwise incurred by a county council in pursuance of this Act shall be paid as general expenses of the county council (*x*).

(3.) The addition made to the county rate in any county for the purpose of defraying contributions for intermediate and technical education under this Act shall not in any year exceed one halfpenny in the pound, on the aggregate amount of the rateable value of the property in the county, as ascertained for the purpose of the levy of the county contributions.

(4.) Every increase of rate levied under this section shall, in all precepts for the levy thereof, be described as a separate item of rate, and when collected from the individual ratepayers shall be specified as a separate item of rate.

Contribution from Treasury.

9.—(1.) The Commissioners of Her Majesty's Treasury shall annually out of moneys provided by Parliament pay in aid of each school aided by the county and subject to a scheme made under this Act such sums as hereinafter mentioned.

(2.) The sums to be so paid shall depend on the efficiency of the schools aided by the county, as ascertained by such annual inspection and report as may be required by the regulations from time to time made by the Treasury for the purposes of this section, and shall be of such amounts as may be fixed by those regulations, and shall be paid in manner provided by those regulations.

(3.) The aggregate amount of the sums paid by the Commissioners of Her Majesty's Treasury in any year in respect of the schools in any county shall not exceed the amount payable in that year in pursuance of this Act out of the county rate.

(4.) The Treasury may from time to time make, and, when made, vary and revoke, regulations for the purposes of this section.

Power to Public Works Loan Commissioners to lend.

10. The purposes for which the governing body of a school may be authorized in pursuance of this Act to borrow money shall be purposes for which the Public Works Loan Commissioners may lend to such governing body.

(*x*) As to general expenses of a county council, see the Local Government Act, 1888, s. 68, *ante*, p. 130. A county council may also contribute for the purposes of this Act any sum received by them in respect of the residue of the English share of the local taxation (customs and excise) duties under the 53 & 54 Vict. c. 60, s. 1, *post*.

Supplemental Provisions. **Sect. 11.**

Duration of powers of joint education committee, and suspension of powers of Charity Commissioners.

11. The powers conferred by this Act on a joint education committee shall not, unless Parliament otherwise directs, be exercised by the committee after the expiration of three years from the date of the commencement of this Act (*y*) and, during the continuance of the powers of the committee under this Act, all powers which otherwise might have been exercised by the Charity Commissioners of making, establishing, or submitting (independently of any scheme submitted by the joint education committee) a scheme for the administration of any educational endowments within the county of such committee, shall, except with the consent of the Education Department, be suspended, and not be exercised by them in relation to such endowments. Nothing in this Act shall prevent any proceedings under the Endowed Schools Acts in relation to any scheme of which a draft has been prepared, published, and circulated before the commencement of this Act, in pursuance of sections thirty-two and thirty-three of the Endowed Schools Act, 1869 (*z*), and such scheme may be proceeded with, submitted for approval, and come into operation as if this Act had not passed.

Description of endowments applicable to purpose of Act.

12.—(1.) An educational endowment within the county of a joint education committee means any educational endowment which is applied in the county or is appropriated for the benefit of the natives or inhabitants of the county, or of some of such natives or inhabitants, or their children or where the benefits of such endowment are divisible between two counties or between the counties in Wales and the county of Monmouth, or any of them, and any place outside of Wales and the county of Monmouth, then means so much of the endowment as the Charity Commissioners may determine to be applicable for the benefit of the county of the joint education committee.

(2.) Any school or endowment of a school to which section seventy-five of the Elementary Education Act, 1870, applies and any endowed school to which section three of the Endowed Schools Act, 1873, applies, shall, if the school is in the county of a joint education committee under this Act, be for the purposes of the Endowed Schools Acts and this Act an educational endowment and endowed school within the county of such committee (*a*).

33 & 34 Vict. c. 75.
36 & 37 Vict. c 87.

(*y*) See note (*n*), *ante*, p. 423.

(*z*) As to s. 32, see note (*o*), *ante*, p. 424. Section 33 provides for the printing and publication of draft schemes by the Charity Commissioners.

(*a*) The governing bodies of schools and endowments excepted from the Act of 1869 as having been in receipt of an annual Parliamentary grant (see s. 8 of that Act) were by s. 75 of the Elementary Education Act, 1870 (33 & 34 Vict. c. 75), empowered to submit schemes to the Education Department, and effect is to be given to such a scheme when approved by that Department as if it had been a scheme under the Act of 1869. A similar provision is made by s. 3 of the Endowed Schools Act, 1873, as to elementary schools, the gross

Sect. 13.

Construction of Act in relation to endowments applicable to purposes thereof.

13. For the purposes of any scheme under this Act every notice relating to the scheme shall be sent to the joint education committee concerned therein in like manner as if they were a governing body, and such committee shall, during the duration of their powers under this Act, have the same power of applying to the Charity Commissioners with respect to any educational endowment within their county as if they were the governing body of that endowment. Nothing in this Act shall authorize the making of any scheme interfering with—

(1.) Any endowment given either by present gift made subsequently to the passing of the Endowed Schools Act, 1869, or by the will of a testator who died subsequently to the passing of the said Act, unless the founder or governing body of such endowment assents to the scheme.

In the case of an endowment or part of an endowment given either by present gift made subsequently to the passing of the Endowed Schools Act, 1869, or by the will of a testator who died subsequently to the passing of the said Act, sections twenty-five and twenty-six of the said Act shall for the purposes of a scheme under this Act, and subject to the provisions of this Act, apply in like manner as if the same and any older endowment or part of an endowment were respectively in the said sections substituted for an endowment or part of an endowment originally given to charitable uses less or more than fifty years before the commencement of the said Act (*b*).

Exemption of schemes from certain provisions of Endowed Schools Acts.

14. Nothing in the Endowed Schools Acts which is inconsistent with any of the provisions of this Act shall apply in the case of any scheme under this Act, but subject to this enactment the powers conferred by this Act shall be in addition to, and not in derogation of, the powers under the said Act.

Report by Charity Commissioners.

15. The Charity Commissioners shall in every year cause to be laid before both Houses of Parliament a report of the proceedings under this Act during the preceding year.

Application of Act to counties and county boroughs.

51 & 52 Vict. c. 41.

16.—(1.) In this Act the expression "county" means an administrative county as defined in the Local Government Act, 1888 (*c*), and includes a county borough within the meaning of that Act, and the expression "county council" includes the council of a county borough.

---

average annual income of the aggregate educational endowments of which during the three years before September 1st, 1873, did not exceed one hundred pounds.

(*b*) Sections 25 and 26 of the Act of 1869 relate to the application of that Act to cases where old and new endowments have become mixed. The sections must be referred to, to explain the provision in the text.

(*c*) "Administrative county" means the area for which a county council is elected in pursuance of the Local Government Act, 1888, and see the definition in s. 100 of that Act, *ante*, p. 172.

(2.) Any sums payable by the council of a county borough in pursuance of this Act shall be paid out of the borough fund or borough rate. Sect. 16 (2).

17. In this Act unless there is something in the context inconsistent therewith— General definitions.

The expression "intermediate education" means a course of education which does not consist chiefly of elementary instruction in reading, writing, and arithmetic, but which includes instruction in Latin, Greek, the Welsh and English language and literature, modern languages, mathematics, natural and applied science, or in some of such studies, and generally in the higher branches of knowledge, but nothing in this Act shall prevent the establishment of scholarships in higher or other elementary schools;

The expression "technical education" includes instruction in—

(i.) Any of the branches of science and art with respect to which grants are for the time being made by the Department of Science and Art;

(ii.) The use of tools, and modelling in clay, wood, or other material;

(iii.) Commercial arthmetic, commercial geography, book-keeping and shorthand;

(iv.) Any other subject applicable to the purposes of agriculture, industries, trade, or commercial life and practice, which may be specified in a scheme, or proposals for a scheme, of a joint education committee, as a form of instruction suited to the needs of the district;

but it shall not include teaching the practice of any trade or industry or employment.

The expression "Endowed Schools Acts" means the Endowed Schools Acts, 1869, 1873, and 1874; 32 & 33 Vict. c. 56. 36 & 37 Vict. c. 87. 37 & 38 Vict. c. 87.

The expression "Education Department" means the Lords of the Committee of Her Majesty's Privy Council on Education;

The expression "Charity Commissioners" means the Charity Commissioners for England and Wales;

The expression "scholarship" includes exhibition or other educational emolument;

The expression "parent" includes guardian and every person who is liable to maintain or has the actual custody of a child;

The expression "scheme under this Act" means a scheme under the Endowed Schools Act as amended by this Act.

PUBLIC BODIES CORRUPT PRACTICES ACT, 1889.

(52 & 53 VICT. CAP. 69.)

An Act for the more effectual Prevention and Punishment of Bribery and Corruption of and by Members, Officers, or Servants of Corporations, Councils, Boards, Commissions, or other Public Bodies. [30th August, 1889.]

WHEREAS it is expedient more effectually to provide for the prevention and punishment of bribery and corruption of and by members, officers, or servants of corporations, councils, boards, commissions, and other public bodies:

* * * * *

Corruption in office a misdemeanor.

1.—(1.) Every person who shall by himself, or by, or in conjunction with any other person, corruptly solicit or receive, or agree to receive (*d*), for himself, or for any other person, any gift, loan, fee, reward, or advantage (*e*) whatever as an inducement to, or reward for, or otherwise on account of any member, officer, or servant of a public body as in this Act defined (*e*), doing or forbearing to do anything in respect of any matter or transaction whatsoever, actual or proposed, in which the said public body is concerned, shall be guilty of a misdemeanor (*f*).

(2.) Every person (*g*) who shall by himself, or by, or in conjunction with any other person, corruptly give, promise, or offer any gift, loan, fee, reward, or advantage (*h*) whatsoever to any person, whether for the benefit of that person or of another person, as an inducement to or reward for, or otherwise on account of any member, officer, or servant of any public body as in this Act defined (*h*), doing or forbearing to do anything in respect of any matter or transaction whatsoever, actual or proposed, in which such public body as aforesaid is concerned, shall be guilty of a misdemeanor (*i*).

Penalty for offences.

2. Any person on conviction for offending as aforesaid shall, at the discretion of the court before which he is convicted (*k*)—

(*d*) This sub-section applies to the person bribed or corrupted. The next sub-section deals with the person bribing. It is not necessary on an indictment for an offence under this sub-section to prove that the accused at the time of the commission of the alleged offence was himself a member, officer, or servant of a public body as defined by this Act, the alleged offence being an attempt to obtain a sum of money for abstaining, or inducing other persons to abstain, from giving evidence on an application to the London County Council for a music and dancing licence. *R.* v. *Edwards*, 59 J. P. 88.

(*e*) For the definition of "advantage," "public body," etc., see s. 7, *infra.*

(*f*) This misdemeanor will be an offence which may be tried on indictment at quarter sessions (s. 6). The penalty is prescribed by s. 2.

(*g*) The word "person" includes a body of persons, such as a firm or joint stock company. See s. 7.

(*h*) See the definition of "advantage," "public body," etc., in s. 7, *infra.*

(*i*) See note (*f*) to the preceding sub-section.

(*k*) The court will be either the court of quarter sessions (see s. 6), or the assizes, or Central Criminal Court. The offence is not punishable summarily.

Sect. 2.

(a.) Be liable to be imprisoned for any period not exceeding two years, with or without hard labour, or to pay a fine not exceeding five hundred pounds, or to both such imprisonment and such fine; and

(b.) In addition, be liable to be ordered to pay to such body (*l*), and in such manner as the court directs, the amount or value of any gift, loan, fee, or reward received by him or any part thereof; and

(c.) Be liable to be adjudged incapable of being elected or appointed to any public office (*m*) for seven years from the date of his conviction, and to forfeit any such office held by him at the time of his conviction; and

(d.) In the event of a second conviction for a like offence, he shall, in addition to the foregoing penalties, be liable to be adjudged to be for ever incapable of holding any public office (*m*), and to be incapable for seven years of being registered as an elector, or voting at an election either of members to serve in Parliament or of members of any public body, and the enactments for preventing the voting and registration of persons declared by reason of corrupt practices to be incapable of voting shall apply to a person adjudged in pursuance of this section to be incapable of voting (*n*); and

(e.) If such person is an officer or servant in the employ of any public body upon such conviction (*o*) he shall, at the discretion of the court, be liable to forfeit his right and

---

(*l*) That is, the public body (as defined by s. 7) concerned in the transaction in respect of which the offence was committed.

(*m*) As to what is a public office, see s. 7.

(*n*) The Corrupt Practices Act, 1883, s. 37, provides that every person who, in consequence of conviction, or of the report of an election court under that Act, or the Municipal Corporations Act, 1882, Part IV., or under any other Act for the time being in force, relating to corrupt practices at an election for any public office, has become incapable of voting at any election, whether a parliamentary election or an election to any public office, is prohibited from voting at any such election, and his vote shall be void. By s. 39, the registration officer (*i.e.*, the clerk of the county council or town clerk) in every county and borough is required annually to make out a list of persons disqualified to vote by reason of corrupt practices, and to send this list to the overseers of every parish in the county or borough, and the overseers are to publish this list, and omit the name of every person named in it from the list of voters prepared by them. By the Municipal Elections (Corrupt Practices) Act, 1884 (47 & 48 Vict. c. 70), s. 24, *ante*, p. 358, the town clerk of every municipal borough is required annually, in July, to make out a list of persons disqualified by corrupt practices to vote at a municipal election in the borough, and to send a copy to the overseers of every parish in the borough, and the overseers must omit the names of the persons named therein from the burgess list. It seems to follow from the text that the lists prepared by clerks of the peace and town clerks under these enactments must include the names of all persons convicted under this Act.

(*o*) This consequence will apparently follow, whether the conviction is for a first or a subsequent conviction.

Sect. 2.

claim to any compensation or pension to which he would otherwise have been entitled.

Savings.

3.—(1.) Where an offence under this Act is also punishable under any other enactment, or at common law, such offence may be prosecuted and punished either under this Act, or under the other enactment, or at common law, but so that no person shall be punished twice for the same offence (*p*).

(2.) A person shall not be exempt from punishment under this Act by reason of the invalidity of the appointment or election of a person to a public office (*q*).

Restriction on prosecution.

4.—(1.) A prosecution for an offence under this Act shall not be instituted except by or with the consent of the Attorney-General (*r*).

(2.) In this section the expression "Attorney-General" means the Attorney or Solicitor-General for England, and as respects Scotland, means the Lord Advocate, and as respects Ireland, means the Attorney or Solicitor-General for Ireland.

Expenses of prosecution.

5. The expenses of the prosecution of an offence against this Act shall be defrayed in like manner as in the case of a felony (*s*).

Jurisdiction of quarter sessions.

6. A court of general or quarter sessions shall in England have jurisdiction to inquire of, hear, and determine an offence under this Act (*t*).

Interpretation.

7. In this Act—

The expression "public body" means any council of a county or county of a city or town, any council of a municipal

---

(*p*) It appears from Com. Dig. "Officer" (N.), that all officers, whether such by the common law, or made pursuant to statute, are punishable for corruption or oppressive proceedings, according to the nature and heinousness of the offence, either by indictment, attachment, action at the suit of the party injured, loss of their offices, etc. It is also stated that bribery of an officer is punishable at common law by fine and imprisonment. It is unlikely, however, that any offence which is within the terms of this Act will be dealt with otherwise than as herein provided.

(*q*) In other words, the Act will apply to the corrupt acts of members, officers, or servants who are such *de facto*, though the validity of their election or appointment may be open to question.

(*r*) It is entirely in the discretion of the Attorney-General to grant or refuse his consent. See *Ex parte Hurter*, 47 J. P. 724; 15 Cox C. C. 166. But for the provision in the text, a prosecution could have been instituted by any person.

(*s*) By 7 Geo. 4, c. 64, s. 22, the court before which any person shall be prosecuted or tried for any felony may order payment of the expenses of the prosecutor and his witnesses in attending before the examining magistrate and the grand jury, and in otherwise carrying on the prosecution. By s. 25, these expenses are payable by the treasurer of the county. By 29 & 30 Vict. c. 52, s. 1, in any case of felony the examining magistrate can make an order for costs and expenses of the prosecutor and his witnesses, though there may have been no committal. And by 30 & 31 Vict. c. 35, the provisions of the preceding Acts were extended to the expenses of witnesses for the defence who were bound over to appear at the trial.

(*t*) It seems doubtful whether any such provision was necessary to give jurisdiction to the quarter sessions. The general rule with regard to indictable offences newly created by statute, is that the quarter sessions has jurisdiction unless it is otherwise expressly provided. "Archbold's Quarter Sessions," p. 912; Com. Dig. "Justice of the Peace," B. (3); and see *R.* v. *Cock*, 4 M. & S. 71

Sect. 7.

borough, also any board, commissioners, select vestry, or other body which has power to act under and for the purposes of any Act relating to local government, or the public health, or to poor law, or otherwise to administer money raised by rates in pursuance of any public general Act, but does not include any public body as above defined existing elsewhere than in the United Kingdom (*u*):

The expression "public office" means any office or employment of a person as a member, officer, or servant of such public body:

The expression "person" includes a body of persons corporate or unincorporate:

The expression "advantage" includes any office or dignity, and any forbearance to demand any money or money's worth or valuable thing, and includes any aid, vote, consent or influence, or pretended aid, vote, consent or influence, and also includes any promise or procurement of or agreement or endeavour to procure, or the holding out of any expectation of any gift, loan, fee, reward, or advantage, as before defined.

8. * * * **9.** * * * (*x*).

10. This Act may be cited as the Public Bodies Corrupt Practices Act, 1889. Short title.

TECHNICAL INSTRUCTION ACT, 1889.

(52 & 53 VICT. CAP. 76) (*y*).

An Act to facilitate the Provision of Technical Instruction.

[30th August, 1889.]

* * * * *

1.—(1.) A local authority may from time to time out of the local rate (*z*) supply or aid the supply of technical or manual

Power for local authority to

(*u*) This definition includes all sanitary authorities, urban and rural.

(*x*) Sections 8 and 9 apply to Scotland and Ireland respectively.

(*y*) This Act enables local authorities (including county councils) to supply or aid the supply of technical or manual instruction as defined by s. 8, *infra*. It is amended or explained by the Technical Instruction Act, 1891 (54 Vict. c. 4), *post*. The Technical and Industrial Institutions Act, 1892 (55 & 56 Vict. c. 29), *post*, facilitates the acquisition and holding of land for the purposes of such institutions, and the Local Taxation (Customs and Excise) Act, 1890 (53 & 54 Vict. c. 60), s. 1, *post*, empowers county councils to make contributions for the purposes of technical education out of sums received by them in respect of the residue of the English share of the local taxation (customs and excise) duties under that Act. Such contributions may be made over and above the limited amount which may be raised by rates under the present Act.

County councils may also acquire schools for science and art and literary and scientific institutions under the 54 & 55 Vict. c. 61, *post*; as to their powers with respect to intermediate education in Wales, see the 52 & 53 Vict. c. 40, *ante*, p. 423.

(*z*) The "local rate," in the case of a county council, is the county fund, s. 4, *infra*.

Sect. 1 (1). instruction (*t*), to such extent and on such terms as the authority think expedient, subject to the following restrictions, namely:—

supply or aid the supply of technical instruction.

(a.) The local authority shall not out of the local rate supply or aid the supply of technical or manual instruction to scholars receiving instruction at an elementary school in the obligatory or standard subjects prescribed by the minutes of the Education Department for the time being in force;

(b.) It shall not be required, as a condition of any scholar being admitted into or continuing in any school aided out of the local rate, and receiving technical or manual instruction under this Act that he shall attend at or abstain from attending any Sunday school or any place of religious worship, or that he shall attend any religious observance or any instruction in religious subjects in the school or elsewhere: Provided that in any school, the erection of which has been aided under this Act, it shall not be required as a condition of any scholar being admitted into or continuing in such school, that he shall attend at or abstain from attending any Sunday school or any place of religious worship, or that he shall attend any religious observance or any instruction in religious subjects in the school or elsewhere;

(c.) No religious catechism or religious formulary, which is distinctive of any particular denomination, shall be taught at any school aided out of the local rate, to a scholar attending only for the purposes of technical or manual instruction under this Act, and the times for prayer or religious worship, or for any lesson or series of lessons on a religious subject, shall be conveniently arranged for the purpose of allowing the withdrawal of such scholar therefrom;

(d.) A local authority may, on the request of the school board for its district or any part of its district, or of any other managers of a school or institution within its district for the time being in receipt of aid from the Department of Science and Art, make, out of any local rate raised in pursuance of this Act, to such extent as may be reasonably sufficient, having regard to the requirements of the district, but subject to the conditions and restrictions contained in this section, provision in aid of the technical and manual instruction for the time being supplied in schools or institutions within its district, and shall distribute the provision so made in proportion to the nature and amount of efficient

(*t*) See the definition, s. 8, *infra*; as to aiding the technical and manual instruction supplied in institutions outside the county, and providing scholarships and paying the fees of students ordinarily resident within the county, see the Technical Instruction Act, 1891, s. 1, *post*.

technical or manual instruction supplied by those schools or institutions respectively (*u*); Sect. 1 (1).

(e.) Where such other managers of a school or institution receive aid from a local authority in pursuance of this section, the local authority shall, for the purposes of this Act, be represented on the governing body of the school or institution in such proportion as will, as nearly as may be, correspond to the proportion which the aid given by the local authority bears to the contribution made from all sources other than the local rate and money provided by Parliament to the cost of the technical or manual instruction given in the school or institution aided;

(f.) If any question arises as to the sufficiency of the provision made under this section, or as to the qualification of any school or institution to participate in any such provision, or as to the amount to be allotted to each school or institution, or as to the extent to which, or mode in which, the local authority is to be represented on the governing body of any such school or institution, the question shall be determined by the Department of Science and Art: Provided that no such provision, out of any rate raised in pursuance of this Act, shall be made in aid of technical or manual instruction in any school conducted for private profit; and

(g.) The amount of the rate to be raised in any one year by a local authority for the purposes of this Act shall not exceed the sum of one penny in the pound.

(2.) A local authority may for the purposes of this Act appoint a committee consisting either wholly or partly of members of the local authority, and may delegate to any such committee any powers exerciseable by the authority under this Act, except the power of raising a rate or borrowing money.

(3.) Nothing in this Act shall be construed so as to interfere with any existing powers of school boards with respect to the provision of technical and manual instruction (*u*).

Provision for entrance examination.

2. It shall be competent for any school board or local authority, should they think fit, to institute an entrance examination for persons desirous of attending technical schools or classes under their management or to which they contribute.

(*u*) A school provided by a school board must be a "public elementary school," that is to say, elementary education must be the principal part of the education there given. See Elementary Education Act, 1870 (33 & 34 Vict. c. 75), ss. 3, 14. This does not necessarily exclude other subjects. It is believed that the law officers of the Crown have advised the Education Department that school boards may provide their scholars with technical or manual instruction, and that these boards commonly provide such instruction and receive aid from the Science and Art Department.

Sect. 3.

Parliamentary grants in aid of technical instruction.

3. The conditions on which parliamentary grants may be made in aid of technical or manual instruction shall be those contained in the minutes of the Department of Science and Art in force for the time being.

Provisions as to local authorities.

4.—(1.) For the purposes of this Act the expression "local authority" shall mean the council of any county or borough and any urban sanitary authority within the meaning of the Public Health Acts.

(2.) The local rate for the purposes of this Act shall be—

(a.) In the case of a county council, the county fund (*x*);

(b.) In the case of a borough council, the borough fund or borough rate;

(c.) In the case of an urban sanitary authority not being a borough council, the district fund and general district rate, or other fund or rate applicable to the general purposes of the Public Health Acts;

(3.) A county council may charge any expenses incurred by them under this Act on any part of their county for the requirements of which such expenses have been incurred (*y*).

(4.) A local authority may borrow for the purposes of this Act—

(a.) In the case of a county council, in manner provided by the Local Government Act, 1888 (*z*); 51 & 52 Vict. c. 41.

(b.) In the case of a borough council, as if the purposes of this Act were purposes for which they are authorised by section one hundred and six of the Municipal Corporations Act, 1882, to borrow; 45 & 46 Vict. c. 50.

(c.) In the case of an urban sanitary authority not being a borough council, as if the purposes of this Act were purposes for which they are authorised to borrow under the Public Health Acts.

Audit of accounts of aided schools.

5. Where the managers of a school or institution receive aid from a local authority in pursuance of this Act, they shall render to the local authority such accounts relating to the application of the money granted in aid, and those accounts shall be verified and audited in such manner as the local authority may require and the managers shall be personally liable to refund to the local authority any money granted under this Act, and not shown to be properly applied for the purposes for which it was granted.

Audit of accounts of urban sanitary authority.

6. The accounts of the receipts and expenditure of an urban sanitary authority under this Act shall be audited in like manner

(*x*) See Local Government Act, 1888, s. 68, *ante*, p. 130.

(*y*) Expenses so charged will be "special expenses." Local Government Act, 1888, s. 68.

(*z*) See Local Government Act, 1888, s. 69, *ante*, p. 132.

and with the like incidents and consequences, as the accounts of their receipts and expenditure under the Public Health Act, 1875. Sect. 6.

7. * * * * * (a).

8. In this Act—

The expression "technical instruction" shall mean instruction in the principles of science and art applicable to industries, and in the application of special branches of science and art to specific industries or employments. It shall not include teaching the practice of any trade or industry or employment, but, save as aforesaid, shall include instruction in the branches of science and art with respect to which grants are for the time being made by the Department of Science and Art, and any other form of instruction (including modern languages and commercial and agricultural subjects), which may for the time being be sanctioned by that Department by a minute laid before Parliament and made on the representation of a local authority that such a form of instruction is required by the circumstances of its district. Meaning of technical and manual instruction.

The expression "manual instruction" shall mean instruction in the use of tools, processes of agriculture, and modelling in clay, wood, or other material.

9. This Act shall not extend to Scotland. Extent of Act.

10. This Act may be cited as the Technical Instruction Act, 1889. Short title.

COUNTY COUNCILS ASSOCIATION EXPENSES ACT, 1890 (b).

(53 Vict. Cap. 3.)

An Act to remove doubts as to the Legality of certain Payments by County Councils. [29th March, 1890.]

Whereas an association of county councils of England and Wales has been formed for the purpose of consultation as to their common interests and the discussion of matters relating to local Government:

* * * * *

1. The council of an administrative county may pay out of the county fund, as general expenses incurred by them in the execution Power to defray expenses in

---

(a) Section 7 relates to Ireland exclusively.

(b) This Act extends to county councils a principle which has been recognized in the Poor Law Conferences Act, 1883 (46 Vict. c. 11), and the Public Health and Local Government Conferences Act, 1885 (48 & 49 Vict. c. 22). In these Acts the usefulness of discussing questions relating to poor law or local government is recognized. The above Act goes a step further in permitting a subscription to the fund of the County Councils Association.

Sect. 1.

connexion with association of county councils. 51 & 52 Vict. c. 41.

of their duties under the Local Government Act, 1888, any sum not exceeding thirty-one pounds and ten shillings in any one year, as an annual or other subscription to the funds of the association, as well as any reasonable expenses of the attendance of representatives, not exceeding in any case four, at meetings of the association.

Short title and extent of Act.

2. This Act may be cited for all purposes as the County Councils Association Expenses Act, 1890.

This Act does not extend to Scotland or Ireland.

LUNACY ACT, 1890.

(53 Vict. Cap. 5.)

An Act to consolidate certain of the Enactments respecting Lunatics (c).
[29th March, 1890.]

* *

Preliminary.

Short title.

1. This Act may be cited as the Lunacy Act, 1890.

Extent of Act.

2. Save as in this Act otherwise expressly provided, this Act shall not extend to Scotland or Ireland.

Commencement.

3. This Act shall come into operation, save as in this Act otherwise expressly provided, on the first day of May one thousand eight hundred and ninety.

* * * * *

Chronic lunatics may be received in workhouses in certain cases.

26.—(1.) The visitors of any asylum may, with the consent of the Local Government Board and the Commissioners, and subject to such regulations as they respectively prescribe, make arrangements with the guardians of any union for the reception into the workhouse of any chronic lunatics, not being dangerous, who are in the asylum and have been selected and certified by the manager of the asylum as proper to be removed to the workhouse (*d*).

(2.) Every lunatic received in a workhouse under this section shall, while he remains there, continue a patient on the books of the asylum for the purposes of this Act so far as it relates to lunatics removed to asylums.

(*c*) This Act, as its title states, consolidates with amendments most of the earlier Acts respecting lunatics. It repeals and re-enacts, for example, certain sections of the Local Government Act, 1888. It has itself been amended by the Lunacy Act, 1891 (54 & 55 Vict. c. 65), *post.* Only those sections of the Act are included here which relate to county councils.

(*d*) The visitors above referred to are the visiting committee appointed in counties by the county councils under s. 169 (*post*). For the definition of the terms "asylum," "commissioners," "managers," etc., see s. **341**, *post.*

Institutions in which Lunatics may be received.

Sect. 27 (1).

Institutions to which lunatics may be removed.

27.—(1.) Subject to the restrictions in this section mentioned, every summary reception order, and every reception order made by two or more commissioners, may authorize the reception of the lunatic named in the order not only into an asylum of the county or borough in which the place from which the lunatic is sent is situate, but also into any other institution for lunatics.

(2.) A lunatic shall not under any such order be sent elsewhere than to an asylum of the county or borough in which the place from which he is sent is situate, unless there is no such asylum, or there is a deficiency of room, or there are some special circumstances by reason whereof the lunatic cannot conveniently be taken to such asylum, and the deficiency of room or special circumstances shall be stated in the order (*e*).

(3.) A pauper lunatic shall not be received under an order into any asylum other than an asylum belonging wholly or in part to the county or borough in which the place from which the lunatic is sent or the parish in which he is adjudged to be settled is situate, unless there is a subsisting contract for the reception of lunatics of such county or borough therein, or such borough otherwise contributes to the asylum into which the pauper is to be received, except the order is endorsed by a visitor of that asylum.

(4.) The manager of a hospital or licensed house shall not be bound to receive any lunatic under any such order except in pursuance of a subsisting contract.

* * * * *

Commissioners and visitors not to sign certificates.

33. A medical practitioner who is a commissioner or a visitor shall not sign any certificate for the reception of a patient into a hospital or licensed house, unless he is directed to visit the patient by a judicial authority under this Act, or by the Lord Chancellor or a Secretary of State, or a committee appointed by the judge in lunacy (*f*).

* * * * *

Duration of Reception Orders.

Duration of reception orders.

38.—(1.) Every reception order dated after or within three months before the commencement of this Act, shall expire at the end of one year from its date, and any such order dated three months or more before the commencement of this Act shall expire at the end of one year after the commencement of this Act unless such orders respectively are continued as herein-after provided.

(*e*) This section is amended by s. 6 of the Lunacy Act, 1891, *post*, to meet the case of a lunatic in a workhouse situate in a county which does not include the union to which the workhouse belongs.

(*f*) This prohibition applies to a member of the visiting committee appointed under s. 169 (*post*). The judicial authority referred to in this section is a justice of the peace specially appointed to sign reception orders under the Act, or a county court judge, or a magistrate as defined by s. 341, *post* (see s. 9).

Sect. 38 (2).

(2.) In the case of any institution for lunatics the commissioners may by order under their seal direct that the reception orders of patients detained therein shall, unless continued as herein-after provided, expire on any quarterly day next after the days on which the orders would expire under the last preceding sub-section.

(3.) An order for the removal of a patient from one custody to another shall not be deemed to be a reception order within this section, but the patient who is removed shall after removal be deemed to be detained under the original reception order as a lunatic, and such order shall expire in accordance with the provisions of this section unless continued as herein-after provided.

(4.) * * * * * (*g*).

(5.) The person sending the special report shall give to the commissioners such further information concerning the patient to whom the special report relates as they require.

(6.) If in the opinion of the commissioners the special report does not justify the accompanying certificate, then—

(a.) In the case of a patient in a hospital or licensed house or under care as a single patient, the commissioners shall make further inquiry, and if dissatisfied with the result they or any two of them may by order direct his discharge:

(b.) In the case of a patient in an asylum, the commissioners shall send a copy of the report, with any other information in their possession relating to the case, to the clerk to the visiting committee of the asylum (*h*), and the committee, or any three of them, shall thereupon investigate the case and may discharge the patient or give such directions respecting him as they may think proper.

(7.) The manager of any institution for lunatics, and any person having charge of a single patient, who detains a patient after he has knowledge that the order for his reception has expired, shall be guilty of a misdemeanor.

(8.) The special reports and certificates under this section may include and refer to more than one patient.

(9.) A certificate under the hand of the secretary to the commissioners that an order for reception has been continued to the date therein mentioned shall be sufficient evidence of the fact.

(10.) This section shall not apply to lunatics so found by inquisition.

(*g*) This sub-section (as to the period for which a reception order is to remain in force) is repealed, and a new sub-section substituted by s. 7 of the Lunacy Act, 1891, *post*.

(*h*) As to the visiting committee, see s. 169, *post*. This section is only material for purposes of this work in so far as it imposes the duty of investigation, as above stated, on that committee.

PART II.

Sect. 39 (1).

CARE AND TREATMENT.

Reports after Reception.

Reports upon and visits to private patients.

39.—(1.) The medical officer of every institution for lunatics, and the medical attendant of every single patient shall at the expiration of one month after the reception of a private patient prepare and send to the commissioners a report as to the mental and bodily condition of the patient, in such form as the commissioners direct (*i*).

* * * * *

(7.) In the case of a private patient in an asylum or hospital the commissioners, after receiving the report, shall either make arrangements for a visit being paid, as soon as conveniently may be, to the patient therein named by one or more of the commissioners, who shall report to the commissioners whether the detention of the patient is or is not proper; or the commissioners shall send a copy of the report to the clerk to the visiting committee of the asylum or to the managing committee of the hospital, and one or more members of the committee shall thereupon, as soon as conveniently may be, visit the patient named in the report and report to the committee whether his detention is or is not proper, and the committee, or any three of them, may upon consideration of such last-mentioned report, by writing under their hands discharge the patient or give such directions with regard to him as they think fit.

(8.) If within a month after the reception of any private patient, the institution for lunatics or house into which he was received is visited by one or more commissioners or by any visitors, and such patient is there seen and examined by him or them, and the propriety of his detention reported on in like manner as by this section provided, no special visit shall necessarily be paid to such patient after the receipt of any such report.

(9.) If the commissioners in any case under this section determine that a patient ought to be discharged they may make an order for his discharge.

* * * *

Absence on Trial or for Health.

Absence on trial or for health.

55.—(1.) Any two visitors of an asylum, with the advice in writing of the medical officer, may permit a patient in the asylum to be absent on trial so long as they think fit.

(2.) The visitors may make an allowance to a pauper lunatic absent from the asylum on trial, not exceeding the charge in the asylum, and that allowance, and no more, shall be paid for him as if he were in the asylum.

* * * * *

(*i*) The omitted sub-sections relate only to licensed houses and single patients. Section 8 of the Act of 1891, *post*, provides that s. 39 shall not apply to lunatics received under a removal order, or so found by inquisition.

Sect. 55 (6).

(6.) A commissioner as regards any hospital or licensed house, and two members of the managing committee of a hospital, and two of the visitors of a house licensed by visitors (*k*), may, of their own authority, permit a pauper patient to be absent upon trial for such period as may be thought proper, and may make or order to be made an allowance to the pauper, not exceeding the charge for him in the hospital or house, which shall be payable as if he were in the hospital or house, but shall be paid over to him or for his benefit as the commissioners or visitors may direct.

* * * * *

(8.) If a person allowed to be absent on trial for any period does not return at the expiration thereof, and a medical certificate certifying that his detention as a lunatic is no longer necessary is not sent to the visitors of the asylum or the manager of the hospital or house, he may at any time within fourteen days after the expiration of the period of trial be retaken as in the case of an escape.

* * * * *

Boarding-out Lunatics.

Maintenance for pauper lunatic taken charge of by relatives.

57.—(1.) Where application is made to the visiting committee of an asylum by any relative or friend of a pauper lunatic confined therein that he may be delivered over to the custody of such relative or friend, the committee may, upon being satisfied that the application has been approved by the guardians of the union to which the lunatic is chargeable or the local authority liable for his maintenance, and, in case the proposed residence is outside the limits of such union or the area subject to such local authority, then also by a justice having jurisdiction in the place where the relative or friend resides, and that the lunatic will be properly taken care of, order the lunatic to be delivered over accordingly.

(2.) Where any such order is made, the authority liable for the maintenance of the lunatic shall pay to the person to whom the lunatic is delivered such allowance for the maintenance of the lunatic, not exceeding the expenses which would be incurred on his account if he were in the asylum, as such authority on the recommendation of the visiting committee of the asylum from which the lunatic was delivered over thinks proper.

(3.) For the purposes of section twenty-four, sub-section (2) (f), of the Local Government Act, 1888, a lunatic boarded out by the authorities of any asylum shall be deemed to be a lunatic maintained in an asylum (*l*).

51 & 52 Vict. c. 41.

(*k*) The word "visitors" was a slip for "justices," and the mistake has been set right by 54 & 55 Vict. c. 65, s. 9 (2), *post*. The same sub-section substitutes for "the commissioners or visitors," "such commissioners or such two visitors."

(*l*) See this sub-section, *ante*, p. 56.

Removal of Lunatics.

* * * * *

61.—(1.) The authority liable for the maintenance of a pauper lunatic detained in a hospital or licensed house may make an order for the removal of the lunatic (*m*), and may direct the mode of removal. Remo al of lunatic in a hospital or licensed house by guardians.

(2.) Upon production to the manager of the hospital or house of a copy of the order he shall forthwith remove the patient or suffer him to be removed.

* * * * *

63. Where the visiting committee of an asylum has made an order for a pauper lunatic in the asylum to be delivered to the custody of a relative or friend (*n*), any two members of the committee may at any time, if they think fit, order the lunatic to be removed to the asylum. Removal of lunatic boarded out into asylum.

64. Any two visitors of an asylum may order a pauper lunatic chargeable to any union within any county or borough to which the asylum wholly or in part belongs, or to such county or to any county for the reception of the pauper lunatics whereof into that asylum there is a subsisting contract, to be removed to that asylum from any other institution for lunatics in which he may be detained. Removal of pauper into county asylum.

65.—(1.) Any two visitors of an asylum may order a pauper lunatic in the asylum to be removed to some other institution for lunatics. Removal of pauper from asylum.

(2.) A lunatic shall not be removed under this section without the consent in writing of two Commissioners, except to—

(a.) An asylum within or belonging wholly or in part to the county within which the asylum from which the lunatic is removed is situate, or to the county in some parish of which the lunatic may have been adjudged to be settled; or

(b.) A hospital or licensed house within any such county as aforesaid; or

(c.) An institution for lunatics into which the lunatic can be received under a subsisting contract.

66. The visitors making an order for the removal of a pauper lunatic may by the order require any relieving officer, or other officer of the union, county or borough to which the lunatic is chargeable, or may authorise any other person, to execute the same. Directions as to execution of order for removal.

67. A pauper lunatic shall not be removed under any order for removal made by two visitors without a medical certificate signed by the medical officer of the institution for lunatics from which the Restriction upon removal of paupers by two visitors.

(*m*) See the amendment to this sub-section in s. 11 of the Lunacy Act, 1891, *post*, specifying the workhouse to which the lunatic is to be removed.

(*n*) See s. 57, *ante*.

Sect. 67.

patient is to be removed, certifying that he is in a fit condition of bodily health to be removed.

* * * * *

Removal orders to be in duplicate.

70.—(1.) Every order for the removal of a lunatic from an institution for lunatics or from the charge of any person and the consent of the commissioners thereto, where required, shall be in duplicate. One duplicate shall be delivered to the manager of the institution for lunatics or the person from whose care the lunatic is removed, and the other to the manager of the institution for lunatics, or the person into whose care the lunatic is removed.

(2.) Every such order, with such consent as aforesaid where required, shall be sufficient authority for the removal and reception of the lunatic, in accordance with the order.

(3.) The manager of the institution from which, or the person from whose care the lunatic is removed under any such order, shall deliver, free of expense, a copy of the reception order and documents accompanying the same to the person executing the order for removal, to be by him delivered to the manager of the institution into which or the person into whose care the lunatic is removed.

(4.) Every such copy shall be certified under the hand of the person whose duty it is to deliver the same.

* * * * *

Discharge of Lunatics.

Discharge of private patient.

72.—(1.) A private patient detained in an institution for lunatics, or under care as a single patient, shall be discharged if the person on whose petition the reception order was made by writing under his hand so directs.

(2.) If that person is dead, or incapable by reason of insanity, absence from England, or otherwise, of signing an order for discharge, or, if a patient having been originally classified as a pauper is afterwards classified as a private patient, the person who made the last payment on account of the patient, or the husband or wife, or if there is no husband or wife, or the husband or wife is incapable as aforesaid, the father, or if there is no father, or he is incapable as aforesaid, the mother of the patient, or, if there is no mother, or she is incapable, then any one of the nearest of kin of the patient, may give the direction for his discharge.

(3.) If there is no person qualified to direct the discharge of a patient under this section, or no person able or willing to act, the commissioners may order his discharge.

Discharge of pauper in hospital or house.

73. The authority liable for the maintenance of a pauper lunatic detained in a hospital or licensed house may make an order for the discharge of the lunatic, and may direct the mode of discharge, and upon production to the manager of the hospital or house of a copy of the order he shall forthwith discharge the patient, or suffer him to be discharged.

Sect. 74.

Restriction on discharge.

74. A patient shall not be discharged under the provisions of the two preceding sections if the medical officer of the institution, or, in the case of a single patient, his medical attendant, certifies in writing that the patient is dangerous and unfit to be at large, together with the grounds on which the certificate is founded, unless two of the visitors of the asylum, or the commissioners visiting the hospital or house, or the visitors of the house, or in the case of a single patient, one of the commissioners, after the certificate has been produced, consent in writing to the patient's discharge.

* * * *

Visitors may discharge patients in asylums.

77.—(1.) Any three visitors of an asylum may order the discharge of any person detained therein whether he is recovered or not.

(2.) Any two such visitors, with the advice in writing of the medical officer, may order the discharge of any person detained in the asylum.

* * * * *

Discharge of pauper on application of relative or friend.

79. When application is made to the visiting committee of an asylum by a relative or friend of a pauper lunatic confined therein, requiring that he may be delivered over to the custody and care of such relative or friend, any two of the visitors may, if they think fit, discharge the lunatic upon the undertaking of the relative or friend, to their satisfaction, that the lunatic shall be no longer chargeable to any union, county, or borough, and shall be properly taken care of and prevented from doing injury to himself or others.

Visiting committee may send notice of intention to discharge pauper lunatic to relieving officer or clerk of local authority.

80.—(1.) When the visitors of an asylum order a pauper lunatic confined therein to be discharged, except on the application of a relative or friend, they may, when they think fit, send a notice in writing, signed by the clerk of the asylum, by post or otherwise, of their intention to discharge the lunatic to a relieving officer of the union to which the lunatic is chargeable, or to the clerk of the local authority liable for his maintenance.

(2.) Upon receipt of such notice, the relieving officer or clerk shall cause the lunatic upon his discharge to be forthwith removed to the workhouse of the union to which the lunatic is chargeable, or, if the lunatic is chargeable to a county or borough (*o*), to the workhouse of the union from which he was sent to the asylum.

PART VI.

VISITORS OF LUNATICS.

* * *

Visiting Committees of Asylums.

Constitution of visiting committee.

169.—(1.) For every asylum there shall be a visiting committee appointed annually by the local authority (*p*), consisting of not less than seven members.

(*o*) A lunatic may be chargeable to a county or borough under s. 290, *post.*

(*p*) A local authority is defined by s. 240, *post.* The expression includes a county council.

Sect. 169 (2).

(2.) The visiting committee of a district asylum (*q*) shall be constituted of the number of members fixed by the agreement under which the asylum is provided.

(3.) Where there is more than one asylum, the local authority (*r*) may appoint one committee for the management and control of all the asylums, and such committee shall appoint a sub-committee for each separate asylum, and may delegate to that sub-committee such powers and duties as the committee from time to time think fit.

(4.) Where a county borough has contributed towards the cost of any county asylum, the council of the borough may, if they so desire, appoint to be members of the visiting committee of the asylum such number of members of the council as may be agreed upon, or in default of agreement be determined by the Commissioners under the Local Government Act, 1888 (*s*), or after they have ceased to hold office, by arbitration under that Act (*t*). Such appointment shall be in substitution for any appointment previously made on the part of the borough.

51 & 52 Vict. c. 41.

(5.) Where a borough, not being a county borough, has contributed towards the cost of any county asylum, and the representatives of the borough on the county council are not entitled to vote for the appointment by the council of visitors of the asylum, the council of the borough may appoint two persons to be members of the committee (*u*).

(6.) During the continuance of a contract for the reception of the pauper lunatics of a county borough or borough specified in the Fourth Schedule into a county asylum, the council of the borough shall appoint a visiting committee to visit the lunatics sent from such county borough or borough in the asylum.

Mode of election of visiting committee.

170. Unless some other day is appointed by the standing orders of the local authority, the visiting committee shall be appointed at the quarterly meeting of the local authority in November (*v*).

Vacancies to be filled up.

171.—(1.) If a visitor dies or resigns, or becomes incapable or disqualified (*x*) to act, the authority by whom he was appointed shall, as soon as possible, appoint in his place some qualified person, and the new appointment shall be made in the same manner as the annual election of visitors.

(*q*) A district asylum is one provided by or for two or more local authorities. See s. 242, *post*.

(*r*) A local authority is defined by s. 240, *post*. The expression includes a county council.

(*s*) See s. 61 of that Act, *ante*, p. 117.

(*t*) See s. 62 of that Act, *ante*, p. 119.

(*u*) Representatives of the borough will not be entitled to vote in the cases provided for by s. 35, sub-s. (6) of Local Government Act, 1888, *ante*, p. 81. *i.e.*, in respect of matters involving expenditure on account of which the parishes in the borough are not, for the time being, liable to be assessed equally with the rest of the county to county contributions.

(*v*) As to the quarterly meeting, see the Municipal Corporations Act, 1882, Sched. 2, rule (2), and the notes thereto, *ante*, p. 335. For "November" in the text it is now necessary to substitute "March," see 54 & 55 Vict. c. 68, s. 1, *post*.

(*x*) As to the disqualification of a member, see s. 174, *post*.

(2.) The continuing members of a visiting committee may act notwithstanding any vacancy in the body. Sect. 171 (2).

172.—(1.) A visiting committee shall hold office until the first meeting of their successors. Duration of office.

(2.) If default is made in electing a visiting committee, the visiting committee last elected shall continue in office as if they had been duly re-elected.

173. The visiting committee of every asylum shall, previously to the month of June in every year, examine the accounts of the treasurer and clerk of the asylum, and shall report the same to the next meeting of the local authority, or of each local authority to whom the asylum wholly or in part belongs. Examination of accounts.

174.—(1.) A member of a visiting committee shall not be interested either in his own name or in the name of any other person in any contract entered into or work done for the committee, and shall not derive any profit or emolument whatsoever from the funds of the asylum. Members of visiting committee not to be interested.

(2.) This provision shall not extend to any interest which a member of a visiting committee may have by reason of his being a shareholder of a company which has entered into any contract with or done any work for the visiting committee, but he shall not be entitled to vote in respect of such contract or work (*y*).

175.—(1.) The provisions of section eighty-two of the Local Government Act, 1888 (*z*), with respect to the proceedings of committees of county councils, shall apply to the proceedings of every visiting committee appointed wholly or partly by a county council, and the chairman of such committee may be elected accordingly. Meetings of visiting committee.

(2.) To other visiting committees the following provisions shall apply :—

(a.) The members of the committee shall within one month after their election meet at some convenient place, to be named in a notice in writing given by two or more of such members, or by the clerk of the outgoing committee by the direction of two or more of such members;

(b.) Notices of meetings shall be given to each member personally, or left at his place of abode, or sent by post seven days at least before the time appointed for the meeting;

(c.) The members shall at the first meeting elect one of their number to be chairman of the committee.

(d.) The chairman shall preside at all meetings at which he is present. In case of his absence from any meeting the members present shall elect one of their member to be chairman of the meeting;

(*y*) The cases cited at p. 253, *ante*, may be referred to on the subject of disqualification by interest.

(*z*) See this section, *ante*, p. 157.

Sect. 175 (2).

(e.) Any meeting may be adjourned from time to time and from place to place;

(f.) The committee shall meet as often as they may think fit;

(g.) A meeting may be adjourned by two members; for all other purposes three members shall be a quorum;

(h.) Every question shall be decided by a majority of the votes of the members present, and in the event of an equality of votes the chairman shall have a second or casting vote;

(i.) The clerk of the committee shall, whenever required in writing by the chairman or any two members of the committee, or by the manager of the asylum, and the chairman may, whenever he thinks fit, summon a meeting of the committee.

Clerk to visiting committee.

176.—(1.) Every visiting committee shall appoint a clerk (who may also be the clerk to the asylum) at such salary as the committee think fit, and a clerk so appointed may be discharged, and in the event of a vacancy in the office a new clerk may be appointed. The clerk to the visiting committee shall, unless he be sooner discharged, continue in office so long as the committee continue in office.

(2.) A visiting committee may sue and be sued in the name of their clerk, and an action by or against a visiting committee shall not abate by the death or removal of the clerk, but the clerk for the time being shall always be deemed the plaintiff or defendant in the action.

* * * * *

Visits by visiting committee.

188. At least two members of the visiting committee shall together, once at least in every two months, inspect every part of the asylum, and see every patient therein, so as to give everyone, as far as possible, full opportunity of complaint, and examine the order and certificate or certificates for the admission of every lunatic admitted since the last visitation and the general books kept in the asylum; and shall enter in the visitors book any remarks they think proper in regard to the condition and management of the asylum and the lunatics therein, and shall sign the book upon every visit.

Visits to lunatics received under a contract.

189.—(1.) During the continuance of a contract for the reception of the pauper lunatics of a county borough or other borough in a county asylum not less than two members of the visiting committee of the borough appointed for the purpose shall together, at least once in every six months, visit the asylum and see and examine the lunatics received under the contract, and shall report the result of their visit to the council of the borough.

(2.) The visitors may, if they think fit, be accompanied by a medical practitioner who is not an officer of the asylum, and they may by order direct payment to such medical practitioner of such a sum as they think fit for his services, and such sum shall upon the production of the order be paid to the medical practitioner by the treasurer of the borough.

(3.) Every report under this section shall be entered among the records of the council of the borough, and may be inspected by the Commissioners, and the Commissioners may, if they think fit, require the town clerk of the borough to transmit to them a copy of any such report. Sect. 189 (3).

190.—(1.) The visiting committee of every asylum shall in every year lay before each local authority to which the asylum belongs, at their quarterly meeting in November, or at such other time as the local authority appoints, a report in writing of the state and condition of the asylum, and as to its sufficiency to provide the necessary accommodation, and as to its management and the conduct of the officers and servants and the care of the patients therein. Reports by visiting committee.

(2.) The committee may in the report make such remarks in relation to any matters connected with the asylum as they think fit.

* * * * *

Application of Fees for Licences.

224.—(1.) All moneys received for licences granted by any justices shall be paid by the clerk of the peace for the county or borough into the county or borough fund. Application of moneys received for licences by clerks of the peace.

(2.) The clerk of the peace for every county or borough shall keep an account of all moneys received and paid by him as aforesaid, and of all moneys otherwise received or paid by him in the execution of this Act.

(3.) Such account shall be made up to the thirty-first day of March in each year, or to such other date as the Local Government Board appoint, and shall be signed by two at least of the visitors for the county or borough; and in the case of the clerk of the peace of a county, shall be audited by the same person, in the same manner, and with the same incidents and consequences as the accounts of officers of the county council under the Local Government Act, 1888 (*a*). 51 & 52 Vict. c. 41.

225.—(1.) The justices of every county or borough in quarter or special sessions may order such sums as may be reasonable for payment of the remuneration or salary of the visitors and their clerk, and of all other expenses incurred by or under the authority of the justices or visitors in the execution of this Act, to be paid to the clerk of the peace of the county or borough out of the county or borough fund. Balance of payments over receipts may be paid out of the funds of the county or borough.

(2.) Every such sum shall be paid out of the county or borough fund by the treasurer thereof, and shall be allowed in his accounts, on the authority of the order by the justices for the payment thereof.

(3.) Every sum ordered to be paid by justices of a county under this section shall be subject to the sanction of the standing joint committee of the county council and quarter sessions as provided by section sixty-six of the Local Government Act, 1888 (*b*).

* * * * *

(*a*) See s. 71 of that Act, *ante*, p. 136. (*b*) See this section, *ante*, p. 128.

Sect. 238 (1).

PART IX.

County and Borough Asylums.

Obligation to provide Asylums.

Local authorities to provide asylums.

238.—(1.) Every local authority, as defined by this Act (*c*), shall provide and maintain an asylum or asylums for the accommodation of pauper lunatics.

(2.) Where the asylum accommodation of a local authority appears to the local authority to be insufficient, the local authority may supply the deficiency by exercising the powers by this Act conferred for providing asylum accommodation, or by rebuilding or enlarging any existing asylum.

(3.) For the purpose of providing asylum accommodation a local authority may purchase any licensed or other houses and land.

51 & 52 Vict. c. 41.

(4.) For the purpose of providing asylum accommodation a local authority not being a county council shall have the same powers as are by section sixty-five of the Local Government Act, 1888, conferred upon a county council (*d*).

Powers to be exercised by a visiting committee.

239. A local authority shall exercise the powers conferred by this Act for providing asylum accommodation by a visiting committee (*e*), subject, if the local authority thinks fit, to their directions as to which of the methods of providing asylum accommodation authorized by this Act shall be adopted.

Local Authority defined.

Local authority defined.

240. The council of every administrative county and county borough respectively constituted under the Local Government Act, 1888, and the council of each of the boroughs specified in the Fourth Schedule, or in the case of the City of London the common council, shall be a local authority for the purposes of this Act (*f*).

Powers for providing Asylums.

Power to provide asylums for pauper and private patients.

241. A local authority may provide asylum accommodation for pauper and private patients, together or in separate asylums, and may provide separate asylums for idiots or patients suffering from any particular class of mental disorder.

Modes in which asylum may be provided.

242.—(1.) For the purpose of providing asylum accommodation, a local authority may do all or any of the following things:—

(a.) Provide and maintain an asylum alone;

(b.) Agree to unite in providing and maintaining a district asylum with any other local authority or local authorities;

(*c*) See s. 240, *post*.

(*d*) See this section, *ante*, p. 126.

(*e*) As to the appointment of the visiting committee, see s. 169, *ante*, p. 447.

(*f*) For the list of county boroughs, see the Fourth Schedule to the Local Government Act, 1888, and the note to the schedule, *ante*, p. 205.

Sect. 242 (1).

(c.) Agree to unite with any other local authority or local authorities upon such terms as to payment and otherwise as may be thought proper for the joint use as a district asylum of any existing asylum, and, if they think fit, for the enlargement of the same.

(2.) Where an agreement to unite has been entered into, an agreement for further union may be entered into between all or any of the local authorities concerned, and for all the purposes of this Act an agreement for further union shall be deemed to be an agreement to unite.

(3.) An agreement to unite shall not be carried into effect without the approval of a Secretary of State.

Contract between council of county borough and visiting committee.

243.—(1.) The council of a county borough may contract with the visiting committee of an asylum for the reception of the pauper lunatics of the borough into the asylum.

(2.) Any such contract may be made for such consideration and upon such terms as to duration, determination, and otherwise as may be agreed between the council of the borough and the visiting committee of the asylum.

(3.) While a contract under this section is in force, making adequate provision for the pauper lunatics of the borough, the council of the borough shall not be required to provide an asylum alone or in union.

(4.) A contract under this section shall not be carried into effect until approved by a Secretary of State.

Provision for case where a county borough has contributed to the cost of a county asylum.

244.—(1.) Where a county borough has contributed to the cost of building and furnishing a county asylum, the existing liability of the borough council shall continue until a new arrangement is made under this section, and the county council shall provide accommodation for and maintain pauper lunatics sent from the borough on the same terms as hitherto.

(2.) Any new arrangement may be made between the county council and all the borough councils concerned, with respect to any such asylum; and if any such new arrangement is made, the borough and county councils may carry into effect any adjustment of property, debts, and liabilities which is the subject of such arrangement. If any council desires to make a new arrangement, and any or all of the other councils refuse to agree to the same, the matter shall be referred to the Commissioners under the Local Government Act, 1888, or, after they have ceased to hold office, to arbitration under that Act (*g*). 51 & 52 Vict. c. 41.

Borough contributing to county asylum exempt.

245.—(1.) Where any borough specified in the Fourth Schedule contributes to a county asylum, such borough shall, so long as it continues to contribute, be deemed to satisfy the requirements of this Act with respect to asylum accommodation.

(*g*) The commissioners have ceased to hold office ; see *ante*, p. 119.

Sect. 245 (2).

(2.) The council of the borough may resolve for the purpose of providing asylum accommodation to separate from the county to which it contributes.

(3.) Notice of the resolution to separate shall be given to the clerk of the county council, and upon the expiration of six months from the date of the notice, the council of the borough shall be subject to the obligations imposed by this Act of providing asylum accommodation.

(4.) Notwithstanding a notice to separate, the council of the borough shall continue liable to contribute to the county asylum, until all the pauper lunatics therein belonging to the borough have been removed.

Where borough contracts with county powers of borough to provide an asylum to cease on determination of contract.

246. Where any borough specified in the Fourth Schedule has contracted for the reception of the lunatics of the borough in the asylum of the county in which the borough is situate, the borough shall, on the determination of the contract, cease to be a local authority under this Act, and [*subject to the enactments providing for an additional charge for the maintenance of lunatics in cases where no contribution has been made towards the cost of building and furnishing an asylum*] (*h*), shall be liable to contribute to the county rate of the county in respect of such lunatic asylum in like manner as the rest of the county.

Power of Secretary of State to enforce Act.

Default by county or borough in providing asylum.

247. If the Commissioners report to a Secretary of State that any local authority has failed to satisfy the requirements of this Act as regards asylum accommodation, the Secretary of State may require the local authority to provide such accommodation in such manner as he may direct, and the local authority shall forthwith carry the requisition into effect.

Agreements to unite.

Provisions to be contained in agreements to unite.

248.—(1.) Agreements to unite shall state—

(a.) The number of visitors to be chosen by each contracting party;

(b.) The proportion in which the expenses of providing the asylum are to be borne by each contracting party, and the basis upon which such proportion is fixed;

Form 21.

(c.) Where the agreement provides for the joint user of an existing asylum, the sum to be paid by each contracting party towards expenses already incurred.

(*h*) The words in italics were repealed by the Lunacy Act, 1891, in consequence of the decision in *Howlett* v. *Maidstone*, [1891] 2 Q. B. 110; 60 L. J. Q. B. 570; 65 L. T. (N.S.) 448; 40 W. R. 116; 55 J. P. 549. The substituted enactments are contained in ss. 13—15 of the Act of 1891, *post*.

Sect. 248 (2).

(2.) Provisions in any agreement to unite, subjecting the visiting committee to any control not provided for by this Act, except the control of the Secretary of State, shall be of no effect (*i*).

Apportionment of expenses.

249. The proportion in which the expenses of providing a district asylum are to be borne, as between the uniting counties and boroughs, may be fixed either according to the extent of the accommodation required for each county and borough, or in proportion to the respective population of each county or borough according to the last census for the time being.

Power to vary agreement to unite.

250. An agreement to unite may with the consent in writing of a majority of the visitors of each contracting local authority and with the sanction of the Secretary of State be altered or varied, but not so as to contain any provision which might not have been contained in an agreement to unite in the first instance.

Agreement to unite to be reported and delivered to clerk of local authority.

251.—(1.) Every agreement to unite shall as soon as possible be reported to the local authorities interested.

(2.) The original of every agreement to unite, and of every agreement varying an agreement to unite, shall be delivered to the clerk of the local authority within whose administrative area the asylum to which the same relates is situate or is intended to be situate, and shall be kept by him among the records of the local authority.

(3.) The original agreement so delivered may be inspected without payment by any Commissioner and by any member of the council of any of the contracting local authorities.

(4.) The clerk of a local authority to whom any such agreement is delivered shall cause copies to be made thereof, and shall within twenty days after delivery to him of the original send one copy to the Commissioners and another copy to each of the contracting local authorities.

Application of money paid for expenses already incurred.

252. Where under an agreement to unite a sum is to be paid towards the expenses already incurred by a local authority in relation to an existing asylum, the sum shall be paid to the treasurer of the local authority as part of the county or borough fund and shall be applied to purposes for which capital is properly applicable.

Visitors to be chosen.

253. When an agreement to unite has been reported, each local authority shall elect out of their body the number of visitors agreed to be chosen by them, and the visitors so chosen shall carry the agreement into effect and shall be the visiting committee of the asylum until the election of a visiting committee in their place (*k*).

Purchase of Land and other incidental Powers.

Powers of committee to provide asylum.

254.—(1.) A visiting committee authorised to provide asylum accommodation may agree upon plans and estimates, and contract

(*i*) A form of agreement to unite is contained in Sched. 2, Form 21, *post*.

(*k*) As to the election of a visiting committee, see s. 169, *ante*, p. 447.

Sect. 254 (1). for the purchase of lands and buildings with or without fittings and furniture, and for the erection, restoration, enlargement, and furnishing of buildings, and for the supply of clothing, and for all the matters necessary for carrying into effect the authority conferred upon them.

(2.) Plans and contracts [for the purchase of lands and buildings and for the erection, restoration, and enlargement of buildings] (*l*) agreed upon by a visiting committee shall not be carried into effect until approved by a Secretary of State.

(3.) A visiting committee shall report to the local authority or local authorities by whom they were elected, all plans, estimates, and contracts agreed upon, and also the amount to be paid by each local authority, and such plans, estimates, and contracts shall be subject to the approval of the local authority, to whom they are to be reported, except where the amount to be expended does not exceed an amount previously fixed by the local authority.

(4.) In the event of a difference between any local authorities as to whether any plan, estimate, or contract ought to be approved, the local authority withholding approval shall, within four months after the plan, estimate, or contract has been reported to them, send to a Secretary of State a statement in writing of their objections, and the Secretary of State may direct the plan, estimate, or contract to be carried into execution, with or without any alterations, or he may direct such other plan, estimate, or contract, as he thinks fit, to be carried into execution, and the decision of a Secretary of State under this section shall be final.

Additions to asylums for private patients.

255. The visiting committee of an asylum, with the consent of each local authority by whom the asylum is provided, and with the approval in writing of a Secretary of State, may make such alterations in or additions to the asylum either by way of detached buildings or blocks of buildings or otherwise as they think fit for the purpose of providing accommodation for private lunatics.

Contracts.

256.—(1.) Every person entering into a contract with a visiting committee shall give sufficient security for due performance of the contract.

(2.) Every such contract and all orders relating thereto shall be entered in a book to be kept by the clerk of the visiting committee, and when the contract is completed the book shall be deposited and kept among the records of the local authority, or, when more than one local authority is interested, then among the records of the local authority which contributes the largest proportion of the expenses of the contract.

(3.) Every such book may be inspected at all reasonable times by any person contributing to the rates of the local authority interested in the contract.

(*l*) The words in brackets are inserted into this sub-section by s. 16 of the Lunacy Act, 1891, *post*.

(4.) A copy of every such book shall be kept at the asylum to which the contract relates. Sect. 256 (4).

257.—A district asylum shall not be enlarged or improved without the consent of all the parties to the agreement under which the same is provided. Enlargement of district asylum.

258.—(1.) The visiting committee of an asylum, with the consent of the local authority by whom they are appointed and of a Secretary of State, may provide for the burial of lunatics dying in the asylum, and of the officers and servants belonging thereto— Burial grounds.

(a.) By appropriating any land already belonging to them or acquiring any land, not exceeding in either case two acres, for enlarging an existing burial ground, or for providing a new burial ground;

(b.) By agreeing with any corporation or persons or body of persons willing to provide for the burial of such lunatics and other persons as aforesaid.

(2.) The committee may procure the consecration of a new or enlarged burial ground, and in the case of a new burial ground, may provide for the appointment of a chaplain therein.

(3.) The incumbent of the parish in which a new or enlarged burial ground provided by a visiting committee is situate, shall not be entitled to any fee for the interment of any person buried therein by direction of the committee.

259. Where a visiting committee undertakes the burial of any pauper lunatic, and the public burial ground of the parish where the death took place is closed or inconveniently crowded, the burial may take place in a public burial ground of some other parish, with the consent of the minister and churchwardens of that parish; and in that case the visiting committee shall pay to the person entitled thereto the burial fees payable under any Act or according to the custom of the place of burial. Burial of lunatics.

260. For the purpose of the purchase of lands by visiting committees the Lands Clauses Acts are hereby incorporated with this Act, except the provisions relating to the purchase of land otherwise than by agreement (*m*), the sale of superfluous lands, the recovery of forfeitures, penalties, and costs and access to the special Act, and the expression "promoters of the undertaking" wherever used in the Lands Clauses Acts shall mean a visiting committee, and the expression "special Act" shall mean this Act. Incorporation of Lands Clauses Acts.

261.—(1.) A visiting committee, instead of purchasing any land or buildings which they are authorised to purchase, may take a lease thereof for any term not less than sixty years at such rent and subject to such covenants as the committee think fit. Power to take land on lease.

(*m*) As to the compulsory purchase of lands, see s. 238, sub-s. (4), *ante*, p. 452.

Sect. 261 (2).

(2.) A visiting committee, with the sanction of each local authority for whom they are authorized to act, may hire or take on lease from year to year, or for any term of years, at such rent and subject to such covenants as they think fit, any land or buildings for the employment of the patients in the asylum, or for the temporary accommodation of any pauper lunatics for whom the accommodation in the asylum is inadequate.

(3.) Lands and buildings hired or taken on lease under this section shall be deemed part of the asylum, and be subject to all existing provisions as to the asylum.

Situation of asylum.

262. The asylum to be provided by any local authority either solely or jointly, may be situate without the limits of the administrative area of the local authority, and if the asylum or any part thereof is so situate, the council and justices of the county, county borough, or borough to which the asylum wholly or in part belongs shall have full power and authority to act in the county or borough in which the asylum is situate, so far as concerns the regulation of the asylum and the powers conferred by this Act, as if the asylum were situate within the proper jurisdiction of such council and justices.

Rating of asylums.

263. Lands and buildings already or to be hereafter purchased or acquired for the purposes of any asylum, and any additional building erected or to be erected thereon, shall, while used for those purposes, be assessed to county, parochial, district and other rates made after the commencement of this Act on the same basis and to the same extent as other lands and buildings in the same parish, township, or district (*n*).

How lands to be conveyed.

264. Any lands acquired for the purposes of this Act may be conveyed to the local authority being a county council, or in cases where the local authority is the council of a borough to the municipal corporation of the borough, or, where more than one local authority is interested, to the local authorities interested as joint tenants.

Power to retain land unsuitable or not required for asylum purposes.

265. Any lands or buildings which have been used for the purposes of an asylum, and have been found unsuitable, or are otherwise not required for such purposes, may, with the consent of a Secretary of State, and subject to such conditions as he thinks fit to impose, be retained by the local authority, and appropriated for

(*n*) This alters the previous law as enacted by 16 & 17 Vict. c. 97, s. 35. In rating the asylum lands, the profit, if any, on the sale of produce, must be taken into account. *R.* v. *Fulbourn* (*Overseers of*), 6 B. & S. 451; 34 L. J. M. C. 106; 12 L. T. (N.S.) 444; 13 W. R. 713. The rates are chargeable to the maintenance account, not to the building and repairs account. *R.* v. *Dolby*, [1892] 2 Q. B. 301; 61 L. J. Q. B. 809; 67 L. T. (N.S.) 296; 56 J. P. 599.

Such parts of an asylum as are occupied by officers having an income of more than 160*l.* are assessable to income tax under Schedule A. *Bray* v. *Lancashire JJ.*, 22 Q. B. D. 484; 58 L. J. M. C. 54; 37 W. R. 392; 53 J. P. 499.

any purposes for which the local authority is empowered to acquire land. Sect. 265.

Repairs, alterations, improvements.

266.—(1.) The visiting committee of an asylum may, of their own authority, order all necessary and ordinary repairs. They may also, of their own authority, order all necessary and proper additions, alterations, and improvements which the asylum may require, to an amount not exceeding four hundred pounds in any one year.

(2.) An order for repairs, additions, alterations, or improvements to an amount exceeding one hundred pounds shall not be given, unless the order is approved and signed by at least three visitors at a meeting of the visiting committee duly summoned upon notice that the proposed expenditure is to be considered thereat.

(3.) Any expenditure incurred, except for repairs, shall be reported by the visiting committee to the local authority on whose behalf the expenditure was incurred.

(4.) In the case of a district asylum, the visiting committee shall apportion expenses incurred under this section in the proportion in which each local authority has contributed to the erection of the asylum, or where any other proportion is fixed by an agreement to unite then in the proportion so fixed; and where any such agreement only provides in what proportion the expense of repairs shall be borne, the expense of additions, alterations, and improvements shall be borne in the same proportion.

(5.) The visiting committee shall make an order for payment of the expenses incurred under this section upon the treasurer of the local authority, or, in the case of a district asylum, shall make an order upon the treasurer of each local authority concerned for payment of the expenses apportioned to that local authority, and the treasurer upon whom the order is made shall pay the amount mentioned in the order out of the county or borough fund.

Dissolution of Agreement to unite.

Power to dissolve a union.

267.—(1.) A visiting committee, with the consent of a Secretary of State, may by a resolution passed by a majority of the whole number of the members of the committee at a meeting summoned upon notice that the resolution is to be proposed thereat dissolve an agreement to unite.

(2.) Every local authority interested under an agreement to unite shall, before a dissolution of the agreement takes effect, elect a committee to provide asylum accommodation in accordance with the provisions of this Act.

(3.) In case an agreement to unite is dissolved between any local authority not having an asylum and a local authority which has an asylum and is in receipt of an annual fixed payment as remuneration for any expenses incurred for the benefit of the local authority making the payment, such last-mentioned local authority may raise

Sect. 267 (3). such a sum of money for compensation to the local authority receiving the payment as may be agreed upon and approved by the visiting committee by whom the union is dissolved.

(4.) Upon the dissolution of an agreement to unite the visiting committee may divide the real and personal property held for the purposes of the agreement among the several local authorities, between whom the agreement existed, in the proportion in which they contributed thereto or are interested therein, or in such proportions as the visiting committee, with the consent of a Secretary of State, think fit. And a sum of money of such amount, and to be raised by any of the local authorities parties to the agreement in such proportions as the committee, with the consent of a Secretary of State, approve, may be awarded to any local authority instead of a share or part of a share in such property.

(5.) Any money to be raised under this section may be raised in the same manner and by the same means as other moneys appointed to be raised for the purposes of this Part of this Act (*o*).

Cancellation of Contracts.

Power to cancel contract.

268.—(1.) Where any lands contracted to be purchased or taken in exchange by a visiting committee are found unsuitable, or are not required, the committee, or any committee appointed in their place, may, with the consent of a Secretary of State, and upon payment of such sum, if any, as a Secretary of State approves, procure a release from the contract and execute a release to the other contracting party.

(2.) The consideration, if any, for such release, and all expenses in relation to the contract and release, shall be raised in the same manner as if the same were payable in respect of the purchase money of lands for the purposes aforesaid.

Admission of Pauper Lunatics from other Counties or Boroughs.

Power to contract for reception of lunatics.

269.—(1.) A visiting committee (*p*) (in this section called the contracting committee) may contract with the manager of a licensed house, or subject as in this section provided with any other visiting committee (in this section called the receiving committee), for the reception into that house, or into the asylum of the receiving committee, of all or any of the pauper lunatics of the local authority for which the contracting committee is acting, or for the use and occupation of the whole or any part of the house, upon such terms as may be agreed.

(*o*) See s. 274, *post*.

(*p*) It does not appear to be competent to the visiting committee of a district asylum appointed under an agreement to unite for the purposes of the district asylum only (see s. 169 (2), *ante*, p. 448) to exercise the power of making reception contracts for boarding out surplus lunatics under this section. These must be made by the visiting committee of the county to which the patients proposed to be boarded out belong.

(2.) Where a contract between a visiting committee and the subscribers to a hospital for the reception of pauper patients into the hospital was subsisting on the twenty-sixth of August one thousand eight hundred and eighty-nine, such contract shall continue in force, and on its expiration a new contract may be entered into with such subscribers subject to the provisions of this section (*q*). **Sect. 269 (2).**

(3.) A contract between a visiting committee and any other visiting committee or the manager of a licensed house or the subscribers to a hospital for the reception of the lunatics of the local authority for which the contracting committee is acting (hereinafter called a reception contract) shall not be made for more than five years, but such contract may be renewed subject to the provisions of this section.

(4.) Where a reception contract has been made, whether before or after the passing of this Act, on behalf of a borough with the visiting committee of an asylum, and the contract is determinable by the parties thereto, or either of them, the contract shall not be determined without the consent of a Secretary of State.

(5.) A reception contract shall not be carried into effect until approved by a Secretary of State, and any reception contract may be determined by a Secretary of State.

(6.) A reception contract with the manager of a licensed house shall determine if the house ceases to be licensed.

(7.) A reception contract shall not exempt the local authority for which the contracting committee is acting from the requirements of this Act as regards asylum accommodation if a Secretary of State determines the contract, although the term for which the contract was entered into has not expired.

(8.) Except as in this section provided a visiting committee shall not after the commencement of this Act enter into a reception contract with subscribers to a hospital.

(9.) Where a reception contract has been made by a visiting committee, the local authority for whom the visiting committee acts shall, while the contract subsists, defray out of the county or borough fund so much of the weekly charge agreed upon for each pauper lunatic as in the opinion of the visiting committee represents the sum due for the accommodation, not exceeding one-fourth of the entire weekly charge, in exoneration to that extent of the union to which the maintenance of any such pauper lunatic is chargeable.

(10.) Where a reception contract has been entered into by the visiting committee of an asylum with the subscribers to a hospital or the manager of a licensed house, the hospital or house may be

---

(*q*) Subsisting contracts between the council of a borough and the subscribers to a hospital are put in the same position by s. 17 of the Lunacy Act, 1891, *post*.

Sect. 269 (10). visited by any members for the time being of the committee of the asylum.

Cases where asylum is more than sufficient for pauper lunatics.

270.—(1.) Where it appears to the visiting committee of an asylum that the asylum is more than sufficient for the pauper lunatics who for the time being can be lawfully received, the committee may by resolution permit any other pauper lunatics to be received into the asylum.

(2.) A resolution under this section may require that no pauper lunatic be admitted thereunder without an undertaking by the minute of the guardians of the union to which the lunatic is chargeable for the payment of the expenses of maintenance of the lunatic, and of his burial if he dies in the asylum, as well as for his removal within six days after notice from the manager of the asylum.

(3.) A resolution under this section may be rescinded or varied.

Admission of Private Patients.

Provisions as to private patients in asylums.

271.—(1.) Private patients may be received into any asylum upon such terms as to payment and accommodation as the visiting committee think fit. All enactments as to the conditions on which such lunatics may be received into hospitals or licensed houses shall be applicable to private patients received into such asylums.

(2.) An account of the amount, by which the sums charged for private patients received in the asylum exceed the weekly charges for pauper lunatics sent from or settled in any place, parish, or borough which has contributed to provide the asylum, shall be made up to the last day of each year, and the surplus, if any, after carrying to the building and repair funds such sums, and providing for such outgoings and expenses as the visiting committee consider proper, shall be paid to the treasurer of the local authority to which the asylum belongs, or in the case of an asylum belonging to several local authorities, to their respective treasurers in the proportions in which such local authorities or the justices of the counties and boroughs whose powers have been transferred to them have contributed to the asylum, and shall be applied as part of the county or borough fund.

Approval of Secretary of State.

Mode of obtaining approval of Secretary of State.

272. For the purpose of procuring the approval of a Secretary of State to any agreement, contract, or plan requiring approval under this Act, the agreement, contract, or plan, with an estimate of the probable cost of carrying it into effect, shall be submitted to the Commissioners, and to the Secretary of State, and the Commissioners shall make such inquiries as they think fit, and shall report thereon to the Secretary of State, who may approve the agreement, contract, or plan, with or without modification, or may refuse his approval.

Provisions for raising Expenses.

Sect. 273.

273. The expenses to be paid and contributed by a local authority for the purposes of this Act shall be paid by the treasurer of the local authority out of the county or borough fund as the case may be to the treasurer of the asylum to which such local authority either alone or jointly pays or contributes.

Borrowing Powers.

Power to borrow.

274.—(1.) For the purpose of paying any money payable under this Act, or for repaying any moneys borrowed under this Act or any former Act, authorising borrowing for purposes of asylum accommodation, the local authority may with the consent of the Local Government Board, and subject to the provisions of the Local Government Act, 1888 (*r*), and the Municipal Corporations Act, 1882, according as the same respectively are applicable to the local authority, borrow on the security of the county or borough fund, and of any revenue of the local authority, or on either such fund or revenues or on any part of the revenues, such money as the local authority requires.

51 & 52 Vict. c. 41. 45 & 46 Vict. c. 50.

(2.) The Public Works Loan Commissioners may, if they see fit, make any loan for the purposes of this Act to the local authority upon the security of any fund or revenues applicable to the purposes of this Act.

Rules and Regulations.

General rules and regulations to be framed.

275.—(1.) The visiting committee of an asylum shall within twelve months after the completion of the asylum prepare and submit to a Secretary of State general rules for the government of the asylum, and such rules when approved by a Secretary of State shall be printed and observed.

(2.) The general rules of every asylum may be altered and varied with the approval of a Secretary of State.

(3.) The visiting committee shall also make regulations (not inconsistent with the general rules) setting forth the number and description of officers and servants and their respective duties and salaries.

(4.) The regulations may provide that any number of beds in such part of the asylum as the committee think fit shall be reserved for the cases specified in the regulations, and in that case the asylum shall for the purposes of this Act, as respects the admission of cases not within the class for which beds are reserved, be deemed full when there are no vacant beds except those so reserved, but the committee may, if they think fit, fill any reserved beds.

(5.) The regulations may also provide for the exclusion of any persons afflicted with any malady which the visiting committee

---

(*r*) See s. 69 of that Act, *ante*, p. 132.

Sect. 275 (5). deem contagious or infectious or coming from a place in which such a malady may be prevalent, and for the absence for a period not exceeding four days of a patient from the asylum by permission of the manager.

(6.) The committee shall also determine the diet of the patients.

Officers of Asylums.

Officers of asylums.

276.—(1.) The visiting committee of every asylum shall appoint:—

(a.) A chaplain, who shall be in priest's orders, and shall be licensed by the bishop of the diocese;

(b.) A medical officer, who shall reside in the asylum and shall not be the clerk or treasurer of the asylum;

(c.) A superintendent of the asylum, or, if there is more than one division, a superintendent of each division of the asylum, who shall be the resident medical officer or one of the resident medical officers of the asylum, or of the division of which he is appointed superintendent, unless a Secretary of State authorise the committee to appoint some other person than a medical officer to be superintendent;

(d.) A clerk;

(e.) A treasurer;

(f.) Such other officers and servants as they think fit.

(2.) The visiting committee may appoint a minister of any religious persuasion to attend patients of the religious persuasion to which the minister belongs.

(3.) The committee may remove any person appointed under this section, and if the office of chaplain, medical officer, superintendent, clerk, or treasurer becomes vacant, the committee shall appoint a person to fill the vacancy subject to the restrictions affecting the original appointment, and they may in their discretion fill any vacancies among other officers and servants of the asylum.

(4.) The committee may also appoint a visiting physician or surgeon to the asylum.

(5.) The salaries, wages, and remuneration of every person appointed under this section shall be fixed by the committee.

277.—(1.) The licence of the chaplain of an asylum shall be revocable by the bishop.

The chaplain.

(2.) The chaplain, or his substitute approved by the committee, shall perform in the chapel of the asylum, or in some other convenient place belonging to the asylum, divine service according to the rites of the Church of England on every Sunday, Christmas-day, and Good-Friday. He shall also perform divine service, and such other services according to the rites of the Church of England as the committee direct, at such times as they appoint.

(3.) If a patient is of a religious persuasion differing from that of the established Church, a minister of his persuasion, at the request of the patient or his friends, may, with the consent of the medical officer and under such regulations as he approves, visit the patient. **Sect. 277 (3).**

278.—(1.) The clerk of the asylum shall keep all books and documents which the visiting committee are required to keep or direct to be kept. Books and accounts.

(2.) He shall also keep an account of the receipts and expenditure on account of the asylum.

(3.) Before the thirtieth day of September in each year, or such other date as the Local Government Board appoint, he shall send an abstract of the account for the previous year, ending on the thirty-first day of March, or such other date as the Local Government Board appoint, to the Local Government Board, and to the Commissioners.

(4.) The abstract shall contain such particulars and be in such form as the Local Government Board direct.

(5.) Within one month from the receipt of the abstract a copy thereof shall be laid before both Houses of Parliament, if Parliament is then sitting, and if not, within one month from the commencement of the next session.

(6.) The treasurer and every officer of an asylum who receives or expends money or goods on account of the asylum shall keep accounts of his receipts and expenditure.

(7.) This section shall not affect any order made by the Local Government Board before the commencement of this Act.

279. * * * * * (*s*).

Pensions.

280.—(1.) The visiting committee may grant to any superintendent, chaplain, matron, or other officer or servant of the asylum, who is incapacitated by confirmed illness, age, or infirmity, or who has been an officer or servant in the asylum for not less than fifteen years and is not less than fifty years old, such superannuation allowance as the committee think fit (*t*). Pensions of officers.

(2.) Where the offices of superintendent and matron are held by man and wife, and a superannuation allowance has been granted to the superintendent, the committee may, if the matron has been an officer of the asylum for not less than twenty years, grant her such

(*s*) Section 279 (as to accounts of county asylums) is repealed by the Lunacy Act, 1891, *post*; s. 18 of that Act being substituted.

(*t*) It was held in *R.* v. *Hereford County Council*, 63 L. T. (N.S.) 245; 38 W. R. 775; 55 J. P. 72, that it was not necessary for the purpose of receiving a superannuation allowance, that the chaplain should reside in the asylum or give his whole time to the duties of his office therein; that there was no distinction between an officer of and an officer in the asylum; and that as the chaplain performed his duties in the asylum, he was an officer in the asylum, and therefore entitled to a superannuation allowance if the visitors in their discretion granted it.

Sect. 280 (2). superannuation allowance as they think fit, although she is not incapacitated by illness, age, or infirmity: Provided that, if any such matron is appointed to a public office or to any office under this Act in respect of which she receives a salary, her superannuation allowance shall, so long as she receives such salary, be suspended or diminished by the amount of the salary according as the salary is or is not greater than the allowance.

(3.) A superannuation allowance shall not exceed two-thirds of the salary paid to the superannuated person at the date of superannuation and such further sum (if any) as the visitors think fit to grant, having regard to the value of the lodgings, rations, and other allowances enjoyed by the superannuated person.

Mode in which pension to be granted.

281.—(1.) A superannuation allowance shall not be granted unless seven clear days' notice of the meeting at which the same is to be granted, and of the intention to determine thereat the question of such grant, has been given, nor unless three visitors concur in and sign the order granting the same.

(2.) A superannuation allowance granted under this Act shall be paid out of the county or borough fund as the case may be.

(3.) A superannuation allowance payable out of the county fund shall not be paid until the grant thereof has been confirmed by the county council.

Service in several asylums of the same local authority.

282. When any officer is transferred from one asylum to another, wholly or in part belonging to the same local authority, his service in all such asylums shall be counted for the purpose of computing his pension, superannuation allowance, or gratuity for length of service, as if all such asylums had constituted only one asylum.

PART X.

Expenses of Pauper Lunatics.

Weekly Expenses.

Weekly sum to be fixed.

283.—(1.) Every visiting committee shall fix a weekly sum, not exceeding fourteen shillings, for the expenses of maintenance and other expenses of each pauper lunatic in the asylum, and of such amount that the total of such weekly sum shall be sufficient to defray such expenses and also the salaries of the officers and attendants of the asylum, and such weekly sum may from time to time be altered (*u*).

(2.) If fourteen shillings a week is found insufficient for the purposes aforesaid, the local authority to whom the asylum belongs may by order direct such addition to be made to the weekly sum

(*u*) Where the visiting committee had in their hands a sum of money, being the excess of receipts over the cost of maintaining lunatics in the asylum, it was held that the guardians of the several unions had no claim to the funds, but that as between the committee and the county council, the latter were entitled. *Proctor* v. *Cheshire County Council*, 56 J. P. 532.

as to the local authority seems necessary, and every such order shall be signed by the clerk of the local authority, and forthwith published in a local newspaper. Sect. 283 (2).

(3.) A committee may fix a greater weekly sum not exceeding fourteen shillings, to be charged in respect of pauper lunatics other than those sent from or settled in a parish or place within the county or borough to which the asylum belongs.

(4.) Any excess created by the payment of such greater weekly sum may, if the visiting committee think fit, be paid over to a building and repair fund, to be applied by the committee to the altering, repairing, or improving the asylum, and the committee shall annually submit to the local authority a detailed statement of the manner in which such fund has been expended (*u*).

Uniform charge where more than one asylum.

284. Where there is more than one asylum under the management and control of a visiting committee, the committee may, subject to any direction given by the local authority, provide that a uniform charge shall be made for the maintenance of lunatics in the several asylums, and that for that purpose any surplus arising on the accounts of one asylum shall be applied to meet the deficit arising on the accounts of another asylum.

* * * * *

Liability for Expenses of Maintenance.

Chargeability of pauper lunatic.

286.—(1.) Where a pauper lunatic is sent to an institution for lunatics, or where a lunatic in an institution for lunatics becomes a pauper, he shall be deemed to be chargeable to the union from which he was sent, until it has been established, as by this Act provided, that the lunatic is settled in some other union, or that it cannot be ascertained in what union the lunatic was settled, and the manager of the institution shall forthwith give to the authority liable for his maintenance notice that the lunatic has become destitute.

(2.) Every pauper lunatic who is chargeable to a union shall, while he resides in an institution for lunatics, be deemed for the purposes of his settlement to be resident in the union to which he is chargeable.

Orders for maintenance of lunatics.

287.—(1.) The justice by whom any pauper lunatic is sent to any institution for lunatics under this Act, or any two justices of the county or borough in which the institution for lunatics where any pauper lunatic is confined is situate, or from any part of which any pauper lunatic has been sent, or any two justices, being visitors of such institution, may make an order upon the guardians of the union to which the lunatic is chargeable, for payment to the treasurer, or manager of the institution, of the reasonable charges of the lodging, maintenance, medicine, clothing, and care (in this Act referred to as the expenses of maintenance) of such lunatic (*x*).

(*x*) An application for an order under this section may be made *ex parte*. *R.* v. *Bruce*, [1892] 2 Q. B. 136 ; 40 W. R. 686 ; 56 J. P. 567.

Sect. 287 (2).

(2.) Any such order may be retrospective or prospective, or partly retrospective and partly prospective.

(3.) An order under this section shall not be subject to appeal (*y*).

Inquiry into settlement.

288. Any two justices for the county or borough in which an institution for lunatics where a pauper lunatic is or has been confined is situate, or to which such institution being an asylum wholly or in part belongs, or from any part of which any pauper lunatic is or has been sent for confinement, may, at any time, inquire into the settlement of the pauper lunatic (*z*).

Adjudication as to settlement.

289. If satisfactory evidence can be obtained as to such settlement in any union, such justices shall, by order, adjudge the settlement, and order the guardians of the union to pay to the guardians of any other union the expenses incurred in or about the examination of the lunatic and the bringing him before a justice or justices, and his removal and conveyance to or from any institution for lunatics (in this Act referred to as the incidental expenses), and all moneys paid by such last-mentioned guardians to the treasurer or manager of the institution for the expenses of maintenance of the lunatic, and incurred within twelve months previous to the date of such order, and, if the lunatic is still in confinement, also to pay to the treasurer or manager of the institution the reasonable expenses of the future maintenance of such lunatic (*a*).

If settlement cannot be ascertained a pauper lunatic may be made chargeable to a borough or county.

290.—(1.) If a pauper lunatic is not settled in the union from which he was sent to an institution for lunatics, and his settlement cannot be ascertained (*b*), and the lunatic was sent from a quarter sessions borough which is free from contributing to the payment of the expenses of pauper lunatics chargeable to the county in which the borough is situate, or from a place not in such a borough, then the relieving officer of the union shall give to the clerk of the local authority within whose area the lunatic is found, ten days' notice to appear before two justices having jurisdiction within such area, at a time and place to be appointed in the notice.

(2.) Upon the appearance of the clerk of the local authority, in person or by deputy, or in case of non-appearance upon proof of due

---

(*y*) An order under this section is ministerial only, and where a claim is made under such an order, the court can go behind it, and inquire whether it was properly made. *Suffolk County Lunatic Asylum* v. *Stow Union*, 76 L. T. (N.S.) 494 ; 45 W. R. 620 ; 61 J. P. 328.

(*z*) The inquiry may be made at any time, even after the discharge or death of the lunatic. See *R.* v. *Manchester (Guardians of)*, 6 E. & B. 919 ; 26 L. J. M. C. 1 ; 28 L.T. (N.S.) 369 ; 20 J.P. 726 ; *Hunslet* v. *Dewsbury*, 26 L. J. M. C. 3 ; 28 L. T. (N.S.) 99. A second order may be made where there has been a change of settlement. *West Derby Union (Guardians of)* v. *Liverpool Select Vestry*, 46 J. P. 372.

(*a*) This order may be made *ex parte*. See *R.* v. *Bruce*, *ante*, p. 467.

(*b*) This applies where the lunatic was born in Scotland or Ireland, and has not acquired a settlement in England. *Somersetshire (Clerk of the Peace for)* v. *Shipham (Overseers of)*, 3 B. & S. 507 ; 32 L. J. M. C. 83 ; 7 L. T. (N.S.) 673 ; 27 J. P. 437.

service of the notice, any two or more such justices may inquire into the circumstances of the case, and adjudge the pauper lunatic to be chargeable to the local authority, and may order the treasurer of the local authority to pay to the guardians of any union the incidental expenses of the lunatic, and all moneys paid by such guardians to the treasurer or manager of the institution for lunatics for the expenses of maintenance of the lunatic, and incurred within twelve months previous to the date of the order, and if the lunatic is still in confinement, to pay to such treasurer or manager the expenses of the future maintenance of the lunatic. Sect. 290 (2).

(3.) Such justices may direct such further inquiries as they think fit to ascertain the union in which any pauper lunatic is settled, and delay their adjudication until after such further inquiries.

(4.) Every local authority to whom a pauper lunatic is adjudged to be chargeable may at any time thereafter inquire as to the union in which the lunatic is settled, and may procure him to be adjudged to be settled in any union (*c*).

Provision for reimbursement of expenses of a lunatic afterwards adjudged to be settled in a union.

291. If after a pauper lunatic has been sent to an institution for lunatics, and has been adjudged chargeable to a local authority, the local authority procure the lunatic to be adjudged to be settled in a union, any two justices of the county or borough in which the institution where the lunatic is confined is situate, or from any part of which the lunatic was sent for confinement, or any two justices, being visitors of the institution, may make an order upon the guardians of the union for payment to the treasurer of the local authority of all expenses of maintenance of the lunatic paid by such treasurer to the treasurer or manager of the institution, and incurred within twelve months previous to the order, and, if the lunatic is still in confinement, also for payment to such treasurer or manager of the expenses of the future maintenance of the lunatic.

Orders as to lunatic paupers.

292.—(1.) Justices by this Act authorised to make orders for payment of expenses upon guardians of unions, may make such orders, although the union is not within the jurisdiction of the justices.

(2.) Orders as to the settlement or chargeability of pauper lunatics and for payment of expenses may be obtained by the guardians of any union.

Order for maintenance to extend to any place where the lunatic is.

293. An order for payment of the future expenses of maintenance of a lunatic shall extend to the payment of such expenses to the treasurer or manager of any institution for lunatics to which he is removed or in which he is for the time being confined.

The costs of pauper lunatics who are irremovable.

294. All incidental expenses and expenses of maintenance of a lunatic removed to an institution for lunatics who would at the time of his removal have been exempt from removal to the parish of his

(*c*) See *All Saints* (*Poplar*) v. *Middlesex* (*Clerk of the Peace of*), 2 E. & E. 829; 29 L. J. M. C. 186; 2 L. T. (N.S.) 215; 24 J. P. 661.

Sect. 294.

9 & 10 Vict. c. 66.

settlement or the country of his birth by reason of some provision of the Poor Removal Act, 1846, as amended by subsequent Acts, shall be paid by the guardians of the union wherein the lunatic has acquired such exemption, and no order shall be made in respect of such lunatic under any provision contained in this or any other Act upon the guardians of the union in which the lunatic is settled while the above-mentioned expenses are to be paid and charged as herein provided (*d*).

Charges may be paid without orders of justices.

295. The guardians upon whom an order might be made under this Act for the payment of any money may pay the same without an order, and may charge the same to such account as they could have done if an order had been made.

The liability of relations of pauper not to be affected.

296. The liability of any relation or person to maintain any lunatic shall not be taken away or affected, where such lunatic is sent to or confined in any institution for lunatics, by any provision herein contained concerning the maintenance of such lunatic.

Expenses of removal, discharge, and burial.

297. The necessary expenses attending the removal, discharge, or burial of a pauper lunatic in any institution for lunatics, shall be borne by the union to which the lunatic is chargeable, or the local authority liable for his maintenance, and shall be paid by the guardians of the union or by the treasurer of the local authority.

Provisions of Act as to expenses to extend to pauper lunatics sent to asylums under any other Act.

298. The provisions of this Act for the payment of expenses in relation to pauper lunatics shall be applicable with respect to persons confined as pauper lunatics sent to any institution for lunatics under any other Act authorizing their reception therein as pauper lunatics, and (save as herein otherwise provided concerning any lunatic who shall appear to have any real or personal property applicable to his maintenance) with respect to all other lunatics sent to any institution for lunatics under any order of a justice or justices made before the commencement of this Act, or under a summary reception order made by a justice under this Act, or under an order made by two or more commissioners before or after the commencement of this Act, as if such last-mentioned lunatics were at the time of being so sent actually chargeable to the union from which they are sent.

Application of Lunatic's Property.

Power to recover expenses against lunatic's estate.

299.—(1.) If it appears to any justice that a lunatic, chargeable to any union, or local authority, has any real or personal property more than sufficient to maintain his family, if any, such justice may by order direct a relieving officer of the union, or the treasurer or some other officer of the local authority, to seize so much of any money,

(*d*) It is beyond the scope of the present work to enter into details of the law relating to the removability of paupers, but as bearing directly on the operation of the above section, reference may be made to *R.* v. *Whitby Union*, L. R. 5 Q. B. 325 ; 39 L. J. M. C. 97 ; 22 L. T. (N.S.) 336 ; 34 J. P. 725 ; *R.* v. *Bruce*, *ante*, p. 467 ; *Hendon* v. *Hampstead*, 62 L. J. M. C. 170.

and to seize and sell so much of any other personal property of the lunatic, and to receive so much of the rents of any land of the lunatic as the justice may think sufficient to pay the expenses of maintenance and incidental expenses respectively incurred or to be incurred in relation to the lunatic (*e*). Sect. 299 (1).

(2.) If any trustee, or the Bank, or any other society or person having possession of any property of a lunatic, shall pay or deliver to a relieving officer of a union, or to the treasurer or other officer of the local authority to which respectively a lunatic is chargeable, any money or other property of the lunatic, to repay the charges in this section mentioned, whether pursuant to an order under this section, or without an order, the receipt of such relieving officer, treasurer, or officer shall be a good discharge (*f*).

Order by county court judge.

300. An order may be made by a judge of county courts upon an application by the guardians of any union for payment of the expenses incurred by them under this Act in relation to a lunatic, and such order may be enforced against any property of the lunatic in the same way as a judgment of the county court.

Appeals.

Persons aggrieved by refusal of an order may appeal to the sessions.

301.—(1.) Any person aggrieved by the refusal of an order by any justice or justices as to any matter within the jurisdiction of a justice or justices under this Part of this Act, may appeal to a court of quarter sessions upon giving to the justice or justices against whom the appeal is made fourteen clear days' notice of appeal.

(2.) The determination of the court upon the appeal shall be final.

Party obtaining order of adjudication to send copy thereof and statement of grounds.

302. The guardians of any union, and the clerk of a local authority, obtaining any order under this Act adjudging the settlement of any lunatic to be in any union, shall, within a reasonable time after the date of the order, send or deliver, by post or otherwise, to the guardians of the union in which the lunatic is adjudged to be settled, a copy of the order, and also a statement in writing under the hand of the clerk to the guardians, or under the hand of the clerk of the local authority, as the case may be, stating the description and address of the guardians or clerk obtaining the order, and the place of confinement of the lunatic, and setting forth the grounds of the adjudication, including the particulars of any settlement relied upon in support thereof; and on the hearing of any appeal against the

---

(*e*) This applies to the case of a lunatic chargeable to a county under s. 290.

(*f*) This sub-section merely enables trustees and others to pay or hand over the property. See *Re Newbegin*, 36 Ch. D. 477; 56 L. J. Ch. 907; 57 L. T. (N.S.) 390; 36 W. R. 69. Whether the justice's order can be enforced at all is not clear, but at all events an injunction will be granted to restrain its being enforced when a receiver in lunacy has been appointed. *Winkle* v. *Bailey*, [1897] 1 Ch. 123; 66 L. J. Ch. 181; 75 L. T. (N.S.) 577; 61 J. P. 135.

Sect. 302. order the respondents shall not give evidence of any other grounds in support of the order than those set forth in such statement (*g*).

Appeal against order of adjudication.

303. If the guardians of any union feel aggrieved by any order adjudging the settlement of a lunatic, they may appeal to the quarter sessions for the county or borough on behalf of which the order has been obtained, or in which the union obtaining the order is situate, or, in case such union extends into several counties, then to the next quarter sessions for the county or borough in which the institution for lunatics where the lunatic is or has been confined is situate, and such sessions, upon hearing the appeal, shall have full power finally to determine the matter.

Copy of depositions to be furnished on application

304.—(1.) The clerk to the justices making an order adjudging the settlement of a lunatic, or the clerk of the peace in the case hereinafter provided for, shall keep the depositions upon which the order was made, and shall, within seven days after application by any party authorised to appeal against the order, furnish a copy of the depositions to the applicant.

(2.) The person applying for a copy of the depositions shall pay for the same at the rate of twopence for every folio of seventy-two words.

(3.) No omission or delay in furnishing a copy of the depositions shall be a ground of appeal against the order.

(4.) On the trial of any appeal no such order shall be quashed or set aside either wholly or in part on the ground that the depositions do not furnish sufficient evidence to support, or that any matter therein contained or omitted raises an objection to the order or grounds on which the same was made.

(5.) If the justices who make any such order have no clerk, they shall send or deliver the depositions to the clerk of the peace of the county or borough to the quarter sessions whereof the appeal lies, and the party obtaining such order shall, in the statement of the grounds of adjudication, state that the justices have no clerk.

No appeal if notice not given within a certain time.

305. No appeal shall be allowed against any such order if notice in writing of the appeal is not sent or delivered by post or otherwise to the party on whose application the order was obtained within twenty-one days after the sending or delivery, as hereinbefore directed, of a copy of the order, and such statement as hereinbefore mentioned, unless within the twenty-one days a copy of the depositions has been applied for by the party intending to appeal, in which case a further period of fourteen days after the sending of such copy shall be allowed for giving notice of appeal.

Grounds of appeal to be stated.

306. In every case where notice of appeal against such order is given the appellant shall, with the notice, or fourteen days at least

(*g*) As to the amendment of the grounds of appeals, see s. 307, *post*, and *R.* v. *Manchester* (*Guardians of*) 6 E. & B. 919; 26 L. J. M. C. 1; 28 L. T. (N.S.) 820; 2 J. P. 726.

before the first day of the sessions at which the appeal is to be tried, send or deliver by post or otherwise to the respondent a statement in writing under his hand, or where the appellants are the guardians of a union, under the hand of the clerk to the guardians, of the grounds of such appeal; and the appellant shall not, on the hearing of any appeal, give evidence of any other grounds of appeal than those set forth in such statement. Sect. 306.

As to the sufficiency of statements of grounds of adjudication or appeal.

307.—(1.) Upon the hearing of any appeal against any such order no objection whatever on account of any defect in the form of setting forth any ground of adjudication or appeal in any such statement shall be allowed, and no objection to the reception of legal evidence offered in support of any such ground alleged to be set forth in any such statement shall prevail, unless the court is of opinion that such alleged ground is so imperfectly or incorrectly set forth as to be insufficient to enable the party receiving the same to inquire into the subject of such statement, and to prepare for trial.

(2.) In all cases where the court is of opinion that any such objection to such statement or to the reception of evidence ought to prevail, the court may, if it thinks fit, cause any such statement to be forthwith amended by some officer of the court, or otherwise, on such terms as to payment of costs to the other party, or postponing the trial to another day in the same sessions, or to the next subsequent sessions, or both payment of costs and postponement, as to the court appears just.

Power for court to amend order on account of omission or mistake.

308.—(1.) If, upon the trial of any appeal against any such order, or upon the return to a writ of certiorari, any objection is made on account of any omission or mistake in drawing up the order, and it is shown to the satisfaction of the court that sufficient grounds were proved before the justices making the order to authorise the drawing up thereof free from the omission or mistake, the court may, upon such terms as to payment of costs as it thinks fit, amend the order and give judgment as if no omission or mistake had existed (*h*).

(2.) No objection on account of any omission or mistake in any such order brought up upon a return to a writ of certiorari shall be allowed, unless the omission or mistake has been specified in the rule for issuing such writ of certiorari.

Power of court as to costs

309.—(1.) Upon every such appeal the court before whom the same is brought may, if it thinks fit, order the party against whom the same is decided to pay to the other such costs and charges as may to the court appear just, and shall certify the amount thereof.

(2.) If either of the parties to the appeal have included in the statement of grounds of adjudication or of appeal sent to the opposite party any grounds in support of the order or of appeal which, in the opinion of the court determining the appeal, are

(*h*) An amendment cannot be made so as to affect new parties not before the court. *R.* v. *Liverpool*, 29 L. J. M. C. 137; 2 L. T. (N.S.) 173; 24 J. P. 646.

Sect. 309 (2). frivolous and vexatious, such party shall be liable, at the discretion of the court, to pay the whole or any part of the costs incurred by the other party in disputing any such grounds.

Decision upon appeal to be final.

310. The decision of the court upon the hearing of any appeal against any such order, as well upon the sufficiency and effect of the statement of the grounds in support of the order and appeal, and of the copy or duplicate of the order sent to the appellant, as upon the amending or refusing to amend the order as aforesaid, or the statement of grounds, shall be final, and shall not be liable to be reviewed in any court by means of a writ of certiorari or mandamus or otherwise.

Abandonment of orders.

311.—(1.) In any case in which an order has been made as aforesaid, and a copy thereof sent as herein required, the party who has obtained the order, whether any notice of appeal against the order has been given or not, and whether any appeal has been entered or not, may abandon the order, by notice in writing under the hand of such party, or, where the order has been obtained by the guardians of a union, under the hand of the clerk to the guardians, to be sent by post or delivered to the appellant or the party entitled to appeal, and thereupon the order and all proceedings consequent thereon shall be void, and shall not be given in evidence, in case any other order for the same purposes is obtained.

(2.) In all cases of such abandonment the party abandoning shall pay to the appellant or the party entitled to appeal the costs which he has incurred by reason of the order and of all subsequent proceedings thereon.

(3.) The proper officer of the court before whom the appeal (if it had not been abandoned) might have been brought shall, upon application, tax and ascertain the costs, at any time, whether the court is sitting or not, upon production to him of the notice of abandonment, and upon proof to him that such reasonable notice of taxation, together with a copy of the bill of costs, has been given to the guardians, or clerk abandoning the order, as the distance between the parties shall in his judgment require; and thereupon the sum allowed for costs, including the usual costs of taxation, which such officer is hereby empowered to charge and receive, shall be endorsed upon the said notice of abandonment, and the said notice so endorsed shall be filed among the records of the said court.

Guardians and officers' interested to have access to the lunatic.

312. In every case of an inquiry, or appeal as to the union in which a pauper lunatic is settled, the guardians, clerks of the guardians, and relieving officers of every union interested in the inquiry or appeal, and every person duly authorised by them respectively, and the clerk of the local authority interested in the inquiry or appeal, and every person duly authorised by him, shall at all reasonable times be allowed free access, in the presence of the medical attendant, to the lunatic to examine him as to the premises.

313. The provisions of section thirty-one of the Summary Jurisdiction Act, 1879, shall not apply to appeals under this part of this Act.

Sect. 313.

Section 31 of 42 & 43 Vict. c. 49. not to apply.

Recovery of Expenses.

314.—(1.) If the treasurer of any local authority, upon whom any order of justices for the payment of money under the provisions of this Act is made, refuses or neglects for twenty days after due notice of such order to pay the money, the money, together with the expenses of recovering the same, shall be recovered by distress and sale of the goods of the treasurer so refusing or neglecting, by warrant under the hands of any two justices authorised to make the order for payment of the money, or by an action at law, or by any other proceeding in a court of competent jurisdiction, against the treasurer.

Money ordered to be paid may be recovered by distress or action.

(2.) If the guardians upon whom any such order is made refuse or neglect for such time as aforesaid to pay the money, the same, together with the expenses of recovering the same, may be recovered by an action at law or by any other proceeding in any such court.

(3.) In case of any such action or proceeding no objection shall be taken to any default or want of form in any order for reception or maintenance, or in any certificate or adjudication under this Act, if such order or adjudication has not been appealed against, or if appealed against has been affirmed.

PART XI.

Penalties, Misdemeanors, and Proceedings.

* * * * *

319. If the manager of an institution for lunatics, or the person having charge of a single patient, omits to send to the coroner notice of the death of a lunatic within the prescribed time, he shall be guilty of a misdemeanor.

Notice to coroner of death.

320. Any person who makes default in sending to the Commissioners or any other person any return, report, extract, copy, statement, notice, plan, or document, or any information within his knowledge or obtainable by him, when required so to do under this Act or any other Act relating to lunacy, or any rules made under this Act or in complying with the said Acts or rules, shall for each day or part of a day during which the default continues be liable to a penalty not exceeding ten pounds, unless a penalty is expressly imposed by this or any other Act for such default: Provided that all or any part of the cumulative penalties may be remitted by the court in any case in which it is made to appear to the satisfaction of the court that the original default or its

Penalty for non-compliance with the Act and rules.

Sect. 320.

continuance during any period of time arose from mere accident or oversight, and not from wilful or culpable neglect on the part of the person sued.

Obstruction.

321.—(1.) Any person who obstructs any Commissioner or Chancery or other visitor in the exercise of the powers conferred by this or any other Act, shall for each offence be liable to a penalty not exceeding fifty pounds, and shall also be guilty of a misdemeanor.

(2.) Any person who wilfully obstructs any other person authorised under this Act by an order in writing under the hand of the Lord Chancellor or a Secretary of State to visit and examine any lunatic or supposed lunatic, or to inspect or inquire into the state of any institution for lunatics, gaol, or place wherein any lunatic or person represented to be lunatic is confined or alleged to be confined, in the execution of such order, and any person who wilfully obstructs any person authorised under this Act by any order of the Commissioners to make any visit and examination or inquiry in the execution of such order, shall (without prejudice to any proceedings, and in addition to any punishment to which such person obstructing the execution of such order would otherwise be subject,) be liable for every such offence to a penalty not exceeding twenty pounds.

Ill-treatment.

322. If any manager, officer, nurse, attendant, servant, or other person employed in an institution for lunatics or any person having charge of a lunatic, whether by reason of any contract, or of any tie of relationship, or marriage, or otherwise, illtreats or wilfully neglects a patient, he shall be guilty of a misdemeanor, and, on conviction on indictment, shall be liable to fine or imprisonment, or to both fine and imprisonment at the discretion of the court, or be liable on summary conviction for every offence to a penalty not exceeding twenty pounds nor less than two pounds.

Penalties for permitting escape and for rescue.

323. If any manager, officer, or servant of an institution for lunatics wilfully permits, or assists, or connives at the escape or attempted escape of a patient, or secretes a patient, he shall for every offence be liable to a penalty not exceeding twenty pounds nor less than two pounds.

Abuse of female lunatic.

324. If any manager, officer, nurse, attendant, or other person employed in any institution for lunatics (including an asylum for criminal lunatics), or workhouse, or any person having the care or charge of any single patient, or any attendant of any single patient, carnally knows or attempts to have carnal knowledge of any female under care or treatment as a lunatic in the institution, or workhouse, or as a single patient, he shall be guilty of a misdemeanor, and, on conviction on indictment, shall be liable to be imprisoned with or without hard labour for any term not exceeding two years; and no consent or alleged consent of such female thereto shall be any defence to an indictment or prosecution for such offence. Sect. 324.

325.—(1.) Except as by this Act otherwise provided, proceedings against any person for offences against this Act may be taken— By whom proceedings to be taken.

(a.) By the secretary of the Commissioners upon their order for any offence;

(b.) By the clerk of the visitors of any licensed house for an offence committed within their jurisdiction;

(c.) By the clerk of the visiting committee of an asylum for any offence by any person employed therein;

and such proceedings shall not abate by the death or removal of the prosecuting secretary or clerk, but the same may be continued by his successor, and in any such proceedings the prosecuting secretary or clerk shall be competent to be a witness.

(2.) Except as by this Act otherwise provided, it shall not be lawful to take such proceedings except by order of the Commissioners, or of visitors having jurisdiction in the place where the offence was committed, or with the consent of the Attorney-General or Solicitor-General.

326. All penalties enforceable under this Act shall be recovered summarily according to the provisions of the Summary Jurisdiction Acts, and shall be paid— Recovery and application of penalties.

a. When recovered by the secretary of the Commissioners, to such secretary;

b. When recovered by the clerk of the visitors of a licensed house, to the clerk of the peace for the county or borough, to be applied in the same way as money received for licences granted by the justices of the county or borough;

c. When recovered by a clerk of the visiting committee of an asylum, to the treasurer of the asylum for the purposes thereof;

d. In all other cases to the treasurer of the county or borough for which the convicting justices acted.

327. Any person aggrieved by an order of justices under this Act, other than orders adjudicating as to the settlement of a lunatic pauper and providing for his maintenance, may appeal to a court of quarter sessions, subject to the conditions and regulations of the Summary Jurisdiction Acts. Appeals.

328. A Secretary of State on the report of the Commissioners or visitors of any institution for lunatics may direct the Attorney-General to prosecute on the part of the Crown any person alleged to have committed a misdemeanor under this Act. Secretary of State may direct prosecution.

329.—(1.) Where any person is proceeded against under this Act on a charge of omitting to transmit or send any copy, list, notice, statement, report or other document required to be transmitted or Evidence upon prosecution.

Sect. 329 (1). sent by such person, the burden of proof that the same was transmitted or sent within the time required shall lie upon such person; but if he proves by the testimony of one witness upon oath that the copy, list, notice, statement, report or document in respect of which the proceeding is taken was properly addressed and put into the post in due time, or (in case of documents required to be sent to the Commissioners or a clerk of the peace or a clerk to guardians) left at the office of the Commissioners or of the clerk of the peace or clerk to guardians, such proof shall be a bar to all further proceedings in respect of such charge.

(2.) In proceedings under this Act, where a question arises whether a house is or is not a licensed house or registered as a hospital, it shall be presumed not to be so licensed or registered unless the licence or certificate of registration is produced, or sufficient evidence is given that a licence or certificate is in force.

Protection to persons putting the Act in force.

330.—(1.) A person who before the passing of this Act has signed or carried out or done any act with a view to sign or carry out an order purporting to be a reception order, or a medical certificate that a person is of unsound mind, and a person who after the passing of this Act presents a petition for any such order, or signs or carries out or does any act with a view to sign or carry out an order purporting to be a reception order, or any report or certificate purporting to be a report or certificate under this Act, or does anything in pursuance of this Act, shall not be liable to any civil or criminal proceedings whether on the ground of want of jurisdiction or on any other ground if such person has acted in good faith and with reasonable care.

(2.) If any proceedings are taken against any person for signing or carrying out or doing any act with a view to sign or carry out any such order, report, or certificate, or presenting any such petition as in the preceding sub-section mentioned, or doing anything in pursuance of this Act, such proceedings may, upon summary application to the High Court or a Judge thereof, be stayed upon such terms as to costs and otherwise as the Court or Judge may think fit, if the Court or Judge is satisfied that there is no reasonable ground for alleging want of good faith or reasonable care.

* * * * *

Commissioners and visitors may summon witnesses.

332.—(1.) The Commissioners, or any two of them, and also the visitors of any licensed house, or any two of them, may, as they see occasion, require, by summons, under the common seal of the Commission, if by the Commissioners, and if by two only of the Commissioners or by two visitors, then under the hands and seals of such two Commissioners or two visitors, as the case may be, any person to appear before them to testify on oath touching any matters respecting which such Commissioners and visitors respectively are by this Act authorised to inquire (which oath such Commissioners or visitors are hereby empowered to administer).

Form 22.

(2.) Every person who does not appear pursuant to the summons, or does not assign some reasonable excuse for not appearing, or who appears and refuses to be sworn or examined, shall, on being convicted thereof before a court of summary jurisdiction for every such neglect or refusal be liable to a penalty not exceeding fifty pounds. Sect. 332 (2).

(3.) Any two or more Commissioners or visitors may, if they think fit, examine on oath any person appearing before them as a witness, without having been summoned.

(4.) Any Commissioners or visitors who summon a person to appear and give evidence, may direct the secretary of the Commissioners or the clerk of such visitors, as the case may be, to pay to such person all reasonable expenses of his appearance and attendance, the same to be considered as expenses incurred in the execution of this Act, and to be taken into account and paid accordingly.

PART XII.

MISCELLANEOUS PROVISIONS, DEFINITIONS, REPEAL.

Indemnity to Bank and others.

333. This Act, and every order purporting to be made under this Act, shall be a full indemnity and discharge to the Bank and every other company and society and their respective officers and servants, and all other persons respectively, for all acts and things done or permitted to be done pursuant thereto, or pursuant to the Rules under this Act, so far as relates to any property in which a lunatic is interested either in his own right, or as trustee or mortgagee, and it shall not be necessary to inquire into the propriety of any order purporting to be made under this Act relating to any such property or the jurisdiction to make the same.

Meaning of word commission in other Acts extended.

334. Where in any Act of Parliament, order or rule of court, or instrument, reference is made to a commission of lunacy, or the inquisition thereon, the general commission and the inquisition, or certificate operating as an inquisition, and the issue and verdict thereon respectively in this Act mentioned, shall be deemed to be included in the reference.

Pension of lunatic payable by public department.

335. When any sum in respect of pay, pension, superannuation, or other allowance, or annuity under the control or management of any public department, is payable to any person, in respect either of service as a civil servant or of military or naval service or of provision for a widow or child of a person employed in civil, military, or naval service, and the person to whom the sum is payable is certified by a justice or minister of religion, and by a medical practitioner, to be unable by reason of mental disability to manage his or her affairs, the public department may pay so much of the said sum as the department may think fit to the institution or person having the care of the disabled person, and may pay the surplus, if any, or such part Forms 16, 17.

Sect. 335.

thereof, as the department may think fit, for or towards the maintenance and benefit of the wife or husband and relatives of the disabled person, and the department shall be discharged from all liability in respect of any sums so paid.

Reception orders before Act.

336. In the case of orders made before the commencement of this Act for the reception of private patients, the person who signed the reception order shall have all the powers and be subject to the obligations by this Act conferred or imposed upon the petitioner for a reception order, and the provisions of this Act relating to persons upon whose petition a reception order was made shall apply in the case of a person who before the commencement of this Act has signed an order for the reception of a private patient, as if the order had been made after the commencement of this Act upon a petition presented by him.

* * * * *

Forms.

339. Subject to rules made under this Act, the forms in the Second Schedule may be used, wherever applicable, with such modifications as circumstances may require, and if used, shall be deemed to be sufficient.

Savings as to criminal lunatics, etc.

340.—(1.) Save as in this Act otherwise expressly provided this Act shall not extend to criminal lunatics.

49 & 50 Vict. c. 25.

(2.) This Act shall not affect the provisions of the Idiots Act, 1886.

Definitions.

341. In this Act, if not inconsistent with the context—

"Asylum" means an asylum for lunatics provided by a county or borough, or by a union of counties or boroughs:

"The Bank" means the Governor and Company of the Bank of England:

"Clerk," in relation to a local authority, means, where the local authority is a county council, the clerk of the council, and where the local authority is a borough council, the town clerk of the borough:

"Commissioners" means the Commissioners in Lunacy:

"Contingent right," as applied to lands, includes a contingent and executory interest, a possibility coupled with an interest, whether the object of the gift or limitation of such interest or possibility be or be not ascertained, also a right of entry, whether immediate or future, and whether vested or contingent:

3 & 4 Will. 4, c. 74.

"Convey" and "conveyance" include the performance of all formalities required to the validity of conveyances by married women and tenants in tail under the "Act for the abolition of fines and recoveries, and for the substitution of more simple modes of assurance," and also surrenders and other acts which a tenant of copyhold lands can perform preparatory to or in aid of a complete assurance of such copyhold lands:

Sect. 341.

"County," for the purpose of the powers exerciseable by justices of a county, does not include a county of a city or county of a town (except the City of London), but includes any county, riding, division, part or liberty of a county having a separate court of quarter sessions:

"County borough" has the same meaning as in the Local Government Act, 1888: 51 & 52 Vict. c. 41.

"Criminal lunatic" has the same meaning as in the Criminal Lunatics Act, 1884: 47 & 48 Vict. c. 64.

"District asylum" means an asylum provided by two or more counties in union, or by any county or counties in union with any borough or boroughs:

"Dividends" includes interest and other annual produce:

"Guardians" means guardians appointed under the Poor Law Amendment Act, 1834, and the Acts amending the same, and includes guardians or other body of persons performing under any local Act the like functions as guardians under the Poor Law Amendment Act, 1834: 4 & 5 Will. 4. c. 76.

"Hospital" means any hospital or part of a hospital or other house or institution (not being an asylum) wherein lunatics are received and supported wholly or partly by voluntary contributions, or by any charitable bequest or gift, or by applying the excess of payments of some patients for or towards the support, provision, or benefit of other patients:

"Inquisition" includes an order, certificate, or verdict operating as an inquisition:

"Institution for lunatics" means an asylum, hospital, or licensed house:

"Justice" means a justice of the peace;

"Land" includes an undivided share of land:

"Lease" includes underlease:

"Lunatic" means an idiot or person of unsound mind:

"Magistrate" means a stipendiary magistrate and any magistrate appointed to act at any of the police courts of the metropolis:

"Manager" in relation to an institution for lunatics means the superintendent of an asylum, the resident medical officer or superintendent of a hospital, and the resident licensee of a licensed house:

"Masters" means the Masters in Lunacy:

"Medical officer" means, in the case of an asylum, the medical superintendent, or if the superintendent is not a medical practitioner the resident medical officer of the asylum, in the case of a hospital the superintendent, and in the case of a licensed house the resident medical practitioner, or if none the medical practitioner who visits the house as the medical attendant thereof:

Sect. 341.

21 & 22 Vict. c. 90.
49 & 50 Vict. c. 48.

"Medical practitioner" means a medical practitioner duly registered under the Medical Act, 1858, and the Acts amending the same, and the Medical Act, 1886 :

"Mortgage" includes every estate, interest, or property in real or personal estate, which is a security for money or money's worth :

"Next of kin" includes heir at law, and the persons entitled under the statutes for the distribution of the estates of intestates :

"Pauper" means a person wholly or partly chargeable to a union, county, or borough :

"Paymaster-General" includes the Assistant Paymaster-General for Supreme Court business :

"Prescribed" means prescribed by this Act or by any rules under this Act :

"Private patient" means a patient who is not a pauper :

"Property" includes real and personal property, whether in possession, reversion, remainder, contingency, or expectancy, and any estate or interest, and any undivided share therein :

"Public department" means the Treasury, the Admiralty, and a Secretary of State, and any other public department of the Government :

"Quarter Sessions" includes general sessions :

"Quarter sessions borough" means a borough having a separate court of quarter sessions :

"Reception order" means an order or authority made or given before or after the commencement of this Act for the reception of a lunatic, whether a pauper or not, in an institution for lunatics or as a single patient, and includes an urgency order :

"Relative" means a lineal ancestor or lineal descendant, or a lineal descendant of an ancestor not more remote than great-grandfather or great-grandmother :

"Stock" includes any fund, annuity, or security transferable in books kept by any company or society, or by instrument of transfer alone, or by instrument of transfer, accompanied by other formalities, and any share or interest therein, and also shares in ships registered under the Merchant Shipping Act, 1854 :

17 & 18 Vict. c. 104.

"Transfer" includes assignment, payment, and other disposition, and the execution, and performance, of every assurance and act to complete a transfer :

"Trust" and "trustee" include implied and constructive trusts, and cases where the trustee has some beneficial interest, and also the duties incident to the office of personal representative of a deceased person, but not the duties incident to an estate conveyed by way of mortgage :

"Union" means any parish or union of parishes for which there is a separate board of guardians :

"Visiting committee" means a committee of visitors of an asylum appointed under this Act: Sect. 341.

"Workhouse" includes an asylum provided for reception and relief of the insane under the Metropolitan Poor Act, 1867, and the managers of every such asylum shall exercise the powers and perform the duties by this Act conferred and imposed upon the guardians of the union to which a workhouse belongs. 30 Vict. c. 6.

342. The Acts mentioned in the Fifth Schedule are hereby repealed to the extent set forth in the third column of the same schedule. Repeal.

Provided that this repeal shall not affect any jurisdiction or practice established, confirmed, or transferred, or salary or compensation or superannuation secured by or under any enactment repealed by this Act.

SCHEDULES.

SECOND SCHEDULE.

* * * Section 248.

FORM 21.

FORM of AGREEMENT for uniting for the purpose of erecting or providing an asylum for the reception of lunatics.

IT is agreed this day of between the visiting committees for the county of and the borough of [*as the case may be*], that the said county and borough [*as the case may be*], shall henceforth be united for the purposes of the Lunacy Act, 1890; and that an asylum for the reception of lunatics, with all necessary buildings, courts, yards, and outlets, shall be immediately provided and properly fitted up and accommodated for the purposes mentioned in the said Act; and that the necessary expenses attending the providing, building, fitting up, repairs, and maintenance of the said asylum shall be defrayed by the said county and borough, so united, in the following proportions, such proportions being fixed according to the probable extent of the accommodation required for the lunatics of the contracting county and borough; (that is to say,)

The county of Five ninths of the said expenses,
The borough of Four ninths of the same,

[*as the case may be, or if the expenses are not fixed with reference to the probable extent of the accommodation, insert instead of the last clause.*]

The expenses shall be from time to time charged upon and raised by such county and borough in proportion to their respective populations as stated in the last return for the time being made of the same under the authority of Parliament.

And it is further agreed, that the committee of visitors to superintend the building, erection, and management of the said asylum shall be appointed in the following proportions; the council for the said county of shall appoint(*i*) , and the council for the borough of shall appoint(*i*) and the proportions in which the said committee of visitors are to be appointed as aforesaid may be from time to time varied, with the consent in writing under the hands of the greater number of visitors of the said county and borough, and with the consent of the Commissioners in Lunacy. And hereunto, we, the undersigned, being the majority of each of the committees appointed by the said councils respectively, do on behalf of the said councils set our hands and seals, this day of .

(*i*) Insert in these blanks either the number or the proportion of visitors: and where the number of the committee of visitors is not fixed in the agreement, but only the proportions, a provision shall be made by the agreement for fixing from time to time the number of such committee.

Schedules.

Sections 169, 240, 245, 246.

FOURTH SCHEDULE.

BOROUGHS, THE COUNCILS OF WHICH ARE LOCAL AUTHORITIES UNDER THIS ACT.

Barnstaple.	Maidstone.
Bedford.	Newark.
Berwick-on-Tweed.	Newbury.
Bridgwater.	Newcastle-under-Lyme.
Bury St. Edmunds.	New Sarum.
Cambridge.	New Windsor.
Colchester.	Penzance.
Doncaster.	Poole.
Dover.	Rochester.
Grantham.	Scarborough.
Gravesend.	Shrewsbury.
Guildford.	Tiverton.
Hereford.	Warwick.
King's Lynn.	Wenlock.
London (City of).	Winchester.

Section 342.

FIFTH SCHEDULE.

Session and Chapter.	Title or Short Title.	Extent of Repeal.
4 & 5 Will. 4, c. 76. -	An Act for the amendment and better administration of the Laws relating to the Poor in England and Wales.	Section forty-five.
8 & 9 Vict. c. 100. -	An Act for the regulation of the care and treatment of lunatics.	The whole Act.
13 & 14 Vict. c. 60. -	The Trustee Act, 1850 - -	Sections three, four, five, six, and fifty-six. Sections twenty, twenty-six, twenty-seven, twenty-eight, thirty-one, forty, forty-one, forty-two, forty-four, forty-five, fifty-one, fifty-two, and fifty-three, so far as they relate to "the Lord Chancellor entrusted as aforesaid." Except so far as the above sections relate to Ireland.
15 & 16 Vict. c. 48. -	An Act for the amendment of the law respecting the property of lunatics.	The whole Act.
15 & 16 Vict. c. 55. -	An Act to extend the provisions of the Trustee Act, 1850.	Sections six and seven, so far as relates to the Lord Chancellor entrusted as aforesaid, and sections ten and eleven. Except so far as the above sections relate to Ireland.
16 & 17 Vict. c. 70. -	The Lunacy Regulation Act, 1853 -	The whole Act.
16 & 17 Vict. c. 96. -	An Act to amend an Act passed in the ninth year of Her Majesty for the regulation of the care and treatment of lunatics.	The whole Act.
16 & 17 Vict. c. 97. -	The Lunatic Asylums Act, 1853 -	The whole Act.
18 Vict. c. 13. - -	An Act to amend and explain the Lunacy Regulation Act, 1853.	The whole Act.
18 & 19 Vict. c. 105. -	An Act to amend the Lunatic Asylums Act, 1853, and the Acts passed in the ninth and seventeenth years of Her Majesty for the Regulation of the Care and Treatment of Lunatics.	The whole Act.
19 & 20 Vict. c. 87. -	An Act to amend the Lunatic Asylums Act, 1853.	The whole Act.

Schedules.

Session and Chapter.	Title or Short Title.	Extent of Repeal.
23 & 24 Vict. c. 127. -	An Act to amend the law relating to attorneys, solicitors, proctors, and certificated conveyancers.	Section twenty-nine.
24 & 25 Vict. c. 55. -	An Act to amend the laws regarding the removal of the poor, and the contribution of parishes to the common fund in unions.	Section seven.
25 & 26 Vict. c. 86. -	The Lunacy Regulation Act, 1862 -	The whole Act.
25 & 26 Vict. c. 111. -	The Lunacy Acts Amendment Act, 1862.	The whole Act.
26 & 27 Vict. c. 110. -	The Lunacy Acts Amendment Act, 1863.	The whole Act.
28 & 29 Vict. c. 80. -	The Lunacy Act Amendment Act, 1865.	The whole Act.
30 Vict. c. 6. - -	The Metropolitan Poor Act, 1867 -	In section thirty, the words "and every such asylum" to the end of the section.
30 & 31 Vict. c. 87. -	The Court of Chancery (Officers) Act, 1867.	Section thirteen.
30 & 31 Vict. c. 106. -	The Poor Law Amendment Act, 1867.	Section twenty-two, except as regards persons suffering from delirium tremens, or from bodily disease of a contagious or infectious character.
31 & 32 Vict. c. 122. -	The Poor Law Amendment Act, 1868.	Section forty-three.
34 & 35 Vict. c. 14. -	The County Property Act, 1871 -	Section two.
38 & 39 Vict. c. 77. -	The Supreme Court of Judicature Act, 1875.	Section seven. In section twenty-six, the words "(including the percentage on estates of lunatics)" and the words "(including the masters and other officers in lunacy)".
45 & 46 Vict. c. 82. -	The Lunacy Regulation Amendment Act, 1882.	The whole Act.
48 & 49 Vict. c. 52. -	The Lunacy Acts Amendment Act, 1885.	The whole Act.
51 & 52 Vict. c. 41. -	The Local Government Act, 1888 -	Section thirty-two, sub-section three, sub-clause (c); section eighty-six, sub-sections one, two, three, four, six, seven, and eight.
52 & 53 Vict. c. 41. -	The Lunacy Acts Amendment Act, 1889.	The whole Act.

CUSTOMS AND INLAND REVENUE ACT, 1890.

(53 VICT. CAP. 8.)

An Act to grant certain Duties of Customs and Inland Revenue, to repeal and alter other Duties, and to amend the Laws relating to Customs and Inland Revenue. [9th June, 1890.]

1. This Act may be cited as the Customs and Inland Revenue Act, 1890. Short title.

* * * * *

7. The following duties of Excise and of Customs, that is to say,— Payment of local taxation (Customs and Excise) duties

(a) the additional duties on spirits imposed by this Act; and

Sect. 7.

to local taxation accounts of England, Scotland and Ireland.
43 & 44 Vict. c. 20.
44 & 45 Vict. c. 12.
52 & 53 Vict. c. 7.

(b) such portion of the duties of Excise and of Customs imposed by section eleven of the Inland Revenue Act, 1880, and section three of the Customs and Inland Revenue Act, 1881, as amended by section three of the Customs and Inland Revenue Act, 1889, in respect of beer, as equals threepence for every thirty-six gallons.

shall be called the local taxation (Customs and Excise) duties, and the proceeds of those duties shall be divided between England, Scotland, and Ireland in the same proportions, and be paid to the same local taxation accounts, and in the like manner and subject to the like regulations of the Treasury, and shall be ascertained as to proportion and otherwise in like manner as the one-half of the proceeds of the probate duties applicable to local purposes is now by law divided, paid, and ascertained, and the proceeds so paid shall be appropriated as Parliament may hereafter direct by any Act passed in the present session (*j*).

* * * * *

OPEN SPACES ACT, 1890.

(53 & 54 Vict. Cap. 15.)

An Act to amend the Open Spaces Act. [25th July, 1890.]

* * * * *

Short title and construction.
40 & 41 Vict. c. 35.
44 & 45 Vict. c. 34.
50 & 51 Vict. c. 32.

1. This Act may be cited as the Open Spaces Act, 1890, and may be read with the Metropolitan Open Spaces Acts, 1877 and 1881, and the Open Spaces Act, 1887 (hereinafter called the principal Acts) as one Act, and this Act and the principal Acts may be cited as the Open Spaces Acts, 1877 to 1890 (*k*).

Definitions.

2. In this Act—

The expression "local authority" shall mean and include any of the public bodies who are empowered by the principal Acts to hold open spaces for the purposes of the Open Spaces Acts, 1877 to 1890 (*l*):

"The court" shall mean the Chancery Division of the High Court of Justice in England and Ireland, and the county court of the district in which the whole or part of any open space may be situated as herein provided.

Transfer to local authority of spaces

3. The trustees of land held upon trust for the purposes of public recreation may, in pursuance of a resolution duly passed as provided

---

(*j*) As to the appropriation of these proceeds, see the 53 & 54 Vict. c. 60, *post*. Section 7 is the only section of this Act bearing on the subject of this work.

(*k*) The earlier Acts will be found set out in Lumley's Public Health.

(*l*) The expression will include the council of a county borough as the urban authority for the borough, but it does not include a county council, except the London County Council, who are the successors of the Metropolitan Board of Works. See 40 & 41 Vict. c. 35, s. 1; 50 & 51 Vict. c. 32, s. 5.

by section two of the Metropolitan Open Spaces Act, 1881 (*m*), transfer by free gift, absolutely or for a limited term, to the local authority of the district in which the whole or the greater part in area of the land is situate, the land so held by them, if such authority is willing to accept such transfer, to be held by the transferees on the trusts and subject to the conditions on which the transferors held the same, or upon such other trusts and subject to such other conditions (so that the land be appropriated to the purposes of public recreation) as may be agreed upon between the transferors and transferees with the approval of the Charity Commissioners for England and Wales, or, as respects Ireland, of the Commissioners of Charitable Donations and Bequests for Ireland. Subject to the obligation of the land so transferred being used for the purposes of public recreation as aforesaid, the local authority may hold the same as and for the purposes of an open space under the Open Spaces Acts, 1877 to 1890. This section shall not apply to any trustees elected or appointed under any local or special Act of Parliament.

Sect. 3. — held by trustees for purposes of public recreation.

4. When any open space (*n*) shall be situate wholly or in part within the district of a local authority, and shall be vested in trustees, other than such trustees as are mentioned in the principal Acts (*o*), or in the last preceding section of this Act, for any charitable purpose, and as part of their trust estate, and it shall appear to the majority of such trustees that such open space is no longer required for the purposes of their trust, or that the same may with advantage to the trust be dealt with under the provisions of this section, it shall be lawful for such trustees, in pursuance of a resolution passed by them in the manner prescribed in the last preceding section of this Act (*p*), and where the open space is subject to the provisions of the Charitable Trusts Acts, 1883 to 1887 (*q*), with such authority or approval as is required by those Acts for a sale of the open space (*r*), and in other cases in pursuance of an order of the court to be obtained as hereinafter provided (*s*), to

Similar power with respect to trustees of other open spaces.

(*m*) The resolution must be passed at a meeting of the trustees summoned by at least one month's notice in writing, left at or sent by post to their last known or usual place of abode, and it must be passed by a majority of not less than two-thirds of those present, and confirmed by a similar majority at a meeting summoned in like manner, and held at an interval of not less than a month after the first meeting.

(*n*) Open space means any land (whether inclosed or uninclosed) which is not built on, and which is laid out as a garden, or is used for purposes of recreation, or lies waste and unoccupied. 44 & 45 Vict. c. 34, s. 1.

(*o*) See 44 & 45 Vict. c. 34, s. 2. These trustees may act under a private or local Act.

(*p*) See note (*m*), *supra*.

(*q*) This should be 1853 to 1887. These Acts are—16 & 17 Vict. c. 137; 18 & 19 Vict. c. 124; 23 & 24 Vict. c. 136; 25 & 26 Vict. c. 112; 32 & 33 Vict. c. 110; 50 & 51 Vict. c. 49. To these must now be added 54 Vict. c. 17; 57 & 58 Vict. c. 35.

(*r*) The authority or approval seems to be that of the Charity Commissioners under 16 & 17 Vict. c. 137, s. 24.

(*s*) See s. 5 of this Act.

Sect. 4. convey or demise such open space to such local authority upon such terms as shall be mutually agreed between them, and the local authority shall thenceforth be entitled to hold the same as an open space upon the terms and under the conditions specified in any such conveyance or demise, or upon such terms and under such conditions as may be so authorised or approved, or as the court shall from time to time order, as the case may be (*t*).

Procedure for obtaining order of court.

5. An order of the court may be made upon application by the trustees, and the court, before making any order, may direct such inquiries to be made, such consents to be obtained, and notice to be given to such persons as to the court shall seem expedient, and may make such order thereon as in its discretion appears proper. Rules for carrying out the preceding provisions of this Act may from time to time be made by the same authority as the General Rules or Orders of the High Court of Justice in England and Ireland, and of the county courts in England, Ireland, and Wales respectively are made (*u*).

Open Spaces Acts to apply outside district of local authority.

6. The Open Spaces Acts, 1877 to 1890, shall be applicable to the whole of any open space which is wholly or partly situated without the district of a local authority in the same manner to all intents and purposes as if the whole of such open space had been situated within such district.

Buildings on open spaces.

7. Where a portion of an area of land not exceeding a twentieth part is covered with a building or buildings, such land may notwithstanding be deemed to be an open space within the meaning of the Open Spaces Acts, 1877 to 1890.

POLICE ACT, 1890.

(53 & 54 VICT. CAP. 45) (*x*).

An Act to make provision respecting the Pensions, Allowances, and Gratuities of Police Constables in England and Wales, and their Widows and Children, and to make other provisions respecting the Police of England and Wales. [14th August, 1890.]

* * * * *

PART I.

Superannuation of Constables.

Right of constables to pensions.

1. Subject to the provisions of this Act, every constable in a police force—

(a) if he has completed not less than twenty-five years approved service (*y*), and, where a limit of age is prescribed by the

---

(*t*) The court is defined by s. 2.

(*u*) No rules have yet been made under this section.

(*x*) This Act repeals all previous statutes relating to police superannuation. The authority charged with the execution of it in a county is the standing joint committee, who are the police authority as defined by the Third Schedule.

(*y*) Approved service as defined by s. 4, *post*.

Sect. 1.

pension scale in force under this Act, is of an age not less than the age so prescribed, shall, on the expiration of such time not exceeding four months after he has given written notice to the police authority of his desire to retire as the police authority may fix, be entitled without a medical certificate to retire and receive a pension for life; and

(b) if after he has completed fifteen years approved service he is incapacited for the performance of his duty by infirmity of mind or body, shall be entitled on a medical certificate to retire and receive a pension for life; and,

(c) if before he has completed fifteen years approved service he is incapacited for the performance of his duty by infirmity of mind or body, shall be entitled on a medical certificate to retire, and thereupon the police authority may, if they think fit, grant him a gratuity; and,

(d) if at any time he is incapacitated for the performance of his duty by infirmity of mind or body occasioned by an injury received in the execution of his duty without his own default, shall be entitled on a medical certificate to retire and receive a pension for life.

Pension allowances and gratuities to widow and children.

2.—(1.) If a constable dies whilst in a police force from the effect of an injury received in the execution of his duty without his own default, the police authority shall grant a pension to his widow, and allowances to his children.

(2.) If a constable dies whilst in a police force from any other cause, the police authority may, if they think fit, grant gratuities to his widow and children or any of them.

(3.) If a constable, to whom a pension has been granted because he was incapacited for the performance of his duty by an injury received in the execution of his duty without his own default, dies from the effects of the injury within twelve months after the grant of the pension, the police authority may, if they think fit, grant a pension to his widow, either for a term of years or otherwise.

(4.) If a constable to whom a pension has been granted dies within twelve months after the grant of the pension, the police authority may, if they think fit, grant gratuities to his widow and children or any of them.

Pension scale.

3.—(1.) The pensions, allowances, and gratuities granted to constables of a police force and to their widows and children shall be in accordance with the pension scale for the force.

(2.) The pension scale for a police force shall be—

(a) as regards ordinary pensions, a fixed scale adopted by the police authority within the maximum and minimum limits set forth in Part I. of the First Schedule to this Act; and

(b) as regards special pensions and allowances and gratuities, the scale set forth in Part II. of that Schedule.

Sect. 3 (3).

(3.) The police authority shall before the first day of January one thousand eight hundred and ninety-one send to the Secretary of State a copy of the scale adopted by them for ordinary pensions.

(4.) If any police authority do not before the said date adopt a fixed scale for ordinary pensions and send a copy thereof to the Secretary of State, the Secretary of State may frame for that authority a fixed scale for ordinary pensions within the maximum and minimum limits set forth in Part I. of the First Schedule to this Act, and that scale shall have the same effect as if it were a scale adopted by the police authority under this section.

(5.) The pension scale for each force shall come into operation on the commencement of this Act.

(6.) A police authority may from time to time adopt and send to the Secretary of State a new scale for ordinary pensions in lieu of the scale for the time being in force, but any such new scale shall not, without the consent of the constable, apply to any constable appointed before the day of its coming into operation.

(7.) The rules contained in Part III. of the First Schedule to this Act shall apply to all pensions, allowances, and gratuities granted under this Act.

Reckoning of service for pension.

4.—(1.) The service of a constable for the purposes of this Act shall be subject to such deductions in respect of sickness, misconduct, or neglect of duty as may be made therefrom in pursuance of the regulations of the force to which the constable belongs; and the expression "approved service" shall for the purposes of this Act mean such service as may after such deductions as aforesaid (if any) be certified under the order of the police authority to have been diligent and faithful service, but shall not, unless the regulations of the police force otherwise prescribe, include service before twenty-one years of age.

(2.) A certificate signed by the chief officer of a police force as to the period of a constable's approved service in that force shall be sufficient evidence thereof.

(3.) Where a deduction is made from a constable's service in respect of sickness, misconduct, or neglect of duty, notice of the deduction shall as soon as may be after the occurrence of the cause for which the deduction is made be given to the constable; and the constable may appeal to the chief officer of his police force against any act of an officer of police superior to the constable which prevents him from reckoning any period of actual service as approved service, and any period of actual service allowed by the chief officer on such appeal shall be deemed to be approved service: Provided that, in the case of a borough having a separate police force, the decision of the chief officer shall be subject to the approval of the watch committee.

(4.) Where a constable has served in more than one police force in any part of the United Kingdom, approved service in any such police force in which he has completed not less than three years approved service, and from which he has with the written sanction of the chief officer of that force removed to another force, shall be reckoned as approved service in the force in which the constable is serving at the time of his retirement. Sect. 4 (4).

(5.) Where a constable with the knowledge of the police authority or of the chief officer of his police force belongs to the army reserve, and is called out for training or for permanent service, he shall be entitled, on returning to the police force after the end of such training or service, to reckon any approved service which he was entitled to reckon at the commencement thereof.

Proof of incapacity for duty liability to serve again, and revision of pension.

5.—(1.) Before granting to a constable an ordinary pension on the ground of his being incapacitated by infirmity for the performance of his duty, the police authority shall be satisfied by the evidence of some legally qualified medical practitioner or practitioners, selected by the police authority, that the constable is so incapacitated, and that the incapacity is likely to be permanent.

(2.) Where the application is for a special pension, the police authority shall also be satisfied that the injury was received by the constable in the execution of his duty, that it was received without the default of the constable, and that the infirmity is attributable to the injury, and shall also determine whether the injury was accidental or not, and whether the disability of the constable for earning his livelihood is total or partial; and for the purpose of determining any of the said questions which ought to be determined on medical grounds shall take the like evidence as above mentioned.

(3.) Where a pension is granted to a constable on the ground of incapacity for the performance of his duty, the police authority shall, yearly or otherwise, until the power under this Act of requiring the constable to serve again ceases, satisfy themselves that the incapacity continues, and, unless they resolve that such evidence is unnecessary, shall satisfy themselves by the like evidence as above mentioned (*z*).

(4.) In the event of the incapacity ceasing before the time at which the constable would, if he had continued to serve, have been entitled without a medical certificate to retire and receive a pension for life, the police authority may cancel his pension and require him to serve again in the police force, in a rank not less than the rank which he held before his retirement, and at a rate of pay not less than the rate which he received before his retirement (*a*).

(5.) Where a constable so serves again, the provisions of this Act as to retirement and pensions, allowances, and gratuities shall apply

---

(*z*) The power hereby conferred cannot be exercised by the police authority for any collateral purpose, such as compelling the constable to come within the jurisdiction of the Bankruptcy Court. The police authority have, however, power to fix the time and place for the examination of the constable. *R.* v. *Lord Leigh, In re Kinchant*, [1897] 1 Q. B. 132.

(*a*) The pension cannot be cancelled without giving the constable an opportunity to serve again. *R.* v. *Lord Leigh, In re Kinchant, supra.*

Sect. 5 (5).

as if he had not previously retired, save that, except in the case of pensions for non-accidental injuries received in the execution of duty, he shall not reckon as approved service the time which elapsed between his former retirement and the commencement of his service again.

(6.) Where a pension is granted to a constable on a scale applicable to total disability for earning a livelihood, it shall be so granted for such period as may be fixed by the police authority, and, if at the expiration of that period the pensioner continues to be totally so disabled, the pension shall, in the discretion of the police authority, either be made permanent or renewed from time to time. If at any time before the pension is made permanent the police authority are satisfied by the evidence of a legally qualified medical practitioner that the pensioner's disability for earning his livelihood has become partial, the pension shall, within the limits allowed by the pension scale, be reduced to the amount allowed by the provisions of the scale applicable to cases of partial disability.

(7.) If a constable fails or refuses, when required by the police authority, to be examined by some legally qualified medical practitioner selected by that authority, the police authority may deal with the constable in all respects as if they were satisfied by the evidence of such a practitioner that the constable is not incapacitated for the performance of his duty or, as the case may be, is only partially disabled.

(8.) The decision of the police authority on the matters above in this section mentioned shall be final, save that in the case of a borough the constable may appeal to the council of the borough, and the decision of the council shall be final.

Power to reduce pension where infirmity partially due to misconduct.

6. Where a constable retires on account of infirmity of mind or body, and the police authority are satisfied on medical evidence that the constable has brought about or contributed to the infirmity by his own default or his vicious habits, the police authority may, in their discretion, reduce the amount of his pension by an amount not exceeding one half of the pension to which he would be otherwise entitled.

Assignment of pensions and regulations as to payment of pensions, etc.

7. The following provisions shall have effect with respect to every pension, allowance, and gratuity (in this section referred to as a "grant") payable by the police authority to any person (in this section referred to as the pensioner):—

(1.) Every assignment of and charge on a grant, and every agreement to assign or charge a grant, shall, except so far as made for the benefit of the family of the pensioner, be void, and on the bankruptcy of the pensioner the grant shall not pass to any trustee or other person acting on behalf of the creditors:

(2.) Where any parochial relief is given to a pensioner or to anyone whom he is liable to maintain, the police authority may pay the whole or any part of the grant to the guardians or other authority giving the relief, and the same, when so paid, may be applied in repayment of any sums expended in such relief, and, subject thereto, shall be paid or applied by the guardians or other authority to or for the benefit of the pensioner: **Sect. 7 (2)**

(3.) If the pensioner neglects to maintain any person whom he is liable to maintain, the police authority may in their discretion pay or apply the whole or any part of the grant to or for the benefit of that person:

(4.) If the pensioner appears to the police authority to be insane or otherwise incapacitated to act, the police authority may pay so much of the grant as the police authority think fit to the institution or person having the care of the pensioner, and may pay the surplus (if any) or such part thereof as the authority think fit for or towards the maintenance and benefit of the wife or relatives of the pensioner:

(5.) On the death of a pensioner to whom a sum not exceeding one hundred pounds is due on account of a grant, then, if the police authority so direct, probate or other proof of the title of the personal representative of the deceased may be dispensed with, and the sum may be paid or distributed to or among the persons appearing to the police authority to be beneficially entitled to the personal estate of the deceased pensioner, or to or among any one or more of those persons, or in case of the illegitimacy of the deceased pensioner, to or among such persons as the police authority may think fit, and the police authority, and any officer of the police authority making the payment, shall be discharged from all liability in respect of any such payment or distribution:

(6.) Any sum payable to a minor on account of a grant may be paid either to the minor or to such person and on such conditions for the benefit of the minor as to the police authority seems expedient:

(7.) Where a payment is made to any person by a police authority in pursuance of this section, the receipt of that person shall be a good discharge to that authority for the sum so paid:

(8.) A police authority may, with the consent of the Secretary of State, make rules with respect to declarations to be taken for any purpose relating to grants payable by that authority, and while any such rules made by a police authority are in force, a person shall not be entitled to receive any sum in respect of a grant payable by that authority until any declaration required by those rules has been made.

Forfeiture of pension or allowance.

8. A pension or allowance under this Act is granted only upon condition that it becomes forfeited, and may be withdrawn by the police authority, in any of the following cases:—

(a) if the grantee is convicted of any offence for which he is sentenced to penal servitude or to imprisonment for a term

Sect. 8 (a).

exceeding three months with hard labour, or to imprisonment for a term exceeding twelve months, whether with or without hard labour; or

(b) if the grantee knowingly associates with thieves or reputed thieves; or

(c) if the grantee refuses to give to the police all information and assistance in his power, for the detection of crime, for the apprehension of criminals, and for the suppression of any disturbance of the public peace; or

(d) if the grantee enters into or continues to carry on any business, occupation, or employment which is illegal, or in which he has made use of the fact of his former employment in the police in a manner which the police authority consider to be discreditable and improper.

Such forfeiture and withdrawal may affect the pension wholly or in part, and may be permanent or temporary, as the police authority may determine.

Punishment for obtaining pension, etc., by fraud.

9. If a person obtains or attempts to obtain for himself or for any other person any pension, gratuity, or allowance under this Act, or any payment on account of any such pension, gratuity, or allowance by means of any false declaration, false certificate, false representation, false evidence, or personation, or by malingering or feigning disease or infirmity, or by maiming or injuring himself, or causing himself to be maimed or injured, or otherwise producing disease or infirmity, or by any other fraudulent conduct, he shall be liable on summary conviction to imprisonment with or without hard labour for a term not exceeding four months or to a fine not exceeding twenty-five pounds, to be paid (notwithstanding anything in any charter or in any other Act whether relating to municipal corporations or otherwise) to the pension fund of the force from which he obtained or attempted to obtain the pension, gratuity, or allowance, and on conviction by a jury to imprisonment, with or without hard labour, for a term not exceeding two years, and also in either case, to forfeit any pension, gratuity, or allowance so obtained.

Saving of right of dismissal and reduction in rank.

10. Nothing in this Act shall prejudice the existing right of any police authority to dismiss any constable, or to reduce him to any lower rank or lower rate of pay, or shall prevent his claim to pension from being refused on account of misconduct, or of negligence in the discharge of his duties, or on account of any of the grounds on which his pension if granted would be liable to be forfeited and withdrawn.

Appeal in case of forfeiture, or refusal of pension or allowance.

11. In any of the following cases—

(a) where a pension after being granted to a constable has subsequently in pursuance of this Act been declared to have been forfeited, and

(b) where a constable is dismissed without a pension to which he would be otherwise entitled, and in any other case where a constable, or the widow or child of a constable, claims a pension or allowance under this Act as of right, and the police authority do not admit the claim,

the constable, widow, or child may apply to the police authority for a re-consideration of the claim to the pension or allowance, and if aggrieved by the decision upon such re-consideration may apply to the next practicable court of quarter sessions for the county within which the constable last served; or if the constable last served in the police force of a borough having a separate police force and a separate court of quarter sessions, then to the next practicable court of quarter sessions for that borough, and that court, after inquiry into the case, may make such order in the matter as appears to the court just, which order shall be final; but nothing in this section shall confer a right to appeal against the exercise of any discretion, or against any decision which is declared by this Act to be final

Application of Act to chief officer of police.

12. The provisions of this Act shall apply to a chief officer of police and to the assistant commissioners of the metropolitan police in like manner, so nearly as circumstances admit, as they apply to any other constable, except that, in the case of a chief officer, the certificate of approved service and the sanction to removal from one force to another may be given by a resolution of the police authority, and that nothing in this section shall make any pension which is now payable out of money provided by Parliament payable from any other source.

Suspension of pension in case of appointment to new office.

13.—(1.) Where a constable in receipt of a pension under this Act from a police authority takes service in any police force, his pension may be suspended by that police authority in whole or in part so long as he remains in that service.

(2.) If a constable in receipt of a pension under this Act is appointed to an office remunerated out of money provided by Parliament, or out of a county or borough rate or fund, he shall not, while holding that office, receive more of the pension than together with the remuneration of that office is equal to one and a half times the remuneration of the office in respect of which the pension was awarded (*b*).

Provision as to service in more than one capacity.

14. Where a person has served in two or all of the following capacities—

(i.) as a civil servant within the meaning of the Superannuation Act, 1887 (*c*); 50 & 51 Vict. c. 67.

(*b*) The provisions of this sub-section apply to any constable in receipt of a pension who is appointed to any office remunerated out of any parochial, district, or other rate. See the Police Act, 1893, s. 4, *post*.

(*c*) A civil servant is defined by s. 12 of the Superannuation Act, 1887, to mean "a person who has served in an established capacity in the permanent civil service of the State within the meaning of section 17 of the Superannuation Act, 1859." By the last-mentioned section it is provided that "no person hereafter to be appointed shall be deemed to have served in the permanent civil service of the State unless such person holds his appointment directly from the Crown or has been admitted into the civil service with a certificate from the Civil Service Commissioners."

Sect. 14.

(ii.) in a police force with a salary paid out of the police fund;

(iii.) in a police force with a salary paid out of money provided by Parliament;

he shall be entitled to reckon his entire period of service in both or all capacities for the purpose of pension, and the pension shall be on the scale and subject to the statutory requirements affecting pensions in the service from which he last retires.

Provided as follows:—

(1.) For the purposes of the pension three years of police service shall be reckoned as equivalent to four years of service as a civil servant, and conversely; and

(2.) The pension shall be payable from money provided by Parliament, and from the police pension fund in such proportions as the Treasury may determine, regard being had to the period of service and the salary received in each capacity.

Rateable deductions from pay to be carried to pension fund.

15.—(1.) The police authority of every police force shall deduct from the pay of every constable in the force—

(a) sums at a rate not exceeding two and a half per cent. per annum on his pay (in this Act referred to as the rateable deduction); and

(b) such stoppages during sickness, and such fines for misconduct, as may be provided by the regulations respecting the force.

(2.) Where a constable has removed to some other force or forces with the written sanction of the chief officer of any force he has removed from, and such constable in due course becomes entitled to and is awarded a pension, the police authority in whose service he then is shall be entitled to call upon the other police authority or authorities with whom he shall have served approved service, and they shall contribute a proportionate part of any pension to such constable reckoned according to the approved service and pay of such constable during his service in such force, and the said proportionate part shall be settled by agreement between the police authorities, or in default of agreement by an arbitrator appointed by the Secretary of State.

Establishment of pension fund, and fines, fees, etc. to be carried to fund.

16.—(1.) There shall be a pension fund of every police force, and there shall be carried to that fund—

(a) the deductions (including stoppages and fines) made in pursuance of this Act from the pay of the constables in the force (*d*); and

(b) the fines imposed by a court of summary jurisdiction, when imposed on constables in the force, or for assaults on constables in the force, and the fines or portions of fines imposed by a court of summary jurisdiction for other

(*d*) See the preceding section.

offences, and awarded to informers being constables in the force; and Sect. 16 (1).

(c) such fines or portions of fines, and such fees payable to or received by constables, as by any Act are directed or authorised to be carried to the superannuation or pension fund of the police force: and

(d) the net sums arising from the sale of worn or cast clothing supplied for the use of constables of the force; and

(e) such proportion of any sum received on account of constables whose services have been lent in consideration of payment as the police authority may consider to be a fair contribution to the pension fund in respect of those constables; and

(f) any payments or contributions payable under the provisions of any local and personal Act to the pension or superannuation fund of any police force, whether out of any fund, rate, or account under the control of the police authority, or payable by any other authority, board, or persons; and

(g) all dividends and other annual sums received in respect of the investments of the pension fund.

(2.) Unless the authority having control of the fund to which the sums hereinafter mentioned would but for this section be carried otherwise resolve, and except so far as the said sums are subject to the foregoing provisions of this section, there shall also be carried to the pension fund of every police force the following sums, namely:—

(h) The net sums received in the police area for pedlars and chimney sweepers certificates (*e*); and

(i) All fees payable to or received by any constable of the force in the execution of his duty as such, or in the execution of any other duty which may be required to be performed by any constable of the force; and

(k) The fines imposed by a court of summary jurisdiction for offences under the Licensing Acts, 1872 and 1874, when committed within the police area, or for any offence under a general or local Act similar to any of the above offences. 35 & 36 Vict. c. 94. 37 & 38 Vict. c. 49.

(3.) The police authority may also direct any sums under the control of the police authority in that capacity, or under the control of the police force, or of any member thereof in that capacity, to be carried to the pension fund, provided that this direction shall not be given in the case of any fund held on a private trust.

(4.) Any resolution passed for the purposes of this section may be revoked or varied.

(*e*) *I.e.*, under 34 & 35 Vict. c. 96, s. 5, and 38 & 39 Vict. c. 70, s. 10. The Chimney Sweepers Act, 1894 (57 & 58 Vict. c. 51), s. 3, provides that all fees received under the last-mentioned section shall be paid to the pension fund of the police force of the police district in which the certificate was issued.

Sect. 16 (5).

(5.) The provisions of this section shall have effect notwithstanding anything in any charter or in any other Act, whether relating to municipal corporations or otherwise.

Distribution of sums granted out of Customs and Excise duties for police superannuation.

17.—(1.) Any annual sum which under an Act passed in the present session (*f*) relating to the distribution of certain duties of Customs and Excise is required to be distributed among the police authorities of the police forces in England and Wales, other than the Metropolitan police force (which sum is in this Act referred to as the Exchequer contribution), shall be distributed according to the following basis of distribution, that is to say:—

(a.) There shall be paid in every financial year to the police authority of every such police force a sum equal to the amount of the rateable deductions made during the year ending the twenty-ninth day of September last preceding the end of the financial year from the pay of the constables belonging to that force, and that sum shall be carried to the pension fund.

(b.) The residue shall at the same time be distributed among the police authorities of those forces in proportion to the amounts paid during the year ending the twenty-ninth day of September last preceding the end of the financial year in respect of pensions, allowances, and gratuities out of their pension funds respectively, and the proportion to be paid to each force shall be carried to the pension fund.

(2.) Provided that a police authority shall not in respect of any year receive any payment under this section unless the Secretary of State gives a certificate that the management and efficiency of the police force under that authority and the administration of the pension fund of that force have during that year been satisfactory; and, if the Secretary of State withholds that certificate as regards any police authority, the amount which would otherwise be payable to that authority under this section shall be forfeited to the Crown and paid into the Exchequer.

(3.) Before any such certificate is finally withheld in respect of any police force, the Secretary of State shall communicate with the police authority of the force, and that authority may address any statement on the subject to the Secretary of State; and in every case in which the certificate is withheld a statement of the grounds on which the Secretary of State has withheld his certificate; together with any such statement of the police authority, shall be laid before Parliament.

(4.) The sums to be paid to each police authority under this section shall be certified by the Secretary of State, who may, if he thinks proper, vary his certificate, but unless it is so varied his certificate shall be conclusive.

(*f*) *I.e.*, 53 & 54 Vict. c. 60, s. 1 (1), *post*.

(5.) Where owing to any special circumstances affecting any particular police force the sum payable to that force under the foregoing provisions of this section would, in the opinion of the Secretary of State, be inequitable as between that force and some other force or forces, the Secretary of State may make such modification in the basis of distribution as appears to him to be necessary to meet the equities of the case. Sect. 17 (5).

(6.) The basis of distribution under this section may also be varied in such manner and in accordance with such conditions as may from time to time be set forth in regulations made by the Secretary of State and submitted to Parliament. All such regulations shall be laid on the table of both Houses of Parliament, and shall not come into operation until they have lain on the table of each House for not less than thirty days on which that House has sat.

(7.) This section shall come into operation on the passing of this Act.

Accounts and investment of pension fund.

18.—(1.) All sums which, in pursuance of this Act, are to be carried to the pension fund of a police force shall be accounted for and paid to the treasurer of that fund (*g*) in such manner as the police authority may direct, and may be dealt with as annual income of the pension fund.

(2.) The pension fund of a police force shall be kept as a separate fund, but the treasurer of the police fund shall be the treasurer of the pension fund, and all enactments and regulations relating to the accounts of the police fund, and to the making up, audit, and publication thereof, and to the power of disallowance and otherwise shall, so nearly as circumstances admit, apply to the pension fund.

(3.) At the end of each financial year the surplus of the annual income of the pension fund above the expenditure thereout shall, as soon as may be, be invested in such name as the police authority direct, and in any manner authorised by law for investments by trustees (*h*), and all investments on account of the fund, under this section or otherwise, are in this Act referred to as the capital of the pension fund.

(4.) The capital of the pension fund shall not be applied for paying any sums payable out of that fund.

Guarantee of pension fund by police fund.

19.—(1.) If at any time the annual income of the pension fund is insufficient to pay the expenses of managing the fund, and the pensions, allowances, gratuities, and other sums payable thereout, the deficiency shall be supplied out of the police fund (*i*).

(2.) In the case of a county divided into districts within the meaning of section twenty-seven of the County Police Act, 1840, as 3 & 4 Vict. c. 88.

(*g*) In a county this officer will be the county treasurer. See s. 34, *post*.

(*h*) The Police Act, 1893, s. 5, *post*, enables the police authority to invest the capital of the pension fund in debentures or mortgages issued or made by a county council in pursuance of s. 69 of the Local Government Act, 1888, *ante*, p. 132.

(*i*) In a county the police fund is the county fund. See the Third Schedule, *post*.

Sect. 19 (2).

19 & 20 Vict. c. 69.

amended by section four of the County and Borough Police Act, 1856, the deficiency shall be supplied by the several districts, as part of the local expenditure thereof, rateably in proportion to the number of constables appointed for each such district (*k*).

(3.) Where the police force of a borough has been consolidated with the police force of a county (*l*), the deficiency shall be supplied out of the police funds of the county and borough respectively in accordance with an agreement between the police authorities for the county and borough made in the same manner and subject to the same conditions as an agreement to consolidate the police force of a borough with the police force of a county can be made, and in default of any such agreement shall be supplied in such manner as may be determined by an arbitrator appointed by the Secretary of State.

(4.) Where the rate which can be levied for the police fund is limited, an addition to that rate may be levied for the purpose of raising the sum required to supply the deficiency.

Power for police authority to make regulations.

20.—(1.) Every police authority may make regulations consistent with this Act with respect to the deductions from a constable's service for sickness, misconduct, or neglect of duty, and with respect to stoppages of pay during sickness and fines for misconduct, and with respect to the mode in which pensions are to be paid, and otherwise for the purpose of giving effect to be provisions of this Act.

(2.) All regulations for a police force made before the commencement of this Act with respect to any of the above matters shall have effect as if made under the powers given by this section.

Power to return rateable deductions on leaving force.

21. If a constable not having been dismissed leaves a police force without a pension or gratuity, the police authority may, if it seems to them just, pay him the whole or part of the rateable deductions which have been made from his pay; but this section shall not apply in the case of his being removed to another force under such circumstances as will enable him to reckon his approved service in the force from which he removes.

Provisional orders by Secretary of State.

22.—(1.) Where it appears to a police authority that the assets of their pension fund exceed the amount required for meeting the liabilities thereon, and that it is expedient to provide for the application of the excess or any part thereof, the police authority may apply to the Secretary of State, and thereupon the Secretary of State may frame and submit to Parliament for confirmation a provisional order authorizing the payment out of the pension fund

(*k*) Under 3 & 4 Vict. c. 88, s. 27, a county may be divided into police districts in cases where the number of constables needed is different in different parts of the same county, and each district pays for its own constables. The 19 & 20 Vict. c 69, s. 4, enables the Queen in Council on petition to order a county to be divided into districts.

(*l*) *I.e.*, under 19 & 20 Vict. c. 69, s. 5.

of such sums, for such purposes, during such period, and subject to such conditions as may seem expedient. Sect. 22 (1).

(2.) Where it appears to a police authority that by reason of their pension fund being sufficient to meet the liabilities thereon it is unnecessary to make any further investments on account of the capital thereof, the police authority may apply to the Secretary of State, and thereupon the Secretary of State may frame and submit to Parliament for confirmation a provisional order authorizing the discontinuance of those investments.

(3.) Where a local Act provides for the payment to members of a special force in any police area of the same pension, superannuation, or other allowances or gratuities as are by that local Act provided for the police force of the area, the authority controlling the special force may apply to the Secretary of State, and thereupon the Secretary of State may frame and submit to Parliament for confirmation a provisional order providing—

(i.) for the adjustment of any financial relations existing at the commencement of this Act between the police force and the special force as regards the payment of pensions, allowances, and gratuities to members of those forces respectively; and

(ii.) for applying with or without modification all or any of the provisions of this Act to the special force.

(4.) A provisional order under this section shall be of no force unless and until it is confirmed by Act of Parliament, but when so confirmed shall have effect with any modifications made therein by Parliament.

(5.) If, while the Bill confirming any such order is pending in either House of Parliament, a petition is presented against any order comprised therein, the Bill, so far as it relates to that order, may be referred to a Select Committee, and the petitioner shall be allowed to appear and oppose as in the case of private Bills.

(6.) All costs charges and expenses incurred by the Secretary of State in relation to any order under this section shall be defrayed by the authority applying for the order.

(7.) For the purposes of this section the expression "special force" means a fire brigade, fire police, or other like force.

PART II.

General Amendment of Acts.

23.—(1.) Every police authority may from time to time, and shall at least once in every five years, submit for approval to a Secretary of State a table of fees payable to constables in respect of the service of summonses, the execution of warrants, and the performance of other occasional duties which may be required of the constables under that authority, and in respect of the performance of any other act done by constables in the execution of their duty, Table of fees.

Sect. 23 (1) and the Secretary of State may approve of the table, with or without modification.

(2.) Every police authority shall also provide for those fees being duly accounted for and being duly paid to the treasurer of that authority, and those fees shall, subject to the provisions of this Act, be applied in manner provided by the enactments relating to the police force of that authority, and so far as those enactments do not extend, then in aid of the police fund of that authority.

(3.) A constable may receive any fee mentioned in a table for the time being approved not more than five years previously by a Secretary of State, but no other fee shall be taken by a constable for any service performed by him.

(4.) Every constable shall duly account in accordance with the provisions made as above mentioned for any fee taken by him.

Amendment of 22 & 23 Vict. c. 32, s. 24, as to amount of gratuity.

24. So much of the County and Borough Police Act, 1859, as limits the amount of the gratuity which may be granted as a reward for a meritorious act done by a constable in the execution of his duty is hereby repealed (*m*).

Assistance by one police force to another.

25.—(1.) Where a police authority deem it expedient for any special emergency or under any exceptional circumstances to strengthen their police force (in this section referred to as the aided force) by constables belonging to another police force, such number of constables belonging to the latter force may be added to the aided force, and for such period, as may be agreed on between the police authorities of the forces; and the constables so added, notwithstanding that they have not been sworn in or taken any declaration as constables of the aided force, shall, during that period, be deemed, save as otherwise provided by the agreement, to be for all purposes constables of the aided force, and shall have the like powers, duties, and privileges (*n*).

(2.) The agreement may be made for a particular occasion or as a standing agreement, and with reference either to recurring or to unforeseen events, or otherwise, as may be thought expedient.

(3.) Any power conferred on a police authority by this section or by any agreement made thereunder may (subject to anything in the agreement to the contrary) be delegated by that authority to their chief officer of police by any general or special order, and with or without any exceptions, restrictions, or conditions.

(4.) An agreement under this section may contain such terms as to the command of the constables added to the aided force, and as

---

(*m*) Under 22 & 23 Vict. c. 32, s. 24, the amount was limited to 3*l*.

(*n*) The county council are bound to pay to a borough council in respect of an aiding force brought into the borough under this sub-section, one half of the cost of the pay and clothing of such aiding force, under the Local Government Act, 1888, s. 24, sub-s. (2) (*j*). *R.* v. *West Riding of Yorkshire*, [1895] 1 Q. B. 885; 64 L. J. M. C. 145; 72 L. T. (N.S.) 520; 43 W. R. 386; 59 J. P. 340.

to the expenses (including the pay and allowances of the constables so added and provision for pensions, gratuities, and allowances in the event of those constables being killed or injured) and otherwise, as may seem expedient. **Sect. 25 (4).**

(5.) An agreement may be made by a police authority with more police authorities than one.

26. A police authority may require every constable at the time of his appointment to appear before a justice of the peace, and make and sign a declaration as to his previous service in a police force or public employment, in the form contained in the Second Schedule to this Act, or to the like effect; and if any constable knowingly makes a false declaration, he shall be liable, on summary conviction, to be imprisoned, with or without hard labour, for any period not exceeding three months. Declaration by constables respecting previous service.

27. Whereas the annual value of property on which contributions for the purposes of the metropolitan police force are calculated is required to be computed according to the last valuation for the time being acted upon in assessing the county rate, and in some cases since the passing of the Local Government Act, 1888, there may be no such valuation: Be it therefore enacted that in the case of any area for which there is no such valuation, the valuation for the purpose of the said computation shall be such as is from time to time agreed upon between the receiver for the metropolitan police district and the rating authority, whether overseers or others, of the said area, or in default of agreement, as may be determined by arbitration of the Local Government Board, and the provisions of the Local Government Act, 1888, respecting the determination of differences by arbitration of the Local Government Board shall apply accordingly (*o*). Computation of annual value in certain cases for the purpose of the metropolitan police.

In the case of any contribution made or required before the commencement of this Act, the receiver and rating authority may agree to adjust the amount according to any valuation made in pursuance of this section, or such other valuation as they may agree under all the circumstances to be just.

28.—(1.) Where in pursuance of the Act of the session held in the first and second years of King William the Fourth, chapter forty-one, intituled "An Act for amending the laws relative to the appointment of special constables, and for the better preservation of the peace," a special constable is appointed by a justice or justices exercising jurisdiction in any part of the metropolitan police district, he shall have all the powers of a constable throughout the whole of the metropolitan police district and the city of London, and the provisions of that Act shall apply to him as if the metropolitan police district were one county; and the allowances and Provision as to special constables.

(*o*) See the Local Government Act, 1888, s. 63, *ante*, p. 121, and 59 Vict. c. 9, *post*.

Sect. 28 (1). expenses mentioned in section thirteen of that Act may, if the Secretary of State so directs, be paid out of the metropolitan police fund.

(2.) Where in pursuance of the same Act a special constable is appointed by a justice or justices having jurisdiction in the city of London, he shall have the powers of a constable throughout the whole of the metropolitan police district.

Provision as to receiver of metropolitan police district.

29. It shall not be necessary for the receiver for the time being of the metropolitan police district to give security for the faithful performance of his duty, and any security already given for this purpose shall cease to be in force.

PART III.

Temporary and Supplemental Provisions.

Application of Act to existing funds and constables.

30. For the purpose of adapting the provisions of Part One of this Act to existing pension or superannuation funds and existing constables (that is to say, to constables appointed to police forces, and to the pension or superannuation funds established for those forces, before the commencement of this Act, whether under any general or local Act, or otherwise) the following provisions shall have effect:

(1.) As soon as may be after the commencement of this Act, the amount of every existing pension or superannuation fund of a police force shall, where it is not already held by the treasurer of the police fund of that force, be transferred by the persons holding the same to such persons as the police authority may direct, to be held and dealt with as part of the pension fund under this Act, and as part of the capital or income thereof, as the case may require:

(2.) Where the Exchequer contribution to the police authority of a police force becomes payable before any existing fund of the force which is required to be so transferred is so transferred, or, in the case of a police force not having any such fund, before a pension fund is established for the force in pursuance of this Act, the payment of the contribution shall be deferred until the Secretary of State has certified that the fund is so transferred or established:

(3.) Where the police force of a borough has been consolidated with the police force of a county, and the existing pension or superannuation fund of the police force of the borough has not been transferred to the county treasurer, that fund shall be transferred in accordance with the foregoing provisions of this section, as soon as may be after the commencement of this Act, by the persons holding the same, and, in the absence of any agreement between the police authorities for the county and borough, the income of that fund shall be applied in paying the superannuation and other allowances charged thereon at the date of the transfer, and, subject thereto, in paying the pensions, allowances, and gratuities to constables employed in the consolidated force, and their widows and children, in such manner as may be determined by an arbitrator appointed by the Secretary of State: Sect. 30 (3).

(4.) In Lincolnshire section twenty-two of the County and Borough Police Act, 1859, and sections six, seven, and eight of the Police Superannuation Act, 1865, as amended by the Lincolnshire Police Superannuation Act, 1888, shall, so far as is consistent with the tenor thereof, apply to the pension fund under this Act in like manner as if it were the superannuation fund in those sections mentioned: 22 & 23 Vict. c. 32. 28 & 29 Vict. c. 35. 51 Vict. c. ix.

(5.) Every police authority shall, within fourteen days after a pension scale has been adopted by or framed for the police authority in pursuance of this Act, cause written notice to be given to every constable in the police force under that authority, requiring him to inform that authority in writing before the date of the commencement of this Act, whether he does or does not accept the provisions of this Act in lieu of the existing enactments respecting superannuation:

(6.) This Act shall not apply to any existing constable who, before the date of the commencement of this Act, whether any such notice has or has not been given to him, declines in writing to accept the provisions of this Act; but save as aforesaid this Act shall apply to all existing constables; and those constables shall be deemed to have surrendered in favour of the police authority all right to any provision made before the commencement of this Act, either wholly or partly, by the police authority for the superannuation of such constables, or, in case of their death, for their widows and children or any of them, whether that provision is made by an annual allowance, insurance, or otherwise:

(7.) If by reason of the police authority not having given such notice as aforesaid an existing constable becomes entitled to a less pension than he would have been entitled to receive if this Act had not passed, he may apply to the police authority, and the police authority may make such order as may seem just for the purpose of preventing the constable from suffering any loss by reason of the notice not having been given:

(8.) In the case of any existing constable to whom this Act applies, his approved service for any period before the commencement of this Act in the force in which he is serving at the time of his retirement shall be reckoned as approved service; and his service for not less than three years either wholly or partly before the commencement of

Sect. 30 (8).

this Act in any police force in any part of the United Kingdom from which he removed with the sanction of the chief officer or police authority of that force to another force, shall (notwithstanding the sanction was not given in writing) be reckoned as approved service for the said period in the last-mentioned force, unless the police authority who give him the notice respecting the acceptance of this Act, inform him in writing at the time of such notice that they refuse to allow the said service to be reckoned, but their refusal shall not prevent the reckoning of that service under any other provision of this section :

(9.) Any description of service before the commencement of this Act, either in a police force or otherwise, which any existing constable to whom this Act applies is at the commencement of this Act entitled to reckon as service for any period towards superannuation out of the existing pension or superannuation fund of his police force, and which is not reckoned under any other provision of this Act, shall be reckoned for the same period for the purposes of pension under this Act: In the case of any existing constable to whom this Act applies, who has served not less than ten years before the commencement of this Act in a police force in which the police authority have heretofore, under the provisions of former Acts, granted pensions of higher amount than authorised by the scale adopted by that police authority under the provisions of this Act, and who becomes entitled to a pension under this Act, then, notwithstanding anything in this Act, the pension may, if the police authority think fit, exceed the amount prescribed in the adopted scale so as it does not exceed the amount which might have been granted if this Act had not passed :

(10.) Provided that if, in the case of any existing constable, rateable deductions or other payments towards superannuation or insurance have not, during the period of the service which he is entitled to reckon for the purpose of calculating his pension under this Act, or for some part of such period not less than ten years, been made, and contributions have not been made from other sources to a superannuation fund in lieu of the rateable deductions not so made, the pension granted under this Act to such constable may, if the police authority think fit, be reduced by an annual amount equal to such deferred annuity as could, according to the tables for the purchase of deferred annuities from the Commissioners for the Reduction of the National Debt through the medium of the Post Office, have been purchased by rateable deductions made at the rate fixed under this Act during the said period of service, or the part thereof during which such deductions or payments were not made.

Sect. 31.

31. The provisions of this Act shall have effect, notwithstanding anything in any other Act, general or local, to the contrary.

Act to supersede local Acts.

32. This Act shall apply to the metropolitan police force, subject as follows :—

Application of Act to metropolitan police.

(1.) Anything authorised or required to be done by a resolution or other act of the police authority may be done by any instrument signed by a Secretary of State :

(2.) Anything authorised or required to be done with the approval of a Secretary of State, or by a Secretary of State on the submission or application of a police authority, may be done by a Secretary of State alone :

(3.) The court of quarter sessions to which an application is to be made with respect to a decision as to a pension or allowance shall be the court of quarter sessions for the county of London :

(4.) Nothing in this Act shall apply to any existing constable who acted as one of the police of any of Her Majesty's dockyards, and upon his transfer to the metropolitan police force did not accept the terms of superannuation of members of that force, or agree to allow the deductions to be made from his pay which have been made towards such superannuation from the pay of other members of that force ; and any such constable shall be entitled to superannuation under the Superannuation Act, 1859, notwithstanding that he obtained no certificate from the Civil Service Commissioners :

22 Vict. c. 26.

(5.) The rate and conditions of pension of the chief commissioner of metropolitan police, and of the assistant commissioners of metropolitan police shall be regulated by the provisions of this Act, and not by the provisions of the Metropolitan Police Staff (Superannuation) Act, 1875, but the said chief commissioner and assistant commissioners shall be entitled to pension under the provisions of this Act in respect of any emoluments in respect of which they are entitled to a superannuation allowance made under the Metropolitan Police Staff (Superannuation) Act, 1875.

38 & 39 Vict. c. 28.

(6.) The rateable deductions from the salary of the chief commissioner of metropolitan police and from the salaries of such of the assistant commissioners of metropolitan police as receive salaries from money provided by Parliament shall be paid into the Exchequer and not to the pension fund.

(7.) The existing chief commissioner and assistant commissioners of metropolitan police shall be deemed existing constables within the meaning of this Act.

33. In this Act, unless the context otherwise requires,—

Police areas and authorities.

The expression "police area" means one of the areas set forth in the first column of the Third Schedule to this Act ; and the expressions "police authority," "chief officer of police,"

Sect. 33.

and "police fund," mean, as respects each police area, the authority, officer, and fund respectively mentioned opposite to that area in the second, third, and fourth columns of that schedule; and the expression "police force" means a force maintained by one of the police authorities mentioned in the said schedule:

Provided as follows:—

(1.) In the case of a county the powers of the police authority under this Act with respect to the accounting for and payment of sums to be carried to the pension fund or police fund, and with respect to investments, shall be exercised by the county council, and any sum payable under this Act by the police authority shall be payable by the county council on the requisition of the standing joint committee of the quarter sessions and the county council;

(2.) Any contributions required to meet payments out of the county fund for the purposes of this Act shall be assessed in like manner as contributions to meet the expenses of the police force;

(3.) The exercise of the powers conferred by this Act on the watch committee of a borough shall be subject to the approbation of the council of the borough.

Definitions

34. In this Act, unless the context otherwise requires,

The expression "treasurer" includes any receiver, chamberlain, or other officer, by whatever name known, who performs the duties of treasurer in relation to any police fund:

The expression "fine" includes a pecuniary penalty:

The expression "fee" does not include any reward paid to an individual constable by direction of the Admiralty, or of any military authority, or of a Secretary of State not acting as the police authority, or any gratuity paid to a constable for a meritorious act done in the execution of his duty.

Saving for existing pensions.

35. Notwithstanding anything in this Act or in any repeal by this Act every person in receipt of any pension, superannuation, or other allowance at the commencement of this Act shall continue to be entitled to receive the same, subject to the same limitations and conditions as before the commencement of this Act, and the same shall not be altered under this Act, and shall, save as otherwise expressly provided by this Act, be paid out of the like funds, as nearly as may be, as if this Act had not passed.

Repeal.

36. The Acts mentioned in the Fourth Schedule to this Act are hereby repealed to the extent in the third column of that schedule mentioned, and so much of any other Act as regulates the superannuation of any police force in England and Wales, or is inconsistent with this Act, is also hereby repealed:

Provided that— Sect. 36 (1).

(1.) This repeal shall not affect the right of any police authority to grant any pension or superannuation or other allowance or gratuity to any existing constable to whom this Act does not apply, or to the widow and child of any such constable, or either of them, and shall not affect the right of any such constable, widow, or child to claim such pension, or superannuation or other allowance or gratuity, and any such pension, allowance or gratuity may be granted and claimed accordingly, and the claim shall be allowed as if this Act had not passed, but the pension, allowance, or gratuity shall be paid out of the pension fund:

(2.) This repeal shall not prevent any constable from reckoning as approved service any service which he is entitled under any enactment hereby repealed to reckon towards pension or superannuation:

(3.) Any table of fees made in pursuance of any enactment hereby repealed shall continue in force in like manner as if it had been at the date of the commencement of this Act approved by the Secretary of State in pursuance of this Act:

(4.) Nothing in this section shall repeal any enactment so far as it relates to any fire brigade, fire police, or other force to which or to the members whereof the provisions of this Act do not apply.

Commencement of Act.

37. This Act shall come into operation on the first day of April one thousand eight hundred and ninety-one, except as to anything which is by this Act required or authorised to be done before that date, and except as to any provision which is expressed to come into operation on the passing of this Act.

Short titles.

38.—(1.) This Act may be cited as the Police Act, 1890.

(2.) The Acts mentioned in the Fifth Schedule to this Act are in this Act referred to and may be cited by the short titles respectively in that schedule mentioned, and may be cited collectively by the short title at the commencement of that schedule mentioned.

(3.) The Metropolitan Police Acts, 1829 to 1887, and this Act may be cited together as the Metropolitan Police Acts, 1829 to 1890.

(4.) The Acts mentioned in the said Fifth Schedule and this Act may be cited together as the Police Acts, 1839 to 1890 (*p*).

Act not to apply to City.

39. This Act shall not apply to the City of London Police

Extent of Act.

40. This Act shall not extend to Scotland or Ireland.

(*p*) To these must be added the Police Act, 1893 ; all may be cited together as the Police Acts, 1839 to 1893.

Schedules.

Section 3.

SCHEDULES.

FIRST SCHEDULE.

Pension Scale.

Part I.

Ordinary Pensions.

(1.) The pension to a constable on retirement shall be within the maximum and minimum limits following; that is to say,

(a) if he has completed fifteen but less than twenty-one years approved service, an annual sum not less than one sixtieth nor more than one fiftieth of his annual pay for every completed year of approved service; and

(b) if he has completed twenty-one but less than twenty-five years approved service, an annual sum not less than twenty sixtieths nor more than twenty fiftieths of his annual pay, with an addition of not less than two sixtieths and not more than two fiftieths of his annual pay for every completed year of approved service above twenty years; and

(c) if he has completed twenty-five years approved service, an annual sum not less than thirty sixtieths nor more than thirty-one fiftieths of his annual pay, with an addition of not less than one sixtieth nor more than three fiftieths of his annual pay for every completed year of approved service above twenty-five years, so however that the pension shall not exceed two thirds of his annual pay.

(2.) Where a limit of age is fixed below which a constable is not to be entitled to retire on a pension without a medical certificate, it shall be not less than fifty years and not more than fifty-five years, or in the case of a constable above the rank of sergeant, not more than sixty years, but it shall not be obligatory on a police authority to fix any such limit.

Part II.

Maximum of Gratuity to Constable.

(3.) Any gratuity on retirement to a constable who is incapacitated for the performance of his duty shall not exceed the amount of one month's pay for every completed year of approved service.

Special Pensions.

(4.) The pension to a constable who is incapacitated for the performance of his duty by infirmity of mind or body occasioned by an injury received in the execution of his duty without his own default, shall vary according as the injury is or is not accidental, and according as the constable is partially or totally disabled from earning his livelihood.

(5.) The amount of pension in such cases shall be in the discretion of the police authority but within the maximum and minimum limits following:—

Scale A.

If the injury is accidental and the constable is partially disabled (*q*)—

(a) if he has completed not more than five years approved service, an annual sum not greater than ten fiftieths and not less than ten sixtieths of his annual pay;

(*q*) Provision is made by the Police Act, 1893, s. 3, *post*, for the increase of a pension where a partial disablement afterwards becomes total.

(b) if he has completed more than five and not more than ten years approved service, an annual sum not greater than twelve fiftieths and not less than twelve sixtieths of his annual pay;

(c) if he has completed more than ten and not more than fifteen years approved service, an annual sum not greater than fifteen fiftieths and not less than fifteen sixtieths of his annual pay; and

(d) if he has completed more than fifteen years approved service, an annual sum not greater than the maximum pension and not less than the minimum pension authorised under Article (1) of this schedule.

Scale B.

If the injury is accidental and the constable is totally disabled—

(a) if he has completed not more than ten years approved service, an annual sum not greater than fifteen fiftieths and not less than fifteen sixtieths of his annual pay;

(b) if he has completed more than ten and not more than fifteen years approved service, an annual sum not greater than twenty fiftieths and not less than twenty sixtieths of his annual pay;

(c) if he has completed more than fifteen years approved service, an annual sum not greater than the maximum pension authorised under Article (1) of this schedule, with an addition equal to five fiftieths of his annual pay, and not less than the minimum pension authorised under the same Article, with an addition equal to five sixtieths of his annual pay, provided that the pension shall not exceed two thirds of his annual pay.

Scale C.

If the injury is not accidental and the constable is partially disabled—

(a) if he has completed not more than ten years approved service, an annual sum not greater than twenty fiftieths and not less than twenty sixtieths of his annual pay;

(b) if he has completed more than ten and not more than fifteen years approved service, an annual sum not greater than twenty-five fiftieths and not less than twenty-five sixtieths of his annual pay;

(c) if he has completed more than fifteen years approved service, an annual sum not greater than the maximum pension authorised under Article (1) of this schedule, with an addition equal to ten fiftieths of his annual pay, and not less than the minimum pension authorised under the same Article, with an addition equal to ten sixtieths of his annual pay, provided that the pension shall not exceed two thirds of his annual pay.

Scale D.

If the injury is not accidental and the constable is totally disabled—

A sum not exceeding full pay and not less than the maximum amount prescribed by Scale C.

Pensions Allowances and Gratuities to Widow and Children.

(6.) Where a constable without his own default loses his life from the effect of an injury received in the execution of his duty, the pension to his widow and the allowances to his children shall be according to the following scale:—

(a.) The pension to the widow shall be an annual sum of fifteen pounds;

Schedules

(b.) The allowance to each child shall be an annual sum of two pounds ten shillings:

Provided that the police authority may, in the case of a constable of a rank higher than that of sergeant, increase the above amounts, so however that the pension for a widow of an inspector do not exceed the annual sum of twenty-five pounds, and the pension for a widow of an officer of a rank higher than that of inspector do not exceed thirty pounds, and the allowance for a child of a constable of a rank higher than that of sergeant do not exceed the annual sum of five pounds.

(7.) Where a constable dies under circumstances which do not entitle his widow and children to a pension or allowance under the preceding article of this schedule, any gratuities to the widow and children shall not exceed in the whole the amount of one month's pay for every completed year of approved service of the deceased constable.

(8.) The gratuities granted to the widow and children of a constable who dies within twelve months after the grant of a pension shall not exceed in the whole the difference between the annual pay of the constable and the amount he has actually received in respect of his pension.

Part III.

General Rules.

(9.) The pension to a widow shall continue only while she remains a widow and is of good character.

(10.) The allowance to a child shall not continue after the child attains the age of fifteen years.

(11.) In estimating any pension, gratuity, or allowance for the purposes of this Act—

(a) a pension or gratuity to a constable shall be calculated according to the amount of his annual pay at the date of his retirement;

(b) a pension or gratuity to the widow and an allowance or gratuity to a child of a constable shall be calculated according to the amount of the constable's annual pay at the date of his death;

(c) but *where a constable has, in the course of the three years next before the date of his retirement or death, been in more than one rank* (r), his annual pay at the date of the retirement or death shall be deemed to be the average annual amount of pay received by him for the said three years, instead of the annual amount actually received by him at that date.

Section 26.

SECOND SCHEDULE.

Declaration.

*Insert according to the circumstances.

I, *A. B.*, now residing in the parish of in the county of , solemnly and sincerely declare that I have* never served in any police force in Great Britain, nor in the Royal Irish Constabulary, nor in the Royal Navy, nor in Her Majesty's army, nor in the militia, nor under the Post

---

(r) The words in italics are repealed, and the following words substituted for them by the Police Act, 1893 (56 & 57 Vict. c. 10), s. 6: "Where a constable at the date of his retirement or death holds a rank to which he has been promoted within the three years previous." The effect of this is that if a constable has been reduced in rank, his pension will be calculated with reference to his pay at the date of his retirement, and this applies to a constable who is bound by the Act of 1890 who retires after 1893. *Ruff* v. *Secretary of State for the Home Department*, 60 J. P. 343.

Office, nor under any public department [*or* that I have served in the police force for years, from to , and in Her Majesty's army for years from to , and am now in the Army Reserve, but have not served in the Royal Irish Constabulary nor in the Royal Navy, nor in the militia, nor under the Post Office, nor under any public department, *or as the case may be*]. Schedules.

Declared before me.

(Signed) *A. B.*

At the day of 18 .

THIRD SCHEDULE.

Section 33.

POLICE AREAS AND AUTHORITIES.

Police Area.	Police Authority.	Chief Officer of Police.	Police Fund.
The Metropolitan Police District.	One of Her Majesty's Principal Secretaries of State.	The commissioner of police of the metropolis.	The funds applicable for defraying the expenses of the metropolitan police force.
A county - - -	The standing joint committee of the quarter sessions and the county council.	The chief constable -	The county fund.
A borough - - -	The watch committee.	The chief or head constable.	The borough fund or borough rate or any fund or rate applicable under any local Act for the expenses of the police force.
A town not being a borough and maintaining a separate police force under any local Act of Parliament.	The authority having the management of the police under the local Act.	The head constable or other officer by whatever name called having the chief command of the police.	The fund or rate applicable under the local Act for the expenses of the police force.
The river Tyne within the limits of the Acts relating to the Tyne Improvement Commissioners.	The Tyne Improvement Commissioners.	The superintendent or other officer having the chief command of the police.	The tonnage rates and dues and other sums applicable under the Acts relating to the improvement of the river Tyne for the expenses of maintaining the police force.

In this schedule the expression "county" means an administrative county within the meaning of the Local Government Act, 1888, but does not include a county borough.

Such parts of any county as are within the Metropolitan Police District, or as form part of any other police area, shall not be deemed for the purposes of this Act to form part of the county police area.

FOURTH SCHEDULE.

Section 36.

ACTS REPEALED.

Session and Chapter.	Title or Short Title.	Extent of Repeal.
10 Geo. 4, c. 44. - -	An Act for improving the police in and near the metropolis.	In section ten, from "and the receiver for the time being," where those words first occur, to "paid to him under this Act."
2 & 3 Vict. c. 47. - -	The Metropolitan Police Act, 1839.	Sections twenty-two and twenty-three.

Schedules.

Session and Chapter.	Title or Short Title.	Extent of Repeal.
2 & 3 Vict. c. 71. - -	An Act for regulating the police courts in the metropolis.	In section forty-six, the words "which "shall be appled towards defraying "the charge of maintaining the "police of the metropolis."
3 & 4 Vict. c. 88. - -	An Act to amend an Act for the establishment of county and district constables.	Sections ten, eleven, and seventeen.
19 & 20 Vict. c. 69. -	An Act to render more effectual the police in counties and boroughs in England and Wales.	Sections eight, ten, eleven, thirteen, twenty-seven, twenty-eight, and twenty-nine.
20 & 21 Vict. c. 64. -	The Metropolitan Police Act, 1857.	Section fifteen.
22 & 23 Vict. c. 32. -	An Act to amend the law concerning the police in counties and boroughs in England and Wales.	Sections eight, nine, ten, twelve, thirteen, fifteen, sixteen, seventeen, nineteen, twenty, twenty-one, twenty-three, and twenty-eight, and in section twenty-four the words "not exceeding three pounds."
24 & 25 Vict. c. 124. -	The Metropolitan Police Act, 1861.	Section six.
28 & 29 Vict. c. 35. -	The Police Superannuation Act, 1865.	Section two, except so far as it relates to the County and Borough Police Act, 1859; and sections three, four, five, and nine.
45 & 46 Vict. c. 50. -	The Municipal Corporations Act, 1882.	Fifth Schedule, Part II., 5 (*b*) from "or as may be awarded" down to "length of service."

Section 38.

FIFTH SCHEDULE.

The Police (England) Acts.

Session and Chapter.	Title.	Short Title.
2 & 3 Vict. c. 93. -	An Act for the establishment of county and district constables by the authority of justices of the peace.	County Police Act, 1839.
3 & 4 Vict. c. 88. -	An Act to amend the Act for the establishment of county and district constables.	County Police Act, 1840.
19 & 20 Vict. c. 69. -	An Act to render more effectual the police in counties and boroughs in England and Wales.	County and Borough Police Act, 1856.
20 Vict. c. 2. - -	An Act to facilitate the appointment of chief constables for adjoining counties, and to confirm appointments of chief constables in certain cases.	County Police Act, 1857.
22 & 23 Vict. c. 32. -	An Act to amend the law concerning the police in counties and boroughs in England and Wales.	County and Borough Police Act, 1859.
28 & 29 Vict. c. 35. -	An Act to amend the law relating to the police superannuation funds in counties and boroughs.	Police Superannuation Act, 1865.

45 & 46 Vict. c. 50.

Sections one hundred and ninety to one hundred and ninety-four (both inclusive) of the Municipal Corporations Act, 1882, shall for the purposes of this Act be deemed to form part of the Acts in this schedule.

LOCAL TAXATION (CUSTOMS AND EXCISE) ACT, 1890.

(53 & 54 VICT. CAP. 60.)

An Act for the Distribution and Application of certain Duties of Customs and Excise; and for other purposes connected therewith. [18th August, 1890.]

WHEREAS certain local taxation (customs and excise) duties have by an Act of the present session (*s*) been directed to be paid to the same local taxation accounts as the local taxation probate duty, and it is expedient to provide for the distribution and application of the duties so paid:

*

Application of English share of customs and excise duties.

1.—(1.) Out of the English share of the local taxation (customs and excise) duties paid to the local taxation account on account of any financial year—

(a.) The sum of three hundred thousand pounds shall be applied for such purposes of police superannuation in England as hereinafter mentioned (*t*);

(b.) The residue shall, unless Parliament otherwise determines, be distributed between county and county borough funds, and carried to the Exchequer contribution accounts of those funds respectively, and applied under the Local Government Act, 1888, as if it were part of the English share of the local taxation probate duty, and shall be the subject of an adjustment between counties and county boroughs, according to section thirty-two of the said Act, by the Commissioners under that Act (*u*). 51 & 52 Vict. c. 41.

(2.) The council of any such county or county borough may contribute any sum received by such council in respect of the residue under this section, or any part of that sum, for the purposes of technical education (*x*) within the meaning of the Technical Instruction Act, 1889 (*y*), and may make that contribution over and above any sum that may be raised by rate under that Act.

(*s*) This Act is the 53 & 54 Vict. c. 8, s. 7, *ante*, p. 485.

(*t*) See s. 4, *post*. As to the distribution of the money by police authorities, see the Police Act, 1890, s. 17, *ante*, p. 498.

(*u*) As to the English share of the local taxation probate duty, see the Local Government Act, 1888, ss. 21—24, *ante*, p. 48.

It is provided by 54 Vict. c. 4, s. 2, *post*, that any moneys received by a county council under this clause, and directed by resolution to be appropriated or set aside for the purposes of technical or manual instruction, shall, although not expended or specifically contributed or allotted in whole or in part before the end of the financial year, remain applicable for such purposes, and shall not be applied in manner provided by s. 23, sub-ss. (2)—(10), of the Local Government Act, 1888, until the county council shall have made an order for such application.

(*x*) This includes both technical and manual instruction within the meaning of the Technical Instruction Acts, 1889 and 1891 (54 Vict. c. 4, s. 3), *post*.

(*y*) 52 & 53 Vict. c. 76, *ante*, p. 435.

Sect. 3 (3).

(3.) A county council may make any such contribution by giving the amount of the contribution or any part of that amount to any town council or other urban sanitary authority in their county for the purpose of the same being applied by such council or authority under the Technical Instruction Act, 1889, over and above any sum which can be raised under that Act by rate by such council or authority (z).

52 & 53 Vict. c. 76.

(4.) The council for any county to which the Welsh Intermediate Education Act, 1889 (a), applies may contribute any sum received by such council under this section in respect of the said residue or any part of that sum towards intermediate and technical education under that Act, in addition to the amount which the council can under that Act contribute for such education.

52 & 53 Vict. c. 40.

* * * * *

Distribution of sums for police superannuation in England and Scotland.

4.—(1.) Out of the annual sum applicable under this Act for police superannuation in England one hundred and fifty thousand pounds shall be paid to the receiver for the Metropolitan police district, and applied in aid of the police superannuation fund for the Metropolitan police force.

(2.) The remaining half of the said annual sum shall be distributed among the police authorities of the other police forces in England other than the police force of the city of London . . . . (b), and the amounts to be so distributed shall be distributed and applied towards the superannuation of the police forces in such manner and in accordance with such conditions and regulations as may be provided by or in pursuance of any Act hereafter passed, and until so distributed and applied shall remain to the credit of the local taxation accounts.

Distribution of local taxation (customs and excise) duties. 51 & 52 Vict. c. 41.

5. All sums paid in respect of the local taxation (customs and excise) duties to any local taxation accounts mentioned in section twenty-one of the Local Government Act, 1888 (c) . . . shall be paid and distributed by the like central authority as in the case of the local taxation probate duty, and the enactments relating to such distribution shall, subject to the express provisions of this Act, apply accordingly; the said accounts are in this Act referred to by the names given them in the said Acts.

* * * * *

Definitions.

6. In this Act, unless the context otherwise requires:—

The expression "local taxation probate duty" means the moiety of probate duties which under section twenty-one of the Local Government Act, 1888, ... is directed to be paid to the several local taxation accounts in England, . . .

(z) See s. 1, sub-s. (1) (g), of that Act, *ante*, p. 437.

(a) See that Act, *ante*, p. 423.

(b) In this and the following sections, clauses relating only to Scotland and Ireland are omitted. As to the distribution of the sums referred to, see s. 17 of the Police Act, 1890, *ante*, p. 498.

(c) *Ante*, p. 48.

The expression "central authority" means as respects England the Local Government Board; . . . Sect. 6.

7. This Act may be cited as the Local Taxation (Customs and Excise) Act, 1890. Short title.

ALLOTMENTS ACT, 1890.

(53 & 54 VICT. CAP. 65) (*d*).

An Act to provide for an Appeal from a Sanitary Authority failing to carry into effect the Allotments Act, 1887.

[18th August, 1890.]

* * * * *

1. This Act shall be construed as one with the Allotments Act, 1887 (in this Act referred to as the principal Act), and the principal Act and this Act may be cited together as the Allotments Acts, 1887 and 1890, and this Act may be cited as the Allotments Act, 1890. Construction and short title. 50 & 51 Vict. c. 48.

2.—(1.) Where such representation (*e*) as is authorised by section two of the principal Act has been made to the sanitary authority with respect to any district or parish, not being within the limits of Appeal to county council by persons

---

(*d*) This Act enables a county council to take steps to provide allotments of land for the labouring population in any urban district or rural parish within their county where the district council have failed in a proper case to provide such allotments under the Allotments Act, 1887. The Act of 1887 and this Act are fully annotated in Mr. Brooke Little's "Law of Allotments"; they are also set out in "Lumley's Public Health." The procedure under these Acts has been affected in several important particulars by the Local Government Act, 1894, *post.*

(*e*) The representation must be made to the sanitary authority, viz., the district council, by any six registered parliamentary electors or ratepayers resident in an urban district or in some parish within a rural district, or (in the case of such a parish) by the parish council, and must state that the circumstances of the urban district or parish are such that it is the duty of the district council to take proceedings under the Allotments Act, 1887. See s. 2 of that Act and s. 6 (3) of the Local Government Act, 1894, *post.*

If the district council are of opinion that there is a demand for allotments for the labouring population in the urban district or parish, and that they cannot be obtained at a reasonable rent (as defined by the Act of 1887) and on reasonable conditions by voluntary arrangement, the district council are required by s. 2 of the Act of 1887, and subject to the provisions of that Act, to purchase or hire suitable land adequate to provide a sufficient number of allotments, and to let it in allotments to persons belonging to the labouring population resident in the district or parish and desiring to take it. They are not, however, to acquire land for allotments save at such price or rent that in their opinion all expenses incurred (except in making public roads) in relation to the allotments may reasonably be expected to be recouped out of the rents.

It is only after a representation has been made under the principal Act and has been ineffectual that a petition may be presented to the county council under the text. Such a petition may, in the case of a rural parish, be presented by the parish council as well as by the persons mentioned in this section. Local Government Act, 1894, s. 6 (3), *post.*

Sect. 2 (1).

entitled to make representation to sanitary authority.

45 & 46 Vict. c. 50.

a borough as defined by the Municipal Corporations Act, 1882, and any six persons qualified to make such representation consider that the circumstances of the district or parish are such as to make it the duty of the sanitary authority to take proceedings under that Act therein, and that the sanitary authority have failed to acquire land adequate and suitable in quality and position to provide a sufficient number of allotments, such persons may petition the county council of the county in which such district or parish is situate, stating the facts and requesting the council to put into force the principal Act for the purpose of providing a sufficient number of allotments for the district or parish.

(2.) The council, if satisfied by the inquiry hereinafter mentioned (*f*) that the circumstances are such that land for allotments should be acquired, shall pass a resolution to that effect, and thereupon the powers and duties of the sanitary authority under the principal Act, so far as regards that district or parish, shall be transferred from the sanitary authority to the county council, and the county council, in substitution for the sanitary authority, shall proceed to acquire land in accordance with the principal Act, and otherwise execute that Act in the said district or parish (*g*).

Provided that this section shall not affect the property in, or any powers or duties of the sanitary authority in relation to, any land which before the passing of the said resolution was acquired by the sanitary authority under the principal Act.

Standing committee.

51 & 52 Vict. c. 41.

3.—(1.) For the purposes of this Act or the principal Act every county council, as soon as is conveniently practicable after the passing of this Act, and annually thereafter at the meeting for the election of chairman, shall appoint under the Local Government Act, 1888, (*h*), a standing committee not exceeding one fourth of their whole body.

(2.) For the purpose of any business under this Act relating to any district or parish wholly or partly situate in an electoral division, the county councillor representing that division shall, if not already appointed, be an additional member of the committee.

(*f*) See s. 3, *post*.

(*g*) But where the land is purchased by the county council for allotments for a parish having a parish council, it is to be conveyed to that council, and the county council will not, it seems, be concerned with laying it out for allotments or with the letting and management of the allotments. See Local Government Act, 1894, s. 9 (14), *post*, which assigns these duties to the parish council. The procedure for the acquisition of land for allotments by a district council under the Act of 1887 is detailed in ss. 3 and 4 of that Act, under which compulsory powers may be obtained by a provisional order of the county council confirmed by Parliament. But a simple method of obtaining compulsory powers is provided by s. 9 of the Local Government Act, 1894, *post*. See also the orders of the Local Government Board, made under that section; Part IV. of this work, *post*.

(*h*) See the Local Government Act, 1888, ss. 28 (2), 75, *ante*, pp. 64, 141, and Municipal Corporations Act, 1882, s. 22, *ante*, p. 260.

Sect. 3 (3).

(3.) Any petition under this Act shall as of course, and without any order of the council, be referred to the standing committee, who, on being satisfied of the bonâ fides of the application, shall forthwith cause a local inquiry into the circumstances to be made, and shall report the result to the council.

(4.) An inquiry under this Act or the principal Act shall be held by such one or more members of the standing committee, or such officer of the county council or other person as the standing committee may appoint to hold the same.

Supplementa provisions on council acquiring powers of sanitary authority.

4. Where the powers of the sanitary authority under the principal Act are, by virtue of this Act, transferred to the county council, the following provisions shall have effect—

(a.) The principal Act shall apply with the modifications necessa for giving effect to this Act:

(b.) The county council may borrow for the purposes of this Act subject to the conditions, in the manner, and on the security of the rate, subject to, in, and on the security of which the sanitary authority might have borrowed under the principal Act, if this Act had not been passed (*i*). The council shall have power to charge the said rate with the repayment of the principal and interest of the loan; and such loan with the interest thereon shall be repaid by the sanitary authority in like manner, and such charge shall have the like effect, as if the loan were lawfully raised and charged on that rate by the sanitary authority:

(c.) The county council shall keep separate accounts of all receipts and expenditure under this Act, and, in the application of sub-section six of section ten of the principal Act, the Local Government Act, 1888, shall be substituted for the Public Health Act, 1875 (*k*):

51 & 52 Vict c. 41.
38 & 39 Vict. c. 55.

(d.) The county council may make a provisional order for the purchase of land on the recommendation of the standing committee, without any petition from the sanitary authority, and the council shall be considered as the promoters of the order (*l*):

(e.) The county council may delegate to the sanitary authority any powers under section six, section seven, or section eight of the principal Act (which sections relate to the management of the allotments, and the letting and use thereof, and the recovery of the rent and of possession

---

(*i*) The borrowing powers of district councils for the purposes of the Allotments Act, 1887, are contained in s. 10 (4) and (5) of that Act, and ss. 233 to 244 of the Public Health Act, 1875. The security is in the case of an urban district, the district fund and general district rate; in the case of a rural parish, the special rate made in that parish.

(*k*) These accounts will therefore be audited as accounts of the county council under s. 71 of the Local Government Act, 1888, *ante*, p. 136.

(*l*) See note (*g*), *supra*, and s. 9 of the Local Government Act, 1894, *post*.

Sect. 4.

thereof); and, subject to the terms of the delegation, all expenses and receipts arising in the exercise of the powers so delegated shall be paid and dealt with as expenses and receipts of the sanitary authority under the principal Act (*m*):

(f.) The county council, on the request of the sanitary authority, may, by order under their seal, transfer to that authority all or any of the powers, duties, property, and liabilities vested in and imposed on the council by virtue of this Act as regards the district of such authority or any part thereof, and the property so transferred shall be deemed to have been acquired by that authority under the principal Act, and that authority shall act accordingly (*m*).

Use of school room free of charge.

5. Any room in a school receiving a grant out of moneys provided by Parliament may, except during ordinary school hours, be used free of charge for the purpose of an inquiry under this Act, or for the purposes of this Act by the county council or any committee appointed under this Act, or, with the consent of any two managers, for the purpose of holding public meetings to discuss any question relating to allotments under this Act or the principal Act, but any damage done to the room and any expense incurred by the person or persons having control over the room on account of its being so used shall be paid by the county council or by the persons calling the meeting.

Nothing in this section shall give any right to hold a public meeting in a schoolroom (a) unless not less than six days before the meeting a notice of the intention to hold the meeting on the day and at the time specified in the notice, signed by the persons calling the meeting, being not less than six in number, and being persons qualified to make a representation to the local authority under the principal Act, has been given, if the school is under a school board, to the clerk of the board, and in any other case to one of the managers of the school; nor (b) if the use of the schoolroom on the said day and at the said time has previously to the receipt of the notice of the meeting been granted for some other purpose; but in that case the clerk or manager, or some one on his behalf, shall forthwith after the receipt of the notice, inform in writing one of the persons signing it that the use of the school has been so granted for some other purpose, and name some other day on which the schoolroom can be used for the meeting.

If the persons calling the meeting fail to obtain the use of a schoolroom under this section, they may appeal to the standing committee under this Act, and the committee shall forthwith decide the

(*m*) See note (*g*), *ante*, p. 518. Where the land is acquired for a rural parish and assured to the parish council under s. 9 (14) of the Local Government Act, 1894, the county council will not possess the powers referred to in clause (e) of this section, nor does it seem that they will have any powers, duties, property, or liabilities to transfer under clause (f).

appeal and make such order respecting the use of the room as seems just (*n*). **Sect. 5.**

6.—(1.) All expenses incurred by the county council in executing the principal Act or this Act in any district or parish on default of a sanitary authority, or incurred by the council in or incidentally to a local inquiry under this Act, shall be paid in the first instance out of the county fund as for general county purposes, and, unless defrayed out of moneys received by the council in respect of any land acquired under this Act otherwise than by sale or exchange, or out of money borrowed as before in this Act mentioned, shall when the powers and duties of the sanitary authority under the principal Act are transferred to the county council in pursuance of this Act, be repaid to the county council as a debt by the sanitary authority (*o*). Expenses.

(2.) All sums payable by a sanitary authority in pursuance of this Act shall be defrayed in like manner as expenses under the principal Act are required to be defrayed, save that in the case of a rural authority they shall, with the exception of the principal and interest of any money borrowed, or the rent of any land hired by the county council be charged as general expenses.

(3.) All sums received by a county council in respect of any land acquired under this Act otherwise than from any sale or exchange, in so far as they are not required for the payment of expenses incurred by them in respect of such land, shall be paid to the sanitary authority, and in the case of a rural sanitary authority shall be credited to the parish on account of which the land was acquired.

HOUSING OF THE WORKING CLASSES ACT, 1890.
(53 & 54 Vict. Cap. 70.)

An Act to consolidate and amend the Acts relating to Artizans and Labourers Dwellings and the Housing of the Working Classes.

[18th August, 1890.]

Be it enacted by the Queen's most Excellent Majesty, by and with the advice and consent of the Lords Spiritual and Temporal, and Commons, in this present Parliament assembled, and by the authority of the same, as follows:

1. This Act may be cited as the Housing of the Working Classes Act, 1890 (*p*). Short title of Act.

* * * * *

(*n*) See also s. 4 of the Local Government Act, 1894, *post*, as to the use of the rooms here referred to by the parochial electors or parish council of a rural parish to discuss any question relating to allotments.

(*o*) Expenses incurred in the preliminary inquiry referred to in s. 3 (3), (4), *supra*, will be defrayed as in this section directed. The costs of an inquiry under s. 9 (3) of the Local Government Act, 1894 (to be held before an order for compulsory acquisition of land is made), will be defrayed as directed by ss. 9 (19) and 72 (4) of that Act.

(*p*) The carrying into effect of this Act is not one of the duties imposed on a county council, except in the case of the London County Council, which is the local authority under Parts I. and III., and is generally concerned in the

PART II.

Unhealthy Dwelling-Houses.

* * * *

Powers of County Councils.

Sect. 45 (1).

Powers of county councils.

45.—(1.) Where the medical officer of health or any inhabitant householders make a representation or complaint (*q*), or give information to any vestry or district board in the administrative county of London or to the local board of Woolwich, or to any rural sanitary authority elsewhere (which vestry, board, or authority is in this Act referred to as the district authority) (*r*) or to the medical officer of such authority either respecting any dwelling-house being in a state so dangerous or injurious to health as to be unfit for human habitation, or respecting an obstructive building, and also where a closing order has been made as respects any dwelling-house, the district authority shall forthwith forward to the county council of the county in which the dwelling-house or building is situate, a copy of such representation, complaint, information, or closing order, and shall from time to time report to the council such particulars as the council require respecting any proceedings taken by the authority with reference to such representation, complaint, information, or dwelling-house.

(2.) Where the county council—

(a) are of opinion that proceedings for a closing order as respects any dwelling-house ought to be instituted, or that an order ought to be made for the demolition of any buildings forming or forming part of any dwelling-house as to which a closing order has been made, or that an order ought to be made for pulling down an obstructive building specified in any representation under this part of this Act; and

(b) after reasonable notice, not being less than one month, of such opinion has been given in writing to the district authority, consider that such authority have failed to institute or properly prosecute proceedings, or to make the order for demolition, or to take steps for pulling down an obstructive building;

---

execution of this Act. The entire Act is set out in Lumley's Public Health. Two sections only (both included in Part II. of the Act) are set out here, namely, s. 45, which enables a county council to assume the powers of a local authority in the case of default by the latter, and s. 52, which enables the county medical officer to make a representation under Part II. of that Act.

(*q*) The representation or complaint here referred to is that made by the medical officer of health of a district, or four householders, that a dwelling-house is unfit for human habitation, or that a building is an obstructive building. See ss. 30, 31, 38 of this Act.

It seems that a representation or complaint made by a parish council under the Local Government Act, 1894, s. 6 (2), *post*, must be reported to the county council under this section.

(*r*) The district authority does not include an urban council, save in the case of the Woolwich Local Board. Consequently an urban council will not

Sect. 45 (2).

the council may pass a resolution to that effect, and thereupon the powers of the district authority as respects the said dwelling-house and building under this part of this Act (otherwise than in respect of a scheme), shall be vested in the county council, and if a closing order or an order for demolition or for pulling down an obstructive building is made, and not disallowed on appeal, the expenses of the council incurred as respects the said dwelling-house and building, including any compensation paid, shall be a simple contract debt to the council from the district authority (*s*).

(3.) Any debt to the council under this section shall be defrayed by the district authority as part of their expenses in the execution of this part of this Act (*t*).

(4.) The county council and any of their officers shall, for the purposes of this section, have the same right of admission to any premises as any district authority or their officers have for the purpose of the execution of their duties under the enactments relating to public health, and a justice may make the like order for enforcing such admission (*u*).

* * *

Report to local authority by county medical officer. 45 & 46 Vict. c. 50.

52. A representation from the medical officer of health of any county submitted to the county council and forwarded by that council to the local authority of any district in the county, not being a borough as defined by the Municipal Corporations Act, 1882, shall, for the purposes of this part of this Act, have the like effect as a representation from the medical officer of health of the district (*x*).

* * * * *

---

have to report to the county council under this sub-section, nor can the county council act under this section in an urban district.

(*s*) The district authority (see the preceeding sub-section) will have the month after notice within which they may themselves proceed to apply for a closing order, to make a demolition order, or as the case may be. After the month their powers will pass to the county council, who may put this part of the Act in operation as if they were the local authority.

(*t*) As to these expenses, see s. 42 of the Act.

(*u*) There is no general enactment in the Public Health Acts relating to the entry of officers upon premises for the performance of their duties. There are several express provisions enabling them to enter for specific purposes, and the provision which seems to be indicated in the text is that in s. 102 of the Public Health Act, 1875. That section enables an officer to enter any premises for the purpose of examining as to the existence of any nuisance therein at any time between the hours of nine a.m. and six p.m. If admission is refused, a justice, upon complaint made to him upon oath, may, by order, authorize the officer to enter. The text may, however, refer to s. 305 of the same Act.

(*x*) This section seems to be intended to provide that the medical officer of a county council appointed under the Local Government Act, 1888, s. 17, *ante*, p. 44, may make a representation to his council with reference to unhealthy dwellings or obstructive buildings in the county, and not in any borough. If he does so the council must forward the representation to the local authority, who must thereupon take proceedings upon it as if it were a representation made to them by their own medical officer.

TECHNICAL INSTRUCTION ACT, 1891.

(54 VICT. CAP. 4) (*y*).

An Act to amend the Law relating to Technical Instruction.

[26th March, 1891.]

* * * * *

Explanation of powers of local authority as to technical instruction. 52 & 53 Vict. c. 76.

1.—(1.) Subject to the conditions and restrictions contained in the Technical Instruction Act, 1889, a local authority (*a*) may—

(a.) Make such provision in aid of the technical or manual instruction for the time being supplied in a school or institution outside its district as may, in the opinion of the authority, be necessary for the requirements of the district in cases where similar provision cannot be so advantageously made by aiding a school or institution within its district (*b*); and

(b.) Provide or assist in providing scholarships for or pay or assist in paying the fees of students ordinarily resident in the district of the local authority at schools or institutions within or outside that district.

(2.) In distributing the provision made in aid of technical or manual instruction, the local authority may consider all the circumstances of the case, and shall not be bound to distribute the provision so made exclusively in proportion to the nature and amount of efficient technical or manual instruction supplied by those schools or institutions respectively.

Application of balances. 53 & 54 Vict. c. 60.

2. Any moneys received by a county council under sub-section (1) (b) of section one of the Local Taxation (Customs and Excise) Act, 1890 (*c*), and directed by resolution of the county council to be appropriated or to be set aside for the purposes of technical or manual instruction, shall, although not expended or specifically contributed or allotted in whole or in part before the end of the financial year, remain applicable for such purposes, and shall not be applied in manner provided by sub-section (2) and the following sub-sections of section twenty-three of the Local Government Act, 1888 (*d*), until the county council shall have made an order for such application.

51 & 52 Vict c. 41.

Where a council shall have referred to a committee the question of appropriating to purposes of technical or manual instruction any sum consisting of the whole or any part of such moneys, this section, unless and until the council otherwise direct, shall, until the committee shall have made their report and the council shall have

---

(*y*) This Act amends and explains the Technical Instruction Act, 1889, *ante*, p. 435.

(*a*) The expression "local authority" includes a county council. See the Act of 1889, s. 4, *ante*, p. 438.

(*b*) Under the Act of 1889, and could only be given to schools and institutions within the district.

(*c*) See this section, *ante*, p. 515.

(*d*) See this section, *ante*, p. 50.

arrived at a decision thereon or the appointment of the committee shall have been rescinded, apply to such sum as if the same had been directed by the council to be appropriated to such purposes. Sect. 2.

3. The expression "technical education" in section one of the Local Taxation (Customs and Excise) Act, 1890 (*c*), shall be deemed to include both technical and manual instruction within the meaning of the Technical Instruction Act, 1889 and 1891. Construction of 53 & 54 Vict. c. 60, s. 1.

4. This Act may be cited as the Technical Instruction Act, 1891, and shall be construed as one with the Technical Instruction Act, 1889, and this Act and the Technical Instruction Act, 1889, may be cited together as the Technical Instruction Acts, 1889 and 1891. Short title and construction.

ELECTORAL DISABILITIES REMOVAL ACT, 1891.

(54 VICT. CAP. 11) (*e*).

An Act to remove certain Disabilities of Persons by reason of absence to be registered as Voters at Parliamentary and Local Elections.

[11th May, 1891.]

* * * * *

1. This Act may be cited as the Electoral Disabilities Removal Act, 1891. Short title.

2. A person shall not be disqualified from being registered— Temporary absence of person in performance of duty not to disqualify as elector.

(a) in the parliamentary register of electors for a county or borough in respect of his inhabitant occupation of a dwelling-house or lodgings or his occupation of any land or tenement; or

(b) in the local government register of electors (*f*) for a county or borough in respect of his occupation of any house, warehouse, counting-house, shop, building, land, or tenement,

by reason only that during part of the qualifying period not exceeding four months at any one time, he has in the performance of any duty arising from or incidental to any office, service, or employment held or undertaken by him been absent from his dwelling-house or lodgings, or not resided in or within the required distance from such county or borough.

(*e*) This Act creates an important exception to the general rule that, for purposes of the old burgess qualification and of the new ten pounds occupation qualification, both of which are extended to county electors, residence during the whole of the qualifying period is necessary. Cases illustrative of this principle will be found in the notes to the Municipal Corporations Act, 1882, s. 9, *ante*, p. 244.

(*f*) This expression means, as respects an administrative county, the county register, and as respects a county or other municipal borough, the burgess roll. See the Interpretation Act, 1889, s. 17.

RAILWAY AND CANAL TRAFFIC (PROVISIONAL ORDERS) AMENDMENT ACT, 1891.

(54 Vict. Cap. 12) (*g*).

An Act to remove doubts as to the Powers of Public Bodies in reference to Provisional Order Bills under the Railway and Canal Traffic Act, 1888. [11th May, 1891.]

35 & 36 Vict. c. 91. Whereas by an Act of the thirty-fifth and thirty-sixth years of the reign of Her present Majesty, chapter ninety-one, intituled "An Act to authorise the application of funds of municipal corporations and other governing bodies in certain cases," herein-after referred to as the Borough Funds Act, authority is given to the council of any municipal borough, the board of health, local board, commissioners, trustees, or other body acting under any general or local Act of Parliament for the management, improvement, cleansing, paving, lighting, and otherwise governing places or districts, to apply the borough fund or rate, or other the public funds or rates under the control of any such governing body, to the payment of the costs, charges, and expenses of promoting or opposing any local and personal Bill or Bills in Parliament:

51 & 52 Vict. c. 41. 52 & 53 Vict. c. 50. And whereas by the Local Government Act, 1888, and the Local Government (Scotland) Act, 1889, the county council of an administrative county has the same powers of opposing Bills in Parliament as are conferred on the council of a municipal borough by the above-recited Act of the thirty-fifth and thirty-sixth years of Victoria, chapter ninety-one:

51 & 52 Vict. c. 53. And whereas by the Borough Funds (Ireland) Act, 1888, similar powers were conferred upon governing bodies in Ireland:

51 & 52 Vict. c. 25. And whereas by the Railway and Canal Traffic Act, 1888, it was, among other things, provided that if while any Bill to confirm a Provisional Order by the Board of Trade under section twenty-four of that Act be pending in either House of Parliament a petition be presented against the Bill, or any classification and schedule comprised therein, the Bill, so far as it relates to the matter petitioned against, should be referred to a select committee, or, if the two Houses of Parliament think fit so to order, to a joint committee of such Houses, and the petitioner should be allowed to appear and

---

(*g*) The object of this Act is fully stated in the preamble. Under the Local Government Act, 1888, s. 15, power was given to a county council to oppose bills in Parliament to the same extent as a borough council might do so under the Borough Funds Act. But the power to oppose under the last-mentioned Act was confined to local and personal bills, while a provisional order under 51 & 52 Vict. c. 25, s. 24, is a public general Act.

The 51 & 52 Vict. c. 25, s. 24, enables the Board of Trade to submit to Parliament a provisional order confirming a revised classification of merchandise traffic, and a revised schedule of maximum rates and charges applicable thereto. The Act under consideration enables a county council to petition and appear against the bill confirming such order, as if it were a local and personal bill.

oppose as in the case of a private Bill; and further, it was by the said Act provided that the Act of Parliament confirming any Provisional Order made under that section should be a public general Act: Preamble.

And whereas doubts have been entertained whether in view of the said enactment governing bodies as defined by the Borough Funds Act and the Borough Funds (Ireland) Act, 1888, respectively and county councils have power to apply the funds or rates under their control in opposing or subscribing towards the opposition of any Bill to confirm any Provisional Order made under section twenty-four of the Railway and Canal Traffic Act, 1888, and it is expedient that such doubts should be removed:

* * * * *

Powers of governing bodies and county councils with reference to Bills for confirming Provisional Orders made under 51 & 52 Vict. c. 25, s. 24.

1. Every governing body within the meaning of the Borough Funds Act or the Borough Funds (Ireland) Act, 1888, and every county council shall be entitled to be a petitioner and to appear and oppose any Bill to confirm any Provisional Order made under section twenty-four of the Railway and Canal Traffic Act, 1888, and to provide or contribute towards providing the expenses of the appearance or opposition of a petitioner out of the funds or rates under their respective control, as if the Bill for confirming such Provisional Order were a local or personal Bill within the meaning of section two of the Borough Funds Act, or of section three of the Borough Funds (Ireland) Act, 1888; and the provisions of the said last-mentioned Acts respectively shall apply to any such appearance or opposition, and to any expenses incurred or to be incurred in relation thereto: Provided that in the case of a county council no consent of owners and ratepayers shall be required.

Short title.

2. This Act may be cited as the Railway and Canal Traffic (Provisional Orders) Amendment Act, 1891.

REGISTRATION OF ELECTORS ACT, 1891.

(54 Vict. Cap. 18.)

An Act for the removal of Doubts arising under the Registration of Electors Acts. [11th June, 1891.]

41 & 42 Vict. c. 26.

Whereas under section thirty of the Parliamentary and Municipal Registration Act, 1878, one half of the expenses and receipts under the Registration of Electors Acts in respect of an area common to a parliamentary borough and a municipal borough are defrayed and applied in accordance with the Parliamentary Registration Acts, and one half are paid out of and to the borough fund:

51 & 52 Vict. c. 10.

And whereas by section four of the County Electors Act, 1888, the said Act, together with other Registration of Electors Acts, is applied to a parish not situate in a municipal borough, with the substitution of "parish" for "municipal borough":

Preamble. And whereas doubts have arisen whether, having regard to the provisions of section eight of the said Act, the provisions of section thirty of the Parliamentary and Municipal Registration Act, 1878, were applied by virtue of the above-recited enactment, and it is expedient to remove such doubts:

* * * * *

Short title and construction.

1. This Act may be cited as the Registration of Electors Act, 1891, and shall be construed as one with the Registration of Electors Acts, 1843 to 1888, which Acts, together with this Act, may be cited as the Registration of Electors Acts, 1843 to 1891.

Application of 41 & 42 Vict. c. 26, s. 30, to expenses in a parish situate in a parliamentary and not in a municipal borough.

2. Where a parish is situate in a parliamentary but not in a municipal borough, one half of the expenses and receipts under the Registration Acts, 1843 to 1888, in respect of such parish shall, as from the passing of the County Electors Act, 1888, be defrayed out of and paid to the county fund, and the other half of such expenses shall be defrayed out of and paid to the rate raised in such parish for the relief of the poor (*h*). The revising barrister shall as part of the business of the revision, if necessary, determine what expenses and receipts are incurred or arise or have been incurred or have arisen under the said Acts in respect of such parish.

FISHERIES ACT, 1891.

(54 & 55 VICT. CAP. 37) (*i*).

An Act to carry into effect an International Declaration respecting the North Sea Fisheries, and to amend the Law relating to Sea Fisheries and Salmon and Freshwater Fisheries.

[21st July, 1891.]

* * *

PART I. (*k*).

* *

PART II.

SEA FISHERIES REGULATION ACT, 1888.

Extension of powers of local fisheries

7. The powers of a local fisheries committee to make bye-laws in pursuance of section two of the Sea Fisheries Regulation Act, 1888 (*l*),

---

(*h*) See s. 8 of the County Electors Act, 1888, *ante*, p. 396.

(*i*) Part II. of this Act is to be read as one with the Sea Fisheries Regulation Act, 1888 (51 & 52 Vict. c. 54), *ante*, p. 401, and with the Sea Fisheries Regulation Act, 1894 (57 & 58 Vict. c. 26), *post*.

(*k*) Part I. relates only to the Belgian Declaration respecting the North Sea Fisheries.

(*l*) See this section, *ante*, p. 402. The local fisheries committee is a committee of a county or borough council, or a joint committee of two or more councils in a sea fisheries district created under the Act of 1888.

shall extend to making bye-laws, to be observed within their district, for restricting or prohibiting, either entirely or subject to any exceptions and regulations, the fishing for or taking of all or any specified kinds of sea fish during any period specified in any such bye-law. Sect. 7. — Committee for making bye-laws. 51 & 52 Vict. c. 54.

8. Where any offence under the Sea Fisheries Regulation Act, 1888, or under any bye-law made in pursuance thereof, is committed on the sea coast or at sea beyond the ordinary jurisdiction of a court of summary jurisdiction and not on or from a ship or boat, it shall be deemed to have been committed within the body of any county abutting on that sea coast, or adjoining that sea, and may be tried and punished accordingly. Jurisdiction as to offences.

9. A local fisheries committee appointed in pursuance of the Sea Fisheries Regulation Act, 1888, may, within their district, enforce the provisions of the Fisheries (Oyster, Crab, and Lobster) Act, 1877, and of any other Act relating to sea fisheries. Powers of local fisheries committee for enforcement of Sea Fisheries Acts.

10. Any county or borough council may, if they think fit, pay or contribute to any expenses incurred by a board of salmon conservators in exercise of their powers under the Sea Fisheries Regulation Act, 1888 (*m*). Power for county council, etc., to pay or contribute to expenses under 51 & 52 Vict. c. 54.

11. This Part of this Act shall be construed as one with the Sea Fisheries Regulation Act, 1888, and that Act and this Part of this Act may be cited collectively as the Sea Fisheries Regulation Acts, 1888 and 1891. Construction and short title of Part of Act.

PART III. (*n*).

* *

PART IV.

GENERAL.

13. The powers conferred by the Sea Fisheries Act, 1883, or this Act, or any other Act relating to sea fisheries, or by any Act relating to salmon and freshwater fisheries, upon any authorities or officers to enforce any such Act shall not be construed as limiting or taking away the power of any other person to take legal proceedings for the enforcement of any such Act or of any bye-law made thereunder. Explanation as to power of taking legal proceedings for enforcing Fisheries Acts.

14. This Act may be cited as the Fisheries Act, 1891. Short title.

(*m*) See s. 12 of the Act of 1888, *ante*, p. 406.

(*n*) Part III. enables the Board of Trade to constitute a fishery district for the River Stour (Suffolk and Essex).

SCHOOLS FOR SCIENCE AND ART ACT, 1891.

(54 & 55 VICT. CAP. 61.) (*o*).

An Act to facilitate the transfer of Schools for Science and Art to Local Authorities. [5th August, 1891.]

* * * * *

Transfer of school for science and art or literary or scientific institution to local authority. 17 & 18 Vict. c. 112. 52 & 53 Vict. c. 76. 33 & 34 Vict. c. 75.

1.—(1.) The managers of any school for science and art, or for science, or for art, or of any institution to which the Literary and Scientific Institutions Act, 1854, applies (*p*), may make an arrangement with any local authority within the meaning of the Technical Instruction Act, 1889 (*q*), for transferring the school or institution to that authority, and the local authority may assent to any such arrangement and give effect thereto, subject to the provisions of that Act.

(2.) The provisions of section twenty-three of the Elementary Education Act, 1870 (*r*), with respect to arrangements for the transfer of schools shall apply in the case of arrangements for the transfer of schools or institutions in pursuance of this section, with this modification, that for the purposes of transfers to a local authority references to the school board shall be construed as references to the local authority and references to the Education Department as references to the Department of Science and Art, and references to a school shall, in the case of an institution not being a school, be construed as references to the institution.

(3.) In this section the expression "managers" includes all persons who have the management of any school or institution,

---

(*o*) This Act permits the managers of schools for science and art, and other similar institutions, to transfer those schools or institutions to local authorities, including county councils. The powers of the body to whom such a transfer is made as to the management of the school or institution, are left somewhat vague by this Act; they are, however, to give effect to the arrangement for the transfer, subject to the provisions of the Technical Instruction Act, 1889 (*ante*, p. 435); and s. 23 of the Elementary Education Act, 1870, as to transfers of schools to school boards, is to apply with certain modifications. It seems, therefore, that the powers of management are to be gathered from those enactments.

(*p*) The institutions here referred to are "every institution for the time being established for the promotion of science, literature, the fine arts, for adult instruction, the diffusion of useful knowledge, the foundation or maintenance of libraries, reading-rooms for general use among the members or open to the public, of public museums and galleries, of paintings and other works of art, collections of natural history, mechanical and philosophical inventions, instruments, or designs," except the Royal Institution and the London Institution for the Advancement of Literature and the Diffusion of Useful Knowledge.

(*q*) This definition includes a county council, see s. 4 of the Act, *ante*, p. 438.

(*r*) The section referred to contains detailed provisions as to voluntary arrangements for the transfer of an elementary school, and the property held in connection with it, to a school board. A school so transferred "shall to such extent and during such times as the school board have, under such arrangement, any control over the school, be deemed to be a school provided by the school board."

whether the legal interest in the site and buildings of the school or institution is or is not vested in them (*s*). Sect. 1 (3)

2. This Act may be cited as the Schools for Science and Art Act, 1891. Short title.

HIGHWAYS AND BRIDGES ACT, 1891.

(54 & 55 Vict. Cap. 63.)

An Act to confer further powers on County Councils and other Authorities with respect to Main Roads and other Highways and Bridges. [5th August, 1891.]

* * * * *

1. This Act may be cited as the Highways and Bridges Act, 1891. Short title

2. This Act shall not apply to Scotland or Ireland or the county of London. Extent of Act.

3. The council of any administrative county, and any highway authority or authorities (*t*), and the council of any adjoining county, may from time to time make and carry into effect agreements (*u*) with each other for or in relation to the construction, reconstruction, alteration or improvement, or the freeing from tolls, of any main road (*v*) or other highway, or of any bridge (including the approaches thereto), wholly or partly situate within the jurisdiction of any one or more of the party or parties to the agreement. Agreement between highway authorities for improvement of roads and bridges.

All expenses incurred by any such county council or highway

(*s*) It is doubtful whether this sub-section enables the managers to convey a legal interest in property which is not vested in them to the local authority. Section 23 of the Elementary Education Act, 1870, provides that "nothing in this section shall authorize the managers to transfer any property which is not vested in them, or a trustee for them, or held in trust for the school."

(*t*) By s. 6, *post*, expressions which are defined by the Local Government Act, 1888, are to have the same meaning in this Act. By s. 100 of that Act, *ante*, p. 174, the expression "highway authority" means as respects an urban sanitary district, the urban sanitary authority, and as respects a highway district, the highway board or authority having the powers of a highway board; and as respects a highway parish, the surveyor or surveyors of highways or other officers performing similar duties. Since the passing of the Local Government Act, 1894, which by s. 25, *post*, p. 621, transfers to rural councils the powers of the highway authorities within their districts, the foregoing definition is out of date, and the highway authorities are practically the urban and rural district councils.

(*u*) The Inland Revenue authorities do not consider that these agreements, or agreements under s. 11 (3) (4) of the Local Government Act, 1888, are made "pursuant to the Highway Acts for or relating to the making, maintaining, or repairing of highways," so as to be chargeable with a sixpenny stamp only under the Stamp Act, 1891. That Act contains no definition of "the Highway Acts"; and neither the Act of 1888 nor this present Act is included in the group of Highway Acts referred to in the Short Titles Act, 1896 (59 & 60 Vict. c. 14), the collective title given being "The Highway Acts, 1835 to 1885."

(*v*) As to main roads, see s. 11 of the Local Government Act, 1888, and the notes to that section, *ante*, p. 21.

Sect. 3.

authority, in pursuance of this section, shall be defrayed as part of the expenses incurred in relation to the maintenance, repair, improvement, or enlargement of bridges, main roads, or other highways by such council or highway authority (*x*), in such proportions as shall be determined by any such agreement as aforesaid, and any powers of borrowing, applicable to the raising of any fund for the payment of any such expenses as aforesaid, shall be applicable accordingly:

Provided that if a highway board (*y*) think it just that any parish or parishes specially benefited by any construction, reconstruction, alteration, or improvement under this section should bear the expense thereof, or any part of such expense, they may, with the approval of the county council of the county within which their highway district is situate, and with the assent of the inhabitants of such parish or parishes in vestry assembled (*z*), charge such expense, or such part thereof as they may think just, exclusively on such parish or parishes.

Power to reduce main road to status of ordinary highway. 41 & 42 Vict. c. 77.

4. Section sixteen of the Highways and Locomotives Amendment Act, 1878, shall apply to any part of a main road in any county, and so much of such section as requires that any order made thereunder shall be provisional, and shall be confirmed as in the said Act mentioned, is hereby repealed, but no such order shall be made in respect of any main road within a municipal borough without the assent of the council of the said borough having been first obtained (*a*).

Contracts for supply of road material not to disqualify for election to county council.

5. No person shall be disqualified for being elected, or for being a member of a county council, by reason only of his having any share or interest in any contract with such county council for the supply from land, of which he is owner or occupier, of stone, gravel, or other materials for making or repairing highways or bridges. Provided always that no such share or interest in any contract shall exceed the amount of fifty pounds in any one year (*b*).

Construction of Act. 51 & 52 Vict. c. 41.

6. Words and expressions to which meanings are assigned by the Local Government Act, 1888, have in this Act the same respective

---

(*x*) In the case of a county council, these expenses will therefore be general expenses. See the Local Government Act, 1888, s. 11, sub-s. (1), *ante*, p. 21.

(*y*) The rural district council has, with few exceptions, now succeeded to all the powers and duties of a highway board within its district. See the Local Government Act, 1894, s. 25, *post*, p. 621.

(*z*) In a rural parish the parish council, or parish meeting (as the case may be), must now give this assent.

(*a*) Section 16 of the Highways and Locomotives Amendment Act, 1878, is set out, *ante*, p. 22.

(*b*) But for this provision a county councillor who had an interest in such a contract would have been disqualified under s. 12, sub-s. (1) (c), of the Municipal Corporations Act, 1882, *ante*, p. 252.

meanings, and in this Act the word "highway" includes any public bridle path or footway (*c*). **Sect. 6.**

LUNACY ACT, 1891.

(54 & 55 VICT. CAP. 65.)

An Act to amend the Lunacy Act, 1890 (*d*). [5th August, 1891.]

* * * * *

1. This Act may be cited as the Lunacy Act, 1891, and this Act shall be construed as one with the Lunacy Act, 1890 (in this Act called the principal Act), and this Act and the principal Act may be cited together as the Lunacy Acts, 1890 and 1891. Short title. 53 & 54 Vict. c. 5.

* * * * *

6. Where a workhouse is situate in a county which does not include the union to which the workhouse belongs, a summary reception order made by a justice of the county in which the workhouse is situate may order a lunatic in the workhouse to be received in any asylum, in which pauper lunatics chargeable to the union, to which the workhouse belongs, may legally be received. Section 27.

7. Sub-section four of section thirty-eight of the principal Act is hereby repealed, and the following sub-section is substituted therefor :— Section 38 (4).

(4.) A reception order shall remain in force for a year after the date by this Act or by an order of the Commissioners appointed for it to expire, and thereafter for two years, and thereafter for three years, and after the end of such periods of one, two, and three years for successive periods of five years, if not more than one month nor less than seven days before the expiration of the period at the end of which, as fixed by this Act or by an order of the Commissioners under sub-section two, the order would expire, and of each subsequent period of one, two, three, and five years respectively, a special report of the medical officer of the institution or of the medical attendant of the single patient as to the mental and bodily condition of the patient with a certificate under his hand certifying that the patient is still of unsound mind and a proper person to be detained under care and treatment is sent to the Commissioners.

8. Section thirty-nine of the principal Act shall not apply to lunatics received under a removal order or to lunatics so found by inquisition. Section 39.

9. * * * * *

(2.) In sub-section six of section fifty-five of the principal Act, Section 55.

(*c*) See s. 100 of the Local Government Act, 1888, *ante*, p. 171.

(*d*) The present Act is set out only so far as it alters or amends the provisions of the Act of 1890 (which are set out, *ante*, p. 440), or otherwise affects county councils.

Sect. 9 (2). for the words "licensed by visitors" shall be substituted the words "licensed by justices," and for the words "the Commissioners or visitors" shall be substituted the words "such Commissioner or such two visitors."

Section 61 (1). **11.** In sub-section one of section sixty-one of the principal Act the words "to the workhouse of the union to which the lunatic is chargeable, or if the lunatic is chargeable to a county or borough (*e*), to the workhouse of the union from which he was sent to the hospital or licensed house" shall be inserted after the words "of the lunatic."

Hospitals may alter regulations.

12. The managing committee of every hospital may, with the approval of a secretary of state, alter the regulations of the hospital.

Boroughs annexed to counties under s. 246 to contribute to expense of asylum.

13.—(1.) Where under section two hundred and forty-six of the principal Act, a borough ceases to be a local authority under that Act, the borough shall for all purposes of that Act be annexed to and treated as part of the county in which the borough is situate, and if or so far as the borough has not contributed towards the expense of providing the asylum of the county, a sum to be paid by the borough towards the expenses already incurred in providing the asylum shall be fixed by agreement between the councils of the county and borough, or in default of agreement by an arbitrator appointed by the parties, or, if the parties cannot agree upon an arbitrator, by an arbitrator appointed by the Local Government Board. In fixing the sum to be paid by the borough, the borough shall be credited with any sums already contributed by the borough for lunacy purposes in excess of its legal liability; and the arbitrator shall take into consideration the amounts that may have been paid by the borough for the reception or maintenance, in the asylum of the county, of the lunatics of the borough.

(2.) Where a borough had before the passing of this Act, by virtue of section eighty-six of the Local Government Act, 1888, and the determination of any contract, become liable to contribute to the county rate of the county in respect of a lunatic asylum, this section shall apply to such borough as if it had immediately after the passing of this Act ceased under section two hundred and forty-six of the principal Act, to be a local authority (*f*).

51 & 52 Vict. c. 41

(*e*) As to the cases in which a lunatic may be chargeable to a county or borough, see s. 290 of the Lunacy Act, 1890, *ante*, p. 468.

(*f*) Section 86 (4) of the Local Government Act, 1888 (repealed by the Lunacy Act, 1890, and substantially re-enacted by s. 246 of that Act, *ante*, p. 454, which is itself partially repealed by s. 26 of this Act, *post*), provided that where at the passing of the Act a borough with separate quarter sessions, and not a county borough, but containing in 1881 a population of 10,000 or upwards,

14. Any question relating to lunatic asylums or the maintenance of lunatics arising between any local authorities under the principal Act and any boroughs not being local authorities under that Act, and any visiting committees or any two or more of such parties respectively, may be referred to an arbitrator appointed by the parties, or, if the parties cannot agree upon an arbitrator, by the Local Government Board.

Sect. 14.

Power to refer questions as to asylums to the court or to arbitration.

15. The provisions of sub-sections five, six, and seven of section sixty-two of the Local Government Act, 1888, shall apply to every sum by virtue of this Act agreed to be paid or awarded by an arbitrator as if such sum had been agreed to be paid or awarded under section sixty-two of the Local Government Act, 1888 (*g*).

Section 62 of 51 & 52 Vict. c. 41 applied.

16. In sub-section two of section two hundred and fifty-four of the principal Act, there shall be added after the word "contracts" the words "for the purchase of lands and buildings and for the erection, restoration, and enlargement of buildings" (*h*).

Amendment of s. 254 of 53 & 54 Vict. c. 5.

17. Where a contract between the council of a borough and the subscribers to a hospital for the reception of pauper lunatics into the hospital was subsisting on the twenty-sixth day of August one thousand eight hundred and eight-nine, such contract, unless determined by the parties or one of them, shall be deemed to have continued in force since that date, and may be renewed subject to the same conditions and with the same consequences as if the contract had been entered into by a visiting committee on behalf of the borough (*i*).

Contracts by town councils and the subscribers to a hospital.

18. The provisions of the Local Government Act, 1888, relating to the accounts of county councils and their officers, and to the

Accounts of county asylums.

---

contracts with the county quarter sessions for the reception of the borough lunatics in the county asylum, such borough, on the determination of the contract, should cease to have power to build an asylum, and should, "subject to the enactments providing for an additional charge for the maintenance of lunatics in cases where no contribution has been made towards the cost of building and furnishing an asylum," be liable to contribute to the county rate in respect of such asylum in like manner as the rest of the county. The provision in the text seems to have been passed in consequence of the decision in *Howlett* v. *Maidstone* (*Mayor, etc., of*), [1891] 2 Q. B. 110; 60 L. J. Q. B. 570; 65 L. T. (N.S.) 448; 40 W. R. 116; 55 J. P. 549, in which it was held that by reason of the above sub-section the visitors of a county asylum had no power (which they formerly had under s. 54 of 16 & 17 Vict. c. 97) of fixing the amount to be paid for the maintenance of a pauper lunatic sent from a borough which had not contributed to the cost of building and furnishing the asylum, but that in case of difference the borough was entitled to have the amount ascertained by arbitration, under s. 62 of the Local Government Act, 1888. Any such arbitration will now be under ss. 14 and 15 of this Act.

(*g*) See s. 62 of the Act of 1888, *ante*, p. 119.

(*h*) See s. 254 of the Act of 1890, *ante*, p. 455.

(*i*) See s. 269 (2) of the Act of 1890, *ante*, p. 461.

Sect. 18.

audit of such accounts, shall apply to the accounts of every asylum belonging wholly or in part to a county council and of the visiting committee and officers thereof (*k*).

Removal of lunatic becoming a pauper.

19.—(1.) Where a lunatic in a hospital or licensed house becomes a pauper, the manager of the hospital or house may, after having given notice to the authority liable for the maintenance of the lunatic (*l*) of his intention so to do, apply to a justice of the peace having jurisdiction in the place where the hospital or house is situate for an order for the removal of the lunatic, and such justice may, if he thinks fit, make an order for the removal of the lunatic to an institution for lunatics to which pauper lunatics for whose maintenance the authority is liable may legally be sent and for the reception of the lunatic therein, and such institution shall be named in the order, and the manager of the hospital or house shall forthwith cause the lunatic to be removed to the institution named in the order. In the case of such removal the original reception order shall remain in force, and shall authorise the classification of the lunatic as a pauper lunatic in the institution to which he is removed.

(2.) The costs of obtaining an order under this section and of the removal of the lunatic shall be repaid to the manager who obtains the order by the authority liable for the maintenance of the lunatic, and any justice having jurisdiction in the place where the hospital or house from which the lunatic was removed is situate shall have power to fix the amount of such costs and to order such authority to repay the same. The provisions of section three hundred and fourteen of the principal Act (*m*) shall apply to every such order for the repayment of costs.

* *

Payment of expenses as to lunatics becoming paupers

22. The provisions of the principal Act for the payment of expenses in relation to pauper lunatics shall be applicable with respect to lunatics in institutions for lunatics who become paupers (*n*).

* *

Repeal.

29. The enactments in the schedule are hereby repealed.

(*k*) This section is in substitution for s. 279 of the Lunacy Act, 1890, which is repealed by s. 26, *post*. As to the accounts of county councils and the audit of those accounts, see the Local Government Act, 1888, s. 71, *ante*, p. 136, and the enactments there referred to.

(*l*) As to the authority liable for the maintenance, see ss. 286 *et seq.*, of the Lunacy Act, 1890, *ante*, p. 467; such authority may be the county or borough council: see s. 290 of the same Act, *ante*, p. 468.

(*m*) See this section, *ante*, p. 475.

(*n*) See Part X. of the Act of 1890, *ante*, p. 466, *et seq.*

SCHEDULE.

Schedule.

ENACTMENTS REPEALED.

Section 29.

Session and Chapter.	Short Title.	Extent of Repeal.
53 & 54 Vict. c. 5. -	The Lunacy Act, 1890 -	Section nine, sub-section one, from "having" to the end of the sub-section. Section ten, in sub-section one the words "within the county and borough respectively," and in sub-section four the words "within the same" occurring twice. Section thirteen, sub-section two, from "within" to "jurisdiction." Section twenty-four, sub-section six, from "that a pauper" to "asylum" where that word next occurs. Section sixty-two. Section ninety-nine, the words "with a jury." Section one hundred and forty-nine. Section two hundred and forty-six, from "subject" to "an asylum." Section two hundred and seventy-nine. Section three hundred and thirty-eight, sub-section two, the words "in lunacy." The Second Schedule, Form 13. The Fourth Schedule, the references to "Dover" and "Maidstone" repealed as from the commencement of the Lunacy Act, 1890.

COUNTY COUNCILS (ELECTIONS) ACT, 1891.

(54 & 55 VICT. CAP. 68.)

An Act to alter the Date of holding County Council Elections, and to remove Doubts respecting the Holding of such Elections.

[5th August, 1891.]

* * * * *

1.—(1.) The ordinary day of election of county councillors in each county shall be such day between the first and eighth day of March as the county council may fix, and, if no date is so fixed, shall be the eighth day of March (*o*). Change of date of elections.

(2.) The ordinary day of retirement of county councillors shall be the eighth day of March in every third year, and on that day the county councillors then in office shall retire together, and their places shall be filled by the newly-elected councillors, who shall come into office on that day.

(3.) The sixteenth day of March or such other day within ten days after the ordinary day of retirement of county councillors as the council of any county may from time to time fix for that county, shall, in substitution for the ninth day of November, be the ordinary day of election of the chairman, and of the aldermen, and the day for holding a quarterly meeting, and if the county council fix any hour for the quarterly meeting, that hour shall be

(*o*) Under the Local Government Act, 1888, s. 75, the ordinary day of election was November 1st.

Sect. 1 (3).

45 & 46 Vict. c. 50.

substituted for the hour specified in the Municipal Corporations Act, 1882 (*p*).

(4.) All periods which, in the enactments of the Municipal Corporations Act, 1882, are computed by reference to the first or ninth day of November shall, so far as those enactments apply to county councils, be computed by reference to such of the above-mentioned days then next following as the case requires (*q*).

The ordinary day of election of councillors shall be fixed by the county council not less than six weeks before the ordinary day of retirement of county councillors.

Nothing shall authorise or require a returning officer to hold an election of a county councillor to fill a casual vacancy which occurs within six months before the ordinary day of retirement of county councillors (*r*).

County registers.

2.—(1.) The county register shall be completed before the twentieth day of December in every year and come into operation on the next first day of January.

(2.) The burgess lists forming the burgess roll, which comes into operation on the first day of November in every year, shall on and after that day until the next first day of January form part of the county register in substitution for the former burgess lists (*s*).

Removal of doubts and amendment as to election of county councillors in boroughs.

3. For the purpose of the election of county councillors for any electoral division which is co-extensive with, or wholly comprised in, a municipal borough, the following provisions shall have effect:—

(a.). The mayor of the borough, or some person appointed by him, or, if the mayor is dead or absent or otherwise incapable of acting, an alderman appointed by the council of the borough, shall be the returning officer, and so far as respects such election shall follow the instructions of, and return the names of the persons elected to, the county returning officer:

51 & 52 Vict. c. 41.

(b.) Nothing in section seventy-five of the Local Government Act, 1888, substituting the returning officer or his deputy for the town clerk, shall extend to any such election (*t*).

(*p*) Under the Local Government Act, 1888, s. 75, sub-s. (13), November 7th was the ordinary day of election of the chairman and county aldermen, and the day for holding a quarterly meeting of the county council. The hour for holding the November quarterly meeting was *noon*. See the Municipal Corporations Act, Sched. 2, r. 2, *ante*, p. 335.

(*q*) The periods here referred to are chiefly those which relate to elections. Thus, under s. 54 of the Municipal Corporations Act, 1882, notice of election must be given nine days at least before the day of election; nomination papers must be delivered seven days at least before that day, etc.

(*r*) This provision is substituted for that in the Local Government Act, 1888, s. 75, sub-s. (16) (a), which is repealed by this Act.

(*s*) This section amends s. 45 of the Municipal Corporations Act, 1882, as applied to county councils. See the notes to that section, *ante*, p. 280.

(*t*) This section is substituted for s. 75, sub-s. (6) of the Local Government Act, 1888.

Sect. 4.

Transitory provisions.

4. The chairmen and vice-chairmen of county councils, and the deputy chairman of the London County Council, county aldermen, and county councillors, and committees (including the members of a joint committee appointed by a county council) whose term of office would but for this Act expire on the ordinary day of election in November next after the passing of this Act, shall go out of office on the next following ordinary day of election or retirement (as the case may be) fixed by this Act, and their term of office shall be extended accordingly; but nothing shall authorise or require the returning officer to hold an election of a county councillor to fill a casual vacancy at any time before the ordinary day of election next after the passing of this Act, and the aldermen whose term of office would, but for this Act, expire at the end of three years after the November next after the passing of this Act shall go out of office on the ordinary day of election next following the end of those years, and their term of office shall be extended accordingly (*u*).

Amendment of 45 & 46 Vict. c. 50. ss. 34, 35; and 51 & 52 Vict. c. 41, s. 75.

5. The declaration required under sections thirty-four and thirty-five of the Municipal Corporations Act, 1882, to be made by a person elected to a corporate office in a county may be made at any time within three months after notice of the election, and such declaration may be made either in the manner prescribed by the Local Government Act, 1888, or before any justice of the peace or commissioner to administer oaths in the Supreme Court of Judicature (*x*).

Returning officer not disqualified for membership of county council.

6. It is hereby declared that a person shall not be disqualified, nor be deemed ever to have been disqualified, under section twelve of the Municipal Corporations Act, 1882, for being a member of a county council by reason only of his being appointed returning officer by that council, except where he has directly or indirectly by himself or his partner received any profit or remuneration in respect of such appointment (*y*).

Repeal.

7. The Act specified in the Schedule to this Act is hereby repealed to the extent in the third column of that schedule mentioned.

Short title and construction.

8. This Act may be cited as the County Councils (Elections) Act, 1891, and shall be construed as one with the Local Government Act, 1888.

(*u*) This section is now spent.

(*x*) See s. 34 of the Municipal Corporations Act, 1882, *ante*, p. 272. Under that section, as amended by the Local Government Act, 1888, s. 75, the period within which the declaration had to be made was ten days.

(*y*) See the notes to s. 12 of the Municipal Corporations Act, 1882, *ante*, p. 253.

Schedule.

SCHEDULE.

ENACTMENTS REPEALED.

Session and Chapter.	Title or Short Title.	Extent of Repeal.
51 & 52 Vict. c. 41. -	The Local Government Act, 1888.	Section seventy-five, from "In a year in which" to "be conducted together," being sub-section one; from "In a borough the returning officer" down to "construed to refer to the town clerk," being sub-section six; and from "The period between" down to "returning officer may fix," being sub-section nine; and from "The seventh of November" to "quarterly meeting of the county council," being sub-section thirteen; and from "shall authorise or require" to "such electoral division or," being paragraph (d) of sub-section sixteen.

MORTMAIN AND CHARITABLE USES ACT AMENDMENT ACT, 1892.

(55 & 56 VICT. CAP. 11.)

An Act to amend the Mortmain and Charitable Uses Act, 1888. [20th June, 1892.]

* * * * *

Extension of 51 & 52 Vict. c. 42, s. 6.

1. Section six of the Mortmain and Charitable Uses Act, 1888, except so much of sub-section (2) thereof as provides that an assurance by deed, made otherwise than in good faith for full and valuable consideration, must be executed not less than twelve months before the death of the assuror, shall apply to any assurance by deed of land to any local authority for any purpose or purposes for which such authority is empowered by any Act of Parliament to acquire land (*z*).

(*z*) Section 6 of the Mortmain and Charitable Uses Act, 1888, exempts from the provisions of Parts I. and II. of that Act assurances by deed of land of any quantity for certain public purposes, but requires that such an assurance, if made otherwise than in good faith, for full and valuable consideration, shall be executed not less than twelve months before the death of the assuror. It also exempts assurances by will of land of certain limited quantities. The effect of the provision of the text is to extend the exemption to assurances by deed to a county council or any other local authority (as defined in s. 2), for any purpose for which they are empowered by Act of Parliament to acquire land, although such assurances be voluntary, and be made within twelve months before the death of the assuror; it does not apply to assurances by will. "Land," in the Mortmain, etc., Act, 1888, includes "tenements and hereditaments, corporeal or incorporeal, of any tenure, but not money secured in land, or other personal estate arising from or connected with land"; Mortmain, etc., Act, 1891 (54 & 55 Vict. c. 73), s. 3, repealing the definition in s. 10 of the Act of 1888. But as by s. 10 of the Act of 1891 nothing in that Act is to limit or affect the exemptions contained in Part III. of the Act of 1888 (which part includes s. 6), it would seem that "land" in the present Act will have the meaning assigned to it by the Interpretation Act, 1889 (52 & 53 Vict. c. 63), s. 3, and will include "messuages, tenements and hereditaments, houses and buildings, of any tenure."

Definitions.

2. For the purpose of this Act "local authority" means any county council, council of a municipal borough, sanitary authority, or any body having power to make a rate for public purposes or by the issue of any precept, certificate, or other document to require payment from some authority or officer of money which may render necessary the making of any such rate; and "assurance" has the same meaning as in the Mortmain and Charitable Uses Act, 1888 (*a*).

Extent of Act.

3. This Act shall not apply to Scotland or Ireland.

Short title.

4. This Act may be cited as the Mortmain and Charitable Uses Act Amendment Act, 1892.

CHARITY INQUIRIES (EXPENSES) ACT, 1892.

(55 & 56 VICT. CAP. 15.)

An Act to authorise the Councils of Counties and County Boroughs to contribute to the Expenses of Inquiries into certain Charities.

[20th June, 1892.]

* * * * *

Power for council of county or county borough to contribute to expenses of charity inquiries.

1.—(1.) The council of any county or county borough may, if they think fit, pay or contribute towards the expenses of any inquiry conducted by the Charity Commissioners into any charities which are by the trusts governing their administration expressly appropriated in whole or in part for the benefit of their county or county borough, or of any part thereof (*b*).

(2.) The payment or contribution may be made out of the county fund (*c*), or in the case of a county borough out of the borough fund or borough rate.

Short title

2. This Act may be cited as the Charity Inquiries (Expenses) Act, 1892.

(*a*) "Assurance" is defined by s. 10 of the Mortmain, etc., Act, 1888, to include "a gift, conveyance, appointment, lease, transfer, settlement, mortgage, charge, incumbrance, devise, bequest, and every other assurance by deed, will, or other instrument." But the present Act, as pointed out in the previous note, applies to assurances by deed only.

(*b*) The powers and duties of the Charity Commissioners as to holding inquiries into the nature and objects of charities, their administration, management, and results, and the value, condition, and application of their property and income are contained in the Charitable Trusts Acts, 1853 to 1894, viz., 16 & 17 Vict. c. 137 (1853); 18 & 19 Vict. c. 124 (1855); 23 & 24 Vict. c. 136 (1860); 25 & 26 Vict. c. 112 (1862); 32 & 33 Vict. c. 110 (1869); 50 & 51 Vict. c. 49 (1887); 54 & 55 Vict. c. 17 (1891); and 57 & 58 Vict. c. 35 (1894).

(*c*) A contribution made by a county council under this Act will be general expenses of the county council. Local Government Act, 1888, s. 68 (2), *ante*, p. 130.

WEIGHTS AND MEASURES (PURCHASE) ACT, 1892.

(55 & 56 VICT. CAP. 18.) (*d*).

An Act for authorising County and Borough Councils to purchase Franchises of Weights and Measures. [20th June, 1892.]

* * * * *

Power for county or borough council to purchase franchise of weights and measures.

1.—(1.) Where the council of a county or borough are the local authority for the execution of the law relating to weights and measures (*e*), the council and the owner of any franchise of weights and measures (*f*) may, with the approval of the Board of Trade, enter into and carry into effect any agreement for the sale to and purchase by the council of all or any of the powers and authorities of the franchise owner within the area under the council as such local authority, and on any such purchase being completed the powers and authorities purchased shall cease to be exercised.

(2.) For the purpose of any such purchase the Lands Clauses Acts shall be incorporated with this Act, except the provisions of those Acts with respect to the purchase and taking of land otherwise than by agreement, and the franchise shall be deemed land within the meaning of those Acts.

51 & 52 Vict. c. 41.

38 & 39 Vict. c. 55.

(3.) A county council may borrow money for the purposes of this Act in accordance with the Local Government Act, 1888 (*g*), and a borough council may borrow money for the purposes of this Act in accordance with the Public Health Act, 1875.

(4.) The expenses incurred by a borough council under this Act shall be defrayed out of the borough fund or borough rate, and any money borrowed by such a council shall be borrowed on the security of the borough fund or borough rate.

(5.) For the purposes of this Act the expression "franchise of weights and measures" shall include the authority which any court-leet for any hundred or manor, or any jury or ward inquest, or the lord or lady of any manor, or any other person, may have for inspecting, examining, regulating, verifying, stamping, adjusting, seizing, breaking, or destroying any weights or measures, or weighing instrument or measuring instrument.

(*d*) See the Weights and Measures Act, 1889, *ante*, p. 409, and the Weights and Measures Act, 1893, and the Weights and Measures (Metric System) Act, 1897, *post*.

(*e*) By virtue of s. 3 (xiii) of the Local Government Act, 1888, *ante*, p. 12, the county council is the local authority under the Weights and Measures Acts, except (i) in a county borough (*ib.* s. 31); (ii) in the larger quarter sessions boroughs (*ib.* s. 35); and (iii) in the larger boroughs not being quarter sessions boroughs mentioned on p. 87, *ante*, in which cases the local authority is the council of the borough. See also the note to the Weights and Measures Act, 1893, *post*, p. 574.

(*f*) The expression "franchise of weights and measures" is defined, sub-s. (5), *infra*.

(*g*) As to borrowing by a county council, see s. 69 of the Local Government Act, 1888, *ante*, p. 132. The expenses of a county council under this Act are "general expenses," *ib.* s. 68 (2).

Sect. 2.

2. Where the council of a county have in pursuance of this Act acquired any franchise of weights and measures in respect of any area within a borough the council of which are not at the time of such acquisition the local authority for the execution of the law relating to weights and measures, the council of that borough shall not become such a local authority (*h*) until they have recouped to the council of the county such proportion of the expenses of the county council in acquiring the franchise and in executing the law relating to weights and measures as may be agreed on between the respective councils, or may, in case of difference, be determined by the Board of Trade. Provision as to certain boroughs.

3. This Act shall not extend to Scotland or Ireland. Extent of Act.

4. This Act may be cited as the Weights and Measures (Purchase) Act, 1892, and shall be read as one with the Weights and Measures Acts, 1878 and 1889. Short title and construction. 41 & 42 Vict. c. 49. 52 & 53 Vict. c. 21.

TECHNICAL AND INDUSTRIAL INSTITUTIONS ACT, 1892.

(55 & 56 Vict. Cap. 29) (*i*).

An Act to facilitate the Acquisition and Holding of Land by Institutions for promoting Technical and Industrial Instruction and Training. [27th June, 1892.]

* * * *

1. This Act may be cited as the Technical and Industrial Institutions Act, 1892. Short title.

2. This Act applies to every institution established, whether before or after the passing of this Act, for effecting all or any of the following purposes, that is to say:— Definition of institution.

(*h*) Having regard to s. 37 of the Local Government Act, 1888, *ante*, p. 82, it appears that a borough council can only *become* the local authority for the purposes of the Weights and Measures Acts, if the borough is constituted into a county borough under s. 54 of that Act.

(*i*) Under this Act a county council may become the governing body of an institution established for any of the purposes mentioned in s. 2, and may acquire any land required for an institution of which they are the governing body. It is to be noticed that the Act does not deal with the question of how funds are to be provided for the purchase of the land, and contains no borrowing powers; it appears, in fact, to contemplate the existence of an endowment applicable for the purpose. If, however, the institution is established for the purpose of giving technical instruction (see s. 2 (i), it would appear that a county council may, under the powers given to them by the Technical Instruction Act, 1889 (*ante*, p. 435), endow it out of the county fund, and borrow money for the purpose of acquiring the land. See s. 4 (4) (a) of that Act. There is no power to take land compulsorily for the purposes of this Act. Voluntary conveyances for the purposes of the Act by limited owners are contemplated by the Act, but subject to restrictions which render this power very difficult to exercise. See s. 7, *infra*.

Sect. 2 (i).

52 & 53 Vict. c. 76.

(i.) To give technical instruction within the meaning of the Technical Instruction Act, 1889 (*k*);

(ii.) To provide the training, mental or physical, necessary for the above purpose.

(iii.) In connection with the purposes before mentioned, to provide workshops, tools, scientific apparatus and plant of all kinds, libraries, reading rooms, halls for lectures, exhibitions, and meetings, gymnasiums, and swimming baths, and also general facilities for mental and physical training, recreation, and amusement, and also all necessary and proper accommodation for persons frequenting the institution;

and every such institution is in this Act referred to as the institution.

Governing body.

3.—(1.) The governing body (*l*) of the institution may be any body corporate, council, public authority, local authority, commissioners, directors, committee, trustees, or other body of persons, corporate or unincorporate, willing to undertake, or elected or appointed for the purpose of undertaking, or having, the government and management of the institution.

(2.) The governing body may make bye-laws and rules for the management and conduct of the institution.

Incorporation of 8 & 9 Vict. c. 18. 23 & 24 Vict. c. 106.

4. The Lands Clauses Consolidation Act, 1845, and the Lands Clauses Consolidation Acts Amendment Act, 1860 (except the provisions of those Acts relating to the purchase and taking of lands otherwise than by agreement, and with respect to the entry upon lands by promoters of the undertaking, and with respect to determining the amount of purchase money by valuation of surveyors), are hereby incorporated in this Act.

Power to take land by agreement.

5. The governing body of the institution may by agreement enter on, take, and use any land required by them for the purposes of the institution, and such land may be conveyed either to the governing body or to trustees for the governing body (*m*).

Conveyance may be by way of sale, exchange, or gift.

6.—(1.) A conveyance of land may be made to the governing body of the institution or to trustees for the governing body either for valuable consideration in money, or in consideration of a rentcharge,

---

(*k*) See this Act, *ante*, p. 435. It would seem that a county council might itself establish an institution for this purpose under the Act of 1889, and might then proceed under this Act with respect to it. But this Act does not itself enable a county council to establish or endow any institution.

(*l*) It seems clear that under this section a county council may be the governing body of an institution to which the Act relates, if the scheme or instrument establishing the institution so provides. If as suggested in note (*k*), *supra*, the institution has been founded by the county council, they may themselves be the governing body, or appoint a committee for that purpose.

(*m*) If the governing body is incorporated, it will probably be found convenient to convey the land to them, and where they are unincorporate, to convey to trustees for them.

or by way of exchange for other land, or, subject as in this Act provided, by way of free gift, and without any consideration. Sect. 6 (1).

(2.) A conveyance under this Act by a person having an equitable estate shall operate to pass any bare outstanding legal estate vested in a trustee (*n*).

Conveyances by limited owners.

7.—(1.) A conveyance under this Act by a person not entitled to dispose absolutely for his own benefit (*o*) of the land proposed to be conveyed (other than a conveyance on a sale or exchange for the best consideration in money, or by way of rentcharge, or in land to be reasonably obtained) shall be subject to the following restrictions and provisions:—

(a.) It shall not in itself, or in addition to any land conveyed under this Act by the same person, comprise more than two acres in the whole in any one county, city, or borough:

(b.) It shall be made either with the consent of the person, if any, entitled to the next estate of freehold in remainder for the time being, or with the approval of the High Court of Justice.

(2.) Every application to the Court for an order approving a conveyance under this Act shall be by summons in chambers, and shall, subject to the Acts regulating the Court, be assigned to the Chancery Division (*p*).

(3.) On any such application the Court may direct notice to be served on such persons, if any, as it thinks fit.

(4.) On any such application the Court shall have regard to the circumstances of the settled estate, the wants of the neighbourhood, and the interests of the persons entitled in remainder, and the Court, if it thinks fit under all the circumstances of the case, may make an order approving the proposed conveyance. Such order, if the Court thinks fit, may be made on such terms and conditions, if any, as the Court thinks proper; but no such order shall be made if the

(*n*) This is a novel provision. Its effect is to make unnecessary the concurrence of the trustee in the conveyance, for the purpose of vesting the bare outstanding legal estate in the governing body or their trustees.

(*o*) This section appears to contemplate, although it does not expressly authorize, voluntary conveyances of lands for the purposes of the Act by limited owners, such as tenants for life. It does not expressly amend or even refer to the Settled Land Act, 1882, under which a tenant for life has large powers of selling the settled land, but subject to the provision that "every sale shall be made at the best price that can reasonably be obtained" (see s. 4 of that Act, and compare s. 74 of the Housing of the Working Classes, 1890). But it imposes certain restrictions on such conveyances (besides the limitation as to quantity contained in clause (a), *infra*) for the purpose of protecting the interests of the remaindermen. The consent either of the person entitled to the next estate, if freehold in remainder, or of the court, must be obtained, and the consent of the court cannot be given if any remainderman opposes, unless the court thinks his opposition unreasonable, or that his interest is so remote that it may properly be disregarded (sub-s. (4), *infra*). It is difficult to see in what circumstances the opposition of a person to a proposal for the giving away of his property could be regarded as unreasonable.

(*p*) As to chambers in the Chancery Division, see Rules of the Supreme Court, Order LV.

Sect. 7 (4).

application is opposed by any person entitled in remainder, unless the Court is of opinion that the opposition is unreasonable, or the interest of the person opposing so remote that it may properly be disregarded (*o*).

Institution to be public.

8. Every institution for which land has been acquired under an exercise of the powers conferred by this Act shall be open generally either to all persons or to all persons within specified limits as to age, qualification (*r*), or otherwise, and either without payment or on specified terms as to times of attendance and payment of subscriptions or fees or otherwise, but so that no preference be given to any person or class of persons within the specified limits.

Site may be sold or exchanged.

9.—(1.) Land acquired under the powers of this Act shall not be used (*s*) otherwise than for the purposes of an institution within the meaning of this Act, but, with the consent of the Charity Commissioners, may be sold or may be exchanged for other land.

(2.) The governing body or their trustees may execute conveyances and do all acts necessary to effectuate a sale or exchange.

(3.) On a sale, the receipt of the governing body or of the trustees for the governing body shall be a sufficient discharge for the purchase money, and such money shall, as soon as convenient, be invested in the purchase of other land.

(4.) Land purchased or taken in exchange under this section shall be devoted to the same purposes and be liable to the same incidents as originally were applicable to or affected the land sold or given in exchange.

(5.) Money arising by sale may, until reinvested in the purchase of land, be invested in the names of the governing body or of trustees for the governing body in any manner in which trust money is for the time being by law authorised to be invested (*t*); and all dividends and income on investments so made and all the resulting income shall be invested in like manner so as to accumulate in the way of compound interest, and be added to capital until the capital is reinvested in the purchase of land.

Parts I. and II. of 51 & 52 Vict. c. 42, and part of 54 & 55 Vict. c. 73, not to apply.

10.—(1.) Parts I. and II. of the Mortmain and Charitable Uses Act, 1888, and so much of the Mortmain and Charitable Uses Act, 1891, as requires that land assured by will shall be sold within one year from the death of the testator, shall not apply to conveyances or to assurances by will made under or for the purposes of this Act,

---

(*r*) This section does not prohibit a religious test; but a county council providing funds under the Technical Instruction Act, 1889, for the purposes of an institution to which the present Act relates would, of course, be bound by the provisions of s. 1 of that Act, *ante*, p. 435.

(*s*) *Scil.*, until it has been sold under this section.

(*t*) The investments authorized for trust funds are stated in the Trustee Act, 1893 (56 & 57 Vict. c. 53), s. 1.

but every such conveyance or assurance shall be enrolled as soon as may be in the books of the Charity Commissioners (*u*). **Sect. 10 (1).**

(2.) Any corporate body may acquire and shall be entitled to hold and retain land for the purposes of this Act without any licence in mortmain.

Extent of Act.

11. This Act shall not extend to Scotland.

SMALL HOLDINGS ACT, 1892.

(55 & 56 Vict. Cap. 31) (*x*).

An Act to facilitate the acquisition of Small Agricultural Holdings.
[27th June 1892.]

* * * *

PART I.

Provision of Small Holdings by County Councils.

Power for county council to acquire land for small holdings.

1.—(1.) If the council of any county are of opinion that there is such a demand for small holdings in their county as justifies them in putting into operation this Part of this Act (*y*), the council may, subject to the provisions of this Act, acquire any suitable land for the purpose of providing small holdings for persons who desire to buy and will themselves cultivate the holdings.

(2.) The expression "small holding" for the purposes of this Act shall mean land acquired by a council under the powers and for the purposes of this Act, and which exceeds one acre and either does not exceed fifty acres, or, if exceeding fifty acres, is of an annual value for the purposes of the income tax not exceeding fifty pounds.

(*u*) This constitutes a wider exemption from the Mortmain Acts than that contained in s. 6 of the Mortmain, etc., Act, 1888, in favour of assurances of land for public parks, school houses, and museums. The quantity of land which may be assured by will under that section is limited, while under the text any quantity of land may be devised for the purposes of this Act, and land so devised is not required to be sold within a year from the death of the testator, as is the case with land assured by will under the Mortmain, etc., Act, 1891. The books of the Charity Commissioners are those kept under s. 42 of the Charitable Trusts Act, 1855 (18 & 19 Vict. c. 124), which section provides for certified copies being received as evidence of the contents of documents so enrolled.

(*x*) This Act enables county councils, subject to certain conditions, to acquire land for the purpose of providing small agricultural holdings, and to sell, or under some circumstances to let such holdings to persons desiring to cultivate them. The expression "small holding" is defined by s. 1 (2). Section 16 of the Act is amended in a small particular by s. 6 (4) of the Local Government Act, 1894, *post*.

(*y*) The question whether the demand exists will be determined by the opinion of the committee appointed under s. 5, *post*. It will be noticed that this whole clause is permissive, and is subject to the other provisions of the Act, including the restriction as to expenditure contained in s. 18, *post*. It may be noticed that the Act does not define the class of the community from which the demand must proceed; the benefits of the Act are not confined to the labouring population as is the case with the Allotments Acts.

Sect. 2.

County council may lease land in lieu of purchasing.

2. Where land through its proximity to a town or suitability for building purposes, or for any other special reason has a prospective value which in the opinion of the county council is too high to make its purchase for agricultural purposes desirable, the council may hire the land on lease or otherwise for the purpose of letting it in small holdings in accordance with the provisions of this Act.

Purchase of land and adaptation of it for small holdings.

3.—(1.) For the purpose of the purchase of land under this Act by a county council the Lands Clauses Acts shall be incorporated with this Act, except the provisions of those Acts with respect to the purchase and taking of land otherwise than by agreement, which provisions shall not apply for the purposes of this Act; and section
38 & 39 Vict. c. 55. one hundred and seventy-eight of the Public Health Act, 1875, shall apply as if the county council were referred to therein (*z*).

(2.) The county council may, if they think fit, before sale or letting adapt for small holdings any land acquired under this Act by dividing and fencing it, making occupation roads, and executing any other works, such as works for the provision of drainage or water supply, which can in the opinion of the council be more economically and efficiently executed for the land as a whole.

(3.) The county council may also, if they think fit, as part of the agreement for the sale or letting of a small holding, adapt the land for a small holding by erecting thereon such buildings, or making such adaptations of existing buildings, as in their opinion are required for the due occupation of the holding, and cannot be made by the purchaser or tenant.

Sale or letting of small holdings.

4.—(1.) The county council shall apportion the total cost of the acquisition of the land, and of any adaptation thereof, among the several holdings in such manner as seems just, and shall, save as herein-after mentioned, offer the small holdings for sale in accordance with rules under this Act (*a*).

(2.) Where the county council are of opinion that any persons desirous of themselves cultivating small holdings are unable to buy on the terms fixed by this Act, or where the land has been hired by the council on lease or otherwise, the council may, in the case of any small holding which either does not exceed fifteen acres in extent, or if exceeding fifteen acres is of the annual value for the purpose of the income tax not exceeding fifteen pounds, instead of offering it for sale, offer to let it in accordance with rules under this Act (*b*).

Provided that a tenant of any small holding may, before the expiration of his tenancy, remove any fruit and other trees and

(*z*) Land cannot be taken compulsorily under this Act. Section 178 of the Public Health Act, 1875, enables the Chancellor and Council of the Duchy of Lancaster to sell lands to a local authority; the text gives them a like power as to the sale of lands for the purposes of this Act.

(*a*) These rules are made by the county council under s. 7, *post*.

(*b*) The primary intention of the Act is that the small holdings shall be sold out and out; it is only where persons desirous of cultivating such holdings are unable to buy, that the power to let them arises.

bushes planted or acquired by him for which he has no claim for compensation, and remove any toolhouse, shed, greenhouse, fowl-house, or pigsty built or acquired by him for which he has no claim for compensation (*c*). Sect. 4 (2).

(3.) The county council shall have power to sell, or, in the case of small holdings which may be let, to let one or more small holdings to a number of persons working on a co-operative system, provided such system be approved by the county council.

(4.) The cost of acquisition and adaptation shall for the purposes of this section include every expense incurred by the council in relation to the land, inclusive of any allowance to any officers of the council for work done in relation thereto.

Committee of and inquiry by council.

5.—(1.) Any county council may, and every county council not being a council of a county borough shall, appoint a committee to consider whether the circumstances of the county justify the council in putting into operation this Part of this Act (*d*).

(2.) Any one or more county electors may present a petition to the council of their county, alleging that there is a demand for small holdings in the county, and praying that this Part of this Act may be put in operation, and thereupon the petition shall be referred to the committee appointed under this section, who, on being satisfied that the petition is presented in good faith and on reasonable grounds, shall forthwith cause an inquiry into the circumstances to be made and shall report the result to the council.

(3.) If any councillor representing or alderman residing in any electoral division of a county in which it is alleged that there is a demand for small holdings is not a member of the committee, he shall be added to the committee for the consideration of the alleged demand.

Regulations as to purchase money and sale.

6.—(1.) The purchase money for each small holding sold by the county council shall include the costs of registration of title, but shall not include any expense incurred by the purchaser for legal or other advice or assistance (*e*).

(*c*) A claim for compensation in respect of the matters here specified might arise under the Agricultural Holdings Act, 1883 (46 & 47 Vict. c. 61), or the Allotments and Cottage Gardens Compensation for Crops Act, 1887 (50 & 51 Vict. c. 26), or possibly under the Market Gardeners' Compensation Act, 1895 (58 & 59 Vict. c. 27). Where a claim for compensation exists, the tenant will not apparently have the rights mentioned in the text.

(*d*) This committee, like that under the Allotments Act, 1890, *ante*, p. 518, is intended to be a standing committee of the county council. It will be noticed that the appointment of this committee is obligatory in the case of every county council, except councils of county boroughs. As to the constitution of the committee for the purposes of considering any particular allegation of a demand under this section, the requirements of sub-section (3) should be noticed.

(*e*) Section 10, *infra*, requires the county council to apply under the Land Transfer Act, 1875, for their registration as proprietors of land purchased by them under this Act, and that section is amended by s. 19 of the Land

Sect. 6 (2).

(2.) Every purchaser shall, within such time, not less than one month after the purchase, as is fixed by rules under this Act, complete the purchase.

(3.) On such completion he shall pay not less than one fifth of the purchase money (*f*).

(4.) A portion representing not more than one fourth of the purchase money may, if the county council think fit, be secured by a perpetual rentcharge which shall be redeemable in manner directed by section forty-five of the Conveyancing and Law of Property Act, 1881, with respect to rentcharges to which that section applies (*g*).

44 & 45 Vict. c. 41.

(5.) The residue (if any) of the purchase money shall be secured by a charge on the holding in favour of the council, and shall either be repaid by half-yearly instalments of principal with such interest, and within such term not exceeding fifty years from the date of the sale, as may be agreed on with the council, or shall if the purchaser so requires, be repaid with such interest and within such term as aforesaid by a terminable annuity payable by equal half-yearly instalments. The amount for the time being unpaid may at any time be discharged, and any such terminable annuity may at any time be redeemed, in accordance with tables fixed by the county council (*h*).

Transfer Act, 1897, *post.* The costs of registration referred to in the text seem to be the costs of the transfer in the Land Registry of the small holding from the county council to the purchaser; these costs are, it seems, to be paid by the county council out of the purchase money, which, of course, should be calculated so as to cover them. The costs of the land certificate to be issued to the purchaser from the county council were (by Rule 21 of the Land Registry (Small Holdings) Rules, 1892) included in the "costs of registration of title," mentioned in the text. But new rules under the Land Transfer Act, 1897, will, no doubt, shortly be issued.

(*f*) There is nothing apparently to prevent the county council from requiring more than a fifth or even the whole of the purchase money to be paid on completion.

(*g*) Section 45 of the Conveyancing Act, 1881, provides for the redemption of rentcharges issuing out of land; the owner of the land (in the present case the purchaser of the small holding) may, in writing, request the Board of Agriculture (formerly the Copyhold Commissioners) to certify the amount of money in consideration whereof the rent may be redeemed. The Board are required to give this certificate (under their seal), and where the owner of the rent is absolutely entitled to it (as would be the case with a county council acting under the text), the owner of the land may, after serving one month's notice on the owner of the rent (viz., the county council), pay or tender to him the certified amount, and on proof to the board that payment or tender has been so made, they must certify that the rent is redeemed; that certificate is final and conclusive, and the land is thereby absolutely freed and discharged from the rent. It is believed that in the absence of special circumstances, twenty-five years' purchase of the rent is the usual price for redemption fixed in this manner.

(*h*) The period of repayment, and the amount of the interest, will practically be fixed by the county council; they are, however, bound to accept repayment of the sum due or redemption (in accordance with their own tables) of the annuity at any time, although the period originally fixed has not expired, and they do not appear to be entitled to any particular length of notice of such repayment or redemption.

Sect. 6 (6).

(6.) The council may, if they think fit, agree to postpone for a term not exceeding five years the time for payment of all or any part of an instalment either of principal or interest or of a terminable annuity, in consideration of expenditure by the purchaser which, in the opinion of the council, increases the value of the holding, but shall do so on such terms as will, in their opinion, prevent them from incurring any loss (*i*).

(7.) A small holding may be sold subject to such rights of way or other rights for the benefit of other small holdings as the council consider necessary or expedient.

Rules as to mode and conditions of sale.

7. Every county council acquiring land under this Act shall make rules for carrying into effect this Act, except as otherwise provided, and in particular—

(a) as to the manner in which holdings are to be sold or let or offered for sale or letting; and

(b) as to the notice to be given of the offer for sale or letting; and

(c) for guarding against any small holding being let or sold to a person who is unable to cultivate it properly, and otherwise for securing the proper cultivation of a holding.

List to be kept by county council.

8. Every county council shall keep a list of the owners and occupiers of small holdings sold or let by them, and a map or plan showing the size, boundaries, and situation of each small holding so sold or let.

Conditions affecting small holdings.

9.—(1.) Every small holding sold by a county council under this Act shall for a term of twenty years from the date of the sale, and thereafter so long as any part of the purchase money remains unpaid, be held subject to the following conditions:—

(a.) That any periodical payments due in respect of the purchase money shall be duly made;

(b.) That the holding shall not be divided, subdivided, assigned, let, or sublet without the consent of the county council;

(c.) That the holding shall be cultivated by the owner or occupier as the case may be, and shall not be used for any purpose other than agriculture;

(d.) That not more than one dwelling-house shall be erected on the holding;

(*i*) It is in the discretion of the county council whether they will act or not under this clause, but if they do so they are bound to make such conditions as will prevent them from incurring loss.

(*k*) At the end of twenty years from the sale, or if the purchase money is not then all paid, then, at the date when it is all paid, a small holding will be freed from these conditions; but see s. 11, *post*, as to the right of repurchase arising in certain circumstances. The conditions do not in terms prohibit the mortgage or settlement of a small holding, but they make such transactions impossible. An entry is made in the register at the Land Registry, showing that the holding registered is subject to then conditions. See the Land Registry (Small Holdings) Rules, 1892, r. 19.

Sect. 9 (1)

(e.) That any dwelling-house erected on the holding shall comply with such requirements as the county council may impose for securing healthiness and freedom from overcrowding;

(f.) That no dwelling-house or building on the holding shall be used for the sale of intoxicating liquors;

(g.) In the case of any holding on which, in the opinion of the county council, a dwelling-house ought not to be erected, that no dwelling-house shall be erected on the holding without the consent of the county council.

(2.) If any such condition is broken, the council may, after giving the owner an opportunity of remedying the breach, if it is capable of remedy, cause the holding to be sold.

(3.) If on the decease of the owner while the holding is subject to the conditions imposed by this section, the holding would, by reason of any devise, bequest, intestacy, or otherwise, become subdivided, the council may require the holding to be sold within twelve months after such decease to some one person, and if default is made in so selling the holding, the council may cause the holding to be sold (*l*).

(4.) Any sale by the county council under this section may be made either subject to the charge in respect of purchase money or free, wholly or partly, from that charge, and in either case the provisions of this Act with respect to the purchase money shall apply in like manner as if the sale were the first sale of a small holding under this Act (*m*).

(5.) The proceeds of the sale shall be applied in discharge of any unpaid purchase money for the holding or redemption of any rent-charge or terminable annuity which is not to continue a charge on the holding, and, subject as aforesaid, shall be paid to the person appearing to the council to be entitled to receive the same (*m*).

(6.) The county council may, under special circumstances, to be recorded in their minutes, sell or consent to the sale under this section of a small holding free from all or any of the conditions

---

(*l*) A devise or bequest of a small holding to one individual is unobjectionable.

(*m*) Under sub-ss. (4) and (5) a holding may be sold subject to the payment of any balance of purchase money remaining payable in respect of it, or free wholly or partly from such charge, and in the latter case, the price must be sufficient to discharge the out-standing purchase money, or, if it has taken the form of an annuity under s. 6 (5), to redeem the annuity. The sale is to be conducted by the county council, and they are, it seems, to receive the purchase money of the new purchaser. After retaining a sum sufficient to discharge any outstanding balance of the original purchase money (or to redeem the annuity), they are to pay the proceeds of sale to the person appearing to them to be entitled thereto. This latter provision throws a somewhat onerous duty on the county council; some provision might have been expected for the protection of the new purchaser who pays his purchase money to the county council, and some power to the county council to deduct from the proceeds of sale, the costs incurred by them in carrying it out, but it is conceived that "proceeds of sale" must be read as meaning net proceeds after paying all expenses.

imposed by this section, and may give such consent on such terms as they think fit (*n*). Sect. 9 (6)

(7.) Every small holding let by a county council under the foregoing provisions of this Act shall be held subject to the conditions on which it would under this section be held if it were sold, except so far as those conditions relate to the purchase money; and if any such condition or any term of the letting is broken the council may, after giving the tenant an opportunity of remedying the breach (if it is capable of remedy) determine the tenancy.

(8.) Nothing in or done under this section shall derogate from the effect of any building or sanitary byelaws for the time being in force.

Registration of title to small holdings.

10.—(1.) When a county council have purchased land under this Act, they shall apply for their registration as proprietors thereof with an absolute title under the Land Transfer Act, 1875 (*o*). 38 & 39 Vict. c. 87.

(2.) Rules under the Land Transfer Act, 1875, may—

(a) adapt that Act to the registration of small holdings, with such modifications as appear to be required; and

(b) on the application and at the expense of a county council provide, by the appointment of local agents or otherwise, for carrying into effect the objects of this section.

Right of purchase, if land diverted from agriculture.

11. If at any time after the restrictive conditions imposed by this Act have ceased to attach to a small holding, the owner of the holding desires to use the holding for purposes other than agriculture, he shall before so doing, whether the holding is situate within a town or built upon or not, offer the holding for sale, first to the county council from whom the holding was purchased, next to the person or persons (if any) then entitled to the lands from which the holding was originally severed, and then to the person or persons whose lands immediately adjoin the holding, and sections one hundred and twenty-seven to one hundred and thirty of the Lands Clauses Consolidation Act, 1845, shall apply as if the owner of the small 8 & 9 Vict. c. 18.

(*n*) "Special circumstances" would, it is conceived, exist where it was found impossible to find a purchaser willing to take the land, subject to the conditions which would attach to it under this section as a small holding.

(*o*) Registration with an absolute title under the Land Transfer Act, 1875, involves a strict investigation of title in the Registry, and is by no means lightly granted. The Land Registry (Small Holdings) Rules, 1892, made under this section, provided for provisional registration with less than an absolute title pending further investigation, and also facilitated registration where the title had been investigated by a conveyancing counsel, and his report is submitted to the Registry. But now under the Land Transfer Act, 1897 (60 & 61 Vict. c. 65), s. 19, *post*, a county council applying for registration under the provision in the text may be registered with any such title as is authorized by the Land Transfer Act, 1875, viz., absolute, qualified, or possessory; a purchaser of a small holding from the county council is to be registered with an absolute title, subject to such incumbrances as may be created under this (Small Holdings) Act. The same section provides for the recovery of damages from the county council by a person claiming by title paramount.

Sect. 11.

holding were the promoter of the undertaking, and the holding were superfluous lands within the meaning of those sections (*p*).

Extension of provisions of 45 & 46 Vict. c. 38.

12. Where a person having the powers of a tenant for life within the meaning of the Settled Land Act, 1882, sells, exchanges, or leases, any settled land to a county council for the purposes of this Act, such sale, exchange, or lease may be made at such a price, or for such consideration, or at such rent as, having regard to the said purposes and to all the circumstances of the case, is the best that can be reasonably obtained (*q*).

Power to limited owner to sell at a fee farm rent.

13. A person having the powers of a tenant for life within the meaning of the Settled Land Act, 1882, may grant the settled land, or a part thereof, to a county council for the purposes of this Act in perpetuity, at a fee farm or other rent secured by condition of re-entry, or otherwise as may be agreed upon (*r*).

Power to attach grazing rights, &c. to small holdings.

14. Where any right of grazing, sheepwalk, or other similar right is attached to land acquired by a county council for the purposes of small holdings, the council may attach any share of the right to any small holding in such manner and subject to such regulations as they think expedient.

Letting of land unsold and sale of

15.—(1.) A county council shall, if practicable, sell or let as small holdings, and in accordance with this Act, any land acquired under

(*p*) It is difficult to see how s. 127 of the Lands Clauses Act, 1845, can apply to a case under this section; it requires the promoter of the undertaking to sell the superfluous lands within a certain period, and in default of his doing so, the lands are to vest in the adjoining owners in certain proportions. The text clearly does not require the owner of the holding to sell the lands, except in the event of one of the options to purchase being exercised. The effect of the other incorporated sections combined with the text is that the owner of the holding before using it for purposes other than agriculture must offer it for sale, in succession, first to the county council, next to the persons then entitled to the lands (if any) from which the holding was originally severed, if they can after diligent inquiry, be found, and then to the adjoining owners, such persons being capable of entering into a contract for the purchase of the lands; where more persons than one are entitled to the right of pre-emption, the owner of the holding may select to which of them he will first make the offer. Each person to whom the offer is made has six weeks in which to accept the offer; if he refuses or does not accept within the six weeks, his right of pre-emption ceases; a written declaration before a justice by a disinterested person that an offer was made and refused, or not accepted with six weeks, or that the person or all the persons entitled to the right of pre-emption were out of the country, or could not after diligent inquiry be found, or were not capable of entering into a contract for purchase, is sufficient evidence of the facts. In the event of any person exercising his right of pre-emption, the price is to be settled in default of agreement by arbitration. See the incorporated sections and notes thereto in Browne and Allan on Compensation, pp. 275—285.

(*q*) This section varies the provisions of the Settled Land Act, 1882, ss. 4, 7, that sales and leases by a tenant for life under that Act must be at the best price, or reserve the best rent that can reasonably be obtained. The limited owners who have the powers of a tenant for life under that Act are enumerated in the Settled Land Act, 1882, s. 58.

(*r*) See note to the preceding section.

this Act, but if the council are of opinion that any such land is not needed for, or is unsuitable for, small holdings, or cannot be sold or let under the foregoing provisions of this Act, or that some more suitable land is available, they may sell or let the land otherwise than under the said provisions, or exchange the land for other land more suitable for small holdings, and may pay or receive money for equality of exchange, and may erect such buildings or execute such other works as will in the opinion of the council enable the land to be sold or let without loss. **Sect. 15 (1).** — Superfluous or unsuitable land.

(2.) The council may also, while any sale of a holding is pending in pursuance of this Act, temporarily let or manage the holding for such time and in such manner as they think expedient.

(3.) Sections one hundred and twenty-eight to one hundred and thirty-two of the Lands Clauses Consolidation Act, 1845 (relating to the right of pre-emption of superfluous lands) shall apply upon any sale in pursuance of this section before any such buildings or works as aforesaid are erected or executed on the land proposed to be sold, but save as aforesaid the provisions of the Lands Clauses Consolidation Act, 1845, with respect to the sale of superfluous lands shall not apply (*s*). 8 & 9 Vict. c. 18.

16.—(1.) Where a county council provide small holdings they may delegate, with or without restrictions, the powers of the county council under this Act with respect to the adaptation of land for any holdings, and the sale, letting, and management of any holdings to a committee consisting of— Provisions as to management of holdings.

The county councillor representing the electoral division in which the holdings are situate; and

Two other members of the county council; and

Two of the allotment managers (if any) under the Allotments Act, 1887, for the parish or area in which the holdings are situate selected by those managers, or if there are no allotment managers, two persons appointed in manner provided by that Act for the appointment of allotment managers (*t*); or 50 & 51 Vict. c. 48.

If the holdings are situate within the limits of a municipal borough, then, instead of the persons selected or appointed as aforesaid, two members of the borough council;

and in the construction of this Act references to the county council shall, in their application to the powers so delegated, include any such committee. Provided that a county council shall not under this section delegate any powers of making or levying a rate or of borrowing money.

(*s*) The effect of ss. 128—130 of the Act of 1845 is stated in note (*p*), *ante*, p. 554. Sections 131 and 132 relate to the conveyance of the superfluous lands to the purchasers.

(*t*) If the parish has a parish council, two members of the parish council (apparently to be selected by that council) are to be members of the committee in substitution for the allotment managers or other persons here mentioned. Local Government Act, 1894, s. 6 (4), *post*.

Sect. 16 (2).

51 & 52 Vict. c. 41.

(2.) The Local Government Act, 1888, shall apply to any committee appointed under this section as if it were appointed under that Act (*u*).

PART II.

Loans by County Councils to Tenants purchasing Small Holdings.

Power of county council to advance money for purchase of small holding.

17.—(1.) Where the tenant of a small holding has agreed with his landlord for the purchase of the holding the county council of the county in which the holding or any part of it is situate may, if they think fit, advance to the tenant on the security of the holding an amount not exceeding four-fifths of the purchase money thereof (*x*).

(2.) The provisions of this Act with respect to the purchase money secured by a charge on a small holding sold by a county council, and with respect to any small holding so sold, shall apply to an advance made, and a holding purchased under this section, as if the advance was the purchase money, save that the county council shall not guarantee the title of the purchaser of the holding (*y*).

(3.) No advance shall be made by a county council under this section, unless they are satisfied that the title to the holding is good, that the sale is made in good faith, and that the price is reasonable.

PART III.

Supplemental.

Restrictions on powers of council.

18.—(1.) A county council shall not acquire land under this Act save at such price that, in the opinion of the council, all expenses incurred by the council in relation to the land will be recouped out of the purchase money for the land sold by the council, or in the case of land let out of the rent, and shall fix the purchase money or rent at such reasonable amount as will, in their opinion, guard them against loss.

(2.) A county council shall not take any proceedings under this Act whereby the charge for the time being on the county rate, for

(*u*) As to committees appointed under the Local Government Act, 1888, see ss. 28, 81, 82 of that Act, *ante*, pp. 64, 155, and s. 22 of the Municipal Corporations Act, 1882, *ante*, p. 260.

(*x*) By the definition of "small holding" in s. 1 (2), *supra*, it must be land acquired by a council under this Act. The present section, however, appears to contemplate under that description a piece of land (perhaps within the limits of size or value mentioned in s. 1 (2)) of which the county council is not the owner.

(*y*) This clause appears to make s. 9 applicable to a holding purchased under this section, but it is difficult to say how far that and other sections are to apply. The reference to a guarantee of title is obscure; there is no guarantee by the county council of the title of the purchaser of a small holding, it is, however, believed that the Bill as originally drafted provided for some such guarantee being given, and the saving provision in the text was retained by error after the provision to which it related had been eliminated. See now s. 19 of the Local Transfer Act, 1897, *post*.

the purposes of this Act, including the annual payments in respect of the loans raised for those purposes, is, in the opinion of the council, likely to exceed in any one year the amount produced by a rate of a penny in the pound, and, where the said charge at any time is equal or nearly equal to that amount, no further land shall be purchased in pursuance of this Act, until the charge has been decreased so as to admit of the further purchase without the charge exceeding the said amount. Sect. 18 (2).

19.—(1.) A county council may borrow money for the purposes of this Act in accordance with the Local Government Act, 1888, or, if the council of a county borough, with the Public Health Act, 1875, except that any money so borrowed shall, notwithstanding anything in either of those Acts, be repaid within such period not exceeding fifty years, as the council, with the consent of the Local Government Board, determine in each case. Provided that money borrowed under this Act shall not be reckoned as part of the total debt of a county for the purpose of section sixty-nine, sub-section two, of the Local Government Act, 1888 (z). Borrowing powers and expenses. 51 & 52 Vict. c. 41. 38 & 39 Vict. c. 55.

(2.) The Public Works Loan Commissioners may, in manner provided by the Public Works Loans Act, 1875, lend any money which may be borrowed by a county council for the purposes of this Act. 38 & 39 Vict. c. 89.

(3.) Every loan by the Public Works Loan Commissioners in pursuance of this Act shall bear such rate of interest not less than three pounds two shillings and sixpence per cent. per annum, as the Treasury may authorise as being in their opinion sufficient to enable such loans to be made without loss to the Exchequer.

(4.) Any capital money received by a county council in payment or discharge of purchase money for land sold by them, or in repayment of an advance made by them, shall be applied, with the sanction of the Local Government Board, either in repayment of debt or for any other purpose for which capital money may be applied.

(5.) The expenses incurred by the council of a county borough under this Act shall be defrayed out of the borough fund or borough rate, and any money borrowed by such a council shall be borrowed on the security of the borough fund or borough rate.

20. For the purposes of this Act—

The expressions "agriculture" and "cultivation" shall include horticulture and the use of land for any purpose of Definitions.

(z) As to borrowing by a county council, see s. 69 of the Local Government Act, 1888, *ante*, p. 132. Sub-section (2) of that section prohibits further borrowing (except under a provisional order confirmed by Parliament) where the total debt exceeds, or with the proposed loan will exceed, one-tenth of the annual rateable value of the county, according to the county rate basis. Loans under this Act are not to be reckoned as part of the total debt for the purpose of that restriction. The thirty years prescribed by sub-s. (5) of that section as the maximum period for repayment is extended in the case of a loan under this Act to fifty years.

As to borrowing by a borough council under the Public Health Act, 1875, see ss. 233 *et seq*, of that Act.

Sect. 20.

husbandry, inclusive of the keeping or breeding of live stock, poultry or bees, and the growth of fruit, vegetables, and the like:

The expression "county" shall mean the area under the authority of a county council:

The expression "county council" shall include the council of a county borough, and the expression "electoral division" in its application to a county borough divided into wards shall mean ward, and in its application to a county borough the expression "county rate" shall mean the borough rate or borough fund:

The expression "county elector" shall include "burgess."

In this Act, and in the enactments incorporated with this Act, the expression "land" shall include any right or easement in or over land.

21. * * **22.** * * **23.** * * **24.** * * (*a*).

Extent of Act.

25. This Act shall not apply to Ireland.

Commencement of Act.

26. This Act shall come into operation on the first day of October, one thousand eight hundred and ninety-two.

Short title.

27. This Act may be cited as the Small Holdings Act, 1892.

POLICE RETURNS ACT, 1892.

(55 & 56 Vict. Cap. 38.)

An Act to alter the period for which certain Police Returns are required to be made. [27th June 1892.]

* * * * *

Amendment of provision as to annual police returns. 19 & 20 Vict. c. 69.

1. The annual statement required by section fourteen of the County and Borough Police Act, 1856, shall be made for each calendar year, and shall be transmitted to one of Her Majesty's principal Secretaries of State as soon as may be after the termination of that year (*b*).

(*a*) These sections apply exclusively to Scotland.

(*b*) The statement referred to is a statement of the number of offences reported to the police within the county, the number of persons apprehended by the police, the nature of the charges against them, the result of the proceedings taken thereupon, and any other particulars relating to the state of crime within the county which the justices think it material to furnish (19 & 20 Vict. c. 69, s. 14). The present statute requires the returns to be made for the calendar year instead of for the year ending September 29th, as under the Act of 1856. The duty of transmitting the statement devolves upon the standing joint committee of the quarter sessions, and the county council under the Local Government Act, 1888, s. 9 (1), *ante*, p. 18.

2. This Act shall come into operation on the first day of January one thousand eight hundred and ninety-three. **Sect. 2.** Commencement.

3. This Act may be cited as the Police Returns Act, 1892. Short title.

MILITARY LANDS ACT, 1892.

(55 & 56 VICT. CAP. 43) (c).

An Act to consolidate and amend certain Enactments relating to the Acquisition of Land for Military Purposes.

[27th June 1892.]

*

PART I.

Acquisition of Land for Military Purposes.

1.—(1.) A Secretary of State may purchase land in the United Kingdom under this Act, for the military purposes of any portion of Her Majesty's military forces. Powers to purchase land.

(2.) A volunteer corps may, with the consent of the Secretary of State, themselves purchase land under this Act for military purposes.

(3.) The council of a county or borough may, at the request of one or more volunteer corps, purchase under this Act, and hold, land (*d*) on behalf of the volunteer corps for military purposes (*d*).

(4.) The Secretary of State shall, before giving his consent to the purchase of any land under this Act by a volunteer corps, send an inspector to the land for the purpose of ascertaining its capabilities of being used for military purposes with due regard to the safety and convenience of the public, and shall give or withhold his consent accordingly.

2. For the purpose of the purchase of land under this Act, the Lands Clauses Acts (*e*) shall be incorporated with this Act, with the exceptions and additions and subject to the provisions following; (that is to say,) Machinery for purchase of land

(1.) There shall not be incorporated with this Act sections sixteen or seventeen of the Lands Clauses Consolidation Act, 1845, or the provisions of that Act with respect to affording access to the special Act.

(*c*) Power is given to a county council by this Act to purchase and hold land on behalf of volunteer or yeomanry corps for military purposes. The Lands Clauses Acts are incorporated with certain exceptions ; the customary powers under those Acts can only be put in force by means of a Provisional Order of the Secretary of State made after the procedure mentioned in this Act has been followed, and also requiring confirmation by Parliament. See s. 2, *infra.*

As to the temporary use of land for military manœuvres, see 60 & 61 Vict. c. 43, *post.*

(*d*) "Military purposes" and "land" are defined by s. 23, *infra.*

(*e*) These Acts are fully annotated in Browne and Allan on Compensation.

Sect. 2 (2).

(2.) In the construction of this Act and the incorporated Acts this Act shall be deemed to be the special Act, and the Secretary of State, volunteer corps, or council of a county or borough, as the case may be (in this section referred to as "the purchaser"), shall be deemed to be the promoters of the undertaking.

(3.) Where the Secretary of State is the purchaser—

(a.) The bond required by section eighty-five of the Lands Clauses Consolidation Act, 1845, shall be under the seal of the Secretary of State, and shall be sufficient without the addition of the sureties in those sections mentioned.

(b.) When compensation has been paid to any person in respect of any estate or interest in land taken under this Act, the land shall vest in the Secretary of State for all the estate and interest of that person, including any estate or interest therein held in trust by that person or capable of being conveyed by him in pursuance of any power. Nevertheless the Secretary of State may require that person to execute any conveyance which he might have been required to execute if this Act had not passed; and nothing in this section shall in any manner invalidate any such conveyance when executed.

(4.) The provisions of the incorporated Acts with respect to the purchase of land compulsorily shall not be put in force until a Provisional Order has been made and the sanction of Parliament has been obtained in manner in this Act mentioned.

(5.) One month at the least before the making of the Provisional Order, if the Secretary of State is the purchaser, and before the application for the Order in any other case, the purchaser shall serve, in manner provided by the Lands Clauses Acts, a notice on every owner or reputed owner, lessee or reputed lessee, and occupier of any land intended to be so purchased, describing the land intended to be taken, and in general terms the purposes to which it is to be applied, and stating the intention of the purchaser to obtain the sanction of Parliament to the purchase thereof, and inquiring whether the person so served assents or dissents to the taking of his land, and requesting him to forward to the purchaser any objections he may have to his land being taken.

(6.) Where the Secretary of State is the purchaser, he shall, at some time after the service of the notice, cause a public local inquiry to be held by a competent officer into the objections made by any persons whose land is required to be taken, and by other persons, if any, interested in the subject matter of the inquiry.

(7.) Where the purchaser is a volunteer corps or the council of a county or borough— Sect. 2 (7).

(a.) The corps or council may, if they think fit, on compliance with the provisions of this section with respect to notices, present a petition to a Secretary of State. The petition shall state the land intended to be taken, and the purposes for which the land is required, and the names of the owners, lessees, and occupiers of land who have assented, dissented, or are neuter in respect of the taking the land, or who have returned no answer to the notice. The petition shall pray that the corps or council may, with reference to the land, be allowed to put in force the powers of the Lands Clauses Acts with respect to the purchase and taking of lands otherwise than by agreement, and the prayer shall be supported by such evidence as the Secretary of State requires:

(b.) On receipt of the petition and on due proof of the proper notices having been served, the Secretary of State shall take the petition into consideration, and may either dismiss the same, or direct a public local inquiry to be held by a competent officer as to the propriety of assenting to the prayer of the petition.

(8.) Before a local inquiry is held in pursuance of this section the Secretary of State shall publish a notice of the intention to hold the inquiry—

(a) by affixing copies conspicuously on or in the immediate neighbourhood of the land proposed to be acquired; and

(b) by advertising the notice once at least in each of two successive weeks in some one and the same local newspaper circulating in the neighbourhood.

(9.) If after the local inquiry has been held the Secretary of State is satisfied that the land ought to be taken, he may make a Provisional Order to that effect, authorising the taking of the land either by himself or by a volunteer corps or by a council of a county or borough, as the case may be, and may submit a Bill to Parliament for the confirmation of the Provisional Order, but the Provisional Order shall not be of any effect unless and until it is confirmed by Parliament.

(10.) If, while the Bill confirming any such order is pending in either House of Parliament, a petition is presented against anything comprised therein, the Bill, so far as relates to the order, may be referred to a select committee, and the petitioner shall be allowed to appear and oppose as in the case of private Bills.

3. Land acquired under this Act may be let by a volunteer corps, or if acquired by the council of a county or borough, by that Power to let land.

Sect. 3.

council, in any manner consistent with the use thereof for military purposes (*f*).

Payment of expenses.

4. Any expenses incurred by the council of a county or borough for the purposes of this Act shall be defrayed by the council of a county out of the county fund (*g*), and by the council of a borough out of the borough fund or borough rate.

Power of volunteer corps to borrow.

5.—(1.) A volunteer corps may, with the consent of the Secretary of State, and subject to such conditions as he may impose, borrow such money as may be required for the purpose of the purchase by them of land under this Act.

(2.) The money shall be borrowed on the security of the land acquired by the volunteer corps, and also on the security of any grant to the corps out of money provided by Parliament (*h*).

Powers of borough council to borrow.

38 & 39 Vict. c. 55.

6. The council of a borough may borrow for the purpose of acquiring land under this Act in like manner as they may borrow for the purposes of the Public Health Act, 1875, and the provisions of that Act shall apply accordingly, but the money shall be borrowed on the security of the borough fund or borough rate.

Power for Public Works Loan Commissioners to lend.

38 & 39 Vict. c. 89.

7.—(1.) The Public Works Loan Commissioners may in manner provided by the Public Works Loans Act, 1875, lend any money which may be borrowed for the purposes of this Act, and may so lend on the security authorised by this Act without requiring any other security.

(2.) Every loan by the Public Works Loan Commissioners under this Act shall be repaid within a period not exceeding fifty years, and shall bear interest at a rate not less than three and a half per centum per annum, or such other rate as may be fixed by a minute of the Treasury under section two of the Public Works Loans Act, 1879.

42 & 43 Vict. c. 77.

Provision as to disbandment of corps, &c.

8.—(1.) If a volunteer corps holding land under this Act is disbanded, the land shall, by virtue and subject to the provisions of this section, vest in the Secretary of State from the date of the disbandment, subject to the repayment of any money borrowed for the purchase of the land, and not already repaid, and the sums required for such repayment shall, if and so far as not provided by the sale of the land, be paid out of moneys provided by Parliament for army services.

(*f*) See the definition, s. 23, *infra.*

(*g*) These will be general expenses, see Local Government Act, 1888, s. 68 (2), *ante*, p. 130. No express power to borrow for the purpose of purchasing land is given to county councils by this Act, as is done in the cases of volunteer corps and borough councils by the next two sections. But having regard to s. 69 (1) (b) of the Local Government Act, 1888, *ante*, p. 132, no further powers appear to be necessary.

(*h*) The borrowing powers of a volunteer corps have been extended by the Military Lands Act, 1897 (60 Vict. c. 6).

(2.) A certificate of the Secretary of State that land has vested in him under this section shall be conclusive evidence of the fact certified. Sect. 8 (2).

(3.) If the volunteer corps on whose behalf land is acquired under this Act by a county or borough council is disbanded, the council may either appropriate the land to any purpose approved by the Local Government Board, or sell it for the best price that can be reasonably obtained, and any money arising from the sale shall be applied towards repaying any money borrowed for the purchase of the land, and so far as not required for that purpose shall be applied to any purpose to which capital moneys are properly applicable, and which is approved by the Local Government Board.

Provided that before so appropriating any such land or before selling any such land, if it is not so appropriated, the council shall offer to sell the same to the person then entitled to the land (if any) from which the same was originally severed, and thereupon sections one hundred and twenty-nine to one hundred and thirty-two, both inclusive, of the Lands Clauses Consolidation Act, 1845, shall apply as if the land were superfluous land and the council were the promoters of the undertaking within the meaning of those sections (*i*). 8 & 9 Vict. c. 18.

Rules as to exercise of powers, &c., by volunteer corps.

9.—(1.) Rules under section twenty-four of the Volunteer Act, 1863, may provide for the exercise of any powers and the performance of any duty under this Act by any officer of the volunteer corps on behalf of the corps, and may provide generally for the carrying into effect of this Act by a volunteer corps. 26 & 27 Vict. c. 65.

(2.) The powers given by section twenty-five of the Volunteer Act, 1863, to the commanding officer for the time being of a volunteer corps and his successors shall include a power to mortgage any land acquired under this Act and to do all things necessary for that purpose.

10. * * * * * (*k*).

Power to lease land held for public purposes.

11.—(1.) Any person, body of persons, or authority holding land for ecclesiastical or public purposes may lease any such land to a Secretary of State or to a volunteer corps for military purposes for any term not exceeding twenty-one years, subject to the following provisions:

(a.) An ecclesiastical corporation sole below the dignity of a bishop shall not grant any such lease without the consent

---

(*i*) See the incorporated sections and notes in Browne and Allan on Compensation, pp. 284—287. Their effect is stated in the notes to ss. 11, 15 of the Small Holdings Act, 1892, *ante*, p. 554.

(*k*) This section does not affect county councils. It confers certain powers of leasing to the Secretary of State, or to a volunteer corps, land which belongs to the Crown, the Duchies of Lancaster and Cornwall, or certain public departments.

Sect. 11 (1).

in writing of the bishop to whose jurisdiction he is subject, and of the patron of the preferment to which the land belongs, or the guardians or trustees of such patron:

(b.) A lease of parochial property shall be granted under and in accordance with the provisions of section three of the Union and Parish Property Act, 1835, and the Acts amending the same:

5 & 6 Will. 4, c. 69.

(c.) Where the land is vested in any trustees, commissioners, or other body of persons, a majority of a meeting of such trustees, commissioners, or other body of persons duly convened may grant a lease under this section and execute any instrument for that purpose:

(d.) Where the land belongs to an administrative county, the county council may grant a lease under this section with the consent of the Local Government Board.

(2.) A lease under this section shall cease to have effect if the land ceases to be used for military purposes (*l*).

Proof that land has ceased to be used for military purposes.

12. Any land leased under this Act shall be deemed to have ceased to be used for military purposes where there has not been such use for a period of one year, and a certificate of the fact of such non-user is given by a Secretary of State; and the certificate shall be conclusive evidence of the fact of such non-user.

Power to stop or divert footpaths.

13.—(1.) Where a footpath crosses or runs inconveniently or dangerously near to any land leased under this Act, that footpath may, with the consent of the vestry of the parish in which the same is situate, and on the certificate of two justices that the footpath to be substituted is convenient for the public, be stopped up or diverted.

5 & 6 Will. 4, c. 50.

(2.) The provisions of the Highway Act, 1835, as to the obtaining of a certificate and the stopping up or diverting a highway where a person other than the inhabitants or vestry are desirous of stopping up, diverting, or turning a highway shall apply so far as practicable to the obtaining of a certificate, and the stopping up or diverting a footpath under this section; with this exception, that the certificate of the justices shall be conclusive in cases where it states the fact of their having viewed the footpath to be stopped up or diverted, and that the proposed new footpath is convenient for the public (*m*).

PART II. (*n*).

Bye-laws as to Land used for Military Purposes.

Power of Secretary of State to

14.—(1.) Where any land belonging to a Secretary of State or to a volunteer corps is for the time being appropriated by or with the

(*l*) See the definition, s. 23, *infra*, and see also s. 12, *infra*.

(*m*) See ss. 84 to 92 of the Highway Act, 1835, and see also s. 13 (1) of the Local Government Act, 1894, *post*.

(*n*) This part (ss. 14 to 18) relates to the making of bye-laws by the Secretary of State as to the use of land held for military purposes, and for securing the consent of a Secretary of State for any military purpose, a Secretary of State may make byelaws for regulating the use of the land for the purposes to which it is appropriated, and for securing the public against danger arising from that use, with power to prohibit all intrusion on the land and all obstruction of the use thereof. Sect. 14 (1).

Power to make bye-laws as to use of land held for military purposes and securing safety of public.

Provided that no byelaws promulgated under this section shall authorise the Secretary of State to take away or prejudicially affect any right of common.

(2.) Where any such byelaws permit the public to use the land for any purpose when not used for the military purpose to which it is appropriated, those byelaws may also provide for the government of the land when so used by the public, and the preservation of order and good conduct thereon, and for the prevention of nuisances, obstructions, encampments, and encroachments thereon, and for the prevention of any injury to the same, or to anything growing or erected thereon, and for the prevention of anything interfering with the orderly use thereof by the public for the purpose permitted by the byelaws.

(3.) For the purposes of this section, "land belonging to a Secretary of State" means land under the management of a Secretary of State, whether vested in Her Majesty or in the Secretary of State, or in a person as trustee for Her Majesty or the Secretary of State; and "land belonging to a volunteer corps" means any land vested in that corps or in any person as trustee for that corps.

15. Where a Secretary of State or a volunteer corps has for the time being the right of using for any military purpose any land vested in another person, this Part of this Act shall apply in like manner as if the land were vested in the Secretary of State or volunteer corps, and the same were appropriated for the said purpose, save that nothing therein or in any byelaws made thereunder shall injuriously affect the private rights of any person further or otherwise than is authorised by the grant of the right to use the land.

Application of byelaws where right of firing acquired.

16.—(1.) A byelaw under this Act shall not interfere with any highway, unless made with the consent of the authority having control of the repair of the roads of the town, district, parish, or other area in which the highway is situate, but where it appears to the authority that any highway crosses or runs inconveniently or dangerously near to any land the use of which can be regulated by byelaws under this Act, the authority may consent to a byelaw providing to such extent as seems reasonable for the temporary diversion from time to time of the highway, or for the restriction from time to time of the use thereof.

Bye-laws as to highways.

---

safety of the public. It does not affect county councils, except as regards their duties as to main roads, which may be affected by s. 16. As to the use of land for military manœuvres, and the powers of a county council in relation thereto, see 60 & 61 Vict. c. 43, *post.*

Sect. 16 (2).

(2.) Any such highway, if a footpath, may (without prejudice to any other power of stopping up or diverting the same) be stopped up or diverted in the manner in which a footpath crossing or running inconveniently or dangerously near to any land leased under Part One of this Act may be stopped up or diverted.

Notice and enforcement of byelaws.

17.—(1.) A Secretary of State, before making any byelaws under this Act, shall cause the proposed byelaws to be made known in the locality, and give an opportunity for objections being made to the same, and shall receive and consider all objections made; and when any such byelaws are made, shall cause the boundaries of the area to which the byelaws apply to be marked, and the byelaws to be published in such manner as appears to him necessary to make them known to all persons in the locality; and shall provide for copies of the byelaws being sold at the price of one shilling for each copy to any person who desires to obtain the same.

(2.) If any person commits an offence against any byelaw under this Act, he shall be liable, on conviction before a court of summary jurisdiction, to a fine not exceeding five pounds, and may be removed by any constable or officer authorised in manner provided by the byelaw from the area, whether land or water, to which the byelaw applies, and taken into custody without warrant, and brought before a court of summary jurisdiction to be dealt with according to law, and any vehicle, animal, vessel, or thing found in the area in contravention of any byelaw, may be removed by any constable or such officer as aforesaid, and on due proof of such contravention, be declared by a court of summary jurisdiction to be forfeited to Her Majesty.

(3.) A byelaw under this Act shall be deemed to be a regulation within the meaning of the Documentary Evidence Act, 1868, and may be proved accordingly.

31 & 32 Vict. c. 37.

Byelaws in case of leased land.

18.—(1.) Where land has been leased under Part One of this Act, a byelaw made in respect of that land shall not be inconsistent with any condition contained in the instrument of lease.

(2.) Where land has been leased under Part One of this Act subject to a condition that byelaws relating to the land shall be made with the consent of the lessor, or shall be made by the lessor subject to the approval of the Secretary of State, that condition shall be observed, and the lessor, acting with the approval of the Secretary of State, shall have the same power of making byelaws in relation to the land as is conferred by this Act on the Secretary of State.

PART III.

Supplemental.

Application of Act to yeomanry corps.

19. This Act shall apply in the case of a yeomanry corps as if it were a volunteer corps; and all land acquired by a yeomanry corps shall vest in the commanding officer of the corps for the time bein and his successors in office with power for him to sue and make contracts and conveyances and to do all other lawful acts relating thereto.

Sect. 19.

Power to have compensation settled by arbitration.

20. Where any land is acquired under this Act or for military purposes under any Act with which the Lands Clauses Acts are incorporated, the person or authority acquiring the land may require that the compensation to be paid for the land be settled by arbitration and not by reference to a jury, and thereupon the provisions of the Lands Clauses Acts with reference to arbitration shall, if not already applicable, apply for the purpose of settling the compensation.

21. * * * * * (*o*)

Saving for acquisition of land under other Acts.

22. All powers given by this Act shall be in addition to any other power to acquire land for military purposes conferred by any Act passed before this Act, and nothing contained in this Act shall prejudicially affect the powers vested in the Secretary of State for War under the Defence Acts and the Acts incorporated therewith.

Interpretation.

23. In this Act the expression "military purposes" includes rifle or artillery practice, the building and enlarging of barracks and camps, the erection of butts, targets, batteries, and other accommodation, the storing of arms, military drill, and any other purpose connected with military matters approved by the Secretary of State.

In this Act and the enactments incorporated therewith the expression "land" includes any easement in or over lands, and for the purpose or Part One of this Act includes any right of firing over lands or other right of user.

24—27. * * * * (*p*).

Repeal.

28. The Acts mentioned in the schedule to this Act are hereby repealed to the extent specified in the third column of that schedule: Provided that land acquired in any manner under any enactment repealed by this Act shall be deemed to have been acquired in a similar manner under this Act, and any byelaws made under any enactment so repealed shall be deemed to have been made under this Act.

Short title.

29. This Act may be cited as the Military Lands Act, 1892.

(*o*) This section enables the Secretary of State to erect alignment marks upon the coast, compensation being payable to the owners of lands injuriously affected.

(*p*) Section 24 contains a saving for the New Forest. Sections 25, 26, 27, relate to the application of the Act to Scotland, Ireland, and the Isle of Man respectively.

Schedule.

SCHEDULE.

ENACTMENTS REPEALED.

Session and Chapter.	Title or Short Title.	Extent of Repeal.
22 Vict. c. 12.	The Defence Act, 1859	Section one.
26 & 27 Vict. c. 65.	The Volunteer Act, 1863	Sections thirty-one to forty inclusive.
34 & 35 Vict. c. 86.	The Regulation of the Forces Act, 1871.	Section seventeen.
48 & 49 Vict. c. 36.	The Artillery and Rifle Ranges Act, 1885.	The whole Act, except section three.
49 & 50 Vict. c. 5.	The Drill Grounds Act, 1886	The whole Act.
53 & 54 Vict. c. 25.	The Barracks Act, 1890	Sections two and three.
54 & 55 Vict. c. 54.	The Ranges Act, 1891	The whole Act, except section eleven so far as that section relates to the acquisition of land under the Defence Act, 1842, and the Acts amending the same.

CORONERS ACT, 1892.

(55 & 56 VICT. CAP. 56.).

An Act to amend the Law in relation to the Appointment of Coroners and Deputy Coroners in Counties and Boroughs.

[28th June 1892.]

* * * * *

Appointment and powers of a deputy coroner of both a county and a borough.

1.—(1.) Every coroner, whether for a county or a borough, shall appoint, by writing under his hand, a fit person approved by the chairman or mayor, as the case may be, of the council who appointed the coroner (*q*), not being an alderman or councillor of such council, to be his deputy, and may revoke such appointment, but such revocation shall not take effect until the appointment of another deputy has been approved as aforesaid.

(2.) A duplicate of every appointment shall be sent to the said council and be kept among the records of the county or borough, as the case may be.

(3.) A deputy may act for the coroner during his illness or during his absence for any lawful or reasonable cause, or at any inquest which the coroner is disqualified for holding, but not otherwise. In the case of a borough coroner the necessity of his so acting shall be certified on each occasion by a justice of the peace, and such certificate shall state the cause of absence of the coroner, be openly read to every inquest jury summoned by the deputy coroner, and be conclusive evidence of the jurisdiction of the deputy to act.

(*q*) The expression "council who appointed the coroner," is explained by sub-s (7), *post.* Where the appointment has been made by or on the recommendation of a joint committee, it seems that the approval of the chairman (or mayor) of one of the councils represented on the committee is sufficient.

(4.) The deputy of a coroner shall, notwithstanding the coroner vacates his office by death or otherwise, continue in office until a new deputy is appointed, and shall act as the coroner while the office is so vacant in like manner as during the illness of the coroner, and one certificate may extend to the period of the vacancy, and he shall be entitled to receive in respect of the period of the vacancy the like remuneration as the vacating coroner. **Sect. 1 (4).**

(5.) For the purpose of an inquest or act which a deputy of a coroner is authorised to hold or do, he shall be deemed to be that coroner, and have the same jurisdiction and powers and be subject to the same obligations, liabilities, and disqualifications as that coroner, and he shall generally be subject to the provisions of the Coroners Act, 1887, and to the law relating to coroners in like manner as that coroner. 50 & 51 Vict. c. 71.

(6.) A council may postpone the appointment of a coroner to fill a vacancy, either generally or in any particular case, for a period not exceeding three months from the date at which that vacancy occurs.

(7.) For the purposes of this section the council who appointed a coroner shall—

(a) where the coroner was, in pursuance of any section of the Local Government Act, 1888, appointed by or on the recommendation of a joint committee, be deemed to be any of the councils who appointed any members of that committee; and 51 & 52 Vict. c. 41.

(b) where a coroner for a district of a county is, in pursuance of subsection four of section thirty-four of the Local Government Act, 1888, appointed by the council of any county borough, be deemed to be that council (*r*).

(8.) In the case of a county coroner who has been elected before the date on which the provisions of the Local Government Act, 1888, as to the appointment of coroners came into force, the council of any county or county borough, in which the district of the coroner is wholly or partially situated, shall for the purposes of this section be deemed to be the council who appointed the coroner.

2. The Acts specified in the schedule to this Act are hereby repealed to the extent in the third column of that schedule mentioned. **Repeal.**

(*r*) As to the appointment of coroners by county councils, and where the coroner's district extends into more administrative counties than one, by joint committees of county councils, see Local Government Act, 1888, s. 5, *ante*, p. 15. Under s. 34 (4) of the same Act, *ante*, p. 75, the council of a county borough appoints a county coroner where district is wholly situate within the county borough; where it is situate partly within and partly without the borough the county (not the borough) council appoints, but is bound to appoint the person recommended by a joint committee of the county and borough councils if there is such a committee for the purpose of considering who is to be elected. And see, as to coroners in Yorkshire, the Yorkshire Coroners Act, 1897, *post*.

Sect. 3.

Construction of Act and short title.

3. This Act shall be construed as one with the Coroners Act, 1887, and this Act and that Act may be cited together as the Coroners Acts, 1887 and 1892, and this Act may be cited separately as the Coroners Act, 1892.

SCHEDULE.

Session and Chapter.	Short Title.	Extent of Repeal.
45 & 46 Vict. c. 50. -	The Municipal Corporations Act, 1882.	Section one hundred and seventy-two.
50 & 51 Vict. c. 71. -	The Coroners Act, 1887 -	Section thirteen, and in section thirty-three the words "and the appointment of a deputy by "such coroner."

SHOP HOURS ACT, 1892.

(55 & 56 VICT. CAP. 62) (*s*).

An Act to amend the law relating to the Employment of Young Persons in Shops. [28th June 1892.]

WHEREAS the health of many young persons employed in shops and warehouses is seriously injured by reason of the length of the period of employment:

* * * * *

Short title.

1. This Act may be cited as the Shop Hours Act, 1892.

Commencement of Act.

2. This Act shall come into operation on the first day of September one thousand eight hundred and ninety-two.

Hours of employment in shops.

3.—(1.) No young person (*t*) shall be employed in or about a shop (*u*) for a longer period than seventy-four hours, including meal times, in any one week.

41 & 42 Vict. c. 16.

(2.) No young person shall, to the knowledge of his employer, be employed in or about a shop, having been previously on the same day employed in any factory or workshop, as defined by the Factory and Workshop Act, 1878, for the number of hours permitted by the said Act or for a longer period than will together with the time

---

(*s*) This Act is amended by 56 & 57 Vict. c. 67, and 58 Vict. c. 5, *post.* A county council is empowered by s. 8, *post*, to appoint inspectors for carrying the Act into execution.

(*t*) See the definition in s. 9, *post.*

(*u*) See the definition of "shop," *post*, s. 9. Where a newsagent occupying a shop for the purposes of his business employed a boy where work was done partly inside the shop and partly in fetching newspapers and delivering them to customers, it was held that the whole employment was "in or about the shop" within the meaning of this section. *Collman* v. *Roberts*, [1896] 1 Q. B. 457; 65 L. J. M. C. 63; 74 L. T. (N.S.) 198; 44 W. R. 445; 60 J. P. 184; 12 T. L. R. 202; 18 Cox C. C. 273.

during which he has been so previously employed complete such number of hours (*x*). Sect. 3.

Notice of hours to be given.

4. In every shop in which a young person is employed a notice shall be kept exhibited by the employer in a conspicuous place referring to the provisions of this Act, and stating the number of hours in the week during which a young person may lawfully be employed in that shop (*y*).

Fine for employing persons contrary to the Act.

5. Where any young person is employed in or about a shop contrary to the provisions of this Act, the employer shall be liable to a fine not exceeding one pound for each person so employed (*z*).

Power of occupier to exempt himself from fine on conviction of actual offender.

6. Where the employer of any young person is charged with an offence against this Act, he shall be entitled upon information duly laid by him to have any other person whom he charges as the actual offender brought before the court at the time appointed for hearing the charge; and if, after the commission of the offence has been proved, the said employer proves to the satisfaction of the court that he has used due diligence to enforce the execution of the Act, and that the said other person has committed the offence in question without his knowledge, consent, or connivance, the said other person shall be summarily convicted of such offence, and the occupier shall be exempt from any fine.

Summary proceedings.

7. All offences under this Act shall be prosecuted, and all fines under this Act shall be recovered in like manner as offences and fines are prosecuted and recovered under the Factory and Workshop Act, 1878, and sections eighty-eight, eighty-nine, ninety, and ninety-one of the said Act, and so much of section ninety-two thereof as relates to evidence respecting the age of any person (*a*) . . . shall have effect as if re-enacted in this Act and in terms made applicable thereto.

Appointment of inspectors.

8. The council of any county or borough, and in the city of London the common council, may appoint such inspectors as they may think necessary for the execution of this Act within the areas of their

---

(*x*) The definitions of "factory" and "workshop" are contained in s. 93 of the Act of 1878. As to the permitted hours of employment, see ss. 10—21 of the same Act.

(*y*) An employer who neglects to exhibit in his shop the notice required by this section does not thereby render himself liable to penalties under s. 5. *Hammond* v. *Pulsford*, [1895] 1 Q. B. 223 ; 64 L. J. M. C. 63 ; 71 L. T. (N.S.) 767 ; 43 W. R. 236 ; 59 J. P. 533. But a penalty is now imposed by the Shop Hours Act, 1895, *post*.

(*z*) This fine is recoverable summarily. See s. 7, *post*. As to the fine for not exhibiting the notice required by s. 4, see the Shop Hours Act, 1895, *post*.

(*a*) These sections were for the most part repealed by the Summary Jurisdiction Act, 1884, before this Act was passed. A question may therefore arise whether the procedure under this Act is regulated by these sections, regarded as unrepealed and incorporated, or by the Summary Jurisdiction Act, 1884. Words are here omitted relating to Scotland and Ireland only.

Sect. 8.

respective jurisdictions, and sections sixty-eight and seventy (*b*) of the Factory and Workshop Act, 1878, shall apply in the case of any such inspector as if he were appointed under that Act, and as if the expression workshop as used in those sections included any shop within the meaning of this Act (*c*).

* * * *

Interpretation.

9. In this Act, unless the context otherwise requires—

"Shop" means retail and wholesale shops, markets, stalls, and warehouses in which assistants are employed for hire, and includes licensed public-houses and refreshment houses of any kind :

"Young person" means a person under the age of eighteen years:

Other words and expressions have the same meanings respectively as in the Factory and Workshop Act, 1878.

41 & 42 Vict. c. 16.

Exemption of members of the same family, and servants.

10. Nothing in this Act shall apply to a shop where the only persons employed are members of the same family, dwelling in the building of which the shop forms part, or to which the shop is attached, or to members of the employer's family so dwelling, or to any person wholly employed as a domestic servant.

POLICE ACT, 1893.

(56 VICT. CAP. 10) (*d*).

An Act to amend the Police Acts. [9th June 1893.]

* * * * *

Constables employed on fire duty to be deemed to be engaged on police duty.

1. Where a constable belonging to any police force, in pursuance of any general or special direction of the police authority, acts as a fireman or assists in the extinguishment of fire, or in protecting life or property from fire, such constable shall be deemed for the purposes of the Police Act, 1890, to be in the execution of his duty.

2. *Borough police may be employed as fire brigade.* 10 *&* 11 *Vict. c.* 89 (*e*).

(*b*) Section 68 of the Act of 1878 gives to the inspectors wide powers as to entering buildings and the like. Section 70 relates to certificates of the appointment of inspectors. The form of certificate to be furnished to an inspector on his appointment is prescribed by Order of the Secretary of State, dated April 21st, 1893 (St. R. & O. p. 470).

(*c*) The remainder of this section relates only to Ireland. As to payment of salaries and expenses out of the county or borough fund, see 56 & 57 Vict. c. 67, *post*.

(*d*) This Act amends the Police Act, 1890, *ante*, p. 488, in several particulars as to police pensions. The sections which relate exclusively to borough police are omitted. Section 5 enables the police pension fund to be invested in the debentures or mortgages of a county council.

(*e*) Section 2 relates to the employment of borough police as firemen.

3.—(1.) Where a pension is in pursuance of the Police Act, 1890, granted to a constable on the scale applicable to partial disability for earning a livelihood, the police authority may, within three years from the grant of the pension, if satisfied by the evidence of some legally qualified medical practitioner or practitioners selected by the police authority that the disability attributable to the injury received in the execution of duty has become total, increase the pension to the amount allowed by the provisions of the scale applicable to total disability (*f*). **Sect. 3 (1).** Power to increase pension.

(2.) This section shall apply in the case of all pensions granted since the commencement of the Police Act, 1890.

4. The provisions of subsection two of section thirteen of the Police Act, 1890, shall apply to any constable in receipt of a pension who is appointed to any office remunerated out of any parochial, district, or other rate (*g*). Amendment of 53 & 54 Vict. c. 45, s. 13 (2).

5. A police authority, in addition to the powers of investment conferred by section eighteen of the Police Act, 1890, may invest the capital of the pension fund in debentures or mortgages issued or made by a county council in pursuance of the powers conferred by section sixty-nine subsection eight of the Local Government Act, 1888 (*h*). Extension of powers of investment of pension fund.

6. In Schedule I. (11) (c) of the Police Act, 1890, for the words ("where a constable has, in the course of the three years next before the date of his retirement or death, been in more than one rank") shall be substituted the words ("where a constable at the date of his retirement or death holds a rank to which he has been promoted within the three years previous") (*i*). Amendment of Schedule I. 53 & 54 Vict. c. 45.

7. This Act shall be read as one with the Police Act, 1890, and nothing in this Act shall interfere with or diminish the powers of the Secretary of State under section seventeen of that Act (*k*). Construction of Act and saving.

(*f*) As to the scales applicable to partial disability, see the Police Act, 1890, and Part II. of the First Schedule to that Act, *ante*, pp. 488, 510.

(*g*) The effect of this section read with s. 13 (2) of the Act of 1890, *ante*, p. 495, is that a constable in receipt of a pension who is appointed to an office remunerated out of moneys provided by Parliament or out of a county or borough rate or fund, or out of a parochial, district, or other rate, he is not to receive more of his pension than, together with the remuneration of that office, is equal to one-and-a-half times the remuneration of the office in respect of which the pension was awarded.

(*h*) See s. 18 of the Act of 1890, *ante*, p. 499, and Local Government Act, 1888, s. 69 (8), *ante*, p. 134.

(*i*) See this schedule, *ante*, p. 512, Rule (11) relates to the method of estimating pensions, gratuities, and allowances.

(*k*) See s. 17 of the Act of 1890, *ante*, p. 498, as to the granting or withholding of the certificate of the Secretary of State as to the satisfactoriness of the management and efficiency of a police force and the administration of the pension fund.

Sect. 8.

8. * * * * * (*l*).

Short title.

9. This Act may be cited as the Police Act, 1893; and the Police Acts, 1839 to 1890, and this Act may be cited together as the Police Acts, 1839 to 1893.

WEIGHTS AND MEASURES ACT, 1893.

(56 & 57 VICT. CAP. 19) (*m*).

An Act to amend the Law relating to Weights and Measures.

[29th June 1893.]

* * * * *

Relief of certain boroughs from contribution to county expenses.
41 & 42 Vict. c. 49.
52 & 53 Vict. c. 21.
55 & 56 Vict. c. 18.

1. Where the mayor, aldermen, and burgesses of a borough, not being a county borough, and not having a separate court of quarter sessions, were, on the first day of January one thousand eight hundred and ninety-three, the legally constituted local authority for the purposes of the Weights and Measures Acts, 1878 to 1892, or for the execution of the law relating to weights and measures under any local Act, they shall be paid by the county council of the county in which the borough is situate, once in every year, the proportionate amount contributed towards the expenses incurred by the county council in the execution of those Acts by the several parishes and parts of parishes within the borough, such proportion being calculated according to the values stated in the basis for county rates in force for the time being. Provided that when the amount received by a county council from the execution of those Acts is in excess of the expenditure thereupon, a proportionate part of such excess amount shall be deducted from any sum due to such borough as a recoupment under the Contagious Diseases (Animals) Acts, or the Sale of Food and Drugs Acts respectively (*n*).

Short title and construction.

2. This Act may be cited as the Weights and Measures Act, 1893, and shall be read as one with the Weights and Measures Acts, 1878 to 1892 (*o*.)

Commencement.

3. This Act shall come into operation on the first day of April, one thousand eight hundred and ninety-four.

(*l*) Section 8 contains an amendment of s. 14 of the Towns Police Clauses Act, 1847, and empowers the Secretary of State to make provisional orders for the amendment of the provisions of local Acts as to fire brigades and fire police.

(*m*) This Act applies to a borough with a population exceeding 10,000, but having no separate quarter sessions, where the council of the borough were the local authority for purposes of weights and measures by reason of their having resolved to be such authority, or by reason of their having before 1878 possessed separate standards. It will be observed that neither s. 35 nor s. 39 of the Local Government Act, 1888, applied to such boroughs so far as regarded the Weights and Measures Acts.

(*n*) The sum here referred to is that which is payable by the county to the borough under the Diseases of Animals Act, 1894 (57 & 58 Vict. c. 57), s. 41, *post*, and under the Sale of Food and Drugs Act, 1879 (42 & 43 Vict. c. 30), s. 9.

(*o*) See also the Weights and Measures (Metric Systems) Act, 1897, *post*.

BARBED WIRE ACT, 1893.

(56 & 57 Vict. Cap. 32) (*p*).

An Act to prevent the use of Barbed Wire for Fences in Roads, Streets, Lanes and other Thoroughfares (*q*). [27th July 1893.]

* * * * *

1. This Act may be cited for all purposes as the Barbed Wire Act, 1893. Short title.

2. In this Act—

The expression "barbed wire" means any wire with spikes or jagged projections; and the expression "nuisance to a Interpretation.

(*p*) This Act concerns county councils in their capacity as highway authorities in respect of main roads. See Local Government Act, 1888, s. 11, *ante*, p. 21. The following cases are in point with reference to the subject matter of this Act, though they were decided before its passing.

A landowner erected upon his own land by the side of a public road in Scotland a fence of barbed wire, and the road trustees brought an action to have it removed on the ground that it was dangerous to persons and cattle lawfully using the road. The fence was placed about three feet from the boundary line between the road and the landowner's property, and stood entirely upon his land. *Held*, that the action lay, but, upon the defendant undertaking so to alter and protect the fence as to remove the danger, the action was dismissed. *Elgin Road Trustees* v. *Innes*, 14 Ct. Sess. Cas. (4th ser.) 48. The occupier of certain land adjoining a public footpath fenced it off from the footpath by barbed wire set back nine feet from the path. *Held*, that he was liable in damages to a man who tore his clothes on the barbs whilst making way for other persons to pass him on the footpath. *Bird* v. *Frost*, 56 J. P. 164. Plaintiff and defendant were adjoining landowners, and defendant was bound to maintain a boundary fence between their lands for their mutual benefit. Defendant caused a gap in the fence to be made up with barbed wire, which was placed three feet within his own boundary. Plaintiff afterwards put a mare into his field, and she injured herself on the wire. *Held*, that the wire was so placed as to be dangerous to cattle lawfully put by the plaintiff into his field, and that defendant was liable in damages for the injury to the mare. *Bennett* v. *Blackmore*, 26 L. J. 228; 90 L. T. 395. Defendants erected a fence of barbed wire between their railway line and plaintiff's farm. Sheep grazing on plaintiff's farm were injured by coming in contact with the wire. *Held*, that the defendants were liable for the damage occasioned to the sheep. *M'Quillan* v. *Crommelin Iron Ore Co.* 26 Ir. L. T. Rep. 15. Lands belonging to plaintiff and defendant, who were adjoining owners, were separated by an old quickset fence. This hedge defendant dug up and replaced by a new one of young quicks, which he protected by a barbed wire fence of a very severe character, set up with plaintiff's acquiescence on plaintiff's land. Plaintiff then turned out a mare to graze on his land, and she was injured. *Held*, that defendant was liable. *Shipton* v. *Lucas*, 92 L. T. 297. Defendant put up a barbed wire fence separating his land from a public footpath, and plaintiff was walking along the footpath when a sudden gust of wind blew his coat against the fence, and it was torn. No negligence or want of skill or care in the erection of the fence was imputed to the defendant, but the county court judge held that the fence as constructed and placed was dangerous to the public using the footpath and a nuisance. This decision was affirmed on appeal to the High Court. *Stewart* v. *Wright*, 57 J. P. 137; affirmed 9 T. L. R. 480.

A valuable collection and review of the American cases on the subject will be found in 95 L. T. 419.

(*q*) This title must not be taken to limit the meaning of the term "highway" as used in the Act. A *cul-de-sac* may be a highway. *Bateman* v. *Bluck*, 18 Q. B. 870; 21 L. J. Q. B. 406; 17 Jur. 386.

Sect. 2.

highway," as applied to barbed wire, means barbed wire which may probably be injurious to persons or animals lawfully using such highway:

In England and Wales the expression "local authority" means any county council, any urban sanitary authority, any sanitary authority in London, any highway board, and any other local authorities existing, or that may be hereafter created by Parliament, having control over highways (*r*).

* * * * *

Removal of barbed wire where nuisance to highway.

3.—(1.) Where there is on any land adjoining a highway within the county or district of a local authority a fence made with barbed wire, or in or on which barbed wire has been placed, and such barbed wire is a nuisance to such highway, it shall be lawful for such local authority to serve notice in writing upon the occupier of such land requiring him within a time therein stated (not to be less than one month nor more than six months after the date of the notice) to abate such nuisance.

(2.) If on the expiration of the time stated in the notice the occupier shall have failed to comply therewith, it shall be lawful for the local authority to apply to a court of summary jurisdiction (*s*), and such court, if satisfied that the said barbed wire is a nuisance to such highway, may by summary order (*t*) direct the occupier to abate such nuisance; and on his failure to comply with such order within a reasonable time the local authority may do whatever may be necessary in execution of the order, and recover in a summary manner the expenses incurred in connexion therewith (*u*).

* * * * *

Proceedings where local authority is occupier of the land.

4. Where the local authority are the occupiers of the land, proceedings under this Act may be taken by any ratepayer within the district of the local authority, and a notice to the local anthority to abate the nuisance shall be deemed to be properly served if it is served upon the clerk of the local authority, and any ratepayer taking proceedings may do all acts and things which a local authority is empowered to do.

Expenses of local authority.

5. Any expenses incurred by a local authority in the execution of this Act shall be defrayed in like manner as the expenses of the local authority incurred in respect of any highways (*x*).

(*r*) The remainder of this section only applies to Scotland and Ireland. Highway boards are now in most cases superseded by rural district councils under s. 25 of the Local Government Act, 1894, *post*, p. 621.

(*s*) As defined by s. 13 (11) of the Interpretation Act, 1889 (52 & 53 Vict. c. 63).

(*t*) Without appeal, except by case stated under s. 33 of the Summary Jurisdiction Act, 1879.

(*u*) The next sub-section relates only to Ireland.

(*x*) In the case of a county council, these expenses will be charged to the general county account. See Local Government Act, 1888, ss. 11 (1), 68, *ante*, pp. 21, 130.

FERTILISERS AND FEEDING STUFFS ACT, 1893.

(56 & 57 VICT. CAP. 56) (y).

An Act to amend the Law with respect to the sale of Agricultural Fertilisers and Feeding Stuffs. [22nd September 1893.]

* * * * *

1.—(1.) Every person who sells for use as a fertiliser of the soil any article manufactured in the United Kingdom or imported from abroad shall give to the purchaser an invoice stating the name of the article and whether it is an artificially compounded article or not, and what is at least the percentage of the nitrogen, soluble and insoluble phosphates, and potash, if any, contained in the article, and this invoice shall have effect as a warranty by the seller of the statements contained therein. Warranty on sale of fertiliser.

(2.) For the purposes of this section an article shall be deemed to be manufactured if it has been subjected to any artificial process.

(3.) This section shall not apply to a sale where the whole amount sold at the same time weighs less than half a hundredweight.

2.—(1.) Every person who sells for use as food for cattle any article which has been artificially prepared shall give to the purchaser an invoice stating the name of the article and whether it has been prepared from one substance or seed, or from more than one substance or seed, and this invoice shall have effect as a warranty by the seller of the statements contained therein. Warranty on sale of feeding stuff.

(2.) Where any article sold for use as food for cattle is sold under a name or description implying that it is prepared from any particular substance, or from any two or more particular substances, or is the product of any particular seed, or of any two or more particular seeds, and without any indication that it is mixed or compounded with any other substance or seed, there shall be implied a warranty by the seller that it is pure, that is to say, is prepared from that substance or those substances only, or is a product of that seed or those seeds only.

(3.) On the sale of any article for use as food for cattle there shall be implied a warranty by the seller that the article is suitable for feeding purposes.

(4.) Any statement by the seller of the percentages of nutritive and other ingredients contained in any article sold for use as food for cattle, made after the commencement of this Act in an invoice of such article or in any circular or advertisement descriptive of such article, shall have effect as a warranty by the seller.

(y) This Act requires every county council to appoint or join with other councils (county or borough) in appointing a district agricultural analyst for the purpose of analysing fertilizers of the soil and feeding stuffs for cattle on the request of a purchaser. The Act creates offences in connection with the adulteration of these articles and enables county councils to institute prosecutions for such offences.

Sect. 3 (1).

Penalties for breach of duty by seller.

3.—(1.) If any person who sells any article for use as a fertiliser of the soil or as food for cattle commits any of the following offences, namely:—

(a.) Fails without reasonable excuse to give, on or before or as soon as possible after the delivery of the article, the invoice required by this Act; or

(b.) Causes or permits any invoice or description of the article sold by him to be false in any material particular to the prejudice of the purchaser; or

(c.) Sells for use as food for cattle any article which contains any ingredient deleterious to cattle, or to which has been added any ingredient worthless for feeding purposes and not disclosed at the time of the sale,

he shall, without prejudice to any civil liability, be liable, on summary conviction, for a first offence to a fine not exceeding twenty pounds and for any subsequent offence to a fine not exceeding fifty pounds.

(2.) In any proceeding for an offence under this section it shall be no defence to allege that the buyer, having bought only for analysis, was not prejudiced by the sale.

(3.) A person alleged to have committed an offence under this section in respect of an article sold by him shall be entitled to the same rights and remedies, civil or criminal, against the person from whom he bought the article as are available to the person who bought the article from him, and any damages recovered by him may, if the circumstances justify it, include the amount of any fine and costs paid by him on conviction under this section, and the costs of and incidental to his defence on such conviction.

Power to appoint analysts.

4.—(1.) The Board of Agriculture shall appoint a chief agricultural analyst (hereafter referred to as the chief analyst), who shall have such remuneration out of moneys provided by Parliament as the Treasury may assign. The chief analyst shall not while holding his office engage in private practice.

(2.) Every county council shall, and the council of any county borough may, appoint or concur with another council or other councils in appointing for the purposes of this Act a district agricultural analyst (hereafter referred to as a district analyst) for its county or borough, or a district comprising the counties or boroughs of the councils so concurring. The remuneration of any such district analyst shall be provided by the council, or in the case of a joint appointment by the respective councils in such proportions as they may agree, and shall be paid, in the case of a county, as general expenses (*z*), and, in the case of a county borough, out of the borough fund or borough rate. The appointment shall be subject to the approval of the Board of Agriculture. Provided that

(*z*) These expenses will be paid out of the county fund. See Local Government Act, 1888, s. 68, *ante*, p. 130.

no person shall while holding the office of district analyst engage in any trade, manufacture, or business connected with the sale or importation of articles used for fertilising the soil or as food for cattle.

Sect. 4 (2).

Power for purchaser to have fertiliser or feeding stuff analysed.

5.—(1.) Every buyer of any article used for fertilising the soil or as food for cattle shall, on payment to a district analyst of a fee sanctioned by the body who appointed the analyst, be entitled, within ten days after delivery of the article to the buyer or receipt of the invoice by the buyer, whichever is later, to have the article analysed by the analyst, and to receive from him a certificate of the result of his analysis.

(2.) Where a buyer of an article desires to have the article analysed in pursuance of this section, he shall, in accordance with regulations made by the Board of Agriculture (*a*), take three samples of the article, and shall in accordance with the said regulations cause each sample to be marked, sealed, and fastened up, and shall deliver or send by post one sample with the invoice or a copy thereof to the district analyst, and shall give another sample to the seller, and shall retain the third sample for future comparison: Provided that a district analyst, or some person authorised by him in that behalf with the approval of the body who appointed the analyst, shall, on request either by the buyer or by the seller, and on payment of a fee sanctioned by the said body, take the samples on behalf of the buyer.

(3.) The certificate of the district analyst shall be in such form and contain such particulars as the Board of Agriculture direct (*b*), and every district analyst shall report to the Board as they direct the result of any analysis made by him in pursuance of this Act.

(4.) If the seller or the buyer objects to the certificate of the district analyst, one of the samples selected, or another sample selected in like manner, may, at the request of the seller, or, as the case may be, the buyer, be submitted with the invoice or a copy thereof to the chief analyst, and the seller, or, as the case may be, the buyer, shall, on payment of a fee sanctioned by the Treasury, be entitled to have the sample analysed by the chief analyst, and to receive from him a certificate of the result of his analysis.

(5.) At the hearing of any civil or criminal proceeding with respect to any article analysed in pursuance of this section, the production of a certificate of the district analyst, or if a sample has been submitted to the chief analyst, then of the chief analyst, shall be sufficient evidence of the facts therein stated, unless the defendant or person charged requires that the analyst be called as a witness.

(*a*) Regulations under this clause were issued by the Board of Agriculture and bear date December 23rd, 1893. They are published in the Statutory Rules and Orders, 1893, p. 295.

(*b*) The form of this certificate was prescribed by an Order of the Board, December 20th, 1893. See Statutory Rules and Orders, 1893, p. 299.

Sect. 5 (6).

(6.) The costs of and incidental to the obtaining of any analysis in pursuance of this section shall be borne by the seller or the buyer in accordance with the results of the analysis, and shall be recoverable as a simple contract debt.

Penalty for tampering.

6. If any person knowingly and fraudulently—

(a) tampers with any parcel of fertiliser or feeding stuff so as to procure that any sample of it taken in pursuance of this Act does not correctly represent the contents of the parcel; or

(b) tampers with any sample taken under this Act;

he shall be liable on summary conviction to a fine not exceeding twenty pounds, or to imprisonment for a term not exceeding six months.

Prosecutions and appeals.

7.—(1.) A prosecution for an offence under this Act may be instituted either by the person aggrieved, or by the council of a county or borough, or by any body or association authorised in that behalf by the Board of Agriculture, but in the case of an offence under section three shall not be instituted by the person aggrieved or by any body or association (*b*) except on a certificate by the Board of Agriculture that there is reasonable ground for the prosecution.

(2.) Any person aggrieved by a summary conviction under this Act may appeal to a court of quarter sessions.

Construction and application.

8.—(1.) For the purposes of this Act the expression "cattle" shall mean bulls, cows, oxen, heifers, calves, sheep, goats, swine, and horses; and the expressions "soluble" and "insoluble" shall respectively mean soluble and insoluble in water.

(2.) This Act shall apply to wholesale as well as retail sales.

9. * * **10.** * * * (*c*).

Commencement of Act.

11. This Act shall come into operation on the first day of January, one thousand eight hundred and ninety-four.

Short title.

12. This Act may be cited as the Fertilisers and Feeding Stuffs Act, 1893.

(*b*) "Body or association" must be taken to mean a body or association authorized by the Board of Agriculture, and not to include a county (or borough) council; these councils may, it appears, institute a prosecution under s. 3 without a certificate from the Board.

(*c*) Sections 9 and 10 relate only to Scotland and Ireland respectively.

PUBLIC AUTHORITIES PROTECTION ACT, 1893.

(56 & 57 Vict. Cap. 61) (*d*).

An Act to generalize and amend certain statutory provisions for the protection of persons acting in the execution of statutory and other public duties. [5th December 1893.]

* * * *

1. Where after the commencement of this Act (*e*) any action, prosecution, or other proceeding (*f*) is commenced in the United Kingdom against any person for any act done in pursuance, or execution, or intended execution of any Act of Parliament (*g*), or of

Protection of persons acting in execution of statutory or other public duty.

(*d*) This Act repeals various enactments relating to proceedings against public authorities and their officers in respect of the performance of their duties. It abolishes notice of action in every case, but it limits the time within which proceedings may be instituted. It will, of course, apply to proceedings against county councils and their officers.

(*e*) Viz., January 1st, 1894; see s. 4, *infra*.

(*f*) It has been held that this Act, unlike the repealed s. 264 of the Public Health Act, 1875, applies to proceedings taken for an injunction to restrain the committing of a nuisance; *Harrop* v. *Ossett* (*Mayor, etc. of*), 1898, 1 Ch. 525; 14 T. L. R. 308. It appears, therefore, that such decisions as *Att.-Gen.* v. *Hackney Local Board*, L. R. 20 Eq. 626; 44 L. J. Ch. 545; 33 L. T. (N.S.) 244; *Flower* v. *Low Leyton Local Board*, 5 Ch. D. 347; 46 L. J. Ch. 621; 36 L. T. (N.S.) 760; 25 W. R. 545; 41 J. P. 548; *Sellors* v. *Matlock Local Board*, 14 Q. B. D. 928; 52 L. T. (N.S.) 782; *Bateman* v. *Poplar District Board of Works*, 33 Ch. D. 360; 55 L. T. (N.S.) 374; *Chapman* v. *Auckland Union* (*Guardians of*), 23 Q. B. D. 294; 58 L. J. Q. B. 504; 61 L. T. (N.S.) 446; 53 J. P. 820; *Pryce* v. *Hole*, 6 T. L. R. 195; *Whitfield* v. *Newquay Local Board*, *Law Times*, March 18th, 1882, p. 349, will not be in point as to the proceedings to which this Act relates. The repealed s. 264 was also held to be inapplicable to an action for the recovery of land: *Foat* v. *Margate* (*Mayor of*), 11 Q. B. D. 299; 47 J. P. 535; *S.C. Holder* v. *Margate* (*Mayor of*), 52 L. J. Q. B. 711; and to an action brought by a contractor against a local board for a breach of contract: *Davies* v. *Swansea* (*Corporation of*), 8 Ex. 808; 22 L. J. Ex. 297; 17 J. P. 649; but this Act may be of wider application. The section was held to apply to an action for money had and received for the recovery from a local board of sums paid by mistake for paving expenses: *Midland Rail. Co.* v. *Withington Local Board*, 11 Q. B. D. 788; 52 L. J. Q. B. 689; 49 L. T. (N.S.) 489; 47 J. P. 789; and to proceedings against a member of a local board for penalties: *Lea* v. *Facey*, 17 Q. B. D. 139; 55 L. J. M. C. 149; 55 L. T. (N.S.) 300; 51 J. P. 20; affirmed C. A., 19 Q. B. D. 352; 56 L. J. Q. D. 536; 35 W. R. 721; 51 J. P. 756.

(*g*) Questions have often arisen as to whether an act complained of was in fact done, or intended to be done, under an Act of Parliament, and so protected by enactments similar to that of the text. See the cases collected in the notes to this section in Lumley's Public Health. *Per* Kelly, C.B., in *Wilson* v. *Halifax* (*Mayor of*), L. R. 3 Ex. 117; 37 L. J. Ex. 44; 17 L. T. (N.S.) 660; 16 W. R. 707; 32 J. P. 230; "It is now settled by authority that an omission to do something that ought to be done in order to the complete performance of a duty imposed upon a public body under an Act of Parliament, or the continuing to leave any such duty unperformed, amounts to an act done or intended be done within the meaning of those clauses requiring notice of action for the protection of public bodies acting in the discharge of public duties under Acts of Parliament." And in *Selmes* v. *Judge*, L. R. 6 Q. B. 724; 40 L. J. Q. B. 287; 24 L. T. (N.S.) 904; 19 W. R. 1110; 35 J. P. 645. Blackburn, J., dealing with a question of notice of action under s. 109 of the Highways Act, 1835 (5 & 6 Will. 4, c. 50), said: "It has long been decided that such a provision is intended to protect persons from the consequences of committing illegal acts which are intended to be done

Sect. 1.

any public duty or authority, or in respect of any alleged neglect or default in the execution of any such Act, duty, or authority, the following provisions shall have effect:

(a.) The action, prosecution, or proceeding shall not lie or be instituted unless it is commenced within six months next after the act, neglect, or default complained of, or, in case of a continuance of injury or damage, within six months next after the ceasing thereof (*h*):

---

under the authority of an Act of Parliament, but which by some mistake are not justified in its terms, and cannot be defended by its provisions."

To an action for slander the defendant pleaded that the words were spoken while he was acting as clerk of the markets, in pursuance of the Acts relating to municipal corporations in Ireland, which statutes entitled him to a month's notice of action for any act done in pursuance of them. The plea was held good on demurrer, for the words spoken while acting in pursuance of the statutes were as much within their protection as acts done. *Murray* v. *McSwinney*, Ir. Rep. 9 C. L. 545. See, however, *Royal Aquarium, etc. Society* v. *Parkinson*, L. R. [1892] 1 Q. B. 431; 61 L. J. Q. B. 409; 66 L. T. (N.S.) 513; 40 W. R. 450; 56 J. P. 404, in which a defamatory statement made by a county councillor in the course of proceedings at a meeting for granting music and dancing licences, was held not to be an act done by him in the execution of his duty, so as to make notice of action necessary under 11 & 12 Vict. c. 44, s. 9.

(*h*) In the *Midland Rail. Co.* v. *Withington Local Board*, 11 Q. B. D. 788; 52 L. J. Q. B. 689; 49 L. T. (N.S.) 489; 47 J. P. 789, an action to recover money paid for paving expenses under s. 150 of the Public Health Act, 1875, under the mistaken belief of both parties that the street was not repairable by the inhabitants, it appeared that the money was paid on October 30th, 1880, so that the six months would expire on April 30th, 1881. On April 13th, the plaintiff's secretary wrote to the defendants for information as to the result of certain proceedings which were to determine whether the road was a highway or not, and stating that if the board were defeated they would expect a return of the money. The defendants replied that they were going to appeal, and would inform the plaintiffs of the result. The action was brought in March, 1882, after a month's notice had been given. It was held that the facts did not disclose a waiver by the defendants of the benefit of the similar provision as to a six months period contained in s. 264 of the Public Health Act, 1875.

As to the computation of the six months, see *Freeman* v. *Read*, 4 B. & S. 174; 32 L. 7. M. C. 226; 8 L. T. (N.S.) 458; 11 W. R. 802; 10 Jur. (N.S.) 149; *Radcliffe* v. *Bartholomew*, [1892] 1 Q. B. 161; 61 L. J. M. C. 63; 65 L. T. (N.S.) 677; 40 W. R. 63; 56 J. P. 262; 8 T. L. R. 43. Where the cause of action is the doing of the act itself, the limitation of time runs from the act; where it is the resulting damage, it runs from the time when the damage results, and where the injurious act is continuing and causes continuous damage, the right of action also continues. See *Whitehouse* v. *Fellowes*, 10 C. B. (N.S.) 765; 30 L. J. C. P. 305; *Bonomi* v. *Backhouse*, E. B. & E. 622; 28 L. J. Q. B. 378: 34 L. J. Q. B. 181.

Where an excavation made by a local authority under a street for the purpose of laying a sewer was not properly filled in, and in consequence a subsidence of the plaintiff's land with injury to houses thereon took place, which began at a period more than six months before and went on continuously down to the commencement of an action by the plaintiff in respect of such subsidence, it was held, on the authority of *Darley Main Colliery Co.* v. *Mitchell*, 11 App. Cas. 127, that the further subsidence, which took place within the six months before action, constituted a distinct cause of action in respect of which the action was maintainable, notwithstanding the provisions of s. 264 of the Act of 1875. *Crumbie* v. *Wallsend Local Board*, L. R. [1891] 1 Q. B. 503; 60 L. J. Q. B. 392; 64 L. T. (N.S.) 490; 55 J. P. 421; 7 T. L. R.

(b.) Wherever in any such action a judgment is obtained by the defendant, it shall carry costs to be taxed as between solicitor and client: **Sect. 1.**

(c.) Where the proceeding is an action for damages, tender of amends before the action was commenced may, in lieu of or in addition to any other plea, be pleaded (*i*). If the action was commenced after the tender, or is proceeded with after payment into court of any money in satisfaction of the plaintiff's claim, and the plaintiff does not recover more than the sum tendered or paid, he shall not recover any costs incurred after the tender or payment, and the defendant shall be entitled to costs, to be taxed as between solicitor and client, as from the time of the tender or payment; but this provision shall not affect costs on any injunction in the action:

(d.) If, in the opinion of the court, the plaintiff has not given the defendant a sufficient opportunity of tendering amends before the commencement of the proceeding the court may award to the defendant costs to be taxed as between solicitor and client.

This section shall not affect any proceedings by any department of the Government against any local authority or officer of a local authority.

2. There shall be repealed as to the United Kingdom so much of any public general Act as enacts that in any proceeding to which this Act applies— Repeal.

(a) the proceeding is to be commenced in any particular place; or

(b) the proceeding is to be commenced within any particular time; or

(c) notice of action is to be given; or

(d) the defendant is to be entitled to any particular kind or amount of costs, or the plaintiff is to be deprived of costs in any specified event; or

(e) the defendant may plead the general issue;

and in particular there shall be so repealed the enactments specified in the schedule to this Act to the extent in that schedule mentioned.

---

229. And see, to the same effect, *Fairbrother* v. *Bury Rural Sanitary Authority*, 37 W. R. 544.

In an action for compensation awarded in respect of damage occasioned by the exercise of powers under the Metropolis Management Acts, it was held to be no defence that the action was commenced more than six months after the damage was sustained, as s. 106 of the Metropolis Management Act, 1862 (which is similar to the text) did not apply to such a claim, and still less to an action on an award made upon such claim. *Delaney* v. *Metropolitan Board of Works*, L. R. 2 C. P. 532; affirmed 3 C. P. 111; 37 L. J. C. P. 59; 17 L. T. (N.S.) 262; 16 W. R. 137; 31 J. P. 788.

(*i*) This seems to imply that the Act applies to proceedings other than actions for damages. It is probable, therefore, that it has a wider application than s. 264 of the Public Health Act, 1875; and see *Harrop* v. *Ossett* (*Mayor, etc. of*), *ante*, p. 581.

Sect. 2.

This repeal shall not affect any proceeding pending at the commencement of this Act (*k*).

3. * * * * * (*l*).

Commencement.

4. This Act shall come into operation on the first day of January one thousand eight hundred and ninety-four.

Short title.

5. This Act may be cited as the Public Authorities Protection Act, 1893.

SCHEDULE (*k*).

SHOP HOURS ACT, 1893.

(56 & 57 VICT. CAP. 67) (*n*).

An Act to amend the Shop Hours Act, 1892.

[21st December 1893.]

* * * * *

Short titles.

1. This Act may be cited as the Shop Hours Act, 1893, and this Act and the Shop Hours Act, 1892, may be cited together as the Shop Hours Acts, 1892 and 1893.

Salaries and expenses.

2.—(1.) Any salaries payable or other expenses incurred by the council of a county or a borough for the purposes of the Shop Hours Act, 1892, shall be defrayed by the council of a county out of the county fund, and by the council of a borough out of the borough fund or borough rate.

* * * * * (*o*).

3. * * * * * (*o*).

ISOLATION HOSPITALS ACT, 1893.

(56 & 57 VICT. CAP. 68) (*p*).

An Act for enabling County Councils to promote the establishment of Hospitals for the reception of Patients suffering from Infectious Diseases. [21st December 1893.]

* * * * *

Short title.

1. This Act may be cited for all purposes as the Isolation Hospitals Act, 1893.

(*k*) The schedule contains a long list of repealed enactments which are not material to the subject of the present work.

(*l*) Section 3 contains a saving as to Scotland only.

(*n*) This Act amends the Shop Hours Act, 1892 (*ante*, p. 570), by providing for the payment of salaries and expenses under that Act, in the case of a county, out of the county fund. The original Act is further amended by 58 Vict. c. 5, *post*.

(*o*) Sub-section (2) of this section applies to Ireland only. Section 3 applies to Scotland only.

(*p*) By s. 131 of the Public Health Act, 1875, both urban and rural district councils have power to provide hospitals for the use of the inhabitants of their districts. This Act enables a county council, upon the application of

Sect. 2.

Limits of Act.

2. This Act shall not extend to Scotland or Ireland, or to the administrative county of London, or to any county borough, or without the consent of the council of the borough to any borough containing, according to the census for the time being in force, a population of ten thousand persons or upwards, or to any borough containing a less population without the like consent, unless the Local Government Board by order direct that the Act shall apply to such borough.

County council to provide for establishment of isolation hospitals on application, &c.

3. The council of every county may, on such application being made to them, and proof adduced, as is in this Act mentioned, provide or cause to be provided in any district within their county a hospital for the reception of patients suffering from infectious diseases (in this Act referred to as "an isolation hospital") (*q*).

Application by whom to be made.

4.—(1.) An application to a county council for the establishment of an isolation hospital may be made by any one or more of the authorities, by this Act defined as local authorities (*r*), having jurisdiction in the county, or any part of the county; and any such application may be made in pursuance of a resolution passed at a meeting of such authority by a majority of the members assembled thereat, and voting in manner in which votes are required by law to be given at a meeting of the authority. Any such meeting shall be called together by notice given in manner in which notices of the meetings of the authority concerned are required to be given by law, and specifying the object of the meeting to be the making an application to the county council under this Act.

(2.) An application for the establishment of an isolation hospital may also be made by any number of ratepayers not less than twenty-five, in any contributory place as defined by this Act (*s*).

Application, how made.

5.—(1.) The application shall be made by petition, and shall state the district for which the isolation hospital is required, and the reasons which the petitioners adduce for its establishment.

---

a local authority (as defined by s. 26), to provide an isolation hospital for any district within their county for persons suffering from infectious diseases. The district for which such a hospital may be provided under this Act is to be fixed by the county council subject to the right of objection under ss. 8 and 20 by the local authority having jurisdiction in the proposed district to the formation or subsequent variation of that district.

(*q*) It will be observed that hospitals to be provided under this Act are for infectious cases only. Infectious diseases within the meaning of the Act are defined by s. 26, *post*.

This section does not, of course, empower a county council to create a nuisance by the establishment of an isolation hospital. See the cases collected under s. 131 of the Public Health Act, 1875, in Lumley's Public Health.

It may be observed that though the text purports to enable a county council to provide a hospital, the Act does not contain provisions for their doing so except through a hospital committee.

(*r*) These are urban and rural district councils and parish councils. See s. 26, *post*. They do not, however, include boroughs, save to the extent mentioned in s. 2, *ante*.

(*s*) For definition of a contributory place, see s. 26, *post*.

Sect. 5 (2).

(2.) The county council shall, by themselves, or by a committee of their body appointed for that purpose, consider the petition, and, if satisfied by the statements of the petition as originally prepared, or by any amendments made therein, that a primâ facie case is made out for a local inquiry, they shall cause such inquiry to be made as to the necessity for the establishment of an isolation hospital.

Effect of report of medical officer of county.

6. The county council may direct an inquiry to be made by the medical officer of health of the county as to the necessity of an isolation hospital being established for the use of the inhabitants of any particular district in the county, and in the event of such medical officer reporting that such an hospital ought to be established for the use of the inhabitants of a district, may take the same proceedings in all respects for the establishment of such hospital as if a petition had been presented by a local authority for the establishment of an isolation hospital for the district named in the report of such medical officer of health (*t*).

Conduct of local inquiry.

7. The county council shall conduct the local inquiry into the necessity for the establishment of an isolation hospital, and as to the proper site for the hospital, and the district for which it is to be established (in this Act called the "hospital district"), by a committee consisting of such number of their members, either with or without the addition of such other persons, or in such other manner as the council think expedient. All expenses properly incurred by any such committee shall be paid as herein-after directed. The local inquiry shall be held subject to such regulations and otherwise as the council thinks fit. Due notice of the time and place at which any inquiry is to be held by the county council shall be given in such manner as the county council may think the best adapted to inform any persons interested (*u*), and such persons may attend and state their case before the members appointed to conduct such inquiry.

Variation of district and appeal.

8.—(1.) Every hospital district constituted under this Act shall consist of a single local area, or two or more local areas, as defined by this Act (*x*).

(2.) The county council may vary any proposed hospital district by adding to it or subtracting from it any local area (*y*). A local area which is already provided with such isolation hospital accommodation as may in the opinion of the county council be sufficient for the reasonable exigencies of such area, shall not, without the assent of

(*t*) This section provides an alternative method for putting the county council in motion. The inquiry by the county medical officer of health does not, however, dispense with the local inquiry directed to be held under th preceding section.

(*u*) These would apparently include the local authorities for the proposed district and the owners of the land proposed to be taken for the site of the hospital, and, probably, also the adjoining owners.

(*x*) For definition of local area, see s. 26, *post*.

(*y*) Compare s. 20, *post*, as to the alteration of an order for the constitution of a hospital district.

the local authority of such area testified by a resolution of such authority, be included in a hospital district under this Act. Sect. 8 (2).

(3.) If any local authority having jurisdiction within any part of the proposed hospital district, object to the formation of such a district, or to the addition or subtraction thereto or therefrom of any local area within their jurisdiction, such authority may at any time within three months from the date of the order appeal to the Local Government Board (*z*), and the decision of such Board shall be conclusive.

Order as to dismissal of petition or constitution of district.

9. On conclusion of a local inquiry by the county council as to the necessity for the establishment of an isolation hospital, the county council shall make an order (*a*), either dismissing the petition, or constituting a hospital district (*b*), and directing an isolation hospital for such district to be established: Provided that the county council shall not take steps for the constitution of a hospital district for one or more contributory places forming a portion of a rural sanitary district within the jurisdiction of the county council, or for one local area, unless the sanitary (*c*) authority of such place or places, or area, assent to the application, or are proved to the satisfaction of the county council to be unable or unwilling to make suitable hospital accommodation for such place, places, or area.

Hospital committee.

10.—(1.) When a hospital district has been constituted, a committee shall be formed by the county council. Any such committee may consist wholly of members of the county council, or partly of members of the county council and partly of representatives of the local area or areas in the district, or wholly of such local representatives. The county council shall make regulations for the election, rotation, and qualification, and for all other matters relating to the constitution of any such committee, subject to these qualifications, that where no contribution is made by the county council to the funds of the hospital (*d*), such committee shall consist, unless the constituent local authorities otherwise desire, wholly of representatives of the local area or local areas of the district, and that if any local authority within the hospital district feels aggrieved by the mode in which any such committee is constituted, it may appeal to the Local Government Board (*e*), and that Board may modify the constitution of any committee so formed by the county council in such manner as the Board think expedient and just.

(2.) A hospital committee shall have all such powers of acquiring land as are herein-after mentioned (*f*), also all such other powers of

---

(*z*) As to appeals to the Local Government Board, see s. 24, *post*.

(*a*) For power to vary the order subsequently, see s. 20.

(*b*) Power to vary the district is given by s. 8, *supra*. As to payment of expenses where the hospital district consists of more than one local area, see s. 18, *post*.

(*c*) *Sic, quære*, "local authority."

(*d*) Power to make such contribution is given by s. 21, *post*.

(*e*) As to appeals to the Local Government Board, see s. 24, *post*.

(*f*) See s. 11, *post*.

Sect. 10 (2). providing a hospital by purchase or otherwise, and managing and maintaining the same when so provided, as the county council may delegate to them: Provided that the county council shall retain to themselves the power of inspecting any such hospital, and of raising money by loan for the purposes of such hospital (*g*).

(3.) A hospital committee shall be a body corporate, having a perpetual succession and a common seal, under such name and style as may be conferred on it by the county council. It shall be capable of acquiring land, by devise, gift, purchase or otherwise, without licence in mortmain.

(4.) Where a hospital district is an area wholly or as to the greater part thereof under the jurisdiction of any corporate local authority (*h*), the county council may, if they think fit, invest such local authority with all the powers of a hospital committee under this Act, and thereupon such authority shall be deemed to be the hospital committee for such district, and shall exercise all the powers of such committee under its original corporate name.

Purchase of land for hospital.

11. Subject to any directions given by the county council, a hospital committee may purchase or lease any land, whether within or without the hospital district, for the purpose of erecting thereon an isolation hospital, and may exercise all the powers conferred on a sanitary authority by the provisions of the Public Health Act, 1875, and the Acts amending the same, relating to the purchase of lands. For the purposes of this section the provisions contained in sections one hundred and seventy-five to one hundred and seventy-eight (inclusive), and sections two hundred and ninety-six to two hundred and ninety-eight (inclusive), of the Public Health Act, 1875, shall, so far as consistent herewith, be incorporated with this Act (*i*).

38 & 39 Vict. c. 55.

Management of hospital, and regulations.

12. A hospital committee may from time to time, make all necessary rules and regulations for the conduct and management of their hospital and the patients therein.

Ambulances to be provided.

13. Every isolation hospital shall be provided with an ambulance or ambulances for the purpose of conveying patients to the hospital, and shall, so far as practicable, be in connexion with the system of telegraphs.

Additional hospital accommodation.

14. A hospital committee may, in expectation of or in the event of an outbreak of any infectious disease (*k*), provide any accommodation

(*g*) Power to raise money by loan is given by s. 22, *post*.

(*h*) This will include urban and rural district councils and parish councils.

(*i*) Sections 175—178 of the Public Health Act, 1875 (see *ante*, p. 126), relate to the purchase of lands by sanitary authorities, and to the sale and letting thereof, and include power to apply to the Local Government Board to make provisional orders putting in force the compulsory clauses of the Lands Clauses Acts, and provisions as to the sale of lands of the Duchy of Lancaster. Sections 296—298 relate to inquiries and provisional orders of the Local Government Board. These sections are set out, *ante*, p. 164.

(*k*) For definition of infectious disease, see s. 26, *post*.

in addition to their existing accommodation, by hiring or otherwise acquiring, any buildings, tents, wooden houses, or other places for the reception of patients. A hospital committee may, in addition to, or instead of, providing a central hospital, establish within their district hospitals in cottages or small buildings, or otherwise as they may think expedient. A hospital committee may also, before they have established a permanent hospital or hospitals, provide for their district such temporary accommodation as is in this section mentioned. **Sect. 14.**

15. Subject to any regulations made by the county council, a hospital committee may make arrangements for the training of nurses for attendance on patients suffering from any infectious disease, either inside or outside the hospital, and may charge for the attendance of such nurses outside the hospital; and the expenses of any such nurses, after deducting any profits derived from their services, shall be establishment expenses of the hospital, within the meaning of this Act (*l*). Training of nurses.

16.—(1.) There shall be charged with respect to every person admitted into the hospital such sum as the hospital committee may think sufficient to defray the expenses in this Act defined as patients' expenses (*m*) incurred in respect of such person; and there shall be added thereto, in the case of persons brought from beyond the hospital district, such sum as the committee may think fit, as a contribution to the structural and establishment expenses (*m*). Charges for patients.

(2.) Persons desirous of being provided with accommodation of an exceptional character may be so provided on their undertaking, to the satisfaction of the committee, to pay for the same a sum fixed by the committee, and also to pay for all other expenses incurred in respect of their maintenance in the hospital, and all expenses so incurred in respect of such a patient are in this Act referred to as "special patients' expenses."

17.—(1.) The expenses to be incurred in respect of any isolation hospital under this Act shall be classified as structural expenses, establishment expenses, and patients' expenses. Classification of expenses.

"Structural expenses" shall include the original cost of providing the hospital, including the purchase (if any) of the site, and the furnishing such hospital with the necessary appliances and furniture required for the purpose of receiving patients; also any permanent extension or enlargement of the hospital, or any alteration or repair of the drainage, and any structural repairs; but shall not include ordinary repairs, painting, cleaning, or the renewal or keeping in order of the appliances and furniture, or the supply of new appliances or furniture.

"Establishment expenses" means the cost of keeping the hospital, its appliances and furniture, in a state requisite for the comfort of

---

(*l*) See as to the different classes of expenses, s. 17, *post*.

(*m*) See s. 17, *post*.

Sect. 17 (1). the patients, also the salaries of the doctors, nurses, servants, and all other expenses for maintaining the hospital in a fit state for the reception of patients.

"Patients' expenses" means the cost of conveying, removing, feeding, providing medicines, disinfecting, and all other things required for patients individually, exclusive of structural and establishment expenses (*n*).

(2.) All expenses incurred by a county council in and about the formation of a hospital district, including the costs of any inquiries, and the expenses of obtaining land and other preliminary expenses, shall be deemed to be structural expenses.

(3.) In the case of any doubt arising as to what are structural expenses, establishment expenses, or patients' expenses within the meaning of this Act, the decision of the hospital committee shall be conclusive.

Payment of expenses.

18. All expenses incurred by a county council or by a hospital committee under this Act, with the exception of patients' expenses, and special patients' expenses, shall, when a hospital district consists of a single local area, be defrayed out of the local rate of that area (*o*). Where the hospital district consists of more than one local area, all the expenses, save as aforesaid, incurred by the hospital committee shall be paid out of a common fund to which all receipts shall be carried, and to which the local authorities (*p*) in the hospital district shall contribute in such proportions as the county council by their order constituting the district (*q*) may determine.

38 & 39 Vict. c. 55.

Section two hundred and eighty-four of the Public Health Act, 1875 (*r*), shall apply to the sums to be contributed by the local authorities under this section as if the same were sums to be contributed by component districts and the hospital committee were a joint board under that Act.

Recovery of patients' expenses.

19.—(1.) Patients' expenses (*s*), in respect of any person who at the time of his reception into the hospital, or at any time within fourteen days previously, is or has been in receipt of poor law relief, shall be a debt due to the hospital committee from the guardians of the union from which he is sent, and shall be recoverable from them in a summary manner (*t*) or otherwise (*u*).

(*n*) As to expenses of burial, see s. 19 (4), *post.*

(*o*) For definitions of local area and local rate, see s. 26, *post.* As to contributions out of the county rate, see s. 21, *post.*

(*p*) Defined in s. 26, *post.*

(*q*) See s. 9, *ante.*

(*r*) The section referred to provides for the issue by the joint board of precepts to the local authorities for the amount of their contributions, and contains provisions for enforcing payment.

(*s*) Defined in s. 17, *supra.*

(*t*) By the civil debt procedure under 42 & 43 Vict. c. 49, ss. 6 and 35.

(*u*) *E.g.*, in the county court. This section removes a difficulty as to the recovery of the expenses of paupers which is not provided for in cases under s. 132 of the Public Health Act, 1875.

(2.) Patients' expenses, in respect of a non-pauper patient, shall be a debt due to the hospital committee, and recoverable in a summary manner from the local authority of the local area from which the patient is sent, and shall be paid out of the local rate *(x)*. Sect. 19 (2).

(3.) Where a patient has been brought from a place beyond the hospital district, any additional charges made by the hospital committee in respect of such patient shall be recoverable as if they were part of the patients' expenses.

(4.) Special patients' expenses *(y)* shall be a debt recoverable in a summary manner from the patient, or from the estate of the patient, in respect of whom the expenses have been incurred.

(5.) The expenses of the burial of any patient dying in the hospital shall be payable in the same manner in which the expenses of his maintenance are payable.

Power of county council to alter order.

20. A county council may, on the application of a hospital committee, and with the assent of any local authority concerned in such alteration, alter any order made by them for the establishment of a hospital *(z)*.

Power of county councils to contribute to hospitals.

21. A county council may, where they deem it expedient so to do for the benefit of the county, contribute out of the county rate a capital or annual sum towards the structural and the establishment expenses of an isolation hospital, or to either class of such expenses *(a)*.

Power to borrow money.

22. A county council may borrow on the security of the county rate, and in manner provided by the Local Government Act, 1888 *(b)*, any money required for the purpose of carrying into effect the provisions of this Act; and any loans so borrowed, and any other money expended by them for the purposes of this Act, together with interest thereon at the rate of four pounds per centum per annum, shall be repaid to the county council out of the local rate, as in this Act directed; and, in the case of a loan, shall be repaid within a period not exceeding that within which the loan is repayable by the county council.

Treatment in hospital not to disqualify.

23. A person shall not by reason of his being admitted into and maintained in an hospital established in pursuance of this Act suffer any disqualification or any loss of franchise or other right or privilege *(c)*.

Inquiries by Local Government Board.

24. Sub-sections one and five of section eighty-seven of the Local Government Act, 1888 *(d)*, shall apply in every case where the

(x) For definitions of local area, local authority, and local rate, see s. 26, *post*. The civil debt procedure will be applicable.

(y) See s. 16 (2), *ante*.

(z) Power to vary the district is given by s. 8 (2), *ante*, p. 586.

(a) As to what are structural and establishment expenses, see s. 17, *ante*. By s. 18 these fall primarily on the local rate.

(b) See s. 69 of that Act, *ante*, p. 132.

(c) An extension of the Medical Relief Disqualification Removal Act, 1885, 48 & 49 Vict. c. 46.

(d) See *ante*, p. 163.

Sect. 25. Local Government Board are authorised to determine any question on appeal to them.

Audit of accounts. **25.** The provisions of sections two hundred and forty-five, two hundred and forty-seven, two hundred and forty-nine, and two hundred and fifty of the Public Health Act, 1875, as amended by the District Auditors Act, 1879, shall apply to the accounts of any hospital committee, and of any officers or assistants of such committee, and to the audit of such accounts, as if such committee were an urban authority other than the council of a borough (*e*).

Definitions. **26.** A "local area" means in this Act any one of the following localities, that is to say, an urban sanitary district, a rural sanitary district, or any contributory place, or where a local area is included in more than one county, the part of the area included in each county (*f*).

38 & 39 Vict. c. 55. A "contributory place" has the same meaning in this Act as in section two hundred and twenty-nine of the Public Health Act, 1875 (*g*).

A "local authority" means in this Act, as respects an urban sanitary district, the urban sanitary authority; as respects a rural sanitary district, the rural sanitary authority, and in the case of any contributory place being a parish, the vestry or other authority in which the powers of the vestry may be vested by any Act of Parliament (*h*), and in the case of any other contributory place situated within the district of a rural sanitary authority, such rural sanitary authority.

The "local rate" means, as respects an urban or rural sanitary district or contributory place, the rate out of which expenses incurred in the execution of the Acts relating to public health are directed to be paid, and in the case of any contributory place the expenses incurred in the execution of this Act shall be deemed to be special expenses (*i*).

52 & 53 Vict. c. 72. The expression "infectious diseases" in this Act has the same meaning as in the Infectious Diseases (Notification) Act, 1889 (*k*), and the provisions of this Act shall apply to the infectious diseases specifically mentioned in that Act, and may be applied to any other infectious disease, by order of the county council, or any committee to whom they have delegated their powers under this section, in like manner as if such council or committee were a local authority acting under that Act (*l*).

(*e*) See the sections referred to, and notes in Lumley's Public Health.

(*f*) Since the Local Government Act, 1894, came into operation, local areas have for the most part been adjusted so that the whole of each area is within the same county.

(*g*) "Contributory place" is defined by the section referred to; the expression includes a rural parish and a special drainage district within a rural district.

(*h*) The powers of the vestry were vested in the parish council by the Local Government Act, 1894, s. 6, *post*.

(*i*) See ss. 207 and 229 of the Public Health Act, 1875.

(*k*) See the enumeration of infectious diseases in s. 6 of that Act.

(*l*) See s. 7 of that Act.

LOCAL GOVERNMENT ACT, 1894.

(56 & 57 VICT. CAP. 73 (*m*).)

An Act to make further provision for Local Government in England and Wales. [5th March 1894.]

* * * * *

PART I.

PARISH MEETINGS AND PARISH COUNCILS.

Constitution of Parish Meetings and Parish Councils.

Constitution of parish meetings and establishment of parish councils.

1.—(1.) There shall be a parish meeting for every rural parish, and there shall be a parish council for every rural parish which has a population of three hundred or upwards; Provided that an order of the county council in pursuance of Part III. of this Act—

(a) shall, if the parish meeting of a rural parish having a population of one hundred or upwards so resolve, provide for establishing a parish council in the parish, and may, with the consent of the parish meeting of any rural parish having a population of less than one hundred, provide for establishing a parish council in the parish; and

(b) may provide for grouping a parish with some neighbouring parish or parishes under a common parish council, but with a separate parish meeting for every parish so grouped, so, however, that no parish shall be grouped without the consent of the parish meeting for that parish (*n*).

(2.) For the purposes of this Act every parish in a rural sanitary district shall be a rural parish.

(3.) Where a parish is at the passing of this Act situate partly within and partly without a rural sanitary district, the part of the parish which is within the district, and the part which is without, shall, as from the appointed day, but subject to any alteration of area made by or in pursuance of this or any other

(*m*) This Act imposes numerous duties upon county councils. Amongst the more important are those relating to the alteration of areas and boundaries under Part III., the making of orders for the compulsory acquisition of land by parish councils (ss. 9, 10), the hearing of and acting upon complaints of defaults by district councils in the performance of their duties (ss. 16, 26), the establishment and dissolution of parish councils, and the grouping of parishes under a common parish council (s. 1 and Part III.) The Act has been fully annotated by the present editors in a separate work. The importance of the Act to county councils is so great that it has been thought impossible to omit it from the present work; but it is proposed only to call attention to some of the points which more particularly affect county councils, and to refer the reader for fuller information to the separate work already alluded to.

(*n*) Further provisions as to orders for establishing parish councils and grouping parishes are contained in ss. 38—40, *post*.

Sect. 1 (3).

Act (*n*), be separate parishes, in like manner as if they had been constituted separate parishes under the Divided Parishes and Poor Law Amendment Act, 1876, and the Acts amending the same (*o*).

39 & 40 Vict. c. 61.

Parish meetings.

2.—(1.) The parish meeting for a rural parish shall consist of the following persons, in this Act referred to as parochial electors, and no others, namely, the persons registered in such portion either of the local government register of electors or of the parliamentary register of electors as relates to the parish.

(2.) Each parochial elector may, at any parish meeting, or at any poll consequent thereon, give one vote and no more on any question, or, in the case of an election, for each of any number of persons not exceeding the number to be elected.

(3.) The parish meeting shall assemble at least once in every year, and the proceedings of every parish meeting shall begin not earlier than six o'clock in the evening.

(4.) Subject to the provisions of this Act as to any particular person being the chairman of a parish meeting, the meeting may choose their own chairman.

(5.) A poll consequent on a parish meeting shall be taken by ballot.

(6.) The reasonable expenses of and incidental to the holding of a parish meeting or the taking of a poll consequent thereon shall be defrayed as hereinafter provided.

(7.) With respect to parish meetings the provisions in the First Schedule to this Act shall have effect.

Constitution of parish council.

3. (*p*)—(1.) The parish council for a rural parish shall be elected from among the parochial electors of that parish or persons who have during the whole of the twelve months preceding the election resided in the parish, or within three miles thereof, and shall consist of a chairman and councillors, and the number of councillors shall be such as may be fixed from time to time by the county council, not being less than five nor more than fifteen.

(2.) No person shall be disqualified by sex or marriage for being elected or being a member of a parish council.

(*n*) The area of the parish might have been altered before this section took effect, by an order of the county council under s. 36, *post*, or s. 57 of the Local Government Act, 1888, *ante*, p. 111. See also the similar provision as to parishes situate in more than one urban district, s. 36 (2), *post*.

(*o*) The effect of a division of a parish under this section is to abolish all poor law settlements previously acquired in the old parish: *Dorking Union (Guardians of)* v. *St. Saviour's Union (Guardians of)*, 14 T. L. R. 213.

(*p*) The duties of a county council under this section (of fixing the number of parish councillors and naming a parish where necessary) were for the most part performed before the Act came into operation. But the number of councillors may be altered from time to time, and the provisions of this section must be borne in mind in framing an order for the establishment of a new parish council.

(3.) The term of office of a parish councillor shall be one year. Sect. 3 (3).

(4.) On the fifteenth day of April in each year (in this Act referred to as the ordinary day of coming into office of councillors) the parish councillors shall go out of office, and their places shall be filled by the newly elected councillors.

(5.) The parish councillors shall be elected by the parochial electors of the parish.

(6.) The election of parish councillors shall, subject to the provisions of this Act, be conducted according to rules framed under this Act for that purpose by the Local Government Board.

(7.) The parish council shall in every year, on or within seven days after the ordinary day of coming into office of councillors, hold an annual meeting.

(8.) At the annual meeting, the parish council shall elect, from their own body or from other persons qualified to be councillors of the parish, a chairman, who shall, unless he resigns, or ceases to be qualified, or becomes disqualified, continue in office until his successor is elected.

(9.) Every parish council shall be a body corporate by the name of the parish council, with the addition of the name of the parish, or if there is any doubt as to the latter name, of such name as the county council after consultation with the parish meeting of the parish direct, and shall have perpetual succession, and may hold land for the purposes of their powers and duties without licence in mortmain; and any act of the council may be signified by an instrument executed at a meeting of the council, and under the hands, or, if an instrument under seal is required, under the hands and seals, of the chairman presiding at the meeting and two other members of the council.

(10.) With respect to meetings of parish councils the provisions in the First Schedule to this Act shall have effect.

Use of schoolroom.

4.—(1.) (*q*). In any rural parish in which there is no suitable public room vested in the parish council or in the chairman of a parish meeting and the overseers which can be used free of charge for the purposes in this section mentioned, the parochial electors and the parish council shall be entitled to use, free of charge, at all reasonable times, and after reasonable notice, for the purpose of—

(a) the parish meeting or any meeting of the parish council; or

---

(*q*) Under clause (b) of this sub-section the rooms referred to may be used for local inquiries by the county council. It will be noticed, however, that the right to use the rooms is given to "the parochial electors and the parish council," and it is conceived that a resolution of the parish meeting or council will be necessary before the use of the rooms can be claimed. See the circular of the Education Department of November 30th, 1894, set out in the appendix to the editors' work on this Act.

Sect. 4 (1).

(b) any inquiry for parochial purposes by the Local Government Board or any other Government department or local authority ; or

(c) holding meetings convened by the chairman of the parish meeting or by the parish council, or if as to allotments in the manner prescribed by the Allotments Act, 1890, or otherwise as the Local Government Board may by rule prescribe, to discuss any question relating to allotments, under the Allotments Acts, 1887 and 1890, or under this Act ; or

53 & 54 Vict. c. 65.

(d) the candidature of any person for the district council or the parish council ; or

(e) any committee or officer appointed, either by the parish meeting or council or by a county or district council, to administer public funds within or for the purposes of the parish

any suitable room in the schoolhouse of any public elementary school receiving a grant out of moneys provided by Parliament, and any suitable room the expense of maintaining which is payable out of any local rate :

Provided that this enactment shall not authorise the use of any room used as part of a private dwelling-house, nor authorise any interference with the schoolhours of an elementary day or evening school, nor, in the case of a room used for the administration of justice or police, with the hours during which it is used for these purposes.

(2.) If, by reason of the use of the room for any of the said purposes, any expense is incurred by the persons having control over the room, or any damage is done to the room or to the building of which the room is part or its appurtenances, or the furniture of the room or the apparatus for instruction, the expense or damage shall be defrayed as part of the expenses of the parish meeting or parish council or inquiry as the case may be ; but when the meeting is called for the purpose of the candidature of any person, such expense or damage shall be reimbursed to the parish meeting or the parish council by the persons by whom or on whose behalf the meeting is convened.

(3.) If any question arises under this section as to what is reasonable or suitable, it may be determined, in the case of a schoolhouse, by the Education Department, in the case of a room used for the administration of justice or police, by a Secretary of State, and in any other case by the Local Government Board.

Powers and Duties of Parish Councils and Parish Meetings.

Parish council to appoint overseers.

5.—(1.) The power and duty of appointing overseers of the poor, and the power of appointing and revoking the appointment of an assistant overseer, for every rural parish having a parish council, shall be transferred to and vested in the parish council, and that council shall in each year, at their annual meeting, appoint the overseers of the parish, and shall as soon as may be fill any casual vacancy occurring in the office of overseer of the parish, and shall in either case forthwith give written notice thereof in the prescribed form to the board of guardians. Sect. 5 (1).

(2.) As from the appointed day—

(a) the churchwardens of every rural parish shall cease to be overseers, and an additional number of overseers may be appointed to replace the churchwardens, and

(b) references in any Act to the churchwardens and overseers shall, as respects any rural parish, except so far as those references relate to the affairs of the church, be construed as references to the overseers, and

(c) the legal interest in all property vested either in the overseers or in the churchwardens and overseers of a rural parish, other than property connected with the affairs of the church, or held for an ecclesiastical charity, shall, if there is a parish council, vest in that council, subject to all trusts and liabilities affecting the same, and all persons concerned shall make or concur in making such transfers, if any, as are requisite for giving effect to this enactment.

Transfer of certain powers of vestry and other authorities to parish council.

6.—(1.) Upon the parish council of a rural parish coming into office, there shall be transferred to that council :—

(a.) The powers, duties, and liabilities of the vestry of the parish (*r*) except—

(i.) so far as relates to the affairs of the church or to ecclesiastical charities ; and

(ii.) any power, duty, or liability transferred by this Act from the vestry to any other authority :

(b.) The powers, duties, and liabilities of the churchwardens of the parish, except so far as they relate to the affairs of the church or to charities, or are powers and duties of overseers, but inclusive of the obligations of the churchwardens with respect to maintaining and repairing closed churchyards wherever the expenses of such maintenance and repair are repayable out of the poor rate under the Burial Act, 1855: Provided that such obligations shall not in the case of any particular parish 18 & 19 Vict. c. 128.

(*r*) It does not follow from this provision that a parish council is liable to indictment for non-repair of a highway. *R.* v. *Shipley*, 13 T. L. R. 486 ; 61 J. P. 488 ; 18 Cox C. C. 531.

Sect. 6 (1).

be deemed to attach, unless or until the churchwardens subsequently to the passing of this Act shall give a certificate, as in the Burial Act, 1855, provided, in order to obtain the repayment of such expenses out of the poor rate.

(c.) The powers, duties, and liabilities of the overseers or of the churchwardens and overseers of the parish with respect to

(i.) appeals or objections by them in respect of the valuation list, or appeals in respect of the poor rate, or county rate, or the basis of the county rate (*rr*) ; and

(ii.) the provision of parish books and of a vestry room or parochial office, parish chest, fire engine, fire escape, or matters relating thereto ; and

(iii.) the holding or management of parish property, not being property relating to affairs of the church or held for an ecclesiastical charity, and the holding or management of village greens, or of allotments, whether for recreation grounds or for gardens or otherwise for the benefit of the inhabitants or any of them ;

(d.) The powers exercisable with the approval of the Local Government Board by the board of guardians for the poor law union comprising the parish in respect of the sale, exchange, or letting of any parish property.

(2.) A parish council shall have the same power of making any complaint or representation as to unhealthy dwellings or obstructive buildings as is conferred on inhabitant householders by the Housing of the Working Classes Act, 1890, but without prejudice to the powers of such householders (*s*).

53 & 54 Vict. c. 70.

(3.) A parish council shall have the same power of making a representation with respect to allotments, and of applying for the election of allotment managers, as is conferred on parliamentary electors by the Allotments Act, 1887, or the Allotments Act, 1890, but without prejudice to the powers of those electors (*t*).

50 & 51 Vict. c. 48.
53 & 54 Vict. c. 65.

(4.) Where any Act constitutes any persons wardens for allotments, or authorises or requires the appointment or election of any wardens committee or managers for the purpose of allotments, then, after a parish council for the parish interested in such allotments comes into office, the powers and duties of the wardens, committee,

---

(*rr*) As to the county rate, see note to s. 3 (i.) of the Local Government Act, 1888, *ante*, p. 5.

(*s*) A complaint or representation under this sub-section is made in the first instance to the district council or their medical officer. But under s. 45 of the Housing of the Working Classes Act, 1890, the matter of the complaint must be brought to the attention of the county council, who may exercise the powers of the district council in the event of that body failing to take proceedings in a proper case. See this section, *ante*, p. 522.

(*t*) See the Allotments Act, 1890, and notes, *ante*, p. 517.

or managers shall be exercised and performed by the parish council, and it shall not be necessary to make the said appointment or to hold the said election, and for the purpose of section sixteen of the Small Holdings Act, 1892, two members of the parish council shall be substituted for allotment managers or persons appointed as allotment managers (*u*).

Sect. 6 (4).

55 & 56 Vict. c. 31.

Transfer of powers under adoptive Acts.

7.—(1.) As from the appointed day, in every rural parish the parish meeting shall, exclusively, have the power of adopting any of the following Acts, inclusive of any Acts amending the same (all which Acts are in this Act referred to as "the adoptive Acts"); namely,—

(a.) The Lighting and Watching Act, 1833; 3 & 4 Will. 4, c. 90.

(b.) The Baths and Washhouses Acts, 1846 to 1882; 9 & 10 Vict. c. 74. 45 & 46 Vict. c. 30.

(c.) The Burial Acts, 1852 to 1885; 15 & 16 Vict. c. 85. 48 & 49 Vict. c. 21.

(d.) The Public Improvements Act, 1860; 23 & 24 Vict. c. 30.

(e.) The Public Libraries Act, 1892. 55 & 56 Vict. c. 53.

(2.) Where under any of the said Acts a particular majority is required for the adoption or abandonment of the Act, or for any matter under such Act, the like majority of the parish meeting or, if a poll is taken, of the parochial electors, shall be required, and where under any of the said Acts the opinion of the voters is to be ascertained by voting papers, the opinion of the parochial electors shall be ascertained by a poll taken in manner provided by this Act.

(3.) Where under any of the said Acts the consent or approval of, or other act on the part of, the vestry of a rural parish is required in relation to any expense or rate, the parish meeting shall be substituted for the vestry, and for this purpose the expression "vestry" shall include any meeting of ratepayers or voters.

(4.) Where there is power to adopt any of the adoptive Acts for a part only of a rural parish, the Act may be adopted by a parish meeting held for that part (*x*).

(5.) Where the area under any existing authority acting within a rural parish in the execution of any of the adoptive Acts is co-extensive with the parish, all powers, duties, and liabilities of that authority shall, on the parish council coming into office, be transferred to that council.

(6.) This Act shall not alter the incidence of charge of any rate levied to defray expenses incurred under any of the adoptive Acts,

---

(*u*) See s. 16 of the Small Holdings Act, 1892, *ante*, p. 555.

(*x*) The "part" of a parish to adopt the adoptive Act must, of course, be such a part as is entitled under the Act in question to adopt it. See, for instance, s. 73 of the Lighting and Watching Act, 1833; ss. 12 and 13 of the Burial Act, 1855; and s. 5 of the Burial Act, 1857. The provision in the text does not give any increased powers of adopting for a part.

Sect. 7 (6).

and any such rate shall be made and charged as heretofore, and any property applicable to the payment of such expenses shall continue to be so applicable (*y*).

(7.) When any of the adoptive Acts is adopted for the whole or part of a rural parish after the appointed day, and the parish has a parish council, the parish council shall be the authority for the execution of the Act.

(8.) For the purposes of this Act the passing of a resolution to provide a burial ground under the Burial Acts, 1852 to 1885, shall be deemed an adoption of those Acts.

Additional powers of parish council.

8.—(1.) (*z*) A parish council shall have the following additional powers, namely, power—

(a) to provide or acquire buildings for public offices and for meetings and for any purposes connected with parish business or with the powers or duties of the parish council or parish meeting ; and

(b) to provide or acquire land for such buildings and for a recreation ground and for public walks ; and

(c) to apply to the board of Agriculture under section nine of the Commons Act, 1876 ; and

39 & 40 Vict. c. 56.

(d) to exercise with respect to any recreation ground, village green, open space, or public walk, which is for the time being under their control, or to the expense of which they have contributed, such powers as may be exercised by an urban authority under section one hundred and sixty-four of the Public Health Act, 1875, or section forty-four of the Public Health Acts Amendment Act, 1890, in relation to recreation grounds or public walks, and sections one hundred and eighty-three to one hundred and eighty-six of the Public Health Act, 1875, shall apply accordingly as if the parish council were a local authority within the meaning of those sections ; and

38 & 39 Vict. c. 55.
53 & 54 Vict. c. 59.

(e) to utilise any well, spring, or stream within their parish and provide facilities for obtaining water therefrom, but so as not to interfere with the rights of any corporation or person ; and

(f) to deal with any pond, pool, open ditch, drain or place containing, or used for the collection of, any drainage, filth, stagnant water, or matter likely to be prejudicial to

(*y*) As to alteration of areas under Adoptive Acts, see ss. 53 and 69 of this Act, *post*, and s. 59 of the Local Government Act, 1888, *ante*, p. 114.

(*z*) The purposes for which a parish council may acquire land under this section must be borne in mind by a county council in considering any application for an order for putting the compulsory clauses of the Lands Clauses Acts into operation under s. 9, *post*.

health, by draining, cleansing, covering it, or otherwise preventing it from being prejudicial to health, but so as not to interfere with any private right or the sewage or drainage works of any local authority; and Sect. 8 (1).

(g) to acquire by agreement any right of way, whether within their parish or an adjoining parish, the acquisition of which is beneficial to the inhabitants of the parish or any part thereof; and

(h) To accept and hold any gifts of property, real or personal, for the benefit of the inhabitants of the parish or any part thereof; and

(i) to execute any works (including works of maintenance or improvement) incidental to or consequential on the exercise of any of the foregoing powers, or in relation to any parish property, not being property relating to affairs of the church or held for an ecclesiastical charity; and

(k) to contribute towards the expense of doing any of the things above-mentioned, or to agree or combine with any other parish council to do or contribute towards the expense of doing any of the things above-mentioned.

(2.) A parish council may let, or, with the consent of the parish meeting, sell or exchange, any land or buildings vested in the council, but the power of letting for more than a year and the power of sale or exchange shall not be exercised, in the case of property which has been acquired at the expense of any rate, or is at the passing of this Act applied in aid of any rate, or would but for want of income be so applied, without the consent of the Local Government Board, or in any other case without such consent or approval as is required under the Charitable Trusts Acts, 1853 to 1891, for the sale of charity estates, provided that the consent or approval required under those Acts shall not be required for the letting for allotments of land vested in the parish council.

(3.) Nothing in this section shall derogate from any obligation of a district council with respect to the supply of water or the execution of sanitary works.

(4.) Notice of any application to the Board of Agriculture in relation to a common shall be served upon the council of every parish in which any part of the common to which the application relates is situate.

Powers for acquisition of land.

9. (*a*)—(1.) For the purpose of the acquisition of land by a parish council the Lands Clauses Acts shall be incorporated with this Act,

(*a*) See the notes to this section in the separate work on this Act already referred to.

Sect. 9 (1).

38 & 39 Vict. c. 55.

except the provisions of those Acts with respect to the purchase and taking of land otherwise than by agreement, and section one hundred and seventy-eight of the Public Health Act, 1875, shall apply as if the parish council were referred to therein.

(2.) If a parish council are unable to acquire by agreement and on reasonable terms suitable land for any purpose for which they are authorised to acquire it, they may represent the case to the county council, and the county council shall inquire into the representation (*b*).

50 & 51 Vict. c. 48. 53 & 54 Vict. c. 65.

(3.) If on any such representation, or on any proceeding under the Allotments Acts, 1887 and 1890, a county council are satisfied that suitable land for the said purpose of the parish council or for the purpose of allotments (as the case may be), cannot be acquired on reasonable terms by voluntary agreement, and that the circumstances are such as to justify the county council in proceeding under this section, they shall cause such public inquiry to be made in the parish, and such notice to be given both in the parish and to the owners, lessees, and occupiers of the land proposed to be taken as may be prescribed (*c*), and all persons interested shall be permitted to attend at the inquiry, and to support or oppose the taking of the land.

(4.) After the completion of the inquiry, and considering all objections made by any persons interested, the county council may make an order for putting in force, as respects the said land or any part thereof, the provisions of the Lands Clauses Acts with respect to the purchase and taking of land otherwise than by agreement (*d*).

(5.) If the county council refuse to make any such order, the parish council, or, if the proceeding is taken on the petition of the district council, then the district council, may petition the Local Government Board, and that Board after local inquiry may, if they think proper, make the order, and this section shall apply as if the order had been made by the county council. Any order made under this subsection overruling the decision of the county council shall be laid before Parliament by the Local Government Board.

(*b*) The inquiry here referred to is a preliminary inquiry, which may or may not lead to the holding of a public inquiry under the next sub-section.

(*c*) "Prescribed," *i.e.*, by the Local Government Board ; s. 75, *post.* Orders prescribing the procedure under this section to be followed by county councils and by councils of county boroughs were made by the Local Government Board on May 22nd and 23rd, 1885, respectively, and are set out, *post.*

(*d*) The order must incorporate the Lands Clauses Acts and parts of the Railways Clauses Act, 1845, "with the necessary adaptations." See sub-s. (10) of this section.

(6.) A copy of any order made under this section shall be served in the prescribed manner (*e*), together with a statement that the order will become final and have the effect of an Act of Parliament, unless within the prescribed period (*e*) a memorial by some person interested is presented to the Local Government Board praying that the order shall not become law without further inquiry. Sect. 9 (6).

(7.) The order shall be deposited with the Local Government Board, who shall inquire whether the provisions of this section and the prescribed regulations have been in all respects complied with; and if the Board are satisfied that this has been done, then, after the prescribed period—

(a.) If no memorial has been presented, or if every such memorial has been withdrawn, the Board shall, without further inquiry, confirm the order:

(b.) If a memorial has been presented, the Local Government Board shall proceed to hold a local inquiry, and shall, after such inquiry, either confirm, with or without amendment, or disallow the order:

(c.) Upon any such confirmation the order, and if amended as so amended, shall become final and have the effect of an Act of Parliament, and the confirmation by the Local Government Board shall be conclusive evidence that the requirements of this Act have been complied with, and that the order has been duly made, and is within the powers of this Act.

(8.) Sections two hundred and ninety-three to two hundred and ninety-six, and subsections (1) and (2) of section two hundred and ninety-seven of the Public Health Act, 1875, shall apply to a local inquiry held by the Local Government Board for the purposes of this section, as if those sections and subsections were herein re-enacted, and in terms made applicable to such inquiry.

(9.) The order shall be carried into effect, when made on the petition of a district council, by that council, and in any other case by the county council.

(10.) Any order made under this section for the purpose of the purchase of land otherwise than by agreement shall incorporate the Lands Clauses Acts and sections seventy-seven to eighty-five of the Railways Clauses Consolidation Act, 1845, with the necessary adaptations, but any question of disputed compensation shall be dealt with in the manner provided by section three of the Allotments Act, 1887, and provisoes (a), (b), and (c) of subsection (4) of that section are incorporated with this section and shall apply 8 & 9 Vict. c. 20.

(*e*) See the orders referred to in the last note. The prescribed period is one calendar month after the making of the order.

Sect. 9 (10). accordingly (*f*): Provided that in determining the amount of disputed compensation, the arbitrator shall not make any additional allowance in respect of the purchase being compulsory.

(11.) At any inquiry or arbitration held under this section the person or persons holding the inquiry or arbitration shall hear any authorities or parties interested by themselves or their agents, and shall hear witnesses, but shall not, except in such cases as may be prescribed, hear counsel or expert witnesses.

(12.) The person or persons holding a public inquiry for the purposes of this section on behalf of a county council shall have the same powers as an inspector or inspectors of the Local Government Board when holding a local inquiry (*g*); and section two hundred and ninety-four of the Public Health Act, 1875, shall apply to the costs of inquiries held by the county council for the purpose of this section as if the county council were substituted for the Local Government Board (*h*).

(*f*) The incorporated provisions of sub-s. (4) of s. 3 of the Allotments Act, 1887, are as follows:—

Sub-section (4)—

"Provided that—

"(a.) Any question of disputed compensation shall be referred to the arbitration of a single arbitrator appointed by the parties, or if the parties do not concur in the appointment of a single arbitrator, then on the application of either of them, by the Local Government Board, and the remuneration to be paid to the arbitrator appointed by the Local Government Board shall be fixed by that Board.

"(b.) If an arbitrator appointed for the purposes of this Act dies or becomes incapable to act before he has made his award, or fails to make his award within two months after he is appointed, his appointment shall determine, and the determination of the compensation shall be referred to another arbitrator appointed in like manner as if no arbitrator had been previously appointed: Provided always, that the same arbitrator may be re-appointed.

"(c.) An arbitrator appointed under this section shall be deemed to be an arbitrator within the meaning of the Lands Clauses Consolidation Act, 1845, and the Acts amending the same, and the provisions of those Acts with respect to an arbitration shall apply accordingly; and further, the arbitrator, notwithstanding anything in the said Acts, shall determine the amount of the costs, and shall have power to disallow as costs in the arbitration the costs of any witness whom he considers to have been called unnecessarily, and any other costs which he considers to have been incurred unnecessarily."

(*g*) Inspectors of the Local Government Board may summon any person to be examined before them or to produce and verify on oath any books, contracts, agreements, accounts, or copies of the same (and not in relation to or involving any question of title to lands except the property of the local authority). They may examine witnesses on oath or require the party examined to make and subscribe a declaration of the truth of his evidence. Disobedience of any summons, refusing to produce, altering or concealing any books, etc., is a misdemeanor, and evidence falsely given before the inspector, is perjury. See Public Health Act, 1875, s. 296; 4 & 5 Will. 4, c. 76, s. 12; and 10 & 11 Vict. c. 109, ss. 20, 21.

(*h*) Section 294 of the Public Health Act, 1875, empowers the Board to make orders as to the costs of inquiries instituted by the Board, and as to the parties by whom, or the rates out of which, such costs shall be borne. See also sub-section (19), *infra*.

(13.) Sub-section (2) of section two, if the land is taken for allotment, and, whether it is or is not so taken, subsections (5), (6), (7), and (8) of section three of the Allotments Act, 1887, and section eleven of that Act, and section three of the Allotments Act, 1890, are incorporated with this section, and shall, with the prescribed adaptations, apply accordingly (*i*). **Sect. 9 (13).** 50 & 51 Vict. c. 48. 53 & 54 Vict. c. 65.

(14.) Where the land is acquired otherwise than for allotments, it shall be assured to the parish council; and any land purchased by a county council for allotments under the Allotments Act, 1887 and 1890, and this Act, or any of them, shall be assured to the parish council, and in that case sections five to eight of the Allotments Act, 1887, shall apply as if the parish council were the sanitary authority (*k*).

(15.) Nothing in this section shall authorise the parish council to acquire otherwise than by agreement any land for the purpose of any supply of water, or of any right of way.

(16.) In this section the expression "allotments" includes common pasture where authorised to be acquired under the Allotments Act, 1887.

(17.) Where, under the Allotments Act, 1890, the Allotments Act, 1887, applies to the purchase of land by the county council, that Act shall apply as amended by this section, and the parish council shall have the like power of petitioning the county council as is given to six parliamentary electors by section two of the Allotments Act, 1890 (*l*).

(18.) This section shall apply to a county borough with the necessary modifications, and in particular with the modification that the order shall be both made and confirmed by the Local Government Board and shall be carried into effect by the council of the county borough (*m*).

(19.) The expenses of a county council incurred under this section shall be defrayed in like manner as in the case of a local inquiry by a county council under this Act (*n*).

Hiring of land for allotments.

10.—(1.) The parish council shall have power to hire land for allotments, and if they are satisfied that allotments are required,

---

(*i*) The incorporated provisions, as adapted by the Local Government Board, are set out in the schedules to the orders referred to in note (*c*), *ante*, p. 602.

(*k*) By this section land acquired for allotments by a county council must be assured to the parish council, and that council is entrusted with the powers given by ss. 5 to 8 of the Allotments Act, 1887, as to the adaptation, management, letting, and use of the allotments, and the recovery of rent and possession. The county council cannot therefore now delegate any of these powers to the district council as they formerly could under s. 4 of the Allotments Act, 1890.

(*l*) See the Allotments Act, 1890, *ante*, p. 517.

(*m*) See note (*c*), *ante*, p. 602.

(*n*) See note (*h*), *ante*, p. 604, and s. 72 (4), *post*.

Sect. 10 (1). and are unable to hire by agreement on reasonable terms suitable land for allotments, they shall represent the case to the county council, and the county council may make an order authorising the parish council to hire compulsorily for allotments, for a period not less than fourteen years nor more than thirty-five years, such land in or near the parish as is specified in the order, and the order shall, as respects confirmation and otherwise, be subject to the like provisions as if it were an order of the county council made under the last preceding section of this Act, and that section shall apply as if it were herein re-enacted with the substitution of "hiring" for "purchase" and with the other necessary modifications (*o*).

(2.) A single arbitrator, who shall be appointed in accordance with the provisions of section three of the Allotments Act, 1887, and to whom the provisions of that section shall apply, shall have power to determine any question—

(a) as to the terms and conditions of the hiring; or

(b) as to the amount of compensation for severance; or

(c) as to the compensation to any tenant upon the determination of his tenancy; or

(d) as to the apportionment of the rent between the land taken by the parish council and the land not taken from the tenant; or

(e) as to any other matter incidental to the hiring of the land by the council, or the surrender thereof at the end of their tenancy;

but the arbitrator in fixing the rent shall not make any addition in respect of compulsory hiring.

(3.) The arbitrator, in fixing rent or other compensation, shall take into consideration all the circumstances connected with the land, and the use to which it might otherwise be put by the owner during the term of hiring, and any depreciation of the value to the tenant of the residue of his holding caused by the withdrawal from the holding of the land hired by the parish council.

(4.) Any compensation awarded to a tenant in respect of any depreciation of the value to him of the residue of his holding caused by the withdrawal from the holding of the land hired by the parish council shall as far as possible be provided for by taking such compensation into account in fixing, as the case may require, the rent to be paid by the parish council for the land hired by them, and the apportioned rent, if any, to be paid by the tenant for that portion of the holding which is not hired by the parish council.

(*o*) As to orders by a county council under this section, see s. 9 and notes, *ante*, and also the notes to this section in the separate work of the editors upon this Act, and see in particular sub-ss. (8), (9), *infra*.

(5.) The award of the arbitrator or a copy thereof, together with a report signed by him as to the condition of the land taken by the parish council, shall be deposited and preserved with the public books, writings, and papers of the parish, and the owner for the time being of the land shall at all reasonable times be at liberty to inspect the same and to take copies thereof. **Sect. 10 (5).**

(6.) Save as herein-after mentioned, sections five to eight of the Allotments Act, 1887, shall apply to any allotment hired by a parish council in like manner as if that council were the sanitary authority and also the allotment managers:

Provided that the parish council—

(a) may let to one person an allotment or allotments exceeding one acre, but, if the land is hired compulsorily, not exceeding in the whole four acres of pasture or one acre of arable and three acres of pasture; and

(b) may permit to be erected on the allotment any stable, cowhouse, or barn; and

(c) shall not break up, or permit to be broken up, any permanent pasture, without the assent in writing of landlord.

(7.) On the determination of any tenancy created by compulsory hiring a single arbitrator who shall be appointed in accordance with the provisions of section three of the Allotments Act, 1887, shall have power to determine as to the amount due by the landlord for compensation for improvements, or by the parish council for depreciation, but such compensation shall be assessed in accordance with the provisions of the Agricultural Holdings (England) Act, 1883. 46 & 47 Vict. c. 61.

(8.) The order for compulsory hiring may apply, with the prescribed adaptations, such of the provisions of the Lands Clauses Acts (including those relating to the acquisition of land otherwise than by agreement) as appear to the county council or Local Government Board sufficient for carrying into effect the order, and for the protection of the persons interested in the land and of the parish council (*p*).

(9.) Nothing in this section shall authorise the compulsory hiring of any mines or minerals, or confer any right to take, sell, or carry away any gravel, sand, or clay, or authorise the hiring of any land which is already owned or occupied as a small holding within the meaning of the Small Holdings Act, 1892. 55 & 56 Vict. c. 31.

(10.) If the land hired under this section shall at any time during the tenancy thereof by the parish council be shown to the

---

(*p*) The adaptations of the Lands Clauses Act are prescribed by an order of the Local Government Board of May 21st, 1895, which is set out, *post*.

Sect. 10 (10). satisfaction of the county council to be required by the landlord for the purpose of working and getting the mines, minerals, or surface minerals thereunder, or for any road or work to be used in connexion with such working or getting, it shall be lawful for the landlord of such land to resume possession thereof upon giving to the parish council twelve calendar months previous notice in writing of his intention so to do, and upon such resumption the landlord shall pay to the parish council and to the allotment holders of the land for the time being such sum by way of compensation for the loss of such land for the purposes of allotments as may be agreed upon by the landlord and the parish council, or in default of such agreement as may be awarded by a single arbitrator to be appointed in accordance with the provisions of section three of the Allotments Act, 1887, and the provisions of that section shall apply to such arbitrator.

The word "landlord" in this subsection means the person for the time being entitled to receive the rent of the land hired by the parish council.

(11.) The Local Government Board shall annually lay before Parliament a report of any proceedings under this and the preceding section.

Restrictions on expenditure.

11.—(1.) A parish council shall not, without the consent of a parish meeting, incur expenses or liabilities which will involve a rate exceeding threepence in the pound for any local financial year, or which will involve a loan.

(2.) A parish council shall not, without the approval of the county council, incur any expense or liability which will involve a loan. (*q*)

(3.) The sum raised in any local financial year by a parish council for their expenses (other than expenses under the adoptive Acts) shall not exceed a sum equal to a rate of sixpence in the pound on the rateable value of the parish at the commencement of the year, and for the purpose of this enactment the expression "expenses" includes any annual charge, whether of principal or interest, in respect of any loan.

(4.) Subject to the provisions of this Act, the expenses of a parish council and of a parish meeting, including the expenses of any poll, shall be paid out of the poor rate; and where there is a parish council that council shall pay the said expenses

(*q*) The consent of the county council to the actual borrowing is required by the next section. The county council ought, it is submitted, before approving the incurring of an expense or liability under this clause, satisfy themselves as to the object for which it is proposed to be incurred, and should require that the consent of the parish meeting be first obtained (under sub-s. (1)), and should see that the parish council are not exceeding the borrowing limit imposed by s. 12 (1), *post*.

of the parish meeting of the parish; and the parish council, and where there is no parish council the chairman of the parish meeting, shall, for the purpose of obtaining payment of such expenses, have the same powers as a board of guardians have for the purpose of obtaining contributions to their common fund. **Sect. 11 (4).**

(5.) The demand note for any rate levied for defraying the expenses of a parish council or a parish meeting, together with other expenses, shall state in the prescribed form the proportion of the rate levied for the expenses of the council or meeting, and the proportion (if any) levied for the purpose of any of the adoptive Acts.

Borrowing by parish council.

12.—(1.) A parish council for any of the following purposes, that is to say—

(a) for purchasing any land, or building any buildings, which the council are authorised to purchase or build; and

(b) for any purpose for which the council are authorised to borrow under any adoptive Acts; and

(c) for any permanent work or other thing which the council are authorised to execute or do, and the cost of which ought, in the opinion of the county council and the Local Government Board, to be spread over a term of years;

may, with the consent of the county council and the Local Government Board, borrow money in like manner and subject to the like conditions as a local authority may borrow for defraying expenses incurred in the execution of the Public Health Acts, and sections two hundred and thirty-three, two hundred and thirty-four, and two hundred and thirty-six to two hundred and thirty-nine of the Public Health Act, 1875, shall apply accordingly, except that the money shall be borrowed on the security of the poor rate and of the whole or part of the revenues of the parish council, and except that as respects the limit of the sum to be borrowed, one half of the assessable value shall be substituted for the assessable value for two years (*r*). 38 & 39 Vict. c. 55.

(*r*) Before giving their consent to borrowing by a parish council, the county council must satisfy themselves (i.) that the purpose is one for which the parish council is authorized to borrow (and in the case of works, that the cost ought to be spread over a term of years); (ii.) that the proposed loan will not bring the existing debt above the prescribed limit; and (iii.) that the consent of the parish meeting under s. 11 (1) has been obtained. It is somewhat doubtful on the construction of this section whether the consent of the county council, as well as of the Local Government Board, to the period of repayment is required. Such consent by the board is required by s. 234 of the Public Health Act, 1875, and the effect of the present section may be to substitute the consent of both bodies for that of the board under the section referred to. Probably if the period were fixed by the county council, the board would adopt that period in their sanction. The maximum period is sixty years from the date of borrowing. A consent by the county council under this section ought, it is thought, to be under their seal.

Sect. 12 (2)

(2.) A county council may lend to a parish council any money which the parish council are authorized to borrow, and may, if necessary, without the sanction of the Local Government Board, and irrespectively of any limit of borrowing, raise the money by loan, subject to the like conditions and in the like manner as any other loan for the execution of their duties, and subject to any further conditions which the Local Government Board may by general or special order impose.(*s*)

(3.) A parish council shall not borrow for the purposes of any of the adoptive Acts otherwise than in accordance with this Act, but the charge for the purpose of any of the adoptive Acts shall ultimately be on the rate applicable to the purposes of that Act.

Footpaths and roads.

13.—(1.) The consent of the parish council and of the district council shall be required for the stopping, in whole or in part, or diversion, of a public right of way within a rural parish, and the consent of the parish council shall be required for a declaration that a highway in a rural parish is unnecessary for public use and not repairable at the public expense, and the parish council shall give public notice of a resolution to give any such consent, and the resolution shall not operate—

(a) unless it is confirmed by the parish council at a meeting held not less than two months after the public notice is given; nor

(b) if a parish meeting held before the confirmation resolve that the consent ought not to be given.

(2.) A parish council may, subject to the provisions of this Act with respect to restrictions on expenditure, undertake the repair and maintenance of all or any of the public footpaths within their parish, not being footpaths at the side of a public road, but this power shall not nor shall the exercise thereof relieve any other authority or person from any liability with respect to such repair or maintenance.

Public property and charities.

14 (*t*).—(1.) Where trustees hold any property for the purposes of a public recreation ground or of public meetings, or of allotments, whether under Inclosure Acts or otherwise, for the benefit of the inhabitants of a rural parish, or any of them, or for any public purpose connected with a rural parish, except for an ecclesiastical

(*s*) As to borrowing by a county council, see s. 69 of the Local Government Act, 1888, *ante*, p. 132. Further conditions as to borrowing by county councils under the provisions in the text have been imposed by a general Order of the Local Government Board of November 5th, 1895, which is set out, *post*.

(*t*) The provisions of this section must be borne in mind by county councils in making orders as to groups of parishes under s. 38, *post*.

charity (*u*), they may, with the approval of the Charity Commissioners, transfer the property to the parish council of the parish, or to persons appointed by that council, and the parish council, if they accept the transfer, or their appointees, shall hold the property on the trusts and subject to the conditions on which the trustees held the same. Sect. 14 (1).

(2.) Where overseers of a rural parish as such are, either alone or jointly with any other persons, trustees of any parochial charity, such number of the councillors of the parish or other persons, not exceeding the number of the overseer trustees, as the council may appoint, shall be trustees in their place, and, when the charity is not an ecclesiastical charity, this enactment shall apply as if the churchwardens as such were specified therein as well as the overseers (*x*).

(3.) Where the governing body of a parochial charity other than an ecclesiastical charity does not include any persons elected by the ratepayers or parochial electors or inhabitants of the parish, or appointed by the parish council or parish meeting, the parish council may appoint additional members of that governing body not exceeding the number allowed by the Charity Commissioners in each case; and if the management of any such charity is vested in a sole trustee, the number of trustees may, with the approval of the Charity Commissioners, be increased to three, one of whom may be nominated by such sole trustee and one by the parish council or parish meeting. Nothing in this subsection shall prejudicially affect the power or authority of the Charity Commissioners, under any of the Acts relating to charities, to settle or alter schemes for the better administration of any charity.

(4.) Where the vestry of a rural parish are entitled, under the trusts of a charity other than an ecclesiastical charity, to appoint any trustees or beneficiaries of the charity, the appointment shall be made by the parish council of the parish, or in the case of beneficiaries, by persons appointed by the parish council.

(5.) The draft of every scheme relating to a charity, not being an ecclesiastical charity, which affects a rural parish, shall on or before the publication of the notice of the proposal to make an order for such scheme in accordance with section six of the Charitable Trusts Act, 1860, be communicated to the council of the parish, and where there is no parish council to the chairman of the parish meeting, and, in the case of a council, the council may, 23 & 24 Vict c. 136.

(*u*) See this expression defined, *post*, s. 75; and see *Re Ross's Charity*, noted *infra*, and *Re Perry Almshouses Charity*, W. N. 1898, p. 14.

(*x*) The effect of the last paragraph of this clause is that the parish council can appoint trustees in place of the churchwardens, where they, whether joined with the overseers or not, are made trustees by the instrument creating a non-ecclesiastical charity. *Re Ross's Charity*, [1897] 2 Ch. 397; 66 L. J. Ch. 662; 77 L. T. (N.S.) 89; 46 W. R. 27; 61 J. P. 742.

Sect. 14 (5). subject to the provisions of this Act with respect to restrictions on expenditure, and to the consent of the parish meeting, either support or oppose the scheme, and shall for that purpose have the same right as any inhabitants of a place directly affected by the scheme.

(6.) The accounts of all parochial charities, not being ecclesiastical charities, shall annually be laid before the parish meeting of any parish affected thereby, and the Charitable Trusts Amendment Act, 1855, shall apply with the substitution in section forty-four of the parish meeting for the vestry, and of the chairman of the parish meeting for the churchwardens, and the names of the beneficiaries of dole charities shall be published annually in such form as the parish council, or where there is no parish council the parish meeting, think fit.

18 & 19 Vict. c. 124.

(7.) The term of office of a trustee appointed under this section shall be four years, but of the trustees first appointed as aforesaid one half, as nearly as may be, to be determined by lot, shall go out of office at the end of two years from the date of their appointment, but shall be eligible for re-appointment.

(8.) The provisions of this section with respect to the appointment of trustees, except so far as the appointment is transferred from the vestry, shall not apply to any charity until the expiration of forty years from the date of the foundation thereof, or, in the case of a charity founded before the passing of this Act by a donor or by several donors any one of whom is living at the passing of this Act, until the expiration of forty years from the passing of this Act, unless with the consent of the surviving donor or donors.

(9.) Whilst a person is trustee of a parochial charity he shall not, nor shall his wife or any of his children, receive any benefit from the charity.

Delegated powers of parish councils.

15. A rural district council may delegate to a parish council any power which may be delegated to a parochial committee under the Public Health Acts, and thereupon those Acts shall apply as if the parish council were a parochial committee, and where such district council appoint a parochial committee consisting partly of members of the district council and partly of other persons, those other persons shall, where there is a parish council, be or be selected from the members of the parish council.

Complaint by parish council of default of district council.

16.—(1.) Where a parish council resolve that a rural district council ought to have provided the parish with sufficient sewers, or to have maintained existing sewers, or to have provided the parish with a supply of water in cases where danger arises to the health of the inhabitants from the insufficiency or unwholesomeness of the existing supply of water, and a proper supply can be got at a reasonable cost, or to have enforced with regard to the parish any provisions of the Public Health Acts which it is their duty to enforce, and have failed so to do, or that they have failed to maintain and repair any highway in a good and substantial manner, the parish council may complain to the county council, and the county council, if satisfied after due inquiry that the district council have so failed as respects the subject-matter of the complaint, may resolve that the duties and powers of the district council for the purpose of the matter complained of shall be transferred to the county council, and they shall be transferred accordingly. Sect. 16 (1).

(2.) Upon any complaint under this section the county council may, instead of resolving that the duties and powers of the rural district council be transferred to them, make such an order as is mentioned in section two hundred and ninety-nine of the Public Health Act, 1875, and may appoint a person to perform the duty mentioned in the order, and upon such appointment sections two hundred and ninety-nine to three hundred and two of the Public Health Act, 1875, shall apply with the substitution of the county council for the Local Government Board (*y*). 38 & 39 Vict. c. 55.

(*y*) Section 299 of the Public Health Act, 1875, provides as follows:— "Where complaint is made to the Local Government Board that a local authority has made default in providing their district with sufficient sewers, or in the maintenance of existing sewers, or in providing their district with a supply of water in cases where danger arises to the health of the inhabitants from the insufficiency or unwholesomeness of the existing supply of water, and a proper supply can be got at a reasonable cost, or that a local authority has made default in enforcing any provisions of this Act which it is their duty to enforce, the Local Government Board, if satisfied, after due inquiry, that the authority has been guilty of the alleged default, shall make an order limiting a time for the performance of their duty in the matter of such complaint. If such duty is not performed by the time limited in the order, such order may be enforced by writ of mandamus or the Local Government Board may appoint some person to perform such duty, and shall by order direct that the expenses of performing the same, together with a reasonable remuneration to the person appointed for superintending such performance, and amounting to a sum specified in the order, together with the costs of the proceedings, shall be paid by the authority in default; and any order made for the payment of such expenses and costs may be removed into the Queen's Bench Division, and be enforced in the same manner as if the same were an order of such court. Any person appointed under this section to perform the duty of a defaulting local authority shall, in the performance and for the purposes of such duty, be invested with all the powers of such authority other than (save as hereinafter provided) the powers of levying rates, and the Local Government Board may from time to time, by order, change any person so appointed."

Sections 300 to 302 make provision for the recovery of the costs and expenses from the defaulting authority, and empower the Local Government Board to obtain a loan for the purposes of such expenses, such loan to be charged upon the local rate and to be a debt due from the defaulting authority. Where a parish council has made a complaint under the provisions in the text to a county council, that body may act in one of two ways: (i.) they may, under sub-s. (1), resolve to exercise the powers of the district council in respect of the matter of the complaint. In this case the provisions of s. 63, *post*, will apply; or (ii.) they may, instead of taking over the dutic

Sect. 16 (3).

(3.) Where a rural district council have determined to adopt plans for the sewerage or water supply of any contributory place within the district, they shall give notice thereof to the parish council of any parish for which the works are to be provided before any contract is entered into by them for the execution of the works.

Parish officers and parish documents.

17.—(1.) A parish council may appoint one of their number to act as clerk of the council without remuneration.

(2.) If no member of the parish council is appointed so to act, and there is an assistant overseer, he, or such one of the assistant overseers, if more than one, as may be appointed by the council, shall be the clerk of the parish council, and the performance of his duties as such shall be taken into account in determining his salary.

(3.) If there is no assistant overseer, the parish council may appoint a collector of poor rates, or some other fit person, to be their clerk, with such remuneration as they may think fit.

(4.) A parish council shall not appoint to the office of vestry clerk.

(5.) When a parish council act as a parochial committee by delegation from the district council they shall have the services of the clerk of the district council, unless the district council otherwise direct.

(6.) The parish council may appoint one of their own number or some other person to act as treasurer without remuneration, and the treasurer shall give such security as may be required by regulations of the county council.

(7.) All documents required by statute or by standing orders of Parliament to be deposited with the parish clerk of a rural parish shall, after the election of a parish council, be deposited with the clerk, or, if there is none, with the chairman, of the parish council, and the enactments with respect to the inspection of, and taking copies of, and extracts from, any such documents shall apply as if the clerk, or chairman, as the case may be, were mentioned therein

(8.) The custody of the registers of baptisms, marriages, and burials, and of all other books and documents containing entries wholly or partly relating to the affairs of the church or to ecclesiastical charities, except documents directed by law to be kept with the public books, writings, and papers of the parish, shall remain as provided by the existing law unaffected by this

---

and powers of the defaulting district council, take similar measures to those which may be taken by the Local Government Board under s. 299 of the Public Health Act, 1875, for compelling the district council to perform their duty in the matter of the complaint; if they adopt this course, they are to have the powers of the Local Government Board under ss. 299 to 302 of the Act referred to.

Sect. 17 (8).

Act. All other public books, writings, and papers of the parish, and all documents directed by law to be kept therewith, shall either remain in their existing custody, or be deposited in such custody as the parish council may direct. The incumbent and churchwardens on the one part, and the parish council on the other, shall have reasonable access to all such books, documents, writings, and papers, as are referred to in this subsection, and any difference as to custody or access shall be determined by the county council.

(9.) Every county council shall from time to time inquire into the manner in which the public books, writings, papers, and documents under the control of the parish council or parish meeting are kept with a view to the proper preservation thereof, and shall make such orders as they think necessary for such preservation, and those orders shall be complied with by the parish council or parish meeting (*z*).

Parish wards.

18.—(1.) A county council may, on application by the parish council, or not less than one tenth of the parochial electors of a parish, and on being satisfied that the area or population of the parish is so large, or different parts of the population so situated, as to make a single parish meeting for the election of councillors impracticable or inconvenient, or that it is desirable for any reason that certain parts of the parish should be separately represented on the council, order that the parish be divided for the purpose of electing parish councillors into wards, to be called parish wards, with such boundaries and such number of councillors for each ward as may be provided by the order (*a*).

(2.) In the division of a parish into wards regard shall be had to the population according to the last published census for the time being, and to the evidence of any considerable change of

(*z*) The jurisdiction of the county council to make orders as to the proper preservation of documents is limited to such documents as have passed under the control of the parish council under the preceding sub-section; but under that sub-section it appears that the county council may be called to decide whether the custody of particular documents ought or ought not to be under the control of the parish council. It has been held that the tithe apportionment map of a parish is a document placed under the control of the parish council by this section, and that an order of a county council that it shall be deposited in such custody as the parish council may direct can be enforced by an order of justices under 23 & 24 Vict. c. 23, s. 28. *Lewis* v. *Poole* (WRIGHT and KENNEDY, JJ.), [1898] 1 Q. B. 164; 67 L. J. Q. B. 73; 77 L. T. (N.S.) 369; 46 W. R. 93; 61 J. P. 776.

(*a*) An order for the division of a parish into wards for the purpose of electing parish councillors can only be made if application be made under this section, and if the county council is satisfied of the existence of the circumstances here referred to. If the parish is divided into wards for the election of rural district councillors (see s. 60, *post*), it is desirable that in any division into wards under the text the same boundaries should be used for both purposes. A county council has also power to make orders preserving the rights of distinct parts of one and the same parish, without dividing the parish into wards. See s. 37, *post*.

Sect. 18 (2).

population since that census, and to area and to the distribution and pursuits of the population, and to all the circumstances of the case.

(3.) Any such order may be revoked or varied by the county council on application by either the council or not less than one tenth of the parochial electors of the parish, but while in force shall have effect as if enacted by this Act.

(4.) In a parish divided into parish wards there shall be a separate election of parish councillors for each ward.

Provisions as to small parishes.

19. In a rural parish not having a separate parish council, the following provisions shall, as from the appointed day, but subject to provisions made by a grouping order(*b*), if the parish is grouped with some other parish or parishes, have effect :—

(1.) At the annual assembly the parish meeting shall choose a chairman for the year ;

(2.) The parish meeting shall assemble not less than twice in each year ;

(3.) The parish meeting may appoint a committee of their own number for any purposes which, in the opinion of the parish meeting, would be better regulated and managed by means of such a committee, and all the acts of the committee shall be submitted to the parish meeting for their approval ;

(4.) All powers, duties, and liabilities of the vestry shall, except so far as they relate to the affairs of the church or to ecclesiastical charities, or are transferred by this Act to any other authority, be transferred to the parish meeting ;

(5.) The power and the duty of appointing the overseers, and of notifying the appointment, and the power of appointing and revoking the appointment of an assistant overseer, shall be transferred to and vest in the parish meeting, and the power given by this Act to a parish council of appointing trustees of a charity in the place of overseers or churchwardens, shall vest in the parish meeting ;

(6.) The chairman of the parish meeting and the overseers of the parish shall be a body corporate by the name of the chairman and overseers of the parish, and shall have perpetual succession, and may hold land for the purposes of the parish without licence in mortmain ; but shall in all respects act in manner directed by the parish meeting,

(*b*) In making a grouping order a county council must take care to show to what extent the provisions of this section are to be altered by the order. So far as they are left unaltered, the powers given by this section to each individual parish composing the group will continue to be exerciseable.

and any act of such body corporate shall be executed under the hands, or if an instrument under seal is required under the hands and seals, of the said chairman and overseers ; Sect. 19 (6).

(7.) The legal interest in all property which under this Act would, if there were a parish council, be vested on the appointed day in the parish council shall vest in the said body corporate of the chairman and overseers of the parish, subject to all trusts and liabilities affecting the same, and all persons concerned shall make or concur in making such transfers (if any) as are requisite to give effect to this enactment ;

(8.) The provisions of this Act with respect to the stopping or diversion of a public right of way, or the declaring of a highway to be unnecessary and not repairable at the public expense, and with respect to a complaint to a county council of a default by a district council, shall apply, with the substitution of the parish meeting for the parish council ;

(9.) A rate levied for defraying the expenses of the parish meeting (when added to expenses under any of the adoptive Acts) shall not exceed sixpence in the pound in any local financial year ;

(10.) On the application of the parish meeting the county council may confer on that meeting any of the powers conferred on a parish council by this Act ;

(11.) Any act of the parish meeting may be signified by an instrument executed at the meeting under the hands, or, if an instrument under seal is required under the hands and seals, of the chairman presiding at the meeting and two other parochial electors present at the meeting.

PART II.

Guardians and District Councils.

20. As from the appointed day the following provisions shall apply to boards of guardians :— Election and qualification of guardians.

(1.) There shall be no ex-officio or nominated guardians :

(2.) A person shall not be qualified to be elected or to be a guardian for a poor law union unless he is a parochial elector of some parish within the union, or has during the whole of the twelve months preceding the election resided in the union, or in the case of a guardian for a parish wholly or partly situate within the area of a borough, whether a county borough or not, is qualified

Sect. 20 (2).

to be elected a councillor for that borough, and no person shall be disqualified by sex or marriage for being elected or being a guardian. So much of any enactment, whether in a public general or local and personal Act, as relates to the qualification of a guardian shall be repealed:

(3.) The parochial electors of a parish shall be the electors of the guardians for the parish, and, if the parish is divided into wards for the election of guardians, the electors of the guardians for each ward shall be such of the parochial electors as are registered in respect of qualifications within the ward:

(4.) Each elector may give one vote and no more for each of any number of persons not exceeding the number to be elected;

(5.) The election shall, subject to the provisions of this Act, be conducted according to rules framed under this Act by the Local Government Board (*c*):

(6.) The term of office of a guardian shall be three years, and one third, as nearly as may be, of every board of guardians shall go out of office on the fifteenth day of April in each year, and their places shall be filled by the newly elected guardians. Provided as follows:—

(a.) Where the county council on the application of the board of guardians of any union in their county consider that it would be expedient to provide for the simultaneous retirement of the whole of the board of guardians for the union, they may direct that the members of the board of guardians for that union shall retire together on the fifteenth day of April in every third year, and such order shall have full effect, and where a union is in more than one county, an order may be made by a joint committee of the councils of those counties (*d*);

(b.) Where at the passing of this Act the whole of the guardians of any union, in pursuance of an order of the Local Government Board, retire together at the end of every third year, they shall continue so to retire, unless the county council, or a joint committee of the county councils, on the application of the board of

---

(*c*) See further as to these rules and the duties devolving upon county councils under them, s. 48, *post*.

(*d*) As to joint committees, see Local Government Act, 1888, s. 81, *ante* p. 155.

guardians or of any district council of a district wholly or partially within the union, otherwise direct. **Sect. 20 (7).**

(8.) A board of guardians may elect a chairman or vice-chairman or both, and not more than two other persons, from outside their own body, but from persons qualified to be guardians of the union, and any person so elected shall be an additional guardian and member of the board. Provided that on the first election, if a sufficient number of persons who have been ex-officio or nominated guardians of the union, and have actually served as such, are willing to serve, the additional members shall be elected from among those persons.

21. As from the appointed day,—

Names of county districts and district councils.

(1.) Urban sanitary authorities shall be called urban district councils and their districts shall be called urban districts; but nothing in this section shall alter the style or title of the corporation or council of a borough:

(2.) For every rural sanitary district there shall be a rural district council whose district shall be called a rural district;

(3.) In this and every other Act of Parliament, unless the context otherwise requires, the expression "district council" shall include the council of every urban district, whether a borough or not, and of every rural district, and the expression "county district" shall include every urban and rural district whether a borough or not.

22. The chairman of a district council unless a woman or personally disqualified by any Act shall be by virtue of his office justice of the peace for the county in which the district is situate, but before acting as such justice he shall, if he has not already done so, take the oaths required by law to be taken by a justice of the peace other than the oath respecting the qualification by estate. **Chairman of council to be justice.**

23. As from the appointed day, where an urban district is not a borough— **Constitution of district councils in urban districts not being boroughs.**

(1.) There shall be no ex-officio or nominated members of the urban sanitary authority:

(2.) A person shall not be qualified to be elected or to be a councillor unless he is a parochial elector of some parish within the district, or has during the whole of the twelve months preceding the election resided in the district, and no person shall be disqualified by sex or marriage for being elected or being a councillor. So much of any

Sect. 23 (2).

enactment whether in a public general or local and personal Act as relates to the qualification of a member of an urban sanitary authority shall be repealed:

(3.) The parochial electors of the parishes in the district shall be the electors of the councillors of the district, and, if the district is divided into wards, the electors of the councillors for each ward shall be such of the parochial electors as are registered in respect of qualifications within the ward:

(4.) Each elector may give one vote and no more for each of any number of persons not exceeding the number to be elected:

(5.) The election shall, subject to the provisions of this Act, be conducted according to rules framed under this Act by the Local Government Board (*e*):

(6.) The term of office of a councillor shall be three years, and one-third, as nearly as may be, of the council, and if the district is divided into wards one-third, as nearly as may be, of the councillors for each ward, shall go out of office on the fifteenth day of April in each year, and their places shall be filled by the newly elected councillors. Provided that a county council may on request made by a resolution of an urban district council, passed by two-thirds of the members voting on the resolution, direct that the members of such council shall retire together on the fifteenth day of April in every third year, and such order shall have full effect.

Rural district councils.

24.—(1.) The district council of every rural district shall consist of a chairman and councillors, and the councillors shall be elected by the parishes or other areas for the election of guardians in the district.

(2.) The number of councillors for each parish or other area in a rural district shall be the same as the number of guardians for that parish or area.

(3.) The district councillors for any parish or other area in a rural district shall be the representatives of that parish or area on the board of guardians, and when acting in that capacity shall be deemed to be guardians of the poor, and guardians as such shall not be elected for that parish or area.

(4.) The provisions of this Act with respect to the qualification, election, and term of office and retirement of guardians, and to the qualification of the chairman of the board of guardians, shall apply to district councillors and to the chairman of the district council of a rural district, and any person qualified to be a guardian

---

(*e*) See note (*c*), *ante*, p. 618.

for a union comprising the district shall be qualified to be a district councillor for the district. Sect. 24 (4).

(5.) Where a rural sanitary district is on the appointed day situate in more than one administrative county, such portion thereof as is situate in each administrative county shall, save as otherwise provided by or in pursuance of this or any other Act, be as from the appointed day a rural district ;(*f*)

Provided that where the number of councillors of any such district will be less than five, the provisions, so far as unrepealed, of section nine of the Public Health Act, 1875, with respect to the nomination of persons to make up the members of a rural authority to five, shall apply, unless the Local Government Board by order direct that the affairs of the district shall be temporarily administered by the district council of an adjoining district in another county with which it was united before the appointed day, and if they so direct, the councillors of the district shall be entitled, so far as regards those affairs, to sit and act as members of that district council, but a separate account shall be kept of receipts and expenses in respect of the district, and the same shall be credited or charged separately to the district. 38 & 39 Vict. c. 55.

(6.) The said provisions of section nine of the Public Health Act, 1875, shall apply to the district council of a rural district to which they apply at the passing of this Act.

(7.) Every district council for a rural district shall be a body corporate by the name of the district council, with the addition of the name of the district, or if there is any doubt as to the latter name, of such name as the county council direct, and shall have perpetual succession and a common seal, and may hold land for the purposes of their powers and duties without licence in mortmain.

Powers of district council with respect to sanitary and highway matters.

25.—(1.) As from the appointed day, there shall be transferred to the district council of every rural district all the powers, duties, and liabilities of the rural sanitary authority in the district, and of any highway authority in the district, and highway boards shall cease to exist, and rural district councils shall be the successors of the rural sanitary authority and highway authority, and shall also have as respects highways all the powers, duties, and liabilities of an urban sanitary authority under sections one hundred and forty-four to one hundred and forty-eight of the Public Health Act, 1875, and those sections shall apply in the case of a rural district and of the council thereof in like manner as in the case of an urban district and an urban authority. Provided that the council of any county may by order postpone within their county 38 & 39 Vict. c. 55.

(*f*) County councils were empowered to deal with these cases by orders under s. 36, *post*.

Sect. 25 (1). or any part thereof the operation of this section, so far as it relates to highways, for a term not exceeding three years from the appointed day or such further period as the Local Government Board may on the application of such council allow (*g*).

(2.) Where a highway repairable ratione tenuræ appears on the report of a competent surveyor not to be in proper repair, and the person liable to repair the same fails when requested so to do by the district council to place it in proper repair, the district council may place the highway in proper repair, and recover from the person liable to repair the highway the necessary expenses of so doing.

(3.) Where a highway authority receives any contribution from the county council towards the cost of any highway under section eleven, sub-section (10), of the Local Government Act, 1888, such contribution may be made, subject to any such conditions for the proper maintenance and repair of such highways, as may be agreed on between the county council and the highway authority (*h*).

51 & 52 Vict. c. 41.

(4.) Where the council of a rural district become the highway authority for that district, any excluded part of a parish under section two hundred and sixteen of the Public Health Act, 1875, which is situate in that district, shall cease to be part of any urban district for the purpose of highways, but until the council become the highway authority such excluded part of a parish shall continue subject to the said section.

(5.) Rural district councils shall also have such powers, duties, and liabilities of urban sanitary authorities under the Public Health Acts or any other Act, and such provisions of any of those Acts relating to urban districts shall apply to rural districts, as the Local Government Board by general order direct.

(6.) The power to make such general orders shall be in addition to and not in substitution for the powers conferred on the Board by section two hundred and seventy-six of the Public Health Act, 1875, or by any enactment applying that section; and every order made by the Local Government Board under this section shall be forthwith laid before Parliament.

(*g*) The period of postponement authorized by this section expired on December 28th, 1897, the date on which the first rural district councils elected under this Act came into office; see s. 84 (4), *post*. But in some cases the Local Government Board has, under the power in the text, allowed county councils to postpone the operation of this section as to highways for a further period; except where this has been done the section is in full operation. An order postponing the operation of the section ought to contain provisions for the election of the highway authorities during the period of postponement. See s. 84 (4), *post*.

(*h*) See the section referred to, *ante*, p. 34, and also the Highways and Bridges Act, 1891, s. 3, *ante*, p. 531.

Sect. 25 (7).

(7.) The powers conferred on the Local Government Board by the said section two hundred and seventy-six, or by any enactment applying that section, may be exercised on the application of a county council, or with respect to any parish or part of a parish on the application of the parish council of that parish (*i*).

Duties and powers of district council as to rights of way, rights of common, and roadside wastes.

26.—(1.) It shall be the duty of every district council to protect all public rights of way, and to prevent as far as possible the stopping or obstruction of any such right of way, whether within their district or in an adjoining district in the county or counties in which the district is situate, where the stoppage or obstruction thereof would in their opinion be prejudicial to the interests of their district, and to prevent any unlawful encroachment on any roadside waste within their district (*k*).

(2.) A district council may with the consent of the county council for the county within which any common land is situate aid persons in maintaining rights of common where, in the opinion of the council, the extinction of such rights would be prejudicial to the inhabitants of the district; and may with the like consent exercise in relation to any common within their district all such powers as may, under section eight of the Commons Act, 1876, be exercised by an urban sanitary authority in relation to any common referred to in that section (*l*); and notice of any application to the Board of Agriculture in relation to any common within their district shall be served upon the district council.

39 & 40 Vict. c. 56.

(3.) A district council may, for the purpose of carrying into effect this section, institute or defend any legal proceedings, and generally take such steps as they deem expedient.

(4.) Where a parish council have represented to the district council that any public right of way within the district or an adjoining district in the county or counties in which the district is situate has been unlawfully stopped or obstructed, or that an unlawful encroachment has taken place on any roadside waste within the district, it shall be the duty of the district council, unless satisfied that the allegations of such representation are incorrect, to take proper proceedings accordingly; and if the

(*i*) Under the provision in the text a county council may apply to the board to make an order investing a rural district council with urban powers in respect of their district or any contributory place therein.

(*k*) The county council has full power to take steps for asserting the right of the public to the use and enjoyment of the wastes at the side of the main roads. Local Government Act, 1888, s. 11 (1), *ante*, p. 21. The powers given by the text to the district council are apparently cumulative. See sub-section (6), *infra*.

(*l*) Under the text a county council may, it seems, sanction the expenditure of money by a district council for the purpose of maintaining or acquiring rights of common for the inhabitants of their district.

Sect. 26 (4.) district council refuse or fail to take any proceedings in consequence of such representation, the parish council may petition the county council for the county within which the way or waste is situate, and if that council so resolve the powers and duties of the district council under this section shall be transferred to the county council (*m*).

(5.) Any proceedings or steps taken by a district council or county council in relation to any alleged right of way shall not be deemed to be unauthorised by reason only of such right of way not being found to exist (*n*).

(6.) Nothing in this section shall affect the powers of the county council in relation to roadside wastes.

(7.) Nothing in this section shall prejudice any powers exerciseable by an urban sanitary authority at the passing of this Act, and the council of every county borough shall have the additional powers conferred on a district council by this section.

Transfer of certain powers of of justices to district councils.

27.—(1.) As from the appointed day the powers, duties, and liabilities of justices out of session in relation to any of the matters following, that is to say,—

(a) the licensing of gang masters;

(b) the grant of pawnbrokers' certificates;

(c) the licensing of dealers in game;

(d) the grant of licences for passage brokers and emigrant runners;

(e) the abolition of fairs and alteration of days for holding fairs;

(f) the execution as the local authority of the Acts relating to petroleum and infant life protection;

when arising within a county district, shall be transferred to the district council of the district.

(2.) As from the appointed day, the powers, duties, and liabilities of quarter sessions in relation to the licensing of knackers' yards within a county district shall be transferred to the district council of the district.

(e.) All fees payable in respect of the powers, duties, and liabilities transferred by this section shall be payable to the district council (*o*).

Expenses of rural district council.

28. The expenses incurred by the council of an urban district in the execution of the additional powers conferred on the council

(*m*) As to the effect of a resolution of the county council transferring to themselves the powers of a district council, see s. 63, *post*.

(*n*) This provision seems intended to prevent the disallowance by the auditor of expenditure incurred in seeking to establish or protect a right of way which in the event proved to be non-existent.

(*o*) As to the application of this section to county boroughs, see s. 32, *post*.

by this Act shall, subject to the provistons of this Act, be defrayed in a borough out of the borough fund or rate, and in any other case out of the district fund and general district rate or other fund applicable towards defraying the expenses of the execution of the Public Health Act, 1875. Sect. 28. 38 & 39 Vict. c. 55.

29. The expenses incurred by the council of a rural district shall, subject to the provisions of this Act, be defrayed in manner directed by the Public Health Act, 1875, with respect to expenses incurred in the execution of that Act by a rural sanitary authority, and the provisions of the Public Health Acts with respect to those expenses shall apply accordingly. Expenses of rural district council.

Provided as follows :

(a.) Any highway expenses shall be defrayed as general expenses :

(b.) When the Local Government Board determine any expenses under this Act to be special expenses and a separate charge on any contributory place, and such expenses would if not separately chargeable on a contributory place be raised as general expenses, they may further direct that such special expenses shall be raised in like manner as general expenses, and not by such separate rate for special expenses as is mentioned in section two hundred and thirty of the Public Health Act, 1875 : 38 & 39 Vict. c. 55.

(c.) A district council shall have the same power of charging highway expenses under exceptional circumstances on a contributory place as a highway board has in respect of any area under section seven of the Highways and Locomotives (Amendment) Act, 1878 : 41 & 42 Vict. c. 77.

(d.) Where highway expenses would, if this Act had not passed, have been in whole or in part defrayed in any parish or other area out of any property or funds other than rates, the district council shall make such provision as will give to that parish or area the benefit of such property or funds by way of reduction of the rates on the parish or area.

30. The provisions of this Part of this Act respecting guardians shall apply to the administrative county of London and to every county borough. Guardians in London and county boroughs.

31.—(1.) The provisions of this Act with respect to the qualification of the electors of urban district councillors, and of the persons to be elected, and with respect to the mode of conducting the election, shall apply as if members of the local board of Provisions as to London vestries and district boards.

Sect. 31 (1). Woolwich and the vestries elected under the Metropolis Management Acts, 1855 to 1890, or any Act amending those Acts, and the auditors for parishes elected under those Acts, and so far as respects the qualification of persons to be elected as if members of the district boards under the said Acts, were urban district councillors, and no person shall, ex officio, be chairman of any of the said vestries. Provided that the Elections (Hours of Poll) Act, 1885, shall apply to elections to the said vestries.

48 Vict. c. 10.

(2.) Each of the said vestries, except those electing district boards, and each of the said district boards and the local board of Woolwich, shall at their first meeting after the annual election of members elect a chairman for the year, and section forty-one of the Metropolis Management Act, 1855, shall apply only in case of the absence of such chairman, and the provisions of this Act with respect to chairmen of urban district councils being justices shall apply as if the said vestries and boards were urban district councils.

18 & 19 Vict. c. 120.

(3.) Nothing in any local and personal Act shall prevent any vestry in the county of London from holding their meeting at such time as may be directed by the vestry.

Application to county boroughs of provisions as to transfer of justices' powers.

32. The provisions of this Part of this Act respecting the powers, duties, and liabilities of justices out of session, or of quarter sessions, which are transferred to a district council, shall apply to a county borough as if it were an urban district, and the county borough council were a district council.

Power to apply certain provisions of Act to urban districts and London.

33.—(1.) The Local Government Board may, on the application of the council of any municipal borough, including a county borough, or of any other urban district, make an order conferring on that council or some other representative body within the borough or district all or any of the following matters, namely, the appointment of overseers and assistant overseers, the revocation of appointment of assistant overseers, any powers, duties, or liabilities of overseers, and any powers, duties, or liabilities of a parish council, and applying with the necessary modifications the provisions of this Act with reference thereto.

(2.) Where it appears to the Local Government Board that, by reason of the circumstances connected with any parish in a municipal borough (including a county borough) or other urban district divided into wards, or with the parochial charities of that parish, the parish will not, if the majority of the body of trustees administering the charity are appointed by the council of the borough or district, be properly represented on that body, they may, by their order, provide that such of those trustees as are appointed by the council, or some of them, shall be appointed on the nomination of the councillors elected for the ward or wards comprising such parish or any part of the parish. Sect. 33 (2).

(3.) Any order under this section may provide for its operation extending either to the whole or to specified parts of the area of the borough or urban district, and may make such provisions as seem necessary for carrying the order into effect.

(4.) The order shalt not alter the incidence of any rate, and shall make such provisions as may seem necessary and just for the preservation of the existing interests of paid officers.

(5.) An order under this section may also be made on the application of any representative body within a borough or district.

(6.) The provisions of this section respecting councils of urban districts shall apply to the administrative county of London in like manner as if the district of each sanitary authority in that county were an urban district, and the sanitary authority were the council of that district.

(7.) The Local Government Board shall consult the Charity Commissioners before making any order under this section with respect to any charity.

Supplemental provisions as to control of overseers in urban districts.

34. Where an order of the Local Government Board under this Act confers on the council of an urban district, or some other representative body within the district, either the appointment of overseers and assistant overseers, or the powers, duties, and liabilities of overseers, that order or any subsequent order of the Board may confer on such council or body the powers of the vestry under the third and fourth sections of the Poor Rate Assessment and Collection Act, 1869. 32 & 33 Vict. c. 41.

Restrictions on application of Act to London, etc.

35. Save as specially provided by this Act, this Part of this Act shall not apply to the administrative county of London or to a county borough.

PART III.

AREAS AND BOUNDARIES.

Duties and powers of county council with respect to areas and boundaries.

36.—(1.) For the purpose of carrying this Act into effect in the case of—

(a) every parish and rural sanitary district which at the passing of this Act is situate partly within and partly without an administrative county; and

(b) every parish which at the passing of this Act is situate partly within and partly without a sanitary district; and

(c) every rural parish which has a population of less than two hundred; and

Sect. 36 (1).

(d) every rural sanitary district which at the passing of this Act has less than five elective guardians capable of acting and voting as members of the rural sanitary authority of the district; and

(e) every rural parish which is co-extensive with a rural sanitary district;

every county council shall forthwith take into consideration every such case within their county, and whether any proposal has or has not been made as mentioned in section fifty-seven of the Local Government Act, 1888, shall as soon as practicable, in accordance with that section, cause inquiries to be made and notices given, and make such orders, if any, as they deem most suitable for carrying into effect this Act in accordance with the following provisions, namely:—

51 & 52 Vict. c. 41.

(i.) the whole of each parish, and, unless the county council for special reasons otherwise direct, the whole of each rural district shall be within the same administrative county;

(ii.) the whole of each parish shall, unless the county council for special reasons otherwise direct, be within the same county district; and

(iii.) every rural district which will have less than five elected councillors shall, unless for special reasons the county council otherwise direct, be united to some neighbouring district or districts.

(2.) Where a parish is at the passing of this Act situate in more than one urban district, the parts of the parish in each such district shall, as from the appointed day, unless the county council for special reasons otherwise direct, and subject to any alteration of area made by or in pursuance of this or any other Act, be separate parishes, in like manner as if they had been constituted separate parishes under the Divided Parishes and Poor Law Amendment Act, 1876, and the Acts amending the same.

39 & 40 Vic c. 61.

(3.) Where a parish is divided by this Act, the county council may by order provide for the application to different parts of that parish of the provisions of this Act with respect to the appointment of trustees or beneficiaries of a charity and for the custody of parish documents, but the order, so far as regards the charity, shall not have any effect until it has received the approval of the Charity Commissioners.

(4.) Where a rural parish is co-extensive with a rural sanitary district, then, until the district is united to some other district or districts, and unless the county council otherwise direct, a separate election of a parish council shall not be held for the parish, but the district council shall, in addition to their own powers, have the powers of, and be deemed to be, the parish council.

(5.) Where an alteration of the boundary of any county or borough seems expedient for any of the purposes mentioned in this section, application shall be made to the Local Government Board for an order under section fifty-four of the Local Government Act, 1888. **Sect. 36 (5).**

(6.) Where the alteration of a poor law union seems expedient by reason of any of the provisions of this Act, the county council may, by their order, provide for such alteration in accordance with section fifty-eight of the Local Government Act, 1888, or otherwise, but this provision shall not affect the powers of the Local Government Board with respect to the alterations of unions.

(7.) Where an order for the alteration of the boundary of any parish or the division thereof, or the union thereof or of any part thereof, with another parish is proposed to be made after the appointed day, notice thereof shall, a reasonable time before it is made, be given to the parish council of that parish, or if there is no parish council, to the parish meeting, and that parish council or parish meeting, as the case may be, shall have the right to appear at any inquiry held by the county council with reference to the order, and shall be at liberty to petition the Local Government Board against the confirmation of the order.

(8.) Where the alteration of the boundary of any parish, or the division thereof or the union thereof or of part thereof with another parish, seems expedient for any of the purposes of this Act, provision for such alteration, division, or union may be made by an order of the county council confirmed by the Local Government Board under section fifty-seven of the Local Government Act, 1888. **51 & 52 Vict. c. 41.**

(9.) Where a parish is by this Act divided into two or more parishes, those parishes shall, until it is otherwise provided, be included in the same poor law union in which the original parish was included.

(10.) Subject to the provisions of this Act, any order made by a county council in pursuance of this Part of this Act shall be deemed to be an order under section fifty-seven of the Local Government Act, 1888, and any board of guardians affected by an order shall have the same right of petitioning against that order as is given by that section to any other authority.

(11.) Where any of the areas referred to in section fifty-seven of the Local Government Act, 1888, is situate in two or more counties, or the alteration of any such area would alter the boundaries of a poor law union situate in two or more counties, a joint committee appointed by the councils of those counties shall, subject to the terms of delegation, be deemed to have and to have always had power to make orders under that section with respect

Sect. 36 (11). to that area ; and where at the passing of this Act a rural sanitary district or parish is situate in more than one county, a joint committee of the councils of those counties shall act under this section, and if any of those councils do not, within two months after request from any other of them, appoint members of such joint committee, the members of the committee actually appointed shall act as the joint committee. Provided that any question arising as to the constitution or procedure of any such joint committee shall, if the county councils concerned failed to agree, be determined by the Local Government Board.

50 & 51 Vict. c. 61.

(12.) Every report made by the Boundary Commissioners under the Local Government Boundaries Act, 1887, shall be laid before the council of any administrative county or borough affected by that report, and before any joint committee of county councils, and it shall be the duty of such councils and joint committees to take such reports into consideration before framing any order under the powers conferred on them under this Act.

(13.) Every county council shall, within two years after the passing of this Act, or within such further period as the Local Government Board may allow either generally or with reference to any particular matter, make such orders under this section as they deem necessary for the purpose of bringing this Act into operation, and after the expiration of the said two years or further period the powers of the county council for that purpose shall be transferred to the Local Government Board, who may exercise those powers (*p*).

Provision as to parishes having parts with defined boundaries.

37. Where it is proved to the satisfaction of the county council that any part of a parish has a defined boundary, and has any property or rights distinct from the rest of the parish, the county council may order that the consent of a parish meeting held for that part of the parish shall be required for any such act or class of acts of the parish council affecting the said property or rights as is specified in the order (*q*).

Orders for grouping parishes and

38.—(1.) Where parishes are grouped, the grouping order shall make the necessary provisions for the name of the group, for the

(*p*) Numerous alterations of areas and boundaries were effected by or under this section in or shortly after the year 1894, and the object aimed at—that each parish should be wholly contained in one county district and each county district in one county—has been for the most part attained, and the section is practically spent. See the notes to this section in the authors' separate work on this Act, and see also as to alterations of boundaries, Part III. of the Local Government Act, 1888, and in particular ss. 57 and 59 of that Act, *ante* pp. 111, 114.

(*q*) A case for an order under this section might arise where the benefits of a charity were confined to the inhabitants of an ancient chapelry or some other definite part of a civil parish, and it was desired to give those inhabitants a separate voice in the choice of any trustees of the charity to be appointed by the parish council under s. 14, *ante*. Section 49 provides for the holding of a "parish meeting" for a part of a parish.

Sect. 38 (1).

dissolving groups.

parish meetings in each of the grouped parishes, and for the election in manner provided by this Act of separate representatives of each parish on the parish council, and may provide for the consent of the parish meeting of a parish to any particular act of the parish council, and for any other adaptations of this Act to the group of parishes, or to the parish meetings in the group (*r*).

(2.) Where parishes are grouped the whole area under each parish council shall, unless the county council for special reasons otherwise direct, be within the same administrative county and county district.

(3.) Where parishes are grouped, the grouping order shall provide for the application of the provisions of this Act with respect to the appointment of trustees and beneficiaries of a charity, and the custody of documents, so as to preserve the separate rights of each parish (*s*).

(4.) The parish meeting of any parish may apply to the county council for a grouping order respecting that parish, and, if the parish has a less population than two hundred, for a parish council (*t*), and any such application shall be forthwith taken into consideration by the county council.

(5.) The county council may, on the application of the council for any group of parishes or of the parish meeting for any parish included in a group of parishes, make an order dissolving the group, and shall by the order make such provision as appears necessary for the election of parish councils of the parishes in the group and for the adjustment of property, rights, and liabilities as between separate parishes and the group (*u*).

Provisions for increase and decrease of population.

39.—(1.) Where the population of a parish not having a separate parish council increases so as to justify the election of such council, the parish meeting may petition the county council, and the county council, if they think proper, may order the election of a parish council in that parish, and shall by the order make such provision as appears necessary for separating the parish from any group of parishes in which it is included, and for the alteration of the parish council of the group, and for the adjustment of property,

(*r*) It must be borne in mind, in making an order under this section, that by s. 19, *ante*, the parish meeting and the corporate body of the chairman and overseers of a parish having no separate parish council, have certain powers and duties which will continue after the grouping order has been made, save so far as they are varied by that order.

(*s*) The provisions of the Act as to charities and custody of documents are contained in ss. 14 and 17, *ante*. These provisions must be applied by the grouping order in such a way that each parish of the group shall retain its rights.

(*t*) The power to apply for a parish council is not limited to parishes having a less population than 300 ; see s. (1) (a), *ante*, p. 593.

(*u*) As to adjustment, see s. 68, *post*.

Sect. 39 (1). rights, and liabilities as between the group and the parish with a separate parish council.

(2.) Where the population of a parish, according to the last published census for the time being, is less than two hundred, the parish meeting may petition the county council, and the county council, if they think proper, may order the dissolution of the parish council, and from and after the date of the order this Act shall apply to that parish as to a parish not having a parish council. The order shall make such provision as appears necessary for carrying it into effect, and for the disposal and adjustment of the property, rights, and liabilities of the parish council. Where a petition for such an order is rejected, another petition for the same purpose may not be presented within two years from the presentation of the previous petition.

Certain orders of county council not to require confirmation.

40. A grouping order, and an order establishing or dissolving a parish council, or dissolving a group of parishes, and an order relating to the custody of parish documents or requiring the approval of the Charity Commissioners, and an order requiring the consent of the parish meeting for any part of the parish to any act or class of acts of the parish council, shall not require submission to or confirmation by the Local Government Board (*x*).

Reduction of time for appealing against county council orders.

41. The time for petitioning against an order under section fifty-seven of the Local Government Act, 1888, shall be six weeks instead of three months after the notice referred to in sub-section three of that section (*y*).

Validity of county council orders.

42. When an order under section fifty-seven of the Local Government Act, 1888, has been confirmed by the Local Government Board, such order shall at the expiration of six months from that confirmation be presumed to have been duly made, and to be within the powers of that section, and no objection to the legality thereof shall be entertained in any legal proceeding whatever (*z*).

PART IV.

SUPPLEMENTAL.

Parish Meetings and Elections.

Removal of disqualification of

43. For the purposes of this Act a woman shall not be disqualified by marriage for being on any local government register

(*x*) The orders referred to are those made under ss. 1 (1), 38, 39, 17, 36 (3), and 37 of this Act, *ante*.

(*y*) See the sub-section referred to, *ante*, p. 112.

(*z*) This provision may be usefully resorted to in case of questions arising as to whether an order was *intra vires* or not.

of electors, or for being an elector of any local authority, provided that a husband and wife shall not both be qualified in respect of the same property (*a*).

Sect. 43. — married women.

Register of parochial electors.

44.—(1.) The local government register of electors and the parliamentary register of electors, so far as they relate to a parish shall, together, form the register of the parochial electors of the parish; and any person whose name is not in that register shall not be entitled to attend a meeting or vote as a parochial elector, and any person whose name is in that register shall be entitled to attend a meeting and vote as a parochial elector unless prohibited from voting by this or any other Act of Parliament.

(2.) Where the parish is in a parliamentary borough, such portion of the parliamentary register of electors for the county as contains the names of persons registered in respect of the ownership of any property in the parish shall be deemed to form part of the parliamentary register of electors for the parish within the meaning of this section.

(3.) The lists and register of electors in any parish shall be framed in parts for wards of urban districts and parishes in such manner that they may be conveniently used as lists for polling at elections for any such wards.

(4.) Nothing in any Act shall prevent a person, if duly qualified, from being registered in more than one register of parochial electors.

(5.) Where in that portion of the parliamentary register of electors which relates to a parish a person is entered to vote in a polling district other than the district comprising the parish, such person shall be entitled to vote as a parochial elector for that parish, and in addition to an asterisk there shall be placed against his name a number consecutive with the other numbers in the list.

(6.) Where the revising barrister in any list of voters for a parish would—

(a.) In pursuance of section seven of the County Electors Act, 1888, place an asterisk or other mark against the name of any person; or 51 Vict. c. 10.

(b.) In pursuance of section four of the Registration Act, 1885, erase the name of any person otherwise than by reason

(*a*) The effect of this provision is, that coverture does not disentitle a married woman who is otherwise qualified to have her name inserted on a local government register of electors, "for the purposes of this Act," viz., as a parochial elector. The disability of coverture still exists with regard to the power to vote as a county elector. See Municipal Corporations Act, 1882, s. 63, and notes, *ante*, p. 290. A married woman is not qualified to be a parochial elector by reason of her ownership of property, there being no ownership qualification for local government electors. *Drax* v. *Ffooks*, [1896] 1 Q. B. 238; 65 L. J. Q. B. 270; 74 L. T. 43; 44 W. R. 393; 60 J. P. 214; 12 T. L. R. 185.

Sect. 44 (6).

of that name appearing] more than once in the lists for the same parish ; or

41 & 42 Vict. c. 26. 48 & 49 Vict. c. 15.

(c.) in pursuance of section twenty-eight of the Parliamentary and Municipal Registration Act, 1878, as amended by section five of the Registration Act, 1885, place against the name of a person a note to the effect that such person is not entitled to vote in respect of the qualification contained in the list,

the revising barrister shall, instead of placing that mark or note, or erasing the name, place against the name, if the person is entitled to vote in respect of that entry as a county elector or burgess, a mark signifying that his name should be printed in division three of the list, or if he is entitled to vote only as a parochial elector, a mark signifying that he is entitled to be registered as a parochial elector, and the name so marked shall not be printed in the parliamentary register of electors, but shall be printed, as the case requires, either in division three of the local government register of electors, or in a separate list of parochial electors.

(7.) Where the name of a person is entered both in the ownership list and in the occupation list of voters in the same parish, and the revising barrister places against that name a mark or note signifying that the name should be printed in division three of the list, an asterisk or other mark shall be there printed against the name, and such person shall not be entitled to vote as a parochial elector in respect of that entry.

(8.) Such separate list shall form part of the register of parochial electors of the parish, and shall be printed at the end of the other lists of electors for the parish, and the names shall be numbered consecutively with the other names on those lists, and the law relating to the register of electors shall, with the necessary modifications, apply accordingly, and the lists shall, for the purposes of this Act, be deemed to be part of such register.

(9.) Any person may claim for the purpose of having his name entered in the parochial electors list, and the law relating to claims to be entered in lists of voters shall apply.

(10.) The clerk of the county council or town clerk, as the case may be, shall, in printing the lists returned to him by the revising barrister, do everything that is necessary for carrying into effect the provisions of this section with respect to the persons whose names are marked by the revising barrister in pursuance of this section.

45. *Supplemental provisions as to parish meetings.*]

Sect. 46 (1).

Disqualifications for parish or district council.

46. (*b*)—(1.) A person shall be disqualified for being elected or being a member or chairman of a council of a parish or of a district other than a borough or of a board of guardians if he—

(a) is an infant or an alien ; or

(b) has within twelve months before his election, or since his election, received union or parochial relief ; or

(c) has, within five years before his election or since his election, been convicted either on indictment or summarily of any crime, and sentenced to imprisonment with hard labour without the option of a fine, or to any greater punishment, and has not received a free pardon, or has, within or during the time aforesaid, been adjudged bankrupt, or made a composition or arrangement with his creditors ; or

(d) holds any paid office under the parish council or district council or board of guardians, as the case may be ; or

(e) is concerned in any bargain or contract entered into with the council or board, or participates in the profit of any such bargain or contract or of any work done under the authority of the council or board.

(2.) Provided that a person shall not be disqualified for being elected or being a member or chairman of any such council or board by reason of being interested—

(a) in the sale or lease of any lands or in any loan of money to the council or board, or in any contract with the council for the supply from land, of which he is owner or occupier, of stone, gravel, or other materials for making or repairing highways or bridges, or in the transport of materials for the repair of roads or bridges in his own immediate neighbourhood ; or

(b) in any newspaper in which any advertisement relating to the affairs of the council or board is inserted ; or

(c) in any contract with the council or board as a shareholder in any joint stock company ; but he shall not vote at any meeting of the council or board on any question in which such company are interested, except that in the case of a water company or other company established for the carrying on of works of a like public nature, this prohibition may be dispensed with by the county council.

(3.) Where a person who is a parish councillor, or is a candidate for election as a parish councillor, is concerned in any such bargain

(*b*) This section may be compared with s. 39 of the Municipal Corporations Act, *ante*, p. 275. It is submitted that the powers of dispensing with the prohibition mentioned in sub-s. (2) (c), and the removal of a disqualification under sub-s. (3), ought to be by order under the seal of the county council

Sect. 46 (3).

or contract, or participates in any such profit, as would disqualify him for being a parish councillor, the disqualification may be removed by the county council if they are of opinion that such removal will be beneficial to the parish.

(4.) Where a person is disqualified by being adjudged bankrupt or making a composition or arrangement with his creditors, the disqualification shall cease, in case of bankruptcy, when the adjudication is annulled, or when he obtains his discharge with a certificate that his bankruptcy was caused by misfortune without any misconduct on his part, and, in case of composition or arrangement, on payment of his debts in full.

(5.) A person disqualified for being a guardian shall also be disqualified for being a rural district councillor (*c*).

* * * * *

Supplemental provisions as to parish councils.

47.—(1.) If at the annual election of parish councillors any vacancies are not filled by election, such number of the retiring councillors as are not re-elected, and are required to fill the vacancies, shall, if willing, continue to hold office. The councillors so to continue shall be those who were highest on the poll at the previous election, or if the numbers were equal or there was no poll, as may be determined by the parish meeting, or if not so determined, by the chairman of the parish council.

(2.) A retiring parish councillor or chairman of a parish council or parish meeting shall be re-eligible.

(3.) A parish councillor may, by notice in writing to the chairman of the council, resign his office, and a chairman of a parish council or parish meeting may resign his chairmanship by notice in writing to the council or meeting.

(4.) A casual vacancy among parish councillors or in the office of chairman of the council shall be filled by the parish council, and where there is no parish council, a casual vacancy in the office of chairman of the parish meeting shall be filled by the parish meeting, and the person elected shall retire from office at the time when the vacating councillor or chairman would have retired.

(5.) If any parish council become unable to act by reason of a want of councillors, whether from failure to elect or otherwise, the county council may order a new election, and may by order make such provision as seems expedient for authorising any person to act temporarily in the place of the parish council and of the chairman thereof (*d*).

(*c*) Sub-sections (6) to (10) do not affect county councils.

(*d*) A similar power as to district councils is given by s. 59 (5), *post*. See also as to the power of a county council to remove difficulties in connection with elections under this Act, s. 48 (5), and the Local Government (Elections) Act, 1896, *post*. In case of a resort to the expedient of authorizing a person

Sect. 48 (1).

Supplemental provisions as to elections, polls, and tenure of office.

48.—(1.) The election of a parish councillor shall be at a parish meeting, or at a poll consequent thereon.

(2.) Rules framed under this Act by the Local Government Board in relation to elections (*e*) shall, notwithstanding anything in any other Act, have effect as if enacted in this Act, and shall provide, amongst other things—

(i.) for every candidate being nominated in writing by two parochial electors as proposer and seconder and no more;

(ii.) for preventing an elector at an election for a union or for a district not a borough from subscribing a nomination paper or voting in more than one parish or other area in the union or district;

(iii.) for preventing an elector at an election for a parish divided into parish wards from subscribing a nomination paper or voting for more than one ward;

(iv.) for fixing or enabling the county council to fix the day of the poll and the hours during which the poll is to be kept open, so, however, that the poll shall always be open between the hours of six and eight in the evening;

(v.) for the polls at elections held at the same date and in the same area being taken together, except where this is impracticable;

(vi.) for the appointment of returning officers for the elections.

(3.) At every election regulated by rules framed under this Act, the poll shall be taken by ballot, and the Ballot Act, 1872, and the Municipal Elections (Corrupt and Illegal Practices) Act, 1884, and sections seventy-four and seventy-five and Part IV. of the Municipal Corporations Act, 1882, as amended by the last-mentioned Act (including the penal provisions of those Acts) shall, subject to adaptations, alterations, and exceptions made by such rules, apply in like manner as in the case of a municipal election. Provided that—

35 & 36 Vict. c. 33. 47 & 48 Vict. c. 70. 45 & 46 Vict. c. 50.

(a) section six of the Ballot Act, 1872, shall apply in the case of such elections, and the returning officer may, in addition to using the schools and public rooms therein referred to free of charge, for taking the poll, use the same, free of charge, for hearing objections to nomination papers and for counting votes; and

---

to act temporarily in the place of the parish council, it is submitted that the powers of the person so authorized should be defined by the order.

(*e*) The practice of the Local Government Board was at first to issue each year separate sets of rules applicable to the annual elections of each of the bodies to whose election this Act applies; but at the beginning of the year 1898 permanent rules were issued for the elections of guardians and district and parish councillors. Under these rules county councils have various powers and duties, such as fixing the day and hours of poll.

Sect. 48 (3).

(b) section thirty-seven of the Municipal Elections (Corrupt and Illegal Practices) Act, 1884, shall apply as if the election were an election mentioned in the First Schedule to that Act.

(4.) The provisions of the Municipal Corporations Act, 1882, and the enactments amending the same, with respect to the expenses of elections of councillors of a borough, and to the acceptance of office, resignation, re-eligibility of holders of office, and the filling of casual vacancies, and section fifty-six of that Act, shall, subject to the adaptations, alterations, and exceptions made by the said rules, apply in the case of guardians and of district councillors of a county district not a borough, and of members of the local board of Woolwich, and of a vestry under the Metropolis Management Acts, 1855 to 1890, and any Act amending the same. Provided that—

(a) the provisions as to resignation shall not apply to guardians, and district councillors of a rural district shall be in the same position with respect to resignation as members of a board of guardians ; and

(b) nothing in the enactments applied by this section shall authorise or require a returning officer to hold an election to fill a casual vacancy which occurs within six months before the ordinary day of retirement from the office in which the vacancy occurs, and the vacancy shall be filled at the next ordinary election ; and

(c) the rules may provide for the incidence of the charge of the expenses of the elections of guardians being the same as heretofore.

(5.) If any difficulty arises as respects the election of any individual councillor or guardian, or member of any such local board or vestry as aforesaid, or auditor, and there is no provision for holding another election, the county council may order a new election to be held and give such directions as may be necessary for the purpose of holding the election.

(6.) Any ballot boxes, fittings, and compartments provided by or belonging to any public authority, for any election (whether parliamentary, county council, municipal, school board, or other), shall, on request, and if not required for immediate use by the said authority, be lent to the returning officer for an election under this Act, upon such conditions and either free of charge or, except in the prescribed cases, for such reasonable charge as may be prescribed.

(7.) The expenses of any election under this Act shall not exceed the scale fixed by the county council, and if at the beginning of one month before the first election under this Act a county council have not framed any such scale for their county, the Local Government Board may frame a scale for the county, and the scale so framed shall apply to the first election, and shall have effect as if it had been made by the county council, but shall not be alterable until after the first election. **Sect. 48 (7).**

(8.) This section shall, subject to any adaptations made by the said rules, apply in the case of every poll consequent on a parish meeting, as if it were a poll for the election of parish councillors.

49. Where a parish meeting is required or authorised in pursuance of this Act to be held for a ward or other part of a parish, then— Provision as to parish meeting for part of parish.

(a) the persons entitled to attend and vote at the meeting, or at any poll consequent thereon, shall be the parochial electors registered in respect of qualifications in that ward or part; and

(b) the provisions of this Act with respect to parish meetings for the whole of a parish, including the provisions with respect to the convening of a parish meeting by parochial electors, shall apply as if the ward or part were the whole parish.

50 (*f*). *Supplemental provisions as to overseers.*]

51 (*f*). *Public notices.*]

52 (*f*). *Supplemental provisions as to transfer of powers.*]

53.—(1.) Where on the appointed day any of the adoptive Acts is in force in a part only of a rural parish, the existing authority under the Act, or the parish meeting for that part, may transfer the powers, duties, and liabilities of the authority to the parish council, subject to any conditions with respect to the execution thereof by means of a committee as to the authority or parish meeting may seem fit, and any such conditions may be altered by any such parish meeting. Supplemental provisions as to adoptive Acts.

(2.) If the area on the appointed day under any authority under any of the adoptive Acts will not after that day be comprised within one rural parish, the powers and duties of the authority shall be transferred to the parish councils of the rural parishes wholly or partly comprised in that area, or, if the area is partly

(*f*) Section 50 relates to the action to be taken by the guardians where default has been made in notifying the appointment of overseers, under ss. 5 or 33, *ante*; s. 51 to the giving of parish notices; and s. 52 contains further provisions as to the transfer of powers to the new parish authorities. These sections do not directly affect county councils.

Sect. 53 (2). comprised in an urban district, to those parish councils and the district council of the urban district, and shall, until other provision is made in pursuance of this Act, be exercised by a joint committee appointed by those councils. Where any such rural parish has not a parish council the parish meeting shall, for the purposes of this provision, be substituted for the parish council.

(3.) The property, debts, and liabilities of any authority under any of the adoptive Acts whose powers are transferred in pursuance of this Act shall continue to be the property, debts, and liabilities of the area of that authority, and the proceeds of the property shall be credited, and the debts and liabilities and the expenses incurred in respect of the said powers, duties, and liabilities, shall be charged to the account of the rates or contributions levied in that area, and where that area is situate in more than one parish the sums credited to and paid by each parish shall be apportioned in such manner as to give effect to this enactment.

(4.) The county council on the application of a parish council may, by order, alter the boundaries of any such area if they consider that the alteration can properly be made without any undue alteration of the incidence of liability to rates and contributions or of the right to property belonging to the area, regard being had to any corresponding advantage to persons subject to the liability or entitled to the right (*g*).

Effect on parish council of constitution of urban district.

54.—(1.) Where a new borough is created, or any other new urban district is constituted, or the area of an urban district is extended, then—

(a) as respects any rural parish or part of a rural parish which will be comprised in the borough or urban district, provision shall be made, either by the constitution of a new parish, or by the annexation of the parish or parts thereof to another parish or parishes, or otherwise, for

---

(*g*) As to the constitution of the joint committee referred to in this section, and the apportionment of the expenses of the adoptive Acts where those Acts are the Burial Acts, see the Local Government (Joint Committees) Act, 1897, *post*. The provisions of this section should be borne in mind by county councils when altering areas in which any of the adoptive Acts (as to which see s. 7, *ante*) are in force. It would seem to be contrary to the spirit of the Act to attempt to set up a special authority under an adoptive Act (*e.g.*, a burial board), this Act having put an end to such authorities in rural parishes. It is conceived that the power given by sub-s. (4) of this section to alter the area under an adoptive Act can rarely be exercised, having regard to the limitations upon its exercise which the sub-section imposes. But where the alteration of the area under any local authority is necessary or proper for the purposes of an order under s. 57 of the Local Government Act, 1888, *ante*, p. 111, the county council has power to alter that area under s. 59 of the same Act, *ante*, p. 114. It has been held that the county council have such power in respect of an area under the Burial Acts. *R.* v. *Durham County Council* (WRIGHT and BRUCE, JJ.), January 13th, 1897; L. G. Chronicle, 1897, p. 70.

the appointment of overseers and for placing the parish or part in the same position as other parishes in the borough or district, and Sect. 54 (1).

(b) as respects any parish or part which remains rural, provision shall be made for the constitution of a new parish council for the same, or for the annexation of the parish or part to some other parish or parishes, or otherwise for the government of the parish or part, and

(c) provision shall also where necessary be made for the adjustment of any property, debts, and liabilities affected by the said creation, constitution, or extension.

(2.) The provision aforesaid shall be made—

(a.) Where a new borough is created, by a scheme under section two hundred and thirteen of the Municipal Corporations Act, 1882; 45 & 46 Vict. c. 50.

(b.) Where any other new urban district is constituted, by an order of the county council under section fifty-seven of the Local Government Act, 1888; 51 & 52 Vict. c. 41.

(c.) Where the area of an urban district is extended, by an order of the Local Government Board under section fifty-four, or of the county council under section fifty-seven, as the case may be, of the Local Government Act, 1888.

(3.) Where the area of an urban district is diminished this section shall apply with the necessary modifications (*h*).

55.—(1.) Where a parish is divided or united or grouped with another parish by an order in pursuance of this Act each new parish or group so formed shall bear such name as the order directs. Power to change name of district or parish.

(2.) Where a parish is divided by this Act, each parish so formed shall bear such name as the county council direct.

(3.) Any district council may, with the sanction of the county council, change their name and the name of their district.

(4.) Every change of name made in pursuance of this section shall be published in such manner as the authority authorising the change may direct, and shall be notified to the Local Government Board.

(*h*) This section must be noted in cases of the formation of part of a rural district into an urban district, or the extension of an urban district by an order of the county council, under s. 57 of the Act of 1888, *ante*, p. 111. It must be seen that each portion of the area affected is included in a properly formed parish, new parishes being created where necessary, and that any portion of the area remaining rural is placed under the jurisdiction of a new, or added to the area of an existing parish council. Provision must be made for the election of representatives upon such parish councils, and the election orders of the Local Government Board will generally require to be applied, with modifications.

Sect. 55 (5).

(5.) Any such change of name shall not affect any rights or obligations of any parish, district, council, authority, or person, or render defective any legal proceedings, and any legal proceedings may be continued or commenced as if there were no change of name.

Committees of parish or district councils.

56.—(1.) A parish or district council may appoint committees, consisting either wholly or partly of members of the council, for the exercise of any powers which, in the opinion of the council, can be properly exercised by committees, but a committee shall not hold office beyond the next annual meeting of the council, and the acts of every such committee shall be submitted to the council for their approval.

Provided that where a committee is appointed by any district council for any of the purposes of the Public Health Acts or Highway Acts, the council may authorise the committee to institute any proceeding or do any act which the council might have instituted or done for that purpose other than the raising of any loan or the making of any rate or contract.

(2.) Where a parish council have any powers and duties which are to be exercised in a part only of the parish, or in relation to a recreation ground, building, or property held for the benefit of a part of a parish, and the part has a defined boundary, the parish council shall, if required by a parish meeting held for that part, appoint annually to exercise such powers and duties a committee consisting partly of members of the council and partly of other persons representing the said part of the parish.

(3.) With respect to committees of parish and district councils the provisions in the First Schedule to this Act shall have effect.

(4.) This section shall not apply to the council of a borough.

Joint committees.

57.—(1.) A parish or district council may concur with any other parish or district council or councils in appointing out of their respective bodies a joint committee for any purpose in respect of which they are jointly interested, and in conferring, with or without conditions or restrictions, on any such committee any powers which the appointing council might exercise if the purpose related exclusively to their own parish or district.

(2.) Provided that a council shall not delegate to any such committee any power to borrow money or make any rate.

(3.) A joint committee appointed under this section shall not hold office beyond the expiration of fourteen days after the next annual meeting of any of the councils who appointed it.

(4.) The costs of a joint committee under this section shall be defrayed by the councils by whom it is appointed in such proportions as they may agree upon, or as may be determined in case of difference by the county council. **Sect. 57 (4).**

(5.) Where a parish council can under this Act be required to appoint a committee consisting partly of members of the council and partly of other persons (*i*), that requirement may also be made in the case of a joint committee, and shall be duly complied with by the parish councils concerned at the time of the appointment of such committee.

58. *Audit of accounts of district and parish councils and inspection.*]

59. (*k*) *Supplemental provisions as to district councils.* 38 & 39 *Vict. c.* 55.]

* * * * *

(5.) If any district council, other than a borough council, become unable to act, whether from failure to elect or otherwise, the county council of the county in which the district is situate may order elections to be held and may appoint persons to form the district council until the newly elected members come into office (*l*).

* * * * *

Miscellaneous.

Supplemental provisions as to guardians.

60.—(1.) The council of each county may, from time to time, by order, fix or alter the number of guardians or rural district councillors to be elected for each parish within their county, and for those purposes may exercise powers of adding parishes to each other and dividing parishes into wards, similar to those which by the Acts relating to the relief of the poor are, for the purpose of the election of guardians, vested in the Local Government Board (*m*).

(*i*) See s. 56 (2), *supra*.

(*k*) The earlier clauses of this section relate to the proceedings of district councils (other than councils of boroughs) and of boards of guardians. Subsection (6) contains a saving for the powers of the Secretary of State as to Aldershot, under 20 & 21 Vict. c. 22.

(*l*) Compare the similar powers as to parish councils under s. 47 (5), *ante*, p. 636.

(*m*) The power to fix and alter the number of guardians formerly belonged to the Local Government Board exclusively, under 4 & 5 Will. 4, c. 76, s. 38, and 7 & 8 Vict. c. 101, s. 18. The same body derived their power of adding parishes to each other from 31 & 32 Vict. c. 122, s. 6. That section provides that the Local Government Board may by order add any parish in a union, the population of which, according to the last census, does not exceed 300, and the annual rateable value of which does not exceed the average rateable value of the parishes in the same union, according to the valuation lists in force for the time being, to some adjoining parish in the same union for the purpose of the election of guardians. By 39 & 40 Vict. c. 61, s. 12, the Local Government Board may by their order divide any parish into wards for the election of guardians, and determine the number of guardians to be elected for every such ward, having due regard to the value of the rateable property therein; and each such ward is, for the purposes of such election, to be deemed a separate parish except so far as the board may otherwise order.

These powers are conferred by the text on county councils, or in the cases mentioned in sub-s. (3), on their joint committees.

Sect. 60 (2).

(2.) The council of each county may for the purpose of regulating the retirement of guardians or rural district councillors, in cases where they retire by thirds, and in order that as nearly as may be one third of the persons elected as guardians for the union, and one third of the persons elected as rural district councillors for the district, shall retire in each year, direct in which year or years of each triennial period the guardians or district councillors for each parish, ward, or other area in the union or rural district shall retire (*n*).

(3.) Where a poor law union is situate in more than one county, the power under this section of fixing or altering the number of guardians or rural district councillors, and of regulating the retirement of guardians and of district councillors, shall be exercised by a joint committee of the councils of the counties concerned, but if any of those councils do not, within two months after request from any other of them, appoint members of such joint committee, the members of the committee actually appointed shall act as the joint committee.

Provided that if any order under this subsection is, within six weeks after the making thereof, objected to by any of the county councils concerned, or by any committee of any of those councils authorised in that behalf, it shall be of no effect until confirmed by the Local Government Board (*o*).

(4.) Where under any local and personal Act guardians of a poor law union are elected for districts, whether called by that name

---

(*n*) Guardians and rural district councillors retire by thirds unless an order has been made for their simultaneous retirement under s. 20, sub-s. (6), *ante*, p. 618. As each parish, ward, or group of united parishes has not three guardians or councillors, but some may have more and others less than that number, it is necessary to provide for the years in which the guardians or councillors of each parish will retire. Thus, in a parish having only one guardian, the election of a guardian can take place only once in three years, though in a parish with three there may be one retirement every year.

(*o*) Although the area of a poor law union may be altered under s. 36, sub-s. (6), *ante*, p. 629, the general scheme of the Act is to leave the area of the union untouched even when it extends into two counties. In that case the powers of fixing and altering the number of guardians and rural district councillors and of regulating the retirement of guardians and rural district councillors are exerciseable by the county councils concerned by means of a joint committee to act for the entire union. It is to be observed that the power of dividing a parish into wards is not given to the joint committee; that power apparently rests with the council of the county in which the parish is situate; but the joint committee will provide for the simultaneous retirement of guardians and rural district councillors under s. 20, sub-s. (6), *ante*, p. 618, and 24, sub-s. (4), *ante*, p. 620.

The number of members appointed by each county council to serve on the joint committee is apparently to be fixed by agreement. See further as to joint committees, s. 81 of the Act of 1888, *ante*. p. 155.

The proviso gives in effect an appeal to the Local Government Board at the instance of a dissenting council.

or not, the provisions of this Act with respect to the election of guardians shall apply as if each of the districts were a parish (*p*). Sect. 60 (4).

(5.) The board of guardians of a union elected in pursuance of this Act shall, save as otherwise provided by an order of the Local Government Board, made on the application of those guardians, have the same powers and duties under any local and personal Act as the existing board of guardians.

(6.) Nothing in this Act shall alter the constitution of the corporation of the guardians of the poor within the city of Oxford, or the election or qualification of the members thereof, except those members who are elected by the ratepayers of parishes.

61. *Place of meeting of parish or district council or board of guardians* (*q*).]

62. *Permissive transfer to urban district council of powers of other authorities.*]

Provisions as to county council acquiring powers of district council.

63.—(1.) Where the powers of a district council are by virtue of a resolution under this Act transferred to a county council, the following provisions shall have effect:—

(a.) Notice of the resolution of the county council by virtue of which the transfer is made shall be forthwith sent to the district council and to the Local Government Board:

(b.) The expenses incurred by the county council shall be a debt from the district council to the county council, and shall be defrayed as part of the expenses of the district council in the execution of the Public Health Acts, and the district council shall have the like power of raising the money as for the defraying of those expenses:

(c.) The county council for the purpose of the powers transferred may on behalf of the district council borrow subject to the like conditions, in the like manner, and on the security of the like fund or rate, as the district council might have borrowed for the purpose of those powers:

(d.) The county council may charge the said fund or rate with the payment of the principal and interest of the loan, and the loan with the interest thereon shall be paid by the district council in like manner, and the charge shall have

(*p*) In a few unions and parishes guardians, or as they sometimes called, governors, of the poor are under local Acts. Where the areas for which separate guardians are elected are not parishes, they are to be deemed parishes so that the county council have the same powers for the purposes of the election of guardians for such areas as if they were parishes.

(*q*) Section 61 prohibits the use of licensed premises for meetings of parish and district authorities, and s. 62 enables an urban district council to transfer to themselves the powers, duties, and liabilities of any authority under the adoptive Acts within their district.

Sect. 63 (1).

the like effect, as if the loan were lawfully raised and charged on that fund or rate by the district council:

(e.) The county council shall keep separate accounts of all receipts and expenditure in respect of the said powers.

(f.) The county council may by order vest in the district council all or any of the powers, duties, property, debts, and liabilities of the county council in relation to any of the said powers, and the property, debts, and liabilities so vested shall be deemed to have been acquired or incurred by the district council for the purpose of those powers(*r*).

(2.) Where a rural district is situate in two or more counties a parish council complaining under this Act may complain to the county council of the county in which the parish is situate, and if the subject-matter of the complaint affects any other county the complaint shall be referred to a joint committee of the councils of the counties concerned, and any question arising as to the constitution of such joint committee shall be determined by the Local Government Board, and if any members of the joint committee are not appointed, the members who are actually appointed shall act as the joint committee(*s*).

(*r*) This sub-section will apply where a county council has resolved, upon the complaint of a parish council of the default of a district council that the duties and powers of the district council for the purpose of the matter complained of shall be transferred to the county council. See s. 16, and s. 26, sub-s. (4), *ante*, pp. 612, 623. It does not appear that under these sections the powers of an urban district council can be transferred to a county council.

As to the defraying of the expenses of a rural district council, see ss. 229 *et seq.* of the Public Health Act, 1875, and s. 29 of this Act, *ante*, p. 625. As to their borrowing powers, see ss. 233 *et seq.* of the Public Health Act, 1875. The county council may borrow under the provisions in the text, for any purpose for which the defaulting district council might have borrowed; the loan will be secured on the fund or rate which the district council might have charged, and will be repayable by the district council. Where the default is in respect of a matter to which s. 26 (4) of this Act relates, the provisions of s. 29, *ante*, as to highway expenses must be borne in mind. Clause (f) enables the county council to hand over any property acquired for the purposes of the exercise of the powers of the district council by the county council, and to put the district council in the same position as regards powers, duties, debts, and liabilities relating to the subject matter of the complaint, as if the powers of the district council had been exercised by that council in the first instance, and no complaint had been made.

(*s*) Where a complaint is referred to a joint committee of county councils under this sub-section, it appears that that joint committee will have power to determine whether or not any action is to be taken in the matter of the complaint, and whether if action is to be taken it is to be taken by the method of taking over the powers of the defaulting district council, or by the method of compelling that council to perform the duty in respect of which the complaint is made, see note to s. 16, *ante*, p. 612.

The body to take action in either of these ways will be, it is submitted, the joint committee of the county councils, and not the county council to whom the complaint was originally made.

Sect. 64.

64. A county council may employ a district council as their agents in the transaction of any administrative business on matters arising in, or affecting the interests of, its own district (*t*).

Power to act through district council.

65. *Saving for harbour powers.*]

66. *Saving for elementary schools* (*u*).]

Transfer of property and debts and liabilities.

67. Where any powers and duties are transferred by this Act from one authority to another authority—

(1.) All property held by the first authority for the purpose or by virtue of such powers and duties shall pass to and vest in the other authority, subject to all debts and liabilities affecting the same; and

(2.) The latter authority shall hold the same for the estate, interest, and purposes, and subject to the covenants, conditions, and restrictions for and subject to which the property would have been held if this Act had not passed, so far as the same are not modified by or in pursuance of this Act; and

(3.) All debts and liabilities of the first authority incurred by virtue of such powers and duties shall become debts and liabilities of the latter authority, and be defrayed out of the like property and funds out of which they would have been defrayed if this Act had not passed.

Adjustment of property and liabilities.

68. (*x*)—(1.) Where any adjustment is required for the purpose of this Act, or of any order, or thing made or done under this Act, then, if the adjustment is not otherwise made, the authorities interested may make agreements for the purpose, and may thereby adjust any property, income, debts, liabilities, and expenses, so far as affected by this Act, or such scheme, order, or thing, of the parties to the agreement.

(2.) The agreement may provide for the transfer or retention of any property, debts, or liabilities, with or without any conditions, and for the joint use of any property, and for payment by either party to the agreement in respect of property, debts, and liabilities

(*t*) See the enumeration of the "administrative business" in s. 3 of the Act of 1888, *ante*, p. 5, but that enumeration does not exhaust the administrative business of a county council.

(*u*) Sections 65 and 66 contain savings for harbour powers, and for the trusteeship, management, or control of elementary schools. See the definition of "elementary school" in s. 75, *post*.

(*x*) As to adjustment, see also s. 62 of the Act of 1888, *ante*, p. 119. A county council may provide for any adjustment which becomes necessary in consequence of an order under s. 57 of that Act by the order itself (see s. 59 (4) (e), *ante*, p. 116); but they may leave the question of adjustment to be settled by the authorities concerned, under s. 62, or if the order is made under this Act, under the provision in the text. As to what matters require adjustment in consequence of such an order, see *Re Llanwonno School Board and Ystradyfodwg School Board*, Times, May 20th, 1898; *Re Rochdale Union and Haslingden Union*, Times, May 21st, 1898.

Sect. 68 (2).

so transferred or retained, or of such joint user, and in respect of the salary or remuneration of any officer or person, and that either by way of an annual payment or, except in the case of a salary or remuneration, by way of a capital sum, or of a terminable annuity for a period not exceeding that allowed by the Local Government Board: Provided that where any of the authorities interested is a board of guardians, any such agreement, so far as it relates to the joint use of any property, shall be subject to the approval of the Local Government Board.

(3.) In default of an agreement, and as far as any such agreement does not extend, such adjustment shall be referred to arbitration in accordance with the Arbitration Act, 1889, and the arbitrator shall have power to disallow as costs in the arbitration the costs of any witness whom he considers to have been called unnecessarily, and any other costs which he considers to have been incurred unnecessarily, and his award may provide for any matter for which an agreement might have provided.

52 & 53 Vict. c. 49.

(4.) Any sum required to be paid by any authority for the purpose of adjustment may be paid as part of the general expenses of exercising their duties under this Act, or out of such special fund as the authority, with the approval of the Local Government Board, direct, and if it is a capital sum the payment thereof shall be a purpose for which the authority may borrow under the Acts relating to such authority, on the security of all or any of the funds, rates, and revenues of the authority, and any such sum may be borrowed without the consent of any authority, so that it be repaid within such period as the Local Government Board may sanction.

(5.) Any capital sum paid to any authority for the purpose of any adjustment under this Act shall be treated as capital, and applied with the sanction of the Local Government Board, either in the repayment of debt or for any other purpose for which capital money may be applied.

Power to deal with matters arising out of alteration of boundaries.

69. Where an alteration of any area is made by this Act, an order for any of the matters mentioned in section fifty-nine of the Local Government Act, 1888, may, if it appears to the county council desirable, be made by the county council, or, in the case of an area situate in more than one county, by a joint committee of county councils, but nothing in this section shall empower a county council or joint committee to alter the boundaries of a county (*y*).

(*y*) See s. 59 of the Act of 1888, *ante*, p. 114. It was held in *R.* v. *Durham County Council*, L. G. Chronicle, 1897, p. 70, that where a parish, having a burial board, had been divided by the operation of ss. 1 (3) and 36 (2) of this Act, *ante*, this section gives the county council power to make an order altering the Burial Acts area.

The alteration of the boundaries of a county can be effected by means of

Sect. 70 (1).

Summary proceeding for determination of questions as to transfer of powers.

70.—(1.) If any question arises, or is about to arise, as to whether any power, duty, or liability is or is not transferred by or under this Act to any parish council, parish meeting, or district council, or any property is or is not vested in the parish council, or in the chairman and overseers of a rural parish, or in a district council, that question, without prejudice to any other mode of trying it, may, on the application of the council, meeting, or other local authority concerned, be submitted for decision to the High Court in such summary manner as, subject to any rules of court, may be directed by the court; and the court, after hearing such parties and taking such evidence (if any) as it thinks just, shall decide the question.

(2.) If any question arises or is about to arise under this Act, as to the appointment of the trustees or beneficiaries of any charity, or as to the persons in whom the property of any charity is vested, such question shall, at the request of any trustee, beneficiary, or other person interested, be determined in the first instance by the Charity Commissioners, subject to an appeal to the High Court brought within three months after such determination. Provided that an appeal to the High Court of Justice from any determination of the Charity Commissioners under this section may be presented only under the same conditions as are prescribed in the case of appeals to the High Court from orders made by the Charity Commissioners under the Charitable Trusts Acts, 1853 to 1891.

(3.) An appeal shall, with the leave of the High Court or Court of Appeal, but not otherwise, lie to the Court of Appeal against any decision under this section.

Supplemental provisions as to county council orders.

71. A copy of every order made by a county council or joint committee in pursuance of this Act shall be sent to the Local Government Board, and, if it alters any local area or name, also to the Board of Agriculture.

Provisions as to local inquiries.

72.—(1.) The expenses incurred by the Local Government Board in respect of inquiries or other proceedings under this Act shall be paid by such authorities and persons and out of such funds and rates as the Board may by order direct, and the Board may certify the amount of the expenses so incurred, and any sum so certified and directed by the Board to be paid by any authority or person shall be a debt from that authority or person to the Crown.

(2.) Such expenses may include the salary of any inspector or officer of the Board engaged in the inquiry or proceeding, not exceeding three guineas a day.

---

a provisional order of the Local Government Board, under s. 54 of the Act of 1888, *ante*, p. 108. A county council may apply to the board for such an order (s. 36, sub-s. (5), *ante*, p. 629).

Sect. 72 (3).

(3.) The Local Government Board and their inspectors shall have for the purposes of an inquiry in pursuance of this Act the same powers as they respectively have for the purpose of an inquiry under the Public Health Act, 1875.

(4.) Where a county council hold a local inquiry under this Act or under the Local Government Act, 1888, on the application of the council of a parish or district, or of any inhabitants of a parish or district, the expenses incurred by the county council in relation to the inquiry (including the expenses of any committee or person authorised by the county council) shall be paid by the council of that parish or district, or, in the case of a parish which has not a parish council, by the parish meeting; but, save as aforesaid, the expenses of the county council incurred in the case of inquiries under this Act shall be paid out of the common fund.

Provision as to Sundays and bank holidays.

73. When the day on which any thing is required by or in pursuance of this Act to be done is Sunday, Christmas Day, or Good Friday, or a bank holiday, that thing shall be done on the next following day, not being one of the days above-mentioned.

74. *Provisions as to Scilly Islands.*]

Construction of Act. 51 & 52 Vict. c. 41.

75.—(1.) The definition of "parish" in section one hundred of the Local Government Act, 1888, (*z*) shall not apply to this Act, but, save as aforesaid, expressions used in this Act shall, unless the context otherwise requires, have the same meaning as in the said Act.

(2.) In this Act, unless the context otherwise requires—

Any reference to population means the population according to the census of one thousand eight hundred and ninety-one.

(*z*) See this section, *ante*, p. 171. It is there enacted that in the Act of 1888 "parish" "means a place for which a separate overseer is or can be appointed, and where part of a parish is situate within and part of it without any county, borough, urban sanitary district, or other area means each such part." The application of this definition being expressly excluded, the definition of "parish" in the Interpretation Act, 1889 (52 & 53 Vict. c. 63), applies, whereby (s. 5) "parish" is defined to mean, "as respects England and Wales, a place for which a separate poor rate is or can be made, or for which a separate overseer is or can be appointed." The part of the definition in the Act of 1888 which relates to parts of parishes would obviously be inapplicable to the present Act, having regard to its provisions as to parishes situate partly within and partly without a larger area; see ss. 1 and 36, and notes, *ante*, pp. 593, 627.

It may be mentioned that the definition of "county" in the Act of 1888, is varied (*infra*, sub-s. (2)), so as to include a "county borough," and that the definition of "district council," and "county district" in the Act of 1888, (definitions which had reference to future legislation which might establish district councils), must now be read as referring to the district councils, which are established by this Act, and to the districts of such councils. See s. 21 *ante*, p. 619.

The expression "parochial elector," when used with reference to a parish in an urban district, or in the county of London or any county borough, means any person who would be a parochial elector of the parish if it were a rural parish. Sect. 75 (2).

The expression "election" includes both the nomination and the poll.

The expression "trustees" includes persons administering or managing any charity or recreation ground, or other property or thing in relation to which the word is used.

The expression "ecclesiastical charity" includes a charity, the endowment whereof is held for some one or more of the following purposes :—

(a) for any spiritual purpose which is a legal purpose ; or

(b) for the benefit of any spiritual person or ecclesiastical officer as such ; or

(c) for use, if a building, as a church, chapel, mission room, or Sunday school, or otherwise by any particular church or denomination ; or

(d) for the maintenance, repair, or improvement of any such building as aforesaid, or for the maintenance of divine service therein ; or

(e) otherwise for the benefit of any particular church or denomination, or of any members thereof as such (*a*).

Provided that where any endowment of a charity, other than a building held for any of the purposes aforesaid, is held in part only for some of the purposes aforesaid, the charity, so far as that endowment is concerned, shall be an ecclesiastical charity within the meaning of this Act ; and the Charity Commissioners shall, on application by any person interested, make such provision for the apportionment and management of that endowment as seems to them necessary or expedient for giving effect to this Act.

The expression shall also include any building which in the opinion of the Charity Commissioners has been erected or provided within forty years before the passing of this Act mainly by or at the cost of members of any particular church or denomination.

(*a*) Where a charity consisted of an annuity to be paid annually "on St. Thomas's Day" to the churchwardens of a parish, and to be laid out by them in the purchase of clothing for six old and poor widows of the parish, with a preference to those who were most constant in their attendance on "the public services of the church," it was held by NORTH, J., affirming the decision of the Charity Commissioners, that the charity was not an ecclesiastical charity, as being for the benefit of members of the Church of England, and that the parish council had power to appoint trustees in place of the churchwardens, under s. 14 (2), *ante*, p. 611. *In re Ross's Charity*, [1897] 2 Ch. 397 ; 66 L. J. Ch. 662 ; 77 L. T. (N.S.) 89 ; 46 W. R. 27 ; 61 J. P. 742 ; *Re Perry Almshouses Charity*, W. N. 1898, p. 14.

Sect. 75 (2).

The expression "affairs of the church" shall include the distribution of offertories or other collections made in any church.

The expression "parochial charity" means a charity the benefits of which are or the separate distribution of the benefits of which is confined to inhabitants of a single parish, or of a single ancient ecclesiastical parish divided into two or more parishes, or of not more than five neighbouring parishes.

The expression "vestry" in relation to a parish means the inhabitants of the parish whether in vestry assembled or not, and includes any select vestry either by statute or at common law.

The expression "rateable value" means the rateable value stated in the valuation list in force, or, if there is no such list, in the last poor rate.

The expression "county" includes a county borough, and the expression "county council" includes the council of a county borough.

33 & 34 Vict. c. 75.

The expression "elementary school" means an elementary school within the meaning of the Elementary Education Act, 1870.

The expression "local and personal Act" includes a Provisional Order confirmed by an Act and the Act confirming the Order.

The expression "prescribed" means prescribed by order of the Local Government Board.

Extent of Act.

76. This Act shall not extend to Scotland or Ireland.

Short title.

77. This Act may be cited as the Local Government Act, 1894.

PART V.

TRANSITORY PROVISIONS (*b*).

First elections to parish councils.

78.—(1.) The overseers of each rural parish shall convene the first parish meeting of the parish at the time fixed by or under this Act for the first election of parish councillors, whether there is or is not a parish council for the parish, and for this purpose the overseers of a parish shall be deemed to be the overseers of every part of the parish.

(*b*) Some of the transitory provisions have been inserted in this work for the reasons that some of them are of permanent effect (*e.g.*, the provisions of s. 81, as to existing officers, and the definition of "appointed day" in s. 84), and others are often of use as containing provisions which may easily be adapted so as to apply in cases of the constitution of new authorities by the order of a county council.

(2.) The chairman of the parish meeting at which the first parish councillors are nominated, or in his default the clerk of the guardians, shall convene the first meeting of the parish council. Sect. 78 (2).

(3.) The first parish councillors and the first chairman of a parish meeting elected under this Act shall retire on the second ordinary day of coming into office of councillors which happens after their election.

79.—(1.) The existing boards of guardians and urban and rural sanitary authorities shall take the necessary measures for the conduct of the first elections of guardians and district councillors respectively under this Act, including any appointment of returning officers required by rules under this Act. First elections of guardians and district councils.

(2.) Where a parish is divided by this Act into two or more new parishes, then, subject to any order made by the county council, there shall be one guardian, and if it is in a rural district, one district councillor for each of such new parishes.

(3.) Of the guardians and urban and rural district councillors first elected under this Act, save as herein-after mentioned, one third as nearly as may be shall continue in office until the fifteenth day of April one thousand eight hundred and ninety-six, and shall then retire; and one third as nearly as may be shall continue in office until the fifteenth day of April one thousand eight hundred and ninety-seven, and shall then retire; and the remainder shall continue in office until the fifteenth day of April one thousand eight hundred and ninety-eight, and shall then retire.

(4.) The guardians and rural district councillors to retire respectively on the fifteenth day of April one thousand eight hundred and ninety-six and on the fifteenth day of April one thousand eight hundred and ninety-seven shall be the guardians and rural district councillors for such parishes, wards, or other areas, as may be determined by the county council for the purpose of the rotation.

(5.) Where guardians or rural district councillors retire together at the end of the triennial period, the guardians and district councillors first elected under this Act shall retire on the fifteenth day of April one thousand eight hundred and ninety-eight.

(6.) Of the first urban district councillors elected under this Act, the third who are respectively to retire on the fifteenth day of April one thousand eight hundred and ninety-six and one thousand eight hundred and ninety-seven shall be determined according to their place on the poll at the election, those that were lowest on the poll retiring first. If there was no poll, or if a question arises in consequence of an equality of votes between two or more councillors, the matter shall be determined by ballot conducted under the direction of the council.

Sect. 79 (7).

(7.) In the case of an urban district divided into wards, the foregoing provisions with respect to retirement shall apply separately to each ward.

(8.) Upon the day on which the first guardians and urban or rural district councillors elected under this Act come into office, the persons who are then members of boards of guardians, and urban and rural sanitary authorities, shall cease to hold office, but until that day the persons who are at the passing of this Act guardians and members of urban sanitary authorities (for urban districts not being boroughs) and of highway boards shall continue in office notwithstanding any want of qualification, as if the term of office for which they were elected expired on that day, and, except for the purpose of filling casual vacancies or electing additional guardians, no further elections shall be held.

(9.) The first meeting of each district council elected under this Act shall be convened by the returning officer.

(10.) The foregoing provisions shall apply to the existing members and first members elected under this Act of the local board of Woolwich and of any vestry under the Metropolis Management Acts, 1855 to 1890, and any Act amending the same, and to the existing and first auditors elected under those Acts in like manner as if they were members of urban sanitary authorities or urban district councillors, as the case may require, except that the date of the annual election shall be substituted for the fifteenth day of April.

(11.) The overseers of any parish divided by this Act shall, until the first appointment of overseers next after the appointed day, continue in office as if they were overseers of each part of the said parish, which by reason of such division becomes a separate parish.

Power of county council to remove difficulties.

80.—(1.) * * * * * (*c*)

(2.) The Local Government Board shall make regulations for expediting and simplifying the procedure under section fifty-seven of the Local Government Act, 1888, in all cases in the year one thousand eight hundred and ninety-four, for the purpose of bringing this Act into immediate operation, and such regulations may dispense with the final approval of an order by the county council in cases where the prescribed notice of the proposed order has been given before it is made by the county council (*d*).

(*c*) This transitory provision has now been superseded by the Local Government (Elections) Act, 1896, *post*.

(*d*) An order under this sub-section was made on March 22nd, 1894, and was in force during the remainder of the year 1894; it was set out in the second edition of Macmorran and Dill's "Local Government Act, 1894," at p. 159. The order of September 14th, 1889 (*post*), came again into force on January 1st, 1895.

81.—(1.) Where the powers and duties of any authority other than justices are transferred by this Act to any parish or district council, the officers of that authority shall become the officers of that council, and for the purposes of this section the body appointing a surveyor of highways shall be deemed to be a highway authority and any paid surveyor to be an officer of that body.

Sect. 81 (1).

Existing officers.

(2.) Where there is in a rural parish an existing vestry clerk appointed under the Vestries Act, 1850, he shall become the clerk of the parish council, and if there is also an assistant overseer in the parish, then, notwithstanding the foregoing provisions of this Act, that assistant overseer shall not, while such vestry clerk holds office, be the clerk of the parish council.

13 & 14 Vict. c. 57.

(3.) Any existing assistant overseer in a parish for which a parish council is elected shall, unless appointed by a board of guardians, become an officer of the parish council.

(4.) Every such officer, vestry clerk, and assistant overseer, as above in this section mentioned shall hold his office by the same tenure and upon the same terms and conditions as heretofore, and while performing the same duties shall receive not less salary or remuneration than heretofore.

(5) Where a parish or rural sanitary district is divided by this Act, any officer for the parish or district so divided shall hold his office as such officer for each parish or district formed by the division, and his salary shall be borne by the respective parishes or districts in proportion to their rateable value at the commencement of the local financial year next after the passing of this Act.

(6.) So much of any enactment as authorises the appointment of assistant overseers by a board of guardians shall be repealed as from the appointed day.

(7.) Section one hundred and twenty of the Local Government Act, 1888, which relates to compensation to existing officers, shall apply in the case of existing officers affected by this Act, whether officers above in this section mentioned or not, as if references in that section to the county council were references to the parish council, or the district council, or board of guardians or other authority whose officer the person affected is when the claim for compensation arises as the case may require. Provided that all expenses incurred by a district council in pursuance of this section shall be paid as general expenses of the council, and any expenses incurred by a board of guardians in pursuance of this section shall be paid out of their common fund, and any expenses incurred by any other authority in pursuance of this section shall be paid out of the fund applicable to payment of the salary of the offices affected.

51 & 52 Vict. c. 41.

82.—(1.) Where before the appointed day the highway expenses were charged on a particular parish or other area and not on a

Provision as to highways.

Sect. 82 (1). district, the district council may determine that the highways in that parish or area shall be placed in proper repair before the expenses of repairing the same become a charge upon the district, and, failing such highways being placed in proper repair to the satisfaction of the district council, the district council may themselves place the highways in proper repair, and the expense incurred by them of placing those highways in proper repair shall be a separate charge on the parish or area, and any question which arises as to whether any such expenses are properly a separate charge on the parish or area shall be determined by the county council.

(2.) Where in pursuance of an order of a county council a parish continues to maintain its own highways after the appointed day, the highway expenses shall not be deemed to be expenses of the parish council or of the parish meeting within the meaning of this Act.

Duty of county council to bring Act into operation.

83. It shall be the duty of every county council to exercise all such of their powers as may be requisite for bringing this Act into full operation within their county as soon as may be after the passing thereof, and a county council may delegate their powers under this Act to a committee.

Appointed day.

84.—(1.) The first elections under this Act shall be held on the eighth day of November next after the passing of this Act, or such later date or dates in the year one thousand eight hundred and ninety-four as the Local Government Board may fix.

(2.) The persons elected shall come into office on the second Thursday next after their election, or such other day not more than seven days earlier or later as may be fixed by or in pursuance of the rules made under this Act in relation to their election.

(3.) Every division into wards or alteration of the boundaries of any parish or union or district which is to affect the first election shall, if it affects the parishes or parts for which the registers of parochial electors will be made, be made so far as practicable before the first day of July next after the passing of this Act, and any such division or alteration which after the appointed day may be made on application by the parish council or any parochial electors of any parish, may be made before the appointed day on application by the vestry or a like number of the ratepayers of the parish.

Provided that—

(a.) If any county council having any such division or alteration under consideration so direct, the lists of voters shall be framed in parts corresponding with such division or alteration so that the parts may serve either for the unaltered parish, union, or district, or for the same when divided or altered ; and (b.) If the county council making such division or alteration on or after the said day and on or before the last day of August one thousand eight hundred and ninety-four so direct, the clerk of the county council shall make such adjustment of the registers of parochial electors as the division or alteration may render necessary for enabling every parochial elector to vote at the first election in the ward, union, or district in which his qualification is situate, and in that case the said division or alteration shall be observed in the case of that election. Sect. 84 (3).

(4.) Subject as in this Act mentioned, "the appointed day" shall,

(a) for the purpose of elections and of parish meetings in parishes not having a parish council, be the day or respective days fixed for the first elections under this Act, or such prior day as may be necessary for the purpose of giving notices or doing other acts preliminary to such elections; and

(b) for the purpose of the powers, duties, and liabilities of councils or other bodies elected under this Act, or other matters not specifically mentioned, be the day on which the members of such councils or other bodies first elected under this Act come into office; and

(c) for the purpose of powers, duties, and liabilities transferred to a council of a borough by this Act, be the first day of November next after the passing of this Act;

and the lists and registers of parochial electors shall be made out in such parts as may be necessary for the purpose of the first elections under this Act.

Provided that where an order of a county council postpones the operation of the section with respect to highways as respects their county or any part thereof the day on which such postponement ceases shall, as respects such county or part, be the appointed day, and the order of postponement shall make such provision as may be necessary for holding elections of highway boards during the interval before the appointed day.

85. *Current rates, etc.*]

86. *Saving for existing securities and discharge of debts.*]

87. *Saving for existing bye-laws.*]

88. *Saving for pending contracts, etc.*]

89. The Acts specified in the Second Schedule to this Act are hereby repealed as from the appointed day to the extent in the third column of that schedule mentioned, and so much of any Act, whether public general or local and personal, as is inconsistent Repeal.

Sect. 89. with this Act is also hereby repealed. Provided that where any wards of an urban district have been created, or any number of members of an urban sanitary authority fixed, by or in pursuance of any local and personal Act, such wards and number of members shall continue and be alterable in like manner as if they had been fixed by an order of the county council under this or any other Act (*e*).

SCHEDULE.

FIRST SCHEDULE (*f*).

RULES AS TO PARISH MEETINGS, PARISH COUNCILS, AND COMMITTEES.

PART ONE.

Section 2.

Rules applicable to Parish Meetings.

(1.) * * * * * * (*g*).

(2.) Not less than seven clear days before any parish meeting, public notice thereof shall be given specifying the time and place of the intended meeting and the business to be transacted at the meeting, and signed by the chairman of the parish council or other conveners of the meeting.

(3.) If the business relates to the establishment or dissolution of a parish council, or the grouping of a parish, or the adoption of any of the adoptive Acts, not less than fourteen days' notice shall be given.

(4.) A parish meeting may discuss parish affairs and pass resolutions thereon.

(5.) Every question to be decided by a parish meeting shall, in the first instance, be decided by the majority of those present and voting on the question, and the chairman shall announce his decision as to the result, and that decision shall be final, unless a poll is demanded.

(*e*) The schedule of repeals has not been inserted, as with the exception of the repeal of a part of s. 36 (1) of the Municipal Elections (Corrupt Practices) Act, 1884 (*ante*, p. 370), the repeals do not affect the subject-matter of this work.

This Act does not give power to a county council to create wards or fix the number of councillors in an urban district, but the meaning of the proviso in the text seems to be that where these matters are provided for by or in pursuance of a local and personal Act the county council shall have the same power of altering them from time to time as that body has in the case of rural districts under this Act (s. 60, sub-s. (1), *ante*, p. 643), and in urban districts under s. 57 of the Act of 1888 (*ante*, p. 111).

(*f*) The schedules relating to the procedure of parish meetings, parish councils, and their committees have been retained, since it is often necessary for county councils, when considering representations by, or making loans to, parish councils, or orders to cure defective elections, or otherwise dealing with parish councils, to satisfy themselves as to the observance of the rules laid down by the Act.

(*g*) Rule (1), as to the annual assembly of the parish meeting, has been repealed by the Local Government Act, 1897 (60 Vict. c. 1), which enacts (s. 2) that that annual assembly "shall be held on some day between the first day of March and the first day of April, both inclusive, in each year."

Schedule 1.

(6.) A poll may be demanded at any time before the conclusion of a parish meeting.

(7.) A poll may be demanded by any one parochial elector in the case of a resolution respecting any of the following matters, namely :—

(a.) Any application, representation, or complaint to a county council or district council ;

(b.) The appointment of a chairman for the year or of a committee, or the delegation of any powers or duties to a committee, or the approval of the acts of a committee ;

(c.) The appointment of an overseer, the appointment or revocation of the appointment or dismissal of an assistant overseer or a parish officer ;

(d.) The appointment of trustees or beneficiaries of a charity ;

(e.) The adoption of any of the adoptive Acts ;

(f.) The formation or dissolution of a school board ;

(g.) The consent or refusal of consent to any act, matter, or thing which cannot by law be done without that consent ;

(h.) The incurring of any expense or liability ;

(i.) The place and time for the assembly of the parish meeting ;

(k.) Any other prescribed matter ;

but, save as aforesaid, a poll shall not be taken unless either the chairman of the meeting assents, or the poll is demanded by parochial electors present at the meeting, not being less than five in number or one third of those present, whichever number is least.

(8.) In case of an equal division of votes at a parish meeting the chairman shall have a second or casting vote.

(9.) Where a parish meeting is held for the election of parish councillors, opportunity shall be given at the meeting for putting questions to such of the candidates as are present, and receiving explanations from them, and any candidate shall be entitled to attend the meeting and speak thereat, but, unless he is a parochial elector, not to vote.

(10.) If the chairman of the parish meeting is absent from or unwilling or unable to take the chair at any assembly of the parish meeting, the meeting may appoint a person to take the chair, and that person shall have, for the purpose of that meeting, the powers and authority of the chairman.

(11.) Any notice required to be given to or served on a parish meeting may be given to or served on the chairman of the parish meeting.

PART TWO.

Rules applicable to Parish Councils.

Section 3.

(1.) Every parish councillor shall, at the first meeting after his election, or if the council at the first meeting so permit, then at a later meeting fixed by the council, sign, in the presence of some member of the council, a declaration that he accepts the office, and if he does not sign such a declaration his office shall be void.

(2.) If any casual vacancy arise in the council, the council shall forthwith be convened for filling the vacancy.

(3.) The first business at the annual meeting shall be to elect a chairman and to appoint the overseers.

(4.) The chairman may at any time convene a meeting of the parish council. If the chairman refuses to convene a meeting of the council after a requisition for that purpose signed by two members of the council has been presented to him, any two members of the council may forthwith, on that refusal, convene a meeting. If the chairman (without so refusing) does

Schedule 1. not within seven days after such presentation, convene a meeting, any two members of the council may, on the expiration of those seven days, convene a meeting.

(5.) Three clear days at least before any meeting of a parish council, notice thereof specifying the time and place of the intended meeting and the business to be transacted at the meeting, and signed by or on behalf of the chairman of the parish council or persons convening the meeting, shall be given to every member of the parish council, and in case of the annual meeting notice specifying the like particulars shall be given to every member of the parish council immediately after his election.

(6.) Any notice required by law to be given to the chairman or any other member of the parish council may be left at or sent by post to the usual place of abode of such chairman or member.

(7.) No business shall be transacted at any meeting of a parish council unless at least one third of the full number of members are present thereat, subject to this qualification, that in no case shall the quorum be less than three.

(8.) The names of the members present at any meeting of the parish council, as well as of those voting on each question on which a division is taken, shall be recorded, so as to show whether each vote given was for or against the question.

(9.) Every question at a meeting of a parish council shall be decided by a majority of votes of the members present and voting on that question.

(10.) In case of an equal division of votes the chairman of the meeting shall have a second or casting vote.

(11.) The parish council may, if they think fit, appoint one of their number to be vice-chairman, and the vice-chairman shall, in the absence or during the inability of the chairman, have the powers and authority of the chairman.

(12.) The proceedings of a parish council shall not be invalidated by any vacancy among their members, or by any defect in the election or qualification of any members thereof.

(13.) A parish council shall hold not less than four meetings in each year, of which one shall be the annual meeting, and every such meeting shall be open to the public unless the council otherwise direct.

(14.) Every cheque or other order for payment of money by a parish council shall be signed by two members of the council.

(15.) Any notice required to be given to or served on a parish council may be given to or served on the clerk to the parish council.

(16.) The parish council may appear before any court or in any legal proceeding by their clerk or by any officer or member authorised generally or in respect of any special proceeding by resolution of the council, and their clerk or any member or officer shall, if so authorised, be at liberty to institute and carry on any proceeding which the parish council are authorised to institute and carry on.

Part Three.

Section 2, 3.

General.

(1.) Minutes of the proceedings of every parish council and parish meeting shall be kept in a book provided for that purpose.

(2.) A minute of proceedings at a meeting of a parish council, or of a committee of a parish or district council, or at a parish meeting, signed at the same or the next ensuing meeting by a person describing himself as or appearing to be chairman of the meeting at which the minute is signed, shall be received in evidence without further proof. **Schedule 1.**

(3.) Until the contrary is proved, every meeting in respect of the proceedings whereof a minute has been so made shall be deemed to have been duly convened and held, and all the members of the meeting shall be deemed to have been duly qualified; and where the proceedings are proceedings of a committee, the committee shall be deemed to have been duly constituted, and to have had power to deal with the matters referred to in the minutes.

(4.) Any instrument purporting to be executed under the hands or under the hands and seals of the chairman and of two other members of a parish council or of a parish meeting shall, until the contrary is proved, be deemed to have been duly so executed.

(5.) Subject to the provisions of this Act, a parish council may make, vary, and revoke standing orders for the regulation of their proceedings and business, and of the proceedings and business at parish meetings for a rural parish having a parish council.

(6.) Where there is no council for a rural parish, the parish meeting may, subject to the provisions of this Act, regulate their own proceedings and business.

PART FOUR.

Proceedings of Committees of Parish or District Councils. Section 56.

(1.) The quorum, proceedings, and place of meeting of a committee, whether within or without the parish or district, and the area (if any) within which the committee are to exercise their authority, shall be such as may be determined by regulations of the council or councils appointing the committee.

(2.) Subject to such regulations, the quorum, proceedings, and place of meeting, whether within or without the parish or district, shall be such as the committee direct, and the chairman at any meeting of the committee shall have a second or casting vote.

SECOND SCHEDULE.

ENACTMENTS REPEALED (*h*).

(*h*) See note to s. 89, *ante*, p. 658.

MUSIC AND DANCING LICENCES (MIDDLESEX) ACT, 1894.

(57 & 58 VICT. CAP. 15) (*i*).

An Act to amend the Law as regards Music and Dancing Licences in Middlesex. [3rd July 1894.]

* * * * *

Short title.

1. This Act may be cited for all purposes as the Music and Dancing Licences (Middlesex) Act, 1894.

Music and dancing licences.

2. For the regulation of places ordinarily used (*k*) for public dancing or music, or other public entertainment of the like kind, the

(*i*) The Disorderly Houses Act, 1751 (25 Geo. 2, c. 36), s. 2, provided that any house, room, garden, or other place kept for public dancing, music, or other public entertainment of the like kind in the cities of London and Westminster, or within 20 miles thereof without a licence from quarter sessions should be deemed a disorderly house or place. Under the Local Government Act, 1888, s. 3, *ante*, p. 7, the powers and duties of the quarter sessions as to licensing for music and dancing were transferred to the county councils in area within the operation of the Act. The Act is now repealed as far as Middlesex is concerned; see s. 2 (12), *post*, and the provisions in the text substituted. The Act may be usefully compared with s. 50 of the Public Health Act, 1890. See Lumley's Public Health, p. 594.

(*k*) The words of 25 Geo. 2, c. 26, s. 2, were "*kept* for public dancing, etc." Here the words are "ordinarily used" and in sub-s. (1) "kept or used." These words probably mean that there must be a habitual keeping or use of the room for public dancing, etc., though the reference in sub-s. (1) to a licence for the purpose of a charitable entertainment seems to indicate that a licence is necessary even for a single entertainment; and see sub-s. (11), *infra*.

The following cases decided under the Act of 1751 may be usefully referred to as showing what amounted to keeping a house for public dancing under that Act.

The statute extends to houses kept for the purpose of private dancing, not to public places only. *Clarke* v. *Searle*, 1 Esp. 25.

A room in which musical performances are regularly exhibited, though it is not kept or used solely for that purpose, is within the statute, and requires a licence. *Bellis* v. *Beale*, 2 Esp. 592.

A room kept by a dancing master for the instruction of his scholars and subscribers, and to which persons are not indiscriminately admitted, is not within the statute. *Bellis* v. *Burghall*, 2 Esp. 722.

To subject a party to the penalties of the statute for keeping a house for illegal dancing and music, it is not necessary that the party who kept the house should take money for admission. *Archer* v. *Willingrice*, 4 Esp. 186.

A temporary use of a room in a public house for the purpose of dancing on a particular festival or occasion does not subject the owner to the penalty of the statute. *Shutt* v. *Lewis*, 5 Esp. 128.

The statute extends to licensed taverns and hotels, and it is no defence that the company frequenting the performance was respectable or that the admission money was not received for the benefit of the keeper of the house. *Green* v. *Bothroyd*, 3 C. & P. 471.

A room used for public music or dancing is within the statute, although it is not exclusively used for those purposes, and although no money is taken for admission; but the mere accidental or occasional use of a room for either or both of these purposes will not be within the statute. *Gregory* v. *Jupp*, 6 C. & P. 271; 1 M. & Rob. 313.

In an action to recover the penalty for keeping an unlicensed house for public dancing, it appeared that music, dancing, etc., had occasionally taken

following provisions shall have effect in the administrative county of Middlesex; namely, Sect. 2.

(1.) After the thirty-first day of December one thousand eight hundred and ninety-four, a house, room, garden, or other

---

place at the defendant's house (a public house), and that no money was taken by him for admission, but the rooms were let to persons who sold tickets and received money for admission at the door; but there was no direct evidence that the defendant knew of this practice :—*Held*, that there was evidence to go to the jury of a keeping of the house by the defendant for the purposes mentioned in the statute, and that the judge was wrong in directing a non-suit. *Marks* v. *Benjamin*, 3 M. & W. 565; 3 Jur. 1194.

No action can be maintained on an agreement to exhibit entertainment for gain in a place where, by the above statute, a licence cannot be obtained. *Levy* v. *Yates*, 8 A. & E. 129.

A room within the limits of the Act kept for public dancing or music without a licence is a disorderly house under 25 Geo. 2, c. 36, s. 2, though no disorderly or improper conduct is allowed in the said room. The preamble does not confine this section to "places of entertainment for the lower sort of people," where robberies are likely to ensue. The defendant when indicted for keeping such house must prove his licence. *R.* v. *Wolfe and Others*, 13 J. P. 428.

A. kept a room which was used as a supper room and place of general refreshment, there being at the end of it a raised platform, on which stood a piano, and where songs were constantly sung. Programmes of the performance were laid about in different parts of the room. The company was respectable, and no money was paid for admission, nor any extra charge made for the articles consumed there. An action having been brought for a penalty under 25 Geo, 2., c. 36, the judge directed the jury to say whether the room was used for the purpose of supplying refreshments in the manner of an hotel, the music and singing being incidental merely, or whether it was used principally for musical performances; and ultimately he directed them to consider whether the room was used for both purposes, in which latter case the informer would be entitled to the verdict. The jury found that the room was used for the purpose of an hotel, and found a verdict for A. :—*Held*, that although the verdict might be against the evidence, there was no misdirection. *Hall* v. *Green*, 2 C. L. R. 427; 23 L. J. M. C. 15; 9 Exch. 247.

Under similar words in a local Act, it was held that to bring a case within the statute the music and dancing must be an essential part of the entertainment, and not merely accessories to it. It is not necessary that the dancing should be by the public. *Quaglieni* v. *Matthews*, 6 B. & S. 474; 34 L. J. M. C. 116; 11 Jur. (N.S.) 636; 29 J. P. 439.

Where a room above the bar of a public-house was used for music and dancing, the keeper of the house was held liable not for having a licence, though the persons using the room paid nothing to him for it. *Frailing* v. *Messenger*, 16 L. T. (N.S.) 497; 31 J. P. 423.

Under the statute the justices have a discretion to grant a licence for music only; and the keeper of a house with a music licence only is liable to a penalty for keeping a house without a licence if he permits public dancing in the house. *Brown* v. *Nugent*, L. R. 6 Q. B. 693; 7 Q. B. 588; 40 L. J. M. C. 166; 26 L. T. (N.S.) 880; 20 W. R. 89; 36 J. P. 22.

C. was lessee of a theatre duly licensed under 6 & 7 Vict. c. 68; he also held a justices' licence under 25 Geo. 2, c. 36, and on Ash Wednesday he gave a concert in the theatre, to which the public were admitted for money. Both his licences contained a regulation that no entertainment should be given on Ash Wednesday. It was held that he did not commit an offence against the 25 Geo. 2, c. 36, as the concert was not a public entertainment *ejusdem generis* with public dancing, and, at all events, the room was not habitually kept for such entertainment. *Syres* v. *Conquest*, 28 L. T. (N.S.) 402; 21 W. R. 524; 37 J. P. 342.

Under similar provisions in a local Act it was held that the justices had an implied right to grant the licence for one year, though no period was mentioned

Sect. 2 (1).

place, whether licensed or not for the sale of wines, spirits, beer, or other fermented or distilled liquors, shall not be kept or used for public dancing, singing, music, or other public entertainment of the like kind, without a licence for the purpose or purposes (*l*) for which the same respectively is to be used first obtained from the County Council of Middlesex and for the registration thereof a fee of five shillings shall be paid by the person applying therefor; provided that such fee shall in no case be payable by any applicant in respect of any licence granted for the purpose of a charitable or other like entertainment:

(2.) The County Council may at any meeting convened with fourteen days' previous notice, or at any adjournment thereof, grant licences to such persons as they think fit to keep or use houses, rooms, gardens, or places for all or any of the purposes aforesaid upon such terms and conditions, and subject to such restrictions, as they by the respective licences determine, and every licence shall be in force for one year or for such shorter period as the County Council on the grant of the licence shall determine, unless the same shall have been previously revoked as hereinafter provided (*m*):

(3.) The County Council may from time to time at any such meeting as aforesaid transfer any such licence to such person as they think fit:

(4.) Each person shall in each case give fourteen days' notice to the clerk of the County Council and to the superintendent of police of the police division in which the house, room, garden, or place is situated, of his intention to apply for any such licence, or for the transfer of any such licence:

(5.) Any house, room, garden, or place kept or used for any of the purposes aforesaid without such licence first obtained

---

in the statute, and that they were entitled to refuse to renew it. *Hoffman* v *Bond*, 32 L. T. (N.S.) 775; 40 J. P. 5.

The defendant kept a skating rink, which was enclosed by a wall, and was partly roofed with canvas and partly open to the air. It was open for skating in the daytime and in the evening. In the daytime there was no music. In the evening a band played operatic and dance music while the skaters skated. The defendant had no licence. It was held that the defendant might be properly convicted of keeping a place of public entertainment of a like kind to music and dancing without a licence, and, *semble*, that he might also be convicted of keeping a place for public music without a licence. *R.* v. *Tucker*, 2 Q. B. D. 417: 46 L. J. M. C. 197; 36 L. T. (N.S.) 478; 25 W. R. 697; 41 J. P. 294.

(*l*) See *Brown* v. *Nugent*, *supra*.

(*m*) Applications for licences must be determined judicially. See *R.* v. *London County Council*, [1892] 1 Q. B. 190; 61 L. J. M. C. 75; 66 L. T. (N.S.) 168; 40 W. R. 285; 56 J. P. 8; *Royal Aquarium Society* v. *Parkinson*, [1892] 1 Q. B. 431; 61 L. J. Q. B. 409; 66 L. T. (N.S.) 513; 40 W. R. 450; 50 J. P. 404. And see the notes to s. 3 (v) of the Local Government Act, 1888, *ante*, pp. 7, 8.

shall be deemed a disorderly house, and the person occupying, or rated as occupier of, the same shall be liable on summary conviction to a penalty not exceeding five pounds for every day on which the same is kept or used for any of the purposes aforesaid; and it shall be lawful for any constable, being thereunto authorised by warrant under the hand of one of Her Majesty's justices of the peace for the county of Middlesex, to enter any such house, room, garden, or place so kept or used without such licence as aforesaid, and to apprehend every person who shall be found therein in order that they may be dealt with according to law (*n*). Sect. 2 (5).

(6.) There shall be affixed and kept up in some conspicuous place on the door or entrance of every house, room, garden, or place so kept or used and so licensed as aforesaid an inscription in large capital letters in the words following: "Licensed in pursuance of Act of Parliament for ," with the addition of words showing the purpose or purposes for which the same is licensed;

(7.) Any house, room, garden or place so kept or used, although so licensed as aforesaid, shall not be opened for any of the said purposes except on the days and between the hours stated in the licence: Provided that no such house, room, garden, or other place so kept or used shall be open for any of the purposes aforesaid after midnight and before the hour of noon; save that if on any special occasion an occasional licence of exemption shall have been granted under the twenty-ninth section of the Licensing Act, 1872, in respect of any house, room, garden, or other place licensed under this Act, no penalty shall be incurred on account of such house, room, garden or other place being kept open for any of the purposes aforesaid on such special occasion from midnight until the hour specified in such occasional licence as the hour for closing (*o*). 35 & 36 Vict c. 94.

(8.) The affixing and keeping up of such inscription as aforesaid, and the observance of the days and hours of opening and closing, shall be inserted in and made a condition of every such licence:

(9.) In case of any breach or disregard of any of the terms or conditions upon or subject to which the licence was granted the holder thereof shall be liable on summary conviction to a

(*n*) The power to enter and arrest is not given by the Public Health Act, 1890. A similar provision is to be found in 25 Geo. 2, c. 36, s. 2, but it does not appear in what way persons merely found in the house are to be "dealt with according to law."

(*o*) This sub-section substantially re-enacts the amendment of 25 Geo. 2, c. 36, s. 3, which is contained in the Public Entertainments Act, 1875 (38 & 39 Vict. c. 21).

Sect. 2 (9).

penalty not exceeding twenty pounds, and in the case of a continuing offence to a daily penalty (*i.e.*, a penalty for each day on which such offence is continued after conviction therefor) not exceeding five pounds, and such licence shall be liable to be revoked by the order of the County Council:

(10.) No notice need be given under sub-section (4) of this section when the application is for a renewal of any existing licence held by the applicant for the same premises:

(11.) The County Council may, if and as they think fit, grant to any person applying for the same a licence to keep or use any house, room, garden, or place for any purpose within the meaning of this section for any period not exceeding fourteen days which they shall specify in such licence, notwithstanding that no notice shall have been given under sub-section (4) of this section:

25 Geo. 2, c. 36. 38 & 39 Vict. c. 21.

(12.) From and after the passing of this Act, sections two and three of the Disorderly Houses Act, 1751, and the whole of the Public Entertainments Act, 1875, shall be repealed so far as relates to the administrative county of Middlesex:

(13.) Nothing in this Act shall be deemed to interfere with any other enactment respecting the prosecution of persons keeping disorderly houses:

(14.) The powers by this Act conferred upon the County Council shall be in addition to and not in derogation of any of the powers of licensing now vested in the County Council (*p*).

WILD BIRDS PROTECTION ACT, 1894.

(57 & 58 VICT. CAP. 24).

An Act to amend the Wild Birds Protection Act, 1880 (*q*).

[20th July 1894.]

* * * * *

Short title and construction. 43 & 44 Vict. c. 35.

1. This Act may for all purposes be cited as the Wild Birds Protection Act, 1894, and shall be construed as one with the Wild Birds Protection Act, 1880 (herein-after referred to as "the principal Act,"), except as herein-after provided.

(*p*) Having regard to the repeal contained in sub-s. (12), it is difficult to understand what other powers of licensing are vested in the county council.

(*q*) See the note to Local Government Act, 1888, s. 3 (xiii.), *ante*, p. 12, and the Wild Birds Protection Act, 1896, *post*, which further amends the Act of 1880, and explains the present Act.

Sect. 2.

Prohibition of taking or destroying eggs.

2. A Secretary of State may, after the passing of this Act, upon application by the county council of any administrative county by order prohibit—

(1.) The taking or destroying of wild birds eggs in any year or years in any place or places within that county; or

(2.) The taking or destroying the eggs of any specified kind of wild birds within that county or part or parts thereof, as recommended by the said county council and set forth in the said order.

(3.) The application by the county council shall specify the limits of the place or places, or otherwise, the particular species of wild birds to which it is proposed that any prohibition in the order is to apply, and shall set forth the reasons on account of which the application is made (*r*).

Order as to application of principal Act to other birds.

3. A Secretary of State may, on the representation of the council of any administrative county (*s*), order that the principal Act shall apply within that county or any part or parts thereof to any species of wild bird not included in the schedule of that Act, as if that species of wild bird were included in the schedule of that Act, and on the making of such order that Act shall apply accordingly.

Publication of order.

4.—(1.) The council of an administrative county (*s*) shall in every year give public notice of any order under this Act which is in force in any place within their county during the three weeks preceding the commencement of the period of the year during which the order operates.

(2.) Public notice under this section shall be given—

(a.) As regards each place in which an order operates, by advertising the order in two local newspapers circulating in or near that place;

(b.) By fixing notices of the order in conspicuous spots within and near each place in which the order operates; and

(c.) In such other manner as the Secretary of State may direct, or as the council may think expedient, with a view to making the order known to the public.

Penalties.

5. Any person who, after the passing of this Act, shall take or destroy, or incite any other person to take or destroy—

(a.) The eggs of any wild birds within any area specified in the order; or

(b.) The eggs of any species of wild bird named in the order, shall, on conviction before any two justices of the peace in

---

(*r*) An order under this section may be limited to particular places, periods, and species of birds; the order must, it appears, follow the application in these respects. The powers of a county council under this Act are exerciseable by the council of a county borough. See 59 & 60 Vict. c. 56, s. 3, *post.*

(*s*) Including the council of a county borough. See last note.

Sect. 5.

England, Wales, or Ireland, or before the sheriff in Scotland, forfeit and pay for every egg so taken or destroyed a sum not exceeding one pound.

Expenses.

51 & 52 Vict. c. 41.
52 & 53 Vict. c. 50.

6. Any expenses incurred by the council of a county under this Act may be defrayed by that council as expenses for general county purposes within the meaning of the Local Government Act, 1888 (*t*), or so far as respects Scotland, the Local Government (Scotland) Act, 1889.

7. *Application to Scotland and Ireland.*]

SEA FISHERIES (SHELL FISH) REGULATION ACT, 1894.

(57 & 58 VICT. CAP. 26.)

An Act to extend the powers of Local Fisheries Committees with respect to Fisheries for Shell Fish. [20th July 1894.]

* * * * *

Extension of powers of local fisheries committees with respect to shell fish.
51 & 52 Vict. c. 54.

1.—(1.) The powers of a local fisheries committee to make bye-laws in pursuance of section two of the Sea Fisheries Regulation Act, 1888, shall extend to making bye-laws to be observed within their district for the regulation, protection, and development of fisheries for all or any specified kinds of shell fish, and any such bye-laws may provide, amongst other things, for

(a.) The fixing of the sizes and condition at which shell fish may not be removed from a fishery, and the mode of determining such sizes; (*x*)

(b.) The obligation to re-deposit in specified localities any shell fish the removal or possession of which is prohibited by or in pursuance of any Act of Parliament;

(c.) The protection of shell fish laid down for breeding purposes;

(d.) The protection of culch and other material for the reception of spat, that is to say, of the spawn or young of any kinds of shell fish; and

(e.) The obligation to re-deposit such culch and other material in specified localities.

(*t*) In the case of the council of a county borough, the expenses are to be defrayed out of the borough fund or borough rate. 59 & 60 Vict. c. 56, s. 3, *post.*

(*u*) This Act extends the powers of a local fisheries committee (formed under the Sea Fisheries Regulation Act, 1888, *ante*, p. 401), with respect to shell fish.

(*x*) For an instance where a bye-law under this section was upheld by the court, see *Thompson* v. *Burns*, 66 L. J. Q. B. 176; 76 L. T. (N.S.) 58; 61 J. P. 84; 14 T. L. R. 114. It was there held that the offence of removing under-sized shell fish from a fishery contrary to a bye-law made under this section is complete when the shell fish have been taken up from any part of the fishery with the intention of wantonly carrying them away.

(2.) A local fisheries committee shall have power to stock or restock any public fishery for shell fish, and for that purpose to incur such expenses as may be sanctioned by the Board of Trade. Sect. 1 (2).

(3.) For the purposes of this Act the expression "shell fish" shall include all kinds of molluscs and crustaceans.

Short title. 51 & 52 Vict. c. 54. 54 & 55 Vict. c. 37.

2. This Act may be cited as the Sea Fisheries (Shell Fish) Regulation Act, 1894, and the Sea Fisheries Regulation Acts, 1888 and 1891, and this Act may be cited collectively as the Sea Fisheries Regulation Acts, 1888 to 1894.

DISEASES OF ANIMALS ACT, 1894.

(57 & 58 VICT. CAP. 57) (z).

An Act to consolidate the Contagious Diseases (Animals) Acts, 1878 *to* 1893. [25th August 1894.]

* * * *

Central and Local Authorities.

Powers of Board of Agriculture in England, Wales, and Scotland. 52 & 53 Vict. c. 30.

1. The powers and duties conferred and imposed by this Act on the Board of Agriculture as regards England and Wales and Scotland, shall be executed and discharged by the Board in manner provided by the Board of Agriculture Act, 1889, and this Act (*a*).

Local authorities to execute Act.

2. The local authorities in this Act described shall execute and enforce this Act and every order of the Board of Agriculture so far as the same are to be executed or enforced by local authorities.

Local authorities in England and Wales. 51 & 52 Vict. c. 41.

3. The Local authorities in England and Wales shall be—

(i) for each borough not being a borough to which section thirty-nine of the Local Government Act, 1888, applies (*b*), the borough council;

(ii) for the residue of each administrative county, the county council (*c*).

(*z*) This Act is administered in a county by the county council; see s. 3, *infra*. It has been amended by 59 & 60 Vict. c. 15, *post*.

(*a*) Under the repealed Acts the central authority was the Privy Council, but the powers of the Privy Council were transferred to the Board of Agriculture by 52 & 53 Vict. c. 30.

(*b*) These are the smaller boroughs with a population of less than 10,000 (see the section referred to, *ante*, p. 86). For the purposes of this Act the smaller boroughs will form part of the administrative county.

(*c*) See the definition of the expression "administrative county" in s. 100 of the Local Government Act, 1888, *ante*, p. 172.

Sect. 3.

Provided that the mayor and commonalty and citizens of the city of London, acting by the mayor, aldermen, and commons of that city in common council assembled, shall be the local authority for the city of London, and shall be the local authority in and for the county of London for the purpose of the provisions of this Act relating to foreign animals (*d*).

Separation of Diseased Animals and Notice to Police.

Separation of diseased animals, and notice to constable.

4.—(1.) Every person having in his possession or under his charge an animal affected with disease shall—

(a.) as far as practicable keep that animal separate from animals not so affected; and

(b.) with all practicable speed give notice of the fact of the animal being so affected to a constable of the police force for the police area wherein the animal so affected is (*e*).

(2.) The constable to whom notice is given, shall forthwith give information thereof to such person or authority as the Board of Agriculture by general order direct.

(3.) The Board may make such orders as they think fit for prescribing and regulating the notice to be given to or by any person or authority in case of any particular disease or in case of the illness of an animal, and for supplementing or varying for those purposes any of the provisions of this section.

Cattle Plague.

Cattle plague infected place.

5.—(1.) Where it appears to an inspector that cattle plague exists, or has within ten days existed, in a cow-shed, field, or other place, he shall forthwith make and sign a declaration thereof.

(2.) He shall serve a notice, signed by him, of that declaration on the occupier of that cow-shed, field, or other place.

(3.) Thereupon that cowshed, field, or other place, with all lands and buildings contiguous thereto in the same occupation, shall become and be a place infected with cattle plague, subject to the determination and declaration of the Board of Agriculture.

(4.) The inspector shall serve a like notice, signed by him, unless in the circumstances this appears to him not to be expedient, on the occupiers of all lands and buildings, any part whereof lies, in his judgment, within one mile in any direction from that cowshed, field, or other place, or on the occupiers of any of those lands and buildings.

(5.) Thereupon all the lands and buildings aforesaid, on the occupiers whereof the inspector serves such a notice, shall become

(*d*) As to foreign animals, see ss. 24, 30, *post.*

(*e*) See the definition of "animal," "disease," "police force," "police area," in s. 59, *post.*

and be part of the place infected with cattle plague, subject to the determination and declaration of the Board. Sect. 5 (6).

(6.) The inspector shall, with all practicable speed, inform the Board and the local authority of his declaration and notices, and shall send to the Board his declaration and a copy of his secondly-mentioned notice (if any).

(7.) The Board shall forthwith on receipt of the information inquire into the correctness of the inspector's declaration.

(8.) If the Board are satisfied of the correctness of that declaration as regards the existence or past existence of cattle plague, they shall by order determine and declare accordingly, and prescribe the limits of the place infected with cattle plague.

(9.) If the Board are not satisfied of the correctness of the inspector's declaration as regards the existence or past existence of cattle plague, they shall by order determine and declare accordingly; and thereupon, as from the time specified in the order, the place comprised in the inspector's declaration and notices shall cease to be a place infected with cattle plague.

(10.) The Board may at any time, if they think fit, on any evidence satisfactory to them, by order—

(a) declare any cow-shed, field, or other place with or without any lands or buildings adjoining or near thereto, to be a place infected with cattle plague; or

(b) extend, contract, or otherwise alter the limits of a place infected with cattle plague; or

(c) declare a place infected with cattle plague or any part thereof to be free from cattle plague.

Cattle plague infected area.

6. The Board of Agriculture may at any time, if they think fit, by order—

(a) declare any area, wherein a place infected with cattle plague is situate, to be an area infected with cattle plague; or

(b) extend, contract, or otherwise alter the limits of an area infected with cattle plague; or

(c) declare an area infected with cattle plague or any part thereof to be free from cattle plague.

Slaughter by Board of Agriculture in cattle plague, and compensation out of public money.

7.—(1.) The Board of Agriculture shall (*f*) cause to be slaughtered—

(i) all animals affected with cattle plague, and

(ii) all animals being or having been in the same shed, stable, herd or flock, or in contact with an animal affected with cattle plague.

(*f*) Under this sub-section, slaughter is compulsory; under the next, it is discretionary.

Sect. 7 (2).

(2.) The Board may, if they think fit, in any case cause to be slaughtered—

(i) any animals suspected of being affected with cattle plague, or being in a place infected with cattle plague,

(ii) any animals being in such parts of an area infected with cattle plague as are not comprised in a place infected with cattle plague (but in this last-mentioned case subject to such regulations as the Treasury think fit to make).

(3.) The Board shall for animals slaughtered under this section pay compensation as follows, out of money provided by Parliament:—

(a.) Where the animal slaughtered was affected with cattle plague, the compensation shall be one half of its value immediately before it became so affected, but so that the compensation does not in any such case exceed twenty pounds; and

(b.) In every other case the compensation shall be the value of the animal immediately before it was slaughtered, but so that the compensation does not in any case exceed forty pounds.

Infected Places, Areas, and Circles for Diseases generally.

Pleuro-pneumonia or foot-and-mouth disease infected place.

8.—(1.) Where it appears to an inspector of a local authority that pleuro-pneumonia or foot-and-mouth disease exists, or has within the period herein-after mentioned existed, in a shed, field, or other place, he shall forthwith make and sign a declaration thereof. For the purposes of this sub-section the period shall be in the case of pleuro-pneumonia fifty-six days, and in the case of foot-and-mouth disease ten days.

(2.) The inspector shall serve a notice, signed by him, of the declaration on the occupier of that shed, field, or other place, and, in the case of foot-and-mouth disease, also on the occupier of any land or buildings contiguous thereto as he may consider necessary.

(3.) Thereupon that shed, field, or other place shall become and be a place infected with pleuro-pneumonia or foot-and-mouth disease, as the case may be, subject to the determination and declaration of the local authority (*g*).

(4.) The inspector shall, with all practicable speed, inform the local authority of his declaration and notice, and shall send his declaration and a copy of his notice to the local authority, and shall, with all practicable speed, inform the Board of Agriculture of his declaration and notice, and send a copy of the same to the Board.

(*g*) *Cf.* s. 5 (3). Under this section the determination is to be that of the local authority.

(5.) The local authority shall forthwith on receipt of that information inquire into the correctness of the inspector's declaration, with the assistance and advice, in the case of pleuro-pneumonia, and if so required by Order of the Board in the case of foot-and mouth disease, of a veterinary inspector, or of a person qualified according to this Act to be such (*h*). Sect. 8 (5).

(6.) If the local authority are satisfied of the correctness of the inspector's declaration as regards the existence or past existence of pleuro-pneumonia or foot-and-mouth disease, they shall by order determine and declare accordingly, and prescribe the limits of the place infected with pleuro-pneumonia or foot-and-mouth disease, and may, if they think fit, include within those limits any lands or buildings adjoining or near to the shed, field, or other place to which the inspector's declaration relates.

(7.) The local authority may include in a place infected with pleuro-pneumonia or foot-and-mouth disease any adjoining part of the district of another local authority, with the previous consent in writing of that authority, but not otherwise.

(8.) If the local authority are not satisfied of the correctness of the inspector's declaration as regards the existence or past existence of pleuro-pneumonia or foot-and-mouth disease, they shall by order determine and declare accordingly; and thereupon, as from the time specified in that behalf in the order, the shed, field or other place to which the inspector's declaration relates, shall cease to be a place infected with pleuro-pneumonia or foot-and-mouth disease, as the case may be.

(9.) The local authority shall forthwith report to the Board the declaration of the inspector, and the proceedings of the local authority thereon, and shall state whether or not it is, in their opinion, expedient that an infected area, comprising the infected place, should be declared, and, if so, what should, in their opinion, be the limits of that area, and whether or not there is within that area any place used for the holding of a market, fair, exhibition, or sale of animals or any specified kind thereof, and, if so, whether or not it is, in their opinion, expedient that the holding in that area, while infected, of a market, fair, exhibition or sale of animals, or such kind thereof, should be prohibited or restricted by order of the Board (*i*).

(10.) This section shall, notwithstanding anything therein contained, be construed and have effect subject to the subsequent section of this Act, whereby the Board are required to make, by order, provision respecting the case of animals found to be affected with pleuro-pneumonia or foot-and-mouth disease while exposed for sale or exhibited in a market, fair, sale-yard, or place of exhibition,

---

(*h*) See the definition of "veterinary inspector" in s. 59, *post*.

(*i*) The board have a general power to prohibit the holding of a market or fair under s. 22 (xix.), *post*. As to infected areas, see s. 9, *post*.

Sect. 8 (10)

and in other circumstances specified in the same section, and generally while being in a place not in the possession or occupation, or under the control, of the owner of the animals (*k*).

(11.) Where a local authority have declared a place to be infected with pleuro-pneumonia or foot-and-mouth disease, they may, if they think fit, having first obtained the assistance and advice of a veterinary inspector, or of a person qualified according to this Act to be such (*l*), at any time after the expiration of the period hereinafter mentioned from the date of the cessation therein of pleuro-pneumonia or foot-and-mouth disease, but not sooner, declare by order that place to be free from pleuro-pneumonia or foot-and-mouth disease. For the purposes of this sub-section the period shall be in the case of pleuro-pneumonia fifty-six days, and in the case of foot-and-mouth disease fourteen days or such longer period not exceeding twenty-eight days as the Board by general order prescribe.

(12.) The Board may at any time, if they think fit, on any evidence satisfactory to them, by order—

(a) declare any shed, field, or other place with or without any lands or buildings adjoining or near thereto, to be a place infected with pleuro-pneumonia or foot-and-mouth disease;

(b) extend, contract, or otherwise alter the limits of any place infected with pleuro-pneumonia or foot-and-mouth disease declared either by the Board or a local authority; or

(c) declare any place which has been declared by the Board or a local authority to be a place infected with pleuro-pneumonia or foot-and-mouth disease, to be free from pleuro-pneumonia or foot-and-mouth disease as the case may be.

Pleuro-pneumonia or foot-and-mouth disease infected area.

9.—(1.) The Board of Agriculture may at any time if they think fit, on any evidence satisfactory to them by order—

(a) declare any area wherein a place infected with pleuro-pneumonia or foot-and-mouth disease is situate to be an area infected with pleuro-pneumonia or foot-and-mouth disease; and

(b) extend the limits of an area infected with pleuro-pneumonia or foot-and-mouth disease; and

(c) when there is not within an area so declared, or within some particular portion thereof, any place infected with pleuro-pneumonia or foot-and-mouth disease, as the case may be, declare that area or that portion thereof to be free from pleuro-pneumonia or foot-and-mouth disease.

(2.) The Board on making any order declaring an area to be an area infected with pleuro-pneumonia or foot-and-mouth disease shall

---

(*k*) The section here referred to is s. 9 (2), *post*.

(*l*) See the definition of "veterinary inspector" in s. 59, *post*.

consider whether it is necessary or expedient to prohibit the holding in that area, while infected, of any market, fair, exhibition, or sale of animals or any specified kind thereof, and shall either prohibit the holding thereof accordingly or allow the same to be held on such terms and conditions, if any, as they think fit to prescribe (*m*). **Sect. 9 (2).**

General provisions as to infected places and areas.

10.—(1.) The Board of Agriculture may make such orders as they think fit, subject and according to the provisions of this Act, for prescribing the cases in which places and areas are to be declared to be infected with a disease other than cattle plague, pleuro-pneumonia, or foot-and-mouth disease (*n*), and the authority, mode, and conditions by, in, and on which declarations in that behalf are to be made, and the effect and consequences thereof, and the duration and discontinuance thereof, and other matters connected therewith.

(2.) Every place or area so declared infected, as well as a place or area declared infected with cattle plague, pleuro-pneumonia, or foot-and-mouth disease, shall be an infected place or area for the purposes of this Act.

(3.) Notwithstanding anything in this Act, where the Board, on inquiry, and after communication with the local authority, but without prejudice to the powers of the Board as regards cattle plague, are satisfied that a declaration of a place being an infected place has been made in error respecting the existence or past existence of disease, or respecting the limits of a place, or respecting any other matter of fact whereon the declaration proceeded, the Board may by order cancel the declaration as regards the infected place, or as regards any part thereof, as they think fit.

(4.) Where, in accordance with the provisions of this Act, a place or an area or a portion of an area is declared free from a disease, or a declaration of a place being an infected place is cancelled as regards the place or as regards any part thereof, then, from the time specified in that behalf by the Board or a local authority, as the case may be, the place, or area or that portion of the area or that part of the place, shall cease to be, or to be in, an infected place or area.

(5.) An order of the Board or of a local authority declaring a place to be an infected place or area, or declaring a place or area, or a portion of an area, to be free from disease, or cancelling a declaration, shall be conclusive evidence to all intents of the existence or past existence or cessation of the disease, or of the error, and of any other matter whereon the order proceeds.

(*m*) The board have a general power to prohibit the holding of a market or fair under s. 22 (xix.), *post*.

(*n*) See the definition of "disease" in s. 59. The board have power under s. 22 (xxxv.) to extend the definition so as to include other diseases.

Sect. 11 (1).

Movement into, within, or out of infected places and areas in case of pleuro-pneumonia and foot-and-mouth disease.

11.—(1.) Cattle (*o*) shall not be moved into, within, or out of a place or area infected with pleuro-pneumonia otherwise than in accordance with the conditions contained in Part I. of the First Schedule to this Act.

(2.) Animals shall not be moved into, within, or out of a place or area infected with foot-and-mouth disease otherwise than in accordance with the conditions contained in Part II. of the First Schedule to this Act.

Provisions as to infected circles.

12.—(1.) Where the Board of Agriculture by order declare that this section shall apply in the case of any disease, then, upon any place becoming, in pursuance of a declaration made and signed by an inspector of a local authority, a place infected with that disease, the whole space lying within a distance of half a mile from any part of the infected place shall become and be a circle infected with that disease: Provided that the Board may, if they think fit, limit the application of any such order to infected places in any particular district or districts.

(2.) Where, under or in pursuance of this Act, the place, in respect of which an infected circle has been constituted in pursuance of this section, ceases to be an infected place, the infected circle shall cease to exist.

(3.) The Board may make such orders as they think fit for giving public notice of the existence of, and for contracting, the limits of, and dissolving infected circles, and for prohibiting or regulating the movement of animals into, within, and out of infected circles, or for any of those purposes, or for authorizing a local authority to make regulations for those purposes or any of them, subject to such conditions, if any, as the Board think fit to prescribe.

(4.) Where two or more circles infected with the same disease adjoin or overlap each other, the whole of the infected circles shall be deemed for the purpose of the movement of animals under any orders or regulations made in pursuance of this section to be one infected circle.

Power to exclude strangers by notice.

13. A person owning or having charge of any animals in a place or area declared infected with any disease may affix, at or near the entrance to a building or inclosure in which the animals are, a notice forbidding persons to enter therein without the permission mentioned in the notice; and thereupon it shall not be lawful for any person, not having by law a right of entry or way into, on, or over that building or inclosure, to enter or go into, on, or over the same without that permission.

(*o*) Note the distinction between "cattle," to which this sub-section relates, and "animals," which are the subjects of the next sub-section. See the definition of these sub-sections in s. 59, *post*.

Slaughter by Board of Agriculture in case of Pleuro-pneumonia, Foot-and-mouth Disease, or Swine-fever.

Sect. 14 (1).

Slaughter by Board of Agriculture in pleuro-pneumonia, and compensation.

14.—(1.) The Board of Agriculture shall (*p*) cause to be slaughtered all cattle affected with pleuro-pneumonia.

(2.) The Board may, if they think fit, in any case cause to be slaughtered :—

(a) any cattle suspected of being affected with pleuro-pneumonia; and

(b) any cattle which are or which have been in the same field, shed, or other place, or in the same herd or otherwise in contact with cattle affected with pleuro-pneumonia, or which appear to the Board to have been in any way exposed to the infection of pleuro-pneumonia.

(3.) The Board shall for cattle slaughtered under this section pay compensation as follows :—

(a) where the animal slaughtered was affected with pleuro-pneumonia, the compensation shall be three-fourths of the value of the animal immediately before it became so affected, but so that the compensation do not in any such case exceed thirty pounds; and

(b) in every other case the compensation shall be the value of the animal immediately before it was slaughtered, but so that the compensation do not in any case exceed forty pounds.

(4.) Where the Board have decided that any head of cattle is to be slaughtered under this section, the Board shall, if the owner of such head of cattle by notice in writing so requires, cause the same to be slaughtered within twenty-one days after the receipt of the notice.

(5.) The costs of the execution of this section in Great Britain shall be paid by the Board out of the moneys standing to the Cattle Pleuro-pneumonia Account for Great Britain.

Slaughter by Board of Agriculture in foot-and mouth disease, and compensation.

15.—(1.) The Board of Agriculture may, if they think fit, in any case cause to be slaughtered—

(a.) Any animals affected with foot-and-mouth disease, or suspected of being so affected; and

(b.) Any animals which are or have been in the same field, shed, or other place, or in the same herd or flock, or otherwise in contact with animals affected with foot-and-mouth disease, or which appear to the Board to have been in any way exposed to the infection of foot-and-mouth disease.

(2.) The Board shall for animals slaughtered under this section pay compensation as follows :—

(i.) Where the animal slaughtered was affected with foot-and-mouth disease the compensation shall be the value of the animal immediately before it became so affected :

(*p*) Here, also, observe the distinction between the imperative language of this sub-section and the permissive words of the next.

Sect. 15 (2).

(ii.) In every other case the compensation shall be the value of the animal immediately before it was slaughtered (*q*).

(3.) The costs of the execution of this section in Great Britain shall be paid by the Board out of the moneys standing to the Cattle Pleuro-pneumonia Account for Great Britain.

Slaughter by Board of Agriculture in swine-fever and compensation.

16.—(1.) The Board of Agriculture may, if they think fit, in any case cause to be slaughtered—

(a.) Any swine affected with swine-fever, or suspected of being so affected; and

(b.) Any swine which are or have been in the same field, pig-sty, shed, or other place, or in the same herd, or otherwise in contact with swine affected with swine fever, or which appear to the Board to have been in any way exposed to the infection of swine-fever.

(2.) The Board shall for animals slaughtered under this section pay compensation as follows:—

(i.) Where the animal slaughtered was affected with swine-fever, the compensation shall be one-half of the value of the animal immediately before it became so affected:

(ii.) In every other case the compensation shall be the value of the animal immediately before it was slaughtered (*r*).

(3.) The costs of the execution of this section in Great Britain, including the costs of such measures under this Act as may seem to the Board necessary for preventing the spread of swine-fever, shall be paid by the Board out of the money standing to the Cattle Pleuro-pneumonia Account for Great Britain.

Additional officers, and expenses for purposes of slaughter.

17. The Board of Agriculture may, for the purposes of the execution of the sections of this Act relating to the slaughter by the Board of cattle, animals, or swine, on account of pleuro-pneumonia, foot-and-mouth disease, or swine fever, employ such additional inspectors, valuers, and other persons, and at such remuneration and may incur such expenses as, subject to the sanction of the Treasury, the Board think necessary; and all costs and expenses incurred under this section shall be paid by the Board out of the money standing to the Cattle Pleuro-pneumonia Account for Great Britain.

Pleuro-pneumonia Account for Great Britain.

18.—(1.) The account opened at the Bank of England under the provisions of section two of the Contagious Diseases (Animals) Pleuro-pneumonia Act, 1890 (and therein and in this Act referred to as the Cattle Pleuro-pneumonia Account for Great Britain), is hereby continued, and there shall be paid to the said account—

(a) such moneys (not exceeding one hundred and forty thousand pounds in any one year) as may be provided by Parliament towards defraying the costs incurred by the Board of

---

(*q*) There is no limit in this section or the next as to the amount of the compensation.

(*r*) See the preceding note.

Sect. 18 (1).

Agriculture in the execution in Great Britain of the provisions of this Act relating to the slaughter of cattle, animals, or swine, on account of pleuro-pneumonia, foot-and-mouth disease, or swine-fever, and such other costs and expenses as are by this Act made payable out of the money standing to the Cattle Pleuro-pneumonia Account for Great Britain; and

(b) all sums received by the Board on the sale of the carcases of cattle, animals, or swine slaughtered by the Board on account of pleuro-pneumonia, foot-and-mouth disease, or swine-fever, after deducting any amounts payable thereout as excess to the owners of the cattle, animals, or swine, under this Act.

Provided that of the money provided by Parliament for the Cattle Pleuro-pneumonia Accounts for Great Britain and Ireland not more than fifty thousand pounds shall be so provided for the costs of the execution of this Act as respects swine-fever in any one year.

(2.) If in any financial year the money standing to the Cattle Pleuro-pneumonia Account for Great Britain is insufficient to defray the costs and expenses by this Act made payable out of the money standing to the Cattle Pleuro-pneumonia Account for Great Britain, the Local Government Board and the Secretary for Scotland shall out of the Local Taxation Account (*s*) and the Local Taxation (Scotland) Account respectively, pay to the Cattle Pleuro-pneumonia Account for Great Britain in the proportions provided in the Second Schedule to this Act such additional sums as may be certified by the Board of Agriculture to be required for defraying those costs and expenses.

(3.) The regulations contained in the Second Schedule to this Act shall apply to the Cattle Pleuro-pneumonia Account for Great Britain.

Slaughter in Disease, and Compensation generally.

Power for Board of Agriculture to provide for slaughter in diseases other than cattle plague.

19. The Board of Agriculture may make such orders as they think fit subject and according to the provisions of this Act for directing or authorising, in case of the existence or suspected existence of any disease other than cattle plague and under such conditions as the Board think fit to prescribe, the slaughter of animals by local authorities, either generally or in particular instances, and in all or any of such cases the payment of compensation for the same by local authorities out of the local rate (*t*); and the Board may by such orders direct or authorise the slaughter both of animals actually affected with disease, and also of animals suspected of disease, or

(*s*) This is the account to which the proceeds of the local taxation licence and part of the estate duty are carried under the Local Government Act, 1888, ss 20—21, *ante*, p. 46, as amended by 57 & 58 Vict. c. 30, s. 19, *ante*, p. 49.

(*t*) For the definition of the local rate, see s. 40, *post*. In a county the local rate is the county rate.

Sect. 19.

being or having been in the same field, shed, or other place, or in the same herd or flock, or otherwise in contact, with animals affected with disease, or being or having been otherwise exposed to the infection thereof.

General provisions relative to slaughter and compensation.

20.—(1.) The Board of Agriculture may, notwithstanding anything in this Act, reserve for observation and treatment an animal liable to be slaughtered under this Act by order of the Board or of a local authority, but subject to payment of compensation by the Board or the local authority, as the case may be, as in case of actual slaughter.

(2.) Where an animal has been slaughtered under this Act by order of the Board or of a local authority, the carcase of the animal shall belong to the Board or to the local authority, as the case may be, and shall be buried, or sold, or otherwise disposed of by the Board or the local authority, or as they direct, as the condition of the animal or carcase and other circumstances may require or admit; and any money received by a local authority on any such sale shall be carried by them to the credit of the local rate (*u*).

(3.) If, in any case, the sum received by the Board or a local authority on sale of a carcase under this section exceeds the amount paid for compensation to the owner of the animal slaughtered, the Board or the local authority, as the case may be, shall pay that excess to the owner, after deducting reasonable expenses.

(4.) Where an animal has been slaughtered under this Act by order of the Board or of a local authority, the Board or the local authority, as the case may be, may use for the burial of the carcase any ground in the possession or occupation of the owner of the animal and suitable in that behalf, or any common or uninclosed land, but, as regards the use by a local authority of common or uninclosed land, not without the approval of the Board.

(5.) If the owner of an animal slaughtered under this Act by order of the Board or of a local authority has an insurance on the animal, the amount of the compensation awarded to him under this Act may be deducted by the insurers from the amount of the money payable under the insurance before they make any payment in respect thereof.

(6.) A local authority shall keep in such manner as the Board by general order direct, a record relative to slaughter, which record shall be admitted in evidence.

(7.) Notwithstanding anything in this Act, the Board or a local authority, as the case may be, may, if they think fit, withhold either wholly or partially, compensation or other payment in respect of an animal slaughtered under this Act by their respective order, where the owner or the person having charge thereof has, in the judgment of the Board or the local authority, as the case may be, been guilty, in relation to the animal, of an offence against this Act,

---

(*u*) See the preceding note.

or where the animal, being a foreign animal, was, in their judgment, diseased at the time of its landing. Sect. 20 (7).

Exceptional Powers for Transit, and in other Cases.

Board of Agriculture to provide for pleuro-pneumonia or foot-and-mouth during transit, etc.

21.—(1.) The Board of Agriculture shall, by order, make such further or other provision as they think necessary or expedient respecting the case of animals found to be affected with pleuro-pneumonia or foot-and-mouth disease—

(i) while exposed for sale or exhibited in a market, fair, sale-yard, place of exhibition, or other place; or

(ii) while placed in a lair or other place before exposure for sale; or

(iii) while in transit or in course of being moved by land or by water; or

(iv) while in a foreign animals wharf or foreign animals quarantine station; or

(v) while being in a slaughter-house or place where animals are slaughtered or are kept with a view to slaughter; or

(vi) while being on common or uninclosed land; or

(vii) generally, while being in a place not in the possession or occupation or under the control of the owner of the animals.

(2.) The Board shall, by orders under this section, make such provision as they think fit for the consequences under this Act of animals being so found in the circumstances aforesaid, as well with regard to the animals as with regard to the places where they are when so found and other places, and with regard to animals being or having been in the same shed or stable, herd or flock, or in contact, with animals so found.

(3.) The Board may, by orders under this section relating to particular places, make such provision as they think fit for the consequences aforesaid.

(4.) Every order under this section shall have full effect notwithstanding any provision of this Act requiring the declaration of a place infected with pleuro-pneumonia or foot-and-mouth disease or relating to any consequence thereof, or to any matter connected herewith, and notwithstanding any other provision whatsoever of this Act.

Disease and Movement, generally.

Power for Board of Agriculture to make orders for prevention or checking of

22. The Board of Agriculture may make such orders as they think fit, subject and according to the provisions of this Act, for the following purposes, or any of them (*v*):

(i) for prescribing and regulating the publication by placards, handbills, or otherwise, in the immediate neighbourhood

---

(*v*) The orders made under this section are too voluminous for inclusion in this work. The following is a list of the general orders under the Diseases of Animals Acts, 1894 and 1896, in force on the January 1st, 1898:—

The Swine-Fever Order of 1894; the Swine-Fever (Movement from Ireland) Temporary Order of 1894; the Glanders or Farcy Order of 1894; the Cattle-Plague Order of 1895; the Pleuro-Pneumonia Order of 1895; the Foot-and-

Sect. 22.

disease, and other purposes.

of a place or area declared infected, of the fact of such declaration;

(ii) for prohibiting or regulating the movement of animals and persons into, within, or out of an infected place or area;

(iii) for prescribing and regulating the isolation or separation of animals being in an infected place or area;

(iv) for prohibiting or regulating the removal of carcases, fodder, litter, utensils, pens, hurdles, dung, or other things into, within, or out of an infected place or area;

(v) for prescribing and regulating the destruction, burial, disposal, or treatment of carcases, fodder, litter, utensils, pens, hurdles, dung, or other things, being in an infected place or area, or removed thereout;

(vi) for prescribing and regulating the cleansing and disinfection of infected places and areas, or parts thereof;

(vii) for prescribing and regulating the disinfection of the clothes of persons coming in contact with or employed about diseased or suspected animals, or being in an infected place, and the use of precautions against the spreading of disease by such persons;

(viii) for prohibiting or regulating the digging up of carcases which have been buried;

(ix) for prohibiting or regulating the exposure of diseased or suspected animals in markets or fairs or sale-yards, or other public or private places, where animals are commonly exposed for sale, and the placing thereof in lairs or other places adjacent to or connected with markets or fairs, or where animals are commonly placed before exposure for sale;

(x) for prohibiting or regulating the sending or carrying of diseased or suspected animals, or of dung or other thing likely to spread disease, or the causing the same to be sent or carried, on railways, canals, rivers, or inland navigations, or in coasting vessels, or otherwise;

(xi) for prohibiting or regulating the carrying, leading, or driving of diseased or suspected animals, or the causing them to be

---

Mouth Disease Order of 1895; the Sheep-Pox Order of 1895; the Sheep-Scab Order of 1895; the Anthrax Order of 1895; the Animals (Transit and General) Order of 1895; the Water Supply on Railways Order of 1895; the Swine-Fever (Infected Areas) Order of 1896; the Swine-Fever (Suspected Zones) Order of 1896; the Foreign Animals Order of 1896; the Channel Islands Animals Order of 1896; the Isle of Man Animals Order of 1896; the Foreign Animals (Quarantine) Order of 1896; the Markets and Fairs (Swine-Fever) Order of 1896; the Rabies Order of 1897; the Importation of Dogs Order of 1897; the Swine-Fever (Movement from Ireland) Temporary Order of 1897 (No. 4); the Foreign Animals (Amendment) Order of 1897.

The right to lay an information for an offence against this Act and the orders made thereunder is not restricted to the local authorities whose duty it is to execute and enforce it, but such an information may be laid by a common informer. *R.* v. *Stewart*, [1896] 1 Q. B. 300; 65 L. J. M. C. 83; 74 L. T. (N.S.) 54; 44 W. R. 368; 60 J. P. 356.

Sect. 22.

carried, led, or driven on highways or thoroughfares, or elsewhere;

(xii) for prohibiting or regulating the placing or keeping of diseased or suspected animals on commons or uninclosed lands, or in fields or other places insufficiently fenced, or on the sides of highways;

(xiii) for prescribing and regulating the seizure, detention, and disposal of a diseased or suspected animal exposed, carried, kept or otherwise dealt with in contravention of an order of the Board; and for prescribing and regulating the liability of the owner or consignor or consignee of such animal to the expenses connected with the seizure, detention and disposal thereof;

(xiv) for prescribing the mode of ascertainment of the value of an animal slaughtered or liable to be slaughtered, by order of the Board or of a local authority;

(xv) for regulating applications for, and the mode of payment of, compensation to be paid out of money provided by Parliament;

(xvi) for prescribing and regulating the destruction, burial, disposal, or treatment of carcases of animals slaughtered by order of the Board or of a local authority, or dying while diseased or suspected;

(xvii) for prohibiting or regulating the movement of animals, and the removal of carcases, fodder, litter, dung, and other things, and for prescribing and regulating the isolation of animals newly purchased;

(xviii) for prescribing and regulating the issue and production of licences respecting movement and removal of animals and things;

(xix) for prohibiting or regulating the holding of markets, fairs, exhibitions, and sales of animals (*w*);

(xx) for prescribing and regulating the cleansing and disinfection of places used for the holding of markets, fairs, exhibitions, or sales of animals, or for lairage of animals, and yards, sheds, stables, and other places used for animals;

(xxi) for prescribing and regulating the cleansing and disinfection of vessels, vehicles, and pens and other places, used for the carrying of animals for hire or purposes connected therewith:

(xxii) for prescribing modes of cleansing and disinfection;

(xxiii) for prohibiting the conveyance of animals by any specified vessel to or from any port in the United Kingdom for such time as the Board may consider expedient:

(*w*) See also s. 8, sub-s. (9), s. 9 (2). The power hereby conferred is not, however, limited by these sections. As to what amounts to a "sale" of animals, see *Maclean* v. *Monk*, 77 L. T. (N.S.) 663.

Sect. 22.

(xxiv) for insuring for animals carried by sea a proper supply of food and water and proper ventilation during the passage and on landing;

(xxv) for protecting them from unnecessary suffering during the passage and on landing;

(xxvi) for protecting animals from unnecessary suffering during inland transit;

(xxvii) for securing a proper supply of water and food to animals during any detention thereof;

(xxviii) for prescribing and regulating the marking of animals;

(xxix) for prohibiting, absolutely or conditionally, the use, for the carrying of animals or for any purpose connected therewith, of a vessel, vehicle, or pen or other place in respect whereof, or of the use whereof, a penalty has been recovered from any person for an offence against this Act;

(xxx) for prescribing and regulating the muzzling of dogs, and the keeping of dogs under control;

(xxxi) for prescribing and regulating the seizure, detention, and disposal (including slaughter) of stray dogs and of dogs not muzzled, and of dogs not being kept under control, and the recovery from the owners of dogs of the expenses incurred in respect of their detention;

(xxxii) for prescribing and regulating the payment and recovery of expenses in respect of animals;

(xxxiii) for prescribing and regulating the form and mode of service or delivery of notices and other instruments;

(xxxiv) for authorising a local authority to make regulations for any of the purposes of this Act or of an order of the Board subject to such conditions, if any, as the Board, for the purpose of securing uniformity and the due execution of the provisions of this Act, think fit to prescribe;

(xxxv) for extending, for all or any of the purposes of this Act, the definition of disease of this Act, so that the same shall for those purposes, or any of them, comprise any disease of animals in addition to the diseases mentioned in this Act;

(xxxvi) for extending, for all or any of the purposes of this Act, the definition of animals in this Act, so that the same shall for those purposes or any of them comprise any kind of four-footed beasts, in addition to the animals mentioned in this Act; and

(xxxvii) generally, for the better execution of this Act, or for the purpose of in any manner preventing the spreading of disease.

Provision of water and food at railway stations.

23.—(1.) Every railway company shall make a provision, to the satisfaction of the Board of Agriculture, of water and food, or either of them, at such stations as the Board, by general or specific description, direct, for animals carried, or about to be or having been carried, on the railway of the company.

Sect. 23 (3).

(2.) The water and food so provided, or either of them, shall be supplied to any such animal by the company carrying it, on the request of the consignor or of any person in charge thereof.

(3.) As regards water, if, in the case of any animal, such a request is not made, so that the animal remains without a supply of water for twenty-four consecutive hours, the consignor and the person in charge of the animal shall each be guilty of an offence against this Act; and it shall lie on the person charged to prove such a request and the time within which the animal had a supply of water.

(4.) But the Board may, if they think fit, by order prescribe any other period, not less than twelve hours, instead of the period of twenty-four hours aforesaid, generally, or in respect of any particular kind of animals.

(5.) The company supplying water or food under this section may make in respect thereof such reasonable charges (if any) as the Board by order approve, in addition to such charges as they are for the time being authorised to make in respect of the carriage of animals. The amount of those additional charges accrued due in respect of any animal shall be a debt from the consignor and from the consignee thereof to the company, and shall be recoverable by the company from either of them, with costs, by proceedings in any court of competent jurisdiction. The company shall have a lien for the amount thereof on the animal in respect whereof the same accrued due, and on any other animal at any time consigned by or to the same consignor or consignee to be carried by the company.

Foreign Animals.

24. * * * * * (*x*).

25. The Board of Agriculture may, whenever they deem it expedient so to do, for the purpose of preventing the introduction of disease into the United Kingdom, make orders for prohibiting the landing of animals or of any specified kind thereof, or of carcases, fodder, litter, dung, or other thing brought from any specified country out of the United Kingdom or any specified part of any such country, and they shall prohibit the landing of such animals whenever they are not satisfied with respect to any such country or any specified part thereof, that having regard to the sanitary condition of the animals therein or imported therefrom, to the laws made by such country for the regulation of the importation and exportation of animals, and for the prevention of the introduction or spreading

Orders prohibiting importation of animals.

(*x*) The Diseases of Animals Act, 1896 (59 & 60 Vict. c. 15), s. 1 (1), provides that for s. 24 of the Act of 1894 there shall be substituted the following section, namely: "The provisions set forth in Part I. (slaughter at port of landing) of the Third Schedule to this Act shall apply to all foreign animals other than (a) foreign animals, the landing of which, is for the time being, prohibited by order of the Board of Agriculture; and (b) foreign animals intended for exhibition or other exceptional purposes, and the landing of which is allowed for the time being by the board, subject to the provisions of Part II. (quarantine) of the Third Schedule to this Act."

Sect. 26.

of disease, and to the administration of such laws, the circumstances are such as to afford reasonable security against the importation therefrom of animals affected with foot-and-mouth disease (*y*).

26. * * * * * (*z*).

Orders admitting animals to quarantine.

27. Notwithstanding anything contained in this Act or in any order of the Board of Agriculture, the Board may make such orders as they think fit for allowing the landing of any foreign animals intended for exhibition, or for other exceptional purposes, and for allowing such animals to be landed without being subject to the provisions of Part I. (slaughter at port of landing) of the Third Schedule to this Act, and the provisions of Part II. (quarantine) of the said Schedule shall apply to any animals so allowed to be landed.

Special provisions as to Channel Islands and Isle of Man.

28. In relation to animals brought from the Channel Islands or the Isle of Man, the Board of Agriculture may, if they think fit, by order or by licence, alter or add to the provisions of the Third Schedule to this Act relating to slaughter or to quarantine, as the case may require.

Orders to be laid before Parliament.

29. Every order made in pursuance of this Act in relation to the landing or conveyance of foreign animals shall be forthwith laid before both Houses of Parliament.

Regulation of ports.

30.—(1.) The Board of Agriculture may make such orders as they think fit, subject and according to the provisions of this Act, for the following purposes, or any of them:

(i) for prescribing the ports at which alone foreign animals may be landed;

(ii) for defining the limits of ports for the purposes of this Act;

(iii) for defining parts of ports;

(iv) for prohibiting or regulating the movement of animals into, within, or out of a defined part of a port;

(v) for prescribing and regulating the inspection and examination, and the mode, time, and conditions of slaughter, of animals in a defined part of a port;

(vi) for prescribing and regulating the disposal of animals, not being foreign animals, and being in a defined part of a port;

(vii) for regulating the removal of carcases, fodder, litter, utensils, dung, or other things into, within, or out of a defined part of a port, and the disposal thereof, when likely to introduce or spread disease;

(viii) for prescribing and regulating the cleansing and disinfection of a defined part of a port or of parts thereof;

(ix) for prescribing and regulating the disinfection or destruction of things being in a defined part of a port or removed thereout;

(*y*) See note (*x*) *supra*.

(*z*) This section was repealed by the Diseases of Animals Act, 1896 (59 & 60 Vict. c. 15), s. 1, sub-s. (2).

(x) for regulating the movement of persons into, within, or out of a defined part of a port; **Sect. 30 (1).**

(xi) for prescribing and regulating the disinfection of the clothes of persons employed or being in a defined part of a port, and the use of precautions against the introduction or spreading by them of disease;

(xii) for prescribing and regulating the seizure and detention of any foreign animal, carcase, fodder, litter, dung, or other thing whereby disease may be introduced or spread; and

(xiii) generally, for the better execution of this Act in relation to foreign animals, carcases, fodder, litter, dung, or other things, or for the purpose of in any manner preventing the introduction or spreading thereby of disease.

(2.) Notwithstanding anything in this Act, a defined part of a port, or any part thereof, shall not be declared to be an infected place, or be made part of an infected place, otherwise than by the Board.

(3.) Where the district or part of a district of a local authority under this Act is or comprises, or is comprised in, a port or part of a port, the Board may, if they think fit, in relation to that port or part of a port, by order, make any body, other than the body constituted the local authority by this Act for such district or part of a district, the local authority for the purposes of the provisions of this Act relating to foreign animals, and, in connexion with the local authority so made, prescribe the local rate, if any, and the clerk of the local authority.

General Provisions as to Local Authorities.

31.—(1.) The provisions in the Fourth Schedule to this Act shall have effect with respect to committees of local authorities, but nothing therein contained shall prejudice or affect the power of a county council to delegate their powers to any committee or body under section twenty-eight of the Local Government Act, 1888 (*a*). **Committees of local authorities.** 51 & 52 Vict. c. 41.

(2.) Provided that the Board of Agriculture, in any order made by them under this Act for authorising a local authority to make regulations, may direct that the power to make such regulations for any purpose specified in that behalf in the order shall be exercised only by the local authority or their executive committee, and shall not be deputed to any other committee nor to a sub-committee.

32.—(1.) A local authority may provide, erect, and fit up wharves, stations, lairs, sheds, and other places for the landing, reception, keeping, sale, slaughter, or disposal of foreign or other animals, carcases, fodder, litter, dung, and other things. **Provision of wharves, stations, lairs, etc.**

(2.) There shall be incorporated with this Act the Markets and Fairs Clauses Act, 1847, except sections six to nine and fifty-one to sixty thereof. 10 & 11 Vict. c. 14.

(*a*) See this section, *ante*, p. 64, and *Huth* v. *Clarke*, cited in the notes to that section.

Sect. 32 (3).

(3.) A wharf or other place provided by a local authority under this section shall be a market within that Act; and this Act shall be the special Act; and the prescribed limits shall be the limits of lands acquired or appropriated for purposes of this section; and bye-laws shall be approved by the Board of Agriculture, which approval shall be sufficient without any other approval or allowance, notice of application for approval being given, and proposed bye-laws being published before application, as required by the Markets and Fairs Clauses Act, 1847.

10 & 11 Vict. c. 14.

(4.) A local authority may charge for the use of a wharf or other place provided by them under this section such sums as may be imposed by bye-laws, and the same shall be deemed tolls authorised by the special Act.

(5.) All sums so received by the local authority shall be carried to a separate account, and shall be applied in payment of interest on money borrowed by them under the Contagious Diseases (Animals) Act, 1869, the Contagious Diseases (Animals) Acts, 1878 to 1893, or this Act, and in repayment of the principal thereof, and, subject thereto, towards discharge of their expenses under this Act.

32 & 33 Vict. c. 70.

(6.) The local authority shall make such periodical returns to the Board of Agriculture of their expenditure and receipts in respect of the wharf or other place as the Board require.

(7.) The Board, if satisfied on inquiry that the tolls taken by the local authority for the wharf or other place may properly be reduced, regard being had to the expenditure and receipts of the local authority in respect thereof, and to any money secured on the tolls, and to the other circumstances of the case, may require the local authority to submit to the Board, for their approval, a new schedule of tolls, and on failure of the local authority to do so to the satisfaction of the Board, may, by order, prescribe such tolls as the Board think fit, in lieu of those before approved by the Board.

(8.) The provisions of this section shall apply to a wharf or other place provided by a local authority under the Contagious Diseases (Animals) Act, 1869, or under the Contagious Diseases (Animals) Acts, 1878 to 1893.

32 & 33 Vict. c. 70.

Power for local authority to acquire land.

33.—(1.) A local authority may purchase, or may by agreement take on lease or at a rent, land for wharves or other places, or for use for burial of carcases, in cases where there is not any ground suitable in that behalf in the possession or occupation of the owner of the animal, or any common or uninclosed land suitable and approved by the Board of Agriculture in that behalf, or for any other purpose of this Act.

(2.) The local authority may (subject to any agreement) dispose of lands so acquired but not required for the purposes of this Act, carrying the money produced thereby to the credit of the local rate (*b*).

(*b*) See s. 40, *post*.

(3.) The regulations contained in section one hundred and seventy-six of the Public Health Act, 1875, shall be observed with respect to the purchase of land by a local authority for purposes of this Act, as if the local authority were a local board, and purposes of this Act were purposes of that Act; provided that the requisite advertisements and notices may be published and served in any two consecutive months, and that the local rate shall be substituted for the rates therein mentioned (*c*). Sect. 33 (3). 38 & 39 Vict. c. 55.

(4.) The powers conferred by this section may be exercised by a local authority with respect to land within or without their district.

34.—(1.) Where a local authority fail to execute or enforce any of the provisions of this Act, or of an order of the Board of Agriculture, the Board may by order empower a person therein named to execute and enforce those provisions, or to procure the execution and enforcement thereof. Proceedings in case of default of local authorities.

(2.) The expenses incurred under any such order or in respect of any such default by or on behalf of the Board, including compensation for animals slaughtered, shall be expenses of the local authority, and the treasurer or other proper officer of the local authority shall pay the amount of such expenses to the Board on demand, and in default of payment a person appointed by the Board to sue in that behalf, may recover the amount of such expenses, with costs, from the local authority.

(3.) For the purposes of this section an order of the Board shall be conclusive in respect of any default, amount of expenses, or other matter therein stated or appearing.

(4.) The provisions of this section shall be without prejudice to the right or power of the Board, or any other authority or any person, to take any other proceedings for requiring a local authority to execute or enforce any of the provisions of this Act, or of an order of the Board (*d*).

35.—(1.) Every local authority shall appoint so many inspectors and other officers as the local authority think necessary for the execution and enforcement of this Act, and shall assign to those inspectors and officers such duties, and salaries or allowances, and may delegate to any of them such authorities and discretion, as to the local authority seem fit, and may at any time revoke any appointment so made. Inspectors and other officers of local authority.

(2.) Every local authority shall keep appointed at all times at least one veterinary inspector (*e*), and shall appoint and at all times keep appointed so many other veterinary inspectors as the Board of

(*c*) Section 176 of the Public Health Act, 1875, is set out *ante*, p. 126. It enables the local authority to purchase land otherwise than by agreement.

(*d*) Having regard to this enactment, the board appear to have power to compel performance by a local authority of its statutory duties by *mandamus*.

(*e*) See s. 59, *post*.

Sect. 35 (2).

Agriculture, having regard to the extent and circumstances of the district of the local authority, direct.

(3.) The Board, on being satisfied on inquiry that an inspector of a local authority is incompetent, or has been guilty of misconduct or neglect, may, if they think fit, direct his removal, and thereupon he shall cease to be an inspector.

Reports to Board of Agriculture.

36. Every local authority and their inspectors and officers shall send and give to the Board of Agriculture such notices, reports, returns, and information as the Board require.

Orders and regulations of local authorities.

37.—(1.) An order or regulation of a local authority may be proved—

(i) by the production of a newspaper purporting to contain the order or regulation as an advertisement; or

(ii) by the production of a copy of the order or regulation purporting to be certified by the clerk of the local authority as a true copy.

(2.) An order or regulation so proved shall be taken to have been duly made, unless and until the contrary is proved.

(3.) An order or regulation of a local authority authorised by this Act or by an order of the Board of Agriculture shall alone be deemed for the purposes of this Act an order or regulation of a local authority.

Powers of local authorities to be for their district.

38. The provisions of this Act conferring powers on, or otherwise relating to, a local authority, or their inspectors or officers, shall, unless otherwise expressed, be read as having reference to the district of the local authority; and powers thereby conferred shall, unless it is otherwise expressed, be exerciseable and shall operate within and in relation to that district only.

Transfer of powers from one local authority to another, or formation of united district.

39.—(1.) Wherever the whole or any part of the district of any local authority is wholly surrounded by or has a common boundary with the district of any other local authority, those two local authorities may by agreement in writing between themselves make and vary and rescind provisions for the exercise by one of them (in this section referred to as the administering authority) of powers under this Act or any order of the Board of Agriculture within the whole or any part of the district of the other (in this section referred to as the surrendering authority) and for ascertaining the proportion of the expenses of the administering authority to be paid by the surrendering authority, such proportion to be fixed with reference to the rateable value of the part of the district of the surrendering authority surrendered to the administering authority as compared with the rateable value of the original area of the district of the administering authority (*d*).

(*d*) This is a useful provision under which a borough, which is of itself a district having a local authority under s. 3, may, for purposes of the Act, be dealt with by the county council; it also enables a county council to administer the Act in a detached or isolated portion of an adjoining county.

(2.) The district or part of a district subjected, in pursuance of an agreement under this section, to the powers of the administering authority, shall, for the purpose of the exercise of such powers, be deemed to be part of the district of the administering authority, and be dealt with accordingly. Sect. 39 (2).

(3.) Any expenses payable by a surrendering authority to an administering authority under this section shall be paid out of the local rate of the surrendering authority.

(4.) Provided that where the surrendering authority is the local authority for a borough and the administering authority is the local authority for a county to the rate of which such borough is assessed, the provision of this Act requiring that the local authority of the borough shall be paid by the local authority of the county the proportionate amount paid by the several parishes or parts of parishes in the borough shall not apply.

(5.) A local authority may by agreement in writing concur with any other local authority or authorities in appointing out of their respective bodies a joint committee consisting of such number of members with such tenure of office as they may determine, and in assigning to the joint committee a district consisting of the whole or such parts of the districts of the constituent authorities as the authorities may determine, and in delegating to the joint committee within their district the whole or any part of the powers of a local authority, and the joint committee shall, in respect of any powers so assigned to them, exercise the same powers and be subject to the same obligations, and this Act and any order of the Board shall, in respect of the district so assigned, take effect, as if such district were the district of a local authority and the joint committee were a local authority within the meaning of this Act.

(6.) All expenses incurred by the joint committee shall be apportioned among the component areas belonging to the different constituent authorities in proportion to the rateable values of such areas, as compared with each other, and shall be paid out of the local rates of the constituent authorities.

(7.) An agreement made under this section shall not be valid unless it has been approved by the Board (*e*).

(8.) The expression "powers" in this section shall not include the power of making or levying a rate, but shall include all other powers, duties, and obligations exerciseable by or imposed on a local authority or its officers under or by this Act, or any order of the Board.

Expenses of Local Authorities.

40.—(1). The expenses of a local authority under this Act shall be defrayed out of the local rate; and such sums as may be necessary Expenses out of local rate.

(*e*) *I.e.*, the Board of Agriculture. See s. 59, *post*.

Sect. 40 (1).

to defray those expenses shall be levied with and as part of the local rate.

(2.) The local rate in England and Wales shall be as follows :—

(i) in the case of the local authority for a county, the county rate with the county fund;

(ii) in the case of the local authority for the City of London, the consolidated rate; and

(iii) in the case of the local authority for a borough, the borough rate with the borough fund.

(3.) Provided that the payment of the expenses of the local authority for the county of London, under this Act, shall be a general county purpose for which the parishes in the City of London shall be liable to be assessed to county contributions (*f*).

Relief of boroughs from contribution to county expenses.

41.—(1.) In England and Wales the council of a borough assessed to the county rate of a county shall be paid by the council of the county the proportionate amount paid by the several parishes and parts of parishes in the borough towards the expenses under this Act of the council of the county (*g*).

(2.) Nothing in this Act shall affect the exemption of any borough which had a separate court of quarter sessions at the date of the passing of the Local Government Act, 1888, from contributing towards the expenses under this Act of the council of the county within which the borough is situate (*h*).

51 & 52 Vict. c. 41.

Power for local authority to borrow.

42.—(1.) Where the amount or proportion of the local rate levied or required for the purposes of this Act exceeds or would exceed in any financial year sixpence in the pound, a local authority may borrow at interest on the credit of the local rate any money necessary for the purposes of this Act, and may secure the repayment thereof, with interest, by mortgaging the local rate for any term not exceeding seven years.

(2.) Where the amount or proportion aforesaid exceeds or would exceed in any financial year ninepence in the pound, the Local Government Board may, if they think fit, on application of the local authority, extend the term to any period not exceeding fourteen years.

(3.) A local authority, borrowing for the purposes of this section, shall borrow subject to the provisions of the Local Loans Act, 1875;

38 & 39 Vict c. 83.

(*f*) Thus the City contributes towards the general rate for the county of London for purposes of this Act, although under s. 3, *ante*, the mayor, etc., of London are themselves a local authority, and their own expenses as such are payable out of the consolidated rate.

(*g*) This appears to apply to all boroughs, although under s. 3 of this Act only the larger quarter sessions boroughs have a local authority of their own. Under the repealed Act of 1878, s. 47 (1), this provision was intelligible, for every borough had a local authority for itself.

(*h*) Under the repealed Act of 1878, s. 47 (2), every quarter sessions borough was exempt, and the Local Government Act of 1888, s. 35, continued this exemption in the case of the larger quarter sessions boroughs only. The text, therefore, applies only to these boroughs.

and every loan raised under this section shall be discharged in manner prescribed by section thirteen of that Act, for which purpose a sinking fund is hereby prescribed, if in any case the Local Government Board so direct, but not otherwise (*i*). Sect. 42 (3).

(4.) The Public Works Loan Commissioners may, on the recommendation of the Local Government Board, advance money to a local authority in manner provided by the Public Works Loans (Money) Act, 1875, and any enactment amending or substituted for that Act, the same to be repaid, with interest, within the term aforesaid, and the local authority may so borrow accordingly. 38 & 39 Vict. c. 58.

(5.) A local authority, borrowing for any of the purposes of this Act, may, if they think fit, give as security, either with the local rate, if any, or separately therefrom, the charges which they are authorised to make for the use of a wharf or other place provided by them under this Act, and any estates, revenues, or funds belonging to them and not otherwise appropriated by law; and in that case the limitations in this section respecting the amount or proportion of rate and term of years shall not operate.

Police.

Duties and authorities of constables.

43.—(1.) The police force of each police area shall execute and enforce this Act and every order of the Board of Agriculture.

(2.) Where a person is seen or found committing, or is reasonably suspected of being engaged in committing, an offence against this Act, a constable may, without warrant, stop and detain him; and, if his name and address are not known to the constable, and such person fails to give them to the satisfaction of the constable, the constable may, without warrant, apprehend him; and the constable may, whether so stopping or detaining or apprehending the person or not, stop, detain, and examine any animal, vehicle, boat, or thing to which the offence or suspected offence relates, and require the same to be forthwith taken back to or into any place or district wherefrom or whereout it was unlawfully removed, and execute and enforce that requisition.

(3.) If any person obstructs or impedes or assists to obstruct or impede a constable or other officer in the execution of this Act or of an order of the Board or of a regulation of a local authority, the constable or officer may without warrant apprehend the offender.

(4.) A person apprehended under this section shall be taken with all practicable speed before a justice, and shall not be detained without a warrant longer than is necessary for that purpose; and all

---

(*i*) The Local Loans Act, 1875, will be found set out *in extenso* in the Appendix to Lumley's Public Health. Under s. 13, a loan may be repaid by means of annuity certificates, debentures, the annual appropriation of a fixed sum to the discharge of part of the loan, or where it is prescribed by a sinking fund. Under the provision in the text, a sinking fund can only be resorted to if the Local Government Board so direct.

Sect. 43 (4). enactments relating to the release of persons on recognizances taken by an officer of police or a constable shall apply in the case of a person apprehended under this section.

(5.) The foregoing provisions of this section respecting a constable extend and apply to any person called by a constable to his assistance.

(6.) A constable shall forthwith make a report in writing to his superior officer of every case in which he stops any person, animal, vehicle, boat, or thing under this section, and of his proceedings consequent thereon.

(7.) Nothing in this section shall take away or abridge any power or authority that a constable would have had if this section had not been enacted.

General Administrative Provisions.

General powers of inspectors.

44.—(1.) An inspector (*j*) shall have, for the purposes of this Act, all the powers which a constable has, under this Act or otherwise, in the place where the inspector is acting.

(2.) An inspector may at any time enter any land or shed to which this Act applies, or other building or place wherein he has reasonable grounds for supposing—

(a) that disease exists or has within fifty-six days existed; or

(b) that the carcase of a diseased or suspected animal is or has been kept, or has been buried, destroyed, or otherwise disposed of; or

(c) that there is to be found any pen, place, vehicle, or thing in respect whereof any person has on any occasion failed to comply with the provisions of this Act, or of an order of the Board of Agriculture, or of a regulation of a local authority; or

(d) that this Act or an order of the Board or a regulation of a local authority has not been or is not being complied with.

(3.) An inspector may at any time enter any pen, vehicle, vessel, or boat in which or in respect whereof he has reasonable grounds for supposing that this Act or an order of the Board or a regulation of a local authority has not been or is not being complied with.

(4.) An inspector entering, as herein-before by this section authorised, shall, if required by the owner, or occupier, or person in charge of the land, building, place, pen, vehicle, vessel, or boat, state in writing his reasons for entering.

(5.) A certificate of a veterinary inspector (*k*) to the effect that an animal is or was affected with a disease specified in the certificate shall for the purposes of this Act be conclusive evidence in all courts of justice of the matter certified.

(*j*) This means an inspector of the board or an inspector of the local authority. See s. 59, *post*.

(*k*) See the definition of "veterinary inspector" in s. 59, *post*.

(6.) An inspector of the Board shall have all the powers of an inspector throughout England or that part thereof for which he is appointed, and in addition to the powers herein-before conferred upon inspectors, an inspector of the Board may at any time, for the purpose of ascertaining whether pleuro-pneumonia, foot-and-mouth disease, or swine-fever exists, or has within fifty-six days existed, in any shed, land, or other place, enter such shed, land, or place. Sect. 45 (6).

45.—(1.) Where an inspector of the Board of Agriculture is satisfied that this Act or an order of the Board or a regulation of a local authority has not been or is not being complied with on board a vessel in a port, then, on the representation in writing to that effect of the inspector, stating particulars of non-compliance, the vessel may be detained until the Board otherwise direct. Power for detention of vessels.

(2.) The officer detaining the vessel shall forthwith deliver to the master or person in charge of the vessel a copy of the representation.

(3.) Section six hundred and ninety-two of the Merchant Shipping Act, 1894, shall apply in the case of such detention as if it were authorised or ordered under that Act. 57 & 58 Vict. c. 60.

46.—(1.) Where a carcase washed ashore is buried or destroyed under the direction of a receiver of wreck with authority from the Board of Trade, the expenses thereof shall be expenses of the local authority, and shall be paid by the local authority to the receiver on demand, and in default of payment shall be recoverable with costs by the receiver from the local authority. Expenses of burial of carcases washed ashore.

(2.) Where a local authority has incurred any expenses under this section on account of the burial or destruction of the carcase of any animal which, or the carcase of which, was thrown or washed from any vessel, the owner of the vessel shall be liable to repay such expenses to the local authority; and the local authority may recover such expenses with costs in the same manner as salvage is recoverable.

47. No stamp duty shall be payable on, and no fee or other charge shall be demanded or made for, any appointment, certificate, declaration, licence, or thing under this Act, or an order of the Board of Agriculture, or a regulation of a local authority, or for any inspection or other act precedent to the granting, making, or doing of a certificate, declaration, licence, or other thing. Exemption from stamp duty and fees.

48.—(1.) In any proceeding under this Act, no proof shall be required of the appointment or handwriting of an inspector or other officer of the Board of Agriculture or of the clerk or an inspector or other officer of a local authority. Evidence and form and service of instruments.

(2.) Every notice under this Act or under any order or regulation made under this Act must be in writing.

(3.) Any notice or other instrument under this Act or under an order of the Board or a regulation of a local authority may be served

Sect. 48 (3). on the person to be affected thereby, either by the delivery thereof to him personally, or by the leaving thereof for him at his last known place of abode or business, or by the sending thereof through the post in a letter addressed to him there.

(4.) A notice or other instrument to be served on the occupier of any building, land, or place may, except when sent by post, be addressed to him by the designation of the occupier of that building, land, or place, without naming or further describing him; and where it is to be served on the several occupiers of several buildings, lands, or places, may, except when sent by post, be addressed to them collectively by the designation of the occupiers of those several buildings, lands, or places, without further naming or describing them, but separate copies thereof being served on them severally.

Provisions respecting Orders of Board of Agriculture.

49.—(1.) The Board of Agriculture may alter or revoke any order of the Board.

(2.) Every order of the Board shall have effect as if it had been enacted by this Act (*l*).

(3.) The Board shall in the case of every order made by them under this Act, publish in the London Gazette a notice that the order has been made, and of the place where copies of the order may be obtained.

(4.) Every local authority shall at their own expense publish every order of the Board, and every licence, or other instrument sent to them by the Board for publication, in such manner as the Board direct, and, subject to and in the absence of any direction, by advertisement in a newspaper circulating in the district of the local authority.

(5.) The validity or effect of an order of the Board, licence, or other instrument issued by the Board shall not be affected by want of or defect or irregularity in any publication thereof.

Yearly return to Parliament.

50. The Board of Agriculture shall make and lay before both Houses of Parliament not later than the thirty-first day of March in each year, a return stating the proceedings and expenditure under this Act of the Board, and, as far as reasonably may be, of all local authorities, in the year ending the thirty-first day of December then last; and showing the number of foreign animals landed and found diseased in that year, specifying separately the different kinds of disease, and the ports of exportation and landing, and the mode of disposal of the animals; and containing such other information respecting the operation of this Act as the Board think fit.

Offences and Legal Proceedings.

Penalties for offences.

51. If any person is guilty of an offence against this Act, he shall for every such offence be liable—

(i) to a fine not exceeding twenty pounds; or

(*l*) As to the effect of this provision, see *Baker* v. *Williams*, [1898] 1 Q. B. 23; 66 L. J. Q. B. 880; 77 L. T. (N.S.) 495; 46 W. R. 64; 62 J. P. 21; 14 T. L. R. 13.

(ii) if the offence is committed with respect to more than four animals, to a fine not exceeding five pounds for each animal; or

(iii) where the offence is committed in relation to carcases, fodder, litter, dung, or other thing (exclusive of animals), to a fine not exceeding ten pounds in respect of every half ton in weight thereof after one half ton, in addition to the first fine of not exceeding twenty pounds.

General offences.

52. If any person, without lawful authority or excuse, proof whereof shall lie on him, does any of the following things, he shall be guilty of an offence against this Act:

(i) if he does anything in contravention of this Act, or of an order of the Board of Agriculture, or of a regulation of a local authority; or

(ii) if, where required by this Act or by an order of the Board to keep an animal separate as far as practicable, or to give notice of disease with all practicable speed, he fails to do so; or

(iii) if he fails to give, produce, observe, or do any notice, licence, rule, or thing which by this Act, or by an order of the Board, or by a regulation of a local authority, he is required to give, produce, observe, or do; or

(iv) if he does anything which by this Act or an order of the Board is made or declared to be not lawful; or

(v) if he does or omits anything, the doing or omission whereof is declared by this Act or by an order of the Board to be an offence by him against this Act; or

(vi) if he refuses to an inspector or other officer, acting in execution of this Act, or of an order of the Board, or of a regulation of a local authority, admission to any land, building, place, vessel, pen, vehicle, or boat which the inspector or officer is entitled to enter or examine, or obstructs or impedes him in so entering or examining, or otherwise in any respect obstructs or impedes an inspector or constable or other officer in the execution of his duty, or assists in any such obstructing or impeding; or

(vii) if he throws or places, or causes or suffers to be thrown or placed, into or in any river, stream, canal, navigation, or other water, or into or in the sea within three miles of the shore, the carcase of an animal which has died of disease, or been slaughtered as diseased or suspected;

and on a further conviction within a period of twelve months for a second or subsequent offence against the same sub-section of this section he shall be liable, in the discretion of the court, to be imprisoned for any term not exceeding one month, with or without hard labour, in lieu of the fine to which he is liable under this Act.

Sect. 53 (1).

Imprisonment instead of fine for use of expired licences, digging up of carcases, and other specified offences.

53.—(1.) If any person does any of the following things, he shall be guilty of an offence against this Act:

(i) if, with intent to unlawfully evade this Act, or an order of the Board of Agriculture, or a regulation of a local authority, he does anything for which a licence is requisite under this Act, or an order of the Board, or a regulation of a local authority, without having obtained a licence: or

(ii) if, where a licence is requisite, having obtained a licence, he, with the like intent, does the thing licensed after the licence has expired: or

(iii) if he uses or offers or attempts to use as such a licence an instrument not being a complete licence, or an instrument untruly purporting or appearing to be a licence, unless he shows to the satisfaction of the court that he did not know of that incompleteness or untruth, and that he could not with reasonable diligence have obtained knowledge thereof: or

(iv) if, with intent to unlawfully evade this Act, or an order of the Board of Agriculture, or a regulation of a local authority, he alters, or falsely makes, or ante-dates, or counterfeits, or offers or utters, knowing the same to be altered, or falsely made, or ante-dated, or counterfeited, a licence, declaration, certificate, or instrument made or issued, or purporting to be made or issued, under or for any purpose of this Act, or of an order of the Board or of a regulation of a local authority: or

(v) if, for the purpose of obtaining a licence, certificate, or instrument, he makes a declaration or statement false in any material particular, unless he shows to the satisfaction of the court that he did not know of that falsity, and that he could not with reasonable diligence have obtained knowledge thereof: or

(vi) if he obtains or endeavours to obtain such a licence, certificate, or instrument by means of a false pretence, unless he shows to the satisfaction of the court that he did not know of that falsity, and that he could not with reasonable diligence have obtained knowledge thereof: or

(vii) if he grants or issues such a licence, certificate, or instrument, being false in any date or other material particular, unless he shows to the satisfaction of the court that he did not know of that falsity, and that he could not with reasonable diligence have obtained knowledge thereof, or if he grants or issues such a licence, certificate, or instrument, having, and knowing that he has, no lawful authority to grant or issue the same: or

(viii) if, with intent to unlawfully evade or defeat this Act, or an order of the Board, or a regulation of a local authority, he grants or issues an instrument being in form a licence, certificate, or instrument made or issued under this Act or an order of the Board or a regulation of a local authority, for permitting or regulating the movement of a particular animal, or the doing of any other particular thing, but being issued in blank, that is to say, not being before the issue thereof so filled up as to specify any particular animal or thing: or

(ix) if he uses or offers or attempts to use for any purpose of this Act, or of an order of the Board, or of a regulation of a local authority, an instrument so issued in blank, unless he shows to the satisfaction of the court that he did not know of it having been so issued in blank, and that he could not with reasonable diligence have obtained knowledge thereof: or

(x) if he by means of any fraud or false pretence obtains, or attempts to obtain, compensation from the Board or a local authority in respect of an animal slaughtered, or aids or abets any person in any such fraud or false pretence: or

(xi) if, without lawful authority or excuse, proof whereof shall lie on him, he digs up, or causes to be dug up, a carcase buried under the direction of the Board or of a local authority or of a receiver of wreck: or

(xii) if, where the Board has by order prohibited, absolutely or conditionally, the use for the carrying of animals, or for any purpose connected therewith, of a vessel, vehicle, or pen, or other place, he, without lawful authority or excuse, proof whereof shall lie on him, does anything so prohibited;

(2.) And in every case in this section specified he shall be liable, on conviction, in the discretion of the court, to be imprisoned for any term not exceeding two months, with or without hard labour, in lieu of the fine to which he is liable under this Act.

Proceedings in court of summary jurisdiction.

54. Any offence against this Act may be prosecuted, and any fine in respect thereof may be recovered, and any money by this Act or an order of the Board of Agriculture made recoverable summarily may be recovered, and any summary orders under this Act or an order of the Board may be made in manner provided by the Summary Jurisdiction Acts; but nothing in this section shall apply to proceedings under the Customs Acts.

Appeal.

55. If any person thinks himself aggrieved by the dismissal of a complaint by, or by any determination or adjudication of, a court of summary jurisdiction under this Act, he may appeal therefrom to a court of quarter sessions.

Proceedings under Customs Acts for unlawful landing or shipping.

56.—(1.) If any person lands or ships or attempts to land or ship an animal or thing in contravention of this Act or of an order of the Board of Agriculture, he shall be liable, under and according to the Customs Acts, to the penalties imposed on persons importing or exporting or attempting to import or export goods the importation or exportation whereof is prohibited by or under the Customs Acts,

Sect. 56 (1). without prejudice to any proceeding against him under this Act for an offence against this Act.

(2.) The animal or thing in respect whereof the offence is committed shall be forfeited under and according to the Customs Acts in like manner as goods the importation whereof is prohibited by or under the Customs Acts.

General provision as to procedure.

57.—(1.) Where the owner or person in charge of an animal is charged with an offence against this Act relative to disease or to any illness of the animal, he shall be presumed to have known of the existence of the disease or illness, unless and until he shows to the satisfaction of the court that he had not knowledge thereof, and could not with reasonable diligence have obtained that knowledge.

(2.) Where a person is charged with an offence against this Act in not having duly cleansed or disinfected any place, vessel, vehicle, or thing belonging to him or under his charge, and a presumption against him on the part of the prosecution is raised, it shall lie on him to prove the due cleansing and disinfection thereof.

(3.) A person charged with an offence against this Act may, if he thinks fit, tender himself to be examined on his own behalf, and thereupon he may give evidence in the same manner and with the like effect and consequences as any other witness.

(4.) Every offence against this Act shall be deemed to have been committed, and every cause of complaint or matter for summary proceeding under this Act or an order of the Board of Agriculture or regulation of a local authority shall be deemed to have arisen, either in any place where the same actually was committed or arose, or in any place where the person charged or complained of or proceeded against happens to be at the time of the institution or commencement of the charge, complaint, or proceeding.

(5.) Notwithstanding anything in any Act relating to the metropolitan police or to municipal corporations or in any other Act, such part not exceeding one half of every fine or forfeiture recovered under this Act (except in proceedings under the Customs Acts) as the court before which it is recovered thinks fit, shall be paid to the person who proceeds for the same, and the residue thereof shall be applied as if this section had not been enacted.

Miscellaneous.

Local authority and local rate in Hove.

58. Notwithstanding anything in this Act the Hove Improvement Act Commissioners shall be the local authority for the Improvement Act District of Hove, and the local rate for that district shall be the rate applicable by the Commissioners to the maintenance of the police, and this Act shall apply to that district as if it were a borough and as if the said Commissioners were the council of the borough.

Sect. 59 (1).

Interpretation and construction.

59.—(1.) In this Act, unless the context otherwise requires, the following terms have the meanings herein-after respectively assigned to them, that is to say:

the expression "cattle" means bulls, cows, oxen, heifers, and calves:

the expression "animals" means, except where it is otherwise expressed, cattle, sheep, and goats, and all other ruminating animals, and swine:

the expression "disease" means cattle plague (that is to say, rinderpest, or the disease commonly called cattle plague), contagious pleuro-pneumonia of cattle (in this Act called pleuro-pneumonia), foot-and-mouth disease, sheep-pox, sheep-scab, or swine-fever (that is to say, the disease known as typhoid fever of swine, soldier purples, red disease, hog cholera or swine-plague):

the expression "diseased" means affected with disease:

the expression "suspected" means suspected of being diseased:

the expression "carcase" means the carcase of an animal, and includes part of a carcase, and the meat, bones, hide, skin, hoofs, horns, offal, or other part of an animal, separately or otherwise, or any portion thereof:

the expression "fodder" means hay or other substance commonly used for food of animals:

the expression "litter" means straw or other substance commonly used for bedding or otherwise for or about animals:

the expression "foreign" applied to animals and things, means brought to the United Kingdom from a country out of the United Kingdom:

the expression "inspector of the Board of Agriculture" or "inspector of a local authority" means a person appointed to be an inspector for purposes of this Act by the Privy Council or the Board of Agriculture, or by a local authority, as the case may be; and the expression "inspector," used alone, means such a person, by whichever authority appointed:

the expression "veterinary inspector" means an inspector being a member of the Royal College of Veterinary Surgeons, or any veterinary practitioner qualified as approved by the Board of Agriculture:

the expressions "police area" and "police force" with respect to the City of London mean the said city and the police thereof, and with respect to any other place have the same meaning as in the Police Act, 1890: 53 & 54 Vict. c. 45.

the expression "district," when used with reference to a local authority, means the area for which the local authority exercises powers under this Act (*m*):

(*m*) See s. 3, *ante*, p. 669.

Sect. 59 (1).

39 & 40 Vict. c. 36.

the expression "the Customs Acts" means the Customs Consolidation Act, 1876, and any enactment amending or substituted for that Act:

the expression "justice" means justice of the peace:

the expression "railway company" includes a company or person working a railway under lease or otherwise:

the expression "Order of Council" means an Order of the Privy Council under the Contagious Diseases (Animals) Acts, 1875 to 1886:

the expression "order of the Board of Agriculture" means an order made by the Board of Agriculture under this Act or under any enactment by this Act repealed.

(2.) In the computation of time for purposes of this Act, a period reckoned by days from the happening of an event or the doing of an act or thing shall be deemed to be exclusive of the day on which the event happens or the act or thing is done.

Special Provisions as to Scotland (*n*).

Special Provisions as to Ireland (*o*).

Supplemental.

Repeal of enactments in schedule.

78.—(1.) The Acts specified in the Fifth Schedule to this Act are hereby repealed to the extent specified in the third column to that schedule.

(2.) Notwithstanding such repeal, every Order of Council and in Council, and every order of the Board of Agriculture, or regulation of a local authority made, and every licence granted, and every committee or sub-committee constituted, and every inspector appointed, under any of the enactments repealed, shall continue and be as if this Act had not been passed; but so that the same may be revoked, altered, cancelled, or otherwise dealt with under this Act, as if it had been made, done, or granted under this Act.

Short title.

79. This Act may be cited as the Diseases of Animals Act, 1894.

SCHEDULES.

FIRST SCHEDULE.

Part I.

Pleuro-Pneumonia.

1. Cattle shall not be moved into or out of a place infected with pleuro-pneumonia, except where, as regards movement into such a place, the cattle

(*n*) Sections 60 to 64 inclusive relate to Scotland only.
(*o*) Sections 65 to 77 inclusive relate to Ireland only.

are affected with pleuro-pneumonia, and except in such other cases as the Board of Agriculture think fit by order to except. Schedule 1.

2. In the cases so excepted by order cattle may be moved into or out of an infected place on conditions prescribed by order of the Board, and not otherwise.

3. Cattle may be moved into, within, or out of such parts of an area infected with pleuro-pneumonia as are not comprised in a place infected with pleuro-pneumonia, by licence of the local authority, granted on conditions prescribed by order of the Board, and not otherwise.

PART II.

Foot-and-Mouth Disease.

1. Animals shall not be moved into or out of a place infected with foot-and-mouth disease except where, as regards movement into such a place, the animals are affected with foot-and-mouth disease, and except in such other cases as the Board of Agriculture think fit by order to except.

2. In the cases so excepted by order animals may be moved into or out of an infected place on conditions prescribed by order of the Board, and not otherwise.

3. Animals may be moved into, within, or out of such parts of an area infected with foot-and-mouth disease as are not comprised in a place infected with foot-and-mouth disease, by licence of the local authority, granted on conditions prescribed by order of the Board, and not otherwise.

SECOND SCHEDULE.

Sections 18, 73.

REGULATIONS AS TO CATTLE PLEURO-PNEUMONIA ACCOUNTS.

1. Notwithstanding anything in this Act the moneys provided by Parliament towards defraying the cost of the execution of the provisions of this Act relating to the slaughter by the Board of Agriculture or the Lord Lieutenant and Privy Council of cattle, animals, or swine, on account of pleuro-pneumonia, foot-and-mouth disease, or swine-fever, may be apportioned between Great Britain and Ireland in such manner as the Treasury in communication with the Board and the Lord Lieutenant may direct.

2. At the end of every financial year, accounts of the receipts and expenditure of the Cattle Pleuro-pneumonia Account for Great Britain and the Cattle Pleuro-pneumonia Account for Ireland shall be made up in such form and with such particulars as may be directed by the Treasury, and such accounts shall be audited by the Comptroller and Auditor-General as public accounts in accordance with such regulations as the Treasury may make, and shall be laid before Parliament, together with his report thereon.

3. If at the end of any financial year the Treasury, after communication with the Board of Agriculture, or the Lord Lieutenant and Privy Council, as the case may be, are satisfied that the balance standing to the credit of either of the said Cattle Pleuro-pneumonia Accounts, or any part of such balance, will not be required for the purposes of this Act, they may—

(a) in the case of the Cattle Pleuro-pneumonia Account for Great Britain direct such balance or part to be paid in the proportions provided by this Schedule into the Local Taxation Account (p) and the Local Taxation (Scotland) Account, in repayment of any sums which have

(p) See note (s) *ante*, p. 679.

Schedule 2.

been paid to the Cattle Pleuro-pneumonia Account out of the said Local Taxation Accounts; and

(b) in the case of the Cattle Pleuro-pneumonia Account for Ireland, direct such balance or part to be paid into the general account of the General Cattle Diseases Fund in repayment of any sums which have been paid out of the said general account for any of the purposes to which the Cattle Pleuro-pneumonia Account is by this Act applicable;

and in either case the Treasury may direct any balance or part which may not be required for such repayment to be paid into the Exchequer.

4. The proportions in which any sum is to be paid out of or into the Local Taxation Account and the Local Taxation (Scotland) Account under this Act shall be eighty-eight per centum of such sum out of or into the Local Taxation Account, and twelve per centum out of or into the Local Taxation (Scotland) Account.

5. All money paid under this Act out of or into the Local Taxation Account shall in account be charged against or credited to the proceeds of the probate duty (*q*).

6. All moneys paid under this Act out of or into the Local Taxation (Scotland) Account shall in account be charged against or credited to the residue of the Scotch share of the local taxation (customs and excise) duties in manner provided by section two of the Local Taxation (Customs and Excise) Act, 1890.

53 & 54 Vict. c. 60.

7. Payments out of or into the said Cattle Pleuro-pneumonia Accounts, and all other matters relating to the accounts and to the moneys standing to the credit of the accounts shall be made and regulated in such manner as the Treasury direct.

THIRD SCHEDULE.

Sections 24, 26, 27.

Foreign Animals.

Part I.

Slaughter at Port of Landing.

1. The animals shall be landed only at a part of a port defined for that purpose by order of the Board of Agriculture, to be called a foreign animals wharf.

2. The animals shall be landed in such manner, at such times, and subject to such supervision and control as the Commissioners of Customs direct.

The animals shall not be moved alive out of the wharf.

Part II.

Quarantine.

1. The animals shall be landed only at a part of a port defined for that purpose by order of the Board of Agriculture, to be called a foreign animals quarantine station.

2. The animals shall be landed in such manner, at such times, and subject to such supervision and control as the Commissioners of Customs direct, and subject to such conditions in respect of the animals, or of the vessel from which they are landed, as the Board by order prescribe.

(*q*) See the Local Government Act, 1888, s. 21, *ante*, p. 48.

Schedule 3.

3. When landed the animals shall be placed in sheds or other receptacles in the quarantine station, prepared by the local authority or the owners of the quarantine station, or the consignees of animals, or other persons, and approved by the Board.

4. The animals shall not be moved out of the quarantine station except on conditions prescribed by order of the Board.

5. Notwithstanding anything in the foregoing provisions of this part of this Schedule the provisions of this Act relating to slaughter in case of the existence of disease, and to compensation or other payment in respect of animals so slaughtered, and to the ownership of carcases of such animals, shall apply to animals within a foreign animals quarantine station.

FOURTH SCHEDULE.

Section 30.

COMMITTEES OF LOCAL AUTHORITIES.

1. Every local authority shall form and keep up a committee or committees, and may appoint the number of members by whom the powers of a committee may be exercised, and may at any time add to or diminish the number of the members of a committee, or otherwise alter the constitution thereof, and fill up or provide for the filling up of vacancies therein, or revoke the appointment thereof and appoint another committee or committees, and lay down rules for the guidance of a committee, who shall act accordingly.

2. A committee may consist wholly of members of the local authority or partly thereof, and partly of other persons, being rated occupiers in the district of the local authority, and otherwise qualified, as the local authority think fit.

3. A local authority may except in so far as it is otherwise provided by order of the Board of Agriculture delegate all or any of their powers, except the power to make a rate, to a committee, with or without conditions or restrictions (*r*).

4. A local authority may revoke or alter any power given by them to a committee.

5. A local authority may, if they think fit, appoint and designate one committee as their executive committee.

6. An executive committee shall have all the powers of the local authority, except the power to make a rate, and may, if they think fit, appoint a sub-committee or sub-committees, and delegate to them [except in so far as it is otherwise provided by order of the Board] all or any of the powers of the executive committee, with or without conditions or restrictions, and revoke or alter any such delegation, and appoint the number of members by whom the powers of a sub-committee may be exercised, and add to or diminish the number of the members of a sub-committee, or otherwise alter the constitution thereof, and fill up or provide for the filling up of vacancies therein, or revoke the appointment thereof and appoint another sub-committee or other sub-committees, and lay down rules for the guidance of a sub-committee who shall act accordingly.

7. Proceedings of a committee or sub-committee shall not be invalidated by any vacancy in the committee or sub-committee.

8. In case of the formation of two or more committees, they shall act according to rules laid down for their guidance by the local authority.

(*r*) See *Huth* v. *Clarke*, *ante*, p. 64.

Schedule 4.

9. A committee, and a sub-committee of an executive committee, may elect a chairman of their meetings.

10. If no chairman is elected, or if the chairman so elected is not present at the time appointed for a meeting, the members then present shall choose a chairman for that meeting.

11. A committee or sub-committee may meet and adjourn as they think proper.

12. Every question at a meeting of a committee or sub-committee shall be determined by a majority of the votes of the members, including the chairman, present and voting on the question; and in case of equal division, the chairman shall have a second vote.

FIFTH SCHEDULE.

Section 78.

ENACTMENTS REPEALED.

Session and Chapter.	Title or Short Title.	Extent of Repeal.
41 & 42 Vict. c. 74. -	The Contagious Diseases (Animals) Act, 1878.	The whole Act, except section thirty-four.
47 & 48 Vict. c. 13. -	The Contagious Diseases (Animals) Act, 1884.	The whole Act.
47 & 48 Vict. c. 47. -	The Contagious Diseases (Animals) Transfer of Parts of Districts Act, 1884.	The whole Act.
49 & 50 Vict. c. 32. -	The Contagious Diseases (Animals) Act, 1886.	The whole Act, except section nine.
52 & 53 Vict. c. 30. -	The Board of Agriculture Act, 1889 -	Section three.
53 & 54 Vict. c. 14. -	The Contagious Diseases (Animals) (Pleuro-pneumonia) Act, 1890.	The whole Act.
55 & 56 Vict. c. 47. -	The Contagious Diseases (Animals) Act, 1892.	The whole Act.
56 & 57 Vict. c. 43. -	The Contagious Diseases (Animals) Act, 1893.	The whole Act.

SHOP HOURS ACT, 1895.

(58 VICT. CAP. 5.)

An Act to amend the Shop Hours Act, 1892 (*s*). [9th April 1895.]

* * * * *

Penalty on failure to comply with 55 & 56 Vict. c. 62, s. 4.

1. If any employer fails to keep exhibited the notice required by section four of the Shop Hours Act, 1892, in manner required by that section, he shall be liable to a fine not exceeding forty shillings (*t*).

(*s*) See the Acts of 1892 and 1893, *ante*, pp. 570 and 584.

(*t*) Under s. 4 of the Act of 1892 (*ante*, p. 571) an employer of young persons is bound to exhibit in a conspicuous place in his shop a notice referring to that Act, and stating the number of hours in the week during which a young person may be lawfully employed in his shop. This Act, however, omitted to provide a penalty for the neglect to exhibit the notice. See *Hammond* v. *Pulsford*, [1895] 1 Q. B. 223; 64 L. J. M. C. 63; 71 L. T. (N.S.) 767; 43 W. R. 236; 59 J. P. 533. This defect is remedied by the text.

Sect. 2.

Short title and construction.

2. This Act may be cited as the Shop Hours Act, 1895, and shall be construed as part of the Shop Hours Act, 1892, and the Shop Hours Acts, 1892 and 1893, and this Act may be cited collectively as the Shop Hours Acts, 1892 to 1895.

LOCAL GOVERNMENT (STOCK TRANSFER) ACT, 1895.

(58 & 59 Vict. Cap. 32.)

An Act to amend the Local Government Act, 1894, *so far as regards the transfer of any stock, share, or security standing in the name of, or dividends payable to, a local authority.* [6th July 1895.]

* * * * *

Alteration of name on transfer of stock standing in the name of local authority.

56 & 57 Vict. c. 73.

51 & 52 Vict. c. 41.

1.—(1.) Where any stock is standing in the books of any company in the name of any local authority the following provisions shall have effect:—

(a.) If by virtue of the Local Government Act, 1894, or anything done under that Act or the Local Government Act, 1888, the name of the local authority is changed (*u*), then upon the request of such authority and the production of a statutory declaration by the clerk of the authority specifying the stock, and verifying the change of name and identity of the authority, the company shall enter such stock in the new name of the local authority in like manner as if the stock had been transferred to the authority under that name, and pay to that authority all dividends accrued and to accrue due thereon:

(b.) If by virtue of the Local Government Act, 1894, or anything done under that Act or the Local Government Act, 1888, any other local authority becomes entitled to the stock or any dividends thereon, a certificate of the clerk of the county council, or the order or award (*x*) under which the local authority becomes so entitled, shall be a sufficient authority to the company to transfer the stock into the name of the local authority specified in that behalf in the order, award, or certificate, and to pay the dividends to such authority:

(c.) If in any other case any other local authority is entitled to the stock or any dividends thereon, the court may on application make an order vesting in such authority or person as the court may direct, the right to transfer the

---

(*u*) See ss. 57 and 59 of the Local Government Act 1888, and ss. 21, 36 and 55 of the Local Government Act, 1894, *ante*.

(*x*) For instance an order of a county council altering an area and establishing a new local authority under ss. 57 and 59 of the Act of 1888, *ante*, pp. 111, 114; or an award under s. 62 of that Act, *ante*, p. 119; or s. 68 of the Act of 1894, *ante*, p. 647.

Sect. 1 (1).

56 & 57 Vict. c. 53.

said stock, or pay such dividends, to the authority in or to whom the same ought to be vested or paid, and the Trustee Act, 1893, shall apply in like manner as if the vesting order where made under section thirty-five of that Act.

(2.) In this Act—

"A local authority" includes any urban or rural sanitary authority, council of a borough, improvement commissioners, local board, urban district council, rural district council, board of guardians, highway board, burial board, parish council, overseers, churchwardens and overseers, and chairman of a parish meeting and overseers:

"County council" includes the council of a county borough:

"Order of a county council" (*y*) means an order made either by a county council or by any joint committee of county councils, and, if such order requires confirmation by the Local Government Board, means the order as confirmed by that Board:

"Company" includes the Bank of England, and any company or person keeping books in which any stock is registered:

"Stock" includes any share, annuity, or other security.

(3.) The jurisdiction of the court under this Act may be exercised by the High Court, or in cases within the jurisdiction of a palatine court or county court, by that court.

Short title.

2. This Act may be cited as the Local Government (Stock Transfer) Act, 1895.

LOCAL GOVERNMENT (ELECTIONS) ACT, 1896.

(59 VICT. CAP. 1) (*z*).

An Act to continue temporarily certain Powers for the Removal of Difficulties at Elections under the Local Government Act, 1894.

[6th March 1896.]

* * * * *

Power of county council to remove difficulties.

1.—(1.) If any difficulty arises with respect to any election of parish or district councillors or of guardians, or to the first meeting after any ordinary election of such councillors or guardians, or if, from an election not being held, or being defective, or otherwise, the council or board has not been properly constituted, the county council

(*y*) It is remarkable that this expression does not occur in this Act; no doubt an order such as is referred to in s. 1 (1) (b) is intended.

(*z*) This Act is substantially a re-enactment of s. 80, sub-s. (1) of the Local Government Act, 1894, which applied to the first elections only. See also as to the powers of county councils to remove difficulties at elections under the Local Government Act, 1894, ss. 47 (5), 48 (5), and 59 (5), *ante*, pp. 636, 638, 643.

may by order make any appointment or do anything which appears to them necessary or expedient for the proper holding of any such election or meeting, and properly constituting the council or board, and may, if it appears to them necessary, direct the holding of an election or meeting, and fix the dates for any such election or meeting. **Sect. 1 (1)**

(2.) Any such order may modify the provisions of the Local Government Act, 1894, and the enactments applied by, or rules framed under, that Act, so far as may appear to the county council necessary or expedient for carrying the order into effect. 56 & 57 Vict. c. 73.

(3.) A county council may delegate their powers under this section to a committee.

2. This Act shall continue in force until the thirty-first day of December, one thousand eight hundred and ninety-seven, and no longer, unless continued by Parliament (*a*). Duration.

3. This Act may be cited as the Local Government (Elections) Act, 1896. Short title.

LOCAL GOVERNMENT (DETERMINATION OF DIFFERENCES) ACT, 1896.

(59 VICT. CAP. 9) (*b*).

An Act to amend certain Provisions of the Local Government Act, 1888, *with respect to the Determination of Differences by the Local Government Board.* [21st May 1896.]

* * * * *

1. The Local Government Act, 1888, shall have effect, as if in sub-sections three and four of section eleven of that Act for the words "be determined by arbitration of the Local Government Board," and in sub-section nine of the same section for the words "be referred to the arbitration of the Local Government Board," were substituted the words "be determined by the Local Government Amendment of 51 & 52 Vict. c. 44, s. 11, as to determination of differences.

(*a*) This Act was continued to December 31st, 1898, by the Expiring Laws Continuance Act, 1897 (60 & 61 Vict. c. 54).

(*b*) This Act appears to have been passed in consequence of the decision in *Re Kent County Council* v. *Sandgate Local Board*, [1895] 2 Q. B. 43; 64 L. J. Q. B. 502; 72 L. T. (N.S.) 725; 43 W. R. 601; 59 J. P. 456; in which it was held that where differences are directed by the Local Government Act, 1888, to be determined by arbitration of the Local Government Board, the board must proceed under s. 63 of that Act, with the consequence that they, or the arbitrator appointed by them, may be compelled under the Arbitration Act, 1889 (52 & 53 Vict. c. 49) s. 24 to state a case for the opinion of the court. This Act makes it optional for the Board in determining differences as to the amount of payments to be made by local authorities and other matters in respect of highways under s. 11 of the Act of 1888 to act as arbitrators or not. If they do not so act they can determine the difference by means of a local inquiry under s. 87 of that Act, and this order made after the inquiry will (under s. 295 of the Public Health Act 1875, which is incorporated by s. 87) be binding and conclusive.

Sect. 1.

Board either as arbitrators or otherwise at the option of the Board," and as if in section sixty-three of that Act for the words "are required in pursuance of this Act to decide," were inserted the words "determine as arbitrators."

Validation of past orders.

2. An order of the Local Government Board made before the passing of this Act and purporting to have been made for the determination of any matter under section eleven of the Local Government Act, 1888, shall not be invalid by reason only of the Board having determined the matter as arbitrators or otherwise, instead of appointing an arbitrator to determine it.

Short title.

3. This Act may be cited as the Local Government (Determination of Differences) Act, 1896.

DISEASES OF ANIMALS ACT, 1896.

(59 & 60 Vict. Cap. 15.)

An Act to amend the Diseases of Animals Act, 1894 (*c*).
[20th July 1896.]

* * *

Slaughter of foreign animals. 57 & 58 Vict. c. 57.

1.—(1.) For section twenty-four of the Diseases of Animals Act, 1894, shall be substituted the following section, namely:—

"The provisions set forth in Part I. (slaughter at port of landing) of the Third Schedule to this Act shall apply to all foreign animals other than—

(a) foreign animals the landing of which is for the time being prohibited by order of the Board of Agriculture; and

(b) foreign animals intended for exhibition or other exceptional purposes, and the landing of which is allowed for the time being by the Board, subject to the provisions of Part II. (quarantine) of the Third Schedule to this Act."

(2.) Section twenty-six of the Diseases of Animals Act, 1894, is hereby repealed.

Commencement of Act.

2. This Act shall come into operation on the first day of January next after the passing thereof.

Short title and construction.

3. This Act may be cited as the Diseases of Animals Act, 1896, and shall be construed as one with the Diseases of Animals Act, 1894, and that Act and this Act may be cited together as the Diseases of Animals Acts, 1894 and 1896.

(*c*) See this Act, *ante*, p. 669.

AGRICULTURAL RATES ACT, 1896.

(59 & 60 Vict. Cap. 16) (*d*).

An Act to amend the Law with respect to the Rating of Occupiers of Agricultural Land in England, and for other purposes connected therewith. [20th July 1896.]

* * * * *

Exemption of agricultural land from half of rates to which this Act applies.

1.—(1.) During the continuance of this Act, that is to say, the period of five years after the thirty-first day of March next after the passing of this Act, the occupier of agricultural land in England shall be liable in the case of every rate to which this Act applies, to pay one half only of the rate in the pound payable in respect of buildings and other hereditaments (*e*).

(2.) This Act shall apply to every rate as defined by this Act, except a rate—

(a) which the occupier of agricultural land is liable, as compared with the occupier of buildings or other hereditaments, to be assessed to or to pay in the proportion of one half or less than one half, or

(b) which is assessed under any commission of sewers or in respect of any drainage, wall, embankment, or other work for the benefit of the land.

Payment out of Local Taxation Account in respect of deficiency arising from exemption.

2.—(1.) In respect of the deficiency which will arise from the provisions of this Act in the produce of rates made by the spending authorities in England, as hereinafter defined, there shall during the continuance of this Act—

(a) be paid to the Local Taxation Account (*f*) an annual sum (in this Act referred to as the annual grant) of such amount as is certified under the provisions hereinafter contained; and

(b) be issued from the Local Taxation Account by half-yearly payments out of the annual grant to each such spending

(*d*) The object of this Act is to make the occupier of agricultural land liable, in the case of certain rates, to the payment on one half only of the rate in the pound payable in respect of buildings and other hereditaments. Amongst the rates to which the Act applies is the county rate leviable by a county council under the County Rate Act, 1852 (15 & 16 Vict. c. 81), and the Local Government Act, 1888, s. 3 (i), *ante*, p. 5. The deficiency caused by the relief of agricultural land from half the rate, is made up to the spending authorities (including county councils) by means of half-yearly payments made out of an annual grant from the proceeds of the estate duty on personal property to the Local Taxation Account. The Act provides machinery for ascertaining the amount of the annual grant (viz., the total deficiency throughout England), payable to the Local Taxation Account and the share of that grant payable to each spending authority in respect of the deficiency arising in the produce of the rates of that authority. The Act is temporary only; see s. 1 (1). It is fully treated in a work by Mr. Walter C. Ryde, 2nd edition, 1896.

(*e*) The definition of "agricultural land," *post*, s. 9, includes "market gardens," but it has been held in a recent case that as to glass-houses erected in a market garden, the occupier is liable to pay the full rate: *Smith* v. *Richmond*, [1898] 1 Q. B. 683, *per* LINDLEY, M.R., and RIGBY, L.J. (VAUGHAN WILLIAMS, L.J., *diss.*), reversing the decision of COLLINS, J. (RIDLEY, J., *diss.*), 77 L. T. (N.S.) 161; 61 J. P. 710.

(*f*) As to the Local Taxation Account, see the Local Government Act, 1888, ss. 20 *et seq.*, *ante*, p. 46.

Sect. 2 (1).

authority a share of that grant of such amount as is certified under the provisions hereinafter contained.

(2.) The Commissioners of Inland Revenue, in such manner, by such payments, and under such regulations, as the Treasury direct, shall pay to the Local Taxation Account, out of the proceeds of the estate duty (*ff*) derived in England from personal property, the annual sum required by this section to be paid to that account.

(3.) The first of those payments shall be made during the six months ending on the thirty-first day of March next after the passing of this Act, so as to make up a half-yearly payment to meet the issues to spending authorities on account of the six ensuing months.

Contributions from more than one parish.

3.—(1.) Where any spending authority require in any half year or other period to raise from two or more parishes a sum by a rate to which this Act applies, they shall, in determining the net amount to be so raised, deduct the sum issuable to them in respect of the said rate on account of their share of the annual grant for the said half year or other period, and the net amount after that deduction shall, where it would otherwise be raised in proportion to the rateable value, be raised in proportion to the assessable value of those parishes.

(2.) For the purposes of this section the assessable value of a parish shall be the rateable value thereof reduced by an amount equal to one half of the rateable value of the agricultural land in the parish (*g*).

Certifying of annual sums payable in respect of deficiency.

4.—(1.) The Local Government Board shall, as soon as may be after the passing of this Act, certify the amount—

(a) of the annual grant to be paid to the Local Taxation Account; and

(b) of the share of such grant to be paid annually to each spending authority,

under this Act, and for that purpose shall determine in the prescribed manner the amount which for the purposes of this Act is to be taken as having been raised during the last year before the passing of this Act by any rate to which this Act applies for the expenditure of each spending authority.

(2.) Such proportion of the whole amount so taken to be raised in respect of any hereditaments or parishes as the Local Government Board estimate to be the proportion of the total rateable value of those hereditaments or parishes which represents the value of agricultural land, shall be taken for the purposes of this Act as the amount raised during the said year, by the said authority, by the said rate, in respect of agricultural land, and one half of that amount shall be taken as the deficiency which will arise from the provisions of this Act in the produce of the said rate.

(*ff*) As to the estate duty, see s. 21 of the Local Government Act, 1888, and notes, *ante*, p. 48.

(*g*) The amount to be raised from the parishes in a county by the county rate will be determined upon the footing prescribed by this section.

Sect. 4 (3).

(3.) A sum equal to the total amount of the deficiencies thus estimated for all the spending authorities in England shall be the amount of the annual grant, and a sum equal to the deficiency thus estimated in the case of each spending authority shall be the share of that spending authority in the annual grant, and the Local Government Board shall certify the same accordingly.

(4.) The Local Government Board, in acting under this section, shall obtain such information and make such inquiries, and in such manner as they think fit.

(5.) The Local Government Board may in case of error amend, or for the purpose of meeting any alteration in an area or authority to which a certificate relates may vary, a certificate under this section, and any such amendment or variation shall have effect from the date of the original certificate, or any later date fixed by the Board; but, save as aforesaid, a certificate shall be final and binding on all persons.

(6.) The Local Government Board may give provisional certificates, if they think necessary for the purpose of enabling the first payments to and out of the Local Taxation Account under this Act to be made, before they have sufficient information to enable them to give final certificates.

Separate statement in valuation lists, etc., of value of agricultural land.

5. In every valuation list and in the basis or standard for any county rate, and in any valuation made by the council of a borough or any other council for the purpose of raising the borough or other rate—

(a) where separate hereditaments are specified therein, the value of agricultural land shall be stated separately from that of any building or other hereditament; and

(b) in every case the total rateable value of the agricultural land in each parish shall be stated separately from the total rateable value of the buildings or other hereditaments in such parish; and whenever a copy of the total of the rateable value of any parish is required to be sent to any person (*h*), such copy shall state both the above-mentioned totals; and

(c) where any hereditament consists partly of agricultural land and partly of buildings, the gross estimated rental of the buildings, when valued separately, in pursuance of this Act, from the agricultural land shall, while the buildings are used only for the cultivation of the said land, be calculated not on structural cost, but on the rent at which they would be expected to let to a tenant from year to year, if they could only be so used; and the total gross estimated rental

(*h*) The basis or standard for the county rate is made according to the value of the rateable property in each parish. See notes to Local Government Act, 1888, s. 3 (i), *ante*, p. 5. A copy of the basis or standard (before it is confirmed) is sent to the overseers of each parish; County Rate Act, 1852, s. 13.

Sect. 5.

of the hereditament shall not be increased by the said separate valuation.

Procedure for ascertaining deficiency and for separation of value of agricultural land from buildings and other hereditaments.

6.—(1.) For the purposes of this Act returns shall be made to the Local Government Board (*i*) in accordance with the prescribed regulations—

(a) by every spending authority in relation to the sums actually received by them or their predecessors during the year next before the passing of this Act from any rate to which this Act applies; and

(b) by every assessment committee or council whose duty it is to revise or make a valuation list, basis, standard or other valuation for any parish, in relation to the gross estimated rental and rateable value of that parish, and the proportion thereof which represents agricultural land; and

(c) by any such authority, committee, or council in relation to any other prescribed information.

(2.) For the purpose of the returns, statements showing the gross estimated rental and rateable value of the agricultural land in a parish, and, in the case of any hereditament separately valued which consists in part of agricultural land and in part of buildings or other hereditaments, of each such part, shall be made by the overseers of every parish, and corrected by the assessment committee, and sent to the surveyor of taxes, and be subject to objection or appeal by the said surveyor and overseers before the assessment committee, and the justices in special sessions, and the court of quarter sessions, and subject to the right of any aggrieved ratepayer to be heard upon the said appeal, in such form, within such times, and generally in such manner, and subject to such provisions, as may be prescribed. These provisions shall conform as nearly as circumstances will permit to the existing statutory law respecting valuation lists, as regards notices, rights to inspect and take extracts, the hearing of objections, and otherwise.

(3.) The Local Government Board may by order make regulations for the purpose of this section, and also generally for carrying into effect this Act, and those regulations shall be laid before both Houses of Parliament, and if neither House of Parliament within ten days passes a resolution adverse to the said order, they shall be binding in law until varied in the same manner, shall have effect as if they were enacted in this Act, and shall amongst other matters provide—

(a) for fixing, with the concurrence of the Treasury, for the purpose of the division in the statements of agricultural land from buildings or other hereditaments, the minimum gross estimated rental and rateable value of the buildings or other hereditaments;

(*i*) The returns required by this section were sent to the Local Government Board in the year 1896, and this part of the section is now spent. They were made pursuant to an order of the Local Government Board, dated 28th July, 1896, which will be found in S. R. O., 1896, p. 497.

Sect. 6 (3).

(b) for giving effect to a notice of objection or appeal by the surveyor of taxes unless it is proved that such notice is unfair or incorrect;

(c) for the temporary adoption by the county council or any other council, of the division in the return between the total rateable value of agricultural land and that of buildings and other hereditaments:

(d) for the alteration of the valuation list in accordance with the statements as finally settled and sending copies of the returns to spending authorities and for applying and adapting any statutory form or procedure respecting the valuation list or poor rate; and

(e) for adapting this Act to cases where there is no valuation list, or where a sum is raised by rate from an area not a parish.

(4.) The regulations may also provide fines for the breach thereof not exceeding forty shillings, or in case of any continuing offence not exceeding forty shillings a day during the continuance of the offence, and any such fine may be recovered as a Crown debt or to an amount not exceeding one hundred pounds before a court of summary jurisdiction.

As to spending authorities.

7.—(1.) Where the spending authority are a school board for a school district which is a parish, or the surveyors of highways, the amount which otherwise would be payable under this Act to the spending authority may be paid to the guardians of the poor law union in which the parish is situate, and, if so paid, shall be paid or credited by them to the spending authority.

(2.) Every sum paid under this Act out of the Local Taxation Account to any spending authority in respect of any rate, shall, for the purpose of its application, of account, and of audit, be deemed to have been raised by the said rate.

(3.) For the purposes of section ninety-seven of the Elementary Education Act, 1870, any amount paid or credited under this Act out of the local taxation account to a school board shall be deemed to have been actually paid by the rating authority, and the amount which would have been raised or been produced by a rate of threepence in the pound on the rateable value shall be calculated in like manner as if this Act had not passed. 33 & 34 Vict. c. 75.

As to limit of rate or expenditure in case of any local authority

8. A limit imposed by any enactment on a rate shall be construed as being only a limit on the amount to be raised by that rate, and where by that limit or otherwise the sum to be raised or expended by a local authority is limited by any enactment by reference to a rate, the limit shall be varied so as to enable the local authority to raise or expend the same sum as they might have done if this Act had not passed, and in the case of a spending authority receiving any sum paid under this Act out of the local taxation account in

Sect. 8. respect of such rate that sum shall be deemed to be part of the sum raised thereby.

Definitions. **9.** In this Act, unless the context otherwise requires :—

The expression "rate" means a rate made during the continuance of this Act, the proceeds of which are applicable to public local purposes, and which is leviable on the basis of an assessment in respect of the yearly value of property, and includes any sum which, though obtained in the first instance by a precept, certificate, or other instrument requiring payment from some authority or officer, is or can be ultimately raised out of a rate as before defined:

The expression "rateable value" in the case of the county rate, or any other rate, levied according to any annual value not being rateable value as stated in the valuation list, means that annual value:

25 & 26 Vict. c. 103; 27 & 28 Vict. c. 39; 32 & 33 Vict. c. 67.

The expression "valuation list" means a valuation list under the Union Assessment Committee Acts, 1862 and 1864, or, in the metropolis, under the Valuation (Metropolis) Act, 1869:

The expression "spending authority" means any of the local authorities in England mentioned in the schedule to this Act:

The expression "occupier" includes owner where the owner is rated in place of the occupier:

51 & 52 Vict. c. 41.

The expression "Local Taxation Account" has the same meaning as in the Local Government Act, 1888 (*k*):

The expression "prescribed" means prescribed by order of the Local Government Board:

The expression "agricultural land" means any land used as arable, meadow, or pasture ground only, cottage gardens exceeding one quarter of an acre, market gardens, nursery grounds, orchards, or allotments, but does not include land occupied together with a house as a park, gardens, other than as aforesaid, pleasure-grounds, or any land kept or preserved mainly or exclusively for purposes of sport or recreation, or land used as a racecourse:

The expression "cottage" means a house occupied as a dwelling by a person of the labouring classes:

The expression "year" means the local financial year, that is to say, the twelve months beginning on the first day of April, or where the spending authority do not make up their accounts to that day on the nearest day thereto to which they do make up their accounts, or on any other prescribed day.

Short title. **10.** This Act may be cited as the Agricultural Rates Act, 1896.

(*k*) See s. 20 of that Act, *ante*, p. 46.

SCHEDULE.

Schedule.

SPENDING AUTHORITIES.

County councils, councils of county boroughs, councils of boroughs and other urban districts and of rural districts, boards of guardians, the receiver of the metropolitan police district, school boards, highway boards, surveyors of highways.

LOCOMOTIVES ON HIGHWAYS ACT, 1896.

(59 & 60 VICT. CAP. 36) (*l*).

An Act to amend the Law with respect to the Use of Locomotives on Highways. [14th August 1896.]

* * * * *

Exemption of light locomotives from certain statutory provisions.

1.—(1.) The enactments mentioned in the schedule to this Act, and any other enactment restricting the use of locomotives on highways and contained in any public general or local and personal Act in force at the passing of this Act, shall not apply to any vehicle propelled by mechanical power if it is under three tons in weight unladen, and is not used for the purpose of drawing more than one vehicle (such vehicle with its locomotive not to exceed in weight unladen four tons), and is so constructed that no smoke or visible vapour is emitted therefrom except from any temporary or accidental cause; and vehicles so exempted, whether locomotives or drawn by locomotives, are in this Act referred to as light locomotives.

Provided that—

(a) the council of any county or county borough shall have power to make bye-laws preventing or restricting the use such locomotives upon any bridge within their area (*m*), where such council are satisfied that such use would be attended with damage to the bridge or danger to the public:

(b) a light locomotive shall be deemed to be a carriage within the meaning of any Act of Parliament, whether public general or local, and of any rule, regulation, or bye-law,

---

(*l*) This Act frees "light locomotives" (as defined by s. 1) from the restrictions imposed upon the use of locomotives by the enactments mentioned in the schedule. Restrictions upon the use of light locomotives are, however, imposed by this Act, and by the regulations of the Local Government Board made under it. The Act affects county councils as highway authorities in respect of main roads, and they are themselves empowered to make bye-laws under it as to the use of light locomotives upon bridges (s. 1 (1) (a)), and to make applications to the Local Government Board as to their use in particular places (s. 6 (2)).

(*m*) Apparently whether a "county bridge" or not. As to the penalty for a breach of the bye-law, see s. 7, *post*.

Sect. 1 (1).

made under any Act of Parliament, and, if used as a carriage of any particular class, shall be deemed to be a carriage of that class, and the law relating to carriages of that class shall apply accordingly.

(2.) In calculating for the purposes of this Act the weight of a vehicle unladen, the weight of any water, fuel, or accumulators, used for the purpose of propulsion, shall not be included.

Regulations as to lights.

2. During the period between one hour after sunset and one hour before sunrise, the person in charge of a light locomotive shall carry attached thereto a lamp so constructed and placed as to exhibit a light in accordance with the regulations to be made by the Local Government Board (*n*).

Locomotives to carry a bell.

3. Every light locomotive shall carry a bell or other instrument capable of giving audible and sufficient warning of the approach or position of the carriage.

Rate of speed.

4. No light locomotive shall travel along a public highway at a greater speed than fourteen miles an hour, or than any less speed that may be prescribed by regulations of the Local Government Board (*n*).

Use of petroleum, etc. 34 & 35 Vict. c. 105. 42 & 43 Vict. c. 47. 44 & 45 Vict. c. 67.

5. The keeping and use of petroleum or of any other inflammable liquid or fuel for the purpose of light locomotives shall be subject to regulations made by a Secretary of State, and regulations so made shall have effect notwithstanding anything in the Petroleum Acts, 1871 to 1881 (*o*).

Local Government Board regulations.

6.—(1.) The Local Government Board may make regulations (*n*) with respect to the use of light locomotives on highways, and their construction, and the conditions under which they may be used.

(2.) Regulations under this section may, if the Local Government Board deem it necessary, be of a local nature and limited in their application to a particular area, and may, on the application of any local authority, prohibit or restrict the use of locomotives for purposes of traction in crowded streets, or in other places where such use may be attended with danger to the public.

All regulations under this section shall have full effect notwithstanding anything in any other Act, whether general or local, or any bye-laws or regulations made thereunder.

Every regulation purporting to be made in pursuance of this section shall be forthwith laid before both Houses of Parliament.

Penalties.

7. A breach of any bye-law or regulation made under this Act, or of any provision of this Act, may, on summary conviction, be punished by a fine not exceeding ten pounds.

(*n*) Regulations of the Local Government Board under this Act were issued on November 9th, 1896. See these regulations and the circular to local authorities which accompanied them, *post*.

(*o*) Regulations under this section were made by the Secretary of State on November 3rd, 1896, and are set out in S. R. O., 1896, p. 173.

8.—(1.) On and after the first day of January next after the passing of this Act there shall be granted, charged, and paid in Great Britain for every light locomotive, which is liable to duty either as a carriage or as a hackney carriage under section four of the Customs and Inland Revenue Act, 1888, an additional duty of excise at the following rate; namely,— **Sect. 8 (1).** Excise duty on certain locomotives. 51 & 52 Vict. c. 8.

	£	s.	d.
If the weight of the locomotive exceeds one ton unladen, but does not exceed two tons unladen - - - - - -	2	2	0
If the weight of the locomotive exceeds two tons unladen - - - - - -	3	3	0

(2.) Every such duty shall be paid together with the duty on the licence for the locomotive as a carriage or hackney carriage, and shall in England be dealt with in manner directed with respect to duties on local taxation licences within the meaning of the Local Government Act, 1888 (*p*). * * * 51 & 52 Vict. c. 41.

9. The requirements of sub-section (4) of section twenty-eight of the Highways and Locomotives Amendment Act, 1878, may be from time to time varied by order of the Local Government Board. Construction of wheels of locomotives on roads.

10. * * * **11.** * * * (*q*).

12. This Act may be cited as the Locomotives on Highways Act, 1896, and shall come into operation on the expiration of three months from the passing thereof. Short title and commencement.

SCHEDULE.

ENACTMENTS WHICH ARE NOT TO APPLY TO LIGHT LOCOMOTIVES.

The Locomotives Act, 1861 (24 & 25 Vict. c. 70), except so much of section one as relates to tolls on locomotives, and sections seven and thirteen.

Section forty-one of the Thames Embankment Act, 1862 (25 & 26 Vict. c. 93).

The Locomotives Act, 1865 (28 & 29 Vict. c. 83).

The Locomotives Amendment (Scotland) Act, 1878 (41 & 42 Vict. c. 58).

Part II. of the Highways and Locomotives (Amendment) Act, 1878 (41 & 42 Vict. c. 77).

Section six of the Public Health (Ireland) Amendment Act, 1879 (42 & 43 Vict. c. 57).

(*p*) As to local taxation licences, see s. 20 of the Local Government Act 1888, *ante*, p. 46, and the First Schedule to that Act, *ante*, p. 203. Light locomotives will not require a licence from the county council under s. 32 of the Highways and Locomotives (Amendment) Act, 1878, that section being contained in Part II. of that Act. See s. 1 (1) of this Act, *ante*, p. 717.

The remainder of this section relates to Scotland only.

(*q*) Sections 10 and 11 relate to Scotland and Ireland respectively.

LIGHT RAILWAYS ACT, 1896.

(59 & 60 VICT. CAP. 48) (*q*).

An Act to facilitate the Construction of Light Railways in Great Britain. [14th August 1896.]

* * * * *

Establishment of Light Railway Commission.

1.—(1.) For the purpose of facilitating the construction and working of light railways (*r*) in Great Britain, there shall be established a commission consisting of three commissioners, to be styled the Light Railway Commissioners, and to be appointed by the President of the Board of Trade.

(2.) It shall be the duty of the Light Railway Commissioners to carry this Act into effect, and to offer, so far as they are able, every facility for considering and maturing proposals to construct light railways.

(3.) If a vacancy occurs in the office of any of the Light Railway Commissioners by reason of death, resignation, incapacity or otherwise, the President of the Board of Trade may appoint some other person to fill the vacancy, and so from time to time as occasion may require.

(4.) There shall be paid to one of the commissioners such salary not exceeding one thousand pounds a year, as the Treasury may direct.

(5.) The Board of Trade may, with the consent of the Treasury as to number and remuneration, appoint and employ such number of officers and persons as they think necessary for the purpose of the execution of the duties of the Light Railway Commissioners under this Act, and may remove any officer or person so appointed or employed (*s*).

(6.) The said salary and remuneration, and all expenses of the Light Railway Commissioners incurred with the sanction of the

---

(*q*) By this Act county councils are empowered to apply to the light railway commissioners for an order authorizing a light railway. Such an order must be submitted to the Board of Trade for confirmation, and may require to be submitted to Parliament. If authorized by the order, a county council may contract and work the railway themselves, or contract for its construction and working, and advance moneys to a light railway company and combine with other councils or persons for these purposes. The Act contains provisions as to the expenses of county councils incurred under the Act, and as to the appointment of joint committees by county councils and other local authorities for the purposes of the Act. Orders made under the Act may contain various provisions for the protection of county councils. The Act expires on December 31st, 1901, unless continued. Full information on this Act and the Acts incorporated therewith as relating to light railways will be found in Dodd and Allan's "Law of Light Railways."

(*r*) The expression "light railway" is not defined by the Act. Some light is thrown on the meaning of the term by ss. 27--29 of the Regulation of Railways Act, 1868 (31 & 32 Vict. c. 119), and the Light Railways (Ireland) Act, 1889 (52 & 53 Vict. c. 67), s. 11.

(*s*) The offices of the commissioners are at No. 23, Great George Street, Westminster.

Treasury in the execution of this Act shall, except so far as provision is made for their payment by or under this Act, be paid out of moneys provided by Parliament. Sect. 1 (6).

(7.) The Commissioners may act by any two of their number.

(8.) The powers of the Light Railway Commissioners shall, unless continued by Parliament, cease on the thirty-first day of December one thousand nine hundred and one.

Application for orders authorising light railways.

2. An application for an order authorising a light railway under this Act shall be made to the Light Railway Commissioners, and may be made—

(a) by the council of any county, borough, or district, through any part of which the proposed railway is to pass (*t*); or

(b) by any individual, corporation, or company; or

(c) jointly by any such councils, individuals, corporations, or companies.

Powers of local authorities under order.

3.—(1.) The council of any county, borough, or district, may if authorised by an order under this Act—

(a) undertake themselves to construct and work, or to contract for the construction or working of the light railway authorised;

(b) advance to a light railway company, either by way of loan or as part of the share capital of the company (*u*), or partly in one way and partly in the other, any amount authorised by the order;

(c) join any other council or any person or body of persons in doing any of the things above mentioned; and

(d) do any such other act incidental to any of the things above mentioned as may be authorised by the order.

(2.) Provided that—

(a) an order authorising a council to undertake to construct and work or to contract for the construction or working of a light railway, or to advance money to a light railway company, shall not be made except on an application by the council made in pursuance of a special resolution passed in manner directed by the First Schedule to this Act; and

(b) a council shall not construct or work or contract for the construction or working of any light railway wholly or

---

(*t*) The application must be in pursuance of a special resolution. See s. 3 (2) (a) and First Schedule, *post*. If the railway is wholly or partly outside the county the provisions of s. 3 (2) (b) *post*, must be noticed. Applications will be received in the months of May and November only. See the rules of the Board of Trade, September 1896, *post*, which regulate the procedure to be followed in such applications. As to advertisements and notices, see also the provisions and procedure contained in s. 7, *post*. As to the documents which must accompany the application, see r. 27, Appendix, *post*.

(*u*) "Light Railway Company" and "share capital" are defined s. 28, *post*.

Sect. 3 (2).

partly outside their area, or advance any money for the purpose of any such railway, except jointly with the council of the outside area, or on proof to the satisfaction of the Board of Trade that such construction, working, or advance is expedient in the interests of the area of the first-mentioned council, and in the event of their being authorised so to do their expenditure shall be so limited by the order as not to exceed such amount as will, in the opinion of the Board of Trade, bear due proportion to the benefit which may be expected to accrue to their area from the construction or working of the railway.

Loans by Treasury.

4.—(1.) Where the council of any county, borough, or district have advanced or agreed to advance any sum to a light railway company, the Treasury may also agree to make an advance to the company by lending them any sum not exceeding one quarter of the total amount required for the purpose of the light railway and not exceeding the amount for the time being advanced by the council.

Provided that the Treasury shall not advance money to a light railway company under this section, unless at least one-half of the total amount required for the purpose of the light railway is provided by means of share capital, and at least one-half of that share capital has been subscribed and paid up by persons other than local authorities.

(2.) Any loan under this section shall bear interest at such rate not less than three pounds two shillings and sixpence per centum per annum as the Treasury may from time to time authorise as being in their opinion sufficient to enable such loans to be made without loss to the Exchequer, and shall be advanced on such conditions as the Treasury determine.

(3.) Where the Treasury advance money to a light railway company under this section, and the advance by the council to the company is made in whole or part by means of a loan, the loan by the Treasury under this section shall rank pari passu with the loan by the council.

Special advances by Treasury.

5.—(1.) Where it is certified to the Treasury by the Board of Agriculture that the making of any light railway under this Act would benefit agriculture in any district, or by the Board of Trade that by the making of any such railway a necessary means of communication would be established between a fishing harbour or fishing village and a market, or that such railway is necessary for the development of or maintenance of some definite industry, but that owing to the exceptional circumstances of the district the railway would not be constructed without special assistance from the State, and the Treasury are satisfied that a railway company existing at the time will construct and work the railway if an advance is made by the Treasury under this section, the Treasury may, subject to the limitation of this Act as to the amount to be expended for the purpose of special advances, agree that the railway be aided out of public money by a special advance under this section. Sect. 5 (1).

Provided that—

(a) the Treasury shall not make any such special advance unless they are satisfied that landowners, local authorities, and other persons locally interested have by the free grant of land or otherwise given all reasonable assistance and facilities in their power for the construction of the railway (*x*); and

(b) a special advance shall not in any case exceed such portion not exceeding one half of the total amount required for the construction of the railway as may be prescribed by rules to be made by the Treasury under this Act; and

(c) where the Treasury agree to make any such special advance as a free grant, the order authorising the railway may make provision as regards any parish that, during a period not exceeding ten years to be fixed by the order, so much of the railway as is in that parish shall not be assessed to any local rate at a higher value than that at which the land occupied by the railway would have been assessed if it had remained in the condition in which it was immediately before it was acquired for the purpose of the railway, but before such provision is made in any order the local and rating authorities of every such parish shall be informed of the intention to insert such provision, and shall be entitled to be heard. The order may authorise the Board of Trade to extend any such period.

(2.) A special advance under this section may be a free grant or a loan or partly a free grant and partly a loan.

(3.) Any free grant or loan for a special advance under this section shall be made on such conditions and at such rate of interest as the Treasury direct.

Limitation on amount of advance and provision of money by National Debt Commissioners.

6.—(1.) The total amount advanced by the Treasury under this Act shall not at any one time exceed one million pounds, of which a sum not exceeding two hundred and fifty thousand pounds may be expended for the purpose of special advances under this Act.

(2.) The National Debt Commissioners may lend to the Treasury, and the Treasury may borrow from the National Debt Commissioners, such money as may be required for the purpose of advances by the Treasury under this Act, on such terms as to interest, sinking fund, and period of repayment (not exceeding thirty years from the date

---

(*x*) *Quære* whether a county council could make a free grant of land vested in them for the purposes of the railway. See s. 19, *post*, and s. 7 of the Lands Clauses Act, 1845, and s. 19 of the Interpretation Act, 1889.

Sect. 6 (2). of the loan) as may be agreed on between the National Debt Commissioners and the Treasury.

(3.) The sums so lent by the National Debt Commissioners shall be repaid out of money provided by Parliament for the purpose, and if and so far as that money is insufficient shall be charged on, and payable out of, the Consolidated Fund, or the growing produce thereof.

Consideration of application by Light Railway Commissioners.

7.—(1.) Where an application for authorizing a light railway under this Act is made to the Light Railway Commissioners, those Commissioners shall, in the first instance, satisfy themselves that all reasonable steps have been taken for consulting the local authorities, including road authorities, through whose areas the railway is intended to pass, and the owners and occupiers of the land it is proposed to take, and for giving public notice of the application, and shall also themselves by local inquiry and such other means as they think necessary possess themselves of all such information as they may consider material or useful for determining the expediency of granting the application.

(2.) The applicants shall satisfy the commissioners that they have

(a) published once at least in each of two consecutive weeks, in some newspaper circulating in the area or some part of the area through which the light railway is to pass, an advertisement describing shortly the land proposed to be taken and the purpose for which it is proposed to be taken, naming a place where a plan of the proposed works and the lands to be taken, and a book of reference to the plan, may be seen at all reasonable hours, and stating the quantity of land required; and

(b) served notice in the prescribed manner on every reputed owner, lessee, and occupier of any land intended to be taken, describing in each case the land intended to be taken, and inquiring whether the person so served assents to or dissents from the taking of his land, and requesting him to state any objections he may have to his land being taken.

The plan and book of reference shall be in the prescribed form, and for the purposes of this section the expression "prescribed" shall mean prescribed by rules made under this Act (*y*).

(3.) The Commissioners shall before deciding on an application give full opportunity for any objections to the application to be laid before them, and shall consider all such objections, whether made formally or informally.

(4.) If after consideration the Commissioners think that the application should be granted, they shall settle any draft order (*z*) submitted to them by the applicants for authorising the railway, and

(*y*) See these rules, *post*.

(*z*) See s. 11, *post*, as to what provisions the order may contain.

see that all such matters (including provisions for the safety of the public and particulars of the land proposed to be taken) are inserted therein, as they think necessary for the proper construction and working of the railway. Sect. 7 (4).

(5.) The order of the Light Railway Commissioners shall be provisional only, and shall have no effect until confirmed by the Board of Trade in manner provided by this Act.

(6.) Where an application for a light railway has been refused by the Light Railway Commissioners, the applicants, if the council of any county, borough, or district, may appeal against such refusal to the Board of Trade (*a*), who may, at any time if they think fit, remit the application or any portion thereof to the said Commissioners for further consideration with or without special instructions.

Submission of order to Board of Trade for confirmation.

8.—(1.) The Commissioners shall submit any order made by them under this Act to the Board of Trade for confirmation, accompanied by such particulars and plans as may be required by the Board, and shall also make and lay before the Board with the order a report stating the objections which have been made to the application, and the manner in which they have been dealt with, and any other matters in reference to the order which the Commissioners may think fit to insert in the report.

(2.) The Board of Trade shall give public notice of any order so submitted to them in such manner as they think best for giving information thereof to persons interested, and shall also state in the notice that any objections to the confirmation of the order must be lodged with the board and the date by which those objections must be lodged.

Consideration of order by Board of Trade.

9.—(1.) The Board of Trade shall consider any order submitted to them under this Act for confirmation with special reference to—

(a) the expediency of requiring the proposals to be submitted to Parliament; and

(b) the safety of the public; and

(c) any objection lodged with them in accordance with this Act.

(2.) The Light Railway Commissioners shall, so far as they are able, give to the Board of Trade any information or assistance which may be required by the Board for the purpose of considering any order submitted to them or any objection thereto.

(3.) If the Board of Trade on such consideration are of opinion that by reason of the magnitude of the proposed undertaking, or of the effect thereof on the undertaking of any railway company existing at the time, or for any other special reason relating to the undertaking, the proposals of the promoters ought to be submitted to Parliament, they shall not confirm the order.

(*a*) As to objecting to the confirmation by the Board of Trade of an order made by the commissioners, see ss. 8 and 9 (5), *post*.

Sect. 9 (4).

(4.) The Board of Trade shall modify the provisions of the order for ensuring the safety of the public in such manner as they consider requisite or expedient.

(5.) If any objection to the order is lodged with the Board of Trade and not withdrawn, the Board of Trade shall consider the objection and give to those by whom it is made an opportunity of being heard, and if after consideration they decide that the objection should be upheld, the Board shall not confirm the order, or shall modify the order so as to remove the objection.

(6.) The Board of Trade may at any time, if they think fit, remit the order to the Light Railway Commissioners for further consideration, or may themselves hold or institute a local inquiry, and hear all parties interested.

Confirmation of order by Board of Trade.

10. The Board of Trade may confirm the order with or without modifications as the case may require, and an order so confirmed shall have effect as if enacted by Parliament, and shall be conclusive evidence that all the requirements of this Act in respect of proceedings required to be taken before the making of the order have been complied with.

Provisions which may be made by the order.

11. An order under this Act may contain provisions consistent with this Act for all or any of the following purposes—

(a) the incorporation, subject to such exceptions and variations as may be mentioned in the order, of all or any of the provisions of the Clauses Acts as defined by this Act (*b*). Provided that where it appears to the Board of Trade that variations of the Lands Clauses Acts are required by the special circumstances of the case, the Board of Trade shall make a special report to Parliament on the subject, and that nothing in this section shall authorise any variation of the provisions of the Lands Clauses Acts with respect to the purchase and taking of land otherwise than by agreement (*c*); and

(b) the application, if and so far as may be considered necessary, of any of the enactments mentioned in the Second Schedule to this Act (being enactments imposing obligations on railway companies with respect to the safety of the public and other matters); and

(c) giving the necessary powers for constructing and working the railway, including power to make agreements with railway and other companies for the purpose; and

(d) giving any railway company any power required for carrying the order into effect; and

---

(*b*) See the definition in s. 28, *post*.

(*c*) Sections 16—68 of the Lands Clauses Act, 1845, are here referred to; they are varied in several important particulars by ss. 13 and 14 of this Act, *post*.

Sect. 11.

(e) the constitution as a body corporate of a company for the purpose of carrying out the objects of the order; and

(f) the representation on the managing body of the railway of any council who advance, or agree to advance, any money for the purpose of the railway; and

(g) authorising a council to advance or borrow morey for the purposes of the railway and limiting the amount to be so advanced or borrowed, and regulating the terms on which any money is to be so advanced or borrowed; and

(h) the manner in which the profits are to be divided, where an advance is made by a council to a light railway company as part of the share capital of the company; and

(i) the proper audit of the accounts of the managing body of the railway where the managing body is not a local authority and the time within which the railway must be constructed; and

(j) fixing the maximum rates and charges for traffic; and

(k) in the case of a new company, requiring the company to make a deposit, and providing for the time of making and the application of the deposit; and

(l) empowering any local authority to acquire the railway; and

(m) any other matters, whether similar to the above or not, which may be considered ancillary to the objects of the order or expedient for carrying those objects into effect.

Application of general Railway Acts.

12.—(1.) The Clauses Acts, as defined by this Act, and the enactments mentioned in the Second Schedule of this Act, shall not apply to a light railway authorised under this Act except so far as they are incorporated or applied by the order authorizing the railway.

(2.) Subject to the foregoing provisions of this Act and to any special provisions contained in the order authorising the railway, the general enactments relating to railways shall apply to a light railway under this Act in like manner as they apply to any other railway; and for the purposes of those enactments, and of the Clauses Acts so far as they are incorporated or applied by the order authorising the railway, the light railway company shall be deemed a railway company, and the order under this Act a special Act, and any provision thereof a special enactment. Provided that a light railway shall not be deemed to be a railway within the meaning of the Railway Passenger Duty Act, 1842, and that no duties shall hereafter be levied in respect of passengers conveyed on a light railway constructed under this Act in respect of the conveyance of such passengers upon such railway.

5 & 6 Vict. c. 79.

Mode of settling purchase-money and compensation for

13.—(1.) Where any order under this Act incorporates the Lands Clauses Acts, any matter which under those Acts may be determined by the verdict of a jury, by arbitration, or by two justices, shall for the purposes of the order be referred to and determined by a single

Sect. 13 (1).

taking of land.

arbitrator appointed by the parties, or if the parties do not concur in the appointment of a single arbitrator then by the Board of Trade, and the provisions of this Act shall apply with respect to the determination of any such matter in lieu of those of the Lands Clauses Acts relating thereto. Provided that in determining the amount of compensation, the arbitrator shall have regard to the extent to which the remaining and contiguous lands and hereditaments belonging to the same proprietor may be benefited by the proposed light railway.

(2.) The Board of Trade may, with the concurrence of the Lord Chancellor, make rules fixing a scale of costs to be applicable on any such arbitration, and may, by such rules, limit the cases in which the costs of counsel are to be allowed.

52 & 53 Vict. c. 49.

(3.) The Arbitration Act, 1889, shall apply to any arbitration under this section.

Payment of purchase money or compensation.

14. Any order under this Act may, notwithstanding anything in the Lands Clauses Acts, authorise the payment to trustees of any purchase money or compensation not exceeding five hundred pounds.

Provisions as to Board of Trade.

37 & 38 Vict. c. 40.

15.—(1.) If the Board of Trade hold a local inquiry for the purposes of this Act, Part I. of the Board of Trade Arbitrations, etc., Act, 1874, shall apply to any inquiry so held as if—

(a) the inquiry was held on an application made in pursuance of a special Act; and

(b) the parties making the application for the order authorising the light railway, and in the case of an inquiry held with reference to an objection made to any such application the persons making the objection in addition, were parties to the application within the meaning of section three of the Act.

(2.) The Board of Trade may make such rules as they think necessary for regulating the procedure under this Act, whether before the Board of Trade or before the Light Railway Commissioners, and any other matters which they may think expedient to regulate by rule for the purpose of carrying this Act into effect (*d*).

(3.) There shall be charged in respect of proceedings under this Act before the Board of Trade or the Light Railway Commissioners such fees as may be fixed by the Treasury on the recommendation of the Board of Trade.

(4.) Any expenses of the Board of Trade under this Act shall, except so far as provision is made for their payment by or under this Act, be defrayed out of moneys provided by Parliament.

(5.) The Board of Trade shall present to Parliament annually a report of their proceedings and of the proceedings of the Light Railway Commissioners under this Act.

(*d*) See the rules set out, *post*, p. 831.

16.—(1.) The council of any county, borough, or district may pay any expenses incurred by them and allowed by the Light Railway Commissioners with reference to any application for an order authorising a light railway under this Act, in the case of a county council as general expenses (*e*), in the case of a borough council out of the borough fund or rate, and in the case of a district council other than a borough council as general expenses under the Public Health Acts. **Sect. 16 (1).** Expenses of local authorities.

Provided that any expenses incurred by a county council under this Act may be declared by the order authorising the railway or, in the event of an unsuccessful application for such an order, by the Light Railway Commissioners, to be exclusively chargeable on certain parishes only in the county, and those expenses shall be levied accordingly as expenses for a special county purpose under the Local Government Act, 1888 (*e*). 51 & 52 Vict. c. 41.

(2.) Where the council of any county, borough, or district are authorised to expend any money by an order authorising a light railway under this Act, they may raise the money required,—

(a) if the expenditure is capital expenditure, by borrowing in manner authorised by the order; and

(b) if the expenditure is not capital expenditure, as if it was on account of the expenses of an application under this Act.

(3.) The Board of Trade may from time to time on the application of any council extend, subject to the limitations of this Act, the limit of the amount which the council are authorised by an order under this Act to borrow, or to advance to a light railway company, and the limit so extended shall be substituted for the limit fixed by the order.

(4.) Where an order under this Act authorises any council to borrow for the purposes of a light railway, suitable provision shall be made in the order for requiring the replacement of the money borrowed within a fixed period not exceeding sixty years, either by means of a sinking fund or otherwise.

(5.) Any profits made by a council in respect of a light railway shall be applied in aid of the rate out of which the expenses of the council in respect of the light railway are payable.

(6.) Where a rate is levied for meeting any expenditure under this Act, the demand note for the rate shall state, in a form prescribed by the Local Government Board, the proportion of the rate levied for that expenditure.

17.—(1.) The councils of any county, borough, or district, may appoint a joint committee for the purpose of any application for an order authorising a light railway under this Act, or for the joint construction or working of a light railway, or for any other purpose Joint committees.

(*e*) As to general expenses of a county council and special county purposes, see s. 68 of the Local Government Act, 1888, *ante*, p. 130.

Sect. 17 (1). in connexion with such a railway for which it is convenient that those councils should combine.

51 & 52 Vict. c. 41. 56 & 57 Vict. c. 73.

(2.) The provisions of the Local Government Act, 1888, or of the Local Government Act, 1894, as the case may be, with respect to joint committees, shall apply to any joint committee appointed for the purpose of this Act by any councils who could appoint a joint committee under those Acts, but where the councils have no power under those Acts to appoint a joint committee the provisions in the Third Schedule to this Act shall apply (*f*).

Working of ordinary railway as light railway.

18. Where a company have power to construct or work a railway, they may be authorised by an order under this Act to construct and work or to work the railway or any part of it as a light railway under this Act.

Power of owners to grant land or advance money for a light railway.

19.—(1.) Where any person has power, either by statute or otherwise, to sell and convey any land for the purpose of any works of a light railway, he may, with the sanction of the Board of Agriculture given under this section, convey the land for that purpose either without payment of any purchase money or compensation or at a price less than the real value, and may so convey it free from all incumbrances thereon (*g*).

27 & 28 Vict. c. 114.

(2.) Whenever any person who is a landowner within the meaning of the Improvement of Land Act, 1864, contributes any money for the purpose of any works of a light railway, the amount so contributed may, with the sanction of the Board of Agriculture given under this section, be charged on the land of the landowner improved by the works in the same manner and with the like effect as in the case of a charge under that Act.

(3.) The Board of Agriculture shall not give their sanction under this section unless they are satisfied that the works for which the land is conveyed or the money is contributed will effect a permanent increase in the value of the land held by the same title or of other land of the same landowner exceeding, in the case of a conveyance of land, that which is, in the opinion of the Board of Agriculture, the real value of the land conveyed or the difference between that value and the price, as the case may be, and in the case of a contribution of money the amount contributed: Provided also, that if the land proposed to be conveyed is subject to incumbrances, the Board of Agriculture, before giving their sanction under this section, shall cause notice to be given to the incumbrancers, and shall consider the objections, if any, raised by them.

(*f*) Joint committees of county councils may be appointed under s. 81 of the Local Government Act, 1888, *ante*, p. 155; of district councils under s. 57 the Local Government Act, 1894, *ante*, p. 642. Joint committees of county and district councils will be appointed under the text, and the provisions of the Third Schedule, *post*, will apply.

(*g*) See note (*x*), *ante*, p. 723.

Sect. 20.

20. The Commissioners of Woods, shall, on behalf of Her Majesty, have the like powers to convey Crown lands as are by this Act conferred upon persons having power, either by statute or otherwise, to sell and convey lands, except that in the case of Crown lands the sanction of the Treasury shall be substituted for the sanction of the Board of Agriculture.

Power to grant Crown lands.

21.—(1.) No land being part of any common, and no easement over or affecting any common, shall be purchased, taken, or acquired under this Act without the consent of the Board of Agriculture, and the Board shall not give their consent unless they are satisfied that, regard being had to all the circumstances of the case, such purchase, taking, or acquisition is necessary, that the exercise of the powers conferred by the order authorising the railway will not cause any greater injury to the common than is necessary, and that all proper steps have been taken in the interest of the commoners and of the public to add other land to the common (where this can be done) in lieu of the land taken, and where a common is divided to secure convenient access from one part of the common to the other.

Provision as to commons.

(2.) The expression " common " in this section shall include any land subject to be enclosed under the Inclosure Acts, 1845 to 1882, any metropolitan common within the meaning of the Metropolitan Commons Acts, 1866 to 1878, and any town or village green.

22. If any objection to any application for authorising a light railway is made to the Light Railway Commissioners, or if any objection to any draft order is made to the Board of Trade on the ground that the proposed undertaking will destroy or injure any building or other object of historical interest, or will injuriously affect any natural scenery, the Commissioners and the Board of Trade respectively shall consider any such objection, and give to those by whom it is made a proper opportunity of being heard in support of it.

Preservation of scenery and objects of historical interest.

23. Any junction of a light railway authorised under this Act with any existing railway shall so far as is in the opinion of the Board of Trade reasonably practicable avoid interference with lines of rails used for passenger traffic.

Junctions with existing railways.

24. An order authorising a light railway under this Act may be altered or added to by an amending order made in like manner and subject to the like provisions as the original order.

Amendment of order.

Provided that—

(a) the amending order may be made on the application of any authority or person; and

(b) the Board of Trade, in considering the expediency of requiring the proposals for amending the order to be submitted to Parliament, shall have regard to the scope and provisions of the original order; and

Sect. 24.

(c) the amending order shall not confer any power to acquire the railway except with the consent of the owners of the railway.

Provision as to telegraphs. 41 & 42 Vict. c. 76.

25. The definition of "Act of Parliament" in the Telegraph Act, 1878, shall include an order authorising a light railway under this Act (*h*).

26. *Application to Scotland.*]

Extent of Act.

27. *Act not to extend to Ireland.*]

Definitions.

28. In this Act, unless the context otherwise requires,—

The expression "light railway company" includes any person or body of persons, whether incorporated or not, who are authorised to construct, or are owners or lessees of, any light railway authorised by this Act, or who are working the same under any working agreement:

The expression "Clauses Acts" means the Lands Clauses Acts, the Railways Clauses Consolidation Act, 1845, and the Railways Clauses Act, 1863, and the Companies Clauses Acts, 1845 to 1889:

The expression "share capital" includes any capital, whether consisting of shares or of stock, which is not raised by means of borrowing.

Short title.

29. This Act may be cited as the Light Railways Act, 1896.

SCHEDULES.

Section 3.

FIRST SCHEDULE.

Mode of Passing Special Resolutions.

1. The resolution approving of the intention to make the application must be passed at a meeting of the council.

2. The resolution shall not be passed unless a month's previous notice of the resolution has been given in manner in which notices of meetings of the council are usually given.

3. The resolution shall not be passed unless two-thirds of the members of the council present and voting concur in the resolution.

(*h*) The effect of this section is to empower the Postmaster-General to establish telegraph lines on a light railway constructed under this Act.

SECOND SCHEDULE.

Schedule 2.

Section 12.

ENACTMENTS RELATING TO SAFETY, ETC.

Session and Chapter.	Title or Short Title.	Enactment referred to.
2 & 3 Vict. c. 45.	An Act to amend an Act of the fifth and sixth years of the reign of his late Majesty King William the Fourth relating to highways.	The whole Act.
5 & 6 Vict. c. 55.	The Railway Regulation Act, 1842	Sections four, five, six, nine, ten.
9 & 10 Vict. c. 57.	An Act for regulating the gauge of railways.	The whole Act.
31 & 32 Vict. c. 119.	The Regulation of Railways Act, 1868	Sections nineteen, twenty, twenty-two, twenty-seven, twenty-eight, and twenty-nine.
34 & 35 Vict. c. 78.	The Regulation of Railways Act, 1871	Section five.
36 & 37 Vict. c. 76.	The Railway Regulation Act (Returns of signal arrangements, working, etc.), 1873.	Sections four and six.
41 & 42 Vict. c. 20.	The Railway Returns (Continuous Brakes) Act, 1878.	The whole Act.
46 & 47 Vict. c. 34.	The Cheap Trains Act, 1883	Section three.
52 & 53 Vict. c. 57.	The Regulation of Railways Act, 1889	The whole Act.

THIRD SCHEDULE. (i)

JOINT COMMITTEES.

(a.) Any council taking part in the appointment of a joint committee may delegate to the committee any power which the council may exercise for the purpose for which the committee is appointed.

(b.) A council shall not be authorised to delegate to a joint committee any power of making a rate or borrowing money.

(c.) Subject to the terms of the delegation the joint committee shall have the same power in all respects with respect to any matter delegated to them, as the councils appointing it or any of them.

(d.) The members of the joint committee may be appointed at such times and in such manner, and shall hold office for such period, as may be fixed by the councils appointing them :

Provided that a member shall not hold office beyond the expiration of fourteen days after the day for the ordinary election of councillors of the council by which he was appointed, or in Scotland after the day for the ordinary election of councillors of the council of the county in which the district is situated.

(e.) The costs of a joint committee shall be defrayed by the councils by whom the committee is appointed, in such proportions as they may agree upon, and in the event of their differing in opinion, as may be determined by the Board of Trade on an application by either council.

(f.) When any of the councils joining in the appointment of a joint committee is a county or district council other than a borough council, the accounts of the joint committee shall be audited in like manner and with the like power to the officer auditing the accounts,

(i) As to the application of this Schedule, see s. 17 (2), *ante* p. 730.

Schedule 3.

and with the like incidents and consequences as the accounts of a county council (*j*).

(g.) The chairman at any meeting of the committee shall have a second or casting vote.

(h.) The quorum, proceedings, and place of meeting of a committee, whether within or without the area within which the committee are to exercise their authority, shall be such as may be determined by regulations jointly made by the councils appointing the committee, and in the event of their differing in opinion as may be determined by the Board of Trade on an application by either council.

(i.) Subject to those regulations the quorum, proceedings, and place of meeting, whether within or without the area within which the committee are to exercise their jurisdiction, shall be such as the committee direct.

WILD BIRDS PROTECTION ACT, 1896.

(59 & 60 VICT. CAP. 56.)

An Act to amend the Wild Birds Protection Acts (*k*).

[14th August 1896.]

* * * * *

Extension of powers under 43 & 44 Vict. c. 35.

1. From and after the passing of this Act the powers exerciseable by the Secretary of State on application (*l*) under section eight of the Wild Birds Protection Act, 1880, shall extend to the making of an order prohibiting, for special reasons mentioned in the application, the taking or killing of particular kinds of wild birds during the whole or any part of that period of the year to which the protection of wild birds under that Act does not extend, or the taking or killing of all wild birds in particular places during the whole or any part of that period.

Publication of orders.

2. Public notice of any order made under this Act shall be given in the manner required by the Wild Birds Protection Act, 1894, with respect to orders made under that Act (*m*).

Explanation of 57 & 58 Vict. c. 24.

3. The powers exerciseable under the Wild Birds Protection Act, 1894, by the county council of an administrative county are hereby declared to be exerciseable by the council of a county borough, and any expenses incurred by the council of a county borough under that Act or this Act may be defrayed out of the borough fund or borough rate.

(*j*) As to the audit of the accounts of a county council, see s. 71 of the Local Government Act, 1888, *ante*, p. 136.

(*k*) See the note to Local Government Act, 1888, s. 3 (xiii.), *ante*, p. 12, and also the Wild Birds Protection Act, 1894, *ante*, p. 666.

(*l*) The application must be made by the county council. See the section referred to and s. 3 (xiii.) of the Local Government Act, 1888, *ante*, p. 12.

(*m*) See s. 4 of that Act, *ante*, p. 667.

Sect. 6.

4. Where any person is convicted of an offence against this Act or the principal Act, the court may, in addition to any penalty that may be imposed, order any trap, net, snare, or decoy bird used by such person for taking any wild bird to be forfeited. Power to forfeit traps, nets, snares, etc.

5. *Application to Scotland.*]

6. *Act not to extend to Ireland.*]

7. This Act may be cited as the Wild Birds Protection Act, 1896, and shall be construed with the Wild Birds Protection Act, 1880, the Wild Birds Protection Act, 1881, and the Wild Birds Protection Act, 1894, and those Acts and this Act may be cited collectively as the Wild Birds Protection Acts, 1880 to 1896. Short title, and collective title.

YORKSHIRE CORONERS ACT, 1897.

(60 & 61 Vict. Cap. 39.)

An Act to constitute the Ridings of Yorkshire separate Counties for all the purposes of the Coroners Acts. [6th August 1897.]

* * * * *

1. For all the purposes of the Coroners Acts, 1844, 1860, 1887, and 1892, the ridings of Yorkshire shall respectively be separate counties, and the county council of each riding shall, to the exclusion of any other authority, be the county authority for all the purposes of those Acts (*n*). Ridings of Yorkshire to be separate counties in respect of the Coroners Acts.

Provided that nothing in this section shall affect the alteration in manner provided by section five, sub-section three, of the Local Government Act, 1888, of the district of any coroner which is at the commencement of this Act situate partly in one and partly in another of the ridings (*o*). 51 & 52 Vict. c. 41.

2. Nothing herein contained shall affect the rights, duties, powers, or liabilities of any county coroner holding office at the commencement of this Act, and if the district of any such coroner is divided into two or more districts, residence in any one of such districts shall be deemed to comply with section five of the Coroners Act, 1844 (*p*). Rights of existing county coroners. 7 & 8 Vict. c. 92.

(*n*) This is an amendment of s. 38 of the Coroners Act, 1887 (50 & 51 Vict. c. 71), which provided that the whole of Yorkshire should be a county for purposes of that Act.

(*o*) See this sub-section, *ante*, p. 15. It enables the joint committee of the county appointed under s. 46, *ante*, p. 99, to alter the district of any coroner so that it should not be situate in more than one riding.

(*p*) An existing coroner will therefore continue to be a coroner for the entire county of Yorkshire under 7 & 8 Vict. c. 92, s. 19, but he will satisfy the requirements of s. 5 of that Act by residing in any part of his present district even if that is divided under s. 5, sub-s. (3) of the Local Government Act, 1888, *ante*, p. 15.

Sect. 3.

Commencement of Act.

3. This Act shall come into operation on the first day of April, one thousand eight hundred and ninety-eight.

Short title.

4. This Act may be cited as the Yorkshire Coroners Act, 1897.

LOCAL GOVERNMENT (JOINT COMMITTEES) ACT, 1897.

(60 & 61 Vict. Cap. 40.)

An Act to amend the Local Government Act, 1894, *with regard to Joint Committees for the purposes of the Burial Acts* (*q*).

[6th August 1897.]

* * * * *

Joint committees for Burial Acts. 56 & 57 Vict. c. 73.

1.—(1.) Where a joint committee is appointed under section fifty-three of the Local Government Act, 1894, for the purposes of the Burial Acts, 1852 to 1885—

(a) any expenses incurred in carrying out those purposes shall be defrayed, any money borrowed for those purposes shall be borrowed, and any receipts arising from those purposes shall be divided, by the councils appointing the committee in such proportion as they may agree upon, or, as in default of agreement, may be determined by the county council, or, if one of the councils so appointing is the council of a county borough, by the Local Government Board;

(b) the consent of the Local Government Board shall be required to the borrowing by any council of any money required to be borrowed for those purposes, but that consent shall be conclusive as to the power of the council to borrow, and no other consent shall be required either under the said Burial Acts, or the Local Government Act, 1894, or any other Act (*r*);

(c) Part IV. of the First Schedule to the Local Government Act, 1894, shall apply to the proceedings of the committee.

(*q*) Section 53 (2) of the Local Government Act, 1894, *ante*, p. 639, provides for the execution of the Burial Acts (amongst other "adoptive Acts") in cases where by the operation of the Act of 1894 a parish in which the Burial Acts were in force became divided into two or more parishes: the powers under the Burial Acts were transferred to the councils of the rural parishes or urban districts which comprised the old Burial Acts area, and were to be exercised by a joint committee appointed by those councils. The section did not provide for the constitution of the joint committee. This Act makes provision for this, as also for the apportionment of the expenses, but it seems doubtful whether it does not create new difficulties as to the area chargeable with the expenses when apportioned having regard to s. 7 (6) and s. 53 (3) of the Act of 1894, *ante*, pp. 599, 640.

(*r*) A parish council borrowing in pursuance of this Act will not require to obtain the consent of the county council under s. 12 (1) of the Local Government Act, 1894, *ante*, p. 609; and as the consent of the Local Government Board is to be conclusive, it appears that the consent of the parish meeting and the approval of the county council (under s. 11 of the same Act) to the incurring by the parish council of expenses involving a loan will not be necessary.

(2.) If any difference arises as to the constitution of any such committee it may be determined by order of the Local Government Board. Sect. 1 (2).

(3.) For the purposes of this section references to a council shall, in the case of a parish not having a parish council, include the parish meeting, and the parish meeting shall have the same power of borrowing for the purposes of the Burial Acts as a parish council would have (*s*).

Short title.

2. This Act shall be construed as one with the Local Government Act, 1894, and may be cited as the Local Government (Joint Committees) Act, 1897.

MILITARY MANŒUVRES ACT, 1897.

(60 & 61 VICT. CAP. 43) (*t*).

An Act to facilitate Military Manœuvres. [6th August 1897.]

* * * * *

Power to authorise execution of military manœuvres.

1.—(1.) Her Majesty may, by Order in Council, authorise the execution of military manœuvres within specified limits and during a specified period not exceeding three months. Provided that the same limits, or any part thereof, shall not be specified more than once in any period of five years.

(2.) Whenever it is proposed to make any such Order a draft thereof shall, not less than six months before the Order is to come into force, be sent to the council of each county, county borough, district, and parish, wholly or partly within the specified limits, and in the case of the New Forest to the court of verderers; and notice of this intention to make the Order shall, not less than three months before the Order is to come into force, be advertised in at least two newspapers circulating generally within the district (*u*).

(*s*) The Act of 1894 does not contemplate any borrowing by a parish meeting; the mortgage could, it seems, be executed, on the direction of the parish meeting, by the chairman and overseers under s. 19 (6) of the Local Government Act, 1894, *ante*, p. 616.

(*t*) This Act affects county councils as highway authorities in respect of main roads, and also as having the duty of appointing members of the military manœuvres commission referred to in ss. 4, *et seq.* It is probably intended also that they shall have power to raise objections to the making an Order in Council under the Act. See s. 1 (2).

(*u*) It may be presumed that the object of this provision is to enable the county councils and other bodies mentioned to make representations to the Privy Council as to the desirability or otherwise of making the order of which the draft is before them for consideration. The order ought, it would seem, to be made a sufficient time before its coming into force to enable the proceedings of the military manœuvres commission mentioned in s. 5, *infra*, to take place.

Sect. 1 (3).

(3.) The draft Order shall not be submitted to Her Majesty in Council until it has lain before each House of Parliament for thirty days on which that House is sitting, nor unless each House presents an address to Her Majesty praying that the Order may be made.

Powers exerciseable for purposes of manœuvres.

2. Where an Order in Council under this Act authorises the execution of military manœuvres, such persons as are under the authority of Her Majesty engaged in the manœuvres (in this Act referred to as the authorised forces) may under the direction of the Secretary of State within the specified limits and during the specified period,

(a) pass over, and encamp, construct military works, not of a permanent character, and execute military manœuvres on any authorised land (*x*) ; and

(b) supply themselves with water from any authorised sources of water (*x*), and, for that purpose, dam up any running water. Provided always, that such damming up of water does not interfere with the carrying on of any trade or industry, and that nothing in this Act shall authorise the taking of water from any source of supply belonging to a private owner, or public authority, except subject to the supply shown to be required by those entitled to use such water supply.

Provided as follows—

(1.) Nothing in this Act shall authorise entry on or interference with (except to the extent of using authorised roads (*x*)) any dwelling-house, place of worship, school, factory, workshop, store or premises, used for the carrying on of any trade, business, or manufacture, farmyard, garden, orchard, pleasure ground or nursery ground, burial ground, ground attached to any place of worship, or school, or any premises enclosed within the curtilage of or attached to any dwelling-house, or any enclosed wood or plantation.

(2.) The officer in command of the authorised forces (*y*) shall take care that there is no interference with earthworks, ruins, or other remains of antiquarian or historical interest, or with any picturesque or valuable timber, or other natural features of exceptional interest or beauty, and shall be empowered to prevent trespass or damage to property by persons not belonging to the forces, and shall cause all lands used under the powers conferred by this Act to be restored as soon and as far as practicable to their previous condition.

(*x*) The expressions "authorized land," "authorized sources," and "authorized roads," are explained by s. 5, *infra*.

(*y*) This expression is defined at the beginning of this section.

(3.) Subject to the provisions of this Act with respect to— Sect. 2 (3).

(a) the closing of roads and footpaths; and

(b) obstruction of or interference with military manœuvres; and

(c) entering or remaining in a camp,

nothing in this Act shall prejudicially affect any public right or any right of common.

Power to close roads

3.—(1.) Two justices of the peace, not being military officers in command of the forces (*z*), may, if they shall think fit, on the application of a commissioned officer in command of the authorised forces or of part thereof, by order, suspend, for a time not exceeding forty-eight hours, any right of way over any road or footpath (*a*) within the specified limits and within their jurisdiction. Provided that any such order shall only be made with regard to any county, or main, or parish, road by at least two justices, not being military officers in command of the forces (*z*), sitting in petty sessions in the petty sessional division or divisions within which such road or part of road to be stopped is situate, and for a time not exceeding twelve hours, and after seven days notice of such intended application published in at least one newspaper circulating generally in the district, and subject to such terms and conditions as may be required by the said justices for the protection of individuals or of the public or of public bodies.

(2.) The officer in command of the authorised forces shall cause such public notice of the order as the justices may require to be given not less than twelve hours before the order comes into force, and shall give all reasonable facilities for traffic whilst the order is in force.

Military Manœuvres Commission.

4.—(1.) Whenever an Order in Council is made (*b*) under this Act a commission (in this Act called the Military Manœuvres Commission) shall be formed consisting of as representative members (a) and (b):

(a) two persons appointed by the council of each county and one person appointed by the council of each county borough (if any) wholly or partly within the specified limits; and

(b) if those limits include any part of the New Forest, two persons appointed by the court of verderers; and

(c) such other persons, being resident owners or occupiers of land within those limits, as may be appointed by the

(*z*) The context seems to require that "forces" should be read as "authorized forces" here.

(*a*) Apparently the road or footway need not be an "authorized road" within s. 5 (1), *infra*.

(*b*) The commission is not to be formed until the order has been actually made; but it appears necessary that they should act before it comes into force. See note (*u*), *ante*, p. 737.

Sect. 4 (1).

Secretary of State. Provided always that the persons appointed under the foregoing provisions of this section exceed in number the persons appointed by the Secretary of State.

(2.) The commission may act by three of their number, and notwithstanding any vacancy in their number.

(3.) Any question arising at any meeting of the commission shall be decided by the majority of those voting on the question, and if the votes are equal the chairman of the meeting shall have a second or casting vote.

Power of Commission to make orders and regulations.

5.—(1.) The Military Manœuvres Commission may make orders for determining what lands, roads, and sources of water are to be authorised lands, roads, and sources within the meaning of this Act (*c*).

(2.) Before any such order is made, a draft thereof shall be sent to the district council for each district wholly or partly within the specified limits, and be deposited by them for public inspection during at least two weeks at their office or some other suitable place fixed by them, and notice of the deposit, stating the mode of objecting to the order (*d*), shall be advertised for two successive weeks in at least two newspapers circulating generally within those limits.

(3.) The commission shall hold at least one public meeting to hear any objections to the draft order, and shall consider all objections made, and shall, if necessary, revise the draft order with reference thereto, and within a week of such meeting serve the revised draft on such district council.

(4.) The commission may also make regulations with respect to—

(a) the protection and maintenance of animals by securing them in folds or farmyards, or otherwise, and

(b) any matter which the commission may deem important for preventing damage to property and for carrying into effect the purposes of this Act.

(5.) Any person who, without reasonable cause, fails to comply with any such regulation shall not be entitled to compensation for any damage caused to his property by reason of his default.

(6.) All orders and regulations made by the commission shall be published in such manner as may appear to the commission most suitable for giving notice thereof to the persons affected thereby.

Compensation for damage.

6.—(1.) Where an Order in Council authorises the execution of military manœuvres, full compensation shall be made out of money to be provided by Parliament for any damage to person or property

(*c*) The lands, roads, and sources must of course be within the limits specified in the Order in Council.

(*d*) The mode of objecting is left to the discretion of the commission, subject to sub-s. (3), *infra*.

or interference with rights or privileges, arising from putting in force any of the provisions of this Act, and whether or not occasioned by the acts or defaults of the authorised forces, including therein all expenses reasonably incurred in protecting persons, property, rights, and privileges, and any damage by reason of excessive weight or extraordinary traffic caused to any highway for the repair of which any public body or any individual is responsible. Sect. 6 (1).

(2.) The Military Manœuvres Commission shall, with the concurrence of the Treasury, appoint a compensation officer or compensation officers to determine as speedily as possible any claim for compensation under this Act, and settle the amount payable.

(3.) The commission may make regulations with respect to the procedure for making and determining claims for compensation, for limiting the time within which claims must be made, and for regulating the mode in which compensation is to be paid.

(4.) If the amount of compensation is not settled by agreement between the compensation officer and the claimant, the difference between them shall be referred to arbitration, and for this purpose the service in manner directed by the regulations of a notice of claim for compensation shall be treated as a submission to arbitration within the meaning of the Arbitration Act, 1889, and that Act shall apply accordingly. 52 & 53 Vict. c. 44.

7.—(1.) If, within the limits and during the period specified in an Order authorising military manœuvres under this Act, any person— Offences.

(a) wilfully and unlawfully obstructs or interferes with the execution of the manœuvres; or

(b) without due authority enters or remains in any camp,

he shall be liable on summary conviction to a fine not exceeding forty shillings, and he and any animal or vehicle under his charge may be removed by any constable, or by, or by order of, any commissioned officer of the authorised forces.

(2.) If within the limits and during the period aforesaid, any person—

(a) without due authority moves any flag or other mark distinguishing, for the purposes of the manœuvres, any lands; or

(b) maliciously cuts or damages any telegraph wire laid down by or for the use of the authorised forces,

he shall be liable on summary conviction to a fine not exceeding five pounds.

8. [*Application to Scotland.*]

9. [*Application to Ireland.*]

10. This Act may be cited as the Military Manœuvres Act, 1897. Short title.

WEIGHTS AND MEASURES (METRIC SYSTEM) ACT, 1897.
(60 & 61 VICT. CAP. 46.)

An Act to legalize the Use of Weights and Measures of the Metric System. [6th August 1897.]

* * * * *

Use of metric weights and measures in trade. 41 & 42 Vict. c. 49.

1. Notwithstanding anything in the Weights and Measures Act, 1878, the use in trade of a weight or measure of the metric system shall be lawful, and nothing in section nineteen of that Act shall make void any contract, bargain, sale, or dealing, by reason only of its being made or had according to weights or measures of the metric system, and a person using or having in his possession a weight or measure of the metric system shall not by reason thereof be liable to any fine (*e*).

Metric standards and equivalents. 41 & 42 Vict. c. 49.

2.—(1.) The Board of Trade standards which may be made under section eight of the Weights and Measures Act, 1878, shall include metric standards derived from the iridio-platinum linear standard metre and iridio-platinum standard kilogram deposited with the Board of Trade and numbered 16 and 18 respectively (*f*).

(2.) It shall be lawful for the Queen by Order in Council to make a table of metric equivalents in substitution for the table in Part I. of the Third Schedule to the Weights and Measures Act, 1878, and, as from the date at which the Order in Council comes into operation, Part I. of the said schedule and sections eighteen and thirty-eight of the said Act shall be repealed (*g*).

Short title.

3. This Act may be cited as the Weights and Measures (Metric System) Act, 1897, and may be cited with the Weights and Measures Acts, 1878 to 1893 (*h*).

(*e*) Section 19 of the Weights and Measures Act, 1878, makes void contracts, bargains, sales and dealings for work, goods, wares, or merchandise, or other things to be done, sold, delivered, carried or agreed for by weight or measure if not made or had according to one of the imperial weights or measures ascertained by that Act, and makes liable to a fine any person selling by any denomination of weight or measure other than one of the imperial weights or measures or some multiple or part thereof. Section 24 renders liable to a fine every person who uses or has in his possession for use for trade a weight or measure not of the denomination of some Board of Trade standard. These and any similar prohibitions in the Act are not to apply to weights or measures of the metric system.

(*f*) The Board of Trade standards (derived from the Imperial standards) are set out in the Second Schedule to the Act of 1878. Section 8 provides for the making of new Board of Trade standards.

(*g*) Section 18 of the Act of 1878 provides that the table of metric equivalents in the Third Schedule may be lawfully used for computing and expressing in weights and measures, weights and measures of the metric system. Section 38 provides for the verification by the Board of Trade of metric weights and measures submitted to them and intended to be used for lawful purposes, not being for the purpose of trade. The table of metric equivalents forms Part I. of the Third Schedule.

(*h*) See the Act of 1893, *ante*, p. 574.

LAND TRANSFER ACT, 1897.

(60 & 61 Vict. Cap. 65) (*i*).

An Act to establish a Real Representative, and to amend the Land Transfer Act, 1875. [6th August 1897.]

Whereas it is expedient to establish a real representative, and to amend the Land Transfer Act, 1875, in this Act referred to as "the principal Act:" 38 & 39 Vict. c. 87.

*

Part I.

Establishment of a Real Representative.

* * *

Part II.

Amendments of the Land Transfer Act, 1875.

* * * *

Registration of small holdings. 55 & 56 Vict. c. 31.

19.—(1.) Where a county council apply in pursuance of section ten of the Small Holdings Act, 1892 (*k*), for registration as proprietors of land, they may be registered as proprietors of that land, with any such title as is authorised by the principal Act.

(2.) Where a county council, after having been so registered, transfer any such land to a purchaser of a small holding, the purchaser shall be registered as proprietor of the land with an absolute title, subject only to such incumbrances as may be created under the Small Holdings Act, 1892, and in any such case the remedy of any person claiming by title paramount to the county council in respect either of title or incumbrances shall be in damages only, and such damages shall be recoverable against the county council (*l*).

(*i*) The bulk of the subject-matter of this Act lies far outside the scope of this work. Part I. of the Act (which is wholly omitted) provides for the vesting of the real estate of a deceased person, like his leaseholds, in his personal representatives. Part II. amends the Land Transfer Act, 1875 (38 & 39 Vict. c. 87), in many particulars, thereby facilitating the registration of the title to land and its transfer in the land registry, and further detailed amendments are set out in the First Schedule. Section 19 is the only clause of Part II. which directly affects county councils (when acting under the Small Holdings Act, 1892, *ante*, p. 547). Part III. relates to the introduction of *compulsory* registration of title; it is included on account of the power given by s. 23 (6) to a county council to place their veto upon the introduction of the compulsory system into their county. Part IV. s. 22 deals with the making of rules and fee orders as to transactions in the land registry; s. 23, relating to the Yorkshire Registries of Deeds, is set out.

(*k*) See this section, *ante*, p. 553, and the note thereto, where the effect of the present section is explained.

(*l*) Whether the title of the county council is absolute, qualified, or possessory, the title of their transferee, the purchaser of a small holding, is to

PART III.

Compulsory Registration and Insurance Fund.

Sect. 20 (1).

Power to require registration of title on sale.

20.—(1.) Her Majesty the Queen may, by Order in Council, declare, as respects any county (*m*) or part of a county mentioned or defined in the Order, that, on and after a day specified in the Order, registration of title to land is to be compulsory on sale, and thereupon a person shall not, under any conveyance on sale executed on or after the day so specified, acquire the legal estate in any freehold land in that county, or part of a county, unless or until he is registered as proprietor of the land (*n*).

(2.) In this section the expression "conveyance on sale" means an instrument executed on sale by virtue whereof there is conferred or completed a title under which an application for registration as first proprietor of land may be made under the principal Act.

38 & 39 Vict. c. 87.

(3.) The title with which a proprietor of freehold land is registered in pursuance of this section shall be not less than a possessory title; but nothing in this section shall prevent any

---

be registered as absolute, and is not to be disturbed even by a person claiming by title paramount to the county council; any such person may, however, recover damages from the county council. It seems desirable, therefore, that the county council should, where possible, obtain registration with an absolute title in the first instance.

(*m*) "County" is defined by sub-s. (11) of this section, *post*.

(*n*) On November 26th, 1897, notice was given to the London County Council (under sub-s. (5), *infra*) of a draft order under this section, making registration of title to land compulsory on sale "as respects the county of London on and after July 1st, 1898." It will be observed that this notice was given before this Act came into operation (see s. 25, *post*), presumably under the power contained in s. 37 of the Interpretation Act, 1889. The county council considered the draft order on February 15th, 1898, and placed no veto upon it. The draft order provided that it might be "amended or added to or repealed by Order in Council." On May 17th, 1898, notice appeared in the "London Gazette" that it was proposed to submit to Her Majesty the draft of an Order in Council declaring that registration of title to land is to be compulsory on sale in the county of London. The draft order accompanying the notice provides for the application of compulsory registration to different portions of the county on different dates as shown by the schedule to the order, which is as follows:—

Portions of the County.	Days on and after which Registration of Title to Land is to be compulsory on sale.
The parishes of Hampstead, Saint Pancras, Saint Marylebone, and George's, Hanover Square - - - - - - - -	September 1st, 1898.
The parishes of Shoreditch, Bethnal Green, Mile End Old Town, Wapping, Saint George's in the East, Shadwell, Ratcliff, Limehouse, Bow, Bromley, and Poplar - - - - -	January 1st, 1899.
The remainder of the county (not including the city of London) north of the centre line of the River Thames except North Woolwich - - - - - - - - - - - - -	October 1st, 1899.
The remainder of the county not including the city of London -	January 1st, 1900.
The city of London - - - - - - - - - -	July 1st, 1900.

This draft order is also expressed to be subject to amendment. It does not appear that any fresh notice was given to the London County Council as to this order; but perhaps it is to be treated as an amendment of the draft already considered by that council, which draft, as above appears, was in wider terms than the later one.

person from being registered with any other title if the registrar is satisfied of his title. Sect. 20 (3).

(4.) It shall be lawful for Her Majesty in Council to revoke or vary any Order made under this section.

(5.) In the case of every Order proposed to be made under this section, notice shall, six months before the Order is made, be given to the council of the county to which such Order is proposed to be applied. A draft of the proposed Order, together with the name of at least one place within or conveniently near to the county where a district registry office will be established, shall accompany the notice, and shall also be published in the Gazette (*o*).

(6.) If within three months after receipt of the draft the county council, at a meeting specially called for the purpose, at which two-thirds of the whole number of the members shall be present, resolve, and communicate to the Privy Council their resolution, that in their opinion compulsory registration of title would not be desirable in their county, the Order shall not be made (*o*).

(7.) The first Order made under this section shall not affect more than one county (*o*).

(8.) Except as to a county or part of a county which shall have signified through the county council of such county, pursuant to a resolution of such council passed at a meeting at which two-thirds of the whole number of the members shall be present, its desire that registration of title shall be compulsorily applied to it, no further Order shall be made under this section, and in any case no further Order shall be made under this section until the expiration of three years from the making of the first Order. Provided that in the case of an Order made under this sub-section the provisions of sub-section (6) shall not apply (*p*).

(9.) Every Order of Council made under this section shall, within thirty days from the date thereof, if Parliament be then sitting, or within twenty days from the commencement of the next session, if Parliament be not sitting, be laid on the table of both Houses of Parliament, and if within forty days of any order being so laid an Address in either House disapproving of such order be carried, such Order shall be void and of no effect.

(10.) Any Order made under this section shall be made with due regard to the utilisation (if practicable) of any land registry existing in the county to which compulsory registration is proposed to be applied or in any adjoining county (*q*).

(*o*) See last preceding note.

(*p*) The effect of this section is that the compulsory provisions cannot be applied beyond the area affected by the order of the year 1898 until the year 1901, and then only upon the request of a county council. The compulsory provisions are experimental only.

(*q*) See note (*n*) *supra*.

Sect. 20 (11).

51 & 52 Vict. c. 41.

(11.) For the purposes of this section the word county shall have the same meaning as in the Local Goverment Act, 1888, and shall include a county borough; and the word county council shall include the council of such borough (*r*).

(12.)—(i.) In the event of any portion of a county or part of a county as regards which an Order has been made under this section being included in another county or in a county borough as regards which no Order has been made under this section, such Order shall cease to be in force within such included portion of the county,

(ii.) In the event of any portion of a county or part of a county as regards which no Order has been made under this section being included in another county or in a county borough as regards which an Order has been made under this section, such Order shall apply to such included portion of the county (*s*).

21. * * * * (*t*).

Part IV.

Miscellaneous.

22. * * * * * (*u*).

Provision for the Yorkshire registries of deeds.

23.—(1.) At any time after the passing of this Act, and subject to the provisions of section twenty of this Act, the Lord Chancellor may enter into an agreement with the county council of any of

(*r*) "County" is not defined by the Local Government Act, 1888, except as *not* including the county of a city or county of a town, *ante*, p. 171; apparently the reference in the text is to the definition in that Act, s. 100, of "administrative county," *ante*, p. 172. It has been doubted whether an order making registration of title compulsory can be made as to the city of London: but if "county" in this Act be taken to mean administrative county it seems that such an order may be made, for the "metropolis" (which includes the city) is an administrative county. See Local Government Act, 1888, s. 40 (1), *ante*, p. 88, and definition of "metropolis" *ib.* s. 100, *ante*, p. 172. It will be observed that the city of London is dealt with in the draft order referred to, *ante*, p. 744, note (*n*).

(*s*) This section provides for the alteration of the area of compulsory registration in cases where the boundaries of a county or borough affected by an order under this section are altered, as they may be under s. 54 of the Local Government Act, 1888, *ante*, p. 108.

(*t*) Section 21 relates to the creation of an insurance fund for providing indemnity in cases of error, etc., in the Land Registry.

(*u*) Section 22 relates mainly to the making of rules and regulations and fee orders under this Act and the Land Transfer Act, 1875. The rules in force at the moment of writing this note are those of December 24th, 1875, January 1st, 1889, and November 23rd, 1891, as modified by the Provisional Land Transfer Rules, 1897, made under both Acts at the end of the year 1897, and set out 42 Sol. J. 146. But general rules under both Acts have been prepared by the rule committee appointed under this section, and will shortly come into force; a draft of these rules appears in the Weekly Notes, April 30th, 1898. They do not appear to make any special provision for the registration of title to Small Holdings or to rescind the Land Registry (Small Holdings) Rules, 1892; but these last mentioned rules appear to require some revision so as to bring them into accordance with the provisions of s. 19 of this Act, *ante*, p. 743.

the three ridings of Yorkshire for the transfer of the business of the local deed registry established in that riding to the office of land registry (*x*). Sect. 23 (1).

(2.) The agreement shall be drawn up in accordance with the principles of sections one, three, and four of the Land Registry (Middlesex Deeds) Act, 1891 (*y*), which provided for the transfer of the Middlesex registry of deeds to the land registry, and shall, after approval by the Treasury, take effect accordingly. 54 & 55 Vict. c. 64.

(3.) The whole of the property, assets, and liabilities of the county council, in relation to the local registry, shall be included in the transfer, and shall be taken over by the State at a price to be specified in or ascertained under the terms of the agreement, but no sum shall be payable for compensation in respect of any future loss of fees consequent upon such transfer.

(4.) Unless and until an agreement as aforesaid is concluded the county council may from time to time, at intervals of five years, in the event of their suffering loss, owing to the business of the local registry being diminished by reason of the principal Act and this Act, apply to the Treasury for compensation, and the Treasury shall award such compensation accordingly.

(5.) The compensation shall be made by the payment of a capital sum to the county fund to be determined in case of dispute by arbitration in the usual way on the basis of the receipts and expenditure in respect of the local registry during the three years previous to the claim being made, and that the county fund shall not be placed in a worse financial position by the operation of the Act.

(6.) All payments under this section shall be made out of moneys to be provided by Parliament.

Interpretation.

24.—(1.) All hereditaments, corporeal and incorporeal, shall be deemed land within the meaning of the principal Act and this Act, except that nothing in this Act shall render compulsory the registration of the title to an incorporeal hereditament, or to mines or minerals apart from the surface, or to a lease having less than forty years to run or two lives yet to fall in, or to an undivided share in land, or to freeholds intermixed and indistinguishable from lands of other tenure, or to corporeal hereditaments parcel of a manor, and included in a sale of the manor as such.

(2.) In this Act the expression "personal representative" means an executor or administrator.

(*x*) As to the Yorkshire registries of deeds (which must not be confounded with registries for registration of titles under the Land Transfer Acts, 1875 and 1897), see Local Government Act, 1888, s. 46 (4) and note *ante*, pp. 100, 101.

(*y*) The sections referred to provide for the transfer of the Middlesex registry of deeds to the Land Registry for the vesting in Her Majesty for the public service of the registers and other property of the Middlesex registry, and for the taking over of necessary officers and for pensions, allowances, etc.

Sect. 25.

Commencement of Act.

25. This Act shall come into operation on the first day of January one thousand eight hundred and ninety-eight.

Short title and construction.

26. This Act may be cited as the Land Transfer Act, 1897, and shall be construed as one with the principal Act, and that Act and this Act may be cited together as the Land Transfer Acts, 1875 and 1897.

SCHEDULES (*z*).

*

(*z*) The First Schedule contains minor amendments of the Land Transfer Act, 1875; the Second Schedule gives a scale of registration fees to be paid in districts where registration is compulsory; this scale is, however, liable to alteration by the rule committee.

PART IV.

Orders, Circulars, and other Official Documents relating to the powers and duties of County Councils.

ADJUSTMENT.

The following is the final report of the Commissioners appointed under the Local Government Act, 1888 (s. 61, *ante,* p. 118).

To the Queen's Most Excellent Majesty.

May it please Your Majesty,

We, the Commissioners appointed under the Local Government Act, 1888, desire humbly to present to Your Majesty a report of our proceedings in executing the several duties laid upon us by that Act and by subsequent legislation.

The duties laid upon us by the Local Government Act were as follows:—

(1.) To make equitable adjustments respecting the distribution of the proceeds of the Local Taxation Licences and Probate Duty Grant, and respecting all other financial relations between the county boroughs specified in the Third Section to the Act and the counties in which, for the purposes of the Act, they were respectively deemed to be situate, should such adjustments not have been made by agreement between the several county and borough councils within twelve months after April 1st, 1889.

(2.) To determine, until final adjustments were made, the proportions in which the payments out of the Local Taxation Account were to be made to such counties and county boroughs.

(3.) In default of agreement, to determine the number of members of the council of a county borough which should be members of the visiting committee of a county lunatic asylum, or to make a new arrangement in respect to any such county asylum, should any of the contributory councils desire it, and the other council or councils refuse to agree to the same.

(4.) In default of agreement between the respective county councils, to apportion the property, debts, and liabilities of the

Report.

counties of Kent, Middlesex, and Surrey between the portions of those counties situate within the Metropolis and the portions situate outside the same.

(5.) To determine in regard to the retention by the justices of any property, should difference arise between the justices and the county council in respect to such retention.

The following additional duties were laid upon us by subsequent legislation, viz.:—

(6.) By the Local Taxation (Customs and Excise) Act, 1890, to make an equitable adjustment between counties and county boroughs respecting the distribution of the proceeds of the residue of the Local Taxation (Customs and Excise) duties.

(7.) By the Local Government Board's Isle of Wight (County) Order, 1889, confirmed by the Local Government Board's Provisional Order Confirmation (No. 2) Act, 1889, to make, in default of agreement within four months after April 1st, 1890, an equitable adjustment of financial relations between the county of Southampton and the county of the Isle of Wight.

(8.) By the Local Government Board's City of Oxford Order, 1889, confirmed by the Local Government Board's Provisional Orders Confirmation Act, 1889, to make, in default of agreement within twelve months after November 9th, 1889, an equitable adjustment respecting the above-mentioned distributions and respecting all other financial relations between the county of Oxford and the county borough of Oxford.

(9.) By the Local Government Board's Borough of Grimsby Order, 1890, to make, in default of agreement within six months after November 9th, 1890, an adjustment similar to the above between the county of Lincoln (parts of Lindsey) and the county borough of Grimsby.

(10.) By the under-mentioned Acts and Orders to make the adjustments necessitated by the extensions of certain county boroughs in default of agreements within the periods therein respectively limited for the purpose, as follows, viz.:—The Burnley Corporation Act, 1889; the Swansea Corporation Act, 1889; the Walsall Corporation Act, 1890; the Local Government Board's City of Canterbury Order, 1890; City of Coventry Order, 1890; City of Manchester Order, 1890; Borough of Great Yarmouth Order, 1890; and Borough of Huddersfield Order, 1890.

(11.) By the Local Government Board's Borough of Newport Order, 1891, to make in default of agreement within three months after November 7th, 1891, an adjustment as directed by such order between the county of Monmouth and county borough of Newport.

The addition made to our duties by the several Acts of Parliament and Provisional Orders last mentioned, and the delay on the part of some of the authorities in bringing their cases before us after the termination of the periods fixed for the making of the adjustments

Report.

by agreement, rendered it necessary that the duration of the Commission, at first limited to December 31st, 1890, should be from time to time extended, and by the Expiring Laws Continuance Act, 1890, it was continued to December 31st, 1891, and, by the same Act of 1891, to June 30th, 1892.

As instances of the magnitude of the interests affected by some of the adjustments, it may be mentioned that out of the 4,805,940*l.* 7*s.* 1*d.** paid from the Local Taxation Account in the financial year ended March 31st, 1890, no less an amount than 3,176,740*l.* 1*s.* 1*d.*† was payable on behalf of the counties and county boroughs between which the distributions were to be severally adjusted. And with regard to the other financial relations between counties and county boroughs, contributions of such large amount were, under the terms of the Act, ceasing to be paid by the boroughs to the county funds, that in the case of the county of Lancaster sums exceeding in the aggregate 350,000*l.* have under our awards been directed to be paid as equitable provision for their cessation. The properties to be apportioned were also in some instances of considerable magnitude. The three lunatic asylums belonging to the county of Middlesex, and now transferred to the county of London, viz. :—Colney Hatch, Hanwell, and Banstead, together with the site and foundations of the new asylum in course of construction at Claybury, were valued by agreement for the purposes of the apportionment at the sum of 1,247,000*l.*

The first of the matters referred to us which demanded our attention was the apportionment to counties and county boroughs of the interim payments out of the Local Taxation Account pending the final settlements. Most of the counties and county boroughs were able to agree in recommending the proportions requisite for this purpose, and the proportions so recommended were temporarily adopted. These proportions are shown in Appendix A. of this report. It subsequently became evident, when we had determined the general principles of adjustment, that in some cases the proportions so adopted were giving a result materially different from that which would be produced by the application of such principles. In these cases the proportions at first adopted were, as soon as possible, varied, and in the final settlement all sums paid under the interim apportionment were brought into account.

	£	*s.*	*d.*
* Local Taxation Licences - - - - -	2,994,419	8	7
Probate Duty Grant - - - - -	1,811,520	18	6
Total - - - - - - -	4,805,940	7	1

	£	*s.*	*d.*
† Local Taxation Licences - - - - -	2,057,683	5	6
Probate Duty Grant - - - -	1,119,056	15	7
Total - - - - - - -	3,176,740	1	1

Report.

At the termination of the twelve months after April 1st, 1889, the period limited by the Local Government Act for the making of settlements by agreements between the several councils, it was found that in five counties only had such settlements been made. Such counties, with the county boroughs therein situate, are as follows:—

Counties.	County Boroughs.
Lincoln (parts of Lindsey)	Lincoln.
Leicester	Leicester.
Northumberland	Newcastle.
Surrey	Croydon.
Worcester	Dudley. Worcester.

We had, therefore, to make the adjustments in the cases of twenty-two out of the twenty-seven counties, and fifty-five out of the sixty-one county boroughs specified in the Third Schedule of the said Act, as well as in the other previously mentioned cases from time to time referred to us by Acts of Parliament and Provisional Orders of the Local Government Board.

Several other of the counties and county boroughs found themselves after the termination of the above-mentioned twelve months in a position to agree upon terms of settlement; and in all cases in which such agreements were made, the terms so arranged were accepted by us for the purpose of our awards, and such agreements are recited or referred to in the Orders by which the final settlements were made. Such orders will be found at the end of the minutes of evidence.

For the purpose of obtaining the necessary information to enable us to make the several adjustments, we invited each of the councils concerned to state in writing the matters upon which our decision was required, and also, should they desire to do so, to send representatives to address us in reference thereto. As the adjustments were of an unprecedented character, and involved issues of the magnitude previously mentioned, and as the directions contained in the statute under which we were acting appeared to be very variously interpreted by the different councils concerned, we acceded to the generally expressed wish of the councils that they should be allowed to appear by counsel.

Our first meeting was held on April 12th, 1889, and we have sat on fifty-eight days. On thirty-nine of these we listened to the arguments addressed to us on behalf of the councils of the counties and county boroughs, the majority of which, as will be seen from the shorthand notes of the proceedings, were represented by eminent counsel. The details of our proceedings on such thirty-nine days are contained in the minutes of evidence annexed to this Report.

Local taxation licenses

In determining the adjustment respecting the distribution of the proceeds of the Local Taxation Licences and Probate Duty Grant,

Report.

and probate duty grant.

we were directed to have regard to the consideration that the county was not to be placed in any worse financial position by reason of the boroughs therein being constituted county boroughs, and that a county borough was not to be placed in a worse financial position than it would have been in if it had remained part of the county, and had shared in the division of the sums received by a county in respect of the licence duties and the probate duty grant.

It was difficult to ascertain what would have been precisely the financial position of a county borough had it remained part of a county; but it was obvious that in sharing in the division of the sums received by a county in respect of the licence duties and probate duty grant, each county borough, where several such boroughs were contained in one county, would have shared upon the same terms as the rest, and that it was therefore necessary to make not only the adjustment between county and county borough directly contemplated by the Act, but also an adjustment between the several county boroughs situate in the county.

The difficulty in ascertaining the precise financial position of a county borough had it remained part of the county, arose from the following facts: By section 23 (2) (ii.) (iii.) of the Local Government Act, the county council would have had to make to or on behalf of the local authorities within the borough the payments specified in sections 24, 26, and 35 (5) of that Act, that is to say, by sections 24 and 35 (5), payments in substitution for all local grants previously received except the grant on account of main roads, and, by section 26, a payment to guardians in respect of the costs of union officers. The remainder of the proceeds of the local taxation licences and probate duty grant would, by section 23 (2) (iv.), have been transferred to the general purposes account of the county fund. By section 11 (1) the whole cost of the maintenance of the main roads in the borough would have been defrayed by the county council as a general county purpose, and under section 35 (4) (*b*), the borough council might have been able to obtain from the county council or from the Local Government Board a declaration that some of the roads within the borough were main roads.

We were of an opinion that an attempt to determine by a number of special inquiries what roads within the county boroughs would have been declared main roads had such boroughs remained parts of the counties in which, for the purposes of the Local Government Act, they were respectively deemed to be situate, and what additional roads within the county area would also have been declared main roads, and to appraise the annual cost of maintenance of such roads, would have caused great delay and expense, and could have produced no satisfactory result.

On the other hand, from an inspection of the amounts received by counties and boroughs in respect of the several grants made out of the Exchequer prior to the passing of the Act, it was apparent to us that if, in making the adjustment, we should take into consideration

Report.

the grants mentioned in the above-mentioned sections 24, 26, and 35 (5), while neglecting the grant formerly received in respect of main roads, we should be giving to the county boroughs and taking away from the counties the grants from which respectively they had in the past derived the greatest benefit.

It appeared to us that it was not the intention of the Local Government Act that any special relief received by a local area from the Exchequer grants prior to the passing of the Act should be excluded from the adjustment.

After careful consideration of the provisions of the Act, and the arguments addressed to us, we determined that an equitable adjustment of the distribution of the proceeds of the Local Taxation Licences and Probate Duty Grant between each county and the county boroughs deemed to be therein situate would be effected by giving to such several authorities in each year the annual amount received prior to the passing of the Local Government Act out of the grants discontinued after the passing of that Act,* together with the amount payable under the above-mentioned section 26, and dividing the remainder in proportion to the rateable values of the county and boroughs. We also determined that the figures of the various amounts should be fixed for a period of five years, or until altered under the provisions of section 32 (6) of the Local Government Act, and for this purpose we adopted for the discontinued grants the figures of the shares certified by the Local Government Board under section 22 of the last-mentioned Act to have been received by the counties and boroughs respectively during the financial year ending March 31st next before the passing of the Act out of the grants theretofore made out of the Exchequer in aid of local rates which ceased to be granted after the passing of the Act; and for the grants to be made under section 26 we adopted the figures of the sums payable by counties and county boroughs in the year ending March 31st, 1890. And, as the salaries of poor-law medical officers would be included in both such grants, we deducted from the discontinued grants, as above defined, the amounts included therein on that behalf. For the ratio of rateable values we adopted the figures agreed for this purpose between the respective councils, or, in default of any such agreed ratio, the figures of the poor rate valuations in force at Lady Day, 1889.

A statement showing all the figures above referred to, and the effect of the adjustments made either by our awards or by the agreements of the councils, in respect of the financial year ended March 31st, 1890, is contained in Appendix B. of this report, and in Appendix C. is a further statement comparing the relief in the £ afforded to the ratepayers by the grants received out of the Exchequer in the year ended March 31st, 1888, and the relief in the £ afforded by the proceeds of the Local Taxation Licences and Probate Duty Grant distributed as shown in the previous tables.

---

* Such grants included the half cost of main roads.

Report.

Local Taxation (Customs and Excise) Duties.

In those cases in which terms of adjustment had been settled by agreement between the parties for the distribution of the proceeds of the residue of the Local Taxation (Customs and Excise) Duties under section 1 (1) (b) of the Local Taxation (Customs and Excise) Act, 1890, we have adopted such terms, and in default of any such agreements we determined that such proceeds should be distributed between the county and borough councils in the same manner as the remainder of the proceeds of the Local Taxation Licences and Probate Duty Grant above referred to, viz., in the ratio of rateable values fixed for the purposes of the adjustment.

Other financial relations.

The adjustment of the financial relations between counties and county boroughs other than the distribution of the proceeds of the Local Taxation Licences and Probate Duty Grant, and of the proceeds of the residue of the Local Taxation (Customs and Excise) Duties, was a matter fraught with special difficulty.

By sub-section (1) of section 32 of the Local Government Act such adjustment was to provide in case of any expenses which might in future be incurred by the county wholly or partly on behalf of the borough for the liability of such borough to contribute, and, save as provided by the Act, any existing liability to contribute or to incur expense was, after the appointed day, to cease, and an equitable provision for such cessation was to be made in the adjustment.

By sub-section (3) of the same section it was directed that in such adjustment regard should be had (1) to the property, debts, and liabilities connected with the financial relations of the county and borough; (2) to the consideration that the county was not to be placed in a worse financial position by reason of the boroughs therein being constituted county boroughs; and (3) to the amount of benefit and value of the services which the borough received in return for existing contributions.

In the majority of cases the amounts contributed by the boroughs appeared to us to exceed the amount of benefit and value of the services rendered to the borough by the county, since the boroughs contributed for several purposes in respect of which they had themselves provided their own separate establishments. On the other hand, had they remained in the counties, they would have continued to be liable to contribute towards the same purposes and in the same manner as before the passing of the Act. Consequently we found it difficult to reconcile the direction that the county was not to be placed in a worse financial position by reason of the boroughs therein being constituted county boroughs, and at the same time to have regard to the amount of benefit and value of the services which the boroughs received in return for existing contributions.

The established rule of construction required that some effect should be given to every consideration to which the Act provided that regard should be had. It appeared to us that this could only be done by making the two considerations meet each other half way.

Report.

With regard to county bridges and with regard to main roads in county boroughs not having separate courts of quarter sessions on April 1st, 1889, we were unable to say that the value of the service rendered to the boroughs by the counties was less than the contribution which the boroughs were liable to make, seeing that access to and from the boroughs was by roads and bridges outside their own boundaries. It therefore appeared to us that the third consideration above referred to did not in this case apply, and that we must have regard only to the consideration that the counties should not be placed in any worse financial position by reason of the boroughs therein being constituted county boroughs.

The conclusions at which we had arrived were communicated to the councils concerned in a memorandum, of which the substance is contained in the following paragraphs, and such councils were invited to settle by agreement the figures requisite for our awards.

As to the salaries of county officers, towards which a county borough had been liable to contribute before the appointed day, if such officers should in future render no service to the county borough, the liability of the borough to contribute would cease, and equitable provision for such cessation was to be made in the adjustment.

We determined that the amount of the annual contribution made by the boroughs towards such salaries should be estimated on an average of the sums contributed on that behalf, and that the payment of a capital sum representing fifteen years' purchase of such amount should constitute an equitable provision for the cessation of liability in respect thereof.

And as to the salaries paid to county officers in respect of services which in future would be rendered partly on behalf of a county borough, the value of the services which the borough would in future receive were to be settled either by agreement or by our decision, and in respect of such value the borough was to continue to contribute.

From the amount of the annual contribution theretofore made, the amount of the continuing annual contribution was to be deducted, and with regard to the remainder, we determined that fifteen years' purchase should constitute an equitable provision for the cessation of liability to contribute.

County bridges.

In the matter of county bridges, we determined that the equitable provision for the cessation of the liability of a borough to contribute and of the county to incur expense should be based upon the principle that each such liability should be valued, and the balance of the cost of the one liability over and above that of the other should be paid by the borough council to the county council, or by the county council to the borough council, as the case might be.

In estimating the respective values of such liabilities, the average annual expenditure of the county for the ten years prior to the appointed day was to be ascertained, and the boroughs were to be

Report.

deemed to have been liable to contribute towards such expenditure in proportion to the rateable values agreed or determined for the purposes of the adjustment, and the county was to be deemed to have been liable to expend upon the county bridges within the borough the average annual amount expended during the same period.

The balance of the cost of the one liability over and above that of the other we declared to be the net annual liability for the cessation of which equitable provision was to be made, and we determined that thirty years' purchase of such annual liability should be the equitable provision for the cessation thereof.

Main roads.

With regard to main roads, we determined that the equitable provision for the cessation of liability should be based upon the same principles as had been laid down in the case of county bridges, and in estimating the respective values of the liabilities, the county boroughs which had not separate courts of quarter sessions on the appointed day should be deemed to have been liable to contribute rateably towards one-fourth part of the total main road expenditure of the entire county (excluding quarter sessional boroughs), and the county should be deemed to have been liable to contribute to the borough one-fourth part of the cost of maintaining the main roads within the borough.

Miscellaneous expenses, including parliamentary registration.

Towards such expenses as would in future be incurred by the county wholly or partly on behalf of a county borough, the borough would remain liable to contribute.

The amount of the continuing annual contribution was to be settled either by agreement or by our decision, and deducted from the amount of the average annual contribution made in respect of such expenses prior to the appointed day. Of the difference between such amounts, we determined that the payment of fifteen years' purchase should constitute an equitable provision for the cessation of liability to contribute.

We determined that the value of the contributions should be calculated upon an average of the three complete financial years prior to April 1st, 1889; but in the case of county bridges we made a distinction, and based our awards upon a ten years' average, upon the ground that, while the number of bridges had remained almost constant throughout that period, the annual expenditure upon them had in some cases varied greatly from year to year.

We determined that the expense in future to be incurred by the county on behalf of a county borough in respect of the registration of parliamentary voters should be estimated in accordance with the apportionment contemplated by section 14 (1) of the Registration Act, 1885.

Continuing contributions.

With regard to any sums which a county borough remained liable to contribute under section 32 of the Local Government Act in respect of expenses which would in future be incurred by a county wholly or partly on behalf of the borough, we intimated that if any agreement were made to commute such contribution for a capital

Report.

sum, we were prepared to make our award in the terms of such agreement. But, in default of any such agreement, we were of opinion that we must decline to make any such commutation.

County property.

Several boroughs having claimed a share in property which, by the operation of the Local Government Act, had become vested in the county council, we declared that such claim existed only in respect of any share of beneficial interest or occupation of which the boroughs had been deprived by the operation of that Act, and that no borough had been deprived of any such share in the case of the following and similar buildings, viz., county hall, courts of justice and offices, judges' house or lodgings, and court-houses.

With regard to militia store-houses and any other county property of which the rents were applied on account of the county rate, we determined that such property should be either retained by the county at a valuation or realised within six months of the date of the award, and that the council of any county borough which had contributed to the cost of such property should receive a proportion of the ascertained value thereof, or of the proceeds of sale, calculated upon the respective rateable values of the county and county borough agreed for the purposes of the adjustment, or, in default of such agreed rateable value, in proportion to the poor rate valuations in force at Lady Day, 1889.

The effect of our communicating our decisions to the parties was that in many cases the amounts to be included in our awards were settled by agreement. Where they could not be so settled we charged our secretary to visit the localities for the purpose of discussing with the parties the several items of the adjustment, and upon his report based our final awards.

In any case in which between any county and county borough an arrangement had been made that any continuing annual contribution, for services still to be rendered by the county, should cease upon agreed terms of redemption, we have included such arrangement in our award.

In the case of any continuing contribution, if the parties could agree to fix the annual amount thereof, we included such fixed amount in our award, bearing in mind that under section 32 (6) of the Local Government Act such amount, should it have become inequitable, might be readjusted after the termination of a period of five years.

Where county boroughs had received grants of separate courts of quarter sessions after the appointed day and before the making of our awards, if the redemption contemplated by section 32 (3) (b) of the Act were arranged by agreement and application made to us to include the terms thereof in our award, we did not in any case refuse to make such inclusion.

County lunatic asylums.

In the absence of an agreement between all the parties, we have not thought it within our province to disturb existing arrangements in regard to county lunatic asylums, if the only object sought were

Report.

to alter the proportions of contribution settled by law. In cases, however, where it appeared to us expedient that one or other of the contributing authorities should provide separate accommodation for its pauper lunatics, we made orders directing that such separate accommodation should be provided, and proper compensation be made to the outgoing authority for the loss of its share in the asylum. In determining the amount of such compensation we had regard to the amount of accommodation of which such authority was being deprived.

Where applications were made to us to fix the number of members of the council of a county borough which should be members of the visiting committee of the county asylum, we fixed such number in proportion to the current annual contribution payable by the borough as compared with that payable by the county towards the building, furnishing, and repairing of the asylum.

The arguments addressed to us in relation to the making of such new arrangements and fixing of such numbers are contained in the minutes of evidence of our fourth, twelfth, thirty-third, and thirty-sixth days' proceedings, and to such minutes of evidence the orders made will be found annexed.

In the case of the Sussex County Lunatic Asylum an important legal question arose as to the extent of the authority conferred upon us by the Local Government Act. This question we deemed it expedient to submit for counsel's opinion, and the case submitted and the opinion given are annexed to the minutes of evidence of our thirty-sixth day's proceedings.

The London and Surrey County Councils were able to settle by agreement the apportionment of property, debts, and liabilities under section 40 (7) of the Local Government Act between the portion of the county of Surrey situate within the metropolis and the portion situate outside the metropolis.

In the apportionment under the same section between the portions of the county of Middlesex, the majority of the items were included in an agreement made between the London and Middlesex County Councils, and in default of complete agreement, the apportionment having been referred to us for settlement, we made an order giving effect to certain parts of the agreement and dealing with the other matters at issue.

The London and Kent County Councils, in default of agreement, applied to us to determine the principles upon which the apportionment should be made, and, after our decision had been given, settled by agreement the details which are included in our order.

County borough extensions

In the adjustment respecting the cost of maintaining the main roads in areas added to county boroughs after April 1, 1889, we took into account the liability of the county for the whole cost of such roads as provided by section 11 of the Local Government Act, and having distributed to each authority out of the proceeds of the Local Taxation Licences and Probate Duty Grant, a sum equivalent to one

Report. half of the yearly cost of the maintenance of main roads in the county area and borough area respectively, we determined that the difference between one half the average annual cost of maintenance of the main roads in the area added to the borough and the rateable share of the said area in one half of the annual cost of the main roads of the county should be the annual liability for the cessation of which equitable provision was to be made.

The sums fixed by the Treasury under the provisions of section 61 (6) of the Local Government Act for the payment of the costs of the Commission, amounting in the aggregate to 5,371*l.*, are shown in Appendix D. All such sums have been received by us from the councils of the counties and county boroughs therein mentioned, and the amounts so received have been paid by us into the Exchequer, as contemplated by the above-mentioned sub-section of the Act.

We have not deemed it necessary to set out in this report the various contentions put forward on behalf of the councils interested in the several adjustments, as such contentions and the arguments by which they were supported are contained in the shorthand notes of our proceedings.

It will suffice to say that careful attention has been given to the various views presented to us, and that in arriving at our decisions regard has been had to the considerations commended to our notice by the Act, and every effort made to render such decisions, within the meaning of the Act, a final settlement of the various matters to which they relate.

The orders giving effect to our decisions, signed by the Chairman of the Commission on our behalf, and issued under our authority, will be found annexed to the minutes of evidence taken in each case.

We desire to express our acknowledgment of the ready and courteous assistance received from the Local Government Board in furnishing the statistical and other information for which we had on frequent occasions to apply to them, and also our sense of the able and assiduous efforts made by the officers of the county and borough councils to bring about a satisfactory settlement of the difficult questions arising in the adjustments and to supply the details of contribution and expenditure necessary for the preparation of our final awards.

We also desire to record our deep sense of the zeal and ability displayed by our secretary, Mr. Gaskell, in the discharge of the onerous and complicated duties which have devolved upon him.

All which we humbly submit to your Majesty's gracious consideration.

DERBY.
August 15th, 1892. GEORGE SHAW LEFEVRE.
JOHN L. WHARTON.
FRANK MOWATT.
JOSEPH JOHN HENLEY.

General Order.

BORROWING,

(*And see* "COUNTY STOCK.")

COUNTY COUNCILS: LOANS FOR PURPOSE OF ADVANCES TO PARISH COUNCILS (*a*).

GENERAL ORDER OF 5TH NOVEMBER, 1895.

To the County Councils of the several Administrative Counties in England and Wales, other than the County Council of London: And to all others whom it may concern.

Whereas by sub-section (2) of section 12 of the Local Government Act, 1894, it is enacted as follows:—

"(2.) A county council may lend to a parish council any money which the parish council are authorised to borrow, and may, if necessary, without the sanction of the Local Government Board, and irrespectively of any limit of borrowing, raise the money by loan, subject to the like conditions and in the like manner as any other loan for the execution of their duties, and subject to any further conditions which the Local Government Board may by general or special order impose."

Now, therefore, We, the Local Government Board, do hereby order that any loan raised by a county council in pursuance of the above-recited sub-section for the purpose of lending to a parish council any money which such parish council are authorised to borrow shall be subject, in addition to the conditions applied by such sub-section, to the following further conditions; namely,—

(1.) The loan raised by the county council shall be discharged within a term ending not later than one year after the date at which the parish council are required to pay off the money lent to them.

(2.) The money lent to the parish council shall be repayable by them to the county council by equal yearly or half-yearly instalments of principal or of principal and interest combined.

(3.) If the whole or any part of an instalment of principal is not paid by the parish council to the county council within six months after the date on which the instalment is due, the county council shall set apart out of the county fund the amount of such instalment by which the parish council are in default, and shall apply the same in repayment of the loan by means of which the moneys lent to the parish council were raised or in redemption of stock if the loan has been raised by stock. If the amount due from the parish council is thereafter received by the county council from the parish council, the amount shall be applied in recouping the county fund the amount set apart out of such fund.

(*a*) See s. 12(2) of the Local Government Act, 1894, *ante*, p. 610.

General Order.

(4.) Subject to article 3, all sums received by the county council from the parish council for principal shall be applied only in repayment of the loan by means of which the moneys lent to the parish council were raised, or in the redemption of stock if the loan has been raised by stock.

(5.) All sums which in pursuance of article 3 or article 4 are required to be applied in redemption of stock shall be transferred to the redemption fund, loans fund, or other fund or account to which, under the provisions of, the Acts or regulations in force for the time being in the county governing the issue and redemption of stock by the county council, sums required to be applied in redemption of stock are to be paid.

(6.) Subject to article 3, all sums received by the county council from the parish council for principal and not forthwith applied as required by article 4 shall be invested by the county council in securities in which sums so applicable may lawfully be invested, and the county council may from time to time vary any such investments.

Given under the Seal of Office of the Local Government Board, this Fifth day of November, in the year One thousand eight hundred and ninety-five.

(L.S.) HENRY CHAPLIN, *President.*

HUGH OWEN, *Secretary.*

THE FOLLOWING CIRCULAR WAS ISSUED WITH THE FOREGOING ORDER :—

SIR,—I am directed by the Local Government Board to draw attention to the power conferred on county councils with respect to lending money to parish councils and to raising loans for this purpose.

Sub-section (2) of section 12 of the Local Government Act, 1894, provides that "a county council may lend to a parish council any money which the parish council are authorised to borrow, and may, if necessary, without the sanction of the Local Government Board, and irrespectively of any limit of borrowing, raise the money by loan, subject to the like conditions and in the like manner as any other loan for the execution of their duties, and subject to any further conditions which the Local Government Board may, by general or special order, impose."

It will be observed that a county council can only lend money to a parish council which the latter are authorised to borrow, and consequently a county council cannot make an advance unless the parish council have obtained the consent of the county council and of the Board to the borrowing of the money as required by sub-section (1) of section 12 of the Act.

When, however, a parish council have obtained these consents, it will be competent for the county council to lend them the money which they are authorised to borrow, and the county council may advance the loan either from money in the county fund at the time or from money obtained by a loan raised for the purpose. If the county council have recourse to a loan, they may borrow without the sanction of the Board, and irrespectively of any limit imposed upon their borrowing by sub-section (2) of section 69 of the Local Government Act, 1888, or otherwise. In other respects the loan must be raised subject to the like conditions and in the like manner as any other loan for the execution of the duties of the county council. The loan, however, is also to be subject to any further conditions which the Board may by general or special order impose, and the Board have thought it desirable to issue a General Order prescribing such further conditions as appear to them to be necessary. Six copies of the Order are enclosed. Circular.

The conditions imposed by the Order are that the loan shall be discharged not later than one year after the date at which the parish council are required to pay off the advance made to them, that the money lent shall be repayable by the parish council by equal yearly or half-yearly instalments of principal or of principal and interest combined, and that if the parish council should fail to pay the whole or part of an instalment within six months after the instalment is due, the county council shall set apart out of the county fund the amount by which the parish council are in default, and shall apply that amount in repayment of the loan raised for the purpose of the advance or in redemption of stock if the loan has been raised by stock. On the receipt from the parish council of the amount by which they were in default, the county fund is to be recouped the amount set apart as above mentioned.

Subject to this, all sums received by the county council from the parish council for principal are to be applied only in repayment of the loan or in redemption of stock, as the case may be. All sums required to be applied in redemption of stock are to be transferred to the fund or account to which under the Acts or regulations in force in the county governing the issue and redemption of stock, sums required to be applied in redemption of stock are to be paid. Any sums received for principal and not forthwith applied in repayment of the loan or in redemption of stock, as the case may be, are to be invested in securities in which such sums may lawfully be invested. The investments may from time to time be varied by the county council for others of a like kind.

I am, Sir,
Your obedient Servant,
HUGH OWEN,
Secretary.

The Clerk to the County Council.

COUNTY STOCK.

Order in Council under section 70 *of the Local Government Act,* 1888, *ante*, p. 135 (*a*).

At the Court at Balmoral, the 26th day of September, 1891.

Present, the Queen's most Excellent Majesty in Council.

Whereas the Local Government Board have, in virtue of the powers conferred upon them by "The Local Government Act, 1888," made certain Regulations apply to the creation, issue, transfer, and redemption of, and other dealings with, any county stock which any County Council create under the Local Government Act, 1888, in exercise of any statutory borrowing powers as defined in the said Regulations:

And whereas the said Regulations have, as required by the said Act, been laid before both Houses of Parliament for the period of

(*a*) The regulations confirmed by this Order are amended by regulations confirmed by an Order of August 3rd, 1897, which is set out, *post*, p. 793.

Order in Council.

thirty days, and no resolution has been passed by either House that such Regulations ought not to be proceeded with:

Now, therefore, Her Majesty having taken the said Regulations (copy whereof is hereunto annexed) into consideration, is pleased, by and with the advice of Her Privy Council, to confirm, and doth hereby confirm, the said Regulations.

C. L. PEEL.

REGULATIONS referred to in the foregoing Order:—

THE LOCAL GOVERNMENT ACT, 1888.

REGULATIONS AS TO ISSUE OF COUNTY STOCK.

To the County Councils of the several Administrative Counties in England and Wales, other than the County Council of London;—

And to all others whom it may concern.

Whereas by sub-section (8) of Section 69 of the Local Government Act, 1888, it is enacted that where the County Council are authorised to borrow any money on loan they may raise such money by stock issued under the said Act or by the other methods mentioned in the said sub-section;

And whereas by Section 70 of the said Act it is enacted as follows:—

"70.—(1.) County Stock may be created, issued, transferred, dealt with, and redeemed in such manner, and in accordance with such regulations, as the Local Government Board may from time to time prescribe.

"(2.) Without prejudice to the generality of the above power, such regulations may provide for the discharge of any loan raised by such stock, and in the case of consolidation of debt for extending or varying the times within which loans may be discharged, and may provide for the consent of limited owners and for the application of the Acts relating to stamp duties and to cheques, and for the disposal of unclaimed dividends, and may apply for the purposes of this section, with or without modifications, any enactments of the Local Loans Act, 1875, and the Acts amending the same, and of any Act relating to stock issued by the Metropolitan Board of Works, or by the corporation of any municipal borough.

(3.) Such regulations shall be laid before each House of Parliament for not less than thirty days during which such House sits, and if either House during such thirty days resolves that such regulations ought not to be proceeded with, the same shall be of no effect, without prejudice, nevertheless, to the making of further regulations.

"(4.) If no such resolution is passed, it shall be lawful for Her Majesty by Order in Council to confirm such regulations, and the same when so confirmed shall be deemed to have been duly made and to be within the powers of this Act, and shall be of the same force as if they were enacted in this Act." **Regulations**

Now, therefore, We, the Local Government Board, in pursuance of the powers given to Us by the above-cited Section, Do hereby Order and Prescribe as follows:—

The Regulations herein-after contained shall, from and after the confirmation thereof as aforesaid, apply to the creation, issue, transfer, and redemption of, and other dealings with any county stock which any County Council create under the Local Government Act, 1888, in exercise of any Statutory borrowing power as defined in Article 1.

Preliminary.

Article 1.—In these Regulations— Interpretation.

The County Council means the County Council exercising under these Regulations the power of borrowing by the creation of stock; "The county council."

Stock, unless the context otherwise requires, means county stock created by the County Council under these Regulations; "Stock."

The Board means the Local Government Board; "The Board."

The Bank of England means the Governor and Company of the Bank of England; "The Bank of England."

Revenues of the County Council includes the revenues of the County Council from time to time arising from any land, undertakings, or other property for the time being of the County Council, and rates or contributions leviable by or on the precept of the County Council; "Revenues of the County Council."

Statutory borrowing power means any power, whether or not coupled with a duty, of borrowing, or continuing on loan, or re-borrowing money, or of redeeming or paying off, or creating or continuing payment of or in respect of any annuity, rentcharge, rent, or other security representing or granted in lieu of consideration money, for the time-being existing under any Act of Parliament, public or local, passed or to be passed, or under any Provisional Order confirmed by Act of Parliament passed or to be passed, or under these Regulations, or under any order or sanction of any Government department made or given, or to be made or given, by authority of any Act of Parliament passed or to be passed; "Statutory borrowing power."

Statutory security means any security in which trustees are for the time being by or under any Act of Parliament passed or to be passed authorised to invest trust money, except any security of the County Council, and any other mortgage, "Statutory security."

Regulations

bond, debenture, stock, annuity, rentcharge, rent, or other security authorised by or under any Act of Parliament passed or to be passed, or under these Regulations, of any Local Authority as defined by Section 34 of the Local Loans Act, 1875 (*b*), except as before excepted, and except securities payable to bearer;

"Interest." Interest includes instalments of an annuity and half-yearly or other payments of or in respect of a rentcharge, rent, or other security.

Creation and Charge of Stock.

Creation of stock.

Article 2.—(1.) Where the County Council have for the time being any statutory borrowing power, then, subject and according to the provisions of these Regulations, the County Council may from time to time by resolution exercise the power by creation of redeemable stock, to be from time to time issued for such amount within the limit of the power, at such price, being not lower than ninety-five per centum, to bear such half-yearly or other dividends, and to be so transferable, that is to say, in books or by deed, as the County Council by the resolution direct: Provided that, subject to any Regulation which the Board may make amending these Regulations, all stock at any time and from time to time so created shall be created on and subject to such terms and conditions as that the same shall form one and the same class of stock, bearing one and the same rate of dividend, and shall become redeemable as herein-after provided after the expiration of the same period from the first creation of the stock (*c*).

(2.) All stock at any time and from time to time so created shall rank equally without any priority or preference by reason of any precedence in the date of any statutory borrowing power, or in the date of creation of any portion of stock, or in the date of issue of any portion of stock, or on any other ground whatsoever, and shall (unless otherwise expressed in the resolution for creation of the stock) also rank equally with all other securities of the County Council created or granted in pursuance of any statutory borrowing power at any time after the date of the first creation of any stock.

(3.) After the expiration of such a period from the creation of the stock as the Board shall determine, the stock shall be redeemable at par, at the option of the County Council, and within such a period (not exceeding forty years) from the first creation of the stock as the

---

(*b*) According to the definitions of "local authority" and "rate" in the section referred to, a parish council appears to be a local authority within this article; so that moneys standing to the credit of the redemption fund account and requiring investment under Article 12, *infra*, may be invested upon the security of a loan to a parish council. See s. 12 of the Local Government Act, 1894, *ante*, p. 610.

(*c*) The creation of stock of different classes is permitted by Article 1 of the amending regulations of 1897, *post*.

Board shall determine, the whole of the stock shall be redeemed or purchased and extinguished. **Regulations**

(4.) Each resolution for creation of stock shall specify after what period the stock thereby created is redeemable at par, and within what period the stock is to be redeemed or purchased and extinguished.

(5.) The stock shall be designated by such name as the County Council in the resolution for creation of the stock shall, with the approval of the Board, determine.

Borrowing power to be exerciseable for actual sum raiseable.

Article 3.—Each statutory borrowing power of the County Council shall be construed to authorise the County Council to create such an amount of stock and from time to time to issue such nominal amounts thereof as will, in the aggregate, according to the price of issue, produce the actual amount of money for the time being lawfully raiseable by the County Council under that power, or some portion of that actual amount, or (as the case may be) the actual amount of money properly payable by the County Council as consideration on payment off or redemption by the County Council of any mortgage, bond, debenture, stock, annuity, rentcharge, rent, or other security.

Charge of stock.

Article 4.—(1.) All stock for the time being issued and the dividends thereon shall be and the same are by virtue of these Regulations charged indifferently on the county fund and all the revenues of the County Council.

(2.) The dividends for the time being payable on all stock shall rank equally with interest on all other securities of the County Council created or granted in pursuance of any statutory borrowing power at any time after the date of the first creation of any stock, and the same dividends and interest shall, subject to all charges existing at that date, be the first charge on the county fund and all the revenues of the County Council.

Consolidation of Loans.

Consolidation of loans

Article 5.—The Board may approve a scheme for the consolidation for the purpose of the repayment of all or any of the loans raised by the County Council under all or any of the statutory borrowing powers of the County Council (*d*), whether existing at the date of these Regulations or not, and any such scheme shall fix the period or periods within which the loans so consolidated shall be discharged, and for that purpose may extend or vary any period allowed for the payment off of such loans by the statutory borrowing powers: Provided that the Board, in approving the period or

(*d*) Loans previously raised by stock and loans included in any previous consolidation scheme may be included in a scheme under this article. See Article 2 of the amending regulations of 1897, *post*.

Regulations — periods as aforesaid, shall have due regard to the amounts of the several loans and the periods allowed for the payment off of such loans respectively by the statutory borrowing powers.

Payment of Dividends.

Payments to dividends funds account.

Article 6.—For the payment of dividends on the stock there shall in each year be carried to an account of the county fund, entitled the Stock (Dividends) Fund Account (herein-after referred to as the dividends fund account) (*e*), a sum or sums equal to the aggregate amount of all dividends payable during the year.

Charge of sums carried to dividends fund account.

Article 7.—Of the sums carried to the dividends fund account such as represent the dividends payable in respect of stock raised for general county purposes shall be charged to the general county account of the county fund, and such as represent the dividends payable in respect of stock raised for any special county purpose shall be charged to the special county account to which expenditure for that purpose is properly chargeable.

Payment and charge of dividends.

Article 8.—The County Council shall, from time to time, pay the dividends on the stock, and charge the same to the dividends fund account.

Redemption of Stock.

Payments to redemption fund account.

Article 9.—For redemption and extinction, or purchase and extinction, of the stock there shall be carried to an account of the county fund, entitled the Stock (Redemption) Fund Account (herein-after referred to as the redemption fund account) (*e*), a sum or sums equal to the aggregate amount of all sums payable in the year for redemption and extinction, or purchase and extinction, of the stock.

Charge of sums carried to redemption fund account.

Article 10.—Of the sums carried to the redemption fund account such as represent sums payable for the redemption or purchase of any amount of stock raised for general county purposes shall be charged to the general county account of the county fund, and such as represent sums payable for the redemption or purchase of stock raised for any special county purpose shall be charged to the special county account to which expenditure for that purpose is properly chargeable.

Amounts to be carried to redemption fund account.

Article 11.—(1.) (*f*) The several amounts to be carried to the redemption fund account (subject to any reduction thereof authorised

---

(*e*) As to the keeping of separate Stock (Dividends) Funds Accounts and Stock (Redemption) Funds Accounts for different classes of stock, see Article 1 (2) (3) of the amending order of 1897, *post*.

(*f*) As to cases in which clauses (1) and (4) of this article will not apply, see Article 3 of the amending regulations of 1897, *post*, p. 795.

by these Regulations) shall be determined by the provisions either of paragraph (a), paragraph (b), or paragraph (c) of this clause, according as the Board shall determine :— Regulations

(a.) The said amounts shall be the same as would under the statutory borrowing power have been payable towards paying off the money represented by the stock, or to a sinking fund for the repayment of the same, if the same had been raised otherwise than by the issue of stock; provided that if the moneys payable as aforesaid were not required to be accumulated, the Board may determine what the several amounts to be carried to the redemption fund account shall be, having regard to the rate at which the moneys carried to the redemption fund account will be accumulated.

(b.) The said amounts shall be such amounts as will, with accumulations at compound interest at a rate per centum per annum to be determined by the Board, be sufficient, after payment of all expenses, to purchase the amount of stock at par within the time within which, under the statutory borrowing power, the money represented by the stock is to be repaid: Provided that the board may from time to time, if they think fit, alter such rate of interest.

(c.) If the statutory borrowing power in exercise of which the stock is issued does not determine the amounts to be paid towards paying off or to a sinking fund in respect of the money to be borrowed thereunder, or the period within which the same is to be repaid, or if the board approve a scheme for the consolidation of all or any of the loans to be raised by the issue of stock, the several amounts to be carried to the redemption fund account shall be such amounts as will, with accumulations at compound interest at a rate per centum per annum to be determined by the Board, be sufficient, after payment of all expenses, to purchase the amount of stock at par within such time, not exceeding forty years from the first creation of the stock, as the Board shall determine; Provided that the Board may from time to time, if they think fit, alter such rate of interest.

(2.) If it appears to the Board at any time that any sum carried to the redemption fund account will not be sufficient to redeem the amount of stock in respect of which the same is carried to the said account within the time allowed for the continuance of the loan represented by the stock, the said sum shall be increased to such extent as the Board may direct; and the Board shall at any time have power to consent to the reduction of any sum to be carried to the redemption fund account as aforesaid, either temporarily or permanently, in any case in which it appears to the Board that the same would be more than sufficient to redeem the amount of stock in

Regulations respect of which it is carried to the said account within the time allowed for the continuance of the loan represented by the stock; and if at any time the amount carried to the redemption fund account is, in the opinion of the Board, sufficient, with the accumulations to arise thereon, to redeem the stock within the time or times allowed for the continuance of the loan or loans represented by the stock, the County Council may, with the consent of the Board, cease to carry any sums to the redemption fund account.

(3.) If the County Council create and issue stock for the purpose of defraying the expenses of the creation and issue of any stock, the amount of stock created and issued for that purpose shall be redeemable and extinguished after and within the same periods after and within which the stock is to be redeemed and extinguished for the purpose of defraying the expenses of which it was so created and issued; and, for the purpose of determining the sums to be carried to the redemption fund account as aforesaid, the amount of the said expenses shall be deemed to be the amount of a loan authorised by a statutory borrowing power, and required to be paid off within the period within which the stock is to be extinguished.

(4.) (*g*) If, before the expiration of the period allowed for the continuance of any loan represented by an amount of stock, the County Council apply, in the redemption or purchase and extinction of stock, to that or any less amount, any part of the money carried to the redemption fund account, then a sum equal to the interest which the part of such moneys so applied would have produced at the rate per centum on which the payments of the redemption fund account are calculated shall, in each year, until the expiration of the said period allowed for the continuance of the loan, be carried to the redemption fund account, and charged to the account of the county fund properly chargeable with the sums carried to the redemption fund account in respect of the amount of stock aforesaid.

Provided that if any amount of stock extinguished by application of part of the moneys carried to the redemption fund account as aforesaid is purchased by the County Council at a rate exceeding One Hundred Pounds sterling for One Hundred Pounds stock, the interest to be carried to the redemption fund account under this part of this Article shall be calculated as if only One Hundred Pounds sterling had been applied out of such moneys for each One Hundred Pounds stock purchased, and the County Council shall either carry to the redemption fund account, during the year in which such purchase is made, an additional sum or sums equal in amount to the sum or sums paid in excess of the said rate for the purchase of stock in such year, or shall, during such year and each succeeding year until the expiration of the period allowed for the continuance of the loan represented by the stock extinguished, carry to the redemption fund account such additional sum as the Board shall approve; and such

(*g*) See note (*f*), *ante*, p. 768.

additional sum or sums shall be charged to the account of the county fund properly chargeable with the sums carried to the redemption fund account in respect of that amount of stock.

Regulations

* * * * * (*h*).

Investment and application of sums carried to redemption fund account.

ARTICLE 12.—The sum standing to the credit of the redemption fund account shall from time to time be applied by the County Council in redeeming stock according to the terms of issue and purchasing stock for extinction, and, pending such application, shall be invested on statutory securities, and the interest and annual proceeds arising from those securities shall be carried to the redemption fund account, and be invested and accumulated in like manner.

Extinction of stock redeemed or purchased.

ARRICLE 13.—The County Council on redeeming or purchasing any stock shall forthwith pass a resolution directing the stock so redeemed or purchased to be cancelled by the registrar, and on such cancellation the same and all dividends thereon which have not already become payable shall be and the same are by virtue of these Regulations extinguished.

CONVERSION OF OTHER SECURITIES INTO STOCK.

Payment off or substitution for existing securities.

ARTICLE 14.—(1.) Where any mortgage, bond, debenture, stock, annuity, rentcharge, or other security granted or created before or after the date of these Regulations under any statutory borrowing power is outstanding or payable, and the County Council have power, with the consent of the holder of that security, or otherwise, to pay off the amount thereby secured or represented, or to redeem the same, they may pay off or redeem the security accordingly with money raised by stock, or they may, with the consent of the holder thereof, issue stock in substitution for the security.

Provided that as regards any loans specified for the purposes of this provision in an Order of the Board, the Board may, in such Order, require the foregoing powers of this Article to be exercised as far as practicable *pari passu* with respect to all such loans and in such a manner as not to extend the period approved under these Regulations for the payment off of such loans on consolidation.

(2.) The County Council may in every such case make such reasonable payment as they may think fit to the holder of any security for his consent, or for otherwise compensating him for the payment off or redemption of or substitution for his security, and any such payment may be either in money or stock, or partly in one and partly in the other (*i*).

(*h*) For the provision substituted for the last paragraph of this article, see Art. 5 of the amending regulations, *post*, p. 796.

(*i*) Stock may be issued for the purpose of raising money to be paid under this clause, but subject to the provisions of Art. 4 of the amending regulations of 1897.

Regulations

(3.) In every such case of payment off redemption or substitution the County Council shall forthwith carry to the redemption fund account the whole or a proportionate part (as the case may require) of any money and securities forming part of any sinking fund applicable to the discharge of the security, and also such further sum, if any, as may be necessary to make the money and securities so paid and transferred equivalent to the amount which should have been in such sinking fund, or should have been paid off, in respect of the security for the payment off or redemption of which or in substitution for which the stock is created.

(4.) Where the holder of the security is one of the persons described in Section 7 of the Lands Clauses Consolidation Act, 1845, and by that Act enabled to sell land thereunder, that person may consent to payment or redemption of, or substitution for, the money secured or represented by that security, and may accept money for giving that consent as if the person so consenting were the absolute owner of that security, and that person is hereby indemnified for so doing, and his receipt shall be a good discharge for the same.

(5.) Money received by the holder of any security as authorised by this Article, and stock issued to him in substitution for any security, shall be subject to the same trusts, powers, testamentary and other dispositions, provisions, and incumbrances, as the money secured or represented by the security was subject to, immediately before the payment off redemption or substitution, and every deed, or other instrument, or any testamentary, or other disposition, shall take effect with reference to the whole, or a proportionate part of the money or stock received, or substituted, as the case may be.

Effect on Borrowing Powers.

Extinction or suspension of power.

Article 15.—On the issue of any portion of stock the statutory borrowing power, in exercise whereof that stock is issued, shall be affected as follows ; namely,—

(a.) If the stock is issued for the whole term limited for the continuance of any loan, or for the continuance of payment of or in respect of any mortgage, bond, debenture, stock, annuity, rentcharge, rent, or other security granted or created under that statutory borrowing power, then that power, to the extent of the money raised by that stock (except in the case herein-after provided for), shall be and the same is by virtue of these Regulations extinguished ; but

(b.) If the stock is issued for part only of that term, then so much of the money raised by that stock as represents the balance which should be outstanding may be re-borrowed by the County Council for the residue of that term, or any part thereof, and so from time to time.

APPLICATION OF MONEY RAISED.

Regulations

General application of money from stock.

ARTICLE 16.—Money raised by stock shall be applied for purposes for which money raiseable under the statutory borrowing power, in exercise whereof the stock is issued, ought by law to be applied, and not otherwise.

Provided that if, after the raising of any money by stock under these Regulations, it shall be found that any part of such money is not required for the purposes to which it is applicable as aforesaid, the County Council shall carry the same to the redemption fund account or apply such money for such other purposes for which the County Council shall have a statutory borrowing power as the Board may, by Order, approve; and if any such money is so carried to the redemption fund account the statutory borrowing power in exercise whereof the stock represented by the money so paid was issued shall, to the amount of the money so paid, be deemed not to have been extinguished; and if any such money is applied for some other purpose as aforesaid the stock represented by the money so applied shall be deemed to have been created and issued under these regulations in exercise or part exercise of *such last-mentioned statutory borrowing power* (*k*).

Temporary investment of money raised by stock.

ARTICLE 17.—The County Council shall from time to time, if required by the Board, and may at any time invest temporarily on statutory securities any sum raised by stock and not for the time being applied to or required for the undertaking or purpose for which it is raised.

REGISTRATION AND CERTIFICATES.

Appointment of registrar

ARTICLE 18.—(1). The County Council shall, on and subject to such terms and instructions not inconsistent with any provision of these Regulations as they think expedient, appoint and keep appointed an officer of the County Council, or any other person, or the Bank of England, or any other bank, or any banking or other company, as registrar for all or any of the purposes of these Regulations (in these Regulations referred to as the registrar).

(2.) The County Council in relation to these Regulations and the registrar shall respectively be deemed a banker within the Bankers Books Evidence Act, 1879.

Stock register.

ARTICLE 19.—(1.) The registrar shall keep books, in which shall be entered the names and addresses of holders from time to time of stock, and the amounts held by them (in these Regulations referred to as the stock register).

(*k*) For the words in italics read "the statutory borrowing power which the County Council could exercise for such other purpose": Art. 6 of the amending regulations of 1897.

Regulations

(2.) The stock register shall be *primâ facie* evidence of any matter entered therein in accordance with these Regulations, and of the title of the persons entered therein as holders of stock.

Certificates of proprietorship of stock.

ARTICLE 20.—(1.) On demand of a holder of stock the County Council may, if they think fit, give to him a certificate of the proprietorship thereof, under their common seal, specifying the amount of stock to which he is entitled (in these Regulations referred to as a stock certificate).

(2.) A stock certificate shall be *primâ facie* evidence of the title of the person therein named, his executors, administrators, successors, or assigns, to the stock therein specified; but the want of a stock certificate, if such want be accounted for to the satisfaction of the County Council, shall not prevent the holder of stock from disposing of and transferring the same.

(3.) If a stock certificate is worn out or damaged the County Council, on production thereof, may cancel it, and give a similar stock certificate to the party in whom the property in the stock certificate and in the stock therein specified is then vested.

(4.) If a stock certificate is lost or destroyed the County Council, on proof thereof to their satisfaction, may give a similar stock certificate to the party entitled to the certificate lost or destroyed.

(5.) An entry of the issue of a stock certificate or a substituted certificate, as the case may be, shall be made in the stock register.

TRANSFER.

Power for stockholder to transfer.

ARTICLE 21.—Subject to the provisions of these Regulations, every stockholder may transfer all or any part of his stock in books or by deed.

Transfer in books.

ARTICLE 22.—(1.) If and where the resolution for creation of any portion of stock makes the same transferable in books and not by deed, the provisions of this Article shall apply and have effect, but not otherwise.

(2.) The registrar shall keep books wherein transfers of stock so transferable shall be entered (in these Regulations referred to as the stock transfer books).

(3.) Every such entry shall be conceived in proper words for the purpose of transfer, and shall be signed by the party making the transfer, or, if he is absent, by his agent thereunto lawfully authorised in writing under his hand attested by a witness.

(4.) Where the Bank of England are the registrar they may, if they think fit, require that the agent be so authorised by power of attorney under the hand and seal of the party making the transfer, attested by two or more credible witnesses.

(5.) The person to whom a transfer is made may, if he thinks fit, underwrite his acceptance thereof.

(6.) Except as otherwise provided by Act of Parliament, and subject to the provisions of these Regulations respecting any portion of stock which the resolution for creation thereof makes transferable by deed and not in books, no mode of transferring stock other than that prescribed in this Article shall be good in law. **Regulations**

ARTICLE 23.—(1.) If and where the resolution for creation of any portion of stock makes the same transferable by deed, and not in books, the provisions of this Article shall apply and have effect, but not otherwise. **Transfer by deed.**

(2.) Every transfer of stock so transferable shall be by deed.

(3.) The deed of transfer shall relate only to the transfer, and shall not contain any recital, trust, power, or proviso whatsoever.

(4.) The deed of transfer, when duly executed, shall be delivered to and kept by the registrar, and the registrar shall enter a memorial thereof in a book to be called the register of transfers of stock, and shall endorse on the deed of transfer a notice of that entry.

(5.) * * * * * (*l*)

(6.) Until the deed of transfer has been so delivered to the registrar, the County Council or the registrar shall not be affected thereby, and the purchaser of the stock shall not be entitled to receive any dividend thereon.

ARTICLE 24.—(1.) The registrar, before allowing any transfer of stock, may, if the circumstances of the case appear to him to make it expedient, require evidence of the title of any person claiming a right to make the transfer. **Evidence on transfer.**

(2.) That evidence shall be a statutory declaration of one or more competent persons, or of such other nature as the registrar, with the approval of the County Council, may require.

ARTICLE 25.—(1.) The registrar, with the approval of the County Council, may, as regards any portion of stock, close the stock transfer books or the register of transfers of stock (as the case may be) on any day in the month next before that in which dividends on that portion of stock are payable, but so that the books be not at any time kept closed for more than fifteen days. **Closing of transfer books.**

(2.) The persons who on the day of such closing are inscribed as stockholders shall, as between them and their transferees of stock, be entitled to the dividend next payable thereon.

ARTICLE 26.—Unless the County Council have compounded for stamp duty, all stock shall, notwithstanding anything in any resolution of the County Council, be transferable by deed, and not in books, and every deed of transfer of stock transferable by deed shall be duly stamped, and the consideration shall be truly stated therein. **Stamp duty on transfers.**

(*l*) For the clause substituted for this clause see Art. 7 of the amending regulations of 1897, *post*, p. 797.

Regulations

TRANSMISSION.

Transmission on death.

ARTICLE 27.—(1.) The interest of a deceased stockholder in stock shall be transferable by his executors or administrators, notwithstanding any specific bequest thereof.

(2.) Where two or more persons are registered as owners of any stock, such persons shall be deemed to be joint owners with right of survivorship between them.

(3.) The County Council or the registrar shall not be required to allow any executors or administrators to transfer any stock until the probate of the will or the letters of administration to the estate of the deceased has or have been left with the registrar for registration, and may require all the executors who have proved the will to join in the transfer.

Transmission otherwise than by death of holder or transfer in books or by deed.

ARTICLE 28.—(1.) If the interest in any stock has become transmitted by any lawful means other than a transfer in books or by deed, or than the death of a stockholder, satisfactory evidence of the transmission shall be furnished to the registrar by a statutory declaration of one or more competent persons, or in such other manner as the registrar may, with the approval of the County Council, require.

(2.) The name of the person entitled under the transmission shall be entered in the stock register.

(3.) Until such evidence has been furnished, the County Council or the registrar shall not be affected by the transmission, and no person claiming by virtue thereof shall be entitled to receive any dividend on the stock.

(4.) In this Article the term transmission includes any case of apparent transmission in consequence of the change of name of the stockholder, although the actual ownership of the stock may remain unaltered.

DIVIDENDS.

Payment of dividends.

ARTICLE 29.—The County Council shall pay by the registrar the dividends on stock.

Dividends to executors, etc.

ARTICLE 30.—The County Council or the registrar shall not be required to pay any executors or administrators any dividend on stock held by their testator or intestate until the probate of the will or the letters of administration has or have been left with the registrar for registration.

Evidence of title.

ARTICLE 31.—The registrar before paying any dividend on any stock may, if the circumstances of the case appear to him to make it expedient, require evidence of the title of any person claiming a right to receive the dividend, and that evidence shall be a statutory declaration of competent persons, or of such other nature as the registrar, with the approval of the County Council, may require.

Regulations — Dividends to joint holders.

Article 32.—(1.) Where more persons than one are registered as joint holders of any stock, any one of them may give an effectual receipt for any dividend thereon, unless notice to the contrary has been given to the registrar by any other of them.

(2.) Where stock is standing in the name of an infant or person of unsound mind jointly with any person not under legal disability, a letter of attorney for receipt of the dividends on the stock shall be sufficient authority in that behalf if given under the hand and seal of the person not under disability attested by two or more credible witnesses, but the registrar before acting on the letter of attorney may, if he think fit, require proof to his satisfaction of the alleged infancy or unsoundness of mind by a statutory declaration of one or more competent persons.

Dividend warrants by post.

Article 33.—(1.) Where a stockholder desires to have his dividends sent to him by post, he may make a request for that purpose to the registrar in writing, signed by him in a form approved by the County Council, and shall give to the registrar an address in the United Kingdom, or in the Channel Islands, or the Isle of Man, to which the letters containing the warrants are from time to time to be sent.

(2.) The posting by the registrar of a letter containing a dividend warrant addressed to a stockholder at his request at the address so given by him shall, as respects the liability of the County Council and of the registrar, be equivalent to the delivery of the warrant to the stockholder himself.

(3.) Every warrant so sent by post shall be deemed a cheque, and the County Council and the registrar shall, in relation thereto, be deemed a banker within the Bills of Exchange Act, 1882.

(4.) Provided that this Article shall not apply to cases to which the provisions of Section 4 of the National Debt Act, 1889, apply.

Stock Certificates with Coupons to Bearer.

Provisions respecting stock certificates with coupons to bearer.

Article 34.—(1.) On demand of a stockholder, the registrar may issue to the stockholder a stock certificate to bearer, that is to say, a certificate of title to his stock or any part thereof, entitling the bearer to the stock therein specified, and transferable by delivery with coupons entitling the bearer of the coupons to the dividends on the stock, but so that no such certificate or coupons shall give a title to dividends beyond the time limited for redemption of the stock.

(2.) A stock certificate to bearer shall not be issued in respect of any sum of stock other than Ten Pounds or a multiple of Ten Pounds.

(3.) No trustee shall apply for, purchase, take, or hold a stock certificate to bearer unless he is in express words authorised to do so by the instrument creating his trust, and any contravention of this provision by a trustee shall be deemed a breach of trust; but this provision shall not impose on the County Council or the registrar

Regulations an obligation to inquire or to take notice whether a person applying for or holding a stock certificate to bearer is or is not a trustee, or subject the County Council or the registrar to any liability in case of his, with or without notice, issuing to a trustee a stock certificate to bearer, or invalidate any stock certificate to bearer issued.

(4.) Where a stock certificate to bearer is outstanding the stock represented thereby shall cease to be transferable in books or by deed.

(5.) The bearer of a stock certificate to bearer may, on delivery up to the registrar of the certificate, and of all unpaid coupons belonging thereto, require to be entered in the stock register as the holder of the stock described in the certificate under which he derives title, and thereupon such stock certificate and coupons shall be cancelled and the stock shall be re-entered in the register as transferable, and shall become and again be transferable in the stock transfer books or by deed, as the case may require, and shall, as regards the mode of payment of the dividends thereon, be in the like condition as if no stock certificate to bearer had been issued in respect thereof.

(6.) The coupons issued with a stock certificate to bearer shall comprise the dividends to be paid in respect of the stock therein specified for such period as the County Council approve.

(7.) At the end of that period fresh coupons may be issued for such further period as the County Council approve, and so for successive periods during the continuance in force of the stock certificate, but the County Council may direct the registrar, in lieu of issuing fresh coupons in respect of any stock certificate, to give in exchange a fresh stock certificate with coupons.

(8.) Payment to the bearer of a coupon of the amount expressed therein shall be a full discharge to the County Council and to the registrar from all liability in respect of that coupon and the dividend represented thereby.

(9.) Where the Bank of England are the registrar coupons shall be payable at the chief establishment of the Bank at the expiration of three clear days from the day of presentation, and at any branch establishment of the Bank situate more than ten miles from the chief establishment at the expiration of five clear days from the day of presentation.

(10.) If a stock certificate to bearer or coupon is worn out or damaged, the registrar, on production and delivery up thereof, may cancel it and issue a new certificate or coupon.

(11.) If a stock certificate to bearer or coupon is lost or destroyed, the registrar may issue a new certificate or coupon on receiving indemnity to the satisfaction of the County Council against the claims of all persons deriving title under the certificate or coupon lost or destroyed.

(12.) All coupons issued under these Regulations in respect of any stock certificate to bearer shall, for the purposes of the Acts relating to stamp duties, be deemed to have been attached to and issued with such stock certificate. Regulations

(13.) Stock specified in a stock certificate to bearer shall be charged on the same securities, and be subject to the same powers of redemption and other powers, and save as regards the mode of transfer and of payments of dividends thereon, and save so far as a stock certificate to bearer is a negotiable instrument, shall be subject to the same incidents in all respects as if that stock had continued to be registered in the stock register as transferable in books or by deed.

General.

Nature of stock: notice of trusts.

Article 35.—(1.) Stock is personal property.

(2.) Stock is not liable to foreign attachment by the custom of London or otherwise.

(3.) No notice of any trust, express, implied, or constructive, in respect of any stock, or of any stock certificate to bearer or coupon, shall be entered in the stock register, or in any other book kept by the County Council or the registrar, or be receivable by the County Council or the registrar, or affect the registrar or the County Council through the registrar or otherwise.

Receiver.

Article 36.—(1.) If at any time any dividend due on any stock remain unpaid for two months after demand in writing the person entitled thereto may apply to the High Court for a receiver, and the Court may, if it thinks fit, appoint a receiver on such terms as it thinks fit.

(2.) The receiver shall have the like power of collecting, receiving, recovering, and applying all money which ought to be carried under these Regulations to the redemption fund account or to the dividends fund account, and of assessing, making, and recovering all rates and contributions for the purpose of obtaining the same, as the County Council or any officer thereof would or might have, and such other powers and such duties as the Court thinks fit, and shall apply all money so collected, after payment of expenses and costs, as the Court directs, for purposes of these Regulations.

(3.) The Court may at any time discharge the receiver, and shall have full jurisdiction over him and all persons interested in his acts.

Protection of holders of stock.

Article 37.—A person taking or holding stock shall not be concerned to inquire or to take notice whether the creation or issue thereof was or was not within any statutory borrowing power of the County Council, or otherwise in accordance with these regulations, or whether or not the County Council or any meeting thereof was properly constituted or convened, or whether or not the proceedings at any meeting of the County Council were legal or regular, or to see to the application of any money raised by stock, or be answerable for any loss or misapplication thereof.

Regulations

Annual Return to Local Government Board.

Article 38.—(1.) Once in every year, at a time appointed by the Board, the Clerk to the County Council shall send to the Board an abstract of the accounts of the County Council relating to stock and of the redemption fund account and subordinate accounts in a form prescribed by the Board: and such abstract shall be verified by a statutory declaration of an officer of the County Council, if and as may be required by the Board, and such abstract shall be made up to such date in each year as the Board may determine.

(2.) Unless and until the Board in any case by Order otherwise direct, the said abstract shall—

(a.) Be made up to the Thirty-first day of March in each year;

(b.) Be forwarded to the said Board within forty-two days after that day;

(c.) Be in the form set forth in the Schedule B. to these Regulations; and

(d.) Be verified by a statutory declaration of the Clerk to the County Council, or of such other officer of the County Council as the Board may, on the application of the Council, approve.

(3.) In case of wilful default therein by the Clerk to or other officer of the County Council, the said Clerk or other officer shall on each occasion be liable to a penalty not exceeding Twenty Pounds, and every fine under this Article shall be recoverable summarily on the prosecution of the Board, and not otherwise.

(4.) If by any such abstract or otherwise it appears to the Board that the County Council have failed to comply with any requisition of these Regulations, or of any order of the Board thereunder, in relation to any payment, application, or investment, or otherwise in relation to stock or the redemption fund account, the Board may by Order require the County Council to make good the default within a time therein limited; and if the default be in respect of any sum to be carried to the redemption fund account, or the misapplication of any part of the moneys carried to that account, the Board may by Order direct that the sum in such Order mentioned, not exceeding double the amount in respect of which default has been made, shall be carried to the redemption fund account and be invested and applied in like manner as required by these Regulations in regard to other sums carried to that account.

Unclaimed dividends.

Article 39.—(1.) If at any time any dividend on any stock is unclaimed at the time for payment thereof the same shall, nevertheless, on demand at any subsequent time whatsoever, be paid to the person showing his right thereto, but without interest in the meantime.

(2.) Where any dividend remains unclaimed for five years from the time for payment thereof the County Council shall cause notice thereof to be sent by post in a registered letter addressed to the stockholder named in their books by the description and at the address therein appearing, and so at the expiration of three other successive periods of five years.

Regulations

(3.) At the end of every successive period of five years from the day when the first dividend becomes payable on stock first issued, the County Council shall publish an advertisement in a newspaper circulating in their County, stating what, if any, dividends on stock have then been unclaimed for more than four years, and the names and addresses appearing in the stock register of the persons entitled to such dividends when the same became due.

(4.) At the end of every successive period of ten years from the day when the first dividend becomes payable on stock first issued the County Council, unless it has been otherwise agreed between them and the registrar, may require the registrar to repay to them all dividends unclaimed during that period and then in his hands, and the County Council shall cause the same or any other dividends unclaimed during that period to be carried to the dividends fund account, and may deal therewith as they are by these Regulations empowered to deal with moneys carried to that account, without prejudice, nevertheless, to the rights of any person to those dividends.

Unclaimed stock.

Article 40.—(1.) If at the end of the period within which any stock is required to be extinguished the County Council, by reason of the holder of any of such stock not being forthcoming, or by reason of any doubt as to the ownership of any such stock, shall not be able to redeem, extinguish, and cancel such stock as required by the Regulations herein-before contained, the County Council shall invest on statutory securities a sum equal to the nominal value of all such stock as cannot be redeemed as aforesaid, such sum to be dealt with as herein-after prescribed, and thereupon such stock shall be deemed to have been extinguished.

(2.) If before the end of the period within which any stock is required to be extinguished the County Council shall have extinguished all the stock, except such as cannot be redeemed as aforesaid, the County Council may invest on statutory securities a sum equal to the nominal value of all such stock as cannot be redeemed as aforesaid, such sum to be dealt with as herein-after prescribed, and thereupon such stock shall be deemed to have been extinguished.

(3.) Any sums invested by the County Council as aforesaid shall, unless sold for the purpose of satisfying any claim in respect of the stock represented by the same, be kept invested on statutory securities for a period of ten years, after which time the County Council may appropriate the said sums and any accumulations thereon for such purposes as the Board may approve, without prejudice, nevertheless, to the rights of any person to the said sums or any part thereof.

Saving for power to borrow otherwise.

Article 41.—Nothing in these Regulations shall affect any power of the County Council to raise otherwise than by stock any money

Regulations — which they do not think fit to raise by stock, but whenever, from time to time after the date of the first creation of stock, the County Council raise money otherwise than by stock, they shall cause to be given to each lender of money so raised notice in writing, signed by the Clerk or other authorised officer of the County Council, of the equality of charge which stock has or may have by virtue of these Regulations.

Saving for power of revocation.

ARTICLE 42.—The County Council may by resolution revoke at any time, in whole or in part, any resolution for creation of stock theretofore passed by the County Council if and as far as the same has not been acted on by the issue of stock thereunder, and notice of such revocation shall forthwith be given to the Board,

Saving for other obligations.

ARTICLE 43.—Except as in these Regulations expressly provided nothing in these Regulations shall relieve the County Council from any obligation imposed on them in relation to any statutory borrowing power by any Act of Parliament under or by which that power for the time being exists or is regulated.

Saving for power to sell lands, etc.

ARTICLE 44.—(1.) Nothing in these Regulations shall affect any power or duty of the County Council to sell, lease, or otherwise dispose of any land or property of the County Council, or to apply any purchase money or other money arising thereby in discharge of any charge on that land or property, or the revenues thereof, other than the charge of stock, or affect any claim of any person under such first-mentioned charge.

(2.) That land or property shall, in the hands of the purchaser or other person taking the same under the sale, lease, or other disposition, be by virtue of these regulations absolutely freed from the charge of stock, and he shall not be concerned to see to the application of that purchase money or other money, or be answerable for any loss or misapplication thereof.

Saving for existing securities.

ARTICLE 45.—Nothing in or done under these Regulations shall affect any security or charge created or granted or payable before and subsisting at the date of the first creation of any stock, and the County Council shall, whenever required by the holder of any security or charge aforesaid, apply all such money, do all such acts, exercise all such powers, collect all such money, and assess, make, and levy all such rates and contributions as they would or ought to have applied, done, exercised, collected, assessed, made, and levied for his benefit and security if these Regulations had not been prescribed.

Forgery.

ARTICLE 46.—(1.) Stock shall be deemed capital stock of a body corporate within the Act of the Session of the twenty-fourth and twenty-fifth years of the reign of Her present Majesty (chapter ninety-eight), "to consolidate and amend the statute law of England and Ireland relating to indictable offences by forgery."

(2.) A stock certificate to bearer and a coupon connected therewith shall be deemed a stock certificate and coupon within the Forgery Act, 1870.

Regulations

ARTICLE 47.—Any determination or directions of the Board under these Regulations may be signified by Order under their Seal, and any Order of the Board may contain such provisions as the Board think necessary or proper for giving effect thereto, and shall be enforceable by writ of mandamus to be obtained by the Board out of the High Court, and may be from time to time cancelled or varied by the Board, as the circumstances of the case may require, but the Board shall not make any such Order without first hearing the County Council, if desirous of being heard, which hearing may be in the form of a public inquiry, with or without a published report, or in such other form as the Board, having regard to the circumstances, think just and expedient, and Sections 294 and 296 of the Public Health Act, 1875, shall apply to hearings, inquiries, and other proceedings to which this Article relates: Provided that the costs of inquiries as to which the Board may make Orders under the said Section 294 may include such reasonable sum, not exceeding three guineas a day, as the Board may determine, for the services of any Inspector holding an inquiry.

Orders of Local Government Board.

ARTICLE 48.—Where the Bank of England are the registrar, they may, with the sanction of the County Council, from time to time issue any forms that may be required for carrying into effect the provisions of these Regulations, and may also from time to time make any Regulations that are not inconsistent with these Regulations relative to the following things, and, when made, may alter, vary, or repeal any such Regulations, and make other Regulations instead thereof, or in addition thereto, and any such Regulations for the time being in force shall be duly observed:—

Regulations by Bank of England.

(a.) The period for which coupons are to be given:

(b.) The mode in which the Bank are to act in issuing stock certificates to bearer, or entering in the transfer books the bearers of stock certificates to bearer:

(c.) The mode of proving the title of or identifying any person applying for a stock receipt or stock certificate, or stock certificate to bearer:

(d.) With respect to anything necessary for carrying into effect the provisions of these Regulations which relate to or affect the Bank.

ARTICLE 49.—The forms given in the Schedule A. to these Regulations may be used for the purposes therein indicated, and the same, or forms to the like effect, with such variations or additions as circumstances require, shall be effectual for those purposes.

Forms.

ARTICLE 50.—Fees not exceeding those specified in the said Schedule A. may be taken by or on behalf of the County Council in the cases therein mentioned.

Fees.

Regulations

Expenses.

Article 51.—(1.) The expenses incurred by the County Council in or about the creation and issue of any amount of stock, *including any sum paid by them for composition for stamp duty thereon and any other expenses* (m) properly chargeable to capital, shall be deemed money raiseable under a statutory borrowing power.

(2.) Expenses of bookkeeping and management and other current expenses from time to time incurred by the County Council in the execution of these Regulations shall be defrayed as the ordinary expenses of the County Council are or may be defrayed, and shall be charged to the several Accounts of the County Fund in such proportions as the County Council, having regard to all the circumstances, may from time to time determine.

SCHEDULES.

SCHEDULE A.

Forms.

(A.)

Resolutions on Creation of Stock.

County of [ ].
[, 189 .]

At a meeting of the County Council of [ ] holden on [day, the day of , 189] at [ ] o'clock in the noon in the [ ].

Present :

].

Resolved first—

That, subject to the regulations of the Local Government Board prescribed under the Local Government Act, 1888, the County Council do hereby in exercise of their powers create stock to be called [ ] Stock, and to be issued to an amount which shall be sufficient for the following purposes, but not exceeding [ ] pounds (£) :—

A. For raising the following sums (amounting in the aggregate to the sum of pounds which has not been raised), that is to say :—

(1.) The sum of pounds on account of the money which the County Council have authority to raise by borrowing under the powers conferred upon them by the [ ] for the purchase money for [ ] and the cost of re-construction of portions thereof ;

(2.) The sum of pounds on account of the money which the County Council have authority to raise by borrowing under the powers conferred upon them by the [ ] for the cost of construction of [ ];

(3.) The sum of pounds on account of the money which the County Council have authority to raise by borrowing under the powers conferred upon them by the [ ] for the construction of [ ];

(4.) The sum of pounds on account of the money which the County Council have authority to raise by borrowing under the powers conferred upon them by the [ ] for the purposes of [ ].

(m) For the words in italics read "so far as they are," Art. 8 of the amending regulations of 1897.

Schedule A.

B. For raising instead of re-borrowing the sum of pounds required by the County Council for the purpose of paying off when due sums amounting to pounds which will fall due before the [, 189], being a portion of their debts now subsisting on the security of outstanding securities granted by the [ ] for raising money for the purposes of the following Acts (that is to say) :—

and which sums the County Council are under those Acts authorised to re-borrow.

C. For raising the sum of pounds for paying off or redeeming statutory securities granted by the [ ] under the following Acts and now outstanding (that is to say) :—

D. For the purpose of issuing stock in substitution for statutory securities granted by the [ ] under the following Acts and now outstanding (that is to say) :—

Resolved secondly :—

That such stock shall be issued at the price, and shall bear the dividends, and be transferable in the manner herein-after specified (that is to say) :—

A. The minimum price of issue to be [£] per cent., the first dividend to be payable on the [1st January 189];

B. Tenders for stock to be made to . A deposit of 5 per cent. on the amount of stock tendered for to be paid at at the time of the delivery of the tender ;

C. The dates for the further payments on account of the said tenders when accepted to be as follows :—On [Wednesday, the 20th day of October, 189 , so much of the amount tendered and accepted as when added to the deposit will leave £75. (sterling) to be paid for each £100. of stock. On Friday, the 26th day of November, 189 , 25 per cent. On Tuesday, the 11th day of January, 189 , 25 per cent. On Tuesday, the 1st day of March, 189 , 25 per cent.] In case of default in the payment of any instalment at its proper date the deposit and instalments previously paid will be liable to forfeiture :

D. Dividends at £ per cent. per annum, payable [quarterly];

E. Dividends on the total amount of stock (calculated from the 1st of October, 189), to be payable on the 1st January, 189 .

F. Stock certificates to bearer with coupons attached for the dividends payable 1st January, 189 , and 1st April, 189 , to be issued in exchange for the provisional receipts.

G. In the event of the receipt of tenders for a larger amount of stock than that proposed to be issued at or above the minimum price, the tenders at the lowest price accepted to be subject to proportionate diminution.

H. Stock to be issued in sums of not less than £10.

J. Stock to be transferable in books and not by deed. (*See, however, Article* 26.)

Resolved thirdly—

That such stock shall be redeemable as follows : *state terms.*

Resolved fourthly—

That such stock shall be redeemed or purchased and extinguished within a period of years from the creation of such stock.

Resolved fifthly—

That an agreement be entered into with the Commissioners of Inland Revenue for the payment to them of composition under the provisions of the Customs and Inland Revenue Act, 1887, for the stamp duty on transfers of stock issued under the foregoing resolutions.

Schedule A.

(B.)

Stock Receipt.

[ ] STOCK (£ per cent.)

Transfer days: Monday, Tuesday, Wednesday, Thursday, Friday, *Holidays excepted.*	RECEIVED this day of , 189 , of herein-after called the said transferee, the sum of being the consideration for interest or share in the [ ] STOCK (per cent.) transferable at the , and all my property and interest in, and right to, the same, and the dividends thereon, by this day transferred unto the said transferee. Witness hand Witness	The Proprietors to protect themselves from FRAUD are recommended to ACCEPT, by themselves or their attorneys, all TRANSFERS made to them. £ *s.* *d.*

[*Indorsement.*]

NOTICE TO HOLDERS OF [ ] STOCK (£ per cent.)

Payment of Dividends.

Dividends are due on [*the* 1*st January,* 1*st April,* 1*st July, and* 1*st October,*] unless the [1*st*] of either of these months falls on a Sunday, in which case the dividends will be payable on the following business day.

Dividends will be paid in one of the following modes :—

I. To the stockholders personally, or to their attorneys at the .

N.B.—Stockholders may arrange for the receipt of their dividends, free of charge, at [ ].

II. By transmission of dividend warrants by post, at the risk of the stockholder, under the following regulations :

1. Any stockholder residing within the United Kingdom, or in the Channel Islands, or the Isle of Man, who desires to have his dividend warrant sent to his address by post, must fill up a form of application, to be obtained at [ ].
2. In the case of joint accounts, the applications must be signed by all the members of the account, directing the warrant to be sent to one of them at a given address.
3. Post dividend warrants will be crossed & *Co.*, and will only be payable through a banker, They will be drawn to the order of the stockholder, and must be endorsed.

☞ Stockholders, whose warrants are sent by post, should give notice to [ ] if they are *not* received on the day on which they ought to be delivered ; but need not acknowledge those that arrive in due course.

Stock Certificates to Bearer.

Stock certificates to bearer, of the denominations of [£. 10 or any multiple of £. 10] with coupons for the quarterly dividends attached, may be obtained in exchange for inscribed stock, except in the case of stock held upon any trust.

(C.)

County Stock Certificate.

County of [ ].

Number

This is to certify that *A.B.* of [ ] is the proprietor of [ ] pounds of [ ] Stock subject to the regulations relating thereto.

Given under the common seal of the County Council of [ ] this [ ] day of [ ] [18].

Schedule A.

(D.)

Transfer in Books.

No.

Entered by

Witness to the identity of

[ ] STOCK (£ per cent,
this day of in the year of our Lord One thousand eight hundred and do assign and transfer interest or share in the [ ] STOCK (£ per cent.) transferable at the , and all my property and interest in, and right to, the same, and the dividends thereon, unto
Executors, administrators, or assigns. Witness hand
Witness
do freely and voluntarily accept the above stock transferred to
Witness

£	s.	d.

(E.)

Application for Issue of Power of Attorney.

, the day of , 189 . From *A.B.* and *C.D.* [*the registered stockholders*________________________________

____

____

£ [ ] STOCK (£ per cent.)

To *G.H.* [*the intended Attorney*]

____

____

____

Examined by	Dr. fol. Posted by	Cr. fol. Posted by	Transfer book.

(F.)

Power of Attorney for Sale and Transfer and for Receipt of Dividends.

Corporate Account.

[ ] STOCK.
ACCEPTANCE, SALE OF £ AND DIVIDENDS.

We
our attorneys and attorney
for us and in our name and on our behalf—

First—to ACCEPT all transfers made or to be made to us of any sum of [ ] Stock.

Secondly—to SELL and TRANSFER all or any part of the sum of said stock standing in our name in the books of the ;

Thirdly—to RECEIVE and GIVE RECEIPTS for all DIVIDENDS OR PAYMENTS due or to become due on any sum of the said stock from time to time standing in our name in the books of the

AND ALSO—to do whatever is necessary or proper to be done for the purposes aforesaid, or any of them.

Schedule A. In witness whereof we have hereunto affixed our corporate seal, this day of , in the year of our Lord one thousand eight hundred and

Sealed with the corporate seal and delivered in the presence of

N.B.—The execution of this letter must be attested by [two witnesses who are] not of the corporate body, and who must be present when the corporate seal is affixed.

Indorsement.

INSTRUCTIONS FOR EXECUTING THE WITHIN LETTER OF ATTORNEY.

Corporate Account.

The *date* must be inserted in *words* and not in figures.

The execution must be attested by [*two credible witnesses* who are] not of the corporate body, and who must add [their addresses and their qualities, professions, or occupations].

A *witness resident in a town* must give the No. of house as well as the name of the street.

If *clerks* or *servants* are witnesses they must give the names and addresses of their employers,

When a witness is a *female* she must state whether she is a *spinster*, *wife*, or *widow*; and if a *wife* she must give her husband's name, address and quality, profession, or occupation.

A *wife* is not a *valid witness* to the execution of this letter of attorney when her husband's name appears in the letter as attorney or transferee.

If any *alteration*, *interlineation*, *or erasure* be made in this letter of attorney, it must be particularly stated in the attestation, subscribed to by the witnesses, that such alteration, interlineation, or erasure was made previously to the execution of the letter.

I demand to act by this letter of attorney, this day of , 18 .

Witness

(G.)

Deed of Transfer.

County of [ ].

I, *A.B.*, of [ ] in consideration of the sum of [ ] pounds paid to me by *C.D.*, of [ ] (herein-after called the said transferee) do hereby transfer to the said transferee the sum of [ ] pounds [ ] stock standing [or part of the stock standing] in my name in the books of the County Council of [ ] to hold unto the said transferee, his executors, administrators, and assigns [*or* successors and assigns], subject to the several conditions on which I hold the same at the time of the execution hereof, and I, the said transferee, do hereby agree to take the said stock subject to the same conditions.

As witness our hands and seals the [ ] day of [ ].

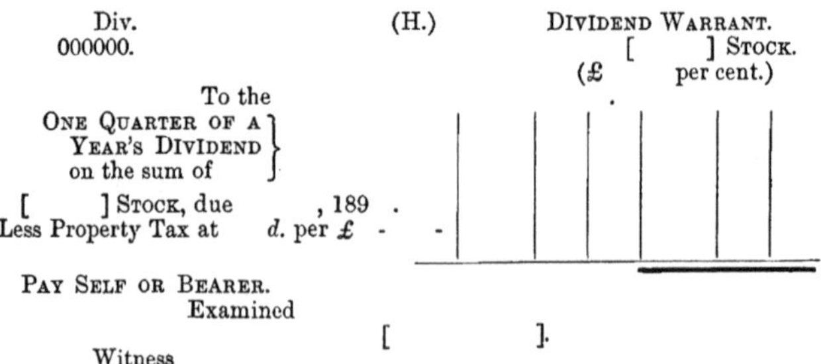

Div. (H.) DIVIDEND WARRANT.

000000. [ ] STOCK.

(£ per cent.)

To the

ONE QUARTER OF A YEAR'S DIVIDEND on the sum of

[ ] STOCK, due , 189 .

Less Property Tax at *d.* per £ - -

PAY SELF OR BEARER.

Examined

[ ].

Witness

(I.)

Schedule A.

Dividend Warrant by Post.

(1.)

[ ] STOCK.
(£ per cent.)

REQUEST FOR TRANSMISSION OF DIVIDEND WARRANTS BY POST.

To the

A sum of £ [ ] STOCK (£ per cent.) is now standing in name, as follows :— Amount. "my" or "our."

______

______ Names, addresses, and descriptions as recorded in the books.

______

______

As the person entitled to the dividends upon the above-mentioned amount of stock hereby authorise [ ] in the name of to draw upon the [ ] for the amount of the quarterly dividends due and to become due on the said amount of stock, or on the amount for the time being standing in name : "I" or "we." "myself" or "our *nominee*." "my" or "our."

And hereby request the said [ ] to send through the post at risk, and until further notice, the warrants so drawn to— "I" or "we." "my" or "our."

Name
Present address

If the account is a sole one, insert here the name and address of the stockholder; If the account is a joint one, insert here the name and address o one of the stockholders as *nominee*.

SIGN HERE.

In the case of joint stockholders, or of co-executors, all must sign.

______

______

______

______

Date 189 .

[*On second half-sheet of same Form.*]

This half-sheet is to be retained by the stockholder. Reference to it will often save unnecessary correspondence.

NOTICE TO HOLDERS OF [ ] STOCK
(£ PER CENT.)

Transmission of Dividend Warrants by Post.

Dividends upon the above-named stock may be transmitted through the post to the *stockholder* in sole accounts, and to *any one of the stockholders* in joint accounts, *at their risk* upon a form of request being duly filled up and forwarded to [ ]. (Forms are obtainable at [ ]).

N.B.—This arrangement does not apply to stockholders whose addresses are beyond the United Kingdom, the Channel Islands, and the Isle of Man.

Persons receiving dividends under letters of attorney cannot have the warrants for such dividends sent to them by post.

A separate form must be used for each separate holding of stock.

When forwarding a form of request, care should be taken to state the number of overdue dividends, if any.

Dividends are payable on [1*st January*, 1*st April*, 1*st July, and* 1*st October*].

When the [1*st*] happens on a Sunday, the dividends are not payable until the [2*nd*].

Forms of request may be delivered at any date, either by hand or through the post; but when received between the day on which the balance for a dividend is struck and the day on which the dividend is payable, the warrants for such *next* dividend will be forwarded as soon as possible, but the [ ] will not guarantee their being posted on the day before the dividend is payable.

For the dividend payable [1*st January*] the balance is struck on or about the [1*st December*].

For the dividend payable [1*st April*] the balance is struck on or about the [1*st March*].

Schedule A. For the dividend payable [1*st July*] the balance is struck on or about the [1*st June*].

For the dividend payable [1*st October*] the balance is struck on or about the [1*st September*].

Warrants for overdue dividends will be forwarded as promptly as possible, but not necessarily by return of post.

Any change of address of the stockholder in sole accounts, or of the nominee in joint accounts, should be notified at once to [ ]. When any such notification reaches less than a fortnight before the next dividend is due, there may be a delay of a few days in the delivery of the warrant for such next dividend.

In the absence of any notification to the contrary, it will be taken for granted that dividend warrants have duly reached their destinations. When they are not received on the correct day, notice should be given to the [ ] without delay.

As postal dividend warrants are made payable to order, they must be indorsed; they are crossed in blank, and consequently are only payable on presentation by a banker. ([ ] will not undertake to cross postal dividend warrants with the names of particular bankers).

Instructions to transmit warrants by post remain in force, although the stock may have been added to, or a part sold.

Stockholders selling stock by attorney, if they wish to continue to receive their dividends through the post, should instruct their bankers, or brokers, to obtain letters of attorney *for sale only*.

All communications with reference to postal dividend warrants should be addressed to [ ], and the postage should be prepaid.

(2.)

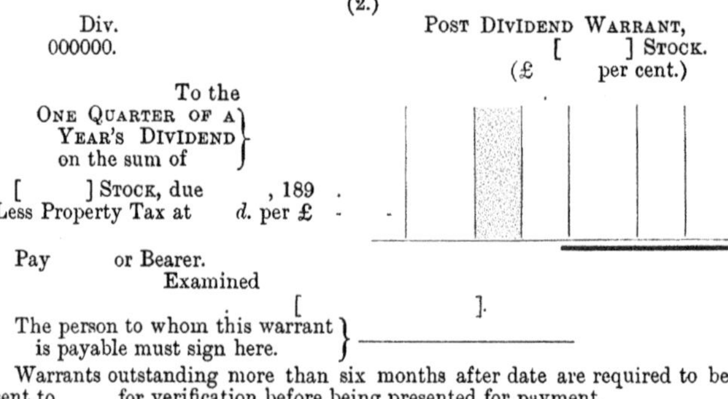
Div.
000000.

POST DIVIDEND WARRANT,
[ ] STOCK.
(£ per cent.)

To the

ONE QUARTER OF A YEAR'S DIVIDEND on the sum of

[ ] STOCK, due , 189 .
Less Property Tax at *d.* per £ - -

Pay or Bearer.

Examined

[ ].

The person to whom this warrant is payable must sign here. } ____________

Warrants outstanding more than six months after date are required to be sent to for verification before being presented for payment.

(K.)

Stock Certificate with Coupons to Bearer.

[ ] STOCK CERTIFICATE TO BEARER.

Dividend at £ per Cent. per annum.

£50 **A00000**

This is to certify that the bearer of this Certificate is entitled to FIFTY POUNDS [ ] Stock with dividend thereon at the rate of £ per Cent. per Annum transferable at [ ].

Dated , 189 .

Signed

Countersigned

A00000 **£50**

The Coupons attached to this Certificate are payable at [ ].

When the Coupons are exhausted this Certificate will be exchanged on presentation at [ ], for a new Certificate with fresh Coupons attached.

Schedule A.

[*Coupons.*]

5 Div. [ ] STOCK.	5 Div.	4 Div. [ ] STOCK.	4 Div.
Coupon for Shillings and Pence, (Less Income Tax) being Three Months' Dividend at £ Per Cent. per Annum. A 00000 Due [1*st January*, 1892] on Certificate for FIFTY POUNDS. [ ] STOCK. £0 0 0 *Payable at* .	[ ] STOCK. *Due* [1*st* *Jan.* 1892]. A 00000 £0 0 0	Coupon for Shillings and Pence, (Less Income Tax) being Three Months' Dividend at £ Per Cent. per Annum. A 00000 Due [1*st October*, 1891] on Certificate for FIFTY POUNDS. [ ] STOCK. £0 0 0 *Payable at* .	[ ] STOCK. *Due* [1*st* *Oct.* 1891]. A 00000 £0 0
3 Div. [ ] STOCK.	3 Div.	2 Div. [ ] STOCK.	2 Div.
Coupon for Shillings and Pence, (Less Income Tax) being Three Months' Dividend at £ Per Cent. per Annum. A 00000 Due [1*st July*, 1891] on Certificate for FIFTY POUNDS. [ ] STOCK. £0 0 0 *Payable at* .	[ ] STOCK. *Due* [1*st* *July*, 1891]. A 00000 £0 0 0	Coupon for Shillings and Pence, (Less Income Tax) being Three Months' Dividend at £ Per Cent. per Annum. A 00000 Due [1*st April*, 1891] on Certificate for FIFTY POUNDS. [ ] STOCK. £0 0 0 *Payable at* .	[ ] STOCK. *Due* [1*st* *April*, 1891]. A 00000 £0 0 0

FEES.

	£	s.	d.
On original issue of stock receipt or stock certificate - -	0	2	6
On any new stock certificate - - - - - - - -	0	2	6
On transfer including certificate - - - - - - -	0	5	0
On any issue of stock certificate to bearer in respect of every *ten* pounds of stock specified therein - - - - - -	0	0	6
On re-entry in stock register of stock specified in stock certificate to bearer - - - - - - - - - - -	0	5	0

SCHEDULE B.

Abstract of Stock and Redemption Fund Accounts, made in pursuance of Article 38 of the Regulations of the Local Government Board issued under Section 70 of the Local Government Act, 1888.

1. Name of County Council. 2. Name of Stock. 3. Period for which Abstract is made, viz., Year ended . 4. Rate of Interest on Stock. 5. Average Price of Issue of Stock.

BORROWING POWERS.									
Purpose in respect of which borrowing power is exercised	Act of Parliament, Provisional Order, or Sanction authorising borrowing.	Amount of borrowing power.	Amount of borrowing power authorised to be exercised by the issue of Stock.	Amount of borrowing power exercised by the issue of Stock up to commencement of Year.	Amount of borrowing power exercised by the issue of Stock up end of Year.	Total borrowing power exercised by the issue of Stock and otherwise up to end of Year.	Period within which Loan is repayable.	Date when first annual payment to Redemption Fund Account became due.	Rate of Interest prescribed for accumulation of sums carried to Redemption Fund Account.
6.	7.	8.	9.	10.	11.	12.	13.	14.	15.
1 to 28		£ s. d.	£ s. d.	£ s. d.	£ s. d.	£ s. d.			

—*Continued.*

STOCK ACCOUNT.					
Amount of Stock issued at commencement of Year, and in respect of which a sum has annually to be carried to Redemption Fund Account.	Amount of Stock issued during Year.	Amount of Stock extinguished up to commencement of Year.	Amount of Stock extinguished during Year.	Amount of Stock unextinguished at end of Year.	
16.	17.	18.	19.	20.	
£ s. d.	£ s. d.	£ s. d.	£ s. d.	£ s. d.	1 to 28

—*Continued.*

REDEMPTION FUND					
Amount, if any, received and carried to Redemption Fund Account during Year from sales of Surplus Land, etc.	Amount having formed part of any Sinking Fund, and carried to Redemption Fund Account during Year.	Amount carried to Redemption Fund Account during the Year as interest on investments.	Amount carried to Redemption Fund Account during the year as interest on part of the sums carried to that Account applied in extinction of Stock.	Amount carried to Redemption Fund Account during the Year and not included in previous Columns.	Fund from which payments in last preceding Column were made.
21.	22.	23.	24.	25.	26.
1 to 28 £ s. d.	£ s. d.	£ s. d.	£ s. d.	£ s. d.	

—*Continued.*

ACCOUNT.						
Total carried to Redemption Fund Account from all sources during Year.	Amount standing to credit of Redemption Fund Account at commencement of Year.	Amount paid for extinction of Stock during Year.	Amount standing to credit of Redemption Fund Account at end of Year.			
			Uninvested.	Invested.	Description of Securities in which invested.	
27.	28.	29.	30.	31.	32.	
£ s. d.	£ s. d.	£ s. d.	£ s. d.	£ s. d.		1 to 28

Given under the Seal of Office of the Local Government Board, this Third day of July, in the year One thousand

Order in Council under section 70 *of the Local Government Act*, 1888, ante, p. 135, *amending the Order last set out.*

At the Court at Osborne House, Isle of Wight, the 3rd day of August, 1897.

Present, the Queen's Most Excellent Majesty in Council.

Whereas the Local Government Board did, in pursuance of the powers conferred upon them by the Local Government Act, 1888, on the 12th day of June 1897, make certain regulations amending the regulations confirmed by Order in Council of 26th September, 1891, applicable to the creation, issue, transfer, and redemption of and other dealings with any County Stock which any County Council create under the Local Government Act, 1888, in exercise of any statutory borrowing power:

And whereas the said amending Regulations have, as required by the said Act, been laid before both Houses of Parliament for a period of 30 days, and no resolution has been passed by either House that such amending Regulations ought not to be proceeded with.

Now, therefore, Her Majesty having taken the said amending regulations (copy whereof is hereunto annexed) into consideration, is pleased, by and with the advice of Her Privy Council, to confirm, and doth hereby confirm the same. C. L. PEEL.

AMENDING REGULATIONS referred to in the foregoing Order.

THE LOCAL GOVERNMENT ACT, 1888.

REGULATIONS AS TO ISSUE OF COUNTY STOCK: AMENDING ORDER.

To the COUNTY COUNCILS of the several Administrative Counties in ENGLAND and WALES, other than the County Council of London —: And to all others whom it may concern.

Whereas by sub-section (8) of Section 69 of the Local Government Act, 1888, it is enacted that where the County Council are authorised to borrow any money on loan they may raise such money by stock issued under the said Act, or by the other methods mentioned in the said sub-section;

And whereas by Section 70 of the said Act it is enacted as follows:

"70.—(1.) County stock may be created, issued, transferred, dealt with, and redeemed in such manner, and in accordance with such regulations as the Local Government Board may from time to time prescribe.

"(2.) Without prejudice to the generality of the above power, such regulations may provide for the discharge of any loan raised by such stock, and in the case of consolidation of debt for extending or varying the times within which loans may be discharged, and may provide for the consent of limited owners and for the application of the Acts relating to stamp duties and to cheques, and for the disposal of unclaimed dividends, and may apply for the purposes of this section, with or without modifications, any enactments of the Local Loans Act, 1875, and the Acts amending the same, and of any Act relating to stock issued by the Metropolitan Board of Works, or by the corporation of any municipal borough.

"(3.) Such regulations shall be laid before each House of Parliament for not less than thirty days during which such House sits, and if either House during such thirty days resolves that such regulations ought not to be proceeded with the same shall be of no effect, without prejudice nevertheless to the making of further regulations.

"(4.) If no such resolution is passed, it shall be lawful for Her Majesty by Order in Council to confirm such regulations, and the same when so confirmed shall be deemed to have been duly made and to be within the powers of this Act, and shall be of the same force as if they were enacted in this Act."

And whereas the Local Government Board by Order dated the 3rd day of July, 1891, made Regulations under the said Section (herein-after called "the Regulations"), and the same were confirmed by Order in Council dated the 26th day of September, 1891;

And whereas it is desirable that the Regulations should be amended as herein-after provided:

Now therefore, We, the Local Government Board, in pursuance of the powers given to Us by the last above-cited Section, do hereby Order and Prescribe as follows:—

From and after the confirmation of these Regulations by Order in Council, the Regulations shall be amended by the additions and alterations herein-after contained, and as so amended shall apply to the creation, issue, transfer, and redemption of, and other dealings with, any stock which any County Council create under the Local Government Act, 1888, in exercise of any statutory borrowing power as defined in Article 1 of the Regulations:

Provided that the said additions and alterations shall not apply to any stock issued before the confirmation of these Regulations, except as herein-after expressly mentioned, or as We may hereafter direct.

ARTICLE 1.—(1.) A County Council who shall have issued stock under the Regulations, whether of one or more classes, and whether before or after the date of this Order, may, if the Board by Order so provide, from time to time, create and issue stock, under and subject to the Regulations as hereby amended, of another class than any stock previously created by the County Council, and so that some or all of the terms and conditions on which the same is issued, including the rate of dividend payable thereon and the period after which the same shall become redeemable, may not be the same as those of any stock previously created, but any such stock shall rank equally with the stock previously issued, and (unless otherwise expressed in the resolution for the creation of the stock) with all other securities of the County Council created or granted in pursuance of any statutory borrowing power at any time after the date of the first creation of any stock.

(2.) A separate Stock (Dividends) Fund Account of the County Fund and a separate Stock (Redemption) Fund Account of the County Fund shall be kept for every class of stock; the accounts for each class of stock being distinguished by number or otherwise.

(3.) In this Order the term "Dividends Fund Account" and "Redemption Fund Account" shall mean as well the Stock (Dividends) Fund Account, and Stock (Redemption) Fund Account under the Regulations, as the Stock (Dividends) Fund Account and the Stock (Redemption) Fund Account for any class of stock created and issued by a County Council under the provisions of this Article.

ARTICLE 2.—In any consolidation scheme, under Article 5 of the Regulations, loans previously raised by stock and loans included in any previous consolidation scheme, whether before or after this Order, may be included.

ARTICLE 3.—(1.) If money to be raised by the issue of stock is to be lent by the County Council, and to be repaid by instalments, or if in any other case the Board think fit, the Board may determine that the amounts of the several contributions to the Redemption Fund Account in respect of such stock (subject to any reduction thereof authorised under the Regulations) shall be determined by the provisions either of paragraph (a), paragraph (b), or paragraph (c) of this clause:—

(a.) The said amounts shall be the same as would, under the statutory borrowing power, have been payable towards paying off the money represented by the stock, or to a non-accumulating sinking fund for the repayment of the same, if the same had been raised otherwise than by the issue of stock.

(b.) The said amounts shall be such equal annual amounts as will be sufficient, after payment of all expenses, to purchase the amount of stock at par within the time within which, under the statutory borrowing power or Order of the Board under the Regulations as hereby amended, the money represented by the stock is to be repaid.

(c.) If the statutory borrowing power in exercise of which the stock is issued does not determine the amounts to be paid towards paying off or to a non-accumulating sinking fund in respect of the money to be borrowed thereunder, or the period within which the same is to be repaid, or if the Board approve a scheme for the consolidation of all or any of the loans raised or to be raised by the issue of stock, the amounts of the several contributions shall be such equal annual amounts as will be sufficient, after payment of all expenses, to purchase the amount of stock at par within such time, not exceeding forty years from the first creation of the stock, as the Board shall determine.

(2.) Except as herein-after provided, the provisions of clause (1) of Article 11 of the Regulations, and so much of clause (4) of that Article as requires interest to be paid into the Redemption Fund

Account or any part of the money carried to that Account and applied in the redemption or purchase and extinction of such stock, and so much of Article 12 of the Regulations as requires the interest and annual proceeds arising from the investment of the sums standing to the credit of the Redemption Fund Account to be invested and accumulated shall not apply to contributions made to the Redemption Fund Account under this Article; provided that (without prejudice to the power reserved to the Board under clause (2) of Article 11 of the Regulations), if the Board shall at any time be of opinion that the contributions made to the Redemption Fund Account under this Article will not, in consequence of the depreciation of the securities in which the same are invested, be sufficient to redeem or purchase the amount of stock in respect of which such contributions are made as required by the Regulations as hereby amended, they may direct that the above-mentioned provisions of clause (4) of Article 11 and of Article 12 shall apply with such modifications as they may prescribe. Provided also, that so long as the above-mentioned provisions of Article 12 shall not apply, the interest and annual proceeds arising from the investment of contributions made to the Redemption Fund Account under this Article may be paid into the Dividends Fund Account, in reduction of the amount to be provided by contributions as required by Article 6 of the Regulations.

ARTICLE 4.—(1.) If the County Council create and issue stock for the purpose of raising any money to be paid under clause (2) of Article 14 of the Regulations, to the holder of any security for his consent to or for otherwise compensating him for the payment off or redemption of his security, or to the substitution of stock for his security, the period within which provision shall be made for the redemption of the amount of stock created and issued for that purpose shall be such period as the Board may determine, not exceeding the period within which the money representing the security paid off or redeemed or for which the stock is substituted is required to be paid off under the statutory borrowing power or under any Order of the Board prescribing the time within which such money is to be paid off or redeemed.

(2.) The amount of any payment under clause (2) of Article 14 of the Regulations which may be raised by the issue of stock shall not exceed the amount which the Board may by Order authorise to be so raised.

ARTICLE 5.—The following provisions shall be substituted for the last paragraph of Article 11 of the Regulations, and shall apply to stock issued before or after this Order:—

"When the County Council redeem or purchase and extinguish stock by the application of any part of the money carried to the Redemption Fund Account, the stock so redeemed or purchased and extinguished shall be deemed to be stock issued in respect of such one or more of the statutory borrowing powers exercised by the issue of stock and, if in respect of more than one, in such proportions as the County Council shall before or within three months after the redemption or purchase direct, or in default of such direction, as the Local Government Board shall determine: Provided that no larger amount of stock shall be deemed to be redeemed or purchased and extinguished in respect of any statutory borrowing power than the amount which, according to the actual price of redemption or purchase, could be redeemed or purchased with the contributions paid into the Redemption Fund Account in respect of that borrowing power and the accumulations (if any) thereon."

ARTICLE 6.—The words "the statutory borrowing power which the County Council could exercise for such other purpose" shall be substituted in Article 16 of the Regulations for the words "such last-mentioned statutory borrowing power." This amendment shall apply to stock issued before or after this Order.

ARTICLE 7.—The following shall be substituted for clause (5) of Article 23 of the Regulations:—

The Registrar shall, after reasonable notice, and on delivery up of the old stock certificate, or on such proof that it cannot be produced, as the Registrar, with the approval of the County Council, may require, deliver to the purchaser a new stock certificate under the seal of the County Council.

ARTICLE 8.—Clause (1) of Article 51 of the Regulations shall be amended by the substitution for the words "including any sum paid by them for composition for stamp duty thereon and any other expenses," of the words "so far as they are."

ARTICLE 9.—These Regulations shall be read as one with the Regulations, and may be cited as "The County Stock Regulations (Amendment), 1897," and with the Regulations as "The County Stock Regulations, 1891 and 1897," and the Regulations may be cited as "The County Stock Regulations, 1891."

Given under the Seal of Office of the Local Government Board, this twelfth day of June, in the year One thousand eight hundred and ninety-seven.

HENRY CHAPLIN,
President.

(L.S.)

HUGH OWEN,
Secretary.

LAND, COMPULSORY HIRING AND PURCHASE OF.

PARISH COUNCILS.

Compulsory Hiring of Land for Allotments (*a*).

Regulations and Adaptations under Section 10 *of the Local Government Act*, 1894.

(GENERAL ORDER, MAY 20TH, 1895.)

To the County Council of every Administrative County in England and Wales, except the Administrative County of London;—
To each Parish Council in England and Wales;—
And to all others whom it may concern.

Whereas by section 9 of the Local Government Act, 1894, it is enacted that—

"9.—(1.) For the purpose of the acquisition of land by a parish council the Lands Clauses Acts shall be incorporated with this Act, except the provisions of those Acts with respect to the purchase and taking of land otherwise than by agreement, and section one hundred and seventy-eight of the Public Health Act, 1875, shall apply as if the parish council were referred to therein.

"(2.) If a parish council are unable to acquire by agreement and on reasonable terms suitable land for any purpose for which they are authorised to acquire it, they may represent the case to the county council, and the county council shall inquire into the representation.

"(3.) If on any such representation, or on any proceeding under the Allotments Acts, 1887 and 1890, a county council are satisfied that suitable land for the said purpose of the parish council, or for the purpose of allotments (as the case may be), cannot be acquired on reasonable terms by voluntary agreement, and that the circumstances are such as to justify the county council in proceeding under this section, they shall cause such public inquiry to be made in the parish, and such notice to be given both in the parish and to the owners, lessees, and occupiers of the land proposed to be taken as may be prescribed, and all persons interested shall be permitted to attend at the inquiry, and to support or oppose the taking of the land.

"(4.) After the completion of the inquiry, and considering all objections made by any persons interested, the county council may make an order for putting in force, as respects the said land or any part thereof, the provisions of the Lands Clauses Acts

(*a*) As to compulsory *purchase* of land by parish councils (and by district councils for allotments), see the Order of May 22nd, 1895, *post*, p. 821; and in connection with the present Order, see the Order of May 21st, 1895, containing adaptations of the Lands Clauses Acts, *post*, p. 805.

with respect to the purchase and taking of land otherwise than by agreement.

"(5.) If the county council refuse to make any such order, the parish council, or, if the proceeding is taken on the petition of the district council, then the district council, may petition the Local Government Board, and that Board after local inquiry may, if they think proper, make the order, and this section shall apply as if the order had been made by the county council. Any order made under this sub-section overruling the decision of the county council shall be laid before Parliament by the Local Government Board.

"(6.) A copy of any order made under this section shall be served in the prescribed manner, together with a statement that the order will become final and have the effect of an Act of Parliament, unless within the prescribed period a memorial by some person interested is presented to the Local Government Board praying that the order shall not become law without further inquiry.

"(7.) The order shall be deposited with the Local Government Board, who shall inquire whether the provisions of this section and the prescribed regulations have been in all respects complied with; and if the Board are satisfied that this has been done, then, after the prescribed period—

"(a.) If no memorial has been presented, or if every such memorial has been withdrawn, the Board shall, without further inquiry, confirm the order:

"(b.) If a memorial has been presented, the Local Government Board shall proceed to hold a local inquiry, and shall, after such inquiry, either confirm, with or without amendment, or disallow the order:

"(c.) Upon any such confirmation the order, and if amended as so amended, shall become final and have the effect of an Act of Parliament, and the confirmation by the Local Government Board shall be conclusive evidence that the requirements of this Act have been complied with, and that the order has been duly made, and is within the powers of this Act.

* * * * *

"(13.) Subsection (2) of section two, if the land is taken for allotments, and, whether it is or is not so taken, subsections (5), (6), (7), and (8) of section three of the Allotments Act, 1887, and section eleven of that Act, and section three of the Allotments Act, 1890, are incorporated with this section, and shall, with the prescribed adaptations, apply accordingly.

* * * * *

And whereas by sub-section (1) of section 10 of the said Act it is enacted that—

"10.—(1.) The parish council shall have power to hire land for allotments, and if they are satisfied that allotments are required, and are unable to hire by agreement on reasonable terms suitable land for allotments, they shall represent the case to the county council, and the county council may make an order authorising the parish council to hire compulsorily for allotments, for a period not less than fourteen years nor more than thirty-five years, such land in or near the parish as is specified in the order, and the order shall, as respects confirmation and otherwise, be subject to the like provisions as if it were an order of the county council made under the last preceding section of this Act, and that section shall apply as if it were herein re-enacted with the substitution of 'hiring' for 'purchase' and with the other necessary modifications."

And whereas by section 75 of the said Act it is enacted, that, in that Act, unless the context otherwise requires, the expression "prescribed" means prescribed by order of the Local Government Board:

Now therefore, We, the Local Government Board, in pursuance of the powers given to Us in that behalf, do, by this Our Order, and until We shall otherwise Direct, Prescribe as follows; that is to say,—

Article I.—In every case in which a County Council on a representation by a Parish Council under sub-section (1) of section ten of the Local Government Act, 1894, propose to proceed under that enactment, and with a view to such proceeding, to cause public Inquiry to be made, the County Council shall, not less than six weeks before the day on which it is proposed that the Inquiry shall be held, cause notice to be given in such form and in such manner as are herein-after prescribed:—

I. The notice shall specify the particulars of the representation, and shall state that the County Council propose to cause public Inquiry to be made.

II. The notice shall further specify, as regards any land proposed to be compulsorily hired, the quantity and description and the situation of the land proposed to be compulsorily hired, the period for which it is proposed that the land shall be compulsorily hired, and the names of the owners, lessees, and occupiers of the said land.

III. A printed copy of the notice shall be sent by post by the County Council to each owner, lessee, and occupier of the land proposed to be compulsorily hired, or, if such owner, lessee, or occupier is absent abroad, to his agent.

Article II.—The County Council, not more than one calendar month and not less than two weeks before the holding of the public Inquiry, shall cause a notice to the like effect as that of the notice prescribed by Article I., and containing also a statement of the day, time, and place appointed for the holding of the Inquiry, and of the person or persons by whom the Inquiry is to be held, to be published and given in accordance with the following requirements; that is to say,—

I. The notice shall be published in the Parish, by posting a printed copy of the notice as a bill or placard in every such place in the Parish as is ordinarily used for posting public or parochial notices.

II. A printed copy of the notice shall be sent by post by the County Council—

To the Parish Council; and

To each owner, lessee, and occupier of the land proposed to be compulsorily hired, or, if such owner, lessee, or occupier is absent abroad, to his agent.

ARTICLE III.—The County Council shall, within ten days after the making of the order (*b*), cause a copy of any order made by them under section ten of the Local Government Act, 1894, to be served by post in accordance with the following requirements; that is to say,—

A copy of the said Order shall be sent by post to the Parish Council, and to each owner, lessee, and occupier of the land proposed to be compulsorily hired, or, if such owner, lessee, or occupier is absent abroad, to his agent.

ARTICLE IV.—Every copy of a notice or order which, in pursuance of any provision in Articles I., II., and III. is required to be sent or served by post to or upon any Parish Council or person therein mentioned shall be so sent or served by a registered letter containing such copy, and properly addressed, prepaid, and posted to such Council, or to such person at his usual or last known place of abode.

ARTICLE V.—The period within which a memorial by a person interested praying that an Order made under section ten of the Local Government Act, 1894, shall not become law without further inquiry may be presented to the Local Government Board shall be the period of one calendar month after the making of the said Order.

ARTICLE VI.—For the purposes of section ten of the said Local Government Act, 1894, the several provisions herein-before mentioned of the Allotments Acts, 1887 and 1890, shall be adapted in the form and manner set forth in the Schedule to this Order.

SCHEDULE.

THE ALLOTMENTS ACT, 1887.

Section 2 (2).

(2.) A Parish Council shall not, under section ten of the Local Government Act, 1894, or in pursuance of an Order made under the said section, acquire land for allotments, save at such price or rent that, in the opinion of the said Council, all expenses, except such expenses

(*b*) As to the adapted provisions of the Lands Clauses Acts which the order may contain, see the Order of the Local Government Board of May 21, 1895, *post*, p. 805.

as are incurred in making roads to be used by the public, incurred by the said Council in acquiring the land and otherwise in relation to the allotments may reasonably be expected to be recouped out of the rents obtained in respect thereof.

Section 3 (5), (6), (7), *and* (8).

(5.) In construing for the purposes of section ten of the Local Government Act, 1894, so far as the said section empowers a Parish Council to hire land by agreement for allotments, and for that purpose provides that section nine of the Local Government Act, 1894, shall apply as if it were therein re-enacted, with certain modifications, the provisions of the Lands Clauses Acts as incorporated, and of section one hundred and seventy-eight of the Public Health Act, 1875, as applied by sub-section (1) of section nine of the Local Government Act, 1894, the last-mentioned Act shall be deemed to be the Special Act, and the Parish Council shall be deemed to be the Local Authority or the promoters of the Undertaking, as the case requires, and the word "land" shall have the same meaning as in the Allotments Act, 1887.

(6.) Where land is hired compulsorily by a Parish Council under an Order in pursuance of section ten of the Local Government Act, 1894, the following provisions shall apply:—

(*a.*) The County Council and the Local Government Board shall not make an Order for the compulsory hiring of any park, garden, pleasure-ground, or other land required for the amenity or convenience of any dwelling-house, or any land the property of a railway or canal company, which is or may be required for the purposes of their undertaking.

(*b.*) The County Council and the Local Government Board shall, in making an Order for the compulsory hiring of land, have regard to the extent of land held in the neighbourhood by any owner and to the convenience of other property belonging to the same owner, and shall, so far as is practicable, avoid taking an undue or inconvenient quantity of land from any one owner.

(7.) For the purpose of the hiring of land by a Parish Council for allotments in pursuance of section ten of the Local Government Act, 1894, any person or body of persons or body corporate authorised to sell land to the Sanitary Authority for the purposes of the Allotments Act, 1887, may, without prejudice to any other power of leasing, lease land to the Parish Council, without any fine or premium, for a term not exceeding thirty-five years.

(8.) The County Council and the Local Government Board shall not make an Order in pursuance of section ten of the Local Government Act, 1894, for the compulsory hiring of any right to coal or metalliferous ore.

Section 11.

(1.) Where a Parish Council are of opinion that any land, or any part of any land, hired by the said Council by agreement, in pursuance of section ten of the Local Government Act, 1894, for the purpose of allotments is no longer needed for such purpose, the said Council may, with the sanction of the County Council, and subject to the terms and conditions of the hiring of such land or part and to the provisions of sub-section (2) of section eight of the Local Government Act, 1894, let such land or part.

(2.) Any money received from the letting of the land may, subject to the provisions of section eight of the Local Government Act, 1894, be applied in aid of the expenses of the Parish Council under the Local Government Act, 1894.

THE ALLOTMENTS ACT, 1890.

Section 3 (2), (3), *and* (4).

(2.) For the purpose of any business under section ten of the Local Government Act, 1894, relating to any parish wholly or partly situate in an electoral division, the County Councillor representing that division shall, if not already appointed, be an additional member of the Standing Committee appointed for the purposes of the Allotments Acts, 1887 and 1890.

(3.) Any representation by a parish council under sub-section (1) of section ten of the Local Government Act, 1894, shall, as of course, and without any Order of the County Council, be referred to the said Standing Committee, who shall forthwith inquire into the circumstances, and shall report the result to the County Council.

(4.) Where the County Council are satisfied that the circumstances are such as to justify them in proceeding under section ten of the Local Government Act, 1894, the public inquiry which, by sub-section (3) of section nine as applied by sub-section (1) of section ten of the said Act, is required to be made shall be held by such one or more members of the said Standing Committee, or such officer of the County Council as the said Standing Committee may appoint to hold the same.

Given under the Seal of Office of the Local Government Board, this Twentieth day of May, in the year One thousand eight hundred and ninety-five.

(L.S.) G. SHAW-LEFEVRE, *President.*

WALTER FOSTER, *Secretary.*

The following Memorandum was issued with the foregoing Order:—

By section 10 (1) of the Local Government Act, 1894, it is enacted that the Parish Council shall have power to hire land for allotments, and if they are satisfied that allotments are required and are unable to hire by agreement on reasonable terms suitable land for allotments, they shall represent the case to the County Council, and the County Council may make an Order authorising the Parish Council to hire compulsorily for allotments for a period not less than 14 years nor more than 35 years, such land in or near the Parish as is specified in the Order.

The Order, as respects confirmation and otherwise, is subject to the like provisions as if it were an Order of the County Council made under section 9 of the Local Government Act, 1894, and that section will apply as if it were re-enacted in sub-section 1 of section 10, with the substitution of "hiring" for "purchase," and with the other necessary modifications.

Section 9, which is thus applied, specifies various matters which must be prescribed by the Local Government Board. Regulations as to such of these matters as are appropriate to the case in which a Parish Council seek power to hire land compulsorily for allotments will be found in the accompanying Order. The Order also prescribes certain adaptations of sub-section (2) of section 2, of sub-sections (5), (6), (7), and (8) of section 3, and of section 11 of the Allotments Act, 1887, and also of section 3 of the Allotments Act, 1890.

A brief explanation of some points arising in connexion with the procedure under section 10 of the Local Government Act, 1894, is appended.

As regards the hiring of land by agreement, the Parish Council will not require the aid of any intermediary authority. The Parish Council in such circumstances are brought into direct relations with the landowner.

As to hiring by agreement, the Parish Council may wish to negotiate for the acquisition of land held by persons entitled as tenants for life, or otherwise as limited owners, or subject to any disability or incapacity which would not attach to an absolute owner in fee simple, and provision has been made for meeting these cases by an enlargement of the powers of owners in this respect. The prescribed adaptation of section 3 (7) of the Allotments Act, 1887, provides that for the purpose of the hiring of land by a Parish Council for allotments in pursuance of section 10 of the Local Government Act, 1894, any person or body of persons or body corporate authorised to sell land to the Sanitary Authority for the purposes of the Allotments Act, 1887, may, without prejudice to any other power of leasing, lease land to the Parish Council without any fine or premium for a term not exceeding 35 years.

The effect of this adaptation is that the persons enabled to sell land by virtue of the Lands Clauses Acts as incorporated with section 3 (1) of the Allotments Act, 1887, are empowered to lease, and their powers, where these under the general law would be more restricted, are enlarged so as to give them authority to grant a lease for a term not exceeding 35 years.

But if the Parish Council are unable to hire by agreement on reasonable terms suitable land for allotments, it will be requisite for the Council, if they desire to carry the matter further, to invoke the aid of the County Council.

To bring the matter before the County Council a representation by the Parish Council will be necessary.

This representation should state fully the circumstances on which the Parish Council rely to show that they are unable to hire suitable land by agreement on reasonable terms. The representation, in pursuance of the prescribed adaptation of section 3 (3) of the Allotments Act, 1890, will, as of course, and without any order of the County Council, be referred to the Standing Committee of the County Council appointed under the last-mentioned Act. It will be incumbent upon the Standing Committee to inquire forthwith into the representation, and to report the result to the County Council.

Upon this inquiry and report the County Council will be in a position to form an opinion as to whether any further action by them will be requisite or expedient.

If the County Council are satisfied that suitable land for allotments cannot be hired by the Parish Council by agreement on reasonable terms, and that the circumstances are such as to justify the County Council in proceeding under section 10 with a view to the making of an order authorising the Parish Council to hire land compulsorily, it will then be the duty of the County Council in the subsequent steps of their procedure to follow the regulations prescribed by the Order of the Board.

Local Government Board,
May 1895.

Compulsory Hiring of Land for Allotments: Adaptations of Lands Clauses Acts.

(General Order, May 21st, 1895.)

To the County Council of every Administrative County in England and Wales, except the Administrative County of London;—

And to all others whom it may concern.

Whereas by sub-sections (1) and (8) of section 10 of the Local Government Act, 1894, it is enacted that—

"10.—(1.) The parish council shall have power to hire land for allotments, and if they are satisfied that allotments are required, and are unable to hire by agreement on reasonable terms suitable land for allotments, they shall represent the case to the county council, and the county council may make an order authorising the parish council to hire compulsorily for allotments, for a period not less than fourteen years nor more than thirty-five years, such land in or near the parish as is specified in the order, and the order shall, as respects confirmation and otherwise, be subject to the like provisions as if it were an order of the county council made under the last preceding section of this Act, and that section shall apply as if it were herein re-enacted with the substitution of 'hiring' for 'purchase' and with the other necessary modifications."

"(8.) The order for compulsory hiring may apply, with the prescribed adaptations, such of the provisions of the Lands Clauses Acts (including those relating to the acquisition of land otherwise than by agreement) as appear to the county council or Local Government Board sufficient for carrying into effect the order, and for the protection of the persons interested in the land and of the parish council."

And whereas by section 75 of the said Act, it is enacted that, in that Act, unless the context otherwise requires, the expression "prescribed" means prescribed by order of the Local Government Board:

Now, therefore, We, the Local Government Board, in pursuance of the powers given to Us in that behalf, Do hereby prescribe as follows; that is to say,—

For the purposes of any Order to be made under section ten of the Local Government Act, 1894, for authorising a Parish Council to hire compulsorily for allotments for a period not less than fourteen years nor more than thirty-five years such land as is specified in the Order, the provisions of the Lands Clauses Act shall be adapted so that the provisions of the Lands Clauses Acts which any such order may apply shall be the provisions of those Acts in the form and with the adaptations contained in the paragraphs numbered one to thirty-five, both inclusive, of the Schedule to this Order, and in the words in the said schedule set forth by way of introduction to and description of the subject-matter of the said paragraphs.

SCHEDULE.

I.

WITH RESPECT TO THE CONSTRUCTION OF THE ADAPTED PROVISIONS.

1. (*II.-III.*) (*a*). The expression "the adapted provisions" means the Lands Clauses Consolidation Act, 1845, as applied, with the prescribed adaptations, in pursuance of section ten of the Local Government Act, 1894; the expression "the Lands Clauses Consolidation Act, 1845," used in the adapted provisions, means the Lands Clauses Consolidation Act, 1845, as applicable to the purchase or taking of lands for any such undertaking as is mentioned in section one of the said Act; the expression "the Order," used in the adapted provisions, means any Order made under sub-section (1) of section ten of the Local Government Act, 1894, which authorises the compulsory hiring of land by a Parish Council; the expression "the Commencement of the Order" means the date at which any such Order becomes final in

(*a*) The roman figures refer to the sections of the Lands Clauses Consolidation Act, 1845.

pursuance of sections nine and ten of the Local Government Act, 1894; the expression "the Undertaking" means the purpose for which by the Order the compulsory hiring of lands by a Parish Council is authorised; the expression "the Parish Council" means the Parish Council by the Order empowered to hire lands compulsorily for the Undertaking; the expression "Lands" has the meaning assigned to the expression "Land" when used in section three of the Allotments Act, 1887, as incorporated and applied by sections nine and ten of the Local Government Act, 1894; the expression "Paymaster General" means Her Majesty's Paymaster General for the time being for and on behalf of the Supreme Court, or the Assistant Paymaster General for Supreme Court business for the time being deputed by the Paymaster General to act on his behalf for such business; the expression "County" has the same meaning as in the Local Government Act, 1894, except that it does not include a County Borough; the expression "Owner" means the person or persons or corporation who, whether under the adapted provisions, or otherwise by reason of his or their estate or interest in the lands, or of the powers of leasing exerciseable by him or them in respect of the lands comprised in the Order, is or are enabled to lease the same for the Undertaking to the Parish Council for the term for which the Parish Council are by the Order authorised to hire the same compulsorily; the expression "Compensation" means any sum of money payable by the Parish Council in respect of the hiring of any lands by the Order authorised to be compulsorily hired, and not being rent or other payment to become due under the lease in respect of the said land; and the expression "the Bank" means the Bank of England.

Unless the contrary intention appears, all words and expressions used in the adapted provisions, and not herein-before specifically defined, shall have the meanings respectively assigned to them by and shall be construed in accordance with the provisions of the Interpretation Act, 1889, and the rules of construction in the Interpretation Act, 1889, contained shall apply to the adapted provisions as if the said provisions were an Act passed after the commencement of the Interpretation Act, 1889.

2. (*V.*) For the purposes of section ten of the Local Government Act, 1894, the incorporation with the Order of the adapted provisions shall be effected by the statement in the Order that the adapted provisions shall be incorporated therewith; and thereupon all the adapted provisions shall form part of the Order, and the Order shall be construed as if the adapted provisions were set forth therein with reference to the matter to which it relates.

II.

As to the Hiring of Lands by Agreement.

3. (*VI.*) Subject to the adapted provisions, the Parish Council may agree with the owner of any lands, by the Order authorised to be

compulsorily hired, for the hiring of any such lands or of such parts thereof as the Parish Council think proper.

4. (*VII.*) All parties seised, possessed of, or entitled to any lands by the order authorised to be compulsorily hired, or of or to any estate or interest therein, may lease or (according to their estate or interest therein) may join in leasing the same to the Parish Council; and all corporations, tenants in tail or for life, married women, tenants by the curtesy or in dower, guardians, committees of lunatics or idiots, trustees, or feoffees in trust for charitable or other purposes, executors and administrators, entitled to the receipt of the rents and profits of any lands by the Order authorised to be compulsorily hired, may lease such lands for the Undertaking to the Parish Council for the term mentioned in the Order, and may exercise this power not only on behalf of themselves and their respective heirs, executors, administrators and successors, but also for and on behalf of every person entitled in reversion, remainder, or expectancy after them or in defeasance of the estates of such persons, and as to such married women, whether they be of full age or not, as if they were sole and of full age, and as to such guardians on behalf of their wards, and as to such committees on behalf of the lunatics or idiots of whom they are the committees, and that to the same extent as such wives, wards, lunatics, and idiots respectively could have exercised the same power under the authority of the adapted provisions if they had respectively been under no disability, or as if any disability to which any such parties may be subject did not extend to the power to lease such lands for the undertaking to the parish council for the term mentioned in the Order, and as to such trustees, executors, and administrators on behalf of their *cestui que trusts*, whether infants, issue unborn, lunatics, femes coverts, or other persons, and that to the same extent as such *cestui que trusts* respectively could have exercised the same powers under the adapted provisions if they had respectively been under no disability, or as if any disability to which any such parties may be subject did not extend to the power to lease such lands for the Undertaking to the Parish Council for the term mentioned in the Order.

5. (*X.*) The Owner of any lands by the Order authorised to be compulsorily hired, if he is entitled, otherwise than under the adapted provisions, to lease the same for the term mentioned in the Order, may agree with the Parish Council as to the terms and conditions of the lease; but if he is not entitled so to lease the same, except under the adapted provisions, the terms and conditions of the lease shall be settled by arbitration; and unless the owner is entitled to dispose of such lands absolutely for his own benefit, the compensation, if any, to be paid for auy permanent damage or injury to such lands shall be settled by arbitration.

III.

With respect to the Hiring of lands otherwise than by Agreement.

6. (*XVIII.*) When the Parish Council require to hire compulsorily any lands by the Order authorised to be hired, they shall give notice thereof to the owner of such lands, or to all the parties interested in such lands, or to such of the said parties as shall, after diligent inquiry, be known to the Parish Council, and by such notice shall demand from such parties the particulars of their estate and interest in such lands, in so far as such particulars are required in order to ascertain the owner thereof; and every such notice shall state the particulars of the lands so required, and the term for which the Parish Council are authorised to hire the same, and that the Parish Council are willing to treat for the hiring thereof.

7. (*XIX.*) Every notice required to be given by the Parish Council to the owner or any party shall either be served personally on such owner or party or sent by post to or left at his usual place of abode in the United Kingdom if any such can, after diligent inquiry, be found, and, in case any such owner or party shall be absent from the United Kingdom, or cannot be found after diligent inquiry, shall be sent by post to or left with any agent ordinarily receiving the rents of the lands on behalf of the owner or other party entitled thereto, and a copy thereof shall also be sent by post to or left with the occupier of the lands to which such notice relates, or, if there be no such occupier, shall be affixed upon some conspicuous part of such lands.

8. (*XX.*) If any such party be a Corporation aggregate such notice shall be sent by post to or left at the principal office of business of such Corporation, or, if no such office can, after diligent inquiry, be found, shall be sent by post to or served on some principal officer, if any, of such Corporation, and such notice shall also be sent by post to or left with the occupier of the lands to which it relates, or, if there be no such occupier, shall be affixed upon some conspicuous part of such lands.

9. (*XXI.*) If the Parish Council cannot after diligent inquiry ascertain the owner of the lands or the parties interested therein, or if for twenty-one days after the giving, sending, leaving, serving, or affixing of such notice any such owner fail to state the particulars of his interest in respect of any such lands, or to treat with the Parish Council in respect thereof, or if such owner and the Parish Council do not agree as to the terms and conditions of the hiring, or as to any other matter mentioned in sub-section (2) of section ten of the Local Government Act, 1894, any question arising as to any such matter shall be determined in the manner provided by sub-section (4) of section three of the Allotments Act, 1887, as amended by sub-section (2) of section ten of the Local Government Act, 1894.

10. (*XXV.*) Every appointment of an arbitrator appointed by the parties in accordance with the provisions of sub-section (4) of section three of the Allotments Act, 1887, as amended by sub-section (2) of section ten of the Local Government Act, 1894, shall be made in writing on the part of the Parish Council by an instrument executed at a meeting of the Council, and under the hands and seals of the Chairman presiding at the meeting and two other members of the Council, and every such appointment on the part of any other party shall be made in writing under the hand of such party, or, if such party be a Corporation aggregate, under the Common Seal of such Corporation.

Every appointment of an arbitrator appointed by the parties, or appointed, if the parties do not concur in the appointment of the arbitrator, by the Local Government Board, shall be delivered or sent to the arbitrator, and shall be deemed a submission to arbitration on the part of the several parties.

11. (*XXXII.*) The arbitrator may call for the production of any documents in the possession or power of either party which he may think necessary for determining the question in dispute, and may examine the parties or their witnesses on oath, and administer the oaths and take the affirmations necessary for that purpose: and if any person so sworn or affirming wilfully and corruptly gives false evidence he shall be guilty of perjury.

12. (*XXXIII.*) Before the arbitrator enters into the consideration of any matters referred to him, he shall, in the presence of a Justice, make and subscribe the following declaration; that is to say,—

"*I, A.B., do solemnly and sincerely declare that I will faithfully and honestly, and to the best of my skill and ability, hear and determine the matters referred to me under the provisions of the*

(naming the Order). *A.B.*

Made and subscribed in the presence of . . . ."

And such declaration shall be annexed to the award when made: and if any arbitrator having made such declaration wilfully act contrary thereto he shall be guilty of a misdemeanour.

13. (*XXXV.*) The arbitrator shall deliver his award to the Parish Council who shall retain the same and shall forthwith on demand, at their own expense, furnish a copy thereof to the other party to the arbitration and to every other person interested in any question determined by the said award.

14. (*XXXVI.*) The submission to any such arbitration may be made a Rule of the Supreme Court on the application of either of the parties.

15. (*XXXVII.*) No award made with respect to any question to be determined by arbitration in pursuance of the provisions of sub-

section (4) of section three of the Allotments Act, 1887, as amended by sub-section (2) of section ten of the Local Government Act, 1894, and in pursuance of such last-mentioned enactment, shall be set aside for irregularity or error in matter of form.

IV.

WITH RESPECT TO COMPENSATION COMING TO PARTIES SEISED IN FEE, OR TO PARTIES HAVING LIMITED INTERESTS, OR PREVENTED FROM TREATING OR REFUSING TO ACCEPT TENDERS, OR REFUSING TO LEASE.

16. (*LVIII.-LXXII.*) Where, in accordance with an agreement made with the parish council in pursuance of the adapted provisions, or in accordance with an award of an arbitrator appointed as herein-before provided, any compensation becomes payable on the hiring by the Parish Council of any lands by the Order authorised to be compulsorily hired, such compensation shall (except as herein-after provided) be paid to the party to whom the same is payable according to such agreement or award within a period of six weeks after the date of the agreement, or after the receipt by the Parish Council of the award of the arbitrator, or if by reason of the absence of such party from the United Kingdom, or of failure to find him after diligent inquiry, the Parish Council are prevented from paying such compensation to such party, or if such party shall, on such compensation being tendered to him, refuse to receive the same, such compensation shall be deposited as soon as conveniently may be in a Post Office Savings Bank established in any town or other place in which the usual or last known place of abode of such party within the United Kingdom is situate, or in some bank to be approved by the Arbitrator, to the account of such party.

Provided that where such compensation shall be payable in respect of breaking up permanent pasture, or in respect of any other permanent damage or injury to the lands to be hired, and such lands are to be hired from any party not seised in fee or entitled to dispose of the lands absolutely for his own benefit, such compensation shall be deposited by the Parish Council within a period of six weeks after they shall have received the award of the arbitrator in the Bank to the account there of the Paymaster General to the credit of the parties interested in such lands (describing them so far as the Parish Council can do) subject to the control and disposition of the Supreme Court, and with respect to compensation so deposited the provisions of sections seventy-four, seventy-eight, seventy-nine, and eighty of the Lands Clauses Consolidation Act, 1845, shall, subject to the provisions of any Act or Rule of Court for the time being in force for regulating moneys paid into the Supreme Court, apply, as nearly as may be, to such compensation as if it were purchase money or compensation payable in respect of any lands or any interest therein purchased or taken under the said Act by the promoters of the undertaking:

Provided also, that, if such compensation payable in respect of breaking up permanent pasture, or in respect of any other permanent damage or injury to the lands to be hired, do not amount to the sum of two hundred pounds, and exceed the sum of twenty pounds, the same shall either be deposited in the Bank in the manner herein-before directed, and when so deposited shall be subject to the provisions herein-before contained, or made applicable to compensation deposited in the bank, or such compensation may be paid to two trustees, to be nominated by the parties entitled to the rents or profits of the lands on the hiring whereof the same is payable, such nomination to be signified by writing under the hands of the parties so entitled; and in the case of a married woman entitled otherwise than as if she were a feme sole, or in the case of the infancy, lunacy, or other incapacity of the parties entitled to such compensation, such nomination may be made by the husband of such married woman, or by the guardian, committee, or trustee of such infant, lunatic, or party subject to incapacity as aforesaid, and the compensation so paid to such trustees, and the produce arising therefrom, shall be by such trustees applied as nearly as may be in the same manner as if such compensation or produce were money, or the produce arising from money, paid to such trustees in pursuance of the provisions of section sixty-nine of the Lands Clauses Consolidation Act, 1845, but it shall not be necessary to obtain any Order of the Court for that purpose:

Provided likewise that if such compensation do not exceed the sum of twenty pounds, the same shall be paid to the parties entitled to the rents and profits of the lands, on the hiring whereof the same shall be payable, for their own use and benefit, or, in the case of a married woman entitled otherwise than as if she were a feme sole, or in the case of the infancy, lunacy, or other incapacity of any such party, such money shall be paid to the husband of such married woman for her use or to the guardian, committee, or trustee of such infant, lunatic, or party subject to incapacity as aforesaid, for the use of such infant, lunatic, or party.

17. (*LXXV.*) Upon payment or upon deposit in a Post Office Savings Bank, in a bank approved by the arbitrator, or in the Bank (according as the circumstances of the case and the adapted provisions applicable thereto allow or require), of any compensation agreed or awarded to be paid by the Parish Council, the owner of the lands authorised to be compulsorily hired shall, when required so to do by the Parish Council, duly lease such lands to the said Council.

18. (*LXXVII.*) In every case in which, in pursuance of the adapted provisions, the compensation agreed or awarded to be paid on the hiring of any lands by the Order authorised to be compulsorily hired has been deposited in a Post Office Savings Bank, or in a bank approved by the arbitrator, or in the Bank, an officer of such Post Office Savings Bank, or a cashier of such bank approved as aforesaid, or of the Bank shall give to the Parish Council, or to the party depositing such compensation

by their direction, a receipt for such compensation. Such receipt shall be prepared by the Parish Council, shall be submitted by the Parish Council, or by the party depositing such compensation by their direction, to such officer or cashier for his signature, and shall specify to whose account such compensation is deposited, and, if the same is deposited in the Bank to the account there of the Paymaster General, to the credit of what parties (describing them so far as the Parish Council can do) and in respect of the hiring of what lands the same shall have been deposited.

19. (*LXXVI-LXXVII.*) When the Parish Council have, in pursuance of the adapted provisions, paid or deposited all compensation agreed or awarded to be paid on the hiring of any lands by the Order authorised to be compulsorily hired, if the owner of the lands refuses, or, after notice in writing by the Parish Council fails within one calendar month to execute a lease of the lands, so framed and containing such covenants and conditions as may have been agreed upon between him and the Parish Council, or, if the terms and conditions of the hiring have been settled by arbitration, if the owner of the lands cannot after diligent inquiry be ascertained, or fails within a like period after such notice to execute the lease delivered by the arbitrator with the award, the Parish Council shall execute such a lease or the said lease in duplicate, and shall forward one copy thereof to the owner of the lands, if he can be found, and shall thereupon be entitled to enter upon the lands and to hold the same under the lease and subject to the covenants and conditions therein contained, and shall be liable to the payment of the rent and be bound by the covenants as if the lease had been duly executed by all parties.

V.

With respect to Leases of Lands.

20. (*LXXXI.*) Every lease in respect of lands by the Order authorised to be compulsorily hired for the Undertaking, shall be so framed and shall contain such covenants and conditions as will give due effect to such terms and conditions of the hiring, and to such other matters as may have been agreed or awarded in relation to such hiring, and if the terms and conditions have been settled by arbitration the lease shall be settled by the arbitrator, and copies of the same in duplicate, duly stamped, shall be delivered with the award, and shall for the purpose of costs be considered as forming part of the award.

21. (*LXXXII.*) The costs of procuring the execution of the lease by the owner shall be borne by the Parish Council.

22. (*LXXXIII.*) If the Parish Council and the party entitled to any such costs do not agree as to the amount thereof, such costs shall be taxed by one of the Taxing Masters of the Supreme Court, upon an Order of the Court, to be obtained upon petition in a summary way by

either of the parties; and the Parish Council shall pay what the said Master shall certify to be due in respect of such costs to the party entitled thereto, or in default thereof the same may be recovered in the same way as any other costs payable under an Order of the Court, and the expense of taxing such costs shall be borne by the Parish Council unless upon such taxation one-sixth part of the amount of such costs be disallowed, in which case the costs of such taxation shall be borne by the party whose costs shall be so taxed, and the amount thereof shall be ascertained by the said Master, and deducted by him accordingly in his certificate of such taxation.

VI.

With respect to the Entry upon Lands by the Parish Council.

23. (*XCI.*) If in any case in which, according to the adapted provisions, the Parish Council are authorised to enter upon and hold any lands by the Order authorised to be compulsorily hired, the owner or occupier of any such lands or any other person refuse to give up the possession thereof, or hinder the Parish Council from entering upon or holding the same, a court of summary jurisdiction, on complaint made by the Parish Council, may require the owner or occupier of such lands or other person to deliver possession of the same to the Parish Council or permit them to enter thereon; and any Order made under these provisions may be enforced as provided by section thirty-four of the Summary Jurisdiction Act, 1879.

VII.

With respect to Copyhold Lands.

24. (*XCV.-XCVIII.*) The power herein-before given to lease lands by the Order authorised to be compulsorily hired shall, in the case of lands of copyhold or customary tenure, extend so as to enable any party herein-before authorised to lease lands, to lease such copyhold or customary lands to the Parish Council for such period as may be authorised by the Order, and subject to such terms and conditions of hiring as may be agreed or awarded, notwithstanding that such person shall not have obtained from the Lord of the Manor, of which the said copyhold or customary lands are held or are parcel, such licence (if any) as would be required to empower such person to make such lease; and the Lord of the Manor whereof the said copyhold or customary lands are held or are parcel may, notwithstanding any custom applicable to the said Manor, or any limitation by Statute or otherwise of the estate or interest of the said Lord, grant a licence which shall be effectual to empower any such person as aforesaid to make any such lease as is herein-before authorised.

Provided that where any such lease is made and the party making the same shall not, prior to the making thereof, have obtained such licence as the Lord is herein-before authorised to grant, the Parish Council shall forthwith apply to the Lord to grant such licence; and any such licence granted upon such application shall be as effectual as if such licence had been granted prior to the making of such lease: Provided further, that if upon such application the Lord refuse to grant such licence the Parish Council may, so far as regards the Lord and his estate or interest, proceed with respect to compensation, and otherwise in pursuance of the adapted provisions; and the adapted provisions shall, as nearly as may be, apply to the case as if the case were one of refusal by the owner of lands to lease such lands:

Provided lastly, that every such lease and the particulars of the grant or refusal of such licence shall be entered on the rolls of the Manor; and the Steward of the Manor shall cause such lease and particulars to be so entered, and shall give to the Parish Council a certificate of such entry on payment to such Steward of the accustomed fees, or if there be no accustomed fees, on payment of such sum as may, by a Court of Summary Jurisdiction, on the application of such Steward or the Parish Council, be adjudged to be payable in respect of such entry and certificate.

VIII.

With respect to Lands subject to Mortgage.

25. (*CVIII.-CXIV.*) If any lands by the Order authorised to be compulsorily hired are subject to any mortgage and the Parish Council are authorised and propose to hire such lands for a longer term than that for which the party in possession (whether mortgagor or mortgagee) is enabled to lease the same except under the adapted provisions, the Parish Council may in accordance with the adapted provisions with respect to the giving of notices to the owner of or to parties interested in lands authorised to be compulsorily hired, give notice to the party not in possession (whether mortgagor or mortgagee) requiring him within a time in the notice mentioned, being not less than one calendar month from the giving thereof, to join in making the lease of such lands, and if within the time specified he refuse or neglect so to join the terms and conditions of the hiring and the compensation (if any) to be paid on the hiring of such lands by the Parish Council in respect of any permanent damage or injury to such lands shall be settled by arbitration in manner provided by sub-section (4) of section three of the Allotments Act, 1887, as amended by sub-section (2) of section ten of the Local Government Act, 1894, and the lease when executed by the mortgagor or mortgagee in possession, or, in the event of his refusal or failure to execute the same, when executed by the Parish Council in pursuance of the adapted provisions in that behalf, shall be valid as against the mortgagee or mortgagor not in possession.

26. (*CVIII.-CXIV.*) In every case where the Parish Council under a lease made in pursuance of the adapted provisions hold lands subject

to a mortgage made before the date of the Order authorising the compulsory hiring of such lands, and the lease is not valid as against the mortgagee, the Parish Council shall for themselves and for every tenant of an allotment upon the said lands be entitled, as against any mortgagee who takes possession, to the compensation to which an occupier of land would be entitled under section two of the Tenants Compensation Act, 1890; and that enactment and the enactments therein referred to shall be construed as applicable to the circumstances of the case, as if the contract of tenancy therein mentioned were for a term of years not exceeding the period for which the said lands may have been authorised to be compulsorily hired.

IX.

WITH RESPECT TO LANDS SUBJECT TO LEASES OR CONTRACTS OF TENANCY.

27. (*CXIX.*) If any lands be comprised in a lease or contract of tenancy for an unexpired term and part only of such lands be by the Order authorised to be compulsorily hired for the undertaking, the owner by the adapted provisions or otherwise empowered to lease such part to the Parish Council, and his lessee or tenant, shall have power to agree as to the apportionment of the rent payable under such lease or contract of tenancy between the lands to be hired by the Parish Council and the residue of the lands comprised in such lease or contract of tenancy.

Every such agreement may contain the necessary stipulations and conditions with respect to any matter which in relation to such apportionment may be made the subject of determination by an award of an arbitrator appointed under sub-section (4) of section three of the Allotments Act, 1887, as amended by sub-section (2) of section ten of the Local Government Act, 1894.

After such apportionment has been settled as aforesaid, the lessee or tenant shall as to all future accruing rent be liable only to so much of the rent as shall be so apportioned in respect of that part of the lands which is not hired by the Parish Council; and as to such part, and as against his lessee or tenant, the owner shall have all the same rights and remedies for the recovery of such portion of rent as previously to such apportionment he had for the recovery of the whole rent reserved by the lease or contract of tenancy, and all the covenants, conditions, and agreements of such lease or contract of tenancy, except as to the amount of rent to be paid and as to any other matter as to which any stipulation or condition is contained in the agreement as to such apportionment, shall remain in force with regard to that part of the lands which is not hired by the Parish Council in the same manner as if such part only of the said lands had been included in the lease or contract of tenancy.

If the owner and his lessee or tenant fail to agree as to the apportionment of the rent payable as aforesaid, or as to any other matter which might be settled by such agreement, the matter or matters in dispute shall be settled by arbitration in manner provided by sub-section (4) of section three of the Allotments Act, 1887, as amended by sub-section (2) of section ten of the Local Government Act, 1894. If any arbitrator be appointed to settle the terms and conditions of the hiring by the Parish Council, or the compensation (if any) to be paid by them, he shall also act as arbitrator for the purpose of this provision, and the lessee or tenant shall be one of the parties to agree to his appointment; but if no such arbitrator be appointed, the arbitrator for the purposes of this provision shall be appointed by the owner and the lessee, or, if they do not concur, by the Local Government Board, in accordance with the provisions of sub-section (4) of section three of the Allotments Act, 1887, and the costs of the arbitration shall be paid by the Parish Council unless the County Council shall otherwise direct.

28. (*CXXI.*) If any lands comprised in a lease or contract of tenancy for an unexpired term, and by the Order authorised to be compulsorily hired by the Parish Council, be in the possession of any person having no greater interest therein than as tenant for a year, or from year to year, and if such person be required to give up possession of all such lands so occupied by him before the expiration of his term or interest therein, he shall be entitled to compensation for the value of his unexpired term or interest in such lands, and for any just allowance which ought to be made to him by an incoming tenant, and for any loss or injury which such person may sustain.

Upon payment or tender of such compensation, as agreed between such person and the Parish Council, or as determined by the award of an arbitrator appointed under sub-section (4) of section three of the Allotments Act, 1887, as amended by sub-section (2) of section ten of the Local Government Act, 1894, such person shall deliver up to the Parish Council all such lands as may be in his possession and as may be required for the Undertaking.

29. (*CXXII.*) If any party claim compensation in respect of an unexpired term or interest under any lease or grant of any lands by the Order authorised to be compulsorily hired, the Parish Council may require such party to produce the lease or grant in respect of which such claim is made, or sufficient evidence thereof, and if, after demand made in writing by the Parish Council, such lease or grant, or such evidence thereof be not produced within twenty-one days, the party so claiming compensation shall be considered as a tenant holding only from year to year, and be entitled to compensation accordingly.

X.

With respect to the Limit of Time for Compulsory Hiring.

30. (*CXXIII.*) The powers of the Parish Council for the compulsory hiring of lands for the Undertaking shall not be exercised after the

expiration of the period prescribed by the Order, and if no period be prescribed by the Order not after the expiration of one year from the commencement of the Order.

XI.

With respect to Lands Hired, but not required for the Undertaking.

31. (*CXXVII.-CXXXII.*) Where the Parish Council are of opinion that any lands by the Order authorised to be compulsorily hired are no longer needed for the Uundertaking, the Parish Council shall, by an instrument executed at a meeting of the Council and under the hands and seals of the Chairman presiding at the meeting and two other members of the Council, declare that the lands are no longer needed for the Undertaking, and shall send by post a copy of such declaration to the party from whom such lands were hired, or any other person for the time being entitled to the receipt of the rent reserved by the lease under which such lands are held by the Parish Council.

Upon the receipt of such declaration, it shall be at the option of such party or other person to act upon the said declaration as if it were an offer of surrender of the unexpired term.

If within a period of two calendar months from the receipt by him of the said declaration such party or other person, by writing under his hand and seal, or, if such party or other person be a Corporation aggregate, under the Common Seal of such Corporation, addressed to the Parish Council, signify his acceptance of the surrender, the unexpired term shall be deemed to have been surrendered by act and operation of law as from the date of acceptance by such party or other person.

If within a period of two calendar months from the receipt by him of the said declaration such party or other person by writing under his hand and seal, or, if such party or other person be a Corporation aggregate, under the Common Seal of such Corporation, signify his refusal of the surrender, or, if within such period he fail to signify in the manner aforesaid his acceptance or refusal, the unexpired term shall not be deemed to have been surrendered by act and operation of law; and thereupon it shall be at the option of the Parish Council to make such offers to let the said lands as in accordance with the adapted provisions they are empowered to make.

32. (*CXXVII.-CXXXII.*) Where in pursuance of the adapted provisions the unexpired term in respect of lands by the Order authorised to be compulsorily hired shall be deemed to have been surrendered by act and operation of law, the Parish Council and the party from whom such lands have been hired, or any other person entitled to the receipt of the rent reserved by the lease under which such lands have been held by the Parish Council, may agree as to the

consideration for such surrender, and as to any matters as to which an arbitrator in relation to the surrender of lands at the end of any tenancy created by compulsory hiring or on the determination of any such tenancy is by sub-sections (2) and (7) of section ten of the Local Government Act, 1894, empowered to determine.

On failure of the parties to agree as to any matter herein-before mentioned, any question in dispute shall be referred to the arbitration of a single arbitrator appointed in accordance with the provisions of sub-section (4) of section three of the Allotments Act, 1887; and for the determination of such question that enactment and the provisions of sub-sections (2) and (7) of section ten of the Local Government Act, 1894, shall apply with the necessary modifications.

33. (*CXXVII.-CXXXII.*) Where in pursuance of the adapted provisions the unexpired term in respect of lands by the Order authorised to be compulsorily hired shall be deemed to have been surrendered by act and operation of law, the surrender shall be deemed to be valid and effectual notwithstanding any disability affecting any party to such surrender; and the adapted provisions with respect to the payment of and other dealing with compensation on the hiring of lands by the Order authorised to be compulsorily hired shall, with the necessary modifications, be deemed to apply to any amount agreed or awarded to be paid by the Parish Council on such surrender as aforesaid.

34. (*CXXVII.-CXXXII.*) Where in pursuance of the adapted provisions it is at the option of the Parish Council, as regards lands which in their opinion are no longer needed for the Undertaking, to make offers to let the said lands, they shall first offer to let the same to the tenant for the time being of the lands (if any) from which the said lands were originally severed.

Every such offer shall be made in writing, and shall specify the terms and conditions of the proposed letting.

If such tenant be desirous of hiring the said lands upon the terms and conditions specified in such offer, and within a period of one calendar month after such offer signify his acceptance thereof to the Parish Council, they shall let the lands to such tenant accordingly; and the parties shall, as soon as conveniently may be, execute such contract of tenancy as the circumstances of the case may require.

If such tenant be not desirous of hiring the said lands upon the terms and conditions specified in such offer, and within a period of one calendar month after such offer signify to the Parish Council his refusal of such offer, or if within such period he fail to signify to the Parish Council his acceptance or refusal of such offer, it shall be at the option of the Parish Council to make the like offer, with the like incidents and consequences, to any tenant for the time being of any lands immediately adjoining such first-mentioned lands.

If such tenant be not desirous of hiring the said lands upon the terms and conditions specified in such offer, and within a period of one calendar month after such offer signify to the Parish Council his refusal of such offer, or if within such period he fail to signify to the Parish Council his acceptance or refusal of such offer, it shall be at the option of the Parish Council to let the said lands to any other person.

Provided that—

1. Every contract of tenancy in pursuance of the foregoing provisions shall be in such form and to such effect as to secure that the said lands when hired shall not, except with the consent of the party from whom the said lands have been compulsorily hired by the Parish Council, or of any other person entitled to receive the rent reserved by the lease under which the said lands have been held by the Parish Council, be used otherwise than for purposes wholly agricultural or wholly pastoral, or for purposes in part agricultural, and as to the residue pastoral, or be in whole or in part cultivated as a market garden, and that the period for which the said lands may be hired shall be less than the unexpired term vested in the Parish Council; and that
2. The terms and conditions of such contract of tenancy shall not impair or prejudicially affect any right, interest, or claim of the party from whom the said lands have been hired by the Parish Council, or any person for the time being entitled to the receipt of the rent payable by the said Council, in respect of any matter mentioned in section ten of the Local Government Act, 1894, and that, notwithstanding any such letting by the Parish Council as is authorised by the adapted provisions, such right or interest shall remain vested in, and such claim may be made by such party or person, as fully and effectually, and with the same incidents and consequences, as if the said lands had remained in the possession of the Parish Council and had been used by them for the Undertaking.

XII.

With respect to certain excepted Lands.

35. (*XCIX.-CVII.*) The adapted provisions and the Order shall not extend and apply to

Any lands belonging to Her Majesty the Queen, her Heirs and successors in right of the Crown, or in right of the Duchy of Lancaster; nor to

Any lands belonging to the Duchy of Cornwall; nor to

Any lands being common or waste lands or in the nature of common or waste lands.

Given under the Seal of Office of the Local Government Board, this Twenty-first day of May, in the year One thousand eight hundred and ninety-five.

(L.S.) G. Shaw Lefevre, *President.*

Walter Foster, *Secretary.*

PARISH AND DISTRICT COUNCILS.

Compulsory Purchase of Land (a).

Regulations and Adaptations under Section 9 *of the Local Government Act*, 1894.

(General Order, 22nd May, 1895.)

To the County Council of every Administrative County in England and Wales, except the Administrative County of London;

To the Urban District Council of each Urban District in England and Wales which is not a County Borough;—

To the Rural District Council of each Rural District in England and Wales:—

To each Parish Council in England and Wales:—

And to all others whom it may concern.

Whereas by section 9 of the Local Government Act, 1894, it is enacted that—

"9.—(1.) For the purpose of the acquisition of land by a parish council the Lands Clauses Acts shall be incorporated with this Act, except the provisions of those Acts with respect to the purchase and taking of land otherwise than by agreement, and section one hundred and seventy-eight of the Public Health Act, 1875, shall apply as if the parish council were referred to therein.

"(2.) If a parish council are unable to acquire by agreement and on reasonable terms suitable land for any purpose for which they are authorised to acquire, they may represent the case to the county council, and the county council shall inquire into the representation.

"(3.) If on any such representation, or on any proceeding under the Allotments Acts, 1887 and 1890, a county council are satisfied that suitable land for the said purpose of the parish council or for the purpose of allotments (as the case may be) cannot be acquired on reasonable terms by voluntary agreement, and that the circumstances are such as to justify the county council in proceeding under this section, they shall cause such public inquiry to be made in the parish, and such notice to be given both in the parish and to the owners, lessees, and occupiers of the land proposed to be taken as may be prescribed, and all persons interested shall be permitted to attend at the inquiry, and to support or oppose the taking of the land.

"(4.) After the completion of the inquiry, and considering all objections made by any person interested, the county council may make an order for putting in force, as respects the said land or

(a) As to the compulsory *hiring* of land by a parish council for allotments, see the Order of May 20th, 1895, *ante*, p. 798.

any part thereof, the provisions of the Lands Clauses Acts with respect to the purchase and taking of land otherwise than by agreement.

"(5.) If the county council refuse to make any such order, the parish council, or, if the proceeding is taken on the petition of the district council, then the district council, may petition the Local Government Board, and that Board after local inquiry may, if they think proper, make the order, and this section shall apply as if the order had been made by the county council. Any order made under this sub-section overruling the decision of the county council shall be laid before Parliament by the Local Government Board.

"(6.) A copy of any order made under this section shall be served in the prescribed manner, together with a statement that the order will become final and have the effect of an Act of Parliament, unless within the prescribed period a memorial by some person interested is presented to the Local Government Board praying that the order shall not become law without further inquiry.

"(7.) The order shall be deposited with the Local Government Board, who shall inquire whether the provisions of this section and the prescribed regulations have been in all respects complied with; and if the Board are satisfied that this has been done, then after the prescribed period—

"(*a*.) If no memorial has been presented, or if every such memorial has been withdrawn, the Board shall, without further inquiry, confirm the order:

* * *

"(10.) Any order made under this section for the purpose of the purchase of land otherwise than by agreement shall incorporate the Lands Clauses Acts and sections seventy-seven to eighty-five of the Railways Clauses Consolidation Act, 1845, with the necessary adaptations, but any question of disputed compensation shall be dealt with in the manner provided by section three of the Allotments Act, 1887, and provisoes (*a*), (*b*), and (*c*) of sub-section (4) of that section are incorporated with this section and shall apply accordingly: Provided that in determining the amount of disputed compensation, the arbitrator shall not make any additional allowance in respect of the purchase being compulsory.

* * * *

"(13.) Sub-section (2) of section two, if the land is taken for allotments, and, whether it is or is not so taken, sub-sections (5), (6), (7), and (8) of section three of the Allotments Act, 1887, and section eleven of that Act, and section three of the Allotments Act, 1890, are incorporated with this section, and shall, with the prescribed adaptations, apply accordingly."

And whereas by section 75 of the said Act it is enacted that, in that Act, unless the context otherwise requires, the expression "prescribed" means prescribed by order of the Local Government Board:

Now therefore, We, the Local Government Board, in pursuance of the powers given to Us in that behalf, do, by this Our Order, and until We shall otherwise Direct, Prescribe as follows; that is to say,—

Article I.—In every case in which a County Council on a representation by a Parish Council under sub-section (2) of section nine of the Local Government Act, 1894, or on any proceeding under the Allotments Acts, 1887 and 1890, propose to proceed under section nine of the Local Government Act, 1894, and with a view to such proceeding, to cause public Inquiry to be made, the County Council shall, not less than six weeks before the day on which it is proposed that the Inquiry shall be held, cause notice to be given in such form and in such manner as are herein-after prescribed:—

I.—The notice shall specify the particulars of the representation or of the proceeding under the Allotments Acts, 1887 and 1890, and shall state that the County Council propose to cause public Inquiry to be made.

II.—The notice shall further specify as regards any land proposed to be taken, the quantity and description, and the situation of the land proposed to be taken, the names of the owners, lessees, and occupiers of the said land, and the purpose for which the said land is proposed to be taken.

III.—A printed copy of the notice shall be sent by post by the County Council to each owner, lessee, and occupier of the land proposed to be taken, or, if such owner, lessee, or occupier is absent abroad, to his agent.

Article II.—The County Council, not more than one calendar month and not less than two weeks before the holding of the public Inquiry, shall cause a notice to the like effect as that of the notice prescribed by Article I., and containing also a statement of the day, time, and place appointed for the holding of the Inquiry, and of the person or persons by whom the Inquiry is to be held, to be published and given in accordance with the following requirements; that is to say,

I.—The notice shall be published in the Parish, or in the case of any proceeding under the Allotments Acts, 1887 and 1890, relating to an Urban District, in the District by posting a printed copy of the notice as a bill or placard in every such place in the Parish or District as is ordinarily used for posting public or parochial notices.

II.—A printed copy of the notice shall be sent by post by the County Council:—

(a.) Where the County Council propose to proceed on a representation of the Parish Council under sub-section (2) of section nine of the Local Government Act, 1894,

to the Parish Council: and

(b.) In the case of any proceeding under the Allotments Acts, 1887 and 1890:

i. Where the proceeding is taken on a petition under section two of the Allotments Act, 1890, by persons qualified as mentioned in that section,—
to each of the petitioners.

ii. Where the proceeding is taken on the petition of the Parish Council,—
to the Parish Council.

iii. Where the proceeding is taken on the petition of the District Council,—
to the District Council: and

(c). In every case to each owner, lessee, and occupier of the land proposed to be taken, or, if such owner, lessee, or occupier is absent abroad, to his agent.

Article III.—1. The County Council shall, within ten days after the making of the Order, cause a copy of any Order made by them under section nine of the Local Government Act, 1894, to be served by post in accordance with the following requirements; that is to say,—

i. Where the Order relates to land proposed to be taken by the Parish Council for any purpose to which sub-section (2) of the said Section applies:

A copy of the said Order shall be sent by post to the Parish Council.

2. Where the Order relates to land proposed to be taken for the purpose of allotments:—

i. If the proceeding is taken upon the petition under section two of the Allotments Act, 1890, of persons qualified as mentioned in that section or upon the petition of the Parish Council,—
to the Parish Council.

ii. If the proceeding is taken upon the petition of the District Council,—
to the District Council.

3. In every case a copy of the said Order shall be sent by post to each owner, lessee, and occupier of the land proposed to be taken, or, if such owner, lessee, or occupier is absent abroad, to his agent.

Article IV.—Every copy of a notice or order which in pursuance of any provision in Articles I., II., and III. is required to be sent or served by post to or upon any council or person therein mentioned shall be so sent or served by a registered letter containing such copy, and properly addressed, prepaid, and posted to such council or to such person at his usual or last known place of abode.

Article V.—The period within which a memorial by a person interested praying that an Order made under section nine of the Local Government Act, 1894, shall not become law without further inquiry may be presented to the Local Government Board shall be the period of one calendar month after the making of the said Order.

ARTICLE VI.—For the purposes of section nine of the Local Government Act, 1894, except so far as by sub-section (18), the said section is rendered applicable to a county borough, the several provisions herein-before mentioned of the Allotments Acts, 1887 and 1890, shall be adapted in the form and manner set forth in the Schedule to this Order.

SCHEDULE.

THE ALLOTMENTS ACT, 1887.

Section 2 (2).

(2.) A County Council or a District Council carrying into effect an Order made under section nine of the Local Government Act, 1894, for putting in force as respects land to be taken for the purpose of allotments the provisions of the Lands Clauses Act with respect to the purchase and taking of land otherwise than by agreement shall not under such Order acquire land for allotments save at such price or rent that in the opinion of the said Council all expenses, except such expenses as are incurred in making roads to be used by the public, incurred by the said Council in acquiring the land and otherwise in relation to the allotments may reasonably be expected to be recouped out of the rents obtained in respect thereof.

Section 3 (5), (6), (7) *and* (8).

(5.) In construing, for the purposes of section nine of the Local Government Act, 1894, the provisions of the Lands Clauses Acts as incorporated with the said section, and the provisions of the said Acts and of sections seventy-seven to eighty-five of the Railways Clauses Consolidation Act, 1845, as incorporated with an Order which has been made and has become final under the said section, the Local Government Act, 1894, together with any such Order, shall be deemed to be the Special Act; and the Parish Council, for any purpose for which the said Council are authorised to acquire land by agreement, or for any purpose in relation to which land authorised to be acquired otherwise than by agreement may be assured by the said Council, and the County Council carrying into effect, for such last-mentioned purpose, any such Order as is herein-before mentioned, and the County Council or the District Council carrying into effect, for the purpose of allotments, any such Order as is herein-before mentioned, shall respectively, as the case requires, be deemed to be the promoters of the Undertaking or the Company, and the word "land" in relation to any purpose for which the Parish Council are authorised to acquire land or in relation to allotments shall have the same meaning as in the Allotments Act, 1887.

(6.) Where land is purchased under an Order in pursuance of section nine of the Local Government Act, 1894, otherwise than by agreement the following provisions shall apply :—

(a.) The County Council and the Local Government Board shall not make an Order for purchasing any park, garden, pleasure-ground, or other land required for the amenity or convenience of any dwelling-house, or any land the property of a railway or canal company which is or may be required for the purposes of their undertaking :

(b.) The County Council and the Local Government Board shall, in making an Order for purchasing land, have regard to the extent of land held in the neighbourhood by any owner, and to the convenience of other property belonging to the same owner, and shall, so far as is practicable, avoid taking an undue or inconvenient quantity of land from any one owner.

(7.) For the purpose of the hiring of land by a Parish Council for a purpose for which the said Council are authorised to acquire land, any person, or body of persons, or body corporate authorised to sell land to the Sanitary Authority for the purposes of the Allotments Act, 1887, may, without prejudice to any other power of leasing, lease land to the Parish Council, without any fine or premium, for a term not exceeding thirty-five years.

(8.) The County Council and the Local Government Board shall not make an Order in pursuance of section nine of the Local Government Act, 1894, for purchasing any right to coal or metalliferous ore.

Section 11.

(1.) Where a Parish Council are of opinion that any land or any part of any land acquired by the said Council by agreement in pursuance of section nine of the Local Government Act, 1894, or assured to the said Council in pursuance of sub-section (14) of section nine of the Local Government Act, 1894, for a purpose for which the said Council are authorised to acquire land, is no longer needed for the purpose for which the said land was acquired, or that any other land more suitable for such purpose is available and may be acquired by the said Council by agreement, the said Council may, with the sanction of the County Council, and subject to the provisions of sub-section (2) of section eight of the Local Government Act, 1894, sell or let such land or part, or exchange the same for other land more suitable for the said purpose, and may pay or receive money for equality of exchange.

(2.) Where a Parish Council are of opinion that any land or any part of any land assured to the said Council in pursuance of sub-section (14) of section nine of the Local Government Act, 1894, for the purpose of allotments is no longer needed for such purpose, the said Council may, with the sanction of the County Council, and subject to the provisions of sub-section (2) of section eight of the Local Government Act, 1894, sell or let such land or part, or exchange the same for other land more suitable for the said purpose, and may pay or receive money for equality of exchange.

(3.) Where a District Council having carried into effect an Order which has been made and has become final under section nine of the Local Government Act, 1894, for putting in force for the purpose of allotments the provisions of the Lands Clauses Acts with respect to the purchase and taking of land otherwise than by agreement, are of opinion that any land or any part of any land acquired by the said Council, is no longer needed for the purpose of allotments, or that any other land more suitable for such purpose is available and may be acquired by agreement, the said Council, with the sanction of the County Council, may sell or let such land or part, or exchange the same for other land more suitable for the said purpose, and may pay or receive money for equality of exchange.

(4.) The proceeds of a sale under the foregoing provisions of any land or any part of any land acquired by or assured to a Parish Council, and any money received by the said Council on any such exchange as aforesaid by way of equality of exchange, shall be applied in discharging, either by way of a sinking fund or otherwise, the debts and liabilities of the said Council in respect of the land acquired or assured as aforesaid, or for any purpose for which capital money may be applied and which is approved by the Local Government Board; and the interest thereon (if any) and any money received from the letting of the land may, subject to the provisions of section eight of the Local Government Act, 1894, be applied in aid of the expenses of the said Council under the Local Government Act, 1894.

(5.) The proceeds of a sale under the foregoing provisions of any land or any part of any land acquired by a District Council carrying into effect an order which has been made and has become final under section nine of the Local Government Act, 1894, for putting in force for the purpose of allotments the provisions of the Lands Clauses Acts with respect to the purchase and taking of land otherwise than by agreement, shall be applied, and any surplus remaining, any interest, and any money received from the letting of the land may or shall be applied, as nearly as may be in the same manner, and with the same incidents and consequences, as if the said land had been acquired and otherwise dealt with in pursuance of the Allotments Act, 1887.

(6.) Sections one hundred and twenty-eight to one hundred and thirty-two (both inclusive) of the Lands Clauses Consolidation Act, 1845 (relating to the right of pre-emption of superfluous lands), shall apply upon any sale of any land in pursuance of the foregoing provisions; but save as aforesaid, the provisions of the Lands Clauses Consolidation Act, 1845, with respect to the sale of superfluous lands shall not be deemed to be incorporated in section nine of the Local Government Act, 1894, or in any Order made under that section.

THE ALLOTMENTS ACT, 1890.

Section 3.

(2.) For the purpose of any business under section nine of the Local Government Act, 1894, relating to any District or Parish wholly or partly situate in an electoral division, the County Councillor representing that division shall, if not already appointed, be an additional member of the Standing Committee appointed for the purposes of the Allotments Acts, 1887 and 1890.

(3.) Any representation by a Parish Council under sub-section (2) of section nine of the Local Government Act, 1894, shall, as of course, and without any Order of the County Council, be referred to the said Standing Committee, who shall forthwith inquire into the circumstances, and shall report the result to the County Council.

(4.) Where the County Council are satisfied that the circumstances are such as to justify them in proceeding under section nine of the Local Government Act, 1894, the public inquiry mentioned in sub-section (3) of the said section shall be held by such one or more members of the said Standing Committee, or such officer of the County Council as the said Standing Committee may appoint to hold the same.

Given under the Seal of Office of the Local Government Board, this Twenty-second day of May, in the year One thousand eight hundred and ninety-five.

(L.S.)

G. SHAW LEFEVRE,
President.

WALTER FOSTER,
Secretary.

The following Memorandum was issued with the foregoing Order.

The provisions of this Order relate to cases of two kinds, viz.: (1) Representations by Parish Councils under section 9 (2) of the Local Government Act, 1894; and (2) certain proceedings under the Allotments Acts, 1887 and 1890.

As to cases of the first description, it may be pointed out that if a Parish Council are unable to purchase by agreement and on reasonable terms suitable land for any purpose (other than allotments) for which they are authorised to purchase land (as, for example, for a purpose within the scope of the powers of the Parish Council under section 8 of the Local Government Act, 1894), they may represent the case to the County Council. If, on any such representation, the County Council are satisfied that suitable land for the purpose of the Parish Council cannot be acquired on reasonable terms by voluntary agreement, and that the circumstances are such as to justify the County Council in proceeding under section 9 of the Local Government Act, 1894, the County Council are then to cause such public inquiry to be made in the parish, and such notice to be given both in the parish and to the owners, lessees, and occupiers of the land proposed to be taken as may be prescribed by the Local Government Board.

In Articles I. and II. of the Order, the Local Government Board have prescribed regulations as to the preliminary notices and as to the public inquiry.

Article III., in pursuance of sub-section 6 of section 9, prescribes the mode of service of Orders made by County Councils under the section.

Article IV. relates to the same matter, and also the mode of serving copies of the notices referred to in Articles I. and II.

Article V. prescribes the period within which a memorial by some person interested, praying that an order made under section 9 shall not become law without further inquiry, may be presented to the Board.

Article VI. prescribes adaptations of the provisions of sub-sections (5), (6), (7), and (8) of section 3, and of section 11 of the Allotments Act, 1887, and of section 3 of the Allotments Act, 1890.

(2.) As regards proceedings under the Allotments Acts, 1887 and 1890, it may be observed that the provisions of the Order relate to proceedings taken on (i.) the petition under section 2 of the Allotments Act, 1890, of persons qualified as mentioned in that section; (ii.) on the petition of the Parish Council: and (iii.) on the petition of the District Council.

(3.) As to cases (i.) and (ii.), the following explanation will show the various steps which are necessary to bring matters to a point at which the County Council may elect to take action under section 9 of the Local Government Act, 1894:—

Under section 2 of the Allotments Act, 1887, on a representation in writing to the District Council of any urban or rural district by any six parliamentary electors or ratepayers resident in the case of an urban district, in that district, and in the case of a rural district, in some parish in that district, that the circumstances of the urban district or parish are such that it is the duty of the District Council to take proceedings therein under that Act, the District Council are to take such representation into consideration.

Where such a representation has been made, and any six persons qualified to make the representation consider that the circumstances of the district or parish are such as to make it the duty of the District Council to take proceedings therein under the Allotments Act, 1887, and that the District Council (not being the town council of a borough) have failed to acquire land adequate and suitable in quality and position to provide a sufficient number of allotments, these persons, under section 2 (1) of the Allotments Act, 1890, may petition the County Council, stating the facts and requesting the County Council to put into force the Act of 1887, for the purpose of providing a sufficient number of allotments for the district or parish.

Where a parish in a rural district has a Parish Council, that Council may exercise the power of the six parliamentary electors in the matter of the preliminary representation; but the power thus conferred upon the Parish Council is additional to and not in substitution for that of the electors; and in the case of such a parish the further power of petitioning the County Council is exerciseable by the Parish Council as well as by the electors.

In an urban district, however, the representation and the petition can only come from the six registered parliamentary electors or ratepayers resident in the district.

But the representation to the District Council is a condition precedent to the exercise of the power of petitioning, and the statement of facts which the petitioners are to make should include a reference to the prior representation as indicating a basis for the action of the petitioners.

For the proper investigation of matters arising upon such petitions the Allotments Act, 1890, provides for the appointment by the County Council of a Standing Committee. Annually, at the meeting for the election of chairman, the County Council are to appoint under the Local Government Act, 1888, a Standing Committee not exceeding one-fourth of the whole council. For business relating to any district or parish wholly or partly situate in an electoral division, the county councillor representing that division is, if not already appointed, to be an additional member of the Committee. The petition is, as of course, and without any order of the Council, to be referred to the Standing Committee. The Committee, on being satisfied of the *bona fides* of the application, are forthwith to cause a local inquiry into the circumstances to be made and to report the result to the Council.

When this report has been received, it will rest with the County Council to decide whether they will proceed further under the Allotments Act, 1890, or whether they will have recourse to the new procedure authorised by section 9 of the Local Government Act, 1894.

It may be added that (1) in a rural parish having a Parish Council, procedure with a view to an order under section 9 of the Local Government Act, 1894, on the petition of parliamentary electors, or ratepayers, or of the Parish Council will not be available unless it can be shown that there has been failure on the part of the District Council to exercise their powers, and that land cannot be acquired on reasonable terms by voluntary agreement; and that (2) in the case of a rural parish not having a Parish Council, the procedure will not be applicable unless the parish meeting has under section 19 of that Act been invested with the powers in this particular of the Parish Council. For without a Parish Council or a meeting invested with its powers there will be nobody to whom the land acquired by the County Council can be assured under sub-section 14 of section 9 of the Local Government Act, 1894.

In relation to procedure under section 9, Article I. prescribes the notice to be given in the parish or in the district (if it be urban), and to the owners, lessees, and occupiers of the land proposed to be taken. Article II. prescribes the notice of the public inquiry; Article III. prescribes the mode of serving copies of Orders made by County Councils; Article IV. relates to the same subject and also to the service of copies of the notices prescribed by Articles I. and II.; Article V. prescribes the period within which a memorial by a person interested, praying that an Order shall not become law without further inquiry, may be presented to the Local Government Board; and Article VI. prescribes adaptations of sub-section (2) of section 2, sub-sections (5), (6), (7), and (8) of section 3, and of section 11 of the Allotments Act, 1887, and section 3 of the Allotments Act, 1890.

(4.) With respect to case (iii), in which proceedings under the Allotments Acts, 1887 and 1890, are taken on the petition of the District Council, it may be said that the occasion for resorting to the procedure which section 9 of the Local Government Act, 1894, authorises, may arise at a stage in proceedings under the Allotments Act, 1887, at which the District Council are met by the difficulty that suitable land sufficient for allotments for their district or any parish in their district cannot be acquired by them by hiring or purchase by agreement at a reasonable price or rent, and subject to reasonable conditions.

At this stage the District Council, under section 3 (2) of the Allotments Act, 1887, may petition the County Council. On the receipt of such a petition it will be referred for investigation and report to the Standing Committee appointed by the County Council under section 3 of the Allotments Act, 1890.

Assuming that on the report of the Standing Committee the County Council consider that the case is one in which they should proceed under section 9 of the Local Government Act, 1894, it will be incumbent upon them in taking the various steps indicated in that enactment to observe the requirements of Articles I.—IV. of the Order. Articles V. and VI. also apply to cases in which District Councils are concerned.

Local Government Board,
May, 1895.

LIGHT RAILWAY (a).

RULES DATED SEPTEMBER, 1896, MADE BY THE BOARD OF TRADE WITH RESPECT TO APPLICATIONS TO THE LIGHT RAILWAY COMMISSIONERS FOR ORDERS AUTHORISING LIGHT RAILWAYS.*

Notice of Proposed Application.

1. Notice of intention to apply to the Light Railway Commissioners for an Order authorising a light railway, or for an amending Order, Notice by advertisement.

* *Official Note.*—These rules will regulate the procedure before the Light Railway Commissioners where a scheme for a light railway has been matured and it is intended to make a formal application for an Order.

The Commissioners will at all times be prepared to give every facility in their power for considering and maturing proposals for the construction of light railways to be submitted to them.

(a) See the Light Railways Act, 1896, *ante*, p. 720.

Rule 1. must be published by advertisement in each of two consecutive weeks in the month of April or of October, in at least one local newspaper circulating in the area or part of the area through which it is proposed to make the railway.

Contents of notice.

2. The notice must describe generally the line of the railway and its termini, and the lands proposed to be taken, stating the quantity and the purpose for which it is proposed to take them; it must state the proposed gauge and motive power of the railway; it must be subscribed with the name of the person, company, or council responsible for the publication of the notice (hereinafter referred to as "the promoters"); and must name a place where a plan of the proposed works and of the lands to be taken and a book of reference to the plan and a section of the proposed works may be seen at all reasonable hours, and where copies of the draft Order can be obtained on payment of not exceeding one shilling per copy.

The notice must state that objections should be made in writing to the Light Railway Commissioners in accordance with Rule 31.

Deposit with local authorities.

3. Copies of the draft Order and of the plan and book of reference and section and of the estimate hereinafter mentioned must be deposited by the promoters during the month of May or of November, with the clerk of the county council, and of every borough, district, and parish council in or through whose county, borough, district, or parish, any part of the railway is proposed to be made; and shall be open to inspection during office hours.

With the above documents there must also be deposited a sheet or sheets of the ordnance map, on the scale of not less than one inch to a mile, with the line of railway indicated thereon, so as to show its general course and direction.

Deposits with government departments.

4. Copies of the draft Order and of all the above documents, must be deposited by the promoters during the month of May or of November, with the Board of Trade, and copies of the draft Order with the Treasury, the Board of Agriculture, the Postmaster-General, the Commissioners of Customs and of Inland Revenue, the Admiralty, the War Office, the Office of Woods and Forests, and the Office of Works, and with the Secretary for Scotland in the case of proposed railways in Scotland.

Provided that as regards the provisions of this Rule and of Rules 1 and 3, in the year 1896 the month of November shall be substituted for the month of October, and the month of December for the month of November.

Plans, Book of Reference, and Sections.

Plan.

5. Every plan must be drawn to a scale of not less than four inches to the mile, and must describe the lands intended to be taken, and the line or situation of the whole of the railway (no alternative line or work being in any case permitted), and the lands in or

through which it is to be made, or through which any communication to or from the railway shall be made. Rule 5.

6. Where it is the intention of the promoters to apply for powers to make any lateral deviation from the line of the proposed railway, the limits of such deviation shall be defined on the plan, and all lands included within such limits shall be marked thereon. As to limits of deviation.

7. Unless the whole of such plan shall be upon a scale of not less than a quarter of an inch to every one hundred feet, an enlarged plan shall be added of any building, yard, courtyard, or land within the curtilage of any building, or of any ground cultivated as a garden, either in the line of the proposed work, or included with the limits of the said deviation, on a scale of not less than a quarter of an inch to every one hundred feet. Buildings, etc. on enlarged scale.

8. The distances from one of the termini must be shown in miles and furlongs on the plan, and a memorandum of the radius of every curve not exceeding one mile in length, shall be noted on the plan in furlongs and chains. Distances to be marked.

9. Where tunnelling as a substitute for open cutting is intended, the same shall be marked by a dotted line on the plan, and no work shall be shown as tunnelling in the making of which it will be necessary to cut through or remove the surface soil. Tunnelling to be marked.

10. If it be intended to divert widen or narrow any public carriage road, navigable river, canal, or railway, the course of such diversion and the extent of such widening or narrowing shall be marked on the plan. Diversion of roads, etc.

11. When a railway is intended to form a junction with an existing or authorised line of railway, the course of such existing or authorised line of railway shall be shown on the deposited plan for a distance of 800 yards on either side of the proposed junction on the same scale as the scale of the general plan. Case of junctions with other lines.

12. If it be intended to lay any part of the railway along a road or street, the plan shall show at what distance from an imaginary straight line drawn along the centre of such road or street it is proposed to lay th Case of rails along road.

13. The book of reference shall contain the names of the owners or reputed owners, lessees or reputed lessees, and occupiers of all lands and houses in the line of the proposed railway or within the limits of deviation as defined on the plan, and shall describe such lands and houses respectively. Book of reference.

The book of reference shall also contain the name of the road authority of any road or street along which it is proposed to lay any part of the railway.

14. The section shall be drawn to the same horizontal scale as the plan, and to a vertical scale of not less than one inch to every one hundred feet, and shall show the surface of the ground marked on the plan, the intended level of the proposed railway, the height of Scale of sections.

Rule 14.

every embankment and the depth of every cutting, and a datum horizontal line, which shall be the same throughout the whole length of the railway or any branch thereof respectively, and shall be referred to some fixed point (stated in writing on the section), near one of the termini of the railway.

In every section the line of the railway marked thereon shall correspond with the upper surface of the rails.

Vertical measures to be marked at change of gradient.

15. Distances on the datum line shall be marked in miles and furlongs, to correspond with those on the plan; a vertical measure from the datum line to the line of the railway shall be marked in feet and inches, or decimal parts of a foot, at the commencement and termination of the railway, and at each change of the gradient or inclination thereof; and the proportion or rate of inclination between every two consecutive vertical measures shall also be marked.

Height of railway over or depth under surface of roads, etc. to be marked.

16. Wherever the line of the railway is intended to cross any public carriage road, navigable river, canal, or railway, the height of the railway over or depth under the surface thereof, and the height and span of every arch of all bridges and viaducts by which the railway will be carried over the same, shall be marked in figures at every crossing thereof, and where the railway will be carried across any such public carriage road or railway, on the level thereof, such crossing shall be so described on the section, and it shall also be stated if such level will be unaltered.

Cross sections in certain cases.

17. If any alteration be intended in the water level of any canal, or in the level or rate of inclination of any public carriage road or railway, which will be crossed by the railway, then the same shall be stated on the section, and each alteration shall be numbered; and cross sections in reference to the numbers, on a horizontal scale of not less than one inch to every three hundred and thirty feet, and on a vertical scale of not less than one inch to every forty feet shall be added which shall show the present surface of such road, canal, or railway, and the intended surface thereof, when altered; and the greatest of the present and intended rates of inclination of the portion of such road or railway intended to be altered shall also be marked in figures thereon, and where any public carriage road is crossed on the level, a cross section of such road shall also be added; and all such cross sections shall extend for two hundred yards on each side of the centre line of the railway.

Embankments and cuttings.

18. Wherever the extreme height of an embankment, or the extreme depth of any cutting, shall exceed five feet, the extreme height over or depth under the surface of the ground shall be marked in figures on the section; and if any bridge or viaduct of more than three arches shall intervene in any embankment, or if any tunnel shall intervene in any cutting, the extreme height or depth shall be marked in figures on each of the parts into which such embankment or cutting shall be divided by such bridge, viaduct, or tunnel.

19. Where tunnelling, as a substitute for open cutting, or a viaduct as a substitute for solid embankment, is intended, the same shall be marked on the section, and no work shall be shown as tunnelling, in the making of which it will be necessary to cut through or remove the surface soil.

Rule 19. Tunnelling and viaduct to be marked.

20. When a railway is intended to form a junction with an existing or authorised line of railway, the gradient of such existing or authorised line of railway shall be shown on the deposited section, and in connection therewith, and on the same scale as the general section, for a distance of 800 yards on either side of the point of junction.

In case of junctions gradient of existing line to be shown on section.

Notices to Owners, Lessees, and Others.

21. During the month of April or of October the promoters must serve a notice on the owners, or reputed owners, lessees, or reputed lessees, and occupiers of all lands intended to be taken or being within the limits of deviation shown on the deposited plan, describing in each case the particular lands intended to be taken or being within such limits, and inquiring whether the person so served assents or dissents to the taking of such lands, and requesting him to state any objections he may have to such lands being taken.

Service of notices on landowners and others.

Every such notice shall be as nearly as may be in the form set out in the schedule to these Rules.

22. During the month of April or October the promoters must also serve a notice of the intended application on the owner, or reputed owner, lessee, or reputed lessee, of any railway, tramway, or canal which will be crossed or otherwise interfered with by the proposed railway; and on the road authority (where other than a county, borough, district, or parish council) of any road or street along which it is proposed to lay any rails, or which will be otherwise interfered with by the proposed railway; and such notice shall state the place or places where a plan or plans of the proposed railway has or have been or will be deposited.

Notice to owners of railway, etc.

Provided that as regards the provisions of this Rule and of Rule 21, in the year 1896 the month of November shall be substituted for the month of October.

23. Where an amending Order proposes to authorise the promoters to vary or to relinquish the whole or any part of a railway authorised by a former Order, the promoters must during the month of April or October serve notice of the proposal on the owners, or reputed owners, lessees, or reputed lessees, and occupiers of the lands in which any part of the said railway is situate.

Notice of relinquishment of works.

24. Where an amending Order proposes to repeal or alter any provision contained in a former Order for the protection or benefit of any person, public body, or company specifically named, the promoters must during the month of April or October serve notice of the intention to repeal or alter such provision on every such person, public body, or company.

Notice of repeal of protective provisions.

Rule 25.

Estimate.

Estimates.

25. An estimate of the expenses of the proposed railway (including the expense of acquiring land and all incidental expenses) must be made and signed by the person making the same.

26. The estimate shall be in the following form or as near thereto as circumstances may permit:—

Estimate of the proposed Light Railway.

			Whether Single or Double.	
Lines No. - - - - - - -				
	miles	fgs. chs.		
Length of line - - -				
Gauge - - - - - -	Cubic Yards.	Price per Yard.	£ s. d.	£ s. d.
Earthworks :				
Cuttings—Rock - - -				
Soft soil -				
Roads - - -				
Total - - -				
Embankments, including roads - -	Cubic yards			
Bridges—Public roads - - - -	Number			
Accommodation bridges and works - - - - -				
Viaducts - - - - - - - - -				
Culverts and drains - - - - - - -				
Metallings of roads and level crossings - - - -				
Gatekeepers' houses at level crossings - - - -				
Permanent way, including fencing : miles fgs. chs. at	Cost per mile. £ s. d.			
Permanent way for sidings, and cost of junctions - - -				
Stations - - - - - - - - -				
Contingencies - - - - - -	Per cent.			
Land and buildings :	a. r. p.			
Total - - -	£			

The same details for each branch, and general summary of total cost.

Application to the Commissioners.

Documents to accompany application.

27. Every application to the Commissioners for an Order must be made in the month of May or of November except in the year 1896, when it must be made in the month of December, and must be in the case of a corporate body under the seal of such body, and in any other case signed by the promoter or promoters, or if there

are more than two then by any three of them, and must be accompanied by— Rule 27

(a) a copy of the advertisement of the intention to apply for the Order;

(b) three copies of the Draft Order and of each of the documents required by these Rules to be deposited:

(c) a statement as to the proposed gauge and motive power of the railway;

(d) a list of the owners, or reputed owners, lessees, or reputed lessees, and occupiers on whom notices have been served, and a statement as far as can then be made whether in each case they assent, dissent, or are neuter;

(e) a list of the county borough district and parish councils in or through any part of whose county district or parish any part of the railway is proposed to be made, and a statement whether or not they have intimated assent or dissent to the proposal;

(f) a list of the railway, tramway, or canal companies (if any) on whom any notice has been served under these Rules, and a statement whether or not they have intimated assent or dissent to the proposal;

(g) a statement whether any consent of the Board of Agriculture required to any grant of land or to the acquisition of any common land proposed to be authorised by the draft Order has been obtained;

(h) a statement whether it is proposed that the Council of any county borough or district shall expend or advance any money, and if so, of the nature and amount of such expenditure or advance;

(i) a statement whether it is proposed to apply to the Treasury for the advance of any money, and if so, of the amount of the advance sought;

(k) a certificate that a fee of 50*l*. has been paid to the Board of Trade.

(l) a certificate, in the case of an application by an existing company, that the members of the company have assented to the application by such a resolution as is required by the Standing Orders of Parliament in the case of an application to Parliament by such company.

General Provisions as to Notices.

28. Notices and other such documents under these Rules may be in writing or print, or partly in writing and partly in print; and shall be sufficiently authenticated if signed by the clerk of the council, or by some principal officer of the company, or by the

Authentication, etc., of notices.

Rule 28.

promoter or any two or more of the promoters, on whose behalf the notice or other document is served.

Service of notices.

29. Notices and any other documents required or authorised to be served under the Rules may be served by delivering the same to or at the residence of the person to whom they are respectively addressed, or where addressed to the owner or occupier of premises by delivering the same or a true copy thereof to some person on the premises; or if there is no person on the premises who can be so served then by fixing the same on some conspicuous part of the premises; they may also be served by post by a prepaid letter, and if served by post shall be deemed to have been served at the time when the letter containing the same would be delivered in the ordinary course of post, and in proving such service it shall be sufficient to prove that the notice or other document was properly addressed and put into the post.

Any notice by these Rules required to be given to the owner or occupier of any premises may be addressed by the description of the "owner" or "occupier" of the premises (naming them) in respect of which the notice is given without further name or description.

Fees.

Fee payable to Board of Trade.

30. Before lodging any application with the Commissioners a fee of 50*l.* must be paid by the promoters to the Board of Trade, by cheque in favour of an Assistant Secretary of the Board of Trade.

General.

31. All communications to the Commissioners should be on foolscap paper and written on one side only, and should be addressed to—

The Secretary,
Light Railway Commission,
23, Great George Street,
London, S.W.

32. In the case of an application for an amending Order, such of the requirements of these Rules as are inapplicable will be dispensed with.

33. These Rules shall remain in force until modified by the Board of Trade.

COURTENAY BOYLE,
Secretary.

The Board of Trade,
September 1896.

SCHEDULE.

Schedule.

Form of Notice to Landowners and others.

SIR,

WE beg to inform you that application is intended to be made to the Light Railway Commissioners for an Order authorising a light railway from to , and that the property mentioned in the annexed schedule or some part thereof, in which we understand you are interested as therein stated, will be required for the purposes of the said railway, according to the line thereof as at present laid out, or may be required to be taken under the usual powers of deviation to the extent of yards on either side of the said line which will be applied for.

We also beg to inform you that a plan and section of the said undertaking, with a book of reference thereto, have been or will be deposited with the clerks of the (*specify county and other councils as the case may be*) on or before the last day of May [*or* November] and that copies of so much of the said plan and section as relates to the (*parish*) in which your property is situate, with a book of reference thereto, have been or will be deposited for public inspection with the (*clerk of the parish, district, or borough council*) on or before the day of on which plan your property is designated by the numbers set forth in the annexed schedule.

As we are required to report whether you assent to or dissent from the proposed undertaking, you will oblige us by writing your answer of assent or dissent in the form left herewith, and by stating any objections you may have to your property being taken, and returning the same to us with your signature on or before the day of next; and if there should be any error or misdescription in the annexed schedule, we shall feel obliged by your informing us thereof at your earliest convenience, that we may correct the same without delay.

We are, etc.,

Schedule referred to in the foregoing notice describing the property therein alluded to:—

—	Parish, Township, Townland, or extra-parochial Place.	Number on Plans.	Description.	Owner.	Lessee.	Occupier.
Property on the line of the proposed work, or within the limits of the deviation intended to be applied for.						

I, the undersigned, assent to [dissent from] my property being taken for the proposed work [and my objections are that].

LOCAL INQUIRIES.

Regulations as to Inquiries and Notices under Section 57 *of the Local Government Act,* 1888, *ante, p.* 111 (14*th September,* 1889).

To the County Councils for the several Administrative Counties in England and Wales;—

And to all others whom it may concern.

Whereas by sub-sections (1), (2), and (3) of section 57 of the Local Government Act, 1888, it is enacted as follows :—

"57.—(1.) Whenever a county council is satisfied that a primâ facie case is made out as respects any county district not a borough, or as respects any parish, for a proposal for all or any of the following things; that is to say,—

"(*a*) the alteration or definition of the boundary thereof;

"(*b*) the division thereof or the union thereof with any other such district or districts, parish or parishes, or the transfer of part of a parish to another parish;

"(*c*) the conversion of any such district or part thereof, if it is a rural district, into an urban district, and if it is an urban district, into a rural district, or the transfer of the whole or any part of any such district from one district to another, and the formation of new urban or rural districts:

"(*d*) the division of an urban district into wards; and

"(*e*) the alteration of the number of wards, or of the boundaries of any ward, or of the number of members of any district council, or of the apportionment of such members among the wards,

"the county council may cause such inquiry to be made in the locality, and such notice to be given, both in the locality, and to the Local Government Board, Education Department, or other Government department as may be prescribed, and such other inquiry and notices (if any) as they think fit, and if satisfied that such proposal is desirable, may make an order for the same accordingly.

"(2.) Notice of the provisions of the order shall be given, and copies thereof shall be supplied in the prescribed manner, and otherwise as the county council think fit, and if it relates to the division of a district into wards, or the alteration of the number of wards or of the boundaries of a ward, or of the number of the members of a district council, or of the apportionment of the members among the wards shall come into operation upon being finally approved by the county council.

"(3.) In any other case the order shall be submitted to the Local Government Board; and if within three months after such notice of the provisions of the order as the Local Government Board determine to be the first notice, the council of any district affected by the order, or any number of county electors registered in that district or in any ward of that district, not being less than one-sixth of the total number of electors in that district or ward, or if the order relates only to a parish, any number of county electors registered in that parish, not being less than one-sixth of the total number of electors in that parish, petition the Local Government Board to disallow the order, the Local Government Board shall cause to be made a local inquiry, and determine whether the order is to be confirmed or not."

And whereas by sub-section (4) of section 87 of the said Act it is enacted that—

"Where any matter is authorised or required by this Act to be prescribed, and no other provision is made, declaring how the same is to be prescribed, the same shall be prescribed from time to time by the Local Government Board."

And whereas in regard to the matters required by the said section 57 to be prescribed no provision other than that contained in the said section 87 is made, declaring how such matters are to be prescribed:

Now therefore, We, the Local Government Board, in pursuance of the powers given to Us in that behalf, do, by this Our Order, and until We shall otherwise Direct, Prescribe and Determine as follows, with respect to the Inquiries to be made and the notices to be given for the purposes of the said section 57 of the Local Government Act, 1888, the manner of giving such notices, and the several other matters to be prescribed and determined for the purposes of the said section; that is to say,—

ARTICLE I.—(1.) Prior to any Order being made by a County Council in regard to a proposal for all or any of the things specified in sub-section (1) of section 57 of the Local Government Act, 1888, a local Inquiry, at which all persons interested may attend and be heard, shall be held in regard to the proposal as the Council may direct, either by a Committee of the County Council, or by some Person appointed by the County Council to hold such Inquiry.

(2.) If the proposal relate to one or more County Districts, the said Inquiry shall be held at some convenient place in such district or in one of such districts; and if the proposal relate to a parish or parishes, the said Inquiry shall be held either in such Parish or in one of such Parishes, or at such place in the neighbourhood as may, in the opinion of the Committee or Person by whom the Inquiry is to be held, be most convenient for the purpose.

(3.) Before the day when the Inquiry is to be held, public notice of the purport of the proposal, and of the day, time, and place fixed for the Inquiry in regard to it, shall be given by the County Council by advertisement in two successive weeks in some local newspaper circulating in the locality to which the proposal relates.

ARTICLE II.—At least fourteen days before the day when the Inquiry is to be held, a printed Notice of the purport of the proposal, and of the day, time, and place for the Inquiry shall also be published in the manner herein-after described, and shall be sent to the several Government Departments and Local or other Authorities herein-after specified; that is to say,—

(1.) A copy of the said Notice shall be posted as a bill or placard in such places in the County District or Districts or Parish or Parishes interested in the proposal as are ordinarily made use of for posting public or parochial notices.

(2.) In any case where the proposal relates to the alteration of or other dealing with any Sanitary District, a copy of the Notice shall be sent by the County Council to the Sanitary Authority of such District.

(3.) In any case where the proposal relates to the alteration of or other dealing with any Parish a copy of the Notice shall be sent by the County Council to the Overseers of the Poor of such Parish; to the Guardians of the Poor of the Union in which such Parish is comprised; to the School Board (if any) for such Parish or for any part thereof; to the Highway Authority or Authorities of the Parish; to the Burial Board (if any) for such Parish or for any part thereof; and to the Urban Sanitary Authority (if any) in whose district such Parish or any part thereof is comprised.

(4.) A copy of the Notice shall be sent by the County Council to any Local Authority which, in the opinion of the County Council, is specially interested in the proposal.

(5.) A copy of every such Notice shall be sent by the County Council to the Local Government Board; and in any case where the proposal relates to all or any of the things mentioned in paragraphs (*a*), (*b*), and (*c*) of sub-section (1) of section 57 of the said Act, a copy of the Notice shall be sent by the County Council to the Public Works Loan Commissioners, the Director General of the Ordnance Survey at Southampton, and to the Registrar General; and in any case where the proposal relates to the alteration or definition of the boundary of any Parish a copy of the Notice shall be sent to the Education Department.

ARTICLE III.—Public notice of the provisions of any Order made by a County Council under sub-section (1) of section 57 of the said Act shall be given by the County Council by advertisement in two successive weeks in some local newspaper circulating in each District or Parish affected by the Order; and the first of such advertisements shall be published within fourteen days after the making of the Order.

The said advertisement shall contain either a copy of the Order or a statement of the effect of the Order, and shall also contain a statement of the time and place or places during and at which copies of the Order may be inspected by any owner or ratepayer in any area affected by the Order during a period of one month from the date of the first publication of such advertisement, and the Order shall be open for such inspection during such period.

Article IV.—A copy of any Order made as aforesaid by a County Council shall, at any time while copies of the Order are open to inspection as aforesaid, and, in the case of an Order which requires to be confirmed by the Local Government Board, at any time before the confirmation of the Order by the Local Government Board, be supplied by the Clerk to the Council to any owner or ratepayer in any area affected by the Order, upon payment by such owner or ratepayer of a sum not exceeding threepence for each hundred words of manuscript if the copy of the Order be in writing, or upon payment of a sum not exceeding threepence for a printed copy of the Order.

Article V.—On or before the date of the first publication of the advertisement in pursuance of Article III. hereof of the provisions of any Order made as aforesaid, and, in the case of any such Order which does not require to be confirmed by the Local Government Board, one month at least before the Order is finally approved by the County Council under the said sub-section (2) of section 57 of the said Act, three copies of the Order shall be forwarded to the Local Government Board and to each of the other Government Departments to whom a copy of the Notice of the Inquiry relative to the proposed Order was, by Article II. of this Order, required to be sent; a copy of the Order shall also be sent to each of the Local or other Authorities to whom a copy of such Notice was so required to be sent, and a copy shall also be posted in like manner as the Notice of the Inquiry was, in pursuance of the same Article, required to be posted.

Article VI.—The first advertisement in pursuance of Article III. hereof of the provisions of any Order made by a County Council under the said sub-section (1) of section 57 of the said Act shall be deemed to be the "first notice" for the purposes of sub-section (3) of that section

Article VII.—The expression "County Council" in this Order shall include a Joint Committee appointed under section 81 of the said Act by any County Councils of Administrative Counties for the purpose of dealing under section 57 of the said Act with a matter in which such Councils are jointly interested.

Given under the Seal of Office of the Local Government Board, this Fourteenth day of September, in the year One thousand eight hundred and eighty-nine.

(L.S.) Chas. T. Ritchie,
President.

Hugh Owen,
Secretary.

LOCOMOTIVES ON HIGHWAYS (a).

Regulations (*9th November*, 1896).

To the County Councils of the several Administrative Counties in England and Wales ;—

To the Councils of the several County Boroughs in England and Wales ;—

To the Sanitary Authorities of the several Sanitary Districts in the Administrative County of London ;—

To the Urban District Councils of the several Urban Districts in England and Wales ;—

To the Rural District Councils acting as the Highway Authorities in Rural Districts in England and Wales ;—

And to all others whom it may concern.

Whereas by section 6 of the Locomotives on Highways Act, 1896 (*b*) (herein-after called "the Act"), it is enacted that—

"(1.) The Local Government Board may make regulations with respect to the use of light locomotives on highways, and their construction, and the conditions under which they may be used.

"(2.) . . . All regulations under this section shall have full effect notwithstanding anything in any other Act, whether general or local, or any bye-laws or regulations made thereunder."

And whereas by section 2 of the Act it is enacted that—

"During the period between one hour after sunset and one hour before sunrise, the person in charge of a light locomotive shall carry attached thereto a lamp so constructed and placed as to exhibit a light in accordance with the regulations to be made by the Local Government Board."

And whereas by section 7 of the Act it is enacted that—

"A breach of any . . . regulation made under this Act, . . . may, on summary conviction, be punished by a fine not exceeding ten pounds."

Now therefore, in pursuance of the powers given to Us by the Act, and by any other Statutes in that behalf, We, the Local Government Board, Do by this Our Order make the following Regulations with respect to the use of Light Locomotives on Highways, and their construction, and the conditions under which they may be used, and Direct that the same shall have effect on and after the Fourteenth day of November, One thousand eight hundred and ninety-six :—

ARTICLE I.—In this Order—

The expression "carriage" includes a waggon, cart, or other vehicle.

(*a*) See as to the construction of wheels of locomotives on highways the Order of November 26th, 1897, *post*, p. 856, which Order does not, like the Order here set out, apply to "Light Locomotives." See as to this the circular of the Local Government Board, *post*, pp. 855, 856.

(*b*) *Ante*, p. 717.

The expression "horse" includes a mule or other beast of draught or burden, and the expression "cattle" includes sheep.

The expression "Light Locomotive" means a vehicle propelled by mechanical power which is under three tons in weight unladen, and is not used for the purpose of drawing more than one vehicle (such vehicle with its locomotive not exceeding in weight unladen four tons), and is so constructed that no smoke or visible vapour is emitted therefrom except from any temporary or accidental cause.

In calculating for the purposes of this Order the weight of a vehicle unladen, the weight of any water, fuel, or accumulators used for the purpose of propulsion shall not be included.

ARTICLE II.—No person shall cause or permit a Light Locomotive to be used on any highway, or shall drive or have the charge of a Light Locomotive when so used, unless the conditions herein-after set forth shall be satisfied, namely,—

(1.) The Light Locomotive, if it exceeds in weight unladen five hundredweight, shall be capable of being so worked that it may travel either forwards or backwards.

(2.) The Light Locomotive shall not exceed six and a half feet in width, such width to be measured between its extreme projecting points.

(3.) The tyre of each wheel of the Light Locomotive shall be smooth and shall, where the same touches the ground, be flat and of the width following, namely,—

(a) if the weight of the Light Locomotive unladen exceeds fifteen hundredweight, but does not exceed one ton, not less than two and a half inches;

(b) if such weight exceeds one ton, but does not exceed two tons, not less than three inches;

(c) if such weight exceeds two tons, not less than four inches.

Provided that where a pneumatic tyre or other tyre of a soft and elastic material is used, the tyre may be round or curved, and there may be upon the same projections or bosses rising above the surface of the tyre if such projections or bosses are of the same material as that of the tyre itself, or of some other soft and elastic material. The width of the tyre shall, for the purpose of this proviso, mean the extreme width of the soft and elastic material on the rim of the wheel when not subject to pressure.

(4.) The Light Locomotive shall have two independent brakes in good working order, and of such efficiency that the application of either to such Locomotive shall cause two of its wheels on the same axle to be so held that the wheels shall be effectually prevented from revolving, or shall have the same effect in stopping the Light Locomotive as if such wheels were so held.

Provided that in the case of a bicycle this Regulation shall apply as if, instead of two wheels on the same axle, one wheel was therein referred to.

(5.) The Light Locomotive shall be so constructed as to admit of its being at all times under such control as not to cause undue interference with passenger or other traffic on any highway.

(6.) In the case of a Light Locomotive drawing or constructed to draw another vehicle or constructed or used for the carriage of goods, the name of the owner and the place of his abode or business, and in every such case and in the case of every Light Locomotive weighing unladen one ton and a half or upwards, the weight of the Light Locomotive unladen shall be painted in one or more straight lines upon some conspicuous part of the right or off side of the Light Locomotive in large legible letters in white upon black or black upon white, not less than one inch in height.

(7.) The Light Locomotive and all the fittings thereof shall be in such a condition as not to cause, or to be likely to cause, danger to any person on the Light Locomotive or on any highway.

(8.) There shall be in charge of the Light Locomotive when used on any highway a person competent to control and direct its use and movement.

(9.) The lamp to be carried attached to the Light Locomotive in pursuance of section 2 of the Act shall be so constructed and placed as to exhibit, during the period between one hour after sunset and one hour before sunrise, a white light visible within a reasonable distance in the direction towards which the Light Locomotive is proceeding or is intended to proceed, and to exhibit a red light so visible in the reverse direction. The lamp shall be placed on the extreme right or off side of the Light Locomotive in such a position as to be free from all obstruction to the light.

Provided that this Regulation shall not extend to any bicycle, tricycle, or other machine to which section 85 of the Local Government Act, 1888, applies.

ARTICLE III.—No person shall cause or permit a Light Locomotive to be used on any highway for the purpose of drawing any vehicle, or shall drive or have charge of a Light Locomotive when used for such purpose unless the conditions herein-after set forth shall be satisfied, namely,—

(1.) Regulations (2), (3), (5), and (7) of Article II. of this Order shall apply as if the vehicle drawn by the Light Locomotive was therein referred to instead of the Light Locomotive itself, and Regulation (6) of the Article shall apply as if such vehicle was a Light Locomotive constructed for the carriage of goods.

(2.) The vehicle drawn by the Light Locomotive, except where the Light Locomotive travels at a rate not exceeding four miles an hour, shall have a brake in good working order of such efficiency that its application to the vehicle shall cause two of the wheels of the vehicle on the same axle to be so held that the wheels shall be effectually prevented from revolving, or shall have the same effect in stopping the vehicle as if such wheels were so held.

(3.) The vehicle drawn by the Light Locomotive shall, when under the last preceding Regulation a brake is required to be attached thereto, carry upon the vehicle a person competent to apply efficiently the brake: Provided that it shall not be necessary to comply with this Regulation if the brakes upon the Light Locomotive by which the vehicle is drawn are so constructed and arranged that neither of such brakes can be used without bringing into action simultaneously the brake attached to the vehicle drawn, or if the brake of the vehicle drawn can be applied from the Light Locomotive independently of the brakes of the latter.

Article IV.—Every person driving or in charge of a Light Locomotive when used on any highway shall comply with the Regulations herein-after set forth; namely,—

(1.) He shall not drive the Light Locomotive at any speed greater than is reasonable and proper having regard to the traffic on the highway, or so as to endanger the life or limb of any person, or to the common danger of passengers.

(2.) He shall not under any circumstances drive the Light Locomotive at a greater speed than twelve miles an hour. If the weight unladen of the Light Locomotive is one ton and a half and does not exceed two tons, he shall not drive the same at a greater speed than eight miles an hour, or if such weight exceeds two tons at a greater speed than five miles an hour.

Provided that whatever may be the weight of the Light Locomotive, if it is used on any highway to draw any vehicle, he shall not under any circumstances drive it at a greater speed than six miles an hour.

Provided also that this Regulation shall only have effect during six months from the date of this Order, and thereafter until We otherwise direct.

(3.) He shall not cause the Light Locomotive to travel backwards for a greater distance or time than may be requisite for purposes of safety.

(4.) He shall not negligently or wilfully cause any hurt or damage to any person, carriage, horse, or cattle, or to any goods conveyed in any carriage on any highway, or, when on the Light Locomotive, be in such a position that he cannot have control over the same, or quit the Light Locomotive without having taken due precautions against its being started in his absence, or allow the Light Locomotive or a vehicle drawn thereby to stand on such highway so as to cause any unnecessary obstruction thereof.

(5.) He shall when meeting any carriage, horse, or cattle keep the Light Locomotive on the left or near side of the road, and when passing any carriage, horse, or cattle proceeding in the same direction keep the Light Locomotive on the right or off side of the same.

(6.) He shall not negligently or wilfully prevent, hinder, or interrupt the free passage of any person, carriage horse, or cattle on any highway, and shall keep the Light Locomotive and any vehicle drawn thereby on the left or near side of the road for the purpose of allowing such passage.

(7.) He shall, whenever necessary, by sounding the bell or other instrument required by section 3 of the Act, give audible and sufficient warning of the approach or position of the Light Locomotive.

(8.) He shall on the request of any police constable, or of any person having charge of a restive horse, or on any such constable or person putting up his hand as a signal for that purpose, cause the Light Locomotive to stop and to remain stationary so long as may be reasonably necessary.

ARTICLE V.—If the Light Locomotive is one to which Regulation (6) of Article II. applies, and the particulars required by that Regulation are not duly painted thereon, or if the Light Locomotive is one to which that Regulation does not apply, the person driving or in charge thereof shall, on the request of any constable, or on the reasonable request of any other person, truly state his name and place of abode, and the name of the owner, and the place of his abode or business.

This Order may be cited as "The Light Locomotives on Highways Order, 1896."

Given under the Seal of Office of the Local Government Board, this ninth day of November, in the year One thousand eight hundred and ninety-six.

(L.S.) HENRY CHAPLIN, *President.*

HUGH OWEN, *Secretary.*

The following circular was issued with the foregoing order :

LOCOMOTIVES ON HIGHWAYS ACT, 1896.

Local Government Board,
Whitehall, S. W.,
10th November, 1896.

Sir,

Order No. 35,520. I am directed by the Local Government Board to draw attention to the provisions of the Locomotives on Highways Act, 1896 (59 & 60

Vict. c. 36), the object of which is to amend the law with respect to the use of locomotives on highways. The Act will come into operation on the 14th instant. (Section 12.)

Light Locomotives.

Exception from certain Enactments.

Regulations of Secretary of State.

Sub-section (1) of section 1 of the Act provides that the enactments mentioned in the Schedule, and any other enactment restricting the use of locomotives on highways, and contained in any public, general, or local and personal Act in force at the passing of the new Act, shall not apply to any vehicle propelled by mechanical power if it is under three tons in weight unladen, and is not used for the purpose of drawing more than one vehicle (such vehicle with its locomotive not to exceed in weight unladen four tons), and is so constructed that no smoke or visible vapour is emitted therefrom except from any temporary or accidental cause. Vehicles so exempted, whether locomotives or drawn by locomotives, are in the Act referred to as Light Locomotives.

In calculating for the purposes of the Act the weight of a vehicle unladen, the weight of any water, fuel, or accumulators, used for the purpose of propulsion, is not to be included. (Section 1 (2).)

The enactments which are mentioned in the Schedule to the Act, and which are not to apply to light locomotives, are the Locomotives Act, 1861 (24 & 25 Vict. c. 70), section 41 of the Thames Embankment Act, 1862 (25 & 26 Vict. c. 93), the Locomotives Act, 1865 (28 & 29 Vict. c. 83), and Part II. of the Highways and Locomotives (Amendment) Act, 1878 (41 & 42 Vict. c. 77). An exception is, however, made as regards so much of section 1 of the Locomotives Act, 1861, as relates to tolls on locomotives, as regards section 7 of that Act, which requires damage caused by locomotives to bridges to be made good, and as regards section 13, which provides that nothing in the Act shall authorise any person to use upon a highway a locomotive engine which shall be so constructed or used as to cause a public or private nuisance, and directs that every person using a locomotive engine on a highway shall, notwithstanding the Act, be liable to an indictment or action for such use, where, but for the passing of the Act, such indictment or action could be maintained. Light Locomotives will not be exempted from these enactments.

Among the enactments from which Light Locomotives will be exempted, and which are included in the Schedule to the new Act, special attention may be directed to the provisions of section 28 of the Highways and Locomotives (Amendment) Act, 1878, regulating the weight of locomotives and the construction of wheels, and to sections 31 and 32 of the same Act, under which various bodies may make bye-laws as to certain matters relating to the use of locomotives. These provisions will not apply to Light Locomotives, and no licence from the council of any county or county borough will be required for the use of these locomotives.

Light Locomotive to be deemed a Carriage.

A Light Locomotive is to be deemed to be a carriage within the meaning of any Act of Parliament, whether public, general or local and of any rule, regulation, or bye-law made under any Act of Parliament, and if used as a carriage of any particular class, is to be deemed to be a carriage of that class and the law relating to carriages of that class is to apply accordingly. (Section 1 (1) (b).) Consequently if, *e.g.*, a Light Locomotive is used as a hackney carriage, all statutory provisions and bye-laws with regard to hackney carriages in force in the place in which the Light Locomotive is used will apply to it.

Excise Duty on Light Locomotives.

Under section 4 of the Customs and Inland Revenue Act, 1888 (51 & 52 Vict. c. 8), certain excise duties are payable for every carriage and every hackney carriage as thereby defined. The definition of carriage includes any carriage, except a hackney carriage, drawn or propelled upon a road or tramway by steam or electricity or any other mechanical power, but does not include a waggon, cart, or other such vehicle which is constructed or adapted for use, and is used, solely for the conveyance of any goods or burden in the course of trade or husbandry, and whereon the christian name and surname and place of abode or place of business of the person, or the name or style and principal or only place of business of the company or firm keeping the same are visibly and legibly painted in letters of not less than one inch in length. Hackney carriage is defined by the section as meaning any carriage standing or plying for hire, and including any carriage let for hire by a coachmaker or other person whose trade or business it is to sell carriages, or to let carriages for hire, provided that such carriage is not let for a period amounting to three months or more.

The duties imposed by the section will be payable for Light Locomotives which are carriages or hackney carriages as above defined, but besides these, where a Light Locomotive is liable to duty, either as a carriage or as a hackney carriage, under section 4 of the Customs and Inland Revenue Act, 1888, an additional excise duty will, on and after the 1st of January next, be payable for it under section 8 of the new Act, at the following rate, namely :—

	£	*s.*	*d.*
If the weight of the Locomotive exceeds one ton unladen, but does not exceed 2 tons unladen - - - - -	2	2	0
If the weight of the Locomotive exceeds 2 tons unladen	3	3	0

Every such duty must be paid together with the duty on the licence for the Locomotive as a carriage or a hackney carriage, and it will be dealt with in manner directed with respect to duties on local taxation licences within the meaning of the Local Government Act, 1888. The duty will accordingly be collected by the Inland Revenue Commissioners, and be paid with the proceeds of the duties on local taxation licences into the Local Taxation Account.

Regulations of Board as to Light Locomotives.

Section 6 of the Act empowers the Board to make regulations with respect to the use of Light Locomotives on highways and their construction, and the conditions under which they may be used. The Board, after communicating with other Government Departments interested, and with a large number of Local Authorities, manufacturers of Locomotives, and other persons and bodies concerned, and considering the suggestions thus obtained, have issued an Order making Regulations in pursuance of the power conferred upon them by the section, and copies of the Order are enclosed.

The Order has been placed on sale and will shortly be obtainable from Messrs. Eyre and Spottiswoode, East Harding Street, Fleet Street, London, E.C., either directly or through any bookseller.

In the Act, as already explained, the term "Light Locomotive" includes vehicles which are exempted from the enactments in the Schedule, whether they are locomotives or are drawn by locomotives. For the purposes of the Order, however, it has been found convenient not to include in the term any vehicle drawn by a Locomotive. Article I. accordingly provides that in the Order the expression "Light Locomotive" shall mean a vehicle propelled by mechanical power which is under three tons in weight unladen, and is not used for the purpose of drawing more than one vehicle (such vehicle with its locomotive not exceeding in weight unladen four tons), and is so constructed that no smoke or visible vapour is emitted therefrom except from any temporary or accidental cause.

In the part of this circular dealing with Regulations made by the Board under the Act, the term "Light Locomotive" is used in this sense.

In calculating for the purposes of the Order, the weight of a vehicle unladen, the weight of any water, fuel, or accumulators used for the purpose of propulsion is not to be included.

Article II. prohibits any person from causing or permitting a Light Locomotive to be used on any highway, or from driving or having charge of a Light Locomotive when so used, unless certain conditions are satisfied. These conditions require that the Light Locomotive, if it exceeds in weight unladen 5 cwt., shall be capable of being so worked that it may travel either forwards or backwards, and relate to the width of the Light Locomotive, the smoothness and width of the tyres of the wheels and to the brakes. They also require that the Light Locomotive shall be so constructed as to admit of its being at all times under such control as not to cause undue interference with passenger or other traffic on any highway, that the Light Locomotive and all its fittings shall be in such a condition as not to cause, or to be likely to cause, danger to any person on the Light Locomotive or on any highway, and that there shall be in charge of the Light Locomotive, when used on any highway, a person competent to control and direct its use and movement.

Regulation (6) of Article I. requires that the name of the owner, and the place of his abode or business, and the weight of the Light Locomotive unladen, shall, in the case of a Light Locomotive drawing or constructed to draw another vehicle, or constructed or used for the carriage of goods, be painted in one or more straight lines upon some conspicuous part of the right or off side of the Light Locomotive in large legible letters, in white upon black or black upon white, not less than one inch in height. Moreover, the weight of the Light Locomotive must in every case, where unladen it amounts to a ton and a half or upwards, be painted on it in a similar manner.

It will be observed that this Regulation will not extend to all Light Locomotives. So far as it relates to the name of the owner and the place of his abode or business, it will only apply to the case of any Light Locomotive drawing or constructed to draw another vehicle, or constructed or used for the carriage of goods, whilst as regards the weight of the Light Locomotive, it will apply to these cases, and also to the case of any Light Locomotive weighing a ton and a half or upwards.

If the Light Locomotive is one to which the Regulation applies and the particulars required are not duly painted on it, or if the Light Locomotive is not one to which the Regulation applies, the person driving or in charge of it is required by Article V. of the Order, on the request of any constable, or on the reasonable request of any other person, to truly state his name and place of abode, and the name of the owner, and the place of his abode or business.

Section 2 of the Act directs that during the period between one hour after sunset and one hour before sunrise the person in charge of a Light Locomotive shall carry attached thereto a lamp so constructed and placed as to exhibit a light in accordance with the regulations to be made by the Board. Regulation (9) of Article I. of the Order accordingly makes it one of the conditions upon which a Light Locomotive can be used on a highway that the lamp to be carried attached to it in pursuance of section 2 of the Act shall be so constructed and placed as to exhibit, during the period between one hour after sunset and one hour before sunrise, a white light visible within a reasonable distance in the direction towards which the Light Locomotive is proceeding or is intended to proceed, and to exhibit a red light, so visible, in the reverse direction. The lamp must be placed on the extreme right or off side of the Light Locomotive in such position as to be free from all obstruction to the light. The Regulation will not extend to bicycles, tricycles, velocipedes, or other similar machines. Section 85 of the Local Government Act, 1888, contains provisions as to the lamp to be carried by these machines.

Article III. of the Order deals with any vehicle drawn by a Light Locomotive, and prohibits any person from causing or permitting a Light Locomotive to be used on a highway for the purpose of drawing any vehicle, or from driving or having charge of a Light Locomotive when used for this purpose, unless certain conditions are satisfied.

The effect of the Article is to make applicable to a vehicle drawn by a Light Locomotive the conditions in Article II. with respect to the width of the Light Locomotive, and to the tyres of the wheels, with respect to the construction of the Light Locomotive so as to secure its being under such control as not to cause undue interference with passenger or other traffic on any highway, and with respect to the Light Locomotive and its fittings being in such a condition as not to cause, or to be likely to cause danger to any person on the Light Locomotive or on any highway. The Regulations in Article II. on these subjects will apply as if the vehicle drawn by a Light Locomotive was therein referred to instead of the Light Locomotive itself. Moreover the name of the owner, and the place of his abode or business, and the weight of the vehicle must be painted on it in the manner directed by Regulation (6) of Article II. in the case of a Light Locomotive constructed for the carriage of goods.

Article III. also directs that any vehicle drawn by a Light Locomotive, except where the Light Locomotive travels at a rate not exceeding four miles an hour, must have a brake of a prescribed efficiency, and requires that the vehicle shall carry upon it a person competent to apply the brake efficiently. It will not, however, be necessary to comply with this last condition, if the brakes upon the Light Locomotive by which the vehicle is drawn are so constructed and arranged that neither of them can be used without bringing into action simultaneously the brake attached to the vehicle drawn, or if the brake of the vehicle drawn can be applied from the Light Locomotive independently of the brakes of the latter.

By Article IV. Regulations are made with which every person driving or in charge of a Light Locomotive when used on any highway is required to comply. These Regulations are intended to prevent injury being caused by any Light Locomotive to any person, carriage, horse, or cattle, or to any goods conveyed in any carriage on a highway, and also to prevent obstruction of the highway by Light Locomotives or vehicles drawn by them, or undue interference with the ordinary traffic. The usual rules applicable where carriages meet or pass each other are required to be observed in the case of Light Locomotives, and any person driving or in charge of a Light Locomotive must, on the request of any police constable or of any person having charge of a restive horse, or on the constable or person putting up his hand as a signal for that purpose, cause the Light Locomotive to stop, and to remain stationary so long as may be reasonably necessary.

The provision in Section 3 of the Act that every Light Locomotive shall carry a bell or other instrument capable of giving audible and sufficient warning of the approach or position of the carriage is supplemented by Regulation (7) of Article IV., which directs that the person driving or in charge of the Light Locomotive shall, whenever necessary, by sounding such bell or other instrument, give audible and sufficient warning of the approach or position of the Light Locomotive.

Speed of Light Locomotives.

Section 4 of the Act directs that no Light Locomotive shall travel along a public highway at a greater speed than 14 miles an hour, or than any less speed that may be prescribed by Regulations of the Board. There is considerable difficulty in laying down definite rules as to the speed of Light Locomotives at the present time, as no experience has been obtained of their use in this country; but the Board have been strongly urged to make some general Regulations on the subject, and they have dealt with it by Article IV. of the Order. That Article directs that a person driving or in charge of a Light Locomotive when used on any highway shall not drive it at any speed greater than is reasonable and proper, regard being had to the traffic on the highway, or so as to endanger the life or limb of any person, or to the common danger of passengers. Regulation (2) of the article further provides that he shall not under any circumstances drive the Light Locomotive at a greater speed than 12 miles an hour. The Board have considered that some further restrictions should be placed on the speed of Light Locomotives of considerable weight. The Article accordingly provides that if the weight of the Light Locomotive unladen is one ton and a half, and does not exceed two tons, it shall not be driven at a greater speed than eight miles an hour, or if such weight exceeds two tons, at a greater speed than five miles an hour.

A low rate of speed is specially necessary where a Light Locomotive is used on any highway to draw another vehicle, and the Article directs that in this case the Light Locomotive shall not under any circumstances be driven at a greater speed than six miles an hour.

The Board are aware that experience may render it desirable that modifications should be made in the rules on this subject, and they have accordingly provided that Regulation (2) of Article IV. shall only have effect for six months from the date of the Order, and thereafter until they otherwise direct.

It will be understood that a person driving a Light Locomotive will not necessarily be entitled to drive it at the rates of speed mentioned in this Regulation (2). He cannot drive at a greater speed than is prescribed by the Regulation, but he must drive at such less speed as is required to enable him not to contravene Regulation (1) of Article IV., which prohibits him from driving at any greater speed than is reasonable and proper, regard being had to the traffic on the highway. or so as to endanger the life or limb of any person, or to the common danger of passengers.

The Regulations which the Board have made are of general application, but sub-section (2) of section 6 of the Act provides that Regulations under the section may, if the Board deem it necessary, be of a local nature and limited in their application to a particular area, and may, on the application of any local authority, prohibit or restrict the use of locomotives for purposes of traction in crowded streets, or in other places where such use may be attended with danger to the public.

It will, of course, be competent to any Local Authority to apply to the Board under this enactment to make Regulations of a local nature as to the speed of Light Locomotives if they consider that the circumstances of their district render further Regulations necessary, but the Board would suggest that any such application should be deferred until some experience has been obtained of the working of the general Regulations on the subject.

Effect of Regulations.

All Regulations made by the Board under the Act will, under section 6 (2) have full effect, notwithstanding anything in any other Act, whether general or local, or any bye-law or regulations made thereunder; but they will not exempt a Light Locomotive, or the owner or person in charge of it, from the operation of any statutory provision or bye-law applicable thereto, and such provision will apply as if the Regulations had not been made.

Regulations of Secretary of State.

Section 5 of the Act provides that the keeping and use of petroleum or of any other inflammable liquid or fuel for the purpose of Light Locomotives shall be subject to Regulations made by a Secretary of State, and that Regulations so made shall have effect notwithstanding anything in the Petroleum Acts, 1871 to 1881. The Secretary of State has made Regulations under this provision and copies of them are enclosed at his request. They have been placed on sale, so that they will shortly be obtainable in the same way as the Regulations made by the Board.

Byelaws by Council of County or County Borough.

Under proviso (*a*) to section 1 (1) of the Act the council of any county or county borough are empowered to make byelaws preventing or restricting the use of Light Locomotives upon any bridge within their area, where the council are satisfied that such use would be attended with damage to the bridge or danger to the public.

Byelaws made under this provision will not require sanction or confirmation by the Board or by any other authority.

Fines.

A breach of any byelaw or Regulation made under the Act, or of any provision of the Act, may, on summary conviction, be punished by a fine not exceeding £10. (Section 7.)

Driving Wheels of Locomotives other than Light Locomotives.

The provisions of the Act for the most part relate to Light Locomotives as thereby defined, but it contains one section which applies to other locomotives on roads. Sub-section (4) of section 28 of the Highways and Locomotives (Amendment) Act, 1878, provides that the driving wheel of a Locomotive shall be cylindrical and smooth-soled, or shod with diagonal cross-bars of not less than three inches in width nor more than three-quarters of an inch in thickness, extending the full breadth of the tyre, and that the space intervening between each such cross-bar shall not exceed three inches. Section 9 of the new Act provides that these requirements may be from time to time varied by Order of the Board. As section 28 of the Act of 1878 is included in Part II. of that Act, and Light Locomotives are exempted from this Part, neither sub-section (4) of section 28 of the Act of 1878 nor section 9 of the Act of 1896 will apply to these Locomotives.

I am, Sir,
Your obedient Servant,
HUGH OWEN,
Secretary.

The Clerk to the County Council,
or other Local Authority.

General Order, 26*th November*, 1897, *varying Provisions as to Construction of Wheels of Locomotives on Highways* (*a*).

To the County Councils of the several Administrative Counties in England and Wales;—

To the Councils of the several County Boroughs in England and Wales;—

To the Sanitary Authorities of the several Sanitary Districts in the Administrative County of London;—

To the Urban District Councils of the several Urban Districts in England and Wales;—

To the Rural District Councils acting as the Highway Authorities in Rural Districts in England and Wales;—

And to all others whom it may concern.

Whereas by section 28 of the Highways and Locomotives (Amendment) Act, 1878, it is enacted that it shall not be lawful to use on any turnpike road or highway a Locomotive constructed otherwise than in accordance with the provisions therein set forth, and by sub-section (4) of that section it is provided as follows; that is to say,—

"The driving wheels of a locomotive shall be cylindrical and smooth-soled, or shod with diagonal cross-bars of not less than three inches in width nor more than three-quarters of an inch in thickness, extending the full breadth of the tyre, and the space intervening between each such cross-bar shall not exceed three inches."

And whereas by section 9 of the Locomotives on Highways Act, 1896, it is enacted that the requirements of the above-cited sub-section (4) of section 28 of the Highways and Locomotives (Amendment) Act, 1878, may be from time to time varied by Order of the Local Government Board:

(*a*) This Order does not apply to "Light Locomotives." See note, *ante*, p. 844, and the last paragraph of the above circular.

Now therefore, in pursuance of the powers given to Us in that behalf, We, the Local Government Board, hereby vary the provisions of sub-section (4) of section 28 of the Highways and Locomotives (Amendment) Act, 1878, as follows :—

A locomotive may be used the driving wheels of which instead of being smooth-soled or shod with cross-bars are shod with wooden blocks, subject to the following conditions :—

1. No block shall be less than five inches in width measured along the circumference of the wheel.
2. The blocks shall not be more than two inches apart similarly measured.
3. The blocks shall be arranged in two or more rows, and so that a straight line drawn through the middle of each block shall pass through the middle of the interval between the blocks of the next row.
4. The width of each block measured across the circumference of the wheel shall be such that the sum of the widths of the blocks shall not be less than the width prescribed by the Act for the tire; provided that no block shall be less than five inches in width measured as last-mentioned.
5. The blocks shall work on efficient springs or other elastic material so as to yield with the pressure of the weight of the Locomotive ; but not so that the surface of the wood block shall be at any time level with or depressed below the tire of the wheel.
6. No such wheel shall be used any block of which is so worn that any metal rim surrounding the block can come in contact with the road.

Given under the Seal of Office of the Local Government Board, this Twenty-sixth day of November, in the year One thousand eight hundred and ninety-seven.

HENRY CHAPLIN,
President.

(L.S.)
HUGH OWEN,
Secretary.

The following circular was issued with the foregoing Order.

Local Government Board,
Whitehall, S.W.,
27th November 1897.

SIR,

I AM directed by the Local Government Board to advert to section 28 of the Highways and Locomotives (Amendment) Act, 1878 (41 & 42 Vict. c. 77) which makes it unlawful to use on any highway a locomotive constructed otherwise than in accordance with the provisions of the section. One of these provisions is contained in sub-section (4), Order, No. 37,058.

which directs that the driving wheels of the locomotive shall be cylindrical and smooth-soled, or shod with diagonal cross-bars of not less than three inches in width nor more than three-quarters of an inch in thickness, extending the full breadth of the tire, and that the space intervening between each such cross-bar shall not exceed three inches.

Section 9 of the Locomotives on Highways Act, 1896 (59 & 60 Vict. c. 36), however, enacts that the requirements of sub-section (4) of section 28 of the Act of 1878 may be from time to time varied by Order of the Board, and representations have been made to the Board as to the expediency of their exercising the power thus conferred upon them.

The Board, after communicating with a number of local authorities and other bodies and persons concerned, and considering the suggestions thus obtained, have issued an Order varying the provisions of sub-section (4) of section 28 of the Act of 1878, so that, subject to the conditions specified in the Order, a locomotive may be used on a highway if the driving wheels, instead of being smooth-soled or shod with cross-bars, are shod with wooden blocks. It will be understood that the Order does not affect the requirements of section 28, except those contained in sub-section (4), and that the other requirements must still be complied with.

Copies of the Order are enclosed. It has been placed on sale and will shortly be obtainable from Messrs. Eyre and Spottiswoode, East Harding Street, Fleet Street, London, E.C., either directly or through any bookseller.

I am, Sir,
Your obedient Servant,
HUGH OWEN,
Secretary.

The Clerk to the County Council,
or other Local Authority.

PARISH COUNCILS.

See "BORROWING," *ante*, p. 761; "LAND: COMPULSORY HIRING AND PURCHASE OF," *ante*, pp. 798—831.

INDEX.

A

INDEX.

B.

C.

D.

E.

F.

G.

H.

I.

J.

K.

L.

M.

P.

Q.

R.

S.

W.

Y.

LONDON: PRINTED BY SHAW AND SONS, FETTER LANE AND CRANE COURT.

Lightning Source UK Ltd.
Milton Keynes UK
UKHW031337031218
333390UK00012B/706/P

WEBSTER'S

UNIVERSAL DICTIONARY & THESAURUS

WEBSTER'S

UNIVERSAL DICTIONARY & THESAURUS

GEDDES & GROSSET

Published 2005 by Geddes & Grosset, David Dale House, New Lanark, ML11 9DJ, Scotland, UK

First published 2003, reprinted 2005

ISBN 1 84205 188 1

Printed and bound in Poland, OZGraf, S.A.

Preface

Webster's Universal Dictionary and Thesaurus is more than just a dictionary and thesaurus – with additional factual material, it forms an ideal reference source for use in home, school and office.

A dictionary is an essential tool for all who wish to communicate, study or enjoy the richness of language. In the world of today, information reaches us by radio, television, computer and the written word, and a comprehensive but concise dictionary is an invaluable aid to a complete understanding and a deeper appreciation of the great literature that is the heritage of all who use the English language. This dictionary will be of use for reference, study and the fuller enjoyment of word games.

The modern lexicographer's prime role in preparing a dictionary is to reflect the changes taking place in contemporary language. Linguistic change can often be so gradual that it is barely noticed, although occasionally there is a sudden realization that a new word or phrase, previously unknown, is in general use, or that a form once considered to be 'wrong' has slowly become 'right'.

In presenting a dictionary in a concise form, the problems that have to be faced regarding which words to include and which words to leave aside are not easy to resolve. Some entries are so familiar to us that the entries may seem unnecessary, yet it is vital that these entries are included. Some words may be little-used and yet merit inclusion because of the other words in the language that have their roots in the lesser-known term.

The advantage of a thesaurus becomes ever more apparent with use. A thesaurus jogs the memory – it offers help to the writer struggling to encapsulate a meaning in a poignant *mot juste* that remains tantalisingly on the verge of memory. It is indispensable to the student, journalist, writer and public speaker; and to the business person who wishes to express himself or herself accurately, effectively and succinctly. A thesaurus is fun to use, and with the fun comes the opportunity to enhance one's personal command of words and increase one's general knowledge. Words that may not be well known to the reader will trigger off investigations in the dictionary and lead him or her to explore the remoter corners of the language. Finally, a thesaurus is a tool that the word-gamester – compiler, player or solver – cannot do without.

Also included in this volume are invaluable appendices of: grammar and usage; a punctuation guide; a list of commonly misspelt words; a list of commonly misused words; English idioms; proverbs, similes and clichés; up-to-date world facts with map diagrams; and leaders of the world. An additional feature is the World Maps section which comprises an up-to-date atlas with full-colour maps and a location key.

Contents

How to use this book

Throughout the book, the order of entries is by strict alphabetical order of headword, disregarding hyphens and spaces. Words spelled identically but with entirely different origins are listed separately with superscript numerals, e.g. **jam**[1], **jam**[2]. Guide words at the top of a page give the first and last entries on that page.

In the dictionary, alternative spellings reflecting differences between American and British English are listed for single headwords, e.g. **ardour**, **ardor**, but not for compounds, e.g. **colour bar**, **colour-blind**. Where the alternative form is close to the main form they are listed together. Where they are separated by more than two entries, they are indicated at the end of the entry, prefixed by *also*, and the alternative listed in its correct alphabetical place, e.g. **colour** ... *—also* **color**.

Irregular plurals of nouns, e.g. **beauty**, **beauties** or **axis, axes,** are given in bold type in parentheses following the part of speech label. Regular plurals are also included where there might otherwise be confusion, e.g. **pistachio**, **pistachios**. Where a noun that appears to be a plural takes a singular verb, this is indicated by the label *n sing*.

Irregular spellings of the comparative and superlative forms of adjectives, and present and past participles and tenses of verbs (where they differ) are also included. Where the present participles and past tenses have variant forms between American and British English these are also indicated, e.g. **travelling**, **travelled** or **traveling**, **traveled**.

Change of part of speech within an entry is marked by an asterisk *, e.g. **pirate** *n* ... **vti*. Part of speech labels are listed in the abbreviations.

The organization of the World Facts section differs slightly from the dictionary and thesaurus. A note on page 834, at the beginning of the World Facts section, explains how to use it to best advantage.

Abbreviations used in this book

abbr	abbreviation	*n*	noun
adj	adjective	*naut*	nautical
adv	adverb	*neut*	neuter
anat	anatomy	*news*	news media
approx	approximately	*nf*	noun feminine
arch	archaic	*npl*	noun plural
archit	architecture	*n sing*	noun singular
astrol	astrology	*obs*	obsolete
asrton	astronomy	*orig*	original, originally, origin
Austral	Australia, Austalasia	*p*	participle
aux	auxiliary	*pers*	person, personal
biol	biology	*philos*	philosophy
bot	botany	*photog*	photography
Brit	Britain, British	*pl*	plural
c	circa, about	*poet*	poetical
cap	capital	*poss*	possessive
cent.	century	*pp*	past participle
chem	chemical, chemistry	*prep*	preposition
compar	comparative	*pres t*	present tense
comput	computing	*print*	printing
conj	conjunction	*pron*	pronoun
demons	demonstrative	*pr p*	present participle
derog	derogatory, derogatorily	*psychol*	psychology
econ	economics	*pt*	past tense
eg	exempli gratia, for example	*RC*	Roman Catholic
elect	electricity	*reflex*	reflexive
esp	especially	*Scot*	Scotland
fig	figuratively	*sing*	singular
geog	geography	*sl*	slang
geol	geology	*superl*	superlative
geom	geometry	*theat*	theater
gram	grammar	*TV*	television
her	heraldry	*UK*	United Kingdom
hist	history	*US*	United States
ie	id est, that is	*USA*	United States of America
imper	imperative	*usu*	usually
incl	including	*vb*	verb
inf	informal	*vb aux*	auxiliary verb
interj	interjection	*vi*	intransitive verb
math	mathematics	*vt*	transitive verb
mech	mechanics	vti	transitive or intransitive verb
med	medicine	vulg	vulgar, vulgarly
mil	military	zool	zoology
myth	mythology		

English Dictionary

A

A *abbr* = ampere(s).
Å *abbr* = ångström(s).
a *adj* the indefinite article; one; any; per.
A1 *adj* (*inf*) in perfect condition; physically fit; excellent.
AA *abbr* = Alcoholics Anonymous; anti-aircraft; Automobile Association.
AAA *abbr* = Automobile Association of America; Amateur Athletics Association.
aardvark *n* a nocturnal African mammal with a long snout that feeds on termites.
aardwolf *n* (*pl* **aardwolves**) the earth wolf, a South African carnivore like a hyena.
ab *prep* from, as in *ab initio*.
ab- *prefix* away, from, apart.
abaca *n* Manila hemp.
aback *adv* **taken aback** startled.
abacus *n* (*pl* **abaci, abacuses**) a frame with sliding beads for doing arithmetic.
Abaddon *n* a destroying angel, the devil; hell.
abaft *adv, prep* (*naut*) behind.
abalone *n* an edible mollusc having an ear-shaped shell lined with mother-of-pearl.
abandon *vt* to leave behind; to desert; to yield completely to an emotion or urge. * *n* freedom from inhibitions.—**abandonment** *n*.
abandoned *adj* (*behaviour*) showing abandon, unrestrained.—**abandonedly** *adv*.
abase *vt* to degrade, humiliate.—**abasement** *n*.
abash *vt* to cause a feeling of shame, embarrassment or confusion.—**abashment** *n*.
abashed *adj* ashamed, embarrassed.
abate *vti* to make or become less; (*law*) to end.—**abatement** *n*.
abatis *n* (*pl* **abatis, abatises**) a defence work of fallen trees with the branches towards the enemy.
abattoir *n* a slaughterhouse.
abbacy *n* (*pl* **abbacies**) the office or rights of an abbot.
abbatial *adj* of an abbey or abbot.
abbé *n* a French ecclesiastic.
abbess *n* the woman who heads a convent of nuns.
abbey *n* a building occupied by monks or nuns; a church built as part of such a building; the community of monks or nuns.
abbot *n* the head of an abbey of monks.
abbreviate *vt* to make shorter, esp to shorten (a word) by omitting letters.
abbreviation *n* the process of abbreviating; a shortened form of a word.
ABC[1] *n* the alphabet; the basic facts of a subject.
ABC[2] *abbr* = American Broadcasting Corporation; Australian Broadcasting Corporation.
abdicate *vti* to renounce an official position or responsibility, etc.—**abdication** *n*.
abdomen *n* the region of the body below the chest containing the digestive organs; the belly; (*insects, etc*) the section of the body behind the thorax.—**abdominal** *adj*.—**abdominally** *adv*.
abducent *adj* (*anat*) (*limb, etc*) drawn from its natural position.
abduct *vt* to carry off (a person) by force; (*anat*) to draw (a limb, etc) from its natural position.—**abduction** *n*.—**abductor** *n*.
abeam *adv* (*naut*) at right angles to a ship's length, abreast.
abecedarian *adj* of the ABC, elementary; arranged alphabetically. * *n* one learning the ABC, a beginner, a learner.
abed *adv* in bed.
abelmosk *n* an Asian herb of the mallow family yielding musk.
aberrant *adj* deviating from that regarded as normal or right.—**aberrance, aberrancy** *n*.
aberration *n* a deviation from the normal; a mental or moral lapse.
abet *vt* (**abetting, abetted**) to encourage or assist, esp to do wrong.—**abetment** *n*.—**abetter,** (*esp law*) **abettor** *n*.
abeyance *n* (*usu preceded by* **in**) (*law, etc*) suspended temporarily.
abhor *vt* (**abhorring, abhorred**) to detest, despise.
abhorrence *n* detestation.
abhorrent *adj* detestable.
abide *vt* (**abiding, abode** *or* **abided**) to endure; to put up with.
abiding *adj* permanent.—**abidingly** *adv*.
abigail *n* a lady's maid.
ability *n* (*pl* **abilities**) the state of being able; power to do; talent; skill.
ab initio (*Latin*) from the beginning.
abiogenesis *n* spontaneous generation.—**abiogenetic** *adj*.
abject *adj* wretched; dejected.—**abjection** *n*.—**abjectly** *adv*.
abjure *vt* to renounce.—**abjuration** *n*.—**abjurer** *n*.
ablactation *n* the act of weaning a child from the breast.
ablate *vti* (**ablating, ablated**) to remove surgically; (*astrophysics*) to melt or vaporize when entering the earth's atmosphere; (*geol*) to erode, to waste or wear away.—**ablation** *n*.
ablative *adj* (*gram*) expressing source, instrumentality, etc; (*astrophysics*) ablating. * *n* one of the cases of Latin nouns, expressing chiefly separation and instrumentality and sometimes place.
ablative absolute *n* a particular construction in Latin of a noun and a participle in the ablative case, agreeing in gender and number, and forming a clause by themselves, but unconnected gramatically with the rest of the sentence.
ablaut *n* (*linguistics*) a vowel permutation, the change of a root vowel in the derivation of a word, as *do, did* or *sing, sang, sung, song*.
ablaze *adj* burning, on fire.
-able *adj suffix* capable of, as in *suitable*.
able *adj* having the competence or means (to do); talented; skilled.—**ably** *adv*.
able-bodied *adj* fit, strong.
able-bodied seaman *n* a trained seaman in the (merchant) navy.—*also* **able seaman.**
abloom *adv* in bloom, blooming.
ablution *n* (*usu pl*) a washing or cleansing of the body by water; the ritual cleansing of vessels or hands.—**ablutionary** *adj*.
ably *adv* in an able manner.
ABM *abbr* = antiballistic missile.
abnegate *vt* to deny oneself (a right, etc); to renounce.—**abnegation** *n*.
abnormal *adj* unusual, not average or typical; irregular.—**abnormality** *n*.—**abnormally** *adv*.
abnormality *n* (*pl* **abnormalities**) deformity; irregularity; difference or departure from a regular type or rule.
aboard *adv* on or in an aircraft, ship, train, etc.—*also prep*.
abode[1] *n* a home, residence.
abode[2] *see* **abide.**
abolish *vt* to bring to an end, do away with.—**abolisher** *n*.—**abolishment** *n*.
abolition *n* the act of abolishing; (*with cap*) in UK, the ending of the slave trade (1807) or slavery (1833), in US, the emancipation of the slaves (1863).
abolitionist *n* one who is in favour of the repeal or abolition of some existing law or custom; (*often with cap*) one in favour of Abolition.
abomasum *n* (*pl* **abomasa**) the fourth stomach of a ruminant animal.—**abomasal** *adj*.
A-bomb *n* atomic bomb.
abominable *adj* despicable, detestable; (*inf*) very unpleasant.—**abominably** *adv*.
abominable snowman *n* a huge creature of legend resembling a man or an animal, said to be found in the Himalayas.—*also* **yeti.**

abominate *vt* to abhor; to regard with feelings of disgust or hatred.—**abominator** *n*.
abomination *n* detestation; a loathsome person or thing.
aboriginal *adj* existing in a place from the earliest times; of aborigines. * *n* the species of animals or plants presumed to have originated within a given area.
aborigine *n* any of the first known inhabitants of a region; (*with cap*) one of the original inhabitants of Australia before the arrival of European settlers.
abort *vti* to undergo or cause an abortion; to terminate or cause to terminate prematurely. * *n* the premature termination of a rocket flight, etc.
abortion *n* the premature expulsion of a foetus, esp if induced on purpose.
abortionist *n* a person who performs abortions, esp illegally.
abortive *adj* failing in intended purpose; fruitless; causing abortion.—**abortively** *adv*.
aboulia *see* **abulia**.
abound *vi* to be in abundance; to have in great quantities.
about *prep* on all sides of; near to; with; on the point of; concerning. * *adv* all around; near; to face the opposite direction.
about-turn, about-face *n* a complete reversal in direction or opinion, etc. * *vi* to make an about-turn.
above *prep* over, on top of; better or more than; beyond the reach of; too complex to understand. * *adv* in or to a higher place; in addition; (*text*) mentioned earlier.
aboveboard *adj, adv* without trickery; in open sight.
abracadabra *n* a cabbalistic word used as a charm, a spell; gibberish.
abradant *adj* having the property of rubbing away. * *n* a substance employed for abrading or scouring.
abrade *vt* to wear or rub away; to remove as by friction or abrasion; to corrode, as by acids.—**abrader** *n*.
abranchiate, abranchial *adj* (*zool*) devoid of gills. * *n* an animal without gills.
abrasion *n* the act or process of rubbing away by friction, etc; a scraped area, esp on the body.
abrasive *adj* causing abrasion; harsh, irritating. * *n* a substance or tool used for grinding or polishing, etc.—**abrasively** *adv*.
abreact *vt* (*psychoanal*) to remove (a complex) by acting it out or talking it out.—**abreaction** *n*.—**abreactive** *adj*.
abreast *adv* side by side and facing the same way; informed (of); aware.
abridge *vt* to shorten by using fewer words but keeping the substance.
abridgment, abridgement *n* the state of being contracted or curtailed; a shortened version of a text; an epitome.
abroach *adj, adv* letting out; broached, pierced so as to let the liquor run.
abroad *adv* in or to a foreign country; over a wide area; out in the open; in circulation, current.
abrogate *vt* to repeal, cancel.—**abrogator** *n*.
abrogation *n* the act of abrogating; the repeal or annulling of a law.
abrupt *adj* sudden; unexpected; curt.—**abruptly** *adv*.—**abruptness** *n*.
abruption *n* a separation with violence; a sudden or abrupt termination.
abscess *n* an inflamed area of the body containing pus.
abscissa *n* (*pl* **abscissas, abscissae**) (*geom*) one of the two coordinates fixing the position of a point.
abscission *n* the act of severance; (*bot*) the shedding of parts; the breaking off in a sentence, leaving the rest to be implied.
abscond *vi* to hide, run away, esp to avoid punishment for a wrongdoing.
abseil *vi* to descend a rock face by means of a double rope attached to a higher point.—**abseiling** *n*.
absence *n* the state of not being present; the time of this; a lack; inattention.
absent[1] *adj* not present; not existing; inattentive.—**absently** *adv*.
absent[2] *vt* to keep (oneself) away.
absentee *n* a person who is absent, as from work or school.
absenteeism *n* persistent absence from work, school, etc.
absently *adv* in an abstracted manner.
absent-minded *adj* inattentive; forgetful.
absinthe, absinth *n* a potent, green, brandy-based liqueur flavoured with wormwood.
absit omen (*Latin*) may the foreboding caused by some unlucky word or event not come to pass.
absolute *adj* unrestricted, unconditional; complete; positive; perfect, pure; not relative; (*monarch, ruler, etc*) authoritarian, despotic; (*inf*) utter, out-and-out.
absolutely *adv* completely; unconditionally; (*inf*) I completely agree, certainly.
absolution *n* forgiveness; remission of sin or its penalty.
absolutism *n* the state of being absolute; the principle or system of absolute government.—**absolutist** *n, adj*.
absolve *vt* to clear from guilt or blame; to give religious absolution to; to free from a duty, obligation, etc.
absolver *n* one who absolves, or pronounces absolution.
absorb *vt* to take in; to soak up; to incorporate; to pay for (costs, etc); to take in (a shock) without recoil; to occupy one's attention or interest completely.—**absorber** *n*.—**absorptive** *adj*.
absorbable *adj* capable of being absorbed.—**absorbability** *n*.
absorbefacient *adj* inducing or causing absorption. * *n* something that causes absorption.
absorbent *adj* capable of absorbing moisture, etc.—**absorbency** *n*.
absorbent cotton *n* raw cotton that has been bleached and sterilized for use as a dressing, etc.—*also* **cotton wool**.
absorbing *adj* engrossing.—**absorbingly** *adv*.
absorption *n* the process or act of absorbing; the state of being absorbed; entire preoccupation of the mind.—**absorptive** *adj*.
absorption lines *npl* dark lines in the spectrum produced by the absorption of cool vapours through which the light has passed.
absorptivity *n* the power of absorption; (*physics*) the rate of absorption of radiation by a material.
abstain *vi* to keep oneself from some indulgence, esp from drinking alcohol; to refrain from using one's vote.
abstainer *n* one who abstains, especially from intoxicants.
abstemious *adj* sparing in consuming food or alcohol.—**abstemiously** *adv*.—**abstemiousness** *n*.
abstention *n* the act of holding off or abstaining; the withholding of a vote.—**abstentious** *adj*.—**abstentionist** *n*.
abstergent *adj* possessing cleansing or purging properties. * *n* that which cleanses or purges; a detergent.
abstinence *n* an abstaining or refraining, esp from food or alcohol.
abstinent *adj* refraining from over-indulgence, esp with regard to food and drink. * *n* an abstainer.—**abstinently** *adv*.
abstract *adj* having no material existence; theoretical; (*art*) non-representational. * *n* (*writing, speech*) a summary or condensed version. * *vt* to remove or extract; to separate; to summarize.
abstracted *adj* not paying attention.—**abstractedly** *adv*.—**abstractedness** *n*.
abstraction *n* preoccupation, inattention; an abstract concept.—**abstractive** *adj*.
abstractionism *n* the theory and art of the abstract, esp non-representational painting.—**abstractionist** *adj, n*.
abstract noun *n* the name of a state or quality considered apart from the object to which it belongs.
abstruse *adj* obscure; hidden; difficult to comprehend; profound.—**abstrusely** *adv*.—**abstruseness** *n*.
absurd *adj* against reason or common sense; ridiculous.—**absurdly** *adv*.
absurdity *n* (*pl* **absurdities**) the state of being absurd; that which is absurd.
abulia *n* (*psychol*) loss of willpower.—*also* **aboulia**.—**abulic** *adj*.
abundance *n* a plentiful supply; a considerable amount.
abundant *adj* plentiful; rich (in).—**abundantly** *adv*.

abuse *vt* to make wrong use of; to mistreat; to insult, attack verbally. * *n* misuse; mistreatment; insulting language; immoderate or illegal use of drugs or other stimulants.—**abuser** *n*.
abusive *adj* insulting.—**abusively** *adv*.—**abusiveness** *n*.
abut *vi* (**abutting, abutted**) to adjoin, border or lean (on, against).
abutment, abuttal *n* that which borders upon something else; the solid structure that supports the extremity of a bridge or arch.
abutter *n* (*law*) the owner of an adjoining property.
abuzz *adv* filled with buzzing sounds; active, alive.
abysm *n* (*arch*) an abyss, a gulf.
abysmal *adj* extremely bad, deplorable.—**abysmally** *adv*.
abyss *n* a bottomless depth; anything too deep to measure; hell.
abyssal *adj* pertaining to oceanic depths.
AC, ac *abbr* = alternating current.
Ac (*chem symbol*) actinium.
a/c *abbr* = account; account current.
ac- *prefix* the form of *ad-* before *c, k, g*.
acacia *n* a genus of shrubby or arboreous leguminous plants of warmer regions with white or yellow flowers, several species of which yield gum.
academic *adj* pertaining to a school, college or university; scholarly; purely theoretical in nature. * *n* a member of a college or university; a scholarly person.
academically *adv* theoretically, unpractically.
academician *n* a member of an Academy.
academy *n* (*pl* **academies**) a school for specialized training; (*Scot*) a secondary school; (*with cap*) a society of scholars, writers, scientists, etc.
Acadian *adj* of Acadia, a region of Canada, Nova-Scotian.
acanthine *adj* pertaining to or resembling the plant acanthus. * *n* ornamentation in the shape of the acanthus leaf.
acanthus *n* (*pl* **acanthuses, acanthi**) a genus of herbaceous plants with sharp-toothed leaves; (*archit*) ornamentation adopted in the capitals of the Corinthian and Composite orders, and resembling the foliage of the acanthus.
a cappella *adv* (*mus*) after the style of church or chapel music, without accompaniment.
acarid *n* a tick or mite of the *Acarina* order of insects, etc, in which the divisions of head, thorax and abdomen are not apparent.—*also adj*.
acarpellous, acarpelous *adj* (*bot*) without carpels.
acarpous *adj* (*bot*) not producing fruit; sterile or barren.
acatalectic *adj* (*verse*) with a complete number of syllables, not catalectic.—*also n*.
acaudal, acaudate *adj* (*zool*) without a tail.
acaulescent *adj* (*bot*) stemless or with a very short stem.—**acaulescence** *n*.
acc. *abbr* = according; account; accusative.
Accadian *see* **Akkadian.**
accede *vi* to take office; to agree or assent to (a suggestion).
accelerando *adv, adj* (*mus*) with gradual increase of speed. * *n* (*pl* **accelerandos**) a piece of music played in this way.
accelerate *vti* to move faster; to happen or cause to happen more quickly; to increase the velocity of (a vehicle, etc).—**accelerative, acceleratory** *adj*.
acceleration *n* the act of accelerating or condition of being accelerated; the rate of increase in speed or change in velocity; the power of accelerating.
accelerator *n* a device for increasing speed; a throttle; (*physics*) an apparatus that imparts high velocities to elementary particles.
accent *n* emphasis on a syllable or word; a mark used to indicate this; any way of speaking characteristic of a region, class, or an individual; the emphasis placed on something; rhythmic stress in music or verse. * *vt* to express the accent, or denote the vocal division of a word by stress or modulation of the voice; to pronounce; to mark or accent a word in writing by use of a sign; to dwell upon or emphasize, as a passage of music.
accentuate *vt* to emphasize.
accentuation *n* the act of accentuating by stress or accent; speaking or writing with emphasis or distinction.
accept *vt* to receive, esp willingly; to approve; to agree to; to believe in; to agree to pay.
acceptable *adj* satisfactory; welcome; tolerable.—**acceptability** *n*.—**acceptably** *adv*.
acceptance *n* the act of accepting; the act of being accepted or received with approbation; agreement; the subscription to a bill of exchange; the bill accepted or the sum contained in it.
acceptation *n* the act of accepting or state of being accepted or acceptable; the meaning or sense of a word or statement in which it is to be understood.
accepter, acceptor *n* one who accepts; the person who accepts a bill of exchange.
access *n* approach, or means of approach; the right to enter, use, etc. * *vt* (*comput*) to retrieve (information) from a storage device; to gain access to.
accessible *adj* able to be reached; open (to).—**accessibility** *n*.—**accessibly** *adv*.
accession *n* the act of reaching or assuming a rank or position.—**accessional** *adj*.
accessory *adj* additional; extra. * *n* (*pl* **accessories**) a supplementary part or item, esp of clothing; a person who aids another in a crime.—**accessorial** *adj*.
acciaccatura *n* (*pl* **acciaccaturas, acciaccature**) a half-note or grace note below the principal note, struck at the same time as the principal note and immediately released while the latter is held.
accidence *n* (*linguistics*) the part of grammar that deals with the inflections of words, which are accidents, not essentials; a book containing the rudiments of grammar; the rudiments themselves.
accident *n* an unexpected event; a mishap or misfortune, esp one resulting in death or injury; chance.
accidental *adj* occurring or done by accident; non-essential; (*mus*) a sign prefixed to a note indicating a departure from the key signature.—**accidentally** *adv*.
accidie *n* sloth, torpor, apathy.
accipiter *n* a generic name for birds of prey, as the common hawk.
accipitrine *adj* hawk-like, rapacious.
acclaim *vt* to praise publicly (the merits of a person or thing); to welcome enthusiastically. * *vi* to shout approval. * *n* a shout of welcome or approval.
acclamation *n* a shout of applause or other demonstration of hearty approval, loud united assent; an outburst of joy or praise; the adoption of a resolution *viva voce*; a mode of papal election.—**acclamatory** *adj*.
acclimatize *vt* to adapt to a new climate or environment * *vi* to become acclimatized.—**acclimatization** *n*.
acclivity *n* (*pl* **acclivities**) an ascent or upward slope of the earth; the talus of a rampart.—**acclivitous** *adj*.
accolade *n* praise; approval; an award; a ceremonial touch on the shoulder with a sword to confer knighthood.
accommodate *vt* to provide lodging for; to oblige, supply; to adapt, harmonize.
accommodating *adj* obliging, willing to help.—**accommodatingly** *adv*.
accommodation *n* lodgings; the process of adapting; willingness to help.
accommodation bill *n* a bill or note endorsed by one or more parties to enable the drawer to raise money upon it.
accommodation ladder *n* a ladder or stairway suspended at the gangway of a ship.
accommodative *adj* disposed or tending to accommodate.
accompaniment *n* an instrumental part supporting a solo instrument, a voice, or a choir; something that accompanies.
accompanist, accompanyist *n* one who plays a musical accompaniment.
accompany *vt* (**accompanying, accompanied**) (*person*) to go with; (*something*) to supplement.

accomplice *n* a partner, esp in committing a crime.
accomplish *vt* to succeed in carrying out; to fulfil.
accomplished *adj* done; completed; skilled, expert; polished.
accomplishment *n* a skill or talent; the act of accomplishing; something accomplished.
accord *vi* to agree; to harmonize (with). * *vt* to grant. * *n* consent; harmony.
accordance *n* agreement; conformity.
accordant *adj* corresponding; of the same mind.
according *prep* as stated by or in; (*with* **to**) in conformity with; (*with* **as**) depending on whether. * *adj* agreeing, harmonious.
accordingly *adv* consequently; therefore; suitably.
accordion *n* a portable keyboard instrument with manually operated folding bellows that force air through metal reeds.—**accordionist** *n*.
accost *vt* to approach and speak to, often to accuse of crime or to solicit sexually.
account *n* a description; an explanatory statement; a business record or statement; a credit arrangement with a bank, department store, etc; importance, consequence. * *vt* to think of as; consider. * *vi* to give a financial reckoning (to); (*with* **for**) to give reasons (for); (*with* **for**) to kill, dispose of.
accountable *adj* liable; responsible; explainable.—**accountability** *n*.—**accountably** *adv*.
accountancy *n* the profession or practice of an accountant.
accountant *n* one whose profession is auditing business accounts.
account book *n* a book for the entering of accounts, or in which particulars of sales, purchases, etc, are kept.
accounting *n* the maintaining or auditing of detailed business accounts; accountancy.
accoutre, accouter *vt* to dress; to equip; to array in military dress; to furnish with accoutrements.—**accoutrement, accouterment** *n*.
accoutrements, accouterments *npl* equipage; dress; military equipment.
accredit *vt* to give credit or authority to; to have confidence in; to authorize; to stamp with authority; to believe and accept as true.—**accreditation** *n*.
accredited *adj* authorized officially; accepted as valid; certified as being of a prescribed quality.
accrescent *adj* (*bot*) increasing; growing.
accrete *vi* to adhere, to grow together; to be added. * *vt* to cause to grow or unite. * *adj* (*bot*) grown into one.
accretion *n* an increase by natural growth; the addition of external parts; the growing together of parts or members naturally separate.—**accretive, accretionary** *adj*.
accrue *vi* (**accruing, accrued**) to come as a natural increase or addition; (*money, etc*) to accumulate or be added periodically.—**accrual, accrument** *n*.
accumbent *adj* (*bot*) reclining or recumbent; (*hist*) of the Roman style of reclining on a couch at meals.—**accumbency** *n*.
accumulate *vti* to collect together in increasing quantities, to amass.
accumulation *n* the act of accumulating or amassing; the addition of interest to principal; the mass accumulated.
accumulative *adj* cumulative; acquisitive.
accumulator *n* a rechargable battery; (*horseracing*) a bet that accumulates in value over successive races; (*comput*) a storage register.
accuracy *n* (*pl* **accuracies**) the quality of being accurate; exactness or correctness.
accurate *adj* conforming with the truth or an accepted standard; done with care, exact.—**accurately** *adv*.
accursed, accurst *adj* under or subject to a curse; ill-fated, doomed to destruction; detestable; execrable.
accusation *n* the act of accusing or being accused; an allegation; the charge of guilt brought against a person.
accusative *n* (*gram*) the case expressing the direct object of a word.
accusatorial, accusatory *adj* accusing, or containing an accusation; (*of legal procedure*) in which prosecutor and judge are not the same (opposite to inquisitorial).
accuse *vt* to charge with a crime, fault, etc; to blame.—**accuser** *n*.—**accusingly** *adv*.
accused *n* (*law*) (*with* **the**) the defendant in court facing a criminal charge.
accuser *n* one who accuses; one who formally charges an offence against another.
accustom *vt* to make used (to) by habit, use, or custom.
accustomed *adj* usual, customary; used to.
ace *n* the one spot in dice, playing cards, dominoes, etc; a point won by a single stroke, as in tennis; an expert. * *adj* (*inf*) excellent.
-acea *n suffix* forming the plural names for orders of animals, eg Crustacea, Crustaceae.
-aceae *n suffix* forming plural names for families of plants, eg Rosaceae.
acedia *n* an abnormal condition of the mind, characterized by lassitude, listlessness, and general indifference.
acentric *adj* away from the centre; having no centre.
acephalous *adj* headless; without a leader; an ovary of a plant that has its style springing from the base instead of the apex.
acerbic *adj* bitter and harsh to the taste; astringent.
acerbity *n* (*pl* **acerbities**) sharpness of speech or manner; (of taste) bitterness.
acerose *adj* (*bot*) like a needle, very narrow, rigid, and tapering to a point.
acervate *adj* growing in closely compacted clusters.
acet-, aceto- *prefix* vinegar.
acetabulum *n* (*pl* **acetabula, acetabulums**) the cavity of the hip bone into which the femur fits; one of the cup-like suckers on the arms of the cuttlefish; the posterior sucker of the leech; the saucer-shaped fructification of certain lichens; the receptacle of various fungi; a cup to hold vinegar.
acetanilide, acetanilid *n* a pungent white powder, formed by the action of acetyl choride on aniline, used in medicine as an antipyretic.
acetate *n* a salt or ester of acetic acid; a fabric made from cellulose acetate.
acetic *adj* of acetic acid or vinegar.
acetic acid *n* a clear liquid with a strong acid taste and sharp smell, present in a dilute form in vinegar.
acetify *vt* (**acetifying, acetifed**) to turn into vinegar.—**acetification** *n*.—**acetifier** *n*.
acetometer *n* an instrument for gauging the strength or purity of vinegar or acetic acid.
acetone *n* a clear flammable liquid used as a solvent.
acetous, acetose *adj* of the nature of vinegar; sour; causing acetification.
acetylene *n* a gas that burns with a hot flame, used for welding, etc.
Achates *n* a faithful friend, from Aeneas's friend in Virgil's *Aeneid*.
ache *n* a dull, continuous pain. * *vi* to suffer a dull, continuous mental or physical pain; (*inf*) to yearn.—**achy** *adj*.
achieve *vt* to perform successfully, accomplish; to gain, win.—**achievable** *adj*.—**achiever** *n*.
achievement *n* a thing achieved, esp by great effort, courage, determination, etc; accomplishment; (*her*) an escutcheon in memory of a distinguished feat.
Achilles' heel *n* a person's vulnerable or weak point.
Achilles' tendon *n* a tendon attaching the heel to the calf muscles.
achlamydeous *adj* having neither calyx nor corolla.
achromatic *adj* colourless; transmitting light without decomposing it.—**achromatically** *adv*.—**achromaticity, achromatism** *n*.
achromatize *vt* to deprive of the power of transmitting colour; to render achromatic.—**achromatization** *n*.
acicula *n* (*pl* **aciculae**) a spine or prickle.
acicular *adj* needle-shaped.
aciculate, aciculated *adj* in the shape of a needle; acicular.
acid *adj* sharp, tart, sour; bitter. * *n* a sour substance; (*chem*) a corrosive substance that turns litmus red; (*sl*) LSD.—**acidly** *adv*.
acid house *n* a party where people take drugs and dance to House music; the style of popular music played.
acidic *adj* containing a large proportion of the acid element; opposed to basic.

acidifier *n* a substance having the property of imparting an acid quality.
acidify *vti* (**acidifying, acidified**) to make or become acid.—**acidification** *n*.
acidimeter *n* an instrument for measuring the strength of acids.—**acidimetric** *adj*.—**acidimetrically** *adv*.—**acidimetry** *n*.
acidity *n* (*pl* **acidities**) the quality or condition of being acid.
acidosis *n* an acid condition of the blood.—**acidotic** *adj*.
acid rain *n* rain made acidic by air pollution from power stations, etc.
acid test *n* a crucial or conclusive test.
acidulate *vt* to render slightly acid. * *adj* acidulous.—**acidulation** *n*.
acidulous, acidulent *adj* somewhat acid; tart; peevish.
acierate *vt* (**acierating, acierated**) to change into steel.—**acieration** *n*.
acinaciform *adj* (*bot*) resembling a scimitar in shape, as an acinaciform leaf or pod.
aciniform *adj* grape-like; clustered like grapes.
-acious *adj suffix* forming adjectives meaning full of, inclined to, as mendacious.
-acity *n suffix* forming corresponding nouns of quality, as mendacity.
acknowledge *vt* to admit that something is true and valid; to show that one has noticed or recognized.
acknowledgment, acknowledgement *n* the act of acknowledging; the admission or recognition of a truth; confession; the expression of appreciation of a favour or benefit conferred; a printed recognition by an author of others' works used or referred to; a receipt.
aclinic line *n* the imaginary point near the equator where the magnetic needle has no dip, the magnetic equator.
acme *n* the peak or highest point; the height of perfection.
acne *n* inflammation of the skin glands producing pimples.
acolyte *n* an assistant or follower, esp of a priest.
aconite, aconitum *n* the plant wolf's-bane or monk's-hood; the drug prepared from the plant.—**aconitic** *adj*.
acorn *n* the nut of the oak tree.
acotyledon *n* (*bot*) a plant with seeds (spores) that have no cotyledons (seed lobes).—**acotyledonous** *adj*.
acoustic, acoustical *adj* of the sense of hearing or sound; of acoustics; (*mus*) not amplified, eg a guitar.—**acoustically** *adv*.
acoustician *n* one skilled in acoustics.
acoustics *npl* (*room, concert hall, etc*) properties governing how clearly sounds can be heard in it; (*in sing*) the physics of sound.—**acoustician** *n*.
acquaint *vt* to make (oneself) familiar (with); to inform; (*with* **with**) to introduce (to).
acquaintance *n* a person whom one knows only slightly.
acquainted *adj* having personal knowledge; (*with* **of, with**) familiar, known.
acquiesce *vi* (*with* **in**) to comply with readily, or put up no opposition to.
acquiescence *n* compliance; assent.—**acquiescent** *adj*.
acquire *vt* to gain by one's own efforts; to obtain.—**acquirable** *adj*.
acquirement *n* the act of acquiring; that which is acquired; mental attainment.
acquisition *n* the act of gaining, acquiring; someone or something that is acquired, often of special worth or talent.
acquisitive *adj* eager or greedy for possessions.—**acquisitively** *adv*.—**acquisitiveness** *n*.
acquit *vt* (**acquitting, acquitted**) to free from an obligation; to behave or conduct (oneself); to declare innocent.
acquittal *n* the act of releasing or acquitting, the state of being acquitted; a judicial discharge from accusation; the performance (of duty).
acquittance *n* a discharge or release from debt or other liability; a receipt barring a further demand.
acre *n* land measuring 4840 square yards.
acreage *n* area measured in acres.
acrid *adj* sharp and bitter of taste or smell; caustic, critical in attitude or speech.—**acridity** *n*.—**acridly** *adv*.
acrimony *n* (*pl* **acrimonies**) bitterness of manner or language.—**acrimonious** *adj*.—**acrimoniously** *adv*.
acro- *prefix* topmost, extreme.
acrobat *n* a skilful performer of spectacular gymnastic feats.—**acrobatic** *adj*.—**acrobatically** *adv*.
acrobatics *npl* acrobatic feats.
acrocarpous *adj* (*bot*) having (like the mosses) the fruit at the end of the primary axis.
acrogen *n* (*bot*) a nonflowering plant increasing by growth from the top, as ferns and mosses.—**acrogenic, acrogenous** *adj*.
acrolith *n* a sculptured figure, with head and extremities of stone and the rest of wood.
acromegaly *n* a hormonal disease resulting in overdeveopment of the extremities.—**acromegalic** *adj*.
acronycal, acronical *adj* (*astron*) (*stars*) rising at sunset and setting at sunrise.
acronym *n* a word formed from the initial letters of other words (as *laser*).
acrophobia *n* dread of heights.—**acrophobe** *n*.—**acrophobic** *adj, n*.
acropolis *n* the highest part or citadel of a Grecian city; the citadel itself.
acrospire *n* (*bot*) the sprout of a seed.
across *prep* from one side to the other of; on or at an angle; on the other side of. * *adv* crosswise; from one side to the other.
across-the-board *adj* (*wage increase, cut, etc*) applying equally to all; (*horseracing*) winning a bet if the horse comes first, second or third.
acrostic *n* a poem or word puzzle in which certain letters of each line spell a complete word, etc.—**acrostically** *adv*.
acrylic *adj* of or derived from acrylic acid. * *n* an acrylic fibre or resin.
act *vi* to perform or behave in a certain manner; to perform a specific function; to have an effect; to perform on the stage; (*with* **up**) (*inf*) to misbehave; to malfunction. * *vt* to portray by actions, esp on the stage; to pretend, simulate; to take the part of, as a character in a play. * *n* something done, a deed; an exploit; a law; a main division of a play or opera; the short repertoire of a comic, etc; something done merely for effect or show.
acting *n* the art of an actor. * *adj* holding an office or position temporarily.
actinia *n* (*pl* **actiniae, actinias**) any of a genus of sea anemones that resemble flowers when the tentacles of the mouth are spread out.
actiniform, actinoid *adj* having the form of rays; star-shaped.
actinism *n* the property of light by which chemical changes are caused, as in photography.—**actinic** *adj*.—**actinically** *adv*.
actinium *n* a radioactive element occurring as a decay product of uranium.
actinozoan *see* **anthozoan**.
action *n* the process of doing something; an operation; a movement of the body, gesture; a land or sea battle; a lawsuit; the unfolding of events in a play, novel, etc; (*inf*) (*with* **the**) the centre of (social) activity.
actionable *adj* providing grounds for legal action.—**actionably** *adv*.
action painting *n* expressionist art produced by daubing, dribbling, splashing, throwing, etc, paint on to the canvas.
activate *vt* to make active; to set in motion; to make radioactive.—**activation** *n*.—**activator** *n*.
active *adj* lively, physically mobile; engaged in practical activities; energetic, busy; (*volcano*) liable to erupt; capable of producing an effect; radioactive; (*armed forces*) in full-time service. * *n* (*gram*) the verb form having as its subject the doer of the action.—**actively** *adv*.—**activeness** *n*.
active service, active duty *n* full-time service in a military force, esp during a war.
activist *n* an advocate of direct or militant action, esp in politics.—**activism** *n*.
activity *n* (*pl* **activities**) the state of being active; energetic, lively action; specific occupations (*indoor activities*).
act of God *n* a direct and unforeseeable act of nature that could not reasonably have been guarded against.
actor *n* a person who acts in a play, film, etc.—**actress** *nf*.

actual *adj* real; existing in fact or reality.
actuality *n* (*pl* **actualities**) the state of being real or actual; that which is in full existence; reality.
actualize *vt* to realize in action; to describe realistically; to make actual.—**actualization** *n*.
actually *adv* as an existing fact, really; strange though it seems.
actuary *n* (*pl* **actuaries**) a person who calculates insurance risks, premiums, etc.—**actuarial** *adj*.
actuate *vt* to move or incite to action; to put in motion; to impel, influence.—**actuation** *n*.—**actuator** *n*.
acuity *n* sharpness of thought or vision.
aculeate *adj* pointed; (*zool*) equipped with a sting; (*bot*) having aculei or sharp prickles.
aculeus *n* (*pl* **aculei**) a prickle.
acumen *n* sharpness of mind, perception.
acuminate *adj* ending in a sharp point. * *vt* (**acuminating, acuminated**) to sharpen.—**acumination** *n*.
acupuncture *n* the insertion of the tips of fine needles into the skin at certain points to treat various common ailments.—**acupuncturist** *n*.
acute *adj* perceptive; sharp-witted; (*hearing*) sensitive; (*pain*) severe; very serious; (*angles*) less than 90 degrees; (*disease*) severe but not long lasting.—**acutely** *adv*.—**acuteness** *n*.
acute accent *n* a mark (;aA) over a vowel in certain languages to indicate emphasis or special quality.
-acy *n suffix* forming nouns of state or quality, eg piracy.
ad[1] *abbr* = advertisement.
ad[2] *prep* to, as in *ad absurdum*.
ad- *prefix* to, as in *adhere*.
AD *abbr* = *anno domini* (in the year of Our Lord) in dates of the Christian era, indicating the number of years since the birth of Christ.
ad absurdum (*Latin*) to absurdity.
adactylous *adj* without toes or fingers.
adage *n* a proverb, old saying.
adagio *adv* (*mus*) slowly, gracefully. * *n* (*pl* **adagios**) a slow movement.
adamant *adj* inflexible, unyielding. * *n* adamantine, an extremely hard substance.
adamantine *adj* made of adamantine; impenetrable, very hard. * *n* an extremely hard substance; the diamond (—*also* **adamant**).
Adamite *n* a child of Adam; a member of a sect who went naked; a nudist.—**Adamitic** *adj*.
Adam's apple *n* the hard projection of cartilage in the front of the neck.
Adam's needle *n* a popular name of the yucca.
adapt *vti* to make or become fit; to adjust to a new purpose or circumstances.—**adaptability** *n*.—**adaptable** *adj*.—**adapter** *n*.
adaptation *n* the process or condition of being adapted; something produced by modification; a version of a literary composition rewritten for a different medium.
adaptor *n* a device that allows an item of equipment to be put to new use; a device for connecting parts of differing size and shape; an electrical plug using one socket for different appliances.
adaxial *adj* towards the axis.
ADC *abbr* = aide-de-camp.
add *vt* to combine (two or more things together); to combine numbers or amounts in a total; to remark or write further. * *vi* to perform or come together by addition.
addax *n* (*pl* **addaxes, addax**) a large North African antelope with twisted horns.
addendum *n* (*pl* **addenda**) a thing to be added; supplementary text appended to a book, etc.
adder *n* the venomous viper.
adder's-tongue *n* a kind of fern whose spike resembles the tongue of a snake.
addict *n* a person who is dependent upon a drug. * *vt* to devote or give oneself up to; to practise sedulously (usu pejorative).—**addiction** *n*.—**addictive** *adj*.
addition *n* the act or result of adding; something to be added; an extra part.
additional *adj* added, extra; supplementary.—**additionally** *adv*.
additive *adj* produced by addition. * *n* a substance added (to food, etc) to improve texture, flavour, etc.
addle *vb* (**addling, addled**) *vt* to make corrupt, putrid or confused. * *vi* to become addled. * *adj* rotten.
addle-headed, addle-pated *adj* stupid, weak-brained; muddled.
address *vt* to write directions for delivery on (a letter, etc); to speak or write directly to; to direct one's skills or attention (to); (*golf*) to adjust one's stance and aim before hitting the ball; * *n* a place where a person or business resides, the details of this on a letter for delivery; a speech, esp a formal one; (*comput*) a specific memory location where information is stored.—**addressable** *adj*.
addressee *n* a person or company to whom a letter is addressed.
Addressograph *n* (*trademark*) an addressing machine.
adduce *vt* to offer as an example or evidence.
adducent *adj* bringing forward or together.
adducible, adduceable *adj* capable of being adduced.
adduct *vt* to pull towards; (*of muscles*) to draw to a common centre.—**adduction** *n*.—**adductive** *adj*.
adductor muscle *n* a muscle that draws certain parts to a common centre.
ademption *n* (*law*) the revocation of a grant; the lapse of a legacy.
aden-, adeno- *prefix* gland.
adenitis *n* inflammation of a gland.
adenoids *npl* enlarged masses of tissue in the throat behind the nose.—**adenoidal** *adj*.
adenoma *n* (*pl* **adenomas, adenomata**) a gland-like benign tumour.
adept *adj* highly proficient. * *n* a highly skilled person.—**adeptly** *adv*.—**adeptness** n.
adequacy *n* adequateness; sufficiency for a particular purpose.
adequate *adj* sufficient for requirements; barely acceptable.—**adequately** *adv*.—**adequateness** *n*.
à deux (*French*) for two; intimate.
adhere *vi* to stick, as by gluing or suction; to give allegiance or support (to); to follow.
adherence *n* the act or state of adhering; unwavering attachment.
adherent *adj* sticking, attached. * *n* a supporter of a political party, idea, etc.
adhesion *n* the action or condition of adhering; the attachment of normally separate tissues in the body.
adhesive *adj* sticky; causing adherence. * *n* a substance used to stick, such as glue, paste, etc.—**adhesiveness** *n*.
ad hoc *adj* for a particular purpose.
ad hominem (*Latin*) to the man, personal.
adiabatic *adj* (*physics*) not gaining or losing heat.—**adiabatically** *adv*.
adiaphorous *adj* (*theol*) tolerant in nonessential points of religion; morally indifferent; (*med*) neither helping nor harming.
adieu *n* (*pl* **adieux, adieus**) farewell, goodbye; good wishes at parting.
ad infinitum *adv* without end, forever.
ad interim (*Latin*) for the meantime.
adipocere *n* a fatty substance resulting from decomposition of animal bodies in moist places.—**adipocerous** *adj*.
adipose *adj* of, like or containing animal fat; fatty.—**adiposity** *n*.
adit *n* an entrance or passage; an entrance to a mine more or less horizontal.
adjacent *adj* nearby; adjoining, contiguous.—**adjacency** *n*.
adjective *n* a word used to add a characteristic to a noun or pronoun.—**adjectival** *adj*.—**adjectivally** *adv*.
adjoin *vt* to unite or join. * *vi* to lie next to.
adjoining *adj* beside, in contact with.
adjourn *vt* to suspend (a meeting) temporarily. * *vi* (*inf*) to retire (to another room, etc).—**adjournment** *n*.
adjournment *n* the act of adjourning; the postponement of a meeting.

adjudge *vt* (**adjudging, adjudged**) to decide or award judicially; to sentence; to determine in a controversy, to adjudicate.—**adjudgment, adjudgement** *n*.
adjudicate *vt* (*law*) to hear and decide (a case). * *vi* to serve as a judge (in or on).—**adjudicator** *n*.
adjudication *n* the act of determining judicially; a judicial sentence; a court's decision.
adjunct *n* something joined or added but inessential.—**adjunctive** *adj*.
adjuration *n* the solemn charging on oath; the oath used.
adjure *vt* to command on oath under pain of a penalty; to charge solemnly, request earnestly.
adjust *vt* to arrange in a more proper or satisfactory manner; to regulate or modify by minor changes; to decide the amount to be paid in settling (an insurance claim). * *vi* to adapt oneself.—**adjustable** *adj*.—**adjuster** *n*.
adjustment *n* the act of adjusting; arrangement.
adjutancy *n* (*pl* **adjutancies**) the office of an adjutant.
adjutant *n* a military staff officer who assists the commanding officer.
adjutant general *n* (*pl* **adjutants general**) the chief staff officer of an army, through whom all orders, etc, are received and issued by the general commanding.
adjuvant *adj* assisting, helpful. * *n* a helper, an auxiliary.
ad-lib *vti* (**ad-libbing, ad-libbed**) (*speech, etc*) to improvise. * *n* an ad-libbed remark. * *adv* spontaneously, freely.—**ad-libber** *n*.
adman *n* (*pl* **admen**) (*inf*) a person who works in the advertising business.
admass *n* the public targeted by or influenced by advertising.
admeasure *vt* (**admeasuring, admeasured**) to measure dimensions; to apportion.
admeasurement *n* a measurement by a rule; adjustment of proportions; dimensions.
admin *n* (*inf*) administration.
administer *vt* to manage, direct; to give out as a punishment; to dispense (medicine, punishment, etc); to tender (an oath, etc).
administrate *vti* to manage or control the affairs of a business, institution, etc.
administration *n* management; the people who administer an organization; the government; (*with cap*) the executive officials of a government, their policies, and term of office.
administrative *adj* of management; executive.—**administratively** *adv*.
administrator *n* a person who manages or supervises; (*law*) one appointed to settle an estate.
admirable *adj* deserving of admiration or approval.—**admirably** *adv*.
admiral *n* the commanding officer of a fleet; a naval officer of the highest rank.
admiralty *n* (*pl* **admiralties**) the department of a government having authority over naval affairs; the building in which naval affairs are transacted; the office of an admiral.
admiration *n* a feeling of pleasurable and often surprised respect or approval; an admired person or thing.
admire *vt* to regard with honour, approval and pleasure; to express admiration for.—**admirer** *n*.—**admiring** *adj*.—**admiringly** *adv*.
admissible *adj* that may be admitted or allowed.—**admissibility, admissibleness** *n*.
admission *n* an entrance fee; a conceding, confessing, etc; a thing conceded, confessed, etc.—**admissive** *adj*.
admit *vb* (**admitting, admitted**) *vt* to allow to enter or join; to concede or acknowledge as true. * *vi* to give access; (*with* **of**) to allow or permit.
admittance *n* the act of admitting; the right to enter.
admittedly *adv* acknowledged as fact, willingly conceded.
admix *vt* to mix with something else; to add as an extra ingredient.
admixture *n* a mixture, a compound of substances mixed together.
admonish *vt* to remind or advise earnestly; to reprove gently.
admonition *n* a friendly reproof or warning.—**admonitory** *adj*.
adnate *adj* (*bot*) with organic cohesion of unlike parts.
ad nauseam *adv* to a sickening degree.
ado *n* fuss, excitement, esp over trivial matters.
adolescence *n* the period of life between puberty and maturity; youth.
adobe *n* a brick made of sun-dried clay; clay for making adobe bricks; a building using such bricks.
adolescent *adj* pertaining to the stage between childhood and maturity; (*inf*) immature. * *n* an adolescent person.
adopt *vt* to take legally into one's family and raise as one's child; to select and pursue, eg a course of action; to take as one's own.—**adoption** *n*.
adoptive *adj* made or related by adoption.
adorable *adj* worthy of being adored; extremely charming.—**adorably** *adv*.
adoration *n* worship, homage; profound regard.
adore *vt* to worship; to love deeply.—**adoringly** *adv*.
adorn *vt* to decorate; to make more pleasant or attractive.—**adornment** *n*.
ad rem *adj, adv* to the point or purpose.
adrenal *adj* of or near the kidney. * *n* an adrenal gland.
adrenal gland *n* one of two glands situated above the kidneys that secretes adrenaline.
adrenaline *n* a hormone that stimulates the heart rate, blood pressure, etc in response to stress and that is secreted by the adrenal glands or manufactured synthetically.
adrift *adj, adv* afloat without mooring, drifting; loose; purposeless.
adroit *adj* skilful and clever, sharp-witted.—**adroitly** *adv*.—**adroitness** *n*.
adscititious *adj* taken in addition; added from without; additional, supplementary.
adsorb *vti* to accumulate on a surface, to collect by adsorption.—**adsorbable** *adj*.
adsorbent *n* an adsorbing substance.
adsorption *n* the action of a solid in condensing and holding a gas upon it.
adulate *vt* to flatter excessively or basely.—**adulator** *n*.—**adulatory** *adj*.
adulation *n* excessive flattery.—**adulatory** *adj*.
adult *adj* fully grown; mature; suitable only for adults, as in pornography, etc. * *n* a mature person, etc.—**adulthood** *n*.
adulterant *adj* adulterating. * *n* the person or thing that adulterates.
adulterate *vt* to make impure or inferior, etc by adding an improper substance.—**adulteration** *n*.—**adulterator** *n*.
adulterer *n* a person who commits adultery.—**adulteress** *nf*.
adulterine *adj* resulting from adulterous intercourse; fake, spurious; illegal.
adulterous *adj* guilty of adultery.
adultery *n* (*pl* **adulteries**) sexual intercourse between a married person and someone other than their legal partner.
adumbral *adj* overshadowing; shady.
adumbrate *vt* to foreshadow; to overshadow; to give a faint semblance of.—**adumbration** *n*.—**adumbrative** *adj*.
ad valorem *adj, adv* according to value; (*customs, duties*) levied on the value of goods as sworn to by the owner.
advance *vt* to bring or move forward; to promote; to raise the rate of; (*money*) to lend. * *vi* to go forward; to make progress; to rise in rank, price, etc. * *n* progress; improvement; a rise in value; payment beforehand; (*pl*) friendly approaches, esp to please. * *adj* in front; beforehand.
advanced *adj* in front; old; superior in development or progress.
advancement *n* promotion to a higher rank; progress in development.
advantage *n* superiority of position or condition; a gain or benefit; (*tennis*) the first point won after deuce. * *vt* to produce a benefit or favour to.
advantageous *adj* producing advantage, beneficial.—**advantageously** *adv*.
advent *n* an arrival or coming; (*with cap*) (*Christianity*) the coming of Christ; the four-week period before Christmas.
Adventist *n* a person who believes in Christ's second coming to set up a kingdom on earth.—**Adventism** *n*.
adventitious *adj* happening by chance; casual; fortuitous; accidental; produced out of normal and regular order; growing in an abnormal position.—**adventitiously** *adv*.—**adventitiousness** *n*.

Advent Sunday *n* the Sunday nearest (before or after) to St Andrew's Day (30 November).

adventure *n* a strange or exciting undertaking; an unusual, stirring, often romantic, experience.

adventure playground *n* a children's playground equipped with materials and objects for building, climbing, hiding in, etc.

adventurer *n* a person who seeks adventure; someone who seeks money or power by unscrupulous means.—**adventuress** *nf.*

adventurous *adj* inclined to incur risk; full of risk; rash; enterprising; daring.—**adventurously** *adv.*

adverb *n* a word that modifies a verb, adjective, another adverb, phrase, clause or sentence and indicates how, why, where, etc.—**adverbial** *adj.*—**adverbially** *adv.*

adversary *n* (*pl* **adversaries**) an enemy or opponent.

adversative *adj* (*words*) denoting opposition or contrariety; expressing opposition.

adverse *adj* hostile; contrary or opposite; unfavourable.—**adversely** *adv.*

adversity *n* (*pl* **adversities**) trouble, misery, misfortune.

advert[1] *vt* to refer (to); to turn attention (to).

advert[2] *n* (*inf*) an advertisement.

advertence, advertency *n* attention; heedfulness.—**advertent** *adj.*

advertently *adv* in an intentional manner.

advertise, advertize *vt* to call public attention to, esp in order to sell something, by buying space or time in the media, etc. * *vi* to call public attention to things for sale; to ask (for) by public notice.—**advertiser, advertizer** *n.*

advertisement, advertizement *n* advertising; a public notice, usu paid for by the provider of a good or service.

advertising, advertizing *n* the promotion of goods or services by public notices; advertisements; the business of producing adverts.

advice *n* recommendation with regard to a course of action; formal notice or communication.

advisable *adj* prudent, expedient.—**advisability** *n.*

advise *vt* to give advice to; to caution; to recommend; to inform. * *vi* to give advice.—**adviser, advisor** *n.*

advised *adj* acting with caution; deliberate; judicious.—**advisedly** *adv.*

advisory *adj* having or exercising the power to advise; containing or giving advice.

advocaat *n* a sweet egg-based liqueur.

advocacy *n* (*pl* **advocacies**) the function of an advocate; a pleading in support (of).

advocate *n* a person who argues or defends the cause of another, esp in a court of law; a supporter. * *vt* to plead in favour of, to recommend.

adynamia *n* want of vital power, prostration, weakness.—**adynamic** *adj.*

adze, adz *n* a type of axe with a blade at right angles to the handle for cutting and shaping wood.

aedile, *n* a Roman magistrate who exercised supervision over the temples, public and private buildings, the markets, public games, sanitation, etc, hence a municipal officer.—*also* **edile.**

aegis *n* protection, sponsorship.—*also* **egis.**

Aeolian *adj* pertaining to Aeolis in Asia Minor or to the Aeolic race; of Aeolus, the Greek god of winds.

aeolian harp *n* a stringed instrument, the wires of which are set in motion and sounded by the wind.

Aeolic *adj* of Aeolis. * *n* the Aeolic dialect of ancient Greece.

aeon *n* a period of immense duration; an age.—*also* **eon.**

aeonian *adj* everlasting.—*also* **eonian.**

aerate *vt* to supply (blood) with oxygen by respiration; to supply or impregnate with air; to combine or charge a liquid with gas.—**aeration** *n.*

aerator *n* an apparatus for making aerated waters.

aerial *adj* belonging to or existing in the air; of aircraft or flying. * *n* a radio or TV antenna.

aerialist *n* a trapeze or high-wire artist.

aerie *see* **eyrie.**

aeriform *adj* having the form of air; gaseous; like air; unsubstantial.

aerify *vt* (**aerifying, aerified**) to combine with air.—**aerification** *n.*

aero- *prefix* aviation; air vessel

aerobatics *npl* stunts performed while flying an aircraft.

aerobe, aerobium *n* (*pl* **aerobes, aerobia**) a microbe that cannot live without air.

aerobic *adj* (*exercise*) that conditions the heart and lungs by increasing the efficient intake of oxygen by the body.

aerobics *npl* aerobic exercises.

aerodrome *n* an airfield.

aerodynamics *n* the study of the forces exerted by air or other gases in motion, esp around solid bodies such as aircraft.—**aerodynamic** *adj.*—**aerodynamically** *adv.*

aerofoil *n* a wing, the lifting surface of an aeroplane.

aerogram, aerogramme *n* a radio telegraphic message.

aerolite *n* a stone falling from the air, a meteorite.

aerology *n* the science that deals with the air and the atmosphere.—**aerologic, aerological** *adj.*—**aerologist** *n.*

aerometer *n* an instrument for weighing the air.—**aerometric** *adj.*

aerometry *n* the branch of physics concerned with air, pneumatics.

aeronaut *n* an aviator; the pilot or navigator of an aircraft.

aeronautical, aeronautic *adj* of or pertaining to aeronatics or an aeronaut.—**aeronautically** *adv.*

aeronautics *n* the science dealing with the operation of aircraft; the art or science of flight.

aeroplane *n* a power-driven aircraft.—*also* **airplane.**

aerosol *n* a suspension of fine solid or liquid particles in gas, esp as held in a container under pressure, with a device for releasing it in a fine spray.

aerospace *n* the earth's atmosphere and the space beyond. * *adj* technology for flight in aerospace.

aerostat *n* a balloon; a balloonist.

aerostatics *n* (*used as sing*) the science that studies the equilibrium of bodies sustained in air; the science of air navigation.—**aerostatic, aerostatical** *adj.*

aerostation *n* ballooning.

aeruginous *adj* of or like verdigris or copper rust.

aery see eyrie.

Aesculapian *adj* of or pertaining to Aesculapius, the Roman god of medicine, or to medicine.

aesthete *n* a person who is or pretends to be highly sensitive to art and beauty.—*also* **esthete.**

aesthetic, aesthetical *adj* of or pertaining to aesthetics; concerned with beauty rather than practicality.—*also* **esthetic, esthetical.**—**aesthetically, esthetically** *adv.*

aestheticism *n* the cult of the beautiful, esp a fantastic art movement at the end of the 19th century.—*also* **estheticism.**

aesthetics *n* the philosophy of art and beauty.—*also* **esthetics.**

aestival *adj* of or occurring in summer.—*also* **estival.**

aestivation *n* (*bot*) the arrangement of petals in a flower bud; (*zool*) the spending of the dry season in a dormant state.—*also* **estivation.**

aet., aetat. *abbr* = *aetatis*, of, at, the age of.

aetiology, aetiological, aetiologist *see* **etiology.**

af- *prefix* the form of *ad-* before *f.*

afar *adv* at, to, or from a great distance.

affable *adj* friendly; approachable.—**affability** *n.*—**affably** *adv.*

affair *n* a thing done or to be done; (*pl*) public or private business; (*inf*) an event; a temporary romantic or sexual relationship.

affaire (de coeur) *n* a love affair.

affect[1] *vt* to have an effect on; to produce a change in; to act in a way that alters or affects the feelings of.

affect[2] *vt* to pretend or feign (an emotion); to incline to or show a preference for.

affect[3] *n* an emotion, feeling or desire associated with a certain stimulus.

affectation *n* a striving after or an attempt to assume what is not natural or real; pretence.

affected *adj* (*manner, etc*) assumed artificially.—**affectedly** *adv*.—**affectedness** *n*.
affecting *adj* having power to excite the emotions; moving; pathetic.—**affectingly** *adv*.
affection *n* tender feeling; liking.—**affectional** *adj*.
affectionate *adj* showing affection, loving.—**affectionately** *adv*.
affective *adj* arousing the emotions, emotional.—**affectivity, affectiveness** *n*.
afferent *adj* conveying inwards or to a part.
affettuoso *adv* (*mus*) with feeling, tender, pathetic.
affiance *vt* to promise in marriage, betroth. * *n* faith, trust; a marriage contract.
affiche *n* a paper affixed to a wall, a poster.
affidavit *n* a statement written on oath.
affiliate *vt* to connect as a subordinate member or branch; to associate (oneself with). * *vi* to join. * *n* an affiliated person, club, etc.—**affiliation** *n*.
affinity *n* (*pl* **affinities**) attraction, liking; a close relationship, esp by marriage; similarity, likeness; (*chem*) a tendency in certain substances to combine.
affirm *vt* to assert confidently or positively; to confirm or ratify; (*law*) to make an affirmation.
affirmation *n* affirming; an assertion; a solemn declaration made by those declining to swear an oath, eg on religious grounds.
affirmative *adj* confirming; indicating agreement. * *n* a positive word or statement, eg *yes*.—**affirmatively** *adv*.
affix *vt* to fasten; to add, esp in writing; to attach.
afflatus *n* a breath or blast of wind; poetic or divine inspiration; creative power.
afflict *vt* to cause persistent pain or suffering to; to trouble greatly.—**afflictive** *adj*.
affliction *n* persistent pain, suffering; a cause of this.
affluence *n* an abundant supply, as of thoughts, words, riches; wealth.
affluent *adj* rich, well provided for.—**affluently** *adv*.
affluenza *n* a psychological disease resulting from an excess of affluence.
afflux *n* a flowing towards; an increase; an influx.
afford *vt* to be in a position to do or bear without much inconvenience; to have enough time, money, or resources for; to supply, produce.
afforest *vt* to plant trees to cover with forest.—**afforestation** *n*.
affranchise *vt* to free from an obligation or slavery; to enfranchise.—**affranchisement** *n*.
affray *n* a noisy fight.
affreightment *n* the hire of a ship for the transportation of goods or freight.
affright *vt* (*arch*) to frighten, to terrify; to alarm; to confuse.
affront *vi* to insult or offend openly or deliberately. * *n* such an insult or offence.
affusion *n* the act of pouring upon, esp in baptism.
Afghan *adj* pertaining to Afghanistan. * *n* a native of Afghanistan (—*also* **Afghani**).
aficionado *n* (*pl* **aficionados**) a devotee of a particular sport, activity, etc.
afield *adv* far away from home; to or at a distance; astray.
afire *adj, adv* on fire.
aflame *adj, adv* flaming, ablaze, in a glow.
afloat *adj* floating; at sea, on board a ship; debt-free; flooded.—*also adv*.
afoot *adj, adv* on foot; astir; on the move; in operation.
afore *adv, prep* in front, before; previously.
aforementioned *adj* mentioned previously.
aforesaid *adj* referred to previously.
aforethought *adj* premeditated.
a fortiori (*Latin*) with stronger reason, more conclusively.
afraid *adj* full of fear or apprehension; regretful.
afreet *n* (*Arabian myth*) an evil demon.
afresh *adv* anew, starting again.
African *adj* pertaining to Africa. * *n* a native of Africa.
African violet *n* any of various African plants popular as houseplants, with purple, pink or white flowers and velvet-textured leaves.
Afrikaans *n* a language derived from Dutch used in South Africa.
Afrikander, Africander *n* (any of) a breed of southern African beef cattle.
Afrikaner *n* a South African native white, esp of Dutch descent.
Afro *n* (*pl* **Afros**) a bushy hairstyle.
Afro- *prefix* Africa or African.
Afro-American *n* a Black American. * *adj* of or relating to Black Americans, or their culture, history, etc.
afrormosia *n* a hard wood similar to teak, used in furniture.
aft *adv* at, near, or towards the stern of a ship or rear of an aircraft.
after *prep* behind in place or order; following in time, later than; in pursuit of; in imitation of; in view of, in spite of; according to; about, concerning; subsequently. * *adv* later; behind. * *conj* at a time later than. * *adj* later, subsequent; nearer the stern of a ship or aircraft.
afterbirth *n* the placenta expelled from the womb after giving birth.
afterbrain *n* that portion of the brain behind the hind-brain, the medulla oblongata.
afterburner *n* a device in a jet engine used to provide extra thrust by igniting additional fuel.
aftercare *n* care following hospital treatment, etc.
afterdamp *n* the carbonic acid found in coal mines after an explosion of fire damp; choke damp.
aftereffect *n* an effect that occurs some time after its cause.
afterglow *n* the glow in the sky after sunset.
afterimage *n* the image that remains momentarily after the eye has been withdrawn from a bright object.
afterlife *n* life after death.
aftermath *n* the result, esp an unpleasant one.
aftermost *adj* hindmost; farthest aft, nearest to the stern.
afternoon *n* the time between noon and sunset or evening.—*also adj*.
afternote *n* the second or unaccented note, which takes its time from the first or accented note.
afterpains *npl* pains after childbirth.
aftershave *n* lotion for use after shaving.
aftertaste *n* the taste that remains after eating or drinking.
afterthought *n* a thought or reflection occurring later.
afterwards, afterward *adv* at a later time.
afterwit *n* wisdom that comes too late.
Ag (*chem symbol*) silver.
ag- *prefix* the form of *ad-* before *g*.
aga *n* in Turkey, a commander or chief officer; a title of respect.—*also* **agha**.
again *adv* once more; besides; on the other hand.
against *prep* in opposition to; unfavourable to; in contrast to; in preparation for; in contact with; as a charge on.
agalloch *n* a fragrant resinous heartwood.—*also* **eaglewood**.
agama *n* a short-tongued lizard found in India and Africa.
agami *n* a South American bird allied to the cranes; a trumpeter bird.
agamic *adj* (*biol*) produced without sexual action, asexual.—**agamically** *adj*.
agamogenesis *n* (*biol*) asexual reproduction.—**agamogenetic** *adj*.—**agamogenetically** *adv*.
agapanthus *n* an ornamental plant with bright blue flowers.
Agape *n* the love feast of the early Christians at communion time.
agape *adj* open-mouthed.
agar *n* a preparation of seaweed used for jelly, glue and bacteria culture.
agaric *n* a mushroom or other fungus of the genus *Agaricus*.
agate *n* stone with striped or clouded colouring used as a gemstone.
agave *n* a genus of plants of which the chief species is the century plant.
age *n* the period of time during which someone or something has lived or existed; a stage of life; later years of life; a historical period; a division of geological time; (*inf: often pl*) a long time. * *vti* (**ageing** *or* **aging, aged**) to grow or make old, ripe, mature, etc.

aged *adj* very old; of a specified age. * *n* (*with* **the**) the elderly.
ageism *n* discrimination on grounds of age.—*also* **agism.—ageist, agist** *adj.*
ageless *adj* timeless; appearing never to grow old.
age-long *see* **age-old.**
agency *n* (*pl* **agencies**) action; power; means; a firm, etc empowered to act for another; an administrative government division.
agenda, agendum *n* (*pl* **agendas, agendums**) a list of items or matters of business that need to be attended to.
agenesis *n* imperfect development of the body.—**agenetic** *adj.*
agent *n* a person or thing that acts or has an influence; a substance or organism that is active; one empowered to act for another; a government representative; a spy.
agent provocateur *n* (*pl* **agents provocateurs**) a person hired to tempt or provoke suspected persons into illegal acts so to incriminate themselves.
age-old *adj* ancient.—*also* **age-long.**
agglomerate *vti* to gather into a heap; to accumulate; to collect into a mass. * *n* a heap or mass; a rock consisting of volcanic fragments.—**agglomeration** *n.*—**agglomerative** *adj.*
agglutinate *vti* to stick or fuse together; to form words into compounds. * *adj* glued together.—**agglutination** *n.*—**agglutinative** *adj.*
agglutination *n* the act or condition of being united or joined together; the formation of words by combination, not inflexion.
aggrandize *vt* to increase the power, rank, wealth, or reputation of.—**aggrandizement** *n.*
aggravate *vt* to make worse; (*inf*) to annoy, irritate.—**aggravation** *n.*
aggravated *adj* (*law*) denoting a grave form of a specified offence.
aggravating *adj* making worse or more heinous; (*inf*) annoying, irritating.
aggregate *adj* formed of parts combined into a mass or whole; taking all units as a whole. * *n* a collection or sum of individual parts; sand, stones, etc mixed with cement to form concrete. * *vt* to collect or form into a mass or whole; to amount to (a total).—**aggregation** *n.*
aggression *n* an unprovoked attack; a hostile action or behaviour.
aggressive *adj* boldly hostile; quarrelsome; self-assertive, enterprising.—**aggressively** *adv.*—**aggressiveness** *n.*
aggressor *n* a person or country that attacks first.
aggrieve *vt* to pain; to injure; to have a grievance; to bear heavily upon; to oppress.—**aggrieved** *adj.*—**aggrievedly** *adv.*
aggro *n* (*sl*) aggression.
agha *see* **aga.**
aghast *adj* utterly horrified.
agile *adj* quick and nimble in movement; mentally acute.—**agility** *n.*
agio *n* (*pl* **agios**) the premium on changing paper money into cash or for exchanging one currency for another.—**agiotage** *n.*
agism *see* **ageism.**
agitate *vt* to shake, move; to disturb or excite the emotions of. * *vi* to stir up public interest for a cause, etc.—**agitation** *n.*—**agitator** *n.*
agitato *adj, adv* (*mus*) in a hurried or agitated manner.
agitator *n* one who starts or keeps up a political or other agitation; an implement for stirring.
aglet *n* a tag (of a shoelace, etc); a spangle, a metallic ornament; a catkin.—*also* **aiglet.**
aglow *adj* radiant with warmth or excitement.
agnail *n* a sore under or near the nail, a hangnail.
agnate *adj* related by the father's side or with the same male ancestor. * *n* a relative by the father's side.—**agnatic** *adj.*
agnomen *n* (*pl* **agnomina**) the fourth name of a person in ancient Rome; an additional name or epithet, as *Milton, the poet.*—**agnominal** *adj.*
agnostic *n* one who believes that knowledge of God is impossible. * *adj* pertaining to the agnostics or their teachings; expressing ignorance.—**agnostically** *adv.*—**agnosticism** *n.*
Agnus Dei *n* a figure of a lamb bearing a banner or cross, symbolic of Christ and associated emblematically with St John the Baptist; the lamb and flag; a medal of wax or precious metal stamped with the figure of the Agnus Dei and blessed by the pope for distribution on Low Sunday.
ago *adv* in the past. * *adj* gone by; past.
agog *adj, adv* in agitation or expectation; eager, on the lookout.
agonic *adj* making no angle.
agonistic *adj* of athletic contests; athletic; polemic; melodramatic; strained; unnatural.
agonize *vti* to suffer or cause to suffer agony; to strive.—**agonizingly** *adv.*
agony *n* (*pl* **agonies**) extreme mental or physical suffering.
agony aunt *n* a person who replies to readers' problem letters in an agony column.
agony column *n* the column of a newspaper devoted to advertisements relating to lost friends, etc; a column in a magazine containing readers' letters with helpful replies to problems.
agoraphobia *n* abnormal fear of crossing open places.—**agoraphobic** *adj, n.*
agouti *n* (*pl* **agoutis, agouties**) a rodent similar to the guinea pig found in the West Indies and South America.
AGR *abbr* = advanced gas-cooled reactor.
agraphia *n* the inability to write due to mental illness.
agrarian *adj* of or relating to fields, or their cultivation; of or relating to farmers or agricultural life. * *n* an advocate of redistribution of property in land.
agrarianism *n* the principle of a uniform division of land; agitation with respect to land tenure.
agree *vb* (**agreeing, agreed**) *vi* to be of similar opinion; to consent or assent (to); to come to an understanding about; to be consistent; to suit a person's digestion; (*gram*) to be consistent in gender, number, case, or person. * *vt* to concede, grant; to bring into harmony; to reach terms on.
agreeable *adj* likeable, pleasing; willing to agree.—**agreeableness** *n.*—**agreeably** *adv.*
agreement *n* harmony in thought or opinion, correspondence; an agreed settlement between two people, etc.
agrestic *adj* rustic; uncouth.
agriculture *n* the science or practice of producing crops and raising livestock; farming.—**agricultural** *adj.*—**agriculturally** *adv.*—**agriculturist, agriculturalist** *n.*
agrimony *n* (*pl* **agrimonies**) a yellow-flowered plant.
agronomics *n* (*used as sing*) the part of economics concerned with the management and distribution of farming lands.—**agronomic, agronomical** *adj.*
agronomy *n* the science of land cultivation and management, husbandry.—**agronomist** *n.*
agrostology *n* the branch of botany that treats of the grasses.
aground *adj, adv* on or onto the shore.
aguardiente *n* an inferior Spanish brandy.
ague *n* malaria, an intermittent fever; the cold fit of the intermittent fever.—**aguish** *adj.*
ah *interj* an exclamation of sudden emotion.
AH *abbr* = *anno Hegira* (in the year of the Hegira) used in dates of the Muslim era.
aha *interj* an exclamation of satisfaction, triumph or mockery.
ahead *adj* in or to the front; forward; onward; in advance; winning or profiting.—*also adv.*
ahem *interj* an exclamation to call attention.
ahoy *interj* a term used in hailing a vessel.
A.I. *abbr* = artificial insemination; artificial intelligence.
ai *n* (*pl* **ais**) a South American three-toed sloth.
AID *abbr* = Agency for International Development; artificial insemination (by) donor.
aid *vti* to help, give assistance to. * *n* anything that helps; a specific means of assistance, eg money, equipment; a helper.
aide *n* an aide-de-camp; assistant.

aide-de-camp *n* (*pl* **aides-de-camp**) a military officer serving as an assistant to a senior officer.
aide-mémoire *n* (*pl* **aides-mémoire**) a summarized document; a memorandum, etc, as an aid to the memory.
AIDS, Aids *n* (*acronym for* acquired immune deficiency syndrome) a condition caused by a virus, in which the body loses its immunity to infection.
AIDS-related complex *n* a condition in which mild symptoms of AIDS (e.g. fever, weight loss) precede development of the full-blown disease.
aiglet *see* **aglet.**
aigrette, aigret *n* a small white heron; a plume arranged in imitation of the feathers of the heron, worn on helmets and as a hat decoration.
aiguille *n* a sharp peak of rock.
aiguillette *n* an ornamental tag or lace worn on uniforms and liveries.
AIH *abbr* = artificial insemination (by) husband.
ail *vt* to give or cause pain. * *vi* to feel pain; to be afflicted with pain.
aileron *n* a hinged section on the wing of an aircraft used for lateral control.
ailing *adj* unwell.
ailment *n* a slight illness.
ailurophobia *n* cat fear; a morbid dread of cats and a consciousness of their presence even when they are not in sight.—**ailurophobe** *n.*
aim *vti* to point or direct towards a target so as to hit; to direct (one's efforts); to intend. * *n* the act of aiming; purpose, intention.
aimless *adj* without purpose or object.—**aimlessly** *adv.*—**aimlessness** *n.*
ain't = am not, is not, are not, has not, have not.
air *n* the mixture of invisible gases surrounding the earth; the earth's atmosphere; empty, open space; a light breeze; aircraft, aviation; outward appearance, demeanour; a pervading influence; (*mus*) a melody; (*pl*) an affected manner. * *vt* to expose to the air for drying, etc; to expose to public notice; (*clothes*) to place in a warm place to finish drying.
airbag *n* a safety device in a motor vehicle that automatically inflates to protect the occupants in the event of an accident.
air base *n* a base for military aircraft.
air bath *n* a lengthened exposure of the body to the action of the air and sun; an arrangement for drying articles by exposing them to air of any regulated temperature.
air bed *n* an inflatable mattress usu of plastic or rubber.
airborne *adj* carried by or through the air; aloft or flying.
air box *n* a tube for conveying fresh air to a mine; a flue supplying air to a furnace; a chamber behind the fire box of a furnace to assist combustion by supply of air.
air brake *n* a brake operated by compressed air.
air brick *n* a brick with holes in the sides through which air for ventilation can pass.
airbrush *n* a device for spraying paint by compressed air.
airbus *n* a jet aircraft designed for short-distance intercity flights.
air conditioning *n* regulation of air humidity and temperature in buildings, etc.
air-cooled *adj* cooled by having air passed over, into, or through.
air course *n* a ventilating passage in a mine.
air cover *n* protection for ground forces given by fighter aircraft; the aircraft giving this protection.
aircraft *n* (*pl* **aircraft**) any machine for travelling through air.
aircraft carrier *n* a warship with a large flat deck, for the carrying, taking off and land of aircraft.
aircrew *n* the crew of an aircraft.
air cushion *n* an inflatable cushion usu of plastic or rubber.
air drop *n* a dropping by parachute of troops and supplies.
Airedale *n* a large rough-coated terrier.
airfield *n* a field where aircraft can take off and land.
air force *n* the aviation branch of a country's armed forces.
air gas *n* an illuminating gas made from air charged with the vapour of petroleum, naphtha, etc.
airgun *n* a gun that fires pellets by compressed air.
airhead *n* (*sl*) a stupid person.
air hostess *n* a stewardess on a passenger aircraft.
airing *n* exposure to the open air for drying or freshening; exercise in the open air; exposure to public view.
airless *adj* stuffy; sultry.—**airlessness** *n.*
air letter *n* a sheet of light writing paper that is folded and sealed for sending by airmail.
airlift *n* the transport of cargo, troops, passengers, etc by air, esp in an emergency.—*also vt.*
airline *n* a system or company for transportation by aircraft; a beeline.
airliner *n* a large passenger aeroplane.
airlock *n* a blockage in a pipe caused by an air bubble; an airtight compartment giving access to a pressurized chamber.
airmail *n* mail transported by aircraft.
airman *n* (*pl* **airmen**) a male civilian or military pilot, etc.—**airwoman** *nf* (*pl* **airwomen**).
airmiss *n* the near collision of aircraft in flight.
airplane *see* **aeroplane.**
air plant *n* a plant that derives its nourishment from the air, an epiphyte.
airplay *n* the playing of a recording over radio or TV.
air pocket *n* a patch of rarefied air causing aircraft to drop abruptly.
airport *n* a place where aircraft can land and take off, with facilities for repair, etc.
air pump *n* a machine for exhausting the air from a receiver; the pump used to exhuast the water and gases from the condenser of a steam engine.
air raid *n* an attack by military aircraft on a surface target.
airs *npl* affected behaviour for the purpose of impressing others.
airship *n* a self-propelled steerable aircraft that is lighter than air.
airsick *adj* nauseated due to the motion of an aircraft.
airspace *n* the space above a nation over which it maintains jurisdiction.
airspeed *n* the speed of an aircraft relative to the outside air.
airstrip *n* an area of land cleared for aircraft to land on; a runway.
airtight *adj* too tight for air or gas to enter or escape; (*alibi, etc*) invulnerable.
airtime *n* (*radio, TV*) the time alotted to a programme, item, commercial, etc; the time at which the broadcast begins.
air-to-air *adj* (*weaponry, communications, etc*) activated between aircraft in flight.
air valve *n* a valve regulating the supply of air to a boiler or pipe.
air vesicle *n* a dilatation of the trachea of certain insects enabling them to ascend or descend by its inflation or expiration; a vesicle filled with air in certain fishes, connected with the swim bladder.
airway *n* an aircraft route; a ventilation passage, as in a mine; a passage for air into the lungs; (*med*) a device to maintain the airway of an unconscious person.
airworthy *adj* safe to fly.—**airworthiness** *n.*
airy *adj* (**airier, airiest**) open to the air; breezy; light as air; graceful; lighthearted; flippant.—**airily** *adv.*—**airiness** *n.*
aisle *n* a passageway, as between rows of seats; a side part of a church.
ait *n* a small island in a river or lake.—*also* **eyot.**
aitch *n* the letter H.
aitchbone *n* the rump bone; the cut of meat lying over it.
ajar *adv* partly open, as a door.
AK *abbr* = Alaska.
aka, a.k.a *or* **AKA** *abbr* = also known as.
akimbo *adv* having the hands on the hips and the elbows bent outwards.
akin *adj* related; essentially similar, compatible.
Akkadian *n* an ancient Babylonian language preserved in cuneiform inscriptions. * *adj* of Akkad or Accad, the Babylonian city.—*also* **Accadian.**
al- *prefix* the form of *ad-* before *l.*
-al *adj suffix* of, of the nature of, as in *mortal, colossal.* * *n suffix* esp of verbal action, as in *approval.*

AL *abbr* = Alabama.
Al (*chem symbol*) = aluminium.
Ala. *abbr* = Alabama.
à la *prep* in the style of.
alabaster *n* a type of soft, chalky stone used in ornaments.—**alabastrine** *adj.*
à la carte *adj* (*menu*) with dishes listed and priced as separate items.
alack *interj* an exclamation of blame, sorrow, or surprise.
alacrity *n* promptness, eager readiness.—**alacritous** *adj.*
alameda *n* a public promenade planted with trees.
à la mode *adv* in the fashion. * *adj* fashionable.
alamode *n* a thin, light, glossy black silk.
alar *adj* of wings; winged; winglike; wing-shaped.—*also* **alary.**
alarm *n* a signal warning of danger; an automatic device to arouse from sleep or to attract attention; the fear arising from the apprehension of danger. * *vt* to give warning of danger; to fill with apprehension or fear.
alarm clock *n* a clock with an apparatus that can be set to ring loudly at a particular time.
alarming *adj* frightening, disconcerting.—**alarmingly** *adv.*
alarmist *n* one who keeps prophesying danger, a panic-monger.—**alarmism** *n.*
alarum *n* (*arch*) an alarm.
alary *see* **alar.**
alas *interj* expressive of misery, unhappiness, grief, etc.
alate *adj* having wings or winglike side appendages.
alb *n* a white priestly vestment reaching to the feet, worn at the celebration of the Eucharist in the RC Church and in some Anglican churches.
albacore *n* a large species of mackerel or tunny found in the Atlantic and Pacific Oceans.
albata *n* an alloy imitating silver; German silver.
albatross *n* any of various large web-footed seabirds; a heavy burden, as of debt, guilt, etc; (*golf*) a score of three under par.
albeit *conj* although, even though, notwithstanding.
albescent *adj* shading into white; whitish; becoming white.—**albescence** *n.*
albino *n* (*pl* **albinos**) a person lacking normal coloration, so that they have white skin and pink eyes; an animal or plant with abnormal pigmentation.
Albion *n* (*arch*) Britain.
album *n* a book with blank pages for the insertion of photographs, autographs, etc; a long-playing record, cassette, or CD.
albumen *n* the white of an egg.
albumenize *vt* to coat (paper) with an albuminous solution.
albuminoid *adj* like albumen. * *n* a class of organic compounds that form the chief part of the organs and tissues of animals and plants; proteids.
albuminous *adj* like, or containing, albumin.
albuminuria *n* the presence of albumin in the kidneys and the urine.
alburnum *n* the white and softer part of wood between the bark and the heartwood; sapwood.
alcahest *see* **alkahest.**
Alcaic *n* a kind of lyric verse form consisting of four lines of four feet devised by the 7th-century bc Greek poet Alcaeus.—*also adj.*
alcaide *n* the commander of a castle in Spain; the warder of a Spanish jail.
alcalde, alcade *n* a magistrate or justice in Spain or Portugal.
alcazar *n* a Spanish or Moorish palace or castle.
alchemist *n* one who studies or practises alchemy.
alchemize *vt* to transmute.
alchemy *n* (*pl* **alchemies**) chemistry as practised during medieval times, with the aim of transmuting base metals into gold.—**alchemic, alchemical** *adj.*—**alchemist** *n.*
alcohol *n* a liquid, generated by distillation and fermentation, that forms the intoxicating agent in wine, beer and spirits; a liquid containing alcohol; a chemical compound of this nature.
alcoholic *adj* of or containing alcohol; caused by alcohol. * *n* a person suffering from alcoholism.
alcoholism *n* a disease caused by excessive consumption of alcohol.
alcoholize *vt* to subject to the influence of alcohol; to rectify (spirits of wine).—**alcoholization** *n.*
alcoholometer *n* an instrument for determining the strength of spirits.
Alcoran *n* the Koran, the Muslim bible.
alcove *n* a recess off a larger room.
aldehyde *n* a volatile fluid with a suffocating smell, obtained from alcohol.
al dente *adj* cooked but still firm to the teeth.
alder *n* a genus of plants growing in moist land and related to the birch.
alderman *n* (*pl* **aldermen**) in US, a member of certain municipal councils; (*formerly*) in England and Wales, a senior councillor.—**aldermanic** *adj.*
ale *n* beer.
aleatory *adj* depending on dice or chance.
alee *adj, adv* (*naut*) on the lee, to leeward.
alegar *n* vinegar made from ale.
alehouse *n* a place where ale is sold.
alembic *n* an apparatus formerly used in distilling.
Alençon *n* a fine lace made at Alençon in France.
alert *adj* watchful; active, brisk. * *n* a danger signal. * *vt* to warn of impending danger, put in a state of readiness.—**alertly** *adv.*—**alertness** *n.*
alexandrine *n* a heroic verse of six iambic feet, or twelve syllables.—*also adj.*
alexia *n* the inability to read, due to mental illness.
alexin *n* a disease-resisting protein in blood serum.
alfalfa *n* a deep-rooted leguminous plant grown widely for hay and forage.—*also* **lucerne.**
alfresco *adj* taking place outside in the open.—*also adv.*
alga *n* (*pl* **algae**) any of a group of chiefly aquatic lower plants classified according to colour.—**algal** *adj.*
algarroba, algaroba *n* the carob tree and bean; St John's bread.
algebra *n* the branch of mathematics dealing with the properties and relations of numbers; the generalization and extension of arithmetic.—**algebraic, algebraical** *adj.*—**algebraist** *n.*
Algerian *adj* pertaining to Algeria or Algiers. * *n* a native of Algeria or Algiers.
Algerine *adj* Algerian.
-algia *n suffix* pain.—**algic** *adj.*
algid *adj* cold, chilly.
ALGOL *n* (*comput*) a high-level programming language used for solving general problems in science and mathematics.
algology *n* the study of algae.—**algologist** *n.*
algor *n* the rigor or chill on the onset of fever.
algorism *n* the arabic (decimal) numeration; arithmetic.—**algorismic** *adj.*
algorithm *n* (*math*) any method or procedure for computation.—**algorithmic** *adj.*—**algorithmically** *adv.*
alias *adv* otherwise called. * *n* (*pl* **aliases**) an assumed name.
alibi *n* (*pl* **alibis**) (*law*) the plea that a person charged with a crime was elsewhere when it was committed; (*inf*) any excuse.
alien *adj* foreign; strange; distasteful to, counter to. * *n* a person from another country, place, etc; a person of foreign birth who has not been naturalized; a being from outer space.
alienable *adj* (*law*) (*property*) that may be transferred.—**alienability** *n.*
alienage *n* the state or legal status of an alien.
alienate *vt* to render hostile or unfriendly; to make less affectionate or interested.
alienation *n* estrangement; transference; diversion to another purpose; mental derangement.
alienee *n* (*law*) one to whom property is transferred.
alienism *n* the study and treatment of mental alienation.—**alienist** *n.*
alienor *n* (*law*) one who transfers property to another.
aliform *adj* wing-shaped.
alight[1] *vi* (**alighting, alighted** *or* **alit**) to come down, as from a bus; to land after a flight.

alight[2] *adj* on fire; lively.

align *vt* to place in a straight line, to bring into agreement, etc. * *vi* to line up.—**alignment** *n*.

alignment *n* the act of laying out or adjusting by a line; the ground plan of a railway or road.

alike *adj* like one another. * *adv* equally; similarly.

aliment *n* food; the necessaries of life generally; an allowance for support by decree of court. * *vt* to make provision for the maintenance of; to make provision for the support of parents or children respectively.—**alimental** *adj*.

alimentary *adj* pertaining to nourishment, food.

alimentary canal *n* the tube extending within the body from the mouth to the anus through which food passes and is absorbed.

alimentation *n* the act of giving nourishment; the function of the alimentary canal.—**alimentative** *adj*.

alimony *n* (*pl* **alimonies**) an allowance for support made by one spouse to the other, esp a man to his wife or former wife, pending or after a legal separation or divorce.—*also* **maintenance.**

aliped *adj* having wing-like limbs, as the bat.

aliphatic *adj* (*chem*) of fat.

aliquant *adj* (*math*) being a part of a number that does not divide it without a remainder, as 8 is the aliquant part of 25.—*also n*.

aliquot *adj* (*math*) being a part of a number of quantity that will divide it without a remainder, as 8 is the aliquot part of 24.—*also n*.

alive *adj* having life; active, alert; in existence, operation, etc.

alizarin *n* a red colouring matter found in madder but now produced from anthracene.

alkahest *n* the supposed universal solvent of the alchemists.—*also* **alcahest.**

alkali *n* (*pl* **alkalis, alkalies**) (*chem*) any salt or mixture that neutralizes acids.—**alkaline** *adj*.

alkalify *vb* (**alkalifying, alkalified**) *vt* to form or convert into alkali. * *vi* to become an alkali.

alkalimeter *n* an instrument used to determine the relative strength of alkalis.

alkalimetry *n* the process of determining the strength of an alkaline mixture or liquid.—**alkalimetric** *adj*.

alkaline *adj* pertaining to, or having the properties of, an alkali.—**alkalinity** *n*.

alkalize *vt* to convert into an alkali or render alkaline.—**alkalizable** *adj*.

alkaloid *n* a body or substance containing alkaline properties; (*pl*) nitrogenous compounds met with in plants in combination with organic acids. * *adj* resembling an alkali in its properties.

alkanet *n* a rich red dye; the plant the root of which yields it.

all *adj* the whole amount or number of; every one of. * *adv* wholly; supremely, completely; entirely. * *n* the whole number, quantity; everyone; everything.

alla breve *adv* (*mus*) in quick time, with one breve to a measure.

Allah *n* the Muslim name of God.

all along *adv* throughout.

allantoid *adj* of or pertaining to the allantois; (*bot*) sausage-shaped. * *n* the allantois.—**allantoidal** *adj*.

allantois *n* (*pl* **allantoides**) a membranous appendage of most vertebrate embryos.

allay *vt* to lighten, alleviate; to pacify or make calm.

all but *adv* almost.

all clear *n* a signal indicating that a danger has passed or that it is safe to proceed.

allegation *n* the act of alleging; assertion; declaration; that which is asserted or alleged; that which is offered as a plea, an excuse, or justification; the statement as yet unproved of a party to a suit.

allege *vt* to assert or declare, esp without proof; to offer as an excuse.

allegedly *adv* asserted without proof.

allegiance *n* the obligation of being loyal to one's country, etc; devotion, as to a cause.

allegorical, allegoric *adj* pertaining to, consisting of, or in the nature of allegory; figurative.—**allegorically** *adv*.

allegorize *vt* to put in the form of an allegory.—**allegorization** *n*.

allegory *n* (*pl* **allegories**) a fable, story, poem, etc in which the events depicted are used to convey a deeper, usu moral or spiritual, meaning.—**allegorist** *n*.

allegretto *adv* (*mus*) moderately fast. * *n* (*pl* **allegrettos**) a piece of music played in this way.

allegro *adv* (*mus*) fast. * *n* (*pl* **allegros**) a piece of music played in this way.

allele *n* (*genetics*) either of a pair of contrasting characteristics one or the other of which is found unmixed in descendants of a cross between parental forms respectively possessing them.—*also* **allelomorph.**—**allelic** *adj*.—**allelism** *n*.

alleluia *see* **hallelujah.**

allemande *n* a German national dance in three-quarter time.

allergen *n* a substance inducing an allergic reaction.

allergenic *adj* causing an allergic reaction.

allergy *n* (*pl* **allergies**) an abnormal reaction of the body to substances (certain foods, pollen, etc) normally harmless; antipathy.—**allergic** *adj*.

allerion *n* (*her*) an eagle displayed without feet or beak.

alleviate *vt* to lessen or relieve (pain, worry, etc).—**alleviation** *n*.—**alleviator** *n*.

alleviative *adj* tending to alleviate. * *n* that which alleviates.

alley *n* a narrow street between or behind buildings; a bowling lane.

all fours *adv* on hands and knees.

All-hallowe'en *n* Hallowe'en.

All-hallows *npl* All Saints' Day, celebrated on 1 November, in honour of all the saints.

alliaceous *adj* of the nature or property of garlic or the onion.

alliance *n* a union by marriage or treaty for a common purpose; an agreement for this; the countries, groups, etc in such an association.

allied *see* **ally.**

alligator *n* a large reptile similar to the crocodile but having a short, blunt snout.

alligator pear *n* the avocado.

all in *adj* (*price, etc*) all-inclusive.

all-in *adj* (*inf*) exhausted.

all-inclusive *adj* including everything.

alliteration *n* the repetition of the same sound at the beginning of two or more words in a phrase, etc.—**alliterative** *adj*.

allocate *vt* to distribute or apportion in shares; to set apart for a specific purpose.

allocation *n* the act of alloting, allocating, or assigning; an allotment or assignment; an allowance made on an account.

allocution *n* a formal address, esp as one delivered by the Pope to his clergy or to the Church generally.

allodial *adj* freehold; not feudal. * *n* land thus held.

allodium, allod *n* (*pl* **allodia, allods**) freehold estate; land that is the absolute property of the owner.

allogamy *n* (*biol*) cross-fertilization.—**allogamous** *adj*.

allograph *n* a signature by one person on behalf of another, opposite of autograph.—**allographic** *adj*.

allomorphism *n* (*chem*) the property in certain substances of assuming a different form while remaining the same in constitution.

all one *adj, n* in effect the same.

allopath, allopathist *n* one who favours or practises allopathy.

allopathy *n* the orthodox medical practice of treating disease by inducing an action opposite to the disease it is sought to cure, opposite of homoeopathy.—**allopathic** *adj*.—**allopathically** *adv*.

allot *vt* (**allotting, allotted**) to distribute, allocate.

allotment *n* allotting; a share allotted; a small area of land rented for cultivation.

allotropy, allotropism *n* the capability shown by certain chemical elements to assume different forms, each characterized by peculiar qualities, as the occurrence of carbon in the form of the diamond, charcoal and plumbago respectively.—**allotropic** *adj*.—**allotropically** *adv*.

allottee *n* one to whom an allotment or share is granted or assigned; a plot-holder.
all out *adv* with maximum capacity.
all-out *adj* using maximum effort.
all-over *adj* covering the whole surface.
allow *vt* to permit; to acknowledge, admit as true; (*money*) to give, grant as an allowance at regular intervals; to estimate as an addition or deduction. * *vi* to admit the possibility (of).
allowable *adj* permissible.—**allowably** *adv*.
allowance *n* an amount or sum allowed or given at regular times; a discount; a portion of income not subject to income tax; permission; admission, concession.
alloy *n* a solid substance comprising a mixture of two or more metals; something that degrades the substance to which it is added. * *vt* to make into an alloy; to degrade or spoil by mixing with an inferior substance.
all-purpose *adj* suitable for many uses.
all right *adv* good enough, acceptable; without doubt. * *adj* satisfactory; safe, well; agreeable. * *interj* (*used to express consent*).—*also* **alright**.
all-round *adj* efficient in all respects, esp sport.
All Saints' Day *n* (*Christian Church*) 1 November, a festival in honour of all the saints.
All Souls' Day *n* (*RC Church*) the day, celebrated 2 November, in honour of the departed.
allspice *n* an aromatic spice made from the berry of a West Indian tree.
all-star *adj* made up entirely of outstanding performers.
all there *adj* (*sl*) not mentally wanting.
all-time *adj* unsurpassed until now.
all told *adv* with all counted; all in all.
allude *vi* to refer indirectly to.
allure *vt* to entice, charm. * *n* fascination; charm.—**allurement** *n*.
alluring *adj* attractive.
allusion *n* alluding; an implied or indirect reference.—**allusive** *adj*.
allusive *adj* having reference to something not definitely expressed.—**allusively** *adv*.—**allusiveness** *n*.
alluvion *n* the wash of the sea or river against a shore; land added to a shore or riverbank by the action of the water; an overflow.
alluvium *n* (*pl* **alluviums, alluvia**) earth, sand, gravel, etc deposited by moving water.—**alluvial** *adj*.
ally *vti* (**allying, allied**) to join or unite for a specific purpose; to relate by similarity of structure, etc. * *n* (*pl* **allies**) a country or person joined with another for a common purpose.
Almagest *n* the great astronomical treatise of Ptolemy of the 2nd century ad; (*without cap*) other similar treatises.
alma mater *n* one's school, college, or university.
almanac *n* a calendar with astronomical data, weather forecasts, etc.
almanack *n* (*arch*) an almanac.
almandine *n* a violet-red variety of garnet, tinged sometimes with blue or yellow.
almighty *adj* all-powerful. * *n* (*with cap*) God, the all-powerful.—**almightly** *adv*.—**almightiness** *n*.
almond *n* the edible kernel of the fruit of a tree of the rose family; the tree bearing this fruit. * *adj* (*eyes, etc*) oval and pointed at one or both ends.
almoner *n* (*formerly*) one who dispenses or distributes alms or charity; an alms purse; a pouch or purse which in early times was suspended from the girdle.
almost *adv* all but, very nearly but not quite all.
alms *npl* money, food, etc given to the poor.
almshouse *n* a house endowed by private or public charity and appropriated to the use of the poor.
aloe *n* (*pl* **aloes**) a succulent plant with tall spikes of flowers.
aloes *n* (*used as sing*) the bitter juice of the aloe plant used in medicine.
aloft *adv* in the air, flying; high up.
alone *adj* isolated; without anyone or anything else; unassisted; unique. * *adv* exclusively.
along *adv* onward, forward; over the length of; in company and together with; in addition. * *prep* in the direction of the length of; in accordance with.
alongside *prep* close beside. * *adv* at the side.
aloof *adv* at a distance; apart. * *adj* cool and reserved.—**aloofness** *n*.
alopecia *n* baldness; loss of hair through skin disease.
aloud *adv* with a normal voice; loudly; spoken.
alow *adv* (*naut*) to or in a lower part; below.
alp *n* a mountain peak.
alpaca *n* a Peruvian llama with long fine wool; a fabric made of this wool.
alpenglow *n* a peculiar purple glow on the snow on the Alps seen just before sunrise and after sunset.
alpenhorn *n* a long and nearly straight horn used by the mountaineers of the Alps.
alpenstock *n* a stout staff with an iron spike, used by mountain climbers.
alpha *n* the first letter of the Greek alphabet.
alphabet *n* the characters used in a language arranged in conventional order.
alphabetical, alphabetic *adj* pertaining to an alphabet; in the order of the alphabet.—**alphabetically** *adv*.
alphabetize *vt* to arrange in alphabetical order.—**alphabetization** *n*.
alphanumeric, alphameric *adj* containing letters of the alphabet and numerals.—**alphanumerically, alphamerically** *adv*.
alpha particle *n* a particle of helium given off by radium.
alpha ray *n* radiation of alpha particles.
alpine *adj* (*with cap*) of the Alps; of high mountains. * *n* a mountain plant, esp a small herb.
alpinist *n* a mountaineer who climbs in the Alps or in areas of similar mountains.—**alpinism** *n*.
Alps *npl* a high mountain range in south central Europe.
already *adv* by or before the time specified; before the time expected.
alright *adv* a frequent spelling of all right.
Alsatian *n* a German shepherd; a native of Alsace.
also *adv* in addition, besides.
also-ran *n* a defeated contestant in a race, an election, etc.
alt *n* (*mus*) the high notes above the treble staff.
Alta. (*abbr*) = Alberta.
Altaic *adj* pertaining to the Altaic mountain regions, partly bounding Russia and China. * *n* the language of the region.
altar *n* a table, etc for sacred purposes in a place of worship.
altarage *n* the offerings placed upon the altar to be devoted to the church, or appropriated by the priest as stipend.
altar cloth *n* a general term for the coverings of the altar.
altar ledge *n* a step or ledge behind the altar of a church, slightly raised above it for holding lights, flowers, and other symbolical ornaments; a retable.
altarpiece *n* a painting, decorative screen, or other work of art, placed over or behind an altar.
altarscreen *n* a screen or partition separating the altar from the choir; a reredos.
altar slab *n* the top of an altar; the consecrated part of an altar (the mensa).
altarwise *adv* placed in the usual position of an altar, with the ends towards the north and south, and the front to the west.
altazimuth *n* an instrument for determining the altitudes and azimuths of the stars and planets.
alter *vti* to make or become different in a small way; to change.—**alterable** *adj*.—**alterability** *n*.
alteration *n* the act of altering or changing; the change or modification effected.
alterative *adj* producing change; having the power to alter. * *n* a medicine that restores the healthy functions of the body.
altercate *vi* to contend in words; to wrangle; to dispute with anger or heat.

altercation *n* an angry or heated quarrel.
alter ego *n* one's other self; a constant companion.
alternant *adj* alternating; composed of alternate layers.
alternate[1] *vt* to do or use by turns. * *vi* to act, happen, etc by turns; to take turns regularly.—**alternation** *n*.
alternate[2] *adj* occurring or following in turns.—**alternately** *adv*.
alternate angles *npl* the internal angles made by two lines with a third on opposite sides of it.
alternating current *n* an electric current that reverses its direction at regular intervals.
alternation *n* the act of alternating, or state of being alternate; reciprocal succession; antiphonal singing or reading.
alternative *adj* presenting a choice between two things. * *n* either of two possibilities.—**alternatively** *adv*.
alternative comedy *n* a form of comedy that avoids conventional humour (e.g. racist and sexist jokes), characterized by aggressively delivered and blackly humourous stand-up routines that usu challenge political and social orthodoxy.
alternative medicine *n* any technique of medical treatment without use of drugs, eg osteopathy, acupuncture, dieting.
alternator *n* an electric generator that produces alternating current.
althaea, althea *n* a genus of plants including the marshmallow and the hollyhock.
althorn *n* a musical instrument of the saxhorn class, frequently used in military bands.
although *conj* though; in spite of that.
altimeter *n* an instrument for measuring altitude.
altimetry *n* the art of measuring altitudes by the use of the altimeter.—**altimetrical** *adj*.
altissimo *adj* (*mus*) of the part or notes situated above F in alt.
altitude *n* height, esp above sea level.—**altitudinal** *adj*.
alto *n* (*pl* **altos**) the range of the highest male voice; a singer with this range; a contralto. * *adj* high.
alto clef *n* the C clef placed on the third line of the staff.
altogether *adv* in all; on the whole; completely.
alto-relievo, alto-rilievo *n* (*pl* **alto-relievos, alto-rilievos**) high relief; figures or other objects that stand out boldly from the background, and having more than half their thickness projecting.
altruism *n* unselfish concern for or dedication to the interests or welfare of others.—**altruist** *n*.—**altruistic** *adj*.—**altruistically** *adv*.
aludel *n* one of the pear-shaped glass or earthenware pots, open at both ends, used in sublimation.
alum *n* a double sulphate formed of aluminium and some other element, usually an alkali metal.
alumina *n* the single oxide of aluminium, the most abundant of the earths; a notable constituent of common clay, alumina is largely used in dyeing and calico printing as a mordant.
aluminiferous *adj* containing or yielding alum, alumina, or aluminium.
aluminous *adj* of, containing or resembling alum or alumina.
aluminium, aluminum *n* a silvery-white malleable metallic element notable for its lightness.
alumna *n* (*pl* **alumnae**) a female graduate or pupil of a university or college.
alumnus *n* (*pl* **alumni**) a former pupil or student.—**alumna** *nf* (*pl* **alumnae**).
alum root *n* a popular name given to certain astringent roots of saxifrages.
alum schist *n* a thin-bedded fissile rock from which alum is procured.
alunite *n* subsulphate of alumina and potash.
alveolar *adj* of tooth sockets.
alveolate *adj* with deep pits or cells resembling the honeycomb.—**alveolation** *n*.
alveolus *n* (*pl* **alveoli**) a small pit, cell, cavity, or socket; the socket in which a tooth is fixed; the cell of a honeycomb.
alvine *adj* pertaining or belonging to the intestines or belly.
always *adv* at all times; in all cases; repeatedly; forever.
Alzheimer's disease *n* a degenerative disorder of the brain resulting in progressive senility.
am *see* **be**.
a.m. *abbr* = *ante meridiem,* before noon.
amadou *n* a styptic and a tinder prepared by steeping the solid portions of a fungus affecting trees in a solution of saltpetre; German tinder.
amah *n* an East Indian nurse or female servant.
amalgam *n* an alloy of mercury and another metal; a mixture.
amalgamate *vt* to combine, unite.
amalgamation *n* the act or process of compounding mercury with another metal; the separation of precious metals from the mother rock by means of quicksilver; the blending or mixing of different elements or things; the union or consolidation of two or more companies or businesses into one concern, a merger.
amanuensis *n* (*pl* **amanuenses**) one who is employed to write at the dictation or direction of another; a secretary.
amaranth *n* an imaginary flower said by poets to be unfading; a plant of the genus *Amarantus*; a colour mixture in which magenta is the chief ingredient; red colouring added to some foods.
amaranthine *adj* pertaining to the amaranth; never-fading, like amaranth; purplish.
amaryllis *n* a genus of bulbous flowering plants to which the belladonna lily and narcissus belong.
amass *vt* to bring together in a large quantity; to accumulate.—**amasser** *n*.—**amassment** *n*.
amateur *n* one who engages in a particular activity as a hobby, and not as a profession. * *adj* of or done by amateurs.—**amateurism** *n*.
amateurish *adj* lacking expertise.—**amateurishly** *adv*.—**amateurishness** *n*.
amatol *n* a high explosive.
amatory, amatorial *adj* relating to or expressive of love.
amaurosis *n* loss or decay of sight due to partial, periodic, or complete paralysis of the optic nerve.—**amaurotic** *adj*.
amaze *vt* to fill with wonder, astonish.—**amazing** *adj*.—**amazingly** *adv*.
amazement *n* the state of being amazed; astonishment; perplexity arising from sudden surprise.
Amazon *n* (*Greek myth*) a race of women warriors; a tall strong athletic woman.—**Amazonian** *adj*.
amazon ant *n* a species of ant found in Europe and America, which seizies the neuters of other species in the pupa stage and brings them up with their own larvae.
amazonite *n* the amazon stone gemstone.
amazon stone *n* a beautiful green feldspar found near the Amazon.
ambary, ambari *n* (*pl* **ambaries, ambaris**) a plant of Asia that produces a jute-like fibre; the fibre.
ambassador *n* the highest-ranking diplomatic representative from one country to another; an authorized messenger.—**ambassadorial** *adj*.—**ambassadress** *nf*.
ambassador extraordinary *n* an ambassador sent on a special mission.
ambassador plenipotentiary *n* an ambassador sent with full powers to make a treaty.
amber *n* a hard yellowish fossil resin, used for jewellery and ornaments, etc; the colour of amber; a yellow traffic light used to signal "caution".
ambergris *n* a waxy substance found in tropical seas, which is secreted by sperm whales and is used in perfumery as a fixative.
amberoid, ambroid *n* pressed amber; synthetic amber.
amber tree *n* the common name for various species of African evergreen shrubs with fragrant leaves.
ambidextrous *adj* able to use the left and the right hand equally well.—**ambidexterity** *n*.
ambience, ambiance *n* surrounding influence, atmosphere.
ambient *adj* surrounding.
ambiguity *n* (*pl* **ambiguities**) double or dubious significance; vagueness.
ambiguous *adj* capable of two or more interpretations; indistinct, vague.—**ambiguously** *adv*.—**ambiguousness** *n*.
ambit *n* a circuit or compass; the line or sum of the lines by which a figure is bounded; the perimeter; sphere of action.
ambition *n* desire for power, wealth and success; an object of ambition.

ambitious *adj* having or governed by ambition; resulting from or showing ambition; requiring considerable effort or ability.—**ambitiously** *adv*.

ambivalent *adj* having mixed feelings toward the same object.—**ambivalence** *n*.

amble *vi* to walk in a leisurely way. * *n* an easy pace. —**ambler** *n*.

amblyopia *n* dimness of vision; amaurosis.—**amblyopic** *adj*.

ambo *n* (*pl* **ambos, ambones**) a pulpit; a reading desk.

amboyna, amboina *n* a beautifully mottled and curled variegated wood used in cabinet work.

ambrosia *n* (*Classical myth*) the food of the gods; anything exquisitely pleasing to taste or smell; a genus of weeds allied to wormwood.—**ambrosial, ambrosian** *adj*.

ambrotype *n* (*photog*) a process by which the light parts of a photograph are produced in silver, the dark parts showing as a background through the clear glass.

ambry *n* (*pl* **ambries**) a recess in a church wall for sacred vessels; a repository for arms; a cupboard for money tools, etc.

ambsace *n* two ones, the lowest throw at dice; bad luck.

ambulacrum *n* (*pl* **ambulacra**) a perforation in the shell of echinoderms through which the tube feet are protruded.—**ambulacral** *adj*.

ambulance *n* a special vehicle for transporting the sick or injured.

ambulance chaser *n* one who attempts to profit from disaster.

ambulant *adj* (*patient*) able to walk, not bed-ridden; moving from place to place.

ambulate *vi* to walk about; to move about; to wander.—**ambulation** *n*.

ambulatory *adj* of or pertaining to walking; movable; temporary; capable of walking. * *n* (*pl* **ambulatories**) a place for walking in; a covered way.

ambuscade *n* a strategic disposition of troops in ambush.

ambush *n* the concealment of soldiers, etc to make a surprise attack; the bushes or other cover in which they are hidden. * *vti* to lie in wait; to attack from an ambush.

ambush marketing *n* the practice of taking advantage of another's official event to advertise one's own products.—*also* **ambushing**.

ameba *see* **amoeba**.

ameer *see* **amir**.

ameliorate *vti* to make or become better.—**ameliorative** *adj*.—**ameliorator** *n*.

amelioration *n* the making or growing better; improvement.

amen *interj* may it be so!

amenable *adj* easily influenced or led, tractable; answerable to legal authority.—**amenability** *n*.—**amenably** *adv*.

amend *vt* to remove errors, esp in a text; to modify, improve; to alter in minor details.—**amendable** *adj*.—**amender** *n*.

amendatory *adj* tending to amend; corrective.

amende honorable *n* (*pl* **amendes honorables**) a public apology and reparation; a punishment formerly inflicted in France on traitors and the sacrilegious.

amendment *n* the act of amending, correction; an alteration to a document, etc.

amends *npl* (*used as sing*) compensation or recompense for some loss, harm, etc.

amenity *n* (*pl* **amenities**) pleasantness, as regards situation, convenience, or service.

amenorrhoea, amenorrhea *n* abnormal absence of menstruation.

ament, amentum *n* (*pl* **aments, amenta**) a catkin, as of the willow.

amentia *n* want of reason; mental deficiency.

amerce *vt* to punish by an arbitrary fine.—**amerceable** *adj*.—**amercement** *n*.

Amerenglish *n* the English language as spoken in the United States.

American *adj* belonging to or characteristic of America. * *n* an inhabitant of the US.

Americanism *n* a form of expression peculiar to the US; a custom peculiar to the US; attachment to the US.

Americanize *vt* to render American; to assimilate to the political and social institutions of the US.—**Americanization** *n*.

americium *n* a white radioactive metallic element derived from plutonium.

Amerindian, Amerind *n* an American Indian.—**Amerindic** *adj*.

ametabolic *adj* (*certain insects*) not undergoing metamorphosis.

amethyst *n* a gemstone consisting of bluish-violet quartz; the colour of an amethyst.—**amethystine** *adj*.

amiable *adj* friendly in manner, congenial.—**amiability** *n*.—**amiably** *adv*.

amianthus *n* earth or mountain flax, a fibrous variety of asbestos.—**amianthine, amianthoid, amianthoidal** *adj*.

amicable *adj* friendly; peaceable.—**amicability, amicableness** *n*.—**amicably** *adv*.

amice *n* a square of white linen formerly worn on the head but now worn about the neck and shoulders by celebrant priests while saying Mass; a pilgrim's cloak.

amicus curiae *n* (*pl* **amici curiae**) (*law*) a friend of the court; a disinterested adviser.

amid, amidst *prep* in or to the middle of; during.

amide *n* any of several compounds produced by the replacement of a hydrogen atom of ammonia by an acid radical or metal atom.

amidships *adv* in the middle of a ship.

amine *n* any of several organic compounds formed by replacing hydrogen atoms of ammonia by one or more univalent hydrocarbon radicals.

amino acid *n* any of a group of organic acids that occur in proteins.

amir *n* (*formerly*) the Muslim ruler of Afghanistan.—*also* **ameer**.

amiss *adj* wrong, improper. * *adv* in an incorrect manner.

amity *n* (*pl* **amities**) friendship.

ammeter *n* an instrument for measuring electric current in amperes.

ammo *n* (*sl*) ammunition.

ammonal *n* a highly explosive compound.

ammonia *n* a pungent colourless gas composed of nitrogen and hydrogen.

ammoniac[1] *n* a gum resin.—*also* **gum ammoniac**.

ammoniacal, ammoniac[2] *adj* of, pertaining to, like or containing ammonia.

ammonite *n* a fossil shell, twisted like a ram's horn; snakestone.—**ammonitic** *adj*.

ammonium *n* the hypothetical base of ammonia.

ammunition *n* bullets, shells, rockets, etc; any means of attack or defence; facts and reasoning used to prove a point in an argument.

amnesia *n* a partial or total loss of memory.—**amnesiac, amnesic** *n, adj*.

amnesty *n* (*pl* **amnesties**) a general pardon, esp of political prisoners; a pardon granted for a limited time. * *vt* (**amnestying, amnestied**) to pardon (an offence).

amniocentesis *n* the extraction by hollow needle of a sample of amniotic fluid from the womb to test for foetal abnormalities.

amnion *n* (*pl* **amnions, amnia**) the thin innermost membrane surrounding the foetus in the womb of mammals, birds, and reptiles.—**amniotic** *adj*.

amoeba *n* (*pl* **amoebae, amoebas**) a unicellular microorganism found in water, damp soil and the digestive tracts of animals.—*also* **ameba**.—**amoebic, amebic** *adj*.

amoebaean, amoebean *adj* (*verse form*) alternately answering.

amok *adj, adv* **run amok** to run about armed, in a state of frenzy, attacking all that come in the way; indiscriminate slaughter; headstrong violence.—*also* **amuck**.

among, amongst *prep* in the number of, surrounded by; in the group or class of; within a group, between; by the joint efforts of.

amontillado *n* (*pl* **amontillados**) a dry kind of light-coloured sherry.

amoral *adj* neither moral nor immoral; without moral sense.—**amorality** *n*.—**amorally** *adv*.

amoretto, amorino *n* (*pl* **amoretti, amorini**) (*art*) a figure of cupid and representations of children.—*also* **putto**.

amorist *n* an amateur in love, a philanderer.

amoroso *adj* (*mus*) in a tender, amatory style.

amorous *adj* displaying or feeling love or desire.—**amorously** *adv*.—**amorousness** *n*.

amor patriae *n* love of one's country.

amorphous *adj* lacking a specific shape, shapeless; unrecognizable, indefinable.—**amorphism** *n*.
amortization *n* the extinction of a debt by means of a sinking fund; the act of alienating lands to a corporation in mortmain.—**amortizement** *n*.
amortize *vt* to put money aside at intervals for gradual payment of (a debt, etc).—**amortization** *n*.
amount *vi* to be equivalent (to) in total, quantity or significance. * *n* the total sum; the whole value or effect; a quantity.
amour *n* a love affair; an intrigue.
amour propre *n* self-love, vanity; self-respect.
amp *n* an ampere; (*inf*) an amplifier.
ampelopsis *n* kinds of vine creeper, incl the Virginia creeper.
amperage *n* the strength of an electric current measured in amperes.
ampere *n* the standard SI unit by which an electric current is measured.
ampersand *n* the sign (&) meaning "and".
amphetamine *n* a drug used esp as a stimulant and to suppress appetite.
amphi- *prefix* of both kinds; on both sides; around.
amphibian *n* an animal living on land but breeding in water; an aircraft that can take off and land on water or land; a vehicle that can travel on land and through water.
amphibious *adj* living on both land and in water; (*mil*) involving both sea and land forces.
amphibology, amphiboly *n* (*pl* **amphibologies, amphibolies**) an ambiguous phrase, as a sentence that may be construed in two distinct ways, as "The duke yet lives that Henry shall depose"; a quibble.
amphibrach *n* (*verse*) a foot of three syllables, the middle long, the first and last short.—**amphibrachic** *adj*.
amphimacer *n* (*verse*) a foot of three syllables, the middle short, the first and last long.
amphimixis *n* (*pl* **amphimixes**) a mingling of male and female gametes in sexual reproduction.
amphioxus *n* (*pl* **amphioxi, amphioxuses**) the name of the lancelet, a fish with a body tapering at both ends, the lowest in organization of the vertebrates.
amphipod *n* any of the *Amphipoda* order of crustaceans having feet for both walking and swimming, including the sandhoppers and sand fleas.
amphiprostyle *adj* (*archit*) with a portico at both ends. * *n* a building of this kind, esp a temple.—**amphiprostylar** *adj*.
amphisbaena *n* (*pl* **amphisbaenae, amphisbaenas**) a fabled serpent with a head at each end; a kind of lizard or worm.—**amphisbaenic** *adj*.
amphitheatre, amphitheater *n* an oval or circular building with rising rows of seats around an open arena.
amphora *n* (*pl* **amphorae, amphoras**) a two-handled vessel of oblong shape, used by the ancients for holding wine, etc; a Greek and Roman liquid measure, the former 9 gallons, the latter 6 gallons.
ample *adj* large in size, scope, etc; plentiful.—**amply** *adv*.
amplification *n* the act of amplifying or expanding; enlargement.
amplifier *n* a device that increases electric voltage, current, or power, or the loudness of sound.
amplify *vt* (**amplifying, amplified**) to expand more fully, add details to; (*electrical signals, etc*) to strengthen.
amplitude *n* largeness of extent, scope; abundance; the maximum deviation of an oscillation from the mean or zero.
amplitude modulation *n* (the transmitting of information by) the modulation of the amplitude of a radio carrier wave in accordance with the amplitude of the signal carried.
ampoule, ampul, ampule *n* a small sealed glass vessel containing liquid, esp for injection.
ampulla *n* (*pl* **ampullae**) an ancient vessel which contained unguents for the bath; a drinking vessel; a vessel for consecrated oil or chrism used in church rites and at the coronation of sovereigns.—**ampullar, ampullary** *adj*.
amputate *vt* to cut off, esp by surgery.—**amputation** *n*.
amuck *see* **amok**.
amulet *n* something worn as a charm against evil.
amuse *vt* to entertain or divert in a pleasant manner; to cause to laugh or smile.—**amusing** *adj*.
amusement *n* that which amuses; the state of being amused; an entertainment; a pastime.
amusement arcade *n* an indoor or roofed area with mechanical games for entertainment.
amusement park *n* an outdoor area with fairground entertainments.
amygdalate *adj* of or belonging to the almond.
amygdalin *n* a white crystalline substance obtained from the kernels of almonds.
amygdaloid *adj* almond shaped. * *n* an igneous rock containing almond-shaped nodules of some mineral.
amyl *n* (*formerly*) the alcohol radical of many chemical compounds.
amylase *n* an enzyme that breaks down starch and glycogen.
amyl nitrite *n* a drug inhaled to relieve spasms.
amylaceous *adj* of starch, starchy.
amylene *n* a hydrocarbon obtained by the removal of water from amyl alcohol.
amyloid *n* a starchy food.
amylopsin *n* a pancreatic ferment converting starch into sugar.
an- *prefix* the form of *ad-* before *n*.
an *adj* the indefinite article ("a"), used before words beginning with the sound of a vowel except "u".
-an, -ain, -ane *adj suffix* of, of the nature of, as in *suburban, certain, humane*.
-ana, -iana *n suffix* sayings of, publications about, as *Shakespeariana*, etc.
ana- *prefix* up, anew, again.
Anabaptist *n* one who believes in the rebaptizing of adults on their profession of faith; one who holds the invalidity of infant baptism; (*pl*) the sect of Baptists.—**Anabaptism** *n*.
anabas *n* a genus of Indian fishes allied to the perch, remarkable for their power of living a long time out of water and of travelling on land.
anabasis *n* (*pl* **anabases**) the name given to Xenophon's account of the expedition of Cyrus the Younger (401 bc); an inland military expedition.
anabatic *adj* (*of wind*) caused by upward current of air.
anabiosis *n* a coming to life again, resuscitation.
anableps *n* (*pl* **anableps**) a genus of the perch family found in Guiana, remarkable for the structure of its eye.
anabolic steroid *n* any of various synthetic steroid hormones that promote rapid muscle growth.
anabolism *n* constructive metabolism, in which simple molecules synthesize into more complex ones.—**anabolic**.
anabranch *n* a stream that leaves a river and rejoins it lower down.
anachronism *n* a person, custom, or idea regarded as out of date or out of its period.—**anachronistic** *adj*.—**anachronistically** *adv*.
anacoluthia *n* want of grammatical sequence, esp in a sentence.—**anacoluthic** *adj*.
anacoluthon *n* (*pl* **anacolutha**) a sentence in which one part belongs to a different construction from the other.
anaconda *n* a large South American semiaquatic snake that kills its prey by constriction.
Anacreontic *adj* after the manner of Anacreon, the Greek poet (6th century bc); amatory, erotic. * *n* a poem in praise of love and wine.
anacrusis *n* (*pl* **anacruses**) (*linguistics*) an unstressed syllable at the beginning of a verse.—**anacrustic** *adj*.
anadiplosis *n* (*rhetoric*) the repetition of the last word of a line or clause at the beginning of the next.
anadromous *adj* (*fish*) ascending from the sea to freshwater rivers to deposit spawn, as the salmon, etc.
anaemia *n* a condition in which the blood is low in red cells or in haemoglobin, resulting in paleness, weakness, etc.—*also* **anemia**.
anaemic *adj* suffering from anaemia; weak; pale; listless.—*also* **anemic**.
anaerobe, anaerobium *n* (*pl* **anaerobes, anaerobia**) a microbe that can live without air.

anaerobiosis *n* life devoid of oxygen.—**anaerobic** *adj*.—**anaerobically** *adv*.
anaesthesia *n* a partial or total loss of the sense of pain, touch, etc.—*also* **anesthesia.**
anaesthetic *n* a drug, gas, etc used to produce anaesthesia, as before surgery. * *adj* of or producing anaesthesia.—*also* **anesthetic.**
anaesthetist *n* a person trained to give anaesthetics.—*also* **anesthetist.**
anaesthetize *vt* to administer an anaesthetic.—*also* **anesthetize.**—**anaesthetization, anesthetization** *n*.
anaglyph *n* an ornament or work of art carved in low relief, as distinguished from intaglio.—**anaglyphic, anaglyphical, anaglyptic, anaglyptical** *adj*.
anagnorisis *n* (*pl* **anagnorises**) the denouement in a drama.
anagoge, anagogy *n* an allegorical or mystical interpretation, a hidden sense.—**anagogic, anagogical** *adj*.—**anagogically** *adv*.
anagram *n* a word or sentence formed by rearranging another word or sentence.—**anagrammatic, anagrammatical** *adj*.—**anagrammatically** *adv*.
anagrammatize *vt* to make into an anagram. * *vi* to construct anagrams.—**anagrammatism** *n*.—**anagrammatist** *n*.
anal *adj* of or situated near the anus.
analects, anelecta *npl* literary passages or extracts selected from published works by different authors.—**analectic** *adj*.
analeptic *adj* restorative. * *n* a restorative drug.
analgesia *n* insensibility to pain without loss of consciousness.
analgesic *adj* relieving pain. * *n* a pain-relieving drug.
analogism *n* a reasoning from the cause to the effect; study and examination of matters and things by reference to their analogies.—**analogist** *n*.
analogize *vt* to reason or expound by reference to analogy, to draw comparisons. * *vi* to treat or investigate by use of analogy.
analogous *adj* corresponding in certain respects (to).—**analogously** *adv*.
analogue, analog *n* a word or thing analogous to something else.
analogy *n* (*pl* **analogies**) a similarity or correspondence in certain respects between two things.—**analogical, analogic** *adj*.
analysand *n* anyone undergoing psychoanalysis.
analysis *n* (*pl* **analyses**) the process of analysing; a statement of the results of this; psychoanalysis.
analyst *n* a person who analyses; a psychoanalyst.
analytic, analytical *adj* pertaining to analysis.—**analytically** *adv*.
analysable, analyzable *adj* capable of being resolved by, or that may be subjected to, analysis.
analyse, analyze *vt* to separate (something) into its constituent parts to investigate its structure and function, etc; to examine in detail; to psychoanalyse.
anamnesis *n* (*pl* **anamneses**) recollection; a patient's case history.—**anamnestic** *adj*.—**anamnestically** *adv*.
anamorphosis *n* (*pl* **anamorphoses**) the irregular and distorted representation of an object as viewed directly, but which is corrected and reduced to its proper proportion when regarded from a different point of view, or reflected by a curved mirror; the abnormal or monstrous development of a portion of a plant or flower; a gradual progression from one type to another.
ananas *n* a genus of tropical plants to which the pineapple belongs.
anandrous *adj* without stamens.
ananthous *adj* without flowers.
anapaest, anapest *n* a foot comprising two short syllables and one long syllable.—**anapaestic, anapestic** *adj*.
anaphora *n* (*rhetoric*) the repetition at the beginning of the succeeding clauses of sentences of the word or words used in beginning the first; that part of the Eucharistic service which starts with the Sursum Corda; the oblique ascension of a star.—**anaphoric** *adj*.—**anaphorically** *adv*.
anaphrodisia *n* impotence of the sexual organs; absence of venereal desire.
anaphrodisiac *adj* tending to diminish sexual desire. * *n* a remedy that produces such an effect.
anaphylaxis *n* excessive sensitivity to a substance or germ due to prior inoculation with it, an allergy.—**anaphylactic** *adj*.—**anaphylactically** *adv*.
anaplasty *n* the repairing of wounds by the transplantation of adjacent healthy tissue, plastic surgery.—**anaplastic** *adj*.
anarchism *n* lawlessness; confusion; anarchy; the doctrines of the anarchists.
anarchist *n* a person who believes that all government is unnecessary and should be abolished.—**anarchistic** *adj*.
anarchy *n* the absence of government; political confusion; disorder, lawlessness.—**anarchic, anarchical** *adj*.
anarthrous *adj* without the article; destitute of joints; without articulated limbs.
anasarca *n* (*med*) dropsy.—**anasarcous** *adj*.
anastigmat *n* a lens corrected of astigmatism.—**anastigmatic** *adj*.
anastomosis *n* (*pl* **anastomoses**) a cross-connection of arteries, rivers, etc.—**anastomotic** *adj*.
anastrophe *n* (*rhetoric*) an inversion of the sequence of words in a sentence, as "echoed the hills", for "the hills echoed".
anathema *n* (*pl* **anathemas**) anything greatly detested; an ecclesiastical curse or denunciation accompanied by excommunication.
anathematize *vt* to pronounce a decree of excommunication against. * *vi* to curse.—**anathematization** *n*.
anatomist *n* one possessing a knowledge of anatomy by dissection.
anatomize *vt* to dissect; to study the structure of; to analyse.—**anatomization** *n*.
anatomy *n* (*pl* **anatomies**) the science of the physical structure of plants and animals; the structure of an organism.—**anatomical** *adj*.—**anatomically** *adv*.
anbury *n* (*pl* **anburies**) a soft wart or tumour on horses and cattle; a disease in turnips.
ANC *abbr* = African National Congress.
-ance *n suffix* denoting quality or action, as in *arrogance, penance*.
ancestor *n* one from whom a person is descended, a forefather; an early animal or plant from which existing types are descended; something regarded as a forerunner.—**ancestress** *nf*.
ancestral *adj* belonging to, or connected with, one's ancestors; derived from one's progenitors; lineal.
ancestry *n* (*pl* **ancestries**) ancestors collectively; lineage.
anchor *n* a heavy metal implement that lodges at the bottom of the sea or a river to hold a ship in position; something that gives support or stability. * *vt* to fix by an anchor; to secure firmly.
anchorage *n* a safe anchoring place for ships; the charge for anchoring.
anchorite *n* one who voluntarily secludes him or herself from society and lives a solitary life devoted to religious or philosophic meditation; a recluse; a hermit.—**anchoress** *nf*.
anchorman *n* (*pl* **anchormen**) (*sport*) the last man in a team to compete and whose contribution is vital; the compere of a television broadcast.
anchor stock *n* the crossbar at the top of the shank, at right angles to the arms.
anchor watch *n* the watch on board ship when at anchor; the seamen on this watch.
anchovy *n* (*pl* **anchovies, anchovy**) a small Mediterranean fish resembling a herring with a very salty taste.
anchovy pear *n* a West Indian fruit like the mango, used as a pickle.
anchylose *see* **ankylose.**
anchylosis *see* **ankylosis.**
ancien régime *n* (*pl* **anciens régimes**) the old order, esp that ruling France before the Revolution.
ancient *adj* very old; dating from the distant past; of the period and civilizations predating the fall of the Roman Empire; old-fashioned. * *n* a person who lived in the ancient period; (*pl*) the members of the classical civilizations of antiquity, esp of Greece and Rome.
Ancient of Days *n* (*Bible*) God, as described in the Book of Daniel.
ancillary *adj* subordinate (to); auxiliary; supplementary. * *n* (*pl* **ancillaries**) a subordinate or auxiliary person or thing.

ancipital, ancipitous *adj* (*biol*) two-edged and sharp.
ancon, ancone *n* (*pl* **ancones**) (*archit*) a bracket or projection for the support of a cornice; the elbow.—**anconal, anconeal** *adj*.
and *conj* in addition to; together with; plus; increasingly; as a consequence, afterwards; expressing contrast.
andalusite *n* a silicate of alumina.
andante *adj* (*mus*) moderately slow; naturally and easily. * *n* a movement written and to be played in andante time.
andantino *adj* rather slower than andante. * *n* (*pl* **andantinos**) a movement slower than an andante.
andesite *n* a silicate of alumina, soda, and lime.
andiron *npl* metal standards used for open fires to support the logs; fire dogs.
androgen *n* a male sex hormone.—**androgenic** *adj*.
androgenous *adj* (*biol*) having only male offspring.
androgynous *adj* combining both sexes or bearing both male and female organs; hermaphroditical.—**androgyne** *n*.—**androgyny** *n*.
android *n* (*science fiction*) a robot in human form.—*also adj*.
androsphinx *n* (*pl* **androsphinxes, androsphinges**) a sphinx with the body of a lion and the head of a man.
anecdotal *adj* relating to anecdotes; (*evidence, etc*) obtained from experience, not scientific.
anecdote *n* a short entertaining account about an amusing or interesting event or person.
anemia *see* **anaemia**.
anemic *see* **anaemic**.
anemograph *n* an instrument for registering the force or direction of the wind.
anemography *n* the scientific description of winds, and the measurement and registration of their force and direction.—**anemographic** *adj*.—**anemographically** *adv*.
anemology *n* the science and literature of the winds.
anemometer *n* an instrument for measuring the force or speed of the wind.
anemone *n* a plant of the buttercup family.
anemophilus *adj* (flowers, etc) fertilized by pollen carried by the wind, wind-pollinated.—**anemophily** *n*.
anemoscope *n* an apparatus for exhibiting the direction of the wind.
anent *prep, adv* (*Scot*) with regard or respect to; concerning.
aneroid *adj* having no liquid, as quicksilver. * *n* a barometer shaped like a watch, the action depending on the varying pressure of the atmosphere on the top of an elastic metal box.
aneroid barometer *n* a barometer that measures air pressure by its effect on the flexible lid of a box containing a partial vacuum.
anesthesia *see* **anaesthesia**.
anesthetic *see* **anaesthetic**.
anesthetist *see* **anaesthetist**.
anesthetize *see* **anaesthetize**.
aneurysm, aneurism *n* the permanent abnormal swelling of an artery.
anew *adv* afresh; again, once more; in a new way or form.
anfractuous *adj* winding, intricate.—**anfractuosity** *n* (*pl* **anfractuosities**).
angary *n* a belligerent's right to seize and use neutral property, for which it pays indemnity.
angel *n* a messenger of God; an image of a human figure with wings and a halo; a very beautiful or kind person; (*inf*) one who gives financial backing to an enterprise.
angel cake *n* a small round cake with a round fruit on the top.
Angeleno *n* (*pl* **Angelenos**) (*inf*) an inhabitant of the city of Los Angeles.
angelfish *n* (*pl* **angelfish, angelfishes**) a species of shark with large pectoral fins, which give to it a winged appearance.
angelic, angelical *adj* belonging to or resembling an angel in nature or function.—**angelically** *adv*.
angelica *n* the candied stalks of a fragrant plant used esp in cake decoration.
Angelus *n* (*RC Church*) a devotional exercise commemorating the Incarnation, during which the Ave Maria is twice repeated, said morning, noon, and night; the bell that is rung to announce the time of such devotions.
anger *n* strong displeasure, often because of opposition, a hurt, etc. * *vti* to make or become angry.
angina *n* sharp stabbing pains in the chest, usu caused by angina pectoris.
angina pectoris *n* a heart disease causing a spasmodic gripping pain in the chest.
angiology *n* the branch of anatomy that deals with the blood vessels and lymphatics.
angioma *n* (*pl* **angiomas, angiomata**) a tumour caused by the enlargement of a blood vessel.—**angiomatous** *adj*.
angiosperm *n* (*bot*) a plant having its seeds protected by a covering.—**angiospermous** *adj*.
angle[1] *n* a corner; the point from which two lines or planes extend or diverge; a specific viewpoint; an individual method or approach (eg to a problem). * *vt* to bend at an angle; to move or place at an angle; to present information, news, etc from a particular point of view.
angle[2] *vi* to fish with a hook and line; to use hints or artifice to get something.—**angler** *n*.
angler *n* one who fishes with rod and line; the name of a fish with filamentary appendage that attracts smaller fish on which it feeds.
Anglican *adj* belonging to or of the Church of England and other churches in communion with it. * *n* a member of the Anglican Church; a ritualist.
Anglicanism *n* the principles and ritual of the Anglican Church.
Anglicism *n* a form of speech, an English idiom; a principle or mannerism peculiar to England.
anglicize *vt* to make or to render into English; to accord with English manners and customs.—**anglicization** *n*.
angling *n* the art or act of fishing with rod and line.
Anglo- *prefix* English, British.
Anglo-American *adj* pertaining to England and the United States conjointly, as to commerce or population. * *n* an American citizen of English descent.
Anglo-Catholic *adj* Catholic according to the teachings and ritual of the English Church; in the strictest Catholic sense; high church. * *n* a member of the English Church, popularly a ritualist or high churchman, who repudiates the term "Protestant".
Anglo-Catholicism *n* the principles and ritual of the Anglican Church interpreted in their strictest Catholic sense.
Anglo-French *adj* English and French. * *n* the old French language introduced into England by the Normans.
Anglo-Indian *adj* pertaining to England and India conjointly. * *n* one of English descent born or residing in India.
Anglo-Irish *adj* pertaining to England and Ireland, or to the English settled in Ireland and their descendants; having the father or mother of English or Irish race. * *npl* English born or resident in Ireland.
Anglomania *n* a predilection carried to excess for everything that is English, in the sense of being peculiar to England.
Anglo-Norman *adj* common to England and Normandy. * *n* one of the Norman settlers in England after the Conquest (ad 1066).
Anglophile *n* a person who loves England or anything English.—*also* **Anglophil**.
Anglophobe *n* one who hates or fears England and the English.
Anglophobia *n* an intense aversion or fear of everything English.—**Anglophobe** *n*.
Anglo-Saxon *adj* pertaining to the Saxon settlers in England prior to the Conquest, or to their language. * *n* one of the Saxon settlers in England as distinguished from those on the Continent; Old English, the language of the settlers; (*pl*) the English race.
angora *n* a long-haired variety of cat, rabbit or goat; fabric made from the hair of angora goats or rabbits.
angostura bark *n* a bitter aromatic bark used for medicinal purposes.
angostura bitters *npl* a bitter flavouring made from the bark of a South American tree.

angry *adj* (**angrier, angriest**) full of anger; inflamed.—**angrily** *adv*.
angst *n* a feeling of anxiety, fear or remorse.
angstrom, ångström *n* one hundred millionth of a centimetre, a unit used in measuring the length of light waves.
anguilliform *adj* shaped like an eel or a serpent.
anguine *adj* snakelike.
anguish *n* agonizing physical or mental distress.
angular *adj* having one or more angles; forming an angle; measured by an angle; stiff and clumsy in manner, thin and bony.
angularity *n* (*pl* **angularities**) the quality of being angular in any sense.
angulate *adj* constructed of angles; having the form of an angle.
angulation *n* the exact measurement of angles; an angular shape.
anhydride *n* an oxygen compound formed by substituting an acid radicle for the whole of the hydrogen in one or two molecules of water.
anhydrite *n* anhydrous sulphate of lime.
anhydrous *adj* without water, applied to minerals in which the water of crystallization is not present.
ani *n* (*pl* **anis**) a tropical American bird of the cuckoo family.
aniconic *adj* (*idols*) not of human or animal form.
anil *n* the indigo plant; a dye yielded by it.
anile *adj* resembling an old woman; aged.—**anility** *n*.
aniline *n* a base used in the formation of many rich dyes obtained from coal tar but more extensively from benzole. * *adj* of or pertaining to aniline.
animadversion *n* the act of observing; capacity for perception; censure; criticism; stricture.
animadvert *vi* to give the mind to; to pass comment or stricture upon, to criticize.
animal *n* any living organism except a plant or bacterium, typically able to move about; a lower animal as distinguished from man, esp mammals; a brutish or bestial person. * *adj* of or like an animal; bestial; sensual.
animalcule, animalculum *n* (*pl* **animalcules, animalcula**) one of a class of minute or microscopic organisms abounding in water and infusions.—**animalcular** *adj*.
animalism *n* the state of being animal, or actuated by animal instincts or appetites; the theory that regards humankind as merely animal; sensuality.—**animalist** *n*.—**animalistic** *adj*.
animality *n* the state or quality of being an animal, or possessing animal characteristics, animal nature.
animalize *vt* to make animal; to impart animal life, form, and attributes; to sensualize or bestialize; to convert into animal substance by assimilation.—**animalization** *n*.
animal kingdom *n* beings endowed with animal life and regarded collectively, one of the three great divisions of nature.
animal liberation *n* freeing animals from captivity and exploitation (eg in laboratories) by humans, action esp associated with organizations such as the Animal Liberation Front.
animal magnetism *n* another name for mesmerism; attractiveness, esp to the opposite sex.
animal rights *n* a movement that seeks to extend certain rights, such as freedom from captivity and exploitation by humans, to animals.
animal spirits *npl* vivacity; liveliness of disposition.
animal worship *n* the worship of animals as symbols of deities, as among the ancient Egyptians, Hindus, etc.
animate *vt* to give life to; to liven up; to inspire, encourage. * *adj* alive; lively.
animated *adj* lively, full of spirit.
animated cartoon *n* a film made by photographing a series of drawings, giving the illusion of movement.
animation *n* liveliness; movement; the skill of making animated films.
animato *adv, adj (mus)* with vigour.
animator, animater *n* an artist who draws and produces animated cartoons.
animé *n* an amber-coloured resin, resembling copal, obtained from a tropical American tree and used in varnish.
animism *n* in primitive religion, the belief that natural effects are due to spirits and that inanimate objects have spirits; the belief in a human apparitional soul, having the form and appearance of the body, existing after death as semi-human.—**animist** *n*.—**animistic** *adj*.
animosity *n* (*pl* **animosities**) strong dislike; hostility.
animus *n* an actuating spirit; a bitter or hostile feeling (against); hostility.
anion *n* the element in a body decomposed by voltaic action, which is evolved at the positive pole or anode.—**anionic** *adj*.
anise *n* the common name for a plant (indigenous in Egypt) yielding the seeds used in aniseed.
aniseed *n* the seed of the anise plant, used as a flavouring.
anisette *n* a liqueur prepared from aniseed.
ankh *n* an Egyptian cross with a loop or handle at the top, the symbol of life.—*also* **crux ansata**.
ankle *n* the joint between the foot and leg, the part of the leg between the foot and calf.
anklet *n* an ornamental chain worn round the ankle.
ankylose *vt* to consolidate or join by bony growth; to stiffen as a joint. * *vi* to grow together; to become stiff.—*also* **anchylose**.
ankylosis *n* (*zool*) the joining or consolidation of parts formerly or normally separate or movable by means of bony growth; (*med*) the stiffening of a joint by fibrous bands or union of bones.—*also* **anchylosis**.—**ankylotic, anchylotic**.
anna *n* an Indian coin, one sixteenth of a rupee.
annals *npl* a written account of events year by year; historical records; periodical reports or records of a society.—**annalist** *n*.—**annalistic** *adj*.
annates *npl* (*RC Church*) the sum paid to the pope by an abbot or bishop on his appointment to a benefice or see and consisting of the first year's revenue of the living, now chiefly supplied by Peter's Pence.
anneal *vt* to fix by heat; to temper and render malleable; to bake or fuse.—**annealer** *n*.
annelid *n* any of a class of invertebrates which includes the worms, whose bodies are composed of numerous segments or ring-like divisions.—**annelidan** *adj*.
annex *vt* to attach, esp to something larger; to incorporate into a state the territory of (another state).
annexation *n* the act of annexing; that which is annexed.—**annexational** *adj*.—**annexationism** *n*.—**annexationist** *n*.
annexe *n* an extension to a main building; something added, a supplement.
annihilate *vt* to destroy completely; (*inf*) to defeat convincingly, as in an argument.—**annihilable** *adj*.—**annihilative** *adj*.—**annihilator** *n*.
annihilation *n* the act of annihilating; nonexistence.
anniversary *n* (*pl* **anniversaries**) the yearly return of the date of some event; a celebration of this.—*also adj*.
anno Domini *adv* (*abbr* ad) in the year of our Lord, dating from the birth of Christ. * *n* (*inf*) advancing age.
annotate *vti* to provide with explanatory notes.—**annotative** *adj*.—**annotator** *n*.
annotation *n* the act of noting or commenting upon; a note, remark, or criticism made in a book.
announce *vt* to bring to public attention; to give news of the arrival of; to be an announcer for. * *vi* to serve as an announcer.
announcement *n* the act of announcing; that which is announced; a proclamation.
announcer *n* a person who reads the news, etc on the radio or TV.
annoy *vt* to vex, tease, irritate, as by a repeated action.—**annoyingly** *adv*.
annoyance *n* the act of annoying or causing vexation; the state of being annoyed; the thing or act that annoys.
annual *adj* of or measured by a year; yearly; coming every year; living only one year or season. * *n* a plant that lives only one year; a periodical published once a year.—**annually** *adv*.
annuitant *n* one who is in receipt of, or is entitled to receive, an annuity.
annuity *n* (*pl* **annuities**) an investment yielding fixed payments, esp yearly; such a payment.
annul *vt* (**annulling, annulled**) to do away with; to deprive of legal force, nullify.

annular *adj* ring-like; in the form of a ring or annulus. * *n* the ring of light surrounding the moon's body in an annular eclipse of the sun
annulate *adj* ringed; having ring-like bands or circles.
annulation *n* a ring-like formation.
annulet *n* a small ring; (*archit*) a small fillet encircling a column.
annulment *n* the act of reducing to nothing; abolition; invalidation.
annulose *adj* composed of a succession of rings; segmented.
annunciate *vt* to make known officially or publicly; to announce, proclaim.—**annunciation** *n*.—**annunciative, annunciatory** *adj*.
Annunciation *n* (*Bible*) the intimation of the Incarnation made by the angel Gabriel to the Virgin Mary (Luke 1:28–33); the Church festival (Lady Day, 25 Mar) commemorating this.
annunciator *n* a signalling apparatus; an indicator connected with bells and telephones, to show where attendance is required.
anode *n* the positive electrode by which electrons enter an electric circuit.
anodyne *n* a drug that relieves pain; anything that relieves pain or soothes.
anoestrus *n* the period of sexual inactivity in mammals between periods of estrus.—*also* **anestrus**.—**anoestrous, anestrous** *adj*.
anoint *vt* to rub with oil; to apply oil in a sacred ritual as a sign of consecration.—**anointment** *n*.
anomalistic year *n* the time occupied by the earth in passing through its orbit (365 days, 6 hours, 13 minutes, 48 seconds), from perihelion to perihelion.
anomalous *adj* deviating from the common order, abnormal.
anomaly *n* (*pl* **anomalies**) abnormality; anything inconsistent or odd.—**annomalistic** *adj*.—**anomalistically** *adv*.
anon *adv* soon; at another time; (*arch*) anonymous.
anonym *n* an unnamed person; an assumed name.
anonymous *adj* having or providing no name; written or provided by an unnamed person; lacking individuality.—**anonymity** *n*.—**anonymously** *adv*.
anopheles *n* (*pl* **anopheles**) any of a genus of mosquitos, which transmits the microbe of malaria.
anorak *n* a waterproof jacket with a hood.
anorexia *n* loss of appetite.—**anorexic** *adj*.
anorexia nervosa *n* the psychological condition causing fear of becoming overweight and reluctance to eat even to the point of starvation and death.
anosmia *n* the inability to smell.—**anosmatic, anosmic** *adj*.
another *adj* a different or distinct (thing or person); an additional one of the same kind; some other.—*also pron*.
ansate *adj* with a handle, as a vase.
Anschluss *n* the union of Nazi Germany with Austria in 1938; the annexation of one territory by another for the benefit of the more powerful.
anserine, anserous *adj* of, relating to or resembling a goose; stupid as a goose.
answer *n* a spoken or written reply or response; the solution to a problem; a reaction, response. * *vt* to speak or write in reply; to satisfy or correspond to (eg a specific need); to justify, offer a refutation of. * *vi* to reply; to act in response (to); to be responsible (for); to conform (to).
answerable *adj* capable of being refuted; (*with* **for** *or* **to**) responsible, accountable.—**answerability** *n*.—**answerableness** *n*.
answering machine *n* an apparatus that records incoming telephone calls.
-ant *adj suffix* as in *repentant*. * *n suffix* denoting agent, as in *celebrant*.
ant *n* any of a family of small, generally wingless insects of many species, all of which form and live in highly organized groups.
anta *n* (*pl* **antae**) (*archit*) a square pilaster at either corner of a building, or at either side of a door.
antacid *n* a substance that counters excessive acidity.
antagonism *n* antipathy, hostility; an opposing force, principle, etc.
antagonist *n* an adversary; an opponent.
antagonistic *adj* acting in opposition; opposed.—**antagonistically** *adv*.
antagonize *vt* to arouse opposition in.—**antagonization** *n*.
antalkali *n* (*pl* **antalkalis, antalkalies**) a substance that counteracts the presence of alkali in the system; an acid.—**antalkaline** *adj, n*.
Antarctic *adj* of the South Pole or its surroundings. * *n* the Antarctic regions; the Antarctic Ocean.
ant bear *n* the aardvark.
ant bird *n* one of an extensive group of South American birds.
ant cow *n* an aphid or similar insect collected by ants for the sweet secretion in its body.
ante *n* a player's stake in poker; (*inf*) money contributed as a share in a joint project.
ante- *prefix* in front of; earlier than.
anteater *n* an ant-eating animal, as the pangolin.
antecede *n* to precede or go before in time or space.
antecedence *n* precedence; going before; priority.
antecedent *adj* prior in time, previous. * *n* a preceding event or happening; (*pl*) ancestry; (*pl*) the previous events of a person's life.
antechamber *n* an anteroom.
antedate *vt* to carry back to an earlier period; to anticipate. * *n* a date esp on a document earlier than the actual date.
antediluvian *adj* of or pertaining to the world before the Flood; belonging to very ancient times; antiquated, primitive. * *n* one who lived before the Flood; an old-fashioned person.
antelope *n* (*pl* **antelopes, antelope**) any of the family of fast-running and graceful deer-like animals of Africa and Asia.
ante meridiem *n* (*abbr* a.m.) the period between midnight and noon.—**antemeridian** *adj*.
antenatal *adj* occurring or present before birth.
antenna *n* (*pl* **antennae**) either of a pair of feelers on the head of an insect, crab, etc; (*pl* **antennas**) a metal device for transmitting and receiving radio waves.
antennule *n* a little antenna.
antependium *n* (*pl* **antependia**) a covering for the front of an altar.
antepenult *n* the last but two, usu of syllables.
antepenultimate *adj* pertaining to the last but two. * *n* that which is last but two, antepenult.
anterior *adj* at or towards the front; earlier; previous.
anteroom *n* an outer room leading into a larger or main room.
anthelion *n* (*pl* **anthelia**) (*meteorol*) a luminous halo, opposite the sun, formed around the shadow of the head of the observer, as projected on a cloud or fog bank.
anthem *n* a religious choral song; a song of praise or devotion, as to a nation.
anther *n* the part of a flower's stamen containing pollen.—**antheral** *adj*.
anthill *n* a mound thrown up by ants or termites in digging their nests.
anthologize *vt* to compile or include in an anthology.
anthology *n* (*pl* **anthologies**) a collection of poetry or prose.—**anthological** *adj*.—**anthologist** *n*.
anthozoan *n* any of a class of radiated soft marine zoophytes, which includes the sea anemones, corals, etc.—*also* **actinozoan**.
anthracene *n* a complex hydrocarbon obtained from coal tar, the source of a red dye.
anthracite *n* a hard coal that gives off a lot of heat and little smoke.—**anthracitic** *adj*.
anthrax *n* (*pl* **anthraces**) a contagious bacterial disease of cattle and sheep, etc that can be transmitted to people.
anthropo- *prefix* man.
anthropocentric *adj* centring in man.—**anthropocentrism** *n*.
anthropoid *adj* resembling man. * *n* one of the higher apes resembling man.—**anthropoidal** *adj*.
anthropology *n* the scientific study of human beings, their origins, distribution, physical attributes and culture.—**anthropological** *adj*.—**anthropologist** *n*.
anthropometry *n* the measurement of the human body; the branch of anthropology relating to such measurement of persons at various ages and in different tribes, races, occupations, etc.—**anthropometric, anthropometrical** *adj*.—**anthropometrist** *n*.

anthropomorphism *n* the ascription of human behaviour to other animals or to things.—**anthropomorphic** *adj*.—**anthropomorphist** *n*.
anthropomorphize *vt* to invest with human qualities.
anthropomorphous *adj* in the form of a human being.
anthropophagi *npl* (*sing* **anthropophagus**) cannibals, men-eaters.
anti- *prefix* opposed to; against.
anti-aircraft *adj* for use against aircraft.
antiar *n* the upas tree of Java; a poison obtained from one species of it.
antibiotic *n* any of various chemical, fungal or synthetic substances used against bacterial or fungal infections.
antibody *n* (*pl* **antibodies**) a protein produced by an organism in response to the action of a foreign body, such as the toxin of a parasite, that neutralizes its effects.
antic *n* a ludicrous action intended to amuse.
Antichrist *n* (*Bible*) an opponent of Christ, esp the great personal opponent expected to appear before the end of the world (1 John 2:22).
Antichristian *n* one who is an opponent of the Christian religion. * *adj* pertaining to Antichrist; opposed to the Christian religion.
anticipant *adj* operating beforehand. * *n* one who looks forward.
anticipate *vt* to give prior thought and attention to; to use, spend, act on in advance; to foresee and take action to thwart another; to expect. * *vi* to speak, act, before the appropriate time.
anticipation *n* the act of taking beforehand; expectation; hope; preconception.
anticlerical *adj* opposed to the power of the clergy or church, esp in secular affairs. * *n* a person opposed to the power of the church.—**anticlericalism** *n*.
anticlimax *n* a sudden drop from the important to the trivial; an ending to a story or series of events that disappoints one's expectations.—**anticlimactic** *adj*.—**anticlimactically** *adv*.
anticlinal *adj* (*strata*) inclining or folding with the convex side upwards; inclined in opposite directions.
anticlockwise *see* **counterclockwise**.
anticoagulant *n* a substance that inhibits blood clotting.
anticyclone *n* a body of air rotating about an area of high atmospheric pressure.—**anticyclonic** *adj*.
antidepressant *n* any of various drugs used to alleviate mental depression.—*also adj*.
antidote *n* a remedy that counteracts a poison; something that counteracts harmful effects.
antifebrile *adj* capable of allaying fever. * *n* a medicine for allaying fever.
antifreeze *n* a substance used, as in a car radiator, to prevent freezing up.
antigen *n* a substance introduced into the blood to stimulate production of antibodies.—**antigenic** *adj*.—**antigenically** *adv*.
antihero *n* (*pl* **antiheroes**) a leading character in a book, film, etc who lacks the conventional heroic attributes.
antihistamine *n* any of a group of drugs that inhibit the action of histamines, used in treating allergic conditions.
antilog *n* an antilogarithm.
antilogarithm *n* a number which a logarithm represents.—**antilogarithmic** *adj*.
antilogy *n* (*pl* **antilogies**) a contradiction.
antimacassar *n* an ornamental covering for chairbacks, etc, to prevent their being soiled (formerly by macassar oil, once used as a pomade).
antimatter *n* matter composed of antiparticles.
antimasque *n* a droll or grotesque interlude between parts of a more serious nature in a masque.
antimere *n* (*biol*) one of two or more corresponding parts or organs on opposite sides of animals.—**antimeric** *adj*.—**antimerism** *n*.
antimonic, antimonous *adj* relating to, composed of, or obtained from antimony.
antimony *n* (*pl* **antimonies**) a brittle metallic element used in making alloys.—**antimonial** *adj, n*.
antinomy *n* (*pl* **antinomies**) contradiction in law or authorities or conclusions; the opposition of one law or part of a law to another.—**antinomic** *adj*.—**antinomically** *adv*.
antiparallel *adj* running parallel, but in an opposite direction. * *n* one of two or more lines making equal angles with two other lines, but in contrary order.
antiparticle *n* an elementary particle with the same mass as its corresponding particle but having an equal and opposite electric charge, resulting in mutual destruction when brought into contact.
antipathetic, antipathetical *adj* possessing or causing a natural antipathy or aversion (to).—**antipathetically** *adv*.
antipathy *n* (*pl* **antipathies**) a fixed dislike; aversion; an object of this.
antiperiodic *adj* preventive of a return in periodic or intermittent disease. * *n* a medicine for periodic diseases.
antipersonnel *adj* (*weapon*) used to destroy people rather than objects.
antiperspirant *n* a substance used to stem excessive perspiration.
antiphlogistic *adj* efficacious in counteracting fever or inflammation. * *n* any remedy that checks inflammatory symptoms.
antiphon *n* a verse or sentence sung by one choir in response to another, as in church services; an anthem.
antiphonal *adj* characterized by responsive singing; sung alternately. * *n* a collection of antiphons.—**antiphonally** *adv*.
antiphonary *n* (*pl* **antiphonaries**) a book of responses used in church services; an antiphonal. * *adj* antiphonal or responsive.
antiphony *n* (*pl* **antiphonies**) the alternate or responsive rendering of psalms or chants by a dual choir; a musical setting of sacred verses arranged for alternate singing.
antiphrasis *n* (*rhetoric*) the use of words in a sense opposite to the true one.
antipodes *npl* the regions on the earth's surface opposite each other; (*with cap preceded by* **the**) Australia and New Zealand.—**antipodean** *adj*.
antipope *n* one who usurps or is elected to the papal office in opposition to a pope canonically elected; a rival pope.
antipyretic *adj* preventive of, or remedial to fever. * *n* a fever-allaying drug.—**antipyresis** *n*.
antipyrine *n* a drug obtained from coal tar and used to relieve neuralgia, etc, and to reduce heat in fevers.
antiquarian *adj* connected with the study of antiquities. * *n* an antiquary.
antiquary *n* (*pl* **antiquaries**) a person who studies or collects antiquities.
antiquated *adj* old-fashioned; obsolete.
antique *adj* from the distant past; old-fashioned. * *n* a relic of the distant past; a piece of furniture, pottery, etc dating from an earlier historical period and sought after by collectors.
antiquity *n* (*pl* **antiquities**) the far distant past, esp before the Middle Ages; (*pl*) relics dating from the far distant past.
antirrhinum *n* snapdragon.
antisabbatarian *adj* opposed to the observance of the Sabbath.—*also n*.
antiscorbutic *n* a remedy against scurvy.—*also adj*.
anti-Semite *n* one who is hostile toward or discriminates against Jews as a religious or racial group.—**anti-Semitic** *adj*.—**anti-Semitism** *n*.
antiseptic *n* a substance that destroys or prevents the growth of disease-producing microorganisms. * *adj* destroying harmful organisms; very clean; (*inf*) unexciting.—**antiseptically** *adv*.
antiserum *n* (*pl* **antiserums, antisera**) blood serum containing antibodies.
antisocial *adj* avoiding the company of other people, unsocial; contrary to the interests of society in general.
antispasmodic *adj* counteractive to or curative of spasms. * *n* a medicine having such an effect.
antistatic *adj* (*material, agent*) counteracting the effects of static electricity.
antistrophe *n* a stanza or movement of a Greek chorus alternating with the strophe, sung in moving to the right.—**antistrophic** *adj*.
antithesis *n* (*pl* **antitheses**) a contrast or opposition, as of ideas; the exact opposite.—**antithetical, antithetic** *adj*.
antitoxin *n* a substance that acts against a specific toxin in the body; a serum containing an antitoxin, injected into a person to prevent disease.—**antitoxic** *adj*.

antitrade *n* a tropical wind blowing steadily in an opposite direction to the trade wind.
antitrust *adj* (*laws, regulations*) restricting or opposing the activities of cartels and monopolies.
antitype *n* that which a type or symbol stands for; that which preceded the type and of which the type is the representation.
antivenin *n* an antidote to snake poison.
antivivisectionist *n* a person who opposes scientific experimentation on live animals.
antler *n* the branched horn of a deer or related animal.—**antlered** *adj*.
antlion *n* a neuropterous insect whose larva constructs a pitfall for ants and other insects.
antonomasia *n* (*rhetoric*) the use of an attribute or epithet, or style of dignity or office, in place of the proper noun, eg "the Stagirite" for Aristotle, or the reverse, of a proper noun for a common noun, eg "some mute inglorious Milton".—**antonomastic** *adj*.—**antonomastically** *adv*.
antonym *n* a word that has the opposite meaning to another.
antrum *n* (*pl* **antra**) (*anat*) a cavity, esp in the upper jawbone.
anurous *adj* (*zool*) tailless.
anus *n* the excretory orifice of the alimentary canal.
anvil *n* the heavy iron block on which metal objects are shaped with a hammer.
anxiety *n* (*pl* **anxieties**) the condition of being anxious; eagerness, concern; a cause of worry.
anxious *adj* worried; uneasy; eagerly wishing; causing anxiety.—**anxiously** *adv*.—**anxiousness** *n*.
any *adj* one out of many, some; every.
anybody *pron* any person; an important person.
anyhow *adv* in any way whatever; in any case.
any more, anymore *adv* now; nowadays.
anyone *pron* any person; anybody.
anything *pron* any object, event, fact, etc. * *n* a thing, no matter what kind.
anyway *adv* in any manner; at any rate; haphazardly.
anywhere *adv* in, at, or to any place.
Anzac *abbr* = Australian and New Zealand Army Corps. * *n* a member of this corps.—*also adj*.
aorist *n* (*gram*) an indeterminate past tense of the verb expressing completed action. * *adj* indefinite; pertaining to the aorist tense.—**aoristic** *adj*.—**aoristically** *adv*.
aorta *n* (*pl* **aortas, aortae**) the main artery that carries blood from the heart to be distributed through the body.—**aortic, aortal** *adj*.
aoudad *n* a wild sheep-like animal of North Africa, somewhat resembling the chamois.
ap- *prefix* the form of *ad-* before *p*.
apace *adv* at a swift pace.
Apache *n* (*pl* **Apaches, Apache**) a tribe of North American Indians.
apache *n* a Parisian street ruffian, a hooligan;
apagoge *n* (*logic*) the establishing of a proposition by demonstrating the untenability of its opposite.—**apagogic, apagogical** *adj*.—**apagogically** *adv*.
apanage *see* **appanage**.
apart *adv* at a distance, separately, aside; into two or more pieces.
apartheid *n* a policy of racial segregation implemented in South Africa.
apartment *n* a room or rooms in a building; a flat.
apathetic *adj* devoid of or insensible to feeling or emotion.—**apathetically** *adv*.
apathy *n* lack of feeling; lack of concern, indifference.—**apathetic** *adj*.—**apathetically** *adv*.
apatite *n* a crystalline phosphate of lime.
ape *n* a chimpanzee, gorilla, orangutan, or gibbon; any monkey; a mimic. * *vt* to imitate.
apeak *adv* (*naut*) nearly vertical in position.
apeman *n* (*pl* **apemen**) an extinct creature supposedly intermediate in development between apes and man.
aperçu *n* a first view; a rapid survey; a brief outline.
aperient *adj* gently laxative; opening the bowels. * *n* a mild laxative medicine.
aperiodic *adj* without periodicity.—**aperiodically** *adv*.—**aperiodicity** *n*.
aperitif, apéritif *n* an alcoholic drink taken before a meal as an appetizer.
aperture *n* an opening; a hole; a slit; in optical instruments, the (diameter of the) opening allowing or controlling the amount of light or radiation to enter.
apery *n* (*pl* **aperies**) mimicry.
apetalous *adj* without petals or corolla.—**apetaly** *n*.
apex *n* (*pl* **apexes, apices**) the highest point, the tip; the culminating point; the vertex of a triangle.
aphaeresis *n* (*pl* **aphaereses**) (*linguistics*) the removal of a letter or syllable from the beginning of a word.—*also* **apheresis**.
aphagia *n* the inability to swallow.
aphasia *n* loss of the power of speech or the appropriate use of words due to disease or injury of the brain.—**aphasic** *adj*.
aphelion *n* (*pl* **aphelia**) that point in the orbit of a planet or a comet which is farthest from the sun.
apheliotropic *adj* (*bot*) turning from the sun.
apheresis *see* **aphaeresis**.
aphesis *n* (*linguistics*) the gradual loss of an unaccented vowel at the beginning of a word, as in "squire" for "esquire".—**aphetic** *adj*.—**aphetically** *adv*.
aphid *n* any of various small insects, such as the greenfly, that suck the juice of plants.
aphis *n* (*pl* **aphides**) an aphid.
aphonia, aphony *n* dumbness, loss of voice.—**aphonic** *adj*.
aphorism *n* a brief, wise saying; an adage.—**aphoristic** *adj*.
aphrodisiac *adj* arousing sexually. * *n* a food, drug, etc that excites sexual desire.
aphtha *n* (*pl* **aphthae**) the small round white ulcers infesting the interior of the mouth; thrush.
aphyllous *adj* (*bot*) without leaves.—**aphylly** *n*.
apian *adj* of, pertaining to, or like bees.
apiarian *adj* of or relating to beekeeping.
apiarist *n* a beekeeper.
apiary *n* (*pl* **apiaries**) a place with hives where bees are kept.
apical *adj* of, pertaining to, belonging to, or at the apex.—**apically** *adv*.
apices *see* **apex**.
apiculate *adj* terminated abruptly by a point, as leaves.
apiculture *n* beekeeping.—**apicultural** *adj*.—**apiculturist** *n*.
apiece *adv* to, by, or for each one.
apish *adj* like an ape in manners; foolish; imitative.—**apishness** *n*.
apivorous *adj* feeding on bees.
aplacental *adj* without a placenta.
aplanatic *adj* (*physics*) free from, or correcting, spherical or chromatic aberration.—**aplanatically** *adv*.
aplastic *adj* without plasticity; not easily moulded.
aplomb *n* poise; self-possession.
apnea, apnoea *n* partial suspension of breathing; suffocation.—**apnoeic** *adj*.
apo- *prefix* off, from, away; un-; quite.
apocalypse *n* a cataclysmic event, the end of the world; revelation, esp that of St John; (*with cap*) the last book of the New Testament.—**apocalyptic** *adj*.—**apocalyptically** *adv*.
apocarpous *adj* (*bot*) having the carpels of the ovary separate or distinct.
apochromat *n* a highly achromatic lens.—**apochromatic** *adj*.
apocopate *vt* to cut off or drop the last letter or syllable of a word.—**apocopation** *n*.
apocope *n* (*linguistics*) the cutting off or deletion of the last letter or syllable of a word.
Apocrypha *npl* (*used as sing*) books of the Old Testament, eg Ecclesiasticus, accepted as an authentic part of the Holy Scriptures by the RC Church but not by Protestants.
apocryphal *adj* doubtful; untrue; invented; (*with cap*) of the Apocrypha.—**apocryphally** *adv*.
apodal *adj* without feet.

apodeictic, apodictic *adj* clearly established, unquestionable true.—**apodeictically, apodictically** *adv*.

apodosis *n* (*pl* **apodoses**) (*gram*) the latter portion, or consequent clause, of a conditional sentence.

apogamy *n* the absence of sexual reproduction; asexual reproduction.—**apogamic** *adj*.—**apogamous** *adj*.

apogee *n* the point in the orbit of the moon or any planet where it is most distant from the earth; the highest point.

apolitical *adj* uninterested or uninvolved in politics.

Apollo *n* (Greek, Roman myth) a sun god and god of music; (*pl* **Apollos**) a young handsome man.

apologetic *adj* expressing an apology; contrite; presented in defence.—**apologetically** *adv*.

apologetics *n* (*used as sing*) the defence and vindication of the principles and laws of Christian belief.

apologia *n* a written defence of one's principles or conduct.

apologist *n* a person who makes an apology; a defender of a cause.

apologize *vi* to make an apology.

apologue *n* a moral fable; a fiction or allegory embodying a moral application, as *Aesop's Fables*.

apology *n* (*pl* **apologies**) an expression of regret for wrongdoing; a defence or justification of one's beliefs, etc; (*with* **for**) a poor substitute.

apophthegm *n* a pithy saying embodying a wholesome truth or precept, a maxim.—*also* **apothegm**.

apophyge *n* (archit) the small hollow curve of a column where it springs from the base or top of the shaft.

apoplectic *adj* of, causing, or exhibiting symptoms of apoplexy; (*inf*) furious.

apoplexy *n* a sudden loss of consciousness and subsequent partial paralysis, usu caused by a broken or blocked artery in the brain.

aport *adv* (*naut*) on or towards the port or left side of a ship.

aposiopesis *n* (*pl* **aposiopeses**) (*rhetoric*) a sudden breaking off in speech for effect, eg "Bertrand is—what I dare not name".—**aposiopetic** *adj*.

apostasy *n* (*pl* **apostasies**) abandonment of one's religion, principles or political party.

apostate *n* a person who commits apostasy.

apostatize *vi* to abandon one's faith, church or party; to change one's religion for another.

a posteriori *adj* (*logic*) inductively, from effect to cause, founded on observation of facts, effects or consequences.

apostil *n* a marginal note.

apostle *n* the first or principal supporter of a new belief or cause; (*with cap*) one of the twelve disciples of Christ.

Apostles' Creed *n* the shortest of the three creeds, so named as containing a summary of apostolic doctrine.

apostle spoon *n* a spoon having a figure of one of the Apostles at the top of the handle.

apostolate *n* the dignity or office of an apostle, now restricted to that of the pope.

apostolic *adj* of or relating to the Apostles or their teachings; of or relating to the pope as successor to the Apostle St Peter.

Apostolic Church, Apostolic See *n* the Christian church as founded and governed by the Apostles on their doctrine and order. The name originally applied to the Churches of Rome, Antioch, Ephesus, Alexandria and Jerusalem.

Apostolic succession *n* the regular and uninterrupted transmission of ministerial authority by bishops from the Apostles.

apostrophe[1] *n* a mark (') showing the omission of letters or figures, also a sign of the possessive case or the plural of letters and figures; a breaking off in speech to appeal to someone dead or absent.—**apostrophic** *adj*.

apostrophe[2] *n* (*rhetoric*) a digression made in a speech or address, esp one directed at a person.

apostrophize *vt* to address by apostrophe; to omit a letter or letters; to mark an omission by the sign ('). * *vi* to make an apostrophe or short digressive address in speaking.

apothecaries' weight *n* a system of weights used for dispensing drugs, comprising the pound (12 oz), the ounce (8 drachms), the drachm (3 scruples), the scruple (20 grains), and the grain.

apothecary *n* (*pl* **apothecaries**) (*arch*) one who prepares and dispenses medicines and drugs, a pharmacist.

apothecium *n* (*pl* **apothecia**) the shield-like receptacle of lichens.—**apothecial** *adj*.

apothegm *see* **apophthegm**.

apotheosis *n* (*pl* **apotheoses**) deification; glorification of a person or thing; the supreme or ideal example.

apotheosize *vt* to exalt to the rank of a god; to deify.

appal, appall *vt* (**appals** *or* **appalls, appalling, appalled**) to fill with terror or dismay.

appalling *adj* shocking, horrifying.—**appallingly** *adv*.

appanage *n* provision for the younger sons of kings, etc; a perquisite; a dependency; an attribute.—*also* **apanage**.

apparatus *n* (*pl* **apparatus, apparatuses**) the equipment used for a specific task; any complex machine, device, or system.

apparel *n* clothing, dress. * *vt* (**apparelling, apparelled** *or* **appareling, appareled**) to dress; to clothe.

apparent *adj* easily seen, evident; seeming, but not real.—**apparently** *adv*.

apparition *n* an appearance or manifestation, esp something unexpected or unusual; a ghost.

appassionato *adj, adv* (*mus*) with passion.

appeal *vi* to take a case to a higher court; to make an earnest request; to refer to a witness or superior authority for vindication, confirmation, etc; to arouse pleasure or sympathy. * *n* the referral of a lawsuit to a higher court for rehearing; an earnest call for help; attraction, the power of arousing sympathy; a request for public donations to a charitable cause.—**appealable** *adj*.—**appealer** *n*.—**appealing** *adj*.

appear *vi* to become or be visible; to arrive, come in person; to be published; to present oneself formally (before a court, etc); to seem, give an impression of being.

appearance *n* the act or occasion of appearing; that which appears; external aspect of a thing or person; outward show, semblance.

appease *vt* to pacify; to allay; to conciliate by making concessions.—**appeasement** *n*.

appellant *n* a person who makes an appeal to a higher court.

appellate *adj* pertaining to appeals; dealing with appeals. * *n* the person appealed against or called upon to appear.

appellation *n* the name, title or designation by which a person or thing is called or known; the act of appealing.

appellative *n* (*gram*) a common, as distinguished from a proper, name; the designation of a class. * *adj* serving to distinguish, as a name or denomination of a group or class; common, as a noun.

appellee *n* the person appealed against; the defendant in an appeal.

append *vt* to attach; to add, esp to the end as a supplement, etc.

appendage *n* something appended; an external organ or part, as a tail.

appendant *adj* attached or annexed; attached in a subordinate capacity to another.* *n* that which is appended or added.

appendicectomy, appendectomy *n* (*pl* **appendicectomies, appendectomies**) surgical removal of the appendix that grows from the intestine.

appendicitis *n* inflammation of the appendix that grows from the intestine.

appendicle *n* a small appendage.

appendix *n* (*pl* **appendixes, appendices**) a section of supplementary information at the back of a book, etc; a small tube of tissue that forms an outgrowth of the intestine (—*also* **vermiform appendix**).

apperception *n* (*psychol*) perception with consciousness of self.—**apperceptive** *adj*.

appertain *vi* to belong or pertain to, as by relation or custom.

appetence, appetency *n* (*pl* **appetences, appetencies**) desire, craving; affinity.

appetite *n* sensation of bodily desire, esp for food; (*with* **for**) a strong desire or liking, a craving.

appetizer *n* a food or drink that stimulates the appetite; something that whets one's interest.
appetizing *adj* stimulating the appetite.—**appetizingly** *adv*.
applaud *vt* to show approval, esp by clapping the hands; to praise.
applause *n* approval expressed by clapping; acclamation.
apple *n* a round, firm, fleshy, edible fruit.
apple brandy *n* a liqueur distilled from cider.
applecart *n* **upset the applecart** to spoil one's plans.
applejack *n* apple brandy.
apple-pie bed *n* a bed made with the sheets folded so that one's legs cannot get down.
apple-pie order *n* perfect order.
apple sauce *n* a sauce of stewed apples usu served with pork; (*sl*) nonsense, flattery.
applicative *adj* capable of being applied.
applicatory *adj* fit to be applied.
appliance *n* a device or machine, esp for household use.
applicable *adj* that may be applied; appropriate, relevant (to).—**applicability** *n*.
applicant *n* a person who applies, esp for a job.
application *n* the act of applying; the use to which something is put; a petition, request; concentration, diligent effort; relevance or practical value.
applicator *n* a device for applying something.
applied *adj* practical.
appliqué *n* ornamental fabricwork applied to another fabric. * *vt* (**appliquéing, appliquéed**) to decorate with appliqué.
apply *vb* (**applying, applied**) *vt* to bring to bear; to put to practical use; to spread, lay on; to devote (oneself) with close attention. * *vi* to make a formal, esp written, request; to be relevant.
appoggiatura *n* (*pl* **appoggiaturas, appoggiature**) (*mus*) a grace note immediately preceding a principal note with which it is connected, and taking its time from the latter.
appoint *vt* to fix or decide officially; to select for a job; to prescribe.
appointed *adj* equipped; furnished.
appointee *n* a person appointed.
appointment *n* an appointing; a job or position for which someone has been selected; an arrangement to meet.
apportion *vt* to divide into shares; allot.—**apportionable** *adj*.—**apportioner** *n*.—**apportionment** *n*.
appose *vt* to apply; to place opposite or in juxtaposition.
apposite *adj* (*remarks*) especially pertinent, appropriate.—**appositely** *adv*.
apposition *n* the act of adding; addition by application, or placing together; (*gram*) the placing of a second noun in the same case in juxtaposition to the first, which it characterizes or explains, as St Mark, the Evangelist.—**appositional** *adj*.
appraisal, appraisement *n* the act of appraising or valuing, esp the putting of a price upon with a view to sale; a valuation.
appraise *vt* to estimate the value or quality of.—**appraiser** *n*.
appreciable *adj* capable of being perceived or measured; fairly large.—**appreciably** *adv*.
appreciate *vt* to value highly; to recognize gratefully; to understand, be aware of; to increase the value of. * *vi* to rise in value.
appreciation *n* gratitude, approval; sensitivity to aesthetic values; an assessment or critical evaluation of a person or thing; a favourable review; an increase in value.—**appreciative** *adj*.
apprehend *vt* to arrest, capture; to understand, to perceive.
apprehension *n* anxiety; the act of arresting; understanding; an idea.
apprehensive *adj* uneasy; anxious.—**apprehensively** *adv*.
apprentice *n* one being taught a trade or craft; a novice. * *vt* to take on as an apprentice.—**apprenticeship** *n*.
apprise, apprize *vt* to give notice to; to inform.
approach *vi* to draw nearer. * *vt* to make a proposal to; to set about dealing with; to come near to. * *n* the act of approaching; a means of entering or leaving; a move to establish relations; the final descent of an aircraft.
approachable *adj* within approaching distance; easy to approach; inviting friendship.—**approachability** *n*.—**approachably** *adv*.
approbation *n* formal approval; sanction.
appropriate *adj* fitting, suitable. * *vt* to take for one's own use, esp illegally; (*money, etc*) to set aside for a specific purpose.—**appropriately** *adv*.—**appropriateness** *n*.
appropriation *n* the act of setting apart or reserving for one's own use; a sum of money set aside for a particular purpose.
approval *n* the act of approving; favourable opinion; official permission.
approve *vt* to express a good opinion of; to authorize. * *vi* (*with* **of**) to consider to be favourable or satisfactory.
approx. *abbr* = approximate(ly).
approximate *adj* almost exact or correct. * *vt* to come near to; to be almost the same as. * *vi* to come close.—**approximately** *adv*.
approximation *n* a close estimate; a near likeness.
appulse *n* a coming towards; (astron) the near approach of a planet to a conjunction with the sun or any fixed star.—**appulsive** *adj*.
appurtenance *n* that which belongs or relates to something else; an adjunct or appendage; that which belongs it, is accessory to; an estate or property.—**appurtenant** *adj, n*.
APR *abbr* = annual percentage rate.
Apr. *abbr* = April.
après-ski *n* social activity after skiing.—*also adj*.
apricot *n* a small, oval, orange-pink fruit resembling the plum and peach.
April *n* the fourth month of the year, having 30 days.
April Fool *n* the victim of a trick played on 1 April, **April Fool's Day.**
a priori (*Latin*) deductively, from cause to effect.
apron *n* a garment worn to protect clothing; anything resembling the shape of an apron used for protection; the paved surface on an airfield where aircraft are parked, etc.
apropos *adv* at the right time; opportunely; appropriately. * *adj* appropriate. * *prep* (*with* **of**) regarding, in reference to.
apse *n* a domed or vaulted recess, esp in a church.
apsis *n* (*pl* **apsides**) (*astron*) one of two points in the orbit of a planet situated at the furthest or the least distance from the central body or sun; the imaginary line connecting these points.—**apsidal** *adj*.
apt adj ready or likely (to); suitable, relevant; able to learn easily.—**aptness** *n*.
apteral *adj* (*archit*) without side columns.
apterous *adj* without wings.
apterygial *adj* lacking wings or fins.
apteryx *n* the kiwi, a New Zealand bird with rudimentary wings and no tail.
aptitude *n* suitability; natural talent, esp for learning.
apyretic *adj* without fever, or with intermission of fever.
aq *abbr* = aqua.
aqua *n* (*pl* **aquae, aquas**) water as used in pharmacy.
aquaculture *n* the cultivation and breeding of fish and other marine organisms.—*also* **aquiculture.**—**aquacultural** *adj*.—**aquaculturist** *n*.
aqua fortis *n* impure nitric acid.
aqualung *n* portable diving gear comprising air cylinders connected to a face mask.
aquamarine *n* a variety of bluish-green beryl used as a gemstone; its colour.
aquaplane *n* a plank towed at high speed. * *vi* to ride on one.
aqua regia *n* a mixture of nitric and hydrochloric acids, capable of dissolving gold.
aquarelle *n* a style of painting in Chinese ink and thin watercolours; a painting so executed.—**aquarellist** *n*.
aquarium *n* (*pl* **aquariums, aquaria**) a tank, pond, etc for keeping aquatic animals or plants; a building where collections of aquatic animals are exhibited.
Aquarius *n* (*astrol*) the eleventh sign of the zodiac, the water-carrier, operative 20 January–18 February.—**Aquarian** *adj, n*.
aquatic *adj* of or taking place in water; living or growing in water.

aquatics *npl* water sports.
aquatint *n* a style of etching resembling a watercolour drawing in Indian ink or in sepia; an engraving produced by this process. * *vt* to etch or engrave in aquatint.
aqua vitae *n* unrectified alcohol; brandy and other ardent spirits.
aqueduct *n* a large pipe or conduit for carrying water; an elevated structure supporting this.
aqueous *adj* of, like, or formed by water.
aqueous humour *n* a limpid fluid of the eye, filling the space between the crystalline lens and the cornea.
aquiculture *n* hydroponics; another name for aquaculture.—**aquicultural** *adj*.—**aquiculturist** *n*.
aquilegia *n* columbine.
aquiline *adj* of or like an eagle; (*nose*) hooked, like an eagle's beak.
ar- *prefix* the form of *ad-* before *r*.
-ar *adj suffix* of, belonging to, as in *angular, popular*.
AR *abbr* = Arkansas.
Ar (*chem symbol*) argon.
Arab *n* a native of Arabia; one of the Arabic races spread over the African and Syrian deserts. * *adj* pertaining to Arabia or the Arabs.
arabesque *n* a decorative design incorporating organic motifs, such as leaves and flowers, in an intricate pattern; (*ballet*) a posture in which the dancer balances on one leg with one arm extending forwards and the other arm and leg extending backwards.
Arabian *adj* of Arabia, Arab. * *n* an Arab.
Arabian camel *n* a camel with a single hump.
Arabic *n* the Arabian language. * *adj* of or pertaining to the Arabic language and the countries in which it is spoken.
Arabic numeral *n* one of the numbers 0, 1, 2, 3, 4, 5, etc.
arable *adj* (*land*) suitable for ploughing or planting crops.—*also n*.
arachnid *n* any of a class of animals including spiders, scorpions, mites and ticks.—**arachnidan** *adj, n*.
arachnoid *adj* pertaining to spiders; resembling the web of a spider. * *n* the enveloping membrane of the brain and spinal cord, between the dura mater and the pia mater.
aragonite *n* a variety of carbonate of lime.
arak *see* **arrack.**
Aramaic *n* the language of Palestine at the time of Christ.
araneid *n* a member of the Arachnida order, the spider family.
araucaria *n* one of a genus of coniferous trees, found principally in South America and Australia, which includes the monkey puzzle.
arbalest *n* a crossbow with a drawing mechanism.
arbiter *n* a person having absolute power of decision or absolute control.
arbitrage *n* the rapid purchase and resale of stocks to maximize price discrepancy, often using confidential knowledge.—*also* **index arbitrage.**
arbitrament *n* an arbiter's judgment; an authoritative decision.
arbitrary *adj* not bound by rules; despotic, absolute; capricious, unreasonable.—**arbitrarily** *adv*.—**arbitrariness** *n*.
arbitrate *vi* to act as an arbitrator. * *vt* to submit to an arbiter; to act as an arbiter upon.
arbitration *n* the settlement of disputes by arbitrating.
arbitrator *n* a person chosen to settle a dispute between contending parties.
arbor[1] *see* **arbour.**
arbor[2] *n* the main support of a machine; an axis, a spindle.
Arbor Day *n* a day legally set apart in certain states of the US for planting trees.
arboraceous *adj* pertaining to, or of the nature of, a tree or trees; living on or among trees.
arboreal *adj* of or living in trees.
arboreous *adj* wooded.
arborescent *adj* growing or formed like a tree.—**arborescence** *n*.
arboretum *n* (*pl* **arboreta, arboretums**) a botanical tree garden where rare trees are cultivated and exhibited.
arboriculture *n* the cultivation of trees and shrubs, forestry.
arborization, arborisation *n* a tree-like appearance.
arbor vitae *n* an evergreen tree extensively cultivated in gardens, etc.
arbour *n* a place shaded by trees, foliage, etc; a bower.—*also* **arbor.**
arbutus *n* (*pl* **arbutuses**) one of a genus of tree-like evergreen shrubs to which the strawberry tree belongs.
ARC *abbr* = AIDS-related complex.
ARC *acronym for* AIDS-related condition.
arc *n* a portion of the circumference of a circle or other curve; a luminous discharge of electricity across a gap between two electrodes or terminals. * *vi* to form an electric arc.
arcade *n* a series of arches supported on columns; an arched passageway; a covered walk or area lined with shops.
Arcadia, Arcady *n* (*poet*) ideal countryside.
Arcadian *adj* of or pertaining to Arcadia, a department of Greece, or its inhabitants; rurally simple. * *n* an inhabitant of Arcadia.
arcane *adj* secret or esoteric.
arcanum *n* (*pl* **arcana**) a secret, a mystery; a valuable elixir.
arch[1] *n* a curved structure spanning an opening; the curved underside of the foot. * *vti* to span or cover with an arch; to curve, bend into an arch.
arch[2] *adj* (*criminal, etc*) principal, expert; clever, sly; mischievous.—**archly** *adv*.—**archness** *n*.
Archaean *adj* of the earliest geological period or strata.—*also* **Archean.**
archaeology *n* the study of past human societies through their extant remains.—*also* **archeology.**—**archaeological, archeological** *adj*.—**archaeologist, archeologist** *n*.
archaeopteryx *n* oldest fossil bird.
archaic *adj* belonging to ancient times; (*language*) no longer in common use.
archaism *n* an archaic word or phrase.—**archaistic** *adj*.
archaize *vti* to affect the archaic; to make archaic.—**archaizer** *n*.
archangel *n* a principal angel.—**archangelic** *adj*.
archbishop *n* a bishop of the highest rank.
archbishopric *n* the jurisdiction, office or see of an archbishop.
archdeacon *n* a clergyman ranking next under a bishop.
archdeaconry *n* (*pl* **archdeaconries**) the office, rank, jurisdiction, or residence of an archdeaon.
archdiocese *n* the diocese of an archbishop.—**archdiocesan** *adj*.
archducal *adj* of or pertaining to an archduchess, an archduchy or an archduke.
archduchess *n* a daughter of the emperor of Austria; the wife or widow of an archduke.
archduchy *n* (*pl* **archduchies**) the territory or rank of an archduke or an archduchess.
archduke *n* a prince of the imperial house of Austria.
Archean *see* **Archaean.**
archegonium *n* (*pl* **archegonia**) (*bot*) the pistillidium or female organ of the higher cryptogams (ferns, etc).
archenemy *n* (*pl* **archenemies**) a principal enemy; Satan.
archeology *see* **archaeology.**
archer *n* a person who shoots with a bow and arrow.
archerfish *n* (*pl* **archerfish, archerfishes**) a scaly-finned fish of the Java seas, which catches insects by darting drops of water upon them.
archery *n* the art or sport of shooting arrows from a bow.
archetype *n* the original pattern or model; a prototype.—**archetypal, archetypical** *adj*.
archfiend *n* a chief fiend; Satan.
archidiaconal *adj* of or pertaining to an archdeacon or to his office.
archidiaconate *n* the office of an archdeacon.
archiepiscopate, archiepiscopacy *n* the rule or dignity of an archbishop.
archiepiscopal *adj* of or pertaining to an archbishop or to his office.
archimagus, archimage *n* the high priest of the Persian magi or fireworshippers; a chief magician.
archil *see* **orchil.**
archimandrite *n* (*Greek Orthodox Church*) the abbot of a monastery, or an abbot-general having the charge and superintendence of several monasteries.

Archimedean screw *n* an instrument for raising water, consisting of a flexible tube wound spirally around or within a cylinder in the form of a screw. When placed in an inclined position, with the lower end immersed in water, by the revolution of the screw the water is raised to the upper end.

archipelago *n* (*pl* **archipelagoes, archipelagos**) a sea filled with small islands; a group of small islands.—**archipelagic, archipelagian** *adj*.

architect *n* a person who designs buildings and supervises their erection; someone who plans something.

architectonic *adj* pertaining to design or construction; skilled in architecture; expert in constructing; of the systematizing of knowledge.—**architectonically** *adv*.

architectonics *n* (*used as sing*) the science of architecture; structure.

architecture *n* the art, profession, or science of designing and constructing buildings; the style of a building or buildings; the design and organization of a computer's parts.—**architectural** *adj*.—**architecturally** *adv*.

architrave *n* an epistyle, the lowest division of an entablature, the part resting immediately on a column; the parts round a door or window.

archives *npl* the location in which public records are kept; the public records themselves.—**archival** *adj*.

archivist *n* a keeper of public records.

archivolt *n* the undercurve of an arch or the moulding on it.

archpriest *n* a chief priest; a rural dean.

archway *n* an arched or vaulted passage, esp that leading into a castle.

arc light *n* light produced by a current of electricity passing between two carbon points placed a short distance from each other.

arctic *adj* (*often with cap*) of, near, or relating to the North Pole or its surroundings; (*inf*) very cold, icy.

Arctic Circle *n* an imaginary circle around the arctic regions parallel to the equator.

arctic fox *n* a small species of fox, whose fine fur is used for muffs, trimmings, etc.

Arctic Ocean *n* the ocean that washes the northern coasts of Europe, Asia and North America.

arcuate *adj* bent or curved in the form of a bow.

arcuation *n* the act of bending; the state of being bent or curved; a method of propagating trees by bending branches to the ground and covering portions of them with earth.

arc welding *n* welding using an electric arc.

ardent *adj* passionate; zealous.—**ardency** *n*.—**ardently** *adv*.

ardent spirits *npl* alocholic beverages, as brandy, whisky, etc.

ardour, ardor *n* warmth of feeling; extreme intensity.

arduous *adj* difficult, laborious; steep, difficult to climb.—**arduously** *adv*.—**arduousness** *n*.

are[1] *see* **be.**

are[2] *n* a metric unit of measure equal to 100 square metres.

area *n* an expanse of land; a total outside surface, measured in square units; a specific part of a house, district, etc; scope or extent.

areca *n* a genus of lofty palms, including the tree from which the betelnut and the astringent juice Catechu are obtained.

arena *n* an area within a sports stadium, etc where events take place; a place or sphere of contest or activity.

arenaceous *adj* sandy; abounding in, or having the properties of, sand.

aren't = are not.

areola *n* (*pl* **areolae, areolas**) a very small area; an interstice in tissue; the coloured circle or halo surrounding the nipple of the breast.—**areolar, areolate** *adj*.—**areolation** *n*.

arête *n* the sharp ridge or spur of a mountain.

argali *n* (*pl* **argalis, argali**) a large wild Asiatic sheep, remarkable for its huge curved horns.

argent *n* (*her*) silver, represented in a drawing or engraving of a coat of arms by a plain white surface, symbolic of purity, beauty, etc. * *adj* made of or resembling silver; silvery white; bright like silver.

argentiferous *adj* producing or containing silver.

argentine *adj* pertaining to or resembling silver; silvery. * *n* a silvery-white slaty variety of calcite; white metal coated with silver, imitation silver.

argil *n* clay, esp potter's clay or earth.

argillaceous *adj* of or containing clay, clayey.

argilliferous *adj* producing or containing clay.

argillite *n* clay-slate.—**argillitic** *adj*.

argol *n* a deposit of crude tartar on the sides of wine vessels; crude tartar from which cream of tartar is prepared.

argon *n* an inert gaseous element.

argosy *n* (*pl* **argosies**) a large, richly laden merchant ship.

argot *n* the special vocabulary of any set of persons, as of lawyers, criminals, etc.—**argotic** *adj*.

arguable *adj* debatable; able to be asserted; plausible.—**arguably** *adv*.

argue *vb* (**arguing, argued**) *vt* to try to prove by reasoning; to debate, dispute; to persuade (into, out of). * *vi* to offer reasons for or against something; to disagree, exchange angry words.—**arguer** *n*.

argufy *vi* (**argufying, argufied**) (*sl*) to argue tediously, to wrangle.

argument *n* a disagreement; a debate, discussion; a reason offered in debate; an abstract, summary.

argumentation *n* systematic reasoning; argument, discussion.

argumentative *adj* prone to arguing.—**argumentatively** *adv*.—**argumentativeness** *n*.

argy-bargy *n* (*pl* **argy-bargies**) a tedious discussion. * *vi* to argue at length.

aria *n* a song for one voice accompanied by instruments, eg in opera.

Arian *adj* pertaining to the doctrines of the Arian sect, which held that Christ is not divine.—**Arianism** *n*.

arid *adj* very dry, parched; uninteresting; dull.—**aridity** *n*.—**aridly** *adv*.

Aries *n* (*astrol*) the first sign of the zodiac, the Ram, operative 21 March–21 April.—**Arian** *adj, n*.

arietta *n* a short aria, song or air.

aright *adv* correctly.

aril *n* (*bot*) an accessory covering or appendage of certain seeds.

arioso *adj, adv* (*mus*) like an air; in a smooth melodious style.

arise *vi* (**arising, arose,** *pp* **arisen**) to get up, as from bed; to rise, ascend; to come into being, to result (from).

arista *n* (*pl* **aristae**) the awn or beard of grasses; a bristle.

aristate *adj* bearded; having a beard or bristle, as certain grasses.

aristocracy *n* (*pl* **aristocracies**) (a country with) a government dominated by a privileged minority class; the privileged class in a society, the nobility; those people considered the best in their particular sphere.

aristocrat *n* a member of the aristocracy; a supporter of aristocratic government; a person with the manners or taste of a privileged class.

aristocratic *adj* relating to or characteristic of the aristocracy; elegant, stylish in dress and manners.—**aristocratically** *adv*.

Aristotelian *adj* pertaining to, or characteristic of, Aristotle (384–322 bc) or his philosophy.

arithmetic *n* (*math*) computation (addition, subtraction, etc) using real numbers; calculation.—**arithmetic, arithmetical** *adj*.—**arithmetically** *adv*.

arithmetician *n* one skilled in the science of numbers.

Ariz. *abbr* = Arizona.

ark *n* (*Bible*) the boat in which Noah and his family and two of every kind of creature survived the Flood; a place of safety; an enclosure in a synagogue for the scrolls of the Torah.

Ark. *abbr* = Arkansas.

ark of the covenant *n* (*Bible*) the chest containing the two stone tablets inscribed with the Ten Commandments.

arm[1] *n* the upper limb from the shoulder to the wrist; something shaped like an arm, as a support on a chair; a sleeve; power, authority; an administrative division of a large organization.

arm[2] *n* (*usu pl*) a weapon; a branch of the military service; (*pl*) heraldic bearings. * *vt* to provide with weapons, etc; to provide with something that protects or strengthens, etc; to set a fuse ready to explode. * *vi* to prepare for war or any struggle.

armada *n* a fleet of warships or aircraft.

armadillo *n* (*pl* **armadillos**) a small animal from South America with a body covering of small bony plates.

Armageddon *n* (*Bible*) the site of the last decisive battle between good and evil; any great decisive battle.

armament *n* (*often pl*) all the military forces and equipment of a nation; all the military equipment of a warship, etc; the process of arming or being armed for war.

armature *n* a piece of iron connecting the poles of a magnet or electro-magnet to preserve and increase the magnetic force; the revolving part of a dynamo; arms, armour, that which serves as a means of defence; iron bars or framework used to strengthen a building; a framework supporting clay, etc, in sculpture or modelling.

armchair *n* a chair with side rests for the arms. * *adj* lacking practical experience.

armed forces *npl* the military forces of a nation.—*also* **armed services**.

armful *n* as much as the arms can hold.

armhole *n* an opening for the arm in an item of clothing.

armiger *n* one entitled to use heraldic bearings, an esquire.—**armigerous** *adj*.

armillary *adj* of or resembling a bracelet; consisting of circles or rings.

armillary sphere *n* a skeleton celestial globe showing the relative positions of the stars, etc.

Arminianism *n* a Christian Protestant doctrine that denies Calvin's doctrine of predestination.—**Arminian** *adj, n*.

armistice *n* a truce, preliminary to a peace treaty.

armlet *n* an ornamental or protective band worn around the arm; a badge worn on the arm; a small arm of the sea.

armorial *adj* pertaining to armour or the arms or escutcheon of a family. * *n* a book or dictionary of heraldic devices and the names of persons entitled to use them.

armour, armor *n* any defensive or protective covering.

armoured, armored *adj* covered or protected with armour; equipped with tanks and armour vehicles.

armourer, armorer *n* the custodian of the arms of a battleship, etc; (formerly) a maker of arms or armour; one who had charge of the armour of another.

armour plate, armor plate *n* a plate of iron or steel affixed to a ship or tank as part of a casing for protection against shellfire.

armoury, armory *n* (*pl* **armouries, armories**) an arsenal; a place where armour or ammunition is stored.

armpit *n* the hollow underneath the arm at the shoulder.

arms *see* **arm**[2].

army *n* (*pl* **armies**) a large organized body of soldiers for waging war, esp on land; any large number of persons, animals, etc.

army worm *n* the larva of a moth that devastates grain and other crops, esp destructive in North America; the larva of a European small two-winged fly.

arnica *n* a genus of perennial herbs, esp mountain tobacco, whose roots and flowers are used to make a tincture for treating bruises.

aroma *n* a pleasant smell; a fragrance.

aromatherapy *n* the massage of fragrant oils into the skin to relieve tension and promote wellbeing.

aromatic *adj* giving out an aroma; fragrant, spicy; odoriferous. * *n* a plant, herb or drug yielding a fragrant smell.—**aromatically** *adv*.

aromatize *vt* to render fragrant, to perfume, to scent.—**aromatization** *n*.

arose *see* **arise**.

around *prep* on all sides of; on the border of; in various places in or on; approximately, about. * *adv* in a circle; in every direction; in circumference; to the opposite direction.

arousal *n* the act of awakening or stimulating; the state of being awakened or stimulated.

arouse *vt* to wake from sleep; to stir, as to action; to evoke.

arpeggio *n* (*pl* **arpeggios**) (*mus*) the playing of notes of a chord in rapid succession, instead of simultaneously; a passage or chord so played.

arquebus *n* an old-fashioned handgun fired from a forked rest.—*also* **harquebus**.

arrack *n* an alcoholic spirit distilled in some Asian countries from rice, molasses, the juice of the date palm, etc.—*also* **arak**.

arraign *vt* to put on trial; to indict, accuse; to censure publicly; to impeach.—**arraigner** *n*.—**arraignment** *n*.

arrange *vt* to put in a sequence or row; to settle, make preparations for; (*mus*) to prepare a composition for different instruments other than those intended.* *vi* to come to an agreement; to make plans.—**arranger** *n*.

arrangement *n* the act of putting in proper form or order; that which is ordered or disposed; the method or style of disposition; a preparatory measure; preparation; settlement; classification; adjustment; adaptation; (*pl*) plans.

arrant *adj* notorious; unmitigated; downright, thorough; shameless.

arras *n* a tapestry; hangings made of a rich figured fabric.

array *n* an orderly grouping, esp of troops; an impressive display; fine clothes; (*comput*) an ordered data structure that allows information to be easily indexed. * *vt* to set in order, to arrange; to dress, decorate.—**arrayal** *n*.

arrears *npl* overdue debts; work, etc still to be completed.

arrest *vt* to stop; to capture, apprehend esp by legal authority; to check the development of a disease; to catch and hold the attention of. * *n* a stoppage; seizure by legal authority.

arrestee *n* one who has been arrested.

arrester *n* one who or that which stops or seizes, or causes to be detained.

arresting *adj* striking or attracting to the mind or eye; impressive.—**arrestingly** *adv*.

arrière-pensée *n* (*pl* **arrière-pensées**) a mental reservation.

arris *n* (*pl* **arris, arrises**) (*archit*) the line or sharp edge in which two curved or straight surfaces, forming an exterior angle, meet each other.

arrival *n* arriving; a person or thing that has arrived.

arrive *vi* to reach any destination; to come; (*with* **at**) to reach agreement, a decision; to achieve success, celebrity.

arriviste *n* an ambitious person, a self-seeker.

arrogance *n* an exaggerated assumption of importance.

arrogant *adj* overbearing; aggressively self-important.—**arrogantly** *adv*.

arrogate *vt* to assume or lay claim to unduly or presumptuously.—**arrogation** *n*.—**arrogative** *adj*.—**arrogator** *n*.

arrondissement *n* a subdivision of a French department; a municipal subdivision of Paris, etc.

arrow *n* a straight, pointed weapon, made to be shot from a bow; a sign used to indicate direction or location.

arrowhead *n* the head or barb of an arrow; an aquatic plant so named from the shape of its leaves.

arrowroot *n* a starch obtained from the rootstocks of several species of West Indian plants.

arrowwood *n* a wood once used for arrows by American Indians.

arroyo *n* a watercourse or rivulet; the dry bed of a small stream.

arse *n* (*vulg*) the buttocks.

arsenal *n* a workshop or store for weapons and ammunition.

arsenate *n* a salt formed by combination of arsenic acid with any base.

arsenic *n* a soft grey metallic element, highly poisonous.

arsenical *adj* pertaining to or containing arsenic.

arsenious, arsenous *adj* pertaining to or containing arsenic.

arsenite *n* a salt of arsenious acid.

arsis *n* (*poet*) the part of a metrical foot where the accent is placed.

arson *n* the crime of using fire to destroy property deliberately.—**arsonist** *n*.

art[1] *n* human creativity; skill acquired by study and experience; any craft and its principles; the making of things that have form and beauty; any branch of this, as painting, sculpture, etc; drawings, paintings, statues, etc; (*pl*) the creative and nonscientific branches of knowledge, esp as studied academically.

art[2] (*arch*) the second person singular indicative mood and present tense of the verb to be.

art deco *n* a style of design and architecture popular in the 1920s and 1930s and characterized by bold geometrical lines.

artefact *see* **artifact.**
artel *n* a workers' guild in the former USSR.
artemisia *n* a large genus of plants to which the common wormwood belongs, yielding a volatile oil (the chief ingredient of absinthe).
arterial *adj* pertaining to an artery or the arteries; contained in an artery; (*blood*) oxygenated, of a lighter red colour than venous blood; (*road*) major, with many branches.
arterialize *vt* to convert as venous blood into arterial blood by exposure to oxygen in the lungs.—**arterialization** *n.*
arteriosclerosis *n* (*med*) hardening of the walls of the arteries due to the action of fatty deposits, which impairs blood circulation.—**arteriosclerotic** *adj.*
artery *n* (*pl* **arteries**) a tubular vessel that conveys blood from the heart; any main channel of transport or communication.
artesian well *n* a well in which water rises to the surface by internal pressure.
artful *adj* skilful at attaining one's ends; clever, crafty.—**artfully** *adv.*—**artfulness** *n.*
arthritis *n* painful inflammation of a joint.—**arthritic** *adj.*
arthropod *n* a member of the largest group of invertebrate animals with jointed legs, such as the butterfly, spider, crab, centipede.
artichoke *n* a thistle-like plant with a scaly flower head, parts of which are eaten as a vegetable.
article *n* a separate item or clause in a written document; an individual item on a particular subject in a newspaper, magazine, etc; a particular or separate item; (*gram*) a word placed before a noun to identify it as definite or indefinite.
articled *adj* apprenticed to, as an articled clerk to a solicitor.
articular *adj* of a joint or structural components in a joint.
articulate *adj* capable of distinct, intelligible speech, or expressing one's thoughts clearly; jointed. * *vti* to speak or express clearly; to unite or become united (as) by a joint.—**articulatedly** *adv.*—**articulateness** *n.*
articulated lorry, articulated truck *n* a large vehicle composed of a tractor and one or more trailers connected by flexible joints for greater manoeuvrability.—*also* **trailer truck.**
articulation *n* the act of jointing; the act of speaking distinctly; a distinct utterance; the state of being articulated; a joint or juncture between bones; the point of separation of organs or parts of a plant; a node or joint of the stem, or the space between two nodes.—**articulatory** *adj.*
articulator *n* one who pronounces distinctly; any organ of the mouth, etc, that moves to produce speech sounds.
artifact *n* a product of human craftsmanship, esp a simple tool or ornament.—*also* **artefact.**
artifice *n* a clever contrivance or stratagem; a trick, trickery.
artificer *n* a skilled or artistic worker; a maker or constructor; an inventor.
artificial *adj* lacking natural qualities; man-made.—**artificiality** *n.*—**artificially** *adv.*
artificial insemination *n* injection of semen into the womb by artificial means so that conception takes place without sexual intercourse.
artificial intelligence *n* (*comput*) the ability to imitate intelligent human behaviour.
artificial respiration *n* the forcing of air into and out of the lungs of somebody whose breathing has stopped.
artillery *n* (*pl* **artilleries**) large, heavy guns; the branch of the army that uses these.
artisan *n* a skilled workman.
artist *n* one who practises fine art, esp painting; one who does anything very well.—**artistic** *adj.*
artiste *n* a professional, usu musical or theatrical, entertainer.
artistic *adj* pertaining to art or to artists; characterized by aesthetic feeling or conformity to the principles of a school of art or design.—**artistically** *adv.*
artistry *n* artistic quality, ability, work, etc.
artless *adj* simple, natural; without art or skill.—**artlessly** *adv.*—**artlessness** *n.*
art nouveau *n* a style of art and decoration that developed in the late 19th century, characterized by flowing curves and designs in imitation of nature.
arty *adj* (**artier, artiest**) (*inf*) having a pretentious or affected interest in art.
arty-crafty, artsy-craftsy *adj* (*inf*) relating to arts and crafts, esp when affecting a simple, traditional style.
arum *n* a genus of plants with small flowers within a hood-shaped leaf.
arundinaceous *adj* pertaining to or resembling a reed or cane.
-ary *adj suffix, n suffix* connected with, as *dictionary.*
Aryan *n* a member of the Indo-European race; according to Nazi belief, a Caucasian, esp of the Nordic type, with no Jewish blood. * *adj* pertaining to the Aryans, or to their language.
As (*chem symbol*) arsenic.
as[1] *adv* equally; for instance; when related in a certain way. * *conj* in the same way that; while; when; because. * *prep* in the role or function of.
as[2] *n* (*pl* **asses**) a Roman weight equivalent to the libra or pound; a Roman copper coin.
asafoetida, asafetida *n* a foul-smelling gum resin obtained from the roots of several large umbelliferous plants and used in medicine.
ASAP, a.s.a.p. *abbr* = as soon as possible.
asbestos, asbestus *n* a fine fibrous mineral used for making incombustible and chemical-resistant materials.
asbestosis *n* (*med*) a disease of the lungs caused by the inhalation of asbestos fibres.
ascend *vti* to go up; to succeed to (a throne).
ascendancy, ascendency *n* governing or dominating influence; power; sway.
ascendant, ascendent *adj* rising upwards; dominant.
ascender *n* one who ascends; the top part of letters such as b, d, h.
ascension *n* the act of ascending or rising.—**ascensional** *adj.*
Ascension *n* the ascent of Christ into heaven after the Resurrection.
Ascension Day *n* a movable feast commemorating the Ascension, celebrated on the Thursday next but one before Whit Sunday.—*also* **Holy Thursday.**
ascent *n* an ascending; an upward slope; the means of, the way of ascending.
ascertain *vt* to acquire definite knowledge of, to discover positively.—**ascertainable** *adj.*
ascetic *adj* self-denying, austere. * *n* a person who practises rigorous self-denial as a religious discipline; any severely abstemious person.—**ascetically** *adv.*—**asceticism** *n.*
ascidian *n* a type of mollusc with a leathery tunic resembling a double-necked bottle, a sea squirt.—*also adj.*
ascidium *n* (*pl* **ascidia**) (*bot*) a pitcher-shaped or flask-shaped organ peculiar to certain plants, as the pitcher plants.
ASCII *acronym* (*comput*) = *A*merican *S*tandard *C*ode for *I*nformation *I*nterchange, a standard code of 128 alphanumeric characters for storing and exchanging information.
ascomycete *n* one of a family of the fungi, including most of the lichens, which form free spores within elongated spore cases.—**ascomyetous** *adj.*
ascorbic acid *n* vitamin C, found esp in citrus fruit and fresh green vegetables.
ascribe *vt* to attribute, impute or refer; to assign.—**ascribable** *adj.*—**ascription, adscription** *n.*
ascus *n* (*pl* **asci**) the spore case of lichens and fungi.
asdic *n* an apparatus for locating submarines; an echo sounder; sonar.
asepsis *n* an absence of disease or putrefaction; a surgical method aiming at this.—**asceptic** *adj.*
asexual *adj* lacking sex or sexual organs; (*reproduction*) produced without the union of male and female germ cells.—**asexuality** *n.*—**asexually** *adv.*
ash[1] *n* a tree with silver-grey bark; the wood of this tree.
ash[2] *n* powdery residue of anything burnt; fine, volcanic lava.
ashamed *adj* feeling shame or guilt.—**ashamedly** *adv.*

ash can *n* a container for household refuse, a garbage can.
ashen *adj* like ashes, esp in colour; pale.
Ashkenazi *n* (*pl* **Ashkenazim**) a Jew from Germany or eastern Europe.
ashlar, ashler *n* a squared stone used in building; masonry of this; thin slabs of building stone squared for facing walls.
ashlaring *n* a wall faced with ashlar; a low wall of a garret, built close to where the rafters reach the floor.
ashore *adv* to or on the shore; to or on land.—*also adj*.
ashram *n* a Hindu religious retreat.
ashtray *n* a small receptacle for tobacco ash and cigarette stubs.
Ash Wednesday *n* the first day of Lent; a special day set apart for fasting.
ashy *adj* (**ashier, ashiest**) of ashes; ash-coloured, pale.
Asian *adj* of or relating to the continent of Asia, its inhabitants or languages.—*also n*.
Asiatic cholera *n* a virulent form of cholera.
aside *adv* on or to the side; in reserve; away from; notwithstanding. * *n* words uttered and intended as inaudible, esp as spoken by an actor to the audience and supposedly unheard by the other actors on the stage.
asinine *adj* silly, stupid.—**asininity** *n*.
ask *vt* to put a question to, inquire of; to make a request of or for; to invite; to demand, expect. * *vi* to inquire about.—**asker** *n*.
askance, askant *adv* with a sideways glance; with distrust.
askew *adv* to one side; awry.—*also adj*.
aslant *adv* not at right angles; obliquely. * *prep* slantingly across, athwart.
asleep *adj* sleeping; inactive; numb. * *adv* into a sleeping condition.
asocial *adj* not capable of or avoiding social contact; antisocial.
asp *n* a small poisonous snake.
asparagus *n* a plant cultivated for its edible young shoots.
aspartame *n* an artificial sweetener derived from an amino acid.
aspect *n* the look of a person or thing to the eye; a particular feature of a problem, situation, etc; the direction something faces; view; (*astrol*) the position of the planets with respect to one another, regarded as having an influence on human affairs.
aspen *n* a species of poplar with leaves that have tremble in the slightest breeze. * *adj* (*arch*) quivering.
aspergillus *n* (*pl* **aspergilli**) a genus of microscopic fungi, to which several of the moulds belong.
asperity *n* (*pl* **asperities**) hardship, severity; sharpness of temper.
asperse *vt* to slander; (*rare*) to besprinkle, to bespatter.—**asperser** *n*.—**aspersive** *adj*.
aspersions *npl* slander; an attack on a person's reputation.
aspersorium *n* (*pl* **aspersoria, aspersoriums**) a vessel containing holy water for sprinkling; a brush or metallic instrument used for sprinkling the water.
asphalt *n* a hard, black bituminous substance, used for paving roads, etc. * *vt* to surface with asphalt.—**asphaltic** *adj*.
asphodel *n* one of several plants of the lily family; (*poet*) the daffodil; (*poet*) an immortal, unfading flower that bloomed in the meadows of Elysium (possibly the narcissus).
asphyxia *n* unconsciousness due to lack of oxygen or excess of carbon dioxide in the blood.
asphyxiate *vt* to suffocate.—**asphyxiation** *n*.—**asphyxiator** *n*.
aspic *n* a savoury jelly used to coat fish, game, etc.
aspidistra *n* an Asian plant with broad leaves, grown as a house plant.
aspirant *n* someone who aspires to something.
aspirate[1] *n* the sound of *h*.
aspirate[2] *vt* to pronounce with an *h*; to suck out using an aspirator.
aspiration *n* strong desire; ambition; the act of aspirating; the act of breathing; the withdrawal of air or fluid from a body cavity.—**aspiratory** *adj*.
aspirator *n* a device used to suck (air, fluid, etc) from a (body) cavity.
aspire *vi* to desire eagerly; to aim at high things.—**aspirer** *n*.—**aspiring** *adj*.
aspirin *n* (*pl* **aspirin, aspirins**) acetylsalicylic acid, a pain-relieving drug.
asquint *adv, adj* with a squint, to or out of the corner of the eye; obliquely.
ass *n* a donkey; a silly, stupid person; (*sl*) the arse, the buttocks.
assagai *see* **assegai**.
assai *adv* (*mus*) very, more, extremely.
assail *vt* to attack violently either physically or verbally.—**assailable** *adj*.—**assailer** *n*.—**assailment** *n*.
assailant *n* an attacker.
assassin *n* a murderer, esp one hired to kill a leading political figure, etc.
assassinate *vt* to kill a political figure, etc; to harm (a person's reputation, etc).—**assassination** *n*.
assault *n* a violent attack; (*law*) an unlawful threat or attempt to harm another physically. * *vti* to make an assault (on); to rape.—**assaulter** *n*.
assault course *n* an obstacle course used for military training.
assay *n* the analysis of the quantity of metal in an ore or alloy, esp the standard purity of gold or silver; a test. * *vt* (**assaying, assayed**) to subject to analysis; to determine the quantity or proportion of one or more of the constituents of a metal.—**assayable** *adj*.—**assayer** *n*.
assegai, assagai *n* (*pl* **assegais, assagais**) (*S Africa*) a light hardwood javelin or spear for casting or stabbing.
assemblage *n* a gathering of persons or things; (*art*) a form of collage.
assemble *vti* to bring together; to collect; to fit together the parts of; (*comput*) to translate using an assembler.
assembler *n* (*comput*) a program that converts low-level mnemonic symbols into machine code.
assembly *n* (*pl* **assemblies**) assembling or being assembled; a gathering of persons, esp for a particular purpose; the fitting together of parts to make a whole machine, etc.
assembly line *n* a series of machines, equipment and workers through which a product passes in successive stages to be assembled.
assemblyman *n* (*pl* **assemblymen**) a member of a legislative assembly.—**assemblywoman** *nf* (*pl* **assemblywomen**)
assent *vi* to express agreement to something. * *n* consent or agreement.—**assentor, assenter** *n*.
assentation *n* compliance with the opinion of another, in flattery or obsequiousness.
assert *vt* to declare, affirm as true; to maintain or enforce (eg rights).—**assertible** *adj*.
assertion *n* an asserting; a statement that something is a fact, usu without evidence.
assertive *adj* self-assured, positive, confident; dogmatic.—**assertively** *adv*.—**assertiveness** *n*.
assess *vt* to establish the amount of, as a tax; to impose a tax or fine; to value, for the purpose of taxation; to estimate the worth, importance, etc of.—**assessable** *adj*.
assessment *n* the act of assessing or determining an amount to be paid; an official valuation of property, or income, for the purpose of taxation; the specific sum levied as tax, or assessed for damages.
assessor *n* a person appointed to assess property or persons for taxation; an expert appointed to assist a judge or magistrate as an adviser on special points of law.—**assessorial** *adj*.
asset *n* anything owned that has value; a desirable thing; (*pl*) all the property, accounts receivable, etc of a person or business; (*pl*) (*law*) property usable to pay debts.
asset-stripping *n* the practice of buying a company in order to sell off its assets at a profit.—**asset-stripper** *n*.
asseverate *vt* to declare solemnly; to affirm or aver positively.—**asseveration** *n*.
asshole *n* (*sl*) a stupid person; (*vulg*) the anus.
assibilate *vt* (*phonetics*) to pronounce with a hissing sound; to alter to a sibilant.—**assibilation** *n*.
assiduity *n* (*pl* **assiduities**) close application, steady attention; diligence; (*usu pl*) constant attentions.
assiduous *adj* persistent or persevering; diligent.—**assiduously** *adv*.—**assiduousness** *n*.
assign *vt* to allot; to appoint to a post or duty; to ascribe; (*law*) to transfer (a right, property, etc).—**assignable** *adj*.—**assigner** *n*.
assignat *n* a money or currency bond secured on state lands, issued by the

French Revolutionary Government (1789–96).
assignation *n* the act of assigning; a meeting, esp one made secretly by lovers.
assignee *n* (*law*) one to whom an assignment of anything is made, either in trust or for his or her own use and enjoyment.
assignment *n* the act of assigning; something assigned to a person, such as a share, task, etc.
assignor *n* (*law*) one who assigns or transfers an interest.
assimilate *vt* to absorb; to digest; to take in and understand fully; to be ascribed; to be like.—**assimilable** *adj*.—**assimilation** *n*.
assimilative, assimilatory *adj* having the power of assimilating, or causing assimilation, tending to produce assimilation.
assist *vti* to support or aid.—**assister** *n*.
assistance *n* help; furtherance; aid; succour; support.
assistant *n* one who or that which assists; a helper; an auxiliary; a subordinate. * *adj* helping; lending aid; auxiliary.
assize *n* (*pl* **assizes**) a court or session of justice for the trial by jury of civil or criminal cases; (*usu pl*) (*formerly*) the sessions held periodically in each county of England by judges of the Supreme Court; (*usu pl*) the time or place of holding the assize.
associable *adj* capable of being joined or associated; liable to be affected by sympathy with kindred parts or organs.
associate *vt* to join as a friend, business partner or supporter; to bring together; to unite; to connect in the mind. * *vi* to combine or unite with others; to come together as friends, business partners or supporters. * *adj* allied or connected; having secondary status or privileges. * *n* a companion, business partner, supporter, etc; something closely connected with another; a person admitted to an association as a subordinate member.
association *n* an organization of people joined together for a common aim; the act of associating or being associated; a connection in the mind, memory, etc.
association football *n* football played with a round ball that is not handled, soccer.
associationism *n* (*psychol*) the mental connection existing between an object and the ideas related to it.
associative *adj* tending to or characterized by association; (*math*) having elements whose result is the same despite the grouping.
assonance *n* a correspondence in sound between words or syllables.—**assonant** *adj*, *n*.—**assonantal** *adj*.
assort *vt* to arrange in groups according to kind. * *vi* to agree in kind.—**assortative, assortive** *adj*.—**assorter** *n*.
assorted *adj* distributed according to sorts; miscellaneous.
assortment *n* a collection of people or things of different sorts.
asst *abbr* = assistant.
assuage *vt* to soften the intensity of; to soothe.—**assuager** *n*.—**assuagement** *n*.—**assuasive** *adj*.
assume *vt* to take on, to undertake; to usurp; to take as certain or true; to pretend to possess.—**assumable** *adj*.—**assumer** *n*.
assuming *adj* presumptuous.
assumption *n* something taken for granted; the taking on of a position, esp of power; (*with cap*) the ascent of the Virgin Mary into heaven; (*RC Church*) the Christian feast in remembrance of this, celebrated 15 August.—**assumptive** *adj*.
assurance *n* a promise, guarantee; a form of life insurance; a feeling of certainty, self-confidence.
assure *vt* to make safe or certain; to give confidence to; to state positively; to guarantee, ensure.—**assurable** *adj*.—**assurer** *n*.
assured *adj* certain; convinced; self-confident.—**assuredness** *n*.
assuredly *adv* certainly.
assurgent *adj* ascending, rising; (*bot*) rising in a curve.
Assyrian *adj* pertaining to Assyria, an ancient kingdom of Mesopotamia, or to its inhabitants or language. * *n* the language spoken in Assyria; an inhabitant of Assyria.
Assyriology *n* the science or study of the extinct language and the antiquities of Assyria.—**Assyriologist** *n*.
astatic *adj* having a tendency not to stand still; unstable.—**astatically** *adv*.—**astaticism** *n*.
astatine *n* a radioactive element.
aster *n* a kind of plant with round composite flowers; a Michaelmas daisy.
-aster *n suffix* petty imitation, as in *poetaster*.
asteriated *adj* (*crystal, etc*) radiated; having the form of a star.
asterisk *n* a sign (*) used in writing or printing to mark omission of words, a footnote or other reference, etc. * *vt* to mark with an asterisk.
asterism *n* a group or cluster of stars; three asterisks placed in the form of a triangle (***) or (***) to direct attention to a particular passage; the star-like appearance in certain crystals.
astern *adv* behind a ship or aircraft; at or towards the rear of a ship, etc; backward.
asternal *adj* (*anat*) (*ribs*) not joined to the sternum or breastbone.
asteroid *n* any of the small planets between Mars and Jupiter. * *adj* star-like; star-shaped (—*also* **asteroidal**).
asthenia *n* debility, weakness.—**asthenic** *adj*.
asthma *n* a chronic respiratory condition causing difficulty with breathing.—**asthmatic** *adj*.—**asthmatically** *adv*.
asthmatic *adj* of or suffering from or good for asthma, * *n* an asthmatic person.—**asthmatically** *adv*.
astigmatism *n* a defective condition of the eye or lens causing poor focusing.—**astigmatic** *adj*.—**astigmatically** *adv*.
astir *adv* moving or bustling about; out of bed.
astomatous *adj* (*biol*) lacking a mouth; without breathing pores.
astonish *vt* to fill with sudden or great surprise.—**astonishing** *adj*.—**astonishment** *n*.
astound *vt* to astonish greatly.—**astounding** *adj*.—**astoundingly** *adv*.
astraddle *adv* astride, straddling.
astragal *n* (*archit*) a small moulding or bead of semicircular form; a ring of moulding round the top or bottom of a column.
astragalus *n* (*pl* **astragali**) the ball of the ankle joint; the lower bone into which the tibia articulates.
astrakhan *n* the dark curly fleece of lambs from Astrakhan in Russia; a cloth with a curled pile made from or imitating this.
astral *adj* of or from the stars.
astray *adv* off the right path; into error.
astride *adv* with a leg on either side. * *prep* extending across.
astringent *adj* that contracts body tissues; stopping blood flow, styptic; harsh; biting. * *n* an astringent substance—**astringency** *n*.
astro- *prefix* (*astrophysics*) of a star or stars.
astrodome *n* a large sports stadium covered with a domed translucent roof.
astrolabe *n* an instrument formerly used for taking altitudes of the sun and stars.
astrology *n* the study of planetary positions and motions to determine their supposed influence on human affairs.—**astrologer, astrologist** *n*.—**astrological** *adj*.—**astrologically** *adv*.
astrometry *n* the art by which the apparent relative magnitude of the stars is determined.—**astrometric, astrometrical** *adj*.
astronaut *n* one trained to make flights in outer space.
astronautics *npl* (*used as sing*) the scientific study of space flight and technology.
astronomical, astronomic *adj* enormously large; of or relating to astronomy.—**astronomically** *adv*.
astronomical clock *n* a clock that keeps sidereal time.
astronomical year *n* a year the length of which is determined by astronomical observations.
astronomy *n* the scientific investigation of the stars and other planets.—**astronomer** *n*.
astrophotography *n* photography of the heavenly bodies.—**astrophotographic** *adj*.
astrophysics *n* (*used as sing*) the branch of astronomy that deals with the physical and chemical constitution of the stars.—**astrophysical** *adj*.—**astrophysicist** *n*.

astute *adj* clever, perceptive; crafty, shrewd.—**astutely** *adv*.—**astuteness** *n*.
asunder *adv* apart in direction or position; into pieces.
asylum *n* a place of safety, a refuge; (*formerly*) an institution for the blind, the mentally ill, etc.
asymmetric, asymmetrical *adj* lacking symmetry.—**asymmetrically** *adv*.
asymmetry *n* a lack of symmetry or proportion between the parts of a thing.
asymptote *n* (*geom*) the line that continually approaches nearer to a given curve without ever meeting it.—**asymptotic, asymptotical** *adj*.
asyndeton *n* (*pl* **asyndetons, asyndeta**) (*gram*) a figure of speech in which conjunctions are omitted, as "I came, I saw, I conquered"; such a figure.
at- *prefix* the form of *ad-* before *t*.
At (*chem symbol*) astatine.
at *prep* on; in; near; by; used to indicate location or position.
ataraxia, ataraxy *n* impassivity; peace of mind.
atavism *n* the appearance in plants or animals of characteristics typical in more remote ancestors; reversion to a more primitive type.—**atavistic** *adj*.—**atavistically** *adv*.
ataxia *n* irregularities in the functions of the body, esp muscular coordination, or in the course of a disease.—**ataxic, atactic** *adj*.
-ate *adj suffix* having or furnished with, as *foliate*. * *n suffix* forming the equivalent of *pp*, as in *associate*.
ate *see* **eat**.
atelier *n* a workshop; the studio of a painter or sculptor.
a tempo, a tempo primo *n* (*mus*) a direction to a musician to restore the original time after acceleration or retardation.
a tempo giusto *n* (*mus*) a direction to a performer to sing or play in strict time.
Athanasian Creed *n* one of the three creeds thus named as containing an exposition of the doctrines of the Trinty and incarnation of Christ, which Athanasius, bishop of Alexandria (*c*. 296–373), defended.
atheism *n* belief in the nonexistence of God.—**atheist** *n*.—**atheistic, atheistical** *adj*.
atheling *n* an Anglo-Saxon title of honour conferred on royal children and young nobles.
athenaeum, atheneum *n* a public institution, club or building devoted to the purposes or study of literature, science and art; a literary club; (*with cap*) the temple of Athena in ancient Athens, where scholars met.
Athenian *adj* pertaining to Athens, the capital of Greece. * *n* a native or citizen of Athens.
athermanous *adj* resisting the passage of heat; nonconducting.—**athermany** *n*.
atherosclerosis *n* (*pl* **atheroscleroses**) a degenerative disease of the arteries characterized by deposition of fatty material on the inner arterial walls.—**atherosclerotic** *adj*.
athirst *adj* thirsty; eager (for).
athlete *n* a person trained in games or exercises requiring skill, speed, strength, stamina, etc.
athlete's foot *n* a fungal infection of the feet.
athletic *adj* of athletes or athletics; active, vigorous.—**athletically** *adv*.—**athleticism** *n*.
athletics *n* (*used as sing or pl*) running, jumping, throwing sports, games, etc.
athwart *prep* across, from side to side. * *adv* crosswise; obliquely; across the course or direction of a ship; adversely (to).
atilt *adv* in the position or with the action of a person making a thrust; tilted.
atlantes *see* **atlas**^{2}.
Atlantic *adj* of, near or relating to the Atlantic Ocean.
atlas^1 *n* a book containing maps, charts and tables.
atlas^2 *n* (*pl* **atlantes**) (*archit*) a figure or half-figure of a man, used in place of a column or pilaster to support an entablature.—*also* **telamon**.
-ation *n suffix* denoting action or its result, as in *flirtation, vacation*.

ATM *abbr* = automated teller machine.
atmo- *prefix* vapour, air, atmosphere.
atmometer *n* an instrument for measuring the rate and amount of evaporation from a moist surface.—**atmometry** *n*.
atmosphere *n* the gaseous mixture that surrounds the earth or the other stars and planets; a unit of pressure equal to the pressure of the atmosphere at sea level; any dominant or surrounding influence; special mood or aura.—**atmospheric, atmospherical** *adj*.
atmospherics *npl* interference in radio reception, etc caused by atmospheric disturbances.
at. no. *abbr* = atomic number.
atoll *n* a coral reef enclosing a central lagoon.
atom *n* the smallest particle of a chemical element; a tiny particle, bit.
atomic *adj* pertaining to or consisting of atoms; extremely minute.—**atomically** *adv*.
atomic bomb *n* a bomb whose explosive power derives from the atomic energy released during nuclear fission or fusion.—*also* **A-bomb**.
atomic energy *n* the energy derived from nuclear fission.
atomicity *n* the number of atoms in a molecule of an element; equivalence; the combining capacity of an element, valency.
atomic theory *n* the theory that elemental bodies consist of ultimate atoms of definite weight, and that atoms of different elements unite chemically with each other in fixed proportions.
atomic weight *n* the weight of the atom of any element as compared with another taken as a standard, usu hydrogen, taken as 1.
atomism *n* the doctrine of atoms, atomic theory.—**atomist** *n*.—**atomistic, atomistical** *adj*.
atomize *vt* to reduce to a fine spray or minute particles.—**atomization** *n*.
atomizer *n* a device for atomizing liquids, usu perfumes or cleaning agents.
atonal *adj* (*mus*) avoiding traditional tonality; not written in any established key.—**atonality** *n*.—**atonally** *adv*.
atone *vi* to give satisfaction or make amends (for).—**atonable, atoneable** *adj*.—**atoner** *n*.
atonement *n* satisfaction, reparation; (*Christianity*: *with cap*) the reconciliation of humankind with God through Christ's self-sacrifice.
atonic *adj* (*word, etc*) unaccented; lacking tone, or vital energy. * *n* an unaccented word or syllable; a medicine to allay excitement.—**atonicity** *n*.
atony *n* lack of tone; debility; weakness of any organ.
atop *adv* on or at the top.
atrip *adv* (*naut*) (*anchor*) just clear of the ground.
atrium *n* (*pl* **atria, atriums**) an auricle of the heart; the unroofed courtyard of a Roman house; an entrance hall that rises up several storeys, often with a glass roof.
atrocious *adj* extremely brutal or wicked; (*inf*) very bad, of poor quality.—**atrociously** *adv*.
atrocity *n* (*pl* **atrocities**) a cruel act; something ruthless, wicked, repellent.
atrophy *n* (*pl* **atrophies**) a wasting away or failure to grow of a bodily organ. * *vti* (**atrophying, atrophied**) to cause or undergo atrophy.
atropine, atropin *n* a crystalline alkaloid of a very poisonous nature extracted from the deadly nightshade (belladonna), having the singular property of producing dilatation of the pupil of the eye.
attacca *n* (*mus*) a direction to a performer at the end of a movement to follow on with the next without pause.
attach *vt* to fix or fasten to something; to appoint to a specific group; to ascribe, attribute. * *vi* to become attached; to adhere.—**attachable** *adj*.—**attacher** *n*.
attaché *n* a technical expert on a diplomatic staff.
attaché case *n* a flat case for carrying documents, etc.
attached *adj* fixed; feeling affection for.
attachment *n* a fastening; affection, devotion; something attached; a device or part fixed to a machine, implement, etc; the act of attaching or being attached.
attack *vt* to set upon violently; to assault in speech or writing; to invade,

as of a disease. * *vi* to make an assault. * *n* an assault; a fit of illness; severe criticism; an enthusiastic beginning of a performance, task, undertaking, etc.—**attacker** *n*.

attain *vt* to succeed in getting or arriving at; to achieve. * *vi* to come to or arrive at by growth or effort.—**attainable** *adj*.—**attainability** *n*.

attainder *n* loss of estate and civil rights following conviction for high treason.

attainment *n* something attained; an accomplishment.

attaint *vt* to subject to attainder; to infect; to stain, to disgrace.

attar *n* a fragrant essential oil extracted from rose petals and used in making perfume.

attempt *vt* to try to accomplish, get, etc. * *n* an endeavour or effort to accomplish; an attack, assault.—**attemptable** *adj*.—**attempter** *n*.

attend *vt* to take care of; to go with, accompany; to be present at. * *vi* to apply oneself (to); to deal with, give attention to.—**attender** *n*.

attendance *n* attending; the number of people present; the number of times a person attends.

attendant *n* a person who serves or accompanies another; someone employed to assist or guide. * *adj* accompanying, following as a result; being in attendance.

attention *n* the application of the mind to a particular purpose, aim, etc; awareness, notice; care, consideration; (*usu. pl*) an act of civility or courtesy; (*usu. pl*) indications of admiration or love; (*mil*) a soldier's formal erect posture.

attentive *adj* observant, diligent; courteous.—**attentively** *adv*.—**attentiveness** *n*.

attenuate *vt* to make thin; to weaken; to reduce the force or severity of. * *vi* to become thin; to weaken.—**attenuation** *n*.

attest *vt* to state as true; to certify, as by oath; to give proof of. * *vi* to testify, bear witness (to).—**attestable** *adj*.—**attestation** *n*.—**attester, attestor** *n*.

attestation *n* the act of attesting; testimony or evidence given on oath or by official declaration; swearing in.

attic *n* the room or space just under the roof; a garret.

Attic *adj* pertaining to Attica in Greece; classical; elegant. * *n* a dialect of ancient Athens.

atticism *n* an elegant expression; (*with cap*) a peculiarity of style or idiom characterizing the Attic rendering of the Greek language.

Attic order *n* a square column of any of the five Greek orders of architecture.

Attic salt, Attic wit *n* delicate wit.

attire *vt* to clothe; to dress up. * *n* dress, clothing.

attitude *n* posture, position of the body; a manner of thought or feeling; behaviour; the position of an aircraft or spacecraft in relation to certain reference points.—**attitudinal** *adj*.

attitudinize *vi* to assume affected postures, to pose for effect.—**attitudinizer** *n*.

attorn *vti* to transfer; to make legal acknowledgment of a new landlord.—**attornment** *n*.

attorney *n* (*pl* **attorneys**) one legally authorized to act for another; a lawyer.

attorney general *n* (*pl* **attorneys general, attorneys generals**) the chief law officer of of a state or nation acting as its legal representative and advising the chief executive on legal matters.

attract *vt* to pull towards oneself; to get the admiration, attention, etc of. * *vi* to be attractive.—**attractable** *adj*.—**attractor** *n*.

attraction *n* the act of attraction; the power of attracting, esp charm; (*physics*) the mutual action by which bodies tend to be drawn together.

attractive *adj* pleasing in appearance, etc; arousing interest; able to draw or pull.—**attractively** *adv*.—**attractiveness** *n*.

attribute *vt* to regard as belonging to; to ascribe, impute (to). * *n* a quality, a characteristic of.—**attributable** *adj*.

attribution *n* the act of attributing, esp a work of art, etc to a particular creator; a designation; a function.—**attributional** *adj*.

attributive *adj* expressing an attribute; (*gram*) qualifying. * *n* a word joined to and describing a noun; an adjective or adjective phrase.—**attributively** *adv*.

attributive *adj* pertaining to, of the nature of, or expressing, an attribute; (*gram*) qualifying. * *n* a word denoting an attribute; a word joined to and describing a noun; an adjective or adjectival phrase.

attrition *n* a grinding down by or as by friction; a relentless wearing down and weakening; natural wastage or reduction of a workforce by not employing replacements for those who resign or leave.—**attritional** *adj*.—**attritive** *adj*.

attune *vt* to bring (a person or thing) into harmony with; to adapt.

at. wt. *abbr* = atomic weight.

atypical *adj* not according to type; without definite typical character.—**atypically** *adv*.

Au (*chem symbol*) gold.

aubade *n* a musical announcement of dawn; a sunrise song.

auberge *n* an inn.

aubergine *n* a plant producing a smooth, dark-purple fruit; this fruit used as a vegetable.—*also* **eggplant**.

aubrietia, aubretia *n* a small purple-flowered perennial plant.

auburn *adj* reddish brown.

au contraire *adv* on the contrary.

au courant *adj* well-informed, esp in current affairs.

auction *n* a public sale of items to the highest bidder. * *vt* to sell by or at an auction.

auction bridge *n* a form of bridge in which the players contract to take a certain number of tricks, with extra tricks counting towards game.

auctioneer *n* one who conducts an auction.

audacious *adj* daring, adventurous; bold; rash; insolent.—**audaciously** *adv*.—**audaciousness** *n*.

audacity *n* (*pl* **audacities**) boldness; daring; spirit; presumptuousness; impudence; effrontery.

audible *adj* heard or able to be heard.—**audibility** *n*.—**audibly** *adv*.

audience *n* a gathering of listeners or spectators; the people addressed by a book, play, film, etc; a formal interview or meeting, esp one in which one's views are heard.

audile *adj* received through hearing.

audio *n* sound; the reproduction, transmission or reception of sound.

audio frequency *n* a frequency audible to the human ear.

audiometer *n* an instrument for gauging the power of hearing.—**audiometric** *adj*.—**audiometrically** *adv*.—**audiometry** *n*.

audiotypist *n* a typist who works from a recording.

audiovisual *adj* using both sound and vision, as in teaching aids.

audit *n* the inspection and verification of business accounts by a qualified accountant. * *vt* to make such an inspection.

audition *n* a trial to test a performer. * *vti* to test or be tested by audition.

auditor *n* a person qualified to audit business accounts.—**auditorial** *adj*.

auditorium *n* (*pl* **auditoriums, auditoria**) the part of a building allotted to the audience; a building or hall for speeches, concerts, etc.

auditory *adj* of or relating to the sense of hearing.

au fait *adj* fully informed about; competent.

au fond (*French*) fundamentally.

auf Wiedersehen *interj*, *n* till we meet again.

Aug. *abbr* = August.

auger *n* a tool for boring holes, a large gimlet.

aught *n* anything; any part. * *adv* (*arch*) in any degree, in any way; at all.—*also* **ought**.

augite *n* a variety of pyroxene of a black or dark green colour.—**augitic** *adj*.

augment *vti* to increase.—**augmentable** *adj*.—**augmenter, augmentor** *n*.

augmentation *n* enlargement, addition, increase; (*mus*) the increase in time value of the notes of a theme; (*her*) an additional charge to a coat of arms bestowed as a mark of honour.

augmentative *adj* having the quality or power of augmenting; (*gram*) increasing in force the idea of a word. * *n* a word or affix that expresses with greater force the idea conveyed by the term from which it is derived, opposite of diminutive.

au gratin *adj* topped with breadcrumbs or breadcrumbs and cheese, and cooked until crisp.

augur *vti* to prophesy; to be an omen (of).—**augural** *adj.*

augury *n* (*pl* **auguries**) the art or practice of foretelling events by reference to natural signs or omens; an omen; prediction; presage.

August *n* the eighth month of the year, having 31 days.

august *adj* imposing; majestic.

Augustan *adj* of or pertaining to Augustus Caesar, emperor of Rome, or his reign, during which Roman literature gained its highest point; of or pertaining to the period of the highest stage of literary excellence in other countries.

auk *n* a northern sea bird with short wings used as paddles.

au lait *adj* with milk.

auld lang syne *n* days of old; long ago.

au naturel *adj, adv* in the natural state; cooked plainly; raw; nude.

aunt *n* a father's or mother's sister; an uncle's wife.

auntie, aunty *n* (*pl* **aunties**) (*inf*) aunt.

au pair *n* a person, esp a girl, from abroad who performs domestic chores, child-minding, etc in return for board and lodging.

aura *n* (*pl* **auras, aurae**) a particular quality or atmosphere surrounding a person or thing.

aural[1] *adj* of the ear or the sense of hearing.—**aurally** *adv.*

aural[2] *adj* of the air or an aura.

aureate *adj* golden; gilded; golden yellow.

aureole, aureola *n* (*art*) a halo, radiance, or luminous cloud encircling the figures of Christ, the virgin and the saints in sacred pictures; anything resembling an aureole.

au revoir *n* goodbye for the present.

auric *adj* of or pertaining to gold.

auricle *n* the external part of the ear; either of the two upper chambers of the heart.

auricula *n* (*pl* **auriculas, auriculae**) a species of primrose with leaves the shape of a bear's ear.

auricular *adj* of or received by the ear; shaped like an ear; spoken privately; relating to the auricles of the heart.

auriculate *adj* ear-shaped; having ears or ear-like appendages.

auriferous *adj* gold-bearing; yielding or containing gold.

aurochs *n* (*pl* **aurochs**) an extinct wild ox of North Africa, Europe and Asia.

aurora *n* (*pl* **auroras, aurorae**) either of the luminous bands seen in the night sky in the polar regions.—*also* **northern lights.**

aurora australis *n* the aurora seen at the South Pole.

aurora borealis *n* the aurora seen at the North Pole.

aurous *adj* of or bearing gold.

auscultate *vt* to examine by auscultation.—**auscultator** *n.*—**auscultatory** *adj.*

auscultation *n* a listening to the sounds of the heart, lungs, etc in the chest for medical diagnosis.

auspex *n* (*pl* **auspices**) one who divined by observation of birds in ancient Rome.

auspice *n* (*pl* **auspices**) an omen; (*pl*) sponsorship; patronage.

auspicious *adj* showing promise, favourable.—**auspiciously** *adv.*

Aussie *n* (*sl*) an Australian.

austere *adj* stern, forbidding in attitude or appearance; abstemious; severely simple, plain.—**austerely** *adv.*—**austereness** *n.*

austerity *n* (*pl* **austerities**) being austere; economic privation.

austral *adj* southern; (*with cap*) Australian.

Australasian *adj* of or pertaining to Australasia (Australia, New Zealand and adjacent islands). * *n* a native or inhabitant of Australasia.

Australian *adj* of or pertaining to Australia. * *n* a native or inhabitant of Australia.

Australoid *adj* of the variety of human population that includes the Australian aborigines. * *n* an Australoid person.

autarchy *n* (*pl* **autarchies**) absolute or autocratic rule or sovereignty; a country governed in such a way; autarky.—**autarchic, autarchical** *adj.*

autarky *n* (*pl* **autarkies**) self-sufficiency, esp in the economic sphere; the policy of encouraging economic self-sufficiency.—**autarkic, autarkical** *adj.*

authentic *adj* genuine, conforming to truth or reality; trustworthy, reliable.—**authentically** *adv.*—**authenticity** *n.*

authenticate *vt* to demonstrate the authenticity of; to make valid; to verify.—**authentication** *n.*—**authenticator** *n.*

author *n* a person who brings something into existence; the writer of a book, article, etc. * *vt* to be the author of.—**authoress** *nf.*—**authorial** *adj.*

authoritarian *adj* favouring strict obedience; dictatorial. * *n* a person advocating authoritarian principles.—**authoritarianism** *n.*

authoritative *adj* commanding or possessing authority; accepted as true; official.—**authoritatively** *adv.*

authority *n* (*pl* **authorities**) the power or right to command; (*pl*) officials with this power; influence resulting from knowledge, prestige, etc; a person, writing, etc cited to support an opinion; an expert.

authorize *vt* to give authority to, to empower; to give official approval to, sanction.—**authorization** *n.*

Authorized Version *n* the version of the Bible published by the sanction of James I of England in 1611 and appointed to be read in churches.—*also* **King James Bible, King James Version.**

authorship *n* the writing profession; origin (of book).

autism *n* (*psychiatry*) a mental state, usu of children, marked by disregard of external reality—**autistic** *adj.*

auto *n* (*pl* **autos**) (*inf*) an automobile.

auto- *prefix* self; by oneself or itself.

autobahn *n* a German, Austrian or Swiss motorway.

autobiography *n* (*pl* **autobiographies**) the biography of a person written by himself or herself.—**autobiographer** *n.*—**autobiographical** *adj.*

autocephalous *adj* having its own head; independent.

autochondriac *n* a person who is preoccupied with his or her car.

autochthon *n* (*pl* **autochthons, autochthones**) an earliest known inhabitant, an aboriginal.

autochthonous, autochthonal *adj* pertaining to primitive inhabitants; indigenous, native to the soil.—**autochthonism, autochthony** *n.*

autoclave *n* a strong container used for chemical reactions at high temperatures and pressures; a device for sterilizing implements using steam at high pressure.

autocracy *n* (*pl* **autocracies**) government by one person with absolute power.

autocrat *n* an absolute ruler; any domineering person.—**autocratic** *adj.*—**autocratically** *adv.*

autocross *n* cross-country motor racing.

Autocue *n* (*trademark*) a prompting device used in TV, etc, which provides speakers with a script that remains invisible to the audience.—*also* **Teleprompter.**

auto-da-fé *n* (*pl* **autos-da-fé**) a public judgment by the Spanish Inquisition upon prisoners tried for heresy and other offences against the religious or civil law; the subsequent execution of such sentences by burning.

autoeroticism, autoerotism *n* self-produced sexual emotion.—**autoerotic** *adj.*

autogamy *n* self-fertilization.—**autogamous** *adj.*

autogenesis, autogeny *n* spontaneous generation.—**autogenetic** *adj.*

autogenous *adj* self-generated; produced independently.

autogyro, autogiro *n* (*pl* **autogyros, autogiros**) an aircraft like a helicopter but with unpowered rotor blades.

autograph *n* a person's signature. * *vt* to write one's signature in or on.—**autographic** *adj.*—**autographically** *adv.*

autography *n* one's own handwriting; a lithographic process by which copies of writings or drawings are reproduced in facsimile.

autolysis *n* the destruction of cells of a body by the action of its own serum.—**autolytic** *adj.*

automaker *n* a manufacturer of automobiles.
automat *n* in US, a restaurant equipped with slot machines for dispensing food and drink; a vending machine.
automate *vt* to control by automation; to convert to automatic operation.
automated telling machine *n* a device that provides cash and other banking services automatically when activated by a plastic card issued to customers; a cash dispenser.—*also* **autoteller.**
automatic *adj* involuntary or reflexive; self-regulating; acting by itself. * *n* an automatic pistol or rifle.—**automatically** *adv*.
automatic pilot *n* a device that can maintain an aircraft or ship on a previously set course.—*also* **autopilot.**
automatic transmission *n* a system in a motor vehicle for changing gears automatically.
automation *n* the use of automatic methods, machinery, etc in industry.
automatism *n* automatic action; involuntary action; mechanical routine; the doctrine that assigns all animal functions to the active operation of physical laws.—**automatist** *n*.
automaton *n* (*pl* **automatons, automata**) any automatic device, esp a robot; a human being who acts like a robot.
automatous *adj* spontaneous; of the nature of an automaton.
automobile *n* a usu four-wheeled vehicle powered by an internal combustion engine.—*also* **motor car.**
automotive *adj* relating to motor vehicles.
autonomy *n* (*pl* **autonomies**) freedom of self-determination; independence, self-government.—**autonomous** *adj*.
autopilot *n* automatic pilot.
autoplasty *n* the process of repairing lesions by application of tissue removed from another part of the same body.—**autoplastic** *adj*.
autopsy *n* (*pl* **autopsies**) a post-mortem examination to determine the cause of death.
autoroute *n* a French motorway.
autostrada *n* an Italian motorway.
autosuggestion *n* (*psychoanal*) self-applied suggestion.—**autosuggestive** *adj*.
autoteller *see* **automated telling machine.**
autotoxin *n* a poisonous substance produced by changes within an organism.—**autotoxic** *adj*.
autumn *n* the season between summer and winter.—*also* **fall.**
autumnal *adj* belonging or peculiar to autumn or fall; produced or gathered in autumn; pertaining to the period of life when middle age is past. * *n* a plant that flowers in autumn.
aux. *abbr* = auxiliary.
auxiliary *adj* providing help, subsidiary; supplementary. * *n* (*pl* **auxiliaries**) a helper; (*gram*) a verb that helps form tenses, moods, voices, etc of other verbs, as *have, be, may, shall,* etc.
AV *abbr* = ad valorem; audiovisual; Authorized Version.
avadavat *n* a small Asian finch-like bird, kept as a caged bird for its song.
avail *vti* to be of use or advantage to. * *n* benefit, use or help.
available *adj* ready for use; obtainable, accessible.—**availability** *n*.—**availably** *adv*.
avalanche *n* a mass of snow, ice, and rock tumbling down a mountainside; a sudden overwhelming accumulation or influx.
avant-garde *n* (*arts*) those ideas and practices regarded as in advance of those generally accepted. * *adj* pertaining to such ideas and practices and their creators.—**avant-gardism** *n*.
avarice *n* greed for wealth.—**avaricious** *adj*.—**avariciously** *adv*.
avast *interj* (*naut*) stop! cease! hold!
avatar *n* (*Hinduism*) the descent to earth of a deity in an incarnate form; manifestation or embodiment; transference of personality.
avdp. *abbr* = avoirdupois.
ave *interj* hail; farewell. * *n* an Ave Maria; a salutation.
Ave, ave *abbr* = avenue.
Ave Maria *n* (*RC Church*) Hail Mary.
avenge *vt* to get revenge for.—**avenger** *n*.
avens *n* (*pl* **avens**) the popular name of plants to which the herb bennet belongs.
aventurine *n* a brown, gold-spangled kind of Venetian glass; a variety of micaceous quartz or feldspar.
avenue *n* a street, drive, etc, esp when broad; means of access; the way to an objective.
aver *vt* (**averring, averred**) to state as true; to assert.—**averment** *n*.
average *n* the result of dividing the sum of two or more quantities by the number of quantities; the usual kind, amount, quality, etc. * *vt* to calculate the average of; to achieve an average number of.
averse *adj* unwilling; opposed (to).
aversion *n* antipathy; hatred; something arousing hatred or repugnance.
avert *vt* to turn away or aside from; to prevent, avoid.—**avertible, avertable** *adj*.
avian *adj* of or pertaining to birds.
aviary *n* (*pl* **aviaries**) a building or large cage for keeping birds.
aviate *vi* to pilot or travel in an aircraft.
aviation *n* the art or science of flying aircraft.
aviator *n* a pilot, esp in the early history of flying.
aviculture *n* the breeding and rearing of birds.—**aviculturist** *n*.
avid *adj* eager, greedy.—**avidly** *adv*.
avidity *n* greediness; eagerness; strong appetite.
avifauna *n* (*pl* **avifaunae**) the birds of a region regarded collectively.—**avifaunal** *adj*.
avionics *n* (*used as sing*) the application of electronics in aviation.—**avionic** *adj*.
avocado *n* (*pl* **avocados**) a thick-skinned, pear-shaped fruit with yellow buttery flesh.
avocet *n* one of several species of wading birds, characterized by very long legs and an extremely slender curved bill.
avoid *vt* to keep clear of, shun; to refrain from.—**avoider** *n*.
avoidable *adj* able to be avoided.
avoidance *n* the act of annulling or making void; the act of shunning; the state of being vacant.
avoirdupois *n* the system of weights based on the pound of 16 ounces; (*inf*) excess weight.
avow *vt* to declare confidently; to acknowledge.—**avowed** *adj*.—**avowedly** *adv*.—**avower** *n*.
avowal *n* an open declaration; a frank acknowledgment; a confession.
avulsion *n* a separation by violence; the sudden removal of land, without change of ownership, caused by a flood, etc.
avuncular *adj* like an uncle.
await *vti* to wait for; to be in store for.
awake *vb* (**awaking, awoke** *or* **awaked,** *pp* **awoken** *or* **awaked**) *vi* to wake; to become aware. * *vt* to rouse from sleep; to rouse from inaction. * *adj* roused from sleep, not asleep; active; aware.
awaken *vti* to awake.
awakening *n* the act of rousing from sleep; a revival of religion, or activity of a particular religious sect. * *adj* rousing; exciting; alarming.
award *vt* to give, as by a legal decision; to give (a prize, etc); to grant. * *n* a decision, as by a judge; a prize.
aware *adj* realizing, having knowledge; conscious; fully conversant with and sympathetic towards (*ecologically aware*).—**awareness** *n*.
awash *adj* filled or overflowing with water.
away *adv* from a place; in another place or direction; off, aside; far. * *adj* absent; at a distance.
awe *n* a mixed feeling of fear, wonder and dread. * *vt* to fill with awe.
aweather *adv* (*naut*) on the weather side, or towards the wind. * *n* opposed to the alee.
aweigh *adj, adv* (*naut*) (*anchor*) atrip, just drawn out of the ground and hanging perpendicularly.
awesome *adj* inspiring awe; (*inf*) marvellous, terrific.
awestricken, awestruck *adj* struck with awe.
awful *adj* very bad; unpleasant. * *adv* (*inf*) very.—**awfulness** *n*.
awfulize *vt* to envisage a situation as being worse than it is.—*also* **catastrophize.**

awfully *adv* in an awful manner; excessively; (*inf*) very.

awhile *adv* for a short time.

awkward *adj* lacking dexterity, clumsy; graceless; embarrassing; embarrassed; inconvenient; deliberately obstructive or difficult to deal with.—**awkwardly** *adv*.—**awkwardness** *n*.

awl *n* a small pointed tool for boring or piercing, used by shoemakers, etc.

awn *n* the beard or bristle-like appendage of the outer glume of wheat, barley, and numerous grasses.

awning *n* a structure, as of canvas, extended above or in front of a window, door, etc to provide shelter against the sun or rain.

awoke *see* **awake**.

AWOL *abbr* = absent without leave.

awry *adv* twisted to one side. * *adj* contrary to expectations, wrong.

axe, ax *n* (*pl* **axes**) a tool with a long handle and bladed head for chopping wood, etc. * *vt* to trim, split, etc with an axe.

axial *adj* of, forming or round an axis.—**axially** *adv*.

axil *n* (*bot*) the angle formed by the upper side of an organ or branch with the stem or trunk to which it is attached.

axile *adj* (*bot*) of, lying or situated in, or attached to, an axis.

axilla *n* (*pl* **axillae, axillas**) the armpit, or cavity in the junction of the arm and shoulder; the axil of a leaf.

axillary *adj* of or pertaining to the armpit; (*bot*) pertaining to, springing from, or situated in, the axil. * *n* (*pl* **axillaries**) a feather from the axilla of a bird.

axiom *n* a widely held or accepted truth or principle.

axiomatic *adj* pertaining to, or of the nature of, an axiom.—**axiomatically** *adv*.

axis[1] *n* (*pl* **axes**) a real or imaginary straight line about which a body rotates; the centre line of a symmetrical figure; a reference line of a coordinate system; (*with cap*) a partnership, alliance, esp of Germany and Italy, 1936 to the end of World War II.—**axial** *adj*.

axis[2] *n* (*pl* **axises**) a small deer of India and Asia with slender antlers.

axle *n* a rod on or with which a wheel turns; a bar connecting two opposite wheels, as of a car.

axletree *n* a bar connecting the opposite wheels of a carriage, on the rounded ends of which the wheels revolve.

axolotl *n* a Mexican amphibian like the salamander, having gills.

ay[1], **aye**[1] *adv* (*arch*) for ever, always; continually.

ayah *n* a native Indian nurse or lady's maid.

ayatollah *n* a Shiite Muslim leader; a title of respect.

aye[2], **ay**[2] *adv, interj* yes; even so; indeed. * *n* (*pl* **ayes**) an affirmative answer or vote in a parliamentary division; the members so voting.

aye-aye *n* a small nocturnal quadruped, native to Madagascar and allied to the lemurs.

AZ *abbr* = Arizona.

azalea *n* a flowering shrub-like plant.

azan *n* the call to public prayers in Islamic countries.

azedarach *n* an Asian tree, the bark or root of which was formerly used as a drug.

Azilian *adj* of a Mesolithic geological stage characterized by bone harpoon heads and painted stone pebbles.

azimuth *n* (*astron*) a vertical arc from the zenith to the horizon; the angular distance of this from the meridian.—**azimuthal** *adj*.

azoic *adj* without life; (*geol*) without fossils, older than the lowermost series of rocks containing traces of organic life.

azote *n* an old name for nitrogen.

AZT *abbr* = azidothymidine, a drug that has been effective in alleviating symptoms in some AIDS sufferers.

Aztec *adj* pertaining to the Aztec race that ruled Mexico before the Spanish conquest. * *n* a member of the Aztec race.

azure *adj* sky-blue.

azurite *n* blue carbonate of copper; blue malachite or chessylite; lazulite.

azygous *adj* (*anat*) single, as a muscle or vein; not one of a pair.

B

B *abbr* = boron.

b *abbr* = born; billion.

BA *abbr* = Bachelor of Arts; British Airways; British Academy.

Ba *abbr* = barium.

baa *n* the bleat of a sheep. * *vi* to bleat as a sheep.

baba *n* a small sponge cake soaked in (usu rum) flavoured syrup.

Babbitt metal *n* an anti-friction alloy of copper, tin and zinc, used in crank and axle bearings, etc.

Babbittry *n* (*derog*) businessman's or middle-class person's standards or blinkered outlook.—**Babbitt** *n*.

babble *vi* to make sounds like a baby; to talk incoherently, endlessly or senselessly; to give away secrets; to murmur, as a brook. * *n* incoherent talk; chatter; a murmuring sound.—**babbler** *n*.

babe *n* a baby; a naive person; (*sl*) a girl or young woman.

Babel *n* (*Bible*) the tower in Shinar (Genesis 11); a lofty structure; a confused and meaningless sound of voices; a scene of confusion and noise.

babirusa, babiruossa, babirussa *n* the wild hog of Eastern Asia.

baboon *n* a large, short-tailed monkey.

babul *n* the rind of the East Indian acacia.

baby *n* (*pl* **babies**) a newborn child or infant; a very young animal; (*sl*) a girl or young woman; a personal project. * *vt* (**babying, babied**) to pamper.—*also adj*.—**babyish** *adj*.

baby boom *n* a sharp rise in the birth rate.

baby-boomer *n* a person born in the period immediately after World War II when the birthrate increased sharply (*baby boom*).

baby break *n* a period, often five years, when a parent raises children before returning to work.

baby burst *n* a sudden fall in birth rate.

baby carriage *n* a perambulator.

baby grand *n* a small grand piano.

Babylonian *adj* of or pertaining to the ancient kingdom of Babylonia; magnificent; luxurious. * *n* an inhabitant of Babylonia; its language.

baby-sit *vti* (**baby-sitting, baby-sat**) to look after a baby or child while the parents are out.—**baby-sitter** *n*.

baby snatcher *n* (*inf*) one who marries or has a liaison with a much younger person; a person who steals a baby.

baby wipe *n* a disposable paper towel, ready moistened.

baccalaureate *n* the university degree awarded to a Bachelor of Arts etc; a commencement address.

baccarat *n* a card game where players bet against the banker.

baccate *adj* having many berries; berry-shaped.

bacchanal *n* a priest of Bacchus, the god of wine; a drunken reveler; a drunken feast.—**bacchanalian** *adj*.

bacchanalia *npl* drunken revels.

bacchant *n* (*pl* **bacchants, bacchantes**) a priest or votary of Bacchus; a drunkard.—**bacchante** *nf* (*pl* **bacchantes**).

Bacchic *adj* pertaining to Bacchus or the feasts in his honour; riotous, or mad with drink.

bacciferous *adj* bearing or producing berries.

bacciform *adj* berry-shaped.

baccivorous *adj* eating or subsisting on berries.

bachelor *n* an unmarried man; a person who holds a degree from a college or university.—**bachelorhood** *n*.

bachelor's buttons *npl* the popular name for a double-flowered buttercup with blossoms resembling buttons.

bacillary, bacillar *adj* of, like, caused by, or consisting of bacilli; rod-shaped.

bacilliform *adj* rod-shaped, like a bacillus.

bacillus *n* (*pl* **bacilli**) any of a genus of rod-shaped bacteria; (*loosely*) bacteria in general.

back[1] *n* the rear surface of the human body from neck to hip; the corresponding part in animals; a part that supports or fits or makes firm the back of anything; the part farthest from the front; (*sport*) a player or position behind the front line. * *adj* at the rear; (*streets, etc*) remote or inferior; (*pay, etc*) of or for the past; backward. * *adv* at or towards the rear; to or towards a former condition, time, etc; in return or requital; in reserve or concealment. * *vti* to move or go backwards; to support; to bet on; to provide or be a back for; to supply a musical backing for a singer; (*with* **down**) to withdraw from a position or claim; (*with* **off**) to move back (or away, etc); (*with* **out**) to withdraw from an enterprise; to evade keeping a promise, etc; (*with* **up**) to support; to move backwards; to accumulate because of restricted movement; (*comput*) to make a copy (of a data file, etc) for safekeeping.

back[2] *n* a large shallow cistern or vat used by brewers, etc, for liquids.

backache *n* an ache or pain in the back.

backbencher *n* in UK, Australia, etc, a member of parliament who does not hold office.

backbite *vt* (**backbiting, backbit,** *pp* **backbitten** *or* **backbit**) to talk spitefully or ill of behind a person's back.—**backbiter** *n*.—**backbiting** *n*.

backboard *n* a board at the back of a cart; a board worn at the back to support the back; a thin wooden backing used for picture frames, mirrors, etc.

backbone *n* the spinal column; main support; strength, courage.

backbreaking *adj* arduous; physically exhausting.

backchat *n* (*inf*) cheeky repartee.

backcomb *vt* (*hair*) to comb towards the roots to give body.

backdate *vt* to declare valid from some previous date.

backdoor *adj* indirect, concealed, devious.

backdown *n* the act of backing down; the withdrawal of a claim, etc.

backdrop *n* a curtain, often scenic, at the back of a stage; background.

back end *n* (*dial*) autumn.

backer *n* a patron; one who bets on a contestant.

backfire *vi* (*cars*) to ignite prematurely causing a loud bang from the exhaust; to have the opposite effect from that intended, usu with unfortunate consequences.—*also n*.

backgammon *n* a board game played by two people with pieces moved according to throws of the dice.

background *n* the distant part of a scene or picture; an inconspicuous position; social class, education, experience; circumstances leading up to an event.

backhand *n* (*tennis, etc*) a stroke played with the hand turned outwards.

backhanded *adj* backhand; (*compliment*) indirect, ambiguous.—*also adv*.—**backhandedly** *adv*.

backhander *n* a backhanded stroke; (*inf*) a backhanded remark; (*sl*) a bribe.

backing *n* support; supporters; a lining to support or strengthen the back of something; musical accompaniment to a (esp pop) singer.

backlash *n* a violent and adverse reaction; a recoil in machinery.

backlist *n* books published in past years that are still in print.

backlog *n* an accumulation of work, etc still to be done.

back number *n* a former issue (of a magazine, etc); an out-of-date person.

backpack *n* a rucksack; an equipment pack carried on the back of an astronaut, etc. * *vi* to travel, hike, etc wearing a backpack.

back pay *n* an increase in wages or salary paid retrospectively.

back-pedal *vi* (**back-pedalling, back-pedalled** *or* **back-pedaling, back-pedaled**) to work the pedals of a bicycle backwards; to modify or withdraw one's original argument or action.

back-seat driver *n* a passenger in a car who irritates the driver with persistent unwanted advice.

backside *n* (*inf*) buttocks.

backslide *vi* (**backsliding, backslid,** *pp* **backslid** *or* **backslidden**) to return to one's (bad) old ways.—**backslider** *n*.

backspace *vi* to move a typewriter carriage or cursor of a word processor back one space.

backspin *n* (*sport*) a backward spin in a ball to slow it down.

backstage *adv* behind the stage of a theatre in areas hidden from the audience; (*inf*) away from public view.—*also adj*.

backstairs *npl* stairs in the back part of a house; stairs for private use. * *adj* indirect; underhand; secret; intriguing.

backstay *n* (*naut*) a long rope extending from the masthead to the side of a ship, supporting the mast.

backstitch *n* an overlapping stitch. * *vt* to sew with this stitch.

backstroke *n* (*swimming*) a stroke using backward circular sweeps of the arms whilst lying face upwards.

backsword *n* a sword with one sharp edge, a broadsword; a stick with a basket handle used in the game of singlestick.

back-to-back *adj* facing in opposite directions, often with the backs touching.

backtrack *vi* to return along the same path; to reverse or recant one's opinion, action, etc.

backup *n* an alternate or auxiliary; support, reinforcement; (*comput*) a copy of a data file, etc.

backward *adj* turned toward the rear or opposite way; shy; slow or retarded. * *adv* backwards.—**backwardness** *n*.

backwards *adv* towards the back; with the back foremost; in a way opposite the usual; into a less good or favourable state or condition; into the past.

backwash *n* water receding from the action of an oar, propeller, etc; the consequences of an event.

backwater *n* a pool of still water fed by a river; a remote, backward place.

backwoods *npl* uncleared forest land; an isolated, thinly populated area.—**backwoodsman** *n* (*pl* **backwoodsmen**).

backyard *n* a yard at the back of a house.

baclava *see* **baklava**.

bacon *n* salted and smoked meat from the back or sides of a pig; **to bring home the bacon** to succeed; to help materially; **to save one's bacon** to have a narrow escape.

bacteria *npl* (*sing* **bacterium**) microscopic unicellular organisms usu causing disease.—**bacterial** *adj*.

bactericide *n* a substance that destroys bacteria.—**bactericidal** *adj*.

bacteriology *n* the scientific study of bacteria.—**bacteriological** *adj*.—**bacteriologist** *n*.

bacteriolysis *n* destruction of bacteria by a serum.—**bacteriolytic** *adj*.

bacterium *see* **bacteria**.

Bactrian camel *n* a camel with two humps.

bad[1] *adj* (**worse, worst**) not good; not as it should be; inadequate or unfit; rotten or spoiled; incorrect or faulty; wicked; immoral; mischievous; harmful; ill; sorry, distressed.—**badness** *n*.

bad[2] *see* **bid**.

bad blood *n* enmity, hostility.

bad debt *n* a debt that is not recoverable.

baddie, baddy *n* (*pl* **baddies**) (*inf*) a villain.

badderlocks *n* a large dark-green edible seaweed.

bade *see* **bid**.

badge *n* an emblem, symbol or distinguishing mark.

badger *n* a hibernating, burrowing black and white mammal related to the weasel. * *vt* to pester or annoy persistently.

badinage *n* light or playful raillery or banter.

badly *adv* (**worse, worst**) poorly; inadequately; unsuccessfully; severely; (*inf*) very much.

badminton *n* a court game for two or four players played with light rackets and a shuttlecock volleyed over a net.

badmouth *vt* (*sl*) to speak ill of; to slander.

baffle *vt* to bewilder or perplex; to frustrate; to make ineffectual. * *n* a plate or device used to restrict the flow of sound, light or fluid.—**bafflement** *n*.—**baffling** *adj*.

bag *n* a usu flexible container of paper, plastic, etc that can be closed at the top; a satchel, suitcase, etc; a handbag; a purse; game taken in hunting; a bag-like shape or part; (*derog*) an old, unpleasant or ugly woman; (*inf: in pl*) plenty (of). * *vti* (**bagging, bagged**) to place in a bag; to kill in hunting; (*inf*) to get; to make a claim on; to hang loosely.

bagasse *n* sugar-cane refuse after crushing, used as a fuel.

bagatelle *n* something of little value; a piece of light music usu for piano; a board game in which balls struck with a cue or by a spring are aimed at holes or pinned spaces.
bagel *n* a ring-shaped bread roll, hard and glazed on the outside, soft in the centre.
bagful *n* (*pl* **bagfuls**) as much as will fill one bag.
baggage *n* suitcases; luggage; **bag and baggage** with one's entire possessions; entirely.
bagging *n* the act of putting into bags; a coarse cloth or other material used for bags; filtration through canvas bags.
baggy *adj* (**baggier, baggiest**) hanging loosely in folds.—**baggily** *adv*.—**bagginess** *n*.
bag lady *n* (*pl* **bag ladies**) a homeless woman who wanders the streets carrying her possessions in shopping bags or carrier bags.
bagman *n* (*pl* **bagmen**) (*formerly*) a travelling salesman who carried his wares in saddlebags; a person who collects or distributes illegally obtained money for another.
bagnio *n* (*pl* **bagnios**) a brothel; a bath house; an oriental prison.
bagpipe *n* (*often pl*) a musical instrument consisting of an air-filled bag fitted with pipes.
bail[1] *n* money lodged as security that a prisoner, if released, will return to court to stand trial; such a release; the person pledging such money. * *vt* to free a person by providing bail; (*with* **out**) to help out of financial or other difficulty; (*government, bank, etc*) to assist a floundering business.—**bailable** *adj*.
bail[2] *vti* (*usu with* **out**) to scoop out (water) from (a boat).
bail[3] *n* (*cricket*) either of two wooden crosspieces that rest on the three stumps; a bar separating horses in an open stable; a metal bar that holds the paper against the roller of a typewriter.
bailee *n* (*law*) the person to whom goods are delivered in trust.
bailey *n* the outer wall of a castle; a castle yard.
Bailey bridge *n* a prefabricated bridge of steel easily and quickly assembled for temporary use.
bailie *n* (*Scot*) a municipal officer corresponding to an alderman.
bailiff *n* in UK, the agent of a landlord or landowner; a sheriff's officer who serves writs and summonses; a minor official in some US courts, usu a messenger or usher.
bailiwick *n* the district within which a bailiff has jurisdiction; a person's special sphere of knowledge or activity or jurisdiction.
bailment *n* (*law*) a delivery of goods in trust to another; the action of becoming surety for one in custody.
bailor *n* (*law*) one who delivers goods in trust.
bail-out *n* assistance by a bank, government, etc, to help (a company) in financial trouble.
bailsman *n* (*pl* **bailsmen**) one who gives bail for another.
bain-marie *n* (*pl* **bains-marie**) a vessel that holds hot water for cooking or warming food.
bairn *n* (*Scot*) a child.
bait *n* food attached to a hook to entice fish or make them bite; any lure or enticement. * *vt* to put food on a hook to lure; to set dogs upon (a badger, etc); to persecute, worry or tease, esp by verbal attacks; to lure, to tempt; to entice.
baize *n* a coarse, green woollen fabric used to cover snooker tables.
bake *vt* (*pottery*) to dry and harden by heating in the sun or by fire; (*food*) to cook by dry heat in an oven. * *vi* to do a baker's work; to dry and harden in heat; (*inf*) to be very hot. * *n* all the food baked at one time or baking; a party or picnic featuring one baked item, eg a *clambake*.
baked beans *npl* cooked haricot beans canned in tomato sauce.
bakehouse *n* a bakery.
Bakelite *n* (*trademark*) a hard synthetic resin used for dishes, etc.
baker *n* a person who bakes and sells bread, cakes, etc.
baker's dozen *n* thirteen.
bakery *n* (*pl* **bakeries**) a room or building for baking; a shop that sells bread, cakes, etc; baked goods.
baking powder *n* a leavening agent containing sodium bicarbonate and an acid-forming substance.
baking soda *n* sodium bicarbonate.
baklava *n* a cake made with thin, flaky pastry, honey and nuts.—*also* **baclava**.
baksheesh *n* a present of money as a bribe or tip to expedite service.
balaclava (helmet) *n* a woollen hood that covers the ears and neck.
balalaika *n* a Russian, three-stringed guitar with a triangular body.
balance *n* a device for weighing, consisting of two dishes or pans hanging from a pivoted horizontal beam; equilibrium; mental stability; the power to influence or control; a remainder.—**in the balance** a state of uncertainty.—**on balance** having considered all aspects or factors. * *vt* to weigh; to compare; to equalize the debit and credit sides of an account. * *vi* to be equal in power or weight, etc; to have the debits and credits equal.—**balanceable** *adj*.—**balancer** *n*.
balance of payments *n* the difference between a country's total receipts from abroad and total payments abroad over a given period.
balancer *n* one who or that which keeps anything in equilibrium; an acrobat; (*pl*) halter.
balance sheet *n* a statement of assets and liabilities.
balance wheel *n* a wheel that regulates the speed of a clock or watch.
balas *n* a variety of spinel ruby of a pale rose-red colour.
balata *n* dried gum from a South American tree, used as a substitute for guttapercha.
balcony *n* (*pl* **balconies**) a projecting platform from an upper storey enclosed by a railing; an upper floor of seats in a theatre, etc, often projecting over the main floor.—**balconied** *adj*.
bald *adj* lacking a natural or usual covering, as of hair, vegetation, or nap; (*tyre*) having little or no tread; (*truth*) plain or blunt; bare, unadorned.—**baldly** *adv*.—**baldness** *n*.
baldachin *n* a canopy, esp over a throne or altar; a rich brocade fabric used for this.
balderdash *n* nonsense.
balding *adj* becoming bald.
baldric *n* a broad belt, often richly ornamented, worn round the waist, or over one shoulder and across the breast.
bale[1] *n* a large bundle of goods, as raw cotton, compressed and bound. * *vt* (*hay etc*) to make into bales. * *vi* (*with* **out**) to parachute from an aircraft, usu in an emergency.
bale[2] *n* a great evil; woe.
baleen *n* whalebone.
baleful *adj* evil; harmful; deadly; ominous.—**balefully** *adv*.—**balefulness** *n*.
balk *see* **baulk**.
ball[1] *n* a spherical or nearly spherical body or mass; a round object for use in tennis, football, etc; a throw or pitch of a ball; a missile for a cannon, rifle, etc; any rounded part or protuberance of the body; (*pl*: *sl*) testicles; nonsense. * *interj* (*pl*) (*sl*) nonsense! * *vti* to form into a ball; (*vulg sl*) to have sexual intercourse with.
ball[2] *n* a formal social dance; (*inf*) a good time.—**ballroom** *n*.—**ballroom dancing** *n*.
ballad *n* a narrative song or poem; a slow, sentimental, esp pop, song.—**balladeer** *n*.—**balladry** *n*.
ballade *n* a poem of (usu) three eight-line stanzas and an envoy, all with the same rhymes and refrain.
balladmonger *n* a dealer in ballads; an inferior poet, a poetaster.
ballast *n* heavy material carried in a ship or vehicle to stabilize it when it is not carrying cargo; crushed rock or gravel, etc used in railway tracks.
ball bearing *n* a device for lessening friction by having a rotating part resting on small steel balls; one of these balls.
ball boy *n* (*tennis*) a boy who retrieves balls that go out of play.—**ball girl** *nf*.
ballcock *n* a device that uses a floating ball to regulate the flow of water in a cistern, tank, etc.
ballerina *n* a female ballet dancer.
ballet *n* a theatrical representation of a story, set to music and performed by dancers; the troupe of dancers.
balletomane *n* an enthusiastic lover of ballet.—**balletomania** *n*.

ballistic *adj* relating to the flight of projectiles.

ballistic missile *n* a missile whose trajectory is initially guided then ballistic.

ballistics *n* (*used as sing*) the scientific study of projectiles and firearms.

ballonet *n* a small balloon; a subdivision of a balloon's or an airship's gasbag for controlling descent.

balloon *n* a large airtight envelope that rises up when filled with hot air or light gases, often fitted with a basket or gondola for carrying passengers; a small inflatable rubber pouch used as a toy or for decoration; a balloon-shaped line enclosing speech or thoughts in a strip cartoon. * *vti* to inflate; to swell, expand; to travel in a balloon.—**balloonist** *n*.

balloon jib, balloon sail *n* (*naut*) a light triangular sail used by yachts in a slight breeze.

ballooning *n* the art or practice of managing balloons or making balloon ascents.

ballot *n* a paper used in voting; the process of voting; the number of votes cast; the candidates offering themselves for election. * *vi* (**balloting, balloted**) to vote.—**balloter** *n*.

ballot box *n* a secure container for ballot papers.

ballpoint pen *n* a pen with a tiny ball, which rotates against an inking cartridge, as its writing tip.

ball valve *n* a valve that is opened or shut by the rising or falling of a ball.

ballyhoo *n* vulgar, noisy publicity or advertisement.

ballyrag *vb* (**ballyragging, ballyragged**) *vt* to hustle, to jeer at. * *vi* to indulge in horseplay.—*also* **bullyrag**.

balm *n* a fragrant ointment used in healing and soothing; anything comforting and soothing.

balm of Gilead *n* any of various fragrant resins, as that of the evergreen terebinth tree of Arabia or the balsam fir; a North American poplar with broad heart-shaped leaves.

balmoral *n* a laced boot; a Scottish bonnet of wool; a petticoat.

balmy *adj* (**balmier, balmiest**) having a pleasant fragrance; soothing; (*weather*) mild, warm.

balneology *n* the science of therapeutic baths and their effect.—**balneological** *adj*.—**balneologist** *n*.

baloney *n* (*inf*) foolish talk; nonsense.—*also* **boloney**.

balsa *n* lightweight wood from a tropical American tree.

balsam *n* a fragrant, resinous substance; the tree yielding it.—**balsamic** *adj*.

balsam fir *n* a North American evergreen pine with flat needles and yielding balsam.

balsamiferous *adj* producing or yielding balsam.

Baltimore oriole *n* an American bird nearly related to the starlings with bright orange and black plumage.

baluster *n* any of the small posts of a railing, as on a staircase.—**balustered** *adj*.

balustrade *n* an ornamental row of balusters joined by a rail.

bambino *n* (*pl* **bambinos, bambini**) a child or baby; (*RC Church*) a figure of the infant Christ wrapped in swaddling clothes, exhibited in churches from Christmas to Epiphany.

bamboo *n* (*pl* **bamboos**) any of various, often tropical, woody grasses, used for furniture.

bamboo shoots *npl* the edible shoots of certain bamboos.

bamboozle *vt* (*inf*) to deceive; to mystify.—**bamboozlement** *n*.—**bamboozler** *n*.

ban[1] *n* a condemnation, an official prohibition. * *vt* (**banning, banned**) to prohibit, esp officially; to forbid.

ban[2] *n* (*feudal*) a public proclamation or summons to arms.

banal *adj* trite, commonplace.—**banally** *adj*.

banality *n* (*pl* **banalities**) anything trite or trivial; a commonplace remark, etc.

banana *n* a herbaceous plant bearing its fruit in compact, hanging bunches.

banana republic *n* (*derog*) a small country, esp in Central America, that is dominated by foreign interests.

banana skin *n* (*inf*) an unforeseen occurrence that causes embarrassment.

banana split *n* ice cream served on a lengthwise sliced banana and topped with syrup, nuts, cream, etc.

banausic *adj* merely mechanical; mean, illiberal.

band[1] *n* a strip of material used for binding; a stripe; (*radio*) a range of wavelengths.

band[2] *n* a group of people with a common purpose; a group of musicians playing together, an orchestra. * *vti* to associate together for a particular purpose.

bandage *n* a strip of cloth for binding wounds and fractures. * *vt* to bind a wound.

bandanna, bandana *n* a large coloured handkerchief.

bandbox *n* a light box of pasteboard, etc, for holding collars or hats.

bandeau *n* (*pl* **bandeaux**) a band for the hair; a fitting band inside a hat.

banderilla *n* a barbed dart, used by a banderillero in bullfights to exasperate the bull.

banderillero *n* (*pl* **banderilleros**) a bullfighter's assistant.

banderole, banderol *n* a long narrow flag with a cleft end; a streamer; a small flag carried at the head of a lance or mast; a scroll or band with an inscription.—*also* **bannerol**.

bandicoot *n* a large rat, native to India and Sri Lanka, very destructive to rice fields and gardens; the name given to rat-like marsupials of several species found in Australia and Tasmania.

bandit *n* (*pl* **bandits, banditti**) a robber.—**banditry** *n*.

bandmaster *n* the conductor of a musical, esp brass, band.

bandoleer, bandolier *n* a belt worn over the chest with pockets for holding ammunition.

bandore, bandora *n* an ancient stringed instrument resembling a zither.—*also* **pandora, pandore**.

band saw *n* a motorized, toothed steel belt used for sawing.

bandsman *n* (*pl* **bandsmen**) a player in a musical, esp brass, band.

bandstand *n* a platform for a musical band.

bandwagon *n* a wagon for carrying a band in a parade; a movement, idea, etc that is (thought to be) heading for success.

bandwidth *n* the range of frequencies within a given waveband for radio or other types of transmission.

bandy[1] *vt* (**bandying, bandied**) to pass to and fro; (*often with* **about**) (*rumours, etc*) to spread freely; to exchange words, esp angrily.

bandy[2] *adj* (**bandier, bandiest**) having legs curved outwards at the knee.

bandy-legged *adj* bandy.

bane *n* a person causing distress or misery; something bringing destruction or death; a poison.—**baneful** *adj*.

baneberry *n* (*pl* **baneberries**) a plant of the buttercup family bearing white or red poisonous berries; its berry.—*also* **herb Christopher, cohosh**.

bang[1] *n* a hard blow; a sudden loud sound. * *vt* to hit or knock with a loud noise; (*door*) to slam. * *vi* to make a loud noise; to hit noisily or sharply. * *adv* with a bang, abruptly; successfully; (*inf*) precisely.

bang[2] *n* (*pl*) hair cut straight across the forehead to form a fringe; false hair so worn. * *vt* to cut the hair across the forehead to form a fringe.

bang[3] *see* **bhang**.

banger *n* an exploding firework; (*sl*) a sausage; (*sl*) an old car.

bangle *n* a bracelet worn on the arm or ankle.

banian *see* **banyan**.

banish *vt* to exile from a place; to drive away; to get rid of.—**banishment** *n*.

banister *n* the railing or supporting balusters in a staircase.—*also* **bannister**.

banjo *n* (*pl* **banjos, banjoes**) a stringed musical instrument with a drum-like body and a long fretted neck.—**banjoist** *n*.

bank[1] *n* a mound or pile; the sloping side of a river; elevated ground in a lake or the sea; a row or series of objects, as of dials, switches. * *vti* to form into a mound; to cover (a fire) with fuel so that it burns more slowly; (*aircraft*) to curve or tilt sideways.

bank[2] *n* an institution that offers various financial services, such as the safekeeping, lending and exchanging of money; the money held by the banker or dealer in a card game; any supply or store for the future, such as a *blood bank*. * *vti* (*cheques, cash, etc*) to deposit in a bank; to work as a banker.

bank account *n* money deposited in a bank and credited to the depositor.
bank bill *n* a note or a bill of exchange of a bank payable on demand or at a future specified time.
bankbook *n* a book in which a record is kept of deposits and withdrawals of money into a personal account.
bank discount *n* a deduction made according to the current rate of interest.
banker *n* a person who runs a bank; the keeper of the bank at a gaming table.
banker's card *see* **cheque card**.
bank holiday *n* in UK, a weekday when banks are officially closed; a day observed as a public holiday.
banking *n* the activity or occupation of running a bank. * *adj* of or concerning a bank.
banknote *n* a promissory note issued by a bank, which serves as money.
bank rate *n* the rate at which a central bank will discount bills.
bankrupt *n* a person, etc legally declared unable to pay his debts; one who becomes insolvent. * *adj* judged to be insolvent; financially ruined; devoid of resources, ideas, etc. * *vt* to make bankrupt.—**bankruptcy** *n*.
banksia *n* any of an Australian genus of flowering shrubs with evergreen leaves.
banner *n* a flag or ensign; a headline running across a newspaper page; a strip of cloth bearing a slogan or emblem carried between poles in a parade.
banneret *n* (*hist*) an order of knighthood conferred on the field of battle for distinguished service or a deed of valour; the person on whom the degree was conferred and who ranked between a baron and a knight.
bannerette *n* a little banner or flag.
bannerol *see* **banderole**.
bannister *see* **banister**.
bannock *n* a thick flat cake made of oatmeal or barley and baked on a griddle.
banns *npl* public declaration of intention, esp in church, to marry.
banquet *n* a feast; an elaborate and sometimes formal dinner in honour of a person or occasion. * *vt* (**banqueting, banqueted**) to hold a banquet.—**banqueter** *n*.
banquette *n* a cushioned bench; a step along the inside of a parapet on which soldiers stood to fire upon the enemy; the footway of a bridge when raised above the carriageway.
banshee *n* (*folklore*) a female fairy whose wail portends a death in the family.
bantam *n* a dwarf breed of domestic fowl; a small, aggressive person; (*boxing*) a bantamweight.
bantamweight *n* a boxing weight (112–118 lbs; 51–53.5 kg) between featherweight and flyweight.
banter *vt* to tease good-humouredly.—**banterer** *n*.
Bantu *n* (*pl* **Bantu, Bantus**) one of a group of Southern African peoples or their language.
banyan *n* an Indian fig tree with vast, rooting branches.—*also* **banian**.
banzai *interj* a Japanese greeting or salute.
baobab *n* an African tree with an enormously thick trunk.
bap *n* a large soft bread roll.
baptism *n* the sprinkling of water on the forehead, or complete immersion in water, as a rite of admitting a person to a Christian church; any initiating experience.—**baptismal** *adj*.—**baptismally** *adv*.
Baptist *n* a member of a Protestant Christian denomination holding that the true church is of believers only, who are all equal, that the only authority is the Bible, and that adult baptism by immersion is necessary.
baptistry, baptistery *n* (*pl* **baptistries, baptisteries**) the part of a church where baptism takes place.
baptize *vt* to christen, to name.—**baptizer** *n*.
bar[1] *n* a straight length of wood or metal; a counter where alcoholic drinks or other refreshments are served; a place with such a counter; an oblong piece, as of soap; anything that obstructs or hinders; a band or strip; a strip or bank of sand or mud near and in line with the shore or across a river or harbour; (*mil*) a badge signifying a second award; (*with cap*) barristers or lawyers collectively; the legal profession; (*mus*) a vertical line dividing a staff into measures; (*mus*) a measure. * *vt* (**barring, barred**) to secure or fasten as with a bar; to exclude or prevent; to oppose. * *prep* except for.
bar[2] *n* a unit of atmospheric pressure.
barathea *n* a type of fine woollen material.
barb *n* the sharp backward point of a fish-hook, etc; one of the sharp parts combined to form barbed wire; a pointed or critical remark; a beard-like growth. * *vt* to provide with a barb.—**barbed** *adj*.
barbarian *n* an uncivilized, primitive person; a cruel vicious person.—*also adj*.
barbaric *adj* of or suitable for barbarians.—**barbarically** *adv*.
barbarism *n* a barbarous act; the state of being a barbarian; an expression or word that is tasteless or not standard; an object or act that offends.
barbarity *n* (*pl* **barbarities**) savage cruelty; a vicious act.
barbarize *vti* to make or become barbarous.
barbarous *adj* uncivilized, cruel, coarse.—**barbarously** *adv*.
Barbary ape *n* a tailless macaque monkey of North Africa and Gibraltar.
barbate *adj* tufted, bearded.
barbecue *n* a metal frame for grilling food over an open fire; an open-air party where barbecued food is served. * *vt* (**barbecuing, barbecued**) to cook on a barbecue.
barbed wire *n* wire with barbs at close intervals.—*also* **barbwire**.
barbel *n* a freshwater fish with beard-like filaments at its mouth; such a filament.—**barbelled** *adj*.
barbell *n* a metal rod with weights at each end, used in weightlifting.
barber *n* a person who cuts hair and shaves beards.
barberry *n* (*pl* **barberries**) a thorny shrub with yellow flowers; its red berry.
barbershop *n* the business premises of a barber.
barbet *n* a tropical bird with tufts of feathers at the base of the bill.
barbette *n* a raised platform for guns to fire over a parapet; a type of armoured turret in a warship.
barbican *n* a defensive tower over the gate or drawbridge of a castle or fortification.
barbitone, barbital *n* a habit-forming, toxic, hypnotic and sedative drug.
barbiturate *n* a sedative drug.
barbule *n* a minute barb; a filament fringing the barb of a feather.
barbwire *see* **barbed wire**.
barcarole, barcarolle *n* a Venetian gondolier's song; an instrumental piece resembling this.
bar code *n* a striped pattern on a package, book cover, etc, containing information about the price that can be read by a computer for stock control, etc.
bard *n* a poet.—**bardic** *adj*.
bare *adj* without covering; unclothed, naked; simple, unadorned; mere; without furnishings. * *vt* to uncover; to reveal.—**bareness** *n*.
bareback *adj* on a horse with no saddle.—*also adv*.
barefaced *adj* with the face shaven or uncovered; shameless.—**barefacedly** *adv*.
barefoot, barefooted *adj* with the feet bare.—*also adv*.
barège, barege *n* a thin gauze-like fabric, usu of silk and worsted.
barehanded *adj* without using weapons.
barely *adv* openly; merely, scarcely.
bargain *n* an agreement laying down the conditions of a transaction; something sold at a price favourable to the buyer; **into the bargain** as well; in addition. * *vt* to make a bargain, to haggle; (*with* **for**) to expect or hope for.
barge *n* a flat-bottomed vessel, used to transport freight along rivers and canals; a large boat for excursions or pleasure trips. * *vi* to lurch clumsily; (*with* **in**) to interrupt (a conversation) rudely; (*with* **into**) to enter abruptly.
bargeboard *n* a board placed at a gable to conceal the roof timbers.
barge couple *n* one of two beams bounding a gable, mortised and tenoned together and used for strengthening a building.

barge course *n* the tiling that projects beyond the principal rafters in a building; a wall coping constructed of bricks set on edge.
bargee *n* the owner of or one employed on a barge; a bargeman.
barilla *n* an alkali made from kinds of marine plant or seaweed.
barite *see* **barytes.**
baritone *n* the adult male voice ranging between bass and tenor; a singer with such a voice.—*also adj.*
barium *n* (*chem*) a white metallic element.
barium sulphate *n* a white insoluble fine heavy powder which is opaque to X-rays, swallowed by a patient before X-ray of the alimentary canal.
bark[1] *n* the harsh or abrupt cry of a dog, wolf, etc; a similar sound, such as one made by a person. * *vi* to make a loud cry like a dog; to speak or shout sharply or angrily.
bark[2] *n* the outside covering of a tree trunk. * *vt* to remove the bark from; to scrape; to skin (the knees, etc).
bark[3] *see* **barque.**
barkentine *see* **barquentine.**
barker *n* one who or that which barks; a person who shouts his wares, etc, usu at a fairground.
barking *n* the process of stripping bark from trees; the process of tanning leather or dyeing with bark.
barley *n* a grain used in making beer and whisky, and for food.
barleycorn *n* a grain of barley; (*formerly*) a measure of length, one-third of an inch (0.85 cm).
barley sugar *n* a transparent amber-coloured sweet.
barm *n* the froth on fermenting liquor used as leaven in breadmaking, yeast.
barmaid *n* a female serving alcohol in a bar.
barman *n* (*pl* **barmen**) a man serving alcohol in a bar.
Barmecide, Barmedcidal *adj* like the Barmecide's feast in *The Arabian Nights*; imaginarily satisfying; unreal, illusory.
bar mitzvah *n* (*Judaism*) the ceremony marking the thirteenth birthday of a boy, who then assumes full religious obligations; the boy himself.
barn *n* a farm building used for storing grain, hay, etc, and sheltering animals.
barnacle *n* a marine crustacean that attaches itself to rocks and ship bottoms.
barnacle goose *n* a wild European grey-winged goose that breeds in the Arctic.
barn dance *n* a social dance featuring several dance forms (as square dancing).
barn owl *n* any of a genus of owl with brownish plumage above and white plumage below.
barnstorm *vi* to tour (rural areas) as an actor, or making speeches in a political campaign, or demonstrating flying stunts.—**barnstormer** *n.*
barograph *n* a self-recording aneroid barometer.—**barographic** *adj.*
barogram *n* the record traced by a barograph.
barometer *n* an instrument for measuring atmospheric pressure and imminent changes in the weather; anything that marks change.—**barometric** *adj.*—**barometrically** *adv.*
baron *n* a member of a rank of nobility, the lowest in the British peerage; a powerful businessman.—**baroness** *nf.*
baronage *n* the whole body of barons; the dignity or rank of a baron.
baronet *n* the lowest hereditary title of honour in Britain.
baronetage *n* the collective body of baronets; the dignity or rank of a baronet.
baronetcy *n* (*pl* **baronetcies**) the dignity or rank of a baronet.
baronial *adj* pertaining to or suitable for a baron.
barony *n* (*pl* **baronies**) the rank or lands of a baron; (*Scot*) a large manor; (*Ir*) a division of a county.
baroque *adj* extravagantly ornamented, esp in architecture and decorative art.
baroscope *n* an instrument for indicating variations in the pressure of the atmosphere without actual measurement of its weight.—**baroscopic** *adj.*
barouche *n* a 19th-century roomy four-wheeled carriage for four with a folding top.
barque *n* (*poet*) a ship; a three-masted vessel with the foremast and main mast square-rigged and the mizzen fore-and-aft.—*also* **bark.**
barquentine, barquantine *n* a three-masted vessel with the foremast square-rigged and the main mast and mizzenmast fore-and-aft or schooner-rigged.—*also* **barkentine.**
barrack *vti* to shout or protest at.—**barracker** *n.*
barracks *n* (*used as sing*) a building for housing soldiers.
barracuda *n* (*pl* **barracuda, barracudas**) a fierce fish with edible flesh.
barrage *n* a man-made dam across a river; heavy artillery fire; (*of protests, questions, etc*) continuous and heavy delivery.
barrage balloon *n* a large balloon anchored to the ground and trailing cables or nets, used as a defence against low-flying enemy aircraft.
barranca, barranco *n* (*pl* **barrancas, barrancos**) a deep mountain gully or ravine.
barratry *n* the defrauding or injury of a ship's owner, freighter or insurer by the master or crew; the practice of inciting and encouraging lawsuits or litigation.—**barrator** *n.*—**barratrous** *adj.*
barre *n* a horizontal rail used for ballet practice.
barred *see* **bar**[1].
barrel *n* a cylindrical container, usu wooden, with bulging sides held together with hoops; the amount held by a barrel; a tubular structure, as in a gun. * *vt* (**barrelling, barrelled** *or* **barreling, barreled**) to put into barrels.
barrel organ *n* a mechanical piano or organ played by a revolving cylinder with pins that operate the keys or valves to produce sound.
barren *adj* infertile; incapable of producing offspring; unable to bear crops; unprofitable; (*with* **of**) lacking in.
barricade *n* a barrier or blockade used in defence to block a street; an obstruction. * *vt* to block with a barricade.
barrier *n* anything that bars passage, prevents access, controls crowds, etc, such as a fence; obstruction; hindrance.
barrier reef *n* an exposed coral reef separated from the shore by a navigable channel.
barring *prep* excepting; leaving out of account.
barrister *n* a qualified lawyer who has been called to the bar in England.
barrow[1] *n* a wheelbarrow or hand-cart used for carrying loads.
barrow[2] *n* a prehistoric burial mound.
Barsac *n* a French white wine.
bar sinister *n* (*her*) in error for **bend sinister**, the badge of illegitimacy.
Bart *abbr* = baronet.
barter *vt* to trade commodities or services without exchanging money. * *vi* to haggle or bargain. * *n* trade by the exchanging of commodities.—**barterer** *n.*
bartizan *n* an overhanging turret at the top of a tower or wall.
barytes *n* a white crystalline mineral of great weight, consisting mainly of barium sulphate.—*also* **barite, heavy spar.**
baryon *n* an elementary particle (nucleon or hyperon) with a mass greater than or equal to that of the proton.
basal *adj* pertaining to, at or forming the base; fundamental. * *n* a basal part.—**basally** *adv.*
basalt *n* hard, compact, dark-coloured igneous rock.—**basaltic** *adj.*
bascule *n* a mechanical arrangement on the seesaw principle by which the lowering of one end raises the other; a kind of drawbridge so operated.
base[1] *n* the bottom part of anything; the support or foundation; the fundamental principle; the centre of operations (eg military); (*baseball*) one of the four corners of the diamond. * *vt* to use as a basis; to found (on); (*with* **at, in**) to place, to station.—**basal** *adj.*
base[2] *adj* low in morality or honour; worthless; menial.—**basely** *adv.*—**baseness** *n.*
baseball *n* the US national game, involving two teams that score runs by hitting a ball and running round four bases arranged in a diamond shape on the playing area.
baseborn *adj* (*arch*) of low or mean birth; illegitimate; mean.
baseless *adj* without a base; unfounded.
baseline *n* the line at each end of a games court marking the limit of play;

(*baseball*) the line between any two consecutive bases; a measured line in a survey area from which triangulations are calculated.

baseman *n* (*pl* **basemen**) (*baseball*) a fielder placed at the first, second, and third bases respectively.

basement *n* the part of a building that is partly or wholly below ground level.

base metal *n* any metal other than the precious metals.

bash *vt* (*inf*) to hit hard; to dent by striking. * *n* (*inf*) a heavy blow; (*inf*) a try or attempt; (*sl*) a party.

bashful *adj* easily embarrassed, shy.—**bashfully** *adv*.—**bashfulness** *n*.

bashibazouk *n* a volunteer or irregular in the Turkish army.

BASIC *n* (*comput*) a simple programming language: *B*eginners' *A*ll-purpose *S*ymbolic *I*nstruction *C*ode.

basic *adj* fundamental; simple. * *n* (*often pl*) a basic principle, factor, etc; the rudiments.—**basically** *adv*.

basicity *n* the state of being a base; (*chem*) the power of an acid to unite with one or more atoms of a base.

basic slag *n* the phosphates of lime and oxidized impurities left as a brittle powder in steelmaking and used as a fertilizer.

basidium *n* (*pl* **basidia**) the cell to which the spores of certain fungi are attached.—**basidial** *adj*.

basify *vt* (**basifying, basified**) to convert into a base, make basic.

basil *n* a plant with aromatic leaves used for seasoning food.

basilar, basilary *adj* (*anat*) pertaining to or situated at the base, esp of the skull.

basilica *n* a church with a broad nave, side aisles, and an apse; (*RC Church*) a church with special ceremonial rites.—**basilican** *adj*.

basilisk *n* a fabulous creature dealing death by its gaze, sometimes identified with the cockatrice; a lizard with an inflatable crest. * *adj* pertaining to the basilisk; penetrating or malignant.

basin *n* a wide shallow container for liquid; its contents; any large hollow, often with water in it; a tract of land drained by a river.

basinet *n* a light steel helmet of medieval times, often with a visor.

basis *n* (*pl* **bases**) a base or foundation; a principal constituent; a fundamental principle or theory.

bask *vi* to lie in sunshine or warmth; to enjoy someone's approval.

basket *n* a container made of interwoven cane, wood strips, etc; the hoop through which basketball players throw the ball to score.

basketball *n* a game in which two teams compete to score by throwing the ball through an elevated net basket or hoop; this ball.

basket hilt *n* the hilt of a sword shaped like a basket.

basking shark *n* a large shark of northern seas, which is harmless and has the habit of basking at the surface in the sun.

basque *n* a woman's jacket with a short skirt.

Basque *n* one of a people inhabiting the western Pyrenees; their language.

bas-relief *n* a low relief; a form of relief in which the figures stand out very slightly from the ground.—*also* **basso-rilievo**.

bass[1] *n* (*mus*) the range of the lowest male voice; a singer or instrument with this range. * *adj* of, for or in the range of a bass.

bass[2] *n* (*pl* **bass**) any of numerous freshwater food and game fishes.

bass clef *n* (*mus*) the character C placed at the beginning of the bass staff.

basset[1], **basset hound** *n* a smooth-haired hound with short legs.

basset[2] *vi* (**basseting, basseted**) (*geol*) to crop out at the surface. * *n* an outcrop.

basset horn *n* a tenor clarinet.

bassinet *n* a wickerwork or wooden cradle with a hood; a pram.

bassist *n* a player of the double bass.

basso *n* (*pl* **bassos, bassi**) one who sings bass.

bassoon *n* an orchestral, deep-toned woodwind instrument.—**bassoonist** *n*.

basso profundo *n* (*pl* **basso profundos**) the lowest bass voice; a singer with such a voice.

basso-rilievo *n* (*pl* **basso-rilievos**) a bas-relief.

bass viol *n* a large stringed instrument of the violin class for playing bass, the violoncello.

bast *n* the tough inner fibrous bark of various trees, especially of the lime; rope or matting made from this bark.

basta *interj* enough!

bastard *n* a person born of unmarried parents; (*offensive*) an unpleasant person; (*inf*) a person (*lucky bastard*); (*inf*) a difficult task, situation, etc. * *adj* illegitimate (by birth); false; not genuine.—**bastardy** *n*.

bastardize *vt* to declare illegitimate; to falsify or corrupt.—**bastardization** *n*.

baste[1] *vt* to drip fat over (roasting meat, etc).

baste[2] *vt* to sew with long loose stitches as a temporary seam.

bastinado *n* (*pl* **bastinadoes**) a caning of the soles of the feet as a form of torture. * *vt*. (**bastinadoing, bastinadoed**) to torture in this way.

bastion *n* a tower at the corner of a fortification; any strong defence; one who strongly upholds or supports a principle, etc.—**bastioned** *adj*.

basuco *n* the dregs of cocaine after refining, which are packaged and sold in Colombia.

bat[1] *n* a wooden club used in cricket, baseball, etc; a batsman; a paddle used in table tennis. * *vb* (**batting, batted**) *vt* to hit as with a bat. * *vi* to take one's turn at bat.

bat[2] *n* a nocturnal, mouse-like flying mammal with forelimbs modified to form wings.

bat[3] *vt* (**batting, batted**) (*one's eyelids*) to wink or flutter.

batch *n* the quantity of bread, etc produced at one time; one set, group, etc; an amount of work for processing by a computer in a single run.

bate *vt* to lessen or reduce; to deduct.

bateau *n* (*pl* **bateaux**) a light boat used esp on Canadian rivers.

bath *n* water for washing the body; a bathing; a bathtub; (*pl*) a building with baths for public use; a municipal swimming pool. * *vti* to give a bath to; to bathe.

bath chair *n* a wheeled chair for invalids.

bathe *vt* to dampen with any liquid. * *vi* to have a bath; to go swimming; to become immersed.—**bather** *n*.

bathometer *n* an apparatus for measuring depths.

bathos *n* anticlimax; descent from the elevated to the ordinary in speech or writing.

bathrobe *n* a loose-fitting garment of absorbent fabric for use after bathing or as a dressing gown.

bathroom *n* a room with a bath or shower and usually a lavatory and washbasin.—*also* **lavatory**.

bathtub *n* a usu fixed tub for bathing.

bathymetry *n* the art or science of sounding or of measuring sea depths.—**bathymetric** *adj*.—**bathymetrically** *adv*.

bathyscaphe *n* a submersible vessel for deep-sea observation and exploration.

bathysphere *n* a hollow steel sphere for descending to great depths in the sea.

batik *n* a method of printing coloured designs on fabric; fabric produced by this method.

batiste *n* a kind of cambric; a fabric like cambric.

batman *n* (*pl* **batmen**) (*mil*) in UK, an officer's servant.

baton *n* a staff serving as a symbol of office; a thin stick used by the conductor of an orchestra to beat time; a hollow cylinder carried by each member of a relay team in succession; a policeman's truncheon.

batrachian *n* one of the amphibians, which includes frogs and toads. * *adj* of or pertaining to frogs or toads.

batsman *n* (*pl* **batsmen**) (*cricket, baseball*) the player whose turn it is to bat.

battalion *n* an army unit consisting of three or more companies; a large group.

batten[1] *n* a strip of wood or metal; a strip of wood put over a seam between boards. * *vt* to fasten or supply with battens.

batten[2] *vt* to make fat by rich living; to fertilize or enrich. * *vi* to grow or become fat; to thrive at the expense of others.

batter *vt* to beat with repeated blows; to wear out with heavy use; to criticize strongly and at length. * *vi* to strike heavily and repeatedly. * *n* a mixture of flour, egg, and milk or water used in cooking.—**batterer** *n*.

battering ram *n* (*hist*) a military machine for breaching the walls of besieged places, consisting of a large beam with an iron head resembling the head of a ram.

battery *n* (*pl* **batteries**) a set of heavy guns; a small unit of artillery; an electric cell that supplies current; an unlawful beating; an arrangement of hens' cages designed to increase egg laying.

battle *n* a combat or fight between two opposing individuals or armies; a contest; any struggle towards a goal. * *vti* to fight; to struggle.—**battler** *n*.

battle-axe, battle-ax *n* (*pl* **battle-axes**) an old-fashioned two-headed axe; (*inf*) a domineering woman.

battle cruiser *n* a heavy-gunned ship with higher speed and lighter armour than a battleship.

battle cry *n* a war cry; a slogan used to rally supporters of a political campaign, etc.

battledore *n* a wooden bat used in washing, baking, etc; a bat used in **battledore and shuttlecock**, a forerunner of badminton.

battlefield *n* the land on which a battle is fought.

battlement *n* a parapet or wall with indentations, from which to shoot.

battle royal *n* (*pl* **battles royal**) a fight with many combatants; a general engagement; a melee.

battleship *n* a large, heavily armoured warship.

battue *n* (*hunting*) the driving up of game by beaters towards the guns; wholesale slaughter.

batty *adj* (**battier, battiest**) (*inf*) crazy; eccentric.—**battiness** *n*.

bauble *n* a showy toy; a shining ball hung on a Christmas tree as a decoration; a worthless trifle or ornament.

baud *n* (*comput*) a unit used in measuring the speed of electronic data transmissions.

baulk *vt* to obstruct or foil. * *vi* to stop and refuse to move and act.—*also* **balk**.

bauxite *n* aluminium ore.

bawd *n* a woman who runs a brothel; a prostitute.

bawdy *adj* (**bawdier, bawdiest**) humorously indecent; obscene, lewd.—**bawdily** *adv*.—**bawdiness** *n*.

bawl *vti* to shout; to weep loudly. * *n* a loud shout; a noisy weeping.—**bawler** *n*.—**bawling** *n*.

bay[1] *n* a type of laurel tree.

bay[2] *n* a wide inlet of a sea or lake; an inward bend of a shore.

bay[3] *n* an alcove or recess in a wall; a compartment used for a special purpose.

bay[4] *vti* to bark (at). * *n* the cry of a hound or a pursuing pack.—**at bay** the position of one forced to turn and fight.

bay[5] *adj* reddish brown. * *n* a horse of this colour.

bayberry *n* (*pl* **bayberries**) any of various shrubs, esp the wax myrtle of North America; the grey waxy berry of the wax myrtle; a West Indian tree with fragrant leaves used in bay rum.

bay leaf *n* the leaf of the laurel dried and used as a flavouring for food.

bayonet *n* a blade for stabbing attached to the muzzle of a rifle. * *vt* (**bayoneting, bayoneted** *or* **bayonetting, bayonetted**) to kill or stab with a bayonet.

bayou *n* in the southern US, the marshy inlet or outlet of a lake or river.

bay rum *n* a perfumed cosmetic obtained from the leaves of the bayberry.

bay window *n* a window projecting from the outside wall of a house.

bazaar *n* a marketplace; a street full of small shops; a benefit sale for a church, etc.

bazooka *n* a portable anti-tank weapon that fires rockets from a long tube.

B and B *abbr* = bed and breakfast.

BBC *abbr* = British Broadcasting Corporation.

BC *abbr* = Before Christ; British Columbia.

BD *abbr* = Bachelor of Divinity.

bdellium *n* a fragrant gum used medicinally and as a perfume; the African and Asian tree yielding it.

be- *prefix* all over, thoroughly, as in *bespatter*; to make, as in *bedim*; to call, as in *bedevil*; to form a transitive verb from an intrasitive, as *bewail*.

Be (*chem symbol*) beryllium.

be *vi* (*pr t* **am, are, is,** *pt* **was, were,** *pp* **been**) to exist; to live; to take place.

beach *n* a flat, sandy shore of the sea. * *vi* to bring (a boat) up on the beach from the sea.

beachcomber *n* a person who hangs about the shore on the lookout for wreckage or plunder; a long curling wave rolling in from the ocean.—**beachcombing** *n*.

beachhead *n* an area of seashore captured from the enemy by an advance force in preparation for a full-scale landing of troops and equipment.

beach music *n* a style of pop music originating on the coast of South Carolina, based on soul music and rhythm and blues.

beacon *n* a light, esp on a high place, tower, etc, for warning or guiding. * *vi* to guide, to act as a beacon.

bead *n* a small ball pierced for stringing; (*pl*) a string of beads; (*pl*) a rosary; a bubble or droplet of liquid; the sight of a rifle.—**beaded** *adj*.

beading *n* moulding or edging in the form of a series of beads; a wooden strip, rounded on one side, used for trimming.—*also* **beadwork**.

beadle *n* an officer of a parish or church; a mace-bearer; (*formerly*) an officer in a law court.

beady *adj* (**beadier, beadiest**) (*eyes*) small, round and bright, sometimes calculating or unfriendly.—**beadily** *adv*.—**beadiness** *n*.

beagle *n* a small hound with short legs and drooping ears.

beak *n* a bird's bill; any projecting part; the nose.—**beaked** *adj*.

beaker *n* a large drinking cup, or the amount it holds; a cylindrical vessel with a pouring lip used by chemists and pharmacists.

beam *n* a long straight piece of timber or metal; the crossbar of a balance; a ship's breadth at its widest point; a slender shaft of light, etc; a radiant look, smile, etc; a steady radio or radar signal for guiding aircraft or ships. * *vt* (*light, etc*) to send out; to smile with great pleasure.

beamy *adj* (**beamier, beamiest**) emitting rays of light; resembling a beam in size and weight; (*ship*) broad; (*inf*) having broad hips.

bean *n* a plant bearing kidney-shaped seeds; a seed or pod of such a plant; any bean-like seed.

bean bag *n* a small cloth bag filled with dried beans and used in games; a larger cloth bag filled with plastic granules and used for sitting on.

bean curd *n* soft cheese made from soya milk.—*also* **tofu**.

beanfeast *n* (*inf*) an annual dinner given by an employer for his employees; (*inf*) any festive meal.

bean sprout *n* the shoot of the mung bean used in Chinese cooking.

bear[1] *vb* (**bearing, bore,** *pp* **borne**) *vt* to carry; to endure; to support, to sustain; to conduct (oneself); to produce or bring forth; (*with* **out**) to show to be true, confirm. * *vi* to be productive; (*with* **down**) to press or weigh down; to overwhelm; (*with* **on** *or* **upon**) to have reference to, be relevant to; (*with* **out**) to confirm the truth of; (*with* **up**) to endure with courage; (*with* **with**) to listen to patiently.

bear[2] *n* (*pl* **bears, bear**) a large mammal with coarse black, brown or white fur, short legs, strong claws and feeding mainly on fruit and insects; a gruff or ill-mannered person; a teddy bear; a speculator who sells stock in anticipation of a fall in price so that he may buy them back at a lower price.

bearable *adj* endurable.—**bearably** *adv*.

bear baiting *n* the former sport of setting dogs to attack captive bears.

beard *n* hair covering a man's chin; similar bristles on an animal or plant. * *vt* to defy, oppose openly.—**bearded** *adj*.

beardless *adj* without a beard; youthful.

bearer *n* a person who bears or presents; a person who carries something (a coffin, etc).

bear garden *n* (*formerly*) a place where bears were kept for sport; any scene or place of tumult or disorder.

bear hug *n* (*wrestling*) a hold in which the opponent's arms and chest are pinned in a tight embrace; any tight embrace.

bearing *n* demeanour; conduct; a compass direction; (*with* **on, upon**) relevance; a machine part on which another part slides, revolves, etc; (*usu pl*) one's position, orientation.

bearing rein *n* a short fixed rein for holding up the head of a horse.—*also* **checkrein**.

bearish *adj* resembling a bear in qualities; rude, surly.—**bearishly** *adv*.—**bearishness** *n*.
bear's breech *n* one of two tall plants of the acanthus genus with purple-tinged white flowers.
bear's ear *see* **auricula**.
bearskin *n* the skin of a bear used as a garment, rug, etc; a tall furry cap worn by a guardsman in the British army.
beast *n* a large, wild, four-footed animal; a brutal, vicious person; (*inf*) something difficult, an annoyance.
beastings *see* **beestings**.
beastly *adj* (**beastlier, beastliest**) (*inf*) disagreeable. * *adv* (*inf*) very (*beastly cold*).
beat *vb* (**beating, beaten,** *pp* **beat**) *vt* to strike, dash or pound repeatedly; to flog; to overcome or counteract; to win against, to arrive first; to find too difficult for; (*mus*) to mark (time) with a baton, etc; (*eggs, etc*) to mix by stirring vigorously; (*esp wings*) to move up and down; (*a path, way, etc*) to form by repeated trampling; (*sl*) to baffle; (*with* **up**) (*inf*) to cause grievous bodily harm to by severe and repeated blows and kicks. * *vi* to hit, pound, etc repeatedly; to throb; (*naut*) to sail against the wind. * *n* a recurrent stroke, pulsation, as in a heartbeat or clock ticking; rhythm in music or poetry; the area patrolled by a police officer.—**beatable** *adj*.
beaten *adj* defeated; (*metal*) shaped or formed by pounding; (*a path*) formed by constant trampling.
beater *n* an implement for beating, such as an attachment for an electric food mixer; one who rouses game birds from cover.
beatific *adj* showing great happiness; making blessed.—**beatifically** *adv*.
beatify *vt* (**beatifying, beatified**) (*RC Church*) to declare that one who has died is among the blessed in heaven; to make blissfully happy.—**beatification** *n*.
beating *n* the act of striking or thrashing; throbbing or pulsation; a defeat.
beatitude *n* blessedness; heavenly happiness; (*with cap*) (*Bible*) one of Christ's eight sayings in the Sermon on the Mount (Matthew 5).
beau *n* (*pl* **beaus, beaux**) a woman's suitor or sweetheart.
Beaufort scale *n* an international system of indicating wind strength, from 0 (calm) to 12 (hurricane).
beau geste *n* (*pl* **beaux gestes**) a fine gesture; a gesture that appears noble but is meaningless.
beau ideal *n* (*pl* **beaux ideals**) ideal excellence, a standard of perfection.
beaujolais *n* (*often with cap*) a popular fruity red or white wine from Burgundy in France.
beau monde *n* the fashionable world.
beaut *adj* (*sl*) good. * *n* (*sl*) beauty.
beauteous *adj* (*poet*) beautiful.
beautician *n* one who works in a beauty salon offering cosmetic treatments.
beautiful *adj* having beauty; very enjoyable.—**beautifully** *adv*.
beautify *vti* (**beautifying, beautified**) to make or become beautiful.—**beautification** *n*.
beauty *n* (*pl* **beauties**) the combination of qualities in a person or object that cause delight or pleasure; a very attractive woman or girl; good looks; a very fine specimen.
beauty salon, beauty parlour, beauty shop *n* an establishment that offers cosmetic beauty treatments.
beauty sleep *n* sleep taken before midnight, supposed to be more restorative than that taken later.
beauty spot *n* a scenic location; a small birthmark or artificial patch on the cheek, regarded as a mark of beauty.
beaver[1] *n* a large semi-aquatic dam-building rodent; its fur; a hat made from beaver fur. * *vi* (*often with* **away**) to work hard (at).
beaver[2] *n* the lower or moveable part of a helmet's face guard.
bebop *see* **bop**.
becalm *vt* to make calm; to make (a ship) motionless from lack of wind.—**becalmed** *adj*.
became *see* **become**.
because *conj* since; for the reason that.
because of *prep* by reason of.
beccafico *n* (*pl beccaficos*) a small bird of the warbler family, eaten as a delicacy in Italy.
béchamel sauce *n* a thick, rich white sauce.
bêche-de-mer *n* (*pl* **bêches-de-mer**) the trepang, a sea slug dried and eaten as a food in China; a form of pidgin English used in the islands of the Pacific (—*also* **beach-la-mar**).
beck[1] *n* a wave or nod with the finger or head.
beck[2] *n* a brook, a mountain stream.
becket *n* (*naut*) a rope loop, a hook, or a bracket for securing sails, tackle, etc.
beckon *vti* to summon by a gesture.—**beckoner** *n*.—**beckoning** *adj*.
becloud *vt* to obscure by clouds, to dim.
become *vb* (**becoming, became,** *pp* **become**) *vi* to come or grow to be. * *vt* to be suitable for.
becoming *adj* appropriate; seemly; suitable to the wearer.—**becomingly** *adv*.
becquerel *n* the SI unit of radiation activity.
bed *n* a piece of furniture for sleeping on; the mattress and covers for this; a plot of soil where plants are raised; the bottom of a river, lake, etc; any flat surface used as a foundation; a stratum. * *vt* (**bedding, bedded**) to put to bed; to embed; to plant in a bed of earth; to arrange in layers.
BEd *abbr* = Bachelor of Education.
bed and breakfast *n* overnight accommodation and breakfast the following morning, as offered in hotels and guesthouses, etc.—**bed-and-breakfast** *adj*.
bedaub *vt* to smear all over.
bedbug *n* a bloodsucking wingless insect that infests dirty bedding.
bedchamber *n* a bedroom.
bedclothes *npl* sheets, blankets, etc for a bed.
bedding *n* bedclothes; litter (straw, etc) for animals; a bottom layer, foundation.
bedding plant *n* a young plant suitable for a garden bed.
bedeck *vt* to cover with finery, to adorn.
bedevil *vt* (**bedevilling, bedevilled** *or* **bedeviling, bedevilled**) to plague or bewilder.—**bedevilment** *n*.
bedew *vt* to moisten, to sprinkle.
bedfellow *n* a sharer of a bed; an associate, ally, etc, esp a temporary one.
bedim *vt* (**bedimming, bedimmed**) to make dim.
bedizen *vt* to adorn or dress gaudily.—**bedizenment** *n*.
bedlam *n* (*arch*) a madhouse; uproar.
Bedouin *n* (*pl* **Bedouins, Bedouin**) an Arab desert nomad; a gypsy.
bedpan *n* a vessel used as a lavatory by a bedridden person; a warming pan.
bedplate *n* the base plate or frame or platform on which a machine is fixed.
bedraggle *vt* to make untidy or dirty by dragging in the wet or dirt.—**bedraggled** *adj*.
bedridden *adj* confined to bed through illness.
bedrock *n* solid rock underlying soil, etc; the base or bottom; fundamentals.
bedroom *n* a room for sleeping in. * *adj* suggestive of sexual relations; (*area, suburb, etc*) inhabited by commuters.
bedside *n* the space beside a bed. * *adj* situated or conducted at the bedside; suitable for someone bedridden.
bedsitter, bedsit, bedsitting room *n* a single room with sleeping and cooking facilities.
bedsore *n* an ulcerous sore caused by pressure, common in bedridden persons.
bedspread *n* a covering for a bed, usu decorative.
bedstead *n* a frame for the spring and mattress of a bed.
bedstraw *n* a plant of the madder family used formerly as straw for stuffing beds.

bee[1] *n* a social, stinging four-winged insect that is often kept in hives to make honey; any of numerous insects that also feed on pollen and nectar and are related to wasps.

bee[2] *n* a social meeting for work on behalf of a neighbour or a charitable object.

bee[3] *n* (*naut*) strips of wood bolted each side of a bowsprit, through which the fore topmast stays are reeved.

beebread *n* a brown bitter substance consisting of the pollen of flowers collected and stored by bees as food for larvae.

beech *n* a tree with smooth silvery-grey bark; its wood.

beechmast *n* beechnuts collectively.

beechnut *n* the triangular nut of the beech, which yields an oil.

bee-eater *n* any of the numerous species of bee-eating birds.

beef *n* (*pl* **beefs**) the meat of a full-grown cow, steer, etc; (*inf*) muscular strength; (*inf*) a complaint, grudge; (*pl* **beeves**) cows, ox, steers, etc bred for their meat. * *vt* (*with* **up**) to add weight, strength or power to.

beefburger *n* a flat grilled or fried cake of minced beef.

beefcake *n* (*sl*) muscular men displayed provocatively, esp in photographs.

beefeater *n* an eater of beef; (*inf*) in UK, a yeoman of the royal guard, attending the sovereign on state occasions.

beef tea *n* stewed beef juice.

beefy *adj* (**beefier, beefiest**) brawny, muscular.

beehive *n* a container for keeping honeybees; a scene of crowded activity.

beekeeper *n* one who keeps bees for producing honey.—**beekeeping** *n*.

beeline *n* the straight course pursued by a bee returning laden to the hive; a direct line or course.

Beelzebub *n* the devil, Satan; a fallen angel, next in power to Satan.

bee moth *n* a moth that lays its eggs in beehives, and whose larvae feed upon the wax.

been *see* **be.**

beep *n* the brief, high-pitched sound of a horn or electronic signal. * *vti* to make or cause to make this sound.

beer *n* an alcoholic drink made from malt, sugar, hops and water fermented with yeast.

beery *adj* (**beerier, beeriest**) smelling or tasting of beer.

beestings *npl* the first milk given by a cow after calving.—*also* **biestings, beastings.**

beeswax *n* wax secreted by bees, refined and used for polishing.

beeswing *n* a gauze-like crust that occurs in port and some other wines, indicative of age.

beet *n* a red, edible root used as a vegetable, in salads, etc; a source of sugar.

beetle[1] *n* any of an order of insects having hard wing covers.

beetle[2] *n* a heavy wooden mallet for driving wedges, etc; a club for beating linen, etc, in washing. * *vt* to use a beetle on; to beat with a heavy wooden mallet.

beetle[3] *vi* to be prominent; to jut out, overhang, as a cliff.—**beetling** *adj*.

beetroot *n* (*pl* **beetroot**) the fleshy root of beet used as a vegetable, in salads, etc.—*also* **red beet.**

beeves *see* **beef.**

beezer *n* (*sl*) a fellow; (*sl*) a nose.

befall *vti* (**befalling, befell,** *pp* **befallen**) to happen or occur to.

befit *vt* (**befitting, befitted**) to be suitable or appropriate for; to be right for.—**befittingly** *adv*.

befog *vt* (**befogging, befogged**) to involve in a fog, to confuse.

befool *vt* to make a fool of.

before *prep* ahead of; in front of; in the presence of; preceding in space or time; in preference to; rather than. * *adv* beforehand; previously; until now. * *conj* earlier than the time that; rather than.

beforehand *adv* ahead of time; in anticipation.

befoul *vt* to make foul, to soil.—**befouler** *n*.—**befoulment** *n*.

befriend *vt* to be a friend to, to favour.

befuddle *vt* to confuse, stupefy, often with drink.

beg *vti* (**begging, begged**) to ask for money or food; to ask earnestly; to implore.

began *see* **begin.**

beget *vt* (**begetting, begot** *or* **begat,** *pp* **begotten or begot**) to become the father of; to cause.—**begetter** *n*.

beggar *n* a person who begs or who lives by begging; a pauper; (*inf*) a person. * *vt* to reduce to poverty; (*description*) to render inadequate.

beggarly *adj* like, or in the condition of, a beggar; poor; mean, contemptible.—**beggarliness** *n*.

beggary *n* the state of a beggar; extreme poverty; beggars collectively.

begin *vti* (**beginning, began,** *pp* **begun**) to start doing, acting, etc; to originate.

beginner *n* one who has just started to learn or do something; a novice.

beginning *n* source or origin; commencement.

begird *vt* (**begirding, begirded** *or* **begirt**) to gird round, to encompass, surround.

begone *interj* go away! be off!

begonia *n* a tropical plant cultivated for its showy petalless flowers and ornamental lopsided leaves.

begorra *interj* by God.

begot, begotten *see* **beget.**

begrime *vt* to make grimy, to soil deeply.

begrudge *vt* to grudge; to envy.—**begrudgingly** *adv*.

beguile *vt* (**beguiling, beguiled**) to cheat or deceive; to charm; to fascinate.—**beguilement** *n*.—**beguiler** *n*.—**beguilingly** *adv*.

beguine *n* a West Indian dance in bolero rhythm; the music for this.

begum *n* a Muslim queen or lady of high rank.

begun *see* **begin.**

behalf *n* **in** *or* **on behalf of** in the interest of; for.

behave *vti* to act in a specified way; to conduct (oneself) properly.

behaviour, behavior *n* way of behaving; conduct or action.—**behavioural, behavioral** *adj*.

behaviourism, behaviorism *n* the doctrine that human action is governed by external stimuli.—**behaviourist, behaviorist** *adj, n*.—**behaviouristic, behavioristic** *adj*.

behead *vt* to cut the head off.

beheld *see* **behold.**

behemoth *n* (*Bible*) an enormous animal described in Job, possibly the hippopotamus.

behest *n* a command; a precept.

behind *prep* at the rear of; concealed by; later than; supporting. * *adv* in the rear; slow; late.

behindhand *adj, adv* late, in arrears.

behold *vb* (**beholding, beheld**) *vt* to look at; to observe. * *vi* to see.—**beholder** *n*.

beholden *adj* indebted to; bound under an obligation.

behoof *n* advantage; interest; profit; use; behalf.

behove, behoove *vt* to be necessary or fit for, to be incumbent.

beige *n* a very light brown.

being *n* life; existence; a person or thing that exists; nature or substance.

bejewel *vt* (**bejewelling, bejewelled** *or* **bejeweling, bejeweled**) to ornament or furnish with jewels.

bel *n* a unit equal to 10 decibels.

belabour, belabor *vt* to beat soundly, to thump; to criticize severely.

belated *adj* coming late.—**belatedly** *adv*.

belay *vti* (**belaying, belayed**) to secure (a rope) by winding it round a spike, piton; to secure by a rope.

belch *vti* to expel gas from the stomach by the mouth; to eject violently from inside.—*also n*.

beleaguer *vt* to besiege, to blockade; to harass.

belemnite *n* a pointed fossil internal bone or shell of an extinct family of cuttlefish.

bel esprit *n* (*pl* **beaux esprits**) a person of wit or genius.

belfry *n* (*pl* **belfries**) the upper part of a tower, in which bells are hung.

Belgian *adj* of or pertaining to Belgium or its inhabitants. * *n* a native or inhabitant of Belgium.

Belial *n* a demon or devil; a fallen angel.

belie *vt* (**belying, belied**) to show to be a lie; to misrepresent; to fail to live up to (a hope, promise).—**belier** *n*.
belief *n* a principle or idea considered to be true; religious faith.
believe *vt* to accept as true; to think; to be convinced of. * *vi* to have religious faith.—**believable** *adj*.—**believer** *n*.
believing *adj* trustful.
belittle *vt* (*a person*) to make feel small; to disparage.—**belittlement** *n*.—**belittler** *n*.—**belittlingly** *adv*.
bell[1] *n* a hollow metal object which rings when struck; anything bell-shaped; the sound made by a bell.
bell[2] *n* the cry of a stag in rut. * *vi* to make this cry.
belladonna *n* the deadly nightshade plant, whose flowers, leaves and stalk are poisonous.
bellbird *n* an American bird whose note resembles a bell; an Australian bird with a similar call.
bell buoy *n* a buoy with a warning bell activated by wave movement.
belle *n* a pretty woman or girl.
belles-lettres *n* (*used as sing*) artistic literature, including poetry, essays, etc.—**belletrist** *n*.—**belletristic** *adj*.
bellfounder *n* a person who casts bells.—**bellfoundry** *n*.
bellhop, bellboy *n* one who carries luggage, runs errands, etc in a hotel or club.
bellicose *adj* war-like; ready to fight.—**bellicosity** *n*.
belligerent *adj* at war; of war; war-like; ready to fight or quarrel.—**belligerence** *n*.—**belligerently** *adv*.
bell jar *n* a protective glass cover in the shape of a bell.
bellman *n* (*pl* **bellmen**) one who uses a bell for public announcement, a town crier.
bell metal *n* an alloy of copper and tin, used for the manufacture of bells.
bellow *vi* to roar; to make an outcry. * *vt* to utter loudly. * *n* the roar of a bull; any deep roar.
bellows *n* (*used as pl or sing*) a device for creating and directing a stream of air by compression of its collapsible sides.
bellpull *n* a rope or handle for a bell.
bell punch *n* a punch with a signal bell used for punching tickets and checking the number of fares issued.
bellpush *n* a button that operates a bell.
bellwether *n* the leading sheep of a flock with a bell round its neck.
belly *n* (*pl* **bellies**) the lower part of the body between the chest and the thighs; the abdomen; the stomach; the underside of an animal's body; the deep interior, as of a ship. * *vti* (**bellying, bellied**) to swell out; to bulge.
bellyache *n* (*inf*) a pain in the stomach. * *vi* (*sl*) to complain constantly.
bellyband *n* a band that encircles the belly of a horse, a saddle girth.
bellybutton *n* (*inf*) the navel.
belly dance *n* a solo dance performed by a woman with sinuous, provocative movements of the belly and hips.—**belly dancer** *n*.
belly-flop *vt* (**belly-flopping, belly-flopped**) to dive in such a way that the body lands almost flat against the water.—**belly flop** *n*.
bellyful *n* (*sl*) as much as one can tolerate of something.
belong *vi* to have a proper place; to be related (to); (*with* **to**) to be a member; to be owned; (*inf*) to fit in socially.
belongings *npl* personal effects, possessions.
beloved *adj* dearly loved. * *n* one who is dearly loved.
below *prep* lower than; unworthy of. * *adv* in or to a lower place; south of; beneath; later (in a book, etc).
belt *n* a band of leather, etc worn around the waist; any similar encircling thing; a belt as an award for skill, eg in boxing, judo; a continuous moving strap passing over pulleys and so driving machinery; a distinctive region or strip; (*sl*) a hard blow. * *vt* to surround, attach with a belt; to thrash with a belt; (*sl*) to deliver a hard blow; (*sl*) to hurry; (*with* **out**) (*sl*) to sing or play loudly; (*with* **up**) to fasten with a belt. * *vi* (*with* **up**) (*inf*) to wear a seat belt; (*sl:often imper*) to be quiet.
Beltane *n* a Celtic festival formerly observed in Scotland on old May Day and in Ireland on June 21 by the kindling of huge bonfires.
beluga *n* a large sturgeon; its caviar; a white whale.
belvedere *n* a raised turret or summerhouse for viewing scenery.
bema *n* the inner part of the chancel in a Greek church; a speaker's platform; a platform in a synagogue from which services are led.
bemire *vt* to soil with mire; to be stuck in mud.
bemoan *vti* to lament.
bemuse *vt* to muddle; to preoccupy.—**bemused** *adj*.—**bemusement** *n*.
ben *n* (*Scot*) a mountain.
bench *n* a long hard seat for two or more persons; a long table for working at; the place where judges sit in a court of law; the status of a judge; judges collectively; (*sport*) the place where reserves, etc, sit during play.
bench mark *n* a surveyor's mark for making measurements; something that serves as a standard.
bencher *n* one who sits on a bench; in UK, a senior member of an Inn of Court, one of a group that has the government of the society.
bench warrant *n* a warrant issued by a court or judge for someone's arrest.
bend *vb* (**bending, bent**) *vt* to form a curve; to make crooked; to turn, esp from a straight line; to adapt to one's purpose, distort. * *vi* to turn, esp from a straight line; to yield from pressure to form a curve; (*with* **over** *or* **down**) to curve the body; to give in. * *n* a curve, turn; a bent part; (*pl: used as sing or pl*) decompression sickness in divers.—**bendable** *adj*.
bend sinister *n* (*her*) a bar or band drawn from the upper corner of the shield at the left (sinister) to the opposite base at the right (dexter), a sign of illegitimacy.
bender *n* one who or that which bends; (*sl*) a bout of drinking.
beneath *prep* underneath; below; unworthy. * *adv* in a lower place; underneath.—*also adj*.
benedict *n* a newly married man, esp if previously a confirmed bachelor.
benedicite *n* a blessing, a grace; (*with cap*) a Christian hymn or canticle sung at morning prayer when the Te Deum is not used.
Benedictine *adj* of or relating to the order of St Benedict. * *n* a monk of the Benedictine order; a kind of liqueur made from herbs and spices.
benediction *n* a blessing; an invocation of a blessing, esp at the end of a church service.—**benedictory** *adj*.
Benedictus *n* the Song of Zacharias (Luke 1) used as a canticle after the second lesson at morning prayer when the Jubilate is not sung.
benefaction *n* the act of doing good; the money or help given.
benefactor *n* a patron.—**benefactress** *nf*.
benefice *n* a church office yielding an income to a clergyman.
beneficence *n* active kindness, the act of doing good; a benefaction.
beneficent *adj* generous; conferring blessings.—**beneficence** *n*.—**beneficently** *adv*.
beneficial *adj* advantageous.—**beneficially** *adv*.
beneficiary *n* (*pl* **beneficiaries**) a person who receives or will receive benefit, as from a will, etc.
benefit *n* advantage; anything contributing to improvement; (*often pl*) allowances paid by a government, insurance company, etc; a public performance, bazaar, etc, the proceeds of which are to help some person or cause. * *vb* (**benefiting, benefited**) *vt* to help. * *vi* to receive advantage.
benefit of clergy *n* a sanctioning by the church; (*hist*) exemption from trial by a secular court.
benefit society, benefit association *n* an association for mutual insurance against sickness, etc.
benevolence *n* inclination to do good; kindness; generosity; (*formerly*) a royal tax levied under the guise of a gratuity to the sovereign.—**benevolent** *adj*.—**benevolently** *adv*.
Bengali *n* a native or inhabitant of the Bengal province of India; the language spoken in Bengal. * *adj* of or pertaining to Bengal, its inhabitants or language.
Bengal light *n* a firework used also for signals, giving a steady bright blue light.
benighted *adj* overtaken by night; in moral darkness or ignorance.
benign *adj* favourable; kindly; gentle or mild; (*med*) not malignant.—**benignly** *adv*.

benignant *adj* kind; benign.—**benignancy** *n*.

benignity *n* (*pl* **benignities**) kindliness.

benison *n* (*arch*) a benediction or blessing.

benne *n* the sesame, an Asian annual cultivated for its seeds, which yield a valuable oil.

bent[1] *see* **bend.**

bent[2] *n* aptitude; inclination of the mind. * *adj* curved or crooked; (*with* **on**) strongly determined; (*sl*) dishonest; sexually deviant.

bent[3] *n* a kind of coarse stiff grass; a withered grass stalk; a heath.

benthos *n* the flora and fauna at the bottom of the sea; the sea bottom itself.—**benthic, benthonic** *adj*.

bentwood *adj* (*furniture*) made of wood that is bent and shaped by heat.

benumb *vt* to make numb.—**benumbed** *adj*.

benzene *n* a mixture of hydrocarbons from petroleum used as a solvent, in the manufacture of plastics, and as motor fuel.

benzine, benzol *n* a volatile mixture of lighter hydrocarbons from petroleum, used as a solvent and as motor fuel.

benzoin *n* a resin of the benjamin tree of Sumtra, used chiefly in cosmetics, perfumes and incense.—**benzoic** *adj*.

bequeath *vt* (*property, etc*) to leave by will; to pass on to posterity.—**bequeathal** *n*.—**bequeather** *n*.

bequest *n* act of bequeathing; something that is bequeathed, a legacy.

berate *vt* to scold severely.

berberine *n* an alkaloid used in dyeing and medicine, and obtained as a bitter yellow substance from the barberry and other plants.

berceuse *n* (*pl* **berceuses**) a cradle song; a tender or soothing musical composition.

bereave *vt* to deprive (of) a loved one through death.—**bereaved** *adj*.—**bereavement** *n*.

bereft *adj* deprived; bereaved.

beret *n* a flat, round, brimless, soft cap.

berg *n* an iceberg.

bergamot *n* a variety of lemon, the rind of which yields a valuable oil used in perfumery; the oil of the bergamot; a variety of pear; a variety of mint; a coarse kind of tapestry.

bergschrund *n* a crevasse between a glacier and the side of its valley.

beriberi *n* a disease of the nervous system, due to lack of vitamin B.

berkelium *n* a radioactive metallic element derived from americium.

berlin *n* a fine dyed knitting wool; an 18th-century four-wheeled carriage with a hood behind.

berm, berme *n* a ledge between a ditch and rampart; a narrow shelf along a slope; a shoulder of a road.

Bermuda grass *n* a valuable variety of pasture grass.

Bermuda-rigged *adj* (*naut*) rigged with a high tapering mainsail.

Bermuda shorts *npl* close-fitting knee-length shorts.

berry *n* (*pl* **berries**) any small, juicy, stoneless fruit (eg blackberry, holly berry). * *vti* (**berrying, berried**) to bear, produce or gather berries.

berserk *adj* frenzied; destructively violent.—*also adv*.

berth *n* a place in a dock for a ship at mooring; a built-in bed, as in a ship or train; (*inf*) a job. * *vt* to put into or furnish with a berth; to moor a ship. * *vi* to occupy a berth.

bertha *n* a wide lace collar.

Bertillon system *n* a method of identifying criminals by body measurements.

beryl *n* a (usu green) precious stone.

beryllium *n* a hard lightweight silvery-white metallic element used in making alloys.

beseech *vt* (**beseeching, beseeched** *or* **besought**) to implore, to entreat; to beg earnestly for.

beset *vt* (**besetting, beset**) to surround or hem in; to attack from all sides; to harass.

besetting *adj* constantly harassing.

beside *prep* at, by the side of, next to; in comparison with; in addition to; aside from; **beside oneself** extremely agitated.

besides *prep* other than; in addition; over and above. * *adv* in addition; also; except for that mentioned; moreover.

besiege *vt* to hem in with armed forces; to close in on; to overwhelm, harass, etc.

besmear *vt* to smear with sticky stuff; to soil.

besmirch *vt* to sully; to make dirty, to soil.

besom *n* a broom made of twigs; (*Scot*) a naughty or silly woman.

besotted *adj* muddled with drunkenness or infatuation; dull, stupid.—**besottedly** *adv*.

besought *see* **beseech.**

bespangle *vt* to adorn with spangles; to dot or sprinkle with something that glitters.

bespatter *vt* to soil by spattering; to spot with mud; to asperse with calumny.

bespeak *vt* (**bespeaking, bespoke,** *pp* **bespoken** *or* **bespoke**) to speak for beforehand; to order or arrange in advance; to be evidence of; to indicate, as by signs or marks.

bespoke *adj* (*clothes*) custom-made; (*tailor*) making such clothes.

besprent *adj* (*poet*) sprinkled; scattered.

besprinkle *vt* to sprinkle over (with).

best *adj* (*superl of* **good**) most excellent; most suitable, desirable, etc; largest; above all others. * *n* one's utmost effort; the highest state of excellence. * *adv* (*superl of* **well**) in or to the highest degree. * *vt* to defeat, outdo.

bestial *adj* brutal; savage.—**bestially** *adv*.

bestiality *n* (*pl* **bestialities**) brutal or brutish behaviour; a brutal or savage action or practice; sexual intercourse by a person with an animal.

bestialize *vt* to make like a beast; to degrade to the level of a brute.

bestiary *n* (*pl* **bestiaries**) a medieval treatise on beasts.

bestir *vt* (**bestirring, bestirred**) to put into brisk or vigorous action; to rouse, exert (oneself).

best man *n* the principal attendant of the bridegroom at a wedding.

bestow *vt* to present as a gift or honour.—**bestowal** *n*.—**bestower** *n*.

bestrew *vt* (**bestrewing, bestrewed,** *pp* **bestrewed** *or* **bestrewn**) to strew or scatter over; to lie scattered over.

bestride *vt* (**bestriding, bestrode,** *pp* **bestridden**) to stand, sit on or mount with the legs astride.

best seller *n* a book or other commodity that sells in vast numbers; the author of such a book.—**best-selling** *adj*.

bet *n* a wager or stake; the thing or sum staked; a person or thing likely to bring about a desired result; (*inf*) belief, opinion. * *vti* (**betting, bet** *or* **betted**) to declare as in a bet; to stake (money, etc) in a bet (with someone).

beta *n* the second letter of the Greek alphabet; (*astron*) the second star in a constellation; (*chem*) the second of two or more isomerous modifications of the same compound; (*biol*) the second subspecies or permanent variety of a species.

beta blocker *n* a drug that subdues cardiac activity, used in the treatment of high blood pressure.

betake *vt* (**betaking, betook,** *pp* **betaken**) to have recourse (to), to resort; to take oneself (to), to go.

beta particle *n* an electron or positron ejected from the nucleus of an atom during radioactive disintegration.

beta ray *n* a stream of penetrating rays emitted by radioactive substances.

beta wave *n* an electrical rhythm of the brain associated with normal waking consciousness.

betel *n* an Asian pepper, the leaves of which are mixed with betel nuts and chewed as a stimulant or narcotic.

betel nut *n* the seed of the betel palm.

betel palm *n* a palm tree of tropical Asia with feathery leaves and scarlet or orange fruit.

bête noir *n* (*pl* **bêtes noires**) pet hate.

bethel *n* a hallowed spot; a seamen's church; in UK, a nonconformist chapel.

betide *vt* to happen to, to befall. * *vi* to come to pass.

betimes *adv* (*arch*) in good time; before it is too late; early; soon.

bêtise *n* folly; an ill-chosen remark.

betoken *vt* to signify, to indicate by signs; to augur, to foreshadow.
betony *n* (*pl* **betonies**) a purple-flowered woodland plant formerly used in medicine and as a dye.
betook *see* **betake**.
betray *vt* to aid an enemy; to expose treacherously; to be a traitor to; to reveal unknowingly.—**betrayal** *n*.—**betrayer** *n*.
betroth *vt* to promise in marriage.
betrothal *n* the state of being engaged to marry; a mutual promise for future marriage made between a man and a woman.
betrothed *adj* affianced, engaged to be married. * *n* a fiancé or fiancée.
better[1] *adj* (*compar of* **good**) more excellent; more suitable; improved in health; larger. * *adv* (*compar of* **well**) in a more excellent manner; in a higher degree; more. * *n* a person superior in position, etc; a more excellent thing, condition, etc. * *vt* to outdo; to surpass.
better[2] *n* someone who bets.
betterment *n* an improvement.
between *prep* the space, time, etc separating (two things); (*bond, etc*) connecting from one or the other.
betweentimes, betweenwhiles *adv* at or during intervals.
betwixt *prep* between; in the space that separates.
bevel *n* an angle other than a right angle; the inclination that one surface makes with another when not at right angles; a tool for setting of angles. * *vb* (**bevelling, bevelled** *or* **beveling, beveled**) *vt* to cut on the slant. * *vi* to slant or incline.
bevel gear *n* a gear in which the axis or shaft of the driving wheel forms an angle with the shaft of the wheel driven.
beverage *n* a drink, esp one other than water.
bevy *n* (*pl* **bevies**) a flock of quails; a large group (esp of girls).
bewail *vt* to mourn or weep aloud for, to lament. * *vi* to express grief.—**bewailer** *n*.—**bewailing** *n*.
beware *vti* to be wary or careful (of).
bewilder *vt* to perplex; to confuse hopelessly.—**bewilderingly** *adv*.—**bewilderment** *n*.
bewitch *vt* to cast a spell over; to fascinate or enchant.
bewitching *adj* fascinating, enchanting, captivating, alluring.—**bewitchingly** *adv*.
bey *n* a Turkish title of respect; a title similar to Mr; (*formerly*) a governor of a province or district in the Turkish dominions.
beyond *prep* further on than; past; later than; outside the reach of (*beyond help*). * *adv* further away. * *n* (*with* **the**) life after death.
bezant *n* a gold coin of Byzantium or Constantinople, issued in the Middle Ages and current in Europe until the fall of the Eastern Empire, 1472; (*her*) a small circle of gold representing the coin.
bezel *n* the sloping edge of a chisel; the rim that holds a gem in its setting; the groove in which the glass of a watch is fitted.
bezique *n* a game of cards for two, three, and four persons using two decks of cards with sixes and cards below omitted.
bezoar *n* a calcareous concretion found in the intestines of certain animals.
bhang *n* the dried leaves of Indian hemp, chewed or smoked as an intoxicant or narcotic, hashish.—*also* **bang**.
bhp *abbr* = brake horsepower.
bi- *prefix* having two; doubly; happening twice during; every two; using two or both; joining or involving two; having twice the amount of acid or base.
Bi (*chem symbol*) bismuth.
biannual *adj* occurring twice a year.—**biannually** *adv*.
bias *n* a slanting or diagonal line, cut or sewn across the grain in cloth; a weight inside a bowl in a game of bowls slanting its course when rolled; partiality; prejudice. * *vt* (**biasing, biased** *or* **biassing, biassed**) to prejudice.
biathlon *n* (*sport*) an athletic event combining cross-country skiing and rifle shooting.
biauriculate, biauricular *adj* having two auricles, as the heart of the higher vertebrates; (*bot*) having two ear-like projections at the base, as a leaf.
biaxial *adj* having two (optic) axes.—**biaxially** *adv*.
bib[1] *n* a cloth or plastic cover tied around a baby or child to prevent food spillage on clothes; the upper part of dungarees or an apron.
bib[2] *vi* (**bibbing, bibbed**) (*arch*) to drink, to tipple.
bib[3] *n* a kind of fish, whiting pout.
bibelot *n* a trinket, a knickknack.
Bible *n* the sacred book of the Christian Church; the Old and New Testaments; (*without cap*) an authoritative book on a particular subject.
biblical *adj* of or referring to the Bible.—**biblically** *adv*.
Biblicist *n* a biblical scholar; a fundamentalist.—**Biblicism** *n*.
biblio- *prefix* book or books.
bibliography *n* (*pl* **bibliographies**) a list of writings on a given subject or by a given author; the study of the history of books and book production.—**bibliographer** *n*.—**bibliographic** *adj*.—**bibliographical** *adj*.
bibliolatry *n* book worship; excessive reverence for the letter of the Bible.—**bibliolater** *n*.—**bibliolatrous** *adj*.
bibliomania *n* a mania for acquiring rare and curious books.—**bibliomaniac** *adj, n*.
bibliophile, bibliophil *n* a book lover.—**bibliophilistic** *adj*.—**bibliophism** *n*.
bibliopole, bibliopolist *n* a bookseller, esp one who deals in rare works.—**bibliopolic** *adj*.—**bibliopoly** *n*.
bibliotheca *n* (*pl* **bibliothecas, bibliothecae**) a library; a list of books.
bibulous *adj* readily absorbing or imbibing fluids; spongy; addicted to drink.—**bibulously** *adv*.—**bibulousness** *n*.
bicameral *adj* (*legislature*) having two chambers.
bicarbonate *n* sodium bicarbonate.
bicentenary *adj* occurring every two hundred years. * *n* (*pl* **bicentenaries**) a two hundredth anniversary or its celebration.
bicentennial *adj* lasting or occurring every two hundred years. * *n* a bicentenary, the two hundredth anniversary of an event, or its celebration.
bicephalous, bicephalic *adj* (*biol*) two-headed.
biceps *n* (*pl* **biceps, bicepses**) the muscle with two points of origin, esp the large muscle in the upper arm.
bichloride *n* (*chem*) a compound of two or more atoms of chlorine combined with a base; dichloride.
bicipital *adj* (*anat*) having two heads, as a biceps muscle; dividing into two parts at either extremity.
bicker *vi* to squabble, quarrel.—*also n*.—**bickerer** *n*.
bicoastal *adj* pertaining to both the west and east coasts of the United States.
biconcave *adj* hollow on both sides.—**biconcavity** *n*.
biconvex *adj* rounded on both sides.
bicorn, bicornuate *adj* having two horns.
bicuspid *adj* having two points or prominences (—*also* **bicuspidate**). * *n* one of the two double-pointed teeth forming the first pair of molars on either side of the jaw, above and below.
bicycle *n* a vehicle consisting of a metal frame on two wheels, driven by pedals and having handlebars and a seat. * *vti* to ride or travel on a bicycle.—**bicyclist, bicycler** *n*.
bid[1] *n* an offer of an amount one will pay or accept; (*cards*) a statement of the number of tricks that a player intends to win. * *vi* (**bidding, bid**) to make a bid.—**bidder** *n*.
bid[2] *vt* (**bidding, bade** *or* **bid**, *pp* **bidden** *or* **bid**) to command or ask; to summon; (*farewell, etc*) to express.
biddable *adj* docile, obedient; worth bidding on.—**biddability** *n*.—**biddably** *adv*.
bidding *n* an order; command; an invitation; the act of offering a price at auction.
biddy[1] *n* (*pl* **biddies**) (*inf*) a woman, esp an old or meddlesome one.
biddy[2] *n* (*pl* **biddies**) (*dial*) a fowl or chicken.
bide *vb* (**biding, bided** *or* **bode**) *vi* to wait; to dwell. * *vt* to endure, suffer; to wait for.
bidentate *adj* having two teeth, or two tooth-like processes.
bidet *n* a low, bowl-shaped bathroom fixture with running water for bathing the crotch and anus.
biennial *adj* lasting two years; occurring every two years. * *n* a plant that lasts for two years.—**biennially** *adv*.

bier *n* a portable framework on which a coffin is put.
biestings *see* **beestings.**
bifacial *adj* having two faces or fronts; (*leaves*) having upper and lower surfaces that are dissimilar; having opposite surfaces alike.
bifarious *adj* (*bot*) two-fold; two-rowed; pointing in two ways.
biff *n* (*sl*) a blow. * *vt* to hit, strike.
bifid *adj* divided by a deep cleft, partially divided into two.—**bifidity** *n.*—**bifidly** *adv*.
bifilar *adj* two-threaded; fitted with two threads.—**bifilarly** *adv*.
bifocal *adj* (*spectacles*) having two different focuses.
bifocals *npl* spectacles with bifocal lenses for near and distant vision.
bifoliate *adj* (*bot*) having two leaves.
bifurcate *vti* to divide into two branches.—**bifurcation** *n*.
big *adj* (**bigger, biggest**) large; of great size; important; influential; grown-up; pregnant; generous; boastful.—**bigness** *n*.
bigamist *n* a person guilty of bigamy.
bigamy *n* (*pl* **bigamies**) the act of marrying a second time when one is already legally married.—**bigamous** *adj*.—**bigamously** *adv*.
big bang theory *n* (*astron*) the theory that the universe originated in a cataclysmic explosion and is still expanding.
big brother *n* an older brother; a person who fills that protective role; (*with caps*) a ruthless and sinister dictator, corporation, etc that wields absolute power.
big business *n* large corporations and enterprises collectively, esp when regarded as exploitative.
big cat *see* **cat.**
big deal *n* an important achievement. * *interj* (*sl*) an expression of scorn or contempt.
big dipper *n* a roller coaster; (*with caps*) the seven main stars in the constellation Ursa Major.
big dry *n* a period of drought longer than normal.
big game *n* large animals or fish hunted for sport; an important, usu risky objective.
biggin[1] *n* a close-fitting child's hood or cap.
biggin[2] *n* a small building; a cottage.
bighead *n* (*inf*) a boastful or conceited person.—**bigheaded** *adj*.
bighorn *n* (*pl* **bighorns, bighorn**) the wild sheep of the Rocky Mountains.
bight *n* a loop or bend of a rope, in distinction from the ends; a bend in a coastline forming an open bay; a small bay between two headlands.
bigmouth *n* (*inf*) a loud-mouthed, bragging or indiscreet person.
big name *n* a famous person, esp in entertainment.
bigot *n* an intolerant person who blindly supports a particular political view or religion.—**bigoted** *adj*.
bigotry *n* (*pl* **bigotries**) the state or condition of a narrow-minded, intolerant person; blind and obstinate attachment to a particular creed, party or opinion; intolerance; fanaticism.
big screen *n* (*inf*) the cinema (industry).
big shot *n* (*inf*) an important person.
big stick *n* the threat of force.
big time *n* the top level in any profession.
big top *n* a large circus tent.
bigwig *n* (*inf*) an important person.
bijou *n* (*pl* **bijoux**) a jewel; any small and elegantly finished article. * *adj* (*often derog*) small and elegant.
bijouterie *n* bijoux collectively, jewellery.
bijugate, bijugous *adj* (*bot*) having two pairs of leaflets; having two heads in profile, one of which overlaps the other.
bike *n* (*inf*) a bicycle; a motorcycle.
bikini *n* (*pl* **bikinis**) a scanty two-piece swimsuit for women.
bilabiate *adj* (*bot*) having two lips, as a flower.
bilateral *adj* having two sides; affecting two parties reciprocally.—**bilaterally** *adv*.
bilberry *n* (*pl* **bilberries**) an edible dark-blue berry.
bilbo *n* (*pl* **bilboes**) a rapier or sword; (*pl*) a long bar of iron with sliding shackles for the feet and a lock at the end, formerly used as fetters.
bile *n* a gall, a thick bitter fluid secreted by the liver; bad temper.
bilge *n* the lowest part of a ship's hull; filth that collects there.
bilge keel *n* a piece of timber secured edgeways under the bottom of a vessel to prevent heavy rolling.
bilge water *n* foul water in a ship's bilge.
bilharzia *n* a tropical disease caused by a parasitic worm.
biliary *adj* of or pertaining to the bile; conveying bile.
bilingual *adj* written in two languages; able to speak two languages.—**bilingualism** *n*.—**bilingually** *adv*.
bilious *adj* suffering from or caused by disorder of the bile; peevish.—**biliously** *adv*.—**biliousness** *n*.
bilirubin *n* an orange or yellow pigment in the bile.
biliverdin *n* a green pigment in the bile, the oxidized form of bilirubin.
bilk *vt* to deceive or defraud, as by evading a payment; to leave in the lurch; (*cribbage*) to spoil the score of an opponent. * *n* a swindler; the act of spoiling the score of an opponent at cribbage.—**bilker** *n*.
bill[1] *n* a bird's beak.
bill[2] *n* a statement for goods supplied or services rendered, the money due for this; a list, as a menu or theatre programme; a poster or handbill; a draft of a proposed law, to be discussed by a legislature; a bill of exchange; a piece of paper money; (*law*) a written declaration of charges and complaints filed. * *vt* to make out a bill of (items); to present a statement of charges to; to advertise by bills; (*a performer*) to book.
billabong *n* an Australian word for a pond or a stagnant pool connected to a river.
billboard *n* a large panel designed to carry outdoor advertising; a hoarding.
billet[1] *n* a written order to provide lodging for military personnel; the lodging; a position or job. * *vt* (**billeting, billeted**) to assign to lodging by billet.
billet[2] *n* a small stick or log of wood, as for fuel; (*archit*) a moulding ornament, resembling a billet of wood.
billet-doux *n* (*pl* **billets-doux**) a love letter.
bill fold *n* a notecase or wallet.
billhook *n* a small curved cutting tool with a hooked point.
billiards *n* a game in which hard balls are driven by a cue on a felt-covered table with raised, cushioned edges.
billing *n* the order in which actors' names are listed.
billingsgate *n* coarse or profane language; virulent abuse.
billion *n* (*pl* **billions, billion**) a thousand millions, the numeral 1 followed by 9 zeros; in UK, a million million, a trillion.—**billionaire** *n*.—**billionth** *adj, n*.
bill of exchange *n* a written order to pay a certain sum of money to the person named.
bill of fare *n* a menu.
bill of health *n* a ship's certificate of health; a report on a situation or condition, usu favourable.
bill of lading *n* a receipt issued to a shipper by a carrier, listing the goods received for shipment.
bill of rights *n* a charter or summary of basic human rights.
bill of sale *n* a written statement transferring ownership by sale.
billon *n* an alloy of gold and silver, with a large proportion of copper or other base metal, used in coinage of low value.
billow *n* a large wave; any large swelling mass or surge, as of smoke. * *vi* to surge or swell in a billow.—**billowy** *adj*.
billposter *n* a person who pastes up bills.
billsticker *n* a billposter.
billy, billycan *n* (*pl* **billies, billycans**) (*Austral*) a can used as a kettle by campers.
billy-goat *n* a male goat.
bilobate, bilobed *adj* divided into two lobes or segments, with two lobes.
bilocular, biloculate *adj* divided into, or containing, two cells.
biltong *n* (*S Africa*) strips of meat, salted and dried in the sun.
bimanous *adj* (*zool*) having two hands.

bimbo *n* (*pl* **bimbos, bimboes**) (*sl*) an attractive, but brainless, young woman, often one who has an affair with a prominent person.
bimetallic *adj* of or containing two metals; of or based on bimetallism.
bimetallism *n* a monetary system using both gold and silver as a standard currency at a fixed relative value.—**bimetallist** *n*.
bimonthly *adj* every two months; loosely twice a month.
bin *n* a box or enclosed space for storing grain, coal, etc; a dustbin. * *vt* (**binning, binned**) to put or store in a bin; (*inf*) to discard, throw away.
binary *adj* made up of two parts; double; denoting or of a number system in which the base is two, each number being expressed by using only two digits, specifically 0 and 1.
binary star *n* a double star or sun whose members revolve round their common centre of gravity.
binate *adj* (*bot*) occurring or growing in pairs.—**binately** *adv*.
binaural *adj* of or used with both ears; (*sound*) transmitted from two sources.—**binaurally** *adv*.
bind *vb* (**binding, bound**) *vt* to tie together, as with rope; to hold or restrain; to encircle with a belt, etc; to fasten together the pages of (a book) and protect with a cover; to obligate by duty, love, etc; (*with* **over**) to compel, as by oath or legal restraint; (*often with* **up**) to bandage. * *vi* to become tight or stiff; to stick together; to be obligatory; (*sl*) to complain. * *n* anything that binds; (*inf*) a difficult situation.
binder *n* a folder for keeping loose papers together; a bookbinder; something used to bind; a sheaf-binding machine.
bindery *n* (*pl* **binderies**) a bookbinder's workshop.
binding *n* the covering of a book holding the pages together.
bindweed *n* a common name for twining plants belonging to the genus Convolvulus.
bine *n* the slender stem of a twining plant, esp hop; one of these plants.
binge *n* (*inf*) a heavy drinking session; immoderate indulgence in anything.
bingo *n* a game of chance in which players cover numbers on their cards according to the number called aloud. * *interj*, *n* a cry of delight, surprise or success.
binnacle *n* a turret-shaped box containing a ship's compass.
binocular *adj* for or using both eyes.
binoculars *npl* a viewing device for use with both eyes, consisting of two small telescope lenses joined together.
binomial *n* (*math*) an expression or quantity consisting of two terms connected by the sign plus (+) or minus (−). * *adj* consisting of two terms; pertaining to binomials; (*biol*) using two names, esp of classification by genus and species.—**binomially** *adv*.
binomial theorem *n* the general algebraic formula, discovered by Newton, by which any power of a binomial quantity may be found with performing the progressive multiplication.
binturong *n* a prehensile-tailed civet of India.
binucleate, binucleated, binuclear *adj* having two nuclei.
bio- *prefix* life.
biochemistry *n* the chemistry of living organisms.—**biochemical** *adj*.—**biochemist** *n*.
biodegradable *adj* readily decomposed by bacterial action.
bioengineering *n* the application of engineering principles in the biological and medical sciences.—**bioengineer** *n*.
biofeedback *n* the practice of monitoring and recording involuntary mental and physiological processes (eg brainwaves) in order to attempt to bring them under conscious control.
biogenesis *n* the theory that only living matter can produce living matter; the science of life development.—**biogenetic** *adj*.—**biogenetically** *adv*.
biography *n* (*pl* **biographies**) an account of a person's life written by another; biographical writings in general.—**biographer** *n*.—**biographical** *adj*.
biology *n* the study of living organisms.—**biological** *adj*.—**biologically** *adv*.—**biologist** *n*.
biometry, biometrics *n* (*used as sing*) the statistics of biology or probable duration of life.—**biometric, biometrical** *adj*.—**biometrically** *adv*.—**biometrician** *n*.
bionics *n* the study of electronically operated mechanical systems that function like living organisms.—**bionic** *adj*.
bionomics *n* (*used as sing*) ecology.—**bionomic, bionomical** *adj*.—**bionomist** *n*.
biophysics *n* the application of physics to biology.—**biophysical** *adj*.—**biophysicist** *n*.
bioplasm *n* living germinal matter, living protoplasm.—**bioplasmic** *adj*.
biopsy *n* (*n* **biopsies**) the removal of parts of living tissue for medical diagnosis.
biorhythm *n* a cyclical pattern in physiological activity said to determine a person's intellectual, emotional and physical moods and behaviour.—**biorhythmic** *adj*.
biosphere *n* the regions of the earth's surface and atmosphere inhabited by living things.
biosynthesis *n* (*pl* **biosyntheses**) the formation of chemical compounds by living organisms.—**biosynthetic** *adj*.—**biosynthetically** *adv*.
biotechnology *n* the commercial and industrial application of biological processes, such as the use of microorganisms to dye cloth.
biotic *adj* of life or specific life conditions.
biotin *n* a factor of the vitamin B group found in liver and egg yolk.
biparous *adj* producing two at once in time or place; (*zool*) producing two at a birth; (*bot*) having two branches.
bipartisan *adj* of, representing or supported by two political parties.—**bipartisanship** *n*.
bipartite *adj* having two parts; involving two.—**bipartition** *n*.
biped *n* an animal having two feet.—*also adj*.—**bipedal** *adj*.
bipinnate *adj* (*bot*) having lobes that are lobed themselves.—**bipinnately** *adv*.
biplane *n* an aeroplane with two sets of wings.
bipod *n* a stand with two legs for supporting a weapon, etc.
bipolar *adj* having two poles or opposite extremities; of or affecting both the earth's poles; having or expressing two directly opposite ideas or qualities.—**bipolarity** *n*.
biquadratic *adj* (*math*) pertaining to the fourth power. * *n* the fourth power, arising from the multiplication of a square number or quantity by itself.
birch *n* a tree with a smooth white bark and hard wood; a bundle of birch twigs used for thrashing. * *vt* to flog.—**birchen** *adj*.
bird *n* any class of warm-blooded, egg-laying vertebrates with a feathered body, scaly legs, and forelimbs modified to form wings; (*sl*) a woman; (*sl*) time in prison; **for the birds** useless, worthless, unimportant; **get** *or* **give the bird** (*inf*) to boo an entertainer off the stage.
birdbrain *n* (*inf*) a stupid or frivolous person.—**bird-brained** *adj*.
birdie *n* (*inf*) a small bird; (*golf*) a score of one stroke under par for a hole.
birdlime *n* a viscous substance used for snaring small birds; a thing that snares. * *vt* to smear or trap with birdlime.
bird of passage *n* a migratory bird; a transient person.
bird of prey *n* a meat-eating bird (as a hawk, owl, falcon, etc) that hunts other animals for food.
birdseed *n* a mixture of seeds for feeding wild or caged birds.
bird's-eye *adj* seen from above; dappled to resemble the eye of a bird. * *n* any of several plants with flowers resembling a bird's eye.
bird watcher *n* one who makes a study of birds in the wild.—**bird watching** *n*.
bireme **n** an ancient galley with two tiers of oars.
biretta *n* a square cap with three corners worn by Roman Catholic clergy.
Biro *n* (*trademark*) (*pl* **Biros**) a ball-point pen.
birr *vi* to make a whirring sound, like that of a spinning wheel. * *n* a whirring sound.
birth *n* the act of being born; childbirth; the origin of something; lineage, ancestry.
birth control *n* the use of contraceptive drugs or devices to limit reproduction.
birthday *n* the day of birth; the anniversary of the day of birth.

birthmark *n* a patch or blemish on the body dating from birth.
birth rate *n* the number of births per thousand of population per year.
birthright *n* privileges or property that a person is believed entitled to by birth.
birthstone *n* a gem symbolizing the month of one's birth.
bis *adv* twice; (*mus*) for a second time; encore.
biscuit *n* a small, flat, dry, sweet or plain cake baked from dough.—*also* **cookie**. * *adj* pale brown in colour.
bise *n* a piercing dry northeast wind prevalent in Switzerland.
bisect *vt* to split into two equal parts; (*geom*) to divide into two equal parts.—**bisection** *n*.
bisector *n* a line bisecting.
bisexual *adj* sexually attracted to both sexes; having the characteristics of both sexes. * *n* a person sexually attracted to both sexes.—**bisexualism, bisexuality** *n*.
bishop *n* a high-ranking clergyman governing a diocese or church district; a chessman that can move in a diagonal direction.
bishopric *n* the office, dignity or jurisdiction of a bishop; a diocese.
bismuth *n* one of the elements, a light reddish-coloured metal of brittle texture.—**bismuthal, bismuthic** *adj*.
bison *n* (*pl* **bison**) a wild ox of Europe and America.—*also* **buffalo**.
bisque[1] *n* a thick cream soup made from shellfish.
bisque[2] *n* an unglazed white porcelain, used for statuettes, etc, biscuit porcelain.
bisque[3] *n* (*croquet, tennis, golf*) a stroke allowed to an inferior player or side.
bissextile *n* a leap year. * *adj* pertaining to a leap year.
bister *see* **bistre**.
bistort *n* a herb with twisted roots, snakeweed.
bistoury *n* (*pl* **bistouries**) a surgeon's knife, a scalpel.
bistre *n* a warm brown pigment made from wood soot. * *adj* of this colour.—*also* **bister**.
bistro *n* (*pl* **bistros**) a small restaurant.
bisulcate *adj* having two furrows or grooves; cloven-footed.
bisulphate, bisulfate *n* a salt of sulphuric acid in which half of its hydrogen is replaced by a positive element.
bisulphite, bisulfite *n* a salt of sulphurous acid, half the hydrogen of which is replaced by the base.
bit[1] *n* a small amount or piece; in US, a small coin worth one eighth of a dollar; a small part in a play, film, etc, a bit part.—**a bit** slightly, rather.
bit[2] *n* a metal mouthpiece in a bridle used for controlling a horse; a cutting or boring attachment for use in a brace, drill, etc. * *vt* (**bitting, bitted**) to put a bridle upon; to put the bit in the mouth of.
bit[3] *n* (*comput*) a unit of information in binary notation equivalent to either of two digits, 0 or 1.
bit[4] *see* **bite**.
bitch *n* a female dog or wolf; (*sl*) a spiteful woman; (*inf*) an unpleasant or difficult situation. * *vi* (*inf*) to grumble; to act spitefully; (*with* **up**) to make a mess of, to ruin.
bite *vb* (**biting, bit,** *pp* **bitten**) *vt* to grip or tear with the teeth; to sting or puncture, as an insect; to cause to smart; to take the bait. * *vi* to press or snap the teeth (into, at, etc); (*with* **back**) to stop oneself from saying something offensive, embarrassing, etc. * *n* the act of biting with the teeth; a sting or puncture by an insect.
biting *adj* severe; critical, sarcastic.—**bitingly** *adv*.—**bitingness** *n*.
bit part *n* a small acting role in a play, film, etc.
bitt *n* (*usu pl*) (*naut*) a post of wood or iron to which cables are made fast. * *vt* to put round the bitts.
bitter *adj* having an acrid or sharp taste; sorrowful; harsh; resentful; cynical; (*weather*) extremely cold.—**bitterly** *adj*.—**bitterness** *n*.
bitter end *n* final extremity.
bittern[1] *n* a wading bird of the heron family, with a booming cry.
bittern[2] *n* the liquid that remains after cystallization of common salt from sea water or the brine of salt springs.
bitters *npl* liquor in which herbs or roots are steeped.
bittersweet *n* the woody nightshade, the roots and leaves of which when chewed produce first a bitter then a sweet taste; a variety of apple. * *adj* simultaneously sweet and bitter; pleasantly sad.
bituminize *vt* to make into or mix with bitumen.—**bituminization** *n*.
bitty *adj* (**bittier, bittiest**) small, tiny; made up of scraps of something.
bitumen *n* any of several substances obtained as residue in the distillation of coal tar, petroleum, etc, or occurring naturally as asphalt.—**bituminous** *adj*.
bivalent *adj* (*chem*) having a valency of two; (*genetics*) having two homologous chromosomes; (*logic*) having two truth values. * *n* an element, one of the atoms of which can replace two atoms of hydrogen; (*genetics*) a pair of homologous chromsomes.—**bivalency** *n*.
bivalve *n* any mollusc having two valves or shells hinged together, as a clam.—**bivalvular** *adj*.
bivouac *n* a temporary camp, esp one without tents or other cover. * *vi* (**bivouacking, bivouacked**) to spend the night in a bivouac.
biweekly *adj* every two weeks; twice a week. * *n* (*pl* **biweeklies**) a periodical published every two weeks.
bizarre *adj* odd, unusual.
Bk (*chem symbol*) berkelium.
blab *vti* (**blabbing, blabbed**) to reveal (a secret); to gossip. * *n* a gossip.—**blabber** *n*.
black *adj* of the darkest colour, like coal or soot; having dark-coloured skin and hair; without light; dirty; evil, wicked; sad, dismal; sullen; angry; (*coffee, etc*) without milk. * *n* black colour; (*often with cap*) a Negro, Australian Aborigine; black clothes, esp when worn in mourning; (*chess, draughts*) black pieces.—**in the black** without debts, in credit. * *vt* to make black; to blacken; (*shoes*) to polish with blacking; to boycott; (*with* **out**) (*lights*) to extinguish, obliterate; (*broadcast*) to prevent transmission. * *vi* (*with* **out**) to lose consciousness or vision.—**blackly** *adv*.—**blackness** *n*.
black-and-blue *adj* livid with bruises.
black and white *n* writing, print; a line drawing; a photograph not in colour. * *adj* black-and-white.
black-and-white *adj* (*film, photography*) in black and white, not colour; (*ideas, etc*) highly simplistic.
black art *n* black magic, witchcraft.
blackball *vt* to ostracize.
black belt *n* a black belt awarded to an expert of the highest skill in judo or karate; a person who holds a black belt.
blackberry *n* (*pl* **blackberries**) a woody bush with thorny stems and berry-like fruit; its black or purple edible fruit (—*also* **bramble**). * *vt* to gather blackberries.
blackbird *n* any of various birds, the male of which is almost all black.
blackboard *n* a black or dark green board written on with chalk.
black book *n* a record of offenders; **in someone's black books** in disfavour; **little black book** (*sl*) an address book with names and telephone numbers of women.
black box *n* a flight recorder on an aircraft.
black bread *n* rye bread.
black bryony *n* a European climbing plant with small green flowers and poisonous red berries.
blackcap *n* the popular name of several black-crested birds.
blackcock *n* the male of the European black grouse or black game.
black comedy *n* a comedy with a tragic theme.
Black Death *n* the name given to the bubonic plague that ravaged Europe and Asia in the 14th century.
black economy *n* undeclared economic activity.
blacken *vt* to make black; to defame.
black eye *n* (*inf*) discoloration around the eye caused by a blow; (*sl*) shame.
blackfish *n* (*pl* **blackfish, blackfishes**) a female salmon immediately after spawning; a common name for several species of British and American fish.
black flag *n* the flag of a pirate with a skull and crossbones emblazoned upon it.

blackfly *n* (*pl* **blackflies**) any of various dark insects, esp a North American fly that sucks the blood of mammals.

black frost *n* a severe frost without a rime that damages vegetation.

blackguard *n* a villain, scoundrel.—**blackguardism** *n*.—**blackguardly** *adj*.

blackhead *n* a small spot or pimple clogging a pore in the skin.

black hole *n* a hypothetical, invisible region in space.

black ice *n* a thin transparent coating of ice on roads or other surfaces.

blacking *n* black shoe polish.

blackish *adj* rather black.—**blackishly** *adv*.—**blackishness** *n*.

blackjack[1] *n* a gambling game with cards in which players try to obtain points better than the banker's but not more than 21.—*also* **pontoon, twenty-one, vingt-et-un.**

blackjack[2] *n* a large leather vessel or drinking cup; a short leather club with a flexible handle. * *vt* to hit with a blackjack.

blackjack (oak) *n* a dark shrubby oak of North America.

black lead *n* plumbago, graphite.

blackleg *n* a person who takes a striker's place, a scab; a person who endeavours to obtain money by cheating at races or cards, a rook; a disease affecting sheep and cattle. * *vti* (**blacklegging, blacklegged**) to act or injure, as a blackleg.

black letter *n* the old English or Gothic type used in early manuscripts and the first printed books. * *adj* written or printed in black letter.

blacklist *n* a list of those censored, refused employment, regarded as suspicious politically or generally not to be trusted. * *vt* to put on such a list.

black magic *n* sorcery, witchcraft.

blackmail *vt* to extort money by threatening to disclose discreditable facts. * *n* the crime of blackmailing.—**blackmailer** *n*.

Black Maria *n* a prison van, a patrol wagon.

black market *n* the illegal buying and selling of goods, esp banned goods, eg drugs, or when rationing is in force.—**black marketeer, black marketer** *n*.

black mass *n* a travesty of the Mass used by Satanists.

blackout *n* the darkness when all lights are switched off; temporary loss of consciousness or electricity; a breakdown of communications between a spacecraft and ground control; a closing down of radio or TV broadcasting due to strike action or government ban.

black power *n* a movement of black people whose goal is political, social and economic equality with whites.

black pudding *n* a dark sausage with a large proportion of blood.

Black Rod *n* in UK, the usher belonging to the order of the Garter and the House of Lords, so called from the black rod of the office.

black sheep *n* a person regarded as disreputable or a disgrace by their family.

Blackshirt *n* a fascist, esp a member of Mussolini's Italian Fascist party.

blacksmith *n* a metal worker, esp one who shoes horses.

black spot *n* an area where traffic accidents frequently happen; a difficult or dangerous place; a disease affecting leaves, esp of roses.

blackthorn *n* the sloe; a walking stick cut from the stem of the sloe.

black widow *n* a poisonous spider found in America, the female of which devours its mate.

bladder *n* a sac that fills with fluid, esp one that holds urine flowing from the kidneys; any inflatable bag.

bladderwort *n* any of a genus of water plants, some of which trap insects.

bladderwrack *n* a type of seaweed with trailing fronds containing small air bladders.

blade *n* the cutting edge of a tool or knife; the broad, flat surface of a leaf; a straight, narrow leaf of grass; the flat part of an oar or paddle; the runner of an ice skate.—**bladed** *adj*.

blah[1] *n* (*sl*) nonsense, exaggeration; a blunder.

blah[2] *adj* (*sl*) boring; mediocre.

blain *n* an inflamed sore, a blister.

blame *vt* to hold responsible for; to accuse. * *n* responsibility for an error; reproof.—**blamable, blameable** *adj*.

blameful *adj* meriting blame; guilty.—**blamefully** *adv*.—**blamefulness** *n*.

blameless *adj* innocent; free from blame.—**blamelessly** *adv*.—**blamelessness** *n*.

blameworthy *adj* deserving blame.—**blameworthiness** *n*.

blanch *vt* to whiten or bleach; to make pale; (*vegetables, almonds, etc*) to scald. * *vi* to turn pale.

blancmange *n* a dessert made from gelatinous or starchy ingredients (as cornflour) and milk.

bland *adj* mild; gentle; insipid.—**blandly** *adv*.—**blandness** *n*.

blandish *vti* to flatter in order to coax; to cajole.

blandishment *n* (*usu pl*) a winning expression or action, an artful caress, cajolery.

blank *adj* (*paper*) bearing no writing or marks; vacant; (*mind*) empty of thought; (*look*) without expression; (*denial, refusal*) utter, complete; (*cheque*) signed but with no amount written in. * *n* an empty space, esp one to be filled out on a printed form; an empty place or time.—**blankly** *adv*.—**blankness** *n*.

blank (cartridge) *n* a powder-filled cartridge without a bullet.

blank cheque, blank check *n* a signed cheque with the amount left blank to be filled by the payee; complete freedom of action.

blanket *n* a large, soft piece of cloth used for warmth, esp as a bed cover; (*of snow, smoke*) a cover or layer. * *adj* applying to a wide variety of cases or situations. * *vt* to cover.

blank verse *n* unrhymed verse.

blare *vti* to sound harshly or loudly. * *n* a loud, harsh sound.

blarney *n* wheedling talk, flattery. * *vt* (**blarneying, blarneyed**) to influence or talk over by soft wheedling speeches; to humbug with flattery.

Blarney Stone *n* a stone in the wall of Blarney Castle, Cork, on kissing which a person is said to become an adept in flattery.

blasé *adj* bored, indifferent; sated with pleasure.

blaspheme *vt* to speak irreverently of (God, a divine being or sacred things). * *vi* to utter blasphemy.—**blasphemer** *n*.

blasphemous *adj* impious, grossly insulting (to God, etc).

blasphemy *n* (*pl* **blasphemies**) impious speaking; speaking irreverently of God, a divine being or sacred things.

blast *n* a sharp gust of air; the sound of a horn; an explosion; an outburst of criticism. * *vt* to wither; to blow up, explode; to criticize sharply. * *vi* to make a loud, harsh sound; to set off explosives, etc; (*with* **off**) to be launched.

blasted *adj* withered; (*inf*) damned.

blastema *n* (*pl* **blastemas, blastemata**) (*biol*) the point of growth of an organ as yet unformed, from which it is developed.—**blastemal, blastemic, blastematic** *adj*.

blast furnace *n* a smelting furnace using compressed air.

blasto- *prefix* bud; germination.

blastoderm *n* a layer of embryonic cells in an egg from which an organism is formed.—**blastodermic** *adj*.

blastoff *n* the launch of a space vehicle or rocket; the time when this takes place.

blastogenesis *n* reproduction by budding.—**blastogenic, blastogenetic** *adj*.

blatant *adj* noisy; glaringly conspicuous.—**blatancy** *n*.—**blatantly** *adv*.

blather *see* **blather**.

blatherskite *n* a blethering or blustering person.

blaze[1] *n* an intensive fire; a bright light; splendour; an outburst (of emotion). * *vi* to burn brightly; to shine with a brilliant light; to be excited, as with anger.

blaze[2] *n* a white mark on the face of a horse or other quadruped; a white mark cut on a tree to serve as a guide. * *vt* to mark, as trees, by removing a portion of the bark; to indicate, as a path or boundary, by blazing trees; **blaze a trail** to act as a pioneer.

blaze[3] *vt* to proclaim, to publish widely.

blazer *n* a lightweight jacket, often in a bright colour representing membership of a sports club, school, etc.

blazon *vt* to proclaim publicly; to adorn; to describe (heraldic or armorial bearings) in technical terms. * *n* the terminology of coats of arms.—**blazoner** *n*.—**blazonment** *n*.

blazonry *n* (*pl* **blazonries**) a heraldic device; the art of describing and explaining coats of arms; decoration, as with heraldic devices; a bright display.

bldg. *abbr* = building.
bleach *vti* to make or become white or colourless. * *n* a substance for bleaching.—**bleachable** *adj*.—**bleacher** *n*.
bleachers *npl* the unroofed seats at a baseball field or sports ground.
bleaching powder *n* a white powder, chloride of lime, used for bleaching.
bleak[1] *adj* cold; exposed; bare; harsh; gloomy; not hopeful.—**bleakly** *adv*.—**bleakness** *n*.
bleak[2] *n* (*pl* **bleak, bleaks**) a small European river fish with brilliant silvery scales.
blear *adj* (*eyes*) sore or dim with inflammation. * *vt* to make (eyes) sore or watery; to dim or blur.
bleary *adj* (**blearier, bleariest**) (*eyesight*) dim with water or tears; obscure, indistinct.—**blearily** *adv*.—**bleariness** *n*.
bleary-eyed *adj* with eyes dulled by tears or tiredness; dull.
bleat *vi* to cry as a sheep, goat or calf; to complain. * *n* a bleating cry or sound.—**bleater** *n*.—**bleatingly** *adv*.
bleb *n* a small blister; a bubble in water or glass.
bleed *vb* (**bleeding, bled**) *vi* to lose blood; to ooze sap, colour or dye; to die for a country or an ideal; to sympathize (often ironically). * *vt* to remove blood or sap from; (*inf*) to extort money or goods from.
bleeder *n* one who bleeds, esp blood from another; (*inf*) a person with haemophilia; (*sl*) an annoying person.
bleep *vi* to emit a high-pitched sound or signal (eg a car alarm). * *n* a small portable electronic radio receiver that emits a bleep to convey a message.—*also* **bleeper**.
blemish *n* a flaw or defect, as a spot. * *vt* to mar; to spoil.
blench *vi* to flinch; to blanch.
blend *vt* (*varieties of tea, etc*) to mix or mingle; to mix so that the components cannot be distinguished. * *vi* to mix, merge; to shade gradually into each other, as colours; to harmonize. * *n* a mixture.
blende *n* any of various minerals composed mainly of metallic sulphides; a yellow to brownish-black zinc ore, sphalerite.
blender *n* something or someone that blends; an electrical device for preparing food.—*also* **liquidizer**.
blenny *n* (*pl* **blennies, blenny**) a small elongated spiny-finned sea fish.
blepharitis *n* inflammation of the eyelids.—**blepharitic** *adj*.
blesbok *n* (*pl* **blesboks, blesbok**) a South African white-faced antelope.
bless *vt* (**blessing, blessed** *or* **blest**) to consecrate; to praise; to call upon God's protection; to grant happiness; to make the sign of the cross over.
blessed *adj* holy, sacred; fortunate; blissful; beatified.—**blessedly** *adv*.—**blessedness** *n*.
blessing *n* a prayer or wish for success or happiness; a cause of happiness; good wishes or approval; a grace said before or after eating.
blest *see* **bless**.
blet *n* a decayed spot in fruit.
blether *vi* (*inf*) to talk foolishly. * *n* (*inf*) foolish talk; one who talks it.—*also* **blather**.
blew *see* **blow**[2].
blight *n* any insect, disease, etc that destroys plants; anything that prevents growth or destroys; somone or something that spoils. * *vt* to destroy; to frustrate.
blimp *n* a small, nonrigid airship; any airship; a soundproof cover for a camera.
blind *adj* sightless; unable to discern or understand; not directed by reason; (*exit*) hidden, concealed; closed at one end. * *n* something that deceives; a shade for a window; (*sl*) a drinking bout. * *vti* to make sightless, to deprive of insight; to dazzle (with facts, a bright light, etc); to deceive.—**blindly** *adv*.—**blindness** *n*.
blind alley *n* a street closed at one end; an occupation or inquiry that leads to nothing.
blind date *n* a date between two individuals who have never met before; either individual on a blind date.
blinder *n* a horse's blinkers.
blindfish *n* (*pl* **blindfish, blindfishes**) a diminutive fish of a pale colour and with rudimentary eyes, which inhabits underground waters.
blindfold *n* a cloth or bandage used to cover the eyes. * *adj* having the eyes covered, so as not to see; reckless. * *vt* to cover the eyes with a strip of cloth, etc; to hamper sight or understanding; to mislead.
blind man's buff *n* a game in which a blindfold person tries to catch and identify others.
blind spot *n* a point on the retina of the eye that is insensitive to light; a place where vision is obscured; a subject on which someone is ignorant.
blindstorey, blindstory *n* (*pl* **blindstoreys, blindstories**) (*archit*) the storey below the clerestory, admitting no light.
blindworm *n* the slowworm, a small, slender limbless lizard with very small eyes.
blini, blinis *npl* (*sing* **blin**) buckwheat pancakes.
blink *vi* to open and close the eyes rapidly; (*light*) to flash on and off; (*with* **at**) to ignore. * *vt* (*with* **at**) to be amazed or surprised. * *n* a glance, a glimpse; a momentary flash.
blinker *n* one who blinks; that which obscures the sight or mental perception; (*pl*) a screen for a horse's eye, to prevent it from seeing sideways; (*sl*) the eyes.
blip *n* a trace on a radar screen; a recurring sound; a temporary setback. * *vi* (**blipping, blipped**) to make a blip.
bliss *n* supreme happiness; spiritual joy.—**blissful** *adj*.—**blissfully** *adv*.
blister *n* a raised patch on the skin, containing water, as caused by burning or rubbing; a raised bubble on any other surface. * *vti* to cause or form blisters; to lash with words.
blistering *adj* (*criticism*) scornful, cruel.
BLit, BLitt *abbr* = Bachelor of Literature.
blithe *adj* happy, cheerful, gay.—**blithely** *adv*.—**blitheness** *n*.
blithering *adj* (*inf*) stupid, idiotic.
blithesome *adj* blithe, merry.—**blithesomely** *adv*.—**blithesomeness** *n*.
blitz *n* heavy aerial bombing; any sudden destructive attack; a determined effort. * *vt* to subject to a blitz.
blitzkrieg *n* warfare in which blitz is employed; any swift combined action.
blizzard *n* a severe storm of wind and snow.
bloat *vti* to swell as with water or air; to puff up, as with pride; to cure or dry (fish) in smoke.—**bloated** *adj*.
bloater *n* a herring or mackerel smoked and partially dried, but not split open.
blob *n* a drop of liquid; a round spot (of colour, etc).
bloc *n* a group of parties, nations, etc united to achieve a common purpose.
block *n* a solid piece of stone or wood, etc; a piece of wood used as a base (for chopping, etc); a group or row of buildings; a number of things as a unit; the main body of a petrol engine; a building divided into offices; an obstruction; a child's building brick; (*sl*) the head. * *vt* to impede or obstruct; to shape; (*often with* **out**) to sketch roughly. * *vi* to obstruct an opponent in sports.—**blocker** *n*.
blockade *n* (*mil*) the obstruction of an enemy seaport by warships; any strategic barrier. * *vt* to obstruct in this way.—**blockader** *n*.
blockage *n* an obstruction.
blockbuster *n* (*sl*) a very heavy bomb of great penetrative power; a conspicuously powerful or effective person or thing; one who engages in blockbusting.
blockbusting *n* the practice of persuading house owners to sell their houses quickly by convincing them that property values will drop.
blockhead *n* a dolt, a stupid person.
blockhouse *n* a small fort, usu of timber; a log house; a concrete fortification with loopholes for observation or firing from.
block letter *n* a handwritten capital letter similar to a printed letter.
block vote *n* at a conference, a total vote represented by one delegate.
bloke *n* (*inf*) a man.
blond, blonde *adj* having light-coloured hair and skin; light-coloured. * *n* a blond person.—**blondness, blondeness** *n*.
blonde lace *n* a silk lace.

blood *n* the red fluid that circulates in the arteries and veins of animals; the sap of a plant; the essence of life; kinship; descent; hatred; anger; bloodshed; guilt of murder.
blood-and-thunder *adj* melodramatic. * *n* a sensational story or play.
blood bank *n* a place where blood is taken from blood donors and stored.
blood bath *n* a massacre.
blood brother *n* one of two men or boys pledged to treat the other as a brother, as confirmed by the ceremonial mingling of blood.
blood cell *n* a red or white cell present in the blood.
blood count *n* the determination of the numbers of red and white corpuscles in a sample of blood.
bloodcurdling *adj* exciting terror, horrifying, chilling.
blood donor *n* a person who donates his or her blood for transfusion.
blooded *adj* having a specific kind of blood (*hot-blooded*); of fine breed; initiated.
blood group *n* any of the classes of human blood.—*also* **blood type**.
blood heat *n* the normal heat of the human blood in health (37°C, 98.4° F).
bloodhound *n* a large breed of hound used for tracking; a detective.
bloodletting *n* phlebotomy; bloodshed, eg a massacre.
bloodless *adj* without blood or slaughter; unfeeling.—**bloodlessly** *adv*.—**bloodlessness** *n*.
blood money *n* money obtained at the cost of another's life; the reward paid for the discovery or capture of a murderer; compensation paid to the next of kin of a person slain by another.
blood poisoning *n* septicaemia.
blood pressure *n* the pressure of the blood in the arterial system.
blood pudding *n* blood sausage.
blood-red *adj* red as blood.
blood relation, blood relative *n* a person related by descent, not marriage.
blood sausage *n* a dark sausage with a large proportion of blood.
bloodshed *n* killing.
bloodshot *adj* (*eye*) suffused with blood, red and inflamed.
blood sport *n* any sport in which an animal is hunted and killed.
bloodstain *n* a stain made by blood.
bloodstained *adj* stained with blood; responsible for killing.
bloodstock *n* thoroughbred horses collectively.
bloodstone *n* a dark green quartz flecked with red jasper; heliotrope.
bloodstream *n* the flow of blood through the blood vessels in the human body.
bloodsucker *n* an animal that sucks blood, a leech; a person who sponges or preys on another, an extortionist.—**bloodsucking** *adj, n*.
blood test *n* an examination of a blood specimen to ascertain blood group, alcohol intake, etc.
bloodthirsty *adj* (**bloodthirstier, bloodthirstiest**) eager for blood, cruel, warlike.—**bloodthirstiness** *n*.
blood type *see* **blood group**.
blood vessel *n* in the body, a vein, artery, or capillary.
bloody *adj* (**bloodier, bloodiest**) stained with or covered in blood; bloodthirsty; cruel, murderous; (*sl*) as an intensifier (*a bloody good hiding*). * *vt* (**bloodying, bloodied**) to cover with blood.—**bloodily** *adv*.—**bloodiness** *n*.
Bloody Mary *n* (*pl* **Bloody Marys**) a drink made with vodka and tomato juice.
bloody-minded *adj* (*inf*) deliberately obstructive.—**bloody-mindedness** *n*.
bloom[1] *n* a flower or blossom; the period of being in flower; a period of most health, vigour, etc; a youthful, healthy glow; the powdery coating on some fruit and leaves. * *vi* to blossom; to be in one's prime; to glow with health etc.
bloom[2] *n* a rough mass of incandescent iron for hammering or rolling into bars. * *vt* to make (iron) into bloom.
bloomer, blooper *n* (*inf*) a stupid mistake.
bloomers *npl* (*inf*) baggy knickers.
blooming *adj* blossoming, flowering; flourishing; (*sl*) confounded, bloody.—**bloomingly** *adv*.
blossom *n* a flower, esp one that produces edible fruit; a state or time of flowering. * *vi* to flower; to begin to develop.—**blossomy** *adj*.
blot *n* a spot or stain, esp of ink; something that diminishes or spoils the beauty of; a blemish in reputation. * *vt* (**blotting, blotted**) to spot or stain; to obscure; to disgrace; to absorb with blotting paper.
blotch *n* a spot or discoloration on the skin; any large blot or stain. * *vt* to cover with blotches.—**blotched** *adj*.—**blotchily** *adv*.—**blotchy** *adj*.
blotter *n* a piece of blotting paper.
blotting paper *n* absorbent paper used to dry freshly written ink.
blotto *adj* (*sl*) very drunk.
blouse *n* a shirt-like garment worn by women.
blow[1] *n* a hard hit, as with the fist; a sudden attack; a sudden misfortune; a setback.
blow[2] *vb* (**blowing, blew,** *pp* **blown**) *vi* to cause a current of air; to be moved or carried (by air, the wind, etc); (*mus*) to make a sound by forcing in air with the mouth; (*often with* **out**) to burst suddenly; to breathe hard; (*with* **out**) to become extinguished by a gust of air; (*gas or oil well*) to erupt out of control; (*with* **over**) to pass without consequence. * *vt* to move along with a current of air; to make a sound by blowing; to inflate with air; (*a fuse, etc*) to melt; (*inf*) to spend (money) freely; (*sl*) to leave; (*sl*) to divulge a secret; (*sl*) to bungle; (*often with* **up**) to burst by an explosion; (*with* **out**) to extinguish by a gust; (*storm*) to dissipate (itself) by blowing; (*with* **over**) to pass over or pass by; (*with* **up**) to enlarge a photograph; (*with* **up**) (*inf*) to lose one's temper.
blow[3] *vi* (**blowing, blew,** *pp* **blown**) to blossom, to flower. * *n* a mass of blossom; the state or condition of flowering.
blow-by-blow *adj* told or shown in great detail.
blow-dry *vi* (**blow-drying, blow-dried**) to style recently washed hair with a hand-held drier.
blower *n* one who blows; a braggart; a device for producing a stream of gas or air.
blowfly *n* (*pl* **blowflies**) a fly that lays its eggs in rotting meat.
blowhole *n* a nostril of a whale; a vent for the escape of gas, air, etc; a hole in ice used for breathing by whales, seals, etc; a hole of gas in metal capturing during the solidifying process.
blow job *n* (*sl*) fellatio.
blowlamp, blowtorch *n* a gas-powered torch that produces a hot flame for welding, etc.
blown *adj* swollen or bloated.
blowout *n* (*inf*) a festive social event; a bursting of a container (as a tyre) by pressure on a weak spot; an uncontrolled eruption of a gas or oil well.
blowpipe *n* a tube through which a current of air or gas is driven upon a flame to concentrate its heat on a substance, eg glass, to fuse it; a long tube of cane or reed used to discharge arrows by the force of the breath.
blowup *n* an explosion; an enlarged photograph; (*sl*) an angry outburst.
blowy *adj* (**blowier, blowiest**) breezy, windy.
blowzy, blowsy *adj* (**blowzier, blowziest** *or* **blowsier, blowsiest**) (*esp a woman*) fat and ruddy, slatternly.—**blowzily, blowsily** *adv*.—**blowziness, blowziness** *n*.
blubber[1] *vi* to weep loudly.
blubber[2] *n* whale fat; excessive fat on the body.
bludgeon *n* a short, heavy stick used for striking. * *vti* to strike with a bludgeon; to bully or coerce.
blue *adj* (**bluer, bluest**) of the colour of the clear sky; depressed; (*film*) indecent, obscene. * *n* the colour of the spectrum lying between green and violet; (*with* **the**) the sky, the sea; (*pl: with* **the**) (*inf*) a depressed feeling; (*pl: with* **the**) a style of vocal and instrumental jazz; a representative in a sport of a university, esp Oxford or Cambridge; the badge worn or honour bestowed; in UK, a member or adherent of the Tory party. * *vt* (**blueing** *or* **bluing, blued**) to make or dye blue; to dip in blue liquid; (*sl*) to squander.
blue baby *n* one born with a heart condition causing a blueness of the skin.

bluebell *n* any of several plants with a one-sided cluster of blue bell-shaped flowers.
bluebird *n* any of various small songbirds prevalent in North America.
blue blood *n* royal or aristocratic descent.
bluebonnet *n* a Scottish cap of blue cloth; a name given to the Scottish troops before the Union, 1707; a Scotsman.
blue book *n* a governmental official report, etc, bound in blue paper covers; a directory of socially prominent persons; a booklet in which students answer examination questions.
bluebottle *n* a large fly; (*inf*) a policeman.
blue cheese *n* cheese with veins of blue mould.
blue chip *adj* (*stocks, shares*) providing a reliable return.
blue-collar *adj* of or pertaining to manual workers.
blue devils *npl* low spirits; mental depression; delirium tremens.
bluegrass *n* any of several rich pasture grasses with bluish green blades, esp in Kentucky; improvisatory country music played on unamplified instruments.
blue gum *n* a lofty eucalyptus tree of Australia, valuable for its timber and essential oil.
blueing *n* the process of imparting a blue tint; the indigo, etc, used by washerwomen.—*also* **bluing.**
bluejacket *n* a seaman in the British or US navy.
blue mould *n* a minute fungus that attacks bread and other foodstuffs.
bluenose *n* a puritanical person; a Nova Scotian.
blue peter *n* a small blue flag with a white square in the centre, hoisted when a ship is about to sail.
blueprint *n* a blue photographic print of plans; a detailed scheme, template of work to be done; basis or prototype for future development.
blue ribbon *n* in UK, the broad ribbon of a dark blue colour worn by members of the order of the Garter; a prized distinction; a mark of success; a thin blue strip worn as a badge of teetotalism.
blue rinse *n* a rinse giving a blue tint to grey hair.
blue-rinse *adj* (*inf*) describing mature, assured, social women and their background.
blues *npl* (*used as sing or pl*) depression, melancholy; a type of melancholy folk music originating among Black Americans.
bluestocking *n* a woman of literary tastes or occupation.
bluestone *n* a grey sandstone used for building, etc; copper sulphate in crystalline form.
blue whale *n* a rorqual, the largest mammal known.
bluey *n* (*Austral*) a bushman's bundle.
bluff[1] *adj* rough in manner; abrupt, outspoken; ascending steeply with a flat front. * *n* a broad, steep bank or cliff.—**bluffness** *n.*
bluff[2] *vti* to mislead or frighten by a false, bold front.* *n* deliberate deception.—**bluffer** *n.*
bluing *see* **blueing.**
blunder *vi* to make a foolish mistake; to move about clumsily. * *n* a foolish mistake.—**blunderer** *n.*—**blundering** *adj.*—**blunderingly** *adv.*
blunderbuss *n* (*hist*) a short gun or firearm with a wide bore, firing many balls; a clumsy person.
blunge *vt* (*pottery*) to mix clay with water.
blunt *adj* not having a sharp edge or point; rude, outspoken, unsubtle. * *vti* to make or become dull.—**bluntly** *adv.*—**bluntness** *n.*
blur *n* a stain, smear; an ill-defined impression. * *vti* (**blurring, blurred**) to smear; to make or become indistinct in shape, etc; to dim.—**blurred** *adj.*—**blurredly** *adv.*—**blurry** *adj.*
blurb *n* a promotional description, as on a book cover; an exaggerated advertisement.
blurt *vt* (*with* **out**) to utter impulsively.
blush *n* a red flush of the face caused by embarrassment or guilt; any rosy colour. * *vi* (*with* **for, at**) to show embarrassment, modesty, joy, etc involuntarily, by blushing; to become rosy.
blusher *n* a cosmetic that gives colour to the cheeks.
blush wine *n* rosé wine, a blend of red and white wines.
bluster *vi* to make a noise like the wind; to bully. * *n* a blast, as of the wind; bullying or boastful talk, often to hide shame or embarrassment.—**blusterer** *n.*—**blustery** *adj.*—**blusteringly, blusterously** *adv.*
Blvd *abbr* = Boulevard.
B-movie *n* (*cinema*) a film made as a supporting feature, esp in the 1940s and 1950s.
BMus *abbr* = Bachelor of Music.
bn *abbr* = battalion; billion.
BO *abbr* = (*inf*) body odour.
boa *n* any of various large South American snakes that crush their prey; a long fluffy scarf of feathers.
boa constrictor *n* the largest boa, remarkable for its length and power of destroying its prey by constriction.
boar *n* a male pig, a wild hog.
board *n* meals, esp when provided regularly for pay; a long, flat piece of sawed wood, etc; a flat piece of wood, etc for some special purpose; pasteboard; a council; a group of people who supervise a company; the side of a ship (*overboard*). * *vt* to provide with meals and lodging at fixed terms; to come onto the deck of (a ship); to get on (a train, bus, etc). * *vi* to provide with meals, or room and meals, regularly for pay; (*with* **up**) to cover with boards; **to take on board** to appoint to a position; to adopt new ideas.
boarder *n* one who is provided with board.
board game *n* a game as chess, chequers, etc, played by moving pieces on a marked board.
boarding *n* light timber collectively; a covering of planks; the act of supplying, or state of being supplied with, food and lodging for a stipulated sum; the act of entering a ship or aircraft.
boarding house *n* a house for boarders.
boarding school *n* a school where the students are boarded.
boardroom *n* a room where meetings of a company's board are held.
board rule *n* a figured scale for finding the number of square feet in a board without calculation.
boardwalk *n* a footway of boards, esp by the sea.
boarish *adj* coarse; brutal; cruel.
boart *see* **bort.**
boast[1] *vi* to brag. * *vt* to speak proudly of; to possess with pride. * *n* boastful talk.—**boaster** *n.*—**boastingly** *adv.*
boast[2] *vt* to dress stone with a broad chisel and mallet; to dress a block in outline for a statue, etc, prior to more detailed or delicate work.
boastful *adj* given to boasting.—**boastfully** *adv.*—**boastfulness** *n.*
boat *n* a small, open, waterborne craft; (*inf*) a ship. * *vi* to travel in a boat, esp for pleasure.
boatbill(ed heron) *n* a South American wading bird with a boat-shaped bill.
boater *n* a stiff flat straw hat.
boathook *n* a hooked pole for drawing a boat to land, fending off, etc.
boathouse *n* a shed for boats.
boating *n* rowing, sailing, etc, for pleasure.
boatman *n* (*pl* **boatmen**) a person who works on, deals in, or operates boats.
boat people *npl* refugees fleeing by boat.
boatswain *n* a ship's officer in charge of hull maintenance and related work.—*also* **bosun.**
boat train *n* a train for steamer or ferry passengers.
bob *vb* (**bobbing, bobbed**) *vi* to move abruptly up and down, often in water; to nod the head; to curtsey. * *vt* (*hair*) to cut short. * *n* a jerking motion up and down; the weight on a pendulum, plumb line, etc; a woman's or girl's short haircut.
bobbery *n* (*pl* **bobberies**) a rumpus, a row, a noisy disturbance; a pack of hunting dogs.
bobbin *n* a reel or spool on which yarn or thread is wound.
bobbinet *n* a machine-made cotton netting or lace in imitation of pillow lace.
bobble *n* a small woolly ball used for ornament or trimming; a bobbing movement; (*inf*) a mistake; a fumble. *vti* to bob up and down; to make a mistake; to fumble with (a ball).

bobby *n* (*pl* **bobbies**) (*sl*) a policeman.
bobby pin *n* a clip for holding hair in position; a hairgrip.
bobcat *n* (*pl* **bobcats, bobcat**) a medium-sized feline of eastern North America with a black-spotted reddish-brown coat and a short tail.
bobolink *n* an American migratory songbird.—*also* **reedbird, ricebird**.
bobsled, bobsleigh *n* a long racing sled. * *vi* (**bobsledding, bobsledded**) to ride or race on a bobsled.
bobstay *n* (*naut*) a rope holding the bowsprit down to the stem.
bobtail *n* a short tail or a tail cut short; an animal with a docked tail; the rabble (*rag-tag and bobtail*). * *adj* with a docked tail.—**bobtailed** *adj*.
Boche *n* (*pl* **Boche**) (*sl*) a German, esp a soldier.
bock *n* a variety of lager beer of double strength; a glass of beer.
bode *vt* to be an omen of.
bodega *n* a wine vault, cellar or shop where wine is sold from the cask; a store specializing in Hispanic groceries.
bodice *n* the upper part of a woman's dress.
bodiless *adj* without a body, incorporeal.—**bodilessness** *n*.
bodily *adj* physical; relating to the body. * *adv* in the flesh; as a whole; altogether.
bodkin *n* a large blunt needle, a tool for piercing holes; a pin for fastening hair; a small dagger.
body *n* (*pl* **bodies**) the whole physical substance of a person, animal, or plant; the trunk of a person or animal; a corpse; the principal part of anything; a distinct mass; substance or consistency, as of liquid; a richness of flavour; a person; a distinct group of people. * *vt* (**bodying, bodied**) to give shape to.
body bag *n* a large plastic sack, usu zipped, to carry a corpse from the scene of a disaster.
bodybuilding *n* strengthening and enlarging the muscles through exercise and diet for competitive display.—**bodybuilder** *n*.
bodyguard *n* a person or persons assigned to guard someone.
body language *n* gestures, unconscious bodily movements, etc, that function as a means of communication.
body politic *n* the collective body of people living under an organized political government.
body-snatcher *n* (*formerly*) one who stole corpses from graves for dissection by anatomists.
body stocking *n* a woman's tight-fitting garment that covers the torso and sometimes the legs.
body warmer *n* a sleeveless, quilted outer garment.
bodywork *n* the outer shell of a motor vehicle.
Boeotian *adj* pertaining to Boeotia in central Greece, noted for its moist and heavy atmosphere; dull, stupid. * *n* an inhabitant of Boeotia; a dull, stupid person.
Boer *n* a Dutch-descended South African.—*also adj*.
boffin *n* (*inf*) a military research scientist.
boffo *adj* (*sl*) wonderful, amazing.
bog *n* wet, spongy ground; quagmire. * *vb* (**bogging, bogged**) *vt* to sink or submerge in a bog or quagmire. * *vi* to sink or stick in a bog.—**boggy** *adj*.
bogey[1] *n* (*pl* **bogeys**) (*golf*) one stroke more than par on a hole.
bogey[2] *n* (*pl* **bogeys**) a goblin; a cause of worry.—*also* **bogy** (*pl* **bogies**).
bogeyman *n* (*pl* **bogeymen**) an imaginary monster commonly used to frighten children.
boggle *vi* to be surprised; to hesitate (at). * *vt* to confuse (the imagination, mind, etc).
bogie *n* an assembly of four or six wheels on a rail carriage.
bogle *n* a goblin, a spectre; a scarecrow.
bogus *adj* counterfeit, spurious.
bogy *see* **bogey**[2].
bohea *n* a black China tea of the lowest quality.
Bohemian *adj* of or pertaining to Bohemia in Czechoslovakia; unconventional. * *n* an inhabitant of Bohemia; a person who disregards social conventions or evinces a wild or roving disposition; a gipsy.
Bohemianism *n* the life or habits of a person, usu artistic or literary, who by natural inclination leads a free and easy unconventional existence.
boil[1] *vi* to change rapidly from a liquid to a vapour by heating; to bubble when boiling; to cook in boiling liquid; to be aroused with anger; (*with* **down**) to reduce by boiling; to condense; (*with* **over**) to overflow when boiling; to burst out in anger. * *vt* to heat to boiling point; to cook in boiling water.—**boilable** *adj*.
boil[2] *n* an inflamed, pus-filled, painful swelling on the skin.
boiler *n* a container in which to boil things; a storage tank in which water is heated and steam generated; a device for providing central heating and hot water.
boilersuit *n* coveralls.
boiling point *n* the temperature at which a liquid boils; the point at which a person loses his temper; the point of crisis.
boisterous *adj* wild, noisy; stormy; loud and exuberant.—**boisterously** *adv*.
bola, bolas *n* a South American hunting implement consisting of two or more balls of iron or stone attached to the ends of a leather cord, used to entangle the legs of an animal.
bold *adj* daring or courageous; fearless; impudent; striking to the eye. * *n* boldface type.—**boldly** *adv*.—**boldness** *n*.
boldface type *n* type characters with thickened, heavy strokes.
bole[1] *n* the trunk or stem of a tree.
bole[2] *n* friable clay or clayey shale, usu coloured by oxide of iron.
bolection *n* (*archit*) a raised moulding on a panel.
bolero *n* (*pl* **boleros**) a lively Spanish dance; the music accompanying such a dance; a short jacket-shaped bodice.
boletus *n* (*pl* **boletuses, boleti**) any of a large genus of thick-stemmed fungi containing edible or poisonous species.
bolide *n* a large meteor that explodes on coming into contact with air, a fire ball.
boll *n* the pod of a plant, esp of cotton or flax.
bollard *n* a strong post on a wharf around which mooring lines are secured; one of a line of posts closing off a street to traffic; an illuminated marker on a traffic island.
bollocks *npl* (*sl*) testicles. * *interj* used to express utter disbelief, ridicule, etc.
boll weevil *n* an American weevil that infests cotton bolls.
bolometer *n* an instrument for measuring radiation.—**bolometric** *adj*.—**bolometrically** *adv*.
boloney *see* **baloney**.
Bolshevik *n* (*pl* **Bolsheviks, Bolsheviki**) a Russian communist; a revolutionary; an opponent of an existing social order.
Bolshevism *n* the doctrines and practices of the Bolsheviks; the communist form of government adopted in Russia in March 1917.—**Bolshevist** *adj, n*.
bolshie, bolshy *adj* (*sl*) left-wing; rebellious. * *n* (*pl* **bolshies**) (*often with cap*) a Bolshevik; a revolutionary.
bolster *n* a long narrow pillow; any bolster-like object or support. * *vt* (*often with* **up**) to support or strengthen.—**bolsterer** *n*.—**bolsteringly** *adv*.
bolt[1] *n* a bar used to lock a door, etc; an arrow for a crossbow; a flash of lightning; a threaded metal rod used with a nut to hold parts together; a roll (of cloth, paper, etc); a sudden dash. * *vt* to lock with a bolt; to eat hastily; to say suddenly; to blurt (out); to abandon (a party, group, etc). * *vi* (*horse*) to rush away suddenly * *adv* erectly upright.—**bolter** *n*.
bolt[2] *vt* to sift or separate coarser from finer particles; to examine with carc, to investigate; to separate.—*also* **boult**.—**bolter** *n*.
bolthole *n* an escape route; a safe and secret hiding place; a person's private refuge.
boltrope *n* (*naut*) a rope to which the edges of sails are sewn.
bolus *n* (*pl* **boluses**) a medicine in the form of a soft rounded mass, larger than an ordinary pill, to be swallowed at once; anything disagreeable, which must be accepted.
bomb *n* a projectile containing explosives, incendiary material, or chemicals used for destruction; (*with* **the**) the hydrogen or atomic bomb; (*sl*) a lot of money. * *vt* to attack with bombs. * *vi* to fail, to flop.

bombard *vt* to attack with bombs or artillery; to attack verbally.—**bombardment** *n*.
bombardier *n* the crew member who releases the bombs in a bomber; in Britain and Canada, a noncommissioned artillery officer.
bombardier beetle *n* any of various coleopterous insects that, when irritated, expel a fluid from the abdomen with a slight report.
bombast *n* pretentious or boastful language.—**bombastic** *adj*.—**bombastically** *adv*.
bombazine *n* a twilled fabric of which the warp is silk and the weft worsted.
bombe *n* a frozen dessert moulded into a round shape.
bomber *n* a person who bombs; an aeroplane that carries bombs.
bomber jacket *n* a waist-length bloused jacket with a zip.
bombshell *n* a shocking surprise.
bombsight *n* a manual or electronic device for aiming bombs.
bomb site *n* an area devastated by bombing; a vacant area cleared after a bombing raid.
bombycid *n* any of a family of moths, including the silkworm moth.
bona fide *adj* in good faith; genuine or real.
bona fides *n* good faith; honourable dealing.
bonanza *n* a rich vein of ore; any source of wealth; unexpected good fortune or luck.
bonbon *n* a small piece of candy, a sweet.
bond *n* anything that binds, fastens, or unites; (*pl*) shackles; an obligation imposed by a contract, promise, etc; the status of goods in a warehouse until taxes are paid; an interest-bearing certificate issued by the government or business, redeemable on a specified date; surety against theft, absconding, etc. * *vt* to join, bind, or otherwise unite; to provide a bond for; to place or hold (goods) in bond; to put together bricks or stones so that they overlap to give strength. * *vi* to hold together by means of a bond.—**bondable** *adj*.—**bonder** *n*.
bondage *n* slavery, captivity.
bondstone *n* a long stone runing through a wall and so binding it.
bone *n* the hard material making up the skeleton; any constituent part of the skeleton; (*pl*) the skeleton; the essentials or basics of anything. * *vti* to remove the bones from, as meat; (*with* **up**) (*inf*) to study hard.—**boneless** *adj*.
bone black *n* a black pigment made partly from charcoal obtained by roasting animal bones.
bone china *n* china made from clay mixed with bone ash.
bone-dry *adj* completely dry.
bonehead *n* (*sl*) a fool.
bone meal *n* fertilizer or feed made of crushed or ground bone.
bone of contention *n* a source of strife.
bonesetter *n* one who treats fractures or dislocated limbs without medical qualification to do so.
bonfire *n* an outdoor fire.
bongo[1] *n* (*pl* **bongos**) either of a pair of small drums of different pitch struck with the fingers.
bongo[2] *n* (*pl* **bongo, bongos**) a large striped African antelope.
bonhomie *n* good-heartedness; a frank good-natured manner.—**bonhomous** *adj*.
bonito *n* (*pl* **bonitos, bonito**) one of several species of warm-sea game fishes allied to the tuna.
bonk *vt* (*inf*) to hit; (*inf*) to have sexual intercourse with.—**bonking** *n*.
bon mot *n* (*pl* **bons mots**) a witty saying, a fitting remark.
bonne *n* a French nursemaid.
bonnet *n* a hat with a chin ribbon, worn by women and children; a case or covering, usu of sheet metal, placed over a motor (—*also* **hood**).
bonny, bonnie *adj* (**bonnier, bonniest**) healthy, attractive looking.
bonsai *n* (*pl* **bonsai**) a miniature tree or shrub that has been dwarfed by selective pruning; the art of cultivating bonsai.
bonspiel *n* (*Scot*) a curling match between players of different clubs.
bontebok *n* (*pl* **bonteboks, bontebok**) a pied antelope of South Africa.
bon ton *n* the style of persons in high life; good breeding; fashionable society; height of fashion.
bonus *n* (*pl* **bonuses**) an amount paid over the sum due as interest, dividend, or wages.
bon vivant *n* (*pl* **bons vivants**) a gourmet.
bon voyage *n*, *interj* an expression used to wish travellers a pleasant trip.
bony *adj* (**bonier, boniest**) of or resembling bones; having large or prominent bones; full of bones.
bonze *n* a Buddhist monk.
boo *interj* an expression of disapproval. * *n* (*pl* **boos**) hooting. * *vb* (**booing, booed**) *vi* to low like an ox; to groan. * *vt* to hoot at.
boob *n* a stupid awkward person; a blunder; (*sl*) a female breast.
booby *n* (*pl* **boobies**) a foolish person; the loser in a game.
booby prize *n* a prize of little value for the lowest score.
booby trap *n* a trap for playing a practical joke on someone; a camouflaged explosive device triggered by an unsuspecting victim.
boodle *n* money paid for votes or undue political influence; graft; lot, caboodle.
boogie *vi* (**boogieing, boogied**) to dance to pop music or jazz. * *n* fast, rhythmic music for dancing.
boogie-woogie *n* a style of jazz piano.
boohoo *vi* (**boohooing, boohooed**) to weep noisily or to pretend to do so. * *n* (*pl* **boohoos**) the sound of noisy weeping.
book *n* a bound set of printed or blank pages; a literary composition of fact or fiction; the script or libretto of a play or musical; (*pl*) written records of transactions or accounts; a book or record of bets. * *vt* to make a reservation in advance; to note a person's name and address for an alleged offence. * *vi* to make a reservation.
bookcase *n* a piece of furniture with shelves for books.
book club *n* an organization that sells books to its members at cheaper prices, usu by mail order.
book end *npl* a prop at the end of a row of books to keep them upright.
bookie *n* (*inf*) a bookmaker.
bookish *adj* fond of reading.—**bookishness** *n*.
bookkeeping *n* the systematic recording of business accounts.—**bookkeeper** *n*.
book learning *n* theoretical, not practical, knowledge.—**book-learned** *adj*.
booklet *n* a small book, usu with a paper cover; a pamphlet.
bookmaker *n* a person who takes bets on horse races, etc and pays out winnings; a manufacturer or publisher of books.
bookman *n* (*pl* **bookmen**) a literary man, a scholar; one who works in publishing.
bookmark(er) *n* a thing to mark a place in a book.
bookplate *n* a label in a book with the owner's name on it.
bookseller *n* a person who sells books.
bookstall *n* a stall for the sale of books, magazines, etc.
bookworm *n* an insect that feeds on books; a person who reads a lot.
Boolean algebra *n* (*math*) a system of symbolic logic used in the manipulation of sets and other mathematical entities, and in computing science.
boom[1] *n* a spar on which a sail is stretched; a barrier across a harbour; a long pole carrying a microphone.
boom[2] *vi* to make a deep, hollow sound. * *n* a resonant sound, as of the sea.
boom[3] *vi* to flourish or prosper suddenly. * *n* a period of vigorous growth (eg in business, sales, prices).
boomer *n* the male of the great kangaroo; one who starts or promotes a boom; (*sl*) a migratory worker.
boomerang *n* a curved stick that, when thrown, returns to the thrower; an action that unexpectedly rebounds and harms the agent.—*also vi*.
boom town *n* a town that suddenly grows and increases in economic prosperity.
boon[1] *n* something useful or helpful; a blessing; a favour.
boon[2] *adj* bountiful; convivial, jolly; specially friendly (*boon companion*).
boondocks *npl* (*sl*) a wild, inhospitable area; a dull, provincial region.—**boondock** *adj*.

boor *n* an ill-mannered or coarse person.—**boorish** *adj*.—**boorishly** *adv*.—**boorishness** *n*.
boost *vt* (*sales, etc*) to increase; to encourage, to improve; to push; to help by advertising or promoting. * *n* a push.
booster *n* a thing or person that increases the effectiveness of another mechanism; the first stage of a rocket, which usually breaks away after launching; a substance that increases the effectiveness of medication.
boosterism *n* the practice of boosting an image or product commercially.
booster shot, booster injection *n* a supplementary dose of medicine, esp a vaccine.
boot[1] *n* a strong covering for the foot and lower part of the leg; (*sl: with* **the**) dismissal from employment; the rear compartment of a car used for holding luggage, etc (*—also* **trunk**). * *vt* to kick; to get rid of by force; (*comput*) to bring a program from a disc into the memory.
boot[2] *n* (*arch*) advantage, use; **to boot** as well. * *vi* (*arch*) to avail.
bootblack *n* one who shines shoes.
booted *adj* wearing boots.
bootee *n* a knitted or soft shoe for a baby.
booth *n* a stall for selling goods; a small enclosure for voting; a public telephone enclosure.
bootjack *n* an appliance for drawing off boots.
bootleg *vt* (**bootlegging, bootlegged**) to smuggle illicit alcohol; to deal in illegally made records and tapes of live music, etc.—**bootlegger** *n*.
bootless *adj* useless, unavailing.—**bootlessly** *adv*.—**bootlessness** *n*.
bootlicker *n* a person who ingratiates himself or herself to gain favour, a toady.
boots *n* (*pl* **boots**) in UK, the servant in an hotel who cleans the boots of the guests.
boots and saddles *n* a cavalry signal to mount.
booty *n* (*pl* **booties**) spoils obtained as plunder.
booze *vi* (*inf*) to drink alcohol excessively. * *n* alcohol.—**boozer** *n*.
boozy *adj* (**boozier, booziest** (*sl*) addicted to drink; drunk.—**boozily** *adv*.
bop *n* a style of 1940s jazz music.*—also* **bebop.**
bora *n* a fierce dry northeast wind that blows on the coasts of the Adriatic Sea.
boracic *see* **boric.**
boracic acid *see* **boric acid.**
borage *n* a blue-flowered herb used in salads, etc.
borax *n* a mineral composed of the sodium salt compounded of boracic acid chiefly from the dried beds of certain lakes, used in the manufacture of glass, enamel, antiseptics, soaps, etc; (*sl*) shoddy merchandise.
Bordeaux *n* any of several red, white or rosé wines from around Bordeaux in France.
bordello *n* (*pl* **bordellos**) a brothel.
border *n* the edge, rim, or margin; a dividing line between two countries; a narrow strip along an edge. * *vi* (*with* **on, upon**) to be adjacent; to approach, to verge on. * *vt* to form a border.
bordereau *n* (*pl* **bordereaux**) a memorandum of contents, a docket.
borderer *n* a dweller on a frontier.
borderland *n* land forming a border or frontier; an uncertain or debatable district; an intermediate state.
borderline *n* a boundary. * *adj* on a boundary; doubtful, indefinite.
bordure *n* (*her*) a border round a shield.
bore[1] to drill so as to form a hole; to weary, by being dull or uninteresting. * *n* a hole made by drilling; the diameter of a gun barrel; a dull or uninteresting person.
bore[2] *see* **bear**[1].
bore[3] *n* a tidal wave that breaks in the estuaries of some rivers and, impeded by a narrowing channel, rises in a ridge and courses along with great force and noise.
boreal *adj* of or pertaining to the north, or to the north wind; situated on the northern side; of a northern character.
Boreas *n* the north wind personified.
boredom *n* tedium.
boric *adj* of or yielding boron.*—also* **boracic.**
boric acid *n* a white solid acid used in manufacturing and as a mild antiseptic.
boring *adj* dull, tedious; making holes.
born *pp* of **bear**[1]. * *adj* by birth, natural.
born-again *adj* having undergone a revival of personal faith or conviction.
borne *see* **bear**[1].
bornite *n* a valuable ore of copper.
boron *n* a nonmetallic element found in borax.
borough *n* a self-governing, incorporated town; an administrative area of a city, as in London or New York.
borough English *n* (*formerly*) a custom existing in some parts of England by which an estate descended to the youngest son instead of the eldest, or, if there were no son, to the youngest brother.
borrow *vt* to obtain (an item) with the intention of returning it; (*an idea*) to adopt as one's own; (*loan, money*) to obtain from a financial institution at definite rates of interest.—**borrower** *n*.
borscht, borsch *n* a type of soup (orig from Russia) made with beetroot.
borstal system *n* (*often cap*) (*formerly*) a reformatory system by which the sentence depended on the prisoner's conduct; now called a youth custody centre.
bort, bortz *n* an imperfect or inferior diamond used for polishing other stones; a fragment of diamond made in the cutting.*—also* **boart.**
borzoi *n* (*pl* **borzois**) a tall hound with a long, silky coat and a long head, a Russian wolfhound.
boscage, boskage *n* ground covered with trees and shrubs; woods; thickets; a wooded landscape.
bosh *n* (*inf*) nonsense.*—also interj*.
bosk *n* a small wood, a thicket.
bosky *adj* (**boskier, boskiest**) wooded, bushy.—**boskiness** *n*.
bosom *n* the breast of a human being, esp a woman; the part of a dress that covers it; the seat of the emotions. * *adj* (*friend*) very dear, intimate.
bosun *see* **boatswain.**
boss[1] *n* (*inf*) the manager or foreman; a powerful local politician. * *vt* to domineer; to be in control.
boss[2] *n* a protuberant part; a stud or knob, an ornamental projection of a ceiling. * *vt* to ornament with studs or knobs.
bossa nova *n* a dance from Brazil similar to the samba; the music for this.
bossy *adj* (**bossier, bossiest**) (*inf*) domineering, fond of giving orders.—**bossily** *adv*.—**bossiness** *n*.
bot *n* the larva of the botfly, which infests horses, cattle, sheep, etc; (*pl*) the disease that it causes.*—also* **bott.**
botanical, botanic *adj* pertaining to plants and botany.—**botanically** *adv*.
botanize *vi* to study plants, esp on a field trip.—**botanizer** *n*.
botany *n* (*pl* **botanies**) the study of plants.—**botanist** *n*.
botch *n* a poorly done piece of work. * *vt* to mend or patch clumsily; to put together without sufficient care.—**botcher** *n*.
botchy *adj* (**botchier, botchiest**) clumsily made or done; marked with botches.—**botchily** *adv*.—**botchiness** *n*.
botfly *n* (*pl* **botflies**) any of many winged insects with larvae parasitic on humans and livestock.
both *adj, pron* the two together; the one and the other. * *conj* together equally.*—also adv*.
bother *vt* to perplex or annoy; to take the time or trouble. * *n* worry; trouble; someone who causes problems, etc.
botheration *n* bother.*—also interj*.
bothersome *adj* causing bother.
bothy *n* (*pl* **bothies**) (*Scot*) a small cottage or hut, esp a hut or barrack serving as farm servants' quarters; a shelter for climbers on mountains.
bo tree *n* the peepul, the sacred tree of the Buddhists.
botryoidal *adj* resembling a bunch of grapes.—**botryoidally** *adv*.
bott *see* **bot.**
bottle[1] *n* a glass or plastic container for holding liquids; its contents; (*sl*) courage, nerve. * *vt* to put in bottles; to confine as if in a bottle.
bottle[2] *n* (*dial*) a quantity of hay or grass bundled up.

bottle green *adj* dark green.

bottleneck *n* a narrow stretch of a road where traffic is held up; a congestion in any stage of a process.

bottlenose *n* a dolphin with a sharp protruding beak; a moderately large toothed whale with a prominent beak.

bottom *n* the lowest or deepest part of anything; the base or foundation; the lowest position (eg in a class); the buttocks; (*naut*) the part of a ship's hull below water; the seabed. * *vt* to be based or founded on; to bring to the bottom, to get to the bottom of. * *vi* to become based; to reach the bottom; (*with* **out**) to flatten off after dropping sharply.

bottomlands *npl* rich flat low-lying land along watercourses in the western states of the US.

bottomless *adj* very deep; without limit.

bottom line *n* the crux; the line at the bottom of a financial report that shows the net profit or loss; the final result.—**bottom-line** *adj*.

bottomry *n* (*pl* **bottomries**) the borrowing of money by the owner on the security of his or her ship. * *vt* to pledge (a ship) thus.

botulism *n* a type of severe food poisoning.

bouclé, boucle *n* a type of looped yarn or fabric.

boudoir *n* a woman's bedroom.

bouffant *adj* puffed out; (*of hair*) backcombed.

bougainvillea, bougainvillaea *n* a tropical plant with large rosy or purple bracts.

bough *n* a branch of a tree.

bought *see* **buy.**

bougie *n* a wax candle; (*med*) a slender flexible tube for inserting into the gullet, etc; a catheter.

bouillabaisse *n* a French fish stew.

bouillon *n* a clear seasoned stock or broth.

boulder *n* a large stone or mass of rock rounded by the action of erosion.

boule[1] *n* an imitation gemstone.

boule[2] *n* in ancient Athens, a higher popular assembly; (*with cap*) the lower house of the modern Greek legislative assembly.

boule[3] *see* **boulle.**

boules *n* (*used as sing*) a French game similar to bowls played with small, hard balls.

boulevard *n* a broad, often tree-lined road.

boulevardier *n* a frequenter of a boulevard, esp a Parisian; a man about town.

bouleversement *n* an overturning, overthrow.

boulle *n* decorative inlaying for cabinetwork, consisting of brass or other metal, tortoiseshell, etc, worked into scrolls or other patterns; the articles so ornamented.—*also* **boule, buhl.**

boult *see* **bolt**[2].

bounce *vi* to rebound; to jump up suddenly; (*sl: cheque*) to be returned because of lack of funds; (*with* **back**) to recover easily, eg from misfortune or ill health. * *vt* to cause a ball to bounce; (*sl*) to put (a person) out by force; (*sl*) to fire from a job. * *n* a leap or springiness; capacity for bouncing; sprightliness; boastfulness, arrogance.

bouncer *n* (*sl*) a man hired to remove disorderly people from nightclubs, etc.

bouncing *adj* big, healthy, etc.

bouncy *adj* able to spring or bound; elastic; vigorous, lively.—**bouncily** *adv*.—**bounciness** *n*.

bound[1] *see* **bind.**

bound[2] *n* (*usu pl*) the limit or boundary. * *vt* to limit, confine or surround; to name the boundaries of.

bound[3] *n* a jump or leap. * *vi* to jump or leap.

bound[4] *adj* (*with* **for**) intending to go to, on the way to.

boundary *n* (*pl* **boundaries**) the border of an area; the limit; (*cricket*) the limit line of a field; a stroke that goes beyond the boundary line.

bounden *adj* (*duty*) obligatory.

bounden duty *n* a moral obligation.

bounder *n* one who or that which bounds; (*inf*) an insolent, ill-bred man, who makes himself disagreeable to those whom he meets.

boundless *adj* unlimited, vast.—**boundlessly** *adv*.—**boundlessness** *n*.

bounteous *adj* giving freely, bountiful, generous; plentiful.—**bounteously** *adv*.—**bounteousness** *n*.

bountiful *adj* generous in giving.—**bountifully** *adv*.—**bountifulness** *n*.

bounty *n* (*pl* **bounties**) generosity in giving; the gifts given; a reward or premium.

bouquet *n* a bunch of flowers; the perfume given off by wine.

bouquet garni *n* (*pl* **bouquets garnis**) herbs tied in a small bundle used for flavouring stews, soups, sauces, etc.

bourbon *n* a whiskey distilled in the US from corn mash.

bourdon *n* the bass drone of the bagpipe; a bass stop of an organ.

bourgeois *n* (*pl* **bourgeois**) a member of the bourgeoisie or middle class; a conventional and unimaginative individual. * *adj* smug, respectable, conventional; mediocre.

bourgeoisie *n* the class between the lower and upper classes, mostly composed of professional and business people.—*also* **middle class.**

bourn, bourne[1] *n* a small stream, a rivulet.

bourn, bourne[2] *n* (*arch*) a boundary; a destination, goal; a realm.

bourrée *n* (*mus*) a composition of a lively character, similar to the gavotte; the music for this.

bourse *n* a stock exchange for the transaction of business; (*with cap*) the stock exchange of Paris.

bouse *vi* (*naut*) to pull or haul hard.—*also* **bowse.**

boustrophedon *n* an ancient mode of writing lines alternately from left to right and from right to left.—**boustrophedonic** *adj*.

bout *n* a spell, a turn, a period spent in some activity; a contest or struggle, esp boxing or wrestling; a time of illness.

boutique *n* a small shop, usually selling fashionable clothing and accessories.

boutonniere, boutonnière *n* a buttonhole; a spray of flowers worn in it.

bouzouki *n* (*pl* **bouzoukis**) a Greek stringed instrument similar to the mandolin.

bovine *adj* relating to cattle; dull; sluggish. * *n* an ox, cow etc.

bow[1] *vi* to bend the knee or to lean the head (and chest) forward as a form of greeting or respect or shame; (*with* **before**) to accept, to submit; (*with* **out**) to withdraw or retire gracefully. * *vt* to bend downwards; to weigh down; to usher in or out with a bow. * *n* a lowering of the head (and chest) in greeting.

bow[2] *n* a weapon for shooting arrows; an implement for playing the strings of a violin; a decorative knot of ribbon, etc. * *vti* to bend, curve.

bow[3] *n* the forward part of a ship.

bow compass *n* (*geom*) a compass with jointed legs.

bowdlerize *vt* to expurgate, to remove indelicate words from.—**bowdlerism** *n*.—**bowdlerization** *n*.

bowel *n* the intestine; (*pl*) entrails; (*pl*) the deep and remote part of anything.

bower[1] *n* an arbour, a shady recess; (*poet*) dwelling.

bower[2] *n* (*naut*) an anchor carried at the bow of a ship.

bower[3] *n* (*cards*) one of the two highest cards in some card games, or the second and third highest (when the joker is used).

bowerbird *n* one of various Australian birds belonging to the starling family.

bowhead *n* an Arctic whale with a large mouth; Greenland whale.

bowie knife *n* a long hunting knife, a sheath knife.

bowing *n* a playing upon an instrument of the violin class with a bow; the particular style of execution.

bowl[1] *n* a wooden ball having a bias used in bowling; (*pl*) a game played on a smooth lawn with bowls. * *vti* to play the game of bowls; (*cricket*) to send a ball to a batsman; to dismiss (a batsman) by hitting the wicket with a bowled ball; (*with* **over**) to knock over; (*inf*) to astonish.

bowl[2] *n* a deep, rounded dish; the rounded end of a pipe; a sports stadium.

bow-legged *adj* having legs that curve outwards between the thigh and the ankle; bandy.

bowler[1] *n* a person who plays bowls; (*cricket*) the player who delivers the ball.

bowler[2] *n* a stiff felt hat.—*also* **derby.**
bowline *n* (*naut*) a knot used in making a fixed end loop; (*naut*) a rope from the weather side of a square sail to the bow to keep the ship near the wind.
bowling *n* a game in which a heavy wooden ball is bowled along a bowling alley at ten wooden skittles; the game of bowls.
bowling alley *n* a long narrow wooden lane, usu one of several in a building designed for them.
bowling green *n* a smooth lawn for bowls.
bowman[1] *n* (*pl* **bowmen**) an archer.
bowman[2] *n* (*pl* **bowmen**) (*naut*) the oarsman nearest the bow.
bowsaw *n* a saw with a blade under tension for cutting curves.
bowse *see* **bouse.**
bowsprit *n* a large boom or spar running out from the stem of a (sailing) ship to carry its sails forward.
bowstring *n* the string of a bow.
bow tie *n* a necktie tied in the shape of a bow.
bow window *n* a curved bay window.
bow-wow *n* a dog's bark; a child's name for a dog. * *vi* to bark like a dog.
bowyer *n* a maker or seller of archery bows.
box[1] *n* a container or receptacle for holding anything; (*theatre*) a compartment with seats; (*inf*) a television set. * *vt* to put into a box; to enclose; (*with* **in**) to restrict.
box[2] *vt* to hit using the hands or fists. * *vi* to fight with the fists.* *n* a blow on the head or ear with the fist.
box[3] *n* an evergreen shrub or small tree yielding a hard close-grained wood; the wood. * *adj* of box or boxwood.
boxcar *n* an enclosed freight car.
boxer *n* a person who engages in boxing; a breed of dog with smooth hair and a stumpy tail.
boxer shorts *npl* loose underpants that resemble the pants worn by boxers.
box girder *n* a girder constructed from rectangular metal plates.
boxing *n* the skill or sport of fighting with the fists.
Boxing Day the weekday following December 25, Christmas, when traditionally presents are given to tradesmen, employees, etc.
box office *n* a theatre ticket office; the popularity of a play, film, actor.—**box-office** *adj*.
box pleat *n* a double pleat in cloth made by two facing folds.
boxwood *n* the hard wood of the box tree; the tree itself.
boy *n* a male child; a son; a lad; a youth. * *interj* an exclamation of surprise or joy.
boyar *n* (*formerly*) a Russian landed proprietor of an old aristocratic order abolished by Peter I.
boycott *vt* to refuse to deal with or trade with in order to punish or coerce.—*also n*.
boyfriend *n* a male friend with whom a person is romantically or sexually involved.
boyhood *n* the time, or state, of being a boy.
boyish *adj* like a boy; puerile; with the appeal of a boy.—**boyishly** *adv*.—**boyishness** *n*.
Boy Scout *n* a scout; (*without cap*) (*inf*) a man with a strong sense of duty.
boysenberry *n* (*pl* **boysenberries**) (the fruit of) a hybrid shrub developed by crossing the loganberry and various blackberries and raspberries.
BP, B/P *abbr* = blood pressure.
Bq (*symbol*) bequerel.
Br *abbr* = British; (*chem symbol*) bromine; brother.
bra *n* a brassiere.
brace *n* a prop; a support to stiffen a framework; a hand tool for drilling; (*pl* **brace**) a pair, esp of game; (*pl*) straps for holding up trousers; a dental appliance for straightening the teeth. * *vt* to steady.
brace and bit *n* a revolving tool for boring.
bracelet *n* an ornamental chain or band for the wrist; (*pl: sl*) handcuffs.
bracer[1] *n* something that braces; a pick-me-up.
bracer[2] *n* a wrist guard in archery.
brachial *adj* of, pertaining to, or like the arm.
brachiate *adj* having arms; (*bot*) having branches in pairs, nearly horizontal and each pair at right angles to the next.—**brachiation.**
brachiopod *n* an animal like a mollusc with two spirally coiled armlike appendages, one on each side of the mouth.
brachy- *prefix* short.
brachycephalic, brachycephalous *adj* (*anat*) having the skull short in proportion to its breadth, short-headed.—**brachycephaly** *n*.
brachylogy *n* (*pl* **brachylogies**) conciseness; a condensed expression.—**brachylogous** *adj*.
brachypterous *adj* (*insects*) short-winged.
brachyuran *adj* of or belonging to a group of ten-footed crustaceans, including the crabs, marked by an undeveloped abdomen (—*also* **brachyurous**) * *n* a member of this group.
bracing *adj* refreshing, invigorating.—**bracingly** *adv*.
bracken *n* a large, coarse fern; a wide area of these growing on hills or moorland.
bracket *n* a projecting metal support for a shelf; a group or category of people classified according to income; (*pl*) a pair of characters ( ), [ ], { }, used in printing or writing as parentheses. * *vt* to support with brackets; to enclose by brackets; (*people*) to group together.
brackish *adj* somewhat salty; nauseating.—**brackishness** *n*.
bract *n* a modified leaf growing from a flower stem or enveloping a head of flowers.—**bracteal** *adj*.
bracteate *adj* (*plant*) furnished with bracts. * *n* a plate or dish made of a thin beaten precious metal and decorated.
brad *n* a slender flat nail with a projection on one side.
bradawl *n* a small boring tool for making holes for brads.
brady- *prefix* slow.
brae *n* (*Scot*) a hillside; sloping ground.
brag *vti* (**bragging, bragged**) to boast. * *n* a boast or boastful talk.—**bragger** *n*.
braggadocio *n* (*pl* **braggadocios**) bragging talk, empty boasting; a boaster, braggart.
braggart *n* a loud arrogant boaster.
Brahma[1] *n* (*Hinduism*) a supreme god; divine essence.
Brahma[2] *n* a useful variety of large domestic fowl with feathered legs.
Brahman[1] *n* (*pl* **Brahmans**) (*Hinduism*) a member of the highest caste, formerly consisting only of priests; Brahma.—**Brahmanic, Brahmanical** *adj*.
Brahman[2] *n* (*pl* **Brahmans, Brahman**) a breed of Indian cattle with a large hump used in crossbreeding beef cattle.
Brahmani *n* (*pl* **Brahmanis**) a female Brahman.
Brahmanism *n* the religion or doctrines of the Brahmans.—**Brahmanist** *n*.
Brahmin *n* a Brahman; a member of an upper-class New England family.
braid *vt* to interweave three or more strands (of hair, straw, etc); to make by such interweaving. * *n* a narrow band made by such interweaving for decorating clothing; a plait.—**braider** *n*.
brail *n* (*naut*) one of certain ropes used to gather up the foot and leeches of a sail prior to furling. * *vt* (*usu with* **up**) to haul in by the brails.
Braille *n* printing for the blind, using a system of raised dots that can be understood by touch.—*also adj*.
brain *n* nervous tissue contained in the skull of vertebrates that controls the nervous system; intellectual ability; (*inf*) a person of great intelligence; (often *pl*) the chief planner of an organization or enterprise. * *vt* to shatter the skull of; (*sl*) to hit on the head.
brainchild *n* (*pl* **brainchildren**) the result of creative thought; a clever and original idea or plan.
brain death *n* the irreversible cessation of brain activity, but not of the heartbeat, widely accepted as a criterion of death.
brain drain *n* the loss of highly skilled scientists, technicians, academics, etc through emigration.
brainless *adj* (*inf*) stupid.—**brainlessness** *n*.
brainpan *n* the cranium.
brainstorm *n* a violent mental disturbance; a brain wave.
brainteaser *n* a mathematical puzzle; a difficult problem.

brainwash *vt* to change a person's ideas or beliefs by physical or mental conditioning, usu over a long period.—**brainwasher** *n*.—**brainwashing** *n*.
brain wave *n* an electrical impulse in the brain; (*inf*) a bright idea.
brainy *adj* (**brainier, brainiest**) (*inf*) having a good mind; intelligent.—**braininess** *n*.
braise *vt* (*meat, vegetables, etc*) to sauté lightly and cook slowly in liquid with the lid on.
brake[1] *n* a device for slowing or stopping the motion of a wheel by friction. * *vt* to retard or stop by a brake. * *vi* to apply the brake on a vehicle; to become checked by a brake.
brake[2] *n* bracken.
brake[3] *n* a place overgrown with brushwood, etc; a thicket.
brake horsepower *n* the rate of work of an engine measured in terms of its resistance to a brake.
brakeman *n* (*pl* **brakemen**) a person in charge of a brake; a guard on a train; the person at the back of a bobsled team.
brake shoe *n* that part of a brake which presses against the wheel.
bramble *n* a prickly shrub or vine, esp of blackberries and raspberries.—**brambly** *adj*.
brambling *n* a migratory European finch with bright plumage.
bran *n* the husks of grain separated by sieving from the flour; a food containing these.
branch *n* an offshoot extending from the trunk or bough of a tree or from the parent stem of a shrub; a separately located subsidiary or office of an enterprise or business; a part of something larger, eg a road or railway. * *vi* to possess branches; to divide into branches; to come out (from a main part) as a branch; (*with* **out**) to extend or enlarge one's interests, activities, etc.
branchia *n* (*pl* **branchiae**) a respiratory organ of fishes and some amphibians, a gill.—**branchial** *adj*.
branchiate *adj* having permanent gills.
branchio- *prefix* gills.
branchiopod *n* one of a group of crustaceans, including the water flea, the gills of which are situated on the feet.
brand *n* an identifying mark on cattle, imprinted with hot iron; a burning piece of wood; a mark of disgrace; a trademark; a particular make (of goods). * *vt* to burn a mark with a hot iron; to fix in the memory; to denounce.
brandish *vt* (*a weapon, etc*) to wave or flourish in a threatening manner.—**brandisher** *n*.
brandling *n* a small brownish-red earthworm used as bait by freshwater anglers.
brand name *n* the name by which a certain commodity is known.—**brand-name** *adj*.
brand-new *adj* entirely new and unused.
brandy *n* (*pl* **brandies**) an alcoholic liquor made from distilled wine or fermented fruit juice.
brant *n* the brent goose, the smallest species of the wild goose.
brash[1] *adj* bold; loud-mouthed; reckless.—**brashly** *adv*.—**brashness** *n*.
brash[2] *n* broken, loose and angular fragments of rock underlying alluvial deposits; small broken pieces of ice; hedge clippings.
brash[3] *n* acid eructation, a fit of sickness; a rash; a burst of rain.
brasilin *see* **brazilin**.
brass *n* an alloy of copper and zinc; (*inf*) impudence; nerve; cheek; money; (*often pl*) the brass instruments of an orchestra or band; (*sl*) officers or officials of high rank.
brassard, brassart *n* armour for the upper arm; an armlet for the upper arm.
brass band *n* a band that uses brass and percussion instruments.
brasserie *n* a bar and restaurant.
brassica *n* any of a group of plants that includes cabbages, turnips and mustards.—**brassicaceous** *adj*.
brassie *n* (*golf*) a wooden club orig with a brass sole, now No. 2 wood.
brassiere *n* a woman's undergarment for protecting and supporting the breasts, a bra.
brass tacks *npl* (*inf*) basic facts.
brassy *adj* (**brassier, brassiest**) like brass; brazen, cheeky.—**brassily** *adv*.—**brassiness** *n*.
brat *n* an ill-mannered, annoying child.
bratpack *n* a group of precociously young actors, writers, etc.
brattice *n* (*mining*) a wooden partition or separating wall in a level or shaft to form an air passage. * *vt* to divide by a brattice.
bratwurst *n* a type of seasoned German sausage made from pork.
bravado *n* (*pl* **bravadoes, bravados**) pretended confidence; swaggering.
brave *adj* showing courage; not timid or cowardly; fearless; handsome; of excellent appearance. * *vt* to confront boldly; to defy. * *n* a North American Indian warrior.—**bravely** *adv*.
bravery *n* (*pl* **braveries**) the quality of being brave; courage, fearlessness; finery, magnificence.
bravo *interj* well done! * *n* (*pl* **bravoes, bravos**) a cry or shout of "bravo!"
bravura *n* bold daring; dash; (*mus*) a passage requiring spirit and technical brilliance.
brawl *n* a loud quarrel; a noisy fight. * *vi* to quarrel loudly.—**brawler** *n*.
brawn *n* strong, well-developed muscles; physical strength; pickled pork.
brawny *adj* (**brawnier, brawniest**) muscular, tough.—**brawnily** *adv*.—**brawniness** *n*.
bray[1] *n* the sound of a donkey; any harsh sound. * *vi* (**braying, brayed**) to make similar sounds.—**brayer** *n*.
bray[2] *vt* (**braying, brayed**) to pound or beat fine or small.
brayer *n* (*print*) a hand roller used to rub down and temper ink.
braze[1] *vt* to solder with an alloy of brass and zinc.—**brazer** *n*.
braze[2] *vt* to cover or ornament with brass; to colour like brass.
brazen *adj* made of brass; shameless. * *vt* (*usu with* **out**) to face a situation boldly and shamelessly.—**brazenness** *n*.
brazier[1] *n* a metal container for hot coals.
brazier[2] *n* a worker in brass.
brazil *n* brazilwood; a dye of various tints of esp red and orange obtained from brazilin.
brazilin *n* the colouring substance extracted from brazilwood.—*also* **brasilin**.
brazil nut *n* a large three-cornered nut, the seed of a tall tree of Brazil.
brazilwood *n* a very heavy wood of a red colour from various species of Central and South American trees.
breach *n* a break or rupture; violation of a contract, promise, etc; a break in friendship. * *vt* to make an opening in.
breach of promise *n* the breaking of a promise to marry.
breach of the peace *n* a public disturbance.
bread *n* a dough, made from flour, yeast and milk, that is baked; nourishment; (*sl*) money; **bread and butter** (*inf*) one's livelihood. * *vt* to coat meat, fish, etc with breadcrumbs before cooking.
bread-and-butter *adj* (*job*) providing a basic income; (*issues, etc*) fundamental, basic; (*letter*) thanking for hospitality.
breadbasket *n* a basket for holding bread; (*sl*) the stomach; a source of food.
breadboard *n* a wooden board for cutting bread on; board used for constructing experimental electric circuits.
breaded *adj* coated with breadcrumbs.
breadfruit *n* (*pl* **breadfruits, breadfruit**) the fruit of a tree growing in the Pacific islands, which, when roasted, is eaten as bread.
breadline *n* a queue for bread ration; **on the breadline** poverty-stricken, only just able to subsist.
breadth *n* measurement from side to side, width; extent; liberality (eg of interests).
breadthways, breadthwise *adv* from side to side.
breadwinner *n* the principal wage-earner of a family.
break *vb* (**breaking, broke,** *pp* **broken**) *vt* to smash or shatter; to tame; (*rules*) to violate; to discontinue; to cause to give up a habit; (*fall*) to lessen the severity of; to ruin financially; (*news*) to impart; to decipher or solve; (*with* **down**) to crush or destroy; to analyse; (*with* **in**) to intervene; to train. * *vi* to fall apart; (*voice*) to assume a lower tone at

puberty; to cut off relations with; to suffer a collapse, as of spirit; (*news*) to become public in a sudden and sensational way; (*with* **down**) to fail completely; to succumb emotionally; (*with* **even**) to suffer neither profit nor loss (after taking certain action); (*with* **in**) to force a way in; (*with* **out**) to appear, begin; to erupt; to throw off restraint, escape; (*with* **up**) to disperse; to separate; to collapse. * *n* a breaking; an interruption; a gap; a sudden change, as in weather; a rest or a short holiday; an escape; (*snooker, billiards*) a continuous run of points; (*sl*) a fortunate opportunity.

breakable *adj* able to be broken. * *n* a fragile object.

breakage *n* the action of breaking; something broken.

breakaway *n* secession, disassociation.

break dancing *n* dancing that involves acrobatic movements.

breakdown *n* a mechanical failure; failure of health; nervous collapse; an analysis.

breakdown truck *n* a vehicle for towing away smashed or damaged cars, etc.

breaker[1] *n* a large wave that crashes onto the shore, reef, etc.

breaker[2] *n* (*naut*) a small cask for holding water.

breakeven *n* the point at which costs are covered but no profit is made.

breakfast *n* the first meal of the morning; the food consumed. * *vi* to have breakfast.

break-in *n* the unlawful entering of premises, esp by thieves.

breakneck *adj* dangerously steep or fast.

break of day *n* dawn.

break-out *n* an escape, esp from prison.

breakthrough *n* the action of breaking through an obstruction; an important advance or discovery.

break-up *n* separation; collapse; dispersal.

breakwater *n* a barrier that protects a harbour or area of coast against the force of the waves.

bream[1] *n* (*pl* **bream**) a freshwater fish.

bream[2] *vt* (*naut*) to clear (a ship's bottom) of shells, seaweed, etc, by heating and scraping.

breast *n* the chest; one of the two mammary glands; the seat of the emotions. * *vt* to oppose, confront; to arrive at the top of; to confess (*make a clean breast of*).

breastbone *n* (*anat*) the flat narrow bone in the centre of the chest that connects the ribs, the sternum.

breast-feed *vt* (**breast-feeding, breast-fed**) to allow a baby to suck milk from the breast.

breastplate *n* armour covering the front of the body; a part of the vestment of a Jewish high priest.

breaststroke *n* a swimming stroke in which both arms are brought out sideways from the chest.

breastwork *n* a hastily constructed work thrown up breast-high for defence; the parapet of a building.

breath *n* the inhalation and exhalation of air in breathing; the air taken into the lungs; life; a slight breeze; (*scandal*) a hint.

Breathalyzer, Breathalyser *n* (*trademark*) a device for measuring the amount of alcohol in a person's breath.

breathe *vi* to inhale and exhale, to respire air; to take a rest or pause; to exist or live; to speak or sing softly; to whisper. * *vt* to emit or exhale; to whisper or speak softly.

breather *n* a pause during exercise to recover one's breath.

breathing *n* respiration; air in gentle motion; a gentle influence; a pause; (*phonetics*) an accent (´) whether an initial vowel is aspirated or not.

breathing space *n* a pause in which to recover, get organized or get going.

breathless *adj* out of breath; panting; gasping; unable to breathe easily because of emotion.—**breathlessly** *adv*.—**breathlessness** *n*.

breathtaking *adj* very exciting.

breathy *adj* (**breathier, breathiest**) (*voice*) not clear sounding.—**breathily** *adv*.—**breathiness** *n*.

breccia *n* a rock of angular fragments cemented by lime, etc.—**brecciated** *adj*.

bred *see* **breed.**

bree *n* (*Scot*) broth; juice or liquor in which something has been steeped or boiled.

breech *n* the back part of a gun barrel.

breech delivery, breech birth *n* the birth of a baby buttocks or feet first.

breeches *npl* trousers extending just below the knee.

breeches buoy *n* a lifebuoy on a hawser to take people off a wreck.

breeching *n* the harness that passes round a horse's hindquarters; a strong rope to check the recoil of a gun.

breechloader *n* a gun loaded at the breach.—**breechloading** *adj*.

breed *vb* (**breeding, bred**) *vt* to engender; to bring forth; (*dogs*) to raise; to give rise to. * *vi* to produce young; to be generated. * *n* offspring; lineage or race; species (of animal).—**breeder** *n*.

breeder reactor *n* a nuclear reactor that produces more fissile material than it consumes.

breeding *n* the bearing of offspring; one's education and training; refined behaviour.

breeze[1] *n* a light gentle wind; something easy to do. * *vi* (*inf*) to move quickly or casually.

breeze[2] *n* sifted ashes and cinders used in burning bricks; house sweepings, refuse.

breeze block *n* a lightweight building brick composed mainly of the ashes of coal and coke.

breezy *adj* (**breezier, breeziest**) windy; nonchalant; light-hearted, cheerful.—**breezily** *adv*.—**breeziness** *n*.

brent (goose) *n* the smallest species of the wild goose.—*also* **brant.**

br'er *n* (*dial*) brother.

brethren *see* **brother.**

Breton *adj* of or relating to Brittany, its people or language. * *n* an inhabitant of Brittany; the Celtic language of Brittany.

breve *n* a mark (˘) used to indicate a short vowel; (*mus*) the longest note now used, equal to two whole notes (two semibreves or four minims).

brevet *n* (*mil*) a commission to an officer in the army conferring a higher rank but without increase of pay; a warrant; a licence. * *adj* conferred by brevet; nominal, honorary. * *vt* (**brevetting, brevetted** *or* **breveting, breveted**) to confer brevet rank on.—**brevetcy** *n*.

brevi- *prefix* short.

breviary *n* (*pl* **breviaries**) (*RC Church*) a book containing the daily offices and prayers.

brevirostrate *adj* (*birds*) short-billed.

brevity *n* (*pl* **brevities**) briefness; conciseness.

brew *vt* to make (beer, ale, etc) from malt and hops by boiling and fermenting; to infuse (tea, etc); to plot, scheme. * *vi* to be in the process of being brewed; to be about to happen. * *n* a brewed drink.

brewage *n* something made by brewing; the brewing process.

brewer *n* a person who brews, usu beer.

brewery *n* (*pl* **breweries**) a place where beer, etc is brewed.

briar *see* **brier.**

bribe *n* money or gifts offered illegally to gain favour or influence; the gift to achieve this. * *vt* to offer or give a bribe to.—**bribable** *adj*.—**briber** *n*.

bribery *n* (*pl* **briberies**) the giving or taking of bribes.

bric-a-brac *n* curios, ornamental or rare odds and ends.

brick *n* a baked clay block for building; a similar shaped block of other material. * *vt* to lay or wall up with brick.

brickbat *n* a piece of brick, esp one used as a weapon; an unfavourable remark.

bricklayer *n* a person who lays bricks.

brick red *n* a greyish red colour.—**brick-red** *adj*.

brickwork *n* a structure formed of bricks.

bridal *adj* relating to a bride or a wedding.

bride *n* a woman about to be married or recently married.

bridegroom *n* a man about to be married or recently married.

bridesmaid *n* a young girl or woman attending the bride during a wedding.

bridge[1] *n* a structure built to convey people or traffic over a river, road, railway line, etc; the platform on a ship where the captain gives directions; the hard ridge of bone in the nose; an arch to raise the strings of

a guitar, etc; a mounting for false teeth.* *vt* to be or act as a bridge; to be a connecting link between.—**bridgeable** *adj*.
bridge[2] *n* a card game for two teams of two players based on whist.
bridgeboard *n* a notched board into which the ends of the steps of wooden stairs are fastened.
bridgehead *n* a defensive work covering the end of a bridge nearest the enemy; a foothold in enemy territory.
bridgework *n* a false tooth or teeth secured to the natural teeth.
bridging *n* a piece of wood between two beams to keep them apart.
bridging loan *n* a loan, usu short-term, advanced to cover the gap between the settlement of two transactions, esp between buying a new house and selling the old one.
bridle *n* the headgear of a horse, controlling its movements; a restraint or check; (*naut*) a mooring cable. * *vt* to put a bridle on (a horse); to restrain or check. * *vi* to draw one's head back as an expression of anger, scorn, etc.—**bridler** *n*.
bridle path *n* a trail suitable for horse riding.
bridoon *n* the light snaffle and rein of a military bridle.
Brie *n* creamy white soft cheese.
brief *n* a summary of a client's case for the instruction of a barrister in a trial at law; an outline of an argument, esp that setting out the main contentions; (*pl*) men's or women's close-fitting underpants or knickers. * *vt* to provide with a precise summary of the facts. * *adj* short, concise.—**briefly** *adv*.—**briefness** *n*.
briefcase *n* a flat case for carrying documents, etc.
brier *n* a plant with a thorny or prickly woody stem; a mass of these; a tobacco pipe made from the root of the brier.—*also* **briar**.—**briery, briary** *adj*.
brig *n* a two-masted square-rigged vessel; a naval prison, esp on a ship.
brigade *n* an army unit, smaller than a division, commanded by a brigadier; a group of people organized to perform a particular function.
brigadier *n* an officer commanding a brigade and ranking next below a major general.
brigand *n* a bandit, usu one of a roving gang.
brigantine *n* a small two-masted vessel, square-rigged on the foremast only and with raking masts.
bright *adj* clear, shining; brilliant in colour or sound; favourable or hopeful; intelligent, illustrious. * *adv* brightly.—**brightly** *adv*.—**brightness** *n*.
brighten *vti* to make or become brighter.—**brightener** *n*.
Bright's disease *n* a kidney disease characterized by the presence of albumin in the urine.
brill *n* (*pl* **brill, brills**) a European flatfish resembling the turbot.
brilliance *n* intense radiance, lustre, splendour.
brilliancy *n* the quality of being brilliant; shining quality, lustrousness, shining brightness.
brilliant *adj* sparkling, bright; splendid; very intelligent.—**brilliantly** *adv*.
brilliantine *n* a cosmetic oil giving a gloss to the hair; a shiny fabric of cotton and mohair.
brim *n* the rim of a hollow vessel; the outer edge of a hat. * *vti* (**brimming, brimmed**) to fill or be filled to the brim; (*with* **over**) to overflow.
brimful *adj* completely full; overflowing.
brimstone *n* sulphur; a yellow butterfly.
brindled *adj* streaked brown or grey, or with flecks of a darker colour.
brine *n* salt water; the sea.
bring *vt* (**bringing, brought**) to fetch, carry or convey "here" or to the place where the speaker will be; to cause to happen (eg rain, relief), to result in; to lead to an action or belief; to sell for; (*with* **about**) to induce, to effect; (*with* **down**) to cause to fall by or as if by shooting; (*with* **forth**) to give birth to; (*with* **forward**) to present something for consideration; to transfer a total figure from the bottom of a page to the top of the next page; (*with* **in**) to yield a profit or return; to return a verdict in court; to introduce (a legislative bill); to earn (an income); (*with* **off**) to achieve a success, often against odds; accomplish; (*with* **out**) to cause to appear; to produce (a play) or publish (a book); to demonstrate clearly, expose to view; to help someone with encouragement; (*with* **over**) to convince a person to change their loyalties; (*with* **round**) to convince a person to change their opinion; to get someone to agree or give support; to restore a person to consciousness, revive; (*with* **up**) to educate, rear a child; to raise (a matter) for discussion; to vomit.—**bringer** *n*.
brink *n* the verge of a steep place; the edge of the sea; the point of onset; the threshold of danger.
brinkmanship, brinksmanship *n* the pursuing of a policy, esp in international relations, that brings serious risk of danger in order to gain advantage.
briny *adj* (**brinier, briniest**) salty. * *n* the sea.—**brininess** *n*.
brio *n* vivacity.
brioche *n* a small, slightly sweet, bread roll.
briony *see* **bryony**.
briquette, briquet *n* a compacted brick usu of fine compressed material, esp charcoal.
brisk *adj* alert; quick; vigorous; sharp in tone.—**briskly** *adv*.—**briskness** *n*.
brisket *n* meat from the breast of an animal.
brisling *n* a small fish like a sardine.
bristle *n* a short, coarse hair. * *vi* to stand up, as bristles; to have the bristles standing up; to show anger or indignation; to be thickly covered (with).
bristly *adj* (**bristlier, bristliest**) covered with bristles; rough.—**bristliness** *n*.
Bristol board *n* a thick smooth white pasteboard.
brit *n* the young of the herring and sprat; small animals upon which whales feed.
Brit *n* (*inf*) a British person.
Brit. *abbr* = Britain; British.
Britannia *n* Britain or its former empire personified.
Britannia metal *n* a white metal alloy of tin, copper, antimony and bismuth, resembling pewter.
Britannic *adj* of Britain; British.
Briticism *n* a word, phrase, etc, peculiar to or characteristic of British English.
British *adj* of or pertaining to Great Britain or its inhabitants; pertaining to the ancient Britons. * *n* the people of Britain; the language of the ancient Britons.
Britisher *n* a British subject.
Britishism *n* a Briticism.
Briton *n* a native of Great Britain, esp before the Anglo-Saxon conquest.
brittle *adj* easily cracked or broken; fragile; sharp-tempered.—**brittleness** *n*.
britzka, britzska *n* an open carriage with a hooded top and space for reclining.
bro *n* (*inf*) mate, buddy.
broach *vt* (*a topic*) to introduce for discussion; to pierce (a container) and draw out liquid.
broad *adj* of large extent from side to side; wide; spacious; giving an overall view or idea; (*humour*) coarse; strongly marked in dialect or pronunciation. * *n* (*sl*) a woman.—**broadly** *adv*.—**broadness** *n*.
broad arrow *n* an arrow with a broad barbed head; a UK government mark to distinguish its property.
broad bean *n* a plant widely grown for its large flat edible seed.
broadcast *n* a programme on radio or television. * *vti* (**broadcasting, broadcast**) to transmit on radio or television; to make known widely; to scatter seed.—**broadcaster** *n*.
Broad Church *n* a section or party intermediate between the High and the Low Church of England; any group that opposes rigid dogma.—**Broad-Church** *adj*.
broadcloth *n* a fine woollen cloth with a smooth finished surface.
broaden *vti* to grow or make broad; to widen.
broadloom *adj* (*carpets*) woven on a wide loom.
broad-minded *adj* tolerant; liberal in outlook.—**broad-mindedly** *adv*.—**broad-mindedness** *n*.
broad seal *n* the official seal of a nation.
broadsheet *n* a large sheet of paper printed on one side only; a large format newspaper, approx 15 by 24 inches (38 by 61 cms).

broadside *n* the entire side of a ship above the waterline; a simultaneous volley from one side of a warship; a sheet printed on one side containing information of a popular nature or an attack on some public person; any verbal or written attack.

broad-spectrum *adj* efficacious against a wide range (of diseases, microorganisms).

broadsword *n* a cutting sword with a broad straight blade.

Brobdingnagian *adj* resembling one of the giant inhabitants of the land of Brobdingnag in Swift's *Gulliver's Travels*; gigantic.

brocade *n* a heavy fabric woven with raised patterns, orig in gold and silver. * *vt* to work with a raised pattern.

brocatelle, brocatel *n* a figured brocade of silky texture; a variegated marble from Italy and Spain.

broccoli *n* (*pl* **broccoli**) a kind of cauliflower with loose heads of tiny green buds.

broch *n* (*Scot*) a dry-built circular tower of the Iron Age.

brochette *n* (food cooked on) a skewer or small spit.

brochure *n* an advertising booklet.

brock *n* (*dial*) a badger.

brogan *n* a sturdy ankle-high work shoe.

brogue *n* a sturdy shoe; a dialectical accent, esp Irish.

broil[1] *vti* to cook by exposure to direct heat; to grill.

broil[2] *n* a noisy quarrel, a tumult. * *vi* to be heated with passion.

broiler *n* a pan, grill, etc for broiling; a bird fit for broiling.

broke *pt* of **break**. * *adj* (*inf*) hard up, having no money.

broken *pp* of **break**. * *adj* splintered, fractured; violated; ruined; tamed; disconnected, interrupted; overwhelmed by sorrow or ill fortune; (*speech*) imperfect.—**brokenly** *adv*.—**brokenness** *n*.

broken-down *adj* extremely infirm; worn out.

brokenhearted *adj* grief-stricken; very sad.

broken-winded *adj* (*horse*) having the heaves.

broker *n* an agent who negotiates contracts of purchase and sale (as of commodities or securities); a power broker; a stockbroker.

brokerage *n* a broker's business; the commission charged by a broker.

bromate *n* a salt of bromic acid.

brome (grass) *n* any of a genus of oat-like grasses with drooping clusters of spikelets.

bromic acid *n* a compound of bromine and oxygen.

bromide *n* a compound of bromine; a sedative; (*sl*) a bore; a trite remark.

bromine *n* an evil-smelling nonmetallic element related to chlorine and iodine.—**bromic** *adj*.

bronchi *see* **bronchus**.

bronchia *npl* (*sing* **bronchium**) the bronchial tubes.

bronchial *adj* of or pertaining to the bronchial tubes.

bronchial tube *n* either of the two main branches of the windpipe.

bronchitis *n* inflammation of the lining of the bronchial tubes.—**bronchitic** *adj*.

bronchopneumonia *n* diffuse inflammation of the lungs and bronchi.

bronchus *n* (*pl* **bronchi**) one of the two principal branches of the windpipe or trachea.

bronco *n* (*pl* **broncos**) a wild or half-tamed horse of North America.

broncobuster *n* a cowboy who breaks in broncos.—**broncobusting** *n*.

brontosaur, brontosaurus *n* (*pl* **brontosauruses**) a large plant-eating dinosaur.—**brontosaurian** *adj*.

Bronx cheer *n* (*inf*) a rude sound made with the lips; a raspberry.

bronze *n* a copper and tin alloy, sometimes other elements; any object cast in bronze; a reddish-brown colour. * *adj* made of, or like, or of the colour of bronze; (*skin*) tanned.—**bronzy** *adj*.

Bronze Age *n* the age succeeding the Stone Age, the ornaments and weapons of that period being made of bronze.

brooch *n* an ornament held by a pin or a clasp.

brood *vi* to incubate or hatch (eggs); to ponder or worry about. * *n* a group having a common nature or origin, esp the children in a family; the number produced in one hatch.

broody *adj* (**broodier, broodiest**) contemplative, moody; (*inf*) wanting to have a baby.—**broodily** *adv*.—**broodiness** *n*.

brook[1] *n* a freshwater stream.

brook[2] *vt* to tolerate.—**brookable** *adj*.

brooklet *n* a small brook.

broom[1] *n* a bundle of fibres or twigs attached to a long handle for sweeping.

broom[2] *n* a shrub bearing large yellow flowers.

broomstick *n* the handle of a broom.

Bros *abbr* = Brothers.

brose *n* (*Scot*) a kind of porridge made by pouring boiling water or milk or meat liquor on oatmeal.

broth *n* a thin or thick soup made by boiling meat, etc in water.

brothel *n* a house where prostitutes work.

brother *n* a male sibling; a friend who is like a brother; a fellow member of a group, profession or association; a lay member of a men's religious order; (*pl* **brethren**) used chiefly in formal address or in referring to the members of a society or sect.

brother-in-law *n* (*pl* **brothers-in-law**) the brother of a husband or wife; the husband of a sister.

Brother Jonathan *n* (*hist*) a humorous personification of the US.

brotherhood *n* the state or quality of being a brother, brotherliness; a fraternity, an association.

brotherly *adj* like a brother; kind; affectionate.—**brotherliness** *n*.

brougham *n* a light closed four-wheeled carriage for one or two horses.

brought *see* **bring**.

brouhaha *n* a fuss; uproar.

brow *n* the forehead; the eyebrows; the top of a cliff; the jutting top of a hill.

browbeat *vt* (**browbeating, browbeat**, *pp* **browbeaten**) to intimidate with threats, to bully.

brown *adj* having the colour of chocolate, a mixture of red, black and yellow; tanned. * *n* a brown colour. * *vti* to make or become brown, esp by cooking.—**brownish** *adj*.—**brownness** *n*.

brown bear *n* a large wild bear of a brownish colour that lives in forests in temperate areas of Asia, North America and Europe.

brown bread *n* bread made from wholemeal flour.

brown coal *n* lignite.

browned-off *adj* (*sl*) fed up, depressed.

Brownian movement *n* a rapid whirling movement frequently seen in microscopic particles suspended in water or other liquids.

brownie *n* a square of flat, rich chocolate cake; a friendly helpful elf; (*with cap*) a member of the junior branch of the Girl Scout or Guide movement.

Brownie point *n* a credit gained by having scored some success.

Browning *n* an automatic or semi-automatic gas-operated rifle; an automatic machine gun.

brown rice *n* unpolished rice.

brownshirt *n* (*often cap*) a member of the Nazi Party; a storm trooper.

brownstone *n* a kind of sandstone; a house built of this.

brown study *n* a reverie.

brown sugar *n* sugar that is unrefined or partially refined.

browse *vti* to nibble, to graze; to examine (a book) at one's leisure or casually.—**browser** *n*.

brucellosis *n* an infectious disease of livestock, esp cattle, which can be passed to human beings.

bruin *n* the brown bear personified.

bruise *vt* to injure and discolour (body tissue, surface of fruit) without breaking the skin; to break down (as leaves and berries) by pounding; to inflict psychological pain on. * *vi* to inflict a bruise; to undergo bruising. * *n* contusion of the skin; a similar injury to plant tissue; an injury, esp to the feelings.

bruiser *n* a tough, pugnacious man; a boxer.

bruit *n* a report; a rumour; fame. * *vt* to report; to noise abroad.

brumal *adj* of or like winter, wintry.

brume *n* fog, mist; a thick vapour.—**brumous** *adj*.

brunch *n* breakfast and lunch combined.

brunette, brunet *adj* having dark-brown or black hair, often with dark eyes. * *n* a brunette person.

brunt *n* the main force or shock of a blow; the hardest part.

brush[1] *n* a device made of bristles set in a handle, used for grooming the hair, painting or sweeping; a short unfriendly meeting or exchange of words; a fox's bushy tail; a light stroke or graze, made in passing. * *vt* to groom or sweep with a brush; to remove with a brush; (*with* **aside**) to ignore, to regard as little account; (*with* **up**) to refresh one's memory of or skill in a subject; to wash and tidy oneself. * *vi* to touch lightly or graze; (*with* **up**) to smarten one's appearance.—**brusher** *n*.

brush[2] *n* brushwood.

brush-off *n* a curt dismissal.

brush-up *n* a smartening of one's appearance; refreshment of memory or skill.

brushwood *n* rough, close bushes; a thicket, a coppice; small wood or twigs suitable for the fire.

brushwork *n* a particular or characteristic style of painting.

brusque *adj* blunt and curt in manner.—**brusquely** *adv*.—**brusqueness** *n*.

Brussels carpet *n* a strong kind of woollen carpet.

Brussels lace *n* a fine, expensive lace with a floral pattern made orig in Brussels.

Brussels sprout *n* a plant of the cabbage family with a small edible green head.

brut *adj* (*wines*) dry, unsweetened.

brutal *adj* inhuman; savage, violent; severe.—**brutally** *adv*.

brutality *n* (*pl* **brutalities**) the quality of being brutal; pitiless cruelty; a brutal act.

brutalize *vt* to treat brutally; to degrade.—**brutalization** *n*.

brute *n* any animal except man; a brutal person; (*inf*) an unpleasant or difficult person or thing. * *adj* (*force*) sheer, physical.

brutish *adj* brutal; stupid; savage, violent; coarse.—**brutishly** *adv*.—**brutishness** *n*.

bryology *n* the scientific study of mosses.—**bryological** *adj*.—**bryologist** *n*.

bryony *n* (*pl* **bryonies**) any of several climbing plants of Europe and North Africa; black bryony; white bryony.—*also* **briony**.

bryozoan *n* any small animal belonging to the class Polyzoa, forming moss-like colonies by budding.

BSc *abbr* = Bachelor of Science.

Bt. *abbr* = Baronet.

bub *n* (*inf*) a boy; brother.

bubble *n* a film of liquid forming a ball around air or gas; a tiny ball of gas or air in a liquid or solid; a transparent dome; a scheme that collapses. * *vi* to boil; to rise in bubbles; to make a gurgling sound.

bubble and squeak *n* meat and vegetables fried together.

bubble bath *n* perfumed crystals or liquid added to a bath to soften the water and produce foam; a bath to which this has been added.

bubble gum *n* chewing gum that can be blown into large bubbles.

bubbly *adj* (**bubblier, bubbliest**) having bubbles, effervescent; cheerful, high-spirited. * *n* (*inf*) champagne.

bubo *n* (*pl* **buboes**) an inflamed swelling in the groin or armpit.—**bubonic** *adj*.

bubonic plague *n* a highly infectious often fatal disease contracted from fleas from infected rats.

bubonocele *n* a rupture or hernia in the groin.

buccal *adj* pertaining to the cheek or the mouth.

buccaneer *n* a sea robber, a pirate. * *vi* to be a pirate.

buccinator *n* a flat muscle of the cheek, also called the trumpeter's muscle from its use in blowing wind instruments.

Buchmanism *see* **Oxford Group**.

buck *n* the male of animals such as the deer, hare, rabbit, antelope; (*inf*) a dashing young man; (*sl*) a dollar. * *vti* (*horse*) to rear upwards quickly; (*inf*) to resist; (*with* **up**) (*inf*) to make or become cheerful; to hurry up.

buckaroo *n* (*pl* **buckaroos**) a cowboy.

buckbean *n* a water plant with pinkish flowers.

buckboard *n* a light four-wheeled carriage with a flexible board bearing the seats.

bucket *n* a container with a handle for carrying liquid or substances in small pieces; (*comput*) a direct-access storage area from which data can be retrieved; (*inf*) a wastepaper bin. * *vt* to drive fast or recklessly; to pour with rain.

bucket seat *n* a single, contoured seat with an adjustable back as in a car, etc.

bucket shop *n* (*sl*) a dishonest brokerage firm; a business that sells cheap airline tickets.

buckeye *n* a North American tree with white or reddish flowers growing in clusters, the American horse chestnut; its nut; a native of Ohio.

buckjumper *n* a vicious untrained horse that endeavours to throw its rider by arching its back and drawing its feet together.

buckle *n* a fastening or clasp for a strap or band; a bend or bulge. * *vti* to fasten with a buckle; to bend under pressure, etc; (*with* **down**) (*inf*) to apply oneself diligently.

buckler *n* a small shield; protection. * *vt* to defend.

bucko *n* (*pl* **buckoes**) (*naut*: *sl*) a swaggering bully; (*Irish*) a young man.

buckpasser *n* (*inf*) one who regularly shifts the blame or responsibility to someone else.

buckram *n* a coarse linen or cotton cloth stiffened with dressing. * *adj* made of, or resembling, buckram; stiff, precise. * *vt* (**buckraming, buckramed**) to stiffen with or bind in buckram.

buckshee *n* (*sl*) an extra allowance, a windfall. * *adj, adv* free, for nothing.

buckshot *n* shot of a large size for shooting game.

buckskin *n* a soft leather of deerskin, etc; (*pl*) breeches or shoes made of this; (*hist*) a native American. * *adj* made of buckskin.

buckthorn *n* any of several shurbs or trees with small greenish flowers, black berries and thorny branches.

bucktooth *n* (*pl* **buckteeth**) a projecting front tooth.

buckwheat *n* a plant cultivated for its triangular seeds, which are ground into meal and used as a cereal.

bucolic *adj* pastoral; rustic. * *n* a pastoral poem; a rustic.—**bucolically** *adv*.

bud[1] *n* an embryo shoot, flower, or flower cluster of a plant; an early stage of development. * *vi* (**budding, budded**) to produce buds; to begin to develop.

bud[2] *n* (*inf*) buddy.

Buddha *n* one who has arrived at the state of perfect enlightenment; an image of Siddharta Gautama, founder of Buddhism.

Buddhism *n* a system of ethics and philosophy based on teachings of Buddha.

Buddhist *n* a follower of Buddhism.

budding *n* being in an early stage of development; promising or showing promise.

buddle *n* an inclined trough in which ore is separated from earth by the action of running water. * *vt* to wash ore in a buddle.

buddleia *n* a shrub with lilac or yellow flowers.

buddy *n* (*pl* **buddies**) (*inf*) a friend; a term of informal address; one who helps and supports another, esp an AIDS sufferer. * *vi* (**buddying, buddied**) to help as a buddy.

budge[1] *vti* to shift or move.

budge[2] *n* lambskin dressed with the wool outwards.

budgerigar *n* a small Australian parrot bred as a cage bird in many varieties of different colours.

budget *n* an estimate of income and expenditure within specified limits of a country, a business, etc; the total amount of money for a given purpose; a stock or supply; **on a budget** restricting one's expenditure. * *vb* (**budgeting, budgeted**) *vi* to make a budget. * *vt* to put on a budget; to plan; (*with* **for**) to allow for or save money for a purpose or aim.—**budgetary** *adj*.

budgie *n* (*inf*) a budgerigar.

buff *n* a heavy, soft, brownish-yellow leather; a dull brownish yellow; (*inf*) a devotee, fan; (*inf*) a person's bare skin. * *adj* made of buff; of a buff colour. * *vt* to clean or shine, orig with leather or a leather-covered wheel.

buffalo *n* (*pl* **buffalo, buffaloes** *or* **buffalos**) a wild ox; a bison.

buffer[1] *n* anything that lessens shock, as of collision; something that serves as a protective barrier; a temporary storage area in a computer.

buffer[2] *n* (*sl*) a good-tempered somewhat foolish person; an elderly man.

buffer zone, buffer state *n* an area intended to separate; a neutral area.

buffet[1] *n* a blow with the hand or fist. * *vb* (**buffeting, buffeted**) *vt* to hit with the hand or fist; to batter (as of the wind). * *vi* to make one's way esp under difficult conditions.—**buffeter** *n*.

buffet[2] *n* a counter where refreshments are served; a meal at which guests serve themselves food.

buffet car *n* a railway coach where light refreshments are served.

buffeting *n* repeated battering.

buffo *n* (*pl* **buffi, buffos**) a comic actor, esp in an opera. * *adj* comic; burlesque.

buffoon *n* a clown, a jester; a silly person.

buffoonery *n* ridiculous behaviour.

bug[1] *n* a continuing source of irritation.

bug[2] *n* an insect with sucking mouth parts; any insect; (*inf*) a germ or virus; (*sl*) a defect, as in a machine; (*sl*) a hidden microphone; an obsession, an enthusiasm. * *vt* (**bugging, bugged**) (*sl*) to plant a hidden microphone; (*sl*) to annoy, anger, etc.

bugbear *n* an object that causes great fear and anxiety.

bugger *n* a sodomite; (*sl*) a contemptible or annoying person or thing. * *vt* to practise buggery with; (*sl*) to ruin; to exhaust; (*with* **off**) to leave. * *interj* an exclamation of annoyance.

buggery *n* anal sexual intercourse.

buggy *n* (*pl* **buggies**) a light four-wheeled, one-horse carriage with one seat; a small pushchair for a baby; a small vehicle.

bughouse *n* (*sl*) a mental home. * *adj* crazy.

bugle[1] *n* a valveless brass instrument like a small trumpet, used esp for military calls. * *vti* to signal by blowing a bugle.—**bugler** *n*.

bugle[2] *n* an elongated glass bead, usu black.

bugle[3] *n* bugleweed.

bugleweed *n* a plant of Europe and Asia with spikes or clusters of small blue or white flowers.

bugloss *n* any of various plants with hairy leaves and stems.

buhl *see* **boulle**.

build *vb* (**building, built**) *vt* to make or construct, to establish, base; (*with* **up**) to create or develop gradually. * *vi* to put up buildings; (*with* **up**) to grow or intensify; (*health, reputation*) to develop. * *n* the way a thing is built or shaped; the shape of a person; the physical appearance or weight or size of a person.—**builder** *n*.

building *adj* the skill or occupation of constructing houses, boats, etc; something built with walls and a roof.

building society *n* a company that pays interest on deposits and issues loans to enable people to buy their own houses.—*also* **savings and loan association**.

built-in *adj* incorporated as an integral part of a main structure; inherent.

built-up *adj* made higher, stronger, etc with added parts; having many buildings on it, eg *built-up area*.

bulb *n* the underground bud of plants such as the onion and daffodil; a glass bulb in an electric light; a rounded shape.—**bulbous** *adj*.

bulbiferous *adj* (*plants*) producing bulbs.

bulbil *n* (*bot*) a small bulb formed at the side of an old one; a small solid or scaly bud, which detaches itself from the stem, becoming an independent plant.

bulbul *n* an Eastern songbird; (*poet*) the Persian nightingale.

bulge *n* a swelling; a rounded projected part; a significant rise in numbers (of population). * *vti* to swell or bend outward.—**bulgy** *adj*.

bulimia *n* insatiable hunger, voracity.

bulimia nervosa *n* an illness characterized by bouts of compulsive eating followed by self-induced vomiting.

bulk *n* magnitude; great mass; volume; the main part; **in bulk** in large quantities. * *adj* total, aggregate; (*goods*) not packaged.

bulk buying *n* the large-scale buying of one commodity usu at a cost reduction; the purchase by one country of the total output of a product of another country.

bulk carrier *n* a ship carrying as cargo one unpackaged commodity.

bulkhead *n* a wall-like partition in the interior of a ship, aircraft or vehicle.

bulky *adj* (**bulkier, bulkiest**) large and unwieldy.—**bulkily** *adv*.—**bulkiness** *adj*.

bull[1] *n* an adult male bovine animal; a male whale or elephant; a speculator who buys in anticipation of reselling at a profit; the bull's-eye; (*sl*) nonsense; bullshit. * *adj* male; rising in price.

bull[2] *n* an official edict issued by the pope, with the papal seal on it.

bull[3] *n* a ludicrous inconsistency in language.—*also* **Irish bull**.

bulla *n* (*pl* **bullae**) a lead seal on a papal document; a blister.—**bullous** *adj*.

bullace *n* a wild European species of plum cultivated as the damson.

bullate *adj* blistered; puffy.

bulldog *n* a variety of dog of strong muscular build, remarkable for its courage and ferocity, formerly used for baiting bulls; a short-barrelled pistol with a large calibre. * *adj* characterized by the courage of a bulldog; tenacious.

bulldog clip *n* a spring clip with a powerful grip.

bulldoze *vt* to demolish with a bulldozer; (*inf*) to force.

bulldozer *n* an excavator with caterpillar tracks for moving earth.

bullet *n* a small metal missile fired from a gun or rifle.

bulletin *n* an announcement; a short statement of news or of a patient's progress.

bulletin board *n* a board on which notices are posted.

bulletproof *adj* providing protection against bullets.

bullfight *n* a combat between armed men and a bull or bulls.

bullfighting *n* the sport of goading and then killing bulls, popular in Spain, etc.—**bullfighter** *n*.

bullfinch *n* a common brightly coloured European songbird.

bullfrog *n* a large North American frog found in marshy places, remarkable for its loud bellowing croak.

bullheaded *adj* stubborn; stupid.—**bullheadedly** *adv*.—**bullheadedness** *n*.

bullion *n* gold or silver in mass before coinage.

bull-necked *adj* having a short thick neck.

bullock *n* a gelded bull; steer.

bullring *n* an arena for bullfighting.

bull's-eye *n* (*darts, archery*) the centre of a target; something resembling this; a direct hit; a large round peppermint boiled sweet.

bullshit *n* (*vulg sl*) nonsense; exaggeration, pretentious talk. * *vti* (**bullshitting, bullshitted**) (*vulg sl*) to claim knowledge that is lacking; to talk boastfully.—**bullshitter** *n*.

bull terrier *n* a dog bred by a cross between the bulldog and the terrier.

bullwhip *n* a whip with a long lash for driving cattle. * *vt* (**bullwhipping, bullwhipped**) to whip with this.

bully *n* (*pl* **bullies**) a person, adult or child, who hurts or intimidates others weaker than himself or herself. * *vb* (**bullying, bullied**) *vt* to intimidate, oppress or hurt. * *vi* (*with* **off**) (*hockey*) to cross sticks in a bully-off to start a match. * *adj* (*inf*) very good, as in *bully for you*.

bully (beef) *n* canned corned beef.

bully boy *n* a hoodlum, a ruffian, usu one hired to beat up someone.

bullyrag *see* **ballyrag**.

bulrush *n* a tall marsh plant.

bulwark *n* a defensive wall or rampart; (*naut*) a fence-like structure projecting above the deck of a ship; an object or person acting as a means of defence.

bum *n* (*inf*) a tramp; an idle person; (*inf*) a devotee, as of skiing or tennis; (*sl*) buttocks or anus. * *adj* broken; useless. * *vti* (**bumming, bummed**) to beg, to sponge; to live as a vagabond; (*with* **around**) to be idle, to loaf about.

bumble *vi* to do or say something clumsily or in a confused way; to stumble.—**bumbler** *n*.

bumblebee *n* a large, furry bee.

bumboat *n* a boat used for conveying provisions, fruit, etc, for sale to vessels lying off shore.

bummer *n* a worthless person who sponges on others; a low politician; an unpleasant experience, esp due to drug taking.

bump *vi* to knock with a jolt. * *vt* to hurt by striking or knocking; (*inf*) to refuse a booked passenger a seat on a flight because of overbooking by the airline; (*with* **into**) to collide with; (*inf*) to meet by chance; (*with* **off**) (*sl*) to kill, murder; (*with* **up**) (*inf*) to increase prices, size or bulk. * *n* a jolt; a knock; the noise made by a bump or a collision; a swelling or lump; one of the bulges on the head supposedly indicating a special faculty.

bumper *n* a shock-absorbing bar fixed to the front and rear of a motor vehicle; a brimming glass for a toast. * *adj* exceptionally large.

bumpkin *n* an awkward or simple country person.

bumptious *adj* offensively conceited or self-assertive.—**bumptiously** *adv*.—**bumptiousness** *n*.

bumpy *adj* (**bumpier, bumpiest**) having many bumps; rough; jolting, jerky.—**bumpily** *adv*.—**bumpiness** *n*.

bum steer *n* (*sl*) false or deceptive information or advice.

bun *n* a roll made of bread dough and currants, spices and sugar; a bun-shaped coil of hair at the nape of the neck.

bunch *n* a cluster; a number of things growing or fastened together; (*inf*) a group of people. * *vi* to group together; * *vt* to make into a bunch.—**bunchy** *adj*.—**bunchiness** *n*.

buncombe *see* **bunkum**.

bund[1], **Bund** *n* (*pl* **bunds, Bünde**) a league, a confederacy.

bund[2] *n* an embankment to protect land against inundation.

bundle *n* a number of things fastened together; a fastened package; (*sl*) a large sum of money. * *vt* to put together in bundles; to push hurriedly into.—**bundler** *n*.

bung *n* a cork or rubber stopper. * *vt* to close up with or as with a bung; (*sl*) to throw, toss.

bungalow *n* a one-storey house.

bungle *n* a mistake or blunder; something carried out clumsily. * *vt* to spoil something through incompetence or clumsiness.—**bungler** *n*.—**bungling** *adj, n*.

bunion *n* a lump on the side of the first joint of the big toe.

bunk[1] *n* a narrow, shelf-like bed; a bunk bed.

bunk[2] *n* (*sl*) a hurried departure.

bunk[3] *n* (*sl*) buncombe.

bunk bed *n* one of two or three single beds arranged one above the other in a compact unit.

bunker *n* a large storage container, esp for coal; a sand pit forming an obstacle on a golf course; an underground shelter.

bunkum *n* idle or showy speech; nonsense.—*also* **buncombe**.

bunny *n* (*pl* **bunnies**) a pet name for a rabbit; a nightclub waitress dressed to resemble a rabbit.

Bunsen burner *n* a burner that mixes gas and air to produce a smokeless flame of great heat.

bunt[1] *vti* (*animal*) to butt; (*baseball*) to tap (the ball) within the infield. * *n* this stroke.

bunt[2] *n* a species of fungus that produces the smut disease in wheat.

bunt[3] *n* the bulge of a sail, net, etc.

bunting[1] *n* a cotton fabric used for making flags; a line of pennants and decorative flags.

bunting[2] *n* a bird allied to the finches and sparrows.

buntline *n* (*naut*) one of the ropes attached to the foot rope of a square sail to draw the sail up to the yard.

buoy *n* a bright, anchored, marine float used for mooring and for making obstacles. * *vt* to keep afloat; (*usu with* **up**) to hearten or raise the spirits of; to mark with buoys.

buoyancy *n* ability to float or rise; cheerfulness; resilience.

buoyant *adj* able to float; light, elastic; not easily depressed, cheerful.—**buoyantly** *adv*.

bur *n* a prickly seed-case of a plant; a person hard to shake off; a rough edge left after drilling or cutting; a burr. * *vt* (**burring, burred**) to pick burs off.

burble *vi* to make a gurgling sound; to speak incoherently, esp from excitement.—**burbler** *n*.

burbot *n* (*pl* **burbot, burbots**) a freshwater fish like the eel.

burden[1] *n* a load; something worrisome that is difficult to bear; responsibility. * *vt* to weigh down, to oppress.

burden[2] *n* the chorus or refrain of a song; a topic dwelt on in speech or writing.

burdensome *adj* onerous; oppresive; heavy.—**burdensomely** *adv*.

burdock *n* a large wayside weed with prickly flowers and rough broad leaves.

bureau *n* (*pl* **bureaus, bureaux**) a writing desk; a chest of drawers; a branch of a newspaper, magazine or wire service in an important news centre; a government department.

bureaucracy *n* (*pl* **bureaucracies**) a system of government where the administration is organized in a hierarchy; the government collectively; excessive paperwork and red tape.

bureaucrat *n* an official in a bureaucracy, esp one who adheres inflexibly to this system.—**bureaucratic** *adj*.—**bureaucratically** *adv*.

burette, buret *n* a graduated glass tube, usu with a tap, for measuring the volume of liquids.

burg *n* a town; (*formerly*) a fortified town.

burgee *n* a swallow-tailed flag or pennant flown on the mast of a yacht to show membership of a club or of a merchant vessel to show ownership.

burgeon *vt* to start to increase rapidly; (*plant*) to bloom copiously.

burger *n* (*inf*) hamburger.

burgess *n* in UK, a citizen or freeman of a borough; (*formerly*) a member of parliament for a borough or university; in US, a representative sent by a town to the colonial legislative body of Virginia or Maryland.

burgh *n* (*Scot*) a borough.—**burghal** *adj*.

burgher *n* a citizen or freeman of a burgh or borough; a prosperous person of the middle classes.

burglar *n* a person who trespasses in a building with the intention of committing a crime, such as theft.

burglary *n* (*pl* **burglaries**) the act or crime of breaking into a house or any building with intent to commit a felony, esp theft.

burgle, burglarize *vti* to commit burglary (in or on).

burgomaster *n* the chief magistrate of a municipal town in Holland, Belgium or Germany.

burgonet *n* a kind of steel cap or helmet of the 16th century.

Burgundy *n* (*pl* **Burgundies**) a dryish wine, red or white, made in the Burgundy region of eastern France; a similar wine produced elsewhere; a dark purplish red colour.

burial *n* the act of burying; interment of a dead body.

burial ground *n* a graveyard.

burin *n* a chisel used for engraving metal, wood or marble; (*archaeol*) a primitive tool with a chisel-shaped head.

burke *vt* to murder by suffocation; to dispose of quietly; to hush up.

burl *n* a small knot or lump in thread or cloth; a knot in wood; a wood veneer with knots in it. * *vt* to pick knots, etc, from, as in finishing cloth.

burlap *n* a coarse fabric made of jute, hemp, etc, used for bagging or in upholstery.

burlesque *n* a caricature; a literary or dramatic satire. * *vti* (**burlesquing, burlesqued**) to make fun of, to caricature. * *adj* of or like burlesque; mockingly imitative.

burly *adj* (**burlier, burliest**) heavily built; sturdy.—**burliness** *n*.

burn[1] *vb* (**burning, burned** *or* **burnt**) *vt* to destroy by fire; to injure by heat. * *vi* to be on fire; to feel hot; to feel passion; (*inf*) to suffer from sunburn; (*with* **off**) to clear ground by burning all vegetation; to get rid of (surplus gas, energy) by burning or using up; (*with* **out**) (*fire*) to go out; (*person*) to lose efficiency through exhaustion, excess or overwork. * *n* a scorch mark or injury caused by burning.

burn[2] *n* (*Scot*) a small stream, a brook.

burner *n* the part of a lamp or stove that produces a flame.

burnet *n* a brown-flowered plant of the rose family.

burning *adj* intense, passionate; urgent.—**burningly** *adj*.

burning glass *n* a double convex lens used to focus the sun's rays on combustible substances to ignite them.

burnish *vt* to make shiny by rubbing; to polish. * *n* lustre; polish.—**burnishable** *adj*.—**burnisher** *n*.

burnous, burnoose *n* a long, hooded cloak worn by Arabs.

burnt *see* **burn**.

burnt offering *n* something offered and burnt upon an altar as a sacrifice or an atonement for sin.

burnt sienna *n* an orange-reddish pigment used in painting.

burro *n* (*pl* **burros**) a donkey.

burp *vi* to belch. * *vt* to pat a baby on the back to cause it to belch. * *n* a belch.

burr[1] *see* **bur**.

burr[2] *n* a whirring sound; a gruff pronunciation of the letter *r*. * *vti* to pronounce with a burr.

burrito *n* a tortilla baked with a savoury filling.

burrow *n* an underground hide or tunnel dug by a rabbit, badger or fox, etc for shelter. * *vi* to dig a burrow; to live in a burrow; to hide (oneself); to grope into the depths of one's pockets.—**burrower** *n*.

burry *adj* (**burrier, burriest**) full of burs; rough; prickly.

bursa *n* (*pl* **bursae, bursas**) (*anat*) a sac or sac-like cavity, esp between joints, full of a fluid that lessens friction.—**bursal** *adj*.

bursar *n* a treasurer; a person in charge of the finances of a college or university; a student holding a bursary.—**bursarial** *adj*.

bursary *n* (*pl* **bursaries**) a scholarship awarded to a student.—**bursarial** *adj*.

burst *vb* (**bursting, burst**) *vt* to break open; to cause to explode. * *vi* to emerge suddenly; to explode; to break into pieces; to give vent to. * *n* an explosion; a burst; a volley of shots; a sudden increase of activity; a spurt.—**burster** *n*.

burton *n* (*naut*) a tackle formed of two or more blocks or pulleys; **go for a burton** to die; to be no longer useful.

bury *vt* (**burying, buried**) (*bone, corpse*) to place in the ground; to inter; to conceal, to cover; to blot out of the mind; **bury the hatchet** to make peace; to be reconciled.

bus *n* (*pl* **buses, busses**) a motor coach for public transport. * *vti* (**busing, bused** *or* **bussing, bussed**) to transport or travel by bus; to take by bus children from one area to another, esp to balance racial numbers.

busby *n* (*pl* **busbies**) a tall, fur hat, esp one worn by a guardsman.

bush[1] *n* a low shrub with many branches; a cluster of shrubs forming a hedge; woodland; (*with* **the**) uncultivated land, esp in Africa, Australia, New Zealand, Canada; a thick growth, eg of hair; a fox's tail or brush.

bush[2] *n* a metal lining of a hole in which an axle turns to reduce wear by friction (—*also* **bushing**). * *vt* to furnish with a bush.

bushbaby *n* (*pl* **bushbabies**) a small tree-dwelling nocturnal lemur from Africa.

bushed *adj* (*inf*) tired, exhausted; (*Austral*) lost in the bush.

bushel[1] *n* a dry measure containing eight gallons (UK) or 64 pints (US); a vessel of such a capacity; a large quantity.

bushel[2] *vt* (**bushelling, bushelled** *or* **busheling, busheled**) to patch or repair, esp clothes.—**busheller, busheler** *n*.

bushfire *n* a fire, often widespread, in bush or scrubland.

bushing *see* **bush**[2].

bushman *n* (*pl* **bushmen**) a woodsman; (*Austral*) a settler in the bush or newly opened country; (*with cap*) one of a tribe of South African aboriginals near the Cape of Good Hope.

bushmaster *n* a large deadly South American snake with brown and grey markings.

bushranger *n* a frontiersman; (*Austral*: *formerly*) a criminal who escaped and lived a lawless life in the bush.

bush telegraph *n* a means of communicating news by drumbeat across a large area; (*inf*) a means of spreading gossip.

bushwhack *vi* to work one's way through the bush; to ambush.

bushwhacker *n* a backwoodsman; a guerrilla fighter; an implement for cutting brushwood.

bushy *adj* (**bushier, bushiest**) covered with bushes; (*hair*) thick.—**bushiness** *n*.

business *n* trade or commerce; occupation or profession; a firm; a factory; one's concern or responsibility; a matter; the agenda of a business meeting.

businesslike *adj* efficient, methodical, practical.

businessman *n* (**businessmen**) a person who works for an industrial or commercial company, esp as an executive.—**businesswoman** *nf* (*pl* **businesswomen**).

busing *see* **bussing**.

busker *n* a street entertainer.—**busking** *n*.

buskin *n* a half boot or high shoe; a high boot once worn by tragic actors to increase their height; a tragic drama.

busman's holiday *n* a holiday spent doing what one usually does at work.

buss *n* a smacking kiss. * *vt* to kiss.

bussing *n* the transport of children to a school in another district to achieve racially balanced classes.—*also* **busing**.

bust[1] *n* the chest or breast of a human being, esp a woman; a sculpture of the head and chest.

bust[2] *vti* (**busting, busted** *or* **bust**) (*inf*) to burst or break; to make or become bankrupt or demoted; to hit; to arrest. * *n* (*inf*) a failure; financial collapse; a punch; a spree; an arrest.

bustard *n* any of a genus of large swift-running birds of Europe and Africa.

buster *n* a person or thing that busts; something very large; a frolic; a violent wind; (*with cap*) (*inf*) boy, man, a form of address.

bustle[1] *vi* to move or act noisily, energetically or fussily. * *n* noisy activity, stir, commotion.—**bustler** *n*.—**bustling** *adj*.

bustle[2] *n* a pad placed beneath the skirt of a dress to cause it to puff up at the back.

bust-up *n* (*inf*) a fight or quarrel; a noisy brawl; the permanent ending of a relationship.

busy *adj* (**busier, busiest**) occupied; active; crowded; full; industrious; (*painting*) having too much detail; (*room, telephone*) engaged, in use. * *vt* (**busying, busied**) to occupy; to make or keep busy (esp oneself).—**busily** *adv*.—**busyness** *n*.

busybody *n* (*pl* **busybodies**) a meddlesome person.

but *prep* save; except. * *conj* in contrast; on the contrary, other than. * *adv* only; merely; just. * *n* an objection.

butane *n* an inflammable gas used as a fuel.

butch *adj* (*sl*) tough; aggressively male; (*often of a woman*) male-looking.

butcher *n* a person who slaughters meat; a retailer of meat; a ruthless murderer. * *vt* to slaughter; to murder ruthlessly; to make a mess of or spoil.

butcherbird *n* any of a genus of shrikes that suspend their slaughtered prey from thorns.

butcher's-broom *n* a low-growing evergreen shrub with rigid branched stems and spiny leaves.

butchery *n* (*pl* **butcheries**) the preparation of meat for sale; slaughter.

butler *n* a manservant, usu the head servant of a household, etc.

butt[1] *vti* to strike or toss with the head or horns, as a bull, etc; (*with* **in**) to interfere, to enter into unasked. * *n* a push with the head or horns.—**butter** *n*.

butt[2] *n* a large cask for wine or beer.

butt[3] *n* a mound of earth behind targets; a person who is the target of ridicule or jokes; (*pl*) the target range.

butt[4] *n* the thick or blunt end; the stump; (*sl*) a cigarette; fag end; (*sl*) the buttocks. * *vti* to join end to end.

butte *n* an abrupt isolated hill or ridge.

butter *n* a solidified fat made from cream by churning. * *vt* to spread butter on; (*with* **up**) (*inf*) to flatter.

butter bean *n* a variety of lima bean cultivated for its large flat pale edible seeds.

buttercup *n* any of various plants with yellow, glossy, cup-shaped flowers.

butterfingers *n* (*used as sing*) a person who lets (a ball, etc) slip through his or her fingers.—**butterfingered** *adj*.

butterfly *n* (*pl* **butterflies**) an insect with a slender body and four usu brightly coloured wings; a swimming stroke.

buttermilk *n* the sour liquid that remains after separation from the cream in buttermaking.

butternut *n* a North American tree of the walnut family; its large oily nut; its hard wood; the colour of the butternut, a brownish grey, the colour of the Confederate uniform in the American Civil War; one who wore the uniform of the Confederate army.

butterscotch *n* a sauce made of melted butter and brown sugar; a kind of hard toffee made from this; its flavour; a brownish-yellow colour.

butterwort *n* a violet-flowered bog plant with leaves that secrete a viscid fluid to entrap small insects.

buttery[1] *adj* like or tasting of butter; insincere.

buttery[2] *n* (*pl* **butteries**) a storeroom for wine or food.

buttock *n* either half of the human rump.

button *n* a disc or knob of metal, plastic, etc used as a fastening; a badge; a small button-like sweet; an electric bell push; a knob at the point of a fencing foil. * *vti* to fasten with a button or buttons.

buttonhole *n* the slit through which a button is passed; a single flower in the buttonhole. * *vt* to make buttonholes; to sew with a special buttonhole stitch; (*person*) to keep in conversation.

buttonhook *n* a tool for fastening buttons on shoes or gloves.

buttress *n* a projecting structure for strengthening a wall. * *vt* to support or prop.

butyraceous *adj* like butter in consistency, appearance or properties.

butyrate *n* a salt of butyric acid.

butyric acid *n* a colourless liquid obtained from butter, also present in cod-liver oil and sweat glands.

buxom *adj* plump and healthy; (*woman*) big-bosomed.—**buxomness** *n.*

buy *vt* (**buying, bought**) to purchase (for money); to bribe or corrupt; to acquire in exchange for something; (*inf*) to believe; (*with* **off**) to pay (someone) to ensure that some undesired action is not taken; (*with* **out**) to purchase a controlling interest in or share of; to secure the release of (e.g. a person from the army) by payment; (*with* **up**) to purchase the total supply of something; to acquire a controlling interest in. * *n* a purchase.

buyer *n* a person who buys; a customer; an employee who buys on behalf of his or her employer, esp a company or store.

buyer's market *n* a market in which, because the supply exceeds the demand, the buyers control the price.

buzz *vi* to hum like an insect; to gossip; to hover (about). * *vt* spread gossip secretly; (*inf*) to telephone. * *vi* (*with* **off**) to go away. * *n* the humming of bees or flies; a rumour; (*sl*) a telephone call; (*sl*) a thrill, a kick.

buzzard *n* a large bird of prey of the hawk family.

buzzer *n* a device producing a buzzing sound.

buzz saw *n* a circular saw.

buzzword *n* (*inf*) a vogue or jargon word; a word or phrase that was once a technical or specialist term and which has suddenly become popular, often used mainly for effect.—*also* **fuzzword.**

bwana *n* (*E Africa*) an employer, a boss; (*with cap*) a form of address.

by-, bye- *prefix* subordinate, side, secret.

by *prep* beside; next to; via; through the means of; not later than. * *adv* near to; past; in reserve, aside.

by and by *adv* presently, before long; later; eventually; in the future.—**by-and-by** *n.*

by and large *adv* on the whole.

by-blow *n* a side blow; a bastard.

bye *n* something subordinate or incidental; an odd man in a knockout competition; (*cricket*) a run scored without the ball being hit by the batsman; (*golf*) holes left after a match is decided; (*lacrosse*) a goal.

bye-bye[1] *interj* (*inf*) goodbye.

bye-bye[2] *n* sleep; bed.

by-election, bye-election *n* an election held other than at a general election.

bygone *adj* past. * *n* (*pl*) past offences or quarrels.

bylaw, bye-law *n* a rule or law made by a local authority or a company.

by-line *n* a line under a newspaper article naming its author.

bypass *n* a main road built to avoid a town; a channel redirecting the flow of something around a blockage; (*med*) an operation to redirect the flow of blood into the heart. * *vt* (**bypassing, bypassed**) to go around; to avoid, to act by ignoring the usual channels.

bypath *n* a secluded path.

byplay *n* action or dumb show aside from the main action.

byproduct, by-product *n* something useful produced in the process of making something else.

byre *n* a shed for cows.

byroad *n* an unfrequented or side road.

byssus *n* (*pl* **byssuses, byssi**) a tuft of long soft silky filaments by which certain molluscs attach themselves to rocks; a fine linen used by the ancient Egyptians for wrapping mummies.

bystander *n* a chance onlooker.

byte *n* (*comput*) a set of eight bits treated as a unit.

by the by, by the bye *adv* incidentally.

by the way *adv* incidentally.

byway *n* a side road; a specialist or abstruse interest or area of study.

byword *n* a well-known saying; a perfect example; an object of derision.

Byzantine *adj* of or pertaining to Byzantium, the ancient capital of the Eastern Roman Empire; (*archit*) in the style of the Eastern Empire. * *n* an inhabitant of Byzantium.

C

C *abbr* = Celsius, centigrade; (*math*) third known quantity; (*roman numerals*) 100; (*chem symbol*) = carbon.

c.[1] *abbr* = carat; cent(s); century.

c.[2] *abbr* = *circa*, about.

© (*symbol*) = copyright.

CA *abbr* = California; Chartered Accountant.

Ca (*chem symbol*) = calcium.

cab *n* a taxicab; the place where the driver sits in a truck, crane, etc.

cabal *n* a conspiracy, a secret plot; a small group of people united in perpetrating this; a clique. * *vi* (**caballing, caballed**) to form a cabal, to plot.

cabala, cabbala *n* a mystic interpretation of Scripture by Jewish rabbis; occult lore.—*also* **kabala, kabbala.**—**cabalism, cabbalism** *n.*—**cabalist, cabbalist** *n.*—**cabalistic, cabbalistic** *adj.*

caballero *n* (*pl* **caballeros**) a Spanish knight or gentleman; a horseman; a Spanish dance.

cabaret *n* entertainment given in a restaurant or nightclub.

cabbage *n* a garden plant with thick leaves formed usu into a compact head, used as a vegetable.

cabbage rose *n* a large full rose.

cabby, cabbie *n* (*pl* **cabbies**) (*inf*) a person who drives a cab for hire.

caber *n* a rough pole, usu cut from a tree, tossed as a trial of strength at Highland games.

cabin *n* a small house, a hut; a room in a ship; the area where passengers sit in an aircraft.

cabin cruiser *n* a powerful motorboat with living accommodation.

cabinet *n* a case or cupboard with drawers or shelves; a case containing a TV, radio, etc; (*often with cap*) a body of official advisers to a government; the senior ministers of a government.

cabinetmaker *n* a person who makes fine furniture.

cable *n* a strong thick rope often of wire strands; an anchor chain; an insulated cord that carries electric current; a cablegram; a bundle of insulated wires for carrying cablegrams, TV signals, etc; (*naut*) a cable length. * *vti* to send a message by cablegram.

cable car *n* a car drawn by a moving cable, as up a steep incline.
cablegram *n* a message transmitted by telephone line, submarine cable, satellite, a cable.
cable-laid *adj* (*rope*) composed of three triple strands.
cable length *n* (*naut*) (*UK*) a unit of length, about 100 fathoms, 608 feet or one tenth of a nautical mile, (*US*) 120 fathoms, 720 feet.
cable stitch *n* a pattern of knitting stitches resembling a cable.
cable television *n* TV transmission to subscribers by cable.
cabman *n* (*pl* **cabmen**) the driver of a cab.
cabochon *n* a precious stone polished but not faceted.
caboodle *n* (*sl*) a lot, a set (*the whole caboodle*).
caboose *n* the guard's car at the rear of a freight train; a kitchen on a ship's deck.
cabriolet *n* a covered carriage with two or four wheels drawn by one horse; a car body with a folding hood and fixed sides.
cacao *n* a tropical tree; its seed, from which cocoa and chocolate are obtained.
cachalot *n* the sperm whale.
cache *n* a secret hiding place; a store of weapons or treasure; a store of food left for use by travellers, etc. * *vt* to place in a cache.
cache (memory) *n* a small high-speed memory for easy access and frequent reference to computer data.
cachepot *n* an ornamental pot to hold a flowerpot.
cachet *n* a mark of authenticity; any distinguishing mark; prestige.
cachexia, cachexy *n* (*med*) a bad state of general health, weakness.—**cachectic** *adj*.
cachinnate *vi* to laugh loudly and unrestrainedly.—**cachinnation** *n*.
cachou[1] *see* **catechu**.
cachou[2] *n* a lozenge for sweetening the breath.
cachucha *n* a quick Spanish dance; the music for it.
cacique *n* a West Indian or American Indian chief; a political boss.
cackle *n* the clucking sound of a hen; shrill or silly talk or laughter. * *vi* to utter with a cackle.
caco- *prefix* bad.
cacodemon, cacodaemon *n* an evil spirit.
cacodyl *n* an evil-smelling compound of arsenic and methyl.
cacoethes *n* a bad habit or propensity of the body or mind; an uncontrollable urge.—**cacoethic** *adj*.
cacography *n* bad handwriting or spelling, the opposite of calligraphy and orthography.—**cacographic** *adj*.
cacophonous *adj* harsh, ill-sounding, discordant.
cacophony *n* (*pl* **cacophonies**) an ugly sound, a discord.
cactus *n* (*pl* **cactuses, cacti**) a plant with a thick fleshy stem that stores water and is often studded with prickles.
cad *n* (*inf*) a man who behaves in an ungentlemanly or dishonourable way.—**caddish** *adj*.—**caddishly** *adv*.—**caddishness** *n*.
cadastre, cadaster *n* a register of the real estate of a district or county as a basis for taxation.—**cadastral** *adj*.
cadaver *n* a dead body.—**cadaveric** *adj*.
cadaverous *adj* gaunt, haggard; pallid, livid.—**cadaverousness** *n*.
caddis *n* the larva of the mayfly used as bait.
caddie, caddy *n* (*pl* **caddies**) a person who carries a golfer's clubs.—*vi* (**caddying, caddied**) to perform as a caddie.
caddy *n* (*pl* **caddies**) a small box or tin for storing tea.
cade *n* a lamb, etc, bred by hand.
cadence *n* a falling of the voice; the intonation of the voice; rhythm; measured movements as in marching.
cadent *adj* rhythmic; falling.
cadenza *n* (*mus*) an ornamental flourish at the close of a movement.
cadet *n* a student at an armed forces academy, police college, etc; a school pupil in a school army training corps.
cadge *vti* to beg or obtain by begging.—**cadger** *n*.
cadi *n* a minor Mohammedan judge.
cadmium *n* a whitish metallic element.
cadre *n* a permanent nucleus or framework of a political or military unit.
caduceus *n* (*pl* **caducei**) the winged wand of Hermes (Mercury) entwined with two serpents, the emblem of the medical profession; an ancient herald's wand.
caducity *n* the quality or condition of being caducous; senility.
caducous *adj* (*biol*) (*parts of a plant*) falling off quickly or before maturity; fleeting; perishable.
caecum *n* (*pl* **caeca**) the pouch at the beginning of the large intestine containing the vermiform appendix.—*also* **cecum.**—**caecal** *adj*.
Caesar *n* the title of Roman emperors, esp Julius Caesar (*c*. 100–44 bc); (*without cap*) any ruler.
Caesarean section, Cesarean section *n* the removal of a child from the womb by a surgical operation involving the cutting of the abdominal wall.
caesium *n* a rare silvery alkaline metal.—*also* **cesium.**
caesura *n* (*pl* **caesuras, caesurae**) a natural pause in the rhythm of a verse line.—**caesural** *adj*.
cafe, café *n* a small restaurant, a coffee bar, a nightclub, etc.
café au lait *n* coffee with milk; a light brown colour.
café noir *n* coffee without milk.
cafeteria *n* a self-service restaurant.
cafetière *n* a usu glass coffee pot with a plunger to press down coffee grounds.
caffeine *n* a stimulant present in coffee and tea.—**caffeinic** *adj*.
caftan *n* a long-sleeved, full-length, voluminous garment originating in the Middle East.—*also* **kaftan.**
cage *n* a box or enclosure with bars for confining an animal, bird, prisoner, etc; a car for raising or lowering miners. * *vt* to shut in a cage, to confine.
cagey, cagy *adj* (**cagier, cagiest**) (*inf*) wary, secretive, not frank.—**cagily** *adv*.—**caginess** *n*.
cahier *n* sheets of paper put loosely together, a notebook.
cahoots *npl* partnership; **in cahoots** in league or partnership.
CAI *abbr* = computer-aided instruction.
caiman *n* (*pl* **caimans**) an alligator of South and Central America.—*also* **cayman.**
caique, caïque *n* a skiff or light rowing boat used on the Bosphorus in Turkey.
cairn *n* a stone mound placed as a monument or marker.
cairngorm *n* (a gemstone of) a yellow or brown variety of quartz or rock crystal.
caisson *n* a watertight chamber used for carrying out underwater repairs or construction work; an apparatus for floating or lifting a vessel.
caitiff *n* (*arch*) a coward; a rascal. * *adj* (*arch*) base, despicable, cowardly.
cajole *vti* to persuade or soothe by flattery or deceit.—**cajoler** *n*.—**cajolingly** *adv*.
cajolery, cajolement *n* (*pl* **cajoleries, cajolements**) the action or practice of cajoling; persuasion by false arts.
Cajun, Cajan *n* an inhabitant of Louisiana descended from 18th-century French-Canadian immigrants; the dialect spoken by Cajuns.
cake *n* a mixture of flour, eggs, sugar, etc baked in small, flat shapes or a loaf; a small block of compacted or congealed matter. * *vti* to encrust; to form into a cake or hard mass.
cakewalk *n* an elaborate step dance; a task accomplished without difficulty.
Cal *abbr* = California; Calorie.
cal *abbr* = calendar; calibre; calorie.
Calabar bean *n* a West African plant; its poisonous bean.
calabash *n* the fruit of the calabash tree of tropical America, used when dried as a vessel for liquids, etc.
calaboose *n* (*inf*) a jail.
calamanco *n* (*pl* **calamancoes, calamancos**) a glossy woollen fabric, brocaded or checkered.
calamander *n* a fine variety of Indian ebony of a very hard texture.
calamari *n* squid eaten as a food.
calamary *n* (*pl* **calamaries**) squid.

calamine *n* a zinc oxide powder used in skin lotions, etc for its soothing effect.
calamint *n* an aromatic herb of the mint family.
calamite *n* a fossil plant resembling a horsetail.
calamitous *adj* producing or resulting from calamity; disastrous.—**calamitously** *adv*.—**calamitousness** *n*.
calamity *n* (*pl* **calamities**) a disastrous event, a great misfortune; adversity.
calamus *n* (*pl* **calami**) any of a genus of palms producing the rattan canes; the sweet flag.
calando *adv* (*mus*) gradually; slower and softer.
calash *n* a light carriage with low wheels and a folding removable top; (*Canada*) a two-wheeled single-seater carriage; a hood formerly worn by women.—*also* **caleche**.
calcar *n* (*pl* **calcaria**) a tube or spur at the base of a petal or sepal; a furnace used in glass-making.
calcareous *adj* of the nature of, or containing, lime.—**calcareousness** *n*.
calceiform, calceolate *adj* (*bot*) slipper-shaped.
calceolaria *n* any of a genus of South American ornamental plants with slipper-shaped flowers.
calcic *adj* of or containing calcium.
calciferous *adj* containing or yielding carbonate of lime.
calcify *vb* (**calcifying, calcified**) *vt* to convert into lime. * *vi* to harden by conversion into lime.
calcimine *n* a white or tinted wash for walls or ceilings.—*also* **kalsomine**.
calcination *n* the act or process of reducing to powder by heat.
calcine *vt* to reduce a substance to chalky powder by the action of heat; to burn to ashes. * *vi* to undergo calcination.
calcite *n* crystallized carbonate of lime.—**calcitic** *adj*.
calcium *n* the chemical element prevalent in bones and teeth.
calcium carbide *n* a fusion of coal or coke with lime in an electrical furnace, which, with water, produces acetylene gas.
calcium carbonate *n* a compound occurring naturally in limestone, chalk, and in bones and shells.
calcsinter *n* a crystalline deposit from lime springs.
calcspar *n* calcite, a crystalline carbonate of lime.
calculate *vti* to reckon or compute by mathematics; to suppose or believe; to plan.—**calculable** *adj*.
calculated *adj* adapted or suited (to); deliberate, cold-blooded, premeditated.—**calculatedly** *adv*.
calculating *adj* shrewd, scheming.—**calculatingly** *adv*.
calculation *n* the act of calculating; the result obtained from this; an estimate.—**calculational** *adj*.
calculator *n* a device, esp a small, electronic, hand-held one, for doing mathematical calculations rapidly; one who calculates.
calculous *adj* stony; gritty.
calculus *n* (*pl* **calculi, calculuses**) an abnormal, stony mass in the body; (*math*) a mode of calculation using symbols.
caldera *n* a deep caldron-like cavity on the summits of extinct volcanoes.
caldron *see* **cauldron**.
caleche *see* **calash**.
Caledonian *adj* pertaining to Caledonia, the ancient name of Scotland; Scottish. * *n* a native of Scotland.
calefacient *adj* producing or exciting heat. * *n* a heat-producing substance.—**calefaction** *n*.
calendar *n* a system of determining the length and divisions of a year; a chart or table of months, days and seasons; a list of particular, scheduled events.
calendar month *n* a solar month reckoned according to the calendar, as distinguished from the lunar month.
calender[1] *n* a press with rollers for finishing the surface of cloth, paper, etc. * *vt* to press in a calender.—**calenderer** *n*.
calender[2] *n* a mendicant dervish.
calends *npl* in the Roman calendar, the first day of each month.—*also* **kalends**.
calendula *n* any of a genus of plants, including the marigold, from which a medical tincture is obtained.
calenture *n* a tropical fever with delirium.
calf[1] *n* (*pl* **calves**) the young of a cow, seal, elephant, whale, etc; the leather skin of a calf.
calf[2] *n* (*pl* **calves**) the fleshy back part of the leg below the knee.
calf love *n* puppy love; an immature infatuation.
calfskin *n* the skin of a calf made into leather.
calibrate *vt* to measure the calibre of a gun; to adjust or mark units of measurement on a measuring scale or gauge.—**calibration** *n*.—**calibrator** *n*.
calibre, caliber *n* the internal diameter of a gun barrel or tube; capacity, standing, moral weight.
calico *n* (*pl* **calicoes, calicos**) a kind of cotton cloth. * *adj* made of this.
calif *see* **caliph**.
Calif. *abbr* = California.
califate *see* **caliphate**.
californium *n* an artificial radioactive metallic element.
calipash *n* the part of a turtle belonging to the upper shell, enclosing a dull greenish gelatinous edible substance.
calipee *n* the part of a turtle belonging to the lower shell, enclosing a light yellow gelatinous edible substance.
caliper *see* **calliper**.
caliph *n* the former title assumed by the successors of Mohammed as rulers; title of a Turkish sultan.—*also* **calif**.
caliphate *n* the office, dignity or government of a caliph.—*also* **califate**.
calisthenics *npl* light gymnastic exercises.—*also*—**callisthenics**. —**calisthenic, callisthenic** *adj*.
calix *n* (*pl* **calices**) a chalice; a cup-like cavity or organ.
calk[1] *see* **caulk**.
calk[2] *n* the part of a horseshoe that projects downwards to prevent slipping; a semicircular piece of iron nailed to the heel of a boot.
call *vi* to shout or cry out; to pay a short visit; to telephone; (*with* **in**) to pay a brief or informal visit; (*with* **on**) to pay a visit; to ask, to appeal to. * *vt* to summon; to name; to describe as specified; to awaken; to give orders for; (*with* **down**) to invoke; (*with* **in**) to summon for advice or help; to bring out of circulation; to demand payment of (a loan); (*with* **off**) to cancel; (*an animal*) to call away in order to stop, divert; (*with* **out**) to cry aloud; to order (workers) to come out on strike; to challenge to a duel; to summon (troops) to action; (*with* **up**) to telephone; to summon to military action, as in time of war; to recall. * *n* a summons; the note of a bird; a vocation, esp religious; occasion; a need; a demand; a short visit; the use of a telephone; a cry, a shout.
calla (lily) *n* an ornamental plant of the arum family with a large white spathe that enfolds a yellow spadix.
callant, callan *n* (*Scot*) a lad, a youth.
call box *n* a telephone booth; a roadside box containing a telephone for making emergency calls.
callboy *n* a prompter's attendant who tells actors when to go on.
caller[1] *n* one who calls, esp by telephone; one who pays a brief visit.
caller[2] *adj* (*Scot*) (*food*) cool, fresh; in season; (*fish*) recently caught.
call girl *n* (*inf*) a prostitute who makes appointments by telephone.
calligraphy *n* handwriting; beautiful writing.—**calligrapher, calligraphist** *n*.—**calligraphic** *adj*.—**calligraphically** *adv*.
calling *n* the act of summoning; a summons or invitation; a vocation, trade or profession; the state of being divinely called.
calliope *n* a steam organ; (*with cap*) the muse of epic poetry.
calliper *n* a metal framework for supporting a crippled or weak leg; paper thickness measured in microns; (*pl*) a two-legged measuring instrument. * *vt* to measure with or use callipers.—*also* **caliper**.
callisthenics *see* **calisthenics**.
call loan *n* a loan subject to recall without notice.
callosity *n* (*pl* **callosities**) the state or quality of being hardened; a callus.
callous *adj* (*skin*) hardened; (*person*) unfeeling.—**calloused** *adj*—**callously** *adv*.—**callousness** *n*.
callow *adj* inexperienced, undeveloped.—**callowness** *n*.

call sign *n* a signal identifying a particular radio transmitter.
call-up *n* a summons to military service.
callus *n* (*pl* **calluses**) a hardened, thickened place on the skin.
calm *adj* windless; still, unruffled; quiet, peaceful. * *n* the state of being calm; stillness; tranquillity. * *vti* to become or make calm.—**calmly** *adv*.—**calmness** *n*.
calmative *adj* (*med*) sedating. * *n* a sedative.
calomel *n* a preparation of mercury used as a purgative.
caloric *adj* of or pertaining to heat or calories.—**calorically** *adv*.
Calorie *n* a unit of heat equalling 1,000 calories.
calorie *n* a unit of heat; a measure of food energy.—*also* **calory**.
calorific *adj* heat-producing; (*inf*) causing fat.—**calorifically** *adv*.
calorimeter *n* an instrument for measuring quantities of heat.—**calorimetric, calorimetrical** *adj*.—**calorimetry** *n*.
calory *see* **calorie**.
calotte *n* a small plain skullcap of satin, etc, worn by priests.
calotype *n* a photographic process in which the image is received on paper prepared with iodide of silver.
caloyer *n* a Greek monk of the order of St Basil.
calpac, calpack *n* a tall brimless sheepskin cap worn by Turks and Armenians.—*also* **kalpak**.
caltrop, caltrap, calthrop *n* any of various plants with prickly fruit; an iron instrument with four spikes, placed in ditches, etc, to hinder the advance of troops.
calumet *n* the tobacco pipe of the North American Indians, smoked as a symbol of peace or to ratify treaties.
calumniate *vt* to accuse falsely and maliciously. * *vi* to utter calumnies.—**calumniation** *n*.—**calumniator** *n*.
calumny *n* (*pl* **calumnies**) a slander; a lie, a false accusation.—**calumnious** *adj*.—**calumniously** *adv*.
calvados *n* apple brandy distilled in Normandy in France.
calvary *n* (*pl* **calvaries**) a place or representation of the crucifixion of Christ; an experience of intense mental suffering; (*with cap*) the place where Christ was crucified.
calve *vti* to give birth to a calf; (*glacier, iceberg*) to break up and release ice.
calves *see* **calf**.
Calvinism *n* the doctrines of John Calvin (1509–64) the French theologian and reformer, esp those relating to predestination and election.—**Calvinist** *n*.—**Calvinistic** *adj*.
calvities *n* (*med*) baldness.
calx *n* (*pl* **calxes, calces**) the powder left when a metal or mineral has been subjected to great heat.
calycine, calycinal *adj* having a calyx; of or on the calyx.
calycle, calyculus *n* (*pl* **calycles, calyculi**) a whorl of small bracts forming a secondary calyx below the true one.
calypso *n* (*pl* **calypsos**) a West Indian folk song that comments on current events or personalities.
calyptra *n* (*bot*) the hood-like covering of the spore case of mosses.—**calyptrate** *adj*.
calyx *n* (*pl* **calyxes, calyces**) the outer series of leaves that form the cup from which the petals of a flower spring.
cam *n* a device to change rotary to reciprocating motion.
camaraderie *n* friendship, comradeship.
camarilla *n* a political clique, a cabal.
camber *n* a slight upward curve in the surface of a road, etc. * *vti* to curve upwards slightly.—**cambered** *adj*.
cambist *n* an expert in exchanges; a dealer in bills of exchange.
cambium *n* (*pl* **cambiums, cambia**) the formative layer of cellular tissue that lies between the young wood and the bark of exogenous trees.—**cambial** *adj*.
Cambrian *adj* of Wales; (*geol*) of the earliest Palaeozoic period, before the Silurian. * *n* the strata underlying the Silurian rocks, now classed with them.
cambric *n* a fine white linen or cotton cloth.
camcorder *n* a portable video recorder with built-in sound recording facilities.
came *see* **come**.
camel *n* a large four-footed, long-necked animal with a humped back; a fawny-beige colour.—*also adj*.
cameleer *n* a camel driver.
camellia *n* an oriental evergreen shrub with showy blooms.—*also* **japonica**.
camelopard *n* the giraffe.
camel's hair, camelhair *n* the hair of a camel; cloth from this; its fawn-tan colour; the hair from a squirrel's tail used as a paintbrush.—**camel's-hair, camelhair** *adj*.
Camembert *n* a soft white cheese originating in Normandy.
cameo *n* (*pl* **cameos**) an onyx or other gem carved in relief, often showing a head in profile; an outstanding bit role, esp in a motion picture; a short piece of fine writing.
camera *n* the apparatus used for taking still photographs or television or motion pictures; a judge's private chamber; **in camera** in private, esp of a legal hearing excluding the public; **off camera** outside the area being filmed; **on camera** being filmed, before the camera.
cameraman *n* (*pl* **cameramen**) a film or television camera operator.
camera obscura *n* a darkened chamber or box in which, by means of lenses, external objects are exhibited on paper, glass, etc.
camera-ready *adj* (*printing*) ready for photographic platemaking.
camera-shy *adj* unwilling to, or against, being filmed or photographed.
camion *n* a heavy truck, a wagon.
camise *n* a light loose robe, a chemise.
camisole *n* a woman or girl's loose sleeveless underbodice.
camlet *n* a kind of light cloth.
camomile *see* **chamomile**.
Camorra *n* a secret terrorist organization in southern Italy; a lawless clique.
camouflage *n* a method (esp using colouring) of disguise or concealment used to deceive an enemy; a means of putting people off the scent. * *vt* to conceal by camouflage.
camp[1] *n* the ground on which tents or temporary accommodation is erected; the occupants of this, such as holiday-makers or troops; the supporters of a particular cause. * *vi* to lodge in a camp; to pitch tents.—**camping** *n*.
camp[2] *adj* (*sl*) theatrical, exaggerated; effeminate; homosexual. * *vi* (*with* **up**) to make or give an exaggerated display of camp characteristics.
campaign *n* a series of military operations; a series of operations with a particular objective, such as election of a candidate or promotion of a product; organized course of action. * *vi* to take part in or conduct a campaign.—**campaigner** *n*.
campanile *n* a bell tower detached from the body of a church.
campanology *n* the art of bell ringing.—**campanologist** *n*.
campanula *n* a plant with bell-shaped flowers.
campanulate *adj* (*flower*) bell-shaped.
camper *n* one who lives in a tent; a person on a camping holiday; a vehicle equipped with all domestic facilities.
campfire *n* an outdoor fire at a camp; a social gathering around such a fire.
camp follower *n* a civilian, esp a prostitute, who provides unofficial services to military personnel; a person who is sympathetic to the aims of a particular group but is not a member.
camphene *n* rectified oil of turpentine.
camphor *n* a solid white transparent essential oil with a pungent taste and smell used to repel insects, as a stimulant in medicine, etc.—**camphoric** *adj*.
camphor tree *n* a species of laurel that yields camphor.
camphorate *vt* to saturate or treat with camphor.
campion *n* any of various wild plants of the pink family, the commonest having red or white flowers.
camp meeting *n* an oudoor religious meeting.

campsite *n* a camping ground, often with facilities for holiday-makers.
campstool *n* a folding stool or seat.
campus *n* (*pl* **campuses**) the grounds, and sometimes buildings, of a college or university.
camshaft *n* the rotating shaft to which cams are fitted to lift valves in engines.
Can *abbr* = Canada; Canadian.
can[1] *vt* (*pt* **could**) to be able to; to have the right to; to be allowed to.
can[2] *n* a container, usu metal, with a separate cover in which petrol, film, etc is stored; a tin in which meat, fruit, drinks, etc are hermetically sealed; the contents of a can; (*sl*) jail; (*sl*) a lavatory; **in the can** (*film*) shot and edited and ready for showing; (*inf*) accomplished, agreed, tied up. * *vti* (**canning, canned**) to preserve (foods) in a can.—**canner** *n*.
Canada balsam *n* a resin obtained from a species of fir.
Canada Day *n* a national Canadian holiday, July 1, commemorating its dominion status (established 1867).
Canada goose *n* a large grey goose with a black head and neck and a white throat patch.
Canadian *adj* of or pertaining to Canada. * *n* a native of Canada.
canaille *n* a rabble, the lowest orders.
canal *n* an artificial waterway cut across land; a duct in the body. * *vt* (**canalling, canalled** *or* **canaling, canaled**) to provide with canals.
canalize, canalise *vt* to provide with a canal or channel. * *vi* to flow in or into a channel; to establish new channels or outlets.—**canalization, canalisation** *n*.
canapé *n* a small piece of pastry, bread or toast with a savoury spread or topping.
canard *n* a false report, an absurd story, a baseless rumour.
canary *n* (*pl* **canaries**) a small finch, usu greenish to yellow in colour, kept as a songbird.
canasta *n* a card game played with two packs of cards, for two to six players.
cancan *n* an energetic dance performed by women, involving high kicks and the lifting of frothy petticoats.
cancel *vt* (**cancelling, cancelled** *or* **canceling, canceled**) to cross out; to obliterate; to annul, suppress; (*reservation, etc*) to call off; to countermand; (*with* **out**) to make up for.—**canceller, canceler** *n*.
cancellation, cancelation *n* the act of cancelling; annulment; something that has been cancelled; the mark made by cancelling.
cancellous, cancellate, cancellated *adj* (*med*) marked with cross lines or ridges.
Cancer *n* (*astron*) the Crab, a northern constellation; (*astrol*) the 4th sign of the zodiac, operative 21 June–21 July.—**Cancerian** *adj*.
cancer *n* the abnormal and uncontrollable growth of the cells of living organisms, esp a malignant tumour; an undesirable or dangerous expansion of something.—**cancerous** *adj*.
cancroid *adj* resembling a cancer; like a crab.
candela *n* a unit of luminous intensity.
candelabrum *n* (*pl* **candelabra**) a branched and ornamented candlestick or lampstand.
candescent *adj* glowing; white-hot.—**candescence** *n*.
candid *adj* frank, outspoken; unprejudiced; (*photograph*) informal.—**candidly** *adv*.—**candidness** *n*.
candidate *n* a person who has nomination for an office or qualification for membership or award; a student taking an examination.—**candidacy** *n*.—**candidature** *n*.
candid camera *n* a small camera for photographing people unexpectedly or unknowingly.
candied *adj* preserved in or encrusted with sugar.
candle *n* a stick of wax with a wick that burns to give light. * *vt* to check the freshness of eggs by examining in front of a light.
candlelight *n* the light produced by a candle or candles.
Candlemas (Day) *n* the Feast of the Purification of the Virgin Mary (2 February).
candlepower *n* a unit of measurement of the intensity of a light source, measured in candelas.
candlestick *n* a holder for one or more candles.
candlewick *n* a cotton fabric with raised pattern of tufted yarn.—*also adj*.
candour, candor *n* sincerity, openness, frankness.
candy *n* (*pl* **candies**) a solid confection of sugar or syrup with flavouring, fruit, nuts, etc, a sweet. * *vb* (**candying, candied**) *vt* to preserve by coating with candy; to encrust with crystals. * *vi* to become candied.
candyfloss *n* a confection of spun sugar.—*also* **cotton candy**.
candy-striped *adj* (*cloth*) with narrow stripes of colour on a white background.
candytuft *n* a plant with pink, white or purple tufted flowers.
cane *n* the slender, jointed stem of certain plants, as bamboo; a plant with such a stem, as sugar cane; (*usu with* **the**) a stick of this used for corporal punishment; strips of this used in furniture making etc or for supporting plants; a walking stick. * *vt* to thrash with a cane; to weave cane into; (*inf*) to beat, eg in a game.
canebrake *n* a thicket of canes.
canella *n* an aromatic and tonic bark of a West Indian tree.
canescent *adj* (*biol*) growing white, hoary.
cane sugar *n* sugar made from sugar cane.
cangue *n* (*formerly*) a square wooden collar worn as a punishment by criminals in China.
canine *adj* of or like a dog; of the family of animals that includes wolves, dogs and foxes; pertaining to a canine tooth. * *n* a dog or other member of the same family of animals; in humans, a pointed tooth next to the incisors.
canister *n* a small box or container usu of metal for storing tea, flour, etc; a tube containing tear gas which explodes and releases its contents on impact.
canker *n* an erosive or spreading sore; a foot disease in horses; an ear disease in cats and dogs; a fungal disease of trees; a corrupting influence.—**cankerous** *adj*.
cankerworm *n* a caterpillar destructive to trees or plants.
canna *n* a showy American tropical plant.
cannabin *n* a narcotic resin extracted from hemp.
cannabis *n* a narcotic drug obtained from the hemp plant; the hemp plant.—*also* **hashish, marijuana**.—**cannabic** *adj*.
canned *adj* stored in sealed tins; recorded for reproduction; (*sl*) drunk.
canned hunt *n* (*sl*) an organized big-game hunt carried out within an area from which the quarry cannot escape.
cannel (coal) *n* a hard bituminous coal burning with a clear bright flame.
cannelloni *npl* stuffed pasta tubes.
cannelure *n* a groove or fluting.
cannery *n* (*pl* **canneries**) a building, etc, where foods are canned.
cannibal *n* a person who eats human flesh; an animal that feeds on its own species. * *adj* relating to or indulging in this practice.—**cannibalism** *n*.—**cannibalistic** *adj*.
cannibalize *vti* to strip (old equipment) of parts for use in other units.—**cannibalization** *n*.
cannikin *n* a small can.
cannon *n* (*pl* **cannon**) a large mounted piece of artillery; an automatic gun on an aircraft; (*pl* **cannons**) (*billiards*) a carom. * vi to collide with great force (with into); to rebound; (*billiards*) to make a carom.
cannonade *n* a heavy, continuous artillery attack. * *vti* to attack with cannon.
cannonball *n* the heavy, round shot fired from a cannon; (*tennis*) a low, fast service stroke. * *vi* to move along at great speed.
cannoneer *n* an artilleryman.
cannon fodder *n* soldiers regarded as expendable in war.
cannonry *n* (*pl* **cannonries**) artillery.
cannot = can not.
cannula *n* (*pl* **cannulas, cannulae**) (*med*) a small tube for inspecting or withdrawing fluids.
canny *adj* (**cannier, canniest**) knowing, shrewd; cautious, careful; thrifty.—**cannily** *adv*.—**canniness** *n*.
canoe *n* a narrow, light boat propelled by paddles.—*also vi* (**canoeing, canoed**).—**canoeist** *n*.

canon *n* a decree of the Church; a general rule or standard, criterion; a list of the books of the Bible accepted as genuine; the works of any author recognized as genuine; a list of canonized saints; a member of a cathedral chapter; a part of the mass containing words of consecration; (*mus*) a round.

canoness *n* (*RC Church*) one of a number of women living under canon law but not compelled to take religious vows.

canonical *adj* pertaining to a rule or canon; according to or established by ecclesiastical laws; belonging to the canon of scripture. * *n* (*pl*) the official dress of the clergy.—**canonically** *adv*.

canonical hour *n* (*RC Church*) one of the hours appointed by ecclesiastical law for daily prayer: matins with lauds, prime, sext, nones, vespers, and compline.

canonist *n* an expert in canon law.—**canonistic** *adj*.

canonize *vt* (*RC Church*) to officially declare (a person) a saint.—**canonization** *n*.

canon law *n* rules or laws relating to faith, morals and discipline that regulate church government, as laid down by popes and councils.

canonry *n* (*pl* **canonries**) the office of a cathedral canon.

canoodle *vti* (*sl*) to cuddle, to fondle.

canopy *n* (*pl* **canopies**) a tent-like covering over a bed, throne, etc; any roof-like structure or projection; the transparent cover of an aeroplane's cockpit; the tops of trees in a forest; the sky regarded as a covering. * *vt* (**canopying, canopied**) to cover with or as with a canopy.

cans *npl* (*sl*) headphones.

cant[1] *n* insincere or hypocritical speech; language specific to a group (eg thieves, lawyers); cliched talk, meaningless jargon. * *vi* to talk in or use cant.

cant[2] *n* an inclination or tilt; a slanting surface, bevel. * *vti* to slant, to tilt; to overturn by a sudden movement.

can't = can not.

cantabile *adv* (*mus*) in a lyrical flowing style.

Cantabrigian *n* a student or graduate of Cambridge University; an inhabitant of Cambridge.—*also adj*.

cantaloupe, cantaloup *n* a variety of melon with orange flesh.

cantankerous *adj* ill-natured, bad-tempered, quarrelsome.—**cantankerously** *adv*.—**cantankerousness** *n*.

cantata *n* (*mus*) a composition for voices of a story or religious text.

cantatrice *n* a female singer, esp one who sings in operas.

canteen *n* a restaurant attached to factory, school, etc, catering for large numbers of people; a flask for carrying water; (a box containing) a set of cutlery.

canter *n* a horse's three-beat gait resembling a slow, smooth gallop.—*also vti*.

Canterbury bell *n* a large variety of campanula with handsome bell-shaped blossoms.

cantharides *npl* (*sing* **cantharis**) (*med*) a diuretic preparation made from dried Spanish flies, formerly considered an aphrodisiac.—*also* **Spanish fly**.

canthus *n* (*pl* **canthi**) the angle made by the meeting of the eyelids.

canticle *n* a song taken from the Bible (eg the Magnificat).

cantilever *n* a projecting beam that supports a balcony, etc.

cantilever bridge *n* a bridge supported by cantilevers springing from piers.

cantle *n* a corner; a piece; the rising rear part of a saddle.

canto *n* (*pl* **cantos**) a division of a long poem.

canton *n* a political and administrative division of Switzerland.—**cantonal** *adj*.

Cantonese *n* (*pl* **Cantonese**) a Chinese language deriving from Canton; an inhabitant or native of Canton.—*also adj*.

cantonment *n* a part of a town or village alloted to a body of troops; in India, a permanent military station.

cantor *n* a singer of liturgical solos in a synagogue; the leader of singing in a church choir.

cantorial *adj* of or pertaining to a precentor's or the north side of the choir of a church.

cantrip *n* a prank, a piece of mischief; a magic spell.

Canuck *n* (*inf*) a Canadian.—*also adj*.

canvas *n* a strong coarse cloth of hemp or flax, used for tents, sails, etc, and for painting on; a ship's sails collectively; a tent or tents; an oil painting on canvas.

canvasback *n* (*pl* **canvasbacks, canvasback**) a North American duck esteemed for the delicacy of its flesh.

canvass *vti* to go through (places) or among (people) asking for votes, opinions, orders, etc.—also *n*.—**canvasser** *n*.

canyon *n* a long, narrow valley between high cliffs.

canzone, canzona *n* (*pl* **canzoni, canzone**) a song or air resembling the madrigal; an instrumental piece in the style of a madrigal.

canzonet, canzonette *n* a short light song.

caoutchouc *n* rubber.—*also adj*.

cap *n* any close-fitting headgear, visored or brimless; the special headgear of a profession, club, etc; the top of a mushroom or toadstool; a cap-like thing, as an artificial covering for a tooth; a top, a cover; a percussion cap in a toy gun; a type of contraceptive device; (*sport*) the head gear presented to a player chosen for a team. * *vt* (**capping, capped**) to put a cap on; to cover (the end of); to award a degree at a university; to seal (an oil or gas well); to equal, outdo or top; to limit the level of a tax increase, etc; (*sport*) to choose a player for a team.

capability *n* (*pl* **capabilities**) the quality of being capable; an undeveloped faculty.

capable *adj* able or skilled to do; competent, efficient; susceptible (of); adapted to.—**capably** *adv*.

capacious *adj* able to hold a great deal; roomy.—**capaciousness** *n*.

capacitance *n* (a measure of) the ability of a system to store an electric charge.

capacitate *vt* to make capable; to enable; to qualify.—**capacitation** *n*.

capacitor *n* a device for storing electric charge.

capacity *n* (*pl* **capacities**) the power of holding or grasping; cubic content; mental ability or power; character; the position held; legal competence; the greatest possible output or content.

cap-a-pie *adv* from head to foot.

caparison *n* an ornamental covering for a horse; rich clothing. * *vt* to cover (a horse) with rich clothing; to adorn with rich dress.

cape[1] *n* a headland or promontory running into the sea.

cape[2] *n* a sleeveless garment fastened at the neck and hanging over the shoulders and back.

capelin, caplin *n* a small sea fish of the smelt family, largely used as bait for cod.

caper[1] *vi* to skip about playfully, to frolic. * *n* a playful leap or skip; (*sl*) an escapade; (*sl*) a criminal activity.

caper[2] *n* a low, prickly Mediterranean shrub; its pickled flower buds, used in cooking (eg caper sauce).

capercaillie, capercailzie *n* the largest Old World grouse.

Capetian *adj* of or pertaining to the dynasty founded by Hugh Capet, who ascended the French throne in 987.

capias *n* (*law*) a writ for arrest.

capillarity *n* (*pl* **capillarities**) the power possessed by porous bodies of drawing up a fluid; surface tension.

capillary *adj* of or as fine as a hair; (*tube, pipe*) of a hair-like calibre; (*anat*) of the capillaries. * *n* (*pl* **capillaries**) one of the very fine blood vessels connecting arteries and veins.

capital[1] *adj* of or pertaining to the head; (*offence*) punishable by death; serious; chief, principal; leading, first-class; of, or being the seat of government; of capital or wealth; relating to a large letter, upper case; (*inf*) excellent. * *n* a city that is the seat of government of a country; a large letter; accumulated wealth used to produce more; stock or money for carrying on a business; a city, town, etc pre-eminent in some special activity.—**capitally** *adv*.

capital[2] *n* the head or top part of a column or pillar.

capital gain *n* the profit made on the sale of an asset.

capital goods *npl* goods (eg machinery) used to produce other goods.

capitalism *n* the system of individual ownership of wealth; the dominance of such a system.

capitalist *n* a person who has money invested in business for profit; a supporter of capitalism. * *adj* of or favouring capitalism.—**capitalistic** *adj*.
capitalize *vti* (with **on**) to use (something) to one's advantage; to convert into money or capital; to provide with capital; to write in or print in capital letters.—**capitalization** *n*.
capitally *adv* in a capital manner; excellently.
capital punishment *n* the death penalty for a crime.
capitate *adj* (*bot*) shaped like a head; head-like.
capitation *n* a direct, uniform tax imposed on each person, a tax per head.
Capitol *n* (*with* **the**) the building where the US Congress meets; the temple of Jupiter on the Capitoline in Rome.
capitular *adj* of or pertaining to a chapter. * *n* a member of a cathedral chapter.
capitulary *n* (*pl* **capitularies**) a statue passed in a chapter, as of knights or canons; (*pl*) the body of statues of a chapter or of an ecclesiastical council.
capitulate *vi* to surrender on terms; to give in.—**capitulation** *n*.—**capitulator** *n*.—**capitulatory** *adj*.
capo *n* (*pl* **capos**) a device attached across the fingerboard of a guitar to raise the pitch of the strings.
capon *n* a castrated cockerel fattened for eating.
caponize *vt* to make a cock a capon by castration.
caporal *n* a French tobacco.
capote *n* a long coarse cloak; a long mantle for women.
cappuccino *n* (*pl* **cappuccinos**) frothy, milky coffee usu served sprinkled with chocolate powder.
capreolate *adj* (*bot*) furnished with tendrils.
capriccio *n* (*pl* **capriccios, capricci**) a light musical composition in a fantastic, whimsical style.
capriccioso *adv* (*mus*) in a free, fantastic style.
caprice *n* a passing fancy; an impulsive change in behaviour, opinion, etc; a whim.
capricious *adj* unstable, inconstant; unreliable.—**capriciously** *adv*.—**capriciousness** *n*.
Capricorn *n* (*astron*) the Goat, a southern constellation; (*astrol*) the tenth sign of the zodiac, operative 21 December–19 January.—**Capricornean** *adj*.
caprification *n* a process of accelerating the ripening of the fig by puncturing it.
caprine *adj* of, pertaining to, or like a goat.
capriole *n* a leap of a horse made without advancing; a caper. * *vi* to execute a capriole, to kick up the heels.
capsaicin *n* an alkaloid extracted from several species of capsicum.
capsicum *n* a tropical plant with bell-shaped fruits containing hot or mild seeds; the fruit of this plant used as a vegetable.—*also* **red** or **green pepper**.
capsize *vti* to upset or overturn.
capstan *n* an upright drum around which cables are wound to haul them in; the spindle in a tape recorder that winds the tape past the head.
capsulate, capsulated *adj* furnished with or enclosed in a capsule.—**capsulation** *n*.
capsule *n* a small gelatin case enclosing a drug to be swallowed; a metal or plastic container; (*bot*) a seed case; the orbiting and recoverable part of a spacecraft.—**capsular** *adj*.
capsulize *vt* to present (information) in a concise or condensed form.—**capsulization** *n*.
captain *n* a chief, leader; the master of a ship; the pilot of an aircraft; a rank of army, naval and marine officer; the leader of a team, as in sports; a leading employer in industry; a policeman responsible for a precinct. * *vt* to be captain of.—**captaincy** *n*.
captaincy, captainship *n* (*pl* **captaincies, captainships**) the rank, post, or commission of a captain.
caption *n* a heading in a newspaper, to a chapter, etc; a legend or title describing an illustration; a subtitle. * *vti* to provide with a caption.
captious *adj* ready to find fault or take offence; carping, quibbling.—**captiously** *adv*.
captivate *vt* to fascinate; to charm.—**captivating** *adj*.—**captivation** *n*.—**captivator** *n*.
captive *n* one kept confined; a prisoner; a person obsessed by an emotion. * *adj* taken or kept prisoner; unable to avoid being addressed (*a captive audience*); unable to refuse (a product) through a lack of choice (*a captive market*); captivated.
captivity *n* (*pl* **captivities**) the state of being a captive; a period of imprisonment.
captor *n* a person or animal who takes a prisoner.
capture *vt* to take prisoner; (*fortress, etc*) to seize; to catch; to gain or obtain by skill, attraction, etc, to win. * *n* the act of taking a prisoner or seizing by force; anything or anyone so taken.
capuche *n* a monk's hood or cowl; the hood of a cloak.
capuchin *n* a monkey with hair resembling a cowl; a pigeon with cowl-like feathers; a woman's cloak and hood; (*with cap*) a Franciscan monk of the mendicant order.
capybara *n* a large South American rodent that lives mostly in water.
car *n* a self-propelled motor vehicle, an automobile, a motorcar; the passenger compartment of a train, airship, lift, cable railway, etc; a railway carriage.
carabineer, carabinier *see* **carbineer**.
carabiner *n* (*climbing*) a type of shackle with a snap link, used to secure a rope.
caracal *n* a kind of lynx; its fur.
caracole, caracol *vi* (*horse*) to make a half turn to the right or left. * *n* a half turn, right or left; a spiral staircase.
carafe *n* an open-topped bottle for serving water or wine at table.
carageen *see* **carrageen**.
caramel *n* burnt sugar, used in cooking to colour or flavour; a type of sweet tasting of this.
caramelize *vti* to turn or be turned into caramel.
carapace *n* the upper shell of the tortoise, turtle, crab, etc.
carat *n* a measure of weight for precious stones; a measure of the purity of gold.—*also* **karat**.
caravan *n* a large enclosed vehicle that is equipped to be lived in and may be towed by a car (—*also* **trailer**); a band of merchants travelling together for safety. * *vi* (**caravanning, caravanned**) to travel with a caravan, esp on holiday.
caravanserai, caravansary *n* (*pl* **caravanserais, caravansaries**) in the East, a large inn surrounding a spacious courtyard, where caravans rest at night.
caravel, caravelle *n* an ancient small light fast Spanish ship with broad bows, a narrow high poop, four masts and lateen sails.—*also* **carvel**.
caraway *n* a biennial plant with pungent aromatic seeds used as a flavouring.
carbide *n* a compound of carbon with another element, esp calcium carbide.
carbine *n* a light, semiautomatic or automatic rifle.
carbineer *n* a mounted soldier armed with a carbine.—*also* **carabineer, carabinier**.
carbo-, carb- *prefix* carbon.
carbohydrate *n* a compound of carbon, hydrogen and oxygen, esp in sugars and starches as components of food. * *npl* starchy foods.
carbolic acid *n* phenol.
carbolize *vt* to sterilize with carbolic acid.
carbon *n* a nonmetallic element, a constituent of all organic matter; a duplicate made with carbon paper.
carbon-12 *n* an isotope of carbon, used as the standard for atomic weight.
carbon-14 *n* a radioisotope used in medicine as a tracer and in carbon dating.
carbonaceous *adj* pertaining to, composed of or resembling carbon.
carbonado *n* (*pl* **carbonadoes, carbonados**) a piece of meat cut crossways for grilling.
carbonate *n* a salt of carbonic acid. * *vt* to treat with carbon dioxide, as in making soft, fizzy drinks.—**carbonated** *adj*.

carbon copy *n* a copy of typed or written material made by using carbon paper; (*inf*) an exact copy of something or someone.
carbon dating *n* a scientific method of dating material by measuring the amount of carbon-14 it contains.
carbon dioxide *n* a gas formed by combustion and breathing and absorbed by plants.
carbonic *adj* of or obtained from carbon.
carbonic acid *n* a weakly acidic solution of carbon dioxide in water.
carboniferous *adj* coal-bearing, yielding carbon; (*with cap*) of or relating to strata of the Palaeozoic Age from which coal is derived.
carbonize *vt* to convert into carbon or a carbon residue.—**carbonization** *n.*
carbon monoxide *n* a colourless, odourless, highly poisonous gas.
carbon paper *n* a sheet of paper covered with a dark, waxy pigment inserted between sheets of paper for making copies of writing or typing.
Carborundum *n* (*trademark*) a compound of carbon and silicon used for polishing and grinding.
carboy *n* a, usu cushioned, container of glass, plastic or metal for the safe transportation of liquids.
carbuncle *n* a red, knob-shaped gemstone, esp a garnet; a large inflamed boil; a pimple.—**carbuncular** *adj.*
carburet *vt* (**carburetting, carburetted** *or* **carbureting, carbureted**) to combine with carbon.
carburetor, carburettor *n* a device in an internal-combustion engine for making an explosive mixture of air and fuel vapour.
carburize *vt* to combine with carbon.—**carburization** n.
carcanet *n* (*arch*) a collar of jewels.
carcass *n* the dead body of an animal; a framework, skeleton or shell; (*derog*) the body of a living person.
carcinogen *n* a substance that produces cancer.—**carcinogenic** *adj.*
carcinoma *n* (*pl* **carcinomas, carcinomata**) a tumour caused by a cancer.
card[1] *n* a small piece of cardboard; a piece of this with a figure or picture for playing games or fortune-telling; a piece of this filed in a card index; a membership card; a piece of card with a person or firm's name, address or with an invitation, greeting, message, etc; (*inf*) an entertaining or eccentric person; a small piece of plastic identifying a person for banking purposes, eg a cheque card, credit card; (*pl*) card games; (*pl*) card playing; (*pl*) employees insurance and tax documents held by the employer.
card[2] *n* a toothed instrument for combing cotton, wool or flax fibres off. * *vt* (*wool, etc*) to comb.
cardamom, cardamum, cardamon *n* a tropical Asian plant the seed pods of which are used as a spice.
cardboard *n* thick stiff paper, often with a clay coating, for boxes, cartons, etc. * *adj* made of this; lacking substance; makeshift.
card-carrying *adj* being an official member of a political party, organization, etc.
card catalogue *n* a catalogue, each item of which is entered on a separate card.
card file *n* a filing system in which each item is entered separately on a single card.
cardi- *prefix* heart.
cardiac *adj* relating to the heart. * *n* a person suffering a disorder of the heart; a drug to stimulate the heart.
cardiac arrest *n* heart failure.
cardialgia *n* heartburn.—**cardialgic** *adj.*
cardigan *n* a knitted sweater fastening up the front.
cardinal *adj* of chief importance, fundamental; of a bright red. * *n* an official appointed by the Pope to his councils; bright red.—**cardinally** *adv.*
cardinalate, cardinalship *n* the office, rank, or dignity of a cardinal; the body of cardinals.
cardinal numbers *npl* numbers that express how many (1, 2, 3, 4 etc).
cardinal points *npl* the four chief points of the compass: north, south, east, west.
cardinal virtues *npl* justice, prudence, temperance, and fortitude.
cardio- *prefix* heart.
cardiogram *n* an electrocardiogram.
cardiograph *n* a device for recording heart movements; an electrocardiograph.
cardiology *n* the branch of medicine concerned with the heart and its diseases.—**cardiological** *adj.*—**cardiologist** *n.*
cardiopulmonary *adj* of or concerned with or affect the heart and lungs.
cardiovascular *adj* of or pertaining to the heart and the blood vessels.
carditis *n* inflammation of the muscular tissue of the heart.
cardoon *n* a plant related to and resembling the artichoke and used as a vegetable in Spain and France.
cards *see* **card**[1].
cardsharp(er) *n* a person who cheats at cards.
care *n* anxiety; concern; serious attention, heed; consideration; charge, protection; the cause or object of concern or anxiety. * *vt* to feel concern; to agree, like, or be willing (to do something); **care of** at the address of, c/o; **in, into care** (*person*) taken charge of by a local authority by court order. * *vi* (*usu with* **for** *or* **about**) to feel affection or regard; to have a desire (for); to provide for, have in one's charge.
careen *vt* to bring (a ship) over on one side for calking, cleansing, or repairing. * *vi* to incline to one side, as a ship under press of sail.
career *n* progress through life; a profession, occupation, esp with prospects for promotion. * *vi* to rush rapidly or wildly.
careerist *n* a person who is ambitious to advance in a chosen profession.
career woman *n* a woman primarily interested in her job and in furthering her career.
carefree *adj* without cares, lively, light-hearted.
careful *adj* painstaking; cautious; thoughtful.—**carefully** *adv.*—**carefulness** *n.*
careless *adj* not careful; unconcerned, insensitive; carefree.—**carelessly** *adv.*—**carelessness** *n.*
carer *n* one who takes on (professionally) the care of a dependent person.
caress *n* any act or expression of affection; an embrace. * *vt* to touch or stroke lovingly.—**caresser** *n.*—**caressingly** *adv.*
caret *n* a mark (^) showing where something omitted in text is to be inserted.
caretaker *n* a person put in charge of a place or thing; (*government*) one temporarily in control.
careworn *adj* showing signs of stress, worry.
cargo *n* (*pl* **cargoes, cargos**) the load carried by a ship, truck, aircraft, etc; freight.
Carib *n* (*pl* **Caribs, Carib**) a member of an Indian people of the Lesser Antilles and neighbouring parts of the South American coast, or of their descendants; their language. * *adj* of or pertaining to the Carib people or language.
Caribbean *adj* of or pertaining to the Caribbean Sea and its islands. * *n* the Caribbean Sea.
caribou *n* (*pl* **caribou, caribous**) a large North American reindeer.
caricature *n* a likeness made ludicrous by exaggeration or distortion of characteristic features. * *vt* to make a caricature of, to parody.—**caricaturist** *n.*
caries *n* (*pl* **caries**) decay of bones or teeth.
carillon *n* a chime of bells diatonically tuned and played by hand or machinery; a simple air adapted for playing on a set of bells.
carina *n* (*pl* **carinae, carinas**) a keel; the two lower petals of a papilionaceous flower (as the furze) partially joined; the keel of the breastbone of birds.
carinate, carinated *adj* shaped like a keel.
caring *adj* compassionate; of or dealing with people's welfare, usu professionally.
carious *adj* affected with caries; decayed.
carling *n* a ship's timber running fore and aft from one transverse deck beam to another, serving as a foundation for the planks of the deck.
Carlovingian *see* **Carolingian.**
carmagnole *n* a popular song and dance of the time of the French Revolution; a costume adapted by the revolutionists; a bombastic report from the French armies during the Revolution.

Carmelite *n* a member of a mendicant order founded on Mount Carmel in the 12th century, a white friar; a variety of pear; a kind of fine woollen cloth. * *adj* of or belonging to the order of Carmelites.

carminative *n* a medicine that expels wind and relieves colic and flatulence. * *adj* expelling wind.

carmine *n* a rich crimson pigment; the essential colouring principle of cochineal.

carnage *n* great slaughter.

carnal *adj* of the flesh; sexual; sensual; worldly.—**carnality** *n*.—**carnally** *adv*.

carnal knowledge *n* sexual intercourse.

carnation *n* a garden flower, the clove pink.

carnelian *see* **cornelian.**

carnet *n* a customs permit or licence, esp for a vehicle; a book of tickets, etc.

carnival *n* public festivities and revelry; a travelling fair with sideshows, etc.

carnivore *n* a flesh-eating mammal.

carnivorous *adj* (*animals*) feeding on flesh; (*plants*) able to trap and digest insects.

carob *n* an edible, sugary pod of a Mediterranean tree.

carol *n* a joyful song or hymn; a Christmas hymn. * *vi* (**carolling, carolled** *or* **caroling, caroled**) to sing carols; to sing with happiness.

Caroline, Carolean *adj* belonging to the period of Charles I or Charles II.

Carolingian *adj* of or pertaining to the medieval Frankish dynasty that once ruled France. * *n* a member of this dynasty.—*also* **Carlovingian.**

Carolinian *adj* of or pertaining to either North or South Carolina.

carom *n* (*billiards*) a shot in which the cue ball hits two others successively. * *vi* to make a carom.—*also* **cannon.**

carotid (artery) *n* one of the two principal arteries, one on either side of the neck, which convey blood from the aorta to the head.—**carotidal** *adj*.

carousal *n* a feast or festival; a noisy drinking bout or revel.

carouse *vi* to drink and have fun.—**carousal** *n*.—**carouser** *n*.

carousel *n* a merry-go-round; a revolving circular platform, as in an airport luggage conveyor.

carp[1] *vi* to find fault, esp continually.

carp[2] *n* (*pl* **carp, carps**) a brown and yellow freshwater fish.

carpal *adj* pertaining to the carpus or wrist.

car park *n* a parking lot.

carpe diem (*Latin*) seize the day; take advantage of a present opportunity.

carpel *n* a simple pistil, or one of the parts of a compound pistil or ovary of a flower.—**carpellary** *adj*.

carpellate *adj* having a carpel.

carpenter *n* a person skilled in woodwork, esp in house building.—**carpentry** *n*.

carpenter bee *n* a bee that makes nests in wood.

carpentry *n* the art of cutting, framing, and joining timber; work done by a carpenter.

carpet *n* a woven fabric for covering floors; any thick covering * *vt* to cover with carpet; (*inf*) to issue a reprimand, to have on the carpet to rebuke.

carpetbag *n* a carrying bag formerly made of carpeting.

carpetbagger *n* an outsider, esp a nonresident who meddles in politics.

carpeting *n* cloth for carpets; carpets in general.

carpet sweeper *n* a mechanical device for removing dirt, etc, from a carpet.

carphone *n* a cellular telephone fitted in and operated from a car.

carpology *n* the branch of botany that treats of the structure of fruits in general.—**carpological** *adj*.—**carpologist** *n*.

carpophore *n* (*bot*) a slender prolongation of the axis that bears the carpels.

carport *n* an open-sided shelter for a car extending from the side of a house.

carpus *n* (*pl* **carpi**) the bones between the forearm and the hand, forming the wrist in man and the corresponding bones in other animals.

carrack *n* a large round-built vessel formerly used by the Portuguese and Spaniards in the East Indian and American trade.

carrageen, carragheen *n* a seaweed very common on the rocks of the Irish coast that, when dried and bleached, is known as Irish moss and is used for blancmanges, soup, etc.—*also* **carageen.**

carrel *n* a small study room or cubicle, esp in a library.

carriage *n* the act of carrying, transport; the cost of this; deportment, bearing; behaviour; a rail coach or compartment; a wheeled coach drawn by horses; a frame with wheels to carry a gun; the moving part of a typewriter.

carriage dog *n* the spotted Dalmatian.

carrick bend *n* (*naut*) a particular kind of knot for splicing two hawsers together.

carrick bitt *n* (*naut*) one of the bitts supporting the windlass.

carrier *n* one who carries or transports goods, esp for hire; a device for carrying; a person or animal transmitting an infectious disease without being affected by it; an aircraft carrier; a plastic or paper bag with handles for holding things; a portable seat for a baby, a carrycot.

carrier pigeon *n* a homing pigeon used to carry messages.

carrier wave *n* an electromagnetic wave that can be modulated in frequency, amplitude, etc, to transmit (radio, TV, etc) signals.

carrion *n* the dead putrefying flesh of an animal.

carrion crow *n* the common crow of Europe.

carronade *n* a short cannon of large bore for close range, formerly used in the navy.

carron oil *n* a mixture of linseed oil and lime water used as a liniment for burns.

carrot *n* a plant grown for its edible, fleshy orange root; an inducement, often illusory.

carroty *adj* orange-red in colour.

carry *vb* (**carrying, carried**) *vt* to convey or transport; to support or bear; to involve, have as a result; to hold (oneself); to extend or prolong; to gain by force; to win over; to stock; to be pregnant; (*with* **away**) to delight; to arouse to extreme enthusiasm; to remove violently; (*with* **forward**) (*book-keeping*) to transfer (a total) to the next column, page, etc; (*with* **off**) to cause to die; to remove by force, capture; (*situation*) to handle successfully; (*with* **out**) to perform (a task, etc); to accomplish; (*with* **over**) to carry forward; (*with* **through**) to complete. * *vi* (*with* **away**) to be filled with joy or emotion; (*with* **on**) to persevere; to conduct a business, etc; (*inf*) to have an affair; (*inf*) to cause a fuss; (*with* **through**) to enable to survive; to persist.

carryall *n* an overnight or holdall bag.

carrycot *n* a baby carrier, a portable cot.

carry-out *n* food or drink sold by a restaurant but consumed elsewhere.—*also adj*.

carsick *adj* ill or queasy from the motion of a moving vehicle.—**carsickness** *n*.

cart *n* a two-wheeled vehicle drawn by horses; any small vehicle for carrying loads. * *vt* to carry in a cart; (*inf*) to transport with effort.

cartage *n* conveyance in a cart; the charge made for this.

carte blanche *n* (*pl* **cartes blanches**) full authority to act as one thinks best.

cartel *n* an association of business firms to coordinate production, prices, etc to avoid competition and maximize profits; a union of political parties to achieve common aims.

Cartesian *adj* pertaining to the French philosopher René Descartes (1596–1650) or his philosophy. * *n* a follower of Descartes or his philosophy.

Carthaginian *adj* pertaining to ancient Carthage, a city of North Africa.

Carthusian *n* one of an order of monks founded (1086) by St Bruno in the Grande Chartreuse, France.

cartilage *n* tough, elastic tissue attached to the bones of animals; gristle.—**cartilaginous** *adj*.

cartload *n* the amount a cart will hold.

cartogram *n* a map showing statistical information in diagrammatic form.
cartography *n* the drawing and publishing of maps.—**cartographer** *n*.—**cartographic, cartographical** *adj*.
carton *n* a cardboard box or container.
cartoon *n* a humorous picture dealing with current events; a comic strip; an animated cartoon; a full-size preparatory sketch for reproduction on a fresco, etc.—**cartoonist** *n*.
cartouche, cartouch *n* a cartridge; a canvas cartridge case; an ornament in the form of an unrolled scroll; on Egyptian monuments, etc, an oval figure containing the name or title of a sovereign or deity.
cartridge *n* the case that contains the explosive charge and bullet in a gun or rifle; a sealed case of film for a camera; the device containing the stylus on the end of the pick-up arm of a record player.
cartridge belt *n* a belt with loops for holding spare cartridges.
cartridge clip *n* a detachable container for cartridges in an automatic firearm.
cartulary *n* (*pl* **cartularies**) a collection or register of charters.—*also* **chartulary**.
cartwheel *n* an acrobatic handspring in which the body revolves with the weight on each hand in turn and the legs spread like the spokes of a wheel.
caruncle *n* a small fleshy excrescence on a bird's head, as the comb or wattle of a fowl; an appendage surrounding the hilum of a seed.—**caruncular, carunculate** *adj*.
carve *vt* to shape by cutting; to adorn with designs; to cut up (meat, etc); (*with* **up**) to cut into pieces or shares; (*sl*) to share out illegal proceeds; to slash someone with a knife or razor.
carvel *see* **caravel.**
carvel-built *adj* (*vessel*) with the outer boards or plates meeting flush, not overlapping.
carving *n* a figure or design carved from wood, stone, etc; the act of carving.
caryatid *n* (*pl* **caryatids, caryatides**) a figure of a woman in long robes supporting an entablature.—**caryatic, caryatidic, caryatidal, caryatidean** *adj*.
caryophyllaceous *adj* (*flowers*) belonging to the pink family.
caryopsis *n* (*pl* **caryopses, caryopsides**) a small dry fruit with the thin pericarp adherent to the seed, as in wheat, etc.
casaba *n* a variety of winter melon with a yellow rind and sweet flesh.—*also* **cassaba.**
Casanova *n* a man of amorous reputation.
cascade *n* a small, steep waterfall; a shower, as of sparks, etc. * *vti* to fall in a cascade.
cascara *n* Californian bark used as an aperient; a bark canoe.
cascarilla *n* the bark of a West Indian shrub, possessing aromatic and bitter properties; the shrub itself, from which is obtained a white bitter crystalline substance, cascarillin.
case[1] *n* a covering; a suitcase; its contents; the binding covering a book.
case[2] *n* an instance; a state of affairs; a condition, circumstance; a lawsuit; an argument for one side; (*sl*) a character; a person of a specific type; (*med*) a patient under treatment; (*gram*) the relationship between nouns, pronouns and adjectives in a sentence; **in case** in order to prevent, lest.
case-harden *vt* to make the surface (of iron or steel) harder than the interior.
case-hardened *adj* with a hard surface; made callous.
case history *n* a record of a person's medical background, etc.
casein *n* a protein in the curd matter of milk.
case knife *n* a sheath knife.
case law *n* law as settled by precedent.
casemate *n* a bomb-proof vault or battery in a fortification; an armoured enclosure for a gun in a warship; a hollow moulding.
casement *n* a window or its frame with a side hinge for opening.
caseous *adj* like cheese, cheesy.
casern, caserne *n* a lodging or barrack for soldiers in a garrison town.
case study *n* an analysis arrived at from studying more than one case history.
casework *n* social work based on the close monitoring of individuals or families.—**caseworker** *n*.
cash[1] *n* money in coins or notes; immediate payment, as opposed to that by cheque or on credit. * *vt* to give or get cash for; (*with* **in**) to exchange something for money; (*inf*) to gain an advantage or seize an opportunity to profit from; (*sl*) to die. * *vi* (*with* **in**) to exploit for profit; to take advantage of.—**cashable** *adj*.
cash[2] *n* (*pl* **cash**) the name of various Eastern coins of low value.
cash and carry *n*, *adj* (a policy of) selling for cash without delivery of goods.
cash-book *n* a book in which a register is kept of money received or paid out.
cash crop *n* a crop grown for market not for consumption.
cashew *n* the small, edible nut of a tropical tree.
cash flow *n* money which is paid into and out of a business during its operations.
cashier[1] *n* a person in charge of the paying and receiving of money in a bank, shop, etc.
cashier[2] *vt* to dismiss (an officer) from military service; to discharge.
cashmere *n* a fine wool from Kashmir goats; a material made from this.
cash on delivery *n* delivery to be paid for to a postman or carrier.
cash register *n* an automatic or electronic machine that shows and records the amount placed in it.
casimere *see* **cassimere.**
casing *n* any protective or outer covering; the material for this.
casino *n* (*pl* **casinos**) a room or building where gambling takes place.
cask *n* a barrel of any size, esp one for liquids; its contents.
casket *n* a small box or chest for jewels, etc; a coffin.
casque *n* (*poet*) a helmet.
cassaba *see* **casaba.**
cassava *n* a plant of tropical America and Africa cultivated for its tuberous roots, which yield a nutritious starch from which cassava bread and tapioca are made.
casserole *n* a covered dish for cooking and serving; the food so cooked and served. * *vt* to cook in a casserole.
cassette *n* a case containing magnetic tape or film for loading into a tape recorder or camera.
cassia *n* one of several tropical leguminous plants, the leaves of several species of which constitute the drug senna.
cassimere *n* a thin twilled woollen cloth used for men's garments.—*also* **casimere.**
cassiterite *n* a native tin dioxide; the principal ore of tin.
cassock *n* a long close-fitting black garment worn by certain clergy and by choristers.
cassowary *n* (*pl* **cassowaries**) a large running bird resembling the ostrich, inhabiting Australia and New Guinea.
cast *vb* (**casting, cast**) *vt* to throw or fling; to throw off or shed; to record; to direct; to shape in a mould; to calculate; to select actors, etc for a play; to throw a fishing line into the water. * *vi* to throw, hurl; (*with* **off**) to untie a ship from its moorings; (*knitting*) to loop off stitches from a needle without letting them unravel; (*with* **on**) to loop the first row of stitches onto a needle. * *n* act of casting; a throw; a plaster form for immobilizing an injured limb; a mould for casting; type or quantity; a tinge of colour; the actors assigned roles in a play; the set of actors; a slight squint in the eye.
castanets *npl* hollow shell-shaped pieces of wood held between the fingers and rattled together, esp to accompany Spanish dancing.
castaway *adj* shipwrecked; discarded. * *n* a shipwrecked person.
cast down *adj* depressed.
caste *n* any of the Hindu hereditary social classes; an exclusive social group.
castellan *n* the governor of a castle.
castellated *adj* having turrets and battlements, as a castle.
caster *see* **castor.**
castigate *vt* to chastise; to punish; to correct.—**castigation** *n*.

casting vote *n* the deciding vote used by the chairman of a meeting when the votes on each side are equal.
cast iron *n* an iron-carbon alloy melted and run into moulds.
cast-iron *adj* made of cast iron; untiring; rigid, unadaptable.
castle *n* a fortified building; a chess piece (*—also* **rook**).
castoff *n* a rejected item; a rough estimate of the number of pages of a finished book, etc.
cast-off *adj* laid aside or rejected.—**castoff** *n*.
castor *n* a small container with a perforated top for sprinkling salt, sugar, etc; a small swivelled wheel on a table leg, etc.*—also* **caster**.
castor oil *n* a vegetable oil used as a cathartic and lubricant.
castrate *vt* to remove the testicles of, to geld.—**castration** *n*.—**castrator** *n*.
castrato *n* (*pl* **castrati, castratos**) a male castrated in childhood to prevent a change of voice at the age of puberty; an artificial male soprano.
casual *adj* accidental, chance; unplanned; occasional; careless, offhand; unmethodical; informal. * *n* someone who works occasionally; (*pl*) informal or leisure clothing, shoes.—**casually** *adv*.—**casualness** *n*.
casualty *n* (*pl* **casualties**) a person injured or killed in a war or in an accident; something damaged or destroyed.
casuarina *n* a tree of Australia and southeast Asia having jointed branches.
casuist *n* one who studies or resolves cases of conscience; one skilled in casuistry.—**casuistic, casuistical** *adj*.—**casuistically** *adv*.
casuistry *n* (*pl* **casuistries**) the study or application of rules of right and wrong; sophistical or equivocal reasoning, esp on moral matters.
casus belli *n* (*pl* **casus belli**) an act or occurrence justifying war.
CAT (*acronym*) computerized axial tomography (*—also* **computer-aided** *or* **computer-assisted tomography**); the production of detailed three-dimensional images from scans of cross-sections of internal organs (**CAT scans**) using a computer-controlled X-ray machine (**CAT scanner**).
cat *n* a small, domesticated feline mammal kept as a pet; a wild animal related to this; lions, tigers, etc (*—also* **big cat**); (*inf*) a spiteful woman; (*sl*) a man.
cata- *prefix* down; wrongly; thoroughly.
catabolism *n* a downward series of changes by which complex bodies are broken down into simpler forms.—**catabolic** *adj*.—**catabolically** *adv*.
catabolize *vti* to subject to or undergo catabolism.
catachresis *n* (*pl* **catachreses**) misapplication of words; formation of words on a false analogy.—**catachrestic** *adj*.—**catachrestically** *adv*.
cataclysm *n* a violent disturbance or disaster.—**cataclysmic** *adj*.
catacomb *n* (*usu pl*) an underground burial place.
catadromous *adj* going down to the sea to spawn.
catafalque *n* a temporary structure erected, usu in a church, to support the coffin on the occasion of a lying in state.
Catalan *adj* of or pertaining to Catalonia, a province of Spain, or to its inhabitants or language. * *n* an inhabitant of Catalonia; the language of Catalonia.
catalectic *adj* (*poetry*) lacking a syllable in the last foot.
catalepsy *n* (*pl* **catalepsies**) a state of temporary rigidity and unconsciousness.—**cataleptic** *adj*.
catalogue, catalog *n* a list of books, names, etc in systematic order. * *vti* to list, to make a catalogue of.—**cataloger, cataloguer** *n*.
catalogue raisonné *n* a catalogue of books, paintings, etc, classed according to their subjects.
catalpa *n* an American tree with trumpet-shaped flowers.
catalyse *vt* to accelerate or retard (a chemical reaction) by catalysis.—**catalyser** *n*.
catalysis *n* (*pl* **catalyses**) the acceleration or retardation of a chemical reaction by the action of a catalyst.—**catalytic** *adj*.
catalyst *n* a substance which accelerates or retards a chemical reaction without itself undergoing any permanent chemical change; a person or thing which produces change.
catalytic converter *n* a filter device in vehicles to reduce pollution from exhaust produced by combustion, eg carbon monoxide, nitrogen oxide, etc.
catamaran *n* a (sailing) boat with twin hulls; a raft of logs.
catamenia *n* menstruation.—**catamenial** *adj*.
catamite *n* a boy kept by a sodomite.
catamount, catamountain *n* the wild cat; the puma, cougar, or mountain lion.
cataplasm *n* a poultice.
cataplexy *n* (*pl* **cataplexies**) a sudden shock to the nerves causing paralysis.
catapult *n* a slingshot; a device for launching aircraft from the deck of an aircraft carrier. * *vt* to shoot forwards as from a catapult.
cataract *n* a waterfall, esp a large sheet one; a disease of the eye causing dimming of the lens and loss of vision.
catarrh *n* inflammation of a mucous membrane, esp in the nose and throat, causing a flow of mucus.—**catarrhal** *adj*.
catarrhine *adj* of or pertaining to a group of monkeys and apes of the Old World, which have the nostrils close together and pointing downwards.
catastrophe *n* a great disaster.—**catastrophic** *adj*.—**catastrophically** *adv*.
catastrophize *vt* to envisage a situation as being worse than it is.*—also* **awfulize.**
catatonia *n* a form of schizophrenia in which a trance-like state is punctuated by periods of hyperactivity.—**catatonic** *adj*.
Catawba *n* (*pl* **Catawba, Catawbas**) a member of a North American Indian people formerly of North and South Carolina; a light red variety of American grape; a light wine made from this grape.
catbird *n* a kind of American thrush.
catboat *n* a small boat with one sail on a single mast near the bows.
cat burglar *n* a burglar who enters by climbing.
catcall *n* a shrill whistle or cry used to express disapproval. * *vt* to express disapproval by a catcall.
catch *vb* (**catching, caught**) *vt* to take hold of, to grasp; to capture; to ensnare or trap; to be on time for; to detect; to apprehend; to become infected with (a disease); to attract (the eye); (*inf*) to see, hear, etc; to grasp (a meaning); (*with* **out**) (*inf*) to detect (a person) in a mistake; (*cricket*) to catch a ball hit by a batsman before it touches the ground, making him "out". * *vi* to become entangled; to begin to burn; (*with* **on**) (*inf*) to become popular; to understand; (*with* **up**) to reach or come level with (eg a person ahead); to make up for lost time, deal with a backlog. * *n* the act of catching; the amount or number caught; a device for fastening; someone worth catching; a hidden difficulty.
catch-all *adj*, *n* (something) intended to cover all eventualities.
catcher *n* (*baseball*) the player who stands behind the batter to catch the ball.
catching *adj* infectious; attractive.
catchment *n* the collecting or the drainage of water.
catchment area *n* the area from which a body of water is fed, eg a river or reservoir; a geographic area served by a particular institution.
catchpenny *n* (*pl* **catchpennies**) an article of little value got up attractively to effect a quick sale.
catch phrase *n* a well-known phrase or slogan, esp one associated with a particular group or person.
catchpole *n* a sheriff's officer; a constable in medieval England.
catch-22 *n* a predicament from which a victim is powerless to escape due to conditions beyond his or her control.
catchup *see* **ketchup.**
catchweight *n* a weight left to the choice of an owner of a horse. * *adv* without being handicapped.
catchword *n* a guide word; a word or expression, briefly popular, representative of a person or point of view; a cue in the theatre.
catchy *adj* (**catchier, catchiest**) easily remembered, as a tune.—**catchiness** *n*.
catechetical, catechetic *adj* instructing orally; proceeding by question and answer; of catechism.—**catechetically** *adv*.
catechin *n* a tannic acid extracted from catechu.
catechism *n* a simple summary of the principles of religion in question and answer form, used for instruction; continuous questioning.—**catechismal** *adj*.

catechize *vt* to instruct by question and answer.—**catechization** *n*.—**catechist, catechizer** *n*.

catechu *n* a brown astringent substance obtained from tropical plants and used in the arts and as a medicine.—*also* **cachou, cutch**.

catechumen *n* one who is under religious instruction prior to receiving baptism; a beginner in the first principles of knowledge.

categorical *adj* unconditional, absolute; positive, explicit.—**categorically** *adv*.

categorical imperative *n* (*philos*) the absolute and unconditional command of moral law.

categorize *vt* to place in a category.—**categorization** *n*.

category *n* (*pl* **categories**) a class or division of things.

catena *n* (*pl* **catenae, catenas**) a series of notions; things connected with each other like the links of a chain; a systematic arrangement of selections from authors to illustrate a doctrine.

catenary *n* (*pl* **catenaries**) a curve formed by a hanging chain. * *adj* of or resembling a chain (—*also* **catenarian**).

catenate *vt* (*biol*) to link together.—**catenation** *n*.

catenulate *adj* (*bot*) consisting of little links.

cater *vi* (*with* **for** *or* **to**) to provide with what is needed or desired, esp food and service, as for parties.—**caterer** *n*.

cateran *n* a kern; a Highland or Irish irregular soldier; a Highland freebooter.

caterpillar *n* the worm-like larvae of a butterfly or moth; the ribbed band in place of wheels on a heavy vehicle; a vehicle (eg tank, tractor) equipped with such tracks.

caterwaul *vi* to make a howling noise like a cat. * *n* such a cry.

catfish *n* (*pl* **catfish, catfishes**) a large, usu freshwater, fish with whisker-like feelers around the mouth.

catgut *n* a strong cord made from animal intestines, used for the strings of musical instruments, sports rackets, and surgical ligatures.

catharsis *n* (*pl* **catharses**) emotional relief given by art, esp tragedy; (*med*) purgation; (*psychoanal*) relief obtained by the uncovering of buried repressions, etc.

cathartic *adj* bringing about catharsis; purgative. * *n* a purgative medicine.—**cathartically** *adv*.

cathead *n* a beam projecting from a ship's bows to which the anchor is secured.

cathedra *n* (*pl* **cathedrae**) a bishop's throne in the cathedral of his diocese; an official or professional chair.

cathedral *n* the chief church of a diocese. * *adj* having or belonging to a cathedral.

Catherine wheel *n* a rotating firework.—*also* **pinwheel**.

catheter *n* a flexible tube inserted into the bladder for drawing off urine.

catheterize *vt* to insert a catheter into.—**catheterization** *n*.

cathode *n* (*elect*) the negative terminal; the electrode by which current leaves.—**cathodal** *adj*.—**cathodic, cathodical** *adj*.

cathode rays *n* (one of the electrons in) a stream of electrons emitted by a cathode in a vacuum tube.

cathode-ray tube *n* a vacuum tube in which electron beams are directed onto a fluorescent screen to produce luminous images, as used in television sets.

Catholic *n* a member of the Roman Catholic Church. * *adj* relating to the Roman Catholic Church; embracing the whole body of Christians.—**Catholicism** *n*.

catholic *adj* universal, all-embracing; broad-minded, liberal; general, not exclusive.

Catholic Epistles *npl* the Epistles of the Apostles addressed to believers generally, ie James 1 and 2, Peter 1, 2 and 3, John, and Jude.

Catholicism *n* the belief of, or adherence to, the Catholic Church or faith, esp to that of the Roman Catholic Church.

catholicity *n* the quality of being catholic; universality, comprehensiveness; accordance with Catholic, esp Roman Catholic, church doctrine.

catholicize *vt* to convert to the Roman Catholic Church.—**catholicization** *n*.

catholicon *n* a universal remedy, a panacea.

cathouse *n* a brothel.

cation *n* a positively charged ion.—**cationic** *adj*.

catkin *n* a hanging spike of small flowers, eg on birch, willow and hazel trees.

cat-like *adj* like a cat; stealthy, noiseless.

catmint, catnip *n* a strongly-scented plant attractive to cats.

catnap *n* a short, light or intermittent sleep, a snooze, a doze.—*also vi* (**catnapping, catnapped**).

cat-o'-nine-tails *n* (*pl* **cat-o'-nine-tails**) a whip with nine lashes of knotted cord, formerly used as a punishment in the army and navy.

catoptric, catoptrical *adj* of or pertaining to mirrors or reflected light.

Cat scan, Cat scanner *see* **CAT**.

cat's cradle *n* a game of making designs with string looped over the fingers.

cat's-eye *n* a hard semi-transparent variety of quartz.

cat's-paw *n* a person used as a tool by another, a dupe; (*naut*) a light breeze that slightly ripples the surface of the water.

catsup *see* **ketchup**.

cattery *n* (*pl* **catteries**) a place for boarding or breeding cats.

cattle *npl* domesticated bovine mammals such as bulls and cows.

cattle-grid *n* a metal grid over a ditch allowing the passage of people and vehicles, but not cattle, sheep, etc.

cattleman *n* (*pl* **cattlemen**) one who tends or drives cattle; a breeder of cattle.

cattle prod *n* an electrified prod for driving cattle.

catty[1] *adj* (**cattier, cattiest**) (*inf*) spiteful, mean.—**cattily** *adv*.—**cattiness** *n*.

catty[2] *n* (*pl* **catties**) an East Indian weight equal to one and a third pounds; a name applied to a Chinese kin or pound; a Siamese coin.

catwalk *n* a narrow, raised pathway on a stage, bridge, etc; fashion modelling (*with* **the**).

Caucasian *adj* of the light-skinned racial group of humankind; of or relating to the Caucasus Mountains. * *n* a Caucasian person.—**Caucasoid** *adj*.

Caucasus *n* a mountain range in the southwest USSR (*with* **the**).—*also* **Caucasus Mountains**.

caucus *n* (*pl* **caucuses**) a private meeting of leaders of a political party or faction, usu to plan strategy.

caudal *adj* of or pertaining to a tail.—**caudally** *adv*.

caudate, caudated *adj* having a tail; having a tail-like appendage.

caudex *n* (*pl* **caudices, caudexes**) the main trunk or axis of a plant.

caudle *n* a warm drink made of wine or ale, spiced or sugared, and mixed with bread, eggs, etc.

caught *see* **catch**.

caul *n* the membrane covering a foetus; part of this covering the head of some infants at birth.

cauldron *n* a large kettle or boiling pot; a state of violent agitation.—*also* **caldron**.

caulescent *adj* having a true stem or stalk.

caulicle *n* a small or rudimentary stem.

cauliflower *n* a kind of cabbage with an edible white flower-head used as a vegetable.

cauliflower ear *n* a thickening condition of the ear, common to boxers, caused by repeated blows.

cauline *adj* of, on or belonging to a stem.

caulk *vt* to make (a boat) watertight by stopping up the seams with pitch.—*also* **calk**.—**caulker, calker** *n*.

causal *adj* forming or being a cause; involving, expressing or implying a cause.—**causally** *adv*.

causality *n* (*pl* **causalities**) the relationship between cause and effect.

causation *n* causality; the act of causing something to happen.—**causational** *adj*.

causative *adj* that causes; effective as a cause; expressing causation.

cause *n* that which produces an effect; reason, motive, purpose, justification; a principle for which people strive; a lawsuit. * *vt* to bring about, to effect; to make (to do something).—**causer** *n*.

cause célèbre *n* (*pl* **causes célèbres**) a famous lawsuit, trial or celebrated issue.
causeless *adj* without cause; groundless.
causerie *n* a discursive conversational article; an informal chat.
causeway *n* a raised road across wet ground or water.
caustic *adj* burning tissue, etc by chemical action; corrosive; sarcastic, cutting. * *n* a caustic substance.—**caustically** *adv*.—**causticness, causticity** *n*.
caustic potash *n* potassium hydroxide, a white substance acting as a powerful bleach, much used in medicine and manufacturing.
caustic soda *n* sodium hydroxide, a white solid substance, largely used in soapmaking.
cauterize *vt* to burn with a caustic substance or a hot iron so as to destroy dead tissue, stop bleeding, etc; to deaden.—**cauterization** *n*.
cautery *n* (*pl* **cauteries**) a burning or searing; an instrument or drug used for such a purpose.
caution *n* care for safety, prudence; a warning, esp a formal one, to a suspect or accused person. * *vt* to warn (against); to admonish.
cautionary *adj* of a warning nature.
cautious *adj* careful, circumspect.—**cautiously** *adv*.—**cautiousness** *n*.
cavalcade *n* a procession of riders on horseback; a dramatic sequence or procession.
cavalier *adj* free and easy, careless; offhand, brusque. * *n* a horseman; a lady's escort; (*with cap*) a royalist in the English Civil War.—**cavalierly** *adv*.
cavalry *n* (*pl* **cavalries**) combat troops originally mounted on horseback.
cavatina *n* (*pl* **cavatine**) a short simple melody.
cave *n* a hollow place inside the earth open to the surface. * *vti* (*with* **in**) to collapse or make collapse; (*inf*) to yield, submit.—**cave-in** *n*.
caveat *n* (*law*) a process to suspend proceedings; a warning.
caveat emptor (*Latin*) let the buyer beware.
cavefish *n* (*pl* **cavefish, cavefishes**) a fish belonging to the family Amblyopsidae, species of which inhabit cave streams of the US.
caveman *n* (*pl* **cavemen**) a prehistoric cave dweller; (*inf*) a person who acts in a primitive or crude manner.
cavern *n* a large cave.—cavernous adj.
cavetto *n* (*pl* **cavetti**) (*archit*) a round concave moulding.
caviar, caviare *n* salted roe of the sturgeon or other large fish.
cavil *vi* (**cavilling, cavilled** *or* **caviling, caviled**) to make trifling objections, to find fault. * *n* a trifling objection.—**caviller** *n*.
caving *n* the sport of exploring caves.—**caver** *n*.
cavity *n* (*pl* **cavities**) a hole; a hollow place, esp in a tooth.
cavort *vi* to frolic, prance.
cavy *n* (*pl* **cavies**) one of several kinds of small rodent including the guinea pig.
caw *n* the cry of the crow, rook, or raven. * *vi* to utter this cry.
cay *n* a small low island.
cayenne, cayenne pepper *n* a hot red pepper made from capsicum.
cayman *see* **caiman.**
Cayuse *n* (*pl* **Cayuse, Cayuses**) a member of an American Indian tribe of Oregon and Washington; their language.
CB *abbr* = citizens' band.
CBC *abbr* = Canadian Broadcasting Corporation.
CD *abbr* = compact disc; corps diplomatique.
Cd (*chem symbol*) = cadmium.
cd *abbr* = candela.
CD-ROM *abbr* = compact disc read only memory: a CD used for distributing text and images in electronic publishing, for computer software, and for permanent storage of computer data.
Ce (*chem symbol*) = cerium.
cease *vti* to stop, to come to an end; to discontinue.
ceasefire *n* a period of truce in a war, uprising, etc.
ceaseless *adj* without ceasing; incessant.—**ceaselessly** *adv*.
cecum *see* **caecum.**
cedar *n* a large coniferous evergreen tree; its wood.—**cedarwood** *n*.
cede *vt* to yield to another, give up, esp by treaty; to assign or transfer the title of.—**ceder** *n*.
cedilla *n* a character written under a c in certain languages (ç) to indicate that it is pronounced as an (s) not (k).
ceil *vt* to overlay or cover the inner surface of a roof; to furnish with a ceiling.
ceiling *n* the inner roof of a room; the lining of this; any upper limit; the highest altitude a particular aircraft can fly.
celadon *n* a soft pale sea-green colour; porcelain or fine earthenware of such a colour. * *adj* having the colour of celadon.
celandine *n* one of several kinds of wild plant with star-shaped yellow flowers.
celebrant *n* one who celebrates, esp the principal officiating priest in offering mass or celebrating the Eucharist.
celebrate *vt* to make famous; to praise, extol; to perform with proper rites; to mark with ceremony; to keep (festival).—**celebrant** *n*.
celebrated *adj* famous.
celebration *n* the act of celebrating; an observance or ceremony to celebrate anything.
celebrity *n* (*pl* **celebrities**) fame; a famous or well-known person.
celeriac *n* a variety of celery with a turnip-like root.
celerity *n* quickness, dispatch.
celery *n* (*pl* **celeries**) a vegetable with long juicy edible stalks.
celesta, celeste *n* a kind of glockenspiel with a keyboard.
celestial *adj* in or of the sky; heavenly; divine.—**celestially** *adv*.
celestite *n* native strontium sulphate.
celiac *see* **coeliac.**
celibacy *n* (*pl* **celibacies**) the unmarried state; complete sexual abstinence.
celibate *n* a person who remains unmarried, esp one who has taken religious vows; a person who abstains from sexual intercourse.—*also adj*.
cell *n* a small room for one in a prison or monastery; a small cavity as in a honeycomb; a device that converts chemical energy into electricity; a microscopic unit of living matter; a small group of people bound by common aims within an organization or political party.—**cellular** *adj*.
cellar *n* a basement; a stock of wines.
cellarage *n* cellars collectively; the space occupied by cellars; a charge for storage in cellars.
cellarer *n* an official in a monastery who superintends the cellar and distribution of provisions; an official of the chapter who has charge of the temporals.
cellarete, cellaret *n* a case for holding bottles of wine or liquor.
cellnet *n* a portable radio telephone used in cellular radio.
cello *n* (*pl* **cellos**) the violoncello, a large four-stringed bass instrument of the violin family, held between the knees.—**cellist** *n*.
cellophane *n* a thin transparent paper made from cellulose, used for wrapping.
Cellphone *n* (*trademark*) a cellular telephone, a portable mobile telephone operated by cellular radio.
cellular *adj* of, resembling or containing cells; (*textiles*) of an open texture.
cellular radio *n* a computer-controlled radio communications system for Cellphones, etc, using a network of transmitters serving small zones called cells, as users move between cells the transmitters/receivers are transferred automatically.
cellule *n* a small cell or cavity.
cellulite *n* a form of fat on the hips, thighs and buttocks that causes puckering of the skin surface.
celluloid *n* a type of plastic made from cellulose nitrate and camphor; a plastic coating on film; cinema film.
cellulose *n* a starch-like carbohydrate forming the cell walls of plants, used in making paper, textiles, film, etc.
cellulose acetate *n* a compound used in the manufacture of artificial textiles, film, and varnishes.
Celsius *adj* pertaining to a thermometer scale with a freezing point of 0 degrees and a boiling point of 100 degrees.
Celt *n* a member of an ancient people who inhabited pre-Roman Britain, Gaul and Spain.

celt *n* a prehistoric edged instrument or weapon of stone or bronze, resembling a chisel or blade of an axe, found in ancient tumuli.

Celtic *adj* of or relating to the Celts; the language of the Celts, including Scots or Irish Gaelic, Manx, Welsh, Cornish and Breton.

Celticist, Celtist *n* a student of Celtic antiquities, languages, etc.

cement *n* a powdered substance of lime and clay, mixed with water, etc to make mortar or concrete, which hardens upon drying; any hard-drying substance. * *vt* to bind or glue together with or as if with cement; to cover with cement.—**cementer** *n*.

cementation *n* the act of cementing; a process for converting iron into steel, glass into porcelain, etc.

cemetery *n* (*pl* **cemeteries**) a place for the burial of the dead.

cenobite *see* **coenobite.**

cenotaph *n* a monument to a person who is buried elsewhere.—**cenotaphic** *adj*.

Cenozoic *adj* of the third geological period, Tertiary.

cense *vt* to perfume with incense.

censer *n* a covered cup-shaped vessel pierced with holes in which incense is burned.

censor *n* an official with the power to examine literature, films, mail, etc and remove or prohibit anything considered obscene, objectionable, etc. * *vt* to act as a censor.—**censorable** *adj*.—**censorial** *adj*.—**censorship** *n*.

censorious *adj* expressing censure; fault-finding.—**censoriously** *adv*.—**censoriousness** *n*.

censure *n* an expression of disapproval or blame. * *vt* to condemn as wrong; to reprimand.—**censurable** *adj*.

census *n* (*pl* **censuses**) an official count of the population, including details of age, sex, occupation, etc; any official count.

cent *n* a hundredth of a dollar; (*inf*) a negligible amount of money.

centaur *n* a fabulous monster, half man, half horse; an expert horseman; (*astron*) a southern constellation.

centaury *n* (*pl* **centauries**) a medicinal herb.

centavo *n* (*pl* **centavos**) the hundredth part of a dollar or peso in use in the South American republics.

centenarian *n* one who is one hundred years old or more.—*also adj*.

centenary *n* (*pl* **centenaries**) a hundredth anniversary or its celebration. * *adj* of a hundred years.

centennial *adj* happening every hundred years. * *n* a centenary.

center *see* **centre.**

centerboard *see* **centreboard.**

centerfold *see* **centrefold.**

centerpiece *see* **centrepiece.**

centesimal *adj* counting or counted by hundredths. * *n* a hundredth part.

centi- *prefix* one hundredth.

centiare, centare *n* a square metre, equal to the hundredth part of an are.

centigrade *adj* Celsius.

centigram, centigramme *n* one hundredth of a gram.

centilitre, centiliter *n* one hundredth of a litre.

centime *n* a small french coin, the hundredth part of a franc.

centimeter, centimetre *n* one hundredth of a metre.

centimetre-gram-second *n* a unit system in which the centimetre, the gram and the mean solar second are taken respectively as the units of length, mass, and time (usu abbreviated **cgs units**).

centipede *n* a crawling creature with a long body divided into numerous segments each with a pair of legs.

centner *n* a weight divisible first into a hundred parts and then into smaller parts; in many European countries the commercial name for a hundredweight.

cento *n* (*pl* **centos**) a literary or musical composition formed by selections from various authors or composers and arranged in a new order.

central *adj* in, at, from or forming the centre; main, principal; important.—**centrally** *adv*.—**centrality** *n*.

central bank *n* a national bank that handles government transactions as opposed to private business.

central heating *n* a system of heating by pipes from a central boiler or other heat source.

centralism *n* the policy or process of bringing under central control.—**centralist** *adj, n*.

centralize *vt* to draw to the centre; to place under the control of a central authority, esp government.—**centralization** *n*.

central nervous system *n* in vertebrates, the brain and spinal cord which coordinates an animal's activity.

central processing unit *n* (*comput*) the part of a computer that performs logical and arithmetical operations on data in accordance with program instructions.

centre *n* the approximate middle point or part of anything, a pivot; interior; point of concentration; a place where a particular activity goes on (*shopping centre*); source; political moderation; (*sport*) a player at the centre of the field, etc, a centre-forward. * *adj* of or at the centre. * *vt* (**centring, centred**) to place in the centre; to concentrate; to be fixed; (*football, hockey*) to kick or hit the ball into the centre of the pitch.—*also* **center.**

centre bit *n* a carpenter's tool turning upon a centre, for boring holes.

centreboard *n* a keel so constructed that it may be raised within the hull of a vessel or lowered, extensively used by racing craft; a yacht with this.—*also* **centerboard.**

centrefold *n* a colour illustration spread across the two facing pages in the middle of a newspaper or magazine.—*also* **centerfold.**

centre of gravity *n* that point of a body through which the resultant of all the forces acting upon it in consequence of the earth's attraction will pass.

centrepiece *n* a central ornament or decoration.—*also* **centerpiece.**

centric, centrical *adj* placed in the centre; central.—**centricity** *n*.

centrifugal *adj* moving away from the centre of rotation.—**centrifugally** *adv*.

centrifugal force *n* an imaginary force which acts outwards on a rotating body or one moving along a curved path.

centrifuge *n* a device used to separate milk, blood, etc, by rotating at very high speed.—**centrifugation** *n*.

centripetal *adj* tending to move towards the centre.—**centripetally** *adv*.

centrist *n* a person of moderate political opinions, etc.—**centrism** *n*.

centrobaric *adj* relating to the centre of gravity or to the method of its determination.

centroid *n* the centre of mass or gravity of a body.

centurion *n* an officer commanding a hundred Roman soldiers.

century *n* (*pl* **centuries**) a period of a hundred years; a set of a hundred; (*cricket*) 100 runs made by a batsman in a single innings; a company of a Roman legion.

century plant *n* a name of the American aloe, from the supposition that it flowered once only in a hundred years.

cep *n* an edible woodland fungus with a shiny brown cap and a white underside.

cephalagia *n* a headache.

cephalic *adj* of the head.

cephalic index *n* the relation of the length of the head to its breadth.

cephalization *n* the tendency in animal development to localize important parts or organs in or near the head.

cephalopod *n* a marine mollusc, such as an octopus, characterized by a well-developed head and eyes and a ring of sucker-bearing tentacles.—**cephalopodan** *n, adj*.

cephalothorax *n* (*pl* **cephalothoraxes, cephalothoraces**) the anterior part of the body in the higher crustaceans, spiders, etc.

ceraceous *adj* resembling wax.

ceramic *adj* of earthenware, porcelain, or brick. * *n* something made of ceramic; (*pl*) the art of pottery.

ceramics *n* (*sing*) work executed wholly or partly in clay and baked; the art of pottery.—**ceramist, ceramicist** *n*.

cerastes *n* (*pl* **cerastes**) the horned viper.

cerate *n* a thick ointment of wax, etc.

ceratodus *n* (*pl* **ceratoduses**) a genus of Australian fishes containing the barramunda, or native salmon.

cere[1] *n* a wax-like membrane at the base of the bill of many birds, as the parrot.
cere[2] *vt* to cover or close with cerecloth.
cereal *n* a grass grown for its edible grain, eg wheat, rice; the grain of such grasses; a breakfast food made from such grains. * *adj* of corn or edible grain.
cerebellum *n* (*pl* **cerebellums, cerebella**) a part of the brain below and behind the cerebrum which coordinates voluntary movements.—**cerebellar** *adj*.
cerebral *adj* of or relating to the cerebrum; intellectual.—**cerebrally** *adv*.
cerebral hemisphere *n* one of the two lateral halves of the cerebrum.
cerebral palsy *n* a disability caused by brain damage before, during or immediately after birth resulting in poor muscle coordination.
cerebrate *vi* to use the brain; to think.
cerebration *n* the conscious or unconscious action of the brain; thought or thinking.
cerebrospinal *adj* of the brain and spinal cord.
cerebrum *n* (*pl* **cerebrums, cerebra**) the front part of the brain of vertebrates; the dominant part of the brain in man, associated with intellectual function; the brain as a whole.
cerecloth *n* a cloth saturated with wax or some gummy substance, used for wrapping embalmed bodies in.
cerement *n* a grave cloth or shroud; (*pl*) grave clothes.
ceremonial *adj* of or with ceremony; formal. * *n* a set of rules for ceremonies.—**ceremonially** *adv*.
ceremonialism *n* adherence to, or fondness for, ceremonial observance; ritualism.—**ceremonialist** *n*.
ceremonious *adj* observant of ceremony; marked by formality; overpolite.—**ceremoniously** *adv*.
ceremony *n* (*pl* **ceremonies**) a sacred rite; formal observance or procedure; behaviour that follows rigid etiquette.
cerise *n* a light and clear red.—*also adj*.
cerium *n* a grey metallic element used in various metallurgical and nuclear applications.
cero- *prefix* wax.
cert *abbr* = certified; certificate; (*sl*) certainty.
certain *adj* sure, positive; unerring, reliable; sure to happen, inevitable; definite, fixed; some; one; unnamed, unspecified.
certainly *adv* without doubt; yes.
certainty *n* (*pl* **certainties**) something undoubted, inevitable; the condition of being certain.
certificate *n* a document formally attesting a fact; a testimonial of qualifications or character.—**certificated** *adj*.
certified public accountant *n* an accountant who has qualified by passing official examinations; a chartered accountant.
certify *vt* (**certifying, certified**) to declare in writing or attest formally; to endorse with authority.—**certification** *n*.
certiorari *n* a writ issuing from a superior court calling for the records of an inferior court, or to remove a case from a court below.
certitude *n* freedom from doubt.
cerulean *adj* deep blue.
cerumen *n* wax of the ear.—**ceruminous** *adj*.
ceruse *n* white lead used as a pigment and from which a cosmetic is prepared.
cervical *adj* of the neck of the womb.
cervical smear *n* (*med*) a sample of cells taken from the cervix for detection of cancer; the taking of the sample.
cervine *adj* of or pertaining to the deer family; of a tawny or fawn colour.
cervix *n* (*pl* **cervixes, cervices**) the neck of the womb.
cesium *see* **caesium.**
cespitose *adj* (*bot*) growing in tufts.
cess[1] *vt* to impose a tax; to assess. * *n* a rate or tax, esp the land tax.
cess[2] *n* (*Irish*) luck or fortune.
cessation *n* a stoppage; a pause.
cession *n* a giving up, a surrender; something ceded.
cessionary *n* (*pl* **cessionaries**) (*law*) a giving or yielding up.
cesspool, cesspit *n* a covered cistern for collecting liquid waste or sewage; (*fig*) a place of sin and depravity.
cestoid *adj* of or pertaining to the Cestoda, an order of parasitic flat worms to which the tapeworms belong. * *n* a flat intestinal worm.
cetacean *n* a member of an order of aquatic, usu marine, mammals that includes whales, dolphins and porpoises. * *adj* belonging to this order (—*also* **cetaceous**).
ceteris paribus (*Latin*) other things being equal.
Cf (*chem symbol*) californium.
cf. *abbr* = compare (Latin *confer*).
CFC *abbr* = chlorofluorocarbon.
cgs *abbr* = centimetre-gram-second.
ch. *abbr* = chapter; church; (*chess*) check.
cha-cha(-cha) *n* a ballroom dance orig from Latin America; the music for this.
chablis *n* (*often with cap*) a dry white wine from Chablis, France.
chacma *n* a South African baboon.
chaconne *n* an old Spanish dance; the music for such a dance.
chad *n* (*comput*) the little scraps of paper or cardboard left by the punching of holes in computer cards or paper tape.
chafe *vti* to restore warmth by rubbing; to make or become sore by rubbing; to irritate; to feel irritation, to fret.
chafer *n* any of various large beetles.
chaff[1] *n* husks of grain separated from the seed by threshing or winnowing; cut hay or straw; worthless stuff.
chaff[2] *vt* to banter; to make a game of. * *vi* to use bantering language. * *n* good-natured teasing, banter.
chaffer *vi* to bargain, haggle. * *n* the act of bargaining.
chaffinch *n* a European songbird.
chaffy *adj* resembling, or full of, chaff; anything light or worthless.
chafing dish *n* a vessel for heating or cooking food on a table; a small portable grate for coals.
chagrin *n* annoyance; vexation; disappointment.
chain *n* a series of connected links or rings; a continuous series; a series of related events; a bond; a group of shops, hotels, etc owned by the same company; a unit of length equal to 66 feet; a range of mountains; a group of islands; (*pl*) anything that restricts or binds; fetters. * *vt* to fasten with a chain or chains.
chain gang *n* a group of prisoners chained together.
chain mail *n* flexible armour formed of metal links interwoven.
chain reaction *n* a process in which a chemical, atomic or other reaction stimulates further reactions, eg combustion or nuclear fission; a series of events, each of which stimulates the next.
chain saw *n* a power-driven saw with teeth linked as in a chain.
chain-smoke *vti* to smoke (cigarettes) one after the other.—**chain-smoker** *n*.
chain stitch *n* an embroidery stitch that resembles the links of a chain.
chain store *n* one of a series of retail stores owned by one company.
chair *n* a separate seat for one, with a back and legs; a seat of authority; a chairman; a professorship; the electric chair. * *vt* to preside as chairman of.
chair lift *n* a series of seats suspended from a cable for carrying sightseers or skiers uphill.
chairman *n* (*pl* **chairmen**) a person who presides at a meeting; the president of a board or committee.—**chairwoman** *nf* (*pl* **chairwomen**).—*also* **chairperson.**
chaise *n* a light two-wheeled carriage; any carriage.
chaise longue *n* (*pl* **chaise longues, chaises longues**) a couch-like chair with a long seat.
chalcedony *n* (*pl* **chalcedonies**) a form of quartz used as a gemstone.
chalco- *prefix* copper.
chalcopyrite *n* a copper ore.

Chaldean, Chaldaean *adj* pertaining to Chaldea, or ancient Babylon, or its language. * *n* the language of ancient Babylon.

chalet *n* a Swiss hut; any similar building used in a holiday camp, as a ski lodge, etc.

chalice *n* a large cup with a base; a communion cup.

chalk *n* calcium carbonate, a soft white limestone; such a stone or a substitute used for drawing or writing. * *vt* to write, mark or draw with chalk; (*with* **up**) (*inf*) to score, get, achieve; to charge or credit.

chalky *adj* (**chalkier, chalkiest**) containing or resembling chalk.—**chalkiness** *n.*

challenge *vt* to summon to a fight or contest; to call in question; to object to; to hail and interrogate; to demand proof of identity. * *n* the act of challenging; a summons to a contest; a calling in question; a problem that stimulates effort.—**challenger** *n.*—**challenging** *adj.*

challis *n* a light all-wool fabric.

chalybeate *adj* (*water*) impregnated with iron.

chamber *n* a room, esp a bedroom; a deliberative body or a division of a legislature; a room where such a body meets; a compartment; a cavity in the body of an organism; part of a gun cylinder holding the cartridge; (*pl*) a judge's office.

chamberlain *n* an official in charge of the household of a monarch or nobleman; a steward, treasurer or factor of a municipal corporation.

chambermaid *n* a woman employed to clean bedrooms in a hotel, etc.

chamber music *n* music for performance by a small group, as a string quartet.

chamber of commerce *n* (*often cap*) an organization of representatives from local businesses formed to promote and protect their interests.

chamber pot *n* a vessel for urine.

chameleon *n* a lizard capable of changing colour to match its surroundings; a person of variable moods or behaviour; an adaptable person.—**chameleonic** *adj.*

chamfer *n* a flat surface made in wood or metal by paring off an angle, a bevel. * *vt* to groove, channel or flute.—**chamferer** *n.*

chamois *n* (*pl* **chamois**) a small antelope found in Europe and Asia; a piece of chamois leather.

chamois leather, chammy (leather) *n* a soft, pliable leather formerly made from chamois skin, and now obtained from sheep, goats and deer; a piece of this for polishing.—*also* **shammy (leather)**.

chamomile *n* an aromatic plant with daisy-like flowers used medicinally for its soothing property and as a hair lightener, and in making camomile tea.—*also* **camomile**.

champ[1] *vti* to munch noisily, chomp; **champ at the bit** to be impatient.

champ[2] *n* (*inf*) a champion.

champagne *n* a sparkling white wine; a pale straw colour.

champaign *n* flat open country, a level expanse. * *adj* level, open.

champerty *n* (*pl* **champerties**) (*law*) the maintenance of a party in a suit on condition that, if successful, the property is shared; the offence of aiding another's lawsuit in order to share in gains from it.—**champertous** *adj.*

champignon *n* an edible mushroom that grows in circular clusters.

champion *n* a person who fights for another; one who upholds a cause; a competitor successful against all others. * *adj* first-class; (*inf*) excellent. * *vt* to defend; to uphold the cause of.

championship *n* the act of championing; the process of determining a champion; a contest held to find a champion.

champlevé *n* enamel bearing indentations filled with colour.—*also adj.*

chance *n* a course of events; fortune; an accident, an unexpected event; opportunity; possibility; probability; risk. * *vti* to risk; to happen; to come upon unexpectedly. * *adj* accidental, not planned.

chancel *n* the part of a church around the altar, for the clergy and the choir.

chancellery, chancellory *n* (*pl* **chancelleries, chancellories**) a chancellor's department or office; an office attached to an embassy.

chancellor *n* a high government official, as, in certain countries, a prime minister; in some universities, the president or other executive officer.—**chancellorship** *n.*

chance-medley *n* (*law*) justifiable homicide in self-defence; inadvertency.

chancery *n* (*pl* **chanceries**) originally in England, next to Parliament the highest court of justice, since 1873 a division of the High Court of Justice; the office for public records; in US a court of equity.

chancre *n* a syphilitic ulcer.—**chancrous** *adj.*

chancy *adj* (**chancier, chanciest**) (*inf*) risky, uncertain.—**chancily** *adv.*

chandelier *n* an ornamental hanging frame with branches for holding lights.

chandler *n* a dealer or merchant, esp in candles, oil, soap, etc.

chandlery *n* (*pl* **chandleries**) a chandler's shop or stock.

change *vt* to make different, to alter; to transform; to exchange; to put fresh clothes on. * *vi* to become different, to undergo alteration; to put on fresh clothes; to continue one's journey by leaving one station, etc, or mode of transport and going to and using another. * *n* alteration, modification; substitution; variety; a fresh set, esp clothes; money in small units; the balance of money returned when given in a larger denomination as payment.—**changer** *n.*

changeable *adj* able to be changed; altering rapidly between different conditions; inconstant.—**changeability** n.—changeably *adv.*

changeful *adj* often changing.

changeless *adj* constant, immutable.—**changelessly** *adv.*—**changelessness** *n.*

changeling *n* a child secretly left in place of another.

change of life *n* the menopause.

changeover *n* a complete change of system, method, state, attitude, etc.

channel[1] *n* the bed or the deeper part of a river, harbour, etc; a body of water joining two larger ones; a navigable passage; a means of passing or conveying or communicating; a band of radio frequencies reserved for a particular purpose, eg television station; a path for an electrical signal; a groove or line along which liquids, etc may flow. * *vt* (**channelling, channelled** *or* **channeling, channeled**) to form a channel in; to groove; to direct.

channel[2] *n* a projection from a ship's side to spread the shrouds and keep them clear of the bulwarks.

chanson *n* (*pl* **chansons**) a song.

chant *vti* to sing; to recite in a singing manner; to sing or shout (a slogan) rhythmically. * *n* sacred music to which prose is sung; sing-song intonation; a monotonous song; a rhythmic slogan, esp as sung or shouted by sports fans, etc.

chanter *n* a person who chants; the tenor or treble pipe of a bagpipe on which the melody is played.

chanterelle *n* an edible yellow mushroom.

chantey, chanty *n* (*pl* **chanteys, chanties**) a shanty.

chanticleer *n* a rooster.

chantry *n* (*pl* **chantries**) a chapel endowed for the saying or singing mass daily for the soul of the founder; such an endowment.

chaology *n* the study of chaos theory.—**chaologist** *n.*

chaos *n* utter confusion, muddle.

chaos theory *n* (*physics*) the theory that the behaviour of dynamic systems is haphazard rather than mathematical.

chaotic *adj* completely without order or arrangement.—**chaotically** *adv.*

chap[1] *vti* (**chapping, chapped**) (*skin*) to make or become split or rough in cold weather. * *n* a chapped place in the skin.

chap[2] *n* (*inf*) a man.

chap[3] *n* (*usu pl*) one of the jaws or its fleshy covering; the mouth of a channel.

chaparejos *npl* a cowboy's leather leg coverings.—*also* **chaps.**

chaparral *n* a dense thicket.

chapatti, chapati *n* (*pl* **chapattis, chapatis**) in Indian cookery, flat unleavened bread.

chapbook *n* a small book of ballads, romances, etc, formerly hawked by a chapman.

chape *n* the metal tip of a scabbard; the part attaching a scabbard to a belt.

chapeau *n* (*pl* **chapeaux, chapeaus**) a hat or head covering.

chapel *n* a building for Christian worship, not as large as a church; an association or trade union of printers in a printing office.

chaperon, chaperone *n* a woman who accompanies a girl at social occasions for propriety. * *vt* to attend as a chaperon.—**chaperonage** *n*.
chapfallen *adj* with the jaw hanging down, dejected, dispirited.—*also* **chopfallen.**
chapiter *n* (*archit*) the upper part or capital of a column.
chaplain *n* a clergyman serving in a religious capacity with the armed forces, or in a prison, hospital, etc.—**chaplaincy** *n*.
chaplet *n* a wreath or garland encircling the head; a rosary; a round moulding carved into beads, olives, etc.—**chapleted** *adj*.
chapman *n* (*pl* **chapmen**) formerly a merchant or trader; a hawker.
chaps *npl* chaparejos.
chapter *n* a main division of a book; the body or meeting of canons of a cathedral or members of a monastic order; a sequence of events; an organized branch of a society or association.
chapterhouse *n* a room for the meetings of a cathedral chapter.
char[1] *n* a charwoman. * *vti* (**charring, charred**) to work as a charwoman.
char[2] *vb* (**charring, charred**) *vt* to burn to charcoal or carbon. * *vti* to scorch.
char[3] *n* (*pl* **char, chars**) a red-bellied fish allied to the salmon.—*also* **charr.**
character *n* the combination of qualities that distinguishes an individual person, group or thing; moral strength; reputation; disposition; a person of marked individuality; an eccentric; (*inf*) a person; a person in a play or novel; a guise, role; a letter or mark in writing, printing, etc.
characterful *adj* full of character, unusual.
characteristic *adj* marking or constituting the particular nature (of a person or thing). * *n* a characteristic or distinguishing feature.—**characteristically** *adv*.
characterize *vt* to describe in terms of particular qualities; to designate; to be characteristic of, mark.—**characterization** *n*.
characterless *adj* ordinary, undistinguished.
charade *n* a travesty; an absurd pretence; (*usu pl*) a game of guessing a word from the acted representation of its syllables and the whole.
charcoal *n* the black carbon matter obtained by partially burning wood and used as fuel, as a filter or for drawing.
chard *n* a type of beet with edible leaves and stalks.
charge *vt* to ask as the price; to record as a debt; to load, to fill, saturate; to lay a task or trust on; to burden; to accuse; to attack at a run; to build up an electric charge (in). * *n* a price charged for goods or service; a build-up of electricity; the amount which a receptacle can hold at one time; the explosive required to fire a weapon; trust, custody; a thing or person entrusted; a task, duty; accusation; an attack.
chargeable *adj* liable to be charged.—**chargeability** *n*.
charge account *n* an account with a store, etc, to which the cost of goods are charged for later payment.
charge card *n* a type of credit card issued by a chain store or other organization.
chargé d'affaires *n* (*pl* **chargés d'affaires**) an ambassador's deputy; a minor diplomat.
charger *n* a cavalry horse; a device for charging a battery.
charily *adv* reluctantly; cautiously.
chariness *n* a being chary.
chariot *n* a two-wheeled vehicle driven by two or more horses in ancient warfare, races, etc.—**charioteer** *n*.
charisma, charism *n* (*pl* **charismata, charisms**) personal quality enabling a person to influence or inspire others; a God-given power or gift.—**charismatic** *adj*.
charitable *adj* of or for charity; generous to the needy, benevolent; lenient in judging others, kindly.—**charitableness** *n*.—**charitably** *adv*.
charity *n* (*pl* **charities**) leniency or tolerance towards others; generosity in giving to the needy; a benevolent fund or institution.
charivari *n* a mock serenade of discordant music; hurly-burly.—*also* **shivaree.**
charlatan *n* a person who pretends to be what he or she is not; one who professes knowledge dishonestly, esp of medicine.—**charlatanism, charlatanry** *n*.
Charleston *n* a lively dance with sidekicks from the knee.
charlock *n* wild mustard.
charlotte *n* a pudding of stewed fruit covered with breadcrumbs.
charlotte russe *n* whipped cream custard enclosed in a sponge cake.
charm *n* an alluring quality, fascination; a magic verse or formula; something thought to possess occult power; an object bringing luck; a trinket on a bracelet. * *vt* to delight, captivate; to influence as by magic.—**charmer** *n*.
charming *adj* delightful, attractive.—**charmingly** *adv*.
charnel house *n* a vault containing corpses or bones.
charpoy *n* a light portable Indian bedstead.
charqui *n* beef cut into strips and sun-dried.
charr *see* **char**[3].
chart *n* a map, esp for use in navigation; an information sheet with tables, graphs, etc; a weather map; a table, graph, etc; (*pl with* **the**) a list of the most popular music recordings. * *vt* to make a chart of; to plan (a course of action).
charter *n* a document granting rights, privileges, ownership of land, etc; the hire of transportation. * *vt* to grant by charter; to hire.
chartered accountant *n* an accountant who has qualified by passing the official examinations; a certified public accountant.
Chartism *n* a democratic reforming movement in England for the extension of political power to the working class, embodied in the People's Charter of 1838.—**Chartist** *adj, n*.
Chartreuse *n* (*trademark*) a yellowish green liqueur; (*without cap*) its colour.
chartulary *see* **cartulary.**
charwoman *n* (*pl* **charwomen**) a woman employed to clean a house.
chary *adj* (**charier, chariest**) cautious; sparing; (*with* **of**) unwilling to risk.
chase[1] *vt* to pursue; to run after; to drive (away); to hunt; (*inf: usu with* **up**) to pursue in a determined manner. * *n* pursuit; a hunt; a quarry hunted; a steeplechase.
chase[2] *n* a frame for securing a page of type; a groove; that part of a cannon in front of the trunnions.
chase[3] *vt* to work or emboss precious metals; to cut a screw.
chaser *n* a horse used in steeplechasing; a person that chases; (*inf*) a drink taken after another, as in beer after a whisky.
chasm *n* a deep cleft, an abyss, a gaping hole; a wide difference in opinions, etc.—**chasmal, chasmic** *adj*.
chassé *n* a rapid gliding step in dancing. * *vi* to perform a chassé.
chasseur *n* a French light-armed foot or cavalry soldier; a domestic dressed in military or hunting costume.
chassis *n* (*pl* **chassis**) the frame, wheels, engine of a car, aeroplane or other vehicle.
chaste *adj* pure, abstaining from unlawful sexual intercourse; virgin; modest; restrained, unadorned.—**chastely** *adv*.—**chasteness** *n*.
chasten *vt* to correct by suffering, discipline; to restrain.—**chastener** *n*.
chastise *vt* to punish; to beat; to scold.—**chastisement** *n*.
chastity *n* sexual abstinence; virginity; purity.
chasuble *n* a rich sleeveless vestment worn over the alb by a priest celebrating mass.
chat *vti* (**chatting, chatted**) to talk in an easy or familiar way; (*with* **up**) (*inf*) to talk in a flirtatious way with another person. * *n* informal conversation.
chateau, château *n* (*pl* **chateaus, châteaux**) a castle or large country estate in France.
chatelaine *n* the lady of a country house; a bunch of chains to which are attached keys, etc, worn at the waist by ladies.
chatoyant *adj* changing in colour or lustre.—**chatoyancy** *n*.
chat show *n* a television or radio programme with informal interviews and conversation.
chattel *n* (*usu pl*) goods, possessions; (*law*) personal property except freehold.
chatter *vi* to talk aimlessly and rapidly; (*animal, etc*) to utter rapid cries; (*teeth*) to rattle together due to cold or fear. * *n* idle rapid talk; the sound of chattering.—**chatterer** *n*.

chatterbox *n* an incessant talker.

chatty *adj* (**chattier, chattiest**) talkative, full of gossip.—**chattily** *adv*.—**chattiness** *n*.

chauffeur *n* a person who drives a car for someone else. * *vt* to drive as a chauffeur.—**chauffeuse** *nf*.

chauvinism *n* aggressive patriotism; excessive devotion to a belief, cause, etc, esp a man's belief in the superiority of men over women.—**chauvinist** *n*.—**chauvinistic** *adj*.

chaw *vt* (*dial*) to chew, to munch, esp tobacco. * *n* a plug of tobacco.

cheap *adj* low-priced, inexpensive; good value; of little worth, inferior; vulgar.—**cheaply** *adv*.—**cheapness** *n*.

cheapen *vti* to make or become cheap; to lower the value, worth or reputation of.

cheap-jack *n* (*inf*) a person who sells cheap or worthless goods. * *adj* worthless, inferior.

cheapskate *n* (*inf*) a mean or dishonourable person.

cheat *vti* to defraud, to swindle; to deceive; to play unfairly. * *n* a fraud, deception; a person who cheats.—**cheater** *n*.

check *vti* to bring or come to a stand; to restrain or impede; to admonish, reprove; to test the accuracy of, verify; (*with* **in**) to sign or register arrival at a hotel, work, an airport, etc; (*with* **out**) to settle the bill and leave a hotel; to investigate. * *n* repulse; stoppage; a pattern of squares; a control to test accuracy; a tick against listed items; a bill in a restaurant; a cheque; (*chess*) a threatening of the king; a money order to a bank (—*also* **check**).

checkbook *see* **chequebook**.

check digit *n* (*comput*) a digit added to data digits to test accuracy and check for corruption.

checker[1] *see* **chequer**.

checker[2] *n* a cashier in a supermarket.

checkerboard *n* a draughtboard.

checkered *see* **chequered**.

check list *n* a list of items, used for reference or verification.

checkmate *n* (*chess*) the winning position when the king is threatened and unable to move; utter defeat. * *vt* (*chess*) to place in checkmate; to defeat, foil.

checking account *n* a bank account, usu with no interest, from which money is withdrawn by cheques or cash cards; a current account.

checkout *n* a place where traffic may be halted for inspection; the place in a store where goods are paid for.

checkpoint *n* a place where visitors' passports or other official documents may be examined.

checkrein *see* **bearing rein**.

checkroom *n* a temporary repository for luggage, coats, etc.

checkup *n* a thorough examination; a medical examination, usu repeated at intervals.

Cheddar *n* a type of hard, white or yellow cheese originally made in Cheddar, England.

cheek *n* the side of the face below the eye; (*sl*) buttock; impudence.

cheeky *adj* (**cheekier, cheekiest**) disrespectful, impudent.—**cheekily** *adv*.—**cheekiness** *n*.

cheep *n* the frail squeak of a young bird. * *vi* to make such a sound.

cheer *n* a shout of applause or welcome; a frame of mind, spirits; happiness. * *vt* to gladden; to encourage; to applaud.

cheerful *adj* in good spirits; happy.—**cheerfully** *adv*.—**cheerfulness** *n*.

cheerleader *n* a person who leads organized cheering, esp at a sports event.

cheerless *adj* dismal, depressing.

cheers *interj* (*inf*) an expression used in offering a toast, as a form of farewell or thanks.

cheery *adj* (**cheerier, cheeriest**) lively, genial, merry.—**cheerily** *adv*.—**cheeriness** *n*.

cheese *n* the curds of milk pressed into a firm or hard mass; a boss or important person (*big cheese*).

cheeseburger *n* a hamburger with melted cheese on top.

cheesecake *n* a cake made with cottage or cream cheese; (*sl*) attractive women or men displayed as sex objects in photographs, etc.

cheesecloth *n* a thin cotton fabric.

cheeseparing *adj* niggardly, mean.

cheesy *adj* (**cheesier, cheesiest**) like cheese.—**cheesiness** *n*.

cheetah *n* a large spotted cat, similar to a leopard.

chef *n* a professional cook.

chef-d'oeuvre *n* (*pl* **chefs-d'oeuvre**) a masterpiece.

cheiro-, chiro- *prefix* hand.

chela *n* (**chelae**) a claw-like pincer of the crab, etc.—**cheliferous** *adj*.

chelonian *n* any of the order of reptiles, including turtles and tortoises.—*also adj*.

chemical *n* a substance used in, or arising from, a chemical process. * *adj* of, used in, or produced by chemistry.—**chemically** *adv*.

chemical engineering *n* the branch of engineering dealing with the design, construction, and manufacture of plant used in industrial chemical processes.

chemical warfare *n* warfare in which poison gases and other chemicals are used.

chemin de fer *n* a gambling game, a kind of baccarat.

chemise *n* a woman's undergarment; a loose-fitting dress.

chemisette *n* a short bodice worn over the breast; lace, etc, filling the neck opening of a dress.

chemist *n* a pharmacy; a manufacturer of medicinal drugs; a person skilled in chemistry.

chemistry *n* (*pl* **chemistries**) the science of the properties of substances and their combinations and reactions; chemical structure.

chemotherapy *n* the treatment of disease, esp cancer, by drugs and other chemical agents.

chenille *n* silk or worsted cord.

cheque *see* **check**.

chequebook *n* a book containing blank cheques to be drawn on a bank.—*also* **checkbook**.

chequer *n* a pattern of squares (—*also* **checker**); a flat counter used in the game of checkers (—*also* **draughtsman**); (*pl*) a game for two players who each move twelve round flat pieces over a checkerboard (—*also* **draughts**).

chequered *adj* marked with a variegated pattern; having a career marked by fluctuating fortunes.—*also* **checkered**.

cherish *vt* to tend lovingly, foster; to keep in mind as a hope, ambition, etc.—**cherisher** *n*.

cheroot *n* a cigar cut square at each end.

cherry *n* (*pl* **cherries**) a small red, pitted fruit; the tree bearing it; a bright red colour.

cherry picker *n* a crane, usu on a truck, with a long elbow-jointed arm carrying a platform that can be raised and lowered.

chersonese *n* (*poet*) a peninsula.

chert *n* an impure flint-like quartz or hornstone.—**cherty** *adj*.

cherub *n* (*pl* **cherubim**) an angel of the second order; a winged child or child's head; (*pl* **cherubs**) an angelic, sweet child.—**cherubic** *adj*.

chervil *n* an aromatic herb used for flavouring.

Cheshire cheese *n* a mild flavoured cheese, originally made in Cheshire, England.

chess[1] *n* a game played by two people with 32 pieces on a chessboard.

chess[2] *n* one of the flooring planks of a pontoon bridge.

chessboard *n* a board chequered with 64 squares in two alternate colours, used for playing chess or draughts.

chessman *n* (*pl* **chessmen**) any of the 16 pieces used by each player in chess.

chest *n* a large strong box; the part of the body enclosed by the ribs, the thorax.

chesterfield *n* a large, stuffed couch with straight ends; a man's overcoat.

chestnut *n* a tree or shrub of the beech family; the edible nut of a chestnut; the wood of the chestnut; a horse with chestnut colouring; (*inf*) an old joke. * *adj* of the colour of a chestnut, a deep reddish brown.

chest of drawers *n* a piece of furniture containing several drawers.
chesty *adj* (**chestier, chestiest**) (*inf*) prone to chest infections; having a large chest or bosom.—**chestily** *adv*.—**chestiness** *n*.
cheval-de-frise *n* (*pl* **chevaux-de-frise**) a fence constructed of a bar armed with long spikes.
cheval glass *n* a full-length mirror which can swivel in its frame.
chevalier *n* a knight; a horseman; a member or knight of an honourable order; the lowest title or rank of the old French nobility; a gallant.
chevet *n* an apse; a group of apses.
cheviot *n* a rough cloth made from the wool of sheep bred on the Cheviot Hills along the border between England and Scotland.
chevron *n* the V-shaped bar on the sleeve of a uniform, showing rank.
chevrotain *n* a small musk deer.
chew *vt* to grind between the teeth, to masticate; (*with* **over**) to ponder, think over; (*with* **up**) to spoil by chewing. * *n* the act of chewing; something to chew, as a sweet or tobacco.—**chewable** *adj*.—**chewer** *n*.
chewing gum *n* a flavoured gum made from chicle, for chewing.
chewed-up *adj* (*sl*) made nervous or worried.
chewy *adj* (**chewier, chewiest**) needing to be chewed.
chez *prep* at the home of.
chi *n* the 22nd letter of the Greek alphabet.
Chianti *n* a dry red or white wine from Italy.
chiaroscuro *n* (*pl* **chiaroscuros**) the effects of light and shade; the treatment of this in painting, drawing, or engraving; the use of contrast and relief in literature. * *adj* pertaining to such treatment.—**chiaroscurism** *n*.—**chiaroscurist** *n*.
chiasma, chiasm *n* (*pl* **chiasmas, chiasmata, chiasms**) the central body of nervous matter formed by the junction and the crossing of the fibres of the optic nerves.—**chiasmal** *adj*.—**chiasmic** *adj*.
chiasmus *n* (*pl* **chiasmi**) a figure of speech by which the order of words in the first of two parallel clauses is reversed in the second, eg "to stop too fearful and too faint to go".—**chiastic** *adj*.
chibouk, chibouque *n* a long Turkish tobacco pipe.
chic *n* elegance, style. * *adj* stylish.
chicane *n* a hand at bridge without trumps; a barrier or obstacle on a motor-racing course; chicanery.
chicanery *n* (*pl* **chicaneries**) underhand dealing, trickery; verbal subterfuge.
Chicano *n* (*pl* **Chicanos**) a Mexican-American.—*also adj*.
chick *n* a young bird; (*sl*) a young attractive woman or girl.
chickadee *n* the American blackcap titmouse.
chickaree *n* the American red squirrel.
chicken *n* a young, domestic fowl; its flesh. * *adj* cowardly, timorous. * *vi* (*with* **out**) (*inf*) to suffer a failure of nerve or courage.
chicken feed *n* poultry food; (*inf*) a trifling amount of money.
chicken-hearted, chicken-livered *adj* cowardly.
chickenpox *n* a contagious viral disease that causes a rash of red spots on the skin.
chicken wire *n* light wire netting with a hexagonal mesh.
chickpea *n* (the seed eaten as a vegetable of) an Asian leguminous plant.
chickweed *n* a small white-flowered plant of the pink family.
chicle *n* the milky gum of a tropical American tree used to make chewing gum.
chicory *n* (*pl* **chicories**) a salad plant; its dried, ground, roasted root used to flavour coffee or as a coffee substitute.
chide *vt* (**chiding, chided** *or* **chid**; *pp* **chided, chid** *or* **chidden**) to rebuke, scold.—**chider** *n*.—**chidingly** *adv*.
chief *adj* principal, most important. * *n* a leader; the head of a tribe or clan.
chiefly *adv* especially; mainly; for the most part.
chieftain *n* the head of a Scottish clan; a chief.
chiffchaff *n* a European warbler.
chiffon *n* a thin gauzy material. * *adj* made of chiffon; (*pie filling, etc*) having a light fluffy texture.
chiffonier, chiffonnier *n* a high chest of drawers; a wide, low cupboard.
chignon *n* a mass of hair worn in a roll at the back of the head, a bun.
chigoe *n* a species of West Indian and South American flea that burrows beneath the skin of the feet, causing irritation and ulcers.—also **jigger**.
Chihuahua *n* a tiny dog with erect ears, originally from Mexico.
chilblain *n* an inflamed swelling on the hands, toes, etc, due to cold.
child *n* (*pl* **children**) a young human being; a son or daughter; offspring; an innocent or immature person.
child abuse *n* physical, mental or sexual maltreatment of a child by parents or any other adult.
childbearing *n* pregnancy and childbirth.—*also adj*.
childbirth *n* the process of giving birth to children.
child care *n* care by an authority of homeless children or those from a disturbed home background.
childe *n* a term formerly applied to the scions of knightly houses before their admission into knighthood; a youth of noble birth.
childhood *n* the period between birth and puberty in humans.
childish *adj* of, like or suited to a child; foolish.—**childishly**.—**childishness** *n*.
child labour *n* illegal employment of children below a certain age.
childless *adj* having no children.
child-like *adj* like a child; innocent, simple, candid.
children *see* **child**.
child's play *n* an easy task.
chili *n* (*pl* **chilies**) the hot-tasting pod of some of the capsicums, dried and used as flavouring.
chiliad *n* a thousand; a thousand years.—**chiliadal, chiliadic** *adj*.
chiliasm *n* the doctrine of the milennium.—**chiliast** *n*.—**chiliastic** *adj*.
chili con carne *n* a spicy stew of minced beef, beans, onions and tomatoes flavoured with chilli powder or chillies.
chill *n* a sensation of coldness; an illness caused by exposure to cold and marked by shivering; anything that dampens or depresses. * *adj* shivering with cold; feeling cold; unemotional, formal. * *vti* to make or become cold; to harden by cooling; to depress.
chillum *n* the bowl of a hookah; a hookah; smoking.
chilly *adj* (**chillier, chilliest**) cold; unfriendly.—**chilliness** *n*.
chilopod *n* any of an order of the class Myriopoda, containing the centipedes.
chime[1] *n* the harmonious sound of a bell; accord; harmony; (*pl*) a set of bells or metal tubes, etc tuned in a scale; their ringing. * *vi* to ring (a bell); (*with* **in**) (*inf*) to join in in agreement; to interrupt a conversation; (*with* **with**) to agree. * *vt* to indicate the hour by chiming, as a clock.
chime[2], **chimb** *n* the rim formed by the ends of the staves of a cask.
chimera, chimaera *n* (*Greek myth*) a fire-breathing monster with body parts from various different animals; a fantastic hybrid; an impossible fancy.
chimere *n* a loose silk robe worn by an Anglican bishop, either sleeveless or with lawn sleeves.
chimerical, chimeric *adj* merely imaginary; fantastic, visionary; unreal.—**chimerically** *adv*.
chimney *n* (*pl* **chimneys**) a passage for smoke, hot air or fumes, a funnel; a chimney stack; the vent of a volcano; a vertical crevice in rock large enough to enter and climb.
chimneypiece *n* a mantelpiece.
chimneypot *n* a pipe extending a chimney at the top.
chimney stack *n* the chimney above roof level.
chimney sweep *n* a person who removes soot from chimneys.
chimp *n* (*inf*) chimpanzee.
chimpanzee *n* an African anthropoid ape.
chin *n* the part of the face below the mouth.
china *n* fine porcelain; articles made from this.
china clay *n* kaolin.
Chinatown *n* the Chinese quarter of any city.
chinch *n* a tropical American insect destructive to corn crops; a bedbug.
chinchilla *n* a small South American rodent with soft grey fur; a breed of domestic cat; a breed of rabbit.

chine *n* the backbone or spine of an animal; a piece of the backbone of an animal with adjacent parts cut for cooking; a ridge; a rocky ravine or large fissure in a cliff.

Chinese *adj* of or pertaining to China. * *n* (*pl* **Chinese**) an inhabitant of China.

Chinese chequers *n* a board game played with marbles.

Chinese gooseberry *see* **kiwi fruit.**

Chinese lantern *n* a collapsible paper lantern.

Chinese puzzle *n* an intricate puzzle based on fitting boxes within boxes; any very difficult puzzle or complex problem.

Chinese restaurant syndrome *n* an ailment characterized by chest pain, dizziness, flushing, allegedly caused by consuming in quantity monosodium glutamate found in Chinese food.

Chinese white *n* a white pigment; white zinc oxide.

chink[1] *n* a narrow opening; a crack or slit.

chink[2] *n* the sound of coins clinking together.

chino *n* (*pl* **chinos**) a strong, hardwearing twilled cotton; (*pl*) trousers made of this fabric.

chinoiserie *n* (an object or objects in) a style of decoration copying Chinese motifs.

Chinook *n* a jargon of native and foreign words used on the northwest Pacific coast by Indians and whites.

chinook *n* a warm dry southwesterly wind of the eastern slopes of the Rocky Mountains; a warm moist wind blowing onto the northwest coast of America.

chinquapin *n* the dwarf chestnut of the US; its nut.

chintz *n* a glazed cotton cloth printed with coloured designs.

chintzy *adj* (**chintzier, chintziest**) of or describing furniture, decor, etc covered in chintz; cheap; tasteless in a flowery way.

chinwag *vi* (**chinwagging, chinwagged**) (*sl*) to talk, to gossip. * *n* (*sl*) a chatty conversation, a gossip.

chip *vt* (**chipping, chipped**) to knock small pieces off; to shape or make by chipping. * *n* a small piece cut or broken off; a mark left by chipping; a thin strip of fried potato, french fry; a potato chip; a counter used in games; a tiny piece of semiconducting material, such as silicon, printed with a microcircuit and used as part of an integrated circuit.

chipboard *n* a thin stiff material made from compressed wood shavings and other waste pieces combined with resin.

chipmunk *n* a small, striped, squirrel-like animal of North America.

Chippendale *adj* of the light style of furniture introduced in the middle of the 18th century by the furniture maker and designer, Thomas Chippendale (1718–79).

chipper *adj* active; lively, cheerful.

chip shot *n* a short, lofted approach shot in golf.

chiro-, cheiro- *prefix* hand.

chirography *n* the art of writing, calligraphy; judgment of character by the handwriting.—**chirographer** *n*.—**chirographic, chirographical** *adj*.

chiromancy *n* palmistry.—**chiromancer** *n*.

chiropody *n* the care and treatment of the feet.—**chiropodist** *n*.

chiropractic *n* the manipulation of joints, esp of the spine, to alleviate nerve pressure as a method of curing disease.—**chiropractor** *n*.

chirp *n* the sharp, shrill note of some birds or a grasshopper. * *vi* to make this sound.—**chirper** *n*.

chirpy *adj* (**chirpier, chirpiest**) lively, cheerful.—**chirpily** *adv*.—**chirpiness** *n*.

chirr *n* the shrill rasping sound of a grasshopper. * *vi* to make this sound.—*also* **churr.**

chirrup *vi* (*birds*) to twitter; to make a clicking sound to a horse. * *n* chirruping sound.—**chirruper** *n*.—**chirrupy** *adj*.

chisel *n* a tool with a square cutting end. * *vt* (**chiselling, chiselled** *or* **chiseling, chiseled**) to cut or carve with a chisel; (*sl*) to defraud.—**chiseller** *n*.

chit[1] *n* a voucher or a sum owed for drink, food, etc; a note; a requisition.

chit[2] *n* a child; (*derog*) an impudent girl.

chitchat *n* gossip, trivial talk.

chitin *n* the white horny substance that forms the outer covering of many invertebrate animals.—**chitinoid** *adj*.—**chitinous** *adj*.

chiton *n* in ancient Greece, a knee-length tunic; a full-length woman's dress; a genus of molluscs.

chitterlings, chitlins, chitlings *npl* the small edible entrails of pigs.

chivalrous *adj* relating to chivalry; war-like; high-spirited; brave, gallant; generous to the weak.—**chivalrously** *adv*.

chivalry *n* (*pl* **chivalries**) the medieval system of knighthood; knightly qualities, bravery, courtesy, respect for women.—**chivalric** *adj*.—**chivalrous** *adj*.—**chivalrously** *adv*.

chive, chives *n* a plant whose onion-flavoured leaves are used in cooking and salads.

chivvy, chivy *vt* (**chivvying, chivvied** *or* **chivying, chivied**) to annoy, harass, nag.

chloral (hydrate) *n* a bitter white crystalline compound used as a sedative or anaesthetic.

chlorate *n* a salt of chloric acid.

chlor-, chloro- *prefix* green.

chloric *adj* pertaining to or containing chlorine.

chloric acid *n* an acid containing hydrogen, oxygen, and chlorine.

chloride *n* any compound containing chlorine.—**chloridic** *adj*.

chloride of lime *n* a compound of chlorine with lime used in bleaching.

chlorinate *vt* to treat or combine with chlorine; to disinfect with chlorine.—**chlorination** *n*.

chlorine *n* a nonmetallic element, a yellowish-green poisonous gas used in bleaches, disinfectants, and in industry.

chloro-, chlor- *prefix* green.

chlorofluorocarbon *n* any of various compounds containing carbon, chlorine, fluorine and hydrogen, used in refrigerants, aerosol propellants, etc, and thought to be harmful to the earth's atmosphere.

chloroform *n* a colourless volatile liquid formerly used as an anaesthetic.

chlorophyll, chlorophyl *n* the green photosynthetic colouring matter in plants.

chlorosis *n* a disease affecting young women, characterized by anaemia.—**chlorotic** *adj*.

chock *n* a block of wood or other material used as a wedge. * *vt* to secure with a chock.

chock-a-block *adj* completely full.—*also* **chock-full.**

chocolate *n* a powder or edible solid made of the roasted, pounded cacao bean; a drink made by dissolving this powder in boiling water or milk; a sweet with a centre and chocolate coating. * *adj* flavoured or coated with chocolate; dark reddish brown.—**chocolaty** *adj*.

chocolate-box *adj* sweetly pretty; oversentimental.

choice *n* act of choosing; the power to choose; selection; alternative; a thing chosen; preference; the best part. * *adj* of picked quality, specially good.—**choicely** *adv*.—**choiceness** *n*.

choir *n* an organized group of singers, esp of a church; the part of a church before the altar used by them.

choirboy *n* one of the young trebles in a choir.

choirmaster *n* one who trains and conducts the singers in a choir.

choke *vti* to stop the breath of, stifle; to throttle; to suffocate; to block (up); to check, esp emotion, to choke back or up. * *n* a fit of choking; a choking sound; a valve that controls the flow of air in a carburettor.

chokebore *n* a shotgun with a bore narrowing towards the muzzle.

chokedamp *n* carbonic acid gas generated in mines.

choker *n* a necklace worn tight round the neck; a high collar.

choler *n* bile; irascibility, anger.

cholera *n* a severe, infectious intestinal disease.

choleric *adj* irascible; tending to anger; angry.

cholesterol, cholesterin *n* a substance found in animal tissues, blood and animal fats, thought to be a cause of hardening of the arteries.

chomp *vt* to chew noisily and with relish, champ.

chondr-, chondri-, chondro- *prefix* cartilage.

chondrify *vti* (**chondrifying, chondrified**) to change into cartilage.—**chondrification** *n*.

choose *vb* (**choosing, chose,** *pp* **chosen**) *vt* to select (one thing) rather than another. * *vi* to decide, to think fit.—**chooser** *n*.

choosy *adj* (**choosier, choosiest**) (*inf*) cautious; fussy, particular.—**choosily** *adv*.—**choosiness** *n*.

chop[1] *vt* (**chopping, chopped**) to cut by striking; to cut into pieces. * *n* a cut of meat and bone from the rib, loin, or shoulder; a downward blow or motion; **get the chop** (*sl*) to be dismissed from one's employment; to be killed.

chop[2] *n* a mark or brand denoting quality.

chopfallen *see* **chapfallen.**

chopper *n* a tool for chopping; a cleaver; a small hand axe; (*sl*) a helicopter.

choppy *adj* (**choppier, choppiest**) (*sea*) running in rough, irregular waves; jerky.—**choppily** *adv*.—**choppiness** *n*.

chops *npl* the jaws or cheeks.

chopsticks *n* a pair of wooden or plastic sticks used in Asian countries to eat with.

chop suey *n* a Chinese-American dish consisting of stir-fried vegetables and meat or seafood served with rice.

choral[1] *adj* relating to, sung by, or written for, a choir or chorus.—**chorally** *adv*.

chorale, choral[2] *n* a slow hymn or psalm sung to a traditional or composed melody, esp by a choir.

chord[1] *n* (*mus*) three or more notes played simultaneously.—**chordal** *adj*.

chord[2] *n* a straight line joining the ends of an arc; a feeling of sympathy, recognition or remembering (*strike a chord*).

chore *n* a piece of housework; a regular or tedious task.

chorea *n* a neurological disorder characterized by jerky involuntary movements, esp of the arms, legs and face.—**choreal, choreic** *adj*.

choreograph *vt* to devise the steps for a ballet, dance, etc.

choreography *n* the art of devising ballets or dances.—**choreographer** *n*.—**choreographic** *adj*.—**choreographically** *adv*.

choric *adj* of or for a Greek chorus.

chorion *n* the exterior membrane of a seed or foetus.—**chorionic, chorial** *adj*.

chorister *n* a member of a choir.

chorizo *n* (*pl* **chorizos**) a spicy pork sausage.

chorography *n* the geographical description of a region.—**chorographer** *n*.—**chorographic, chorographical** *adj*.

choroid *n* the vascular membrane of the retina.

chorology *n* the study of the geographical distribution of plants and animals.

chortle *vi* to chuckle exultantly.—*also n*.

chorus *n* (*pl* **choruses**) a group of singers and dancers in the background to a play, musical, etc; a group of singers, a choir; music sung by a chorus; a refrain; an utterance by many at once. * *vt* (**chorusing, chorused**) to sing, speak or shout in chorus.

chorus girl *n* one who sings and dances in the chorus of a musical.—**chorus boy** *nm*.

chose, chosen *see* **choose.**

chough *n* a red-legged crow.

chow *n* a breed of thick-coated dog, originally from China (—*also* **chow chow**); (*sl*) food.

chowder *n* a thick clam and potato soup.

chow mein *n* a Chinese-American dish of fried, crispy noodles with meat and vegetables.

chrestomathy *n* (*pl* **chrestomathies**) a collection of extracts for learning a foreign language; a phrasebook; an anthology.

chrism *n* consecrated oil.—**chrismal** *adj*.

chrisom *n* an infant's baptismal robe.

Christ *n* Jesus of Nazareth, regarded by Christians as the Messiah.

christen *vt* to enter the Christian Church by baptism; to give a name to; (*inf*) to use for the first time.—**christener** *n*.—**christening** *n*.

Christendom *n* all Christians, or Christian countries regarded as a whole.

Christian *n* a person who believes in Christianity. * *adj* relating to, believing in, or based on the doctrines of Christianity; kind, gentle, humane.

Christian Era *n* the present era reckoned from the birth of Christ.

Christianity *n* the religion based on the teachings of Christ.

Christianize *vt* to convert to Christianity.—**Christianization** *n*.—**Christianizer** *n*.

Christianly *adj* like or befitting a Christian.

Christian name *n* a name given when one is christened; (*loosely*) any forename.

Christian Science *n* a system of religion founded by Mary Baker Eddy, 1866, in which sin and disease are regarded as mental errors to be overcome by faith.—**Christian Scientist** *n*.

Christlike *adj* resembling Christ.

Christmas *n* (*pl* **Christmases**) an annual festival (25 December) in memory of the birth of Christ.

Christmas card *n* a greeting card, usu decorative, sent at Christmas.

Christmas Eve *n* the day and esp the night before Christmas Day.

Christmas rose *n* the black hellebore.

Christmastide *n* Christmas Eve (24 December) to Epiphany (6 January).

Christmas tree *n* an evergreen tree decorated at Christmas; an imitation tree.

Christology *n* the branch of theology that studies Christ's nature.—**Christological** *adj*.—**Christologist** *n*.

chrom-, chromo- *prefix* colour.

chromate *n* a salt or ester of chromic acid.

chromatic *adj* of or in colour; (*mus*) using tones outside the key in which the passage is written.—**chromatically** *adv*.—**chromaticism** *n*.

chromatics *n* (*sing*) the science of colour.

chromatic scale *n* a twelve-note musical scale that proceeds by semitones.

chromatin *n* a protoplasmic substance in a cell nucleus forming chromosomes.—**chromatinic** *adj*.

chromatography *n* the separation of the components of a substance by passing it over or through a substance that absorbs selectively.—**chromatograph** n.—**chromatographer** *n*.—**chromatographic** *adj*.—**chromatographically** *adv*.

chrome *n* chromium; a chromium pigment; something plated with an alloy of chromium.

-chrome *adj suffix* coloured. * *n suffix* colour, pigment.

chrome green *n* a green pigment made from a compound of chromium.

chrome red *n* a red pigment made from a compound of chromium.

chrome yellow *n* a yellow pigment made from a compound of chromium.

chromic *adj* of chromium.

chromium *n* a hard metallic element used in making steel alloys and electroplating to give a tough surface.

chromo-, chrom- *prefix* colour.

chromogen *n* the colouring matter of plants.—**chromogenic** *adj*.

chromolithography *n* the art of printing in colours from stone.—**chromolithograph** *n*.—**chromolithographer** *n*.—**chromolithographic** *adj*.

chromosome *n* any of the microscopic rod-shaped bodies bearing genes.

chromosphere *n* the rose-coloured outer gaseous envelope of the sun above the photosphere.—**chromospheric** *adj*.

chron-, chrono- *prefix* time.

chronic *adj* (*disease*) long-lasting; regular; habitual;.—**chronically** *adv*.—**chronicity** *n*.

chronicle *n* a record of events in chronological order; an account; a history. * *vt* to record in a chronicle.—**chronicler** *n*.

chronogram *n* an inscription which includes in it the date of some event.—**chronogrammatic, chronogrammatical** *adj*.

chronograph *n* an instrument for recording minute intervals of time; a stopwatch.—**chronographer** *n*.—**chronographic** *adj*.

chronological, chronologic *adj* arranged in order of occurrence.—**chronologically** *adv*.

chronology *n* (*pl* **chronologies**) the determination of the order of events, eg in history; the arrangement of events in order of occurrence; a table of events listed in order of occurrence.—**chronologist** *n*.

chronometer *n* a very accurate instrument for measuring time exactly.

chronometry *n* the scientific measurement of time.—**chronometric, chronometrical** *adj*.—**chronometrically** *adv*.

chronoscope *n* an instrument for measuring by electricity the velocity of a projectile.—**chronoscopic** *adj*.

chrys-, chryso- *prefix* gold.

chrysalis *n* (*pl* **chrysalises, chrysalides**) the pupa of a moth or butterfly, enclosed in a cocoon.
chrysanthemum *n* a plant with a brightly coloured flower head.
chryselephantine *adj* composed (or overlaid) partly with gold and partly with ivory.
chrysoberyl *n* a yellowish-green gem.
chrysolite *n* a green-coloured and sometimes transparent gem.—**chrysolitic** *adj*.
chrysoprase *n* a variety of chalcedony of an apple-green colour.
chthonian, chthonic *adj* (*Greek gods*) of the underworld, as opposed to Olympian.
chub *n* (*pl* **chub, chubs**) a small freshwater fish of the carp family.
chubby *adj* (**chubbier, chubbiest**) plump.—**chubbiness** *n*.
chuck[1] *vt* to throw, to toss; (*inf*) to stop, to give up. * *n* (*usu with* **the**) a giving up; dismissal.
chuck[2] *n* a device on a lathe, etc, that holds the work or drill; a cut of beef from the neck to the ribs.
chuck[3] *vt* to make a noise like a hen calling to her chickens. * *n* a hen's call.
chuck[4] *n* (*dial*) darling.
chuckle *vt* to laugh softly; to gloat. * *n* a quiet laugh.—**chuckler** *n*.
chuck wagon *n* a provision cart.
chuff[1] *n* a surly fellow, a boor.
chuff[2] *vi* to make a puffing sound, as a steam engine. * *n* such a sound.
chug *n* the explosive sound of a car exhaust, etc. * *vi* (**chugging, chugged**) to make such a sound.
chukker, chukka *n* each period of play in a game of polo.
chum *n* (*inf*) a close friend, esp of the same sex. * *vi* (**chumming, chummed**) to be friendly (with); to room together.
chummy *adj* (**chummier, chummiest**) friendly, close to.—**chummily** *adv*.—**chumminess** *n*.
chump *n* (*inf*) a stupid person; a fool.
chunk *n* a short, thick piece or lump, as wood, bread, etc.—**chunky** *adj*.
chunky *adj* (**chunkier, chunkiest**) short and thick; (*clothing*) of heavy material.—**chunkily** *adv*.—**chunkiness** *n*.
Chunnel *n* (*inf*) the Channel Tunnel linking England and France.
church *n* a building for public worship, esp Christian worship; the clerical profession; a religious service; (*with cap*) all Christians; (*with* **the**) a particular Christian denomination.
churchgoer *n* one who goes to church regularly.—**churchgoing** *adj, n*.
churchman *n* (*pl* **churchmen**) a member of the Church; a clergyman.—**churchwoman** *n* (*pl* **churchwomen**).
churchwarden *n* in the Anglican church, an elected lay representative who administers the secular matters of a parish church.
churchyard *n* the yard around a church often used as a burial ground.
churl *n* formerly one of the lowest orders of freemen; a peasant; a surly ill-bred person.
churlish *adj* surly, ill-mannered.—**churlishly** *adv*.—**churlishness** *n*.
churn *n* a large metal container for milk; a device that can be vigorously turned to make milk or cream into butter. * *vt* to agitate in a churn; to make (butter) this way; to stir violently; (*with* **out**) (*inf*) to produce quickly or one after the other or without much effort.
churr *see* **chirr**.
chute *n* an inclined trough or a passage for sending down water, logs, rubbish, etc; a fall of water, a rapid; an inclined slide for children; a slide into a swimming pool.
chutney *n* a relish of fruits, spices, and herbs.
chutzpah, chutzpa *n* shameless audacity, presumption, or gall.
chyle *n* a milk-like fluid separated from digested matter in the stomach, absorbed by the lacteal vessels and assimiliated into the blood.—**chylaceous, chylous** *adj*.
chyme *n* the pulpy mass of digested food prior to the separation of the chyle.
Ci (*symbol*) curie.
CIA *abbr* = Central Intelligence Agency.
ciao *interj* (*Italian*) used to express greeting or farewell.
ciborium *n* (*pl* **ciboria**) a covered chalice for holding the sacrament; a canopy over an altar.
cicada, cicala *n* (*pl* **cicadas, cicadae** *or* **cicalas, cicale**) a large fly-like insect with transparent wings, the male producing a loud chirp or drone.
cicatrix *n* (*pl* **cicatrices**) the scar remaining after a wound has healed; a scarlike mark.—**cicatricial** *adj*.—**cicatricose** *adj*.
cicatrize *vt* to heal a wound by inducing the skin to form a cicatrix; to mark with scars.—**cicatrization** *n*.—**cicatrizer** *n*.
cicely *n* (*pl* **cicelies**) a species of umbelliferous plants allied to chervil.
cicerone *n* (*pl* **cicerones, ciceroni**) a guide who explains the antiquities and chief features of a place.
CID *abbr* = Criminal Investigation Department.
-cide *n suffix* killing, or killer of, as in *regicide*.
cider *n* fermented apple juice as a drink.
cigar *n* a compact roll of tobacco leaf for smoking.
cigarette *n* shredded tobacco rolled in fine paper for smoking.
cilia *npl* (*sing* **cilium**) the hair of the eyelids; long minute hair-like appendages on the margins of vegetable bodies; the minute vibrating filaments lining or covering certain organs.—**ciliated** *adj*.
cilice *n* haircloth.
Cimmerian *adj* intensely dark; gloomy; pertaining to the Cimmerii, a legendary people mentioned by Homer as living in perpetual darkness.
C in C *abbr* = Commander in Chief.
cinch *n* (*sl*) a firm hold, an easy job; a saddle band or girth.
cinchona *n* a South American tree that yields quinine and other drugs.
cinchonism *n* a medical condition characterized by buzzing in the ears, deafness, etc, caused by the excessive use of quinine.
cincture *n* a belt or girdle worn round the waist; a raised or carved ring at the bottom and top of a pillar.
cinder *n* a tiny piece of partly burned wood, etc; (*pl*) ashes from wood or coal.—**cindery** *adj*.
cine- *prefix* motion picture or cinema, as in *cinecamera, cinefilm*.
cineast, cineaste *n* a film enthusiast.
cinema *n* a place where motion pictures are shown; film as an industry or art form.—**cinematic** *adj*.—**cinematically** *adv*.
cinematography *n* the art or science of motion-picture photography.—**cinematographic** *adj*.—**cinematographer** *n*.
cinéma vérité *n* cinema photography of real-life scenes and situations, etc, to create realism.
cineraria *n* a genus of garden plants of the aster family with bright flowers.
cinerarium *n* (*pl* **cineraria**) a place for keeping a person's ashes after cremation.
cinerary *adj* of, pertaining to, or containing, ashes.
cinereous *adj* ash-grey.
cingulum *n* (*pl* **cingula**) belt.
cinnabar *n* red sulphide of mercury. * *adj* vermilion.
cinnamon *n* a tree of the laurel family; its aromatic edible bark; a spice made from this; a yellowish-brown colour. * *adj* yellowish brown.—**cinnamonic, cinamic** *adj*.
cinnamon stone *n* a variety of the garnet.
cinque *n* a five at dice or cards.
cinquecento *n* the 16th century and Italian fine art of that period. * *adj* designed or executed in such Italian style.
cinquefoil *n* a plant with leaves divided into five lobes; (*archit*) ornamentation resembling five leaves.
cipher *n* the numeral 0, zero; any single Arabic numeral; a thing or person of no importance, a nonentity; a method of secret writing. * *vt* to convert (a message) into cipher.—*also* **cypher**.
circa *prep* about.
circadian *adj* of or pertaining to biological processes that occur in 24-hour cycles.
circinate *adj* (*leaf*) rolled up with the tip inwards.
circle *n* a perfectly round plane figure; the line enclosing it; anything

(built) in the form of a circle; the curved seating area above the stalls in a theatre; a group, set or class (of people); extent, scope, as of influence. * *vti* to encompass; to move in a circle; to revolve (round); to draw a circle round.—**circler** *n*.

circlet *n* a small circle; a circular band or hoop.

circuit *n* a distance round; a route or course; an area so enclosed; the path of an electric current; a visit to a particular area by a judge to hold courts; the area itself; a chain or association, eg of cinemas controlled by one management; sporting events attended regularly by the same competitors and at the same venues; a motor-racing track.—**circuital** *adj*.

circuit breaker *n* a switch that interrupts an electric circuit under certain abnormal conditions.

circuitous *adj* roundabout, indirect.—**circuitously** *adv*.

circuitry *n* (*pl* **circuitries**) the plan of an electric circuit; the components of a circuit.

circular *adj* shaped like a circle, round; (*argument*) using as evidence the conclusion which it is seeking to prove; moving round a circle. * *n* an advertisement, etc addressed to a number of people.—**circularity, circularness** *n*.

circularize *vt* to make circular; to send circulars to; to canvass.—**circularization** *n*.—**circularizer** *n*.

circular saw *n* a power-driven saw with a circular blade.

circulate *vti* to pass from hand to hand or place to place; to spread or be spread about; to move round, finishing at the starting point.—**circulative** *adj*.—**circulator** *n*.—**circulatory** *adj*.

circulating decimal *n* the recurring decimal.

circulating library *n* a lending library.

circulation *n* the act of circulating; a movement to and fro; the regular cycle of blood flow in the body; the number of copies sold of a newspaper, etc; currency.

circum- *prefix* round, about.

circumambient *adj* enclosing, or being surrounded, on all sides.—**circumambience, cicumambiency** *n*.

circumcise *vt* to cut off the foreskin of (a male) or the clitoris of (a female), esp as a religious rite.

circumcision *n* the act of circumcising; spiritual purification.

circumference *n* the line bounding a circle, a ball, etc; the length of this line.—**circumferential** *adj*.

circumflex *n* an accent (^) placed over a vowel to indicate contraction, length, etc.—**circumflexion** *n*.

circumfuse *vt* to pour or spread around; to bathe (with).—**circumfusion** *n*.

circumlocution *n* the use of more words than are necessary; a roundabout or evasive expression.—**circumlocutory** *adj*.

circumnavigate *vt* to sail or fly completely round (the world).—**circumnavigable** *adj*.—**circumnavigation** *n*.—**circumnavigator** *n*.

circumnutate *vi* (*bot*) to turn successively to all points of the compass.—**circumnutation** *n*.

circumpolar *adj* near the north or south pole; (*astron*) always above the horizon.

circumscribe *vt* to draw a line around; to enclose; to limit or restrict.—**circumscription** *n*.

circumspect *adj* prudent, cautious; careful; discreet.—**circumspection** *n*.—**circumspective** *adj*.

circumstance *n* an occurrence, an incident; a detail; ceremony; (*pl*) a state of affairs; condition in life.

circumstantial *adj* detailed; incidental; (*law*) strongly inferred from direct evidence.—**circumstantially** *adv*.

circumstantiality *n* (*pl* **circumstantialities**) the state of being circumstantial; fullness of detail.

circumstantiate *vt* to describe or verify in detail.—**circumstantiation** *n*.

circumvallate *vt* to surround with a rampart.—**circumvallation** *n*.

circumvent *vt* to evade, bypass; to outwit.—**circumventer, circumventor** *n*.—**circumvention** *n*.

circumvolution *n* the act of rolling round; the state of being rolled round; a coil.—**circumvolutory** *adj*.

circus *n* (*pl* **circuses**) a large arena for the exhibition of games, feats of horsemanship, etc; a travelling show of acrobats, clowns, etc; a company of people travelling round giving displays; houses built in a circle; an open space in a town where streets meet; (*inf*) noise, disturbance; loud, extravagant behaviour.

cirque *n* a natural amphitheatre or ring.

cirrhosis *n* a hardened condition of the tissues of an organ, esp the liver.—**cirrhosed** *adj*.—**cirrhotic** *adj*.

cirriped, cirripede *adj* having feet resembling cirri; pertaining to the Cirripedia, a subclass of parasitic crustaceans, as the barnacles and acorn shells.

cirrocumulus *n* (*pl* **cirrocumuli**) a cloud broken up into small fleecy masses.

cirrostratus *n* (*pl* **cirrostrati**) a horizontal or slightly inclined light fleecy cloud.

cirrouse, cirrous *adj* terminating in a curl, tuft, or tendril.

cirrus *n* (*pl* **cirri**) thin, wispy clouds.

CIS *abbr* = Commonwealth of Independent States: a federation of former Soviet republics, such as Russia, Ukraine, who wish to retain voluntary links with one another.

cis- *prefix* on this side of.

cisalpine *adj* this side of the Alps with regard to Rome, south of the Alps.

cisco *n* (*pl* **ciscoes, ciscos**) the Canadian lake herring.

cismontane *adj* on this (northern) side of the Alps.

cist *n* a prehistoric stone tomb consisting of two rows of stone and covered with a flat stone slab; a box or chest.

Cistercian *n* one of a Benedictine order of monks, founded 1098 at Citeaux, France. * *adj* pertaining to the Cistercians.

cistern *n* a tank or reservoir for storing water, esp in a toilet.

citadel *n* a fortress in or near a city.

citation *n* a quotation; a source or authority cited; a commendation, esp for bravery; (*law*) a summons to appear.

cite *vt* to summon officially to appear in court; to quote; to give as an example or authority.—**citable, citeable** *adj*.

cithara *n* an ancient lyre.—*also* **kithara.**

citify *vt* (**citifying, citifed**) to assume city ways, habits, dress.

citizen *n* a member of a city, state or nation.—**citizenship** *n*.

citizenry *n* (*pl* **citizenries**) citizens collectively.

citizen's band *n* a shortwave band reserved for private radio communication.

citrate *n* a salt or ester of citric acid.

citric *adj* of or obtained from citrus fruits or citric acid.

citric acid *n* a sour acid found in fruits and used as a flavouring.

citrine *adj* lemon-coloured.

citron *n* a large fruit-like a lemon; the tree bearing it; a yellow-green colour.

citronella *n* a fragrant Asian grass which yields an aromatic oil used in soap, perfumes, and in insect repellents.

citrus *n* (*pl* **citruses**) a genus of trees including the lemon, orange, etc; the fruit of these trees. * *adj* of or relating to citrus trees or shrubs or their fruit.

cittern *n* a medieval stringed instrument.

city *n* (*pl* **cities**) an important or cathedral town; a town created a city by charter; the people of a city; business circles, esp financial services.—*also adj*.

city editor *n* the editor in charge of local news.

city fathers *npl* the people who take part in running a city.

city hall *n* the townhall; the government of a city or its officers; (*inf*) bureaucracy.

city slicker *n* (*inf*) one who adopts city ways; a suave, unreliable person.

city-state *n* (*hist*) a sovereign state comprising a city and its surrounding territory.

civet *n* a cat-like animal of central Africa and South Asia; the pungent substance secreted by this animal used in perfumery.

civic *adj* of a city, citizen or citizenship. * *npl* the principles of good citizenship; the study of citizenship.—**civically** *adv*.
civil *adj* of citizens or the state; not military or ecclesiastical; polite, obliging; (*law*) relating to crimes other than criminal ones or to private rights.—**civilly** *adv*.
civil defence *n* the organization of civilians against enemy attack.
civil disobedience *n* refusal to pay taxes, etc, as part of a political campaign; nonviolent protest to achieve an end.
civil engineer *n* an engineer who designs and constructs roads, bridges, etc.
civilian *n* a person who is not a member of the armed forces.
civility *n* (*pl* **civilities**) good manners, politeness.
civil rights *npl* the personal rights of a citizen.
civil service *n* those employed in the service of a state apart from the military.—**civil servant** *n*.
civil war *n* a war between citizens of the same state or country.
civilization *n* the state of being civilized; the process of civilizing; an advanced stage of social culture; moral and cultural refinement.
civilize *vt* to bring out from barbarism; to educate in arts and refinements.—**civilizer** *n*.
civilized *adj* no longer in a savage or uncultured state.
civvy *adj* (*sl*) civilian. * *n* (*pl* **civvies**) (*sl*) civilian clothes.
Cl (*chem symbol*) = chlorine.
cl *abbr* = centilitre(s).
clack *vt* to make a sudden, sharp sound; to chatter rapidly and continuously. * *n* a sudden, sharp sound as of wood striking wood.
clad[1] *see* **clothe**.
clad[2] *vt* (**cladding, clad**) to bond one material to another for protection (*iron cladding*).—**cladding** *n*.
claim *vt* to demand as a right; to call for; to require; to profess (to have); to assert; to declare to be true. * *n* the act of claiming; a title, right to something; a thing claimed, esp a piece of land for mining.—**claimable** *adj*.—**claimer** *n*.
claimant *n* a person who makes a claim.
clairvoyance *n* the power of seeing things not present to the senses, second sight.
clairvoyant *n* a person with the gift of clairvoyance. * *adj* possessing clairvoyance; having remarkable insight.
clam *n* an edible marine bivalve mollusc. * *vb* (**clamming, clammed**) *vt* to gather clams. * *vi* (*with* **up**) (*inf*) to remain silent, refuse to talk.
clamant *adj* insistent, crying; clamorous.
clambake *n* clams baked with seaweed; a picnic at which baked clams form the chief dish.
clamber *vi* to climb with difficulty, using the hands as well as the feet. * *n* a climb performed in this way.—**clamberer** *n*.
clammy *adj* (**clammier, clammiest**) damp and sticky.—**clammily** *adv*.—**clamminess** *n*.
clamour, clamor *n* a loud confused noise; an uproar; an insistent demand. * *vi* to demand loudly; to make an uproar.—**clamorous** *adj*.
clamp *n* a device for gripping objects tightly together. * *vt* to grip with a clamp; to attach firmly. * *vi* (*with* **down**) to put a stop to forcefully. * *vt* to attach a wheelclamp to a wheel to immobilize an illegally parked car.
clan *n* a group of people with a common ancestor, under a single chief; people with the same surname; a party or clique.
clandestine *adj* done secretly; surreptitious; sly.—**clandestinely** *adv*.
clang *n* a loud metallic sound. * *vti* to make or cause to make a clang.
clangour, clangor *n* a sharp clang; repeated clanging.—**clangourous, clangorous** *adj*.—**clangourously, clangorously** *adv*.
clank *n* a short, harsh metallic sound. * *vt* to make or cause to make a clank.
clannish *adj* closely united and excluding others.—**clannishly** *adv*.
clansman *n* (*pl* **clansmen**) a member of a clan.—**clanswoman** *nf* (*pl* **clanswomen**).
clap[1] *vti* (**clapping, clapped**) to strike (the hands) together sharply; to applaud in this way; to slap; to flap (wings) loudly; to put or place suddenly or vigorously. * *n* the sound of hands clapping; a sudden sharp noise; a sudden sharp slap.
clap[2] *n* (*vulg*) venereal disease, gonorrhoea.
clapboard *n* a narrow, thin board used for building by overlapping each piece.
clapper *n* the tongue of a bell.
claptrap *n* flashy display, empty words.
claque *n* an organized body of people paid to applaud or express disapproval at theatres; interested admirers.
clarence *n* a closed four-wheeled carriage with a curved front.
claret *n* a dry red wine of Bordeaux in France; its purple-red colour.
claret cup *n* a summer drink composed of iced claret, lemon, brandy, etc.
clarify *vti* (**clarifying, clarified**) to make or become clear or intelligible; to free or become free from impurities.—**clarification** *n*.—**clarifier** *n*.
clarinet *n* an orchestral woodwind instrument.—**clarinettist** *n*.
clarion *n* a shrill trumpet formerly used in war; a rousing sound. * *adj* ringing.
clarity *n* clearness.
clarkia *n* a bright-flowered garden plant.
clary *n* (*pl* **claries**) meadow and wild sage.
clash *n* a loud noise of striking weapons, cymbals, etc; a contradiction, disagreement; a collision. * *vti* to make or cause to make a clash by striking together; to conflict; to collide; to be at variance (with); (*colours*) to be unsuitable or not pleasing when put together.—**clasher** *n*.
clasp *n* a hold, an embrace; a catch or buckle. * *vt* to grasp firmly, to embrace; to fasten with a clasp.—**clasper** *n*.
clasp knife *n* a knife with a blade or blades that shut into the handle.
class *n* a division, a group; a kind; a set of students who are taught together; a grade of merit or quality; standing in society, rank; (*inf*) high quality, excellence; style. * *vt* to put into a class.
class-conscious *adj* aware of and taking part in the conflict between labouring and other classes.—**class-consciousness** *n*.
classic *adj* of the highest class or rank, esp in literature; of the best Greek and Roman writers; of music conforming to certain standards of form, complexity, etc; traditional; authoritative. * *n* a work of literature, art, cinema, etc of the highest excellence; a definitive work of art.
classical *adj* influenced by, of or relating to ancient Roman and Greek art, literature and culture; traditional; serious; refined.—**classicality** *n*.—**classically** *adv*.
classicism, classicalism *n* the use of ancient Roman and Greek style.
classicist, classicalist *n* a scholar of the classics.—**classicistic** *adj*.
classics *n* (*with* **the**) the study of ancient Greek and Roman literature; any literature considered to be a model of its type.
classification *n* the organization of knowledge into categories; a category or a division of a category into which knowledge or information has been put.—**classificational** *adj*.—**classificatory** *adj*.
classified *adj* arranged by a system of classification; (*information*) secret and restricted to a select few; (*advertisements*) grouped according to type.
classify *vt* (**classifying, classified**) to arrange in classes, to categorize; to restrict for security reasons.—**classifiable** *adj*.—**classifier** *n*.
classless *adj* not divided into classes; not belonging to a particular class.—**classlessness** *n*.
classmate *n* a member of the same class in a school, college, etc.
classroom *n* a room where pupils or students are taught.
classy *adj* (**classier, classiest**) (*sl*) stylish; elegant.—**classily** *adv*.—**classiness** *n*.
clastic *adj* (*geol*) composed of fragments.
clatter *n* a rattling noise; noisy talk. * *vti* to make or cause a clatter.—**clattery** *adj*.
clause *n* a single article or stipulation in a treaty, law, contract, etc; (*gram*) a short sentence; a division of a sentence.—**clausal** *adj*.
claustral *adj* of or pertaining to a cloister, cloistral.
claustrophobia *n* a morbid fear of confined spaces.—**claustrophobe** *n*.—**claustrophobic** *adj*.—**claustrophobically** *adv*.
clavate, claviform *adj* club-shaped.
clavichord *n* a medieval keyboard instrument, the predecessor of the piano.—**clavichordist** *n*.

clavicle *n* one of the two bones that connect the shoulder blades with the breast bone, the collarbone.—**clavicular** *adj*.
clavier *n* a musical instrument with a keyboard; the keyboard.
claw *n* the sharp hooked nail of an animal or bird; the pointed end or pincer of a crab, etc; a claw-like thing. * *vti* to seize or tear with claws or nails; to clutch or scratch (at); (*with* **back**) to recover (something) with difficulty; to get back money by taxing; to take back part of what was handed out, esp by taxation.—**clawer** *n*.
claw hammer *n* a hammer with a claw for drawing out nails.
clay *n* a sticky ductile earthy material.—**clayey** *adj*.
claymore *n* a large two-edged sword formerly used in Scotland.
clay pigeon *n* a brittle clay disc or other object propelled into the air as a shooting target; someone in a vulnerable position.
clean *adj* free from dirt or impurities; unsoiled; morally or ceremonially pure; complete, decisive; free of errors; free of suggestive language; not carrying firearms or drugs. * *adv* entirely; outright; neatly. * *vti* to remove dirt from; (*with* **out**) to remove dirt out of; (*sl*) to take away everything from someone, esp money; (*with* **up**) to leave clean; (*sl*) to get rid of corrupt people, a system, etc; to gain a large profit.—**cleanable** *adj*.—**cleanness** *n*.
clean-cut *adj* sharply defined, clear-cut; well-shaped.
cleaner *n* a substance or device used for cleaning; a person employed to clean; (*pl*) a dry cleaner.
clean-limbed *adj* having well-proportioned or shapely limbs.
cleanly *adj* (**cleanlier, cleanliest**) clean in habits or person; pure; neat. * *adv* in a clean manner.—**cleanliness** *n*.
cleanse *vt* to make clean or pure.—**cleansable** *adj*.
cleanser *n* something that cleanses, esp a detergent, face cream, etc.
clear *adj* bright, not dim; transparent; without blemish; easily seen or heard; unimpeded, open; free from clouds; quit (of); plain, distinct, obvious; keen, discerning; positive, sure; without debt. * *adv* plainly; completely; apart from. * *vti* to make or become clear; to rid (of), remove; to free from suspicion, vindicate; to disentangle; to pass by or over without touching; to make as a profit; (*with* **off**) (*inf*) to depart; (*with* **up**) to explain; to tidy up; (*weather*) to become fair.—**clearness** *n*.
clearance *n* the act of clearing; permission, authority to proceed; the space between two objects in motion.
clear-cut *adj* having a sharp, clearly defined outline, as if chiselled; straightforward and open.
clear-headed *adj* showing sense, alertness, judgment.—**clear-headedly** *adv*.—**clear-headedness** *n*.
clearing *n* a tract of land cleared of trees, etc for cultivation.
clearing bank *n* a bank that uses a clearing house to exchange cheques and credits with other banks.
clearing house *n* an office where cheques are sorted and exchanged by the clearing banks; a central agency for the collection, classification and distribution of information.
clearly *adv* in a clear manner; evidently.
clear-sighted *adj* discerning, objective.
clearstory *see* **clerestory**.
cleat *n* a wedge; a strip of wood nailed crossways to a footing, etc; a projection for making ropes fast to.
cleavage *n* the way a thing splits; divergence; the hollow between the breasts.
cleave[1] *vti* (**cleaving, cleft, cleaved** *or* **clove,** *pp* **cleft, cleaved** *or* **cloven**) to divide by a blow; split; to sever.—**cleavable** *adj*.
cleave[2] *vi* (**cleaved, clave**) to be faithful to; to stick.
cleaver *n* a butcher's heavy chopper.
cleavers *n* goose-grass.
cleek *n* an iron-headed golf club with a narrow straight face; (*Scot*) a large hook or crook.
clef *n* a sign on a music stave that indicates the pitch of the notes.
cleft *n* a fissure or crack.
cleft palate *n* a congenital fissure of the hard palate in the roof of the mouth.
cleistogamy *n* (bot) self-fertilization without opening of the flower.—**cleistogamous, cleistogamic** *adj*.
clematis *n* a climbing plant with large colourful flowers.
clemency *n* (*pl* **clemencies**) mercy, leniency; mildness, esp of weather.
clement *adj* merciful, gentle; (*weather*) mild.
clench *vt* (*teeth, fist*) to close tightly; to grasp. * *n* a firm grip.
clerestory *n* (*pl* **clerestories**) the upper story, with windows, of the nave of a church.—*also* **clearstory**.—**clerestoried, clearstoried** *adj*.
clergy *n* (*pl* **clergies**) ministers of the Christian church collectively.
clergyman *n* (*pl* **clergymen**) a member of the clergy.
cleric *n* a member of the clergy.
clerical *adj* of or relating to the clergy or a clergyman; of or relating to a clerk or a clerk's work.—**clerically** *adv*.
clerical collar *n* a narrow stiff white collar buttoned at the back and worn by the clergy.—*also* **dog collar**.
clericalism *n* clerical influence, esp of an undue kind.
clerihew *n* a short nonsensical or satirical poem, usu in four lines of varying length, eg Sir Christopher Wren / Said, "I'm going to dine with some men. / If anyone calls, / Say I'm designing St Paul's."
clerk *n* an office worker who types, keeps files, etc; a layman with minor duties in a church; a public official who keeps the records of a court, town, etc.—**clerkdom** *n*.—**clerkship** *n*.
clerkly *adj* (**clerklier, clerkliest**) pertaining to a clerk, or to penmanship. * *adv* in a scholarly manner.
clever *adj* able; intelligent; ingenious; skilful, adroit.—**cleverly** *adv*.—**cleverness** *n*.
clew *n* a ball of thread; the corner of a sail to which a sheet is attached. * *vt* to truss up (sails) to the yard of a ship.
cliché *n* a hackneyed phrase; something that has become commonplace.—**cliché'd, clichéd** *adj*.
click *n* a slight, sharp sound. * *vi* to make such a sound; (*inf*) to establish immediate friendly relations with; to succeed; (*inf*) to become plain or evident; to fall into place.—**clicker** *n*.
client *n* a person who employs another professionally; a customer.—**cliental** *adj*.
clientele *n* clients, customers.
cliff *n* a high steep rock face.
cliffhanger *n* the perilous situation at the climax of each episode of a serialized film or book; any dramatic or suspenseful situation.—**cliffhanging** *adj*.
climacteric *n* a critical period, a turning point, esp in the life of an individual; the male menopause. * *adj* forming a crisis (—*also* **climacterical**).
climate *n* the weather characteristics of an area; the prevailing attitude, feeling, atmosphere.—**climatic, climatical, climatal** *adj*.
climatology *n* the science of climates.—**climatologic, climatological** *adj*.—**climatologist** *n*.
climax *n* the highest point; a culmination; sexual orgasm; the highlight or most interesting part of a story, drama or music. * *vti* to reach, or bring to a climax.—**climactic, climactical** *adj*.
climb *vti* to mount with an effort; to ascend; to rise; (*plants*) to grow upwards by clinging onto walls, fences or other plants; (*with* **down**) to descend from a higher level; to retreat from a position previously held, eg in a debate or argument; to yield. * *n* an ascent.
climber *n* a mountaineer or rock climber; a climbing plant; a socially ambitious person.
clime *n* (*poet*) a country, region, or tract.
clinch *vt* (*argument, etc*) to confirm or drive home. * *vi* (*boxing*) to grip the opponent with the arms to hinder his punching. * *n* the act of clinching; (*inf*) an embrace.
clincher *n* a decisive point in an argument.
cling *vi* (**clinging, clung**) to adhere, to be attached (to); to keep hold by embracing or entwining.—**clinger** *n*.
clingstone *n* a fruit, eg the peach, with pulp adhering to the stone.—*also adj*.
clinic *n* a place where outpatients are given medical care or advice; a place where medical specialists practise as a group; a private or

specialized hospital; the teaching of medicine by treating patients in the presence of students.

clinical *adj* of or relating to a clinic; based on medical observation; plain, simple; detached, cool, objective.—**clinically** *adv*.

clink[1] *n* a slight metallic ringing sound. * *vti* to make or cause to make such a sound.

clink[2] *n* (*sl*) prison.

clinker *n* very hard-burnt brick; a mass of partly vitrified brick; slag; a fine specimen.

clinker-built *adj* built so that the planks of a boat overlap each other like weather-boarding.

clinkstone *n* an igneous rock that emits a clinking sound when struck.

clinometer *n* an instrument for measuring the angles of slopes or the dip of rock strata; a kind of plumb level.—**clinometric, clinometrical** *adj*.—**clinometry** *n*.

clinquant *adj* glittering. * *n* tinsel.

clip[1] *vt* (**clipping, clipped**) to cut or trim with scissors or shears; to punch a small hole in, esp a ticket; (*words*) to shorten or slur; (*inf*) to hit sharply. * *n* the piece clipped off; a yield of wool from sheep; an extract from a film; (*inf*) a smart blow; speed.

clip[2] *vt* (**clipping, clipped**) to hold firmly; to secure with a clip. * *n* any device that grips, clasps or hooks; a magazine for a gun; a piece of jewellery held in place by a clip.

clipboard *n* a writing board with a spring clip for holding paper.

clip joint *n* (*sl*) a place, such as nightclub or restaurant, that overcharges or defrauds its customers.

clipper *n* a fast sailing ship.

clippers *n* a hand tool, sometimes electric, for cutting hair; nail clippers.

clipping *n* an item cut from a publication, film, etc, a cutting.

clique *n* a small exclusive group, a set.—**cliquey, cliquish** *adj*.

clitoridectomy *n* (*pl* **clitoridectomies**) the excision of the clitoris.

clitoris *n* a small sensitive erectile organ of the vulva.—**clitoral** *adj*.

cloaca *n* (*pl* **cloacae**) a sewer; the cavity receiving the alimentary canal and urinary duct in birds, reptiles, many fishes, and the lower mammals.—**cloacal** *adj*.

cloak *n* a loose sleeveless outer garment; a covering; something that conceals, a pretext. * *vt* to cover as with a cloak; to conceal.

cloak-and-dagger *adj* involving intrigue or espionage; undercover.

cloakroom *n* a room where overcoats, luggage, etc, may be left.

clobber *vt* (*sl*) to hit hard and repeatedly; to defeat; to criticize severely.

cloche *n* a bell-shaped glass or plastic cover for food or outdoor plants; a woman's bell-shaped hat.

clock[1] *n* a device for measuring time; any timing device with a dial and displayed figures; a dandelion head after flowering. * *vt* to time (a race, etc) using a stopwatch or other device; (*inf*) to register a certain speed; (*sl*) to hit; (*with* **off, out**) to stop work, esp by registering the time of one's departure on a card; (with **on, in**) to start work, esp by registering the time of one's arrival on a card.

clock[2] *n* a woven or embroidered ornament on a sock or stocking.

clockwise *adv* moving in the direction of a clock's hands.—*also adj*.

clockwork *n* the mechanism of a clock or any similar mechanism with springs and gears. * *adj* mechanically regular.

clod *n* a lump of earth or clay; a stupid person.

cloddish *adj* stupid; phlegmatic.

clodhopper *n* (*inf*) a clumsy person; (*usu pl*) a large heavy shoe.

clog *n* a wooden-soled shoe. * *vt* (**clogging, clogged**) to cause a blockage in; to impede, obstruct.

cloggy *adj* (**cloggier, cloggiest**) lumpy, clogging; adhesive, sticky.—**clogginess** *n*.

cloisonné *n* enamel decoration with the colours of the pattern set in spaces partitioned off by wires. * *adj* inlaid with partitions; decorated in outline with bands of metal.

cloister *n* a roofed pillared walk, usu with one side open, in a convent, college, etc; a religious retreat. * *vt* to confine or keep apart as if in a convent.

cloistered *adj* solitary, secluded.

cloistral *adj* pertaining to or confined in a cloister; secluded; claustral.

clone *n* a group of organisms or cells derived asexually from a single ancestor; an individual grown from a single cell of its parent and genetically identical to it; (*inf*) a person or thing that resembles another. * *vt* to propagate a clone from; to make a copy of.—**clonal** *adj*.

clonus *n* (*pl* **clonuses**) (*med*) a series of convulsive spasms.—**clonic** *adj*.—**clonicity** *n*.

close[1] *adj* near; reticent, secret; nearly alike; nearly even or equal; dense, compact; cut short; sultry, airless; narrow; careful; restricted. * *adv* closely; near by. * *n* a courtyard; the entrance to a courtyard; the precincts of a cathedral.—**closely** *adv*.—**closeness** *n*.

close[2] *vt* to make closed; to stop up (an opening); to draw together; to conclude; to shut; (*with* **down**) to wind up, eg a business. * *vi* to come together; to complete; to finish. * *n* a completion, end.

close call *n* a close shave, a narrow escape.

close(d) corporation *n* a corporation in which vacancies are filled up by its members.

closed *adj* shut up; with no opening; restricted; not open to question or debate; not open to the public, exclusive.

closed book *n* something too difficult to understand; something put aside for ever.

closed circuit *n* the transmission of TV signals by cable to receivers connected in a particular circuit.

closed shop *n* a firm employing only members of a trade union.

close-fisted *adj* mean with money.

close-hauled *adj* with sails trimmed to keep as near to the wind as possible.

close(d) season *n* certain months in the year in which it is illegal to kill certain game, protected wild birds, fish, etc.

close shave, close thing *n* a close call, a narrow escape.

closet *n* a small room or a cupboard for clothes, supplies, etc; a small private room. * *vt* to enclose in a private room for a confidential talk.

close-up *n* a film or television shot taken from very close range; a close examination.

closure *n* closing; the condition of being closed; something that closes; (*parliament, etc*) a decision to end further debate and move to an immediate vote.

clot *n* a thickened mass, esp of blood; (*sl*) an idiot.* *vti* (**clotting, clotted**) to form into clots, to curdle, coagulate.

cloth *n* (*pl* **cloths**) woven, knitted or pressed fabric from which garments, etc are made; a piece of this; a tablecloth; clerical dress; (*with* **the**) the clergy.

cloth binding *n* a book binding of linen over cardboard.

clothe *vt* (**clothing, clothed** *or* **clad**) to cover with garments; to dress; to surround, endow (with).

clothes *npl* garments, apparel.

clotheshorse *n* a wooden or metal frame for drying linen, etc; a dressy person.

clothesline *n* a rope on which washing is hung to dry.

clothespin *n* a plastic, wooden or metal clip for attaching washing to a line.

clothier *n* one who manufactures or sells cloth and clothes.

clothing *n* clothes.

cloud *n* a visible mass of water vapour floating in the sky; a mass of smoke, etc; a threatening thing, a gloomy look; a multitude; **on cloud nine** (*inf*) blissfully happy; **under a cloud** suspected of wrongdoing, disgraced. * *vt* to darken or obscure; to confuse; to depress.—**cloudless** *adj*.

cloudberry *n* (*pl* **cloudberries**) a species of wild dwarf raspberry.

cloudburst *n* a sudden rainstorm.

cloud chamber *n* (*physics*) a chamber filled with vapour used for detecting the tracks of high-energy particles.

cloud-cuckoo-land *n* a realm of fantasy, imagination and impossible dreams.

cloudlet *n* a small cloud.

cloudy *adj* (**cloudier, cloudiest**) of or full of clouds; not clear; gloomy.—**cloudily** *adv*.—**cloudiness** *n*.

clout *n* a blow; (*sl*) power, influence.
clove[1] *see* **cleave.**
clove[2] *n* a segment of a bulb, as garlic.
clove[3] *n* the dried flower bud of a tropical tree, used as a spice.
clove hitch *n* a knot used to secure a rope around a spar or pole.
cloven *adj* divided; split.—*see also* **cleave.**
cloven hoof *n* the split hoof of oxen, sheep, etc; the mark of the Devil; an evil influence.
clove pink *n* the carnation.
clover *n* a low-growing plant with three leaves used as fodder; a trefoil; **in clover** (*inf*) luxury.
cloverleaf *n* connecting roads built in the shape of a clover leaf.
clown *n* a person who entertains with jokes, antics, etc, esp in a circus; a clumsy or boorish person. * *vi* to act the clown, behave comically or clumsily.—**clownish** *adj.*
cloy *vt* to sicken with too much sweetness or pleasure.—**cloyingly** *adv.*
club *n* a heavy stick used as a weapon; a stick with a head for playing golf, etc; an association of people for athletic, social, or common purposes; its premises; a suit of playing cards with black clover-like markings. * *vb* (**clubbing, clubbed**) *vt* to beat with or use as a club. * *vi* to form into a club for a common purpose.
clubbable, clubable *adj* suitable for a club, sociable.
clubfoot *n* a congenital malformation of the foot.
clubhaul *vt* (*naut*) to tack by dropping the lee anchor as soon as the wind is out of the sails, bringing the ship's head to the wind.
clubhouse *n* premises used by a club.
club moss *n* the lycopodium.
club sandwich *n* a three-layered sandwich.
cluck *n* the call of a hen. * *vi* to make such a noise.
clue *n* a guide to the solution of a mystery or problem. * *vt* (**cluing, clued**) (*with* **in, up**) to provide with helpful information.
clueless *adj* (*inf*) stupid, incompetent.
clumber *n* a breed of spaniel, a field spaniel.
clump *n* a cluster of trees; a cluster of bacteria; a lump; (*of hair*) a handful; the sound of heavy footsteps.
clumsy *adj* (**clumsier, clumsiest**) unwieldy; awkward; lacking tact, skill or grace.—**clumsily** *adv.*—**clumsiness** *n.*
clung *see* **cling.**
clunk *n* a dull metallic sound. * *vi* to make this sound.
clupeid *n* one of the genus of fishes to which the herring belongs.—*also adj.*
cluster *n* a bunch, esp of things growing or tied together; a swarm; a group. * *vti* to form or arrange in a cluster.—**clustery** *adj.*
clutch[1] *vt* to seize, to grasp tightly; to snatch at. * *n* a tight grip; a device for throwing parts of a machine into or out of action; the pedal operating this device; (*pl*) power.
clutch[2] *n* a nest of eggs; a brood of chicks.
clutter *n* a disordered mess; confusion. * *vti* to litter; to put into disorder.
Clydesdale *n* a heavy breed of carthorse.
clypeal, clypeate *adj* shield-shaped.
clypeus *n* (*pl* **clypei**) a shield-like part of an insect's head.
clyster *n* a liquid injected into the lower intestines by a syringe, an enema.
Cm (*chem symbol*) curium.
cm *abbr* = centimetre.
CNN *abbr* = Cable News Network.
CO *abbr* = Colorado; Commanding Officer.
Co (*chem symbol*) = cobalt.
Co. *abbr* = Company; County.
co- *prefix* together with, jointly.
c/o *abbr* = care of.
coach *n* a long-distance bus; a railway carriage; a large, covered four-wheeled horse-drawn carriage; a sports instructor; a tutor in a specialized subject. * *vti* to teach or train.
coach dog *n* a Dalmatian dog.
coachman *n* (*pl* **coachmen**) the driver of a horse carriage.
coaction *n* compulsion; an acting together.—**coactive** *adj.*—**coactivity** *n.*
coadjutor *n* a helper; an assistant to a bishop.—**coadjutrix** *nf.*
coadunate *adj* (*bot*) united, growing together.—**coadunation** *n.*—**coadunative** *adj.*
coagulant *n* a substance that causes coagulation.
coagulate *vti* to change from a liquid to partially solid state, to clot, curdle.—**coagulation** *n.*—**coagulative** *adj.*—**coagulator** *n.*
coagulum *n* (*pl* **coagula**) a clot (of blood); a curdled mass.
coal *n* a black mineral used for fuel; a piece of this; an ember.
coalesce *vi* to come together and form one, to merge.—**coalescence** *n.*—**coalescent** *adj.*
coalfield *n* a region yielding coal.
coalfish *n* (*pl* **coalfish, coalfishes**) the pollock.
coal gas *n* gas obtained from coal and formerly used for lighting and heating.
coalition *n* a temporary union of parties or states.—**coalitional** *adj.*—**coalitionist, coalitioner** *n.*
Coal Measure *n* that part of the Carboniferous series in which coal is found.
coal oil *n* petroleum; kerosene.
coal tar *n* a thick opaque liquid distilled from bituminous coal and from which many rich dye colours are obtained.
coaming *n* the raised wood or iron border round the outside of a ship's hatch.
coaptation *n* the adjustment or adaptation of parts to one another.
coarse *adj* rough; large in texture; rude, crude; inferior.—**coarsely** *adv.*—**coarseness** *n.*
coarse-grained *adj* having a coarse grain; ill-tempered; gross.
coarsen *vti* to make or become coarse.
coast *n* an area of land bordering the sea; the seashore. * *vi* to sail along a coast; to travel down a slope without power; to proceed with ease.—**coastal** *adj.*
coaster *n* a ship engaged in coastal trade; a tray for a decanter; a small mat for drinks; a roller coaster.
coastguard *n* an organization which monitors the coastline and provides help for ships in difficulties, prevents smuggling, etc.
coastline *n* the outline of the shore.
coat *n* a sleeved outer garment; the natural covering of an animal; a layer. * *vt* to cover with a layer or coating.
coat hanger *n* a piece of wood, wire or plastic curved to fit the shoulders for hanging a garment from a hook.
coati, coatimundi *n* a raccoon-like South American animal.
coating *n* a surface coat or layer; material for coats.
coat of arms *n* the heraldic bearings of a family, city, institution, etc.
coat of mail *n* chain mail.
coax *vt* to persuade gently; to obtain by coaxing; to make something work by patient effort.—**coaxer** *n.*—**coaxingly** *adv.*
coaxial *adj* having a common axis.
coaxial cable *n* a transmission cable having a double conductor separated by insulating material, as for a television.
cob[1] *n* a sturdy riding horse; a corn cob; a round lump of coal; a male swan.
cob[2] *n* a composition of clay and straw used for building.
cobalt *n* a metallic element; a deep blue pigment made from it.
cobalt-60 *n* a radioisotope used in radiotherapy.
cobalt-blue *n* a greenish-blue pigment derived from cobalt.
cobalt bomb *n* a radioisotope (cobalt-60) used in radiotherapy; a nuclear weapon made from a hydrogen bomb encased in cobalt.
cobber *n* (*Austral*) (*sl*) a chum, a pal.
cobble[1] *n* a cobblestone, a rounded stone used for paving. * *vt* to pave with cobblestones.
cobble[2] *vt* to repair, to make (shoes); to put together roughly or hastily.
cobbler *n* a person who mends shoes; a clumsy workman.
cobbler[2] *n* an iced drink of wine or spirits, fruit and sugar; fruit covered with a rich crust as a pudding.

cobelligerent *n* a power cooperating with another in carrying on a war.
cobnut *n* a large hazelnut.
Cobol *n* (*comput*) a high-level programming language for general business use (Common Business Orientated Language).
cobra *n* a venomous hooded snake of Africa and India.
cobweb *n* a spider's web; a flimsy thing; an entanglement.—**cobwebbed** *adj*.—**cobwebby** *adj*.
coca *n* either of two South American shrubs; their leaves, chewed as a stimulant.
Coca-Cola *n* (*trademark*) a brown-coloured carbonated soft drink flavoured with coca leaves, etc.
cocaine, cocain *n* an intoxicating addictive drug obtained from coca leaves, used in anaesthesia.
cocainism *n* a morbid state resulting from excess of cocaine.
cocainize *vt* to subject to, or render insensible by, cocaine; to treat with cocaine.—**cocainization** *n*.
cocci *see* **coccus**.
coccus *n* (*pl* **cocci**) a spherical bacterium; one of the separable carpels of a dry fruit.—**coccal, coccoid** *adj*.
coccyx *n* (*pl* **coccyges**) a small triangular bone at the base of the spine.—**coccygeal** *adj*.
cochineal *n* a scarlet dye obtained from dried insects.
cochlea *n* (*pl* **cochleae**) the spiral-shaped cavity of the inner ear.
cochleate, cochleated *adj* shell-shaped, screw-like.
cock[1] *n* the adult male of the domestic fowl; the male of other birds; a tap or valve; the hammer of a gun; a cocked position; (*vulg*) the penis. * *vt* to set erect, to stick up; to set at an angle; to bring the hammer (of a gun) to firing position; (*with* **up**) to make a complete mess of.—**cockup** *n*.
cock[2] *n* a small pile of hay.
cockade *n* a rosette worn on the hat as a badge.
cock-a-hoop *adj* elated, exultant.
Cockaigne *n* an imaginary land of plenty.—*also* **Cockayne**.
cock-a-leekie *n* soup made of chicken boiled with leeks, etc.
cockalorum *n* a young cock; a perky or self-important person.
cock-and-bull story *n* an incredible story.
cockatoo *n* (*pl* **cockatoos**) a large crested parrot.
cockatrice *n* a fabulous serpent possessing the power of killing by a glance of its eye, a basilisk.
Cockayne *see* **Cockaigne**.
cockchafer *n* a large winged beetle.
cockcrow *n* the time of dawn, early morning.
cocked hat *n* a hat with turned-up brims pointed in front and behind; **to knock into a cocked hat** to beat easily.
cockerel *n* a young cock, rooster.
cocker spaniel *n* a small breed of spaniel.
cockeyed *adj* (*inf*) having a squint; slanting; daft, absurd.
cockfight *n* an organized fight between gamecocks.
cockhorse *n* a rocking horse.
cockle[1] *n* an edible shellfish with a rounded shell.
cockle[2] *vti* to curl up, to pucker. * *n* a wrinkle, a bulge.
cockle[3] *n* a purple-flowered weed, the plant corncockle or darnel.
cockleshell *n* the shell of a cockle; a frail boat.
cockloft *n* a small upper loft; a garret.
cockney *n* (*pl* **cockneys**) a person born in the East End of London; the dialect of this area.
cockpit *n* the compartment of a small aircraft for the pilot and crew, the flight deck; an arena for cock fighting; the driver's seat in a racing car.
cockroach *n* a nocturnal beetle-like insect.
cockscomb *n* a cock's crest; a jester's cap resembling a cock's comb; a decorative plant with red or yellow flowers; a vain young fop.—*also* **coxcomb**.
cockshy *n* (*pl* **cockshies**) a thing set up to be thrown at; a throw at a cockshy.
cocksure *adj* quite certain; over-confident.
cocktail *n* an alcoholic drink containing a mixture of spirits or other liqueurs; an appetizer, usu containing shellfish, served as the first course of a meal.
cocky *adj* (**cockier, cockiest**) cheeky; conceited; arrogant.—**cockily** *adv*.—**cockiness** *n*.
coco *n* (*pl* **cocos**) the coconut palm.
cocoa *n* a powder of ground cacao seeds; a drink made from this.
cocoa bean *n* the seed of the cacao plant.
cocoa butter *n* a waxy substance derived from cocoa beans and used in perfumery, confectionery, etc.
coconut matting *n* rough matting made from the fibrous outer husks of coconuts.
coconut *n* the fruit of the coconut palm.
coconut palm *n* a tall palm tree that is grown widely in the tropics for its fruit, the coconut.
coconut shy *n* a fairground stall where coconuts are set up as targets.
cocoon *n* a silky case spun by some insect larvae for protection in the chrysalis stage; a cosy covering. * *vt* to wrap in or as in a cocoon; to protect oneself by cutting oneself off from one's surroundings.
cocotte[1] *n* a small fireproof dish for cooking and individual serving of food.
cocotte[2] *n* a promiscuous woman.
COD *abbr* = cash on delivery; collect on delivery.
cod *n* (*pl* **cod, cods**) a large edible fish of the North Atlantic.
coda *n* (*mus*) a passage at the end of a composition or section to give a greater sense of finality; a supplementary section at the end of a novel.
coddle *vt* to treat as an invalid, to pamper; to cook (eggs) in lightly boiling water.—**coddler** *n*.
code *n* a system of letters, numbers or symbols used to transmit secret messages, or to simplify communication; a systematic body of laws; a set of rules or conventions; (*comput*) a set of program instructions. * *vt* to put into code.
codeine *n* an analgesic substance.
codeword, codename *n* a word used in planning and when referring to a secret operation.
codex *n* (*pl* **codices**) a volume of ancient manuscripts.
codger *n* (*sl*) a buffer, an old man.
codicil *n* an addition to a will modifying, adjusting, or supplementing its contents.—**codicillary** *adj*.
codify *vt* (**codifying, codified**) to collect or arrange (laws, rules, regulations, etc) into a system.—**codifier** *n*.—**codification** *n*.
codlin *n* a kind of stewing apple.
codling *n* a young cod.
cod-liver oil *n* oil derived from the livers of cod and related fish which is rich in vitamins A and D.
codpiece *n* a baggy appendage once worn in front of men's breeches.
codswallop *n* (*sl*) nonsense.
co-ed *adj* (*inf*) coeducational. * *n* (*inf*) a girl attending a coeducational school or college.
coeducation *n* the teaching of students of both sexes in the same institution.—**coeducational** *adj*.—**coeducationally** *adv*.
coefficient *n* (*math*) a numerical or constant factor in an algebraic term.
coelacanth *n* a type of primitive fish that is extinct except for one species.
coelenterate *n* any of a group of aquatic creatures with a bulbous or tube-shaped body and a mouth surrounded by tentacles, such as sea anemones, jellyfish and corals.—*also adj*.
coeliac *adj* of or pertaining to the abdomen. * *n* a person with celiac disease.—*also* **celiac**.
coeliac disease *n* a chronic digestive disease of young children, causing malnutrition and diarrhoea.
coenobite *n* one of a religious order living in a convent or in community.—*also* **cenobite**.
coequal *adj* having complete equality.—**coequality** *n*.—**coequally** *adv*.
coerce *vt* to compel; to force by threats.—**coercible** *adj*.—**coercion** *n*.
coercion *n* the act of coercing; forcible compulsion; government by force.—**coercionary** *adj*.—**coercionist** *n*.

coercive *adj* having the power to force; compelling.—**coerciveness** *n.*
coessential *adj* of the same substance.—**coessentiality, coessentialness** *n.*
coeternal *adj* equally eternal.—**coeternally** *adv.*
coeval *adj* contemporaneous. * *n* a person of the same age, a contemporary.—**coevality** *n.*—**coeally** *adv.*
coexist *vi* to exist together at the same time; to live in peace together.—**coexistence** *n.*—**coexistent** *adj.*
coextensive *adj* extending over the same space or time; equally extensive.
C of E *abbr* = Church of England.
coffee *n* a drink made from the seeds of the coffee tree; the seeds, or the shrub; a light-brown colour.
coffee bean *n* the seed of the coffee plant.
coffee house, coffee bar, coffee shop *n* a refreshment house where coffee is served.
coffee mill *n* a machine for grinding coffee beans.
coffeepot *n* a pot for making coffee in.
coffee table *n* a low table for holding drinks, books, etc.
coffee table book *n* a large book for display, not reading.
coffer *n* a strong chest for holding money or valuables.
cofferdam *n* a watertight structure enclosing a submerged area which can be pumped dry to allow construction or essential repair work.
coffin *n* a box for a dead body to be buried or cremated in.
coffin bone *n* a bone inside a horse's hoof.
coffle *n* a gang of slaves, animals, etc chained together.
cog[1] *n* a tooth-like projection on the rim of a wheel.
cog[2] *vti* (**cogging, cogged**) to load dice in order to cheat. * *n* a trick.
cogent *adj* persuasive, convincing.—**cogently** *adv.*—**cogency** *n.*
cogitate *vi* to think deeply, to ponder.—**cogitation** *n.*—**cogitator** *n.*
cognac *n* a superior grape brandy distilled in France.
cognate *adj* having a common source or origin; kindred, related.—**cognation** *n.*
cognition *n* the mental act of perceiving; knowledge.—**cognitive** *adj.*
cognizable *adj* knowable; (*law*) within the cognizance of a court.
cognizance *n* judicial knowledge or notice; extent of knowledge; awareness, perception; (*her*) a distinctive crest or badge.
cognizant *adj* aware, informed (of).
cognize *vt* to have cognition of.
cognomen *n* (*pl* **cognomens, cognomina**) a surname; a nickname.
cognoscente *n*(*pl* **cognoscenti**) (*usu pl*) a connoisseur.
cogwheel *n* a wheel with a toothed rim for gearing.
cohabit *vi* to live together as husband or wife.—**cohabitant, cohabiter** *n.*—**cohabitation** *n.*
cohere *vi* to stick together; to remain united; to be consistent.
coherent *adj* cohering; capable of intelligible speech; consistent.—**coherently** *adv.*—**coherence** *n.*
cohesion *n* the act of cohering or sticking together; the force that causes this; interdependence.—**cohesive** *adj.*
cohort *n* a tenth part of a Roman legion; any group of persons banded together; a follower, a comrade.
coif *n* a close-fitting cap.
coiffeur *n* a hairdresser.—**coiffeuse** *nf.*
coiffure *n* a hairstyle.
coil[1] *vti* to wind in rings or folds; to twist into a circular or spiral shape. * *n* a coiled length of rope; a single ring of this; (*elect*) a spiral wire for the passage of current; an intrauterine contraceptive device.—**coiler** *n.*
coil[2] *n* (*arch*) tumult, disturbance.
coin *n* a piece of legally stamped metal used as money. * *vt* to invent (a word, phrase); to make into money, to mint; to make a lot of money quickly.
coinage *n* the act of coining; the issue of coins, currency; a coined word.
coincide *vi* to occupy the same portion of space; to happen at the same time; to agree exactly, to correspond.
coincidence *n* the act of coinciding; the occurrence of an event at the same time as another without apparent connection.
coincident *adj* coinciding.
coincidental *adj* happening by coincidence.—**coincidentally** *adv.*
coin-op *n* a self-service launderette, etc where the machines are operated by coins.
Cointreau (*trademark*) *n* a clear liqueur with orange flavouring.
coir *n* the prepared fibre of the husks of coconuts.
coitus, coition *n* sexual intercourse.—**coital** *adj.*
coitus interruptus *n* the interruption of coitus by withdrawal of the penis before ejaculation.
Coke *n* (*trademark*) short for Coca-Cola.
coke[1] *n* coal from which gas has been expelled. * *vt* to convert (coal) into coke.
coke[2] *n* (*sl*) cocaine.
col *n* a pass between mountain peaks; an atmospheric depression between two anticyclones.
col- *prefix* the form of *com-* before *l*.
Col. *abbr* = Colonel.
cola[1] *see* **colon**[1].
cola[2] *n* a carbonated drink flavoured with extracts from the kola nut and coca leaves.—*also* **kola.**
colander *n* a bowl with holes in the bottom for straining cooked vegetables, pasta, etc.
cola nut *see* **kola nut.**
colcannon *n* an Irish dish of boiled cabbage and potatoes mashed together and seasoned with salt, pepper, etc.
colchicum *n* meadow saffron; a narcotic made from its seeds.
colcothar *n* red peroxide of iron used as a pigment.
cold *adj* lacking heat or warmth; lacking emotion, passion or courage; unfriendly; dead; (*scent*) faint; (*sl*) unconscious. * *adv* (*inf*) without prior knowledge or preparation; completely. * *n* absence of heat; the sensation caused by this; cold weather; a virus infection of the respiratory tract.—**coldish** *adj.*—**coldly** *adv.*—**coldness** *n.*
cold-blooded *adj* having a body temperature that varies with the surrounding air or water, as reptiles and fish; without feeling; callous; ruthless; in cold blood.—**cold-bloodedness** *n.*
cold chisel *n* a tempered chisel for cutting cold iron.
cold cream *n* a creamy preparation for cleansing and softening the skin.
cold feet *n* (*inf*) fear.
cold frame *n* an unheated plant frame with a glass top for protecting seedlings, etc.
cold front *n* the forward edge of a cold air mass approaching a warmer mass.
cold-shoulder *vt* (*inf*) to treat with indifference or hostility.—**cold shoulder** *n.*
cold sore *n* one or more blisters appearing near the mouth, caused by the virus herpes simplex.
cold storage *n* storage in refrigerated areas; (*with* **in**) (*inf*) abeyance, being set aside for future use.
cold sweat *n* a cooling and moistening of the skin usually associated with fear or shock.
cold turkey *n* (*sl*) sudden withdrawal of narcotic drugs from an addict as a cure; the symptoms (eg nausea, vomiting, cramps) resulting from this withdrawal.
cold war *n* enmity between two nations characterized by military tension and political hostility.
cole *n* cabbage plants in general.
coleopteran *n* (*pl* **coleopterans, coleoptera**) any of the beetles, an order of insects having the outer pair of wings formed into hard sheathes for the inner pair.—**coleopterous** *adj.*
coleslaw *n* raw shredded cabbage, carrots, onions in a dressing, used as a salad.
coleus *n* (*pl* **coleuses**) a plant cultivated for its variegated foliage.
colic *n* acute spasmodic pain in the abdomen.—**colicky** *adj.*
coliseum *n* a large building, such as a stadium, used for sports events and other public entertainments; (*with cap*) the Colosseum.
colitis *n* inflammation of the colon.—**colitic** *adj.*
collaborate *vi* to work jointly or together, esp on a literary project; to side

with the invaders of one's country.—**collaboration** *n*.—**collaborator** *n*.—**collaborative** *adj*.
collage *n* art made up from scraps of paper, material and other odds and ends pasted onto a hard surface.
collagen *n* a protein present in connective tissue and bones which yields gelatin when boiled.
collapse *vi* to fall down; to come to ruin, to fail; to break down physically or mentally. * *n* the act of collapsing; a breakdown, prostration.
collapsible, collapsable *adj* designed to fold compactly.—**collapsibility** *n*.
collar *n* the band of a garment round the neck; a decoration round the neck, a choker; a band of leather or chain put round an animal's neck. * *vt* to put a collar on; (*inf*) to seize; to arrest.
collarbone *n* one of the two bones that connect the shoulder blades with the breast bone, the clavicle.
collate *vt* to examine and compare (manuscripts, etc); to put (pages) together in sequence; (*bishop*) to appoint to a benefice.—**collation** *n*.—**collator** *n*.
collateral *n* security pledged for the repayment of a loan. * *adj* side by side; accompanying but secondary; descended from the same ancestor but not directly.—**collaterally** *adv*.
collation *n* the act of collating, a comparison; a light meal; the presentation to a benefice by a bishop, who is the patron.
colleague *n* an associate in the same profession or office; a fellow worker.
collect[1] *vti* to bring together, gather or assemble; to regain command of (oneself); to concentrate (thoughts, etc); to ask for or receive money or payment. * *adj* (*telephone call*) paid for by the person called.
collect[2] *n* a short comprehensive prayer for a particular occasion.
collectible, collectable *adj* (*antiques, etc*) of interest to a collector. * *n* an object worth collecting.
collectanea *npl* passages selected from various authors; a miscellany.
collected *adj* self-possessed, cool.—**collectedly** *adv*.
collection *n* act of collecting; an accumulation; money collected at a meeting, etc; a group of things collected for beauty, interest, rarity or value; the periodic showing of a designer's fashions; a regular gathering of post from a postbox.
collective *adj* viewed as a whole, taken as one; combined, common; (*gram*) used in the singular to express a multitude. * *n* a collective enterprise, as a farm.—**collectively** *adv*.
collective bargaining *n* negotiations on working conditions between representatives of employees and management.
collective farm *n* a farm or number of smallholdings run on a cooperative basis, usually under state supervision.
collective noun *n* a singular noun covering a number of person or things (eg *family*, *flock*).
collectivism *n* the political or economic theory of collective ownership of the means of production and distribution by the state or people.—**collectivist** *n*.—**collectivistic** *adj*.
collectivize *vt* to bring into public ownership in accordance with the principle of collectivism.—**collectivization** *n*.
collector *n* a person who collects things, eg stamps, butterflies, as a hobby or so as to inspect them, as tickets.
colleen *n* (*Irish*) a girl.
college *n* an institution of higher learning; a school offering specialized knowledge; the buildings housing a college; an organized body of professionals.
collegian *n* a student or recent graduate of a college.
collegiate, collegial *adj* of or belonging to a college; containing, connected with or having the status of a college.
collet *n* the part of a ring in which the stone is set.
collide *vi* to come into violent contact (with); to dash together; to conflict; to disagree.
collie *n* a breed of dog with a pointed muzzle and long hair, used as a sheepdog.
colligate *vt* to bind together; to bring (isolated facts) under a general principle.—**colligation** *n*.—**colligative** *adj*.
collimate *vt* to bring into the same line; to make parallel.—**collimation** *n*.
collinear *adj* in the same straight line.—**collinearity** *n*.
collision *n* state of colliding together; a violent impact of moving bodies, a crash; a clash of interests, etc.
collision course *n* one that, if continued on, will end in disaster.
collocate *vt* to place together; to arrange.
collocation *n* a placing in a particular order; an arrangement, relative situation.
collodion *n* a preparation of soluble pyroxylin with ether, used in photography.
colloid *adj* like glue or jelly; (*chem*) of a gummy noncrystalline kind. * *n* a viscid inorganic transparent substance.—**colloidal** *adj*.—**colloidality** *n*.
collop *n* a slice of meat.
colloquial *adj* used in familiar but not formal talk, not literary.—**colloquially** *adv*.
colloquialism *n* a colloquial word or phrase.
colloquium *n* (*pl* **colloquiums, colloquia**) a conference, seminar.
colloquy *n* (*pl* **colloquies**) a conversation; a written dialogue.
collotype *n* a gelatine photographic plate used for printing from in ink.—**collotypic** *adj*.
collude *vi* to act together; to conspire, esp to defraud.
collusion *n* the act of colluding; an agreement to commit fraud or deception.—**collusive** *adj*.
collyrium *n* (*pl* **collyria, collyriums**) an eye salve.
collywobbles *npl* (*sl*) abdominal pain or discomfort; nervousness.
colobus *n* any of a genus of long-tailed African monkeys with shortened or absent thumbs.
colocynth *n* a kind of cucumber; the pulp it yields dried and powdered and used as a purgative.
cologne *n* eau-de-Cologne, a scented liquid.
colon[1] *n* (*pl* **colons, cola**) the part of the large intestine from the caecum to the rectum.—**colonic** *adj*.
colon[2] *n* (*pl* **colons**) a punctuation mark (:) between the semicolon and the full stop, usu written before an explanation or a list.
colonel *n* a commissioned officer junior to a brigadier but senior to a lieutenant colonel.—**colonelcy, colonelship** *n*.
colonial *adj* of or pertaining to a colony or colonies; (*with cap*) pertaining to the thirteen British colonies that became the US. * *n* a person who takes part in founding a colony, a settler.—**colonially** *adv*.
colonialism *n* the policy of acquiring and governing colonies.—**colonialist** *adj, n*.
colonist *n* a person who settles in a colony.
colonize *vt* to establish a colony in; to settle in a colony.—**colonization** *n*.—**colonizer** *n*.
colonnade *n* a range of columns placed at regular intervals; a similar row, as of trees.
colony *n* (*pl* **colonies**) an area of land acquired and settled by a distant state and subject to its control; a community of settlers; a group of people of the same nationality or interests living in a particular area; a collection of organisms in close association.
colophon *n* a publisher's imprint or decorative device on a book; (*formerly*) an inscription at the end of a book giving the printer's or writer's name.
color *see* **colour**.
colorable *see* **colourable**.
colored *see* **coloured**.
colorfast *see* **colourfast**.
colorful *see* **colourful**.
coloring *see* **colouring**.
colorist *see* **colourist**.
colorize *see* **colourize**.
colorless *see* **colourless**.
Colorado beetle *n* a yellowish beetle with ten longitudinal black stripes on its back, destructive to potatoes.
colorant *n* a colouring matter.

coloration *n* colouring.

coloratura, colorature *adj* (*mus*) highly ornamented or florid. * *n* a vocal passage sung in this way.

colorific *adj* producing colour.

colorimeter *n* an instrument for measuring the intensity of colour, strength of dyes, etc.—**colorimetric, colorimetrical** *adj*.—**colorimetry** *n*.

Colosseum *n* a large amphitheatre in Rome built in the 1st century.

colossal *adj* gigantic, immense; (*inf*) amazing, wonderful.—**colossally** *adv*.

colossus *n* (*pl* **colossi, colossuses**) a gigantic statue; something immense.

colostomy *n* (*pl* **colostomies**) a surgical opening into the bowl forming an artificial anus.

colostrum *n* the first milk secreted after parturition; biestings.—**colostral** *adj*.

colotomy *n* (*pl* **colotomies**) an incision in the colon.

colour *n* the eye's perception of wavelengths of light with different colours corresponding to different wavelengths; the attribute of objects to appear different according to their differing ability to absorb, emit, or reflect light of different wavelengths; colour of the face or skin; pigment; dye; paint; (*literature*) use of imagery, vividness; (*mus*) depth of sound; (*pl*) a flag; a symbol of a club, team, etc. * *vt* to give colour to, paint; to misrepresent; to influence. * *vi* to emit colour; (*face*) to redden in anger or embarrassment; to blush; to change colour, to ripen.—*also* **color**.

colourable *adj* capable of being coloured; specious, plausible.—*also* **colorable.**

colour bar *n* discrimination based on race, esp by White races against other races.

colour-blind *adj* unable to distinguish colours, esp red and green.—**colour blindness** *n*.

colour code *n* a system of identifying by colours, eg of electrical wires.

coloured *adj* possessing colour; biased, not objective; of a darker skinned race. * *n* a person of a darker skinned race.—*also* **colored.**

colourfast *adj* of a material made with non-running or non-fading colours after washing.—*also* **colorfast.**

colour filter *n* (*photog*) a thin plate or layer for adjusting depth and brightness of required colours.

colourful *adj* full of colour; vivid.—*also* **colorful.**—**colourfully** *adv*.

colouring *n* appearance in term of colour; disposition or use of colour; a substance for giving colour.—*also* **coloring.**

colourist *n* an artist whose works are characterized by beauty of colour.—*also* **colorist.**—**colouristic** adj.

colourize *vt* to add colour to a black-and-white film using a special device.—*also* **colorize.**

colourless *adj* lacking colour; dull, uninteresting, characterless.—*also* **colorless.**—**colourlessly** *adv*.—**colourlessness** *n*.

colporteur *n* a person who hawks books, esp bibles.

colt *n* a young male horse; a young, inexperienced person; an inexperienced player of a sport.

colter *see* **coulter.**

coltish *adj* like a colt; frisky; inexperienced.

coltsfoot *n* (*pl* **coltsfoots**) a yellow-flowered weed.

colubrine *adj* of, like or pertaining to snakes.

columbarium *n* (*pl* **columbaria**) a dovecote; a place with niches for cinerary urns.

Columbian *adj* pertaining to the US.

Columbine *n* a female character or dancer in a pantomime, sweetheart of Harlequin.

columbine[1] *adj* pertaining to or like a dove or pigeon.

columbine[2] *n* a garden plant, aquilegia.

columbium *n* a metallic element now called niobium.

Columbus Day *n* a legal holiday in most US states, 12 October, commemorating Columbus' landing in the Americas, 1492.

columella *n* (*pl* **columellae**) (*biol*) a central axis or column.—**columellar** *adj*.

column *n* a round pillar for supporting or decorating a building; something shaped like this; a vertical division of a page; a narrow-fronted deep formation of troops; a long line of people; a feature article appearing regularly in a newspaper, etc.—**columnar** *adj*.—**columned, columnated** *adj*.

columnist *n* a journalist who contributes a regular newspaper or magazine column.

colza *n* rape seed.

colza oil *n* an oil made from rape seed.

coma[1] *n* (*pl* **comas**) deep prolonged unconsciousness.

coma[2] *n* (*pl* **comae**) (*astron*) the nebulous hair-like envelope around the nucleus of a comet; (*bot*) the silky hairs at the end of a seed; the branches forming the leafy head of a tree.—**comal** *adj*.

comate *adj* (*bot*) hairy.

comatose *adj* in a coma; lethargic, sleepy.

comb *n* a toothed instrument for separating hair, wool, etc; a part of a machine like this; the crest of a cock; a honeycomb. * *vt* to arrange (hair) or dress (wool) with a comb; to seek for thoroughly.

combat *vti* to strive against, oppose; to do battle. * *n* a contest; a fight; struggle.—**combatable** *adj*.—**combater** *n*.

combatant *adj* fighting. * *n* a person engaged in a fight or contest.

combative *adj* aggressive, keen to fight.

comber *n* a wool-combing machine; a long curling wave, a breaker.

combination *n* the act of combining; a union of separate parts; persons allied for a purpose; a sequence of numbers which opens a combination lock; a motorcycle and sidecar.

combination lock *n* a lock which can only be opened by moving a set of dials to show a specific sequence of numbers.

combinations *npl* an all-in-one undergarment also covering the arms and legs.

combine *vti* to join together; to unite intimately; to possess together; to cooperate; (*chem*) to form a compound with. * *n* an association formed for commercial or political purposes; a machine for harvesting and threshing grain.—**combinable** *adj*.—**combiner** *n*.

combo *n* (*pl* **combos**) a small jazz band; (*inf*) any small group.

combust *vt* to burn.

combustible *adj* capable of burning; easily set alight; excitable. * *n* a combustible thing.—**combustibility, combustibleness** *n*.

combustion *n* the process of burning; the process in which substances react with oxygen in air to produce heat.

combustion chamber *n* the space in the cylinder of an engine in which the gas compressed by the piston is exploded.

come *vi* (**coming, came,** *pp* **come**) to approach; to arrive; to reach; to happen (to); to originate; to turn out (to be); to occur in a certain order; to be derived or descended; to be caused; to result; to be available; (*sl*) to experience a sexual orgasm; (*with* **about**) to happen; (*naut*) to change to a new tack; (*with* **across**) to meet with unexpectedly; to communicate the intended information or impression; to provide what is expected; (*sl*) to pay up; (*with* **along**) to make progress; (*with* **at**) to find out; to attack; (*with* **away**) to get detached; to leave with; (*with* **between**) to cause the estrangement of (two people); (*with* **by**) to obtain, esp by chance; to pass; (*with* **down**) to descend; to fall; to suffer an illness; to leave university; (*with* **down on**) to reprimand; (*with* **forward**) to offer oneself for some duty, volunteer; (*with* **from**) (*inf*) to have an awareness of the circumstances causing one's attitudes or actions; to understand what someone means; (*with* **in**) to enter, arrive; (*race*) to finish in a certain position; to perform a certain function; to become popular or fashionable; (*money*) to be received as income; to turn out to be; (with **into**) to enter; to receive as an inheritance; (*with* **of**) to result from; (*with* **off**) to become detached; to fall from; to emerge from or finish something in a specified way; to succeed; to be reduced in price, etc; (*inf*) to happen; (*inf*) to have the intended effect; (*with* **on**) to advance, make progress; (*electricity, etc*) to begin functioning; to enter on to the stage or set; (*with* **out**) to become public or be published; to go on strike; to declare oneself in public; to present oneself openly as homosexual; to transpire; to make one's debut;

(*with* **over**) to change sides; to communicate effectively; to make an impression; (*inf*) to become affected with a certain feeling; (*with* **round, around**) to recover one's normal state; to look in as a visitor; to regain consciousness; to change one's opinion, accede to something; (*with* **to**) to regain consciousness, revive; (*total*) to amount to; (*with* **through**) to overcome; to survive; (*with* **under**) to be subjected to; to be classed among; (*with* **up**) to approach; to grow; to come to a higher place or rank; (*sun*) to rise; to occur; to arise for discussion, etc; (*with* **upon**) to discover or meet unexpectedly; (*with* **up with**) to overtake; to put forward for discussion.

comeback *n* (*inf*) a return to a career or to popularity; (*inf*) a witty answer.

comedian *n* an actor of comic parts; an entertainer who tells jokes; a person who behaves in a humorous manner.

comedienne *nf* a female comedian.

comedown *n* a downfall; a disappointment.

comedy *n* (*pl* **comedies**) an amusing play or film; drama consisting of amusing plays; an amusing occurrence; humour.—**comedic** *adj*.

comehither *adj* (*sl*) flirtatious; charmingly seductive.

comely *adj* (**comelier, comeliest**) pleasing to the eye, good-looking.—**comeliness** *n*.

come-on *n* (*inf*) an enticement, lure.

comer *n* (*inf*) a person or thing showing promise of success.

comestible *n* (*usu pl*) anything to eat.

comet *n* a celestial body that travels round the sun, with a visible nucleus and a luminous tail.—**cometary, cometic** *adj*.

comeuppance *n* (*inf*) a deserved retribution.

comfit *n* a candy; a sugared almond.

comfort *vti* to bring consolation to; to soothe; to cheer. * *n* consolation; relief; bodily ease; (*pl*) things between necessities and luxuries.—**comforting** *adj*.

comfortable *adj* promoting comfort; at ease; adequate; (*inf*) financially well off.—**comfortably** *adv*.

comforter *n* one who comforts; a woollen scarf; a baby's dummy teat; a quilted bedcover.

comfort station *n* (*inf*) a public lavatory.

comfrey *n* a tall bell-flowered hairy plant.

comfy *adj* (**comfier, comfiest**) (*inf*) comfortable.

comic *adj* of comedy; causing amusement. * *n* a comedian; an entertaining person; a paper or book with strip cartoons.

comical *adj* funny, laughable; droll, ludicrous.—**comically** *adv*.

comic book *n* a book or magazine containing stories told in strip cartoons.

comic opera *n* a musical play with a comic theme.

comic relief *n* a humorous scene or character in a tragedy that alleviates tension.

comic strip *n* a series of drawings that depict a story in stages.

coming *adj* approaching next; of future importance or promise.

comitia *n* (*pl* **comitia**) one of the three Roman public assemblies for passing laws, declaring war, etc.

comity *n* (*pl* **comities**) civility, politness; acts of international courtesy.

comma *n* a punctuation mark (,) that indicates a slight pause or break in a sentence or separates items in a list.

command *vti* to order; to bid; to control; to have at disposal; to evoke, compel; to possess knowledge or understanding of; to look down over; to be in authority (over), to govern. * *n* an order; control; knowledge; disposal; position of authority; something or someone commanded; an instruction to a computer.

commandant *n* an officer in command of troops or a military establishment, esp a fortress.

commandeer *vt* to seize for military purposes; to appropriate for one's own use.

commander *n* a person who commands, a leader; a naval officer ranking next below a captain.—**commandership** *n*.

commander in chief *n* the commander of a state's entire forces.

commanding *adj* in command; dominating; impressive.

commandment *n* a command; a divine law, esp one of the Ten Commandments in the Bible.

command module *n* the operational part of a spacecraft.

commando *n* (*pl* **commandos, commandoes**) a member of an elite military force trained to raid enemy territory.

comme il faut (*French*) as it should be; correct; well bred.

commemorate *vt* to keep in the memory by ceremony or writing; to be a memorial of.—**commemoration** *n*.—**commemorative, commemoratory** *adj*.—**commemorator** *n*.

commence *vti* to begin.

commencement *n* a start; a ceremony of conferring degrees; the day of this.

commend *vt* to speak favourably of, to praise; to recommend; to entrust.—**commendable** *adj*.—**commendably** *adv*.—**commendatory** *adj*.

commendation *n* the act of commending, praise; an award.

commensal *adj* (*biol*) living together, but not at the expense of another; (*person, organization*) living and feeding with another. * *n* one of two commensal plants or animals; a dinner companion.—**commensalism, commensality** *n*.

commensurable *adj* measurable by the same standard; divisible without a remainder by the same quantity; proportionate (to).—**commensurability** *n*.

commensurate *adj* having the same extent or measure; proportionate.—**commensuration** *n*.

comment *n* a remark, observation, criticism; an explanatory note; talk, gossip. * *vi* to make a comment (upon); to annotate.—**commenter** *n*.

commentary *n* (*pl* **commentaries**) a series of explanatory notes or remarks; a verbal description on TV or radio of an event as it happens, esp sport (—*also* **running commentary**).—**commentarial** *adj*.

commentate *vt* to act as a commentator.

commentator *n* one who reports and analyses events, trends, etc, as on television.

commerce *n* trade in goods and services on a large scale between nations or individuals.

commercial *adj* of or engaged in commerce; sponsored by an advertiser; intended to make a profit. * *n* a broadcast advertisement.—**commerciality** *n*.—**commercially** *adv*.

commercial art *n* art designed for use in all aspects of advertising and packaging.—**commercial artist** *n*.

commercialism *n* commercial methods or principle.—**commercialist** *n*.—**commercialistic** *adj*.

commercialize *vt* to put on a business basis; to exploit for profit.—**commercialization** *n*.

commercial traveller *n* a sales representative or travelling salesman.

commie *n* (*pl* **commies**) (*derog*) a communist.

commination *n* a threatening of divine punishment and vengeance, denunciation, cursing.—**comminatory** *adj*.

commingle *vti* to mix together, to mingle.

comminute *vt* to reduce to minute particles or powder.—**comminution** *n*.

commiserate *vti* to sympathize (with); to feel pity for.—**commiseration** *n*.—**commiserator** *n*.

commissar *n* (*formerly*) a head of a government department in the USSR.

commissariat *n* a supply of provisions; the department in charge of this, as for an army.

commissary *n* (*pl* **commissaries**) a store, as in an army camp, where food and supplies are sold; a restaurant in a film studio, factory, etc.—**commissarial** *adj*.

commission *n* authority to act; a document bestowing this; appointment as a military officer of the rank of lieutenant or above; a body of people appointed (by government) for specified duties; a task or duty or business committed to someone; a special order for something, esp a picture or other art object; a percentage on sales paid to a salesman or agent; brokerage. * *vt* to empower or appoint by commission; to employ the service of; to authorize.—**commissional, commissionary** *adj*.

commissioner *n* a person empowered by a commission; various types of civil servant; a member of a commission.

commissure *n* (*anat*) a line of junction, a seam; the point of union between two bodies.—**commissural** *adj*.
commit *vti* (**committing, committed**) to entrust; to consign (to prison); to do, to perpetrate a crime, etc; to pledge, to involve.—**committer** *n*.
commitment *n* the act of committing; an engagement that restricts freedom; an obligation; an order for imprisonment or confinement in a mental institution (—*also* **committal**).
committed *adj* dedicated; pledged by a commitment.
committee *n* a body of people appointed from a larger body to consider or manage some matter.
commode *n* a chamber pot enclosed in a stool; a chest of drawers.
commodious *adj* roomy; (*arch*) useful.
commodity *n* (*pl* **commodities**) an article of trade; a useful thing; (*pl*) goods.
commodore *n* a naval officer ranking below a rear admiral and above a captain; the senior commander of a fleet; the president of a yacht club.
common *adj* belonging equally to more than one; public; usual, ordinary; widespread; familiar; frequent; easily obtained, not rare; low, vulgar; (*noun*) applying to any of a class. * *n* a tract of open public land; (*pl*) the common people; the House of Commons.—**commonality** *n*.—**commonly** *adv*.—**commonness** *n*.
commonage *n* the right of pasturing on common land.
commonalty, commonality *n* (*pl* **commonalties, commonalities**) the common people.
common chord *n* a note accompanied by its third and fifth.
common denominator *n* a common multiple of the denominators of two or more fractions; a characteristic in common.
commoner *n* an ordinary person, not a member of the nobility.
common law *n* the body of law developed in England based on custom and judicial precedents, as distinct from statute law. * *adj* denoting a marriage recognized in law not by an official ceremony, but after a man and woman have cohabited for a number of years.
common market *n* a grouping of nations formed to facilitate trade by removing tariff barriers; (*with caps*) the European Economic Community.
common measure *n* a number that will divide two or more numbers without a remainder.
commonplace *adj* ordinary, unremarkable. * *n* a platitude; an ordinary thing.
Commons *n* (*with* **the**) the House of Commons, the lower House of the British Parliament.
common sense *n* ordinary, practical good sense.—**common-sense** *adj*.
common time *n* (*mus*) two or four beats in a bar.
commonweal *n* the public good.
commonwealth *n* a political community; a sovereign state, republic; a federation of states; (*with cap*) an association of sovereign states and dependencies ruled or formerly ruled by Britain.
commotion *n* a violent disturbance; agitation; upheaval.—**commotional** *adj*.
communal *adj* of a commune or community; shared in common.—**communality** *n*.—**communally** *adv*.
communalism *n* a political system based on local self-government.—**communalist** *n*.—**communalistic** *adj*.
communalize *vt* to make over to a community.—**communalization** *n*.
communard *n* one who advocates government by communes.
commune[1] *n* a group of people living together and sharing possessions; the smallest administrative division in several European countries.
commune[2] *vi* to converse intimately; to communicate spiritually.
communicable *adj* able to be communicated; (*disease*) easily passed on.—**communicability, communicableness** *n*.
communicant *n* a person who receives Holy Communion.
communicate *vti* to impart, to share; to succeed in conveying information; to pass on; to transmit, esp a disease; to be connected.—**communicator** *n*.—**communicatory** *adj*.
communication *n* the act of communicating; information; a connecting passage or channel; (*pl*) connections of transport; (*pl*) means of imparting information, as in newspapers, radio, television.
communications satellite *n* an artificial satellite orbiting the earth used to relay telephone, radio and TV signals.
communicative *adj* inclined to talk and give information.
communion *n* common possession, sharing; fellowship; an emotional bond with; union in a religious body; (*with cap*) Holy Communion, the Christian sacrament of the Eucharist when bread and wine are consecrated and consumed.—**communional** *adj*.
communiqué *n* an official communication, esp to the press or public.
communism *n* a social system under which private property is abolished and the means of production are owned by the people; (*with cap*) a political movement seeking the overthrow of capitalism based on the writings of Karl Marx; the system as instituted in the former USSR and elsewhere.—**communistic** *adj*.
communist *n* a supporter of communism; (*with cap*) a member of a Communist party.
community *n* (*pl* **communities**) an organized political or social body; a body of people in the same locality; the general public, society; any group having work, interests, etc in common; joint ownership; common character; a group of plants and animals of a region, dependent on each other for life and survival.
community centre *n* a place providing social and recreational facilities for a local community.
commutative *n* relating to or involving substitution; (*math*) having a result that is independent of the order in which the elements are combined; (*addition, etc*) showing this property.
commutator *n* a device for reversing the direction of electric current.
commute *vti* to travel a distance daily from home to work; to exchange (for); to change (to); to reduce (a punishment) to one less severe.—**commutable** *adj*.—**commutation** *n*.
commuter *n* a person who commutes to and from work.
comose *adj* hairy; tufted.
compact[1] *n* an agreement; a contract, a treaty.
compact[2] *adj* closely packed; condensed; terse; firm; taking up space neatly. * *vt* to press or pack closely; to compose (of). * *n* a small cosmetic case, usu containing face powder and a mirror.—**compacter** *n*.—**compactly** *adv*.—**compactness** *n*.
compact disc *n* a small mirrored disc containing music (or audio-visual material) encoded digitally in metallic pits which are read optically by a laser beam.
compact video disc *n* a laser disc, similar to an audio compact disc, which plays sound and pictures.
companion[1] *n* an associate in an activity; a partner; a friend; one of a pair of matched things; a low-ranking member of an order of knighthood.—**companionship** *n*.
companion[2] *n* a wooden shelter over a companionway.
companionable *adj* friendly, sociable.—**companionability** *n*.—**companionably** *adv*.
companionway *n* a ladder or staircase on a ship.
company *n* (*pl* **companies**) any assembly of people; an association of people for carrying on a business, etc; a society; a military unit; the crew of a ship; companionship, fellowship; a guest, visitor(s).
comparable *adj* able or suitable to be compared (*with* **with**); similar.—**comparably** *adv*.—**comparability** *n*.
comparative *adj* estimated by comparison; relative, not absolute; (*gram*) expressing more.—**comparatively** *adv*.
compare *vt* to make one thing the measure of another; to observe similarity between, to liken; to bear comparison; (*gram*) to give comparative and superlative forms of (an adjective). * *vi* to make comparisons; to be equal or alike.—**comparer** *n*.
comparison *n* the act of comparing; an illustration; a likeness; (*gram*) the use of *more* or *er* with an adjective.
compartment *n* a space partitioned off; a division of a railway carriage; a

separate section or category.—**compartmental** *adj*.—**compartmented** *adj*.

compartmentalize *vt* to divide into categories, esp excessively.—**compartmentalization** *n*.

compass *n* a circuit, circumference; an extent, area; the range of a voice; an instrument with a magnetic needle indicating north, south, east, west; (*often pl*) a two-legged instrument for drawing circles, etc.—**compassable** *adj*.

compassion *n* sorrow for another's sufferings; pity.

compassionate *adj* showing compassion; merciful.—**compassionately** *adv*.

compass points *n* north, south, east, west, etc.

compatible *adj* agreeing or fitting in (with); of like mind; consistent; (*body organ*) able to be transplanted successfully.—**compatibly** *adv*.—**compatibility** *n*.

compatriot *n* a fellow countryman.—*also adj*.—**compatriotic** *adj*.

compeer *n* an equal; a companion.

compel *vt* (**compelling, compelled**) to force, constrain; to oblige; to obtain by force.—**compeller** *n*.

compelling *adj* evoking powerful feelings, eg interest, admiration.

compendious *adj* containing much in a small space, succinct.

compendium *n* (*pl* **compendiums, compendia**) an abridgement; a summary; a collection; an assortment of things in one box.

compensate *vti* to counterbalance; to make up for; to recompense.—**compensator** *n*.—**compensatory, compensative** *adj*.

compensation *n* the act of compensating; a sum given to compensate, esp for loss or injury; an exaggerated display of ability in one area as a cover-up for a lack in another.

compete *vi* to strive; to contend; to take part in a competition, esp sporting.

competence *n* the quality of being capable; sufficiency; capacity; an adequate income to live on.

competency *n* (*pl* **competencies**) competence; (*law*) the capacity to testify in court.

competent *adj* fit, capable; adequate; with enough skill for; legally qualified.—**competently** *adv*.

competition *n* act of competing; rivalry; a contest in skill or knowledge; a match.

competitive *adj* of, or involving, competition; of sufficient value in terms of price or quality to ensure success against rivals.—**competitively** *adv*.—**competitiveness** *n*.

competitor *n* a person who competes; an opponent; a rival.

compile *vt* to collect or make up from various sources; to amass; to gather data, etc for a book; (*comput*) to translate high-level program instructions into machine code using a compiler.—**compilation** *n*.

compiler *n* a person who compiles a book, etc; (*comput*) a program that translates high-level program instructions into machine code.

complacency, complacence *n* (*pl* **complacencies, complacences**) self-satisfaction; gratification.

complacent *adj* self-satisfied.—**complacently** *adv*.—**complacency, complacence** *n*.

complain *vi* to find fault, to grumble; to be ill; (*poet*) to express grief, to make a mourning sound.—**complainer** *n*.

complainant *n* (*law*) a plaintiff.

complaint *n* a statement of some grievance; a cause of distress or dissatisfaction; an illness.

complaisant *adj* disposed to please, obliging; compliant.–**complaisance** *n*.

complement *n* something making up a whole; a full allowance (of equipment or number); the entire crew of a ship, including officers. * *vt* to make complete.

complementary *adj* completing; together forming a balanced whole.

complete *adj* entire; free from deficiency; finished; thorough. * *vt* to make complete; to finish.—**completeness** *n*.—**completer** *n*.—**completive** *adj*.

completely *adv* entirely, utterly.

completion *n* the act of completing; accomplishment; fulfilment.

complex *adj* having more than one part; intricate, not simple; difficult. * *n* a complex whole; a collection of interconnected parts, buildings or units; a group of mostly unconscious impulses, etc strongly influencing behaviour; (*inf*) an undue preoccupation; a phobia.—**complexity** *n* (*pl* **complexities**).

complex fraction *n* (*math*) a fraction with fractions for the numerator or denominator or both.

complexion *n* a colour, texture and look of the skin; aspect, character.

complexity *n* (*pl* **complexities**) the state of being complex, complexness.

complex number *n* (*math*) a number having both real and imaginary parts.

complex sentence *n* a sentence with one principal clause and one or more subordinate clauses.

compliance, compliancy *n* the act of complying with another's wishes; acquiescence.

compliant *adj* yielding, submissive.—**compliantly** *adv*.

complicate *vt* to make intricate or involved; to mix up.

complicated *adj* intricately involved; difficult to understand.

complication *n* a complex or intricate situation; a circumstance that makes (a situation) more complex; (*med*) a condition or disease following an original illness.

complicity *n* (*pl* **complicites**) partnership in wrongdoing.

compliment *n* a polite expression of praise, a flattering tribute; (*pl*) a formal greeting or expression of regard. * *vt* to pay a compliment to, to flatter; to congratulate (on).

complimentary *adj* conveying or expressing a compliment; given free of charge.

complin, compline *n* (*RC Church*) the last service of the day following vespers.

comply *vi* (**complying, complied**) to act in accordance (with); to yield, to agree.—**complier** *n*.

compo *n* (*pl* **compos**) a mixture of plaster, stucco, etc; (*sl*) compensation.

component *adj* going to the making of a whole, constituent. * *n* a component part.—**componential** *adj*.

comport *vti* to conduct (oneself); to be compatible, to accord (with).—**comportment** *n*.

compose *vt* to make up, to form; to construct in one's mind, to write; to arrange, to put in order; to settle, to adjust; to tranquillize; (*print*) to set up type * *vi* to create musical works, etc.

composed *adj* calm, self-controlled.—**composedly** *adv*.

composer *n* a person who composes, esp music.

composite *adj* made up of distinct parts or elements; (*archit*) blending Ionic and Corinthian orders; (*bot*) having many flowers in the guise of one, as the daisy. * *n* a composite thing or flower.

composition *n* the act or process of composing; a work of literature or music, a painting; a short written essay; the general make-up of something; a chemical compound.—**compositional** *adj*.

compositor *n* a person who puts together, or sets up, type for printing.

compos mentis *adj* of sound mind, sane.

compost *n* a mixture of decomposed organic matter for fertilizing soil.

composure *n* the state of being composed, calmness.

compote *n* fruit preserved in syrup.

compound[1] *n* a substance or thing made up of a number of parts or ingredients, a mixture; a compound word made up of two or more words. * *vt* to combine (parts, elements, ingredients) into a whole, to mix; to intensify by adding new elements; to settle (debt) by partial payment. * *vi* to become joined in a compound; to come to terms of agreement. * *adj* compounded or made up of several parts; not simple.—**compounder** *n*.

compound[2] *n* an enclosure in which a building stands.

compound eye *n* the eye in insects consisting of numerous separate visual units.

compound fracture *n* a fracture in which the shattered bone protrudes through the skin.

compound interest *n* interest paid on the principal sum of capital and the interest that it has accrued.

compound sentence *n* a sentence with more than one principal clause.

comprador *n* a native agent for a foreign company in China or Japan.
comprehend *vt* to grasp with the mind, to understand; to include, to embrace.—**comprehendible** *adj*.—comprehension *n*.
comprehensible *adj* capable of being understood.—**comprehensibly** *adv*.—**comprehensibility** *n*.
comprehensive *adj* wide in scope or content, including a great deal; (*car insurance policy*) covering most risks including third party, fire, theft. * *n* a comprehensive school.—**comprehensively** *adv*.—**comprehensiveness** *n*.
compress *vt* to press or squeeze together; to bring into a smaller bulk; to condense. * *n* a soft pad for compressing an artery, etc; a wet or dry bandage or pad for relieving inflammation or discomfort.—**compressed** *adj*.—**compressible** *adj*.—**compressive** *adj*.
compression *n* the act of compressing; the increase in pressure in an engine to compress the gases so that they explode.—**compressional** *adj*.
compressor *n* a machine for compressing air or other gases.
comprise *vt* to consist of, to include.—**comprisable** *adj*.—**comprisal** *n*.
compromise *n* a settlement of a dispute by mutual concession; a middle course or view between two opposed ones. * *vti* to adjust by compromise; to lay open to suspicion, disrepute, etc.—**compromiser** *n*.
compromised *adj* (*reputation*) open to disrepute, tarnished.
comptroller *n* the form of controller used in some titles.
compulsion *n* the act of compelling; something that compels; an irresistible urge.
compulsive *adj* compelling; acting as if compelled.—**compulsively** *adv*.
compulsory *adj* enforced, obligatory, required by law, etc; involving compulsion; essential.—**compulsorily** *adv*.
compunction *n* pricking of the conscience; remorse; scruple.—**compunctious** *adj*.
computation *n* the act or process of computing; a reckoning, an estimate.—**computational** *adj*.
compute *vt* to determine mathematically; to calculate by means of a computer. * *vi* to reckon; to use a computer.—**computability** *n*.—**computable** *adj*.—**computation** *n*.
computer *n* an electronic device that processes data in accordance with programmed instructions.
computer-aided tomography, computer-asisted tomography *see* **CAT**.
computer game *n* a game on cassette or disk to play on a home computer by means of operating the keys according to the images appearing on the screen.
computer graphics *n* the production and manipulation of pictorial images on a computer screen.
computerize *vt* to equip with computers; to control or perform (a process) using computers; to store or process data using a computer.—**computerization** *n*.
computerized axial tomography *see* **CAT**.
computer language *n* a code used to provide instructions and data to a computer.
computer literate *adj* capable of or proficient in using computers.
computer virus *n* a program introduced into a computer system with the intention of sabotaging or destroying data.
comrade *n* a companion; a fellow member of a Communist party.—**comradely** *adv*.—**comradeship** *n*.
comsat *n* communications satellite.
con[1] *vt* (**conning, conned**) (*inf*) to swindle, trick. * *n* (*inf*) a confidence trick.
con[2] *n* against, as in **pro and con**.
con[3] *prep* with.
con[4] *vt* (**conning, conned**) to direct the course of (a ship).
con[5] *vt* (**conning, conned**) to study; to learn by heart.
con[6] *n* (*sl*) a convict.
con- *prefix* com-.
con amore *adj, adv* (*mus*) with love.
conation *n* (*psychol*) the faculty of voluntary agency, including volition and desire.
conative *adj* (*verb*) expressing endeavour or effort; pertaining to the faculty of conation.
con brio *adj, adv* (*mus*) with spirit.
concatenate *vt* to link together. * *adj* linked.
concatenation *n* a string of connected ideas or events.
concave *adj* curving inwards, hollow. * *n* a concave line or surface.—**concavity** *n* (*pl* **concavities**).
concavo-concave *adj* hollow on both surfaces, as a lens.
concavo-convex *adj* concave on one side, convex on the other.
conceal *vt* to hide, to keep from sight; to keep secret.—**concealment** *n*.
concede *vt* to grant; to admit to be true, to allow; to agree to be certain in outcome.—**conceder** *n*.
conceit *n* an over-high opinion of oneself; vanity; a far-fetched comparison, a quaint fancy.
conceited *adj* full of conceit, vain.—**conceitedly** *adv*.
conceivable *adj* capable of being imagined or believed; possible.—**conceivably** *adv*.
conceive *vti* to become pregnant (with); to form in the mind; to think out, to imagine; to understand; to express.
concenter *see* **concentre**.
concentrate *vt* to bring or converge together to one point; to direct to a single object or purpose; to collect one's thoughts or efforts; (*chem*) to increase the strength of by diminishing bulk, to condense. * *n* a concentrated product, esp a food reduced in bulk by eliminating fluid; a foodstuff relatively high in nutrients.—**concentrator** *n*.
concentration *n* the act or process of concentrating; the direction of attention to a single object; a drawing together of forces; the simultaneous firing of many weapons.—**concentrative** *adj*.
concentration camp *n* a camp where persons (as prisoners of war, political prisoners, and refugees) are detained or confined.
concentre *vti* to bring or come to a common centre.—*also* **concenter**.
concentric, concentrical *adj* having a common centre.—**concentrically** *adv*.—**concentricity** *n*.
concept *n* a general idea, esp an abstract one.
conceptacle *n* (*bot*) that which holds anything; a follicle.
conception *n* the act of conceiving; the fertilizing of an ovum by a sperm; a thing conceived; an idea, a notion.—**conceptional** *adj*.
conceptual *adj* of mental conception or concepts.
conceptualism *n* (*philos*) the theory that universal truths exist in the mind apart from any concrete embodiment.—**conceptualist** *n*.—**conceptualistic** *adj*.
conceptualize *vt* to form a concept of in the mind based on evidence, experience, etc.—**conceptualization** *n*.
concern *vt* to relate or apply to; to fill with anxiety; to interest (oneself) in; to take part, to be mixed up (in). * *n* a thing that concerns one; anxiety, misgiving; interest in or regard for a person or thing; a business or firm.
concerned *adj* troubled, worried; interested.—**concernedly** *adv*.
concerning *prep* about; regarding.
concert *n* a musical entertainment; harmony; agreement or union; **in concert** working together; (*musicians*) playing together.
concerted *adj* planned or arranged by mutual agreement; combined; (*mus*) arranged in separate parts for musicians or singers.
concertina *n* a hexagonal musical instrument, similar to an accordion, which produces sound by squeezing bellows which pass air over metal reeds.
concertino *n* (*pl* **concertini**) a short concerto.
concerto *n* (*pl* **concertos, concerti**) a musical composition for a solo instrument and orchestra.
concert pitch *n* a pitch slightly above normal; a state of exceptional efficiency.
concession *n* the act of conceding; something conceded; a grant of rights, land, etc by a government, corporation, or individual; the sole right to sell a product within an area; a reduction in price (of admission, travel, etc) for certain people.—**concessionary** *adj*.—**concessible** *adj*.

concessionaire, concessioner *n* a person holding a concession.
concessive *adj* of or expressing concession.
conch *n* (*pl* **conchs, conches**) a tropical marine spiral shell, sometimes used as a trumpet.
concha *n* (*pl* **conchae**) the external ear or its cavity; (*archit*) the dome of a semicircular apse.—**conchal** *adj*.
conchiferous *adj* producing shells.
conchology *n* the branch of zoology that studies molluscs and their shells.—**conchological** *adj*.—**conchologist** *n*.
concierge *n* a resident doorkeeper or janitor, esp in France.
conciliar *adj* of or pertaining to ecclesiastical councils.
conciliate *vt* to win over from hostility; to make friendly; to appease; to reconcile.—**conciliation** *n*.—**conciliator** *n*.—**conciliatory** *adj*.
concinnity *n* (*pl* **concinnities**) neatness, elegance, esp in speech or writing.—**concinnous** *adj*.
concise *adj* brief, condensed, terse.—**concisely** *adv*.—**conciseness** *n*.
concision *n* conciseness; (*arch*) mutilation.
conclave *n* a private or secret meeting; a meeting of cardinals in seclusion to choose a pope; the meeting place.—**conclavist** *n*.
conclude *vti* to bring or come to an end, to finish; to effect, to settle; to infer; to resolve.
conclusion *n* concluding; the end or close; an inference; a final opinion; (*logic*) a proposition deduced from premises.
conclusive *adj* decisive; convincing, removing all doubt.—**conclusively** *adv*.
concoct *vt* to make by combining ingredients; to devise, to plan; to invent (a story).—**concocter, concoctor** *n*.—**concoctive** *adj*.
concoction *n* the act of concocting; something concocted; a mixture; a lie.
concomitance *n* the state of being concomitant; coexistence.
concomitant *n* an accompanying thing or circumstance.—*also adj*.
concord *n* agreement, harmony; a treaty; grammatical agreement.—**concordant** *adj*.
concordance *n* agreement; an alphabetical index of words in a book or in the works of an author with their contexts.
concordant *adj* agreeing, harmonious.
concordat *n* a compact or agreement, esp between church and state.
concourse *n* a crowd; a gathering of people or things, eg events; an open space or hall where crowds gather, eg a railway or airport terminal.
concrescence *n* (*biol*) a growing together, coalescence.—**concrescent** *adj*.
concrete *adj* having a material existence; (*gram*) denoting a thing, not a quality, not abstract; actual, specific (*a concrete example*); made of concrete. * *n* anything concrete; a mixture of sand, cement, etc with water, used in building. * *vti* to form into a mass, to solidify; to build or cover with concrete.
concretion *n* a solidified mass; a stone-like mass found in some parts of the body, calculus.—**concretionary** *adj*.
concubinage *n* the act of living with a woman without being legally married.
concubine *n* a secondary wife (in polygamous societies); (*formerly*) a mistress of a king or nobleman.—**concubinage** *n*.
concupiscence *n* sexual desire, lust.—**concupiscent** *adj*.
concur *vi* (**concurring, concurred**) to happen together, to coincide; to cooperate; to be of the same opinion, to agree.—**concurrence** *n*.
concurrence *n* the act of concurring; agreement; consent.
concurrent *adj* existing, acting or occurring at the same time; coinciding.—**concurrently** *adv*.
concuss *vt* to shake violently, to agitate; to cause concussion of the brain to.
concussion *n* the violent shock of an impact or explosion; loss of consciousness caused by a violent blow to the head.—**concussive** *adj*.
condemn *vt* to express strong disapproval of; to find guilty; to blame or censure; to declare unfit for use; to force into unwillingly.—**condemnable** *adj*.—**condemnation** *n*.—**condemnatory** *adj*.—**condemner** *n*.
condense *vt* to reduce to a smaller compass, to compress; to change from a gas into a liquid; to concentrate; to express in fewer words. * *vi* to become condensed.—**condensable, condensible** *adj*.—**condenser** *n*.—**condensation** *n*.
condensed milk *n* milk that has been sweetened and reduced by evaporation.
condenser *n* an apparatus for reducing gases or vapour to a liquid or solid form; a device for storing electricity; a lens for concentrating light.
condescend *vi* to waive one's superiority; to deign, to stoop; to act patronizingly.—**condescension** *n*.
condescending *adj* kindly in a lordly fashion to inferiors; patronizing.
condescension *n* a condescending act or manner.
condign *adj* deserved, merited; suitable.
condiment *n* a seasoning or relish.
condition *n* the state or nature of things; anything required for the performance, completion or existence of something else; physical state of health; an abnormality, illness; a prerequisite; (*pl*) attendant circumstances. * *vt* to be essential to the happening or existence of; to stipulate; to agree upon; to make fit; to make accustomed (to); to bring about a required effect by subjecting to certain stimuli.
conditional *adj* depending on conditions; not absolute; (*gram*) expressing condition. * *n* a conditional clause or conjunction.—**conditionality** *n*.—**conditionally** *adv*.
conditioner *n* a person or thing that conditions; a creamy substance for bringing the hair into a glossy condition.
conditioning *n* a bringing into a required state or state of fitness for an objective.
condo *n* (*pl* **condos, condoes**) (*inf*) a condominium.
condole *vt* (*with* **with**) to express sympathy for another.—**condolatory** *adj*.—**condoler** *n*.
condolence, condolement *n* sympathy.
con dolore *adv* (*mus*) mournfully.
condom *n* a sheath for the penis, used as a contraceptive and to prevent infection.
condominium *n* (*pl* **condominiums**) a block of apartments, each apartment being individually owned; joint rule; a country ruled by more than one other country.
condone *vt* to overlook, to treat as nonexistent; to pardon an offence.—**condonation** *n*.—**condoner** *n*.
condor *n* a large South American vulture.
condottiere *n* (*pl* **condottieri**) a military adventurer, a captain of mercenaries.
conduce *vi* to tend to bring about, to contribute (to).—**conducer** *n*.
conducive *adj* leading to or helping to cause or produce a result.
conduct *vti* to lead; to guide; to convey; to direct (an orchestra); to carry on or manage (a business); to transmit (electricity, heat); to behave (oneself). * *n* management, direction; behaviour.—**conductible** *adj*.—**conductibility** *n*.
conductance *n* the ability of a specified system to conduct electricity.
conduction *n* the conducting or transmission of heat or electricity through a medium; the transmission of nerve impulses.
conductive *adj* having the power to transmit heat or electricity.—**conductivity** *n* (*pl* **conductivities**).
conductor *n* a person who conducts an orchestra; one in charge of passengers on a train, or who collects fares on a bus; a substance that conducts heat or electricity.—**conductress** *nf*.
conduit *n* a channel or pipe that carries water, etc.
conduplicate *adj* (*bot*) folded lengthwise along the middle.—**conduplication** *n*.
condyle *n* the rounded head at the end of a bone fitting into another bone.—**condylar** *adj*.
condyloid *adj* shaped like, resembling or connected with a condyle.
cone *n* a solid pointed figure with a circular or elliptical base; any cone-shaped object (*an ice-cream cone*); a warning ballard on roads, etc; the scaly fruit of the pine, fir, etc.
coney *see* **cony**.
confab *n* (*inf*) an informal talk, chat.
confabulate *vi* to talk familiarly together.—**confabulation** *n*.—**confabulator** *n*.—**confabulatory** *adj*.

confection *n* candy, ice cream, preserves, etc; anything overfussy, fanciful or ornate.

confectionary *n* (*pl* **confectionaries**) a place where confectionery is made or sold. * *adj* of or pertaining to confectionery.

confectioner *n* a person who makes or sells confectionery.

confectionery *n* (*pl* **confectioneries**) candies.

confederacy *n* (*pl* **confederacies**) a union of states, an alliance; a combination of persons for illegal purposes; (*with cap*) the Confederate States of America.

confederate *adj* banded together by treaty, united in confederation. * *vti* to bring or come into alliance or confederacy. * *n* a member of a confederacy; a partner in design, an accomplice; an ally.

Confederate States *npl* in US history, the eleven Southern States that seceded from the Union in 1861, leading to the Civil War in which they were defeated in 1865.

confederation *n* the act or state of confederating; an alliance of individuals, organizations, states or cantons (as in Switzerland).—**confederationism** *n*.—**confederationist** *n*.

confer *vt* (**conferring, conferred**) to grant or bestow; to compare views or take counsel; to consult.—**conferment, conferral** *n*.—**conferrable** *adj*.—**conferrer** *n*.

conferee, conferree *n* one on whom something is conferred; a member of a conference.

conference *n* a meeting for discussion or consultation.—**conferential** *adj*.

conferva *n* (*pl* **confervae, confervas**) a genus containing green freshwater algae.—**conferval** *adj*.—**confervoid** *adj*.

confess *vt* to acknowledge or admit; to disclose (sins) to a confessor; (*priest*) to hear confession of. * *vi* to make or hear a confession.

confessedly *adv* avowedly.

confession *n* admission or acknowledgement of a fault or sin, esp to a confessor; a thing confessed; a statement of one's religious beliefs, creed.—**confessionary** *adj*.

confessional *n* an enclosure in a church where a priest hears confessions.

confessor *n* a priest who hears confessions and grants absolution; one who confesses.

confetti *npl* small bits of coloured paper thrown at weddings.

confidant *n* a person trusted with one's secrets.—**confidante** *nf*.

confide *vti* to put confidence (in); to entrust; to impart a confidence or secret.—**confider** *n*.

confidence *n* firm trust, faith; belief in one's own abilities; boldness; something revealed confidentially.

confidence trick *n* the persuading of a victim to hand over valuables as proof of confidence.

confident *adj* full of confidence; positive, assured.—**confidently** *adv*.

confidential *adj* spoken or written in confidence, secret; entrusted with secrets.—**confidentiality, confidentialness** *n*.—**confidentially** *adv*.

confiding *adj* unsuspicious.—**confidingly** *adv*.

configuration *n* arrangement of parts; external shape, general outline; aspect; (*astrol*) the relative position of the planets; the make-up of a computer system.—**configurational, configurative** *adj*.

confine *vt* to restrict, to keep within limits; to keep shut up, as in prison, a sickbed, etc; to imprison. * *n* (*pl*) borderland, edge, limit.—**confinable, confineable** *adj*.

confined *adj* narrow, enclosed, of limited space.

confinement *n* a being confined; the period of childbirth.

confirm *vt* to make stronger; to establish firmly; to make valid, to ratify; to corroborate; to administer rite of confirmation to.

confirmation *n* the act of confirming; convincing proof; the rite by which people are admitted to full communion in Christian churches.

confirmatory, confirmative *adj* giving extra proof; corroborative.

confirmed *adj* habitual; settled in belief, mode of life, etc; having undergone the rite of confirmation.

confiscate *vt* to appropriate to the state as a penalty; to seize by authority.—**confiscable** *adj*.—**confiscation** *n*.—**confiscator** *n*.—**confiscatory** *adj*.

conflagration *n* a massively destructive fire.—**conflagrative** *adj*.

conflation *n* a fusing together; a combining of two variant readings of a text into one.—**conflate** *vt*.

conflict *n* a fight; a contest; strife, quarrel; emotional disturbance. * *vi* to be at variance; to clash (with); to struggle.—**confliction** *n*.—**conflictive, conflictory** *adj*.

conflicting *adj* contradictory.

confluence, conflux *n* the point where two rivers meet; a coming together.

confluent *adj* flowing or running together. * *n* a tributary river or stream.

confocal *adj* having a common focus.

conform *vi* to comply, to be obedient (to); to act in accordance with. * *vt* to adapt; to make like.—**conformer** *n*.

conformable *adj* compliant; corresponding, adapted (to); in parallel order.—**conformability, conformableness** *n*.—**conformably** *adv*.

conformation *n* arrangement of parts, structure; adaptation.

conformist *n* one who conforms to established rules, standards, etc; compliance with the rites and doctrines of an established church.—**conformism** *n*.

conformity, conformance *n* (*pl* **conformities, conformances**) correspondence; agreement; conventional behaviour; compliance.

confound *vt* to mix up, to obscure; to perplex, to astound; to overthrow; to mistake one thing for another.—**confounder** *n*.

confounded *adj* astonished; confused; annoying; (*inf*) damned.—**confoundedly** *adv*.

confraternity *n* (*pl* **confraternities**) a brotherhood or society of men associated for a common purpose.—**confraternal** *adj*.

confrère *n* an associate, a colleague.

confront *vt* to stand in front of, to face; to bring face to face (with); to encounter; to oppose.—**confronter** *n*.

confrontation *n* the coming face to face with; hostility without actual warfare, esp between nations.

Confucian *adj* pertaining to Confucius, the Chinese philosopher. * *n* a follower of the teachings of Confucius.

confuse *vt* to throw into disorder; to mix up; to mistake one thing for another; to perplex, to disconcert; to embarrass; to make unclear.—**confusable** *adj*.—**confusing** *adj*.—**confusingly** *adv*.

confused *adj* perplexed; disordered; mentally unbalanced.—**confusedly** *adv*.

confusion *n* the act or state of being confused; disorder; embarrassment, discomfiture; lack of clarity.

confute *vt* (*argument, etc*) to prove wrong; to convict of error; to overcome in argument.—**confutation** *n*.—**confutative** *adj*.—**confuter** *n*.

conga *n* a Cuban dance in which the dancers move along in a long line; music for this. * *vi* (**congaing, congaed**) to do this dance.

congé *n* dismissal; (*arch*) a formal bow, esp at parting.

congeal *vti* to change from a liquid to a solid by cooling, to jell.—**congealment** *n*.

congelation *n* the act of congealing; a congealed state or substance.

congener *n* a person or thing of the same kind as another.

congeneric *adj* of the same genus or origin.

congenial *adj* of a similar disposition or with similar tastes, kindred; suited, agreeable (to).—**congenially** *adv*.—**congeniality, congenialness** *n*.

congenital *adj* existing or dating since birth, as in certain defects.—**congenitally** *adv*.

conger eel *n* a large marine eel.

congeries *n* (*used as sing or pl*) a gathered mass, a heap; a conglomeration.

congest *vt* to overcrowd. * *vi* (*med*) to affect with congestion.—**congested** *adj*.—**congestible** *adj*.

congestion *n* an overcrowding; (*med*) an excessive accumulation of blood in any organ; an accumulation of traffic causing obstruction.—**congestive** *adj*.

conglobate *vti* to form into a mass.—**conglobation** *n*.

conglomerate *adj* stuck together in a mass. * *vt* to gather into a ball. * *n* a coarse-grained rock of embedded pebbles; a large corporation consisting of companies with varied and often unrelated interests.—**conglomeratic, conglomeritic** *adj*.

conglomeration *n* the act of conglomerating; a mass stuck together; a miscellaneous collection.

conglutinate *vt* to glue together. * *adj* glued together; united by an adhesive substance.—**conglutination** *n*.—**conglutinative** *adj*.

congou *n* a kind of black Chinese tea.

congratulate *vt* to express sympathetic pleasure at success or good fortune of, to compliment; to feel satisfied or pleased with oneself.—**congratulation** *n*.—**congratulator** *n*.—**congratulatory** *adj*.

congratulations *npl* an expression of joy or pleasure.

congregate *vti* to flock together, to assemble; to gather into a crowd or mass.—**congregator** *n*.

congregation *n* a gathering, an assembly; a body of people assembled for worship.

congregational *adj* of a congregation; (*with cap*) of or pertaining to Congregationalism.

Congregationalism *n* a form of church government in which each congregation has management of its own affairs.—**Congregationalist** *adj, n*.

congress *n* an association or society; an assembly or conference, esp for discussion and action on some question; (*with cap*) the legislature of the US, comprising the Senate and the House of Representatives.

congressional *adj* of, or relating to, a congress.—**congressionalist** *n*.

Congressman *n* (*pl* **Congressmen**) a member of Congress.—**Congresswoman** *nf* (*pl* **Congresswomen**).

congruent *adj* in agreement; harmonious; (*geom*) having identical shape and size so that all parts correspond.—**congruence, congruency** *n*.

congruous *adj* accordant; fit.—**congruity** *n*.

conic, conical *adj* of a cone; cone-shaped.

conics *n* (*used as sing*) the branch of geometry that deals with conic sections.

conic section *n* a curve formed from a cone—an ellipse, a parabola, or a hyperbola.

conidium (*pl* **conidia**) a reproductive cell formed of certain fungi.—**conidial** adj.

conifer *n* any evergreen trees and shrubs with true cones (as pines) and others (as yews).—**coniferous** *adj*.

coniferous *adj* bearing fruit cones.

conine, conin *n* a very poisonous alkaloid existing in the hemlock.

conium *n* a genus of biennial poisonous plants including the hemlock.

conjectural *adj* depending on conjecture, doubtful.—**conjecturally** *adv*.

conjecture *n* a guess, guesswork. * *vt* to make a conjecture, to guess, surmise.—**conjecturer** *n*.—**conjecturable** *adj*.—**conjectural** *adj*.

conjoin *vt* to join together; to connect or associate. * *vi* to be joined.—**conjoinedly** *adv*.—**conjoiner** *n*.

conjoint *adj* united, combined; cooperating.—**conjointly** *adv*.

conjugal *adj* of or relating to marriage.—**conjugality** *n*.—**conjugally** *adv*.

conjugate *vt* to give the parts of (a verb); to unite.—**conjugable** *adj*.—**conjugation** *n*.—**conjugator** *n*.—**conjugative** *adj*.

conjugation *n* the act of conjugating; a group of verbs with the same inflections; the union of cells in reproduction.—**conjugational** *adj*.

conjunct *adj* joined together; associated.

conjunction *n* (*gram*) a word connecting words, clauses or sentences; a union; a simultaneous occurrence of events; the apparent proximity of two or more planets.—**conjunctional** *adj*.

conjunctiva *n* (*pl* **conjunctivas, conjunctivae**) the mucous membrane that lines the inner surface of the eyelids and the exposed area of the eyeball.—**conjunctival** *adj*.

conjunctive *adj* serving to unite; closely connected; (*gram*) of or pertaining to conjunctions. * *n* a conjunction.—**conjunctively** *adv*.

conjunctivitis *n* inflammation of the conjunctiva.

conjuncture *n* a combination of many circumstances or causes; a critical time.—**conjunctural** *adj*.

conjuration *n* the act of conjuring or invoking; an incantation; an enchantment; a solemn entreaty.

conjure *vti* to practise magical tricks; to call up (spirits) by invocation.

conjurer, conjuror *n* one who conjures or is skilled in sleight of hand.

conk *n* (*sl*) the nose or head. * *n* a blow to the nose or head. * *vt* to hit, esp on the head. * *vi* (*with* **out**) (*sl*) (*machine*) to break down entirely; to collapse suddenly from exhaustion.

conker *n* (*inf*) the horse chestnut; (*pl*) a children's game using conkers on a string.

con man *n* (*inf*) a swindler, one who defrauds by means of a confidence trick.

con moto *adj* (*mus*) spirited.

connate *adj* inborn, congenital; (*leaves*) united at the base.

connatural *adj* congenital; having the same nature.

connect *vti* to fasten together, to join; to relate together, to link up; (*trains, buses, etc*) to be timed to arrive as another leaves so that passengers can continue their journey; to establish a link by telephone; (*sl*) to punch or kick; to uncover (a source of drugs).—**connectible, connectable** *adj*.—**connector, connecter** *n*.

connection *n* the act of connecting; the state of being connected; a thing that connects; a relationship, bond; a train, bus, etc timed to connect with another; an opportunity to transfer between trains, buses, etc; context; a link between components in an electric circuit; a relative; (*sl*) a supply or the supplier of illicit drugs; (*pl*) clients, customers.—**connectional** *adj*.

connective *adj* serving to connect.—**connectively** *adv*.

connectivity *n* the ability of computers of different kinds to communicate.

conning tower *n* the armoured pilot house of a submarine.

conniption *n* (*sl*) a fit of hysteria or rage.

connivance *n* the act of conniving; pretence of ignorance; passive cooperation in a crime or fault; collusion.

connive *vi* to permit tacitly; to wink (at); to plot.—**conniver** *n*.

connivent *adj* converging.

connoisseur *n* a trained discriminating judge, esp of the fine arts.

connotation *n* a consequential meaning, an implication—**connotative, connotive** *adj*.

connote *vt* to imply; to indicate; to mean.

connubial *adv* of or relating to marriage.—**connubiality** *n*.—**connubially** *adv*.

conoid *n* (*geom*) a solid formed by revolution of a conic section about its axis. * *adj* somewhat conical (*—also* **conoidal**).

conquer *vt* to gain victory (over), to defeat; to acquire by conquest; to overcome, to master. * *vi* to be victor.—**conqueror** *n*.

conquest *n* conquering; the winning of a person's affection; a person or thing conquered.

conquistador *n* (*pl* **conquistadors, conquistadores**) a member of the Spanish forces that conquered Mexico and Peru in the 16th century.

consanguineous, consanguine *adj* related by blood or birth.—**consanguinity** *n*.

conscience *n* the knowledge of right and wrong that affects action and behaviour; the sense of guilt or virtue induced by actions, behaviour, etc; an inmost thought; conscientiousness.

conscience clause *n* a clause in an act giving relief to persons having religious scruples to some requirement in it.

conscience investment *n* the investment in companies whose activities do not offend the investor's moral principles.*—also* **ethical investment.**

conscience money *n* money paid, usu anonymously, to atone for some dishonest act or illegal monetary gain.

conscience-stricken *adj* feeling extreme guilt or remorse.

conscience-stricken *adj* feeling pangs of guilt.

conscientious *adj* following the dictates of the conscience; scrupulous; careful, thorough.—**conscientiously** *adv*.—**conscientiousness** *n*.

conscientious objector *n* a person who refuses to serve in the military forces on moral or religious grounds.

conscionable *adj* governed by conscience, just.—**conscionably** *adv*.

conscious *adj* aware (of); awake to one's surroundings; (*action*) realized by the person who does it, deliberate.—**consciously** *adv*.

consciousness *n* the state of being conscious; perception; the whole body of a person's thoughts and feelings.
conscript *adj* enrolled into service by compulsion; drafted. * *n* a conscripted person (as a military recruit). * *vt* to enlist compulsorily.
conscription *n* compulsory military or naval service; the persons enrolled.—**conscriptional** *adj*.
consecrate *vt* to set apart as sacred, to sanctify; to devote (to).—**consecration** *n*.—**consecrator** *n*.—**consecratory, consecrative** *adj*.
consecration *n* the act of consecrating; a setting apart or devoting to a sacred use or office; (*with cap*) (*RC Church*) the part of Mass when the bread and wine are blessed.
consecution *n* a following on; a logical sequence.
consecutive *adj* following in regular order without a break; successive; (*gram*) expressing consequence.—**consecutively** *adv*.
consensual *adj* caused by sympathetic action.
consensus *n* an opinion held by all or most; general agreement, esp in opinion.
consent *vi* to agree (to); to comply; to acquiesce * *n* agreement, permission; concurrence.—**consenter** *n*.
consequence *n* a result, an outcome; importance; (*pl*) an unpleasant result of an action; a game in which each player writes part of a story without knowing what has gone before.
consequent *adj* occurring as a result.
consequential *adj* pompous, self-important; resultant.—**consequentiality, consequentialness** *n*.—**consequentially** *adv*.
consequently *adv* as a result, therefore.
conservancy *n* (*pl* **conservancies**) in UK, an authority controlling a river or port; conservation.
conservation *n* the act of conserving; preservation of the environment and natural resources.—**conservational** *adj*.—**conservationist** *n*.
conservation of energy *n* the fact that the amount of energy in a closed system remains the same although its form changes.
conservatism *n* opposition to change; a political ideology favouring preservation and defence of tradition.
conservative *adj* traditional, conventional; cautious; moderate. * *n* a conservative person; (*with cap*) a member of the Conservative Party in Britain and other countries.—**conservatively** *adv*.
conservatoire *n* an institution for instruction in music.
conservator *n* a custodian, a keeper; a preserver; a member of a conservancy.
conservatory *n* (*pl* **conservatories**) a greenhouse attached to a house; a conservatoire.
conserve *vt* to keep from loss or injury; to preserve (a foodstuff) with sugar. * *n* a type of jam using whole fruit.—**conservable** *adj*.—**conserver** *n*.
consider *vti* to reflect (upon), to contemplate; to examine, to weigh the merits of; to take into account; to regard as; to be of the opinion; to act with respect; to allow for.—**considerer** *n*.
considerable *adj* a fairly large amount; worthy of respect.—**considerably** *adv*.
considerate *adj* careful of the feelings of others.—**considerately** *adv*.
consideration *n* the act of considering; deliberation; a point of importance; an inducement; thoughtfulness; deference; a payent.
considered *adj* well thought out.
considering *prep* in view of. * *adv* all in all. * *conj* seeing that.
consign *vt* to hand over, to commit; to send goods addressed (to).—**consignable** *adj*.—**consignation** *n*.
consignee *n* the person to whom goods are consigned.
consignment *n* consigning; goods, etc consigned.
consignor *n* the person by whom goods are consigned.
consist *vi* to be made up (of); to be comprised (of).
consistency *n* (*pl* **consistencies**) degree of density, esp of thick liquids; the state of being consistent.
consistent *adj* compatible, not contradictory; uniform in thought or action.—**consistently** *adv*.
consistory *n* a solemn assembly or the place where it meets; the ecclesiastical court of the pope and cardinals, of an Anglican bishop, or of Presbyterian presbyters.—**consistorial, consistorian** *adj*.
consolation *n* someone or something that offers comfort in distress.—**consolatory** *adj*.
consolation prize *n* a prize for the runner up or loser in a competition.
console[1] *vt* to bring consolation to, to cheer in distress.—**consolable** *adj*.—**consoler** *n*.
console[2] *n* a desk containing the controls of an electronic system; the part of an organ containing the pedals, stops, etc; an ornamental bracket supporting a shelf or table.
consolidate *vti* to solidify; to establish firmly, to strengthen; to combine into a single whole.—**consolidator** *n*.
consolidation *n* the act of consolidating; solidification.
consols *npl* British government securities consolidated into a single stock.
consommé *n* a clear soup made from meat stock.
consonance, consonancy *n* (*pl* **consonance, consonancies**) agreement of sounds; harmony; concord.
consonant *n* a letter of the alphabet that is not a vowel; the sound representing such a letter. * *adj* consistent, in keeping (with).—**consonantal** *adj*.
consort *n* a husband or wife, esp of a reigning queen or king; a ship sailing with another. * *vti* to associate, to keep company with (often dubious companions).—**consorter** *n*.
consortium *n* (*pl* **consortia**) an international banking or financial combination.—**consortial** *adj*.
conspectus *n* a general sketch or digest of some subject, a synopsis.
conspicuous *adj* easily seen, prominent; outstanding, eminent.—**conspicuousness** *n*.—**conspicuously** *adv*.
conspiracy *n* (*pl* **conspiracies**) a secret plan for an illegal act; the act of conspiring.
conspirator *n* one who conspires.—**conspiratorial, conspiratory** *adj*.—**conspiratorially** *adv*.
conspire *vti* to combine secretly for an evil purpose; to plot, to devise.
con spirito *adj, adv* (*mus*) with spirit.
constable *n* in UK, a policeman or policewoman of the lowest rank; a governor of a royal castle.
constabulary *n* (*pl* **constabularies**) in UK, a police force.—*also adj*.
constancy *n* being constant; steadfastness; fidelity.
constant *adj* fixed; unchangeable; unchanging; faithful; firm and steadfast; continual. * *n* (*math, physics*) a quantity that does not vary.
constantly *adv* continually, continuously, often.
constellate *vti* to form into a constellation.
constellation *n* a group of fixed stars; an assembly of the famous.—**constellatory** *adj*.
consternate *vt* to dismay.
consternation *n* surprise and alarm; shock; dismay.
constipate *vt* to cause constipation in.—**constipated** *adj*.
constipation *n* infrequent and difficult movement of the bowels.
constituency *n* (*pl* **constituencies**) a body of electors; the voters in a particular district or area.
constituent *adj* forming part of a whole, component; having the power to revise the constitution. * *n* a component part; a member of an elective body; a voter in a district.
constitute *vt* to set up by authority, to establish; to frame, to form; to appoint; to compose, to make up.—**constituter, constitutor** *n*.
constitution *n* fundamental physical condition; disposition; temperament; structure, composition; the system of basic laws and principles of a government, society, etc; a document stating these specifically.
constitutional *adj* of or pertaining to a constitution; authorized or limited by a constitution, legal; inherent, natural. * a walk for the sake of one's health.—**constitutionally** *adv*.—**constitutionality** *n*.
constitutionalism *n* constitutional government; adherence to constitutional principles.—**constitutionalist** *n*.
constitutive *adj* having the power to enact, constituent; elemental; essential; productive.

constrain *vt* to compel, to force; to hinder by force; to confine, to imprison.—**constrainer** *n*.
constrained *adj* enforced; embarrassed, inhibited; showing constraint.
constraint *n* compulsion; forcible confinement; repression of feeling; embarrassment; a condition that restricts freedom.
constrict *vt* to draw together, to squeeze, to compress.
constricted *adj* narrowed, cramped.
constriction *n* compression; tightness.—**constrictive** *adj*.
constrictor *n* a constrictive muscle; a snake that crushes its prey.
construct *vt* to make, to build, to fit together; to compose. * *n* a structure; an interpretation; an arrangement, esp of words in a sentence.—**constructible** *adj*.—**constructor, constructer** *n*.
construction *n* a constructing; anything constructed; a structure, building; interpretation, meaning; (*gram*) two or more words grouped together to form a phrase, clause or sentence.—**constructional** *adj*.
constructive *adj* helping to improve, promoting development.—**constructively** *adv*.
constructivism *n* nonrepresentational art, esp sculpture based on movement and using machine-made materials.
construe *vti* (**construing, construed**) to translate word for word; to analyse grammatically; to take in a particular sense, to interpret.—**construer** *n*.
consubstantiation *n* the doctrine that the body and blood of Christ are in a mysterious manner substantially present in the Eucharistic elements after Consecration.
consuetude *n* an established custom.—**consuetudinary** *adj*.
consul *n* a government official appointed to live in a foreign city to attend to the interests of his country's citizens and business there.—**consular** *adj*.
consulate *n* the official residence of a consul; the office of a Roman consul.
consult *vti* to seek advice from, esp a doctor or lawyer; to seek information from, eg a work of reference; to deliberate, to confer.—**consulter, consultor** *n*.
consultant *n* a specialist who gives professional or technical advice; a senior physician or surgeon in a hospital; a person who consults another.—**consultancy** *n* (*pl* **consultancies**).
consultation *n* the act of consulting; a conference, esp with a professional adviser.—**consultative, consultatory, consultive** *adj*.
consultative, consultatory *adj* advisory; deliberative.
consumable *adj* able to be consumed. * *n* (*usu pl*) something bought to be used.
consume *vti* to destroy; to use up; to eat or drink up; to waste away; to utilize economic goods.
consumer *n* a person who uses goods and services, the end user.
consumer goods *npl* commodities for domestic consumption which are not used for the production of other goods and services.
consumerism *n* protection of the interests of consumers; encouragement to buy consumer goods.
consumer price index *n* an index of the prices of the food, clothing and housing necessary for life.
consummate[1] *vt* to bring to perfection, to be the crown of; (*marriage*) to complete by sexual intercourse.—**consummation** *n*.—**consummative, consummatory** *adj*.—**consummator** *n*.
consummate[2] *adj* complete, perfect, highly skilled.
consumption *n* the act of consuming; the state of being consumed or used up; (*econ*) expenditure on goods and services by consumers; tuberculosis.
consumptive *adj* tending to consume; affected with consumption. * *n* a person with tuberculosis.
contact *n* touch, touching; connection; an acquaintance, esp one willing to provide help or introductions in business, etc; a connection allowing the passage of electricity; (*med*) a person who has been in contact with a contagious disease.* *vti* to establish contact with.—**contactual** *adj*.
contact lens *n* a thin correctional lens placed over the cornea of the eye.
contagion *n* the communicating of a disease by contact; a disease spread in this way; a corrupting influence.
contagious *adj* (*disease*) spread by contact; capable of spreading disease by contact; (*influence*) catching, infectious.—**contagiousness** *n*.
contain *vt* to hold, to enclose; to comprise, to include; to hold back or restrain within fixed limits.
container *n* a receptacle, etc designed to contain goods or substances; a standardized receptacle used to transport commodities.
containerize *vt* to put or convey (cargo) in large standardized containers.
containment *n* the prevention of the expansion of a hostile power; the prevention of the release of dangerous quantities of radioactive material from a nuclear reactor.
containment building *n* a building enclosing a nuclear reactor to limit the spread of radiation, esp in the event of an accident.
contaminate *vt* to render impure by touch or mixing, to pollute, esp by radioactive contact.—**contaminant** *n*.—**contaminator** *n*.
contamination *n* the act of contaminating; the state of being contaminated; a thing that contaminates.
conte *n* a short story.
contemn *vt* to despise; to disregard scornfully.—**contemner, contemnor** *n*.—**contemnible** *adj*.
contemplate *vti* to look at steadily; to reflect upon, to meditate; to have in view, to intend.—**contemplator** *n*.
contemplation *n* the act of contemplating; pious meditation; intention.
contemplative *adj* thoughtful, meditative, of or given to contemplation; dedicated to religious contemplation.—**contemplatively** *adv*.—**contemplativeness** *n*.
contemporaneous *adj* existing or occurring at the same time; of the same period.—**contemporaneously** *adv*.—**contemporaneity** *n*.
contemporary *adj* living or happening at the same time; of about the same age; present day; of or following present-day trends in style, art, fashion, etc. * *n* (*pl* **contemporaries**) a person living at the same time; a person of the same age.—**contemporarily** *adv*.
contempt *n* the feeling one has towards someone or something considered low, worthless etc; the condition of being despised; disregard.
contemptible *adj* deserving contempt.—**contemptibly** *adv*.—**contemptibility** *n*.
contemptuous *adj* showing or feeling contempt; disdainful.—**contemptuously** *adv*.—**contemptuousness** *n*.
contend *vti* to take part in a contest, to strive (for); to quarrel; to maintain (that), to assert or argue strongly for.—**contender** *n*.
content[1] *n* (*usu pl*) what is in a container; (*usu pl*) what is in a book; substance or meaning.
content[2] *adj* satisfied (with), not desiring more; willing (to); happy; pleased. * *n* quiet satisfaction. * *vt* to make content; to satisfy.—**contentment** *n*.
contented *adj* content; gratified, satisfied.—**contentedly** *adv*.
contention *n* contending, struggling, arguing; a point in dispute; an assertion in an argument.—**contentional** *adj*.
contentious *adj* tending to argue; likely to cause dispute, controversial.—**contentiously** *adv*.
conterminous *adj* having a common boundary (with), contiguous.—*also* **coterminous**.
contest *vti* to call in question, to dispute; to fight to gain, to compete for; to strive. * *n* a struggle, an encounter; a competition; a debate; a dispute.—**contestable** *adj*.—**contestation** *n*.—**contester** *n*.
contestant *n* a competitor in a contest; a person who contests.
context *n* the parts of a written work or speech that precede and follow a word or passage, contributing to its full meaning; associated surroundings, setting.—**contextual** *adj*.—**contextually** *adv*.
contextualize *vt* to place in or treat as part of a context.
contexture *n* a structure; a fabric; a style of composition.—**contextural** *adj*.
contiguous *adj* touching, adjoining; near; adjacent.—**contiguity** *n*.
continent[1] *n* one of the six or seven main divisions of the earth's land; (*with cap*) the mainland of Europe, excluding the British Isles; a large extent of land.

continent[2] *adj* able to control urination and defecation; practising self-restraint; chaste.—**continence, continency** *n*.

continental *adj* of a continent; (*with cap*) of or relating to Europe, excluding the British Isles; of or relating to the former thirteen British colonies later forming the USA. * *n* an inhabitant of the Continent.—**continentalism** *n*.—**continentalist** *n*.—**continentally** *adv*.

continental breakfast *n* a light morning meal of coffee and rolls.

continental drift *n* (*geol*) the (theoretical) gradual process of separation of the continents from their original solid land mass.

continental shelf *n* the sea bed, under relatively shallow seas, bordering a continent.

contingency *n* (*pl* **contingencies**) a possibility of a future event or condition; something dependent on a future event.

contingent *adj* possible, that may happen; chance; dependent (on); incidental (to). * *n* a possibility; a quota of troops.—**contingently** *adv*.

continual *adj* frequently repeated, going on all the time.—**continuality** *n*.—**continually** *adv*.

continuance *n* uninterrupted succession; duration.

continuant *n* a consonant whose sound can be prolonged, as *f*, *v*.

continuation *n* a continuing; prolongation; resumption; a thing that continues something else, a sequel, a further instalment.

continue *vt* to go on (with); to prolong; to extend; to resume, to carry further. * *vi* to remain, to stay; to last; to preserve.—**continuable** *adj*.—**continuer** *n*.—**continuingly** *adv*.

continuity *n* (*pl* **continuities**) continuousness; uninterrupted succession; the complete script or scenario in a film or broadcast.

continuous *adj* continuing; occurring without interruption.—**continuously** *adv*.—**continuousness** *n*.

continuum *n* (*pl* **continua, continuums**) a continuous and homogeneous whole.

contort *vti* to twist out of a normal shape, to pull awry.—**contorted** *adj*.—**contortion** *n*.—**contortional** *adj*.

contortionist *n* a person who can twist his or her body into unusual postures, esp as entertainment.—**contortionistic** *adj*.

contour *n* the outline of a figure, land, etc; the line representing this outline; a contour line. * *adj* made according to a shape or form (*contour chair*).

contour line *n* a line on a map that passes through all points at the same altitude.

contra *n* a thing that may be argued against.

contra- *prefix* against.

contraband *n* smuggled goods; smuggling. * *adj* illegal to import or export.—**contrabandist** *n*.

contraband of war *n* certain commodities used in warfare; the traffic in them with belligerent states; goods supplied to one belligerent and seizable by another.

contrabass *n* an instrument sounding an octave lower than another instrument of the same class; the largest instrument of the violin class, the double bass.—**contrabassist** *n*.

contrabassoon *n* the largest instrument of the oboe class.—**contrabassoonist** *n*.

contraception *n* the deliberate prevention of conception, birth control.

contraceptive *n* a contraceptive drug or device.—*also adj*.

contract *vt* to draw closer together; to confine; to undertake by contract; (*debt*) to incur; (*disease*) to become infected by; (*word*) to shorten by omitting letters. * *vi* to shrink; to become smaller or narrower; to make a contract; (*with* **out**) to decide not to take part in or join, eg a pension scheme. * *n* a bargain; an agreement to supply goods or perform work at a stated price; a written agreement enforceable by law.—**contractibility** *n*.—**contractible** *adj*.

contract bridge *n* a form of bridge in which the players contract to take a certain number of tricks.

contractile *adj* able or causing to grow smaller.—**contractility** *n*.

contraction *n* the act of contracting; the state of being contracted; a contracted word; a labour pain in childbirth.—**contractional** *adj*.—**contractive** *adj*.

contractor *n* a person who makes a business contract, esp a builder; something that draws together, eg a muscle.

contractual *adj* of a contract.—**contractually** *adv*.

contradance *see* **contredanse**.

contradict *vti* to assert the contrary or opposite of; to deny; to be at variance (with); to lack consistency.—**contradictable** *adj*.—**contradicter, contradictor** *n*.

contradiction *n* the act of contradicting; a denial.—**contradictory** *adj*.

contradistinction *n* a distinction by opposite qualities.—**contradistinctive** *adj*.

contradistinguish *vt* to mark the difference between two things by contrasting their opposite qualities.

contralto *n* (*pl* **contraltos**) a singing voice having a range between tenor and mezzo-soprano; a person having this voice.

contraposition *n* opposition, antithesis.

contraption *n* (*inf*) a device, a gadget.

contrapuntal *adj* of or according to counterpoint.—**contrapuntally** *adv*.

contrapuntist *n* one skilled in the rules of counterpoint.

contrariety *n* (*pl* **contrarieties**) opposition; inconsistency, discrepancy.

contrariwise *adv* on the other hand; conversely.

contrary *adj* opposed; opposite in nature; wayward, perverse. * *n* (*pl* **contraries**) the opposite. * *adv* in opposition to; in conflict with.—**contrarily** *adv*.—**contrariness** *n*.

contrast *vi* to show marked differences. * *vt* to compare so as to point out the differences. * *n* the exhibition of differences; difference of qualities shown by comparison; the degree of difference between colours or tones when put together.

contravene *vt* to infringe (a law), to transgress; to conflict with, to contradict.—**contravener** *n*.—**contravention** *n*.

contredanse *n* a dance in which the partners are arranged in opposite lines; the music for this.—*also* **contradance**.

contretemps *n* (*pl* **contretemps**) a confusing, embarrassing or awkward occurrence.

contribute *vti* to give to a common stock or fund; to write (an article) for a magazine or newspaper; to furnish ideas, etc.—**contributive** *adj*.

contribution *n* the act of contributing; something contributed; a literary article; a payment into a collection.

contributor *n* a person who contributes, esp the writer of an article for a newspaper, etc; a factor, a contributory cause.—**contributorial** *adj*.

contributory *adj* giving, donating; partly responsible, sharing in.

con trick *n* (*inf*) confidence trick.

contrite *adj* deeply repentant, feeling guilt.—**contritely** *adv*.—**contrition** *n*.

contrivance *n* something contrived, esp a mechanical device, invention; inventive ability; an artificial construct; a stratagem.

contrive *vt* to plan ingeniously; to devise, to design, to manage; to achieve, esp by some ploy or trick; to scheme.—**contriver** *n*.

contrived *adj* skilful but overdone; (*writing*) not spontaneous or natural or flowing.

control *n* restraint; command, authority; a check; a means of controlling; a standard of comparison for checking an experiment; (*pl*) mechanical parts by which a car, aeroplane, etc is operated. * *vt* (**controlling, controlled**) to check; to restrain; to regulate; to govern; (*experiment*) to verify by comparison.

controllable *adj* able to be controlled.—**controllably** *adv*.

controller *n* a person who controls, esp one in charge of expenditure or finances.

control tower *n* a tower at an airport from which flight directions are given.

controversial *adj* causing controversy, open to argument.—**controversialism** *n*.—**controversialist** *n*.—**controversially** *adv*.

controversy *n* (*pl* **controversies**) a discussion of contrary opinions; dispute, argument.

controvert *vt* to contend against; to refute; to disprove.—**controverter** *n*.—**controvertible** *adj*.

contumacious *adj* resisting authority, insubordinate; obstinate.

contumacy *n* (*pl* **contumacies**) stubborn resistance to authority, esp contempt of court.—**contumacious** *adj*.
contumelious *adj* haughtily contemptuous or offensive; supercilious.
contumely *n* (*pl* **contumelies**) haughty and contemptuous rudeness; scornful and insolent abuse; reproach, disgrace.
contuse *vt* to wound or bruise without breaking the skin.—**contusive** *adj*.
contusion *n* a wound that does not break the skin, a bruise.—**contusioned** *adj*.
conundrum *n* a riddle involving a pun; a puzzling question.
conurbation *n* a vast urban area around and including a large city.
convalesce *vi* to recover health and strength after an illness; to get better.—**convalescence** *n*.
convalescent *adj* recovering health; aiding the recovery of full health. * *n* a patient recovering after an illness.
convection *n* the transmission of heat through a liquid by currents; the process whereby warmer air rises while cooler air drops.—**convectional** *adj*.—**convective** *adj*.
convector *n* a heater that circulates warm air.
convene *vti* to call together for a meeting.—**convenable** *adj*.—**convener** *n*.
convenience *n* what suits one; a useful appliance.
convenience food *n* food that is easily and quickly prepared.
convenient *adj* handy; suitable; causing little or no trouble.—**conveniently** *adv*.
convent *n* a house of a religious order, esp an establishment of nuns.
conventicle *n* a meeting house; a secret meeting; an assembly for worship, usu by a schism; (*formerly*) a prohibited meeting of Nonconformists or Covenanters.
convention *n* a political or ecclesiastical assembly or meeting; an agreement between nations, a treaty; established usage, social custom.
conventional *adj* of or based on convention or social custom; not spontaneous; lacking imagination or originality; following accepted rules; (*weapons*) non-nuclear.—**conventionality** *n* (*pl* **conventionalities**).—**conventionally** *adj*.
conventionalism *n* that which is received as established by usage, etc; adherence to established usage.—**conventionalist** *n*.
conventionalize *vt* to make conventional.—**conventionalization** *n*.
conventual *adj* belonging to a convent. * *n* a member or inmate of a convent.
converge *vti* to come or bring together.—**convergence, convergency** *n*.—**convergent** *adj*.
conversable *adj* disposed to converse, sociable.
conversant *adj* well acquainted; proficient; familiar (with).—**conversance, conversancy** *n*.
conversation *n* informal talk or exchange of ideas, opinions, etc between people.—**conversational** *adj*.—**conversationally** *adv*.
conversationalist, conversationist *n* a person who is good at conversation.
conversation piece *n* originally an 18th-century picture showing a group in an outdoor or indoor setting; something unusual or novel that provokes conversation; a play that focuses interest on dialogue as much as on action.
conversazione *n* (*pl* **conversazioni, conversaziones**) a meeting for conversation, esp on literary or scientific topics.
converse[1] *vi* to engage in conversation (with). * *n* familiar talk, conversation.—**converser** *n*.
converse[2] *adj* opposite, contrary. * *n* something that is opposite or contrary.—**conversely** *adv*.
conversion *n* change from one state, or from one religion, to another; something converted from one use to another; an alteration to a building undergoing a change in function; (*rugby*) a score after a try by kicking the ball over the crossbar.—**conversional, conversionary** *adj*.
convert *vt* to change from one thing, condition or religion to another; to alter; to apply to a different use; (*rugby*) to make a conversion after a try. * *n* a converted person, esp one who has changed religion.
converter, convertor *n* one who converts; an iron retort used for converting pig iron into steel in the Bessemer process; a kind of electrical induction coil.
converter reactor *n* a nuclear reactor that changes fertile material to fissile material.
convertible *adj* able to be converted. * *n* an automobile with a folding or detachable roof.—**convertibility** *n*.
convex *adj* curving outward like the surface of a sphere.—**convexly** *adv*.—**convexity** *n*.
convexo-concave *adj* convex on one side, concave on the other.
convexo-convex *adj* curving outwards on both sides, as a lens.
convey *vt* to transport; to conduct, to transmit; to make known, to communicate; (*law*) to make over (property).—**conveyable** *adj*.—**conveyor, conveyer** *n*.
conveyance *n* the act of conveying; a means of transporting, a vehicle; (*law*) the act of transferring property.—**conveyancer** *n*.
conveyancing *n* the business of drawing up deeds, leases, etc, and investigating titles to property.
conveyor belt *n* a continuous moving belt or linked plates for moving objects in a factory.
convict *vt* to prove or pronounce guilty. * *n* a convicted person serving a prison sentence.
conviction *n* act of convicting; a settled opinion; a firm belief.
convince *vt* to persuade by argument or evidence; to satisfy by proof.—**convincer** *n*.—**convincible** *adj*.
convincing *adj* compelling belief.—**convincingly** *adv*.
convivial *adj* sociable, jovial.—**conviviality** *n*.—**convivially** *adv*.
convocation *n* the act of convoking an assembly, esp of bishops, clergy or heads of a university; an assembly of clergy.—**convocational** *adj*.—**convocator** *n*.
convoke to call or summon together; to convene.—**convoker** *n*.
convolute *vt* to form into a rolled or coiled shape. * *adj* (*bot*) rolled upon itself; coiled.
convoluted *adj* twisted; coiled; complicated, difficult to understand.
convolution *n* a rolling together, a coiling; a fold, a twist; a complicated or confused matter.
convolve *vt* to roll together.
convolvulus *n* (*pl* **convolvuluses, convolvuli**) a twining plant with bell-shaped flowers.
convoy *n* a group of ships or vehicles travelling together for protection. * *vt* to travel thus.
convulse *vt* to agitate violently; to shake with irregular spasms. * *vi* (*inf*) to cause to shake with uncontrollable laughter.—**convulsive** *adj*.—**convulsively** *adv*.
convulsion *n* a violent involuntary contraction of a muscle or muscles; an agitation, tumult; (*pl*) a violent fit of laughter.
cony, coney *n* (*pl* **conies, coneys**) rabbit, or the skin or fur of a rabbit used in making clothes.
coo *n* the note of the pigeon; a soft murmuring sound. * *vt* (**cooing, cooed**) to utter the cry of a dove or pigeon; to speak softly; to act or murmur in a loving manner.
cook *vt* to prepare (food) by heat; (*inf*) to fake (accounts, etc); to subject to great heat. * *vi* to be a cook; to undergo cooking; (*with* **up**) to plot; to make up a story. * *n* a person who cooks; one whose job is to cook.—**cookable** *adj*.
cookbook, cookery book *n* a book of recipes and other information for preparing food.
cook-chill *n* (*catering*) a method in which meals are pre-cooked, chilled rapidly and then reheated as required.
cooker *n* an electric or gas appliance for cooking.
cookery *n* the art or practice of cooking.
cookhouse *n* a kitchen, esp outdoors.
cookie, cooky *n* (*pl* **cookies**) a small flat sweet cake; (*sl*) a person.
cookout *n* a meal cooked and eaten outdoors, a barbecue.
cool *adj* moderately cold; calm; indifferent; unenthusiastic; cheeky. * *vti* to make or become cool. * *n* coolness; composure.—**coolly** *adv*.—**coolness** *n*.
coolant *n* a fluid or other substance for cooling machinery.

cooler *n* that which cools; a vessel for cooling liquids, etc; a drink of spirits; (*sl*) prison.
cool-headed *adj* not easily excited.
coolie, cooly *n* (*pl* **coolies**) an Indian or Chinese hired labourer.
cooling tower *n* a tall hollow construction used in some industries, in which water is cooled and reused.
coon *n* a raccoon; (*derog*) a black person.
cooncan *n* a card game for two.
coop *n* a small pen for poultry. * *vt* to confine as in a coop.
co-op *n* a cooperative.
cooper *n* one who makes and repairs barrels, etc.
cooperage *n* the business or workshop of a cooper; the price for a cooper's work.
cooperate *vi* to work together, to act jointly.—**cooperation** *n*.—**cooperator** *n*.
cooperative *adj* willing to cooperate; helpful. * *n* an organization or enterprise owned by, and operated for the benefit of, those using its services.—**cooperatively** *adv*.
co-opt *vt* to elect or choose as a member by the agreement of the existing members.—**co-optation, co-option** *n*.—**co-optative, co-optive** *adj*.
coordinate *vt* to integrate (different elements, etc) into an efficient relationship; to adjust to; to function harmoniously. * *n* an equal person or thing; any of a series of numbers that, in a given frame of reference, locate a point in space; (*pl*) separate items of clothing intended to be worn together. * *adj* equal in degree or status.—**coordinately** *adv*.—**coordinator** n.
coordination *n* the act of coordinating; the state of being coordinated; balanced and harmonious movement of the body.
coot *n* a European water-bird with dark plumage and a white spot on the forehead; a silly person.
cootie *n* (*sl*) a louse.
cop[1] *vb* (**copping, copped**) *vt* (*sl*) to arrest, catch. * *vi* (*with* **out**) (*sl*) to fail to perform, to renege. * *n* (*sl*) capture; a policeman.
cop[2] *n* a conical ball of thread on a spindle.
copaiba *n* an aromatic resinous balsam from various South American and West Indian trees.
copal *n* a gum resin used in varnishes.
coparcenary *n* joint heirship.
coparcener *n* a coheir.
copartner *n* a joint partner.—**copartnership** *n*.
cope[1] *vi* to deal successfully with; to contend on even terms (with).
cope[2] *n* a large semicircular ecclesiastical vestment worn by bishops and priests over the surplice; a canopy, esp of heaven.
Copernican *adj* of or relating to Copernicus and his teaching that the earth and planets revolve around the sun.
copestone *n* the top stone of a structure; a crowning touch.
copier *n* a copying machine, a photocopier.
copilot *n* a second pilot in an aircraft.
coping *n* the top masonry of a wall.
coping saw *n* a saw with a U-shaped frame and narrow blade used for cutting outlines in wood.
copious *adj* plentiful, abundant.—**copiously** *adv*.—**copiousness** *n*.
cop-out *n* (*sl*) an evasion; a means of avoiding responsibility.
copper[1] *n* a reddish ductile metallic element; a bronze coin. * *adj* made of, or of the colour of, copper. * *vt* to cover with copper.—**coppery** *adj*.
copper[2] *n* (*sl*) a police officer.
copper-bottomed *adj* to be trusted; financially sound.
copperhead *n* a South American snake.
copperplate *n* a polished plate of copper for engraving or printing; a print from this; copybook writing.
coppersmith *n* a worker in copper.
copra *n* the dried kernel of the coconut after the oil has been removed.
copro- *prefix* dung.
coprolite *n* fossil dung.—**coprolitic** *adj*.
coprophagous *adj* feeding on dung, as certain beetles.—**coprophagy** *n*.
coprophilia *n* an abnormal interest in faeces; love of obscenity.
coprophilous *adj* growing in dung.
copse *n* a thicket of small trees and shrubs.
Copt *n* a native Egyptian Christian.
copter *n* a helicopter.
Coptic *adj* pertaining to the Copts, their church or their language. * *n* the language spoken by Copts.
copula *n* (*pl* **copulas, copulae**) a link, a connecting part; (*gram*) a word that joins the subject and predicate in a sentence or proposition.—**copular** *adj*.
copulate *vi* to have sexual intercourse.—**copulation** *n*.—**copulatory** *adj*.
copulative *adj* joining, uniting; (*gram*) serving as a copula; uniting ideas as well as words. * *n* a copulative conjunction.
copy *n* (*pl* **copies**) a reproduction; a transcript; a single specimen of a book; a model to be copied; a manuscript for printing; newspaper text; text for an advertisement; subject matter for a writer. * *vt* (**copying, copied**) to make a copy of, to reproduce; to take as a model, to imitate.
copybook *n* a book of handwriting exercises.
copy-edit *vt* to correct and prepare text for printing.
copyhold *n* (*English law*) a tenure of estate by copy of the court roll or custom of the manor.
copyholder *n* a tenant by copyhold; (*print*) a reader's assistant.
copyist *n* one who copies.
copyright *n* the exclusive legal right to the publication and sale of a literary, dramatic, musical, or artistic work in any form. * *adj* protected by copyright.
copywriter *n* a writer of advertising or publicity copy.—**copywriting** *n*.
coq au vin *n* a dish of chicken cooked in wine.
coquet *vi* (**coquetting, coquetted**) to flirt with; to seek to attract attention or admiration; to trifle.
coquetry *n* (*pl* **coquetries**) the act of coquetting; flirtatious behaviour.
coquette *n* a woman who trifles with men's affections.—**coquettish** *adj*.
coquito *n* (*pl* **coquitos**) a tall Chilean palm producing edible nuts and palm honey.
coracle *n* a boat with a wicker frame covered with leather.
coracoid *n* a hook-like process of the scapula or bladebone.
coral *n* the hard skeleton secreted by certain marine polyps. * *adj* made of coral, esp jewellery; of the colour of coral, deepish pink.
coralline, coralloid *adj* consisting of, or like, coral; of a colour like coral.* *n* a coral-like seaweed or animal.
coral reef *n* a formation or bank of coral.
coral tree *n* an American tree with blood-red flowers.
corban *n* an offering to God in fulfilment of a vow.
corbeil *n* (*archit*) a sculptured basket of flowers, fruit, etc.
corbel *n* a stone or timber projection from a wall to support something. * *vt* (**corbelling, corbelled** *or* **corbeling, corbeled**) to furnish with or support by corbel.
corbicula *n* (*pl* **corbiculae**) the receptacle for pollen in the honey bee.
cord *n* a thick string or thin rope; something that binds; a slender electric cable; a ribbed fabric, esp corduroy; (*pl*) corduroy trousers; any part of the body resembling string or rope (*spinal cord*).
cordage *n* a quantity of cords or ropes; ropes and rigging collectively.
cordate *adj* heart-shaped.
cordial *adj* hearty, warm; friendly; affectionate. * *n* a fruit-flavoured drink.—**cordially** *adv*.—**cordialness** *n*.
cordiality *n* (*pl* **cordialities**) sincere sympathethic geniality; sincerity; heartiness.
cordiform *adj* heart-shaped.
cordillera *n* a continuous ridge or chain of mountains, esp of the Andes mountains.
cordite *n* an explosive used in bullets and shells.
cordless *adj* (*electrical device*) operated by a battery.
cordon *n* a chain of police or soldiers preventing access to an area; a piece of ornamental cord or ribbon given as an award. * *vt* (*with* **off**) (*area*) to prevent access to.

cordon bleu *n* the highest distinction in any profession; a first-class cook.—*also adj*.

cordon sanitaire *n* a barrier around an infected area; a buffer zone.

cordovan *n* a Spanish leather made of goatskin or split horsehide, tanned and dressed.—*also* **cordwain.**

cords *npl* (*inf*) corduroy trousers.

corduroy *n* a strong cotton fabric with a velvety ribbed surface; (*pl*) trousers of this.

corduroy road *n* a roadway formed of logs laid crosswise across swampy ground, etc.

cordwain *see* **cordovan.**

cordwainer *n* (*arch*) a worker in leather; a shoemaker.

core *n* the innermost part, the heart; the inner part of an apple, etc containing seeds; the region of a nuclear reactor containing the fissile material; (*comput*) a form of magnetic memory used to store one bit of information. * *vt* to remove the core from.—**corer** *n.*

coreopsis *n* a kind of plant with rayed flowers and seeds with two small horns at the end.

corespondent *n* (*law*) a person named as having committed adultery with the husband or wife from whom a divorce is sought.—**corespondency** *n.*

corgi *n* (*pl* **corgis**) a Welsh breed of dog with short legs and a sturdy body.

coriaceous *adj* of leather; leathery.

coriander *n* a plant with aromatic seeds used for flavouring food.

Corinthian *adj* of or pertaining to Corinth, a Greek city noted for its luxury and licentiousness; luxurious; conducted by amateurs; (*archit*) denoting the Corinthian order. * *n* a man about town; a gentleman yachtsman or sportsman.

Corinthian order *n* the lightest and most ornate of the classic orders of architecture, with a bell-shaped capital and ornamented with acanthus leaves.

corium *n* (*pl* **coria**) the innermost layer of skin of the cuticle.

cork *n* the outer bark of the cork oak used esp for stoppers and insulation; a stopper for a bottle, esp made of cork. * *adj* made of cork. * *vt* to stop up with a cork; to give a taste of cork to (wine).

corkage *n* a charge made by a restaurant for serving wine, esp when brought in by the customer from outside.

corked *adj* (*wine*) contaminated by a decayed cork.

corker *n* (*sl*) something conclusive or superlatively good; a flagrant lie.

corkscrew *n* a tool for drawing corks from wine bottles. * *adj* spiral-shaped, resembling a corkscrew.

corky *adj* made of, or like, cork.

corm *n* the bulb-like underground stem of the crocus, etc; a solid bulb.—**cormous** *adj.*

cormel *n* a new corm developing from a mature one.

cormorant *n* a large voracious sea bird with dark plumage and webbed feet.

corn[1] *n* a grain or seed of a cereal plant; plants that yield grain; maize; (*sl*) something corny.

corn[2] *n* a small hard painful growth on the foot.

corn[3] *vt* to preserve or cure, as with salt.

corn(ed) beef *n* cooked salted beef.

corn circle *see* **crop circle.**

corncob *n* the central part of an ear of maize to which the corn kernels are attached; a corncob pipe.

corncockle *n* a plant with purplish flowers that grows among corn.

corncrake *n* a bird with a harsh cry, the landrail.

corncrib *n* a storehouse for corn.

cornea *n* (*pl* **corneas, corneae**) the transparent membrane in front of the eyeball.—**corneal** *adj.*

cornel *n* the cornelian cherry or dogwood, yielding an acrid edible red berry.

cornelian *n* a dull-red semi-transparent form of chalcedony.—*also* **carnelian.**

corneous *adj* horny.

corner *n* the point where sides or streets meet; an angle; a secret or confined place; a difficult or dangerous situation; (*football, hockey*) a free kick from the corner of the pitch; a monopoly over the supply of a good or service giving control over the market price; one of the opposite angles in a boxing ring. * *vt* to force into a corner; to monopolize supplies of (a commodity). * *vi* to turn round a corner; to meet at a corner or angle.

cornerstone *n* the principal stone, esp one at the corner of a foundation; an indispensable part; the most important thing or person.

cornet *n* a tapering valved brass musical instrument; a cone-shaped wafer for ice cream.

cornetist, cornettist *n* a performer on the cornet.

cornfield *n* a field planted with corn or other cereal plants.

cornflakes *npl* a breakfast cereal made from split and toasted maize.

cornflour *n* a type of corn or maize flour used for thickening sauces.—*also* **cornstarch.**

cornflower *n* a blue-flowered wild plant growing in cornfields.

cornice *n* a plaster moulding round a ceiling or on the outside of a building.

corniche *n* a coastal road, esp one along a cliff offering spectacular views.

corniculate *adj* horned; spurred.

Corn Laws *npl* British laws (1436–1834) for regulating the import and export of corn, repealed 1846–9.

corn pone *n* a type of Indian cornbread made with milk and eggs.

cornstalk *n* a stem of corn; (*sl*) a youth or girl of Australian birth.

cornstarch *see* **cornflour.**

cornucopia *n* a horn-shaped container overflowing with fruits, flowers, etc; great abundance, an inexhaustible store.

cornute, cornuted *adj* (*biol*) horned; horn-like.

corny *adj* (**cornier, corniest**) (*inf*) hackneyed; banal; trite; overly sentimental.—**cornily** *adv.*—**corniness** *n.*

corolla *n* the inner envelope of a flower composed of two or more petals.

corollary *n* (*pl* **corollaries**) an additional inference from a proposition already proved; a result.

corona *n* (*pl* **coronas, coronae**) a top; a crown; a luminous halo or envelope round the sun or moon; the flat projecting part of a cornice.

coronal *adj* pertaining to the corona. * *n* a crown or garland.

coronary *adj* pertaining to the arteries supplying blood to the heart. * *n* (*pl* **coronaries**) a coronary artery; coronary thrombosis.

coronary thrombosis *n* blockage of one of the coronary arteries by a blood clot.

coronation *n* the act or ceremony of crowning a sovereign.

coroner *n* a public official who inquires into the causes of sudden or accidental deaths.—**coronership** *n.*

coronet *n* a small crown; an ornamental headdress.

corpora *see* **corpus.**

corporal[1] *n* a noncommissioned officer below the rank of sergeant.—**corporalship** *n.*

corporal[2] *adj* of or relating to the body; physical, not spiritual.—**corporality** *n.*—**corporally** *adv.*

corporal[3] *n* a communion cloth.

corporate *adj* legally united into a body; of or having a corporation; united.—**corporately** *adv.*

corporation *n* a group of people authorized by law to act as one individual; a city or town council.—**corporative** *n.*

corporator *n* a member of a corporation.

corporeal *adj* having a body or substance, material.—**corporeality, corporealness** *n.*—**corporeally** *adv.*

corposant *n* a flame-like electric discharge from a ship's mast and rigging in thundery weather, St Elmo's fire.

corps *n* (*pl* **corps**) an organized subdivision of the military establishment; a group or organization with a special function (*medical corps*).

corps de ballet *n* all the dancers in a ballet company.

corps diplomatique *n* all the ambassadors at a particular capital, the diplomatic corps.

corpse *n* a dead body. * *vi* (*theat sl*) to laugh or create laughter mischievously on stage.

corpulent *adj* fleshy, fat.—**corpulence, corpulency** *n*.
corpus *n* (*pl* **corpora**) a body or collection, esp of written works; the chief part of an organ.
Corpus Christi *n* (*RC Church*) a festival in honour of the Eucharist, held on the Thursday after Trinity Sunday.
corpuscle *n* a red or white blood cell.—**corpuscular** *adj*.
corpus delicti *n* (*law*) the essence of a crime charged.
corral *n* a pen for livestock; an enclosure with wagons; a strong stockade. * *vt* (**corralling, corralled**) to form a corral; to put or keep in a corral.
correct *vt* to set right, to remove errors from; to reprove, to punish; to counteract, to neutralize; to adjust. * *adj* free from error; right, true, accurate; conforming to a fixed standard; proper.—**correctable, correctible** *adj*.—**correctly** *adv*.—**correctness** *n*.—**corrector** *n*.
correction *n* the act of correcting; punishment.—**correctional** *adj*.
correctitude *n* correctness, esp of conduct.
corrective *adj* serving to correct or counteract. * *n* that which corrects.—**correctively** *adv*.
correlate *vti* to have or to bring into mutual relation; to correspond to one another. * *n* either of two things so related that one implies the other.—**correlation** *n*.—**correlative** *adj*.
correlation *n* reciprocal relation; similarity or parallelism of relation or law; the interdependence of functions, organs, natural forces, or phenomena.—**correlational** *adj*.
correlative *adj* having or expressing reciprocal or mutual relation. * *n* the antecedent to a pronoun.—**correlativeness, correlativity** *n*.
correspond *vi* to answer, to agree; to be similar (to); to tally; to communicate by letter.
correspondence *n* communication by writing letters; the letters themselves; agreement.
correspondence school *n* an institution offering tuition (**correspondence courses**) by post.
correspondent *n* a person who writes letters; a journalist who gathers news for newspapers, radio or television from a foreign country. * *adj* similar, analogous.
corridor *n* a long passage into which compartments in a train or rooms in a building open; a strip of land giving a country without a coastline access to the sea.
corrie *n* (*Scot*) a round hollow on a hillside.
corrigendum *n* (*pl* **corrigenda**) an error in a book, etc, for which a correction slip is printed.
corrigible *adj* capable of being amended, correct, or reformed.—**corrigibility** *n*.
corroborant *adj* corroborating. * *n* a corroborating fact.
corroborate *vt* to confirm; to make more certain; to verify.—**corroboration** *n*.—**corroborative** *adj*.—**corroborator** *n*.
corroboree *n* an Australian festivity and dance.
corrode *vti* to eat into or wear away gradually, to rust; to disintegrate.—**corrodant, corrodent** *n*.—**corroder** *n*.—**corrodible** *adj*.—**corrosion** *n*.
corrosion *n* the act of corroding; a corroded condition.
corrosive *adj* causing corrosion. * *n* a corrosive substance, as acid.—**corrosively** *adv*.—**corrosiveness** *n*.
corrosive sublimate *n* a poisonous compound of mercury.
corrugate *vt* to form into parallel ridges and grooves.—**corrugated** *adj*.—**corrugation** *n*.
corrugated iron *n* sheet iron pressed in alternate parallel ridges and grooves and galvanized.
corrugated paper *n* paper used for packaging with one surface in parallel ridges.
corrupt *adj* dishonest; taking bribes; depraved; rotten, putrid. * *vti* to make or become corrupt; to infect; to taint.—**corrupter, corruptor** *n*.—**corruptive** *adj*.—**corruptly** *adv*.—**corruptness** *n*.
corruptible *adj* open to corruption.—**corruptibility** *n*.
corruption *n* the act of corrupting; the state of being corrupted; physical dissolution.—**corruptionist** *n*.
corsage *n* a small bunch of flowers for pinning to a dress; the part of a woman's dress covering the bust.
corsair *n* a pirate; a pirate ship.
corse *n* (*poet*) a corpse.
corselet, corslet *n* light body armour, esp for the breast.
corset *n* a close-fitting undergarment, worn to support the torso.
corsetière *n* a woman who makes and fits corsets.—**corsetier** *nm*.
cortege, cortège *n* a train of attendants; a retinue; a funeral procession.
Cortes *n* the national and legislative assembly of Spain and (formerly) Portugal.
cortex *n* (*pl* **cortices**) an outer layer of tissue of any organ, eg the outer grey matter of the brain; the outer tissue of a plant stem; bark of a tree.—**cortical** *adj*.
corticate, corticated *adj* covered with bark or a bark-like substance.—**cortication** *n*.
cortisone *n* a hormone produced by the adrenal glands, the synthetic version of which is used to treat arthritis, allergies and skin disorders, etc.
corundum *n* a hard mineral of many colours used as an abrasive and as gemstones.
coruscate *vi* to sparkle, to flash.—**coruscation** *n*.
corvée *n* the exacting of unpaid labour in the feudal system.
corves *see* **corf**.
corvette *n* a fast escort warship.
corvine *adj* of or pertaining to a crow or raven.
corymb *n* an inflorescence with the flowers all nearly at the same level and the lower stalks are the longest.—**corymbose, corybous** *adj*.
coryphaeus *n* (*pl* **coryphaei**) the leader of the chorus in ancient Greek drama.
coryphée *n* a ballet dancer.
coryza *n* a severe cold in the head with inflammation of the mucous membrane of the nose.
cos *abbr* = cosine.
cosec *abbr* = cosecant.
cosecant *n* (*geom*) the secant of the complement of the given angle or arc of 90°.
coseismal, coseismic *adj* showing simultaneous shocks of an earthquake.
cosh *vt* (*sl*) to bludgeon.
cosher *vt* to pamper, to coddle.
cosignatory *n* a person signing along with another.
cosine *n* a trigonometrical function of an angle that in a right-angled triangle is equal to the ratio of the length of the adjacent side to the hypotenuse.
cosmetic *n* a preparation for improving the beauty, esp of the face. * *adj* beautifying or correcting faults in the appearance.—**cosmetically** *adv*.
cosmetic surgery *n* surgery carried out to improve the appearance.
cosmic, cosmical *adj* of or pertaining to the universe and the laws that govern it; vast in extent, intensity, or comprehensiveness.—**cosmically** *adv*.
cosmo- *prefix* universe.
cosmogony *n* (*pl* **cosmogonies**) the origin of the universe; a theory or treatise on this.—**cosmogonal** *adj*.—**cosmogonic, cosmogonical** *adj*.—**cosmogonist** *n*.
cosmography *n* the description and mapping of the universe or the earth as a whole.—**cosmographer, cosmographist** *n*.—**cosmographic, cosmographical** *adj*.
cosmology *n* the science of the nature, origins, and development of the universe.—**cosmological, cosmologic** *adj*.—**cosmologist** *n*.
cosmonaut *n* a Russian astronaut.
cosmopolitan *adj* of all parts of the world; free from national prejudice; at home in any part of the world. * *n* a well-travelled person; a person without national prejudices.—**cosmopolitanism** *n*.
cosmopolite *n* a citizen of the world, a person without patriotism; an animal or plant found worldwide.—**cosmopolitism** *n*.
cosmos *n* the universe as an ordered whole; any orderly system.
Cossack *n* a member of a Russian people skilled as horsemen. * *adj* pertaining to Cossacks.
cosset *vt* to make a pet of; to pamper.

cost *vt* (**costing, cost**) to involve the payment, loss, or sacrifice of; to have as a price; to estimate and fix the price of. * *n* a price; an expense; expenditure of time, labour, etc; a loss, a penalty; (*pl*) the expenses of a lawsuit.

costa *n* (*pl* **costae**) a rib.—**costal** *adj*.

costard *n* a large kind of English apple; (*arch*) a head.

costate *adj* ribbed.

cost-effective *adj* giving a satisfactory return for the amount spent on outlay.

costive *adj* constipated.

costly *adj* (**costlier, costliest**) expensive; involving great sacrifice.—**costliness** *n*.

costmary *n* (*pl* **costmaries**) a perennial plant with fragrant leaves, formerly used for flavouring ale.

cost-of-living index *n* consumer price index.

costume *n* a style of dress, esp belonging to a particular period, fashion, etc; clothes of an unusual or historical nature, as worn by actors in a play, etc; fancy dress.

costume jewellery *n* imitation gems or cheap jewellery worn for decorative effect.

costumer, costumier *n* a dealer in fancy dress for the theatre, etc.

cosy *adj* (**cosier, cosiest**) warm and comfortable; snug; friendly for an ulterior motive. * *n* a cover to keep a thing warm.—*also* **cozy.**—**cosily** *adv*.—**cosiness** *n*.

cot[1] *n* a child's box-like bed; a narrow collapsible bed.

cot[2] *abbr* = cotangent.

cotangent *n* a trigonometrical function of an angle that in a right-angled triangle is equal to the ratio of the length of the adjacent side to the opposite side.

cot death *n* the sudden death of a baby during sleep from an unexplained cause.—*also* **crib death.**

cote *n* a shed or shelter for animals or birds, esp doves.

cotenant *n* a joint tenant.—**cotenancy** *n*.

coterie *n* a small circle of people with common interests; a social clique.

coterminous *see* **conterminous.**

cotidal *adj* (*chart lines*) joining those places where high tide occurs at the same time.

cotillion *n* a brisk, lively dance for eight or more people; music for such a dance; a formal ball.

cotoneaster *n* an ornamental shrub of the rose family with red or orange berries.

cotta *n* (*pl* **cottae, cottas**) a short surplice.

cottage *n* a small house, esp in the country.

cottage cheese *n* a soft cheese made from loose milk curds.

cottage industry *n* manufacture carried out in the home, eg weaving, basketry.

cottager *n* a person who lives or holidays in a cottage.

cotter[1], **cottar** *n* a farm labourer who has the use of a cottage for which he works in lieu of rent.

cotter[2] *n* a bolt, wedge, etc used to secure parts of machinery to prevent movement.

cotter pin *n* a split pin that secures (a cotter, etc) by spreading the ends after insertion.

cotton *n* soft white fibre of the cotton plant; fabric or thread made of this; thread. * *adj* made of cotton. * *vi* (*with* **on**) (*inf*) to realize the meaning of, to understand; to take a liking to.—**cottony** *adj*.

cotton candy *see* **candyfloss.**

cotton grass *n* a plant with long silky hairs.

cottontail *n* an American rabbit.

cotton wool *n* raw cotton that has been bleached and sterilized for use as a dressing, etc; absorbent cotton; a state of being protected.

cotyledon *n* a seed lobe or rudimentary leaf or leaves of an embryo; kinds of plant, chiefly evergreens.—**cotyledonal** *adj*.—**cotyledonary** *adj*.—**cotyledonous, cotyledonoid** *adj*.

cotyloid, cotyloidal *adj* cup-shaped.

couch *n* a piece of furniture, with a back and armrests, for seating several persons; a bed, esp as used by psychiatrists for patients. * *vt* to express in words in a particular way; to lie down; to deposit in a bed or layer; (*arch*) to crouch ready for springing; to depress or remove (a cataract in the eye).—**coucher** *n*.

couchant *adj* (*her*) lying down with the head up.

couch grass *n* a kind of coarse grass that spreads rapidly.

couching *n* the operation of removing a cataract from the eye by depressing or removing the crystalline lens; a stye of embroidery.

couch potato *n* (*sl*) a person who would rather watch television in leisure time than participate in sports, etc.

cougar *n* a puma.

cough *vi* to expel air from the lungs with a sudden effort and noise; (*with* **up**) (*inf*) to hand over or tell unwillingly. * *n* the act of coughing; a disease causing a cough.

cough drop *n* a lozenge that when sucked relieves a cough.

cough syrup *n* a medicinal liquid to relieve coughing.

could *see* **can**[1].

couldn't = could not.

coulee *n* a dry ravine with sloping sides; a flow of lava.

coulisse *n* a piece of grooved timber in which anything slides; one of the side scenes of a stage; (*pl*) the space between the side scenes.

couloir *n* a steeply ascending gorge in a mountainside.

coulomb *n* an SI unit of electric charge; the quantity of electricity conveyed by a current of one ampere in one second.

coulter *n* a vertical blade at the front of a ploughshare.—*also* **colter.**

coumarin *n* an aromatic crystalline substance obtained from the tonka bean and used in perfumes and medicines.—**coumaric** adj.

council *n* an elected or appointed legislative or advisory body; a central body uniting a group of organizations; an executive body whose members are equal in power and authority.—**councillor, councilor** *n*.—**councillorship, councilorship** *n*.

councillor, councilor *n* a member of a council.—**councillorship, councilorship** *n*.

councilman *n* (*pl* **councilmen**) a member of a council, a councillor.

counsel *n* advice; consultation, deliberate purpose or design; a person who gives counsel, a lawyer or a group of lawyers; a consultant. * *vb* (**counselling** *or* **counseling, counselled** *or* **counseled**) *vt* to advise; to recommend. * *vi* to give or take advice.

counselling, counseling *n* professional guidance for an individual or a couple from a qualified person.

counsellor, counselor *n* an adviser; a lawyer.

counsellor, counselor *n* one who gives advice, esp legal advice, an adviser.

count[1] *n* a European noble.

count[2] *vt* to number, to add up; to reckon; to consider to be; to call aloud (beats or time units); to include or exclude by counting; (*with* **against**) to have an adverse effect. * *vi* to name numbers or add up items in order; to mark time; to be of importance or value; to rely (upon); (*with* **on**) to rely on: (*with* **out**) (*inf*) to exclude, leave out; to pronounce after a count a floored boxer to be the loser. * *n* an act of numbering or reckoning; the total counted; a separate and distinct charge in an indictment; rhythm.

countdown *n* the descending count backwards to zero, eg to the moment a rocket lifts off.

countenance *n* the whole form of the face; appearance; support. * *vt* to favour, give approval to.

counter[1] *n* one who or that which counts; a disc used for scoring, a token; a table in a bank or shop across which money or goods are passed.

counter[2] *adv* contrary; adverse; in an opposite direction; in the wrong way. * *adj* opposed; opposite. * *n* a return blow or parry; an answering move. * *vti* to oppose; to retort; to give a return blow; to retaliate.

counter- *prefix* rival; opposed; reversed; matched.

counteract *vt* to act in opposition to so as to defeat or hinder; to neutralize.—**counteraction** *n*.—**counteractive** *adj*.

counterattack *n* an attack in response to an attack. * *vt* to make a counterattack.

counterattraction *n* a rival attraction; attraction in an opposite direction.
counterbalance *n* a weight balancing another. * *vt* to act as a counterbalance; to act against with equal power.
counterchange *vti* to interchange; to chequer.
countercharge *n* an opposing charge, esp by an accused person against his or her accuser. * *vt* to charge in opposition to another.
countercheck *n* a check on a check; an opposing check; (*arch*) a retort.
counterclaim *n* an opposing claim, esp by a defendant in a lawsuit.—**counterclaimant** *n*.
counterclockwise *adj* moving in a direction contrary to the hands of a clock as viewed from the front.—*also adv*.—*also* **anticlockwise**.
counterespionage *n* spying on or exposing enemy spies.
counterfeit *vt* to imitate; to forge; to feign, simulate. * *adj* made in imitation, forged; feigned, sham. * *n* an imitation, a forgery.—**counterfeiter** *n*.
counterfoil *n* a detachable section of a cheque or ticket, kept as a receipt or record; a stub.
counterintelligence *n* activities intended to frustrate enemy espionage and intelligence-gathering operations.
counterirritant *n* an application or action irritating the body surface to relieve internal inflammation.—**counterirritation** *n*.
countermand *vt* to revoke or annul, as an order or command; to cancel the orders of another. * *n* a command cancelling another.
countermarch *vti* to march in the reverse direction. * *n* such a march.
countermeasure *n* an action taken to neutralize or retaliate against some threat or danger, etc.
countermine *n* a mine made to intercept that of an enemy. * *vi* to make a countermine; to counterplot.
counteroffensive *n* a counterattack, esp by defenders of a position.
counterpane *n* a bedspread.
counterpart *n* a thing exactly like another, a duplicate; a corresponding or complementary part or thing.
counterplot *n* a plot to defeat another plot. * *vi* (**counterplotting, counterplotted**) to plot in retaliation.
counterpoint *n* (*mus*) a melody added as an accompaniment to another. * *vt* to set in contrast.
counterpoise *n* a weight, force or influence that balances another; equilibrium. * *vt* to counterbalance.
counterproductive *adj* producing a contrary effect on productivity or usefulness; hindering the desired end.
Counter-Reformation *n* the reforming movement in the Roman Catholic Church following the Protestant Reformation.
counter-revolution *n* a revolution undoing the work of a previous one.—**counter-revolutionary** *adj*, *n*.
countersign *vt* to authenticate a document by an additional signature. * *n* an additional signature to a document to attest it; a word to be given in answer to a sentry's challenge; an additional mark.—**countersignature** *n*.
countersink *vt* (**countersinking, countersunk**) to enlarge the upper part of a hole so that the screw head will sit flush with, or below, the surface; to drive (a screw) into such a hole. * *n* a tool for countersinking.
countertenor *n* a high tenor voice with an alto range; a person who sings countertenor.
counterterrorism *n* terrorist act(s) perpetrated in revenge for former terrorist act(s).
countervail *vt* to counterbalance, compensate for.
counterweight *n* a counterbalancing weight or power.
countess *n* a woman with the rank of count or earl; the wife or widow of a count.
counting house *n* a book-keeping office or department.
countless *adj* innumerable.
countrified, countryfied *adj* in the manner of the country; rural.
country *n* (*pl* **countries**) a region or district; the territory of a nation; a state; the land of one's birth or residence; rural parts; country-and-western. * *adj* rural.
country-and-western *n* a style of white folk music of the southeastern US.—*also* **country music**.
country club *n* a social and sporting facility in a rural setting.
country dance *n* a dance with the couples face to face in two lines.
country house *n* a gentleman's country residence.
countryman *n* (*pl* **countrymen**) a person who lives in the country; a person from the same country as another.—**countrywoman** *nf* (*pl* **countrywomen**).
countryside *n* a rural district.
county *n* (*pl* **counties**) in US, an administrative subdivision of a state; in UK, an administrative subdivision for local government.—*also adj*.
county palatine *n* a county having royal powers in the administration of justice.
county town, county seat *n* the capital of a county.
coup *n* a sudden telling blow; a masterstroke; a coup d'état.
coup de grâce *n* (*pl* **coups de grâce**) a finishing or fatal blow.
coup d'état *n* (*pl* **coups d'état**) a sudden and unexpected bold stroke of policy; the sudden overthrow of a government.
coup de théâtre *n* (*pl* **coups de théâtre**) a sudden dramatic or sensational action.
coupé *n* a closed, four-seater, two-door automobile with a sloping back.
couple *n* two of the same kind connected together; a pair; a husband and wife; a pair of equal and parallel forces. * *vt* to link or join together. * *vi* to copulate.
couplet *n* two consecutive lines of verse that rhyme with each other.
coupling *n* a device for joining parts of a machine or two railway carriages.
coupon *n* a detachable certificate on a bond, presented for payment of interest; a certificate entitling one to a discount, gift, etc.
courage *n* bravery; fortitude; spirit.—**courageous** *adj*.—**courageously** *adv*.—**courageousness** *n*.
courgette *n* a zucchini.
courier *n* a messenger, esp diplomatic; a tourist guide; a carrier of illegal goods between countries.
course *n* a race; a path or track; a career; a direction or line of motion; a regular sequence; the portion of a meal served at one time; conduct; behaviour; the direction a ship is steered; a continuous level range of brick or masonry of the same height; the chase of a hare by greyhounds; a length of time; an area set aside for a sport or a race; a series of studies; any of the studies. * *vt* to hunt. * *vi* to move swiftly along an indicated path; to chase with greyhounds.
courser *n* one who courses; a dog trained for coursing; (*poet*) a swift and spirited horse.
coursing *n* the sport of pursuing game with hunting dogs.
court *n* an uncovered space surrounded by buildings or walls; a short street; a playing space, as for tennis, etc; a royal palace; the retinue of a sovereign; (*law*) a hall of justice; the judges, etc engaged there; address; civility; flattery. * *vt* to seek the friendship of; to woo; to flatter; to solicit; to risk. * *vi* to carry on a courtship.
courteous *adj* polite; obliging.—**courteously** *adv*.—**courteousness** *n*.
courtesan *n* (*formerly*) a prostitute, or mistress of a courtier.
courtesy *n* (*pl* **courtesies**) politeness and kindness; civility; a courteous manner or action.
courthouse *n* a public building that houses law courts.
courtier *n* one in attendance at a royal court.
courtly *adj* (**courtlier, courtliest**) well-mannered, polite; of a court.—**courtliness** *n*.
court martial *n* (*pl* **courts martial, court martials**) a court of justice composed of naval or military officers for the trial of disciplinary offences.
court-martial *vt* (**court-martialling, court-martialled** *or* **court-martialing, court-martialed**) to try by court martial.
court plaster *n* a superior kind of sticking plaster, originally used by ladies at court for ornamental patches on the face.
courtship *n* the act of wooing.
courtyard *n* an enclosed space adjoining or in a large building.
couscous *n* a North African dish of cracked wheat steamed and served with a meat and vegetable stew.

cousin *n* the son or daughter of an uncle or aunt.—**cousinly** *adj*.—**cousinship**
couture *n* the design and manufacture of expensive fashion clothes.
couturier *n* a designer of expensive fashion clothes.—**couturière** *nf*.
couvade *n* a primitive custom by which when a child is born the father takes to his bed, where he receives the attentions usu given to the mother.
cove *n* a small sheltered bay or inlet in a body of water; a curved moulding at the juncture of a wall and ceiling (*—also* **coving**).
coven *n* an assembly of witches.
covenant *n* a written agreement; a solemn agreement of fellowship and faith between members of a church; an agreement to pay annually a sum to a charity. * *vt* to promise by a covenant. * *vi* to enter into a formal agreement.—**covenantal** *adj*.—**covenanted** *adj*.
covenantee *n* one in whose favour a covenant is made.
covenantor *n* one who enters into a covenant.
cover *vt* to overspread the top of anything with something else; to hide; to save from punishment; to shelter; to clothe; to understudy; to insure against damage, loss, etc; to report for a newspaper; to include; to make a journey over; (*male animal*) to copulate. * *vi* to spread over, as a liquid does; to provide an excuse or alibi (for); to work, eg as a salesman, in a certain area; to have within firing range. * *n* that which is laid on something else; a bedcover; a shelter; a covert; an understudy; something used to hide one's real actions, etc; insurance against loss or damage; a place laid at a table for a meal.—**coverer** *n*.
coverage *n* the amount, extent, etc covered by something; the amount of reporting of an event for newspaper, television, etc.
coverall *n* (*usu pl*) a one-piece garment that completely covers and protects one's clothing.
cover charge *n* a charge made by a restaurant over and above the cost of the food and service.
cover girl *n* an attractive girl whose picture is used on magazine covers.
covering *n* that which covers or protects; dress.
covering letter *n* a letter containing an explanation of an accompanying item.
coverlet *n* a bedspread.
coversine *n* the versed sine of the complement of an angle or arc.
covert *adj* covered; secret, concealed. * *n* a place that protects or shelters; a thicket; shelter for game.—**covertly** *adv*.
coverture *n* a cover; shelter; (*law*) the status of a married woman.
cover-up *n* something used to hide one's real activities, etc; a concerted effort to keep an act or situation from being made public.
covet *vt* to desire earnestly; to lust after; to long to possess (what belongs to another).—**coveter** *n*.—**covetous** *adj*.—**covetousness** *n*.
covetous *adj* avaricious, grasping, acquisitive.—**covetousness** *n*.
covey *n* a hatch or brood of birds, esp partridges.
coving *n* a curved moulding at the juncture of a wall and ceiling.—*also* **cove**.
cow[1] *n* the mature female of domestic cattle; the mature female of various other animals, as the whale, elephant, etc; (*sl*) a disagreeable woman.
cow[2] *vt* to take the spirit out of, to intimidate.
coward *n* a person lacking courage; one who is afraid.
cowardice *n* lack of courage.
cowardly *adj* of, or like, a coward.—**cowardliness** *n*.
cowbane *n* water hemlock.
cowbird *n* an American blackbird so called from its accompanying cattle.
cowboy *n* a person who tends cattle or horses (*—also* **cowhand**); (*inf*) one who is engaged in dubious business activities.
cowcatcher *n* a wedge-shaped iron frame on the front of a locomotive to push aside obstacles.
cower *vi* to crouch or sink down through fear, etc; to tremble.
cowfish *n* (*pl* **cowfish, cowfishes**) a name given to various fishes and other marine animals, as the dolphin.
cowgirl *n* a woman who works as a cowhand.
cowherd *n* a person employed to tend cattle.
cowhide *n* the tanned and dressed skins of cows; a stout flexible whip made of rawhide.
cowl *n* a hood; the hooded habit of a monk; the draped neckline of a woman's dress or sweater; a chimney corner.
cowlick *n* a tuft of hair turned up or brushed over the forehead.
cowling *n* the metal covering of an aeroplane engine.
coworker *n* a fellow worker.
cow pat *n* a piece of cow dung.
cow pony *n* a mustang used by cowboys.
cowpox *n* a disease of cows that produces vesicles from which the vaccine for inoculation against smallpox is obtained.
cowpuncher, cowpoke *n* a cowboy.
cowry, cowrie *n* (*pl* **cowries**) a marine mollusc with a glossy, brightly speckled shell.
cowslip *n* a common wild plant with small fragrant yellow flowers.
cox *n* a coxswain. * *vt* to act as a coxswain.
coxa *n* (*pl* **coxae**) the hip joint.—**coxal** *adj*.
coxalgia *n* a pain in, or disease of, the hip joint.—**coxalgic** *adj*.
coxcomb *n* a cockscomb; a vain conceited person, a fop.
coxcombry *n* (*pl* **coxcombries**) affected airs, foppishness.
coxswain *n* a person who steers a boat, esp a lifeboat or racing boat.—*also* **cockswain**.
coy *adj* playfully or provocatively demure; bashful.—**coyly** *adv*.—**coyness** *n*.
coyote *n* (*pl* **coyotes, coyote**) a small prairie wolf of North America.
coypu *n* (*pl* **coypus, coypu**) an aquatic beaver-like animal, originally from South America.
coz *n* (*arch*) cousin.
cozen *vt* to cheat, to beguile; to act deceitfully.—**cozenage** *n*.—**cozener** *n*.
cozy *see* **cosy**.
CP *abbr* = Communist Party.
cp. *abbr* = compare.
Cpl *abbr* = Corporal.
CPU *abbr* = central processing unit.
Cr (*chem symbol*) chromium.
cr. *abbr* = credit; creditor.
crab *n* any of numerous chiefly marine broadly built crustaceans. * *vi* (**crabbing, crabbed**) to fish for crabs; to complain.
crab-apple *n* a wild apple.
crabbed *adj* bad-tempered, morose; (*writing*) cramped; hard to decipher.
crabby *adj* bad-tempered.—**crabbily** *adv*.—**crabbiness** *n*.
crab louse *n* a species of body louse.
crabstick *n* a cudgel; a surly person.
crack *vt* to burst, break or sever; to utter a sharp, abrupt cry; to injure; to damage mentally; to open a bottle; (*sl*) to make (a joke); (*inf*) to break open (a safe); to decipher (a code). * *vi* to make a sharp explosive sound; (*inf*) to lose control under pressure; to shift erratically in vocal tone; (*with* **up**) (*inf*) to be unable to cope; (*sl*) to take the drug crack. * *n* a chink or fissure; a narrow fracture; a sharp sound; a sharp resonant blow; an altered tone of voice; a chat, gossip; a wisecrack; (*inf*) an attempt; an expert; (*sl*) the drug cocaine packaged in the form of pellets.
crackbrained *adj* crazy.
crackdown *n* repressive action to quell disorder, etc.
cracked *adj* split, broken; blemished; insane; legally imperfect.
cracker *n* a firework that explodes with a loud crack; a paper tube that when pulled explodes harmlessly and releases a paper hat and plastic toy; a thin, crisp biscuit; (*sl*) a person or thing of great ability or excellence.
crackerjack *n* (*sl*) a fine specimen.
crackers *adj* (*sl*) crazy.
crackhead *n* (*sl*) a person who is addicted to the drug crack.
crack house *n* (*sl*) a place where the drug crack is made available by dealers.
cracking *adj* (*inf*) fast-moving; excellent. * *n* the act of hacking into computer games; **to get cracking** to start to do something with vim and vigour.

crackle *vi* to make a slight, sharp explosive noise. * *vt* to cover with a delicate network of minute cracks. * *n* a noise of frequent and slight cracks and reports; a surface glaze on glass or porcelain.—**crackly** *adj*.
crackling *n* (*usu pl*) the browned crisp rind of roast pork.
cracknel *n* a thick puffy dry fancy biscuit.
crackpot *n* (*inf*) an eccentric, a crazy person. * *adj* (*inf*) crazy, unpractical.
cracksman *n* (*pl* **cracksmen**) a burglar.
-cracy *n suffix* government by, as in *democracy*.
cradle *n* a baby's crib or a small bed, often on rockers; infancy; birthplace or origin; a case for a broken limb; a framework of timbers, esp for supporting a boat; the rest for a telephone handset. * *vt* to rock or place in a cradle; to nurse or train in infancy.
cradlesong *n* a lullaby.
cradling *n* the open timbers or ribs of a vaulted ceiling.
craft *n* manual skill; a skilled trade; the members of a skilled trade; cunning; (*pl* **craft**) a boat, ship, or aircraft.
craftsman *n* (*pl* **craftsmen**) a person skilled in a particular craft.—**craftsmanship** *n*.—**craftswoman** *nf* (*pl* **craftswomen**).
crafty *adj* (**craftier, craftiest**) cunning, wily.—**craftily** *adv*.—**craftiness** *n*.
crag *n* a rough steep rock or cliff.
craggy, cragged *adj* (**craggier, craggiest**) full of crags; rugged.—**cragginess** *n*.
crake *n* the corncrake.
cram *vb* (**cramming crammed**) *vt* to pack tightly, to stuff; to fill to overflowing; (*inf*) to prepare quickly for an examination. * *vi* to eat greedily.
crambo *n* (*pl* **cramboes**) a game in which rhymes have to be found for a given word.
cramp *n* a spasmodic muscular contraction of the limbs; (*pl*) abdominal spasms and pain; a clamp. * *vt* to affect with muscular spasms; to confine narrowly; to hamper; to secure with a cramp. * *vi* to suffer from cramps.
cramped *adj* restricted, narrow; (*handwriting*) small and irregular.
crampon, crampoon *n* a metal frame with spikes attached to boots for walking or climbing on ice.
cranberry *n* (*pl* **cranberries**) a small red sour berry; the shrub it grows on.
crane *n* a large wading bird with very long legs and neck, and a long straight bill; a machine for raising, shifting, and lowering heavy weights. * *vti* to stretch out (the neck).
crane fly *n* the daddy-longlegs.
cranesbill *n* a kind of wild geranium.
craniology *n* the scientific study of skulls and their characteristics.—**craniological** *adj*.—**craniologist** *n*.
craniometer *n* an instrument for measuring the skull.
craniometry *n* the measurement and study of skulls.—**craniometric, craniometrical** *adj*.
craniotomy *n* (*pl* **craniotomies**) the operation of crushing the head of a dead fetus for facilitating delivery; the operation of opening the skull for neurosurgery.
cranium *n* (*pl* **craniums, crania**) the skull, esp the part enclosing the brain.—**cranial** *adj*.
crank *n* a right-angled arm attached to a shaft for turning it; (*inf*) an eccentric person, usu one with strange or unorthodox opinions; an irritable or rude person. * *vt* to provide with a crank; to turn or wind; (*with* **up**) (*engine*) to start with a crank handle; (*inf*) to speed up; (*sl*) to inject a narcotic drug.
crankcase *n* the housing for a crankshaft in an internal combustion engine, etc.
crankpin *n* a cylindrical pin parallel with the shaft axis of a crank upon which the connecting rod acts to turn the crank.
crankshaft *n* a shaft with one or more cranks for transmitting motion.
cranky *adj* (**crankier, crankiest**) (*inf*) eccentric; shaky; cross.—**crankily** *adv*.—**crankiness** *n*.
cranny *n* (*pl* **crannies**) a fissure, crack, crevice.
crap *n* (*sl*) nonsense; (*vulg*) faeces. * *vi* (**crapping, crapped**) (*vulg*) to defecate.—**crappy** *adj*.
crape *n* crepe; a black gauze-like crimped silk material used for mourning.
craps *n* (*sing or pl*) a gambling game played with two dice.
crapshooter *n* a player of craps.
crapulence *n* sickness from drinking to excess.—**crapulent, crapulous** *adj*.
craquelure *n* a network of tiny cracks found on old paintings caused by cracking of the varnish.
crash *n* a loud, sudden confused noise; a violent fall or impact; a sudden failure, as of a business or a computer; a collapse, as of the financial market. * *adj* done with great speed, suddenness or effort. * *vti* to clash together with violence; to make a loud clattering noise; (*aircraft*) to land with a crash; to involve a car in a collision with one or more other vehicles or with a hard object; to collapse, to ruin; (*inf*) to intrude into (a party); (*with* **out**) *vi* (*sl*) to fall asleep; to pass out; to stay the night somewhere other than home.
crash dive *n* an emergency dive by a submarine.
crash helmet *n* a cushioned helmet worn by airmen, motorcyclists, etc for protection.
crash-land *vti* (*aircraft*) to make an emergency landing without lowering the undercarriage, or to be landed in this way.—**crash-landing** *n*.
crass *adj* gross; dense; very stupid.—**crassly** *adv*.—**crassness, crassitude** *n*.
-crat *n suffix* a supporter or member of a particular form of government or class.
cratch *n* a rack for fodder.
crate *n* an open box of wooden slats, for shipping; (*sl*) an old vehicle or aircraft. * *vt* to pack in a crate.
crater *n* the mouth of a volcano; a cavity caused by the landing of a meteorite, the explosion of a bomb, shell, etc; an ancient Greek goblet.—**craterous** *adj*.
cravat *n* a neckcloth.
crave *vt* to have a strong desire (for); to ask humbly, to beg.—**craving** *n*.
craven *adj* spiritless, cowardly. * *n* a coward.
craw *n* a bird's crop.
crawfish *n* (*pl* **crawfish**) a crayfish; the spiny lobster.
crawl *vi* to move along the ground on hands and knees; to move slowly and with difficulty; to creep; (*inf*) to seek favour by servile behaviour; to swarm (with). * *n* the act of crawling; a slow motion; a racing stroke in swimming.—**crawler** *n*.
crayfish *n* (*pl* **crayfish**) any of numerous freshwater crustaceans; the spiny lobster.
crayon *n* a stick or pencil of coloured chalk; a drawing done with crayons. * *vt* to draw with a crayon.—**crayonist** *n*.
craze *n* a passing infatuation; excessive enthusiasm; a crack in pottery glaze. * *vt* to produce cracks; to render insane.—**crazed** *adj*.
crazy *adj* (**crazier, craziest**) (*inf*) mad, insane; foolish; ridiculous; unsound; madly in love with; (*paving*) composed of irregular pieces.—**crazily** *adv*.—**craziness** *n*.
creak *vi* to make a shrill grating sound. * *n* such a sound.
creaky *adj* (**creakier, creakiest**) apt to creak.—**creakiness** *n*.
cream *n* the rich, fatty part of milk; the choicest part of anything; a yellowish white colour; a type of face or skin preparation; any preparation of the consistency of cream (eg *shoe cream*). * *vt* to add or apply cream to; to beat into a soft, smooth consistency; to skim cream from; to remove the best part of. * *vi* to form cream or scum; to break into a creamy froth.
cream cheese *n* soft cheese made from soured milk or cream.
creamer *n* a machine or dish for separating cream from milk; a jug for cream or milk; a powder used as a substitute for cream in drinks.
creamery *n* (*pl* **creameries**) a place where dairy products are made or sold.
cream of tartar *n* purified tartar or argol, potassium bitartrate.
creamy *adj* (**creamier, creamiest**) like cream.—**creaminess** *n*.
crease *n* a line made by folding; a wrinkle; (*cricket*) a line made by a batsman or bowler marking the limits of their position. * *vti* to make or form creases; to become creased; (*sl*) to find something very funny.
create *vt* to cause to come into existence; to form out of nothing. * *vi* to make something new, to originate; (*sl*) to make a fuss.
creatine, creatin *n* a white crystalline substance in muscular tissue.

creation *n* the act of creating; the thing created; the whole world or universe; a production of the human mind; (*with cap*) the universe as created by God.—**creational** *adj*.
creationism *n* the belief in special creation, not evolution; the belief that God creates a soul for every human being at birth.—**creationist** *adj, n*.
creative *adj* of creation; having the power to create; imaginative, original, constructive.—**creatively** *adv*.—**creativeness** *n*.—**creativity** *n*.
creator *n* one who creates, esp God.
creature *n* a living being; a created thing; one dependent on the influence of another.—**creatural, creaturely** *adj*.
crèche *n* a day nursery for very young children.
credence *n* belief or trust, esp in the reports or testimony of another.
credentials *npl* documents proving the identity, honesty or authority of a person.
credibility gap *n* a gap between what is claimed in official statements and the true facts of a situation.
credible *adj* believable; trustworthy.—**credibility, credibleness** *n*.—**credibly** *adv*.
credit *n* belief; trust; honour; good reputation; approval; trust in a person's ability to pay; time allowed for payment; a sum at a person's disposal in a bank; the entry in an account of a sum received; the side of the account on which this is entered; (*educ*) a distinction awarded for good marks in an examination; (*pl*) a list of those responsible for a film, television programme, etc. * *vt* to believe; to trust; to have confidence in; to attribute to; to enter on the credit side of an account.
creditable *adj* worthy of praise.—**creditableness, creditability** *n*.—**creditably** *adv*.
credit card *n* a card issued by a bank, department store, etc authorizing the purchase of goods and services on credit.
creditor *n* a person to whom money is owed.
credit rating *n* an appraisal of a person's or a business's creditworthiness.
credits *npl* a list of those involved in the production of a film or television show.
creditworthy *adj* worthy of being given credit as judged by the capacity to earn, repay debts promptly, etc.—**creditworthiness** *n*.
credo *n* (*pl* **credos**) a creed.
credulous *adj* over-ready to believe; easily imposed on.—**credulously** *adv*.—**credulity** *n*.
creed *n* a system of religious belief or faith; a summary of Christian doctrine; any set of principles or beliefs.—**creedal, credal** *adj*.
creek *n* a natural stream of water smaller than a river.
creel *n* a wicker fishing basket; a wickerwork cage.
creep *vi* (**creeping, crept**) to move slowly along the ground, as a worm or reptile; (*plant*) to grow along the ground or up a wall; to move stealthily or slowly; to fawn; to cringe; (*flesh*) to feel as if things were creeping over it. * *n* (*inf*) a dislikable or servile person; (*pl: inf*) shrinking horror.
creeper *n* a creeping or climbing plant.
creepy *adj* (**creepier, creepiest**) making one's flesh crawl; causing fear or disgust.—**creepily** *adv*.—**creepiness** *n*.
creepy-crawly *n* (*pl* **creepy-crawlies**) (*inf*) a small crawling insect.
cremate *vt* to burn (a corpse) to ashes.—**cremation** *n*.—**cremationism** *n*.—**cremationist** *n*.
crematorium *n* (*pl* **crematoriums, crematoria**) a place where bodies are cremated.
crematory *adj* pertaining to cremation. * *n* (*pl* **crematories**) a place for burning the dead, a crematorium.
crème, creme *n* cream.
crème de la crème *n* the cream of the cream, the very best.
crème de menthe *n* a green-coloured peppermint liqueur.
crenate, crenated *adj* (*leaves*) scalloped.—**crenation, crenature** *n*.
crenellated, crenelated *adj* having battlements.—**crenellation, crenelation** *n*.
crenulate, crenulated *adj* (*leaves*) finely notched, indented.—**crenulation** *n*.
Creole *n* a descendant of European settlers in the West Indies or South America; a white descendant of French settlers in the southern US; a person of mixed European and Negro ancestry; the language of any of these groups.
creole *n* a language combining two or more original languages, one of which is European.
creosol *n* an oily liquid resembling phenol, a constituent of creosote.
creosote *n* an oily substance derived from tar used as a wood preservative. * *vt* to treat with creosote.—**creosotic** *adj*.
crepe, crêpe *n* a thin, crinkled cloth of silk, rayon, wool, etc (—*also* **crape**) ; thin paper like crepe; a thin pancake.
crepe de Chine *n* a silk crepe.
crepe paper, crêpe paper *n* a thin soft coloured paper that resembles crepe.
crepe rubber *n* a type of ribbed rubber used for the soles of shoes.
crêpe suzette *n* (*pl* **crêpes suzettes**) a thin orange-flavoured pancake with a hot liqueur sauce.
crepitate *vi* to make a slight, sharp crackling noise.—**crepitation** *n*.
crept *see* **creep.**
crepuscular *adj* pertaining to or resembling twilight; active at twilight, as certain animals.
crescendo *adv* (*mus*) gradually increasing in loudness or intensity; moving to a climax. * *n* (*pl* **crescendos, crescendi**) a crescendo passage or effect.
crescent *n* the figure of the moon in its first or last quarter; a narrow, tapering curve; a curving street. * *adj* crescent-shaped; (*arch*) increasing.—**crescentic** *adj*.
cresol *n* a phenol obtained from coal and wood tar.
cress *n* any of various plants with pungent leaves, used in salads.
cresset *n* a light set on a beacon; an open frame of iron containing fire, used as a torch.
crest *n* a plume of feathers on the head of a bird; the ridge of a wave; the summit of a hill; a distinctive device above the shield on a coat of arms. * *vti* to mount to the top of; to take the form of a crest; to provide or adorn with a crest, to crown.—**crested** *adj*.
crestfallen *adj* dejected.
cresting *n* an ornamental finish, esp along a rooftop; ornamentation on top of furniture, a mirror, etc.
Cretaceous *n* a geological group between the Jurassic and Tertiary formations. * *adj* of the last Mesozoic era.
cretaceous *adj* composed of or like chalk; chalky.
Cretan *adj* of or pertaining to Crete or its inhabitants.
cretin *n* a person suffering from mental and physical retardation due to a thyroid disorder; (*inf*) an idiot.—**cretinism** *n*.—**cretinoid, cretinous** *adj*.
cretonne *n* an unglazed cotton fabric printed with coloured patterns on one side.
crevasse *n* a deep cleft in a glacier; a deep crack.
crevice *n* a crack, a fissure.
crew *n* the people operating a ship or aircraft; a group of people working together. * *vi* to act as a member of the crew of a ship, etc.
crewcut *n* a very short hairstyle for men.
crewel *n* a fine twisted or worsted yarn used in embroidery.—**crewelist** *n*.
crew neck *n* a plain closely-fitting neckline in sweaters.
crib *n* a rack for fodder, a manger; a child's cot with high sides; a model of the manger scene representing the birth of Jesus; (*inf*) something copied from someone else; (*inf*) a literal translation of foreign texts used (usu illicitly) by students in examinations, etc. * *vti* (**cribbing, cribbed**) (*inf*) to copy illegally, plagiarize.
cribbage *n* a card game for two to four players.
crib death *see* **cot death.**
cribellum *n* (*pl* **cribella**) a spinning organ in front of the spinnerets of certain spiders.
cribriform adj with small holes like a sieve.
crick *n* a painful stiffness of the muscles of the neck. * *vt* to produce a crick in.
cricket[1] *n* a leaping grasshopper-like insect.
cricket[2] *n* a game played with wickets, bats, and a ball, by eleven players on each side.—**cricketer** *n*.
cried *see* **cry.**

crier *n* one who cries; an officer who makes public proclamations.
crime *n* a violation of the law; an offence against morality or the public welfare; wrong-doing; (*inf*) a shame, disappointment.
criminal *adj* of the nature of, or guilty of, a crime. * *n* a person who has committed a crime.—**criminality** *adv*.—**criminally** *adv*.
criminal conversation *n* (*formerly*) a legal action for damages for illegal sexual intercourse; adultery.
criminology *n* the scientific study of crime.—**criminological, criminologic** *adj*.—**criminologist** *n*.
crimp[1] *vt* to press into small folds; to frill; to corrugate; (*hair*) to curl.—**crimper** *n*.
crimp[2] *n* a person luring or pressganging sailors aboard a vessel. * *vt* to decoy thus.
crimson *n* a deep-red colour inclining to purple. * *adj* crimson-coloured. * *vti* to dye with crimson; to blush.
cringe *vi* to shrink in fear or embarrassment; to cower; to behave with servility; to fawn.
cringle *n* a loop of rope containing a metal ring for another rope to pass through.
crinite *adj* hairy.
crinkle *vt* to wrinkle; to corrugate; to crimp; to rustle. * *vi* to curl; to be corrugated or crimped. * *n* a wrinkle.—**crinkly** *adj*.
crinoid *adj* lily-shaped. * *n* a stone lily, a kind of sea urchin.
crinoline *n* a hooped skirt made to project all round; a stiff fabric for stiffening a garment.
crinum *n* any of several handsome tropical plants.
cripple *vt* to deprive of the use of a limb; to disable. * *n* a lame or otherwise disabled person. * *adj* lame.
crippling *adj* harmful; unbearable.
crisis *n* (*pl* **crises**) a turning point; a critical point in a disease; an emergency; a time of serious difficulties or danger.
crisp *adj* dry and brittle; bracing; brisk; sharp and incisive; decided; very clean and tidy. * *n* a potato snack; in US, a potato chip. * *vt* to make crisp.—**crisply** *adv*.—**crispness** *n*.
crispate, crispated *adj* curled; (*bot*) with a wavy margin.—**crispation** *n*.
crispy *adj* (**crispier, crispiest**) crisp.—**crispily** *adv*.—**crispiness** *n*.
crisscross *vti* to intersect; to mark with cross lines. * *n* an intersecting; a mark of a cross; a game of noughts and crosses. * *adj* crossing; in cross lines. * *adv* crosswise.
cristate, cristated *adj* crested; tufted.
criterion *n* (*pl* **criteria**) a standard, law or rule by which a correct judgment can be made.
critic *n* a person skilled in judging the merits of literary or artistic works; one who passes judgment; a fault-finder.
critical *adj* skilled in criticism; censorious; relating to the turning point of a disease; crucial.—**critically** *adv*.
criticism *n* being critical; an adverse comment; a review or analysis of a book, play, work of art, etc by a critic.
criticize *vt* to pass judgment on; to find fault with; to examine critically.—**criticizer** *n*.
critique *n* a critical article or review.
critter *n* (*dial*) a creature.
croak *n* a deep hoarse discordant cry. * *vti* to utter a croak; (*inf*) to die, to kill.—**croakily** *adv*.—**croakiness** *n*.—**croaky** *adj*.
Croatian, Croat *adj* of or pertaining to Croatia, its people or language. * *n* an inhabitant of Croatia; the language of Croatia, a dialect of Serbo-Croatian.
crochet *n* a kind of knitting done with a hooked needle. * *vti* (**crocheting, crocheted**) to do this; to make crochet articles.—**crocheter** *n*.
crocidolite *n* blue asbestos.
crock[1] *n* an earthenware pot.
crock[2] *n* a broken-down horse; (*sl*) a worn-out or unfit person. * *vti* to become or make unfit.
crock[3] *n* soot on a kettle, etc. * *vt* to blacken with soot.
crockery *n* china dishes, earthenware vessels, etc.
crocket *n* a small curved ornament on the angles of spires, canopies, etc.
crocodile *n* a large amphibious reptile, similar to an alligator; its skin, used to make handbags, shoes, etc; a line of schoolchildren walking in pairs.
crocodile tears *npl* insincere grief.
crocodilian *adj* pertaining to crocodiles. * *n* any of the order of reptiles that includes alligators and crocodiles.
crocus *n* (*pl* **crocuses**) a bulbous plant with yellow, purple, or white flowers.
croft *n* a small plot of land with a rented farmhouse, esp in Scotland.—**crofter** *n*.
croissant *n* a rich bread roll.
Cro-Magnon man *n* a race of man living in late Palaeolithic times.
cromlech *n* a prehistoric monument of rough stones in a circle and usu surrounding a lofty pillar of stone.
crone *n* a withered old woman.
crony *n* (*pl* **cronies**) an intimate friend.
crook *n* a shepherd's hooked staff; a bend, a curve; a swindler, a dishonest person. * *adj* (*sl*) unwell. * *vti* to bend or to be bent into the shape of a hook.
crooked *adj* bent, twisted; dishonest.—**crookedly** *adv*.—**crookedness** *n*.
croon *vi* to hum in a low gentle voice. * *vt* to sing songs in a soft gentle manner.—**crooner** *n*.
crop *n* a year's or a season's produce of any cultivated plant; harvest; any collection of things appearing at the same time; a pouch in a bird's gullet; a hunting whip; hair cut close or short. * *vti* (**cropping, cropped**) to clip short; to bite off or eat down (grass); (*land*) to yield; to sow, to plant; (*geol*) to come to the surface; to sprout; (*with* **up**) (*inf*) to occur or appear by chance or unexpectedly.
crop circle *n* a circular patch of corn in a cornfield that has been flattened by an as yet unexplained whirling movement.
crop-eared *adj* with clipped ears; short-haired.
cropper *n* a thing that crops; a cloth-facing machine; a pouter pigeon; (*sl*) a heavy fall.
croquet *n* a game played with mallets, balls and hoops. * *vt* (**croqueting, croqueted**) to drive away an opponent's ball by striking one's own placed in contact with it.
croquette *n* a ball of minced meat, fish or potato seasoned and fried brown.
crosier *n* the pastoral staff of a bishop.—*also* **crozier**.
cross *n* a figure formed by two intersecting lines; a wooden structure, consisting of two beams placed across each other, used in ancient times for crucifixion; the emblem of the Christian faith; a symbol or mark (X); a focal point in a town; a burden, or affliction; a device resembling a cross; a cross-shaped medal; a hybrid. * *vti* to pass across; to intersect; to meet and pass; to place crosswise; to mark with a cross; to make the sign of the cross over; to thwart, to oppose; to modify (a breed) by intermixture (with). * *adj* transverse; reaching from side to side; intersecting; out of temper, peevish.—**crosser** *n*.—**crossly** *adv*.—**crossness** *n*.
crossbar *n* a horizontal bar, as that across goal posts or a bicycle frame.
crossbill *n* a bird whose mandibles cross when the bill is closed.
crossbow *n* a bow set crosswise on the stock from which bolts are shot along a groove.
crossbreed *vt* (**crossbreeding, crossbred**) to breed animals by mating different varieties. * *n* an animal produced in this way.
crosscheck *vt* to verify by checking different opinions or sources.
cross-country *adj* across fields; denoting cross-country racing or skiing.—also *n*.
crosscurrent *n* a current that flows across another in water or air; ideas running counter to those generally held.
crosse *n* a long-handled racket in which the ball is caught and carried in lacrosse.
cross-examine *vt* to question closely; (*law*) to question (a witness) who has already been questioned by counsel on the other side.—**cross-examiner** *n*.—**cross-examination** *n*.
cross-eyed *adj* squinting.—**cross-eye** *n*.

cross-fertilization *n* fertilization of the ovules of a flower by the pollen of another.
cross-fertilize *vt* to fertilize (a plant) with pollen from another.
crossfire *n* converging gunfire from two or more positions; animated debate or argument.
cross-grained *adj* contrary or awkward; with an irregular grain or fibre.
crosshatch *vt* to shade with crossed lines.
crossing *n* an intersection of roads or railway lines; a place for crossing a street; the crossbreeding of animals and plants.
cross-legged *adj* seated with one leg crossed over the other.
crosspatch *n* (*inf*) a bad-tempered person.
crosspiece *n* a transverse piece.
cross-purpose *n* a contrary purpose; **be at cross-purposes** to talk without either party realizing that the other is talking about a different thing.
cross-question *vt* to question to elicit details or test the accuracy of an account already given.—**cross-questioning** *n*.
cross-refer *vt* to mark (text, a book, etc) in such a way as to direct the reader to another page, etc with more information.
cross-reference *n* a note directing the reader to a different section of a book or document.
crossroad *n* a road crossing another; (*pl*) where two roads cross; (*fig*) the time when a decisive action has to be made.
cross section *n* a cutting at right angles to length; the surface then shown; a random selection of the public.—**cross-sectional** *adj*.
cross-stitch *n* a stitch formed of two stitches of the same length, one crossing the other.
crosstalk *n* interference in lines of communication, esp telephone lines; a quick-witted flow of conversation; repartee.
crosstie *n* a railway sleeper.
crosstree *n* (*naut*) one of several pieces of timber across the head of a lower mast to support the mast above.
crosswalk *n* a street crossing for pedestrians.
crosswind *n* a side or unfavourable wind.
crosswise, crossways *adv* in the manner of a cross.
crossword (puzzle) *n* a puzzle in which interlocking words to be inserted vertically and horizontally in a squared diagram are indicated by clues.
crotch *n* the region of the body where the legs fork, the genital area; any forked region.
crotchet *n* (*mus*) a note equal to the duration of a half-minim.—*also* **quarter note**.
crotchety *adj* peevish, ill-tempered.—**crotchetiness** *n*.
crouch *vi* to squat or lie close to the ground; to cringe, to fawn.
croup[1] *n* inflammation of the windpipe causing coughing and breathing problems, esp in children.—**croupous, croupy** *adj*.
croup[2], **croupe** *n* the rump or buttocks of certain animals; the place behind the saddle of a horse.
croupier *n* a person who presides at a gaming table and collects or pays out the money won or lost.
crouton *n* a small piece of fried or toasted bread sprinkled onto soups.
crow *n* any of various usu large, glossy, black birds; a cawing cry, the shrill sound of a cock. * *vi* (**crowing, crowed** *or* **crew**) to make a sound like a cock; to boast in triumph; to utter a cry of pleasure.—**crower** *n*.
crowbar *n* an iron bar for use as a lever.
crowd *n* a number of people or things collected closely together; a dense multitude, a throng; (*inf*) a set; a clique. * *vti* to press closely together; to fill to excess; to push, to thrust; to importune.—**crowded** *adj*.
crowfoot *n* (*pl* **crowfoots**) any of several kinds of buttercup with yellow or white flowers and leaves like a crow's foot.
crown *n* a wreath worn on the head; the head covering of a monarch; regal power; the sovereign; the top of the head; the top of a tree; a summit; a reward; the part of a tooth above the gum. * *vt* to invest with a crown; to adorn or dignify; to complete; to reward; to put an artificial crown on a tooth; (*sl*) to strike on the head.
crown colony *n* a British colony subject to the control of the home government.
crown glass *n* a fine, thick kind of glass.
crown land *n* in the UK, land or real property belonging to the sovereign.
crown prince *n* the heir apparent to a throne.
crown princess *n* the heiress apparent to a throne; the wife of a crown prince.
crown saw *n* a kind of circular saw.
crownwork *n* the covering or replacement of the crown of a tooth; the making of crowns; a fortified outwork.
crow's-foot *n* (*pl* **crow's-feet**) a wrinkle at the corner of the eye; an arrangement of cords to suspend an awning; a decorative embroidery stitch.
crow's-nest *n* a lookout or watchtower on the main topmast of a sailing vessel.
crozier *see* **crosier**.
CRT *abbr* = cathode-ray tube.
cruces *see* **crux**.
crucial *adj* decisive; severe; critical.—**crucially** *adv*.
cruciate *adj* (*bot*) cross-shaped.
crucible *n* a heat-resistant container for melting ores, etc.
crucifer *n* any of many plants with four petals arranged like a cross, as the mustard, etc; the bearer of a large cross in a religious procession.
crucifier *n* one who crucifies.
crucifix *n* a cross with the sculptured figure of Christ.
crucifixion *n* a form of execution by being nailed or bound to a cross by the hands and feet; (*with cap*) the death of Christ in this manner.
cruciform *adj* cross-shaped.
crucify *vt* (**crucifying, crucified**) to put to death on a cross; to cause extreme pain to; to defeat utterly in an argument; to ridicule mercilessly.
crud *n* (*sl*) a deposit of encrusted filth; nuclear waste; a contemptible person.
crude *adj* in a natural state; unripe; raw; immature; harsh in colour; unfinished, rough; lacking polish; blunt; vulgar. * *n* crude oil.—**crudely** *adv*.—**crudeness** *n*.
crude oil *n* unrefined petroleum.
crudités *npl* coarsely chopped raw vegetables eaten with a dip.
crudity *n* (*pl* **crudities**) crudeness; a crude act or expression.
cruel *adj* (**crueller, cruellest**) disposed to give pain to others; merciless; hard-hearted; fierce; painful; unrelenting.—**cruelly** *adv*.—**cruelty** *n*.
cruelty *n* (*pl* **cruelties**) inhumanity; savageness; a cruel act.
cruet *n* a small glass bottle for vinegar and oil, used at the table; a set of containers holding salt, pepper, vinegar.
cruise *vi* to sail to and fro; to wander about; to move at the most efficient speed for sustained travel. * *vt* to cruise over or about. * *n* a voyage from place to place for military purposes or in a liner for pleasure.
cruise missile *n* a subsonic low-flying guided missile.
cruiser *n* fast warship smaller than a battleship; a pleasure yacht or motorboat.
crumb *n* a fragment of bread; the soft part of bread; a little piece of anything; (*sl*) a despicable person. * *vi* to cover food with breadcrumbs before cooking.
crumble *vt* to break into crumbs; to cause to fall into pieces. * *vi* to disappear gradually, to disintegrate.—**crumbly** *adj*.
crumby *adj* (**crumbier, crumbiest**) in crumbs; soft.—**crumbiness** *n*.
crummy *adj* (**crummier, crummiest**) (*sl*) dirty, squalid, worthless; slightly ill.—**crumminess** *n*.
crump *n* a bursting shell; the crunching or exploding sound of this. * *vi* to explode. * *vt* to shell; to hit (a ball) hard.
crumpet *n* a soft cake with holes on one side, often eaten toasted; (*sl*) a sexually attractive woman.
crumple *vti* to twist or crush into wrinkles; to crease; to collapse. * *n* a wrinkle or crease made by crumpling.—**crumply** *adj*.
crunch *vti* to crush with the teeth; to tread underfoot with force and noise; to make a sound like this; to chew audibly. * *n* the sound or act of crunching; (*with* **the**) (*inf*) the crucial moment, the time of vital decision.
crunchy *adj* (**crunchier, crunchiest**) crisp; able to be crunched.—**crunchily** *adv*.—**crunchiness** *n*.

crupper *n* a looped leather band attached to the back of a saddle and passing under the horse's tail; the hindquarters of a horse.
crural *adj* of the leg or thigh; leg-shaped.
crus *n* (*pl* **crura**) the leg proper; a part resembling a leg.
crusade *n* a medieval Christian military expedition to recover the Holy Land; a vigorous concerted action for the defence of a cause or the advancement of an idea. * *vi* to engage in a crusade.—**crusader** *n*.
cruse *n* a small earthenware pot or dish for holding liquids.
crush *vt* to press between two opposite bodies; to squeeze; to break by pressure; to bruise; to ruin; to quell, to defeat; to mortify. * *vi* to be pressed out of shape or into a smaller compass. * *n* a violent compression or collision; a dense crowd; (*inf*) a large party; a drink made from crushed fruit; (*sl*) an infatuation.—**crushable** *adj*.—**crusher** *n*.
crust *n* any hard external coating or rind; the exterior solid part of the earth's surface; a shell or hard covering; (*sl*) a means of livelihood. * *vti* to cover or become covered with a crust.—**crusty** *adj* (**crustier, crustiest**).—**crustily** *adv*.—**crustiness** *n*.
crustacean *n* any aquatic animal with a hard shell, including crabs, lobsters, shrimps, and barnacles.—*also adj*.—**crustaceous** *adj*.
crutch *n* a staff with a crosswise head to support the weight of a lame person; something that supports; a prop; the crotch.
crux *n* (*pl* **cruxes, cruces**) a difficult problem; the essential or deciding point.
cry *vb* (**crying, cried**) *vi* to call aloud; to proclaim; to exclaim vehemently; to implore; to shed tears; (*with* **off**) (*inf*) to cancel (an agreement, arrangement, etc), to renege; (*with* **out**) to shout due to fear or pain. * *vt* to utter loudly and publicly; (*with* **out for**) to be in dire need of. * *n* (*pl* **cries**) an inarticulate sound; an exclamation of wonder or triumph; an outcry; clamour; an urgent appeal; a spell of weeping; a battle cry; a catchword; the particular sound made by an animal or bird.
crybaby *n* (*pl* **crybabies**) a child who weeps easily; a person who cries or complains often.
cryo- *prefix* frost; freezing.
cryoextraction *n* the extraction of juice from grapes that have been frozen before pressing to obtain a higher level of sugar and fruitier taste.
cryogen *n* a substance for producing freezing temperatures.
cryogenics *n* (*sing*) the science of very low temperatures and their effects.
cryolite *n* a mineral from which aluminium is produced.
cryometer *n* an instrument for measuring very low temperatures.—**cryometry** *n*.
cryonic suspension *n* the process of freezing a corpse in the hope that it may be restored to life in the future.
cryonics *n* (*sing*) the use of extreme cold to preserve living tissue (eg organs) for future use.
cryosurgery *n* surgery involving freezing to destroy or remove diseased tissue.
crypt *n* an underground chamber or vault, esp under a church, used as a chapel or for burial.
crypt-, crypto- *prefix* hidden.
cryptaesthesia, cryptesthesia *n* clairvoyance; extrasensory perception.
cryptic, cryptical *adj* hidden, secret; mysterious.
cryptogam *n* a plant without stamens or pistil, a non-flowering plant, as mosses, ferns, etc.—**cryptogamic, cryptogamous** *adj*.
cryptogram *n* a coded message, cipher.
cryptograph *n* a piece of writing in cipher.
cryptography *n* the art of code writing and breaking.—**cryptographer** *n*.—**cryptographic** *adj*.
cryptozoology *n* the study of creatures whose existence has yet to be proved, eg the yeti, the Loch Ness monster.
crystal *n* a solid piece, eg of quartz, geometrically shaped owing to regular arrangement of its atoms; very clear, brilliant glass; articles of such glass, as goblets; (*sl*) the drug methamphetamine packaged and sold as a stimulant in powdered form (—*also* **crystal meth**). * *adj* made of crystal.—**crystalline** *adj*.
crystal gazing *n* fortune telling by peering into a ball of crystal.
crystalline *adj* pertaining to or having the form of a crystal; clear; transparent.—**crystallinity** *n*.
crystalline lens *n* a transparent biconvex solid body enclosed in a capsule between the vitreous and acqueous humours of the eye.
crystallize *vti* to form crystals; to give definite form; to express clearly the theme and content of an argument, proposition, etc.—**crystallization** n.
crystallography *n* the science of the forms and structure of crystals.—**crystallographer** *n*.—**crystallographic** *adj*.
crystalloid *adj* resembling a crystal; of a crystalline structure, opposite to colloid. * *n* a crystalloid substance; one of certain bodies that in solution diffuse readily through animal membranes.
Cs (*chem symbol*) = caesium.
c/s *abbr* = cycles per second.
CS gas *n* an irritant gas used in quelling riots and disturbances.
CST *abbr* = Central Standard Time.
CT *abbr* = Connecticut.
ct *abbr* = carat; cent; court.
ctenidium *n pl* **ctenidia**) one of the respiratory organs of molluscs.
ctenoid *adj* having a comb-like margin.
Cu (*chem symbol*) = copper.
cu. *abbr* = cubic.
cub *n* a young carnivorous mammal; a young, inexperienced person; (*with cap*) a Cub Scout. * *vi* (**cubbing, cubbed**) to bring forth cubs.
cubage, cubature *n* the act of determining the contents of a solid; the contents so measured.
cubbyhole *n* a small or snug place; a pigeonhole.
cube *n* a solid body with six equal square sides or faces; a cube-shaped block; the product of a number multiplied by itself twice. * *vt* to raise (number) to the third power, or cube; to cut into cube-shaped pieces.
cubeb *n* a species of pepper of Asia; its small spicy berry dried and used as a stimulant.
cube root *n* the number that gives the stated number when cubed.
cubic *adj* having the form or properties of a cube; three-dimensional.
cubical *adj* of or pertaining to volume; cube-shaped.
cubicle *n* a small separate sleeping compartment in a dormitory, etc.
cubiculum *n* (*pl* **cubicula**) a burial chamber in a catacomb.
cubism *n* a style of painting in which objects are depicted as fragmented and reorganized geometrical forms.—**cubist** *n*.—**cubistic** *adj*.—**cubistically** *adv*.
cubit *n* an ancient measure of about 18 inches; the forearm from the elbow to the wrist.
cubital *adj* of the forearm.
cuboid *adj* like a cube. * *n* a regular solid contained by parallelograms.
Cub Scout *n* a junior branch of the Scout Association.
cuckold *n* a man whose wife has committed adultery.—**cuckoldry** *n*.
cuckoo *n* a bird with a dark plumage, a curved bill and a characteristic call that lays its eggs in the nests of other birds. * *adj* (*inf*) crazy, silly.
cuckoo clock *n* a clock that strikes the hours with a cuckoo call.
cuckoopint *n* a European plant with large leaves, purple flowers and bearing red berries.
cuckoo spit *n* a white froth exuded by froghopper larvae on the leaves of plants.
cucullate, cucullated *adj* hooded; hood-shaped.
cucumber *n* a long juicy fruit used in salads and as a pickle; the creeping plant that bears it.
cucurbit *n* any of an order of succulent, climbing, tendril-bearing plants with a fleshy fruit, including cucumbers, pumpkins, melons, etc.
cud *n* the food that a ruminating animal brings back into the mouth to chew again; **chew the cud** to consider and mull over.
cudbear *n* a purple dye made from lichens.
cuddle *vt* to embrace or hug closely. * *vt* to nestle together. * *n* a close embrace.
cuddlesome *adj* tempting to cuddle.
cuddly *adj* (**cuddlier, cuddliest**) given to cuddling; tempting to cuddle.

cuddy *n* (**cuddies**) (*naut*) the cabin of a half-decked boat; a small cabin, a galley.
cudgel *n* a short thick stick for beating. * *vt* (**cudgelling, cudgelled** *or* **cudgeling, cudgeled**) to beat with a cudgel.—**cudgeller, cudgeler** *n*.
cudweed *n* a plant with a fine down, belonging to the aster family.
cue[1] *n* the last word of a speech in a play, serving as a signal for the next actor to enter or begin to speak; any signal to do something; a hint. * *vt* (**cueing** *or* **cuing, cued**) to give a cue to.
cue[2] *n* a tapering rod used in snooker, billiards, and pool to strike the cue ball.
cue ball *n* (*snooker, etc*) the ball that a player strikes in order to hit other balls.
cuff[1] *n* a blow with the fist or the open hand. * *vt* to strike such a blow.
cuff[2] *n* the end of a sleeve; a covering round the wrist; the turn-up on a trouser leg.
cufflink *n* a decorative clip for fastening the edges of a shirt cuff.
cuirass *n* defensive armour for the breast and back, a breastplate.
cuirassier *n* a cavalry soldier armed with a cuirass.
cuisine *n* a style of cooking or preparing food; the food prepared.
cuisse *n* defensive armour for the thighs.
culch *n* materials forming a spawning bed for oysters; oyster spawn.
cul-de-sac *n* (*pl* **culs-de-sac, cul-de-sacs**) a street blocked off at one end; a blind alley; a position, job leading nowhere.
-cule *n suffix* forming diminutives, as *animalcule*.
culinary *adj* of or relating to cooking.
cull *vt* to select; to pick out, gather. * *n* the selection of certain animals with the intention of killing them.—**culler** *n*.
cullet *n* broken or refuse glass for recycling.
culm[1] *n* the stem of grasses.
culm[2] *n* inferior anthracite coal.
culminate *vti* to reach the highest point of altitude, rank, power, etc; (*astron*) to reach the meridian; to bring to a head or the highest point.—**culminant** *adj*.—**culmination** *n*.
culottes *npl* a women's flared trousers that resemble a skirt.
culpable *adj* deserving censure; criminal; blameworthy.—**culpably** *adv*.—**culpability** *n*.
culprit *n* a person accused, or found guilty, of an offence.
cult *n* a system of worship; devoted attachment to a person, principle, etc; a religion regarded as unorthodox or spurious; its body of adherents; a current fashion.—**cultic** *adj*.—**cultism** *n*.—**cultist** *n*.
cultivate *vt* to till and plant; to improve by care, labour, or study; to seek the society of; to civilize or refine.—**cultivated** *adj*.
cultivation *n* the act of cultivating; the state of being cultivated; tillage; culture.
cultivator *n* a machine for breaking up soil for cultivation; someone who cultivates.
cultrate, cultrated *adj* (*bot*) shaped like a pruning knife; pointed and sharp-edged.
cultural *adj* pertaining to culture.—**culturally** *adv*.
culture *n* appreciation and understanding of the arts; the skills, arts, etc of a given people in a given period; the entire range of customs, beliefs, social forms, and material traits of a religious, social, or racial group; the scientific cultivation of plants to improve them and find new species; improvement of the mind, manner, etc; a growth of bacteria, etc in a prepared substance.* *vt* to cultivate bacteria for study or use.
cultured *adj* educated to appreciate the arts; having good taste; artificially grown, as cultured pearls.
cultured pearl *n* a pearl induced to grow artificially by the injection of a foreign body into the closed shell.
culture shock *n* loss of bearings and distress caused by an uprooting from a familiar environment or culture.
culverin *n* a 16th-century long cannon with serpent-shaped handles.
culvert *n* a drain or conduit under a road.
cum *prep* with.
cumarin *see* **coumarin**.
cumber *vt* to hamper, to burden. * *n* a hindrance.
cumbersome *adj* inconveniently heavy or large, unwieldy.
cumin, cummin *n* a plant cultivated for its seeds which are used as a spice.
cummerbund *n* a sash worn as a waistband, esp with a man's tuxedo.
cumshaw *n* in China, a present or bonus.
cumulate *vt* to accumulate; to combine into one; to build up by adding new material.—**cumulation** *n*.
cumulative *adj* augmenting or giving force; growing by successive additions; gathering strength as it grows.—**cumulatively** *adv*.
cumulative voting *n* a system of voting in which each voter has as many votes as there are candidates, and may give all to one candidate.
cumulus *n* (*pl* **cumuli**) a cloud form having a flat base and rounded outlines.
cuneate *adj* wedge-shaped.
cuneiform *adj* wedge-shaped (—*also* **cuneal**). * *n* the wedge-shaped characters of ancient Assyrian and Persian writing.
cunnilingus *n* sexual stimulation of the female genitals by the tongue.
cunning *adj* ingenious; sly; designing; subtle. * *n* slyness, craftiness.
cunt *n* (*vulg*) the female genitals, the vagina; (*derog*) a woman; (*offensive*) an obnoxious person.
cup *n* a small, bowl-shaped container for liquids, usu with a handle; the amount held in a cup; a drink made from a mixture of drinks with one main ingredient (eg *claret cup*); one of two shaped supporting parts of a brassiere; an ornamental cup used as a trophy. * *vt* (**cupping, cupped**) to take or put as in a cup; to curve (the hands) into the shape of a cup.
cupbearer *n* one who serves wine at a banquet, esp an officer of a royal household.
cupboard *n* a closet or cabinet with shelves for cups, plates, utensils, food etc.
cupel *n* a small flat vessel used to assay precious metals. * *vt* (**cupelling, cupelled** *or* **cupeling, cupeled**) to refine precious metals from lead in a cupel.
cupful *n* (*pl* **cupfuls**) as much as a cup will contain.
Cupid *n* the god of love in Roman mythology.
cupidity *n* greed of gain; covetousness.
cupola *n* a dome, esp of a pointed or bulbous shape; a furnace for melting metals.—**cupolated** *adj*.
cupreous *adj* of or like copper; coppery.
cupric, cuprous *adj* containing copper.
cupriferous *adj* yielding copper.
cuprite *n* red oxide of copper.
cupule *n* (*biol*) a cup-shaped part, as of the acorn.
cur *n* a mongrel dog; a despicable person.
curable *adj* able to be cured, remediable.—**curability** *n*.—**curably** *adv*.
curaçao *n* an orange-flavoured liqueur.
curacy *n* (*pl* **curacies**) the office or district of a curate.
curare, curari *n* a substance extracted from vines and used by South American Indians to poison arrows.
curarine *n* an alkaloid extract of curare used as a muscle relaxant.
curarize *vt* to poison with curare.—**curarization** *n*.
curassow *n* a large turkey-like bird of South America.
curate *n* an assistant of a vicar or rector.
curative *adj* tending to cure. * *n* a curative agent or drug.
curator *n* a superintendent of a museum, art gallery, etc.—**curatorial** *adj*.
curb *vt* to restrain; to check; to keep in subjection. * *n* that which checks, restrains, or subdues; a line of raised stone forming the edge of a pavement (—*also* **kerb**).
curbing *n* curbstones collectively; material for curbstones.—*also* **kerbing**.
curb roof *n* a roof with a double slope, the lower being steeper.
curbstone *n* the stone edge of a path.—*also* **kerbstone**.
curcuma *n* one of several kinds of plant including turmeric.
curd *n* the coagulated part of soured milk, used to make cheese.—**curdy** *adj*.—**curdiness** *n*.
curdle *vti* to turn into curds; to coagulate; (*with* **the blood**) to cause terror.—**curdler** *n*.

cure *n* the act or art of healing; a remedy; restoration to health. * *vt* to heal; to rid of; to preserve meat or fish by drying, salting, etc.
curé *n* a French parish priest.
curettage *n* surgical scraping to remove growths or dead tissue, etc.
curette, curet *n* a surgical instrument for scraping a body cavity. **vt* (**curetting, curetted**) to scrape with this.
curfew *n* a signal, as a bell, at a fixed evening hour as a sign that everyone must be indoors; the signal or hour.
curia *n* (*pl* **curiae**) the papal court; a senate house of ancient Rome; one of the divisions of the Roman people; a medieval court of justice.
curie *n* a unit of radioactivity.
curio *n* (*pl* **curios**) an item valued as rare or unusual.
curiosity *n* (*pl* **curiosities**) the quality of being curious; inquisitiveness; a strange, rare or interesting object.
curious *adj* anxious to know; prying, inquisitive; strange, remarkable, odd.—**curiously** *adv*.—**curiousness** *n*.
curium *n* an artificially made radioactive metallic element derived from plutonium.
curl *vti* to form into a curved shape, to coil; to twist into ringlets; to proceed in a curve, to bend; to play at curling; (*with* **up**) to rest with the body in a curved shape and the legs drawn up; to relax in a comfortable place; (*inf*) to give up; to be embarrassed and sickened by. * *n* a ringlet of hair; a spiral form, a twist; a bend or undulation.
curler *n* a small pin or roller used for curling the hair; a person who plays curling.
curlew *n* a bird with a long curved bill and long legs.
curlicue *n* an exaggerated ornamental curl.
curling *n* a Scottish game in which two teams slide large smooth stones on ice into a target circle.
curling stone *n* a heavy round flat stone with a handle used in curling.
curling tongs *n* a pair of tongs heated to curl hair.
curly *adj* (**curlier, curliest**) full of curls.—**curliness** *n*.
curmudgeon *n* an ill-natured churlish person; a miser.—**curmudgeonly** *adj*.
currant *n* a small variety of dried grape; a shrub that yields a red or black fruit.
currency *n* (*pl* **currencies**) the time during which a thing is current; the state of being in use; the money current in a country.
current *adj* generally accepted; happening now; presently in circulation. * *n* a body of water or air in motion, a flow; the transmission of electricity through a conductor; a general tendency.
current account *n* a bank account, usu with no interest, from which money is withdrawn by cheques or cash cards; a checking account.
currently *adv* at the present time.
curricle *n* a two-wheeled open carriage drawn by two horses abreast.
curriculum *n* (*pl* **curricula, curriculums**) a prescribed course of study.—**curricular** *adj*.
curriculum vitae *n* (*pl* **curricula vitae**) a brief survey of one's career.
currier *n* a leather dresser.—**curriery** *n*.
currish *adj* snappy; quarrelsome; rude.
curry[1] *n* (*pl* **curries**) a spicy dish with a hot sauce; curry seasoning. * *vt* (*pl* **currying, curried**) to flavour with curry.
curry[2] *vt* (**currying, curried**) to rub down and groom (a horse); to dress leather after tanning; to beat; (*with* **favour**) to use flattery to ingratiate.
currycomb *n* a metal comb for grooming horses.
curse *n* a calling down of destruction or evil; a profane oath; a swear word; a violent exclamation of anger; a scourge. * *vti* to invoke a curse on; to swear, to blaspheme; to afflict, to torment.
cursed *adj* damnable.
cursive *adj* running; flowing. * *n* a script with the letters joined, as in handwriting.
cursor *n* a flashing indicator on a computer screen indicating position; the transparent slide on a slide rule.
cursorial *adj* (*bird*) with limbs adapted for running or walking.
cursory *adj* hasty, passing; superficial, careless.—**cursorily** *adv*.
curt *adj* short; abrupt; concise; rudely brief.—**curtly** *adv*.—**curtness** *n*.
curtail *vt* to cut short; to reduce; to deprive of part (of).—**curtailment** *n*.
curtain *n* a cloth hung as a screen at a window, etc; the movable screen separating the stage from the auditorium; (*pl: sl*) the end, death. * *vt* to enclose in, or as with, curtains.
curtain call *n* (*theat*) a call from the audience for performers to appear at the end to receive applause.
curtain lecture *n* a private reprimand from a wife to her husband.
curtain-raiser *n* a short play preceding the main one; an introductory item.
curtilage *n* (*law*) a yard, garden or enclosure of a house, included in the same fence.
curtsy, curtsey *n* (*pl* **curtsies, curtseys**) a formal gesture of greeting or respect, involving bending the knees, made by women. * *vi* (**curtsying, curtsied** *or* **curtseying, curtseyed**) to make a curtsy.
curvaceous *adj* (*inf*) having an attractive body with shapely curves.
curvature *n* a bending; a curved form.
curve *n* a bending without angles; a bent form or thing; (*geom*) a line of which no part is straight. * *vti* to form into a curve, to bend.—**curvy** *adj* (**curvier, curviest**).
curvet *n* a particular leap of a horse; a frisk or bound. **vi* (**curvetting, curvetted** *or* **curveting, curveted**) to leap as a horse; to frisk or bound.
curvilinear, curvilineal *adj* consisting of or bounded by curved lines.—**curvilinearity** *n*.
cusec *n* a unit of flow of one cubic foot of water per second.
cushion *n* a case stuffed with soft material for resting on; the elastic border around a snooker table; the air mass supporting a hovercraft. * *vt* to furnish with cushions; to protect by padding; to give protection against difficulties, etc; to soften the effect of.—**cushiony** *adj*.
cushy *adj* (**cushier, cushiest**) (*inf*) easy, comfortable.
cusp *n* an apex or point; the point at each end of a crescent moon; (*astrol*) the transitional point of a house; (*archit*) the pointed intersection between two arcs; a cone-shaped point on a tooth; a fold or flap of a heart valve.
cuspid *n* a canine tooth.
cuspidate, cuspidal *adj* of, like or having a cusp; (*leaves, etc*) ending in a point.
cuspidor *n* a spittoon.
cuss *n* (*sl*) an annoying person; a curse. * *vt* (*sl*) to curse.
cussed *adj* (*sl*) cursed; stubborn, perverse.
cussedness *n* (*sl*) contrariness.
custard *n* a sauce mixture of milk, eggs and sugar.
custard apple *n* a West Indian tree; its dark fruit with a soft edible pulp.
custodian *n* one who has the care of anything; a keeper; a caretaker.
custody *n* (*pl* **custodies**) guardianship; imprisonment; security.—**custodial** *adj*.
custom *n* a regular practice; usage; traditions of a people or a society; frequent repetition of the same act; business patronage; (*pl*) duties on imports.
customary *adj* habitual; conventional; common.—**customarily** *adv*.
custom-built *adj* made to a customer's specifications.
customer *n* a person who buys from a shop or business, esp regularly; (*inf*) a person.
custom house *n* an office or building where duties are paid on exported or imported goods and vessels are entered and cleared.
cut *vb* (**cutting, cut**) *vt* to cleave or separate with a sharp instrument; to make an incision in; to wound with a sharp instrument; to divide; to trim; to intersect; to abridge; to diminish; to pass deliberately without recognition; to wound the feelings deeply; to reduce or curtail; to grow a new tooth through the gum; to divide (a pack of cards) at random; to switch off (a light, an engine); (*inf*) to stay away from class, school, etc; (*with* **back**) to prune vegetation; to economize; (*with* **down**) to fell a tree; to reduce expenditure, consumption, etc; to make a smaller garment from an old one; to kill; (*with* **off**) to take away by cutting or slicing; to stop abruptly, esp a telephone conversation; to sever relations; to be so placed as to foil something, eg an escape; (*with* **out**) to delete; to cut into shapes; (*inf*) to force out a rival; to give up an indulgence

or habit; (*with* **up**) to cut into pieces; to wound with a knife; (*inf*) to affect deeply. * *vi* to make an incision; to perform the work of an edged instrument; to grow through the gums; (*cinema*) to change to another scene, to stop photographing; (*with* **in**) to butt in; to interpose oneself; to interrupt with comments; to drive between two vehicles, leaving insufficient space; (*with* **out**) (*engine*) to stop working. * *n* an incision or wound made by a sharp instrument; a gash; a sharp stroke; a sarcastic remark; a passage or channel cut out; a slice; a block on which an engraving is cut; the fashion or shape of a garment; the deliberate ignoring of an acquaintance; the division of a pack of cards; a diminution in price below another merchant; (*sl*) a share, as of profits. * *adj* divided or separated; gashed; having the surface ornamented or fashioned; not wrought or hand-made; reduced in price.

cutaneous *adj* pertaining to the skin.

cutaway *n* a drawing (of a machine) with part of the exterior covering cut away to show the internal mechanism; (*film*) a scene shot separately from but relevant to the main action.

cutback *n* a reduction, esp in expenditure; a flashback.

cutch *see* **catechu.**

cute *adj* (*inf*) acute, shrewd; pretty or attractive, esp in a dainty way.—**cutely** *adv*.—**cuteness** *n*.

cut glass *n* flint glass cut into facets or figures.

cuticle *n* the skin at the base of the fingernail or toe nail; epidermis.—**cuticular** *adj*.

cutie *n* (*sl*) a bright smart girl.

cutis *n* (*pl* **cutes, cutises**) the vascular layer of the skin, below the epidermis.

cutlass *n* a sailor's short heavy sword.

cutler *n* a maker of or dealer in knives.

cutlery *n* knives, forks, etc for eating and serving food.

cutlet *n* a neck chop of lamb, etc; a small slice cut off from the ribs or leg; minced meat in the form of a cutlet.

cutoff *n* a short or straight road; a new shorter channel cut by a river across a bend; a device for stopping steam from entering a cylinder.

cutout *n* a switch to cut off an electric light from a circuit.

cutpurse *n* a pickpocket.

cutter *n* someone or something that cuts; a small, swift sailing vessel; a light boat carried by larger ships.

cutthroat *n* a murderer. * *adj* merciless; (*razor*) having a long blade in a handle.

cutting *n* a piece cut off or from; an incision; a newspaper clipping; a slip from a plant for propagation; a passage or channel cut out; the process of editing a film or recording; a recording. * *adj* (*wind*) sharp, biting; (*remarks*) hurtful.

cuttlebone *n* the internal bone of the cuttlefish, used for polishing, etc.

cuttlefish *n* (*pl* **cuttlefish, cuttlefishes**) a marine creature with a flattened body that squirts ink when threatened.

cutwater *n* the fore part of a ship's prow.

cutwork *n* appliqué work.

CV *abbr* = curriculum vitae.

cwt. *abbr* = hundredweight.

cyan *n* a blue colour, one of the primary colours.

cyanamide, cyanamid *n* a chemical compound of calcium carbide and nitrogen, used as a fertilizer.

cyanate *n* a compound of cyanic acid with a base.

cyanic acid *n* a strong acid composed of cyanogen and oxygen.

cyanide *n* a poison.

cyanogen *n* a colourless poisonous gas burning with a purple flame and with the odour of peach blossom.

cyanosis *n* a condition of the body in which its surface becomes blue due to insufficient aeration of the blood.—**cyanotic** *adj*.

cyanotype *n* a photographic process in which the picture is taken in Prussian blue; a blueprint.

cybernetics *n* (*sing*) the study of communication and control functions in living organisms, and in mechanical and electronic systems.—**cybernetic** *adj*.

cyberphobia *n* a morbid fear or intense dislike of computers.—**cyberphobic** *adj*.

cyclamen *n* a plant of the primrose family, with pink, purple or white flowers.

cycle *n* a recurring series of events or phenomena; the period of this; a body of epics or romances with a common theme; a group of songs; a bicycle, motorcycle, or tricycle. * *vi* to go in cycles; to ride a bicycle or tricycle.

cyclic, cyclical *adj* moving or recurring in cycles.—**cyclically** *adv*.

cyclist *n* a person who rides a bicycle.

cycloid *n* a curve traced by a point on a circle as it rolls along a straight line.—**cycloidal** *adj*.

cyclometer *n* an instrument for registering the revolutions of a wheel.—**cyclometry** *n*.

cyclone *n* a violent circular storm; an atmospheric movement in which the wind blows spirally round towards a centre of low barometric pressure.—**cyclonic** *adj*.

Cyclopean *adj* pertaining to the Cyclops, the legendary one-eyed giant; one-eyed; huge and rough; vast, massive; (*archit*) built of huge stones without mortar.

cyclopedia, cyclopaedia *n* an encyclopedia.—**cyclopedic, cyclopaedic** *adj*.

cyclorama *n* a series of moving pictures extended circularly so as to appear in natural perspective to the viewer standing in the centre.—**cycloramic** *adj*.

cyclotron *n* an apparatus for accelerating charged particles in a magnetic field.

cygnet *n* a young swan.

cylinder *n* a hollow figure or object with parallel sides and circular ends; an object shaped like a cylinder; any machine part of this shape; the piston chamber in an engine.—**cylindrical** *adj*.—**cylindrically** *adv*.

cylindroid *adj* like a cylinder. * *n* a solid body resembling a cylinder but with the ends elliptical.

cyma *n* (*pl* **cymae, cymas**) (*archit*) ogee moulding of a cornice.

cymbal *n* (*mus*) one of a pair of two brass plates struck together to produce a ringing or clashing sound.—**cymbalist** *n*.

cyme *n* a flower cluster in which the main stem ends in a flower, while from each side of the main stem secondary stems branch off to end a flower, and tertiary stems from those, etc.—**cymose** *adj*.

Cymric *adj* pertaining to the Cymry, or the Welsh. * *n* the Welsh language.

cynic *n* a morose, surly, or sarcastic person; a sceptic about people, motives and actions; one of a sect of ancient Greek philosophers.—**cynicism** *n*.

cynical *adj* sceptical of or sneering at goodness; shameless in admitting unworthy motives.—**cynically** *adv*.

cynosure *n* a centre of attraction or admiration.

cypher *see* **cipher.**

cypress *n* an evergreen tree with hard wood.

Cyprian *adj* of Cyprus; of Aphrodite, the Greek goddess of love; wanton, lascivious. * *n* a native of Cyprus; a prostitute.

cyprinid *n* any of a family of freshwater fishes, including the carp.

cyprinoid *adj* of or resembling a cyprinid; carp-like.

Cypriot *adj* pertaining to Cyprus, or to its inhabitants. * *n* a native of Cyprus.

Cyrillic *adj* of or pertaining to St Cyril, or to the Slavonic alphabet. * *n* the alphabet of the Slavonic languages.

cyst *n* a closed sac developing abnormally in the structure of plants or animals.—**cystic** *adj*.

cystic fibrosis *n* a congenital disorder in young children characterized by chronic respiratory and digestive problems.

cystitis *n* inflammation of the urinary bladder.

cystocele *n* a hernia caused by protrusion of the bladder.

cystoid *adj* cyst-like. * *n* a growth resembling a cyst.

cystolith *n* a stone in the bladder.

cystoscope *n* an instrument for examining the urinary bladder.—**cystoscopic** *adj*.—**cystoscopy** *n*.

cystotomy *n* (*pl* **cystotomies**) the opening of the human bladder for the removal of a stone, etc.
cyt-, cyto- *prefix* cell.
cytogenesis, cytogeny *n* cell formation in plants and animals.
cytology *n* the scientific study of cells; cell structure.—**cytological** *adj*.—**cytologist** *n*.
cytoplasm *n* the substance of a cell as opposed to its nucleus.—**cytoplasmic** *adj*.
cytoscreening *n* the examination of smear tests for indications of cervical cancer.
czar *see* **tsar.**
czardas *n* a Hungarian national dance with varying tempos; the music for it.
czarevitch *see* **tsarevitch.**
czarina, czaritsa *see* **tsarina, tsaritsa.**
Czech *n* a native, or the language, of the Czech Republic.

D

D (*symbol*) (*mus*) the second note of the C major scale; (*chem*) deuterium; five hundred.
d. *abbr* = penny or pennies (*UK currency before 1971*).
DA *abbr* = District Attorney.
dab[1] *vt* (**dabbing, dabbed**) to touch lightly with something moist or soft. * *n* a quick light tap; a small lump of anything moist or soft.—**dabber** *n*.
dab[2] *n* a species of European flounder.
dab[3] *n* (*inf*) a dab hand.
dabble *vi* to move hands, feet, etc gently in water or another liquid; (*usu with* **at, in, with**) to do anything in a superficial or dilettante way. * *vt* to splash.—**dabbler** *n*.
dabchick *n* a water bird, the little grebe.
dab hand *n* (*inf*) an adept person, an expert.
da capo *adj, adv* (*mus*) from the beginning.
dace *n* (*pl* **dace**) a small freshwater fish of the carp family.
dacha *n* in Russia, a house in the country used as a holiday and summer residence.
dachshund *n* a breed of short-legged, long-bodied hound.
dacoit *n* one of a group of robbers in India and Burma, who plunder in bands.—*also* **dakoit.**
dactyl *n* a poetic foot of three syllables, one long and two short.—**dactylic** *adj, n*.
dactylogram *n* a fingerprint.
dactylography *n* the science of fingerprints.—**dactylographer** *n*.—**dactylographic** *adj*.
dactylology *n* the art of communicating ideas with the fingers; sign language.
dad *n* (*inf*) father.
Dada *n* a school of art and literature that aims at suppressing all relations between thought and expression.—**Dadaism** *n*.—**Dadaist** *n*.—**Dadaistic** *adj*.
daddy *n* (*pl* **daddies**) (*inf*) father.
daddy longlegs *n* (*inf*) any of various spiders or insects with long, slender legs, esp a crane fly.
dado *n* (*pl* **dadoes**) the lower part of a room wall when separately panelled or decorated.
daff *vi* (*Scot*) to sport, to play.
daffodil *n* a yellow spring flower, a narcissus; its pale yellow colour.
daft *adj* (*inf*) silly, weak-minded; giddy; mad.—**daftly** *adv*.—**daftness** *n*.
dagger *n* a short weapon for stabbing; a reference mark used in printing (†) (—*also* **obelisk**).
dago *n* (*pl* **dagos, dagoes**) (*offensive*) a foreigner, esp from Spain or Portugal.
daguerreotype *n* an early photographic process using a copper plate; a picture taken by this process.—**daguerreotypy** *n*.
dahlia *n* a half-hardy tuberous perennial of the aster family grown for its colourful blooms.
daily *adj, adv* (happening) every day; constantly, progressively. * *n* (*pl* **dailies**) a newspaper published every weekday; (*inf*) a charwoman.
dainty *adj* (**daintier, daintiest**) delicate; choice; nice, fastidious. * *n* (*pl* **dainties**) a titbit, a delicacy.—**daintily** *adv*.—**daintiness** *n*.
daiquiri *n* (*pl* **daiquiris**) a cocktail of rum, sugar and lime juice.
dairy *n* (*pl* **dairies**) a building or room where milk is stored and dairy products made; a shop selling these; a company supplying them.
dairy cattle *npl* cows reared for milk production.
dairying *n* the business or occupation of a dairy farmer.
dairyman *n* (*pl* **dairymen**) a person who works in a dairy or deals in dairy products.
dairy products *npl* milk and products made from it, eg butter, cheese, yogurt.
dais *n* a low platform at one end of a hall or room.
daisy *n* (*pl* **daisies**) any of various plants with a yellow centre and white petals.
daisywheel *n* (*comput*) a flat, wheel-shaped, printing device with characters at the ends of spokes.
dal *n* a split-grain pulse commonly used in Indian cooking.—*also* **dhal.**
Dalai Lama *n* the chief lama of Tibet.
dale *n* a valley.
dalliance *n* idle or frivolous time-wasting; trifling; flirtation.
dally *vi* (**dallying, dallied**) to lose time by idleness or trifling; to play or trifle (with); to flirt.—**dallier** *n*.
dallymoney *n* (*sl*) alimony paid by one partner in a former sexual relationship to the other.
Dalmatian *n* a large short-haired dog with black spot-like markings on a white body.
dalmatic *n* a loose vestment with open sides worn esp by a bishop.
dam[1] *n* an artificial embankment to retain water; water so contained. * *vt* (**damming, dammed**) to retain (water) with such a barrier; to stem, obstruct, restrict.
dam[2] *n* the mother of a four-footed animal.
damage *n* injury, harm; loss; (*inf*) price, cost; (*pl*) (*law*) payment in compensation for loss or injury. * *vt* to do harm to, to injure.—**damageable** *adj*.—**damager** *n*.—**damaging** *adj*.
damask *n* a reversible, figured, woven fabric, esp linen or silk. * *adj* made of this; having a pinkish colour like a damask rose.
damask rose *n* a rose with greyish-pink blooms and a sweet fragrance used in perfume making.
dame *n* the comic, female role in a pantomime usu played by a man; (*sl*) a woman; (*with cap*) the title of a woman who has been awarded an order of chivalry equivalent to the title of a Knight; the wife of a knight or baronet.
dammar, damar *n* a resin used for varnish.
damn *vt* to condemn, censure; to ruin; to curse; to consign to eternal punishment. * *vti* to prove guilty. * *interj* (*sl*) expressing irritation or annoyance. * *n* (*sl*) something having no value. * *adj, adv* damned.
damnable *adj* deserving damnation; despicable; hateful; offensive; wicked; (*inf*) annoying.—**damnably** *adv*.
damnation *n* the state of being condemned to hell; the act of damning. * *interj* expressing annoyance, irritation, etc.
damnatory *adj* assigning to, or containing a threat of, damnation.
damned *adj* (*inf*) damnable; extremely.—*also adv*.
damnify *vt* (**damnifying, damnified**) (*law*) to cause loss or damage to.
damp *n* humidity, moisture; in mines, poisonous or foul gas. * *adj* slightly wet, moist. * *vt* to moisten; (*with* **down**) to stifle, reduce.—**damply** *adv*.—**dampness** *n*.
dampen *vti* to make or become damp. * *vt* to stifle.—**dampener** *n*.
damper *n* a depressive influence; a metal plate in a flue for controlling combustion; (*mus*) a device for stopping vibration in stringed instruments; (*Austral*) unleavened bread.
damsel *n* (*formerly*) a girl.

damselfly *n* (*pl* **damselflies**) an insect resembling the dragonfly but having wings that fold when at rest.

damson *n* a small, dark-purple variety of plum; the colour of this; the tree on which this fruit grows.

dance *vti* to move rhythmically, esp to music; to skip or leap lightly; to execute (steps); to cause to dance or to move up and down. * *n* a piece of dancing; a dance performance of an artistic nature; a party with music for dancing; music for accompanying dancing.—**dancer** *n*.—**dancing** *adj*, *n*.

D and C *n* (*med*) dilation (of the cervix) and curettage (of the womb).

dandelion *n* a common wild plant with ragged leaves, a yellow flower and a fluffy seed head.

dander[1] *n* scurf from various animals, eg cats, dogs, that may be allergenic; temper; fighting spirit.

dander[2] *vi* (*Scot*) to saunter. * *n* a sauntering stroll.

Dandie Dinmont *n* a breed of terrier.

dandify *vt* to give the character or style of a dandy to; to make trim or smart like a dandy.—**dandification** *n*.

dandle *vt* to play with (a baby) on the knee, to fondle.—**dandler** *n*.

dandruff *n* scales of skin on the scalp, under the hair, scurf.—**dandruffy** *adj*.

dandy *n* (*pl* **dandies**) a man who likes to dress too fashionably. * *adj* (**dandier, dandiest**) (*inf*) excellent, fine.—**dandyish** *adj*.—**dandyism** *n*.

dandy-brush *n* a stiff brush for grooming horses.

Dane *n* a native or citizen of Denmark.

Danegeld *n* an annual tax imposed in England in the reign of Ethelred II to maintain forces against the Danes.

Danelaw, Danelagh *n* the code of laws established by the Danes on their settlement in England; that part of the country where these laws were in force.

dang *adj*, *adv*, *interj*, *n* a euphemistic form of **damn**.

danger *n* exposure to injury or risk; a source of harm or risk.

dangerous *adj* involving danger; unsafe; perilous.—**dangerously** *adv*.—**dangerousness** *n*.

dangle *vi* to hang and swing loosely. * *vt* to carry something so that it hangs loosely; to display temptingly.—**dangler** *n*.

Danish *adj* of the people or language of Denmark. * *n* the language of Denmark.

Danish pastry *n* a sweet pastry topped with fruity icing and nuts.

dank *adj* disagreeably damp.—**dankly** *adv*.—**dankness** *n*.

danseur *n* a professional dancer, a ballet dancer.—**danseuse** *nf*.

dap *vb* (**dapping, dapped**) *vi* to drop bait gently into water. * *vt* to dip lightly; to bounce (a ball). * *n* a bounce.

daphne *n* a genus of small evergreen shrubs with fragrant flowers, allied to the laurel.

dapper *adj* nimble; neat in appearance, spruce.

dapple *vti* to mark with or show patches of a different colour; to variegate. * *adj* marked in such a way. * *n* something so marked.

dapple-grey *adj* mottled with darker grey. * *n* a horse of this colour.

Dardanian, Dardan *adj* pertaining to Dardania, an ancient city of Troy, in Asia Minor, or its people. * *n* a Trojan.

dare *vti* (**daring, dared** *or* **durst**) to be bold enough; to venture, to risk; to defy, to challenge. * *n* a challenge.—**darer** *n*.

daredevil *n* a rash, reckless person. * *adj* daring, bold; courageous.—**daredevilry, daredeviltry** *n*.

daring *adj* fearless; courageous; unconventional. * *n* adventurous courage.—**daringly** *adv*.

dark *adj* having little or no light; of a shade of colour closer to black than white; (*person*) having brown or black skin or hair; gloomy; (*inf*) secret, unknown; mysterious. * *n* a dark state or colour; ignorance; secrecy.—**darkly** *adv*.—**darkness** *n*.

darken *vti* to make or become dark or darker.—**darkener** *n*.

dark horse *n* a competitor about whom little is known; a person of reserved character; a surprise political candidate.

darkish *adj* quite dark.

darkroom *n* a room for processing photographs in darkness or safe light.

darksome *adj* gloomy.

darling *n* a dearly loved person; a favourite. * *adj* lovable; much admired.

darn[1] *vt* to mend a hole in fabric or a garment with stitches. * *n* an area that has been darned.—**darner** *n*.

darn[2] *interj* a form of **damn** as a mild oath.—*also adj*.

darnel *n* a kind of rye grass.

darning *n* a patch made by darning; material, garments, etc to be darned.

dart *n* a small pointed missile; a sudden movement; a fold sewn into a garment for shaping it; (*pl*) an indoor game in which darts are thrown at a target. * *vti* to move rapidly; to send out rapidly.

dartboard *n* a circular cork or wooden target used in the game of darts.

darter *n* one of several kinds of bird or fish.

Darwinian *adj* pertaining to Charles Darwin, the naturalist (1809–82) or Darwinism. * *n* an evolutionist.

Darwinism *n* the theory of natural selection advocated by Darwin.—**Darwinist** *n*.

dash *vti* to fling violently; to rush quickly; (*hopes*) to shatter; (*one's spirits, etc*) to depress, confound; to write quickly. * *n* a short race; a rush; a small amount of something added to food; a tinge; a punctuation mark (—); a dashboard; vigour, verve; display.

dashboard *n* an instrument panel in a car.

dasher *n* one who or that which dashes; a dashing person; the part of a churn that agitates cream.

dashing *adj* debonair; spirited, stylish, dapper.—**dashingly** *adv*.

dastard *n* a malicious coward.

dastardly *adj* mean, cowardly; base.—**dastardliness** *n*.

dasyure *n* a small carnivorous Australian marsupial.

DAT *abbr* = digital audio tape.

data *npl* (*sing* **datum**) (*often used as sing*) facts, statistics, or information either historical or derived by calculation or experimentation.

data bank, database *n* a large store of information for analysis, esp one held in a computer.

data capture *n* the process of translating information into computer-readable form.

data processing *n* the analysis of information stored in a computer for various uses, eg stock control, statistical research, mathematical modelling, etc.

date[1] *n* a day or time of occurrence; a statement of this in a letter, etc; a period to which something belongs; a duration; an appointment, esp with a member of the opposite sex. * *vt* to affix a date to; to note the date of; to reckon the time of; (*inf*) to make a date with; (*inf*) to see frequently a member of the opposite sex. * *vi* to reckon from a point in time; to show signs of belonging to a particular period.—**datable, dateable** *adj*.—**dater** *n*.

date[2] *n* the sweet fruit of the date palm, a palm tree of tropical regions.

dated *adj* old-fashioned; out of style; bearing a date.—**datedness** *n*.

dateless *adj* without a date; timeless; classic.

dateline *n* a line on a newspaper story giving the date and place of writing. * *vt* to provide with a dateline.

date line *n* the line running north to south along the 180-degree meridian, east of which is one day earlier than west of it.—*also* **International Date Line.**

dative *adj* (*gram*) denoting an indirect object. * *n* the dative case.—**datival** *adj*.—**datively** *adv*.

datum *n* (*pl* **data**) a single unit of information; a thing given or taken for granted; something known or assumed as fact and made the basis of reasoning or calculation; an assumption or premise from which inferences are drawn; (*pl* **datums**) (*geol*) a level, line or point used as a reference in surveying.

datura *n* any of several kinds of strongly scented narcotic plant.

daub *vt* to smear or overlay (with clay, etc); to paint incompetently. * *n* a smear; a poor painting.—**dauber** *n*.

daughter *n* a female child or descendant; a female member of a family, race, etc; a woman in relation to her native country or place; (*physics*) a nucleus, particle, etc, produced from another by radioactive decay; (*biol*) a cell produced by the division of another.

daughter-in-law *n* (*pl* **daughters-in-law**) the wife of one's son.

daughterly *adj* of or befitting a daughter.—**daughterliness** *n*.

daunt *vt* to intimidate; to discourage.—**daunter** *n*.—**dauntingly** *adv*.

dauntless *adj* incapable of being discouraged; intrepid, fearless.—**dauntlessly** *adv*.—**dauntlessness** *n*.

dauphin *n* the title of the eldest son of the king of France, 1349–1830.

dauphine, dauphiness *n* the wife of the dauphin.

davenport *n* a large sofa, often able to be converted into a bed; a small ornamental writing desk.

davit *n* a small crane with tackle for raising or lowering a lifeboat, etc over a ship's side.

Davy Jones *n* the spirit of the sea.

Davy Jones's locker *n* the seabed, the deep, esp as the grave of those who die at sea.

daw *n* a bird of the crow family; a jackdaw.

dawdle *vi* to move slowly and waste time, to loiter.—**dawdler** *n*.

dawn *vi* (*day*) to begin to grow light; to begin to appear. * *n* daybreak; a first sign.

day *n* the time when the sun is above the horizon; the twenty-four hours from midnight to midnight; daylight; a particular period of success or influence; (*usu pl*) a period, an epoch.

daybook *n* a diary; an account book for recording the day's transactions.

daybreak *n* the first appearance of daylight, dawn.

daydream *n* a reverie. * *vi* to have one's mind on other things; to fantasize.—**daydreamer** *n*.

daylight *n* the light of the sun; dawn; publicity; a visible gap; the dawning of sudden realization or understanding.

days *adv* during the day regularly.

daytime *n* the time of daylight.

day-to-day *adj* daily; routine.

daze *vt* to stun, to bewilder. * *n* confusion, bewilderment.—**dazedly** *adv*.—**dazedness** *n*.

dazzle *vt* to confuse the sight of or be partially blinded by strong light; to overwhelm with brilliance. * *n* the act of dazzling; a thing that dazzles; an overpoweringly strong light; bewilderment.—**dazzlement** *n*.—**dazzler** *n*.—**dazzlingly** *adv*.

dB, db *abbr* = decibels.

DBS *abbr* = direct broadcasting by satellite.

DC District of Columbia.

dc, DC *abbr* = direct current.

DD *abbr* = Doctor of Divinity.

D-day *n* the date (June 6, 1944) of the Allied cross-channel invasion of France during World War II; any date set aside for an important event.

DDT *abbr* = dichlorodiphenyltrichloroethane, a chemical used as an insecticide.

de *prep* from, concerning; of.

de- *prefix* down; off; completely; un-.

de-accessioning *n* the disposal, usu by selling, of an artefact or painting in a public collection.

deacon *n* (*Anglican, RC churches*) an ordained member of the clergy ranking below a priest; (*Presbyterian churches*) a lay church officer who assists the minister.—**deaconship** *n*.

deaconess *n* a churchwoman appointed to do work in a parish; a member of an institution or order trained to carry on systematic charitable work; in a convent, the nun who attends to the altar.

deactivate *vt* (*bomb*) to make inactive or harmless.—**deactivation** *n*.—**deactivator** *n*.

dead *adj* without life; inanimate, inert; no longer used; lacking vegetation; emotionally or spiritually insensitive; without motion; (*fire, etc*) extinguished; (*limb, etc*) numb; (*colour, sound etc*) dull; (*a ball*) out of play; complete, exact; unerring. * *adv* in a dead manner; completely; utterly. * *n* a dead person; the quietest time.—**deadness** *n*.

deadbeat *n* (*inf*) a lazy or socially inept person; a vagrant.

dead duck *n* (*sl*) a person or thing destined to fail.

deaden *vt* to render numb or insensible; to deprive of vitality; to muffle.—**deadener** *n*.—**deadeningly** *adv*.

dead end *n* a cul-de-sac; a hopeless situation.

dead-end *adj* (*job*) holding no chance of advancement; having no hope of success in the future (*dead-end kids*).

deadening *n* material for soundproofing a room.

deadeye *n* an expert marksman; (*naut*) a round, laterally flattened wooden block pierced with three holes through which the lanyards are passed, used for extending the shrouds.

deadfall *n* a trap with a falling weight, which can kill or disable; a tangled mass of fallen trees.

deadhead *n* a person who has a free pass on trains or to places of amusement, etc; a transport vehicle travelling empty. * *vt* to remove dead flower heads from (a plant); to provide free admission to. * *vi* to travel or gain admission without payment; to drive an empty transport vehicle.

dead heat *n* a race in which two or more finish equal, a tie.

dead letter *n* a law or rule that is no longer enforced; a letter that cannot be delivered and is returned to the sender.

deadlight *n* (*naut*) a storm shutter for a cabin window; a skylight not made to open.

deadline *n* the time by which something must be done.

deadlock *n* a clash of interests making progress impossible; a standstill.—*also vt*.

deadly *adj* (**deadlier, deadliest**) fatal; implacable; (*inf*) tedious. * *adv* death-like; intensely.—**deadliness** *n*.

deadly nightshade *n* a poisonous plant with purple flowers and black berries.—*also* **belladonna**.

deadpan *adj* (*inf*) deliberately expressionless or emotionless.—*also adv*.

dead reckoning *n* the taking of a ship's position by log and compass, not astronomical observations.

dead set *adv* with determination.

dead weight *n* a very heavy load; an oppressive burden.

dead wood *n* (*inf*) a useless person or thing.

deaf *adj* unable to hear; hearing badly; not wishing to hear.—**deafly** *adv*.—**deafness** *n*.

deafen *vt* to deprive of hearing.—**deafeningly** *adv*.

deaf-mute *n* a deaf and dumb person.

deal[1] *vb* (**dealing, dealt**) *vt* (*a blow*) to deliver, inflict; (*cards, etc*) to distribute; (*with* **with**) to do business with; (*problem, task*) to solve. * *vi* to do business (with); to trade (in). * *n* a portion, quantity; (*inf*) a large amount; a dealing of cards; a business transaction.

deal[2] *n* fir or pine wood.—*also adj*.

dealer *n* a trader; a person who deals cards; (*sl*) a seller of illegal drugs.

dealings *npl* personal or business transactions.

dealt *see* **deal**.

dean *n* the head of a cathedral chapter; a college fellow in charge of discipline; the head of a university or college faculty.—**deanship** *n*.

deanery *n* (*pl* **deaneries**) the office or residence of a dean.

dear *adj* loved, precious; charming; expensive; a form of address in letters. * *n* a person who is loved. * *adv* at a high price.—**dearness** *n*.

dearie, deary *n* (*pl* **dearies**) (*inf*) a darling, a dear.

dearly *adv* with great affection; at a high price or rate.

dearth *n* scarcity, lack.

death *n* the end of life, dying; the state of being dead; the destruction of something.

deathbed *n* the bed in which a person dies or is about to die.

deathblow *n* a blow causing death.

death duty *n* a tax paid on an inheritance after a death.—*also* **death tax**.

deathless *adj* immortal.—**deathlessly** *adv*.—**deathlessness** *n*.

deathly *adj* like death, pale, still; deadly. * *adv* in a manner causing or tending to death; to a degree resembling death; (*inf*) extremely (*deathly quiet*).—**deathliness** *n*.

death mask *n* a plaster cast of a face taken immediately after death.

death rate *n* the yearly proportion of deaths to population.—*also* **mortality rate.**
death rattle *n* a deep gurgling noise sometimes made by a dying person.
death row *n* the section of a prison housing inmates sentenced to death.
death's head *n* a skull or representation of a skull, emblematic of death.
death's-head moth *n* a large moth with skull-like markings.
death tax *see* **death duty.**
deathtrap *n* an unsafe place, thing or structure.
death warrant *n* official authorization for the execution of a person condemned to death; anything that guarantees the destruction of hope or expectation.
deathwatch beetle *n* a small beetle that makes a ticking sound, superstitiously supposed to forebode death.
deathwatch *n* a vigil beside a dying person; a guard over a criminal prior to execution.
death wish *n* a usu unconscious wish for one's own death or that of another.
deb *n* (*inf*) a debutante.
debacle *n* a sudden disastrous break-up or collapse; a break-up of river ice.
debar *vt* (**debarring, debarred**) to exclude, to bar.—**debarment** *n.*
debark *vti* to land from a ship, to disembark.—**debarkation** *n.*
debase *vt* to lower in character or value; (*coinage*) to degrade.—**debasement** *n.*—**debaser** *n.*
debatable *adj* open to question, disputed.—**debatably** *adv.*
debate *n* a formal argument; a discussion, esp in parliament. * *vt* to consider, contest. * *vi* to discuss thoroughly; to join in debate.—**debater** *n.*
debauch *vti* to corrupt, dissipate; to lead astray, to seduce.—**debaucher** *n.*
debauchee *n* a dissolute person, a libertine.
debauchery *n* (*pl* **debaucheries**) depraved over-indulgence; corruption; profligacy.
debenture *n* a bond with guaranteed interest and forming a first charge on assets; a certificate acknowledging a debt; a certificate entitling a refund of customs duty.
debilitate *vt* to weaken, to enervate.—**debilitation** *n.*—**debilitative** *adj.*
debility *n* (*pl* **debilities**) weakness, infirmity.
debit *n* the entry of a sum owed, opposite to the credit; the left side of a ledger used for this. * *vt* to charge to the debit side of a ledger.
debonair, debonnaire *adj* having a carefree manner; courteous, gracious, charming.—**debonairly** *adv.*
debouch *vi* to march or to flow out from a narrow space to open ground.—**debouchment** *n.*
debrief *vt* (*diplomat, etc*) to make a report following a mission; to obtain such information.—**debriefing** *n.*
debris *n* (*pl* **debris**) broken and scattered remains, wreckage.
debt *n* a sum owed; a state of owing; an obligation.
debtor *n* a person, company, etc who owes money to another.
debug *vt* (**debugging, debugged**) (*inf*) (*room, etc*) to clear of hidden microphones; (*machine, program, plan, etc*) to locate and remove errors from; to remove insects from.
debunk *vt* (*inf*) (*claim, theory*) to expose as false.—**debunker** *n.*
debut *n* a first appearance as a public performer or in society. * *vi* to make one's debut.
debutant *n* one making a debut, esp a sportsman.
debutante *n* a young woman making her first appearance in upper-class society; a young woman regarded as wealthy, aristocratic and indolent.
Dec. *abbr* = December.
decade *n* a period of ten years; a group of ten.—**decadal** *adj.*
decadence, decadency *n* a state of deterioration in standards, esp of morality.
decadent *adj* deteriorating; self-indulgent.—**decadently** *adv.*
decaffeinated *adj* (*coffee, tea, carbonated drinks, etc*) with caffeine reduced or removed.
decagon *n* a ten-sided plane figure.—**decagonal** *adj.*
decahedron *n* a solid with ten faces.—**decahedral** *adj.*
decalcify *vt* (**decalcifying, decalcified**) to deprive (bone etc) of its lime.
decalitre, decaliter *n* a unit of ten litres.
Decalogue *n* the Ten Commandments.
decametre, decameter *n* a unit of ten metres.
decamp *vi* to leave suddenly or secretly.—**decampment** *n.*
decanal *adj* of a dean or his office; of the south side of the choir of a church, etc.
decant *vt* (*wine, etc*) to pour from one vessel to another, leaving sediment behind.—**decantation** *n.*
decanter *n* an ornamental bottle (usu glass) for holding wines, etc.
decapitate *vt* to behead.—**decapitation** *n.*—**decapitator** *n.*
decapod *adj* having ten feet or ten arms. * *n* a ten-footed crustacean, or ten-armed cephalopod.—**decapodal, decapodan, decapodous** *adj.*
decarbonate *vt* to deprive of carbon dioxide.—**decarbonation** *n.*
decarbonize *vt* take carbon or carbon deposit from.—**decarbonization** *n.*
decare *n* a measure of 1,000 square metres.
decasyllable *n* a ten-syllabled line or word.—**decasyllabic** *adj, n.*
decathlon *n* a track-and-field contest consisting of ten events.—**decathlete** *n.*
decay *vti* to rot, to decompose; to deteriorate, to wither. * *n* the act or state of decaying; a decline, collapse.
decease *n* death. * *vi* to die.
deceased *adj* dead. * *n* the dead person.
deceit *n* the act of deceiving; cunning; treachery; fraud.
deceitful *adj* treacherous; insincere; misleading.—**deceitfully** *adv.*—**deceitfulness** *n.*
deceive *vt* to cheat; to mislead; to delude; to impose upon.—**deceivable** *adj.*—**deceiver** *n.*—**deceivingly** *adv.*
decelerate *vt, vi* to reduce speed.—**deceleration** *n.*—**decelerator** *n.*
December *n* the twelfth and last month of the year with 31 days.
Decembrist *n* one of the conspirators who took part in the insurrection against Tsar Nicholas I of Russia, on his accession, December 1825.
decency *n* (*pl* **decencies**) being decent; conforming to accepted standards of proper behaviour.
decennial *adj* lasting for, or occurring, every ten years.—**decennially** *adv.*
decennium *n* (*pl* **decenniums, decennia**) a ten-year period, a decade.
decent *adj* respectable, proper; moderate; not obscene; (*inf*) quite good; (*inf*) kind, generous.—**decently** *adv.*
decentralize *vt* (*government, organization*) to divide among local centres.—**decentralist** *adj, n.*—**decentralization** *n.*
deception *n* the act of deceiving or the state of being deceived; illusion; fraud.
deceptive *adj* apt to mislead; ambiguous; unreliable.—**deceptively** *adv.*—**deceptiveness** *n.*
deci- *prefix* one tenth.
decibel *n* a unit for measuring sound level.
decide *vti* to determine, to settle; to give a judgment on; to resolve.—**decidable** *adj.*
decided *adj* unhesitating; clearly marked.
decidedly *adv* definitely, certainly.
decider *n* a deciding round, a final heat.
deciduous *adj* (*trees, shrubs*) shedding all leaves annually, at the end of the growing season.—**deciduousness** *n.*
decilitre, deciliter *n* a unit equal to one-tenth of a litre.
decillion *n* in UK, the tenth power of a million, a unit followed by 60 zeros; in US, the eleventh power of a thousand, a unit followed by 33 zeros.—**decillionth** *adj.*
decimal *adj* of tenths, of numbers written to the base 10. * *n* a tenth part; a decimal fraction.—**decimally** *adv.*
decimal classification *see* **Dewey Decimal System.**
decimal currency *n* currency in which units are divisible by ten.
decimal fraction *n* a fraction whose denominator is ten or a power of ten, indicated by figures after a decimal point.
decimalize *vt* to express as a decimal or to convert to a decimal system.—**decimalization** *n.*

decimal point *n* a dot written before the numerator in a decimal fraction (eg 0.5 = 1/2).
decimal system *n* a system of weights and measures in which units are related in multiples or submultiples of ten.
decimate *vt* to kill every tenth person; to reduce by one tenth; to kill a great number.—**decimation** *n*.—**decimator** *n*.
decimetre, decimeter *n* a measure of length, one tenth of a metre.
decipher *vt* to decode; to make out (indistinct writing, meaning, etc).—**decipherable** *adj*.—**decipherer** *n*.—**decipherment** *n*.
decision *n* a settlement; a ruling; a judgment; determination, firmness; (*boxing*) a win on points.—**decisional** *adj*.
decisive *adj* determining the issue, positive; conclusive, final.—**decisively** *adv*.—**decisiveness** *n*.
deck *n* the floor on a ship, aircraft, bus or bridge; a pack of playing cards; the turntable of a record-player; the playing mechanism of a tape recorder; (*sl*) the ground, the floor. * *vt* to cover; to adorn.
deck chair *n* a folding chair made of canvas suspended in a frame.
deck hand *n* a seaman who performs manual tasks.
deckle edge *n* the ragged edge, as on handmade paper.—**deckle-edged** *adj*.
deckle *n* a gauge on a papermaking machine for determining the width.
declaim *vti* to state dramatically; to recite.—**declaimer** *n*.
declamation *n* the art of declaiming according to rhetorical rules; impassioned oratory; distinct and correct enunciation of words in vocal music.
declamatory *adj* pertaining to, or characterized by, declamation; noisy in style; appealing to the passions.—**declamatorily** *adv*.
declaration *n* the act of declaring or proclaiming; that which is declared; an assertion; publication; a statement reduced to writing.
declarative *adj* making a declaration.—**declaratively** *adv*.
declaratory *adj* declarative; explanatory, affirmative.—**declaratorily** *adv*.
declare *vt* to affirm, to proclaim; to admit possession of (dutiable goods). * *vi* (*law*) to make a statement; (*with* **against, for**) to announce one's support.—**declarable** *n*.
déclassé *adj* fallen in the social scale.
declassify *vt* (**declassifying, declassified**) to remove a document, etc from the list of official secrets.—**declassification** *n*.
declension *n* (*gram*) variation in the form of a noun and its modifiers to show case and number; a complete set of such variations of a noun, etc.—**declensional** *adj*.
declination *n* a downward bend; (*astron*) the angular distance of a star and the celestial equator; (*compass*) the angle between true north and the magnetic north.—**declinational** *adj*.
decline *vi* to refuse; to move down; to deteriorate, fall away; to fail; to diminish; to draw to an end; to deviate. * *vt* to reject, to refuse; (*gram*) to give the cases of a declension. * *n* a diminution; a downward slope; a gradual loss of physical and mental faculties.—**declinable** *adj*.—**decliner** *n*.
declivity *n* (*pl* **declivities**) a downward slope.—**declivitous** *adj*.
decoct *vt* to boil anything to extract its essence.
decoction *n* an extract obtained by boiling or digesting in hot water; the act of decocting.
decode *vt* to translate a code into plain language.
decoder *n* one who decodes; (*comput*) a device for converting data from one form to another, eg binary to decimal.
decollate *vt* to separate (collated papers); (*arch*) to behead.—**decollator** *n*.
decollation *n* the act of decollating; (*art*) a representation of a beheading, esp of St John the Baptist.
décolletage *n* a low-cut dress or neckline.
décolleté *adj* having a low neckline.
decolonize *vt* to allow a colony to become independent.
decolorize *vt* to remove colour from, to bleach.—**decoloration** *n*.—**decolorization** *n*.
decompose *vti* to separate or break up into constituent parts, esp as part of a chemical process; to resolve into its elements. * *vi* to decay.—**decomposable** *adj*.—**decomposition** *n*.
decompress *vt* to decrease the pressure on, esp gradually; to return (a diver, etc) to a condition of normal atmospheric pressure.—**decompression** *n*.—**decompressive** *adj*.—**decompressor** *n*.
decompression sickness *n* a condition affecting divers, astronauts, etc, resulting from too rapid a return from high pressure to atmosphere and characterized by cramps and paralysis.
decongestant *n* a medical preparation that relieves congestion, eg catarrh.
deconsecrate *vt* to transfer (a church) from ecclesiastical use.—**deconsecration** *n*.
decontaminate *vt* to free from (radioactive, etc) contamination.—**decontamination** *n*.—**decontaminator** *n*.
decontrol *vt* (**decontrolling, decontrolled**) to release from control, esp government control.
décor, decor *n* general decorative effect, eg of a room; scenery and stage design.
decorate *vt* to ornament; to paint or wallpaper; to honour with a badge or medal.
decoration *n* decorating; an ornament; a badge or an honour.
decorative *adj* ornamental, pretty to look at.—**decoratively** *adv*.—**decorativeness** *n*.
decorator *n* a person who decorates, esp houses.
decorous *adj* proper, decent; showing propriety and dignity.—**decorously** *adv*.—**decorousness** *n*.
decorticate *vt* to remove the bark, rind, or husk from; to remove the cortex of an organ by surgery. * *vi* to peel or come off, as bark, skin.—**decortication** *n*.—**decorticator** *n*.
decorum *n* what is correct in outward appearance, propriety of conduct, decency.
decoy *vt* to lure into a trap. * *n* anything intended to lure into a snare.—**decoyer** *n*.
decrease *vti* to make or become less. * *n* a decreasing; the amount of diminution.—**decreasingly** *adv*.
decree *n* an order, edict or law; a judicial decision. * *vt* (**decreeing, decreed**) to decide by sentence in law; to appoint.—**decreeable** *adj*.—**decreer** *n*.
decrement *n* a decrease; the amount of this; (*math*) a negative increment of a variable.—**decremental** *adj*.
decrepit *adj* worn out by the infirmities of old age; in the last stage of decay.—**decrepitly** *adv*.
decrepitate *vti* to heat (a salt, mineral) until it crackles; to crackle under extreme heat.—**decrepitation** *n*.
decrepitude *n* the state or condition of being decrepit; feebleness and decay, esp that due to old age.
decrescendo *n* (*pl* **decrescendos**) (*mus*) a sign (>) that the volume of sound is to be gradually reduced; a gradual decrease in force of tone or a passage where this occurs. * *adj* gradually diminishing in loudness.—*also* **diminuendo**.
decrescent *adj* growing less; (*moon*) waning.—**decrescence** *n*.
decretal *n* (*RC Church*) a papal decree; a book of edicts. * *adj* of a decree or decretal.
decry *vt* (**decrying, decried**) to disparage, to censure as worthless.—**decrial** *n*.—**decrier** *n*.
dectet *n* a group of eight musicians or voices.
decumbent *adj* lying down, prostrate, reclining; (*bot*) resting on the ground, trailing.—**decumbence, decumbency** *n*.
decuple *adj* tenfold. * *n* a number repeated ten times. * *vt* to increase tenfold.
decurion *n* a Roman officer commanding ten men.
decurrent *adj* (*plant*) running or extending downward.
decussate *vti* to intersect in the form of an X. * *adj* X-shaped; (*leaves*) in pairs, at right angles to those above and below.—**decussation** *n*.
dedicate *vt* to consecrate (to some sacred purpose); to devote wholly or chiefly; to inscribe (to someone).—**dedicatee** *n*.—**dedicator** *n*.—**dedicatory, dedicative** *adj*.

dedicated *adj* devoted to a particular cause, profession, etc; single-minded; assigned to a particular function.

dedication *n* the act of dedicating; a dedicatory inscription in a book, etc; devotion to a cause, ideal, etc.

deduce *vt* to derive (knowledge, a conclusion) from reasoning; infer.—**deducible** *adj*.

deduct *vt* to take (from); to subtract.

deductible *adj* capable of being deducted; allowable as a deduction against income tax.—**deductibility** *n*.

deduction *n* deducting; the amount deducted; deducing; a conclusion that something is true because it necessarily follows from a set of general premises known to be valid.—**deductive** *adj*.—**deductively** *adv*.

deed *n* an act; an exploit; a legal document recording a transaction.

deem *vti* to judge; to think, to believe.

deep *adj* extending or placed far down or far from the outside; fully involved; engrossed; profound, intense; heartfelt; penetrating; difficult to understand; secret; cunning; sunk low; low in pitch; (*colour*) of high saturation and low brilliance. * *adv* in a deep manner; far in, into. * *n* that which is deep; the sea.—**deeply** *adv*.—**deepness** *n*.

deepen *vt* to make deeper in any sense; to increase. * *vi* to become deeper.—**deepener** *n*.

deepfreeze *n* a refrigerator in which food is frozen and stored.

deep-freeze *vt* (**deep-freezing, deep-froze** *or* **deep-freezed,** *pp* **deep-frozen, deep-freezed**) to freeze (food) so that it keeps for a long period of time; to store in a freezer. * *n* a freezer.

deep-fry *vt* (**deep-frying, deep-fried**) to fry food in deep fat in order to cook or brown it without turning.—**deep-fryer** *n*.

deep-laid *adj* (*plans, etc*) secret and elaborate.

deep-rooted *adj* (*feelings, opinions, etc*) firmly established; ingrained; deep-seated.

deep-seated *adj* having its seat far beneath the surface; deep-rooted.

Deep South *n* the southeastern states of the USA.

deep space *n* the region of outer space beyond our solar system.

deer *n* (*pl* **deer, deers**) a four-footed animal with antlers, esp on the males, including stag, reindeer, etc.

deerhound *n* a large rough-haired greyhound.—*also* **Scottish deerhound**.

deerstalker *n* a person who hunts deer; a soft hat peaked at the front and back.

de-escalate *vti* to reduce the intensity of.—**de-escalation** *n*.

deface *vt* to disfigure; to obliterate.—**defaceable** *adj*.—**defacement** *n*.—**defacer** *n*.

de facto *adv* in fact; in reality.—*also adj*.

defalcate *vi* to embezzle money held in trust.—**defalcation** *n*.—**defalcator** *n*.

defamation *n* the act of injuring someone's good name or reputation without justification, either orally or in writing; the condition of being defamed.

defamatory *adj* containing that which is injurious to the character or reputation of someone.—**defamatorily** *adv*.

defame *vt* to destroy the good reputation of; to speak evil of.—**defamer** *n*.

default *n* neglect to do what duty or law requires; failure to fulfil a financial obligation; (*comput*) a basic setting or instruction to which a program reverts. * *vi* to fail in one's duty (as honouring a financial obligation, appearing in court).

defaulter *n* one who defaults; one who fails to appear in court when required, or to make a proper account of money or property entrusted to his charge; on the Stock Exchange, one who fails to meet his engagements.

defeasance *n* (*law*) annulment; a condition annexed to a deed, which being performed renders the deed void.

defeasible *adj* able to be annulled.—**defeasibility** *n*.

defeat *vt* to frustrate; to win a victory over; to baffle. * *n* a frustration of plans; overthrow, as of an army in battle; loss of a game, race, etc.—**defeater** *n*.

defeatism *n* disposition to accept defeat.—**defeatist** *n, adj*.

defecate *vi* to empty the bowels. * *vt* (*chem*) to free from impurities, to refine.—**defecation** *n*.—**defecator** *n*.

defect *n* a deficiency; a blemish, fault. * *vi* to desert one's country or a cause, transferring one's allegiance (to another).—**defector** *n*.

defection *n* desertion of duty or allegiance.

defective *adj* having a defect; faulty; incomplete. * *n* a person defective in physical or mental powers.—**defectively** *adv*.—**defectiveness** *n*.

defence, defense *n* resistance or protection against attack; a means of resisting an attack; protection; vindication; (*law*) a defendant's plea; the defending party in legal proceedings; (*sport*) defending (the goal, etc) against the attacks of the opposing side; the defending players in a team.—**defenceless, defenseless** *adj*.—**defencelessness, defenselessness** *n*.

defend *vt* to guard or protect; to maintain against attack; (*law*) to resist, as a claim; to contest (a suit).—**defendable** *adj*.—**defender** *n*.

defendant *n* a person accused or sued in a lawsuit.

defensible *adj* able to be defended or justified.—**defensibly** *adv*.—**defensibility** *n*.

defensive *adj* serving to defend; in a state or posture of defence.—**defensively** *adv*.—**defensiveness** *n*.

defer[1] *vt* (**deferring, deferred**) to put off to another time; to delay.—**deferrable, deferable** *adj*.—**deferrer** *n*.

defer[2] *vi* (**deferring, deferred**) to yield to another person's wishes, judgment or authority.

deference *n* a deferring or yielding in judgment or opinion; polite respect.

deferent *adj* deferential (*anat*) conveying (a fluid, etc) away.

deferential *adj* expressing deference or respect.—**deferentially** *adv*.

deferment *n* a delay; postponement.

deferral *n* a deferment.

deferred *adj* postponed; (*stock, shares*) having its dividend payable after other shares.

defiance *n* the act of defying; wilful disobedience; a challenge.

defiant *adj* characterized by defiance; challenging.—**defiantly** *adv*.

deficiency *n* (*pl* **deficiencies**) being deficient; lack, shortage; deficit.

deficient *adj* insufficient, lacking.—**deficiently** *adv*.

deficit *n* the amount by which an amount falls short of what is required; excess of expenditure over income, or liabilities over assets.

defilade *vt* to raise (a rampart) to protect defensive lines from guns placed in a high position. * *n* protection provided in this way.

defile[1] *vt* to pollute or corrupt.—**defilement** *n*.—**defiler** *n*.

defile[2] *n* a long, narrow pass or way, through which troops can pass only in single file. * *vt* to march in single file.

define *vt* to fix the bounds or limits of; to mark the limits or outline of clearly; to describe accurately; to fix the meaning of.—**definable** *adj*.—**definer** *n*.

definite *adj* defined; having distinct limits; fixed; exact; clear.—**definiteness** *n*.

definitely *adv* certainly; distinctly. * *interj* used to agree emphatically.

definition *n* a description of a thing by its properties; an explanation of the exact meaning of a word, term, or phrase; sharpness of outline.—**definitional** *adj*.

definitive *adj* defining or limiting; decisive, final.—**definitively** *adv*.—**definitiveness** *n*.

definitude *n* the quality of being definite; definiteness, precision.

deflagrate *vt* to set fire to. * *vi* to cause to burn with sudden and sparkling combustion.—**deflagration** *n*.

deflate *vt* to release gas or air from; to reduce in size or importance; to reduce the money supply, restrict credit, etc to reduce inflation in the economy.—**deflator** *n*.

deflation *n* deflating; a reduction in the supply of money, causing a fall in prices.—**deflationary** *adj*.—**deflationist** *adj, n*.

deflect *vti* to turn or cause to turn aside from a line or proper course.—**deflective** *adj*.—**deflector** *n*.

deflection *n* the action of deflecting or the state of being deflected from a straight line or regular path; deviation; the turning of a magnetic needle away from its zero; the amount of this.

defloration *n* a deflowering.

deflower *vt* to deprive of virginity; to corrupt the beauty, innocence of.—**deflowerer** *n*.

defoliant *n* a chemical that kills foliage.

defoliate *vt* to strip (a plant or tree) of its leaves.—**defoliation** *n*.—**defoliator** *n*.

deforce *vt* (*law*) to keep (property) out of the legal owner's possession by force; (*Scots law*) to resist (an officer of law in execution of his duty).—**deforcement** *n*.

deforest *vt* to clear of trees.—**deforestation** *n*.—**deforester** *n*.

deform *vt* to spoil the natural form of; to put out of shape.—**deformer** *n*.

deformation *n* the act of deforming; a change for the worse; a perverted form of word.

deformed *adj* misshapen; warped.

deformity *n* (*pl* **deformities**) the condition of being deformed; a deformed part of the body; a defect.

defraud *vt* to remove (money, rights, etc) from a person by cheating or deceiving.—**defraudation** *n*.—**defrauder** *n*.

defray *vt* to provide money (to pay expenses, etc).—**defrayable** *adj*.—**defrayal** *n*.—**defrayer** *n*.

defrock *vt* to expel from the priesthood, to unfrock.

defrost *vt* to unfreeze; to free from frost or ice.* *vi* to become unfrozen.

deft *adj* skilful, adept; nimble.—**deftly** *adv*.—**deftness** *n*.

defunct *adj* no longer being in existence or function or in use.—**defunctive** *adj*.

defuse *vt* to disarm an explosive (bomb or mine) by removing its fuse; to decrease tension in a (crisis) situation.

defy *vt* (**defying, defied**) to resist openly and without fear; to challenge (a person) to attempt something considered dangerous or impossible; to resist attempts at, to elude.—**defier** *n*.

dégagé *adj* unconstrained, at ease.

degauss *vt* to neutralize or remove a magnetic field.—**degausser** *n*.

degeneracy *n* (*pl* **degeneracies**) the condition or quality of being degenerate; an instance of degeneracy; something that is degenerate.

degenerate *adj* having declined in physical or moral qualities; sexually deviant. * *vi* to become or grow worse. * *n* a degenerate person.—**degenerately** *adv*.

degeneration *n* the act, state, or process of growing worse; degeneracy; decline; the morbid impairment of any structural tissue or organ.

degenerative *adj* of the nature of, or tending to, degenerate.—**degeneratively** *adv*.

deglutinate *vt* to extract gluten from; to unglue.—**deglutination** *n*.

deglutition *n* the power to swallow, a swallowing.

degradable *adj* capable of being broken down by biological or chemical action.

degradation *n* a degrading or being degraded in quality, rank or status; a degraded state; (*geol*) a lowering of land by erosion; (*RC Church*) the unfrocking of a priest.

degrade *vt* to reduce in rank or status; to disgrace; to decompose; to be lowered by erosion.—**degrader** *n*.

degrading *adj* humiliating; (*geol*) eroding.—**degradingly** *adv*.

degree *n* a step in an ascending or descending series; a stage in intensity; the relative quantity in intensity; a unit of measurement in a scale; an academic title awarded as of right or as an honour.

degression *n* a going down; a decrease, esp in taxation rate.—**degressive** *adj*.

dehisce *vi* (*fruits, seed pods, etc*) to burst open.

dehiscent *adj* (*fruits*) opening to release seeds.—**dehiscence** *n*.

dehorn *vt* to cut back, or deprive of, horns.—**dehorner** *n*.

dehumanize *vt* to remove human qualities from; to deprive of personality or emotion, to render mechanical.—**dehumanization** *n*.

dehydrate *vt* to remove water from. * *vi* to lose water, esp from the bodily tissues.—**dehydration** *n*.—**dehydrator** *n*.

dehypnotize *vt* to rouse from a hypnotic state.

de-ice *vt* to prevent the formation of or to remove ice from a surface.—**de-icer** *n*.

deicide *n* the killing of a god; the killer of a god.—**deicidal** *adj*.

deictic *adj* (*gram*) demonstrative; (*logic*) proving directly.—**deictically** *adv*.

deific *adj* making, or tending to make, divine.

deify *vt* (**deifying, deified**) to make into a god; to worship as a god, glorify.—**deification** *n*.—**deifier** *n*.

deign *vi* to condescend; to think it worthy to do (something).

deil *n* (*Scot*) the devil.

deism *n* belief in the existence of God, but not religious revelation.—**deist** *n*.—**deistic, deistical** *adj*.

deity *n* (*pl* **deities**) a god or goddess; the rank or essence of a god; (*with cap and* **the**) God.

déjà vu *n* the illusion that you have already experienced the present situation.

deject *vt* to have a depressing effect on.

dejecta *npl* excrement, droppings.

dejected *adj* morose, depressed.—**dejectedly** *adv*.—**dejectedness** *n*.

dejection *n* depression; lowness of spirits.

de jure *adv* according to the law, by right.

delaine *n* a light fabric of wool and cotton.

delate *vt* (*formerly*) to inform against (a person); to report (an offence).—**delation** *n*.—**delator** *n*.

delay *vt* to postpone; to detain, obstruct. * *vi* to linger. * *n* a delaying or being delayed; the time period during which something is delayed.—**delayer** *n*.

dele *vt* (**deleing, deled**) (*print*) to take out a letter, etc, in proofreading. * *n* a mark that a letter, etc, is to be deleted.

delectable *adj* delightful, delicious.—**delectability** *n*.—**delectably** *adv*.

delectation *n* delight, enjoyment.

delegate *vt* to appoint as a representative; to give powers or responsibilities to (an agent or assembly). * *n* a deputy or an elected representative.—**delegable** *adj*.

delegation *n* the act of delegating; a group of people empowered to represent others.

delete *vt* to strike out (something written or printed); to erase.

deleterious *adj* harmful or destructive.

deletion *n* the act of deleting; a word, passage, etc, deleted from a text; the absence of a normal part of a chromosome.

delft, delftware *n* a type of blue-glazed earthenware, originally from Delft in Holland.

deli *n* (*pl* **delis**) (*inf*) a delicatessen.

deliberate *vt* to consider carefully. * *vi* to discuss or debate thoroughly; to consider. * *adj* well thought out; intentional; cautious.—**deliberately** *adv*.—**deliberateness** *n*.—**deliberator** *n*.

deliberation *n* careful consideration; thorough discussion; caution.

deliberative *adj* of or appointed for deliberation; as a result of deliberation.—**deliberatively** *adv*.

delicacy *n* (*pl* **delicacies**) delicateness; sensibility; a luxurious food.

delicate *adj* fine in texture; fragile, not robust; requiring tactful handling; of exquisite workmanship; requiring skill in techniques.—**delicately** *adv*.—**delicateness** *n*.

delicatessen *n* a store selling prepared foods, esp imported delicacies.

delicious *adj* having a pleasurable effect on the senses, esp taste; delightful.—**deliciously** *adv*.—**deliciousness** *n*.

delict *n* a legal offence.

delight *vt* to please greatly. * *vi* to have or take great pleasure (in). * *n* great pleasure; something that causes this.—**delighter** *n*.

delighted *adj* very pleased; filled with delight.—**delightedly** *adv*.—**delightedness** *n*.

delightful *adj* giving great pleasure.—**delightfully** *adv*.—**delightfulness** *n*.

delimit, delimitate *vt* to fix or mark the boundaries of.—**delimitation** *n*.—**delimitative** *adj*.

delineate *vt* to describe in great detail; to represent by drawing.—**delineation** *n*.—**delineative** *adj*.

delineator *n* one who delineates; an adjustable tailor's pattern.

delinquency *n* (*pl* **delinquencies**) neglect of or failure in duty; a misdeed; a fault; antisocial or illegal behaviour, esp by young people (—*also* **juvenile delinquency**).

delinquent *adj* negligent; guilty of an offence. * *n* a person guilty of a misdeed, esp a young person who breaks the law.

deliquesce *vi* to melt and become liquid by absorbing moisture from the atmosphere.—**deliquescence** *n*.—**deliquescent** *adj*.

delirious *adj* mentally confused, light-headed; wildly excited.—**deliriously** *adv*.—**deliriousness** *n*.

delirium *n* (*pl* **deliriums, deliria**) a state of mental disorder, esp caused by a feverish illness; wild enthusiasm.

delirium tremens *n* a disorder of the brain, causing delusions and violent trembling, as the result of excessive drinking.

deliver *vt* (*goods, letters, etc*) to transport to a destination; to distribute regularly; to liberate, to rescue; to give birth; to assist at a birth; (*blow*) to launch; (*baseball*) to pitch; (*speech*) to utter.—**deliverable** *adj*.—**deliverer** *n*.

deliverance *n* the act of rescuing or liberating.

delivery *n* (*pl* **deliveries**) the act of delivering; anything delivered or communicated; the manner of delivering (a speech, etc); the manner of bowling in cricket, etc; the act of giving birth.

dell *n* a small hollow, usu with trees.

delocalize *vt* to deprive of local character; to remove from a locality.—**delocalization** *n*.

delouse *vt* to rid the lice from.

Delphic, Delphian *adj* relating to the ancient Greek city or its famous oracle which imparted enigmatic prophecies; obscure or ambiguous in meaning.

delphinium *n* a garden plant with spikes of, usu blue, flowers.

delta *n* the fourth letter of the Greek alphabet; an alluvial deposit at the mouth of a river.—**deltaic** *adj*.

delta wing *n* a triangular-shaped aircraft wing.

deltoid *adj* of the shape of the letter delta; triangular. * *n* (*anat*) a muscle that lifts the upper arm.

delude *vt* to mislead, to deceive.—**deluder** *n*.

deluge *n* a flood; anything happening in a heavy rush. * *vt* to inundate.

delusion *n* a false belief; a persistent false belief that is a symptom of mental illness.—**delusional** *adj*.

delusive *adj* deluding or tending to delude; deceptive; false.—**delusively** *adv*.

delusory *adj* delusive.

deluxe *adj* luxurious, of superior quality.

delve *vti* to search deeply; to dig.—**delver** *n*.

demagnetize *vt* to remove the magnetic properties of.—**demagnetization** *n*.—**demagnetizer** *n*.

demagogic, demagogical *adj* of, pertaining to, or characteristic of a demagogue.—**demagogically** *adv*.

demagogue, demagog *n* a political orator who derives power from appealing to popular prejudices.

demagoguery *n* demagogy; the rhetoric of a demagogue.

demagogy *n* the principles or practice of a demagogue; rule by a demagogue.

demand *vt* to ask for in an authoritative manner. * *n* a request or claim made with authority for what is due; an urgent claim; desire for goods and services shown by consumers.—**demandable** *adj*.—**demander** *n*.

demandant *n* a plaintiff.

demanding *adj* constantly making demands; requiring great skill, concentration or effort.—**demandingly** *adv*.

demantoid *n* an emerald green garnet used as a gem.

demarcate *vt* to delimit; to define or mark the bounds of.—**demarcator** *n*.

demarcation, demarkation *n* the act of marking off a boundary or setting a limit to; a limit; the strict separation of the type of work done by members of different trade unions.

démarche *n* a diplomatic announcement of policy or plan.

demark *vt* to demarcate.

dematerialize *vti* to deprive of or give up material form.—**dematerialization** *n*.

deme *n* a territorial subdivision or township of ancient Greece; (*biol*) a group within a species with similar cell structure, etc.

demean *vt* to lower in dignity.—**demeaning** *adj*.

demeanour, demeanor *n* behaviour; bearing.

dement *vt* to make insane, to drive mad.

demented *adj* crazy, insane.—**dementedly** *adv*.

dementia *n* the failure or loss of mental powers.

demerge *vt* to separate a previously merged business corporation into several companies.—**demerger** *n*.

demerit *n* a fault, a defect; a mark recording poor work by a student, etc.

demersal *adj* (*zool*) found in deep water or on the sea bottom.

demesne *n* (*law*) one's own land; (*hist*) a landed estate attached to a manor; a domain.

demi- *prefix* half.

demigod *n* a being that is part mortal part god; a god-like individual.—**demigoddess** *nf*.

demijohn *n* a large bottle, often in a wicker case.

demilitarize *vt* to remove armed forces, weapons systems, etc from.—**demilitarization** *n*.

demimondaine *n* a member of the demimonde, a courtesan.

demimonde *n* a class of women not recognized by society, esp in 19th-century France, because of promiscuity; any socially disreputable group.

demise *n* (*formal*) death; termination, end. * *vt* to give or grant by will. * *vi* to pass by bequest or inheritance.—**demisable** *adj*.

demisemiquaver *n* (*mus*) a note with a time value of half a semiquaver.—*also* **thirty-second note**.

demitasse *n* a small cup (of black coffee).

demiurge *n* in Platonic philosophy, the creator of the world; in Gnostic philosophy, an agent of the Supreme Being in the creation of man and the material universe; in ancient Greece, the chief magistrate of some states.—**demiurgic** *adj*.

demo *n* (*pl* **demos**) (*inf*) a demonstration.

demob *vt* (**demobbing, demobbed**) (*inf*) to demobilize. * *n* (*inf*) demobilization.

demobilize *vt* to discharge from the armed forces.—**demobilization** *n*.

democracy *n* (*pl* **democracies**) a form of government by the people through elected representatives; a country governed by its people; political, social or legal equality.

democrat *n* a person who believes in or promotes democracy; (*with cap*) a member of the Democratic Party in the US.

democratic *adj* of, relating to, or supporting the principles of democracy; favouring or upholding equal rights; (*with cap*) of or pertaining to the Democratic Party in the US.—**democratically** *adv*.

democratize *vt* to make democratic. * *vi* to become democratic.—**democratization** *n*.

démodé *adj* out of fashion.

demodulate *vt* to extract a modulating (radio, video, etc) wave or signal from a modulated carrier wave.—**demodulator** *n*.—**demodulation** *n*.

demography *n* the study of population statistics concerning birth, marriage, death and disease.—**demographer, demographist** *n*.—**demographic** *adj*.—**demographically** *adv*.

demoiselle *n* a damsel; a small crane of North Africa, southeast Europe and central Asia.

demolish *vt* (*a building*) to pull down or knock down; (*an argument*) to defeat; (*inf*) to eat up.—**demolisher** *n*.—**demolishment** *n*.

demolition *n* a demolishing or being demolished, esp by explosives.—**demolitionist** *adj, n*.

demon *n* an evil spirit; a cruel person; someone who is very skilled, energetic, hard-working, etc.—**demonic** *adj*.—**demonically** *adv*.

demonetize *vt* to withdraw (coin) from circulation; to abandon (gold etc) as a currency.—**demonetization** *n*.

demoniac, demoniacal *adj* of or like a demon; possessed by evil; frenzied, energetic. * *n* a person possessed by a demon.—**demoniacally** *adv*.

demonism *n* belief in demons; the nature of a demon.—**demonist** *n.*
demonize *vt* to make into or represent as a demon.
demonolater *n* a demon worshipper.—**demonolatry** *n.*
demonology *n* the study of demons and superstitions about them.—**demonologist** *n.*
demonstrable *adj* able to be demonstrated or proved.—**demonstrability** *n.*—**demonstrably** *adv.*
demonstrate *vt* to indicate or represent clearly; to provide certain evidence of, prove; to show how something (a machine, etc) works. * *vi* to show one's support for a cause, etc by public parades and protests; to act as a demonstrator of machinery, etc.—**demonstrational** *adj.*
demonstration *n* proof by evidence; a display or exhibition; a display of feeling; a public manifestation of opinion, as by a mass meeting, march, etc; a display of armed force.
demonstrative *adj* displaying one's feelings openly and unreservedly; indicative; conclusive; (*gram*) describing an adjective or pronoun indicating the person or thing referred to.—**demonstratively** *adv.*—**demonstrativeness** *n.*
demonstrator *n* a person who shows consumer goods to the public; one who or that which shows how a machine, etc works; a person who takes part in a public protest.
demoralize *vt* to lower the morale of, discourage.—**demoralization** *n.*—**demoralizer** *n.*
demos *n* in ancient Greece, the common people of a state; the population personified.
demote *vt* to reduce in rank or position.—**demotion** *n.*
demotic *adj* pertaining to the people; in the simplified style of ancient Egyptian writing.
demulcent *adj* softening; soothing. * *n* a medicine that allays irritation.
demur *vi* (**demurring, demurred**) to raise objections.—**demurral** *n.*
demure *adj* modest, reserved; affectedly quiet and proper; coy.—**demurely** *adv.*—**demureness** *n.*
demurrage *n* a charge for keeping a ship, truck, etc beyond the time agreed for unloading.
demurrer *n* (*law*) a plea that an opponent's facts are irrelevant; exception taken.
demy *n* (*pl* **demies**) a size of paper for printing (22½ x 17½ ins) or writing (20 x 15½ ins).
demystify *vt* (**demystifying, demystified**) to remove the mystery from; clarify.—**demystification** *n.*
den *n* a cave or lair of a wild beast; a place where people gather for illegal activities; a room in a house for relaxation or study.
denarius *n* (*pl* **denarii**) in ancient Rome, a silver coin; a gold coin worth 25 silver denarii.
denary *adj* of ten; decimal.
denationalize *vt* to transfer (industry, etc) from state control to private ownership.—**denationalization** *n.*
denaturalize *vt* to make unnatural; to deprive of acquired citizenship.—**denaturalization** *n.*
denature *vt* to modify the nature of; to change the properties of (a protein) by the action of an acid or heat; to render (alcohol) unfit for consumption.—**denaturant** *n.*—**denaturation** *n.*
dendriform *adj* branching, like a tree.
dendrite *n* a stone or mineral with tree-like markings; a fine branch of one of the nerve cells that conduct impulses.—**dendritic** *adj.*
dendrochronology *n* the dating of past events by studying the annual growth rings in trees.—**dendrochronological** *adj.*
dendroid *adj* resembling a tree in appearance.
dendrology *n* the scientific study of trees.—**dendrologic, dendrological** *adj.*—**dendrologist** *n.*
dene *n* a low sandy tract near sea, a dune.
denegation *n* a denial.
dengue *n* a tropical disease transmitted by the mosquito, causing fever and pain in the joints.
deniable *adj* able to be denied; questionable.—**deniably** *adv.*
denial *n* the act of denying; a refusal of a request, etc; a refusal or reluctance to admit the truth of something.
denier[1] *n* a unit of weight used to measure the fineness of silk, nylon or rayon fibre, esp as used in women's tights, etc.
denier[2] one who denies.
denigrate *vt* to disparage the character of; to belittle.—**denigration** *n.*—**denigrator** *n.*
denim *n* a hard-wearing cotton cloth, esp used for jeans; (*pl*) denim trousers or jeans.
denizen *n* an inhabitant, resident; an animal or plant established in a region where it is not native.
denominate *vt* to give a name to; to designate.
denomination *n* a name or title; a religious group comprising many local churches, larger than a sect; one of a series of related units, esp monetary.
denominational *adj* of, belonging to or controlled by a religious denomination.—**denominationally** *adv.*
denominationalism *n* denominational spirit, policy or principles; adherence to these.—**denominationalist.**
denominative *adj* giving a name; (*gram*) formed from a substantive or adjectival stem; connotative. * *n* a verb formed from a substantive or adjectival stem.
denominator *n* the part of a fractional expression written below the fraction line.
denotation *n* the action of denoting; expression by marks, signs or symbols; a sign, indication; a mark by which a thing is made known; designation, meaning.
denotative *adj* having the power to denote or point out; significant.—**denotatively** *adv.*
denote *vt* to indicate, be the sign of; to mean.—**denotement** *n.*
denouement, dénouement *n* the resolution of a plot or story; the solution, the outcome.
denounce *vt* to condemn or censure publicly; to inform against; to declare formally the ending of (treaties, etc).—**denouncement** *n.*—**denouncer** *n.*
dense *adj* difficult to see through; massed closely together; dull-witted, stupid.—**densely** *adv.*—**denseness** *n.*
density *n* (*pl* **densities**) the degree of denseness or concentration; stupidity; the ratio of mass to volume.
dent *n* a depression made by pressure or a blow. * *vti* to make a dent or become dented.
dental *adj* of or for the teeth.—**dentally** *adv.*
dental floss *n* waxed thread for cleaning between the teeth.
dental hygienist *n* a professionally trained and qualified person who checks and cleans teeth.—*also* **hygienist.**
dentate *adj* toothed, notched.
denticle *n* a small tooth or tooth-like projection.
denticulate *adj* (*leaf*) having small teeth.
dentiform *adj* tooth-shaped.
dentifrice *n* toothpowder or toothpaste.
dentil *n* (*arch*) a small, square, projecting block on a moulding.
dentin, dentine *n* the hard, bone-like substance forming the main part of teeth.
dentist *n* a person qualified to treat tooth decay, gum disease, etc.
dentistry *n* the area of medicine dealing with the care of teeth and the treatment of diseases of the teeth and gums; the practice of this as a profession.
dentition *n* the process or period of cutting the teeth; the arrangement of the teeth.
dentoid *adj* tooth-shaped.
denture *n* (*usu pl*) a set of artificial teeth.
denude *vt* to make naked; to deprive, strip.—**denudation** *n.*—**denuder** *n.*
denunciate *vt* (*rare*) to denounce.—**denunciator** *n.*
denunciation *n* the act of denouncing; a threat.—**denunciator** *n.*—**denunciatory** *adj.*

deny *vt* (**denying, denied**) to declare to be untrue; to repudiate; to refuse to acknowledge; to refuse to assent to a request, etc.
deodand *n* (*law*) (*hist*) a chattel that, having caused death, was forfeited to the crown.
deodar *n* a tall Himalayan cedar tree yielding a valuable timber.
deodorant *n* a substance that removes or masks unpleasant odours.
deodorize *vt* to remove the odour or smell from.—**deodorization** *n*.—**deodorizer** *n*.
deoxidize *vt* to deprive of oxygen.
depart *vi* to go away, leave; to deviate (from).
departed *adj* (*time, etc*) long past; (*person*) recently dead.
department *n* a unit of specialized functions into which an organization or business is divided; a province; a realm of activity.
departmental *adj* of, having, or organized into departments.—**departmentally** *adv*.
departmentalism *n* departmental structure, esp a bureaucratic one.
departmentalize *vt* to split into departments; to subdivide.—**departmentalization** *n*.
department store *n* a large store divided into various departments selling different types of goods.
departure *n* a departing; a deviating from normal practice; a new venture, course of action, etc.
depend *vi* to be determined by or connected with anything; to rely (on), put trust (in); to be reliant on for support, esp financially.
dependable *adj* able to be relied on.—**dependably** *adv*.—**dependability** *n*.
dependant, dependent *n* a person who is dependent on another, esp financially.
dependence, dependance *n* the state of being dependent; reliance, trust; a physical or mental reliance on a drug, person, etc.
dependency *n* (*pl* **dependencies**) dependence; a territory controlled by another country.
dependent, dependant *adj* relying on another person, thing, etc for support, money, etc; contingent; subordinate.
depersonalize *vt* to eliminate the individual character from a person, organization, etc; to make impersonal.—**depersonalization** *n*.
depict *vt* to represent pictorially; to describe.—**depicter, depictor** *n*.—**depiction** *n*.
depilate *vt* to remove hair from.—**depilation** *n*.—**depilator** *n*.
depilatory *n* (*pl* **depilatories**) a substance for removing superfluous hair. * *adj* removing hair.
deplane *vti* to alight or unload from an aircraft.
deplete *vt* to use up a large quantity of.—**depletion** *n*.—**depletive** *adj*.
deplorable *adj* shocking; extremely bad.—**deplorably** *adv*.
deplore *vt* to regret deeply; to complain of; to deprecate.—**deplorer** *n*.—**deploringly** *adv*.
deploy *vt* (*military forces*) to distribute and position strategically. * *vi* to adopt strategic positions within an area.—**deployment** *n*.
deplume *vt* to strip of feathers, to pluck; to strip of position, honour, etc.—**deplumation** *n*.
depolarize *vt* to deprive of or counteract the polarity of.—**depolarization** *n*.
depone *vti* (*Scot*) to testify upon oath, to depose.
deponent *adj* (*gram*) (*verb*) passive in form but active in meaning. * *n* (*gram*) a deponent verb; (*law*) one who makes a deposition.
depopulate *vt* to reduce the population of.—**depopulation** *n*.—**depopulator** *n*.
deport *vt* to expel (an undesirable person) from a country; to behave (in a certain manner).—**deportable** *adj*.
deportation *n* forcible removal from a country, esp of an undesirable person.
deportee *n* a deported person.
deportment *n* manners; bearing; behaviour.
depose *vt* to remove from power; to testify, esp in court.—**deposable** *adj*.—**deposer** *n*.
deposit *vt* to place or lay down; to pay money into a bank or other institution for safekeeping, to earn interest, etc; to pay as a first instalment; to let fall, leave. * *n* something deposited for safekeeping; money put in a bank; money given in part payment or security; material left in a layer, eg sediment.
depositary *n* (*pl* **depositaries**) the person to whom something is entrusted; a depository.
deposition *n* the act of depositing or deposing; a being removed from office or power; a sworn testimony, esp in writing.
depositor *n* a person who deposits money in a bank, etc.
depository *n* (*pl* **depositories**) a place where anything is deposited; a depositary.
depot *n* a warehouse, storehouse; a place for storing military supplies; a military training centre; a bus or railway station.
deprave *vt* to pervert; to corrupt morally.—**depravation** *n*.—**depraver** *n*.
depraved *adj* morally debased; corrupt; made bad or worse.—**depravedly** *adv*.
depravity *n* (*pl* **depravities**) moral corruption; extreme wickedness.
deprecate *vt* to criticize, esp mildly or politely; to belittle.—**deprecation** *n*.—**deprecative** *adj*.—**deprecator** *n*.
deprecative *adj* deprecatory.
deprecatory *adj* apologetic; disapproving, belittling.
depreciate *vti* to make or become lower in value.—**depreciator** *n*.—**depreciatory, depreciative** *adj*.
depreciation *n* a fall in value, esp of an asset through wear and tear; an allowance for this deducted from gross profit; disparagement.
depredate *vt* to pillage; to rob; to lay waste; to prey upon.—**depredator** *n*.
depredation *n* plundering; pillage.
depress *vt* to push down; to sadden, dispirit; to lessen the activity of.—**depressing** *adj*.—**depressingly** *adv*.
depressant *adj* causing depression. * *n* a substance that reduces the activity of the nervous system; a drug that acts as a depressant.
depressed *adj* cast down in spirits; lowered in position; flattened from above, or vertically.
depression *n* excessive gloom and despondency; an abnormal state of physiological inactivity; a phase of the business cycle characterized by stagnation, widespread unemployment, etc; a falling in or sinking; a lowering of atmospheric pressure, often signalling rain.
depressive *adj* depressing; tending to suffer from mental depression.—**depressively** *adv*.
depressor *n* one who or that which depresses; a muscle that draws down an organ or part.
deprive *vt* to take a thing away from; to prevent from using or enjoying.—**deprivation** *n*.
deprived *adj* lacking the essentials of life, such as adequate food, shelter, education, etc.
dept. *abbr* = department.
depth *n* deepness; the distance downwards or inwards; the intensity of emotion or feeling; the profundity of thought; intensity of colour; the mid point of the night or winter; the lowness of sound or pitch; the quality of being deep.
depth charge *n* a bomb designed to explode under water, used against submarines.
depurate *vti* to free or become free from impurities.—**depuration** *n*.—**depurative** *adj*.—**depurator** *n*.
deputation *n* a person or group appointed to represent others.
depute *vt* to appoint as one's representative; to delegate.
deputize *vi* to act as deputy.—**deputization** *n*.
deputy *n* (*pl* **deputies**) a delegate, representative, or substitute.
deracinate *vt* to tear up by the roots.—**deracination** *n*.
derail *vti* (*train*) to cause to leave the rails.—**derailment** *n*.
derailleur *n* a system of gearing on a bicycle.
derange *vt* to throw into confusion; to disturb; to make insane.—**deranged** *adj*.—**derangement** *n*.
derby *n* (*pl* **derbies**) a bowler hat.
deregulate *vt* to remove (eg government) regulations or controls from (an industry, etc).—**deregulation** *n*.
derelict *adj* abandoned, deserted and left to decay; negligent. * *n* a person abandoned by society; a wrecked ship or vehicle.

dereliction *n* neglect (of duty); abandonment.
deride *vt* to scorn, mock.
de rigueur *adj* required by fashion or etiquette.
derisible *adj* open to derision.
derision *n* ridicule.
derisive *adj* full of derision; mocking, scornful.—**derisively** *adv*.—**derisiveness** *n*.
derisory *adj* showing or deserving of derision.
derivation *n* the tracing of a word to its root; origin; descent.—**derivational** *adj*.
derivative *adj* derived from something else; not original. * *n* something that is derived; a word formed by derivation; (*math*) the rate of change of one quantity with respect to another.—**derivatively** *adv*.
derive *vt* to take or receive from a source; to infer, deduce (from). * *vi* to issue as a derivative (from).—**derivable** *adj*.—**deriver** *n*.
dermal *adj* of the skin; consisting of skin.
dermatitis *n* inflammation of the skin.
dermatology *n* the science of the skin and its diseases.—**dermatologic, dermatological** *adj*.—**dermatologist** *n*.
dermic *adj* dermal.
dermis *n* the fine skin below the epidermis containing blood vessels.
derogate *vti* to detract (from); to lose face; to degenerate; to take a part (from).—**derogation** *n*.
derogatory *adj* disparaging; deliberately offensive.—**derogatorily** *adv*.
derrick *n* any crane-like apparatus; a tower over an oil well, etc, holding the drilling machinery.
derring-do *n* bravery, reckless valour.
derringer *n* a pocket pistol with a short barrel of very large calibre.
dervish *n* a member of a Muslim religious order vowing chastity and poverty, noted for frenzied, whirling dancing.
desalinate *vt* to remove the salt from (seawater, etc).—**desalination** *n*.—**desalinator** *n*.
descant *n* a musical accompaniment sung or played in counterpoint to the main melody.—*also vi*.
descend *vi* to come or climb down; to pass from a higher to a lower place or condition; (*with* **on, upon**) to make a sudden attack upon, or visit unexpectedly; to sink in morals or dignity; to be derived. * *vt* to go, pass, or extend down.
descendant *n* a person who is descended from an ancestor; something derived from an earlier form.
descendent *adj* descending; sinking.
descendible *adj* (*law*) that may be inherited; transmissible.
descent *n* a descending; a downward motion or step; a way down; a slope; a raid or invasion; lineage, ancestry.
describe *vt* to give a verbal account of; to trace out.—**describable** *adj*.—**describer** *n*.
description *n* a verbal or pictorial account; a sort, a kind.
descriptive *adj* tending to or serving to describe.—**descriptively** *adv*.—**descriptiveness** *n*.
descry *vt* (**descrying, descried**) to catch sight of.
desecrate *vt* to violate a sacred place by destructive or blasphemous behaviour.—**desecration** *n*.—**desecrator, desecrater** *n*.
desegregate *vt* to abolish (racial or sexual) segregation in.—**desegregation** *n*.
desert[1] *n* (*often pl*) a deserved reward or punishment.
desert[2] *vt* to leave, abandon, with no intention of returning; to abscond from the armed forces without permission.—**deserter** *n*.—**desertion** *n*.
desert[3] *n* a dry, barren region, able to support little or no life; a place lacking in some essential quality.
desertification *n* the transformation of fertile land into arid waste or desert through soil erosion, overcultivation, etc.
desertion *n* deserting; being forsaken.
deserve *vt* to merit or be suitable for (some reward, punishment, etc).
deserved *adj* justly earned, merited.—**deservedly** *adv*.—**deservedness** *n*.
deserving *adj* worthy of support, esp financially.
deshabille *see* **dishabille**.
desiccate *vti* to dry or become dried up; to preserve (food) by drying.—**desiccation** *n*.—**desiccative** *adj*.
desiccator *n* an apparatus for drying foods and other substances.
desiderate *vt* to feel the lack of, to desire earnestly.—**desideration** *n*.—**desiderative** *adj*.
desideratum *n* (*pl* **desiderata**) anything desired; a want or desire generally felt and recognized.
design *vt* to plan; to create; to devise; to make working drawings for; to intend. * *n* a working drawing; a mental plan or scheme; the particular form or disposition of something; a decorative pattern; purpose; (*pl*) dishonest intent.
designate *vt* to indicate, specify; to name; to appoint to or nominate for a position, office. * *adj* (*after noun*) appointed to office but not yet installed.—**designator** *n*.
designation *n* the act of designating; nomination; a distinguishing name or title.
designedly *adv* intentionally.
designer *n* a person who designs things; a person who is renowned for creating high-class fashion clothes. * *adj* (*inf*) trendy, of the latest, esp expensive, fashion.
designer drug *n* a synthetic narcotic or hallucinogenic substance which mimics the chemical structure and effects of banned drugs but is not yet covered by anti-drug laws.
designing *adj* crafty, scheming. * *n* the art or practice of making designs.
desirable *adj* arousing (sexual) desire; advisable or beneficial; worth doing.—**desirability** *n*.—**desirably** *adv*.
desire *vt* to long or wish for; to request, ask for. * *n* a longing for something regarded as pleasurable or satisfying; a request; something desired; sexual craving.
desirous *adj* desiring; craving.
desist *vi* to stop (doing something).—**desistance** *n*.
desk *n* a piece of furniture with a writing surface and usu drawers; a counter behind which a cashier, etc sits; the section of a newspaper responsible for a particular topic.
desktop publishing *n* the use of a microcomputer with sophisticated page-layout programs and a laser printer to produce professional-looking printed matter.
desman *n* (*pl* **desmans**) a small amphibious animal similar to a mole.
desmoid *adj* having the characteristics of, or resembling, a ligament; (*tumour*) fibrous.
desolate *adj* solitary, lonely; devoid of inhabitants; laid waste; forlorn, disconsolate; overwhelmed with grief. * *vt* to depopulate; to devastate, lay waste; to make barren or unfit for habitation; to leave alone, forsake, abandon; to overwhelm with grief.—**desolately** *adv*.—**desolateness** *n*.—**desolator, desolater** *n*.
desolated *adj* wretched, lonely, miserable.
desolation *n* destruction, ruin; a barren state; loneliness; wretchedness.
despair *vi* to have no hope. * *n* utter loss of hope; something that causes despair.
despatch *see* **dispatch**.
desperado *n* (*pl* **desperadoes, desperados**) a violent criminal.
desperate *adj* (almost) hopeless; reckless through lack of hope; urgently requiring (money, etc); (*remedy*) extreme, dangerous.—**desperately** *adv*.—**desperateness** *n*.
desperation *n* loss of hope; recklessness from despair.
despicable *adj* contemptible, worthless.—**despicableness** *n*.—**despicably** *adv*.
despise *vt* to regard with contempt or scorn; to consider as worthless, inferior.
despite *prep* in spite of.
despoil *vt* to plunder, rob.—**despoiler** *n*.—**despoilment** *n*.
despoliation *n* despoilment; pillage.
despond *vi* to lose hope, to be dejected. * *n* despondency.
despondency, despondence *n* a being despondent; depression or dejection of spirits through loss of resolution or hope.
despondent *adj* dejected, depressed.—**despondently** *adv*.

despot *n* a ruler possessing absolute power; a tyrant.

despotic, despotical *adj* of, pertaining to, or of the nature of a despot or of despotism; arbitrary, tyrannical.—**despotically** *adv*.

despotism *n* absolute power, tyranny; a state governed by a despot.

desquamate *vti* to peel or scale off.—**desquamation** *n*.

dessert *n* the sweet course at the end of a meal.

dessertspoon *n* a spoon in between a teaspoon and a tablespoon in size, used for eating desserts.

destination *n* the place to which a person or thing is going.

destine *vt* to set aside for some specific purpose; to predetermine; intend.

destiny *n* (*pl* **destinies**) the power supposedly determining the course of events; the future to which any person or thing is destined; a predetermined course of events.

destitute *adj* (*with* **of**) lacking some quality; lacking the basic necessities of life, very poor.

destitution *n* extreme poverty.

destroy *vt* to demolish, ruin, to put an end to; to kill.

destroyer *n* one who or that which destroys; a fast small warship.

destruct *vt* to destroy deliberately (a missile, etc). * *n* the act of destructing (a missile, etc).

destructible *adj* subject to destruction; able to be destroyed.—**destructibility** *n*.

destruction *n* the act or process of destroying or being destroyed; ruin.

destructionist *n* an anarchist.

destructive *adj* causing destruction; (*with* **of** *or* **to**) ruinous; (*criticism*) intended to discredit, negative.—**destructively** *adv*.—**destructivity** *n*.

destructor *n* a furnace for burning up rubbish, etc; an explosive device for blowing up a malfunctioning rocket, etc.

desuetude *n* disuse, discontinuance.

desultory *adj* going aimlessly from one activity or subject to another, not methodical.—**desultorily** *adv*.—**desultoriness** *n*.

detach *vt* to release; to separate from a larger group; (*mil*) to send off on special assignment.

detachable *adj* able to be detached.—**detachability** *n*.—**detachably** *adv*.

detached *adj* separate; free from bias or emotion; (*house*) not joined to another; aloof.

detachment *n* indifference; freedom from emotional involvement or bias; the act of detaching; a thing detached; a body of troops detached from the main body and sent on special service.

detail *vt* to describe fully; (*mil*) to set apart for a particular duty. * *n* an item; a particular or minute account; (*art*) treatment of smaller parts; a reproduction of a smaller part of a picture, statue, etc; a small detachment for special service.

detailed *adj* giving full details; thorough.

detain *vt* to place in custody or confinement; to delay.—**detainment** *n*.

detainee *n* a person who is held in custody.

detainer *n* the (wrongful) detaining of person or goods; a writ for holding on another charge a person already arrested.

detect *vt* to discover the existence or presence of; to notice.

detectable *adj* able to be detected.—**detectability** *n*.

detection *n* a discovery or a being discovered; the job or process of detecting.

detective *n* a person or a police officer employed to find evidence of crimes.

detector *n* a device for detecting the presence of something.

detent *n* a catch for locking machinery or regulating the striking of a clock.

détente, detente *n* relaxation of tension between countries.

detention *n* the act of detaining or withholding; a being detained; confinement; the act of being kept in (school after hours) as a punishment.

deter *vt* (**deterring, deterred**) to discourage or prevent (from acting).—**determent** *n*.

deterge *vt* to cleanse, as a wound.

detergent *n* a cleaning agent, esp one made from a chemical compound rather than fats, as soap. * *adj* having cleaning power.

deteriorate *vt* to make or become worse.—**deterioration** *n*.—**deteriorative** *adj*.

determinable *adj* capable of being definitely ascertained; defined with clearness; terminable.—**determinability** *n*.—**determinably** *adv*.

determinant *adj* determining. * *n* something that determines, a decisive factor; (*math*) an algebraic term expressing the sum of certain products arranged in a square or matrix.

determinate *adj* definitely bounded in time, space, position, etc; fixed; clearly defined; distinct; resolute, decisive; (*bot*) having the terminal flower bud opening first, followed by those on lateral branches.—**determinately** *adv*.—**determinateness** *n*.

determination *n* the act or process of making a decision; a decision resolving a dispute; firm intention; resoluteness.

determinative *adj* determining, limiting, or defining; tending to define the genus or species * *n* that which serves to determine the quality or character of something else; a demonstrative pronoun; an ideograph.—**determinatively** *adv*.

determine *vt* to fix or settle officially; to find out; to regulate; to impel. * *vi* to come to a decision.

determined *adj* full of determination, resolute.—**determinedly** *adv*.—**determinedness** *n*.

determiner *n* one who or that which determines; (*gram*) a word that limits the meaning of a noun, esp an article or possessive pronoun.

determinism *n* the theory that all events, including human actions, are determined by preceding causes, thereby precluding free will.—**determinist** *n*.—**deterministic** *adj*.—**deterministically** *adv*.

deterrent *n* something that deters; a nuclear weapon that deters attack through fear of retaliation. * *adj* deterring.—**deterrence** *n*.

detest *vt* to dislike intensely.—**detester** *n*.

detestable *adj* intensely disliked, abhorrent.—**detestably** *adv*.

detestation *n* extreme dislike; a detestable person or thing.

dethrone *vt* to remove from a throne, to depose.—**dethronement** *n*.—**dethroner** *n*.

detinue *n* (*law*) a writ for recovery of property wrongfully detained.

detonate *vti* to explode or cause to explode rapidly and violently.

detonation *n* a sudden explosion with a loud report.

detonator *n* a device that sets off an explosion.

detour *n* a deviation from an intended course, esp one serving as an alternative to a more direct route. * *vti* to make or send by a detour.

detoxification centre *n* an institution that treats alcoholism or drug addiction.

detoxify *vt* (**detoxifying, detoxified**) to extract poison or toxins from.—**detoxification** *n*.

detract *vt* to take away. * *vi* to take away (from).—**detractor** *n*.

detraction *n* defamation; slander; depreciation.—**detractive** *adj*.—**detractively** *adv*.

detrain *vt, vi* to set down or alight from a train.—**detrainment** *n*.

detriment *n* (a cause of) damage or injury.

detrimental *adj* harmful.—**detrimentally** *adv*.

detrition *n* a wearing down by rubbing or friction.

detritus *n* debris; loose matter, esp formed by rubbing away or erosion of a larger mass (eg a rock).—**detrital** *adj*.

de trop *adj* too much; out of place; (*person*) not wanted.

detumescence *n* the diminution of a swelling, esp of an erect penis.—**detumescent** *adj*.

deuce[1] *n* a playing card or dice with two spots; (*tennis*) the score of forty-all.

deuce[2] *interj* (*inf*) the devil!—an exclamation of surprise or annoyance.

deuced *adj* (*inf*) confounded.

deus ex machina *n* divine intervention; an artificial solution of difficulties, esp in a play.

deuter(o)- *prefix* second.

deuteragonist *n* (*Greek drama*) the second principal actor.

deuterium *n* heavy hydrogen, used as a moderator in nuclear reactors to slow the rate of fission.

deuterocanonical *adj* of or belonging to a second canon or to the Apocrypha.

deuterogamy *n* a second marriage.
deuteron *n* the nucleus of a heavy hydrogen atom.
deutoplasm *n* the albuminous part of the yolk that provides food for the embryo in an egg.—**deutoplasmic** *adj*.
Deutschmark, Deutsche Mark *n* the monetary unit of Germany.
deutzia *n* a small shrub of the saxifrage family with clusters of white flowers.
deva *n* (*Hinduism*) a god.
devaluate *vt* to devalue.
devalue *vt* (**devaluing, devalued**) to reduce the exchange value of (a currency).—**devaluation** *n*.
devastate *vt* to lay waste; to destroy; to overwhelm.—**devastatingly** *adv*.—**devastation** *n*.—**devastator** *n*.
develop *vt* to evolve; to bring to maturity; to show the symptoms of (eg a habit, a disease); to treat a photographic film or plate to reveal an image; to improve the value of. * *vi* to grow (into); to become apparent.
developer *n* a person who develops; a person or organization that develops property; a reagent for developing photographs.
developing country *n* a poor country that is attempting to improve its social conditions and encourage industrial growth.
development *n* the process of growing or developing; a new situation that emerges; a piece of land or property that has been developed.—**developmental** *adj*.
deviant *adj* that which deviates from an accepted norm. * *n* a person whose behaviour deviates from the accepted standards of society.—**deviance, deviancy** *n*.
deviate *vi* to diverge from a course, topic, principle, etc.—**deviator** *n*.
deviation *n* a deviating from normal behaviour, official ideology, etc; deflection of a compass needle by magnetic disturbance; (*statistics*) difference from a mean.
device *n* a machine, implement, etc for a particular purpose; an invention; a scheme, a plot.
devil *n* (*with cap*) in Christian and Jewish theology, the supreme spirit of evil, Satan; any evil spirit; an extremely wicked person; (*inf*) a reckless, high-spirited person; (*inf*) someone or something difficult to deal with; (*inf*) a person. * *vb* (**devilling, devilled** *or* **deviling, deviled**) *vt* to cook food with a hot seasoning. * *vi* to act as a drudge to someone; to do research for an author or barrister.
devilfish *n* (**devilfish, devilfishes**) the manta, a very large ray; a large species of octopus.
devilish *adj* fiendish; mischievous. * *adv* (*inf*) very.—**devilishly** *adv*.—**devilishness** *n*.
devil-may-care *adj* audacious, contemptuous of authority.
devilment *n* mischievous behaviour.
devilry *n* (*pl* **devilries**) wickedness; malicious mischief.
devil's advocate *n* a person who advocates an opposing cause, esp for the sake of argument.
devious *adj* indirect; not straightforward; underhand, deceitful.—**deviously** *adv*.—**deviousness** *n*.
devisable *adj* capable of being imagined; (*law*) (*real estate*) capable of being bequeathed.—**devisability** *n*.
devise *vt* to invent, contrive; to plan; (*law*) to leave (real estate) by will. * *n* (*law*) a bequest (of real estate); property so bequeathed.—**deviser** *n*.
devisee *n* (*law*) a person to whom (real estate) has been bequeathed.
devisor *n* (*law*) a person who bequeathes, esp real estate.
devitalize *vt* to deprive of vitality or vigour.—**devitalization** *n*.
devitrify *vt* (**devitrifying, devitrified**) to deprive of glassy quality, to make opaque.—**devitrification** *n*.
devoid *adj* (*with* **of**) lacking; free from.
devoirs *npl* civilities; one's best.
devolution *n* a transfer of authority, esp from a central government to regional governments; a passing on from one person to another.
devolve *vti* to hand on or be handed on to a successor or deputy.—**devolvement** *n*.
devote *vt* to give or use for a particular activity or purpose.
devoted *adj* zealous; loyal; loving.—**devotedly** *adv*.—**devotedness** *n*.
devotee *n* (*with* **of** *or* **to**) a person who is enthusiastically or fanatically devoted to something; a religious zealot.
devotion *n* given to religious worship; piety; strong affection or attachment (to); ardour; (*pl*) prayers.
devotional *adj* of devotions; devout. * *n* a brief religious service.
devour *vt* to eat up greedily; to consume; to absorb eagerly by the senses or mind.
devout *adj* very religious, pious; sincere, dedicated.—**devoutly** *adv*.—**devoutness** *n*.
dew *n* air moisture, deposited on a cool surface, esp at night.
dew point *n* the air temperature at which dew forms.
dewberry *n* (*pl* **dewberries**) a kind of trailing blackberry plant; its dark blue fruit.
dewclaw *n* a rudimentary toe above a dog's paw or above the hoof of a deer, etc.
Dewey Decimal System *n* a method of classifying library books into ten main subject areas.—*also* **decimal classification**.
dewlap *n* a flap of skin hanging under the throat of some animals, eg cows; loose skin on the throat of an elderly person.
dewy *adj* (**dewier, dewiest**) wet with dew.—**dewily** *adv*.—**dewiness** *n*.
dewy-eyed *adj* sentimental, naive.
dexter *adj* right; (*her*) to the viewer's left and the wearer's right.
dexterity *n* manual skill, adroitness.
dexterous *adj* possessing manual skill; quick, mentally or physically; adroit; clever.—**dexterously** *adv*.—**dexterousness** *n*.
dextral *adj* on the right-hand side; right-handed; (*shell*) with whorls going to the right.—**dextrality** *n*.—**dextrally** *adv*.
dextrin, dextrine *n* a white gummy substance found in plant sap, etc, and used as gum and a thickening agent.
dextrorotation *n* right-handed or clockwise rotation.—**dextrorotary, dextrorotatory** *adj*.
dextrorse *adj* (*bot*) twining spirally from left to right.—**dextrorsely** *adv*.
dextrose *n* a form of glucose found in fruit, honey and animal tissues.
dextrous *adj* dexterous.
DFC *abbr* = Distinguished Flying Cross.
dhak *n* an Indian tree with brilliant red flowers.
dhal *see* **dal**.
dharma *n* (*Hinduism, Buddhism*) the law requiring virtue and righteousness; its practice in daily life.
dhobi *n* (*pl* **dhobis**) in India, a laundryman.
dhole *n* (*pl* **dholes, dhole**) an Asian wild dog that hunts in packs.
dhoti *n* (*pl* **dhotis**) a loincloth worn by men in India.
dhow *n* an Arab coastal vessel with a triangular sail.
di- *prefix* two; twice; double.
diabase *n* dolerite, a dark coloured igneous rock.
diabetes *n* a medical disorder marked by the persistent and excessive discharge of urine.
diabetes mellitus *n* a breakdown in the body's ability to absorb carbohydrates caused by a deficiency of insulin, which results in abnormally high levels of sugar in the blood and urine.
diabetic *adj* of or suffering from diabetes. * *n* a person with diabetes.
diablerie *n* a devil's work, sorcery; devil-lore; mischief.
diabolic *adj* devilish; cruel, wicked.—**diabolically** *adv*.—**diabolicalness** *n*.
diabolical *adj* diabolic; (*inf*) extremely bad or annoying.
diabolism *n* devil worship; witchcraft.—**diabolist** *n*.
diabolize *vt* to make into or represent as a devil.
diaconal *adj* of or pertaining to a deacon.
diaconate *n* the office or dignity of a deacon; deacons collectively.
diacritic *adj* diacritical. * *n* a diacritical mark.
diacritical *adj* distinguishing, distinctive, esp of accents, etc attached to letters to indicate pronunciation.—**diacritically** *adv*.
diacritical mark *n* a mark, such as an accent, used above or below a letter to indicate differences in sound.
diactinic *adj* transparent to actinic rays.—**diactinism** *n*.

diadelphous *adj* (*flowers*) with stamens in two bundles.
diadem *n* a crown or jewelled headband worn by royalty.
diaeresis *see* **dieresis.**
diagnose *vt* to ascertain by diagnosis.—**diagnosable, diagnoseable** *adj.*
diagnosis *n* (*pl* **diagnoses**) the identification of a disease from its symptoms; the analysis of the nature or cause of a problem.—**diagnostician** *n.*
diagnostic *adj* of or aiding diagnosis; characteristic. * *n* a symptom distinguishing a disease; a characteristic; (*pl*: *used as sing*) the art of diagnosing.—**diagnostically** *adv.*
diagonal *adj* slanting from one corner to an opposite corner of a polygon. * *n* a straight line connecting opposite corners.—**diagonally** *adv.*
diagram *n* a figure or plan drawn in outline to illustrate the form or workings of something. * *vt* (**diagramming, diagrammed** *or* **diagraming, diagramed**) to demonstrate in diagram form.
diagrammatic, diagrammatical *adj* having the form or nature of a diagram; of or pertaining to diagrams.—**diagrammatically** *adv.*
diagraph *n* an instrument for enlarging maps, etc mechanically.
dial *n* the face of a watch or clock; a graduated disk with a pointer used in various instruments; the control on a radio or television set indicating wavelength or station; the numbered disk on a telephone used to enter digits to connect calls; an instrument for telling the time by the sun's shadow. * *vt* (**dialling, dialled** *or* **dialing, dialed**) to measure or indicate by a dial; to make a telephone connection by using a dial or numbered keypad.
dialect *n* the form of language spoken in a particular region or social class.—**dialectal** *adj.*—**dialectally** *adv.*
dialectic *n* the pursuit of truths in philosophy through logical debate.—**dialectical** *adj.*—**dialectically** *adv.*
dialectology *n* the study of dialects.—**dialectological** *adj.*—**dialectologist** *n.*
dialogue, dialog *n* a conversation, esp in a play or novel; an exchange of opinions, negotiation.
dial tone *n* a sound heard over the telephone indicating that the line is clear.
dialyse, dialyze *vt* to separate crystalline from colloid parts of a mixture by filtration.—**dialysation, dialyzation** *n.*
dialyser, dialyzer *n* a machine for dialysing, esp one that act as a kidney.
dialysis *n* (*pl* **dialyses**) the removal of impurities from the blood by filtering it through a membrane.—**dialytic** *adj.*—**dialytically** *adv.*
diamagnetic *adj* cross-magnetic, tending to point east and west.—**diamagnetically** *adv.*
diamagnetism *n* the property of certain bodies when under the influence of magnetism and freely suspended of taking a position at right angles to the magnetic meridian.
diamanté *adj* glittering with rhinestones, sequins or imitation jewels. * *n* a material ornamented in this way.
diameter *n* a straight line bisecting a circle; the length of this line.
diametric, diametrical *adj* of or along a diameter; completely opposed.—**diametrically** *adv.*
diamond *n* a valuable gem, a crystallized form of pure carbon; (*baseball*) the playing field, esp the infield; a suit of playing cards denoted by a red lozenge. * *adj* composed of, or set with diamonds; shaped like a diamond; denoting the 60th (or 75th) anniversary of an event.
diamondback *n* a large rattlesnack with diamond-shaped markings.
dianthus *n* (*pl* **dianthuses**) any of a large genus of ornamental plants, including carnations and pinks.
diapason *n* the entire compass of a voice or instrument; a recognized musical standard of pitch; the foundation stops of an organ.
diaper *n* a nappy.
diaphanous *adj* (*fabrics*) delicate, transparent.—**diaphanously** *adv.*—**diaphanousness** *n.*
diaphoretic *adj* causing profuse perspiration. * *n* a diaphoretic drug.
diaphragm *n* the midriff, a muscular structure separating the chest from the abdomen; any thin dividing membrane; a device for regulating the aperture of a camera lens; a contraceptive cap covering the cervix; a thin vibrating disk used in a telephone receiver, microphone, etc.—**diaphragmatic** *adj.*—**diaphragmatically** *adv.*
diarchy *n* (*pl* **diarchies**) government by two independent authorities.—*also* **dyarchy**.
diarist *n* one who keeps a diary; the author of a diary.
diarrhoea, diarrhea *n* excessive looseness of the bowels.—**diarrhoeal, diarrheal, diarrhoeic, diarrheic** *adj.*
diary *n* (*pl* **diaries**) a daily record of personal thoughts, events, or business appointments; a book for keeping a daily record.
Diaspora *n* the dispersion of the Jews after the Babylonian captivity; the Jewish communities outside Israel; (*without cap*) the dispersion of any peoples outside their native area.
diastase *n* any enzyme that converts starch into sugar.—**diastatic, diastasic** *adj.*
diastole *n* the dilation of the chambers of the heart during which they fill with blood.—**diastolic** *adj.*
diatessaron *n* the combination of the four Gospels into a single narrative.
diathermancy *n* the property of transmitting radiant heat.—**diathermanous** *adj.*
diathermic *adj* having diathermancy; allowing heat rays to pass freely.
diathermy *n* the use of electric current to warm or destroy body tissues as part of medical treatment.
diathesis *n* (*pl* **diatheses**) a constitutional tendency, esp to disease; a predisposing factor.
diatom *n* a microscopic alga found in fresh and seawater and in soil.—**diatomaceous** *adj.*
diatomite *n* soft earth formed from the shells of diatoms and used as a filter, etc.
diatonic *adj* (*mus*) using only the major and minor scales, as opposed to the chromatic scale.—**diatonically** *adv.*—**diatonicism** *n.*
diatribe *n* a lengthy and abusive verbal attack.
dib *vti* (**dibbing, dibbed**) to dibble; (*fishing*) to drop bait gently into water; to dip lightly.
dibasic *adj* containing two atoms of hydrogen replaceable by a basic radical.—**dibasicity** *n.*
dibber *n* a dibble.
dibble *n* a pointed tool used to make holes in the ground for seedlings. * *vt* to make a hole in the ground with a dibber.
dicast *n* in ancient Athens, a juryman.
dice *n* (*the pl of* **die**[2] *but used as sing*) a small cube with numbered sides used in games of chance. * *vt* to gamble using dice; to cut (food) into small cubes.
dicentra *n* a member of a genus of perennial plants with heart-shaped flowers.
dicephalous *adj* two-headed.
dicey *adj* (**dicier, diciest**) (*inf*) risky.
dichloride *see* **bichloride.**
dichogamous, dichogamic *adj* (*bot*) with stamens and pistils maturing at different times, preventing self-fertilization.—**dichogamy** *n.*
dichotomy *n* (*pl* **dichotomies**) a division into two parts.—**dichotomous, dichotomic** *adj.*
dichroic, dichroitic *adj* (*crystal*) showing two colours; dichromatic.
dichroism *n* the property by which a crystallized body exhibits different colours according to the direction of light transmitted through it.
dichromatic *adj* two-coloured (—*also* **dichroic**); being able to see only two of the three primary colours, colour-blind; (*biol*) having one of two varieties of seasonal coloration.—**dichromatism** *n.*
dichromic *adj* seeing only two of the three primary colours, dichromatic.
dick *n* (*sl*) a detective; (*sl*) a person; (*vulg*) a penis.
dickens *interj* (*inf*) the devil.
dicker *vi* to barter or trade on a small scale; to haggle.* *n* a barter; a deal; haggling.
dicky, dickey[1] *n* (*pl* **dickies, dickeys**) a false shirt-front; a seat at the back of a sports car.
dicky, dickey[2] *adj* (**dickier, dickiest**) (*sl*) shaky, unsound.

dicrotic *adj* having a double or secondary pulse beat.—**dicrotism** *n*.
dicta *see* **dictum.**
Dictaphone *n* (*trademark*) a machine that records dictation and later reproduces it for typing.
dictate *vt* to say or read for another person to write or for a machine to record; to pronounce, order with authority. * *vi* to give dictation; to give orders (to). * *n* an order, rule, or command; (*usu pl*) an impulse, ruling principle.
dictation *n* the act of dictating words to be written down by another; the thing dictated; an authoritative utterance.
dictator *n* a ruler with absolute authority, usu acquired by force.
dictatorial *adj* like a dictator; tyrannical; domineering.—**dictatorially** *adv*.
dictatorship *n* the office or government of a dictator; a country governed by a dictator; absolute power.
diction *n* a way of speaking, enunciation; a person's choice of words.
dictionary *n* (*pl* **dictionaries**) a reference book containing the words of a language or branch of knowledge alphabetically arranged, with their meanings, pronunciation, origin, etc.
Dictograph *n* (*trademark*) a sound recording instrument used for recording or monitoring telephone conversations.
dictum *n* (*pl* **dictums, dicta**) an authoritative pronouncement.
did *see* **do.**
Didache *n* the title of a 2nd-century ad treatise on Christian doctrine and order, discovered 1883.
didactic *adj* intended to teach; instructive; in a lecturing manner.—**didactically** *adv*.—**didacticism** *n*.
didactics *n* (*used as sing*) the art of teaching.
diddle *vi* (*sl*) to cheat.—**diddler** *n*.
didn't = did not.
didymium *n* a mixture of rare earths, formerly thought to be an element, used for colouring glass.
didymous *adj* (*biol*) growing in pairs; paired or double.
die[1] *vb* (**dying, died**) *vi* to cease existence; to become dead; to stop functioning; to feel a deep longing; (*with* **out**) to become extinct. * *vi* to experience a particular form of death.
die[2] *n* a dice.
die[3] *n* (*pl* **dies**) an engraved stamp for pressing coins; a casting mould; a tool used in cutting the threads of screws or bolts, etc.
diecious *see* **dioecious.**
diehard *n* a person who prolongs futile resistance, usu an extreme conservative.
dielectric *adj* nonconducting * *n* any medium, as glass, that transmits electric force by induction.
dieresis *n* (*pl* **diereses**) a sign (¨) placed over the second of two separate vowels to show that each has a separate sound in pronuniation, as *Zoë*; a division in a line of verse.—*also* **diaeresis.**—**dieretic, diaeretic** *adj*.
diesel *n* a vehicle driven by a diesel engine.
diesel engine *n* an internal combustion engine in which ignition is produced by the heat of highly compressed air alone.
diesel oil *n* a form of petroleum for diesel engines, ignited by the heat of compression.
diesis (*pl* **dieses**) *n* the double dagger used in printing (•); (*mus*) the difference between a greater and lesser semitone.
diet[1] *n* food selected to adjust weight, to control illness, etc; the food and drink usually consumed by a person or animal. * *vt* to put on a diet. * *vi* to eat according to a special diet.—**dieter** *n*.
diet[2] *n* a legislative assembly in some countries.
dietary *adj* pertaining to a diet.
dietetic, dietetical *adj* regulating food or diet.—**dietetically** *adv*.
dietetics *n* (*used as sing*) the science of diet.
dietetics *n* (*used as sing*) the scientific study of diet and nutrition.
differ *vi* to be unlike, distinct (from); to disagree.
difference *n* the act or state of being unlike; disparity; a distinguishing feature; the amount or manner of being different; the result of the subtraction of one quantity from another; a disagreement or argument.
different *adj* distinct, separate; unlike, not the same; unusual.—**differently** *adv*.
differentia *n* (*pl* **differentiae**) (*logic*) what distinguishes a thing from others, esp one subclass from another of the same class.
differential *adj* of or showing a difference; (*math*) relating to increments in given functions. * *n* something that marks the difference between comparable things; the difference in wage rates for different types of labour, esp within an industry.—**differentially** *adv*.
differential calculus *n* the branch of calculus dealing with the rate of change of given functions with respect to their variables.
differential gear *n* a type of gear that allows powered wheels in a motor vehicle to turn at different speeds (eg when cornering).
differentiate *vt* to make different; to become specialized; to note differences; (*math*) to calculate the derivative of.
differentiation *n* the act of differentiating; (*biol*) specialization; (*math*) the calculation of a differential.
difficult *adj* hard to understand; hard to make, do, or carry out; not easy to please.
difficulty *n* (*pl* **difficulties**) the state of being difficult; a problem, etc that is hard to deal with; an obstacle; a troublesome situation; a disagreement.
diffidence *n* lack of confidence in one's own ability; shyness, modesty.
diffident *adj* shy, lacking self-confidence, not assertive.—**diffidently** *adv*.
diffract *vti* to cause, or cause to undergo, diffraction.—**diffractive** *adj*.
diffraction *n* the breaking up of a ray of light into coloured bands of the spectrum, or into a series of light and dark bands.
diffuse *vt* to spread widely in all directions. * *vti* (*gases, fluids, small particles*) to intermingle. * *adj* spread widely, not concentrated; wordy, not concise.—**diffusely** *adv*.
diffusion *n* the act of diffusing; a spreading abroad; the passing by osmosis through animal membranes.
diffusive *adj* extending; spreading widely.—**diffusively** *adv*.—**diffusiveness** *n*.
dig *vt* (**digging, dug**) to use a tool or hands, claws, etc in making a hole in the ground; to unearth by digging; to excavate; to investigate; to thrust (into); to nudge; (*sl*) to understand, approve. * *n* (*sl*) a thrust; an archaeological excavation; a cutting remark.
digamist *n* one who marries for a second time.—**digamous** *adj*.—**digamy** *n*.
digamma *n* a letter of the ancient Greek alphabet, in sound approaching that of V or W.
digastric *adj* (*muscle*) with two swollen ends. * *n* a neck muscle that helps lower the jaw.
digenesis *n* (*biol*) an alternating process of reproduction, sexual in one generation, asexual in the following.—**digenetic** *adj*.
digest[1] *vt* to convert (food) into assimilable form; to reduce (facts, laws, etc) to convenient form by classifying or summarizing; to form a clear view of (a situation) by reflection. * *vi* to become digested.
digest[2] *n* an abridgment of any written matter; a periodical synopsis of published or broadcast material.
digester *n* one who makes a digest; a thing that digests; an apparatus for extracting the essence of a substance by heat.
digestible *adj* capable of being digested.—**digestibility, digestibly** *adv*.
digestion *n* the act or process of digesting.—**digestional** *adj*.
digestive *adj* pertaining to, performing, or aiding, digestion. * *n* a thing that aids digestion; a sweet wholemeal biscuit.
digger *n* an implement or machine for digging; (*inf*) an Australian or New Zealander (used as a form of address).
digit *n* any of the basic counting units of a number system, including zero; a human finger or toe.
digital *adj* of, having or using digits; using numbers rather than a dial to display measurements; of or pertaining to a digital computer or digital recording.—**digitally** *adv*.
digital audio tape *n* a magnetic tape capable of being used in digital recording, giving high-quality audio reproduction.
digital clock *n* a clock that displays the time in figures.

digital computer *n* a computer that processes information in the form of characters and digits in electronic binary code.
digitalin *n* a poison extracted from foxglove leaves.
digitalis *n* a drug derived from foxglove leaves, used as a heart stimulant.
digital recording *n* the conversion of sound into discrete electronic pulses (representing binary digits) for recording.
digital watch *n* a watch that displays the time in figures.
digitate, digitated *adj* having separate fingers or toes.—**digitation** *n*.
digitigrade *adj* (cats, dogs, etc) walking on the toes. * *n* an animal that walks in this way.
digitize *vt* (*data, images*) to translate into digital form for input into a computer.—**digitization** *n*.
diglot *adj* bilingual. * *n* a book with the text in two languages.
dignified *adj* possessing dignity; noble; serious.—**dignifiedly** *adv*.
dignify *vt* (**dignifying, dignified**) to confer dignity; to exalt; to add the appearance of distinction (to something).
dignitary *n* (*pl* **dignitaries**) a person in a high position or rank.
dignity *n* (*pl* **dignities**) noble, serious, formal in manner and appearance; sense of self-respect, worthiness; a high rank, eg in the government.
digraph *n* a combination of two sounds or characters to represent one simple sound, as *ph* in *phone*.—**digraphic** *adj*.—**digraphically** *adv*.
digress *vi* to stray from the main subject in speaking or writing.—**digression** *n*.
digressive *adj* tending to digress; deviating from the subject.—**digressively** *adv*.—**digressiveness** *n*.
dihedral *adj* (*angle*) having two intersecting plane faces or sides. * *n* a dihedral angle; the angle between aircraft wings for improving stability.
dik-dik *n* a small East African antelope.
dike *see* **dyke**[2].
dike[1] *n* an embankment to prevent flooding or form a barrier to the sea; a ditch; a causeway.—*also* **dyke.**
dilapidate *vt* to bring into partial ruin by neglect or misuse. * *vi* to become dilapidated.
dilapidated *adj* in a state of disrepair; shabby.
dilapidation *n* a state of damage or disrepair.
dilatation *n* a dilating, esp as part of a medical procedure; an abnormal enlargement of an organ, etc.—**dilatational** *adj*.
dilatation and curettage *n* a surgical procedure for opening the cervix and scraping the uterus.
dilate *vti* to make wider or larger; to increase the width of; to expand, amplify, enlarge; to extend in time, protract, prolong, lengthen. * *vi* to become wider or larger; to spread out, widen, enlarge, expand; to discourse or write at large; to enlarge.—**dilatable** *adj*.—**dilatabilty** *n*.
dilation *n* the action or process of dilating; something dilated.
dilator *n* that which dilates; a surgical instrument for opening or expanding an orifice; a muscle that dilates the parts on which it acts.
dilatory *adj* tardy; causing or meant to cause delay.—**dilatorily** *adv*.—**dilatoriness** *n*.
dildo *n* (*pl* **dildos**) an artificial penis used for sexual stimulation.
dilemma *n* a situation where each of two alternative courses is undesirable; any difficult problem or choice.—**dilemmatic** *adj*.
dilettante *n* (*pl* **dilettantes, dilettanti**) a person who dabbles in a subject for amusement only.
diligence[1] *n* careful attention; assiduity; industry.
diligence[2] *n* (*formerly*) a French stagecoach.
diligent *adj* industrious; done with proper care and effort.—**diligently** *adv*.
dill *n* a yellow-flowered herb whose leaves and seeds are used for flavouring and in medicines.
dillydally *vi* (**dillydallying, dillydallied**) (*inf*) to dawdle, loiter.
dilute *vt* to thin down, esp by mixing with water; to weaken the strength of. * *adj* diluted.—**diluter, dilutor** *n*.—**diluteness** *n*.
dilution *n* the act of diluting; a weak liquid.
diluvial, diluvian *adj* pertaining to, produced by, or resulting from, a deluge or flood, esp the Flood of the Bible.
diluvium (*pl* **diluviums, diluvia**) *n* (*formerly*) geological deposits caused by water action, drift.
dim *adj* (**dimmer, dimmest**) faintly lit; not seen, heard, understood, etc clearly; gloomy; unfavourable; (*inf*) stupid. * *vti* (**dimming, dimmed**) to make or cause to become dark.—**dimly** *adv*.—**dimness** *n*.
dime *n* a US or Canadian coin worth ten cents.
dimension *n* any linear measurement of width, length, or thickness; extent; size.
dimensional *adj* of or pertaining to dimension or magnitude; (*geom*) of or pertaining to (a specified number of) dimensions.—**dimensionality** *n*.—**dimensionally** *adv*.
dimerous *adj* (*flowers*) having two members in each whorl; (*insects*) having a foot composed of two parts.
dimeter *n* (a line of) verse of two measures, a measure being one or two feet, according to the metre.
diminish *vti* to make or become smaller in size, amount, or importance.—**diminishable** *adj*.—**diminishment** *n*.
diminuendo *see* **decrescendo.**
diminution *n* act or process of being made smaller.
diminutive *adj* very small. * *n* a word formed by a suffix to mean small (eg *duckling*) or to convey affection (eg *Freddie*).
dimity (*pl* **dimities**) *n* a light, strong striped or figured cotton cloth used for curtains, etc.
dimmer *n* a switch for reducing the brightness of an electric light.
dimorphism *n* the quality of assuming, crystallizing or existing in two forms.—**dimorphic, dimorphous** *adj*.
dimple *n* a small hollow, usu on the cheek or chin. * *vti* to make or become dimpled; to reveal dimples.—**dimply** *adj*.
dimwit *n* (*inf*) an idiotic person, a fool.—**dimwitted** *adj*.—**dimwittedly** *adv*.—**dimwittedness** *n*.
din *n* a loud persistent noise. * *vt* (**dinning, dinned**) to make a din; (*with* **into**) to instil by continual repetition.
dinar *n* the monetary unit of Yugoslavia and various North African countries.
dine *vi* to eat dinner. * *vt* to entertain to dinner.
diner *n* a person who dines; a dining car on a train; a small, cheap eating place.
dinette *n* a small area in a house for eating in.
ding *vi* to sound, as a bell, with a continuous monotonous tone. * *vt* to impress by noisy repetition. * *n* the ringing sound of a bell.
ding-dong *n* the sound of a metallic body produced by blows, as a bell; (*inf*) a violent argument. * *adj* characterized by a rapid succession of blows; (*insults, etc*) vigorously maintained. * *vi* to ring as or like a bell. * *vt* to assail with constant repetition; to repeat with mechanical regularity.
dinghy *n* (*pl* **dinghies**) a small open boat propelled by oars or sails; a small inflatable boat.
dingle *n* a small wooded hollow.
dingo *n* (*pl* **dingoes**) an Australian wild dog.
dingy *adj* (**dingier, dingiest**) dirty-looking, shabby.—**dingily** *adv*.—**dinginess** *n*.
dining car *n* a restaurant car on a train.
dining room *n* a room used for eating meals.
dinkum *adj* genuine, honest.
dinky *adj* (**dinkier, dinkiest**) (*inf*) small; of no consequence, unimportant; (*Scot*) neat and attractive, smart.
dinner *n* the principal meal of the day; a formal meal in honour of a person or occasion.
dinner jacket *n* a tuxedo.
dinosaur *n* any of an order of extinct reptiles, typically enormous in size; (*inf*) a person or thing regarded as outdated.
dinothere *n* a huge, extinct animal like an elephant.
dint *n* (*arch*) a mark left by a blow, a dent; **by dint of** by force of. * *vt* make a dint in.
diocesan *adj* of or pertaining to a diocese; the bishop of a diocese.
diocese *n* the district over which a bishop has authority.

diode *n* a semiconductor device for converting alternating to direct current; a basic thermionic valve with two electrodes.

dioecious *adj* (*bot, zool*) having male and female organs respectively in separate individuals.—*also* **diecious.**

dioptase *n* a vitreous emerald green ore of copper.

dioptre, diopter *n* a unit for measuring the refractive power of a lens.

dioptric, dioptrical *adj* assisting vision by means of the refraction of light in viewing distant objects.

dioptrics *n* (*used as sing*) the area of optics dealing with the refraction of light.

diorama *n* a miniature three-dimensional scene, esp in a museum; any small-scale model with figures; a device for producing changing effects using special lighting on a translucent picture.—**dioramic** *adj*.

diorite *n* a granite-like rock consisting of felspar and hornblende.

dioxide *n* an oxide with two molecules of oxygen to one molecule of the other constituents.

dip *vt* (**dipping, dipped**) to put (something) under the surface (as of a liquid) and lift quickly out again; to immerse (as a sheep in an antiseptic solution). * *vi* to go into water and come out quickly; to suddenly drop down or sink out of sight; to read superficially; to slope downwards. * *n* a dipping of any kind; a sudden drop; a mixture in which to dip something.

dip., Dip. *abbr* = diploma.

diphtheria *n* an acute infectious disease causing inflammation of the throat and breathing difficulties.—**diphtherial** *adj*.

diphtheritic, diphtheric *adj* of or like diphtheria; affected by diphtheria.

diphthong (*n* the union of two vowel sounds pronounced in one syllable; a ligature.—**diphthongal** *adj*.

diphyllous *adj* (*bot*) having two leaves.

diploblastic *adj* (*zool*) with two germ layers.

diplodocus *pl* **diplodocuses**) *n* an extinct reptile with a very long tail and neck and a small head.

diploe *n* the soft spongy tissue between the two layers of the skull.—**diploic** *adj*.

diploma *n* (*pl* **diplomas**) a certificate given by a college or university to its graduating students; the course of study leading to a diploma; (*pl often* **diplomata**) an official document, a charter.

diplomacy *n* (*pl* **diplomacies**) the management of relations between nations; skill in handling affairs without arousing hostility.

diplomat *n* a person employed or skilled in diplomacy.

diplomatic, diplomatical *adj* of diplomacy; employing tact and conciliation; tactful.—**diplomatically** *adv*.

diplomatic corps *n* all the ambassadors at a particular capital, the corps diplomatique.

diplomatic immunity *n* the exemption from local laws and taxes accorded to foreign diplomats in the country where they are stationed.

diplomatist *n* a diplomat.

dipole *n* two equal and opposite electric charges or magnetic poles a small distance apart; a molecule in which the centres of negative and positive charge do not coincide; a directional aerial consisting of two metal rods.—**dipolar** *adj*.

dipper *n* a ladle; any of various diving birds.

dippy *n* (**dippier, dippiest**) (*sl*) eccentric; crazy.

dipso *n* (*pl* **dipsos**) (*inf*) a dipsomaniac.

dipsomania *n* a compulsive craving for alcohol.

dipsomaniac *n* a person with an uncontrollable craving for alcohol. * *adj* of or having dipsomania.—**dipsomaniacal** *adj*.

dipstick *n* a rod with graduated markings to measure fluid level.

dipteral *adj* (*archit*) having a double row of columns, as a temple, etc.

dipteran *n* any of a large order of insects including flies, mosquitoes, midges, having one pair of true wings and piercing or sucking mouthparts.

dipterous *adj* (*insects*) two-winged; (*seeds*) with appendanges resembling wings.

diptych *n* a pair of paintings or carvings on two panels hinged together.

dire *adj* dreadful; ominous; desperately urgent.—**direly** *adv*.—**direness** *n*.

direct *adj* straight; in an unbroken line, with nothing in between; frank; truthful. * *vt* to manage, to control; to tell or show the way; to point to, to aim at; (*a letter or parcel*) to address; to carry out the organizing and supervision of; to train and lead performances; to command. * *vi* to determine a course; to act as a director.—**directness** *n*.

direct current *n* an electric current that flows in one direction only.

direction *n* management, control; order, command; a knowing or telling what to do, where to go, etc; any way in which one may face or point; (*pl*) instructions.

directional *adj* relating to direction in space; (*aerial*) transmitting in one direction only.—**directionality** *n*.—**directionally** *adv*.

direction finder *n* a device used to locate the direction of incoming radio signals, used in navigation.

directive *adj* directing; authoritatively guiding or ruling. * *n* an order, instruction.

directly *adv* in a direct manner; immediately; in a short while.

Directoire *adj* of or imitating the low-necked high-waisted dress or curving oriental furniture of the Directoire period in France (1795–99).

director *n* person who directs, esp the production of a show for stage or screen; one of the persons directing the affairs of a company or an institution.—**directorial** *adj*.—**directorship** *n*.

directorate *n* a board of directors; the position of a director (—*also* **directorship**).

directory *n* (*pl* **directories**) an alphabetical or classified list, as of telephone numbers, members of an organization, charities, etc.

direct tax *n* a tax paid by the actual person or organization on which it is levied.

direful *adj* dreadful, dire.—**direfully** *adv*.

dirge *n* a song or hymn played or sung at a funeral; a slow, mournful piece of music.

dirigible *adj* able to be steered. * *n* an airship.

dirk *n* a small dagger, esp as formerly worn by Scottish Highlanders.

dirndl *n* a woman's full skirt with a tight waistband.

dirt *n* filth; loose earth; obscenity; scandal. * *adj* made of dirt.

dirt-cheap *adj* (*inf*) very cheap.

dirty *adj* (**dirtier, dirtiest**) filthy; unclean; dishonest; mean; (*weather*) stormy; obscene. * *vti* (**dirtying, dirtied**) to make or become dirty.—**dirtily** *adv*.—**dirtiness** *n*.

dis- *prefix* not, the reverse of; away from, apart; deprive of.

disability *n* (*pl* **disabilities**) a lack of physical, mental or social fitness; something that disables, a handicap.

disable *vt* to make useless; to cripple; (*law*) to disqualify.—**disablement** *n*.

disabled *adj* having a physical handicap.

disabuse *vt* to free from a mistaken impression.

disaccord *vi* to disagree, to be at variance. * *n* disagreement, incongruity.

disadvantage *n* an unfavourable condition or situation; loss, damage. * *vt* to put at a disadvantage.

disadvantaged *adj* deprived or discriminated against in social and economic terms.

disadvantageous *adj* causing disadvantage; unfavourable.—**disadvantageously** *adv*.

disaffected *adj* discontented, no longer loyal.—**disaffectedly** *adv*.—**disaffection** *n*.

disaffirm *vt* (*law*) to set aside, to reverse.—**disaffirmation** *n*.

disafforest *vt* to change from the legal state of forest to that of ordinary land; to remove forest from.—**disafforestation** *n*.

disagree *vi* (**disagreeing, disagreed**) to differ in opinion; to quarrel; (*with* **with**) to have a bad effect on.—**disagreement** *n*.

disagreeable *adj* nasty, bad tempered.—**disagreeableness** *n*.—**disagreeably** *adv*.

disagreement *n* refusal to agree; a difference; a quarrel or dispute.

disallow *vt* to refuse to allow or to accept the truth or value of.—**disallowance** *n*.

disannul *vt* (**disannulling, disannulled**) to annul completely; to make void.

disappear *vi* to pass from sight completely; to fade into nothing.—**disappearance** *n*.

disappoint *vt* to fail to fulfil the hopes of (a person).—**disappointed** *adj*.—**disappointing** *adj*.—**disappointingly** *adv*.

disappointment *n* the frustration of one's hopes; annoyance due to failure; a person or thing that disappoints.

disapprobation *n* disapproval, condemnation.

disapproval *n* the action or fact of disapproving; condemnation of what is wrong.

disapprove *vti* to express or have an unfavourable opinion (of).—**disapprovingly** *adv*.

disarm *vt* to deprive of weapons or means of defence; to defuse (a bomb); to conciliate. * *vi* to abolish or reduce national armaments.

disarmament *n* the reduction or abolition of a country's armed forces and weaponry.

disarming *adj* allaying opposition, conciliating; ingratiating, endearing.—**disarmingly** *adv*.

disarrange *vt* to make untidy; to disorganize.—**disarrangement** *n*.

disarray *n* disorder, confusion; undress. * *vt* to put into disorder.

disarticulate *vt* to separate, to take to pieces.—**disarticulation** *n*.—**disarticulator** *n*.

disaster *n* a devastating and sudden misfortune; utter failure.—**disastrous** *adj*.—**disastrously** *adv*.

disavow *vt* to deny, disclaim; to repudiate.—**disavowal** *n*.—**disavower** *n*.

disband *vt* to disperse; to break up and separate.—**disbandment** *n*.

disbar *vt* (**disbarring, disbarred**) to deprive (a barrister) of the right to practice.—**disbarment** *n*.

disbelief *n* a disbelieving; mental rejection of a statement or assertion; positive unbelief.

disbelieve *vt* to believe to be a lie. *vi* to have no faith (in).—**disbeliever** *n*.

disburden *vt* to throw off a burden; to relieve of anything annoying or oppressive * *vi* to ease one's mind.—**disburdenment** *n*.

disburse *vt* to pay out.—**disburser** *n*.

disbursement *n* a paying out (of money); expenditure.

discalced *adj* (*friars, etc*) barefoot, wearing sandals.

discard *vti* to cast off, get rid of; (*cards*) to throw away a card from one's hand. * *n* something discarded; (*cards*) a discarded card.

disc brake, disk brake *n* a brake in which two flat discs press against a central plate on the wheel hub.

discern *vt* to perceive; to see clearly.—**discernible** *adj*.—**discernibly** *adv*.

discerning *adj* discriminating; perceptive.—**discerningly** *adv*.—**discernment** *n*.

discharge *vt* to unload; to send out, emit; to release, acquit; to dismiss from employment; to shoot a gun; to fulfil, as duties. * *vi* to unload; (*gun*) to be fired; (*fluid*) to pour out. * *n* the act or process of discharging; something that is discharged; an authorization for release, acquittal, dismissal, etc.

disciple *n* a person who believes in and helps to spread another's teachings, a follower; (*with cap*) one of the twelve apostles of Christ.—**discipleship** *n*.

disciplinarian *n* a person who insists on strict discipline.

disciplinary *adj* of or for discipline.

discipline *n* a field of learning; training and conditioning to produce obedience and self-control; punishment; the maintenance of order and obedience as a result of punishment; a system of rules of behaviour. * *vt* to punish to enforce discipline; to train by instruction; to bring under control.—**disciplinable** *adj*.—**disciplinal** *adj*.

disc jockey *n* (*inf*) a person who announces records on a programme of broadcast music, or in discotheques.

disclaim *vi* to deny connection with; to renounce all legal claim to.

disclaimer *n* a denial of legal responsibility; a written statement embodying this.

disclose *vt* to bring into the open, to reveal.—**disclosure** *n*.

disclosure *n* the act of revealing anything secret; discovery; an uncovering.

disco *n* (*pl* **discos**) (*inf*) a discotheque.

discography *n* (*pl* **discographies**) a classified list or survey of gramophone records or CDs.—**discographer** *n*.

discoid *adj* round and flat like a disc (—*also* **discoidal**). * *n* anything with the shape of a disc.

discolour, discolor *vti* to ruin the colour of; to fade, stain.—**discolouration** *n*.

discomfit *vt* to defeat; to rout; to frustrate; to thwart; to disconcert.

discomfiture *n* defeat; disappointment; confusion.

discomfort *n* uneasiness; something causing this. * *vt* to make uncomfortable; to make apprehensive or uneasy.

discommode *vt* to put to inconvenience.

discompose *vt* to disturb the calmness of; to ruffle.—**discomposure** *n*.

disconcert *vt* to confuse; to upset; to embarrass.—**disconcerting** *adj*.—**disconcertingly** *adv*.

disconnect *vt* to separate or break the connection of.—**disconnection** *n*.

disconnected *adj* not connected, detached; disjointed; incoherent.—**disconnectedly** *adv*.—**disconnectedness** *n*.

disconsolate *adj* miserable; dejected.—**disconsolately** *adv*.—**disconsolation** *n*.

discontent *n* lack of contentment, dissatisfaction (—*also* **discontentment**). * *adj* not content; dissatisfied; discontented. * *vt* to deprive of contentment; to dissatisfy.

discontented *adj* feeling discontent; unhappy, unsatisfied.—**discontentedly** *adv*.

discontinuance *n* a discontinuing or breaking off; interruption; (*law*) the termination of a suit by the plaintiff.

discontinuation *n* a discontinuing; discontinuance; a breach or interruption of continuity.

discontinue *vti* to stop or come to a stop; to give up, esp the production of something; (*law*) to terminate (a suit).

discontinuity *n* (*pl* **discontinuities**) a being discontinuous; lack or failure of continuity or sequence; a break or gap in a structure; (*geol*) a point at which the character of the earth alters abruptly; (*math*) a function that is discontinuous.

discontinuous *adj* not continuous, incoherent, intermittent; (*math*) of a function that varies discontinously and whose differential coefficient may therefore become infinite.—**discontinuously** *adv*.

discord *n* lack of agreement, strife; (*mus*) a lack of harmony; harsh clashing sounds.

discordant *adj* at variance; inharmonious; jarring; incongruous.—**discordance, discordancy** *n*.—**discordantly** *adv*.

discotheque, discothèque *n* an occasion when people gather to dance to recorded pop music; a club or party, etc where this takes place; equipment for playing such music.

discount *n* a reduction in the amount or cost; the percentage charged for doing this. * *vt* to deduct from the amount, cost; to allow for exaggeration; to disregard; to make less effective by anticipation. * *vi* to make and give discounts.—**discountable** *adj*.—**discounter** *n*.

discountenance *vt* to refuse moral support to; to discourage, frown upon.

discourage *vt* to deprive of the will or courage (to do something); to try to prevent; to hinder.—**discouragingly** *adv*.

discouragement *n* the action or fact of discouraging; the state or feeling of being discouraged; something that discourages; a disheartening or deterring influence.

discourse *n* a formal speech or writing; conversation. * *vi* to talk or write about.

discourteous *adj* lacking in courtesy, rude.—**discourteously** *adv*.—**discourteousness** *n*.

discourtesy *n* (*pl* **discourtesies**) lack of courtesy or consideration; rudeness; an inconsiderate or rude act.

discover *vt* to see, find or learn of for the first time.—**discoverable** *adj*.—**discoverer** *n*.

discovert *adj* (*law*) (*single woman, divorcée, widow*) without a husband.—**discoverture** *n*.

discovery *n* (*pl* **discoveries**) the act of discovering or state of being discovered; something discovered; (*law*) a process obliging on the parties to an action to disclose relevant facts or documents.

discredit *n* damage to a reputation; doubt; disgrace; lack of credibility. * *vt* to damage the reputation of; to cast doubt on the authority or credibility of.

discreditable *adj* bringing discredit or disgrace.—**discreditably** *adv*.
discreet *adj* wisely cautious, prudent; unobtrusive.—**discreetly** *adv*.—**discreetness** *n*.
discrepancy *n* (*pl* **discrepancies**) difference; a disagreement, as between figures in a total.
discrepant *adj* inconsistent; not tallying.—**discrepantly** *adv*.
discrete *adj* individually distinct; discontinuous.—**discretely** *adv*.—**discreteness** *n*.
discretion *n* the freedom to judge or to choose; prudence; wise judgment; skill.
discretionary *adj* left to or done at one's own discretion.
discriminate *vi* to be discerning in matters of taste or judgment; to make a distinction; to treat differently, esp unfavourably due to prejudice.
discriminating *adj* judicious; discerning; discriminatory.—**discriminatingly** *adv*.
discrimination *n* prejudicial treatment of a person, minority group, etc, based on sex, religion, race, etc; penetration, discernment.
discriminative *adj* serving to discriminate or distinguish; discerning; discriminatory.—**discriminatively** *adv*.
discriminator *n* one who or that which discriminates; (*electronics*) a circuit that converts a property of a signal into an amplitude variation.
discriminatory *adj* discriminating; showing prejudice or favouritism; biased.—**discriminatorily** *adv*.
discursive *adj* wandering from one subject to another; digressive.—**discursively** *adv*.—**discursiveness** *n*.
discus *n* (*pl* **discuses, disci**) a heavy disk with a thickened middle, thrown by athletes.
discuss *vt* to talk over; to investigate by reasoning or argument.—**discussible, discussable** *adj*.
discussion *n* an argument; a debate; the airing of a question.
disdain *vt* to scorn, treat with contempt. * *n* scorn; a feeling of contemptuous superiority.—**disdainful** *adj*.—**disdainfully** *adv*.
disdainful *adj* showing or feeling disdain; contemptuous; haughty.—**disdainfully** *adv*.—**disdainfulness** *n*.
disease *n* an unhealthy condition in an organism caused by infection, poisoning, etc; sickness; a harmful condition or situation.—**diseased** *adj*.
disembark *vti* to land from a ship, debark.—**disembarkation** *n*.
disembarrass *vt* to free from embarrassment; to relieve (of); to disentangle.—**disembarrassment** *n*.
disembody *vi* (**disembodying, disembodied**) to free (a soul, spirit, etc) from the body.—**disembodiment** *n*.
disembogue *vti* (**disemboguing, disembogued**) (*river etc*) to discharge, pour forth (its water).
disembowel *vt* (**disembowelling, disembowelled** *or* **disemboweling, disemboweled**) to remove the entrails of; to remove the substance of.—**disembowelment** *n*.
disenchant *vt* to disillusion.—**disenchantment** *n*.
disencumber *vt* to free from burden or hindrance.
disendow *vt* to deprive (a church) of endowments.—**disendowment** *n*.
disenfranchise *see* **disfranchise**.
disengage *vt* to separate or free from engagement or obligation; to detach, to release.—**disengaged** *adj*.—**disengagement** *n*.
disentail *vt* to release from entail.—*also n*.
disentangle *vt* to untangle; to free from complications.—**disentanglement** *n*.
disenthrall, disenthral *vt* (**disenthralling, disenthralled**) to free from bondage, to emancipate.
disestablish *vt* to displace from a settled position; to sever (church) from connection with the state.—**disestablishment** *n*.
disesteem *vt* to regard with disfavour, to dislike. * *n* lack of favour or regard.
diseur *n* a reciter of monologues for entertainment.—**diseuse** *nf*.
disfavour, disfavor *n* dislike; disapproval. * *vt* to treat with disfavour.
disfeature *vt* to disfigure.
disfigure *vt* to spoil the beauty or appearance of.—**disfigurer** *n*.
disfigurement, disfiguration *n* the act of disfiguring; a disfigured state; a thing that disfigures; a blemish, a defect.
disfranchise *vt* to deprive of the right to vote.—*also* **disenfranchise**.—**disfranchisement, disenfranchisement** *n*.
disgorge *vt* to emit violently from the throat, to vomit; to empty; to surrender (eg stolen property).—**disgorgement** *n*.
disgrace *n* a loss of trust, favour, or honour; something that disgraces. * *vt* to bring disgrace or shame upon.—**disgracer** *n*.
disgraceful *adj* causing or deserving disgrace, shameful.—**disgracefully** *adv*.—**disgracefulness** *n*.
disgruntled *adj* dissatisfied, resentful.—**disgruntlement** *n*.
disguise *vt* to hide what one is by appearing as something else; to hide what (a thing) really is. * *n* the use of a changed appearance to conceal identity; a false appearance.—**disguisedly** *adv*.—**disguiser** *n*.
disgust *n* sickening dislike; repugnance; aversion. * *vt* to cause disgust in.—**disgustedly** *adv*.
dish *n* any of various shallow concave vessels to serve food in; the amount of food served in a dish; the food served; a shallow concave object, as a dish aerial; (*inf*) an attractive person. * *vt* (*with* **out**) (*inf*) to distribute freely; (*with* **up**) to serve food at mealtimes; (*inf*) to present (eg facts).
dishabille *n* a partly clad state, undress.—*also* **deshabille**.
dish aerial, dish antenna *n* a microwave antenna used in radar, telescopes, telecommunications, etc having a concave reflector.
disharmonize *vt* to put out of harmony; to set at variance.
disharmony *n* (*pl* **disharmonies**) a lack of harmony between sounds; discord; a discordant situation, etc.—**disharmonious** *adj*.
dishcloth *n* a cloth for washing dishes.
dishearten *vt* to discourage.—**dishearteningly** *adv*.—**disheartenment** *n*.
dishevelled, disheveled *adj* rumpled, untidy.—**dishevelment** *n*.
dishonest *adj* not honest.—**dishonestly** *adv*.—**dishonesty** *n*.
dishonour, dishonor *n* loss of honour; disgrace, shame. * *vt* to bring shame on, to disgrace; to refuse to pay, as a cheque.
dishonourable, dishonorable *adj* lacking honour, disgraceful.—**dishonourably, dishonorably** *adv*.
dishtowel *n* a towel for drying dishes.
dishwasher *n* an appliance for washing dishes; a person employed to wash dishes.
dishwater *n* water used for washing dishes; something that looks like or tastes like this.
dishy *adj* (**dishier, dishiest**) (*inf*) physically attractive, good-looking.
disillusion *vt* to free from (mistaken) ideals or illusions. * *n* the state of being disillusioned.—**disillusionment** *n*.
disincentive *n* a discouragement to action or effort.
disinclination *n* reluctance, unwillingness.
disinclined *adj* unwilling.
disinfect *vt* to destroy germs.—**disinfection** *n*.
disinfectant *n* any chemical agent that inhibits the growth of or destroys germs.
disinformation *n* false information given out by intelligence agencies to mislead foreign spies.
disingenuous *adj* insincere, not candid or straightforward.—**disingenuously** *adv*.—**disingenuousness** *n*.
disinherit *vt* to deprive of the right to an inheritance.—**disinheritance** *n*.
disintegrate *vti* to break or cause to break into separate pieces.—**disintegration** *n*.—**disintegrator** *n*.
disinter *vt* (**disinterring, disinterred**) to take out of a grave; to bring out from obscurity, to unearth.—**disinterment** *n*.
disinterest *n* lack of partiality or bias. * *vt* to cease to concern (oneself).
disinterested *adj* impartial; objective.—**disinterestedly** *adv*.—**disinterestedness** *n*.
disjoin *vt* to separate. * *vi* to become detached.
disjoint *vt* to dislocate; to take to pieces. * *adj* (*math*) having no elements in common; (*obs*) disjointed.
disjointed *adj* incoherent, muddled, esp of speech or writing.—**disjointedly** *adv*.—**disjointedness** *n*.

disjunction *n* severance, disconnection (—*also* **disjuncture**); (*logic*) a compound proposition presenting alternative terms only one of which is true.

disjunctive *adj* disjoining; alternative; (*gram*) marking an adverse or oppositional sense; syntactically independent; (*logic*) presenting alternative terms.—**disjunctively** *adv*.

disk[1] *n* a disc; a cylindrical pad of cartilage between the vertebrae; a gramophone record.

disk[2] *n* any flat, thin circular body; something resembling this, as the sun; (*comput*) a storage device in a computer, either floppy or hard.

disk brake *see* **disc brake.**

disk drive *n* (*comput*) a mechanism that allows a computer to read data from, and write data to, a disk.

dislike *vt* to consider unpleasant. * *n* aversion, distaste.—**dislikable, dislikeable** *adj*.

dislocate *vt* to put (a joint) out of place, to displace; to upset the working of.

dislocation *n* the act of dislocating; a joint put out of its socket; an imperfection in a crystalline structure; (*geol*) a displacement of stratified rocks, a fault.

dislodge *vt* to force or move out of a hiding place, established position, etc.—**dislodgment, dislodgement** *n*.

disloyal *adj* unfaithful; false to allegiance, disaffected.—**disloyally** *adv*.

disloyalty (*pl* **disloyalties**) *n* the state of being unfaithful; a disloyal act.

dismal *adj* gloomy, miserable, sad; (*inf*) feeble, worthless.—**dismally** *adv*.

dismantle *vt* to pull down; to take apart.—**dismantlement** *n*.

dismast *vt* to deprive (a ship) of a mast or masts.

dismay *n* apprehension, discouragement. * *vt* to fill with dismay.

dismember *vt* to cut or tear off the limbs from; to cut or divide into pieces.—**dismemberment** *n*.

dismiss *vt* to send away; to remove from an office or employment; to stop thinking about; (*law*) to reject a further hearing (in court); (*cricket*) to bowl a batsman or side out.—**dismissible** *adj*.

dismissal *n* the act of dismissing; a removal from office, etc.

dismissive *adj* rejecting; offhand.—**dismissively** *adv*.

dismount *vti* to alight from a horse or bicycle; to remove from a mount or setting.

disobedience *n* the withholding of obedience; a refusal to obey; violation of a command by omitting to conform to it, or of a prohibition by acting in defiance of it; an instance of this.

disobedient *adj* failing or refusing to obey.—**disobediently** *adv*.

disobey *vt* (**disobeying, disobeyed**) to refuse to follow orders.

disoblige *vt* to ignore the wishes of; to inconvenience.—**disobligingly** *adv*.

disorder *n* lack of order; untidiness; a riot; an illness or interruption of the normal functioning of the body or mind. * *vt* to throw into confusion; to upset.

disorderly *adj* untidy; unruly, riotous.—**disorderliness** *n*.

disorganize *vt* to confuse or disrupt an orderly arrangement.—**disorganization** *n*.

disorient, disorientate *vt* to cause the loss of sense of time, place or identity; to confuse.—**disorientation** *n*.

disown *vt* to refuse to acknowledge as one's own.

disparage *vt* to belittle.—**disparagingly** *adv*.—**disparagement** *n*.

disparate *adj* unequal, completely different.—**disparately** *adv*.—**disparateness** *n*.

disparity *n* (*pl* **disparities**) essential difference; inequality.

dispassionate *adj* unemotional; impartial.—**dispassionately** *adv*.—**dispassionateness** *n*.

dispatch *vt* to send off somewhere; to perform speedily; to kill. * *n* a sending off (of a letter, a messenger etc); promptness; haste; a written message, esp of news.—*also* **despatch.**—**dispatcher** *n*.

dispel *vt* (**dispelling, dispelled**) to drive away and scatter.

dispensable *adj* able to be done without; unimportant.—**dispensability** *n*.

dispensary *n* (*pl* **dispensaries**) a place in a hospital, a chemist shop, etc where medicines are made up and dispensed; a place where medical treatment is available.

dispensation *n* the act of distributing or dealing out; exemption from a rule, penalty, etc.

dispense *vt* to deal out, distribute; to prepare and distribute medicines; to administer.

dispenser *n* a person who dispenses medicines; a machine, etc, that dispenses measured quanitites or units of something.

dispermous *adj* (*bot*) two-seeded.

dispersal *n* the act of dispersing; dispersion.

disperse *vt* to scatter in different directions; to cause to evaporate; to spread (knowledge); to separate (light, etc) into different wavelengths. * *vi* to separate, become dispersed.—**dispersedly** *adv*.

dispersion *n* a dispersing, or state of being dispersed; (*physics*) the separation of light into colours by diffraction or refraction; (*statistics*) the scattering of data about a mean.

dispersive *adj* tending to disperse; producing dispersion.—**dispersively** *adv*.

dispirit *vt* to depress the spirits of; to dishearten; to render cheerless.

dispirited *adj* depressed, discouraged.—**dispiritedly** *adv*.

displace *vt* to take the place of, to oust; to remove from a position of authority.

displaced person *n* a person who has become a refugee from their own country, eg due to war or famine.

displacement *n* the act of displacing; substitution; apparent change of position; the weight of water displaced by a solid body immersed in it.

display *vt* to show, expose to view; to exhibit ostentatiously. * *n* a displaying; an eye-catching arrangement, exhibition; a computer monitor for presenting visual information.

displease *vt* to cause offence or annoyance to.

displeasure *n* a feeling of being displeased; dissatisfaction.

disport *vt* to amuse or divert (oneself). * *vi* to display gaily.

disposable *adj* designed to be discarded after use; available for use. * *n* something disposable, eg a baby's nappy.

disposal *n* a disposing of something; order, arrangement.

dispose *vt* to place in order, arrange; to influence. * *vi* to deal with or settle; to give, sell or transfer to another; to throw away.

disposed *adj* inclined (towards something).

disposition *n* a natural way of behaving towards others; tendency; arrangement.—**dispositional** *adj*.

dispossess *vt* to deprive, rid (of); to eject.—**dispossession** *n*.—**dispossessor** *n*.

dispraise *vt* to disparage; to censure. * *n* depreciation; a reproach.—**dispraisingly** *adv*.

disproof *n* a disproving or refuting; evidence that refutes.

disproportion *n* a lack of symmetry, a being out of proportion. * *vt* to render or make out of due proportion.—**disproportional** *adj*.—**disproportionally** *adv*.

disproportionate *adj* out of proportion.—**disproportionately** *adv*.

disprove *vt* to prove (a claim, etc) to be incorrect.—**disprovable** *adj*.

disputable *adj* likely to cause dispute, arguable.—**disputability** *n*.—**disputably** *adv*.

disputant *n* a person involved in a dispute.

disputation *n* an argument; an exercise in debate.

disputatious *adj* fond of argument, contentious.—**disputatiously** *adv*.—**disputatiousness** *n*.

dispute *vt* to make the subject of an argument or debate; to query the validity of. * *vi* to argue. * *n* an argument; a quarrel.

disqualify *vt* (**disqualifying, disqualified**) to make ineligible because of a violation of rules; to make unfit or unsuitable, to disable.—**disqualifier** *n*.—**disqualification** *n*.

disquiet *vt* to trouble, disturb; to make uneasy or restless. * *n* disturbance; uneasiness, anxiety, worry; restlessness. * *adj* restless; uneasy; disturbed.—**disquieting** *adj*.

disquietude *n* restlessness; disturbance; a feeling, occasion or cause of disquiet.

disquisition *n* a careful examination of a subject.
disregard *vt* to pay no attention to; to consider as of little or no importance. * *n* lack of attention, neglect.
disrelish *vt* to dislike.—*also n.*
disrepair *n* a worn-out condition through neglect of repair.
disreputable *adj* of bad reputation; not respectable; discreditable.—**disreputably** *adv*.
disrepute *n* disgrace, discredit.
disrespect *n* lack of respect, rudeness.—**disrespectful** *adj*.—**disrespectfully** *adv*.
disrobe *vti* to undress; to uncover.
disrupt *vti* to break up; to create disorder or confusion; to interrupt.—**disruption** *n*.
disruptive *adj* causing disruption.—**disruptively** *adv*.
dissatisfaction *n* disapproval; discontent; something that dissatisfies.
dissatisfactory *adj* unsatisfactory.
dissatisfy *vt* (**dissatisfying, dissatisfied**) to fail to please, to make discontented.
dissect *vt* to cut apart (a plant, an animal, etc) for scientific examination; to analyse and interpret in fine detail.—**dissection** *n*.—**dissector** *n*.
disseise, disseize *vt* to deprive of possession; to dispossess unlawfully.—**disseisor, disseizor** *n*.
disseisin, disseizin *n* the act of unlawfully dispossessing a person or an estate.
dissemble *vti* to pretend or to conceal (eg true feelings) by pretence.—**dissemblance** *n*.—**dissembler** *n*.
disseminate *vt* to spread or scatter (ideas, information, etc) widely.—**dissemination** *n*.—**disseminator** *n*.
dissension *n* disagreement, esp when resulting in conflict.
dissent *vi* to hold a different opinion; to withhold assent. * *n* a difference of opinion.—**dissenter** *n*.
dissentient *adj* disagreeing with the majority. * *n* a person who dissents.
dissepiment *n* (*biol*) a calcareous or membraneous partition, a septum.
dissertate *vi* to hold forth, to discourse.—**dissertator** *n*.
dissertation *n* a written thesis, esp as required for a university degree, etc.
disservice *n* an ill turn, a harmful action.
dissever *vti* to cut apart, to disunite.—**disseverance, disseverment** *n*.
dissident *adj* disagreeing. * *n* a person who disagrees strongly with government policies, esp one who suffers harassment or imprisonment as a result.—**dissidence** *n*.
dissimilar *adj* unlike, different.—**dissimilarly** *adv*.
dissimilarity *n* (*pl* **dissimilarities**) lack of similarity; a difference, distinction.
dissimulate *vt* to dissemble.—**dissimulation** *n*.—**dissimulator** *n*.
dissipate *vt* to scatter, dispel; to waste, squander (money, etc). * *vi* to separate and vanish.—**dissipater, dissipator** *n*.
dissipated *adj* dissolute, indulging in excessive pleasure; scattered, wasted.—**dissipatedly** *adv*.—**dissipatedness** *n*.
dissipation *n* dispersion; wastefulness; frivolous or dissolute living.
dissociate *vti* to separate or cause to separate the association of (people, things, etc) in consciousness; to repudiate a connection with.—**dissociation** *n*.
dissociation *n* a dissociating or being dissociated; (*chem*) decomposition of a molecule into single atoms, etc; (*psychol*) the separation of an attitude, belief, etc, from the rest of the personality.
dissoluble *adj* soluble.—**dissolubility** *n*.
dissolute *adj* lacking moral discipline, debauched.—**dissolutely** *adv*.—**dissoluteness** *n*.
dissolution *n* separation into component parts; the dissolving of a meeting or assembly (eg parliament); the termination of a business or personal relationship; death; the process of dissolving.
dissolve *vt* to cause to pass into solution; to disperse (a legislative assembly); to melt; (*partnership, marriage*) to break up legally, annul. * *vi* to become liquid; to fade away; to be overcome by emotion.—**dissolvable** *adj*.—**dissolver** *n*.
dissolvent *adj* able to dissolve. * *n* a substance that dissolves.
dissonance *n* a harsh or inharmonious sound; discord; lack of agreement; (*mus*) an incomplete or unfulfilled chord requiring resolution into harmony.
dissonant *adj* inharmonious; discordant; disagreeing; (*mus*) producing dissonance.—**dissonantly** *adv*.
dissuade *vt* to prevent or discourage by persuasion.—**dissuasion** *n*.—**dissuasive** *adj*.
dissyllable *n* a word of two syllables.—*also* **disyllable**.—**dissyllabic, disyllabic** *adj*.
dissymmetry (**dissymmetries**) *n* an absence or lack of symmetry; symmetry in opposite directions, like right and left hands.—**dissymmetrical, dissymmetric** *adj*.
distaff line *n* the female line of a family.
distaff *n* the stick on which wool for flax is wound for spinning; (*arch*) a woman, women.
distal *adj* (*anat*) relatively distant from the centre of the body or point of attachment.—**distally** *adv*.
distance *n* the amount of space between two points or things; a distant place or point; remoteness, coldness of manner. * *vt* to place at a distance, physically or emotionally; to outdistance in a race, etc.
distant *adj* separated by a specific distance; far-off in space, time, place, relation, etc; not friendly, aloof.—**distantly** *adv*.
distaste *n* aversion; dislike.
distasteful *adj* unpleasant, offensive.—**distastefully** *adv*.—**distastefulness** *n*.
distemper *n* an infectious and often fatal disease of dogs and other animals; a type of paint made by mixing colour with egg or glue instead of oil; a painting made with this.
distend *vti* to swell or cause to swell, esp from internal pressure.
distensible *adj* able to be distended.
distension, distention *n* a distending or being distended; a swelling.
distich *n* (*pl* **distichs**) (*poetry*) a couplet.
distichous *adj* (*bot*) arranged in two rows on opposite sides of an axis.—**distichously** *adv*.
distil, distill *vti* (**distils** *or* **distills, distilling, distilled**) to treat by, or cause to undergo, distillation; to purify; to extract the essence of; to let or cause to fall in drops.
distillate *n* a product of distillation.
distillation *n* the conversion of a liquid into vapour by heat and then cooling the vapour so it condenses again, separating out the liquid's constituents or purifying it in the process; a distillate.—**distillatory** *adj*.
distiller *n* an individual or organization that distils, eg a brewery.
distillery *n* (*pl* **distilleries**) a place where distilling, esp of alcoholic spirits, is carried on.
distinct *adj* different, separate (from); easy to perceive by the mind or senses.—**distinctly** *adv*.—**distinctness** *n*.
distinction *n* discrimination, separation; a difference seen or made; a distinguishing mark or characteristic; excellence, superiority; a mark of honour.
distinctive *adj* clearly marking a person or thing as different from another; characteristic.—**distinctively** *adv*.—**distinctiveness** *n*.
distingué *adj* of superior manner, distinguished, striking.
distinguish *vt* to see or recognize as different; to mark as different, characterize; to see or hear clearly; to confer distinction on; to make eminent or known. * *vi* to perceive a difference.—**distinguishable** *adj*.
distinguished *adj* eminent, famous; dignified in appearance or manners.
Distinguished Flying Cross *n* a US military decoration for gallantry or heroism in flying operations.
distort *vt* to pull or twist out of shape; to alter the true meaning of, misrepresent.
distortion *n* a distorting or being distorted; a distorted feature; (*optics*) a faulty image; (*electronics*) an unwanted change in a signal, etc.—**distortional** *adj*.
distract *vt* to draw (eg the mind or attention) to something else; to confuse.—**distractingly** *adv*.

distracted *adj* bewildered, confused.—**distractedly** *adv*.
distraction *n* something that distracts the attention; an amusement; perplexity; extreme agitation.—**distractive** *adj*.—**distractively** *adv*.
distrain *vt* to seize and hold goods or chattels as security for payment of a debt.—**distrainer, distrainor** *n*.—**distrainment** *n*.
distrainee *n* a person who is distrained upon.
distraint *n* the act of distraining for debt; seizure.
distrait *adj* absent-minded, preoccupied.
distraught *adj* extremely distressed.
distress *n* physical or emotional suffering, as from pain, illness, lack of money, etc; a state of danger, desperation. * *vt* to cause distress to.—**distressingly** *adv*.
distressful *adj* suffering or causing distress.—**distressfully** *adv*.—**distressfulness** *n*.
distributary *n* (**distributaries**) a river branch that does not return to the main stream.
distribute *vt* to divide and share out; to spread, disperse throughout an area.—**distributable** *adj*.
distribution *n* a distributing or a being distributed; allotment; a thing distributed; diffusion; the geographical range or occurence of an organism; classification; (*law*) the apportioning of an estate among the heirs; (*commerce*) the marketing of goods to customers, their handling and transport; (*statistics*) the way numbers denoting characteristics in a statistical population are distributed.—**distributional** *adj*.
distributor *n* an agent who sells goods, esp wholesale; a device for distributing current to the spark plugs in an engine.
district *n* a territorial division defined for administrative purposes; a region or area with a distinguishing character.
district attorney *n* in US a lawyer who is the state's prosecutor in a judicial district.
District of Columbia *n* a federal area whose boundary is that of Washington, the capital.
distrust *n* suspicion, lack of trust. * *vt* to withhold trust or confidence from; to suspect.—**distrustful** *adj*.—**distrustfully** *adv*.—**distrustfulness** *n*.
disturb *vt* to interrupt; to cause to move from the normal position or arrangement; to destroy the quiet or composure of.
disturbance *n* a disturbing or being disturbed; an interruption; an outbreak of disorder and confusion.
disturbed *adj* showing symptoms of emotional illness.
disulphate, disulfate *n* a sulphate containing one atom of hydrogen, replaceable by a basic element.
disulphide, disulfide *n* a sulphide in which two atoms of sulphur are contained.
disunite *vt* to divide, disrupt. * *vi* to separate.
disuse *n* the state of being neglected or unused.—**disused** *adj*.
disyllable *see* **dissyllable**.
ditch *n* any long narrow trench dug in the ground. * *vt* to make a ditch in; (*sl*) to drive (a car) into a ditch; (*sl*) to make a forced landing of (an aircraft); (*sl*) to get rid of.
dither *vi* to hesitate, vacillate. * *n* a state of confusion; uncertainty.—**ditherer** *n*.
dithyramb *n* a hymn sung in honour of Dionysus, the Greek god of wine; an impassioned speech or writing.—**dithyrambic** *adj, n*.—**dithyrambically** *adv*.
dittany (*pl* **dittanies**) *n* an aromatic pink-flowered plant of the mint family formerly considered to have magical properties.
ditto *n* (*pl* **dittos**) the same again, as above—used in written lists and tables to avoid repetition. * *vt* (**dittoing, dittoed**) to repeat.
ditto marks *npl* two small marks (") placed under an item repeated.
ditty *n* (*pl* **ditties**) a simple song.
diuretic *n* a substance or drug that acts to increase the discharge of urine.—*also adj*.
diurnal *adj* occurring daily; of the daytime; having a daily cycle.—**diurnally** *adv*.
diva *n* (*pl* **divas, dive**) an accomplished female opera singer; a prima donna.
divalent *adj* (*chem*) having a valence of two.
divan *n* a long couch without back or sides; a bed of similar design.
dive *vi* (**diving, dived** *or* **dove, dived**) to plunge headfirst into water; (*aircraft*) to descend or fall steeply; (*diver, submarine*) to submerge; to plunge (eg the hand) suddenly into anything; to dash headlong, lunge. * *n* a headlong plunge; a submerging of a submarine, etc; a sharp descent; a steep decline; (*sl*) a disreputable public place.
dive bomber *n* an aircraft designed to release its bombs during a steep dive for superior accuracy.—**dive-bomb** *vt*.
diver *n* a person who dives; a person who works or explores underwater from a diving bell or in a diving suit; any of various aquatic birds.
diverge *vi* to branch off in different directions from a common point; to differ in character, form, etc; to deviate from a path or course.—**divergence** *n*.—**divergent** *adj*.
divers *adj* (*arch*) various; sundry.
diverse *adj* different; assorted, various.—**diversely** *adv*.—**diverseness** *n*.
diversify *vb* (**diversifying, diversified**) *vt* to vary; to invest in a broad range of securities to lessen risk of loss. * *vi* to engage in a variety of commercial operations to reduce risk.—**diversification** *n*.
diversion *n* turning aside from a course; a recreation, amusement; a drawing of attention away from the principal activity; a detour when a road is temporarily closed to traffic.—**diversionary** *adj*.
diversity *n* (*pl* **diversities**) the condition or quality of being diverse; unlikeness; a difference, distinction; variety.
divert *vt* to turn aside from one course onto another; to entertain, amuse.
diverticulitis *n* inflammation of a diverticulum.
diverticulum *n* (*pl* **diverticula**) a pocket or side branch off a passage or cavity in the body, esp the intestine.
divertimento *n* (*pl* **divertimenti, divertimentos**) a light, pleasant vocal or instrumental composition.
divertissement *n* an amusement; a recreation, a light entertainment, a ballet, etc, as an interlude between the acts of a play; an entr'acte; (*mus*) a divertimento.
divest *vt* to strip of clothing, equipment, etc; to deprive of rights, property, power, etc.—**divestiture, divestment** *n*.
divide *vt* to break up into parts; to distribute, share out; to sort into categories; to cause to separate from something else; to separate into opposing sides; (*parliament*) to vote or cause to vote by division; (*math*) to ascertain how many times one quantity contains another. * *vi* to become separated; to diverge; to vote by separating into two sides. * *n* a watershed; a split.—**dividable** *adj*.
divided highway *see* **dual carriageway**.
dividend *n* a number which is to be divided; the money earned by a company and divided among the shareholders; a bonus derived from some action.
divider *n* something that divides; a screen, furniture or plants, etc used to divide up a room; (*pl*) measuring-compasses.
divi-divi (*pl* **divi-divis**) *n* a South American tropical plant; its astringent husks used for dyeing and tanning.
divination *n* the art of foretelling the future or discovering hidden knowledge by supernatural means; intuitive perception.—**divinatory** *adj*.
divine *adj* of, from, or like God or a god; (*inf*) excellent. * *n* a clergyman; a theologian. * *vt* to foretell the future by supernatural means; to discover intuitively; to dowse. * *vi* to practise divination.—**divinely** *adv*.—**diviner** *n*.
diving bell *n* an open-bottomed chamber for working under water, supplied with compressed air.
diving board *n* a platform or springboard for diving from.
diving suit *n* a watertight suit with a helmet and air supply, used by divers.
divining rod *n* a forked twig used for dowsing.
divinity *n* (*pl* **divinities**) any god; theology; the quality of being God or a god.
divisible *adj* able to be divided.—**divisibility** *n*.
division *n* a dividing or being divided; a partition, a barrier; a portion or section; a military unit; separation; (*Parliament*) a separation into two

opposing sides to vote; a disagreement; (*math*) the process of dividing one number by another.—**divisional** *adj*.

divisive *adj* creating disagreement or disunity.—**divisively** *adv*.—**divisiveness** *n*.

divisor *n* a number that is to be divided into another number (the dividend).

divorce *n* the legal dissolution of marriage; separation. * *vt* to terminate a marriage by divorce; to separate.

divorcé, divorcee *n* a divorced person.—**divorcée** *nf*.

divorcement *n* the act or process of divorcing.

divot *n* a lump of turf dug from the ground while making a golf swing, etc.

divulge *vt* to tell or reveal.—**divulgence** *n*.

divvy *n* (*pl* **divvies**) in the UK, a dividend; in the US, a portion. * *vt* (**divvying, divvied**) (*usu with* **up**) to share out.

Dixie *n* the southern States of the US.

Dixieland *n* Dixie; a New Orleans jazz style.

dizzy *adj* (**dizzier, dizziest**) confused; causing giddiness or confusion; (*sl*) silly; foolish. * *vt* to make dizzy; to confuse.—**dizzily** *adv*.—**dizziness** *n*.

DJ *abbr* = disc jockey; dinner jacket.

dl *abbr* = decilitre.

DM *abbr* = Deutschmark.

dm *abbr* = decimetre.

DMus *abbr* = Doctor of Music.

DMZ *abbr* = demilitarized zone.

DNA *abbr* = deoxyribonucleic acid, the main component of chromosomes that stores genetic information.

do *vt* (*pres t* **does, doing, did,** *pp* **done**) to perform; to work; to end, to complete; to make; to provide; to arrange, to tidy; to perform; to cover a distance; to visit; (*sl*) to serve time in prison; (*sl*) to cheat, to rob; (*sl*) to assault; (*with* **in**) (*inf*) to kill; to tire out. * *vi* to act or behave; to be satisfactory; to manage. * *n* (*pl* **dos, do's**) (*inf*) a party; (*inf*) a hoax. *Do* has special uses where it has no definite meaning, as in asking questions (*Do you like milk?*), emphasizing a verb (*I do want to go*), and standing for a verb already used (*My dog goes where I do*).

DOA *abbr* = dead on arrival.

Doberman (pinscher) *n* a breed of dog with a smooth glossy black-and-tan coat and docked tail.

doc *n* (*inf*) doctor.

docent *n* a person licensed to teach in a university, but of lower grade and authority than a professor.

docile *adj* easily led; submissive.—**docilely** *adv*.—**docility** *n*.

dock[1] *vt* (*an animal's tail*) to cut short; (*wages, etc*) to deduct a portion of.

dock[2] *n* a wharf; an artificial enclosed area of water for ships to be loaded, repaired, etc; (*pl*) a dockyard. * *vt* to come or bring into dock; to join (spacecraft) together in space.

dock[3] *n* an enclosed area in a court of law reserved for the accused.

dockage *n* the provision of accommodation for the docking of vessels; money paid for the use of a dock.

docker *n* a labourer who works at the docks.—*also* **longshoreman** *n*.

docket *n* a label or document recording the contents of a package, delivery instructions, payment advice, or details of payment of customs duties; in US, a list of lawsuits to be tried by a court. * *vt* (*goods*) to put a docket on; (*lawsuit*) to enter on a docket.

dockyard *n* an area with docks and facilities for repairing and refitting ships.

doctor *n* a person qualified to treat diseases or physical disorders; the highest academic degree; the holder of such a degree. * *vt* to treat medically; (*machinery, etc*) to patch up; to tamper with, falsify; (*inf*) to castrate or spay.—**doctoral** *adj*.

doctorate *n* the highest degree in any discipline given by a university, conferring the title of doctor.

doctrinaire *adj* obsessed by theory rather than by experience. * *n* a person so obsessed.—**doctrinairism** *n*.

doctrine *n* a principle of belief.—**doctrinal** *adj*.—**doctrinally** *adv*.

document *n* a paper containing information or proof of anything. * *vt* to provide or prove with documents.—**documental** *adj*.—**documentation** *n*.

documentary *adj* consisting of documents; presenting a factual account of an event or activity. * *n* (*pl* **documentaries**) a nonfiction film.

dodder *vt* to tremble or shake through old age or weakness; to walk slowly and shakily.—**dodderer** *n*.—**doddery** *adj*.

dodecagon *n* a geometric figure with twelve angles and sides.

dodecahedron *n* a solid figure with twelve faces.—**dodecahedral** *adj*.

dodge *vi* to move quickly in an irregular course. * *vt* to evade (a duty) by cunning; to avoid by a sudden movement or shift of position; to trick. * *n* a sudden movement; (*inf*) a clever trick.—**dodger** *n*.

dodgy *adj* (**dodgier, dodgiest**) (*inf*) cunning; risky.

dodo *n* (*pl* **dodos, dodoes**) a large, clumsy bird, now extinct.

doe *n* (*pl* **does, doe**) a female deer, rabbit, or hare.

doer *n* a person who acts, as opposed to thinking or talking; an active energetic person.

does *see* **do**.

doeskin *n* the skin of a doe; a fine woollen cloth with a smooth finish.

doesn't = does not.

doff *vt* to take off (esp one's hat) in greeting or as a sign of respect.

dog *n* a canine mammal of numerous breeds, commonly kept as a domestic pet; the male of the wolf or fox; a despicable person; a device for gripping things. * *vt* (**dogging, dogged**) to pursue relentlessly.—**dog-like** *adj*.

dogcart *n* a light, two-wheeled carriage with cross seats back to back.

dog collar *n* a collar for a dog; (*inf*) a clerical collar.

dog days *npl* the warmest days of the year.

doge *n* (*formerly*) the chief magistrate in republican Venice and Genoa.

dog-eared *adj* worn, shabby; (*book*) having the corners of the pages turned down.—**dog-ear** *vt*.

dogfight *n* (*loosely*) a fiercely disputed contest; combat between two fighter planes, esp at close quarters.

dogfish *n* (*pl* **dogfish, dogfishes**) any of various small shark-like fish.

dogged *adj* tenacious.—**doggedly** *adv*.—**doggedness** *n*.

doggerel *n* trivial or worthless verse.

doggish *adj* like a dog, surly; (*sl*) showily stylish.—**doggishly** *adv*.—**doggishness** *n*.

doggo *adv* (*sl*) silent and still; **lie doggo** to lie low, stay hidden.

doggone *interj* (*sl*) darn, damn. * *adj* (*sl*) cursed, confounded. * *vt* (*sl*) to damn.

doggy *adj* (**doggier, doggiest**) of or like a dog; fond of dogs; (*sl*) showily stylish. * *n* (*pl* **doggies**) a pet name for a dog; a little dog (—*also* **doggie**).

doghouse *n* a dog kennel; **in the doghouse** (*inf*) in disgrace.

dogleg *n* something having a sharp angle or a sharp bend, as a road or fairway on a golf course. * *adj* crooked like a dog's hind leg (—*also* **doglegged**).

dogma *n* (*pl* **dogmas, dogmata**) a belief taught or held as true, esp by a church; a doctrine; a belief.

dogmatic, dogmatical *adj* pertaining to a dogma; forcibly asserted as if true; overbearing.—**dogmatically** *adv*.

dogmatics *n* (*used as sing*) the study of religious dogmas; doctrinal theology.

dogmatize *vt* to assert in a dogmatic manner.—**dogmatism** *n*.—**dogmatist** *n*.

do-gooder *n* a well-meaning person, esp if naive or ineffectual.—**do-gooding** *n*.

dog paddle *n* an elementary form of swimming in which the arms and legs paddle rapidly in the water.—**dog-paddle** *vi*.

dog rose *n* a prickly wild rose.

dogsbody *n* (*pl* **dogsbodies**) (*inf*) a drudge.

dogtooth (*pl* **dogteeth**) *n* a canine tooth; (*archit*) a small conical ornament resembling a petal in Early English architecture.

dogtrot *n* a gentle trot; a covered passageway.

dogwatch *n* (*naut*) one of two watches on board ship of two hours each, between 4 and 8 pm.

dogwood *n* any of several shrubs with clusters of small flowers.

doily *n* (*pl* **doilies**) a small ornamented mat, laid under food on dishes, eg cakes.—*also* **doyley**.

doing *n* an action or its result; (*pl*) things done; actions.

doit *n* a small old Dutch copper coin; a thing of little value.
do-it-yourself *n* domestic repairs, woodwork, etc undertaken as a hobby or to save money.—*also adj*.—**do-it-yourselfer** *n*.
dolabriform, dolabrirate *adj* (*bot*) hatchet-shaped.
Dolby *n* (*trademark*) an electronic noise-reduction system used in sound-recording and playback systems.
dolce *adj* soft. * *adv* (*mus*) gently.
doldrums *npl* inactivity; depression; boredom; the regions of the ocean about the equator where there is little wind.
dole *n* (*inf*) money received from the state while unemployed; a small portion. * *vt* to give (out) in small portions.
doleful *adj* sad, gloomy.—**dolefully** *adv*.—**dolefulness** *n*.
dolerite *n* a dark-coloured basic igneous rock composed of augite, felspar and iron; basaltic greenstone.
dolichocephalic *adj* with a skull long in proportion to its breadth, long-headed.—**dolichocephaly** *n*.
doll *n* a toy in the form of a human figure; a ventriloquist's dummy; (*sl*) a woman
dollar *n* the unit of money in the US, Canada, Australia and many other countries.
dollop *n* (*inf*) a soft mass or lump; a portion, serving.
dolly *n* (*pl* **dollies**) (*inf*) a child's word for a doll; a wheeled platform for a camera. * *vi* (**dollying, dollied**) to manoeuvre a camera dolly.
dolman *n* (*pl* **dolmans**) a loose robe; a short cloak.
dolman sleeve *n* a full, wide sleeve narrowing to a wristband.
dolmen *n* a prehistoric structure of two or more erect stones supporting a horizontal slab.
dolomite *n* a white mineral obtained from sedimentary rock; a sedimentary rock similar to limestone.—**dolomitic** *adj*.
doloroso *adv* (*mus*) sadly.
dolorous *adj* mournful, doleful.—**dolorously** *adv*.—**dolorousness** *n*.
dolour, dolor *n* grief, sorrow, distress.
dolphin *n* a marine mammal with a beak-like snout, larger than a porpoise but smaller than a whale.
dolphinarium *n* (*pl* **dolphinariums, dolphinaria**) a large pool or aquarium for keeping and displaying dolphins.
dolt *n* a dull or stupid person.—**doltish** *adj*.—**doltishly** *adv*.—**doltishness** *n*.
Dom *n* (*RC Church*) the title of certain dignitaries; a former Portuguese title of rank, as Don.
domain *n* an area under the control of a ruler or government; a field of thought, activity, etc.
dome *n* a large, rounded roof; something high and rounded.—*also vt*.
domed *adj* having, or shaped like, a dome.
domesday *n* the day of God's Last Judgment of mankind.—*also* **doomsday**.
Domesday Book *n* the record of William I's survey of England in 1086.
domestic *adj* belonging to the home or family; not foreign; (*animals*) tame. * *n* a servant in the home.—**domestically** *adv*.
domestic science *n* the study of household skills; home economics.
domesticate *vt* to tame; to make home-loving and fond of household duties.—**domestication** *n*.
domesticity *n* (*pl* **domesticities**) home life; being domestic.
domicile *n* a house; a person's place of residence. * *vt* to establish, to settle permanently.—**domiciliary** *adj*.
domiciliate *vt* to domicile.—**domiciliation** *n*.
dominant *adj* commanding, prevailing over others; overlooking from a superior height. * *n* (*mus*) the fifth note of a diatonic scale.—**dominance** *n*.—**dominantly** *n*.
dominate *vt* to control or rule by strength; to hold a commanding position over; to overlook from a superior height.—**domination** *n*.—**dominator** *n*.
domineer *vti* to act in an arrogant or tyrannical manner.—**domineeringly** *adv*.
dominical *adj* pertaining to Christ as Lord, or to Sunday.
dominie *n* (*Scot*) a schoolteacher; (*inf*) a clergyman.
dominion *n* a territory with one ruler or government; the power to rule; authority.
domino *n* (*pl* **dominoes, dominos**) a flat oblong tile marked with up to six dots; (*pl*) a popular game usu using a set of 28 dominoes; a loose cloak, usu worn with an eye mask, at masquerades.
Don *n* a Spanish title for a gentleman or nobleman.—**Doña** *nf*.
don[1] *vt* (**donning, donned**) to put on; to invest with; to assume.
don[2] *n* a head, fellow or tutor at Oxford or Cambridge universities; (*loosely*) any university teacher; a Mafia leader.
donate *vt* to give as a gift or donation, esp to a charity.—**donator** *n*.
donation *n* a donating; a contribution or gift, esp to a charity.
donative *n* a gift; largess, a donation. * *adj* given by donation.
done[1] *see* **do**.
done[2] *adj* completed; cooked sufficiently; socially acceptable; (*with* **for**) (*sl*) doomed; dead; exhausted; discarded.
donee *n* a person to whom a gift is made.
donjon *n* the central tower of a castle, a keep.
donkey *n* (*pl* **donkeys**) a small animal resembling a horse.
donkey engine *n* a portable auxiliary engine.
donkey jacket *n* a thick waterproof jacket, esp worn by labourers.
donkey's years *npl* (*inf*) a very long time.
donkey-work *n* the groundwork; drudgery.
Donna *n* a term of respect to a lady in Italy.
donnish *adj* (*inf*) resembling a university don.—**donnishly** *adv*.—**donnishness** *n*.
donor *n* a person who donates something, a donator; a person who gives their blood, organs, etc for medical use.
don't = do not.
donut *n* (*sl*) a doughnut.
doodad *n* (*inf*) a small item whose name is lost or forgotten.
doodle *vi* to scribble aimlessly. * *vt* to draw (something) absentmindedly. * *n* a meaningless drawing or scribble.—**doodler** *n*.
doom[1] *n* a grim destiny; ruin. * *vt* condemn to failure, destruction, etc.
doom[2] *see* **doum**.
doomsday *n* the day of God's Last Judgment of mankind.—*also* **domesday**.
door *n* a movable barrier to close an opening in a wall; a doorway; a means of entry or approach.
doorjamb *n* one of the two vertical sides of a door frame; a doorpost.
doorkeeper *n* a person guarding a door.
doorman *n* (*pl* **doormen**) a uniformed attendant stationed at the entrance to large hotels, offices, etc.
doormat *n* a mat placed at the entrance to a doorway for wiping one's feet; (*inf*) a submissive or easily bullied person.
doornail *n* (*formerly*) a large nail with which doors were studded; **dead as a doornail** most certainly dead.
doorplate *n* a plate with the name of the occupant of a building.
doorpost *n* the straight vertical side-post of a door, jamb.
doorstop *n* a device for preventing a door from moving or fixed to the bottom of a door to prevent it hitting a wall when opening, etc.
doorway *n* an opening in a wall, etc filled by a door.
dope *n* a thick pasty substance used for lubrication; (*inf*) any illegal drug, such as cannabis or narcotics; (*sl*) a stupid person; (*sl*) information. * *vt* to treat with dope. * *vi* to take addictive drugs.
dopey, dopy *adj* (**dopier, dopiest**) (*sl*) stupid; (*inf*) half asleep.—**dopiness** *n*.
doppelgänger, doppelganger *n* a ghostly double of a living person.
Dorian *adj* of or relating to an early Greek race that overthrew the Mycenaean civilization. * *n* a member of that race.
Doric *adj* of the Dorians or their dialect; of or belonging to the oldest and simplest style of Greek architecture. * *n* the dialect of the Dorians; any broad dialect.
dormant *adj* sleeping; quiet, as if asleep; inactive.—**dormancy** *n*.
dormer *n* an upright window that projects from a sloping roof.
dormitory *n* (*pl* **dormitories**) a large room with many beds, as in a boarding school.
dormouse *n* (*pl* **dormice**) a small mouse-like creature that hibernates in winter.

dorp *n* (*S Africa*) a small town.
dorsal *adj* of, on, or near the back.—**dorsally** *adv*.
dorsiventral *adj* (*leaves*) having a differentiated back and front.
dory[1] *n* (*pl* **dories**) a light flat-bottomed boat with a sharp bow and high sides.
dory[2] *n* (*pl* **dories**) an edible yellow seafish.—*also* **John Dory**.
dosage *n* the administration of a medicine in doses; the size of a dose; the operation of dosing.
dose *n* the amount of medicine, radiation, etc administered at one time; a part of an experience; (*sl*) a venereal disease. * *vt* to administer a dose (of medicine) to.
doss *vi* (*sl*) to sleep, esp in a dosshouse.
dossal, dossel *n* a hanging of silk or damask at the back and sides of an altar.
dosshouse *n* (*sl*) a cheap lodging house.
dossier *n* a collection of documents about a subject or person, a file.
dot *n* a small round speck, a point; the short signal in Morse code. * *vt* (**dotting, dotted**) to mark with a dot; to scatter (about).—**dotter** *n*.
dotage *n* weakness and infirmity caused by old age.
dotard *n* a person in their dotage.
dote *vi* (*with* **on** *or* **upon**) to show excessive affection.—**doter** *n*.
dot matrix printer *n* (*comput*) a printer in which each printed character is formed by pins selected from a rectangular array.
dotted *see* **dot**.
dotterel, dottrel *n* a small plover of Europe and Asia, now rare; a similar Australian bird.
dottle *n* a remnant of tobacco left in a smoked pipe.
dotty *adj* (**dottier, dottiest**) (*inf*) eccentric, slightly mad.—**dottily** *adv*.—**dottiness** *n*.
double *adj* twice as large, as strong, etc; designed or intended for two; made of two similar parts; having two meanings, characters, etc; (*flowers*) having more than one circle of petals. * *adv* twice; in twos. * *n* a number or amount that is twice as much; a person or thing identical to another; (*film*) a person closely resembling an actor and who takes their place to perform stunts, etc; (*pl*) a game between two pairs of players. * *vti* to make or become twice as much or as many; to fold, to bend; to bend sharply backwards; to sail around; to have an additional purpose.—**doubly** *adv*.
double agent *n* a spy secretly acting for two governments at the same time.
double-barrelled, double-barreled *adj* (*gun*) having two barrels; (*surname*) having two parts; (*question*) serving a double purpose.
double bass *n* the largest instrument of the violin family.—**double bassist** *n*.
double boiler *n* two saucepans fitting into each other so that the contents of the upper are cooked while boiling in the lower.
double-breasted *adj* (*suit*) having one half of the front overlap the other.
double cream *n* cream with a high fat content.
double-cross *vt* to betray an associate, to cheat. * **double cross** *n*.—**double-crosser** *n*.
double-dealing *n* treachery, deceit.—**double-dealer** *n*.
double-edged *adj* acting in two ways; (*remarks*) having two possible meanings (eg well-meaning or malicious).
double entendre *n* a word or phrase with two meanings, one of which is usu indecent.
double entry *n* (*bookkeeping*) a system where each transaction is entered as a debit in one account and a credit in another.—**double-entry** *adj*.
double-faced *adj* having two faces; hypocritical.
double-jointed *adj* having joints which allow the limbs, figures, etc an unusual degree of flexibility.
double-park *vt* to park alongside a car which is already parked beside the kerb.
double-quick *adj, adv* very quick. * *vti* to march quickly.
double standard *n* a principle that is applied more strictly to one person or group than to another.
doublet *n* (*formerly*) a man's close-fitting jacket; one of a pair of similar things.
doublethink *n* a belief in two conflicting ideas, principles, etc.
doubleton *n* two cards only of a suit (in a player's hand).
doubloon *n* an old Spanish gold coin.
doubt *vi* to be uncertain or undecided. * *vt* to hold in doubt; to distrust; to be suspicious of. * *n* uncertainty; (*often pl*) lack of confidence in something, distrust.—**doubter** *n*.
doubtful *adj* feeling doubt; uncertain; suspicious.—**doubtfully** *adv*.—**doubtfulness** *adv*.
doubtless *adv* no doubt; probably. * *adj* assured; certain.—**doubtlessly** *adv*.—**doubtlessness** *n*.
douce *adj* (*Scot*) sober; sedate; prudent; modest.
douceur *n* a gift for services rendered, or to secure favour; a bribe.
douche *n* a jet of water directed on or into a part of the body; a device for applying this. * *vt* to cleanse or treat with a douche.
dough *n* a mixture of flour and water, milk, etc used to make bread, pastry, or cake; (*inf*) money.
doughboy *n* a boiled dumpling; (*sl*) a soldier.
doughnut *n* a small, fried, usu ring-shaped, cake.—*also* **donut**.
doughty *adj* (**doughtier, doughtiest**) valiant; strong.—**doughtily** *adv*.—**doughtiness** *n*.
doughy (**doughier, doughiest**) *adj* soft, like dough.—**doughiness** *n*.
doum, doom *n* an Egyptian palm tree.
dour *adj* stern; sullen; grim.—**dourly** *adv*.—**dourness** *n*.
douse *vt* to plunge into or soak with water; to put out, extinguish.
dove[1] *see* **dive**.
dove[2] *n* a small bird of the pigeon family; (*politics, diplomacy*) an advocate of peace or a peaceful policy.
dovecote, dovecot *n* a shelter and breeding place for domesticated pigeons.
dovetail *n* a wedge-shaped joint used in woodwork. * *vt* to fit or combine together.
dowager *n* a widow possessing property or title from her husband; (*inf*) a dignified elderly woman.
dowdy *adj* (**dowdier, dowdiest**) poorly dressed, not stylish.—**dowdily** *adv*.—**dowdiness** *n*.
dowel *n* a headless wooden or metal pin used for fastening wood or stone. * *vt* (**doweling, doweled** *or* **dowelling, dowelled**) to fasten with dowels.
dower *n* a widow's share of her husband's estate.
down[1] *n* soft fluffy feathers or fine hairs.
down[2] *adv* towards or in a lower physical position; to a lying or sitting position; toward or to the ground, floor, or bottom; to a source or hiding place; to or in a lower status or in a worse condition; from an earlier time; in cash; to or in a state of less activity. * *adj* occupying a low position, esp lying on the ground; depressed, dejected. * *prep* in a descending direction in, on, along, or through. * *n* a low period (as in activity, emotional life, or fortunes); (*inf*) a dislike, prejudice. * *vti* to go or cause to go or come down; to defeat; to swallow.
down[3] *n* (*usu pl*) a tract of bare hilly land used for pasturing sheep; banks or rounded hillocks of sand.
downbeat *adj* (*mus*) the first beat in the bar, the downward gesture of a conductor's baton; (*inf*) dismal; relaxed.
downcast *adj* dejected; (*eyes*) directed downwards.
downer *n* (*sl*) a depressant drug, esp a barbiturate; a depressing experience or situation.
downfall *n* a sudden fall (from power, etc); a sudden or heavy fall of rain or snow.
downgrade *n* a descending slope. * *vt* to reduce or lower in rank or position; to disparage.
down payment *n* a deposit.
downpour *n* a heavy fall of rain.
downright *adj* frank; absolute. * *adv* thoroughly.
downscale, down-market *adj* (*goods, services*) of inferior quality.

downside *n* the less appealing or advantageous aspect of something.
downsize *vt* to produce a smaller version of (eg a car); to reduce the numbers in a workforce by means of redundancy.
Down's syndrome *n* a chromosomal abnormality resulting in a flat face, slanting eyes and mental retardation.
downstage *adv* to the front of the stage.
downstairs *adv* to or on a lower floor. * *adj* on the ground floor or a lower floor. * *n (used as sing or pl)* the lower part of a house, the ground floor.
down-to-earth *adj* practical, sensible.
downtown *n* the main business district of a town or city.—*also adj.*
downtrodden *adj* oppressed, trampled underfoot.
downturn *n* a decline in (economic) activity or prosperity.
down under *n (inf)* Australia or New Zealand.
downward *adj* moving from a higher to a lower level, position or condition. * *adv* towards a lower place, position, etc; from an earlier time to a later (—*also* **downwards**)
downwind *adv* in the direction the wind is blowing.—*also adj.*
downy *adj* (**downier, downiest**) like, covered with, or made of, down.
dowry *n* (*pl* **dowries**) the money or possessions that a woman brings to her husband at marriage.
dowse *vi* to search for water, treasure, etc with a divining rod.—**dowser** *n.*
doxology *n* (*pl* **doxologies**) a hymn of praise to God.
doxy *n* (*pl* **doxies**) (*arch*) a sweetheart, a prostitute.
doyen *n* a senior member of a group; an expert in a field; the oldest example of a category.—**doyenne** *nf.*
doyley *see* **doily.**
doze *vi* to sleep lightly. * *n* a light sleep, a nap.—**dozer** *n.*
dozen *n* a group of twelve.—**dozenth** *adj.*
dozy *adj* (**dozier, doziest**) drowsy; (*inf*) stupid.—**dozily** *adv.*—**doziness** *n.*
DPhil, D.Phil *abbr* = Doctor of Philosophy.
Dr *abbr* = Doctor; debtor.
drab *adj* (**drabber, drabbest**) dull, uninteresting; of a dull brown colour. * *n* a dull yellowy brown colour; cloth of this colour.—**drably** *adv.*—**drabness** *n.*
drabble *vt* to make wet or dirty by dragging through mud or water.
dracaena *n* any of a genus of tropical liliaceous palm-like plants.
drachm *n* in UK, a unit of capacity (^{1}/8th fluid ounce); in US, a dram; a drachma.
drachma *n* (*pl* **drachmas, drachmae**) the monetary unit of Greece.
draconian *adj* (*laws, etc*) very cruel, severe; (*with cap*) of the 7th-century Athenian statesman Draco or his extremely harsh laws.
draft *n* a rough plan, preliminary sketch; an order for the payment of money by a bank; a smaller group selected from a larger for a specific task; conscription. * *vt* to draw a rough sketch or outline of; to select for a special purpose; to conscript.—*also* **draught.**
draftboard, draftsboard *see* **draughtboard.**
draftee *n* a conscript.
draftsman *see* **draughtsman.**
drafty *see* **draughty.**
drag *vb* (**dragging, dragged**) *vt* to pull along by force; to draw slowly and heavily; to search (in water) with a dragnet or hook. * *vi* to trail on the ground; to move slowly and heavily; (*sl*) to draw on a cigarette. * *n* something used for dragging, a dragnet, a heavy harrow; something that retards progress; a braking device; (*sl*) something boring or tedious; (*sl*) women's clothes worn by a man; (*sl*) a draw at a cigarette.
dragée *n* a coated nut or ball of sugar; a silver coated ball used as a cake decoration; a pill coated with sugar.
draggle *vt* to wet or soil by dragging in the mud or along the ground * *vi* to become dirty or wet by dragging.
dragnet *n* a net for scouring a riverbed, pond, etc to search for anything; a coordinated hunt for an escaped criminal, etc.
dragon *n* a mythical winged reptile; an authoritarian or grim person, esp a woman.
dragonfly *n* (*pl* **dragonflies**) an insect with a long slender abdomen, large eyes and iridescent wings.
dragoon *n* a soldier on horseback, a cavalryman. * *vt* to force into submission by bullying commands.
drail *n* a weighted fishhook for dragging through water.
drain *vt* to draw off liquid gradually; to make dry by removing liquid gradually; to exhaust physically or mentally; to drink the entire contents of a glass * *vi* to flow away gradually; to become dry as liquid trickles away. * *n* a sewer, pipe, etc by which water is drained away; something that causes exhaustion or depletion.—**drainer** *n.*
drainage *n* a draining; a system of drains; something drained off.
draining board, drainboard *n* a sloping, usu grooved, surface beside a sink for draining washed dishes.
drainpipe *n* a pipe that carries waste liquid, sewage, etc out of a building.
drake *n* a male duck.
dram *n* a small drink of spirits; a small amount; a unit of capacity (^{1}/8th fluid ounce); a unit of weight (avoirdupois 27.243 grains or 0.00265 ounce/apothecaries' weight 3 scruples or 60 grains).
drama *n* a play for the stage, radio or television; dramatic literature as a genre; a dramatic situation or a set of events.
dramatic *adj* of or resembling drama; exciting, vivid.—**dramatically** *adv.*
dramatics *n* (*used as sing or pl*) the producing or performing of plays; (*used as sing*) exaggerated behaviour, histrionics.
dramatis personae *n* the characters in a play.
dramatist *n* a person who writes plays.
dramatization *n* the action or process of dramatizing; an event or novel, etc, adapted to the form of a play.
dramatize *vt* to write or adapt in the form of a play; to express in an exaggerated or dramatic form.—**dramatizer** *n.*
dramaturge, dramaturg *n* a playwright; a literary adviser; an expert in dramaturgy.
dramaturgy *n* the art of dramatic composition; representation and stage effect.—**dramaturgic, dramaturgical** *adj.*
drank *see* **drink.**
drape *vt* to cover or hang with cloth; to arrange in loose folds; to place loosely or untidily. * *n* a hanging cloth or curtain; (*pl*) curtains.
draper *n* a seller of cloth.
drapery *n* (*pl* **draperies**) fabrics or curtains, esp as arranged in loose folds; the trade of a draper.
drastic *adj* acting with force and violence.—**drastically** *adv.*
drat *interj* (*sl*) a euphemism for damn.
dratted *adj* (*sl*) confounded; annoying.
draught *n* a current of air, esp in an enclosed space; the pulling of a load using an animal, etc; something drawn; a dose of medicine or liquid; an act of swallowing; the depth of water required to float a ship; beer, wine, etc stored in bulk in casks; a flat counter used in the game of draughts; (*pl*) (*used as sing*) a game for two players using 24 round pieces on a draughboard.
draughtboard *n* a square board identical to a chessboard used for playing draughts.—*also* **draftboard, draftsboard.**
draughtsman[1] *n* (*pl* **draughtsmen**) a person who makes detailed drawings or plans.—*also* **draftsman.**—**draughtsmanship, draftsmanship** *n.*
draughtsman[2] *n* (*pl* **draughtsmen**) *n* a flat counter used in the game of draughts.—*also* **checker, draftsman.**
draughty *adj* (**draughtier, draughtiest**) letting in or exposed to drafts of air.—*also* **drafty.**—**draughtiness, draftiness** *n.*
Dravidian *adj* pertaining to an ancient race and their languages, spoken in southern India and Sri Lanka. * *n* a member of this race; a family of languages spoken by the Dravidians.
draw *vti* (**drawing, drew,** *pp* **drawn**) to haul, to drag; to cause to go in a certain direction; to pull out; to attract; to delineate, to sketch; to receive (as a salary); to bend (a bow) by pulling back the string; to leave (a contest) undecided; to write up, to draft (a will); to produce or allow a current of air; to draw lots; to get information from; (*ship*) to require a certain depth to float; (*with* **on**) to approach; to use (a resource); to withdraw (money) from (an account, etc); to put on (clothes); (*with* **out**) to extract; to prolong, extend; to cause (someone) to speak freely;

to take (money) from an account; (*with* **up**) to bring or come to a standstill; to draft (a document); to straighten oneself; to form soldiers into an array. * *n* the act of drawing; (*inf*) an event that attracts customers, people; the drawing of lots; a drawn game.

drawback *n* a hindrance, handicap.

drawbridge *n* a bridge (eg over a moat) designed to be drawn up.

drawee *n* one on whom an order, bill of exchange, or a draft is drawn.

drawer *n* a person who draws; a person who draws a cheque; a sliding box-like compartment (as in a table, chest, or desk); (*pl*) knickers, underpants.

drawing *n* a figure, plan, or sketch drawn by using lines.

drawing pin *n* a thumbtack.

drawing room *n* a room where visitors are entertained, a living room.

drawl *vt* to speak slowly and with elongated vowel sounds. * *n* drawling speech.—**drawler** *n*.—**drawlingly** *adv*.

drawn[1] *see* **draw.**

drawn[2] *adj* looking strained because of tiredness or worry.

drawstring *n* a string or tape threaded through fabric which when pulled gathers it up or closes an opening (eg in a purse).

dray *n* a low, stoutly built cart used for heavy loads.

dread *n* great fear or apprehension. * *vt* to fear greatly.

dreadful *adj* full of dread; causing dread; extreme (*dreadful tiredness*); (*sl*) bad, disagreeable.—**dreadfully** *adv*—**dreadfulness** *n*.

dreadlocks *npl* hair worn in long matted strands by male Rastafarians.

dreadnought, dreadnaught *n* a battleship with main armament entirely of big guns; a heavy cloth; an overcoat of this cloth.

dream *n* a stream of thoughts and images experienced during sleep; a day-dreaming state, a reverie; an ambition; an ideal. * *vb* (**dreaming, dreamt** or **dreamed**) *vi* to have a dream during sleep; to fantasize. * *vt* to dream of; to imagine as a reality; (*with* **up**) to devise, invent.—**dreamer** *n*.

dreamy *adj* (**dreamier, dreamiest**) given to dreaming, unpractical; (*inf*) attractive, wonderful.—**dreamily** *adv*.—**dreaminess** *n*.

dreary *adj* (**drearier, dreariest**) dull; cheerless.—**drearily** *adv*.—**dreariness** *n*.

dredge[1] *n* a device for scooping up material from the bottom of a river, harbour, etc. * *vt* to widen, deepen, or clean with a dredge; to scoop up with a dredge; (*with* **up**) (*inf*) to discover, reveal, esp through effort.

dredge[2] *vt* to coat (food) by sprinkling.

dredger[1] *n* a vessel fitted with dredging equipment.

dredger[2] *n* a container with a perforated lid for sprinkling.

dreggy (**dreggier, dreggiest**) *adj* full of dregs; like dregs.

dregs *npl* solid impurities that settle on the bottom of a liquid; residue; (*inf*) a worthless person or thing.

drench *vt* to soak, saturate.

dress *n* clothing; a one-piece garment worn by women and girls comprising a top and skirt; a style or manner of clothing. * *vt* to put on or provide with clothing; to decorate; (*wound*) to wash and bandage; (*animal*) to groom; to arrange the hair; to prepare food (eg poultry, fish) for eating by cleaning, gutting, etc; (*with* **up**) to attire in best clothes; to improve the appearance of. * *vi* to put on clothes; to put on formal wear for an occasion; (*with* **up**) to put on fancy dress, etc.

dressage *n* the training of a horse in deportment and obedience.

dress circle *n* the first tier of seats in a theatre above the stalls.

dresser *n* a person who assists an actor to dress; a type of kitchen sideboard.

dressing *n* a sauce or stuffing for food; manure spread over the soil; dress or clothes; the bandage, ointment, etc applied to a wound.

dressing-down *n* a severe scolding.

dressing gown *n* a loose garment worn when one is partially clothed.

dressmaker *n* a person who makes clothes.—**dressmaking** *n*.

dress rehearsal *n* rehearsal in full costume.

dressy *adj* (**dressier, dressiest**) stylish; elaborate; showy.—**dressily** *adv*.—**dressiness** *n*.

drew *see* **draw.**

dribble *vi* to flow in a thin stream or small drips; to let saliva trickle from the mouth. * *vt* (*soccer, basketball, hockey*) to move (the ball) along little by little with the foot, hand, stick, etc. * *n* the act of dribbling; a thin stream of liquid.—**dribbler** *n*.

driblet *n* a small amount; a drop, trickle.

dried *see* **dry.**

drier *see* **dry, dryer.**

drift *n* a heap of snow, sand, etc deposited by the wind; natural course, tendency; the general meaning or intention (of what is said); the extent of deviation (of an aircraft, etc) from a course; an aimless course; the action or motion of drifting. * *vt* to cause to drift.* *vi* to be driven or carried along by water or air currents; to move along aimlessly; to be piled into heaps by the wind.

driftage *n* matter that drifts ashore; deviation from a course caused by air or sea currents.

drifter *n* a person who wanders aimlessly.

driftwood *n* wood cast ashore by tides.

drill[1] *n* an implement with a pointed end that bores holes; the training of soldiers, etc; repetitious exercises or training as a teaching method; (*inf*) correct procedure or routine. * *vt* to make a hole with a drill; to instruct or be instructed by drilling.

drill[2] *n* a machine for planting seeds in rows; a furrow in which seeds are planted; a row of seeds planted in this way.—*also vt*.

drilling platform *n* the fixed or mobile structure supporting the equipment and accommodation facilities, etc for drilling an offshore oil well.

drilling rig *n* the machinery required to drill an oil well.

drily *see* **dry.**

drink *vb* (**drinking, drank**, *pp* **drunk**) *vt* to swallow (a liquid); to take in, absorb; to join in a toast. * *vi* to consume alcoholic liquor, esp to excess. * *n* liquid to be drunk; alcoholic liquor; (*sl*) the sea.—**drinker** *n*.

drip *vti* (**dripping, dripped**) to fall or let fall in drops. * *n* a liquid that falls in drops; the sound of falling drops; (*med*) a device for administering a fluid slowly and continuously into a vein; (*inf*) a weak or ineffectual person.—**dripper** *n*.

drip-dry *adj* (*clothing*) drying easily and needing relatively little ironing.—*also vti*.

dripping *n* fat that drips from meat during roasting.

drive *vb* (**driving, drove**, *pp* **driven**) *vt* to urge, push or force onward; to direct the movement or course of; to convey in a vehicle; to carry through strongly; to impress forcefully; to propel (a ball) with a hard blow. * *vi* to be forced along; to be conveyed in a vehicle; to work, to strive (at). * *n* a trip in a vehicle; a stroke to drive a ball (in golf, etc); a driveway; a military attack; an intensive campaign; dynamic ability; the transmission of power to machinery.

drive-in *n* a cinema, restaurant, etc, where customers are served in their cars.—*also adj*.

drivel *n* nonsense. * *vi* (**drivelling, drivelled** *or* **driveling, driveled**) to talk nonsense.—**driveller, driveler** *n*.

driven *see* **drive.**

driver *n* one who or that which drives; a chauffeur; (*golf*) a wooden club used from the tee.

driveway *n* a road for vehicles, often on private property.

drizzle *n* fine light rain.—*also vi*.—**drizzly** *adj*.

drogue *n* a sea anchor; a small parachute that slows down or stabilizes something (as a jet aircraft); a funnel-shaped device that enables an aeroplane to be refuelled from a tanker plane while in flight; a buoy at the end of a harpoon line; a windsock.

droit *n* equity; a right of ownership, esp in land; custom; duty.

droll *adj* oddly amusing; whimsical.—**drollness** *n*.—**drolly** *adv*.

drollery *n* (*pl* **drolleries**) the quality of being droll; buffoonery; a droll act.

dromedary *n* (*pl* **dromedaries**) a one-humped camel.

drone *n* a male honey-bee; a lazy person; a deep humming sound; a monotonous speaker or speech; an aircraft piloted by remote control. * *vi* to make a monotonous humming sound; to speak in a monotonous manner.

drool *vi* to slaver, dribble; to show excessive enthusiasm for.

droop *vi* to bend or hang down; to become weak or faint. * *n* the act or an instance of drooping.

droopy *adj* (**droopier, droopiest**) drooping; tending to droop; (*sl*) tired, depressed.—**droopily** *adv*.—**droopiness** *n*.

drop kick *n* a kick made by dropping the ball onto the ground and kicking as it bounces.—**drop-kick** *vt*.

drop *n* a small amount of liquid in a roundish shape; something shaped like this, as a sweet; a tiny quantity; a sudden fall; the distance down; (*pl*) liquid medicine, etc dispensed in small drops. * *vb* (**dropping, dropped**) *vi* to fall in drops; to fall suddenly; to go lower, to sink; to come (in); (*with* **in**) to visit (with) informally; (*with* **out**) to abandon or reject (a course, society, etc). * *vt* to let fall, to cause to fall; to lower or cause to descend; to set down from a vehicle; to mention casually; to cause (the voice) to be less loud; to give up (as an idea).—**dropper** *n*.

droplet *n* a tiny drop (as of liquid).

dropout *n* a student who abandons a course of study; a person who rejects normal society.

droppings *npl* animal dung.

dropsy *n* an unnatural accumulation of serious fluid in any cavity of the body or its tissues.—**dropsical** *adj*.

droshky, drosky *n* (*pl* **droshkies, droskies**) a light four-wheeled open Russian carriage.

dross *n* a surface scum on molten metal; rubbish, waste matter.

drought *n* a long period of dry weather.—**droughty** *adj*.

drove[1] *see* **drive**.

drove[2] *n* a group of animals driven in a herd or flock, etc; a large moving crowd of people.

drover *n* a person whose occupation is to drive cattle.

drown *vti* to die or kill by suffocation in water or other liquid. * *vt* to flood; to drench; to become deeply immersed in some activity; to blot out (a sound) with a louder noise; to remove (sorrow, etc) with drink.

drowse *vi* to be nearly asleep.

drowsy *adj* (**drowsier, drowsiest**) sleepy; soporific; lethargic; inactive.—**drowsily** *adv*.—**drowsiness** *n*.

drub *vt* (**drubbing, drubbed**) to thrash; to defeat convincingly.

drudge *vi* to do boring or very menial work. * *n* a person who drudges, esp a servant.—**drudger** *n*.—**drudgingly** *adv*.

drudgery *n* (*pl* **drudgeries**) dull, boring work.

drug *n* any substance used in medicine; a narcotic. * *vt* (**drugging, drugged**) to administer drugs to; to stupefy.

drugget *n* a coarse woollen or cotton fabric; a rug made of this.

druggist *n* a pharmacist.

drugstore *n* a retail store selling medicines and other miscellaneous articles such as cosmetics, film, etc.

druid *n* (*often with cap*) a priest of the ancient inhabitants (probably Celtic) of Britain, Gaul and Germany; a member of a modern society reviving druidism.—**druidic, druidical** *adj*.

druidism *n* the beliefs, manners, rites and customs of the druids.

drum *n* a round percussion instrument, played by striking a membrane stretched across a hollow cylindrical frame; the sound of a drum; anything shaped like a drum, as a container for liquids. * *vb* (**drumming, drummed**) *vi* to play a drum; to beat or tap rhythmically. * *vt* (*with* **in**) to instil (knowledge) into a person by constant repetition; (*with* **up**) to summon as by drum; to create (business, etc) by concerted effort; to originate.

drumhead *n* the membrane stretched across the end of a drum.

drummer *n* a person who plays a drum; (*inf*) a travelling salesman.

drumstick *n* a stick for beating a drum; the lower part of a cooked leg of poultry.

drunk[1] *see* **drink**.

drunk[2] *adj* intoxicated with alcohol. * *n* a drunk person.

drunkard *n* an habitual drunk.

drunken *adj* intoxicated; caused by excessive drinking.—**drunkenly** *adv*.—**drunkenness** *n*.

drupe *n* a fleshy fruit with a stone, as a plum.—**drupaceous** *adj*.

drupelet *n* a small drupe in a compound fruit, eg. raspberry.

druse *n* a crust of crystals; a rock cavity lined with this.

Druse, Druze *n* a member of a fanatical politico-religious sect in Syria and Lebanon.

dry *adj* (**drier, driest**) free from water or liquid; thirsty; marked by a matter-of-fact, ironic or terse manner of expression; uninteresting, wearisome; (*bread*) eaten without butter, etc; (*wine*) not sweet; not selling alcohol. * *vti* (**drying, dried**) to make or become dry; (*with* **out**) to be treated for alcoholism or drug addiction.—**drily, dryly** *adv*.—**dryness** *n*.

dryad *n* (*pl* **dryads, dryades**) (*Greek myth*) a wood nymph.

dry-clean *vt* to clean with solvents as opposed to water.—**dry-cleaner** *n*.—**dry-cleaning** *n*.

dry dock *n* a dock that can be drained of water to make ship repairs easier.

dryer *n* a device for drying, as a tumble-drier; a clothes horse.—*also* **drier**.

dry ice *n* solid carbon dioxide.

dry rot *n* decay of timber caused by a fungus; any form of moral decay or corruption.

dry run *n* (*inf*) a rehearsal.

dry-salt *vt* to cure (meat, etc) by salting and drying.

drysalter *n* (*formerly*) a dealer in dyes, oils, etc.—**drysaltery** *n*.

DSC *abbr* = Distinguished Service Cross.

DSM *abbr* = Distinguished Service Medal.

DSO *abbr* = Distinguished Service Order.

dt, DT *abbr* = delirium tremens.

DTP *abbr* = desktop publishing.

dual *adj* double; consisting of two.

dual carriageway *n* a road with traffic travelling in oposite directions separated by a central reservation.—*also* **divided highway**.

dualism *n* a twofold division; (*philos*) the doctrine that the universe is based on two principles, eg good and evil, mind and matter.—**dualist** *n*.—**dualistic** *adj*.—**dualistically** *adv*.

duality *n* (*pl* **dualities**) the condition or quality of being two or in two parts, dualism; dichotomy.

dub[1] *vt* (**dubbing, dubbed**) to confer knighthood on; to nickname.

dub[2] *vt* (**dubbing, dubbed**) to replace the soundtrack of (a film), eg with one in a different language; to add sound effects or music to (a film, broadcast, etc); to transfer (a recording) to a new tape.

dubbin, dubbing *n* a grease for softening and waterproofing leather.

dubiety *n* (*pl* **dubieties**) doubtfulness, uncertainty; a matter of doubt.

dubious *adj* doubtful (about, of); uncertain as to the result; untrustworthy.—**dubiously** *adv*.—**dubiousness** *n*.

ducal *adj* of or pertaining to a duke, a dukedom or a duchy.—**ducally** *adv*.

ducat *n* a gold or silver coin formerly in use in Europe; (*pl*) (*sl*) money.

duce *n* a chief, a leader; (*with cap*) the title used by the Italian Fascist dictator, Benito Mussolini (1922–43).

duchess *n* the wife or widow of a duke; a woman having the same rank as a duke in her own right.

duchy *n* (*pl* **duchies**) the territory of a duke, a dukedom.

duck[1] *vt* to dip briefly in water; to lower the head suddenly, esp to avoid some object; to avoid, dodge. * *vi* to dip or dive; to move the head or body suddenly; to evade a duty, etc. * *n* a ducking movement.

duck[2] *n* (*pl* **ducks, duck**) a water bird related to geese and swans; the female of this bird; its flesh used as food.

duck[3] *n* a plain cotton cloth; (*pl*) trousers or light clothes made from this and worn in hot climates.

duckbill, duck-billed platypus *n* an Australian egg-laying furred mammal with webbed feet and a broad bill.—*also* **platypus**.

duckboard *n* a path of wooden slats laid over muddy or wet ground.

duckling *n* a young duck.

duckweed *n* a common floating freshwater plant.

ducky, duckie *adj* (**duckier, duckiest**) (*inf*) fine; satisfactory; cute. * *n* (*pl* **duckies**) (*inf*) a term of endearment, darling.

duct *n* a channel or pipe for fluids, electric cable, etc; a tube in the body for fluids to pass through.
ductile *adj* malleable; yielding.
dud *adj* (*sl*) worthless. * *n* (*sl*) anything worthless; an ineffectual person.
dude *n* a dandy; a city person on holiday in a ranch.
dudeen *n* a short clay tobacco pipe.
dudgeon *n* resentment, indignation; (*arch*) the hilt of a dagger.
due *adj* owed as a debt; immediately payable; fitting, appropriate; appointed or expected to do or arrive. * *adv* directly, exactly. * *n* something due or owed; (*pl*) fees.
duel *n* combat with weapons between two persons over a matter of honour, etc; conflict of any kind between two people, sides, ideas, etc. * *vi* (**duelling, duelled** *or* **dueling, dueled**) to fight in a duel.—**duellist, duelist** *n*.
duello *n* (*pl* **duellos**) the duelists' code.
duenna *n* an older woman acting as a chaperone of young women in Spanish or Portuguese families.
duet *n* a musical composition for two performers.—**duettist** *n*.
duffel, duffle *n* a coarse, heavy woollen cloth.
duffel bag, duffle bag *n* a large cylindrical drawstring bag for personal belongings.
duffel coat, duffle coat *n* a heavy, hooded overcoat, fastened with toggles.
duffer *n* an incompetent person, esp an elderly one.
dug *see* **dig**.
dugong *n* an aquatic herbivorous mammal resembling the seal and walrus; the sea cow.
dugout *n* a boat made from the hollowed out tree trunk; a rough underground shelter.
duiker *n* (*pl* **duikers, duiker**) a small South African antelope.
duke *n* the highest order of British nobility; the title of a ruler of a European duchy.
dukedom *n* a duchy; the rank, position or title of a duke.
dulcet *adj* sweet-sounding, melodious.—**dulcetly** *adv*.
dulcimer *n* a musical instrument with wire strings that are struck with a hammer; a folk-music instrument with usu three strings that are played by plucking (—*also* **dulcimore**).
dulia *n* the veneration paid to saints and angels as the servants of God.
dull *adj* not sharp or pointed; not bright or clear; stupid; boring; not active. * *vti* to make or become dull.—**dully** *adv*.—**dullness** *n*.
dullard *n* a slow-witted person.
dulse *n* a red edible seaweed found on rocks.
duly *adv* properly; suitably.
dumb *adj* not able to speak; silent; (*inf*) stupid.—**dumbly** *adv*.—**dumbness** *n*.
dumbbell *n* one of a pair of heavy weights used for muscular exercise; (*sl*) a fool.
dumbfound, dumfound *vti* to astonish, surprise.
dumbwaiter *n* a stand with revolving shelves for holding food; a revolving tray for holding food; a small elevator or lift for carrying food, etc, between floors.
dum-dum *n* (*sl*) a foolish person.
dumdum (bullet) *n* a soft-nosed, expanding bullet.
dumdum *n* (*sl*) a stupid person; a dummy.
dummy *n* (*pl* **dummies**) a figure of a person used to display clothes; (*sl*) a soother or pacifier for a baby; a stupid person; an imitation; (*bridge*) the exposed cards of the dealer's partner.
dump *vt* to drop or put down carelessly in a heap; to deposit as rubbish; to abandon or get rid of; to sell goods abroad at a price lower than the market price abroad; (*with* **on**) (*sl*) to censure strongly the words or actions of others. * *n* a place for refuse; a temporary store; (*inf*) a dirty, dilapidated place; (*pl*) (*inf*) despondency, low spirits.—**dumper** *n*.
dumpling *n* a rounded piece of dough cooked by boiling or steaming; a short, fat person.
dumpster *n* a large garbage can.
dumpy *adj* (**dumpier, dumpiest**) short and thick.—**dumpily** *adv*.—**dumpiness** *n*.
dun[1] *adj* (**dunner, dunnest**) greyish-brown.—**dunness** *n*.
dun[2] *vt* (**dunning, dunned**) to press persistently for payment of a debt.
dunce *n* a person who is stupid or slow to learn.
dunderhead *n* a stupid person, a dunce.—**dunderheaded** *adj*.
dune *n* a hill of sand piled up by the wind.
dung *n* excrement; manure; filth. * *vt* to spread with manure.—**dungy** *adj*.
dungaree *n* a coarse cotton cloth; (*pl*) overalls or trousers made from this.
dungeon *n* an underground cell for prisoners.
dunghill *n* a heap of dung.
dunk *vti* to dip (cake, etc) into liquid, eg coffee.
dunlin *n* a small red-backed sandpiper of northern regions.
dunnage *n* loose wood, etc, used to pack cargo or keep it out of bilge water in a ship's hold; baggage.
dunnite *n* a powerful explosive used esp in shells.
duo *n* (*pl* **duos, dui**) a pair of performers; (*inf*) two persons connected in some way.
duodecimal *adj* of twelve; proceeding by twelves. * *n* a twelfth; a system of computing by twelves.
duodecimo *n* (*pl* **duodecimos**) a book of sheets folded into twelve leaves; this book size.—*also* **twelvemo**.
duodenary *adj* duodecimal.
duodenum *n* (*pl* **duodena, duodenums**) the first part of the small intestine.—**duodenal** *adj*.
duologue *n* a play with two actors; a conversation between two people.
dup *vt* (**dupping, dupped**) (*arch*) to open.
dupe *n* a person who is cheated. * *vt* to deceive; to trick.—**dupable** *adj*.—**duper** *n*.—**dupery** *n*.
duple *adj* double; (*mus*) of two beats to the bar.
duplex *adj* having two parts, double. * *n* a flat or apartment on two floors.—**duplexity** *n*.
duplicate *adj* in pairs, double; identical; copied exactly from an original. * *n* one of a pair of identical things; a copy. * *vt* to make double; to make an exact copy of; to repeat.—**duplicable** *adj*.
duplication *n* the act of duplicating; a copy; multiplication by two.—**duplicative** *adj*.
duplicator *n* a machine for making copies, esp of a document.
duplicity *n* (*pl* **duplicities**) treachery; deception.—**duplicitous** *adj*.
durable *adj* enduring, resisting wear, etc.—**durability** *n*.—**durably** *adv*.
duralumin *n* a strong alloy of aluminium with copper, magnesium, manganese and silicon.
dura mater *n* the tough outer membrane that envelops the brain and spinal cord.
duramen *n* the inner heartwood of a tree.
durance *n* imprisonment.
duration *n* the time in which an event continues.
durbar *n* (*formerly*) a state levee or reception in India and Africa.
duress *n* compulsion by use of force or threat; unlawful constraint; imprisonment.
durian, durion *n* an oval fruit with a foul smell and a pleasant taste; the Asian tree that bears it.
during *prep* throughout the duration of; at a point in the course of.
durmast *n* a dark European oak yielding a tough wood.
durst *see* **dare**.
dusk *n* (the darker part of) twilight.
dusky *adj* (**duskier, duskiest**) having a dark colour.—**duskily** *adv*.—**duskiness** *n*.
dust *n* fine particles of solid matter. * *vt* to free from dust; to sprinkle with flour, sugar, etc.
dustbin *n* a container for household refuse.—*also* **garbage can, trash can**.
dust bowl *n* a drought area subject to dust storms.
dust cover *n* a dust jacket.
duster (coat), dustcoat *n* a coat for keeping off dust, worn esp by early motorists.
duster *n* a cloth for dusting; a device for dusting; a duster coat; a light housecoat.

dustman *n* (*pl* **dustmen**) a garbageman.
dust jacket *n* a paper cover for a book.
dust wrapper *n* a dust jacket.
dusty *adj* (**dustier, dustiest**) covered with dust.—**dustily** *adv*.—**dustiness** *n*.
Dutch *adj* pertaining to Holland, its people, or language. * *n* the Dutch language.
Dutch courage *n* courage obtained from alcohol; alcoholic drink.
Dutch elm disease *n* a fungal disease which withers the foliage of elm trees and eventually kills them.
Dutch oven *n* a metal box for cooking before an open fire.
Dutch treat *n* a meal, etc, where each pays for himself or herself.
Dutch uncle *n* a person with stern kindness.
duteous *adj* (*poet*) dutiful.—**duteously** *adv*.—**duteousness** *n*.
dutiable *adj* (*goods, etc*) subject to duty.—**dutiability** *n*.
dutiful *adj* performing one's duty; obedient.—**dutifully** *adv*.—**dutifulness** *n*.
duty *n* (*pl* **duties**) an obligation that must be performed for moral or legal reasons; respect for one's elders or superiors; actions and responsibilities arising from one's business, occupation, etc; a tax on goods or imports, etc.
duty-free *adj* free from tax or duty.
duumvir *n* (*pl* **duumvirs, duumviri**) in ancient Rome, either of two officers of high rank acting together in one capacity or public function; either member of a duumvirate.
duumvirate *n* a governing body of two; two such people.
duvet *n* a thick, soft quilt used instead of bedclothes.—*also* **continental quilt.**
dwarf *n* (*pl* **dwarfs, dwarves**) a person, animal or plant of abnormally small size. * *vt* to stunt; to cause to appear small.
dwarfish *adj* like a dwarf; very small.—**dwarfishness** *n*.
dwell *vi* (**dwelling, dwelt** *or* **dwelled**) to live (in a place); (*with* **on**) to focus the attention on; to think, talk, or write at length about.—**dweller** *n*.
dwelling *n* the house, etc where one lives, habitation.
dwindle *vi* to shrink, diminish; to become feeble.
Dy (*chem symbol*) dysprosium.
dyad *n* a pair; (*chem*) a bivalent atom, element, or radical.—**dyadic** *adj*.
dyarchy *see* **diarchy.**
dye *vt* (**dyeing, dyed**) to give a new colour to. * *n* a colouring substance, esp in solution; a colour or tint produced by dyeing.—**dyer** *n*.
dyeing *n* the process or work of giving colour to fabrics using dyes.
dyed-in-the-wool *adj* uncompromising in attitude or opinion.
dyestuff *n* material yielding a dye.
dying[1] *see* **die**[1].
dying[2] *adj* passing away from life; decaying physically; drawing to a close; expiring. * *n* death.
dyke[1] *see* **dike**[1].
dyke[2] *n* (*derog*) a lesbian.
dynamic *adj* relating to force that produces motion; (*person*) forceful, energetic.—**dynamically** *adv*.
dynamics *n* (*used as sing*) the branch of science that deals with forces and their effect on the motion of bodies.
dynamism *n* dynamic influence or power; (*philos*) the theory that the universe is constituted of forces.—**dynamist** *n*.—**dynamistic** *adj*.
dynamite *n* a powerful explosive; a potentially dangerous situation; (*inf*) an energetic person or thing. * *vt* to blow up with dynamite.—**dynamiter** *n*.
dynamo *n* (*pl* **dynamos**) a device that generates electric current.
dynamoelectric, dynamoelectrical *adj* of or denoting the production of electricity from mechanical energy or of mechanical energy from electricity.
dynamometer *n* an instrument for measuring energy expended.
dynast *n* a ruler, usu a hereditary one.
dynasty *n* (*pl* **dynasties**) a line of hereditary rulers or leaders of any powerful family or similar group.—**dynastic** *adj*.—**dynastically** *adv*.
dyne *n* a unit of force, causing in one gram an acceleration per second of one centimetre per second; the unit of force in the cgs system.
dys- *prefix* bad, unfavourable.
dysentery *n* painful inflammation of the large intestine with associated diarrhoea.—**dysenteric** *adj*.
dysergy *n* (*business*) the possibility that the merger of two companies will produce a combined operation of less productivity and efficiency, the opposite of synergy.
dysfunction *n* a failure in normal functioning.—**dysfunctional** *adj*.
dysgenic *adj* having a bad effect on the hereditary qualities of a race.
dysgenics *n* (*used as sing*) the study of the causes of reduction in quality of a race.
dyslexia *n* impaired ability in reading or spelling.—**dyslexic** *adj, n*.
dysmenorrhoea, dysmenorrhea *n* painful menstruation.—**dysmenorrhoeal, dysmenorrheal** *adj*.
dyspepsia *n* indigestion, esp chronic.
dyspeptic *adj* of or afflicted with indigestion. * *n* a dyspeptic sufferer.
dysphagia *n* difficulty in swallowing.—**dysphagic** *adj*.
dysphasia *n* a deficiency in the use or understanding of language.—**dysphasic** *adj*.
dysphoria *n* morbid restlessness, fidgets.—**dysphoric** *adj*.
dyspnoea, dyspnea *n* shortness of breath, difficulty in breathing.—**dyspnoeal, dyspneal, dyspneic, dyspnoeic** *adj*.
dysprosium *n* a soft metallic element used in lasers and magnetic alloys.
dystrophy *n* various hereditary disorders causing progressive weakening of the muscles (*muscular dystrophy*).—**dystrophic** *adj*.
dysuria *n* difficulty in passing urine.—**dysuric** *adj*.

E

E. *abbr* = east; eastern; Ecstacy.
E- *prefix* used to indicate a standard system (for packaging, weight, content, etc) within the European Community.
each *adj* every one of two or more.
eager *adj* enthusiastically desirous (of); keen (for); marked by impatient desire or interest.—**eagerly** *adv*.—**eagerness** *n*.
eager beaver *n* (*inf*) an exceptionally diligent person.
eagle *n* a bird of prey with keen eyes and powerful wings; (*golf*) a score of two strokes under par.
eagle-eyed *adj* having very sharp eyesight.
eagle owl *n* a type of large owl, also known as the great horned owl.
eaglet *n* a young eagle.
ear[1] *n* (the external part of) the organ of hearing; the sense or act of hearing; attention; something shaped like an ear.
ear[2] *n* the part of a cereal plant (eg corn, maize) that contains the seeds.
earache *n* a pain in the ear.
eardrum *n* the membrane within the ear that vibrates in response to sound waves.
eared *adj* having ears.
earing *n* (*naut*) a rope attaching the upper corner of a sail to a yard or stanchion.
earl *n* a member of the British nobility ranking between a marquis and a viscount.—**countess** *nf*.
earldom *n* the position or estate of an earl.
early *adj* (**earlier, earliest**) before the expected or normal time; of or occurring in the first part of a period or series; of or occurring in the distant past or near future.—*also adv*.—**earliness** *n*.
earmark *vt* to set aside for a specific use; to put an identification mark on. * *n* a distinguishing mark.
earn *vt* to gain (money, etc) by work or service; to acquire; to deserve; to earn interest (on money invested, etc).
earnest *adj* sincere in attitude or intention.—**earnestly** *adv*.—**earnestness** *n*.
earnings *npl* wages or profits; something earned.

earphone *n* a device held to or worn over the ear, through which sound is transmitted; a headphone.
earpiece *n* a telephone earphone.
earplug *n* a piece of wadding or wax inserted in the ear to prevent noise or water penetration.
earring *n* an ornament worn on the ear lobe.
earshot *n* hearing distance.
ear-splitting *adj* very loud.
earth *n* the world that we inhabit; solid ground, as opposed to sea; soil; the burrow of a badger, fox, etc; a connection between an electric device or circuit with the earth; (*inf*) a large amount of money. * *vt* to cover with or bury in the earth; to connect an electrical circuit or device to earth.
earthborn *adj* mortal.
earthbound *adj* confined to the earth; heading towards the earth.
earthen *adj* composed of earth; made of baked clay.
earthenware *n* pottery, etc made from baked clay.
earthly *adj* (**earthlier, earthliest**) of the earth; material, worldly.—**earthliness** *n*.
earthquake *n* a violent tremor of the earth's crust.
earth science *n* any of the sciences (eg geology) concerned with the nature and composition of the earth.
earthwards, earthward *adv* towards the earth.
earthwork *n* an excavation of earth; a fortification.
earthworm *n* any of various common worms that live in the soil.
earthy *adj* (**earthier, earthiest**) of or resembling earth; crude.—**earthiness** *n*.
earwax *n* cerumen, the brown wax found in the ear.
earwig *n* a small insect with a pincer-like appendage at the end of its body.
ease *n* freedom from pain, discomfort or disturbance; rest from effort or work; effortlessness; lack of inhibition or restraint, naturalness. * *vt* to relieve from pain, trouble, or anxiety; to relax, make less tight, release; to move carefully and gradually. * *vi* (*often with* **off**) to become less active, intense, or severe.
easeful *adj* restful.
easel *n* a supporting frame, esp one used by artists to support their canvases while painting.
easement *n* relief; something that gives ease or relief; (*law*) right of way over someone else's land.
easily *adv* with ease; by far; probably.
east *n* the direction of the sunrise; the compass point opposite west; (*with cap preceded by* **the**) the area of the world east of Europe. * *adj, adv* in, towards, or from the east.
Easter *n* the Christian festival observed on a Sunday in March or April in commemoration of the resurrection of Christ.
easterly *adj* situated towards or belonging to the east, coming from the east. * *n* (*pl* **easterlies**) a wind from the east.
eastern *adj* of or in the east.
easterner *n* someone from the east.
easternmost *adj* farthest to the east.
easting *n* the distance travelled by a vessel eastwards from a given meridian.
eastward *adj* towards the east.—**eastwards** *adv*.
easy *adj* (**easier, easiest**) free from pain, trouble, anxiety; not difficult or requiring much effort; (*manner*) relaxed; lenient; compliant; unhurried; (*inf*) open to all alternatives. * *adv* with ease.—**easiness** *n*.
easy chair *n* a comfortable chair.
easygoing *adj* placid, tolerant, relaxed.
eat *vt* (**eating, ate,** *pp* **eaten**) to take into the mouth, chew and swallow as food; to have a meal; to consume, to destroy bit by bit; (*also with* **into**) to corrode; (*inf*) to bother, cause anxiety to; (*with* **up**) to consume completely; (*inf*) to listen or absorb avidly; (*inf*) to preoccupy. * *vi* (*with* **out**) to eat away from home, esp in a restaurant. * *n* (*pl: inf*) food.—**eater** *n*.
eatable *adj* suitable for eating; fit to be eaten. * *n* (*pl*) food.
eau de Cologne *n* (*pl* **eaux de Cologne**) a perfume originally from Cologne.
eau de vie *n* brandy.
eaves *npl* the overhanging edge of a roof.
eavesdrop *vi* (**eavesdropping, eavesdropped**) to listen secretly to a private conversation.—**eavesdropper** *n*.
ebb *n* the flow of the tide out to sea; a decline. * *vi* (*tide water*) to flow back; to become lower, to decline.
ebon *n* (*poet*) ebony.
ebonite *n* a hard black rubber substance.
ebonize *vt* to make black by staining like ebony.
ebony *n* (*pl* **ebonies**) a hard heavy wood. * *adj* black as ebony.
ebracteate *adj* without bracts.
ebullient *adj* exuberant, enthusiastic; boiling.—**ebullience, ebulliency** *n*.—**ebulliently** *adv*.
ebullition *n* boiling; an outburst (of passion, feeling, etc).
EC *abbr* = European Community; East Central.
eccentric *adj* deviating from a usual or accepted pattern; unconventional in manner or appearance, odd; (*circles*) not concentric; off centre; not precisely circular. * *n* an eccentric person.—**eccentrically** *adv*.
eccentricity *n* (*pl* **eccentricities**) strangeness of behaviour; an eccentric or unusual habit.
ecclesiastic[1] *n* a member of the clergy.
ecclesiastic[2], **ecclesiastical** *adj* of or relating to the Christian Church or clergy.—**ecclesiastically** *adv*.
ecclesiasticism *n* excessive attachment to the forms, usages, organization and privileges of the Christian Church.
ecclesiology *n* the study of the Christian Church and its development; the study of church architecture and decoration.—**ecclesiological** *adj*.—**ecclesiologist** *n*.
ecdysis (*pl* **ecdyses**) *n* sloughing of skin, moulting.
ECG *abbr* = electrocardiogram.
echelon *n* a stepped formation of troops, ships, or aircraft; a level (of authority) in a hierarchy.
echidna *n* (*pl* **echidnas, echidnae**) an Australian nocturnal, toothless, spiny, egg-laying animal.
echinoderm *n* one of a class of animals which includes starfish and sea urchins.
echinus *n* (*pl* **echini**) a sea urchin.
echo *n* (*pl* **echoes**) a repetition of sound caused by the reflection of sound waves; imitation; the reflection of a radar signal by an object. * *vb* (**echoing, echoed**) *vi* to resound; to produce an echo. * *vt* to repeat; to imitate; to send back (a sound) by an echo.
echo chamber *n* a room with walls that reflect sound, used for making acoustic measurements and creating special sound effects.
echoic *adj* like an echo; imitative.
echolocation *n* finding unseen objects by means of reflected sound waves.
echo sounder *n* an instrument for determining the depth beneath a ship using sound waves.—**echo sounding** *n*.
éclair *n* a small oblong shell of choux pastry covered with chocolate and filled with cream.
eclampsia *n* (*med*) a serious condition occurring in the last three months of pregnancy, caused by toxins in the blood and causing convulsions.
éclat *n* success; applause; striking effect; social distinction.
eclectic *adj* selecting from or using various styles, ideas, methods, etc; composed of elements from a variety of sources. * *n* a person who adopts an eclectic method.—**eclectically** *adv*.—**eclecticism** *n*.
eclipse *n* the obscuring of the light of the sun or moon by the intervention of the other; a decline into obscurity, as from overshadowing by others. * *vt* to cause an eclipse of; to overshadow, darken; to surpass.—**eclipser** *n*.
ecliptic *n* the apparent path of the sun's motion relative to the stars.—**ecliptically** *adv*.
eclogue *n* a short, esp pastoral poem.
eco- *prefix* ecology; ecological.
ecology *n* (the study of) the relationships between living things and their environments.—**ecological** *adj*.—**ecologist** *n*.

econometrics *n* (*sing*) the application of mathematical and statistical methods in economics.
economic *adj* pertaining to economics or the economy; (*business, etc*) capable of producing a profit.
economical *adj* thrifty.—**economically** *adv*.
economics *n* (*sing*) the social science concerned with the production, consumption and distribution of goods and services; (*pl*) financial aspects.
economist *n* an expert in economics.
economize *vti* to spend money carefully; to save; to use prudently.—**economization** *n*.
economy *n* (*pl* **economies**) careful use of money and resources to minimize waste; an instance of this; the management of the finances and resources, etc of a business, industry or organization; the economic system of a country.
ecosphere *n* the parts of the universe where life can exist.
ecosystem *n (ecology)* a system comprising a community of living organisms and its surroundings.
ecru *n* beige.
ecstasy *n* (*pl* **ecstasies**) intense joy; (*sl: often with cap*) the synthetic amphetamine-based drug MDMA, which reduces social and sexual inhibitions.—**ecstatic** *adj*.—**ecstatically** *adv*.
ECT *abbr* = electroconvulsive therapy.
ecto-, ect- *prefix* outside.
ectoderm *n* the outer layer of an embryo or skin.
ectomorph *n* a person with a lightly built physique.—**ectomorphic** *adj*.—**ectomorphy** *n*.
-ectomy *n suffix* denoting surgical removal of a part.
ectopic *adj* (*anat*) in an abnormal position; (*fertilized egg*) developing abnormally outside the uterus.
ectoplasm *n* the outer layer of the cytoplasm of a cell; a substance supposedly exuded from the body of spiritualist mediums during trances.—**ectoplasmic** *adj*.
ectype *n* a reproduction or imitation of an original design.
ECU *abbr* = European currency unit.
ecumenical *adj* of the whole Christian Church; seeking Christian unity worldwide.—**ecumenicalism, ecumenicism** *n*.—**ecumenically** *adv*.
eczema *n* inflammation of the skin causing itching and the formation of scaly red patches.—**eczematous** *adj*.
edacious *adj* gluttonous, greedy.—**edacity** *n*.
Edam *n* a mild-flavoured round Dutch cheese, usu with a red waxy rind.
eddy *n* (*pl* **eddies**) a swiftly revolving current of air, water, fog, etc. * *vi* (**eddying, eddied**) to move round and round.
edelweiss *n* a small white-flowered alpine herb.
edema *see* **oedema.**
Eden *n* (*Bible*) the garden where Adam and Eve lived after the creation; a paradise.
edentate *adj* (*zool*) toothless.
edge *n* the border, brink, verge, margin; the sharp cutting side of a blade; sharpness, keenness; force, effectiveness. * *vt* to supply an edge or border to; to move gradually.—**edger** *n*.
edgeways, edgewise *adv* with the edge forwards; sideways.
edging *n* any border for decoration or strengthening.
edgy *adj* (**edgier, edgiest**) irritable.—**edgily** *adv*.—**edginess** *n*.
edible *adj* fit or safe to eat.—**edibility, edibleness** *n*.
edict *n* a decree; a proclamation.—**edictal** *adj*.
edifice *n* a substantial building; any large or complex organization or institution.—**edificial** *adj*.
edify *vt* (**edifying, edified**) to improve the moral character or mind of (a person).—**edification** *n*.—**edifier** *n*.—**edifyingly** *adv*.
edile *see* **aedile.**
edit *vt* to prepare (text) for publication by checking facts, grammar, style, etc; to be in charge of a publication; (*cinema*) to prepare a final version of a film by selection and arrangement of photographed sequences.
edition *n* a whole number of copies of a book, etc printed at a time; the form of a particular publication.
editio princeps (*pl* **editiones principes**) *n* the first printed edition of a book.
editor *n* a person in charge of a newspaper or other publication; a person who edits written material for publication; one who prepares the final version of a film; a person in overall charge of the form and content of a radio or television programme.—**editorship** *n*.
editorial *adj* of or produced by an editor.* *n* an article expressing the opinions of the editor or publishers of a newspaper or magazine.—**editorialist** *n*.—**editorially** *adv*.
EDP *abbr* = electronic data processing.
educable, educatable *adj* able to be educated.
educate *vt* to train the mind, to teach; to provide schooling for.—**educator** *n*.
education *n* the process of learning and training; instruction as imparted in schools, colleges and universities; a course or type of instruction; the theory and practice of teaching.—**educational** *adj*.—**educationally** *adv*.
educationalist, educationist *n* an expert in education.
educative *adj* educating.
educe *vt* to elicit (information, etc); to infer.—**educible** *adj*.
edulcorate *vt* to free from acids and other impurities by washing.—**edulcoration** *n*.
EEC *abbr* = European Economic Community (now European Community).
EEG *abbr* = electroencephalogram.
eel *n* a snake-like fish.
eelpout *n* a type of freshwater fish, found in Europe, North America and Asia; another name for the burbot.
e'en *n* (*poet*) evening.
e'er *adv* (*poet*) ever.
eerie *adj* (**eerier, eeriest**) causing fear; weird.—**eerily** *adv*.—**eeriness** *n*.
efface *vt* to rub out, obliterate; to make (oneself) humble or inconspicuous.—**effaceable** *adj*.—**effacement** *n*.—**effacer** *n*.
effect *n* the result of a cause or action by some agent; the power to produce some result; the fundamental meaning; an impression on the senses; an operative condition; (*pl*) personal belongings; (*pl: theatre, cinema*) sounds, lighting, etc to accompany a production. * *vt* to bring about, accomplish.—**effecter** *n*.—**effectible** *adj*.
effective *adj* producing a specified effect; forceful, striking in impression; actual, real; operative.—**effectively** *adv*.—**effectiveness** *n*.
effectual *adj* able to produce the desired effect.—**effectuality, effectualness** *n*.—**effectually** *adv*.
effectuate *vt* to make happen.—**effectuation** *n*.
effeminate *adj* (*man*) displaying what are regarded as feminine qualities.—**effeminacy, effeminateness** *n*.
effendi (*pl* **effendis**) *n* a Turkish title of respect, equivalent to sir or Mr.
efferent *adj* (*anat*) conveying or discharging outwards.
effervesce *vt* (*liquid*) to froth and hiss as bubbles of gas escape; to be exhilarated.—**effervescence** *n*.—**effervescent** *adj*.—**effervescible** *adj*.
effete *adj* decadent, weak.—**effeteness** *n*.
efficacious *adj* achieving the desired result.—**efficacy, efficaciousness** *n*.
efficient *adj* achieving results without waste of time or effort; competent.—**efficiently** *adv*.—**efficiency** *n* (*pl* **efficiencies**).
effigy *n* (*pl* **effigies**) a sculpture or portrait; a crude figure of a person, esp for exposure to public contempt and ridicule.
effloresce *vi* to blossom; (*chem*) to turn to powder when exposed to air, to crystallize; to become encrusted with crystals as a result of loss of water.—**efflorescence** *n*.—**efflorescent** *adj*.
effluence, efflux *n* something that flows out.
effluent *adj* flowing out. * *n* that which flows out, esp sewage.
effluvium *n* (*pl* **effluvia, effluviums**) an offensive vapour or smell.—**effluvial** *adj*.
effort *n* exertion; an attempt, try; a product of great exertion.—**effortful** *adj*.
effortless *adj* done with little effort, or seemingly so.—**effortlessly** *adv*.—**effortlessness** *n*.
effrontery *n* (*pl* **effronteries**) impudent boldness, insolence.

effulgent *adj* radiant, brilliant.—**effulgence** *n.*
effuse *vt* (*liquid, words*) to flow or pour out.
effusion *n* a pouring out; an unrestrained outpouring, as of emotion; something poured out.
effusive *adj* gushing, emotionally unrestrained; demonstrative.—**effusiveness** *n.*
eft *n* a newt.
e.g., eg, eg. *abbr* = for example (Latin *exempli gratia*).
egad *interj* (*arch*) an exclamation of surprise, pleasure or admiration.
egalitarian *adj* upholding the principle of equal rights for all.—*also n.*—**egalitarianism** *n.*
egest *vt* to excrete.—**egestion** *n.*
egesta *npl* excrement.
egg[1] *n* the oval hard-shelled reproductive cell laid by birds, reptiles and fish; the egg of the domestic poultry used as food; ovum.—**eggy** *adj.*
egg[2] *vt* (*with* **on**) to incite (someone to do something).
egger *n* a type of large moth.
egghead *n* (*inf*) an intellectual.
eggnog *n* a drink made from egg, beaten up with hot milk, sugar and brandy.
eggplant *see* **aubergine.**
eggshell *n* the hard outer covering of an egg. * *adj* fragile; (*paint*) having a slight sheen.
egis *see* **aegis.**
eglantine *n* the sweetbrier; the wild rose.
ego *n* (*pl* **egos**) the self; self-image, conceit.
egocentric *adj* self-centred.—**egocentricity** *n.*
egoism *n* self-concern; self-centredness.—**egoist** *n.*—**egoistic, egoistical** *adj.*—**egoistically** *adv.*
egotism *n* excessive reference to oneself; conceit.—**egotist** *n.*—**egotistic, egotistical** *adj.*—**egotistically** *adv.*
ego trip *n* (*inf*) an activity undertaken to boost one's own self-esteem or importance in the eyes of others.—**ego-trip** *vi.*
egregious *adj* outstandingly bad.—**egregiousness** *n.*
egress *n* the way out, exit.
egression *n* the act of going out or emerging; egress.
egret *n* a type of heron.
Egyptology *n* the study of Egyptian antiquities and hieroglyphics.—**Egyptologist** *n.*
eh *interj* an exclamation of inquiry or surprise.
eider *n* a large marine duck, the down of which has commercial value as a filling for quilts etc.
eiderdown *n* the down of the eider duck used for stuffing quilts, etc; a thick quilt with a soft filling.
eidolon *n* (*pl* **eidolons, eidola**) *n* an apparition or phantom.
eight *n, adj* one more than seven; the symbol for this (8, VIII, viii); (the crew of) an eight-oared rowing boat.
eighteen *n, adj* one more than seventeen; the symbol for this (18, XVIII, xviii).—**eighteenth** *adj.*
eighteenmo (*pl* **eighteenmos**) *n* a book whose sheets are folded into eighteen leaves.
eightfold *adj, adv* consisting of eight units; being eight times as great or many.
eighth *adj, n* one after seventh; one of eight equal parts.
eighty *n* (*pl* **eighties**) eight times ten; the symbol for this (80, LXXX, lxxx); (*pl*) the numbers from 80 to 89.—**eightieth** *adj, n.*
einsteinium *n* an artificial radioactive element.
eisteddfod *n* (*pl* **eisteddfods, eisteddfodau**) a Welsh competitive festival of the arts, esp singing.—**eisteddodic** *adj.*
either *adj, n* the one or the other of two; each of two. * *conj* correlative to *or.*
ejaculate *vti* to emit a fluid (as semen); to exclaim.—**ejaculation** *n.*—**ejaculator** *n.*—**ejaculatory** *adj.*
eject *vt* to turn out, to expel by force. * *vi* to escape from an aircraft or spacecraft using an ejector seat.—**ejection** *n.*—**ejector** *n.*
ejecta *npl* matter discharged by an erupting volcano.
ejector seat *n* an escape seat, esp in combat aircraft, that can be ejected with its occupant in an emergency by means of explosive bolts.
eke *vt* (*with* **out**) to supplement; to use (a supply) frugally; to make (a living) with difficulty.
elaborate *adj* highly detailed; planned with care and exactness. * *vt* to work out or explain in detail.—**elaborateness** *n.*—**elaboration** *n.*—**elaborative** *adj.*—**elaborator** *n.*
élan *n* verve, spirit.
eland *n* an African antelope with spirally twisted horns.
elapse *vi* (*time*) to pass by.
elasmobranch *n* (*pl* **elasmobranchs**) a member of a class of fish that includes sharks and skates.
elastic *adj* returning to the original size and shape if stretched or squeezed; springy; adaptable. * *n* fabric, tape, etc incorporating elastic thread.—**elastically** *adv.*—**elasticity** *n.*
elasticated *adj* made elastic by the use of elastic thread.
elate *vt* to fill with happiness or pride.—**elated** *adj.*—**elatedness** *n.*—**elation** *n.*
elbow *n* the joint between the forearm and upper arm; the part of a piece of clothing covering this; any sharp turn or bend, as in a pipe. * *vt* to shove away rudely with the elbow; to jostle.
elbow grease *n* (*inf*) effort, hard work.
elbowroom *n* space to move, scope.
elder[1] *n* a tree or shrub with flat clusters of white or pink flowers.
elder[2] *n* an older person; an office bearer in certain churches.—**eldership** *n.*
elderberry *n* (*pl* **elderberries**) (the fruit of) an elder.
elderly *adj* quite old.—**elderliness** *n.*
eldest *n* oldest, first born.
El Dorado, eldorado *n* an imaginary land of vast wealth.
eldritch, eldrich *adj* (*Scot*) weird; hideous.
elecampane *n* a plant of the aster family, from the roots of which a tonic medicine is made.
elect *vti* to choose by voting; to make a selection (of); to make a decision on. * *adj* chosen for an office but not installed.
election *n* the public choice of a person for office, esp a politician.
electioneer *vi* to work on behalf of a candidate for election.—**electioneering** *n.*
elective *adj* pertaining to, dependant on, or exerting the power of, choice.—**electivity, electiveness** *n.*
elector *n* a person who has a vote at an election.—**electorship** *n.*
electoral *adj* of elections or electors.
electorate *n* the whole body of qualified electors.
electric *adj* of, producing or worked by electricity; exciting, thrilling. * *npl* electric fittings.
electrical *adj* of or relating to electricity.—**electrically** *adv.*
electric chair *n* a chair used in executing condemned criminals by electrocution.
electric eel *n* an eel-like fish capable of giving an electric shock.
electric eye *n* a photoelectric cell.
electric guitar *n* a guitar that is electronically amplified.
electrician *n* a person who installs and repairs electrical devices.
electricity *n* a form of energy comprising certain charged particles, such as electrons and protons; an electric current.
electrify *vt* (**electrifying, electrified**) to charge with electricity; to modify or equip for the use of electric power; to astonish or excite.—**electrifiable** *adj.*—**electrification** *n.*—**electrifier** *n.*
electro-, electr- *prefix* of or by electricity.
electrocardiogram *n* the tracing made by an electrocardiograph.
electrocardiograph *n* a device for recording the electrical activity of the heart.—**electrocardiographic, electrocardiographical** *adj.*—**electrocardiography** *n.*
electrochemistry *n* the area of chemistry dealing with chemical changes caused by electricity.—**electrochemical** *adj.*—**electrochemist** *n.*

electroconvulsive therapy *n* treatment of certain types of mental illness by passing an electric current through the brain.

electrocute *vt* to kill or execute by electricity.—**electrocution** *n*.

electrode *n* a conductor through which an electric current enters or leaves an electrolyte, gas discharge tube or thermionic valve.

electrodynamics *n* (*sing*) the area of physics dealing with electric currents.—**electrodynamic, electrodynamical** *adj*.

electroencephalogram *n* the tracing produced by an electroencephalograph.

electroencephalograph *n* a device for recording the electrical activity of the brain.—**electro-encephalographic** *adj*.—**electroencephalographically** *adv*.—**electroencephalography** *n*.

electrokinetics *n* (*sing*) the area of physics dealing with electricity in motion.—**electrokinetic** *adj*.

electrolysis *n* the passage of an electric current through an electrolyte to effect chemical change; the destruction of living tissue, esp hair roots, by the use of an electric current

electrolyte *n* a solution that conducts electricity.

electrolyze *vt* to cause to undergo electrolysis.—**electrolyzation** *n*.—**electrolyzer** *n*.

electromagnet *n* a metal core rendered magnetic by the passage of an electric current through a surrounding coil.

electromagnetic *adj* pertaining to, or produced by, electromagnetism.—**electromagnetically** *adv*.

electromagnetism *n* magnetism produced by an electric current; the area of science dealing with the relations between electricity and magnetism.

electrometallurgy *n* metallurgy using a slow electric current to precipitate certain metals from their solutions, or to separate metals from their ores.—**electrometallurgical** *adj*.—**electrometallurgist** *n*.

electrometer *n* an instrument for measuring electricity.—**electrometric, electrometrical** *adj*.—**electrometry** *n*.

electromotive *adj* producing an electric current.

electromotive force *n* a source of energy producing an electric current; the amount of energy drawn from such a source per unit current of electricity passing through it, measured in volts.

electron *n* a negatively charged elementary particle that forms the part of the atom outside the nucleus.

electronegative *adj* with a negative electrical charge.

electronic *adj* of or worked by streams of electrons flowing through semiconductor devices, vacuum or gas; of or concerned with electrons or electronics.—**electronically** *adv*.

electronic mail *n* messages, etc, sent and received via computer terminals.

electronic publishing *n* the publication of information on CD-ROM, magnetic disks, on-line databases, etc, for access by computer.

electronics *n* (*sing*) the study, development and application of electronic devices; (*pl*) electronic circuits.

electron microscope *n* a powerful microscope that uses a stream of electrons instead of light to produce magnified images.

electronvolt *n* a unit of energy equivalent to the energy gained by an electron that has been accelerated through a potential difference of one volt.

electrophorus *n* (*pl* **electrophori**) an instrument for generating static electricity by induction.

electroplate *vt* to plate or cover with metal (eg silver) by electrolysis. * *n* electroplated objects.—**electroplater** *n*.

electropositive *adj* with a positive electrical charge.

electroscope *n* an instrument for showing the presence or quality of electricity.—**electroscopic** *adj*.

electrostatics *n* (*sing*) the branch of physics concerned with static electric charges.—**electrostatic** *adj*.—**electrostatically** *adv*.

electrotherapeutics *n* (*sing*) the area of medicine dealing with the use of electrotherapy.

electrotherapy *n* the treatment of disease using electricity.—**electrotherapist** *n*.

electrotype *n* (*print*) a facsimile made by covering a mould or plate of the original with a coating of copper or nickel. * *vt* to make a copy in this way.—**electrotyper** *n*.

electrum *n* an alloy of gold and silver.

electuary *n* (*pl* **electuaries**) a medicinal drug mixed with honey or syrup.

eleemosynary *adj* dependent on charity; (*money*) given as charity.

elegant *adj* graceful; refined; dignified and tasteful in manner and appearance.—**elegance, elegancy** *n*.—**elegantly** *adv*.

elegiac *adj* characteristic of elegy; mournful.

elegize *vt* to write an elegy about.—**elegist** *n*.

elegy *n* (*pl* **elegies**) a slow mournful song or poem.

element *n* a constituent part; any of the 105 known substances composed of atoms with the same number of protons in their nuclei; a favourable environment for a plant or animal; a wire that produces heat in an electric cooker, kettle, etc; any of the four substances (earth, air, fire, water) that in ancient and medieval thought were believed to constitute the universe; (*pl*) atmospheric conditions (wind, rain, etc); (*pl*) the basic principles, rudiments.

elemental *adj* of elements or primitive natural forces.—**elementally** *adv*.

elementary *adj* concerned with the basic principles of a subject.—**elementariness** *n*.

elementary particle *n* any of the subatomic particles, such as electrons, protons and neutrons, not made up of other particles.

elemi *n* (*pl* **elemis**) a resin used in medicines and varnishes.

elenchus *n* (*pl* **elenchi**) (*logic*) refutation of an argument.—**elenctic** *adj*.

elephant *n* (*pl* **elephants, elephant**) a large heavy mammal with a long trunk, thick skin, and ivory tusks.—**elephantoid** *adj*.

elephantiasis *n* (*pl* **elephantiases**) a disease in which the limbs or scrotum become enormously enlarged.—**elephantiasic** *adj*.

elephantine *adj* of or like elephants; very big or clumsy.

elevate *vt* to lift up; to raise in rank; to improve in intellectual or moral stature.

elevated *adj* raised; (*fig*) inflated; (*inf*) tipsy.

elevation *n* a raised place; the height above the earth's surface or above sea level; the angle to which a gun is aimed above the horizon; a drawing that shows the front, rear, or side view of something.

elevator *n* a cage or platform for moving something from one level to another; a moveable surface on the tailplane of an aircraft to produce motion up and down; a lift; a building for storing grain.

eleven *adj, n* one more than ten; the symbol for this (11, XI, xi); (*soccer, etc*) a team of eleven players.—**eleventh** *adj, n*.

elf *n* (*pl* **elves**) a mischievous fairy.—**elfin** *adj*.—**elfish, elvish** *adj*.

elflock *n* an intricately twisted lock of hair.

elicit *vt* to draw out (information, etc).—**elicitable** *adj*.—**elicitation** *n*.—**elicitor** *n*.

elide *vt* (*linguistics*) to cut off a syllable or vowel.

eligible *adj* suitable to be chosen, legally qualified; desirable, esp as a marriage partner.—**eligibility** *n*.—**eligibly** *adv*.

eliminate *vt* to expel, get rid of; to eradicate completely; (*sl*) to kill; to exclude (eg a competitor) from a competition, usu by defeat.—**eliminable** *adj*.—**elimination** *n*.—**eliminative, eliminatory** *adj*.—**eliminator** *n*.

elision *n* (*linguistics*) the cutting off of a syllable or vowel.

elite, élite *n* a superior group; (*typewriting*) a letter size having twelve characters to the inch.

elitism *n* leadership or rule by an elite; advocacy of such a system.—**elitist** *n*.

elixir *n* (*alchemy*) a substance thought to have the power of transmuting base metals into gold, or of conferring everlasting life; any medicine claimed as a cure-all; a sweet syrup containing a medicine.

Elizabethan *adj* pertaining to Queen Elizabeth I of England and her reign (1558–1603), esp its architecture and literature; pertaining to Queen Elizabeth II of Great Britain and her reign (1952–). * *n* a person alive in the reign of Elizabeth I.

elk *n* (*pl* **elks, elk**) the largest existing deer of Europe and Asia.

ell *n* an old measure of length used for cloth, based on the length of a man's arm, approximately equal to 45 inches (1.15 metres).

ellipse *n* (*geom*) a closed plane figure formed by the plane section of a right-angled cone; a flattened circle.

ellipsis *n* (*pl* **ellipses**) the omission of words needed to complete the grammatical construction of a sentence; the mark (. . .) used to indicate such omission.

ellipsoid *n* (*geom*) an elliptical spheroid; an oval.—**ellipsoidal** *adj*.

elliptic, elliptical *adj* of or like an ellipse; having a part understood.—**elliptically** *adv*.

ellipticity *n* (*geom*) the extent of deviation of an oval from a circle or sphere.

elm *n* a tall deciduous shade tree with spreading branches and broad top; its hard heavy wood.

elocution *n* skill in public speaking.—**elocutionary** *adj*.—**elocutionist** *n*.

elongate *vti* to make or become longer.—**elongation** *n*.

elope *vi* to run away secretly with a lover, esp to get married.—**elopement** *n*.—**eloper** *n*.

eloquence *n* skill in the use of words; speaking with fluency, power or persuasiveness.

eloquent *adj* (*speaking, writing, etc*) fluent and powerful.

else *adv* besides; otherwise.

elsewhere *adv* in another place.

elucidate *vt* to make clear, to explain.—**elucidation** *n*.—**elucidative, elucidatory** *adj*.—**elucidator** *n*.

elude *vt* to avoid stealthily; to escape the understanding or memory of a person.—**eluder** *n*.—**elusion** *n*.

elusive *adj* escaping; baffling; solitary, difficult to contact.—**elusiveness** *n*.

elver *n* a young eel.

elves, elvish *see* **elf**.

Elysian *adj* of or resembling Elysium; paradisiacal, blissful.

Elysium *n* the ancient Greek paradise; a condition of perfect happiness.

elytron, elytrum *n* (*pl* **elytra**) one of the hard wing cases of a beetle.—**elytroid, elytrous** *adj*.

em *n* (*print*) a measure of width, equal to one sixth of an inch (approx 4 mm).

emaciate *vti* to make or become very thin and weak.—**emaciated** *adj*.—**emaciation** *n*.

emanate *vi* to issue from a source.—**emanative** *adj*.—**emanator** *n*.—**emanatory** *adj*.

emanation *n* something coming from or caused by something else.—**emanational** *adj*.

emancipate *vt* to liberate, esp from bondage or slavery.—**emancipative** *adj*.—**emancipator** *n*.—**emancipatory** *adj*.

emancipation *n* the act of freeing; freedom, liberation.—**emancipationist** *n*.

emarginate, emarginated *adj* (*leaf*) notched at the edges or tip.—**emargination** *n*.

emasculate *vt* to castrate; to deprive of vigour, strength, etc.—**emasculation** *n*.—**emasculative, emasculatory** *adj*.—**emasculator** *n*.

embalm *vt* to preserve (a dead body) with drugs, chemicals, etc.—**embalmer** *n*.—**embalmment** *n*.

embank *vt* to enclose or protect with an embankment.

embankment *n* an earth or stone mound made to hold back water or to carry a roadway.

embargo *n* (*pl* **embargoes**) an order of a government forbidding ships to enter or leave its ports; any ban or restriction on commerce by law; a prohibition, ban. * *vt* (**embargoing, embargoed**) to lay an embargo on; to requisition.

embark *vti* to put or go on board a ship or aircraft to begin a journey; to make a start in any activity or enterprise.—**embarkation** *n*.—**embarkment** *n*.

embarrass *vt* to make (a person) feel confused, uncomfortable or disconcerted.—**embarrassing** *adj*.—**embarrassment** *n*.

embassy *n* (*pl* **embassies**) a person or group sent to a foreign government as ambassadors; the official residence of an ambassador.

embattle *vt* to arrange troops for battle; to prepare for battle.—**embattled** *adj*.

embay *vt* to bring or drive a ship into a bay.

embed *vt* (**embedding, embedded**) to fix firmly in surrounding matter.—**embedment** *n*.

embellish *vt* to decorate, to adorn.—**embellisher** *n*.—**embellishment** *n*.

ember *n* a piece of glowing coal or wood in a fire; (*pl*) the smouldering remains of a fire.

embezzle *vt* to steal (money, securities, etc entrusted to one's care).—**embezzlement** *n*.—**embezzler** *n*.

embitter *vt* to cause to feel bitter.—**embitterment** *n*.

emblazon *vt* to make bright with colour; to ornament with heraldic devices.—**emblazonment** *n*.

emblazonry *n* heraldic decoration, blazonry.

emblem *n* a symbol; a figure adopted and used as an identifying mark.

emblematic, emblematical *adj* of emblems; symbolic.—**emblematically** *adv*.

emblements *npl* (*law*) the annual crops produced by the labour of the cultivator; the profit from these crops.

embody *vt* (**embodying, embodied**) to express in definite form; to incorporate or include in a single book, law, system, etc.—**embodiment** *n*.

embolden *vt* to inspire with courage; to make bold.

embolism *n* the obstruction of a blood vessel by a blood clot, air bubble, etc.—**embolismic** *adj*.

embolus *n* (*pl* **emboli**) material obstructing a blood vessel, eg a blood clot or air bubble.

embonpoint *n* plumpness.

emboss *vt* to ornament with a raised design.—**embosser** *n*.—**embossment** *n*.

embouchure *n* the mouth of a river; (*mus*) the mouthpiece of a wind instrument; the correct positioning of the mouth when playing a wind instrument.

embowel *vt* (**embowelling, embowelled** *or* **emboweling, emboweled**) (*arch*) to remove the intestines from, disembowel; to embed, to bury.

embower *vt* (*arch*) to cover with, or as with, a bower.

embrace *vt* to take and hold tightly in the arms as a sign of affection; to accept eagerly (eg an opportunity); to adopt (eg a religious faith); to include. * *n* the act of embracing, a hug.—**embraceable** *adj*.—**embracement** *n*.

embracer *n* one who embraces; (*law*) one who attempts to influence a jury corruptly.

embracery *n* (*law*) the act of attempting to corrupt or influence a jury.

embranchment *n* the act of branching out.

embrasure *n* an opening in a wall or parapet from which to fire guns; a window or door having its sides slanted on the inside.

embrocate *vt* to rub a diseased or injured part of the body with a lotion.

embrocation *n* a liniment for applying to, or rubbing, an injured part of the body.

embroider *vt* to ornament with decorative stitches; to embellish (eg a story).—**embroiderer** *n*.

embroidery *n* (*pl* **embroideries**) decorative needlework; elaboration or exaggeration (of a story, etc).

embroil *vt* to involve (a person) in a conflict, argument, or problem.—**embroiler** *n*.—**embroilment** *n*.

embryo *n* (*pl* **embryos**) an animal during the period of its growth from a fertilized egg up to the third month; a human product of conception up to about the second month of growth; a thing in a rudimentary state.—**embryoid** *adj*.

embryology *n* the scientific study of embryos.—**embryological, embryologic** *adj*.—**embryologist** *n*.

embryonic, embryonal *adj* immature, existing at an early stage.—**embryonically** *adv*.

emend *vt* to correct mistakes in written material.—**emendable** *adj*.—**emendation** *n*.

emerald *n* a rich green gemstone; its colour.

emerge *vi* to appear up out of, to come into view; to be revealed as the result of investigation.—**emergence** *n*.—**emergent** *adj*.

emergency *n* (*pl* **emergencies**) an unforeseen situation demanding immediate action; a serious medical condition requiring instant treatment.

emeritus *adj* retired but still holding one's title or rank.—*also n*.
emersed *adj* (*bot*) rising out of water.
emersion *n* the act of emerging.
emery *n* a hard granular mineral used for grinding and polishing; a hard abrasive powder.
emery board *n* a nailfile made from cardboard covered with powdered emery.
emery paper *n* a stiff paper covered with powdered emery.
emetic *n* a medicine that induces vomiting.—*also adj*.—**emetically** *adv*.
emf, EMF *abbr* = electromotive force.
emigrant *n* a person who emigrates.
emigrate *vi* to leave one's country for residence in another.—**emigration** *n*.
émigré *n* an emigrant, usually someone forced to emigrate.
eminence, eminency *n* (*pl* **eminences, eminencies**) high rank or position; a person of high rank or attainments; (*with cap*) the title for a cardinal of the RC Church; a raised piece of ground, a high place.
eminent *adj* famous; conspicuous; distinguished.—**eminently** *adv*.
emir *n* a ruler in parts of Africa and Asia.
emirate *n* the territory governed by an emir.
emissary *n* (*pl* **emissaries**) a person sent on a mission on behalf of another, esp a government.
emit *vt* (**emitting, emitted**) to send out (light, heat, etc); to put into circulation; to express, to utter.—**emission** *n*.—**emissive** *adj*.—**emitter** *n*.
Emmenthal(er), Emmental *n* a hard Swiss cheese with lots of holes.
emmet *n* (*dial*) an ant.
emollient *adj* softening and soothing, esp the skin. * *n* a preparation used for skin care.—**emollience** *n*.
emolument *n* a fee received, salary.
emote *vi* to display emotion theatrically.
emotion *n* a strong feeling of any kind.
emotional *adj* of emotion; inclined to express excessive emotion.—**emotionality** *n*.—**emotionally** *adv*.—**emotionalism** *n*.
emotive *adj* characterized by or arousing emotion.—**emotiveness, emotivity** *n*.
empale *see* **impale**.
empanel *vt* (**empanelling, empanelled** *or* **empaneling, empaneled**) (*law*) to enrol (for a jury); to enter on a jury list.—*also* **impanel**.
empathize *vi* to treat with or feel empathy.
empathy *n* the capacity for participating in and understanding the feelings or ideas of another.—**empathic, empathetic** *adj*.
emperor *n* the sovereign ruler over an empire.—**emperorship** *n*.
emperor penguin *n* an Antarctic penguin, the largest species known.
empery *n* (*pl* **emperies**) (*arch*) power, dominion.
emphasis *n* (*pl* **emphases**) particular stress or prominence given to something; force or vigour of expression; clarity of form or outline.
emphasize *vt* to place stress on.
emphatic *adj* spoken, done or marked with emphasis; forceful, decisive.—**emphatically** *adv*.—**emphaticalness** *n*.
emphysema *n* a medical condition marked by the distension of the air sacs in the lungs, causing breathlessness.—**emphysematous** *adj*.
empire *n* a large state or group of states under a single sovereign, usu an emperor; nations governed by a single sovereign state; a large and complex business organization.
empiric *adj* empirical. * *n* an empirical worker; a quack.
empirical *adj* based on observation, experiment or experience only, not theoretical.—**empirically** *adv*.—**empiricalness** *n*.
empiricism *n* (*philos*) the theory that experience is the only source of knowledge; the use of empirical methods.—**empiricist** *n*.
emplacement *n* a position prepared for a gun or artillery.
emplane *vti* to put on board a plane; to board a plane.
employ *vt* to give work and pay to; to make use of.—**employable** *adj*.
employee *n* a person who is hired by another person for wages.
employer *n* a person, business, etc that employs people.
employment *n* an employing; a being employed; occupation or profession.
empoison *vt* to taint, corrupt.
emporium *n* (*pl* **emporiums, emporia**) a large shop carrying many different items.
empower *vt* to give official authority to.—**empowerment** *n*.
empress *n* the female ruler of an empire; the wife or widow of an emperor.
empty *adj* (**emptier, emptiest**) containing nothing; not occupied; lacking reality, substance, or value; hungry. * *vb* (**emptying, emptied**) *vt* to make empty; to transfer or discharge (the contents of something) by emptying. * *vi* to become empty; to discharge contents. * *n* (*pl* **empties**) empty containers or bottles.—**emptily** *adv*.—**emptiness** *n*.
empty-handed *adj* with nothing in one's hands; without gain.
empty-headed *adj* scatterbrained.
empyema *n* (*pl* **empyemata**) a collection of pus, esp in the chest.—**empyemic** *adj*.
empyrean *n* (*arch*) the highest heaven. * *adj* pertaining to the highest heaven; celestial.
EMS *abbr* = European Monetary System.
EMU *abbr* = European Monetary Union.
emu *n* a fast-running Australian bird, related to the ostrich.
emulate *vt* to try to equal or do better than; to imitate; to rival or compete.—**emulation** *n*.—**emulative** *adj*.—**emulator** *n*.
emulous *adj* wanting to excel; competitive.
emulsify *vti* (**emulsifying, emulsified**) to make or become an emulsion.—**emulsification** *n*.—**emusifier** *n*.
emulsion *n* a mixture of mutually insoluble liquids in which one is dispersed in droplets throughout the other; a light-sensitive substance on photographic paper or film.—**emulsive** *adj*.
emunctory *n* (*pl* **emunctories**) (*anat*) an excretory duct or canal. * *adj* excretory.
en *n* (*print*) a measure of width, equal to half an em.
enable *vt* to give the authority or means to do something; to make easy or possible.—**enabler** *n*.
enact *vt* to make into law; to act (a play, etc).—**enactive** *adj*.—**enactment** *n*.—**enactor** *n*.—**enactory** *adj*.
enamel *n* a glass-like substance used to coat the surface of metal or pottery; the hard outer layer of a tooth; a usu glossy paint that forms a hard coat. * *vt* (**enamelling, enamelled** *or* **enameling, enameled**) to cover or decorate with enamel.—**enameller, enameler, enamellist, enamelist** *n*.—**enamelwork** *n*.
enamour, enamor *vt* to inspire with love.—**enamoured, enamored** *adj*.
enarthrosis *n* (*pl* **enarthroses**) (*anat*) a ball-and-socket joint.
en bloc *adv* in a mass.
encage *vt* to shut up in, or as in, a cage.
encamp *vt* to place or stay in a camp.—**encampment** *n*.
encapsulate *vt* to enclose or be enclosed in, as a capsule; to summarize.—**encapsulation** *n*.
encase *vt* to enclose (as if) in a case.—**encasement** *n*.
encaustic *adj* (*ceramics*) with colours burned in. * *n* the art of painting in melted wax; a piece of work done by this method.
enceinte *adj* pregnant.
encephalic *adj* of the brain.
encephalitis *n* inflammation of the brain.—**encephalitic** *adj*.
encephalogram *n* an electroencephalogram.—**encephalograph** *n*.
enchain *vt* to hold fast with, or as with, a chain.—**enchainment** *n*.
enchant *vt* to bewitch, to delight.—**enchanter** *n*.—**enchantment** *n*.—**enchantress** *nf*.
enchase *vt* to engrave, to emboss.
encircle *vt* to surround; to move or pass completely round.—**encirclement** *n*.
enclasp *vt* to clasp.
enclave *n* an area of a country's territory entirely surrounded by foreign territory.
enclitic *adj* (*linguistics*) attached to the preceding word and treated as a suffix, *eg* "thee" in "prithee". * *n* an enclitic word.—**enclitically** *adv*.
enclose *vt* to shut up or in; to put in a wrapper or parcel, usu together with a letter.—**enclosable** *adj*.—**encloser** *n*.

enclosure *n* an enclosing; an enclosed area; something enclosed with a letter, in a parcel, etc.
encomiast *n* a composer of an encomium.—**encomiastic** *adj*.
encomium *n* (*pl* **encomiums, encomia**) a usu formal expression of high praise in speech or writing.
encompass *vt* to encircle or enclose; to include.—**encompassment** *n*.
encore *interj* once more! * *n* a call for the repetition of a performance.—*also vt*.
encounter *vt* to meet, esp unexpectedly; to fight, engage in battle with; to be faced with (problems, etc). * *n* a meeting; a conflict, battle.
encourage *vt* to inspire with confidence or hope; to urge, incite; to promote the development of.—**encouragement** *n*.—**encourager** *n*.—**encouragingly** *adv*.
encroach *vi* to infringe another's territory, rights, etc; to advance beyond an established limit.—**encroacher** *n*.—**encroachingly** *adv*.—**encroachment** *n*.
encrust *vt* to cover with a hard crust; to form a crust on the surface of; to decorate a surface with jewels.—**encrustation** *n*.
encumber *vt* to weigh down; to hinder the function or activity of.—**encumberingly** *adv*.
encumbrance *n* something that is a hindrance or burden.
encumbrancer *n* a person who has a legal claim on an estate.
encyclical *adj* circulated widely (—*also* **encyclic**). * *n* a letter addressed by the pope to all Roman Catholic bishops.
encyclopedia, encyclopaedia *n* a book or series of books containing information on all branches of knowledge, or treating comprehensively a particular branch of knowledge, usu in alphabetical order.
encyclopedic, encyclopaedic *adj* comprehensive.—**encyclopedically, encyclopaedically** *adv*.
encyclopedist, encyclopaedist *n* a compiler of an encyclopedia.
encyst *vti* (*biol*) to enclose, or become enclosed in, a cyst or vesicle.—**encystment** *n*.
end *n* the last part; the place where a thing stops; purpose; result, outcome. * *vt* to bring to an end; to destroy. * *vi* to come to an end; to result (in). * *adj* final; ultimate.
end-, endo- *prefix* within.
endanger *vt* to put in danger.—**endangerment** *n*.
endear *vt* to make loved or more loved.—**endearing** *adj*.—**endearingly** *adv*.
endearment *n* something that endears; a word or words of affection.
endeavour, endeavor *vi* to try or attempt (to). * *n* an attempt.
endemic *adj* (*disease*) locally prevalent; (*plant*) peculiar to a locality. * *n* an endemic disease; an endemic plant.—**endemicity** *n*.—**endemically** *adv*.
ending *n* reaching or coming to an end; the final part.
endive *n* an annual or biennial herb widely cultivated as a salad plant; a variety of chicory used in salads.
endless *adj* unending; uninterrupted; extremely numerous.—**endlessly** *adv*.—**endlessness** *n*.
endo-, end- *prefix* within.
endocarditis *n* inflammation of the endocardium.—**endocarditic** *adj*.
endocardium *n* (*pl* **endocardia**) the membrane lining the heart cavities.
endocarp *n* the inner coat or shell of a fruit.—**endocarpal, endocarpic** *adj*.
endocrine *adj* secreting internally, specifically producing secretions that are distributed in the body by the bloodstream (—*also* **endocrinal**). * *n* an endocrine gland.
endocrine gland *n* a gland that secretes hormones directly into the bloodstream, eg the pituitary and thyroid.
endocrinology *n* the scientific study of endocrine glands and hormones.—**endocrinologic, endocrinological** *adj*.—**endocrinologist** *n*.
endoderm *n* the inner layer of embryonic cells in an egg from which an organism is formed.—*also* **entoblast, entoderm**.—**endodermal, endodermic, entodermal, entodermic** *adj*.
endogamy *n* the practice of marrying only within the same tribe.—**endogamous** *adj*.
endogenous *adj* growing from or on the inside.—**endogeny** *n*.
endomorph *n* a mineral enclosed within another mineral; a person with a heavily built physique.—**endomorphic** *adj*.—**endomorphy** *n*.
endomorphism *n* (*geol*) metamorphosis of molten rock within older rock.
endoparasite *n* an internal parasite.—**endoparasitic** *adj*.
endoplasm *n* (*biol*) the inner layer of protoplasm.
endorse *vt* to write one's name, comment, etc on the back of to approve; to record an offence on a driving licence; to support.—**endorsable** *adj*.—**endorsee** *n*.—**endorsement** *n*.—**endorser** *n*.
endoscope *n* a medical instrument for examining the interior of the body.—**endoscopic** *adj*.—**endoscopist** *n*.—**endoscopy** *n*.
endosmosis *n* (*biol*) osmosis inwards through the porous membrane of a cell, etc, by a surrounding liquid.
endosperm *n* the albumen of a seed.—**endospermic** *adj*.
endothelium *n* (*pl* **endothelia**) (*anat*) a tissue which lines blood vessels.
endow *vt* to give money or property to provide an income for; to provide with a special power or attribute.—**endower** *n*.
endowment *n* an endowing; an income, etc settled on an individual or organization; a natural quality or gift.
endpaper *n* either of two folded sheets of paper pasted against the inside covers of a book and attached to the first and last pages.
end product *n* the final result of a manufacturing or other process.
endue *vt* (**enduing, endued**) to provide with a quality or power.—*also* **indue**.
endurance *n* the ability to withstand pain, hardship, strain, etc.
endure *vt* to undergo, tolerate (hardship, etc) esp with patience. * *vi* to continue in existence, to last out.—**endurable** *adj*.—**endurability** *n*.—**endurably** *adv*.
enduring *adj* lasting, permanent.—**enduringly** *adv*.
endways *adv* on end, with the end foremost.
enema *n* (*pl* **enemas, enemata**) the injection of a liquid into the rectum to void the bowels; the liquid injected.
enemy *n* (*pl* **enemies**) a person who hates or dislikes and wishes to harm another; a military opponent; something harmful or deadly.
energetic *adj* lively, active; done with energy.—**energetically** *adv*.
energetics *n* (*sing*) the science of energy.
energize *vt* to fill with energy; to invigorate; to apply an electric current to.—**energizer** *n*.
energy *n* (*pl* **energies**) capacity of acting or being active; vigour, power; (*physics*) capacity to do work.
enervate *vt* to lessen the strength or vigour of; to enfeeble in mind and body.—**enervation** *n*.—**enervative** *adj*.—**enervator** *n*.
enface *vt* to write or stamp on the face of a document.
enfant terrible *n* (*pl* **enfants terribles**) a person who makes awkward remarks.
enfeeble *vt* to make feeble.—**enfeeblement** *n*.—**enfeebler** *n*.
enfeoff *vt* (*law*) to give a freehold property to; to convey.—**enfeoffment** *n*.
enfilade *n* gunfire directed (at troops, etc) in a line from end to end.—*also vt*.
enfold *vt* to wrap up; to hug in the arms.—**enfolder** *n*.—**enfoldment** *n*.
enforce *vt* to compel obedience by threat; to execute with vigour.—**enforceable** *adj*.—**enforcement** *n*.—**enforcer** *n*.
enfranchise *vt* to admit to citizenship; to grant the vote to.—**enfranchisement** *n*.—**enfranchiser** *n*.
engage *vt* to pledge as security; to promise to marry; to keep busy; to hire; to attract and hold, esp attention or sympathy; to cause to participate; to bring or enter into conflict; to begin or take part in a venture; to connect or interlock, to mesh.—**engager** *n*.
engaged *adj* entered into a promise to marry; reserved, occupied or busy.
engagement *n* the act or state of being engaged; a pledge; an appointment agreed with another person; employment; a battle.
engaging *adj* pleasing, attractive.—**engagingly** *adv*.—**engagingness** *n*.
engender *vt* to bring into existence.—**engenderment** *n*.
engine *n* a machine by which physical power is applied to produce a physical effect; a locomotive; (*formerly*) a mechanical device, such as a large catapult, used in war.

engineer *n* a person trained in engineering; a person who operates an engine, etc; a member of a military group devoted to engineering work; a designer or builder of engines. * *vt* to contrive, plan, esp deviously.

engineering *n* the art or practice of constructing and using machinery; the art and science by which natural forces and materials are utilized in structures or machines.

English *adj* of, relating to, or characteristic of England, the English people, or the English language. * *n* the language of the English people, the US and many areas formerly under British control; English language and literature as a subject of study.

engorge *vt* to congest with blood; to consume (food) greedily.—**engorgement** *n*.

engrained *see* **ingrained.**

engrave *vt* to produce by cutting or carving a surface; to cut to produce a representation that may be printed from; to lodge deeply (in the mind, etc).—**engraver** *n*.

engraving *n* a print made from an engraved surface.

engross *vt* to occupy (the attention) fully; to copy in large handwriting; to prepare the final text of.—**engrossing** *adj*.—**engrossment** *n*.

engulf *vt* to flow over and enclose; to overwhelm.—**engulfment** *n*.

enhance *vt* to increase in value, importance, attractiveness, etc; to heighten.—**enhancement** *n*.—**enhancer** *n*.

enigma *n* someone or something that is puzzling or mysterious.—**enigmatic, enigmatical** *adj*.—**enigmatically** *adv*.

enjoin *vt* to command, order someone with authority; to forbid, to prohibit.—**enjoiner** *n*.—**enjoinment** *n*.

enjoy *vt* to get pleasure from, take joy in; to use or have the advantage of; to experience.—**enjoyment** *n*.

enjoyable *adj* giving enjoyment.—**enjoyably** *adv*.

enkindle *vt* to set on fire; (*fig*) to inflame.

enlace *vt* to entwine; to enfold.—**enlacement** *n*.

enlarge *vti* to make or grow larger; to reproduce (a photograph) in a larger form; to speak or write at length (on).

enlargement *n* an act, instance, or state of enlarging; a photograph, etc that has been enlarged.

enlarger *n* a device for making photographic enlargements.

enlighten *vt* to instruct; to inform.—**enlightening** *adj*.—**enlightenment** *n*.

enlightened *adj* well-informed, tolerant, unprejudiced.

enlist *vt* to engage for service in the armed forces; to secure the aid or support of. * *vi* to register oneself for the armed services.—**enlistee** *n*.—**enlistment** *n*.

enliven *vt* to make more lively or cheerful.—**enlivening** *adj*.—**enlivenment** *n*.

en masse *adv* all together; in a large group.

enmesh *vt* to catch in a net; to entangle.—*also* **inmesh, immesh.**

enmity *n* (*pl* **enmities**) hostility, esp mutual hatred.

ennage *n* (*print*) the number of ens in a text.

ennea- *prefix* nine.

ennead *n* a set of nine.—**enneadic** *adj*.

enneagon *n* a plane figure with nine sides and nine angles.

ennoble *vt* to make noble, dignify; to raise (a person) to a rank of nobility.—**ennoblement** *n*.—**ennobler** *n*.

ennui *n* boredom, apathy.

enology *see* **oenology.**

enormity *n* (*pl* **enormities**) great wickedness; a serious crime; huge size, magnitude.

enormous *adj* extremely large.—**enormously** *adv*.

enough *adj* adequate, sufficient. * *adv* so as to be sufficient; very; quite. * *n* a sufficiency. * *interj* stop!

enounce *vt* to proclaim, to enunciate.

en passant *adv* in passing.

enquire, enquirer *see* **inquire.**

enquiry *see* **inquiry.**

enrage *vt* to fill with anger.—**enraged** *adj*.—**enragement** *n*.

enrapture *vt* to fill with pleasure or delight.

enrich *vt* to make rich or richer; to ornament; to improve in quality by adding to.—**enricher** *n*.—**enrichment** *n*.

enrol, enroll *vti* (**enrols** *or* **enrolls, enrolling, enrolled**) to enter or register on a roll or list; to become a member of a society, club, etc; to admit as a member.—**enrollee** *n*.—**enroller** *n*.—**enrolment, enrollment** *n*.

en route *adv* along or on the way.

ensanguine *vt* to smear or cover with blood.

ensconce *vt* to establish in a safe, secure or comfortable place.

ensemble *n* something regarded as a whole; the general effect; the performance of the full number of musicians, dancers, etc; a complete harmonious costume.

enshrine *vt* to enclose (as if) in a shrine; to cherish as sacred.—*also* **inshrine.**—**enshrinement** *n*.

enshroud *vt* to cover with, or as with, a shroud.

ensiform *adj* sword-shaped.

ensign *n* a flag; the lowest commissioned officer in the US Navy.

ensilage *n* storage in a pit or silo; silage.

ensile *vt* to store in a silo.—**ensilability** *n*.

enslave *vt* to make into a slave; to subjugate.—**enslavement** *n*.—**enslaver** *n*.

ensnare *vt* to trap in, or as in, a snare.—**ensnarement** *n*.

ensue *vi* (**ensuing, ensued**) to occur as a consequence or in time.—**ensuing** *adj*.

en suite *adv, adj* in a single unit.

ensure *vt* to make certain, sure, or safe.—**ensurer** *n*.

enswathe *vt* to wrap, swathe.

ENT *abbr* = ear, nose, and throat.

entablature *n* the part of a building resting on top of columns.

entablement *n* a platform for a statue, above the dado and base.

entail *vt* to involve, necessitate as a result; to restrict the inheritance of property to a designated line of heirs. * *n* the act of entailing or the estate entailed.—**entailer** *n*.—**entailment** *n*.

entangle *vt* to tangle, complicate; to involve in a tangle or complications.—**entanglement** *n*.—**entangler** *n*.

entelechy *n* (*pl* **entelechies**) (*philos*) actuality.

entente (cordiale) *n* a friendly understanding or relationship between two or more countries.

enter *vi* to go or come in or into; to come on stage; to begin, start; (*with* **for**) to register as an entrant. * *vt* to come or go into; to pierce, penetrate; (*an organization*) to join; to insert; (*proposal, etc*) to submit; to record (an item) in a diary, etc.—**enterable** *adj*.—**enterer** *n*.

enteric, enteral *adj* intestinal.—**enterally** *adv*.

enteritis *n* inflammation of the intestines, usu causing diarrhoea.

enteron (*pl* **entera**) the alimentary canal.

enterotomy *n* (*pl* **enterotomies**) dissection of, or an incision into, the bowels.

enterprise *n* a difficult or challenging undertaking; a business project; readiness to engage in new ventures.—**enterpriser** *n*.

enterprising *adj* adventurous, energetic and progressive.—**enterprisingly** *adv*.

entertain *vt* to show hospitality to; to amuse, please (a person or audience); to have in mind; to consider.

entertainer *n* a person who entertains in public, esp professionally.

entertaining *adj* amusing; diverting.—**entertainingly** *adv*.

entertainment *n* entertaining; amusement; an act or show intended to amuse and interest an audience, etc.

enthral, enthrall *vt* (**enthrals** *or* **enthralls, enthralling, enthralled**) to captivate.—**enthralment, enthrallment** *n*.

enthrone *vt* to install ceremonially, as a monarch or bishop.—**enthronement** *n*.

enthuse *vti* to fill with or express enthusiasm.

enthusiasm *n* intense interest or liking; something that arouses keen interest.

enthusiast *n* a person filled with enthusiasm for something.

enthusiastic *adj* filled with enthusiasm.—**enthusiastically** *adv*.

enthymeme *n* (*logic*) a syllogism in which one premise is suppressed.

entice *vt* to attract by offering some pleasure or reward.—**enticement** *n*.—**enticer** *n*.—**enticing** *adj*.
entire *adj* whole; complete.—**entireness** *n*.
entirely *adv* fully; completely.
entirety *n* (*pl* **entireties**) completeness; the total.
entitle *vt* to give a title to; to give a right (to).—**entitlement** *n*.
entity *n* (*pl* **entities**) existence, being; something that has a separate existence.
entoblast, entoderm *see* **endoderm.**
entomb *vt* to place in, or as in, a tomb.—**entombment** *n*.
entomic *adj* of insects.
entomo-, entom- *prefix* insect.
entomology *n* the branch of zoology that deals with insects.—**entomological, entomologic** *adj*.—**entomologist** *n*.
entomophagous *adj* insect-eating.
entomophilous *adj* fertilized by insects.
entopic *adj* (*anat*) in a normal position.
entourage *n* a retinue, group of attendants.
entozoic *adj* living within an animal.
entozoan *n* (*pl* **entozoa**) a parasite which lives inside an animal.
entr'acte *n* a light entertainment, a ballet, etc, as an interlude between the acts of a play or opera.
entrails *npl* the insides of the body, the intestines.
entrain *vti* to put or get onto a train.
entrance[1] *n* the act of entering; the power or authority to enter; a means of entering; an admission fee.
entrance[2] *vt* to put into a trance; to fill with great delight.—**entrancement** *n*.—**entrancing** *adj*.
entrant *n* a person who enters (eg a competition, profession).
entrap *vt* (**entrapping, entrapped**) to catch, as if in a trap; to lure into a compromising or incriminatory situation.—**entrapment** *n*.—**entrapper** *n*.
entreat *vt* to request earnestly; to implore, beg.—**entreaty** *n* (*pl* **entreaties**).
entrecôte *n* a boned cut of beef from between the ribs.
entrée, entree *n* a dish served before the main meal; in US, the principal dish of a meal; the right or power of admission.
entremets *n* (*pl* **entremets**) a dessert.
entrench *vt* to dig a trench as a defensive perimeter; to establish (oneself) in a strong defensive position.—**entrencher** *n*.—**entrenchment** *n*.
entrepôt *n* an intermediate centre of trade and transhipment.
entrepreneur *n* a person who takes the commercial risk of starting up and running a business enterprise.—**entrepreneurial** *adj*.—**entrepreneurship** *n*.
entresol *n* a floor between the ground and first floor, a mezzanine.
entropy *n* (*pl* **entropies**) a measure of the unavailable energy in a closed thermodynamic system; disorder, disorganization.
entrust *vt* (*usu with* **with**) to confer as a responsibility, duty, etc; (*usu with* **to**) to place something in another's care.—**entrustment** *n*.
entry *n* (*pl* **entries**) the act of entering; a place of entrance; an item recorded in a diary, journal, etc; a person or thing taking part in a contest.
entwine *vt* to twine together or around.—**entwinement** *n*.
enucleate *vt* to remove the nucleus from.
E number *n* a series of numbers with the prefix E used to identify food additives within the European Community.
enumerate *vt* to count; to list.—**enumeration** *n*.—**enumerator** *n*.
enunciate *vt* to state definitely; to pronounce clearly.—**enunciation** *n*.—**enunciator** *n*.—**enunciative** *adj*.
enure *see* **inure.**
enuresis *n* urinary incontinence; bedwetting.—**enuretic** *adj*.
envelop *vt* to enclose completely (as if) with a covering.—**envelopment** *n*.
envelope *n* something used to wrap or cover, esp a gummed paper container for a letter; the bag containing the gas in a balloon or airship.
envemon *vt* to put poison into; (*fig*) to embitter.
enviable *adj* causing envy; fortunate.—**enviably** *adv*.
envious *adj* filled with envy.—**enviously** *adv*.
environ *vt* to surround or enclose.
environment *n* external conditions and surroundings, esp those that affect the quality of life of plants, animals and human beings.—**environmental** *adj*.—**environmentally** *adv*.
environmentalist *n* a person who is concerned with improving the quality of the environment.—**environmentalism** *n*.
environs *npl* the surrounding area or outskirts of a district or town.
envisage *vt* to have a mental picture of.—**envisagement** *n*.
envoy *n* a diplomatic agent; a representative.
envy *n* (*pl* **envies**) resentment or discontent at another's achievements, possessions, etc; an object of envy. * *vt* (**envying, envied**) to feel envy of.—**envier** *n*.
enwrap *vt* to wrap up.
enzootic *adj* (*disease*) affecting animals in a particular district.
enzyme *n* a complex protein, produced by living cells, that induces or speeds chemical reactions in plants and animals.
eon *see* **aeon.**
eonian *see* **aeonian.**
eonism *n* (*psychiatry*) a tendency in a male to adopt female clothing and mannerisms, transvestitism.
eosin, eosine *n* a pink coal tar dye.—**eosinic** *adj*.
EP *abbr* = extended play (gramophone record).
epact *n* (*astron*) the difference between the solar and the lunar month, about eleven days in the year.
eparch *n* (*Greek Orthodox Church*) a metropolitan or other bishop; a governor of an eparchy.
eparchy, eparchate *n* (*pl* **eparchies, eparchates**) a Greek province; the diocese of an eparch.—**eparchial** *adj*.
epaulette, epaulet *n* a piece of ornamental fabric or metal worn on the shoulder, esp on a uniform.
épée *n* a sword used in fencing.—**épéeist** *n*.
epenthesis *n* (*pl* **epentheses**) *n* (*linguistics*) the insertion of a letter or syllable in the middle of a word.
epergne *n* a branched centrepiece or ornamental stand for a dinner table.
epexegesis *n* (*pl* **epexegeses**) (*linguistics*) the use of additional words to clarify a meaning.—**epexegetic, epexegetical** *adj*.
ephah *n* a Hebrew dry measure, equal to about one bushel (33 litres).
ephebe *n* a young citizen (aged 18 to 20) of ancient Greece.
ephedrine *n* an alkaloid used to treat asthma and hay fever.
ephemeral *adj* existing only for a very short time. * *n* an ephemeral thing or organism.—**ephemerality, empheralness** *n*.
ephemeris *n* (*pl* **ephemerides**) an astronomical almanac showing the daily positions of the sun, moon and planets.
ephod *n* a vestment worn by a Jewish priest.
ephor *n* (*pl* **ephors, ephori**) a magistrate in ancient Greece.
epi-, ep- *prefix* upon, at, in addition.
epiblast *n* the outer layer of the embryonic cells in an egg from which an organism is formed.—**epiblastic** *adj*.
epic *n* a long poem narrating the deeds of a hero; any literary work, film, etc in the same style. * *adj* relating to or resembling an epic.
epicarp *n* the outer skin of a fruit.
epicene *adj* having characteristics of both sexes; lacking characteristics of either sex, sexless.
epicentre, epicenter *n* the area of the earth's surface directly above the focus of an earthquake.—**epicentral** *adj*.
epicure *n* a person who has cultivated a refined taste in food, wine, literature, etc.—**epicurism, epicureanism** *n*.
epicurean *adj* given to sensuous enjoyment.
epicycle *n* (*geom*) a small circle, the centre of which is situated on the circumference of a larger circle.—**epicyclic** *adj*.
epicycloid *n* (*geom*) a curve described by a point in the circumference of one circle which rolls round the circumference of another circle.
epidemic *adj, n* (a disease) attacking many people at the same time in a community or region.—**epidemical** *adj*.
epidemiology *n* the area of medicine dealing with epidemic diseases.—**epidemiological** *adj*.—**epidemiologist** *n*.

epidermis *n* an outer layer, esp of skin.—**epidermal, epidermic, epidermoid** *adj*.

epidiascope *n* a projector for magnifying opaque as well as transparent pictures.

epidural *n* a spinal anaesthetic used for the relief of pain during childbirth.

epigastrium *n* (*pl* **epigastria**) the upper part of the abdomen.

epigenesis *n* the theory that an organism is created by the division or segmentation of a fertilized egg cell; a form of geological metamorphism of rock brought about by outside forces; the depositing of ore in already formed rock.—**epigenesist, epigenist** *n*.—**epigenetic** *adj*.—**epigentically** *adv*.

epiglottis *n* (**epiglottises, epiglottides**) a thin flap of cartilaginous tissue over the entrance to the larynx.—**epiglottal, epiglottic** *adj*.

epigram *n* a short witty poem or saying.—**epigrammatic** *adj*.—**epigrammatically** *adv*.

epigrammatize *vti* to compose an epigram (about).—**epigrammatist** *n*.

epigraph *n* a quotation at the beginning of a book or chapter; an inscription on a building or monument.—**epigraphic, epigraphical** *adj*.

epigraphy *n* the study of inscriptions.—**epigraphist, epigrapher** *n*.

epilepsy *n* a disorder of the nervous system marked typically by convulsive attacks and loss of consciousness.

epileptic *adj* of or affected with epilepsy. * *n* a person affected with epilepsy.—**epileptically** *adv*.

epilogue *n* the concluding section of a book or other literary work; a short speech addressed by an actor to the audience at the end of a play.—**epilogist** *n*.

epiphany *n* (*pl* **epiphanies**) a moment of sudden revelation or insight; (*with cap*) a festival of the Christian Church in commemoration of the coming of the Magi to Christ.

epiphenomenon *n* (*pl* **epiphenomena**) a by-product; (*med*) an attendant symptom.

epiphyte *n* (*bot*) a plant which grows on another plant but is not fed by it.—**epiphytic** *adj*.

episcopacy *n* (*pl* **episcopacies**) the system of church government by bishops.

episcopal *adj* of bishops; governed by bishops.—**episcopally** *adv*.

episcopalian *adj* pertaining to episcopacy * *n* a member or supporter of an episcopal church.—**episcopalianism** *n*.

episcopate *n* the office of a bishop.

episiotomy *n* (*pl* **episiotomies**) a cut made in the perineum during childbirth to prevent tearing.

episode *n* a piece of action in a dramatic or literary work; an incident in a sequence of events.

episodic, episodical *adj* happening at irregular intervals; digressive.—**episodically** *adv*.

epispastic *adj* producing a blister.

epistaxis *n* (*med*) nosebleed.

epistemology *n* the science of the processes and grounds of knowledge.

epistle *n* (*formal*) a letter; (*with cap*) a letter written by one of Christ's Apostles to various churches and individuals.

epistler *n* someone who reads the Epistle in the communion service; one who writes an epistle.

epistolary *adj* pertaining to, contained in, or conducted by letters.

epistrophe *n* (*rhetoric*) the practice of ending several successive clauses or sentences with the same word.

epistyle *n* an architrave.

epitaph *n* an inscription in memory of a dead person, usu on a tombstone.—**epitaphic** *adj*.—**epitaphist** *n*.

epithalamium *n* (*pl* **epithalamia**) a nuptial song or poem.—**epithalamic** *adj*.

epithelioma *n* (*pl* **epitheliomas, epitheliomata**) a cancer of the epithelium.—**epitheliomatous** *adj*.

epithelium *n* (*pl* **epithelia**) any of the cells that line the surface of the membranes of the body.—**epithelial** *adj*.

epithet *n* a descriptive word or phrase added to or substituted for a person's name (*Vlad the Impaler*).—**epithetic, epithetical** *adj*.

epitome *n* a typical example; a paradigm; personification; a condensed account of a written work.—**epitomic, epitomical** *adj*.—**epitomist** *n*.

epitomize *vt* to be or make an epitome of.—**epitomization** *n*.—**epitomizer** *n*.

epoch *n* a date in time used as a point of reference; an age in history associated with certain characteristics; a unit of geological time.—**epochal** *adj*.

epode *n* a kind of lyric poem; the last part of a lyric ode.

eponym *n* a person after whom something is named; a name so derived.—**eponymous, eponymic** *adj*.—**eponymy** *n*.

epopee *n* an epic poem; epic poetry.

EPOS *abbr* = electronic point of sale.

epos *n* early unwritten epic poetry; an epic poem; the subject of an epic poem.

epoxy *adj* (*chem*) of or containing an oxygen atom and two other groups, usually carbon, which are themselves linked with other groups.

epoxy resin *n* a strong synthetic resin containing epoxy groups, used in laminates and adhesives.

epsilon *n* the 5th letter of the Greek alphabet.

equable *adj* level, uniform; (*climate*) free from extremes of hot and cold; even-tempered.—**equability, equableness** *n*.—**equably** *adv*.

equal *adj* the same in amount, size, number, or value; impartial, regarding or affecting all objects in the same way; capable of meeting a task or situation. * *n* a person that is equal. * *vt* (**equalling, equalled** *or* **equaling, equaled**) to be equal to, esp to be identical in value; to make or do something equal to.—**equally** *adv*.

equality *n* (*pl* **equalities**) being equal.

equalize *vti* to make or become equal; (*games*) to even the score.—**equalization** *n*.—**equalizer** *n*.

equanimity *n* (*pl* **equanimities**) evenness of temper; composure.—**equanimous** *adj*.

equate *vt* to make, treat, or regard as comparable. * *vi* to correspond as equal.

equation *n* an act of equalling; the state of being equal; a usu formal statement of equivalence (as in logical and mathematical expressions) with the relations denoted by the sign =; an expression representing a chemical reaction by means of chemical symbols.—**equational** *adj*.

equator *n* an imaginary circle passing round the globe, equidistant from the North and South poles.—**equatorial** *n*.

equerry *n* (*pl* **equerries**) an officer in the British royal household.

equestrian *adj* pertaining to horses and riding; on horseback. * *n* a skilled rider.—**equestrienne** *nf*.—**equestrianism** *n*.

equi- *prefix* equal.

equiangular *adj* having equal angles.

equidistant *adj* at equal distances.—**equidistance** *n*.

equilateral *adj* having all sides equal.

equilibrate *vti* to balance.—**equilibration** *n*.—**equilibrator** *n*.

equilibrist *n* a tightrope walker; an acrobat.—**equilibristic** *adj*.

equilibrium *n* (*pl* **equilibriums, equilibria**) a state of balance of weight, power, force, etc.

equine *adj* of or resembling a horse.

equinox *n* the two times of the year when night and day are equal in length (around 21 March and 23 September).—**equinoctial** *adj*.

equip *vt* (**equipping, equipped**) to provide with all the necessary tools or supplies.—**equipper** *n*.

equipage *n* a carriage with horses and liveried attendants.

equipment *n* the tools, supplies and other items needed for a particular task, expedition, etc.

equipoise *n* balance, equilibrium.

equipollent *adj* equal in power.—**equipollence** *n*.

equiponderant *vti* to make or be equal in weight.—**equiponderant** *adj*.

equisetum *n* (*pl* **equisetums, equiseta**) a plant of the group that includes horsetails.

equitable *adj* just and fair; (*law*) pertaining to equity as opposed to common or statute law.—**equitableness** *n*.—**equitably** *adv*.

equitation *n* horsemanship.
equity *n* (*pl* **equities**) fairness; (*law*) a legal system based on natural justice developed into a body of rules supplementing the common law; (*pl*) ordinary shares in a company.
equivalence, equivalency *n* (*pl* **equivalences, equivalencies**) equality of value or power; (*chem*) the property of having equal valency.
equivalent *adj* equal in amount, force, meaning, etc; virtually identical, esp in effect or function. * *n* an equivalent thing.
equivocal *adj* ambiguous; uncertain; questionable; arousing suspicion.—**equivocality, equivocacy** *n*.—**equivocally** *adv*.
equivocate *vi* to use ambiguous language, esp in order to confuse or deceive.—**equivocation** *n*.—**equivocator** *n*.—**equivocatory** *adj*.
equivoque, equivoke *n* a pun; an ambiguous expression.
Er (*chem symbol*) erbium.
era *n* an historical period typified by some special feature; a chronological order or system of notation reckoned from a given date as a basis.
eradiate *vti* to emit rays, to radiate.—**eradiation** *n*.
eradicate *vt* to obliterate.—**eradicable** *adj*.—**eradication** *n*.—**eradicator** *n*.
erase *vt* to rub out, obliterate; to remove a recording from magnetic tape; to remove data from a computer memory or storage medium.—**erasable** *adj*.—**erasion** *n*.
eraser *n* a piece of rubber, etc for rubbing out marks or writing.
erasure *n* an erasing; something rubbed out.
erbium *n* a soft metallic element of the rare earth group.
ere *prep, conj* (*poet*) before.
erect *adj* upright; not leaning or lying down; (*sexual organs*) rigid and swollen with blood from sexual stimulation. * *vt* to construct, set up.—**erectable** *adj*.—**erecter, erector** *n*.—**erectness** *n*.
erectile *adj* (*penis, clitoris, etc*) able to become enlarged and rigid through sexual stimulation.—**erectility** *n*.
erection *n* construction; something erected, as a building; swelling, esp of the penis, due to sexual excitement.
erector *n* a person who, or a thing that, erects; a muscle that erects.
eremite *n* a hermit.—**eremitic, eremitical** *adj*.—**eremitism** *n*.
erethism *n* (*med*) an abnormal degree of excitement in an organ or tissue of the body.
erg *n* the unit for measuring work or energy.
ergo *adv* therefore.
ergometer *n* an instrument for measuring work performed or force produced.
ergonomics *n* (*sing*) the study of the interaction between people and their working environment with the aim of improving efficiency.—**ergonomic** *adj*.—**ergonomically** *adv*.—**ergonomist** *n*.
ergot *n* a disease of rye and other cereals caused by a fungus; this fungus; a medicine derived from an ergot fungus.
ergotism *n* a toxic condition in humans caused by ergot fungus or chronic excessive use of an ergot drug.
erica *n* a genus of flowering plants, including the heaths.
ericaceous *adj* of the heath family.
eristic, eristical *adj* (*logic*) seeking to win an argument rather than find the truth.
ermine *n* (*pl* **ermines, ermine**) the weasel in its winter coat; the white fur of the winter coat; a rank or office whose official robe is edged with ermine.
erne, ern *n* the sea eagle.
erode *vt* to eat or wear away gradually.
erogenous *adj* sexually arousing; sensitive to sexual stimulation.
erosion *n* the act of eroding; gradual destruction or eating away; an eroded part.—**erosive, erosional** *adj*.
erotic, erotical *adj* of sexual love; sexually stimulating.—**erotically** *adv*.
erotica *n* sexually explicit literature or art.
eroticism, erotism *n* erotic nature; sexually arousing themes in literature and art; sexual desire.
erotomania *n* excessive sexual desire.—**erotomaniac** *n*.
err *vi* to be or do wrong.
errand *n* a short journey to perform some task, usu on behalf of another; the purpose of this journey.
errant *adj* going astray, esp doing wrong; moving aimlessly.
errantry *n* (*pl* **errantries**) the state or conduct of a knight errant.
erratic *adj* capricious; irregular; eccentric, odd.—**erratically** *adv*.
erratum *n* (*pl* **errata**) a written or printed error; a page bearing a list of corrigenda (—*also* **corrigendum**).
erroneous *adj* incorrect; mistaken.—**erroneously** *adv*.
error *n* a mistake, an inaccuracy; a mistaken belief or action; (*statistics*) the difference between an approximation of a value and the actual value, usu expressed as a percentage.
ersatz *adj* made in imitation; synthetic.
Erse *n* Scottish Gaelic; Irish Gaelic.—*also adj*.
erstwhile *adv* formerly. * *adj* former.
eructation *n* the act of belching.
erudite *adj* scholarly, having great knowledge.—**eruditely** *adv*.—**erudition** *n*.
erupt *vi* to burst forth; to break out into a rash; (*volcano*) to explode, ejecting ash and lava into the air.—**eruptible** *adj*.
eruption *n* the ejection of lava from a volcano; an outbreak; a rash, pimples.—**eruptional** *adj*.—**eruptive** *adj*.
eryngo, eringo *n* (*pl* **eryngoes, eryngos, eringoes, eringos**) one of a genus of plants including the sea holly.
erysipelas *n* an acute bacterial disease, characterized by a fever and skin inflammation.—**erysipelatous** *adj*.
erythema *n* (*med*) a superficial patchy redness of the skin.—**erythematic, erythematous, erythemic** *adj*.
erythrocyte *n* a red blood corpuscle.—**erythrocytic** *adj*.
Es (*chem symbol*) einsteinium.
escalade *n* the act of scaling the walls of a fortified place by ladders.
escalate *vi* to increase rapidly in magnitude or intensity.—**escalation** *n*.
escalator *n* a motorized set of stairs arranged to ascend or descend continuously.
escallop *n* a scallop.
escalope *n* a thin cut of meat, esp veal.
escapade *n* a wild or mischievous adventure.
escape *vt* to free oneself from confinement, etc; to avoid, remain unnoticed; to be forgotten. * *vi* to achieve freedom; (*gas, liquid*) to leak. * *n* an act or instance of escaping; a means of escape; a leakage of liquid or gas; a temporary respite from reality.—**escapable** *adj*.—**escaper** *n*.
escapee *n* a person who has escaped, esp a prisoner.
escapement *n* a device in a watch or clock by which the motions of the pendulum or balance are regulated.
escape velocity *n* the minimum velocity required for a rocket, etc to escape the gravitational pull of the earth or other celestial body.
escapism *n* the tendency to avoid or retreat from reality into fantasy.—**escapist** *n, adj*.
escapologist *n* a performer who escapes from handcuffs, locked boxes, etc.—**escapology** *n*.
escargot *n* a snail prepared as food.
escarp *n* a steep bank in front of a rampart.
escarpment *n* a steep side of a ridge or plateau.
eschatology *n* (*pl* **eschatologies**) the study of death, judgment, heaven and hell, and how humanity relates to them.
escheat *n* (*law*) (*formerly*) the lapsing of property to the state in the absence of an heir or by forfeiture; property that passes to the state in this way. * *vt* to confiscate property by escheat. * *vi* to revert to the state by escheat.
eschew *vt* to avoid as habit, esp on moral grounds.—**eschewal** *n*.—**eschewer** *n*.
escort *n* a person, group, ship, aircraft, etc accompanying a person or thing to give protection, guidance, or as a matter of courtesy; a person who accompanies another on a social occasion. * *vt* to attend as escort.
escritoire *n* a writing desk.
escrow *n* (*law*) a contract kept by a third party until the fulfilment of a condition.

escudo *n* (*pl* **escudos**) the monetary unit of Portugal.
esculent *adj* edible.
escutcheon *n* a shield bearing a coat of arms.
esker, eskar *n* (*geol*) a ridge of gravel, glacially deposited.
Eskimo *n* (*pl* **Eskimos, Eskimo**) the Inuit people; a group of peoples of eastern Siberia; a member of these peoples; their language.—*also adj*.
Eskimo dog *n* a powerful type of dog with a thick coat bred to pull sledges.
esophagus *see* **oesophagus.**
esoteric *adj* intended for or understood by a select few; secret; private.—**esoterically** *adv*.—**esotericism** *n*.
ESP *abbr* = extrasensory perception.
esp. *abbr* = especially.
espadrille *n* a flat shoe usu having a fabric upper and rope soles.
espalier *n* a plant (as a fruit tree) trained to grow flat against a support; the trellis on which such plants are trained.
esparto *n* (*pl* **espartos**) either of two Spanish and Algerian grasses used esp in paper-making.
especial *adj* notably special, unusual; particular to one person or thing.—**especially** *adv*.
Esperanto *n* an artificial international language.
espionage *n* spying or the use of spies to obtain information.
esplanade *n* a level open space for walking or driving, esp along a shore.
espouse *vt* to adopt or support a cause.—**espousal** *n*.—**espouser** *n*.
espresso *n* (*pl* **espressos**) coffee brewed by forcing steam through finely ground darkly roasted coffee beans; an apparatus for making espresso.
esprit *n* wit; liveliness.
esprit de corps *n* a sense of loyalty and attachment to a group to which one belongs.
espy *vt* (**espying, espied**) to catch sight of.—**espial** *n*.—**espier** *n*.
Esq *abbr* = esquire.
esquire *n* a general courtesy title used instead of Mr in addressing letters.
essay *n* a short prose work usu dealing with a subject from a limited or personal point of view; an attempt. * *vt* (**essaying, essayed**) to try, to attempt.
essayist *n* an essay writer.
essence *n* that which makes a thing what it is; a substance distilled or extracted from another substance and having the special qualities of the original substance; a perfume.
essential *adj* of or containing the essence of something; indispensable, of the greatest importance. * *n* (*often pl*) indispensable elements or qualities.—**essentiality, essentialness** *n*.—**essentially** *adv*.
essential oil *n* any of various plant oils used in perfumery.
establish *vt* to set up (eg a business) permanently; to settle (a person) in a place or position; to get generally accepted; to place beyond dispute, prove as a fact.—**establisher** *n*.
established *adj* (*church, religion*) officially recognized as the national church or religion of a country.
establishment *n* the act of establishing; a commercial organization or other large institution; the staff and resources of an organization; a household; (*with cap*) those people in institutions such as the government, civil service and commerce who use their power to preserve the social, economic and political status quo.
establishmentarian *adj*, *n* of an established church; supporting the established church system. * *n* a person who advocates official recognition of a church or religion.—**establishmentarianism** *n*.
estaminet *n* a café.
estancia *n* a cattle ranch in Latin America.
estate *n* landed property; a large area of residential or industrial development; a person's total possessions, esp at their death; a social or political class.
estate agent *see* **realtor.**
estate car *n* a car with extra carrying space reached through a rear door.—*also* **station wagon.**
esteem *vt* to value or regard highly; to consider or think. * *n* high regard, a favourable opinion.
ester *n* (*chem*) a compound of acid and alcohol.
esthete, esthetics *see* **aesthete, aesthetics.**
estheticism *see* **aestheticism.**
estimable *adj* worthy of esteem; calculable.
estimate *vt* to judge the value, amount, significance of; to calculate approximately. * *n* an approximate calculation; a judgment or opinion; a preliminary calculation of the cost of a particular job.—**estimative** *adj*.
estimation *n* estimating; an opinion, judgment; esteem.
estimator *n* someone or something that estimates.
estival *see* **aestival.**
estivation *see* **aestivation.**
estivation *see* **aestivation.**
estop *vt* (**estopping, estopped**) (*law*) to prohibit by estoppel.
estoppel *n* (*law*) a legal impediment arising as a result of one's previous action.
estrange *vt* to alienate the affections or confidence of.—**estranged** *adj*.—**estrangement** *n*.
estrogen *see* **oestrogen.**
estrus *see* **oestrus.**
estuarine *adj* pertaining to, or formed in, an estuary.
estuary *n* (*pl* **estuaries**) an arm of the sea at the mouth of a river.
esurient *adj* voracious, greedy.—**esurience** *n*.
ETA *abbr* = estimated time of arrival.
eta *n* the 7th letter of the Greek alphabet.
étagère *n* an ornamental stand.
et al *abbr* = *et alii*, and others.
etc, etc. *abbr* = et cetera.
et cetera, etcetera *n* and so forth.
etceteras *npl* the usual extra things or persons.
etch *vti* to make lines on (metal, glass) usu by the action of acid; to produce (as a design) by etching; to delineate clearly.—**etcher** *n*.
etching *n* the art or process of producing designs on and printing from etched plates; an impression made from an etched plate.
ETD *abbr* = estimated time of departure.
eternal *adj* continuing forever without beginning or end, everlasting; unchangeable; (*inf*) seemingly endless.—**eternality, eternalness** *n*.—**eternally** *adv*.
eternalize *vt* to make eternal.—**eternalization** *n*.
eternity *n* (*pl* **eternities**) infinite time; the timelessness thought to constitute life after death; (*inf*) a very long time.
etesian *adj* (*winds*) blowing from the northwest in the Mediterranean for about forty days each summer.
ethane *n* a colourless gaseous hydrocarbon found in natural gas and used esp as fuel.
ethene *see* **ethylene.**
ether *n* (*chem*) a light flammable liquid used as an anaesthetic or solvent; the upper regions of space, the invisible elastic substance formerly believed to be distributed evenly through all space.—**etheric** *adj*.
ethereal *adj* delicate; spiritual; celestial.—**ethereality, etherealness** *n*.—**ethereally** *adv*.
etherealize *vt* to make ethereal; to regard as ethereal.—**etherealization** *n*.
etherize *vt* (*patient*) to anaesthetize, using ether.—**etherization** *n*.
ethic *n* a moral principle or set of principles. * *adj* ethical.
ethical *adj* of or pertaining to ethics; conforming to the principles of proper conduct, as established by society, a profession, etc; (*med*) legally available only on prescription.—**ethically** *adv*.—**ethicalness, ethicality** *n*.
ethical investment *n* the investment in companies whose activities do not offend the investor's moral principles.—*also* **conscience investment.**
ethics *n* (*sing*) the philosophical analysis of human morality and conduct; system of conduct or behaviour, moral principles.—**ethicist** *n*.
Ethiopian *adj* of or pertaining to Ethiopia, its languages or people.—*also n*.
ethmoid *adj* (anat) denoting a light, spongy bone that forms the roof of the nose (—*also* **ethmoidal**). * *n* the ethmoid bone.

ethnic, ethnical *adj* of races or large groups of people classed according to common traits and customs.—**ethnically** *adv.*

ethno- *prefix* indicating race; people; culture.

ethnography *n* the area of anthropology dealing with the scientific description of human races.—**ethnographer** *n.* **ethnographic, ethnographical** *adj.*

ethnology *n* the scientific study of the origins and culture, etc of different races and peoples.—**ethnologic, ethnological** *adj.*—**ethnologist** *n.*

ethology *n* the scientific study of animal behaviour.—**ethologic, ethological** *adj.*—**ethologist** *n.*

ethos *n* the distinguishing character, sentiment, moral nature, or guiding beliefs of a person, group, or institution.

ethyl *n* the radical from which common alcohol and ether are derived.

ethylene *n* a colourless sweet-smelling gaseous hydrocarbon obtained from petroleum and used to manufacture chemicals including polythene.—*also* **ethene.**

etiolate *vti* (*green plants*) to bleach by depriving of light; to make or become pale and sickly.—**etiolation** *n.*

etiology *n* (*pl* **etiologies**) the study of causation, esp causes of diseases.—*also* **aetiology.**—**etiological** *adj.*—**etiologist** *n.*

etiquette *n* the form of conduct or behaviour prescribed by custom or authority to be observed in social, official or professional life.

Etruscan *n* an inhabitant of ancient Etruria (now Tuscany); the language of ancient Etruscans.—*also adj.*

étude *n* (*mus*) a short study or exercise for a solo instrument.

étui *n* (*pl* **étuis**) a pocket case for sewing implements and other small articles.

etymology *n* (*pl* **etymologies**) the study of the source and meaning of words; an account of the source and history of a word.—**etymological, etymologic** *adj.*—**etymologist** *n.*

etymon *n* (*pl* **etymons, etyma**) the root of a word, or its original meaning.

Eu (*chem symbol*) europium.

eucalyptol *n* a liquid contained in eucalyptus oil.

eucalyptus, eucalypt *n* (*pl* **eucalyptuses, eucalypti** *or* **eucalypts**) any of a genus of mostly Australian evergreen trees cultivated for their resin, oil, and wood; a type of oil obtained from its leaves.

Eucharist *n* the Christian sacrament of communion in which bread and wine are consecrated; the consecrated elements in communion.—**Eucharistic, Eucharistical** *adj.*

euchre *n* a card game for two, three or four players.

Euclidean *adj* pertaining to or accordant with the geometrical principles of Euclid, the Greek mathematician (*fl* 3rd century bc).

eudemonism, eudaemonism *n* the ethical doctrine that regards happiness as the chief end in moral conduct.

eudiometer *n* an instrument for measuring the amount of oxygen in the air.

eugenics *n* (*sing*) the science of improving the human race by selective breeding.—**eugenic** *adj.*—**eugenically** *adv.*—**eugenicist** *n.*

euhemerism *n* the theory that the classical deities are deified heroes and that the myths connected with them are based on real history.—**euhemerist** *n.*—**euhemeristic** *adj.*—**euhemeristically** *adv.*

eulogize *vt* to extol in speech or writing.—**eulogist, eulogizer***n.*—**eulogistic, eulogistical** *adj.*—**eulogistically** *adv.*

eulogy *n* (*pl* **eulogies**) a speech or piece of writing in praise or celebration of someone or something.

eunuch *n* a castrated man.

euonymus *n* a genus of small trees, containing the spindle tree.

euphemism *n* a mild or inoffensive word substituted for a more unpleasant or offensive term; the use of such inoffensive words.—**euphemistic** *adj.*—**euphemistically** *adv.*

euphonic, euphonical *adj* sounding pleasant to the ear.—**euphonically** *adv.*

euphonium *n* a brass musical instrument with its oval bell pointed backwards.

euphony *n* (*pl* **euphonies**) a pleasing sound, esp words.—**euphonious** *adj.*

euphorbia *n* a member of the large genus of plants of the spurge family.

euphoria *n* a feeling of elation.—**euphoric** *adj.*—**euphorically** *adv.*

euphuism *n* an affected style of prose using elaborate antithesis, alliteration, and conceits; the pedantic or affected use of words or language.—**euphuist** *n.*—**euphuistic, euphuistical** *adj.*

Eurasian *adj* of Europe and Asia (Eurasia) taken as one continent; of mixed European and Asian descent.—*also n.*

eureka *interj* used to express triumph on a discovery.

eurhythmics *see* **eurythmics.**

Euro- *prefix* Europe; European.

Eurocrat *n* a member of the administration of the European Community.

Europe *n* a continent extending from Asia in the east to the Atlantic Ocean in the west.

European *adj* relating to or native to Europe. * *n* a native or inhabitant of Europe; a person of European descent.

European Economic Community *or* **European Community** *n* the official name of the European Common Market, whose members aim to eliminate all obstacles to the free movement of goods, services, capital and labour between the member countries and to set up common external commercial, agricultural, and transport policies.

europium *n* a soft metallic element of the rare earth group.

eurythmics *npl* the art of representing musical harmony by physical gestures.—*also* **eurhythmics.**

Eustachian tube *n* a tube that leads from the middle ear to the pharynx.

euthanasia *n* the act or practice of killing painlessly, esp to relieve incurable suffering.

eV *abbr* = electronvolt.

evacuate *vti* to move (people, etc) from an area of danger to one of safety; to leave or make empty; to discharge wastes from the body.—**evacuation** *n.*—**evacuative** *adj.*—**evacuator** *n.*

evacuee *n* an evacuated person.

evade *vt* to manage to avoid, esp by dexterity or slyness.—**evadable** *adj.*—**evader** *n.*

evaluate *vt* to determine the value of; to assess.—**evaluation** *n.*—**evaluator** *n.*

evanescent *adj* fading away, vanishing; ephemeral.—**evanescence** *n.*

evangel *n* the Christian gospel.

evangelical *adj* of or agreeing with Christian teachings, esp as presented in the four Gospels; pertaining to various Christian sects that believe in salvation through personal conversion and faith in Christ.—**evangelicalism** *n.*

evangelism *n* preaching the Christian gospel; missionary zeal.

evangelist *n* a person who preaches the gospel; one of the writers of the four Gospels.—**evangelistic** *adj.*—**evangelistically** *adv.*

evangelize *vt* to preach or spread the gospel; to seek converts to a particular cause.—**evangelization** *n.*—**evangelizer** *n.*

evaporate *vti* to change into a vapour; to remove water from; to give off moisture; to vanish; to disappear.—**evaporable** *adj.*—**evaporation** *n.*—**evaporative** *adj.*—**evaporator** *n.*

evaporated milk *n* tinned unsweetened milk thickened by evaporation.

evasion *n* the act of evading; a means of evading, esp an equivocal reply or excuse.—**evasive** *adj.*—**evasively** *adv.*—**evasiveness** *n.*

eve *n* the evening or the whole day, before a festival; the period immediately before an event; (*formerly*) evening.

evection *n* (*astron*) a periodical irregularity of the moon's motion.

even *adj* level, flat; smooth; regular, equal; balanced; exact; divisible by two. * *vti* to make or become even; (*with* **up**) to balance (debts, etc). * *adv* exactly; precisely; fully; quite; at the very time; used as an intensive to emphasize the identity of something (*he looked content, even happy*), to indicate something unexpected (*she refused even to look at him*), or to stress the comparative degree (*she did even better*).—**evenly** *adv.*—**evenness** *n.*

even-handed *adj* impartial, fair.—**even-handedness** *n.*

evening *n* the latter part of the day and early part of the night.

evening primrose *n* a plant with yellow flowers that open in the evening.

evens *npl* (*bet*) winning the same as the stake if successful; offered at such odds, as a horse.—*also* **even money.**

evensong *n* vespers; evening prayers.

event *n* something that happens; a social occasion; contingency; a contest in a sports programme.
even-tempered *adj* calm.
eventful *adj* full of incidents; momentous
eventide *n* (*formerly*) evening.
eventual *adj* happening at some future unspecified time; ultimate.—**eventually** *adv*.
eventuality *n* (*pl* **eventualities**) a possible occurrence.
eventuate *vi* to result.—**eventuation** *n*.
ever *adv* always, at all times; at any time; in any case.
evergreen *adj* (*plants, trees*) having foliage that remains green all year.—*also n*.
everlasting *adj* enduring forever; (*plants*) having flowers that may be dried without loss of form or colour.—**everlastingly** *adv*.
evermore *adv* forever.
evert *vt* to turn inside out.—**eversible** *adj*.—**eversion** *n*.
every *adj* being one of the total.
everybody, everyone *pron* every person.
everyday *adj* happening daily; commonplace; worn or used on ordinary days.
everything *pron* all things, all; something of the utmost importance.
everywhere *adv* in every place.
evict *vt* to expel from land or from a building by legal process; to expel.—**eviction** *n*.—**evictor** *n*.
evidence *n* an outward sign; proof, testimony, esp matter submitted in court to determine the truth of alleged facts. * *vt* to demonstrate clearly; to give proof or evidence for.
evident *adj* easy to see or understand.—**evidently** *adv*.
evidential *adj* relating to, providing, or based on evidence.—**evidentially** *adv*.
evil *adj* wicked; causing or threatening distress or harm. * *n* a sin; a source of harm or distress.—**evilly** *adv*.—**evilness** *n*.
evildoer *n* a wicked person.—**evildoing** *n*.
evil eye *n* a stare superstitiously believed to inflict harm; the power to cause harm in this manner.
evince *vt* to indicate that one has (eg a quality); to demonstrate.—**evincible** *adj*.—**evincive** *adj*.
eviscerate *vt* to take out the intestines of, disembowel.—**evisceration** *n*.—**eviscerator** *n*.
evocative *adj* serving to evoke.—**evocatively** *n*.
evoke *vt* to call forth or up.—**evocable** *adj*.—**evocation** *n*.—**evoker** *n*.
evolution *n* a process of change in a particular direction; the process by which something attains its distinctive characteristics; a theory that existing types of plants and animals have developed from earlier forms.—**evolutionary, evolutional** *adj*.
evolutionist *adj* pertaining to evolution. * *n* someone who believes in the theory of evolution.
evolve *vi* to develop by or as if by evolution.—**evolvable** *adj*.—**evolvement** *n*.
ewe *n* a female sheep.
ewer *n* a large pitcher or jug with a wide spout.
ex[1] *n* (*inf*) a former husband, wife, etc.
ex[2] *prep* out of, from.
ex- *prefix* out, forth; quite, entirely; formerly.
exacerbate *vt* to make more violent, bitter, or severe.—**exacerbatingly** *adv*.—**exacerbation** *n*.
exact *adj* without error, absolutely accurate; detailed. * *vt* to compel by force, to extort; to require.—**exactable** *adj*.—**exactness** *n*.—**exactor, exacter** *n*.
exacting *adj* greatly demanding; requiring close attention and precision.—**exactingness** *n*.
exaction *n* the extortion of money, etc; an outrageous demand; something exacted.
exactitude *n* (the state of) being exact.
exactly *adv* in an exact manner; precisely. * *interj* quite so!
exaggerate *vt* to enlarge (a statement, etc) beyond what is really so or believable.—**exaggeration** *n*.—**exaggerative** *adj*.—**exaggerator** *n*.
exalt *vt* to raise up, esp in rank, power, or dignity.—**exalted** *adj*.—**exalter** *n*.
exaltation *n* elevation; rapture; a flock of larks.
exam *n* (*inf*) an examination.
examination *n* an examining, close scrutiny; a set of written or oral questions designed as a test of knowledge; the formal questioning of a witness on oath.—**examinational** *adj*.
examine *vt* to look at closely and carefully, to investigate; to test, esp by questioning.—**examinable** *adj*.—**examiner** *n*.
examinee *n* a person who is being tested in an examination.
example *n* a representative sample; a model to be followed or avoided; a problem to be solved in order to show the application of some rule; a warning to others.
exanimate *adj* dead, defunct, lifeless.—**exanimation** *n*.
exarch *n* a bishop of the Eastern Orthodox Church; the governor of a province under the Byzantine Empire.
exarchate, exarchy *n* the area of jurisdiction of an exarch.
exasperate *vt* to annoy intensely.—**exasperatedly** *adv*.—**exasperating** *adj*.—**exasperation** *n*.
Excalibur *n* in legend, King Arthur's sword.
ex cathedra *adj* with authority.
excavate *vt* to form a hole or tunnel by digging; to unearth; to expose to view (historical remains, etc) by digging away a covering.—**excavation** *n*.—**excavator** *n*.
exceed *vt* to be greater than or superior to; to go beyond the limit of.—**exceedable** *adj*.—**exceeder** *n*.
exceedingly *adv* very, extremely.
excel *vb* (**excelling, excelled**) *vt* to outdo, to be superior to. * *vi* (*with* **in, at**) to do better than others.
excellence *n* that in which one excels; superior merit or quality; (*with cap*) a title of honour given to certain high officials (—*also* **Excellency**).
excellent *adj* very good, outstanding.—**excellently** *adv*.
excelsior *interj* higher. * *n* soft wood shavings for stuffing.
except *vt* to exclude, to take or leave out. * *prep* not including; other than.—**exceptable** *adj*.
excepting *prep* except, not including.
exception *n* the act of excepting; something excepted; an objection.
exceptionable *adj* open to objection.—**exceptionably** *adv*.
exceptional *adj* unusual, forming an exception; superior.—**exceptionally** *adv*.
excerpt *n* an extract from a book, film, etc. * *vt* to select or quote (a passage from a book).—**exerptible** *adj*.—**exerption** *n*.
excess *n* the exceeding of proper established limits; the amount by which one thing or quantity exceeds another; (*pl*) overindulgence in eating or drinking; unacceptable conduct.
excessive *adj* greater than what is acceptable, too much.—**excessively** *adv*.—**excessiveness** *n*.
exchange *vt* to give and take (one thing in return for another); to give to and receive from another person. * *n* the exchanging of one thing for another; the thing exchanged; the conversion of money in one currency into a sum of equivalent value in another currency; the system of settling commercial debts between foreign governments, eg by bills of exchange; a place where things and services are exchanged, esp a marketplace for securities; a centre or device in which telephone lines are interconnected.—**exchangeable** *adj*.—**exchangeability** *n*.—**exchanger** *n*.
exchange rate *n* the rate at which one foreign currency may be exchanged for another.
exchequer *n* (*with cap*) the British governmental department in charge of finances; (*inf*) personal finances.
excise[1] *n* a tax on the manufacture, sale, or use of certain articles within a country.—**excisable** *adj*.
excise[2] *vt* to remove by cutting out.—**excision** *n*.
exciseman *n* (*pl* **excisemen**) (*formerly*) an officer employed to collect and enforce excise.
excitable *adj* easily excited.—**excitability, excitableness** *n*.
excitant *n* a stimulant. * *adj* stimulating.
excitation *n* the act of exciting; the state of excitement.—**excitative, excitatory** *adj*.

excite *vt* to arouse the feelings of, esp to generate feelings of pleasurable anticipation; to cause to experience strong emotion; to stir up, agitate; to rouse to activity; to stimulate a physiological response, eg in a bodily organ.

excited *adj* experiencing or expressing excitement.—**excitedly** *adv*.—**excitedness** *n*.

excitement *n* a feeling of strong, esp pleasurable, emotion; something that excites.

exciting *adj* causing excitement; stimulating.—**excitingly** *adv*.

exclaim *vti* to shout out or utter suddenly and with strong emotion.—**exclaimer** *n*.

exclamation *n* a sudden crying out; a word or utterance exclaimed.—**exclamational** *adj*.

exclamation point, exclamation mark *n* the punctuation mark (!) placed after an exclamation.

exclamatory *adj* of or expressing exclamation.—**exclamatorily** *adv*.

exclave *n* a small part of a country lying within the territory of another country.

exclude *vt* to shut out, to keep out; to reject or omit; to eject.—**excluder** *n*.—**exclusion** *n*.

exclusive *adj* excluding all else; reserved for particular persons; snobbishly aloof; fashionable, high-class, expensive; unobtainable or unpublished elsewhere; sole, undivided.—**exclusively** *adv*.—**exclusiveness** *n*.—**exclusivity** *n*.

excogitate *vt* to devise, to invent; to discover by thinking.—**excogitation** *n*.—**excogitative** *adj*.

excommunicate *vt* to bar from association with a church; to exclude from fellowship.—**excommunication** *n*.—**excommunicative** *adj*.—**excommunicator** *n*.

excoriate *vt* to strip of the skin; to flay.—**excoriation** *n*.

excrement *n* waste matter discharged from the bowels.—**excremental, excrementitious** *adj*.

excrescence *n* an outgrowth, esp abnormal, from a plant or animal; a disfigurement.

excrescent *adj* pertaining to excrescence; superfluous.

excreta *npl* waste matter discharged from the body, faeces, urine.

excrete *vt* to eliminate or discharge wastes from the body.—**excreter** *n*.—**excretion** *n*.—**excretive, excretory** *adj*.

excruciate *vt* to inflict severe pain upon; to torture.—**excruciation** *n*.

excruciating *adj* intensely painful or distressful; (*inf*) very bad.—**excruciatingly** *adv*.

exculpate *vt* to free (a person) from alleged fault or guilt.—**exculpable** *adj*.—**exculpation** *n*.

exculpatory *adj* tending or serving to exculpate.

excurrent *adj* (*bot*) (*leaf*) having a midrib running beyond the edge; (*tree*) having a projecting stem; (*zool*) having a duct, etc, whose contents flow out.

excursion *n* a pleasure trip; a short journey.

excursionist *n* someone going on an excursion.

excursive *adj* digressing, rambling.—**excursively** *adv*.

excursus *n* (*pl* **excursuses, excursus**) a dissertation added as a supplement to a work, giving additional information on certain points; a digression from the main subject of a work.

excusable *adj* able to be excused.—**excusably** *adv*.

excuse *vt* to pardon; to forgive; to give a reason or apology for; to be a reason or explanation of; to let off. * *n* an apology, a plea in extenuation.

ex-directory *adj* (*telephone number*) not listed in the telephone directory by request.

execrable *adj* appalling.—**execrableness** *n*.

execrate *vt* to denounce as evil; to abhor.—**execration** *n*.—**execrative, execratory** *adj*.

executant *n* a person who executes or performs, esp an artist, musician, etc.

execute *vt* to carry out, put into effect; to perform; to produce (eg a work of art); to make legally valid; to put to death by law.—**executable** *adj*.—**executer** *n*.

execution *n* the act or process of executing; the carrying out or suffering of a death sentence; the style or technique of performing, eg music.

executioner *n* a person who executes a death sentence upon a condemned prisoner.

executive *n* a person or group concerned with administration or management of a business or organization; the branch of government with the power to put laws, etc into effect. * *adj* having the power to execute decisions, laws, decrees, etc.

executor *n* a person appointed by a testator to see the terms of a will implemented.—**executorial** *adj*.—**executorship** *n*.

executory *adj* (*law*) pertaining to the execution of laws; to be carried out at a future date.

executrix *n* (*pl* **executrices, executrixes**) a female executor.

exegesis *n* (*pl* **exegeses**) an explanation or interpretation of a text or passage, esp of the Bible.

exegetic, exegetical *adj* expository; interpretative.

exegetics *n* (*sing*) the study of exegesis.

exemplar *n* a model; a typical instance or example.

exemplary *adj* deserving imitation; serving as a warning.—**exemplarily** *adv*.—**exemplariness** *n*.

exemplify *vt* (**exemplifying, exemplified**) to illustrate by example; to be an instance or example of.—**exemplification** *n*.—**exemplifier** *n*.

exempt *adj* not liable, free from the obligations required of others. * *vt* to grant immunity (from).—**exemptible** *adj*.—**exemption** *n*.

exercise *n* the use or application of a power or right; regular physical or mental exertion for health, amusement or acquisition of some skill; something performed to develop or test a specific ability or skill; (*often pl*) manoeuvres carried out for military training and discipline. * *vt* to use, exert, employ; to engage in regular physical activity to strengthen the body, etc; to train (troops) by means of drills and manoeuvres; to engage the attention of; to perplex.—**exercisable** *adj*.

exergue *n* the space below the principal design on a coin or medal for the insertion of a date, etc.—**exergual** *adj*.

exert *vt* to bring (eg strength, influence) into use.

exertion *n* an exerting; a strenuous effort.—**exertive** *adj*.

exeunt (*Latin*) they go off, a stage direction.

exfoliate *vi* to flake off; (*tree*) to shed bark.—**exfoliation** *n*.

ex gratia *adj* given as a favour or where no legal obligation exists.

exhalant *adj* exhaling. * *n* a duct, organ, etc used for exhaling.

exhale *vt* to breathe out.—**exhalation** *n*.

exhaust *vt* to use up completely; to make empty; to use up, tire out; (*subject*) to deal with or develop completely. * *n* the escape of waste gas or steam from an engine; the device through which these escape.—**exhausted** *adj*.—**exhauster** *n*.—**exhaustible** *adj*.—**exhausting** *adj*.

exhaustion *n* the act of exhausting or being exhausted; extreme weariness.

exhaustive *adj* comprehensive, thorough.—**exhaustively** *adv*.

exhibit *vt* to display, esp in public; to present to a court in legal form. * *n* an act or instance of exhibiting, something exhibited; something produced and identified in court for use as evidence.—**exhibitor** *n*.—**exhibitory** *adj*.

exhibition *n* a showing, a display; a public show; an allowance made to a student.

exhibitioner *n* a student who holds an exhibition.

exhibitionism *n* an excessive tendency to show off one's abilities; a compulsion to expose oneself indecently in public.—**exhibitionist** *n*.—**exhibitionistic** *adj*.

exhilarant *adj* exhilarating. * *n* something that exhilarates.

exhilarate *vt* to make very happy; to invigorate.—**exhilarating** *adj*.—**exhilaration** *n*.—**exhilarator** *n*.

exhort *vt* to urge or advise strongly.—**exhortation** *n*.—**exhortative, exhortatory** *adj*.—**exhorter** *n*.

exhume *vt* to dig up (a dead person) for detailed examination.—**exhumation** *n*.—**exhumer** *n*.

exigency, exigence *n* (*pl* **exigencies, exigences**) a pressing need; emergency.

exigent *adj* urgent; exacting.—**exigently** *adv*.

exigible *adj* (*debt etc*) liable to be exacted.
exiguous *adj* very small in amount, meagre.—**exiguity, exiguousness** *n*.
exile *n* prolonged absence from one's own country, either through choice or as a punishment; an exiled person. * *vt* to banish, to expel from one's native land.—**exilic, exilian** *adj*.
exist *vi* to have being; to just manage a living; to occur in a specific place under specific conditions.
existence *n* the state or fact of existing; continuance of life; lifestyle; everything that exists.
existent *adj* real, actual; existing; current.
existential *adj* of or pertaining to existence; existentialist.
existentialism *n* (*philos*) a movement stressing personal freedom and responsibility in relation to existence.—**existentialist** *n, adj*.
exit *n* a way out of an enclosed space; death; a departure from a stage. * *vi* to leave, withdraw; to go offstage.
ex libris *adj* from the library of. * *n* (*pl* **ex libris**) a book plate.
exocrine *adj* secreting though a duct; of or relating to exocrine glands or their secretions.
exocrine gland *n* a gland that releases secretions through a duct, eg a sweat gland.
exoderm *see* **ectoderm.**
exodus *n* the departure of many people; (*with cap*) the departure of the Israelites from Egypt led by Moses; (*Bible*) the second book of the Old Testament.
ex officio *adv, adj* by virtue of an official position.
exogamy *n* the practice of marrying only outside one's own tribe.—**exogamous** *adj*.
exogenous *adj* (*biol*) produced by external growth; a used or influenced by external factors.—**exogenously** *adv*.
exonerate *vt* to absolve from blame; to relieve from a responsibility, obligation.—**exoneration** *n*.—**exonerative** *adj*.—**exonerator** *n*.
exophthalmos, exophthalmus *n* protrusion of the eyeball.—**exophthalmic** *adj*.
exorbitant *adj* (*prices, demands, etc*) unreasonable, excessive.—**exorbitance** *n*.
exorcise, exorcize *vt* to expel an evil spirit (from a person or place) by ritual and prayer.—**exorciser, exorcizer** *n*.—**exorcism** *n*.—**exorcist** *n*.
exordium *n* (*pl* **exordiums, exordia**) the opening part of a speech or composition.—**exordial** *adj*.
exoteric *adj* accessible to ordinary people; external.—**exoterically** *adv*.—**exotericism** *n*.
exotic *adj* foreign; strange; excitingly different or unusual.—**exotically** *adv*.—**exoticism** *n*.—**exoticness** *n*.
exotica *npl* exotic items, esp as a collection.
expand *vt* to increase in size, bulk, extent, importance; to describe in fuller detail. * *vi* to become larger; to become more genial and responsive.—**expandable, expandible** *adj*.—**expander** *n*.
expanse *n* a wide area of land, etc; the extent of a spread-out area.
expansible *adj* capable of expansion, or of being expanded.—**expansibility** *n*.
expansile *adj* capable of expansion, or of causing expansion.
expansion *n* the act of expanding or being expanded; something expanded; the amount by which something expands; the fuller development of a theme, etc.—**expansionary** *adj*.
expansive *adj* able to or having the capacity to expand or cause expansion; comprehensive; (*person*) genial, communicative.—**expansively** *adv*.—**expansiveness** *n*.
ex parte *adj* (*law*) on behalf of one side only; partisan.
expatiate *vi* to speak or write at length; to enlarge.—**expatiation** *n*.—**expatiator** *n*.
expatriate *adj* living in another country; self-exiled or banished. * *n* an expatriate person. * *vti* to exile (oneself) or banish (another person). —**expatriation** *n*.
expect *vt* to anticipate; to regard as likely to arrive or happen; to consider necessary, reasonable or due; to think, suppose.
expectant *adj* expecting, hopeful; filled with anticipation; pregnant.—**expectantly** *adv*.—**expectancy, expectance** *n*.
expectation *n* the act or state of expecting; something that is expected to happen; (*pl*) prospects for the future, esp of inheritance.—**expectative** *adj*.
expectorant *n* a medicine that promotes expectoration.
expectorate *vti* to bring up (mucus) from the respiratory tract by coughing; to spit.—**expectoration** *n*.—**expectorator** *n*.
expediency, expedience *n* (*pl* **expediencies, expediences**) fitness, suitability; an inclination towards expedient methods.—**expediential** *adj*.
expedient *adj* suitable or desirable under the circumstances. * *n* a means to an end; a means devised or used for want of something better.—**expediently** *adv*.
expedite *vt* to carry out promptly; to facilitate.—**expediter, expeditor** *n*.
expedition *n* a journey to achieve some purpose, as exploration, etc; the party making this journey; speedy efficiency, promptness.
expeditionary *adj* of or constituting an expedition.
expeditious *adj* speedy; efficient.—**expeditiously** *adv*.
expel *vt* (**expelling, expelled**) to drive out, to eject; to banish.—**expellable** *adj*.—**expellee** *n*.—**expeller** *n*.
expend *vt* to spend (money, time, energy, etc); to use up, consume.—**expender** *n*.
expendable *adj* able to be consumed, not worth keeping; available for sacrifice to achieve some objective.—**expendability** *n*.
expenditure *n* the act or process of expending money, etc; the amount expended.
expense *n* a payment of money for something, expenditure; a cause of expenditure; (*pl*) money spent on some activity (eg travelling on business); reimbursement for this.
expense account *n* an account of expenses to be reimbursed to an employee.
expensive *adj* causing or involving great expense; costly.—**expensively** *adv*.—**expensiveness** *n*.
experience *n* observation or practice resulting in or tending towards knowledge; knowledge gained by seeing and doing; a state of being affected from without (as by events); an affecting event. * *vt* to have experience of.
experienced *adj* wise or skilled through experience.
experiential *adj* of or based on experience.
experiment *n* any test or trial to find out something; a controlled procedure carried out to discover, test, or demonstrate something. * *vi* to carry out experiments.—**experimentation** *n*.—**experimenter** *n*.
experimental *adj* of, derived from, or proceeding by experiment; empirical; provisional.—**experimentalism** *n*.—**experimentally** *adv*.
expert *adj* thoroughly skilled; knowledgeable through training and experience. * *n* a person with special skills or training in any art or science.—**expertly** *adv*.—**expertness** *n*.
expertise *n* expert knowledge or skill.
expiate *vt* to pay the penalty for; to make amends for.—**expiation** *n*.—**expiator** *n*.—**expiatory** *adj*.
expire *vti* to come to an end; to lapse or become void; to breathe out; to die.—**expiration** *n*.—**expirer** *n*.
expiry *n* (*pl* **expiries**) the ending of a period of validity, eg of a passport.
explain *vt* to make plain or clear; to give a reason for, account for.—**explainable** *adj*.—**explainer** *n*.
explanation *n* an act or process of explaining; something that explains, esp a statement.
explanatory, explanative *adj* serving as an explanation.—**explanatorily** *adv*.
expletive *n* a violent exclamation or swearword.
explicable *adj* able to be explained.
explicate *vt* to analyse the implications of; to explain in great detail.—**explication** *n*.—**explicative, explicatory** *adj*.—**explicator** *n*.
explicit *adj* clearly stated, not merely implied; outspoken, frank; graphically detailed.—**explicitly** *adv*.—**explicitness** *n*.

explode *vti* to burst or cause to blow up with a loud noise, as in the detonation of a bomb; (*emotions*) to burst out; (*population*) to increase rapidly; to expose (a theory, etc) as false.—**exploder** *n*.

exploit *n* a bold achievement. * *vt* to utilize, develop (raw materials, etc); to take unfair advantage of, esp for financial gain.—**exploitable** *adj*.—**exploitation** *n*.—**exploitative** *adj*.

exploratory, explorative *adj* for the purpose of exploring or investigating.

explore *vti* to examine or inquire into; to travel through (a country) for the purpose of (geographical) discovery; to examine minutely.—**exploration** *n*.—**explorer** *n*.

explosion *n* an act or instance of exploding; a sudden loud noise caused by this; an outburst of emotion; a rapid increase or expansion.

explosive *adj* liable to or able to explode; liable or threatening to burst out with violence and noise. * *n* an explosive substance.—**explosively** *adv*.

exponent *n* a person who explains or interprets something; a person who champions, advocates, or exemplifies; (*math*) an index of the power to which an expression is raised.

exponential *adj* of, relating to or having an exponent; (*math*) having a variable in an exponent; able to be expressed by an exponential function. * *n* an exponential function.—**exponentially** *adv*.

exponential function *n* a mathematical function in which the constant quantity of the expression is raised to the power of a variable quantity, i.e. the exponent.

export *vt* to send out (goods) of one country for sale in another. * *n* the act of exporting; the article exported.—**exportable** *adj*.—**exportation** *n*.—**exporter** *n*.

exposé *n* a revelation of crime, dishonesty, etc.

expose *vt* to deprive of protection or shelter; to subject to an influence (as light, weather); to display, reveal; to uncover or disclose.—**exposable** *adj*.—**exposal** *n*.—**exposer** *n*.

exposed *adj* open to view; not shielded or protected.—**exposedness** *n*.

exposition *n* a public show or exhibition; a detailed explanation; a speech or writing explaining a process, thing, or idea.—**expositional** *adj*.

expositive, expository *adj* of, pertaining to or conveying exposition; explanatory.—**expositively, expositorily** *adv*.

ex post facto *adj* (*law*) enacted retrospectively. * *adv* after the fact.

expostulate *vi* to argue with, esp to dissuade.—**expostulation** *n*.—**expostulator** *n*.—**expostulatory, expostulative** *adj*.

exposure *n* an exposing or state of being exposed; time during which light reaches and acts on a photographic film, paper or plate; publicity.

expound *vt* to explain or set forth in detail.—**expounder** *n*.

express *vt* to represent in words; to make known one's thoughts, feelings, etc; to represent by signs, symbols, etc; to squeeze out. * *adj* firmly stated, explicit; (*train, bus, etc*) travelling at high speed with few or no stops. * *adv* at high speed, by express service. * *n* an express train, coach, etc; a system or company for sending freight, etc at rates higher than standard.—**expresser** *n*.—**expressible** *adj*.

expression *n* an act of expressing, esp by words; a word or phrase; a look; intonation; a manner of showing feeling in communicating or performing (eg music); (*math*) a collection of symbols serving to express something.—**expressional** *adj*.—**expressionless** *adj*.

expressionism *n* a style of art, literature, music, etc that seeks to depict the subjective emotions aroused in the artist by objects and events, not objective reality.—**expressionist** *n*.—**expressionistic** *adj*.

expressive *adj* serving to express; full of expression.—**expressively** *adv*.—**expressiveness** *n*.

expressly *adv* explicitly; for a specific purpose.

expressway *n* a motorway.

expropriate *vt* to remove (property) from its owner, to dispossess.—**expropriable** *adj*.—**expropriation** *n*.—**expropriator** *n*.

expulsion *n* the act of expelling or being expelled.—**expulsive** *adj*.

expunge *vt* to obliterate, to erase.—**expunction** *n*.—**expunger** *n*.

expurgate *vt* to cut from a book, play, etc any parts supposed to be offensive or erroneous.—**expurgation** *n*.—**expurgator** *n*.—**expurgatory, expurgatorial** *adj*.

exquisite *adj* very beautiful, refined; sensitive, showing discrimination; acutely felt, as pain or pleasure.—**exquisitely** *adv*.

exsanguinate *vt* to drain of blood.—**exsanguination** *n*.

exsanguine *adj* bloodless.

exscind *vt* to cut off; to cut out, excise.

exsert *vt* to thrust outwards.—**exsertile** *adj*.—**exsertion** *n*.

exsiccate *vt* to dry up.—**exsiccation** *n*.

extant *adj* still existing.

extemporaneous, extemporary *adj* spoken, acted, etc without preparation.—**extemporaneously, extemporarily** *adv*.

extempore *adv, adj* without preparation, impromptu.

extemporize *vi* to do something extemporaneously.—**extemporization** *n*.

extend *vt* to stretch or spread out; to stretch fully; to prolong in time; to cause to reach in distance, etc; to enlarge, increase the scope of; to hold out (eg the hand); to accord, grant; to give, offer, (eg sympathy). * *vi* to prolong in distance or time; to reach in scope.

extended family *n* a family with three or more generations of blood relations living as a unit.

extendible, extendable *adj* able to be extended.—**extendibility, extendability** *n*.

extensible, extensile *adj* extendible.—**extensibility, extensibleness** *n*.

extension *n* the act of extending or state of being extended; extent, scope; an added part, eg to a building; an extra period; a programme of extramural teaching provided by a college, etc; an additional telephone connected to the principal line.

extensive *adj* large; having a wide scope or extent.—**extensively** *adv*. —**extensiveness** *n*.

extensometer *n* a type of micrometer for measuring the expansion of a body.

extensor *n* a muscle that extends or straightens a limb.

extent *n* the distance over which a thing is extended; the range or scope of something; the limit to which something extends.

extenuate *vt* to make (guilt, a fault, or offence) seem less.—**extenuating** *adj*.—**extenuator** *n*.—**extenuatory** *adj*.

extenuation *n* an extenuating or being extenuated, partial justification; something that extenuates, an excuse.

exterior *adj* of, on, or coming from the outside; external; (*paint, etc*) suitable for use on the outside. * *n* the external part or surface; outward manner or appearance.

exteriorize *vt* to externalize; (*med*) to move (an organ, etc) out of the body, usu to facilitate surgery.

exterminate *vt* to destroy completely.—**exterminable** *adj*.—**extermination** *n*.—**exterminatory** *adj*.

exterminator *n* one who or that which exterminates; a person who is employed to destroy pests, etc.

extern, externe *n* a non-resident doctor.

external *adj* outwardly perceivable; of, relating to, or located on the outside or outer part. * *n* an external feature.—**externally** *adv*.

externality *n* (*pl* **externalities**) a being external or externalized; something external; (*philos*) a being external to the perceiving mind.

externalize *vt* to make external; to attribute an external existence to; to express (feelings, etc) esp in words; (*psychol*) to project (opinions, feelings) onto others or one's surroundings.—**externalization** *n*.

exterritorial *adj* extraterritorial.—**exterritoriality** *n*.

extinct *adj* (*animals*) not alive, no longer existing; (*fire*) not burning, out; (*volcano*) no longer active.—**extinction** *n*.

extine *n* (*bot*) the outer coat of the pollen grain.

extinguish *vt* to put out (a fire, light, etc); to bring to an end.—**extinguishable** *adj*.—**extinguishment** *n*.

extinguisher *n* a device for putting out a fire.

extirpate *vt* to destroy totally, as by uprooting.—**extirpation** *n*.—**extirpative** *adj*.—**extirpator** *n*.

extol, extoll *vt* (**extols** *or* **extolls, extolling, extolled**) to praise highly.—**extoller** *n*.—**extollment, extolment** *n*.

extort *vt* to obtain (money, promises, etc) by force or improper pressure.—**extorter** *n*.—**extortive** *adj*.

extortion *n* the act or practice of extorting; the criminal instance of this; oppressive or unjust exaction.—**extortionary** *adj*.—**extortioner, extortionist** *n*.

extortionate *adj* exorbitant; excessively high in price.—**extortionately** *adv*.

extra *adj* additional. * *adv* unusually; in addition. * *n* something extra or additional, esp a charge; a special edition of a newspaper; a person who plays a non-speaking role in a film.

extra- *prefix* outside, beyond.

extract *vt* to take or pull out by force; to withdraw by chemical or physical means; to abstract, excerpt. * *n* the essence of a substance obtained by extraction; a passage taken from a book, play, film, etc.—**extractable, extractible** *adj*.—**extractability, extractibility** *n*.

extraction *n* the act of extracting; lineage; something extracted.

extractive *adj* tending or serving to extract.

extractor *n* one who extracts; a thing that extracts, esp a device for removing teeth or delivering a baby; a device for extracting stale air or fumes from a room (—*also* **extractor fan**).

extracurricular *adj* not part of the regular school timetable; beyond one's normal duties or activities.

extradite *vt* to surrender (an alleged criminal) to the country where the offence was committed.—**extraditable** *adj*.—**extradition** *n*.

extrados *n* (*pl* **extrados, extradoses**) (*archit*) the upper or outer curve of an arch.

extragalactic *adj* outside the Galaxy.

extrajudicial *adj* out of the ordinary course of legal proceedings.

extramarital *adj* occurring outside marriage, esp sexual relationships.

extramundane *adj* beyond the material world.

extramural *adj* (*course, studies*) outside the usual courses run by a university, etc; outside a city's walls or boundaries.—**extramurally** *adv*.

extraneous *adj* coming from outside; not essential.—**extraneously** *adv*.

extraordinary *adj* not usual or regular; remarkable, exceptional.—**extraordinarily** *adv*.—**extraordinariness** *n*.

extrapolate *vti* to infer (unknown data) from known data.—**extrapolation** *n*.—**extrapolator** *n*.

extrasensory perception *n* the claimed ability to obtain information by means other than the ordinary physical senses.

extraterritorial *adj* outside territorial boundaries; (*embassy etc*) outside the jurisdiction of the country in which it is.—*also* **exterritorial**.

extraterritoriality *n* exemption granted to foreign diplomats from the legal jurisdiction of the country to which they are posted; a country's jurisdiction over its nationals abroad.

extravagant *adj* lavish in spending; (*prices*) excessively high; wasteful; (*behaviour, praise, etc*) lacking in restraint, flamboyant, profuse.—**extravagantly** *adv*.—**extravagance** *n*.

extravaganza *n* an elaborate musical production; a spectacular show, play, film, etc.

extravagate *vi* (*arch*) to wander; to be extravagant.—**extravagation** *n*.

extravasate *vt* (*anat*) to force blood, etc out of its proper vessel; to exude. * *vi* to flow out.—**extravasation** *n*.

extraversion *see* **extroversion**.

extravert *see* **extrovert**.

extreme *adj* of the highest degree or intensity; excessive, immoderate, unwarranted; very severe, stringent; outermost. * *n* the highest or furthest limit or degree; (*often pl*) either of the two points marking the ends of a scale or range.—**extremely** *adv*.—**extremeness** *n*.

extremist *n* a person of extreme views, esp political.—**extremism** *n*.

extremity *n* (*pl* **extremities**) the utmost point or degree; the most remote part; the utmost violence, vigour, or necessity; the end; (*pl*) the hands or feet.

extricable *adj* able to be extricated.

extricate *vt* to release from difficulties; to disentangle.—**extrication** *n*.

extrinsic *adj* external; not inherent or essential.—**extrinsically** *adv*.

extrorse *adj* (*bot*) turned outwards.

extroversion *n* the state of having thoughts and activities directed towards things other than oneself.—*also* **extraversion**.

extrovert *n* a person more interested in the external world than his own thoughts and feelings.—*also* **extravert**.—**extroverted, extraverted** *adj*.

extrude *vt* to force or push out; to mould (metal or plastic) by forcing through a shaped die.—**extrusion** *n*.—**extrusive** *adj*.

exuberant *adj* lively, effusive, high-spirited; profuse.—**exuberance** *n*.—**exuberantly** *adv*.

exuberate *vi* to be exuberant; (*arch*) to abound.

exudate *n* exuded matter, eg sweat.

exudation *n* an exuding or being exuded; exuded matter, eg sweat.—**exudative** *adj*.

exude *vt* to cause or allow to ooze through pores or incisions, as sweat, pus; to display (confidence, emotion) freely.

exult *vi* to rejoice greatly.—**exultation** *n*.

exultant *adj* exulting, joyful; triumphant.—**exultantly** *adv*.

exuviae *npl* the cast-off skins, shells, etc, of animals.—**exuvial** *adj*.

exuviate *vt* (*skin*) to shed, slough.—**exuviation** *n*.

eyas *n* a young hawk.

eye *n* the organ of sight; the iris; the faculty of seeing; the external part of the eye; something resembling an eye, as the hole in a needle, the leaf-bud on a potato, etc. * *vt* (**eyeing** *or* **eying, eyed**) to look at; to observe closely.

eyeball *n* the ball of the eye. * *vt* (*sl*) to stare at.

eyebright *n* a plant with small white and purplish flowers, formerly used as a lotion to treat disorders of the eye.

eyebrow *n* the hairy ridge above the eye.

eye-catching *adj* attractive or striking in appearance.—**eye-catcher** *n*.

eyeful *adj* (*inf*) a close look, gaze; an attractive vision, esp a woman.

eyeglass *n* a lens for correcting defective vision, a monocle.

eyeglasses *npl* spectacles.

eyelash *n* the fringe of fine hairs along the edge of each eyelid.

eyeless *adj* without eyes; blind.

eyelet *n* a small hole for a rope or cord to pass through, as in sails, garments, etc.

eyelid *n* the lid of skin and muscle that moves to cover the eye.

eye-liner *n* a cosmetic used to apply a line round the eye.

eye-opener *n* something that comes as a shock or surprise.

eyepiece *n* the lens or lenses at the end nearest the eye of an optical instrument, eg a telescope.

eyeprint *n* the pattern of veins in the retina, which is unique to an individual and used as a means of identification.

eye-shadow *n* a coloured powder applied to accentuate or decorate the eyelids.

eyeshot *n* seeing distance.

eyesight *n* the faculty of seeing.

eyesore *n* anything offensive to the sight.

eyespot *n* a rudimentary visual organ; (*on butterflies, etc*) a marking resembling an eye.

eyetooth *n* (*pl* **eyeteeth**) a canine tooth in the upper jaw.

eyewash *n* (*inf*) nonsense, drivel.

eye-witness *n* a person who sees an event, such as an accident or a crime, and can describe what happened.

eyrie *n* the nest of an eagle or other bird of prey; any high inaccessible place or position.—*also* **aerie**.

F

F *abbr* = Fahrenheit; (*chem symbol*) fluorine.

f, F *n* the 6th letter of the English alphabet.

fa *n* (*music*) the fourth note in the sol-fa musical notation.—*also* **fah**.

fabaceous *adj* (*bot*) bean-like.

Fabian *adj* pertaining to the tactics of the Roman general, Fabius Maximus; cautiously persistent; watchful. * *n* a member of the Fabian Society.

Fabian Society *n* a society seeking socialism by moral persuasion.

fable *n* a story, often with animal characters, intended to convey a moral; a lie, fabrication; a story involving mythical, legendary or supernatural characters or events.

fabled *adj* related in fables; fictitious.

fabric *n* cloth made by knitting, weaving, etc; framework, structure.

fabricate *vt* to construct, manufacture; to concoct (eg a lie); to forge.—**fabrication** *n*.—**fabricator** *n*.

fabulist *n* a writer of fables; a liar.

fabulous *adj* told in fables; incredible, astonishing; (*inf*) very good.—**fabulously** *adv*.

façade, facade *n* the main front or face of a building; an outward appearance, esp concealing something hidden.

face *n* the front part of the head containing the eyes, nose, mouth, chin, etc; facial expression; the front or outer surface of anything; external show or appearance; dignity, self respect; impudence, effrontery; a coal face. * *vt* to be confronted by (a problem, etc); to deal with (an opponent, problem, etc) resolutely; to be opposite to; to turn (a playing card) face upwards; to cover with a new surface. * *vi* to turn the face in a certain direction; to be situated in or have a specific direction.

face card *n* the king, queen or jack in a pack of cards.

faceless *adj* lacking a face; anonymous.

face-lift *n* plastic surgery to smooth and firm the face; an improvement or renovation, esp to the outside of a building.

facer *n* someone who, or something which, faces; (*inf*) an unexpected setback.

face-saving *adj* allowing the preservation of dignity and prevention of humiliation.

facet *n* a small plane surface (as on a cut gem); an aspect of character, a problem, issue, etc.

facetiae *npl* witty sayings; books characterized by coarse wit.

face-time *n* (*sl*) a spell of duty, esp by US Secret Service agents guarding the President or others.

facetious *adj* joking, esp in an inappropriate manner.—**facetiously** *adv*.—**facetiousness** *n*.

face value *n* the value indicated on the face of (e.g. a coin or share certificate); apparent worth or significance.

facia *see* **fascia**.

facial *adj* of or pertaining to the face. * *n* a beauty treatment for the face.—**facially** *adv*.

facies *n* (*pl* **facies**) the general appearance of a person or a group of plants, animals or rocks; the face.

facile *adj* easy to do; superficial.

facilitate *vt* to make easier; to help forward.—**facilitator** *n*.—**facilitation** *n*.

facility *n* (**facilities**) the quality of being easily done; aptitude, dexterity; something, eg a service or equipment, that makes it easy to do something.

facing *n* a lining at the edge of a garment; a covering on a surface for decoration or protection.

facsimile *n* an exact copy of a book, document, etc; a method of transmitting printed matter (text and graphics) through the telephone system.—*also* **fax**.

fact *n* a thing known to have happened or to exist; reality; a piece of verifiable information; (*law*) an event, occurrence, etc as distinguished from its legal consequences.

faction[1] *n* a small group of people in an organization working together in a common cause against the main body; dissension within a group or organization.—**factional** *adj*.—**factionally** *adv*.—**factious** *adj*.

faction[2] *n* a book, film, etc based on facts but presented as a blend of fact and fiction.

factitious *adj* contrived, artificial.—**factitiously** *adv*.

factitive *adj* (*gram*) causative.

factor *n* any circumstance that contributes towards a result; (*math*) any of two or more numbers that, when multiplied together, form a product; a person who acts for another.

factor 8 *n* a blood-clotting agent used in the treatment of haemophilia.

factorage *n* a factor's commission.

factorial *n* (*math*) an integer multiplied by all lower integers, *eg* 4 x 3 x 2 x 1.

factorize *vt* to reduce to factors.—**factorization** *n*.

factory *n* (*pl* **factories**) a building or buildings where things are manufactured.

factory farm *n* a farm which rears livestock intensively using modern manufacturing processes.—**factory farming** *n*.

factory ship *n* a ship that processes the catch of a fishing fleet.

factotum *n* a person employed to do all kinds of work.

facts of life *npl* knowledge of human sexual reproduction.

factual *adj* based on, or containing, facts; actual.—**factually** *adv*.

facula *n* (*pl* **faculae**) a bright spot or streak on the surface of the sun.

facultative *adj* enabling; optional; contingent.

faculty *n* (*pl* **faculties**) any natural power of a living organism; special aptitude; a teaching department of a college or university, or the staff of such a department.

fad *n* a personal habit or idiosyncrasy; a craze.—**faddish, faddy** *adj*.—**faddism** *n*.—**faddist** *n*.

fade *vi* to lose vigour or brightness of colour gradually; to vanish gradually. * *vt* to cause (an image or a sound) to increase or decrease in brightness or intensity gradually.—*also n*.

fadeless *adj* unfading.

fading *n* decay; loss of colour; (*radio*) a deterioration in quality of reception.

faeces *npl* excrement.—*also* **feces**.—**faecal, fecal** *adj*.

faerie, faery *n* (*pl* **faeries**) (*arch*) the fairy world; enchantment.

Faeroese *n* (*pl* **Faeroese**) an inhabitant of the Faeroes in the North Atlantic; the language of the Faeroes.—*also adj*.—*also* **Faroese**.

fag *vti* (**fagging, fagged**) to become or cause to be tired by hard work. * *n* (*formerly*) a British public schoolboy who performs chores for senior pupils; (*inf*) drudgery; (*sl*) a homosexual; (*sl*) a cigarette.

fag-end *n* the useless remains of anything; (*sl*) a cigarette-end.

faggot[1], **fagot** *n* a bundle of sticks for fuel; (*sl*) a nasty old woman.

faggot[2] *n* (*sl*) in US, a male homosexual.

faggoting, fagoting *n* a method of decorating textile fabrics.

fah *see* **fa**.

Fahrenheit *adj* of, using, or being a temperature scale with the freezing point of water marked at 32∓ and the boiling point at 212∓.

faïence, faience *n* a type of decorated earthenware.

fail *vi* to weaken, to fade or die away; to stop operating; to fall short; to be insufficient; to be negligent in duty, expectation, etc; (*exam, etc*) to be unsuccessful; to become bankrupt. * *vt* to disappoint the expectations or hopes of; to be unsuccessful in an exam, etc; to leave, to abandon; to grade (a candidate) as not passing a test, etc. * *n* failure in an examination.

failing *n* a fault, weakness. * *prep* in default or absence of.

faille *n* a soft silk, used for dresses and hat trimmings.

fail-safe *adj* designed to operate safely even if a fault develops; foolproof.

failure *n* failing, non-performance, lack of success; the ceasing of normal operation of something; a deficiency; bankruptcy; an unsuccessful person or thing.

fain *adv* (*arch*) willingly; gladly. * *adj* willing; glad.

fainéant, faineant *adj* indolent.

faint *adj* dim, indistinct; weak, feeble; timid; on the verge of losing consciousness. * *vi* to lose consciousness temporarily from a decrease in the supply of blood to the brain, as from shock. * *n* an act or condition of fainting.—**faintly** *adv*.—**faintness** *n*.

faint-hearted *adj* lacking courage and resolution.

fainting *n* a sudden and temporary loss of consciousness.

fair[1] *adj* pleasing to the eye; clean, unblemished; (*hair*) light-coloured; (*weather*) clear and sunny; (*handwriting*) easy to read; just and honest; according to the rules; moderately large; average. * *adv* in a fair manner; squarely.—**fairness** *n*.

fair[2] *n* a gathering for the sale of goods, esp for charity; a competitive exhibition of farm, household, or manufactured goods; a fun-fair.
fair game *n* a legitimate target for attack or ridicule.
fairground *n* an open area where fairs are held.
fairing *n* a structure attached to the exterior of an aircraft, ship, motor vehicle, etc to reduce drag.
fairly *adv* in a fair manner; justly; moderately.
fair play *n* justice, honesty; impartiality.
fairway *n* a navigable channel; the mowed part of a golf course between the tee and the green.
fair-weather *adj* (*friend*) unreliable in troubled times.
fairy *n* (*pl* **fairies**) an imaginary supernatural being, usu in human form; (*sl*) a male homosexual.
fairyland *n* the country of fairies; a beautiful, enchanting place.
fairy ring *n* a dark or bare ring in grass caused by fungi.
fairy story, fairy tale *n* a story about fairies; an incredible story; a fabrication.
fait accompli *n* (*pl* **faits accomplis**) something already done; an irreversible act.
faith *n* trust or confidence in a person or thing; a strong conviction, esp a belief in a religion; any system of religious belief; fidelity to one's promises, sincerity.
faithful *adj* loyal; true; true to the original, accurate.—**faithfully** *adv*.—**faithfulness** *n*.
faithless *adj* treacherous, disloyal; untrustworthy.—**faithlessly** *adv*.—**faithlessness** *n*.
fake *vt* to make (an object) appear more real or valuable in order to deceive; to pretend, simulate. * *n* a faked article, a forgery; an impostor. * *adj* counterfeit, not genuine.—**faker** *n*.
fakir *n* a Muslim or Hindu religious mendicant or ascetic.
Falangist *n* a supporter of the Spanish Falange, a fascist party founded in 1933.
falbala *n* a flounce on a dress.
falcate, falciform *adj* sickle-shaped.
falchion *n* a broad, curved sword.
falcon *n* a type of hawk trained for use in falconry.
falconer *n* a person who hunts with, or who breeds and trains hawks for hunting.—**falconry** *n*.
falconet *n* a small falcon.
falderal *n* a trifling ornament.
faldstool *n* an armless chair, used by a bishop.
fall *vi* (**falling, fell,** *pp* **fallen**) to descend by force of gravity; to come as if by falling; to collapse; to drop to the ground; to become lower, weaker, less; to lose power, status, etc; to lose office; to slope in a downward direction; to be wounded or killed in battle; to pass into a certain state; to become pregnant; to take place, happen; to be directed by chance; to come by inheritance; (*with* **about**) to laugh uncontrollably; (*with* **back**) to retreat; (*with* **behind**) to fail to keep up with; to become in arrears with; (*with* **for**) to fall in love with; to be fooled by (a lie, trick, etc); (*with* **out**) to quarrel; to leave one's place in a military formation; (*with* **through**) to fail to happen. * *n* act or instance of falling; something which falls; the amount by which something falls; a decline in status, position; overthrow; a downward slope; a decrease in size, quantity, value; (*US*) autumn; (*wrestling*) a scoring move by pinning both shoulders of an opponent to the floor at once.
fallacious *adj* misleading.—**fallaciously** *adv*.—**fallaciousness** *n*.
fallacy *n* (*pl* **fallacies**) a false idea; a mistake in reasoning.
fallal *n* a piece of finery, an ornament.
fallen *adj* sunk to a lower state or condition; overthrown.
fall guy *n* (*inf*) a person who is easily cheated; a scapegoat
fallible *adj* liable to make mistakes.—**fallibly** *adv*.—**fallibility** *n*.
Fallopian tube *n* either of the two tubes through which the egg cells pass from the ovary to the uterus.
fall-out *n* a deposit of radioactive dust from a nuclear explosion; a by-product.
fallow[1] *adj* (*land*) ploughed and left unplanted for a season or more.
fallow[2] *adj* yellowish-brown.
fallow deer *n* a small European deer with a brownish-yellow coat which becomes spotted with white in summer.
false *adj* wrong, incorrect; deceitful; artificial; disloyal, treacherous; misleading, fallacious.—**falsely** *adv*.—**falseness** *n*.
falsehood *n* a being untrue; the act of deceiving; a lie.
falsetto *n* (*pl* **falsettos**) an artificial tone higher in key than the natural compass of the voice.
falsify *vt* (**falsifying, falsified**) to misrepresent; to alter (a document, etc) fraudulently; to prove false.—**falsification** *n*.
falsity *n* (*pl* **falsities**) the quality of being false; an error, a lie.
falter *vi* to move or walk unsteadily, to stumble; to hesitate or stammer in speech; to be weak or unsure, to waver.—**falteringly** *adv*.
fame *n* the state of being well known; good reputation.—**famed** *adj*.
familiar *adj* well-acquainted; friendly; common; well-known; too informal, presumptuous. * *n* a spirit or demon supposed to aid a witch, etc; an intimate.—**familiarly** *adv*.—**familiarity** *n*.
familiarize *vt* to make well known or acquainted; to make (something) well known.—**familiarization** *n*.
family *n* (*pl* **families**) parents and their children; a person's children; a set of relatives; the descendants of a common ancestor; any group of persons or things related in some way; a group of related plants or animals; a unit of a crime syndicate (as the Mafia).
family circle *n* close relatives.
family name *n* a surname.
family planning *n* birth control.
family tree *n* a genealogical diagram.
famine *n* an acute scarcity of food in a particular area; an extreme scarcity of anything.
famish *vti* to make or be very hungry.
famous *adj* renowned; (*inf*) excellent.—**famously** *adv*.
famulus *n* (*pl* **famuli**) a magician's assistant.
fan[1] *n* a handheld or mechanical device used to set up a current of air. * *vt* (**fanning, fanned**) to cool, as with a fan; to ventilate; to stir up, to excite; to spread out like a fan.
fan[2] *n* an enthusiastic follower of some sport, hobby, person, etc.
fanatic *n* a person who is excessively enthusiastic about something.—**fanatical** *adj*.—**fanatically** *adv*.
fanaticism *n* excessive enthusiasm.
fanaticize *vti* to make or become fanatical.
fan belt *n* the belt that drives the cooling fan in a car engine.
fancied *adj* imaginary.
fancier *n* a person with a special interest in something, esp plant or animal breeding.
fanciful *adj* not factual, imaginary; indulging in fancy; elaborate or intricate in design.—**fancifully** *adv*.
fan club *n* an organized group of followers of a celebrity.
fancy *n* (*pl* **fancies**) imagination; a mental image; a whim; fondness. * *adj* (**fancier, fanciest**) not based on fact, imaginary; elegant or ornamental. * *vt* (**fancying, fancied**) to imagine; to have a fancy or liking for; (*inf*) to be sexually attracted to.
fancy dress *n* a costume worn at masquerades or parties, usu representing an animal, historical character, etc.
fancy-free *adj* uncommitted, carefree.
fancy man *n* (*sl*) a woman's lover; a pimp.
fancy woman *n* (*sl*) a mistress, prostitute.
fancywork *n* ornamental needlework.
fandango *n* (*pl* **fandangos**) a Spanish dance, music for this dance, tomfoolery.
fanfare *n* a flourish of trumpets.
fang *n* a long sharp tooth, as in a canine; the long hollow tooth through which venomous snakes inject poison.
fanlight *n* a semicircular window with radiating bars like the ribs of a fan.
fanny *n* (*pl* **fannies**) (*vulg*) the female genitals; (*US sl*) the buttocks.

fantail *n* a pigeon with a tail that opens out like a fan.
fantan *n* a Chinese gambling game in which players make guesses about hidden counters.
fantasia *n* an improvised musical or prose composition.
fantasize *vt* to imagine in an extravagant way. * *vi* to daydream.
fantast *n* a visionary or dreamer.
fantastic *adj* unrealistic, fanciful; unbelievable; imaginative; (*inf*) wonderful.—**fantastically** *adv*.
fantasy *n* (*pl* **fantasies**) imagination; a product of the imagination, esp an extravagant or bizarre notion or creation; an imaginative poem, play or novel.
fanzine *n* a magazine produced by and for the fans of a celebrity, football club, etc.
FAO *abbr* = Food and Agricultural Organization.
far *adj* (**farther, farthest** *or* **further, furthest**) remote in space or time; long; (*political views, etc*) extreme * *adv* very distant in space, time, or degree; to or from a distance in time or position, very much.—**farness** *n*.
farad *n* a unit of electrical capacitance.
faradic *adj* pertaining to the phenomenon of induced electricity, or to faradization.
faradize *vt* to treat by use of a faradic current.—**faradization** *n*.—**faradizer** *n*
farandole *n* a lively dance, originating in Provence.
faraway *adj* distant, remote; dreamy.
farce *n* a style of light comedy; a drama using such comedy; a ludicrous situation.—**farcical** *adj*.—**farcically** *adv*.
farceur, farceuse *n* a writer of or actor in a farce; a wit.
farcy *n* (*pl* **farcies**) a disease of horses, closely allied to glanders.
fardel *n* (*arch*) a bundle or burden.
fare *n* money paid for transportation; a passenger in public transport; food. * *vi* to be in a specified condition.
Far East *n* the countries of East and Southeast Asia including China, Japan, North and South Korea, Indochina, eastern Siberia and adjacent islands.
farewell *interj* goodbye.—*also n*.
far-fetched *adj* unlikely.
far-flung *adj* spread over a wide area; remote.
farina *n* flour or meal obtained by grinding the seeds of cereals and leguminous plants; starch.
farinaceous *adj* consisting of, or made from, farina; mealy.
farinose *adj* producing farina; resembling farina.
farm *n* an area of land (with buildings) on which crops and animals are raised. * *vt* to grow crops or breed livestock; to cultivate, as land; to breed fish commercially; (*with* **out**) to put out (work, etc) to be done by others, to subcontract.
farmer *n* a person who manages or operates a farm.
farm hand *n* a worker on a farm.
farmhouse *n* a house on a farm.
farming *adj* pertaining to, or engaged in, agriculture. * *n* the business or practice of agriculture.
farmstead *n* a farm with the buildings belonging to it.
farmyard *n* a yard close to or surrounded by farm buildings.
faro *n* a gambling card game.
farouche *adj* sullen; unsociable.
far-out *adj* (*sl*) weird, bizarre; fantastic, wonderful. * *interj* used to express delight.
farrago *n* (*pl* **farragoes**) a confused collection.—**farraginous** *adj*.
far-reaching *adj* having serious or widespread consequences.
farrier *n* a person who shoes horses.
farrow *n* a litter of pigs. * *vti* to give birth to (pigs).
far-seeing *adj* having foresight.
fart *vi* (*vulg*) to expel wind from the anus.—*also n*.
farther *adj* at or to a greater distance. * *adv* to a greater degree.
farthest *adj* at or to the greatest distance. * *adv* to the greatest degree.
farthing *n* a former British monetary unit.
farthingale *n* a hooped support worn beneath a skirt to expand it at the hip line.
fasces *npl* a bundle of rods with an axe used in ancient Rome as a symbol of authority.
fascia *n* (*pl* **fasciae**) the instrument panel of a motor vehicle, the dashboard; the flat surface above a shop front, with the owner's name, etc.—*also* **facia**.
fascicle *n* one part of a book published by instalments (—*also* **fascicule**); a small collection, group or bundle; (*bot*) a cluster of leaves, roots, etc.
fascicular, fasciculate *adj* (*bot*) arranged in fascicles.
fascicule *n* a fascicle.
fasciculus *n* (*pl* **fasciculi**) (*anat*) a bundle of nerve fibres; a fascicle.
fascinate *vt* to hold the attention of, to attract irresistibly.—**fascination** *n*.
fascinating *adj* having great interest or charm.
fascine *n* a long bundle of sticks bound together, used for fortifying ditches, building earthworks, etc.
Fascism *n* a system of government characterized by dictatorship, belligerent nationalism, racism, and militarism.—**Fascist** *n, adj*.
fash *vti* (*Scot*) to bother, worry. * *n* worry; trouble.
fashion *n* the current style of dress, conduct, speech, etc; the manner or form of appearance or action. * *vt* to make in a particular form; to suit or adapt.—**fashioner** *n*.
fashionable *adj* conforming to the current fashion; attracting or frequented by people of fashion.—**fashionably** *adv*.
fast[1] *adj* swift, quick; (*clock*) ahead of time; firmly attached, fixed; (*colour, dye*) non-fading; wild, promiscuous. * *adv* firmly, thoroughly, rapidly, quickly.
fast[2] *vi* to go without all or certain foods. * *n* a period of fasting.
fastback *n* a car with a roof that slopes to the back.
fast breeder reactor *n* a nuclear reactor that produces more fissile material than it uses.
fasten *vti* to secure firmly; to attach; to fix or direct (the eyes, attention) steadily.
fastener, fastening *n* a clip, catch, etc for fastening.
fast food *n* food, such as hamburgers, kebabs, pizzas, etc prepared and served quickly.
fast-forward *vt* to move (video or music tape, etc) on at high speed.
fastidious *adj* hard to please; daintily refined; over-sensitive.—**fastidiously** *adv*.—**fastidiousness** *n*.
fastigiate *adj* (*biol*) narrowing at the apex.
fastness *n* swiftness; colourfast quality; a stronghold.
fast track *n* a hectic and competitive lifestyle or career.—**fast-track** *adj*.
fat *adj* (**fatter, fattest**) plump; thick; fertile; profitable. * *n* an oily or greasy material found in animal tissue and plant seeds; the richest or best part of anything; a superfluous part.—**fatness** *n*.
fatal *adj* causing death; disastrous (to); fateful.—**fatally** *adv*.
fatalism *n* belief that all events are predetermined by fate and therefore inevitable; acceptance of this doctrine.—**fatalist** *n*.—**fatalistic** *adj*.
fatality *n* (*pl* **fatalities**) a death caused by a disaster or accident; a person killed in such a way; a fatal power or influence.
fat cat *n* (*sl*) a rich person.
fate *n* the ultimate power that predetermines events, destiny; the ultimate end, outcome; misfortune, doom, death.
fated *adj* doomed; destined by fate.
fateful *adj* having important, usu unpleasant, consequences.—**fatefully** *adv*.
Fates *npl* (*Greek myth*) the three goddesses of destiny, Atropos, Clotho and Lachesis.
fathead *n* (*inf*) an idiot.
father *n* a male parent; an ancestor; a founder or originator; (*with cap*) God; a title of respect applied to monks, priests, etc. * *vt* to be the father of; to found, originate.—**fatherhood** *n*.
father-in-law *n* (*pl* **fathers-in-law**) the father of one's husband or wife.
fatherland *n* one's native country.
fatherless *adj* without a living father.
fatherly *adj* pertaining to a father; kind, affectionate, as a father. * *adv* like a father.

fathom *n* a nautical measure of 6 feet (1.83 m). * *vt* to measure the depth of; to understand.
fatidic, fatidical *adj* having the gift of prophecy.
fatigue *n* tiredness from physical or mental effort; the tendency of a material to break under repeated stress; any of the menial or manual tasks performed by military personnel; (*pl*) the clothing worn on fatigue or in the field. * *vti* (**fatiguing, fatigued**) to make or become tired.
fatling *n* a young animal fattened for slaughter.
fatten *vt* to make fat or fleshy; to make abundant.—**fattening** *adj*.
fat transfer *n* a cosmetic surgery procedure to take fat from parts of the body, eg hips, and insert it in the face to reduce wrinkling.
fatty acid *n* any of various organic carboxylic acids (e.g. palmitic, stearic and oleic) present in fats and oils.
fatty *adj* (**fattier, fattiest**) resembling or containing fat. * *n* (*pl* **fatties**) (*inf*) a fat person.
fatuous *adj* foolish, idiotic.—**fatuously** *adv*.—**fatuousness** *n*.—**fatuity** *n*.
fatwa, fatwah *n* a decision by a mufti or Muslim judge.
faubourg *n* a suburb, esp of Paris in France.
faucal *adj* (*anat*) of the fauces; (*sound*) deeply guttural.
fauces *n* (*pl* **fauces**) (*anat*) the upper part of the throat.
faucet *n* a fixture for draining off liquid (as from a pipe or cask); a device controlling the flow of liquid through a pipe or from a container (—*also* **tap**).
faugh *interj* an expression of disgust or abhorrence.
fault *n* a failing, defect; a minor offence; (*tennis, etc*) an incorrect serve or other error; a fracture in the earth's crust causing displacement of strata. * *vt* to find fault with, blame. * *vi* to commit a fault.
fault-finding *adj* censorious, critical.—**fault-finder** *n*.
faultless *adj* without fault; perfect; blameless.—**faultlessly** *adv*.—**faultlessness** *n*.
faulty *adj* (**faultier, faultiest**) imperfect; defective; wrong.—**faultily** *adv*.—**faultiness** *n*.
faun *n* (*Roman myth*) a woodland deity, half man, half beast.
fauna *n* (*pl* **faunas, faunae**) the animals of a region, period, or specific environment.
faute de mieux in the absence of anything better.
fauteuil *n* an armchair; a stall in a theatre.
faux pas *n* (*pl* **faux pas**) an embarrassing social blunder.
faveolate *adj* honeycombed.
favonian *adj* of or pertaining to the west wind; (*poet*) favourable.
favour, favor *n* goodwill; approval; a kind or helpful act; partiality; a small gift given out at a party; (*usu pl*) a privilege granted or conceded, esp sexual. * *vt* to regard or treat with favour; to show support for; to oblige (with); to afford advantage to, facilitate.
favourable, favorable *adj* expressing approval; pleasing; propitious; conducive (to).—**favourably, favorably** *adv*.
favourite, favorite *n* a favoured person or thing; a competitor expected to win. * *adj* most preferred.
favouritism, favoritism *n* the showing of unfair favour.
fawn[1] *n* a young deer; a yellowish-brown colour. * *adj* fawn-coloured.
fawn[2] *vi* (*dogs, etc*) to crouch, etc in a show of affection; to flatter in an obsequious manner.—**fawner** *n*.—**fawning** *n*.
fax *n* a document sent by facsimile transmission; a device for sending faxes. * *vt* to send (a document) by facsimile transmission.
fay *n* a fairy.
faze *vt* (*inf*) to disturb; to discompose, to disconcert; to daunt.
FBI *abbr* = Federal Bureau of Investigation.
FC *abbr* (Brit) = Football Club.
Fe (*chem symbol*) iron.
fealty *n* (*pl* **fealties**) (*feudal society*) the loyalty due from a vassal to his feudal lord.
fear *n* an unpleasant emotion excited by danger, pain, etc; a cause of fear; anxiety; deep reverence. * *vt* to feel fear, be afraid of; to be apprehensive, anxious; to be sorry. * *vi* to be afraid or apprehensive.—**fearless** *adj*.—**fearlessly** *adv*.—**fearlessness** *n*.
fearful *adj* causing intense fear; timorous; apprehensive (of); (*inf*) very great, very bad.—**fearfully** *adv*.
fearless *adj* brave, intrepid.—**fearlessly** *adv*.—**fearlessness** *n*.
fearnought, fearnaught *n* a strong woollen cloth.
fearsome *adj* causing fear, frightful.
feasible *adj* able to be done or implemented, possible.—**feasibly** *adv*.—**feasibility** *n*.
feast *n* an elaborate meal prepared for some special occasion; something that gives abundant pleasure; a periodic religious celebration. * *vi* to have or take part in a feast. * *vt* to entertain with a feast.—**feaster** *n*.
feat *n* an action of remarkable strength, skill, or courage.
feather *n* any of the light outgrowths that form the covering of a bird, consisting of a hollow central shaft with a vane of fine barbs on each side; a plume; something resembling a feather; the water thrown up by the turn of the blade of an oar. * *vt* to ornament with feathers; to turn (an oar or propeller blade) so that the edge is foremost.—**feathering** *n*.—**feathery** *adj*.
feather bed *n* a mattress stuffed with feathers.
featherbrain, featherhead *n* (*inf*) a silly, forgetful person.
featherbrained *adj* frivolous, giddy.
featheredge *n* a thin piece of board with one wedge-shaped side.
featherstitch *n* a zigzag stitch with a featherlike appearance.
featherweight *n* a lightweight thing or person; an insignificant thing or person; a boxer weighing from 118–126 lbs (53.5–57 kg); a wrestler weighing from 127–137 lbs (58–62 kg).
feathery *adj* like or covered with feathers.—**featheriness** *n*.
feature *n* any of the parts of the face; a characteristic trait of something; a special attraction or distinctive quality of something; a prominent newspaper article, etc; the main film in a cinema programme. * *vti* to make or be a feature of (something).
featureless *adj* lacking prominent or distinctive features.
Feb. *abbr* = February.
febrifuge *n* a drug that reduces fever.—**febrifugal** *adj*.
febrile *adj* of fever; feverish.
February *n* (*pl* **Februaries**) the second month of the year, having 28 days (or 29 days in leap years).
feces *see* **faeces**.
feckless *adj* incompetent, untrustworthy.—**fecklessly** *adv*.—**fecklessness** *n*.
feculent *adj* muddy, turbid; full of dregs or sediment.—**feculence** *adj*.
fecund *adj* fertile, prolific.—**fecundity** *n*.
fecundate *vt* to impregnate.—**fecundation** *n*.
fed *see* **feed**.
fedayee *n* (*pl* **fedayeen**) an Arab commando or guerrilla.
federal *adj* designating, or of a union of states, etc, in which each member surrenders some of its power to a central authority; of a central government of this type.—**federalism** *n*.—**federalist** *n*.—**federally** *adv*.
federalize *vt* to unite (states, etc) in a federal union; to put under federal authority.—**federalization** *n*.
federate *vti* to unite in a federation. * *adj* united in a league; on a federal basis.—**federative** *adj*.
federation *n* a union of states, groups, etc, in which each subordinates its power to a central authority; a federated organization.
fedora *n* a soft felt hat with a curled brim and a crown creased lengthways.
fee *n* the price paid for the advice or service of a professional; a charge for some privilege, as membership of a club; (*law*) an inheritance in land.
feeble *adj* weak, ineffective.—**feebly** *adv*.—**feebleness** *n*.
feeble-minded *adj* mentally defective; of low intelligence.
feed *vb* (**feeding, fed**) *vt* to give food to; to give as food to; to supply with necessary material; to gratify. * *vi* to consume food. * *n* food for animals; material fed into a machine; the part of a machine supplying this material.

feedback *n* a return to the input of part of the output of a system; information about a product, service, etc returned to the supplier for purposes of evaluation.

feeder *n* a person or thing that feeds; a baby's feeding-bottle; a device for supplying material to a machine; a subsidiary road, railway, etc acting as a link with the central transport network.

feel *vb* (**feeling, felt**) *vt* to perceive or explore by the touch; to find one's way by cautious trial; to be conscious of, experience; to have a vague or instinctual impression of; to believe, consider. * *vi* to be able to experience the sensation of touch; to be affected by; to convey a certain sensation when touched. * *n* the sense of touch; feeling; a quality as revealed by touch.

feeler *n* a tactile organ (as a tentacle or antenna) of an animal; a tentative approach or suggestion to test another person's reactions.

feeling *n* the sense of touch; mental or physical awareness; a physical or mental impression; a state of mind; sympathy; emotional sensitivity; a belief or opinion arising from emotion; (*pl*) emotions, sensibilities.

feet *see* **foot.**

feign *vt* to invent; to pretend.

feint *n* a pretended attack, intended to take the opponent off his guard, as in boxing.—*also vi.*

feldspar *n* any member of the group of hard rock-forming minerals.—*also* **felspar.**—**feldspathic, felspathic** *adj.*

felicitate *vt* to congratulate.—**felicitation** *n.*

felicitous *adj* (*words, etc*) apt, well-chosen; agreeable in manner; happy.—**felicitously** *adv.*

felicity *n* (*pl* **felicities**) happiness; apt and pleasing style in writing, speech, etc.

feline *adj* of cats; cat-like.—**felinity** *n.*

fell[1] *see* **fall.**

fell[2] *vt* to cut, beat, or knock down; to kill, to sew (a seam) by folding one raw edge under the other.

fell[3] *n* a skin, hide, pelt.

fell[4] *adj* (*poet*) cruel, fierce, bloody, deadly.

fellah *n* (*pl* **fellahs, fellahin, fellaheen**) an Arab peasant.

fellatio *n* sexual stimulation of the penis with the mouth.

felloe, felly *n* (*pl* **felloes, fellies**) one of the curved pieces of wood which form the outer section of a wheel; the outer section of a wheel, the circumference.

fellow *n* an associate; a comrade; an equal in power, rank, or position; the other of a pair, a mate; a member of the governing body in some colleges and universities; a member of a learned society; (*inf*) a man or boy. * *adj* belonging to the same group or class.

fellowship *n* companionship; a mutual sharing; a group of people with the same interests; the position held by a college fellow.

felo de se *n* (*pl* **felones de se, felos de se**) the act of suicide; a person who commits suicide.

felon *n* a person guilty of a felony.

felonious *adj* done with the intention of committing a crime; criminal; malignant.—**feloniously** *adv.*—**feloniousness** *n.*

felony *n* (*pl* **felonies**) (*formerly*) a grave crime.

felspar *see* **feldspar.**

felt[1] *see* **feel.**

felt[2] *n* a fabric made from woollen fibres, often mixed with fur or hair, pressed together. * *vti* to make into or become like felt.

felting *n* the material from which felt is made; the process of manufacturing felt.

felucca *n* a small boat with oars and lateen sails, used in the Mediterranean.

female *adj* of the sex that produces young; of a woman or women; (*pipe, plug, etc*) designed with a hollow part for receiving an inserted piece. * *n* a female animal or plant.

feminine *adj* of, resembling, or appropriate to women; (*gram*) of that gender to which words denoting females belong.—**femininity** *n.*

feminism *n* the movement to win political, economic and social equality for women.—**feminist** *adj, n.*

feminize *vti* to make or become feminine.—**feminization** *n.*

femme de chambre *n* (*pl* **femmes de chambre**) a chambermaid.

femme fatale *n* (*pl* **femmes fatales**) a dangerously seductive woman.

femur *n* (*pl* **femurs, femora**) the thighbone.—**femoral** *adj.*

fen *n* an area of low-lying marshy or flooded land.

fence *n* a barrier put round land to mark a boundary, or prevent animals, etc from escaping; a receiver of stolen goods. * *vt* to surround with a fence; to keep (out) as by a fence. * *vi* to practise fencing; to make evasive answers; to act as a fence for stolen goods.—**fencer** *n.*

fencing *n* fences; material for making fences; the art of fighting with foils or other types of sword.

fend *vi* (*with* **for**) to provide a livelihood for.

fender *n* anything that protects or fends off something else, as old tyres along the side of a vessel, or the part of a car body over the wheel.

fenestrated, fenestrate *adj* having windows.

fenestration *n* the design and arrangement of windows in a building.

fennec *n* a type of small fox, found in Africa.

fennel *n* a European herb of the carrot family grown for its foliage and aromatic seeds; a herb grown for its edible bulbous stem tasting of aniseed.

fennelflower *n* one of a variety of Mediterranean plants, with white, blue or yellow flowers.—*also* **love-in-a-mist.**

fenny *adj* marshy.

fenugreek *n* a Mediterranean plant with white flowers and pungent seeds.

feoff *see* **fief.**

fer-de-lance *n* a yellowish, highly poisonous snake of tropical America.

feral, ferine *adj* wild, untamed; like a wild beast.

feretory *n* (*pl* **feretories**) a shrine for the relics of a saint; a chapel for keeping this.

ferial *adj* (*RC: Church*) (*a day*) ordinary, not a festival or a fast.

ferment *n* an agent causing fermentation, as yeast; excitement, agitation. * *vti* to (cause to) undergo fermentation; to (cause to) be excited or agitated.—**fermentable** *adj.*—**fermenter** *n.*

fermentation *n* the breakdown of complex molecules in organic components caused by the influence of yeast or other substances.

fermentative *adj* of or pertaining to fermentation; capable of or causing fermentation.

fermion *n* a type of subatomic particle.

fermium *n* an artificially-produced radioactive metallic element.

fern *n* any of a large class of nonflowering plants having roots, stems, and fronds, and reproducing by spores.—**ferny** *adj.*

fernery *n* (*pl* **ferneries**) a place for growing ferns.

ferny *adj* (**fernier, ferniest**) full of ferns; of or characteristic of ferns.

ferocious *adj* savage, fierce.—**ferociously** *adv.*—**ferocity, ferociousness** *n.*

ferrate *n* a salt of ferric acid.

ferret *n* a variety of the polecat, used in unearthing rabbits. * *vt* to drive out of a hiding-place; (*with* **out**) to reveal by persistent investigation. * *vi* to hunt with ferrets.—**ferreter** *n.*—**ferrety** *adj.*

ferriage *n* the act of conveying by ferry; the fare paid for this.

ferric *adj* of or containing iron.

ferriferous *adj* yielding iron.

Ferris wheel *n* a large upright revolving wheel with suspended seats, popular in amusement parks.

ferroconcrete *n* reinforced concrete.

ferrocyanic acid *n* an acid formed by the union of iron and cyanogen.

ferromagnetism *n* magnetism possessed by iron, and some other metals, which is retained even after the removal of the magnetizing field.—**ferromagnetic** *adj.*

ferromanganese *n* an alloy of iron and manganese.

ferrotype *n* a photograph taken on a sensitized iron plate.

ferrous *adj* containing iron.

ferruginous *adj* containing, or impregnated with, iron; rust-coloured, reddish brown.

ferrule *n* a metal ring or cap on a cane, umbrella, etc, to keep it from splitting.—*also* **ferule.**

ferry *vt* (**ferrying, ferried**) to convey (passengers, etc) over a stretch of water; to transport from one place to another, esp along a regular route. * *n* (*pl* **ferries**) a boat used for ferrying; a ferrying service; the location of a ferry.—**ferryman** *n* (*pl* **ferrymen**).

fertile *adj* able to bear offspring; (*land*) easily supporting plants and vegetation; (*animals*) capable of breeding; (*eggs*) able to grow and develop; prolific; (*mind, brain*) inventive.—**fertility, fertileness** *n*.

fertility *n* the state or quality of being fertile.

fertilize *vt* to make (soil) fertile by adding nutrients; to impregnate; to pollinate.—**fertilization** *n*.

fertilizer *n* natural organic or artificial substances used to enrich the soil.

ferula *n* (*pl* **ferulas, ferulae**) a genus of plants of the parsley family, from one of which asafoetida is produced.

ferule *see* **ferrule.**

fervency *n* earnestness; ardour.

fervent, fervid *adj* passionate; zealous.—**fervently, fervidly** *adv*.—**fervency** *n*.

fervour, fervor *n* intensity of feeling; zeal; warmth.

fescue *n* a kind of grass, often grown for pasture and fodder.

fesse *n* (*her*) a broad horizontal band across the middle of a shield.

festal *adj* of a feast or holiday; festive.—**festally** *adv*.

fester *vti* to become or cause to become infected; to suppurate; to rankle.

festival *n* a time of celebration; performances of music, plays, etc given periodically.

festive *adj* merry, joyous.—**festively** *adv*.—**festiveness** *n*.

festivity *n* (*pl* **festivities**) a festive celebration.

festoon *n* a decorative garland of flowers, etc hung between two points. * *vt* to adorn as with festoons.—**festoonery** *n*.

feta *n* a type of white goat's milk cheese, esp popular in Greece.

fetal *adj* pertaining to the fetus.—*also* **foetal.**

fetch[1] *vt* to go for and bring back; to cause to come; (*goods*) to sell for (a certain price); (*inf*) to deal (a blow, slap, etc); (*with* **up**) to come to stand, arrive at; **fetch and carry** to run errands for another.—**fetcher** *n*.

fetch[2] *n* an apparition of a living person, a wraith; a person's double.

fetching *adj* attractive.—**fetchingly** *adv*.

fête, fete *n* a festival; a usu outdoor sale, bazaar or entertainment in aid of charity. * *vt* to honour or entertain (as if) with a fête.

fetial *n* (*pl* **fetiales**) a priestly herald in ancient Rome who performed rites accompanying a declaration of war or peace.

feticide *n* the destruction of a fetus in the womb.—*also* **foeticide.**

fetid *adj* stinking.—*also* **foetid.**

fetish, fetich *n* an object believed by primitive peoples to have magical properties; any object or activity regarded with excessive devotion.

fetishism, fetichism *n* the transfer of sexual desire to an inanimate object, or to some part of the body other than the sexual organs; worship of, or belief in, fetishes—**fetishist, fetichist** *n*.

fetlock, fetterlock *n* the joint on a horse's leg behind and above the hoof.

fetter *n* (*usu pl*) a shackle for the feet; anything that restrains. * *vt* to put into fetters; to impede, restrain.—**fetterer** *n*.

fettle *n* good condition or repair.

fettucine, fettuccine, fettucini *n* a kind of pasta cut in strips.

fetus *n* (*pl* **fetuses**) the unborn young of an animal, esp in its later stages; in humans, the offspring in the womb from the fourth month until birth.—*also* **foetus** (*pl* **foetuses**).—**fetal, foetal** *adj*.

feud *n* a state of hostilities, esp between individuals, families, or clans; a dispute.—*also vi*.

feudal *adj* pertaining to feudalism; (*inf*) old-fashioned, redundant.

feudalism *n* the economic and social system in medieval Europe, in which land, worked by serfs, was held by vassals in exchange for military and other services to overlords.—**feudalist** *n*.—**feudalistic** *adj*.

feudality *n* (*pl* **feudalities**) the state of being feudal; a feudal estate.

feudalize *vt* to make feudal.—**feudalization** *n*.

feudatory *adj* pertaining to, or held by, feudal tenure.

feudist *n* someone taking part in a feud or argument.

feuilleton *n* in France, etc, the section of a newspaper containing reviews, fiction, etc; an article in this; serialization in a newspaper.—**feuilletonist** *n* —**feuilletonistic** *adj*

fever *n* an abnormally increased body temperature; any disease marked by a high fever; a state of restless excitement.—**fevered** *adj*.

feverfew *n* a perennial European herb, formerly used to reduce fevers.

feverish, feverous *adj* having a fever; indicating a fever; restlessly excited.—**feverishly** *adv*.—**feverishness** *n*.

few *adj, n* a small number, not many.—**fewness** *n*.

fey *adj* strange and unusual.—**feyness** *n*.

fez *n* (*pl* **fezzes**) a red brimless high cap, usu with black tassel, worn esp by men in eastern Mediterranean countries.

ff *abbr* = and the following pages; (mus) fortissimo—very loud.

fiacre *n* a type of horse-drawn carriage.

fiancé *n* a person engaged to be married.—**fiancée** *nf*.

fiasco *n* (*pl* **fiascos, fiascoes**) a complete and humiliating failure.

fiat *n* an order by authority; a decree.

fib *n* a lie about something unimportant. * *vi* (**fibbing, fibbed**) to tell a gib.—**fibber** *n*.

fibre, fiber *n* a natural or synthetic thread, eg from cotton or nylon, which is spun into yarn; a material composed of such yarn; texture; strength of character; a fibrous substance, roughage.—**fibred, fibered** *adj*.

fibreglass, fiberglass *n* glass in fibrous form, often bonded with plastic, used in making various products.

fibre optics, fiber optics *n* (*sing*) the transmission of information in the form of light signals along thin transparent fibres of glass.—**fibre-optic, fiber-optic** *adj*.

fibril, fibrilla *n* (*pl* **fibrils, fibrillae**) a small fibre.—**fibrilar, fibrillar, fibrillose** *adj*

fibrillation *n* the rapid and irregular twitching of muscle fibres, esp in the heart.

fibrin *n* a white protein in the blood, which causes coagulation.

fibrinous *adj* composed of, or resembling,fibrin.

fibroid *adj* (*anat*) containing or resembling fibre. * *n* a benign tumour in the uterus.

fibroin *n* a protein that is the main constituent of silk and cobwebs.

fibroma *n* (*pl* **fibromata, fibromas**) a benign fibrous tumour.

fibrosis *n* the abnormal growth of fibrous tissue in an organ or part of the body.

fibrositis *n* inflammation of fibrous tissues, esp muscles.

fibrous *adj* composed of fibres.—**fibrousness** *n*.

fibula *n* (*pl* **fibulae, fibulas**) the outer of the two bones of the lower leg.—**fibular** *adj*.

fiche *n* (*pl* **fiche**) a microfiche.

fichu *n* a woman's light three-cornered scarf worn over the neck and shoulders.

fickle *adj* inconstant; capricious.—**fickleness** *n*.

fictile *adj* moulded from clay; able to be moulded from clay.

fiction *n* an invented story; any literary work with imaginary characters and events, as a novel, play, etc; such works collectively.—**fictional** *adj*.—**fictionally** *adv*.

fictitious *adj* imaginary, not real; feigned.—**fictitiously** *adv*.

fictive *adj* pertaining to fiction; creating or created by the imagination.—**fictively** *adv*.

fid *n* (*naut*) an iron or wooden bar used to support a topmast; a pin used to open the strands of a rope.

fid. *abbr* = fidelity.

fiddle *n* (*inf*) a violin; (*sl*) a swindle. * *vt* (*inf*) to play on a violin; (*sl*) to swindle; to falsify. * *vi* to handle restlessly, to fidget.—**fiddler** *n*.

fiddle-de-dee *interj* an expression of incredulity or impatience.

fiddle-faddle *n* nonsense; trifles. * *vi* to fuss over unimportant matters.

fiddlehead *n* an ornament at the prow of a ship.

fiddler *n* one who fiddles; (*inf*) a violinist.

fiddlestick *n* a bow for playing the violin.

fiddlesticks *interj* nonsense!

fiddling *adj* trifling, petty.

fidelity *n* (*pl* **fidelities**) faithfulness, loyalty; truthfulness; accuracy in reproducing sound.
fidget *vi* to (cause to) move restlessly. * *n* nervous restlessness; a fussy person.—**fidgetingly** *adv*.—**fidgety** *adj*.
fiducial *adj* (*physics*) taken as a standard of reference; based on trust or faith.—**fiducially** *adv*.
fiduciary *adj* of, held or given in trust; (*paper currency*) depending on public confidence for value. * *n* a trustee.
fie *interj* for shame; an expression of disgust or dismay.
fief *n* (*feudalism*) heritable land held by a vassal; an area in which one has control or influence.—*also* **feoff**.
field[1] *n* an area of land cleared of trees and buildings, used for pasture or crops; an area rich in a natural product (eg gold, coal); a battlefield; a sports ground; an area affected by electrical, magnetic or gravitational influence, etc; the area visible through an optical lens; a division of activity, knowledge, etc; all competitors in a contest; (*comput*) a section of a record in a database. * *vt* (*cricket, baseball, etc*) to catch or stop and return the ball as a fielder; to put (eg. a team) into the field to play; (*inf*) to handle (eg questions) successfully.
field[2] *see* **fjeld.**
field day *n* a day of sports and athletic competition; (*inf*) any day of unusual happenings or success.
fielder *n* (*cricket, baseball, etc*) a person who is not in the batting side, a person who fields.—*also* **fieldsman** (*pl* **fieldsmen**).
field event *n* (*usu pl*) an athletic competition involving jumping or throwing, as opposed to running.
fieldfare *n* a European thrush, which migrates to Britain for winter.
field glasses *npl* small, portable binoculars for use outdoors.
field hockey *n* an outdoor game played by two teams of 11 players with a ball and clubs curved at one end —*also* **hockey.**
fieldmouse *n* a small, noctural mouse that lives in woods and fields.
fieldwork *n* research done outside the laboratory or place of work by scientists, archaeologists, social workers, etc.—**fieldworker** *n*.
fiend *n* an evil spirit; an inhumanly wicked person; (*inf*) an avid fan.—**fiendish** *adj*.—**fiendishly** *adv*.
fierce *adj* ferociously hostile; angry, violent; intense; strong, extreme.—**fiercely** *adv*.—**fierceness** *n*.
fiery *adj* (**fierier, fieriest**) like or consisting of fire; the colour of fire; intensely hot; spicy; passionate, ardent; impetuous; irascible.—**fierily** *adv*.—**fieriness** *n*.
fiesta *n* a religious celebration, a festival, esp in Spain and Latin America.
fife *n* a type of small flute with a shrill sound used esp in military music to accompany drums.—**fifer** *n*.
fife rail *n* (*naut*) a rail round the mast holding belaying pins.
fifteen *adj, n* one more than fourteen; the symbol for this (15, XV, xv); the first point scored by a side in a game of tennis; a rugby football team.—**fifteenth** *adj, n*.
fifth *adj, n* last of five; (being) one of five equal parts; (*mus*) an interval of three tones and a semitone; a gear in a motor vehicle used when driving at speed.—**fifthly** *adv*.
fifth column *n* a subversive organization within a country, which is ready to give help to an enemy.—**fifth columnist** *n*.
fifty *adj, n* (*pl* **fifties**) five times ten; the symbol for this (50, L, l).—**fiftieth** *adj*.
fifty-fifty *adj, adv* (*inf*) evenly, equally; (*chance*) an equal possibility of winning.
fig *n* a tree yielding a soft, pear-shaped fruit; a thing of little or no importance.
fig. *abbr* = figure; figuratively.
fight *vb* (**fighting, fought**) *vi* to engage in battle in war or in single combat; to strive, struggle (for). * *vt* to engage in or carry on a conflict with; to achieve (one's way) by fighting; to strive to overcome; (*with* **off**) to repel; to ward off or repress through effort. * *n* fighting; a struggle or conflict of any kind; a boxing match.—**fighting** *n*.
fighter *n* a person who fights; a person who does not yield easily; an aircraft designed to destroy enemy aircraft.
fighting chance *n* a small chance of success given supreme effort.
figment *n* something imagined or invented.
figurant *n* a ballet dancer who performs as one of a group.—**figurante** *nf*.
figuration *n* the giving of form; representation; a figure, a shape; (*mus*) the use of florid counterpoint.
figurative *adj* metaphorical, not literal; using or full of figures of speech; emblematic; pictorial.—**figuratively** *adv*.
figure *n* a character representing a number; a number; value or price; bodily shape or form; a graphic representation of a thing, person or animal; a design; a geometrical form; a statue; appearance; a personage; (*dancing, skating*) a set of steps or movements; (*pl*) arithmetic. * *vt* to represent in a diagram or outline; to imagine; (*inf*) to consider; (*inf*) to believe; (*with* **out**) (*inf*) to solve. * *vi* to take a part (in), be conspicuous (in); to calculate.—**figurer** *n*.
figured *adj* depicted as a figure; adorned with figures.
figurehead *n* a carved figure on the bow of a ship; a nominal head or leader.
figure of speech *n* an expression not intended to be taken literally, as a metaphor or simile.
figure skating *n* ice skating in which prescribed figures are outlined.
figurine *n* a statuette.
filagree *see* **filigree.**
filament *n* a slender thread or strand; a fibre; the fine wire in an electric light bulb that is made incandescent by current; (*bot*) the anther-bearing stalk of a stamen.—**filamentary, filamentous** *adj*.
filar *adj* of or pertaining to thread; (*microscope, etc*) having fine threads in the eyepiece for measuring tiny distances.
filature *n* the reeling of silk from cocoons; a place where this is done.
filbert *n* the edible nut of the cultivated hazel.
filch *vt* to steal (something of little value), to pilfer.—**filcher** *n*.
file[1] a container for keeping papers, etc, in order; an orderly arrangement of papers; a line of persons or things; (*comput*) a collection of related data under a specific name. * *vt* to dispatch or register; to put on public record. * *vi* to move in a line; to apply.—**filer** *n*.
file[2] *n* a tool, usu steel, with a rough surface for smoothing or grinding. * *vt* to cut or smooth with, or as with, a file; to polish, improve.—**filer** *n*.
filefish *n* (*pl* **filefish, filefishes**) a tropical fish, of the family of triggerfish, with a narrow body and rough skin.
filester *see* **fillister.**
filet *n* a net with a square mesh.
filial *adj* of, or expected from, a son or daughter.—**filially** *adv*.—**filialness** *n*.
filiation *n* the relation of child to father; lineage, line of descent; the formation of branches of a society, etc; a branch so formed.
filibeg *n* a kilt.—*also* **philabeg.**
filibuster *n* a member of a legislature who obstructs a bill by making long speeches. * *vti* to obstruct (a bill) by such methods.—**filibusterer** *n*.
filiform *adj* threadlike.
filigree *n* a kind of lace-like ornamental work in precious metal. * *vt* (**filigreeing, filigreed**) to decorate with filigree.—*also* **filagree.**
filing *n* a particle rubbed off with a file.
Filipino *n* (*pl* **Filipinos**) a native or inhabitant of the Philippines.—*also adj*.
fill *vt* to put as much as possible into; to occupy wholly; to put a person into (a position or job, etc); (*US*) to supply the things called for (in an order, etc); to close or plug (holes, etc); (*with* **in**) to complete (a form, design, etc) by writing or drawing; (*inf*) to provide with the latest news or facts; (with **out**) to make fuller or heavier; to fill in (a form, etc). * *vi* to become full; (*with* **in**) to act as a substitute for; (*with* **out**) to become fuller or heavier. * *n* enough to make full or to satisfy; anything that fills.
filler *n* one who or that which fills; a substance used to plug a hole or increase the bulk of something.
fillet *n* a thin boneless strip of meat or fish; a ribbon, etc worn as a headband;

(*archit*) a narrow band used between mouldings. * *vt* to bone and slice (fish or meat).

filling *n* a substance used to fill a tooth cavity; the contents of a sandwich, pie, etc. * *adj* (*meal, etc*) substantial.

filling station *n* a place where petrol is sold to motorists, a service station.

fillip *n* a blow with the nail of the finger; a stimulus.

fillister, filister *n* a plane used to cut grooves, rabbets, etc.—*also* **filester**.

filly *n* (*pl* **fillies**) a young female horse, usu less than four years.

film *n* a fine, thin skin, coating, etc; a flexible cellulose material covered with a light-sensitive substance used in photography; a haze or blur; a motion picture. * *vti* to cover or be covered as with a film; to photograph or make a film (of).—**filmic** *adj*.

film card *see* **microfiche.**

film star *n* a leading cinema actor or actress.

filmy *adj* (**filmier, filmiest**) gauzy, transparent; blurred, hazy.—**filmily** *adv*.—**filminess** *n*.

filose *adj* threadlike.

filter *n* a device or substance straining out solid particles, impurities, etc, from a liquid or gas; a device for removing or minimizing electrical oscillations, or sound or light waves, of certain frequencies; a traffic signal at certain road junctions that allows vehicles to turn left or right while the main lights are red. * *vti* to pass through or as through a filter; to remove with a filter.—**filterable, filtrable** *adj*.

filter tip *n* the porous tip of a cigarette designed to reduce the intake of tar during smoking.—**filter-tipped** *adj*.

filth *n* dirt; obscenity.

filthy *adj* (**filthier, filthiest**) dirty, disgusting; obscene; (*inf*) extremely unpleasant.—**filthily** *adv*.—**filthiness** *n*.

filtrate *vt* to filter. * *n* a liquid that has been filtered.—**filtration** *n*.

fimbriate, fimbriated *adj* (*bot*) fringed.

fin *n* an organ by which a fish, etc steers itself and swims; a rubber flipper used for underwater swimming; any fin-shaped object used as a stabilizer, as on an aircraft or rocket. * *vb* (**finning, finned**) *vi* (*fish, whale. etc*) to agitate the fins. * *vt* to furnish with fins.

finable, fineable *adj* liable to a fine.

finagle *vt* (*inf*) to obtain or achieve through cunning or deceit; to use trickery or deceit on someone.

final *adj* of or coming at the end; conclusive. * *n* (*often pl*) the last of a series of contests; a final examination.—**finally** *adv*.

finale *n* the concluding part of any public performance; the last section in a musical composition.

finalist *n* a contestant in a final.

finality *n* (*pl* **finalities**) the state or quality of being final; completeness, conclusiveness.

finalize *vt* to make complete, to bring to an end.—**finalization** *n*.

finally *adv* at last; lastly; completely.

finance *n* the management of money; (*pl*) money resources. * *vt* to supply or raise money for.

financial *adj* of finance.—**financially** *adv*.

financier *n* a person skilled in finance.

finback *n* a whale with a prominent dorsal fin; the rorqual.

finch *n* any of numerous songbirds of the *Fringillidae* family.

find *vb* (**finding, found**) *vt* to discover by chance; to come upon by searching; to perceive; to recover (something lost); to reach, attain; to decide and declare to be; (*with* **out**) to discover; to solve; to detect in an offence. * *vi* to reach a decision (as by a jury). * *n* a discovery, something found.—**findable** *adj*.

finder *n* one who or that which finds; a discoverer; a device for sighting the field of view of a camera, telescope, etc.

fin de siècle *adj* of or typical of the end of a century, esp the 19th century. * *n* the end of a century.

finding *n* a discovery; the conclusion reached by a judicial enquiry.

fine[1] *adj* very good; with no impurities, refined; (*weather*) clear and bright; not heavy or coarse; very thin or small; sharp; subtle; elegant. * *adv* in a fine manner; (*inf*) very well.—**finely** *adv*.—**fineness** *n*.

fine[2] *n* a sum of money imposed as a punishment. * *vt* to punish by a fine.—**finable, fineable** *adj*.

fine arts *npl* painting, sculpture, engraving, etc valued for their aesthetic qualities.

fine-draw *vt* (**fine-drawing, fine-drew,** *pp* **fine-drawn**) to sew up (a darn) so neatly that the join cannot be noticed; to draw out (wire) to an extreme fineness.—**fine-drawn** *adj*.

finely *adv* in a fine manner; discriminatingly; subtly; in tiny pieces.

fineness *n* the state or quality of being fine; the quantity of pure metal contained in an alloy.

finery *n* (*pl* **fineries**) elaborate clothes, jewellery, etc.

finespun *adj* delicate, fine; over-subtle.

finesse *n* delicacy or subtlety of performance; skilfulness, diplomacy in handling a situation; (*bridge*) an attempt to take a trick with a card lower than a higher card held by an opponent. * *vt* to achieve by finesse; to play (a card) as a finesse.

fine-tooth(ed) comb *n* a comb with closely set fine teeth for trapping nits, etc.

fine-tune *vt* to make fine adjustments to something in order to improve its effectiveness.

finger *n* one of the digits of the hand, usu excluding the thumb; anything shaped like a finger; (*inf*) the breadth of a finger. * *vt* to touch with fingers; (*mus*) to use the fingers in a certain way when playing; to mark this way on music; (*sl*) to inform against.—**fingerer** *n*.

fingerboard *n* the part of a violin, guitar, etc against which the strings are pressed by the fingers.

finger bowl *n* a small bowl containing water for rinsing the fingers at the table.

fingered *adj* marked by handling; having a finger or fingers; (*mus*) marked to show how the fingers are used.

fingering[1] *n* the manner of using the fingers in playing a musical instrument; the indication of this in a musical score.

fingering[2] *n* a fine knitting yarn.

fingerling *n* a young fish, esp a trout.

fingernail *n* the nail on a finger.

fingerpost *n* a direction post in the shape of a pointing finger.

fingerprint *n* the impression of the ridges on a fingertip, esp as used for purposes of identification.—*also vt*.

fingerstall *n* a protective covering for a finger.

finial *n* (*archit*) a pointed ornament at the top of a spire, gable, etc.—**finialed** *adj*.

finical *adj* fastidious, over-particular, fussy; affectedly fine.—**finicality** *n*.—**finically** *adv*.

finicky, finicking *adj* too particular, fussy.

fining *n* the act or process of clarifying or refining; a liquid used to clarify wine, beer, etc.

finis *n* the end, used at the conclusion of books, films, etc.

finish *vt* to bring to an end, to come to the end of; to consume entirely; to perfect; to give a desired surface effect to. * *vi* to come to an end. * *n* the last part, the end; anything used to finish a surface; the finished effect; means or manner of completing or perfecting; polished manners, speech, etc.—**finisher** *n*.

finishing school *n* a private school for girls which teaches social etiquette.

finite *adj* having definable limits; (*verb form*) having a distinct grammatical person and number.—**finitely** *adv* —**finiteness** *n*.

Finn *n* a native of Finland.

finnan haddock, Finnan haddie *n* a kind of smoked haddock, named after *Findon*, a Scottish fishing village.

finned *adj* having a fin or fins.

Finnish *adj* of or relating to Finland or its language. * *n* the language of Finland.

finny *adj* (**finnier, finniest**) pertaining to, or abounding in, fish; having a fin or fins.

fino *n* (*pl* **finos**) a dry sherry.

fiord *see* **fjord.**

fir *n* a kind of evergreen, cone-bearing tree; its timber.

fire *n* the flame, heat and light of combustion; something burning; burning fuel in a grate to heat a room; an electric or gas fire; a destructive burning; a strong feeling; a discharge of firearms. * *vti* to ignite; to supply with fuel; to bake (bricks, etc) in a kiln; to excite or become excited; to shoot (a gun, etc); to hurl or direct with force; to dismiss from a position.—**fireable** *adj*.—**firer** *n*.

fire alarm *n* a device that uses a bell, hooter, etc to warn of a fire.

firearm *n* a handgun.

fireball *n* a ball of fire; a meteor; the hot gas cloud created by a nuclear explosion.

firebox *n* the furnace in a steam locomotive.

firebrand *n* a piece of burning wood; a person who starts trouble.

firebreak *n* a strip of land cleared of vegetation to halt the spread of a fire.

firebrick *n* a brick made of fireclay to withstand the action of fire.

fire brigade *n* an organized body specially trained and equipped for fighting fires.

firebug *n* (*inf*) an arsonist.

fireclay *n* a fire-resisting clay.

firecracker *n* a small explosive firework.

firedamp *n* a combustible mine gas, chiefly methane.

firedog *n* a metal standard used for open fires to support the logs; andirons.

fire-eater *n* a performer who pretends to eat fire; a quarrelsome person.—**fire-eating** *adj, n*.

fire engine *n* a vehicle equipped for fire-fighting.

fire escape *n* a means of exit from a building, esp a stairway, for use in case of fire.

fire extinguisher *n* a container with a spray nozzle, holding water or chemicals for putting out a fire

firefighter *n* a person who fights fires, esp a member of a fire department; fireman.

firefly *n* (*pl* **fireflies**) a winged nocturnal beetle whose abdomen glows with a soft intermittent light.

fireguard *n* a protective grating placed in frontof a fire.

fire insurance *n* insurance against loss by fire.

fire irons *npl* tools for tending a domestic fire, esp a poker, tongs, and shovel.

firelighter *n* a prepared block of ignitable material used for lighting a fire.

firelock *n* a flintlock.

fireman *n* (*pl* **firemen**) a member of a fire brigade; firefighter; a person employed to tend furnaces.

fireplace *n* a place for a fire, esp a recess in a wall; the area surrounding this.

fireplug *n* a connection in a water main for a hose; a hydrant.

fire power *n* the amount of fire that a military unit can deliver on a target.

fireproof *adj* not easily destroyed by fire. * *vt* to make fireproof.

fire raiser *n* an arsonist.—**fire raising** *n*.

firescreen *n* a movable ornamental screen for keeping the heat of a fire off the face; a screen for decorating an empty fireplace.

fireship *n* a ship filled with explosives to set an enemy's ships on fire.

fireside *n* the area in a room nearest the fireplace; home.

fire station *n* a building where firemen and fire-fighting equipment are based.—*also* **firehouse, station house**.

firetrap *n* a building easily set on fire or hard to get out of if on fire.

firewarden *n* an officer responsible for protecting forests.against fire.

firewater *n* (*inf*) strong alcoholic drink.

firewood *n* wood for fuel.

firework *n* a device packed with explosive and combustible material used to produce noisy and colourful displays; (*pl*) such a display; (*pl*) a fit of temper, an outburst of emotions.

firing *n* baking in intense heat, esp of clay; fuel; the act of discharging a firearm; the act of adding fuel to a fire.

firing line *n* the front line of a military position; the forefront of any activity.

firing squad *n* a detachment with the task of firing a salute at a military funeral or carrying out an execution.

firkin *n* a small wooden barrel containing butter, etc; (*Brit*) a measure of one quarter of a barrel (41 litres/9 gallons).

firm[1] *adj* securely fixed; solid, compact; steady; resolute; definite. * *vti* to make or become firm.—**firmly** *adv*.—**firmness** *n*.

firm[2] *n* a business partnership; a commercial company.

firmament *n* the sky, viewed poetically as a solid arch or vault.—**firmamental** *adj*.

first *adj* before all others in a series; 1st; earliest; foremost, as in rank, quality, etc. * *adv* before anyone or anything else; for the first time; sooner. * *n* any person or thing that is first; the beginning; the winning place, as in a race; low gear; the highest award in a university degree.

first aid *n* emergency treatment for an injury, etc, before regular medical aid is available.

first-born *adj* eldest. * *n* the eldest child in a family.

first-class *adj* of the highest quality, as in accommodation, travel. * *n* the best accommodation on a plane, train, etc; the highest class in an examination, etc.

first-degree burn *n* (*med*) a mild burn causing a painful reddening of the skin but no blistering or charring.

first fruits *npl* fruit which is the first to ripen; the earliest returns or results from an enterprise.

firsthand *adj* obtained directly from a source.

First Lady *n* the wife of the US president.

firstling *n* the first offspring.

firstly *adv* in the first place.

first night *n* the opening performance of a play.

first person *n* (*gram*) pronouns and verbs referring to the person speaking.

first-rate *adj, adv* of the best quality; (*inf*) excellent.

firth *n* an arm of the sea, esp a river mouth.—*also* **frith**.

fiscal *adj* of or relating to public revenue; financial. * *n* a prosecuting official in some countries.

fish[1] *n* (*pl* **fish, fishes**) any of a large group of cold-blooded animals living in water, having backbones, gills for breathing and fins; the flesh of fish used as food. * *vi* to catch or try to catch fish; (*with* **for**) to try to obtain by roundabout methods. * *vt* (*often with* **out**) to grope for, find, and bring to view.—**fishable** *adj*.

fish[2] *n* a rigid strip of wood or metal used to strengthen a mast, joint, etc. * *vt* to strengthen or join with a fish.

fish-eye lens *n* a wide-angled lens with a curved protruding front.

fisher *n* a person who fishes; (*zool*) another name for the pekan, a marten found in North America.

fisherman *n* (*pl* **fishermen**) a person who fishes for sport or for a living; a ship used in fishing.

fishery *n* (*pl* **fisheries**) the fishing industry; an area where fish are caught.

fishfinger *n* a small oblong piece of fish covered in breadcrumbs.—*also* **fish stick**.

fishing *n* the art, sport or business of catching fish.

fishing rod *n* a wooden, metal or fibreglass rod used with a line to catch fish.

fish meal *n* granules of dried fish used as fertilizer and food for livestock.

fishmonger *n* a shop that sells fish.

fishnet *n* a coarse open-mesh fabric.—*also adj*.

fishplate *n* an iron plate, one of a pair used to join railway rails.

fishpond *n* a pond in which fish are kept.

fish stick *see* **fishfinger**.

fishwife *n* (*pl* **fishwives**) a woman who guts or sells fish; a coarse, scolding woman.

fishy *adj* (**fishier, fishiest**) like a fish in odour, taste, etc; (*inf*) creating doubt or suspicion.—**fishily** *adv*.—**fishiness** *n*.

fissile *adj* capable of undergoing nuclear fission; easily split.—**fissility** *n*.

fission *n* a split or cleavage; the reproductive division of biological cells; the splitting of the atomic nucleus resulting in the release of energy, nuclear fission.—**fissionable** *adj*.

fissiparous *adj* multiplying or propagating by fission.

fissiped, fissipedal *adj* (*zool*) having the toes separated, eg dogs, cats, etc.
fissirostral *adj* (*birds*) with a deeply cleft beak, eg swallows.
fissure *n* a narrow opening or cleft. * *vti* to split.
fist *n* the hand when tightly closed or clenched.
fistic *adj* (*joc*) of or pertaining to boxing.
fisticuffs *npl* a fight with the fists.
fistula *n* (*pl* **fistulas, fistulae**) an abnormal passage, as from an abscess to the skin.
fistulous *adj* resembling a fistula; hollow, like a pipe.
fit[1] *adj* (**fitter, fittest**) suited to some purpose, function, etc; proper, right; healthy; (*sl*) inclined, ready. * *n* the manner of fitting. * *vb* (**fitting, fitted**) *vt* to be suitable to; to be the proper size, shape, etc, for; to adjust so as to fit; (*with* **out**) to equip, to outfit. * *vi* to be suitable or proper; to have the proper size or shape.—**fittable** *adj*.—**fitly** *adv*.—**fitness** *n*.
fit[2] *n* any sudden, uncontrollable attack, as of coughing; an outburst, as of anger; a short period of impulsive activity; a seizure involving convulsions or loss of consciousness.
fitch *n* the polecat; the hair of a polecat; a brush made of this.
fitful *adj* marked by intermittent activity; spasmodic.—**fitfully** *adv*.—**fitfulness** *n*.
fitment *n* a piece of equipment, esp fixed furniture.
fitter *n* a person who specializes in fitting clothes; a person skilled in the assembly and operation of a particular piece of machinery.
fitting *adj* appropriate; suitable, right. * *n* an act of one that fits, esp a trying on of altered clothes; a small often standardized electrical part.—**fittingly** *adv*.—**fittingness** *n*.
five *adj, n* one more than four; the symbol for this (5, V, v).
fivefold *adj, adv* having five units or members; being five times as great or as many.
fiver *n* (*inf*) in UK, a £5 note; in US, a $5 bill.
fives *n* (*sing*) a ball game similar to squash, played in a walled court.
fix *vt* to fasten firmly; to set firmly in the mind; to direct (one's eyes) steadily at something; to make rigid; to make permanent; to establish (a date, etc) definitely; to set in order; to repair; to prepare (food or meals); (*inf*) to influence the result or action of (a race, jury, etc) by bribery; (*inf*) to punish. * *vi* to become fixed; (*inf*) to prepare or intend. * *n* the position of a ship, etc, determined from the bearings of two known positions; (*inf*) a predicament; (*inf*) a situation that has been fixed; (*inf*) something whose supply becomes continually necessary or greatly desired, as a drug, entertainment, activity, etc.—**fixable** *adj*.
fixated *adj* having a fixation.
fixation *n* a fixing; (*psychol*) an unhealthy obsession, esp one leading to arrested emotional development.
fixative *n* a substance used to fix things in position; a substance that prevents (colours, perfumes, etc) fading or evaporating.
fixed *adj* firm; not moving; lasting; intent.—**fixedly** *adv*.—**fixedness** *n*.
fixer *n* a chemical that fixes photographs, making the image permanent; (*sl*) a person who fixes something, esp by illegal means.
fixings *npl* trimmings.
fixity *n* (*pl* **fixities**) the state of being fixed; stability; permanence.
fixture *n* what is fixed to anything, as to land or to a house; a fixed article of furniture; a firmly established person or thing; a fixed or appointed time or event.
fizz *vi* to make a hissing or sputtering sound. * *n* this sound; any effervescent drink.—**fizzy** *adj*.—**fizziness** *n*.
fizzle *vi* to make a weak fizzing sound; (*with* **out**) (*inf*) to end feebly, die out, esp after a promising start.
fjeld *n* in Scandinavia, a high, barren plateau.—*also* **field**.
fjord *n* a long, narrow inlet of the sea between high cliffs, esp in Norway.—*also* **fiord**.
fl. *abbr* = fluid; floor; *floruit* (flourished).
flab *n* (*inf*) fat.
flabbergast *vt* (*inf*) to astonish, startle.
flabby *adj* (**flabbier, flabbiest**) fat and soft; weak and ineffective.—**flabbily** *adv*.—**flabbiness** *n*.
flabellate, flabelliform *adj* (*bot*) fan-shaped.
flabellum *n* (*pl* **flabella**) (*RC*) a large fan.
flaccid *adj* not firm or stiff; limp, weak.—**flaccidity** *n*.
flack *see* **flak.**
flacon *n* a small bottle or flask.
flag[1] *vi* (**flagging, flagged**) to grow limp; to become weak, listless.
flag[2] *n* a piece of cloth, usu with a design, used to show nationality, party, a particular branch of the armed forces, etc, or as a signal. * *vt* (**flagging, flagged**) to decorate with flags; to signal to (as if) with a flag; (*usu with* **down**) to signal to stop.
flag[3] *n* a hard, flat stone used for paving, a flagstone. * *vt* (**flagging, flagged**) to pave with flagstones.
flag[4] *n* a plant with a sword-shaped leaf, the iris; a long thin plant blade.
flag day *n* a day on which charitable donations are solicited in exchange for small flags; (*with caps*) in US, 14 June, the anniversary of the adoption of the stars and stripes, 1777.
flagellant *n* a person who scourges himself or herself or others as a sign of religious penance or for sexual gratification.—**flagellantism** *n*.
flagellate *vt* to scourge, to whip.—**flagellation** *n*.—**flagellator** *n*.
flagelliform *adj* long, tapering and flexible; shaped like the thong of a whip.
flagellum *n* (*pl* **flagella, flagellums**) (*biol, zool*) a whiplike appendage; (*bot*) a runner.
flageolet[1] *n* a small flute resembling the treble recorder.
flageolet[2] *n* a type of edible bean.
flagging *n* a pavement of flagstones.
flagitious *adj* atrocious, abominably wicked.—**flagitiously** *adv*.—**flagitiousness** *n*.
flag of convenience *n* a flag of a country flown by a ship registered there by the owners to benefit from less rigorous taxes or safety regulations.
flagon *n* a pottery or metal container for liquids with a handle and spout and often a lid.
flagrant *adj* conspicuous, notorious.—**flagrancy, flagrance** *n*.—**flagrantly** *adv*.
flagrante delicto *adv* in the very act, red-handed.
flagrante delicto *see* **in flagrante delicto.**
flagship *n* the ship that carries the admiral and his flag; the most important vessel of a shipping line; the chief or leading item of a group or collection.
flagstaff, flagpole *n* a pole on which a flag is displayed.
flagstone *n* hard, evenly stratified rock easily split into slabs for paving.
flag-waver *n* an excessively patriotic person, a jingoist.
flail *n* a tool for threshing by hand. * *vt* to beat with a flail. * *vi* (*usu with* **about**) to wave (the arms, etc) wildly.
flair *n* natural ability, aptitude; discernment; (*inf*) stylishness, sophistication.
flak *n* shells fired by anti-aircraft guns; criticism, opposition.—*also* **flack.**
flake *n* a small piece of snow; a small thin layer chipped from a larger mass of something. * *vt* to form into flakes. * *vi* (*with* **out**) (*inf*) to collapse or fall asleep from exhaustion.—**flaker** *n*.
flaky *adj* (**flakier, flakiest**) of or resembling flakes; liable to flake; (*sl*) nervous; (*sl*) odd, eccentric.—**flakily** *adv*.—**flakiness** *n*.
flam *vt* (**flamming, flammed**) (*dial*) to deceive.
flambé, flambée *adj* (*food*) covered with flaming brandy or other spirit.—*also vt*.
flambeau *n* (*pl* **flambeaux, flambeaus**) a lighted, flaming torch; a large ornamental candlestick.
flamboyant *adj* brilliantly coloured; ornate; strikingly elaborate; dashing, exuberant.—**flamboyance, flamboyancy** *n*.—**flamboyantly** *adv*.
flame *n* the burning gas of a fire, appearing as a tongue of light; the state of burning with a blaze; a thing like a flame; an intense emotion; (*inf*) a sweetheart. * *vi* to burst into flame; to become bright red with emotion.
flamen *n* (*pl* **flamens, flamines**) in ancient Rome, a priest devoted to the service of a special deity.

flamenco *n* (*pl* **flamencos**) a type of vigorous Spanish dance and music of gipsy origin.

flame-thrower *n* a weapon that shoots a jet of flaming liquid.

flaming *adj* emitting flames; very hot; gaudy; exaggerated; intense.—**flamingly** *adv*.

flamingo *n* (*pl* **flamingos, flamingoes**) any of several wading birds with rosy-pink plumage and long legs and neck.

flammable *adj* easily set on fire.—**flammability** *n*.

flamy *adj* (**flamier, flamiest**) resembling flame; flame-coloured.

flan *n* an open case of pastry or sponge cake with a sweet or savoury filling.

flânerie *n* idleness.

flâneur an idle person, a lounger.

flange *n* a raised edge, as on a wheel rim to keep it on a rail; a projecting rib. * *vt* to provide with a flange.—**flanged** *adj*.

flank *n* the fleshy part of the side from the ribs to the hip; the side of anything; the right or left side of a formation of troops. * *vt* to attack the flank of; to skirt the side of; to be situated at the side of.

flanker *n* (*mil*) a soldier or fortification used to protect a flank.

flannel *n* a soft light cotton or woollen cloth; a small cloth for washing the face and hands; (*sl*) nonsense, equivocation; (*pl*) trousers of such cloth. * *vt* (**flannelling, flannelled** *or* **flanneling, flanneled**) to wash with a flannel; (*inf*) to flatter.—**flannelly** *adj*.

flannelette *n* a soft cotton fabric.

flap *vi* (**flapping, flapped**) to move up and down, as wings; to sway loosely and noisily, as curtains in the wind, etc; to move or hang like a flap; (*inf*) to get into a panic or fluster. * *n* the motion or noise of a flap; anything broad and flexible, either hinged or hanging loose; a light blow with a flat object; (*inf*) agitation, panic.

flapdoodle *n* (*inf*) nonsense.

flapjack *n* a kind of pancake; a cake made with oats and syrup.

flapper *n* someone who, or something which, flaps; (*inf*) a fashionable young woman of the 1920s.

flare *vi* to burn with a sudden, bright, unsteady flame; to burst into emotion, esp anger; to widen out gradually. * *n* an unsteady flame; a sudden flash; a bright light used as a signal or illumination; a widened part or shape.

flare-up *n* a sudden burst of fire; (*inf*) a sudden burst of emotion.

flash *n* a sudden, brief light; a brief moment; a sudden brief display; (*TV, radio*) a sudden brief news item about an important event; (*photog*) a device for producing a brief intense light; a sudden onrush of water; **flash in the pan** a misfire; a showy start not followed up. * *vi* to send out a sudden, brief light; to sparkle; to come or pass suddenly; (*sl*) to expose the genitals indecently. * *vt* to cause to flash; to send (news, etc) swiftly; (*inf*) to show off. * *adj* (*inf*) flashy.—**flasher** *n*.

flashback *n* an interruption in the continuity of a story, etc, by telling or showing an earlier episode.

flashboard *n* a board placed on a dam to increase its height and hence the depth of the water contained.

flashbulb *n* a small bulb giving an intense light used in photography.

flash flood *n* a sudden brief flood caused by a heavy rainfall.

flash gun *n* (*photog*) a device for holding and operating a flashbulb.

flashing *n* a piece of lead or other metal, used to keep a roof watertight.

flashlight *n* an electric torch; a flash of electric light used to take photographs in dark conditions.

flashpoint *n* the lowest temperature at which vapour, as from oil, will ignite with a flash; the point where a situation will erupt into violence.

flashy *adj* (**flashier, flashiest**) pretentious; showy, gaudy.—**flashily** *adv*.—**flashiness** *n*.

flask *n* a slim-necked bottle; a vacuum flask.

flasket *n* a small flask; a long, shallow basket.

flat *adj* (**flatter, flattest**) having a smooth level surface; lying spread out; broad, even, and thin; not fluctuating; (*tyre*) deflated; dull, tedious; (*drink*) not fizzy; (*battery*) drained of electric current. * *adv* in a flat manner or position; exactly; (*mus*) below true pitch. * *n* anything flat, esp a surface, part, or expanse; a flat tyre; a set of rooms on one floor of a building (—*also* **apartment**).—**flatly** *adv*.—**flatness** *n*.

flatcar *n* an open, sideless rail truck.

flatfish *n* (*pl* **flatfish, flatfishes**) any of an order of marine fishes that as adults have both eyes on one side.

flatfoot *n* a condition in which the arch of the instep is flattened; (*pl* **flatfeet, flatfoots**) (*sl*) a policeman.

flat-footed *adj* having flatfoot; (*inf*) awkward; (*inf*) unprepared; (*inf*) determined, blunt.—**flat-footedly** *adv*.—**flat-footedness** *n*.

flatiron *n* an iron used for clothes, linen, etc, heated by being placed upon a hot stove, etc.

flat spin *n* a spin or manoeuvre in which an aircraft is more horizontal than vertical; (*inf*) a confused or agitated state.

flatten *vti* to make or become flat.—**flattener** *n*.

flatter *vt* to praise excessively or insincerely, esp out of self-interest or to win favour; to display to advantage; to represent as more attractive, etc than reality; to gratify the vanity of; to encourage falsely.—**flatterer** *n*.—**flattering** *adj*.—**flatteringly** *adv*.

flattery *n* (*pl* **flatteries**) compliments; insincere praise.

flattie *n* (*inf*) a woman's shoe with a flat heel.

flatting *n* (*metallurgy*) the process of rolling metal into flat sheets.

flatulence, flatulency *n* wind in the stomach; windiness, verbosity; pomposity.

flatulent *adj* causing or affected with intestinal gas; pretentious, vain.—**flatulently** *adv*.

flatways, flatwise *adv* flat side downwards.

flatworm *n* any of various parasitic worms having a flattened body.

flaunt *vi* to move or behave ostentatiously; (*flag*) to wave in the wind. * *vt* to display.—**flaunter** *n*.—**flauntingly** *adv*.

flaunty *adj* (**flauntier, flauntiest**) inclined to flaunting.

flautist *n* a flute player.—*also* **flutist**.

flavescent *adj* turning yellow; yellowish.

flavin, flavine *n* a yellow dye and antiseptic.

flavorous *adj* tasty.

flavour, flavor *n* the taste of something in the mouth; a characteristic quality. * *vt* to give flavour to.—**flavourer, flavorer** *n*.—**flavoursome, flavorsome** *adj*.

flavouring, flavoring *n* any substance used to give flavour to food.

flaw[1] *n* a defect; a crack. * *vti* to make or become flawed.

flaw[2] *n* a gust of wind, a squall.

flawless *adj* perfect.—**flawlessly** *adv*.—**flawlessness** *n*.

flax *n* a blue-flowered plant cultivated for its fibre and seed; the fibre of this plant.

flaxen, flaxy *adj* made of flax; pale yellow.

flaxseed *n* the seed of the flax plant, from which linseed oil is obtained.

flay *vt* to strip off the skin; to berate, criticize severely.—**flayer** *n*.

flea *n* a small wingless jumping bloodsucking insect.

fleabane *n* a plant of the aster family.

fleabite *n* the bite of a flea; a minor inconvenience.

fleabitten *adj* marked with fleabites; (*inf*) shabby, wretched; (*horses*) flecked with red spots on a light ground.

fleam *n* a lancet used for bleeding cattle.

flea market *n* an open-air street market, usu selling second-hand articles.

fleapit *n* (*inf*) a shabby cinema or theatre.

flèche *n* (*archit*) a slender spire, esp at the intersection of the nave and transept.

fleck *n* a spot or speckle of colour; a tiny particle. * *vt* to mark with flecks.

flection *see* **flexion**.

fled *see* **flee**.

fledge *vt* (*birds*) to rear until ready to fly; to cover or provide with feathers, esp an arrow.

fledgling, fledgeling *n* a young bird just fledged; an inexperienced person, a trainee.

flee *vti* (**fleeing, fled**) to run away from danger, etc; to pass away quickly, to disappear.—**fleer** *n*.

fleece *n* the woollen coat of sheep or similar animal. * *vt* to remove wool from; to defraud.
fleecy *adj* (**fleecier, fleeciest**) like a fleece, woolly.—**fleecily** *adv.*—**fleeciness** *n.*
fleer *n* a derisive look, sneer. * *vti* to sneer (at), to mock.
fleet[1] *n* a number of warships under one command; (*often with cap*) a country's navy; any group of cars, ships, buses, etc, under one control.
fleet[2] *adj* swift moving; nimble.—**fleetly** *adv.*—**fleetness** *n.*
fleeting *adj* brief, transient.—**fleetingly** *adv.*
Fleming *n* a native or inhabitant of Flanders.
Flemish *adj* of the people of Flanders, or their language.
flense, flench *vt* (*whale, seal*) to strip blubber from.
flesh *n* the soft substance of the body, esp the muscular tissue; the pulpy part of fruits and vegetables; meat; the body as distinct from the soul; all mankind; a yellowish-pink colour. * *vt* (*usu with* **out**) to give substance to.
fleshings *npl* flesh-coloured tights.
fleshly *adj* (**fleshlier, fleshliest**) having to do with the body and its desires, material, sensual.—**fleshliness** *n.*
flesh wound *n* a superficial wound.
fleshy *adj* (**fleshier, fleshiest**) of or resembling flesh; plump; succulent; sensual.—**fleshiness** *n.*
fleur-de-lis, fleur-de-lys *n* (*pl* **fleurs-de-lis, fleurs-de-lys**) a heraldic lily, the emblem of France.
fleury *adj* (*her*) decorated with a fleur-de-lis.—*also* **flory.**
flew *see* **fly.**
flews *npl* the pendulous lips of a bloodhound, etc.
flex *vti* to bend (a limb or joint, etc); to contract (a muscle). * *n* an insulated cable used to connect electric appliances to the mains (—*also* **cord**).
flexible *adj* easily bent, pliable; adaptable, versatile; docile.—**flexibility** *n.*—**flexibly** *adv.*
flexile *adj* supple; docile; flexible.—**flexility** *n.*
flexion *n* the act or process of bending; a curve; (*gram*) an inflection.—*also* **flection.**
flexitime, flextime *n* the staggering of working hours to enable each employee to work the full quota of time but at periods most convenient for the individual.
flexor *n* a muscle that acts to bend a joint or limb.
flexuous, flexose *adj* winding, sinuous; unsteady.—**flexuosity** *n.*
flexure *n* the act of bending; the state of being bent; (*math*) the curving of a line or surface.—**flexural** *adj*
flibbertigibbet *n* an impish, flighty or gossipy person.
flick *n* a light stroke or blow; (*inf*) a cinema film. * *vt* to strike or propel with a flick; a flicking movement.
flicker *vi* to burn unsteadily, as a flame; to move quickly to and fro. * *n* a flickering moment of light or flame; a flickering movement.—**flickeringly** *adv.*—**flickery** *adj.*
flick knife *n* a knife with a retractable blade released by pressing a button.
flier *see* **flyer.**
flies *see* **fly.**
flight[1] *n* the act, manner, or power of flying; distance flown; a group of creatures or things flying together; an aircraft scheduled to fly a certain trip; a trip by aircraft; a set of stairs, as between landings; a mental act of soaring beyond the ordinary; a set of feathers on a dart or arrow.
flight[2] *n* an act or instance of fleeing.
flight-deck *n* the cockpit of an aircraft.
flightless *adj* (*birds, insects*) incapable of flying.
flight recorder *n* a device that records information about the flight performance of an aircraft.
flighty *adj* (**flightier, flightiest**) irresponsible, capricious, frivolous.—**flightily** *adv.*—**flightiness** *n.*
flimflam *vt* (**flimflamming, flimflammed**) to deceive. * *n* nonsense; a trick.
flimsy *adj* (**flimsier, flimsiest**) weak, insubstantial; light and thin; (*excuse etc*) unconvincing. * *n* (*pl* **flimsies**) thin paper; copy written on this.—**flimsily** *adv.*—**flimsiness** *n.*
flinch *vi* to draw back, as from pain or fear; to wince.—**flincher** *n.*—**flinchingly** *adv.*
flinders *npl* fragments.
fling *vb* (**flinging, flung**) *vt* to cast, throw aside, esp with force; to put or send suddenly or without warning. * *vi* to kick out violently; to move or rush quickly or impetuously. * *n* the act of flinging; a lively dance; a period of pleasurable indulgence.—**flinger** *n.*
flint *n* a very hard rock that produces sparks when struck with steel; an alloy used for producing a spark in lighters.
flint glass *n* a lustrous kind of glass; lead glass.
flintlock *n* a type of old-fashioned gun fired by sparks from a flint.
flinty *adj* (**flintier, flintiest**) like flint, hard; cruel.—**flintily** *adv.*—**flintiness** *n.*
flip[1] *n* a drink made from any alcoholic beverage sweetened and mixed with beaten egg.
flip[2] *vb* (**flipping, flipped**) *vt* to toss with a quick jerk, to flick; to snap (a coin) in the air with the thumb; to turn or turn over. * *vi* to move jerkily; (*inf*) to burst into anger.
flip-flop *n* a backward handspring; an electronic circuit that can assume either of two states when activated; a rubber-soled sandal with a strap that fits between the toes (—*also* **thong**).
flippant *adj* impertinent; frivolous.—**flippancy** *n.*—**flippantly** *adv.*
flipper *n* a limb adapted for swimming; a flat rubber shoe expanded into a paddle, used in underwater swimming.
flip side *n* the reverse side of a gramophone record; the less attractive or well-known aspect of a person or thing.
flirt *vi* to make insincere amorous approaches; to trifle or toy (eg with an idea). * *n* a person who toys amorously with the opposite sex.—**flirtation** *n.*—**flirter** *n.*—**flirtingly** *adv.*
flirtatious *adj* fond of flirting, coquettish.—**flirtatiously** *adv.*
flit *vi* (**flitting, flitted**) to move lightly and rapidly; to vacate (a premises) stealthily. * the act of flitting, a removal.
flitch *n* a side of bacon, salted and cured; a plank cut from a tree.
flitter *vi* to flit about; to flicker, flutter.
flivver *n* (*sl*) an old or cheap car.
float *vi* to rest on the surface of or be suspended in a liquid; to move lightly; to wander aimlessly. * *vt* to cause to float; to put into circulation; to start up a business, esp by offering shares for sale. * *n* anything that floats; a cork or other device used on a fishing line to signal that the bait has been taken; a low flat vehicle decorated for exhibit in a parade; a small sum of money available for cash expenditures.—**floatable** *adj.*
floatage *see* **flotage.**
floatation *see* **flotation.**
floater *n* something that floats; a person lacking strong political convictions; (*inf*) a blunder.
floating *adj* swimming, or buoyed up, on the surface of a liquid; (*anat*) displaced; (*vote, etc*) not settled; (*capital*) in circulation, available for use.
floccose *adj* tufted.
floccule *n* a mass of fleecy material; a small tuft or flake.
flocculent *adj* woolly or flaky.—**flocculence, flocculency** *n.*
flocculus *n* (*pl* **flocculi**) a tufted mass; (*astron*) a mass of gas appearing as a mark on the sun (—*also* **plage**).
floccus *n* (*pl* **flocci**) down, such as that found on young birds; a tuft of hair.
flock[1] *n* a group of certain animals as birds, sheep, etc, living and feeding together; a group of people or things. * *vi* to assemble or travel in a flock or crowd.
flock[2] *n* a tuft of wool or cotton fibre; woollen or cotton waste used for stuffing furniture.—**flocky** *adj.*
floe *n* a sheet of floating ice.
flog *vt* (**flogging, flogged**) to beat harshly with a rod, stick or whip; (*sl*) to sell.—**flogger** *n.*—**flogging** *n.*
flong *n* (*printing*) paper used for stereotyping.
flood *n* an overflowing of water on an area normally dry; the rising of the

tide; a great outpouring, as of words. * *vt* to cover or fill, as with a flood; to put too much water, fuel, etc on or in. * *vi* to gush out in a flood; to become flooded.—**floodable** *adj*.—**flooder** *n*.

floodgate *n* a gate for controlling the flow of water, a sluice.

floodlight *n* a strong beam of light used to illuminate a stage, sports field, stadium, building exterior, etc. * *vt* (**floodlighting, floodlit**) to illuminate with floodlights.

flood tide *n* the rising or inflowing tide.

floor *n* the inside bottom surface of a room, flooring; the bottom surface of anything, as the ocean; a storey in a building; the area in a legislative assembly where the members sit and debate; the lower limit, the base. * *vt* to provide with a floor; to knock down (a person) in a fight; (*inf*) to defeat; (*inf*) to shock, to confuse.

floorage *n* the area of a floor.

floorboard *n* one of the boards making up a floor.

flooring *n* material for making or covering a floor; a floor.

floor plan *n* a scale drawing of the layout of a floor of a building.

floor show *n* entertainment with singers and dancers, etc in a nightclub.

floozy, floozie, floosie *n* (*pl* **floozies, floosies**) (*sl*) a disreputable woman.

flop *vi* (**flopping, flopped**) to sway or bounce loosely; to move in a heavy, clumsy or relaxed manner; (*inf*) to fail. * *n* a flopping movement; a collapse; (*inf*) a complete failure.

floppy *adj* (**floppier, floppiest**) limp, hanging loosely. * *n* (*pl* **floppies**) a floppy disk.—**floppily** *adv*.—**floppiness** *n*.

floppy disk *n* (*comput*) a flexible magnetic disk in a protective casing used for data storage and retrieval.

flora *n* (*pl* **floras, florae**) the plants of a region or a period.

floral *adj* pertaining to flowers.—**florally** *adv*.

Florentine *n* a native or inhabitant of Florence.—*also adj*.

florescence *n* the process, state or time of flowering.

floret *n* one of the small flowers forming the head of a plant.

floriated, floreated *adj* ornamented with floral decorations; flowery.

floribunda *n* any of several varieties of hybrid roses with large clusters of flowers.

floriculture *n* the cultivation of flowers.—**floricultural** *adj*.—**floriculturist** *n*

florid *adj* flowery; elaborate; (*complexion*) ruddy.—**floridity** *n*.—**floridly** *adv*.

florist *n* a person who sells or grows flowers and ornamental plants.

flory *see* **fleury.**

floss *n* a mass of short silky fibres, as from the rough outside of the silkworm's cocoon; fine silk used in embroidery; dental floss.

flossy *adj* (**flossier, flossiest**) like floss, silky, downy; (*sl*) flashy.

flotage *n* flotation; a craft afloat; flotsam.—*also* **floatage.**

flotation *n* the act or process of floating; the launching of a business venture.—*also* **floatation.**

flotilla *n* a small fleet of ships.

flotsam *n* wreckage or debris found floating in the sea.

flounce[1] *vi* to move in an emphatic or impatient manner.* *n* the act of flouncing, a plunge.

flounce[2] *n* a frill of material sewn to the skirt of a dress. * *vt* to add flounces to.

flouncing *n* a material used for making flounces.

flounder[1] *vi* to move awkwardly and with difficulty; to be clumsy in thinking or speaking.

flounder[2] *n* (*pl* **flounder, flounders**) a small flatfish used as food.

flour *n* the finely ground powder of wheat or other grain. * *vt* to sprinkle with flour.—**floury** *adj*.

flourish *vi* (*plants*) to grow luxuriantly; to thrive, prosper; to live and work at a specified time. * *vt* to brandish dramatically. * *n* embellishment; a curve made by a bold stroke of the pen; a sweeping gesture; a musical fanfare.—**flourisher** *n*.

flout *vt* to treat with contempt, to disobey openly. * *n* an insult.—**flouter** *n*.—**floutingly** *adv*.

flow *vi* (*liquids*) to move (as if) in a stream; (*tide*) to rise; to glide smoothly; (*conversation, etc*) to continue effortlessly; to be characterized by smooth and easy movement; to hang free or loosely; to be plentiful. * *n* a flowing; the rate of flow; anything that flows; the rising of the tide.

flow chart *n* a diagram representing the sequence of and relationships between different steps or procedures in a complex process, eg manufacturing.

flower *n* the seed-producing structure of a flowering plant, blossom; a plant cultivated for its blossoms; the best or finest part. * *vt* to cause to bear flowers. * *vi* to produce blossoms; to reach the best stage.

floweret *n* a little flower.

flowerpot *n* a pot used to contain a growing plant.

flowery *adj* full of or decorated with flowers; (*language*) full of elaborate expressions.—**floweriness** *n*.

flown *see* **fly.**

fl. oz. *abbr* = fluid ounce.

flu *n* (*inf*) influenza.

fluctuate *vi* (*prices, etc*) to be continually varying in an irregular way.—**fluctuation** *n*.

flue[1] *n* a shaft for the passage of smoke, hot air, etc, as in a chimney.

flue[2] *n* soft downy matter; fluff.

flue[3] *n* a type of fishing net.

fluent *adj* able to write and speak a foreign language with ease; articulate, speaking and writing easily and smoothly; graceful.—**fluency** *n*.—**fluently** *adv*.

fluff *n* soft, light down; a loose, soft mass, as of hair; (*inf*) a mistake, bungle. * *vt* to pat or shake until fluffy; (*inf*) to forget, to bungle.

fluffy *adj* (**fluffier, fluffiest**) like fluff; soft and downy; feathery.—**fluffily** *adv*.—**fluffiness** *n*.

fluid *n* a substance able to flow freely, as a liquid or gas does. * *adj* able to flow freely; able to change rapidly or easily.—**fluidal** *adj*.—**fluidity** *n*.—**fluidly** *adv*.

fluid ounce *n* a US unit of capacity equal to one sixteenth of a US pint; a UK unit of capacity equal to one twentieth of an imperial pint

fluke[1] *n* a flatfish; a flattened parasitic worm.

fluke[2] *n* the part of an anchor that fastens in the sea bed, river bottom, etc; the barbed end of a harpoon; one of the lobes of a whale's tail.

fluke[3] *n* a stroke of luck. * *vti* to make or score by a fluke.

fluky, flukey *adj* (**flukier, flukiest**) obtained by luck; uncertain.—**flukiness** *n*.

flume *n* a channel for water; a ravine with a stream; a chute with a flow of water into a swimming pool. * *vt* to transport or divert by a flume.

flummery *n* (*pl* **flummeries**) (*inf*) an empty compliment; a pudding, a kind of custard or blancmange.

flummox *vt* (*inf*) to bewilder, perplex.

flung *see* **fling.**

flunk *vti* (*sl*) to fail, as in school work; to shirk.

flunky, flunkey *n* (*pl* **flunkies, flunkeys**) a servile person, toady; a person who does menial work; a liveried servant.

fluor *see* **fluorspar.**

fluoresce *vi* to display fluorescence.

fluorescence *n* the property of producing light when acted upon by radiant energy; light so produced.—**fluorescent** *adj*.

fluorescent lamp *n* a glass tube coated with a fluorescent substance that emits light when acted upon by ultraviolet radiation.

fluoridate *vt* to add fluoride to drinking water to reduce tooth decay.—**fluoridation** *n*.

fluoride *n* any of various compounds of fluorine.

fluorinate *vt* to treat or mix with fluorine.—**fluorination** *n*.

fluorine, fluorin *n* a chemical element, a pale greenish-yellow corrosive gas.

fluoroscope *n* an instrument with a fluorescent screen, used for studying X-ray images.—**fluoroscopy** *n*.

fluorspar *n* a transparent, or semi-transparent, material, composed of calcium fluoride.—*also* **fluor.**

flurry *n* (*pl* **flurries**) a sudden gust of wind, rain, or snow; a sudden commotion. * *vti* (**flurrying, flurried**) to (cause to) become flustered.

flush[1] *n* a rapid flow, as of water; sudden, vigorous growth; a sudden excitement; a blush; a sudden feeling of heat, as in a fever. * *vi* to flow rapidly; to blush or glow; to be washed out by a sudden flow of water. * *vt* to wash out with a sudden flow of water; to cause to blush; to excite. * *adj* level or in one plane with another surface; (*inf*) abundant, well-supplied, esp with money.—**flusher** *n*.

flush[2] *vt* to make game birds fly away suddenly.—**flusher** *n*.

flush[3] *n* (*poker, etc*) a hand of cards all of the same suit.

fluster *vti* to make or become confused. * *n* agitation or confusion.

flute *n* an orchestral woodwind instrument in the form of a straight pipe (with finger holes and keys) held horizontally and played through a hole located near one end; a decorative groove. * *vi* to play or make sounds like a flute; to cut grooves in.—**fluty** *adj*.

fluter *n* a person who makes flutes; a tool used in making flutes; a flute player.

fluting *n* decorative channels or grooves in pillars, etc; pleats like this in a skirt, etc.

flutist *n* a flute player, flautist.

flutter *vi* (*birds*) to flap the wings; to wave about rapidly; (*heart*) to beat irregularly or spasmodically. * *vt* to cause to flutter. * *n* rapid, irregular motion; nervous excitement; commotion, confusion; (*inf*) a small bet.—**flutterer** *n*.—**fluttery** *adj*.

fluty *adj* (**flutier, flutiest**) soft and clear like the sound of a flute.—**flutily** *adv*,—**flutiness** *n*.

fluvial, fluviatile *adj* of or found in streams and rivers.

flux *n* a continual flowing or changing; a substance used to help metals fuse together, as in soldering.

fluxion *n* a flowing; an excessive flow; (*math*) differential calculus.—**fluxional, fluxionary** *adj*.

fly[1] *n* (*pl* **flies**) a two-winged insect; a natural or imitation fly attached to a fish-hook as bait.

fly[2] *vb* (**flying, flew,** *pp* **flown**) *vi* to move through the air, esp on wings; to travel in an aircraft; to control an aircraft; to take flight, flee; to pass quickly; (*inf*) to depart quickly. * *vt* to cause to fly, as a kite; to escape, flee from; to transport by aircraft. * *n* a flap that conceals buttons, a zip, etc on trousers; material forming the outer roof of a tent; a device for regulating machinery, a flywheel.—**flyable** *adj*.

fly[3] *adj* (*inf*) sly, astute.

flyaway*adj* (*hair etc*) loose; (*person*) flighty.

flyblow *n* the egg or larva of a fly. * *vt* (**flyblowing, flyblew,** *pp* **flyblown**) to contaminate (meat, etc) by laying eggs (esp of a blowfly) in it.

flyby *n* (*pl* **flybys**) a flight past a target, esp by a spacecraft past a celestial body to collect scientific data.

fly-by-night *adj* (*inf*) unreliable, untrustworthy; transitory. * *n* an untrustworthy person, esp one who evades responsibilities or debts by flight.

flycatcher *n* a bird that catches insects on the wing.

flyer *n* something that flies or moves very fast; a pilot.—*also* **flier**.

fly fishing *n* fishing using artificial flies as lures.—**fly-fish** *vi*.

flying *adj* capable of flight; fleeing; fast-moving. * *n* the act of flying an aircraft, etc.

flying boat *n* a sea plane in which the boat forms the fuselage and float.

flying buttress *n* a buttress connected to a wall by an arch, serving to resist outward pressure.

flying colours *npl* great success; triumph.

flying doctor *n* a doctor who visits patients (e.g. in isolated communities) by aircraft.

flying fish *n* any of numerous fishes of warm seas with winglike fins used in gliding through the air.

flying fox *n* a large fruit bat of Africa and Asia.

flying saucer *n* an unidentified flying disc-shaped object, purportedly from outer space.

flying squad *n* a small detachment of police officers mobilized for swift action.

flying squirrel *n* a nocturnal squirrel with folds of skin joining its legs, enabling it to glide.

flying start *n* a start in a race when the competitor is already moving when passing the starting line; a promising start in anything.

flyleaf *n* (*pl* **flyleaves**) the blank leaf at the beginning or end of a book.

flyover *n* a bridge that carries a road or railway over another; a fly-past.

flypaper *n* paper with a sticky poisonous coating that is hung up to trap and kill flies.

fly-past *n* a processional flight of aircraft.

flyte *see* **flite**.

flytrap *n* any of various insect-eating plants; a device for catching flies.

flyweight *n* a boxer weighing not more than 112 pounds (51 kg).

flywheel *n* a heavy wheel which stores energy by inertia, used to regulate machinery.

FM *abbr* = Field Marshal; frequency modulation.

Fm (*chem symbol*) fermium.

f-number *n* (*photog*) a number used to calculate the ratio of light passing through a lens.

FO *abbr* = Foreign Office.

foal *n* the young of the horse or a related animal. * *vti* to give birth to a foal.

foam *n* froth or fine bubbles on the surface of liquid; something like foam, as frothy saliva; a rigid or springy cellular mass made from liquid rubber, plastic, etc. * *vi* to cause or emit foam.

foamy *adj* (**foamier, foamiest**) of, like, or covered with foam.—**foamily** *adv*.—**foaminess** *n*.

f.o.b. *abbr* = free on board.

fob[1] *n* the chain or ribbon for attaching a watch to a waistcoat; any object attached to a watch chain; a small pocket in a waistcoat for a watch.

fob[2] *vt* (**fobbing, fobbed**) (*with* **off**) to cheat; to put off; to palm off (upon).

focal *adj* of or pertaining to a focus.—**focally** *adv*.

focalize *vti* to (cause to) focus.—**focalization** *n*.

focal length *n* the distance between the focal point and optical centre of a lens or mirror.

fo'c's'le, fo'c'sle *see* **forecastle**.

focus *n* (*pl* **focuses, foci**) a point where rays of light, heat, etc meet after being bent by a lens, curved mirror, etc; correct adjustment of the eye or lens to form a clear image; a centre of activity or interest. * *vt* (**focusing, focused** *or* **focussing, focussed**) to adjust the focus of; to bring into focus; to concentrate.—**focusable** *adj*.—**focuser** *n*.

fodder *n* dried food for cattle, horses, etc.

FOE *abbr* = Friends of the Earth.

foe *n* an enemy, an adversary.

foehn *see* **föhn**.

foeman *n* (*arch*) an adversary in war.

foetal *see* **fetal**.

foeticide *see* **feticide**.

foetid *see* **fetid**.

foetus *see* **fetus**.

fog[1] *n* (a state of poor visibility caused by) a large mass of water vapour condensed to fine particles just above the earth's surface; a state of mental confusion; (*photog*) cloudiness on a developed photograph. * *vti* (**fogging, fogged**) to make or become foggy.

fog[2] *n* a second growth of grass in autumn; winter pasture; (*Scot*) moss.

fogbound *n* unable to function due to fog.

fogey, fogy *n* (*pl* **fogeys, fogies**) a person of old-fashioned or eccentric habits.—**fogeyish, fogyish** *adj*.

foggy *adj* (**foggier, foggiest**) thick with fog; mentally confused; indistinct, opaque.—**foggily** *adv*.—**fogginess** *n*.

foghorn *n* a horn (in a ship, etc) sounded in a fog as a warning.

fogy *see* **fogey**.

föhn *n* a warm, dry, Alpine wind.—*also* **foehn**.

foible *n* a slight weakness or failing; an idiosyncrasy; the weakest part of the blade of a sword.

foil[1] *vt* to defeat; to frustrate; to trample a trail to spoil scent. * *n* (*arch*) the trail of hunted game.—**foilable** *adj*.

foil[2] *n* a very thin sheet of metal; a backing for a mirror or gem; anything that sets off or enhances another by contrast; (*archit*) a small arc or

space in the tracery of a window. * *vt* to cover, back or adorn with foil; to set off.
foil[3] *n* a long, thin blunted sword used for fencing.
foison *n* (*arch*) an abundance.
foist *vt* (*with* **in** *or* **into**) to introduce stealthily or without permission; (*with* **off** *or* **on**) to pass off as genuine.
folacin *see* **folic acid.**
fold[1] *vt* to cover by bending or doubling over so that one part covers another; to wrap up, envelop; to interlace (one's arms); to clasp (one's hands); to embrace; to incorporate (an ingredient) into a food mixture by gentle overturnings. * *vi* to become folded; to fail completely; to collapse, esp to go out of business. * *n* something folded, as a piece of cloth; a crease or hollow made by folding.—**foldable** *adj*.
fold[2] *n* a pen for sheep; a group of people or institutions having a common belief, activity, etc. * *vt* to pen in a fold.
-fold *suffix* times repeated, eg *tenfold*.
foldaway *adj* (*bed, etc*) collapsible.
folder *n* a folded cover or large envelope for holding loose papers.
folderol *see* **falderal.**
folding *n* the act or process of folding. * *adj* which folds or can be folded.
foliaceous *adj* resembling or having leaves; (*rock*) having thin layers.
foliage *n* leaves, as of a plant or tree.
foliar *adj* of or pertaining to leaves.
foliate *adj* resembling or having leaves. * *vti* to beat (metal) into foil; to divide into thin layers; to produce leaves; (*archit*) to decorate with foils; to number the leaves of (a book).
foliation *n* (*bot*) the act of producing leaves or the state of having leaves; the act or process of beating a metal into thin plates.
folic acid *n* a B-complex vitamin used in treating anaemia.—*also* **folacin.**
folio *n* (*pl* **folios**) a large sheet of paper folded once to make two leaves of a book; a book of sheets in this size, the largest commonly used; the number of a page in a book. * *vt* (**folioing, folioed**) to number the pages of.
foliose *adj* (*bot*) having many leaves; of or resembling leaves.
folk *n* (*pl* **folk, folks**) a people of a country or tribe; people in general, esp those of a particular area; relatives; folk music. * *adj* of or originating among the ordinary people.—**folkish** *adj*.
folk etymology *n* the perversion of a word in an attempt to explain it, as "sparrow grass" for "asparagus."
folklore *n* the traditional beliefs, customs, legends, etc of a people; the study of these.—**folkloric, folkloristic** *adj*.—**folklorist** *n*.
folk music *n* traditional music.
folk song *n* a traditional song.
folksy *adj* (**folksier, folksiest**) (*inf*) simple, plain; friendly.—**folksiness** *n*.
folktale *n* an anonymous, timeless, and placeless tale circulated orally among a people.
follicle *n* any small sac, cavity, or gland.—**follicular, folliculate, folliculated** *adj*.
follow *vt* to go or come after; to pursue; to go along (a path, road, etc); to copy; to obey; to adopt, as an opinion; to watch fixedly; to focus the mind on; to understand the meaning of; to monitor the progress of; to come or occur after in time; to result from; (*with* **through**) to pursue (an aim) to a conclusion; (*with* **up**) to pursue a question, inquiry, etc, that has been started. * *vi* to go or come after another; to result; (*with* **on**) (*cricket*) to take a second innings immediately after a first; (*with* **suit**) to play a card of the same suit; to do the same thing; (*with* **through**) (*sport*) to continue a stroke or motion of a bat, club, etc after the ball has been struck; (*with* **up**) to pursue steadily; to supplement.—**followable** *adj*.
follower *n* a disciple or adherent; a person who imitates another.
following *n* a body of adherents or believers. * *adj* next after; now to be stated.
follow-on *n* (*cricket*) an immediate return to bat by a side which has scored a certain number of runs fewer than its opponents in the first innings.
follow-through *n* (*golf, tennis, etc*) the continuation of a swing after hitting the ball.
follow-up *n* the continuing after a beginning; a steady pursuit.
folly *n* (*pl* **follies**) a lack of sense; a foolish act or idea; an extravagant and fanciful building which serves no practical purpose.
foment *vt* to stir up (trouble); to bathe with warm water or lotions.—**fomenter** *n*.
fomentation *n* the act of formenting; instigation; the application of a warm lotion to ease pain or swelling.
fond *adj* loving, affectionate; doting, indulgent; (*arch*) overcredulous, simple; (*with* **of**) having a liking for.—**fondly** *adv*.—**fondness** *n*.
fondant *n* a soft sugar mixture for sweets and icings; a sweet made from this.
fondle *vt* to caress.—**fondler** *n*.—**fondlingly** *adv*.
fondue *n* melted cheese used as a dip with small pieces of bread.
font[1] *n* a receptacle for baptismal water; a receptacle for holy water.—**fontal** *adj*.
font[2] *see* **fount**[1].
fontanameter *n* a device for measuring the pressure within the skull of a foetus in the womb.
fontanelle, fontanel *n* one of the open spaces in between the bones of an infant's skull.
food *n* any substance, esp a solid, taken in by a plant or animal to enable it to live and grow; anything that nourishes.
foodie *n* (*pl* **foodies**) (*inf*) a person who takes great delight in cooking and eating.
food poisoning *n* an acute illness caused by harmful bacteria or toxins in food.
food processor *n* an electric appliance used to perform various functions when preparing food, as chopping, mixing and grating.
foodstuff *n* a substance used as food.
fool *n* a person lacking wisdom or common sense; (*Middle Ages*) a jester; a dupe; a cold dessert made from whipped cream mixed with fruit purée. * *vt* to deceive, make a fool of. * *vi* to act jokingly; to spend time idly; to tease or meddle with.
foolery *n* (*pl* **fooleries**) foolish behaviour, buffoonery.
foolhardy *adj* (**foolhardier, foolhardiest**) foolishly bold; rash.—**foolhardiness** *n*.
foolish *adj* unwise; ridiculous; ill-judged.—**foolishly** *adv*.—**foolishness** *n*.
foolproof *adj* proof against failure; easy to understand; easy to use.
foolscap *n* a large size of writing paper.
fool's errand *n* a pointless undertaking.
fool's paradise *n* illusory happiness.
foot *n* (*pl* **feet**) the end part of the leg, on which one stands; anything a resembling foot, as the lower part of a chair, table, etc; the lower part or edge of something, bottom; a measure of length equal to 12 inches (30.48 cm); the part of a garment that covers the foot; an attachment on a sewing machine that grips the fabric; a group of syllables serving as a unit of metre in verse. * *vi* to dance. * *vt* to walk, dance over or on; to pay the entire cost of (a bill).
footage *n* measurement in feet, esp film exposed.
foot-and-mouth disease *n* a contagious disease of cattle.
football *n* a field game played with an inflated leather ball by two teams; the ball used.—**footballer** *n*.
footboard *n* a treadle on a machine; a step on a carriage.
footbridge *n* a narrow bridge for pedestrians.
footer *n* (*sl*) football.
footfall *n* the sound of a footstep.
foot-fault *n* (*tennis*) overstepping the base line when serving. * *vi* to commit a foot-fault.
footgear *n* shoes and socks, etc.
foothill *n* a hill at the foot of higher hills.
foothold *n* a ledge, etc for placing the foot when climbing, etc; a place from which further progress may be made.
footie *see* **footy.**
footing *n* the basis upon which something rests; status, relationship; a foothold; (*archit*) a projecting course at the base of a wall.
footle *vi* to potter.

footlights *npl* a row of lights in front of a stage floor.
footling *adj* trifling.
footloose *adj* free, untramelled.
footman *n* (*pl* **footmen**) a liveried servant or attendant.
footmark *n* a footprint.
footnote *n* a note or comment at the foot of a page.
footpad *n* (*arch*) a highwayman on foot.
footpath *n* a narrow path for pedestrians.
foot-pound *n* a unit of energy, equal to the work required to raise a one pound weight through one foot; equivalent to 0.042 joule.
footprint *n* the impression left by a foot.
foot-rot *n* an inflammation of the feet of sheep and cattle; a plant disease affecting stalks and trunks; (*sl*) athlete's foot.
foots *npl* the sediment of oil or sugar.
footsie *n* (*inf*) amorous touching together of feet; (*inf*) clandestine dealings.
footslog *vt* (**footslogging, footslogged**) (*inf*) to march.
footsore *adj* having painful feet from excessive walking.
footstalk *n* (*bot*) the supporting stem of a plant or flower; (*zool*) the attachment of a barnacle.
footstall *n* a woman's stirrup (used on a sidesaddle)
footstool *n* a stool for the feet of a seated person.
footwear *n* shoes and socks, etc.
footwork *n* skilful use of the feet in boxing, football, dancing, etc.
footy *n* (*sl*) football.—*also* **footie.**
foozle *n* (*golf*) a bungled shot. * *vi* to bungle (a shot).
fop *n* someone obsessed with fashion and appearance.
foppery *n* (*pl* **fopperies**) the appearance, manner or dress of a fop.
foppish *adj* affected in dress and manners.—**foppishly** *adv*.—**foppishness** *n*.
for *prep* because of, as a result of; as the price of, or recompense of; in order to be, to serve as; appropriate to, or adapted to; in quest of; in the direction of; on behalf of; in place of; in favour of; with respect to; notwithstanding, in spite of; to the extent of; throughout the space of; during. * *conj* because.
for- *prefix* expressing prohibition or neglect; bad effect; intensity.
forage *n* food for domestic animals, esp when taken by browsing or grazing; a search for provisions. * *vi* to search for food.—**forager** *n*.
foramen *n* (*pl* **foraminia, foramens**) a short passage or opening, esp in a bone.
foraminifer *n* a member of a group of protozoa having a shell with very minute apertures, through which parts of its body pass.
forasmuch as *conj* seeing that, since.
foray *n* a sudden raid. * *vti* to plunder.—**forayer** *n*.
forbad, forbade *see* **forbid.**
forbear *vb* (**forbearing, forbore,** *pp* **forborne**) *vi* to endure, to avoid. * *vt* to hold oneself back from.—**forbearer** *n*.—**forbearingly** *adv*.
forbearance *n* patience; self-control.
forbid *vt* (**forbidding, forbad** *or* **forbade,** *pp* **forbidden** *or* **forbid**) to command (a person) not to do something; to render impossible, prevent.—**forbiddance** *n*.—**forbidder** *n*.
forbidding *adj* unfriendly, solemn, strict.—**forbiddingly** *adv*.
forbore, forborne *see* **forbear.**
force *n* strength, power, effort; (*physics*) (the intensity of) an influence that causes movement of a body or other effects; a body of soldiers, police, etc prepared for action; effectiveness; violence, compulsion; legal or logical validity. * *vt* to compel or oblige by physical effort, superior strength, etc; to achieve by force; to press or drive against resistance; to produce with effort; to break open, penetrate; to impose, inflict; to cause (plants, animals) to grow at a greater rate than normal.—**forceable** *adj*.—**forcer** *n*.
forced *adj* compulsory; strained.—**forcedly** *adv*.—**forcedness** *n*.
force-feed *vt* (**force-feeding, force-fed**) to compel a person to swallow food.
forceful *adj* powerful, effective.—**forcefully** *adv*.—**forcefulness** *n*.
force majeure *n* compelling force, unavoidable circumstances.
forcemeat *n* finely chopped meat, seasoned and used as a stuffing.
force pump *n* a pump that forces water beyond the range of atmospheric pressure.
forceps *n* (*pl* **forceps, forcipes**) an instrument for grasping and holding firmly, or exerting traction upon objects, esp by jewellers and surgeons.
forcible *adj* powerful; done by force.—**forcibleness** *n*.—**forcibly** *adv*.
ford *n* a shallow crossing place in a river, stream, etc. * *vt* to wade across.—**fordable** *adj*.
fore *adj* in front. * *n* the front. * *adv* in, at or towards the front. * *interj* (*golf*) a warning cry to anybody who may be hit by the ball.
fore- *prefix* in front; beforehand.
fore-and-aft *adj* (*naut*) (situated) at both bow and stern.
forearm[1] *n* the arm between the elbow and the wrist.
forearm[2] *vt* to arm in advance.
forebear *n* (*usu pl*) an ancestor.
forebode *vt* to be a sign or warning (of trouble, etc) in advance; to have a premonition of (an event).—**foreboder** *n*.
foreboding *n* a feeling that evil is going to happen, a presentiment.
forecast *vt* (**forecasting, forecast** *or* **forecasted**) to predict (an event, the weather, etc) through rational analysis; to serve as a forecast of. * *n* a prediction, esp of weather; foresight.—**forecaster** *n*.
forecastle *n* the forward part of a ship containing the crew's quarters.—*also* **fo'c's'le, fo'c'sle**
foreclose *vt* to remove the right of redeeming (a mortgage); to bar, exclude; to hinder.—**foreclosable** *adj*.—**foreclosure** *n*.
forecourt *n* an enclosed space in front of a building, as in a filling station.
forefather *n* (*usu pl*) an ancestor.
forefinger *n* the finger next to the thumb.
forefoot *n* (*pl* **forefeet**) a front foot of an animal; (*naut*) the foremost piece of the keel.
forefront *n* the very front, vanguard.
foregather *see* **forgather.**
forego[1] *see* **forgo.**
forego[2] *vt* (**foregoing, forewent,** *pp* **foregone**) to precede.—**foregoer** *n*.
foregoing *adj* going before, preceding.
foregone conclusion *n* an inevitable result, easily predictable.
foreground *n* the part of a picture or view nearest the spectator's vision.
forehand *n* (*tennis, etc*) a stroke made with the hand facing forwards; the part of a horse in front of the rider. * *adj* (*tennis stroke*) made with the palm leading.
forehanded *adj* thrifty; well-off.—**forehandedness** *n*.
forehead *n* the part of the face above the eyes.
foreign *adj* of, in, or belonging to another country; involving other countries; alien in character; introduced from outside.
foreigner *n* a person from another country; a stranger.
foreignism *n*.a foreign mannerism, custom or saying, or an imitation of any of these.
foreign office *n* the government department which handles foreign affairs.—*also* **state department.**
forejudge *vti* to judge before hearing evidence.
foreknow *vt* (**foreknowing, foreknew,** *pl* **foreknown**) to know beforehand.—**foreknowledge** *n*.
foreland *n* a promontory, a headland.
foreleg *n* a front leg of an animal.
forelock *n* the lock of hair growing above the forehead.
foreman *n* (*pl* **foremen**) a person who supervises workers in a factory, etc; the spokesperson of a jury.—**forewoman** *nf* (*pl* **forewomen**).
foremast *n* the mast nearest the bow of a sailing vessel.
foremost *adj* first in importance; most advanced in rank or position. * *adv* in the first place.
forenoon *n* time before midday; morning.
forensic *adj* of, belonging to or used in courts of law.—**forensicality** *n*.—**forensically** *adv*.
forensic medicine *n* the application of medical expertise to legal and criminal investigations.

foreordain *vt* to arrange in advance; to predestine.—**foreordainment, foreordination** *n*.
forepeak *n* (*naut*) the end of a ship's hold in the angle of the bow.
foreplay *n* mutual sexual stimulation before intercourse.
forerun *vt* (**forerunning, foreran,** *pp* **forerun**) to precede, to foreshadow.
forerunner *n* a person or thing that comes in advance of another; a portent.
foresail *n* (*naut*) the largest sail on the foremast of a sailing vessel.
foresee *vt* (**foreseeing, foresaw,** *pp* **foreseen**) to be aware of beforehand.—**foreseeable** *adj*.—**foreseer** *n*.
foreshadow *vt* to represent or indicate beforehand.—**foreshadower** *n*.
foresheet *n* a rope for controlling a foresail; (*pl*) the inner part of a boat's bows.
foreshore *n* a strip of land next to the shore; the shore between the high and low water marks.
foreshorten *vt* in drawing, etc, to shorten some lines of (an object) to give the illusion of proper relative size.
foresight *n* foreseeing; the power to foresee; prudent provision for the future.—**foresighted** *adj*.—**foresightedness** *n*.
foreskin *n* the loose skin that covers the end of the penis.
forest *n* a thick growth of trees, etc covering a large tract of land; something resembling a forest. * *vt* to plant with trees; to make into forest.—**forestal, forestial** *adj*.
forestall *vt* to prevent by taking action beforehand; to anticipate.—**forestaller** *n*.—**forestalment, forestallment** *n*.
forestation *n* the planting of trees over a large area.
forestay *n* (*naut*) a strong rope reaching from the top of the foremast to the bow of a vessel.
forester *n* a person trained in forestry.
forestry *n* the science of planting and cultivating forests.
foretaste *n* partial experience in advance; anticipation. * *vt* to taste before possession; to have a foretaste of.
foretell *vt* (**foretelling, foretold**) to forecast, to predict.—**foreteller** *n*.
forethought *n* thought for the future; provident care.—**forethoughtful** *adj*.
foretime *n* the past, old times.
foretoken *vt* to portend, foreshadow. * *n* an omen.
foretop *n* (*naut*) a platform at the head of the foremast.
fore-topgallant mast *n* the mast above the fore-topmast, carrying the fore-topgallant sail.
fore-topmast *n* (*naut*) the mast immediately above the foremast, carrying the fore-topsail.
for ever, forever *adv* for all future time; continually.
for evermore, forevermore *adv* for ever.
forewarn *vt* to warn beforehand.—**forewarner** *n*.—**forewarningly** *adv*.
forewent *see* **forego**[2].
forewind *n* (*naut*) a favourable wind.
forewoman *n* (*pl* **forewomen**) a person who supervises workers in a factory, etc; the spokesperson of a jury.
foreword *n* an introduction to a book to explain its purpose, often by someone other than the author.
forfeit *n* something confiscated or given up as a penalty for a fault; (*pl*) a game in which a player redeems a forfeit by performing a ludicrous task. * *vt* to lose or be penalized by forfeiture.—**forfeiter** *n*.—**forfeiture** *n*.
forfend *vt* to protect; (*arch*) to avert, ward off.
forficate *adj* (*zool*) scissor-shaped, forked.
forgather *vi* to assemble, meet.—*also* **foregather**.
forgave *see* **forgive**.
forge[1] *n* (a workshop with) a furnace in which metals are heated and shaped.* *vt* to shape (metal) by heating and hammering; to counterfeit (eg a signature). * *vi* to commit forgery.—**forgeable** *adj*.—**forger** *n*.
forge[2] *vt* to move steadily forward with effort.
forgery *n* (*pl* **forgeries**) fraudulently copying; a forged copy; a spurious thing.
forget *vti* (**forgetting, forgot,** *pp* **forgotten**) to be unable to remember; to overlook or neglect; **forget oneself** to lose self-control; to act unbecomingly.—**forgettable** *adj*.—**forgetter** *n*.
forgetful *adj* apt to forget, inattentive.—**forgetfully** *adv*.—**forgetfulness** *n*.
forget-me-not *n* a plant with bright-blue or white flowers.
forgive *vt* (**forgiving, forgave,** *pp* **forgiven**) to cease to feel resentment against (a person); to pardon. * *vi* to be merciful or forgiving.—**forgivable** *adj*.—**forgiveness** *n*.—**forgiver** *n*.
forgiving *adj* willing to forgive; merciful, kind.—**forgivingly** *adv*.
forgo *vt* (**forgoing, forwent,** *pp* **forgone**) to give up, abstain from.—*also* **forego**.—**forgoer** *n*.
forgot, forgotten *see* **forget**.
fork *n* a small, usu metal, instrument with two or more thin prongs set in a handle, used in eating and cooking; a pronged agricultural or gardening tool for digging, etc; anything that divides into prongs or branches; one of the branches into which a road or river divides; the point of separation. * *vi* to divide into branches; to follow a branch of a fork in a road, etc. * *vt* to form as a fork; to dig, lift, etc with a fork; (*with* **out**) (*sl*) to pay or hand over (money, goods, etc).
forked *adj* shaped like a fork; branching, opening into two or more parts; zigzag, eg lightning.
fork-lift truck *n* a vehicle with power-operated prongs for raising and lowering loads.
forlorn *adj* alone; wretched.—**forlornly** *adv*.
forlorn hope *n* a faint hope; a desperate enterprise.
form[1] *n* general structure; the figure of a person or animal; a mould; a particular mode, kind, type, etc; arrangement; a way of doing something requiring skill; a conventional procedure; a printed document with blanks to be filled in; a class in school; condition of mind or body; a chart giving information about racehorses; changed appearance of a word to show inflection; (*sl*) a criminal record. * *vt* to shape; to train; to develop (habits); to constitute. * *vi* to be formed.—**formable** *adj*.
form[2] *see* **forme**.
formal *adj* in conformity with established rules or habits; regular; relating to the outward appearance only; ceremonial; punctilious; stiff.—**formally** *adv*.
formaldehyde *n* a colourless pungent gas used in solution as a disinfectant and preservative.
formalin *n* an aqueous solution of formaldehyde used as an antiseptic or preservative.—*also* **formol**.
formalism *n* strict observance of outward form or conventional usage.—**formalist** *n*.—**formalistic** *adj*.
formality *n* (*pl* **formalities**) strict observance of established rules or customs; an act or procedure required by law or convention.
formalize *vt* to make formal; to clothe with legal formality.—**formalization** *n*.
format *n* the size, form, shape in which books, etc are issued; the general style or presentation of something, eg a television programme; (*comput*) the arrangement of data on magnetic disk, etc for access and storage. * *vt* (**formatting, formatted**) to arrange in a particular form, esp for a computer.
formate *n* a salt of formic acid.
formation *n* form of making or producing; that which is formed; structure; regular array or prearranged order; (*geol*) a group of strata with common characteristics.—**formational** *adj*.
formative *adj* pertaining to formation and development; shaping; (*gram*) used in forming words.—**formatively** *adv*.—**formativeness** *n*.
forme *n* a frame with type assembled in it for printing.—*also* **form**.
former *adj* of or occurring in a previous time; the first mentioned (of two).—**formerly** *adv*.
formerly *adv* previously; heretofore.
formic *adj* of or pertaining to ants or formic acid.
Formica *n* (*trademark*) a heat-resistant laminated sheeting.
formic acid *n* a colourless pungent liquid found esp in ants and many plants.
formicary, formicarium *n* (*pl* **formicaries, formicaria**) an anthill.
formication *n* an irritation of the skin, resembling the sensation made by insects crawling over it.

formidable *adj* causing fear or awe; difficult to defeat or overcome; difficult to handle.—**formidability** *n*.—**formidably** *adv*.

formless *adj* without distinct form, shapeless.—**formlessness** *n*.

formol *see* **formalin.**

formula *n* (*pl* **formulas, formulae**) a set of symbols expressing the composition of a substance; a general expression in algebraic form for solving a problem; a prescribed form; a formal statement of doctrines; a list of ingredients, as for a prescription or recipe; a fixed method according to which something is to be done; a prescribed recipe for baby food.—**formulaic** *adj*.

formularize *vt* to formulate.—**formularization** *n*.—**formularizer** *n*.

formulary *n* (*pl* **formularies**) a book of prescribed forms, or of prayers, ritual, etc; (*med*) a book giving details of the formulas and preparation of pharmaceutical products. * *adj* of formulas or ritual.

formulate *vt* to express in a formula; to devise.—**formulation** *n*.—**formulator** *n*.

formulism *n* adherence to formulas.—**formulist** *adj, n*.

fornicate[1] *vi* to have sexual intercourse without being married.—**fornication** *n*.—**fornicator** *n*.

fornicate[2], **fornicated** *adj* (*archit*) vaulted, arched.

fornix *n* (*pl* **fornices**) (*anat*) an arch-shaped part.

forsake *vt* (**forsaking, forsook,** *pp* **forsaken**) to desert; to give up, renounce.—**forsaker** *n*.

forsooth *adv* (*arch*) in truth.

forswear *vb* (**forswearing, forswore,** *pp* **foresworn**) *vt* to reject, renounce; to deny; to perjure (oneself).

forsythia *n* a widely cultivated, yellow-flowered shrub.

fort *n* a fortified place for military defence.

forte[1] *n* something at which a person excels.

forte[2] *adv* (*mus*) loudly.

forte-piano *adj, adv* (*music*) loud, then soft.

forth *adv* forwards; onwards; out; into view; **and so forth** and the like.

forthcoming *adj* about to appear; readily available; responsive.—**forthcomingness** *n*.

forthright *adv* frank, direct, outspoken; decisive.—**forthrightly** *adv*.—**forthrightness** *n*.

forthwith *adv* immediately, without delay.

fortification *n* the act or process of fortifying; a wall, barricade, etc built to defend a position.

fortify *vt* (**fortifying, fortified**) to strengthen physically, emotionally, etc; to strengthen against attack, as with forts; to support; (*wine, etc*) to add alcohol to; (*milk*) to add vitamins to.—**fortifiable** *adj*.—**fortifier** *n*.

fortissimo *adv* (*mus*) very loud. * *n* (*pl* **fortissimos, fortissimi**) (*mus*) a passage played very loudly.

fortitude *n* courage in adversity; patient endurance, firmness.—**fortitudinous** *adj*.

fortnight *n* a period of two weeks or fourteen consecutive days.

fortnightly *adj, adv* once a fortnight.

Fortran *n* (*comput*) a high-level programming language used for scientific and mathematical problem-solving.

fortress *n* a strong fort or fortified town.

fortuitous *adj* happening by chance.—**fortuitously** *adv*.—**fortuitousness** *n*.

fortuity *n* (*pl* **fortuities**) fortuitousness; accident, chance.

fortunate *adj* having or occurring by good luck.—**fortunately** *adv*.

fortune *n* the supposed arbitrary power that determines events; luck; destiny; prosperity, success; vast wealth.

fortune hunter *n* someone who seeks to become rich, esp by marrying for money.

fortune-teller *n* a person who claims to foretell a person's future.—**fortune-telling** *n*.

forty *n* (*pl* **forties**) four times ten, the symbol for this (40, XL, xl).—*also adj*.—**fortieth** *adj*.

forty-five *n* a gramophone record played at 45 revolutions per minute; (*with cap*) the Jacobite rebellion of 1745.

forty-niner *n* a pioneer who went to California in 1849 to look for gold.

forty winks *n* (*sing or pl*) a nap.

forum *n* (*pl* **forums, fora**) an assembly or meeting to discuss topics of public concern; a medium for public debate, as a magazine; the marketplace and centre of public affairs in ancient Rome.

forward *adj* at, toward, or of the front; advanced; onward; prompt; bold; presumptuous; of or for the future. * *vt* to promote; to send on. * *n* (*sport*) an attacking player in various games. * *adv* toward the front; ahead.—**forwardness** *n*.

forwardly *adv* pertly; promptly; forwards.

forwards *adv* towards the front, in an onward direction

forwent *see* **forgo.**

forzando *adv* (*music*) with sudden emphasis.

fossa *n* (*pl* **fossae**) (*anat*) a groove, pit or cavity.

fosse, foss *n* a ditch or moat, esp in a fortification.

fossick *vt* to search for by picking over, to rummage.—**fossicker** *n*.

fossil *n* the petrified remains of an animal or vegetable preserved in rock; (*inf*) a thing or person regarded as outmoded or redundant. * *adj* of or like a fossil; dug from the earth.

fossiliferous *adj* containing fossils.

fossilize *vti* to change or become changed into a fossil.—**fossilization** *n*.

fossorial *adj* (*zool*) used for digging.

foster *vt* to encourage; to bring up (a child that is not one's own). * *adj* affording, giving, sharing or receiving parental care although not related.—**fosterer** *n*.

fosterage *n* the act of fostering.

fosterling *n* a foster child.

foudroyant *adj* sudden and overwhelming; dazzling, like lightning.

fought *see* **fight.**

foul *adj* stinking, loathsome; extremely dirty; indecent; wicked; (*language*) obscene; (*weather*) stormy; (*sports*) against the rules. * *adv* unfairly. * *vt* to make filthy; to dishonour; to obstruct; to entangle (a rope, etc); to make a foul against, as in a game; (*with* **up**) to contaminate; to ruin, bungle; to cause to become blocked or entangled. * *vi* to be or become fouled; (*with* **up**) to become blocked or entangled. * *n* (*sports*) a hit, blow, move, etc that is foul.—**foully** *adv*.—**foulness** *n*.

foulard *n* a light silk, or silk-cotton, fabric; a scarf made of this fabric.

foul-mouthed *adj* using abusive or obscene language.

foul play *n* fouls in sport; violent crime, murder.

found[1] *see* **find.**

found[2] *vt* to bring into being; to establish (as an institution) often with provision for future maintenance.

found[3] *vt* to melt and pour (metal) into a mould to produce castings.

foundation *n* an endowment for an institution; such an institution; the base of a house, wall, etc; a first layer of cosmetic applied to the skin; an underlying principle, etc; a supporting undergarment, as a corset.—**foundational** *adj*.—**foundationary** *adj*.

founder[1] *n* one who founds an institution, a benefactor.

founder[2] *n* a person who casts metal.

founder[3] *vi* (*ship*) to fill with water and sink; to collapse; to fail.

foundling *n* a deserted child whose parents are unknown.

foundry *n* (*pl* **foundries**) a workshop or factory where metal castings are produced.

fount[1] *n* a set of printing type or characters of one style and size.—*also* **font.**

fount[2] *n* a source.

fountain *n* a natural spring of water; a source; an artificial jet or flow of water; the basin where this flows; a reservoir, as for ink. * *vti* to (cause to) flow or spurt like a fountain.

fountainhead *n* a spring from which a stream flows; a first source.

fountain pen *n* a pen with an internal reservoir or cartridge of ink which supplies the nib.

four *n* one more than three; the symbol for this (4, IV, iv) ; the fourth in a series or set; something having four units as members (as a four-cylinder engine); a four-oared boat or its crew.—*also adj*.

fourchette *n* (*anat*) a fold of skin situated at the rear of the vulva.

four flush *n* a poker hand with four cards of one suit.
four-flusher *n* a bluffer.
fourfold *adj* having four units or members; being four times as great or as many.—*also adv*.
fourhanded *adj* for four players; (*mus*) for two players.
four-letter word *n* any of various words regarded as offensive or obscene typically containing four letters.
four-poster *n* a bed with four posts and a canopy.
fourscore *n* eighty.
foursome *n* a group or set of four; (*golf*) a game between two pairs in which each pair has one ball.
foursquare *adj* square; firm. * *adv* squarely; firmly.
four-stroke *adj* (*internal-combustion engine*) having a piston that operates a cycle of four strokes for every explosion.
fourteen *n, adj* four and ten; the symbol for this (14, XIV, xiv).—**fourteenth** *adj*.
fourth *adj* next after third. * *n* one of four equal parts of something.—**fourthly** *adv*.
fourth dimension *n* time as added to the three spatial dimensions (length, breadth, depth).
fourth estate *n* journalists or the press in general.
Fourth of July *n* Independence Day of U.S.A.
fowl *n* any of the domestic birds used as food, as the chicken, duck, etc; the flesh of these birds. * *vi* to hunt or snare wildfowl.—**fowler** *n*.—**fowling** *n*.
fox *n* (*pl* **foxes, fox**) any of various small, alert wild mammals of the dog family; the fur of the fox; a sly, crafty person. * *vt* to deceive by cunning. * *vi* (*inf*) to bemuse, puzzle.
foxglove *n* a tall plant with spikes of purple or white flowers.
foxhole *n* a pit dug in the ground as a protection against enemy fire.
foxhound *n* any of various large swift powerful hounds of great endurance used in hunting foxes.
foxtail *n* a type of grass found in Europe, Asia and South America.
fox-terrier *n* any of a breed of small lively terriers formerly used to dig out foxes.
foxtrot *n* a dance for couples in 4/4 time. * *vi* (**foxtrotting, foxtrotted**) to dance the foxtrot.
foxy *adj* (**foxier, foxiest**) reddish-brown; crafty; resembling a fox; physically attractive.—**foxily** *adv*.—**foxiness** *n*.
foyer *n* an anteroom; an entrance hallway, as in a hotel or theatre.
FP *abbr* = (*US*) fireplug; former pupil.
Fr (*chem symbol*) francium.
fr *abbr* = franc.
Fra *n* (*title*) a friar.
fracas *n* (*pl* **fracas, fracases**) uproar; a noisy quarrel.
fraction *n* a small part, amount, etc; (*math*) a quantity less than a whole, expressed as a decimal or with a numerator and denominator.—**fractionary** *adj*.—**fractionally** *adv*.
fractional *adj* of or pertaining to fractions; inconsiderable, very small.
fractional distillation *n* the process used for separating a mixture of liquids into component parts by distillation.
fractionate *vt* to separate (elements of a mixture) by distillation.—**fractionation** *n*.
fractionize *vt* to divide into fractions.—**fractionization** *n*.
fractious *adj* quarrelsome; peevish.—**fractiously** *adv*.—**fractiousness** *n*.
fracture *n* the breaking of any hard material, esp a bone. * *vti* to break; to cause or suffer a fracture.—**fracturable** *adj*.—**fractural** *adj*.
fragile *adj* easily broken; frail; delicate.—**fragilely** *adv*.—**fragility, fragileness** *n*.
fragment *n* a piece broken off or detached; an incomplete portion. * *vti* to break or cause to break into fragments.—**fragmentation** *n*.
fragmentary *adj* consisting of fragments; incomplete.—**fragmentarily** *adv*.—**fragmentariness** *n*.
fragrance, fragrancy *n* (*pl* **fragrances, fragrancies**) a pleasant scent, a perfume.
fragrant *adj* sweet-scented.—**fragrantly** *adv*.
frail[1] *adj* physically or morally weak; fragile.—**frailly** *adv*.—**frailness** *n*.
frail[2] *n* a rush basket; the quantity of fruit held in a frail.
frailty *n* (*pl* **frailties**) physical or moral weakness; infirmity; a failing.
fraise *n* a palisade of pointed sticks, used in a rampart; a type of neck ruff; a tool used to enlarge a drill hole.
framboesia, frambesia *n* an infectious tropical disease, causing red skin eruptions and joint pain.—*also* **yaws**.
frame *vt* to form according to a pattern; to construct; to put into words; to enclose (a picture) in a border; (*sl*) to falsify evidence against (an innocent person). * *n* something composed of parts fitted together and united; the physical make-up of an animal, esp a human body; the framework of a house; the structural case enclosing a window, door, etc; an ornamental border, as around a picture; (*snooker*) a triangular mould for setting up balls before play; (*snooker*) a single game.—**framable, frameable** *adj*.—**framer** *n*.
frame of reference *n* an arbitrary system of axes for describing the position or motion of something or from which physical laws are derived; a set or system (as of facts and ideas) serving to orient; a viewpoint, a theory.
frame-up *n* (*sl*) a conspiracy to have someone falsely accused of a crime.
framework *n* a structural frame; a basic structure (as of ideas); frame of reference.
franc *n* a unit of money in France, Belgium, and Switzerland.
franchise *n* the right to vote in public elections; authorization to sell the goods of a manufacturer in a particular area. * *vt* to grant a franchise.—**franchisement** *n*.
Franciscan *n* a member of the Order of Friars Minor founded by St Francis of Assisi in 1209.
francium *n* a radioactive metallic element.
Franco- *prefix* France; French.
francolin *n* a kind of partridge, found in Africa and Asia.
Francophile *n* a lover of France or its customs, etc.
frangible *adj* fragile, easily broken.—**frangibility** *n*.
frangipane *n* a paste or cake made with almonds and cream.
frangipani *n* (*pl* **frangipanis, frangipani**) a tropical American shrub, the flowers of which are used to make a perfume.
Frank *n* a member of a West Germanic people who conquered Gaul in the 4th century ad.—**Frankish** *adj*.
frank *adj* free and direct in expressing oneself; honest, open. * *vt* to mark letters, etc with a mark denoting free postage. * *n* a mark indicating free postage.—**frankly** *adv*.**frankness** *n*.
Frankenstein *n* a work that ruins its originator.
frankfurter *n* a type of smoked sausage.
frankincense *n* a fragrant gum resin.
franklin *n* a middle-class landowner in 14th and 15th century England.
frantic *adj* violently agitated; furious, wild.—**frantically, franticly** *adv*.
frap *vt* (**frapping, frapped**) (*naut*) to bind tightly.
frappé *adj* iced; chilled.
frater[1] *n* a friar.
frater[2] *n* (*arch*) a refectory.
fraternal *adj* of or belonging to a brother or fraternity; friendly, brotherly.—**fraternalism** *n*.—**fraternally** *adv*.
fraternity *n* (*pl* **fraternities**) brotherly feeling; a society of people with common interests.
fraternize *vt* to associate in a friendly manner.—**fraternization** *n*.
fratricide *n* the murder of a brother; a person guilty of this.—**fratricidal** *adj*.
Frau *n* (*pl* **Frauen, Fraus**) (a title of) a married German woman.
fraud *n* deliberate deceit; an act of deception; (*inf*) a deceitful person; an impostor.
fraudulent *adj* deceiving or intending to deceive; obtained by deceit.—**fraudulence, fraudulency** *n*.—**fraudulently** *adv*.
fraught *adj* filled or loaded (with); (*inf*) anxious; difficult.
Fraülein *n* (*pl* **Fraülein, Fraüleins**) (a title of) an unmarried German woman.

fraxinella *n* a white-flowered Eurasian plant.
fray[1] *n* a fight, a brawl.
fray[2] *vti* (*fabric, etc*) to (cause to) wear away into threads, esp at the edge of; (*nerves, temper*) to make or become irritated or strained.
frazil *n* the ice that forms in a stream.
frazzle *vt* to exhaust; to fray, tatter. * *n* (*inf*) a state of exhaustion.
freak[1] *n* an unusual happening; any abnormal animal, person, or plant; (*inf*) a person who dresses or acts in a notably unconventional manner; an ardent enthusiast. * *vi* (*with* **out**) (*inf*) to hallucinate under the influence of drugs; to experience intense emotional excitement.—**freakish** *adj*.
freak[2] *vt* to variegate; to spot or streak.
freakish *adj* very unusual; changing suddenly.—**freakishly** *adv*.—**freakishness** *n*.
freckle *n* a small, brownish spot on the skin. * *vti* to make or become spotted with freckles.—**freckled, freckly** *adj*.
free *adj* (**freer, freest**) not under the control or power of another; having social and political liberty; independent; able to move in any direction; not burdened by obligations; not confined to the usual rules; not exact; generous; frank; with no cost or charge; exempt from taxes, duties, etc; clear of obstruction; not fastened. * *adv* without cost; in a free manner. * *vt* (**freeing, freed**) to set free; to clear of obstruction, etc.—**freely** *adv*.
freebie *n* (*sl*) something provided free of charge.
freeboard *n* the part of the side of a ship between the upper side of the deck and the water-line.
freebooter *n* a pirate; a plunderer.
freeborn *adj* born of free parents, as opposed to in slavery.
freedman *n* (*pl* **freedmen**) an emancipated slave.
freedom fighter *n* a person violently resisting an oppressive political regime.
freedom *n* being free; exemption from obligation; unrestricted use; a right or privilege.
free enterprise *n* the freedom of business from government intervention or control.
free fall *n* the descent of a body under the force of gravity alone, as a parachutist before the parachute opens.
free fight *n* an indiscriminate contest, a melée.
free-for-all *n* (*inf*) a disorganized fight or brawl involving as many participants as are willing.
free hand *n* freedom to act as desired.
freehand *adj* (*drawing, etc*) drawn by the hand without the aid of instruments.
freehanded *adj* generous; liberal.—**freehandedly** *adv*.—**freehandedness** *n*.
freehold *n* tenure without rent; absolute ownership; an estate so held.—**freeholder** *n*.
free house *n* in the UK, a public house which is allowed to sell drinks from more than one brewer.
free kick *n* (*soccer, rugby*) a place kick awarded because of a foul or infringement by an opponent.
freelance *n* a person who pursues a profession without long-term commitment to any employer (—*also* **freelancer**). * *vt* to work as a freelance.
free-living *n* (*organisms*) not parasitic.—**free-liver** *n*.
freeload *vi* to impose upon another's hospitality.—**freeloader** *n*.
free love *n* sexual intercourse without the restraints of marriage.
freeman *n* (*pl* **freemen**) someone who is not a slave; someone with civic rights.
freemartin *n* a sexually imperfect and sterile cow calf, born as the twin of a bull calf.
Freemason *n* a member of the secretive fraternity (Free and Accepted Masons) dedicated to mutual aid.
freemasonry *n* mutual help between persons of similar interests.
free port *n* a port where goods are received and shipped free of customs duty.
free-range *adj* (*hens*) allowed to roam freely, not confined in a battery; (*eggs*) produced by hens raised in this way.
freesheet *n* a newspaper distributed free of charge.
freesia *n* a sweet-scented African plant of the iris family.
freespoken *adj* outspoken, blunt.—**freespokenness** *n*.
freestanding *adj* (*furniture*) standing on its own; not attached.
freestone *n* a type of limestone or sandstone that is suitable for working.
freestyle *n* a swimming competition in which the competitor chooses the stroke.
freethinker *n* a person who rejects authority in religion, etc; a sceptic.
free trade *n* trade based on the unrestricted international exchange of goods with tariffs used only as a source of revenue.—**free-trader** *n*.
free verse *n* verse without a fixed metrical pattern.
freeway *n* in North America, a fast road, a motorway.
freewheel *n* a device for temporarily disconnecting and setting free the back wheel of a bicycle from the driving gear. * *vi* to ride a bicycle with the gear disconnected; to drive a car with the gear in neutral.—**freewheeler** *n*.
free will *n* voluntary choice or decision; freedom of human beings to make choices that are not determined by prior causes or by divine intervention.
freeze *vb* (**freezing, froze,** *pp* **frozen**) *vi* to be formed into, or become covered by ice; to become very cold; to be damaged or killed by cold; to become motionless; to be made speechless by strong emotion; to become formal and unfriendly. * *vt* to harden into ice; to convert from a liquid to a solid with cold; to make extremely cold; to act towards in a stiff and formal way; to act on usu destructively by frost; to anaesthetize by cold; to fix (prices, etc) at a given level by authority; to make (funds, etc) unavailable to the owners by authority.—**freezable** *adj*.
freeze-dry *vt* (**freeze-drying, freeze-dried**) to preserve (food) by rapid freezing and then drying in a vacuum.
freeze-frame *n* a frame of a motion picture or television film that is repeated to give the illusion of a static picture.
freezer *n* a compartment or container that freezes and preserves food for long periods.
freezing *adj* very cold.
freezing point *n* the temperature at which a liquid solidifies.
freight *n* the transport of goods by water, land, or air; the cost for this; the goods transported. * *vt* to load with freight; to send by freight.
freightage *n* the conveyance of cargo; the cargo conveyed; a charge made for transporting cargo.
freight car *n* a rail truck for carrying freight.
freighter *n* one who freights; a ship or aircraft carrying freight.
French *adj* of France, its people, culture, etc. * *n* the language of France.
French bread *n* bread in a long, slender loaf.
French chalk *n* a soapstone used as a dry lubricant and to mark cloth, etc.
French doors *see* **French windows.**
French dressing *n* a salad dressing made from vinegar, oil and seasonings.
French fries, french fries *npl* thin strips of potato fried in oil, etc, chips.
French horn *n* an orchestral brass instrument with a narrow conical tube wound twice in a circle, a funnel shaped mouthpiece, and a flaring bell.
Frenchify *vti* (**Frenchifies, Frenchifying, Frenchified**) (*inf*) to make or become French.
French leave *n* leave taken without permission; a hasty or secret departure.
French letter *n* a condom.
French polish *n* a shellac varnish for furniture.
French roof *n* a mansard roof.
French toast *n* toast with one side buttered and the other toasted; bread soaked in milk and batter and fried lightly.
French windows *npl* a pair of casement windows extending to the floor that are placed in an outside wall and open on to a patio, garden, etc.—*also* **French doors.**
frenetic *adj* frantic, frenzied.—**frenetically** *adv*.
frenzy *n* (*pl* **frenzies**) wild excitement; violent mental derangement. * *vt* (**frenzying, frenzied**) to infuriate, to madden.—**frenzied** *adj*.—**frenziedly** *adv*.

frequency *n* (*pl* **frequencies**) repeated occurrence; the number of occurrences, cycles, etc in a given period.
frequency modulation *n* the transmission of signals by radio waves whose frequency varies according to the amplitude of the signal.
frequent *adj* coming or happening often. * *vi* to visit often; to resort to.—**frequenter** *n*.—**frequently** *adv*.
frequentative *adj* (*gram*) expressing repetition and intensity (of a verb). * *n* a frequentative verb.
fresco *n* (*pl* **frescos, frescoes**) a picture painted on walls covered with damp freshly laid plaster. * *vt* (**frescoing, frescoed**) to paint in fresco.
fresh *adj* recently made, grown, etc; not salted, pickled, etc; not spoiled; lively, not tired; not worn, soiled, faded, etc; new, recent; inexperienced; cool and refreshing; (*wind*) brisk; (*water*) not salt; (*inf*) presumptuous, impertinent. * *adv* newly.—**freshly** *adv*.—**freshness** *n*.
freshen *vi* to make or become fresh.—**freshener** *n*.
fresher *n* (*pl* **freshers**) a freshman.
freshet *n* a flood caused by melting snow or heavy rain; a stream of fresh water.
freshman *n* (*pl* **freshmen**) a first year student at university, college or high school.
freshwater *adj* of a river; not sea-going.
fret[1] *vti* (**fretting, fretted**) to make or become worried or anxious; to wear away or roughen by rubbing.
fret[2] *n* a running design of interlacing small bars. * *vt* (**fretting, fretted**) to furnish with frets.
fret[3] *n* any of a series of metal ridges along the finger-board of a guitar, banjo, etc used as a guide for depressing the strings.
fretful *adj* troubled; peevish; irritable; impatient.—**fretfully** *adv*.—**fretfulness** *n*.
fretsaw *n* a narrow saw held under tension in a frame used for cutting intricate designs in wood or metal.
fretwork *n* decorative carving consisting of frets.
Freudian *adj* of or pertaining to the psychoanalytic theories of Sigmund Freud. * *n* a psychoanalyst who follows the theories of Freud.—**Freudianism** *n*.
Freudian slip *n* a slip of the tongue said to betray an unconscious feeling.
Fri. *abbr* = Friday.
friable *adj* easily crumbled.—**friability** *n*.
friar *n* a member of certain Roman Catholic religious orders.
friarbird *n* an Australasian songbird with a tongue specially adapted to extract nectar.
friary *n* (*pl* **friaries**) a monastery of friars.
fribble *vt* to fritter away. * *vi* to trifle.—**fribbler** *n*.
fricandeau, fricando *n* (*pl* **fricandeaus, fricandeaux, fricandoes**) a dish made from spiced, stewed veal.
fricassee *n* a dish made of stewed poultry, rabbit, etc in a white sauce. * *vt* (**fricasseeing, fricasseed**) to cook in this way.
fricative *n* (*phonetics*) a sound, eg "f," produced by the friction of breath in a narrow opening. * *adj* pertaining to a fricative.
friction *n* a rubbing of one object against another; conflict between differing opinions, ideas, etc; the resistance to motion of things that touch.—**frictional** *adj*.
friction clutch *n* a clutch that transmits motion by friction.
Friday *n* the sixth day of the week.
fridge *n* (*inf*) a refrigerator.
fried *see* **fry**[1].
friend *n* a person whom one knows well and is fond of; an ally, supporter, or sympathizer. * *vt* (*arch*) to befriend.—**friendless** *adj*.—**friendship** *n*.
friendly *adj* (**friendlier, friendliest**) like a friend; kindly; favourable. * *n* a sporting game played for fun, not in competition.—**friendlily** *adv*.—**friendliness** *n*.
friendly society *n* an association for mutual insurance against sickness, etc.
friendship *n* the state of being friends; intimacy united with affection or esteem; mutual attachment; goodwill.
frier *see* **fry**[1].
frieze[1] *n* a decorative band along the top of the wall of a room; (*archit*) the part of an entablature between the architrave and cornice, often filled with sculpture.
frieze[2] *n* a coarse woollen cloth with a rough shaggy nap on one side.
frigate *n* a warship smaller than a destroyer used for escort, anti-submarine, and patrol duties.
frigate bird *n* a swift-flying tropical sea bird.
fright *n* sudden fear; a shock; (*inf*) something unsightly or ridiculous in appearance.
frighten *vt* to terrify, to scare; to force by frightening.—**frightener** *n*.—**frighteningly** *adv*.
frightful *adj* terrible, shocking; (*inf*) extreme, very bad.—**frightfully** *adv*.—**frightfulness** *n*.
frigid *adj* extremely cold; not warm or friendly; unresponsive sexually.—**frigidity** *n*.—**frigidly** *adv*.
Frigid Zone *n* either of the areas within the Arctic or Antarctic circles.
frigorific *adj* (*arch*) causing cold.
frijol *n* (*pl* **frijoles**) a type of bean, widely cultivated for eating in Mexico.
frill *n* a piece of pleated or gathered fabric used for edging; something superfluous, an affectation. * *vt* to decorate with a frill or frills.—**frilled** *adj*.—**frilly** *adj*.
fringe *n* a decorative border of hanging threads; hair hanging over the forehead; an outer edge; a marginal or minor part. * *vt* to be or make a fringe for. * *adj* at the outer edge; additional; minor; unconventional.
fringe benefit *n* a benefit given by an employer to supplement an employee's wages; any additional advantage.
frippery *n* (*pl* **fripperies**) cheap, gaudy clothes or ornaments; trivia.
Frisbee *n* (*trademark*) a plastic disc that is spun through the air for recreation or sport.
frisette *n* a curly fringe, esp of false hair.—*also* **frizette**.
frisk *vi* to leap playfully. * *vt* (*inf*) to search (a person) by feeling for concealed weapons, etc. * *n* a gambol, dance, or frolic.—**frisker** *n*.
frisky *adj* (**friskier, friskiest**) lively, playful.—**friskily** *adv*.—**friskiness** *n*.
frisson *n* an emotional thrill, a shiver of excitement.
frit, fritt *n* the mixture of sand and fluxes from which glass is made. * *vt* (**fritting, fritted**) to make into frit.
frith *see* **firth**.
frit fly *n* a small fly destructive to grain.
fritillary *n* (*pl* **fritillaries**) a flowering plant of the lily kind,the petals of which are variegated with purple, dice-shaped marks; a butterfly with brownish wings spotted with black or silver.
fritt *see* **frit**.
fritter[1] *n* a slice of fruit or meat fried in batter.
fritter[2] *vt* (*with* **away**) to waste; to break into tiny pieces.—**fritterer** *n*.
frivol *vb* (**frivolling, frivolled** *or* **frivoling, frivoled**) *vi* to behave in a frivolous way; to trifle. * *vt* to squander.
frivolity *n* (*pl* **frivolities**) a trifling act, thought, or action.
frivolous *adj* irresponsible; trifling; silly.—**frivolously** *adv*.—**frivolousness** *n*.
frizette *n see* **frisette**.
frizz *vti* (*hair*) to (cause to) form into small tight curls. * *n* hair that is frizzed.—**frizzer** *n*.
frizzle[1] *vt* to frizz. * *n* a small tight curl.—**frizzler** *n*.
frizzle[2] *vti* to sizzle, as in frying; to scorch by frying.
frizzy, frizzly *adj* (**frizzier, frizziest** *or* **frizzlier, frizzliest**) (*hair*) in tight wiry curls.—**frizziness, frizzliness** *n*.
fro *adv* away from; backward; **to and fro** back and forward.
frock *n* a dress; a smock; a loose wide-sleeved gown worn by a monk. * *vt* to put on a frock; to invest with the office of priest.
frock coat *n* a double-breasted skirted coat for men.
frog[1] *n* a small tailless web-footed jumping amphibian; (*offensive*) a French person.
frog[2] *n* a decorative loop used to fasten clothing; an attachment on a belt for carrying a sword.—**frogged** *adj*.

frog[3] *n* a section of rail where two lines cross.

frog[4] *n* a tender horny substance growing in the middle of the sole of a horse's foot.

frogfish *n* (*pl* **frogfish, frogfishes**) a variety of angler fish.

froggy *adj* (**froggier, froggiest**) resembling or containing a frog or frogs.

froghopper *n* a small jumping insect whose larvae secrete a spittle-like protective covering.

frogman *n* (*pl* **frogmen**) a person who wears rubber suit, flippers, oxygen supply, etc and is trained in working underwater.

frogmarch *vt* to carry an unwilling person by the legs and arms face down; to move (a person) by force.—*also n.*

frolic *n* a lively party or game; merriment, fun. * *vi* (**frolicking, frolicked**) to play happily.—**frolicker** *n.*

frolicsome, frolicky *adj*.fond of frolicking; playful.

from *prep* beginning at, starting with; out of; originating with; out of the possibility or use of.

fromage frais *n* a smooth white curd cheese eaten plain or with added fruit as a dessert.

fromenty *see* **frumenty.**

frond *n* a large leaf with many divisions, esp of a palm or fern.

frondescence *n* (*bot*) the act of producing leaves; foliage.—**frondescent** *adj.*

frons *n* (*pl* **frontes**) a plate found on the head of an insect.

front *n* outward behaviour; (*inf*) an appearance of social standing; etc; the part facing forward; the first part; a forward or leading position; the promenade of a seaside resort; the advanced battle area in warfare; a person or group used to hide another's activity; an advancing mass of cold or warm air. * *adj* at, to, in, on, or of the front. * *vti* to face; to stand or be situated opposite to or over against; to serve as a front (for); to have the front turned in a particular direction.

frontage *n* the front part of a building or plot of land; the width or extent of the front of a shop, building, piece of land, etc.

frontal *adj* of or belonging to the front; of or pertaining to the forehead. * *n* a decorative covering for the front of an altar; a small pediment over a window or door.—**frontally** *adv.*

front bench *n* in the British House of Commons, either of the two rows of benches occupied by the leading figures (**front benchers**) in the Government or Opposition.

front door *n* a main entrance to a building.

frontier *n* the border between two countries; the limit of existing knowledge of a subject.

frontispiece *n* an illustration opposite the title page of a book; (*archit*) the main face of a building.

frontlet *n* a band worn on the forehead; an animal's forehead.

frontrunner *n* the favourite to win a race, election, etc.

frontwards, frontward *adj, adv* towards the front.

frost *n* temperature at or below freezing point; a coating of powdery ice particles; coldness of manner. * *vt* to cover (as if) with frost or frosting; to give a frost-like opaque surface to (glass).

frostbite *n* injury to a part of the body by exposure to cold.—**frostbitten** *adj.*

frosting *n* icing for a cake.

frosty *adj* (**frostier, frostiest**) cold with frost; cold or reserved in manner, chilly, distant.—**frostily** *adv.*—**frostiness** *n.*

froth *n* foam; foaming saliva; frivolity. * *vi* to emit or gather foam.

frothy *adj* (**frothier, frothiest**) full of or composed of froth; frivolous; insubstantial.—**frothily** *adv.*—**frothiness** *n.*

froufrou *n* the rustling sound made by the material, esp silk, of a dress etc, when in motion.

froward *adj* (*arch*) obstinate; wayward.

frown *vi* to contract the brow as in anger or thought; (*with* **upon**) to regard with displeasure or disapproval. * *n* a wrinkled brow; a stern look.—**frowner** *n.*—**frowningly** *adv.*

frowst *n* (*inf*) a close, stuffy atmosphere.

frowsty *adj* stuffy; musty.

frowzy, frowsy *adj* (**frowzier, frowziest** *or* **frowsier, frowsiest**) dirty and untidy; unkempt.

froze *see* **freeze.**

frozen[1] *see* **freeze.**

frozen[2] *adj* formed into or covered by ice; damaged or killed by cold; (*food, etc*) preserved by freezing; motionless; made speechless by strong emotion; formal and unfriendly; extremely cold; (prices, wages, etc) fixed at a given level; (funds, etc) unrealizable.

FRS *abbr* = Fellow of the Royal Society.

fructiferous *adj* (*plant etc*) bearing fruit.

fructify *vb* (**fructifies, fructifying, fructified**) *vt* to make fruitful, fertilize. * *vi* to bear fruit; to become fruitful.—**fructification** *n.*

fructose *n* a type of sugar found in ripe fruit and honey.

fructuous *adj* fruitful.

frugal *adj* economical, thrifty; inexpensive, meagre.—**frugality** *n.*—**frugally** *adv.*

frugivorous *adj* fruit-eating.

fruit *n* the seed-bearing part of any plant; the fleshy part of this used as food; the result or product of any action. * *vti* to bear or cause to bear fruit.

fruitage *n* the process of bearing fruit; a collective term for all fruits.

fruiter *n* a fruit grower; a fruit tree.

fruiterer *n* a dealer in fruit.

fruitful *adj* producing lots of fruit; productive.—**fruitfully** *adv.*—**fruitfulness** *n.*

fruition *n* a coming to fulfilment, realization.

fruitless *adj* unproductive; pointless; useless.—**fruitlessly** *adv.*—**fruitlessness** *n.*

fruit machine *n* a coin-operated gambling machine, using symbols of fruit to indicate a winning combination.

fruit salad *n* a dish of various fruits sliced and mixed.

fruity *adj* (**fruitier, fruitiest**) like, or tasting like, fruit; (*inf*) (*voice*) mellow; (*inf*) salacious.—**fruitiness** *n.*

frumenty *n* a sort of porridge, made from hulled wheat and boiled milk.—*also* **fromenty, furmenty.**

frump *n* a drab and dowdy woman.—**frumpish, frumpy** *adj.*

frustrate *vt* to prevent from achieving a goal or gratifying a desire; to discourage, irritate, tire; to disappoint.—**frustrater** *n.*—**frustratingly** *adv.*—**frustration** *n.*

frustule *n* the shell of a diatom.

frustum *n* (*pl* **frustums, frusta**) (*geom*) the part of a cone, pyramid, etc, left after the top is cut off.

frutescent *adj* pertaining to, having the form of, or resembling a shrub.

fruticose *adj* resembling a shrub.

fry[1] *vti* (**frying, fried**) to cook over direct heat in hot fat. * *n* (*pl* **fries**) a dish of things fried.

fry[2] *n* (*pl* **fries**) recently hatched fishes; the young of a frog, etc.

fryer *n* a person who fries; a pan, etc, for frying in; a piece of meat for frying.—*also* **frier.**

f-stop *n* any of the standard settings of the aperture in a camera lens.

ft. *abbr* = foot or feet.

fuchsia *n* any of a genus of decorative shrubs with purplish-red flowers.

fuchsine, fuchsin *n* a crystalline substance, made into a dark red dye.

fuck *vti* (*vulg*) to have sexual intercourse with. * *n* (*vulg*) an act of sexual intercourse. * *interj* (*vulg*) expressing anger, frustration, etc.

fucus *n* (*pl* **fuci, fucuses**) a kind of large brown flat seaweed.—**fucoid, fucoidal** *adj.*

fuddle *vt* to make drunk; to make confused.

fuddy-duddy *n* (*pl* **fuddy-duddies**) a person with old-fashioned or staid views.

fudge[1] *n* a soft sweet made of butter, milk, sugar, flavouring, etc; (*print*) a piece of late matter inserted in the stop-press column of a newspaper; a made-up story. * *vi* to refuse to commit oneself; to cheat; to contrive by imperfect or improvised means. * *vt* to fake; to fail to come to grips with; to make or do anything in a bungling, careless manner.

fudge[2] *n* nonsense. * *interj* expressing annoyance or disbelief.
fuehrer *see* **führer.**
fuel *n* material burned to supply heat and power, or as a source of nuclear energy; anything that serves to intensify strong feelings. * *vti* (**fuelling, fuelled** *or* **fueling, fueled**) to supply with or obtain fuel.—**fueller, fueler** *n*.
fug *n* (*inf*) a hot, stale atmosphere.
fugacious *adj* fleeting; elusive; volatile; (*bot*) (*petals, etc*) falling off very early.—**fugaciously** *adv*.—**fugaciousness** *n*.
fugacity *n* fugaciousness; the property of a gas to escape or expand.
fugitive *n* a person who flees from danger, pursuit, or duty. * *adj* fleeing, as from danger or justice; fleeting, transient; not permanent.—**fugitively** *adv*.
fugleman *n* (*pl* **fuglemen**) (*formerly*) a soldier who stands in front of others to demonstrate drill; a ringleader.
fugue *n* a polyphonic musical composition with its theme taken up successively by different voices.—**fugal** *adj*.—**fugally** *adv*.
fuguist *n* a composer of fugues.
führer *n* (*German*) a leader, esp a dictator; (*with cap*) the title of Adolf Hitler (1889–1945), leader of the German Nazi party.
-ful *adj suffix* full of, eg *doleful*. * *n suffix* the amount needed to fill, eg *cupful*.
fulcrum *n* (*pl* **fulcrums, fulcra**) the fixed point on which a lever turns; a critical factor determining an outcome.
fulfil, fulfill *vt* (**fulfils** *or* **fulfills, fulfilling, fulfilled**) to carry out (a promise, etc); to achieve the completion of; to satisfy; to bring to an end, complete.—**fulfiller** *n*.—**fulfilment, fulfillment** *n*.
fulgent *adj* (*poet*) shining, radiant.—**fulgency** *n*.—**fulgently** *adv*.
fulgurate *vi* to flash (like lightning).—**fulgurant** *adj*.
fulgurite *n* rock or sand that has been vitrified by lightning.
fuliginous *adj* sooty, smoky.—**fuliginously** *adv*.
full[1] *adj* having or holding all that can be contained; having eaten all one wants; having a great number (of); complete; having reached to greatest size, extent, etc. * *n* the greatest amount, extent etc. * *adv* completely, directly, exactly.
full[2] *vt* to clean and thicken (cloth) by beating.
fullback *n* (*football, rugby, hockey, etc*) one of the defensive players at the back; the position held by this player.
full-blooded *adj* vigorous, hearty.—**full-bloodedly** *adv*.
full-blown *adj* in full bloom; matured, fully developed.
full-bodied *adj* (*flavour*) characterized by richness and fullness.
full dress *n* dress worn for formal or ceremonial occasions.—**full-dress** *adj*.
fuller[1] *n* someone who fulls cloth.
fuller[2] *n* a tool used for grooving and shaping iron; a groove made by this.
fuller's earth *n* a type of clay used for fulling.
full face *adj, adv* seen from in front.
full-frontal *adj* (*inf*) (*nude person or photograph*) with the genitals clearly visible; unrestrained.—**full frontal** *n*.
full house *n* (*poker*) a hand with three cards of the same value and a pair (—*also* **full hand**); (*theatre, etc*) a performance for which all seats are sold; (*bingo*) a complete set of winning numbers.
full moon *n* the moon at its phase when the whole disc is illuminated; the period of this.
fullness *n* the state of being full; **fullness of time** the proper or destined time.—*also* **fulness.**
full-scale *adj* actual size.
full-stop *n* the punctuation mark (.) at the end of a sentence.—*also* **period.**
full time *n* the finish of a match.
full-time *adj* working or lasting the whole time.—**full-timer** *n*.
fully *adv* thoroughly, completely; at least.
fully-fledged *adj* (*bird*) mature; having full status.—*also* **full-fledged.**
fulmar *n* an Arctic sea bird.
fulminant *adj* fulminating; sudden; (*pain*) sharp, piercing.
fulminate *vi* to issue protests with violence or threats; to inveigh (against). * *vt* to utter or exclaim, as a denunciation. * *n* an explosive compound of fulminic acid.—**fulmination** *n*.—**fulminator** *n*.—**fulminatory** *adj*.
fulminic acid *n* an unstable acid composed of cyanogen and oxygen.
fulness *see* **fullness.**
fulsome *adj* excessively praising, obsequious.—**fulsomely** *adv*.—**fulsomeness** *n*.
fulvous *adj* tawny.
fumarole *n* a small hole in a volcano from which gases issue.
fumatorium *n* (*pl* **fumatoriums, fumatoria**) an airtight room where insects, plants, etc, are fumigated.
fumble *vi* to grope about. * *vt* to handle clumsily; to say or act awkwardly; to fail to catch (a ball) cleanly. * *n* an awkward attempt.—**fumbler** *n*.—**fumblingly** *adv*.
fume *n* (*usu pl*) smoke, gas or vapour, esp if offensive or suffocating. * *vi* to give off fumes; to express anger. * *vt* to subject to fumes.—**fumer** *n*.—**fumingly** *adv*.
fumigate *vt* to disinfect or exterminate (pests, etc) using fumes.—**fumigation** *n*.—**fumigator** *n*.
fumitory *n* (*pl* **fumitories**) a plant, found mainly in Europe, the leaves of which were formerly used as a treatment for skin diseases.
fun *n* (what provides) amusement and enjoyment. * *vi* (**funning, funned**) to joke.
funambulist *n* a tightrope walker.
function *n* the activity characteristic of a person or thing; the specific purpose of a certain person or thing; an official ceremony or social entertainment; (*math*) a quantity whose value depends on the varying value of another. * *vi* to perform a function; to act, operate.
functional *adj* of a function or functions; practical, not ornamental; (*disease*) affecting the functions only, not organic.—**functionally** *adv*.
functionalism *n* the theory and practice of design for practical application.—**functionalist** *adj, n*.
functionary *n* (*pl* **functionaries**) a person in an official capacity.
fund *n* a supply that can be drawn upon; a sum of money set aside for a purpose; (*pl*) ready money. * *vt* to provide funds for; to convert (a debt) into stock; to place in a fund.
fundament *n* foundation, basis; (*euphemism*) the buttocks; the anus.
fundamental *adj* basic; essential. * *n* that which serves as a groundwork; an essential.—**fundamentality, fundamentalness** *n*. —**fundamentally** *adv*.
fundamentalism *n* belief in the literal truth of the Bible, Koran etc.—**fundamentalist** *adj, n*.—**fundamentalistic** *adj*.
fundus *n* (*pl* **fundi**) (*anat*) the base or deepest part of an organ.
funeral *n* the ceremony associated with the burial or cremation of the dead; a procession accompanying a coffin to a burial.
funeral director *n* a person who manages funerals.
funereal *adj* suiting a funeral, dismal, mournful.—**funereally** *adv*.
fungal *adj* of or pertaining to a fungus; caused by a fungus.
fungible *adj* (*law*) replaceable by another, similar specimen. * *n* a fungible thing, eg a coin.
fungicide *n* a substance that destroys fungi.—**fungicidal** *adj*.
fungiform *adj* resembling a mushroom
fungoid *adj* resembling a fungus.
fungous *adj* of, pertaining to or like fungi; fungal; developing suddenly.
fungus *n* (*pl* **fungi, funguses**) any of a major group of lower plants, as mildews, mushrooms, yeasts, etc, that lack chlorophyll and reproduce by spores.—**fungic** *adj*.
funicular *adj* of rope or its tension. * *n* a cable railway ascending a mountain.
funiculus *n* (*pl* **funiculi**) (*anat*) a small cord, ligature or fibre.
funk *n* (*inf*) panic, fear; a coward; funky music. * *vti* (*inf*) to show fear; to shirk.—**funker** *n*.
funky[1] *adj* (**funkier, funkiest**) panicky; fearful.
funky[2] *adj* (**funkier, funkiest**) (*inf*) (*pop, jazz music, etc*) soulful, bluesy; fashionable.—**funkiness** *n*.
funnel *n* an implement, usually a cone with a wide top and tapering to a narrow tube, for pouring fluids, powders, into bottles, etc; a metal chimney for the escape of smoke, steam, etc. * *vti* (**funnelling, funnelled** *or* **funneling, funneled**) to pour or cause to pour through a funnel.

funny *adj* (**funnier, funniest**) causing laughter; puzzling, odd; (*inf*) unwell, queasy. * *n* (*pl* **funnies**) a joke; (*pl*) comic strips, esp in a newspaper.—**funnily** *adv*.—**funniness** *n*.

funny bone *n* the part of the elbow where a sensitive nerve rests close to the bone, producing a tingling sensation if struck.

fur *n* the short, soft, fine hair on the bodies of certain animals; their skins with the fur attached; a garment made of fur; a fabric made in imitation of fur; a fur-like coating, as on the tongue. * *vti* (**furring, furred**) to cover or become covered with fur.

furbelow *n* a flounce or other trimming on clothing.

furbish *vt* to polish, to burnish; to renovate.—**furbisher** *n*.

furcate *vi* to fork, divide. * *adj* forked, branching.—**furcation** *n*.

furfur *n* (*pl* **furfures**) scurf, dandruff.

furfuraceous *adj*. resembling bran; resembling dandruff.

Furies *see* **fury**.

furioso *adv* (*mus*) wildly.

furious *adj* full of anger; intense; violent, impetuous.—**furiously** *adv*.—**furiousness** *n*.

furl *vt* to roll up (a sail, flag, etc) tightly and make secure; to fold up, close.—**furlable** *adj*.—**furler** *n*.

furlong *n* 220 yards, one-eighth of a mile (201 metres).

furlough *n* leave of absence from duty, esp for military personnel. * *vt* to grant a furlough to.

furmenty *see* **frumenty**.

furnace *n* an enclosed chamber in which heat is produced to burn refuse, smelt ore, etc.

furnish *vt* to provide (a room, etc) with furniture; to equip with what is necessary; to supply.—**furnisher** *n*.

furnishings *npl* furniture, carpets, etc.

furniture *n* the things in a room, etc that equip it for living, as chairs, beds, etc; equipment.

furore, furor *n* fury, indignation; widespread enthusiasm.

furrier *n* a dealer in furs.

furriery *n* (*pl* **furrieries**) the fur trade; a collective name for furs.

furrow *n* the groove in the earth made by a plough; a groove or track resembling this; a wrinkle. * *vti* to make furrows in; to wrinkle.—**furrower** *n*.—**furrowy** *adj*.

furry *adj* (**furrier, furriest**) like, made of, or covered with, fur.—**furrily** *adv*.—**furriness** *n*.

further *adv* at or to a greater distance or degree; in addition. * *adj* more distant, remote; additional. * *vt* to help forward, promote.—**furtherer** *n*.

furtherance *n* a helping forward.

furthermore *adv* moreover, besides.

furthermost *adj* most remote.

furthest *adj* at or to the greatest distance.

furtive *adj* stealthy; sly.—**furtively** *adv*.—**furtiveness** *n*.

furuncle *n* (*med*) a boil.—**furuncular** *adj*.

fury *n* (*pl* **furies**) intense rage; a frenzy; a violently angry person; (*with cap*) (*Greek, Roman myth*) one of the three winged goddesses of vengeance with serpents for hair, Alecto, Megaera, and Tisiphone.

furze *n* gorse.

fuscous *adj* dark-coloured, esp brownish-black.

fuse *vti* to join or become joined by melting; to (cause to) melt by the application of heat; to equip a plug, circuit, etc with a fuse; to (cause to) fail by blowing a fuse. * *n* a tube or wick filled with combustible material for setting off an explosive charge; a piece of thin wire that melts and breaks when an electric current exceeds a certain level.—*also* **fuze**.

fusee *n* a large-headed match; a conical spindle in a clock, around which the chain is wound.—*also* **fuzee**.

fuselage *n* the body of an aircraft.

fusel oil *n* a poisonous liquid mixture of various alcohols, formed as a byproduct of distillation.

fusible *adj* able to be fused; (*metal, alloy*) having a melting point below 148.9°C (300°F) and used in fuses, etc.—**fusibility** *n*.—**fusibly** *adv*.

fusiform *adj* spindle-shaped.

fusil *n* a light flintlock musket.

fusilier, fusileer *n* (*formerly*) a British soldier armed with a flintlock musket; a soldier in certain infantry regiments.

fusillade *n* a firing of shots in continuous or rapid succession; an outburst, as of criticism. * *vt* to attack or shoot down by fusillade.

fusion *n* the act of melting, blending or fusing; a product of fusion; union, partnership; nuclear fusion.

fuss *n* excited activity, bustle; a nervous state; (*inf*) a quarrel; (*inf*) a showy display of approval. * *vi* to worry over trifles; to whine, as a baby.—**fusser** *n*.

fussy *adj* (**fussier, fussiest**) worrying over details; hard to please; fastidious; over-elaborate.—**fussily** *adv*.—**fussiness** *n*.

fustian *n* a kind of coarse twilled cotton cloth, eg corduroy; ranting language, bombast. * *adj* made of fustian; turgid.

fustic *n* a large tropical American tree; its wood; the yellow obtained from it.

fusty *adj* (**fustier, fustiest**) smelling of mould or damp; outmoded in ideas or opinions.—**fustily** *adv*.—**fustiness** *n*.

futhark, futharc, futhork, futhorc *n* a phonetic alphabet made up of runes.

futile *adj* useless; ineffective.—**futilely** *adv*.—**futility** *n*.

futon *n* a light cotton mattress.

futtock *n* (*naut*) one of the upright curved ribs of a ship, springing from the keel.

future *adj* that is to be; of or referring to time yet to come. * *n* the time to come; future events; likelihood of eventual success; (*gram*) the future tense; (*pl*) commodities purchased at a prescribed price for delivery at some future date.

futurism *n* a movement in art, music, and literature begun in Italy about 1909 marked by an effort to give formal expression to the energy of mechanical processes; a point of view that finds meaning or fulfillment in the future.—**futurist** *adj*, *n*.

futuristic *adj* forward-looking in design, appearance, intention, etc.—**futuristically** *adv*.

futurity *n* (*pl* **futurities**) time or events yet to come.

futurology *n* the forecasting of future trends in human affairs.—**futurologist** *n*.

fuze *see* **fuse**.

fuzee *see* **fusee**.

fuzz *n* fine light particles of fibre (as of down or fluff); a blurred effect; fluff; (*sl*) police. * *vi* to fly off in minute particles; to become blurred.

fuzzword *see* **buzzword**.

fuzzy *adj* (**fuzzier, fuzziest**) like fuzz; fluffy; blurred.—**fuzzily** *adv*.—**fuzziness** *n*.

-fy *vb suffix* to make, eg *solidify*.

G

G (*symbol*) (*mus*) the 5th note of the scale of C; gravitational constant; (*physcs*) conductance; giga; (*sl*) grand ($1000 or £1000).

g *abbr* = gallons(s); gram(s); gravity; acceleration due to gravity.

Ga (*chem symbol*) gallium.

GA, Ga. (*US*) *abbr* = Georgia.

gab *vi* (**gabbing, gabbed**) (*inf*) to talk in a rapid or thoughtless manner, chatter. * *n* (*inf*) idle talk.—**gabber** *n*.

gabardine *n* a firm cloth of wool, rayon, or cotton; gaberdine.

gabble *vti* to talk or utter rapidly or incoherently; to utter inarticulate or animal sounds.—**gabbler** *n*.

gabbro *n* (*pl* **gabbros**) a dark igneous rock like granite.—**gabbroic** *adj*.

gabby *adj* (**gabbier, gabbiest**) (*inf*) talkative.

gabelle *n* (*formerly*) a tax on salt in France.

gaberdine *n* (*formerly*) a long, loose upper garment worn by pilgrims, Jews etc; a raincoat; gaberdine.

gabion *n* (*formerly*) a large cylindrical basket filled with earth or stones, used in military defence; a similar metal container used in engineering and underwater construction.

gable *n* the triangular upper part of a wall enclosed by the sloping ends of a pitched roof.—**gabled** *adj*.
gablet *n* a small ornamental gable used for the summit of niches etc.
gad *vi* (**gadding, gadded**) (*usu with* **about**) to wander restlessly or idly in search of pleasure.—**gadder** *n*.
gadabout *n* (*inf*) a person that wanders restlessly in search of pleasure or amusement.
gadfly *n* (*pl* **gadflies**) any of various flies that bite or annoy livestock; an irritating person.
gadget *n* a small, often ingenious, mechanical or electronic tool or device.—**gadgety** *adj*.
gadgetry *n* gadgets; the use of gadgets.
gadoid *adj, n* (a fish) of the cod family.
gadolinite *n* a silicate of yttrium.
gadolinium *n* a magnetic metallic element of the rare earth group.—**gadolinic** *adj*.
gadroon *n* an ornamental edge of inverted fluting; a decorative border, esp on silver.
gadwall *n* (*pl* **gadwalls, gadwall**) a large freshwater duck, prized as game.
Gael *n* a person who speaks Gaelic, esp a Scottish Highlander or Irishman.
Gaelic *n* the Celtic language of Ireland, the Scottish Highlands, and the Isle of Man.—*also adj*.
gaff *n* a pole with a sharp hook for landing large fish; (naut) a hgh boom or yard for hoisting a sail aft of a mast; (*sl*) one's home. * *vt* to land (a fish) with a gaff.
gaffe *n* a social blunder.
gaffer *n* an old man, often a countryman; an overseer or foreman; the senior electrician of a film crew.
gaff-topsail *n* (*naut*) a light sail set above a gaff.
gag *n* something put over or into the mouth to prevent talking; any restraint of free speech; a joke. * *vb* (**gagging, gagged**) *vt* to cause to retch; to keep from speaking, as by stopping the mouth of. * *vi* to retch; to tell jokes.
gaga *adj* (*inf*) senile; slightly crazy.
gage *see* **gauge.**
gaggle *n* a flock of geese when not in flight; (*inf*) a disorderly collection of people.
gahnite *n* a greenish and dark-brown mineral.
gaiety *n* (*pl* **gaieties**) happiness, liveliness; colourful appearance.
gaige *n* the Chinese word for "radical reform" or peristroika.
gaily *adv* in a cheerful manner; with bright colours.
gain *vt* to obtain, earn, esp by effort; to win in a contest; to attract; to get as an addition (esp profit or advantage); to make an increase in; to reach. * *vi* to make progress; to increase in weight. * *n* an increase esp in profit or advantage; an acquisition.
gainful *adj* profitable.—**gainfully** *adv*.—**gainfulness** *n*.
gainsay *vt* (**gainsaying, gainsaid**) (*formal*) to dispute; to deny.—**gainsayer** *n*.
gait *n* a manner of walking or running; the sequence of footsteps made by a moving horse.
gaiter *n* a cloth or leather covering for the lower leg.
gal[1] *n* (*sl*) a girl.
gal[2], **gall.** *abbr* = gallon.
gala *n* a celebration, festival.
galactic *adj* of a galaxy; huge.
galago *n* (*pl* **galagos**) an African genus of lemurs; a bushbaby.
galantine *n* a dish composed of chicken, veal or other white meat, boned, seasoned, tied up, boiled, shaped and served cold in its own jelly.
galatea *n* a cotton fabric, often with blue and white stripes.
Galatians *n sing* (*New Testament*) the epistles of St Paul addressed to the Galatians.
galavant *see* **gallivant.**
galaxy *n* (*pl* **galaxies**) any of the systems of stars in the universe; any splendid assemblage; (*with cap*) the galaxy containing the Earth's solar system; the Milky Way.
galbanum *n* an odorous and bitter gum resin used in medicine.
gale *n* a strong wind, specifically one between 32 to 63 mph; an outburst.
galea *n* (*pl* **galeae**) (*bot, zool*) a helmet-like structure.—**galeate, galeated** *adj*.
galena *n* a sulphide of lead.
Galenic *adj* of Galen (*c.* ad 130*c.* 200), the Greek physician and philosopher, or his works.
Galilean[1] *adj* of Galilee or its inhabitants * *n* a native of Galilee; (*often pl*) a Christian; (*with* **the**) Jesus Christ.
Galilean[2] *adj* of or pertaining to Galileo (1564–1642), the Italian astronomer and mathematician.
galilee *n* a small chapel or porch at the western entrance to a church.
galingale, galangal *n* a kind of sedge; the aromatic root of an Asian plant.
galiot, galliot *n* a heavily built two-masted Dutch trading vessel; (*formerly*) a small light galley used in the Mediterranean.
galipot *n* a white resinous juice that exudes from pine trees.
galivant *see* **gallivant.**
gall[1] *n* bile; bitter feeling; (*inf*) impudence.
gall[2] *n* a diseased growth on plant tissue produced by fungi, insect parasites, or bacteria.
gall[3] *n* a skin sore caused by rubbing. * *vt* to chafe or hurt by rubbing; to irritate.
gallant *adj* dignified, stately; brave; noble; (*man*) polite and chivalrous to women.—**gallantly** *adv*.—**gallantness** *n*.—**gallantry** *n* (*pl* **gallantries**).
gallantry *n* (*pl* **gallantries**) (an act of) bravery, dashing courage; courtliness, a polite act.
gall bladder *n* a membranous sac attached to the liver in which bile is stored.
galleass *n* a large low-built three-masted vessel propelled by sails and oars, and carrying twenty or more guns.
galleon *n* a large sailing ship of the 15th–18th centuries.
gallery *n* (*pl* **galleries**) a covered passage for walking; a long narrow outside balcony; a balcony running along the inside wall of a building; (the occupants of) an upper area of seating in a theatre; a long narrow room used for a special purpose, eg shooting practice; a room or building designed for the exhibition of works of art; the spectators at a golf tournament, tennis match, etc.—**galleried** *adj*.
galley *n* a long, usu low, ship of ancient or medieval times, propelled by oars; the kitchen of a ship, aircraft; (*print*) a shallow tray for holding type; proofs printed from such type (—*also* **galley proof**).
galliard *n* a lively dance in triple time.
Gallic *adj* of or pertaining to France; of ancient Gaul or its people.
gallic *adj* of or made of gallnuts; (*chem*) of or containing gallium in the trivalent state.
Gallican *adj* of the Roman Catholic Church in France.
Gallicanism *n* the doctrine of the national party in the French Roman Catholic Church, tending to restrict papal control, opposed to Ultramontanism.
Gallice *adv* in French.
Gallicism *n* a French expression or idiom.
Gallicize, Gallicise *vt* to make French in manners, idiom etc.
galligaskins *n pl* trousers, leggings worn in the 16th and 17th centuries.
gallimaufry *n* (*pl* **gallimaufries**) a medley, a hotch-potch.
gallinaceous *adj* of or relating to a group of heavy-bodied largely land-loving birds including pheasants and domestic fowl.
galling *adj* irritating, exasperating.
gallipot *n* a small glazed pot, esp for medicine.
gallium *n* a metallic element that is liquid at room temperature and is used in thermometers, semiconductor devices, etc.
gallivant *vi* (*inf*) to go about in search of amusement.—*also* **galivant, galavant.**
galliwasp *n* a West Indian lizard.
gallnut *n* a round excrescence produced on the oak by the puncturing of the leaf buds by an insect, the gall beetle.
gallon *n* a unit of liquid measure comprising 4 quarts or 3.78 liters (in UK, 4.54 liters); (*pl*) (*inf*) a large amount.

galloon *n* a narrow braid or trimming of silk, gold lace, embroidery etc.
gallop *n* the fastest gait of a horse, etc; a succession of leaping strides; a fast pace. * *vti* to go or cause to go at a gallop; to move swiftly.—**galloper** *n*.
gallowglass *n* a heavily armed footsoldier; a chief's retainer in Ireland in the 13th–16th centuries.
gallows *n* (*pl* **gallowses, gallows**) a wooden frame used for hanging criminals.
gallstone *n* a small solid mass in the gall bladder.
Gallup poll *n* a sampling of public opinion, esp to help forecast an election.
galop *n* a dance.
galore *adv* in great quantity; in plentiful supply.
galosh *n* a waterproof overshoe.
galumph *vi* (*inf*) to prance triumphantly, or clumsily.
galvanic *adj* producing electricity by chemical action; stimulating (people) into action.—**galvanically** *adv*.
galvanism *n* (*arch*) electricity produced by the chemical action of certain bodies or an acid on a metal; the medical use of this.
galvanize *vt* to apply an electric current to; to startle; to excite; to plate (metal) with zinc.—**galvanization** *n*.—**galvanizer** *n*.
galvanometer *n* an instrument for detecting or measuring small electric currents.—**galvanometric, galvanometrical** *adj*.—**galvanometry** *n*.
galvanoscope *n* an instrument for measuring the direction and presence of electricity by movements of a magnetic needle.
gam[1] *n* a school of whales; a visit by one captain of a whaler to another; * *vb* (**gams, gammed, gamming**) *vt* to call upon the captain of a whaler. * *vi* (*whales*) to gather together in schools.
gam[2] *n* (*sl*) a well-shaped leg.
gambado (*pl* **gambados, gambadoes**) *n* a kind of leather legging used by horsemen; a flourish or curvet.
gambier, gambir *n* a vegetable extract used medicinally as an astringent, and also for tanning and dyeing.
gambit *n* (*chess*) an opening in which a piece is sacrificed to gain an advantage; any action to gain an advantage.
gamble *vi* to play games of chance for money; to take a risk for some advantage. * *vt* to risk in gambling, to bet. * *n* a risky venture; a bet.—**gambler** *n*.—**gambling** *n*.
gamboge *n* a yellow gum resin from SE Asia, used as a pigment and as a purgative (—*also* **cambogia**); a bright yellow colour.
gambol *vi* (**gambolling, gambolled** *or* **gamboling, gamboled**) to jump and skip about in play; to frisk. * *n* a caper, a playful leap.
gambrel *n* the hock of a horse; a bent stick of wood or metal resembling a horse's leg, used by butchers; a gambrel roof.
gambrel roof *n* a curved roof with a small gable at each end; a roof with a double slope on each side so that each side is shaped like a horse's leg.
game[1] *n* any form of play, amusement; activity or sport involving competition; a scheme, a plan; wild birds or animals hunted for sport or food, the flesh of such animals. * *vi* to play for a stake. * *adj* (*inf*) brave, resolute; (*inf*) willing.—**gamely** *adv*.—**gameness** *n*.
game[2] *adj* (*limbs*) injured, crippled, lame.
gamecock *n* (*formerly*) a cock bred and trained for fighting.
gamekeeper *n* a person who breeds and takes care of game birds and animals, as on an estate.—**gamekeeping** *n*.
game point *n* (*tennis*) the situation when the next point scored wins the game for one side or player.
gamesmanship *n* (*inf*) the art of winning games by questionable acts just short of cheating.
gamesome *adj* sportive.
gamester *n* a gambler.
gamete *n* a reproductive cell that unites with another to form the cell that develops into a new individual.—**gametal, gametic** *adj*.
gamic *adj* (*zool*) having a sexual character.
gamin *n* a mischievous urchin.
gamine *n* a boyish girl or woman with impish appeal.
gaming *n* the act of playing games for stakes; gambling. —*also adj*.
gamma *n* the third letter of the Greek alphabet.
gamma radiation, gamma rays *n* shortwave electromagnetic radiation from a radioactive substance.
gammer *n* (*rare*) (*usu humorous*) an old woman.
gammon *n* cured or smoked ham; meat from the hindquarters of a side of bacon.
gamogenesis *n* (*bot*) sexual reproduction.
gamopetalous *adj* with petals united at the base.
gamophyllous *adj* (*flowers*) with leaves cohering at the edges.
gamosepalous *adj* (*flowers*) with sepals united at the edges to form a calyx.
gamut *n* a complete range or series; (*mus*) the whole range of notes of a voice or instrument.
gamy, gamey *adj* (**gamier, gamiest**) having the strong smell or flavour of cooked game; (*inf*) spirited, lively.—**gaminess** *n*.
-gamy *n suffix* marriage; sexual union.
gander *n* an adult goose; (*inf*) a quick look.
gang *n* a group of persons, esp labourers, working together; a group of persons acting or associating together, esp for illegal purposes. * *vti* to form into or act as a gang.—**ganged** *adj*.
gangland *n* the criminal fraternity.
gangling, gangly *adj* tall, thin and awkward in appearance and movement.
ganglion *n* (*pl* **ganglia, ganglions**) a mass of nerve cells from which nerve impulses are transmitted.—**ganglionic** *adj*.
gangplank *n* a moveable ramp by which to board or leave a ship.
gangrene *n* death of body tissue when the blood supply is obstructed.—**gangrenous** *adj*.
gangster *n* a member of a criminal gang.
gangue, gang *n* the earth or matrix in which ore is found
gangway *n* a passageway, esp an opening in a ship's side for loading, etc; a gangplank.
ganister, gannister *n* a kind of silicious clay rock or hard sandstone; a refractory material used for lining furnaces.
ganja *n* marijuana.
gannet *n* any of various large voracious fish-eating sea birds.
ganoid *adj* (*fish*) having enamelled bony scales, like the sturgeon. * *n* a ganoid fish.
gantlet *see* **gauntlet.**
gantry *n* (*pl* **gantries**) a metal framework, often on wheels, for a travelling crane; a wheeled framework with a crane, platforms, etc for servicing a rocket to be launched.
gaol, gaolbird, gaoler *see* **jail, jailbird, jailer.**
gap *n* a break or opening in something, as a wall or fence; an interruption in continuity, an interval; a mountain pass; a divergence, disparity. * *vt* (**gapping, gapped**) to make a gap in.—**gappy** *adj*.
gape *vi* to open the mouth wide; to stare in astonishment, esp with the mouth open; to open widely. * *n* the act of gaping; a wide opening.—**gaping** *adj*.—**gapingly** *adv*.
gaper *n* a person who gapes; one of various types of shellfish that have a space between the valves.
gar *n* (*pl* **gar, gars**) a garfish.
garage *n* an enclosed shelter for motor vehicles; a place where motor vehicles are repaired and serviced, and fuel sold. * *vt* to put or keep in a garage.
garage sale *n* a sale of unwanted household goods, held in a garage or other part of the house.
garb *n* clothing, style of dress. * *vt* to clothe.
garbage *n* food waste; unwanted or useless material; rubbish; (*comput*) useless data.
garbageman *n* (*pl* **garbagemen**) a person employed to remove garbage.
garble *vt* to distort (a message, story, etc) so as to mislead.—**garbler** *n*.
garboard (strake) *n* (*naut*) the plank or plate on a ship's bottom next to the keel.
garbology *n* the study of the disposal of waste material.—**garbologist** *n*.
garçon *n* a waiter.

garden *n* an area of ground for growing herbs, fruits, flowers, or vegetables; a yard; a fertile, well-cultivated region; a public park or recreation area, usu laid-out with plants and trees. * *vi* to make, or work in, a garden.—**gardener** *n*.—**gardening** *n*.

gardenia *n* a tree or shrub with beautiful fragrant white or yellow flowers.

garfish *n* (*pl* **garfish, garfishes**) a long, slender freshwater fish with a spearlike snout and a thick-scaled body.

gargantuan *adj* colossal, prodigious.

garget *n* a disease in cattle.

gargle *vti* to rinse the throat by breathing air from the lungs through liquid held in the mouth. * *n* a liquid for this purpose; the sound made by gargling.—**gargler** *n*.

gargoyle *n* a grotesquely carved face or figure, usu acting as a spout to drain water from a gutter; a person with an ugly face.—**gargoyled** *adj*.

garibaldi *n* a type of loose blouse, orig red.

garish *adj* crudely bright, gaudy.—**garishly** *adv*.—**garishness** *n*.

garland *n* a wreath of flowers or leaves worn or hung as decoration. * *vt* to decorate with a garland.

garlic *n* a bulbous herb cultivated for its compound bulbs used in cookery; its bulb.—**garlicky** *adj*.

garment *n* an item of clothing.

garner *vt* to gather, store.

garnet *n* a semiprecious stone, red, yellow or green in colour.

garnish *vt* to decorate; to decorate (food) with something that adds colour or flavour. * *n* something used to garnish food.—**garnisher** *n*.—**garniture** *n*.

garnishee *vt* (**garnisheeing, garnisheed**) (*law*) to warn by garnishment. * *n* (*law*) the person into whose hands the property of another is attached pending the satisfaction of the claims of a third party.

garnishment *n* embellishment; (*law*) notice to holder of another's attached property not to give it to him but to account for it in court; a summons; (*arch*) notice to third party to appear in suit.

garniture *n* embellishment, trimmings (esp on a dish of food).

garpike *n* the garfish.

garret *n* an attic.

garrison *n* troops stationed at a fort; a fortified place with troops. * *vt* to station (troops) in (a fortified place) for its defence.

garrotte, garrote, garotte *n* a method of execution by strangling with an iron collar; the iron collar used. * *vt* to execute by garrotte; to half-throttle and rob.—**garrotter, garroter, garotter** *n*.

garrulous *adj* excessively talkative.—**garrulously** *adv*.—**garrulousness, garrulity** *n*.

garter *n* an elasticated band used to support a stocking or sock.

garth *n* a courtyard surrounded by a cloister; (*arch*) a yard, garden or paddock.

gas *n* (*pl* **gases, gasses**) an air-like substance with the capacity to expand indefinitely and not liquefy or solidify at ordinary temperatures; any mixture of flammable gases used for lighting or heating; any gas used as an anaesthetic; any poisonous substance dispersed in the air, as in war; (*inf*) empty talk; gasoline. * *vt* (**gases** *or* **gasses, gassing, gassed**) to poison or disable with gas; (*inf*) to talk idly and at length.

gasbag *n* (*inf*) an idle talker.

gas chamber *n* an airtight room where animals or people are killed by poisonous gas.

gasconade *n* (*rare*) boastful or blustering talk. * *vi* to bluster, to boast.

gaseous *adj* having the form of or being gas; of or being related to gases; lacking substance or solidity.—**gaseousness** *n*.

gash *n* a long, deep, open cut. * *vt* to cut deep.

gasholder *n* a circular hollow tank, open at the bottom and closed at the top, for storing gas prior to distribution

gasify *vti* (**gasifying, gasified**) to turn into gas.—**gasification** *n*.

gasket *n* a piece or ring of rubber, metal, etc sandwiched between metal surfaces to act as a seal.

gaslight *n* a type of lamp using a jet of gas to provide illumination.

gasman *n* (*pl* **gasmen**) an employee of a gas company who reads meters, etc.

gasolier, gaselier *n* a branched hanging support for gas lights.

gasoline, gasolene *n* (*US*) a liquid fuel or solvent distilled from petroleum.—*also* **petrol**.—**gasolinic** *adj*.

gasometer *n* an instrument for measuring gas; a gasholder.

gasometry *n* the science or process of measuring gas.

gasp *vi* to draw in the breath suddenly and audibly, as from shock; to struggle to catch the breath. * *vt* to utter breathlessly. * *n* the act of gasping.—**gaspingly** *adv*.

gassy *adj* (**gassier, gassiest**) impregnated with or like a gas; given to pretentious talk; inflated.

gastr-, gastro- *prefix* stomach.

gastric *adj* of, in, or near the stomach.

gastric juice *n* digestive fluid secreted by glands in the stomach lining.

gastric ulcer *n* an ulcer of the lining of the stomach.

gastritis *n* inflammation of the stomach.—**gastritic** *adj*.

gastroenteric *adj* of or pertaining to the stomach or intestinal tract.

gastroenteritis *n* inflammation of the mucous membrane of the stomach and intestines.—**gastroenteritic** *adj*.

gastrointestinal *adj* of or pertaining to the stomach or intestines.

gastrology, gastroenterology *n* the study of diseases of the stomach and intestinal tract.

gastronome, gastronomer, gastronomist *n* a connoisseur of food.

gastronomy *n* the art and science of good eating.—**gastronomic, gastronomical** *adj*.—**gastronomically** *adj*.

gastropod *n* any of a large class of molluscs (as snails) with a flattened foot for moving and usu with stalk-like sense organs.—**gastropodan** *adj, n*.—**gastropodous** *adj*.

gastrula *n* (*pl* **gastrulas, gastrulae**) the fertilized ovum at a certain period in its development.

gasworks *n sing* a place where gas is manufactured.

gate *n* a movable structure controlling passage through an opening in a fence or wall; a gateway; a movable barrier; a structure controlling the flow of water, as in a canal; a device (as in a computer) that outputs a signal when specified input conditions are met; the total amount or number of paid admissions to a football match, etc. * *vt* to supply with a gate; to keep within the gates (of a university) as a punishment.

gâteau, gateau *n* (*pl* **gâteaux, gateaux**) a large cream cake.

gate-crasher *n* a person who attends a party, etc without being invited.—**gatecrash** *vi*.

gatefold *n* an oversize page in a book or magazine that is folded in.

gatehouse *n* a house built over or beside a gate.

gatekeeper *n* a person who controls entrance to a gate.

gate-leg(ged) table *n* a table with drop leaves supported by movable legs.

gatepost *n* a post on which a gate is hung, or to which it is attached when closed.

gateway *n* an opening for a gate; a means of entrance or exit.

gather *vt* to bring together in one place or group; to get gradually; to collect (as taxes); to harvest; to draw (parts) together; to pucker fabric by pulling a thread or stitching; to understand, infer. * *vi* to come together in a body; to cluster around a focus of attention; (*sore*) to swell and fill with pus.—**gatherable** *adj*.—**gatherer** *n*.

gathering *n* the act of gathering or assembling together; an assembly; folds made in a garment by gathering.

Gatling gun *n* a machine gun with clustered barrels, which are discharged in succession by turning a handle.

GATT *abbr* = General Agreement on Tariffs and Trade.

gauche *adj* socially inept; graceless, tactless.—**gauchely** *adv*.—**gaucheness** *n*.

gaucherie *n* awkwardness, tactlessness; a tactless or awkward act.

gaucho *n* (*pl* **gauchos**) a cowboy of the pampas of South America.

gaud *n* a piece of finery, a trinket or ornament.

gaudery *n* (*pl* **gauderies**) cheap, showy finery.

gaudy *adj* (**gaudier, gaudiest**) excessively ornamented; tastelessly bright.—**gaudily** *adv*.—**gaudiness** *n*.

gauffer *see* **goffer.**

gauge *n* measurement according to some standard or system; any device for measuring; the distance between rails of a railway; the size of the bore of a shotgun; the thickness of sheet metal, wire, etc. * *vt* to measure the size, amount, etc of.—*also* **gage.—gaugeable, gagable** *adj*.—**gauger, gager** *n*.

Gaul *n* an ancient region of Western Europe corresponding roughly to modern France and Belgium; a native of Gaul.

Gaullism *n* the policies pertaining to General de Gaulle, first president of the Fifth Republic in France (1959–69); the political movement based on de Gaulle's policies and principles.—**Gaullist** *n, adj*.

gaunt *adj* excessively thin as from hunger or age; looking grim or forbidding.—**gauntness** *n*.

gauntlet[1] *n* a knight's armoured glove; a long glove, often with a flaring cuff.—*also* **gantlet** *n*.

gauntlet[2] *n* (*formerly*) a type of military punishment in which a victim was forced to run between two lines of men who struck him as he passed.

gaur *n* a large fierce, dark-coloured ox found in SE Asia and India.

gauss *n* (*pl* **gauss, gausses**) the unit of measurement for magnetic flux density.

gauze *n* any very thin, loosely woven fabric, as of cotton or silk; a firm woven material of metal or plastic filaments; a surgical dressing.

gauzy *adj* (**gauzier, gauziest**) like gauze, thin, transparent.—**gauzily** *adv*.—**gauziness** *n*.

gave *see* **give.**

gavel *n* a hammer used by a chairman, auctioneer, judge, etc to command proceedings.

gavial *n* an Indian crocodile with a long narrow snout.

gavotte *n* a lively dance of French peasant origin.

gawk *vi* to stare at stupidly.

gawky *adj* (**gawkier, gawkiest**) clumsy, awkward, ungainly.—**gawkily** *adv*.—**gawkiness** *n*.

gay *adj* joyous and lively; colourful; homosexual. * *n* a homosexual.—**gayness** *n*.

gaze *vi* to look steadily. * *n* a steady look.—**gazer** *n*.

gazebo *n* (*pl* **gazebos, gazeboes**) a summerhouse or belvedere, elevated to command a wide view.

gazelle *n* (*pl* **gazelles, gazelle**) any of numerous small swift Asian or African antelopes.

gazette *n* a newspaper, now mainly in newspaper titles; an official publication listing government appointments, legal notices, etc.

gazetteer *n* an index of geographical place names.

gazpacho *n* a Spanish soup of tomatoes and other vegetables, served cold.

GB *abbr* = Great Britain.

Gd (*chem symbol*) gadolinium.

GDP *abbr* = Gross Domestic Product.

Ge (*chem symbol*) germanium.

gear *n* clothing; equipment, esp for some task or activity; a toothed wheel designed to mesh with another; (*often pl*) a system of such gears meshed together to transmit motion; a specific adjustment of such a system; a part of a mechanism with a specific function. * *vt* to connect by or furnish with gears; to adapt (one thing) to conform with another.

gearbox *n* a metal case enclosing a system of gears.

gearing *n* a particular arrangement of gears.

gearshift *n* a lever used to engage or change gear, esp in a motor vehicle.

gearwheel *n* a cogwheel.

gecko *n* (*pl* **geckos, geckoes**) a small lizard of warm regions that feeds on insects.

gee *vi* (**geeing geed**) (*often with* **up**) to make a horse go faster. * *interj* a mild oath.

geese *see* **goose.**

geezer *n* (*sl*) an old man.

Geiger counter *n* an electronic device for detecting and measuring radioactive emissions.

geisha *n* (*pl* **geisha, geishas**) a Japanese girl trained as an entertainer to serve as a hired companion to men.

gel *n* a jelly-like substance, as that applied to style and sculpt hair before drying it. * *vti* (**gelling, gelled**) to become or cause to become a gel.—*also* **jell.**

gelatin, gelatine *n* a tasteless, odourless substance extracted by boiling bones, hoofs, etc and used in food, photographic film, medicines, etc.

gelatinize *vt* to make or become gelatinous; to coat with gelatin.—**gelatinization** *n*.—**gelatinizer** *n*.

gelatinous *adj* of or like gelatin; jelly-like in consistency.

gelation *n* solidification (of liquids) by cold.

geld *vt* (**gelding, gelded** *or* **gelt**) to castrate, esp a horse.

gelding *n* a castrated horse.

gelid *adj* intensely cold; icy.—**gelidity** *n*.

gelignite *n* an explosive consisting of nitroglycerin absorbed in a base of wood pulp mixed with sodium or potassium nitrate.

gem *n* a precious stone, esp when cut and polished for use as a jewel; a person or thing regarded as extremely valuable or beloved. * *vt* (**gemming, gemmed**) to decorate or set with gems.

geminate, geminated *adj* growing or occurring in pairs.

gemination *n* duplication; (*rhetoric*) the repetition of a word, etc, for effect.

Gemini *n* the third sign of the zodiac, represented by the twins Castor and Pollux, operative 21 May–20 June.—**Geminian** *adj*.

gemma *n* (*pl* **gemmae**) a growth on an animal or plant budding off as a separate individual.

gemmate *vi* to have buds; to propagate by gemmae.—**gemmation** *n*.—**gemmiparous** *adj*.

gemmule *n* a small bud or gemma; an ovule; a cell produced by certain moulds.

gemot, gemote *n* an assembly or local court in pre-Norman England.

gemsbok *n* (*pl* **gemsbok, gemsboks**) a large, straight-horned South African antelope with a broad black stripe along its length.

gemstone *n* a mineral or substance used as a gem.

gendarme *n* an armed policeman in France and Belgium.

gendarmerie, gendarmery *n* a force of gendarmes.

gender *n* the classification by which words are grouped as feminine, masculine, or neuter; (*inf*) the sex of a person.

gene *n* any of the complex chemical units in the chromosomes by which hereditary characteristics are transmitted.

genealogy *n* (*pl* **genealogies**) a recorded history of one's ancestry; the study of family descent; lineage.—**genealogical** *adj*.—**genealogist** *n*.

genera *see* **genus.**

generable *adj* capable of being generated.

general *adj* not local, special, or specialized; of or for a whole genus, relating to or covering all instances or individuals of a class or group; widespread, common to many; not specific or precise; holding superior rank, chief. * *n* something that involves or is applicable to the whole; a commissioned officer above a lieutenant general; a leader, commander; the title of the head of some religious orders.—**generalness** *n*.

general anaesthetic *n* an anaesthetic effecting the whole body and producing unconsciousness.

general delivery *n* the department of a post office that will hold mail until it is called for.—*also* **poste restante.**

general election *n* a national election to choose representatives in every constituency.

generalissimo *n* (*pl* **generalissimos**) a military commander of combined air, naval and ground forces.

generality *n* (*pl* **generalities**) the quality or state of being general; a vague or inadequate statement.

generalization *n* general inference; induction; a general notion formed by attributing the characteristic(s) of a particular part or member (of a class, community etc) to the whole.

generalize *vti* to form general conclusions from specific instances; to talk (about something) in general terms.—**generalization** *n*.—**generalizer** *n*.

generally *adv* widely; popularly; usually; not specifically.

general practitioner *n* a non-specialist doctor who treats all types of illnesses in the community.

general-purpose *adj* having all kinds of uses.

generalship *n* the office of general; military skill; management skill.

general staff *n* officers who advice and assist a military commander.

general strike *n* a strike of all workers in a city, region or country.

generate *vt* to bring into existence; to produce.

generation *n* the act or process of generating; a single succession in natural descent; people of the same period; production, as of electric current.

generation gap *n* the difference in attitudes and understanding between one generation and another.

generative *adj* pertaining to generation; having the power to generate.

generator *n* one who or that which generates; a machine that changes mechanical energy to electrical energy.

generic *adj* of a whole class, kind, or group.—**generically** *adv*.

generosity *n* (*pl* **generosities**) the quality of being generous; liberality; munificence; a generous act.

generous *adj* magnanimous; of a noble nature; willing to give or share; large, ample.—**generously** *adv*.—**generousness** *n*.

genesis *n* (*pl* **geneses**) the beginning, origin; (*with cap*) the first book of the Old Testament.

genet *n* an animal of southern Europe, western Asia and Africa, related to the civet and valued for its fur; any fur made in imitation of genet.

genetic, genetical *adj* of or relating to the origin, development or causes of something; of or relating to genes or genetics.—**genetically** *adv*.

genetic code *n* the order of genetic information in a cell, which determines hereditary characteristics.

genetic engineering *n* the modification of genetic information in the cell of a plant or animal to improve yield, performance, etc.

genetic fingerprinting *n* the analysis of bodily tissue or fluids to identify the unique genetic character of an individual, as used in criminal investigations, the determination of paternity, etc.

genetics *n sing* the branch of biology dealing with heredity and variation in plants and animals.—**geneticist** *n*.

genial[1] *adj* kindly, sympathetic and cheerful in manner; mild, pleasantly warm.—**geniality, genialness** *n*.—**genially** *adv*.

genial[2] *adj* of the chin.

geniculate, geniculated *adj* having knee-like joints; bent at a sharp angle.

genie *n* (*pl* **genies, genii**) (*fairy tales*) a spirit with supernatural powers which can fulfil your wishes.—*also* **jinni**.

genital *adj* of reproduction or the sexual organs.

genitals, genitalia *npl* the (external) sexual organs.—**genitalic** *adj*.

genitive *adj* (*gram*) of or belonging to the case of nouns, pronouns and adjectives expressing ownership or relation. * *n* the genitive case.—**genitival** *adj*.

genius *n* (*pl* **geniuses**) a person possessing extraordinary intellectual power; (*with* **for**) natural ability, strong inclination.

genocide *n* the systematic killing of a whole race of people.—**genocidal** *adj*.

genre *n* a distinctive type or category, esp of literary composition; a style of painting in which everyday objects are treated realistically.

gens *n* (*pl* **gentes**) in ancient Rome, a clan or house; one of a number of related families claiming a common ancestor or having a name or religious rites etc in common.

gent *n* (*inf*) a gentleman.

genteel *adj* polite or well-bred; affectedly refined.—**genteelly** *adv*.—**genteelness** *n*.

gentes *see* **gens**.

gentian *n* an alpine plant, usu with blue flowers.

gentian violet *n* a crystalline substance used as an antiseptic.

gentile *n* a person who is not a Jew.—*also adj*.

gentility *n* (*pl* **gentilities**) refinement, good manners.

gentle *adj* belonging to a family of high social station; refined, courteous; generous; kind; kindly; patient; not harsh or rough.—**gentleness** *n*.—**gently** *adv*.

gentleman *n* (*pl* **gentlemen**) a man of good family and social standing; a courteous, gracious and honourable man; a polite term of address.—**gentlemanly** *adj*.

gentleman-at-arms *n* (*pl* **gentlemen-at-arms**) one of the bodyguard of the UK sovereign on state occasions.

gentlewoman *n* (*pl* **gentlewomen**) a woman of noble or gentle birth; a lady.

gentrify *vt* (**gentrifying, gentrified**) to convert a working-class house or district to more expensive middle-class tastes.—**gentrification** *n*.

gentry *n* people of high social standing; (*formerly*) landed proprietors not belonging to the nobility.

genuflect *vi* to act in a servile way; to bend the knee in worship or respect.—**genuflection** *n*.—**genuflector** *n*.

genuine *adj* not fake or artificial, real; sincere.—**genuinely** *adv*.—**genuineness** *n*.

genus *n* (*pl* **genera**) (*biol*) a taxonomic division of plants and animals below a family and above a species; a class of objects divided into several subordinate species.

geo- *prefix* earth.

geocentric *adj* viewed as from the centre of the earth; having the earth as a centre.—**geocentrically** *adj*.

geod *abbr* = geodesic; geodesy; geodetic.

geode *n* a cavity lined with crystals, usu within a rock.

geodesic *adj* geodetic (—*also* **geodesical**). * *n* (*math*) the shortest distance between two points on a cruved surface, determined by triangulation.

geodesic dome *n* a lightweight domed structure made of interlocking polygons.

geodesy *n* the mathematical determination of the exact positions of geographical points and the shape and size of the earth.—**geodesic** *adj*.—**geodic** *adj*.

geodetic, geodetical *adj* of, pertaining to, determined by, or carried out by geodesy.

geography *n* (*pl* **geographies**) the science of the physical nature of the earth, such as land and sea masses, climate, vegetation, etc, and their interaction with the human population; the physical features of a region.—**geographer** *n*.—**geographical, geographic** *adj*.—**geographically** *adv*.

geologize *vti* to study geology or the geology of.

geology *n* the science relating to the history and structure of the earth's crust, its rocks and fossils.—**geological, geologic** *adj*.—**geologically** *adv*.—**geologist, geologer** *n*.

geomancy *n* divination by figures or lines.—**geomancer** *n*.—**geomantic** *adj*.

geometer, geometrician *n* one who studies or is skilled in geometry.

geometric, geometrical *adj* pertaining to, or done by, geometry; (*design, etc*) consisting of simple geometric shapes.—**geometrically** *adv*.

geometric progression *n* a sequence in which the terms differ by a constant ratio (e.g. 1, 2, 4, 8, 16 . . .).

geometrize *vti* to work or make by geometrical methods; to study geometry.

geometry *n* the branch of mathematics dealing with the properties, measurement, and relationships of points, lines, planes, and solids.—**geometric, geometrical** *adj*.—**geometrically** *adv*.

geophagy, geophagia, geophagism *n* the practice of eating certain kinds of clay, earth or chalk.—**geophagist** *n*.—**geophagous** *adj*.

geophysics *n sing* the physics of the earth.—**geophysical**.—*adj*.—**geophysicist** *n*.

geopolitics *n sing* the study of the relationship between the geographical situation of a nation and its politics; the study of the effect of a nation's geography on its politics, esp in relation to that nation's relationship with other nations.

geoponic *adj* agricultural.

geoponics *n sing* the scientific study of agriculture.

georgette *n* a thin silk fabric.

Georgian *adj* of the times or reigns of the four Georges (1714–1830) or of George V (1910–36) who ruled Britain; pertaining to Georgia in the

US; pertaining to Georgia in the Caucasus. * *n* a person from Georgia; a person who lived in Georgian times; one who lives as if he or she belonged to Georgian times.

georgic, georgical *adj* of or pertaining to husbandry; rural. * *n* a poem on agriculture; (*with cap: pl*) a poem on agriculture by Virgil.

geothermal, geothermic *adj* of, relating to, or using the heat of the earth's interior.

geotropism *n* (*bot*) a tendency in the roots of certain plants to turn in the direction of the earth.—**geotropic** *adj.*—**geotropically** *adv.*

geranium *n* a garden plant with red, pink or white flowers.

gerbil, gerbille *n* a type of burrowing desert rodent of Asia and Africa.—*also* **jerbil.**

gerent *n* (*rare*) a ruler, a manager.

gerfalcon *see* **gyrfalcon.**

geriatric *adj* relating to geriatrics or old people; (*inf*) old, decrepit. * an aged person.

geriatrics *n sing* a branch of medicine dealing with the diseases and care of old people.—**geriatrician, geriatrist** *n.*

germ *n* a simple form of living matter capable of growth and development into an organism; any microscopic, disease-causing organism; an origin or foundation capable of growing and developing.

German *adj* of or relating to Germany, its people or their language. * *n* a native of Germany.

german *adj* of the same stock or parentage; germane.

germander *n* a plant of the mint family.

germane *adj* relevant.—**germanely** *adv.*—**germaneness** *n.*

Germanic *adj* of Germans or Germany or of a German-speaking nation. * *n* the family of languages derived from Indo-European that comprises the English, Dutch, German, Scandinavian and Gothic languages.

Germanism *n* a German idiom, custom, or characteristic.

germanium *n* a rare metallic element used in transistors.

Germanize *vti* to make or become German in language, custom, manners etc.—**Germanization** *n.*

German measles *n* (*sing*) a mild contagious disease similar to measles.—*also* **rubella.**

Germanophile *n* a lover of Germany or its customs, etc.

Germanophobe *n* a person who has an irrational fear of Germany.—**Germanophobia** *n.*

German shepherd *n* any of a breed of large smooth-haired dogs often used by the police and for guarding property.—*also* **Alsatian.**

German silver *n* an alloy of nickel, copper and zinc.—*also* **nickel silver.**

germ cell *n* a reproductive cell.

germicide *n* a substance used to destroy germs.—**germicidal** *adj.*

germinal *adj* incipient; of or pertaining to a germ or germs or seed buds; in the French revolutionary calendar, the seventh month (March 22–April 20).

germinate *vti* to start developing; to sprout, as from a seed.—**germinable, germinative** *adj.*—**germination** *n.*—**germinator** *n.*

germ warfare *n* the use of disease-causing bacteria against enemy forces.

gerontocracy *n* (*pl* **gerontocracies**) government by old men.—**gerontocratic** *adj.*

gerontology *n* the study of aging and its effects and problems.—**gerontological** *adj.*—**gerontologist** *n.*

gerrymander *vt* to rearrange the boundaries of (voting districts) to favour a particular party or candidate.

gerund *n* the participle of a verb used as a noun.—**gerundial** *adj.*

gerundive *adj* of or like a gerund. * *n* a passive verbal adjective.

gesso *n* (*pl* **gessoes**) a prepared ground of plaster for painting on; plaster of Paris.

gestalt *n* (*pl* **gestalts, gestalten**) an integral pattern or system of phenomena forming a functional unit in which the whole is more than the sum of its parts.

Gestapo *n* the secret police of Nazi Germany.

gestate *vt* to carry (young) in the womb during pregnancy; to develop (a plan, etc) gradually in the mind.—**gestational, gestative** *adj.*—**gestatory** *adj.*

gestation *n* the act or period of carrying young in the womb; pregnancy.

gesticulate *vi* to make expressive gestures, esp when speaking.—**gesticulation** *n.*—**gesticulative** *adj.*—**gesticulator** *n.*

gesture *n* movement of part of the body to express or emphasize ideas, emotions, etc. * *vi* to make a gesture.—**gestural** *adj.*—**gesturer** *n.*

get *vb* (**getting, got,** *pp* **got, gotten**) *vt* to obtain, gain, win; to receive; to acquire; to go and bring; to catch; to persuade; to cause to be; to prepare; (*inf*) (*with vb aux* **have** *or* **has**) to be obliged to; to possess; (*inf*) to strike, kill, baffle; defeat, etc; (*inf*) to understand; (*with* **across**) to cause to be understood; (*with* **in**) to bring in; (*crops, etc*) to gather; to insert; (*with* **off**) to acquit, to secure favourable treatment of; (*letters*) to post; (*with* **out**) to cause to leave or escape; to cause to become known or published; (*with* **out of**) to avoid doing; (*with* **over**) to communicate effectively. * *vi* to come; to go; to arrive; to come to be; to manage or contrive; (*with* **about, around**) to be up and on one's feet, esp after being unwell; to be socially active; (*news, gossip*) to become circulated; (*with* **across**) to be understood; (*with* **at**) to reach; (*inf*) to mean, imply; to irritate, pester relentlessly; (*inf*) to criticize; (*inf*) to corrupt, bribe, influence illegally; (*with* **away**) to escape; (*with* **by**) (*inf*) to manage, to survive; (*with* **in**) (*vehicle, etc*) to enter; to arrive; (*university, college, etc*) to be offered a place; (*with* **off**) to come off, down, or out of; to be acquitted; to escape the consequences of; to begin, depart; (*with* **on**) to go on or into; to put on; to proceed; to grow older; to become late; to manage; to succeed; (*with* **on with**) to establish a friendly relationship; (*with* **out**) to go out or away; to leave or escape; to take out; to become known or published; (*with* **over**) to overcome; to recover from; to forget; (*with* **round, around**) to evade, circumvent; to coax, cajole; (*with* **through**) to use up, spend, consume; to finish; to manage to survive; (*examination, test*) to succeed or pass; to contact by telephone; (*with* **up**) to rise to one's feet; to get out of bed; (*inf*) to organize; (*inf*) to dress in a certain style; (*inf*) to be involved in (mischief, etc).—**getable, gettable** *adj.*

get-at-able *adj* accessible.

getaway *n* the act of escaping; a start in a race, etc.

get-together *n* (*inf*) an informal social gathering or meeting.

get-up *n* (*inf*) dress, costume.

get-up-and-go *n* (*inf*) energy, enthusiasm.

getter *n* one who gets or acquires.

geum *n* a genus of the rose family, with yellow, orange, red or white flowers.

gewgaw *n* a showy ornament; a trinket.

geyser *n* a natural spring from which columns of boiling water and steam gush into the air at intervals; a water heater.

gharry, gharri *n* (*pl* **gharries**) a cart or carriage in India that is available for hire.

ghastly *adj* (**ghastlier, ghastliest**) terrifying, horrible; (*inf*) intensely disagreeable; pale, unwell looking.—**ghastliness** *n.*

ghat, ghaut *n* in India, a mountain pass or a chain of mountains; a landing-place with steps; a flight of steps to a river or a temple.

ghazi *n* (*pl* **ghazies**) a Muslim slayer of infidels; a Turkish title bestowed on distinguished commanders; a warrior champion.

ghee *n* clarified butter.

gherkin *n* a small cucumber used for pickling.

ghetto *n* (*pl* **ghettos, ghettoes**) a section of a city in which members of a minority group live, esp because of social, legal or economic pressure.

ghetto blaster *n* (*inf*) a large portable stereo cassette player and radio with built-in speakers.

ghillie *n* (*pl* **ghillies**) a gillie.

ghost *n* the supposed disembodied spirit of a dead person, appearing as a shadowy apparition; a faint trace or suggestion; a false image in a photographic negative. * *vt* to ghostwrite.

ghostly *adj* (**ghostlier, ghostliest**) of or like a ghost.—**ghostliness** *n.*

ghost town *n* a town abandoned by most or all of its inhabitants.

ghostwrite *vt* (**ghostwriting, ghostwrote,** *pp* **ghostwritten**) to writes books, speeches, articles, etc for another who professes to be the author.—**ghostwriter** *n*.

ghoul *n* (*Muslim folklore*) an evil spirit that robs graves and feeds on the dead; a person with macabre tastes or interests.—**ghoulish** *adj*.—**ghoulishly** *adv*.

GHQ *abbr* = General Headquarters.

GI *n* (*pl* **GI's, GIs**) (*inf*) a private soldier in the US Army.

giant *n* a huge legendary being of great strength; a person or thing of great size, strength, intellect, etc. * *adj* incredibly large.—**giantess** *nf*.

giant panda *n* a large black and white bear-like herbivore.—*also* **panda.**

giaour *n* (*derog*) a Muslim term for an unbeliever, esp a Christian.

gibber *vi* to utter meaningless or inarticulate sounds.

gibberish *n* unintelligible talk, nonsense.

gibbet *n* a gallows; a structure from which bodies of executed criminals were hung and exposed to public scorn.

gibbon *n* a small tailless ape of southeastern Asia and the East Indies.

gibbous *adj* protuberant; humped; irregularly rounded; (*moon*) between full and half.

gibe *n* a taunt, sneer. * *vti* to jeer, scoff (at).—*also* **jibe.**—**giber, jiber** *n*.—**gibingly, jibingly** *adv*.

giblets *npl* the edible internal organs of a bird.

gid *n* a disease in sheep, marked by staggering.

giddy *adj* (**giddier, giddiest**) frivolous, flighty; having a feeling of whirling around as if about to lose balance and fall; causing giddiness. * *vti* (**giddying, giddied**) to make giddy, to become giddy.—**giddily** *adv*.—**giddiness** *n*.

gie *vt* (*Scot*) to give.

GIFT (*acronym*) Gamete Intra-Fallopian Transfer: a technique that helps infertile couples to have children.

gift *n* something given; the act of giving; a natural ability. * *vt* to present with or as a gift.—**giftedness** *n*.

gifted *adj* having great natural ability.

gig[1] *n* a light two-wheeled horse-drawn carriage; a long, light boat.

gig[2] *n* (*inf*) a single booking for a jazz or pop band, etc; a single night's performance. * *vi* (**gigging, gigged**) to perform a gig.

giga- *prefix* one billion (10^9); (*comput*) 2^{30}.

gigantesque *adj* as if by or for a giant.

gigantic *adj* exceedingly large.—**gigantically** *adv*.—**giganticness** *n*.

giggle *vi* to laugh in a nervous or silly manner. * *n* a laugh in this manner; (*inf*) a prank, a joke.—**giggler** *n*.—**giggly** *adj*.

gigolo *n* (*pl* **gigolos**) a man paid to be a woman's escort.

gigot *n* a leg of mutton.

gigue *n* a lively tune; a dance similar to a jig.

gild[1] *see* **guild.**

gild[2] *vt* (**gilding, gilded** *or* **gilt**) to coat with gold leaf; to give a deceptively attractive appearance to.—**gilder** *n*

gilder *see* **guilder.**

gilding *n* the art or process of overlaying or covering with gold leaf; gold leaf applied to a surface; a superficial covering.

gill[1] *n* an organ, esp in fish, for breathing in water.

gill[2] *n* in US a liquid measure equal to 4 fluid ounces (0.25 pint) or 23.6 millimeters; in UK, 5 fluid ounces (0.25 pint) or 28.4 millimeters.

gillie, gilly *n* (*pl* **gillies**) (*Scot*) a Highland attendant, esp one who accompanies a shooting or fishing party.—*also* **ghillie.**

gills *npl* the wattle below the beak of a bird, as in certain domestic fowl; one of the radiating plates under the cap of a mushroom; a person's cheeks or jowls.

gillyflower *n* one of various scented plants of the mustard family, eg wallflower, stock, etc.

gilt[1] *see* **gild.**

gilt[2] *n* gilding; a substance used for this.

gilt-edged *adj* (*securities*) considered a secure investment.

gimbal *n* (*usu pl*) one of two rings moving within each other at right angles, used to suspend a ship's compass, etc.

gimcrack *adj* showy, cheap and useless.

gimlet *n* a small tool with a screw point for boring holes.

gimmick *n* a trick or device for attracting notice, advertising or promoting a person, product or service.—**gimmickry** *n*.—**gimmicky** *adj*.

gimp *n* an interlaced silk twist or trimming interwoven with wire or cord, used for furniture, dresses etc.—*also* **guimpe.**

gin[1] *n* an alcoholic spirit distilled from grain and flavoured with juniper berries.

gin[2] *n* a trap for catching small animals; a type of crane; a machine for separating the seeds from raw cotton. * *vt* (**ginning, ginned**) to trap with a gin; to separate seeds from cotton.

ginger *n* a tropical plant with fleshy roots used as a flavouring; the spice prepared by drying and grinding; (*inf*) vigour; a reddish-brown.—**gingery** *adj*.

ginger ale, ginger beer *n* a carbonated soft drink flavoured with ginger.

gingerbread *n* a cake flavoured with ginger.

gingerly *adv* with care or caution. * *adj* cautious.—**gingerliness** *n*.

ginger snap *n* a ginger-flavoured biscuit.

gingham *n* a cotton fabric with stripes or checks.

gingival *adj* of the gums.

gingivitis *n* inflammation of the gums.

ginglymus *n* (*pl* **ginglymi**) (*anat*) a joint like a hinge.

gink *n* (*sl*) a boy or man, esp an eccentric one.

ginkgo *n* (*pl* **ginkgoes**) a Japanese tree with handsome fan-shaped foliage; the maidenhair tree.

ginseng *n* a plant found in China and North America; its root, said to have an invigorating effect on the mind and body.

gip *see* **gyp.**

Gipsy *see* **Gypsy.**

giraffe *n* (*pl* **giraffes, giraffe**) a large cud-chewing mammal of Africa, with very long legs and neck.

girandole, girandola *n* a branched chandelier; a revolving firework or water jet; a pendant or earring with small stones around a larger one; one of several mines connected in a group.

girasol, girosol, girasole *n* a variety of opal; the fire opal.

gird *vt* (**girding, girded** *or* **girt**) to encircle or fasten with a belt; to surround; to prepare (oneself) for action.

girder *n* a large steel beam for supporting joists, the framework of a building, etc.

girdle *n* a belt for the waist.

girl *n* a female child; a young woman; (*inf*) a woman of any age.—**girlhood** *n*.—**girlish** *adj*.

girlfriend *n* a female friend, esp with whom one is romantically involved.

Girl Guide *n* a member of the Girl Guides, a scouting organization founded in Britain in 1910.

girlie *n* a little girl; a young woman; (*inf*) a woman.

girlie magazine *n* a magazine that contains photographs of nude or semi-nude females.

girlish *adj* of or like a girl.—**girlishly** *adv*.—**girlishness** *n*.

Girl Scout *n* a member of the Girl Scouts, a youth organization founded in the US in 1912.

giro (*pl* **giros**) a credit-transfer system between financial organizations; a payment so made.

Girondist *n* a member of the Gironde, the moderate Republican party during the Revolution in France (1791–93).

girt *see* **gird.**

girt[2] *adj* (*naut*) moored so taut by two cables as not to swing to the wind or tide.

girth *n* the thickness round something; a band put around the belly of a horse, etc to hold a saddle or pack.

gist *n* the principal point or essence of anything.

gîte *n* self-catering holiday accommodation in France.

give *vb* (**giving, gave,** *pp* **given**) *vt* to hand over as a present; to deliver; to hand over in or for payment; to pass (regards etc) along; to act as host or sponsor of; to supply; to yield; (*advice*) to offer; (*punishment, etc*) to inflict; to sacrifice; to perform; (*with* **away**) to make a gift of; to give (the bride) to the bridegroom; to sell cheaply; to reveal, betray; (*with* **in**) to deliver, hand in (a document, etc); (*with* **off**) to emit (fumes, etc); (*with* **out**) to discharge; to make public, to announce; to emit; to distribute; (*with* **over**) to devote time to a specific activity; to cease (an activity); to transfer to another; to set aside for a particular purpose; (*with* **up**) to hand over; to stop, renounce; to cease; to resign (a position); to stop trying; to despair of; to surrender; to devote oneself completely (to). * *vi* to bend, move, etc from force or pressure; (*inf*) to be happening; (*with* **in**) to concede, admit defeat; (*with* **out**) to become used up or exhausted; to fail; (*with* **over**) (*inf*) to stop (an activity). * *n* capacity or tendency to yield to force or strain; the quality or state of being springy; (*with* **in**) to submit; (*with* **out**) to become worn out; (*with* **up**) to accept defeat or failure to do something, to surrender.—**givable, giveable** *adj*.

give-and-take *n* mutual concessions; free-flowing exchange of ideas and conversation.

giveaway *n* (*inf*) an unintentional revelation; a free gift to encourage sales; a freesheet.

given[1] *see* **give**.

given[2] *adj* accustomed (to) by habit, etc; specified; assumed; granted.

giver *n* a person who gives.

gizzard *n* the second stomach of a bird, used for grinding food.

glabrous *adj* without hair, smooth-skinned.

glacé *adj* candied, covered in icing, as fruit. * *vt* (**glacéing, glacéed**) to cover with icing; to candy.

glacial *adj* extremely cold; of or relating to glaciers or a glacial epoch.—**glacially** *adv*.

glaciate *vti* to subject to glacial action; to cover or become covered with glaciers.—**glaciation** *n*.

glacier *n* a large mass of snow and ice moving slowly down a mountain.

glacis *n* (*pl* **glacis**) a sloping bank of earth in front of a fortification for its defence; a slope (on a tank) to throw off hostile shot.

glad *adj* (**gladder, gladdest**) happy; causing joy; very willing; bright.—**gladly** *adv*.—**gladness** *n*.

gladden *vti* to make or become glad.—**gladdener** *n*.

glade *n* an open space in a wood or forest.

gladiate *adj* sword-shaped.

gladiator *n* (*ancient Rome*) a person trained to fight with men or beasts in a public arena.—**gladiatorial** *adj*.

gladiolus *n* (*pl* **gladiolus, gladioli**) any of a genus of the iris family with sword-like leaves and tall spikes of funnel-shaped flowers.

gladsome *adj* joyous.

glair *n* white of egg; size made from this; a sticky substance; any sticky or glairy matter * *vt* to smear with glair.—**glaireous** *adj*.

glairy *adj* (**glairier, glairiest**) like or smeared with glair.—**glairiness** *n*.

glamorize, glamourize *vt* to make glamorous.—**glamorization, glamourization** *n*.—**glamorizer, glamourizer** *n*.

glamour, glamor *n* charm, allure; attractiveness, beauty.—**glamorous, glamourous** *adj*.—**glamorousness, glamourousness** *n*.

glance *vi* to strike obliquely and go off at an angle; to flash; to look quickly. * *n* a glancing off; a flash; a quick look.—**glancingly** *adv*.

gland *n* an organ that separates substances from the blood and synthesizes them for further use in, or for elimination from, the body.

glanders *n* (*sing or pl*) a contagious bacterial disease esp of horses, often fatal.—**glandered** *adj*.—**glanderous** *adj*.

glandular *adj* of, having or resembling glands; (*plants*) covered with hairs tipped with glands.

glare *n* a harsh uncomfortably bright light, esp painfully bright sunlight; an angry or fierce stare. * *vi* to shine with a steady, dazzling light; to stare fiercely.

glaring *adj* dazzling; obvious, conspicuous.—**glaringly** *adv*.—**glaringness** *n*.

glasnost *n* the Russian word for "openness," now applied to the policy, initiated by President Gorbachev of the former USSR, of greater frankness and openness in Soviet affairs.—**glasnostian** *adj*.

glass *n* a hard brittle substance, usu transparent; glassware; a glass article, as a drinking vessel; (*pl*) spectacles or binoculars; the amount held by a drinking glass. * *adj* of or made of glass. * *vt* to equip, enclose, or cover with glass.

glass-blowing *n* the art, skill or process of blowing air into molten glass and shaping it.—**glass-blower** *n*.

glassware *n* objects made of glass, esp drinking vessels.

glasswort *n* a fleshy plant of marshy areas, from which soda was formerly obtained for use in making glass.

glassy *adj* (**glassier, glassiest**) resembling glass; smooth; expressionless, lifeless.—**glassily** *adv*.—**glassiness** *n*.

glaucoma *n* a disease of the eye caused by pressure.—**glaucomatous** *adj*.

glaucous *adj* sea-green; covered with bloom of a blueish-white colour, green with a bluish-grey tinge.

glaze *vt* to provide (windows etc) with glass; to give a hard glossy finish to (pottery, etc); to cover (foods, etc) with a glossy surface. * *vi* to become glassy or glossy. * *n* a glassy finish or coating.—**glazer** *n*.

glazier *n* a person who fits glass in windows.—**glaziery** *n*.

glazing *n* a glaze; the operation of setting glass or applying a glaze; windowpanes; glass; semi-transparent colours passed thinly over other colours to tone down their effect.

gleam *n* a subdued or moderate beam of light; a brief show of some quality or emotion, esp hope. * *vi* to emit or reflect a beam of light.—**gleamingly** *adv*.

glean *vti* to collect (grain left by reapers); to gather (facts, etc) gradually.—**gleanable** *adj*.—**gleaner** *n*.

gleaning *n* the act of collecting after reapers; (*often pl*) that which is collected laboriously from various sources.

glee *n* joy and gaiety; delight; (*mus*) a song in parts for three or more male voices.—**gleeful** *adj*.—**gleefully** *adv*.—**gleefulness** *n*.

gleeful *adj* merry, joyous; triumphant.—**gleefully** *adv*.—**gleefulness** *n*.

gleet *n* a thin mucous discharge, esp from the urethra, resulting from gonorrhoeal disease.

glen *n* a narrow valley.

glengarry *n* (*pl* **glengarries**) (*often cap*) a boat-shaped cap originating in Scotland.

glib *adj* (**glibber, glibbest**) speaking or spoken smoothly, to the point of insincerity; lacking depth and substance.—**glibly** *adv*.—**glibness** *n*.

glide *vti* to move smoothly and effortlessly; to descend in an aircraft or glider with little or no engine power. * *n* a gliding movement.—**glidingly** *adv*.

glider *n* an engineless aircraft carried along by air currents.

gliding *n* the sport of flying gliders.

glim *n* (*sl*) a light, a candle.

glimmer *vi* to give a faint, flickering light; to appear faintly. * *n* a faint gleam; a glimpse, an inkling.

glimmering *n* a faint gleam; a glimpse, an inkling.

glimpse *n* a brief, momentary view. * *vt* to catch a glimpse of.—**glimpser** *n*.

glint *n* a brief flash of light; a brief indication. * *vti* to (cause to) gleam brightly.

glioma *n* (*pl* **gliomata, gliomas**) a tumour of rapid growth on the brain, spinal cord, or auditory nerve.

glissade *vi* to slide down a snow-covered slope without the aid of skis. * *n* a sliding ballet step.—**glissader** *n*.

glissando *n* (*pl* **glissandi, glissandos**) (*mus*) a run by sliding the fingers over the keys of a piano; a quick slur on a violin.

glisten *vi* to shine, as light reflected from a wet surface.—**glisteningly** *adv*.

glister *vi* (*poet*) to sparkle, to glitter.—*also n*.

glitch *n* a malfunction in a, usu electronic, system.

glitter *vi* to sparkle; (*usu with* **with**) to be brilliantly attractive. * *n* a sparkle; showiness, glamour; tiny pieces of sparkling material used for decoration.—**glittering** *adj*.—**glittery** *adj*.

glitz *n*(*sl*) gaudiness; ostentatious glamour.—**glitzy** *adj* (**glitzier, glitziest**)

gloaming *n* twilight.

gloat *vi* to gaze or contemplate with wicked or malicious satisfaction.—**gloater** *n*.—**gloatingly** *adv*.

global *adj* worldwide; comprehensive.—**globally** *adv*.

global warning *n* the process caused by a blanket of 'greenhouse gases' building up around the earth trapping heat from the sun. Carbon dioxide, released by burning fossil fuels is one of the main causes.—*see* **greenhouse effect.**

globate, globated *adj* globe-shaped.

globe *n* anything spherical or almost spherical; the earth, or a model of the earth.

globeflower *n* a plant with round yellow flowers.

globetrotter *n* a person who travels widely.—**globetrotting** *n, adj*.

globin *n* a constituent of red blood corpuscles.

globoid *adj* nearly globular. * *n* a globoid figure.

globose, globous *adj* globe-like, spherical.

globosity, globoseness *n*

globular *adj* spherical.

globule *n* a small spherical particle; a drop, pellet; a blood corpuscle.

globulin *n* an albuminous protein forming one of the constituents of blood, muscle, and the cellular tissue of plants.

glockenspiel *n* an orchestral percussion instrument with tuned metal bars, played with hammers.

glomerate *adj* gathered into a roundish head or mass; compactly clustered.

glomerule *n* a clustered flowerhead.

gloom *n* near darkness; deep sadness. * *vti* to look sullen or dejected; to make or become cloudy or murky.

gloomy *adj* (**gloomier, gloomiest**) almost dark, obscure; depressed, dejected.—**gloomily** *adv*.—**gloominess** *n*.

gloria *n* a halo or aureole; a light fabric of silk, etc; (*with cap*) a prayer of praise, esp the *Gloria in excelsis* and *Gloria patri*; a musical setting of these.

glorify *vt* (**glorifying, glorified**) to worship; to praise, to honour; to cause to appear more worthy, important, or splendid than in reality.—**glorifiable** *adj*.—**glorification** *n*.—**glorifier** *n*.

glorious *adj* having or deserving glory; conferring glory or renown; beautiful; delightful.—**gloriously** *adv*.—**gloriousness** *n*.

glory *n* (*pl* **glories**) great honour or fame, or its source; adoration; great splendour or beauty; heavenly bliss. * *vi* (**glorying, gloried**) (*with* **in**) to exult, rejoice proudly.

gloss[1] *n* the lustre of a polished surface; a superficially attractive appearance. * *vt* to give a shiny surface to; (*with* **over**) to hide (an error, etc) or make seem right or inconsequential.—**glosser** *n*.

gloss[2] *n* an explanation of an unusual word (in the margin or between the lines of a text); a misleading explanation; a glossary. * *vt* to provide with glosses; to give a misleading sense of.—**glosser** *n*.

glossa *n* (*pl* **glossae, glossas**) the tongue, esp of insects.—**glossal** *adj*.

glossary *n* (*pl* **glossaries**) a list of specialized or technical words and their definitions.—**glossarial** *adj*.—**glossarist** *n*.

glossitis *n* inflammation of the tongue.

glossography *n* the making of glossaries or glosses.—**glossographer** *n*.

glossy *adj* (**glossier, glossiest**) having a shiny or highly polished surface; superficial; (*magazines*) lavishly produced. * *n* (*pl* **glossies**) a magazine with many colour pictures, printed on coated paper, esp a fashion magazine.—**glossily** *adv*.—**glossiness** *n*.

glottal *adj* of, pertaining to, or produced by the glottis.

glottis *n* (**glottises, glottides**) the opening between the vocal cords in the larynx.—**glottidean** *adj*.

glove *n* a covering for the hand; a baseball player's mitt; a boxing glove. * *vt* to cover (as if) with a glove.

glover *n* a maker or seller of gloves.

glow *vi* to shine (as if) with an intense heat; to emit a steady light without flames; to be full of life and enthusiasm; to flush or redden with emotion. * *n* a light emitted due to intense heat; a steady, even light without flames; a reddening of the complexion; warmth of emotion or feeling.

glower *vi* to scowl; to stare sullenly or angrily. * *n* a scowl, a glare.—**gloweringly** *adv*.

glow-worm *n* a beetle that emits light from the abdomen.

gloxinia *n* a tropical plant with showy bell-shaped flowers, cultivated as a houseplant.

glucose *n* a crystalline sugar occurring naturally in fruits, honey, etc.

glue *n* a sticky, viscous substance used as an adhesive. * *vt* (**gluing, glued**) to join with glue.—**gluer** *n*.

gluey *adj* (**gluier, glueist**) like glue, sticky.

glum *adj* (**glummer, glummest**) sullen; gloomy.—**glumly** *adv*.—**glumness** *n*.

glumaceous *adj* bearing or resembling glumes.

glume *n* the husk of corn or grasses.

glut *vt* (**glutting, glutted**) to over-supply (the market). * *n* a surfeit, an excess of supply.

gluteal *adj* pertaining to the buttocks.

gluten *n* a sticky elastic protein substance, esp of wheat flour, that gives cohesiveness to dough.—**glutenous** *adj*.

gluteus *n* (*pl* **glutei**) any of the three muscles that form the buttocks.

glutinous *adj* resembling glue, sticky.—**glutinousness, glutinosity** *n*.

glutton *n* a person who eats and drinks to excess; a person who has a tremendous capacity for something (eg for work); a wolverine.—**gluttonous** *adj*.

gluttony *n* the act or habit of eating and drinking to excess.

glyceride *n* an ester of glycerol.

glycerin, glycerine *n* the popular and commercial name for glycerol.

glycerol *n* a colourless, syrupy liquid made from fats and oils, used in making skin lotions, explosives, etc.—**glyceric** *adj*.

glycogen *n* a white insoluble starch-like substance obtained from the livers of animals and humans.

glycol *n* a viscid liquid intermediate between glycerine and alcohol; antifreeze.

glycosuria *n* a disease marked by excess sugar in the urine.—**glycosuric** *adj*.

glyph *n* (*arch*) a perpendicular fluting.—**glyphic** *adj*.

glyptic *adj* pertaining to engraving on gems; figured. * *n* the art of engraving designs on precious stones, ivory, etc.

glyptography *n* the art of cutting designs or engraving on a gem.

gm *abbr* = gram(s).

G-man *n* (*pl* **G-men**) (*inf*) an agent of the FBI.

GMT *abbr* = Greenwich Mean Time.

gnarl *n* a knot on the trunk or branch of a tree.

gnarled *adj* (*tree trunks*) full of knots; (*hands*) rough, knobbly; crabby in disposition.

gnash *vti* to grind (the teeth) in anger or pain. * *n* a grinding of the teeth.—**gnashingly** *adv*.

gnat *n* any of various small, two-winged insects that bite or sting.

gnathic, gnathial *adj* of or pertaining to jaws.

gnaw *vti* (**gnawing, gnawed,** *pp* **gnawed** *or* **gnawn**) to bite away bit by bit; to torment, as by constant pain.—**gnawable** *adj*.—**gnawer** *n*.

gneiss *n* a granite-like rock formed by layers of quartz, mica, etc.—**gneissic, gneissoid, gneissose** *adj*.

gnocchi *npl* small dumplings made from flour, semolina or potatoes.

gnome *n* (*folklore*) a dwarf who dwells in the earth and guards its treasure; a small statue of a gnome used as a garden decoration; a small and ugly person; (*sl*) an international banker or financier.—**gnomish** *adj*.

gnomic *adj* dealing in or containing pithy or sententious sayings; didactic.—**gnomically** *adv*.

gnomon *n* the indicator on a sundial that casts a shadow to indicate the time of day.—**gnomonic** *adj*.—**gnomonically** *adv*.

gnosis *n* (*pl* **gnoses**) higher knowledge, mysticism or insight.

gnostic *adj* of, pertaining to, or having knowledge; (*with cap*) pertaining to the Gnostics or Gnosticism (*— also* **gnostical**). * *n* (*with cap*) a member of an early Christian sect seeking salvation by knowledge, not faith.

Gnosticism *n* the doctrine of the Gnostics.
GNP *abbr* = Gross National Product.
gnu *n* (*pl* **gnus, gnu**) either of two large African antelopes with an ox-like head.—*also* **wildebeest.**
go[1] *vb* (**going, went,** *pp* **gone**) *vi* to move on a course; to proceed; to work properly; to act, sound, as specified; to result; to become; to be accepted or valid; to leave, to depart; to die; to be allotted or sold; to be able to pass (through); to fit (into); to be capable of being divided (into); to belong; (*with* **about**) to handle (a task, etc) efficiently; to undertake (duties, etc); (*sailing*) to change tack; (*with* **into**) to enter; to become a member of; to examine or investigate; to discuss; (*with* **off**) to explode; to depart; (*food, etc*) to become stale or rotten; to fall asleep; to proceed, occur in a certain manner; to take place as planned; to stop liking (something or someone); (*with* **on**) to continue; to happen; to talk effusively; to nag; to enter on stage; (*with* **out**) to depart; (*light, fire, etc*) to become extinguished; to cease to be fashionable; to socialize; (*radio or TV show*) to be broadcast; to spend time with, esp a person of the opposite sex; (*with* **over**) to change one's loyalties (to); to be received or regarded in a certain way; to examine and repair (something); (*with* **round**) to circulate; to be sufficient for everyone; (*with* **slow**) to work at a slow rate as part of an industrial dispute; (*with* **through**) to continue to the end (with); to be approved; to use up completely; to experience (an illness, etc); to search thoroughly; (*with* **together**) to match, to be mutually suited; (*inf*) to associate frequently, esp as lovers; (*with* **up**) in the UK, to enter or return to college or university; (*with* **with**) to match; to accompany; to associate frequently, esp as lovers; (*with* **without**) to be deprived of or endure the lack of (something). * *vt* to travel along; (*inf*) to put up with. * *n* (*pl* **goes**) a success; (*inf*) a try; (*inf*) energy.
go[2] *n* a Japanese board game.
goa *n* an Asian gazelle, the male of which has horns that curve backwards.
goad *n* a sharp-pointed stick for driving cattle, etc; any stimulus to action. * *vt* to drive (as if) with a goad; to irritate, nag persistently.
go-ahead *n* (*inf*) permission to proceed. * *adj* (*inf*) enterprising, ambitious.
goal *n* the place at which a race, trip, etc is ended; an objective; the place over or into which the ball or puck must go to score in some games; the score made.
goalie *n* (*inf*) a goalkeeper.
goalkeeper *n* a player who defends the goal.—**goalkeeping** *n.*
goat *n* a mammal related to the sheep that has backward curving horns, a short tail, and usu straight hair; a lecherous man.
goatee *n* a small pointed beard.
goatherd *n* a person who looks after goats.
goatish *adj* pertaining to or like a goat; (*arch*) lustful; rank-smelling.—**goatishly** *adv.*—**goatishness** *n.*
goatsbeard, goat's-beard *n* a European grass-like plant with yellow flowers; an American plant with compound leaves and small white flowers.
goatskin *n* the skin of a goat; a bottle or garment made of this.
goatsucker *n* a nocturnal bird with dull mottled plumage.—*also* **nightjar.**
gob[1] *n* (*sl*) the mouth.
gob[2] *n* a lump or clot of something; (*inf*) spittle. * *vi* (**gobbing, gobbed**) (*inf*) to spit.
gobbet *n* a lump of something.
gobble *vt* to eat greedily; (*often with* **up**) to take, accept or read eagerly. * *vi* to make a throaty gurgling noise, as a male turkey.
gobbledygook, gobbledegook *n* (*sl*) nonsense, pretentious jargon.
gobbler *n* (*inf*) a turkey cock.
go-between *n* a messenger, an intermediary.
goblet *n* a large drinking vessel with a base and stem but without a handle.
goblin *n* an evil or mischievous elf.
goby *n* (*pl* **goby, gobies**) a sea fish with a large head and a long thin body.
go-cart *n* a small cart for children to play in or pull; a stroller; a handcart.
god *n* any of various beings conceived of as supernatural and immortal, esp a male deity; an idol; a person or thing deified; (*with cap*) in monotheistic religions, the creator and ruler of the universe.
godchild *n* (*pl* **godchildren**) the child a godparent sponsors.
goddaughter *n* a female godchild.
goddess *n* a female deity; a woman of superior charms or excellence.
godfather *n* a male godparent; the head of a Mafia crime family or other criminal organization.
god-fearing *adj* religious.
godforsaken *adj* desolate, wretched.
godhead *n* the divine nature, deity; God.
godhood *n* the quality or condition of being a god; divinity.
godless *adj* irreligious; wicked.—**godlessly** *adv.*—**godlessness** *n.*
godlike *adj* like a god, divine.
godly *adj* (**godlier, godliest**) religious; holy; devout; devoted to God.—**godliness** *n.*
godmother *n* a female godparent.
godown *n* in India and China, a warehouse or storeroom.
godparent *n* a person who sponsors a child, as at baptism or confirmation, taking responsibility for its faith.
godsend *n* anything that comes unexpectedly and when needed or desired.
godson *n* a male godchild.
Godspeed *n* success, good luck.
godwit *n* any of a genus of wading birds with a long bill, related to the snipes but resembling curlews.
goer *n* a regular attender; something, as a car, that goes fast; an enthusiastic person.
gofer *n* (*inf*) a person who runs errands, as in an office.
goffer *vt* to make wavy or frilly with a hot iron, to crimp.—*also* **gauffer.**
go-getter *n* (*inf*) an ambitious person.
goggle *vi* to stare with bulging eyes. * *npl* large spectacles, sometimes fitting snugly against the face, to protect the eyes.
goggle-eyed *adj* with wide staring eyes.
go-go dancer *n* a scantily-clad dancer employed in a disco or nightclub.
going *n* an act or instance of going, a departure; the state of the ground, eg for walking, horse-racing; rate of progress. * *adj* that goes; commonly accepted; thriving; existing.
going-over *n* (*pl* **goings-over**) (*inf*) a thorough inspection; (*sl*) a beating.
goings-on *npl* events or actions, esp when disapproved of.
goiter, goitre *n* an abnormal enlargement of the thyroid gland.—**goitrous** *adj.*
gold *n* a malleable yellow metallic element used esp for coins and jewellery; a precious metal; money, wealth; a yellow colour. * *adj* of, or like, gold.
goldbeater's skin *n* a membrane prepared from the large intestine of an ox used to separate layers of gold in goldbeating.
goldbeating *n* the process of beating gold until it is very thin.—**goldbeater** *n.*
gold card *n* a credit card that entitles the cardholder to extra benefits.
gold-digger *n* a person who mines gold; (*inf*) a woman who uses feminine charms to extract money or gifts from men.—**gold-digging** *adj.*
golden *adj* made of or relating to gold; bright yellow; priceless; flourishing.—**goldenly** *adv.*—**goldenness** *n.*
golden age *n* the fabled early age of innocence and perfect human happiness; the flowering of a nation's civilization or art.
golden calf *n* (*Bible*) a golden calf made by Aaron and worshipped by the Israelites; wealth worshipped as a god.
golden eagle *n* a large eagle of the Northern hemisphere.
golden fleece *n* (*Greek myth*) the ram's fleece in search of which Jason sailed with the Argonauts; an order of knighthood in Austria and Spain.
golden handcuffs *npl* financial incentives to induce an employee to remain in a particular job for an agreed period.
golden handshake *n* (*inf*) financial compensation awarded an employee for loss of employment.

golden mean *n* neither too much nor too little; moderation.
goldenrod *n* a tall plant of the aster family with yellow flowers.
golden rule *n* a guiding principle.
goldfield *n* a district containing gold deposits and diggings.
gold-filled *adj* coated with gold.
goldfinch *n* a common European finch with yellow and black wings.
goldfish *n* (*pl* **goldfish, goldfishes**) a small gold-coloured fish of the carp family, kept in ponds and aquariums.
goldilocks *n* any of various plants with yellow flowers, eg the buttercup; (*with cap*) a name for someone, usu female, with golden hair.
gold leaf *n* gold beaten into very thin sheets, used for gilding.
gold mine *n* a mine where gold is extracted; (*inf*) a source of wealth.
gold plate *n* vessels of gold; a thin covering of gold.—**gold-plated** *adj*.
gold rush *n* a rush to a new gold field, as to the Yukon in 1897.
goldsmith *n* a worker in gold; a dealer in gold plate.
gold standard *n* a monetary standard in which the basic currency unit equals a specified quantity of gold.
golf *n* an outdoor game in which the player attempts to hit a small ball with clubs around a turfed course into a succession of holes in the smallest number of strokes.—**golfer** *n*.
golf ball *n* a hard dimpled ball used in golf; the spherical printing head in some typewriters.
golf club *n* a club with a wooden or metal head used in golf; a golf association or its premises.
golf course, golf links *n* a tract of land laid out for playing golf.
golliard *n* a medieval wandering jester or scholar.
golliwog, golliwogg *n* a cloth doll with a black face.
golly[1] *n* (*inf*) a golliwog.
golly[2] *interj* expressing surprise.
gonad *n* a primary sex gland that produces reproductive cells, such as an ovary or testis.—**gonadal, gonadic** *adj*.
gondola *n* a long, narrow, black boat used on the canals of Venice; a cabin suspended under an airship or balloon; an enclosed car suspended from a cable used to transport passengers, esp skiers up a mountain; a display structure in a supermarket, etc.
gondolier *n* a person who propels a gondola with a pole.
gone[1] *see* **go**[1].
gone[2] *adj* departed; dead; lost; (*inf*) in an excited state; (*inf*) pregnant for a specified period.
goner *n* (*sl*) a person or thing that is ruined, dead, or about to die.
gonfalon *n* a banner, usu with streamers, hung from a crossbar, used in ecclesiastical processions; a military flag or standard with a pointed edge.
gong *n* a disk-shaped percussion instrument struck with a usu padded hammer; (*sl*) a medal. * *vi* to sound a gong.
Gongorism *n* (a passage of) a florid pedantic Spanish literary style resembling euphuism.
goniometer *n* an instrument for measuring solid angles; an instrument used to determine the location of a distant radio station.—**goniometry** *n*.
gonorrhoea, gonorrhea *n* a venereal disease causing a discharge of mucous and pus from the genitals.—**gonorrhoeal, gonorrheal, gonorrhoeic, gonorrheic** *adj*.
goo *n* (*sl*) sticky matter; sickly sentimentality.
good *adj* (**better, best**) having the right or proper qualities; beneficial; valid; healthy or sound; virtuous, honourable; enjoyable, pleasant, etc; skilled; considerable. * *n* something good; benefit; something that has economic utility; (*with* **the**) good persons; (*pl*) personal property; commodities; (*pl*) the desired or required articles. * *adv* (*inf*) well; fully.—**goodish** *adj*.
goodbye *interj* a concluding remark at parting; farewell.—*also n*.
good-for-nothing *adj* useless, worthless. * a worthless person.
Good Friday *n* the Friday before Easter, commemorating the Crucifixion of Christ.
good-humoured *adj* genial, cheerful.—**good-humouredly** *adv*.—**good-humouredness** *n*.
good-looking *adj* handsome.
goodly *adj* (**goodlier, goodliest**) considerable; ample.—**goodliness** *n*.
goodman *n* (*pl* **goodmen**) (*formerly*) the master of a house, a husband; a man not born into the aristocracy.
good-natured *adj* amiable, easy-going.—**good-naturedly** *adv*.—**good-naturedness** *n*.
goodness *n* the state of being good; the good element in something; kindness; virtue. * *interj* an exclamation of surprise.
Good Samaritan *n* a person who helps those in distress (after the compassionate figure mentioned in the Bible.—Luke 10:33).
good-tempered *adj* having a pleasant and kindly nature.
good turn *n* a favour; an act of kindness.
goodwill *n* benevolence; willingness; the established custom and reputation of a business.
goodwoman *n* (*pl* **goodwomen**) (*formerly*) the mistress of a house, a wife; a woman not born into the aristocracy.
goody *n* (*pl* **goodies**) something pleasant or sweet; a goddy-goody. * *interj* an expression (usu used by a child) signifying pleasure.
goody-goody *adj* insufferably virtuous. * *n* (*pl* **goody-goodies**) a goody-goody person.
gooey *adj* (**gooier, gooiest**) (*inf*) soft and sticky; sweet; sentimental.
goof *n* (*sl*) a stupid person; a blunder. * *vi* (*sl*) to bungle.
goofy *adj* (**goofier, goofiest**) (*sl*) silly, stupid.—**goofily** *adv*.—**goofiness** *n*.
goon *n* (*sl*) a thug; a stupid person.
goop *n* (*sl*) any sticky, semi-liquid substance; (*sl*) a rude person.
goosander *n* a web-footed migratory waterfowl.
goose[1] *n* (*pl* **geese**) a large, long-necked, web-footed bird related to swans and ducks; its flesh as food; a female goose as distinguished from a gander; (*inf*) a foolish person.
goose[2] *vt* (*sl*) to poke (a person) between the buttocks.
gooseberry *n* (*pl* **gooseberries**) the acid berry of a shrub related to the currant and used esp in jams and pies.
goose bumps, goose pimples, goose flesh *n* a roughening of the skin caused usu by cold or fear.
goosegrass *n* a species of creeping plant on which geese feed.
gooseneck *n* (*naut*) a bent iron fitted to the extremity of a boom or yard.
goose step *n* a stiff-legged marching step used by some armies when passing in review.
goose-step *vi* (**goose-stepping, goose-stepped**) to march in a stiff-legged manner using the goose step.
gopher *n* a North American burrowing, rat-like rodent; a ground squirrel; a burrowing tortoise.
gopherwood *n* the wood Noah's Ark is reputed to have been made from, possibly cypress; the yellowwood.
gore[1] *n* (clotted) blood from a wound.
gore[2] *n* a tapering section of material used to shape a garment, sail, etc.
gore[3] *vt* to pierce or wound as with a tusk or horns.
gorge *n* a ravine. * *vt* to swallow greedily; to glut. * *vi* to feed gluttonously.—**gorgeable** *adj*.—**gorger** *n*.
gorgeous *adj* strikingly attractive; brilliantly coloured; (*inf*) magnificent.—**gorgeously** *adv*.—**gorgeousness** *n*.
Gorgon *n* (*Greek myth*) one of three female monsters with live snakes for hair whose looks turned the beholder to stone; (*without cap*) any ugly or formidable woman.
gorgonian *n* any of a genus of flexible branching coral.
Gorgonzola *n* a semi-hard blue-veined cheese with a rich flavour, originating in Italy.
gorilla *n* an anthropoid ape of western equatorial Africa related to the chimpanzee but much larger.
gormand *see* **gourmand**.
gormandize *vti* to eat like a glutton.—**gormandizer** *n*.
gorse *n* a spiny yellow-flowered European shrub.
gory *adj* (**gorier, goriest**) bloodthirsty; causing bloodshed; covered in blood.—**gorily** *adv*.—**goriness** *n*.
gosh *interj* an exclamation of surprise.

goshawk *n* any of several long-tailed hawks with short rounded wings.
gosling *n* a young goose.
go-slow *n* a deliberate slowing of the work rate by employees as a form of industrial action.
gospel *n* the life and teachings of Christ contained in the first four books of the New Testament; (*with cap*) one of these four books; anything proclaimed or accepted as the absolute truth.
gospeller, gospeler *n* the reader of the gospel in a communion service; an evangelist.
gossamer *n* very fine cobwebs; any very light and flimsy material. * *adj* light as gossamer.
gossip *n* one who chatters idly about others; such talk. * *vi* to take part in or spread gossip.—**gossiper** *n*.—**gossipingly** *adv*.—**gossipy** *adj*.
gossipmonger *n* a gossip.
got *see* **get**.
Goth *n* any member of a Germanic people that conquered most of the Roman Empire in the 3rd–5th centuries ad.
Gothic *adj* of a style of architecture with pointed arches, steep roofs, elaborate stonework, etc. * *n* German black letter type; a bold type style without serifs.—**Gothically** *adv*.
gotten *see* **get**.
gouache *n* a method of painting with opaque watercolours.
Gouda *n* a type of large flat round Dutch cheese.
gouge *n* a chisel with a concave blade used for cutting grooves. * *vt* to scoop or force out (as if) with a gouge.
gouger *n* one who or that which gouges; a swindler.
goujons *npl* narrow fried strips of fish or chicken in breadcrumbs.
goulash *n* a rich stew made with beef or veal seasoned with paprika.
gourami *n* (*pl* **gourami, gouramis**) an oriental fish cultivated for food.
gourd *n* any trailing or climbing plant of a family that includes the squash, melon, pumpkin, etc; the fruit of one species or its dried, hollowed-out shell, used as a cup, bowl, etc or ornament.
gourmand *n* a person who likes good food and drink, often to excess.—*also* **gormand**.—**gourmandism** *n*.
gourmandise, gormandise *n* the (sometimes excessive) love of good food.
gourmet *n* a person who likes and is an excellent judge of fine food and drink.
gout *n* a disease causing painful inflammation of the joints; esp of the great toe.—**gouty** *adj*.—**goutiness** *n*.
Gov., gov *abbr* = government; governor.
govern *vti* to exercise authority over; to rule, to control; to influence the action of; to determine.—**governable** *adj*.—**governability, governableness** *n*.
governance *n* the action, function, or power of government.
governess *n* a woman employed in a private home to teach and train the children.
government *n* the exercise of authority over a state, organization, etc; a system of ruling, political administration, etc; those who direct the affairs of a state, etc.—**governmental** *adj*.
governor *n* a person appointed to govern a province, etc; the elected head of any state of the US; the director or head of a governing body of an organization or institution; (*sl*) an employer; a mechanical device for automatically controlling the speed of an engine.—**governorship** *n*.
Govt, govt *abbr* = government.
gowan *n* (*Scot*) the daisy.
gown *n* a loose outer garment, specifically a woman's formal dress, a nightgown, a long, flowing robe worn by clergymen, judges, university teachers, etc; a type of overall worn in the operating room. * *vt* to dress in a gown, to supply with a gown.
goy *n* (*pl* **goyim, goys**) (*sl*) Jewish for Gentile.
GP *abbr* = general practitioner.
GPO *abbr* = general post office.
Gr. *abbr* = Grecian; Greece; Greek.
grab *vt* (**grabbing, grabbed**) to take or grasp suddenly; to obtain unscrupulously; (*inf*) to catch the interest or attention of. * *n* a sudden clutch or attempt to grasp; a mechanical device for grasping and lifting objects.—**grabber** *n*.
grabble *vi* to feel about, to grope.—**grabbler** *n*.
grace *n* beauty or charm of form, movement, or expression; good will; favour; a delay granted for payment of an obligation; a short prayer of thanks for a meal. * *vt* to decorate; to dignify.
graceful *adj* having beauty of form, movement, or expression.—**gracefully** *adv*.—**gracefulness** *n*.
graceless *adj* unattractive; lacking sense of what is proper; clumsy.—**gracelessly** *adv*.—**gracelessness** *n*.
grace note *n* (*mus*) an ornamental note.
Graces *npl* (*Greek myth*) the three sister goddesses who are the givers of charm and beauty.
gracile *adj* slender.—**gracility** *n*.
gracious *adj* having or showing kindness, courtesy, etc; compassionate; polite to supposed inferiors; marked by luxury, ease, etc; *interj* an expression of surprise.—**graciously** *adv*.—**graciousness** *n*.
grackle *n* an Asian bird like a starling; an American bird with shiny black plumage; the crow blackbird.
grad *n* (*sl*) a graduate.
gradate *vti* to change or cause to change gradually from one stage, degree, colour, etc to another; to arrange by grade or degree.
gradation *n* a series of systematic steps in rank, degree, intensity, etc; arranging in such stages; a single stage in a gradual progression; progressive change.—**gradational** *adj*.
grade *n* a stage or step in a progression; a degree in a scale of quality, rank, etc; a group of people of the same rank, merit, etc; the degree of slope; a sloping part; a mark or rating in an examination, etc. * *vt* to arrange in grades; to give a grade to; to make level or evenly sloping.
grade crossing *n* a place where a road and rail line or two rail lines cross at the same level, a level crossing.
gradient *n* a sloping road or railway; the degree of slope in a road, railway, etc.
gradin, gradine *n* one of a tier of seats; a ledge at the back of an altar.
gradual *adj* taking place by degrees.—**gradually** *adv*.—**gradualness** *n*.
graduate *n* a person who has completed a course of study at a school, college, or university; a receptacle marked with figures for measuring contents. * *adj* holding an academic degree or diploma; of or relating to studies beyond the first or bachelor's degree.—**graduator** *n*.
graduation *n* graduating or being graduated; the ceremony at which degrees are conferred by a college or university; an arranging or marking in grades or stages.
Graeco- *see* **Greco-**.
graffiti *npl* (*sing* **graffito**) inscriptions or drawings, often indecent, on a wall or other public surface.
graft *n* a shoot or bud of one plant inserted into another, where it grows permanently; the transplanting of skin, bone, etc; the getting of money or advantage dishonestly.—**grafter** *n*.—**grafting** *n*.
grail *n* in medieval legend, the dish or chalice that was used by Christ at the Last Supper, and the object of many knights' quests.—*also* **Holy Grail**.
grain *n* the seed of any cereal plant, as wheat, corn, etc; cereal plants; a tiny, solid particle, as of salt or sand; a unit of weight, 0.0648 gram; the arrangement of fibres, layers, etc of wood, leather, etc; the markings or texture due to this; natural disposition. * *vt* to form into grains; to paint in imitation of the grain of wood, etc. * *vi* to become granular.—**grainer** *n*.
grainy *adj* (**grainier, grainiest**) resembling grains in form or texture.—**graininess** *n*.
gram[1] *n* the basic unit of weight in the metric system, equal to one thousandth of a kilogram (one twenty-eighth of an ounce).
gram[2] *n* any of various leguminous plants grown for their edible seeds.
gram. *abbr* = grammar; grammatical.
grama (grass) *n* a low pasture grass of western and southwestern USA and South America.

gramarye, gramary *n* (*arch*) magic, necromancy.

gramercy *interj* (*arch*) an expression of great thanks; expressing great surprise.

gramineous *adj* of or like grass; grassy.

graminivorous *adj* feeding on grasses.

grammar *n* the study of the forms of words and their arrangement in sentences; a system of rules for speaking and writing a language; a grammar textbook; the use of language in speech or writing judged with regard to correctness of spelling, syntax, etc.

grammarian *n* one who studies grammar; the author of a grammar.

grammatical *adj* conforming to the rules of grammar.—**grammatically** *adv*.

gramophone *n* a record player, esp an old mechanical model with an acoustic horn.—*also* **phonograph**.

grampus *n* (*pl* **grampuses**) a marine mammal, as the blackfish or killer whale.

granadilla *n* a passion-fruit.

granary *n* (*pl* **granaries**) a building for storing grain.

grand *adj* higher in rank than others; most important; imposing in size, beauty, extent, etc; distinguished; illustrious; comprehensive; (*inf*) very good; delightful. * *n* a grand piano; (*inf*) a thousand pounds or dollars.—**grandly** *adv*.—**grandness** *n*.

grand-aunt *n* a father's or mother's aunt.—*also* **great-aunt**.

grandchild *n* (*pl* **grandchildren**) the child of a person's son or daughter.

granddad *n* (*inf*) grandfather; an old man.

granddaughter *n* the daughter of a person's son or daughter.

grand duke *n* the ruler of a state or principality.

grandee *n* a high-ranking person.

grandeur *n* splendour; magnificence; nobility; dignity.

grandfather *n* the father of a person's father or mother.

grandfather clock *n* a large clock with a pendulum in a tall, upright case.

grandiloquent *adj* using pompous words.—**grandiloquence** *n*.

grandiose *adj* having grandeur; imposing; pompous and showy.—**grandiosely** *adv*.—**grandiosity** *n*.

grand jury *n* a jury in the US that examines evidence in a case to determine whether an indictment should be made.

grandma, grandmama *n* (*inf*) grandmother.

grand mal *n* severe epilepsy.

grandmaster *n* an expert player (as of chess) who has scored consistently well in international competition.

grandmother *n* the mother of a person's father or mother.

grandnephew *n* a nephew's or niece's son.—*also* **great-nephew**.

grandniece *n* a nephew's or niece's daughter.—*also* **great-niece**.

grand opera *n* opera in which the whole text is set to music.

grandpa, grandpapa *n* (*inf*) grandfather.

grandparent *n* a grandfather or grandmother.

grand piano *n* a large piano with a horizontal harp-shaped case.

Grand Prix *n* (*pl* **Grand Prix**) any of a series of formula motor races held in different countries throughout the season; an important contest in other sports, including horse racing, tennis, and athletics.

grand slam *n* (*tennis, golf*) a winning of all the major international championships in a season; (*bridge*) a bidding for and winning all the tricks in a deal; (*baseball*) a home run hit when there is a runner on each base.

grandson *n* the son of a person's son or daughter.

grandstand *n* the main structure for seating spectators at a sporting event.

grand tour *n* (*formerly*) a trip round Europe taken by the sons of wealthy Englishmen to complete their education; (*inf*) a sightseeing or educational tour.

grand-uncle *n* a father's or mother's uncle.—*also* **great-uncle**.

grange *n* a country house with outbuildings etc; a local lodge of a powerful agricultural association; (*with* **the**) this association; (*formerly*) an outlying farm building where a monastery or local lord stored crops or tithes; (*arch*) a granary.

grangerize *vt* interleave (a book) with illustrations taken from other books; to remove illustrations, etc, from books for this purpose.—**grangerism** *n*.—**grangerization** *n*.

granite *n* a hard, igneous rock consisting chiefly of feldspar and quartz; unyielding firmness of endurance.—**granitic, granitoid** *adj*.

granivorous *adj* grain-eating; living on seeds.—**granivore** *n*.

granny, grannie *n* (*pl* **grannies**) (*inf*) a grandmother; (*inf*) an old woman.

granny knot *n* a wrongly tied reef knot, which is insecure.

grant *vt* to consent to; to give or transfer by legal procedure; to admit as true. * *n* the act of granting; something granted, esp a gift for a particular purpose; a transfer of property by deed; the instrument by which such a transfer is made.

grantee *n* the person to whom property is transferred by deed, etc.

granter *n* one who grants.

grantor *n* one who transfers property by deed, etc.

granular *adj* consisting of granules; having a grainy texture.—**granularity** *n*.

granulate *vt* to form or crystallize into grains or granules. * *vi* to collect into grains or granules; to become roughened and grainy in surface texture.—**granulation** *n*.—**granulative** *adj*.—**granulator, granulater** *n*.

granule *n* a small grain or particle.

grape *n* a small round, juicy berry, growing in clusters on a vine; a dark purplish red.—**grapey, grapy** *adj*.

grape fern *n* a fern with cresent-shaped fronds, moonwort.

grapefruit *n* (*pl* **grapefruit, grapefruits**) a large, round, sour citrus fruit with a yellow rind.

grape hyacinth *n* any of various small plants of the lily family bearing tight clusters of blue grape-like flowers.

grapeshot *n* cannon shot packed in layers, scattering when fired.

grapevine *n* a type of woody vine on which grapes grow; an informal means of communicating news or gossip.

graph *n* a diagram representing the successive changes in the value of a variable quantity or quantities. * *vt* to illustrate by graphs.

-graph *n suffix* a writing or recording device; something written, drawn or recorded.

-grapher *n suffix* denoting a person with specified skills; denoting a person who writes or draws in a certain way.

graphic, graphical *adj* described in realistic detail; pertaining to a graph, lettering, drawing, painting, etc.—**graphically** *adv*.—**graphicalness, graphicness** *n*.

graphic arts *npl* the fine and applied arts involving design, illustration and printing.

graphics *n sing or pl* the use of drawings and lettering; the drawings, illustrations, etc used in a newspaper, magazine, television programme, etc; information displayed in the form of diagrams, illustrations and animation on a computer monitor.

graphite *n* a soft, black form of carbon used in pencils, for lubricants, etc.—**graphitic** *adj*.

graphology *n* the study of handwriting, esp as a clue to character.—**graphological** *adj*.—**graphologist** *n*.

graph paper *n* ruled paper for drawing graphs and diagrams.

-graphy *n suffix* denoting a form of writing, representation or description.

grapnel *n* a small anchor with multiple claws.

grapple *vt* to seize or grip firmly. * *vi* to struggle hand-to-hand with; to deal or contend with. * *n* a grapnel; an act of grappling, a wrestle; a grip.—**grappler** *n*.

grappling iron, grappling hook *n* an iron bar with claws at one end for anchoring a boat, securing a ship alongside or raising sunken objects.

grasp *vt* to grip, as with the hand; to seize; to understand. * *vi* to try to clutch, seize; (*with* **at**) to take eagerly. * *n* a firm grip; power of seizing and holding; comprehension.—**graspable** *adj*.—**grasper** *n*.

grasping *adj* greedy, avaricious.—**graspingly** *adv*.—**graspingness** *n*.

grass *n* any of a large family of plants with jointed stems and long narrow leaves including cereals, bamboo, etc; such plants grown as lawn; pasture; (*sl*) marijuana; (*sl*) an informer. * *vi* to cover with grass; (*sl*) to inform, betray.

grasshopper *n* any of a group of plant-eating, winged insects with powerful hind legs for jumping.

grassland *n* land reserved for pasture; land, such as prairie, where grass dominates.
grass roots *npl* (*inf*) the common people, the ordinary members of a political or other organization; the basic level, the essentials.
grass snake *n* a small nonpoisonous European snake with a greenish body and yellow markings.
grass widow, grass widower *n* (*inf*) a person whose spouse is frequently absent.
grassy *adj* (**grassier, grassiest**) abounding in, covered with, or like, grass.—**grassiness** *n*.
grate[1] *n* a frame of metal bars for holding fuel in a fireplace; a fireplace; a grating.
grate[2] *vt* to grind into particles by scraping; to rub against (an object) or grind (the teeth) together with a harsh sound; to irritate. * *vi* to rub or rasp noisily; to cause irritation.
grateful *adj* appreciative; welcome.—**gratefully** *adv*.—**gratefulness** *n*.
grater *n* a metal implement with a jagged surface for grating food.
gratification *n* the act of gratifying; satisfaction; pleasure; (*arch*) a reward or recompense.
gratify *vt* (**gratifying, gratified**) to please; to indulge.—**gratification** *n*.—**gratifier** *n*.—**gratifyingly** *adv*.
grating[1] *n* a open framework or lattice of bars placed across an opening.
grating[2] *adj* harsh; irritating.—**gratingly** *adv*.
gratis *adj, adv* free of charge.
gratitude *n* a being thankful for favours received.
gratuitous *adj* given free of charge; done without cause, unwarranted.—**gratuitously** *adv*.—**gratuitousness** *n*.
gratuity *n* (*pl* **gratuities**) money given for a service, a tip.
grav *n* a unit of acceleration equal to standard free fall (1 grav = 9.8 metres (32 feet) per second).
gravamen *n* (*pl* **gravamens, gravamina**) the principal part of a legal complaint or accusation.
grave[1] *n* a hole dug in the ground for burying the dead; any place of burial, a tomb.
grave[2] *adj* serious, important; harmful; solemn, sombre; (*sound*) low in pitch. * *n* an accent (ˊ) over a vowel.—**gravely** *adv*.—**graveness** *n*.
gravel *n* coarse sand with small rounded stones. * *vt* (**gravelling, gravelled** *or* **graveling, graveled**) to cover or spread with gravel.—**gravelish** *adj*.
gravelly *adj* like gravel; (*voice*) deep and rough-sounding.
graven *adj* engraved; fixed indelibly.
graven image *n* an idol.
graver *n* an engraving tool.
gravestone *n* a stone marking a grave, usu inscribed with the name and details of the deceased.
graveyard *n* a burial-ground, cemetery.
gravid *adj* pregnant.—**gravidity, gravidness** *n*.—**gravidly** *adv*.
gravimeter *n* an instrument for measuring the specific gravity of liquid or solid bodies; an instrument for measuring gravity at particular geographical locations.—**gravimetry** *n*.
gravimetric, gravimetrical *adj* of or relating to measurement by weight; determined by weight.—**gravimetrically** *adv*.
gravitate *vi* to move or tend to move under the force of gravitation.—**gravitater** *n*.
gravitation *n* a natural force of attraction that tends to draw bodies together.—**gravitational** *adj*.—**gravitationally** *adv*.
gravitative *adj* pertaining to or determined by gravitation; likely to gravitate, causing something to gravitate.
gravity *n* (*pl* **gravities**) importance, esp seriousness; weight; the attraction of bodies toward the centre of the earth, the moon, or a planet.
gravy *n* (*pl* **gravies**) the juice given off by meat in cooking; the sauce made from this juice; (*sl*) money easily obtained.
gravy boat *n* a small boat-shaped dish for holding and serving gravy or sauces.
gravy train *n* (*sl*) a source of easy money.
gray *n* any of a series of neutral colours ranging between black and white; something (as an animal, garment, cloth, or spot) of a grey colour. * *adj* grey in colour; having grey-coloured hair; darkish; dreary; vague, indeterminate.—*also* **grey**.—**grayish** *adj*.—**grayness** *n*.
graybeard *n* an old man, esp one considered to be wise; an earthenware jug.—*also* **greybeard**.
graylag (goose) *n* the common wild goose of Europe and Asia.
grayling *n* (*pl* **grayling, graylings**) a freshwater fish.
gray matter *n* grey-coloured nerve tissue of the brain and spinal cord; (*inf*) brains, intelligence.
gray squirrel *n* a common squirrel with grey fur orig from North America.
graywacke *n* a hard conglomerate rock of pebbles and sand.—*also* **greywacke**.
graze[1] *vi* to feed on growing grass or pasture. * *vt* to put (animals) to feed on growing grass or pasture.—**grazer** *n*.
graze[2] *vt* to touch lightly in passing; to scrape, scratch. * *n* an abrasion, esp on the skin, caused by scraping on a surface.—**grazingly** *adv*.
grazier *n* a person who grazes cattle and prepares them for the market.
grazing *n* pasture; the crops, plants, etc, growing on this for animals to feed from.
grease *n* melted animal fat; any thick, oily substance or lubricant. * *vt* to smear or lubricate with grease.
greasepaint *n* make-up used by actors.
greaser *n* (*sl*) a mechanic; a motorcyclist, often a member of a gang; a member of the engine room crew on a commercial ship; (*derog*) an unpleasant, fawning person, (*derog*) a person from Latin America or Mexico.
greasy *adj* (**greasier, greasiest**) covered with grease; full of grease; slippery; oily in manner.—**greasily** *adv*.—**greasiness** *n*.
great *adj* of much more than ordinary size, extent, etc; much above the average; intense; eminent; most important; more distant in a family relationship by one generation; (*often with* **at**) (*inf*) skilful; (*inf*) excellent; fine. * *n* (*inf*) a distinguished person.—**greatly** *adv*.—**greatness** *n*.
great-aunt *n* a parent's aunt.—*also* **grand-aunt**.
greatcoat *n* a large heavy coat.
Great Dane *n* a breed of very large smooth-haired dogs.
great divide *n* a watershed between major drainage systems; a significant point of division, esp death.
great-nephew *n* a nephew's or niece's son.—*also* **grandnephew**.
great-niece *n* a nephew's or niece's daughter.—*also* **grandniece**.
great-uncle *n* a parent's uncle.—*also* **grand-uncle**.
great tit *n* a common yellow, black and white Eurasian tit.
Great War *n* the First World War 1914–18.
greave *n* armour for the lower leg.
greaves *npl* the sediment of melted tallow; (*often sing*) armour to protect the legs from the ankle to the knee.
grebe *n* any of a family of swimming and diving birds.
Grecian *adj* pertaining to Greece; in the Greek style; Greek. * *n* a native or inhabitant of Greece; a Greek scholar.
Grecism *n* a Greek idiom, phrase, spirit or style; a reverent imitation of these, eg in architecture or literature.
Grecize *vti* to give a Greek form to; to imitate Greek.
Greco- *prefix* Greek.
Greco-Roman *adj* of or relating to the ancient Greek and Romans.
greed *n* excessive desire, esp for food or wealth.
greedy *adj* (**greedier, greediest**) wanting more than one needs or deserves; having too strong a desire for food and drink.—**greedily** *adv*.—**greediness** *n*.
Greek *adj* of Greece, its people, or its language. * *n* a native of Greece; the language used by Greeks; (*inf*) something unintelligible.
Greek cross *n* a cross with four equal arms.
Greek fire *n* (*ancient history*) a weapon used in sea battles consisting of an unidentified substance that ignited on contact with water.
green *adj* of the colour green; covered with plants or foliage; having a sickly appearance; unripe; inexperienced, naive; not fully processed or treated; concerned with the conservation of natural resources; (*inf*)

jealous. * *n* a colour between blue and yellow in the spectrum; the colour of growing grass; something of a green colour; (*pl*) green leafy vegetables, as spinach, etc; (*often with cap*) a person concerned with the future of the earth's environment; a grassy plot, esp the end of a golf fairway.—**greenish** *adj*.—**greenly** *adv*.—**greenness** *n*.—**greeny** *adj*.
greenback *n* a legal-tender note of US currency.
green bean *n* any of various beans with narrow edible pods.
green belt *n* a belt of parkland, farms, etc surrounding a community, designed to prevent urban sprawl.
greenery *n* (*pl* **greeneries**) green vegetation.
green-eyed *adj* jealous.
green-eyed monster *n* jealousy.
greenfinch *n* a European and Asian bird with yellow and green plumage.
green fingers *n* gardening expertise. Us and Canadian equivalent—**green thumb.**
greenfly *n* (*pl* **greenflies**) an insect pest that infests garden plants and crops.
greengage *n* a small greenish sweet variety of plum.
greenheart *n* a tropical American tree that yields a dark durable timber; the timber.
greenhorn *n* an inexperienced person; a person easily duped.
greenhouse *n* a heated building, mainly of glass, for growing plants.
greenhouse effect *n* action of radiant heat from the sun passing through the glass of greenhouses etc., warming the contents inside, where such heat is thus trapped; application of the same effect to a planet's atmosphere.—*see* **global warming.**
greening[1] *n* a type of cooking apple that is green when ripe.
greening[2] *n* growing awareness of the environment.
green light *n* permission to proceed with a plan, etc.
green pepper *n* the unripe fruit of the sweet pepper eaten raw or cooked.
greenroom *n* the actors' rest room in a theatre, the room where they can receive visitors.
greensand *n* a green sandstone
greenshank *n* a large European wading bird with greenish legs and feet.
greenstone *n* New Zealand jade; any green igneous rock that contains chlorite or epidote.
green thumb *see* **green fingers.**
greensward *n* (*arch*) (a stretch of) turf.
green tea *n* a drink made from dried unfermented tea leaves.
Greenwich Mean Time *n* the time of the meridian of Greenwich, England, used as the basis of worldwide standard time.
greenwood *n* leafy woodland.
greet *vt* to address with friendliness; to meet (a person, event, etc) in a specified way; to present itself to.—**greeter** *n*.
greeting *n* the act of welcoming with words or gestures; an expression of good wishes; (*pl*) a message of regards.
gregarious *adj* (*animals*) living in flocks and herds; (*people*) sociable, fond of company.—**gregariously** *adv*.—**gregariousness** *n*.
Gregorian *adj* pertaining to or established by Gregory, the name of various popes.
Gregorian calendar *n* the reformed calendar introduced in 1582 by Pope Gregory XIII and currently in use.
gremlin *n* an imaginary creature blamed for disruption of any procedure or of malfunction of equipment, esp in an aircraft.
grenade *n* a small bomb thrown manually or projected (as by a rifle or special launcher).
grenadier[1] *n* a soldier of the British Grenadier Guards, the first regiment of the household infantry; (*formerly*) a foot soldier who threw grenades; (*formerly*) a company made up of the tallest and strongest soldiers in the regiment.
grenadier[2] *n* a sea fish with a large head and a long, narrow tail.
grenadine[1] *n* a gauze-like dress fabric.
grenadine[2] *n* a syrup made from pomegranates; a red-orange colour.
gressorial *adj* adapted for walking; (*birds*) having three toes of the feet forward, two of them connected, and one behind.
grew *see* **grow.**
grey *see* **gray.**
greybeard *see* **graybeard.**
greyhound *n* any of a breed of tall and slender dogs noted for its great speed and keen sight.
greywracke *see* **graywracke.**
grid *n* a gridiron, a grating; an electrode for controlling the flow of electrons in an electron tube; a network of squares on a map used for easy reference; a national network of transmission lines, pipes, etc for electricity, water, gas, etc.
griddle *n* a flat metal surface for cooking.
griddlecake *n* a pancake.
gridiron *n* a framework of iron bars for cooking; anything resembling this, as a field used for American football.
gridlock *n* a traffic jam that halts all traffic at a street crossing; the breakdown of an organization or a system.
grief *n* extreme sorrow caused as by a loss; deep distress.
grief-stricken *adj* full of sorrow.
grievance *n* a circumstance thought to be unjust and cause for complaint.
grieve *vti* to feel or cause to feel grief.—**griever** *n*.—**grieving** *adj*, *n*.
grievous *adj* causing or characterized by grief; deplorable; severe.—**grievously** *adv*.—**grievousness** *n*.
griffin, griffon *n* a mythical animal with the body and tail of a lion and an eagle's beak and wings.—*also* **gryphon.**
griffon *n* a small dog with a wire-haired coat; a large hawk with a pale body and black wings, found in Africa, Asia and warm parts of Europe.
grig *n* an extravagantly vivacious person; the sandeel; a young eel; a hen with short legs; heather.
grill *vt* to broil by direct heat using a grill or gridiron; (*inf*) to question relentlessly. * *n* a device on a cooker that radiates heat downward for broiling or grilling; a gridiron; broiled or grilled food; a grille; a grillroom.—**griller** *n*.
grillage *n* an arrangement of planks and crossbeams forming a foundation in loose or marshy soil.
grille, grill *n* an open grating forming a screen.
grillroom *n* a restaurant that specializes in grilled food.
grilse *n* (*pl* **grilses, grilse**) a young salmon returning from the sea to spawn for the first time.
grim *adj* (**grimmer, grimmest**) hard and unyielding, stern; appearing harsh, forbidding; repellent, ghastly in character.—**grimly** *adv*.—**grimness** *n*.
grimace *n* a contortion of the face expressing pain, anguish, humour, etc. * *vi* to contort the face in pain, etc.—**grimacer** *n*.—**grimacingly** *adv*.
grimalkin *n* an old she-cat; a spiteful, bad-tempered old woman.
grime *n* soot or dirt, rubbed into a surface, as the skin. * *vt* to dirty, soil with grime.
grimy *adj* (**grimier, grimiest**) dirty, soiled.—**griminess** *n*.
grin *vi* (**grinning, grinned**) to smile broadly as in amusement; to show the teeth in pain, scorn, etc. * *n* a broad smile.—**grinner** *n*.
grind *vb* (**grinding, ground**) *vt* to reduce to powder or fragments by crushing; to wear down, sharpen, or smooth by friction; to rub (the teeth) harshly together; to oppress, tyrannize; to move or operate by a crank. * *vi* to be crushed, smoothed, or sharpened by grinding; to jar or grate; to work monotonously; to rotate the hips in an erotic manner. * *n* the act or sound of grinding; hard monotonous work.
grinder *n* someone or something that grinds; a molar tooth.
grindstone *n* a circular revolving stone for grinding or sharpening tools.
gringo *n* (*pl* **gringos**) (*offensive*) among Hispanics, a foreigner, esp North Americans.
grip *n* a secure grasp; the manner of holding a bat, club, racket, etc; the power of grasping firmly; mental grasp; mastery; a handle; a small travelling bag. * *vt* (**gripping, gripped**) to take firmly and hold fast.
gripe *vt* to cause sharp pain in the bowels of; (*sl*) to annoy. * *vi* (*sl*) to complain.—**griper** *n*.—**gripingly** *adv*.
grippe *n* (*formerly*) influenza.

gripper *n* one who or that which grips; a mechanical device for seizing and holding.

grisaille *n* a method of painting in grey tints so as to represent a solid body in relief; a decorative painting in grey monochrome, esp on glass.

griseous *adj* bluish-grey.

grisette *n* a lively young French working girl, esp a flirtatious one; an edible toadstool.

griskin *n* the lean part of a loin of pork.

grisly *adj* (**grislier, grisliest**) terrifying; ghastly; arousing horror.—**grisliness** *n*.

grison *n* a carnivorous mammal of Central and South America, which resembles a weasel.

grist *n* grain that is to be or has been ground; matter forming the basis of a story or analysis.

gristle *n* cartilage, esp in meat.—**gristly** *adj*.—**gristliness** *n*.

grit *n* rough particles, as of sand; firmness of spirit; stubborn courage. * *vt* (**gritting, gritted**) to clench or grind together (eg the teeth); to spread grit on (eg an icy road).

grits *npl* oats, hulled and coarsely ground; coarsely ground maize, boiled in water or milk as a food (—*also* **hominy grits**).

gritty *adj* (**grittier, grittiest**) composed of, containing, or resembling, grit; courageous.—**grittily** *adv*.—**grittiness** *n*.

grivet *n* a green and white Ethiopian monkey with a long tail.

grizzle *vt* (*inf*) to fret; to complain. * *vti* to (cause to) become grey * *n* a grey colour; hair that is, or is becoming, grey; a wig of grey hair.—**grizzled** *adj*.

grizzled *adj* streaked with grey; grey-haired.

grizzly *adj* (**grizzlier, grizzliest**) greyish; grizzled. * *n* (*pl* **grizzlies**) the grizzly bear.

grizzly bear *n* a large powerful bear of North America.

groan *vi* to utter a deep moan; to make a harsh sound (as of creaking) under sudden or prolonged strain. * *n* a deep moan; a creaking sound.—**groaner** *n*.—**groaningly** *adv*.

groat *n* (*formerly*) a British silver coin worth fourpence; a trifling sum.

groats *npl* hulled grain broken into fragments, esp oats.

grocer *n* a dealer in food and household supplies.

grocery *n* (*pl* **groceries**) a grocer's shop; (*pl*) goods, esp from a grocer.

grog *n* rum diluted with water, often spiced and served hot.

groggy *adj* (**groggier, groggiest**) (*inf*) weak and unsteady, usu through illness, exhaustion or alcohol.—**groggily** *adv*.—**grogginess** *n*.

grogram *n* a coarse cloth of silk or silk and mohair or wool.

groin *n* the fold marking the junction of the lower abdomen and the thighs; the location of the genitals.

grommet *n* a plastic or rubber ring used to protect wire, a cable, etc passing through a hole; a ring formed of a strand of rope laid round, used in pipe joints or sails (—*also* **grummet**); (*formerly*) a cannon-wad made of rope, and rammed between the powder and the ball.

gromwell *n* a herb of the borage family.

groom *n* a person employed to care for horses; a bridegroom. * *vt* to clean and care for (animals); to make neat and tidy; to train (a person) for a particular purpose.—**groomer** *n*.—**grooming** *n*.

groomsman *n* (*pl* **groomsmen**) one who attends a bridegroom; a best man.

groove *n* a long, narrow channel; a spiral track in a gramophone record for the stylus; a settled routine. * *vt* to make a groove in.

groovy *adj* (**groovier, grooviest**) (*sl*) excellent.

grope *vi* to search about blindly as in the dark; to search uncertainly for a solution to a problem. * *vt* to find by feeling; (*sl*) to fondle sexually. * *n* the act of groping.—**groper** *n*.—**gropingly** *adv*.

grosbeak *n* any finch-like bird of Europe or America with a large stout conical bill.

groschen *n* (*pl* **groschen**) a 10-penning coin used in Germany; a silver coin formerly current in Germany; in Austria, a coin with a value of one hundredth of a schilling.

grosgrain *n* a stout double-corded silk; a fabric or ribbon of this.

gros point *n* a large needlepoint stitch covering two vertical and two horizontal threads; a piece of needlework done in this.

gross *adj* fat and coarse-looking; flagrant, dense, thick; lacking in refinement; earthy; obscene; total, with no deductions. * *n* (*pl* **grosses**) an overall total; (*pl* **gross**) twelve dozen. * *vt* to earn as total revenue.—**grossly** *adv*.—**grossness** *n*.

gross domestic product *n* the total value of goods and services produced by a country in one year.

gross national product *n* the gross domestic product plus income earned from abroad.

grot[1] *n* (*poet*) a grotto.

grot[2] *n* (*Brit sl*) unpleasant mess.—**grotty** *adj* (**grottier, grottiest**) nasty, unattractive; in bad condition; unsatisfactory.

grotesque *adj* distorted or fantastic in appearance, shape, etc; ridiculous; absurdly incongruous. * *n* a grotesque person or thing; a decorative device combining distorted plant, animal and human forms.—**grotesquely** *adv*.—**grotesqueness** *n*.

grotesquery, grotesquerie *n* (*pl* **grotesqueries**) *n* something that is fantastic or distorted in shape, etc.

grotto *n* (*pl* **grottoes, grottos**) a cave, esp one with attractive features.

grotty *see* **grot**.

grouch *vi* (*inf*) to grumble or complain. * *n* (*inf*) a grumble; a person who grumbles.—**groucher** *n*.

grouchy *adj* (**grouchier, grouchiest**) bad-tempered.—**grouchily** *adv*.—**grouchiness** *n*.

ground *n* the solid surface of the earth; soil; the background, as in design; the connection of an electrical conductor with the earth; (*pl*) a basis for belief, action, or argument; the area about and relating to a building; a tract of land; sediment. * *vti* to set on the ground; to run aground or cause to run aground; to base, found, or establish; to instruct in the first principles of; to prevent (aircraft) from flying.

ground control *n* the communications and tracking equipment and staff that monitor aircraft and spacecraft in flight and during takeoff and landing.

ground cover *n* low-growing shrubs, plants and other foliage on the ground.

ground floor *n* the floor of a building on a level with the ground.

ground hog *n* a woodchuck.

grounding *n* basic general knowledge of a subject.

ground ivy *n* a trailing Eurasian plant with bluish-purple flowers.

groundless *adj* without reason.—**groundlessly** *adv*.

groundnut *n* a climbing plant of North America with an underground nut; a peanut.

ground rule *n* a fundamental rule or principle.

groundsel *n* a weed of the aster family with yellow flowers.

groundsheet *n* a waterproof sheet placed on the ground in, or as part of, a tent.

groundsman *n* (*pl* **groundsmen**) a man who looks after a cricket pitch, football pitch, park, etc.

groundswell *n* a large rolling wave; a wave of popular feeling.

groundwork *n* foundation, basis.

group *n* a number of persons or things considered as a collective unit; a small musical band of players or singers; a number of companies under single ownership; two or more figures forming one artistic design. * *vti* to form into a group or groups.

grouper *n* (*pl* **grouper, groupers**) an edible sea fish.

groupie *n* a devoted fan.

group therapy *n* (*psychol*) the simultaneous treatment of patients with similar problems through mutual discussion and exchange of experiences.

grouse[1] *n* (*pl* **grouse, grouses**) a game bird; its flesh as food.

grouse[2] *vi* (*inf*) to complain.—**grouser** *n*.

grout *n* a thin mortar used as between tiles. * *vt* to fill with grout.—**grouter** *n*.

grove *n* a small wood, generally without undergrowth.

grovel *vi* (**grovelling, grovelled** *or* **groveling, groveled**) to lie and crawl in a prostrate position as a sign of respect, fear or humility.—**groveller, groveler** *n*.—**grovellingly, grovelingly** *adv*.

grow *vb* (**growing, grew,** *pp* **grown**) *vi* to come into being; to be produced naturally; to develop, as a living thing; to increase in size, quantity, etc; (*with* **on**) to become more accustomed or acceptable to; (*with* **up**) to mature; to arise, develop. * *vt* to cause or let grow; to raise, to cultivate.—**growable** *adj*.—**grower** *n*.

growing pains *npl* muscular discomfort sometimes experienced by growing children; difficulties experienced in the early stages of a project.

growl *vi* to make a rumbling, menacing sound such as an angry dog makes. * *vt* to express in a growling manner. * *n* a growling noise; a grumble.—**growler** *n*.

growler *n* one who growls; (*arch*) a four-wheeled cab; a small iceberg; a beer jug or beer can.

grown-up *n* a fully grown person, an adult. * *adj* mature, adult; fit for an adult.

growth *n* the act or process of growing; progressive increase, development; something that grows or has grown; an abnormal formation of tissue, as a tumour.

groyne *n* a timber structure to stop the shifting of sand on a beach.

grub *vb* (**grubbing, grubbed**) *vi* to dig in the ground; to work hard. * *vt* to clear (ground) of roots; to uproot. * *n* the worm-like larva of a beetle; (*sl*) food.

grubber *n* one who or that which grubs; a grub hoe.

grubby *adj* (**grubbier, grubbiest**) dirty.—**grubbily** *adv*.—**grubbiness** *n*.

grudge *n* a deep feeling of resentment or ill will. * *vt* to be reluctant to give or admit something.—**grudger** *n*.—**grudging** *adj*.—**grudgingly** *adv*.

gruel *n* a thin porridge cooked in water or milk.

grueling, gruelling *adj* severely testing, exhausting.

gruesome *adj* causing horror or loathing.

gruff *adj* rough or surly; hoarse.—**gruffly** *adv*.—**gruffness** *n*.

grugru *n* the larva of a South American weevil, cooked for food as a delicacy; the palm tree on which this lives.

grumble *vti* to mutter in discontent; to make a rumbling sound. * *n* a complaint; a grumbling sound.—**grumbler** *n*.—**grumblingly** *adv*.

grump *n* (*inf*) a bad-tempered person.

grumpy *adj* (**grumpier, grumpiest**) bad-tempered, peevish.—**grumpily** *adv*.—**grumpiness** *n*.

grunt *vi* to make a gruff guttural sound like a pig; to say or speak in such a manner. * *n* a low gruff sound; (*sl*) a US infantry man.

grunter *n* one who or that which grunts; an edible marine American fish; a pig; (*Austral sl*) a woman who is promiscuous.

Gruyère *n* a hard, pale yellow Swiss cheese usu with holes.

gryphon *see* **griffin.**

G-string *n* a string on an instrument tuned to the note G; a string or strip worn round the waist and between the legs.

G-suit *n* a (gravity) suit designed to counteract the physiological effects of acceleration on airmen and astronauts.

GT *abbr* = *gran turismo*, a sporty touring car.

guaco *n* (*pl* **guacos**) a tropical American plant, used as an antidote to snakebites.

guaiacum *n* any of various tropical and West Indian shrubs or trees; the wood from these; a gum obtained from them, used medicinally and in the manufacture of varnishes.

guan *n* an American bird similar to a turkey.

guanaco *n* (*pl* **guanacos, guanaco**) the wild llama of South America.

guanine *n* a nitrogenous base component of the nucleic acids, DNA and RNA, also found in guano.

guano *n* (*pl* **guanos**) dung of sea birds used as manure; a similar artificially produced fertilizer.

guarantee *n* a pledge or security for another's debt or obligation; a pledge to replace something if it is substandard, etc; an assurance that something will be done as specified; something offered as a pledge or security; a guarantor. * *vt* (**guaranteeing, guaranteed**) to give a guarantee for; to promise.

guarantor *n* a person who gives a guaranty or guarantee.

guaranty *n* (*pl* **guaranties**) (*law*) a guarantee.

guard *vt* to watch over and protect; to defend; to keep from escape or trouble; to restrain. * *vi* to keep watch (against); to act as a guard. * *n* defence; protection; a posture of readiness for defence; any device to protect against injury or loss; a person or group that guards; (*boxing, fencing, cricket*) a defensive attitude; a railway official in charge of a train; (*with cap: pl*) a regiment of British or European household troops.—**guardable** *adj*.—**guarder** *n*.

guarded *adj* discreet; cautious.—**guardedly** *adv*.—**guardedness** *n*.

guardhouse *n* a building used by a military guard when not walking a post; a military jail for temporary confinement.

guardian *n* a custodian; a person legally in charge of a minor or someone incapable of taking care of their own affairs.—**guardianship** *n*.

guardrail *n* a railing, eg at the side of a road, to prevent falling; a short metal rod placed inside the rails to keep a train's wheels on the track.

guardsman *n* (*pl* **guardsmen**) an officer or soldier of the British Guards; an officer or solider of the US National Guard.

guard's van *n* the railway carriage where the guard travels, usu at the back of a train.—*also* **caboose.**

guava *n* a tropical American shrubby tree widely cultivated for its sweet acid yellow fruit.

gubernatorial *adj* pertaining to a governor or to his office.

gudgeon *n* a small edible freshwater fish; a fish used as bait in fishing; a person who is easily imposed upon; an iron pin or shaft on which a wheel revolves; (*naut*) one of the sockets into which a rudder is fixed.

guelder-rose *n* a cultivated variety of cranberry bush with large heads of sterile flowers.

Guelph, Guelf *n* a member of a powerful Italian political party in the Middle Ages, which supported the pope and sought the independence of Italy; a member of a secret society in 19th-century Italy, supporting Italian independence.

guerdon *n* (*poet*) reward. * *vt* to reward, to recompense.

guernsey *n* a particular breed of dairy cattle originally from the island of Guernsey; a close-fitting knitted woollen jersey; (*Austral*) a woollen top worn by a football player.

guerrilla, guerilla *n* a member of a small force of irregular soldiers, making surprise raids.—*also adj*.

guess *vt* to form an opinion of or state with little or no factual knowledge; to judge correctly by doing this; to think or suppose. * *n* an estimate based on guessing.—**guessable** *adj*.—**guesser** *n*.

guesstimate *n* (*inf*) an estimate based mainly on guesswork.

guesswork *n* the process or result of guessing.

guest *n* a person entertained at the home, club, etc of another; any paying customer of a hotel, restaurant, etc; a performer appearing by special invitation.

guesthouse *n* a private home or boarding-house offering accommodation.

guestroom *n* a room kept for guests.

guffaw *n* a crude noisy laugh. * *vi* to laugh boisterously.

guidance *n* leadership; advice or counsel.

guide *vt* to point out the way for; to lead; to direct the course of; to control. * *n* a person who leads or directs others; a person who exhibits and explains points of interest; something that provides a person with guiding information; a device for controlling the motion of something; a book of basic instruction; a Girl Guide.—**guidable** *adj*.—**guider** *n*.—**guiding** *adj, n*.

guidebook *n* a book containing directions and information for tourists.

guided missile *n* a military missile whose course is controlled by radar or internal instruments, etc.

guideline *n* a principle or instruction which determines conduct or policy.

guidepost *n* a direction post; a guiding principle.

guidon *n* a forked or pointed military flag, used esp by troops of light cavalry.

guild *n* a club, society; an association of people with common interests formed for mutual aid and protection, as craftsmen in the Middle Ages.—*also* **gild.**

guilder *n* a coin of the Netherlands, or of Netherlands Antilles and Surinam; a gold or silver coin formerly in circulation in Germany, Austria and the Netherlands.—*also* **gilder, gulden.**
guildhall *n* the meeting place of a guild or corporation.
guile *n* craftiness, deceit.—**guileful** *adj*.—**guilefully** *adv*.—**guilefulness** *n*.
guileless *adj* without guile; ingenuous.—**guilelessly** *adv*.—**guilelessness** *n*.
guillemot *n* a small sea bird of the auk family.
guilloche *n* (*archit*) an ornament resembling braided ribbons.
guillotine *n* an instrument for beheading by a heavy blade descending between grooved posts; a device or machine for cutting paper; a rule for limiting time for discussion in a legislature. * *vt* to execute (someone) by guillotine.—**guillotiner** *n*.
guilt *n* the fact of having done a wrong or committed an offence; a feeling of self-reproach from believing one has done a wrong.
guiltless *adj* innocent.
guilty *adj* (**guiltier, guiltiest**) having guilt; feeling or showing guilt.—**guiltily** *adv*.—**guiltiness** *n*.
guimpe *n* a short blouse worn under a pinafore dress; a piece of cloth used to disguise a low-cut neckline; the starched cloth that covers the shoulders and front of a nun's habit; gimp.
guinea *n* a former English gold coin equal to 21 shillings (£1.05).
guinea fowl *n* a domestic African bird of the pheasant family.
guinea pig *n* a rodent-like animal commonly kept as a pet, and often used in scientific experiments; a person or thing subject to an experiment.
guipure (lace) *n* a coarse lace in which the pattern is supported by bars connecting the motifs rather than founded on a net base; a kind of gimp.
guise *n* an external appearance, aspect; an assumed appearance or pretence.
guitar *n* a stringed musical instrument with a long, fretted neck, and a flat body, which is plucked with a plectrum or the fingers.—**guitarist** *n*.
gular *adj* of, in or pertaining to the gullet or throat.
gulch *n* a deep, narrow ravine.
gulden *see* **guilder.**
gules *n* (*her*) the colour red, also indicated by vertical parallel lines.
gulf *n* a large area of ocean reaching into land; a wide, deep chasm; a vast separation.
Gulf Stream *n* a warm ocean current flowing from the Gulf of Mexico northward towards Europe.
gulfweed *n* brown seaweed with air bladders which floats in dense masses in warm Atlantic waters.—*also* **sargasso, sargasso weed.**
gull *n* any of numerous long-winged web-footed sea birds.
gullet *n* the esophagus; the throat.
gullible *adj* easily deceived.—**gullibility** *n*.—**gullibly** *adv*.
gully *n* (*pl* **gullies**) a narrow trench cut by running water after rain; (*cricket*) a fielding position between the slips and point. * *vt* (**gullying, gullied**) to make gullies in.
gulp *vt* to swallow hastily or greedily; to choke back as if swallowing. * *n* a gulping or swallowing; a mouthful.—**gulper** *n*.—**gulpingly** *adv*.
gum[1] *n* the firm tissue that surrounds the teeth.
gum[2] *n* a sticky substance found in certain trees and plants; an adhesive; chewing gum. * *vb* (**gumming, gummed**) *vt* to coat or unite with gum. * *vi* to become sticky or clogged; (*with* **up**) (*inf*) to mess up, prevent from working properly.
gum ammoniac *n* a gum resin.—*also* **ammoniac.**
gum arabic *n* the gum obtained from certain species of acacia trees and used in the manufacture of adhesives and in pharmacy.
gumbo *n* (*pl* **gumbos**) a rich soup thickened with okra.
gumboil *n* an abscess in the gum.
gumboot *n* a rubber, waterproof boot, a wellington.
gumma *n* (*pl* **gummas, gummata**) a syphilitic tumour.—**gummatous** *adj*.
gummy *adj* (**gummier, gummiest**) sticky; revealing the gums, toothless.—**gummily** *adv*.—**gumminess** *n*.
gumption *n* (*inf*) shrewd practical common sense; initiative.
gum resin *n* a mixture of gum and resin exuded from certain plants and trees.
gumtree *n* a eucalyptus, or one of various other trees that yield gum.
gun *n* a weapon with a metal tube from which a projectile is discharged by an explosive; the shooting of a gun as a signal or salute; anything like a gun. * *vb* (**gunning, gunned**) *vi* to shoot or hunt with a gun; (*with* **for**) to search out in order to hurt or kill. * *vt* (*inf*) to shoot (a person); (*sl*) to advance the throttle of an engine.
gunboat *n* a small armed ship.
gunboat diplomacy *n* the threat of force used to back diplomatic activity.
guncotton *n* a highly explosive substance formed by the action of nitric and sulphuric acid upon cotton, or some other vegetable fibre.
gun dog *n* a dog trained to flush out or retrieve game shot by hunters.
gunfire *n* repeated and consecutive gunshots; the use of guns, etc, rather than other military options.
gunk *n* (*inf*) dirty, greasy, matter; gunge.
gunman *n* (*pl* **gunmen**) an armed gangster; a hired killer.
gunmetal *n* bronze with a dark tarnish; its dark-grey colour.
gunnel *see* **gunwale.**
gunner *n* a soldier, etc who helps fire artillery; a naval warrant officer in charge of a ship's guns.
gunnery *n* the science of the design and operation of large guns.
gunny *n* (*pl* **gunnies**) a strong coarse fabric made from jute used for sacking.
gunpoint *n* the muzzle of a gun; the threat of being shot.
gunpowder *n* an explosive powder used in guns, for blasting, etc.
gunrunning *n* the smuggling of firearms into a country.—**gunrunner** *n*.
gunshot *n* the range of a gun; the instance of shooting a gun or the shot fired from it.
gun-shy *adj* afraid of a loud noise; markedly distrustful.
gunslinger *n* (*sl*) a gunman or gunfighter.
gunstock *n* the wooden or metal mounting of a gun barrel.
gunwale *n* the upper edge of a ship's or boat's side.—*also* **gunnel.**
guppy *n* (*pl* **guppies**) a small vividly-coloured fish of South America and the West Indies popular for aquariums.
gurgitation *n* a whirling motion, a surging.
gurgle *vi* (*liquid*) to make a low bubbling sound; to utter with this sound. * *n* a bubbling sound.—**gurglingly** *adv*.
gurnard *n* (*pl* **gurnard, gurnards**) a spiny sea fish with an armoured head.
guru *n* (*pl* **gurus**) a Hindu or Sikh spiritual teacher; an influential leader or teacher, esp of a religious cult.
gush *vi* to issue plentifully; to have a sudden flow; to talk or write effusively. * *vt* to cause to gush. * *n* a sudden outpouring.—**gushingly** *adv*.
gusher *n* an effusive person; an oil well from which oil spouts forth.
gushy *adj* (**gushier, gushiest**) expressing excessive admiration.—**gushily** *adv*.—**gushiness** *n*.
gusset *n* a small triangular piece of cloth inserted in a garment to strengthen or enlarge a part.
gust *n* a sudden brief rush of wind; a sudden outburst. * *vi* to blow in gusts.
gustation *n* the act of tasting; the ability to taste; taste.—**gustatory** *adj*.
gusto *n* great enjoyment, zest.
gusty *adj* (**gustier, gustiest**) windy; irritable.—**gustily** *adv*.—**gustiness** *n*.
gut *n* (*often pl*) the bowels or the stomach; the intestine; tough cord made from animal intestines; (*pl*) (*sl*) daring; courage. * *vt* (**gutting, gutted**) to remove the intestines from; to destroy the interior of.
gutless *adj* (*inf*) cowardly, lacking determination.—**gutlessness** *n*.
gutsy *adj* (**gutsier, gutsiest**) (*sl*) brave, courageous; passionate; greedy.
gutta *n* (*pl* **guttae**) (*archit*) a small loop-like ornament, esp in a Doric entablature; (*med*) (*formerly*) a drop.
gutta-percha *n* the flexible hardened juice of a tropical tree; one of several trees yielding this.
guttate, guttated *adj* (*plants*) spotted; drop-like.
gutter *n* a channel for carrying off water, esp at a roadside or under

the eaves of a roof; a channel or groove to direct something (as of a bowling alley); the lowest condition of human life. * *adj* marked by extreme vulgarity or indecency. * *vt* to provide with a gutter. * *vi* to flow in rivulets; (*candle*) to melt unevenly; (*candle flame*) to flutter.—**guttering** *n*.

guttering *n* the system of gutters, pipes, etc, on exterior walls for carrying off rainwater; material for making gutters.

guttersnipe *n* a dirty child who plays in the streets, esp slum areas.

guttural *adj* formed or pronounced in the throat; harsh-sounding.—**gutturally** *adv*.—**gutturalness, gutturality, gutturalism** *n*.

gutturalize *vt* to form (a sound) in the throat; to speak in a harsh manner.—**gutturalization** *n*.

guy[1] *n* a rope, chain, etc, for fixing or steadying anything. * *vt* to fix or steady with a guy.

guy[2] *n* an effigy of Guy Fawkes made from old clothes stuffed with newspapers, etc burnt on the anniversary of the Gunpowder Plot (5 November); (*inf*) a man or boy; (*pl*) (*inf*) men or women; a shabby person. * *vt* to tease.

guzzle *vti* to gulp down food or drink greedily.—**guzzler** *n*.

gybe *vti* (*sail, boom*) to swing over from one side to the other; (*yacht*) to alter course in this way.—*also* **jibe**.

gym *n* (*inf*) a gymnasium.

gymkhana *n* a meeting featuring sports contests or athletic skills, esp horse-riding.

gymnasium *n* (*pl* **gymnasiums, gymnasia**) a room or building equipped for physical training and sports.

gymnast *n* a person skilled in gymnastics.

gymnastic *adj* pertaining to gymnastics.—**gymnastically** *adv*.

gymnastics *n sing* training in exercises devised to strengthen the body; (*pl*) gymnastic exercises; (*pl*) feats of dexterity or agility.

gymnosophist *n* one of a class of ancient Hindu philosophers who lived bare-footed and lightly clothed or naked.

gymnosperm *n* a plant whose seeds are not enclosed in a covering; a conifer or a conifer-like plant.—**gymnospermous** *adj*.

gynaecocracy, gynecocracy *n* (*pl* **gynaecocracies, gynecocracies**) female rule or supremacy.—**gynaecocratic, gynecocratic** *adj*.

gynaecology, gynecology *n* the branch of medicine that deals with the diseases and disorders of the female reproductive system.—**gynaecological, gynecological, gynaecologic, gynecologic** *adj*.—**gynaecologist, gynecologist** *n*.

gynarchy *n* (*pl* **gynarchies**) gynaecocracy.

gynoecium *n* (*pl* **gynoecia**) (*bot*) the female organs of a flower.

gynopathy *n* the condition of feeling threatened by women.—**gynopathic** *adj*.

gynophore *n* the long stalk on which the pistil is situated, as in the passion flower.—**gynophoric** *adj*.

gyp *vt* (**gypping, gypped**) (*sl*) to cheat (someone). * *n* a swindle; a swindler; a college servant at Cambridge University; (*sl*) acute pain.—*also* **gip**.

gypsum *n* a chalk-like mineral used to make plaster of Paris and fertilizer.—**gypseous, gypsiferous** *adj*.

Gypsy *n* (*pl* **Gypsies**) a member of a travelling people, orig from India, now spread throughout Europe and North America; (*without cap*) a person who looks or lives like a Gypsy.—*also* **Gipsy** (*pl* **Gipsies**).

gyral *adj* rotatory, whirling; pertaining to a gyrus.

gyrate *vi* to revolve; to whirl or spiral.—**gyration** *n*.—**gyratory** *adj*.

gyre *vt* (*poet*) to gyrate. * (*poet*) a gyration.

gyrfalcon *n* a large northern falcon, often used for hunting.—*also* **gerfalcon**.

gyro *n* (*pl* **gyros**) (*inf*) a gyroscope; a gyrocompass.

gyrocompass *n* a compass mounted on a gyroscope to keep it stable.

gyroscope *n* a wheel mounted in a ring so that its axis is free to turn in any direction, so that when spinning rapidly it keeps its original plane of rotation.—**gyroscopic** *adj*.

gyrose *adj* (*bot*) turned round like a crook.

gyrostabilizer *n* a device of two or more gyroscopes to prevent rolling of a ship or aircraft.

gyrostat *n* a gyrostabilizer.

gyrus *n* (*pl* **gyri**) a convolution (of the brain).

gyve *vt* to fetter * *n* (*usu pl*) shackles.

H (*chem symbol*) hydrogen.

ha *interj* used to express surprise, triumph, etc.—*also* **hah**.

ha. *abbr* = hectare(s).

Habakkuk *n* (*Bible*) one of the minor Old Testament book of prophets.

habeas corpus *n* a writ requiring that a prisoner be brought before a court, esp to ascertain the legality of his or her detention.

haberdasher *n* a dealer in sewing accessories; a dealer in men's clothing.—**haberdashery** *n*.

habergeon *n* a sleeveless coat of chain mail covering the neck and breast.

habile *adj* skillful.

habiliment *n* (*often pl*) clothing, attire.

habilitate *vi* to qualify for a post. * *vt* to provide working capital for a mine.—**habilitation** *n*.—**habilitator** *n*.

habit *n* a distinctive costume, as of a nun, etc; a thing done often and hence easily; a usual way of doing things; an addiction, esp to narcotics. * *vt* to clothe.

habitable *adj* capable of being lived in.—**habitability** *n*.—**habitably** *adv*.

habitat *n* the normal environment of an animal or plant.

habitation *n* the act of inhabiting; a dwelling or residence.—**habitational** *adj*.

habited *adj* wearing a habit or a dress.

habit-forming *adj* addictive.

habitual *adj* having the nature of a habit; regular.—**habitually** *adv*.—**habitualness** *n*.

habituate *vt* to accustom.—**habituation** *n*.

habitude *n* a custom or tendency; familiarity.—**habitudinal** *adj*.

habitué *n* a frequent visitor to a place.

hacienda *n* (in Spanish-speaking countries) a large estate or ranch; the main house on such an estate.

hack[1] *vt* to cut or chop (at) violently; to clear (vegetation) by chopping; (*comput*) to gain illegal access to confidential data. * *n* a gash or notch; a harsh, dry cough.

hack[2] *n* a riding horse for hire; an old worn-out horse; a mediocre or unexceptional writer; a coach for hire; (*inf*) a taxicab. * *vti* to ride a horse cross-country. * *adj* banal, hackneyed.

hackbut *n* a type of arquebus.—*also* **hagbut**.

hacker *n* a person who hacks; (*inf*) (*comput*) a person who uses computers as a hobby, esp one who uses a personal computer to gain illegal access to the computer systems of government departments or large corporations.

hacking *adj* (*cough*) short, dry, spasmodic.

hackles *npl* the hairs on the back of a dog, cat, etc, which stick out when the animal is angry or afraid.

hackney *n* a horse for driving or riding; any of an English breed of high-stepping horses; a carriage or vehicle for hire.

hackneyed *adj* made trite or banal through overuse.

hacksaw *n* a fine-toothed saw for cutting metal.

had *see* **have**.

haddock *n* (*pl* **haddocks, haddock**) an important Atlantic food fish related to the cod.

Hades *n* (*Greek myth*) the home of the dead; (*inf*) hell.—**Hadean** *adj*.

Hadith *n* (*pl* **Hadith, Hadiths**) the traditions surrounding Muhammed and his sayings; an appendix to the Koran.

hadj *n* (*pl* **hadjes**) a pilgrimage to Mecca, required of all Muslims.—*also* **hajj** (*pl* **hajjes**).

hadji *n* (*pl* **hadjis**) a Muslim who has made the pilgrimage to Mecca.—*also* **haji, hajji** (*pl* **hajjis, hajis**).
hadn't = had not.
haema-, haemo- *prefix* blood.
haemal *adj* of or relating to the blood, blood vessels or the part of the body that contains the heart.
haematic *adj* of, containing, acting on, or relating to blood. * *n* a drug that increases the level of haemoglobin in blood.
haematite *n* native ferric oxide, an important iron ore.
haematoid *adj* relating to blood; blood-like.
haemoptysis *n* the spitting or coughing up of blood or mucus containing blood.
hafiz *n* a Muslim who knows the Koran by heart; a title of respect; the guardian of the Mosque.
hafnium *n* a silvery metallic element found in zirconium.
haft *n* the handle of a weapon or tool.
hag *n* an ugly or unpleasant old woman; a witch.—**haggish** *adj*.—**haggishness** *n*.
Haggadah *n* (*pl* **Haggadoth**) (*Judaisim*) a parable or illustration of a commentary on Scripture; a book containing the order for the traditional Passover feast; a narrative of the flight from Egypt that is the main part of the Passover feast.
haggard *n adj* having an exhausted, untidy look.—**haggardly** *adv*.—**haggardness** *n*.
haggis *n* (*pl* **haggises, haggis**) a traditional Scottish dish made of minced offal with suet, onions, oatmeal, seasonings, etc.
haggle *vi* to bargain; barter; to dispute over terms; to cavil. * *n* the act of haggling.—**haggler** *n*.
hagiography *n* (*pl* **hagiographies**) the history or legends of the saints; an uncritical biography.—**hagiographer, hagiographist** *n*.—**hagriographic, hagiographical** *adj*.
hah *see* **ha**.
ha-ha[1] *interj* an exclamation of mockery; an outburst of laughter.—*also* **haw-haw**.
ha-ha[2] *n* a fence sunk in the ground as a boundary of a park or garden.
haiku *n* (*pl* **haiku**) a Japanese verse form of three lines.
hail[1] *vt* to greet; to summon by shouting or signalling, as a taxi; to welcome with approval, to acclaim. * *vi* (*with* **from**) to come from. * *interj* an exclamation of tribute, greeting, etc. * *n* a shout to gain attention; a distance within which one can be heard calling.—**hailer** *n*.
hail[2] *n* frozen raindrops; something, as abuse, bullets, etc, sent forcefully in rapid succession. * *vti* to pour down like hail.
hailstone *n* a pellet of hail.
hailstorm *n* a sudden storm of hail.
hair *n* a threadlike growth from the skin of mammals; a mass of hairs, esp on the human head; a threadlike growth on a plant.
haircut *n* a shortening and styling of hair by cutting it; the style of cutting.
hairdo *n* (*pl* **hairdos**) a particular style of hair after cutting, etc.
hairdresser *n* a person who cuts, styles, colours, etc, hair.—**hairdressing** *n*.
hairgrip *n* a clip for holding hair in position; a bobby pin.
hairless *adj* without hair; having little hair.
hairline *n* a very thin line; the outline of the hair on the head.
Hail Mary *n* (*RC Church*) a prayer to the Virgin Mary beginning with these words.
hairnet *n* a net used to keep the hair in place.
hairpiece *n* a wig or toupee; an additional piece of hair attached to a person's real hair.
hairpin *n* U-shaped pin used to hold hair in place.
hairpin bend *n* a sharply curving bend in a road, etc.
hair-raising *adj* terrifying, shocking.
hair's-breadth *n* a very small space or amount.
hairsplitting *adj* making petty distinctions; quibbling. * *n* the act of making petty distinctions.—**hairsplitter** *n*.
hairspring *n* a slender, hair-like coil spring, as in a watch.
hairstyle *n* the way in which hair is arranged.—**hairstylist** *n*.
hairweaving *n* the technique of attaching strands of false hair to the follicles of the head.
hairy *adj* (**hairier, hairiest**) covered with hair; (*inf*) difficult, dangerous.—**hairiness** *n*.
haji, hajji *see* **hadji**.
hajj *see* **hadj**.
hake *n* (*pl* **hake, hakes**) a marine food fish related to the cod.
hakim *n* a judge, administrator or governor of an Islamic country; a Muslim physician.
Halakah, Halacha *n* (*pl* **Halakoth, Halachoth**) (*Judaism*) traditional law containing minor precepts in addition to the Mosaic law; legal literature in general.
halal *n* meat from animals butchered according to Muslim law. * *adj* of or pertaining to such meat.—*also* **hallal**.
halation *n* (*photog, TV*) a halo-like appearance round an object, caused by light reflection.
halberd, halbert *n* a medieval weapon consisting of a long staff to which an axe with a spear-like point was affixed.
halberdier *n* a soldier armed with a halberd.
halcyon *adj* calm, gentle, peaceful. * *n* a fabled bird (probably the kingfisher) that nested at sea and calmed it.
hale *adj* healthy and strong.
half *n* (*pl* **halves**) either of two equal parts of something; (*inf*) a half-price ticket for a bus, etc; (*inf*) half a pint. * *adj* being a half; incomplete; partial. * *adv* to the extent of a half; (*inf*) partly.
half-and-half *n* something half one thing and half another, esp a mixture of mild and bitter beer. * *adj* partly one thing and partly another. * *adv* in two equal parts.
halfback *n* (*football, hockey*) a player occupying a position between the forwards and the fullbacks; a player in this position in other sports.
half-baked *adj* (*inf*) poorly planned or thought-out; (*inf*) stupid.
half-brother *n* a brother through one parent only.
half-caste *n* a person whose parents are of different races.
half cock *n* the middle position of a gun's hammer; **at half cock** not prepared.—**half-cocked** *adj*.
half-hearted *adj* with little interest, enthusiasm, etc.—**half-heartedly** *adv*.—**half-heartedness** *n*.
half-hour *n* 30 minutes; the point 30 minutes after the beginning of an hour.
half-life *n* the time taken for half the atoms in a radioactive substance to decay.
half-mast *n* the position to which a flag is lowered as a sign of mourning.
half-measure *n* (*often pl*) an inadequate action; a compromise.
half-moon *n* the moon at its phase when half the disc is illuminated; something shaped like this. * *adj* in the shape of a half-moon.
half-nelson *n* a wrestling hold, pinning the arm of an opponent behind the back from behind.
half note *n* (*mus*) a note with the time value of half of a semibreve.—*also* **minim**.
halfpenny (*pl* **halfpence**) *n* a bronze coin worth two farthings in predecimal British currency.
half-sister *n* a sister through one parent only.
half title *n* a short title on the page before the title page of a book, a bastard title.
half-term *n* a short holiday in the middle of a school term.
half-time *n* (*sport*) an interval between two halves of a game.
halftone *n* an illustration printed from a relief plate, showing light and shadow by means of minute dots.
half-track *n* a (military) vehicle with wheels in front but driven by caterpillar tracks at the rear.
half-truth *n* a statement that is only partly true.
half volley *n* (*tennis, etc*) the striking of the ball the instant it bounces.
halfway *adj* midway between two points, etc.
halfwit *n* a stupid or silly person; a mentally retarded person.—**halfwitted** *adj*.—**halfwittedly** *adv*.—**halfwittedness** *n*.
halibut *n* (*pl* **halibut, halibuts**) a large marine flatfish used as food.

halide *n* a compound containing halogen; a haloid.

halitosis *n* bad-smelling breath.

hall *n* a public building with offices, etc; a large room for exhibits, gatherings, etc; the main house on a landed estate; a college building, esp a dining room; a vestibule at the entrance of a building; a hallway.

hallal *see* **halal.**

Hallel *n* (*Judaism*) Psalms 113–118 chanted as part of morning services during Passover and other festivals.

hallelujah, halleluiah *interj* an exclamation of praise to God. * *n* a praising of God; a musical composition having this as its theme.—*also* **alleluia.**

halliard *see* **halyard.**

hallmark *n* a mark used on gold, silver or platinum articles to signify a standard of purity, weight, date of manufacture; a mark or symbol of high quality; a characteristic feature. * *vt* to stamp with a hallmark.

hallo *see* **hello.**

hallow *vt* to make or regard as holy.—**hallowed** *adj*.—**hallowedness** *n*.—**hallower** *n*.

Hallowe'en, Halloween *n* the eve of All Saints' Day, October 31.

Hallowmas *n* (*formerly*) All Saints' Day, November 1.

Hallstatt, Hallstadt *adj* of or denoting the final period of the Bronze Age and the first period of the Iron Age (9th–4th centuries bc).

hallucinate *vti* to have or cause to have hallucinations.—**hallucinator** *n*.

hallucination *n* the apparent perception of sights, sounds, etc, that are not actually present; something perceived in this manner.—**hallucinational, hallucinative** *adj*.—**hallucinatory** *adj*.

hallucinogen *n* a drug that produces hallucinations.—**hallucinogenic** *adj*.

hallux (*pl* **halluces**) the big toe; the first digit on the back foot of an amphibian, bird, mammal, or reptile.

halm *see* **haulm.**

halo *n* (*pl* **haloes, halos**) a circle of light, as around the sun; a symbolic ring of light around the head of a saint in pictures; the aura of glory surrounding an idealized person or thing. * *vt* (**haloing, haloed**) to surround with a halo.

halogen *n* any of the five chemical elements fluorine, chlorine, bromine, iodine and astatine.—**halogenous** *adj*.

halt[1] *n* a temporary interruption or cessation of progress; a minor station on a rail line. * *vti* to stop or come to a stop.

halt[2] *vi* to falter; to hesitate.—**halting** *adj*.

halter *n* a rope or strap for tying or leading an animal; a style of women's dress top tied behind the neck and waist leaving the back and arms bare. * *vt* to put a halter on (a horse, etc).

halve *vt* to divide equally into two; to reduce by half; (*golf*) to play one hole in the same number of strokes as one's opponent.

halves *see* **half.**

halyard *n* a line for hoisting or lowering a sail, yard, or flag.—*also* **halliard.**

ham *n* the upper part of a pig's hind leg, salted, smoked, etc; the meat from this area; (*inf*) the back of the upper thigh; (*inf*) an actor who overacts; (*inf*) a licensed amateur radio operator. * *vti* (**hamming, hammed**) to speak or move in an exaggerated manner, to overact.

hamadryad *n* (*pl* **hamadryads, hamadryades**) (*Greek myth*) a wood nymph; a giant cobra, the king cobra.

hamadryas *n* a North African baboon, the male of which has a heavy mane of silvery hair.

hamal *n* a porter in several Muslim countries.—*also* **hammal, hammaul.**

Hamburg *n* a rich, black grape; a breed of black domestic fowl.

hamburger *n* ground beef; a cooked patty of such meat, often in a bread roll with pickle, etc.

hame[1] *n* either of two curved bars for the traces on the collar of a draught horse.

hame[2] *n* (*Scot*) home.

ham-handed, ham-fisted *adj* (*inf*) clumsy.

Hamite *n* a descendant of Ham, son of Noah; a member of the Hamitic race.

Hamitic *adj* relating to Ham, the races descended from him, or the languages they speak. * *n* any of a group of languages spoken in North Africa.

hamlet *n* a very small village.

hammal, hammaul *see* **hamal.**

hammer *n* a tool for pounding, driving nails, etc, having a heavy head and a handle; a thing like this in shape or use, as the part of the gun that strikes the firing pin; a bone of the middle ear; a heavy metal ball attached to a wire thrown in athletic contests; **hammer and tongs** with great force. * *vti* to strike repeatedly, as with a hammer; to drive, force, or shape, as with hammer blows; (*inf*) to defeat utterly.—**hammerer** *n*.

hammerhead *n* a shark with a mallet-shaped head.

hammock *n* a length of strong cloth or netting suspended by the ends and used as a bed.

hammy *adj* (**hammier, hammiest**) (*inf*) overacting; exaggerated.

hamper[1] *vt* to hinder; to interfere with; to encumber.—**hamperer** *n*.

hamper[2] *n* a large, usu covered, basket for storing or transporting food and crockery, etc.

hamster *n* a small short-tailed rodent with cheek pouches.

hamstring *n* any of the tendons at the back of the thigh that flex and rotate the leg. * *vt* (**hamstringing, hamstrung**) to cripple by severing the hamstring of; to render useless, to thwart.

hamulus (*pl* **hamuli**) *n* a small hook-like projection at the end of the bones or between the fore and hind wings of a bee or bee-like insect.—**hamular** *adj*.

hand *n* the part of the arm below the wrist, used for grasping; a side or direction; possession or care; control; an active part; a promise to marry; skill; one having a special skill; handwriting; applause; help; a hired worker; a source; one of a ship's crew; anything like a hand, as a pointer on a clock; the breadth of a hand, four inches when measuring the height of a horse; the cards held by a player at one time; a round of card play; (*inf*) applause. * *adj* of, for, or controlled by the hand. * *vt* to give as with the hand; to help or conduct with the hand. * *vi* (*with* **on**) to pass to the next.

handbag *n* a woman's small bag for carrying personal items.—*also* **bag, pocket book, purse.**

handbill *n* a small printed notice to be passed out by hand.

handbook *n* a book containing useful instructions.

handcart *n* a small cart pulled or pushed by hand.

handcuff *n* (*usu pl*) either of a pair of connected steel rings for shackling the wrists of a prisoner. * *vt* to manacle.

handed *adj* having or involving (a specified kind or number of) hands.

handfast *vt* (*formerly*) to pledge or betroth; to grip with the hand. * *n* a contract of betrothal.

handful *n* as much as will fill the hand; a few; (*inf*) a person who is difficult to handle or control.

handicap *n* a mental or physical impairment; a contest in which difficulties are imposed on, or advantages given to, contestants to equalize their chances; such a difficulty or advantage; any hindrance. * *vt* (**handicapping, handicapped**) to give a handicap to; to hinder.—**handicapper** *n*.

handicapped *adj* mentally or physically disabled.

handicraft *n* a skill involving the hands, such as basketwork, pottery, etc; an item of pottery, etc made by hand.

handiwork *n* handmade work; something done by a person or thing.

handkerchief *n* a small cloth for blowing the nose, etc.

handle *vt* to touch, hold, or move with the hand; to manage or operate with the hands; to manage, deal with; to buy and sell (goods). * *vi* to react in a specified way. * *n* a part of anything designed to be held or grasped by the hand.—**handleable** *adj*.—**handling** *n*.

handlebar *n* (*often pl*) the curved metal bar with a grip at each end used to steer a bicycle, etc; a bushy moustache with curved ends.

handler *n* a person who trains or controls animals, such as a police dog.

handless *adj* awkward, clumsy.

handmade *adj* made by hand, carefully crafted.

handmaid(en) *n* a female servant.

hand-out *n* an item of food, clothing, etc, given free to the needy; a statement given to the press to replace or supplement an oral presentation.

hand-picked *adj* carefully selected.

handrail *n* a narrow rail for gripping as a support.
hands-on *adj* involving active participation and operating experience.
handsaw *n* any saw that is used in one hand only.
handsel *n* (*formerly*) a good-luck gift on beginning something; a house-warming present; a New Year gift. * *vt* to give a handsel to; to inaugurate; to be first to use something.
handset *n* a telephone earpiece and mouthpiece as a single unit.
handshake *n* a grasping and shaking of a person's hand as a greeting or when concluding an agreement.
handsome *adj* good-looking; dignified; generous; ample.—**handsomely** *adv*.—**handsomeness** *n*.
handspike *n* an iron-shod bar or pipe used as a lever.
handspring *n* (*gymnastics*) a leaping forwards or backwards from a standing position into a handstand then back onto the feet.
handstand *n* the act of supporting the body on the hands with the feet in the air.
hand-to-hand *adj* (*fighting*) at close quarters.
hand-to-mouth *adj* having barely enough food or money to survive.—*also adv*.
handwriting *n* writing done by hand; a style of such writing.—**handwritten** *adj*.
handy *adj* (**handier, handiest**) convenient, near; easy to use; skilled with the hands.—**handily** *adv*.—**handiness** *n*.
handyman *n* (*pl* **handymen**) a person who does odd jobs.
hang *vb* (**hanging, hung**) *vt* to support from above, esp by a rope, chain, etc, to suspend; (*door, etc*) to attach by hinges to allow to swing freely; to decorate with pictures, or other suspended objects; (*wallpaper*) to stick to a wall; to exhibit (works of art); to prevent (a jury) from coming to a decision; (*pt, pp* **hanged**) to put to execute or kill by suspending by the neck. * *vi* to be suspended, so as to dangle loosely; (*clothing, etc*) to fall or flow in a certain direction; to lean, incline, or protrude; to depend; to remain in the air; to be in suspense; to fall or droop; (*pt, pp* **hanged**) to die by hanging; (*with* **about, around**) to loiter; (*with* **back**) to hesitate, be reluctant; (*with* **out**) to meet regularly at a particular place. * *n* the way in which anything hangs; (*sl*) a damn.
hangar *n* a large shelter where aircraft are built, stored or repaired.—*also vt*.
hangbird *n* the Baltimore oriole; any North American bird that builds a hanging nest.
hangdog *adj* abject or ashamed in appearance or manner.
hanger *n* a device on which something is hung; one who hangs things.
hanger-on *n* (*pl* **hangers-on**) a sycophantic follower.
hang-glider *n* an unpowered aircraft consisting of a metal frame over which a lightweight material is stretched, with a harness for the pilot suspended below.—**hang gliding** *n*.
hanging *n* the act of executing a person by suspending them by the neck; something hung, as a picture; (*pl*) decorative draperies hung on walls. * *adj* suspended in the air; undecided; overhanging; situated on a steep slope.
hangman *n* (*pl* **hangmen**) a person who executes prisoners by hanging them.
hangnail *n* a thin strip of torn skin at the root of a fingernail.
hangout *n* a favourite meeting place.
hangover *n* the unpleasant after-effects of excessive consumption of alcohol; something surviving from an earlier time.
hang-up *n* an emotional preoccupation with something.
hank *n* a coiled or looped bundle of wool, rope, etc.
hanker *vi* (*with* **after, for**) to desire longingly.—**hankerer** *n*.—**hankering** *n*.
hanky, hankie *n* (*pl* **hankies**) (*inf*) a handkerchief.
hanky-panky *n* (*inf*) foolish behaviour; dishonesty; illicit sexual relations.
Hansard *n* the official, printed verbatim reports of British parliamentary proceedings.
hanse *n* a medieval guild of merchants; a fee paid by new members of such a guild; (*with cap*) a town of the Hanseatic League; the Hanseatic League.—**hanseatic** *adj*.
Hanseatic League *n* a confederacy of merchants or commercial towns in northern Germany and elsewhere, which lasted from the 14th–19th centuries.
hansom (cab) *n* a light two-wheeled covered horse-drawn carriage, with the driver's seat raised behind.
hap *vb* (**happing, happed**) *vi* (*arch*) to happen or befall. * *vt* to cover up; to wrap up warmly. * *n* (*arch*) chance; luck; a fortunate accident; a covering of any kind.
haphazard *adj* not planned; random. * *adv* by chance.—**haphazardly** *adv*.—**haphazardness** *n*.
hapless *adj* unfortunate, unlucky.—**haplessness** *n*.
haploid *adj* (*cell nucleus, organism*) possessing only half the normal number of chromosomes. * *n* a single set of unpaired chromosomes.
haply *adv* (*formerly*) by chance.
happen *vi* to take place; to be, occur, or come by chance.
happening *n* an occurrence; an improvization.
happy *adj* (**happier, happiest**) fortunate; having, expressing, or enjoying pleasure or contentment; pleased; appropriate, felicitous.—**happily** *adv*.—**happiness** *n*.
happy-go-lucky *adj* irresponsible; carefree.
happy hour *n* a particular time of day when a bar, hotel, etc, sells drinks at reduced prices
happy medium *n* a middle course between extremes.
hapteron *n* (*pl* **haptera**) the tissue in seaweed and related plants that enables them to attach themselves to a host object.
haptic *adj* of or relating to the sense of touch.
harakiri *n* ritual suicide by disembowelment.—*also* **harikari**.
harangue *n* a tirade; a lengthy, forceful speech. * *vti* to make a harangue, to address vehemently.—**haranguer** *n*.
harass *vt* to annoy, to irritate; to trouble (an enemy) by constant raids and attacks.—**harasser** *n*.—**harassment** *n*.
harbinger *n* a person or thing that announces or presages the arrival of another, a forerunner.
harbour, harbor *n* a protected inlet for anchoring ships; any place of refuge. * *vt* to shelter or house; (*grudge, etc*) to keep in the mind secretly. * *vi* to take shelter.—**harbourer, harborer** *n*.
harbourage, harborage *n* a port or anchorage for ships.
hard *adj* firm, solid, not easily cut or punctured; difficult to comprehend; difficult to accomplish; difficult to bear, painful; severe, unfeeling, ungenerous; indisputable, intractable; (*drugs*) addictive and damaging to health; (*weather*) severe; (*currency*) stable in value; (*news*) definite, not speculative; (*drink*) very alcoholic; (*water*) having a high mineral content that prevents lathering with soap; (*colour, sound*) harsh. * *adv* with great effort or intensity; earnestly, with concentration; so as to cause hardness; with difficulty; with bitterness or grief; close, near by.—**hardness** *n*.
hardback *n* a book bound with a stiff cover.—*also adj*.
hard-bitten *adj* (*inf*) tough, seasoned.
hardboard *n* a stiff board made of compressed wood chips.
hard-boiled *adj* (*eggs*) boiled until solid; (*inf*) unfeeling.
hard cash *n* payment in coins and notes as opposed to cheque, credit card, etc.
hard copy *n* output (as from microfilm or a computer) on paper.
hard core *n* the stubborn inner group in an organization that is resistant to change; the heavy foundation material for a road.
hard-core *adj* of a hard core; utterly entrenched; (*pornography*) showing sexual acts in explicit detail.
hard disk *n* (*comput*) a rigid magnetic disk in a sealed unit capable of much greater storage capacity than a floppy disk.
harden *vti* to make or become hard.—**hardener** *n*.
hard-headed *adj* shrewd and unsentimental; practical.—**hard-headedly** *adv*.—**hard-headedness** *n*.
hardhearted *adj* unfeeling; cruel.—**hardheartedly** *adv*.—**hardheartedness** *n*.
hard-hitting *adj* forcefully effective.
hard line *n* an aggressive, unyielding policy.—**hard-line** *adj*.—**hardliner** *n*.
hardly *adv* scarcely; barely; with difficulty; not to be expected.

hardpan *n* a hard, impervious layer of clay below the soil; a solid foundation.
hard sell *n* an aggressive selling technique.
hardship *n* something that causes suffering or privation.
hard shoulder *n* in UK, a raised strip of land alongside a motorway for vehicles to make emergency stops.
hardtack *n* a hard, saltless biscuit formerly eaten by seamen.
hard-up *adj* (*inf*) short of money.
hardware *n* articles made of metal as tools, nails, etc; (*comput*) the mechanical and electronic components that make up a computer system.
hardwood *n* the close-grained wood of deciduous trees.
hardy *adj* (**hardier, hardiest**) bold, resolute; robust; vigorous; able to withstand exposure to physical or emotional hardship.—**hardily** *adv*.—**hardiness** *n*.
hare *n* (*pl* **hare, hares**) any of various timid, swift, long-eared mammals, resembling but larger than the rabbit.
harebell *n* the bluebell; the wild hyacinth.
harebrained *adj* flighty; foolish.
harelip *n* a congenital deformity of the upper lip in the form of a vertical fissure.—**harelipped** *adj*.
harem *n* the usu secluded part of a Muslim household where the women live; the women in a harem.
haricot *n* a type of French bean with an edible light-coloured seed.
harikari *see* **harakiri.**
hark *vi* to listen; (*with* **back**) to retrace a course; to revert (to).
harken *see* **hearken.**
harlequin *n* the performer in a pantomime who wears parti-coloured garments and carries a wand. * *adj* fantastic or full of trickery; colourful.
harlequinade *n* a play or the part of a pantomime in which Harlequin plays a leading role; buffoonery.
harlot *n* (*formerly*) a prostitute.—**harlotry** *n*.
harm *n* hurt; damage; injury. * *vt*. to inflict hurt, damage, or injury upon.—**harmer** *n*.
harmattan *n* a hot dust-laden wind that blows from the interior to the west coast of Africa.
harmful *adj* hurtful.—**harmfully** *adv*.—**harmfulness** *n*.
harmless *adj* not likely to cause harm.—**harmlessly** *adv*.—**harmlessness** *n*.
harmonic *adj* (*mus*) of or in harmony. * *n* an overtone; (*pl*) the science of musical sounds.—**harmonically** *adv*.
harmonica *n* a small wind instrument that produces tones when air is blown or sucked across a series of metal reeds; a mouth-organ.
harmonious *adj* fitting together in an orderly and pleasing manner; agreeing in ideas, interests, etc; melodious.—**harmoniously** *adv*.
harmonium *n* a keyboard musical instrument whose tones are produced by thin metal reeds operated by foot bellows.
harmonize *vi* to be in harmony; to sing in harmony. * *vt* to make harmonious.—**harmonization** *n*.
harmony *n* (*pl* **harmonies**) a pleasing agreement of parts in colour, size, etc; agreement in action, ideas, etc; the pleasing combination of musical tones in a chord; a collation of parallel narratives, esp of the Gospels, with a commentary.
harness *n* the leather straps and metal pieces by which a horse is fastened to a vehicle, plough, etc; any similar fastening or attachment, eg for a parachute, hang-glider. * *vt* to put a harness on; to control so as to use the power of.—**harnesser** *n*.
harp *n* a stringed musical instrument played by plucking. * *vi* (*with* **on** *or* **upon**) to talk persistently (on some subject).—**harpist, harper** *n*.
harpoon *n* a barbed spear with an attached line, for spearing whales, etc. * *vt* to strike with a harpoon.—**harpooner** *n*.
harpsichord *n* a musical instrument resembling a grand piano whose strings are plucked by a mechanism rather than struck.—**harpsichordist** *n*.
harpy *n* (*pl* **harpies**) a grasping, vicious person.
harquebus *see* **arquebus.**
harridan *n* a disreputable, shrewish old woman.
harrier *n* a small breed of hound used for hunting hares; a cross-country runner.
harrow *n* a heavy frame with spikes, spring teeth, or disks for breaking up and levelling ploughed ground. * *vt* to draw a harrow over (land); to cause mental distress to.—**harrower** *n*.—**harrowing** *adj, n*.—**harrowment** *n*.
harry *vt* (**harrying, harried**) to torment or harass.
harsh *adj* unpleasantly rough; jarring on the senses or feelings; rigorous; cruel.—**harshly** *adv*.—**harshness** *n*.
hart *n* (*pl* **hart, harts**) a male deer, especially the red deer, aged five years or more.
hartal *n* (*Hinduism*) the closing of shops as a sign of mourning or as a political gesture.
hartebeest, hartbeest *n* the South African antelope.
hartshorn *n* the antler of a hart; sal volatile.
harum-scarum *adj* (*inf*) rash, reckless. * *n* a giddy rash person.
haruspex *n* (*pl* **haruspices**) in ancient Rome, a soothsayer who foretold events by inspecting the entrails of sacrificial animals.
harvest *n* (the season of) gathering in the ripened crops; the yield of a particular crop; the reward or product of any exertion or action. * *vti* to gather in (a crop). * *vt* to win by achievement.—**harvester** *n*.—**harvesting** *n*.
harvester *n* a person who harvests; a harvesting machine esp a combine harvester.
harvest moon *n* the full moon nearest the time of the September equinox.
has *see* **have.**
has-been *n* (*inf*) a person or thing that has lost its former popularity or celebrity status.
hash[1] *n* a chopped mixture of reheated cooked meat and vegetables. * *vt* to chop up (meat or vegetables) for hash; to mix or mess up.
hash[2] *n* (*inf*) hashish.
hashish *n* resin derived from the leaves and shoots of the hemp plant, smoked or chewed as an intoxicant.
hasn't = has not.
hasp *n* a hinged fastening for a door, etc, esp a metal piece fitted over a staple and fastened as by a bolt or padlock.
hassock *n* a firm cushion used as a footstool or seat.
hast (*arch*) *the second person sing of* **have,** used with **thou.**
hastate *adj* spear-shaped (of a leaf).
haste *n* quickness of motion; urgency. * *vi* (*poet*) to hasten.
hasten *vt* to accelerate; to cause to hurry. * *vi* to move or act with speed.—**hastener** *n*.
hasty *adj* (**hastier, hastiest**) done in a hurry; rash, precipitate.—**hastily** *adv*.—**hastiness** *n*.
hat *n* a covering for the head. * *vt* (**hatting, hatted**) to cover with a hat.
hatband *n* a band or ribbon around the base of a hat; a black cloth band worn as a token of mourning.
hatbox *n* a box or case for a hat or hats.
hatch[1] *n* a small door or opening (as on an aircraft or spaceship); an opening in the deck of a ship or in the floor or roof of a building; a lid for such an opening; a hatchway.
hatch[2] *vt* to produce (young) from the egg, esp by incubating; to devise (eg a plot). * *vi* to emerge from the egg; to incubate.—**hatchable** *adj*.—**hatcher** *n*.
hatch[3] *vt* (*drawing, engraving*) to shade using closely spaced parallel lines or incisions.—**hatching** *n*.
hatchback *n* a sloping rear end on a car with a door; a car of this design.
hatchery *n* (*pl* **hatcheries**) a place for hatching eggs, esp of fish.
hatchet *n* a small axe with a short handle.
hatchet job *n* (*inf*) devastating or malicious verbal or written criticism.
hatchet man *n* a person hired to perform unpleasant tasks; a critic specializing in invective.
hatchment *n* (*her*) a diamond-shaped tablet bearing a dead person's armorial bearings, placed on a house or tomb.
hatchway *n* an opening in a ship's deck or in a floor or roof; a passage giving access to an enclosed space (as a cellar).

hate *vt* to feel intense dislike for. * *vi* to feel hatred; to wish to avoid. * *n* a strong feeling of dislike or contempt; the person or thing hated.—**hater** *n*.

hateful *adj* deserving or arousing hate.—**hatefully** *adv*.—**hatefulness** *n*.

hath (*arch*) *the third person sing of* **have**.

hatred *n* intense dislike or enmity.

hatter *n* a person who makes or sells hats.

hat trick *n* (*cricket*) the taking of three wickets with three successive bowls; the scoring of three successive goals, points, etc in any game.

hauberk *n* a coat of armour, often sleeveless, formed of chain mail, which reached below the knees.

haugh *n* (*Scot*) a small, low-lying riverside meadow.

haughty *adj* (**haughtier, haughtiest**) having or expressing arrogance.—**haughtily** *adv*.—**haughtiness** *n*.

haul *vti* to move by pulling; to transport by truck, etc. * *n* the act of hauling; the amount gained, caught, etc, at one time; the distance over which something is transported.

haulage *n* the transport of commodities; the charge for this.

hauler *n* a person or business that transports goods by road.

haulm *n* the stalk of potatoes, peas, etc, esp after the crop has been gathered.—*also* **halm**.

haunch *n* the part of the body around the hips; the leg and loin of a deer, sheep, etc.—**haunched** *adj*.

haunt *vt* to visit often or continually; to recur repeatedly to. * *vi* to linger; to appear habitually as a ghost. * *n* a place often visited.—**haunter** *n*.

haunted *adj* supposedly visited by ghosts; obsessed; anxious, worried.

haunting *adj* constantly recurring in the mind; unforgettable.—**hauntingly** *adv*.

Hausa *n* a member of the negroid people of West Africa living chiefly in Nigeria; the language of these people.

haustellum *n* (*pl* **haustella**) the tip of the proboscis of the housefly or similar insects used for sucking foods.

hautbois, hautboy *n* (*pl* **hautbois, hautboy**) (*arch*) the oboe.

haute couture *n* high fashion.

haute cuisine *n* high-class cooking.

hauteur *n* arrogance, haughtiness.

Havana (cigar) *n* a cigar rolled from Cuban tobacco.

have *vt* (**has, having,** *pp* **had**) to have in one's possession; to possess as an attribute; to hold in the mind; to experience; to give birth to; to allow, or tolerate; to arrange or hold; to engage in; to cause, compel, or require to be; to to be obliged; (*sl*) to have sexual intercourse with; to be pregnant with; (*inf*) to hold at a disadvantage; (*inf*) to deceive; to accept or receive; to consume food, drink, etc; to show some quality; to perplex.

haven *n* a place where ships can safely anchor; a refuge.

haven't = have not.

haver *vi* (*Scot*) to talk foolishly or in consequently; to dither. * *n* (*pl*) nonsense.

haversack *n* a canvas bag similar to a knapsack but worn over one shoulder.

havoc *n* widespread destruction or disorder. * *vt* (**havocking, havocked**) to lay waste.

haw *n* (the berry of) the hawthorn.

Hawaiian *adj* pertaining to Hawaii, its inhabitants or its language. * *n* an inhabitant of Hawaii; a Polynesian language spoken in Hawaii.

hawfinch *n* a rare European finch with a stout bill, brown plumage and black-and-white wings.

haw-haw *see* **ha-ha**[1].

hawk[1] *n* any of numerous birds of prey; a person who advocates aggressive or intimidatory action. * *vti* to hunt with a hawk; to strike like a hawk.—**hawkish** *adj*.—**hawkishly** *adv*.

hawk[2] *vti* to clear the throat (of) audibly. * *n* the sound of this.

hawk[3] *vt* to offer goods for sale, as in the street; to spread gossip. * *vi* to peddle.

hawker *n* a person who goes about offering goods for sale; a person who hunts with a trained hawk.

hawk-eyed *adj* keen-sighted; vigilant.

hawkweed *n* a yellow-flowered plant of the aster family.

hawse *n* (*naut*) the part of a ship's bows where the hawseholes are situated; the distance from the bow of an anchored ship to the anchor. * *vi* (*naut*) to pitch violently when at anchor.

hawsehole *n* (*naut*) one of the two holes in the upper part of a ship's bows through which the anchor cables pass when the vessel is moored.

hawser *n* (*naut*) a heavy rope for towing, mooring, etc.

hawthorn *n* any of a genus of spring-flowering spiny shrubs or trees with white or pink flowers and red fruit.

hay *n* grass cut and dried for fodder.

haybox *n* an airtight box packed with hay or any other natural insulating material used to keep partially cooked food warm and allow to cook by retained heat.

haycock *n* a conical pile of hay left in the fields to dry out.

hay fever *n* an allergic reaction to pollen, causing irritation of the nose and eyes.

haymaker *n* one who lifts and spreads hay; either of two machines used in haymaking; a wild punch.

haystack, hayrick *n* a pile of stacked hay ready for storing.

haywire *adj* (*inf*) out of order; disorganized.

hazard *n* a risk; a danger; an obstacle on a golf course. * *vt* to risk; to venture.—**hazardable** *adj*.

hazardous *adj* dangerous; risky.—**hazardously** *adv*.—**hazardousness** *n*.

haze *n* a thin vapour of fog, smoke, etc. in the air; slight vagueness of mind. * *vti* to make or become hazy.

hazel *n* a tree with edible nuts; a light-brown colour. * *adj* light-brown.

hazelnut *n* the edible nut of the hazel.

hazy *adj* (**hazier, haziest**) misty; vague.—**hazily** *adv*.—**haziness** *n*.

H-bomb *n* a hydrogen bomb.

HC *abbr* = Holy Communion; House of Commons.

HCF *abbr* = highest common factor.

HDTV *abbr* = high-definition television.

HE *abbr* = high explosive; His Eminence; His (or Her) Excellency.

He (*chem symbol*) helium.

he *pron* the male person or animal named before; a person (male or female). * *n* a male person or animal.

head *n* the part of an animal or human body containing the brain, eyes, ears, nose and mouth; the top part of anything; the foremost part; the chief person; (*pl*) a unit of counting; the striking part of a tool; mind; understanding; the topic of a chapter, etc; crisis, conclusion; pressure of water, steam, etc; the source of a river, etc; froth, as on beer. * *adj* at the head, top or front; coming from in front; chief, leading. * *vt* to command; to lead; to cause to go in a specified direction; to set out; to travel (in a particular direction); to strike (a football) with the head.—**headless** *adj*.

headache *n* a continuous pain in the head; (*inf*) a cause of worry or trouble.—**headachy** *adj*.

headband *n* a ribbon or band worn around the head; a narrow strip of cloth stitched to the top of the spine of a book for protection or decoration.

headboard *n* a board that forms the head of a bed, etc.

headdress *n* a decorative covering for the head.

headed *adj* having (a specified kind of) head; having a heading.

header *n* a dive with the head first; (*scoccer*) the action of striking the ball with the head.

headfirst *adj* with the head in front; recklessly.—*also adv*.

headgear *n* a covering for the head, a hat, cap, etc.

head-hunt *vt* to cut off and preserve the heads of enemies as trophies; a person who recruits executive personnel.—**head-hunter** *n*.—**head-hunting** *n*.

heading *n* something forming the head, top, or front; the title, topic, etc of a chapter, etc; the direction in which a vehicle is moving.

headland *n* a promontory; unploughed land at the ends of a furrow.
headless *adj* being without a head; leaderless.
headlamp, headlight *n* a light at the front of a vehicle.
headline *n* printed lines at the top of a newspaper article giving the topic; a brief news summary. * *vt* to give featured billing or publicity to.
headlong *adj, adv* with the head first; with uncontrolled speed or force; rashly.
headman *n* (*pl* **headmen**) the chieftain or leader of a tribe; a foreman or overseer.
headmaster, headmistress *n* the principal of a school.—**headmastership, headmistress-ship** *n*.
headmost adj foremost
head-on *adj, adv* with the head or front foremost; without compromise.
head over heels *adv* as if somersaulting; completely, utterly, deeply.
headphone *n* one of two radio receivers held to the head by a band.
headquarters *n* the centre of operations of one in command, as in an army; the main office in any organization.
headrest *n* a support for the head.
headroom *n* space overhead, as in a doorway or tunnel.
heads-up *adj* self-assured and excellent.
headset *n* a set of headphones, usu with a microphone.
headshrinker *n* (*sl*) a psychiatrist.
headstall *n* the part of a bridle that fits round a horse's head.
head start *n* an early start; any other competitive advantage.
headstone *n* a marker placed at the head of a grave.
headstrong *adj* determined to do as one pleases; obstinate.
head waiter *n* the head of the dining-room staff in a restaurant.
headwaters *npl* the small streams that are the source of a river.
headway *n* forward motion; progress.
headwind *n* a wind blowing against the direction of a ship or aircraft.
headword *n* a term placed at the beginning (as of an entry in a dictionary).
headwork *n* mental work; the decoration on the keystone of an arch.
heady *adj* (**headier, headiest**) (*alcoholic drinks*) intoxicating; invigorating, exciting; impetuous.—**headily** *adv*.—**headiness** *n*.
heal *vti* to make or become healthy; to cure; (*wound, etc*) to repair by natural processes.—**healable** *adj*.—**healer** *n*.—**healingly** *adv*.
health *n* physical and mental well-being; freedom from disease, etc; the condition of body or mind; a wish for one's health and happiness, as in a toast.
health farm *n* a residential establishment for improving health through a strict regime of diet and exercise.
health foods *npl* foods that are organically grown, unprocessed and additive-free.
healthful *adj* healthy.—**healthfully** *adv*.—**healthfulness** *n*.
healthy *adj* (**healthier, healthiest**) having or producing good health; beneficial; sound.—**healthily** *adv*.—**healthiness** *n*.
heap *n* a mass or pile of jumbled things; (*pl*) (*inf*) a large amount. * *vt* to throw in a heap; to pile high; to fill (a plate, etc) full or to overflowing.—**heaper** *n*.
hear *vb* (**hearing, heard**) *vt* to perceive by the ear; to listen to; to conduct a hearing of (a law case, etc); to be informed of; to learn. * *vi* to be able to hear sounds; (*with* **of** *or* **about**) to be told.—**hearable** *adj*.—**hearer** *n*.
hearing *n* the sense by which sound is perceived by the ear; an opportunity to be heard; the distance over which something can be heard, earshot.
hearing aid *n* a small electronic amplifier worn behind the ear to improve hearing.
hearken *vi* to listen to.—*also* **harken**.—**hearkener** *n*.
hearsay *n* rumour, gossip.
hearse *n* a vehicle for transporting a coffin to a funeral.
heart *n* the hollow, muscular organ that circulates the blood; the central, vital, or main part; the human heart as the centre of emotions, esp sympathy, courage, etc; a conventional design representing a heart; one of a suit of playing cards marked with such a symbol in red.
heartache *n* sorrow or grief.
heart attack *n* a sudden instance of abnormal heart functioning, esp coronary thrombosis.
heartbeat *n* the rhythmic contraction and dilation of the heart.
heartbreak *n* overwhelming sorrow or grief.—**heartbreaker** *n*.
heartbreaking *adj* causing heartbreak; pitiful.—**heartbreakingly** *adv*.
heartbroken *adj* overcome by sorrow or grief.—**heartbrokenly** *adv*.—**heartbrokenness** *n*.
heartburn *n* a burning sensation in the lower chest.
hearten *vt* to encourage; to cheer up.—**hearteningly** *adv*.
heart failure *n* the inability of the heart to supply enough blood to the body; a cessation of heart activity leading to death.
heartfelt *adj* deeply felt; sincere.
hearth *n* the floor of a fireplace and surrounding area; this as symbolic of house and home.
hearthstone *n* a stone forming a hearth; soft stone used to whiten hearths, floors, steps, etc.
heartily *adv* in a vigorous or enthusiastic way; sincerely.
heartland *n* the central or most vital part of an area, region, etc.
heartless *adj* lacking compassion; unfeeling.—**heartlessly** *adv*.—**heartlessness** *n*.
heart-rending *adj* causing much mental anguish.
heartsease *n* the wild pansy
heartsick *adj* extremely unhappy, despondent.—**heartsickness** *n*.
heartstrings *npl* deepest feelings.
heart-throb *n* (*inf*) the object of a person's infatuation; a heartbeat.
heart-to-heart *n* an intimate conversation. * *adj* intimate; candid.
heartwood *n* the central older wood of a tree, usu harder and darker than the outer rings.—*also* **duramen**.
hearty *adj* (**heartier, heartiest**) warm and friendly; (*laughter, etc*) unrestrained; strong and healthy; nourishing and plentiful.—**heartiness** *n*.
heat *n* energy produced by molecular agitation; the quality of being hot; the perception of hotness; hot weather or climate; strong feeling, esp ardour, anger, etc; a single bout, round, or trial in sports; the period of sexual excitement and readiness for mating in female animals; (*sl*) coercion. * *vti* to make or become warm or hot; to make or become excited.
heated *adj* made hot; excited, impassioned.—**heatedly** *adv*.—**heatedness** *n*.
heater *n* a device that provides heat; (*sl*) a pistol.
heath *n* an area of uncultivated land with scrubby vegetation; any of various shrubby plants that thrive on sandy soil, eg heather.
heathen *n* (*pl* **heathens, heathen**) anyone not acknowledging the God of Christian, Jew, or Muslim belief; a person regarded as irreligious, uncivilized, etc. * *adj* of or denothing a heathen; irreligious; pagan.—**heathendom** *n*.
heathenish *adj* relating to or resembling a heathen or heathenish culture; rude, ignorant or uncultured.—**heathenishly** *adv*.—**heathenishness** *n*.
heathenism *n* ignorance of God; paganism; idolatry.
heather *n* a common evergreen shrub of northern and alpine regions with small sessile leaves and tiny usu purplish pink flowers.—**heathery** *adj*.
heating *n* a system of providing heat, as central heating; the warmth provided.
heat wave *n* a prolonged period of unusually hot weather.
heave *vb* (**heaving, heaved**) *vt* to lift or move, esp with great effort; to utter (a sigh, etc) with effort; (*inf*) to throw. * *vi* to rise and fall rhythmically; to vomit; to pant; to gasp; to haul; (**heaving, hove**) (*with* **to**) (*ship*) to come to a stop. * *n* the act or effort of heaving.—**heaver** *n*.
heaven *n* (*usu pl*) the visible sky; (*sometimes cap*) the dwelling place of God and his angels where the blessed go after death; any place or state of great happiness; (*pl*) *interj* an exclamation of surprise.
heavenly *adj* of or relating to heaven or heavens; divine; (*inf*) excellent, delightful.—**heavenliness** *n*.
heavy *adj* (**heavier, heaviest**) hard to lift or carry; of more than the usual, expected, or defined weight; to an unusual extent; hard to do; stodgy, hard to digest; cloudy; (*industry*) using massive machinery to produce

basic materials, as chemicals and steel; (*ground*) difficult to make fast progress on; clumsy; dull, serious. * *n* (*pl* **heavies**) (*theatre*) a villain; (*sl*) a person hired to threaten violence, a thug.—**heavily** *adv*.—**heaviness** *n*.

heavy duty *adj* made to withstand heavy strain or rough usage.

heavy-handed *adj* clumsy; tactless; oppressive.—**heavy-handedly** *adv*.—**heavy-handedness** *n*.

heavy metal *n* a type of rock music characterized by a heavy beat and reliance on loudly amplified instruments.

heavy spar *see* **barium sulphate**.

heavy water *n* deuterium oxide, water in which the normal hydrogen content has been replaced by deuterium.

heavyweight *n* a professional boxer weighing more than 175 pounds (79 kg) or wrestler weighing over 209 pounds (95 kg); (*inf*) a very influential or important individual.

hebdomad *n* (*formerly*) seven; a group of seven; a week.

hebdomadal *adj* weekly.—**hebdomadally** *adv*.

Hebe *n* (*Greek myth*) the goddess of youth.

hebetate *vti* to make or become dull. * *adj* (*plant*) having a blunt or soft point.—**hebetation** *n*.

hebetude *n* mental dullness or lethargy.—**hebetudinous** *adj*.

Hebraic, Hebraical *adj* of or pertaining to the Hebrews, Jewish language or literature.—**Hebraically** *adv*.

Hebraism *n* a linguistic usage, custom or idiom borrowed from and characteristic of the Hebrew language, or to the Jewish people or culture.

Hebraist *n* one who studies or is learned in the Hebrew language and culture.—**Hebraistic, Hebraistical** *adj*.—**Hebraistically** *adv*.

Hebrew *n* a member of an ancient Semitic people; an Israelite; a Jew; the ancient Semitic language of the Hebrews; its modern form. * *adj* pertaining to the Hebrew people; Jewish.

Hecate *n* (*Greek myth*) a goddess of the underworld.

hecatomb *n* in ancient Greece, the ritual sacrifice of 100 oxen; any large sacrifice or slaughter.

heck *interj* an expression of surprise or grief.

heckle *vti* to harass (a speaker) with questions or taunts.—**heckler** *n*.

hect-, hecto- *prefix* hundred.

hectare *n* a metric measure of area, equivalent to 10,000 square metres (2.47 acres).

hectic *adj* involving intense excitement or activity.—**hectically** *adv*.

hectogram *n* a metric unit of mass equivalent to 100 grams (3.527 ounces).

hectograph *n* a process for copying a manuscript by transferring it onto a layer of gelatin coated with glycerin; the machine that uses this process. * *vt* to copy in this way.—**hectographic** *adj*.—**hectographically** *adv*.

hector *vt* to bully; to annoy. * *n* a bully.

he'd = he had, he would.

hedge *n* a fence consisting of a dense line of bushes or small trees; a barrier or means of protection against something, esp financial loss; an evasive or noncommittal answer or statement. * *vt* to surround or enclose with a hedge; to place secondary bets as a precaution. * *vi* to avoid giving a direct answer in an argument or debate.—**hedger** *n*.—**hedgy** *adj*.

hedgehog *n* a small insectivorous mammal with sharp spines on the back.

hedgerow *n* a line of shrubs or trees separating or enclosing fields.

hedonism *n* the doctrine that personal pleasure is the chief good.—**hedonistic** *adj*.—**hedonist** *n*.

heebie-jeebies *npl* (*sl*) nervousness, jitters.

heed *vt* to pay close attention (to). * *n* careful attention.—**heeder** *n*.

heedful *adj* paying attention; mindful.—**heedfully** *adv*.—**heedfulness** *n*.

heedless *adj* inattentive; thoughtless.—**heedlessly** *adv*.—**heedlessness** *n*.

heehaw *n* (an imitation of) the bray of a donkey, a crude laugh. * *vi* to bray like a donkey.

heel[1] *n* the back part of the foot, under the ankle; the part covering or supporting the heel in stockings, socks, etc, or shoes; a solid attachment forming the back of the sole of a shoe; (*inf*) a despicable person. * *vt* to furnish with a heel; to follow closely; (*inf*) to provide with money, etc. * *vi* to follow along at the heels of someone.—**heelless** *adj*.

heel[2] *vti* to tilt or become tilted to one side, as a ship.

heelball *n* a black, waxy substance used to blacken the heels and soles of shoes; a waxy substance used in brass rubbing.

heeler *n* a person who works for a local political organization, esp a ward heeler; (*Austral*) a dog that herds cattle by snapping at their heels.

heeltap *n* a small layer of leather in the heel of a shoe; the dregs of an alcoholic drink left at the bottom of a glass.

heft *vt* to asses the weight of an object by holding it in the hand; to lift; to become used to. * *n* weight; the main part.

hefty *adj* (**heftier, heftiest**) (*inf*) heavy; large and strong; big.—**heftily** *adv*.—**heftiness** *n*.

Hegelian *adj* relating to or pertaining to the German philosopher Georg Hegel (1770–1831) or his theories.—**Hegelianism** *n*.

hegemony *n* (*pl* **hegemonies**) leadership, domination, esp of one nation over others.—**hegemonic** *adj*.

Hegira *n* the flight of Mohammed from Mecca in ad 622, marking the start of the Muslim era.—*also* **Hejira**.

heifer *n* a young cow that has not calved.

height *n* the topmost point; the highest limit; the distance from the bottom to the top; altitude; a relatively great distance above a given level; an eminence; a hill.

heighten *vti* to make or come higher or more intense.—**heightener** *n*.

heinous *adj* outrageously evil; wicked.—**heinously** *adj*.—**heinousness** *n*.

heir *n* a person who inherits or is entitled to inherit another's property, title, etc.—**heirless** *adj*.

heirdom *n* succession by right of blood; inheritance.

heiress *n* a woman or girl who is an heir, esp to great wealth.

heirloom *n* any possession handed down from generation to generation.

heist *n* (*sl*) a robbery. * *vt* (*sl*) to steal.—**heister** *n*.

Hejira *see* **Hegira**.

held *see* **hold**[1].

heliacal *adj* emerging from or passing into the light of the sun.

helianthus *n* any of a genus of plants with large yellow flowers, including the sunflower and Jerusalem artichoke.

helical *adj* like a helix, spiral.—**helically** adv.

helicoid *adj* resembling a flattened spiral. * *n*. a spirally curved geometrical figure.

helicopter *n* a kind of aircraft lifted and moved, or kept hovering, by large rotary blades mounted horizontally.

heliculture *n* the rearing of snails for food.

helio- *prefix* sun.

heliocentric *adj* having the sun as the centre; measured or viewed from the sun's centre.—**heliocentrically** *adv*.—**heliocentricity, heliocentricism** *n*.

heliochrome *n* a photograph in natural colours.

heliograph *n* a signalling device using the sun's rays reflected by a mirror.—**heliographer** *n*.—**heliographic** *adj*.—**heliography** *n*.

heliogravure *n* photogravure, the process of photo-engraving or etching.

heliolatry *n* sun worship.

heliometer *n* a refracting telescope used to measure small angular distances between celestial bodies.

heli-skiing *n* the use of helicopters to take skiers to high, uncrowded off-piste slopes.

heliostat *n* an instrument that sends signals by reflecting the light of the sun in a constant direction.

heliotrope *n* a genus of plants whose flowers follow the course of the sun; a green-hued variety of chalcedony with small red spots; a bloodstone; the bluish-pink colour of the flower heliotrope; an instrument used in geodetic surveying.—**heliotropic** *adj*.

heliotropism *n* the movement of flowers or leaves towards the sun.—**heliotropic** *adj*.

heliport, helipad *n* a landing and takeoff place for a helicopter.

helium *n* a light nonflammable gaseous element.

helix *n* (*pl* **helices, helixes**) a spiral line, as a line coiled round; (*zool*) a snail or its shell; (*anat*) the folded rim of the external ear; (*archit*) a small volute on a capital.

hell *n* (*Christianity*) the place of punishment of the wicked after death; the home of devils and demons; any place or state of supreme misery or discomfort; (*inf*) a cause of this. * *interj* (*inf*) an exclamation of anger, surprise, etc.

he'll = he will.

hellbent *adj* (*inf*) rashly determined.

hellebore *n* any of a genus of mostly poisonous plants, including the Christmas rose.

Hellene, Hellenian *n* a Greek.

Hellenic *adj* of or relating to classical Greece and the Greeks; relating to classical and modern Greeks and their language. * *n* a branch of the Indo-European family of languages made up of Greek and its dialects.

Hellenism *n* the national character of the Greeks; the ideals and principles of classical Greece; the love of Greek culture and art.

Hellenist *n* a non-Greek, especially a Jew, who spoke Greek in classical times; a student of Greek culture and language.

Hellenistic *adj* relating to or characteristic of classical Greece; relating to Greeks or to Hellenism.

Hellenize *vt* to adopt classical Greek culture or customs; to use or study the Greek language.—**Hellenization** *n*.—**Hellenizer** *n*.

hellish *adj* of, pertaining to, or resembling hell; very wicked; (*inf*) very unpleasant.—**hellishly** *adv*.—**hellishness** *n*.

hello *interj* an expression of greeting. * *n* (*pl* **hellos**) the act of saying "hello."—*also* **hallo, hullo** (*pl* **hallos, hullos**).

helm[1] *n* (*naut*) the tiller or wheel used to steer a ship; any position of control or direction, authority. * *vt* to steer; to control.

helm[2] *n* (*arch*) a helmet. * *vt* to provide or cover with a helmet.

helmet *n* protective headgear worn by soldiers, policemen, divers, etc.—**helmeted** *adj*.

helminth *n* a worm, esp an intestinal one, a fluke.

helminthic *adj* pertaining to worms. * *n* a drug used to treat intestinal worms.

helminthoid *adj* worm-shaped.

helminthology *n* the study of parasitic worms

helmsman *n* (*pl* **helmsmen**) a person who steers.—**helmswoman** *nf* (*pl* **helmswomen**).

helot *n* a serf or slave; (*with cap*) in ancient Sparta, a state-owned slave.

helotry *n* slavery or serfdom; the class of slaves or serfs.

help *vt* to make things better or easier for; to aid; to assist; to remedy; to keep from; to serve or wait on. * *vi* to give aid; to be useful.—*interj* used to ask for assistance. * *n* the action of helping; aid; assistance; a remedy; a person that helps, esp a hired person.—**helper** *n*.

helpful *adj* giving help; useful.—**helpfully** *adv*.—**helpfulness** *n*.

helping *n* a single portion of food.

helpless *adj* unable to manage alone, dependent on others; weak and defenceless.—**helplessly** *adv*.—**helplessness** *n*.

helpmate, helpmeet *n* a helpful companion, esp a wife or husband.

helter-skelter *adv* in confused haste. * *adj* disorderly. * *n* a tall spiral slide usu found in an amusement park.

helve *n* the handle of a tool.

Helvetia *n* the Latin name for Switzerland.

Helvetian *adj* of or relating to Helvetia; Swiss. * *n* a native or citizen of Switzerland.

hem *n* the edge of a garment, etc, turned back and stitched or fixed. * *vt* (**hemming, hemmed**) to finish (a garment) with a hem; (*with* **in**) to enclose, confine.—**hemmer** *n*.

he-man *n* (*pl* **he-men**) (*inf*) an excessively masculine or strongly built male.

hematite *n* native ferric oxide, an important iron ore.—*also* **haematite**.

hematology *n* the branch of medicine dealing with blood and its diseases.—**hematologic, hematological** *adj*.—**hematologist** *n*.

hemi- *prefix* half; partial.

hemicycle *n* a half-circle, semicircle.—**hemicyclic** *adj*.

hemidemisemiquaver *n* (*mus*) a sixty-fourth note.

hemihedral *adj* (*crystal*) having only half the normal number of faces.

hemiplegia *n* paralysis of one side.—**hemiplegic** *adj, n*.

hemisphere *n* half of a sphere or globe; any of the halves (northern, southern, eastern, or western) of the earth.—**hemispheric, hemispherical** *adj*.—**hemispherically** *adv*.

hemistitch *n* half of a line of verse.

hemline *n* the bottom edge of a skirt or dress.

hemlock *n* a poisonous plant with small white flowers; a poison made from this plant.

hemmer *n* one who stitches hems; a machine for hemming.

hemoglobin *n* the oxygen-carrying red colouring matter of the red blood corpuscles.

hemophilia *n* a hereditary condition in which the blood fails to clot normally.—**hemophiliac, hemophile** *n*.—**hemophilic** *adj*.

hemorrhage *n* the escape of blood from a blood vessel; heavy bleeding. * *vi* to bleed heavily.—**hemorrhagic** *adj*.

hemorrhoids *npl* swollen or bleeding veins around the anus.—*also* **piles**.—**hemorrhoidal** *adj*.

hemp *n* a widely cultivated Asian herb of the mulberry family; its fibre, used to make rope, sailcloth, etc; a narcotic drug obtained from different varieties of this plant (—*also* **cannabis, marijuana**).—**hempen** *adj*.

hemstitch *n* an ornamental stitch.—**hemstitcher** *n*.

hen *n* the female of many birds, esp the chicken.

henbane *n* a poisonous, sticky, hairy plant of the nightshade family.

hence *adv* from here; from this time; from this reason.

henceforth, henceforward *adv* from now on.

henchman *n* (*pl* **henchmen**) a trusted helper or follower.

hendecagon *n* an eleven-sided plane figure.—**hendecagonal** *adj*.

hendecasyllable *n* a verse of eleven syllables.—**hendecasyllabic** *adj*.

hendiadys *n* the use of two connected words to express one idea, as "with might and main."

henna *n* a tropical plant; a reddish-brown dye extracted from its leaves used to tint the hair or skin. * *vt* to dye with henna.

hennery *n* (*pl* **henneries**) a poultry farm.

henotheism *n* the worship of one god while recognizing the existence of others.—**henotheist** *n, adj*.—**henotheistic** *adj*.

henpeck *vt* to nag and domineer over (one's husband).—**henpecked** *adj*.

henry *n* (*pl* **henries, henrys**) a unit of electrical inductance.

hent *vt* (*arch*) to seize; to grasp. * *n* (*arch*) a clutching; intention; anything that has been gasped by the mind.

hepat-, hepato- *prefix* liver.

hepatic *adj* of, like, or pertaining to the liver. * *n* a drug for treating the liver.

hepatitis *n* inflammation of the liver.

heptad *n* a group of seven; the number seven; an atom or element with the valency of seven.

heptagon *n* a polygon of seven angles and seven sides.—**heptagonal** *adj*.

heptahedron *n* (*pl* **heptahedrons, heptahedra**) a solid figure with seven plane faces.—**heptahedral** *adj*.

heptameter *n* a verse line of seven metrical feet.

heptarchy *n* (*pl* **heptarchies**) government by seven rulers; a state divided into seven regions each with its own ruler; the seven kingdoms of Anglo-Saxon England.

Heptateuch *n* (*Bible*) the first seven books of the Old Testament.

her *pron* the objective and possessive case of the personal pronoun **she**. * *adj* of or belonging to a female.

herald *n* a person who conveys news or messages; a forerunner, harbinger; (*Middle Ages*) an official at a tournament. * *vt* to usher in; to proclaim.

heraldic *adj* of a herald or heraldry.—**heraldically** *adv*.

heraldry *n* (*pl* **heraldries**) the study of genealogies and coats of arms; ceremony; pomp.—**heraldist** *n*.

herb *n* any seed plant whose stem withers away annually; any plant used as a medicine, seasoning, etc.

herbaceous *adj* of or like herbs; green and leafy.
herbage *n* pasturage; the succulent parts of herbs.
herbal *adj* of herbs. * *n* a book listing and describing plants with medicinal properties.
herbalist *n* a person who practises healing by using herbs; a person who grows or deals in herbs.
herbarium *n* (*pl* **herbariums, herbaria**) a (place or container for a) systematic collection of dried plants.—**herbarial** *adj*.
herb Christopher *see* **baneberry.**
herbicide *n* a substance for destroying plants.—**herbicidal** *adj*.
herbivore *n* a plant-eating animal.
herbivorous *adj* herb-eating; (*animals*) plant-eating.—**herbivorousness** *n*.
herby *adj* (**herbier, herbiest**) herb-like; rich in herbs.
herculean *adj* of extraordinary strength, size, or difficulty; (*with cap*) of or like the Roman god Hercules.
herd *n* a large number of animals, esp cattle, living and feeding together. * *vi* to assemble or move animals together. * *vt* to gather together and move as if a herd; to tend, as a herdsman.—**herder** *n*.
herdsman *n* (*pl* **herdsmen**) a person who tends a herd of animals.
here *adv* at or in this place; to or into this place; now; on earth.
hereabout, hereabouts *adv* in this area.
hereafter *adv* after this, in some future time or state. * *n* (*with* **the**) the future, life after death.
hereat *adv* (*arch*) because of this.
hereby *adv* by this means.
hereditable *adj* that may be inherited, heritable.—**hereditability** *n*.—**hereditably** *adv*.
hereditament *n* (*law*) property capable of being inherited.
hereditary *adj* descending by inheritance; transmitted to offspring.—**hereditarily** *adv*.—**hereditariness** *n*.
heredity *n* (*pl* **heredities**) the transmission of genetic material that determines physical and mental characteristics from one generation to another.
herein *adv* (*formal*) in this place, document, etc.
hereinafter *adv* (*formerly*) afterwards of this.
hereof *adv* of this.
heresiarch *n* the leader or fonder of a heretical movement or sect.
heresy *n* (*pl* **heresies**) a religious belief regarded as contrary to the orthodox doctrine of a church; any belief or opinion contrary to established or accepted theory.
heretic *n* a dissenter from an established belief or doctrine.—**heretical** *adj*.—**heretically** *adv*.
hereto *adv* (*formal*) to this matter, document, etc.
heretofore *adv* (*formal*) until now.
hereunder *adv* (*formal*) below.
hereupon *adv* (*formal*) on this matter, issue, etc; immediately after this.
herewith *adv* (*formal*) with this.
heriot *n* a tribute, usu cattle, paid to a feudal lord on the death of a tenant by his heir.
heritable *adj* able to be inherited, hereditable.—**heritably** *adv*.
heritage *n* something inherited at birth; anything deriving from the past or tradition; historical sites, traditions, practices, etc regarded as the valuable inheritance of contemporary society.
heritor *n* (*law*) one who inherits; a proprietor.
hermaphrodite *n* an animal or organism with both male and female reproductive organs; a plant with stamens and pistils in the same floral envelope.—**hermaphroditic** *adj*.—**hermaphroditically** *adv*.
hermaphrodite brig *n* a brig square-rigged forward and schooner-rigged aft.
hermaphroditism, hermaphrodism *n* the state of being an hermaphrodite.
hermeneutics *n sing* the science of interpretation, esp of the Bible.—**hermeneutic, hermeneutical** *adj*.—**hermeneutically** *adv*.
hermetic, hermetical *adj* perfectly closed and airtight; of alchemy, magical.—**hermetically** *adv*.
hermit *n* a person who lives in complete solitude, esp for religious reasons; a recluse.—**hermitic, hermitical** *adj*.—**hermitically** *adv*.
hermitage *n* the dwelling place of a hermit; a secluded retreat.
hern *n* (*arch*) the heron.
hernia *n* (*pl* **hernias, herniae**) the protrusion of an organ, esp part of the intestine, through an opening in the wall of the cavity in which it sits; a rupture.—**hernial** *adj*.—**herniated** *adj*.
hero *n* (*pl* **heroes**) a person of exceptional bravery; a person admired for superior qualities and achievements; the central male character in a novel, play, etc.
heroic *adj* of, worthy of, or like a hero; having the qualities of a hero; daring, risky; (*poetry*) of or about heroes and their deeds, epic; (*language*) grand, high-flown. * *n* heroic verse; (*pl*) melodramatic talk or behaviour.—**heroically** *adv*.
heroic age *n* the age in which the legendary heroes of a nation, esp ancient Greece and Rome, are fabled to have lived in.
heroic couplet *n* a rhyming couplet in iambic pentameter, used in English heroic verse.
heroic verse *n* a verse form used in epic poetry, ie the hexameter in Greek and Latin poetry, the iambic pentameter in English, and the Alexandrine in French.
heroin *n* a powerfully addictive drug derived from morphine.
heroine *n* a woman with the attributes of a hero; the leading female character in a novel, film or play.
heroism *n* the qualities or conduct of a hero; bravery.
heron *n* a slim wading bird with long legs and neck.
heronry *n* (*pl* **heronries**) a heron rookery; a breeding place for herons.
herpes *n* any of several virus diseases marked by small blisters on the skin or mucous membranes.—**herpetic** *adj*.
herpetology *n* the study of snakes and amphibians.—**herpetologist** *n*.
Herr *n* (*pl* **Herren**) a title, the German equivalent of Mister or Sir.
herring *n* (*pl* **herrings, herring**) a small food fish of commercial importance.
herringbone *n* a kind of cross-stitch; a zigzag pattern used in brickwork; (*skiing*) a method of walking uphill with the skis pointing outwards. * *vt* to work in cross-stitch; to decorate with a herringbone pattern. * *vi* to ascend a ski slope in herringbone fashion.
hers *pron* something or someone belonging to her.
herself *pron* the reflexive form of **she** or **her**.
hertz *n* (*pl* **hertz**) the unit of frequency equal to one cycle per second.
he's = he is; he has.
Hesiodic *adj* pertaining to or in the style of Hesiod, a Greek didactic poet of the 8th century bc.
hesitancy *n* (*pl* **hesitancies**) an act of hesitating; the state of being hesitant; indecision.
hesitant *adj* hesitating; indecisive; reluctant; shy.—**hesitantly** *adv*.
hesitate *vi* to be slow in acting due to uncertainty or indecision; to be reluctant (to); to falter or stammer when speaking.—**hesitater** *n*.—**hesitatingly** *adv*.
hesitation *n* the act of hesitating; a pause in speech.
Hesperian *adj* of or relating to the Hesperides; western. * *n* a native or inhabitant of a western land.
Hesperides *n* (*Greek myth*) (*pl*) the nymphs who guarded the golden apples given by Gaia to Hera on her marriage to Zeus; (*sing*) the garden containing the golden apples.
Hesperus *n* the evening star, esp Venus.
Hessian *adj* pertaining to the German state of Hesse. * *n* a native or inhabitant of Hesse; a mercenary soldier.
hessian *n* a coarse cloth made of jute.
hest *n* (*arch*) a behest; a command.
hetaera, hetaira *n* (*pl* **hetaerae, hetaeras, hetairai**) a female prostitute or courtesant, esp in ancient Greece.—**hetaeric, hetairic** *adj*.
heter-, hetero- *prefix* another; abnormal; different, other; unequal.
heterocercal *adj* (*fish*) having the upper lobe of the tail longer than the lower lobe.

heterochromatic *adj* of different colours.
heteroclite *n* an irregularly inflected or unusual word; an unusual person or thing. * *adj* irregular; deviating from the ordinary (*—also* **heteroclitic**).
heterodox *adj* contrary to established beliefs or opinions; unorthodox; heterical.
heterodoxy *n* (*pl* **heterodoxies**) the state of being heterodox; an unorthodox doctrine or opinion; heresy.
heterodyne *vt* to impose (a radio frequency wave) on a transmitting wave to produce pulsations of audible frequency. * *adj* having or produced by combining waves of different lengths.
heterogamous *adj* (*bot*) bearing two kinds of flowers that differ sexually.
heterogeneous *adj* opposite or dissimilar in character, quality structure, etc; not homogeneous; disparate.—**heterogeneity** *n*.—**heterogeneously** *adv*.
heterogenesis *n* the production by certain organisms of offspring differing in structure and habit from the parent, but reverting in subsequent generations to the original type.—**heterogenetic** *adj*.
heterogenous *adj* (*biol*) originating outside the body; foreign.—**heterogeny** *n*.
heterologous *adj* (*biol*) abnormal in type or structure; derived from a different species; consisting of the same elements in varying proportions.—**heterology** *n*.
heteromorphism *n* (*biol*) deviation from the natural form or structure.—**heteromorphic** *adj*.
heteronomous *adj* differing from the normal type; subject to external law, rule or authority.—**heteronomously** *adv*.
heteronym *n* a word spelled in the same way as another or others but having a different meaning, as *brake* (in a vehicle) and *brake* (fern).—**heteronymous** *adj*.
heterophyllous *adj* (*plants*) having leaves of different forms on the same stem.—**heterophylly** *n*.
heterosexual *adj* sexually attracted to the opposite sex. * *n* a heterosexual person.—**heterosexuality** *n*.—**heterosexually** *adv*.
hetman *n* (*pl* **hetmen**) (*formerly*) a Cossack prince or general.
het-up *adj* (*inf*) agitated, annoyed.
heulandite *n* a vitreous transparent brittle mineral.
heuristic *adj* assisting or leading to discovery or invention.—**heuristically** *adv*.
hew *vb* (**hewing, hewed,** *pp* **hewed, hewn**) *vt* to strike or cut with blows using an axe, etc; to shape with such blows. * *vi* to conform (to a rule, principle, etc).—**hewer** *n*.
hex *vt* to bewitch; to bring bad luck. * *n* a magic spell; a curse; a witch.
hex-, hexa- *prefix* six.
hexachord *n* (*mus*) a diatonic series of six notes with a semitone between third and fourth.
hexad *n* a group or series of six; the number or sum of six; a chemical element, atom, or radical that can be combined with, or replaced by, six atoms of hydrogen.—**hexadic** *adj*.
hexagon *n* a polygon having six sides and six angles.—**hexagonal** *adj*.—**hexagonally** *adv*.
hexagram *n* a plane figure having six angles and six sides; a six-pointed star formed by two intersecting triangles; a group of six lines which may be combined into 64 different patterns in I Ching.
hexahedron *n* a solid bounded by six plane faces.—**hexahedral** *adj*
hexameter *n* a line of Greek or Latin verse consisting of six feet the last usually being a spondee; a verse line consisting of six metric feet.—**hexametric, hexametrical** *adj*.
hexapod *n* any of a large class of anthropods; an animal with six legs; an insect. * *adj* having six legs (*—also* **hexapodous**).
Hexateuch *n* (*Bible*) the first six books of the Old Testament.
hey *interj* an expression of joy, surprise or to call attention.
heyday *n* a period of greatest success, happiness, etc.
HF *abbr* = high frequency.
Hf (*chem symbol*) = hafnium.
Hg (*chem symbol*) = mercury.
HGV *abbr* = heavy goods vehicle.
hi *interj* an exclamation of greeting.
hiatus *n* (*pl* **hiatuses, hiatus**) a break in continuity; a lacuna; (*med*) an aperture; (*phonetics*) the concurrence of two vowels in two successive syllables.—**hiatal** *adj*.
hibernaculum *n* (*pl* **hibernacula**) the winter quarters of a hibernating animal; the bud-scales of a winter bud.
hibernal *adj* of or happening in winter; wintry.
hibernate *vi* to spend the winter in a dormant condition like deep sleep; to be inactive.—**hibernation** *n*.—**hibernator** *n*.
Hibernian *adj* relating to Ireland. * *n* a native or inhabitant of Ireland.
hibiscus *n* any plant of a tropical or subtropical genus of plants with large showy flowers.
hiccup, hiccough *n* a sudden involuntary spasm of the diaphragm followed by inhalation and closure of the glottis producing a characteristic sound; (*inf*) a minor setback. * *vt* (**hiccuping, hiccuped** or **hiccupping, hiccupped**) to have hiccups.
hic jacet *n* (*Latin* here lies) an inscription on tombstones.
hick *n* (*inf*) an unsophisticated person, esp from a rural area.
hickory *n* (*pl* **hickories**) a North American tree of the walnut family; its wood; its smooth-shelled edible nut.
hid *see* **hide**[1].
hidalgo *n* (*pl* **hidalgoes**) a low-ranking Spanish nobleman.
hidden *adj* concealed or obscured.
hide[1] *vb* (**hiding, hid,** *pp* **hidden, hid**) *vt* to conceal, put out of sight; to keep secret; to screen or obscure from view. * *vi* to conceal oneself. * *n* a camouflaged place of concealment used by hunters, bird-watchers, etc.—**hider** *n*.
hide[2] *n* the raw or dressed skin of an animal; (*inf*) the human skin.
hide[3] *n* an ancient English measure of land.
hide-and-seek *n* a children's game in which one player must find the others, who have hidden themselves.
hidebound *adj* obstinately conservative and narrow-minded; (*animals*) having a tight or contracted hide that impedes movement; (*trees*) having a tight bark that restricts growth.
hideous *adj* visually repulsive; horrifying.—**hideously** *adv*.—**hideousness** *n*.
hiding[1] *n* (*inf*) a thrashing, a beating.
hiding[2] *n* concealment.
hiding place *n* a place of concealment.
hidrosis *n* perspiration; any skin disease affecting the sweat glands.
hidrotic *adj* of or promoting perspiration. * *n* a drug that stimulates sweating.
hie *vti* (**hieing** *or* **hying, hied**) (*poet*) to speed; to hasten.
hier-, hiero- *prefix* sacred.
hierarch *n* the chief ruler of an ecclesiastical body; a person at a high level of hierarchy.
hierarchism *n* hierarchical principles; government by a hierarchy.—**hierarchist** *n*.
hierarchy *n* (*pl* **hierarchies**) a group of persons or things arranged in order of rank, grade, etc.—**hierarchical, hierarchic** *adj*.—**hierarchically** *adv*.
hieratic *adj* of or relating to priests; sacred; consecrated; of or relating to a cursive form of hieroglyphics used by priests in ancient Egypt. * *n* the Egyptian hieratic script.—**hieratically** *adv*.
hierocracy *n* (*pl* **hierocrocies**) government by priests or ecclesiastics.
hieroglyph *n* a character used in a system of hieroglyphic writing.
hieroglyphic *n* a sacred character or symbol; (*pl*) the picture writings of the ancient Egyptians and others. * *adj* pertaining to hieroglyphs; emblematic.—**hieroglyphically** *adv*.
hierology (*pl* **hierologies**) the sacred literature of people; a biography of a saint.
hierophant *n* in ancient Greece, a priest who initiated novices into the sacred mysteries; a person who explains arcane mysteries.
hifalutin *see* **highfalutin**.
hi-fi *n* (*inf*) high fidelity; equipment for reproducing high quality musical sound.

higgle *vi* to dispute over trifling matters; to haggle.
higgledy-piggledy *adj, adv* (*inf*) in confusion; jumbled up.
high *adj* lofty, tall; extending upward a (specified) distance; situated at or done from a height; above others in rank, position, etc; greater in size, amount, cost, etc than usual; raised or acute in pitch; (*meat*) slightly bad; (*inf*) intoxicated; (*inf*) under the influence of drugs. * *adv* in or to a high degree, rank, etc. * *n* a high level, place, etc; an area of high barometric pressure; (*inf*) a euphoric condition induced by alcohol or drugs.
high and dry *adj* helpless; stranded; (*ship*) out of the water.
high and mighty *adj* (*inf*) arrogant.
highball *n* a cool drink with spirits, soda, etc, served in a tall glass.
highborn *adj* of noble birth.
highboy *n* (*US*) a chest of drawers on legs; a tallboy.
highbrow *n* (*inf*) an intellectual. * *adj* (*inf*) interested in things requiring learning.
High Church *n* the part of the Anglican Church that attaches great importance to the authority of the Church, its sacraments and priesthood.—**High-Church** *adj*.
high-class *adj* of good quality; of or appropriate to the upper social classes.
higher *adj* more high. * *adv* in or to a higher position.
higher education *n* education at college or university level.
higher-up *n* (*inf*) a person of higher rank.
high explosive *n* a very powerful chemical explosive, such as gelignite.
highfalutin, highfaluting *adj* (*inf*) pretentious; pompous.—*also* **hifalutin.**
high fidelity *n* the high quality reproduction of sound.
high-five *n* a form of greeting or congratulation when the hands of two people are joined, palms together, above their heads.
high-flown *adj* extravagantly ambitious; bombastic.
high-flyer, high-flier *n* an ambitious person; a person of great ability in any profession.—**high-flying** *adj*.
high frequency *n* any radio frequency between 3 and 30 megahertz.
high-handed *adj* overbearing, arbitrary.—**high-handedly** *adv*.—**high-handedness** *n*.
high-hat *vti* (**high-hatting, high-hatted**) to affect superiority; to treat patronizingly. * *n* a person who behaves in this way.
highjack, highjacker *see* **hijack.**
high jinks *npl* (*inf*) mischievous sport or tricks.
high jump *n* an athletic event in which a competitor jumps over a high bar; (*inf*) (*with* **the**) a severe reprimand.
highland *adj* of or in mountains. * *n* a region with many hills or mountains; (*pl*) mountainous country; (*with cap*) the mountainous region occupying most of northern Scotland.
highlander *n* a person who lives in a highland area; (*with cap*) an inhabitant of the Scottish Highlands.
Highland fling *n* a lively Scottish dance by one person.
highlife *n* (*W Africa*) a style of jazz music combining American and African elements.
high life *n* fashionable society; its manner of living.—**high-life** *adj*.
highlight *n* the lightest area of a painting, etc; the most interesting or important feature; (*pl*) a lightening of areas of the hair using a bleaching agent. * *vt* to bring to special attention; to give highlights to.
highly *adv* highly, very much; favourably; at a high level, wage, rank, etc.
highly strung *adj* nervous and tense; excitable; high-strung.
High Mass *n* (*RC Church*) a ceremonial mass, usu at the high altar, at which a deacon or subdeacon assist the celebrant.
high-minded *adj* having high ideals, etc.—**high-mindedness** *n*.
highness *n* the state or quality of being high; (*with cap and poss pron*) a title used in speaking to or of royalty.
high-pitched *adj* (*sound*) shrill; (*roof*) steep.
high-powered, high-power *adj* (*lens, etc*) producing great magnification; energetic; powerful; highly competent.
high priest *n* a chief priest, esp the principal priest of the Jewish hierarchy; an unofficial leader of fashion, etc.
high-rise *adj* (*building*) having multiple storeys.* *n* a building of this kind.
highroad *n* a chief road, a highway; an easy course or method.
high roller *n* a gambler; an extravagant person; a leader of fashion.—**high rolling** *adj, n*.
high school *n* a secondary school.
high seas *npl* open ocean waters outside the territorial limits of any nation.
high season *n* the busiest time of the year for a holiday resort, etc.
high-sounding *adj* imposing, pompous.
high-spirited *adj* courageous; lively.—**high-spiritedness** *n*.
high-strung *adj* strung to a high pitch; extremely sensitive; highly strung.
hightail *vi* to leave in a great rush.
high tide *n* the tide at its highest level; the time of this; an acme.
high time *adv* (*inf*) fully time. * *n* an especially good or enjoyable time.
high treason *n* treason against the ruler or state.
high-up *n* (*inf*) a person of high status or position.
high water *n* high tide.—**highwater** *adj*.
highwater mark *n* the highest point reached by a high tide; any maximum.
highway *n* a public road; a main thoroughfare.
highwayman *n* (*pl* **highwaymen**) one who robs travellers on a highway.
high wire *n* a high tightrope.
hijack *vt* to steal (goods in transit) by force; to force (an aircraft) to make an unscheduled flight. * *n* an act of hijacking.—*also* **highjack.**—**hijacker, highjacker** *n*.
hike *vi* to take a long walk. * *vt* (*inf*) to pull up, to increase. * *n* a long walk; a tramp.—**hiker** *n*.
hilarious *adj* highly amusing.—**hilariously** *adv*.—**hilariousness** *n*.—**hilarity** *n*.
hilarity *n* mirth; merriment; cheerfulness.
hill *n* a natural rise of land lower than a mountain; a heap or mound; an slope in a road, etc. *vt* to bank up; to draw earth around (plants) in mounds.
hillbilly *n* (*pl* **hillbillies**) (*inf*) a person from the mountainous areas of southeastern US; country music.—*also adj*.
hillock *n* a small hill.—**hillocked, hillocky** *adj*.
hilly *adj* (**hillier, hilliest**) abounding with or characterized by hills; rugged.—**hilliness** *n*.
hilt *n* the handle of a sword, dagger, tool, etc.
hilum *n* (*pl* **hila**) a scar on the surface of a seed indicating where it was attached to the seed grain; the nucleus of a starch grain.
him *pron* the objective case of **he.**
himation *n* (*pl* **himatia**) in ancient Greece, a square-shaped cloak draped around the body.
himself *pron the reflexive* (he killed himself) *or emphatic* (he himself was lucky) *form of* **he, him.**
Himyaritic *n* an extinct language of the Semitic family of the Afro-Asian family; an Arabian dialect. * *adj* of or relating to the Hymarite people of Arabia or their language.
hind[1] *adj* (**hinder, hindmost** *or* **hindermost**) situated at the back; rear.
hind[2] *n* (*pl* **hinds, hind**) a female deer.
hinder *vt* to obstruct, delay or impede. * *vi* to impose instructions or impediments. * *adj* belonging to or constituting the back or rear of anything.—**hinderer** *n*.
Hindi *n* the official language of India; a group of dialects of northern India.
hindmost, hindermost *adj* farthest behind.
hindquarters *npl* the hind legs and accompanying parts of a quadruped.
hindrance *n* the act of hindering; an obstacle, impediment.
hindsight *n* understanding an event after it has occurred.
Hindu *n* (*pl* **Hindus**) any of several peoples of India; a follower of Hinduism.
Hinduism *n* the dominant religion of India, characterized by an emphasis on religious law, a caste system and belief in reincarnation.
hinge *n* a joint or flexible part on which a door, lid, etc turns; a natural joint, as of a clam; a small piece of gummed paper for sticking stamps in an album. * *vti* to attach or hang by a hinge; to depend.

hinny *n* (*pl* **hinnies**) the sterile offspring of a male horse and a female donkey or ass. * *vi* to neigh.
hint *n* an indirect or subtle suggestion; a slight mention; a little piece of practical or helpful advice. * *vt* to suggest or indicate indirectly. * *vi* to give a hint.—**hinter** *n.*
hinterland *n* the land behind that bordering a coast or river; a remote area.
hip[1] *n* either side of the body below the waist and above the thigh.
hip[2] *n* the fruit of the wild rose.
hip[3] *interj* used as part of a cheer (*hip, hip, hurrah*).
hip[4] *adj* (*sl*) stylish, up-to-date.
hippie, hippy *n* (*pl* **hippies**) (*sl*) a person who adopts an alternative lifestyle, eg involving mysticism, psychedelic drugs, or communal living, to express alienation from conventional society.
hippo *n* (*pl* **hippos**) (*inf*) a hippopotamus.
hippocras *n* an old English cordial of spiced wine.
Hippocratic oath *n* an oath taken by a doctor to observe the code of medical ethics derived from Hippocrates, a Greek physician of the 5th century bc.
hippodrome *n* a dance hall, music hall, etc; in ancient Greece, a stadium for horse and chariot races.
hippogriff *n* (*Greek myth*) a monster with a griffin's head, wings and claws, and the body of a horse.
hippopotamus *n* (*pl* **hippopotamuses, hippopotami**) a large African water-loving mammal with thick dark skin, short legs, and a very large head and muzzle.
hircine *adj* of or resembling a goat; smelling like a goat.
hire *vt* to pay for the services of (a person) or the use of (a thing). * *n* the payment for the temporary use of anything; the fact or state of being hired.—**hirable, hireable** *adj.*—**hirer** *n.*
hireling *n* a person who works only for money, esp for doing something unpleasant.
hire-purchase *n* a system by which a person takes possession of an article after paying a deposit and then becomes the owner only after payment of a series of instalments is completed.
hirsute *adj* covered in hair; of or pertaining to hair.—**hirsuteness** *n.*
his *poss pron* of or belonging to *him.—also adj.*
Hispanic *adj* of or derived from Spain, Spanish or Spanish-speaking countries. * *n* a person of Hispanic descent, esp in the US.
Hispanicism *n* a word or expression borrowed from Spanish.
hispid *adj* bristly; covered with stiff hairs.—**hispidity** *n.*
hiss *vi* to make a sound resembling a prolonged *s*; to show disapproval by hissing. * *vt* to say or indicate by hissing. * *n* the act or sound of hissing.—**hisser** *n.*
hist. *abbr* = history; historian; historical.
hist-, histo- *prefix* tissue.
histamine *n* a substance released by the tissues in allergic reactions, acting as an irritant.—**histaminic** *adj.*
histogenesis *n* the formation of organic tissue.—**histogenetic** *adj.*—**histogenetically** *adv.*
histogram *n* a statistical diagram representing frequency distribution in terms of columns.
histology *n* the study of the microscopic structure of animal and plant tissues.—**histologic, histological** *adj.*—**histologically** *adv.*—**histologist** *n.*
historian *n* a person who writes or studies history.
historic *adj* (potentially) important or famous in history.
historical *adj* belonging to or involving history or historical methods; concerning actual events as opposed to myth or legend; based on history.—**historically** *adv.*—**historicalness** *n.*
historicity *n* historical authenticity; genuineness.
historiography *n* the principles of historical writing, esp that based on the use of primary sources and techniques of research; the study of methods of historical research and writing.—**historiographic, historiographical** *adj.*—**historiographically** *adv.*
historiographer *n* a writer of history, esp an official historian.
history *n* (*pl* **histories**) a record or account of past events; the study and analysis of past events; past events in total; the past events or experiences of a specific person or thing; an unusual or significant past.
histrionic, histrionical *adj* of actors or the theatre; melodramatic.—**histrionically** *adv.*
histrionics *n* (*used as sing or pl*) the art of theatrical representation; melodramatic behaviour or tantrums to attract attention.
hit *vti* (**hitting, hit**) to come against (something) with force; to give a blow (to), to strike; to strike with a missile; to affect strongly; to arrive at; (*with* **on**) to discover by accident or unexpectedly. * *n* a blow that strikes its mark; a collision; a successful and popular song, book, etc; (*inf*) an underworld killing; (*sl*) a dose of a drug.
hit-and-run *n* a motor vehicle accident in which the driver leaves the scene without stopping or informing the authorities.
hitch *vt* to move, pull, etc with jerks; to fasten with a hook, knot, etc; to obtain a ride by hitchhiking. * *vi* to hitchhike. * *n* a tug; a hindrance, obstruction; a kind of knot used for temporary fastening; (*inf*) a ride obtained from hitchhiking.—**hitcher** *n.*
hitchhike *vt* to travel by asking for free lifts from motorists along the way.—**hitchhiker** *n.*
hither *adv* (*formal*) to or towards this place.
hitherto *adv* (*formal*) until this time.
hit list *n* (*sl*) a list of people to be eliminated, etc.
hit man *n* a hired assassin.
Hittite *n* a member of an ancient people of Asia Minor; the language of these people. * *adj* of or pertaining to the Hittite people or their language or inscriptions.
HIV *abbr* = human immunodeficiency virus, the virus that causes Aids.
hive *n* a shelter for a colony of bees; a beehive; the bees of a hive; a crowd of busy people; a place of great activity. * *vt* to gather (bees) into a hive. * *vi* to enter a hive; (*with* **off**) to separate from a group.
hives *n* (*used as sing or pl*) a rash on the skin often caused by an allergy; nettle rash.
hiya *interj* an exclamation of greeting.
HM *abbr* = Her (or His) Majesty('s).
HMS *abbr* = Her (or His) Majesty's Ship.
Ho (*chem symbol*) = holmium.
ho *interj* an exclamation used to attract attention.
hoard *n* an accumulation of food, money, etc, stored away for future use. * *vti* to accumulate and store away.—**hoarder** *n.*
hoarding *n* a temporary screen of boards erected around a construction site; a billboard.
hoarfrost *n* a covering of minute ice crystals.—*also* **white frost.**
hoarse *adj* (*voice*) rough, as from a cold; (*person*) having a hoarse voice.—**hoarsely** *adv.*—**hoarseness** *n.*
hoary *adj* (**hoarier, hoariest**) white or grey with age; having whitish or greyish hairs; (*joke, etc*) ancient, hackneyed.—**hoarily** *adv.*
hoax *n* a deception; a practical joke. * *vt* to deceive by a hoax.—**hoaxer** *n.*
hob *n* a ledge near a fireplace for keeping kettles, etc hot; a flat surface on a cooker incorporating hot plates or burners.
hobble *vi* to walk unsteadily, to limp. * *vt* to fasten the legs of (horses, etc) loosely together to prevent straying. * *n* a limp; a rope, etc, used to hobble a horse.—**hobbler** *n.*
hobbledehoy *n* (*arch*) (*pl* **hobbledehoys**) an inexperienced and awkward young person.
hobby *n* (*pl* **hobbies**) a spare-time activity carried out for personal amusement; (*arch*) a hobbyhorse.—**hobbyist** *n.*
hobbyhorse *n* a child's toy comprising a stick with a horse's head; a rocking horse; a favourite topic for discussion.
hobgoblin *n* a mischievous goblin.
hobnail *n* a short nail with a wide head, used on the soles of heavy shoes.—**hobnailed** *adj.*
hobnob *vi* (**hobnobbing, hobnobbed**) to spend time with in a friendly manner.

hobo *n* (*pl* **hoboes, hobos**) a migrant labourer; a tramp.—**hoboism** *n*.
hock[1] *vt* (*sl*) to give something in security for a loan.—**hocker** *n*.
hock[2] *n* the joint bending backward on the hind leg of a horse, etc.
hock[3] *n* a variety of German white wine.
hockey *n* an outdoor game played by two teams of 11 players with a ball and clubs curved at one end (—*also* **field hockey**); ice hockey.
hockshop *n* (*inf*) a pawnshop.
hocus *vt* (**hocusses, hocussing, hocussed** *or* **hocuses, hocusing, hocused**) to cheat or trick; to dupe; to doctor alcohol in order to stupefy a person so as to cheat him or her; to stupefy with a drug. * *n* a trick; drugged alcohol.
hocus-pocus *n* meaningless words used by a conjurer; sleight of hand; deception. * *vti* (**hocus-pocuses, hocus-pocusing, hocus-pocused** *or* **hocus-pocusses, hocus-pocussing, hocus-pocussed**) to play tricks (on).
hod *n* a trough on a pole for carrying bricks or mortar on the shoulder; a coal scuttle.
hodgepodge *n* a jumble.
hoe *n* a long-handled tool for weeding, loosening the earth, etc. * *vti* (**hoeing, hoed**) to dig, weed, till, etc, with a hoe.
hog *n* a domesticated male pig raised for its meat; (*inf*) a selfish, greedy, or filthy person. * *vt* (**hogging, hogged**) to take more than one's due; to hoard greedily.
hogfish *n* (*pl* **hogfish, hogfishes**) a fish with a bristled head of warm Atlantic waters; the wrasse.
Hogmanay *n* (*Scot*) New Year's Eve.
hogshead *n* a large cask or barrel; one of several measures of liquid capacity, esp one of 63 gallons (238.5 litres).
hogwash *n* swill fed to pigs; rubbishy or nonsensensical writing or speech.
hoi polloi *n* (*often derog*) the common people; the masses.
hoist *vt* to raise aloft, esp with a pulley, crane, etc. * *n* a hoisting; an apparatus for lifting to a higher flower; a lift, elevator.—**hoister** *n*.
hoity-toity *adj* arrogant or haughty. * *interj* an exclamation of surprise.
hokey-pokey *n* hocus-pocus; a cheap ice cream sold in slabs.
hol-, holo- *prefix* whole.
hold[1] *vb* (**holding, held**) *vt* to take and keep in one's possession, to grasp; to maintain in a certain position or condition; to retain; to contain; to own, to occupy; to support, sustain; to remain firm; to carry on, as a meeting; to regard; to believe, to consider; to bear or carry oneself; (*with* **back**) to withhold; to restrain; (*with* **down**) to restrain; (*inf*) to manage to retain one's job, etc; (*with* **forth**) to offer (eg an inducement); (*with* **off**) to keep apart; (*with* **up**) to delay; to hinder; to commit an armed robbery. * *vi* to go on being firm, loyal, etc; to remain unbroken or unyielding; to be true or valid; to continue; (*with* **back**) to refrain; (*with* **forth**) to speak at length; (*with* **off**) to wait, to refrain; (*with* **on**) to maintain a grip on; to persist; (*inf*) to keep a telephone line open. * *n* the act or manner of holding; grip; a dominating force on a person.—**holdable** *adj*.—**holder** *n*.
hold[2] *n* the storage space in a ship or aircraft used for cargo.
holdall *n* a portable container for miscellaneous articles.—*also* **carryall**.
holder *n* one who holds; a device for holding things; a person who has control of something; one who is in possession of a financial document.
holdfast *n* a hook or clamp; the act of gripping strongly; the organ by which seaweed and related plants attach themselves to a host object.
holding *n* (*often pl*) legally held property, esp land, stocks, and bonds.
hold-up *n* a delay; an armed robbery.
hole *n* a hollow place; a cavity; a pit; an animal's burrow; an aperture; a perforation; a small, squalid, dingy place; (*inf*) a difficult situation; (*golf*) a small cavity into which the ball is hit; the tee, the fairway, etc leading to this. * *vti* to make a hole in (something); to drive into a hole; (*with* **up**) to hibernate; (*inf*) to hide oneself.
holey *adj* full of holes.
holiday *n* a period away from work, school, etc for travel, rest or recreation; a day of freedom from work, etc, esp one set aside by law. * *vi* to spend a holiday.—*also* **vacation**.
holiday-maker *n* a vacationer.
holily *adv* in a holy manner.
holiness *n* sanctity; (*with cap and poss pron*) the title of the Pope.
holism *n* (*philos*) the creation by creative evolution of wholes that are greater than the sum of the parts; (*med*) consideration of the whole body in the treatment of disease.—**holistic** *adj*.—**holistically** *adv*.
holland *n* an unbleached linen either glazed or unglazed used for furnishing.
hollandaise sauce *n* a rich sauce of egg yolks, lemon juice, butter, etc.
Hollands *n* a kind of Dutch gin sold in stone bottles.
hollow *adj* having a cavity within or below; recessed, concave; empty or worthless. * *n* a hole, cavity; a depression, a valley.* *vti* to make or become hollow.—**hollowly** *adv*.—**hollowness** *n*.
hollow-eyed *adj* with the eyes deep-set or sunken from tiredness, etc.
holly *n* (*pl* **hollies**) an evergreen shrub with prickly leaves and red berries.
hollyhock *n* a tall-stemmed plant with spikes of large flowers.
holmium *n* a malleable white metallic element.
holoblastic *adj* wholly germinal.
holocaust *n* a great destruction of life, esp by fire; (*with cap and* **the**) the mass extermination of European Jews by the Nazis 1939–45.—**holocaustal, holocaustic** *adj*.
hologram *n* an image made without the use of a lens on photographic film by means of interference between two parts of a laser beam, the result appearing as a meaningless pattern until suitably illuminated, when it shows as a three-dimensional image.
holograph *n* a document wholly in the handwriting of the author.
holography *n* the technique of making or using holograms.—**holographic** *adj*.—**holographically** *adv*.
holohedral *adj* showing all the planes necessary for the perfect symmetry of the crystal system.
holophrastic *adj* (*linguistics*) descriping the stage in language development where most utterances are single words; having the force of a whole phrase; polysynthetic.
holothurian *n* any echinoderm of the class that contains the sea cumcumber. * *adj* of, related or belonging to the holothurians.
holpen *vb* (*arch*) a past participle of *help*.
holster *n* a leather case attached to a belt for a pistol.—**holstered** *adj*.
holt *n* an otter's den; the burrowed lair of any animal; (*poet*) a wood; a wooded hill.
holus-bolus *adv* (*inf*) at a gulp, all at once.
holy *adj* (**holier, holiest**) dedicated to religious use; without sin; deserving reverence. * *n* (*pl* **holies**) a holy place, innermost shrine.
Holy Communion *n* the celebration of the Eucharist.
Holy Ghost *n* (*Christianity*) the third person of the Trinity.
Holy Grail *n* in medieval legend, the dish or chalice that was used by Christ at the Last Supper, and the object of many knights' quests.
Holy Land *n* Palestine.
Holy Spirit *n* the Holy Spirit.
holystone *n* sandstone used by sailors to scour ships' decks. * *vt* to scrub a ship's deck with holystone.
Holy Thursday *see* **Ascension Day**.
Holy Week *n* the week before Easter Sunday.
hom-, homo- *prefix* same; like.
homage *n* a public demonstration of respect or honour towards someone or something.
hombre *n* (*sl*) a man.
homburg *n* a man's soft felt hat with a dented crown.
home *n* the place where one lives; the city, etc where one was born or reared; a place thought of as home; a household and its affairs; an institution for the aged, orphans, etc. * *adj* of one's home or country; domestic. * *adv* at, to, or in the direction of home; to the point aimed at. * *vi* (*birds*) to return home; to be guided onto a target; to head for a destination; to send or go home.
home economics *n* (*sing or pl*) the art and science of household management, nutrition, etc.

home-grown *adj* grown or produced at home or nearby; characteristic of a particular locale.
homeland *n* the country where a person was born.
homely *adj* (**homelier, homeliest**) simple, everyday; crude; not good-looking.—**homeliness** *n.*
home-made *adj* made, or as if made, at home.
homeopathy *n* the system of treating disease by small quantities of drugs that cause symptoms similar to those of the disease.—**homeopath, homeopathist** *n.*—**homeopathic** *adj.*—**homeopathically** *adv.*
homer *n* (*baseball*) a home run; a homing pigeon; (*inf*) work done on an informal basis, without declaring the earnings.
Homeric *adj* pertaining to the poet Homer, or his works; heroic.—**Homerically** *adv.*
home run *n* (*baseball*) a hit that allows the batter to touch all bases and score a run.
homesick *adj* longing for home.—**homesickness** *n.*
homespun *adj* cloth made of yarn spun at home; coarse cloth like this.
homestead *n* a farmhouse with land and buildings.—**homesteader** *n*
home stretch, home straight *n* the part of a race track between the last turn and the finish line; the final part.
home truth *n* an unpleasant fact that a person has to face about himself or herself.
homeward *adj* going towards home. * *adv* homewards.
homewards *adv* towards home.
homework *n* work, esp piecework, done at home; schoolwork to be done outside the classroom; preliminary study for a project.
homey, homeyness *see* **homy.**
homicidal *adj* characterized by homicide; likely to commit suicide.
homicide *n* the killing of a person by another; a person who kills another.—**homicidal** *adj.*—**homicidally** *adv.*
homiletic, homiletical *adj* of or relating to a homily or sermon; of or relating to homiletics.—**homiletically** *adv.*
homiletics *n sing* the art of writing or preaching sermons.
homily *n* (*pl* **homilies**) a sermon; moralizing talk or writing.—**homilist** *n.*
homing *adj* (*pigeon*) trained to fly home after being transported long distances; (*missile, etc*) designed to guide itself onto a target.
hominid *adj* of or relating to the zoological species that includes present-day man and his ancestors. * *n* a member of this species.
hominoid *adj* resembling man; of or belonging to primates.
hominy (grits) *n* ground maize boiled in water to make a thin porridge.
homo[1] *n* any member of the genus *Homo* that includes modern man.
homo[2] *n* (*pl* **homos**) (*inf*) a male homosexual.
homocentric *adj* concentric; having the same centre.
homogeneous *adj* composed of parts that are of identical or a similar kind or nature; of uniform structure.—**homogeneity, homogeneousness** *n.*
homogenize *vt* to break up the fat particles (in milk or cream) so they do not separate; to make or become homogeneous.—**homogenization** *n.*—**homogenizer** *n.*
homograph *n* a word spelled the same as another word but with a different meaning and derived from a different root.
homologous *adj* corresponding in relative position, structure, and descent.
homologue, homolog *n* something that exhibits homology.
homology *n* (*pl* **homologies**) a similarity often attributed to a common origin; affinity of structure.—**homological** *adj.*—**homologically** *adv.*
homonym *n* a word with the same spelling or pronunciation as another, but a different meaning.—**homonymic** *adj.*—**homonymy** *n.*
Homoousian *n* a Christian who believes that Jesus is of the same essence as God.
homophobia *n* fear and hatred of homosexuals; persecution of homosexuals.—**homophobe** *n.*—**homophobic** *adj.*
homophone *n* a letter or group of letters having the same sound as another letter or group of letters; one of a group of words with identical pronunciations but with different meanings or spellings or both.—**homophony** *n.*
homophonous adj alike in sound but different in meaning; relating to or denoting a homophone.
homoplastic *adj* similar in structure; derived from a donating individual of a tissue graft of the same species as the recipient.
Homo sapiens *n* the species designating mankind.
homosexual *adj* sexually attracted towards a person of the same sex. * *n* a homosexual person.—**homosexuality** *n.*—**homosexually** *adv.*
homunculus *n* (*pl* **homunculi**) a dwarf; a miniature man.
homy *adj* (**homier, homiest**) cosy, home-like.—*also* **homey.**—**hominess, homeyness** *n.*
Hon. *abbr* = Honourable.
hon. *abbr* = honorary; honourable.
hone *n* a stone for sharpening cutting tools. * *vt* to sharpen (as if) on a hone.
honest *adj* truthful; trustworthy; sincere or genuine; gained by fair means; frank, open.—**honestness** *n.*
honestly *adv* in an honest manner; really.
honesty *n* (*pl* **honesties**) the quality of being honest; a European plant with purple flowers that forms transparent seed pods.
honey *n* (*pl* **honeys**) a sweet sticky yellowish substance that bees make as food from the nectar of flowers; sweetness; its colour; (*inf*) darling. * *adj* of, resembling honey; much loved.
honeybee *n* the common bee of the genus that produces honey.
honeycomb *n* the structure of six-sided wax cells made by bees to hold their honey, eggs, etc; anything arranged like this. * *vt* to fill with holes like a honeycomb.
honeydew *n* a sugary deposit on leaves secreted by aphids; a variety of melon with yellowish skin and pale green flesh.—**honeydewed** *adj.*
honeyed, honied *adj* flattering; of, containing, or resembling honey.—**honeyedly, honiedly** *adv.*
honeymoon *n* the vacation spent together by a newly married couple.—*also vi.*—**honeymooner** *n.*
honeysuckle *n* a climbing shrub with small fragrant flowers.
hong *n* (*formerly*) in China, a factory or warehouse, or a commercial establishment owned by a foreigner.
honk *n* (a sound resembling) the call of the wild goose; the sound made by an old-fashioned motor horn. * *vti* to cry like a goose; to sound (a motor horn); (*sl*) to be sick.
honky, honkie *n* (*pl* **honkies**) (*offens*) a white person.
honky-tonk *n* a style of ragtime piano playing.
honorarium *n* (*pl* **honorariums, honoraria**) a voluntary payment for professional services for which no fees are nominally due.
honorary *adj* given as an honour; (*office*) voluntary, unpaid.
honorific *adj* conferring honour.—**honorifically** *adv.*
honour, honor *n* high regard or respect; glory; fame; good reputation; integrity; chastity; high rank; distinction; (*with cap*) the title of certain officials, as judges; cards of the highest value in certain card games. * *vt* to respect greatly; to do or give something in honour of; to accept and pay (a cheque when due, etc).—**honourer, honorer** *n.*
honourable, honorable *adj* worthy of being honoured; honest; upright; bringing honour; (*with cap*) a title of respect for certain officials, as Members of Parliament, when addressing each other.—**honourably, honorably** *adv.*
hooch *n* (*US sl*) alcoholic liquor, esp when illicitly distilled or obtained.
hood[1] *n* a loose covering to protect the head and back of the neck; any hood-like thing as the (folding) top of a car, etc; (*US*) the hinged metal covering over an automobile engine—*see* **bonnet.**
hood[2] *n* (*inf*) a hoodlum.
hoodlum *n* a gangster; a young hooligan.—**hoodlumism** *n.*
hoodoo *n* (*pl* **hoodoos**) voodoo; a person or thing thought to bring bad luck. * *vt* (**hoodooing, hoodooed**) to bring ill luck to.—**hoodooism** *n.*
hoodwink *vt* to mislead by trickery.—**hoodwinker** *n.*
hooey *n* nonsense; humbug. * *interj* conveying disbelief.
hoof *n* (*pl* **hoofs, hooves**) the horny covering on the ends of the feet of certain animals, as horses, cows, etc.

hook *n* a piece of bent or curved metal to catch or hold anything; a fish-hook; something shaped like a hook; a strike, blow, etc, in which a curving motion is involved. * *vt* to seize, fasten, hold, as with a hook; (*rugby*) to pass the ball backwards from a scrum.

hookah *n* an oriental tobacco-pipe with a long tube connected to a container of water, which cools the smoke as it is drawn through.

hooked *adj* shaped like a hook; (*sl*) addicted.—**hookedness** *n*.

hooker *n* (*sl*) a prostitute; (*rugby football*) a player in the scrum whose task is to hook the ball.

hookworm *n* a parasitic worm with hooked mouthparts that can bore through the skin and cause disease.

hooky *n* truancy from school.

hooligan *n* a lawless young person.—**hooliganism** *n*.

hoop *n* a circular band of metal or wood; an iron band for holding together the staves of barrels; anything like this, as a child's toy or ring in a hoop skirt. * *vt* to bind (as if) with hoops.—**hooped** *adj*.

hooper *n* a cooper; the wild swan.

hoopla *n.* (*inf*) noise; bustle; (*inf*) misleading publicity.

hoopoe *n* a bird with a fanlike crest and pinky brown plumage.

hooray, hoorah *see* **hurrah**.

hoosegow *n* (*sl*) jail.

Hoosier *n* the nickname used for a native or resident of Indiana.

hoot *n* the sound that an owl makes; a similar sound, as made by a train whistle; a shout of scorn; (*inf*) laughter; (*inf*) an amusing person or thing. * *vi* to utter a hoot; to blow a whistle, etc. * *vt* to express (scorn) of (someone) by hooting.—**hooter** *n*.

hooves *see* **hoof**.

hop[1] *vi* (**hopping, hopped**) to jump up on one leg; to leap with all feet at once, as a frog, etc; (*inf*) to make a quick trip. * *n* a hopping movement; (*inf*) an informal dance; a trip, esp in an aircraft.

hop[2] *n* a climbing plant with small cone-shaped flowers; (*pl*) the dried ripe cones, used for flavouring beer.

hope *n* a feeling that what is wanted will happen; the object of this; a person or thing on which one may base some hope. * *vt* to want and expect. * *vi* to have hope (for).—**hoper** *n*.

hopeful *adj* filled with hope; inspiring hope or promise of success. * *n* a person who hopes to or looks likely to be a success.—**hopefulness** *n*.

hopefully *adv* in a hopeful manner; it is hoped.

hopeless *adj* without hope; offering no grounds for hope or promise of success; impossible to solve; (*inf*) incompetent.—**hopelessly** *adv*.—**hopelessness** *n*.

hoplite *n* in ancient Greece, a heavily armed foot soldier.

hopper *n* a hopping insect; a funnel-shaped container with an opening at the bottom from which its contents can be discharged into a receptacle.

hopscotch *n* a children's game in which the players hop through a sequence of squares drawn on the ground.

horary *adj* of or pertaining to or lasting an hour; noting the hours; hourly.

Horatian *adj* of or pertaining to the Roman poet Horace (658 bc) or his works.

horde *n* a crowd or throng; a swarm.

horizon *n* the apparent line along which the earth and sky meet; the limit of a person's knowledge, interest, etc.

horizontal *adj* level; parallel to the plane of the horizon.—**horizontally** *adv*.—**horizontalness** *n*.

hormone *n* a product of living cells formed in one part of the organism and carried to another part, where it takes effect; a synthetic compound having the same purpose.—**hormonal** *adj*.

horn *n* a bony outgrowth on the head of certain animals; the hard substance of which this is made; any projection like a horn; a wind instrument, esp the French horn or trumpet; a device to sound a warning. * *vt* to wound with a horn; (*with* **in**) to intrude.

hornbeam *n* a tree of the birch family.

hornbill *n* a tropical bird with a horny protuberance on its large beak.

hornblende *n* a dark mineral of silica with magnesium, lime or iron.

hornbook *n* a framed child's primer made of a thin slab of wood or paper on which numbers, the alphabet and the Lord's Prayer were printed and protected with a covering of transparent horn; any elementary primer.

horned *adj* having horns.

hornet *n* a large wasp with a severe sting.

hornpipe *n* a lively dance, formerly associated with British sailors; the music for such a dance; an obsolete wind instrument.

hornswoggle *vt* to deceive; to swindle.

horny *adj* (**hornier, horniest**) like horn; hard; callous; (*sl*) sexually aroused.—**hornily** *adv*.—**horniness** *n*.

horologe *n* any instrument that tells the time; a timepiece.

horology *n* the science of measuring time; the art of making clocks, watches, etc.—**horologic, horological** *adj*.—**horologist, horologer** *n*.

horoscope *n* a chart of the zodiacal signs and positions of planets, etc, by which astrologers profess to predict future events, esp in the life of an individual.

horrendous *adj* horrific; (*inf*) disagreeable.—**horrendously** *adv*.

horrible *adj* arousing horror; (*inf*) very bad, unpleasant, etc.—**horribleness** *n*.—**horribly** *adv*.

horrid *adj* terrible; horrible.—**horridly** *adv*.—**horridness** *n*.

horrific *adj* arousing horror; horrible.—**horrifically** *adv*.

horrify *vt* (**horrifying, horrified**) to fill with horror; to shock.—**horrification** *n*.—**horrifyingly** *adv*.

horripilation *n* gooseflesh; the bristling of the skin caused by chill or fright.

horror *n* the strong feeling caused by something frightful or shocking; strong dislike; a person or thing inspiring horror. * *adj* (*film, story, etc*) designed to frighten.

hors de combat *adj* excluded from competition; unrivalled; unequalled; disabled.

hors d'oeuvre *n* (*pl* **hors d'oeuvre, hors d'oeuvres**) an appetizer served at the beginning of a meal.

horse *n* a four-legged, solid-hoofed herbivorous mammal with a flowing mane and a tail, domesticated for carrying loads or riders, etc; cavalry; a vaulting horse; a frame with legs to support something.

horsebox *n* a trailer used for transporting a horse.

horse brass *n* a decorative brass ornament attached to a horse's harness.

horse chestnut *n* a large tree with large palmate leaves and erect clusters of flowers.

horseflesh *n* horses; the flesh of a horse, esp for eating.

horsehair *n* hair from the mane or the tail of a horse, used for padding, etc.

horse latitude *n* either of two oceanic regions between 30 degrees north and 30 degrees south latitude, marked by calms.

horse laugh *n* a boisterous, usu derisive laugh.

horseleech *n* a large carnivorous leech; an insatiable person.

horseman *n* (*pl* **horsemen**) a person skilled in the riding or care of horses.—**horsemanship** *n*.

horseplay *n* rough, boisterous fun.

horsepower *n* (*pl* **horsepower**) a unit for measuring the power of engines, etc, equal to 746 watts or 33,000 foot-pounds per minute.

horseradish *n* a tall herb of the mustard family; a sauce or relish made with its pungent root.

horse sense *n* common sense.

horseshoe *n* a flat U-shaped, protective metal plate nailed to a horse's hoof; anything shaped like this.

horsetail *n* a plant with jointed stems and whorls of small dark toothlike leaves; the tail of a horse, esp when used as a symbol of rank or as a standard.

horse-trade *n* a negotiation marked by shrewd bargaining and mutual concessions.—*also vi*.

horsewhip *n* a whip with a long thong used on horses. * *vt* (**horsewhipping, horsewhipped**) to flog with a horsewhip.

horsewoman *n* (*pl* **horsewomen**) a woman skilled at riding.
horsy, horsey *adj* (**horsier, horsiest**) of or resembling a horse; preoccupied with horses, horse racing, etc.—**horsily** *adv*.—**horsiness** *n*.
hortatory, hortative *adj* exhorting; encouraging.—**hortatorily** *adv*.
horticulture *n* the art or science of growing flowers, fruits, and vegetables.—**horticultural** *adj*.—**horticulturally** *adv*.—**horticulturist** *n*.
hosanna, hosannah *interj* an exclamation of praise to God. * *n* the cry of hosanna; a shout of praise.
hose[1] *n* a flexible tube used to convey fluids. * *vt* to spray with a hose.
hose[2] *n* (*pl* **hose, hosen**) stockings, socks, tights collectively.
Hosea *n* (*Bible*) an Old Testament book containing the oracles of Hosea, a Hebrew prophet of the 8th century bc.
hosier *n* a person who sells stockings, socks, etc.
hospice *n* a home for the care of the terminally ill; a place of rest and shelter for travellers.
hospitable *adj* offering a generous welcome to guests or strangers; sociable.—**hospitableness** *n*.—**hospitably** *adv*.
hospital *n* an institution where the sick or injured are given medical treatment.
hospitality *n* (*pl* **hospitalities**) the act, practice, or quality of being hospitable.
hospitalize *vt* to place in a hospital.—**hospitalization** *n*.
hospitaler, hospitaller *n* (*often cap*) a member of a medieval charitable religious order, esp one who worked in a hospital.
host[1] *n* a person who receives or entertains a stranger or guest at his house; an animal or plant on or in which another lives; a compere on a television or radio programme. * *vti* to act as a host (to a party, television programme, etc).
host[2] *n* a very large number of people or things.
host[3] *n* the wafer of bread used in the Eucharist or Holy Communion.
hostage *n* a person given or kept as security until certain conditions are met.
hostel *n* a lodging place for the homeless, travellers, or other groups.—**hosteler, hosteller** *n*.—**hosteling, hostelling** *n*.
hostelry *n* (*pl* **hostelries**) (*formerly*) an inn.
hostess *n* a woman acting as a host; a woman who entertains guests at a nightclub, etc.
hostile *adj* of or being an enemy; unfriendly.—**hostilely** *adv*.
hostility *n* (*pl* **hostilities**) enmity, antagonism; (*pl*) deliberate acts of warfare.
hostler *see* **ostler**.
hot *adj* (**hotter, hottest**) of high temperature; very warm; giving or feeling heat; causing a burning sensation on the tongue; full of intense feeling; following closely; electrically charged; (*inf*) recent, new; (*inf*) radioactive; (*inf*) stolen. * *adv* in a hot manner.—**hotly** *adv*.—**hotness** *n*.
hot air *n* (*sl*) empty talk.
hotbed *n* a bed of heated earth enclosed by low walls and covered by glass for forcing plants; ideal conditions for the growth of something, esp evil.
hot-blooded *adj* easily excited.—**hot-bloodedness** *n*.
hotchpotch *n* a thick meat and vegetable stew; a hodgepodge.
hot dog *n* a sausage, esp a frankfurter, served in a long soft roll.
hotel *n* a commercial establishment providing lodging and meals for travellers, etc.
hotelier *n* the owner or manager of a hotel.
hotfoot *adv* with all speed; quickly.
hothead *n* an impetuous person.—**hot-headed** *adj*.—**hot-headedly** *adv*.—**hot-headedness** *n*.
hothouse *n* a heated greenhouse for raising plants; an environment that encourages rapid growth.
hot line *n* a direct telephone link between heads of government for emergency use.
hotplate *n* a heated surface for cooking or keeping food warm; a small portable heating device.
hotpot *n* a dish of meat cooked with potatoes in a tight-lidded pot.
hot seat *n* (*inf*) a dangerous position; (*sl*) the electric chair.
Hottentot *n* (*pl* **Hottentots, Hottentot**) a member of a people of the Cape of Good Hope region of South Africa, with pale brown skin; any of the languages spoken by these people.
hot water *n* (*inf*) trouble.
houmous, houmus *see* **hummus**.
hound *n* a dog used in hunting; a contemptible person. * *vt* to hunt or chase as with hounds; to urge on by harassment.—**hounder** *n*.
hour *n* a period of 60 minutes, a 24th part of a day; the time for a specific activity; the time; a special point in time; the distance covered in an hour; (*pl*) the customary period for work, etc.
hourglass *n* an instrument for measuring time by trickling sand in a specified period.
houri *n* (*pl* **houris**) a beautiful woman of the Muslim paradise; a voluptuous young woman.
hourly *adj* occurring every hour; done during an hour; frequent. * *adv* at every hour; frequently.
house *n* a building to live in, esp by one person or family; a household; a family or dynasty including relatives, ancestors and descendants; the audience in a theatre; a business firm; a legislative assembly; house music. * *vt* to provide accommodation or storage for; to cover, encase.
house arrest *n* detention in one's own house, as opposed to prison.
houseboat *n* a boat furnished and used as a home.
housebound *adj* confined to the house through illness, injury, etc.
housebreaker *n* a burglar; a person employed to demolish buildings.—**housebreaking** *n*.
house-broken *adj* (*dogs, cats, etc*) trained not to mess in the house; (*inf*) well-mannered.
housefly *n* (*pl* **houseflies**) a common fly found in houses, which is attracted by food and can spread disease.
household *n* all those people living together in the same house. * *adj* pertaining to running a house and family; domestic; familiar.
householder *n* the person who owns or rents a house.
housekeeper *n* a person who runs a home, esp one hired to do so.
housekeeping *n* the daily running of a household; (*inf*) money used for domestic expenses; routine maintenance of equipment, records, etc in an organization.
housel *n* (*formerly*) the Eucharist.
houseleek *n* a plant with a rosette of succulent leaves and pink flowers that grows on walls.
housemaid *n* a female servant employed to do housework.
houseman *n* (*pl* **housemen**) an intern.
housemaster *n* a male teacher at a boarding school responsible for the pupils in his house.
house martin *n* a type of swallow with a forked tail.
house music *n* a pop music style, using electronic bass and synthesizers, a fast hypnotic beat and sporadic vocals, that originated in Chicago.
house party *n* a party, usu in a large house, where the guests stay over for several days; the guests themselves.
house plant *n* an indoor plant.
houseproud *adj* concerned with tidiness and cleanliness, often to excess.
house warming *n* a party given to celebrate moving into a new house.
housewife *n* (*pl* **housewives**) the woman who keeps house.—**housewifely** *adj*.—**housewifeliness** *n*.—**housewifery** *n*.
housework *n* the cooking, cleaning, etc, involved in running a home.—**houseworker** *n*.
housing *n* houses collectively; the provision of accommodation; a casing enclosing a piece of machinery, etc; a slot or groove in a piece of wood, etc, to receive an insertion.
hove *see* **heave**.
hovel *n* a small miserable dwelling. * *vt* (**hoveling, hoveled** *or* **hovelling, hovelled**) to shelter in a hovel.
hover *vi* (*bird, etc*) to hang in the air stationary; to hang about, to linger.—**hoverer** *n*.—**hoveringly** *adv*.
hovercraft *n* a land or water vehicle that travels supported on a cushion of air.

how *adv* in what way or manner; by what means; to what extent; in what condition.
howbeit *conj* (*arch*) though; although.
howdah *n* a seat fixed on the back of an elephant or camel.
how do you do *interj* a formal greeting, esp when meeting for the first time.
how-do-you-do, how-d'ye-do *n* (*inf*) a difficult situation, mess.
howdy *n* (*inf*) how do you do; hello.
however *adv* in whatever way or degree; still, nevertheless.
howitzer *n* a short cannon that fires shells at a steep trajectory.
howl *vi* to utter the long, wailing cry of wolves, dogs, etc; to utter a similar cry of anger, pain, etc; to shout or laugh in pain, amusement, etc. * *vt* to utter with a howl; to drive by howling. * *n* the wailing cry of a wolf, dog, etc; any similar sound.
howler *n* (*inf*) a stupid mistake.
howsoever *conj* still; nevertheless. * *adv* by whatever means; in whatever manner.
hoy *n* a coastal vessel; a freight barge. * *interj* a cry used to call attention.
hoya *n* a plant with pink, yellow or white flowers.
hoyden *n* a tomboy; a wild girl.—**hoydenish** *adj*.
HP *abbr* = hire purchase; horsepower; high pressure; Houses of Parliament.
HQ *abbr* = headquarters.
hr *abbr* = hour.
HRH *abbr* = His or Her Royal Highness.
HT *abbr* = high tension.
hub *n* the centre part of a wheel; a centre of activity.
hubba *n* (*sl*) a piece of the drug crack.
hubba-hubba *interj* an exclamation of delight.
hubble-bubble *n* a bubbling noise; confused talk; a hookah.
hubbub *n* a confused noise of many voices; an uproar.
hubby *n* (*pl* **hubbies**) (*inf*) a husband.
hubcap *n* a metal cap that fits over the hub of a car wheel.
hubris *n* arrogance, presumption.—**hubristic** *adj*.
huckaback *n* an absorbent linen or cotton fabric used for towels, etc.
huckleberry *n* (*pl* **huckleberries**) a North American shrub with dark-blue berries; the fruit of this plant.
huckster *n* a person using aggressive or questionable methods of selling.—**hucksterism** *n*.
huddle *vti* to crowd together in a confined space; to curl (oneself) up. * *n* a confused crowd or heap.—**huddler** *n*.
Hudibrastic *adj* mock-heroic, in the style of *Hudibras*, a poem by Samuel Butler (161–280).
hue *n* colour; a particular shade or tint of a colour.
hued *adj* having a colour or hue as specified.
huff *n* a state of smouldering resentment. * *vi* to blow; to puff.
huffish *adj* prone to fits of anger or petulance.
huffy *adj* (**huffier, huffiest**) disgruntled, moody.—**huffily** *adv*.—**huffiness** *n*.
hug *vb* (**hugging, hugged**) *vt* to hold or squeeze tightly with the arms; to cling to; to keep close to. * *vi* to embrace one another. * *n* a strong embrace.—**huggable** *adj*.—**hugger** *n*.
huge *adj* very large, enormous.—**hugely** *adv*.—**hugeness** *n*.
huggermugger *n* secrecy, concealment; confusion. * *adj* secret, clandestine; confused, jumbled. * *adv* in confusion. * *vt* to conceal, to hush up. * *vi* to muddle.
hula, hula-hula *n* a Polynesian dance performed by men or women; the music for this.
hulk *n* the body of a ship, esp if old and dismantled; a large, clumsy person or thing.
hulking, hulky *adj* unwieldy, bulky.
hull *n* the outer covering of a fruit or seed; the framework of a ship. * *vt* to remove the hulls of; to pierce the hull of (a ship, etc).—**huller** *n*.—**hull-less** *adj*.
hullabaloo, hullaballoo *n* (*pl* **hullabaloos, hullaballoos**) a loud commotion, uproar.
hullo *see* **hello**.
hum *vb* (**humming, hummed**) *vi* to make a low continuous vibrating sound; to hesitate in speaking and utter an inarticulate sound; (*inf*) to be lively, busy; (*sl*) to stink. * *vt* to sing with closed lips. * *n* a humming sound; a murmur; (*sl*) a stink.
human *adj* of or relating to human beings; having the qualities of humans as opposed to animals; kind, considerate. * *n* a human being.—**humanness** *n*.
human being *n* a member of the races of *Homo sapiens*; a man, woman or child.
humane *adj* kind, compassionate, merciful.—**humanely** *adv*.—**humaneness** *n*.
human immunodeficiency virus *n* either of two strains of a virus that inhibits the body from developing resistance to diseases and can lead to the development of Aids.
human interest *adj* (*newspaper story, etc*) appealing to the emotions.
humanism *n* belief in the promotion of human interests, intellect and welfare.
humanist *n* one versed in the knowledge of human nature; a student of the humanities.—**humanistic** *adj*.
humanitarian *adj* concerned with promoting human welfare. * *n* a humanitarian person.—**humanitarianism** *n*.—**humanitarianist** *n*.
humanity *n* (*pl* **humanities**) the human race; the state or quality of being human or humane; philanthropy; kindness; (*pl*) the study of literature and the arts, as opposed to the sciences.
humanize *vti* to make or become human.—**humanization** *n*.—**humanizer** *n*.
humankind *n* the human species; humanity.
humanly *adv* in a way characteristic of humans; within the limits of human capabilities.
humanoid *adj* resembling a human being in appearance or character. * *n* a humanoid thing.
humble *adj* having a low estimation of one's abilities; modest, unpretentious; servile. * *vt* to lower in condition or rank; to humiliate.—**humbleness** *n*.—**humbly** *adv*.
humblebee *n* the bumblebee.
humble pie *n* apology, usu under pressure.
humbug *n* fraud, sham, hoax; an insincere person; a peppermint-flavoured sweet. * *vt* (**humbugging, humbugged**) to cheat or impose upon; to hoax.—**humbugger** *n*.—**humbuggery** *n*.
humdinger *n* (*inf*) a remarkable person or thing.
humdrum *adj* dull, ordinary, boring.—**humdrumness** *n*.
humerus *n* (*pl* **humeri**) the bone extending from the shoulder to the elbow in humans.—**humeral** *adj*.
humid *adj* (*air*) moist, damp.—**humidly** *adv*.—**humidness** *n*.
humidifier fever *n* a collection of symptoms, thought to be caused by micro-organisms found in humidifiers and including lethargy, headache and eye irritation, that affect those who work in totally air-conditioned buildings.—*also* **sick building syndrome**.
humidify *vt* (**humidifying, humidified**) to make humid.—**humidification** *n*.—**humidifier** *n*.
humidity *n* (a measure of the amount of) dampness in the air.
humidor *n* a humid cabinet or room where cigars are kept moist.
humiliate *vt* to cause to feel humble; to lower the pride or dignity of.—**humiliatingly** *adv*.—**humiliator** *n*.—**humiliatory** *adj*.
humiliation *n* the act of humiliation; the state of being humiliated; mortification; abasement.
humility *n* (*pl* **humilities**) the state of being humble; modesty.
hummingbird *n* a tiny brightly coloured tropical bird with wings that vibrate rapidly, making a humming sound.
hummock *n* a hillock.—**hummocky** *adj*.
hummus *n* a dip or appetizer of puréed chick peas, sesame seeds and garlic.—*also* **houmous, houmus**.
humoresque *n* a light musical piece.
humorist *n* a person who writes or speaks in a humorous manner.—**humoristic** *adj*.
humorous *adj* funny, amusing; causing laughter.—**humorously** *adv*.—**humorousness** *n*.

humour, humor *n* the ability to appreciate or express what is funny, amusing, etc; the expression of this; temperament, disposition; state of mind; (*formerly*) any of the four fluids of the body (blood, phlegm, yellow and black bile) that were thought to determine temperament. * *vt* to indulge; to gratify by conforming to the wishes of.—**humourful, humorful** *adj*.

humourless, humorless *adj* done or said without humour; lacking a sense of humour.—**humourlessness, humorlessness** *n*.

humourology, humorology *n* the study of humour.

hump *n* a rounded protuberance; a fleshy lump on the back of an animal (as a camel or whale); a deformity causing curvature of the spine. * *vt* to hunch; to arch.

humpback *n* a hunchback.—**humpbacked** *adj*.

humph *interj* expressing annoyance.

humus *n* dark brown or black organic matter in the soil formed from partially decomposed leaves, plants, etc.

Hun *n* one of the ancient Tartar races that overran Europe in the 4th and 5th centuries; a vandal; (*derog*) a German.

hunch *n* a hump; (*inf*) an intuitive feeling. * *vt* to arch into a hump. * *vi* to move forward jerkily.

hunchback *n* a person with curvature of the spine.

hunchbacked *adj* having an abnormal convex curvature of the thoracic spine.

hundred *adj, n* (*pl* **hundreds, hundred**) ten times ten; the symbol for this (100, C, c); the hundredth in a series or set.

hundredfold *adj, adv* one hundred times as great or many.

hundredth *adj* the last of a hundred.

hundredweight *n* (*pl* **hundredweight, hundredweights**) a unit of weight, equal to 110 pounds in US and 112 pounds in the UK.

hung *see* **hang.**

Hungarian *adj* pertaining to Hungary, its inhabitants, or language. * *n* an inhabitant of Hungary; the language spoken in Hungary.

hunger *n* (a feeling of weakness or emptiness from) a need for food; a strong desire. * *vi* to feel hunger; to have a strong desire (for).

hunger strike *n* refusal to take food as a protest.

hung-over *adj* (*sl*) suffering from a hangover.

hungry *adj* (**hungrier, hungriest**) desiring food; craving for something; greedy.—**hungrily** *adv*.—**hungriness** *n*.

hunk *n* (*inf*) a large piece, lump, etc; (*sl*) a sexually attractive man.—**hunky** *adj*.

hunker *vi* to squat, crouch down. * *npl* the haunches or buttocks.

hunkydory *adj* first-rate.

hunt *vti* to seek out to kill or capture (game) for food or sport; to search (for); to chase. * *n* a chase; a search; a party organized for hunting.

hunter *n* a person who hunts; a horse used in hunting.—**huntress** *nf*.

hunting *n* the art or practice of one who hunts; a pursuit; a search.

huntsman *n* (*pl* **huntsmen**) a person who manages a hunt and looks after the hounds.

hurdle *n* a portable frame of bars for temporary fences or for jumping over by horses or runners; an obstacle. (*pl*) a race over hurdles.—**hurdler** *n*.

hurdy-gurdy *n* (*pl* **hurdy-gurdies**) a mechanical instrument such as a barrel organ.

hurl *vt* to throw violently; to utter vehemently. * *n* a violent throw; a ride in a car.—**hurler** *n*.

hurling, hurley *n* an Irish form of field hockey.

hurly-burly *n* (*pl* **hurly-burlies**) uproar; confusion.

hurrah *interj* an exclamation of approval or joy.—*also* **hooray, hoorah.**

hurricane *n* a violent tropical cyclone with winds of at least 74 miles (119 kilometres) per hour.

hurried *adj* performed with great haste.—**hurriedly** *adv*.—**hurriedness** *n*.

hurry *n* (*pl* **hurries**) rush; urgency; eagerness to do, go, etc. * *vb* (**hurrying, hurried**) *vt* to cause to move or happen more quickly. * *vi* to move or act with haste.—**hurryingly** *adv*.

hurt *vb* (**hurting, hurt**) *vt* to cause physical pain to; to injure, damage; to offend. * *vi* to feel pain; to cause pain.—**hurter** *n*.

hurtful *adj* causing hurt, mischievous.—**hurtfully** *adv*.—**hurtfulness** *n*.

hurtle *vti* to move or throw with great speed and force.

husband *n* a man to whom a woman is married. * *vt* to conserve; to manage economically.—**husbander** *n*.

husbandman *n* (*pl* **husbandmen**) a farmer.

husbandry *n* management of resources; farming.

hush *vti* to make or become silent. * *n* a silence or calm.

hush-hush *adj* (*inf*) secret.

hush money *n* (*sl*) money paid to a person to keep a discreditable fact secret.

husk *n* the dry covering of certain fruits and seeds; any dry, rough, or useless covering. * *vt* to strip the husk from.—**husker** *n*.

husky[1] *adj* (**huskier, huskiest**) (*voice*) hoarse; rough-sounding; hefty, strong.—**huskily** *adv*.—**huskiness** *n*.

husky[2] *n* (*pl* **huskies**) an Arctic sled dog.

hussar *n* a member of any of various European light cavalry regiments, usu with an elegant dress uniform.

hussy *n* (*pl* **hussies**) a cheeky woman; a promiscuous woman.

hustings *n* (*pl or sing*) the process of, or a place for, political campaigning.

hustle *vt* to jostle or push roughly or hurriedly; to force hurriedly; (*sl*) to obtain by rough or illegal means. * *vi* to move hurriedly. * *n* an instance of hustling.—**hustler** *n*.

hut *n* a very plain or crude little house or cabin.

hutch *n* a pen or coop for small animals; a hut.

huzzah *interj* (*formerly*) hurrah.

hyacinth *n* a plant of the lily family with spikes of bell-shaped flowers; the orange gemstone jacinth; a light violet to moderate purple.—**hyacinthine** *adj*.

Hyades *n* (*Greek myth*) five nymphs, the daughters of Atlas; the five stars in the constellation Taurus.

hyaline *adj* glassy; transparent.

hybrid *n* the offspring of two plants or animals of different species; a mongrel. * *adj* crossbred.—**hybridism** *n*.—**hybridity** *n*.

hybridize *vti* to produce hybrids; to interbreed.—**hybridizable** *adj*.—**hybridization** *n*.—**hybridizer** *n*.

hydatid *n* a watery cyst in animal tissue; a large bladder containing the larvae of the tapeworm.—*also adj*.

hydr-, hydro- *prefix* water, fluids.

hydra *n* (*pl* **hydras, hydrae**) (*usu with cap*) a legendary many-headed water serpent; any of numerous freshwater polyps having a mouth surrounded by tentacles.

hydrangea *n* a shrub with large heads of white, pink, or blue flowers.

hydrant *n* a large pipe with a valve for drawing water from a water main; a fireplug.

hydrate *n* a chemical compound of water with some other substance. * *vt* to (cause to) combine with or absorb water.—**hydration** *n*.—**hydrator** *n*.

hydraulic *adj* operated by water or other liquid, esp by moving through pipes under pressure; of hydraulics.—**hydraulically** *adv*.

hydraulics *n sing* the science dealing with the mechanical properties of liquids, as water, and their application in engineering.

hydric *adj* of or containing hydrogen; of or containing water.

hydride *n* any compound of hydrogen and another element.

hydriodic *adj* composed of hydrogen and iodine.

hydro *n* (*pl* **hydros**) a hotel or resort offering hydropathic treatment.

hydrocarbon *n* any organic compound containing only hydrogen and carbon.

hydrocele *n* an accumulation of fluid in a body cavity, esp in the scrotum.

hydrocephalus, hydrocephaly *n* an accumulation of fluid in the brain.—**hydrocephalic** *adj*.

hydrochloric acid *n* a strong, highly corrosive acid that is a solution of the gas hydrogen chloride in water.

hydrochloric *adj* composed of hydrogen and chlorine.

hydrocyanic *adj* composed of hydrogen and cyanic.

hydrodynamics *n sing* the science of the mechanical properties of fluids.—**hydrodynamic** *adj*.—**hydrodynamically** *adv*.

hydroelectricity *n* electricity generated by water power.—**hydroelectric** *adj*.

hydrofluoric *adj* composed of hydrogen and fluorine.

hydrofoil *n* a vessel equipped with vanes that lift the hull out of the water to allow fast cruising speeds.

hydrogen *n* a flammable, colourless, odourless, tasteless, gaseous chemical element, the lightest substance known.

hydrogenate *vt* to combine with or treat with hydrogen.—**hydrogenation** *n*.—**hydrogenator** *n*.

hydrogen bomb *n* a powerful bomb that produces explosive energy through the fusion of hydrogen nuclei.

hydrography *n* the study, surveying and mapping of the oceans, seas, lakes, and rivers as on a chart.—**hydrographer** *n*.—**hydrographic, hydrographical** *adj*.

hydrokinetics *n sing* the branch of physics concerned with the study of fluids in motion.

hydrology *n* the science of the properties of water and its distribution on the earth and in the atmosphere.—**hydrologic, hydrological** *adj*.—**hydrologist** *n*.

hydrolysis *n* the chemical breakdown of organic compounds by interaction with water.

hydrolyze *vti* to decompose by hydrolysis.—**hydrolyzation** *n*.—**hydrolyzer** *n*.

hydromechanics *n sing* the science of the use of fluids as motive power also called hydrodynamics.

hydromel *n* a mixture of honey and water that is fermented to make mead.

hydrometer *n* a device for measuring the densities of liquids.—**hydrometric, hydrometrical** *adj*.—**hydrometry** *n*.

hydropathy *n* the use of water to treat diseases.—**hydropathic, hydropathical** *adj*.—**hydropathist, hydropath** *n*.

hydrophane *n* a partially opaque, white type of opal that becomes translucent in water.

hydrophobia *n* a morbid fear of water; rabies.—**hydrophobic** *adj*.

hydrophone *n* an instrument that detects sound through water.

hydrophyte *n* a plant that will grow only in water or sodden soil.—**hydrophitic** *adj*.

hydroplane *n* a light motor boat that skims through the water at high speed with its hull raised out of the water; a fin that directs the vertical movement of a submarine; an attachment to an aircraft that enables it to glide along the surface of water. * *vi* (of a boat) to rise out of the water in the manner of a hydroplane.

hydroponics *n sing* the growing of plants in chemical nutrients without soil.—**hydroponically** *adv*.

hydroscope *n* any instrument that makes observations of underwater objects.

hydrosphere *n* the moisture-bearing envelope that surrounds the earth.

hydrostatics *n sing* the branch of physics concerned with the study of fluids at rest.—**hydrostatic** *adj*.

hydrotherapy *n* (*pl* **hydrotherapies**) the treatment of certain diseases and physical conditions by the external application of water.—**hydrotherapist** *n*.

hydrous *adj* containing water.

hyena *n* a nocturnal, carnivorous, scavenging mammal like a wolf.—*also* **hyaena**.

Hygeia *n* (*Greek myth*) the goddess of health.

hygiene *n* the principles and practice of health and cleanliness.—**hygienic** *adj*.—**hygienically** *adv*.

hygienist *n* a person skilled in the practice of hygiene.

hygrometer *n* an instrument for measuring the humidity of the atmosphere.—**hygrometric** *adj*.—**hygrometrically** *adv*.—**hygrometry** *n*.

hygroscope *n* an instrument that shows changes in the humidity of the atmosphere.

hygroscopic *adj* readily absorbing and retaining moisture from the air.—**hygroscopically** *adv*.

hylozoism *n* (*philos*) the doctrine that life is a property of matter; materialism.—**hylozoic** *adj*.—**hylozoist** *n*.

Hymen *n* (*Greek myth*) the god of marriage.

hymen *n* the mucous membrane partly closing the vaginal orifice.—**hymenal** *adj*.

hymeneal *adj* of marriage, nuptial.

hymenopteran *n* (*pl* **hymenopterans, hymenopterana**) any of a large order of insects that have two pairs of membranous wings.—**hymenopterous** *adj*.

hymn *n* a song of praise to God or other object of worship.

hymnal *n* a hymn book.

hymn book *n* a book of hymns.

hymnology *n* the study of the composition of hymns.—**hymnologist** *n*.

hyoid *adj* U-shaped; of or relating to the hyoid bone at the base of the tongue.

hyoscine *see* **scopolamine.**

hyp-, hypo- *prefix* below; slightly.

hype[1] *n* (*sl*) a hypodermic needle. * *vi* (*sl*) to inject a narcotic drug with a needle.

hype[2] *n* (*sl*) deception; aggressive or extravagant publicity. * *vt* to publicize or promote a product, etc in this manner.

hyped-up *adj* aggressively publicized; (*sl*) stimulated as if by injection of a drug.

hyper- *prefix* above; too; exceeding.

hyperactive *adj* abnormally active.—**hyperactivity** *n*.

hyperesthesia, hyperaesthesia *n* increased sensitivity of any of the sense organs.—**hyperaesthetic** *adj*.

hyperbola *n* (*pl* **hyperbolas, hyperbolae**) (*geom*) a curve formed by a plane intersecting a cone at a greater angle to its base than its side.

hyperbole *n* a figure of speech using absurd exaggeration.

hyperbolic, hyperbolical *adj* pertaining to or containing hyperbole, exaggerated; pertaining to or of the nature of a hyperbola.

hyperborean *adj* of or relating to the extreme north. * *n* an inhabitant of the extreme north; (*Greek myth*) (*with cap*) one of the people who lived in the sunny land beyond the north wind.

hypercritical *adj* excessively critical.—**hypercritically** *adv*.—**hypercriticism** *n*.

hypermetric *adj* beyond the normal metre of a line; having one syllable too many

hypersensitive *adj* extremely vulnerable; abnormally sensitive to a drug, pollen, etc.—**hypersensitivity** *n*.

hypersonic *adj* travelling at speeds at least five times faster than sound; of sound frequencies above 1,000 megahertz.—**hypersonics** *n*.

hypertension *n* abnormally high blood pressure.—**hypertensive** *adj*.

hyperthyroidism *n* the overproduction of the thyroid hormone by the thyroid gland.—**hyperthyroid** *adj, n*.

hypertrophy *n* (*pl* **hypertrophies**) abnormal enlargement of an organ or part.—**hypertrophic** *adj*.

hypervitaminosis *n* the pathological condition that results from the excessive intake of vitamins.

hyphen *n* a punctuation mark (-) used to join two syllables or words, or to divide words into parts. * *vt* to hyphenate.

hyphenate *vt* to join by a hyphen.—**hyphenation** *n*.

hypnosis *n* (*pl* **hypnoses**) a relaxed state resembling sleep in which the mind responds to external suggestion.

hypnotherapy *n* the use of hypnosis in treatment of emotional and psychological disorders.

hypnotic *adj* of or producing hypnosis; (*person*) susceptible to hypnosis. * *n* a drug causing sleep; a person susceptible to hypnosis.—**hypnotically** *adv*.

hypnotism *n* the act of inducing hypnosis; the study and use of hypnosis.—**hypnotist** *n*.

hypnotize *vt* to put in a state of hypnosis; to fascinate.—**hypnotizer** *n*.

hypo- *prefix* below; slightly.

hypocaust *n* the hot-air chamber under a Roman bath.

hypochondria *n* chronic anxiety about health, often with imaginary illnesses.

hypochondriac *n* a person suffering from hypochondria. * *adj* pertaining to or affected with hypochrondria.—**hypochondriacally** *adv*.

hypocorism *n* a diminutive pet name; a euphemism.—**hypocoristic, hypocoristical** *adj*.

hypocrisy *n* (*pl* **hypocrisies**) a falsely pretending to possess virtues, beliefs, etc; an example of this.—**hypocritical** *adj*.—**hypocritically** *adv*.

hypocrite *n* a person who pretends to be what he or she is not.

hypocycloid *n* (*geom*) a curve traced by the point on the circumference of a circle, which rolls on to the inside of another circle.
hypodermic *adj* injected under the skin. * *n* a hypodermic needle, syringe or injection.
hypodermic syringe *n* a syringe with a hollow (hypodermic) needle through which blood samples can be drawn.
hypogastrium *n* (*pl* **hypogastria**) the middle part of the lower region of the abdomen.
hypogeal, hypogean, hypogeous *adj* (*bot*) underground; occuring or living underground.
hypogene *adj* (*rocks*) formed under the surface of the ground.
hypostasis *n* (*pl* **hypostates**) the essential personality of a substance; (*Christianity*) any of the three persons of the Godhead which together make up the Holy Trinity; (*med*) an excess of blood in the organs as the result of poor circulation.—**hypostatic** *adj*.
hypostatize *vt* to regard as real; to embody or personify.—**hypostatization** *n*.
hypostyle *n* a roof supported by columns; a covered colonnade; a pillared hall or court.
hypotenuse *n* the side opposite to the right angle in a right-angled triangle.
hypothecate *vt* to pledge (a property) without delivery of title or possession.—**hypothecation** *n*.—**hypothecator** *n*.
hypothermia *n* an abnormally low body temperature.
hypothesis *n* (*pl* **hypotheses**) something assumed for the purpose of argument; a theory to explain some fact that may or may not prove to be true; supposition; conjecture.
hypothesize *vti* to form or assume as a hypothesis.
hypothetical *adj* based on hypothesis, conjectural.—**hypothetically** *adv*.
hypothyroidism *n* deficient activity of the thyroid glands.
hypsometry *n* the science of measuring altitude.—**hypsometric** *adj*.
hyrax *n* (*pl* **hyraxes, hyraces**) a small African hamster-like mammal related to the elephant.
hyson *n* Chinese green tea.
hyssop *n* an aromatic plant with blue flowers formerly used in medicine.
hysterectomy *n* (*pl* **hysterectomies**) surgical removal of the womb.
hysteresis *n*. (*pl* **hystereses**) magnetic inertia.—**hysteretic** *adj*.
hysteria *n* a mental disorder marked by excitability, anxiety, imaginary organic disorders, etc; frenzied emotion or excitement.
hysteric *n* a hysterical person; (*pl*) fits of hysteria; (*inf*) uncontrollable laughter.
hysterical *adj* caused by hysteria; suffering from hysteria; (*inf*) extremely funny.—**hysterically** *adv*.
hysterotomy *n* (*pl* **hysterotomies**) a surgical incision into the womb.
Hz *abbr* = hertz.

I

I[1] *pron* the person who is speaking or writing, used in referring to himself or herself.
I[2] (*chem symbol*) iodine.
I. *abbr* = island(s); isle(s).
IAEA *abbr* = International Atomic Energy Authority.
iamb, iambus *n* (*pl* **iambi, iambs, iambuses**) a metrical foot consisting of two syllables, the first short or unstressed and the second long or stressed.—**iambic** *adj*.
-iana, -ana *n suffix* sayings of, publications about, as *Shakespeariana*, etc.
-iatric, -iatrical *adj* pertaining to doctors and medicine.
Iberian *adj* pertaining to Spain and Portugal; pertaining to Iberia, the ancient name of the southwest European peninsula now comprising Spain and Portugal.
ibex *n* (*pl* **ibexes, ibices, ibex**) any of various wild mountain goats with large horns.
ibid *abbr* = *ibidem*, in, in the same book, page, etc.
ibis *n* (*pl* **ibises, ibis**) a wading bird with a curved bill.
Ibo *n* (*pl* **Ibo, Ibos**) a member of a Black people of southern Nigeria; their language.
ICBM *abbr* = intercontinental ballistic missile.
ice *n* water frozen solid; a sheet of this; a portion of ice cream or water ice; (*sl*) diamonds; (*sl*) the drug methamphetamine packaged and sold as a stimulant in smokeable form. * *vti* (*often with* **up** *or* **over**) to freeze; to cool with ice; to cover with icing.
ice age *n* a period when much of the earth's surface was covered in glaciers; (with caps) the Pleistocene glacial epoch.
iceberg *n* a great mass of mostly submerged ice floating in the sea.
iceblink *n* a streak of whiteness on the horizon, caused by the reflection of light from masses of ice in the distance.
icebound *adj* (*ship, etc*) surrounded, and immobilized, by ice.
icebox *n* a compartment in a refrigerator for making ice.
icebreaker, iceboat *n* a powerful and reinforced vessel for breaking a channel through ice.
icecap *n* a mass of slowly spreading glacial ice.
ice cream *adj* a sweet frozen food, made from flavoured milk or cream.
ice dance *n* a type of ballroom dancing by skaters on ice.
icefall *n* a steep part of a glacier, resembling a frozen waterfall.
ice field *n* an extensive field of floating ice.
ice floe *n* a sheet of floating ice.
ice hockey *n* an indoor or outdoor hockey game played on ice by two teams of six skaters with curved sticks and a flat disk called a puck.
Icelander *n* a native or inhabitant of Iceland.
Icelandic *adj* of or pertaining to Iceland or its language, literature and people. * *n* the language of Iceland.
ice pack *n* a field of broken and drifting ice, consisting of great masses packed together; a cloth or small bag filled with crushed ice for soothing sores and swellings on the body.
ice pick *n* a pointed awl with a handle for chipping or breaking up ice.
ice plant *n* a type of plant with leaves that glisten as if covered with ice.
ice skate *n* a boot with a steel blade fixed to the sole for skating on ice.—*also vi*.—**ice skater** *n*.
ichneumon *n* a North African mongoose.
ichneumon fly *n* an insect that lays its eggs in the bodies of other insects.
ichnite, ichnolite *n* a fossil footprint.
ichor *n* (*Greek myth*) the ethereal fluid believed to run, instead of blood, in the veins of the classical gods.—**ichorous** *adj*.
ichtny-, icthyo- *prefix* fish.
ichthyic *adj* pertaining to fishes.
ichthyoid, ichthyoidal *adj* resembling a fish.
ichthyology *n* the study of fish.—**ichthyologic, ichthyological** *adj*.—**ichthyologist** *n*.
ichthyophagous *adj* fish-eating.—**ichthyophagy** *n*.
ichthyornis *n* an extinct species of toothed fish-eating bird.
ichthyosaur, ichthyosaurus *n* (*pl* **ichthyosaurs, ichthosauri**) a gigantic, extinct, marine reptile.
ichthyosis *n* a disease in which the skin becomes dry and scaly.
icicle *n* a hanging tapering length of ice formed when dripping water freezes.—**icicled** *adj*.
icily *adv* in an icy manner, coldly.
iciness *n* the state of being icy, coldness.
icing *n* a semi-solid sugary mixture used to cover cakes, etc.—*also* **frosting**.
icon *n* an image; (*Eastern Church*) a sacred image, usu on a wooden panel.—*also* **ikon**.—**iconic, iconical** *adj*.
iconoclast *n* a person who attacks revered or traditional beliefs, opinions, etc.—**iconoclasm** *n*.—**iconoclastic** *adj*.—**iconoclastically** *adv*.
iconography *n* (*pl* **iconographies**) the art of representation by means of images (statues), pictures, or engravings; the study of this art.—**iconographer** *n*.—**iconographic, iconographical** *adj*.
iconolatry *n* the worship of images.
iconology *n* the study of icons.

icosahedron *n* (*pl* **icosahedrons, icosahedra**) (*geom*) a solid bounded by 20 plane faces.

icterus *n* jaundice.—**icteric** *adj*.

ictus *n* (*pl* **ictuses, ictus**) a stress in verse.

icy *adj* (**icier, iciest**) full of, made of, or covered with ice; slippery or very cold; cold in manner.

ID *abbr* = identification.

ID card *n* an identity card.

I'd = I had; I should; I would.

id *n* (*psychoanal*) the primitive psychological instincts in the unconscious which are the source of psychic activity.

ide *n* a small European fish.

idea *n* a mental impression of anything; a vague impression, notion; an opinion or belief; a scheme; a supposition; a person's conception of something; a significance or purpose.

ideal *adj* existing in the mind or as an idea; satisfying an ideal, perfect. * *n* the most perfect conception of anything; a person or thing regarded as perfect; a standard for attainment or imitation; an aim or principle.—**ideally** *adv*.—**idealness** *n*.

idealism *n* the pursuit of high ideals; the conception or representation of things in their ideal form as against their reality.—**idealist** *n*.—**idealistic** *adj*.—**idealistically** *adv*.

ideality *n* (*pl* **idealities**) the quality of being ideal; the faculty to form ideals.

idealize *vt* to consider or represent as ideal.—**idealization** *n*.—**idealizer** *n*.

ideate *vti* to imagine.

idée fixe *n* (*pl* **idées fixes**) a fixed idea; an obsession.

identical *adj* exactly the same; having the same origin.—**identically** *adv*.—**identicalness** *n*.

identifiable *adj* able to be identified.—**identifiableness** *n*.

identification *n* the act of identifying; the state of being identified; that which identifies.

identify *vt* (**identifying, identified**) to consider to be the same, equate; to establish the identity of; to associate closely; to regard (oneself) as similar to another.—**identifier** *n*.

identity *n* (*pl* **identities**) the state of being exactly alike; the distinguishing characteristics of a person, personality; the state of being the same as a specified person or thing.

identity card *n* a card carrying personal details, a photograph, etc of an individual as carried by staff of an organization, journalists, etc.

ideogram, ideograph *n* a symbol, as in Chinese writing, used instead of a word to represent an idea or thing; a graphic sign.

ideography *n* the direct representation of ideas by symbols.—**ideographic, ideographical** *adj*.

ideologist, ideologue *n* one occupied with ideals or ideals; a theorist.

ideology *n* (*pl* **ideologies**) the doctrines, beliefs or opinions of an individual, social class, political party, etc.—**ideological, ideologic** *adj*.

ides *n* the 15th day of March, May, July, or October and the 13th day of any other month in the ancient Roman calender.

idiocy *n* (*pl* **idiocies**) mental deficiency; stupidity, imbecility; something stupid or foolish.

idiom *n* an accepted phrase or expression with a different meaning from the literal; the usual way in which the words of a language are used to express thought; the dialect of a people, region, etc; the characteristic style of a school of art, literature, etc—**idiomatic, idiomatical** *adj*.—**idiomatically** *adv*.

idiopathy *n* a disease whose cause is unknown.—**idiopathic** *adj*.

idiosyncrasy *n* (*pl* **idiosyncrasies**) a type of behaviour or characteristic peculiar to a person or group; a quirk, eccentricity.—**idiosyncratic** *adj*.—**idiosyncratically** *adv*.

idiot *n* a severely mentally retarded adult; (*inf*) a foolish or stupid person.

idiot board *n* an autocue.

idiotic *adj* stupid; senseless.—**idiotically** *adv*.

idle *adj* not employed, unoccupied; not in use; averse to work; useless; worthless. * *vt* to waste or spend (time) in idleness. * *vi* to move slowly or aimlessly; (*engine*) to operate without transmitting power.—**idleness** *n*.—**idler** *n*.—**idly** *adv*.

idler *n* someone who idles; a lazy person.

idol *n* an image or object worshipped as a god; a person who is intensely loved, admired or honoured.

idolatry *n* the worship of idols; excessive admiration or devotion.—**idolatrous** *adj*.—**idolater** *n*.

idolize *vt* to make an idol of, for worship; to love to excess.—**idolization** *n*.—**idolizer** *n*.

idyll, idyl *n* a short simple poem, usu evoking the romance and beauty of rural life; a romantic or picturesque event or scene; a romantic or pastoral musical composition.—**idyllist** *n*.

idyllic *adj* pertaining to or of the nature of an idyll, pastoral; romantic, picturesque.—**idyllically** *adv*.

i.e. *abbr* = *id est*, that is.

if *conj* on condition that; in the event that; supposing that; even though; whenever; whether.

iffy *adj* (*inf*) uncertain, unreliable.

igloo *n* (*pl* **igloos**) an Eskimo house built of blocks of snow and ice.

igneous *adj* of fire; (*rocks*) produced by volcanic action or intense heat beneath the earth's surface.

ignite *vti* to set fire to; to catch fire; to burn or cause to burn.—**ignitable** *adj*.

ignition *n* an act or instance of igniting; the starting of an internal combustion engine; the mechanism that ignites an internal combustion engine.

ignoble *adj* dishonourable, despicable; base, of low birth.—**ignobly** *adv*.

ignominious *adj* bringing disgrace or shame; humiliating, degrading.—**ignominiously** *adv*.

ignominy *n* (*pl* **ignominies**) disgrace, dishonour; a cause of ignominy, a disgraceful act.

ignoramus *n* (*pl* **ignoramuses**) an ignorant person.

ignorance *n* the state of being ignorant; a lack of knowledge.

ignorant *adj* lacking knowledge; uninformed, uneducated; resulting from or showing lack of knowledge.—**ignorance** *n*.—**ignorantly** *adv*.

ignore *vt* to disregard; to deliberately refuse to notice someone.—**ignorable** *adj*.—**ignorer** *n*.

iguana *n* any of a family of large lizards of tropical America.—**iguanian** *adj, n*.

iguanodon *n* a gigantic, extinct, herbivorous lizard.

ihram *n* the distinctive white robes worn by Muslims on pilgrimage to Mecca.

ikebana *n* the Japanese art of flower arranging.

ikon *see* **icon**.

ileac, ileal *adj* (*anat*) pertaining to the ileum.

ileum *n* (*anat*) the lower part of the small intestine.

ilk *n* a type or sort.

ill *adj* (**worse, worst**) not in good health; harmful; bad; hostile; faulty; unfavourable. * *adv* badly, wrongly; hardly, with difficulty. * *n* trouble; harm; evil.

ill. *abbr* = illustrated; illustration.

I'll = I shall; I will.

ill-advised *adj* unwise.

ill at ease *adj* uneasy, embarrassed.

ill-bred *adj* bad-mannered.—**ill-breeding** *n*.

ill-considered *adj* lacking consideration; not thought out properly.

ill-disposed *adj* unfavourably inclined (towards).

illegal *adj* against the law.—**illegally** *adv*.—**illegality** *n*.

illegible *adj* impossible to read.—**illegibility, illegibleness** *n*.—**illegibly** *adv*.

illegitimate *adj* born of parents not married to each other; contrary to law, rules, or logic.—**illegitimacy, illegitimateness** *n*.—**illegitimately** *adv*.

ill-fated *adj* unlucky.

ill-favoured, ill-favored *adj* unattractive; unpleasant.

ill-founded *adj* not based on reliable facts; unsubstantiated.

ill-gotten *adj* illegally or dishonestly acquired.

ill-humoured, ill-humored *adj* bad tempered; sullen.—**ill-humour, ill humor** *n.*
illiberal *adj* narrow-minded; mean.—**illiberality, illiberalness** *n*—**illiberally** *adv.*
illicit *adj* improper; unlawful.—**illicitly** *adv.*
illimitable *adj* limitless, infinite.—**illimitability** *n.*
illiterate *adj* uneducated, esp not knowing how to read or write. * *n* an illiterate person.—**illiteracy** *n.*—**illiterately** *adv.*
ill-mannered *adj* rude.
ill-natured *adj* spiteful.
illness *n* a state of ill-health; sickness.
illogical *adj* not logical or reasonable.—**illogicality, illogicalness** *n.*—**illogically** *adv.*
ill-starred *adj* unlucky.
ill-timed *adj* occurring or done at an unsuitable time.
ill-treat *vt* to treat unkindly, unfairly, etc.—**ill-treatment** *n.*
illume *vt* (*poet*) to light up, illuminate.
illuminant *n* a substance or device that illuminates.
illuminate *vt* to give light to; to light up; to make clear; to inform; to decorate as with gold or lights.—**illumination** *n.*—**illuminative** *adj.*—**illuminator** *n.*
illuminati *npl* (*sing* **illuminato**) a name given to persons professing special spiritual or intellectual enlightenment.
illumination *n* a supply of light; the act of illuminating; the state of being illuminated; (*Brit, esp pl*) decorative coloured lights used in public places.
illumine *vt* (*poet*) to illuminate.
illuminism *n* the belief in and profession of special spiritual and intellectual enlightenment.
ill-usage *n* ill-use, abuse.
ill-use *vt* to treat badly, etc. * *n* abuse.
illusion *n* a false idea or conception; an unreal or misleading image or appearance.—**illusional, illusionary** *adj.*
illusionism *n* (*philos*) a disbelief in objective existence.
illusionist *n* a magician or conjuror.—**illusionism** *n.*
illusory, illusive *adj* deceptive; based on illusion.—**illusorily** *adv.*—**illusoriness** *n.*
illustrate *vt* to explain, as by examples; to provide (books, etc) with explanatory pictures, charts, etc; to serve as an example.—**illustratable** *adj.*—**illustrative** *adj.*—**illustrator** *n.*
illustration *n* the act of illustrating; the state of being illustrated; an example that explains or corroborates; a picture or diagram in a book, etc.—**illustrational** *adj.*
illustrious *adj* distinguished, famous.—**illustriousness** *n.*
ill-will *n* antagonism, hostility.
I'm = I am.
image *n* a representation of a person or thing; the visual impression of something in a lens, mirror, etc; a copy; a likeness; a mental picture; the concept of a person, product, etc held by the public at large. * *vt* to make a representation of; to reflect; to imagine.
imagery *n* (*pl* **imageries**) the work of the imagination; mental pictures; figures of speech; images in general or collectively.
imaginable *adj* able to be imagined.—**imaginably** *adv.*
imaginal *adj* pertaining to an image; pertaining to an imago.
imaginary *adj* existing only in the imagination.—**imaginarily** *adv.*
imagination *n* the image-forming power of the mind, or the power of the mind that modifies the conceptions, esp the higher form of this power exercised in art and poetry; creative ability; resourcefulness in overcoming practical difficulties, etc.
imaginative *adj* having or showing imagination; produced by imagination.—**imaginatively** *adv.*
imagine *vt* to form a mental image of; to believe falsely; (*inf*) to suppose; to guess. * *vi* to employ the imagination.—**imaginer** *n.*
imagist *n* a member of a group of poets, active between 1912 and 1917, who sought clarity of expression through use of precise images.
imago *n* (*pl* **imagoes, imagines**) an insect in its fully developed state; an idealized mental image of oneself or another.
imam *n* a leader of prayer in a mosque; a title given to various Muslim religious leaders.
imamate *n* a region controlled by an imam; the rank or term of office of an imam.
imaret *n* a hostel in Turkey giving accommodation to pilgrims or travellers.
imbalance *n* a lack of balance, as in proportion, emphasis, etc.
imbecile *n* an adult with a mental age of a three- to eight-year-old child; an idiotic person. * *adj* stupid or foolish.
imbecility *n* (*pl* **imbecilities**) mental or physical weakness.
imbed *vt* (**imbedding, imbedded**) to embed.
imbibe *vti* to drink, esp alcoholic liquor; to absorb mentally.—**imbiber** *n.*
imbibition *n* (*chem*) the process of a gel or solid absorbing a liquid; (*photog*) the process, used in colour printing, of using gelatine to absorb dyes.
imbricate, imbricated *adj* (*tiles, leaves*) overlapping.—**imbrication** *n.*
imbroglio *n* (*pl* **imbroglios**) a complicated, confusing situation; a confused misunderstanding.
imbrue *vt* (**imbruing, imbrued**) to wet or moisten; to soak; to drench, esp in blood.—*also* **embrue.**
IMF *abbr* = International Monetary Fund.
imitable *adj* able to be imitated.—**imitability, imitableness** *n.*
imitate *vt* to try to follow as a pattern or model; to mimic humorously, impersonate; to copy, reproduce.—**imitator** *n.*
imitation *n* an act or instance of imitating; a copy; an act of mimicking or impersonation.—**imitational** *adj.*
imitative *adj* imitating or inclined to imitate; characterized by imitation; copying an original, esp something superior.
immaculate *adj* spotless; flawless; pure, morally unblemished.—**immaculacy, immaculateness** *n.*—**immaculately** *adv.*
Immaculate Conception *n* (*RC Church*) the doctrine that the Virgin Mary was conceived without original sin.
immanent *adj* (*qualities*) inherent; (*God*) pervading the universe.—**immanence, immanency** *n.*
immaterial *adj* spiritual as opposed to physical; unimportant.—**immateriality, immaterialness** *n.*
immaterialism *n* (*philos*) the doctrine that matter has no existence independent of the mind.—**immaterialist** *n.*
immaterialize *vt* to make immaterial.
immature *adj* not mature.—**immaturity, immatureness** *n.*
immeasurable *adj* not able to be measured; immense, limitless.—**immeasurably** *adv.*
immediate *adj* acting or occurring without delay; next, nearest, without intervening agency; next in relationship; in close proximity, near to; directly concerning or touching a person or thing.—**immediacy, immediateness** *n.*
immediately *adv* without delay; directly; near, close by. * *conj* as soon as.
immemorial *adj* existing in the distant past, beyond the reach of memory.—**immemorially** *adv.*
immense *adj* very large in size or extent; limitless; (*inf*) excellent.—**immensely** *adv.*
immensity *n* (*pl* **immensities**) the character of being immense; immeasurableness; infinite space; vastness in extent or bulk.
immensurable *adj* immeasurable.
immerse *vt* to plunge into a liquid; to absorb or engross; to baptize by total submergence.—**immersible** *adj.*
immersion *n* the act of immersing; the state of being immersed; baptism by dipping the whole person into water.
immesh *see* **enmesh.**
immethodical *adj* without method or order.
immigrant *n* a person who immigrates; a person recently settled in a country but not born there.
immigrate *vi* to come into a new country, esp to settle permanently.—**immigration** *n.*—**immigrator** *n.*—**immigratory** *adj.*

imminent *adj* about to happen; impending.—**imminence** *n.*—**imminently** *adv.*
immiscible *adj* incapable of being mixed.—**immiscbility** *n.*
immobile *adj* not able to be moved; motionless.—**immobility** *n.*
immobilize *vt* to make immobile.—**immobilization** *n.*
immoderate *adj* excessive, unrestrained.—**immoderately** *adv.*—**immoderation, immoderateness** *n.*
immodest *adj* lacking in modesty or decency.—**immodestly** *adv.*—**immodesty** *n.*
immolate *vt* to kill as a sacrifice.—**immolation** *n.*—**immolator** *n.*
immoral *adj* against accepted standards of proper behaviour; sexually degenerate; corrupt; wicked.—**immorally** *adv.*
immorality *n* (*pl* **immoralities**) the quality of being immoral; an immoral act or practice.
immortal *adj* living for ever; enduring; having lasting fame. * *n* an immortal being or person; (*pl*) the gods of classical mythology.—**immortality** *n.*—**immortally** *adv.*
immortalize *vt* to render immortal; to bestow lasting fame upon.—**immortalization** *n.*
immortelle *n* a type of flower that retains its colour when dried.
immovable *adj* firmly fixed; impassive, unyielding; (*property*) land, buildings, etc.—**immovability, immovableness** *n.*—**immovably** *adv.*
immune *adj* not susceptible to a specified disease through inoculation or natural resistance; conferring immunity; exempt from a certain obligation, tax, duty, etc.
immunity *n* (*pl* **immunities**) the state of being immune.
immunize *vt* to make immune, esp against infection.—**immunization** *n.*
immuno- *prefix* immunity.
immunology *n* the branch of medical science dealing with immunity to disease.—**immunologic, immunological** *adj.*—**immunologist** *n.*
immure *vt* to enclose within walls; to shut up (in prison), confine.
immutable *adj* not capable of change; unalterable.—**immutability, immutableness** *n.*—**immutably** *adv.*
imp *n* a mischievous child; a little devil.
impact *n* violent contact; a shocking effect; the force of a body colliding with another. * *vt* to force tightly together. * *vi* to hit with force.—**impaction** *n.*
impacted *adj* (*tooth*) unable to emerge through the gum because of an obstruction, esp proximity to another tooth.
impair *vt* to make worse, less, etc.—**impairer** *n.*—**impairment** *n.*
impala *n* (*pl* **impalas, impala**) a type of African antelope.
impale *vt* to fix on, or pierce through, with something pointed.—**impalement** *n.*—**impaler** *n.*
impalpable *adj* not able to be sensed by touch; difficult to apprehend or grasp with the mind.—**impalpability** *n.*—**impalpably** *adv.*
impanel *see* **empanel.**
imparity *n* (*pl* **imparities**) inequality; disproportion; disparity.
impart *vt* to give, convey; to reveal, disclose.—**imparter** *n.*
impartial *adj* not favouring one side more than another, unbiased.—**impartiality, impartialness** *n.*—**impartially** *adv.*
impartible *adj* (*law*) which cannot be partitioned.
impassable *adj* (*roads, etc*) incapable of being travelled through or over.—**impassability, impassableness** *n.*—**impassably** *adv.*
impasse *n* a situation from which there is no escape; a deadlock.
impassioned *adj* passionate; ardent.—**impassionedly** *adv.*
impassive *adj* not feeling or showing emotion; imperturbable.—**impassively** *adv.*—**impassiveness, impassivity** *n.*
impaste *vt* (*art*) to paint (onto canvas) in thick layers.—**impastation** *n.*
impasto *n* (*art*) the effect produced by applying thick layers of paint to a canvas; the technique of applying paint in thick layers.
impatiens *n* (*pl* **impatiens**) one of a genus of plants of this name, including balsam and touch-me-not.
impatient *adj* lacking patience; intolerant of delay, etc; restless.—**impatience** *n.*—**impatiently** *adv.*
impeach *vt* to question a person's honesty; to try (a public official) on a charge of wrongdoing.—**impeachable** *adj.*—**impeacher** *n.*—**impeachment** *n.*
impearl *vt* (*arch*) to adorn with pearls; to make like pearls.
impeccable *adj* without defect or error; faultless.—**impeccability** *n.*—**impeccably** *adv.*
impecunious *adj* having little or no money.—**impecuniousness, impecuniosity** *n.*
impedance *n* the total resistance in an electric circuit to the flow of alternating current.
impede *vt* to obstruct or hinder the progress of.—**impeder** *n.*—**impedingly** *adv.*
impediment *n* something that impedes; an obstruction; a physical defect, as a stammer that prevents fluency of speech.—**impedimental** *adj.*
impedimenta *npl* heavy items of baggage, esp military equipment.
impel *vt* (**impelling, impelled**) to urge or force into doing something; to propel.—**impeller** *n.*
impend *vi* to be imminent; to threaten.—**impending** *adj.*
impenetrable *adj* unable to be pierced or penetrated; incomprehensible; unable to be seen through.—**impenetrability** *n.*—**impenetrably** *adv.*
impenitent *adj* not sorry or feeling guilty; unrepentant.—**impenitence, impenitency** *n.*
imperative *adj* urgent, pressing; authoritative; obligatory; designating or of the mood of a verb that expresses a command, entreaty, etc. * *n* a command; (*gram*) the imperative mood of a verb.
imperator *n* (*ancient Rome*) a commander-in-chief; a title given to a victorious general; a title given to the head of state.
imperceptible *adj* not able to be detected by the mind or senses; slight, minute, gradual.—**imperceptibility** *n.*—**imperceptibly** *adv.*
impercipient *adj* lacking perception.
imperfect *adj* having faults, flaws, mistakes, etc; defective; incomplete; (*gram*) designating a verb tense that indicates a past action or state as incomplete or continuous. * (*gram*) an imperfect tense.
imperfection *n* the state or quality of being imperfect; a defect, fault.
imperforate *adj* not perforated; (*anat*) without the normal opening.
imperial *adj* of an empire, emperor, or empress; majestic; of great size or superior quality; of the British non-metric system of weights and measures.—**imperially** *adv.*
imperialism *n* the policy of forming and maintaining an empire, as by subjugating territories, establishing colonies, etc.—**imperialist** *n.*—**imperialistic** *adj.*—**imperialistically** *adv.*
imperil *vt* (**imperiling, imperiled** *or* **imperilling, imperilled**) to put in peril, to endanger.
imperious *adj* tyrannical; arrogant.—**imperiously** *adv*
imperishable *adj* indestructible, not subject to decay; permanently enduring.—**imperishability** *n.*
imperium *n* (*pl* **imperia**) supreme power; an empire.
impermanent *adj* not permanent.—**impermanence, impermanency** *n.*
impermeable *adj* not allowing fluids to pass through; impervious.—**impermeability** *n.*
impermissible *adj* not permissible.
impersonal *adj* not referring to any particular person; cold, unfeeling; not existing as a person; (*verb*) occurring only in the third person singular, usu with "it" as subject.—**impersonality** *n.*—**impersonally** *adv.*
impersonate *vt* to assume the role of another person as entertainment or for fraud.—**impersonation** *n.*—**impersonator** *n.*
impertinent *adj* impudent; insolent; irrelevant.—**impertinence** *n.*—**impertinently** *adv.*
imperturbable *adj* not easily disturbed; calm; impassive.—**imperturbability** *n.*—**imperturbably** *adv.*—**imperturbation** *n.*
impervious *adj* incapable of being penetrated, as by water; not readily receptive (to) or affected (by).
impetigo *n* (*pl* **impetigos**) a contagious bacterial skin disease.—**impetiginous** *adj.*
impetrate *vt* to obtain by supplication, esp by prayer.—**impetration** *n.*
impetuous *adj* acting or done suddenly with impulsive energy.—**impetuosity** *n.*—**impetuously** *adv.*

impetus *n* (*pl* **impetuses**) the force with which a body moves against resistance; driving force or motive.

impiety *n* (*pl* **impieties**) want of piety; ungodliness; an act of irreverence or wickedness.

impinge *vi* (*with* **on, upon**) to have an impact; to encroach.—**impingement** *n*.—**impinger** *n*.

impious *adj* showing lack of reverence; wicked.—**impiously** *adv*.

impish *adj* of or like an imp.—**impishly** *adv*.—**impishness** *n*.

implacable *adj* not able to be appeased or pacified; inflexible, inexorable.—**implacability** *n*.—**implacably** *adv*.

implant *vt* to plant firmly; to fix (ideas, etc) firmly in the mind. * *n* something implanted in tissue surgically.—**implantation** *n*.—**implanter** *n*.

implausible *adj* not plausible.—**implausibility** *n*.—**implausibly** *adv*.

implead *vt* to sue, prosecute.

implement *n* something used in a given activity. * *vt* to carry out, put into effect.—**implemental** *adj*.—**implementation** *n*.—**implementer, implementor** *n*.

implicate *vt* to show to have a part, esp in a crime; to imply.—**implicative** *adj*.

implication *n* an implicating or being implicated; that which is implied; an inference not expressed but understood; deduction.

implicit *adj* implied rather than stated explicitly; unquestioning, absolute.—**implicitly** *adv*.—**implicitness, implicity** *n*.

implode *vi* to collapse inwards.

implore *vt* to request earnestly; to plead, entreat.—**imploration** *n*.—**implorer** *n*.—**imploringly** *adv*.

imply *vt* (**implying, implied**) to hint, suggest indirectly; to indicate or involve as a consequence.

impolite *adj* not polite, rude.—**impolitely** *adv*.—**impoliteness** *n*.

impolitic *adj* contrary to good policy; unwise; injudicious; indiscreet.—**impoliticly** *adv*.

imponderable *adj* not able to be weighed or measured. * *n* something difficult to measure or assess.—**imponderability** *n*.—**imponderably** *adv*.

import *vt* to bring (goods) in from a foreign country for sale or use; to mean; to signify. * *vi* to be of importance, to matter. * *n* something imported; meaning; importance.—**importable** *adj*.—**importer** *n*.

importance *n* the quality of being important; a high place in public estimation; high self-esteem.

important *adj* having great significance or consequence; (*person*) having power, authority, etc.—**importantly** *adv*.

importation *n* the act or business of importing; imported goods.

importunate *adj* persistent in asking or demanding.

importune *vt* to ask urgently and repeatedly.—**importuner** *n*.—**importuning** *n*.

importunity *n* (*pl* **importunities**) persistent solicitation or demand; incessant insistence; urgency.

impose *vt* to put (a burden, tax, punishment) on or upon; to force (oneself) on others; to lay pages of type or film and secure them. * *vi* (*with* **on** *or* **upon**) to take advantage of; to cheat or defraud.—**imposable** *adj*.—**imposer** *n*.

imposing *adj* impressive because of size, appearance, dignity, etc.—**imposingly** *adv*.

imposition *n* the act of imposing; something imposed, as a tax; an unfair burden; (*print*) the arrangement of pages of type or film in the correct order.

impossibility *n* (*pl* **impossibilites**) the character of being impossible; that which cannot be, or be supposed to be, done.

impossible *adj* not capable of existing, being done, or happening; (*inf*) unendurable, outrageous.—**impossibly** *adv*.

impost *n* a tax or duty, esp imposed by customs.

impostor, imposter *n* a person who acts fraudulently by impersonating another.

imposture *n* a fraud, deception.

impotent *adj* lacking in necessary strength, powerless; (*man*) unable to engage in sexual intercourse.—**impotence, impotency** *n*.—**impotently** *adv*.

impound *vt* to take legal possession of; to shut up (an animal) in a pound.—**impoundage, impoundment** *n*.—**impounder** *n*.

impoverish *vt* to make poor; to deprive of strength.—**impoverishment** *n*.

impracticable *adj* not able to be carried out, not feasible.—**impracticability** *n*.—**impracticably** *adv*.

impractical *adj* not practical; not competent in practical skills.—**impracticality** *n*.—**impractically** *adv*.

imprecate *vti* to invoke evil (on); to curse or utter curses.—**imprecatory** *adv*.

imprecation *n* a curse.

imprecise *adj* not precise; ill-defined.—**imprecisely** *adv*.—**imprecision** *n*.

impregnable, impregnatable *adj* secure against attack, unyielding.—**impregnability** *n*.—**impregnably** *adv*.

impregnate *vt* to cause to become pregnant, to fertilize; to saturate, soak (with); to imbue, pervade.—**impregnation** *n*.—**impregnator** *n*.

impresario *n* (*pl* **impresarios**) the manager of an opera, a concert series, etc.

impress[1] *vt* to make a strong, usu favourable, impression on; to fix deeply in the mind; to stamp with a mark; to imprint. * *n* an imprint.—**impresser** *n*.—**impressible** *adj*.

impress[2] *vt* to coerce into military service.—**impressment** *n*.

impression *n* the effect produced in the mind by an experience; a mark produced by imprinting; a vague idea, notion; the act of impressing or being impressed; a notable or strong influence on the mind or senses; the number of copies of a book printed at one go (—*also* **printing**); an impersonation or act of mimicry.—**impressional** *adj*.

impressionable *n* easily impressed or influenced.—**impressionability** *n*.—**impressionably** *adv*.

impressionism *n* painting, writing, etc in which objects are painted or described so as to reproduce only their general effect or impression without selection or elaboration of details.—**impressionist** *adj, n*.—**impressionistic** *adj*.

impressive *adj* tending to impress the mind or emotions; arousing wonder or admiration.—**impressiveness** *n*.

impressment *n* the act of seizing (things) for public use or conscripting (people) into public service.

imprest *n* a sum of money advanced.

imprimatur *n* permission or licence to publish a book, etc; an authoritative mark of approval; sanction.

imprint *vt* to stamp or impress a mark on, etc; to fix firmly in the mind. * *n* a mark made by imprinting; a lasting effect; a note in a book giving the facts of publication.—**imprinter** *n*.

imprison *vt* to put in a prison; to confine, as in a prison.—**imprisoner** *n*.—**imprisonment** *n*.

improbable *adj* unlikely to be true or to happen.—**improbability** *n*.—**improbably** *adv*.

improbity *n* (*pl* **improbities**) wickedness, dishonesty.

impromptu *adj, adv* unrehearsed, unprepared. * *n* something impromptu, as a speech.

improper *adj* lacking propriety, indecent; incorrect; not suitable or appropriate.—**improperly** *adv*.

improper fraction *n* a fraction in which the numerator is greater than or equal to the denominator, as 4/3.

impropriety *n* (*pl* **improprieties**) the quality of being improper; indecency; an improper act, etc.

improve *vt* to make or become better.—**improvable** *adj*.—**improver** *n*.—**improvingly** *adj*.

improvement *n* the act of improving or being improved; an alteration that improves or adds to the value of something.

improvident *adj* lacking foresight or thrift; wanting care to provide for the future; careless.—**improvidence** *n*.

improvisation *n* the act of improvising; the act of composing poetry, music, etc, extemporaneously; an impromptu.—**improvisational** *adj*.

improvise *vti* to compose, perform, recite, etc without preparation; to make or do with whatever is at hand.—**improviser** *n*.

imprudent *adj* rash, lacking discretion; unwise.—**imprudence** *n.*—**imprudently** *adv.*
impudent *adj* disrespectfully bold; impertinent.—**impudence** *n.*—**impudently** *adv.*
impugn *vt* to oppose or challenge as false; to discredit.—**impugnation, impugnent** *n.*—**impugner** *n.*
impuissant *adj* powerless, weak.—**impuissance** *n.*
impulse *n* a sudden push or thrust; a stimulus transmitted through a nerve or a muscle; a sudden instinctive urge to act.
impulsion *n* the act of impelling; the state of being impelled; impetus; an irrational urge, compulsion.
impulsive *adj* tending to act on impulse; forceful, impelling; acting momentarily.—**impulsively** *adv.*—**impulsiveness** *n.*
impunity *n* (*pl* **impunities**) exemption or freedom from punishment or harm.
impure *adj* unclean; adulterated.
impurity *n* (*pl* **impurities**) a being impure; an impure substance or constituent.
impute *vt* to attribute (esp a fault or misbehaviour) to another.—**imputable** *adj.*—**imputation** *n.*—**imputative** *adj.*—**imputer** *n.*
In (*chem symbol*) indium.
in. *abbr* = inch(es).
in *prep* inside; within; at; as contained by; during; at the end of; not beyond; affected by; being a member of; wearing; using; because of; into. * *adv* to or at a certain place; so as to be contained by a certain space, condition, etc; (*games*) batting, in play. * *adj* that is in power; inner; inside; gathered, counted, etc; (*inf*) currently smart, fashionable, etc.
inability *n* (*pl* **inabilities**) lack of ability.
in absentia *adv* in the absence of.
inaccessible *adj* not accessible, unapproachable.—**inaccessibility** *n.*—**inaccessibly** *adv.*
inaccurate *adj* not accurate, imprecise.—**inaccuracy** *n.*—**inaccurately** *adv.*
inaction *n* idleness, inertia.
inactive *adj* not active.—**inactively** *adv.*—**inactivity** *n.*
inadequate *adj* not adequate; not capable.—**inadequacy** *n.*—**inadequately** *adv.*
inadmissible *adj* not admissible, esp as evidence.—**inadmissibility** *n.*—**inadmissibly** *adv.*
inadvertent *adj* not attentive or observant, careless; due to oversight.—**inadvertence, inadvertency** *n.*—**inadvertently** *adv.*
inadvisable *adj* not advisable; inexpedient.—**inadvisability** *n.*—**inadvisably** *adv.*
inalienable *adj* that cannot or should not be surrendered or transferred to another.—**inalienability** *n.*—**inalienably** *adv.*
inalterable *adj* unalterable.—**inalterability** *n.*
inamorata *n* (*pl* **inamoratas**) a woman with whom one is in love; a sweetheart.
inamorato *n* (*pl* **inamoratos**) a man who is in love, a lover.
inane *adj* lacking sense, silly.—**inanely** *adv.*
inanimate *adj* not animate; showing no signs of life; dull.—**inanimately** *adv.*—**inanimateness, inanimation** *n.*
inanition *n* emptiness; exhaustion from lack of nourishment.
inanity *n* (*pl* **inanities**) (*arch*) emptiness; silliness; frivolity; a silly action or remark.
inapplicable *adj* not applicable.—**inapplicability** *n.*
inapposite *adj* not apposite, unsuitable.—**inappositely** *adv.*
inappreciable *adj* not to be appreciated or estimated; of no consequence.
inappreciative *adj* unappreciative.
inapproachable *adj* not approachable, inaccessible.
inappropriate *adj* unsuitable.—**inappropriately** *adv.*—**inappropriateness** *n.*
inapt *adj* inappropriate; unfit, unskilful.—**inaptitude** *n.*
inarticulate *adj* not expressed in words; incapable of being expressed in words; incapable of coherent or effective expression of ideas, feelings, etc.—**inarticulately** *adv.*
inartistic *adj* not artistic; not appreciative of art.—**inartistically** *adv.*
inasmuch *adv* in like degree; (*with* **as**) seeing that; because.
inattentive *adj* not attending; neglectful.—**inattention** *n.*
inaudible *adj* unable to be heard.—**inaudibility** *n.*—**inaudibly** *adv.*
inaugural *n* of or pertaining to an inauguration; a speech made at an inauguration.
inaugurate *vt* to admit ceremonially into office; to open (a building, etc) formally to the public; to cause to begin, initiate.—**inauguration** *n.*—**inaugurator** *n.*
inauspicious *adj* ill-starred; unlucky; unfavourable; unfortunate.
inboard *adv, adj* towards the centre or within an aircraft, ship, etc.
inborn *adj* present from birth; hereditary.
inbred *adj* innate; produced by inbreeding.
inbreed *vti* (**inbreeding, inbred**) to breed by continual mating of individuals of the same or closely related stocks.
in-built *adj* built in.
Inc. *abbr* = Incorporated.
incalculable *adj* beyond calculation; unpredictable.—**incalculability** *n.*—**incalculably** *adv.*
incalescent *adj* (*chem*) increasing in heat.—**incalescence** *n.*
in camera *adv* in private; in a judge's chamber as opposed to open court.
incandesce *vi* to glow with heat.
incandescent *adj* glowing or luminous with intense heat.—**incandescence** *n.*
incantation *n* words chanted in magic spells or rites.—**incantational, incantatory** *adj.*
incapable *adj* lacking capability; not able or fit to perform an activity.—**incapability** *n.*—**incapably** *adv.*
incapacitate *vt* to weaken, to disable; to make ineligible.—**incapacitation** *n.*
incapacity *n* (*pl* **incapacities**) lack of power or strength, inability; ineligibility.
incarcerate *vt* to put in prison, to confine.—**incarceration** *n.*—**incarcerator** *n.*
incarnate *adj* endowed with a human body; personified. * *vt* to give bodily form to; to be the type or embodiment of.—**incarnation** *n.*
incautious *adj* not cautious, reckless.—**incautiously** *adv.*—**incautiousness, incaution** *n.*
incendiarism *n* the act of burning illegally; arson.
incendiary *adj* pertaining to arson; (*bomb*) designed to start fires; tending to stir up or inflame. * *n* (*pl* **incendiaries**) a person that sets fire to a building, etc maliciously, an arsonist; an incendiary substance (as in a bomb); a person who stirs up violence, etc.
incense[1] *vt* to make extremely angry.
incense[2] *n* a substance that gives off a fragrant odour when burned; the fumes so produced; any pleasant odour.
incentive *n* a stimulus; a motive. * *adj* serving as a stimulus to action.
incept *vt* (*biol*) to ingest.
inception *n* the beginning of something.
inceptive *adj* noting a beginning, initial.
incertitude *n* doubt, uncertainty.
incessant *adj* never ceasing; continual, constant.—**incessancy** *n.*—**incessantly** *adv.*
incest *n* sexual intercourse between persons too closely related to marry legally.
incestuous *adj* involving incest; guilty of incest.
inch *n* a measure of length equal to 1/12 foot (2.54 cm); a very small distance or amount. * *vti* to move very slowly, or by degrees.
inchmeal *adv* inch by inch, gradually.
inchoate *adj* just begun; at a very early stage.—**inchoation** *n.*—**inchoative** *adj.*
incidence *n* the degree or range of occurrence or effect.
incident *adj* likely to happen as a result; falling upon or affecting. * *n* something that happens; an event, esp a minor one; a minor conflict.
incidental *adj* happening in connection with something more important; happening by chance. * *npl* miscellaneous items, minor expenses.
incidental music *n* background music for a film, play, etc.

incidentally *adv* in passing, as an aside.
incinerate *vt* to reduce to ashes.—**incineration** *n*.
incinerator *n* a furnace for burning rubbish.
incipient *adj* beginning to be or appear; initial.—**incipience, incipiency** *n*.
incise *vt* to cut or carve into a surface; to engrave.—**incised** *adj*.
incision *n* incising; a cut made into something, esp by a surgeon into a body.
incisive *adj* keen, penetrating; decisive; biting.—**incisively** *adv*.—**incisiveness** *n*.
incisor *n* any of the front cutting teeth at the front of the mouth.
incite *vt* to urge to action; to rouse.—**incitement** *n*.—**inciter** *n*.—**incitingly** *adv*.
incivility *n* (*pl* **incivilities**) lack of civility or courtesy; impoliteness.
incl. *abbr* = including; inclusive.
inclement *adj* (*weather*) rough, stormy; lacking mercy; harsh.—**inclemency** *n*.
inclination *n* a propensity or disposition, esp a liking; a deviation from the horizontal or vertical; a slope; inclining or being inclined; a bending movement, a bow.—**inclinational** *adj*.
incline *vi* to lean, to slope; to be disposed towards an opinion or action. * *vt* to cause to bend (the head or body) forwards; to cause to deviate, esp from the horizontal or vertical. * *n* a slope.—**inclinable** *adj*.—**incliner** *n*.
inclinometer *n* an instrument used to measure the angle made by an aircraft with the horizontal.
include *vt* to enclose, contain; to comprise as part or a larger group, amount, etc.—**includable, includible** *adj*.—**inclusion** *n*.
inclusive *adj* comprehensive; including the limits specified.—**inclusively** *adv*.
incognito *adj, adv* under an assumed name or identity. * *n* (*pl* **incognitos**) a person appearing or living incognito; the name assumed by such a person.—**incognita** *nf* (*pl* **incognitas**).
incognizant *adj* (*usu with* **of**) unaware.—**incognizance** *n*.
incoherent *adj* lacking organization or clarity; inarticulate in speech or thought.—**incoherence, incoherency** *n*.—**incoherently** *adv*.
incombustible *adj* not able to be burned or ignited. * *n* an incombustible substance.—**incombustibility** *n*.—**incombustibly** *adv*.
income *n* the money etc received for labour or services, or from property, investments, etc.
incomer *n* one who comes in; one who succeeds, as a tenant
income tax *n* a tax levied on the net income of a person or business.
incoming *adj* coming; accruing. * *n* the act of coming in; that which comes in; income.
incommensurable *adj* not able to be measured or judged comparatively.—**incommensurability** *n*.—**incommensurably** *adv*.
incommensurate *adj* not commensurate; disproportionate; inadequate; incommensurable.
incommode *vt* to give inconvenience or trouble to; to disturb.—**incommodious** *adj*.
incommunicable *adj* not capable of being communicated.—**incommunicability** *n*.—**incommunicably** *adv*.
incommunicado *adj* not allowed to communicate with others.
incommunicative *adj* not disposed to give information, reserved.
incommutable *adj* which cannot be exchanged or commuted.
incomparable *adj* beyond comparison, matchless; not amenable to comparison.—**incomparability** *n*.—**incomparably** *adv*.
incompatible *adj* not able to exist together in harmony; antagonistic; inconsistent.—**incompatibility** *n*.—**incompatibly** *adv*.
incompetent *adj* lacking the necessary ability, skill, etc. * *n* an incompetent person.—**incompetence, incompetency** *n*.—**incompetently** *adv*.
incomplete *adj* unfinished; lacking a part or parts.—**incompletely** *adv*.—**incompleteness, incompletion** *n*.
incomprehensible *adj* not to be understood or grasped by the mind; inconceivable.—**incomprehensibility** *n*.—**incomprehensibly** *adv*.
incomprehension *n* failure to understand.
incompressible *adj* incapable of being reduced in volume by pressure; resisting pressure.—**incompressibility** *n*.—**incompressibly** *adv*.
incomputable *adj* incalculable, which cannot be reckoned.
inconceivable *adj* impossible to comprehend; (*inf*) unbelievable.—**inconceivably** *adv*.
inconclusive *adj* leading to no definite result; ineffective; inefficient.—**inconclusively** *adv*.—**inconclusiveness** *n*.
incondensable, incondensible *adj* which cannot be condensed or compressed.
inconformity *n* lack of conformity.
incongruity *n* (*pl* **incongruities**) unsuitableness of one thing to another, inconsistency; absurdity.
incongruous *adj* lacking harmony or agreement of parts; unsuitable; inappropriate.—**incongruously** *adv*.—**incongruousness, incongruence** *n*.
inconsequential, inconsequent *adj* not following logically; irrelevant.—**inconsequence** *n*.—**inconsequentiality** *n*.—**inconsequentially, inconsequently** *adv*.
inconsiderable *adj* trivial.—**inconsiderably** *adv*.
inconsiderate *adj* uncaring about others; thoughtless.—**inconsiderately** *adv*.—**inconsideration** *n*.
inconsistency *n* (*pl* **inconsistencies**) the quality of being inconsisteng; incongruity.—**inconsistently** *adv*.
inconsistent *adj* not compatible with other facts; contradictory; irregular, fickle.
inconsolable *adj* not able to be comforted.—**inconsolability** *n*.—**inconsolably** *adv*.
inconsonant *adj* not in harmony or agreement.—**inconsonance** *n*.
inconspicuous *adj* not conspicuous.—**inconspicuously** *adv*.—**inconspicuousness** *n*.
inconstant *adj* subject to change; unstable; variable; fickle; capricious.—**inconstancy** *n*.
inconsumable *adj* which cannot be consumed or used up.
incontestable *adj* not admitting of question or doubt; incontrovertible.—**incontestability** *n*.—**incontestably** *adv*.
incontinent *adj* unable to control the excretion of bodily wastes; lacking self-restraint.—**incontinence** *n*.
incontrovertible *adj* not admitting of controversy; indisputable.—**incontrovertibility** *n*.—**incontrovertibly** *adv*.
inconvenience *n* want of convenience; unfitness; that which incommodes; disadvantage. * *vt* to put to inconvenience; to annoy.—**inconvenient** *adj*.
inconvertible *adj* incapable of being converted into or exchanged for something else.—**inconvertibility** *n*.—**inconvertibly** *adv*.
inconvincible *adj* unable or unwilling to be convinced.
incoordination *n* lack of coordination.
incorporate *vt* to combine; to include; to embody; to merge; to form into a corporation. * *vi* to unite into one group or substance; to form a corporation. * *adj* united; formed into a corporation.—**incorporation** *n*.—**incorporative** *adj*.—**incorporator** *n*.
incorporeal *adj* not corporeal, without substance; spiritual; (*law*) intangible, and existing only in contemplation of the law.—**incorporeally** *adv*.—**incorporeity, incorporeality** *n*.
incorrect *adj* faulty; inaccurate; improper.—**incorrectly** *adv*.—**incorrectness** *n*.
incorrigible *adj* not able to be corrected, reformed or altered.—**incorrigibility** *n*.—**incorrigibly** *adv*.
incorrupt, incorrupted *adj* free from physical or moral taint; unimpaired; upright, esp above the influence of corruption or bribery; honest.
incorruptible *adj* incapable of physical corruption, decay or dissolution; incapable of being bribed; not liable to moral perversion or contamination.—**incorruptibility** *n*.—**incorruptibly** *adv*.
increase *vti* to make or become greater in size, quality, amount, etc. * *n* increasing or becoming increased; the result or amount by which something increases.—**increasable** *adj*.—**increaser** *n*.—**increasingly** *adv*.

incredible *adj* unbelievable; (*inf*) wonderful.—**incredibility** *n*.—**incredibly** *adv*.
incredulity *n* scepticism; disbelief.
incredulous *adj* not able or willing to accept as true; unbelieving.—**incredulously** *adv*.—**incredulousness** *n*.
increment *n* (the amount of) an increase; an addition.—**incremental** *adj*.
increscent *adj* (*moon*) waxing, growing.
incriminate *vt* to involve in or indicate as involved in a crime or fault.—**incrimination** *n*.—**incriminator** *n*.—**incriminatory** *adj*.
incubate *vti* to sit on and hatch (eggs); to keep (eggs, embryos, etc) in a favourable environment for hatching or developing; to develop, as by planning.—**incubation** *n*.—**incubative, incubatory** *adj*.
incubator *n* an apparatus in which eggs are hatched by artificial heat; an apparatus for nurturing premature babies until they can survive unaided.
incubus *n* (*pl* **incubi, incubuses**) an evil spirit believed in folklore to have intercourse with women as they sleep; something oppressive or disturbing, as a nightmare.
inculcate *vt* to teach by frequent repetition or urging.—**inculcation** *n*.—**inculcator** *n*.
inculpate *vt* to blame, censure; to incriminate.—**inculpation** *n*.—**inculpative, inculpatory** *adj*.
incumbency *n* (*pl* **incumbencies**) a duty or obligation; a term of office.
incumbent *adj* resting (on or upon) one as a duty or obligation; currently in office. * *n* the holder of an office, etc.
incunabulum *n* (*pl* **incunabula**) any book printed before 1500; the early stages of anything.—**incunabular** *adj*.
incur *vt* (**incurring, incurred**) to bring upon oneself (something undesirable).—**incurrable** *adj*.
incurable *adj* incapable of being cured; beyond the power of skill or medicine; lacking remedy; incorrigible. * *n* a person diseased beyond cure.—**incurability** *n*.—**incurably** *adv*.
incurious *adj* indifferent, heedless.—**incuriosity** *n*.
incursion *n* an invasion or raid into another's territory, etc.—**incursive** *adj*.
incurvate *vti* to curve inwards. * *adj* curved or bent inwards.—**incurvation** *n*.
incus *n* (*pl* **incudes**) a bone found in the middle ear.
incuse *n* a design stamped onto a coin.
indebted *adj* in debt; obliged; owing gratitude.—**indebtedness** *n*.
indecency *n* (*pl* **indecencies**) lack of decency, modesty, or good manners; something indecent, vulgar, or obscene.
indecent *adj* offending against accepted standards of decent behaviour.—**indecently** *adv*.
indecent assault *n* a sexual assault not involving rape.
indecent exposure *n* the offence of deliberately exposing one's genitals in public.
indeciduous *adj* (*bot*) not deciduous; evergreen.
indecipherable *adj* which cannot be deciphered; illegible.
indecision *n* not able to make a decision; hesitation.
indecisive *adj* inconclusive; irresolute.—**indecisively** *adv*.—**indecisiveness** *n*.
indeclinable *adj* (*gram*) which cannot be declined, having no inflected forms.
indecorous *adj* violating decorum, or any accepted rule of conduct.—**indecorum** *n*.
indeed *adv* truly, certainly. * *interj* expressing irony, surprise, disbelief, etc.
indefatigable *adj* tireless.—**indefatigability** *n*.—**indefatigably** *adv*.
indefeasible *adj* not to be defeated or made void, as a title.—**indefeasibility** *n*.—**indefeasibly** *adv*.
indefensible *adj* unable to be defended or justified.—**indefensibility** *n*.—**indefensibly** *adv*.
indefinable *adj* that cannot be defined.—**indefinably** *adv*.
indefinite *adj* not certain, undecided; imprecise, vague; having no fixed limits.—**indefinitely** *adv*.—**indefiniteness** *n*.
indefinite article *n* the word "a" or "an."
indehiscent *adj* (*bot*) not opening when mature.—**indehiscence** *n*.
indelible *adj* not able to be removed or erased; (*pen, ink, etc*) making an indelible mark.—**indelibility** *adv*.—**indelibly** *adv*.
indelicacy *n* (*pl* **indelicacies**) lack of delicacy; something offensive to modesty or refined taste.
indelicate *adj* improper; rough, crude; tactless.—**indelicately** *adv*.
indemnify *vt* (**indemnifying, indemnified**) to insure against loss, damage, etc; to repay (for damage, loss, etc).—**indemnification** *n*.—**indemnifier** *n*.
indemnity *n* (*pl* **indemnities**) compensation for damage or loss; insurance against future loss or injury.
indemonstrable *adj* which cannot be demonstrated or proved.
indent *vt* to make notches in; to begin (a line of text) farther in from the margin than the rest. * *vi* to form an indentation. * *n* a dent or notch.—**indentor** *n*.
indentation *n* a being indented; a notch, cut, inlet, etc; a dent; a spacing in from the margin (—*also* **indention, indent**).
indenture *n* a written agreement, a contract binding one person to work for another. * *vt* to bind by indentures.
independence *n* the state of being independent.
Independence Day *n* the anniversary of the adoption of the American Declaration of Independence on 4 July 1776.
independency *n* (*pl* **independencies**) a self-governing political unit.
independent *adj* freedom from the influence or control of others; self-governing; self-determined; not adhering to any political party; not connected with others; not depending on another for financial support. * *n* a person who is independent in thinking, action etc.—**independently** *adv*.
in-depth *adj* detailed, thorough.
indescribable *adj* unable to be described; too beautiful, horrible, intense, etc for words.—**indescribability** *n*.—**indescribably** *adv*.
indestructible *adj* not able to be destroyed.—**indestructibility** *n*.—**indestructibly** *adv*.
indeterminable *adj* which cannot be ascertained, settled or classified.
indeterminate *adj* vague, uncertain; not defined or fixed in value.—**indeterminancy, indetermination** *adv*.—**indeterminately** *adv*.
indeterminism *n* (*philos*) the doctrine that the will has a certain freedom, independent of motives.
index *n* (*pl* **indexes, indices**) an alphabetical list of names, subjects, items, etc mentioned in a printed book, usu listed alphabetically at the end of the text; a figure showing ratio or relative change, as of prices or wages; any indication or sign; a pointer or dial on an instrument; the exponent of a number. * *vt* to make an index of or for.—**indexer** *n*.
index arbitrage *see* **arbitrage**.
index finger *n* the forefinger.
Indiaman *n* (*pl* **Indiamen**) (*formerly*) a commercial sailing vessel involved in trade with India.
Indian *n* a native of India; an American Indian, the original inhabitants of the continent of America.
Indian corn *n* maize.
Indian file *n* single file.
Indian ink *n* a solid black pigment; a black ink made from this.—*also* **India ink**.
Indian summer *n* a period of unusually warm weather in the autumn.
indiarubber *n* an elastic gummy substance obtained from the milky juice of several tropical trees and used for rubbing out pencil marks.
Indic *adj* a term sometimes applied to the Indo-European languages of India, eg Sanskrit, Hindi, Bengali, etc.
indicant *n* something which indicates.
indicate *vt* to point out; to show or demonstrate; to be a sign or symptom of; to state briefly, suggest.—**indicatable** *adj*.—**indication** *n*.—**indicatory** *adj*.
indicative *adj* serving as a sign (of); (*gram*) denoting the mood of the verb that affirms or denies.
indicator *n* a thing that indicates or points; a measuring device with a pointer, etc; an instrument showing the operating condition of a piece of machinery, etc; a device giving updated information, such as a departure board in a railway station or airport; a flashing light used to warn of a change in direction of a vehicle.

indices *see* **index.**
indicia *npl* (*sing* **indicium**) distinguishing markings.
indict *vt* to charge with a crime; to accuse.
indictable *adj* subject to being indicted; making one liable to indictment.
indictment *n* a formal written statement framed by a prosecuting authority charging a person of a crime.
indifferent *adj* showing no concern, uninterested; unimportant; impartial; average; mediocre.—**indifference** *n*.—**indifferently** *adv*.
indifferentism *n* systematic indifference, esp with regard to religion.—**indifferentist** *n*.
indigen, indigene *n* a native (person, animal, etc).
indigenous *adj* existing naturally in a particular country, region, or environment; native.
indigent *adj* poor, needy.—**indigence** *n*.
indigestible *adj* difficult or impossible to digest.—**indigestibility** *n*.
indigestion *n* a pain caused by difficulty in digesting food.
indigestive *adj* pertaining to, or having, indigestion.
indign *adj* (*arch*) unworthy; disgraceful.
indignant *adj* expressing anger, esp at mean or unjust action.—**indignantly** *adv*.
indignation *n* anger at something regarded as unfair, wicked, etc.
indignity *n* (*pl* **indignities**) humiliation; treatment making one feel degraded, undignified.
indigo *n* (*pl* **indigos, indigoes**) a deep blue dye or colour.
indirect *adj* not straight; roundabout; secondary; dishonest.—**indirectly** *adv*.—**indirectness** *n*.
indirect evidence *n* circumstantial or inferential evidence.
indirection *n* indirect means or procedure; lack of direction; deceit.
indirect object *n* (*gram*) a person or thing affected by a verb but less directly than the object.
indirect speech *n* reported speech.
indirect tax *n* a tax levied on goods and services (which increases prices) rather than directly on individuals or companies.
indiscernible *adj* not discernible.—**indiscernibly** *adv*.
indiscipline *n* lack of discipline.
indiscreet *adj* not discreet; tactless.—**indiscreetly** *adv*.
indiscrete *adj* not separated into distinct parts.
indiscretion *n* an indiscreet act; rashness.—**indiscretionary** *adj*.
indiscriminate *adj* not making a careful choice; confused; random; making no distinctions.—**indiscriminately** *adv*.—**indiscrimination** *n*.—**indiscriminative** *adj*.
indispensable *adj* absolutely essential.—**indispensability** *n*.—**indispensably** *adv*.
indispose *vt* to make unfit or unwell; to disincline.
indisposed *adj* ill or sick; reluctant; disinclined.
indisposition *n* disinclination; a slight illness.
indisputable *adj* unquestionable; certain.—**indisputability** *n*.—**indisputably** *adv*.
indissoluble *adj* permanent; not able to be dissolved or destroyed.—**indissolubility** *n*.—**indissolubly** *adv*.
indistinct *adj* not clearly marked; dim; not distinct.—**indistinctly** *adv*.—**indistinctness** *n*.
indistinctive *adj* not capable of making distinctions; lacking distinctive characteristics.—**indistinctiveness** *n*.
indistinguishable *adj* not distinguishable; lacking identifying characteristics.—**indistinguishability** *n*.—**indistinguishably** *adv*.
indite *vt* (*arch*) to write.
indium *n* a soft metallic element used in alloys and electronic circuitry.
individual *adj* existing as a separate thing or being; of, by, for, or relating to a single person or thing. * *n* a single thing or being; a person.
individualist *n* a person who thinks or behaves with marked independence.—**individualism** *n*.—**individualistic** *adj*.—**individualistically** *adv*.
individuality *n* (*pl* **individualities**) the condition of being individual; separate or distinct existence; distinctive character.
individualize *vt* to mark as distinct, particularize; to distinguish individually.—**individualization** *n*.
individually *adv* in a distinctive manner; one by one; separately; personally.
individuate *vt* to individualize.—**individuation** *n*.
indivisible *adj* not divisible.—**indivisibility** *n*.—**indivisibly** *adv*.
indocile *adj* unteachable; intractable.—**indocility** *n*.
indoctrinate *vt* to systematically instruct in doctrines, ideas, beliefs, etc.—**indoctrination** *n*.—**indoctrinator** *n*.
Indo-European *adj* of a family of languages (including English) spoken in most of Europe and Asia as far east as northern India.—*also n*.
indolent *adj* idle; lazy.—**indolence** *n*.—**indolently** *adv*.
indomitable *adj* not easily discouraged or defeated.—**indomitability** *n*.—**indomitably** *adv*.
indoor *adj* done, used, or situated within a building.
indoors *adv* in or into a building.
indorse *see* **endorse.**
indraft *n* an inlet or inward current.
indubitable *adj* not capable of being doubted.—**indubitability** *n*.—**indubitably** *adv*.
induce *vt* to persuade; to bring on; to draw (a conclusion) from particular facts; to bring about (an electric or magnetic effect) in a body by placing it within a field of force.—**inducer** *n*.—**inducible** *adj*.
inducement *n* something that induces; a stimulus; a motive.
induct *vt* to place formally in an office, a society, etc; to enrol (esp a draftee) in the armed forces.
inductance *n* the property of an electric circuit by which an electromotive force is produced by a variation in the current in the same or a neighbouring circuit; the measure of inductance in an electric circuit.
inductile *adj* not ductile, not pliant.
induction *n* the act or an instance of inducting, eg into office; reasoning from particular premises to general conclusions; the inducing of an electric or magnetic effect by a field of force.—**inductional** *adj*.
inductive *adj* proceeding by or producing induction; operating by induction; susceptible to being acted on by induction.
inductor *n* one who inducts; (*elect*) that part of an apparatus that acts inductively.
indue *see* **endue.**
indulge *vt* to satisfy (a desire); to gratify the wishes of; to humour. * *vi* to give way to one's desire.—**indulger** *n*.
indulgence *n* indulging or being indulged; a thing indulged in; a favour or privilege; (*RC Church*) a remission of punishment still due for a sin after the guilt has been forgiven.
indulgent *adj* indulging or characterized by indulgence; lenient.—**indulgently** *adv*.
induline, indulin *n* a dark blue dye.
indult *n* (*RC Church*) a licence from the Pope authorizing something not sanctioned by Church law.
induplicate, induplicated *adj* (*bot*) bent inwards.
indurate *vt* to make hard or callous. * *vi* to grow hard or callous.—**induration** *n*.—**indurative** *adj*.
indusium *n* (*pl* **indusia**) (*bot*) the covering of the growing spores in many ferns.—**indusial** *adj*.
industrial *adj* relating to or engaged in industry; used in industry; having many highly developed industries.—**industrially** *adv*.
industrialism *n* social and economic organization characterized by large industries, machine production, urban workers, etc.
industrialist *n* a person who owns or manages an industrial enterprise.
industrialize *vti* to make or become industrial.—**industrialization** *n*.
industrial relations *n* the relations between employees and employers.
industrious *adj* hard-working.—**industriously** *adv*.—**industriousness** *n*.
industry *n* (*pl* **industries**) organized production or manufacture of goods; manufacturing enterprises collectively; a branch of commercial enterprise producing a particular product; any large-scale business activity; the owners and managers of industry; diligence.
indwelling *vti* (**indwelling, indwelt**) to dwell (in).

inebriate *vt* to intoxicate, esp with alcoholic drink. * *n* a drunkard. * *adj* inebriated.—**inebriation** *n*.
inebriated *adj* drunken.
inedible *adj* not fit to be eaten.—**inedibility** *n*.
inedited *adj* unpublished; not edited.
ineducable *adj* impossible to educate, esp due to mental deficiency.
ineffable *adj* too intense or great to be spoken; unutterable; too sacred to be spoken.—**ineffability** *n*.—**ineffably** *adv*.
ineffaceable *adj* which cannot be effaced.—**ineffaceability** *n*.
ineffective *adj* not effective.—**ineffectively** *adv*.—**ineffectiveness** *n*.
ineffectual *adj* not effectual; futile.—**ineffectuality** *n*.—**ineffectually** *adv*.
inefficacious *adj* not having the power to produce a desired effect.—**inefficacy** *n*.
inefficiency *n* (*pl* **inefficiences**) the quality or condition of being inefficient; an instance of inefficiency or incompetence.
inefficient *adj* not efficient.—**inefficiently** *adv*.
inelastic *adj* not elastic; inflexible, unyielding.—**inelastically** *adv*.—**inelasticity** *n*.
inelegant *adj* ungraceful; lacking refinement or polish.—**inelegance** *n*.
ineligible *adj* not eligible.—**ineligibility** *n*.
ineluctable *adj* not possible to escape from or avoid.—**ineluctably** *adv*.
inept *adj* unsuitable; unfit; foolish; awkward; clumsy.—**ineptitude** *n*.—**ineptly** *adv*.
inequality *n* (*pl* **inequalities**) lack of equality in size, status, etc; unevenness.
inequitable *adj* unjust, unfair.—**inequitably** *adv*.
inequity *n* (*pl* **inequities**) lack of equity; injustice.
ineradicable *adj* which cannot be eradicated.
inert *adj* without power to move or to resist; inactive; dull; slow; with few or no active properties.—**inertly** *adv*.—**inertness** *n*.
inertia *n* (*physics*) the tendency of matter to remain at rest (or continue in a fixed direction) unless acted on by an outside force; disinclination to act.
inertial *adj* of, or pertaining to, inertia.
inescapable *adj* which cannot be escaped, inevitable.
inessential *adj* not essential.
inestimable *adj* not to be estimated; beyond measure or price; incalculable; invaluable.—**inestimably** *adv*.
inevitable *adj* sure to happen; unavoidable. * *n* something that is inevitable.—**inevitability** *n*.—**inevitably** *adv*.
inexact *adj* not strictly true or correct.—**inexactitude** *n*.—**inexactly** *adv*.
inexcusable *adj* without excuse; unpardonable.—**inexcusably** *adv*.
inexhaustible *adj* not to be exhausted or spent; unfailing; unwearied.—**inexhaustibility** *n*.—**inexhaustibly** *adv*.
inexorable *adj* unable to be persuaded by persuasion or entreaty, relentless.—**inexorability** *n*.—**inexorably** *adv*.
inexpedient *adj* unsuitable to circumstances; inadvisable.—**inexpedience, inexpediency** *n*.
inexpensive *adj* cheap.—**inexpensively** *adv*.
inexperience *n* want of experience or of the knowledge that comes by experience.
inexperienced *adj* lacking experience; unpractised; unskilled; unversed.
inexpert *adj* unskilled; lacking the knowledge or dexterity derived from practice.
inexpiable *adj* which cannot be expiated.
inexplicable *adj* not to be explained, made plain, or intelligible; not to be interpreted or accounted for.—**inexplicability** *n*.—**inexplicably** *adv*.
inexplicit *adj* not clear.
inexpressible *adj* incapable of being expressed, uttered, or described.—**inexpressibly** *adv*.
inexpressive *adj* lacking expression or distinct significance.
inextensible *adj* which cannot be extended.—**inextensibility** *n*.
inextinguishable *adj* which cannot be extinguished, unquenchable.
in extremis *adv* close to death; in a very difficult situation.
inextricable *adj* that cannot be disentangled, solved, or escaped from.—**inextricably** *adv*.
infallible *adj* incapable of being wrong; dependable; reliable.—**infallibility** *n*.—**infallibly** *adv*.
infamous adj having a bad reputation; notorious; causing a bad reputation; scandalous.
infamy *n* (*pl* **infamies**) ill fame; public disgrace; ignominy.
infancy *n* (*pl* **infancies**) early childhood; the beginning or early existence of anything.
infant *n* a very young child; a baby.
infanta *n* a title for a Spanish princess, not the heir apparent.
infante *n* a title for a Spanish prince, not the heir apparent.
infanticide *n* the killing of an infant; a person who does this.—**infanticidal** *adj*.
infantile *adj* of infants; like an infant, babyish.
infantile paralysis *n* poliomyletis.
infantry *n* (*pl* **infantries**) soldiers trained to fight on foot.
infatuate *vt* to inspire with intense, foolish, or short-lived passion.—**infatuated** *adj*.—**infatuatedly** *adv*.
infatuation *n* an extravagant passion.
infect *vt* to contaminate with disease-causing microorganisms; to taint; to affect, esp so as to harm.—**infective** *adj*.
infection *n* an infecting or being infected; an infectious disease; a diseased condition.
infectious *adj* (*disease*) able to be transmitted; causing or transmitted by infection; tending to spread to others.—**infectiousness** *n*.
infectious hepatitis *n* an infectious disease which causes inflammation of the liver.
infectious mononucleosis *n* an infectious disease characterized by inflammation of the lymph glands.—*also* **glandular fever**.
infelicitous *adj* unfortunate; unhappy; inappropriate; ill-timed.
infelicity *n* (*pl* **infelicities**) misfortune; unhappiness; inapproriateness; an infelicitous act or expression.
infer *vt* (**inferring, inferred**) to conclude by reasoning from facts or premises; to accept as a fact or consequence.—**inferable** *adj*.—**inferrer** *n*.
inference *n* an inferring; something inferred or deduced; a reasoning from premises to a conclusion.—**inferential** *adj*.
inferior *adj* lower in position, rank, degree, or quality. * *n* an inferior person.—**inferiority** *n*.
inferiority complex *n* (*psychol*) an acute sense of inferiority expressed by a lack of confidence or in exaggerated aggression.
infernal *adj* of hell; hellish; fiendish; (*inf*) irritating, detestable.—**infernally** *adv*.
inferno *n* (*pl* **infernos**) hell; intense heat; a devastating fire.
infertile *adj* not fertile.—**infertility** *n*.
infest *vt* to overrun in large numbers, usu so as to be harmful; to be parasitic in or on.—**infestation** *n*.—**infester** *n*.
infidel *n* a person who does not believe in a certain religion; a person who has no religion.
infidelity *n* (*pl* **infidelities**) unfaithfulness, esp in marriage.
infield *n* (*cricket*) the area of the ground near the wicket; (*baseball*) the area of the field enclosed by the baselines.
infielder *n* (*baseball, cricket*) a player in an infield position.
infighting *n* (*boxing*) exchanging punches at close quarters; intense competition within an organization.—**infighter** *n*.
infiltrate *vti* to filter or pass gradually through or into; to permeate; to penetrate (enemy lines, etc) gradually or stealthily, eg as spies.—**infiltration** *n*.—**infiltrator** *n*.
infinite *adj* endless, limitless; very great; vast.—**infinitely** *adv*.
infinitesimal *adj* immeasurably small.—**infinitesimally** *adv*.
infinitive *n* (*gram*) the form of a verb without reference to person, number or tense.—**infinitival** *adj*.
infinitude *n* the condition or quality of being infinite; infinity.
infinity *n* (*pl* **infinities**) the condition or quality of being infinite; an unlimited number, quantity, or time period.
infirm *adj* physically weak, esp from old age or illness; irresolute.
infirmary *n* (*pl* **infirmaries**) a hospital or place for the treatment of the sick.

infirmity *n* (*pl* **infirmities**) being infirm; a physical weakness.
infix *vt* to fix or insert in.
in flagrante delicto *adv* in the very act of commiting the crime, red-handed.—*also* **flagrante delicto.**
inflame *vti* to arouse, excite, etc, or to become aroused, excited, etc; to undergo or cause to undergo inflammation.—**inflamingly** *adv*.
inflammable *adj* able to catch fire, flammable; easily excited.—**inflammability** *n*.
inflammation *n* an inflaming or being inflamed; redness, pain, heat, and swelling in the body, due to injury or disease.
inflammatory *adj* rousing excitement, anger, etc; of or caused by inflammation.—**inflammatorily** *adv*.
inflatable *adj* able to be inflated.
inflate *vti* to fill or become filled with air or gas; to puff up with pride; to increase beyond what is normal, esp the supply of money or credit.—**inflatedly** *adv*.—**inflater, inflator** *n*.
inflation *n* an inflating or being inflated; an increase in the currency in circulation or a marked expansion of credit, resulting in a fall in currency value and a sharp rise in prices.
inflationary *adj* pertaining to or causing inflation.
inflationist *n, adj* (someone) in favour of a policy of an increased issue of money and availability of credit, with inflation as a consequence.
inflect *vt* to change the form (of a word) by inflection; to vary the tone of (the voice).—**inflective** *adj*.—**inflector** *n*.
inflection *n* a bend; the change in the form of a word to indicate number, case, tense, etc; a change in the tone of the voice.—**inflectional** *adj*.
inflexible *adj* not flexible; stiff, rigid; fixed; unyielding.—**inflexibility** *n*.—**inflexibly** *adv*.
inflict *vt* to impose (pain, a penalty, etc) on a person or thing.—**inflicter, inflictor** *n*.—**infliction** *n*.
inflorescence *n* the producing of blossoms; the arrangement of flowers on a stem; a flower cluster; flowers collectively.—**inflorescent** *adj*.
inflow *n* something which flows in.
influence *n* the power to affect others; the power to produce effects by having wealth, position, ability, etc; a person with influence. * *vt* to have influence on.—**influenceable** *adj*.
influent *adj* flowing in.
influential *adj* having or exerting great influence.—**influentially** *adv*.
influenza *n* a contagious feverish virus disease marked by muscular pain and inflammation of the respiratory system.—**influenzal** *adj*.
influx *n* a sudden inflow of people or things to a place.
info *n* (*sl*) information.
inform *vt* to provide knowledge of something to. * *vi* to give information to the police, etc, esp in accusing another.
informal *adj* not formal; not according to fixed rules or ceremony, etc; casual.—**informally** *adv*.
informality *n* (*pl* **informalities**) the lack of regular, customary, or legal form; an informal act.
informant *n* a person who gives information.
information *n* something told or facts learned; news; knowledge; data stored in or retrieved from a computer.—**informational** *adj*.
information technology *n* (the study of) the collection, retrieval, use, storage and communication of information using computers and micro-electronic systems.
information theory *n* mathematical and statistical analysis of information communication systems.
informative, informatory *adj* conveying information, instructive.—**informatively** *adv*.
informer *n* a person who informs on another, esp to the police for a reward.
infra- *prefix* below; within; beneath; after.
infraction *n* a violation of a law, pact, etc.
infra dig *adj* (*inf*) beneath one's dignity.
infrangible *adj* unbreakable; inviolable.—**infrangibility** *n*.
infrared *n* (*radiation*) having a wavelength longer than light but shorter than radio waves; of, pertaining to, or using such radiation.
infrasonic *adj* (*soundwaves*) having a frequency below the audible range.—**infrasound** *n*.
infrastructure *n* the basic structure of any system or organization; the basic installations, such as roads, railways, factories, etc that determine the economic power of a country.
infrequent *adj* seldom occurring; rare.—**infrequence, infrequency** *n*.—**infrequently** *adv*.
infringe *vt* to break or violate, esp an agreement or a law.—**infringement** *n*.
infundibular, infundibulate *adj* funnel-shaped.
infuriate *vt* to enrage; to make furious.—**infuriating** *adj*.—**infuriatingly** *adv*.
infuse *vt* to instil or impart (qualities, etc); to inspire; to steep (tea leaves, etc) to extract the essence.—**infuser** *n*.
infusible[1] *adj* incapable of being fused or melted.—**infusibility** *n*.
infusible[2] *adj* capable of being infused.—**infusibility** *n*.
infusion *n* the act of infusing; something obtained by infusing.
infusorial earth *n* a silicious deposit composed chiefly of the shells of microscopic vegetable organisms called diatoms, used as a polishing powder and in the manufacture of dynamite.
ingenious *adj* clever, resourceful, etc; made or done in an original or clever way.—**ingeniously** *adv*.—**ingeniousness** *n*.
ingénue *n* a naive young woman.
ingenuity *n* (*pl* **ingenuities**) skill in contriving or inventing; resourcefulness.
ingenuous *adj* naive, innocent; candid.—**ingenuously** *adv*.—**ingenuousness** *n*.
ingest *vt* to take (as food) into the body.—**ingestion** *n*.—**ingestive** *adj*.
ingle *n* (*arch*) a fireplace.
inglenook *n* (a seat in) a recess by a large open fireplace.
inglorious *adj* disgraceful, shameful; obscure.
ingot *n* a brick-shaped mass of cast metal, esp gold or silver.
ingrain *vt* to make a deep impression upon; (*arch*) to dye.—*also* **engrain.**
ingrained *adj* (*habits, feelings, etc*) firmly established; (*dirt*) deeply embedded.—*also* **engrained.**
ingrate *adj* (*arch*) ungrateful. * *n* an ungrateful person.
ingratiate *vt* to bring oneself into another's favour.—**ingratiating, ingratiatory** *adj*.—**ingratiation** *n*.
ingratitude *n* absence of gratitude; insensibility to kindness.
ingredient *n* something included in a mixture; a component.
ingress *n* entrance.
in-group *n* a group favouring its own members at the expense of members of other groups.
ingrowing *adj* (*toe nail, etc*) growing abnormally into the flesh.
ingrowth *n* the process of growing inwards; something which grows inwards.
inguinal *adj* of the groin or its vicinity.
ingurgitate *vt* to swallow greedily.—**ingurgitation** *n*.
inhabit *vt* to live in; to occupy; to reside.
inhabitable *adj* fit for habitation.—**inhabitability** *n*.—**inhabitation** *n*.
inhabitant *n* a person or animal inhabiting a specified place.—**inhabitancy, inhabitance** *n*.
inhalant *n* a medicine, etc that is inhaled.
inhalation *n* the act of inhaling.
inhale *vti* to breathe in.
inhaler *n* a device that dispenses medicines in a fine spray for inhalation.
inharmonic, inharmonious *adj* lacking harmony; discordant.
inhere *vi* to be inherent.
inherent *adj* existing as an inseparable part of something.—**inherence, inherency** *n*.—**inherently** *adv*.
inherit *vt* to receive (property, a title, etc) under a will or by right of legal succession; to possess by genetic transmission. * *vi* to receive by inheritance; to succeed as heir.—**inheritor** *n*.
inheritable *adj* capable of being inherited.
inheritance *n* the action of inheriting; something inherited.

inhibit *vt* to restrain; to prohibit.—**inhibitor, inhibiter** *n*.
inhibition *n* an inhibiting or being inhibited; a mental process that restrains or represses an action, emotion, or thought.
inhospitable *adj* not hospitable; affording no shelter; barren; cheerless.—**inhospitably** *adv*.—**inhospitality** *n*.
in-house *adj* within an organization.
inhuman *adj* lacking in the human qualities of kindness, pity, etc; cruel, brutal, unfeeling; not human.
inhumane *adj* not humane; inhuman.
inhumanity *n* (*pl* **inhumanites**) the quality of being inhuman; cruelty.
inhume *vt* to bury, inter.—**inhumation** *n*.—**injumer** *n*.
inimical *adj* hostile; adverse, unfavourable.—**inimically** *adv*.
inimitable *adj* impossible to imitate; matchless.—**inimitably** *adv*.
iniquitous *adj* marked by iniquity.
iniquity *n* (*pl* **iniquities**) wickedness; great injustice.
initial *adj* of or at the beginning. * *n* the first letter of each word in a name; a large letter at the beginning of a chapter, etc. * *vt* (**initialing, initialed** *or* **initialling, initialled**) to sign with initials.—**initialer, initialler** *n*.—**initially** *adv*.
initialize *vt* (*comput*) to format (a disk) to suit a particular processor.—**initialization** *n*.
initiate *vt* to bring (something) into practice or use; to teach the fundamentals of a subject to; to admit as a member into a club, etc, esp with a secret ceremony. * *n* an initiated person.—**initiator** *n*.—**initiatory** *adj*.
initiation *n* the act of initiating; a formal, often secret, ceremony of admission.
initiative *n* the action of taking the first step; ability to originate new ideas or methods.
inject *vt* to force (a fluid) into a vein, tissue, etc, esp with a syringe; to introduce (a remark, quality, etc), to interject.—**injectable** *adj*.
injection *n* an injecting; a substance that is injected.—**injective** *adj*.
injector *n* someone who, or something which, injects; a device for injecting fuel into an internal combustion engine; a device for filling the boiler of a steam engine with water.
injudicious *adj* not judicious; indiscreet; unwise.
injunction *n* a command; an order; a court order prohibiting or ordering a given action.—**injunctive** *adj*.
injure *vt* to harm physically or mentally; to hurt, do wrong to.—**injurer** *n*.
injurious *adj* causing injury.
injury *n* (*pl* **injuries**) physical damage; harm.
injury time *n* (*sport*) time added to compensate for stoppages through injuries to players.
injustice *n* the state or practice of being unfair; an unjust act.
ink *n* a coloured liquid used for writing, printing, etc; the dark protective secretion of an octopus, etc. * *vt* to cover, mark, or colour with ink.
inkhorn *n* (*formerly*) a container for ink.
inkling *n* a hint; a vague notion.
inkstand *n* a stand for an ink bottle.
inkwell *n* a container for ink.
inky *adj* (**inkier, inkiest**) like very dark ink in colour; black; covered with ink.—**inkiness** *n*.
inlaid *see* **inlay**.
inland *adj* of or in the interior of a country. * *n* an inland region. * *adv* into or toward this region.—**inlander** *n*.
in-law *n* a relative by marriage.
inlay *vt* (**inlaying, inlaid**) to decorate a surface by inserting pieces of metal, wood, etc. * *n* inlaid work; material inlaid.—**inlaid** *adj*.
inlet *n* a narrow strip of water extending into a body of land; an opening; a passage, pipe, etc for liquid to enter a machine, etc. * *vt* (**inletting, inletted**) to inlay; to insert.
in loco parentis (*Latin*) in the place of a parent.
inmate *n* a person confined with others in a prison or institution.
in memoriam (*Latin*) in memory of.
inmost *adj* farthest within; most secret.
inn *n* a small hotel; a restaurant or tavern, esp in the countryside.
innards *npl* (*inf*) the stomach and intestines, internal organs.
innate *adj* existing from birth; inherent; instinctive.—**innately** *adv*.
inner *adj* further within; inside, internal; private, exclusive. * *n* (*archery*) the innermost ring on a target.
inner city *n* the central area of a city, esp as affected by overcrowding and poverty.
innermost *adj* furthest within.
inner tube *n* the separate inflatable tube within a pneumatic tire.
innervation *n* the arrangement of nerve filaments in the body; special activity or stimulus in any part of the nervous system.
inning *n* (*baseball*) a team's turn at bat.
innings *n* (*pl* **innings**) (*cricket*) a turn at bat for a batsman or side; the number of runs scored at this time; an opportunity to demonstrate one's abilities.
innkeeper *n* a person who owns or manages an inn.
innocence *n* the condition or quality of being innocent.
innocent *adj* not guilty of a particular crime; free from sin; blameless; harmless; inoffensive; simple, credulous, naive. * *n* an innocent person, as a child.—**innocence** *n*.—**innocently** *adv*.
innocuous *adj* harmless.—**innocuously** *adv*.—**innocuousness** *n*.
innominate *adj* without a name.
innovate *vi* to introduce new methods, ideas, etc; to make changes.—**innovation** *n*.—**innovative, innovatory** *adv*.
innovator *n* one who introduces, or seeks to introduce, new things.
innoxious *adj* harmless.
innuendo *n* (*pl* **innuendos, innuendoes**) a hint or sly remark, usu derogatory; an insinuation.
Innuit *see* **Inuit**.
innumerable, innumerous *adj* too many to be counted; very numerous.—**innumerability** *n*.—**innumerably** *adv*.
innumerate *adj* lacking knowledge or understanding of mathematics and science; not numerate.—*also n*.
inobservance *n* inattention; failure to observe (law, etc).—**inobservant** *adj*.
inoculate *vt* to inject a serum or a vaccine into, esp in order to create immunity; to protect as if by inoculation.—**inoculation** *n*.—**inoculative** *adj*.
inodorous *adj* without odour.
inoffensive *adj* harmless, not offensive.
inofficious *adj* contrary to moral duty.
inoperable *adj* not suitable for surgery.—**inoperability** *n*.
inoperative *adj* not working; producing no effect.
inopportune *adj* unseasonable; untimely.—**inopportuneness, inopportunity** *n*.
inordinate *adj* excessive.—**inordinately** *adv*.
inorganic *adj* not having the structure or characteristics of living organisms; denoting a chemical compound not containing carbon.—**inorganically** *adv*.
inorganic chemistry *n* the chemistry of all substances except those containing carbon.
inosculate *vti* (*anat, of blood vessels, fibres, etc*) to join closely, be closely joined.—**inosculation** *n*.
inpatient *n* a patient being treated while remaining in hospital.
in perpetuum *adv* perpetually, forever.
in posse *adj, adv* having a possible but not an actual existence, potential.
input *n* what is put in, as power into a machine, data into a computer, etc. * *vt* (**inputting, input** *or* **inputted**) to put in; to enter (data) into a computer.
inquest *n* a judicial inquiry held by a coroner, esp into a case of violent or unexplained death; (*inf*) any detailed inquiry or investigation.
inquietude *n* unease, disquiet.
inquiline *n* (*zool*) an animal which lives in the abode of another but does not harm it, eg a hermit crab.—**inquilinous** *adj*.
inquire *vi* to request information about; (*usu with* **into**) to investigate. * *vt* to ask about.—*also* **enquire**.—**inquirer, enquirer** *n*.
inquiry *n* (*pl* **inquiries**) the act of inquiring; a search by questioning; an investigation; a question; research.—*also* **enquiry**.

inquisition *n* a detailed examination or investigation; (*with cap and* **the**) (*RC Church*) formerly the tribunal for suppressing heresy.—**inquisitional** *adj*.

inquisitive *adj* eager for knowledge; unnecessarily curious; prying.—**inquisitively** *adv*.—**inquisitiveness** *n*.

inquisitor *n* a person who questions searchingly or forcefully; (*often cap*) a member of the Inquisition.

inquisitorial *adj* of or resembling an inquisitor; prying.—**inquisitorially** *adv*.

in re *prep* in the matter of.

inroad *n* a raid into enemy territory; an encroachment or advance.

inrush *n* a sudden inward flow or influx.

insalivate *vt* to mix (food) with saliva while chewing.—**insalivation** *n*.

insalubrious *adj* (*climate, place*) unhealthy.—**insalubrity** *n*.

insane *adj* not sane, mentally ill; of or for insane people; very foolish.—**insanely** *adv*.

insanitary *adj* unclean, likely to cause infection or ill-health.—**insanitariness, insanitation** *n*.

insanity *n* (*pl* **insanities**) derangement of the mind or intellect; lunacy; madness.

insatiable *adj* not easily satisfied; greedy.—**insatiability** *n*.—**insatiability** *adv*.—**insatiably** *adv*.

insatiate *adj* insatiable.

inscribe *vt* to mark or engrave (words, etc) on (a surface); to add (a person's name) to a list; to dedicate (a book) to someone; to autograph; to fix in the mind.—**inscribable** *adj*.

inscription *n* an inscribing; words, etc inscribed on a tomb, coin, stone, etc.—**inscriptional** *adj*.

inscrutable *adj* hard to understand, incomprehensible; enigmatic.—**inscrutability** *n*.—**inscrutably** *adv*.

insect *n* any of a class of small arthropods with three pairs of legs, a head, thorax, and abdomen and two or four wings.

insectary *n* (*pl* **insectaries**) a place for keeping insects.

insecticide *n* a substance for killing insects.—**insecticidal** *adj*.

insectivore *n* an order of mammals that are small, nocturnal, and feed on insects or other invertebrates; any insect-eating plant or animal.—**insectivorous** *adj*.

insecure *adj* not safe; feeling anxiety; not dependable.—**insecurely** *adv*.

insecurity *n* (*pl* **insecurities**) the condition of being insecure; lack of confidence or sureness; instability; something insecure.

inseminate *vt* to fertilize; to impregnate.—**insemination** *n*.—**inseminator** *n*.

insensate *adj* not feeling sensation; stupid; without regard or feeling; cold.

insensible *adj* unconscious; unaware; indifferent; imperceptible.—**insensibility** *n*.—**insensibly** *adv*.

insensitive *adj* not sensitive, unfeeling.

insentient *adj* inert; inanimate.

inseparable *adj* not able to be separated; closely attached, as romantically.—**inseparability** *n*.—**inseparably** *adv*.

insert *vt* to put or fit (something) into something else. * *n* something inserted.—**insertion** *n*.

insertion *n* the act of inserting; something which is inserted.

in-service *adj* (*training*) given during employment.

insessorial *adj* (*ornithology*) adapted for perching.

inset *n* something inserted within something larger; an insert. * *vt* (**insetting, inset**) to set in, insert.—**insetter** *n*.

inshore *adj, adv* near or towards the shore.

inshrine *see* **enshrine**.

inside *n* the inner side, surface, or part; (*pl*: *inf*) the internal organs, stomach, bowels. * *adj* internal; known only to insiders; secret. * *adv* on or in the inside; within; indoors; (*sl*) in prison. * *prep* in or within.

inside job *n* (*inf*) a crime committed with the help of someone connected with the victim or premises involved.

inside out *adj* reversed; with the inner surface facing the outside.

insider *n* a person within a place or group; a person with access to confidential information.

insidious *adj* marked by slyness or treachery; more dangerous than seems evident.—**insidiously** *adv*.—**insidiousness** *n*.

insight *n* the ability to see and understand clearly the inner nature of things, esp by intuition; an instance of such understanding.—**insightful** *adj*.

insignia *n* (*pl* **insignias, insignia**) a mark or badge of authority; a distinguishing characteristic.

insignificant *adj* having little or no importance; trivial; worthless; small, inadequate.—**insignificance, insignificancy** *n*.—**insignificantly** *adv*.

insincere *adj* not sincere; hypocritical.—**insincerely** *adv*.—**insincerity** *n*.

insinuate *vt* to introduce or work in slowly, indirectly, etc; to hint.—**insinuator** *n*.

insinuation *n* the act of insinuating; an indirect or sly hint.

insipid *adj* lacking any distinctive flavour; uninteresting, dull.—**insipidity, insipidness** *n*.—**insipidly** *adv*.

insist *vi* (*often with* **on** *or* **upon**) to take and maintain a stand. * *vt* to demand strongly; to declare firmly.—**insister** *n*.

insistent *adj* insisting or demanding.—**insistence, insistency** *n*.—**insistently** *adv*.

in situ *adj* in the original or natural place or position.

insobriety *n* drunkenness.

in so far, insofar *adv* to such a degree or extent.

insole *n* the innser sole of a shoe, etc; a thickness of material used as a inner sole.

insolent *adj* disrespectful; impudent, arrogant; rude.—**insolence** *n*.—**insolently** *adv*.

insoluble *adj* incapable of being dissolved; impossible to solve or explain.—**insolubility** *n*.—**insolubly** *adv*.

insolvent *adj* unable to pay one's debts; bankrupt.—**insolvency** *n*.

insomnia *n* abnormal inability to sleep.

insomniac *n* a person who suffers from insomnia.

insomuch *adv* (*with* **as** *or* **that**) to such an extent; (*with* **as**) inasmuch.

insouciant *adj* calm and unconcerned, carefree.—**insouciance** *n*.

inspect *vt* to look at carefully; to examine or review officially.—**inspection** *n*.—**inspectional** *adj*.—**inspective** *adj*.

inspector *n* an official who inspects in order to ensure compliance with regulations, etc; a police officer ranking below a superintendent.—**inspectorate** *n*.—**inspectoral, inspectorial** *adj*.—**inspectorship** *n*.

inspectorate *n* the office, district or rank of an inspector; a body of inspectors.

inspiration *n* an inspiring; any stimulus to creative thought; an inspired idea, action, etc.—**inspirational** *adj*.

inspiratory *adj* pertaining to inhalation.

inspire *vt* to stimulate, as to some creative effort; to motivate by divine influence; to arouse (a thought or feeling) in (someone); to cause.—**inspiring** *adj*.—**inspiringly** *adv*.

inspirit *vt* to put life into, invigorate; to animate, cheer.

inst. *abbr* = instant (this month).

instability *n* (*pl* **instabilities**) lack of stability; inconstancy.

install, instal *vt* (**installs** *or* **instals, installing, installed**) to formally place in an office, rank, etc; to establish in a place; to settle in a position or state.—**installer** *n*.

installation *n* the act of installing or being installed; machinery, equipment, etc that has been installed.

installment, instalment *n* a sum of money to be paid at regular specified times; any of several parts, as of a magazine story or television serial.

instance *n* an example; a step in proceeding; an occasion. * *vt* to give as an example.

instant *adj* immediate; (*food*) concentrated or precooked for quick preparation. * *n* a moment; a particular moment.

instantaneous *adj* happening or done very quickly.—**instantaneously** *adv*.—**instantaneousness, instantaneity** *n*.

instanter *adv* (*law*) immediately.

instantly *adv* immediately.

instate *vt* to install in an office or rank.

instead *adv* in place of the one mentioned.

instep *n* the upper part of the arch of the foot, between the ankle and the toes.

instigate *vt* to urge on, goad; to initiate.—**instigation** *n*.—**instigator** *n*.

instill, instil *vt* (**instills** *or* **instils, instilling, instilled**) to put (an idea, etc) in or into (the mind) gradually.—**instillation** *n*.—**instiller** *n*.

instinct *n* the inborn tendency to behave in a way characteristic of a species; a natural or acquired tendency; a knack.

instinctive, instinctual *adj* of, relating to, or prompted by instinct.—**instinctively, instinctually** *adv*.

institute *vt* to organize, establish; to start, initiate. * *n* an organization for the promotion of science, art, etc; a school, college, or department of a university specializing in some field.—**institutor, instituter** *n*.

institution *n* an established law, custom, etc; an organization having a social, educational, or religious purpose; the building housing it; (*inf*) a long-established person or thing.

institutional *adj* of or resembling an institution; dull, routine.

institutionalize *vt* to make or become an institution; to place in an institution; to make a person dependent on an institutional routine and unable to cope on their own.—**institutionalization** *n*.

instruct *vt* to provide with information; to teach; to give instructions to; to authorize.—**instructible** *adj*.—**instructor** *n*.—**instructress** *nf*.

instruction *n* an order, direction; the act or process of teaching or training; knowledge imparted; (*comput*) a command in a program to perform a particular operation; (*pl*) orders, directions; detailed guidance.—**instructional** *adj*.

instructive *adj* issuing or containing instructions; giving information, educational.—**instructively** *adv*.

instructor *n* someone who instructs; a teacher.

instrument *n* a thing by means of which something is done; a tool or implement; any of various devices for indicating, measuring, controlling, etc; any of various devices producing musical sound; a formal document. * *vt* to orchestrate.

instrument panel *n* a panel in a vehicle or machine in which instruments monitoring speed, engine status, etc are mounted.

instrumental *adj* serving as a means of doing something; helpful; of, performed on, or written for a musical instrument or instruments.—**instrumentality** *n*.—**instrumentally** *adv*.

instrumentalist *n* a person who plays a musical instrument.

instrumentation *n* the arrangement of a musical composition for different instruments; the use or provision of tools or instruments.

insubordinate *adj* not submitting to authority; rebellious.—**insubordination** *n*.

insubstantial *adj* unreal, imaginary; weak or flimsy.—**insubstantiality** *n*.—**insubstantially** *adv*.

insufferable *adj* intolerable; unbearable.—**insufferably** *adv*.

insufficient *adj* not sufficient.—**insufficiency, insufficience** *n*.—**insufficiently** *adv*.

insufflate *vt* to blow (air, powder) into or onto.—**insufflation** *n*.—**insufflator** *n*.

insular *adj* of or like an island or islanders; narrow-minded; illiberal.—**insularity, insularism** *n*.

insulate *vt* to set apart; to isolate; to cover with a nonconducting material in order to prevent the escape of electricity, heat, sound, etc.—**insulation** *n*.—**insulator** *n*.

insulation *n* the act of insulating; the material used for insulating.

insulator *n* something which insulates; a non-conductor of electricity, heat or sound.

insulin *n* a hormone that controls absorption of sugar by the body, secreted by islets of tissue in the pancreas.

insult *vt* to treat with indignity or contempt; to offend. * *n* an insulting remark or act.—**insulter** *n*.

insuperable *adj* unable to be overcome.—**insuperability** *n*.—**insuperably** *adv*.

insupportable *adj* unbearable, intolerable.

insurable *adj* able to be insured.

insurance *n* insuring or being insured; a contract purchased to guarantee compensation for a specified loss by fire, death, etc; the amount for which something is insured; the business of insuring against loss.

insure *vt* to take out or issue insurance on; to ensure. * *vi* to contract to give or take insurance.

insurer *n* someone who insures, an underwriter; a company which sells insurance.

insurgent *adj* rebellious, rising in revolt. * *n* a person who fights against established authority, a rebel.—**insurgence** *n*.—**insurgency** *n*.

insurmountable *adj* which cannot be overcome, insuperable.

insurrection *adj* a rising or revolt against established authority.—**insurrectional** *adj*.—**insurrectionary** *n, adj*.—**insurrectionism** *n*.—**insurrectionist** *n*.

intact *adj* unimpaired; whole.

intaglio *n* (*pl* **intaglios**) a design carved or engraved below the surface; a printing technique using engraved surfaces.—**intagliated** *adj*.

intake *n* the place in a pipe, etc where a liquid or gas is taken in; a thing or quantity taken in, as students, etc; the process of taking in.

intangible *adj* that cannot be touched, incorporeal; representing value but without material being, as good will; indefinable. * *n* something that is intangible.—**intangibility** *n*.—**intangibly** *adv*.

integer *n* any member of the set consisting of the positive and negative whole numbers and zero, such as –5, 0, 5.

integral *adj* necessary for completeness; whole or complete; made up of parts forming a whole. * *n* the result of a mathematical integration.—**integrally** *adv*.

integral calculus *n* (*maths*) the determination of definite and indefinite integrals and their use in the solution of differential equations.

integrant *adj* component, making part of a whole.

integrate *vti* to make whole or become complete; to bring (parts) together into a whole; to remove barriers imposing segregation upon (racial groups); to abolish segregation; (*math*) to find the integral of.—**integration** *n*.—**integrative** *adj*.

integrated circuit *n* a small electronic circuit assembled from microcomponents mounted on chips of semiconducting material.

integrator *n* someone who, or something which, integrates.

integrity *n* honesty, sincerity; completeness, wholeness; an unimpaired condition.

integument *n* a natural covering as skin, a rind, a husk, etc.—**integumental, integumentary** *adj*.

intellect *n* the ability to reason or understand; high intelligence; a very intelligent person.—**intellective** *adj*.

intellection *n* thought.

intellectual *adj* of, involving, or appealing to the intellect; requiring intelligence. * *n* an intellectual person.—**intellectuality** *n*.—**intellectually** *adv*.

intellectualism *n* the use of the intellect; (*philos*) the theory that all knowledge is derived from the intellect; (*derog*) excessive emphasis on the value of the intellect.—**intellectualist** *n*.

intellectualize *vt* to make intellectual; to use the intellect on. * *vi* to become intellectual; to use the intellect.—**intellectualization** *n*.

intelligence *n* the ability to learn or understand; the ability to cope with a new situation; news or information; those engaged in gathering secret, esp military, information.

intelligence quotient *n* a measure of a person's intelligence, calculated by dividing mental age by actual age and multiplying by 100.

intelligent *adj* having or showing intelligence; clever, wise, etc.—**intelligently** *adv*.

intelligentsia *n* intellectuals collectively.

intelligible *adj* able to be understood; clear.—**intelligibility** *n*.—**intelligibly** *adv*.

intemperate *adj* indulging excessively in alcoholic drink; unrestrained; (*climate*) extreme.—**intemperance** *n*.—**intemperately** *adv*.

intend *vt* to mean, to signify; to propose, have in mind as an aim or purpose.—**intender** *n*.

intendancy *n* (*pl* **intendancies**) the rank or office of an intendant.

intendant *n* a superintendent or manager (esp under a monarch in France, Spain and Portugal).
intended *adj* planned. * *n* (*inf*) a fiancé or fiancée.
intendment *n* the true meaning of something, as fixed by law.
intense *adj* very strong, concentrated; passionate, emotional.—**intensely** *adv*.
intensify *vti* (**intensifying, intensified**) to make or become more intense.—**intensification** *n*.
intensity *n* (*pl* **intensities**) the state or quality of being intense; density, as of a negative plate; the force or energy of any physical agent.
intensive *adj* of or characterized by intensity; thorough; denoting careful attention given to patients right after surgery, etc.—**intensively** *adv*.
intensive care *n* 24-hour monitoring and treatment of acutely ill patients in hospital; the specialized unit administering this.
intent *adj* firmly directed; having one's attention or purpose firmly fixed. * *n* intention; something intended; purpose or meaning.—**intently** *adv*.—**intentness** *n*.
intention *n* a determination to act in a specified way; anything intended.
intentional *adj* done purposely.—**intentionality** *n*.—**intentionally** *adv*.
inter *vt* (**interring, interred**) to bury.
inter- *prefix* between, among.
interact *vi* to act upon each other.—**interaction** *n*.—**interactional** *adj*.
interactive *adj* interacting; allowing two-way communication between a device, such as a computer or compact video disc, and its user.—**interactivity** *n*.
inter alia *adv* among other things.
interbreed *vti* (**interbreeding, interbred**) to breed within the same breed or family; to breed by crossing one species with another.
intercalary *adj* inserted into the calendar to harmonize it with the solar year, eg February 29 as inserted in the leap year.
intercalate *vt* to insert (an intercalary day) into the calendar.—**intercalation** *n*.
intercede *vi* to intervene on another's behalf; to mediate.—**interceder** *n*.
intercellular *adj* lying between cells.
intercept *vt* to stop or catch in its course. * *n* a point of intersection of two geometric figures; interception by an interceptor.—**interception** *n*.—**interceptive** *adj*.
interceptor, intercepter *n* a high-speed fighter aircraft used to intercept and destroy enemy aircraft.
intercession *n* the act of interceding, esp by prayer; mediation.—**intercessional, intercessory** *adj*.—**intercessor** *n*.—**intercessorial** *adj*.
interchange *vt* to give and receive one thing for another; to exchange, to put (each of two things) in the place of the other; to alternate. * *n* an interchanging; a junction on a motorway designed to prevent traffic intersecting.
interchangeable *adj* able to be interchanged.—**interchangeability** *n*.—**interchangeably** *adv*.
intercollegiate *adj* between or among colleges or universities.
intercolumniation *n* the distance between pillars; the spacing between pillars.—**intercolumniar** *adj*.
intercom *n* (*inf*) a system of intercommunicating, as in an aircraft.
intercommunicate *vi* to have mutual communication; to have passage to each other.—**intercommunicable** *adj*.—**intercommunication** *n*.
interconnect *vti* to connect by reciprocal links.—**interconnection** *n*.
intercontinental *adj* between continents.
intercostal *adj* (*anat*) lying between the ribs.
intercourse *n* a connection by dealings or communication between individuals or groups; sexual intercourse, copulation.
intercross *vti* to crossbreed.
intercurrent *adj* occurring at the same time; (*disease*) occurring during the course of another.—**intercurrence** *n*.
interdependence, interdependency *n* dependence on each other.—**interdependent** *adj*.
interdict *vt* to prohibit (an action); to restrain from doing or using something. * *n* an official prohibition.—**interdiction** *n*.—**interdictory** *adj*.
interdisciplinary *adj* involving two or more different branches of knowledge.
interest *n* a feeling of curiosity about something; the power of causing this feeling; a share in, or a right to, something; anything in which one has a share; benefit; money paid for the use of money; the rate of such payment. * *vt* to excite the attention of; to cause to have a share in; to concern oneself with.
interested *adj* having or expressing an interest; affected by personal interest, not impartial.—**interestedly** *adv*.
interesting *n* engaging the attention.
interface *n* a surface that forms the common boundary between two things; an electrical connection between one device and another, esp a computer. * *vt* (*elect*) to modify the input and output configurations of (devices) so that they may connect and communicate with each other; to connect using an interface; to be interactive (with).—**interfacial** *adj*.—**interfacially** *adv*.
interfacing *n* a layer of fabric between the neck, etc of a garment and its facing to give body.
interfere *vi* to clash; to come between; to intervene; to meddle; to obstruct.—**interfering** *adj*.
interference *n* an interfering; (*radio, TV*) the interruption of reception by atmospherics or by unwanted signals.
interferometer *n* (*physics*) an instrument used to measure the length of light waves by interference phenomena.
interferon *n* a protein, produced by cells in response to a virus, which then prevents the virus from growing.
interfuse *vti* to mix, blend.—**interfusion** *n*.
intergalactic *adj* occurring or existing between galaxies.
interglacial *adj* occurring between two glacial periods.
intergrade *vi* (*usu biol*) to change form gradually.—**intergradation** *n*.
interim *n* an intervening period of time. * *adj* provisional, temporary. * *adv* meanwhile.
interior *adj* situated within; inner; inland; private. * *n* the interior part, as of a room, country, etc.
interior angle *n* the angle between two adjacent sides of a polygon.
interior design *n* the art or business of an interior designer—*also* **interior decoration**.
interior designer *n* a person whose profession is the planning of the decor and furnishings of the interiors of houses, offices, etc.—*also* **interior decorator**.
interj. *abbr* = interjection.
interject *vt* to throw in between; to interrupt with.—**interjector** *n*.—**interjectory** *adj*.
interjection *n* an interjecting; an interruption; an exclamation.—**interjectional** *adj*.—**interjectionally** *adv*.
interlace *vti* to combine (as if) by lacing or weaving together.—**interlacement** *n*.
interlard *vt* to insert something foreign into.
interleaf *n* (*pl* **interleaves**) an additional, blank leaf inserted into a book.
interleave *vti* to insert an extra page (usu blank) in a book.
interline *vt* to write between lines.—**interlinear** *adj*.—**interlineation** *n*.
interlining *n* an extra lining between the lining and the outer fabric of a garment, etc; the material for this.
interlink *vt* to link together.
interlock *vti* to lock or become locked together; to join with one another.
interlocution *n* dialogue, discussion.
interlocutor *n* a person who takes part in a conversation.—**interlocutress, interlocutrix** *nf*.
interlocutory *adj* conversational; (*law*) pronounced during legal proceedings.
interlope *vi* to intrude in a matter in which one has no real concern.
interloper *n* a person who meddles; an intruder.
interlude *n* anything that fills time between two events, as music between acts of a play.
interlunar *adj* coming between the old and the new moon.

intermarry *vi* (**intermarrying, intermarried**) (*different races, religions, etc*) to become connected by marriage; to marry within one's close family.—**intermarriage** *n*.
intermediary *n* (*pl* **intermediaries**) a mediator. * *adj* acting as a mediator; intermediate.
intermediate *adj* in the middle; in between.
interment *n* burial.
intermezzo *n* (*pl* **intermezzos, intermezzi**) a short musical composition between parts of an opera, play, etc; a movement between sections of an extended instrumental work; a similar composition intended as an independent work.
interminable *adj* lasting or seeming to last forever; endless.—**interminably** *adv*.
intermingle *vti* to mingle or mix together.
intermission *n* an interval of time between parts of a performance.
intermit *vb* (**intermitting, intermitted**) *vt* to cause to cease for a time; to suspend. * *vi* to cease for a time; to be suspended.
intermittent *adj* stopping and starting again at intervals; periodic.—**intermittence, intermittency** *n*.—**intermittently** *adv*.
intermix *vti* to mix together.
intermixture *n* the act of mixing together; a mixture.
intern[1] *vt* to detain and confine within an area, esp during wartime.—**internment** *n*.
intern[2] *n* a doctor serving in a hospital, usu just after graduation from medical school, a houseman.
intern[3], **interne** *n* an apprentice journalist, teacher, etc.
internal *adj* of or on the inside; of or inside the body; intrinsic; domestic.—**internality** *n*.—**internally** *adv*.
internal combustion engine *n* an engine producing power by the explosion of a fuel-and-air mixture within the cylinders.
international *adj* between or among nations; concerned with the relations between nations; for the use of all nations; of or for people in various nations. * *n* a sporting competition between teams from different countries; a member of an international team of players.—**internationality** *n*.—**internationally** *adv*.
International Date Line *n* the line running north to south along the 180-degree meridian, east of which is one day earlier than west of it.
internationalism *n* an attitude, belief, or policy favouring the promotion of cooperation and understanding between nations.—**internationalist** *n*.
interne *see* **intern**[3].
internecine *adj* extremely destructive to both sides.
internee *n* a person who is interned.
internist *n* a physician who specializes in internal diseases.
internode *n* (*bot*) the space on a plant stem between two nodes or leaf joints.—**internodal** *adj*.
internuncial *adj* pertaining to an internuncio; (*anat*) transmitting nervous signals.
internuncio *n* a representative of the Pope.
interpellate *vt* to question (an official) about government policy or about personal conduct.—**interpellation** *n*.—**interpellator** *n*.
interpenetrate *vt* to penetrate thoroughly. * *vi* to penetrate each other.—**interpenetration** *n*.—**interpenetrative** *adj*.
interplanetary *adj* between or among planets.
interplay *n* the action of two things on each other, interaction.
interplead *vi* (**interpleading, interpleaded, interplead, interpled**) (*law*) to discuss a point incidentally arising, or concerning a third party.
interpleader *n* (*law*) the discussion of a point incidentally arising or concerning a third party.
Interpol (*acronym*) International Criminal Police Organization.
interpolate *vt* to change (a text) by inserting new material; to insert between or among others; (*math*) to estimate a value between two known values.—**interpolator** *n*.—**interpolation** *n*.
interpose *vti* to place or come between; to intervene (with); to interrupt (with).—**interposer** *n*.—**interposition** *n*.
interpret *vt* to explain; to translate; to construe; to give one's own conception of, as in a play or musical composition. * *vi* to translate between speakers of different languages.—**interpretational** *adj*.
interpretation *n* an act or instance of interpreting; an explanation; a rendering (of a piece of music, theatre, etc).
interpreter *n* a person who translates orally for persons speaking in different languages; (*comput*) a program that translates an instruction into machine code.
interracial *adj* between or among races.
interregnum *n* (*pl* **interregnums, interregna**) the period between two reigns, governments, etc; a suspension of normal government; a pause in a continuous series.
interrelate *vti* to be or place in a mutually dependant or reciprocal relationship.—**interrelation** *n*.—**interrelationship** *n*.
interrogate *vti* to question, esp formally.—**interrogation** *n*.—**interrogational** *adj*.—**interrogator** *n*.
interrogative *adj* asking a question. * *n* a word used in asking a question.—**interrogatively** *adv*.
interrogatory *adj* questioning. * *n* (*pl* **interrogatories**) examination by questions.—**interrogatorily** *adv*.
interrupt *vt* to break into (a discussion, etc) or break in upon (a speaker, worker, etc); to make a break in the continuity of. * *vi* to interrupt an action, talk, etc.—**interrupter** *n*.—**interruptive** *adj*.
interruption *n* the act of interrupting; a hindrance; a remark interposed in a conversation, etc.
intersect *vti* to cut or divide by passing through or crossing; (*lines, roads, etc*) to meet and cross each other.
intersection *n* an intersecting; the place where two lines, roads, etc meet or cross.—**intersectional** *adj*.
interspace *n* a space between things.
intersperse *vt* to scatter or insert among other things; to diversify with other things scattered here and there.—**interspersion** *n*.
interstate *adj* between or among different states of a federation.
interstellar *adj* between or among stars.
interstice *n* a crack; a crevice; a minute space.
interstitial *adj* occurring in interstices.
intertexture *n* the act or product of interweaving.
intertribal *adj* between or among tribes.
intertwine *vti* to twine or twist closely together.
interval *n* a space between things; the time between events; (*mus*) the difference of pitch between two notes.
intervene *vi* to occur or come between; to occur between two events, etc; to come in to modify, settle, or hinder some action, etc.—**intervener, intervenor** *n*.—**intervention** *n*.—**interventional** *adj*.
interventionist *n* a person who favours intervention. * *adj* of or in favour of intervention.—**interventionism** *n*.
interview *n* a meeting in which a person is asked about his or her views, etc, as by a newspaper or television reporter; a published account of this; a formal meeting at which a candidate for a job is questioned and assessed by a prospective employer. * *vt* to have an interview with.—**interviewer** *n*.
interviewee *n* a person who is interviewed.
interweave *vti* (**interweaving, interwove** *or* **interweaved,** *pp* **interwoven** *or* **interweaved**) to weave together, interlace; to intermingle.
interwind *vt* (**interwinding, interwound**) to wind together.
intestate *adj* having made no will. * *n* a person who dies intestate.—**intestacy** *n*.
intestine *n* the lower part of the alimentary canal between the stomach and the anus.—**intestinal** *adj*.
intifada *n* the Arabic word for "uprising," esp the uprising in Israel in 1987 of Palestinian inhabitants.
intimacy *n* (*pl* **intimacies**) close or confidential friendship; familiarity; sexual relations.
intimate *adj* most private or personal; very close or familiar, esp sexually; deep and thorough. * *n* an intimate friend. * *vt* to indicate; to make known; to hint or imply.—**intimately** *adv*.

intimation *n* the act of intimating; a notice, announcement.
intimidate *vt* to frighten; to discourage, silence, etc esp by threats.—**intimidation** *n*.—**intimidator** *n*.
intinction *n* (*Eastern Church*) the practice of administering both parts of Holy Communion at the same time by dipping the bread into the wine.
into *prep* to the interior or inner parts of; to the middle; to a particular condition; (*inf*) deeply interested or involved in.
intolerable *adj* unbearable.—**intolerably** *adv*.
intolerance *n* lack of toleration of the opinions or practices of others; inability to bear or endure.—**intolerant** *adj*.
intonate *vti* to recite in a singing voice, chant.
intonation *n* intoning; variations in pitch of the speaking voice; an accent.—**intonational** *adj*.
intone *vti* to speak or recite in a singing tone; to chant.—**intoner** *n*.
in toto *adv* completely; as a whole; entirely.
intoxicant *n* something that intoxicates, esp a drug or an alcoholic drink.—*also adj*.
intoxicate *vt* to make drunken; to elate; to poison.—**intoxicatingly** *adv*.
intoxication *n* drunkenness; great excitement; poisoning.
intra- *prefix* within.
intracranial *adj* within the skull.
intractable *adj* unmanageable, uncontrollable; (*problem, illness, etc*) difficult to solve, alleviate, or cure.—**intractability** *n*.—**intractably** *adv*.
intrados *n* (*pl* **intrados, intradoses**) the inner and lower curve of an arch.
intramural *adj* (*education*) within an institution or organization;
intransigent *adj* unwilling to compromise, irreconcilable.—**intransigence** *n*.—**intransigently** *adv*.
intransitive *adj* (*gram*) denoting a verb that does not take a direct object.—**intransitively** *adv*.
intrauterine *adj* inside the uterus.
intrauterine device *n* a small loop or coil inserted into the uterus as a contraceptive.
intravenous *adj* into a vein.—**intravenously** *adv*.
in-tray *n* a tray holding documents, etc, awaiting attention.
intrench *see* **entrench**.
intrepid *adj* bold; fearless; brave.—**intrepidity** *n*.—**intrepidly** *adv*.
intricate *adj* difficult to understand; complex, complicated; involved, detailed.—**intricacy** *n*.—**intricately** *adv*.
intrigue *n* a secret or underhand plotting; a secret or underhanded plot or scheme; a secret love affair. * *vb* (**intriguing, intrigued**) *vi* to carry on an intrigue. * *vt* to excite the interest or curiosity of.—**intriguer** *n*.
intrinsic *adj* belonging to the real nature of a person or thing; inherent.—**intrinsically** *adv*.
intro- *prefix* within, into.
intro *n* (*pl* **intros**) (*inf*) introduction.
introduce *vt* to make (a person) acquainted by name (with other persons); to bring into use or establish; to present (legislation, etc) for consideration or approval; to present a radio or television programme; to bring into or insert.—**introducer** *n*.
introduction *n* an introducing or being introduced; the presentation of one person to another; preliminary text in a book; a preliminary passage in a musical composition.
introductory *adj* serving as an introduction; preliminary.—**introductorily** *adv*.
introit *n* (*RC Church, Church of England*) a psalm or passage of scripture sung by the choir as the priest approaches the altar before Mass or Holy Communion.
intromission *n* insertion; introduction.
intromit *vt* to insert.—**intromittent** *adj*.
introspect *vi* to examine one's own thoughts and feelings.
introspection *n* examination of one's own mind and feelings, etc.—**introspectional, introspective** *adj*.
introversion *n* the act of introverting; the state of being introverted; the direction of, or tendancy to direct, one's thoughts and concerns inward.
introvert *vt* to turn or direct inward. * *vi* to produce introversion in. * *n* a person who is more interested in his or her own thoughts, feelings, etc than in external objects or events. * *adj* characterized by introversion.—**introversive** *adj*.
intrude *vti* to force (oneself) upon others unasked.—**intruder** *n*.—**intrudingly** *adj*.
intrusion *n* the act or an instance of intruding; the forcible entry of molten rock into and between existing rocks.—**intrusional** *adj*.
intrusive *adj* intruding; tending to intrude; (*rocks*) formed by intrusion.—**intrusively** *adv*.
intrust *see* **entrust**.
intubate *vt* (*med*) to insert a tube into (the larynx, etc).—**intubation** *n*.
intuit *vt* to know by intuition.
intuition *n* a perceiving of the truth of something immediately without reasoning or analysis; a hunch, an insight.—**intuitional** *adj*.—**intutionally** *adv*.
intuitive *adj* perceiving or perceived by intuition.—**intuitively** *adv*.
intuitivism *n* the doctrine that ethical principles are matters of intuition.—**intuitivist** *n*.
intuitonism, intuitionalism *n* the doctrine that the immediate perception of truth is by intuition.—**intuitionist, intuitionalist** *n*.
intumescence, intumescency *n* a swelling up; a tumid state.—**intumescent** *adj*.
intussusception *n* (*med*) the protrusion of the upper part of the intestinal canal into the lower part; (*biol*) the expansion of a cell.
intwine *see* **entwine**.
Inuit *n* (*pl* **Inuit, Inuits**) an Eskimo from Greenland or North America.—*also* **Innuit**.
inulin *n* a starchy constituent of many plants.
inunction *n* the act of applying ointment; the act of anointing or smearing with oil.
inundate *vt* to cover as with a flood; to deluge.—**inundation** *n*.—**inundator** *n*.
inure *vt* to accustom to, esp to something unpleasant.—*also* **enure**.—**inurement, enurement** *n*.
inurn *vt* to put (ashes) in an urn.
inutile *adj* useless.
invade *vt* to enter (a country) with hostile intentions; to encroach upon; to penetrate; to crowd into as if invading.—**invader** *n*.
in vacuo *adv* in a vacuum.
invaginate *vt* (*anat*) to fold back a part of a tubular organ on itself so that it is sheathed.
invagination *n* the process of invaginating; the state of being invaginated.
invalid[1] *adj* not valid.
invalid[2] *n* a person who is ill or disabled. * *vt* to cause to become an invalid; to disable; to cause to retire from the armed forces because of ill-health or injury.
invalidate *vt* to render not valid; to deprive of legal force.—**invalidation** *n*.
invalidity *n* (*pl* **invalidities**) a lack of validity; a state of illness or disability.
invaluable *adj* too valuable to be measured in money.—**invaluably** *adv*.
Invar *n* (*trademark*) an alloy of nickel and steel, used in scientific instruments because of its invariability.
invariable *adj* never changing; constant.—**invariability** *n*.—**invariably** *adv*.
invasion *n* the act of invading with military forces; an encroachment, intrusion.
invasive *adj* marked by military aggression; tending to spread; tending to infringe.
invective *n* the use of violent or abusive language or writing.
inveigh *vi* to speak violently or bitterly (against).—**inveigher** *n*.
inveigle *vt* to entice or trick into doing something.—**inveiglement** *n*.—**inveigler** *n*.
invent *vt* to think up; to think out or produce (a new device, process, etc); to originate; to fabricate (a lie, etc).—**inventible, inventable** *adj*.—**inventor** *n*.
invention *n* something invented; inventiveness.—**inventional** *adj*.

inventive *adj* pertaining to invention; skilled in inventing.—**inventiveness** *n.*
inventory *n* (*pl* **inventories**) an itemized list of goods, property, etc, as of a business; the store of such goods for such a listing; a list of the property of an individual or an estate. * *vt* (**inventorying, inventoried**) to make an inventory of; to enter in an inventory.—**inventoriable** *adj.*—**inventorial** *adj.*
inveracity *n* (*pl* **inveracities**) untruthfulness.
inverse *adj* reversed in order or position; opposite, contrary. * *n* an inverse state or thing.—**inversely** *adv.*
inversion *n* an inverting or being inverted; something inverted.—**inversive** *adj.*
invert *vt* to turn upside down or inside out; to reverse in order, position or relationship.—**invertible** *adj.*
invertebrate *adj* without a backbone (*—also* **invertebral**). * *n* an animal without a backbone.
inverted comma *n* a quotation mark.
invest *vt* to commit (money) to property, stocks and shares, etc for profit; to devote effort, time, etc on a particular activity; to install in office with ceremony; to furnish with power, authority, etc. * *vi* to invest money.
investigate *vti* to search (into); to inquire, examine.—**investigative, investigatory** *adj.*
investigation *n* the act of investigating; an inquiry; a search to uncover facts, etc.—**investigational** *adj.*
investigator *n* one who investigates, esp a private detective.
investiture *n* the act or right of giving legal possession; the ceremony of investing a person with an office, robes, title, etc.
investment *n* the act of investing money productively; the amount invested; an activity in which time, effort or money has been invested.
investor *n* a person who invests money.
inveterate *adj* firmly established, ingrained; habitual.—**inveteracy** *n.*—**inveterately** *adv.*
invidious *adj* tending to provoke ill-will, resentment or envy; (*decisions, etc*) unfairly discriminating.—**invidiously** *adv.*—**invidiousness** *n.*
invigorate *vt* to fill with vigour and energy; to refresh.—**invigorating** *adj.*—**invigoration** *n.*—**invigorative** *adj.*—**invigorator** *n.*
invincible *adj* unconquerable.—**invincibility** *n.*—**invincibly** *adv.*
inviolable *adj* not to be broken or harmed.—**inviolability** *n.*—**inviolably** *adv.*
inviolate *adj* not violated; unbroken, unharmed.—**inviolacy** *n.*
invisible *adj* unable to be seen; hidden.—**invisibility** *n.*—**invisibly** *adv.*
invitation *n* a message used in inviting.
invite *vt* to ask to come somewhere or do something; to ask for; to give occasion for; to tempt; to entice. * *n* (*inf*) an invitation.
inviting *adj* attractive, enticing.—**invitingly** *adv.*
in vitro *adv, adj* (*biological experiments, etc*) occurring outside the living body and in an artificial environment.
in vivo *adv, adj* (*biological processes, etc*) occurring inside the living body.
invocation *n* the act of invoking; a formula used in invoking.—**invocatory** *adj.*
invoice *n* a document listing goods dispatched, usu with particulars of their price and quantity; to demand due settlement. * *vt* to submit an invoice for or to.
invoke *vt* to call on (God, etc) for help, blessing, etc; to resort to (a law, etc) as pertinent; to implore.
involucel *n* (*bot*) a bract around part of a flower head.
involucre *n* (*bot*) a ring of bracts around the base of a flower cluster.
involuntary *adj* not done by choice; not consciously controlled.—**involuntarily** *adv.*—**involuntariness** *n.*
involute, involuted *adj* intricate; (*bot*) folded or rolled inwards (eg leaves, flowers); curled spirally.
involution *n* something which is involute; the act of involving; involvement, complication; (*anat*) the return of an organ or tissue to its normal size after distension; (*math*) the process of raising an arithmetical or algebraic quantity to a given power.
involve *vt* to affect or include; to require; to occupy, to make busy; to complicate; to implicate.—**involvement** *n.*
invulnerable *adj* not capable of being wounded or hurt in any way.—**invulnerability** *n.*—**invulnerable** *adj.*
inward **adj** situated within or directed to the inside; relating to or in the mind or spirit. * *adv* inwards.
inwardly *adv* within; in the mind or spirit; towards the inside or centre.
inwards *adv* towards the inside or interior; in the mind or spirit.
inweave *vt* (**inweaving, inwove** *or* **inweaved,** *pp* **inwoven** *or* **inweaved**) to weave in.
inwrought *adj* worked into or onto (fabric, etc); adorned with figures or patterns.
Io (*chem symbol*) ionium.
iodic *adj* pertaining to, or containing, iodine.
iodide *n* a compound of iodine.
iodine *n* a nonmetallic element, found in seawater and seaweed, whose compounds are used in medicine and photography.
iodism *n* poisoning caused by overdoses of iodine.
iodize *vt* to treat or combine with iodine.
iodoform *n* a compound of iodine, used as an antiseptic.
ion *n* an electrically charged atom or group of atoms formed through the gain or loss of one or more electrons.
Ionic *adj* of a Greek style of architecture that is characterized by ornamental scrolls on the tops of columns.
ionic *adj* of or occurring in the form of ions.
ionize *vti* to change or become changed into ions.—**ionization** *n.*
ionosphere *n* the series of ionized layers high in the stratosphere from which radio waves are reflected.—**ionospheric** *adj.*
iota *n* the ninth letter of the Greek alphabet; a very small quantity; a jot.
IOU *n* (*pl* **IOUs**) a written note promising to pay a sum of money to the holder.
IPA *abbr* = International Phonetic Alphabet.
ipecac, ipecacuanha *n* a South American plant, the root of which is made into a medicine used as an emetic and purgative.
ipso facto *adv* by the fact or act itself.
IQ *abbr* = Intelligence Quotient.
Ir (*chem symbol*) iridium.
IRA *abbr* = Irish Republican Army.
Iranian *n* a native or inhabitant of Iran; a branch of the Indo-European group of languages including Persian; modern Persian.—*also adj.*
irascible *adj* easily angered; hot-tempered.—**irascibility** *n.*—**irascibly** *adv.*
irate *adj* enraged, furious.—**irately** *adv.*
ire *n* anger; wrath.
irenic, irenical *adj* aiming at peace.
iridaceous *adj* (*bot*) of, or pertaining to, the iris family.
iridescent *adj* exhibiting a spectrum of shimmering colours, which change as the position is altered.—**iridescence** *n.*
iridium *n* a metallic element that is extraordinarily resistant to corrosion.
iris[1] *n* (*pl* **irises, irides**) the round, pigmented membrane surrounding the pupil of the eye.
iris[2] *n* (*pl* **irises**) a perennial herbaceous plant with sword-shaped leaves and brightly coloured flowers.
Irish *adj* of Ireland or its people. * *n* the Celtic language of Ireland.
Irish bull *see* **bull**[3].
Irish coffee *n* coffee mixed with Irish whiskey and topped with fresh cream.
Irish moss *see* **carrageen.**
Irish stew *n* a stew of mutton, onions and potatoes.
iritis *n* (*med*) inflammation of the iris.
irk *vt* to annoy, irritate.
irksome *adj* tedious; tiresome.
iron *n* a metallic element, the most common of all metals; a tool, etc of this metal; a heavy implement with a heated flat underface for pressing cloth; (*pl*) shackles of iron; firm strength; power; any of certain golf clubs with angled metal heads. * *adj* of iron; like iron, strong and firm. * *vti* to press with a hot iron; (*with* **out**) to correct or settle a problem through negotiation or similar means.—**ironer** *n.*

Iron Age *n* the period when most tools and weapons were made of iron, following the Bronze Age in around 1100 bc.

ironbark *n* a type of eucalyptus tree.

ironbound *adj* bound with iron; unyielding.

ironclad *adj* covered in iron; difficult to change or break.

iron curtain *n* the name of the physical and ideological barrier which once separated the former Soviet Union and Communist Eastern Europe from the rest of Europe.

iron gray *adj* a slightly greenish dark grey.

ironic, ironical *adj* of or using irony.—**ironically** *adv*.

ironing *n* the act of ironing; items of clothing, etc, for ironing.

ironing-board *n* a narrow flat surface to iron clothes on.

iron lung *n* a large respirator that encloses all of the body but the head.

iron maiden *n* a medieval instrument of torture consisting of a hinged coffin-like box fitted with spikes which was closed around the victim.

ironmonger *n* a dealer in metal utensils, tools, etc; a hardware shop.—**ironmongery** *n*.

iron rations *npl* emergency food rations for military use.

ironstone *n* a type of iron ore; a type of hardwearing earthenware.

ironwood *n* a name given to the timber of certain trees, which is of exceptional hardness and durability.

ironwork *n* articles made of iron, esp decorative railings, etc.

ironworks *n* (*pl or sing*) a factory where iron is smelted, cast, or wrought.

irony *n* (*pl* **ironies**) an expression in which the intended meaning of the words is the opposite of their usual sense; an event or result that is the opposite of what is expected.

irradiance *n* the act of emitting rays of light; lustre.

irradiant *adj* emitting rays of light; shining brightly.

irradiate *vt* to shine upon; to light up; to enlighten; to radiate; to expose to X-rays or other radiation. * *vi* to emit rays; to shine.—**irradiative** *adj*.—**irradiator** *n*.

irradiation *n* the act of irradiating; the condition of being irradiated; the apparent extension of the edges of an illuminated object seen against a dark background; the use of radiation in medicine.

irrational *adj* not rational, lacking the power of reason; senseless; unreasonable; absurd.—**irrationality** *n*.—**irrationally** *adv*.

irrational number *n* a real number (eg p) that cannot be expressed as the result of dividing one integer by another.

irreclaimable *adj* which cannot be reclaimed.

irreconcilable *adj* not able to be brought into agreement; incompatible.—**irreconcilability** *n*.—**irreconcilably** *adv*.

irrecoverable *adj* beyond recovery.—**irrecoverably** *adv*.

irrecusable *adj* which must be accepted.

irredeemable *adj* not able to be redeemed.—**irredeemably** *adv*.

irredentist *n* an advocate of the return of a country of neighbouring regions claimed by another on language and other grounds.—**irredentism** *n*.

irreducible *adj* unable to be reduced from one form, state, degree, etc to another.—**irreducibility** *n*.—**irreducibly** *adv*.

irrefragable *adj* irrefutable, unanswerable.

irrefrangible *adj* inviolable; (*physics*) which cannot be refracted.

irrefutable *adj* unable to deny or disprove; indisputable.—**irrefutability** *adv*.—**irrefutably** *adv*.

irregular *adj* not regular, straight or even; not conforming to the rules; imperfect; (*troops*) not part of the regular armed forces.—**irregularly** *adv*.

irregularity *n* (*pl* **irregularities**) departure from a rule, order or method; crookedness.

irrelative *adj* unconnected, unrelated.

irrelevant *adj* not pertinent; not to the point.—**irrelevance, irrelevancy** *n*.—**irrelevantly** *adv*.

irreligion *n* lack of religious belief; disregard for, or hostility towards, religion.

irreligious *adj* impious, irreverent.

irremediable *adj* which cannot be remedied.

irremissible *adj* unpardonable; (*obligation*) binding.

irremovable *adj* not removable.—**irremovability** *adv*.—**irremovably** *adv*.

irreparable *adj* that cannot be repaired, rectified or made good.—**irreparably** *adv*.

irreplaceable *adj* unable to be replaced.—**irreplaceability** *n*.

irrepressible *adj* unable to be controlled or restrained.—**irrepressibly** *adv*.

irreproachable *adj* blameless; faultless.—**irreproachability** *adv*.—**irreproachably** *adv*.

irresistible *adj* not able to be resisted; overpowering; fascinating; very charming, alluring.—**irresistibility** *adv*.—**irresistibly** *adv*.

irresolute *adj* lacking resolution, uncertain, hesitating.—**irresolutely** *adv*.—**irresoluteness, irresolution** *n*.

irresolvable *adj* which cannot be resolved or solved.

irrespective *adj* (*with* **of**) regardless.—**irrespectively** *adv*.

irresponsible *adj* not showing a proper sense of the consequences of one's actions; unable to bear responsibility.—**irresponsibility** *n*.—**irresponsibly** *adv*.

irresponsive *adj* not responsive.

irretentive *adj* not retentive.

irretrievable *adj* that cannot be recovered; irreparable.—**irretrievability** *n*.—**irretrievably** *adj*.

irreverent, irreverential *adj* not reverent, disrespectful.—**irreverence** *n*.—**irreverently** *adv*.

irreversible *adj* not able to be reversed; unable to be revoked or altered.—**irreversibility** *n*.—**irreversibly** *adv*.

irrevocable *adj* unable to be revoked, unalterable.—**irrevocability** *n*.—**irrevocably** *adv*.

irrigate *vt* to supply (land) with water as by means of artificial ditches, pipes, etc; (*med*) to wash out (a cavity, wound, etc).—**irrigable** *adj*.—**irrigation** *n*.—**irrigative** *adj*.—**irrigator** *n*.

irritable *adj* easily annoyed, irritated, or provoked; (*med*) excessively sensitive to a stimulus.—**irritability** *n*.—**irritably** *adv*.

irritant *adj* irritating; causing irritation. * *n* something that causes irritation.

irritate *vt* to provoke to anger; to annoy; to make inflamed or sore.—**irritative** *adj*.—**irritator** *n*.

irritation *n* the act of irritating; the state of being irritated; someone who, or something which, irritates.

irrupt *vi* to enter forcibly or suddenly.—**irruption** *n*.

is *see* **be**.

ISBN **abbr** = international standard book number.

isinglass *n* a gelatin prepared from fish bladders; mica, esp in thin sheets.

Islam *n* the Muslim religion, a monotheistic religion founded by Mohammed; the Muslim world.—**Islamic** *adj*.

island *n* a land mass smaller than a continent and surrounded by water; anything like this in position or isolation.

islander *n* a native or inhabitant of an island.

isle *n* an island, esp a small one.

islet *n* a small island.

-ism *n suffix* indicating a system or doctrine, as *Protestantism*; a state or condition, as *barbarism*; action, as *criticism*; a peculiarity or idiom, as *archaism*, *gallicism*; a morbid condition caused by abuse of drugs, as *alcoholism*.

isn't = is not.

isobar *n* a line on a map connecting places of equal barometric pressure.—**isobaric** *adj*.—**isobarism** *n*.

isochromatic *adj* of the same colour; (*photog*) giving equal intensity to different colours.

isochronal, isochronous *adj*

isoclinal, isoclinic *adj* having the same dip or inclination.

isodynamic *adj* having equal force.

isogon *n* (*geom*) a figure with equal angles.

isohel *n* a line on a map, linking places with the same hours of sunshine.

isohyet *n* a line on a map, linking places with the same rainfall.

isolate *vt* to set apart from others; to place alone; to quarantine a person or animal with a contagious disease; to separate a constituent substance from a compound.—**isolator** *n*.

isolation *n* the state of being isolated; the act of isolating.

isolationism *n* a policy of refraining from involvement in international affairs.—**isolationist** *adj, n.*
isomer *n* any of two or more chemical compounds whose molecules contain the same atoms but in different arrangements.—**isomeric** *adj.*—**isomerism** *n.*
isometric, isometrical *adj* having equality of measure; relating to muscular contraction involving little shortening of the muscle; (*drawing*) projecting an image to scale in three dimensions with the axis equally inclined.—**isometrically** *adv.*
isometrics *n* (*sing or pl*) physical exercises in which muscles are contracted against each other or in opposition to fixed objects.
isomorphism *n* (*biol*) similarity in form; (*chem*) the quality of having the same crystalline form despite being formed of different elements.—**isomorphic, isomorphous** *adj.*
isopod *n* a type of crustacean with seven pairs of equal legs, eg the woodlouse.
isosceles *adj* denoting a triangle with two equal sides.
isoseismic, isoseismal *adj* pertaining to points at which earthquake shock is of the same intensity. * *n* a line on a map, linking these points.
isotherm *n* a line on a map connecting points of the same temperature.—**isothermal** *adj.*
isotope *n* any of two or more forms of an element having the same atomic number but different atomic weights.—**isotopic** *adj.*—**isotopically** *adv.*
Israelite *n* (*Bible*) a descendant of the Hebrew patriarch Jacob.
issuable *adj* which can be issued.
issuance *n* the act of issuing.
issue *n* an outgoing; an outlet; a result; offspring; a point under dispute; a sending or giving out; all that is put forth at one time (an issue of bonds, a periodical, etc). * *vb* (**issuing, issued**) *vi* to go or flow out; to result (from) or end (in); to be published. * *vt* to let out; to discharge; to give or deal out, as supplies; to publish.
isthmian *adj* of or pertaining to an isthmus.
isthmus *n* (*pl* **isthmuses, isthmi**) a narrow strip of land having water at each side and connecting two larger bodies of land.—**isthmoid** *adj.*
istle *n* a tough fibre made from a species of Mexican agave, used to make cord.—*also* **ixtle**.
it *pron* the thing mentioned; the subject of an impersonal verb; a subject or object of indefinite sense in various constructions. * *n* the player, as in tag, who must catch another.
it'll = it will; it shall.
it's = it is; it has.
Italian *adj* of Italy or its people. * a native of Italy; the Italian language.
Italianate *adj* Italian in style or character.
Italic *adj* (*language*) of ancient Italy.
italic *adj* denoting a type in which the letters slant upward to the right (*this is italic type*). * *n* (*usu pl*) italic type or handwriting.
italicize *vi* to write in italics. * *vt* to underline a word to indicate italics.—**italicization** *n.*
itch *n* an irritating sensation on the surface of the skin causing a need to scratch; an insistent desire. * *vi* to have or feel an irritating sensation in the skin; to feel a restless desire.
itchy *adj* (**itchier, itchiest**) pertaining to or affected with an itch.—**itchiness** *n.*
item *n* an article; a unit; a separate thing; a bit of news or information.
itemize *vt* to specify the items of; to set down by items.—**itemization** *n.*
iterate *vt* to say or do again or repetitively.—**iteration** *n.*—**iterative** *adj.*
ithyphallic *adj* (*poet*) in the manner of the rites or hymns to Bacchus.
itinerancy, itineracy *n* (*pl* **itinerancies, itineracies**) the act of travelling from place to place, esp to carry out an official duty.
itinerant *adj* travelling from place to place. * *n* a traveller.
itinerary *n* (*pl* **itineraries**) a route; a record of a journey; a detailed plan of a journey.
its *poss pron* relating to or belonging to **it**.
itself *pron* the reflexive and emphatic form of **it**.
IUD *abbr* = intrauterine device.
I've = I have
IVF *abbr* = in vitro fertilization: a technique for helping infertile couples to have children, in which a woman's eggs are fertilized by the father's sperm in a laboratory and then re-implanted in the womb.
ivory *n* (*pl* **ivories**) the hard, creamy-white substance forming the tusks of elephants, etc; any substance like ivory; creamy white. * *adj* of or like ivory; creamy white.
ivory tower *n* a place or situation which excludes the realities of everyday life.—**ivory towered** *adj.*
ivy *n* (*pl* **ivies**) a climbing or creeping vine with a woody stem and evergreen leaves.—**ivied** *adj.*
ixtle *see* **istle**.

J

J *abbr* = joule(s).
jab *vti* (**jabbing, jabbed**) to poke or thrust roughly; to punch with short, straight blows. * *n* a sudden thrust or stab; (*inf*) an injection with a hypodermic needle.
jabber *vti* to speak or say rapidly, incoherently, or foolishly. * *n* such talk.—**jabberer** *n.*
jabiru *n* a stork-like bird of tropical America; an Australian stork.
jaborandi *n* a tropical American plant that yields an alkoloid used to stimulate perspiration and as a diuretic.
jabot *n* an ornamental frill worn down the front of a blouse or shirt.
jacamar *n* a South American bird similar to a kingfisher.
jacana, jaçana *n* a small tropical wading bird.
jacaranda *n* a South American tree with hard, heavy wood; any one of several similar trees; the fragrant wood from such trees.
jacinth *n* a reddish-orange gem, a variety of zircon.
jack *n* any of various mechanical or hydraulic devices used to lift something heavy; a playing card with a knave's picture on it, ranking below the queen; a small flag flown on a ship's bow as a signal or to show nationality; (*bowls*) a small white ball used as a target. * *vt* (*with* **in**) (*sl*) to abandon (an attempt at something); (*with* **up**) to raise (a vehicle) by means of a jack; to increase (prices, etc); (*sl*) to inject a narcotic drug.
jackal *n* (*pl* **jackals, jackal**) any of various wild dogs of Africa and Asia.
jackanapes *n* a conceited or upstart person; a pert child; (*arch*) a monkey.
jackass *n* a male donkey; a fool.
jackboot *n* a leather military boot extending above the knee; authoritarian rule, oppression.
jackdaw *n* a black bird like the crow but smaller.
jackeroo, jackaroo (*pl* **jackeroos, jackaroos**) (*Austral sl*) a young person training to be a manager on a sheep or cattle station.
jacket *n* a short coat; an outer covering, as the removable paper cover of a book. * *vt* to cover with a jacket or cover.—**jacketed** *adj.*
jackfruit *n* an East Indian tree or its fruit, which is similar to breadfruit.
jack-in-the-box *n* a toy consisting of a box from which a figure on a spring pops out when the lid is lifted.
jackknife *n* (*pl* **jackknives**) a pocket-knife; a dive in which the diver touches his feet with knees straight and then straightens out. * *vi* to dive in this way; (*articulated truck*) to lose control so that the trailer and cab swing against each other.
jack-of-all-trades *n* (*pl* **jacks-of-all-trades**) a person who does many different types of work.
jack-o'-lantern *n* a lantern made from a hollowed-out pumpkin with holes cut in it to resemble a face; a will-o'-the-wisp.
jackpot *n* the accumulated stakes in certain games, as poker; **hit the jackpot** (*sl*) to win; to gain an enormous amount.
jack rabbit *n* a large hare with long ears, common in North America.
jacksnipe *n* (*pl* **jacksnipes, jacksnipe**) a kind of small snipe; a sandpiper.
jack-tar *n* (*inf*) a sailor.
Jacobean *adj* pertaining to the time or reign of James I of England and VI of Scotland. * *n* a person of this period, esp a poet.

Jacobin *n* a French Dominican friar; a member of a violent democratic faction that exercised a powerful influence in the French Revolution; an extreme revolutionary.—**Jacobinic, Jacobinical** *adj.*—**Jacobinism** *n.*

Jacobite *n* a supporter of James II of England and VII of Scotland after his abdication or of his descendants.—*also adj.*—**Jacobitism** *n.*

jaconet *n* a fine soft white cotton material resembling cambric.

jacquard *n* a loom for weaving patterns; a pattern woven on a jacquard loom.

jactitation *n* boasting; (*med*) a restless, feverish tossing of the body in illness; (*law*) a false pretence of being married to another, or likely to harm another person.

Jacuzzi *n* (*trademark*) a device that swirls water in a bath; a bath containing such a device.

jade *n* a hard, ornamental semiprecious stone; its light green colour.

jaded *adj* tired, exhausted; satiated.—**jadedly** *adv.*—**jadedness** *n.*

jadeite *n* a form of jade found in Burma.

jag[1] *n* a sharp, tooth-like notch or projection. * *vt* (**jagging, jagged**) to cut into notches; to prick.

jag[2] *n* (*sl*) intoxication from drugs or alcohol; (*sl*) a drinking spree.

jagged *adj* having sharp notches or projecting points; notched or ragged.—**jaggedly** *adv.*—**jaggedness** *n.*

jaggery, jaggary, jagghery *n* a coarse East Indian sugar made from palm sap.

jaggy *adj* (**jaggier, jaggiest**) jagged.

jaguar *n* (*pl* **jaguars, jaguar**) a large American black-spotted yellow wild cat similar to the leopard.

jail *n* a prison; imprisonment. * *vt* to send to or confine in prison.

jailbird *n* a person who is or has been confined in jail.

jailer, jailor *n* a person in charge of prisoners in a jail.

Jain *n* an adherent of Jainism. * *adj* pertaining to the Jains or their religious system (—*also* **Jaina, Jainist**).

Jainism *n* a Hindu religion of India similar to Buddhism.

jalap, jalop *n* the root of a Mexican plant used formerly as a purgative; the plant itself or similar plants; the resin from the plant.—**jalapic** *adj.*

jalopy *n* (*pl* **jalopies**) an old battered vehicle.

jalousie *n* a blind with slats like a Venetian blind or a louvred shutter; a louvre window.

jam[1] *n* a preserve made from fruit boiled with sugar until thickened; (*inf*) something easy or desirable.

jam[2] *vb* (**jamming, jammed**) *vt* to press or squeeze into a confined space; to crowd full with people or things; to cause (machinery) to become wedged and inoperable; to cause interference to a radio signal rendering it unintelligible. * *vi* to become stuck or blocked; (*sl*) to play in a jam session. * *n* a crowded mass or congestion in a confined space; a blockage caused by jamming; (*inf*) a difficult situation.—**jammer** *n.*

jamb *n* the straight vertical side-post of a door, fireplace, etc.

jamboree *n* a large party or spree; a large, usu international, gathering of Scouts.

jam-packed *adj* filled to capacity.

jam session *n* (*sl*) an unrehearsed performance by jazz, rock or other musicians, usu for their own enjoyment.

Jan. *abbr* = January.

jangle *vi* to make a harsh or discordant sound, as bells. * *vt* to cause to jangle; to irritate.—*also n.*

janitor *n* a person who looks after a building, doing routine maintenance, etc.—**janitorial** *adj.*

janizary, janissary (*pl* **janizaries, janissaries**) *n* (*formerly*) a foot-guard of the Turkish sultans; a Turkish infantryman.

Jansenism *n* the doctrine of sovereign and irresistible grace, promulgated in the 17th century in opposition to the Jesuits; the religion based on these doctrines.—**Jansenist** *n, adj.*—**Jansenistic** *adj.*

January *n* (*pl* **Januaries**) the first month of the year, having 31 days.

Jap *n* (*sl*) a Japanese.

japan *vt* (**japanning, japanned**) to cover with a hard black glossy lacquer.

Japanese *adj* of Japan, its people or language. * *n* the language of Japan; an inhabitant of Japan.

jape *n* a joke, jest.—**japer** *n.*—**japery** *n.*

japonica *n* any of various species of Japanese plants, Japanese quince, pear, etc; the camellia.

jar[1] *vb* (**jarring, jarred**) *vi* to make a harsh, discordant noise; to have an irritating effect (on one); to vibrate from an impact; to clash. * *vt* to jolt. * *n* a grating sound; a vibration due to impact; a jolt.

jar[2] *n* a short cylindrical glass vessel with a wide mouth; (*inf*) a pint of beer.

jardiniere *n* an ornamental flower-stand of porcelain or metal; mixed diced vegetables stewed in a sauce and served around a meat dish.

jargon[1] *n* the specialized or technical vocabulary of a science, profession, etc; obscure and usu pretentious language. * *vi* to talk in jargon.—**jargonistic** *adj.*

jargon[2], **jargoon** *n* a translucent, colourless, yellowish, or smoky kind of zircon.

jargonize *vti* to put into or talk in jargon.—**jargonization** *n.*

jarl *n* an Old Norse chief, a noble.

jasmine, jasmin *n* any of a genus of climbing shrubs with fragrant white or yellow flowers.

jasper *n* an opaque, many-shaded variety of quartz that, when polished, is made into a variety of ornamental articles and jewellery; a style of porcelain with a dull surface of green or blue.

jaundice *n* a condition characterized by yellowing of the skin, caused by excess of bile in the bloodstream; bitterness; resentment; prejudice.

jaundiced *adj* affected with jaundice; jealous, envious, disillusioned.

jaunt *n* a short journey, usu for pleasure. * *vi* to make such a journey.

jaunty *adj* (**jauntier, jauntiest**) sprightly or self-confident in manner.—**jauntily** *adv.*—**jauntiness** *n.*

Javanese *n* (*pl* **Javanese**) a native or inhabitant of Java; the language of Java.—*also adj.*

javelin *n* a light spear, esp one thrown some distance in a contest.

jaw *n* one of the bones in which teeth are set; either of two movable parts that grasp or crush something, as in a vice; (*sl*) a friendly chat, gossip; argument. * *vi* (*sl*) to talk boringly and at length.

jawbone *n* a bone of the jaw, esp of the lower jaw.

jawbreaker *n* a machine for crushing rocks, etc; (*inf*) a word that is difficult to pronounce.

jay *n* any of several birds of the crow family with raucous voices, roving habits, and destructive behaviour to other birds.

jaycee *n* a young member of a Junior Chamber of Commerce.

jaywalk *vi* to walk across a street carelessly without obeying traffic rules or signals.—**jaywalker** *n.*

jazz *n* a general term for American popular music, characterized by syncopated rhythms and embracing ragtime, blues, swing, jive, and bebop; (*sl*) pretentious or nonsensical talk or actions. * *vt* (*with* **up**) (*inf*) to play (a piece of music) in a jazz style; to enliven, add colour to.

jazzerati *npl* famous or accomplished jazz musicians.

jazzy *adj* (**jazzier, jazziest**) of or like jazz; (*sl*) lively.—**jazzily** *adj.*—**jazziness** *n.*

jealous *adj* apprehensive of or hostile toward someone thought of as a rival; envious of, resentful; anxiously vigilant or protective.—**jealously** *adv.*—**jealousness** *n.*

jealousy *n* (*pl* **jealousies**) suspicious fear or watchfulness, esp the fear of being supplanted by a rival.

jean *n* a hardwearing twilled cotton cloth; (*pl*) trousers made from this or denim.

jeep *n* a small robust vehicle with heavy duty tires and four-wheel drive for use on rough terrain, esp by the military.

jeer *vt* to laugh derisively. * *vi* to scoff (at). * *n* a jeering remark.—**jeerer** *n.*—**jeeringly** *adv.*

jehad *see* **jihad.**

Jehovah *n* (*Bible*) God.

jejune *adj* lacking significance, dull; naive; lacking in nourishment.—**jejunely** *adv.*—**jejuneness** *n.*

jell *vti* to become or make into jelly; to crystallize, as a plan.—*also* **gel.**

jello *n* (*US*) a sweet edible gelatin; jelly, jam.

jelly *n* (*pl* **jellies**) a soft, gelatinous food made from fruit syrup or meat juice; any substance like this. * *vt* (**jellying, jellied**) to turn into jelly, to congeal.—**jellied** *adj*.
jellyfish *n* (*pl* **jellyfish, jellyfishes**) a sea creature with a nearly transparent body and long tentacles.
jennet *n* a small Spanish horse; a female donkey.
jenny *n* (*pl* **jennies**) a machine for spinning; a female of some animals, as a wren or donkey.
jeopardize *vt* to endanger, put at risk.
jeopardy *n* (*pl* **jeopardies**) great danger or risk.
jequirity *n* (*pl* **jequirities**) an Indian shrub with parti-coloured seeds.
jerbil *see* **gerbil**.
jerboa *n* a small desert rodent with long hind legs and a long tail.
jeremiad *n* a long mournful lament or complaint.
jerk[1] *n* a sudden sharp pull or twist; a sudden muscular contraction or reflex; (*inf*) a stupid person. * *vti* to move with a jerk; to pull sharply; to twitch.
jerk[2] *vt* to preserve (meat) by cutting it into long strips and drying it in the sun. * *n* jerked meat (*—also* **jerky**).
jerkin *n* a close-fitting sleeveless jacket.
jerkiness *n*.
jerky[1] *see* **jerk**[2].
jerky[2] *adj* (**jerkier, jerkiest**) moving with jerks.—**jerkily** *adv*.—**jerkiness** *n*.
jeroboam *n* a huge bottle four times ordinary size, esp for champagne.
jerry-built *adj* cheaply and flimsily constructed.—**jerry-builder** *n*.—**jerry-building** *n*.
jerry can *n* a flat-sided container for liquids, esp fuel or water, with a capacity of about five gallons (25 litres).
jersey *n* (*pl* **jerseys**) any plain machine-knitted fabric of natural or artificial fibres; a knitted sweater.
Jerusalem artichoke *n* (the edible tuber of) the North American sunflower.
jess, jesse *n* a short leather strap fixed to the leg of a hawk or falcon.
jest *n* a joke; a thing to be laughed at. * *vi* to jeer; to joke.
jester *n* a person who makes jokes, esp an entertainer employed in a royal household in the Middle Ages.
Jesuit *n* a member of the Catholic Society of Jesus, founded by Ignatius Loyola in 1534; an insidious, crafty intriguer.—**Jesuitic, Jesuitical** *adj*.
Jesuitism, Jesuitry *n* (a following of) the principles, system, or practices of the Jesuits; subtle duplicity; disingenuousness.
Jesus (Christ) *n* the Jewish religious teacher and founder of Christianity.
Jesus freak *n* (*sl*) a fervent Christian, esp a young member of an evangelical group.
jet[1] *n* a hard black compact mineral that can be polished and is used in jewellery; a lustrous black.—**jet-black** *adj*.
jet[2] *n* a stream of liquid or gas suddenly emitted; a spout for emitting a jet; a jet-propelled aircraft. * *vti* (**jetting, jetted**) to gush out in a stream; (*inf*) to travel or convey by jet.
jet engine *n* an engine, such as a gas turbine, producing jet propulsion.
jet lag *n* fatigue caused by disruption of the daily bodily rhythms, associated with crossing time zones at high speed.—**jet-lagged** *adj*.
jet propulsion *n* propulsion of aircraft, boats, etc, by the discharge of gases from a rear vent.—**jet-propelled** *adj*.
jetsam *n* cargo thrown overboard from a ship in distress to lighten it, esp such cargo when washed up on the shore.
jet set *n* the wealthy and fashionable social elite who travel widely for pleasure.—**jetsetter** *n*.
jet stream *n* the jet of exhaust gases from a jet engine; high-altitude winds.
jettison *vt* to abandon, to throw overboard.
jetty *n* (*pl* **jetties**) a wharf; a small pier.
Jew *n* a person descended, or regarded as descended, from the ancient Israelites; a person whose religion is Judaism.
jewel *n* a precious stone; a gem; a piece of jewellery; someone or something highly esteemed; a small gem used as a bearing in a watch. * *vt* (**jewelling, jewelled** *or* **jeweling, jeweled**) to adorn or provide with jewels.
jeweller, jeweler *n* a person who makes, repairs or deals in jewellery, watches, etc.
jewellery, jewelry *n* jewels such as rings, brooches, etc, worn for decoration.
Jewish *adj* of or like Jews.
Jewry *n* (*pl* **Jewries**) the Jewish people.
jew's harp *n* a small metal musical instrument that makes a twanging sound when held between the lips and plucked.
Jezebel *n* a woman of abandoned or licentious demeanour.
jib[1] *n* a triangular sail extending from the foremast in a ship. * *vti* (jibbing, jibbed) to pull (a sail) round to the other side; (*sail*) to swing round.—**jibber** *n*.
jib[2] *n* the projecting arm of a crane.
jib[3] *vi* to refuse to go on; to balk.
jibe *see* **gybe**.
jiffy, jiff *n* (*pl* **jiffies, jiffs**) (*inf*) a very short time.
jig *n* a lively springing dance; the music for this; a device used to guide a tool. * *vt* (**jigging, jigged**) to dance in lively manner, as in a jig; to jerk up and down rapidly.
jigger[1] *see* **chigoe**.
jigger[2] *n* any of various mechanical devices that operate with a jigging motion; a small glass for spirits; a person or thing that jigs; (*naut*) small tackle, a small sail.
jiggermast *n* the stern mast in a two-masted sailing vessel; a small aftermost mast in a four-master.
jiggery-pokery *n* (*inf*) underhand work; trickery.
jiggle *vt* to jerk; to move (something) up and down lightly. * *n* a jerky movement.
jigsaw *n* a saw with a narrow fine-toothed blade for cutting irregular shapes. * *vt* to cut with a jigsaw.
jigsaw (puzzle) *n* a picture mounted on wood or stiff cardboard and then cut up into irregular pieces, which are then assembled for amusement.
jihad *n* a holy war waged by Muslims against nonbelievers; a crusade for or against a cause.—*also* **jehad**.
jilt *vt* to discard (a lover) unfeelingly, esp without warning.—**jilter** *n*.
jimjams *npl* (*sl*) delirium tremens; nervous jitters.
jingle *n* a metallic tinkling sound like a bunch of keys being shaken together; a catchy verse or song with easy rhythm, simple rhymes, etc. * *vti* (to cause) to make a light tinkling sound.—**jingler** *n*.
jingly *adj* (**jinglier, jingliest**) tinkling.
jingo (*pl* **jingoes**) *n* a blustering patriot, a warmonger.
jingoism *n* advocacy of an aggressive foreign policy.—**jingoist** *adj*, *n*.—**jingoistic** *adj*.—**jingoistically** *adv*.
jink *n* a rapid swerve from side to side in order to dodge; (*pl*) high spirits. * *vti* to move nimbly; to dodge.
jinni (*pl* **jinn**) (*fairy tales*) a spirit with supernatural powers that can fulfil your wishes.—*also* **genie**.
jinx *n* (*inf*) someone or something thought to bring bad luck.
JIT *abbr* = just-in-time.
jitter *vi* (*inf*) to feel nervous or to act nervously. * *npl* (*inf*) (*with* **the**) an uneasy nervous feeling; fidgets.
jitterbug *n* a fast acrobatic dance for couples, esp popular in the 1940s. * *vi* (**jitterbugging, jitterbugged**) to dance the jitterbug.
jittery *adj* (*inf*) nervous.—**jitteriness** *n*.
jive *n* improvised jazz played at a fast tempo; dancing to this music; (*sl*) foolish, exaggerated, or insincere talk. * *vti* to dance the jive.
Jnr, jnr *abbr* = Junior.
job *n* a piece of work done for pay; a task; a duty; the thing or material being worked on; work; employment; (*sl*) a criminal enterprise; (*inf*) a difficult task. * *adj* hired or done by the job. * *vti* (**jobbing, jobbed**) to deal in (goods) as a jobber; to sublet (work, etc).
jobber *n* a person who jobs; a person who buys and sells goods as a middleman; in UK, a broker.
jobbery *n* profiting personally from a public office.
jobless *adj* unemployed. * *n* unemployed people collectively.—**joblessness** *n*.

job lot *n* a miscellaneous collection of items sold as one lot; any miscellaneous collection of cheap items.
jock *n (inf)* a jockey; a jockstrap; a male athlete; a disc jockey.
jockey *n (pl* **jockeys**) a person whose job is riding horses in races. * *vti* (**jockeying, jockeyed**) to act as a jockey; to manœuvre for a more advantageous position; to swindle or cheat.
jockstrap *n* a support for the genitals worn by men participating in sport, an atheletic supporter.
jocose *adj* playful, humorous.—**jocosely** *adv*.—**jocoseness** *n*.
jocosity *n (pl* **jocosities**) a being jocose; a playful action; a humorous remark.
jocular *adj* joking; full of jokes.—**jocularity** *n*.—**jocularly** *adv*.
jocund *adj* merry, cheerful; jovial.—**jocundity** *n*.—**jocundly** *adv*.
jodhpurs *npl* riding breeches cut loose at the hips but close-fitting from knee to ankle.
joey *n (pl* **joeys**) *(Austral inf)* a young kangaroo; any young animal or a small child.
jog *vb* (**jogging, jogged**) *vt* to give a slight shake or nudge to; to rouse, as the memory. * *vi* to move up and down with an unsteady motion; to run at a relaxed trot for exercise; *(horse)* to run at a jogtrot. * *n* a slight shake or push; a nudge; a slow walk or trot.—**jogger** *n*.
joggle *vti* to move or shake slightly. * *n* a slight jolt.
jogtrot *n* a slow even-paced trot. * *vi* (**jogtrotting, jogtrotted**) to move at a slow even-paced trot.
john *n (sl)* a toilet; a prostitute's male customer; an easy prey.
John Barleycorn *n* a personification of malt liquor.
John Dory *n* an edible yellow seafish, the dory.
joie de vivre *n* great enjoyment of life.
join *vti* to bring and come together (with); to connect; to unite; to become a part or member of (a club, etc); to participate (in a conversation, etc); *(with* **up**) to enlist in the armed forces; to unite, connect. * *n* a joining; a place of joining.
joinder *n* the act of joining; *(law)* the coupling of two or more causes of action into the same declaration; the coupling of two issues or two parties.
joiner *n* a carpenter, esp one who finishes interior woodwork; *(inf)* a person who is involved in many clubs and activities, etc.
joinery *n* the trade of a joiner; the work of a joiner.
joint *n* a place where, or way in which, two things are joined; any of the parts of a jointed whole; the parts where two bones move on one another in an animal; a division of an animal carcass made by a butcher; *(sl)* a cheap bar or restaurant; *(sl)* a gambling or drinking den; *(sl)* a cannabis cigarette. * *adj* common to two or more; sharing with another. * *vt* to connect by a joint or joints; to divide (an animal carcass) into parts for cooking.
joint account *n* a bank account accessible to two or more people, for deposting or withdrawing funds.
jointer *n* a tool for pointing; a kind of plane; someone or something that forms joints.
jointly *adv* in common; together.
joint stock *n* capital held in common and distributed as shares among the owners.
joint-stock company *n* a company whose capital is owned jointly by stockholders who may sell their individual shares.
jointure *n* landed estate or other property settled on a woman in consideration of her marriage, to be enjoyed by her after the death of her husband; the provision made to enable this; *(arch)* a joining or being joined.
joint venture *n* the sharing of expertise or commercial risk by two or more businesses, etc.
joist *n* any of the parallel beams supporting floorboards or the laths of a ceiling.
jojoba *n* a broad-leaved evergreen shrub with edible seeds yielding a valuable oil.
joke *n* something said or done to cause laughter; a thing done or said merely in fun; a person or thing to be laughed at. * *vi* to make jokes.—**jokingly** *adv*.
joker *n* a person who jokes; *(sl)* a person; an extra playing card made use of in certain games.
jokey, joky *adj* (**jokier, jokiest**) full, or fond, of jokes.
jollify *vti* (**jollifying, jollified**) to make merry, esp with drink; to make jolly.—**jollification** *n*.
jollity *n (pl* **jollities**) the state of being jolly.
jolly *adj* (**jollier, jolliest**) merry; full of fun; delightful; *(inf)* enjoyable. * *vti* (**jollying, jollied**) *(inf)* to try to make (a person) feel good; to make fun of (someone).
Jolly Roger *n* a pirate's flag with a white skull and crossbones on a black background.
jolt *vt* to give a sudden shake or knock to; to move along jerkily; to surprise or shock suddenly. * *n* a sudden jar or knock; an emotional shock.—**joltingly** *adv*.—**jolty** *adj*.
jonquil *n* a species of narcissus.
jooal *see* **joual**.
jorum *n* a large drinking vessel; its contents, esp punch.
josh *vi (sl)* to tease gently. * *n (sl)* friendly teasing; a teasing joke.—**josher** *n*.—**joshingly** *adv*.
joss *n* a Chinese god or idol.
joss stick *n* a stick of incense.
jostle *vti* to shake or knock roughly; to collide or come into contact (with); to elbow for position. * *n* a jostling; a push.
jot *n* a very small amount. * *vt* (**jotting, jotted**) to note (down) briefly.—**jotter** *n*.
jotting *n* something noted down, esp a memorandum.
joual *n* a French Canadian dialect also spoken in Maine that has non-standard French grammar and pronunciation with English syntax and a substantial English vocabulary.—*also* **jooal**.
joule *n (physics)* a unit of energy equal to work done when a force of one newton acts over a distance of one metre.
jounce *vti* to bump; to jolt (someone or something). * *n* a bump, a jolt.
journal *n* a daily record of happenings, as a diary; a newspaper or periodical; *(bookkeeping)* a book of original entry for recording transactions; that part of a shaft or axle that turns in a bearing.
journalese *n* a facile style of writing found in many magazines, newspapers, etc.
journalism *n* the work of gathering news for or producing a newspaper, magazine or news broadcast.
journalist *n* a person who writes for or edits a newspaper, etc; one who keeps a diary.—**journalistic** *adj*.—**journalistically** *adv*.
journalize *vt* to enter in a journal; to keep a daily record.—**journalization** *n*.—**journalizer** *n*.
journey *n (pl* **journeys**) a travelling or going from one place to another; the distance covered when travelling. * *vi* (**journeying, journeyed**) to make a journey.—**journeyer** *n*.
journeyman *n (pl* **journeymen**) a person whose apprenticeship is completed and who is employed by another; a reliable workman.
joust *n* a fight on horseback between two knights with lances. * *vi* to engage in a joust, to run at the tilt.—**jouster** *n*.
Jove *n* the Roman god Jupiter; **by Jove** a mild oath; an exclamation of surprise.
jovial *adj* full of cheerful good humour.—**joviality** *n*.—**jovially** *adv*.
Jovian *adj (Roman myth)* of or like Jove or Jupiter.
jowl[1] *n* the lower jaw; *(usu pl)* the cheek.
jowl[2] *n* the loose flesh around the throat; the similar flesh in an animal, as a dewlap.
jowly *adj* (**jowlier, jowliest**) having heavy jowls.—**jowliness** *n*.
joy *n* intense happiness; something that causes this; its expression.
joyful *adj* filled with, expressing, or causing joy, glad.—**joyfully** *adv*.—**joyfulness** *n*.
joyless *adj* not occasioning joy, unhappy; bleak.—**joylessly** *adv*.—**joylessness** *n*.
joyous *adj* joyful, very happy.—**joyously** *adv*.—**joyousness** *n*.

joyride *n* (*inf*) a car ride, often in a stolen vehicle and at reckless speed, just for pleasure.—**joy-rider** *n*.—**joyriding** *n*.
joystick *n* (*inf*) the control lever of an aircraft; (*comput*) a device for controlling cursor movement on a monitor usu for computer games.
JP *abbr* = Justice of the Peace.
Jr., jr *abbr* = Junior.
jt *abbr* = joint.
jubilant *adj* triumphant; expressing joy; rejoicing.—**jubilance** *n*.—**jubilantly** *adv*.
Jubilate *n* (*Bible*) the 100th psalm, esp as a canticle in morning service; (*mus*) a setting of the 100th psalm.
jubilate *vi* to exult, to show joy.—**jubilation** *n*.
jubilee *n* a 50th or 25th anniversary; a time of rejoicing.
Judaic, Judaical *adj* of the Jews or Judaism.—**Judaically** *adv*
Judaism *n* the religion of the Jews, based on the Old Testament and the Talmud.—**Judaist** *n*.—**Judaistic** *adj*.
Judaize *vi, vt* to make or become Judaistic in belief, customs, precepts, etc.—**Judaization** *n*.
Judas *n* a traitor who pretends to be a friend; (*without cap*) a peephole, as in a cell door.
judder *vi* to vibrate violently. * *n* a spasmodic or rapid shaking.
Judean *adj* of, pertaining to, or from, the ancient region of Judaea.
judge *n* a public official with authority to hear and decide cases in a court of law; a person chosen to settle a dispute or decide who wins; a person qualified to decide on the relative worth of anything. * *vti* to hear and pass judgment (on) in a court of law; to determine the winner of (a contest) or settle (a dispute); to form an opinion about; to criticize or censure; to suppose, think.—**judgeable** *adj*.—**judgingly** *adv*.
judgeship *n* the office of a judge; his or her jurisdiction.
judgment, judgement *n* a judging; a deciding; a legal decision; an opinion; the ability to come to a wise decision; censure.
judgmental, judgemental *adj* of or depending on judgment; tending to make moral or personal judgments.—**judgmentally, judgementally** *adv*.
Judgment Day *n* (*Christianity*) the time of God's final judgment of mankind; (*without cap*) a final judgment; a day of reckoning.
judicable *adj* that may be judged; liable to be judged.
judicator *n* one who judges.
judicatory *n* (*pl* **judicatories**) a system of courts, a judiciary. * *adj* of or pertaining to the administration of justice.
judicature *n* a court or courts of justice; the power of dispensing justice by legal trial and judgment; jurisdiction; a body of judges; a tribunal.
judicial *adj* of judges, courts, or their functions.—**judicially** *adv*.
judiciary *adj* of judges or courts. * *n* (*pl* **judiciaries**) the part of government that administers justice; a system of courts in a country; judges collectively.
judicious *adj* possessing or characterized by sound judgment.—**judiciously** *adv*.—**judiciousness** *n*.
judo *n* a Japanese system of unarmed combat, adapted as a competitive sport from jujitsu.—**judoist** *n*.
jug *n* a vessel for holding and pouring liquids, with a handle and curved lip; a pitcher; (*sl*) prison. * *vt* (**jugging, jugged**) to stew meat (esp hare) in an earthenware pot; (*sl*) to put into prison.—**jugful** *n*.
jugate *adj* coupled together; (*bot*) having leaflets in pairs.
juggernaut *n* a terrible, irresistible force; a large heavy truck; (*with cap*) a Hindu god; his idol, dragged annually in processional car, under whose wheels devotees formerly threw themselves.
juggle *vi* to toss up balls, etc and keep them in the air. * *vt* to manipulate skilfully; to manipulate so as to deceive. * *n* the act of juggling; manipulation.—**jugglery** *n*.
juggler *n* one who juggles, a conjurer; a manipulator, a cheat.
jugular *adj* (*anat*) of the neck or throat. * *n* a jugular vein.
jugular vein *n* (*anat*) any of the large veins in the neck carrying blood from the head.
juice *n* the liquid part of fruit, vegetables or meat; liquid secreted by a bodily organ; (*inf*) vitality; (*inf*) electric current; (*inf*) engine fuel.
juicer *n* a mechanical or electrical device for extracting juice from fruit and vegetables; (*sl*) a person who drinks to excess.
juicy *adj* (**juicier, juiciest**) full of juice; (*inf*) very interesting; (*inf*) highly profitable.—**juicily** *adv*.—**juiciness** *n*.
jujitsu *n* a traditional Japanese system of unarmed defence in which an opponent's strength is used against him.
juju *n* an object of superstitious worship in West Africa used as a fetish or charm; the magic attributed to this.—**jujuism** *n*.
jujube *n* a gelatinous, fruit-flavoured lozenge; the fruit of any of several small trees of the buckthorn family; the trees themselves.
jukebox *n* a coin-operated automatic record or CD player.
Jul. *abbr* = July.
julep *n* a tall drink of bourbon or brandy and sugar over crushed ice, garnished with mint.
Julian *adj* of or pertaining to Julius Caesar or to the Julian calendar.
Julian calendar *n* a calendar introduced in 46 bc by Julius Caesar, in which the year was made to consist of 365 days with a leap year of 366 days every fourth year.
julienne *adj* (*vegetables*) cut into very thin strips. * *n* a clear soup containing such vegetable.
July *n* (*pl* **Julies**) the seventh month of the year, having 31 days.
jumble *vt* (*often with* **up**) to mix together in a disordered mass. * *n* items mixed together in a confused mass; articles for a jumble sale.—**jumbly** *adj*.
jumbo *n* (*pl* **jumbos**) something very large of its kind. * *adj* very large.
jumbo jet *n* a very large jet airliner.
jumbuck *n* (*Austral*) a sheep.
jump *vi* to spring or leap from the ground, a height, etc; to jerk; to pass suddenly, as to a new topic; to rise suddenly, as prices; (*sl*) to be lively; (*often with* **at**) to act swiftly and eagerly; (*with* **at**) to accept or agree too eagerly; (*with* **on**) (*inf*) to reprimand or criticize harshly. * *vt* to leap or pass over (something); to leap upon; to cause (prices, etc) to rise; to fail to turn up (for trial when out on bail); (*inf*) to attack suddenly; (*inf*) to react to prematurely; (*sl*) to leave suddenly; * *n* a jumping; a distance jumped; a sudden transition; an obstacle; a nervous start.
jumper *n* a knitted garment for the upper body; a sleeveless dress for wearing over a blouse, etc.
jumper cable, jump lead *n* one of two cables for transferring electric charge from one battery to another, used to start a car with a flat battery by using the battery of another vehicle.
jump jet *n* (*inf*) a jet aircraft that can take off and land vertically.
jump-start *vt* to start a motor vehicle by pushing it in low gear so the engine turns over or by using jump leads; (*inf*) to set (a sluggish system, etc) in motion.
jumpsuit *n* a one-piece garment, as worn by paratroopers.
jumpy *adj* (**jumpier, jumpiest**) moving in jerks, etc; apprehensive; easily startled.—**jumpily** *adv*.—**jumpiness** *n*.
Jun. *abbr* = June.
jun., Jun. *abbr* = junior.
junction *n* a place or point where things join; a place where roads or railway lines, etc meet, link or cross each other.—**junctional** *adj*.
juncture *n* a junction; a point of time; a crisis.
June *n* the sixth month of the year, having 30 days.
jungle *n* an area overgrown with dense tropical trees and other vegetation, etc; any scene of wild confusion, disorder, or of ruthless competition for survival.
jungly *adj* (**junglier, jungliest**) pertaining to or covered with jungle.
junior *adj* younger in age; of more recent or lower status; of juniors. * *n* a person who is younger, of lower rank, etc; a young person employed in minor capacity in an office; a student in the third year of college or school; (*US inf*) (*with cap*) the younger son, often used after the name if the same as the father's.
junior miss *n* a girl in her teens; a clothes size for girls and slim women.
juniper *n* an evergreen shrub that yields purple berries.

junk[1] *n* a flat-bottomed sailing vessel prevalent in the China Seas.

junk[2] *n* discarded useless objects; (*inf*) rubbish, trash; (*sl*) any narcotic drug, such as heroin. * *vt* (*inf*) to scrap. * *adj* cheap, worthless; showy but without substance.

junk bond *n* an interest-bearing certificate held without security, used in junk debt.

junk debt *n* a method of funding takeovers by lending money unsecured in return for a higher yield and other benefits.—*also* **mezzanine debt**.

Junker *n* (*formerly*) a member of the Prussian aristocracy known for its political conservatism and militarism.

junker *n* (*sl*) a jalopy.

junket *n* curdled milk, sweetened and flavoured; a picnic; an excursion, esp one by an official at public expense. * *vi* to go on a junket.

junketeer *n* to make a practice of going on free trips. * *vi* someone who does this.

junk food *n* a snack or fast food with little nutritional value.

junkie, junky *n* (*pl* **junkies**) (*sl*) an addict of a particular activity, food, etc; a drug addict.

junk mail *n* unsolicited mail, eg advertising leaflets.

Juno *n* (*Roman myth*) the queen of the gods, sister and wife of Jupiter; a queenly woman.—**Junoesque** *adj*.

junta *n* a group of people, esp military, who assume responsibility for the government of a country following a coup d'état or revolution.

Jupiter *n* (*Roman myth*) the king of the gods, Jove; (*astron*) the largest planet in the solar system.

jural *adj* of law; of moral rights and obligations.—**jurally** *adv*.

Jurassic *adj* (geol) of or pertaining to the middle system of the Mesozoic Era marked by the existence of dinosaurs and the appearance of birds and mammals. * *n* the Jurassic period.

jurat *n* (law) a record of the time, place, etc, of an affidavit.

juridical, juridic adj of judicial proceedings or law.—**juridically** *adv*.

jurisconsult *n* one learned in law, a jurist.

jurisdiction *n* the right or authority to apply the law; the exercise of such authority; the limits of territory over which such authority extends.—**jurisdictional** *adj*.—**jurisdictionally** *adv*.

jurisprudence *n* the science or philosophy of law; a division of law.—**jurisprudential** *adj*.—**jurisprudentially** *adv*.

jurisprudent *adj, n* (a person) skilled in law.

jurist *n* an expert on law; a judge.—**juristic** *adj*.—**juristically** *adv*.

juror *n* a member of a jury; a person who takes an oath.

jury[1] *n* (*pl* **juries**) a body of usu 12 people sworn to hear evidence and to deliver a verdict on a case; a committee or panel that decides winners in a contest.

jury[2] *adj* (*naut*) makeshift, temporary.

juryman *n* (*pl* **jurymen**) a male juror.

jury-rigged *adj* (*yacht, etc*) rigged in a temporary or makeshift way.

jurywoman *n* (*pl* **jurywomen**) a female juror.

jussive *adj* (*gram*) imperative, expressing command. * *n* (*gram*) a jussive word, mood or form.

just *adj* fair, impartial; deserved, merited; proper, exact; conforming strictly with the facts. * *adv* exactly; nearly; only; barely; a very short time ago; immediately; (*inf*) really; justly, equitably; by right.—**justly** *adv*.—**justness** *n*.

justice *n* justness, fairness; the use of authority to maintain what is just; the administration of law; a judge.

justice of the peace *n* a magistrate who summarily tries minor cases within his or her jurisdiction.

justiciable *adj* subject to trial; able to be settled by law.—**justiciability** *n*.

justiciar *n* (*formerly*) in England, the administrator of justice, chief justice.

justiciary *n* (*pl* **justiciaries**) an officer who administers justice; a justiciar. * *adj* of or pertaining to the administration of justice.

justifiable *adj* capable of being justified or defended.—**justifiability** *n*.—**justifiably** *adv*.

justification *n* the act of justifying; vindication or defence; a showing adequate reason; absolution; (*print*) the spacing out of type to the full length of a line.

justify *vt* (**justifying, justified**) to prove or show to be just or right; to vindicate; to space out (a line of type) so that it fills the required length.

just-in-time *adj* pertaining to a method of inventory control in production industries, where components are delivered just before they are needed.

jut *vti* (**jutting, jutted**) to project; to stick out. * *n* a part that projects.

jute *n* the fibre of either of two tropical plants used for making sacking, etc.

juvenescent *adj* becoming young.—**juvenescence** *n*.

juvenile *adj* young; immature; of or for young persons. * *n* a young person.

juvenile delinquency *n* (*pl* **delinquencies**) antisocial or illegal behaviour by young people usu under 18.—**juvenile delinquent** *n*.

juvenilia *npl* works produced in an artist's or author's youth.

juvenility *n* (*pl* **juvenilities**) the state of being juvinile; youthfulness; a childish act.

juxtapose *vt* to place side by side, esp for comparison.—**juxtaposition** *n*.

K

K *abbr* = kelvin(s); one thousand; (*comput*) 1024 words, bits or bytes; (*chem symbol*) potassium.

kabbala, kabala *see* **cabbala**.

kabuki *n* classical Japanese theatre.

Kabyle *n* (*pl* **Kabyles, Kabyle**) an Algerian Berber, or his dialect.

Kaddish *n* (*pl* **Kaddishim**) a Jewish daily prayer, used by mourners for the year following, and on the anniversary of, someone's death.

Kaffir, Kafir *n* (*pl* **Kaffirs, Kaffir, Kafirs, Kafir**) (*S Africa*) (*offensive*) any black native African; a native of Kafiristan in Asia; (*pl*) South African mine shares; the language of a Southern African people chiefly found in Cape Province of the Republic of South Africa; (*offensive*) among Muslims, an infidel; a type of sorghum.

kaftan *see* **caftan**.

kaiak *see* **kayak**.

kainite *n* a mineral fertilizer.

Kaiser *n* (*formerly*) the title of the emperors of Germany and Austria.

kaka *n* a New Zealand parrot with a long beak.

kakapo *n* an owl-like parrot, a flightless nocturnal bird nesting in burrows in New Zealand.

kakemono *n* a Japanese hanging picture of paper or silk, mounted on rollers.

kaki *n* (*pl* **kakis**) *n* the Japanese persimmon.

kale, kail *n* a variety of cabbage with crinkled leaves.

kaleidoscope *n* a small tube containing bits of coloured glass reflected by mirrors to form symmetrical patterns as the tube is rotated; anything that constantly changes.—**kaleidoscopic** *adj*.—**kaleidoscopically** *adv*.

kalends *see* **calends**.

kaleyard, kailyard *n* (*Scot*) a kitchen garden.

Kali *n* (*Hindu myth*) the goddess of destruction.

kalif, khalif *see* **caliph**.

kalmia *n* the American mountain laurel.

Kalmuck, Kalmyk *n* (*pl* **Kalmucks, Kalmuck, Kalmyks, Kalmyk**) *n* a member of a Mongolian Buddhist people; the variety of the Mongolian language. * *adj* of or pertaining to the Kalmuck or their language.

kalong *n* a large Indonesian or tropical fruitbat; a flying fox.

kalpak *see* **calpac**.

kalsomine *see* **calcimine**.

Kamasutra *n* an ancient Hindu manual on erotic love.

kame *n* (*Scot*) an elongated gravel or sand mound or hill of glacial origin; a comb.

kami *n* (*pl* **kami**) a divinity or demigod in the Shinto religion of Japan, from whom the Japanese emperors were supposed to have been descended.

kamikaze *n* (*World War II*) a Japanese aircraft packed with explosives for making a suicidal crashing attack; the pilot of such an aircraft.

kamseen, kamsin *see* **khamsin.**

kangaroo *n* (*pl* **kangaroos**) an Australian marsupial with short forelegs and strong, large hind legs for jumping.

kangaroo court *n* an illegal court operated by an unauthorized body, which perverts the proper course of justice.

Kantian *adj* of the German philosopher Immanuel Kant (1724–1804) or his philosophy.

kaolin *n* a white clay used in porcelain, etc.

kapellmeister *n* (*pl* **kapellmeister**) the musical director of an orchestra etc, esp in an 18th-century aristocratic household.

kapok *n* the silky fibres around the seeds of a tropical tree, used for stuffing cushions, etc.

kappa *n* the tenth letter of the Greek alphabet.

kaput *adj* (*sl*) broken, ruined.

karabiner *n* (*mountaineering*) a spring-loaded hook for securing ropes.

karakul *n* (the black fur of) a breed of sheep from the Bukhara region of central Asia.

karaoke *n* a CD music system that plays recordings of popular songs with the vocal part removed to allow amateurs to sing along.

karat *n* a measure of weight for precious stones; a measure of the purity of gold.—*also* **carat.**

karate *n* a Japanese system of unarmed combat using sharp blows of the feet and hands.

Karen *n* (*pl* **Karens, Karen**) *n* a member of a Thai people in Burma, or their language.

karma *n* (*Buddhism, Hinduism*) the sum of a person's actions during one of their existences, held to determine their destiny in the next; (*inf*) a certain aura that a person or place is felt to possess.—**karmic** *adj.*

karoo, karroo *n* (*pl* **karoos, karroos**) (*S Africa*) (*sometimes with a cap*) a series of clayey tablelands, usu barren except in the wet season; a system of rocks in , or a period; of this period.

kart *n* a small motorized vehicle used in racing.—*also* **go-kart.**

karting *n* kart racing.

karyo- *prefix* = nucleus.

katydid *n* a large green North American insect like a grasshopper.

kauri (*pl* **kauris**) a New Zealand pine with oval leaves from which a resinous gum is extracted; the wood or gum from this tree.

kava *n* a Polynesian shrub; an intoxicating and narcotic drink made from it.

kayak *n* an Eskimo canoe made of skins on a wooden frame.—*also* **kaiak.**

kazoo *n* (*pl* **kazoos**) a small tube-shaped musical instrument through which one hums to vibrate a membrane-covered hole at the end or side

KB *abbr* = kilobyte

KBE *abbr* = Knight Commander of the Order of the British Empire.

kc *abbr* = kilocycle.

kcal *abbr* = kilocalorie.

KCB *abbr* = Knight Commander of the Order of the Bath.

KE *abbr* = kinetic energy.

kebab *n* small cubes of grilled meat and vegetables, usu served on a skewer.

keck *vi* to make a sound as if about to vomit; to feel or express loathing.

keddah *n* in India and Burma, an enclosure for catching wild elephants.

kedge *n* a small anchor for kedging a ship. * *vt* to move (a ship) by hauling on a cable attached to a kedge.

kedgeree *n* a dish containing fish, rice and hard-boiled eggs.

keef *see* **kif.**

keek *vt* (*Scot*) to peep cheekily.

keel *n* one of the main structural members of a ship extending along the bottom from stem to stern to which the frame is attached; any structure resembling this. * *vti* (to cause) to turn over.

keelhaul *vt* (*formerly*) to drag under water beneath the bottom of a ship from one side to the other; to reprimand sternly.

keelson *n* a beam of timber laid on the middle of the floor timbers over the keel of a vessel to strengthen it.—*also* **kelson.**

keen[1] *adj* eager, enthusiastic; intellectually acute, shrewd; having a sharp point or fine edge; (*senses*) perceptive, penetrating; extremely cold and piercing; intense; (*prices*) very low so as to be competitive.—**keenly** *adv.*—**keenness** *n.*

keen[2] *n* a dirge or lament for the dead. * *vi* to lament the dead.

keep *vb* (**keeping, kept**) *vt* to celebrate, observe; to fulfil; to protect, guard; to take care of; to preserve; to provide for; to make regular entries in; to maintain in a specified state; to hold for the future; to hold and not let go; (*with* **at**) to harass (a person) into continuing (some task, etc); (*with* **back**) to refuse to disclose; to restrain; (*with* **down**) to repress; to subdue; (*with* **from**) to abstain or restrain from; to preserve as a secret (from someone); (*with* **to**) to cause to adhere strictly to; (*with* **up**) to persist in; to continue; to maintain in good condition. * *vi* to stay in a specified condition; to continue, go on; to refrain or restrain oneself; to stay fresh, not spoil; (*with* **at**) to persist; (*with* **away**) to prevent from approaching; (*with* **down**) to stay hidden; (*with* **on**) to talk or nag continuously; (*with* **to**) to (cause to) adhere strictly to; (*with* **up**) to maintain the same pace, level of knowledge, etc as another; to stay informed; to continue relentlessly. * *n* food and shelter; care and custody; the inner stronghold of a castle.

keeper *n* one who guards, watches, or takes care of persons or things.

keeping *n* care, charge; observance; agreement, conformity.

keepsake *n* something kept in memory of the giver.

kef *see* **kif.**

keg *n* a small barrel.

kelp *n* a large brown seaweed.

kelpie (*pl* **kelpies**) *n* in Scottish folklore, a malevolent water sprite, supposed to take the form of a horse.

Keltic *see* **Celtic.**

kelvin *n* a unit of temperature of the Kelvin scale.

Kelvin scale *n* temperature on a scale where absolute zero (−273.15° Celsius) is taken as zero degrees.

ken *n* understanding; view; sight. * *vt* (**kenning, kenned** *or* **kent**) to know; to recognize at sight.

kendo *n* a Japanese style of fencing with bamboo staves.

kennel *n* a small shelter for a dog, a doghouse; (*often pl*) a place where dogs are bred or kept. * *vt* (**kennelling, kennelled** *or* **kenneling, kenneled**) to keep in a kennel.

keno *n* a game of chance, similar to bingo, played with numbered balls and cards.

kenosis *n* (*theology*) the self-limitation of Christ in laying aside his divinity and becoming man.—**kenotic** *adj.*

kentledge *n* (*naut*) ballast of scrap metal.

kepi *n* (*pl* **kepis**) a French military peaked cap.

kept *see* **keep.**

keratin *n* a tough, fibrous protein, the substance of hair, nails, feathers, etc.

keratitis *n* inflammation of the cornea.

keratose *adj* (*sponges*) having a horn-like skeleton.

kerb *n* a line of raised stone forming the edge of a pavement; a curb.

kerbing *n* kerbstones collectively; material for kerbstones, curbing.

kerbstone *n* the stone edge of a path, curbstone.

kerchief *n* a piece of square cloth worn on the head.

kerf *n* a cut or slit made by a saw, etc.

kermes *n* the dried bodies of female scale insects from which a dye of a deep cherry red colour is obtained; an oak tree found in Europe and Asia, on which these insects live.

kermis *n* an open-air festival or fair.

kern[1], **kerne** *n* (*formerly*) a lightly armed Irish or Scottish medieval footsoldier; a troop of these; (*arch*) a peasant.

kern[2] *n* (*print*) the part of a type or character that overhangs the following piece of type or character.

kernel *n* the inner edible part of a fruit or nut; the essential part of anything.

kerosene, kerosine *n* a fuel oil distilled from petroleum, paraffin.

kersey *n* a coarse smooth-faced woollen cloth.

kerseymere *n* a twilled cloth of fine wool.

kestrel *n* a type of small falcon.
ketch *n* a small two-masted sailing vessel.
ketchup *n* any of various thick sauces, esp one made from puréed tomato, for meat, fish, etc.—*also* **catchup, catsup**
ketone *n* a class of chemical compounds, the simplest being acetone.
kettle *n* a container with a handle and spout for boiling water.
kettledrum *n* a musical instrument consisting of a hollow metal body with a parchment head, the tension of which controls the pitch and is adjusted by screws.
kevel *n* (*naut*) a cleat for belaying ropes.
key[1] *n* a device for locking and unlocking something; a thing that explains or solves, as the legend of a map, a code, etc; a controlling position, person, or thing; one of a set of parts or levers pressed in a keyboard or typewriter, etc; (*mus*) a system of related tones based on a keynote and forming a given scale; style or mood of expression; a roughened surface for improved adhesion of plaster, etc; an electric circuit breaker. * *vt* to furnish with a key; to bring into harmony. * *adj* controlling; important.
key[2] *n* a low island or reef.
keyboard *n* a set of keys in a piano, organ, microcomputer, etc.
keyhole *n* an opening (in a lock) into which a key is inserted.
keyhole surgery *n* surgery performed through small incisions in the body using fibre-optic tubes both for internal examination and as conduits for tiny surgical instruments.
Keynesianism *n* the economic theories based on the works of the English economist John Maynard Keynes (1883–1946).—**Keynesian** *adj*.
keynote *n* the basic note of a musical scale; the basic idea or ruling principle. * *vt* to give the keynote of; to give the keynote speech at.
keypad *n* a small usu hand-held keyboard of numbered buttons used to tap in a telephone number, operate a calculator, etc.
key signature *n* the sharps or flats at the beginning of a musical stave to indicate the key.
keystone *n* the middle stone at the top of an arch, holding the stones or other pieces in place.
keystroke *n* the depressing of a key on a typewriter, computer keyboard, etc.
kg *abbr* = kilogram(s).
KGB *abbr* = (*formerly*) the secret police of the USSR.
khaddar, khadi *n* an Indian homespun cotton cloth.
khaki *adj* dull yellowish-brown. * *n* (*pl* **khakis**) strong, twilled cloth of this colour; (*often pl*) a khaki uniform or trousers.
khamsin *n* a hot southerly wind, esp in Egypt, that blows for about 50 days in spring.—**kamseen, kamsin**.
khan *n* the title of a ruler, prince, or governor in Asia.
khanate *n* the rule or jurisdiction of a khan.
khedive *n* the title of the viceroy of Egypt (1867–1914).
khoraschot *n* the policy in the former USSR, initiated by President Gorbachev, of the decentralized economic accountability of managers in industrial production and other enterprises.
kHz *abbr* = kilohertz.
kiang *n* a wild ass of Tibet.
kibble *vt* to grind coarsely. * *n* a raiseable bucket used in wells, mines etc.
kibbutz *n* (*pl* **kibbutzim**) an agricultural commune in Israel.
kibbutznik *n* a person who lives in a kibbutz.
kibe *n* ulcerated chilblain, esp one on the heel.
kiblah, kibla *n* the point to which Muslims turn at prayer, Mecca.
kibosh *n* (*sl*) nonsense.
kick *vt* to strike with the foot; to drive, force, etc as by kicking; to score (a goal, etc) by kicking; (*with* **about, around**) (*inf*) to abuse physically or mentally; to discuss or analyse (a problem, etc) in a relaxed unsystematic manner; (*with* **out**) (*inf*) to eject, dismiss; (*with* **up**) (*inf*) to cause (trouble, etc). * *vi* to strike out with the foot; to recoil, as a gun; (*inf*) to complain; (*with* **about, around**) (*inf*) to wander idly; to be unused or forgotten; (*with* **off**) (*football*) to give the ball the first kick to start play; (*inf*) to start. * *n* an act or method of kicking; a sudden recoil; (*inf*) a thrill; (*inf*) an intoxicating effect.—**kicker** *n*.
kickback *n* a recoil; (*inf*) a returning of part of a sum of money received in payment.
kickoff *n* (*football*) a kick putting the ball into play; the beginning or start of proceedings, eg a discussion.
kickshaw *n* a trifle, trinket; (*arch*) a small, light, fancy dish, a delicacy.
kickstand *n* a retractable stand for parking a bicycle or motorbike.
kid *n* a young goat; soft leather made from its skin; (*inf*) a child. * *vti* (**kidding, kidded**) (*inf*) to tease or fool playfully; (*goat*) to bring forth young.—**kidder** *n*.
kiddy, kiddie *n* (*pl* **kiddies**) (*inf*) a child.
kidnap *vt* (**kidnapping, kidnapped** *or* **kidnaping, kidnaped**) to seize and hold to ransom, as of a person.—**kidnapper, kidnaper** *n*.
kidney *n* (*pl* **kidneys**) either of a pair of glandular organs excreting waste products from the blood as urine; an animal's kidney used as food.
kidney bean *n* any of various cultivated beans, esp a large dark red bean seed.
kidney stone *n* a hard mineral deposit in the kidney.
kidskin *n* a soft leather made from the skin of a young goat.
kief *see* **kif**.
kier *n* a vat in which cloth is boiled for bleaching.
kieselguhr *n* mineral remains of algae, used for filtering and insulation purposes etc.
kif *n* a drowsy state of well-being produced by marijuana; marijuana itself; any drug producing a similar state.—*also* **keef, kef, kief**.
kill *vt* to cause the death of; to destroy; to neutralize (a colour); to spend (time) on trivial matters; to turn off (an engine, etc); (*inf*) to cause severe discomfort or pain to. * *n* the act of killing; an animal or animals killed.—**killer** *n*.
killer whale *n* a carnivorous black-and-white toothed whale.
killick, killock *n* (*naut*) a heavy stone used as an anchor; a small anchor.
killing *adj* (*inf*) tiring; very amusing; causing death, deadly. * *n* the act of killing, murder; (*inf*) a sudden (financial) success.—**killingly** *adv*.
killjoy *n* a person who spoils other people's enjoyment.
kiln *n* a furnace or large oven for baking or drying (lime, bricks, etc).
kilo *n* (*pl* **kilos**) kilogram; kilometre.
kilo- *prefix* one thousand.
kilobyte *n* 1024 bytes.
kilocalorie *n* a Calorie.
kilocycle *n* a kilohertz.
kilogram *n* a unit of weight and mass, equal to 1000 grams or 2.2046 pounds.
kilohertz *n* one thousand cycles per second, 1000 hertz.
kilolitre, kiloliter *n* one thousand litres.
kilometre, kilometer *n* a unit of length equal to 1000 metres or 0.62 mile.—**kilometric** *adj*.
kiloton *n* a unit of explosive force equal to 1000 tons of TNT.
kilowatt *n* a unit of electrical power, equal to 1000 watts.
kilowatt-hour *n* a unit of energy equal to work done by one kilowatt in one hour.
kilt *n* a knee-length skirt made from tartan material pleated at the sides, worn as part of the Scottish Highland dress for men and women.
kilter *n* good working order; good condition (*out of kilter*).
kimono *n* (*pl* **kimonos**) a loose Japanese robe.
kin *n* relatives; family.—*see* **kith**.
kind[1] *n* sort; variety; class; a natural group or division; essential character.
kind[2] *adj* sympathetic; friendly; gentle; benevolent.—**kindness** *n*.
kindergarten *n* a class or school for very young children.
kind-hearted *adj* benevolent; kind, warm.—**kind-heartedly** *adv*.
kindle *vt* to set on fire; to excite (feelings, interest, etc). * *vi* to catch fire; to become aroused or excited.
kindling *n* material, such as bits of dry wood, for starting a fire.
kindly *adj* (**kindlier, kindliest**) kind; gracious; agreeable; pleasant. * *adv* in a kindly manner; favourably.—**kindliness** *n*.
kindred *n* a person's family or relatives; family relationship; resemblance. * *adj* related; like, similar.

kine *n* (*pl*) (*arch*) cattle.
kinematic *adj* of pure motion, without reference to force etc.
kinematics *n* (*sing*) the science of pure motion.
kinetic *adj* of or produced by movement.—**kinetically** *adv*.
kinetic art *n* sculpture, etc that moves or has moving parts.
kinetic energy *n* energy derived from motion.
kinetics *n* (*used as sing*) the science of the effects of forces in producing or changing motion; the study of the mechanisms and rates of chemical reactions.
king *n* the man who rules a country and its people; a man with the title of ruler, but with limited power to rule; man supreme in a certain sphere; something best in its class; the chief piece in chess; a playing card with a picture of a king on it, ranking above a queen; (*draughts*) a piece that has been crowned.
King Charles spaniel *n* a small breed of spaniel with black and brown markings.
kingcup *n* the marsh marigold; any of various yellow-flowered, five-petalled plants, such as the buttercup or clematis.
kingdom *n* a country headed by a king or queen; a realm, domain; any of the three divisions of the natural world: animal: vegetable, mineral.
kingfisher *n* a short-tailed diving bird that feeds chiefly on fish.
King James Bible, King James Version *n* the version of the Bible published by the sanction of James I of England and VI of Scotland in 1611 and appointed to be read in churches.—*also* **Authorized Version**.
kinglet *n* a minor king; a small bird with a yellow crown found throughout North America.
kingly *adj* (**kinglier, kingliest**) of, resembling, or fit for a king.—**kingliness** *n*.
king-of-arms *n* (*pl* **kings-of-arms**) chief officer of the Heralds' College.
kingpin *n* (*sl*) the chief person in a company, group, etc; the pin in a car, etc that attaches the stub axle to the axle beam and allows limited movement to the stub axle; the foremost pin in tenpin bowling; the central pin in ninepins; the crux of an argument.
kingship *n* the office or authority of a king; the art of ruling as king.
king-size, king-sized *adj* larger than standard size.
kink *n* a tight twist or curl in a piece of string, rope, hair, etc; a painful cramp in the neck, back, etc; a minor problem in some course of action; a personality quirk; (*Brit sl*) a sexual deviation; (*pl*) (*Scot*) a convulsive fit of laughter; (*US*) a bright, original idea. * *vt* to form kinks.
kinkajou *n* nocturnal long-tailed quadruped of Central and Southern America similar to a racoon(—*also* **honeybear**); a short-tailed primate with spiny protrusions from the neck (—*also* **potto**).
kinky *adj* (**kinkier, kinkiest**) full of kinks; (*inf*) eccentric; (*inf*) sexually bizarre.—**kinkiness** *n*.
kinnikinnick, kinnikinic *n* a mixture of dried leaves and bark smoked by American Indians; any of the plants used for this.
kino (gum) *n* an astringent vegetable gum of a dark red colour, used in medicine, tanning etc.
kinsfolk *n* blood relations.
kinship *n* blood relationship; close connection.
kinsman, kinswoman *n* (*pl* **kinsmen, kinswomen**) a relative, esp by blood.
kiosk *n* a small open structure used for selling newspapers, confectionery, etc; a public telephone booth.
kip *vi* (**kipping, kipped**) (*sl*) to sleep. * *n* (*sl*) sleep, a lodging.
kipper *n* a kippered herring, etc. * *vt* to cure (fish) by salting and drying or smoking.
kirk *n* (*Scot*) a church.
kirsch, kirschwasser *n* a type of brandy made from cherries.
kismet *n* fate, destiny.
kiss *vti* to touch with the lips as an expression of love, affection or in greeting; to touch the lips with those of another person as a sign of love or desire; to touch lightly. * *n* an act of kissing; a light, gentle touch.—**kissable** *adj*.
kissagram *n* a celebratory telegram or message delivered with a kiss.
kiss-and-tell *adj* (*inf*) pertaining to the publication of memoirs that reveal hitherto secret details.
kisser *n* one who kisses; (*sl*) the mouth or face.
kiss of life *n* mouth-to-mouth resuscitation.
kist *n* (*Scot*) a chest or box; (*arch*) a cist; (*S Africa*) a large chest or box used for storing linen, esp for a trousseau.
kit *n* clothing and personal equipment, etc; tools and equipment for a specific purpose; a set of parts with instructions ready to be assembled. * *vt* (**kitting, kitted**) (*usu with* **out** *or* **up**) to provide with kit.
kitchen *n* a place where food is prepared and cooked.
kitchenette *n* a small kitchen.
kitchen garden *n* a garden where vegetables are grown for domestic use.
kite *n* a bird of prey with long narrow wings and a forked tail; a light frame covered with a thin covering for flying in the wind.
kith *n* friends and relations, now only in **kith and kin**.
kithara *see* **cithara**.
kitsch *n* art, literature, etc regarded as pretentious, inferior, or in poor taste.—*also adj*.—**kitschy** *adj*.
kitten *n* a young cat; the young of other small mammals. * *vti* to give birth to kittens.
kittenish *adj* like a kitten, playful; (*woman*) flirtatious.
kittiwake *n* either of two types of gull with black-tipped wings.
kittle *adj* (*Scot*) difficult to manage, capricious. * *vt* (*Scot*) to tickle; to cause (someone) to be puzzled or to bother someone.
kitty *n* (*pl* **kitties**) the stakes in a game of poker or other gambling game; a shared fund of money; affectionate name for a cat or kitten.
kiwi *n* (*pl* **kiwis**) a flightless bird of New Zealand; (*inf*) a New Zealander.
kiwi fruit *n* a fruit of an Asian vine.—*also* **Chinese gooseberry**.
KKK *abbr* = Ku Klux Klan.
kl *abbr* = kiloliter.
klaxon *n* a type of old-fashioned motor horn.
kleptomania *n* an uncontrollable impulse to steal.—**kleptomaniac** *n*.
klipspringer *n* a small antelope of South Africa.
kloof *n* a ravine, a deep narrow valley, in South Africa.
klystron *n* an electronic device that generates and amplifies microwaves.
km *abbr* = kilometre(s).
knack *n* an ability to do something easily; a trick; a habit.
knacker *n* one who buys worn-out horses or old houses, ships, etc, for destruction.
knackwurst *n* a type of spicy German sausage.
knap (knapping, knapped) *vt* to break, snap or hit something.
knapsack *n* a bag for carrying equipment or supplies on the back.
knapweed *n* a purple-flowered weed.
knar *see* **knur**.
knave *n* (*formerly*) a tricky or dishonest man; the jack in a pack of playing cards.—**knavish** *adj*.—**knavishly** *adv*.
knavery *n* (*pl* **knaveries**) dishonesty; fraud; deceit.
knead *vt* to squeeze and press together (dough, clay, etc) into a uniform lump with the hands; to make (bread, etc) by kneading; to squeeze and press with the hands.—**kneader** *n*.
knee *n* the joint between the thigh and the lower part of the human leg; anything shaped like a bent knee. * *vt* (**kneeing, kneed**) to hit or touch with the knee.
kneecap *n* the small bone covering and protecting the front part of the knee-joint. * *vt* (**kneecapping, kneecapped**) to maim by shooting into the kneecap.
knee-deep *adj* deep enough to cover the knees; deeply involved.
knee jerk *n* an involuntary jerk when the tendon below the knee is tapped.
kneejerk *adj* responding automatically.
kneel *vi* (**kneeling, kneeled** *or* **knelt**) to go down on one's knee or knees; to remain in this position.—**kneeler** *n*.
knell *n* the sound of a bell rung slowly and solemnly at a death or funeral; a warning of death, failure, etc. * *vi* (*bell*) to ring a knell; to summon, announce, etc (as if) by a knell.
knelt *see* **kneel**.
knew *see* **know**.
Knickerbocker *n* a New Yorker; a descendant of the founders of the original city.

knickerbockers *npl* baggy breeches fastened by a band at the knee.

knickers *npl* an undergarment covering the lower body and having separate leg holes, worn by women and girls.

knickknack *n* a small ornament or trinket.—*also* **nicknack.**

knife *n* (*pl* **knives**) a flat piece of steel, etc, with a sharp edge set in a handle, used to cut or as a weapon; a sharp blade forming part of a tool or machine. * *vt* to cut or stab with a knife.

knife edge *n* the sharp edge of a knife; anything resembling this, such as the blade of an ice skate; a sharp wedge used as a pivot for a balance; a critical or precarious situation.

knight n (*Middle Ages*) a medieval mounted soldier; a man who for some achievement is given honorary rank entitling him to use "Sir" before his given name; a chessman shaped like a horse's head. * *vt* to make (a man) a knight.—**knightly** *adj*.—**knightliness** *n*.

knight-errant *n* (*pl* **knights-errant**) a quixotic person; (*Middle Ages*) a knight who went in quest of adventure, to show his prowess, chivalry etc.

knight-errantry *n* the practices or customs of knights-errant; quixotic behaviour.

knighthood *n* the character, rank, or dignity of a knight; the order of knights.

knit *vb* (**knitting, knitted** *or* **knit**) *vt* to form (fabric or a garment) by interlooping yarn using knitting needles or a machine; to cause (eg broken bones) to grow together; to link or join together closely; to draw (the brows) together. * *vi* to make knitted fabric from yarn by means of needles; to grow together; to become joined or united. * *n* a knitted garment or fabric.—**knitter** *n*.

knitting *n* work being knitted.

knitting needle *n* a long thin eyeless needle, usu made of plastic or steel, used in knitting.

knitwear *n* knitted clothing.

knives *see* **knife.**

knob *n* a rounded lump or protuberance; a handle, usu round, of a door, drawer, etc.

knobby *adj* (**knobbier, knobbiest**) full of knobs.

knobkerrie *n* a round-headed stick used as a weapon in South Africa.

knock *vi* to strike with a sharp blow; to rap on a door; to bump, collide; (*engine*) to make a thumping noise; (*with* **off**) (*inf*) to finish work; (*with* **up**) (*tennis, etc*) to practise before a match. * *vt* to strike; (*inf*) to criticize; (*with* **about, around**) to wander around aimlessly; to treat roughly; (*with* **back**) (*inf*) to drink, swallow quickly; to reject, refuse; (*with* **down**) to indicate a sale at an auction; (*with* **down** *or* **off**) to hit so as to cause to fall; (*with* **off**) (*inf*) to do or make hastily and without effort; to reduce in price; to discontinue, esp work; (*sl*) to kill; (*sl*) to steal; (*with* **out**) to make unconscious or exhausted; to eliminate in a knockout competition; (*inf*) to amaze; (*with* **up**) (*inf*) to make or arrange hastily; (*cricket*) to score a certain number of runs; to rouse; (*sl*) to make pregnant. * *n* a knocking, a hit, a rap.

knockabout *adj* rough, boisterous.

knockdown *adj* cheap; (*furniture*) easy to dismantle.

knocker *n* a device hinged against a door for use in knocking; (*sl*: *usu pl*) a woman's breasts.

knock-kneed *adj* having inward-curving legs.

knockout *n* a punch or blow that produces unconsciousness; a contest in which competitors are eliminated at each round; (*inf*) an attractive or extremely impressive person or thing.

knoll *n* a small round hill.

knot *n* a lump in a thread, etc formed by a tightened loop or tangling; a fastening made by tying lengths of rope, etc; an ornamental bow; a small group, cluster; a hard mass of wood where a branch grows out from a tree, which shows as a roundish, cross-grained piece in a board; a unit of speed of one nautical mile per hour; something that ties closely, esp the bond of marriage. * *vti* (**knotting, knotted**) to make or form a knot (in); to entangle or become entangled.—**knotter** *n*.

knotgrass *n* a weed with a jointed stem and green flowers; any of various similar plants.

knothole *n* a hole in wood once filled by a knot.

knotting *n* a kind of lace work made with knots; a sealer applied to knots before priming wood as protection from sap.

knotty *adj* (**knottier, knottiest**) full of knots; hard to solve; puzzling.—**knottiness** *n*.

know *vt* (**knowing, knew,** *pp* **known**) to be well informed about; to be aware of; to be acquainted with; to recognize or distinguish.—**knowable** *adj*.

know-all *n* a know-it-all.

know-how *n* practical skill, experience.

knowing *adj* having knowledge; shrewd; clever; implying a secret understanding.—**knowingly** *adv*.—**knowingness** *n*.

know-it-all *n* a person who acts as if they know about everything.

knowledge *n* what one knows; the body of facts, etc accumulated over time; fact of knowing; range of information or understanding; the act of knowing.

knowledgeable *adj* having knowledge or intelligence; well-informed.—**knowledgeably** *adv*.

known *see* **know.**

knuckle *n* a joint of the finger, esp at the roots of the fingers; the knee of an animal used as food. * *vi* (*with* **down**) (*inf*) to apply oneself in earnest (to some task, duty, etc); (*with* **under**) to submit, to give in.

knuckle-duster *n* a metal device that fits over the knuckles, used for inflicting severe injury by punching.

knur, knurr *n a k*not either in a tree trunk or in wood; a hard lump.—*also* **knar.**

knurl *n* a small ridge, esp one of a series on a metal surface to prevent slippage.

KO *abbr* = knockout.

koa *n* a Hawaiian tree; the hard wood it produces used in making furniture.

koala *n* an Australian tree-dwelling marsupial with thick, grey fur.

koan *n* an insoluble riddle used as a meditation exercise in Zen Buddhism.

kob *n* a South African water antelope.

kobold *n* a household goblin or elf; a spirit of mines and other underground places.

Kohinoor, Koh-i-nor *n* a famous, very large Indian diamond, which has belonged to the British Crown since 1849.

kohl *n* a fine powder, as of antimony, used for darkening the eyelids.

kohlrabi *n* (*pl* **kohlrabies**) a variety of cabbage with a thick stem, used as a vegetable.

kola nut *n* the seed of either of two tropical trees which has stimulant properties and is chewed or used in making sweet drinks.—*also* **cola nut.**

kolinsky *n* (*pl* **kolinskies**) *n* an Asian mink; its fur.

kolkhoz *n* a collective farm in Russia.

koodoo *n* an African striped antelope with long spiral horns.—*also* **kudu.**

kook *n* (*inf*) a person regarded as silly, eccentric, etc.

kookaburra *n* an Australian kingfisher with a harsh cry like loud laughter.

kooky, kookie *adj* (**kookier, kookiest**) (*inf*) crazy; eccentric.

kop *n* (*S Africa*) an isolated hill.

kopeck, kopek *n* a Russian coin, one hundred of which comprise one ruble.

kopje *n* (*S Africa*) a hillock or small hill.

Koran *n* the sacred book of the Muslims.—**Koranic** *adj*.

Korean *n* a native or inhabitant of Korea; the language spoken in North and South Korea.* *adj* of or pertaining to Korea, its language or people.

kosher *adj* (*Judaism*) clean or fit to eat according to dietary laws; (*inf*) acceptable, genuine. * *n* kosher food.

koto *n* (*pl* **kotos**) *n* a Japanese musical instrument with silk strings, similar to a zither.

kowtow *vi* to show exaggerated respect (to) by bowing.

kph *abbr* = kilometres per hour.

Kr (*chem symbol*) krypton.

kraal *n* an African village consisting of a group of huts surrounded by a pallisade; a sheepfold, or cattle pen. * to pen sheep or cattle in a kraal.

krait *n* a deadly Asian rock snake.
kraken *n* a gigantic fabled sea monster supposed to live in the sea off Norway.
kremlin *n* a Russian citadel; (*with cap and* **the**) the citadel in Moscow, housing the former palace, cathedrals, and the Russian government; (*with cap*) the central government of Russia.
kriegspiel *n* (*sometimes with cap*) (*mil*) a game with blocks or models representing the various sections of an army as if in actual warfare, used in training; a chess game for two players, each playing on their own board with their own pieces, unseen by the other, with the moves regulated by a third person also with a board unseen by either player.
krill *n* (*pl* **krill**) the tiny shrimp-like plankton eaten by many whales.
kris *n* a Malaysian or Indonesian knife or dagger with a wavy blade.—*also* **crease, creese.**
Krishna *n* a great deity of later Hinduism.—**Krishnaism** *n*.
krona *n* (*pl* **kronor**) the monetary unit of Sweden.
króna *n* (*pl* **krónur**) the monetary unit of Iceland.
krone *n* (*pl* **kroner**) the monetary unit of Denmark and Norway.
krypton *n* a colourless, odourless gas used in fluorescent lights and lasers.
Kt *abbr* = Knight.
kudos *n* (*used as sing*) (*inf*) fame, glory, prestige.
kudu *see* **koodoo.**
Kufic *see* **Cufic.**
Ku Klux Klan *n* an American secret society hostile to Blacks, Jews, Catholics, etc.
kulak *n* an independent well-to-do peasant in Russia.
kumiss *n* a spirit made in central Asia from fermented mare's milk and sometimes used as a medicine.
kümmel *n* a liqueur flavoured with caraway seeds.
kumquat *n* a small fruit like an orange with a sweet rind.
kung fu *n* a Chinese system of unarmed combat.
Kurd *n* a native of Kurdistan, an area of plateaus and mountains covering eastern Turkey, northern Iraq, western Iran, and Armenia.
Kurdish *adj* pertaining to the Kurds or to their language. * *n* the language of the Kurds.
kvass, kvas *n* a Russian rye beer that has stale bread as one of its ingredients.—*also* **quass.**
kw. *abbr* = kilowatt(s).
kwashiorkor *n* a disease, esp of children, caused by protein deficiency and characterized by a distended stomach and changes in skin pigmentation.
kwh *abbr* = kilowatt-hour(s).
kyanize *vt* to preserve wood from dry rot by injecting corrosive sublimate.—**kyanization** *n*.
kymograph *n* an instrument for recording pressure, oscillations, sound waves, etc, eg an apparatus for determining the pressure of blood, by means of a stylus on a continually rotating drum of paper; (*phonetics*) an instrument to measure muscular strength in the tongue, lips, etc; an instrument that records the angular oscillations of an aircraft in the air.—*also* **cymograph.**
Kyrie (eleison) *n* a prayer, part of a mass; a musical setting of this; the response in an Anglican communion service.

L

l *abbr* = litre(s).
L, l *n* the 12th letter of the English alphabet; something shaped like an L.
La (*chem symbol*) lanthanum.
la *n* the name given to the sixth note of the diatonic scale in solmization.
laager *n* (*S Africa*) a camp in a circle of wagons.—*also* **lager.**
lab *n* (*inf*) laboratory.
labarum *n* (*pl* **labara**) a banner used in Christian processions.
label *n* a slip of paper, cloth, metal, etc attached to anything to provide information about its nature, contents, ownership, etc; a term of generalized classification. * *vt* (**labelling, labelled** *or* **labeling, labeled**) to attach a label to; to designate or classify (as).—**labeller, labeler** *n*.
labellum *n* (*pl* **labella**) the lower petal of an orchid.
labia *npl* (*sing* **labium**) the lips of the female genitals, comprising the outer pair (*labia majora*) and the inner pair (*labia minora*).
labial *adj* of the lips or labia.
labialize *vt* (*phonetics*) to pronounce (a sound) by rounding one's lips.—**labialization** *n*.
labiate *adj*, *n* (*bot*) (a plant) with the corolla or calyx divided into two parts, resembling lips.
labile *adj* (*chem*) unstable.
labiodental *adj* (*phonetics*) (*sound*) formed by the lips and teeth.
labionasal *adj* (*phonetics*) (*sound*) formed by the lips and nose.
labium *see* **labia.**
labor *see* **labour.**
Labor Day *n* the first Monday in September in US and Canada, a legal holiday honouring labour.
laboratory *n* (*pl* **laboratories**) a room or building where scientific work and research is carried out.
laborious *adj* requiring much work; hard-working; laboured.—**laboriously** *adv*.—**laboriousness** *n*.
labour, labor *n* work, physical or mental exertion; a specific task; all wage-earning workers; workers collectively; the process of childbirth. * *vi* to work; to work hard; to move with difficulty; to suffer (delusions, etc); to be in childbirth. * *vt* to develop in unnecessary detail.
laboured, labored *adj* done with effort; strained.—**labouredly, laboredly** *adv*.
labourer, laborer *n* a person who labours, esp a person whose work requires strength rather than skill.
labour or labor union *n* an organized association of employees of any trade or industry for the protection of their income and working conditions.
Labrador retriever *n* a breed of large, smooth-coated sporting dog.
labradorite *n* a type of feldspar.
labret *n* a shell, etc, worn as an ornament in the lip.
labrum *n* (*pl* **labra**) the liplike shield of an insect's mouth.
laburnum *n* a small tree or shrub with hanging yellow flowers.
labyrinth *n* a structure containing winding passages through which it is hard to find one's way; a maze.—**labyrinthine** *adj*.
lac[1] *n* a resinous substance secreted by certain insects.
lac[2] *see* **lakh.**
lace *n* a cord, etc used to draw together and fasten parts of a shoe, a corset, etc; a delicate ornamental fabric of openwork design using fine cotton, silk, etc. * *vt* to fasten with a lace or laces; to intertwine, weave; to fortify (a drink, etc) with a dash of spirits.
lacerate *vt* to tear jaggedly; to wound (feelings, etc).—**laceration** *n*.
laches *n* (*law*) undue delay in claiming one's rights, etc.
lachrimatory *n* (*pl* **lachrimatories**) a vessel used to hold tears, found in ancient Roman tombs.
lachrymal *adj* of tears; relating to the glands that secrete tears.—*also* **lacrimal.**
lachrymose *adj* tending to shed tears; sad.—**lachrymosity** *n*.
laciniate, laciniated *adj* (*biol*) cut into narrow lobes, fringed.
lack *n* the fact or state of not having any or not having enough; the thing that is needed. * *vti* to be deficient in or entirely without.
lackadaisical *adj* showing lack of energy or interest; listless.—**lackadaisically** *adv*.
lackey *n* a male servant of low rank; a servile hanger-on.
lackluster, lacklustre *adj* lacking in brightness or vigour; dull.
laconic *adj* using few words; concise.—**laconically** *adv*.—**laconicism** *n*.
lacquer *n* a glossy varnish. * *vt* to coat with lacquer, to make glossy.
lacrimal *see* **lachrymal.**
lacrosse *n* a game played by two teams of 10 players with the aim of throwing a ball through the opponents' goal using a long stick topped with a netted pouch for catching and carrying the ball.

lact-, lacto- *prefix* milk.
lactate *vi* (*mammals*) to secrete milk.
lactation *n* the secretion of milk.—**lactational** *adj*.
lacteal *adj* pertaining to, or resembling, milk; (*anat*) conveying chyle.
lactescent *adj* milky; (*plant, insect*) yielding a milky juice.—**lactescence** *n*.
lactic *adj* of or relating to milk; obtained from sour milk or whey; involving the production of lactic acid.
lactic acid *n* an organic acid normally present in sour milk.
lactiferous *adj* producing milk, or a milky juice.
lacto-, lact- *prefix* milk.
lactometer *n* an instrument used for determining the quality of milk.
lactose *n* a sugar present in milk.
lacuna *n* (*pl* **lacunas, lacunae**) a gap, esp a missing portion in a text.—**lacunary** *adj*.
lacustrine *adj* pertaining to lakes; growing by lakesides.
lacy *adj* (**lacier, laciest**) resembling lace.—**lacily** *adv*.—**laciness** *n*.
lad *n* a boy; a young man; a fellow, chap.
ladder *n* a portable metal or wooden framework with rungs between two vertical supports for climbing up and down; something that resembles a ladder in form or use.
ladder back chair *n* a type of chair with a tall slatted back.
laddie *n* a boy; a young lad.
lade *vt* (**lading, laded,** *pp* **laden** *or* **laded**) (*ship*) to load (with cargo); (*with* **with**) to burden; to spoon up (liquid), eg with a ladle.
laden *adj* loaded with cargo; burdened.
la-di-da, la-de-da *adj* (*inf*) affected; foppish. * *n* an affected or foppish person.
ladies' room *n* a public lavatory for women.
lading *n* the act of loading; that which is loaded; cargo; freight.
ladle *n* a long-handled, cup-like spoon for scooping liquids; a device like a ladle in shape or use. * (*with* **out**) (*inf*) to give (money, etc) generously.—**ladleful** *n*.
lady *n* (*pl* **ladies**) a polite term for any woman; (*with cap*) a title of honour given to various ranks of women in the British peerage.
Lady Day *n* 25 March, the feast of the Annunciation.
ladybug, ladybird *n* a small, usu brightly coloured beetle.
lady-in-waiting *n* (*pl* **ladies-in-waiting**) a female member of a royal household, who attends upon a queen or princess.
lady-killer *n* (*inf*) a man who is or thinks he is particularly attractive to women.
ladylike *adj* like or suitable for a lady; refined, polite.
ladylove *n* (*arch*) a sweetheart.
ladyship *n* a title used in speaking to or of a woman with the rank of Lady.
lady-slipper *n* an orchid with flowers resembling slippers.
lady's-smock *n* a flowering plant, also known as the cuckooflower.
laevorotation *see* **levorotation.**
laevulose *see* **levulose.**
lag[1] *vi* (**lagging, lagged**) to fall behind, hang back; to fail to keep pace in movement or development; to weaken in strength or intensity. * *n* a falling behind; a delay.
lag[2] *vt* (**lagging, lagged**) to insulate (pipes, etc) with lagging.
lag[3] *n* (*sl*) a convict; a term of imprisonment.
lagan *n* goods, or wreckage, lying on the seabed.—*also* **ligan.**
lager[1] *n* a light beer that has been aged for a certain period.
lager[2] *see* **laager.**
laggard *n* a person who lags behind; a loiterer. * *adj* backward, slow.—**laggardly** *adv*.
lagging *n* insulating material used to lag pipes, boilers, etc.
lagoon *n* a shallow lake or pond, esp one connected with a larger body of water; the water enclosed by a circular coral reef.
laic, laical *adj* non-clerical, lay; secular.
laicize *vt* to make non-clerical or lay; to open to lay persons.—**laicization** *n*.
laid *see* **lay**[2].
laid-back *adj* relaxed, easy-going.
laid paper *n* paper impressed with fine lines from the wires on which the pulp is laid.
lain *see* **lie**[2].
lair *n* the dwelling or resting place of a wild animal; (*inf*) a secluded place, a retreat.
laird *n* (*Scot*) a landowner.
laissez-faire, laisser-faire *n* the policy of non-interference with individual freedom, esp in economic affairs.—**laissez-faireism, laisser-faireism** *n*.
laity *n* laymen, as opposed to clergymen.
lake[1] *n* a large inland body of water.
lake[2] *n* a purplish-red pigment, originally made from lac.
Lake Wobegon effect *n* a propensity to attribute quality to the average, from the novel by Garrison Keillor.
lakh *n* (*India*) 100,000, esp rupees.
lam[1] *vt* (**lamming, lammed**) (*inf*) to beat or thrash.
lam[2] *n* a sudden flight, esp to evade capture by the authorities.
lama *n* a monk or priest of Lamaism.
Lamaism *n* a form of Buddhism in Tibet and Mongolia.—**lamaist** *n*.—**Lamaistic** *adj*.
lamasery *n* (*pl* **lamaseries**) a monastery of lamas.
lamb *n* a young sheep; its flesh as food; (*inf*) an innocent or gentle person. * *vi* to give birth to a lamb; to tend (ewes) at lambing time.
lambada *n* (the music for) a lively erotic dance of Brazilian origin, in which couples dance with their stomachs touching.
lambast, lambaste *vt* (*inf*) to beat or censure severely.
lambda *n* the Greek letter L.
lambdoid *adj* shaped like lambda.
lambent *adj* (*flame*) playing lightly over a surface; marked by radiance; brilliant.—**lambency** *n*.
lambert *n* a measure of brightness, the brightness of a surface radiating one lumen per square centimetre.
lambkin *n* a little lamb.
lambrequin *n* a short hanging over a door, mantelpiece, etc.
lambrusco *n* a sparkling red Italian wine.
lambskin *n* the skin of a lamb with the wool on or as leather, for making clothes, etc.
lame *adj* disabled or crippled, esp in the feet or legs; stiff and painful; weak, ineffectual. * *vt* to make lame.—**lamely** *adv*.—**lameness** *n*.
lamé *n* a fabric interwoven with metallic threads.
lame duck *n* a weak, ineffectual person; an elected official serving between the end of his or her term and the inauguration of a successor.
lamella (*pl* **lamellae, lamellas**) a thin plate, scale, or film.—**lamellar, lamellate, lamellose** *adj*.
lamelliform *adj* lamella-shaped.
lament *vti* to feel or express deep sorrow (for); to mourn. * *n* a lamenting; an elegy, dirge, etc mourning some loss or death.—**lamenter** *n*.
lamentable *adj* distressing, deplorable.—**lamentably** *adv*.
lamentation *n* a lamenting; a lament, expression of grief.
lamented *adj* grieved for.
lamia *n* (*pl* **lamias, lamiae**) (*myth*) a monster, half snake, half woman.
lamina *n* (*pl* **laminae, laminas**) a thin plate, scale or layer; the expanded part of a foliage leaf.—**laminose** *adj*.
laminate *vt* to cover with one or more thin layers; to make by building up in layers. * *n* a product made by laminating. * *adj* laminated.—**laminator** *n*.
laminated *adj* built in thin sheets or layers; covered by a thin film of plastic, etc.
lamination *n* divisibility, or division, into thin plates.
Lammas *n* (*RC Church*) a feast held on August 1; (*formerly*) a harvest festival celebrated on August 1.
lammergeier, lammergeyer *n* a vulture found in southern Europe, Africa and Asia, the bearded vulture.
lamp *n* any device producing light, either by electricity, gas, or by burning oil, etc; a holder or base for such a device; any device for producing therapeutic rays.

lampas *n* a disease of horses, which causes swelling in the roof of the mouth; a type of flowered silk.
lampblack *n* fine charcoal or soot.
lampion *n* a small lamp.
lamplighter *n* (*formerly*) someone who lit street lamps.
lampoon *n* a piece of satirical writing attacking someone. * *vt* to ridicule maliciously in a lampoon.—**lampooner** *n*.—**lampoonery** *n*.
lamppost *n* a post supporting a street lamp.
lamprey *n* (*pl* **lamprey, lampreys**) an animal resembling an eel but having a jawless, round sucking mouth.
LAN (*acronym*) local area network: a number of computers in close proximity linked together in order to transfer information and share peripherals such as printers.
lanate *adj* woolly.
lance *n* a long wooden spear with a sharp iron or steel head. * *vt* to pierce (as if) with a lance; to open a boil, etc with a lancet.
lance corporal *n* a noncommissioned officer of the lowest rank in the British army.
lanceolate *adj* (*bot*) tapering to a point at either end.
lancer *n* a cavalry soldier formerly armed with a lance; (*pl*) a kind of dance, a quadrille.
lancet *n* a small, usu two-edged, pointed surgical knife.
lancet arch *n* a sharply pointed arch.
lanceted *adj* (*archit*) with one or more lancet arches or windows.
lancet window *n* a tall narrow window with a lancet arch.
lancewood *n* a tough, elastic wood.
land *n* the solid part of the earth's surface; ground, soil; a country and its people; property in land. * *vt* to set (an aircraft) down on land or water; to put on shore from a ship; to bring to a particular place; to catch (a fish); to get or secure (a job, prize, etc); to deliver (a blow). * *vi* to go ashore from a ship; to come to port; to arrive at a specified place; to come to rest.
landamman *n* (*Switzerland*) the chief official in some cantons.
landau *n* a four-wheeled horse-drawn carriage with a roof that folds down.
landaulet, landaulette *n* a small landau.
landed *adj* consisting of land; owning land.
landfall *n* a sighting of land, esp from a ship at sea; the land sighted.
landfill *n* a large pit in which refuse is buried between layers of soil.—*also adj*.
landgrave *n* (*formerly*) a title given to certain counts in Germany.
landgravine *n* the wife of a landgrave; the title given to a woman landgrave.
landing *n* the act of coming to shore or to the ground; the place where persons or goods are loaded or unloaded from a ship; a platform at the end of a flight of stairs.
landing craft *n* a small military vessel designed for landing troops and equipment ashore.
landing gear *n* the undercarriage of an aircraft.
landing stage *n* a platform for landing goods or people from a ship.
landing strip *n* an airstrip.
landlady *n* (*pl* **landladies**) a woman who owns and rents property; a woman who owns and runs a boarding house, pub, etc.
landlocked *adj* surrounded by land.
landlord *n* a man who owns and rents property; a man who owns and runs a boarding house, pub, etc.
landlubber *n* a person who has had little experience of the sea.
landmark *n* any prominent feature of the landscape distinguishing a locality; an important event or turning point.
landmass *n* a large expanse of land.
land mine *n* an explosive charge shallowly buried in the ground, usu detonated by stepping or driving on it.
landowner *n* a person who owns land.—**landowning** *adj, n*.
landscape *n* an expanse of natural scenery seen in one view; a picture of natural, inland scenery. * *vt* to make (a plot of ground) more attractive, as by adding lawns, bushes, trees, etc.
landscape gardening *n* the decorative design and planting of gardens and grounds in imitation of natural scenery.—**landscape gardener** *n*.
landscapist *n* an artist who paints landscapes.
landslide *n* the sliding of a mass of soil or rocks down a slope; an overwhelming victory, esp in an election.
landsman *n* (*pl* **landsmen**) a person who resides and works on land, as opposed to the sea.
Landtag *n* (*Germany, Austria*) the parliament of an individual state.
landward *adv, adj* towards the land.—**landwards** *adv*.
lane *n* a narrow road, path, etc; a path or strip specifically designated for ships, aircraft, cars, etc; one of the narrow strips dividing a running track, swimming pool, etc for athletes and swimmers; one of the narrow passages along which balls are bowled in a bowling alley.
langlauf *n* cross-country skiing.—**langläufer** *n*.
langouste *n* the spiny lobster.
langoustine *n* a large prawn or small lobster.
langsyne *adv* (*Scot*) long ago.
language *n* human speech or the written symbols for speech; any means of communicating; a special set of symbols used for programming a computer; the speech of a particular nation, etc; the particular style of verbal expression characteristic of a person, group, profession, etc.
langue d'oc *n* a form of medieval French spoken in the South of France.
languid *adj* lacking energy or vitality; apathetic; drooping, sluggish.—**languidly** *adv*.—**languidness** *n*.
languish *vi* to lose strength and vitality; to pine; to suffer neglect or hardship; to assume a pleading or melancholic expression.—**languisher** *n*.—**languishment** *n*.
languor *n* physical or mental fatigue or apathy; dreaminess; oppressive stillness.—**languorous** *adj*.
langur *n* a long-tailed monkey, found in South Asia.
laniard *n see* **lanyard.**
laniary *n* (*pl* **laniaries**) a canine tooth.
laniferous, lanigerous *adj* wool-bearing.
lank *adj* tall and thin; long and limp.—**lankly** *adv*.—**lankness** *n*.
lanky *adj* (**lankier, lankiest**) lean, tall, and ungainly.—**lankily** *adv*.—**lankiness** *n*.
lanner *n* a falcon found in Mediterranean countries, North Africa and South Asia; the female of this species.
lanneret *n* the male lanner falcon.
lanolin, lanoline *n* wool grease used in cosmetics, ointments, etc.
lantern *n* a portable transparent case for holding a light; a structure with windows on top of a door or roof to provide light and ventilation; the light-chamber of a lighthouse.
lantern jaw *n* a long thin jaw.
lanthanide *n* any of a series of related chemical elements with atomic numbers from 57 (lanthanum) to 71 (lutetium).
lanthanum *n* a metallic element.
lanyard *n* a rope used for fastening things on board a ship; a cord worn round the neck to hold a knife, whistle, etc.
laodicean *adj* indifferent, esp towards religion.
lap[1] *vti* (**lapping, lapped**) to take in (liquid) with the tongue; (*waves*) to flow gently with a splashing sound.
lap[2] *n* the flat area from waist to knees formed by a person sitting; the part of the clothing covering this.
lap[3] *n* an overlapping; a part that overlaps; one complete circuit of a race track. * *vb* (**lapping, lapped**) *vt* to fold (over or on); to wrap. * *vi* to overlap; to extend over something in space or time.
laparotomy *n* (*pl* **laparotomies**) (*med*) the operation of cutting the abdominal wall.
lapdog *n* a dog small and docile enough to be held on the lap.
lapel *n* a part of a suit, coat, jacket, etc folded back and continuous with the collar.—**lapelled** *adj*.
lapidary *adj* of or relating to stones; inscribed on stone; concise, like an inscription. * *n* (*pl* **lapidaries**) a cutter or engraver of gems.—**lapidarian** *adj*.

lapidate *vt* to stone (to death).—**lapidation** *n*.
lapidify *vti* (**lapidifying, lapidified**) to turn to stone.
lapis lazuli *n* an azure, opaque, semi-precious stone.
lap of honour *n* a ceremonial circuit of the field by a winning person or team.
lappet *n* a small, loose flap.
lapse *n* a small error; a decline or drop to a lower condition, degree, or state; a moral decline; a period of time elapsed; the termination of a legal right or privilege through disuse. * *vi* to depart from the usual or accepted standard, esp in morals; to pass out of existence or use; to become void or discontinued; (*time*) to slip away.—**lapsable, lapsible** *adj*.—**lapser** *n*.
lapsus *n* (*pl* **lapsus**) a slip or error.
laptop *n* a small portable computer that can comfortably be used on the lap.
lapwing *n* a crested plover.
larboard *n* (*naut*) (*formerly*) the port or left side of a ship.
larceny *n* (*pl* **larcenies**) the theft of someone else's property.—**larcenist, larcener** *n*.—**larcenous** *adj*.
larch *n* a cone-bearing tree of the pine family.
lard *n* melted and clarified pig fat. * *vt* to insert strips of bacon or pork fat (in meat) before cooking; to embellish.
larder *n* a room or cupboard where food is stored.
lares *npl* (*Roman myth*) the household gods.
large *adj* great in size, amount, or number; bulky; big; spacious; bigger than others of its kind; operating on a big scale.—**largeness** *n*.
large intestine *n* the section of the digestive system comprising the caecum, colon and rectum.
largely *adv* much, in great amounts; mainly, for the most part.
largen *vt* to make larger, to enlarge.
large-scale *adj* drawn on a big scale to reveal much detail; extensive.
largess, largesse *n* the generous distribution of money, gifts, favours, etc; generosity.
larghetto *adv* (*mus*) slowly. * *n* (*pl* **larghettos**) a passage of music played in this way.
largish *adj* quite large.
largo *adv* (*mus*) slow and dignified. * *n* (*pl* **largos**) a passage of music played in this way.
lariat *n* a rope for tethering grazing horses; a lasso.
lark[1] *n* any of a family of songbirds.
lark[2] *n* a playful or amusing adventure; a harmless prank. * *vi* (*usu with* **about**) to have fun, frolic.—**larky** *adj*.
larkspur *n* an annual delphinium.
larrigan *n* a knee-high leather boot worn by trappers.
larrikin *n* (*Austral sl*) a hooligan.
larrup *vt* (*dial*) to thrash, flog.
larva *n* (*pl* **larvae**) the immature form of many animals after emerging from an egg before transformation into the adult state, eg a caterpillar.—**larval** *adj*.
laryngeal *adj* pertaining to, or situated near, the larynx.
laryngitis *n* inflammation of the larynx.—**laryngitic** *adj*.
laryngo-, laryng- *prefix* larynx.
laryngology *n* the medical study of the larynx.—**laryngologist** *n*.
laryngoscope *n* a medical instrument for examining the larynx.—**laryngoscopy** *n*.
laryngotomy *n* (*pl* **laryngotomies**) (*med*) the operation of cutting into the larynx.
larynx *n* (*pl* **larynxes, larynges**) the structure at the upper end of the windpipe, containing the vocal cords.
lasagna, lasagne *n* pasta formed in thin wide strips; a dish of lasagne baked in layers with cheese, minced meat and tomato sauce.
lascar *n* an East Indian sailor.—*also* **lashkar**.
lascivious *adj* lecherous, lustful; arousing sexual desire.—**lasciviously** *adv*.—**lasciviousness** *n*.
lase *vi* (*gem, gas*) able to act as a laser.
laser *n* a device that produces an intense monochromatic beam of coherent light or other electromagnetic radiation.
laser printer *n* a computer printer that uses a laser beam and photoconductive drum to produce high quality text output.
lasertripsy *n* a medical procedure for removing kidney stones, etc, by the use of laser beams.
lash *vt* to strike forcefully (as if) with a lash; to fasten or secure with a cord, etc; to attack with criticism or ridicule. * *vi* to move quickly and violently; (*rain, waves, etc*) to beat violently against; (*with* **out**) to attack suddenly either physically or verbally; (*inf*) to spend extravagantly (on). * *n* the flexible part of a whip; an eyelash; a stroke (as if) with a whip.—**lasher** *n*.
lashkar *see* **lascar**.
lass, lassie *n* a young woman or girl.
Lassa fever *n* an infectious viral disease of Africa.
lassitude *n* weariness.
lasso *n* (*pl* **lassos, lassoes**) a long rope or leather thong with a running noose for catching horses, cattle, etc. * *vt* (**lassoes** *or* **lassos, lassoing, lassoed**) to catch (as if) with a lasso.—**lassoer** *n*.
last[1] *n* a shoemaker's model of the foot on which boots and shoes are made or repaired. * *vt* to shape with a last.
last[2] *vi* to remain in existence, use, etc; to endure. * *vt* to continue during; to be enough for.
last[3] *adj* being or coming after all the others in time or place; only remaining; the most recent; least likely; conclusive. * *adv* after all the others; most recently; finally. * *n* the one coming last.
last-ditch *adj* being a final effort to avoid disaster.
last hurrah *n* a final appearance; a swan song.
lasting *adj* enduring.—**lastingly** *adv*.
lastly *adv* at the end, in the last place, finally.
last-minute *adj* at the last possible time when something can be done.
last rites *npl* the sacraments prescribed for a person near death.
last straw *n* a final addition to one's burdens that results in collapse or defeat.
last word *n* the final remark in an argument; a definitive statement; the latest fashion.
Lat. *abbr* = Latin.
lat. *abbr* = latitude.
latch *n* a fastening for a door, gate, or window, esp a bar, etc that fits into a notch. * *vti* to fasten with a latch.
latchet *n* (*arch*) a strap or lace for fastening a shoe.
latchkey *n* the key of an outer door.
late *adj, adv* after the usual or expected time; at an advanced stage or age; near the end; far on in the day or evening; just prior to the present; deceased; not long past; until lately; out of office.—**lateness** *n*.
latecomer *n* a person or thing that arrives late.
lateen *n* a triangular sail used on boats in the Mediterranean.—**lateen-rigged** *adj*.
lately *adv* recently, in recent times.
latent *adj* existing but not yet visible or developed.—**latency** *n*.—**latently** *adv*.
later *adv* subsequently; afterwards.—*also compar of* **late**.
lateral *adj* of, at, from, towards the side.—**laterally** *adv*.
lateral thinking *n* a solving of problems by employing unorthodox thought processes.
latest *adj* most recent or fashionable. * *n* (*inf*: *with* **the**) the most up-to-date fashion, news, etc.—*also superl of* **late**.
latex *n* (*pl* **latexes, latices**) the milky juice produced by certain plants, used in the manufacture of rubber.
lath *n* (*pl* **laths**) a thin narrow strip of wood used in constructing a framework for plaster, etc.
lathe *n* a machine that rotates wood, metal, etc for shaping.
lather *n* a foam made by soap or detergent mixed with water; frothy sweat; a state of excitement or agitation. * *vti* to cover with or form lather.—**lathery** *adj*.

lathi *n* a long, heavy stick, carried by policemen in India.

Latin *adj* of ancient Rome, its people, their language, etc; denoting or of the languages derived from Latin (Italian, Spanish, etc), the peoples who speak them, their countries, etc. * *n* a native or inhabitant of ancient Rome; the language of ancient Rome; a person, as a Spaniard or Italian, whose language is derived from Latin.

Latinate *adj* of, resembling or derived from Latin.

Latinist *n* a Latin scholar.

Latinity *n* Latin style.

Latinize *vt* to translate into Latin; to give Latin characteristics to.—**Latinization** *n*.—**Latinizer** *n*.

Latino *n* a person of Latin American origin living in the US.

latish *adj* somewhat late.

latitude *n* the distance from north or south of the equator, measured in degrees; a region with reference to this distance; extent; scope; freedom from restrictions on actions or opinions.—**latitudinal** *adj*.—**latitudinally** *adv*.

latitudinarian *adj* claiming or showing freedom of thought, esp regarding religion. * *n* a person with such an outlook.—**latitudinarianism** *n*.

latria *n* (*RC Church*) supreme worship, offered to God alone.

latrine *n* a lavatory, as in a military camp.

-latry *n suffix* worship, esp excessively.

latter *adj* later; more recent; nearer the end; being the last mentioned of two.

latter-day *adj* present-day; modern.

latterly *adv* recently.

lattice *n* a network of crossed laths or bars.—**latticed** *adj*.

laud *vt* to praise; to extol.

laudable *adj* praiseworthy.—**laudability** *n*.—**laudably** *adv*.

laudanum *n* (*formerly*) any of various opium preparations; a solution of opium in alcohol.

laudation *n* praise.

laudatory, laudative *adj* expressing praise.

laugh *vi* to emit explosive inarticulate vocal sounds expressive of amusement, joy or derision. * *vt* to utter or express with laughter; (*with* **off**) to dismiss as of little importance, make a joke of. * *n* the act or sound of laughing; (*inf*) an amusing person or thing.—**laugher** *n*.—**laughing** *adj, n*.—**laughingly** *adv*.

laughable *adj* causing laughter; ridiculous.—**laughably** *adv*.

laughing gas *n* nitrous oxide.

laughing stock *n* an object of ridicule.

laughter *n* the act or sound of laughing.

launch[1] *vt* to throw, hurl or propel forward; to cause (a vessel) to slide into the water; (*rocket, missile*) to set off; to put into action; to put a new product onto the market. * *vi* to involve oneself enthusiastically. * *n* the act or occasion of launching.

launch[2] *n* an open, or partly enclosed, motor boat.

launch pad, launching pad *n* a platform from which a spacecraft is launched.

launder *vti* to wash and iron clothes. * *vt* to legitimize (money) obtained from criminal activity by passing it through foreign banks, or investing in legitimate businesses, etc.—**launderer** *n*.

launderette *n* an establishment equipped with coin-operated washing machines and driers for public use.

laundress *n* a woman who earns her living by doing laundry.

Laundromat *n* (*trademark*) a launderette.

laundry *n* (*pl* **laundries**) a place where clothes are washed and ironed; clothes sent to be washed and ironed.

laureate *adj* crowned with laurel leaves as a mark of honour. * *n* the recipient of an honour or distinction; a poet laureate.—**laureateship** *n*.

laurel *n* an evergreen shrub with large, glossy leaves; the leaves used by the ancient Greeks as a symbol of achievement.

lava *n* molten rock flowing from a volcano; the solid substance formed as this cools.

lavabo *n* (*pl* **lavaboes, lavabos**) (*RC Church*) the ritual washing of the celebrant's hands at the Eucharist; a washbasin.

lavation *n* the act of washing.

lavatory *n* (*pl* **lavatories**) a sanitary device for the disposal or faeces and urine; a room equipped with this.—*also* **bathroom, toilet.**

lavender *n* the fragrant flowers of a perennial shrub dried and used in sachets; a pale purple.

laver *n* an edible seaweed.

lavish *vt* to give or spend freely. * *adj* abundant, profuse; generous; extravagant.—**lavishly** *adv*.—**lavishness** *n*.

law *n* all the rules of conduct in an organized community as upheld by authority; any one of such rules; obedience to such rules; the study of such rules, jurisprudence; the seeking of justice in courts under such rules; the profession of lawyers, judges, etc; (*inf*) the police; a sequence of events occurring with unvarying uniformity under the same conditions; any rule expected to be observed.

law-abiding *adj* obeying the law.

lawbreaker *n* a person who violates the law.—**lawbreaking** *adj, n*.

lawful *adj* in conformity with the law; recognized by law.—**lawfully** *adv*.—**lawfulness** *n*.

lawgiver *n* a maker of a code of laws.

lawless *adj* not regulated by law; not in conformity with law, illegal.—**lawlessly** *adv*.—**lawlessness** *n*.

lawmaker *n* a maker of laws, a legislator.

lawn[1] *n* a fine sheer cloth of linen or cotton.—**lawny** *adj*.

lawn[2] *n* land covered with closely cut grass, esp around a house.

lawn darts *n* an outdoor game of darts using a lawn as a board, at which are fired foot-long metal darts.

lawn mower *n* a hand-propelled or power-driven machine to cut lawn grass.

lawn tennis *n* tennis played on a grass court.

lawrencium *n* a radioactive metallic element.

lawsuit *n* a suit between private parties in a law court.

lawyer *n* a person whose profession is advising others in matters of law or representing them in a court of law.

lax *adj* slack, loose; not tight; not strict or exact.—**laxly** *adv*.—**laxness** *n*.

laxative *n* a substance that promotes emptying of the bowels.—*also adj*.

laxity *n* the state or quality of being lax, laxness.

lay[1] *see* **lie**[2].

lay[2] *vt* (**laying, laid**) to put down; to allay or suppress; to place in a resting position; to place or set; to place in a correct position; to produce (an egg); (*sl*) to have sexual intercourse with; to devise; to present or assert; to stake a bet; (*with* **down**) to put down; to surrender, relinquish; to begin to build; to establish (guidelines, rules, etc); to store, esp wine; to record tracks in a music studio; (*with* **in**) to store, to stockpile; (*with* **off**) to suspend from work temporarily or permanently; (*with* **on**) to supply, provide; to install (electricity, etc); (*with* **out**) to plan in detail; to arrange for display; to prepare (a corpse) for viewing; (*inf*) to spend money, esp lavishly; (*with* **up**) to store for future use; to disable or confine through illness. * *vi* (*inf*) to leave (a person or thing) alone; (*with* **into**) to attack physically or verbally. * *n* a way or position in which something is situated; (*sl*) an act of sexual intercourse; a sexual partner.

lay[3] *n* a simple narrative poem, esp as intended to be sung; a ballad.

lay[4] *adj* of or pertaining to those who are not members of the clergy; not belonging to a profession.

layabout *n* a loafer, lazy person.

lay-by *n* (*Austral*) a deposit payment system that reserves an article for a purchaser until full settlement; (*Brit*) a pull-in place for motorists to stop at the side of a main road.—**lay by** *vt* to set aside or save for future needs.

layer *n* a single thickness, fold, etc; the runner of a plant fastened down to take root; a hen that lays. * *vti* to separate into layers; to form by superimposing layers; to (cause to) take root by propagating a plant shoot still attached to its parent.

layette *n* a complete set of clothes, equipment and accessories for a newborn baby

lay figure *n* a jointed model of the human body used by artists for hanging drapery on; a person regarded as a puppet or nonentity.

laying *n* a sitting of eggs; the first coat of plaster.

layman *n* (*pl* **laymen**) a person who is not a member of the clergy; a non-specialist, someone who does not possess professional knowledge.—**laywoman** *nf* (*pl* **laywomen**).

layoff *n* a period of involuntary unemployment.

layout *n* the manner in which anything is laid out, esp arrangement of text and pictures on the pages of a newspaper or magazine, etc; the thing laid out.

layover *n* (*US*) a stop on a journey.

lazar *n* (*arch*) a leper.

lazaretto, lazaret, lazarette *n* (*pl* **lazarettos, lazarets, lazarettes**) (*naut*) a part of a ship's hold; (*formerly*) a hospital for people suffering from infectious diseases.

laze *vti* to idle or loaf.

lazulite *n* an azure blue mineral.

lazy *adj* (**lazier, laziest**) disinclined to work or exertion; encouraging or causing indolence; sluggishly moving.—**lazily** *adv*.—**laziness** *n*.

lazybones *n* a lazy person.

lb *abbr* = pound(s) weight.

lbw *abbr* = (*cricket*) leg before wicket.

LCD *abbr* = liquid-crystal display; (*also without cap*) lowest common denominator.

lea[1] *n* (*poet*) a meadow, grassland.

lea[2] *n* a measure of yarn, varying from 80 yards (approx 73 metres) for wool to 300 yards (approx 274 metres) for linen.

leach *vt* to wash (soil, ore, etc) with a filtering liquid; to extract (a soluble substance) from some material. * *vi* to lose soluble matter through a filtering liquid.—**leacher** *n*.

lead[1] *vb* (**leading, led**) *vt* to show the way, esp by going first; to direct or guide on a course; to direct by influence; to be head of (an expedition, orchestra, etc); to be ahead of in a contest; to live, spend (one's life); (*with* **on**) to lure or entice, esp into mischief. * *vi* to show the way, as by going first; (*with* **to**) to tend in a certain direction; to be or go first. * *n* the role of a leader; first place; the amount or distance ahead; anything that leads, as a clue; the leading role in a play, etc; the right of playing first in cards or the card played.

lead[2] *n* a heavy, soft, bluish-grey, metallic element; a weight for sounding depths at sea, etc; bullets; a stick of graphite, used in pencils; (*print*) a thin strip of metal used to space lines of type. * *adj* of or containing lead. * *vt* (**leading, leaded**) to cover, weight, or space out with lead.

leaden *adj* made of lead; very heavy; dull grey; gloomy.—**leadenly** *adv*.

leader *n* the person who goes first; the principle first violin-player in an orchestra; the director of an orchestra; the inspiration or head of a movement, such as a political party; a person whose example is followed; the leading editorial in a newspaper; the leading article.

leadership *n* the act of leading; the ability to be a leader; the leaders of an organization or movement collectively.

lead glass *n* flint glass.

lead-in *n* introductory material; the connection between a radio transmitter or receiver with an aerial or transmission cable.

leading[1] *adj* capable of guiding or influencing; principal; in first position.

leading[2] *n* a covering of lead; (*print*) the body of a type, larger than the size, giving space.

leading article *n* an article in a newspaper stating editorial opinion on a given subject; the leader.

leading light *n* the most important member of a group or organization.

leading question *n* a question worded so as to suggest the desired answer.

leadsman *n* (*pl* **leadsmen**) a sailor who heaves the lead.

lead time *n* the period between the design of a product and its manufacture.

leaf *n* (*pl* **leaves**) any of the flat, thin (usu green) parts growing from the stem of a plant; a sheet of paper; a very thin sheet of metal; a hinged or removable part of a table top. * *vi* to bear leaves; (*with* **through**) to turn the pages of.

leafage *n* foliage.

leafless *adj* without leaves.

leaflet *n* a small or young leaf; a sheet of printed information (often folded), esp advertising matter distributed free. * *vi* to distribute leaflets (to).

leaf mold *n* compost or soil composed of decaying leaves and other vegetable matter; any of various fungal diseases of plants.

leafy *adj* (**leafier, leafiest**) having many or broad leaves; resembling leaves.—**leafiness** *n*.

league[1] *n* an association of nations, groups, etc for promoting common interests; an association of sports clubs that organizes matches between members; any class or category. * *vti* (**leaguing, leagued**) to form into a league.

league[2] *n* (*formerly*) a varying measure of distance, averaging about three miles (5 km).

leak *n* a crack or hole through which liquid or gas may accidentally pass; the liquid or gas passing through such an opening; confidential information made public deliberately or accidentally. * *vi* to (let) escape though an opening; to disclose information surreptitiously.—**leaker** *n*.

leakage *n* the act of leaking; that which enters or escapes by leaking.

leaky *adj* (**leakier, leakiest**) leaking or likely to leak.—**leakiness** *n*.

leal *adj* (*Scot*) loyal.

lean[1] *adj* thin, with little flesh or fat; spare; meagre. * *n* meat with little or no fat.—**leanness** *n*.

lean[2] *vb* (**leaning, leaned** *or* **leant**) *vi* to bend or slant from an upright position; to rest supported (on or against); to rely or depend for help (on). * *vt* to cause to lean.

leaning *n* inclination, tendency.

leant *see* **lean**[1].

lean-to *n* (*pl* **lean-tos**) a building whose rafters rest on another building.

leap *vb* (**leaping, leaped** *or* **leapt**) *vi* to jump; (*with* **at**) to accept something offered eagerly. * *vt* to pass over by a jump; to cause to leap. * *n* an act of leaping; bound; space passed by leaping; an abrupt transition.—**leaper** *n*.

leapfrog *n* a game in which one player vaults over another's bent back. * *vi* (**leapfrogging, leapfrogged**) to vault in this manner; to advance in alternate jumps.

leap year *n* a year with an extra day (29 February) occurring every fourth year.

learn *vti* (**learning, learned** *or* **learnt**) to gain knowledge of or skill in; to memorize; to become aware of, realize.—**learner** *n*.

learned *adj* having learning; erudite; acquired by study, experience, etc.—**learnedly** *adv*.

learning *n* a gaining of knowledge; the acquiring of knowledge or skill through study.

lease *n* a contract by which an owner lets land, property, etc to another person for a specified period. * *vt* to grant by or hold under lease.—**leaseable** *adj*.—**leaser** *n*.

lease-back *n* the process of selling an asset, esp a building, and then renting it.

leasehold *n* the act of holding by lease; the land, buildings, etc held by lease.—**leaseholder** *n*.

leash *n* a cord, strap, etc by which a dog or animal is held in check. * *vt* to hold or restrain on a leash.

least *adj* smallest in size, degree, etc; slightest. * *adv* to the smallest degree. * *n* the smallest in amount.

leastways *adv* at least.

leather *n* material made from the skin of an animal prepared by removing the hair and tanning; something made of leather. * *vt* to cover with leather; to thrash.

leatherback *n* the largest existing sea turtle, having a flexible shell.

Leatherette *n* (*trademark*) an imitation leather.

leatherjacket *n* a tropical fish with a leathery skin; the larva of the cranefly.

leathern *adj* (*arch*) made of, or resembling, leather.
leatherneck *n* (*sl*) a member of the US Marine Corps.
leathery *adj* like leather; tough and flexible.
leave[1] *n* permission to do something; official authorization to be absent; the period covered by this.
leave[2] *vb* **(leaving, left)** *vt* to depart from; to cause or allow to remain in a specified state; to cause to remain behind; to refrain from consuming or dealing with; to have remaining at death, to bequeath; to have as a remainder; to allow to stay or or continue doing without interference; to entrust or commit to another; to abandon. * *vi* to depart; (*with* **off**) to stop, desist.—**leaver** *n*.
leaved *adj* having leaves.
leaven *n* a substance to make dough rise, esp yeast; something that changes or enlivens. * *vt* to raise with leaven; to modify, to enliven.—**leavening** *n*.
leaves *see* **leaf**.
leave-taking *n* a departure, farewell.
leavings *npl* leftovers; remnants; refuse.
leben *n* a food made from soured milk, eaten in North Africa and the Levant.
Lebensraum *n* a piece of territory claimed by another country on the basis that it is needed to accommodate the country's expanding population.
lech *vt* (*sl*) to lust after.
lecher *n* a lecherous man.
lecherous *adj* characterized by or encouraging lechery.
lechery *n* (*pl* **lecheries**) unrestrained sexuality; debauchery.
lecithin *n* any of a group of fatty compounds found in plant and animal tissues, used as an emulsifier and antioxidant.
lectern *n* a reading stand in a church; any similar reading support.
lection *n* a reading from scripture for a particular day; a variant reading of a text.
lectionary *n* (*pl* **lectionaries**) a book listing lessons from scripture to be read at religious services on particular days.
lector *n* a lecturer or reader at a university.
lecture *n* an informative talk to a class, etc; a lengthy reprimand. * *vti* to give a lecture (to); to reprimand.—**lecturer** *n*.
lectureship *n* the position of lecturer.
LED *abbr* = light-emitting diode.
led *see* **lead**[1].
lederhosen *npl* leather shorts with braces worn by men in Austria and Bavaria.
ledge *n* a narrow horizontal surface resembling a shelf projecting from a wall, rock face, etc; an underwater ridge of rocks; a rock layer containing ore.—**ledgy**, *adj*.
ledger *n* a book in which a record of debits, credits, etc is kept.
ledger line *n* a short line added above or below a musical staff to extend its range.—*also* **leger line**.
lee *n* a shelter; the side or part away from the wind.
leech *n* a blood-sucking worm; a person who clings to or exploits another.
leek *n* a vegetable that resembles a greatly elongated green onion.
leer *n* a sly, oblique or lascivious look. * *vi* to look with a leer.—**leeringly** *adv*.
leery *adj* **(leerier, leeriest)** (*with* **of**) suspicious, wary.
lees *npl* sediment in the bottom of a wine bottle, etc.
leeward *adj*, *n* (*naut*) (in) the quarter towards which the wind blows.
leeway *n* the distance a ship or aircraft has strayed sideways of its course; freedom of action as regards expenditure of time, money, etc.
left[1] *see* **leave**[2].
left[2] *adj* of or on the side that is towards the west when one faces north; worn on the left hand, foot, etc. * *n* the left side; (*often cap*) of or relating to the left in politics; the left hand; (*boxing*) a blow with the left hand.
left-hand *adj* of or towards the left side of a person or thing; for use by the left hand.
left-handed *adj* using the left hand in preference to the right; done or made for use with the left hand; ambiguous, backhanded. * *adv* with the left hand.—**left-handedly** *adv*.—**left-handedness** *n*.
left-hander *n* a left-handed person; a blow delivered with the left fist.
left-luggage office *n* (*Brit*) a place at an airport, railway station, etc., where luggage may be left for a small charge with an attendant for safekeeping; a checkroom in the US.
leftist *adj* tending to the left in politics. * *n* a person tending towards the political left.—**leftism** *n*.
leftovers *npl* unused portions of something, esp uneaten food.
leftward *adj, adv* on or toward the left.—**leftwards** *adv*.
left-wing *adj* of or relating to the liberal faction of a political party, organization, etc.—**left-winger** *n*.
lefty *n* (*pl* **lefties**) (*inf*) a left-winger; (*US sl*) a left-handed person.
leg *n* one of the limbs on which humans and animals support themselves and walk; the part of a garment covering the leg; anything shaped or used like a leg; a branch or limb of a forked object; a section, as of a trip; any of a series of games or matches in a competition.
legacy *n* (*pl* **legacies**) money, property, etc left to someone in a will; something passed on by an ancestor or remaining from the past.
legal *adj* of or based on law; permitted by law; of or for lawyers.—**legally** *adv*.
legalese *n* legal language as used in documents.
legalism *n* observance of the letter rather than the spirit of the law, red tape.—**legalist** *n*.—**legalistic** *adj*.—**legalistically** *adv*.
legality *n* (*pl* **legalities**) conformity with the law.
legalize *vt* to make lawful.—**legalization** *n*.
legal tender *n* a currency which a creditor is legally bound to accept in payment of a debt.
legate *n* an envoy, esp from the Pope; an official emissary.—**legatine** *adj*.
legatee *n* a person to whom a legacy is bequeathed.
legation *n* a diplomatic minister and staff; the headquarters of a diplomatic minister.—**legationary** *adj*.
legato *adj, adv* (*mus*) smoothly and evenly.
leg before wicket *n* (*cricket*) the dismissal of a batsman for illegally preventing the ball from hitting the wicket by obstructing it with his or her leg.
leg bye *n* (*cricket*) a run made when the ball touches any part of the batsman except the hand.
legend *n* a story handed down from the past; a notable person or the stories of his or her exploits; an inscription on a coin, etc; a caption; an explanation of the symbols used on a map.—**legendry** *n*.
legendary *adj* of, based on, or presented in legends; famous, notorious.
legerdemain *n* trickery, sleight of hand.
leger line *see* **ledger line**.
legged *adj* having legs.
leggings *npl* protective outer coverings for the lower legs; a leg-hugging fashion garment for women.
leggy *adj* **(leggier, leggiest)** having long and shapely legs.—**legginess** *n*.
leghorn *n* fine plaited straw; a hat made of this; (*with cap*) a breed of domestic fowl.
legible *adj* able to be read.—**legibility** *n*.—**legibly** *adv*.
legion *n* an infantry unit of the ancient Roman army; a large body of soldiers; a large number, a multitude.
legionary *adj* of a legion. * *n* (*pl* **legionaries**) a member of a legion; a soldier in a legion of the ancient Roman army.
legionnaire *n* a member of certain military forces or associations.
Legionnaire's disease *n* a serious and sometimes fatal bacterial infection which causes symptoms like pneumonia (first identified after an outbreak at an American Legion convention in 1976).
legislate *vi* to make or pass laws * *vt* to bring about by legislation.
legislation *n* the act or process of law-making; the laws themselves.
legislative *adj* of legislation or a legislature; having the power to make laws.
legislator *n* a member of a legislative body.
legislature *n* the body of people who have the power of making laws.
legist *n* someone versed in the law.

legit *adj* (*sl*) legimitate.
legitimate *adj* lawful; reasonable, justifiable; conforming to accepted rules, standards, etc; (*child*) born of parents married to each other.—**legitimacy** *n*.—**legitimately** *adv*.
legitimatize *vt* to legitimize.
legitimist *n* a supporter of a hereditary title to a monarchy.—**legitimism** *n*.
legitimize *vt* to make or declare legitimate.—**legitimization** *n*.
legume *n* any of a large family of plants having seeds growing in pods, including beans, peas, etc; the pod or seed of such a plant used as food.
leguminous *adj* (*bot*) belonging to a family of flowering and pod-bearing plants.
legwork *n* (*inf*) work that involves a lot of walking.
lei *n* a garland of flowers worn around the neck, given as a token of affection in Hawaii.
leister *n* a pronged spear used for catching salmon.
leisure *n* ease, relaxation, esp freedom from employment or duties. * *adj* free and unoccupied.—**leisured** *adj*.
leisurely *adj* relaxed, without hurry.
leitmotif, leitmotiv *n* a dominant theme.
lemma *n* (*pl* **lemmas, lemmata**) (*logic*) a premise believed to be true.
lemming *n* a small arctic rodent; one of a group wilfully heading on a course for destruction.
lemon *n* (a tree bearing) a small yellow oval fruit with an acid pulp; pale yellow; (*sl*) a person or thing considered disappointing or useless.—**lemony** *adj*.
lemonade *n* a lemon-flavourced drink.
lemon grass *n* a tropical grass with lemon-scented leaves used in cooking and which yields an aromatic oil.
lemur *n* a Madagascan arboreal primate related to the monkey.
lemuroid, lemurine *adj* pertaining to, or resembling, a lemur.
lend *vb* (**lending, lent**) *vt* to give the use of something temporarily in expectation of its return; to provide (money) at interest; to give, impart. * *vi* to make loans.—**lender** *n*.
length *n* the extent of something from end to end, usu the longest dimension; a specified distance or period of time; something of a certain length taken from a larger piece; a long expanse; (*often pl*) the degree of effort put into some action.
lengthen *vti* to make or become longer.
lengthwise, lengthways *adv* in the direction of the length.
lengthy *adj* (**lengthier, lengthiest**) long, esp too long.—**lengthily** *adv*.—**lengthiness** *n*.
lenient *adj* not harsh or severe; merciful.—**leniency, lenience** *n*.—**leniently** *adv*.
lenitive *adj* easing pain.
lenity *n* (*pl* **lenities**) clemency, mercy; leniency.
leno *n* (*pl* **lenos**) a way of weaving fabric; a fabric woven in this way.
lens *n* a curved piece of transparent glass, plastic, etc used in optical instruments to form an image; any device used to focus electromagnetic rays, sound waves, etc; a similar transparent part of the eye that focuses light rays on the retina.
Lent *n* the forty weekdays from Ash Wednesday to Easter, observed by Christians as a period of fasting and penitence.—**Lenten** *adj*.
lent *see* **lend**.
lentamente *adv* (*mus*) slowly.
lenticular *adj* doubly convex.
lentigo *n* (*pl* **lentigines**) a freckle.
lentil *n* any of several leguminous plants with edible seeds; their seed used for food.
lento *adj, adv* (*mus*) slow, slowly. * *n* (*pl* **lentos**) a piece of music played in this way.
Leo *n* (*astrol*) the fifth sign of the zodiac, in astrology operative July 22–August 21; (*astron*) the Lion, a constellation in the northern hemisphere.
Leonid *n* (*pl* **Leonids, Leonides**) (*astron*) one of the meteors that fall in showers during the November of certain years, their chief point being in the constellation of Leo.
leonine *adj* of or like a lion.
leopard *n* a large tawny feline with black spots found in Africa and Asia.—*also* **panther**.—**leopardess** *nf*.
leotard *n* a skintight one-piece garment worn by dancers and others engaged in strenuous exercise.
leper *n* a person with leprosy.
lepidopteran *n* (*pl* **lepidopterans, lepidoptera**) any of a large order of insects, such as moths or butterflies, that as adults have four wings covered with minute, often coloured, scales and that as larvae are caterpillars.—**lepidopterous** *adj*.
lepidopterist *n* an expert on moths and butterflies.
lepidosiren *n* an eel-like mudfish found in South America
leporine *adj* pertaining to hares; hare-like.
leprechaun *n* (*Irish folklore*) a fairy.
leprosy *n* a chronic infectious bacterial disease of the skin, often resulting in disfigurement.—**leprous** *adj*.
lepton *n* (*phys*) any of various elementary particles, such as electrons and muons, that participate in weak interactions with other elementary particles.
lesbian *n* a female homosexual. * *adj* of or characteristic of lesbians.—**lesbianism** *n*.
lèse-majesté, lese-majesty *n* high treason; a crime against royalty.
lesion *n* any change in an organ or tissue caused by injury or disease; an injury.
less *adj* not so much, not so great, etc; fewer; smaller. * *adv* to a smaller extent. * *n* a smaller amount. * *prep* minus.
lessee *n* a person who holds property under a lease.
lessen *vti* to make or become less.
lesser *adj* less in size, quality or importance.
lesson *n* something to be learned or studied; something that has been learned or studied; a unit of learning or teaching; (*pl*) a course of instruction; a selection from the Bible, read as a part of a church service.
lessor *n* a person who lets property on a lease.
lest *conj* in order, or for fear, that not; that.
let[1] *n* a stoppage; (*tennis*) a minor obstruction of the ball that requires a point to be replayed.
let[2] *vb* (**letting, let**) *vt* to allow, permit; to rent; to assign (a contract); to cause to run out, as blood; as an auxiliary in giving suggestions or commands (*let us go*); (*with* **down**) to lower; to deflate; to disappoint; to untie; to lengthen; (*with* **off**) to allow to leave (a ship, etc); to cause to explode or fire; to release, excuse from (work, etc); to deal leniently with, refrain from punishing; to allow (gas, etc) to escape; (*with* **out**) to release; to reveal; to rent out; to make a garment larger; (*with* **up**) to relax; to cease. * *vi* to be rented; (*with* **on**) (*inf*) to pretend; (*inf*) to reveal (a secret, etc); to pretend. * *n* the letting of property or accommodation.
let-down *n* a disappointment.
lethal *adj* deadly.—**lethality** *n*.—**lethally** *adv*.
lethargy *n* (*pl* **lethargies**) an abnormal drowsiness; sluggishness; apathy.—**lethargic** *adj*.—**lethargically** *adv*.
let's = let us.
letter *n* a symbol representing a phonetic value in a written language; a character of the alphabet; a written or printed message; (*pl*) literature; learning; knowledge; literal meaning. * *vt* to mark with letters.
letter bomb *n* an explosive device concealed in an envelope and sent through the post.
letter box *n* a slit in the doorway of a house or building through which letters are delivered; a postbox.
lettered *adj* literate; highly educated; marked with letters.
letterhead *n* a name, address, etc printed as a heading on stationery; stationery printed with a heading.
lettering *n* the act or process of inscribing with letters; letters collectively; a title; an inscription.
letterpress *n* a method of printing; the printed matter of a book, as opposed to the illustrations.

lettuce *n* a plant with succulent leaves used in salads.
letup *n* a relaxation of effort.
leukemia, leukaemia *n* a chronic disease characterized by an abnormal increase in the number of white blood cells in body tissues and the blood.
leukocyte *n* a white blood cell.
leukoma *n* a white, opaque scar on the cornea of the eye.
leukorrhea *n* a mucous discharge from the vagina.
leukotomy *n* (*pl* **leukotomies**) the severing of nerve fibres in the frontal lobes of the brain formerly used to relieve certain severe mental disorders.
lev *n* (*pl* **leva**) the monetary unit of Bulgaria.
levanter *n* an easterly wind in the Mediterranean.
levantine *n* a kind of reversible silk cloth.
levator *n* (*anat*) a muscle that serves to raise a part of the body.
levee[1] *n* a reception of visitors formerly held by a sovereign or other important person on rising from bed; a reception usu in honour of a particular person.
levee[2] *n* an embankment beside a river.
level *n* a horizontal line or plane; a position in a scale of values; a flat area or surface; an instrument for determining the horizontal. * *adj* horizontal; having a flat surface; at the same height, rank, position, etc; steady. * *vti* (**leveling, leveled** *or* **levelling, levelled**) to make or become level; to demolish; to raise and aim (a gun, criticism, etc).—**levelly** *adv*.
level crossing *n* (*Brit*) a place where a road crosses a railway line on the same level esp where gates or barriers close the road to allow trains to pass; a grade crossing in the US.
leveler, leveller *n* one who levels; an advocate of social equality.
level-headed *adj* having an even temper and sound judgment.—**level-headedly** *adv*.
lever *n* a bar used for prising or moving something; a means to an end; a device consisting of a bar turning about a fixed point; any device used in the same way, eg to operate machinery. * *vt* to raise or move (as with) a lever.
leverage *n* the action of a lever; the mechanical advantage gained by the use of a lever; power, influence.
leveret *n* a hare less than a year old.
leviable *adj* subject to a levy; (*goods*) which may be levied upon or seized.
leviathan *n* something huge.
levigate *vt* to grind to a fine powder.
Levis *n* (*trademark*) jeans made from (blue or black) denim.
levitate *vti* to rise or cause to rise into the air and float without support.—**levitation** *n*.
levity *n* (*pl* **levities**) excessive frivolity; lack of necessary seriousness.
levorotation *n* left-handed or counterclockwise rotation.—*also* **laevorotation.-mevorotatory** *adj*.
levulose *n* a fruit found in sugar.—*also* **laevulose**.
levy *vt* (**levying, levied**) to collect by force or authority, as a tax, fine, etc; an amount levied; to enrol or conscript troops; to prepare for or wage war. * *n* (*pl* **levies**) a levying; the amount levied.—**levier** *n*.
lewd *adj* indecent; lustful; obscene.—**lewdly** *adv*.—**lewdness** *n*.
lewis *n* an appliance for lifting heavy blocks of stone.
lewisite *n* a blistering liquid obtained from arsenic and acetylene, used in gas form in chemical warfare.
lexical *adj* of or pertaining to words in a language; of a lexicon or dictionary.—**lexically** *adv*.
lexicographer *n* a person skilled in lexicography.
lexicography *n* the process of writing or compiling a dictionary; the principles and practices of dictionary making.—**lexicographic, lexicographical** *adj*.—**lexicographically** *adv*.
lexicology *n* the branch of linguistics dealing with the meaning and use of words.—**lexicological** *adj*.—**lexicologist** *n*.
lexicon *n* a dictionary; a special vocabulary, as of a specific language, branch of knowledge, etc.
lexis *n* the total of words or vocabulary in a language.
ley, ley-line *n* a straight line joining two landmarks, supposedly of prehistoric origin.
LF *abbr* = low frequency.
Li (*chem symbol*) lithium.
li *n* the Chinese equivalent of a mile, equivalent to approximately 590 yards.
liability *n* (*pl* **liabilities**) a being liable; something for which one is liable; (*inf*) a handicap, disadvantage; (*pl*) debts, obligations, disadvantages.
liable *adj* legally bound or responsible; subject to; likely (to).
liaise *vi* to form a connection and retain contact with.
liaison *n* intercommunication as between units of a military force; an illicit love affair; a thickening for sauces, soups, etc, as egg yolks or cream.
liana, liane *n* a climbing plant found in tropical forests.
liar *n* a person who tells lies.
Lias *n* (*geol*) the lowest division of rocks of the Jurassic system.—**Liassic** *adj*.
lib *n* (*inf*) liberation.
libation *n* the act of pouring wine or oil on the ground, as a sacrifice; the liquod so poured out; a drink.
libel *n* any written or printed matter tending to injure a person's reputation unjustly; (*inf*) any defamatory or damaging assertion about a person. * *vt* (**libeling, libeled** *or* **libelling, libelled**) to utter or publish a libel against.—**libeler, libeller** *n*.—**libelous, libellous** *adj*.
liberal *adj* ample, abundant; not literal or strict; tolerant; (*education*) contributing to a general broadening of the mind, non-specialist; favouring reform or progress. * *n* a person who favours reform or progress.—**liberally** *adv*.
liberalism *n* liberal opinions, principles or politics.
liberality *n* (*pl* **liberalities**) generosity; breadth of mind.
liberalize*vti* to make or become less strict.—**liberalization** *n*.
liberate *vt* to set free from foreign occupation, slavery, etc.—**liberator** *n*.
liberation *n* the act of liberating; the state of being liberated; the pursuit of social, political or economic equality by or on behalf of those being discriminated against.
liberation priest *n* a priest who is active in working for social and political justice.
liberation theology *n* the belief that Christianity requires commitment to social and political change, as well as faith, esp in South America.
libertarian *n* a person who advocates liberty, esp in conduct or thought; a believer in free will.—**libertarianism** *n*.
liberticide *n* a destroyer of liberty; the destruction of liberty.
libertine *n* a dissolute person; a freethinker. * *adj* unrestrained, morally or socially; licentious.—**libertinism, libertinage** *n*.
liberty *n* (*pl* **liberties**) freedom from slavery, captivity, etc; the right to do as one pleases, freedom; a particular right, freedom, etc granted by authority; an impertinent attitude; authorized leave granted to a sailor.
libidinous *adj* lustful, lascivious.
libido *n* (*pl* **libidos**) the sexual urge.—**libidinal** *adj*.
Libra *n* (*astrol*) the 7th sign of the zodiac, operative 24 September–23 October; a constellation represented as a pair of scales.—**Libran** *n*, *adj*.
librarian *n* a person in charge of a library or trained in librarianship.
librarianship, library science *n* the profession of organizing collections of books, etc for reference by others.
library *n* (*pl* **libraries**) a collection of books, tapes, records, photographs, etc for reference or borrowing; a room, building or institution containing such a collection; (*comput*) a set of, usu general purpose, programs or subroutines for use in programming.
librate *vi* to waver; to balance.—**libratory** *adj*.
libration *n* the act of oscillating; the act of balancing; an apparent irregularity in the motion of the moon or a satellite.
librettist *n* a writer of a libretto.
libretto *n* (*pl* **libretti, librettos**) the text to which an opera, oratorio, etc is set.—**librettist** *n*.
Libyan *n* a native or inhabitant of Libya.—*also adj*.
lice *see* **louse**.

license *n* a formal or legal permission to do something specified; a document granting such permission; freedom to deviate from rule, practice, etc; excessive freedom, an abuse of liberty (*—also* **licence**). **vt* to grant a license to or for; to permit.—**licenser, licensor** *n*.

license plate *n* (*US*) a plate on the front or rear of a motor vehicle that displays its registration number.—*also* **numberplate**.

licensee *n* a person who is granted a licence.

licentiate *n* a person holding a certificate of competence in a profession; a degree between that of bachelor and doctor in some universities; one licensed to preach.—**licentiateship** *n*.

licentious *adj* morally unrestrained; lascivious.—**licentiousness** *n*.

lichee *see* **litchi**.

lichen *n* any of various small plants consisting of an alga and a fungus living in symbiotic association, growing on stones, trees, etc.

lichenology *n* the study of lichens.

lich gate *n* (*Brit*) a roofed gate of a churchyard, under which a coffin can be rested.—*also* **lych gate**.

lichi *see* **litchi**.

licit *adj* lawful.—**licitly** *adv*.

lick *vt* to draw the tongue over, esp to taste or clean; (*flames, etc*) to flicker around or touch lightly; (*inf*) to thrash; (*inf*) to defeat. * *vi* (*sl*) to take the drug crack. * *n* a licking with the tongue; (*inf*) a sharp blow; (*inf*) a short, rapid burst of activity.

lickerish *adj* (*arch*) lustful; greedy.

lickety-split *adv* very fast.

licking *n* (*inf*) a severe beating; a defeat.

lickspittle *n* a servile flatterer.

licorice *n* a black extract made from the root of a European plant, used in medicine and confectionery; a licorice-flavoured sweet.—*also* **liquorice**.

lictor *n* an official serving a magistrate in ancient Rome.

lid *n* a removable cover as for a box, etc; an eyelid.—**lidded** *adj*.

lido *n* (*pl* **lidos**) an open air swimming pool and recreational complex for public use.

lie[1] *n* an untrue statement made with intent to deceive; something that deceives or misleads. * *vi* (**lying, lied**) to speak untruthfully with an intention to deceive; to create a false impression.

lie[2] *vi* (**lying, lay,** *pp* **lain**) to be or put oneself in a reclining or horizontal position; to rest on a support in a horizontal position; to be in a specified condition; to be situated; to exist. * *n* the way in which something is situated.

lied *n* (*pl* **lieder**) a German song or ballad.

lie detector *n* a polygraph device used by police and security services that monitors sharp fluctuations in involuntary physiological responses as evidence of stress, guilt, etc when deliberately lying.

lief *adv* (*arch*) willingly.

liege *n* (*feudalism*) a lord or sovereign (*—also* **liege lord**); a subject or vassal.

lien *n* (*law*) a right to keep another's property pending payment of a debt due to the holder.

lierne *n* (*archit*) a cross-rib or branch rib in vaulting.

lieu *n* place; stead (esp *in lieu of*, in place of, instead of).

lieutenant *n* a commissioned army officer ranking below a captain; a naval officer next below a lieutenant commander; a deputy, a chief assistant to a superior.—**lieutenancy** *n*.

life *n* (*pl* **lives**) that property of plants and animals (ending at death) that enables them to use food, grow, reproduce, etc; the state of having this property; living things collectively; the time a person or thing exists; one's manner of living; one's animate existence; vigour, liveliness; (*inf*) a life sentence; a biography. * *adj* of animate being; lifelong; using a living model; of or relating to or provided by life insurance.

life-belt *n* an inflatable ring to support a person in the water; a safety belt.

lifeblood *n* the blood necessary to life; a vital element.

lifeboat *n* a small rescue boat carried by a ship; a specially designed and equipped rescue vessel that helps those in distress along the coastline.

life buoy *n* a ring-shaped buoyant device to keep a person afloat.

life cycle *n* a sequence of stages through which a living being passes during its lifetime

lifeguard *n* an expert swimmer employed to prevent drownings.

life jacket *n* a sleeveless jacket or vest of buoyant material to keep a person afloat.

lifeless *adj* dead; unconscious; dull.—**lifelessly** *adv*.—**lifelessness** *n*.

lifelike *adj* resembling a real life person or thing.

lifeline *n* a rope for raising or lowering a diver; a rope for rescuing a person, eg as attached to a lifebelt; a vitally important channel of communication or transport.

lifelong *adj* lasting one's whole life.

life peer *n* a British peer whose title lapses with death.

life preserver *n* a club used as a weapon of self-defence; a lifebelt or life jacket.

lifer *n* (*sl*) a person sentenced to prison for life.

life raft *n* a raft kept on board ship for use in emergencies.

lifesaving *adj* something (as drugs) designed to save lives. * *n* the skill or practice of saving lives, esp from drowning.—**lifesaver** *n*.

life science *n* a science dealing with living organisms and life processes, such as biology, zoology, etc.

life sentence *n* imprisonment for life, or a long period, as punishment for a grave offence.

life-size, life-sized *adj* of the size of the original.

lifestyle *n* the particular attitudes, living habits, etc of a person.

lifetime *n* the length of time that a person lives or something lasts.

lift *vt* to bring to a higher position, raise; to raise in rank, condition, etc; (*sl*) to steal; to revoke. * *vi* to exert oneself in raising something; to rise; to go up; (*fog, etc*) to disperse; (*with* **off**) (*rocket, etc*) to take off. * *n* act or fact of lifting; distance through which a thing is lifted; elevation of mood, etc; elevated position or carriage; a ride in the direction in which one is going; help of any kind; (*Brit*) a cage or platform for moving something from one level to another (*—also* **elevator**); upward air pressure maintaining an aircraft in flight.—**lifter** *n*.

liftoff *n* the vertical thrust of a spacecraft, etc at launching; the time of this.

ligament *n* a band of tissue connecting bones; a unifying bond.

ligan *see* **lagan**.

ligate *vt* to tie up (with a ligature).—**ligation** *n*.

ligature *n* a tying or binding together; a tie, bond, etc; two or more printed letters joined together, as œ; a thread used to suture a blood vessel, etc in surgery.

light[1] *n* the agent of illumination that stimulates the sense of sight; electromagnetic radiation such as ultraviolet, infrared or X-rays; brightness, illumination; a source of light, as the sun, a lamp, etc; daylight; a thing used to ignite something; a window; knowledge, enlightenment; aspect or appearance. * *adj* having light; bright; pale in colour. * *adv* palely. * *vt* (**lighting, lit** *or* **lighted**) to ignite; to cause to give off light; to furnish with light; to brighten, animate.

light[2] *adj* having little weight; not heavy; less than usual in weight, amount, force, etc; of little importance; easy to bear; easy to digest; happy; dizzy, giddy; not serious; moderate; moving with ease; producing small products. * *adv* lightly. * *vi* (**lighting, lit** *or* **lighted**) to come to rest after travelling through the air; to dismount, to alight; to come or happen on or upon; to strike suddenly, as a blow.—**lightly** *adv*.—**lightness** *n*.

lighten[1] *vti* to make or become light or lighter; to shine, flash.—**lightener** *n*.

lighten[2] *vti* to make or become lighter in weight; to make or become more cheerful; to mitigate.—**lightener** *n*.

lighter[1] *n* a small device that produces a naked flame to light cigarettes.

lighter[2] *n* a large barge used in loading or unloading larger ships.

lighterage *n* the transport of goods by lighter; the price paid for the service; lighters collectively.

light-fingered *adj* thievish.

light-headed *adj* dizzy; delirious.—**light-headedly** *adv*.

light-hearted *adj* carefree.—**light-heartedly** *adv*.

lighthouse *n* a tower with a bright light to guide ships.
lighting *n* the process of giving light; equipment for illuminating a stage, television set, etc; the distribution of light on an object, as in a work of art.
lightning *n* a discharge or flash of electricity in the sky. * *adv* fast, sudden.
lightning conductor or **rod** *n* a metal rod placed high on a building and grounded to divert lightning from the structure.
light opera *n* an operetta.
light pen *n* a pen-shaped photoelectric device used to communicate with a computer by pointing at the monitor; a similar device used for reading bar codes.
lightship *n* a ship equipped with a warning beacon and moored at a place dangerous to navigation.
lightsome *adj* (*arch, poet*) carefree; graceful, nimble.
lights out *n* (a signal indicating) the time prescribed for retiring to bed, as in a military barracks.
lightweight *adj* of less than average weight; trivial, unimportant. * *n* a person or thing of less than average weight; a professional boxer weighing 130–135 pounds (59–61 kg); a person of little importance or influence.
light-year *n* the distance light travels in one year.
lignaloes *see* **eaglewood.**
ligneous *adj* of or like wood.
ligniform *adj* resembling wood.
lignify *vti* (**lignifies, lignifying, lignified**) (*bot*) to make or become wood, or woody.—**lignification** *n.*
lignin *n* a woody fibre.
lignite *n* a soft brownish-black coal with the texture of the original wood.—**lignitic** *adj.*
lignum vitae *n* the heavy hard wood of the South American guaiacum tree.
ligroin *n* a solvent distilled from petroleum.
ligulate *adj* (*bot*) strap-shaped.
ligule *n* (*bot*) a membranous appendage at the top of a sheathing petiole in grasses; one of the rays of a composite plant.
likable, likeable *adj* attractive, pleasant, genial, etc.—**likably, likeably** *adv.*
like[1] *adj* having the same characteristics; similar; equal. * *adv* (*inf*) likely. * *prep* similar to; characteristic of; in the mood for; indicative of; as for example. * *conj* (*inf*) as; as if. * *n* an equal; counterpart.
like[2] *vt* to be pleased with; to wish. * *vi* to be so inclined.
likelihood *n* probability.
likely *adj* (**likelier, likeliest**) reasonably to be expected; suitable; showing promise of success.* *adv* probably.—**likeliness** *n.*
like-minded *adj* sharing the same tastes, ideas, etc.—**likemindedness** *n.*
liken *vt* to compare.
likeness *n* a being like; something that is like, as a copy, portrait, etc; appearance, semblance.
likewise *adv* the same; also.
liking *n* fondness; affection; preference.
lilac *n* a shrub with large clusters of tiny, fragrant flowers; a pale purple. * *adj* lilac coloured.
Lilliputian *adj* tiny; petty. * *n* a tiny person, a midget.
Li-Lo *n* (*pl* **Li-Los**) (*trademark*) an inflatable rubber or plastic mattress.
lilt *n* a light rhythmic song or tune; a springy motion. * *vi* (*music, song*) to have a lilt; to move buoyantly.—**lilting** *adj.*
lily *n* (*pl* **lilies**) a bulbous plant having typically trumpet-shaped flowers; its flower.
lily-livered *adj* cowardly.
lily of the valley *n* a small plant of the lily family with white bell-shaped flowers.
lily-white *adj* pure white; (*inf*) pure, incorruptible.
lima bean *n* a kind of bean that produces flat, edible pale green seeds; its edible seed.
limb *n* a projecting appendage of an animal body, as an arm, leg, or wing; a large branch of a tree; a participating member, agent; an arm of a cross.—**limbless** *adj.*
limbate *adj* (*bot*) with a border of a different colour.
limber[1] *adj* flexible, able to bend the body easily. * *vt* to make limber. * *vi* to become limber; (*with* **up**) to stretch and warm the muscles in readiness for physical exercise.
limber[2] *n* the detachable wheeled section of a gun carriage.
limbo[1] *n* (*pl* **limbos**) (*Christianity*) the abode after death assigned to unbaptized souls; a place for lost, unwanted, or neglected persons or things; an intermediate stage or condition between extremes.
limbo[2] *n* (*pl* **limbos**) a West Indian dance that involves bending over backwards and passing under a horizontal bar that is progressively lowered.
lime[1] *n* a white calcium compound used for making cement and in agriculture. * *vt* to treat or cover with lime.
lime[2] *n* a small yellowish-green fruit with a juicy, sour pulp; the tree that bears it; its colour.
lime[3] *n* the linden tree.
limekiln *n* a furnace for making lime.
limelight *n* intense publicity; a type of lamp, formerly used in stage lighting, in which lime was heated to produce a brilliant flame.
limen *n* (*pl* **limens, limina**) (*psychol*) the point at which the effect of a stimulus is just discernible.
limerick *n* a type of humorous verse consisting of five lines.
limestone *n* a type of rock composed mainly of calcium carbonate.
limey *n* (*pl* **limeys**) (*US sl*) a British person.
limit *n* a boundary; (*pl*) bounds; the greatest amount allowed; (*inf*) as much as one can tolerate. * *vt* to set a limit to; to restrict.—**limitable** *adj.*
limitary *adj* restrictive; restricted.
limitation *n* the act of limiting or being limited; a hindrance to ability or achievement.
limited *adj* confined within bounds; lacking imagination or originality.
limited liability *n* in UK, responsibility for the debts of a company only to the extent of the amount of capital stock held.
limitless *adj* boundless, immense.—**limitlessly** *adv.*—**limitlessness** *n.*
limn *vt* to paint or draw.—**limner** *n.*
limnology *n* the scientific study of freshwater bodies (e.g. lakes and ponds) in terms of their support for plant and animal life, physical geography, chemical composition, etc.
limo *n* (*inf*) **limousine.**
limousine *n* (*sl*) a large luxury car.
limp[1] *vi* to walk with or as with a lame leg. * *n* a lameness in walking.—**limper** *n.*—**limpingly** *adv.*
limp[2] *adj* not firm; lethargic; wilted; flexible.—**limply** *adv.*—**limpness** *n.*
limpet *n* a mollusc with a low conical shell that clings to rocks.
limpid *adj* perfectly clear; transparent.—**limpidity** *n.*
limpkin *n* a kind of American wading bird.
limy *adj* (**limier, limiest**) containing, or resembling, lime.
linage *n* the number of written or printed lines on a page.
linchpin *n* a pin passed through an axle to keep a wheel in position; a person or thing regarded as vital to an organization, project, etc.
linden *n* a tree with deciduous heart-shaped leaves and small fragrant yellow flowers.
line[1] *vt* (**lining, lined**) to put, or serve as, a lining in.
line[2] *n* a length of cord, rope, or wire; a cord for measuring, making level; a system of conducting fluid, electricity, etc; a thin threadlike mark; anything resembling such a mark, as a wrinkle; edge, limit, boundary; border, outline, contour; a row of persons or things, as printed letters across a page; a succession of persons, lineage; a connected series of things; the course a moving thing takes; a course of conduct, actions, etc; a whole system of transportation; a person's trade or occupation; a field of experience or interest; (*inf*) glib, persuasive talk; a verse; the forward combat position in warfare; fortifications, trenches or other defences used in war; a stock of goods; a piece of information; a short letter, note; (*pl*) all the speeches of a character in a play; (*sl*) a measure of the drug cocaine laid in a strip, ready for sniffing. * *vb* (**lining, lined**) *vt* to mark with lines; to form a line along; to cover with lines; to arrange in a line. * *vi* to align.

lineage *n* direct descent from an ancestor; ancestry.
lineal *adj* hereditary; direct; linear.—**lineally** *adv*.
lineament *n* (*usu pl*) a facial feature.
linear *adj* of, made of, or using a line or lines; narrow and long; in relation to length only.—**linearity** *n*.—**linearly** *adv*.
linear accelerator *n* a device for accelerating elementary particles in a straight line by successively activating electric fields at regular intervals along their path.
lineate *adj* marked with lines.
lineation *n* the drawing, or arrangement, of lines.
line drawing *n* a drawing made with solid lines.
lineengraving *n* an engraving with fine lines; the art of this type of engraving.
linen *n* thread or cloth made of flax; household articles (sheets, cloths, etc) made of linen or cotton cloth.
line-out *n* (*Rugby Union*) the method of restarting a game after the ball has been put into touch, the forwards forming two opposing parallel lines at right angles to the touch-line and jumping for the ball that is thrown in.
line printer *n* a high-speed computer printer that prints each line as a single unit instead of character by character.
liner *n* a large passenger ship or aircraft travelling a regular route.
linesman *n* (*pl* **linesmen**) an official in certain games who assists the referee in deciding when the ball is out of play, etc.
lineup *n* an arrangement of persons or things in a line, eg for inspection.
ling. *abbr* = linguistics.
ling[1] *n* a type of heather.
ling[2] *n* (*pl* **ling, lings**) a sea fish of northern waters used as food.
linger *vi* to stay a long time; to delay departure; to dawdle or loiter; to dwell on in the mind; to remain alive though on the point of death.—**lingerer** *n*.—**lingering** *adj*.—**lingeringly** *adv*.
lingerie *n* women's underwear and nightclothes.
lingo *n* (*pl* **lingoes**) (*inf*) a dialect, jargon, etc.
lingua franca *n* (*pl* **lingua francas, linguae francae**) a language used for communication between speakers of different languages.
lingual *adj* of, or pronounced with, the tongue.—**lingually** *adv*.
linguiform *adj* tongue-shaped.
linguist *n* a person who is skilled in speaking foreign languages.
linguistic *adj* of or pertaining to language or linguistics.—**linguistically** *adv*.
linguistics *n* (*used as sing*) the science of language.
lingulate *adj* tongue-shaped.
liniment *n* a soothing medication, usu applied to the skin.
lining *n* a material used to cover the inner surface of a garment, etc; any material covering an inner surface.
link *n* a single loop or ring of a chain; something resembling a loop or ring or connecting piece; a person or thing acting as a connection, as in a communication system, machine or organization. * *vti* to connect or become connected.
linkage *n* a linking; a series or system of links.
linkboy *n* (*formerly*) someone who guided others through dark streets with a torch.
linkman *n* (*pl* **linkmen**) (*radio, TV*) a presenter who links items, reports, etc, esp on a sports programme.
links *npl* (*also used as sing*) flat sandy soil; a golf course, esp by the sea.
linkup *n* a linking together.
linn *n* (*Scot*) a waterfall; the pool beneath a waterfall; a ravine.
Linnaean, Linnean *adj* pertaining to the Swedish naturalist Linnaeus or to his system of classification.
linnet *n* a small brown or grey songbird.
lino *n* (*inf*) (*pl* **linos**) linoleum.
linocut *n* a design cut in relief on a piece of linoleum; a print made from this.
linoleum *n* a floor covering of coarse fabric backing with a smooth, hard decorative coating.
Linotype *n* (*trademark*) a typesetting machine that casts lines in one piece.
linsang *n* a type of civet, found in Indonesia and Borneo.
linseed *n* the seed of flax, from which linseed oil is made.
linseed oil *n* oil made from flax seeds, used in paint and varnish.
linsey-woolsey *n* a sturdy coarse fabric of linen or cotton and wool mixed.
linstock *n* (*formerly*) a staff holding a match, used to light a cannon.
lint *n* scraped and softened linen used to dress wounds; fluff.
lintel *n* the horizontal crosspiece spanning a doorway or window.
lintwhite *n* (*Scot, arch*) a linnet.
lion *n* a large, flesh-eating feline mammal with a shaggy mane in the adult male; a person of great courage or strength.—**lioness** *nf*.
lionhearted *adj* extremely brave.
lionize *vt* to treat as or make famous.—**lionization** *n*.—**lionizer** *n*.
lip *n* either of the two fleshy flaps that surround the mouth; anything like a lip, as the rim of a jug; (*sl*) insolent talk. * *vt* (**lipping, lipped**) to touch with the lips; to kiss; to utter.
lipid *n* an organic compound in fats, which is soluble in solvents but insoluble in water.
lipo-, lip- *prefix* fat, fatty.
lipoid, lipoidal *adj* fatty, resembling fat. * *n* a fat-like substance.
liposuction *n* cosmetic surgery involving the removal of fat from under the skin of the thighs, stomach, etc using a suction device inserted through an incision.
lipped *adj* having lips or rounded edges.
lip-read *vt* (**lip-reading, lip-read**) to understand another's speech by watching their lip movements.
lip service *n* support expressed but not acted upon.
lipstick *n* a small stick of cosmetic for colouring the lips; the cosmetic itself.
lip-sync, lip-synch *vt* to move the lips in time with a prerecorded soundtrack (of dialogue or music) on film or television.
liquate *vt* to melt (metals) to separate or purify them.—**liquation** *n*.
liquefacient *adj* serving to liquefy. * *n* something that liquefies.
liquefy *vti* (**liquefying, liquefied**) to change to a liquid.—**liquefaction** *n*.—**liquefier** *n*.
liquescent *adj* becoming liquid.
liqueur *n* a sweet and variously flavoured alcoholic drink.
liquid *n* a substance that, unlike a gas, does not expand indefinitely and, unlike a solid, flows readily. * *adj* in liquid form; clear; limpid; flowing smoothly and musically, as verse; (*assets*) readily convertible into cash.—**liquidity** *n*.
liquidate *vt* to settle the accounts of; to close a (bankrupt) business and distribute its assets among its creditors; to convert into cash; to eliminate, kill.
liquidation *n* the act of liquidating or paying off; the settlement of the affairs of a bankrupt person or business.
liquidator *n* an official who winds up a business.
liquidize *vt* to make liquid.
liquidizer *n* a domestic appliance for liquidizing and blending foods.
liquid paraffin *n* an oily distillate of petroleum used as a laxative.—*also* **mineral oil**.
liquor *n* an alcoholic drink; any liquid, esp that in which food has been cooked.
liquorice *n see* **licorice**.
liquor store *n* a place where alcohol is sold for consumption off the premises.—*also* **off-licence, package store**.
lira *n* (*pl* **lire, liras**) the monetary unit of Italy and Turkey.
lisle *n* a fine tightly-twisted cotton thread.
lisp *vi* to substitute the sounds *th* (as in *thin*) for *s* or *th* (as in *then*) for *z*; a speech defect or habit involving such pronunciation; to utter imperfectly. * *vt* to speak or utter with a lisp.—*also n*.—**lisper** *n*.
lissom *adj* lithe; supple; agile, etc.—**lissomeness** *n*.
list[1] *n* a series of names, numbers, words, etc written or printed in order. * *vt* to make a list of; to enter in a directory, etc.
list[2] *vti* to tilt to one side, as a ship. * *n* such a tilting.

listed *adj* (*company, etc*) having its shares quoted on a stock exchange; (*building*) of architectural interest and protected from demolition or alteration without permission.
listed building *n* in UK, a building officially designated as of historic or architectural interest and protected from alteration or demolition.
listen *vi* to try to hear; to pay attention, take heed; (*with* **in**) to intercept radio or telephone communications; to tune into a radio broadcast; to eavesdrop.
listener *n* a person who listens; a person listening to a radio broadcast.
listeriosis *n* chronic food poisoning caused by the bacteria *Listeria*.
listing *n* a list, or an individual entry therein; the act of making a list; (*pl*) a guide giving details of events, eg music, theatre, taking place in a particular area, published in a newspaper or magazine.
listless *adj* lacking energy or enthusiasm because of illness, dejection, etc; languid.—**listlessly** *adv*.—**listlessness** *n*.
lit *see* **light**[1], **light**[2].
lit. *abbr* = literal; literary; literature; litre.
litany *n* (*pl* **litanies**) a type of prayer in which petitions to God are recited by a priest and elicit set responses by the congregation; any tedious or automatic recital.
litchi *n* a fruit consisting of a soft, sweet white pulp in a thin brown shell; the tree that bears this fruit.—*also* **lichee, lichi.**
-lite *n suffix* stone; mineral; fossil.
liter *see* **litre.**
literacy *n* the ability to read and write.
literal *adj* in accordance with the exact meaning of a word or text; in a basic or strict sense; prosaic, unimaginative; real.—**literalness, literality** *n*.—**literally** *adv*.
literalism *n* adherence to the literal sense of a word or saying.—**literalist** *n*.
literary *adj* of or dealing with literature; knowing much about literature.—**literarily** *adv*.—**literariness** *n*.
literate *adj* able to read and write; educated.—*also n*.
literati *npl* educated people.
literatim *adv* letter for letter.
literature *n* the writings of a period or of a country, esp those valued for their excellence; of style or form; all the books and articles on a subject; (*inf*) any printed matter.
-lith *n suffix* stone or rock.
litharge *n* an oxide of lead.
lithe *adj* supple, flexible.—**litheness** *n*.
lithesome *adj* lithe, supple.
lithia *n* an oxide of lithium.
lithic *adj* of or pertaining to stone.
lithium *n* the lightest metallic element.
litho *n* (*pl* **lithos**) a lithograph; lithography.
lithograph *n* a print, etc made by lithography.—**lithographic** *adj*.—**lithographically** *adv*
lithography *n* printing from a flat stone or metal plate, parts of which have been treated to repel ink.—**lithographer** *n*.
lithoid, lithoidal *adj* stonelike.
lithology *n* the study of rocks and their physical characteristics.—**lithologic, lithological** *adj*.
lithophyte *n* a stony polyp; a plant which grows on a rocky surface.
lithosphere *n* the solid outer part of the earth.
lithotomy *n* (*pl* **lithotomies**) (*med*) the operation of cutting into the bladder to remove a stone.—**lithotomic** *adj*.
lithotripter, lithotriptor *n* an instrument that fragments kidney or bladder stones, etc by ultrasound without the need for invasive surgery.
lithotrity *n* (*pl* **lithotrities**) (*med*) the operation of crushing a stone in the bladder.
litigant *n* a person engaged in a lawsuit.
litigate *vti* to bring or contest in a lawsuit.—**litigator** *n*.
litigation *n* the act or processs of carrying on a lawsuit; a judicial contest.
litigious *adj* of or causing lawsuits; fond of engaging in lawsuits; contentious.—**litigiousness** *n*.
litmus *n* a colouring material obtained from certain lichens that turns red in acid solutions and blue in alkaline solutions.
litotes *n* (*pl* **litotes**) (*rhetoric*) understatement for effect.
litre, liter *n* a measure of liquid capacity in the metric system, equivalent to 1.76 pints.—*also* **litre.**
Litt.D, Lit.D *abbr* = Doctor of Letters; Doctor of Literature.
litter *n* rubbish scattered about; young animals produced at one time; straw, hay, etc used as bedding for animals; a stretcher for carrying a sick or wounded person. * *vt* to make untidy; to scatter about carelessly.
littérateur *n* a writer.
litterbug *n* a person who drops refuse in public places.
little *adj* not great or big, small in size, amount, degree, etc; short in duration; small in importance or power; narrow-minded. * *n* small in amount, degree, etc. * *adv* less, least, slightly; not much; not in the least.
little people *npl* (*folklore*) supernatural beings such as fairies, elves and leprechauns.
littoral *adj* of or along the seashore.
liturgics *n* (*sing*) the study of liturgies.
liturgist *n* someone who studies or composes liturgies.
liturgy *n* (*pl* **liturgies**) the prescribed form of service of a church.—**liturgical** *adj*.—**liturgically** *adv*.
livable *adj* worth living; suitable for living in.
live[1] *vi* to have life; to remain alive; to endure; to pass life in a specified manner; to enjoy a full life; to reside; (*with* **in, out**) (*employee*) to reside at (or away from) one's place of work; (*with* **together**) (*unmarried couple*) to cohabit. * *vt* to carry out in one's life; to spend; pass; (*with* **down**) to survive or efface the effects of (a crime or mistake) by waiting until it is forgotten or forgiven.
live[2] *adj* having life; of the living state or living beings; of present interest; still burning; unexploded; carrying electric current; broadcast during the actual performance.
liveable *see* **livable.**
livelihood *n* employment; a means of living.
livelong *adj* of the whole length of (the day).
lively *adj* (**livelier, liveliest**) full of life; spirited; exciting; vivid; keen. * *adv* in a lively manner.—**liveliness** *n*.
liven *vti* to make or become lively.—**livener** *n*.
liver *n* the largest glandular organ in vertebrate animals, which secretes bile, etc and is important in metabolism; the liver of an animal used as food; a reddish-brown colour.
liveried *adj* wearing a livery.
liverish *adj* suffering from liver disorder; peevish.
liverwort *n* a cryptogamous plant, found in wet places.
liverwurst *n* sausage made with liver.
livery *n* (*pl* **liveries**) an identifying uniform, as that worn by a servant.
liveryman *n* (*pl* **liverymen**) a keeper of a livery stable; a member of a livery company.
lives *see* **life.**
livestock *n* (farm) animals raised for use or sale.
live wire *n* (*inf*) a lively, energetic person.
livid *adj* (*skin*) discoloured, as from bruising; greyish in colour; (*inf*) extremely angry.—**lividly** *adv*.—**lividness, lividity** *n*.
living *adj* having life; still in use; true to life, vivid; of life, for living in. * *n* a being alive; livelihood; manner of existence.
living room *n* a room in a house used for general entertainment and relaxation.
living wage *n* a wage sufficient to maintain a reasonable standard of comfort.
lixiviate *vt* to wash (soil, ore, etc) with a filtering liquid; to extract (a soluble substance) from some material.—**lixiviation** *n*.
lizard *n* a reptile with a slender body, four legs, and a tapering tail.
llama *n* a South American animal, related to the camel, used for carrying loads and as a source of wool.
llano *n* (*pl* **llanos**) one of the vast, level plains of South America.

LLB *abbr* = Bachelor of Laws.
LLD *abbr* = Doctor of Laws.
LLM *abbr* = Master of Laws.
lm *abbr* = lumen.
LNG *abbr* = liquefied natural gas.
lo *interj* behold!, see!
loach *n* an edible freshwater fish.
load *n* an amount carried at one time; something borne with difficulty; a burden; *(often pl)* *(inf)* a great amount. * *vt* to put into or upon; to burden; to oppress; to supply in large quantities; to alter, as by adding a weight to dice or an adulterant to alcoholic drink; to put a charge of ammunition into (a firearm); to put film into (a camera); *(comput)* to install a program in memory. * *vi* to take on a load.—**loader** *n*.
loaded *adj* *(sl)* having plenty of money; drunk; under the influence of drugs.
loadstar *see* **lodestar**.
loadstone *see* **lodestone**.
loaf[1] *n* *(pl* **loaves**) a mass of bread of regular shape and standard weight; food shaped like this; *(sl)* the head.
loaf[2] *vi* to pass time in idleness.—**loafer** *n*.
loam *n* rich and fertile soil.
loamy *adj* (**loamier, loamiest**) consisting of or full of loam.—**loaminess** *n*.
loan *n* the act of lending; something lent, esp money. * *vti* to lend.—**loanable** *adj*.—**loaner** *n*.
loath *adj* unwilling.—*also* **loth**.—**loathly** *adv*.
loathe *vt* to dislike intensely; to detest.—**loather** *n*.—**loathing** *n*.
loathsome *adj* giving rise to loathing; detestable.—**loathsomeness** *n*.
loaves *see* **loaf**[1].
lob *vti* (**lobbing, lobbed**) to toss or hit (a ball) in a high curve. * *n* a high-arching throw or kick.
lobar *adj* of or relating to a lobe.
lobate *adj* having lobes; lobelike.
lobby *n* *(pl* **lobbies**) an entrance hall of a public building; a person or group that tries to influence legislators. * *vti* (**lobbying, lobbied**) to try to influence (legislators) to support a particular cause or take certain action.
lobbyist *n* someone employed to lobby.
lobe *n* a rounded projection, as the lower end of the ear; any of the divisions of the lungs or brain.
lobelia *n* a genus of garden plants, usually with blue flowers.
loblolly *n* *(pl* **loblollies**) a type of American pine tree; *(naut)* gruel.
lobotomy *n* *(pl* **lobotomies**) surgical incision into the lobe of an organ; a leukotomy.
lobscouse *n* a sailor's dish of meat, vegetables and ship's biscuit.
lobster *n* *(pl* **lobsters, lobster**) any of a family of edible sea crustaceans with four pairs of legs and a pair of large pincers.
lobule *n* a small lobe.—**lobular, lobulate** *adj*.
local *adj* of or belonging to a particular place; serving the needs of a specific district; of or for a particular part of the body. * *n* an inhabitant of a specific place; *(inf)* a pub serving a particular district.—**locally** *adv*.—**localness** *n*.
locale *n* a place or area, esp in regard to the position or scene of some event.
localism *n* a word, idiom or custom restricted to a particular locality; narrowness of outlook.
locality *n* *(pl* **localities**) a neighbourhood or a district; a particular scene, position, or place; the fact or condition of having a location in space and time.
localize *vt* to limit, confine, or trace to a particular place.—**localization** *n*.
locate *vt* to determine or indicate the position of something; to set in or assign to a particular position.
location *n* a specific position or place; a locating or being located; a place outside a studio where a film is (partly) shot; *(comput)* an area in memory where a single item of data is stored.
locative *adj*, *n* (a grammatical case) indicating place.
loc. cit. *abbr* = loco citato (Latin *in the place cited*).
loch *n* *(Scot)* a lake.
loci *see* **locus**.
lock[1] *n* a fastening device on doors, etc, operated by a key or combination; part of a canal, dock, etc in which the level of the water can be changed by the operation of gates; the part of a gun by which the charge is fired; a controlling hold, as used in wrestling. * *vt* to fasten with a lock; to shut; to fit, link; to jam together so as to make immovable. * *vi* to become locked; to interlock.—**lockable** *adj*.
lock[2] *n* a curl of hair; a tuft of wool, etc.
lockage *n* a system of canal locks; the act of going through a lock; the fee paid for so doing.
locker *n* a small cupboard, chest, etc that can be locked, esp one for storing possessions in a public place.
locker room *n* room equipped with lockers for storing possessions in a public place.
locket *n* a small ornamental case, usu holding a lock of hair, photograph or other memento, hung from the neck.
lockjaw *n* tetanus.
lockout *n* the exclusion of employees from a workplace by an employer, as a means of coercion during an industrial dispute.
locksmith *n* a person who makes and repairs locks and keys.
lockup *n* a jail; a garage or storage room.
loco *adj* *(sl)* crazy.
locomotion *n* motion, or the power of moving, from one place to another.
locomotive *n* an electric, steam, or diesel engine on wheels, designed to move a railway train. * *adj* of locomotion.
locomotor *adj* of or pertaining to locomotion. locomotive.
locular, loculate *adj* *(biol)* split into compartments.
loculus, locule *n* *(pl* **loculi, locules**) *(biol)* a small cavity or cell.
locum *n* *(inf)* a locum tenens.
locum tenens *n* *(pl* **locum tenentes**) a person who stands in for a professional colleague, esp for a doctor, chemist or clergyman.
locus *n* *(pl* **loci**) a place; *(math)* the path of a point or curve, moving according to some specific rule; the aggregate of all possible positions of a moving or generating element.
locust *n* a type of large grasshopper often travelling in swarms and destroying crops; a type of hard-wooded leguminous tree.
locution *n* a word, phrase or expression; an act or mode of speaking.
lode *n* an ore deposit.
lodestar *n* a star, usu the North Star, used to guide navigation.—*also* **loadstar**.
lodestone *n* a magnetic oxide of iron; a piece of this oxide, used as a magnet or a crude compass.—*also* **loadstone**.
lodge *n* a small house at the entrance to a park or stately home; a country house for seasonal leisure activities; a resort hotel or motel; the local chapter or hall of a fraternal society; a beaver's lair. * *vt* to house temporarily; to shoot, thrust, etc firmly (in); to bring before legal authorities; to confer upon. * *vi* to live in a place for a time; to live as a paying guest; to come to rest and stick firmly (in).
lodger *n* a person who lives in a rented room in another's home.
lodging *n* a temporary residence; *(pl)* accommodation rented in another's house.
lodgment, lodgement *n* the act of lodging; the state of being lodged; an accumulation of something deposited; *(mil)* a foothold in enemy territory.
loess *n* a light brown deposit of fine silt and clay found in Asia, Europe and America.—**loessial, loessal** *adj*,
loft *n* a space under a roof; a storage area under the roof of a barn or stable; a gallery in a church or hall. * *vt* to send into a high curve.
lofty *adj* (**loftier, loftiest**) *(objects)* of a great height, elevated; *(person)* noble, haughty, superior in manner.—**loftily** *adv*.—**loftiness** *n*.
log[1] *n* a section of a felled tree; a device for ascertaining the speed of a ship; a record of speed, progress, etc, esp one kept on a ship's voyage or aircraft's flight. * *vb* (**logging, logged**) *vt* to record in a log; to sail or

fly (a specified distance). * *vi* (*with* **on, off**) (*comput*) to establish or disestablish communication with a mainframe computer from a remote terminal in a multi-user system.—**logger** *n*.

log[2] *n* a logarithm.

loganberry *n* (*pl* **loganberries**) a hybrid developed from the blackberry and the red raspberry.

logarithm *n* the exponent of the power to which a fixed number (the base) is to be raised to produce a given number, used to avoid multiplying and dividing when solving mathematical problems.—**logarithmic** *adj*.—**logarithmically** *adv*.

logbook *n* an official record of a ship's or aircraft's voyage or flight; an official document containing details of a vehicle's registration.

loge *n* a box in a theatre.

loggerhead *n* (*arch*) a blockhead; (*pl*) a dispute, confrontation (*to be at loggerheads with someone*); (*zool*) a type of turtle.

loggia *n* (*pl* **loggias, loggie**) a covered open gallery or balcony on the side of a building.

logging *n* the business of cutting down timber.

logic *n* correct reasoning, or the science of this; way of reasoning; what is expected by the working of cause and effect.—**logician** *n*.

logical *adj* conforming to the rules of logic; capable of reasoning according to logic.—**logically** *adv*.—**logicality** *n*.

logician *n* someone versed in logic.

logistics *n* (*used as sing*) the science of the organization, transport and supply of military forces; the planning and organization of any complex activity.—**logistic** *adj*.—**logistically** *adv*.

log jam *n* a blockage of logs floating in a watercourse; a deadlock, standstill.

logo *n* (*pl* **logos**) (*inf*) a logotype.

logo- *prefix* word, speech.

logogram, logograph *n* a sign or letter representing a word or phrase.

logographer *n* an annalist or writer of speeches in ancient Greece.

logography *n* a method of printing in which a type represents a word instead of a letter.

logogriph *n* a word puzzle based on an anagram.

logomachy *n* (*pl* **logomachies**) a dispute over words.

loggorhea *n* excessive or incoherent talkativeness.

Logos *n* (*Christianity*) the Divine Word; the second person of the Trinity, Jesus Christ.

logotype *n* a printed symbol representing a corporation, product, etc; a trademark, emblem.

logrolling *n* in US, the undemocratic trading of votes between politicians to ensure the passage of legislation of mutual interest.

-logue, -log *n suffix* indicating a particular type of speech or writing, as in monologue, travelogue.

logwood *n* a wood of a deep-red colour, used in dyeing.

-logy *n suffix* science, theory or doctrine of, eg *astrology*; type of writing or discourse, eg *phraseology*.

logy *adj* (**logier, logiest**) dull, sluggish.

loin *n* (*usu pl*) the lower part of the back between the hipbones and the ribs; the front part of the hindquarters of an animal used for food.

loincloth *n* a cloth worn around the loins.

loiter *vi* to linger or stand about aimlessly.—**loiterer** *n*.

loll *vi* to lean or recline in a lazy manner, to lounge; (*tongue*) to hang loosely.—**loller** *n*.

lollapalooza, lollapaloosa *n* (*sl*) something or someone exceptional.

Lollard *n* (*hist*) a follower of the 14th-century English religious reformer, John Wycliff.

lollipop *n* a flat boiled sweet at the end of a stick.

lollop *vi* to run or walk with an ungainly, bouncing rhythm.

lolly *n* (*pl* **lollies**) (*inf*) a lollipop; (*Brit sl*) money.

loment *n* a plant pod that breaks at maturity into single-seeded joints.

London Pride *n* a type of saxifrage plant with pink flowers.

lone *adj* by oneself; isolated; without companions, solitary.—**loneness** *n*.

lonely *adj* (**lonelier, loneliest**) isolated; unhappy at being alone; (*places*) remote, rarely visited.—**loneliness** *n*.

loner *n* a person who avoids the company of others.

lonesome *adj* having or causing a lonely feeling.—**lonesomely** *adv*.

long. *abbr* = longitude.

long[1] *adj* measuring much in space or time; having a greater than usual length, quantity, etc; tedious, slow; far-reaching; well-supplied. * *adv* for a long time; from start to finish; at a remote time.

long[2] *vi* to desire earnestly, esp for something not likely to be attained.

longanimity *n* long-suffering, forbearance.

longboat *n* the largest boat carried aboard a ship.

longbow *n* a large hand-drawn bow.

longcloth *n* a fine cotton fabric.

long-distance *adj* travelling or communicating over long distances.

longe *see* **lunge**[2].

longeron *n* the principal longitudinal spar of an aircraft's fuselage.

longevity *n* long life.

longhand *n* ordinary handwriting, as opposed to shorthand.

long-headed *adj* shrewd.

longhorn *n* a breed of long-horned cattle.

longicorn *n* a type of beetle with long antennae.

longing *n* an intense desire.—**longingly** *adv*.

longitude *n* distance east or west of the prime meridian, expressed in degrees or time.

longitudinal *adj* of or in length; running or placed lengthways; of longitude.—**longitudinally** *adv*.

long johns *npl* (*inf*) warm underpants with long legs.

long jump *n* an athletic event consisting of a horizontal running jump.

long-lived *adj* having or tending to live a long time.

long-playing *adj* of or relating to an LP record.

long-range *adj* reaching over a long distance or period of time.

longshore *adj* found on, or pertaining to, the shore.

longshoreman *n* (*pl* **longshoremen**) a person who loads and unloads ships at a port.

long shot *n* a wild guess; a competitor, etc who is unlikely to win; a project that has little chance of success.

long-sighted *adj* only seeing distant objects clearly.—**long-sightedly** *adv*.

long-standing *adj* having continued for a long time.

long-suffering *adj* enduring pain, provocation, etc patiently.

long-term *adj* of or extending over a long time.

longueur *n* a tedious period of time.

long wave *n* a radio wave of a frequency less than 300 kHz.

longways, longwise *adv* in the direction of the length (of something), lengthways.

long-winded *adj* speaking or writing at great length; tiresome.—**long-windedly** *adv*.—**long-windedness** *n*.

loo *n* (*pl* **loos**) (*Brit inf*) a lavatory, a toilet.

looby *n* (*pl* **loobies**) a clumsy, stupid person.

loofah *n* the fibrous skeleton of a type of gourd used as a sponge for scrubbing.—*also* **luffa**.

look *vi* to try to see; to see; to search; to appear, seem; to be facing in a specified direction; (*with* **in**) to pay a brief visit; (*with* **up**) to improve in prospects. * *vt* to direct one's eyes on; to have an appearance befitting. * *n* the act of looking; a gaze, glance; appearance; aspect; (*with* **after**) to take care of; (*with* **over**) to examine; (*with* **up**) to research (for information, etc) in book; to visit.

look-alike *n* a person that looks like another.

looker *n* (*inf*) an attractive woman.

looker-on *n* (*pl* **lookers-on**) a spectator.

look-in *n* a brief visit.

looking glass *n* a mirror.

lookout *n* a place for keeping watch; a person assigned to watch.

look-see *n* (*inf*) a brief inspection.

loom[1] *n* a machine or frame for weaving yarn or thread. * *vt* to weave on a loom.

loom[2] *vi* to come into view indistinctly and often threateningly; to come ominously close, as an impending event.

loon[1] *n* a large fish-eating diving bird.

loon[2] *n* (*sl*) a clumsy or stupid person; a crazy person.

loony, looney *n* (*pl* **loonies**) (*sl*) a lunatic. * *adj* (**loonier, looniest**) (*sl*) crazy, demented.—**looniness** *n*.

loop *n* a figure made by a curved line crossing itself; a similar rounded shape in cord, rope, etc crossed on itself; anything forming this figure; (*comput*) a set of instructions in a program that are executed repeatedly; an intrauterine contraceptive device; a segment of film or magnetic tape. * *vt* to make a loop of; to fasten with a loop. * *vi* to form a loop or loops.

looper *n* a caterpillar that crawls by arching itself into loops.

loophole *n* a means of evading an obligation, etc; a slit in a wall for looking or shooting through.

loopy *adj* (**loopier, loopiest**) (*inf*) slightly mad, cracked.

loose *adj* free from confinement or restraint; not firmly fastened; not tight or compact; not precise; inexact; (*inf*) relaxed. * *vt* to release; to unfasten; to untie; to detach; (*bullet*) to discharge. * *vi* to become loose.—**loosely** *adv*.—**looseness** *n*.

loose cannon *n* a person who acts independently and often obstreperously.

loose-leaf *adj* having pages or sheets that can easily be replaced or removed.

loosen *vti* to make or become loose or looser.—**loosener** *n*.

loosestrife *n* a kind of plant with golden or purple flowers.

loot *n* goods taken during warfare, civil unrest, etc; (*sl*) money. * *vti* to plunder, pillage.—**looter** *n*.

lop *vt* (**lopping, lopped**) to sever the branches or twigs from a tree; to cut off or out as superfluous.

lope *vi* to move or run with a long bounding stride.—*also n*.—**loper** *n*.

lop-eared *adj* having drooping ears.

lophobranchiate *adj* (*fish*) with gills arranged in tufts.

lopsided *adj* having one side larger in weight, height, or size than the other; badly balanced.—**lopsidedly** *adv*.—**lopsidedness** *n*.

loquacious *adj* talkative.—**loquaciously** *adv*.—**loquacity** *n*.

loquat *n* an evergreen tree found in China and Japan; its edible fruit.

loquitur (*theatre*) (*formerly*) he or she speaks (as a stage direction).

lord *n* a ruler, master or monarch; a male member of the nobility; (*with cap and* **the**) God; a form of address used to certain peers, bishops and judges.

lordling *n* a young or minor lord.

lordly *adj* (**lordlier, lordliest**) noble; haughty; arrogant.—**lordliness** *n*.

Lord Mayor *n* the mayor of the City of London and certain other UK boroughs and towns—*also* **Lord Provost** in Scotland.

lordosis *n* forward curvature of the spine.

Lord Privy Seal *n* a British cabinet minister without specific responsibilities.

Lord Provost *see* **Lord Mayor**.

Lord's Day *n* (*with* **the**) Sunday.

lordship *n* the rank or authority of a lord; rule, dominion; (*with* **his** *or* **your**) a title used in speaking of or to a lord.

Lord's Prayer *n* (*with* **the**) the prayer taught by Jesus to His disciples beginning 'Our Father'.

lords spiritual *npl* the bishops and archbishops who are members of the British House of Lords.

lords temporal *npl* the peers other than bishops and archbishops in the British House of Lords.

lore *n* knowledge; learning, esp of a traditional nature; a particular body of tradition.

lorgnette *n* a long-handled opera glass; a pair of spectacles fixed to a long handle, into which they fold.

lorica *n* (*pl* **loricae**) the hard outer shell of certain animals.—**loricate, loricated** *adj*.

lorikeet *n* a small, brightly coloured parrot.

loris *n* (*pl* **loris**) a small, nocturnal, climbing primate, found in South and South-East Asia.

lorn *adj* (*poet*) forsaken; forlorn.

lorry *n* (*pl* **lorries**) (*esp Brit*) a large motor vehicle for transporting heavy loads.—*also* **truck**.

lory *n* (*pl* **lories**) a small parrot with brilliant plumage.

lose *vb* (**losing, lost**) *vt* to have taken from one by death, accident, removal, etc; to be unable to find; to fail to keep, as one's temper; to fail to see, hear, or understand; to fail to have, get, etc; to fail to win; to cause the loss of; to wander from (one's way, etc); to squander. * *vi* to suffer (a) loss.—**losable** *adj*.—**loser** *n*.

losel *n* (*dial*) a worthless person.

loss *n* a losing or being lost; the damage, trouble caused by losing; the person, thing, or amount lost.

loss leader *n* an item sold at a price below its value in order to attract customers.

lost *adj* no longer possessed; missing; not won; destroyed or ruined; having wandered astray; wasted.

lot *n* an object, such as a straw, slip of paper, etc drawn from others at random to reach a decision by chance; the decision thus arrived at; one's share by lot; fortune; a plot of ground; a group of persons or things; an item or set of items put up for auction; (*often pl*) (*inf*) a great amount; much; (*inf*) sort. * *vt* (**lotting, lotted**) to divide into lots.

lota, lotah *n* a brass or copper water pot.

loth *see* **loath**.

Lothario *n* (*pl* **Lotharios**) a libertine.

lotion *n* a liquid for cosmetic or external medical use.

lottery *n* (*pl* **lotteries**) a system of raising money by selling numbered tickets that offer the chance of winning a prize; an enterprise, etc which may or may not succeed.

lotto *n* a game of chance based on the drawing of prize numbers.

lotus *n* a type of waterlily; (*Greek legend*) a plant whose fruit induced contented forgetfulness.

lotus-eater *n* a person dedicated to a life of idle pleasure.

lotus position *n* an erect sitting position in yoga with the legs crossed close to the body.

louche *adj* untrustworthy, shady.

loud *adj* characterized by or producing great noise; emphatic; (*inf*) obtrusive or flashy.—**loudly** *adv*.—**loudness** *n*.

louden *vi* to grow louder. * *vt* to make louder.

loudspeaker *n* a device for converting electrical energy into sound.

lough *n* (*Irish*) a lake; an arm of the sea.

louis, louis d'or *n* (*pl* **louis, louis d'or**) (*formerly*) a French gold coin, with a value of 20 francs.

lounge *vi* to move, sit, lie, etc in a relaxed way; to spend time idly. * *n* a room with comfortable furniture for sitting, as a waiting room at an airport, etc; a comfortable sitting room in a hotel or private house.

lounger *n* a comfortable couch or chair for relaxing on; a person who lounges.

lour *vi* to look sullen; to become dark, gloomy, threatening.—*also* **lower**.—**louringly, loweringly** *adv*.

louse *n* (*pl* **lice**) any of various small wingless insects that are parasitic on humans and animals; any similar but unrelated insects that are parasitic on plants; (*inf*) (*pl* **louses**) a mean, contemptible person.

lousy *adj* (**lousier, lousiest**) infested with lice; (*sl*) disgusting, of poor quality, or inferior; (*sl*) well supplied (with).—**lousily** *adv*,—**lousiness** *n*.

lout *n* a clumsy, rude person.—**loutish** *adj*.

louver, louvre *n* one of a set of slats in a door or window set parallel and slanted to admit air but not rain.—**louvered, louvred** *adj*.

lovable *adj* easy to love or feel affection for.—**lovability** *n*.—**lovably** *adv*.

lovage *n* a European herb used as a seasoning in food.

love *n* a strong liking for someone or something; a passionate affection for another person; the object of such affection; (*tennis*) a score of zero. * *vti* to feel love (for).

love affair *n* a romantic or sexual relationship between two people.
lovebird *n* any of various small parrots.
love child *n* an illegitimate child.
love-in-a-mist *n* a flowering garden plant, fennelflower.
loveless *adj* without love; not feeling or receiving love.—**lovelessly** *adv*.
lovelock *n* a curl worn on the forehead.
lovelorn *adj* pining from love.
lovely *adj* (**lovelier, loveliest**) beautiful; (*inf*) highly enjoyable. * *n* (*pl* **lovelies**) a lovely person.—**loveliness** *n*.
lovemaking *n* sexual activity, esp intercourse, between lovers.
lover *n* a person in love with another person; a person, esp a man, having an extramarital sexual relationship; (*pl*) a couple in love with each other; someone who loves a specific person or thing.
lovesick *adj* languishing through love.—**lovesickness** *n*.
lovey-dovey *adj* (*sl*) displaying affection in an excessive or exaggerated manner.
loving *adj* affectionate.—**lovingly** *adv*.—**lovingness** *n*.
loving cup *n* a large cup with two or more handles passed round a group for all to drink from.
low[1] *n* the sound a cow makes, a moo. * *vi* to make this sound.
low[2] *adj* not high or tall; below the normal level; less in size, degree, amount, etc than usual; deep in pitch; depressed in spirits; humble, of low rank; vulgar, coarse; not loud. * *adv* in or to a low degree, level, etc. * *n* a low level, degree, etc; a region of low barometric pressure.
lowborn, lowbred *adj* of humble birth.
lowboy *n* a table with drawers.
lowbrow *n* (*inf*) a person regarded as uncultivated and lacking in taste.—*also adj*.
low comedy *n* comedy reliant on farce or physical slapstick.
lowdown *n* (*sl: with* **the**) the true, pertinent facts
low-down *adj* (*inf*) mean, contemptible.
lower case *n* small letters (not capitals) used for printing.
lower class *n* the class of people having the lowest status in society.
lower house, lower chamber *n* one of the two chambers in a bicameral legislature, such as the US House of Representatives or the British House of Commons.
lower[1] *adj* below in place, rank, etc; less in amount, degree, etc. * *vt* to let or put down; to reduce in height, amount, etc; to bring down in respect, etc. * *vi* to become lower.—**lowerable** *adj*.
lower[2] *see* **lour.**
lowermost *adj* lowest.
low frequency *n* a radio frequency between 300 and 30 kilohertz.
low-key, low-keyed *adj* of low intensity, subdued.
lowland *n* low-lying land; (*pl*) a flat region. * *adj* of or pertaining to lowlands.—**lowlander** *n*.
low-level language *n* (*comput*) a programming language that corresponds more to machine language than human language.
lowlife *n* (*pl* **lowlifes**) (*sl*) a criminal.
lowly *adj* (**lowlier, lowliest**) humble, of low status; meek.—**lowliness** *n*.
Low Mass *n* a Mass without music or elaborate ritual.
low-rise *adj* (*building*) having only one or two storeys.—*also n*.
low spirited *adj* unhappy, depressed.
low-tech *adj* of or involving low technology.
low technology *n* unsophisticated technology limited to the provision of basic human needs.
low tension *adj* using, conveying, or operating at a low voltage.
low tide *n* (the time of) the tide when it is at its lowest level; a low point.
low water *n* low tide.
lox[1] *n* a type of smoked salmon.
lox[2] *n* liquid oxygen.
loyal *adj* firm in allegiance to a person, cause, country, etc, faithful; demonstrating unswerving allegiance.—**loyally** *adv*.—**loyalty** *n*.
loyalist *n* a person who supports the established government, esp during a revolt.—**loyalism** *n*.
lozenge *n* a four-sided diamond-shaped figure; a cough drop, sweet, etc, originally diamond-shaped.
LP *n* a long-playing record, usu 12 inches (30.5 cm) in diameter and played at a speed of 33 1/3 revolutions per minute.
LPG *abbr* = liquefied petroleum gas.
Lr (*chem symbol*) lawrencium.
LSD *n* a powerful hallucinatory drug (lysergic acid diethylamide).
Lt *abbr* = lieutenant.
Ltd *abbr* = limited liability (used by private companies only).
LU (*chem symbol*) lutetium.
luau *n* a sumptuous feast in Hawaii; a warm welcome; an unexpected source of wealth; a bonanza.
lubber *n* a clumsy person.
lubricant *n* a substance that lubricates.
lubricate *vt* to coat or treat (machinery, etc) with oil or grease to lessen friction; to make smooth, slippery, or greasy. * *vi* to act as a lubricant.—**lubrication** *n*.
lubricator *n* person who or thing that lubricates; a device used for oiling machines.
lubricity *n* slipperiness; evasiveness; lewdness.
lucarne *n* a dormer window, esp in a spire.
lucent *adj* bright, shining.—**lucency** *n*.
lucerne *see* **alfalfa.**
lucid *adj* easily understood; sane.—**lucidly** *adv*.—**lucidity** *n*.
Lucifer *n* Satan.
luck *n* chance; good fortune.
luckless *n* unfortunate, unlucky.—**lucklessly** *adv*.—**lucklessness** *n*.
lucky *adj* (**luckier, luckiest**) having or bringing good luck.—**luckily** *adv*.—**luckiness** *n*.
lucrative *adj* producing wealth or profit; profitable.—**lucratively** *adv*.—**lucrativeness** *n*.
lucre *n* (*derog*) riches, money.
lucubrate *vi* to study, esp by night.—**lucubrator** *n*.
lucubration *n* study, esp nocturnal; (*often pl*) a literary compositon produced as the result of protracted study.
ludicrous *adj* absurd, laughable.—**ludicrously** *adv*.
luff *n* (*naut*) the part of ship towards the wind. * *vti* (*naut*) to turn (a ship) into the wind.
luffa *see* **loofah.**
Luftwaffe *n* the German Air Force.
lug[1] *vt* (**lugging, lugged**) to pull or drag along with effort.
lug[2] *n* an ear-like projection by which a thing is held or supported.
luge *n* a small one-person toboggan.
luggage *n* the suitcases and other baggage containing the possessions of a traveller.
lugger *n* a small vessel rigged with one or more lugsails.
lugsail *n* a square sail, with no boom or lower yard, which hangs nearly at right angles to the mast.
lugubrious *adj* mournful, dismal.—**lugubriously** *adv*.
lugworm *n* a marine worm used as bait.
lukewarm *adj* barely warm, tepid; lacking enthusiasm.
lull *vt* to soothe, to calm; to calm the suspicions of, esp by deception. * *n* a short period of calm.
lullaby *n* (*pl* **lullabies**) a song to lull children to sleep.
lulu *n* (*inf*) a wonderful or remarkable person or thing.
lumbago *n* rheumatic pain in the lower back.
lumbar *adj* of or in the loins.
lumber[1] *n* timber, logs, beams, boards, etc, roughly cut and prepared for use; articles of unused household furniture that are stored away; any useless articles. * *vi* to cut down timber and saw it into lumber. * *vt* to clutter with lumber; to heap in disorder.
lumber[2] *vi* to move heavily or clumsily.—**lumberer** *n*.
lumbering[1] *adj* moving clumsily and heavily.—**lumberingly** *adv*.
lumbering[2] *n* the cutting down and sawing of trees into timber as a business.

lumberjack *n* a person employed to fell trees and transport and prepare timber.
lumbrical *adj* wormlike.
lumen *n* (*pl* **lumina, lumens**) the SI unit of light flux; (*anat*) a duct within a tubular organ.
luminary *n* (*pl* **luminaries**) a body that gives off light, such as the sun; a famous or notable person.
luminescent *adj* emitting light but not heat.—**luminescence** *n*.
luminosity *n* (*pl* **luminosities**) the quality of being luminous; something luminous; (*astron*) the degree of light emitted by a star when compared with the sun.
luminous *adj* emitting light; glowing in the dark; clear, easily understood.—**luminously** *adv*.
lump *n* a small, compact mass of something, usu without definite shape; an abnormal swelling; a dull or stupid person. * *adj* in a lump or lumps. * *vt* to treat or deal with in a mass. * *vi* to become lumpy.
lumper *n* a docker.
lumpfish *n* (*pl* **lumpfish, lumpfishes**) a sea fish found in the North Atlantic, with horny spines and a sucker with which it clings to objects.
lumpish *adj* like a lump; heavy; dull, stupid.
lump sum *n* a sum of money (esp cash) paid as a whole and not in instalments.
lumpy *adj* (**lumpier, lumpiest**) filled or covered with lumps.—**lumpily** *adv*.—**lumpiness** *n*.
lunacy *n* (*pl* **lunacies**) insanity; utter folly.
lunar *adj* of or like the moon.
lunar eclipse *n* an eclipse when the earth passes between the sun and the moon.
lunar month *n* a month measured by the complete revolution of the moon, 29.5 days.
lunar year *n* a year of twelve lunar months, 354.33 days.
lunate, lunated *adj* crescent-shaped.
lunatic *adj* insane; utterly foolish. * *n* an insane person.
lunatic fringe *n* the members of an organization regarded as being fanatical or extreme.
lunation *n* a lunar month, the time taken for the moon to revolve once around the earth.
lunch *n* a light meal, esp between breakfast and dinner; **out to lunch** (*sl*) crazy; eccentric. * *vi* to eat lunch.—**luncher** *n*.
luncheon *n* lunch, esp a formal lunch.
luncheon meat *n* processed meat in tins ready to eat.
lune *n* (*geom*) a figure formed on a plane or sphere by two intersecting arcs of circles.
lunette *n* anything shaped like a crescent; an arched opening in a vaulted roof to admit light.
lung *n* either of the two sponge-like breathing organs in the chest of vertebrates.
lunge[1] *n* a sudden forceful thrust, as with a sword; a sudden plunge forward. * *vti* to move, or cause to move, with a lunge.—**lunger** *n*.
lunge[2] *n* a long halter for training a horse; the use of this in training horses. * *vt* to train with a lunge.—*also* **longe**.
lungfish *n* (*pl* **lungfish, lungfishes**) a freshwater fish with lungs as well as gills.
lungi *n* a long piece of cloth worn as a skirt or loincloth by Indian men.
lungwort *n* a Eurasian plant with dark-coloured leaves spotted with white.
lunisolar *adj* pertaining to the sun and moon; produced by the sun and moon in unison.
lunula, lunule *n* (*pl* **lunulae, lunules**) the white crescent-shaped part near the root of the fingernail.
lupine[1] *n* a garden plant of the pea family.
lupine[2] *adj* of or resembling a wolf.
lupulin *n* a powder, obtained from hops, used as a sedative.
lupus *n* any of several diseases marked by lesions of the skin.
lurch *vi* to lean or pitch suddenly to the side. * *n* a sudden roll to one side.—**lurchingly** *adv*.
lurdan *adj* (*arch*) stupid. * *n* a stupid person.
lure *n* something that attracts, tempts or entices; a brightly coloured fishing bait; a device used to recall a trained hawk; a decoy for wild animals. * *vt* to entice, attract, or tempt.—**luringly** *adv*.
lurid *adj* vivid, glaring; shocking; sensational.—**luridly** *adv*.—**luridness** *n*.
lurk *vi* to lie hidden in wait; to loiter furtively.—**lurker** *n*.
luscious *adj* delicious; richly sweet; delighting any of the senses.—**lusciously** *adv*.—**lusciousness** *n*.
lush[1] *adj* tender and juicy; of or showing abundant growth.—**lushly** *adv*.—**lushness** *n*.
lush[2] *n* (*sl*) an alcoholic.
lust *n* strong sexual desire (for); an intense longing for something. * *vi* to feel lust.—**lustful** *adj*.—**lustfully** *adv*.
lustral *adj* of or relating to ceremonial purification; of or relating to a lustrum.
lustrate *vt* to purify by sacrifice or ceremonial washing.—**lustration** *n*.
lustre, luster *n* gloss; sheen; brightness; radiance; brilliant beauty or fame; glory; a chandelier with pendants of cut glass; a fabric with a lustrous surface; a substance used to give lustre to an object; a metallic glaze on pottery; the quality and intensity of light reflected from the surface of minerals.—**lusterless** *adj*.—**lustrous** *adj*.
lustreware, lusterware *n* earthenware decorated with luster.
lustrum *n* (*pl* **lustrums, lustra**) a period of five years.
lusty *adj* (**lustier, lustiest**) strong; vigorous; healthy.—**lustily** *adv*.—**lustiness** *n*.
lute[1] *n* an old, round-backed stringed musical instrument plucked with the fingers.
lute[2] *n* clay or cement used to make joints airtight, etc.
lutenist, lutist *n* a lute player.
luteous *adj* greenish-yellow.
lutetium *n* a metallic element.
Lutheran *adj* pertaining to Martin Luther 1483–1546), the German religious reformer, or to the Lutheran Church and its doctrines. * *n* a follower of Martin Luther; a member of the Lutheran Church.—**Lutheranism** *n*.
Lutheran Church *n* the Protestant church founded by Martin Luther in Germany in the 16th century.
lux *n* (*pl* **lux**) a unit of illumination.
luxate *vt* to put out of joint.—**luxation** *n*.
luxuriant *adj* profuse, abundant; ornate; fertile.—**luxuriance** *n*.
luxuriate *vi* to enjoy immensely, to revel (in).—**luxuriation** *n*.
luxurious *adj* constituting luxury; indulging in luxury; rich, comfortable.—**luxuriously** *adv*.—**luxuriousness** *n*.
luxury *n* (*pl* **luxuries**) indulgence and pleasure in sumptuous and expensive food, accommodation, clothes, etc; (*often pl*) something that is costly and enjoyable but not indispensable. * *adj* relating to or supplying luxury.
lx *abbr* = lux.
lycanthrope *n* a werewolf; (*med*) a sufferer from lycanthropy.
lycanthropy *n* the supposed power of changing from a human being into a werewolf; (*med*) a form of mental illness in which the sufferer believes himself or herself to be a wolf.
lycée *n* (*pl* **lycées**) a state secondary school in France.
lyceum *n* a public lecture hall.
lychee *see* **lichee**.
lych gate *see* **lich gate**.
lychnis *n* a genus of flowering plants, including the ragged robin and campion.
lycopod *n* a kind of moss, also known as the club moss.
lycopodium *n* any of a genus of perennial plants, the club mosses; an inflammable yellow powder in the spore cases of certain species, used in fireworks.
Lycra *n* (*trademark*) an elastic synthetic material used for tight-fitting garments, such as bicycle shorts and swimwear.
lyddite *n* a powerful explosive, composed chiefly of picric acid.

lye *n* an alkaline solution.
lying *see* **lie**[1], **lie**[2].
lying-in *n* (*pl* **lyings-in, lying-ins**) childbirth.
Lyme disease *n* an infectious disease, carried by ticks, that produces fever, pains in the joints and a rash, and can result in paralysis or chronic fatigue, and, rarely, death.
lymph *n* a clear, yellowish body fluid, found in intercellular spaces and the lymphatic vessels.
lymphatic *adj* of, relating to, or containing lymph; sluggish. * *n* a vessel that contains or conveys lymph.
lymph node *n* any of numerous nodules of tissue distributed along the course of lymphatic vessels that produce lymphocytes.
lympho- *prefix* lymph; lymph tissue; lymphatic system.
lymphocyte *n* a white blood cell formed in the lymph nodes, which helps to protect against infection.—**lymphocytic** *adj*.
lymphoid *adj* relating to lymph glands; resembling lymph.
lymphoma *n* (*pl* **lymphomata**) a tumour of the lymphoid tissue.
lyncean *adj* pertaining to or resembling the lynx; sharp-eyed.
lynch *vt* to murder (an accused person) by mob action, without lawful trial, as by hanging.—**lyncher** *n*.—**lynching** *n*.
lynx *n* (*pl* **lynxes, lynx**) a wild feline of Europe and North America with spotted fur.
lynx-eyed *adj* keen-sighted.
lyonnaise *adj* (*cooking*) with onions.
lyrate, lyrated *adj* lyre-shaped.
lyre *n* an ancient musical instrument of the harp family.
lyrebird *n* an Australian bird with a tail shaped like a lyre.
lyric *adj* denoting or of poetry expressing the writer's emotion; of, or having a high voice with a light, flexible quality. * *n* a lyric poem; (*pl*) the words of a popular song.
lyrical *adj* lyric; (*inf*) expressing rapture or enthusiasm.—**lyrically** *adv*.
lyricism *n* lyrical quality or expression.
lyricist *n* a person who writes lyrics, esp for popular songs.
lyrist *n* a lyric poet; a lyre player.
lysergic acid *see* **LSD**.
lysin *n* a specific antibody in blood that can destroy cells.
lysin *n* a substance, esp an antibody, that kills living cells or bacteria.
lysine *n* an amino acid formed by the digestion of dietary protein.
-lysis *n suffix* disintegration; decomposition.
lysis *n* (*pl* **lyses**) (*biol*) the process of destroying cells with a lysin; (*med*) the gradual abatement of an acute disease.
-lyte *n suffix* denoting a substance able to be disintegrated or decomposed.
-lytic *adj suffix* indicating a disintegration or decomposition.

M *abbr* = mega-; medium; motorway.
M. *abbr* = Master; Monsieur
m *abbr* = metre(s); mile(s); million(s).
MA *abbr* = Master of Arts; Massachusetts.
ma *n* (*inf*) mother.
ma'am *n* madam (used as a title of respect, esp when addressing royalty).
macabre *adj* gruesome; grim; of death.
macaco *n* (*pl* **macacos**) one of various lemurs, esp the ruffled lemur and the ring-tailed lemur.
macadam *n* a road surface composed of successive layers of small stones compacted into a solid mass.
macadamia *n* an Australian tree bearing white flowers and an edible seed (**macadamia nut**).
macadamize *vt* to surface (a road) with macadam.—**macadamization** *n*.
macaque *n* a short-tailed monkey of Asia and Africa.
macaroni *n* (*pl* **macaronis, macaronies**) a pasta made chiefly of fine wheat flour and made into tubes; an 18th-century dandy who copied continental mannerisms etc.
macaronic *adj* (*verse*) using words from more than one language, or a mixture of everyday words and Latin words or words with Latin endings. * *n* (*often pl*) macaronic verse.
macaroon *n* a small cake or biscuit made with sugar, egg whites and ground almonds or coconut.
macaw *n* a large parrot with brightly coloured plumage.
Maccabean *adj* pertaining to the Maccabees, a family of Jewish patriots who led a successful revolt against the Syrians, or to its most famous member, Judas Maccabaeus.
maccaboy *n* a kind of snuff, usu rose-scented.
mace[1] *n* a staff used as a symbol of authority by certain institutions.
mace[2] *n* an aromatic spice made from the external covering of the nutmeg.
macédoine *n* a dish of mixed fruits, served hot or cold; a dish of diced vegetables, usu in jelly or syrup; any mixture.
macerate *vti* to soften or become soft or separated through soaking; to make or become thin.—**maceration** *n*.—**macerator** *n*.
Mach *see* **Mach number**.
machete *n* a large knife used for cutting, or as a weapon.
Machiavellian *adj* cunning; deceitful.
machicolation *n* (*arch*) a projecting parapet, usu found on medieval castles, with openings for dropping stones, etc, on assailants; such an opening.—**machicolated** *adj*.
machinate *vti* to scheme, plan, esp to do harm.—**machinator** *n*.
machination *n* (*usu pl*) an artifice; an intrigue; a plot; the act of plotting or intriguing.
machine *n* a structure of fixed and moving parts, for doing useful work; an organization functioning like a machine; the controlling group in a political party; a device, as the lever, etc that transmits, or changes the application of energy. * *vt* to shape or finish by machine-operated tools. * *adj* of machines; done by machinery.
machine code, machine language *n* (*comput*) programming instructions in binary or hexadecimal code.
machine gun *n* an automatic gun, firing a rapid stream of bullets.—*also vt*.
machine-readable *adj* directly usable by a computer.
machinery *n* machines collectively; the parts of a machine; the framework for keeping something going.
machine tool *n* a mechanized tool for cutting or shaping metals, wood, etc.
machinist *n* one who makes, repairs, or operates machinery.
machismo *n* strong or assertive masculinity; virility.—**macho** *adj*.
Mach number *n* the ratio of the speed of a body in a particular medium to the speed of sound in the same medium. Mach 1 is equal to the speed of sound.
mackerel *n* (*pl* **mackerel, mackerels**) a common oily food fish.
Mackinaw (coat) *n* a short, double-breasted coat made of a heavy woollen plaid material.
mackintosh *n* a waterproof raincoat.
mackle *n* (*printing*) a blurred or imprecise impression, which produces the effect of a double printing.—*also* **macule**.
macle *n* a type of crystal in two parts, containing carbon impurities, sometimes used as a gemstone.
macramé *n* (the art of) knotting or weaving coarse thread to produce ornamental work.
macro- *prefix* = long, large.
macrobiotic *adj* (*diet*) composed of an extremely restricted range of foods, usu vegetables and whole grains.
macrocephalic *adj* having an unusually large skull.—*also* **megacephalic** *adj*.—**macrocephaly** *n*.
macrocosm *n* the universe; any complex system.—**macrocosmic** *adj*.
macroeconomics *n* (*used as sing*) the study of the economy in terms of total national income, production and investment.—**macroeconomic** *adj*.
macron *n* a mark placed over a letter to indicate a stressed or long vowel (¯).

macropterous *adj* (*zool*) large-winged.
macroscopic *adj* visible to the naked eye; regarded in terms of large elements.
macrospore *see* **megaspore.**
macula *n* (*pl* **maculae**) a spot or mark on the skin; a coloured area near the retina, where vision is esp sharp.—**macular** *adj*.—**maculation** *n*.
macule' *see* **mackle.**
mad *adj* (**madder, maddest**) insane; frantic; foolish and rash; infatuated; (*inf*) angry.
madam *n* a polite term of address to a woman; a woman in charge of a brothel; (*inf*) a precocious little girl.
madame *n* (*pl* **mesdames**) the title of a married French woman; used as a title equivalent to Mrs.
madcap *adj* reckless, impulsive.—*also n.*
madden *vti* to make or become insane, angry, or wildly excited.—**maddening** *adj*.—**maddeningly** *adv*.
madder[1] *see* **mad.**
madder[2] *n* a plant of the genus from whose root a red dye and pigment are extracted; the red dye so obtained; a synthetic pigment used in paints and inks.
madding *adj* (*arch*) raging; furious; causing (someone or something) to be raging.
made *see* **make.**
Madeira *n* a rich, strong, white wine made in the North Atlantic island of Madeira.
madeleine *n* a small sponge cake with a coating of red jam covered with coconut.
mademoiselle *n* (*pl* **mesdemoiselles**) the title of an unmarried French girl or woman; used as a title equivalent to Miss; a French teacher or governess.
made-to-order *adj* produced to a customer's specifications; being ideally suited for a particular purpose.
madhouse *n* (*inf*) as mental institution; a state of uproar or confusion.
madly *adv* in an insane manner; at great speed, force; (*inf*) excessively.
madman *n* (*pl* **madmen**) an insane person.
madness *n* insanity; foolishness; excitability.
Madonna *n* the Virgin Mary, esp as seen in pictures or statues.
madras *n* a strong cotton or silk material, usu striped.
madrepore *n* any of several corals, often forming tropical coral reefs.—**madreporic** *adj*.
madrigal *n* a 16th-century love song or pastoral poem in the form of an unaccompanied part-song; 14th-century Italian song derived from a pastoral poem.—**madrigalist** *n*.
maduro *adj* (*cigar*) dark and full-flavoured. * *n* (*pl* **maduros**) such a cigar.
madwoman *n* (*pl* **madwomen**) an insane person.
madwort *n* a small herb with yellow or white flowers, formerly reputed to cure madness; a type of small, low-growing, flowering plant with hairy leaves and blue flowers.
maelstrom *n* a whirlpool; a state of turbulence or confusion.
maenad *n* (**maenads, maenades**) (*Greek myth*) a female adherent of Dionysus; a frantic, agitated woman.—*also* **menad.**
maestoso *adj, adv* (*mus*) in a majestic manner.
maestro *n* (*pl* **maestros**) a master of an art, esp a musical composer, conductor, or teacher.
mae west *n* (*inf*) an inflatable life jacket.
Mafia *n* a secret society composed chiefly of criminal elements, originating in Sicily.
mafioso *n* (*pl* **mafiosos, mafiosi**) a member of the Mafia.
mag. *abbr* = magazine.
magazine *n* a military store; a space where explosives are stored, as in a fort; a supply chamber, as in a camera, a rifle, etc; a periodical publication containing articles, fiction, photographs, etc.
magdalen, magdalene *n* a reformed prostitute; (*rare*) an institution for housing and reforming prostitutes.
magenta *n* a purplish-red dye; purplish red.—*also adj.*
maggot *n* a wormlike larva, as of the housefly.—**maggoty** *adj*.—**maggotiness** *n*.
magi, magian *see* **magus.**
magic *n* the use of charms, spells, etc to supposedly influence events by supernatural means; any mysterious power; the art of producing illusions by sleight of hand, etc. * *adj* of or relating to magic; possessing supposedly supernatural powers; (*inf*) wonderful. * *vt* (**magicking, magicked**) to influence, produce or take (away) by or as if by magic.—**magical** *adj*.—**magically** *adv*.
magician *n* one skilled in magic; a conjurer.
magisterial *adj* of, or suitable for a magistrate; authoritative.—**magisterially** *adv*.
magistracy *n* (*pl* **magistracies**) the office, jurisdiction or dignity of a magistrate; magistrates collectively.
magistral *adj* or or pertaining to a master or teacher, magisterial; (*med*) specially prescribed; (*fortification*) in a strategic position.
magistrate *n* a public officer empowered to administer the law.—**magistrateship, magistrature** *n*.
magma *n* (*pl* **magmas, magmata**) a stratum of hot molten rock within the earth's crust, which solidifies on the surface as lava.
Magna Carta, Magna Charta *n* in England, the Great Charter, forming the basis of civil liberty, granted by King John to the barons, church and freemen in 1215.
magnanimity *n* (*pl* **magnanimities**) generosity.
magnanimous *adj* noble and generous in conduct or spirit, not petty.—**magnanimously** *adv*.
magnate *n* a very wealthy or influential person.
magnesia *n* a magnesium compound used as a mild laxative.
magnesium *n* a white metallic element that burns very brightly.
magnet *n* any piece of iron or steel that has the property of attracting iron; anything that attracts.
magnetic *adj* of magnetism or a magnet; producing or acting by magnetism; having the ability to attract or charm people.—**magnetically** *adv*.
magnetic declination *n* deviation of the magnetic needle from true north; the measure of this.
magnetic equator *n* the imaginary point near the equator where the magnetic needle has no dip, the aclinic line.
magnetic field *n* any space in which there is an appreciable magnetic force.
magnetic needle *n* a thin piece of magnetized iron, steel, etc, used in a compass and other instruments, that indicates the direction of a magnetic field.
magnetic north *n* the northerly direction of the earth's magnetic field, as pointed to by a compass needle.
magnetic pole *n* either of the two variable points in the regions of the earth's northern and southern poles to which a magnetic needle points.
magnetic resonance imaging *n* a method of viewing the body's internal organs by the use of radio waves.
magnetics *n sing* the science of magnetism.
magnetic tape *n* a thin plastic ribbon with a magnetized coating for recording sound, video signals, computer data, etc.
magnetism *n* the property, quality, or condition of being magnetic; the force to which this is due; personal charm.
magnetize *vt* to make magnetic; to attract strongly.—**magnetization** *n*.—**magnetizer** *n*.
magneto *n* (*pl* **magnetos**) a small generator with permanent magnets for generating high voltages, esp the ignition spark in an internal combustion engine.
magnetoelectricity *n* electric phenomena produced by magnetism.
magnetometer *n* an instrument for measuring and comparing magnetic fields.
magneton *n* one of two units of magnetic moment.
magnet school *n* a school in which resources are devoted to developing excellence in one particular field, eg science.

Magnificat *n* the hymn of the Virgin Mary (Luke 1:46–55); a musical setting of this; (*without cap*) any hymn of praise.
magnification *n* magnifying or being magnified; the degree of enlargement of something by a lens, microscope, etc.
magnificence *n* grandeur of appearance; splendour; pomp.
magnificent *adj* splendid, stately or sumptuous in appearance; superb, of very high quality.—**magnificently** *adv*.
magnifico *n* (*pl* **magnificoes**) a person of importance or high rank; (*formerly*) a title of a Venetian nobleman.
magnify *vt* (**magnifying, magnified**) to exaggerate; to increase the apparent size of (an object) as (with) a lens.—**magnifiable** *adj*.—**magnifier** *n*.
magniloquent *adj* pompous in style or speech, bombastic.—**magniloquence** *n*.—**magniloquently** *adv*.
magnitude *n* greatness of size, extent, etc; importance; (*astron*) the apparent brightness of a star.
magnolia *n* a spring-flowering shrub or tree with evergreen or deciduous leaves and showy flowers.
magnum *n* (*pl* **magnums**) a wine bottle that holds twice the normal quantity.
magnum opus *in* (*pl* **magna opera**) the great or chief work of an artist or author.
magpie *n* a black and white bird of the crow family; a person who chatters; an acquisitive person.
maguey *n* any of several species of a tropical American plant, esp one from which fibre is obtained or that is used in the production of alcoholic drinks; the fibre from such a plant.
magus *n* (*pl* **magi**) a Zoroastrian priest; (*with cap*) any of the three wise men who paid homage to Christ at His birth; a magician, sorcerer.—**magian** *adj, n*.
Magyar *adj* pertaining to the Hungarian or Magyar race or language; (*sleeve*) cut as part of the bodice, with no armhole seam.
Mahabharata *n* a great Hindu epic that narrates the dynastic wars of ancient India.
maharajah, maharaja *n* the former title of an Indian prince.
maharani, maharanee *n* the wife of a maharajah.
mahatma *n* (*Hinduism, Buddhism*) a wise man, a sage; (*with cap*) (*Hinduism*) a title or respect for a man of great spirituality.
mahi-mahi *n* either of two dolphin fish (genus *Coryphaena*) of the Pacific Ocean, a food fish.
mahjong, mah-jongg *n* an orig Chinese game for four people played with decorative tiles.
mahlstick *see* **maulstick**.
mahogany *n* (*pl* **mahoganies**) the hard, reddish-brown wood of a tropical tree; a reddish-brown colour.
Mahometan *see* **Muhammedan**.
mahout *n* (*India*) an elephant driver.
maid *n* a maiden; a woman servant.
maiden *n* a girl or young unmarried woman. * *adj* unmarried or virgin; untried; first.—**maidenhood** *n*.
maidenhair (fern) *n* a delicate-leafed fern with small light green leaflets.
maidenhead *n* the hymen.
maidenly *adj* like or suitable to a maiden; modest; gentle.—**maidenliness** *n*.
maiden name *n* the surname of a woman before marriage.
maiden over *n* (*cricket*) an over during which no runs are scored.
maid of honour *n* the principal unmarried attendant of a bride; a small almond-flavoured tart.
maidservant *n* a female servant.
maieutic *adj* of the Socratic method of teaching by means of questions.
mail[1] *n* a body armour made of small metal rings or links.
mail[2] *n* letters, packages, etc transported and delivered by the post office; a postal system. * *vt* to send by mail.—**mailable** *adj*.
mailman *n* (*pl* **mailmen**) a person who collects or delivers mail.—*also* **postman.**
mail order *n* an order for goods to be sent by post.
maim *vt* to cripple; to mutilate.
main *adj* chief in size, importance, etc; principal. * *n* (*often pl but used a sing*) a principal pipe in a distribution system for water, gas, etc; the essential point.
mainframe *n* a large computer that can handle multiple tasks concurrently.
mainland *n* the principal land mass of a continent, as distinguished from nearby islands.
mainline *n* the principal road, course, etc. * *vt* (*sl*) (*drugs*) to inject directly into a vein.
mainly *adv* chiefly, principally.
mainmast *n* (*naut*) the principal mast of a sailing ship with more than one mast.
mainsail *n* (*naut*) the principal lowermost sail on the mainmast.
mainsheet *n* (*naut*) one of the ropes by which the mainsail is extended and fastened, controlling its angle.
mainspring *n* the principal spring in a clock, watch, etc; the chief incentive, motive, etc.
mainstay *n* a chief support.
mainstream *n* a major trend, line of thought, etc.—*also adj*.
maintain *vt* to preserve; to support, to sustain; to keep in good condition; to affirm.—**maintainable** *adj*.—**maintainer** *n*.
maintenance *n* upkeep; (*financial*) support, esp of a spouse after a divorce.
maintop *n* (*naut*) the platform on top of the mainmast.
maisonette *n* a small house; self-contained living quarters, usu on two floors with its own entrance, as part of a larger house.
maître d'hôtel *n* (*pl* **maîtres d'hôtel**) *n* a head waiter; a hotel manager or owner; a house steward.
maize *n* corn; a light yellow colour.
Maj *abbr* (*mil*) = major.
majestic *adj* dignified; imposing.—**majestically** *adv*.
majesty *n* (*pl* **majesties**) grandeur; (*with cap*) a title used in speaking to or of a sovereign.
majolica *n* a fine, soft, enamelled kind of pottery of Italian origin, with a glaze of bright metallic oxides.
major *adj* greater in size, importance, amount, etc; (*surgery*) very serious, life-threatening; (*mus*) higher than the corresponding minor by half a tone. * *vi* to specialize (in a field of study). * *n* in US, an officer ranking just above a captain, in UK, a lieutenant-colonel; (*mus*) a major key, chord or scale.
major-domo *n* (*pl* **major-domos**) a head steward; a butler.
majority *n* (*pl* **majorities**) the greater number or part of; the excess of the larger number of votes cast for a candidate in an election; full legal age; the military rank of a major.
majuscule *n* a capital letter used in printing or in writing. * *adj* of, pertaining to or written in such letters.—**majuscular** *adj*.
make *vb* (**making, made**) *vt* to cause to exist, occur, or appear; to build, create, produce, manufacture, etc; to prepare for use; to amount to; to have the qualities of; to acquire, earn; to understand; to do, execute; to cause or force; to arrive at, reach; (*with* **believe**) to imagine, pretend; (*with* **good**) to make up for, pay compensation; (*with* **out**) to write out; to complete (a form, etc) in writing; to attempt to understand; to discern, identify; (*with* **up**) to invent, fabricate, esp to deceive; to prepare; to make complete; to put together; to settle differences between. * *vi* (*with* **do**) to manage with what is available; (*with* **for**) to go in the direction of; to bring about; (*with* **good**) to become successful or wealthy; (*with* **off**) to leave in haste; (*with* **out**) to pretend; to fare, manage; (*with* **up**) to become reconciled; to compensate for; to put on make-up for the stage. * *n* style, brand, or origin; manner of production.—**maker** *n*.
make-believe *adj* imagined, pretended.—*also n*.
makeshift *adj* being a temporary substitute.—*also n*.
make-up *n* the cosmetics, etc used by an actor; cosmetics generally; the way something is put together, composition; nature, disposition.
makeweight *n* something added to make up the required weight; anything of little value added to fill a lack.
making *n* the act or process of making, creation; (*pl*) earnings; (*pl*) potential; (*pl*) (*sl*) the materials for rolling a cigarette.

Makkah *see* **mecca.**
mal- *prefix* = bad or badly, wrong, ill.
malacca *n* the tough stem of a species of climbing palm, rattan; a brown walking stick made of this (*also* **malacca cane**).
malachite *n* copper carbonate occurring as a green mineral, used as an ore and for making ornaments.
malacology *n* the science of molluscs.—**malacological** *adj*.—**malacologist** *n*.
malacostracan *adj* (*crustacean*) soft-shelled.
maladjusted *adj* poorly adjusted, esp to the social environment.—**maladjustment** *n*.
maladministration *n* corrupt or incompetent management of public affairs.—**maladminister** *vb*.
maladroit *adj* clumsy.—**maladroitness** *n*.
malady *n* (*pl* **maladies**) a disease, illness.
Malaga *n* a sweet, white dessert wine from the Spanish port of Malaga.
Malagasy *n* (*pl* **Malagasy, Malagasies**) a native of Madagascar; the language of Madagascar.* *adj* pertaining to Madagascar, its language or people.
malaise *n* a feeling of discomfort or of uneasiness.
malamute *n* a powerful Alaskan dog with a dense grey coat used to pull sledges.—*also* **malemute.**
malanders *n sing* a disease in horses, the main symptom of which is an eczema-like patch on the horse's leg.
malapert *adj* (*arch*) impudent; pert; saucy.
malapropism *n* a ludicrous misuse of words.—**malapropian** *adj*.
malapropos *adj* out of place, ill-timed. * *adv* in an inapproriate way; unseasonably.
malar *adj* of or relating to the cheek or cheekbone. * *n* the cheekbone.
malaria *n* an infectious disease caused by mosquito bites, and characterized by recurring attacks of fevers and chills.—**malarial** *adj*.
malcontent *adj* discontented and potentially rebellious.—*also n*.
mal de mer *n* seasickness.
male *adj* denoting or of the sex that fertilizes the ovum; of, like, or suitable for men and boys; masculine. * *n* a male person, animal or plant.—**maleness** *n*.
malediction *n* a curse, an imprecation; a denunciation of evil; a slander.—**maledictory** *adj*.
malefactor *n* a criminal, an evildoer.—**malefaction** *n*.
maleficent *adj* harmful, causing evil; mischief-making.—**maleficently** *adv*.—**maleficence** *n*.
malemute *see* **malamute.**
malevolent *adj* ill-disposed toward others; spiteful, malicious.—**malevolence** *n*.—**malevolently** *adv*.
malfeasance *n* (*law*) an illegal action, official misconduct.—**malfeasant** *adj, n*.
malformation *n* faulty or abnormal formation of a body or part.—**malformed** *adj*.
malfunction *n* faulty functioning. * *vi* to function wrongly.
malgré lui *adv* (*French*) against one's wishes, despite oneself.
malic acid *adj* a colourless crystalline acid derived from fruit, esp apples.
malice *n* active ill will, intention to inflict injury upon another.—**malicious** *adj*.—**maliciously** *adv*.—**maliciousness** *n*.
malign *adj* harmful; evil. * *vt* to slander; to defame.—**malignity** *n*.—**malignly** *adv*.
malignant *adj* having a wish to harm others; injurious; (*disease*) rapidly spreading, resistant to treatment, esp of a tumour.—**malignancy** *n*.—**malignantly** *adv*.
malignity *n* (*pl* **malignities**) the state of being malignant or deadly; (*often pl*) (an act of) malice; virulence.
malinger *vi* to feign illness in order to evade work, duty.—**malingerer** *n*.
malison *n* (*arch*) a curse, execration.
mall *n* a shaded avenue, open to the public; a shopping street for pedestrians only; an enclosed shopping centre.
mallard *n* (*pl* **mallard, mallards**) a common wild duck, the ancestor of domestic breeds of duck.
malleable *adj* pliable; capable of being shaped.—**malleability** *n*.
mallee *n* a dwarf eucalyptus found in Australia; (*with* **the**) a sparsely populated area in Australia, the bush.
mallemuck *n* any of various sea birds, incl the fulmar and petrel.
malleolar *adj* pertaining to the ankle.
mallet *n* a small, usu wooden-headed, short-handled hammer; a long-handled version for striking the ball in the games of polo and croquet.
mallow *n* any of a widely found genus of plants with pink flowers and palm-shaped leaves; a similar plant, eg marshmallow.
malm *n* soft friable limestone rock; a loamy soil derived from this; a clay and chalk mixture used as an ingredient in brickmaking.
malmsey *n* (*pl* **malmseys**) a strong, full-flavoured sweet wine orig from Greece but now also made in Madeira, Spain, etc.
malnutrition *n* lack of nutrition.
malodorous *adj* having a foul smell, bad-smelling.—**malodorously** *adv*.—**malodorousness** *n*.
Malpighian *adj* (*anat*) pertaining to various structures, such as the capillary system, discovered by the Italian anatomist Marcello Malpighi (1628–94).
malpractice *n* professional misconduct, esp by a medical practitioner.
malt *n* a cereal grain, such as barley, which is soaked and dried and used in brewing; (*inf*) malt liquor, malt whisky.—**malty** *adj*.
maltha *n* a natural black bitumen; a mineral wax.
Malthusian *adj* of or pertaining to the British political economist Thomas Malthus (1766–1834) or his theory, which maintains that population tends to outgrow its means of subsistence and should be checked by means of birth control. * *n* an advocate of this theory.—**Malthusianism** *n*.
maltose *n* a sugar obtained from starch by the action of diatase or malt and used in bacteriological cultures and baby foods.
maltreat *vt* to treat roughly or badly.—**maltreatment** *n*.
maltster *n* a maker of or dealer in malt.
malvoisie *n* a French dessert wine similar to malmsey.
mama *n* (*inf*) mother.—*also* **mamma.**
mamba *n* a partly tree-living green or black poisonous snake of tropical and southern Africa.
Mameluke *n* (*formerly*) a member of the ruling class in Egypt.
mamma[1] *see* **mama.**
mamma[2] *n* (*pl* **mammae**) the milk-secreting organ of female mammals, such as the udder of a cow, or breast of a woman.—**mammary** *adj*.
mammal *n* any member of a class of warm-blooded vertebrates that suckle their young with milk.—**mammalian** *adj*.
mammalogy *n* the branch of zoology involving the study of mammals.—**mammalogical** *adj*.—**mammalogist** *n*.
mammee *n* a tropical American tree with edible fruit; the large red-skinned fruit from this tree (—*also* **mamee apple**).
mammiferous *adj* having breasts.
mammilla *n* (*pl* **mamillae**) *n* a nipple; a nipple-shaped thing.
mammillary *adj* of or like the breast or a nipple.
mammock *vt* (*inf*) to break in pieces; to shred. * *n* a small piece.
mammon *n* riches regarded as an object of worship and greedy pursuit; (*with cap*) (*Bible*) the pursuit of wealth personified as a false god.—**mammonism** *n*.—**mammonist** *n*.
mammoth *n* an extinct elephant with long, curved tusks. * *adj* enormous.
mammy (*pl* **mammies**) *n* (*inf*) mother, as used by a child; (*offensive*) a black nurse to white children.
man *n* (*pl* **men**) a human being, esp an adult male; the human race; an adult male with manly qualities, eg courage, virility; a male servant; an individual person; a person with specific qualities for a task, etc; an ordinary soldier, as opposed to an officer; a member of a team, etc; a piece in games such as chess, draughts, etc; a husband. * *vt* (**manning, manned**) to provide with men for work, defence, etc.
manacle *n* (*usu pl*) a handcuff. * *vt* to handcuff; to restrain.
manage *vt* to control the movement or behaviour of; to have charge of; to direct; to succeed in accomplishing. * *vi* to carry on business; to contrive to get along.—**manageable** *adj*.

management *n* those carrying out the administration of a business; the managers collectively; the technique of managing or controlling.
manager *n* a person who manages a company, organization, etc; an agent who looks after the business affairs of an actor, writer, etc; a person who organizes the training of a sports team; a person who manages efficiently.
manageress *n* a woman who manages a business, shop, etc.
managerial *adj* of or pertaining to a manager or management.—**managerially** *adv*.
manakin *n* any of a genus of small South American birds with bright plumage and short beaks; a manikin.
mañana *adv* tomorrow; by and by. * *n* an unspecified time in the future.
man-at-arms *n* (*pl* **men-at-arms**) *n* an armed soldier, esp of medieval times.
manatee *n* a large aquatic animal resembling a whale found in tropical seas, the sea cow.
manchineel *n* a poisonous tropical American tree.
manciple *n* in UK, a catering official or steward, esp in a monastery, college, or Inn of Court.
Mancunian *adj* of Manchester. * *n* a citizen of Manchester.
mandamus *n* (*pl* **mandamuses**) (*law*) (*formerly*) a writ issued by a superior court directing the person or inferior court to whom it is issued to perform some specified act or public duty.
mandarin *n* (*formerly*) a high-ranking bureaucrat of the Chinese empire; any high-ranking official, esp one given to pedantic sometimes obscure public pronouncements; (*with cap*) the Beijing dialect that is the official pronunciation of the Chinese language; the fruit of a small spiny Chinese tree that has been developed in cultivation (—*also* **tangerine**).
mandarin collar *n* a narrow, stand-up collar, open in front.
mandatary *n* (*pl* **mandataries**) a person or nation to whom a mandate is given.
mandate *n* an order or command; the authority to act on the behalf of another, esp the will of constituents expressed to their representatives in legislatures. * *vt* to entrust by mandate.
mandatory *adj* of, containing, or having the nature of a mandate; required by mandate; compulsory; (*nation*) holding a mandate. * *n* a mandatary.—**mandatorily** *adv*.
mandible *n* the lower jaw of a vertebrate; the mouth parts of an insect; either jaw of a beaked animal.—**mandibular** *adj*.
mandolin *n* a stringed instrument similar to a lute, with four or five pairs of strings.
mandragora *n* (*poet*) mandrake; a narcotic obtained from it.
mandrake *n* a plant of the nightshade family with narcotic properties that, in folklore, shrieked when uprooted; the May apple.
mandrel, mandril *n* the shank of a lathe, to which work is fixed while turned; the revolving arbor of a circular saw or other machine tool; the spindle that drives the headstock of a lathe.
mandrill *n* a large baboon of West Africa, the male having a red and blue backside.
manducate *vt* (*poet*) to chew, eat.
mane *n* long hair that grows on the back of the neck of the horse, lion, etc.
man-eater *n* an animal that eats human flesh.
manège, manege *n* a school for training horses and teaching horsemanship; the movements of a trained horse.
manes *n* (*pl:often cap*) in Ancient Rome, ancestral spirits, shades; gods of the lower world; (*sing*) the spirit of a dead person.
maneuver *see* **manoeuvre**.
manful *adj* showing courage and resolution.—**manfully** *adv*.
mangabey *n* (*pl* **mangabeys**) a large, slender, arboreal, African monkey.
manganate *n* a salt of manganic acid.
manganese *n* a hard brittle metallic element; its oxide.
manganic *adj* pertaining to, resembling, or containing manganese in the trivalent state.
mange *n* a skin disease affecting mainly domestic animals, which causes itching.
mangel-wurzel *n* a variety of beet used as cattle-fodder.
manger *n* a trough in a barn or stable for livestock fodder.
mangle[1] *vt* to crush, mutilate; to spoil, ruin.
mangle[2] *n* a machine for drying and pressing sheets, etc between rollers. * *vt* to smooth through a mangle.
mango *n* (*pl* **mangoes**) a yellow-red fleshy tropical fruit with a firm central stone.
mangonel *n* an ancient military engine for hurling stones.
mangosteen *n* a tropical Indian tree; its red-brown, sweet, juicy fruit about the size of an orange.
mangrove *n* a tropical tree or shrub with root-forming branches.
mangy *adj* (**mangier, mangiest**) having mange; scruffy, shabby.—**manginess** *n*.
manhandle *vt* to handle roughly; to move by human force.
manhole *n* a hole through which one can enter a sewer, drain, etc.
manhood *n* the state or time of being a man; virility; courage, etc.
man-hour *n* the time unit equal to one hour of work done by one person.
manhunt *n* a hunt for a fugitive.—**manhunter** *n*.
mania *n* a mental disorder displaying sometimes violent behaviour and great excitement; great excitement or enthusiasm; a craze.
maniac *n* a madman; a person with wild behaviour; a person with great enthusiasm for something.—**maniacal** *adj*.
manic *adj* affected with, characterized by, or relating to mania.
manic-depressive *adj* of a mental disorder characterized by alternating periods of mania and deep depression. * *n* a person suffering from this.
Manichaeism, Manicheism the doctrine of the Manicheans, who held the dualistic theory of two eternal equal beings or principles, light (God), the author of all good, and darkness (Evil or Satan), the author of all evil, locked in a constant struggle for ascendancy; any similar doctrine.—**Manichaean, Manichean** *n, adj*.
Manichee *n* one of the sect of Manicheans.
manicure *n* trimming, polishing etc of fingernails.—*also vt*.—**manicurist** *n*.
manifest *adj* obvious, clearly evident. * *vt* to make clear; to display, to reveal. * *n* a list of a ship's or aircraft's cargo; a list of passengers on an aircraft.—**manifestation** *n*.—**manifestly** *adv*.
manifestation *n* the act of manifesting; the state of being manifested; the demonstration of the reality or existence of a quality, person, etc; the form of revelation of an idea, divine being, etc.
manifesto *n* (*pl* **manifestoes, manifestos**) a public printed declaration of intent and policy issued by a government or political party.
manifold *adj* having many forms, parts, etc; of many sorts. * *n* a pipe (eg in an engine) with many inlets and outlets. * *vt* to make copies of.—**manifolder** *n*.
manikin *n* a little man, a dwarf; an anatomical model of the body; a mannequin.—*also* **mannikin**.
manila, manilla *n* a strong, buff-coloured paper originally made from hemp from the Philippines.
manioc *n* cassava, a tropical plant from the roots of which tapioca and cassava are prepared.
maniple *n* (*formerly*) a band worn on the left arm by a priest at mass; a company of a Roman legion.
manipulate *vt* to work or handle skilfully; to manage shrewdly or artfully, often in an unfair way.—**manipulation** *n*.—**manipulative** *adj*.—**manipulator** *n*.
manipulation *n* the act or process of manipulating; the state of being manipulated; the movement of bones, etc, by a physiotherapist; shrewd or knowing management of others for one's own ends.—**manipulatory** *adj*.
manitou, manitu (*pl* **manitous, manitus, manitou, manitu**) *n* an American Indian spirit of good or evil.
mankind *n* the human race.
manly *adj* (**manlier, manliest**) appropriate in character to a man; strong; virile.—**manliness** *n*.
man-made *adj* manufactured or created by man; artificial, synthetic.
manna *n* (*Bible*) the food miraculously given to the ancient Israelites in the wilderness; any help that comes unexpectedly.

manned *adj* performed by a person; (*spacecraft, etc*) having a human crew.

mannequin *n* a model in a fashion show; a life-size model of the human body, used to fit or display clothes.

manner *n* a method of way of doing something; behaviour; type or kind; habit; (*pl*) polite social behaviour.

mannered *adj* full of mannerisms; artificial, stylized, etc.

mannerism *n* an idiosyncracy; an affected habit or style in dress, behaviour or gesture; (*with cap*) a post-Reformation movement in art that held that beauty should be represented as an ideal and used exaggeration and distortion of naturalistic forms to attain this.—**mannerist** *adj, n*.

mannerless *n* rude, bad-mannered.

mannerly *adj* polite; respectful. * *adv* politely; respectfully.—**mannerliness** *n*.

mannikin *see* **manikin.**

mannish *adj* like or pertaining to a man; (*woman*) masculine, aping men.—**mannishly** *adv*.—**mannishness** *n*.

manoeuvre *n* a planned and controlled movement of troops, warships, etc; a skilful or shrewd move; a stratagem. * *vti* to perform or cause to perform manoeuvres; to manage or plan skilfully; to move, get, make, etc by some scheme.—*also* **maneuver.**—**maneuverable, manoeuvrable** *adj*.—**maneuverer, manoeuvrer** *n*.

man-of-war *n* (*pl* **men-of-war**) a (sailing) warship.

manometer *n* an instrument for measuring the pressure of gases and liquids.—**manometric, manometrical** *adj*.

manor *n* a landed estate; the main house on such an estate; (*sl*) a police district.—**manorial** *adj*.

manpower *n* power furnished by human strength; the collective availability for work of people in a given area.

manqué *adj* potential; unsuccessful, failed.

mansard (roof) *n* a roof with a break in its slope, the lower part being steeper than the upper.

manse *n* a nonconformist clergyman's house; (*Scot*) the house of a minister, esp a Church of Scotland parish minister; (*arch*) a large house.

manservant *n* (*pl* **menservants**) a male servant, esp a valet.

mansion *n* a large, imposing house.

manslaughter *n* the killing of a human being by another, esp when unlawful but without malice.

mansuetude *n* (*arch*) gentleness, mildness.

manta (ray) *n* a very large fish with a flattened body and wing-like fins.

mantel *n* the facing above a fireplace; the shelf above a fireplace.—*also* **mantelpiece.**

mantelet *n* a woman's short cape of the mid-19th century; a movable, protective screen, formerly used by besiegers, gunners, pioneers, etc (—*also* **mantlet**).

mantic *adj* of, having the power of, or pertaining to divination.

manticore *n* a fabulous beast with a human head, the body of a lion, and the tail of a scorpion.

mantilla *n* a scarf, usu of lace, worn as a headdress in Spain and South America; a woman's light cloak or hood.

mantis *n* (*pl* **mantises, mantes**) an insect that preys on other insects.—*also* **praying mantis.**

mantissa *n* (*math*) the decimal part of a logarithm.

mantle *n* a loose cloak; anything that envelops or conceals; a fine mesh cover on a gas or oil lamp that emits light by incandescence. * *vt* to cover as with a mantle. * *vi* to be or become covered.

mantlet *see* **mantelet.**

mantra *n* (*Hinduism, Buddhism*) a devotional incantation used in prayer, meditation and in certain forms of yoga.

mantua *n* a woman's loose gown of the 17th and 18th centuries, worn with the front of the skirt caught up or back to show an underskirt.

manual *adj* of the hands; operated, done, or used by the hand; involving physical skill or hard work rather than the mind. * *n* a handy book for use as a guide, reference, etc; a book of instructions.—**manually** *adv*.

manufactory *n* (*pl* **manufactories**) *n* (*obs*) a factory, workshop.

manufacture *vt* to make, esp on a large scale, using machinery; to invent, fabricate. * *n* the production of goods by manufacturing.—**manufacturer** *n*.

manumit *vt* (**manumitting, manumitted**) to release from slavery; to free.—**manumission** *n*.—**manumitter** *n*.

manure *n* animal dung used to fertilize soil. * *vt* to spread manure on.

manus *n* (*pl* **manus**) (*zool*) the hand or that part of the anatomy corresponding to the hand; in ancient Roman law, the fact of a woman's legal subjugation to her husband.

manuscript *n* a book or document that is handwritten or typewritten as opposed to printed; an author's original handwritten or typewritten copy as submitted to a publisher before typesetting and printing.

many *adj* (**more, most**) numerous. * *n* a large number of persons or things.

manyplies *n sing* a ruminant's third stomach, the omasum.

many-sided *adj* with many aspects; versatile.—**many-sidedness** *n*.

Maori *n* (*pl* **Maoris, Maori**) a member of the indigenous peoples of New Zealand; their language.—*also adj*.

map *n* a representation of all or part of the earth's surface, showing either natural features as continents and seas, etc or man-made features as roads, railways etc. * *vt* (**mapping, mapped**) to make a map of.

maple *n* a tree with two-winged fruits, grown for shade, wood, or sap; its hard light-coloured wood; the flavour of the syrup or sugar made from the sap of the sugar maple.

Mar. *abbr* = March.

mar *vt* (**marring, marred**) to blemish, to spoil, to impair.

marabout[1], **marabou** *n* a large African stork with handsome feathers and a short neck; its down, used as trimming, etc; a material produced from a fine raw silk.

marabout[2] *n* in North Africa, a Muslim hermit or saint; the shrine or burial place of a marabout.

maraca *n* a dried gourd or plastic shell filled with beans, pebbles, etc and shaken as a rhythm instrument.

maraschino *n* a strong sweet liqueur made from a type of wild cherry.

maraschino cherry *n* a cherry preserved in maraschino.

marasmus *n* emaciation or atrophy, esp in babies.—**marasmic** *adj*.

marathon *n* a foot race of 26 miles, 385 yards (42.195 km); any endurance contest.

maraud *vi* to roam in search of plunder.—**marauder** *n*.—**marauding** *adj*.

marble *n* a hard limestone rock that takes a high polish; a block or work of art made of marble; a little ball of stone, glass, etc; (*pl*) a children's game played with such balls; (*pl*) (*sl*) wits. * *adj* of or like marble.—**marbly** *adj*.

marbled *adj* veined or mottled like marble; (*meat*) streaked with fat.

marc *n* (*winemaking*) the refuse from pressed fruit; a brandy derived from this.

marcasite *n* white iron pyrites; a white metal, esp steel, cut and polished for use in jewellery.

marcel (wave) *n* a style of artificially waving the hair, popular in the 1920s and 1930s. * *vt* (**marcelling, marcelled**) to style in regular waves.

marcescent *adj* (*bot*) withering without falling off.—**marcescence** *n*.

March *n* the third month of the year having 31 days.

march *vi* to walk with regular steps, as in military formation; to advance steadily. * *vt* to make a person or group march. * *n* a steady advance; a regular, steady step; the distance covered in marching; a piece of music for marching.—**marcher** *n*.

marching orders *npl* official orders for infantry to move to a particular destination; (*inf*) a notice of dismissal.

marchioness *n* the wife or widow of a marquess; a woman of the rank of marquess.

Mardi gras *n* the last day before Lent, Shrove Tuesday, a day of carnival in some cities, esp New Orleans.

mare *n* a mature female horse, mule, donkey.

mare clausum *n* (*law*) a body of water under one country's jurisdiction and closed to foreign ships.

mare liberum *n* (*law*) a body of water open to ships of all countries.

maremma (*pl* **maremme**) *n* an unhealthy marshy coastal district, esp in Italy.

mare's-tail *n* an aquatic plant with tiny flowers and tapering leaves; a wisp of trailing alto-cirrus cloud indicating strong winds at high altitude.
margaric *adj* pertaining to, or like, a pearl.
margarine *n* a butter substitute made from vegetable and animal fats, etc.
margarite *n* a pearly translucent mineral related to mica; a bead-like rock formation.
margay *n* a South American tiger cat.
margin *n* a border, edge; the blank border of a printed or written page; an amount beyond what is needed; provision for increase, error, etc; (*commerce*) the difference between cost and selling price.
marginal *adj* written in the margin; situated at the margin or border; close to the lower limit of acceptability; very slight, insignificant; (*Brit politics*) denoting a constituency where the sitting MP has only a small majority. * *n* a marginal constituency.—**marginally** *adv*.
marginalia *npl* notes written in the margin of a book, etc.
marginalize *vt* to transfer someone away from the centre of affairs in order to render them powerless.
marginate *adj* (*biol*) having a margin. * *vt* to border something with a margin.—**margination** *n*.
margrave *n* (*formerly*) a German nobleman, one rank above a count.
margraviate, margravate *n* the domain or jurisdiction of a margrave.
margravine a female margrave; a margrave's wife or widow.
marguerite *n* a large daisy with white or yellow flowers.
Marian *adj* pertaining to the Virgin Mary, or to Mary, Queen of England, or to Mary, Queen of Scots. * *n* one who worships the Virgin Mary; a partisan of Mary, Queen of England or Mary, Queen of Scots.
marigold *n* a plant with a yellow or orange flower.
marijuana, marihuana *n* a narcotic obtained by smoking the dried flowers and leaves of the hemp plant.—*also* **cannabis, pot.**
marimba *n* a South American xylophone.
marina *n* a small harbour with pontoons, docks, services, etc for yachts and pleasure craft.
marinade *n* a seasoning liquid in which meat, fish, etc is soaked to enhance flavour or to tenderize it before cooking. * *vt* to soak in a marinade.—*also* **marinate.**
marine *adj* of, in, near, or relating to the sea; maritime; nautical; naval. * *n* a soldier trained for service on land or sea; naval or merchant ships.
mariner *n* a seaman, sailor.
Mariolatry *n* the exaggerated worship of the Virgin Mary.
marionette *n* a little jointed doll or puppet moved by strings or wires.
marital *adj* of marriage, matrimonial.
maritime *adj* on, near, or living near the sea; of navigation, shipping, etc.
marjoram *n* a fragrant herb used in cooking and salads.
mark[1] *n* a spot, scratch, etc on a surface; a distinguishing sign or characteristic; a cross made instead of a signature; a printed or written symbol, as a punctuation mark; a brand or label on an article showing the maker, etc; an indication of some quality, character, etc; a grade for academic work; a standard of quality; impression, influence, etc; a target; (*sl*) a potential victim for a swindle.* *vt* to make a mark or marks on; to identify as by a mark; to show plainly; to heed; to grade, rate; (*Brit football*) to stay close to an opponent so as to hinder his play.
mark[2] *n* the basic monetary unit of Germany.
marked *adj* having a mark or marks; noticeable; obvious.—**markedly** *adv*.
marker *n* one that marks; something used for marking.
market *n* a meeting of people for buying and selling merchandise; a space or building in which a market is held; the chance to sell or buy; demand for (goods, etc); a region where goods can be sold; a section of the community offering demand for goods. * *vti* to offer for sale; to sell, buy domestic provisions.—**marketability** *n*.—**marketable** *adj*.
marketing *n* act of buying or selling; all the processes involved in moving goods from the producer to the consumer.
market-making *n* the activity of buying and selling stocks, shares, bonds, securities, etc.—**market-maker** *n*.
marketplace *n* a market in a public square; the world of economic trade and activity; a sphere in which ideas, opinions, etc compete for acceptance.
market research *n* the gathering of factual information from consumers concerning their preferences for goods and services.
marking *n* the conferring of a mark or marks; the characteristic arrangement of marks, as on fur or feathers.
marksman *n* (*pl* **marksmen**) one who is skilled at shooting.—**marksmanship** *n*.
markup *n* a selling at an increased price; the amount of increase.—*also vt*.
marl[1] *n* a mixture of clay and carbonate of lime, used as a manure. * *vt* to manure with marl.—**marly** *adj*.
marl[2] *vt* (*naut*) to wind with marlines, securing with a hitch at each turn.
marline, marlin, marling *n* (*naut*) a two-stranded cord, often tarred, used for winding round ropes, splicing, etc.
marlinespike, marlinspike, marlingspike *n* a pointed piece of iron used for opening the strands of a rope in splicing, etc.
marmalade *n* a jam-like preserve made from oranges, sugar and water.
marmoreal, marmorean *adj* of or like marble.
marmoset *n* a small monkey of South and Central America.
marmot *n* a widely distributed rodent with rough fur, a bushy tail and short legs.
maroon[1] *n* a dark brownish red (—*also adj*); a type of distress rocket.
maroon[2] *vt* to abandon alone, esp on a desolate island; to leave helpless and alone.
marque *n* a brand of a product, esp a car.
marquee *n* a large tent used for entertainment; a canopy over an entrance, as to a theatre.
marquess *n* In UK, a title of nobility ranking between a duke and an earl.
marquetry, marqueterie *n* (*pl* **marquetries, marqueteries**) decorative inlaid veneers of wood, ivory, etc used esp in furniture.
marquis *n* (*pl* **marquises, marquis**) (*Europe*) a nobleman equivalent in rank to a British marquess.
marquisate *n* the estate, dignity, or lordship of a marquis.
marquise *n* a marchioness; a gemstone or ring setting cut in an oval pointed form.
marriage *n* the legal contract by which a woman and man become wife and husband; a wedding, either religious or civil; a close union.
marriageable *adj* of an age to marry.—**marriageability** *n*.
marron glacé *n* (*pl* **marrons glacés**) *n* a cooked chestnut coated with sugar.
marrow *n* the fatty tissue in the cavities of bones; the best part or essence of anything; a widely grown green fruit eaten as a vegetable.
marrowbone *n* a bone containing marrow used in cooking.
marrowfat, marrow pea *n* a late variety of pea that has large seeds; the seed of one of these.
marry[1] *vb* (**marrying, married**) *vt* to join as wife and husband; to take in marriage; to unite. * *vi* to get married.
marry[2] *interj* (*arch*) indeed, forsooth.
Mars *n* the Roman god of war; the planet next to Earth, further away from the sun; (*alchemy*) iron.
Marsala *n* a sweet fortified wine from Sicily.
Marseillaise *adj* pertaining to the city of Marseilles in France or to its inhabitants. * *n* the French national anthem, orig a well-known song of the French Revolution, composed in 1792.
marsh *n* an area of boggy, poorly drained land.—**marshiness** *n*.—**marshy** *adj*.
marshal *n* in some armies, a general officer of the highest rank; an official in charge of ceremonies, parades, etc. * *vt* (**marshalling, marshalled** or **marshaling, marshaled**) (*ideas, troops*) to arrange in order; to guide.—**marshaller** *n*.
marsh mallow *n* a perennial plant with a pink flower and a mucilaginous root used in confectionery and medicine.
marshmallow *n* a soft spongy confection made of sugar, gelatin, etc; (*formerly*) a sweet paste made from the root of the marsh mallow.
marsupial *adj* of an order of mammals that carry their young in a pouch. * *n* an animal of this kind, as a kangaroo, opossum.
marsupium *n* (*pl* **marsupia**) in female marsupials, an external pouch for carrying and nurturing young.

mart *n* a market.
martagon *n* a variety of lily with purple-red flowers found in Europe and Asia; a Turk's-cap lily.
Martello tower *n* (*formerly*) a small round fort used for coastal defence.
marten *n* (*pl* **martens, marten**) a carnivorous tree-dwelling weasel-like mammal.
martial *adj* warlike; military.—**martially** *adv.*
martial arts *npl* systems of self-defence, usu from the Orient, practised as sports, as karate or judo.
martial law *n* rule by military authorities over civilians, as during a war or political emergency.
Martian *adj* of or relating to the planet Mars. * *n* an inhabitant of Mars.
martin *n* one of various types of bird similar to the swallow, with a characteristic shape of tail; the house martin.
martinet *n* one who exerts strong discipline.—**martinetish, martinettish** *adj.*
martingale, martingal *n* a broad strap passing from the noseband to the girth of a horse between its forelegs to keep its head down and prevent it from rearing; a gambling system of doubling successive stakes; (*naut*) a short spar under the bowsprit used as a lower stay for the jib boom or flying jib boom.
martini *n* (*trademark*) (*often with cap*) Italian vermouth; a cocktail of gin and vermouth
Martinmas *n* St Martin's Day, November 11, a Christian festival; one of the Scottish quarter days.
martlet *n* (*arch*) a martin; (*her*) a bird without legs or beak.
martyr *n* a person tortured for a belief or cause; a person who suffers from an illness. * *vt* to kill as a martyr; to make a martyr of.—**martyrdom** *n.*
martyrize *vt* to martyr.
martyrology *n* (*pl* **martyrologies**) *n* a register or history of martyrs; the study of the lives of the martyrs.—**martyrological, martyrologic** *adj.*—**martyrologist** *n.*
martyry *n* (*pl* **martyries**) *n* a shrine in honour of a martyr.
marvel *n* anything wonderful; a miracle. * *vti* (**marvelling, marvelled** *or* **marveling, marveled**) to become filled with wonder, surprise, etc.—**marvellous, marvelous** *adj.*
Marxian *n* a student or advocate of Marxism.—*also adj.*
Marxism *n* the theory and practice developed by Karl Marx and Friedrich Engels advocating public ownership of the means of production and the dictatorship of the proletariat until the establishment of a classless society.—**Marxist** *adj, n.*
marzipan *n* a paste made from ground almonds, sugar and egg white, used to coat cakes or make confectionery.
mascara *n* a cosmetic for darkening the eyelashes.
mascle *n* (*her*) a lozenge perforated with a lozenge shape; a voided lozenge.
mascot *n* a person, animal or thing thought to bring good luck.
masculine *adj* having characteristics of or appropriate to the male sex; (*gram*) of the male gender.—**masculinity** *n.*
MASH *abbr* = mobile army surgical hospital.
mash *n* any soft, pulpy mass; crushed malt and hot water for brewing; (*inf*) mashed potatoes. * *vt* to crush into a mash.
mashie *n* (*formerly*) an iron golf club with a deep, short blade, more or less lofted.
mask[1] *n* a covering to conceal or protect the face; a moulded likeness of the face; anything that conceals or disguises; a respirator placed over the nose and mouth to aid or prevent inhalation of a gas; (*surgery*) a protective gauze placed over the nose and mouth to prevent the spread of germs; (*photog*) a screen used to cover part of a sensitive surface to prevent exposure by light. * *vt* to cover or conceal as with a mask; to disguise one's intentions or character.—**masked** *adj.*
mask[2] *see* **masque.**
masker *n* a masked person; a participant in a masque or masquerade.—*also* **masquer.**
masochism *n* abnormal pleasure, esp sexual, obtained from having physical or mental pain inflicted on one by another person.—**masochist** *n.*—**masochistic** *adj.*
mason *n* a person skilled in working or building with stone; (*with cap*) a Freemason.
masonic *adj* (*often cap*) relating to Freemasonry.
masonry *n* (*pl* **masonries**) stonework.
Masora, Masorah *n* a critical work in Hebrew by the rabbis of the 6–10th cents., indicating how the verbal text of the Bible is to be written in accordance with ancient rules; the critical notes and commentaries of this.—**Masoretic** *adj.*
masque *n* a poetic drama with pageantry, pantomime, dance, song, etc, popular in 16th and 17th-century England; the words and music for one of these; a masquerade.—*also* **mask.**
masquer *see* **masker.**
masquerade *n* a ball or party at which fancy dress and masks are worn; a pretence, false show. * *vi* to take part in a masquerade; to pretend to be what one is not.—**masquerader** *n.*
Mass. *abbr* = Massachusetts.
Mass *n* (*RC Church*) the celebration of the Eucharist.
mass *n* (*pl* **masses**) a quantity of matter of indefinite shape and size; a large quantity or number; bulk; size; the main part; (*physics*) the property of a body expressed as a measure of the amount of material contained in it; (*pl*) the common people, esp the lower social classes. * *adj* of or for the masses or for a large number. * *vti* to gather or form into a mass.
massacre *n* the cruel and indiscriminate killing of many people or animals. * *vt* to kill in large numbers.
massage *n* a kneading and rubbing of the muscles to stimulate the circulation of the blood.* *vt* to give a massage to.
massé shot *n* in billiards, a stroke with the cue held upright, usu to cause the ball to curve round another ball before it hits the intended ball.
masseur *n* a man who gives a massage professionally.—**masseuse** *nf.*
massif *n* a central mountain mass; a large plateau with distinct edges.
massive *adj* big, solid, or heavy; large and imposing; relatively large in comparison to normal; extensive.—**massively** *adv.*—**massiveness** *n.*
mass media *npl* newspapers, radio, television, and other means of communication with large numbers of people.
mass production *n* quantity production of goods, esp by machinery and division of labour.
massy *adj* (**massier, massiest**) (*arch*) massive.
mast *n* a tall vertical pole used to support the sails on a ship; a vertical pole from which a flag is flown; a tall structure supporting a television or radio aerial.
mastaba, mastabah *n* an early Egyptian tomb with a flat roof, the prototype of the pyramids.
mast cell *n* a large blood-borne cell that has a fast-acting role in the body's immune system in fighting inflammation.
mastectomy *n* (*pl* **mastectomies**) the removal of a breast by surgery.
master *n* a man who rules others or has control over something, esp the head of a household; an employer; an owner of an animal or slave; the captain of a merchant ship; a male teacher in a private school; an expert craftsman; a writer or painter regarded as great; an original from which a copy can be made, esp a phonograph record or magnetic tape; (*with cap*) a title for a boy; one holding an advanced academic degree. * *adj* being a master; chief; main; controlling. * *vt* to be or become master of; (*in art, etc*) to become expert.—**mastership** *n.*
master-at-arms *n* (*pl* **masters-at-arms**) a ship's chief petty officer with responsibility for policing, administration, etc.
masterful *adj* acting the part of a master; domineering; expert; skilful.—**masterfully** *adv.*—**masterfulness** *n.*
masterly *adj* expert; skilful.—**masterliness** *n.*
mastermind *n* a very clever person, esp one who plans or directs a project. * *vt* to be the mastermind of.
masterpiece *n* a work done with extraordinary skill; the greatest work of a person or group.

masterstroke *n* brilliant stroke of policy, skill, etc.
masterwork *n* a masterpiece.
mastery *n* control as by a master; victory; expertise.
masthead *n* the top of a mast; the title and ownership details, etc of a newspaper or periodical printed on the front page.
mastic *n* an aromatic resin from mastic trees used chiefly in varnishes; a type of putty used for sealing wood, plaster, etc.
masticate *vt* to chew food before swallowing; to reduce to a pulp.—**mastication** *n*.—**masticator** *n*.
masticatory *adj* adapted for, or pertaining to, chewing. * *n* (*pl* **masticatories**) (*med*) something chewed in order to promote the flow of saliva.
mastiff *n* a breed of large, thickset dogs used chiefly as watchdogs.
mastitis *n* an inflammation of a female breast or an udder.
mastodon *n* any of an extinct genus of mammals allied to the elephant.—**mastodonic** *adj*.
mastoid *n* the bony prominence behind the ear.
masturbate *vi* to manually stimulate one's sexual organs to achieve orgasm without sexual intercourse.—**masturbation** *n*.
mat[1] *n* a piece of material of woven fibres, etc, used for protection, as under a vase, etc, or on the floor; a thick pad used in wrestling, gymnastics, etc; anything interwoven or tangled into a thick mass. * *vti* (**matting, matted**) to cover as with a mat; to interweave or tangle into a thick mass.
mat[2] *adj* without lustre, dull.—*also* **matt**.
matador *n* the bullfighter who kills the bull with a sword.
match[1] *n* a thin strip of wood or cardboard tipped with a chemical that ignites under friction.
match[2] *n* any person or thing equal or similar to another; two persons or things that go well together; a contest or game; a mating or marriage. * *vt* to join in marriage; to put in opposition (with, against); to be equal or similar to; (*one thing*) to suit to another. * *vi* to be equal, similar, suitable, etc.
matchboard *n* one of a number of thin planks tongued and grooved to fit together, used for panelling, etc.
matchbox *n* a small box for holding matches.
matchless *adj* unequalled.—**matchlessly** *adv*.
matchmaker *n* a person who arranges marriages for people; one who schemes to bring about the marriage of two others; a maker of matches.
match play *n* (*golf*) scoring by the number of holes won as opposed to strokes played.
match point *n* (*tennis, badminton, etc*) the situation where the winner of the next point wins the match.
matchwood *n* wood suitable for making matches; wood splinters or fragments.
maté *n* an evergreen South American shrub, related to holly; an infusion of its dried leaves which makes a mildly stimulating tea,.—*also* **Paraguay tea**.
mate[1] *n* an associate or colleague; (*inf*) a friend; one of a matched pair; a marriage partner; the male or female of paired animals; an officer of a merchant ship, ranking below the master. * *vti* to join as a pair; to couple in marriage or sexual union.
mate[2] *vt* to checkmate.
matelote *n* a stew of fish cooked with wine, etc.
mater *n* (*sl*) mother.
materfamilias *n* (*pl* **matresfamilias**) the mother of a family or mistress of a household.
material *adj* of, derived from, or composed of matter, physical; of the body or bodily needs, comfort, etc, not spiritual; important, essential, etc. * *n* what a thing is, or may be made of; elements or parts; cloth, fabric; (*pl*) tools, etc needed to make or do something; a person regarded as fit for a particular task, position, etc.
materialism *n* concern with money and possessions rather than spiritual values; the doctrine that everything in the world, including thought, can be explained only in terms of matter.—**materialist** *n*.—**materialistic** *adj*.
materiality *n* (*pl* **materialities**) the quality or state of being material; material existence; substance.
materialize *vt* to give material form to. * *vi* to become fact; to make an unexpected appearance.—**materialization** *n*.
materially *adv* physically; to a great extent; substantially.
materia medica *n* the science of substances used in medicine incl pharmacology, pharmacy, etc; a substance employed as a medicine or in making drugs.
materiel, matériel *n* the baggage, munitions, and provisions of an army or of any other organization.
maternal *adj* of, like, or from a mother; related through the mother's side of the family.—**maternally** *adv*.
maternity *n* motherhood; motherliness. * *adj* relating to pregnancy.
matey *n* a crony or companion (often used when directly addressing such). * *adj* (**matier, matiest**) (*inf*) friendly, sociable.—**mateyness, matiness** *n*.—**matily** *adv*.
math *n* (*inf*) mathematics.
mathematical, mathematic *adj* of, like or concerned with mathematics; exact and precise.—**mathematically** *adv*.
mathematics *n* (*used as sing*) the science dealing with quantities, forms, space, etc and their relationships by the use of numbers and symbols; (*sing or pl*) the mathematical operations or processes used in a particular problem, discipline, etc.—**mathematician** *n*.
maths *n* (*inf*) mathematics.
matin, matinal *adj* of or pertaining to the morning or to matins.
matinée *n* a daytime, esp an afternoon performance of a play, etc.
matins *n sing or pl* (*Anglican Church*) a morning prayer; (*RC Church*) one of the canonical hours of prayer; (*poet*) a bird's morning song.
matriarch *n* a woman who heads or rules her family or tribe.—**matriarchal, matriarchic** *adj*.
matriarchy *n* (*pl* **matriarchies**) form of social organization in which the mother is the ruler of the family or tribe and in which descent is traced through the mother.
matrices *see* **matrix**.
matricide *n* a person who kills his (her) mother; the killing of one's mother.—**matricidal** *adj*.
matriculate *vti* to enrol, esp as a student.—**matriculation** *n*.
matrimony *n* (*pl* **matrimonies**) the act or rite of marriage; the married state.—**matrimonial** *adj*.—**matrimonially** *adv*.
matrix *n* (*pl* **matrices, matrixes**) the place, substance, etc from which something originates; a mould; the connective intercellular substance in bone, cartilage, or other tissue; (*math*) a rectangular grid of quantities in rows and columns used in solving certain problems.
matron *n* a wife or widow, esp one of mature appearance and manner; a woman in charge of domestic and nursing arrangements in a school, hospital or other institution.—**matronal** *adj*.
matronly *adj* pertaining to or suitable for a matron; sedate, dignified; (*figure*) plump.—**matronliness** *n*.
matronymic *see* **metronymic**.
matt *see* **mat**[2].
matter *n* what a thing is made of; material; whatever occupies space and is perceptible to the senses; any specified substance; content of thought or expression; a quantity; a thing or affair; significance; trouble, difficulty; pus. * *vi* to be of importance.
matter-of-fact *adj* relating to facts, not opinions, imagination, etc.
matting *n* a coarse material, such as woven straw or hemp, used for making mats.
mattock *n* a pick with one head like an axe, the other like an adze.
mattress *n* a casing of strong cloth filled with cotton, foam rubber, coiled springs, etc, used on a bed.
maturate *vti* (*med*) to discharge pus, to fester; (*arch*) to bring or come to maturation.—**maturative** *adj*.
maturation *n* the process of ripening or coming to maturity; (*biol*) the progressive generation of cells already present in the ovary and testis, mitosis; (*rare*) the act of discharging pus, suppuration.

mature *adj* mentally and physically well-developed, grown-up; (*fruit, cheese, etc*) ripe; (*bill*) due; (*plan*) completely worked out. * *vti* to make or become mature; to become due.—**maturely** *adv*.—**matureness** *n*.
maturity *n* the state of being mature; full development; the date a loan becomes due.
matutinal *adj* of, happening during, or pertaining to the morning; early.—**matutinally** *adv*.
maud *n* (*Scot*) a grey-striped woollen plaid worn by shepherds.
maudlin *adj* foolishly sentimental; tearfully drunk.
maul *vt* to bruise or lacerate; to paw.
maulstick *n* a long stick used by painters as a rest for the hand while painting.—*also* **mahlstick**.
maund *n* any of various Asian units of weight, varying from 25 pounds (11 kilograms) to 82 pounds (37 kilograms), according to locality.
maunder *vi* to speak, act or move listlessly or purposelessly.—**maunderer** *n*.
Maundy Thursday the Thursday before Good Friday, in remembrance of the Last Supper.
mausoleum *n* (*pl* **mausoleums, mausolea**) a large tomb.
mauve *n* any of several shades of pale purple. * *adj* of this colour.
maverick *n* an independent-minded or unorthodox individual; an unbranded animal, eg a stray calf.
mavis *n* the song thrush.
mavourneen, mavournin *n* (*Irish*) my darling.
maw *n* the stomach, crop or throat of animals, esp those who require large quantities of food; (*inf*) the throat and stomach of a person who eats food indiscriminately and in large quantities.
mawkish *adj* maudlin; insipid.—**mawkishly** *adv*.—**mawkishness** *n*.
max. *abbr* = maximum.
maxilla *n* (*pl* **maxillae, maxillas**) the upper jawbone; in some insects, any of several parts of the mouth used as a secondary jaw.—**maxillar, maxillary** *adj*.
maxim *n* a concise rule of conduct; a precept.
maxima *see* **maximum**.
maximal *adj* of, consisting of, or pertaining to a maximum; (*math*) last in order. * *n* (*math*) in an ordered set, the member last in order.—**maximally** *adv*.
maximalist *n* one who insists on maximum demands without compromise; (*often with cap*) one who advocates direct action as a means of accomplishing something, esp social and political ends.
maximize *vt* to increase to a maximum.—**maximization** *n*.
maximum *n* (*pl* **maxima, maximums**) the greatest quantity, number, etc. * *adj* highest; greatest possible reached.
maxixe *n* a Brazilian round dance similar to the tango, and like the two-step in rhythm.
maxwell *n* a unit of magnetic flux in the cgs system.
May *n* the fifth month of the year having 31 days.
may *vb aux* (*past* **might**) expressing possibility; permission; wish or hope.
maya *n* (*Hinduism*) illusion, esp that of the world as experienced by the senses as non-material.
May apple *n* an American plant with an egg-shaped edible fruit; its fruit.
maybe *adv* perhaps.
May Day *n* the first day of May, celebrated as a traditional spring festival; observed in many countries as a labour holiday.
Mayday *n* the international radio-telephone signal indicating a ship or aircraft in distress.
mayhem *n* violent destruction, confusion.
mayn't = may not.
mayonnaise *n* a salad dressing made from egg yolks whisked with oil and lemon juice or vinegar.
mayor *n* the chief administrative officer of a municipality.—**mayoral** *adj*.—**mayorship** *n*.
mayoralty *n* (*pl* **mayoralties**) the office or term of office of a mayor.
mayoress *n* the wife of a mayor; a female mayor.
maypole *n* a flower-decked pole hung with ribbons around which May Day festivities are held.
Mazdaism *n* Zoroastrianism.
maze *n* a confusing, intricate network of pathways, esp one with high hedges in a garden; a labyrinth; a confused state.—*adj* **maze like.**
mazer *n* (*arch*) a large drinking cup of hard wood or metal.
mazuma *n* (*sl*) money.
mazurka, mazourka *n* a Polish folk dance in triple time; a musical composition for or imitating this.
mazy, mazier, maziest *adj* intricate, winding; perplexing.—**mazily** *adv*.—**maziness** *n*.
MB *abbr* = Bachelor of Medicine; megabyte.
MBA *abbr* = Master of Business Administration.
MD *abbr* = Maryland; Doctor of Medicine; Managing Director.
Md (*chem symbol*) mendelevium.
MDMA *abbr* = methylene dioxymethamphetamine, a synthetic drug used as the stimulant Ecstasy.
me *pers pron* the objective case of I.
ME[1] *abbr* = myalgic encephalomyelitis.
ME[2], **Me** *abbr* = Maine.
mead *n* a wine made from a fermented solution of honey and spices.
meadow *n* a piece of land where grass is grown for hay; low, level, moist grassland.
meadowlark *n* one of two North American yellow-breasted songbirds related to the Baltimore oriole; any of several birds of South, Central and North America.
meadowsweet *n* a fragrant white-flowered plant of Europe and Asia.
meagre, meager *adj* thin, emaciated; lacking in quality or quantity.—**meagerly, meagrely** *adv*.—**meagerness, meagreness** *n*.
meal[1] *n* any of the times for eating, as lunch, dinner, etc; the food served at such a time.
meal[2] *n* any coarsely ground edible grain; any substance similarly ground.—**mealiness** *n*.—**mealy** *adj*.
mealy-mouthed *adj* not outspoken and blunt; euphemistic; devious in speech.
mean[1] *adj* selfish, ungenerous; despicable; shabby; bad-tempered; (*sl*) difficult; (*sl*) expert.—**meanly** *adv*.—**meanness** *n*.
mean[2] *adj* halfway between extremes; average. * *n* what is between extremes.
mean[3] *vb* (**meaning, meant**) *vt* to have in mind; to intend; to intend to express; to signify. * *vi* to have a (specified) degree of importance, effect, etc.
meander *n* a winding path esp a labyrinth; a winding of a stream or river. * *vi* (*river*) to wind; to wander aimlessly.—**meandering** *adj*.
meanie *n* (*inf*) one who is mean, selfish, etc.—*also* **meanie** *pl* **meanies**).
meaning *n* sense; significance; import. * *adj* significant.—**meaningful** *adj*.—**meaningless** *adj*.
means *npl* that by which something is done; resources; wealth.
meant *see* **mean**[3].
meantime, meanwhile *adv* in or during the intervening time; at the same time. * *n* the intervening time.
meany *see* **meanie.**
measles *n* (*used as sing*) an acute, contagious viral disease, characterized by small red spots on the skin.
measly *adj* (**measlier, measliest**) (*inf*) slight, worthless; having measles.
measure *n* the extent, dimension, capacity, etc of anything; a determining of this, measurement; a unit of measurement; any standard of valuation; an instrument for measuring; a definite quantity measured out; a course of action; a statute, law; a rhythmical unit. * *vt* to find out the extent, dimensions etc of, esp by a standard; to mark off by measuring; to be a measure of. * *vi* to be of specified measurements.—**measurable** *adj*.—**measurably** *adv*.
measured *adj* set or marked off by a standard; rhythmical, regular; carefully planned or considered.
measureless *adj* infinite, without limit.—**measurelessly** *adv*.

measurement *n* a measuring or being measured; an extent or quantity determined by measuring; a system of measuring or of measures.

meat *n* animal flesh; food as opposed to drink; the essence of something.

meatball *n* a small ball of ground meat usu mixed with breadcrumbs and spices; (*inf*) a stupid or foolish person.

meatus *n* (*pl* **meatuses, meatus**) any passage in the body, eg the ear canal.

meaty *adj* (**meatier, meatiest**) full of meat; full of substance.

mecca *n* a place of pilgrimage or a goal of aspiration; a resort or attraction that is visited by a large number of people; (*with cap*) Islam's holiest city, the birthplace of Muhammed (*c*. ad 570) (—*also* **Makkah**).

mechanic *n* a person skilled in maintaining or operating machines, cars, etc.

mechanical *adj* of or using machinery or tools; produced or operated by machinery; done as if by a machine, lacking thought or emotion; of the science of mechanics.—**mechanically** *adv*.

mechanician, *n* a person skilled in mechanics or machinery; a technician; a mechanist.

mechanics *n* (*used as sing*) the science of motion and the action of forces on bodies; knowledge of machinery; (*pl*) the technical aspects of something.

mechanism *n* the working parts of a machine; any system of interrelated parts; any physical or mental process by which a result is produced.

mechanist *n* an expert in mechanics, a mechanician; an advocate of mechanistic philosophy.

mechanistic *adj* of or pertaining to mechanics; of or relating to mechanism; attributing phenomena to physical or biological causes.—**mechanistically** *adv*.

mechanize *vt* to make mechanical; to equip with machinery or motor vehicles.—**mechanization** *n*.—**mechanized** *adj*.

meconium *n* the first faeces of a baby; the juice of the poppy; opium.

MEd *abbr* = Master of Education.

medal *n* a small, flat piece of inscribed metal, commemorating some event or person or awarded for some distinction.—**medallic** *adj*.

medallion *n* a large medal; a design, portrait, etc shaped like a medal; a medal worn on a chain around the neck.

medallist, medalist *n* one awarded a medal.

meddle *vi* to interfere in another's affairs.—**meddler** *n*.—**meddlesome** *adj*.

Mede *n* an inhabitant of Media, an ancient country in southwest Asia to the south of the Caspian Sea.—**Median** *n, adj*.

media *see* **medium.**

mediaeval *see* **medieval.**

mediaevalism, mediaevalist *see* **medievalism.**

medial *adj* of or in the middle; mean, average; (*math*) pertaining to or denoting an average; median; (*phonetics*) denoting a sound made by using an average amount of muscular tension, neither strongly vocalized nor gently pronounced.

median *adj* middle; intermediate. * *n* a median number, point, line, etc.

mediant *n* (*mus*) the third of any scale.—*also adj*.

mediastinum *n* (*pl* **mediastina**) (*anat*) a membranous partition, esp that between the lungs; the part of the body between the lungs containing the heart and associated valves, etc.—**mediastinal** *adj*.

mediate *vt* to intervene (in a dispute); to bring about agreement. * *vi* to be in an intermediate position; to be an intermediary. * *adj* involving an intermediary, not direct or immediate.—**mediately** *adv*.—**mediative** *adj*.

mediation *n* the act of mediating; reconciliation; intervention, esp by a neutral nation seeking a settlement between warring nations.

mediatize *vt* to annex (a state) while leaving its ruler his title.—**mediatization** *n*.

mediator *n* one who or that which mediates; a person who acts as an intermediary; an intercessor.—**mediatory** *adj*.

medic *n* (*inf*) a medical student; (*inf*) a physician or surgeon.

medicable *adj* potentially curable.

medical *adj* relating to the practice or study of medicine. * *n* (*inf*) a medical examination.—**medically** *adv*.

medicament *n* a medicine or healing application.

medicate *vt* to treat with medicine; to impregnate (soap, shampoo, etc) with medication.—**medicative** *adj*.

medication *n* treatment with drugs, medicines, etc; a drug, medicine, or remedy.

medicine *n* any substance used to treat or prevent disease; the science of preventing, treating or curing disease.—**medicinal** *adj*.—**medicinally** *adv*.

medico *n* (*inf*) a doctor or medical student.

medieval *adj* of or like the Middle Ages.—*also* **mediaeval.**

medievalism *n* the spirit, esp in religion and art, customs, etc, characteristic of the Middle Ages; a study of these; any one of these extant since the Middle Ages, or a contemporary imitation of it.—*also* **mediaevalism.**—**medievalist, mediaevalist** *n*.

medigap *n* health insurance taken out by an individual to pay for treatment excluded by government schemes.

mediocre *adj* average; ordinary; inferior.—**mediocrity** *n*.

meditate *vi* to think deeply; to reflect; to empty the mind in order to concentrate on nothing or on one thing, esp as a religious exercise.—**meditator** *n*.

meditation *n* the act of meditating; contemplation of spiritual or religious matters.

meditative *adj* expressing or characterized by meditation; thoughtful.—**meditatively** *adv*.—**meditativeness** *n*.

Mediterranean *n* the Mediterranean Sea. * *adj* of, or relating to (the area around) the Mediterranean Sea; denoting a subdivision of the Caucasian race characterized by a slender build and dark complexion; (*climate*) characterized by hot, dry summers and warm, wet winters.

medium *n* (*pl* **media, mediums**) the middle state or condition; a substance for transmitting an effect; any intervening means, instrument, or agency; (*pl* **media**) a means of communicating information (eg newspapers, television, radio); (*pl* **mediums**) a person claiming to act as an intermediary between the living and the dead. * *adj* midway; average.

medlar *n* a small fruit tree of Europe and Asia; its apple-like fruit; any one of several trees similar to this; the fruit from one of these.

medley *n* (*pl* **medleys**) a miscellany; a musical piece made up of various tunes or passages.

Médoc *n* a red wine from the Bordeaux region of France.

medulla *n* (*pl* **medullas, medullae**) (*anat*) the marrow of bones; inner tissue; (*bot*) the pith of plants.—**medular, medullary** *adj*.

medulla oblongata *n* (*pl* **medulla oblongatas, medullae oblongatae** the nervous tissue of the lower part of the cranium, which governs respiration, the action of the heart, etc.

medusa *n* (*pl* **medusas, medusae**) a jellyfish; one of two coelenterate life cycles, when it has a sac-like, umbrella-shaped body that is capable of moving freely in water (—*also* **medusan, medusoid**).—**medusan** *adj*.

meed *n* (*poet*) recompense, reward.

meek *adj* patient, long-suffering; submissive.—**meekly** *adv*.—**meekness** *n*.

meerschaum *n* a creamy claylike silicate of magnesium from which pipe bowls and building stones are made; a tobacco pipe with a bowl made of this.

meet[1] *vb* (**meeting, met**) *vt* to encounter, to come together; to make the acquaintance of; to contend with, deal with; to experience; to be perceived by (the eye, etc); (*demand, etc*) to satisfy; (*bill, etc*) to pay. * *vi* to come into contact with; to be introduced. * *n* a meeting to hunt or for an athletics competition.

meet[2] *adj* (*arch*) fit, suitable.

meeting *n* a coming together; a gathering.

mega- *prefix* great, large; a million of; (*inf*) greatest.

megabyte *n* (*comput*) a unit of information, approximately equal to one million bytes.

megacephalic *see* **macrocephalic.**

megacycle *n* a megahertz.

megahertz *n* a unit of frequency equal to one million hertz.

megalith *n* a huge stone, esp part of a prehistoric monument.—**megalithic** *adj*.

megalomania *n* a mental illness characterized by delusions of grandeur; (*inf*) a lust for power.—**megalomaniac** *n, adj*.—**megalomaniacal** *adj*.
megaphone *n* a device to amplify and direct the voice.
megapode any of a family of birds of Australia and the South Pacific that builds mounds of sand, etc, to incubate its eggs.
megaspore *n* the protective covering containing the embryo in flowering plants (—*also* **macrospore**); the larger spore of certain mosses, ferns and fungi, which forms the female gametophyte.
megass, megasse *n* a type of paper produced from the residue left after the extraction of sugar from cane.
megathere *n* a huge extinct animal allied to the sloth.—**megatherian** *adj*.
megaton *n* a unit of explosive force equivalent to one million tons of TNT.
megavolt *n* a million volts.
megawatt *n* one million watts.
megilp *n* a mixture of linseed oil and mastic varnish or turpentine, used as a base in oil colours.
megohm *n* a million ohms.
megrim *n* (*arch*) a sick or neuralgic headache, usu of one side of the head, a migraine; a whim, caprice; (*pl*) a disease of horses or cattle, characterized by vertigo, the staggers.
meiosis *n* (*pl* **meioses**) *n* (*biol*) the process of cell division where a nucleus splits into four, each new nucleus having half the number of chromosomes that the orig one had; a rhetorical understatement, esp one where a negative is used instead of its opposite, eg "a not inconsiderable amount" instead of "a large amount"; litotes; (*rare*) any division or separation.—**meiotic** *adj*.—**meiotically** *adv*.
Meistersinger *n* (*pl* **Meistersinger, Meistersingers**) a member of one of the various guilds in German cities of the 14th–16th cents., which instituted the development of poetry and music by establishing competitive standards.
melamine *n* a resinous material used for adhesives, coatings, and laminated products.
melancholy *n* gloominess or depression; sadness. * *adj* sad; depressed.—**melancholia** *n*.—**melancholic** *adj*.
mélange *n* a (confused) mixture; a medley; (*geol*) a hotchpotch of variously shaped rocks of different periods and sizes.
melanin *n* a dark brown pigment in the skin, hair, and eyes of humans and animals.
melanism, melanosis *n* dark coloration of the skin in pale-skinned people or dark-coloured feathers, etc, in birds and animals, caused by abnormal deposits of black or dark pigment in skin tissue, the opposite of albinism.—**melanistic, melanotic** *adj*.
melanoma *n* (*pl* **melanomas, melanomata**) a skin tumour composed of darkly pigmented cells.
melee, mêlée *n* a confused, noisy struggle.
melic *adj* (*poem*) meant to be sung, often used of ancient Greek lyric poetry.
melilot *n* a species of sweet-scented trefoil or clover, with clusters of small yellow or white flowers.—*also* **sweet clover**.
melinite *n* a high explosive similar to lyddite.
meliorate *vti* to improve; to grow better; to make (something) better.—**meliorable** *adj*.—**meliorative** *adj, n*.—**meliorator** *n*.
melioration *n* the process of improving; the state of being improved; an improvement.
meliorism *n* the doctrine that in nature there is a tendency to gradual improvement and this may be accelerated by human effort.
melliferous *adj* forming or yielding honey.
mellifluous, mellifluent *adj* (*voice, sounds*) sweetly flowing, smooth.—**mellifluously** *adv*.—**mellifluousness** *n*.
mellow *adj* (*fruit*) sweet and ripe; (*wine*) matured; (*colour, light, sound*) soft, not harsh; kind-hearted and understanding. * *vti* to soften through age; to mature.—**mellowness** *n*.
melodeon *n* a kind of accordion; a small reed organ.
melodic *adj* pertaining to or having melody.—**melodically** *adv*.
melodious *adj* full of melody, tuneful, musical; sweet-sounding.—**melodiously** *adv*.—**melodiousness** *n*.
melodist *n* a singer; a composer of melodies.
melodize *vti* to make (something) melodious; to compose a melody (for something); to sing a melody.
melodrama *n* a play, film, etc filled with overdramatic emotion and action; drama of this genre; sensational events or emotions.—**melodramatic** *adj*.—**melodramatically** *adv*.—**melodramatist** *n*.
melody *n* (*pl* **melodies**) a tune; a pleasing series of sounds.—**melodic** *adj*.—**melodious** *adj*.
melon *n* the large juicy many-seeded fruit of trailing plants, as the watermelon, cantaloupe.
melt *vti* (**melting, melted,** *pp* **molten**) to make or become liquid; to dissolve; to fade or disappear; to soften or be softened emotionally.—**melting** *adj*.—**meltingly** *adv*.
meltdown *n* the melting of the fuel core of a nuclear reactor; the drastic collapse of almost anything.
melting point *n* the temperature at which a solid melts.
melting pot *n* a place, situation, or product of mixing many different races, traditions, cultures, etc.
melton *n* a kind of thick woollen cloth, with a surface nap, often used for overcoats.
meltwater *n* water derived from the melting of snow or ice.
member *n* a person belonging to a society or club; a part of a body, such as a limb; a representative in a legislative body; a distinct part of a complex whole.
membership *n* the state of being a member; the number of members of a body; the members collectively.
membrane *n* a thin pliable sheet or film; the fibrous tissue that covers or lines animal organs.—**membranous, membranaceous** *adj*.
memento *n* (*pl* **mementos, mementoes**) a reminder, esp a souvenir.
memento mori *n* (*pl* **memente mori**) (an object that serves as) a reminder of death.
memo *n* (*pl* **memos**) a memorandum.
memoir *n* an historical account based on personal experience; (*pl*) an autobiographical record.
memorabilia *npl* (*sing* **memorabile**) things worthy of remembrance or record; clothing, letters, manuscripts, notes, etc, once belonging to or written by famous people or connected with famous events and thought worthy of collection.
memorable *adj* worth remembering; easy to remember.—**memorably** *adv*.
memorandum *n* (*pl* **memorandums**) an informal written communication as within an office; (*pl* **memoranda**) a note to help the memory.
memorial *adj* serving to preserve the memory of the dead. * *n* a remembrance; a monument.
memorialist *n* one who prepares, signs or presents a memorial; one who writes memoirs.
memorialize *vt* to commemorate; to honour by means of a memorial.—**memorialization** *n*.—**memorializer** *n*.
memorize *vt* to learn by heart, to commit to memory.—**memorization** *n*.
memory *n* (*pl* **memories**) the process of retaining and reproducing past thoughts and sensations; the sum of things remembered; an individual recollection; commemoration; remembrance; the part of a computer that stores information (—*also* **store**).
memsahib *n* (*formerly*) a form of address for a European married woman in India.
men *see* **man**.
menace *n* a threat; (*inf*) a nuisance. * *vt* to threaten.—**menacing** *adj*.—**menacingly** *adv*.
menad *see* **maenad**.
ménage *n* a household.
ménage à trois *n* (*pl* **ménages à trois**) a relationship in which a married couple and a lover of one of them live together.
menagerie *n* a place where wild animals are kept for exhibition; a collection of wild animals.

mend *vt* to repair; (*manners, etc*) to reform, improve. * *vi* to become better. * *n* the act of mending; a repaired area in a garment, etc.

mendacity *n* (*pl* **mendacities**) telling lies; a falsehood.—**mendacious** *adj*.—**mendaciously** *adv*.

mendelevium *n* an artificially produced radioactive metallic element.

Mendelism *n* the theories of the Austrian monk and geneticist Gregor Mendel (1822–84) respecting heredity, as set out in Mendel's laws with later modifications.—**Mendelian** *adj*.

mendicant *adj* begging; (*religious orders*) reliant on alms. * *n* a mendicant friar.—**mendicancy, mendicity** *n*.

mending *n* garments requiring to be repaired.

menhaden *n* (*pl* **menhadens, menhaden**)*n* an inedible American fish, yielding a valuable oil.

menhir *n* a tall, monolithic obelisk, sometimes crudely carved, dating from the Bronze Age in the UK or the Neolithic Age in Europe.

menial *adj* consisting of work of little skill; servile. * *n* a domestic servant; a servile person.

meninges *npl* (*sing* **meninx**) the three membranes covering and protecting the brain and the spinal cord.—**meningeal** *adj*.

meningitis *n* inflammation of the membranes enveloping the brain or spinal cord.

meniscus *n* (*pl* **menisci, meniscuses**) a crescent; the crescent-shaped surface of a liquid contained in a tube; a lens convex on one side and concave on the other; (*anat*) the cartilage between the bones of joints, esp at the knee.

menology *n* (*pl* **menologies**) an ecclesiastical calendar; a calendar of saints, esp in the Orthodox Church.

menopause *n* the time of life during which a woman's menstrual cycle ceases permanently.—**menopausal** *adj*.

menorrhagia *n* an excessive menstrual flow.

menses *n* (*pl* **menses**) menstruation; the monthly discharge of blood, etc, from the uterus; the days during which this occurs.

Menshevik *n* (*pl* **Mensheviks, Mensheviki**) (*hist*) a member of the more moderate Russian socialist party (1903–17) or of a liberal opposition party set up after the Revolution.—**Menshevism** *n*.—**Menshevist** *adj, n*.

menstruation *n* the monthly discharge of blood from the uterus.—**menstrual** *adj*.—**menstruate** *vi*.

menstruum *n* (*pl* **menstruums, menstrua**) a solvent, esp if used in making drugs.

mensurable *adj* measurable; (*mus*) of a fixed rhythm.—**mensurability** *n*.

mensuration *n* the science of measurement; the act or process of measuring or taking the dimensions of anything; measurement.

mental *adj* of, or relating to the mind; occurring or performed in the mind; having a psychiatric disorder; (*inf*) crazy, stupid.—**mentally** *adv*.

mentality *n* (*pl* **mentalities**) intellectual power; disposition, character.

menthol *n* peppermint oil.—**mentholated** *adj*.

mention *n* a brief reference to something in speech or writing; an official recognition or citation. * *vt* to refer to briefly; to remark; to honour officially.—**mentionable** *adj*.

mentor *n* a wise and trusted adviser.

menu *n* the list of dishes served in a restaurant; a list of options on a computer display.

meow *n* the cry of a cat; a spiteful remark.—*also vi*.

Mephistophelean, Mephistophelian *adj* pertaining to or like Mephistopheles, the devil of the Faust legend; fiendish, cynical; diabolic.

mephitis *n* a noxious gas emitted from the ground; a foul stench.—**mephitic, mephitical** *adj*.

mercantile *adj* of merchants or trade.

mercantilism *n* a theory popular in 17th and 18th century Europe suggesting that the wealth of a nation increases in proportion to the level of the foreign trade surplus, therefore trade and commerce with other countries, the founding of colonies, a merchant navy etc should be encouraged; (*rare*) commercialism—**mercantilist** *n, adj*.

mercenary *adj* working or done for money only. * *n* (*pl* **mercenaries**) a soldier hired to fight for a foreign army.—**mercenarily** *adv*.—**mercenariness** *n*.

mercer *n* a dealer in textiles, esp silk and velvet.

mercerize *vt* to treat cotton thread so as to strengthen it and make it resemble silk.—**mercerization** *n*.

merchandise *n* commercial goods. * *vti* to sell, to trade; to promote sales by display or advertising.—**merchandiser** *n*.

merchandising *n* the display of goods in a store, etc; the exploitation of a fictional character, pop group, etc, by the production of goods with their image, name, etc.

merchant *n* a trader; a retailer; (*sl*) a person fond of a particular activity.

merchantable *adj* marketable.

merchantman *n* (*pl* **merchantmen**) a trading ship.

merchant marine, merchant navy *n* commercial shipping.

merciful *adj* compassionate, humane.—**mercifulness** *n*.

mercifully *adv* in a merciful way; (*inf*) thank goodness.

merciless *adj* cruel, pitiless; without mercy.—**mercilessly** *adv*.—**mercilessness** *n*.

mercurial *adj* of, containing, or caused by mercury; lively, sprightly; volatile.—**mercurially** *adv*.

mercuric *adj* (*chem*) of or containing bivalent mercury.

mercurous *adj* (*chem*) of or containing monovalent mercury.

Mercury *n* the innermost planet, and the smallest; the Roman god of thieves, traders etc; in ancient Rome, the messenger of the gods.

mercury *n* a heavy silvery liquid metallic element used in thermometers etc.

mercy *n* clemency; compassion; kindness; pity.

mere *adj* nothing more than; simple, unmixed.

merely *adv* simply; solely.

meretricious *adj* tawdry, superficially attractive; insincere.

merganser *n* (*pl* **mergansers, merganser**) *n* a large, diving fish-eating duck with a long narrow bill with serrated edges; a sawbill.

merge *vti* to blend or cause to fuse together gradually; to (cause to) combine, unite.

merger *n* a combining together, esp of two or more commercial organizations.

meridian *n* the imaginary circle on the surface of the earth passing through the north and south poles.

meridional *adj* of a meridian; of the south.—**meridionally** *adv*.

meringue *n* a mixture of egg whites beaten with sugar and baked; a small cake or shell made from this, usu filled with cream.

merino *n* (*pl* **merinos**) a breed of sheep with fine silky wool; the wool or the cloth made from it.

merit *n* excellence; worth; (*pl*) (*of a case*) rights and wrongs; a deserving act. * *vt* to be worthy of, to deserve.

meritocracy *n* (*pl* **meritocracies**) rule by those most skilled or talented; a social system or government based on this; the most talented group in a society.

meritorious *adj* deserving of merit or honour.—**meritoriously** *adv*.—**meritoriousness** *n*.

merle *n* (*Scot*) a blackbird. * *adj* (*dog, esp a collie*) having blue-grey fur with black tinges or streaks.

merlin *n* a small dark-coloured falcon, often used in falconry.

merlon *n* the part of a parapet or battlement between two embrasures.

mermaid *n* (*legend*) a woman with a fish's tail.—**merman** *nm* (*pl* **mermen**).

meroblastic *adj* (*biol*) (*fertilized egg*) of or pertaining to the splitting of cells in the white only and not the entire ovum.

Merovingian *adj* pertaining to the first Frankish dynasty of French kings (*c.* 500–751). * *n* a member or adherent of this dynasty.

merry *adj* (**merrier, merriest**) cheerful; causing laughter; lively; (*inf*) slightly drunk.—**merrily** *adv*.—**merriment** *n*.

merry-go-round *n* a revolving platform of hobbyhorses, etc, a carousel.

merrymaking *n* festivity, fun.—**merrymaker** *n*.

merrythought *n* (*rare*) the forked bone of a chicken's breast, the wishbone.

mes-, meso- *prefix* middle.

mesa *n* a rocky plateau with steep sides usu found in arid regions.

mésalliance *n* a misalliance; a marriage with one of lower social position.

mescaline *n* a hallucinogenic drug derived from the mescal cactus.
mesdames *see* **madame.**
mesdemoiselles *see* **mademoiselle.**
mesembryanthemum *n* one of a genus of flowering, succulent plants with thick and fleshy leaves and showy flowers.
mesentery *n* (*pl* **mesenteries**) the membrane attaching the small intestines to the abdominal wall.—**mesenteric** *adj.*
mesh *n* an opening between cords of a net, wires of a screen, etc; a net; a network; a snare; (*geared wheels, etc*) engagement. * *vt* to entangle, ensnare. * *vi* to become entangled or interlocked.
mesial *adj* (*anat*) in or toward the middle line of the body.—**mesially** *adv.*
mesmerism *n* hypnotism.—**mesmerist** *n.*
mesmerize *vt* to hypnotize; to fascinate.—**mesmeric** *adj.*—**mesmerizer** *n.*
mesne *adj* (*law*) intervening, intermediate.
meso-, mes- *prefix* middle.
mesoblast *n* (*biol*) the middle germinal layer of an ovum, the basis of muscles, bones, blood etc.—*also* **mesoderm.**
mesocarp *n* the middle layer of the seed vessel of a fruit.
mesocephalic *adj, n* (*person*) with a head or skull of medium proportions.
mesoderm *see* **mesoblast.**
mesogastrium *n* the membrane that supports the embryonic stomach.—**mesogastric** *adj.*
Mesolithic *n, adj* of or pertaining to the archaeological era between the Palaeolithic and Neolithic (*c.* 12000–3000 bc).
meson *n* an unstable elementary particle having a mass between that of proton and an electron.
mesophyll *n* the internal tissues of a leaf that are between the upper and lower epidermal layers and contain chlorophyll.—**mesophyllic, mesophyllous** *adj.*
mesophyte *n* a plant requiring an average water supply.—**mesophytic** *adj.*
mesothorax *n* (*pl* **mesothoraxes, mesothoraces**) *n* the middle ring of an insect's thorax, with the second pair of walking legs and the front pair of wings.
Mesozoic *adj* pertaining to the era of geological time lasting from about 248 to 65 million years ago. * *n* this era.
mesquite, mesquit *n* a small pod-bearing tree of the southwest US whose pods are used as fodder.
mess *n* a state of disorder or untidiness, esp if dirty; a muddle; an unsightly or disagreeable mixture; a portion of soft and pulpy or semi-liquid food; a building where service personnel dine; a communal meal. * *vti* to make a mess (of), bungle; to eat in company; to potter (about).
message *n* any spoken, written, or other form of communication; the chief idea that the writer, artist, etc seeks to communicate in a work.
messenger *n* a person who carries a message.
Messiah *n* the promised saviour of the Jews; Jesus Christ.—**Messianic** *adj.*
messieurs *see* **monsieur.**
Messrs *pl* of Mr.
messuage *n* (*law*) a dwelling house with its adjacent buildings and land for the use of the household.
messy *adj* (**messier, messiest**) dirty; confused; untidy.—**messily** *adv.*—**messiness** *n.*
mestizo *n* (*pl* **mestizos, mestizoes**) a person of mixed parentage, esp the child of a Spanish American and an American Indian.
met *see* **meet.**
meta-, met- *prefix* after, with, or implying change.
metabolism *n* the total processes in living organisms by which tissue is formed, energy produced and waste products eliminated.—**metabolic** *adj.*
metabolize *vt* to process by metabolism; to assimilate.
metacarpal *adj* pertaining to the metacarpus. * *n* a bone of the metacarpus.
metacarpus *n* (*pl* **metacarpi**) the bones of that part of the hand that is between the wrist and the fingers, or the corresponding part in other animals.
metacenter, metacentre *n* the point in a floating body where the verticals intersect when the body is tilted and on the position of which its equilibrium or stability depends.—**metacentric** *adj.*
metage *n* the official weighing or measuring of the contents of something; the fee paid for this.
metagenesis *n* the alternation of sexual and asexual generations.—**metagenetic** *adj.*—**metagenetically** *adv.*
metal *n* any of a class of chemical elements which are often lustrous, ductile solids, and are good conductors of heat, electricity, etc, such as gold, iron, copper, etc; any alloy of such elements as brass, bronze, etc; anything consisting of metal.—**metalled** *adj.*
metallic *adj* of, relating to, or made of metal; similar to metal.
metalliferous *adj* yielding metal or metallic ores.
metalline *adj* metallic; impregnated with or yielding metal.
metallize, metalize *vt* to give metallic qualities to; to coat or treat with metal.
metallography *n* the science or description of the structure of metals and alloys; (*print*) lithography using metal plates to print an image.
metalloid *n* a nonmetallic element that possesses some of the chemical properties associated with metals. * *adj* of or having the properties of a metalloid; resembling a metal (—*also* **metalloidal**).
metallurgy *n* the science of separating metals from their ores and preparing them for use by smelting, refining, etc.—**metallurgical** *adj.*—**metallurgist** *n.*
metamere *n* a segment of a body, as in earthworms, crayfish, etc.
metameric *adj* (*zool*) of or having metameres; (*chem*) having the same elements and molecular weight but different properties.—**metamerism** *n.*
metamorphism *n* the change in the structure of rocks through heat, pressure, etc.
metamorphosis *n* (*pl* **metamorphoses**) a complete change of form, structure, substance, character, appearance, etc; transformation; the marked change in some animals at a stage in their growth, eg chrysalis to butterfly.—**metamorphic** *adj.*—**metamorphose** *vi.*
metaphor *n* a figure of speech in which a word or phrase is used for another of which it is an image.—**metaphoric, metaphorical** *adj.*—**metaphorically** *adv.*
metaphrase *n* a word-for-word translation, the opposite of paraphrase. * *vt* to alter the wording of something, esp to alter the meaning; to translate literally.
metaphrast *n* one who alters text, esp one who changes the form, as from verse to prose.—**metaphrastic, metaphrastical** *adj.*
metaphysical *adj* of or pertaining to metaphysics; abstruse, abstract; supernatural; (*poetry*) fantastic or over-subtle in style.—**metaphysically** *adv.*
metaphysics *n sing* the branch of philosophy that seeks to explain the nature of being and reality; speculative philosophy in general.—**metaphysician** *n.*
metaplasm *n* (*biol*) that part of the contents of a cell consisting of inert matter; (*gram*) a change in a word by the adding or dropping of a letter.—**metaplasmic** *adj.*
metastasis *n* (*pl* **metastases**) *n* a change or shift in the location of a disease, often used of the spreading of cancer cells; a transformation or change; (*rare*) metabolism—**metastatic** *adj.*
metatarsal *adj* pertaining to the metatarsus. * *n* one of the bones of the metatarsus.
metatarsus *n* (*pl* **metatarsi**) (*anat*) in humans, the instep, the middle part of the foot between the tarsus and the toes; in other animals, the part corresponding to this.
metathesis *n* (*pl* **metatheses**) the transposition of the letters or syllables of a word; (*chem*) a reaction between two compounds in which the first and second parts of one unite with the second and first parts of the other.—**metathetic, metathetical** *adj.*
metathorax *n* (*pl* **metathoraxes, metathoraces**) *n* the hindmost segment of an insect's thorax, with the third pair of walking legs and the second pair of wings.

metazoan *n* an animal belonging to a division of the animal kingdom in which the body is made up of a large number of cells, ie all animals except sponges and protozoans.
mete *vt* to allot; to portion (out).
metempsychosis *n* (*pl* **metempsychoses**) the transmigration of the soul after the death of the body to another body or form.
meteor *n* a small particle of matter which travels at great speed through space and becomes luminous through friction as it enters the earth's atmosphere; a shooting star.
meteoric *adj* of or relating to a meteor; dazzling, transitory.
meteorite *n* a meteor that has fallen to earth without being completely vaporized.—**meteoritic** *adj*.
meteorograph *n* an instrument for recording various meteorological conditions simultaneously.
meteoroid *n* a small body moving through space, often orbiting the sun which can be seen as a meteor if it enters the earth's atmosphere.
meteorology *n* a study of the earth's atmosphere, particularly weather and climate.—**meteorological** *adj*.—**meteorologist** *n*.
-meter *suffix* denoting a device for measuring; metre(s) in length.
meter[1] *n* a device for measuring and recording a quantity of gas, water, time, etc supplied; a parking meter. * *vt* to measure using a meter.
meter[2] *see* **metre**[1], **metre**[2].
methane *n* a colourless, odourless, flammable gas formed by the decomposition of vegetable matter, as in marshes.
methinks *vb* (*pt* **methought**) (*arch*) it appears or seems to me.
method *n* the mode or procedure of accomplishing something; orderliness of thought; an orderly arrangement or system.
methodical *adj* orderly, systematic.—**methodically** *adv*.
Methodist *n* a member of a Christian denomination founded by John Wesley.—**Methodism** *n*.
methodize *vt* to reduce to method; systematize.
methodology *n* (*pl* **methodologies**) the methods and procedures used by a science or discipline; the philosophical analysis of method and procedure.
methought *see* **methinks**.
meths *n* (*inf*) methylated spirit.
Methuselah *n* a wine bottle eight times the size of an ordinary bottle; (*Old Testament*) a patriarch reputed to have been 969 years old when he died; a very old person.
methyl *n* a compound composed of organic material and metals in which metal groups are bound directly to a metal atom.
methylated spirit *n* a form of alcohol, adulterated to render it undrinkable, used as a solvent.
methylene *n* a bivalent organic radical found in unsaturated hydrocarbons; an inflammable liquid obtained from the distillation of wood.
meticulous *adj* very precise about small details.—**meticulously** *adv*.—**meticulousness** *n*.
métier *n* a person's calling or trade, esp if that person has a natural leaning toward it; a strong point, forte.
métis *n* (*pl* **métis**) *n* (*often cap*) an offspring of mixed parentage; in Canada, one who is the child or a descendant of a French Canadian and an American Indian; one of a group of such people forming a political and national entity, who settled in Manitoba and Saskatchewan.—**métisse** *nf*.
Metol *n* (*trademark*) a colourless, soluble organic substance used as a photographic developer.
metonymy *n* (**metonymies**) a figure of speech in which a thing is replaced by its attribute, eg "the pen is mightier than the sword."—**metonym** *n*.—**metonymical, metonymic** *adj*.
metope *n* (*archit*) the space between two triglyphs of a Doric frieze.
metre[1] *n* rhythmic pattern in verse, the measured arrangement of syllables according to stress; rhythmic pattern in music.—*also* **meter**.
metre[2] *n* the basic unit of length in the metric system, consisting of 100 centimetres and equal to 39.37 inches.—*also* **meter**.
metric *adj* based on the metre as a standard of measurement; of, relating to, or using the metric system.
metrical *adj* of, relating to, or composed in rhythmic metre.—**metrically** *adv*.
metrication *n* conversion of an existent system of units into the metric system.
metrics *n sing* the study of verse form; the art of composing verse.
metric system *n* a decimal system of weights and measures based on the metre, litre and the kilogram.
metro *n* (*pl* **metros**) an urban underground railway system, such as in Paris and other cities.
metrology *n* (*pl* **metrologies**) *n* the science of weights and measures or units of measurement; any of the various systems of units.
metronome *n* an instrument that beats musical tempo.—**metronomic** *adj*.
metronymic *adj* (*name*) derived from one's mother or a female ancestor. * *n* such a name.—*also* **matronymic**.
metropolis *n* the main city, often a capital of a country, state, etc; any large and important city.—**metropolitan** *adj*.
mettle *n* courage, spirit.
mettled *adj* mettlesome.
mettlesome *adj* high-spirited, full of courage.
meunière *adj* (*fish*) coated with flour, cooked in butter and served with parsley and lemon juice.
mew[1] *vi* (*cat*) to emit a high-pitched cry. * *n* the cry of a cat.
mew[2] *n* a gull found in northern areas.
mew[3] *n* a cage for hawks. * *vti* (*hawk*) to shed (feathers), to moult; to put in a mew, to confine.
mewl *vi* (*baby*) to cry feebly, to whimper; to mew. * *n* a whimper.
mews *n sing or pl* a yard or road lined with buildings formerly used stables and later converted into living accommodation.
mezzanine *n* an intermediate storey between others; a theatre balcony.
mezzanine debt *see* **junk debt**.
mezzo *adv* (*mus*) moderately; quite. * *n* (*pl* **mezzos**) a mezzo-soprano.
mezzo-relievo *n* (*pl* **mezzo-relievos**) a carving in half-relief, where the figures project in neither high relief nor low relief from the background.
mezzo-soprano *n* (*pl* **mezzo-sopranos**) (*mus*) a singer, or a part, between soprano and contralto.
mezzotint *n* a method of engraving on copper in which lights are made by scraping a roughened surface; a print so made. * *vt* to engrave a copper plate using this method.
mfr *abbr* = manufacture; manufacturer.
Mg (*chem symbol*) magnesium.
mg *abbr* = milligram.
Mgr *abbr* = manager.
MHR *abbr* = Member of the House of Representatives.
MHz *abbr* = megahertz.
MI *abbr* = Michigan; military intelligence; myocardial infarction.
mi. *abbr* = mile; mill.
MIA *abbr* = missing in action.
miasma *n* (*pl* **miasmas, miasmata**) an unwholesome, foreboding atmosphere; an unpleasant vapour, as from decaying swamp matter.—**miasmal, miasmatic, miasmic** *adj*.
mica *n* a mineral that crystallizes in thin, flexible layers, resistant to heat.—**micaceous** *adj*.
mice *see* **mouse**.
Mich. *abbr* = Michigan.
Michaelmas *n* a church festival commemorating the archangel Michael, celebrated on September 29.
micra *see* **micron**.
micro *n* (*pl* **micros**) a microwave oven; (*comput*) a microcomputer, a microprocessor.
micro-, micr- *prefix* small.
microbe *n* a microscopic organism, esp a disease-causing bacterium.—**microbial, microbic** *adj*.
microbiology *n* the biology of bacteria and other microorganisms and their effects.—**microbiological, microbiologic** *adj*.—**microbiologically** *adv*.—**microbiologist** *n*.

microbus *n* (*pl* **microbuses, microbusses**) a station wagon that resembles a small bus.
microcephalic, microcephalous *adj* having an unusually small head.—**microcephaly** *n.*
microchip *n* a small wafer of silicon, etc, containing electronic circuits.—*also* **chip.**
microcircuit *n* a miniature electronic circuit, esp an integrated circuit.—**microcircuitry** *n.*
microclimate *n* the climate of a restricted specific place within an area as opposed to the climate of the area.—**microclimatic** *adj.*
micrococcus *n* (**micrococci**) a round bacterium, a source of fermentation and of zymotic disease.—**micrococcal** *adj.*
microcomputer *n* a computer in which the central processing unit is contained in one or more microprocessors.
microcosm *n* a miniature universe or world.—**microcosmic, microcosmical** *adj.*—**microcosmically** *adv.*
microcyte *n* an unusually small red blood corpuscle, often present in disease.—**microcytic** *adj.*
microdot *n* a photographic reproduction of a document, plan, etc reduced to a tiny dot, esp for reasons of espionage.
microeconomics *n sing* the branch of economics concerned with the activities of consumers, firms, and commodities.—**microeconomic** *adj.*
microfiche *n* (*pl* **microfiche, microfiches**) a sheet of microfilm containing pages of printed matter.—*also* **film card.**
microfilm *n* film on which documents, etc, are recorded in reduced scale. * *vt* to record on microfilm.
microfloppy *n* (*pl* **microfloppies**) a floppy disk of 3.5 inches diameter contained in a hard covering.
micrograph *n* a photograph of something as seen through a microscope; a device for executing minute engraving or writing.
micrography *n* the description, study or representation of microscopic objects; the process of writing in miniature.—**micrographic** *adj.*
micrometer[1] *n* any of various instruments for measuring minute distances, angles, thicknesses, or apparent diameters, sometimes used with a microscope.
micrometer[2], **micrometre** *n* a unit of length of one thousandth of a millimetre, a micron.
micrometry *n* the measurement of tiny objects, distances, etc, by a micrometer.—**micrometric, micrometrical** *adj.*—**micrometrically** *adv.*
micron *n* (*pl* **microns, micra**) one millionth of a metre, a micrometer.
microorganism *n* an organism visible only through a microscope.
microphone *n* an instrument for transforming sound waves into electric signals, esp for transmission, or recording.—**microphonic** *adj.*
microphotograph *n* a photograph taken through a microscope or of microscopic size, in which the details cannot be distinguished by the naked eye; a photomicrograph.—**microphotographic** *adj.*—**microphotography** *n.*
microphyte *n* a microscopic vegetable growth, esp a parasitic one.—**microphytic** *adj.*
microprocessor *n* a computer processor contained on one or more integrated circuits.
microscope *n* an optical instrument for making magnified images of minute objects by means of a lens or lenses.
microscopic *adj* of, with, like, a microscope; visible only through a microscope; very small.—**microscopically** *adv.*
microscopy *n* (*pl* **microscopies**) the use of microscopes; microscopic investigation.—**microscopist** *n.*
microseism *n* a faint earth tremor, probably not related to earthquakes.—**microseismic** *adj.*
microtome *n* an instrument for cutting thin sections for microscopic examination, used particularly in biology.
microwave *n* an electromagnetic wave between 1 and 100 centimetres in length; (*inf*) a microwave oven. * *vt* to cook (food) in a microwave oven.—**microwavable, microwaveable** *adj.*
microwave oven *n* a cooker in which food is cooked or heated by microwaves.
micturate *vi* to urinate.—**micturition** *n.*
mid *adj* middle. * *prep* amid.
mid. *abbr* = middle.
mid- *prefix* middle.
midday *n* the middle of the day, noon.
midden *n* a dunghill, a refuse heap.
middle *adj* halfway between two given points, times, etc; intermediate; central. * *n* the point halfway between two extremes; something intermediate; the waist. * *vt* to put in the middle; (*naut*) to fold (a sail) in the middle.
middle age *n* the time between youth and old age, *c.* 40–60.—**middle-aged** *adj.*
Middle Ages *npl* the period of European history between about ad 500 and 1500.
middle class *n* the class between the lower and upper classes, mostly composed of professional and business people.—**middle-class** *adj.*
Middle East *n* a general term applied currently to an area extending from the eastern Mediterranean to the Gulf of Arabia; (formerly) that part of Southern Asia from the Tigris and Euphrates to Burma.
middleman *n* (*pl* **middlemen**) a dealer between producer and consumer; an intermediary.
middle-of-the-road *adj* avoiding extremes, esp political extremes.—**middle-of-the-roader** *n.*
middleweight *n* an professional boxer weighing 154–160 pounds (70–72.5 kilograms); a wrestler weighing usu 172–192 pounds (78–87 kilograms).
middling *adj* of medium quality, size, etc; second-rate. * *adv* moderately.—**middlingly** *adv.*
middy *n* (*pl* **middies**) *n* (*inf*) a midshipman; a middy blouse; (*Austral*) a glass of beer, usu containing half a pint.
middy blouse *n* a loose blouse with a sailor collar.
midge *n* a small gnat-like insect with a painful bite.
midget *n* a very small person, a dwarf; something small of its kind.—*also adj.*
midi *n* a coat or skirt that reaches to mid calf.
midland *n* the middle part of a country; (*pl*) (*with cap*) central England; the industrial and manufacturing area of that part of England. * *adj* of or in midland; inland.
midlife *n* (*pl* **midlives**) middle age.—*also adj.*
midmost *adj* in or nearest the middle. * *adv* in the middle.
midnight *n* twelve o'clock at night.
Midrash *n* (*pl* **Midrashim**) a critical exposition of or a sermon on the Jewish scriptural law or some portion of it; one of the various collections of these originating between ad 400 and 1200.
midrib *n* the principal central vein of a leaf.
midriff *n* the middle part of the torso between the abdomen and the chest.—*also adj.*
midship *adj* (*naut*) of or pertaining to the middle part of a ship.
midshipman *n* (*pl* **midshipmen**) in some navies, a noncommissioned officer ranking immediately below a sublieutenant; this naval rank; (*formerly*) a naval cadet officer; an American fish with light-producing organs.
midships *adv* (*naut*) at, near or toward the middle of a ship, amidships.
midst *n* middle. * *prep* amidst, among.
midsummer *n* the middle of summer.—*also adj.*
Midsummer Day *n* June 24, celebrated as the summer solstice or in commemoration of the birth of St John the Baptist.
Midsummer Eve *n* the day before Midsummer Day, June 23.
midway *adv* halfway. * *n* a middle course of action; the area of a carnival where the sideshows are.
midwife *n* (*pl* **midwives**) a person trained to assist women before, during, and after childbirth.—**midwifery** *n.*
mien *n* the expression of the face; demeanour.
miff *n* (*inf*) a petty quarrel, a tiff; a sulky mood. * *vti* to take offence; to offend.
miffy *adj* (**miffier, miffiest**) (*inf*) touchy, huffy; over-sensitive.—**miffiness** *n.*
might[1] *see* **may.**

might[2] *n* power, bodily strength.
mightn't = might not.
mighty *adj* (**mightier, mightiest**) powerful, strong; massive; (*inf*) very.—**mightily** *adv*.—**mightiness** *n*.
mignonette *n* a sweet-scented plant with spikes of small green- white flowers; a greyish-green colour; a delicate bobbin lace.
migraine *n* an intense, periodic headache, usu limited to one side of the head.
migrant *n* a person or animal that moves from one region or country to another; an itinerant agricultural labourer. * *adj* migrating.
migrate *vi* to settle in another country or region; (*birds, animals*) to move to another region with the change in season.—**migration** *n*.—**migratory** *adj*.
mikado *n* (*sl* **mikados**) (*arch*) (*often with cap*) the Japanese emperor.
mike *n* (*inf*) a microphone. * *vt* to provide with a microphone; to transmit by microphone.
mil *n* a unit of length of one thousandth of an inch; (*gunnery*) an angle of one sixty-four-hundredth of a circumference; a milliliter.
mil. *abbr* = military; militia.
milady *n* (*pl* **miladies**) *n* (*formerly*) a word used in Europe for an aristocratic Englishwoman.
milage *see* **mileage.**
milch *adj* yielding milk, used esp of cattle.
milch cow *n* a cow from which milk is obtained for human consumption; a ready source of gain.
mild *adj* (*temper*) gentle; (*weather*) temperate; bland; feeble.—**mildly** *adv*.—**mildness** *n*.
mildew *n* a fungus that attacks some plants or appears on damp cloth, etc as a whitish coating. * *vti* to affect or be affected with mildew.—**mildewy** *adj*.
mile *n* a unit of linear measure equal to 5,280 feet (1.61 km); the nautical mile is 6,075 feet (1.85 km).
mileage *n* total miles travelled; an allowance per mile for travelling expenses; the average number of miles that can be travelled, as per litre of fuel.—*also* **milage.**
milestone *n* a stone marking the number of miles to a place; an important event in life, history, etc.
milfoil *n* a yarrow plant; one of various pond plants with feather-like leaves and small flowers.
miliaria *n* a skin disease resulting from blocked sweat glands and characterized by an acute itchiness, heat rash.—**miliarial** *adj*.
miliary *adj* (*growth, lesion*) very small; (*skin disease*) marked by small lesions resembling millet seeds.
milieu *n* (*pl* **milieus, milieux**) environment, esp social setting.
militant *adj* ready to fight, esp for some cause; combative.—*also n*.—**militance, militancy** *n*.—**militantly** *adv*.
militarism *n* military spirit; a policy of aggressive military preparedness.
militarist *n* a believer in militarism; a student of military science.—**militaristic** *adj*.—**militaristically** *adv*.
militarize *vt* to equip and prepare for war.—**militarization** *n*.
military *adj* relating to soldiers or to war; warlike. * *n* (*pl* **militaries**) the armed forces.
militate *vt* to have influence or force; to produce an effect or change.
militia *n* an army composed of civilians called out in time of emergency.—**militiaman** *n* (*pl* **militiamen**).
milk *n* a white nutritious liquid secreted by female mammals for feeding their young. * *vt* to draw milk from; to extract money, etc, from; to exploit.—**milker** *n*.
milkmaid *n* a girl or woman who milks cows or works in a dairy.
milkman *n* (*pl* **milkmen**) a person who sells or delivers milk to homes.
milk run *n* (*sl*) a routine journey.
milksop *n* a weak cowardly man or boy.—**milksoppy** *adj*.
milk toast *n* toasted bread soaked in warm milk, often eaten by babies and invalids.
milk tooth *n* any of the first teeth of a mammal.
milkweed *n* a plant found mainly in North America yielding a milky sap and with pointed pods containing tufted seeds; any plant with a milky sap.—*also* **silkweed.**
milkwort *n* a kind of plant with small blue, pink or white flowers.
milky *adj* (**milkier, milkiest**) of, filled with, consisting of, yielding, or resembling milk; timid.—**milkily** *adv*.—**milkiness** *n*.
Milky Way *n* (*with* **the**) the galaxy to which the Earth belongs; the system of stars, nebulae, etc, that can be seen in the night sky as a trailing ribbon of light and forms part of the Galaxy.
mill[1] *n* an apparatus for grinding by crushing between rough surfaces; a building where grain is ground into flour; a factory. * *vt* to produce or grind in a mill; (*coins*) to put a raised edge on. * *vi* to move around confusedly.—**miller** *n*.
mill[2] *n* a unit of money equal to one tenth of a cent.
millboard *n* a thick pasteboard, often black or grey, that forms the front and back covers and spine of a book, usu covered by the book binding.
millenarian *adj* consisting of or pertaining to a thousand years; pertaining to the millennium or to millenarianism. * *n* a believer in the millennium; an advocate of millenarianism.
millenarianism *n* (*Christianity*) the belief that the Second Coming of Christ will be preceded or followed by a thousand years of holiness.
millenary *adj* of or pertaining to a thousand; millenarian. * *n* (*pl* **millenaries**) a thousandth anniversary; one thousand as a total, esp one thousand years; a millenarian.
millennium *n* (*pl* **millennia, millenniums**) a period of a thousand years; (*Christianity*) a period of a thousand years of holiness preceding or following the Second Coming of Christ; a coming time of happiness.—**millennial** *adj*.—**millennially** *adv*.
millepede *see* **millipede.**
millepore *n* a tropical coelenterate resembling a coral, with a smooth surface perforated with very small pores.
miller *n* one who or that which mills; an owner of a mill; a moth with a floury appearance.
millesimal *adj* pertaining to a thousandth. * *n* a thousandth.
millet *n* a cereal grass used for grain and fodder.
milli- *prefix* a thousandth part.
milligram *n* a thousandth of a gramme.
milliliter, millilitre *n* a thousandth (.001) of a litre.
millimetre, millimeter *n* a thousandth (.001) of a metre.
milliner *n* a designer or seller of women's hats.—**millinery** *n*.
milling *n* the act of grinding in or passing through a dressing mill; the process of making a serrated edge on a coin, etc; the serrated edge of such a coin; a stratagem to stop cattle stampeding.
million *n* (*pl* **million, millions**) a thousand thousands, the number one followed by six zeros: 1,000,000; (*inf*) a very large number.—**millionth** *adj*.
millionaire *n* a person who owns at least a million of money; one who is extremely rich.
millipede *n* a wormlike arthropod with many legs and a segmented body.—*also* **millepede.**
millpond *n* a reservoir of water for driving a mill; any stretch of calm water.
millrace *n* a current of water that drives a mill; the channel in which this flows.
millstone *n* a stone used for grinding corn; a heavy burden.
millwright *n* a person who designs, builds, and repairs mills or mill parts.
milord *n* (*formerly*) a word used in Europe for an aristocratic or rich Englishman.
milt *n* the sperm of a male fish; its reproductive glands when filled with this; the spleen of some animals. * *vt* to fertilize (the roe of female fish), esp artificially.
milter *n* a male fish in the breeding season.
Miltonic, Miltonian *adj* pertaining to, characteristic of, or resembling the writings of the English poet John Milton (1608–74).
mime *n* a theatrical technique using action without words; a mimic. * *vi* to act or express using gestures alone; (*singers, musicians*) to perform as if singing or playing live to what is actually a prerecorded piece of music.—**mimer** *n*.

mimeograph *n* a machine for making multiple copies of a letter, drawing, etc, by means of a stencil fixed to an inked drum, and masking the non-printing areas; a copy produced from this machine; * *vti* to produce copies (of something) by using this machine.

mimesis *n* (*art, literature, etc*) the realistic representation of objects, people, everyday life, etc; (*biol*) mimicry; (*med*) a condition characterized by symptoms that occur in other diseases but that cannot be found by objective medical testing; a disease that mimics the symptoms of another disease.

mimetic *adj* of or given to imitation or mimicry; (*biol*) pertaining to or having the ability to mimic.—**mimetically** *adv*.

mimic *n* a person who imitates, esp an actor skilled in mimicry. * *adj* related to mimicry; make-believe; sham. * *vt* (**mimicking, mimicked**) to imitate or ridicule.—**mimicker** *n*.

mimicry *n* (*pl* **mimicries**) practice, art, or way of mimicking; (*biol*) the resemblance of an animal to its environment, another animal, etc, to provide protection from predators, mimesis.

mimosa *n* any of a genus of leguminous plants, usu with clustered yellow flowers, whose leaves and stems fold when touched or when exposed to light; the sensitive plant; any of several related or similar plants.

Min. *abbr* = Minister; Ministry.

min. *abbr* = minimum; minute(s).

mina[1] *n* (*pl* **minas, minae**) a weight and coin, current in ancient Anatolia, equal to one sixtieth of a talent.

mina[2] *see* **myna.**

minaret *n* a high, slender tower on a mosque from which the call to prayer is made.

minatory, minatorial *adj* threatening.—**minatorily** *adv*.

mince *vt* to chop or cut up into small pieces; to diminish or moderate one's words. * *vi* to speak or walk with affected daintiness.—**mincer** *n*.—**mincing** *adj*.—**mincingly** *adv*.

mincemeat *n* a mixture of chopped apples, raisins, etc, used as a pie filling; finely chopped meat.

mind *n* the faculty responsible for intellect, thought, feelings, speech; memory; intellect; reason; opinion; sanity. * *vt* to object to, take offence to; to pay attention to; to obey; to take care of; to be careful about; to care about. * *vi* to pay attention; to be obedient; to be careful; to object.

mind-bending *adj* (*inf*) (*drugs, etc*) unbalancing the mind; (*inf*) stretching credibility to the limits.—**mind-bender** *n*.—**mind-bendingly** *adv*.

mind-blowing *adj* (*inf*) (*drugs*) hallucinatory.

mind-boggling *adj* (*inf*) astonishing, bewildering.—**mind-boggler** *n*.

minded *adj* disposed, inclined; (in compounds) having a mind as described, eg small-minded.—**mindedness** *n*.

minder *n* a person who looks after or protects another.

mind-expanding *adj* producing awareness; psychedelic, distorting.

mindful *adj* heedful, not forgetful.—**mindfully** *adv*.—**mindfulness** *n*.

mindless *adj* unthinking, stupid; requiring little intellectual effort.—**mindlessly** *adv*.—**mindlessness** *n*.

mindset *n* attitude, esp when fixed or rigid; a habit.

mind's eye *n* the visual memory or imagination.

mine[1] *poss pron* belonging to me.

mine[2] *n* an excavation from which minerals are dug; an explosive device concealed in the water or ground to destroy enemy ships, personnel, or vehicles that pass over or near them; a rich supply or source. * *vt* to excavate; to lay explosive mines in an area. * *vi* to dig or work a mine.

mine detector *n* a device for indicating the whereabouts of explosive mines.—**mine detection** *n*.

minefield *n* an area sown with explosive mines; a situation containing hidden problems.

minelayer *n* a ship or aircraft for laying mines.

miner *n* a person who works in a mine.

mineral *n* an inorganic substance, found naturally in the earth; any substance neither vegetable nor animal. * *adj* relating to or containing minerals.

mineralize *vt* to convert (something) into a mineral; to impregnate (something) with mineral matter; to change something into a fossil-like object. * *vi* (*gases, etc, in molten rock*) to transform a metal into an ore.—**mineralization** *n*.

mineral kingdom *n* the group of natural substances that consist of only inorganic matter.

mineralogy *n* the science of minerals.—**mineralogical** *adj*.—**mineralogically** *adv*.—**mineralogist** *n*.

mineral water *n* water containing mineral salts or gases, often with medicinal properties.

minestrone *n* a soup of vegetables with pieces of pasta.

minesweeper *n* a ship for clearing away explosive mines.—**minesweeping** *n*.

mingle *vti* to mix; to combine.—**mingler** *n*.

mingy *adj* (**mingier, mingiest**) (*inf*) meagre in quantity; miserly, mean.

mini *n* (*pl* **minis**) something smaller than others of its type; a miniskirt.

mini- *prefix* small.

miniature *adj* minute, on a small scale. * *n* a painting or reproduction on a very small scale.—**miniaturist** *n*.

miniaturize *vt* to greatly reduce the size of.—**miniaturization** *n*.

minibar *n* a small refrigerator in a hotel bedroom, stocked with alcoholic drinks.

minibus *n* (*pl* **minibuses, minibusses**) a small bus for carrying up to twelve passengers.

minicab *n* a saloon car used as a taxi, which can be booked by telephone but not hailed.

minicar *n* a very small car.

minicomputer *n* a computer intermediate in size and processing power between a mainframe and a microcomputer.

minim *n* a unit of fluid measure of one sixtieth of a fluid dram (0.0616 ml) in the US and one twentieth of a scruple (0.592 ml) in the UK; (*mus*) a half note.

minima *see* **minimum.**

minimal *adj* very minute; least possible.—**minimality** *n*.—**minimally** *adv*.

minimalism *n* a style in the creation of art, music, etc, that uses the fewest possible elements to achieve the greatest effect.—**minimalist** *n, adj*.

minimize *vt* to reduce to or estimate at a minimum.—**minimization** *n*.

minimum *n* (*pl* **minimums, minima**) the least possible amount; the lowest degree or point reached.

mining *n* the act, process, or industry of excavating from the earth; (*mil*) the laying of explosive mines.

minion *n* a servile flatterer or dependant; an obsequious person acting on behalf of or carrying out the wishes of another. * *adj* dainty, graceful.

miniseries *n* (*pl* **miniseries**) (*TV*) the dramatization of a novel, etc, shown in several episodes; (*sport*) a short series.

miniskirt *n* a very short skirt.

minister *n* a clergyman serving a church; an official heading a government department; a diplomat. * *vi* to serve as a minister in a church; to give help (to).—**ministerial** *adj*.—**ministerially** *adv*.

ministrant *adj* serving as a minister. * *n* a person who ministers.

ministration *n* the act or process of giving aid; the act of ministering religiously.

ministry *n* (*pl* **ministries**) the act of ministering; the clergy; the profession of a clergyman; a government department headed by a minister; the building housing a government department.

minium *n* red oxide of lead, used as a pigment in paints; red lead.

miniver *n* a white fur, orig from the Siberian squirrel, used as a trimming on ceremonial robes, etc.

mink *n* (*pl* **mink, minks**) any of several carnivorous weasel-like mammals valued for its durable soft fur.

Minn. *abbr* = Minnesota.

minnesinger *n* any of the German lyric poets and musicians of the 12th–14th centuries who sang about love and beauty.

minnow *n* (*pl* **minnow, minnows**) a small, slender freshwater fish.

minor *adj* lesser in size, importance, degree, extent, etc; (*mus*) lower than the corresponding major by a half step. * *n* (*law*) a person under full legal age; (*education*) a secondary area of study requiring fewer credits; (*mus*) a minor key, interval, or scale; (*sport*) a minor league, esp in baseball. * *vi* (*with* **in**) to take a subject requiring fewer credits.

Minorite, Minorist *n* a Franciscan friar, esp one of the order of Friars Minor.

minority *n* (*pl* **minorities**) the smaller part or number; a political or racial group smaller than the majority group; the state of being under age.

Minotaur *n* (*Greek myth*) a monster with the head of a bull and the body of a man, which ate human flesh.

minster *n* a large and important church, often with cathedral status.

minstrel *n* a travelling entertainer and musician in the Middle Ages; a performer in a minstrel show.

minstrel show *n* a variety show with performers singing and dancing wearing black face make-up.

minstrelsy *n* (*pl* **minstrelsies**) the art or occupation of minstrels; minstrels collectively; a collection of ballad poetry.

mint[1] *n* the place where money is coined; a large amount of money; a source of supply. * *adj* unused, in perfect condition. * *vt* (*coins*) to imprint; to invent.—**minter** *n*.

mint[2] *n* an aromatic plant whose leaves are used for flavouring.—**minty** *adj*.

mintage *n* a coin, etc, produced in a mint; the process of producing coins, etc, in a mint; the fee paid to a mint for coining gold or silver; an official mark on a coin.

mint julep *n* a tall drink of bourbon or brandy and sugar over crushed ice, garnished with mint.

minuend *n* (*math*) the number from which another number is to be subtracted.

minuet *n* (the music for) a slow, graceful dance in triple time.

minus *prep* less; (*inf*) without. * *adj* involving subtraction; negative; less than. * *n* a sign (-), indicating subtraction or negative quantity.

minute[1] *n* the sixtieth part of an hour or a degree; a moment; (*pl*) an official record of a meeting. * *vt* to record or summarize the proceedings (of).

minute[2] *adj* tiny; detailed; exact.—**minuteness** *n*.

minutely[1] *adj* occurring every minute. * *adv* every minute.

minutely[2] *adv* in a minute manner; precisely.

minuteman *n* (*pl* **minutemen**) (*sometimes cap*) a member of the militia in the War of American Independence, ready to fight at a minute's notice.

minutiae *npl* (*sing* **minutia**) small or unimportant details.

minx *n* a pert, forward girl; (*arch*) a prostitute.—**minxish** *adj*.

Miocene *adj* pertaining to the middle division of the Tertiary formation after the Olicene and before the Pliocene eras, marked by the appearance of grasses and grazing mammals. * *n* this division or rock formation.

miosis *n* abnormal contraction of the pupil of the eye.—*also* **myosis**.—**miotic** *adj*, *n*.

miracle *n* an extraordinary event attributed to the supernatural; an unusual or astounding event; a remarkable example of something.

miraculous *adj* supernatural; wonderful; able to work miracles.—**miraculously** *adv*.—**miraculousness** *n*.

mirage *n* an optical illusion in which a distant object or expanse of water seems to be nearby, caused by light reflection from hot air; anything illusory or fanciful.

mire *n* an area of wet, soggy, or muddy ground. * *vt* to sink in mire; to dirty; to embroil in difficulties.

mirk *see* **murk**.

mirky *see* **murky**.

mirror *n* a smooth surface that reflects images; a faithful depiction. * *vt* (**mirroring, mirrored**) to reflect or depict faithfully.

mirth *n* merriment, esp with laughter.

mirthful *adj* full of merriment.—**mirthfully** *adv*.—**mirthfulness** *n*.

mirthless *adj* lacking laughter; miserable.—**mirthlessly** *adv*.—**mirthlessness** *n*.

mis-[1] *prefix* wrong(ly); bad(ly); no, not.

mis-[2] *see* **miso-**.

misadventure *n* an unlucky accident; bad luck.

misalliance *n* an unsuitable alliance, usu by marriage with a person of lower social status; a mésalliance.

misanthrope, misanthropist *n* a person who hates or distrusts mankind.

misanthropic *adj* of or characterized by hatred of his or her fellow human beings.—**misanthropically** *adv*.—**misanthropy** *n*.

misogynist *n* a hater or distruster of women. *—**misogynistic** *adj*.

misapprehend *vt* to misunderstand; to misconceive.—**misapprehension** *n*.

misappropriate *vt* to appropriate wrongly or dishonestly; to use illegally; to embezzle.—**misappropriation** *n*.

misbehave *vi* to behave badly. * *vt* to behave (oneself) badly.—**misbehavior, misbehaviour** *n*.

misc. *abbr* = miscellaneous.

miscalculate *vti* to calculate wrongly.—**miscalculation** *n*.

miscarriage *n* the spontaneous expulsion of a foetus prematurely; mismanagement or failure.

miscarry *vi* (**miscarrying, miscarried**) to spontaneously expel a foetus from the uterus; to be unsuccessful; to fail.

miscellaneous *adj* consisting of various kinds; mixed.—**miscellaneously** *adv*.—**miscellaneousness** *n*.

miscellany *n* (*pl* **miscellanies**) a mixed collection; a book comprising miscellaneous writings, etc.

mischance *n* bad luck; an unlucky event.

mischief *n* wayward behaviour; damage.

mischievous *adj* harmful, prankish.—**mischievously** *adv*.—**mischievousness** *n*.

miscible *adj* (*chem*) (*liquids*) capable of being mixed.—**miscibility** *n*.

misconceive *vt* to conceive wrongly; to misjudge; to misapprehend; to misunderstand.—**misconceiver** *n*.

misconception *n* a mistaken idea; misunderstanding.

misconduct *n* dishonest management; improper behaviour. * *vt* to conduct (oneself) badly; to manage dishonestly.

misconstrue *vt* (**misconstruing, misconstrued**) to misinterpret.—**misconstruction** *n*.

miscreant *n* an unscrupulous villain; (*arch*) a heretic. * *adj* unscrupulous; (*arch*) heretical.

misdeed *n* a wrong or wicked act; crime; sin, etc.

misdemeanour, misdemeanor *n* (*law*) a minor offence, a misdeed.

miser *n* a greedy, stingy person who hoards money for its own sake.

miserable *adj* wretched; unhappy; causing misery; bad, inadequate; pitiable.—**miserableness** *n*.—**miserably** *adv*.

Miserere *n* the 51st Psalm, appointed for penitential acts; a musical setting of this psalm; (*without cap*) a misericord in a choir stall.

misericord, misericorde *n* a small ledge, often carved, on the underside of a folding seat in the stall of a church against which a worshipper can lean when standing; in the Middle Ages, a small dagger for giving a death thrust to a seriously wounded person, esp a knight; (*Christianity*) the relaxation of monastic rules for elderly or infirm monks or nuns; a room in a monastery for those with such a dispensation.

miserly *adj* like a miser; tending to hoard; very mean.—**miserliness** *n*.

misery *n* (*pl* **miseries**) extreme pain, unhappiness, or poverty; a cause of such suffering.

misfeasance *n* (*law*) the wrong performance of something that is itself legal.—**misfeasor** *n*.

misfire *vi* (*engine, etc*) to fail to ignite, start; to fail to succeed.—*also* *n*.

misfit *n* something that fits badly; a maladjusted person.

misfortune *n* ill luck; trouble; a mishap; bad luck.

misgiving *n* a feeling of misapprehension, mistrust.

misguided *adj* foolish; mistaken.—**misguidedly** *adv*.

mishap *n* an unfortunate accident.

mishmash *n* a confused mixture, hotchpotch.

Mishnah, Mishna *n* (*Judaism*) the oral law; the written form of this, which was collected in the 2nd century and forms the text of the earlier part of the Talmud.

misinform *vt* to supply with wrong information.—**misinformant, misinformer** *n*.—**misinformation** *n*.
misjudge *vt* to judge wrongly, to form a wrong opinion.—**misjudgment** *n*.
mislay *vt* (**mislaying, mislaid**) to lose something temporarily; to put down or install improperly.—**mislayer** *n*.
mislead *vt* (**misleading, misled**) to deceive; to give wrong information to; to lead into wrongdoing.—**misleader** *n*.
misleading *adj* deceptive; confusing.—**misleadingly** *adv*.
misnomer *n* an incorrect or unsuitable name or description.—**misnomered** *adj*.
miso-, mis- *prefix* hatred of.
misogamy *n* hatred of marriage.—**misogamic** *adj*.—**misogamist** *n*.
misogynist *n* a hater or distruster of women. * *adj* of or characterized by hatred of women.—**misogynistic** *adj*.
misogyny *n* hatred of women.—**misogynic** *adj*.
misplace *vt* to put in a wrong place; (*trust, etc*) to place unwisely.—**misplacement** *n*.
misprint *vt* to print incorrectly. * *n* an error in printing.
misprision *n* (*law*) the concealment of a seriously criminal act; the knowledge of the commission of treason and the failure to report this; (*arch*) contempt; the disparagement or undervaluing of something
mispronounce *vt* to pronounce wrongly.—**mispronunciation** *n*.
misquote *vt* to quote wrongly.—**misquotation** *n*.
misread *vt* (**misreading, misread**) to read or to interpret wrongly.
misrepresent *vt* to represent falsely; to give an untrue idea of.—**misrepresentation** *n*.—**misrepresentative** *adj*.
misrule *n* bad government. * *vt* to govern badly; to govern in an inhumane manner or with injustice.
miss[1] *n* (*pl* **misses**) a girl; (*with cap*) a title used before the surname of an unmarried woman or girl.
miss[2] *vt* to fail to reach, hit, find, meet, hear; to omit; to fail to take advantage of; to regret or discover the absence or loss of. * *vi* to fail to hit; to fail to be successful; to misfire, as an engine. * *n* a failure to hit, reach, obtain, etc.
Miss. *abbr* = Mississippi.
missal *n* a book containing the prayers for Mass.
misshapen *adj* badly shaped; deformed.
missile *n* an object, as a rock, spear, rocket, etc, to be thrown, fired, or launched.
missing *adj* absent; lost; lacking.
missing link *n* something required to complete a series; a hypothetical animal supposedly intermediate between the anthropoid apes and man.
mission *n* a group of people sent by a church, government, etc to carry out a special duty or task; the sending of an aircraft or spacecraft on a special assignment; a vocation. * *adj* of a mission; (*archit*) of a style of church building established by Spanish missioners in the southwest USA.
missionary *n* (*pl* **missionaries**) a person who tries to convert unbelievers to his or her religious faith, esp abroad; one sent on a mission. * *adj*.of a religious mission; tending to propagandize.
missionary position *n* (*inf*) a position for sexual intercourse with the partners face to face and the man on top.
mission control *n* a command centre that controls space flights from the ground.
missioner *n* a missionary; a person in charge of a parochial mission.
missis *n* (*inf*) (*usu with* **the**) one's wife; (*inf*) a name used when directly addressing a woman.—*also* **missus.**
missive *n* (*formal*) a letter or message, often official. * *adj* (*rare*) sent specially, or intended to be sent.
misspent *adj* wasted, frittered away.
missus *see* **missis.**
mist *n* a large mass of water vapour, less dense than a fog; something that dims or obscures. * *vti* to cover or be covered, as with mist.
mistake *vb* (**mistaking, mistook,** *pp* **mistaken**) * *vt* to misunderstand; to misinterpret; * *vi* to make a mistake. * *n* a wrong idea, answer, etc; an error of judgment; a blunder; a misunderstanding.—**mistakable** *adj*.—**mistakably** *adv*.
mistaken *adj* erroneous, ill-judged.—**mistakenly** *adv*.
mister *n* (*inf*) sir; (*with cap*) the title used before a man's surname.
mistime *vt* to do or say at the wrong time; to time wrongly.
mistletoe *n* an evergreen parasitic plant with white berries used as a Christmas decoration.
mistreat *vt* to treat wrongly or badly.—**mistreatment** *n*.
mistress *n* a woman who is head of a household; a woman with whom a man is having a prolonged affair; a female schoolteacher; (*with cap*) the title used before a married woman's surname.
mistrust *n* lack of trust. * *vti* to doubt; to suspect.—**mistrustful** *adj*.—**mistrustfully** *adv*
misty *adj* (**mistier, mistiest**) full of mist; dim, obscure.—**mistily** *adv*.—**mistiness** *n*.
misunderstand *vt* (**misunderstanding, misunderstood**) to fail to understand correctly.
misunderstanding *n* a mistake as to sense; a quarrel or disagreement.
misunderstood *adj* not fully understood; not appreciated properly.
misuse *vt* to use for the wrong purpose or in the wrong way; to ill-treat, abuse. * *n* improper or incorrect use.
mite *n* any of numerous very small parasitic or free-living insects; (*money, etc*) a very small amount.
miter *see* **mitre.**
mitigate *vti* to become or make less severe.—**mitigable** *adj*.—**mitigation** *n*.—**mitigator** *n*.
mitosis *n* (*pl* **mitoses**) *n* a process by which plant or animal cells divide, in which the nucleus of a somatic cell splits into nuclei, each with the same number of chromosomes as there were in the orig cell.—**mitotic** *adj, adv*.
mitral *adj* of or like a mitre; (*anat*) pertaining to the mitral valve.
mitral valve *n* a valve of the heart between the left atrium and the left ventricle.
mitre, miter *n* the headdress of a bishop; a diagonal joint between two pieces of wood to form a corner. * *vt* to join with a mitre corner.—**miterer** *n*.
mitt *n* a glove covering the hand but only the base of the fingers; (*sl*) a hand; a boxing glove; a baseball glove.
mitten *n* a glove with a thumb but no separate fingers.
mix *vt* to blend together in a single mass; to make by blending ingredients, as a cake; to combine; (*with* **up**) to make into a mixture; to make disordered; to confuse or mistake. * *vi* to be mixed or blended; to get along together. * *n* a mixture.—**mixable** *adj*.
mixed *adj* blended; made up of different parts, classes, races, etc; confused.
mixed bag *n* (*inf*) a collection of diverse things or people.
mixed economy *n* an economic system containing both state-owned industries and private enterprise.
mixed-up *adj* (*inf*) perplexed, mentally confused.
mixer *n* a device that blends or mixes; a person considered in terms of their ability (good or bad) to get on with others; a soft drink added to an alcoholic beverage.
mixture *n* the process of mixing; a blend made by mixing.
mix-up *n* a mistake; confusion, muddle; (*inf*) a fight.
mizzen, mizen *n* (*naut*) the lowest sail on the mizzenmast of a vessel; the mizzenmast. * *adj* pertaining to something used with the mizzenmast.
mizzenmast, mizenmast *n* (*naut*) the aftermost mast when there are three masts on a ship; the aftermast on other ships.
mizzle *vi* to rain in very minute drops, to drizzle. * *n* a very fine rain.
mkt *abbr* = market.
ml *abbr* = mile; milliliter.
Mlle(s) *abbr* = mademoiselle, mesdemoiselles.
MM *abbr* = Messieurs.
mm *abbr* = millimeter.
MN *abbr* = Minnesota.

Mn (*chem symbol*) manganese.
mnemonic *adj* of or aiding memory.—*n* a device to aid the memory.—**mnemonically** *adv*.
mnemonics *n sing* a technique of assisting the memory by using formulae to remember things.
Mnemosyne *n* (*Greek myth*) the goddess of memory.
MO *abbr* = Missouri.
Mo (*chem symbol*) molybdenum.
moa *n* any one of several extinct species of large, wingless birds of New Zealand.
Moabite *adj* pertaining to the ancient kingdom of Moab, now part of Jordan. * *n* an inhabitant of Moab.
moan *n* a low mournful sound as of sorrow or pain. * *vti* to utter a moan; to complain.—**moaner** *n*.—**moaningly** *adv*.
moat *n* a deep ditch surrounding a fortification or castle, usu filled with water.
mob *n* a disorderly or riotous crowd; a contemptuous term for the masses; (*sl*) a gang of criminals. * *vt* (**mobbing, mobbed**) to attack in a disorderly group; to surround.—**mobbish** *adj*.
mobcap *n* a plain cap, usu surrounded with a frill, worn indoors by women in the 18th century.
mobile *adj* movable, not fixed; easily changing; characterized by ease in change of social status; capable of moving freely and quickly; (*inf*) having transport. * *n* a suspended structure of wood, metal, etc with parts that move in air currents.—**mobility** *n*.
mobilize *vt* to prepare for action, esp war by readying troops for active service; to organize for a particular reason; to put to use.—**mobilization** *n*.
mobocracy *n* (*pl* **mobocracies**) political rule or ascendancy of the mob; a ruling mob.—**mobocrat** *n*.—**mobocratic** *adj*.—**mobocratically** *adv*.
mobster *n* (*sl*) a gangster.
moccasin *n* a flat shoe based on Amerindian footwear; any soft, flexible shoe resembling this.
mocha *n* a type of coffee, orig from Arabia; a flavouring made from coffee and chocolate.—*also adj*.
mock *vt* to imitate or ridicule; to behave with scorn; to defy; (*with* **up**) to make a model of. * *n* ridicule; an object of scorn. * *adj* false, sham, counterfeit.—**mocker** *n*.—**mockingly** *adv*.
mockery *n* (*pl* **mockeries**) derision, ridicule, or contempt; imitation, esp derisive; someone or something that is mocked; an inadequate person, thing, or action.
mock-heroic *adj* parodying the heroic style of literature or, particularly, poetry, esp when the subject matter is unheroic. * *n* a burlesque imitation of an epic poem or of the heroic style in general.—**mock-heroically** *adv*.
mockingbird *n* a grey American bird with the ability to imitate with exactness the call of other birds.
mockup, mock-up *n* a full-scale working model of a machine, etc.
mod *n* (*often with cap*) a member of a British youth group of the mid-1960s who wore highly fashionable clothes and opposed the rockers, another youth group; a member of a revival of this group, in the late 1970s and early 1980s, whose opposition was to skinheads.
mod. *abbr* = moderate, moderato, modern.
modal *adj* of mode or form, not substance; (*gram*) expressing mood; (*philos*) asserting with qualification; (*mus*) of or composed in a mode.—**modality** *n*.—**modally** *adv*.
mode *n* a way of acting, doing or existing; a style or fashion; form; (*mus*) any of the scales used in composition; (*statistics*) the predominant item in a series of items; (*gram*) mood.
model *n* a pattern; an ideal; a standard worth imitating; a representation on a smaller scale, usu three-dimensional; a person who sits for an artist or photographer; a person who displays clothes by wearing them. * *adj* serving as a model; representative of others of the same style. * *vb* (**modelling, modelled** *or* **modeling, modeled**) *vt* (*with* **after, on**) to create by following a model; to display clothes by wearing. * *vi* to serve as a model for an artist, etc.—**modeler, modeller** *n*.
modem *n* a device that links two computers via the telephone network for transmitting data.
moderate *vti* to make or become moderate; to preside over. * *adj* having reasonable limits; avoiding extremes; mild, calm; of medium quality, amount, etc. * *n* a person who holds moderate views.—**moderately** *adv*.—**moderateness** *n*.
moderation *n* moderateness; freedom from excess; equanimity.
moderato *adv* (*mus*) moderately.
moderator *n* a mediator; (*physics*) a substance that slows the speed of neutrons in a nuclear reactor; (*Presbyterian Church*) a minister who presides at a court, assembly, synod, etc.
modern *adj* of the present or recent times; up-to-date.—**modernity** *n*.—**modernly** *adv*.
modernism *n* modern view, methods or usage; the theory or practice of modern art, literature, etc; (*Christianity*) rationalistic theology.—**modernist** *adj, n*.—**modernistic** *adj*.—**modernistically** *adv*.
modernize *vti* to make or become modern.—**modernization** *n*.
modest *adj* moderate; having a humble opinion of oneself; unpretentious.—**modestly** *adv*.
modesty *n* (*pl* **modesties**) the quality or state of being modest; propriety of behaviour or manner; diffidence; moderation.
modicum *n* (*pl* **modicums, modica**) a small quantity.
modification *n* a modifying or being modified; the result of this; a modified form; an adjustment, alteration; (*biol*) a change in an organism caused by environmental factors but not passed on.—**modificator** *n*.—**modificatory, modificative** *adj*.
modifier *n* one who or that which modifies; (*gram*) a word, clause or phrase that qualifies or limits the meaning of another word, etc, a qualifier.
modify *vt* (**modifying, modified**) to lessen the severity of; to change or alter slightly; (*gram*) to limit in meaning, to qualify.—**modifiable** *adj*.—**modifiability** *n*.
modillion *n* (*archit*) an ornamental bracket under a cornice in the Corinthian order.
modiolus (*pl* **modioli**) *n* (*anat*) the pillar of the cochlea of the internal ear.
modish *adj* fashionable, stylish.—**modishly** *adv*.—**modishness** *n*.
modiste *n* a person who makes fashionable dresses or hats.
modulate *vti* to adjust; to regulate; to vary the pitch, intensity, frequency, etc, of.—**modulator** *n*.—**modulatory** *adj*.
modulation *n* a modulating or being modulated; a change in pitch or intensity of the voice; (*gram*) inflection, esp to change meaning; (*mus*) a transition from one key to another by progression; (*electronics*) the variation of amplitude, frequency or phase of a signal or wave in response to another signal or wave, esp in the transfer to carrier waves.
module *n* a unit of measurement; a self-contained unit, esp in a spacecraft; (*archit*) a semi-diameter of a shaft, etc, used as a standard for regulating other proportions; (*education*) one of a set of learning units making up a course of study.—**modular** *adj*.
modulus *n* (*pl* **moduli**) a quantity expressing the measure of some function or property, eg elasticity.
modus operandi *n* (*pl* **modi operandi**) a method of operating, procedure.
modus vivendi *n* (*pl* **modi vivendi**) a compromise, as between two parties in dispute; a way of living.
mofette, moffette *n* a fissure in an almost extinct volcano from which carbon dioxide and other gases issue; the gases.
mogul, moghul *n* (*inf*) an important person, a magnate; (*with cap*) a ruler of the former Moghul Empire in India.
mohair *n* the long, fine hair of the Angora goat; the silk cloth made from it.
Mohammedan *n, adj* a former word for Muslim.
Mohave *n* (*pl* **Mohaves, Mohave**) one of a North American Indian people who occupied the land along the Colorado river.—*also* **Mojave**.
Mohawk *n* (*pl* **Mohawks, Mohawk**) one of a North American Indian people who occupied the area from the St Lawrence to the Mohawk river. * *n* the language of the Mohawk people.
Mohican *see* **Mahican**.

mohican *n* a hairstyle in which the sides of the head are shaved, leaving a central band of hair, often dyed or in spikes, from the forehead to the nape of the neck.

moidore *n* an ancient Portuguese gold coin.

moiety *n* (*pl* **moieties**) one of two parts or shares; a half.

moiré *n* a fabric, usu silk, that has a surface pattern suggesting rippling water; such a pattern impressed on a fabric.

moiré effect *n* a pattern created when the same pattern is superimposed on another version of itself.

moist *adj* damp; slightly wet.—**moistly** *adv*.—**moistness** *n*.

moisten *vti* to make or become moist.—**moistener** *n*.

moisture *n* liquid in a diffused, absorbed, or condensed state.

moisturize *vt* (*skin, air, etc*) to add moisture to.—**moisturizer** *n*.

Mojave *see* **Mohave**.

moke *n* (*sl*) a boring person; (*Br*) a donkey; (*Austral*) a horse not of the top class.

molar[1] *n* a back tooth, used for grinding food.

molar[2] *adj* of or in the whole mass of matter as distinguished from the properties or motions of atoms or molecules.

molasses *n* (*pl* **molasses**) the thick brown sugar that is produced during the refining of sugar; treacle.

mold[1] *n* a fungus producing a furry growth on the surface of organic matter. * *vi* to become moldy.—*also* **mould**.

mold[2] *n* a hollow form in which something is cast; a pattern; something made in a mold; distinctive character. * *vt* to make in or on a mold; to form, shape, guide.—*also* **mould**.—**moldable** *adj*.—**molder** *n*.

molder *vi* to decay to rot, to crumble to dust.

molding *n* anything made in a mould; a shaped strip of wood or plaster, as around the upper walls of a room.—*also* **moulding**.

moldy *adj* (**moldier, moldiest**) containing or covered with mould; musty, stale; antiquated; (*sl*) dull, boring.—*also* **mouldy**.—**moldiness** *n*.

mole[1] *n* a spot on the skin, usu dark-coloured and raised.

mole[2] *n* a small burrowing insectivore with soft dark fur; a spy within an organization.

mole[3] *n* a large breakwater.

mole[4] *n* the basic SI unit of substance.

molecular *adj* of or inherent in molecules.

molecular biology *n* the branch of biology dealing with the molecular basis of heredity and of protein synthesis.

molecular formula the chemical formula that indicates both the number and type of any atom present in a molecular substance.

molecular weight *n* the total of the atomic weights of all the atoms present in a molecule; the average mass per molecule of any substance relative to one-twelfth the mass of an atom of carbon-12.

molecule *n* the simplest unit of a substance, retaining the chemical properties of that substance; a small particle.

molehill *n* a mound of earth thrown up by a burrowing mole.

moleskin *n* the fur of a mole; a twilled cotton cloth with a soft surface resembling a mole's fur, used for work clothes; (*pl*) trousers made of moleskin.

molest *vt* to annoy; to attack or assault, esp sexually.—**molestation** *n*.—**molester** *n*.

moll *adj* (*sl*) a female partner of a thief or other criminal; a prostitute.

mollify *vt* (**mollifying, mollified**) to make less severe or violent; to soften.—**mollification** *n*.—**mollifier** *n*.—**mollifyingly** *adv*.

mollusk, mollusc *n* an invertebrate animal usu enclosed in a shell, as oysters, etc.—**molluscan, molluskan** *adj, n*.

mollycoddle *vti* to care for someone in an indulgent way; to coddle, pamper. * *n* someone so treated.—**mollycoddler** *n*.

moloch *n* a spiny Australian lizard with a horned head, found in desert areas; (*with cap*) (*Old Testament*) an ancient Semitic fire god to whom children were offered as a sacrifice.

molt *vi* to shed hair, skin, horns, etc prior to replacement of new growth. * *n* a moulting.—*also* **moult**.—**molter** *n*.

molten *adj* melted by heat.

molto *adj* (*mus*) very (modifying another musical direction).

moly *n* (*pl* **molies**) (*Greek myth*) a herb with a black root and a white flower with the power of counteracting the spells of Circe.

molybdenum *n* a metallic element used in alloys, esp strengthening steel.—**molybdous, molybdic** *adj*.

mom *n* (*inf*) mother.

moment *n* an indefinitely brief period of time; a definite point in time; a brief time of importance.

momenta *see* **momentum**.

momentarily *adv* for a short time; in an instant; at any moment.

momentary *adj* lasting only for a moment.—**momentariness** *n*.

momentous *adj* very important.—**momentously** *adv*.—**momentousness** *n*.

momentum *n* (*pl* **momenta, momentums**) the impetus of a moving object, equal to the product of its mass and its velocity.

momma *n* mama.

mommy *n* (*pl* **mommies**) (*inf*) mother.

Mon. *abbr* = Monday.

mon-, mono- *prefix* alone, sole, single.

monachism *n* monasticism; the monastic life or system.—**monachal** *adj*.

monad *n* a unit, number one; (*philos*) the ultimate unit of being or evolution in Leibniz's theory; (*chem*) a radical or atom with a valency of one; (*biol*) a single-celled organism.—**monadic, monadical** *adj*.—**monadically** *adv*.

monadelphous *adj* (*bot*) having stamens in one bundle of filaments wrapped around the style.

monadism *n* (*philos*) the theory, esp as propounded by Leibniz, that the real universe is composed of monads.

monandrous *adj* having only one husband or male partner at a time; (*flowers*) having one stamen only; (*plants*) having flowers with only one stamen.

monandry *n* the custom of having only one husband at a time; (*bot*) a being monandrous.

monarch *n* a sovereign who rules by hereditary right; a powerful or dominant thing or person.—**monarchal, monarchic, monarchical** *adj*.—**monarchically** *adv*.

monarchism *n* the principles of, or devotion to, monarchy.—**monarchist** *n, adj*.—**monarchistic** *adj*.

monarchy *n* (*pl* **monarchies**) a government headed by a monarch; a kingdom.

monastery *n* (*pl* **monasteries**) the residence of a group of monks, or nuns.—**monasterial** *adj*.

monastic, monastical *adj* of monks or monasteries. * *n* a monk; a recluse.—**monastically** *adv*.—**monasticism** *n*.

Monday *n* the second day of the week.

monecious *see* **monoecious**.

monetarism *n* (*economics*) the theory that control of the money supply is the key to achieving low inflation and economic growth.—**monetarist** *n, adj*.

monetary *adj* of the coinage or currency of a country; of or relating to money.—**monetarily** *adv*.

monetize *vt* to convert into money; to give a standard of current value to.—**monetization** *n*.

money *n* (*pl* **moneys, monies**) coins or paper notes authorized by a government as a medium of exchange; property; wealth.

moneychanger *n* one who changes money into other coinage at fixed rate; a machine that dispenses coins.

moneyed *adj* rich.—*also* **monied**.

moneylender *n* a person who lends money for interest, esp as a business.—**moneylending** *n*.

monger *n* a dealer.

mongoose *n* (*pl* **mongooses**) a small predatory mammal of Africa and Asia.

mongrel *n* an animal or plant of mixed or unknown breed, esp a dog. * *adj* of mixed breed or origin.—**mongrelism** *n*.—**mongrelly** *adj*.

mongrelize *vt* to render mongrel.—**mongrelization** *n*.

monied *see* **moneyed.**
monies *see* **money.**
moniker, monicker *n* (*sl*) a name; a nickname.
moniliform *adj* (*biol*) shaped like a necklace.
monism *n* (*philos*) the theory that there is only one kind of being and that matter and mind are ultimately identical.—**monist** *n, adj*.—**monistic** *adj*.—**monistically** *adv*.
monition *n* an admonition; a formal notice from an ecclesiastical court to an offender; a summons; a warning.
monitor *n* a student chosen to help the teacher; any device for regulating the performance of a machine, aircraft, etc; a screen for viewing the image being produced by a television camera; a display screen connected to a computer. * *vti* (*TV or radio transmissions, etc*) to observe or listen to for political or technical reasons; to watch or check on; to regulate or control, a machine, etc.—**monitorial** *adj*.
monitory *adj* conveying a warning. * *n* (*pl* **monitories**) a letter containing an admonition or warning, esp a papal letter.
monk *n* a male member of a religious order living in a monastery.
monkey *n* any of the primates except man and the lemurs, esp the smaller, long-tailed primates; a mischievous child; (*sl*) £500 or $500. * *vi* (**monkeying, monkeyed**) (*inf*) to play, trifle, or meddle.
monkey business *n* (*inf*) mischief; underhand dealings.
monkey wrench *n* a large wrench with an adjustable jaw.
monkfish *n* (*pl* **monkfish, monkfishes**) an angelfish.
monkhood *n* the character or condition of a monk; monks collectively.
monkish *adj* pertaining to or resembling a monk; monastic.—**monkishly** *adv*.—**monkishness** *n*.
monkshood, monk's-hood *n* a poisonous plant, aconite.
mono *adj* (*inf*) monophonic. * *n* (*pl* **monos**) (*inf*) monophonic sound.
mono-, mon- *prefix* alone, sole, single.
monobasic *adj* (*chem*) having one base or atom of a base.
monocarp *n* a monocarpic plant.
monocarpic, monocarpous *adj* (*bot*) bearing fruit only once.
monochord *n* a one-stringed musical instrument with a sound box for determining musical intervals.
monochromatic *adj* consisting of one colour.—**monochromatically** *adv*.
monochrome *n* a painting, drawing, or print in a single colour. * *adj* in one colour or shades of one colour; black and white—**monochromic** *adj*.
monocle *n* a single eyeglass held in place by the face muscles.—**monocled** *adj*.
monocline *n* a geological formation in which the strata are tilted one way only.—**monoclinal** *adj*.
monocotyledon *n* any plant with one seed leaf and three-part flowers, incl grasses, lilies and orchids.—**monocotyledonous** *adj*.
monocrat *n* one who governs alone; an advocate of autocracy or monarchy.—**monocracy** *n*.
monocular *adj* pertaining to, for, or with one eye only; adapted for use with one eye.
monodrama *n* a dramatic piece for one actor.—**monodramatic** *adj*.
monody *n* (*pl* **monodies**) in Greek tragedy, a lyrical poem sung by one actor alone; a plaintive poem or song for one voice, a dirge, an elegy; (*mus*) a composition for one voice, usu accompanied.—**monodic, monodical** *adj*.—**monodist** *n*.
monoecious *adj* (*bot*) having stamens and pistils on the same plant but on different flowers; (*zool*) hermaphroditic.—*also* **monecious.**—**monoeciously** *adv*.
monogamy *n* the practice of being married to only one person at a time.—**monogamist** *n*.—**monogamous** *adj*.
monogenesis *n* derivation from a single cell, resulting in an organism like the adult of the species; asexual reproduction from a single cell; the supposed descent of all organisms from one orig cell; the supposed descent of all human beings from one orig pair.—**monogenous** *adj*.
monogenetic *adj* pertaining to or having the property of monogenesis; (*animals*) born, living and dying on a single host; (*rocks*) originating from a single source or by a single process.
monogram *n* the embroidered or printed initials of one's name on clothing, stationery, etc.—**monogrammed** *adj*.—**monogrammatic** *adj*.
monograph *n* a learned paper written on one particular subject. * *vt* to write such a paper on.—**monographer** *n*.—**monographic** *adj*.—**monographically** *adv*.
monolith *n* a single large block of stone; any massive, unyielding structure.—**monolithic** *adj*.—**monolithically** *adv*.
monologue, monolog *n* a long speech; a soliloquy, a skit, etc for one actor only.—**monologuist, monologist** *n*.
monomania *n* an irrational obsession with a single subject, object, idea, etc.—**monomaniac** *n*.—**monomaniacal** *adj*.
monometallic *adj* containing only one metal; of monometallism.
monometallism *n* the use of a single metal, often gold or silver, as a standard of currency; the economic system underpinning such a standard.—**monometallist** *n*.
monomial *n* (*math*) an expression consisting of one term; (*biol*) a taxonomic classification consisting of one term.—*also adj*.
monomorphic, monomorphous *adj* (*species*) of one type or structure or with parts that have only one type or structure; (*individual organism*) unchanging in shape throughout its life cycle; (*chem*) denoting a chemical compound with a single crystalline form.
monopetalous *adj* (*bot*) (*flowers*) having the corolla in one piece; possessing a single petal.
monophobia *n* an overwhelming fear of being alone.—**monophobic** *adj*.
monophonic *adj* (*sound reproduction*) using one channel only for transmission.—**monophonically** *adv*.
monophthong *n* a simple single vowel sound; two different written vowels pronounced as a single sound.—**monophthongal** *adj*.
monoplane *n* an aeroplane with a single pair of wings.
monoplegia *n* paralysis affecting one limb or one group of muscles only.—**monoplegic** *adj, n*.
monopolize *vt* to get, have, or exploit a monopoly of; to get full control of.—**monopolization** *n*.—**monopolizer** *n*.
monopoly *n* (*pl* **monopolies**) exclusive control in dealing in a particular commodity or supplying a service; exclusive use or possession; that which is exclusively controlled; such control granted by a government.—**monopolism** *n*.—**monopolist** *n*.—**monopolistic** *adj*.—**monopolistically** *adv*.
monorail *n* a single track railway, often with suspended carriages.
monosepalous *adj* (*bot*) (*flowers*) having the calyx undivided; possessing a single sepal.
monosodium glutamate *n* a chemical additive used to give food a meaty taste.
monospermous, monospermal *adj* (*plants*) one-seeded.
monostich *n* a poem in one line.—**monostichic** *adj*.
monosyllabic *adj* (*word*) having one syllable; characterized by or made up of one syllable; terse; curt.—**monosyllabically** *adv*.
monosyllable *n* a word of one syllable.
monotheism *n* the doctrine of or belief in the existence of only one God.—**monotheist** *n*.—**monotheistic** *adj*.—**monotheistically** *adv*.
monotone *n* an utterance or musical tone without a change in pitch; a tiresome sameness of style, colour, etc.—**monotonic** *adj*.—**monotonically** *adv*.
monotonous *adj* unvarying in tone; with dull uniformity, wearisome.—**monotonously** *adv*.—**monotonousness** *n*.
monotony *n* (*pl* **monotonies**) lack of variety; irksome sameness.
monotreme *n* one of a primitive order of Australian egg-laying mammals, with a single vent for digestive, urinary and genital organs.—**monotrematous** *adj*.
Monotype *n* (*trademark*) a hot-metal typesetting machine that casts each character separately; type so cast.
monotype *n* (*print*) one print from a metal or glass plate with a painted image; (*biol*) a genus or species that has only a single type.—**monotypic** *adj*.
monovalent *adj* (*chem*) with a valency of one; univalent.—**monovalence, monovalency** *n*.

monoxide *n* an oxide with one oxygen atom in each molecule.
Monseigneur *n* (*pl* **Messeigneurs**) a French title given to princes, prelates and bishops.
monsieur *n* (*pl* **messieurs**) the French equivalent of sir in address and of Mr with a name.
Monsignor *n* (*pl* **Monsignors, Monsignore**) (*RC Church*) a title given, usu by the Pope, to some prelates or offices.
monsoon *n* a seasonal wind of southern Asia; the rainy season.
monster *n* any greatly malformed plant or animal; an imaginary beast; a very wicked person; a very large animal or thing. * *adj* very large, huge.
monstrance *n* (*RC Church*) a transparent vessel, usu set in a gold or silver frame, in which the consecrated Host is carried in procession or exhibited.
monstrosity *n* (*pl* **monstrosities**) the state or quality of being monstrous; an ugly, unnatural or monstrous thing or person.
monstrous *adj* abnormally developed; enormous; horrible.—**monstrously** *adv*.—**monstrousness** *n*.
montage *n* a rapid sequence of film shots, often superimposed; the art or technique of assembling various elements, esp pictures or photographs; such an assemblage.
montane *adj* of or inhabiting mountains or mountainous terrain.
monte (bank) *n* a gambling card game orig played with dice or cards in Spain.
Montessori method *n* a system of educating very young children, through play, based on free discipline, with each child developing at his own pace.
month *n* any of the twelve divisions of the year; a calendar month.
monthly *adj* continuing for a month; done, happening, payable, etc every month. * *n* a monthly periodical. * *adv* once a month; every month.
monticule *n* a hillock; a small mound resulting from a volcanic eruption.
monument *n* an obelisk, statue or building that commemorates a person or an event; an exceptional example.
monumental *adj* of, like, or serving as a monument; colossal; lasting.—**monumentality** *n*.—**monumentally** *adv*.
moo *n* the long deep sound made by a cow. * *vi* (*cattle*) to low; to make a deep long noise like a cow.
mooch *vt* (*sl*) to wander around aimlessly; (*sl*) to cadge, steal.—**moocher** *n*.
mood *n* a temporary state of mind or temper; a gloomy feeling; a predominant feeling or spirit; (*gram*) that form of a verb indicating mode of action; (*mus*) mode.
moody *adj* (**moodier, moodiest**) gloomy; temperamental.—**moodily** *adv*.—**moodiness** *n*.
moon *n* the natural satellite that revolves around the earth and shines by reflected sunlight; any natural satellite of another planet; something shaped like the moon. * *vi* to behave in an idle or abstracted way.
moonbeam *n* a ray of moonlight.
mooncalf *n* (*pl* **mooncalves**) a born fool; an idler; (*arch*) a monster.
moonflower *n* any of a family of climbing or creeping plants with trumpet-shaped flowers that bloom at night; a tropical plant, orig found in Mexico, with white flowers that bloom at night.
moonlight *n* the light of the moon. * *vi* (*inf*) to have a secondary (usu night-time) job.—**moonlighter** *n*.
moonlit *adj* lit by the moon.
moonraker, moonsail *n* (*naut*) a small sail carried above a skysail.
moonshine *n* moonlight; (*inf*) nonsense, foolish talk; (*sl*) illegally distilled spirits.
moonshiner *n* (*sl*) a distiller of illicit whiskey; a whiskey smuggler.
moonstone *n* a translucent yellowish or yellowish-white stone that exhibits pearly blue-tinged reflections, used as a gemstone.
moonstruck, moonstricken *adj* besotted with love or sentiment; demented.
moonwort *n* a fern with crescent-shaped fronds, grape fern; honesty.
moony *adj* (**moonier, mooniest**) of or like the moon; crescent-shaped; round; listless, dreamy; absent-minded.
Moor *n* a North African Muslim of mixed Arab and Berber ancestry.
moor[1] *n* a tract of open wasteland, usu covered with heather and often marshy.
moor[2] *vti* (*a ship*) to secure or be secured by cable or anchor.
moorage *n* the act of mooring a vessel; a place or charge for mooring.
moorcock *n* the male red grouse.
moorfowl *n* (*arch*) red grouse collectively.
moorhen *n* an aquatic dark-coloured bird with a red bill and a characteristic red mark above the bill, found in ponds and lakes; the female red grouse.
mooring *n* the act of mooring; the place where a ship is moored; (*pl*) the lines, cables, etc by which a ship is moored.
Moorish *adj* pertaining to the Moors; denoting a Spanish architectural style of the 13th–16th centuries, one of the distinguishing features of which is the horseshoe arch.
moorland *n* a stretch of moors.
moose *n* (*pl* **moose**) the largest member of the deer family, native to North America.
moot *adj* debatable; hypothetical. * *vt* (**mooting, mooted**) to propose for discussion.
mop *n* a rag, sponge, etc fixed to a handle for washing floors or dishes; a thick or tangled head of hair. * *vt* (**mopping, mopped**) to wash with a mop.
mope *vi* to be gloomy and apathetic. * *n* a person who mopes, a moper.—**moper** *n*.—**mopey** *adj*.—**mopingly** *adv*.
moped *n* a light, motor-assisted bicycle.
moppet *n* a pet name for a small child, esp a girl; (*arch*) a rag doll.
moquette *n* a material with short velvety pile used for carpets and upholstery.
MOR *abbr* = middle-of-the-road.
moraine *n* a mass of earth, stones, etc, deposited by a glacier.—**morainal, morainic** *adj*.
moral *adj* of or relating to character and human behaviour, particularly as regards right and wrong; virtuous, esp in sexual conduct; capable of distinguishing right from wrong; probable, although not certain; psychological, emotional. * *n* a moral lesson taught by a fable, event, etc; (*pl*) principles; ethics.
morale *n* moral or mental condition with respect to courage, discipline, confidence, etc.
moralism *n* moralizing; a moral attitude or maxim; the practice of or belief in a system of morals independent of religion.
moralist *n* a teacher or student of morals; one for whom morality needs no religious sanction; one concerned with the morals of others.—**moralistic** *adj*.—**moralistically** *adv*.
morality *n* (*pl* **moralities**) virtue; moral principles; a particular system of moral principles.
morality play *n* a medieval allegorical play.
moralize, moralise *vt* to explain or interpret morally; to give a moral direction to. * *vi* to make moral pronouncements.—**moralization, moralisation** *n*.—**moralizer, moraliser** *n*.
morally *adv* in a moral manner, ethically; virtually, practically.
moral philosophy *n* ethics.
Moral Rearmament *n* an international evangelical movement, founded in the US by Frank Buchman (1938), that seeks moral and spiritual revival following conservative Christian principles.—*also* **Buchmanism**.
morass *n* a bog, marsh.
moratorium *n* (*pl* **moratoria, moratoriums**) a legally authorized delay in the payment of money due; an authorized delay or suspension of any activity.—**moratory** *adj*.
morbid *adj* diseased, resulting as from a diseased state of mind; gruesome.—**morbidly** *adv*.—**morbidness** *n*.
morbidity *n* the state of being morbid; the relative incidence of disease.
morbific *adj* causing or producing disease.
morceau *n* (*pl* **morceaux**) a small piece, a morsel; a short work, usu a musical one.
mordacious *adj* biting; sarcastic; cutting.—**mordaciously** *adv*.—**mordacity** *n*.
mordant *adj* biting, caustic; corrosive. * *n* a chemical fixative; a corrosive substance.—**mordancy** *n*.—**mordantly** *adv*.

mordent *n* (*mus*) a trill created by one note rapidly alternating with another one degree below it, used as an ornament

more *adj* (*superl* **most**) greater; further; additional (*—also compar of* **many, much**). * *adv* to a greater extent or degree; again; further.

moreen *n* a stout woollen fabric used esp for furnishings, often embossed or figured with a watered pattern.

morel[1] *n* an edible mushroom with a brownish cap.

morel[2] *n* a nightshade, esp the black nightshade.

morello *n* (*pl* **morellos**) a small dark-red cherry with a tart flavour.

moreover *adv* in addition to what has been said before; besides.

mores *npl* customs so fundamentally established that they have the force of law.

Moresque *adj* (*archit*) Moorish style. * *n* an example of such decoration or architecture; a design in this style.

morganatic *adj* (*marriage*) between a royal person and one of lower rank the children of which are legitimate but neither they nor the morganatic wife or husband share royal rank or property.—**morganatically** *adv*.

morgue *n* a place where the bodies of unknown dead or those dead of unknown causes are temporarily kept prior to burial; a collection of reference materials, eg newspaper clippings.

MORI *abbr* = Market and Opinion Research Institute.

moribund *adj* in a dying state; near death.—**moribundity** *n*.

morion *n* a 16th-century hat-shaped helmet without beaver or visor.

Mormon *n* a member of the Church of Latter-Day Saints whose authority is the Bible and the Book of Mormon, revelations to Joseph Smith in 1827.—**Mormonism** *n*.

morn *n* (*poet*) dawn, morning; (*Scot*) tomorrow.

mornay *n* a white sauce flavoured with cheese. * *adj* (*eggs, etc*) cooked with this sauce.

morning *n* the part of the day from midnight or dawn until noon; the early part of anything. * *adj* of or in the morning.

morning coat *n* a tailcoat, usu grey, with a cutaway front.

morning-glory *n* (*pl* **morning-glories**) any of various twining plants with showy blue bell-shaped flowers.

morning sickness *n* a period of nausea and vomiting in the early stages of pregnancy.

morning star *n* a planet, esp Venus, rising before the sun.

morning suit *n* a man's formal suit of a morning coat and striped trousers.

morning watch *n* (*naut*) a watch on board ship from 4 am to 8 am.

morocco *n* (*pl* **moroccos**) a fine kind of grained leather of goatskin or sheepskin, used in bookbinding and for shoes.

moron *n* an adult mentally equal to a 8 to 12-year-old child; (*inf*) a very stupid person.—**moronic** *adj*.—**moronically** *adv*.—**moronism, moronity** *n*.

morose *adj* sullen, surly; gloomy.—**morosely** *adv*.—**moroseness** *n*.

morpheme *n* the smallest meaningful unit of language as a base, prefix or suffix.—**morphemic** *adj*.—**morphemically** *adv*.

Morpheus *n* (*Greek myth*) the god of dreams and of sleep.

morphine, morphia *n* an alkaloid derived from opium, used as an anaesthetic and sedative.—**morphinic** *adj*.

morphinism *n* addiction to morphine; poisoning caused by the excessive use of morphine.

morphogen *n* that substance in an embryo that determines what the structure will become.

morphology *n* a branch of biology dealing with the form and structure of organisms; the study of word formation in a language.—**morphological** *adj*.—**morphologist** *n*.

morris (dance) *n* a traditional English dance accompanied by tambourines, bells, castanets, violin, concertina, etc, and usu performed by men in costumes representing the Robin Hood legend or other characters from English folklore.

morrow *n* (*arch, poet*) morning; the following day.

morse *n* a jewelled clasp on a cope.

Morse code *n* a code in which letters are represented by dots and dashes or long and short sounds, and are transmitted by visual or audible signals.

morsel *n* a small quantity of food; a small piece of anything.

mort[1] *n* a note or notes sounded on a hunting horn to notify a kill.

mort[2] *n* (*dial*) a great amount or number (of).

mort[3] *n* a salmon in its third year.

mortal *adj* subject to death; causing death, fatal; hostile; very intense. * *n* a human being.—**mortally** *adv*.

mortality *n* (*pl* **mortalities**) state of being mortal; death on a large scale, as from war; number or frequency of deaths in a given period relative to population.

mortality rate *n* the yearly proportion of deaths to population.*—also* **death rate**.

mortar *n* a mixture of cement or lime with sand and water used in building; an artillery piece that fires shells at low velocities and high trajectories; a bowl in which substances are pounded with a pestle.

mortarboard *n* a small square board for holding mortar; a square black college or university cap with a tassel.

mortgage *n* a transfer of rights to a piece of property usu as security for the payment of a loan or debt that becomes void when the debt is paid. * *vt* to make over as a security or pledge; to put an advance claim on.

mortgagee *n* one to whom a mortgage is made or given.

mortgagor, mortgager *n* one who grants a mortgage.

mortician *n* a person who manages funerals.

mortification *n* the act of mortifying; gangrene; (*Christianity*) subjugation of passions and appetite by abstinence; humiliation; vexation, chagrin caused by something that injures one's pride; (*Scots law*) a charitable bequest of lands.

mortify *vti* (**mortifying, mortified**) to subdue by repression or penance; to humiliate or shame; to become gangrenous.—**mortifier** *n*.—**mortifyingly** *adv*.

mortise, mortice *n* a hole in a piece of wood to receive a projection of another piece made to fit.

mortise lock *n* a lock fitted into a mortise in the frame of a door.

mortmain *n* (*law*) a tenure of land held by a corporation, ecclesiastical or other, which cannot transfer ownership.

mortuary *n* (*pl* **mortuaries**) a place of temporary storage for dead bodies.

morula *n* (*pl* **morulas, morulae**) the spherical mass of cells produced by the splitting of the ovum in its primary stage.—**morular** *adj*.

Mosaic, Mosaical *adj* pertaining to Moses, the lawgiver of the Bible, or to the law, institutions, etc, given through him, or to his writings.

mosaic *n* a surface decoration made by inlaying small pieces (of glass, stone, etc) to form figures or patterns; a design made in mosaic. * *adj* of or made of mosaic. * *vt* (**mosaicking, mosaicked**) to adorn with or make into mosaic.—**mosaicist** *n*.

moschatel *n* a plant with a pale-green flower and a musky smell.

Moselle, Mosel *n* a German dry white wine from the Moselle valley.

mosey *vi* (*inf*) (*often with* **along, on down**) to go, to saunter, to amble.

Moslem *see* **Muslim.**

mosque *n* a place of worship for Muslims.

mosquito *n* (*pl* **mosquitoes, mosquitos**) a small two-winged bloodsucking insect.

moss *n* a very small green plant that grows in clusters on rocks, moist ground, etc.

mossback *n* (*sl*) a turtle or a crab, lobster, oyster, etc, that is so old that it has moss growing on its back; (*inf*) an out-of-date or provincial person.

mosstrooper *n* one of a gang of marauders that ravaged the borderland of England and Scotland in the mid-17th century.

mossy *adj* (**mossier, mossiest**) overgrown with, or like, moss.—**mossiness** *n*.

most *adj* (*compar* **more**) greatest in number; greatest in amount or degree; in the greatest number of instances (*—also superl of* **many, much**). * *adv* in or to the greatest degree or extent. * *n* the greatest amount or degree; (*with pl*) the greatest number (of).

-most *adj suffix* forming a superlative, eg *hindmost*.

mostly *adv* for the most part; mainly, usually.

mot juste *n* (*pl* **mots justes**) exactly the right word.

mote[1] *n* a very small particle, a speck (of dust); a mite.
mote[2] *vi* (*arch*) might, must.
motel *n* an hotel for motorists with adjacent parking.
motet *n* (*mus*) (*RC Church*) a short sacred vocal composition, an anthem, usu unaccompanied.
moth *n* a four-winged chiefly night-flying insect related to the butterfly.
mothball *n* a small ball of camphor or naphthalene used to protect stored clothes from moths.
moth-eaten *adj* eaten into by moths; dilapidated; outmoded.
mother *n* a female who has given birth to offspring; an origin or source. * *adj* of or like a mother; native. * *vt* to be the mother of or a mother to.
motherhood *n* the state of being a mother; the qualities of feelings of being a mother; mothers collectively.
mother-in-law *n* (*pl* **mothers-in-law**) the mother of one's spouse.
motherland *n* a person's native land or the country of a person's forebears.
motherly *adj* of, proper to a mother; like a mother.—**motherliness** *n*.
mother-of-pearl *n* the iridescent lining of the shell of the pearl oyster.
motif *n* a recurrent theme in a musical composition—*also* **motive**.
motile *adj* (*biol*) able to move without outside aid; exhibiting movement. * *n* (*psychol*) a person whose perception of the material world comprises, to a very strong degree, the imagery of movement, esp his own.—**motility** *n*.
motion *n* activity, movement; a formal suggestion made in a meeting, law court, or legislative assembly; evacuation of the bowels. * *vti* to signal or direct by a gesture.
motionless *adj* not moving, still.—**motionlessness** *n*.
motion picture *n* a film, movie.
motivate *vt* to supply a motive to; to instigate.—**motivator** *n*.
motivation *n* a motivating or being motivated; incentive; (*psychol*) the mental function or instinct that produces, sustains and regulates behaviour in humans and animals.—**motivational** *adj*.
motive *n* something (as a need or desire) that causes a person to act; a motif in music. * *adj* moving to action; of or relating to motion.—**motiveless** *adj*.—**motivity** *n*.
motley *adj* multicoloured; composed of diverse elements.
motmot *n* any of various tropical American blue and brownish-green, long-tailed birds similar to the jay, of the same family as the kingfisher.
motor *n* anything that produces motion; a machine for converting electrical energy into mechanical energy; a motor car. * *adj* producing motion; of or powered by a motor; of, by or for motor vehicles; of or involving muscular movements. * *vi* to travel by car.
motorbike *n* a motorcycle.
motorboat *n* a boat propelled by an engine or motor.
motorbus *n* (*pl* **motorbuses, motorbusses**) a bus driven by a motor engine.
motorcade *n* a procession of motor vehicles.
motorcar *n* a usu four-wheeled vehicle powered by an internal combustion engine.—*also* **automobile**.
motorcycle *n* a two-wheeled motor vehicle.—**motorcyclist** *n*.
motorist *n* a person who drives a car.
motorize *vt* to equip with a motor; to equip with motor vehicles.—**motorization** *n*.
motorman *n* (*pl* **motormen**) the driver of a tram or an underground train, or other vehicle powered by electricity; a person who operates a motor.
motor scooter *n* a small-wheeled motorcycle with an enclosed engine.
motorway *n* a road with controlled access for fast-moving traffic.—*also* **freeway**.
mottle *vt* to mark with coloured blotches or spots, to variegate. * *n* a pattern of coloured blotches of spots, as on marble; one of the coloured blotches in such a pattern.
mottled *adj* marked with blotches of various colours.
motto *n* (*pl* **mottoes, mottos**) a short saying adopted as a maxim or ideal; a slogan on a heraldic crest; a quotation prefixed to a book, etc; verses, etc, in a Christmas cracker.
mouflon, moufflon *n* (*pl* **mouflons, mouflon, moufflons, moufflon**) a wild large-horned sheep with a short fleece, found in Corsica and Sardinia.
mouillé *adj* softened in sound, palatalized, eg *gl* in *seraglio*.
moujik *see* **muzhik**.
mould *see* **mold**[1], **mold**[2].
moulder *see* **molder**.
moulding *see* **molding**.
mouldy *see* **moldy**.
moulin *n* a deep crack in a glacier through which water and debris drain.
moult *see* **molt**.
mound *n* an artificial bank of earth or stones; a heap or bank of earth. * *vt* to form into a mound.
mount[1] *n* a high hill.
mount[2] *vi* to increase. * *vt* to climb, ascend; to get up on (a horse, platform, etc); to provide with horses; (*a jewel*) to fix on a support; (*a picture*) to frame. * *n* a horse for riding; (*for a picture*) a backing.—**mountable** *adj*.—**mounter** *n*.
mountain *n* a land mass higher than a hill; a vast number or quantity. * *adj* of or in mountains.
mountaineer *n* one who climbs mountains.
mountaineering *n* the technique of climbing mountains.
mountainous *adj* having many mountains; very high; huge.—**mountainously** *adv*.—**mountainousness** *n*.
mountebank *n* (*formerly*) an itinerant quack doctor; a boastful pretender, a charlatan, an impostor.
mounted *adj* seated on horseback or on a bicycle, etc; serving on horseback, as a policeman; placed on a suitable support.
mourn *vti* (*someone dead*) to grieve for; (*something regrettable*) to feel or express sorrow for.—**mourner** *n*.
mournful *adj* expressing grief or sorrow; causing sorrow.—**mournfully** *adv*.—**mournfulness** *n*.
mourning *adj* grieving. * *n* the expression of grief; dark clothes worn by mourners.
mousaka *see* **moussaka**.
mouse *n* (*pl* **mice**) a small rodent with a pointed snout, long body and slender tail; a timid person; a hand-held device used to position the cursor and control software on a computer screen.
mouser *n* an animal that is skilled at catching mice, esp a cat.
moussaka, mousaka *n* a Greek dish comprising aubergines, minced lamb and tomatoes topped with a cheese or white sauce.
mousse *n* a chilled dessert made of fruit, eggs, and whipped cream; a similar savoury dish made with meat or fish; a foamy substance applied to the hair to help it keep its style.
mousseline *n* a sheer fabric resembling muslin, made of rayon or silk; mousseline sauce.
mousseline sauce *n* a white sauce to which whipped cream or the white of an egg has been added.
moustache *see* **mustache**.
mousy, mousey *adj* (**mousier, mousiest**) mouse-like; grey-brown in colour; quiet, stealthy; timid, retiring.—**mousily** *adv*.—**mousiness** *n*.
mouth *n* (*pl* **mouths**) the opening in the head through which food is eaten, sound uttered or words spoken; the lips; opening, entrance, as of a bottle, etc. * *vt* to say, esp insincerely; to form words with the mouth without uttering sound. * *vi* to utter pompously; to grimace.—**mouther** *n*.
mouthful *n* (*pl* **mouthfuls**) as much (food) as fills the mouth; a word or phrase that is difficult to say correctly; (*sl*) a pertinent remark.
mouth organ *n* a harmonica.
mouthpiece *n* the part of a musical instrument placed in the mouth; a person, periodical, etc that expresses the views of others.
mouth-to-mouth resuscitation *n* a method of artificial respiration in which air is forced into the victim's lungs by blowing into the mouth.
mouthwash *n* a flavoured, often antiseptic liquid for rinsing the mouth.
mouthwatering *adj* appetizing; tasty.

movable, moveable *adj* that may be moved. * *npl* personal property.—**movably** *adv*.—**movability** *n*.

move *vt* (**moving, moved**) to shift or change place; to set in motion; to rouse the emotions; to put (a motion) formally. * *vi* to go from one place to another; to walk, to carry oneself; to change place; to evacuate the bowels; to propose a motion as in a meeting; to change residence; (*chess, draughts, etc*) to change the position of a piece on the board. * *n* the act of moving; a movement, esp in board games; one's turn to move; a premeditated action.

movement *n* act of moving; the moving part of a machine, esp a clock; the policy and activities of a group; a trend, eg in prices; a division of a musical work; tempo.

mover *n* one who moves; (*inf*) a driving force, an innovator; a proposer of a motion.

movie *n* a cinema film, motion picture; (*pl*) the showing of a motion picture; the motion-picture medium or industry.

moving *adj* arousing the emotions; changing position; causing motion.—**movingly** *adv*.

mow *vti* (**mowing, mowed,** *pp* **mowed** *or* **mown**) (*grass, etc*) to cut from with a sickle or lawn mower; (*with* **down**) to cause to fall like cut grass.—**mower** *n*.

moxa *n* down obtained from plants, used in Oriental medicine as a counterirritant or for cauterizing by burning on the skin; any plant that yields such down.

mozzarella *n* a moist curd cheese noted for its elasticity when melted.

MP *abbr* = Member of Parliament; Military Police.

mpg *abbr* = miles per gallon.

mph *abbr* = miles per hour.

Mr *n* (*pl* **Messrs**) used as a title before a man's name or an office he holds.

MRI *abbr* = magnetic resonance imaging.

MRM *abbr* = mechanically removed meat.

Mrs *n* (*pl* **Mrs** *or* **Mesdames**) used as a title before a married woman's name.

MS *abbr* = (*pl* **MSS**) manuscript; multiple sclerosis.

Ms *n* the title used before a woman's name instead of Miss or Mrs.

MSc *abbr* = Master of Science.

MSG *abbr* = monosodium glutamate.

MT *abbr* = Montana.

Mt *abbr* = mount.

much *adj* (*compar* **more,** *superl* **most**) plenty. * *adv* considerably; to a great extent.

muchness *n* (*arch*) bulk, greatness; **much of a muchness** just about the same.

mucilage *n* a adhesive prepared for use; a sticky substance obtained from some plants.—**mucilaginous** *adj*.

muck *n* moist manure; black earth with decaying matter; mud, dirt, filth. * *vt* to spread manure; to make dirty; (*with* **out**) to clear of muck. * *vi* to move or load muck; (*with* **about, around**) to engage in useless activity.

mucker *n* (*mining*) a person who clears broken rocks or other waste; (*Br sl*) a friend; (*US sl*) a coarse person.

muckworm *n* a grub or larva bred in manure or mud; (*inf*) a skinflint, a hoarder.

mucky *adj* (**muckier, muckiest**) of or like muck; muddy; filthy.—**muckily** *adv*.—**muckiness** *n*.

mucous *adj* slimy, sticky; like mucus.—**mucosity** *n*.

mucous membrane *n* the mucus-secreting lining of body cavities.

mucus *n* the slimy secretion that keeps mucous membranes moist.

mud *n* soft, wet earth. * *vt* (**muds, mudding, mudded**) to muddy; to throw mud at; to vilify.

muddle *vt* to confuse; to mix up. * *n* confusion, mess.

muddleheaded *adj* silly; confused; absent-minded.—**muddleheadedness** *n*.

muddy *adj* (**muddier, muddiest**) like or covered with mud; not bright or clear; confused. * *vti* (**muddying, muddied**) to make or become dirty or unclear.—**muddily** *adv*.—**muddiness** *n*.

mudguard *n* a screen on a wheel to catch mud splashes.

mudlark *n* (*formerly*) a person who worked or dabbled in mud, esp a scavenger on the banks of tidal rivers; (*arch sl*) a mischievous, poorly dressed child who frequented city streets.(*Austral sl*) a horse that performs well on wet, muddy ground.

muesli *n* a mixture of rolled oats, dried fruit, nuts, etc eaten with milk.

muezzin *n* a Muslim official who proclaims from the minaret of a mosque the hour of prayer, and summons the faithful to worship.

muff[1] *n* a warm soft fur cover for warming the hands.

muff[2] *n* a bungling performance; failure to hold a ball when trying to catch it. * *vti* to bungle.

muffin *n* baked yeast roll.

muffle *vt* to wrap up for warmth or to hide; (*sound*) to deaden by wrapping up.

muffler *n* a long scarf; any means of deadening sound; a device for reducing the noise of a vehicle exhaust.

Mufti *n* (*pl* **Muftis**) an official expounder of Muslim law.

mufti *n* civilian dress worn by a naval or military officer when off duty.

mug *n* a cylindrical drinking cup, usu of metal or earthenware; its contents; (*sl*) the face; (*sl*) a fool. * *vb* (**mugging, mugged**) *vt* to assault, usu with intent to rob.

mugger[1] *n* a person who assaults with intent to rob.

mugger[2], **muggar, muggur** *n* a broad-snouted Asian crocodile that lives in marshes and pools.

muggins *n* (*sl*) an idiot. * *pron* oneself (used deprecating).

muggy *adj* (**muggier, muggiest**) (*weather*) warm, damp and close.—**mugginess** *n*.

mugwump *n* an independent in politics; (*formerly*) a chief, a bigwig.

mujik *see* **muzhik**.

mulatto *n* (*pl* **mulattos, mulattoes**) a person with one black parent and one white parent.

mulberry *n* (*pl* **mulberries**) a tree on whose leaves silkworms feed; its berry.

mulch *n* loose, organic, strawy dung providing a protective covering around the roots of plants. * *vt* to spread mulch.

mulct *vt* to punish with a fine; to acquire money, etc, by fraud or deception. * *n* a fine, esp for some misdemeanour.

mule[1] *n* the offspring of a male donkey and a female horse; a machine for spinning cotton; an obstinate person; (*sl*) a person used to smuggle drugs.

mule[2] *n* a slipper without a heel.

muleteer *n* a mule driver.

muliebrity *n* (*formal*) womanhood; the qualities of womanhood.

mulish *adj* like a mule; stubborn, intractable, wilful.—**mulishly** *adv*.—**mulishness** *n*.

mull[1] *vti* (*inf*) to ponder (over).

mull[2] *vt* (*wine, etc*) to heat, sweeten and spice.—**mulled** *adj*.

mullah, mulla (*formerly*) a Muslim theologian or teacher; a Muslim title of respect.

muller *n* a flat-bottomed pestle for grinding (drugs, paints) on a slab.

mullet *n* (*pl* **mullets, mullet**) any of various types of food fish.

mulligatawny *n* a curry-flavoured meat soup.

mullion *n* an upright bar or division between the panes of a window or the panels of a screen, etc, esp in a Gothic arch; a projecting ridge on a rock face. * *vt* to provide with or divide by mullions.

mullock *n* (*Austral*) a rock containing no gold or from which gold has been extracted, rubbish; (*dial*) disorder.

mult-, multi- *prefix* much, many.

multangular, multiangular *adj* many-angled.

multeity *n* multiplicity.

multicolored, multicoloured *adj* many-coloured.

multifarious *adj* multiform; diversified, of great variety; manifold.—**multifariously** *adv*.—**multifariousness** *n*.

multifid, multifidous *adj* (*bot*) cleft into many parts or lobe-like elements.

multifoil *n* (*archit*) an ornament with over five leaf-like divisions.—*also adj*.

multiform *adj* having many shapes; of many kinds.—**multiformity** *n*.
multilateral *adj* having many sides; with several nations or participants.—**multilaterally** *adv*.
multilingual *adj* speaking or in more than two languages.—**multilingually** *adv*.
multimillionaire *n* a person with two or more millions of money.
multinational *n* a business operating in several countries.—*also adj*.
multinomial *n* (*math*) an expression that consists of the sum of several terms, a polynomial.—*also adj*.
multiplane *n* an aeroplane with two or more pairs of wings.
multiple *adj* of many parts; manifold; various; complex. * *n* (*math*) a number exactly divisible by another.
multiple sclerosis *n* a disease of the nervous system with loss of muscular coordination, etc.
multiplex *adj* (*radio, telecommunications*) the use of a single channel of communication to transmit more than one signal; in map-making, the use of three or more cameras so that the end product appears to be rendered in three dimensions; manifold, multiple. * *vi* to transmit messages or send signals in a multiplex system. * *vt* to send (several signals) simultaneously on one frequency.
multipliable, multiplicable *adj* able to be multiplied.
multiplicand *n* a number to be multiplied by another.
multiplicate *adj* (*rare*) consisting of many.
multiplication *n* the act of multiplying; the process of repeatedly adding a quantity to itself a certain number of times, or any other process which has the same result.—**multiplicational** *adj*.
multiplicative *adj* relating to the mathematical operation of mutiplication; tending to multiply; able to multiply.
multiplicity *n* (*pl* **multiplicities**) a great number or variety (of).
multiplier *n* a thing or person that multiplies; the number by which another is to be multiplied.
multiply *vti* (**multiplying, multiplied**) to increase in number, degree, etc; to find the product (of) by multiplication.
multitude *n* a large number (of people).
multitudinous *adj* of a multitude; very many; having innumerable elements.—**multitudinously** *adv*.—**multitudinousness** *n*.
mum[1] *n* (*inf*) mother.
mum[2] *adj* silent, not speaking. * *n* silence, * *vi* (**mumming, mummed**) to act as a mummer (—*also* **mumm**).
mumble *vti* to speak indistinctly, mutter. * *n* a mumbled utterance.—**mumbler** *n*.—**mumblingly** *adv*.
mumbo jumbo *n* (*pl* **mumbo jumbos**) meaningless ritual, talk, etc.
mumchance *adj* (*arch*) silent; tongue-tied.
mumm *see* **mum**[2].
mummer *n* a person who acts in a play without words; an actor.
mummery *n* (*pl* **mummeries**) performance by mummers; ridiculous ceremonial, pretentious display.
mummify *vt* (**mummifying, mummified**) to embalm (a body) as a mummy; to shrivel, to desiccate.—**mummification** *n*.
mummy[1] *n* (*pl* **mummies**) (*inf*) mother.
mummy[2] *n* (*pl* **mummies**) a carefully preserved dead body, esp an embalmed corpse of ancient Egypt.
mumps *n sing or pl* an acute contagious virus disease characterized by swelling of the salivary glands.
munch *vti* to chew steadily.—**muncher** *n*.
muncipalize *vt* to bring under municipal control; to constitute a place as a municipality.—**municipalization** *n*.
mundane *adj* routine, everyday; banal; worldly.—**mundanely** *adv*.
mungo *n* (*pl* **mungos**) a cheap woollen material made from cloth waste.
municipal *adj* of or concerning a city, town, etc or its local government.—**municipally** *adv*.
municipality *n* (*pl* **municipalities**) a city or town having corporate status and powers of self-government; the governing body of a municipality.
munificent *adj* extremely generous, bountiful.—**munificence** *n*.—**munificently** *adv*.
muniment *n* (*rare*) a defence, a fortification; (*pl*) (*law*) deeds, charters, and other papers for proving title to land.
munition *vt* to equip with arms. * *n* (*pl*) war supplies, esp weapons and ammunition.
muntjac, muntjak *n* any of various small, brown Asian deer with small antlers and a cry similar to that of a dog.
mural *adj* relating to a wall. * *n* a picture or design painted directly onto a wall.—**muralist** *n*.
murder *n* the intentional and unlawful killing of one person by another; (*inf*) something unusually difficult or dangerous to do or deal with. * *vti* to commit murder (upon), to kill; to mangle, to mar.—**murderer** *n*.—**murderess** *nf*.
murderous *adj* capable of or bent on murder; deadly.—**murderously** *adv*.—**murderousness** *n*.
murex *n* (*pl* **murices, murexes**) any of a genus of marine gasteropods, one species of which yields a purple dye used in ancient Greece and Rome.
murine *adj* pertaining to or resembling a mouse or rat; affected, caused or transmitted by rats or mice. * *n* any animal belonging to the same family as rats and mice.
murk *n* indistinct gloom, darkness. * *adj* (*arch*) dark, obscured by fog or mist.—*also* **mirk**.
murky *adj* (**murkier, murkiest**) dark, gloomy; darkly vague or obscure.—*also* **mirky**.—**murkily** *adv*.—**murkiness** *n*.
murmur *n* a continuous low, indistinct sound; a mumbled complaint; (*med*) an abnormal sound made by the heart. * *vti* to make a murmur; to say in a murmur.—**murmurer** *n*.—**murmurous** *adj*.
murphy *n* (*pl* **murphies**) (*inf*) a potato.
murrain *n* any infectious disease of cattle, such as foot-and-mouth disease; (*arch*) a plague.
murrhine, murrine *n* of or pertaining to an unknown substance (possibly jade or porcelain) used to make delicate pottery in ancient Rome. * *n* this substance (—*also* **murra**).
murther *n* (*arch*) murder.—**murtherer** *n*.
muscadine *n* a type of woody plant that produces a grape used to make wine.
muscat *n* any of various types of sweet white grapes used to make wine; muscatel.
muscatel, muscadel *n* a sweet wine made from muscat grapes.
muscle *n* fibrous tissue that contracts and relaxes, producing bodily movement; strength; brawn; power. * *vi* (*inf*) to force one's way (in).
muscle-bound *adj* having some of the muscles abnormally enlarged and lacking in elasticity as from too much exercise; inflexible, rigid.
muscovado, muscavado *n* raw sugar left after the molasses has evaporated from sugar cane.
Muscovite *n* a person who lives in, or originates from, Moscow; (*arch*) a Russian. * *adj* (*arch*) Russian.
muscovite *n* a type of mica often found in granite and sedimentary rocks.
Muscovy (duck) *n* a green-brown duck with white markings and a characteristic red fleshy growth on its beak.—*also* **musk duck**.
muscular *adj* of or done by a muscle; having well-developed muscles; strong, brawny.—**muscularity** *n*.—**muscularly** *adv*.
musculature *n* the entire system of muscles in a living thing; the system of muscles in an organ or a part of this system.
muse *vti* to ponder, meditate; to be lost in thought. * *n* a fit of abstraction.—**muser** *n*.
museum *n* a building for exhibiting objects of artistic, historic or scientific interest.
mush *n* a thick porridge of boiled meal; any thick, soft mass; (*inf*) sentimentality.
mushroom *n* a fleshy fungus with a capped stalk, some varieties of which are edible. * *vi* to gather mushrooms; to spread rapidly, to increase.
mushy *adj* (**mushier, mushiest**) soft, pulpy; (*sl*) sentimental, soppy.—**mushily** *adv*.—**mushiness** *n*.
music *n* the art of combining tones into a composition having structure and continuity; vocal or instrumental sounds having rhythm, melody or harmony; an agreeable sound.

musical *adj* of or relating to music or musicians; having the pleasant tonal qualities of music; having an interest in or talent for music. * *n* a play or film incorporating dialogue, singing and dancing.—**musicality** *n*.—**musically** *adv*.
musicale *n* a musical party.
musician *n* one skilled in music, esp a performer.—**musicianly** *adj*.—**musicianship** *n*.
musicology *n* the study of the history, forms, etc of music.—**musicological** *adj*.—**musicologist** *n*.
musing *adj* meditative; lost in thought.—**musingly** *adv*.
musk *n* an animal secretion with a strong odour, used in perfumes; the odour of musk; a plant with a similar odour.
musk duck *see* **Muscovy.**
muskellunge *n* (*pl* **muskellunges, muskellunge**) a large North American game fish similar to the pike.
musket *n* a long-barrelled, smoothbore shoulder gun formerly used by infantrymen.
musketeer *n* (*formerly*) a soldier armed with a musket.
musketry *n* small-arm fire; practice in this; muskets or musketeers collectively.
muskmelon *n* any of several varieties of widely cultivated melon with a netted or ribbed skin and sweet light-coloured or green flesh and a musky smell; any one of several types of melon related to the honeydew and cantaloupe.
muskrat *n* (*pl* **muskrats, muskrat**) a large North American aquatic rodent, related to the vole, that emits a musky secretion; the fur from this.—*also* **musquash.**
musky *adj* (**muskier, muskiest**) like or smelling of musk; sweet-smelling.—**muskiness** *n*.
Muslim *n* an adherent of Islam. * *adj* of Islam, its adherents and culture.—*also* **Moslem.**
muslin *n* a fine cotton cloth.
musquash *n* the fur of the muskrat; the muskrat.
muss *vt* (*often with* **up**) (*inf*) to disarrange, to rumple. * *n* a state of disorder.
mussel *n* an edible marine bivalve shellfish.
must[1] *aux vb expressing*: necessity; probability; certainty. * *n* (*inf*) something that must be done, had, etc.
must[2] *n* newly pressed grape juice, unfermented or partially fermented wine; the pulp and skin of crushed grapes.
must[3] *see* **musth.**
must[4] *see* **musty.**
mustache *n* the hair on the upper lip.—*also* **moustache.**
mustachio *n* (*pl* **mustachios**) (*often pl*) a moustache, usu bushy or shaped.
mustang *n* a small hardy semi-wild horse of the American prairies.
mustard *n* the powdered seeds of the mustard plant used as a condiment; a brownish-yellow colour; (*sl*) zest.
muster *vt* to assemble or call together, as troops for inspection or duty; to gather. * *vi* to be assembled, as troops. * *n* gathering; review; assembly.
musth, must *n* a state of sexual frenzy in the males of elephants and certain other large mammals. * *adj* denoting an animal in musth.
musty *adj* (**mustier, mustiest**) mouldy, damp; stale.—**mustily** *adv*.—**mustiness, must** *n*.
mutable *adj* able or tending to change or be changed; fickle, inconstant.—**mutability** *n*.—**mutably** *adv*.
mutant *n* a mutation; an organism whose structure has undergone mutation. * *adj* mutating.
mutate *vti* to experience or cause to experience change or alteration.
mutation *n* the act or process of mutating; alteration; (*biol*) a sudden change in some inheritable characteristic of a species; (*linguistics*) a change in a vowel sound when assimilated with another, esp an umlaut.—**mutational** *adj*.
mutatis mutandis (*Latin*) with the necessary changes.
mute *adj* silent; dumb; (*colour*) subdued. * *n* a person who is unable to speak; a device that softens the sound of a musical instrument. * *vt* to lessen the sound of a musical instrument.—**mutely** *adv*.—**muteness** *n*.
mutilate *vt* to maim; to damage by removing an essential part of.—**mutilation** *n*.—**mutilative** *adj*.—**mutilator** *n*.
mutineer *n* a person who takes part in a mutiny.
mutinous *adj* threatening mutiny, rebellious; taking part in a mutiny.—**mutinously** *adv*.
mutiny *vi* (**mutinying, mutinied**) to revolt against authority, esp in military service. * *n* (*pl* **mutines**) a rebellion against authority, esp by soldiers and sailors against officers.
mutism *n* the inability to speak; dumbness; silence; (*psychiatry*) a state in which a person remains silent although there is no physical cause for this.
mutt *n* (*sl*) a fool; a mongrel dog.
mutter *vti* to utter in a low tone or indistinctly; to grumble.—**mutterer** *n*.—**mutteringly** *adv*.
mutton *n* the edible flesh of sheep.
muttonchops *n* whiskers on the side of the face, narrow at the top, broad at the bottom.
mutual *adj* given and received in equal amount; having the same feelings one for the other; shared in common.—**mutuality** *n*.—**mutually** *adv*.
mutule *n* (*archit*) a projecting block under the corona of the Doric cornice.
muzhik *n* a peasant in pre-Revolutionary Russia.—*also* **mujik, moujik.**
muzz *vt* (*inf*) to make (anything) muzzy.
muzzle *n* the projecting nose or mouth of an animal; a strap fitted over the jaws to prevent biting; the open end of a gun barrel. * *vt* to put a muzzle on; to silence or gag.—**muzzler** *n*.
muzzy *adj* (**muzzier, muzziest**) confused, dazed; dizzy; blurred; dull.—**muzzily** *adv*.—**muzziness** *n*.
MW *abbr* = medium wave; megawatt.
Mx *abbr* = maxwell.
my *poss adj* of or belonging to me.
myalgia *n* pain, stiffness or cramp in the voluntary muscles or in one muscle.
myalgic encephalomyelitis *n* a viral condition affecting the nervous system, characterized by fatigue and muscle pains.—*also* **post-viral syndrome.**
mycelium *n* (*pl* **mycelia**) a cellular spawn of fungi.
mycetoma *n* (*pl* **mycetomas, mycetomata**) a fungoid disease, usu of feet, often caused by a wound.
mycology *n* the science of fungi or mushrooms; the fungi found in a particular area.—**mycologist** *n*.
mycosis *n* (*pl* **mycoses**) the presence of, or a disease caused by, a parasitic fungus.
mydriasis *n* excessive dilatation of the pupil of the eye.
mydriatic *adj* causing mydriasis. * *n* a drug that induces mydriasis.
myelitis *n* inflammation of the spinal cord or of bone marrow.
myna (bird) *n* any of severalAsian birds resembling the starling, some species of which can imitate speech.—*also* **mina (bird).**
Mynheer *n* a Dutch title used before a name, as "Mister" as a term of respect.
myocarditis *n* an inflammation of the myocardium.
myocardium *n* (*pl* **myocardia**) the muscular parts of the heart.—**myocardial** *adj*.
myology *n* a branch of medicine concerned with studying the muscles or the diseases affecting them.
myope *n* a short-sighted person.
myopia *n* short-sightedness.—**myopic** *adj*.—**myopically** *adv*.
myosis *see* **miosis.**
myosotis, myosote *n* any of various small plants with blue, pink, or white flowers, incl the forget-me-not.
myriad *n* a great number of persons or things. * *adj* innumerable.
myriapod *n* an arthropod with many legs and a segmented body, incl millipedes and centipedes.—**myriapodan** *adj, n*.—**myriapodous** *adj*.
myrica *n* the root bark of the candleberry or wax myrtle.
myrmecology *n* the scientific study of ants.—**myrmecological** *adj*.—**myrmecologist** *n*.
myrmecophagous *adj* feeding on ants; (*jaws, etc*) adapted for eating ants.
Myrmidon *n* (*pl* **Myrmidons, Myrmidones**) (*Greek myth*) one of a tribe of Thracian warriors formed by Zeus from an anthill who accompanied

Achilles to the Trojan war; a brutal, unprincipled or unquestioning follower or subordinate.—*also adj.*
myrobalan *n* any of several tropical trees containing tannin and bearing a fruit that when dried was used medicinally and in dyeing and tanning; the dye from such a fruit.
myrrh *n* a fragrant gum resin used in perfume, incense, etc.
myrtaceous *adj* of the myrtle family, incl eucalyptus, clove and guava, with leaves that secrete oil.
myrtle *n* an evergreen shrub with fragrant leaves; a trailing periwinkle.
myself *pron* emphatic and reflexive form of I; in my normal state.
mystagogue *n* an initiator into or interpreter of mysteries—**mystagogic** *adj*.—**mystagogy** *n*.
mysterious *adj* difficult to understand or explain, obscure; delighting in mystery.—**mysteriously** *adv*.—**mysteriousness** *n*.
mystery *n* (*pl* **mysteries**) something unexplained and secret; a story about a secret crime, etc; secrecy.
mystic *n* one who seeks direct knowledge of God or spiritual truths by self-surrender. * *adj* mystical.
mystical *adj* having a meaning beyond normal human understanding; magical.—**mystically** *adv*.
mysticism *n* the beliefs or practices of a mystic; belief in a reality accessible by intuition, not the intellect; obscurity of thought or doctrine.
mystify *vt* (**mystifying, mystified**) to puzzle, bewilder, to confuse.—**mystification** *n*.—**mistifier** *n*.—**mistifyingly** *adv*.
myth *n* a fable; a fictitious event; a traditional story of gods and heroes, taken to be true.—**mythic** *adj*.
mythical *adj* imaginary, unreal, untrue; having to do with myths, mythic.—**mythically** *adv*.
mythicize *vt* to treat as myth; to interpret mythically; to turn (something) into myth.
mythologist *n* a student of myths; a writer of myths.
mythology *n* (*pl* **mythologies**) myths collectively; the study of myths.—**mythological** *adj*.
mythopoeic *adj* producing or creating myths.—**mythopoeia, mythopoeisis** *n*.
myxedema, myxoedema *n* an illness leading to physical and mental degeneration due to underactivity of the thyroid gland and thus severe thyroxine deficiency
myxomycete *n* any of various organisms forming a network of creamy filaments on decaying wood, leaves, etc, and displaying characteristics of both plants and animals.

N

N (*chem symbol*) nitrogen. * *abbr* = North.
N, n *n* the 14th letter of the English alphabet; an indefinite number.
n/a *abbr* (*in commerce*) = no account.
NA *abbr* = North America.
Na (*chem symbol*) sodium.
nab *vt* (**nabbing, nabbed**) (*sl*) to catch, arrest.
nabob *n* in India, a deputy or administrator under the Mogul Empire; one who has amassed wealth in India; a very wealthy man.
nacelle *n* the car of an aircraft.
nacho *n* a Mexican snack consisting of a tortilla chip often served grilled with melted cheese, chilli, etc.
nacre *n* mother-of-pearl; the shellfish that yields it.
nacreous *adj* having an iridescent lustre; resembling mother of pearl.
nadir *n* the point opposite the zenith; the lowest point; the depths of despair.
naevus *see* **nevus.**
nag[1] *vti* (**nagging, nagged**) to scold constantly; to harass; to be felt persistently. * *n* a person who nags.
nag[2] *n* (*inf*) a horse.
Naga *n* (*pl* **Nagas, Naga**) (*Hindu myth*) a deified serpent, esp the cobra; a member of the Naga tribes; a class of mendicant Hindus. * *adj* pertaining to an ancient race who invaded India about the 6th century bc, or to certain Burmese border tribes.
nagana *n* a disease caused by the tsetse-fly.
Nagari *n* the name of the Sanskrit alphabet.
nagelflue *n* a peculiar alpine conglomerate rock, interspersed with nail-like pebbles.
nagor *n* a Senegal antelope.
Nahum *n* one of the prophetical books of the Old Testament.
naiad *n* (*pl* **naiads, naiades**) a water nymph; (*pl*) an order of aquatic plants; a family of freshwater bivalves.
naiant *adj* (*her*) representing fishes swimming in a horizontal position.
naif, naïf *adj* naive.
nail *n* a horny plate covering the end of a human finger or toe; a thin pointed metal spike for driving into wood as a fastening or hanging device. * *vt* to fasten with nails; to fix, secure; (*inf*) to catch or hit; (*inf*) to arrest.
nailfile *n* a small metal file or strip of cardboard coated with emery used for trimming and shaping the nails.
nail polish *n* a lacquer for giving a clear or coloured shiny surface to nails.
nainsook *n* a kind of closely woven muslin originally Indian.
naissant *adj* (*her*) issuing forth or rising from some ordinary, and showing only the foreparts of the body.
naive, naïve *adj* inexperienced; unsophisticated; (*argument*) simple.—**naively, naïvely** *adv*.
naiveté, naïveté, naivety *n* natural, unaffected simplicity or ingenuousness.
naked *adj* bare, without clothes; without a covering; without addition or ornament; (*eye*) without optical aid.—**nakedness** *n*.
namby-pamby *adj* weakly sentimental or affectedly pretty or fine. * *n* (*pl* **namby-pambies**) an affected person.
name *n* a word or term by which a person or thing is called; a title; reputation; authority. * *vt* to give a name to; to call by name; to designate; to appoint to an office; (*a date, price, etc*) to specify.
name-calling *n* verbal abuse, esp in place of reasoned debate.
name-dropping *n* the practice of mentioning the names of famous or important people as if they were friends, in order to impress others.—**name-dropper** *n*.
nameless *adj* without a name; obscure; anonymous; unnamed; indefinable; too distressing or horrifying to be described.
namely *adv* that is to say.
nameplate *n* a small plate on a door of a room, house, etc displaying the name of the occupant.
namesake *n* a person or thing with the same name as another.
nan bread, naan bread *n* a type of slightly leavened Indian bread in a flattened oval shape.
nance *n* (*derog*) an effeminate man.
nankeen, nankin *n* a buff-coloured cotton cloth, originally from China.
nanny *n* (*pl* **nannies**) a child's nurse.
nanny goat *n* a female domestic goat.
nano- *prefix* one thousand millionth (10^{-9}) part of, eg *nanosecond*.
nap[1] *n* a short sleep, doze. * *vi* (**napping, napped**) to take a nap.
nap[2] *n* a hairy surface on cloth or leather; such a surface.
napalm *n* a substance added to petrol to form a jelly-like compound used in firebombs and flame-throwers. * *vt* to attack or burn with napalm.
nape *n* the back of the neck.
napery *n* household linen, esp for the table.
naphtha *n* a clear, volatile, inflammable bituminous liquid hydrocarbon exuding from the earth or distilled from coal tar, etc; rock oil.
naphthalene *n* a white crystalline hydrocarbon distilled from coal tar, used in making dyes, explosives and in mothballs.
napiform *adj* turnip-shaped.
napkin *n* a square of cloth or paper for wiping fingers or mouth or protecting clothes at table, a serviette.
napoleon *n* a gold coin formerly current in France, value 20 francs.

Napoleonic *adj* of or like Emperor Napoleon I.
nappy[1] *adj* (**nappier, nappiest**) covered with nap or pile.
nappy[2] *n* (*pl* **nappies**) a diaper.
narceine *n* an alkaloid obtained from opium and used as a sedative.
narcissism *n* excessive interest in one's own body or self.—**narcissistic** *adj.*
narcissus *n* (*pl* **narcissi, narcissuses**) a spring-flowering bulb plant, esp the daffodil.
narco- *prefix* indicating torpor or narcotics.
narcodollars *npl* (*sl*) US dollars earned by a country by the export of illegal drugs.
narcosis *n* (*pl* **narcoses**) a state of unconsciousness or drowsiness produced by narcotics.
narcotic *adj* inducing sleep. * *n* a drug, often addictive, used to relieve pain and induce sleep.
narcotism *n* a morbid dependence on narcotics.
narcotize *vt* to use a narcotic upon.—**narcotization** *n.*
nard *n* spikenard, an aromatic plant; an aromatic unguent prepared from it.
nardoo *n* a genus of Australian acotyledonous aquatic plants, Australian pillwort, the spore cases of which are used as bread.
narghile *n* a small hookah pipe.
narrate *vt* (*a story*) to tell, relate; to give an account of; (*film, TV*) to provide a spoken commentary for.
narration *n* the act of narrating; a statement, written or verbal.
narrative *n* a spoken or written account of a sequence of events, experiences, etc; the art or process of narration.—*also adj.*
narrator *n* one who narrates.
narrow *adj* small in width; limited; with little margin; (*views*) prejudiced or bigoted. * *n* (*usu pl*) the narrow part of a pass, street, or channel. * *vti* to make or grow narrow; to decrease; to contract.—**narrowly** *adv.*—**narrowness** *n.*
narrow gauge *adj* denoting the distance of less than standard gauge (4 feet, 8.5 inches/1.44 metres) between rail metals.
narrow-minded *adj* prejudiced, bigoted; illiberal.—**narrow-mindedness** *n.*
narthex *n* in Early Christian churches the western portico, railed off for catechumens and penitents
narwhal *n* an Arctic whale, the male of which has a long spiral tusk.
nary = never a, ne'er a.
NASA *abbr* = National Aeronautics and Space Administration.
nasal *adj* of the nose; sounded through the nose. * *n* a sound made through the nose.—**nasally** *adv.*
nascent *adj* just starting to grow or develop.
naseberry *n* (*pl* **naseberries**) sapodilla plum tree.
naso- *prefix* nose.
nasturtium *n* an ornamental garden plant with bright flowers, a pungent odour, and edible leaves.
nasty *adj* (**nastier, nastiest**) unpleasant; offensive; ill-natured; disagreeable; (*problem*) hard to deal with; (*illness*) serious or dangerous.—**nastily** *adv.*—**nastiness** *n.*
nat. *abbr* = national; native; natural.
natal *adj* pertaining to one's birth or birthday; indigenous.—**natality** *n.*
natant *adj* swimming; (*her*) (*fish*) floating on the surface.
natation *n* the act or art of swimming.—**natational** *adj.*
natatorial, natatory *adj* swimming or adapted for swimming.
nates *npl* (*sing* **natis**) the buttocks.
nation *n* people of common territory, descent, culture, language, or history; people united under a single government.
national *adj* of a nation; common to a whole nation, general. * *n* a citizen or subject of a specific country.—**nationally** *adv.*
national anthem *n* a patriotic song or hymn adopted officially by a nation for ceremonial and public occasions.
national debt *n* the total money currently on loan to the government of a nation.
National Guard *n* in US, state militia that can be called into federal service.
nationalism *n* patriotic sentiments, principles, etc; a policy of national independence or self-government; fanatical patriotism, chauvinism.—**nationalist** *n.*—**nationalistic** *adj.*
nationality *n* (*pl* **nationalities**) the status of belonging to a nation by birth or naturalization; a nation or national group.
nationalize *vt* to make national; to convert into public or government property.—**nationalization** *n.*
national park *n* an area designated by a government as of important scenic, historical, or environmental value.
native *adj* inborn; natural to a person; innate; (*language, etc*) of one's place of birth; relating to the indigenous inhabitants of a country or area; occurring naturally. * *n* a person born in the place indicated; a local inhabitant; an indigenous plant or animal; an indigenous inhabitant, esp a non-White under colonial rule.
nativism *n* (*philos*) the doctrine of innate ideas; in US, the advocacy of the claim of native as opposed to that of naturalized Americans.—**nativist** *adj, n.*—**nativistic** *adj.*
nativity *n* (*pl* **nativities**) birth; a horoscope at the time of one's birth; (*with cap*) the birth of Christ.
NATO *abbr* = North Atlantic Treaty Organization.
natrolite *n* a hydrated silicate of aluminium and soda.
natron *n* a native carbonate of soda.
natter *vi* (*inf*) to chat, talk aimlessly.—*also n.*
natty *adj* (**nattier, nattiest**) tidy, neat, smart.—**nattily** *adv.*—**nattiness** *n.*
natural *adj* of or produced by nature; not artificial; innate, not acquired; true to nature; lifelike; normal; at ease; (*mus*) not flat or sharp. * *n* (*inf*) a person or thing considered to have a natural aptitude (for) or to be an obvious choice (for); (*inf*) a certainty; (*mus*) a natural note or a sign indicating one.—**naturalness** *n.*
natural childbirth *n* giving birth using techniques of relaxation, controlled breathing, etc rather than with anaesthetics.
natural gas *n* gas trapped in the earth's crust, a combustible mixture of methane and hydrocarbons extracted for fuel.
natural history *n* the study of nature, esp the animal, mineral, and vegetable world.
naturalism *n* (*art, literature*) the theory or practice of describing nature, character, etc in realistic detail; (*philos*) a theory of the world based on scientific as opposed to spiritual or supernatural explanations.—**naturalistic** *adj.*
naturalist *n* a person who studies natural history; a person who advocates or practises naturalism.
naturalization *n* the act of investing a foreigner with the rights and privileges of a natural-born citizen.
naturalize *vt* to confer citizenship upon (a person of foreign birth); (*plants*) to become established in a different climate. * *vi* to become established as if native.
natural law *n* law based on innate moral sense.
naturally *adv* in a natural manner, by nature; of course.
natural number *n* any of the whole numbers starting with 1.
natural philosophy *n* physics.
natural resource *n* a naturally occurring source of wealth as in land, oil, coal, water power, etc.
natural science *n* the study of material things.
natural selection *n* the principle that evolution is determined by the survival of the fittest.
nature *n* the phenomena of physical life not dominated by man; the entire material world as a whole, or forces observable in it; the essential character of anything; the innate character of a person, temperament; kind, class; vital force or functions; natural scenery.
nature worship *n* the worship of the deified forces of nature.
naught *see* **nought.**
naughty *adj* (**naughtier, naughtiest**) mischievous or disobedient; titillating.—**naughtily** *adv.*—**naughtiness** *n.*
naumachia, naumachy *n* (*pl* **naumachias** *or* **naumachiae, naumachies**) a sea fight; a show representing a sea fight.
nausea *n* a desire to vomit; disgust.

nauseate *vti* to arouse feelings of disgust; to feel nausea or revulsion.—**nauseating** *adj*.
nauseous *adj* causing nausea; disgusting.—**nauseously** *adv*.—**nauseousness** *n*.
nautch *n* in India, a dance performed by girls; a dancing exhibition.
nautical *adj* of ships, sailors, or navigation.
nautically *adv* in a nautical manner.
nautical mile *n* an international unit of measure for air and sea navigation equal to 6,075 feet (1.85 km).
nautilus *n* (*pl* **nautiluses, nautili**) a genus of cephalopods, including those furnished with a chambered spinal univalve shell/a shellfish with webbed arms once supposed to sail upon the sea; a kind of diving bell.
naval *adj* of the navy; of ships.
nave[1] *n* the central space of a church, distinct from the chancel and aisles.
nave[2] *n* the central block of a wheel, the hub.
navel *n* the small scar in the abdomen caused by severance of the umbilical cord; a central point.
navigability *n* the quality or state of being navigable.
navigable *adj* (*rivers, seas*) that can be sailed upon or steered through.—**navigably** *adv*.
navigate *vti* to steer or direct a ship, aircraft, etc; to travel through or over (*water, air, etc*) in a ship or aircraft; to find a way through, over, etc, and to keep to a course.
navigation *n* the act, art or science of navigating; the method of calculating the position of a ship, aircraft, etc.—**navigational** *adj*.
navigator *n* one who navigates; one skilled in the science of navigation.
navvy *n* (*pl* **navvies**) (*Brit*) a labourer, esp one who works on roads or railways.
navy *n* (*pl* **navies**) (*often with cap*) the warships of a nation; a nation's entire sea force, including ships, men, stores, etc; navy blue.
navy blue *n* an almost black blue.
nawab *n* an Indian viceroy; a nabob.
nay *adv* (*arch*) no; not only so; yet more; or rather, and even. * *n* a refusal or denial.
Nazarene *n* a native of Nazareth, applied to Jesus Christ, his followers, and the early Christians as a term of contempt; in the early Church, one of a sect of Judaising Christians.
Nazarite, Nazirite *n* a native of Nazareth; a Jew devoted by vow to God to a life of abstinence and purity (Numbers 6).
Nazi *n* (*pl* **Nazis**) a member of the German National Socialist party (1930s).—*also adj*.
NB *abbr* = nota bene (note well); New Brunswick.
Nb (*chem symbol*) niobium.
NBC *abbr* = National Broadcasting Company.
NC *abbr* = North Carolina.
NCO *abbr* = noncommissioned officer.
ND *abbr* = North Dakota.
Nd (*chem symbol*) neodymium.
NE *abbr* = Nebraska; northeast, northeastern.
Ne (*chem symbol*) neon.
Neanderthal *adj* denoting or characteristic of Neanderthal man; primitive.
Neanderthal man *n* a type of primitive human inhabiting Europe in Palaeolithic times.
neap *adj* of either of the lowest high tides in the month. * *n* a neap tide.
Neapolitan *adj* pertaining to Naples or to its inhabitants.
Neapolitan ice cream *n* brick ice cream in layers of different colours and flavours.
near *adj* (**nearer, nearest**) close, not distant in space or time; closely related, intimate; approximate; (*escape, etc*) narrow. * *adv* to or at a little distance; close by; almost. * *prep* close to. * *vti* to approach; to draw close to.—**nearness** *n*.
nearby *adj* neighbouring; close by in position.
Near East *n* Southeast Europe; (formerly) included Turkey, the Balkans and the area of the Ottoman Empire.
nearly *adv* almost, closely.
near miss *n* a bomb, mortar, etc that just fails to hit the target; any type of shot that misses its target; a situation in which two aircraft narrowly avoid a midair collision.
near-sighted *adj* short-sighted, myopic.—**near-sightedness** *n*.
neat[1] *adj* clean and tidy; skilful; efficiently done; well made; (*alcoholic drink*) undiluted; (*sl*) nice, pleasing, etc.—**neatly** *adv*.—**neatness** *n*.
neat[2] *n* cattle of the bovine genus. * *adj* pertaining to bovine animals.
neaten *vt* to make tidy and neat.
neath *prep* (*poet*) beneath.
neb *n* (*Scot*) a bird's beak; a mouth; a nose or snout; a projecting part, a point.
nebula *n* (*pl* **nebulae, nebulas**) a gaseous mass or star cluster in the sky appearing as a hazy patch of light.—**nebular** *adj*.
nebular hypothesis *n* the theory that the solar system in its primal condition existed in the form of a nebula, from which the sun, planets, and satellites were produced by condensation.
nebulosity *n* (*pl* **nebulosities**) the state or quality of being nebulous.
nebulous *adj* indistinct; formless.
necessarily *adv* as a natural consequence.
necessary *adj* indispensable; required; inevitable. * *n* (*pl* **necessaries**) something necessary; (*pl*) essential needs.
necessitarianism *n* (*philos*) the doctrine of necessity, or that man cannot control his actions by his own free will; fatalism.—**necessitarian** *n*.
necessitate *vt* to make necessary; to compel.
necessitous *adj* urgent; pressing; needy.
necessity *n* (*pl* **necessities**) a prerequisite; something that cannot be done without; compulsion; need.
neck *n* the part of the body that connects the head and shoulders; that part of a garment nearest the neck; a neck-like part, esp a narrow strip of land; the narrowest part of a bottle; a strait. * *vti* (*sl*) to kiss and caress.
neckerchief *n* a cloth square worn around the neck.
necklace *n* a string or band, often of precious stones, beads, or pearls, worn around the neck.
neckline *n* the line traced by the upper edge of a garment below the neck.
necktie *n* a man's tie.
necro-, necr- *prefix* corpse.
necrobiosis *n* the decay of living tissue.—**necrobiotic** *adj*.
necrology *n* (*pl* **necrologies**) a register or account of the dead.—**necrological** *adj*.
necromancer *n* one who practises necromancy; a conjurer; a wizard.
necromancy *n* predicting the future by alleged communication with the dead; sorcery.—**necromantic** *adj*.
necrophagous *adj* (*animal*) feeding on carrion.
necrophilia *n* erotic interest in or copulation with corpses.—*also* **necromania**.—**necrophile** *n*.—**necrophiliac** *n*.
necropolis *n* (*pl* **necropolises, necropoleis**) a cemetery.
necropsy *n* (*pl* **necropsies**) a post-mortem examination.
necrosis *n* mortification and death of a bone; gangrene; a disease in plants, characterized by small black spots.—**necrotic** *adj*.
nectar *n* a sweetish liquid in many flowers, used by bees to make honey; any delicious drink.
nectareous, nectarous *adj* producing, or sweet, like nectar.
nectarine *n* a smooth-skinned peach.
nectary *n* (*pl* **nectaries**) that part of a flower which secretes a saccharine fluid.
nee, née *adj* (*literally*) born: indicating the maiden name of a married woman.
need *n* necessity; a lack of something; a requirement; poverty. * *vt* to have a need for; to require; to be obliged.
needful *adj* necessary, required, vital. * *n* (*inf*) what is required, esp money.—**needfulness** *n*.
needle *n* a small pointed piece of steel for sewing; a larger pointed rod for knitting or crocheting; a stylus; the pointer of a compass, gauge, etc;

the thin, short leaf of the pine, spruce, etc; the sharp, slender metal tube at the end of a hypodermic syringe. * *vt* to goad, prod, or tease.

needlepoint *n* a type of embroidery worked on canvas; point lace.

needless *adj* not needed, unnecessary; uncalled for, pointless.—**needlessly** *adv*.—**needlessness** *n*.

needlework *n* sewing, embroidery.

needn't = need not.

needs *adv* necessarily; indispensably.

needy *adj* (**needier, neediest**) in need, very poor.

neep *n* (*Scot*) a turnip.

ne'er *adv* (*poet*) never.

ne'er-do-well *adj* good-for-nothing; improvident; lazy. * *n* an irresponsible person.

nefarious *adj* wicked, evil.

neg. *abbr* = negative(ly).

negate *vt* to nullify; to deny.

negation *n* a negative statement, denial; the opposite or absence of something; a contradiction.

negative *adj* expressing or meaning denial or refusal; lacking positive attributes; (*math*) denoting a quantity less than zero, or one to be subtracted; (*photog*) reversing the light and shade of the original subject, or having the colours replaced by complementary ones; (*elect*) of the charge carried by electrons; producing such a charge. * *n* a negative word, reply, etc; refusal; something that is the opposite or negation of something else; (*in debate, etc*) the side that votes or argues for the opposition; (*photog*) a negative image on transparent film or a plate. * *vt* to refuse assent, contradict; to veto.—**negatively** *adv*.

neglect *vt* to pay little or no attention to; to disregard; to leave uncared for; to fail to do something. * *n* disregard; lack of attention or care.

neglectful *adj*.careless; heedless; slighting.—**neglectfully** *adv*.

negligee *n* a woman's loosely fitting dressing gown.

negligence *n* lack of attention or care; an act of carelessness; a carelessly easy manner.

negligent *adj* careless, heedless.—**negligently** *adv*.

negligible *adj* that need not be regarded; unimportant; trifling.

negotiable *adj* able to be legally negotiated; (*bills, drafts, etc*) transferable.—**negotiability** *n*.

negotiate *vti* to discuss, bargain in order to reach an agreement or settlement; to settle by agreement; (*fin*) to obtain or give money value for (a bill); (*obstacle, etc*) to overcome.

negotiation *n* the act of negotiating or transacting business; a treaty.

negotiator *n* one who negotiates.

Negrillo *n* (*pl* **Negrillos, Negrilloes**) one of a pigmy Negroid race found in Africa.

Negrito *n* (*pl* **Negritos, Negritoes**) one of a diminutive Negroid race of the Philippines and Polynesia.

Negro *n* (*pl* **Negroes**) a member of the dark-skinned, indigenous peoples of Africa; a member of the Negroid group; a person with some Negro ancestors.—*also adj*.—**Negress** *nf*.

Negroid *adj* denoting, or of, one of the major groups of humankind, including most of the peoples of Africa south of the Sahara.

Negus *n* (*pl* **Neguses**) a title of the ruler of Ethiopia.

negus *n* (*pl* **neguses**) a beverage of hot water and wine, sweetened and spiced.

neigh *vi* (**neighing, neighed**) to whinny; to make a sound like the cry of a horse. * *n* the cry of a horse; a whinny.

neighbour, neighbor *n* a person who lives near another; a person or thing situated next to another; a fellow human being. * *vt* to be near, to adjoin.

neighbourhood, neighborhood *n* a particular community, area, or district; the people in an area.

neighbouring, neighboring *adj* adjoining, nearby.

neighbourly, neighborly *adj* characteristic of a neighbour, friendly. * *adv* in a neighbourly or social manner.—**neighbourliness, neighborliness** *n*.

neither *adj, pron* not one or the other (of two); not either. * *conj* not either; also not.

nek *n* (*S Africa*) a depression or pass in a mountain range.

nekton *n* a collective term for minute forms of organic life found at various depths in seas and lakes.—**nektonic** *adj*.

nelson *n* (*wrestling*) a type of hold in which the arms are placed under an opponent's arms from behind so that pressure can be exerted by the palms on the back of the opponent's neck.

nemato-, nemat- *prefix* thread, fibre.

nematode *adj* thread-like * *n* a threadworm.

nem. con. *adv* no one contradicting.

nem. diss. *adv* no one dissenting.

Nemean *adj* pertaining to the Nemea valley of ancient Greece or to the games held there.

nemesis *n* (*pl* **nemeses**) retribution; just punishment; an agent of defeat.

neo- *prefix* new, newly.

neodymium *n* a silvery-white metallic element used in alloys, etc.

Neolithic *adj* of the later Stone Age, marked by the use of polished stone implements.

neologism *n* a new word; the coining of new words, neology; the introduction of new doctrines.—**neologistic, neologistical** *adj*.

neologist *n* an innovator in language or religion, esp one who holds doctrinal views opposed to the orthodox interpretation of revealed religion.

neologize *vt* to introduce new words, phrases, or religious doctrines.

neology *n* neologism; doctrines or rationalistic theological interpretation at variance with orthodox belief.

neon *n* an inert gaseous element that gives off a bright orange glow, used in lighting and advertisements.

neophyte *n* a novice; one recently baptised; a convert. * *adj* recently entered.

neoplasm *n* tissue growth more or less distinct from that in which it occurs.

neoplastic *adj* newly formed.

neoplasty *n* the restoration of tissue by plastic surgery.

NeoPlatonism *n* a system of eclectic philosophy combining the doctrines of Plato with Oriental mysticism in the 3rd century ad.—**NeoPlatonist** *n*.

neoteric *adj* recent in origin; newfangled, modern.—**neoterically** *adv*.

Neotropical *adj* of tropical or South America.

Neozoic *adj* noting rocks from the Trias to the present time.

Nepalese *n, adj* (a) Nepali.

Nepali *n* (*pl* **Nepali, Nepalis**) a native or inhabitant of Nepal; the language of Nepal.—*also adj*.

nepenthe *n* a drug supposed by the ancient Greeks to have the power of causing forgetfulness of sorrow.—**nepenthean** *adj*.

nephew *n* the son of a brother or sister.

nephology *n* the study of clouds.—**nephological** *adj*.—**nephologist** *n*.

nephralgia *n* pain or disease in the kidneys.—**nephralgic** *adj*.

nephrite *n* jade.

nephritic *adj* of or pertaining to the kidneys or kidney disease; affected with disease of the kidneys.

nephritis *n* inflammation of the kidneys.

nephro- *or* **nephr-** *prefix* kidney; kidneys.

nephrology *n* study of the kidneys.

nephrotomy *n* (*pl* **nephrotomies**) incision into the kidney.

ne plus ultra *n* (*Latin*) the farthest attainable point; the acme, the perfect state.—*also* **non plus ultra**.

nepotism *n* undue favouritism shown to relatives, esp in securing jobs.

Neptune *n* the Roman god of the sea; the sea personified; the 8th planet from the sun.

Neptunian *adj* pertaining to the classical deity Neptune, god of the sea, or to the sea; deposited by the agency of the sea.

neptunium *n* a radioactive metallic element.

nerd *n* (*sl*) a boring, straight-laced person; a creep,

Nereid *n* (*pl* **Nereides**) (*Greek myth*) a sea nymph.

nereis *n* (*zool*) a sea worm.

neroli *n* the essential oil of orange flowers.
nervate *adj* (*bot*) ribbed.
nervation *n* (*bot*) the arrangement of veins, venation.
nerve *n* any of the fibres or bundles of fibres that transmit impulses of sensation or of movement between the brain and spinal cord and all parts of the body; courage, coolness in danger; (*inf*) audacity, boldness; (*pl*) nervousness, anxiety. * *vt* to give strength, courage, or vigour to.
nerve cell *n* a cell transmitting impulses in nerve tissue.—*also* **neuron, neurone.**
nerve centre, nerve center *n* a group of closely connected cells; (*mil, etc*) a centre of control from which instructions are sent out.
nerve gas *n* a poison gas that affects the nervous system.
nerveless *adj* calm, cool; weak, feeble.—**nervelessly** *adv*.
nerve-racking, nerve-wracking *adj* straining the nerves, stressful.
nervous *adj* excitable, highly strung; anxious, apprehensive; affecting or acting on the nerves or nervous system.
nervous breakdown *n* a (usu temporary) period of mental illness resulting from severe emotional strain or anxiety.
nervous system *n* the brain, spinal cord, and nerves collectively.
nervure *n* the veins of leaves; the horny ribs supporting the membranous wings of an insect.
nervy *adj* (**nervier, nerviest**) (*inf*) anxious, agitated; (*inf*) impudent, cheeky.
nescience *n* ignorance; agnosticism.—**nescient** *adj*.
ness *n* a headland or cape, a promontory.
-ness *suffix* state, quality of being.
nest *n* a structure or place where birds, fish, mice, etc, lay eggs or give birth to young; a place where young are nurtured; a swarm or brood; a lair; a cosy place; a set of boxes, tables, etc of different sizes, designed to fit together. * *vi* to make or occupy a nest.
nest egg *n* money put aside as a reserve or to establish a fund.
nestle *vti* to rest snugly; to lie snugly, as in a nest; to lie sheltered or half-hidden.
nestling *n* a young bird that has not left the nest.
Nestor *n* (*Greek myth*) a Greek sage of the Trojan war; a wise old man.
Nestorianism *n* the 5th-century doctrine of Nestorius, Bishop of Constantinople, who taught that there were two natures in Christ, one human and one divine, which did not unit and form one person; also that the Virgin Mary was not the Mother of God.—**Nestorian** *n, adj*.
net[1] *n* an openwork material of string, rope, or twine knotted into meshes; a piece of this used to catch fish, to divide a tennis court, etc; a snare. * *vti* (**netting, netted**) to snare or enclose as with a net; to hit (a ball) into a net or goal.
net[2], **nett** *adj* clear of deductions, allowances or charges. * *n* a net amount, price, weight, profit, etc. * *vt* (**netting, netted**) to clear as a profit.
nether *adj* lower or under.
nether world *n* the underworld, hell.
nethermost *adj* lowest.
netsuke *n* a Japanese ornamental toggle for fastening the front of a garment.
netting *n* netted fabric.
nettle *n* a wild plant with stinging hairs. * *vt* to irritate, annoy.
nettle rash *n* a cutaneous skin eruption resembling the effects of a nettle sting.
network *n* an arrangement of intersecting lines; a group of people who co-operate with each other; a chain of interconnected operations, computers, etc; (*radio, TV*) a group of broadcasting stations connected to transmit the same programme simultaneously. * *vt* to broadcast on a network; (*comput*) to interconnect systems so that information, software, and peripheral devices, such as printers, can be shared.
networking *n* the making of contacts and trading information as for career advancement; the interconnection of computer systems.
neur-, neuro- *prefix* nerve.
neural *adj* of or pertaining to the nerves.
neuralgia *n* pain along a nerve.—**neuralgic** *adj*.
neuralgic *adj* pertaining to neuralgia.
neurasthenia *n* brain and nerve exhaustion, as from influenza, etc.
neurectomy *n* (*pl* **neurectomies**) excision of a nerve.
neuritis *n* inflammation of a nerve.
neuro-, neur- *prefix* nerve.
neuroglia *n* the delicate connective tissue between the nerve fibres of the brain and spinal cord.
neurology *n* the branch of medicine studying the nervous system and its diseases.—**neurological** *adj*.—**neurologist** *n*.
neuroma *n* (*pl* **neuromas, neuromata**) a fibrous tumour occuring in nerve tissue.
neuron, neurone *see* **nerve cell.**
neuropathic *adj* pertaining to, or suffering from, nervous disease; affecting the nerves.—**neuropath** *n*.—**neuropathically** *adv*.
neuropathology *n* the study of diseases of the nervous system.—**neuropathologist** *adj*.
neuropathy *n* disease of the nervous system.
neuropteran *n* (*pl* **neuropterans**) any of an order of insects characterized by four transparent, finely reticulated, membranous wings. * *adj* with four wings marked with a network of nerves (—*also* **neuropterous**).
neurosis *n* (*pl* **neuroses**) a mental disorder with symptoms such as anxiety and phobia.
neurosurgery *n* the branch of surgery dealing with the nervous system.—**neurosurgical** *adj*.
neurotic *adj* suffering from neurosis; highly strung; of or acting upon the nerves. * *n* someone with neurosis.
neurotomy *n* (*pl* **neurotomies**) dissection of the nerves.
neurotransmitter *n* a chemical by which nerves cells communicate with each other or with muscles.
neuter *adj* (*gram*) of gender, neither masculine nor feminine; (*biol*) having no sex organs; having undeveloped sex organs in the adult. * *n* a neuter person, word, plant, or animal. * *vt* to castrate or spay.
neutral *adj* nonaligned; not taking sides with either party in a dispute or war; having no distinctive characteristics; (*colour*) dull; (*chem*) neither acid nor alkaline; (*physics*) having zero charge. * *n* a neutral state, person, or colour; a position of a gear mechanism in which power is not transmitted.
neutrality *n* the state of being neutral.
neutralize *vt* to render ineffective; to counterbalance; to declare neutral.—**neutralization** *n*.—**neutralizer** *n*.
neutrally *adv* in a neutral manner.
neutrino *n* (*pl* **neutrinos**) (*phsyics*) a stable elementary particle with almost zero mass and spin 1/2.
neutron *n* an elementary particle with no electric charge and the same mass approximately as a proton.
neutron bomb *n* a nuclear bomb with a small blast that releases neutrons, destroying life but leaving property undamaged.
neutron number *n* the number of neutrons in the nucleus of an atom.
neutron star *n* a star composed solely of densely packed neutrons that has collapsed under its own gravity.
névé *n* the granular compressed snow that forms glacier ice.
never *adv* at no time, not ever; not at all; in no case; (*inf*) surely not.
nevermore *adv* never again.
never-never *adj* imaginary, ideal.
nevertheless *adv* all the same, notwithstanding; in spite of, however.
nevus *n* (*pl* **nevi**) a birthmark, a mole.—*also* **naevus.**—**nevoid** *adj*.
new *adj* recently made, discovered, or invented; seen, known, or used for the first time; different, changed; recently grown, fresh; unused; unaccustomed; unfamiliar; recently begun. * *adv* again; newly; recently.
new blood *n* a recent arrival in an organization expected to bring new ideas and revitalize the system.
newborn *adj* newly born; reborn.
newcomer *n* a recent arrival.

New Deal *n* the economic and social measures introduced into the USA by President Roosevelt in 1933 to combat the great economic crisis that began in 1929.
newel *n* the central pillar of a spiral staircase; the end post of a banister.
New England *n* six northeastern states of the USA.
newfangled *adj* (*contemptuous*) new; novel, very modern.
Newfoundland *n* a large variety of dog, originally from Newfoundland.
newly *adv* recently, lately.
newlywed *n* a recently married person.
new moon *n* the moon when first visible as a crescent.
news *npl* current events; recent happenings; the mass media's coverage of such events; a programme of news on television or radio; information not known before.
newscast *n* radio or television news broadcast.—**newscaster** *n*.
newsdealer, newsagent *n* a retailer of newspapers, magazines, etc.
newsflash *n* an important news item broadcast separately and often interrupting other programmes.
newsletter *n* a bulletin regularly distributed among the members of a group, society, etc, containing information and news of activities, etc.
newspaper *n* a printed periodical containing news published daily or weekly.
newsprint *n* an inexpensive paper on which newspapers are printed.
newsreel *n* a short film presenting news of current events with a commentary.
newsroom *n* the department of a newspaper or broadcasting system that prepares news for publication or broadcasting; a room, etc, where newspapers, magazines, etc, may be read.
New Style calendar *n* the Gregorian or present style of computing the calendar, which replaced the Julian calendar.
newsworthy *adj* timely and important or interesting.
newt *n* any of various small amphibious lizard-like creatures.
New Testament *n* the second part of the Bible including the story of the life and teachings of Christ.
newton *n* the SI unit of force that when acting for 1 second on a mass of 1 kilogram imparts an acceleration of 1 metre per second.
Newtonian *adj* pertaining to, discovered by, or invented by, Sir Isaac Newton, the philosopher, or to his system.
new town *n* in UK, any of various towns built since 1946 as planned units sponsored by government to house overspill population from nearby cities, aid urban redevelopment, etc.
New World *n* the Americas.
New Year's (Day) *n* the first day of a new year; 1 January, a legal holiday in many countries.
New Year's Eve *n* the evening of the last day of the year; 31 December.—*also* **Hogmanay**.
next *adj* nearest; immediately preceding or following; adjacent. * *adv* in the nearest time, place, rank, etc; on the first subsequent occasion.
next of kin *n* the nearest relative of a person.
nexus *n* (*pl* **nexus, nexuses**) a connecting principle or link.
NH *abbr* = New Hampshire.
NI *abbr* = Northern Ireland.
Ni (*chem symbol*) nickel.
nib *n* a pen point. * *vt* (**nibbing, nibbed**) to furnished with a nib; to cut or insert a pen nib.
nibble *vti* to take small bites at (food, etc); to bite (at) lightly and intermittently.—**nibbler** *n*.
Nibelungenlied *n* a medieval German epic poem.
niblick *n* a golf club with a heavy head, used for lofting.
nice *adj* pleasant, attractive, kind, good, etc; particular, fastidious; delicately sensitive.—**nicely** *adv*.
nice-looking *adj* pretty, handsome.
Nicene Creed *n* the creed, one of the three held by the Anglican Church, drawn up by the Ecumenical Council of the Early Christian Church at the Council of Nicaea in Asia Minor in 325 ad, with additions made at the Council of Constantinople 381.
niceness *n* the state or quality of being nice; delicacy of perception or touch.
nicety *n* (*pl* **niceties**) a subtle point of distinction; refinement.
niche *n* a shallow recess in a wall for a statue, etc; a place, use, or work for which a person or thing is best suited.
nick *n* a small cut, chip, etc, made on a surface; (*Brit sl*) a police station, prison. * *vt* to make a nick in; to wound superficially; (*Brit sl*) to steal; (*Brit sl*) to arrest.
nickel *n* a silvery-white metallic element used in alloys and plating; a US or Canadian coin worth five cents.
nickelodeon *n* an early type of jukebox.
nickel silver *n* an alloy of nickel, copper and zinc.—*also* **German silver**.
nicker *vi* to neigh, to snigger.—*also n*.
nicknack *see* **knickknack**.
nickname *n* a substitute name, often descriptive, given in fun; a familiar form of a proper name. * *vt* to give as a nickname.
nicotiana *n* any of the *Nicotiana* genus of plants of Australia and America, eg tobacco.
nicotine *n* a poisonous alkaloid present in tobacco.
nictitate, nictate *vi* to wink.—**nictitation, nictation** *n*.
nictitating membrane *n* a membrane that can be drawn over the eye beneath the eyelid present in many birds, reptiles, fish and some mammals.
nidificate *vi* to build a nest.
nidification *n* the act of building a nest, rearing young, etc.
nidify *vi* (**nidifying, nidified**) to nidificate.
nidus *n* (*pl* **nidi, niduses**) the developing place of spores, seeds, germs, insects' eggs, etc; an accumulation of eggs, tubercles, etc; a nest or hatching place.
niece *n* the daughter of a brother or sister.
niello *n* (*pl* **nielli, niellos**) an ornamental engraving in black on silver, gold, brass, etc; a black alloy used in this. * *vt* (**nielloing, nielloed**) to engrave or decorate with niello.
Niflheim *n* (*Scandinavian myth*) the region of eternal mist and cold.
nifty *adj* (**niftier, niftiest**) (*sl*) neat, stylish.—**niftily** *adv*.—**niftiness** *n*.
niggard *adj* meanly covetous; parsimonious; miserly; niggardly. * *n* one who is meanly covetous; a stingy person, a miser.
niggardliness *n* the state of being niggardly; stinginess.
niggardly *adj* giving grudgingly, ungenerous. * *adv* like a niggard.
nigger *n* (*offensive*) a Negro, Black person; a dark-skinned person.
niggle *vi* to waste time on petty details; to be finicky.
niggler *n* one who trifles at handiwork.
niggling *adj* finicky, fussy; petty; gnawing, irritating.—**nigglingly** *adv*.
nigh *adj, adv, prep* near.
night *n* the period of darkness from sunset to sunrise; nightfall; a specified or appointed evening.
night blindness *n* poor vision in near darkness.
nightcap *n* a cap worn in bed; (*inf*) an alcoholic drink taken just before going to bed.
nightclothes *npl* clothes for wearing in bed, as a nightgown, pyjamas, etc.
nightclub *n* a place of entertainment for drinking, dancing, etc, at night.
nightdress *n* a loose garment worn in bed by women and girls.
nightfall *n* the close of the day.
nightflower *n* a flower that opens at night.
nightglass *n* a short telescope for night use.
nightgown *n* a nightdress.
nightie *n* (*inf*) a nightdress, nightgown.—*also* **nighty**.
nightingale *n* a songbird celebrated for its musical song at night.
nightjar *n* a nocturnal bird with dull mottled plumage.
night life *n* social entertainment at night, esp in towns.
night-light *n* a dim light kept burning at night.
nightlong *adj* lasting through the night.
nightly *adj, adv* done or happening by night or every night.
nightmare *n* a frightening dream; any horrible experience.—**nightmarish** *adj*.
night owl *n* (*inf*) a person who stays up late at night.
night school *n* an educational institution where classes are held in the evening.

nightshade *n* a flowering plant related to the potato and tomato, esp deadly nightshade (belladonna).
nightshirt *n* a long shirt for sleeping in.
nightspot *n* (*inf*) a nightclub.
nightstick *n* (*US*) a short club carried by a policeman or policewoman; a truncheon.
nighttime *n* night.
night watch *n* a watch by night or the person keeping it; (*pl*) nighttime.
night watchman *n* the person who guards a building at night.
nighty *n* (*pl* **nighties**) (*inf*) a nightie.
nigrescent *adj* blackish, growing black.—**nigrescence** *n*.
nihil *n* (*Latin*) nothing, nil.
nihil ad rem *adj* (*Latin*) irrelevant.
nihilism *n* the belief that nothing has real existence, scepticism; the rejection of customary beliefs in morality, religion, etc.
nihilist *n* a supporter of nihilism.—**nihilisitic** *adj*.
nihility *n* nonexistence.
nil *n* nothing.
nilgai, nilgau *n* (*pl* **nilgai, nilgais, nilgau, nilgaus**) a large short-horned Indian antelope.
Nilometer *n* a graduated pillar for measuring the rise of water in the river Nile during its floods; a river gauge.
Nilotic *adj* pertaining to the River Nile.
nimble *adj* agile; quick.—**nimbly** *adv*.
nimbus *n* (*pl* **nimbi, nimbuses**) (*art*) the halo or cloud of light surrounding the heads of divinities, saints, and sovereigns; a rain cloud.
nimby *abbr* = not in my back yard.
niminy-piminy *adj* mincing, prim.
Nimrod *n* a distinguished hunter, from Nimrod, "the mighty hunter" (Genesis 10.9).
nincompoop *n* a stupid, silly person.
nine *adj*, *n* one more than eight. * *n* the symbol for this (9, IX, ix); the ninth in a series or set; something having nine units as members.
ninefold *adj* having nine units or members; being nine times as great or as many.
ninepins *see* **skittles**.
nineteen *adj*, *n* one more than eighteen. * *n* the symbol for this (19, XIX, xix).—**nineteenth** *adj*.
nineteenth *adj* being one of 19 equal parts. * *n* a nineteenth part.
nineteenth hole *n* (*golf*) (*sl*) the bar in the clubhouse.
ninetieth *adj* next after 89. * *n* a ninetieth part.
ninety *adj*, *n* nine times ten. * *n* the symbol for this (90, XC, xc); (*in pl*) **nineties**; the numbers from 90 to 99; the same numbers in a life or century.
ninja *n* a Japanese warrior trained in ninjutsu.—*also adj*.
ninjutsu *n* an ancient Japanese martial art which practises techniques of stealth or invisibility, orig for the purpose of espionage and political assassination.
ninny *n* (*pl* **ninnies**) a person of weak character or mind, a simpleton.
ninon *n* a light silk material.
ninth *adj*, *n* next after eighth; one of nine equal parts of a thing.
Niobe *n* an inconsolable bereaved woman; (*Greek myth*) a heroine who was turned to stone while weeping for her slain children.—**Niobean** *adj*.
niobic *adj* of or containing pentavalent niobium.
niobium *n* a metallic element used in alloys.
nip[1] *vt* (**nipping, nipped**) to pinch, pinch off; to squeeze between two surfaces; (*dog*) to give a small bite; to prevent the growth of; (*plants*) to have a harmful effect on because of cold. * *n* a pinch; a sharp squeeze; a bite; severe frost or biting coldness.
nip[2] *n* a small drink of spirits. * *vti* (**nipping, nipped**) to drink in nips.
nipa *n* an East Indian palm.
nipper *n* a person or thing that nips; the pincer of a crab or lobster; (*pl*) pliers, pincers, etc; (*Brit inf*) a small child.
nipple *n* the small protuberance on a breast or udder through which the milk passes, a teat; a teat-like rubber part on the cap of a baby's bottle; a projection resembling a nipple.
nippy *adj* (**nippier, nippiest**) (*weather*) frosty; (*Brit inf*) quick, nimble.
nirvana *n* (*Buddhism*) the highest religious state, when all desire of existence and worldly good is extinguished, and the soul is absorbed into the Deity.
nisi *adj* (*decree, order, rule, etc*) valid unless cause is shown be the contrary by a fixed datc, at which it is made absolute.
nisi prius *n* (*law*) a writ, beginning with these words, directing a sheriff to empanel a jury; the name of certain courts for the trial of civil actions in the counties. a trial of civil causes by judges of assize.
nit *n* the egg of a louse or other parasitic insect.
niter *see* **nitre**.
niton *n* a gaseous radioactive element, radon.
nit-picking *n* (*inf*) concern with petty details in order to find fault.—*also adj*.
nitr-, nitro- *prefix* containing nitrogen; made with nitric acid.
nitrate *n* a salt of nitric acid; a fertilizer made of this.—**nitration** *n*.
nitre *n* potassium nitrate, saltpetre.—*also* **niter**.
nitric *adj* containing nitrogen.
nitric acid *n* a corrosive, caustic liquid used to make explosives, fertilizers, etc.
nitride *n* a compound of nitrogen with a metal, also with phosphorus, silicon or boron.
nitrification *n* the process of converting into nitre.
nitrify *vti* (**nitrifying, nitrified**) to make or become nitrous.
nitrite *n* a salt of nitrous acid.
nitro-, nitr- *prefix* containing nitrogen; made with nitric acid.
nitrogen *n* a gaseous element forming nearly 78 per cent of air.
nitrogenize *vt* to impregnate with nitrogen.—**nitrogenization** *n*.
nitrogenous *adj* pertaining to, or containing, nitrogen.
nitroglycerin, nitroglycerine *n* a powerful explosive made by adding glycerine to a mixture of nitric and sulphuric acids.
nitrous *adj* resembling, obtained from, or impregnated with, nitre.
nitrous acid *n* a compound of four volumes of nitrogen and one of oxygen.
nitrous oxide *n* a compound of one volume of oxygen and two volumes of nitrogen; laughing gas.
nitty-gritty *n* (*sl*) basic elements; harsh realities; practical details.
nitwit *n* (*inf*) a stupid person.
nival *adj* of or pertaining to snow.
niveous *adj* resembling snow, snow-like.
nix[1] *n* (*German myth*) a water sprite; (*Scot*) a kelpie.—**nixie** *nf*.
nix[2] *n* (*sl*) nothing. * *interj* (*sl*) look out! be careful!
nizam *n* (*with cap*) a title of the ruler of Hyderabad, India; a Turkish army soldier.
NJ *abbr* = New Jersey.
NLQ *abbr* = (*comput*) near letter quality.
NM *abbr* = New Mexico.
No[1] (*chem symbol*) nobelium.
No[2], **no**[1] *abbr* = number.
No[3], **Noh** *n* (*pl* **No, Noh**) Japanese classic dance-drama.
no *adv* (*used to express denial or disagreement*) not so, not at all, by no amount. * *adj* not any; not a; not one, none; not at all; by no means. * *n* (*pl* **noes, nos**) a denial; a refusal; a negative vote or voter.
Noachian, Noachic *adj* pertaining to the patriarch Noah, the deluge, or his times.
nob[1] *n* a knob; (*sl*) the head.
nob[2] *n* (*at cribbage*) knave of suit of turn-up card.
nob[3] *n* (*Brit sl*) a member of the upper classes; a wealthy person.
nobble *vt* (*Brit sl*) to tamper with (a racehorse) to prevent its winning; to obtain (money) by dishonest means; to suborn (a juror, etc) by bribes or threats; to defeat by underhand methods; to steal; to kidnap.
nobelium *n* a radioactive metallic element.
Nobel prize *n* an annual international prize given for distinction in one of six areas: physics, chemistry, physiology and medicine, economics, literature, and promoting peace.

nobility *n* (*pl* **nobilities**) nobleness of character, mind, birth, or rank; the class of people of noble birth.
noble *adj* famous or renowned; excellent in quality or character; of high rank or birth. * *n* a person of high rank in society.
nobleman *n* (*pl* **noblemen**) a peer.—**noblewoman** *nf* (*pl* **noblewomen**).
nobleness *n* the state of quality of being noble.
noblesse oblige *n* rank has its obligations.
nobly *adv* in a noble manner; of noble rank.
nobody *n* (*pl* **nobodies**) a person of no importance. * *pron* no person.
nock *n* a notch in a bow or arrow for the string; (*naut*) the forward upper corner of some sails. * *vt* to fit (an arrow) to string.
nocti-, noct- *prefix* night.
noctiluca *n* (*pl* **noctilucae**) a phosphorescent animalcule.
noctule *n* the largest British kind of bat.
nocturn *n* (*RC Church*) a part of matins.
nocturnal *adj* of, relating to, night; active by night.—**nocturnally** *adv*.
nocturne *n* a picture of a night scene; a musical composition appropriate to the night; a lullaby.
nocuous *adj* hurtful.
nod *vti* (**nodding, nodded**) to incline the head quickly, esp in agreement or greeting; to let the head drop, be drowsy; to indicate by a nod; (*with* **off**) (*inf*) to fall asleep. * *n* a quick bob of the head; a sign of assent or command.
nodal *adj* pertaining to nodes.
noddy *n* (*pl* **noddies**) a simpleton; a tropical sea bird; a four-wheeled carriage with a door at the back
node *n* a knob; a knot; a point of intersection; (*med*) a swelling; (*bot*) the joint of a stem and leaf or leaves; (*astron*) two points at which the orbit of a planet intersects he ecliptic; (*math*) the point at which a curve crosses itself; the point of rest in a vibrating body.
nodical *adj* (*astron*) pertaining to nodes.
nodose *adj* having knots or nodes, knotty, knobbed.—**nodosity** *n*.
nodular, nodulose, nodulous *adj* pertaining to, or like, a nodule.
nodule *n* a small lump or tumour.—**nodular** *adj*.
nodus *n* (*pl* **nodi**) a knotty point, a complication in the plot of a story, etc.
noel, noël *n* Christmas, esp in carols.
noetic *adj* pertaining to, performed by, or originating in, the mind or intellect, intellectual, abstract. * *n* the science of the intellect [(—*also* **noemics**).]
no-fault *adj* (*insurance*) providing damages without blame being fixed; (*divorce*) concluded without blame being charged.
nog[1] *n* a wooden peg or block; a stump. * *vt* (**nogging, nogged**) to secure with nogs.
nog[2] *n* an East Anglian strong beer.
nog[3] *n* (an) eggnog.
noggin *n* a small quantity of alcoholic drink; (*inf*) the head.
nogging *n* a partition formed of timber scantlings filled up with bricks.
no-go area *n* an area that certain individuals or groups are forbidden to enter.
nohow *adv* in no way, by no means.
noil *n* a short wool-combing.
noise *n* a sound, esp a loud, disturbing or unpleasant one; a din; unwanted fluctuations in a transmitted signal; (*pl*) conventional sounds, words, etc made in reaction, such as sympathy. * *vt* to make public.
noiseless *adj* making no sound, silent.—**noiselessly** *adv*.—**noiselessness** *n*.
noisette *n* a small round piece of meat.
noisome *adj* harmful, noxious; foul-smelling.
noisy *adj* (**noisier, noisiest**) making much noise; turbulent, clamorous.—**noisily** *adv*.—**noisiness** *n*.
nolens volens *adv* (*Latin*) willingly or unwillingly, willy-nilly.
noli me tangere *n* (*Latin*) a warning not to meddle; an erosive ulcer, lupus; a wild cucumber; a picture of Christ as he appeared to Mary Magdalen at the sepulchre.
nolle prosequi *n* an English legal term indicating the plaintiff's abandonment of his suit.
nolo episcopari *n* (*Latin*) unwillingness to accept office.
nomad *n* one of a people or tribe who move in search of pasture; a wanderer.—**nomadic** *adj*.
nomadic *adj* wandering; leading a wandering life; pastoral.—**nomadically** *adv*.
no-man's-land *n* an unclaimed piece of land; a strip of land, esp between armies, borders; an ambiguous area, subject, etc.
nombril *n* (*her*) the centre of an escutcheon.
nom de guerre *n* (*pl* **noms de guerre**) a pseudonym, an assumed name.
nom de plume *n* (*pl* **noms de plume**) a pseudonym.
nome *n* a province of modern Greece; a territorial division in ancient Egypt.
nomenclator *n* an ancient Roman slave who named persons met; one who gives names to things, an inventor of names.
nomenclature *n* a system of names, terminology, used in a science, etc, or for parts of a device, etc.
nominal *adj* of or like a name; existing in name only; having minimal real worth, token.
nominalism *n* (*philos*) the doctrine that general notions exist only in the mind or in name, opposite to realism.
nominalist *n* one who holds the doctrine of nominalism.—**nominalistic** *adj*.
nominally *adv* in name only.
nominate *vt* to appoint to an office or position; (*candidate*) to propose for election.—**nominator** *n*.
nomination *n* the act or right of nominating; the state of being nominated.
nominative *adj* (*gram*) denoting the case of the subject of a verb; appointed, not elected. * *n* (*gram*) the nominative case or a word in it.
nominee *n* a person who is nominated.
nomo-, nom- *prefix* law.
nomography *n* (*pl* **nomographies**) the art of drawing up laws.—**nomographic, nomographical** *adj*.
nomology *n* the science of the laws of the mind.—**nomological** *adj*.—**nomologist** *n*.
nomothetic, nomothetical *adj* legislative, founded on a system of laws.
non- *prefix* not, reversing the meaning of a word.
nonage *n* minority, legal infancy; an early stage.
nonagenarian *n* a person who is in his or her nineties.
nonagon *n* a plane figure with 9 sides and 9 angles.—**nonagonal** *adj*.
nonalcoholic *adj* (*drinks, etc*) containing little or no alcohol.
nonaligned *adj* not in alliance with any side, esp in power politics.
nonce *n* **for the nonce** for this time only.
nonce word *n* a word coined for one occasion.
nonchalance *n* coolness; indifference.
nonchalant *adj* calm; cool, unconcerned, indifferent.—**nonchalantly** *adv*.
noncombatant *n* a member of the armed forces whose duties do not include fighting, as a doctor or chaplain; a civilian during wartime.
noncommissioned officer *n* (*mil*) a subordinate officer, as a corporal, sergeant, etc, appointed from the ranks.
noncommittal *adj* not revealing one's opinion.—**noncommittally** *adv*.
non compos mentis *adj* (*Latin*) of unsound mind, not responsible.
nonconductor *n* a substance that will not conduct electricity or heat.
nonconformist *n* a person who does not conform to prevailing attitudes, behaviour, etc; (with cap) in Britain, a Protestant who does not belong to the established church.—*also adj*.
nonconformity *n* (*with cap*) refusal to conform to the established church; a want of conformity, irregularity.
noncooperation *n* refusal to cooperate, esp with government decree, etc.—**noncooperative** *adj*.
nondescript *adj* hard to classify, indeterminate; lacking individual characteristics. * *n* a nondescript person or thing.
none *pron* no one; not anyone; (*pl verb*) not any; no one. * *adv* not at all.
noneffective *adj* not effective; (*soldier, sailor*) not qualified for active service.—*also n*.
nonentity *n* (*pl* **nonentities**) a person or thing of no significance.
nones *npl* in the ancient Roman calendar the ninth day before the Ides, reckoned inclusively, ie 7th of March, May, July, October, and the 5th

of the other months; (*RC Church*) the devotional office for the ninth hour or 3 p.m.

nonesuch *n* an unrivalled person or thing, a nonpareil; a plant like clover used for fodder.—*also* **nonsuch.**

nonet *n* a group of nine connected objects or people; (*mus*) a piece for nine players.

nonetheless *conj* nevertheless.

nonevent *n* an event or experience that is unexpectedly disappointing.

nonfeasance *n* (*law*) the omission of an obligatory act.

nonferrous *adj* containing no iron.

nonflammable *adj* not easily set on fire.

nonillion *n* in the US and France, tenth power of a thousand (1 followed by 30 ciphers); in Britain, the ninth power of one million (1 followed by 54 ciphers).—**nonillionth** *adj.*

nonintervention *n* the policy of refusing to interfere in the affairs of others, esp nations.—**noninterventionist** *adj.*

nonjuror *n* one who refused to take the oath of allegiance to William and Mary in 1689.

non-lethal *adj* (*international affairs*) pertaining to foreign aid given to provide medicine, clothing or food rather than weapons.

nonmetal *n* a chemical element (eg carbon) that is not a metal.

nonmoral *adj* unconcerned with morality; without moral standards.

nonpareil *adj* without an equal; (*person or thing*) unrivalled, matchless, unsurpassed. * *n* unequalled excellence; (*print*) a 6-point type; a variety of apple; a kindof bird, moth, wheat, etc.

nonpartisan *adj* not aligned to one particular political party.

nonparty *adj* free from party obligations.

nonplus *vt* (**nonplusses, nonplussing, nonplussed** *or* **nonpluses, nonplusing, nonplused**) to cause to be so perplexed that one cannot, go, speak, act further. * *n* (*pl* **nonpluses**) a state of perplexity, a standstill.

non plus ultra *see* **ne plus ultra.**

non-profit *adj* (*organization*) not conducted for the purpose of making money.

nonproliferation *n, adj* (placing) restriction on the acquisition or production of, esp nuclear weapons.

nonrepresentational *adj* (*art*) abstract.

nonsense *n* words, actions, etc, that are absurd and have no meaning.—*also adj*. * *interj* absurd!

nonsensical *adj* absurd; unmeaning.—**nonsensically** *adv.*

non sequitur *n* a statement that has no relevance to what has preceded it.

nonstarter *n* a person who is unlikely to succeed; (*horse, racing car, etc*) withdrawn at the last moment.

nonstick *adj* (*saucepans*) coated with a surface that prevents food from sticking.

nonstop *adj* (*train, plane, etc*) not making any intermediate stops; not ceasing. * *adv* without stopping or pausing.

nonsuch *see* **nonesuch.**

nonsuit *n* the withdrawal of a suit during trial either voluntarily or by judgment of the court on the discovery of error or defect in the pleadings. * *vt* to pronounce a nonsuit against.

nonunion *adj* not belonging to a trade union.

nonviolence *n* the abstaining from physical force to achieve civil rights.—**nonviolent** *adj.*

noodle[1] *n* (often *pl*) pasta formed into a strip.

noodle[2] *n* (*inf*) a foolish person; (*sl*) the head.

nook *n* a secluded corner, a retreat; a recess.

noon *n* midday; twelve o'clock in the day. * *adj* pertaining to noon.

noonday, noontide, noontime *adj* pertaining to noon, or midday. * *n* noon.

no one *pron* nobody.

noose *n* a loop of rope with a slipknot, used for hanging, snaring, etc. * *vt* to tie in a noose; to make a noose in or of.

nopal *n* an American cactus, the food of the cochineal insect.

nope *adv* (*sl*) no.

nor *conj* and not; not either.

Nor *abbr* = Norman; north; Norway; Norwegian.

Nordic *adj* (*physical type*) characterized by tall stature, long head, light skin and hair, and blue eyes; (skiing) including cross-country runs and jumping.

Norfolk jacket *n* a man's loose jacket with a belt.

noria *n* a water-raising apparatus in Spain, etc, a waterwheel.

norm *n* a standard or model, esp the standard of achievement of a large group.—**normative** *adj.*

normal *adj* regular; usual; stable mentally. * *n* anything normal; the usual state, amount, etc.—**normalcy** *n.*—**normality** *n.*—**normally** *adv.*

normalize *vti* to make or become normal.—**normalization** *n.*

normal school *n* (*US*) a school for the training of teachers for elementary schools.

Norman *n* any of the people of Normandy who conquered England in 1066; a native or inhabitant of Normandy in France. * *adj* pertaining to the Normans or Normandy; (*archit*) of a style introduced into England by the Normans, characterized by rounded arches and massive square towers (—*also* **Normanesque**).

Norn *n* (*Scand myth*) one of the three fates, Urd, Verdande and Skuld, representing the past, the present and the future.

Norse *adj* of ancient Scandinavia or its inhabitants; of Norway. * *n* the language of Norway.

Norseman *n* (*pl* **Norsemen**) any of the ancient Scandinavian people, the Vikings.

north *n* one of the four points of the compass, opposite the sun at noon, to the right of a person facing the sunset; the direction in which a compass needle points; (*often with cap*) the northern part of one's country or the earth. * *adj* in, of, or towards the north; from the north. * *adv* in or towards the north.

northeast *adj, n* (of) the direction midway between north and east.

northeaster *n* a northeast wind.

northeasterly *adj* towards or coming from the northeast. * *n* (*pl* **northeasterlies**) a northeast wind or storm.

northeastern *adj* belonging to the northeast, or in that direction.

northeastward *adj* towards or in the northeast.—*also adv.*—**northeastwards** *adv.*

norther *n* a wind or storm from the north, esp a strong gale that prevails in the Gulf of Mexico from September to March.

northerly *adj* in, from, or towards the north. * *n* (*pl* **northerlies**) a northerly wind.

northern *adj* of or in the north.

northerner *n* a native or inhabitant of the north.

Northern Hemisphere *n* the half of the earth north of the Equator.

northern lights *npl* the aurora borealis.

northernmost *adj* farthest north.

northing *n* distance northward.

North Pole *n* the northern end of the axis of the earth at a latitude of 90 degrees north.

north star *n* the polar star.

northward *adj* towards or in the north.—*also adv.*—**northwards** *adv.*

northwest *adj, n* (of) the direction midway between north and west.

northwester *n* a northwest wind.

northwesterly *adj* towards or coming from the northwest. * *n* (*pl* **northwesterlies**) a northwest wind or storm.

northwestern *adj* belonging to the northwest, or in that direction.

northwestward *adj* towards or in the northwest.—*also adv.*—**northwestwards** *adv.*

Norwegian *adj, n* (of or relating to) the language, people, etc, of Norway.

nose *n* the part of the face above the mouth, used for breathing and smelling, having two nostrils; the sense of smell; anything like a nose in shape or position. * *vt* to discover as by smell; to nuzzle; to push (away, etc) with the front forward. * *vi* to sniff for; to inch forwards; to pry.

nosebag *n* a bag containing fodder hung from a horse's head.

noseband *n* the part of a bridle that covers the horse's nose.

nosebleed *n* a bleeding from the nose.

nose dive *n* a swift downward plunge of an aircraft, nose first; any sudden sharp drop, as in prices.—**nose-dive** *vi*.
nosegay *n* a bouquet.
nose job *n* (*sl*) cosmetic plastic surgery to reshape the nose.
nosey *see* **nosy.**
nosh *n* (*sl*) food, a meal. * *vt* to chew. * *vi* to eat.
nosing *n* the rounded edge of a step, etc, or the metal shield for it.
noso- *prefix* disease.
nosography *n* the systematic description of diseases.
nosology *n* the classification of the diseases of animals and plants.—**nosological** *adj*.—**nosologically** *adv*.—**nosologist** *n*.
nostalgia *n* yearning for past times or places.
nostalgic *adj* feeling or expressing nostalgia; longing for one's youth.—**nostalgically** *adv*.
nostology *n* the study of senility or ageing, gerontology.—**nostologic** *adj*.
nostril *n* one of the two external openings of the nose for breathing and smelling.
nostrum *n* a quack remedy, patent medicine.
nosy *adj* (**nosier, nosiest**) (*inf*) inquisitive, snooping.—**nosily** *adv*.—**nosiness** *n*.—*also* **nosey.**
nosy parker *n* (*inf*) a prying person, busybody.
not *adv expressing* denial, refusal, or negation.
nota bene note this.—*abbr* = **NB.**
notabilia *npl* things worthy of note.
notability *n* (*pl* **notabilities**) the quality of being notable; a notable person or thing.
notable *adj* worthy of being noted or remembered; remarkable, eminent. * *n* an eminent or famous person.—**notably** *adv*.
notandum *n* (*pl* **notanda**) a thing to be noted.
notarial *adj* pertaining to, or done by, a notary.
notary *n* (*pl* **notaries**) a notary public.
notary public *n* (*pl* **notaries public**) a public official authorized to certify deeds, contracts, etc.
notation *n* a system of symbols or signs to represent quantities, etc, esp in mathematics, music, etc.
notch *n* a V-shaped cut in an edge or surface; (*inf*) a step, degree; a narrow pass with steep sides. * *vt* to cut notches in.
note *n* a brief summary or record, written down for future reference; a memorandum; a short letter; notice, attention; an explanation or comment on the text of a book; a musical sound of a particular pitch; a sign representing such a sound; a piano or organ key; the vocal sound of a bird. * *vt* to notice, observe; to write down; to annotate.
notebook *n* a book with blank pages for writing in.
noted *adj* celebrated, well-known.
note paper *n* paper for writing letters.
noteworthy *adj* outstanding; remarkable.
nothing *n* no thing; not anything; nothingness; a zero; a trifle; a person or thing of no importance or value. * *adv* in no way, not at all.
nothingness *n* the state of being nothing; unconsciousness; worthlessness.
notice *n* an announcement; a warning; a placard giving information; a short article about a book, play, etc; attention, heed; a formal warning of intention to end an agreement at a certain time. * *vt* to observe; to remark upon. * *vi* to be aware of.
noticeable *adj* easily noticed or seen.—**noticeably** *adv*.
notice board *n* a board on which notices are posted.
notifiable *adj* (*infectious diseases*) that must be reported to health authorities.
notification *n* the act of notifying; a notice or paper bearing it.
notify *vt* (**notifying, notified**) to inform; to report, give notice of.
notion *n* a general idea; an opinion; a whim;.
notional *adj* hypothetical, abstract; imaginary.
notions *npl* small useful articles, as thread, needles, etc; haberdashery.
noto- *prefix* back.
notochord *n* the rudimentary form of the vertebral column; a band forming the basis of the spinal column.—**notochordal** *adj*.
notoriety *n* the state of being notorious; disrepute, infamy; public exposure.
notorious *adj* widely known, esp unfavourably.—**notoriously** *adv*.
notornis *n* the gigantic short-winged coot of New Zealand.
nototherium *n* (*pl* **nototheria**) an extinct gigantic marsupial of Australia.
notwithstanding *prep* in spite of. * *adv* nevertheless. * *conj* although.
nougat *n* a chewy sweet consisting of sugar paste with nuts.
nought *n* nothing; a zero. * *adv* in no degree.—*also* **naught.**
noughts and crosses *see* **tick-tack-toe.**
noumenon *n* (*pl* **noumena**) an object of purely intellectual intuition; (*philos*) the substance or real existing under the phenomenal.—**noumenal** *adj*.
noun *n* (*gram*) a word that names a person, a living being, an object, action etc; a substantive.
nourish *vt* to feed; to encourage the growth of; to raise, bring up.
nourishing *adj* containing nourishment; health-giving; beneficial.
nourishment *n* food; the act of nourishing.
nous *n* pure intellect; common sense.
nouveau riche *n* (*pl* **nouveaux riches**) the new rich, a parvenu.—*also adj*.
Nov *abbr* = November.
nova *n* (*pl* **novas, novae**) a new star that explodes into bright luminosity before subsiding.
Novatian *adj* pertaining to the doctrines of the Novatians, a 3rd-century sect who held that the Church should not re-admit the lapsed, and that second marraiges were of the nature of sin.
novel *n* a relatively long prose narrative that is usually fictitious and in the form of a story. * *adj* new and unusual.
novelette *n* a short novel.—**novelettish** *adj*.
novelist *n* a writer of novels.
novelize *vt* to turn (a play, film, etc) into a novel.—**novelization** *n*.
novella *n* (*pl* **novellas, novelle**) a short novel.
novelty *n* (*pl* **novelties**) a novel thing or occurrence; a new or unusual thing; (*pl*) cheap, small objects for sale.
November *n* the eleventh month, having 30 days.
novena *n* (*pl* **novenae**) (*RC Church*) a prayer made for nine days to obtain a request through intercession of the Virgin or saint.
novice *n* a person on probation in a religious order before taking final vows; a beginner.
novitiate, noviciate *n* a probationary period, initiation; a novice; a place where novices live.
now *adv* at the present time; by this time; at once; nowadays. * *conj* since; seeing that. * *n* the present time. * *adj* of the present time.
nowadays *adv* in these days; at the present time.
noway *adv* not at all. * *interj* (**no way**) used to express emphatic denial or refusal.
nowhere *adv* not in, at, or to anywhere.
nowise *adv* not in any manner or degree.
noxious *adj* harmful, unhealthy.—**noxiously** *adv*.—**noxiousness** *n*.
noyade *n* execution by drowning, esp that system of capital punishment for political offenders employed by the French revolutionists of 1789.
noyau *n* (*pl* **noyaux**) a liqueur flavoured with bruised bitter almonds.
nozzle *n* the spout at the end of a hose, pipe, etc.
Np (*chem symbol*) neptunium.
NT *abbr* = New Testament.
-n't = not.
nth *adj* (*maths*) of or having an unspecified number; (*inf*) utmost, extreme.
nu *n* the 13th letter of the Greek alphabet.
nuance *n* a subtle difference in meaning, colour, etc.
nub *n* a lump or small piece; (*inf*) the central point or gist of a matter.
nubbin *n* a small or imperfect ear of maize; undeveloped fruit.
nubecula *n* (*pl* **nubeculae**) the Magellanic clouds, a small galaxy; cloudy appearance; a light film on the eye.
nubile *adj* (*girl*) marriageable; attractive.
nuclear *adj* of or relating to a nucleus; using nuclear energy; having nuclear weapons.
nuclear bomb *n* a bomb whose explosive power derives from uncontrolled nuclear fusion or fission.

nuclear energy *n* energy released as a result of nuclear fission or fusion.
nuclear family *n* father, mother and children.
nuclear fission *n* the splitting of a nucleus of an atom either spontaneously or by bombarding it with particles.
nuclear fusion *n* the combining of two nuclei into a heavier nucleus, releasing energy in the process.
nuclear power *n* electrical or motive power produced by a nuclear reactor.
nuclear reactor *n* a device in which nuclear fission is maintained and harnessed to produce energy.
nuclear waste *n* radioactive waste.
nucleate *adj* having a nucleus.
nucleic acid *n* DNA, RNA or similar complex acid present in all living cells.
nucleo-, nucle- *prefix* nucleus; nucleic acid.
nucleolus *n* (*pl* **nucleoli**) a minute body inside a nucleus.
nucleonics *n* (*used as sing*) the physics and technology of the applications of nuclear energy.
nucleus *n* (*pl* **nuclei, nucleuses**) the central part or the core around which something may develop, or be grouped or concentrated; the centrally positively charged portion of an atom; the part of an animal or plant cell that contains genetic material.
nude *adj* naked; bare; undressed. * *n* a naked human figure, esp in a work of art; the state of being nude.—**nudity** *n*.
nudge *vt* to touch gently with the elbow to attract attention or urge into action; to push slightly. * *n* a gentle touch, as with the elbow.
nudibranch *n* any of the order Nudibranchia of shell-less molluscs with naked gills.
nudism *n* the practice of going nude, esp in groups at designated places and times.
nudist *n* one who believes in going nude.—*also adj*.
nudity *n* (*pl* **nudities**) nakedness.
nugatory *adj* trifling, worthless; inoperative, not valid; useless.
nugget *n* a small lump, esp of gold in its natural state.
nuisance *n* a person or thing that annoys or causes trouble.
nuke *vt* (*sl*) to attack and destroy with a nuclear weapon; (*sl*) to cook or heat (food) in microwave oven. * *n* a nuclear weapon.
null *adj* without legal force; invalid.
nullah *n* in the East Indes, a watercourse or canal; a ravine.
nulla-nulla *n* (*Austral*) a hard wooden club.
nullifier *n* one who nullifies.
nullify *vt* (**nullifying, nullified**) to make null, to cancel out.—**nullification** *n*.
nullipara *n* (*pl* **nulliparae**) a woman who has never given birth to a child, esp if not a virgin.
nullipore *n* a marine coral-like plant with calcareous fronds.
nullity *n* (*pl* **nullities**) the state of being null; a legally invalid document or act; something ineffectual, worthless, etc.
num *abbr* = number; numeral.
numb *adj* deadened; having no feeling (due to cold, shock, etc). * *vt* to make numb.—**numbness** *n*.
number *n* a symbol or word indicating how many; a numeral identifying a person or thing by its position in a series; a single issue of a magazine; a song or piece of music, esp as an item in a performance; (*inf*) an object singled out; a total of persons or things; (*gram*) the form of a word indicating singular or plural; a telephone number; (*pl*) arithmetic; (*pl*) numerical superiority. * *vti* to count; to give a number to; to include or be included as one of a group; to limit the number of; to total.
numberless *adj* too many to count.
number one *n* the first in a list, series, etc; (*inf*) oneself or one's own interests; (*inf*) the most important person or thing; (*inf*) a best-selling pop record. * *adj* most important, urgent, etc.
numberplate *n* a license plate.
Number Ten *n* 10 Downing Street, the London residence of the British prime minister.
numbles *npl* humbles, entrails, esp of a deer.
numbskull *see* **numskull**.
numerable *adj* countable.—**numerably** *adv*.
numeral *n* a symbol or group of symbols used to express a number (eg two = 2 or II, etc).
numerate *adj* having a basic understanding of arithmetic. * *vt* to reckon or enumerate; to point or read, as figures.
numerati *npl* people, esp financiers, who are proficient at arithmetic.
numeration *n* the act of numbering; the art of reading in words numbers expressed by symbols.
numerator *n* the number above the line in a fraction.
numerical, numeric *adj* of or relating to numbers; expressed in numbers.
numerology *n* the study of the supposed occult meaning of numbers.
numerous *adj* many, consisting of many items.
numismatics *n* (*used as sing*) the study of coins, medals, etc.—*also* **numismatology**.—**numismatic** *adj*.
numismatist *n* one skilled in numismatics / a student of coins.
nummular *adj* pertaining to, or like, coins.
nummulite *n* a many-chambered fossil foraminifer resembling a coin.—**nummulitic** *adj*.
numskull *n* a dolt, a blockhead.—*also* **numbskull**.
nun *n* a woman belonging to a religious order.
Nunc Dimittis *n* a canticle.
nunciature *n* the office of a nuncio; the tenure of it.
nuncio *n* (*pl* **nuncios**) the pope's ambassador at a foreign court.
nuncupate *vt* to declare, to make a will verbally, not in writing.
nuncupative *adj* (*law*) verbal, not written; nominal.
nunnery *n* (*pl* **nunneries**) a convent of nuns.
nuptial *adj* relating to marriage. * *npl* a wedding ceremony; marriage.
nurse *n* a person trained to care for the sick, injured or aged; a person who looks after another person's child or children. * *vt* to tend, to care for; (*baby*) to feed at the breast; (*hatred*) to foster; to tend with an eye to the future.
nursemaid *n* a woman in charge of children, a nanny.
nursery *n* (*pl* **nurseries**) a room set aside for children; a place where children may be left in temporary care; a place where young trees and plants are raised for transplanting.
nurseryman *n* (*pl* **nurserymen**) a person who owns or works in a plant nursery.
nursery rhyme *n* a short traditional poem or song for children.
nursery school *n* a school for young children, usu under five.
nursery slope *n* a gently inclined slope for novice skiers.
nursing *n* the profession of a nurse.
nursing home *n* an establishment providing care for convalescent, chronically ill, or disabled people.
nursling, nurseling *n* an infant; one who is nursed.
nurture *vt* to feed; to bring up, educate. * *n* the act of bringing up a child; nourishment.
nut *n* a kernel (sometimes edible) enclosed in a hard shell; a usu metallic threaded block screwed on the end of a bolt; (*sl*) a mad person; (*sl*) a devotee, fan. * *vt* (**nutting, nutted**) to gather nuts.
nutant *adj* (*bot*) having the top bent downward.
nutation *n* nodding; the periodic vibratory movement of the axis of the earth; (*bot*) the turning of flowers towards the sun.—**nutational** *adj*.
nut-brown *adj* coloured like a ripe hazelnut.
nut case *n* (*sl*) a crazy or foolish person.
nutcracker *n* (usu *pl*) a tool for cracking nuts; a bird with speckled plumage.
nuthatch *n* a small climbing bird feeding on nuts.
nutmeg *n* the aromatic kernel produced by a tree, grated and used as a spice.
nutria *n* the fur or skin of the coypu, a South American beaver.
nutrient *n* a substance that nourishes. * *adj* promoting growth.
nutriment *n* nourishing food, nourishment.
nutrition *n* the act or process by which plants and animals take in and assimilate food in their systems; the study of the human diet.—**nutritional** *adj*.

nutritionist *n* a specialist who studies and advises on the human diet.
nutritious *adj* efficient as food; health-giving, nourishing.
nutritive *adj* serving as good. * *n* an article of food.—**nutritively** *adv*.
nuts *adj* (*inf*) very keen (on); (*inf*) crazy.
nuts and bolts *npl* (*inf*) the basic facts or details.
nutshell *n* the hard covering of a nut; a tiny receptacle; a compact way of expression.
nutting *n* nut-gathering.
nutty *adj* (**nuttier, nuttiest**) tasting of or containing nuts; (*sl*) very enthusiastic; (*sl*) crazy, mad, etc.
nux vomica *n* the fruit of an East Indian plant (*Strychnos Nux vomica*), which yields the deadly poison strychnine.
nuzzle *vti* to push (against) or rub with the nose or snout; to nestle, snuggle.
NV *abbr* = Nevada.
NW *abbr* = northwest, northwestern.
NWT *abbr* = Northwest Territories (of Canada).
NY *abbr* = New York.
nyctalopia *n* night blindness; the inability to see clearly except at night.
nyctitropism *n* (*bot*) the so-called sleep of plants, turning in certain direction at night.—**nyctitropic** *adj*.
nylon *n* any of numerous strong, tough, elastic, synthetic materials used esp in plastics and textiles; (*pl*) stockings made of nylon.
nymph *n* (*myth*) a spirit of nature envisaged as a maiden; (*poet*) a lovely young maiden; the chrysalis of an insect.—**nymphean** *adj*.
nymphet *n* a sexually desirable pre-adolescent girl.
nympho *n* (*pl* **nymphos**) (*inf*) a nymphomaniac.
nympholepsy *n* (*pl* **nympholepsies**) frenzy caused by desire of the unattainable.
nympholept *n* one inspired by violent enthusiasm for an ideal.—**nympholeptic** *adj*.
nymphomania *n* uncontrollable sexual desire in women.—**nymphomaniac** *adj, n*.—**nymphomaniacal** *adj*.
nystagmus *n* a condition of the eye, with spasmodic movement of the eyeballs.—**nystagmic** *adj*.
NZ *abbr* = New Zealand.

O

O, o *n* the 15th letter of the English alphabet; something shaped like the letter O; nought, nothing, zero. nothing, zero.
O., o. *abbr* = octavo; old; only.
O (*chem symbol*) oxygen. * *interj* an exclamation of wonder, pain, etc.
O' *prefix* (in *Irish surnames*) descendant of.
o' *prep* (*inf, arch*) short for *of* or *on*.
-o *n, adj suffix* (*inf*) indicating a diminutive, *cheapo;* (*inf*) forming an interjection, *cheerio*.
oaf *n* (*pl* **oafs**) a loutish or stupid person.—**oafish** *adj*.—**oafishly** *adv*
oak *n* a tree with a hard durable wood, having acorns as fruits.
oak apple *n* a spongy excrescence growing on the leaves or young branches of the oak, caused by the gallfly.
oaken *adj* made of or consisting of oak.
oakum *n* a loose fibre obtained by unpicking old rope and used for caulking.
O & M *abbr* = organization and method(s).
OAP *abbr* = (*Brit*) Old age pensioner, senior citizen.
oar *n* a pole with a flat blade for rowing a boat; an oarsman.
oarlock *n* (*US*) a rowlock.
oarsman *n* (*pl* **oarsmen**) a person who rows a boat.—**oarsmanship** *n*.
OAS *abbr* = Organization of American States.
oasis *n* (*pl* **oases**) a fertile place in a desert; a refuge.
oast *n* a kiln for drying hops or barley.
oatcake *n* a thin broad cake of oatmeal.
oaten *adj* made of oats.
oath *n* (*pl* **oaths**) a solemn declaration to a god or a higher authority that one will speak the truth or keep a promise; a swear word; a blasphemous expression.
oatmeal *n* ground oats; a porridge of this; a pale greyish-brown colour.
oats *npl* a cereal grass widely cultivated for its edible grain; the seeds.
OAU *abbr* = Organization of African Unity.
ob. *abbr* = (*Latin*) *obiit*, died.
ob- *prefix* before, against, toward, in front of, reversed.
obbligato *adj* (*mus*) forming an integral part of a musical composition. * *n* (*pl* **obbligatos, obbligati**) an indispensable instrumental part or accompaniment written especially for the instrument named.—*also* **obligato** (*pl* **obligatos, obligati**).
obcordate *adj* (*bot*) inversely cordate.
obdurate *adj* hard-hearted; unyielding, stubborn.—**obduracy** *n*.—**obdurately** *adv*.
OBE *abbr* = Order of the British Empire.
obeah *see* **obi.**
obedience *n* the condition of being obedient; observance of orders, instructions, etc; respect for authority.
obedient *adj* obeying; compliant; submissive to authority, dutiful.—**obediently** *adv*.
obeisance *n* a bow or curtsey; an act of reverence or homage.
obelisk *n* a four-sided tapering pillar usu with a pyramidal top; a reference mark used in printing (†) (—*also* **dagger**).
obelize *vt* to mark with an obelus.
obelus *n* (*pl* **obeli**) a mark (— *or* ÷ *or* †) used in old MSS to indicate a doubtful or spurious reading; in modern writing, a break (—).
obese *adj* very fat.—**obesity** *n*.
obey *vti* (**obeying, obeyed**) to carry out (orders, instructions); to comply (with); to submit (to).
obfuscate *vt* to bewilder or confuse, to darken.—**obfuscation** *n*.
OB-GYN *abbr* = obstetrician and gynaecologist.
obi[1] *n* (*pl* **obis, obi**) a Japanese woman's sash.
obi[2] *n* (*pl* **obis**) in the West Indes and Africa, a system of secret sorcery or magical rites.—*also* **obeah.**
obit *n* (*inf*) an obituary.
obiter dictum *n* (*pl* **obiter dicta**) (*Latin*) a casual remark or opinion expressed incidentally, as by a judge or writer.
obituary *n* (*pl* **obituaries**) an announcement of a person's death, often with a short biography.—**obituarist** *n*.
object *n* something that can be recognized by the senses; a person or thing toward which action, feeling, etc, is directed; a purpose or aim; (*gram*) a noun or part of a sentence governed by a transitive verb or a preposition. * *vti* to state or raise an objection; to oppose; to disapprove.—**objector** *n*.
object ball *n* (*billiards*) the ball meant to be hit by the cue ball.
object glass *n* the lens of a microscope or telescope nearest to the object to be observed and forming the image.
objectify *vt* (**objectifying, objectified**) to render objective; to embody; to materialize.—**objectification** *n*.
objection *n* the act of objecting; a ground for, or expression of, disapproval.
objectionable *adj* causing an objection; disagreeable.—**objectionably** *adv*.
objective *adj* relating to an object; not influenced by opinions or feelings; impartial; having an independent existence of its own, real; (*gram*) of, or appropriate to an object governed by a verb or a preposition. * *n* the thing or placed aimed at; (*gram*) the objective case.—**objectively** *adv*.
objectivism *n* (*philos*) the doctrine that the knowledge of the non-ego is anterior to that of the ego; (*art, literature*) the representation of persons and incidents as they really appear.—**objectivist** *adj, n*.—**objectivistic** *adj*.

objectivity *n* the state or quality of being objective.
object lesson *n* a convincing practical illustration of some principle.
object program *n* (*comput*) a computer program derived from the conversion of a source program into machine code by a compiler or assembler.
objet d'art *n* (*pl* **objets d'art**) a small decorative object.
objurgate *vt* to chide or reprove, to scold.—**objurgation** *n*.
objurgatory *adj* containing reproof or censure.
oblanceolate *adj* (*bot*) lanceolate in the reversed order.
oblate[1] *n* (*RC Church*)a secular priest who has devoted himself and his property to the monastery he has entered. *adj* dedicated to a monastic or religious life.
oblate[2] *adj* (*spheroid*) depressed or flattened at the poles; orange-shaped.
oblation *n* an offering or sacrifice; anything presented in religious worship, esp the Eucharist.—**oblatory, oblational** *adj*.
obligate *vt* to bind by a contract, promise, sense of duty, etc.
obligation *n* the act of obligating; a moral or legal requirement; a debt; a favour; a commitment to pay a certain amount of money; the amount owed under such an obligation.
obligato *see* **obbligato.**
obligatory *adj* binding, not optional; compulsory.
oblige *vt* to compel by moral, legal, or physical force; (*person*) to make grateful for some favour; to do a favour for.
obligee *n* (*law*) a person in whose favour a bond is made; a creditor.
obliging *adj* ready to do favours, agreeable.—**obligingly** *adv*.
obligor *n* (*law*) a person who is bound by a bond; a debtor.
oblique *adj* slanting, at an angle; diverging from the straight; indirect, allusive. * *n* an oblique line.—**obliquely** *adv*.
oblique angle *n* an angle greater or less than a right angle.
oblique case *n* (*gram*) any case except the nominative and vocative.
obliquity *n* (*pl* **obliquities**) obliqueness; a slanting direction; deviation from a moral code.
obliterate *vt* to wipe out, to erase, to destroy.—**obliteration** *n*.
oblivion *n* a state of forgetting or being forgotten; a state of mental withdrawal.
oblivious *adj* forgetful, unheeding; unaware (of).
oblong *adj* rectangular. * *n* any oblong figure.
obloquy *n* (*pl* **obloquies**) reproachful language, detraction; calumny; slander, disgrace.
obnoxious *adj* objectionable; highly offensive.—**obnoxiously** *adv*.—**obnoxiousness** *n*.
oboe *n* an orchestral woodwind instrument having a mouthpiece with a double reed.—**oboist** *n*.
obolus, obol *n* (*pl* **oboli, obols**) an ancient Greek silver coin; a modern Greek weight = 1/10th of a gram.
obovate *adj* (*bot*) inversely ovate.
obs *abbr* = observation; obsolete.
obscene *adj* indecent, lewd; offensive to a moral or social standard.—**obscenely** *adv*.
obscenity *n* (*pl* **obscenities**) the state or quality of being obscene; an obscene act, word, etc.
obscurant *adj, n* (a person) opposed to enlightenment, reactionary.—**obscurantism** *n*.—**obscurantist** *adj, n*.
obscure *adj* not clear; dim; indistinct; remote, secret; not easily understood; inconspicuous; unimportant, humble. * *vt* to make unclear, to confuse; to hide.—**obscurely** *adv*.
obscurity *n* (*pl* **obscurities**) the state or quality of being obscure; an obscure thing or person.
obsequies *npl* (*sing* **obsequy**) funeral rites, a funeral.
obsequious *adj* subservient; fawning.—**obsequiously** *adv*.
observable *adj* worthy of observation; remarkable.—**observably** *adv*.
observance *n* the observing of a rule, duty, law, etc; a ceremony or religious rite.
observant *adj* watchful; attentive, mindful.—**observantly** *adv*.
observation *n* the act or faculty of observing; a comment or remark; careful noting of the symptoms of a patient, movements of a suspect, etc prior to diagnosis, analysis or interpretation.—**observational** *adj*.—**observationally** *adv*.
observatory *n* (*pl* **observatories**) a building for astronomical observation; an institution whose primary purpose is making such observations.
observe *vt* to notice; to perceive; (*a law, etc*) to keep to or adhere to; to arrive at as a conclusion; to examine scientifically. * *vi* to take notice; to make a comment (on).—**observable** *adj*.
observer *n* a person who observes; a delegate who attends a formal meeting but may not take part; an expert analyst and commentator in a particular field.
obsess *vt* to possess or haunt the mind of; to preoccupy.—**obsessive** *adj, n*.—**obsessively** *adv*.
obsession *n* a fixed idea, often associated with mental illness; a persistent idea or preoccupation; the condition of obsessing or being obsessed.
obsidian *n* a hard glassy dark-coloured volcanic lava.
obsolescent *adj* becoming obsolete, going out of date.—**obsolescence** *n*.
obsolete *adj* disused, out of date.
obstacle *n* anything that hinders something; an obstruction.
obstetrics *n sing* the branch of medicine concerned with the care and treatment of women during pregnancy and childbirth.—**obstetric, obstetrical** *adj*.—**obstetrician** *n*.
obstinate *adj* stubborn, self-willed; intractable; persistent.—**obstinacy** *n*.—**obstinately** *adv*.
obstreperous *adj* unruly, turbulent, noisy.
obstruct *vt* to block with an obstacle; to impede; to prevent, hinder; to keep (light, etc) from.
obstruction *n* that which obstructs; the act or an example of obstructing; a hindrance, obstacle.
obstructionism *n* the systematic hindering of political business, etc.—**obstructionist** *adj, n*.
obstructive *adj* tending to obstruct; preventing, hindering.—**obstructively** *adv*.—**obstructiveness** *n*.
obtain *vt* to get, to acquire, to gain. * *vi* to be prevalent, hold good.—**obtainable** *adj*.—**obtainment** *n*.
obtect *adj* (*pupa*) protected by a hard outer case.
obtrude *vti* to push (an opinion, oneself) on others uninvited; to intrude.—**obtruding** *adj*.
obtrusion *n* the act of obtruding; an unwelcome intrusion.
obtrusive *adj* apt to obtrude, pushy; protruding, sticking out.—**obtrusively** *adv*.—**obtrusiveness** *n*.
obtund *vt* (*med*) to blunt, to deaden.
obturate *vt* to stop, to block or seal up; (*gun breech*) to close.—**obturation** *n*.—**obturator** *n*.
obtuse *adj* mentally slow; not pointed; dull, stupid; (*geom*) greater than a right angle.—**obtusely** *adv*.—**obtuseness** *n*.
obverse *n* the front or top side; (*coin*) the head; a counterpart. * *adj* facing the viewer; with the top wider than the base.—**obversely** *adv*.
obversion *n* (*logic*) the immediate inference by which we deny the opposite of anything affirmed.
obvert *vt* (*logic*) to infer by obversion; to turn toward, to face.
obviate *vt* to make unnecessary; (*danger, difficulty*) to prevent, clear away.—**obviation** *n*.
obvious *adj* easily seen or understood; evident.—**obviously** *adv*.—**obviousness** *n*.
obvolute *adj* arranged so as to overlap, as the margins of an organ or part of a plant.
oc- *prefix* the form of *ob-* before *c*.
ocarina *n* an egg-shaped wind instrument played like a flute.
occasion *n* a special occurrence or event; a time when something happens; an opportunity; reason or grounds; a subsidiary cause. * *vt* to cause; to bring about.
occasional *adj* infrequent, not continuous; intermittent; produced for an occasion; (*a cause*) incidental.
occasionalism *n* (*philos*) the Cartesian theory of occasional causes, that bodily actions are caused and controlled by divine agency and not by

the human will. The Cartesian doctrine that apparent action of mind on matter is due to the invervention of God.

occasionally *adv* intermittently; now and then; infrequently.

occident *n* the west; (*with cap*) specifically Europe and America; the countries west of Asia and Turkey in Europe.—**Occidental, occidental** *adj*.

occipital *adj* of or pertaining to the occiput.

occiput *n* (*pl* **occipita, occiputs**) (*anat*) the back part of the skull or head.

occlude *vti* to shut out or in; to stop up, close; (*chem*) to absorb and retain.

occluded front *n* (*meteorol*) the phenomenon formed by a cold front overtaking a warm front and lifting the warm air above the earth's surface.

occlusion *n* the act of occluding; (*dentistry*) the position of the teeth when the jaws are closed; an occluded front.

occult *adj* supernatural, magical; secret.—*also n*.

occultation *n* (*astron*) a temporary disappearance or obscuration, as the eclipse of a star or planet by the moon, etc.

occulted *adj* (*astron*) hidden from the vision, as a star, etc.

occultism *n* mysticism, spiritualism, theosophy, etc.—**occultist** *n*.

occult sciences *npl* magic, alchemy and astrology.

occupancy *n* (*pl* **occupancies**) the act of taking and holding in possession; the time of possession.

occupant *n* a person who occupies, resides in, holds a position or place, etc.

occupation *n* the act of occupying; the state of being occupied; employment or profession; a pursuit.—**occupational** *adj*.

occupational therapy *n* therapy by means of work in the arts and crafts, to aid recovery from disease or injury.—**occupational therapist** *n*.

occupier *n* an occupant.

occupy *vt* (**occupying, occupied**) to live in; (*room, office*) to take up or fill; (*a position*) to hold; to engross (one's mind); (*city, etc*) to take possession of.

occur *vi* (**occurring, occurred**) to happen; to exist; to come into the mind of.

occurrence *n* a happening, an incident, an event; the act or fact of occurring.

ocean *n* a large stretch of sea, esp one of the earth's five oceans; a huge quantity or expanse.

oceangoing *adj* (*vessel*) designed and equipped for travelling on the open ocean.

oceanarium *n* (*pl* **oceanariums, oceanaria**) a large seawater aquarium for displays of marine life.

Oceania *n* the Pacific islands.—**Oceanic** *adj*.

oceanic *adj* of or relating to the ocean; formed or found in the ocean.

Oceanid *n* (*pl* **Oceanids, Oceanides**) (*Greek myth*) a sea nymph.

oceanography *n* the study of the oceans including their physical and chemical make-up, marine biology, and their exploitation.—**oceanographer** *n*.

ocellate, ocellated *adj* marked with small spots or eyes.

ocellus *n* (*pl* **ocelli**) the facet of a compound eye; an eye-like spot, as on a peacock's tail, etc.

ocelot *n* a medium-sized spotted wildcat of North and South America.

och *interj* (*Scot, Irish*) expressing of surprise, contempt, disagreement, disappointment, etc.

ocher, ochre *n* a yellow to orange-coloured clay used as a pigment.

ochlo-, ochl- *prefix* mob.

ochlocracy *n* (*pl* **ochlocracies**) mob rule.—**ochlocrat** *n*.—**ochlocratic** *adj*.

o'clock *adv* indicating the hour; indicating a relative direction or position, twelve o'clock being directly ahead or above.

OCR *abbr* = optical character reader; optical character recognition.

Oct *abbr* = October.

octa- *prefix* eight.

octachord *n* an eight-stringed musical instrument; a series of eight notes, diatonic scale.—**octachordal** *adj*.

octad *n* a group of eight; the number eight; (*chem*) an element or radical with a valency of eight.—**octadic** *adj*.

octagon *n* a plane figure having eight equal sides.—**octagonal** *adj*.

octahedral *adj* having eight equal sides.

octahedron *n* (*pl* **octahedrons, octahedra**) a solid figure contained by eight equal equilateral triangles.

octal *n* (*comput*) a number system with 8 as its base, one digit being equivalent to three bits.

octameter *n* an eight-foot verse.

octane *n* a hydrocarbon found in petrol.

octane number, octane rating *n* a measure of the anti-knock quality of a liquid motor fuel expressed as a percentage.

octant *n* the eighth part of a circle; an instrument for measuring angles; (*astron*) an aspect of two planets, etc, when 45 degrees apart.

octave *n* (*mus*) the eighth full tone above or below a given tone, the interval of eight degrees between a tone and either of its octaves, or the series of tones within this interval.

octavo *n* (*pl* **octavos**) a sheet of printing paper folded in eight leaves or 16 pages (8 vo); this size, average 9 1/2 × 6 ins). * *adj* having eight leaves or 16 pages to the sheet.

octennial *adj* recurring every eighth year; continuing eight years.—**octennially** *adv*.

octet, octette *n* a group of eight (performers, lines of a sonnet); a composition for eight instruments or voices.

octillion *n* the eighth power of a million (1 with 48 ciphers; in US and France, the ninth power of a thousand (1 with 27 ciphers).—**octillionth** *adj*.

octo- *prefix* eight.

October *n* the tenth month of the year, having 31 days.

octodecimo *adj* consiting of 18 leaves or 36 pages to a sheet. * *n* (*pl* **octodecimos**) a book of such size (18 mo).

octogenarian *n* a person who is in his or her eighties.

octopod *n* an animal with eight feet; an eight-armed mollusc.—*also adj*.

octopus *n* (*pl* **octopuses, octopi**) a mollusc having a soft body and eight tentacles covered with suckers.

octoroon *n* the offspring of a white person and a quadroon.

octosyllable *n* a word or verse of eight syllables.—**octosyllabic** *adj*.

octroi *n* in France and Belgium, a tax levied upon articles brought into the gates of a city; duty on goods.

octuple *adj* eight-fold.

ocular *adj* of, by, or relating to the eye; resembling an eye in form or function.

oculist *n* (*formerly*) an opththalmologist.

OD *n* (*inf*) an overdose of a drug, esp a narcotic. * *vi* (**OD'ing, OD'd**) to take an overdose.

od *n* a hypothetical natural force once used to explain magnetism, mesmerism, etc.

odalisque, odalisk *n* a female slave or concubine in the harem of a sultan; (*art*) the depiction of a woman in eastern garments reclining.

odd *adj* eccentric; peculiar; occasional; not divisible by two; with the other of the pair missing; extra or left over. * *npl* probability; balance of advantage in favour of one against another; excess of one number over another, esp in betting; likelihood; disagreement; strife; miscellaneous articles, scraps.—**oddly** *adv*.—**oddness** *n*.

oddball *n* (*sl*) an eccentric person. * *adj* bizarre.

Odd Fellow *n* a member of the order of the benevolent society of the Odd Fellows, a friendly society similar to freemasons.

oddity *n* (*pl* **oddities**) the state of being odd; an odd thing or person; peculiarity.

odd man out *n* a person left when others pair off.

oddment *n* an odd piece left over, esp of fabric.

odds and ends *npl* miscellaneous articles, scraps.

odds-on *adj* (*horse, etc*) (judged to be) having a better than even chance of winning; likely to happen, succeed, win, etc.

ode *n* a lyric poem marked by lofty feeling and dignified style.

odeum *n* (*pl* **odeums, odea**) a hall for musical performances.

odious *adj* causing hatred or offence; disgusting.—**odiously** *adv*.—**odiousness** *n*.
odium *n* general dislike.
odometer *n* an instrument attached to the axle of a vehicle to measure the distance it travels.
odonto-, odont-*prefix* tooth.
odontoglossum *n* a tropical orchid.
odontoid *adj* tooth-shaped, tooth-like.
odontology *n* dental science.—**odontological** *adj*.—**odontologist** *n*.
odor *n* smell; scent; aroma; a characteristic or predominant quality.—*also* **odour.**
odoriferous *adj* diffusing fragrance; (*sl*) smelly.
odorless *adj* without odour.
odorous *adj* having or emitting a scent; smelly; fragrant.
odour *see* **odor.**
odyssey *n* (*pl* **odysseys**) a long adventurous journey; an intellectual or spiritual quest.
Oe (*symbol*) oersted.
OECD *abbr* = Organization for Economic Cooperation and Development.
oecumenical *adj* a rare spelling of **ecumenical.**
OED *abbr* = Oxford English Dictionary.
oedema *n* (*pl* **oedemata**) a swelling in a body or plant caused by excess fluid.—*also* **edema.**—**oedematous** *adj*.
Oedipus complex *n* (*psychoanal*) a complex arising from the relationship of a son to his parents.
oeil de boeuf *n* a small round or oval window in the roof or frieze of a large building.
oeillade *n* a suggestive glance or ogle.
oeno-, oen- *prefix* wine.
oenology *n* the science of wines.—*also* **enology.**—**oenological, enological** *adj*.—**oenologist, enologist** *n*.
o'er *prep, adv* (*poet*) over.
oersted *n* the cgs unit of magnetic field strength.
oesophagus *n* (*pl* **oesophagi**) that part of the alimentary canal that takes food, etc, from the pharynx to the stomach.—*also* **esophagus.**
oestrogen *n* a hormone that develops and maintains female characteristics of the body.—*also* **estrogen.**
oestrus, oestrum *n* violent desire, frenzy; the period of ovulation of mammals, heat.—**oestrous** *adj*.—*also* **estrus, estrum.**
oeuvre *n* (*pl* **oeuvres**) a work of art, literature, music, etc; the life's work of an artist, writer or composer.
of *prep* from; belonging or relating to; concerning; among; by; during; owing to.
of- *prefix* the form of *ob-* before *f*.
off *adv* away, from; detached, gone; unavailable; disconnected; out of condition; entirely. * *prep* away from; not on. * *adj* distant; no longer operating; cancelled; (*food or drink*) having gone bad; on the right-hand side; (*runners, etc*) having started a race.
offal *n* the entrails of an animal eaten as food.
offbeat *adj* unconventional, eccentric.
off-Broadway *adj* denoting a type of small scale, experimental and generally noncommercial theatre situated outside theatrical Broadway in New York.
off-colour *adj* unwell; risqué.
offend *vt* to affront, displease; to insult. * *vi* to break a law.—**offender** *n*.
offense, offence *n* an illegal action, crime; a sin; an affront, insult; a cause of displeasure or anger.
offensive *adj* causing offence; repulsive, disagreeable; insulting; aggressive. * *n* an attack; a forceful campaign for a cause, etc.—**offensively** *adv*.—**offensiveness** *n*.
offer *vt* to present for acceptance or rejection; to show willingness (to do something); to present for consideration; to bid; (*a prayer*) to say. * *vi* to present itself; to declare oneself willing. * *n* something offered; a bid or proposal.
offering *n* a gift, present; a sacrifice.
offertory *n* (*pl* **offertories**) (*Anglican Church*) the sentences read in the Communion service during the collection of the alms; the alms collecting; (*RC Church*) an anthem chanted during Mass while the priest prepares the elements. a church collection; the part of the service when it is taken.
offhand *adv* impromptu; without thinking. * *adj* inconsiderate; curt, brusque; unceremonious.
office *n* a room or building where business is carried out; the people there; (*with cap*) the location, staff, of authority of a Government department, etc; a task or function; a position of authority; a duty; a religious ceremony, rite.
officer *n* an official; a person holding a position of authority in a government, business, club, military services, etc; a policeman.
official *adj* of an office or its tenure; properly authorized; formal. * *n* a person who holds a public office.—**officially** *adv*.
officialdom *n* a body of officials.
officialese *n* the jargon of official documents or as expressed by officials.
officiant *n* an officiating clergyman.
officiate *vi* to conduct a ceremony; to act in an official capacity; to perform the functions of a priest, minister, rabbi, etc.
officious *adj* interfering, meddlesome; offering unwanted advice.—**officiously** *adv*.—**officiousness** *n*.
offing *n* the near or foreseeable future.
offish *adj* (*inf*) distant, stiff.
off-key *adj* sung or played in the wrong key; out of tune; out of step.
off-licence *n* in UK, a licence to sell alcohol for consumption off the premises; a place so licensed (—*also* **liquor store, package store**).
off-line *adj* (*comput*) not connected to the central processor; disconnected.
off-load *vt* to unload; to get rid off.
off-piste *adj* pertaining to skiing in areas away from the normal runs.
offprint *n* a separately printed copy or part of a publication.
off-putting *adj* discouraging, daunting.
off-roading *n* the sport or hobby of driving on dirt tracks or other rugged terrain.—**off-roader** *n*.
offscourings *npl* refuse, dregs.
offset *vt* (**offsetting, offset**) to compensate for, counterbalance. * *n* compensation; a method of printing in which an image is transferred from a plate to a rubber surface and then to paper; a sloping ledge on the face of a wall.
offset printing *n* printing in which the impression is transferred from a plate to a rubber surface and then to paper.
offshoot *n* a branch or shoot growing from the main stem; something derivative.
offshore *adv* at sea some distance from the shore.
offside *adj, adv* illegally in advance of the ball.
offspring *n* a child, progeny; a result.
offstage *adj, adv* out of sight of the audience; behind the scenes.
off-the-peg *adj* (*clothes*) produced ready to wear in standard sizes.
off-the-wall *adj* (*sl*) innovative, unusual, unexpected.
off-white *n, adj* (a) white tinged with yellow or grey.
oft *adv* (*poet*) often.
often *adv* many times, frequently.
ogdoad *n* eight, a set of eight.
ogee *n* an architectural wave-like moulding shaped like an S.
Ogen melon *n* a type of small melon similar to a cantaloupe with sweel orange flesh.
ogham, ogam *n* an ancient British alphabet, the letters formed by notches; a character in it.
ogive *n* a diagonal groin of a vault; a pointed arch.—**ogival** *adj*.
ogle *vti* (**ogling, ogled**) to gape at; to make eyes at; to look at lustfully.—**ogler** *n*.
Ogpu *n* the secret police of Soviet Russia (1923–34).
ogre *n* a man-eating giant; a hideous person.
OH *abbr* = Ohio.

oh *interj* expressing surprise, delight, pain, etc.
ohm *n* a unit of electrical resistance.
ohmmeter *n* an instrument for measuring electrical resistance.
oho *interj* an exclamation of surprise.
-oid *suffix* like, as in *spheroid*.
oil *n* any of various greasy, combustible liquid substances obtained from animal, vegetable, and mineral matter; petroleum; an oil painting; (*pl*) paint mixed by grinding a pigment in oil * *vt* to smear with oil, lubricate.—**oiled** *adj*.
oilcake *n* a cattle food of linseed.
oilcan *n* a container with a long spout for releasing oil for lubricating in individual drops.
oilcloth *n* a waterproof fabric impregnated with oil or synthetic resin.
oil color *n* a colour in which oil is used as a vehicle for pigement.
oiler *n* an oilcan; a greaser.
oil field *n* an area on land or under the sea that produces petroleum.
oilman *n* (*pl* **oilmen**) a dealer in oils.
oil painting *n* a painting in oils; the art of painting in oils.
oil palm *n* an African palm whose fruit yields an edible oil.
oil rig *n* a drilling rig for extracting oil or natural gas.
oilskin *n* fabric made waterproof by treatment with oil; a waterproof garment of oilskin or a plastic-coated fabric.
oil slick *n* a mass of oil floating on the surface of water.
oil well *n* a well from which petroleum is extracted.
oily *adj* (**oilier, oiliest**) like or covered with oil; greasy; too suave or smooth, unctuous.—**oiliness** *n*.
oink *n* (*inf*) the grunt of a pig.—*also vi*.
ointment *n* a fatty substance used on the skin for healing or cosmetic purposes; a salve.
Oireachtas *n* the legislature of Ireland, consisting of the president, the Dáil Eireann (the Chamber of Deputies) and the Seanad Eireann (the Senate).
OK[1] *abbr* = Oklahoma.
OK[2], **okay** *adj*, *adv* (*inf*) all right; correct(ly). * *n* (*pl* **OK's, okays**) approval; * *vt* (**OK'ing, OK'ed** *or* **okaying, okayed**) to approve, sanction as OK.
okapi *n* (*pl* **okapis, okapi**) an African animal allied to the giraffe but smaller and with a shorter neck.
okay *see* **OK**.
okra *n* a tall annual plant yielding long seed-pods used as a vegetable.
old *adj* aged; elderly, not young; having lived or existed for a long time; long used, not new; former; of the past, not modern; experienced; worn out; of long standing.
Old Bailey *n* the central criminal court of England.
old boy *n* a former pupil of a school; (*inf*) a friendly form of address; an old person.—**old girl** *nf*.
old boy network *n* (*inf*) the monopoly of power by a privileged elite who attended the best public schools and universities.
Old Catholic *n* one of a body of Roman Catholics who refused to accept the dogma of papal infallibility (1870).
old country *n* the birthplace of an immigrant or an immigrant's ancestors.
olden *adj* relating to a bygone era.
Old English *n* the English language during the 7th to the 11th centuries.—*also* Anglo-Saxon.
Old English sheepdog *n* a breed of sheepdog with an extremely long shaggy coat.
old-fashioned *adj* out of date; in a fashion of an older time.
Old French *n* the French language from the 7th to the early 14th centuries.
Old Glory *n* the Stars and Stripes.
old gold *adj* of the colour of tarnished gold.
old guard *n* the (original) conservative elements within a political party or other organization.
old hat *adj* old-fashioned, cliched.
old lady *n* (*inf*) one's wife or mother.
old maid *n* (*derog*) a woman, esp an older woman who has never married; a prim, prudish, fussy person.
old man *n* (*inf*) father, husband; (*inf*) someone in charge, esp the captain of a ship.
old master *n* a painting by one of the best painters working in Europe in ther 16th and 17th centuries; one of these painters.
Old Nick *n* (*inf*) the Devil.
old school *n* supporters of traditional or conservative values and practices.
old school tie *n* a distinctive tie which indicates which school one attended; the elitism and solidarity use associated with British public schools and their products.
Old Style *n* the old mode of reckoning time acording to the Julian year of 365 and a quarter days.
Old Testament *n* the Christian designation for the Holy Scriptures of Judaism, the first of the two general divisions of the Christian Bible.
old-time *adj* of an earlier period; old-fashioned.
old-timer *n* an old man; a veteran; a person who has been in the same job, position, etc, for many years.
old wives' tale *n* a belief sustained by tradition, not accuracy.
Old World *n* Europe, Asia, and Africa.
old-world *adj* traditional, quaint; antiquated.
oleaginous *adj* oily; unctuous.
oleander *n* a poisonous evergreen shrub with handsome fragrant flowers.
oleaster *n* the wild olive; a yellow-flowered shrub like it.
oleate *n* a salt of oleic acid.
olefin, olefine *n* a ßhydrocarbon containing two atoms of hydrogen and one atom of carbon.—**olefinic** *adj*.
oleic *adj* obtained from oil.
oleic acid *n* an oily acid obtained from the saponiication of linseed and other oils, or in the making of soap.
olein *n* the pure liquid part of oil or fat.
oleo- *prefix* oil.
oleograph *n* a lithograph in oil colours.
olfactory *adj* relating to the sense of smell. * *n* (*pl* **olfactories**) (*usu pl*) an organ of smell.
olibanum *n* a gum resin used in incense; the frankincense of the ancients.
oligarch *n* a member of an oligarchy.
oligarchy *n* (*pl* **oligarchies**) government by a small group of people; the members of such a government; a state ruled in this way.—**oligarchic, oligarchical** *adj*.
oligo-, olig- *prefix* few, small.
Oligocene *n* (*geol*) a term used to denote certain strata intermediate between the Eocene and Miocene.
olio *n* (*pl* **olios**) a hotchpotch, a stew; a miscellany.
olivaceous *adj* olive-green.
olivary *adj* olive-shaped, oval.
olive *n* an evergreen tree cultivated for its edible hard-stoned fruit and oil; its fruit; a yellow-green colour. * *adj* of a yellow-green colour.
olive branch *n* a gesture of reconciliation of desire to make peace.
olive drab *n* the colour of the US service uniform.
olive oil *n* an edible yellow oil obtained from the fruit of the olive by pressing.
olivine *n* a variety of chrysolite.
olla podrida *n* a mixed stew or hash of meat and vegetables, a favourite Spanish dish; any incongruous mixture.
ology *n* (*pl* **ologies**) (*sl*) a branch of knowledge, a science.
Olympiad *n* in ancient Greece, the interval (four years) between the celebration of the Olympic games; a system of chronology reckoning from the first Olympiad, 776 bc.
Olympian *adj* of Olympus, home of the Greek gods; Olympic; stately; condescending. * *n* a great person.
Olympic *adj* pertaining to Olympia in Elis, where the Olympic games were celebrated.
Olympic Games *n sing or pl* an ancient athletic contest revived in 1896 as an international meeting held every four years in a different country.—*also* **Olympics**.

OM *abbr* = Order of Merit.

om *n* (*Hinduism*) the mystic name of the supreme being uttered when invoking Brahma; (*modern occultism*) spiritual essence, supreme truth and virtue.

-oma *n suffix* indicating a tumour.

omasum *n* (*pl* **omasa**) the third stomach of ruminant animals.

omber, ombre *n* an old card game for three players.

ombudsman *n* (*pl* **ombudsmen**) an official appointed to investigate citizens' or consumers' complaints.

omega *n* the last letter of the Greek alphabet.

omelet, omelette *n* eggs beaten and cooked flat in a pan.

omen *n* a sign or warning of impending happiness or disaster.

omentum *n* (*pl* **omenta, omentums**) (*anat*) the caul or adipose membrane attached to the stomach.

omerta *n* a conspiracy of silence, esp as practised by the Mafia.

omicron *n* the 15th letter of the Greek alphabet.

ominous *adj* relating to an omen; foreboding evil; threatening.—**ominously** *adv*.

omission *n* something that has been left out or neglected; the act of omitting.

omit *vt* (**omitting, omitted**) to leave out; to neglect to do, leave undone.

omni- *prefix* all; universally.

omnibus *n* (*pl* **omnibuses**) (*formal*) a bus; a book containing several works usu by one author.

omnifarious *adj* of all kinds.

omnipotent *adj* all-powerful, almighty; having very great power.—**omnipotence** *n*.

omnipresent *adj* present everywhere, uniquitous.—**omnipresence** *n*.

omniscient *adj* knowing all things.—**omnisciently** *adv*.—**omniscience** *n*.

omnium-gatherum *n* a miscellaneous collection of persons or things.

omnivore *n* an omniverous animal or person.

omnivorous *adj* eating any sort of food; taking in everything indiscriminately.

omophagic, omophagous *adj* eating raw flesh.—**omophagia** *n*.

omphalos *n* centre, hub; (*ancient Greece*) a boss on a shield.

on *prep* in contact with the upper surface of; supported by, attached to, or covering; directed toward; at the time of; concerning, about; using as a basis, condition or principle; immediately after; (*sl*) using; addicted to. * *adv* (so as to be) covering or in contact with something; forward; (*device*) switched on; continuously in progress; due to take place; (*actor*) on stage; on duty. * *adj* (*cricket*) designating the part of the field on the batsman's side in front of the wicket. * *n* (*cricket*) the on side.

onager *n* (*pl* **onagri, onagers**) the wild ass.

onanism *n* masturbation; coitus interruptus.—**onanist** *n, adj*.

once *adv* on one occasion only; formerly; at some time. * *conj* as soon as. * *n* one time.

once-over *n* a preliminary survey.

onco- *prefix* swelling, tumour.

oncology *n* the branch of medicine dealing with tumours.—**oncologist** *n*.

oncoming *adj* approaching.

one *adj* single; undivided, united; the same; a certain unspecified (time, etc). * *n* the first and lowest cardinal number; an individual thing or person; (*inf*) a drink; (*inf*) a joke. * *pron* an indefinite person, used to apply to many people; someone.

one-armed bandit *n* (*inf*) a slot machine for gambling, operated by pulling down a lever on its side.

one-horse *adj* (*sl*) paltry.

oneiro- *prefix* dream.

one-liner *n* (*inf*) a brief joke or witty comment.

oneness *n* unity, singleness, concord.

one-night stand *n* a performance given for one night only in a certain place; (*inf*) (a partner in) a sexual liaison that lasts one night only.

one-off *n, adj* (*Brit*) (something) performed or made only once.

onerous *adj* oppressive, burdensome; troublesome.

oneself *pron reflex form of* one.

one-sided *adj* favouring one side; unequal.

one-time *adj* sometime, former.

one-track *adj* with a single line of rails; with room for only one idea at a time.

one-upmanship *n* the skill of being one jump ahead of or going one better than someone or something else.

one-way *adj* (*traffic*) restricted to one direction; requiring no reciprocal action or obligation.

ongoing *adj* progressing, continuing.

onion *n* an edible bulb with a pungent taste and odour.

on-line *adj* referring to equipment that is connected to and controlled by the central processor of a computer.

onlooker *n* a spectator.

only *adj* alone of its kind; single, sole. * *adv* solely, merely; just; not more than. * *conj* except that, but.

onoma- *prefix* name.

onomastic *adj* of or pertaining to a name or names.

onomastics *n sing* the study of proper names.

onomatopoeia *n* the formation of a word to imitate a sound.—**onomatopoeic** *adj*.

onrush *n* a powerful rushing forwards.

onset *n* a beginning; an assault, attack.

onshore *adj, adv* towards the land; on land, not the sea.

onslaught *n* a fierce attack.

onto *prep* to a position on.

onto- *prefix* being.

ontogeny, ontogenesis *n* (*biol*) the history of the evolution of individual organisms.—**ontogenic, ontogenetic** *adj*.

ontology *n* (*philos*) the logic of pure being or reality; metaphysics.—**ontological** *adj*.—**ontologically** *adv*.

onus *n* (*pl* **onuses**) responsibility, duty; burden.

onward *adj* advancing, forward. * *adv* to the front, ahead, forward.

onwards *adv* onward.

onyx *n* a limestone similar to marble with layers of colour.

oo- *prefix* egg.

oodles *npl* (*sl*) an abundance.

oogamous *adj* heterogamous.

oogenesis *n* the formation of an ovum.—**oogenetic** *adj*.

ooh *interj* expressing surprise, delight, pain, etc.

oolite *n* a limestone composed of grains like the roe of a fish.—**oolitic** *adj*.

oology *n* the scientific study of birds' eggs; a treatise on birds' eggs.—**oological** *adj*.—**oologist** *n*.

oolong *n* a Chinese black tea the flavour of which resembles green tea.

oomiak *see* **umiak**.

oompah *n* an imitation of the deep sound of a brass instrument such as the tuba.

oomph *n* (*inf*) energy, verve; sex appeal.

oops *interj* expressing surprise or apology, esp when making a mistake.

oosperm *n* a fertilized ovum.

ootheca *n* (*pl* **oothecae**) the egg case of certain molluscs and insects containing the eggs.—**oothecal** *adj*.

ooze *vti* to flow or leak out slowly; to seep; to exude. * *n* soft mud or slime.

op. *abbr* = opera; operation; operator; optical; opposite; opus.

op- *prefix* form of *ob-* before *p*.

opacity *n* (*pl* **opacities**) the state of being opaque; obscurity.

opah *n* a bright-coloured sea fish like the mackerel, the kingfish.

opal *n* a white or bluish stone with a play of iridescent colours.

opalescent *adj* resembling opal in its reflection of light, iridescent.—**opalescence** *n*.

opaline *adj* pertaining to or resembling the opal.

opaque *adj* not letting light through; neither transparent nor translucent.—**opaquely** *adv*.—**opaqueness** *n*.

op. cit. *abbr* = (*Latin*) in the work cited.

OPEC *abbr* = Organization of Petroleum Exporting Countries.

open *adj* not closed; accessible; uncovered, unprotected; not fenced; free from trees; spread out, unfolded; public; lacking reserve; (*a person*) forthcoming; generous; readily understood; liable (to); unrestricted; (*syllable*) ending with a vowel; (*consonant*) made without stopping the stream of breath. * *vti* to make or become accessible; to unfasten; to begin; to expand, unfold; to come into view. * *n* a wide space; (*sport*) a competition that any player can enter.—**openness** *n*.

open air *n* outdoors.

open-and-shut *adj* easily solved; straightforward.

opencast mining *see* **strip mining.**

open-ended *adj* with no fixed limit of time or amount.

open-eyed *adj* vigilant.

opener *n* a device for opening cans or bottles.

openhanded *adj* generous.—**openhandedness** *n*.

openhearted *adj* responsive to emotional appeal, frank.—**openheartedness** *n*.

open-heart surgery *n* surgery on the heart whilst its function is performed temporarily by a heart-lung machine.

opening *n* a gap, aperture; a beginning; a chance; a job opportunity. * *adj* initial.

open letter *n* a letter addressed to an individual but published in a newspaper for all to see.

openly *adv* frankly; publicly.

open-minded *adj* unprejudiced.—**open-mindedness** *n*.

open-mouthed *adj* having the mouth open in surprise; gaping, expectant.

open secret *n* a supposed secret which is actually widely known.

open sesame *n* a way of getting into something usually inaccessible.

openwork *n* a pattern with interstices.

opera *n* a dramatic work represented through music and song; plural form of **opus.**

operable *adj* capable of being put into action, practicable; (*med*) capable of being operated upon.

opera bouffe *n* a comic or farcical opera.

opera glasses *n* a small binocular telescope used in theatres, etc.

opera hat *n* a man's collapsible top hat.

opera house *n* a theatre for opera.

operate *vi* to work, to function; to produce a desired effect; to carry out a surgical operation. * *vt* (*a machine*) to work or control; to carry on, run.

operatic *adj* of or relating to opera; exaggerated, overacting.

operating system *n* the software in a computer which controls basic operations such as accepting keyboard input, printing, file handling and displaying error messages.

operation *n* a method of operating; a procedure; a military action; a surgical procedure.

operational *adj* of or relating to an operation; functioning; ready for use; involved in military activity.—**operationally** *adv*.

operations research, operational research *n* the application of mathematical techniques to the analysis of business methods.

operative *adj* functioning; in force, effective; of, by surgery. * *n* a mechanic; a secret agent; a private detective.

operator *n* a person who operates or works a machine, esp a telephone switchboard; a person who owns or runs a business; a person who manipulates.

operculum *n* (*pl* **opercula, operculums**) (*biol*) a cap, lid, or cover; the plate closing the orifice of a univalve; a shell; the gill cover of a fish.—**opercular, operculate** *adj*.

operetta *n* a light opera.

ophidian *n* any of the Ophidia, an order of reptiles including the snakes.—*also adj*.

ophiology *n* that branch of natural history which treats of snakes.—**ophiological** *adj*.—**ophiologist** *n*.

ophite *n* serpentine marble.

ophthalmia *n* inflammation of the eye.

ophthalmic *adj* of, relating to, or situated near, the eye.

ophthalmo-, ophthalm- *prefix* eye or eyeball.

ophthalmology *n* the branch of medicine dealing with diseases of the eye.—**ophthalmologist** *n*.

ophthalmoscope *n* an instrument for examining the interior of the eye.

ophthalmoscopy *n* examination of the eye.—**ophthalmoscopic** *adj*.

-opia *n suffix* indicating a visual defect.

opiate *n* a narcotic drug that contains opium; something that induces sleep or calms feelings.

opine *vt* to hold or express the opinion (that).

opinicus *n* (*her*) a fabulous winged animal with the head and wings of a griffin, the body of a lion, and the tail of a camel.

opinion *n* a belief that is not based on proof; judgment; estimation, evaluation; a formal expert judgment; professional advice.

opinionated *adj* unduly confident in one's opinions, dogmatic.

opinionative *adj* fond of preconceived ideas; self-conceited.—**opinionatively** *adv*.

opium *n* a narcotic drug produced from an annual Eurasian poppy.

opossum *n* (*pl* **opossums, opossum**) a small nocturnal and arboreal marsupial.

oppidan *adj* urban, town-dwelling.

oppilate *vt* (*med*) to block up, to obstruct.—**oppilation** *n*.

opponent *n* a person who opposes another; an adversary, antagonist. * *adj* opposing.

opportune *adj* well-timed; convenient.—**opportunely** *adv*.

opportuneness *n* seasonableness.

opportunist *n* a person who forms or adapts his or her views or principles to benefit from opportunities; to seize opportunities as they may arise.—**opportunism** *n*.

opportunity *n* (*pl* **opportunities**) chance; a favourable combination of circumstances.

opposable *adj* that may be opposed.—**opposability** *n*.—**opposably** *adv*.

oppose *vt* to put in front of or in the way of; to place in opposition; to resist; to fight against; to balance against.—**opposer** *n*.

opposite *adj* placed on opposed sides of; face to face; diametrically different; contrary. * *n* a person or thing that is opposite; an antithesis. * *prep, adv* across from.

opposite number *n* a person in a corresponding position on the other side; a counterpart.

opposition *n* the act of opposing or the condition of being opposed; resistance; antithesis; hostility; a political party opposing the government; (*astron*) the diametrically opposite position of two heavenly bodies, when 180 degrees apart.

oppress *vt* to treat unjustly; to subjugate; to weigh down in the mind.—**oppressor** *n*.

oppression *n* the act of oppressing; the state of being oppressed; persecution; physical or mental distress.

oppressive *adj* tyrannical; burdensome; (*weather*) sultry, close.—**oppressively** *adv*.—**oppressiveness** *n*.

opprobrious *adj* abusive; infamous.

opprobrium *n* a reproach with disdain or contempt; disgrace, ignominy.

oppugn *vt* to reason against, to controvert; to resist.—**oppugnant** *adj, n*.—**oppugner** *n*.

opsonin *n* a chemical agent in blood serum, which makes bacteria vulnerable to phagocytic activity.—**opsonic** *adj*.

opt *vi* to choose, to exercise an option; (*with* **in**) to choose to participate in something; (*with* **out**) to choose not to participate in something.

optative *adj* (*gram*) expressing a desire or wish. * *n* an optative mood or form of a verb.

optic *adj* relating to the eye or sight. * *n* (*inf*) the eye; a device for dispensing a standard measure of spirits, etc.

optical *adj* of or relating to the eye or light; optic; aiding or correcting vision; visual.—**optically** *adv*.

optical character reader *n* a device that allows printed characters, figures, etc to be scanned and input to a computer, by a process of optical character recognition, the identification of printed text by photoelectric means.

optical disc *n* a compact disc used as a high-capacity storage medium for computers.

optical fiber *n* thin glass fiber through which light can be transmitted.

optician *n* a person who makes or sells optical aids.

optics *n sing* the branch of physics dealing with light and vision.

optimal *adj* optimum.—**optimally** *adv*.

optimism *n* a tendency to take the most cheerful view of things; hopefulness; the belief that good must ultimately prevail.—**optimist** *n*.—**optimistic** *adj*.—**optimistically** *adv*.

optimum *n* (*pl* **optima, optimums**) the best, most favourable condition.—*also adj*.

option *n* the act of choosing; the power to choose; a choice; the right to buy, sell or lease at a fixed price within a specified time.

optional *adj* left to choice; not compulsory.—**optionally** *adv*.

optometer *n* an instrument for measuring the limits of distinct vision.

opulent *adj* wealthy; luxuriant.—**opulence** *n*.

opuntia *n* any of a genus of cacti; the Indian fig.

opus *n* (*pl* **opuses, opera**) an artistic or literary work; a musical composition, esp any of the numbered works of a composer.

OR *abbr* = Oregon.

or[1] *conj denoting* an alternative; the last in a series of choices.

or[2] *n* (*her*) gold, denoted by small engraved dots.

ora *see* **os**[1].

orach, orache *n* mountain spinach.

oracle *n* a place in ancient Greece where a deity was consulted; the response given (often ambiguous); a wise adviser; sage advice.—**oracular** *adj*.

oral *adj* of the mouth; spoken, not written; (*drugs*) taken by mouth. * *n* a spoken examination.—**orally** *adv*.

oral history *n* the history of past events as recorded from interviews with people living at the time.

orange *n* a round, reddish-yellow, juicy, edible citrus fruit; the tree bearing it; its colour. * *adj* orange-coloured.

orangeade *n* a drink made with the juice of oranges.

Orangeman *n* (*pl* **Orangemen**) a member of an Irish protestant political party named after William of Orange.

orangery *n* (*pl* **orangeries**) a hothouse for the cultivation of oranges; an orange garden.

orange stick *n* a small thin pointed stick, orig orangewood, used in manicuring the nails.

orangutan, orangoutang *n* a large, long-armed, herbivorous anthropoid ape.

orate *vi* to make an oration; (*inf*) to hold forth.

oration *n* a formal or public speech.

orator *n* an eloquent public speaker.—**oratorical** *adj*.

oratorio *n* (*pl* **oratorios**) a sacred story set to music for voices and instruments.

oratory *n* (*pl* **oratories**) the art of public speaking; eloquence; a place for prayer.

orb *n* a sphere or globe; an ornamental sphere surmounted by a cross, esp as carried by a sovereign at a coronation.

orbicular, orbiculate, orbiculated *adj* orb-shaped, spherical.—**orbicularity** *n*.

orbit *n* (*astron*) a curved path along which a planet or satellite moves; a field of action or influence; the eye socket; (*physics*) the path of an electron around the nucleus of an atom. * *vti* to put (a satellite, etc) into orbit; to circle round.—**orbital** *adj*.

orc *n* a grampus; the killer whale; a sea monster.

orchard *n* an area of land planted with fruit trees.

orchestra *n* a group of musicians playing together under a conductor; their instruments; the space (or pit) in a theatre where they sit; the stalls of a theatre.—**orchestral** *adj*.

orchestrate *vt* to arrange music for performance by an orchestra; to arrange, organize to best effect.—**orchestration** *n*.—**orchestrator** *n*.

orchestrion *n* a large automatic barrel organ.

orchid *n* a plant with unusually shaped flowers in brilliant colours comprising three petals of uneven size.

orchil *n* a red or violet dye obtained from lichen; the lichen.—*also* **archil**.

orchis *n* a genus of wild orchid with curiously shaped roots and flowers.

orcinol, orcin *n* a substance obtained from lichens yielding dye.

ordain *vti* to confer holy orders upon; to appoint; to decree; to order, to command.—**ordainer** *n*.—**ordainment** *n*.

ordeal *n* a severe trial or test; an exacting experience.

order *n* arrangement; method; relative position; sequence; an undisturbed condition; tidiness; rules of procedure; an efficient state; a class, group, or sort; a religious fraternity; a style of architecture; an honour or decoration; an instruction or command; a rule or regulation; a state or condition, esp with regard to functioning; a request to supply something; the goods supplied; (*zool*) divisions between class and family or genus. * *vti* to put or keep (things) in order; to arrange; to command; to request (something) to be supplied.

ordered *adj* marked by regularity and discipline; being arranged or identifiable according to a rule; being labelled by ordinal numbers.

orderly *adj* in good order; well-behaved; methodical. * *n* (*pl* **orderlies**) a hospital attendant; a soldier attending an officer.—**orderliness** *n*.

ordinal *adj* showing position in a series. * *n* an ordinal number.

ordinal number *n* a number denoting its order in a sequence, as first, second, etc.

ordinance *n* a decree, a law; a rite.

ordinary *adj* normal, usual; common; plain, unexceptional.* *n* (*pl* **ordinaries**) a meal for all comers at fixed charges and a fixed time, an inn providing this; archbishop in province, bishop in diocese; prescribed form of service; an ecclesiastical judge; a prison chaplain; (*her*) that part of the escutcheon contained between straight and other lines / one of the simple charges.—**ordinarily** *adv*.

ordinary seaman *n* a seaman of the lowest rank, below able-bodied seaman

ordinate *n* (*geom*) one of the co-ordinates of a point; a straight line in a curve terminated on both sides by the curve and bisected by the diameter.

ordination *n* the act of ordaining or being ordained; admission to the ministry.

ordnance *n* military stores; artillery.

Ordovician *adj* (*geol*) of the period between the Cambrian and Silurian.

ordure *n* excrement; dung.

ore *n* a substance from which minerals can be extracted.

öre *n* (*pl* **öre**) a monetary unit in Sweden, (ø) Denmark and Norway.

oread *n* a mountain nymph (Greek).

Oreg. *abbr* = Oregon.

oregano *n* an aromatic herb whose leaves, either fresh of dried, are used to flavour food.

organ *n* a usu large and complex musical wind instrument with pipes, stops, and a keyboard; a part of an animal or plant that performs a vital or natural function; the means by which anything is done; a medium of information or opinion, a periodical.

organdy, organdie *n* (*pl* **organdies**) a light transparent, usu stiffened cotton fabric.

organ grinder *n* the player of a barrel organ.

organic *adj* of or relating to bodily organs; (disease) affecting a bodily organ; of, or derived from, living organisms; systematically arranged; structural; (*chem*) of the class of compounds that are formed from carbon; (vegetables, etc) grown without the use of artificial fertilizers or pesticides.—**organically** *adv*.

organism *n* an animal or plant, any living thing; an organized body.

organist *n* a person who plays an organ.

organization *n* the act or process of organizing; the state of being organized; arrangement, structure; an organized body or association.

organize *vt* to arrange in an orderly way; to establish; to institute; to persuade to join a cause, group, etc; to arrange for.—**organizer** *n*.

organogenesis *n* organic development.—**organogenetic** *adj*.—**organogenetically** *adv*.
organography *n* a scientific description of the organs of animals or plants.—**organographic** *adj*.
organology *n* that branch of physiology which treats of animal organs.—**organological** *adj*.—**organologist** *n*.
organon *n* (*pl* **organa, organons**) a body of rules for regulating scientific or philosophical investigation / a method of thought, a logical system.
organotherapy *n* the treatment of disease with organic extracts.
organzine *n* a strong silk thread of a very fine texture; a fabric made from it.
orgasm *n* the climax of sexual excitement.—**orgasmic** *adj*.
orgeat *n* a drink made of barley water flavoured with almonds.
orgy *n* (*pl* **orgies**) a wild party or gathering of people, with excessive drinking and indiscriminate sexual activity; over-indulgence in any activity.—**orgiastic** *adj*.
oriel *n* a projecting angular recess with a window; the window.
Orient *n* the East, or Asia, esp the Far East.
orient, orientate *vti* to adjust (oneself) to a particular situation; to arrange in a direction, esp in relation to the points of the compass; to face or turn in a particular direction.
oriental *adj* (*often cap*) of the Orient, its people or languages.
Orientalism *n* an idiom or custom characteristic of the East.
Orientalist *n* an expert in Oriental languages, history, etc.
orientation *n* arrangement; alignment; position relative to a compass direction; one's way of thinking or direction of interest.
orienteering *n* the sport of racing on foot over difficult country using a map and compass
orifice *n* an opening or mouth of a cavity.
oriflamme *n* the ancient royal standard of France, a red flag split at one end and forming flame-shaped streamers; a party symbol; a blaze of colour.
orig. *abbr* = origin; original(ly).
origami *n* the Japanese art of paper folding to make complicated shapes.
origin *n* the source or beginning of anything; ancestry or parentage.
original *adj* relating to the origin or beginning; earliest, primitive; novel; unusual; inventive, creative. * *n* an original work, as of art or literature; something from which copies are made; a creative person; an eccentric.—**originality** *n*.—**originally** *adv*.
original sin *n* the inherent tendency of mankind to sin, derived from Adam and imputed to his descendants.
originate *vti* to initiate or begin; to bring or come into being.—**origination** *n*.—**originator** *n*.
orinasal *adj* (*vowel*) sounded with both the mouth and nose.—*also n*.
oriole *n* kinds of yellow, black-winged bird.
orison *n* (*arch*) a prayer.
orle *n* (*her*) an ordinary in the form of a fillet round a shield; (*archit*) a fillet under the capital of a column.
Orlon *n* (*trademark*) an acrylic fibre.
orlop *n* the lowest deck of a ship with three or more decks.
ormer *n* a mollusc, sea ear.
ormolu *n* an imitation gold made of copper and tin alloy, used for decoration.
ornament *n* anything that enhances the appearance of a person or thing; a small decorative object. * *vt* to adorn, to decorate with ornaments.
ornamental *adj* serving as an ornament; decorative, not useful.—**ornamentally** *adv*.
ornamentation *n* the act or process of ornamenting; something that decorates.
ornate *adj* richly adorned; (*style*) highly elaborate.—**ornately** *adv*.—**ornateness** *n*.
ornery *adj* (*sl*) of a bad disposition, hard to manage.
ornitho-, ornith- *prefix* bird.
ornithology *n* the study of birds.—**ornithological** *adj*.—**ornithologically** *adv*.—**ornithologist** *n*.
ornithopter *n* an aircraft with flapping wings.
ornithorhynchus *n* an Australian genus of monotremes, including the platypus.
oro- *prefix* mountain.
orogeny, orogenesis *n* the formation of mountains.—**orogenic, orogenetic** *adj*.
orography, orology *n* the geography of mountains and mountain systems, their mapping, etc.—**orographic, orological** *adj*.
oroide *n* a gold-coloured alloy of tin and copper.
orotund *adj* (*voice*) full, resonant; (*style*) pompous, high-flown.
orphan *n* a child whose parents are dead. * *vt* to cause to become an orphan.—*also adj*.
orphanage *n* a residential institution for the care of orphans.
Orphean *adj* of or pertaining to Orpheus, the celebrated bard of Classic mythology, or his music; melodious, enchanting.
Orphic *adj* of Orpheus or his cult; mystical.
orphrey *n* an embroidered band or bands of gold or silver on the front of an ecclesiastical vestment from the neck downward, esp on a cope.
orpiment *n* a yellow compound of arsenic, used as a pigment.
orpine *n* a succulent plant with fleshy leaves and purple flowers.
orrery *n* (*pl* **orreries**) a moving model of the solar system, which illustrates by balls mounted on rods the motions, magnitudes, and positions of the planets.
orris *n* a kind of iris.
orrisroot *n* the dried roots of the Florentine orris, used in perfumery and medicine.
ortho- *prefix* straight, right, true.
orthocephalic, orthocephalous *adj* (*anat*) with a skull of medium proportions, between brachycephalic and dolichocephalic.
orthochromatic *adj* (*photog*) giving the correct relative tones to colours, isochromatic.
orthoclase *n* potash feldspar.
orthodontics *n sing* the branch of dentistry dealing with the correction of irregularities in the teeth.—**orthodontic** *adj*.—**orthodontist** *n*.
orthodox *adj* conforming with established behaviour or opinions; not heretical; generally accepted, conventional; (*with cap*) of or relating to a conservative political or religious group.
orthodoxy *n* (*pl* **orthodoxies**) the state or quality of being orthodox; an orthodox practice or belief.
orthoepy *n* the science of correct pronunciation.—**orthoepic** *adj*.—**orthoepist** *n*.
orthogenesis *n* evolution following a definite line, determinate variation.—**orthogenetic** *adj*.
orthognathous *adj* having an upright jaw, neither receding nor protruding.—**orthognathism** *n*.
orthogonal *adj* rectangular.—**orthogonally** *adv*.
orthography *n* (*pl* **orthographies**) the art of spelling and writing words with grammatical correctness; a map projection with a point of sight supposedly infinitely distant.—**orthographer** *n*.—**orthographic, orthographical** *adj*.
orthopedics, orthopaedics *n* the study and surgical treatment of bone and joint disorders.—**orthopedic** *adj*.—**orthopedist** *n*.
orthopteran *n* (*pl* **orthopterans, orthoptera**) any of the Orthoptera order of insects, having their two outer wings overlapping at the top when shut, as in grasshoppers.—**orthopterous** *adj*.
orthoptic *adj* of correct seeing. * *n* the peep-sight of a rifle.
orthotropism *n* vertical growth in plants.—**orthotropic** *adj*.—**orthotropous** *adj*.
ortolan *n* a small bird, allied to the bunting, much esteemed for its flesh.
oryx *n* (*pl* **oryxes, oryx**) a straight-horned African antelope.
OS *abbr* = ordinary seaman; Ordnance Survey (national mapping agency in the UK).
Os (*chem symbol*) osmium.
os[1] *n* (*pl* **ossa**) (*anat*) bone.
os[2] *n* (*pl* **ora**) (*anat*) the mouth.

Oscar *n* any of several small gold statuettes awarded annually by the US Academy of Motion Picture Arts and Sciences for outstanding achievements.
oscillate *vi* to swing back and forth as a pendulum; to waver, vacillate between extremes of opinion, etc.—**oscillation** *n*.
oscillator *n* a device for producing alternating current.
oscillatory *adj* swinging; vibrating.
oscilloscope *n* a device for viewing oscillations on a display screen of a cathode-ray tube.
osculate *vti* (*species*) to have features in common; (*geom*) to make contact (with); (*humorous*) to kiss, to touch.—**osculation** *n*.
osculatory *adj* pertaining to kissing. * *n* a tablet or board on which the picture of Christ or the Virgin Mary are painted for worshippers to kiss.
-ose *suffix* full of.
osier *n* a willow, the twigs of which are used in basket-making.
Osiris *n* the best loved of the Egyptian gods, husband of Iris and father of Horus.
-osis *n suffix* indicating a particular state, esp a diseased condition, *thrombosis;* increase, development of *fibrosis.*
Osmanli *adj* of or pertaining to the Ottoman Empire.—*also n*.
osmium *n* a hard bluish-white metallic element used in alloys.
osmometry *n* the measurement of smells.
osmosis *n* (*pl* **osmoses**) the percolation and intermixture of fluids separated by a porous membrane.—**osmotic** *adj*.—**osmotically** *adv*.
osmunda, osmund *n* the flowering fern of the genus Osmunda.
osnaburg *n* a coarse linen cloth.
osprey *n* (*pl* **ospreys**) a large fish-eating bird of prey.
ossa *see* **os**[2].
ossein *n* gelatinous tissue in bone.
osseous *adj* pertaining to, consisting of, or like, bone.
ossicle *n* a little bone, esp of the ear; (*pl*) hard structures of small size, as the calcareous plates of the starfish.—**ossicular** *adj*.
ossiferous *adj* producing or containing bone.
ossification *n* conversion of soft animal tissue into bone.
ossifrage *n* an old name for the osprey or lammergeier.
ossify *vb* (**ossifying, ossified**) *vt* to convert into bone or into a bone-like substance; to harden. * *vi* to become bone; to grow rigid and unprogressive.
ossuary *n* (*pl* **ossuaries**) an urn for bones.
osteal *adj* osseous.
osteitis *n* inflammation of the bone.
ostensible *adj* apparent; seeming; pretended.—**ostensibly** *adv*.
ostensive *adj* showing, exhibiting.
ostentation *n* a showy, pretentious display.—**ostentatious** *adj*.—**ostentatiously** *adv*.
osteo-, oste- prefix bone.
osteoarthritis *n* painful inflammation of the joints, esp the hips, knees and olhers that bear weight.—**osteoarthritic** *adj*.
osteology *n* that part of anatomy treating of bones, their structure, etc; a bony structure.—**osteological** *adj*.—**osteologist** *n*.
osteoma *n* (*pl* **osteomas, osteomata**) a bone tumour.
osteomalacia *n* softening of the bones.
osteomyelitis *n* an infectious disease causing inflammation of the bone marrow.
osteopathy *n* the treatment of disease by manipulation of the bones and muscles, often as an adjunct to medical and surgical measures.—**osteopath** *n*.
osteophyte *n* an abnormal growth from a bone.—**osteophytic** *adj*.
osteoplasty *n* (*pl* **osteoplasties**) surgery involving bone replacement and grafting.—**osteoplastic** *adj*.
osteoporosis *n* the development of brittle bones due to a calcium deficiency in the bone matrix.—**osteoporotic** *adj*.
osteotome *n* an instrument used in dissecting bones.—**osteotomy** *n*.
ostiary *n* (*pl* **ostiaries**) (*RC Church*) a church door-keeper.
ostler *n* (*formerly*) a man who attended to horses at an inn, a hostler.
ostracize *vt* to exclude, banish from a group, society, etc.—**ostracism** *n*.
ostrich *n* (*pl* **ostriches, ostrich**) a large, flightless, swift-running African bird.
Ostrogoth *n* an eastern Goth.
OT *abbr* = Old Testament.
otalgia *n* earache.
other *adj* second; remaining; different; additional. * *pron* the other one; some other one.
other-directed *adj* guided primarily by the influence or example of others.
otherness *n* diversity.
otherwhere *adv* (*arch*) elsewhere.
otherwhile *adv* (*arch*) at another time.
otherwise *adv* if not, or else; differently.
otherworldly *adj* spiritual; unworldly.—**otherworldliness** *n*.
otic *adj* of the ear.
otiose *adj* superfluous, serving no practical purpose; futile; at leisure.—**otiosity** *n*.
otitis *n* inflammation of the ear.
oto- *prefix* ear.
otolith *n* a chalky concretion in the ear.—**otolithic** *adj*.
otology *n* that part of anatomy which treats of the ear, its structure, etc.—**otological** *adj*.—**otologist** *n*.
otoscope *n* an instrument for examining the interior of the ear.
OTT *abbr* = over the top.
ottava rima *n* (*poet*) an Italian stanza of eight lines of five accents each with three rhymes, the seventh and eighth forming a couplet. A stanza of eight five-foot lines rhyming abababcc.
otter *n* (*pl* **otters, otter**) a fish-eating mammal with smooth fur and a flat tail.
ottoman *n* an upholstered, backless chair or couch. * *adj* (*with cap*) of or relating to a former Turkish dynasty and empire; Turkish.
oubliette *n* an underground dungeon with its entrance in the roof in which prisoners condemned to perpetual imprisonment or secret death were confined.
ouch[1] *interj* an exclamation of pain or annoyance.
ouch[2] *n* a clasp, a jewel; the setting of a gem.
ought[1] *aux vb* expressing obligation or duty; to be bound, to be obliged (to); a variant spelling of **aught**.
ought[2] *see* **aught**.
Ouija *n* (*trademark*) a board with letters and symbols used to obtain messages at seances.
ounce[1] *n* a unit of weight, equal to one sixteenth of a pound or 28.34 grams; one sixteenth of a pint, one fluid ounce.
ounce[2] *n* the snow leopard; (*poet*) the lynx or an animal like it.
our *poss adj, pron* relating or belonging to us.
ours *pron* belonging to us.
ourselves *pron* emphatic and reflexive form of we.
-ous *suffix* full of, as in *joyous*; (*chem*) containing in lower proportion, as in *ferrous* as opposed to *ferric*.
ousel *see* **ouzel**.
oust *vt* to eject, expel, esp by underhand means; to remove forcibly.
out *adv* not in; outside; in the open air; to the full extent; beyond bounds; no longer holding office; ruled out, no longer considered; loudly and clearly; no longer included (in a game, fashion, etc); in error; on strike; at an end; extinguished; into the open; published; revealed; (*radio conversation*) transmission ends. * *prep* out of; out through; outside. * *adj* external; outward. * *n* an exit; means of escape.
out- *prefix* out, outside, away from; external; separate; more, longer.
out-and-out *adj* thoroughgoing; absolute; complete.
outback *n* a remote area inland, esp in Australia.
outbalance *vt* to exceed in weight.
outbid *vt* (**outbidding, outbid,** *pp* **outbidden** *or* **outbid**) to bid higher than.
outboard *adj* (*engine*) outside a ship, etc. * *n* an engine attached to the outside of a boat.
outbrave *vt* to excel in bravery; to defy.

outbreak *n* a sudden eruption (of disease, strife, etc).
outbuilding *n* a detached subsidiary building.
outburst *n* a bursting out; a spurt; an explosion of anger, etc.
outcast *n* a person who is rejected by society.
outcaste *n* one who has lost caste, a pariah. * *vt* to expel from a caste.
outclass *vt* to surpass or excel greatly.
outcome *n* the result, consequence.
outcrop *n* an exposed rock surface. * *vi* (**outcropping, outcropped**) to crop out at the surface.
outcry *n* (*pl* **outcries**) protest; uproar.
outdated *n* obsolete, old-fashioned.
outdistance *vt* to get well ahead of.
outdo *vt* (**outdoing, outdid,** *pp* **outdone**) to surpass, to do more than, to excel.
outdoor *adj* existing, taking place, or used in the open air.
outdoors *adv* in or into the open air; out of doors. * *n* the open air, outside world.
outer *adj* further out or away.
outermost *adj* furthest out; most distant.
outer space *n* any region of space beyond the earth's atmosphere.
outface *vt* to stare down or out of countenance; to defy.
outfall *n* the lower end of a watercourse; a point of discharge.
outfield *n* the outer part of a cricket or baseball field.
outfit *n* the equipment used in an activity; clothes worn together, an ensemble; a group of people associated in an activity. * *vt* (**outfitting, outfitted**) to provide with an outfit or equipment.
outfitter *n* a supplier of equipment or clothes.
outflank *vt* to get round the side of (an enemy); to circumvent.
outflow *n* a flowing out; something that flows out.
outfox *vt* to outwit by superior cunning.
outgeneral *vt* to outdo in strategy.
outgo *vt* (**outgoing, outwent,** *pp* **outgone**) to go beyond; to surpass.
outgoing *adj* departing; retiring; sociable, forthcoming. * *n* an outlay; (*pl*) expenditure.
outgrow *vt* (**outgrowing, outgrew,** *pp* **outgrown**) to become too big for; to grow taller than; to grow out of.
outgrowth *n* an offshoot.
outgun *vt* (**outgunning, outgunned**) to defeat by greater firepower; (*inf*) to surpass.
outhouse *n* a shet, etc, adjoining a main house.
outing *n* a pleasure trip; an excursion.
outlandish *adj* unconventional; strange; fantastic.
outlast *vt* to endure longer than.
outlaw *vt* to declare illegal. * *n* an outlawed person; a habitual or notorious criminal.
outlay *n* a spending (of money); expenditure.
outlet *n* an opening or release; a means of expression; a market for goods or services.
outlier *n* a part of a rock or stratum detached at some distance from the principal mass.
outline *n* a profile; a general indication; a rough sketch or draft.—*also vt.*
outlive *vt* to live longer than, outlast; to live through; to survive.
outlook *n* mental attitude; view; prospect.
outlying *adj* detached; remote, distant.
outmaneuver, outmanoeuvre*vt* to outwit in tactics.
outmatch *vt* to be more than a match for.
outmoded *adj* old-fashioned.
outmost *adj* outermost.
outnumber *vt* to exceed in number.
out-of-date *adj* no longer valid, unfashionable; outmoded.
out-of-pocket *adj* (*expenses*) paid for in cash; having lost money. **outpoint** *vt* to accumulate more points than.
out-of-the-way *adj* uncommon; secluded.
outpatient *n* a person treated at, but not resident in, a hospital.
outpoint *vt* to accumulate more points than.
outport *n* a part of harbour at some distance from the chief port.
outpost *n* (*mil*) a post or detachment at a distance from a main force.
outpouring *n* an effusion, an emotional speech.
output *n* the quantity (of goods, etc) produced, esp over a given period; information delivered by a computer, esp to a printer; (*elect*) the useful voltage, current, or power delivered.—*also vt.*
outrage *n* an extremely vicious or violent act; a grave insult or offence; great anger, etc, aroused by this.—*also vt.*—**outrageous** *adj.*
outrageous *adj* flagrant; atrocious; violent; excessive.—**outrageously** *adv.*—**outrageousness** *n.*
outrank *vt* to be of a higher rank than; to be of a higher priority.
outré *adj* outraging decorum; eccentric, unconventional; extravagant.
outride *vt* (**outriding, outrode,** *pp* **outridden**) to ride faster or farther than; to keep afloat through (a storm).
outrider *n* a mounted escort who goes in advance of a carriage, car, etc.
outrigger *n* a projecting spar for a sail, etc; a projection with a float extending from a canoe to prevent capsizing; a canoe of this type; a projecting frame to support the elevator or tail of an aircraft or the rotor of a helicopter.
outright *adj* complete, downright, direct. * *adv* at once; without restrictions.
outrun *vt* (**outrunning, outran,** *pp* **outran**) to run faster than; to exceed, to go beyond; to escape by running.
outset *n* the start, beginning.
outshine *vt* (**outshining, outshone**) to outdo in brilliance, ability; to shine longer and brighter than.
outside *n* the outer part or surface, the exterior. * *adj* outer; outdoor; (*chance, etc*) slight. * *adv* on or to the outside. * *prep* on or to the exterior of; beyond.
outsider *n* a person or thing not included in a set, group, etc, a non-member; a contestant, esp a horse, not thought to have a chance in a race.
outsize *adj* of a larger than usual size.
outskirts *npl* districts remote from the centre, as of a city.
outsmart *vt* to outwit.
outspan *vt* (**outspanning, outspanned**) (*S Africa*) to unyoke ox teams from a wagon; to encamp. * *n* a halting place.
outspoken *adj* candid in speech, frank, blunt.
outstanding *adj* excellent; distinguished, prominent; unpaid; unresolved, still to be done.
outstation *n* a distant post or station.
outstay *vt* to stay longer than or too long.
outstrip *vt* (**outstripping, outstripped**) to surpass; to go faster than.
outtalk *vt* to talk down.
outvote *vt* to defeat by a higher number of votes.
outward *adj* directed toward the outside; external; clearly apparent. * *adv* toward the outside.
Outward Bound movement *n* (in UK) an educational scheme to promote youth adventure training.
outwardly *adv* externally.
outwards *adv* outward.
outwear *vt* (**outwearing, outwore,** *pp* **outworn**) to outlast; to wear out.
outweigh *vt* to count for more than, to exceed in value, weight, or importance.
outwent *see* **outgo.**
outwit *vt* (**outwitting, outwitted**) to get the better of, defeat, by wit or cunning.
outwork *n* a defence constructed beyond the main body of a fort, etc; work done outside a factory.
ouzel *n* kinds of small bird; a blackbird.—*also* **ousel.**
ouzo *n* a Greek aniseed-flavoured spirit.
ova *see* **ovum.**
oval *adj* egg-shaped; elliptical. * *n* anything oval.
ovariotomy *n* (*pl* **ovariotomies**) the surgical operation of removing a tumour from the ovary.

ovaritis *n* inflammation of the ovary.
ovary *n* (*pl* **ovaries**) one of the two female reproductive organs producing eggs.—**ovarian** *adj*.
ovate *adj* (*bot*) oval, egg-shaped.
ovation *n* enthusiastic applause or public welcome.
oven *n* an enclosed, heated compartment for baking or drying.
ovenbird *n* a kind of bird with a dome-shaped nest; a fowl for cooking.
oven-ready *adj* (*food*) prepared for immediate cooking in the oven.
ovenware *n* attractive heat-resistant dishes in which food can be cooked and served.
over *prep* higher than; on top of; across; to the other side of; above; more than; concerning. * *adv* above; across; in every part; completed; from beginning to end; up and down; in addition; too. * *adj* upper; excessive; surplus; finished; remaining. * *n* (*cricket*) the number of balls bowled before changing ends.
over- *prefix* in excess, too much; above.
overact *vti* to act in an exaggerated manner, to overdo a part.
overactive *adj* abnormally or excessively active.—**overactivity** *n*.
overall *adj* including everything. * *adv* as a whole; generally. * *n* a loose protective garment; (*pl*) a one-piece protective garment covering body and legs.
overarch *vti* to form an arch (over).
overarm *adj, adv* (*sport*) bowled, thrown, performed, etc with the arm raised above the shoulder.
overawe *vt* to restrain by awe, daunt.
overbalance *vti* to fall over; to upset; to outweigh. * *n* a surplus.
overbear *vt* (**overbearing, overbore,** *pp* **overborne**) to dominate, to repress, to bear down.
overbearing *adj* domineering; overriding.—**overbearingly** *adv*.
overblown *adj* excessive, pretentious.
overboard *adv* over the side of a ship, etc; (*inf*) to extremes of enthusiasm.
overbook *vti* to sell tickets (for) in excess of the available seats or space.
overburden *vt* to load too heavily.
overcall *vti* (*bridge*) to bid more on (a hand) than it is worth; to take a bid away from (a partner).
overcame *see* **overcome**.
overcapitalize *vt* to float (a company) with too great a capital.—**overcapitalization** *n*.
overcast *adj* clouded over.
overcharge *vt* (*battery*) to overload; to fill to excess; to demand too high a price (from). * *n* an excessive or exorbitant charge or load.
overcloud *vti* to cover or become covered with clouds; to make or become dark or depressed.
overcoat *n* a warm, heavy topcoat.
overcome *vti* (**overcoming, overcame,** *pp* **overcome**) to get the better of, to prevail; to render helpless or powerless, as by tears, laughter, emotion, etc; to be victorious; to surmount obstacles, etc.
overcompensation *n* (*psychoanal*) an excess of compensation, often resulting in an overbearing manner.—**overcompensatory** *adj*.
overcrop *vt* (**overcropping, overcropped**) to exhaust (land) by excessive cultivation.
overcrowd *vti* to make or become too crowded.
overdo *vt* (**overdoing, overdid,** *pp* **overdone**) to do to excess; to overact; to cook (food) too much.—**overdone** *adj*.
overdose *n* an excessive dose —*also vti*.
overdraft *n* an overdrawing, an amount overdrawn, at a bank.
overdraw *vti* (**overdrawing, overdrew,** *pp* **overdrawn**) to draw in excess of a credit balance; to exaggerate in describing; to make an overdraft.
overdress *vti* to dress too warmly, too showily, or too formally.
overdrive *n* a high gear in a motor vehicle to reduce wear for travelling at high speed. * *vt* (**overdriving, overdrove,** *pp* **overdriven**) to drive too hard, overtax.
overdue *adj* past the time for payment, return, performance, etc; in arrears; delayed.
overeat *vi* (**overeating, overate,** *pp* **overeaten**) to eat too much.
overestimate *vt* to set too high an estimate on or for. * *n* an excessive estimate.—**overestimation** *n*.
overexpose *vt* (*phot*) to expose (a film) to light for too long.—**overexposure** *n*.
overflow *vti* (**overflowing, overflowed,** *pp* **overflown**) to flow over, flood; to exceed the bounds (of); to abound (with emotion, etc). * *n* that which overflows; surplus, excess; an outlet for surplus water, etc.
overgrow *vti* (**overgrowing, overgrew,** *pp* **overgrown**) to cover with growth; to grow too big or fast (for); to outgrow.—**overgrowth** *n*.
overgrown *adj* grown beyond the normal size; rank; ungainly.
overhand *adj, adv* (*sport*) bowled, thrown, performed, etc with the hand above the shoulder.
overhang *vti* (**overhanging, overhung**) to hang or project over. * *n* a projecting part.
overhaul *vt* to examine for, or make, repairs; to overtake.—*also n*.
overhead *adj, adv* above the head; in the sky. * *n* (often *pl*) the general, continuing costs of a business, as of rent, light, etc.
overhear *vt* (**overhearing, overheard**) to hear without the knowledge of the speaker.
overheat *vti* to make or become excessively hot; to stimulate unduly.
overjoyed *adj* highly delighted.
overkill *n* the capability to employ more weapons, etc than are necessary to destroy an enemy; excess capacity for a task.
overland *adj, adv* by, on, or across land.
overlap *vt* (**overlapping, overlapped**) to extend over (a thing or each other) so as to coincide in part.—*also n*.
overlay *vt* (**overlaying, overlaid**) to cover with a coating, to spread over. * *n* a coating.
overleaf *adv* on the other side of the leaf of a book.
overlie *vt* (**overlying, overlay,** *pp* **overlain**) to lie on top of; to stifle thus.
overload *vt* to put too great a burden on; (*elect*) to charge with too much current.
overlong *adj, adv* too long.
overlook *vt* to fail to notice; to look at from above; to excuse.
overlord *n* a lord ranking above other lords; an absolute or supreme ruler.
overman *vt* (**overmanning, overmanned**) to supply with too many workers.
overmaster *vt* to dominate wholly, to overpower.
overmuch *adj, adv* too much.
overnice *adj* too particular.
overnight *adv* for the night; in the course of the night; suddenly. * *adj* done in the night; lasting the night.
overpass *n* a road crossing another road, path, etc, at a higher level; the upper level of such a crossing. * *vt* (**overpassing, overpassed,** *pp* **overpast**) to pass beyond, to overstep; to surpass.
overplay *vt* to place too much emphasis on; to behave in an exaggerated or affected manner.
overplus *n* a surplus, an excess.
overpower *vt* to overcome by superior force, to subdue; to overwhelm.
overpowering *adj* overwhelming; compelling; unbearable.
overproduction *n* supply in excess of the demand.
overqualified *adj* having more qualifications or experience that required for a particular job.
overrate *vt* to value or assess too highly.
overreach *vt* to extend beyond; to circumvent, outwit; to fail by trying too much or being too subtle.
overreact *vi* to show an excessive reaction to something.
override *vt* (**overriding, overrode,** *pp* **overridden**) to ride over; to nullify; to prevail.
overrule *vt* to set aside by higher authority; to prevail over.
overrun *vt* (**overrunning, overran,** *pp* **overrun**) to attack and defeat; to swarm over; to exceed (a time limit, etc).
overseas *adj, adv* across or beyond the sea; abroad.
oversee *vt* (**overseeing, oversaw,** *pp* **overseen**) to supervise; to superintend. * *n* **overseer** *n*.

oversell *vt* (**overselling, oversold**) to sell more than can be delivered, esp stocks.
overset *vti* (**oversetting, overset**) to upset, to disturb; to overthrow.
oversew *vt* (**oversewing, oversewed,** *pp* **oversewn**) to stitch over again to reinforce; to stitch over an edge to prevent fraying.
overshadow *vt* to throw a shadow over; to appear more prominent or important than.
overshoe *n* a galosh.
overshoot *vt* (**overshooting, overshot**) to shoot or send beyond (a target, etc); (*aircraft*) to fly or taxi beyond the end of a runway when landing or taking off.—*also n*.
oversight *n* a careless mistake or omission; supervision.
oversize, oversized *adj* of larger than average size.
overslaugh *n* (*mil*) the passing over of an ordinary duty because of a special one.
oversleep *vi* (**oversleeping, overslept**) to sleep beyond the intended time.
overspend *vt* (**overspending, overspent**) to spend more than necessary; to wear out, tire. * *vi* to spend more than one can afford.
overstate *vt* to state too strongly, to exaggerate.—**overstatement** *n*.
overstay *vt* to remain longer than or beyond the limits of.
overstep *vt* (**overstepping, overstepped**) to exceed; (*a limit*) to step beyond.
overstock *vt* to lay in too large a stock of or for, to glut.—*also n*.
overstrung *adj* too highly strung; too sensitive.
oversubscribe *vt* to apply for more shares in (an issue) than can be allotted.
overt *adj* openly done, unconcealed; (*law*) done with evident intent, deliberate.—**overtly** *adv*.
overtake *vt* (**overtaking, overtook,** *pp* **overtaken**) to catch up with and pass; to come upon suddenly.
overtax *vt* to make too great demands on; to tax too heavily.
overthrow *vt* (**overthrowing, overthrew,** *pp* **overthrown**) to throw over, overturn; (*government, etc*) to bring down by force.—*also n*.
overtime *adv* beyond regular working hours. * *n* extra time worked; payment for this.
overtone *n* an additional subtle meaning; an implicit quality; (*mus*) a harmonic; the colour of light reflected (as by a paint).
overtook *see* **overtake.**
overtop *vt* (**overtopping, overtopped**) to be higher than, to tower above.
overtrain *vti* to train too hard.
overtrump *vt* to play a higher trump than (the card that has trumped another).
overture *n* an initiating of negotiations; a formal offer, proposal; (*mus*) an instrumental introduction to an opera, etc.
overturn *vti* to upset, turn over; to overthrow.
overview *n* a general survey.
overweening *adj* arrogant, presumptuous, conceited.
overweight *adj* weighing more than the proper amount. * *n* excess weight.
overwhelm *vt* to overcome totally; to submerge; to crush; to overpower with emotion.
overwhelming *adj* irresistible; uncontrollable; vast; vastly superior; extreme.
overwork *vti* to work or use too hard or too long.
overwrite *vt* (**overwriting, overwrote, overwritten**) to write in an overly elaborate style; to write too much; to write data to a computer disk thereby erasing the existing contents.
overwrought *adj* over-excited; too elaborate.
ovi- *prefix* egg.
oviduct *n* the tube which conducts the ovum from the ovary to the uterus.
oviferous *adj* egg-carrying.
oviform *adj* egg-shaped.
ovine *adj* pertaining to sheep.
oviparous *adj* producing young by eggs.—**oviparity** *n*.
oviposit *vi* to lay or deposit eggs.—**oviposition** *n*.
ovipositor *n* the organ in certain insects by which its eggs are deposited.
ovisac *n* the cavity in the ovary which contains the ovum.
ovoid *adj* egg-shaped.
ovolo *n* (*pl* **ovoli**) (*archit*) a round or convex egg-shaped moulding.
ovoviviparous *adj* producing eggs containing the young in a living state, as certain animals.—**ovoviviparity** *n*.
ovulate *vi* to discharge or produce eggs from an ovary.—**ovulation** *n*.
ovule *n* the germ borne by the placenta of a plant and subsequently developing into a seed.—**ovular** *adj*.
ovum *n* (*pl* **ova**) an unfertilized female egg cell.
owe *vti* to be in debt; to be obliged to pay; to feel the need to give, do, etc, as because of gratitude.
owing *adj* due, to be paid; owed; (*with* **to**) because of, on account of.
owl *n* a nocturnal bird of prey with a large head and eyes; a person of nocturnal habits, solemn appearance, etc.—**owlish** *adj*.
owlet *n* a young owl.
own[1] *vti* to possess; to acknowledge, admit; to confess to.
own[2] *adj* belonging to oneself or itself, often used reflexively (*my own, their own*).
owner *n* one who owns, a possessor, a proprietor.—**ownership** *n*.
ox *n* (*pl* **oxen**) a cud-chewing mammal of the cattle family; a castrated bull.
oxalate *n* a salt of oxalic acid.
oxalic acid *n* a poisonous acid obtained from oxalis.
oxalis *n* wood sorrel.
oxbow *n* a horseshoe loop in a stream; the U-shaped collar of a yoke.
Oxbridge *n, adj* (of) the British universities of Oxford and Cambridge.
oxen *see* **ox.**
oxeye *n* a kind of flower; a large eye.
Oxfam (*acronym*) the Oxford Committee for Famine Relief.
Oxford Group *n* a former name of Moral Rearmament.
Oxford movement *n* an Anglican high-church movement begun in Oxford in 1833.
oxidation *n* the operation of converting into an oxide.
oxide *n* a compound of oxygen with another element.
oxidize *vti* to cause to undergo a chemical reaction with oxygen; to rust.—**oxidization** *n*.
oxlip *n* a variety of primula; a hybrid between primrose and cowslip.
Oxon. *abbr* = (*degrees, etc*) of Oxford.
Oxonian *adj* pertaining to Oxford. * *n* a graduate or member of Oxford University.
oxtail *n* the tail of an ox, esp skinned and used for stews, soups, etc.
oxy- *prefix* sharp; oxygen.
oxyacetylene *n* a mixture of oxygen with acetylene used in a blowlamp to cut or weld metal.—*also adj*.
oxygen *n* a colourless, odourless, tasteless, highly reactive gaseous element forming part of air, water, etc, and essential to life and combustion.—**oxygenic, oxygenous** *adj*.
oxygenate *vt* to combine or supply with oxygen.—**oxygenation** *n*.
oxygenize *vt* to oxygenate.—**oxygenizer** *n*.
oxygen tent *n* a canopy over a hospital bed, etc, within which a supply of oxygen is maintained.
oxyhemoglobin, oxyhaemoglobin *n* a loose compound of oxygen and haemoglobin.
oxyhydrogen *n* a mixture of oxygen with acetylene and hydrogen, as in a blowlamp, by which an intense heat is produced by the combination of gases.
oxymoron *n* (*pl* **oxymora**) a figure of speech combining contradictory words, e.g. "faith unfaithful kept him falsely true."
oxytone *adj* (*linguistics*) having an acute sound; having the last syllable accented. * *n* an acute sound; a word with the acute accent on the last syllable.
oyez, oyes *interj* the introductory cry of an official or public crier demanding attention or silence.
oyster *n* an edible marine bivalve shellfish.
oystercatcher *n* a wading sea bird.
oz *abbr* = ounce(s).
Oz *n* (Austral sl) Australia.
ozokerite, ozocerite *n* a waxy fossil resin used for candles.

ozone *n* a condensed form of oxygen; (*inf*) bracing seaside air.—**ozonic, ozonous** *adj*.
ozone layer *n* a layer of ozone in the stratosphere that absorbs ultraviolet rays from the sun.
ozonize *vt* to charge with ozone.—**ozonization** *n*.—**ozonizer** *n*.

P

P[1] *abbr* = parking; (*chess*) pawn.
P[2] (*chem symbol*) phosphorus.
p *abbr* = page; penny, pence.
PA *abbr* = Panama; Pennsylvania; personal assistant; public address (system).
Pa (*chem symbol*) protactinium.
pa *n* (*inf*) father, papa.
p.a. *abbr* = per annum.
paca *n* a burrowing rodent found in Central and South America.
pace[1] *n* a single step; the measure of a single stride; speed of movement. * *vti* to measure by paces; to walk up and down; to determine the pace in a race; to walk with regular steps.—**pacer** *n*.
pace[2] *prep* with the permission of; with due respect to.
pacemaker *n* a person who sets the pace in a race; an electronic device inserted in the heart, used to regulate heartbeat.
pacer *n* a horse trained to pace; a pacemaker.
pacha *see* **pasha.**
pachinko *n* a Japanese variation on pinball.
pachisi *n* an Indian game, similar to backgammon.
pachouli *see* **patchouli.**
pachyderm *n* any large thick-skinned mammal, esp an elephant.—**pachydermatous** *adj*.
pacific *adj* promoting peace; mild, conciliatory.—**pacifically** *adv*.
pacifier *n* a person or thing that pacifies; a baby's dummy.
pacifism *n* opposition to the use of force under any circumstances, specifically the refusal to participate in war.—**pacifist** *n*.
pacify *vt* (**pacifying, pacified**) to soothe; to calm; to restore peace to.—**pacification** *n*.
pack *n* a load or bundle (esp one carried on the back); a set of playing cards; a group or mass; a number of wild animals living together; an organized troop (as of Cub Scouts); a compact mass (as of snow); a small package used as a container for goods for sale. * *vt* to put together in a bundle or pack; (*suitcase*) to fill; to crowd; to press tightly so as to prevent leakage; to carry in a pack; to send (off); (*sl: gun, etc*) to carry; (*sl: punch*) to deliver with force. * *vi* (*snow, ice*) to form into a hard mass; to assemble one's belongings in suitcases or boxes. * *adj* used for carrying packs, loads, etc.—**packer** *n*.
package *n* a parcel, a wrapped bundle; several items, arrangements, etc offered as a unit. * *vt* to make a parcel of; to group together several items, etc.—**packager** *n*.
package holiday, package tour *n* a holiday or tour with all the fares, accommodation, food, etc, arranged for an all-inclusive price.
package store *n* (*US*) a place where alcohol is sold for consumption off the premises.—*also* **liquor store.**
packaging *n* the wrapping round a product offered for sale; the presentation of a product.
pack animal *n* an animal, such as a mule or camel, used for carrying loads.
packed out *adj* (*inf*) crowded.
packet *n* a small box or package; (*sl*) a considerable sum; a vessel carrying mail, etc, between one port and another.
packhorse *n* a horse used for carrying goods.
pack ice *n* sea ice formed into a mass by the crushing together of floes, etc.
packing *n* material for protecting packed goods or for making airtight or watertight; the act of filling a suitcase, box, etc.
packsaddle *n* a saddle for carrying goods.
pact *n* an agreement or treaty.
pad[1] *n* the dull sound of a footstep. * *vi* (**padding, padded**) to walk, esp with a soft step.
pad[2] *n* a piece of a soft material or stuffing; several sheets of paper glued together at one edge; the cushioned thickening of an animal's sole; a piece of folded absorbent material used as a surgical dressing; a flat concrete surface; (*sl*) one's own home or room. * *vt* (**padding, padded**) to stuff with soft material; to fill with irrelevant information.
padding *n* stuffing; anything unimportant or false added to achieve length or amount.
paddle[1] *vi* to wade about or play in shallow water.
paddle[2] *n* a short oar with a wide blade at one or both ends; a implement shaped like this, used to hit, beat or stir. * *vti* (*canoe, etc*) to propel by a paddle; to beat as with a paddle; to spank.—**paddler** *n*.
paddock *n* an enclosed field in which horses are exercised.
Paddy *n* (*pl* **Paddies**) (*derog*) a nickname for an Irishman.
paddy[1] *n* (*pl* **paddies**) threshed unmilled rice; a rice field.
paddy[2] *n* (*pl* **paddies**) (*sl*) rage, a fit of temper.
pademelon, paddymelon *n* (*Austral*) a small wallaby.
padlock *n* a detachable lock used to fasten doors etc. * *vt* to secure with a padlock.
padre *n* a military chaplain.
padrone *n* an innkeeper, esp in Italy.
paduasoy *n* a silk fabric.
paean *n* a song of triumph or thanks; praise.—*also* **pean.**
paediatrics *n sing* the branch of medicine dealing with children and their diseases.—*also* **pediatrics.**—**paediatric** *adj*.—**paediatrician** *n*.
paedo- *prefix* child.—*also* **pedo-**.
paedology *n* the study of children.—*also* **pedology.**—**paedologic, paedological** *adj*.—**paedologically** *adv*.—**paedologist** *n*.
paedophilia *n* sexual attraction towards children.—*also* **pedophilia.**—**paedophiliac, paedophilic** *adj*.—**paedophile** *n*.
paeon *n* a four-syllabled metrical foot, comprising, in any order, three short and one long syllable.
pagan *n* a heathen; a person who has no religion.* *adj* irreligious; heathen, non-Christian.—**paganism** *n*.—**paganist** *adj, n*.
paganize *vt* to make pagan. * *vi* to become pagan.
page[1] *n* a boy attendant at a formal function (as a wedding); a uniformed boy employed to run errands. * *vt* to summon by messenger, loudspeaker, etc.
page[2] *n* a sheet of paper in a book, newspaper etc. * *vt* (*a book*) to number the pages of (—*also* **paginate**).
pageant *n* a spectacular procession or parade; representation in costume of historical events; a mere show.
pageantry *n* (*pl* **pageantries**) grand or formal display; pomp.
pageboy *n* a page; a medium-length hairstyle with the ends of the hair turned under.
pager *n* a device carried on a person so he or she can be summoned.—*also* **bleeper.**
paginal *adj* consisting of pages; page for page.
paginate *see* **page**[2].
pagination *n* the act of numbering the pages of a book; the arrangement and number of pages.
pagoda *n* an oriental temple in the form of a tower.
Pahlavi *n* the Persian dialect in which Zoroastrian scriptures were written.
paid *see* **pay.**
pail *n* a bucket.
pain *n* physical or mental suffering; hurting; (*pl*) trouble, exertion. * *vt* to cause distress to.
pained *adj* hurt, offended.
painful *adj* giving pain, distressing.—**painfully** *adv*.—**painfulness** *n*.
painkiller *n* a drug that relieves pain.
painless *adj* without pain.—**painlessly** *adv*.
painstaking *adj* very careful, laborious.—**painstakingly** *adv*.
paint *vt* (*a picture*) to make using oil pigments, etc; to depict with paints;

to cover or decorate with paint; to describe. * *vi* to make a picture. * *n* a colouring pigment; a dried coat of paint.
painter[1] *n* a person who paints, esp an artist.
painter[2] *n* a bow rope for tying up a boat.
painting *n* the act or art of applying paint; a painted picture.
pair *n* a set of two things that are equal, suited, or used together; any two persons or animals regarded as a unit. * *vti* to form a pair (of); to mate.
paisley *n* an intricate pattern of curved shapes; a soft woollen fabric with this design; a shawl made of this material. * *adj* of this pattern or material.
pajamas *see* **pyjamas.**
pakeha *n* (*New Zealand*) a non-Maori, esp a white person.
pal *n* a close friend. * *vi* (**palling, palled**) (*with* **up**) (*inf*) to make friends (with).
palace *n* the official residence of a sovereign, president or bishop; a large stately house or public building.
paladin *n* a knight-errant, esp of the court of Charlemagne.
palatable *adj* (*taste*) pleasant; (*fig*) pleasant or acceptable.—**palatability** *n.*—**palatably** *adv.*
palate *n* the roof of the mouth; taste; mental relish.
palatial *adj* of or like a palace.—**palatially** *adv.*—**palatialness** *n.*
palaver *n* idle chatter; flattery; cajolery. * *vt* to flatter, cajole. * *vi* to talk idly.
palaeo- *prefix* old; ancient; prehistoric.
palaeobotany *n* the study of fossil plants.—*also* (*US*) **paleobotany.**
palaeography *n* the study of ancient writing and manuscripts.—*also* (*US*) **paleography.**—**palaeographic, palaeographical** *adj.*—**palaeographer** *n.*
Palaeolithic *adj* pertaining to the early Stone Age.—*also* (*US*) **Paleolithic.**
palaeontology *n* the study of fossils.—*also* (*US*) **paleontology.**—**palaeontological** *adj.*—**palaeontologist** *n.*
Palaeozoic *adj* pertaining to the geological period in which fossils of the earliest forms of life appear which began 600 million years ago and ended 225 million years ago.—*also* (*US*) **Paleozoic.**
palaeozoology *n* the study of fossil animals.—*also* (*US*) **paleozoology.**—**palaeozoological** *adj.*—**palaeozoologist** *n.*
pale[1] *n* a fence stake; a boundary; (*her*) a vertical stripe in the middle of a shield.
pale[2] *adj* (*complexion*) with less colour than usual; (*colour, light*) faint, wan, dim. * *vti* to make or become pale.—**palely** *adv.*—**paleness** *n.*
paleface *n* (*derog*) a term for a white person, supposedly used by Native Americans.
paleo- *see* **palaeo-.**
paleobotany *see* **palaeobotany.**
paleography *see* **palaeography.**
Paleolithic *see* **Palaeolithic.**
Paleozoic *see* **Palaeozoic.**
paleozoology *see* **palaeozoology.**
palette *n* a small, wooden board on which coloured paints are mixed.
palette knife *n* (*pl* **palette knives**) a thin knife used for mixing colours; a round-ended, flexible knife used in cookery.
palfrey *n* (*arch*) a saddle horse, esp for a woman.
palimony *n* (*inf*) the payment of alimony from one partner in a formal long-term sexual relationship to the other.
palimpsest *n* a manuscript which has been written on more than once, the former writing being still discernible in spite of erasure.
palindrome *n* a word or sentence reading the same forwards as backwards, eg "Able was I ere I saw Elba".—**palindromic** *adj.*
paling *n* a row of stakes in a fence; a railing.
palingenesis *n* (*pl* **palingeneses**) (*theology*) spiritual rebirth through baptism.—**palingenetic** *adj.*
palinode *n* a poem retracting a former poem.
palisade *n* a fence made of pointed stakes driven into the ground; a pointed stake used in a fence of this kind.
palish *adj* somewhat pale.
pall[1] *n* a heavy cloth over a coffin; (*of smoke*) a mantle.
pall[2] *vi* to become boring; to become satiated.
Palladian *adj* (*archit*) in the pseudo-classical style of the architect Andrea Palladio (1518–80).
palladium *n* a rare greyish-white metal found with platinum.
pallbearer *n* someone who carries the coffin at a funeral.
pallet[1] *n* a portable platform for lifting and stacking goods.
pallet[2] *n* a straw bed.
palletize, palletise *vt* to stack, transport or store on pallets.—**palletization, palletisation** *n.*
palliasse *n* a straw mattress.—*also* **paillasse.**
palliate *vt* to extenuate, to excuse; to alleviate without curing.—**palliation** *n.*—**palliator** *n.*
palliative *adj* alleviating without curing; excusing, extenuating. * *n* a thing that palliates.
pallid *adj* wan, pale.—**pallidness** *n.*
pallium *n* (*pl* **pallia, palliums**) a white woollen scarf worn by an archbishop; (*anat*) the cerebral cortex and surrounding matter; (*zool*) a mollusc's outer fold of skin.
pallor *n* paleness, esp of the face.
pally *adj* (**pallier, palliest**) friendly with; intimate.
palm[1] *n* the underside of the hand between fingers and wrist. * *vt* to conceal in or touch with the palm; (*with* **off**) to pass off by fraud, foist.
palm[2] *n* a tropical branchless tree with fan-shaped leaves; a symbol of victory.
palmaceous *adj* of the palm family.
palmar *adj* of or in the palm of the hand.
palmate, palmated *adj* like an open hand; (*bot*) having leaves with lobes radiating from a common point; (*zool*) web-footed.—**palmation** *n.*
palmer *n* (*formerly*) a pilgrim returning from the Holy Land, carrying a palm branch as a token of the pilgrimage.
palmetto *n* (*pl* **palmettos, palmettoes**) a species of small palm tree.
palmistry *n* foretelling the future from lines of the hand.—**palmist** *n.*
Palm Sunday *n* the Sunday before Easter.
palm-top *n* a portable computer small enough to fit in the palm of the hand.
palmy *adj* (**palmier, palmiest**) abounding in palm trees; (*fig*) flourishing, prosperous.
palmyra *n* a palm found in Asia, the leaves of which are used for matting and thatching.
palomino *n* (*pl* **palominos**) a horse with a golden or cream-coloured coat and a white mane and tail.
palp, palpus *n* (*pl* **palps, palpi**) a jointed feeler attached to the mouth parts of an insect.
palpable *adj* tangible; easily perceived, obvious.—**palpability** *n.*—**palpably** *adj.*
palpate *vt* to examine by touch, esp medically.—**palpation** *n.*
palpebral *adj* of the eyelids.
palpitate *vi* (*heart*) to beat abnormally fast; to tremble, flutter.—**palpitation** *n.*
palsy *n* (*pl* **palsies**) paralysis; a condition marked by an uncontrollable tremor of a part of the body. * *vt* (**palsying, palsied**) to paralyse; to make helpless.
palter *vi* to be insincere.
paltry *adj* (**paltrier, paltriest**) almost worthless; trifling.—**paltrily** *adv.*—**paltriness** *n.*
pampas *npl* the treeless, grassy plains of South America.
pampas grass *n* a tall-stemmed South American grass growing in thick tussocks.
pamper *vt* to overindulge; to coddle, spoil.—**pamperer** *n.*
pampero *n* (*pl* **pamperos**) a cold south or south west wind which blows across the pampas.
pamphlet *n* a thin, unbound booklet, esp one attacking or advocating a cause, etc; a brochure.—**pamphleteer** *n.*
Pan *n* (*Greek myth*) the god of woods and fields.—**Pandean** *adj.*
pan[1] *n* a wide metal container, a saucepan; (*of scales*) a tray; a depression in the earth filled with water; severe criticism; the bowl of a lavatory. * *vb* (**panning, panned**) **vi* (*with* **out**) (*inf*) to turn out, esp to turn out

well; to succeed. * *vt* to wash gold-bearing gravel in a pan; (*inf*) to disparage, find fault with.

pan[2] *n* a betel leaf; a mixture of betel nuts and lime wrapped in a betel leaf used for chewing.

pan[3] *vti* (**panning, panned**) (*film camera*) to move horizontally to follow an object or provide a panoramic view.—*also n*.

pan- *prefix* all; general.

panacea *n* a cure-all, universal remedy.—**panacean** *adj*.

panache *n* flair; sense of style.

panada *n* (*cooking*) bread boiled to a pulp and flavoured, used as a sauce base or as stuffing.

panama *n* a hat of a fine, straw-like material.

Pan-American *adj* of or pertaining to North, South and Central America collectively; advocating unity among American countries.

panatella *n* a long, slim cigar.

pancake *n* a round, thin cake made from batter and cooked on a griddle; a thing shaped thus. * *vi* (*aircraft*) to descend vertically in a level position.

panchromatic *adj* (*photog*) sensitive to light of all colours.

pancreas *n* a large gland secreting a digestive juice into the intestine and also producing insulin.—**pancreatic** *adj*.

pancreatin *n* a clear fluid secreted by the pancreas, often extracted from animals and used in medicine.

panda *n* a large black and white bear-like herbivore (*also* **giant panda**); a related reddish-brown raccoon-like animal with a ringed tail (—*also* **lesser panda**).

Pandean *adj* pertaining to the god Pan.

pandemic *adj* epidemic over a large region, universal.

pandemonium *n* (*pl* **pandemoniums**) uproar; chaos.

pander *n* a go-between in sexual liaisons; a pimp. * *vi* (*usu with* **to**) to gratify or exploit a person's desires or weaknesses, etc.—**panderer** *n*.

pandit *see* **pundit.**

P & L *abbr* = profit and loss.

pane *n* a sheet of glass in a frame of a window, door, etc.—**paned** *adj*.

panegyric *n* an ovation or eulogy in praise of a person or event.—**panegyrical** *adj*.—**panegyrist** *n*.

panegyrize *vti* to compose a panegyric (about); to praise highly.

panel *n* a usu rectangular section or division forming part of a wall, door, etc; a board for instruments or controls; a lengthwise strip in a skirt, etc; a group of selected persons for judging, discussing, etc. * *vt* (**panelling, panelled** *or* **paneling, paneled**) to decorate with panels.

panelling, paneling *n* panels collectively; sheets of wood, plastic, etc used for panels.

panellist, panelist *n* a member of a panel.

panelology *n* the collection of comic books as a hobby.

pang *n* a sudden sharp pain or feeling.

pangenesis *n* (*formerly*) the theory that reproductive cells contain particles from all parts of the parents.—**pangenetic** *adj*.

pangolin *n* an insectivorous mammal, also known as the spiny anteater, found in Africa and Asia.

panhandle[1] *n* a narrow, projecting tongue of land.

panhandle[2] *vi* (*inf*) to beg, esp from passers-by. * *vt* (*inf*) to obtain by begging.

panic *n* a sudden overpowering fright or terror.—*also adj*. * *vti* (**panicking, panicked**) to affect or be affected with panic.—**panicky** *adj*.

panic button *n* a switch for setting off an alarm; (*sl*) a frenzied response.

panicle *n* (*bot*) an irregularly bunched flower cluster.

panic-stricken, panic-struck *adj* affected by panic.

paniculate, paniculated *adj* (*bot*) arranged in panicles.

panjandrum *n* a pompous official.

panne *n* a soft, velvet-like fabric.

pannier *n* a large basket for carrying loads on the back of an animal or the shoulders of a person; a bag or case slung over the rear wheel of a bicycle or motorcycle.

pannikin *n* a small metal drinking-cup.

panoply *n* (*pl* **panoplies**) a complete array; a full suit of armour.—**panoplied** *adj*.

panorama *n* a complete view in all directions; a comprehensive presentation of a subject; a constantly changing scene.—**panoramic** *adj*.—**panoramically** *adv*.

panpipes *npl* a wind instrument consisting of short hollow tubes of different lengths, originally of reed, bound together.

pansy *n* (*pl* **pansies**) a garden flower of the violet family, with velvety petals; (*sl*) an effeminate boy or man.

pant *vi* to breathe noisily, gasp; to yearn (for or after something). * *vt* to speak while gasping.

pantalets, pantalettes *npl* a woman's long ruffled drawers.

pantaloon *n* (*pantomine*) a foolish old man on whom the clown plays tricks.

pantaloons *npl* (*hist*) a man's tight breeches fastened at the calf or the foot; (*inf*) baggy trousers.

pantheism *n* the doctrine that the universe in its totality is God; willingness to worship all, or several gods.—**pantheist** *n*.—**pantheistic, pantheistical** *adj*.

pantheon *n* a temple to all the gods; a building in which the famous dead of a nation are buried or remembered; a group of famous persons.

panther *n* (*pl* **panther, panthers**) a leopard, esp one with a black unspotted coat; a puma.

pantihose *n* women's tights.—*also* **panty hose**.

panties *npl* (*inf*) short underpants.

pantile *n* a roof tile with an S-shaped cross-section.

panto *n* (*pl* **pantos**) (*Brit inf*) a pantomime.

pantograph *n* an instrument for copying drawings, maps, etc, to scale.

pantomime *n* (*Brit*) a Christmas theatrical entertainment with music and jokes; a drama without words, using only actions and gestures; mime. * *vti* to mime.—**pantomimic** *adj*.

pantomimist *n* a person who performs in a pantomime; one who composes a pantomime.

pantoum *n* a verse form of four-lined rhyming stanzas.

pantry *n* (*pl* **pantries**) a small room or cupboard for storing cooking ingredients and utensils, etc.

pants *npl* trousers; underpants.

panty hose *see* **pantihose.**

panzer *adj* (*division*) armoured. * *n* a tank, or other armoured vehicle, from a panzer division; (*pl*) armoured troops.

pap *n* soft, bland food for infants, invalids, etc; any oversimplified or insipid writing, ideas, etc.

papa *n* (*inf*) father.

papacy *n* (*pl* **papacies**) the office or authority of the pope; papal system of government.

papal *adj* of the pope or the papacy.—**papally** *adv*.

paparazzo *n* (*pl* **paparazzi**) a freelance photographer who pursues celebrities for sensational or candid shots for publication in newspapers and magazines.

papaveraceous *adj* (*bot*) pertaining or belonging to the poppy family.

papaw *n* (the small edible fruit of) a North American tree of the custard-apple family.—*also* **pawpaw.**

papaya *n* (a West Indian tree bearing) an elongated melon-like fruit with edible yellow flesh and small black seeds.

paper *n* the thin, flexible material made from pulped rags, wood, etc which is used to write on, wrap in, or cover walls; a single sheet of this; an official document; a newspaper; an essay or lecture; a set of examination questions; (*pl*) personal documents. * *adj* like or made of paper. * *vt* to cover with wallpaper.

paperback *n* a book bound in a flexible paper cover. * *adj* pertaining to such a book or the publication of such books.

papering *n* the process of covering with paper; paper so used.

paperknife *n* (*pl* **paperknives**) a blunt knife for opening letters or cutting folded paper.

paper money *n* banknotes; paper currency authorized by a government as representing value.
paperweight *n* a small heavy object for keeping papers in place.
paperwork *n* clerical work of any kind.
papery *adj* like paper in appearance or consistency.—**paperiness** *n*.
papeterie *n* a case containing paper and writing materials.
papier-mâché *n* a substance made of paper pulp mixed with size, glue, etc and moulded into various objects when moist.
papilla *n* (*pl* **papillae**) a small, nipple-like protuberance.—**papillary, papillate, papillose** *adj*.
papist *n* (*derog*) a Roman Catholic.—**papistic** *adj*.—**papistry** *n*.
papoose *n* an American Indian young child.
pappus *n* (*pl* **pappi**) (*bot*) the feathery substance on the seeds of some plants, eg dandelion, thistle.
pappy *adj* (**pappier, pappiest**) semi-liquid, like pap.
paprika *n* a mild red condiment ground from the fruit of certain peppers.
Pap test, Pap smear *n* a technique for the early detection of cancer by examining specially stained cells from the cervix, etc.
papule, papula *n* (*pl* **papules, papulae**) a small, solid elevation of the skin.—**papular** *adj*.
papyrology *n* the study of papyri.—**papyrologist** *n*.
papyrus *n* (*pl* **papyri, papyruses**) an aquatic plant; paper made from this plant, as used in ancient times.
par *n* the standard or normal level; the established value of a currency in foreign-exchange rates; the face value of stocks, shares, etc; (*golf*) the score for a hole required by an expert player; equality.
par-, para- *prefix* beside; against; irregular; abnormal; associated in a subsidiary or accessory capacity.
para *n* (*pl* **paras**) (*inf*) a paragraph; a paratrooper.
parabasis *n* (*pl* **parabases**) (*classical Greek comedy*) an address to the audience by the chorus.
parable *n* a short story used to illustrate a religious or moral point.—**parabolist** *n*.
parabola *n* (*pl* **parabolas**) (*maths*) the curve formed by the cutting of a cone by a plane parallel to its side.
parabolic[1] *adj* of or like a parabola; parabolical.
parabolic[2], **parabolical** *adj* of or expressed in a parable.—**parabolically** *adv*.
paraboloid *n* (*geom*) a solid formed by the revolution of a parabola on its axis.
parachronism *n* an error in chronology, esp in postdating an event.
parachute *n* a fabric umbrella-like canopy used to retard speed of fall from an aircraft. * *vti* to drop, descend by parachute.—**parachutist** *n*.
paraclete *n* a mediator.
parade *n* a ceremonial procession; an assembly of troops for review; ostentatious display; public walk, promenade. * *vti* to march or walk through, as for display; to show off; to assemble in military order.
paradigm *n* a pattern or model; a list of grammatical inflexions of a word.—**paradigmatic** *adj*.—**paradigmatically** *adv*.
paradise *n* heaven; (*Bible*) the Garden of Eden; any place of perfection.
paradisiacal, paradisiac *adj* like, or pertaining to, paradise.
paradox *n* a self-contradictory statement that may be true; an opinion that conflicts with common beliefs; something with seemingly contradictory qualities or phases.—**paradoxical** *adj*.—**paradoxically** *adv*.
paraesthesia *n* (*med*) an abnormal tickling sensation on the skin.—*also* **paresthesia**.—**paraesthetic** *adj*.
paraffin *n* a white waxy tasteless substance obtained from shale, wood, etc; a distilled oil used as fuel, kerosene.—**paraffinic** *adj*.
paragenesis, paragenesia *n* (*geol*) the sequence of formation of the various minerals in a mass of rock—**paragenetic** *adj*.
paragoge, paragogue *n* (*linguistics*) the addition of a letter or a syllable to a word.
paragon *n* a model of excellence or perfection.
paragraph *n* a subdivision in a piece of writing used to separate ideas, marked by the beginning of a new line; a brief mention in a newspaper. * *vt* to divide into paragraphs.—**paragraphic** *adj*.—**paragraphically** *adv*.
Paraguay tea *n* an infusion of the dried leaves of maté, which makes a mildly stimulating tea.—*also* **yerba maté**.
parakeet *n* a small parrot.
paraldehyde *n* a colourless liquid used as a sedative.
paraleipsis, paralipsis *n* (*pl* **paraleipses, paralipses**) (*rhetoric*) drawing attention to something by deliberately understating it.
parallax *n* the apparent angular shifting of an object caused by a change in position of the observer; (*astron*) the difference in the apparent position of a heavenly body and its true place.
parallel *adj* equidistant at every point and extended in the same direction; side by side; never intersecting; similar, corresponding. * *n* a parallel line, surface, etc; a likeness, counterpart; comparison; a line of latitude. * *vt* (**paralleling, paralleled**) to make or be parallel; to compare.
parallelepiped *n* a regular solid figure bounded by six parallelograms, of which the opposite pairs are equal and parallel.
parallelism *n* the state or quality of being parallel.
parallelogram *n* a four-sided plane figure whose opposite sides are parallel.
paralogism *n* (*logic*) a fallacy in reasoning made unconsciously by the reasoner.
paralyse, paralyze *vt* to affect with paralysis; to bring to a stop.—**paralysation** *n*.
paralysis *n* (*pl* **paralyses**) a partial or complete loss of voluntary muscle function or sensation in any part of the body; a condition of helpless inactivity.—**paralytic** *adj*, *n*.
paramatta *n* a light fabric of cotton and wool.—*also* **parramatta**.
paramedic *n* a a person trained to provide emergency medical treatment and to support professional medical staff.
paramedical *adj* (*services*) supplementing and assisting the work of professional medical staff.
parameter *n* (*math*) an arbitrary constant, the value of which influences the content but not the structure of an expression; (*inf*) a limit or condition affecting action, decision, etc.—**parametric** *adj*.—**parametrically** *adv*.
paramilitary *adj* (*forces*) organized on a military pattern and ancillary to military forces.
paramo *n* (*pl* **paramos**) a high bleak plateau in the Andes.
paramount *adj* of great importance.
paramour *n* an illicit lover.
parang *n* a heavy Malay sheath knife.
paranoia *n* a mental illness characterized by delusions of grandeur and persecution; (*inf*) unfounded fear, suspicion.—**paranoiac** *adj*, *n*.
paranoid *adj* of or like paranoia; (*inf*) highly suspicious or fearful.—*also n*.
paranormal *adj* beyond the scope of normal experience or scientific explanation.—**paranormally** *adv*.
parapet *n* a low, protective wall along the edge of a roof, balcony, or bridge, etc.—**parapeted** *adj*.
paraph *n* a mark or flourish after a signature.
paraphernalia *npl* personal belongings; accessories; (*law*) what a wife possesses in her own right.
paraphrase *n* expression of a passage in other words in order to clarify meaning. * *vt* to restate.—**paraphrastic** *adj*.
paraplegia *n* paralysis of the lower half of the body.—**paraplegic** *adj*.
parasailing *n* the sport of gliding through the air attached to an open parachute and towed by a speedboat.—**parasailer, parasailor** *n*.
parascending *n* a form of parachuting in which participants wearing open parachutes are towed into the air by a vehicle or speedboat and then released to glide to the ground.—**parascender** *n*.
paraselene *n* (*pl* **paraselenae**) (*astron*) a bright spot on a lunar halo.
parasite *n* an organism that lives on and feeds off another without rendering any service in return; a person who sponges off another.—**parasitic** *adj*.—**parasitically** *adv*.
parasiticide *n* a substance which kills parasites.
parasitism *n* the parasite-host relationship; the state or behaviour of a parasite.

parasitize *n* to infest with parasites.
parasitology *n* the study of parasites.—**parasitologist** *n.*
parasol *n* a lightweight umbrella used as a sunshade.
parasynthesis *n* (*gram*) derivation from a compound plus affix, eg faint-hearted, which is made up from faint + heart + -ed.
parataxis *n* (*gram*) use of successive clauses without connecting words.
parathyroid *adj* (*anat*) lying near the thyroid gland. * *n* a gland near the thyroid that secretes a hormone that regulates the body's calcium levels.
paratroops *npl* troops dropped by parachute into the enemy area.—**paratrooper** *n.*
paravane *n* a device shaped like a torpedo, with serrated teeth for destroying the moorings of sea mines.
parboil *vt* to boil briefly as a preliminary cooking procedure.
parbuckle *n* a rope sling for raising or lowering casks.
parcel *n* a tract or plot of land; a wrapped bundle; a package; a collection or group of persons, animals, or things. * *vt* (**parcelling, parcelled** *or* **parceling, parceled**) to wrap up into a parcel; (*with* **out**) to apportion.
parcenary *n* joint heirship.
parcener *n* a coheir.
parch *vti* to make or become hot and dry, thirsty; to scorch, roast.—**parched** *adj.*
parchment *n* the skin of a sheep, etc prepared as a writing material; paper like parchment.
pard *n* (*arch*) a leopard.
pardon *vt* to forgive; to excuse; to release from penalty. * *n* forgiveness; remission of penalty.—**pardonable** *adj.*—**pardonably** *adv.*
pardoner *n* one who pardons; (*hist*) a person licensed to sell papal indulgences.
pare *vt* to cut or shave; to peel; to diminish.
paregoric *n* (*formerly*) an opium-based drug used to treat diarrhoea and coughs.
parenchyma *n* (*bot*) the soft cellular tissue or pith of plants; (*anat*) the soft tissue of the glandular organs of the body.—**parenchymatous, parenchymal** *adj.*
parent *n* a father or a mother; an organism producing another; a source.—**parental** *adj.*—**parentally** *adv.*—**parenthood** *n.*
parentage *n* descent, extraction from parents.
parenthesis *n* (*pl* **parentheses**) an explanatory comment in a sentence contained within brackets and set in a sentence, independently of grammatical sequence; the brackets themselves ( ).—**parenthetic, parenthetical** *adj.*—**parenthetically** *adv.*
parenthesize, parenthesise *vt* to insert as a parenthesis; to enclose in parentheses.
parenting *n* the act of being a parent; the role of a parent in relation to a child; that role in relation to someone who is not the child of a parent.
paresis *n* partial or slight paralysis.—**paretic** *adj.*
par excellence *adv* pre-eminently; to the highest degree.
parfait *n* a rich iced dessert of whipped cream, eggs, etc served in a tall glass; layers of ice cream served in a tall glass.
parget *n* a type of plaster. * *vt* to cover with parget.
parhelion *n* (*pl* **parhelia**) a bright spot on a solar halo.
pariah *n* a social outcast; a member of a low caste in southern India and Burma.
parietal *adj* (*anat*) pertaining to the wall of a cavity of the body; pertaining to the large lateral bones of the skull.
paring *n* the act of paring; what is pared off, rind.
pari-mutuel *n* (*pl* **pari-mutuels, paris-mutuels**) a mechanical betting system in which the losers' stakes, less a deduction for the management, are divided among the winners.
pari passu *adv* (*law*) with equal pace, together; in equal degree.
parish *n* an ecclesiastical area with its own church and clergy; the inhabitants of a parish.
parishioner *n* an inhabitant of a parish.
parisyllabic *adj* (*inflected noun or verb*) having an equal number of syllables in all or most inflected forms.
parity *n* (*pl* **parities**) equality; equality of value at a given ratio between different kinds of money, etc; being at par.
park *n* land kept as a game preserve or recreation area; a piece of ground in an urban area kept for ornament or recreation; an enclosed stadium, esp for ball games; a large enclosed piece of ground attached to a country house. * *vti* (*vehicle*) to leave in a certain place temporarily; to manoeuvre into a parking space.
parka *n* a warm hooded garment, often of fur, for wear in arctic conditions.
parking lot *n* a car park.
parking meter *n* a coin-operated machine that registers the purchase of parking time for a motor vehicle.
Parkinsonism *n* Parkinson's disease.
Parkinson's disease *n* a progressive nervous disease resulting in tremor, muscular rigidity, partial paralysis and weakness.
Parkinson's Law *n* any of various humorous observations on human behaviour framed as economic laws, esp the notion that work expands to fill the time available for its completion (named after the English writer C. N. Parkinson b. 1909).
parlance *n* a manner of speech, idiom.
parley *n* a conference, esp with an enemy. * *vi* to discuss, esp with an enemy with a view to bringing about a peace.
parliament *n* a legislative assembly made up of representatives of a nation or part of a nation; (*with cap*) the supreme governing and legislative body of various countries, esp the UK.
parliamentarian *n* a skilled parliamentary debater; an expert on parliamentary rules; (*with cap*) (*hist*) a supporter of the English Parliament against Charles I.
parliamentary *adj* of, used in, or enacted by a parliament; conforming to the rules of a parliament; having a parliament.
parlour *n* a room in a house used primarily for conversation or receiving guests; a room or a shop used for business.
parlour game *n* a game usually played indoors.
parlous *adj* (*arch*) dangerous; shrewd.—**parlously** *adv.*—**parlousness** *n.*
parmales *n* any of the order Parmales of single-celled algae found in the polar regions.
Parmesan *n* a hard cheese with a sharp flavour used, esp grated, as a garnish.
parochial *adj* of or relating to a parish; narrow; provincial in outlook.—**parochially** *adv.*
parochialism *n* narrow-mindedness.
parody *n* (*pl* **parodies**) a satirical or humorous imitation of a literary or musical work or style. * *vt* (**parodying, parodied**) to make a parody of.—**parodic** *adj.*—**parodist** *n.*
paroicous, paroecious *adj* (*bot*) with the two sexes developing in close proximity.
parole *n* word of honour; the release of a prisoner before his sentence has expired, on condition of future good behaviour. * *vt* to release on parole.
parolee *n* a person on parole.
paronomasia *n* a pun or play on words.
paronym *n* (*gram*) a paronymic word.
paronymic, paronymous *adj* (*gram*) with the same derivation; with the same sound but different spelling and meaning.
parotid *adj* (*anat*) situated near the ear. * *n* a parotid gland.
parotitis, parotiditis *n* mumps.
paroxysm *n* a sudden attack of a disease; a violent convulsion of pain or emotion; an outburst of laughter.—**paroxysmal** *adj.*
parquet *n* an inlaid hard wood flooring; the stalls of a theatre below the balcony. * *vt* to furnish (a room) with a parquet floor.
parquetry *n* mosaic woodwork used to cover floors.
parr *n* (*pl* **parrs, parr**) a young salmon.
parramatta *see* **paramatta.**
parrot *n* a tropical or subtropical bird with brilliant plumage and the ability to mimic human speech; one who repeats another's words without understanding. * *vt* to repeat mechanically.

parrotfish *n* (*pl* **parrotfish, parrotfishes**) a brightly coloured tropical fish, with mouth parts resembling a parrot's beak.

parry *vt* (**parrying, parried**) to ward off, turn aside. * *n* (*pl* **parries**) a defensive movement in fencing.

parse *vti* (*words*) to classify; (*sentences*) to analyse in terms of grammar; to give a grammatical description of a word or group of words.

parsec *n* (*astron*) a unit of measure for stellar distances equal to 3.26 light years, approx 19 million miles.

Parsee *n* an Indian adherent of the Zoroastrian religion.—**Parseeism** *n*.

parsimony *n* extreme frugality; meanness, stinginess.—**parsimonious** *adj*.

parsley *n* a bright green herb used to flavour or garnish some foods.

parsnip *n* a biennial plant cultivated for its long tapered root used as a vegetable.

parson *n* an Anglican clergyman in charge of a parish; (*inf*) any, esp Protestant, clergyman.

parsonage *n* the house provided for a parson by his church.

part *n* a section; a portion (of a whole); an essential, separable component of a piece of equipment or a machine; the role of an actor in a play; a written copy of his/her words; (*mus*) one of the melodies of a harmony; the music for it; duty, share; one of the sides in a conflict; a parting of the hair; (*pl*) qualities, talent; the genitals; a region, land or territory. * *vt* to separate; to comb the hair so as to leave a parting. * *vi* to become separated; to go different ways.

partake *vi* (**partaking, partook**; *pp* **partaken**) to participate (in); (*food or drink*) to have a portion of.

partan *n* (*Scot*) a crab.

parterre *n* an ornamental flower garden; the area of a ground floor of a theatre that lies underneath the balconies.

parthenocarpy *n* (*bot*) the formation of fruit without seeds having been formed or fertilized.

parthenogenesis *n* reproduction without sexual union; virgin birth.—**parthenogenetic** *adj*.

partial *adj* incomplete; biased, prejudiced; (*with* **to**) having a liking or preference for.—**partially** *adv*.

partiality *n* (*pl* **partialities**) biased judgment; (*with* **for**) liking, fondness.

partible *adj* able to be divided or separated.

participant *n* one who participates; a sharer.

participate *vi* to join in or take part with others (in some activity).—**participator** *n*.—**participatory** *adj*.

participation *n* the act of participating; the state of being related to a larger whole.

participle *n* (*gram*) a verb form used in compound forms or as an adjective.—**participial** *adj*.—**participially** *adv*.

particle *n* a tiny portion of matter; a speck; a very small part; (*gram*) a word that cannot be used alone, a prefix, a suffix.

parti-coloured *adj* differently coloured in different parts, variegated.

particular *adj* referring or belonging to a specific person or thing; distinct; exceptional; careful; fastidious. * *n* a detail, single item; (*pl*) detailed information.

particularism *n* exclusive devotion to one party or sect; the principle of political freedom for each state in a federation; the theological doctrine that salvation is only for the elect.—**particularist** *n*.

particularity *n* (*pl* **particularities**) the quality of being particular, as distinguished from universal; exactness; fastidiousness.

particularize *vt* to describe in detail; to mention one by one.—**particularization** *n*.

particularly *adv* very; especially; in detail.

parting *n* a departure; a breaking or separating; a dividing line in combing hair. * *adj* departing, esp dying; separating; dividing.

partisan, partizan *n* a strong supporter of a person, party, or cause.—*also adj*.—**partisanship, partizanship** *n*.

partite *adj* (*bot*) divided almost to the base.

partition *n* division into parts; that which divides into separate parts; a dividing wall between rooms. * *vt* to divide.

partitive *adj* (*gram*) denoting a part or partition. * *n* a partitive word.

partizan *see* **partisan.**

partly *adv* in part; to some extent.

partner *n* one of two or more persons jointly owning a business who share the risks and profits; one of a pair who dance or play a game together; either member of a married or non-married couple. * *vt* to be a partner (in or of); to associate as partners.

partnership *n* a contract between two or more people involved in a joint business venture; the state of being a partner.

part of speech *n* each of the categories (eg verb, noun, adjective) into which words are divided according to their grammatical and semantic functions.

partook *see* **partake.**

partridge *n* (*pl* **partridge, partridges**) a stout-bodied game bird of the grouse family.

part song *n* a song with two or more voice parts.

part-time *adj* working fewer than the full number of hours.—**part-timer** *n*.—**part time** *adv*.

parturient *adj* pertaining to childbirth; about to give birth, in labour.

parturition *n* the act of childbirth.

party *n* (*pl* **parties**) a group of people united for political or other purpose; a social gathering; a person involved in a contract or lawsuit; a small company, detachment; a person consenting, accessory; (*inf*) an individual. * *vb* (**partying, partied**) *vi* to attend social parties. * *vt* to give a party for. * *adj* of or for a party.

party line *n* a telephone line shared by two or more subscribers; the policies of a political body.

parvenu *n* someone regarded as vulgar or an upstart, following a rise in his social or economic status.—**parvenue** *nf*.

pas *n* (*pl* **pas**) (*ballet*) a step or series of steps; a dance sequence.

PASCAL *n* a high-level computer programming language used esp for teaching.

pascal *n* the SI unit of pressure.

pas de deux *n* (*pl* **pas de deux**) a ballet sequence for two dancers.

pasha *n* a Turkish title given to a high official; (*formerly*) a provincial governor in the Ottoman Empire.—*also* **pacha.**

pasque-flower *n* a type of anemone which flowers around Easter.

pasquinade *n* a lampoon or rude satire.

pass *vb* (**passing, passed**) *vi* to go past; to go beyond or exceed; to move from one place or state to another; (*time*) to elapse; to go; to die; to happen; (*with* **for**) to be considered as; (*in exam*) to be successful; (*cards*) to decline to make a bid; (*law*) to be approved by a legislative assembly. * *vt* to go past, through, over, etc; (*time*) to spend; to omit; (*law*) to enact; (*judgment*) to pronounce; to excrete; (*in test, etc*) to gain the required marks; to approve. * *n* a narrow passage or road; a permit; (*in a test, etc*) success; transfer of (a ball) to another player; a gesture of the hand; (*inf*) an uninvited sexual approach.

passable *adj* fairly good, tolerable; (*a river, etc*) that can be crossed.—**passably** *adv*.

passage *n* act or right of passing; transit; transition; a corridor; a channel; a route or crossing; a lapse of time; a piece of text or music.

passageway *n* a narrow way, esp flanked by walls, that allows passage; a corridor.

passbook *n* a bankbook.

passé *adj* past its best; outdated.

passementerie *n* a decorative trimming of gold or silver lace, braid, beads, etc.

passenger *n* a traveller in a public or private conveyance; one who does not pull his/her weight.

passe-partout *n* a frame for a picture in which the picture, glass and backing are held together by gummed paper; a master key.

passer-by *n* (*pl* **passers-by**) one who happens to pass or go by.

passerine *adj* pertaining to the order of birds which perch.—*also n*.

passim *adv* here and there; throughout.

passing *adj* transient; casual. * *n* departure, death.

passion *n* compelling emotion, such as love, hate, envy; ardent love, esp sexual desire; (*with cap*) the suffering of Christ on the cross; the object of any strong desire.—**passionless** *adj*.
passional *adj* pertaining to passion; due to passion.
passionate *adj* moved by, showing, strong emotion or desire; intense; sensual.—**passionately** *adv*.
passionflower *n* a chiefly tropical climbing vine.
passion fruit *n* the edible fruit of a passion flower.
Passion play *n* a play representing Christ's Passion.
Passion Sunday *n* the second Sunday before Easter.
passive *adj* acted upon, not acting; submissive; (*gram*) denoting the voice of a verb whose subject receives the action.—**passively** *adv*.—**passivity** *n*.
passive resistance *n* nonviolent noncooperation with the authorities.
passive smoking *n* the involuntary inhalation of smoke from others' cigarettes.
Passover *n* (*Judaism*) a spring holiday, celebrating the liberation of the Israelites from slavery in Egypt.
passport *n* an official document giving the owner the right to travel abroad; something that secures admission or acceptance.
password *n* a secret term by which a person is recognized and allowed to pass; any means of admission; a sequence of characters required to access a computer system.
past *adj* completed; ended; in time already elapsed. * *adv* by. * *prep* beyond (in time, place, or amount). * *n* time that has gone by; the history of a person, group, etc; a personal background that is hidden or questionable.
pasta *n* the flour paste from which spaghetti, noodles, etc is made; any dish of cooked pasta.
paste *n* a soft plastic mixture; flour and water forming dough or adhesive; a fine glass used for artificial gems. * *vt* to attach with paste; (*sl*) to beat, thrash.
pasteboard *n* a stiff board made from sheets of paper pasted together. * *adj* flimsy.
pastel *n* a dried mixture of chalk, pigments and gum used for drawing; a drawing made with such; a soft, pale colour. * *adj* delicately coloured.
pastelist *n* an artist who uses pastels.
pastern *n* the part of a horse's foot between the fetlock and the hoof.
Pasteur treatment *n* (*med*) a method of inoculation against rabies by successive injections of vaccine.
pasteurize *vt* (*milk, etc*) to sterilize by heat or radiation to destroy harmful organisms.—**pasteurization** *n*.
pastiche *n* (*pl* **pastiches**) a literary, musical, or artistic work in imitation of another's style, or consisting of pieces from other sources.—*also* **pasticcio** (*pl* **pasticci**).
pastille, pastil *n* an aromatic or medicated lozenge.
pastime *n* a hobby; recreation, diversion.
pastor *n* a clergyman in charge of a congregation.
pastoral *adj* of shepherds or rural life; pertaining to spiritual care, esp of a congregation.—**pastorally** *adv*.
pastorale *n* a musical composition with a pastoral subject.
pastorate *n* the office or jurisdiction of a pastor; a collective term for pastors.
pastrami *n* highly seasoned smoked beef.
pastry *n* (*pl* **pastries**) dough made of flour, water, and fat used for making pies, tarts, etc; (*pl*) baked foods made with pastry.
pasturage *n* the right to graze animals; pasture.
pasture *n* land covered with grass for grazing livestock; the grass growing on it. * *vt* (*cattle, etc*) to put out to graze in a pasture.
pasty[1] *n* (*pl* **pasties**) meat, etc enclosed in pastry and baked.
pasty[2] *adj* (**pastier, pastiest**) like paste; pallid and unhealthy in appearance.—**pastily** *adv*.—**pastiness** *n*.
pat[1] *vti* (**patting, patted**) to strike gently with the palm of the hand or a flat object; to shape or apply by patting. * *n* a light tap, usu with the palm of the hand; a light sound; a small lump of shaped butter.
pat[2] *adj* apt; exact; glib.—*also adv*.
patagium *n* (*pl* **patagia**) (*zool*) the wing membrane of a bat.
patch *n* a piece of cloth used for mending; a scrap of material; a shield for an injured eye; a black spot of silk, etc worn on the face; an irregular spot on a surface; a plot of ground; a bandage; an area or spot. * *vt* to repair with a patch; to piece together; to mend in a makeshift way.—**patchable** *adj*.—**patcher** *n*.
patchouli, patchouly *n* an Asian plant which yields an essential oil from which a perfume is made.
patchwork *n* needlework made of pieces sewn together; something made of various bits.
patchy *adj* (**patchier, patchiest**) irregular; uneven; covered with patches.—**patchily** *adv*.—**patchiness** *n*.
pate *n* the head.
pâté *n* a rich spread made of meat, fish, herbs, etc.
pâté de foie gras *n* (*pl* **pâtés de foie gras**) a rich paste made from goose liver.
patella *n* (*pl* **patellae**) (*anat*) the kneecap.—**patellar** *adj*.
paten *n* (*Christian Church*) a plate used for the bread at the Eucharist.
patent *adj* plain; apparent; open to public inspection; protected by a patent. * *n* a government document, granting the exclusive right to produce and sell an invention, etc for a certain time; the right so granted; the thing protected by such a right. * *vt* to secure a patent for.—**patentable** *adj*.
patentee *n* a holder of a patent.
patent leather *n* leather with a hard, glossy finish.
patent medicine *n* a medicine made and sold under patent and available without a prescription.
patent office *n* an office which issues patents.
patently *adv* obviously, openly.
patentor *n* the grantor of a patent.
paterfamilias *n* (*pl* **patresfamilias**) the (male) head of a family.
paternal *adj* fatherly in disposition; related through the father.—**paternally** *adv*.
paternalism *n* a system that provides for human needs but allows no individual responsibility.—**paternalist** *adj, n*.—**paternalistic** *adj*.—**paternalistically** *adv*.
paternity *n* fatherhood; origin or descent from a father.
paternity suit *n* a lawsuit to determine whether a particular man is the father of a particular child.
paternity test *n* a blood test to establish whether a man is or is not the father of a particular child.
paternoster *n* the Lord's Prayer in Latin; every eleventh bead in a rosary; a fishing line with hooks at intervals; an elevator consisting of a continuously revolving belt of linked compartments.
path *n* (*pl* **paths**) a way worn by footsteps; a track for people on foot; a direction; a course of conduct.
-path *n suffix* denoting an expert in a specific area of medicine; denoting a person suffering from a specified disorder.
pathetic *adj* inspiring pity; (*sl*) uninteresting, inadequate.—**pathetically** *adv*.
pathetic fallacy *n* the attribution of human emotions to inanimate objects.
pathfinder *n* a person who discovers a way; a person who explores untraversed regions to mark out a new route; a person or thing that marks a spot; a radar device for homing on to a target or navigating.—**pathfinding** *n*.
patho- *prefix* disease.
pathogen *n* an agent, such as a microorganism, that causes disease.—**pathogenic** *adj*.
pathogenesis, pathogeny *n* the origin and development of a disease.—**pathogenetic** *adj*.
pathognomonic *adj* characteristic of a particular disease.
pathological, pathologic *adj* of pathology; of the nature of, caused or altered by disease; (*inf*) compulsive.—**pathologically** *adv*.
pathologist *n* a medical specialist who diagnoses by interpreting the changes in tissue and body fluid caused by a disease.

pathology *n* (*pl* **pathologies**) the branch of medicine that deals with the nature of disease, esp its functional and structural effects; any abnormal variation from a sound condition.

pathos *n* a quality that excites pity or sadness; an expression of deep feeling.

pathway *n* a path; (*chem*) a sequence of enzyme-catalyzed reactions.

-pathy *n suffix* feeling; disease; medical treatment.

patience *n* the capacity to endure or wait calmly; a card game for one (—*also* **solitaire**).

patient *adj* even-tempered; able to wait or endure calmly; persevering. * *n* a person receiving medical, dental, etc treatment.—**patiently** *adv*.

patina *n* a green incrustation on old bronze; a surface appearance of something grown beautiful by age or use; a superficial covering or exterior.

patio *n* (*pl* **patios**) an inner, usu roofless, courtyard; a paved area adjoining a house, for outdoor lounging, dining, etc.

patisserie *n* a pastry shop; pastries.

patois *n* (*pl* **patois**) a dialect.

patriarch *n* the father and head of a family or tribe; a man of great age and dignity.—**patriarchal** *adj*.

patriarchate *n* the office, rank or jurisdiction of a patriarch; people ruled by a patriarch.

patriarchy *n* (*pl* **patriarchies**) government by the head of a family, tribe, etc; a community ruled in this way.

patrician *n* (*ancient Rome*) a member of the nobility. * *adj* aristocratic; oligarchic.

patricide *n* the unlawful killing of one's father; a person who kills his or her father.—**patricidal** *adj*.

patrimony *n* (*pl* **patrimonies**) an estate or right inherited from a father or one's ancestors; an ecclesiastical endowment or estate.—**patrimonial** *adj*.

patriot *n* one who strongly supports and serves his or her country.—**patriotic** *adj*.—**patriotically** *adv*.

patriotism *n* love for or loyalty to one's country.

patristic, patristical *adj* pertaining to the theology and writings of the fathers of the early Christian church.

patrol *vti* (**patrolling, patrolled**) to walk around a building or area in order to watch, guard, inspect. * *n* the act of going the rounds; a unit of persons or vehicles employed for reconnaissance, security, or combat; a subdivision of a Scout or Guide group.—**patroller** *n*.

patrolman *n* (*pl* **patrolmen**) (*chiefly US*) a policeman who patrols a particular area.

patron *n* a regular client or customer; a person who sponsors and supports the arts, charities, etc; a protector.—**patronal** *adj*.

patronage *n* the support given or custom brought by a patron; clientele; business; trade; the power to grant political favours; such favours.

patronize *vt* to treat with condescension; to sponsor or support; to be a regular customer of.—**patronization** *n*.

patronizing *adj* condescending.—**patronizingly** *adv*.

patronymic *adj* derived from the name of an ancestor. * *n* a name derived from an ancestor.

patsy *n* (*pl* **patsies**) (*sl*) a gullible person; a sucker.

patten *n* a wooden shoe on a metal ring, worn as a protection from the damp.

patter[1] *vi* to make quick tapping sounds, as if by striking something; to run with light steps. * *n* the sound of tapping or quick steps.

patter[2] *vi* to talk rapidly and glibly; to mumble (prayers, etc) mechanically. * *vt* to repeat speech mechanically, to gabble. * *n* rapid speech, esp that of a salesman, comedian, etc; glib speech; chatter; jargon.

pattern *n* a decorative arrangement; a model to be copied; instructions to be followed to make something; a regular way of acting or doing; a predictable route, movement, etc. * *vt* to make or do in imitation of a pattern.—**patterned** *adj*.

patty *n* (*pl* **patties**) a small pie; a flat cake of ground meat, fish, etc, usu fried.

patulous *adj* (*bot*) spreading, extended.

paucity *n* fewness; lack of; scarcity.

paulownia *n* a member of a Japanese genus of trees, with heart-shaped leaves and purple flowers.

paunch *n* the belly, esp a potbelly.

paunchy *adj* (**paunchier, paunchiest**) having a big belly.—**paunchiness** *n*.

pauper *n* a very poor person; (*formerly*) a person dependent on charity.—**pauperism** *n*.

pauperize, pauperise *vt* to reduce to pauperism.

pause *n* a temporary stop, esp in speech, action or music. * *vi* to cease in action temporarily, wait; to hesitate.

pavage *n* a tax paid for paving streets.

pavane, pavan *n* (the music for) an old stately dance.

pave *vt* (*a road, etc*) to cover with concrete to provide a hard level surface; **pave the way** to prepare a smooth easy way; to facilitate development.—**paving** *n*.

pavement *n* flat slabs, tiles, etc forming a surface, esp on a public thoroughfare.

pavilion *n* an annexe; a temporary building for exhibitions; a large ornate tent.

pavonine *adj* pertaining to peacocks; resembling a peacock.

paw *n* a foot of a mammal with claws; (*sl*) a hand. * *vti* to touch, dig, hit, etc with paws; to maul; to handle clumsily or roughly.

pawky *adj* (**pawkier, pawkiest**) (*Scot*) having a dry sense of humour.

pawn[1] *n* the piece of lowest value in chess; a person used to advance another's purpose.

pawn[2] *vt* to deposit an article as security for a loan; to wager or risk. * *n* a thing pawned; the state of being given as a pawn.—**pawner** *n*.

pawnbroker *n* a person licensed to lend money at interest on personal property left with him as security.—**pawnbroking** *n*.

pawnshop *n* a pawnbroker's shop.

pawpaw *see* **papaw**.

paxwax *n* a strong tendon in an animal's neck.

pay *vti* (**paying, paid**) to give (money) to in payment for a debt, goods or services; to give in compensation; to yield a profit; to bear a cost; to suffer a penalty; (*homage, attention*) to give. * *n* payment for services or goods; salary, wages.—**paying** *adj*.—**payer** *n*.

payable *adj* that must be paid, due; to be paid on a specified date.

pay dirt *n* soil, gravel, etc worth mining for minerals; (*inf*) a source of wealth.

PAYE *abbr* = pay-as-you-earn; the deduction of income tax from wages or salaries at source.

payee *n* one to whom money is paid.

payload *n* cargo that earns revenue; the total load of an aircraft, spacecraft, satellite, etc.

paymaster *n* a person in charge of paying wages and salaries.

payment *n* the act of paying; amount paid; reward.

paynim *n* (*arch*) a heathen; a Muslim.

payola *n* a bribe paid for the clandestine promotion of a product, esp one paid to a disc jockey to play a particular record; a system of such bribes.

payphone *n* a coin-operated telephone.

payroll *n* a list of employees and their wages; the actual money for paying wages.

Pb (*chem symbol*) lead.

PBX *abbr* = private branch exchange.

PBS (*US*) *abbr* = Public Broadcasting System.

PC *abbr* = personal computer; police constable; political correctness, politically correct.

pc, p.c. *abbr* = per cent; postcard.

PCB *abbr* = polychlorinated biphenyl; printed circuit board.

P.D. (*US*) *abbr* = Police Department; postal district.

Pd (*chem symbol*) palladium.

pd *abbr* = paid.

p.d.q. *abbr* = pretty damn quick.

PE *abbr* = Prince Edward Island; physical education.

pea *n* the edible, round, green seed of a climbing leguminous annual plant.

peace *n* tranquillity, stillness; freedom from contention, violence or war; a treaty that ends a war.

peaceable *adj* inclined to peace.—**peaceably** *adv*.—**peaceableness** *n*.

Peace Corps *n* a US government organization that sends volunteers to work on social, educational, agricultural, etc projects in developing countries.

peace dividend *n* the increase in funds for domestic civil expenditure from a reduction in the defence budget.

peaceful *adj* having peace; tranquil; quiet.—**peacefully** *adv*.—**peacefulness** *n*.

peacemaker *n* one who makes or restores peace; one who reconciles enemies.—**peacemaking** *adj*, *n*.

peace offering *n* a conciliatory gift.

peace pipe *n* a tobacco pipe smoked by American Indians as a sign of peace.

peach *n* a round, sweet, juicy, downy-skinned stone-fruit; the tree bearing it; a yellowish pink colour; (*sl*) a well-liked person or thing.

peachy *adj* (**peachier, peachiest**) of or resembling a peach; (*inf*) great, excellent.—**peachily** *adv*.—**peachiness** *n*.

peacock *n* (**peacocks, peacock**) a male peafowl with a large brilliantly coloured fan-like tail; a person who is a show-off.

peafowl *n* (**peafowls, peafowl**) a peacock or a peahen.

pea-green *adj* bright green.

peahen *n* a female peafowl.

peak *n* the summit of a mountain; the highest point; the pointed end of anything; maximum value; the eyeshade of a cap, visor. * *vti* (*politician, actor, etc*) to reach or cause to reach the height of power, popularity; (*prices*) to reach and stay at the highest level.

peaked *adj* pointed; having a peak; peaky.

peaky *adj* (**peakier, peakiest**) drawn, emaciated; sickly; peaked.

peal *n* a reverberating sound as of thunder, laughter, bells, etc; a set of bells, the changes rung on them. * *vti* to sound in peals, ring out.

pean *see* **paean**.

peanut *n* a leguminous plant with underground pods containing edible seeds; the pod or any of its seeds; (*pl*) (*sl*) a trifling thing or amount.

peanut butter *n* a food paste made by grinding roasted peanuts.

pear *n* a common juicy fruit of tapering oval shape; the tree bearing it.

pearl *n* the lustrous white round gem produced by oysters; mother-of-pearl; anything resembling a pearl intrinsically or physically; one that is choice and precious; a bluish medium grey. * *vti* to fish for pearls; to form drops (on), to bespangle.—**pearler** *n*.—**pearliness** *n*.

pearl button *n* a button covered with mother-of-pearl.

pearl diver *n* a person who dives for pearl oysters.

pearl oyster *n* any of various marine bivalve molluscs that yield pearls.

pearly *adj* (**pearlier, pearliest**) clear, lustrous, like a pearl; covered with pearls; bluish grey. * *n* (*pl* **pearlies**) (*pl*) a London costermonger's dress covered with pearl buttons.

Pearly Gates *npl* (*inf*) the gates of Heaven.

pearmain *n* a variety of apple.

peasant *n* (*inf*) a countryman or countrywoman; an agricultural labourer; (*derog*) a lout.

peasantry *n* peasants as a class.

pease *n* (*arch*) a pea.

peashooter *n* a toy blowpipe through which peas, etc, are blown.

peasouper *n* (*sl*) a thick yellow fog.

peat *n* decayed vegetable matter from bogs, which is dried and cut into blocks for fuel or used as a fertilizer.—**peaty** *adj*.

pebble *n* a small rounded stone; an irregular, grainy surface.—**pebbled** *adj*.—**pebbly** *adj*.

pecan *n* a hickory tree widely grown in the US and Mexico for its edible nuts; its wood; its thin-shelled nut.

peccable *adj* liable to sin.—**peccability** *n*.

peccadillo *n* (*pl* **peccadilloes, peccadillos**) a trifling misdeed, indiscretion.

peccary *n* (*pl* **peccaries, peccary**) an American wild piglike mammal.

peccavi *n* (*pl* **peccavis**) a confession of guilt.

peck *vt* to strike with the beak or a pointed object; to pick at one's food; (*inf*) to kiss lightly; to nag.—*also n*.

pecker *n* something, esp a bird, that pecks; (*sl*) penis.

pecking order *n* a social hierarchy in groups of some birds (eg hens), characterized by the pecking of those lower in the scale and submitting to being pecked by those higher; any social hierarchy.

peckish *adj* (*inf*) hungry; irritable.—**peckishly** *adv*.—**peckishness** *n*.

pecten *n* (*pl* **pectens, pectines**) (*zool*) a comblike membrane on the eyes of birds and some reptiles.

pectin *n* a carbohydrate found in fruits and vegetables, yielding a gel that is used to set jellies.—**pectic** *adj*.

pectoral *adj* of or relating to the breast, chest. * *n* the muscle in the chest; something worn on the breast.

peculate *vt* to appropriate money entrusted to one's care, to embezzle.—**peculation** *n*.—**peculator** *n*.

peculiar *adj* belonging exclusively (to); special; distinct; characteristic; strange.—**peculiarly** *adv*.

peculiarity *n* (*pl* **peculiarities**) an idiosyncrasy; a characteristic; an oddity.

pecuniary *adj* of or consisting of money.—**pecuniarily** *adv*.

pedagogue *n* a schoolteacher.—**pedagogic, pedagogical** *adj*.

pedagogy *n* the art or science of teaching.

pedal[1] *n* a lever operated by the foot. * *vt* (**pedalling, pedalled** *or* **pedaling, pedaled**) to operate or propel by pressing pedals with the foot.—**pedaller, pedaler** *n*.

pedal[2] *adj* (*zool*) pertaining to the foot or feet.

pedalo *n* (*pl* **pedalos**) a small pedal-operated pleasure boat.

pedant *n* a person who attaches too much importance to insignificant details.

pedantic *adj* of, relating to, or being a pedant; narrowly learned.—**pedantically** *adv*.

pedantry *n* (*pl* **pedantries**) an ostentatious display of learning; the state of being a pedant.

pedate *adj* (*bot*) having lateral sections divided into lobes; (*zool*) having, or resembling, feet.

peddle *vt* to go from place to place selling small items; to sell (drugs, etc) illegally.

peddler *n* a person who peddles goods; a person who sells drugs illegally.

pederast *n* a person who practises pederasty.

pederasty *n* sex between a man and a boy.

pedestal *n* the base that supports a column, statue, etc. * *vt* to set on a pedestal; to serve as a pedestal for.

pedestrian *adj* on foot; dull, commonplace. * *n* a person who walks.

pedestrianism *n* walking, or a fondness for walking; the quality of being dull or commonplace.

pedestrianize *vti* to convert (an area) for use by pedestrians only.—**pedestrianization** *n*.

pedicab *n* a pedal-driven rickshaw.

pedicular, pediculous *adj* pertaining to lice; infested with lice.—**pediculosis** *n*.

pedicure *n* cosmetic care of the feet, toes, and nails; a person trained to care for feet in this way.

pediform *adj* foot-shaped.

pedigree *n* a line of descent of an animal; a recorded purity of breed of an individual; a genealogy; lineage; derivation. * *adj* having a known ancestry.—**pedigreed** *adj*.

pediment *n* a triangular ornament crowning the front of a classical building, esp a Greek temple.—**pedimental, pedimented** *adj*.

pedometer *n* an instrument for measuring the distance walked by recording the number of steps taken.

peduncle *n* a flower stalk.—**peduncular** *adj*.

pedunculate, pedunculated *adj* having, or growing upon, a peduncle.

pee *vi* (*sl*) to urinate. * *n* urination; urine.

peek *vi* to look quickly or furtively.—*also n*.

peekaboo *n* a child's game in which one person hides behind his or her hands then peeps out suddenly, shouting, "peekaboo!".

peel *vt* to remove skin or rind from; to bare. * *vi* to flake off, as skin or paint. * *n* rind, esp that of fruit and vegetables.—**peeling** *n*.
peeler *n* a device for peeling; (*sl*) a stripteaser.
peen *n* the pointed or thin end of a hammer-head.
peep[1] *vi* to make shrill noises as a young bird. * *n* a peeping sound.
peep[2] *vi* to look hastily or furtively; to look through a slit or narrow opening; to be just showing. * *n* a furtive or hurried glance, a glimpse; (*of day*) the first appearance.
peeper *n* one who peeps; (*sl*) the eye; (*sl*) a private detective.
peephole *n* a small hole, esp in a door, to spy through.
peeping Tom *n* a person who peeps furtively, a voyeur.
peepshow *n* a small show, esp of erotic pictures, viewed through a hole with a lens; a live show with a nude model, viewed from a booth.
peepul *n* an Indian fig tree, sacred to Buddhists.—*also* **pipal**.
peer[1] *vi* to look closely; to look with difficulty; to peep out.
peer[2] *n* an equal in rank, ability, etc; a nobleman.—**peeress** *nf*.
peerage *n* the rank or title of a peer; peers collectively; a book with a list of peers.
peer group *n* a group of people of the same age, background, education, interests, etc.
peerless *adj* having no equal, matchless.
peeve *vt* (*inf*) to annoy.
peeved *adj* annoyed, resentful.
peevish *adj* fretful, irritable.—**peevishly** *adv*.—**peevishness** *n*.
peg *n* a tapered piece (of wood) for securing or hanging things on, for marking position; a predetermined level at which (a price) is fixed; (*mus*) one of the movable parts for tuning the string of an instrument. * *vti* (**pegging, pegged**) to fasten or mark with a peg; (*a price*) to keep steady; (*with* **away at**) to work steadily, persevere.
Pegasus *n* (*Greek myth*) the winged horse ridden by Bellerophon.
peignoir *n* a woman's dressing gown.
pejorative *adj* (*word, etc*) disparaging, derogatory. * *n* a disparaging word.—**pejoratively** *adv*.
peke *n* (*sl*) a Pekingese dog.
Pekingese, Pekinese *n* (*pl* **Pekingese, Pekinese**) a breed of small dog with long, silky hair, short legs, and a pug nose.
pekoe *n* a scented black Chinese tea.
pelage *n* the hair, wool or fur of an animal.
pelagian *adj* (*marine life*) of or inhabiting the open sea.—*also n*.—**pelagic** *adj*.
pelargonium *n* a member of a widely cultivated genus of flowering plants, including geraniums.
pelf *n* (*derog*) money, wealth.
pelican *n* a large fish-eating waterbird with an expandable pouched bill.
pelisse *n* a woman's long cloak, usu trimmed with fur.
pellagra *n* a disease affecting the skin and nervous system caused by a deficiency of nicotinic acid.—**pellagrous** *adj*.
pellet *n* a small ball of paper, bread, etc; a pill; a small ball of hair, bones, etc regurgitated by a bird of prey; a piece of shot. * *vt* to form into pellets.
pellicle *n* a thin skin or film.—**pellicular** *adj*.
pellitory *n* (*pl* **pellitories**) a European flowering plant, growing in walls.
pell-mell *adv, adj* in a disorderly rush; confusedly; headlong.
pellucid *adj* (*water, etc*) transparent; (*speech, writing, etc*) clear, lucid.—**pellucidity, pellucidness** *n*.
pelmet *n* a canopy for a window frame to hide a curtain rail, etc; a valance.
pelota *n* a Basque ball game similar to tennis, played with basket-shaped rackets against a wall.
pelt[1] *vt* to throw missiles, or words, at. * *vi* (*rain*) to fall heavily; to hurry, rush. * *n* a rush.—**pelter** *n*.
pelt[2] *n* a usu undressed skin of an animal with its hair, wool, or fur.
peltry *n* (*pl* **peltries**) a collective term for the pelts of animals.
pelvis *n* (*pl* **pelvises, pelves**) the bony cavity that joins the lower limbs to the body; the bones forming this.—**pelvic** *adj*.
pemmican, pemican *n* a cake of dried lean meat formerly used by North American Indians; a mixture of beef and suet used as emergency rations.
pemphigus *n* a rare skin disease, characterized by watery blisters.—**pemphigoid, pemphigous** *adj*.
pen[1] *n* an implement used with ink for writing or drawing. * *vt* (**penning, penned**) to write, compose.
pen[2] *n* a small enclosure for cattle, poultry, etc; a small place of confinement. * *vt* (**penning, penned**) to enclose in a pen, shut up.
pen[3] *n* a female swan.
pen[4] *n* (*sl*) a penitentiary.
penal *adj* relating to, liable to, or prescribing punishment; punitive.—**penally** *adv*.
penal code *n* a code of laws concerning crimes and offences and their punishment.
penalize *vt* to impose a penalty; to put under a disadvantage.—**penalization** *n*.
penalty *n* (*pl* **penalties**) a punishment attached to an offence; suffering or loss as a result of one's own mistake; a disadvantage imposed for breaking a rule as in sports; a fine.
penalty area *n* (*soccer*) the area in front of goal in which a foul by a defending player results in the award of a penalty kick.
penalty box *n* (*ice hockey*) an area of the ice where players are sent as a penalty.
penance *n* voluntary suffering to atone for a sin; a sacramental rite consisting of confession, absolution, and penance. * *vt* to impose a penance on.
pence *see* **penny**.
penchant *n* inclination, strong liking (for).
pencil *n* a pointed rod-shaped instrument with a core of graphite or crayon for writing, drawing, etc; a set of convergent light rays or straight lines; a fine paintbrush. * *vt* (**pencilling, pencilled** *or* **penciling, penciled**) to write, draw, or colour with a pencil; (*with* **in**) to commit tentatively.—**penciller, penciler** *n*.
pendant, pendent *n* a hanging ornament, esp a jewel on a necklace, bracelet, etc; a light-fitting suspended from a ceiling. * *adj* (*usu* **pendent**) hanging; projecting; undecided.—**pendency** *n*.
pendentive *n* (*archit*) a portion of a dome supported by a single pillar.
pending *adj* undecided; unfinished; imminent. * *prep* during; until, awaiting.
pendragon *n* (*hist*) a chief of the ancient Britons or Welsh.
pendulous *adj* hanging downwards and swinging freely.—**pendulously** *adv*.
pendulum *n* a weight suspended from a fixed point so as to swing freely; such a device used to regulate the movement of a clock; something that swings to and fro.
peneplain, peneplane *n* (*geol*) a tract of land which is almost a plain.
penetrable *adj* able to be penetrated.—**penetrability** *n*.
penetralia *npl* the inner parts of a temple, etc; mysteries.
penetrant *adj* penetrating. * *n* something which, or someone who, penetrates.
penetrate *vti* to thrust, force a way into or through something; to pierce; to permeate; to understand.—**penetrator** *n*.—**penetrative** *adj*.
penetrating *adj* acute, discerning; (*voice*) easily heard through other sounds.—**penetratingly** *adv*.
penetration *n* the capability, act, or action of penetrating; acute insight.
penguin *n* a flightless, marine bird with black and white plumage, usu found in the Antarctic.
penicillate *adj* (*biol*) having, or forming, small tufts.
penicillin *n* an antibiotic produced naturally and synthetically from moulds.
penile *adj* of, like, or affecting the penis.
peninsula *n* a piece of land almost surrounded by sea.—**peninsular** *adj*.
penis *n* (*pl* **penises, penes**) the male copulative and urinary organ in mammals.

penitence *n* sorrow for committing a sin, repentance.
penitent *adj* feeling regret for sin, repentant, contrite. * *n* a person who atones for sin.—**penitently** *adv*.
penitential *adj* of or expressing penance; being penitent.—**penitentially** *adv*.
penitentiary *n* (*pl* **penitentiaries**) (*US*) a state or federal prison. * *adj* pertaining to penance; pertaining to the reformatory treatment of prisoners.
penknife *n* (*pl* **penknives**) a small knife, usu with one or more folding blades, that fits into the pocket.
penman *n* (*pl* **penmen**) a writer.
penmanship *n* the art, or style, of writing.
Penn, Penna *abbr* = Pennsylvania.
pen name *n* a literary pseudonym.—*also* **nom de plume**.
pennant *n* a long tapering flag used for identifying vessels and for signalling; such a flag symbolizing a championship.
penniless *adj* having no money; poor.—**pennilessly** *adv*.—**pennilessness** *n*.
pennon *n* a small, pointed or swallow-tailed flag of a medieval knight; a long tapering streamer on a ship.
penny *n* (*pl* **pence** *denoting sum*, **pennies** *denoting separate coins*) a bronze coin of the UK worth one hundredth of a pound; (*formerly*) a bronze coin of the UK worth one twelfth of a shilling, or one two hundred and fortieth of a pound; (*US*) a one cent coin.
pennyroyal *n* an aromatic plant of the mint family.
pennyweight *n* a weight, equivalent to 24 grains or 1/20 of an ounce (troy).
pennywort *n* a kind of round-leafed plant, growing variously in walls or in marshes.
pennyworth *n* a penny's worth (of a purchase); a small amount.
penology *n* the study of the punishment and prevention of crime.—*also* **poenology**.—**penological** *adj*.—**penologist** *n*.
pen pal *n* a friend with whom one is in contact only through correspondence.
pensile *adj* suspended; pendulous.
pension *n* a periodic payment to a person beyond retirement age, or widowed, or disabled; a periodic payment in consideration of past services. * *vt* to grant a pension to; (*with* **off**) to dismiss or retire from service with a pension.—**pensionable** *adj*.
pensionary *adj* by way of pension. * *n* (*pl* **pensionaries**) a pensioner.
pensioner *n* a person who receives a pension; a senior citizen.
pensive *adj* thoughtful, musing; wistful, melancholic.—**pensively** *adv*.—**pensiveness** *n*.
pentacle *see* **pentagram**.
pentad *n* a group of five; the number five.
pentadactyl *adj* (*zool*) having five fingers or toes.
pentagon *n* (*geom*) a polygon with five sides; (*with cap*) the pentagonal headquarters of the US defence establishment; the US military leadership collectively.—**pentagonal** *adj*.
pentagram *n* a five-pointed star, often used as a magic symbol.—*also* **pentacle**.
pentahedron *n* (*pl* **pentahedrons, pentahedra**) a solid figure with five faces.
pentamerous *adj* (*bot, zool*) with five parts.
pentameter *n* a verse of five metrical feet.
pentangle *n* a pentagram.
Pentateuch *n* the collective name for the first five books of the Old Testament.
pentathlon *n* an athletic contest involving participation by each contestant in five different events.—**pentathlete** *n*.
pentatonic *adj* (*mus*) of five notes.
pentavalent *adj* (*chem*) with a valency of five.
Pentecost *n* a Christian festival on the seventh Sunday after Easter; Whit Sunday.
Pentecostal *adj* denoting a mainly Protestant Christian movement, now with various organized forms, emphasizing the immediate presence of God in the Holy Spirit; of Pentecost or the influence of the Holy Spirit. * *n* a member of a Pentecostal church.—**Pentecostalist** *adj, n*.
penthouse *n* an apartment on the roof or in the top floor of a building.
pentstemon *n* a flowering garden plant of the family including the beardtongues.—*also* (*chiefly US*) **penstemon**.
pent-up *adj* (*emotion*) repressed, confined.
penult *n* the penultimate syllable of a word. * *adj* last but one.
penultimate *adj* last but one.—*also adj*.
penumbra *n* (*pl* **penumbrae, penumbras**) a shaded region around the shadow of an opaque object, esp the shadow of the moon or earth in an eclipse; the lighter outer part of a sunspot; (*art*) the boundary of light and shade in a picture.—**penumbral** *adj*.
penurious *adj* grudging with money, stingy; poor; scanty.—**penuriously** *adv*.—**penuriousness** *n*.
penury *n* (*pl* **penuries**) extreme poverty; want.
peon *n* a Spanish American labourer; (*formerly*) a Spanish American labourer compelled to work to pay off debts.
peonage, peonism *n* the condition of being a peon; the system of compelling someone to work for a creditor to pay off debts.
peony *n* (*pl* **peonies**) a plant with large, showy, red, pink or white flowers.
people *n* the body of enfranchised citizens of a state; a person's family, relatives; the persons of a certain place, group, or class; persons considered indefinitely; human beings; (*pl*) all the persons of a racial or ethnic group, typically having a common language, institutions, homes, and culture. * *vt* to populate with people.
pep *n* (*inf*) energy, vigour; bounce. * *vt* (**pepping, pepped**) (*usu with* **up**) to enliven by injecting with pep.
pepper *n* a sharp, hot condiment made from the fruit of various plants; the fruit of the pepper plant, which can be red, yellow, or green, sweet or hot, and is eaten as a vegetable. * *vt* to sprinkle or flavour with pepper; to hit with small shot; to pelt; to beat.
peppercorn *n* a dried pepper berry.
pepper mill *n* hand mill for grinding peppercorns.
peppermint *n* a pungent and aromatic mint plant; its oil used for flavouring; a sweet flavoured with peppermint.
pepperoni *n* a spicy beef and pork sausage.
pepperwort *n* a form of aquatic or marsh fern; a type of cress.
peppery *adj* of, like, full of, pepper; fiery; hot-tempered.—**pepperiness** *n*.
peppy *adj* (**peppier, peppiest**) full of bounce; lively.—**peppiness** *n*.
pepsin, pepsine *n* a digestive enzyme contained in gastric juice.
pep talk *n* (*inf*) a vigorous talk made with the intention of arousing enthusiasm, increasing confidence, etc.
peptic *adj* of or promoting digestion; of, producing, or caused by the action of the digestive juices.
peptic ulcer *n* an ulcer of the stomach lining or duodenum.
peptone *n* a product of the action of pepsin on proteins.
peptonize *vt* to convert into peptone.
per *prep* for or in each; through, by, by means of; (*inf*) according to.
peradventure *adv* (*arch*) by chance; perhaps.
perambulate *vti* to walk around.—**perambulation** *n*.—**perambulatory** *adj*.
perambulator *n* one who or that which perambulates; (*Brit formal*) a pram.
per annum *adv* yearly; each year.
percale *n* a cotton fabric, often used for sheets.
per capita *adj, adv* of or for each person.
perceive *vt* to become aware of, apprehend, through the senses; to recognize.—**perceivable** *adj*.—**perceivably** *adv*.
per cent, percent *adv* in, for each hundred. * *n* a percentage.
percentage *n* rate per hundred parts; a proportion; (*inf*) profit, gain.
percept *n* something which is perceived.
perceptible *adj* able to be perceived; discernible.—**perceptibility** *n*.—**perceptibly** *adv*.
perception *n* the act or faculty of perceiving; discernment; insight; a way of perceiving, view.—**perceptional** *adj*.
perceptive *adj* able to perceive; observant.—**perceptively** *adv*.—**perceptivity, perceptiveness** *n*.
perch[1] *n* (*pl* **perch, perches**) a spiny-finned chiefly freshwater edible fish.
perch[2] *n* a pole on which birds roost or alight; an elevated seat or position. * *vti* to alight, rest, on a perch; to balance (oneself) on; to set in a high position.

perchance *adv* (*arch*) by chance; perhaps.
Percheron *n* a sturdy breed of draughthorse.
percipient *adj* perceiving; perceptive. * *n* a person who perceives.—**percipience** *n*.
percolate *vt* (*liquid*) to pass through a filter or pores; to brew coffee. * *vi* to ooze through; to spread gradually.—**percolation** *n*.
percolator *n* a coffeepot in which boiling water is forced through ground coffee beans.
percuss *vt* to tap sharply; (*med*) to tap (the patient's body) gently to find out the condition of an internal organ by sound.
percussion *n* impact, collision; musical instruments played by striking with sticks or hammers, eg cymbals, drums, etc; such instruments regarded as a section of an orchestra; (*med*) tapping the body to discover the condition of an organ by the sounds.—**percussive** *adj*.
percussionist *n* a person who plays a percussion instrument.
percutaneous *adj* (*med*) done through the skin.
per diem *adv, adj* every day. * *n* a daily allowance, as for expenses.
perdition *n* utter loss of the soul; eternal damnation; (*arch*) total destruction, ruin.
peregrinate *vti* to travel, roam about.—**peregrinator** *n*.—**peregrination** *n*.
peregrine *n* a type of falcon common to most areas of the world.
peremptory *adj* urgent; absolute; dogmatic; dictatorial.—**peremptorily** *adv*.—**peremptoriness** *n*.
perennial *adj* perpetual; lasting throughout the year. * *n* (*bot*) a plant lasting more than two years.—**perennially** *adv*.
perestroika *n* the Russian word for "reform, reconstruction," applied to the policy, initiated by President Gorbachev of the former USSR, of dismantling the monolithic state institutions and replacing them with democratic forms of legislation and administration.—**perestroikan** *adj*.
perfect *adj* faultless; exact; excellent; complete. * *n* (*gram*) a verb form expressing completed action or designating a present state that is the result of an action in the past. * *vt* to improve; to finish; to make fully accomplished in anything.—**perfecter** *n*.—**perfectness** *n*.
perfectible *adj* capable of being made perfect.—**perfectibility** *n*.
perfection *n* the act of perfecting; the quality or condition of being perfect; great excellence; faultlessness; the highest degree; a perfect person or thing.
perfectionist *n* one who demands the highest standard.—**perfectionism** *n*.
perfectly *adv* thoroughly, completely; quite well; in a perfect manner.
perfecto *n* (*pl* **perfectos**) a large cigar, tapered at both ends.
perfervid *adj* (*arch*) very fervid, ardent.
perfidious *adj* treacherous, faithless; deceitful.—**perfidiously** *adv*.—**perfidiousness** *n*.
perfidy *n* (*pl* **perfidies**) breach of faith; treachery.
perfoliate *adj* (*bot*) with a stalk which apparently passes through the leaf.
perforate *vt* to pierce; to make a hole or row of holes, by boring through. * *adj* perforated.—**perforatory** *adj*.—**perforator** *n*.
perforation *n* the act of perforating; the condition of being perforated; a hole; a row of holes to facilitate tearing.
perforce *adv* (*arch*) by necessity.
perform *vti* to carry out, do; to put into effect; to act; to execute; to act before an audience; to play a musical instrument.—**performable** *adj*.—**performing** *adj*.
performance *n* the act of performing; a dramatic or musical production; an act or action; (*inf*) a fuss; the capabilities of a vehicle, aircraft, etc. * *adj* high-performance.
performer *n* a person who performs, esp one who entertains an audience.
perfume *n* a pleasing odour; fragrance; a mixture containing fragrant essential oils and a fixative. * *vt* to scent; to put perfume on.—**perfumer** *n*.
perfumery *n* (*pl* **perfumeries**) a place where perfume is sold; perfume in general.
perfunctory *adj* superficial, hasty; done merely as a matter of form, halfhearted; performed carelessly; indifferent.—**perfunctorily** *adv*.—**perfunctoriness** *n*.
perfuse *vt* (*with* **with**) to suffuse, permeate.—**perfusion** *n*.—**perfusive** *adj*.
pergola *n* an arbour or walk arched by a latticework structure supporting climbing plants.
perhaps *adv* possibly, maybe.
peri- *prefix* around; near.
perianth *n* the outer part of a flower, comprising the calyx and corolla together.
periapt *n* an amulet.
pericarditis *n* inflammation of the pericardium.
pericardium *n* (*pl* **pericardia**) the membrane enclosing the heart.—**pericardiac, pericardial** *adj*.
pericarp *n* the part of a fruit developed from the wall of the ovary.—**pericarpial** *adj*.
perichondrium *n* (*pl* **perichondria**) the membrane covering a cartilage.
periclase *n* magnesium oxide as a mineral in crystal or grain form.
pericranium *n* (*pl* **pericrania**) the membrane surrounding the cranium.
peridot *n* a pale green semi-precious form of olivine.
perigee *n* the point of the moon's, or a planet's, orbit, when it is nearest the earth.—**perigean** *adj*.
perihelion *n* (*pl* **perihelia**) the point of a planet's or comet's orbit when it is nearest the sun.
peril *n* danger, jeopardy; risk, hazard.
perilous *adj* dangerous.—**perilously** *adv*.
perimeter *n* a boundary around an area; (*math*) the curve or line bounding a closed figure; the length of this.—**perimetric** *adj*.—**perimetry** *n*.
perineum *n* the area between the genitals and the anus.—**perineal** *adj*.
period *n* a portion of time; menstruation; an interval of time as in an academic day, playing time in a game, etc; an age or era in history, epoch; a stage in life; (*gram*) a full stop (.); (*astron*) a planet's time of revolution. * *interj* an exclamation used for emphasis.
periodic *adj* relating to a period; recurring at regular intervals, cyclic; intermittent.—**periodically** *adv*.—**periodicity** *n*.
periodical *adj* periodic. * *n* a magazine, etc issued at regular intervals.
periodic table *n* a list of chemical elements tabulated by their atomic number.
periodontics *n sing* the branch of dentistry dealing with disorders of the gums and tissues around the teeth.—**periodontal** *adj*.—**periodontist** *n*.
periosteum *n* (*pl* **periostea**) the membrane covering the bones.
periostitis *n* inflammation of the periosteum.
peripatetic *adj* itinerant; (*teacher*) travelling from one school to another.—*also n*.
peripheral *adj* incidental, superficial; relating to a periphery; (*equipment*) for connection to a computer. * *n* a device such as a printer, scanner, etc used with a computer.—**peripherally** *adv*.
periphery *n* (*pl* **peripheries**) the outer surface or boundary of an area; the outside surface of anything.
periphrasis *n* (*pl* **periphrases**) a roundabout way of speech; circumlocution.
periphrastic *adj* using periphrasis; circumlocutory.—**periphrastically** *adv*.
peripteral *adj* (*archit*) with a row of columns on every side.
periscope *n* a device with mirrors that enables the viewer to see objects above or around an obstacle or above water, as from a submarine.
periscopic *adj* (*lens*) with a view around; of a periscope.—**periscopically** *adv*.
perish *vi* to be destroyed or ruined; to die, esp violently; (*rubber, etc*) to deteriorate, rot. * *vt* to cause to rot or perish.
perishable *adj* liable to spoil or decay. * *n* something perishable, esp food.—**perishability** *n*.
peritoneum *n* (*pl* **peritoneums, peritonea**) a membrane that lines the walls of the abdomen.—**peritoneal** *adj*.
peritonitis *n* inflammation of the peritoneum.—**peritonitic** *adj*.
periwinkle[1] *n* any of various edible small marine gastropods with spiralled shells.
periwinkle[2] *n* any of various evergreen trailing plants with blue or white flowers.

perjure *vt* to commit perjury, swear falsely.—**perjurer** *n*.
perjury *n* (*pl* **perjuries**) (*law*) the crime of giving false witness under oath, swearing to what is untrue.
perk[1] *n* (*usu pl*) (*inf*) a perquisite.
perk[2] *vti* (*usu with* **up**) to recover self-confidence; to become lively or cheerful; to prick up, as of a dog's ears; to smarten up.
perky *adj* (**perkier, perkiest**) pert, cheeky; lively, jaunty.—**perkily** *adv*.—**perkiness** *n*.
perm *n* a straightening or curling of hair by use of chemicals or heat lasting through many washings. * *vt* (*hair*) to give a perm to.—*also* **permanent wave.**
permafrost *n* subsoil that is permanently frozen.
permanence *n* the condition or quality of being permanent.
permanency *n* (*pl* **permanencies**) permanence; a person or thing that is permanent.—**permanently** *adv*.
permanent *adj* lasting, or intended to last, indefinitely.
permanent wave *n* a perm.
permanganate *n* a salt of an acid of manganese, esp permanganate of potash.
permeable *adj* admitting the passage of a fluid.—**permeability** *n*.—**permeably** *adv*.
permeate *vti* to fill every part of, saturate; to pervade, be diffused (through); to pass through by osmosis.—**permeation** *n*.
permissible *adj* allowable.—**permissibility** *n*.
permission *n* authorization; consent.
permissive *adj* allowing permission; lenient; sexually indulgent.—**permissively** *adv*.—**permissiveness** *n*.
permit *vti* (**permitting, permitted**) to allow to be done; to authorize; to give opportunity. * *n* a licence.—**permitter** *n*.
permutation *n* any radical alteration; a change in the order of a series; any of the total number of groupings within a group; an ordered arrangement of a set of objects.—**permutational** *adj*.
permute *vt* to put into a different order.
pernicious *adj* destructive; very harmful.—**perniciously** *adv*.—**perniciousness** *n*.
pernickety *see* **persnickety.**
perorate *vi* to speak at length.
peroration *n* the final part of a speech or discourse.
peroxide *n* hydrogen peroxide; a colourless liquid used as an antiseptic and as a bleach.
perpendicular *adj* upright, vertical; (*geom*) at right angles (to). * *n* a perpendicular line, position or style.—**perpendicularity** *n*.—**perpendicularly** *adv*.
perpetrate *vt* (*something evil, criminal, etc*) to do; (*a blunder, etc*) to commit.—**perpetration** *n*.—**perpetrator** *n*.
perpetual *adj* continuous; everlasting; (*plant*) blooming continuously throughout the season.—**perpetually** *adv*.
perpetuate *vt* to cause to continue; to make perpetual.—**perpetuation** *n*.—**perpetuator** *n*.
perpetuity *n* (*pl* **perpetuities**) endless duration, eternity; perpetual continuance; an annuity payable forever.
perplex *vt* to puzzle, bewilder, confuse; to complicate.
perplexity *n* (*pl* **perplexities**) bewilderment, a being at a loss; a perplexing thing, a dilemma.
perquisite *n* an expected or promised privilege, gain, or profit incidental to regular wages or salary; a tip, gratuity; something claimed as an exclusive right.—*also* **perk.**
perron *n* a flight of steps outside a building, leading to the first floor.
perry *n* (*pl* **perries**) a cider-like drink made from pears.
per se *adv* by itself; by its very nature, intrinsically.
persecute *vt* to harass, oppress, esp for reasons of race, religion, etc; to worry persistently.—**persecutor** *n*.
persecution *n* a persecuting or being persecuted; unfair or cruel treatment for reasons of race, religion, etc; a time of persecution.
perseverance *n* persisting efforts of belief, esp in the face of opposition; steadfastness; (*Christianity*) continuance in grace.—**perseverant** *adj*.
persevere *vi* to persist, maintain effort, steadfastly, esp in face of difficulties.—**perseveringly** *adv*.
persiennes *npl* outside window shutters with horizontal louvres.
persiflage *n* frivolous talk, banter.
persimmon *n* one of a species of tropical American trees; the fruit of such a tree.
persist *vi* to continue in spite of obstacles or opposition; to persevere; to last.—**persister** *n*.
persistence, persistency *n* a persisting; tenacity of purpose.
persistent *adj* persevering; stubborn.—**persistently** *adv*.
persnickety *adj* (*inf*) fussy, fastidious; over-attentive to detail.—*also* **pernickety.**
person *n* (*pl* **persons**) a human being, individual; the body (including clothing) of a human being; (*in a play*) a character; one who is recognized by law as the subject of rights and duties; (*gram*) one of the three classes of personal pronouns and verb forms, referring to the person(s) speaking, spoken to, or spoken of.
persona *n* (*pl* **personae**) a person; a character in a play, etc; (*pl*) public role or image.
personable *adj* pleasing in personality and appearance.—**personableness** *n*.—**personably** *adv*.
personage *n* a distinguished person.
persona grata *n* (*pl* **personae gratae**) a person who is acceptable or welcome, esp a diplomat to a foreign government.
personal *adj* concerning a person's private affairs, or his or her character, habits, body, etc; done in person; (*law*) of property that is movable; (*gram*) denoting person.
personality *n* (*pl* **personalities**) one's individual characteristics; excellence or distinction of social and personal traits; a person with such qualities; a celebrity.
personalize *vt* to mark with name, initials, etc; to endow with personal characteristics; to take personally; to personify.—**personalization** *n*.
personally *adv* in person; in one's own opinion; as though directed to oneself.
personalty *n* (*pl* **personalties**) (*law*) personal property.
persona non grata *n* (*pl* **personae non gratae**) a person who is not acceptable or welcome, esp to a foreign government.
personate *vt* to play the part of (in a play etc); (*law*) to pretend to be (someone else) for fraudulent purposes.—**personation** *n*.—**personator** *n*.
personification *n* representation of an abstract idea or a thing as a person; an embodiment, a type; a perfect example.
personify *vt* (**personifying, personified**) to think of, represent, as a person; to typify.—**personifier** *n*.
personnel *n* the employees of an organization or company; the department that hires them.
perspective *n* objectivity; the art of drawing so as to give an impression of relative distance or solidity; a picture so drawn; relation, proportion, between parts of a subject; vista, prospect. * *adj* of or in perspective.
perspicacious *adj* of clear understanding; shrewd; discerning.—**perspicaciously** *adv*.—**perspicacity** *n*.
perspicuous *adj* clearly expressed, lucid.—**perspicuity** *n*.
perspiration *n* the salty fluid excreted on to the surface of the skin, sweat; the act of perspiring.
perspire *vti* to excrete (moisture) through the pores of the skin to cool the body, to sweat.—**perspiringly** *adv*.
persuadable, persuasible *adj* able to be persuaded.—**persuadability, persuasibility** *n*.
persuade *vt* to convince; to induce by argument, reasoning, advice, etc.—**persuader** *n*.
persuasion *n* the act of persuading; a conviction or opinion; a system of religious beliefs; a group adhering to such a system.
persuasive *adj* able to persuade; influencing the mind or emotions.—**persuasively** *adv*.—**persuasiveness** *n*.

pert *adj* impudent, cheeky; sprightly.—**pertly** *adv*.—**pertness** *n*.
pertain *vi* to belong to; to be appropriate to; to have reference to.
pertinacious *adj* persistent; unyielding; obstinate.—**pertinacity, pertinaciousness** *n*.
pertinent *adj* relevant, apposite; to the point.—**pertinence** *n*.—**pertinently** *adv*.
perturb *vt* to trouble; to agitate; to throw into confusion; (*astron*) to cause to undergo perturbation.—**perturbable** *adj*.—**perturbably** *adv*.—**perturbingly** *adv*.
perturbation *n* the state of being troubled, mental agitation; (*astron*) an irregularity or deviation in a regular orbit produced by some additional force.
peruse *vt* to read carefully, to examine.—**perusal** *n*.
pervade *vt* to permeate or spread through; to be rife among.—**pervasion** *n*.
pervasive *adj* able or tending to pervade.—**pervasively** *adv*.—**pervasiveness** *n*.
perverse *adj* deviating from right or truth; persisting in error; wayward; contrary.—**perversely** *adv*.—**perverseness** *n*.
perversion *n* an abnormal way of obtaining sexual gratification, eg sadism; a perverted form or usage of something.
perversity *n* (*pl* **perversities**) a being perverse; a disposition to thwart or annoy; a perverse act.
pervert *vt* to corrupt; to misuse; to distort. * *n* a person who is sexually perverted.—**perverter** *n*.—**pervertible** *adj*.
perverted *adj* wrong; harmful; unnatural; sexually deviant.—**pervertedly** *adv*.
pervious *adj* giving passage, permeable; open to new ideas.
pesade *n* (*dressage*) a position in which the horse is standing on its hind legs and raises its forelegs.
peseta *n* the unit of currency in Spain.
pesky *adj* (**peskier, peskiest**) (*inf*) troublesome, annoying.
peso *n* (*pl* **pesos**) a unit of currency in several Latin American countries and the Philippines.
pessary *n* (*pl* **pessaries**) (*med*) a surgical appliance or suppository inserted into the vagina.
pessimism *n* a tendency to see in the world what is bad rather than good; a negative outlook that always expects the worst.—**pessimist** *n*.—**pessimistic** *adj*.—**pessimistically** *adv*.
pest *n* anything destructive, esp a plant or animal detrimental to man as rats, flies, weeds, etc; a person who pesters or annoys.
pester *vt* to annoy or irritate persistently.—**pesterer** *n*.
pesticide *n* any chemical for killing pests.—**pesticidal** *adj*.
pestiferous *adj* spreading infection; (*fig*) physically or morally noxious.
pestilence *n* an outbreak of a fatal epidemic disease; anything regarded as harmful.
pestilent *adj* irritating; likely to cause a fatal epidemic.—**pestilently** *adv*.
pestilential *adj* of the nature of or conveying pestilence; harmful; annoying.—**pestilentially** *adv*.
pestle *n* a usu club-shaped tool for pounding or grinding substances in a mortar. * *vt* to beat, pound, or pulverize with a pestle.
pet *n* a domesticated animal kept as a companion; a person treated as a favourite. * *adj* kept as a pet; spoiled, indulged; favourite; particular. * *vti* (**petting, petted**) to stroke or pat gently; to caress; (*inf*) to kiss, embrace, etc in making love.
petal *n* any of the leaf-like parts of a flower's corolla.—**petaline** *adj*.—**petalled** *adj*.
petard *n* (*formerly*) a small bomb used to blow in a door, etc.
peter *vi* (*with* **out**) to come to an end; to dwindle to nothing.
petersham *n* a thick corded ribbon used in dressmaking as a stiffening; a thick woollen fabric used for overcoats, etc.
Peter's Pence *n* (*RC Church*) voluntary contributions to the papal treasury; (*formerly*) in England, an annual tax, until its abolishment by Henry VIII, of one penny levied on every house and paid to the Pope.
petiolate *adj* (*bot*) growing on a petiole.
petiole *n* (*bot*) a leaf stalk.
petit *adj* (*esp law*) of lesser importance.
petite *adj* (*woman*) small and trim in figure.
petition *n* a formal application or entreaty to an authority; a written demand for action by a government, etc, signed by a number of people. * *vti* to present a petition to; to ask humbly.—**petitionary** *adj*.—**petitioner** *n*.
petit mal *n* a mild form of epilepsy.
petit point *n* a fine stitch used in needlepoint.
petrel *n* a dark-coloured sea bird capable of flying far from land.
petrifaction, petrification *n* the process of changing animal or vegetable material into stone.
petrify *vti* (**petrifying, petrified**) to turn or be turned into stone; to stun or be stunned with fear, horror, etc.
petro- *prefix* rock, stone; petroleum.
petrochemical *n* any chemical obtained from natural gas or petroleum.
petrodollar *n* a notional unit of money earned by the export of petroleum.
petroglyph *n* a rock carving or drawing.
petrography *n* the scientific description and classification of rocks.—**petrographer** *n*.—**petrographic, petrographical** *adj*.
petrol *n* fuel obtained from petroleum; (*US*) gasoline.
petrolatum *n* a greasy, jelly-like substance obtained from petroleum and used for ointments, etc.
petroleum *n* a crude oil consisting of hydrocarbons occurring naturally in certain rock strata and distilled to yield petrol, paraffin, etc.
petrology *n* (*pl* **petrologies**) the study of rocks and their structure.
petrous *adj* of, or like, rock.
petticoat *n* an underskirt; a slip; (*inf*) woman.
pettifog *vi* to be, or behave like, a pettifogger.
pettifogger *n* an inferior or crooked lawyer; someone who quibbles over details.
pettish *adj* peevish, sulky.
pettitoes *npl* pig's trotters, esp as food.
petty *adj* (**pettier, pettiest**) trivial; small-minded; minor.—**pettily** *adv*.—**pettiness** *n*.
petty officer *n* a noncommissioned officer in the navy.
petulant *adj* showing impatience or irritation; bad-humoured.—**petulance** *n*.—**petulantly** *adv*.
petunia *n* a plant with funnel-shaped purple or white flowers.
petuntse *n* a fine white clay used with kaolin in the manufacture of porcelain.
pew *n* a wooden, bench-like seat in a church, often enclosed; (*sl*) a chair.
pewit *n* the lapwing.—*also* **peewit**.
pewter *n* an alloy of tin and lead with a silvery-grey colour; dishes, etc, made of pewter.—**pewterer** *n*.
PFC (*US*) *abbr* = private first class.
pfennig *n* (*pl* **pfennigs, pfennige**) a unit of currency in Germany worth one hundredth of a Deutschmark.
PG *abbr* = parental guidance: denoting a motion-picture suitable for all ages, but advising parental guidence.
PGA *abbr* = Professional Golfers' Association.
phaeton *n* a light, open, four-wheeled horse-drawn carriage.
phagocyte *n* a white corpuscle which devours harmful micro-organisms and other foreign bodies.
phagocytosis *n* the process by which a phagocyte devours foreign bodies.
phalange *see* **phalanx**.
phalangeal *adj* (*anat*) of or pertaining to a phalanx.
phalanger *n* a small tree-living marsupial of Australasia, with a long tail and bushy fur.
phalanx *n* (*pl* **phalanxes, phalanges**) a massed body or rank of people; (*pl* **phalanges**) a bone of a finger or toe.
phalarope *n* a small wading bird, with a straight bill and webbed feet.
phallic *adj* pertaining to, or resembling, a phallus.
phallicism, phallism *n* the worship of the phallus as the emblem of the generative power in nature.
phallus *n* (*pl* **phalli, phalluses**) the male reproductive organ.

phanerogam *n* (*bot*) a flowering plant.—**phanerogamic, phanerogamous** *adj*.
phantasm *n* a phantom; a vision of an absent person.
phantasmagoria, phantasmagory *n* a series of shifting images, like those seen in a dream.—**phantasmagoric, phantasmagorical** *adj*.
phantom *n* a spectre or apparition. * *adj* illusionary.
pharaoh *n* (*also with cap*) the title of the kings of ancient Egypt.—**pharaonic** *adj*.
Pharisaic, Pharisaical *adj* pertaining to, or characteristic of, the Pharisees; (*fig*) hypocritical.
Pharisee *n* a member of a Jewish religious sect, characterized by its strict observance of the letter of the law; (*fig*) a self-righteous person, a hypocrite.
pharmaceutical *adj* of, relating to pharmacy or drugs. * *n* a medicinal drug.
pharmaceutics *n sing* the science of pharmacy.
pharmacist *n* one licensed to practise pharmacy.
pharmacology *n* the science dealing with the effects of drugs on living organisms.—**pharmacological** *adj*.—**pharmacologist** *n*.
pharmacopoeia *n* a book containing a list of drugs with directions for their use.—**pharmacopoeial** *adj*.
pharmacy *n* (*pl* **pharmacies**) the preparation and dispensing of drugs and medicines; a drugstore.
pharyngeal, pharyngal *adj* pertaining to, or situated near, the pharynx.
pharyngitis *n* inflammation of the pharynx.
pharyngology *n* the medical study of the pharynx.
pharyngoscope *n* an instrument used for looking at the pharynx.
pharyngotomy *n* (*pl* **pharynotomies**) the surgical operation of making an incision into the pharynx.
pharynx *n* (*pl* **pharynges, pharynxes**) the cavity leading from the mouth and nasal passages to the larynx and oesophagus.
phase *n* (*pl* **phases**) an amount of the moon's or a planet's surface illuminated at a given time; a characteristic period in a regularly recurring sequence of events or stage in a development. * *vt* to do by stages or gradually; (*with* **out**) (*making, using, etc*) to stop gradually.—**phasic** *adj*.
PhD *abbr* = Doctor of Philosophy.
pheasant *n* a richly coloured game bird.
phellem *n* (*bot*) cork.
phenacetin *n* a drug used for the relief of pain and fever.
Phenobarbital *n* (*trademark*) a crystalline barbiturate used as a hypnotic and sedative.
phenol *n* carbolic acid.
phenology *n* the study of the influence of climate on certain recurrent phenomena of animal and plant life.
phenomenal *adj* perceptible through the senses; remarkable; outstanding.—**phenomenally** *adv*.
phenomenalism *n* (*philos*) the doctrine that all knowledge is derived from sense impressions.—**phenomenalist** *n*.
phenomenon *n* (*pl* **phenomena, phenomenons**) anything perceived by the senses as a fact; a fact or event that can be scientifically described; a remarkable thing or person.
phenyl *n* the hydrocarbon radical of phenol.
pheromone *n* a molecule that functions as a chemical communication signal between individuals of the same species.
phew *interj* an exclamation of relief, surprise, etc.
phi *n* the 21st letter of the Greek alphabet.
phial *n* a small glass bottle; a vial.
Phi Beta Kappa *n* (*US*) (a member of) the oldest college fraternity.
phil-, philo- *prefix* loving.
philander *vi* (*man*) to flirt with women for amusement.—**philanderer** *n*.
philanthropist *n* a person who tries to benefit others.
philanthropy *n* (*pl* **philanthropies**) love of mankind, esp as demonstrated by benevolent or charitable actions.—**philanthropic, philanthropical** *adj*.—**philanthropically** *adv*.
philatelist *n* a person who collects or studies stamps.
philately *n* the study and collecting of postage and imprinted stamps; stamp collecting.—**philatelic** *adj*.—**philatelically** *adv*.
philharmonic *adj* loving music.
philhellene *n* a lover or supporter of Greece.
philippic *n* a bitter denunciation, an invective.
philistine *n* a person with no feeling for culture; an uncultured, conventional person; (*with cap*) a member of a warlike race hostile to ancient Israel. * *adj* uncultured.—**philistinism** *n*.
philogyny *n* fondness for women.—**phylogynous** *adj*.—**phylogynist** *n*.
philology *n* the study, esp comparative, of languages and their history and structure.—**philological** *adj*.—**philologist, philologer** *n*.
philomel *n* (*poet*) a nightingale.
philosopher *n* a person who studies philosophy; a person who acts calmly and rationally.
philosophical, philosophic *adj* of, relating to, or according to philosophy; serene; temperate; resigned.—**philosophically** *adv*.
philosophize *vi* to reason like a philosopher; to speculate, moralize.—**philosophizer** *n*.
philosophy *n* (*pl* **philosophies**) the study of the principles underlying conduct, thought, and the nature of the universe; general principles of a field of knowledge; a particular system of ethics; composure; calmness.
philtre, philter *n* a love potion.
phlebitis *n* (*med*) an inflammation of a vein.—**phlebitic** *adj*.
phlebotomize *vti* (*med*) to practise phlebotomy (on).
phlebotomy *n* (*pl* **phlebotomies**) a surgical incision into a vein to let blood.—**phlebotomist** *n*.
phlegm *n* a thick mucus discharged from the throat, as during a cold; sluggishness; apathy.
phlegmatic, phlegmatical *adj* unemotional, composed; sluggish.—**phlegmatically** *adv*.
phloem *n* (*bot*) the tissue which carries food around a plant.
phlogiston *n* (*chem*) an inflammable element once believed to exist in all combustible bodies.
phlox *n* (*pl* **phlox, phloxes**) a North American flowering plant.
phobia *n* an irrational, excessive, and persistent fear of some thing or situation.—**phobic** *adj, n*.
phoenix *n* a mythical bird that set fire to itself and rose from its ashes every 500 years; a symbol of immortality.
phon *n* a unit of loudness.
phonate *vi* to utter vocal sounds.—**phonation** *n*.
phone *n, vti* (*inf*) (to) telephone.
phone book *n* (*inf*) telephone book.
phone-in *n* a radio programme in which questions or comments by listeners are broadcast.
phonetic *adj* relating to, or representing, speech sounds.—**phonetically** *adv*.
phonetician *n* a student of, or expert in, phonetics.
phonetics *n sing* the science concerned with pronunciation and the representation of speech sounds.
phonetist *n* a phonetician; an advocate of phonetic spelling.
phoney, phony *adj* (**phonier, phoniest**) (*inf*) not genuine. * *n* (*pl* **phoneys, phonies**) a fake; an insincere person.—**phoneyness, phoniness** *n*.
phonics *n sing* a phonetics-based method of teaching reading.—**phonic** *adj*.
phonogram *n* (*phonetics*) a written character representing a particular sound.
phonograph *n* a device for reproducing sounds from a vinyl disc.
phonography *n* spelling based on pronunciation; a system of shorthand writing based on sound.
phonology *n* (*pl* **phonologies**) the study of speech sounds and their development, and of the sound systems of language.—**phonological** *adj*.—**phonologist** *n*.
phony *see* **phoney**.
phosgene *n* a poisonous gas used in chemical warfare and in industry.
phosphate *n* a compound of phosphorus.—**phosphatic** *adj*.
phosphene *n* the sensation of luminous rings seen when a closed eye is pressed.

phosphide *n* a compound of phosphorus with another element.
phosphite *n* a salt of phosphorous acid.
phosphorescence *n* the property of giving off light without noticeable heat, as phosphorus does; such light.—**phosphorescent** *adj.*
phosphorous *adj* containing phosphorus in lower or higher proportions.
phosphorus *n* a highly reactive, poisonous nonmetallic element; a phosphorescent substance or body, esp one that glows in the dark.
photic *adj* of, or pertaining to, light.
photo *n* (*pl* **photos**) a photograph.
photo- *prefix* light; a photographic process.
photocell *n* a photoelectric cell.
photochemical *adj* of or relating to the effect of radiant energy, esp light.
photochemistry *n* the branch of chemistry concerned with the effect of radiant energy in producing chemical changes; photochemical properties or processes.
photocopy *n* (*pl* **photocopies**) a photographic reproduction of written or printed work. * *vt* (**photocopying, photocopied**) to copy in this way.—**photocopier** *n.*
photoelectric cell *n* a cell whose electrical properties are affected by light; any device in which light controls an electric circuit that operates a mechanical device, as for opening doors.—*also* **photocell.**
photoengraving *n* any photomechanical process of making printing plates.
photo finish *n* the finish of a race where the decision on the winner has to be determined by a photograph as the contestants are so close; any race where the winning margin is small.
photogenic *adj* likely to look attractive in photographs; (*biol*) generating light.—**photogenically** *adv.*
photograph *n* an image produced by photography.—*also* **photo.**
photographic *adj* of or like a photograph; minutely accurate like a photograph; (*memory*) capable of retaining facts, etc, after reading for only a brief time.—**photographically** *adv.*
photography *n* the art or process of recording images permanently and visibly by the chemical action of light on sensitive material, producing prints, slides or film.—**photographer** *n.*
photogravure *n* a printing process using an intaglio plate photographically produced; printed matter so produced.
photojournalism *n* a form of news reporting in which the story is presented mainly through photographs.—**photojournalist** *n.*
photolithograph *n* a picture produced by photolithography.
photolithography *n* (*print*) lithography using plates made from photographs.
photomechanical *adj* of or relating to a printing process that utilizes photography in plate-making.—**photomechanically** *adv.*
photometer *n* an instrument for measuring the intensity of light.
photometry *n* the area of physics concerned with the measurement of light; the use of a photometer.
photomicrograph *n* a photograph taken through a microscope.—**photomicrography** *n.*
photophobia *n* (*med*) oversensivity (of the eyes) to light; (*psychol*) fear or, or aversion to, sunlight.
photosphere *n* the surface of a star, esp the sun.
Photostat *n* (*trademark*) a device for making photographic copies of documents, etc; a copy made in this way. * *vt* (*often without cap*) to copy in this way.—**Photostatic** *adj.*
photosynthesis *n* (*bot*) the process by which a green plant manufactures sugar from carbon dioxide and water in the presence of light.—**photosynthetic** *adj.*—**photosynthetically** *adv.*
photosynthesize *vti* (*plants, etc*) to produce by or carry on photosynthesis.
phototelegraphy *n* the telegraphic transmission of photographs and drawings.
phrasal *adj* of or consisting of a phrase or phrases.—**phrasally** *adv.*
phrasal verb *n* (*gram*) a usu simple verb that combines with a preposition or adverb, or both, to convey a meaning more than the sum of its parts, eg *come out.*
phrase *n* a group of words that does not contain a finite verb but which expresses a single idea by itself; a pointed saying; a high-flown expression; (*mus*) a short, distinct musical passage. * *vt* to express orally, put in words; (*mus*) to divide into melodic phrases.
phrase book *n* a book containing idiomatic expressions of a foreign language and their translations.
phraseogram *n* a shorthand symbol representing a phrase.
phraseology *n* (*pl* **phraseologies**) mode of expression, wording; phrases used by a particular group.—**phraseological** *adj.*
phrasing *n* the wording of a speech or a piece of writing; (*mus*) the division of a melodic line, etc, into musical phrases.
phrenetic *see* **frenetic.**
phrenic *adj* (*anat*) of, or pertaining to, the diaphragm.
phrenology *n* the belief that intelligence and ability may be judged from the shape of a person's skull; study of the shape of the skull based on this belief.—**phrenological** *adj.*—**phrenologist** *n.*
phthisis *n* a wasting disease, esp tuberculosis of the lungs.
phycology *n* the study of algae.
phylactery *n* (*pl* **phylacteries**) (*Judaism*) a small case containing Hebrew texts, worn by Jewish men during prayers.
phyletic *adj* relating to the racial development of an animal or plant type.
phyllode *n* (*bot*) a flattened petiole with the functions of a leaf.
phyllotaxy, phyllotaxis *n* (*pl* **phyllotaxies, phyllotaxes**) (*bot*) the arrangement of leaves on a stem.
phylloxera *n* (*pl* **phylloxeras, phylloxerae**) an insect which attacks vines.
phylogeny, phylogenesis *n* (*pl* **phylogenies, phylogeneses**) (*biol*) the racial evolution of an animal or plant type.—**phylogenic, phylogenetic** *adj.*
phylum *n* (*pl* **phyla**) a major division of the animal or plant kingdom.
physic *vt* (**physicking, physicked**) (*arch*) to administer medicine to.
physical *adj* relating to the world of matter and energy, the human body, or natural science. * *n* a general medical examination.—**physically** *adv.*
physical chemistry *n* the branch of chemistry concerned with the effect of chemical structure on physical properties and of physical changes brought about by chemical reactions.
physical education *n* education in fitness and cure of the body, stressing athletics and hygiene.
physical therapy *n* the treatment of disorders and disease by physical and mechanical means (as massage, exercise, water, heat, etc).—*also* **physiotherapy.**
physician *n* a doctor of medicine.
physicist *n* a specialist in physics.
physics *n* the branch of science concerned with matter and energy and their interactions in the fields of mechanics, acoustics, optics, heat, electricity, magnetism, radiation, atomic structure and nuclear phenomena; the physical processes and phenomena of a particular system.
physio- *prefix* nature.
physiocrat *n* a supporter of the doctine of government according to a natural order based on land as the sole form of wealth.
physiognomy *n* (*pl* **physiognomies**) the art of judging character from facial features; facial expression, face; physical features generally.—**physiognomic, physiognomical** *adj.*—**physiognomist** *n.*
physiography *n* the study of the earth's natural features, physical geography.—**physiographer** *n.*
physiology *n* the science of the functioning and processes of living organisms.—**physiological** *adj.*—**physiologist** *n.*
physiotherapy *n* physical therapy.—**physiotherapist** *n.*
physique *n* bodily structure and appearance; build.
phytogenesis, phytogeny *n* the study of plant evolution.
phyton *n* (*bot*) the smallest unit of a plant capable of growing into a new plant.
pi[1] *n* the 16th letter of the Greek alphabet; (*math*) the Greek letter (p) used as a symbol for the ratio of the circumference to the diameter of a circle, approx. 3.14159.
pi[2] *n* (*pl* **pis**) (*print*) a jumble of type; any disorder. * *vt* to mix, disarrange (type). * *vi* to become mixed up.—*also* **pie.**
piacular *adj* expiatory; sinful.

piaffe *n* (*dressage*) a slow trot.

pia mater *n* (*anat*) the inner membrane enclosing the brain.

pianissimo *adv* (*mus*) very softly.

pianist *n* a person who plays the piano.

piano *n* (*pl* **pianos**) a large stringed keyboard instrument in which each key operates a felt-covered hammer that strikes a corresponding steel wire or wires.

pianoforte *n* (*pl* **pianofortes**) a piano.

piastre, piaster *n* a unit of currency in Egypt, Lebanon, Sudan, Syria and South Vietnam.

piazza *n* in Italy, a public square; a covered walkway or gallery; a veranda.

pibroch *n* a kind of music composed for Scottish bagpipes.

pica *n* (*print*) a standard measurement, equal to 12 points.

picaresque *adj* pertaining to a genre of fiction describing the exploits of rogues.

picaroon *n* (*arch*) a robber, pirate or marauder.

picayune *adj* (*inf*) of little value.

piccalilli *n* a kind of pickle made with cauliflower, onions, etc.

piccaninny *n* (*pl* **piccaninnies**) (*offensive*) a black baby or child.

piccolo *n* (*pl* **piccolos**) a small shrill flute.

pick *n* a heavy tool with a shaft and pointed crossbar for breaking ground; a tool for picking, such as a toothpick or icepick; a plectrum; right of selection; choice; best (of). * *vti* to break up or remove with a pick; to pluck at; to nibble (at), eat fussily; to contrive; to choose; (*fruit, etc*) to gather; to steal from a pocket; (*lock*) to force open; (*with* **up**) to lift; to acquire; to call for; to recover; (*inf*) to make the acquaintance of casually; to learn gradually; to resume; to give a lift to; to increase speed.

pickaback *see* **piggyback**.

pickaninny *n* (*pl* **pickaninnies**) varient (*usu US*) spelling of **piccaninny**.

pickaxe, pickax *n* (*pl* **pickaxes**) a pick with a long pointed head for breaking up hard ground, etc.

pickerel *n* (*pl* **pickerel, pickerels**) a North American freshwater fish of the pike family.

picket *n* a pointed stake; a patrol or group of men selected for a special duty; a person posted by strikes outside a place of work to persuade others not to enter. * *vt* (**picketing, picketed**) to tether to a picket; to post as a military picket; to place pickets, or serve as a picket (at a factory, etc).

pickings *npl* gleanings, perquisites.

pickle *n* vegetables preserved in vinegar; (*inf*) a plight, mess. * *vt* to preserve in vinegar.

pickled *adj* preserved in pickle; (*sl*) drunk.

picklock *n* an instrument for picking locks; someone, esp a thief, who picks locks.

pick-me-up *n* a tonic.

pickpocket *n* a person who steals from pockets.

pick-up *n* the act of picking up; a person or thing picked up; (*elect*) a device for picking up current; the power to accelerate rapidly; the balanced arm of a record player; a pickup truck.

pickup truck *n* a light truck with an enclosed cab and open body.

picnic *n* a usu informal meal taken on an excursion and eaten outdoors; an outdoor snack; the food so eaten; an easy or agreeable task. * *vi* (**picnicking, picnicked**) to have a picnic.—**picnicker** *n*.

picot *n* a small loop of thread used as an edging to lace.

picotee *n* a type of small carnation.

picric acid *n* a toxic acid used as a dye and an explosive.

pictograph *n* a picture representing a word or idea.

pictorial *adj* relating to pictures, painting,or drawing; containing pictures; expressed in pictures; graphic.—**pictorially** *adv*.

picture *n* drawing, painting, photography, or other visual representation; a scene; an impression or mental image; a vivid description; a cinema film. * *vt* to portray, describe in a picture; to visualize.

picturesque *adj* striking, vivid, usually pleasing; making an effective picture.—**picturesquely** *adv*.—**picturesqueness** *n*.

piddle *vt* to squander. * *vi* (*inf*) to idle; to urinate.

piddling *adj* (*inf*) trifling, insignificant.

piddock *n* a bivalve, boring, shellfish.

pidgin *n* a jargon for trade purposes, using words and grammar from two or more different languages.

pie[1] *n* a baked dish of fruit, meat, etc, with an under or upper crust of pastry, or both.

pie[2] *see* **pi**[2].

piebald *adj* covered with patches of two colours. * *n* a piebald horse, etc.

piece *n* a distinct part of anything; a single object; a literary, dramatic, artistic, or musical composition; (*sl*) a firearm; a man in chess or draughts; an opinion, view; a short distance. * *vt* to fit together, join.—**piecer** *n*.

pièce de résistance *n* (*pl* **pièces de résistance**) the most important item or dish.

piecemeal *adv* gradually; bit by bit.

piecework *n* work paid for according to the quantity produced.

pied *adj* of mixed colours, mottled

pied-à-terre *n* (*pl* **pieds-à-terre**) a flat for occasional use; a second home.

pier *n* a structure supporting the spans of a bridge; a structure built out over water and supported by pillars, used as a landing place, promenade, etc; a heavy column used to support weight.

pierce *vt* to cut or make a hole through; to force a way into; (*fig*) to touch or move. * *vi* to penetrate.

piercing *adj* penetrating; keen; (*cold, pain*) acute.—**piercingly** *adv*.

Pierrot *n* (*pantomime*) a male character, usu in a loose white costume with a whitened face; a clown in such a costume.

pietà *n* a picture or sculpture of the Virgin mourning over the dead Christ.

piety *n* (*pl* **pieties**) religious devoutness; the characteristic of being pious.

piezoelectricity *n* the production of electricity in certain types of crystal through the application of mechanical stress.—**piezoeletric, piezoelectrical** *adj*.—**piezoelectrically** *adv*.

piffle *n* (*inf*) silly stuff, nonsense. * *vi* to talk nonsense.

pig *n* a domesticated animal with a broad snout and fat body raised for food; a hog; a greedy or filthy person; an oblong casting of metal poured from the smelting furnace; (*sl*) a policeman. * *vi* (**pigging, pigged**) (*sow*) to give birth; (*inf*) to live in squalor.

pigeon *n* a bird with a small head and a heavy body; (*inf*) a person who is easily conned.

pigeonhole *n* a small compartment for filing papers, etc; a category usu failing to reflect actual complexities. * *vt* to file, classify; to put aside for consideration, shelve.

pigeon-toed *adj* having the toes turned inward.

piggery *n* (*pl* **piggeries**) a place where pigs are reared; a pigsty.

piggish *adj* greedy, dirty, selfish, like a pig.—**piggishly** *adv*.—**piggishness** *n*.

piggy *n* (*pl* **piggies**) a child's name for a young or little pig. * *adj* (**piggier, piggiest**) piggish.

piggyback *n* a ride on the shoulders or back of a person. * *adv* carried on the shoulders or back; transported on top of a larger object.—*also* **pickaback**.

piggy bank *n* a container for coins, often shaped like a pig.

pigheaded *adj* stupidly stubborn.—**pigheadedly** *adv*.—**pigheadedness** *n*.

piglet *n* a young pig.

pigment *n* paint; a naturally occurring substance used for colouring.—**pigmentary** *adj*.

pigmentation *n* (*biol*) coloration of the tissues of plants and animals caused by pigment; the depositing of pigments by cells.

pigmy *see* **pygmy**.

pignut *n* an earthnut.

pigskin *n* leather made from the skin of a pig.

pigsticker *n* a person who goes pigsticking.

pigsticking *n* the hunting of wild boar with a spear, usu on horseback.

pigsty *n* (*pl* **pigsties**) a pen for pigs; a dirty hovel.

pigtail *n* a tight braid of hair.—**pigtailed** *adj*.

pike[1] *n* a sharp point or spike; the top of a spear. * *vt* to pierce or kill with a pike.

pike[2] *n* (*pl* **pike, pikes**) a long-snouted fish, important as a food and game fish.
pike perch *n* (**pike perch, pike perches**) any of various fishes of the perch family resembling the pike.
pikestaff *n* the shaft of a pike.
pilaf, pilaff *n* a dish of spiced rice cooked in stock with, optionally, meat or fish.—*also* **pilau.**
pilaster *n* a rectangular pillar, usu set in a wall.
pilch *n* (*arch*) a triangular flannel wrap for a baby.
pilchard *n* a fish of the herring family.
pile[1] *n* a heap or mound of objects; a large amount; a lofty building; a pyre; (*sl*) a fortune. * *vt* (*with* **up, on**) to heap or stack; to load; to accumulate. * *vi* to become heaped up; (*with* **up, out, on**) to move confusedly in a mass.
pile[2] *n* a vertical beam driven into (the ground) as a foundation for a building, etc. * *vt* to support with piles; to drive piles into.
pile[3] *n* the nap of a fabric or carpet; soft, fine fur or wool.
pileate, pileated *adj* (*biol*) crested.
piledriver *n* a machine for driving in piles.
piles *npl* haemorrhoids.
pile-up *n* an accumulation of tasks, etc; (*inf*) a collision of several vehicles.
pilfer *vti* to steal in small quantities.—**pilferage** *n*.—**pilferer** *n*.
pilgrim *n* a person who makes a pilgrimage.
pilgrimage *n* a journey to a holy place as an act of devotion; any long journey; a life's journey.
piliferous *adj* (*esp bot*) hairy.
piliform *adj* (*bot*) in the form of or like a hair.
pill *n* medicine in round balls or tablet form; (*with cap*) an oral contraceptive.
pillage *n* looting, plunder. * *vti* to plunder, esp during war.—**pillager** *n*.
pillar *n* a slender, vertical structure used as a support or ornament; a column; a strong supporter of a cause.
pillar box *n* in UK, a mailbox in the shape of a pillar.
pillbox *n* a box for pills, esp a decorative one; a small round hat without a brim; (*mil*) a small, fortified, concrete shelter.
pillion *n* a seat behind the driver for a passenger on a motorcycle, etc.
pillory *n* (*pl* **pillories**) (*formerly*) stocks in which criminals were put as punishment. * *vt* (**pillorying, pilloried**) to expose to public scorn and ridicule.
pillow *n* a cushion that supports the head during sleep; something that supports to equalize or distribute pressure. * *vti* to rest on, serve as, a pillow.
pillowcase, pillowslip *n* a removable cover for a pillow.
pilose *adj* (*biol*) hairy.
pilot *n* a person who operates an aircraft; one who directs ships in and out of harbour; a guide; a television show produced as a sample of a proposed series. * *vt* to direct the course of, act as pilot; to lead or guide.
pilotage *n* the work or fee of a pilot.
pilot light *n* a burning gas flame used to light a larger jet; an electric indicator light.
pilule *n* a small pill.—**pilular** *adj*.
pimento *n* (*pl* **pimentos**) allspice; a pimiento.
pimiento *n* a sweet red pepper (capiscum) used in salads and cooked dishes.
pimp *n* a prostitute's agent.—*also vt*.
pimpernel *n* a primulaceous plant with small scarlet, blue or white flowers.
pimple *n* a small, raised, inflamed swelling of the skin.—**pimpled** *adj*.
pimply *adj* (**pimplier, pimpliest**) covered with pimples.
PIN *abbr* = personal identification number (issued by a bank to a customer to validate electronic transactions).
pin *n* a piece of metal or wood used to fasten things together; a small piece of pointed wire with a head; an ornament or badge with a pin or clasp for fastening to clothing; (*bowling*) one of the clubs at which the ball is rolled. * *vt* (**pinning, pinned**) to fasten with a pin; to hold, fix; (*with* **down**) to get (someone) to commit himself or herself as to plans, etc; (*a fact, etc*) to establish.
pinafore *n* a sleeveless garment worn over a dress, blouse, etc.
pinaster *n* a Southern European pine tree.
pince-nez *n* (*pl* **pince-nez**) eyeglasses clipped to the nose by a spring.
pincers *npl* a tool with two handles and jaws used for gripping and drawing out nails, etc; a grasping claw, as of a crab.
pinch *vti* to squeeze or compress painfully; to press between the fingers; to nip; (*sl*) to steal; (*sl*) to arrest. * *n* a squeeze or nip; what can be taken up between the finger and thumb, a small amount; a time of stress; an emergency.
pinchbeck *n* a copper and zinc alloy, used as imitation gold.
pinched *adj* appearing to be squeezed; drawn by cold or stress.
pincushion *n* a pad for holding pins.
Pindaric *adj* (*ode*) associated with the poet Pindar.
pine[1] *n* an evergreen coniferous tree with long needles and well-formed cones; a tree of the pine family; its wood.
pine[2] *vi* to languish, waste away through longing or mental stress; (*with* **for**) to yearn.
pineal gland *n* a pea-sized gland in the brain.
pineapple *n* a tropical plant; its juicy, fleshy, yellow fruit.
pinfold *n* a pound for stray cattle. * *vt* to shut into, or as if into, such a pound.
ping *n* a high-pitched ringing sound. * *vti* to strike with a ping, emit a ping.—**pinger** *n*.
ping-pong *n* a name for table tennis; (*with caps*) (*trademark*) table tennis equipment.
pinion[1] *n* the outer joint of a bird's wing; a wing feather. * *vt* to cut off a pinion; to bind arms to sides, restrain.
pinion[2] *n* a cogwheel.
pink[1] *n* any of various garden plants with a fragrant flower, including carnations; a pale red colour; a huntsman's red coat; the highest type. * *adj* pink-coloured; (*inf*) radical in political views.
pink[2] *vt* to stab, pierce; (*cloth, etc*) to cut a zigzag edge on; to perforate with pinking shears.
pinkeye *n* an inflammation of the conjunctiva, affecting animals and humans.
pinkie, pinky *n* (*pl* **pinkies**) the little finger on the human hand.
pinking shears *npl* shears with notched edges for pinking edges of cloth.
pin money *n* money given to a woman by her husband for personal expenses.
pinna *n* (*pl* **pinnae, pinnas**) (*biol*) the fin of a fish; the feather or wing of a bird; the leaflet of a pinnate leaf.
pinnace *n* (*naut*) a small light schooner-rigged vessel with oars; an eight-oared small boat belonging to a warship.
pinnacle *n* a slender tower crowning a roof, etc; a rocky peak of a mountain; the highest point, climax.
pinnate, pinnated *adj* shaped like a feather; (*leaf*) divided into leaflets.
pinniped *adj* (*zool*) with fin-like feet or flippers.
pinny *n* (*pl* **pinnies**) (*sl*) a pinafore.
pinochle, pinocle *n* a card game.—*also* **pinuchle.**
pinpoint *vt* to locate or identify very exactly.
pinprick *n* a small puncture as made by a pin; a trivial annoyance.
pins and needles *npl* a tingling feeling in the fingers, toes, etc, caused by impeded blood circulation returning to normal; (*with* **on**) in an anxious or expectant state.
pinstripe *n* a very narrow stripe in suit fabrics, etc.
pint *n* a liquid measure equal to half a quart or one eighth of a gallon (0.47 litres); (*inf*) a drink of beer.
pintail *n* (*pl* **pintails, pintail**) a type of duck.
pintle *n* a bolt or pin esp comprising a pivot.
pinto *n* (*pl* **pintos**) a piebald horse.
pinuchle *see* **pinochle.**
pin-up *n* (*sl*) a photograph of a naked or partially naked person; a person who has been so photographed; a photograph of a famous person.

pioneer *n* a person who initiates or explores new areas of enterprise, research, etc; an explorer; an early settler; (*mil*) one who prepares roads, sinks mines, etc. * *vti* to initiate or take part in the development of; to act as a pioneer (to); to explore (a region).

pious *adj* devout; religious; sanctimonious.—**piously** *adv*.—**piousness** *n*.

pip[1] *n* the seed in a fleshy fruit, eg apple, orange.

pip[2] *n* a spot with a numerical value on a playing card, dice, etc; (*inf*) insignia on a uniform showing an officer's rank; a signal on a radar screen.

pip[3] *vi* (**pipping, pipped**) (*bird*) to chirp, to peep; (*hatching bird*) to pierce (its shell).

pipal *see* **peepul.**

pipe *n* a tube of wood, metal etc for making musical sounds; (*pl*) the bagpipes; a stem with a bowl for smoking tobacco; a long tube or hollow body for conveying water, gas, etc. * *vt* to play on a pipe; (*gas, water, etc*) to convey by pipe; to lead, summon with the sound of a pipe(s); to trim with piping. * *vi*.(*sl*) to take the drug crack.

pipeclay *n* a white clay, used to make tobacco pipes and to whiten leather, etc. * *vt* to whiten using pipeclay.

pipeline *n* a pipe (often underground) used to convey oil, gas, etc; a direct channel for information; the processes through which supplies pass from source to user.

piper *n* a person who plays a pipe, esp bagpipes.

pipette, pipet *n* a hollow glass tube into which liquids are sucked for measurement.

piping *n* a length of pipe, pipes collectively; a tube-like fold of material used to trim seams; a strip of icing, cream, for decorating cakes, etc; the art of playing a pipe or bagpipes; a high-pitched sound. * *adj* making a high-pitched sound.

piping hot *adj* very hot.

pipistrelle, pipistrel *n* a small brown bat.

pipit *n* a type of songbird.

pipkin *n* a small earthenware pot.

pippin *n* one of several types of eating apple.

pipsqueak *n* (*inf*) a contemptible or insigificant person.

piquant *adj* strong-tasting; pungent, sharp; stimulating.—**piquancy** *n*.—**piquantly** *adv*.

pique *n* resentment, ill-feeling. * *vt* (**piquing, piqued**) to cause resentment in; to offend.

piqué *n* a corded cotton fabric.

piquet *n* a card game for two.

piracy *n* (*pl* **piracies**) robbery at sea; the hijacking of a ship or aircraft; infringement of copyright; unauthorized use of patented work.

piragua *see* **pirogue.**

piranha *n* a small voracious freshwater fish of tropical America with sharp teeth and a strong jaw.

pirate *n* a person who commits robbery at sea; a hijacker; one who infringes copyright. * *vti* to take by piracy; to publish or reproduce in violation of a copyright.—**piratical, piratic** *adj*.

pirogue *n* a dugout canoe.—*also* **piragua.**

pirouette *n* a spin on the toes in ballet.—*also vi.*

piscatorial, piscatory *adj* of, or pertaining to, fish or fishing.

Pisces *n* the Fishes, in astrology the twelfth sign of the zodiac, operative from 19 February–20 March.—**Piscean** *adj, n*.

pisciculture *n* the controlled rearing and breeding of fish.—**piscicultural** *adj*.—**pisciculturist** *n*.

piscina *n* (*pl* **piscinae, piscinas**) (*RC Church*) a basin with a drain in a church wall, used for rinsing sacred vessels after Mass.

piscine *adj* pertaining to fish.

piscivorous *adj* fish-eating.

pisiform *adj* pea-shaped.

pismire *n* an ant.

piss *vi* (*vulg*) to urinate. * *n* urine.

pistachio *n* (*pl* **pistachios**) a tree found in Mediterranean countries and West Asia; the edible nut of this tree.

piste *n* a ski trail of packed snow; (*fencing*) the rectangular area where a bout takes place.

pistil *n* the seed-bearing part of a flower.

pistillate *adj* (*bot*) having a pistil; with a pistil but no stamens.

pistol *n* a small, short-barrelled handgun. * *vt* (**pistolling, pistolled** *or* **pistoling, pistoled**) to shoot with a pistol.

pistole *n* (*formerly*) a gold coin used in Europe.

piston *n* a disc that slides to and fro in a close-fitting cylinder, as in engines, pumps.

pit *n* a deep hole in the earth; a (coal) mine; a scooped-out place for burning something; a sunken or depressed area below the adjacent floor area; a space at the front of the stage for the orchestra; the area in a securities or commodities exchange in which members do the trading; the scar left by smallpox, etc; the stone of a fruit; a place where racing cars refuel. * *vti* (**pitting, pitted**) to set in competition; to mark or become marked with pits; to make a pit stop.

pit-a-pat *adv* with quick, light steps or beats. * *n* quick, light steps or beats. * *vi* (**pit-a-patting, pit-a-patted**) to make quick, light steps or beats.

pitch[1] *vti* (*tent, etc*) to erect by driving pegs, stakes, etc, into the ground; to set the level of; (*mus*) to set in key; to express in a style; to throw, hurl; to fall heavily, plunge, esp forward. * *n* a throw; height, intensity; a musical tone; a place where a street trader or performer works; distance between threads (of a screw); amount of slope; a sound wave frequency; a sports field; (*cricket*) the area between the wickets; sales talk.

pitch[2] *n* the black, sticky substance from distillation of tar, etc; any of various bituminous substances. * *vt* to smear with pitch.

pitch-black *adj* black, or extremely dark.

pitchblende *n* a black mineral, composed largely of uranium oxide, that also yields radium.

pitch-dark *adj* completely dark.

pitcher *n* a large water jug; (*baseball*) the player who pitches the ball.

pitchfork *n* a long-handled fork for tossing hay, etc. * *vt* to lift with this; to thrust suddenly or willy-nilly into.

pitchy *adj* (**pitchier, pitchiest**) resembling, or smeared with, pitch.

piteous *adj* arousing pity; heart-rending.—**piteously** *adv*.—**piteousness** *n*.

pitfall *n* concealed danger; unexpected difficulty.

pith *n* the soft tissue inside the rind of citrus fruits; the gist, essence; importance.

pithy *adj* (**pithier, pithiest**) like or full of pith; concise and full of meaning.—**pithily** *adv*.—**pithiness** *n*.

pitiable *adj* deserving pity, lamentable, wretched.—**pitiableness** *n*.—**pitiably** *adv*.

pitiful *adj* causing pity, touching; contemptible, paltry.—**pitifully** *adv*.—**pitifulness** *n*.

pitiless *adj* without pity, ruthless.—**pitilessly** *adv*.—**pitilessness** *n*.

pitman *n* (*pl* **pitmen**) a miner.

pittance *n* a very small quantity or allowance of money.

pituitary *adj* of or pertaining to the pituitary gland; (*arch*) of or secreting mucus. * *n* (*pl* **pituitaries**) the pituitary gland.

pituitary gland *n* a ductless gland at the base of the brain that affects growth and sexual development.

pity *n* (*pl* **pities**) sympathy with the distress of others; a cause of grief; a regrettable fact. * *vt* (**pitying, pitied**) to feel pity for.—**pityingly** *adv*.

pityriasis *n* (*pl* **pityriases**) a skin disease characterized by scaly, pink eruptions.

pivot *n* a pin on which a part turns, fulcrum; a key person upon whom progress depends; a cardinal point or factor. * *vt* to turn or hinge (on) a pivot; to attach by a pivot. * *vi* to run on, or as if on, a pivot.—**pivotal** *adj*.

pixel *n* any of the tiny units that form an image (as on a television screen, computer monitor).

pixie, pixy *n* (*pl* **pixies**) a fairy or elf.

pixilated *adj* acting as if influenced by pixies; unconventional, eccentric, whimsical; (*sl*) drunk.

pizza *n* a baked dough crust covered with cheese, tomatoes, etc.
pizzeria *n* a pizza restaurant.
pizzicato *n* (*pl* **pizzicati, pizzicatos**) (*mus*) a note or passage played by plucking the string of a violin or other bowed instrument.—*also adj*.
placable *adj* easily to placate.—**placability** *n*.
placard *n* a poster or notice for public display.
placate *vt* to appease; to pacify.—**placation** *n*.—**placatory** *adj*.
place *n* a locality, spot; a town or village; a building, residence; a short street, a square; space, room; a particular point, part, position, etc; the part of space occupied by a person or thing; a position or job; a seat; rank, precedence; a finishing position in a race. * *vt* to put; to put in a particular place; to find a place or seat for; to identify; to estimate; to rank; (*order*) to request material from a supplier. * *vi* to finish second or among the first three in a race.
placebo *n* (*pl* **placebos, placeboes**) something harmless given by a doctor to fool a patient into thinking he is undergoing treatment.
place mat *n* a small mat serving as an individual table cover for a person at a meal.
placement *n* a placing or being placed; location or arrangement.
place name *n* the name of a geographical locality.
placenta *n* (*pl* **placentas, placentae**) the organ in the uterus of a female mammal that nourishes the foetus.—**placental** *adj*.
placer *n* a deposit containing a valuable mineral found in a river, etc.
placid *adj* calm, tranquil.—**placidity** *n*.—**placidly** *adv*.
placket *n* a slit at the waist of a dress or skirt to make it easy to put on or take off.
placoid *adj* platelike.
plafond *n* a ceiling, esp one of elaborate design; a card game.
plagal *adj* (*musical composition*) having its principal notes between the fifth of the key and its octave.
plagiarism *n* the act of stealing from another author's work, literary theft; that which is plagiarized.—**plagiarist** *n*.—**plagiaristic** *adj*.
plagiarize *vt* to appropriate writings from another author.—**plagiarizer** *n*.
plague *n* a highly contagious and deadly disease; (*inf*) a person who is a nuisance. * *vt* (**plaguing, plagued**) to afflict with a plague; (*inf*) to annoy, harass.
plaguy, plaguey *adj* (*arch*) (*inf*) troublesome, vexatious.
plaice *n* (*pl* **plaice, plaices**) any of various flatfishes, esp a flounder.
plaid *n* a long wide piece of woollen cloth used as a cloak in Highland dress; cloth with a tartan or chequered pattern.
plain *adj* level, flat; understandable; straightforward; manifest, obvious; blunt; unadorned; not elaborate; not coloured or patterned; not beautiful; ugly; pure; unmixed. * *n* a large tract of level country.—**plainness** *n*.
plain clothes *npl* ordinary clothes, not uniform, as worn by a policeman on duty.—*also adj*.
plainly *adv* clearly, intelligibly.
plain sailing *n* easy progress over an unobstructed course.
plainsman *n* (*pl* **plainsmen**) an inhabitant of a plain.
plainsong *n* an old, plain kind of church music chanted in unison.
plain-spoken *adj* frank, outspoken.
plaint *n* (*poet*) lamentation, sad song; (*law*) formal statement of grievance.
plaintiff *n* (*law*) a person who brings a civil action against another.
plaintive *adj* sad, mournful.—**plaintively** *adv*.—**plaintiveness** *n*.
plait *n* intertwined strands of hair, straw, etc; a pigtail. * *vti* (**plaiting, plaited**) to twist strands (of hair) together into a plait.
plan *n* a scheme or idea; a drawing to scale of a building; a diagram, map; any outline or sketch. * *vti* (**planning, planned**) to make a plan of; to design; to arrange beforehand, intend; to make plans.
planar *adj* of or located in a plane; flat.
planarian *n* a type of flatworm.
planchet *n* a plain metal disc from which a coin is made.
planchette *n* a heart-shaped board on wheels, holding a pencil which is supposed to write automatically, giving messages from spirits, when a hand is rested upon it.
plane[1] *n* a tall tree with large broad leaves.
plane[2] *n* a tool with a steel blade for smoothing level wooden surfaces. * *vt* to smooth with a plane.
plane[3] *n* any level or flat surface; a level of attainment; one of the main supporting surfaces of an aeroplane; an aeroplane. * *adj* flat or level. * *vi* to fly while keeping the wings motionless; to skim across the surface of water; to travel by aeroplane.
planet *n* a celestial body that orbits the sun or other star.
planetarium *n* (*pl* **planetariums, planetaria**) a machine used to exhibit the planets, their motions around the sun and their relative distances and magnitudes; a building for housing this instrument; a model of the solar system.
planetary *adj* (*astrol*) under the influence of one of the planets; terrestrial; wandering, erratic.
planetoid *n* an asteroid.
plangent *adj* (*sound*) loud and deep; resounding.—**plangency** *n*.
planimeter *n* an instrument for measuring the area of an irregular plane figure.
planimetry *n* the measurement of plane figures.
planish *vt* (*metal*) to smooth and flatten with a hammer or between rollers.
planisphere *n* a sphere projected on a plane or a map of the heavens.
plank *n* a long, broad, thick board; one of the policies forming the platform of a political party. * *vt* to cover with planks.
planking *n* planks collectively; the act of laying boards.
plankton *n* the microscopic organisms that float on seas, lakes, etc.
planner *n* a person who plans; in UK, an official who plans architectural development and land use.—**planning** *n*.
planoconcave *adj* (*lens*) with one side flat and the other concave.
planoconvex *adj* (*lens*) with one side flat and the other convex.
plant *n* a living organism with cellulose cell walls, which synthesizes its food from carbon dioxide, water and light; a soft-stemmed organism of this kind, as distinguished from a tree or shrub; the machinery, buildings, etc of a factory, etc; (*sl*) an act of planting; (*sl*) something or someone planted. * *vt* (*seeds, cuttings*) to put into the ground to grow; to place firmly in position; to found or establish; (*sl*) to conceal something in another's possession in order to implicate.
plantain[1] *n* a low-growing weed with tough leaves.
plantain[2] *n* a tropical broad-leaved tree yielding an edible fruit similar to the banana.
plantar *adj* (*anat*) pertaining to the sole of the foot.
plantation *n* a large cultivated planting of trees; an estate where tea, rubber, cotton, etc, is grown, cultivated by local labour.
planter *n* a person who owns or runs a plantation; a machine that plants; a decorative container for plants.
plantigrade *adj* (*zool*) walking on the sole of the foot. * *n* a plantigrade animal.
plaque *n* an ornamental tablet or disc attached to or inserted in a surface; a film of mucus on the teeth that harbours bacteria.
plash *n* a splash; a marshy pool or puddle.—**plashy** *adj* (**plashier, plashiest**).
plasm *n* a kind of protoplasm; plasma.
plasma *n* the colourless liquid part of blood, milk, or lymph; a collection of charged particles resembling gas but conducting electricity and affected by a magnetic field.
plasmodium *n* (*pl* **plasmodia**) (*biol*) a mass of protoplasm formed by the union of single-cell organisms; (*med*) any of a genus of parasitic protozoa which cause malaria.
plasmolysis *n* (*biol*) the shrinkage of the protoplasm of a plant cell occurring as a result of loss of water.
plasmolyze *vt* to subject to plasmolysis.
plaster *n* an adhesive dressing for cuts; a mixture of sand, lime and water that sets hard and is used for covering walls and ceilings. * *vt* to cover as with plaster; to apply like a plaster; to make lie smooth and flat; to load to excess.—**plasterer** *n*.
plasterboard *n* a thin board formed by layers of plaster and paper, used in wide sheets for walls, etc.

plaster cast *n* a rigid dressing of gauze impregnated with plaster of Paris; a sculptor's model in plaster of Paris.

plastered *adj* (*sl*) intoxicated.

plaster of Paris *n* gypsum and water made into a quick-setting paste.

plastic *adj* able to be moulded; pliant; made of plastic; (*art*) relating to modelling or moulding. * *n* any of various nonmetallic compounds, synthetically produced, that can be moulded, cast, squeezed, drawn, or laminated into objects, films, or filaments.—**plastically** *adv*.

plasticity *n* the ability to be moulded or altered; the ability to retain a shape attained by pressure deformation.

plastic surgery *n* surgery to repair deformed or destroyed parts of the body.

plastron *n* a breastplate; a trimming on a dress front; a shirt front; a bony plate on the underside of a tortoise or turtle.

plat *n* (*US*) a small plot of ground; a map, esp of land divided into lots for building. * *vt* (**platting, platted**) to make a map of.

platan *n* a plane tree.

plate *n* a flat sheet of metal on which an engraving is cut; an illustration printed from it; a full-page illustration separate from text; a sheet of metal photographically prepared with text, etc, for printing from; a sheet of glass with sensitized film used as a photographic negative; a trophy as prize at a race; a coating of metal on another metal; utensils plated in silver or gold; plated ware; a flat shallow dish from which food is eaten; a helping of food; the part of a denture that fits the palate; (*inf*) a denture. * *vt* (*a metal*) to coat with a thin film of another metal; to cover with metal plates.

plateau *n* (*pl* **plateaus, plateaux**) a flat, elevated area of land; a stable period; a graphic representation showing this.

plated *adj* coated with metal, esp silver or gold.

plate glass *n* rolled, ground, and polished sheet glass.

platelet *n* a small disc-shaped cell in the blood involved in the process of blood clotting.

platen *n* the roller on a typewriter; (*print*) a plate which presses the paper against the type.

plater *n* someone who, or something which, plates; a mediocre racehorse.

platform *n* a raised floor for speakers, musicians, etc; a stage; a place or opportunity for public discussion; the raised area next to a railway line where passengers board trains; a statement of political aims.

plating *n* the act or process of plating; a thin coating of metal; a coating of metal plates.

platinize *vt* to coat with platinum.

platinum *n* a valuable, silvery-white metal used for jewellery, etc.

platinum-blond *adj* (*hair*) silvery blond. * *n* someone with hair of this colour.—**platinum-blonde** *nf*.

platitude *n* a dull truism; a commonplace remark.—**platitudinous** *adj*.

platitudinize *vi* to utter platitudes.

platonic *adj* (*love*) spiritual and free from physical desire; (*with cap*) relating to Plato, the Greek philosopher, or his teachings.—**platonically** *adv*.

platoon *n* a military unit divided into squads or sections.

platter *n* an oval flat serving dish.

platy- *prefix* flat.

platyhelminth *n* a type of flatworm.

platypus *n* (*pl* **platypuses**) a small aquatic egg-laying mammal of Australia and Tasmania, with webbed feet, a bill like a duck's, dense fur, and a broad flat tail.—*also* **duck-billed platypus**.

platyrrhine, platyrrhinian *adj* (*zool*) broad-nosed.

plaudit *n* (*usu pl*) a commendation; a round of applause.

plausible *adj* apparently truthful or reasonable.—**plausibility** *n*.—**plausibly** *adv*.

play *vi* to amuse oneself (with toys, games, etc); to act carelessly or trifle (with somebody's feelings); to gamble; to act on the stage or perform on a musical instrument; (*light*) to flicker, shimmer; (*water*) to discharge or direct on. * *vt* to participate in a sport; to be somebody's opponent in a game; to perform a dramatic production; (*instrument*) to produce music on; (*hose*) to direct; (*fish*) to give line to; to bet on. * *n* fun, amusement; the playing of, or manner of playing, a game; the duration of a game; a literary work for performance by actors; gambling; scope, freedom to move.—**playable** *adj*.

playact *vi* to behave affectedly or overdramatically; to make believe, pretend; to act in a play.—**playacting** *n*.—**playactor** *n*.

playback *n* the act of reproducing recorded sound or pictures, esp soon after they are made; a mechanism in an audio or video recorder for doing this.—*also vt*.

playbill *n* a poster advertising a theatrical performance.

playboy *n* a person who lives for pleasure.

player *n* a person who plays a specified game or instrument; an actor.

playfellow *see* **playmate.**

playful *adj* full of fun; humorous; sportive; fond of sport or amusement.—**playfully** *adv*.—**playfulness** *n*.

playgoer *n* a person who goes to the theatre, esp one who attends frequently or regularly.—**playgoing** *adj*, *n*.

playground *n* an area outdoors for children's recreation.

playhouse *n* a theatre.

playing card *n* one of a set of 52 cards used for playing games, each card having an identical pattern on one side and its own symbol on the reverse.

playing field *n* a place for playing sport.

playlet *n* a short play.

playmate *n* a friend in play.—*also* **playfellow.**

playpen *n* a portable usu collapsible enclosure in which a young child may be left to play safely.

plaything *n* a toy; a thing or person treated as a toy.

playtime *n* a time for recreation, esp at a school.

playwright *n* a writer of plays.

plaza *n* a public square in a town or city; (*US*) an area for the parking and servicing of cars.

plea *n* (*law*) an answer to a charge, made by the accused person; a request; an entreaty.

plead *vti* (**pleading, pleaded, plead** *or* **pled**) to beg, implore; to give as an excuse; to answer (guilty or not guilty) to a charge; to argue (a law case).—**pleadable** *adj*.—**pleader** *n*.

pleading *n* advocacy of a cause in a court of law; one of the allegations and counter allegations made alternately, usu in writing, by the parties in a legal action; the act or instance of making a plea; a sincere entreaty. * *adj* begging, imploring.—**pleadingly** *adv*.

pleasant *adj* agreeable; pleasing.—**pleasantly** *adv*.—**pleasantness** *n*.

pleasantry *n* (*pl* **pleasantries**) a polite or amusing remark.

please *vti* to satisfy; to give pleasure to; to be willing; to have the wish. * *adv* as a word to express politeness or emphasis in a request; an expression of polite affirmation.

pleased *adj* gratified.

pleasing *adj* giving pleasure; agreeable.—**pleasingly** *adv*.

pleasurable *adj* gratifying, delightful.—**pleasurably** *adv*.

pleasure *n* enjoyment, recreation; gratification of the senses; preference.

pleat *n* a double fold of cloth, etc pressed or stitched in place. * *vt* to gather into pleats.

pleb *n* a plebeian; (*sl*) a common person.

plebeian *adj* relating to the common people; base, vulgar. * *n* a commoner of ancient Rome; a vulgar, coarse person.—**plebeianism** *n*.

plebiscite *n* a direct vote of the electorate on a political issue such as annexation, independent nationhood, etc.

plectrum *n* (*pl* **plectra, plectrums**) a thin piece of metal, etc for plucking the strings of a guitar, etc.

pledge *n* a solemn promise; security for payment of a debt; a token or sign; a toast. * *vt* to give as security; to pawn; to bind by solemn promise; to drink a toast to.

pledgee *n* someone to whom a pledge is given.

pledget *n* a small pad of lint, etc, used to apply pressure to wounds.

pleiad *n* a brilliant group (of people).
Pleiades *npl* a cluster of seven stars in the constellation Taurus.
plein-air *adj* (*art*) depicting the effects of light and atmosphere outdoors.
Pleistocene *adj* (*geol*) pertaining to the earliest division of the Quaternary Period.
plenary *adj* full, complete; (*assembly, etc*) attended by all the members.—**plenarily** *adv*.
plenipotentiary *adj* possessing full powers. * *n* (*pl* **plenipotentiaries**) an envoy with authority to act at his own discretion.
plenitude *n* abundance.
plenteous *adj* abundant.
plentiful *adj* abundant, copious.—**plentifully** *adv*.—**plentifulness** *n*.
plenty *n* an abundance; more than enough; a great number. * *adv* (*sl*) quite.
plenum *n* (*pl* **plenums, plena**) a full assembly; a space filled with matter.
pleonasm *n* (*rhetoric*) the use of unnecessary words, eg "he is blind and cannot see".—**pleonastic** *adj*.
plesiosaurus, plesiosaur *n* a large, extinct, long-necked swimming reptile.
plessor *see* **plexor.**
plethora *n* overabundance, glut; (*med*) an excess of red corpuscles in the blood.—**plethoric** *adj*.
pleura *n* (*pl* **pleurae**) the membrane enclosing the lungs.—**pleural** *adj*.
pleurisy *n* inflammation of the membranes enclosing the lungs.—**pleuritic** *adj*.
pleuropneumonia *n* an inflammation of both the pleura and the lung.
Plexiglas *n* (*trademark*) a transparent thermoplastic.
plexor *n* (*med*) a small hammer used in percussion and for testing reflexes.—*also* **plessor.**
plexus *n* (*pl* **plexuses, plexus**) a network, esp of nerves or blood vessels.
pliable *adj* easily bent or moulded; easily influenced.—**pliability** *n*.—**pliably** *adv*.
pliant *adj* easily bent or influenced; supple; flexible, yielding.—**pliancy** *n*.—**pliantly** *adv*.
plicate, plicated *adj* pleated; folded in the form of a fan.
pliers *npl* a tool with hinged arms and jaws for cutting, shaping wire.
plight[1] *n* a dangerous situation; a predicament.
plight[2] *vt* to pledge, vow solemnly. * *n* a pledge; an engagement.—**plighter** *n*.
Plimsoll line *n* a system of markings on the hull of ships to ensure there is no overloading and that cargo is balanced.—*also* **load line.**
plimsolls, plimsoles *npl* (*Brit*) rubber-soled canvas shoes, sneakers.
Pliocene *adj* (*geol*) pertaining to the latest division of the Tertiary Period.
PLO *abbr* = Palestine Liberation Organization.
plod *vi* (**plodding, plodded**) to walk heavily and slowly, to trudge; to work or study slowly and laboriously.—**plodder** *n*.—**ploddingly** *adv*.
plop *vti* (**plopping, plopped**) to fall into water without a splash. * *n* the sound of this. * *adv* with a plop.
plot *n* a small piece of land; a secret plan or conspiracy; the story in a play or novel, etc. * *vt* (**plotting, plotted**) to conspire; (*route*) to mark on a map; (*points*) to mark (on a graph) with coordinates.—**plotter** *n*.
plough, plow *n* a farm implement for turning up soil; any implement like this, as a snowplough. * *vt* to cut and turn up with a plough; to make a furrow (in), to wrinkle; to force a way through; to work at laboriously; (*with* **into**) to run into; (*with* **back**) to reinvest; (*sl*) to fail an examination.—**ploughable** *adj*.—**plougher** *n*.
ploughman, plowman *n* (*pl* **ploughmen, plowmen**) one who ploughs; a farm-worker.
ploughshare, plowshare *n* the part of a plough which cuts the soil.
plover *n* a wading bird with a short tail and a straight bill.
ploy *n* a tactic or manoeuvre to outwit an opponent; an occupation or job; an escapade.
pluck *vt* to pull off or at; to snatch; to strip off feathers; (*fruit, flowers, etc*) to pick; (*person*) to remove from one situation in life and transfer to another. * *vi* to make a sharp pull or twitch. * *n* a pull or tug; heart, courage; dogged resolution.—**plucker** *n*.
plucky *adj* (**pluckier, pluckiest**) brave, spirited.—**pluckily** *adv*.—**pluckiness** *n*.
plug *n* a stopper used for filling a hole; a device for connecting an appliance to an electricity supply; a cake of tobacco; a kind of fishing lure; (*inf*) a free advertisement usu incorporated in other matter. * *vti* (**plugging, plugged**) to stop up with a plug; (*sl*) to shoot or punch; (*inf*) to seek to advertise by frequent repetition; (*with* **at**) (*inf*) to work doggedly.
plum *n* an oval smooth-skinned sweet stone-fruit; a tree bearing it; a reddish-purple colour; a choice thing.
plumage *n* a bird's feathers.
plumb *n* a lead weight attached to a line, used to determine how deep water is or whether a wall is vertical; any of various weights. * *adj* perfectly vertical. * *adv* vertically; in a direct manner; (*inf*) entirely. * *vt* to test by a plumb line; to examine minutely and critically; to weight with lead; to seal with lead; to supply with or install as plumbing. * *vi* to work as a plumber.
plumbago *n* (*pl* **plumbagos**) graphite; one of a genus of flowering plants.
plumber *n* a person who installs and repairs water or gas pipes.
plumbing *n* the system of pipes used in water or gas supply, or drainage; the plumber's craft.
plumbism *n* lead poisoning.
plume *n* a large or ornamental bird's feather; a feathery ornament or thing; something resembling a feather in structure or density. * *vt* (*feathers*) to preen; to adorn with feathers; to indulge (oneself) with an obvious display of self-satisfaction.
plummet *n* a plumb. * *vi* (**plummeting, plumeted**) to fall in a perpendicular manner; to drop sharply and abruptly.
plummy *adj* (**plummier, plummiest**) like, full of, plums; (*inf*) rich, desirable; (*inf*) (*voice*) deep, drawling, rich-sounding.
plump[1] *adj* rounded, chubby. * *vti* to make or become plump; to swell.—**plumply** *adv*.—**plumpness** *n*.
plump[2] *vti* to fall, drop or sink, or come into contact suddenly and heavily; (*someone, something*) to favour or give support. * *n* a sudden drop or plunge or the sound of this. * *adv* straight down, straight ahead; abruptly; bluntly.
plum pudding *n* a rich boiled or steamed pudding with suet, dried fruit, spices, etc.
plumule *n* (*zool*) a down feather; (*bot*) the embryonic stem of a plant.
plumy *adj* (**plumier, plumiest**) feathery; feathered.
plunder *vt* to steal goods by force, to loot. * *n* plundering; booty.—**plunderer** *n*.
plunge *vti* to immerse, dive suddenly; to penetrate quickly; to hurl oneself or rush; (*horse*) to start violently forward.
plunger *n* a solid cylinder that operates with a plunging motion, as a piston; a larger rubber suction cup used to free clogged drains.
plunk *vt* (*mus*) to pluck. * *vti* to throw or fall heavily. *n* the sound produced by something being plucked, or falling in this way.
pluperfect *adj, n* (*gram*) (a tense) denoting an action completed before a past point of time.
plural *adj* more than one; consisting of or containing more than one kind or class. * *n* (*gram*) the form referring to more than one person or thing.—**plurally** *adv*.
pluralism *n* the simultaneous holding of more than one office or benefice; a theory that reality is composed of a plurality of entities; a theory that there are at least two levels of ultimate reality; the coexistence in society of people of distinct ethnic, cultural or religious groups, each preserving their own traditions; a doctrine or policy advocating this condition.—**pluralist** *n*.—**pluralistic** *adj*.—**pluralistically** *adv*.
plurality *n* (*pl* **pluralities**) being plural; a majority; a large number; another term for pluralism.
plus *prep* added to; in addition to. * *adj* indicating addition; positive. * *n* the sign (+) indicating a value greater than zero; an advantage or benefit; an extra.
plush *n* a velvet-like fabric with a nap. * *adj* made of plush; (*inf*) luxurious.

Pluto *n* (*Greek myth*) the god of the underworld; (*astron*) the planet farthest from the sun, discovered in 1930.
plutocracy *n* (*pl* **plutocracies**) government or rule by the wealthy; a wealthy class.—**plutocratic** *adj*.—**plutocratically** *adv*.
plutocrat *n* a person who has power through wealth; a rich person.
Plutonian *adj* pertaining to Pluto or the underworld; infernal.
plutonic *adj* (*geol*) formed from magma cooling beneath the earth's surface.
plutonium *n* a highly toxic transuranic element used as fuel in nuclear power stations and in nuclear weapons.
pluvial *adj* caused by the action of rain; rainy.
pluviometer *n* an instrument used to measure rainfall.—*also* **rain gauge**.
ply[1] *vti* (**plying, plied**) to work at diligently and energetically; to wield; to subject to persistently; (*goods*) to sell; to go to and fro, run regularly; to keep busy.
ply[2] *n* (*pl* **plies**) a layer or thickness, as of cloth, plywood, etc; any of the twisted strands in a yarn, etc. * *vt* (**plying, plied**) to twist together.
plywood *n* a building material consisting of several thin layers of wood glued together.
PM *abbr* = post-mortem; Prime Minister.
Pm (*chem symbol*) promethium.
p.m. *abbr* = post meridiem.
PMS *abbr* = premenstrual syndrome.
PMT *abbr* = premenstrual tension.
pneumatic *adj* concerning wind, air, or gases; operated by or filled with compressed air.—**pneumatically** *adv*.
pneumatics *n sing* the science dealing with the mechanical properties of air.
pneumatology *n* the theological study of the Holy Spirit.
pneumatometer *n* an instrument for measuring the amount of air exhaled in one breath.
pneumatophore *n* the breathing organ of a marsh plant.
pneumonia *n* acute inflammation of the lungs.—**pneumonic** *adj*.
PO *abbr* = Personnel Officer; Petty Officer; Pilot Officer; post office; postal order.
Po (*chem symbol*) polonium.
poach[1] *vt* to cook (an egg without its shell, fish, etc) in or over boiling water.
poach[2] *vti* to catch game or fish illegally; to trespass for this purpose; to encroach on, usurp another's rights, etc; to steal another's idea, employee, etc.—**poaching** *n*.
poacher[1] *n* a pan with shallow cups for poaching eggs; a dish for poaching fish, etc.
poacher[2] *n* a person who poaches another's property.
pochard *n* (*pl* **pochards, pochard**) a red-headed European duck.
pock *n* an eruptive pustule on the skin, esp as a result of smallpox.
pocket *n* a small bag or pouch, esp in a garment, for carrying small articles; an isolated or enclosed area; a deposit (as of gold, water, or gas). * *adj* small enough to put in a pocket. * *vt* to put in one's pocket, to steal; (*ball*) to put in a pocket; to envelop; to enclose; (*money*) to take dishonestly; to suppress.
pocketbook *n* a small folder or case for letters, money, credit cards, etc; a woman's purse, a handbag; monetary resources; a small esp paperback book.
pocketful *n* (*pl* **pocketfuls**) as much as a pocket holds.
pocketknife *n* (*pl* **pocketknives**) a small knife with one or more blades that fold into the handle.
pocket money *n* money for occasional expenses; a child's allowance.
poco *adv* (*mus*) a little.
pococurante *n, adj* (someone who is) indifferent.
pod *n* a dry fruit or seed vessel, as of peas, beans, etc; a protective container or housing; a detachable compartment on a spacecraft. * *vi* (**podding, podded**) to remove the pod from.
podagra *n* gout, esp in the feet.—**podagral, podagric, podagrous** *adj*.
podgy *adj* (**podgier, podgiest**) short and fat, squat.—*also* **pudgy**.—**podginess** *n*.
podium *n* (*pl* **podiums, podia**) a platform used by lecturers, etc; a low wall around the arena of an amphitheatre.
podophyllin *n* a purgative resin obtained from the root of the May apple and mandrake.
poem *n* an arrangement of words, esp in metre, often rhymed, in a style more imaginative than ordinary speech; a poetic thing.
poesy *n* (*pl* **poesies**) the art of writing poetry.
poet *n* the writer of a poem; a person with imaginative power and a sense of beauty.—**poetess** *nf*.
poetaster *n* an inferior poet.
poetic, poetical *adj* of poets or poetry; written in verse; imaginative, romantic, like poetry.—**poetically** *adv*.
poetic justice *n* an outcome in which vice is punished and virtue rewarded in an appropriate manner.
poetic licence *n* latitude allowed to a poet in grammar, facts, etc.
poetics *n sing* the theory, or study, of poetry.
poetize *vt* to make poetic; to compose poetry about. * *vi* to compose poetry.
poet laureate *n* (*pl* **poets laureate**) a poet officially appointed by the British sovereign to write poems celebrating national events, etc.
poetry *n* the art of writing poems; poems collectively; poetic quality or spirit.
pogo stick *n* a stilt with a powerful spring used to hop along the ground.
pogrom *n* an organized extermination of a minority group.
poignant *adj* piercing; incisive; deeply moving.—**poignancy** *n*.—**poignantly** *adv*.
poinsettia *n* a South American plant, widely cultivated as a house plant for its red bracts, which resemble petals.
point *n* a dot or tiny mark used in writing or printing (eg a decimal point, a full stop); a location; a place in a cycle, course, or scale; a unit in scoring or judging; the sharp end of a knife or pin; a moment of time; one of thirty-two divisions of the compass; a fundamental reason or aim; the tip; a physical characteristic; a railway switch; a unit of size in printing equal to one seventy-second of an inch; a unit used in quoting the prices of stocks, bonds and commodities; a headland or cape. * *vti* to give point to; to sharpen; to aim (at); to extend the finger (at or to); to indicate something; to call attention (to).
point-blank *adj* aimed straight at a mark; direct, blunt.—*also adv*.
pointed *adj* having a point; pertinent; aimed at a particular person or group; conspicuous.—**pointedly** *adv*.—**pointedness** *n*.
pointer *n* a rod or needle for pointing; an indicator; a breed of hunting dog.
pointillism *n* in painting, the practice of applying small strokes or dots of colour to a surface so that from a distance they blend together.—**pointillist** *n, adj*.
pointless *adj* without a point; irrelevant, aimless.—**pointlessly** *adv*.—**pointlessness** *n*.
poise[1] *vt* to balance; to hold supported without motion; (*the head*) to hold in a particular way; to put into readiness. * *vi* to become drawn up into readiness; to hover. * *n* a balanced state; self-possessed assurance of manner; gracious tact; bearing, carriage.
poise[2] *n* a centimetre-gram-second unit of viscosity equivalent to one dyne-second per square metre.
poison *n* a substance that through its chemical action usu destroys or injures an organism; any corrupt influence; an object of aversion or abhorrence. * *vt* to administer poison in order to kill or injure; to put poison into; to influence wrongfully.—**poisoner** *n*.
poison gas *n* a poisonous gas, or a liquid or solid giving off poisonous vapours, used in warfare.
poison ivy *n* a climbing plant with ivory-coloured berries and an acutely irritating oil that causes an intensely itchy skin rash; the rash caused by poison ivy.
poisonous *adj* being or containing poison; toxic; having a harmful influence; (*inf*) unpleasant.—**poisonously** *adv*.—**poisonousness** *n*.
poke *vt* to thrust (at), jab or prod; (*hole, etc*) to make by poking; (*sl*) to hit. * *vi* to jab (at); to pry or search (about or around). * *n* a jab; a prod or nudge; a thrust.

poker[1] *n* a metal rod for poking or stirring fire.
poker[2] *n* a card game in which a player bets that the value of his hand is higher than that of the hands held by others.
poker face *n* an expressionless face, concealing a person's thoughts or feelings.—**poker-faced** *adj*.
poky, pokey *adj* (**pokier, pokiest**) small and uncomfortable.—**pokily** *adv*.—**pokiness** *n*.
polar *adj* of or near the North or South Pole; of a pole; having positive and negative electricity; directly opposite.
polar angle *n* the angle between the positive (polar) axis and the radius vector in polar coordinates.
polar bear *n* a large creamy-white bear that inhabits arctic regions.
polar coordinates *npl* either of a pair of coordinates that determine the position of points in space by measuring their distance along a fixed line from the origin or other given point and their angle, which lies between the fixed line and a single axis.
polarimeter *n* an instrument for measuring the polarization of light.
Polaris *n* (*astron*) the brightest star in the Ursa Minor constellation, also known as the Pole Star.
polariscope *n* an instrument used to detect polarized light.
polarity *n* (*pl* **polarities**) the condition of being polar; the magnet's property of pointing north; attraction towards a particular object or in a specific direction; (*elect*) the state, positive or negative, of a body; diametrical opposition; an instance of such opposition.
polarization *n* the production or acquirement of polarity; (*optics*) the process of causing light waves to vibrate in a uniform circular, elliptical or linear pattern; (*elect*) the separation of positive and negative charges; the grouping about opposing factions.
polarize *vt* (*light waves*) to cause to vibrate in a definite pattern; to give physical polarity to; to break up into opposing factions; to concentrate.—**polarizable** *adj*.—**polarizer** *n*.
Polaroid *n* (*trademark*) a transparent material used esp in sunglasses and lamps to prevent glare; a camera that produces a print in seconds.
polder *n* (*Netherlands*) a piece of land reclaimed from the sea.
pole[1] *n* a long slender piece of wood, metal, etc; a flagstaff. * *vt* to propel, support with a pole.
pole[2] *n* either end of an axis, esp of the earth; either of two opposed forces, parts, etc, as the ends of a magnet, terminals of a battery, etc; either of two opposed principles.
poleaxe, poleax *n* a long-handled battle axe; a type of axe used to slaughter cattle. * *vt* to hit or knock down with, or as if with, such an axe.
pole bean *n* a climbing plant that produces long green edible pods, a runner bean.
polecat *n* (*pl* **polecats, polecat**) a small, dark-brown animal, found in Europe, North Africa and Asia, related to the weasel and known for its unpleasant smell.
polemic *n* a controversy or argument over doctrine; strong criticism; a controversialist. * *adj* involving dispute; controversial (—*also* **polemical**).—**polemically** *adv*.—**polemicist** *n*.
polemics *n sing* the art of controversial debate.
polenta *n* an Italian porridge of maize, barley or chestnut meal.
pole vault *n* a field event in which competitors jump over a high bar using a long flexible pole.—**pole-vault** *vi*.—**pole-vaulter** *n*.
police *n* the government department for keeping order, detecting crime, law enforcement, etc; (*pl*) the members of such a department; any similar organization. * *vt* to control, protect, etc with police or a similar force.
policeman *n* (*pl* **policemen**) a member of a police force.—**policewoman** *nf* (*pl* **policewomen**).
police officer *n* a policeman or policewoman.
policy[1] *n* (*pl* **policies**) a written insurance contract.
policy[2] *n* (*pl* **policies**) political wisdom, statecraft; a course of action selected from among alternatives; a high-level overall plan embracing the general principles and aims of an organization, esp a government.
policyholder *n* a person who has an insurance policy.
polio *n* poliomyelitis.
poliomyelitis *n* an acute infectious virus disease marked by inflammation of nerve cells in the spinal cord, causing paralysis.
Polish *adj* of or pertaining to Poland, its inhabitants, language or culture. * *n* the Slavic language of Poland.
polish *vti* to make or become smooth and shiny by rubbing (with a cloth and polish); to give elegance or culture to; (*with* **off**) (*inf*) to finish completely. * *n* smoothness; elegance of manner; a finish or gloss; a substance, such as wax, used to polish.—**polisher** *n*.
polished *adj* accomplished; smoothly or professionally done or performed; (*rice*) having had the husk removed.
polite *adj* courteous; well-bred; refined.—**politely** *adv*.—**politeness** *n*.
politesse *n* (excessively) formal politeness.
politic *adj* expedient; shrewdly tactful; prudent.
political *adj* relating to politics or government; characteristic of political parties or politicians.—**politically** *adv*.
political correctness *n* a movement aimed at removing discrimination against women, ethnic minorities, gays and lesbians, etc by combating sexist and racist language or policies in education, the arts, media and government.—**politically correct** *adj*.
political economy *n* the former name for the science of economics.
politician *n* a person engaged in politics, often used with implications of seeking personal or partisan gain, scheming, etc.
politico *n* (*sl*) a politician.
politics *n* (*sing or pl*) the science and art of government; political activities, beliefs or affairs; factional scheming for power.
polity *n* (*pl* **polities**) the form or constitution of the government of a state; a constitution.
polka *n* a lively dance; the music for this. * *vi* to dance the polka.
polka dot *n* any of a pattern of small round dots forming a pattern on cloth.
poll *n* a counting, listing, etc of persons, esp of voters; the number of votes recorded; an opinion survey; (*pl*) a place where votes are cast. * *vti* to receive the votes (of); to cast a vote; to canvass or question in a poll.—**poller** *n*.
pollack *n* (*pl* **pollacks, pollack**) a type of food fish.—*also* **pollock** (*pl* **pollocks, pollock**).
pollan *n* an Irish freshwater fish.
pollard *n* a tree with its branches pruned to encourage growth; an animal which has cast its horns or antlers, or had them removed.
pollen *n* the yellow dust, containing male spores, that is formed in the anthers of flowers.—**pollinic** *adj*.
pollex *n* (*pl* **pollices**) a thumb or similar first digit.
pollinate *vti* to fertilize by uniting pollen with seed.—**pollinator** *n*.
pollination *n* the transfer of pollen from the anthers of a flower to the stigma, esp by insects.
polliwog, pollywog *n* a tadpole.
pollock *see* **pollack**.
pollster *n* a person who conducts a poll or compiles data obtained from a poll.
poll tax *n* a tax of a fixed amount per person levied on adults.
pollute *vt* to contaminate with harmful substances; to make corrupt; to profane.—**polluter** *n*.
pollution *n* the act of polluting; the state of being polluted; contamination by chemicals, noise, etc.
polo *n* a game played on horseback by two teams, using a wooden ball and long-handled mallets.
polonaise *n* a slow, stately dance in three-four time; the music for such a dance; an outfit with a one-piece bodice and a skirt looped up at the sides.
polo shirt *n* a sports shirt made of a knitted fabric.
polonium *n* a radioactive element.
poltergeist *n* a spirit believed to move heavy objects about and to make noises.
poltroon *n* (*arch*) a coward.

poly- *prefix* many.

polyandry *n* the practice of a woman having more than one husband at the same time.—**polyandrous** *adj*.

polyanthus *n* (*pl* **polyanthuses**) a hybrid garden primrose; a narcissus with small yellow or white flowers in clusters.

polyatomic *adj* with more than two atoms in the molecule.

polybasic *adj* (*chem*) having more than two bases or atoms of a base.

polychaete, poltchete *n* a type of marine worm. * *adj* pertaining to this type of worm (—*also* **polychaetous**).

polychromatic, polychromic, polychromous *adj* having many colours; exhibiting a play of colours; (*physics*) (*light, etc*) having a mixture of wavelengths.—**polychromatism** *n*.

polychrome *adj* made with, or decorated in, many colours. * *n* a work of art in several colours; a painted statue.

polyclinic *n* a general hospital.

polydactyl *n, adj* (an animal or person) with more than the normal number of fingers or toes.

polyester *n* any of a number of synthetic polymeric resins used for adhesives, plastics, and textiles.

polyethylene *n* a light, plastic, multipurpose synthetic material resistant to moisture and chemicals.—*also* **polythene**.

polygamist *n* a person who advocates or practises polygamy.

polygamy *n* the practice of being married to more than one person at a time; (*bot*) the condition of having staminate, pistillate and hermaphrodite flowers on one plant; (*zool*) the practice of having more than one mate.—**polygamous** *adj*.—**polygamously** *adv*.

polygenesis *n* the derivation of a species or race from many origins.—**polygenetic** *adj*.

polyglot *adj* having command of many languages; composed of numerous languages; containing matter in several languages; composed of elements from different languages. * *n* a person who speaks several languages.

polygon *n* a closed plane figure bound by three or more straight lines.—**polygonal** *adj*.

polygonum *n* one of a family of flowering plants including knotgrass.

polygraph *n* an instrument for detecting and measuring involuntary changes in blood pressure, breathing, etc, often used as a lie detector.—**polygraphic** *adj*.

polygyny *n* the practice of a man having more than one wife at the same time.—**polygynous** *adj*.

polyhedron *n* (*pl* **polyhedrons, polyhedra**) a solid with many (usu more than six) plane faces.—**polyhedral** *adj*.

polymath *n* someone learned in many subjects.

polymer *n* (*chem*) a compound that has large molecules composed of many simpler molecules.—**polymeric** *adj*.—**polymerism** *n*.

polymerize *vti* to (cause to) form a polymer.

polymorph *n* a polymorphous organism.

polymorphous, polymorphic *adj* having, or assuming, many different forms.

polynomial *n* (*math*) an expression consisting of a sum of terms each of which is a product of a constant and one or more variables raised to a positive or zero integral power; (*biol*) a species name of more than two terms. * *adj* composed of or expressed as one or more polynomials.

polyp *n* a small water animal with tentacles at the top of a tube-like body; a growth on mucous membrane.—**polypoid** *adj*.

polyphagous *adj* voracious; (*zool*) feeding on various kinds of food.

polyphone *n* (*linguistics*) a polyphonic letter or symbol

polyphonic *adj* many-voiced; (*mus*) contrapuntal; (*phonetics*) representing more than one sound.

polyphony *n* (*pl* **polyphonies**) being polyphonic; using polyphones; (*mus*) counterpoint.

polypod *n, adj* (an animal) with many legs.

polypody *n* (*pl* **polypodies**) a type of fern.

polypus *n* (*pl* **polypi**) (*med*) a tumour with branching roots, found in the nose or womb.

polystyrene *n* a rigid plastic material used for packing, insulating, etc.

polysyllable *n* a word of many syllables.—**polysyllabic** *adj*.—**polysyllabically** *adv*.

polytechnic *n* an institution that provides instruction in many applied sciences and technical subjects.

polytheism *n* belief in many gods, or more than one god.—**polytheist** *n*.—**polytheistic** *adj*.

polythene *see* **polyethylene**.

polyunsaturated *adj* denoting any of certain plant and animal fats and oils with a low cholesterol content.

polyurethane *n* any of various polymers that are used esp in flexible and rigid foams, resins, etc.

pomace *n* crushed apples for making cider; the crushed apples left after making cider.

pomaceous *adj* pertaining to pomes.

pomade *n* a scented ointment for the hair.

pomander *n* an aromatic ball or powder formerly carried for its pleasant smell or as protection against infection; a container for this.

pome *n* the stoneless fruit of the apple and related plants.

pomegranate *n* an edible fruit with many seeds; the widely cultivated tropical tree bearing it.

Pomeranian *n* a breed of small dog.

pomiculture *n* fruit growing.

pommel *n* the rounded, upward-projecting front part of a saddle; a knob on the hilt of a sword. * *vt* (**pommelling, pommelled** *or* **pommeling, pommeled**) to pummel.

pommy, pommie *n* (*pl* **pommies**) (*Austral sl*) a British person.

pomology *n* the study of fruit growing.—**pomological** *adj*.—**pomologist** *n*.

Pomona *n* (*Roman myth*) the goddess of fruit trees.

pomp *n* stately ceremony; ostentation.

pompadour *n* an 18th century hairstyle.

pompano *n* (*pl* **pompano, pompanos**) an edible American sea fish.

pom-pom *n* a quick-firing automatic anti-aircraft gun.

pompon, pompom, *n* an ornamental ball or tuft of fabric strands used on clothing as an ornament; a small tufted flower on some varieties of chrysanthemum and dahlia.

pomposity *n* (*pl* **pomposities**) the state of being pompous; self-importance; a pompous utterance or act.

pompous *adj* stately; self-important.—**pompously** *adv*.—**pompousness** *n*.

poncho *n* (*pl* **ponchos**) a blanket-like cloak with a hole in the centre for the head.

pond *n* a body of standing water smaller than a lake.

ponder *vti* to think deeply; to consider carefully.

ponderable *adj* capable of being evaluated; capable of being weighed.—**ponderability** *n*.

ponderous *adj* heavy; awkward; dull; lifeless.—**ponderously** *adv*.—**ponderousness** *n*.

pone *n* (*US*) corn pone; maize bread.

pong *n* (*Brit sl*) an unpleasant smell. * *vi* (*Brit sl*) to stink.

pongee *n* a thin, unbleached, Chinese silk.

pontifex *n* (*pl* **pontifices**) (*ancient Rome*) a pontiff or high priest.

pontiff *n* the Pope; a bishop; a pontifex.

pontifical *adj* of a pontiff; pompous. * *npl* a bishop's robes.—**pontifically** *adv*.

pontificate *vi* to speak sententiously, pompously or dogmatically; to officiate at a pontifical mass.—**pontificator** *n*.

pontoon[1] *n* a boat or cylindrical float forming a support for a bridge.

pontoon[2] *n* a card game.

pony *n* (*pl* **ponies**) a small horse, a bronco, mustang, etc; (*inf*) a racehorse.

ponytail *n* a style of arranging hair to resemble a pony's tail.

poodle *n* a breed of dog of various sizes with a curly coat.

pool[1] *n* a small pond; a puddle; a small collection of liquid; a swimming pool.

pool[2] *n* a game played on a billiards table with six pockets; a combination of resources, funds, supplies, people, etc for some common purpose; the parties forming such a combination. * *vti* to contribute to a common fund, to share.

poop *n* (*naut*) the stern of a ship; the raised deck in the stern of a ship.
poor *adj* having little money, needy; deserving pity, unfortunate; deficient; disappointing; inferior. * *n* those who have little.—**poorness** *n.*
poorhouse *n* (*formerly*) a public institution housing poor people.
poorly *adv* insufficiently, badly. * *adj* not in good health.
pop[1] *n* a short, explosive sound, a shot; any carbonated, nonalcoholic beverage. * *vti* (**popping, popped**) to make or cause a pop; to shoot; to go or come quickly (in, out, up); (*corn, maize*) to roast until it pops; to put suddenly; (*eyes*) to bulge.
pop[2] *adj* in a popular modern style. * *n* pop music; pop art; pop culture.
pop[3] *n* (*inf*) father; (*inf*) a name used to address an old man.
pop art *n* a realistic art style using techniques and subjects from commercial art, comic strips, posters, etc.
popcorn *n* a kind of corn or maize, which when heated pops or puffs up.
pope *n* the bishop of Rome, head of the RC Church.—**popedom** *n.*
popery *n* (*derog*) Roman Catholicism.
pop-eyed *adj* with bulging eyes; (*fig*) astonished.
popgun *n* a toy gun firing pellets with a popping noise.
popinjay *n* a conceited person.
popish *adj* (*derog*) pertaining to Roman Catholicism.
poplar *n* a slender, quick-growing tree of the willow family.
poplin *n* a sturdy corded fabric.
poppet *n* a term of endearment.
poppet valve *n* a valve opened by being lifted from its seat.
poppy *n* (*pl* **poppies**) an annual or perennial plant with showy flowers, one of which yields opium; a strong reddish colour.
poppycock *n* (*inf*) nonsense.
populace *n* the common people; the masses; all the people in a country, region, etc.
popular *adj* of the people; well liked; pleasing to many people; easy to understand.—**popularly** *adv.*
popularity *n* the condition or quality of being popular.
popularize *vt* to make popular; to make generally accepted or understood.—**popularization** *n.*—**popularizer** *n.*
populate *vt* to inhabit; to supply with inhabitants.
population *n* all the inhabitants or the number of people in an area.
populism *n* any movement based on belief in the rights, wisdom, or virtue of the common people.
populist *n* an advocate of populism; one who claims to represent the people; (*with cap*) a member of the Populist or People's Party in the US (1891–1904) aiming at public control of utilities, etc.
populous *adj* densely inhabited.—**populously** *adv.*—**populousness** *n.*
porbeagle *n* a type of shark.
porcelain *n* a hard, white, translucent variety of ceramic ware. * *adj* made of porcelain.—**porcellaneous** *adj.*
porch *n* a covered entrance to a building; an open or enclosed gallery or room on the outside of a building.
porcupine *n* a large rodent covered with protective quills.
pore[1] *n* a tiny opening, as in the skin, plant leaves, stem, etc, for absorbing and discharging fluids.
pore[2] *vti* (*with* **over**) to look with steady attention; to study closely.
porgy *n* (*pl* **porgy, porgies**) an edible sea fish.
pork *n* the flesh of a pig used as food.
porker *n* a pig, esp a fattened one.
porky *adj* (**porkier, porkiest**) of or like pork; (*sl*) impertinent; (*sl*) obese, fat.—**porkiness** *n.*
porno *n* (*sl*) pornography—*also* **porn.** * *adj* pornographic.
pornography *n* writings, pictures, films, etc, intended primarily to arouse sexual desire.—**pornographer** *n.*—**pornographic** *adj.*—**pornographically** *adv.*
porous *adj* having pores; able to absorb air and fluids, etc.—**porously** *adv.*—**porousness** *n.*
porphyry *n* (*pl* **porphyry**) a reddish igneous rock, containing crystals of feldspar.
porpoise *n* (*pl* **porpoise, porpoises**) any of several small whales, esp a black blunt-nosed whale of the north Atlantic and Pacific; any of several bottle-nosed dolphins.
porridge *n* a thick food, usu made by boiling oats or oatmeal in water or milk.
porringer *n* a small dish for porridge, etc.
port[1] *n* a harbour; a town with a harbour where ships load and unload cargo; airport; a place where goods may be cleared through customs.
port[2] *n* a porthole; an opening, as in a valve face, for the passage of steam, etc; a hole in an armoured vehicle for firing a weapon; a circuit in a computer for inputting or outputting data.
port[3] *n* the left of an aircraft or ship looking forward.—*also adj.*
port[4] *n* a strong, sweet, fortified dark red wine.
portable *adj* capable of being carried or moved about easily.—**portability** *n.*
portage *n* a carrying of boats and supplies overland between navigable rivers, lakes, etc; any route over which this is done. * *vti* (*boats, etc*) to carry over a portage.
portal *n* an impressive gate or doorway.
portamento *n* (*mus*) a continuous glide from one note to another.
portcullis *n* a grating that can be lowered to bar entrance to a castle.
portend *vt* to give warning of, to foreshadow.
portent *n* an omen, warning.
portentous *adj* ominous; pompous, self-important.—**portentously** *adv.*—**portentousness** *n.*
porter[1] *n* a doorman or gatekeeper.
porter[2] *n* a person who carries luggage, etc, for hire at a station, airport, etc; a railway attendant for passengers; a dark brown beer.
porterage *n* the hire of a porter; the charge for this.
porterhouse *n* a choice cut of beef steak; (*formerly*) an eating place.
portfolio *n* (*pl* **portfolios**) a flat case for carrying papers, drawings, etc; a collection of work; the office of a cabinet minister or minister of state; a list of stocks, shares, etc.
porthole *n* an opening (as a window) with a cover or closure esp in the side of a ship or aircraft; a port through which to shoot; an opening for intake or exhaust of a fluid.
portico *n* (*pl* **porticoes, porticos**) a covered walkway with columns supporting the roof.
portière *n* a heavy curtain over a door or doorway.
portion *n* a part, a share, esp an allotted part; a helping of food; destiny. * *vt* to share out.
portly *adj* (**portlier, portliest**) dignified; stout.—**portliness** *n.*
portmanteau *n* (*pl* **portmanteaus, portmanteaux**) a large oblong travelling case with two compartments.
portmanteau word *n* a word combining the sound and sense of two other words, eg brunch.
portrait *n* a painting, photograph, etc, of a person, esp of the face; (*of person*) a likeness; a vivid description.
portraitist *n* a maker of portraits by painting, photography, etc.
portraiture *n* the drawing of portraits; a portrait; a description in words; portraits collectively.
portray *vt* to make a portrait of; to depict in words; to play the part of in a play, film, etc.—**portrayable** *adj.*—**portrayer** *n.*
portrayal *n* the act or process of portraying; a description; a representation.
portress *n* a female porter.
pose *n* a position or attitude, esp one held for an artist or photographer; an attitude deliberately adopted for effect. * *vti* to propound, assert; to assume an attitude for effect; to sit for a painting, photograph; to set oneself up (as).
poser *n* a person who poses; a difficult problem.
poseur *n* an affected, insincere person.
posh *adj* (*inf*) elegant; fashionable.
posit *vt* to assume as fact, postulate.
position *n* place, situation; a position occupied; posture; a job; state of affairs; point of view. * *vt* to place or locate.
positional *adj* related to, or fixed by position; involving little movement; dependent on context, environment or position.

positive *adj* affirmative; definite; sure; marked by presence, not absence, of qualities; expressed clearly, or in a confident manner; constructive; empirical; (*elect*) charged with positive electricity; (*math*) greater than zero, plus; (*gram*) of adjective or adverb, denoting the simple form; (*photog*) having light, shade, colour as in the original. * *n* a positive quality or quantity; a photographic print made from a negative.

positively *adv* in a positive way; decidedly.

positiveness *n* the condition or quality of being positive; confidence; certainty.

positivism *n* a philosophy recognizing only matters of fact and experience; the quality of being positive.—**positivist** *n, adj*.—**positivistic** *adj*.—**positivistically** *adv*.

positron *n* (*physics*) a particle of the same size as an electron, but with a positive charge.

posology *n* the area of medicine dealing with evaluation of doses.

posse *n* a body of people summoned by a sheriff to assist in keeping the peace, etc; (*sl*) a group of criminals, usu of Jamaican origin and in New York.

possess *vt* to own, have, keep; to dominate or control the mind of.—**possessor** *n*.—**possessory** *adj*.

possessed *adj* owned; controlled as if by a demon.

possession *n* ownership; something possessed; (*pl*) property.

possessive *adj* of or indicating possession; (*gram*) denoting a case, form or construction expressing possession; having an excessive desire to possess or dominate.—**possessively** *adv*.—**possessiveness** *n*.

posset *n* a hot drink of milk curdled with wine or ale.

possibility *n* (*pl* **possibilities**) the state of being possible; a possible occurrence, a contingency.

possible *adj* that may be or may happen; feasible, practicable.—**possibly** *adv*.

possum *n* (*inf*) an opossum; a phalanger; **play possum** to pretend to be asleep or dead; to remain silent.

post[1] *n* a piece of wood, metal, etc, set upright to support a building, sign, etc; the starting or finishing point of a race. * *vt* (*poster, etc*) to put up; to announce by posting notices; (*name*) to put on a posted or published list.

post[2] *n* a fixed position, esp where a sentry or group of soldiers is stationed; a position or job; a trading post; a settlement. * *vt* to station in a given place.

post[3] *n* the official conveyance of letters and parcels, mail; letters, parcels, etc, so conveyed; collection or delivery of post, mail. * *vt* to send a letter or parcel; to keep informed.—**postal** *adj*.

post- *prefix* after.

postage *n* the charge for sending a letter, etc, as represented by stamps.

postage stamp *n* an adhesive or imprinted stamp issued or authorized by a government and used on mail as evidence of prepayment of postage.

postal card *n* (*US*) a card with a stamp issued by the government for mailing at low rates; a post card.

postcard *n* a card, usu decorative, for sending messages by post; a postal card.

post chaise *n* (*formerly*) a light, closed, horse-drawn carriage used for carrying both post and passengers.

postcode *n* in UK, letters and digits to denote an address and assist sorting.

postdate *vt* to write a future date on a letter or cheque.

postdiluvian, postdiluvial *adj* occurring after the Flood (of the Old Testament).

poster *n* a usu decorative or ornamental printed sheet for advertising.

poste restante *n* the department of a post office that will hold mail until it is called for, general delivery.

posterior *adj* later in time or order; at the rear. * *n* the buttocks.—**posteriorly** *adv*.

posterity *n* future generations; all of a person's descendants.

postern *n* a back or side entrance; a small private door.

postfix *vt* to append as a suffix. * *n* a suffix.

post-free *adj* postpaid.

postglacial *adj* existing after a glacial period.

postgraduate *n* a person pursuing study after graduating from a high school or college. * *adj* (*study*) continued after the taking of a degree.

posthaste *adv* with all possible speed.

posthumous *adj* (*child*) born after its father's death; (*award, etc*) given after one's death.—**posthumously** *adv*.

postiche *adj* artificial; superfluous; inappropriate. * *n* an ornament added, esp inappropriately, to finished work; a wig; an imitation.

postilion, postillion *n* someone who rides one of the horses drawing a carriage and guiding the team.

postimpressionism *n* a 19th-century school of painting which sought to express the artist's conception of things rather than their outward appearance.—**postimpressionist** *n, adj*.

postliminium, postliminy *n* (*law*) the right of a prisoner of war or exile to resume his or her former privileges on return to his or her own country.

postlude *n* (*mus*) a closing movement.

postman *n* (*pl* **postmen**) a mailman.

postmark *n* the post office mark cancelling the stamp on a letter by showing the date, place of posting.

postmaster *n* the manager of a post office.

postmeridian *adj* of or taking place in the afternoon.

post meridiem = p.m. (Latin for *after noon*).

postmortem *n* an examination of a corpse to determine the cause of death; an autopsy.—*also adj*.

postnatal *adj* occurring immediately after birth.

post-obit *adj* (*law*) after death. * *n* a bond in which a borrower undertakes to repay a loan on the death of someone from whom he or she expects to receive a legacy.

post office *n* the building where postage stamps are sold and other postal business conducted; a public department handling the transmission of mail.

postpaid *adj* with a charge for postage, post free.

postpone *vt* to put off, delay to a future date.—**postponable** *adj*.—**postponement** *n*.—**postponer** *n*.

postprandial *adj* after-dinner.

postscript *n* a note added to a letter after completion.

postulant *n* someone making a request; a candidate for admission to a religious order.

postulate *vt* to assume to be true; to demand or claim. * *n* a position taken as self-evident; (*math*) an unproved assumption taken as basic; an axiom.—**postulation** *n*.

posture *n* a pose; a body position; an attitude of mind; an official stand or position. * *vti* to pose in a particular way; to assume a pose.—**postural** *adj*.—**posturer** *n*.

post-viral syndrome *n* the viral condition myalgic encephalomyelitis that affects the nervous system.

posy *n* (*pl* **posies**) a small bunch of flowers.

pot[1] *n* a deep, round cooking vessel; an earthenware or plastic container for plants; a framework for catching fish or lobsters; (*inf*) a large amount (as of money); (*inf*) all the money bet at a single time. * *vb* (**potting, potted**) *vt* to put or preserve in a pot. * *vi* to take a pot shot, shoot.

pot[2] *n* (*sl*) cannabis.

potable *adj* drinkable.

potash *n* potassium carbonate.

potassium *n* a soft silvery-white metallic element.—**potassic** *adj*.

potation *n* the act of drinking; a draught or drink.

potato *n* (*pl* **potatoes**) a starchy, oval tuber eaten as a vegetable.

potbelly *n* (*pl* **potbellies**) a protruding belly.—**potbellied** *adj*.

potboiler *n* an inferior literary or artistic work done simply to earn money.

potboy *n* (*formerly*) in UK, an assistant in a public house.

poteen *n* (*Irish*) illicitly distilled whiskey.

potency *n* (*pl* **potencies**) the quality or condition of being potent; power; strength.

potent *adj* powerful; influential; intoxicating; (*a male*) able to have sexual intercourse.—**potently** *adv*.

potentate *n* a person with great power; a ruler; a monarch.

potential *adj* possible, but not yet actual. * *n* the unrealized ability to do something.—**potentially** *adv*.

potentiality *n* (*pl* **potentialities**) latent capacity for development or growth; something with this.

potentiate *vt* to make possible; to give power to.

potentilla *n* a flowering plant of the rose family.

pother *n* a bustle or turmoil; a turmoil.

pothole *n* a hole worn in a road by traffic; (*geol*) a deep hole or cave in rock caused by the action of water.

pothouse *n* (*formerly*) in UK, a public house.

pothunter *n* someone who hunts for the sake of the game caught, not for the sport.

potion *n* a mixture of liquids, such as poison.

potpourri *n* (*pl* **potpourris**) a mixture of scented, dried flower petals; a collection; a medley or miscellany.

potsherd, potshard *n* a piece of broken earthenware.

pot shot *n* a random or easy shot.

pottage *n* a thick broth.

potted *adj* in a pot; preserved (in a pot); (*version, history*) abridged.

potter[1] *n* a person who makes earthenware vessels.

potter[2] *vi* to busy oneself idly; (*US*) to putter.—**potterer** *n*.

pottery *n* (*pl* **potteries**) earthenware vessels; a workshop where such articles are made.

potto *n* (*pl* **pottos**) a West African lemur; a kinkajou.

potty[1] *adj* (**pottier, pottiest**) (*inf*) slightly crazy; trivial, petty.—**pottiness** *n*.

potty[2] *n* (*pl* **potties**) (*inf*) a chamber pot.

pouch *n* a small bag or sack; a bag for mail; a sacklike structure, as that on the abdomen of a kangaroo, etc, for carrying young.—**pouched** *adj*.

poult *n* a young fowl.

poultice *n* a hot moist dressing applied to a sore part of the body.

poultry *n* domesticated birds kept for meat or eggs.

pounce *vi* to swoop or spring suddenly (upon) in order to seize; to make a sudden assault or approach.—*also n*.

pound[1] *n* a unit of weight equal to 16 ounces; a unit of money in the UK and other countries, symbol £.

pound[2] *vt* to beat into a powder or a pulp; to hit hard. * *vi* to deliver heavy blows repeatedly (at or on); to move with heavy steps; to throb; (*with* **away**) to work hard and continuously.—**pounder** *n*.

pound[3] *n* a municipal enclosure for stray animals; a depot for holding impounded personal property until claimed; a place or condition of confinement.

poundage *n* a charge per pound of weight; weight in pounds; the act of impounding; the state of being impounded.

poundal *n* a unit of force, giving to a mass of one pound an acceleration of one foot per second per second.

pour *vti* to cause to flow in a stream; to flow continuously; to rain heavily; to serve tea or coffee.—**pourer** *n*.

pourboire *n* a tip or gratuity.

pout *vti* to push out (the lips); to look sulky. * *n* a thrusting out of the lips; (*pl*) a fit of pique.—**poutingly** *adv*.

pouter *n* someone who pouts; a breed of pigeon with a prominent crop.

poverty *n* the condition of being poor; scarcity.

poverty-stricken *adj* very poor, impoverished.

POW *abbr* = prisoner of war.

powder *n* any substance in tiny, loose particles; a specific kind of powder, esp for medicinal or cosmetic use; fine dry light snow. * *vti* to sprinkle or cover with powder; to reduce to powder.—**powderer** *n*.

powdered *adj* sprinkled or covered with powder; reduced to power.

powdered sugar *n* (*US*) icing sugar.

powdery *adj* like powder; easily crumbled.

power *n* ability to do something; political, social or financial control or force; a person or state with influence over others; legal force or authority; physical force; a source of energy; (*math*) the result of continued multiplication of a quantity by itself a specified number of times. * *adj* operated by electricity, a fuel engine, etc; served by an auxiliary system that reduces effort; carrying electricity. * *vt* to supply with a source of power.—**powered** *adj*.

powerful *adj* mighty; strong; influential.—**powerfully** *adv*.—**powerfulness** *n*.

powerhouse *n* a power station; (*inf*) a strong or energetic person, team, etc.

powerless *adj* without power; helpless; feeble.—**powerlessly** *adv*.—**powerlessness** *n*.

power station, power plant *n* a building where electric power is generated.

power-striding *n* brisk walking as a means of improving fitness.

powwow *n* an American Indian ceremony (as for invoking victory in war); (*inf*) any conference or get-together. * *vi* to confer, chat.

pox *n* a virus disease marked by pustules; (*arch*) smallpox; syphilis; a plague; a curse.

pozzuolana, pozzolana *n* volcanic ashes used in hydraulic cement.

pp *abbr* = past participle; (*mus*) pianissimo.

pp. *abbr* = pages.

p.p. *abbr* = per pro.

ppm *abbr* = (*chem*) parts per million.

PPS *abbr* = post (additional) postscript.

PQ *abbr* = Quebec.

PR *abbr* = public relations; proportional representation.

Pr (*chem symbol*) praseodymium.

practicable *adj* able to be practised; possible, feasible.—**practicability** *n*.—**practicably** *adv*.

practical *adj* concerned with action, not theory; workable; suitable; trained by practice; virtual, in effect.

practicality *n* (*pl* **practicalities**) the condition of being practical; a practical feature or aspect.

practical joke *n* a prank intended to embarrass or to cause discomfort.

practically *adv* in a practical manner; virtually.

practice *n* action; habit, custom; repetition and exercise to gain skill; the exercise of a profession.

practise *vti* to repeat an exercise to acquire skill; to put into practice; to do habitually or frequently; (*profession*) to work at.

practised *adj* acquired by practice; proficient; experienced.

practitioner *n* a person who practises a profession.

praedial *adj* pertaining to land or landed property.—*also* **predial**.

praetor *n* (*ancient Rome*) a magistrate, ranking next to a consul.

pragmatic *adj* practical; testing the validity of all concepts by their practical results.—**pragmatically** *adv*.

pragmatics *n sing* the study of the relationship of signs and symbols and their use; (*linguistics*) the study of meaning derived from context.

pragmatism *n* the judging of events or actions by their results, esp in politics; pragmatic behaviour; (*philos*) a theory that judges the truth of a doctrine by the conduct resulting from belief in it.—**pragmatist** *n*.—**pragmatistic** *adj*.

prairie *n* a large area of level or rolling land predominantly in grass; a dry treeless plateau.

prairie dog *n* a burrowing rodent related to the marmot.

prairie wolf *n* the coyote.

praise *vt* to express approval of, to commend; to glorify, to worship. * *vi* to express praise. * *n* commendation; glorification.—**praiser** *n*.

praiseworthy *adj* deserving praise; commendable.—**praiseworthily** *adv*.—**praiseworthiness** *n*.

praline *n* a confection made of nuts and sugar.

prance *vi* (*horse*) to spring on the hind legs, bound; (*person*) to walk or ride in a showy manner; to swagger. * *n* a prancing; a caper.—**prancer** *n*.—**prancingly** *adv*.

prank[1] *n* a mischievous trick or joke; a ludicrous act.—**prankster** *n*.

prank[2] *vti* to adorn, to deck; to dress up showily.

prase *n* a green, transparent form of quartz.

praseodymium *n* a silvery-white metallic element.
prate *vti* to chatter, talk idly.—**prater** *n*.
pratincole *n* a bird resembling a swallow.
prattle *vti* to talk in a childish manner; to babble. * *n* empty chatter.—**prattler** *n*.
prawn *n* an edible marine shrimp-like crustacean. * *vi* to fish for prawns.—**prawner** *n*.
praxis *n* (*pl* **praxises, praxes**) practice; an example, or set of examples, for an exercise.
pray *vti* to offer prayers to God; to implore.
prayer[1] *n* supplication, entreaty, praise or thanks to God; the form of this; the act of praying; (*pl*) devotional services; something prayed for.
prayer[2] *n* one who prays.
prayerful *adj* given to prayer; devout.—**prayerfully** *adv*.
pre- *prefix* before, beforehand; previous to; surpassingly.
preach *vi* to advocate in an earnest or moralizing way. * *vt* to deliver a sermon; (*patience, etc*) to advocate.
preacher *n* one who preaches, esp a Protestant clergyman.
preachify *vi* (*inf*) to hold forth tediously.—**preachification** *n*.
preachy *adj* (**preachier, preachiest**) (*inf*) fond of moralizing or preaching.
preamble *n* an introductory part to a document, speech, or story, stating its purpose.—**preambulary** *adj*.
prearrange *vt* to arrange beforehand.—**prearrangement** *n*.
prebend *n* a stipend granted to a canon or member of the chapter by a cathedral.—**prebendal** *adj*.
prebendary *n* (*pl* **prebendaries**) someone who holds a prebend.
precancerous *adj* likely to become cancerous.
precarious *adj* dependent on chance; insecure; dangerous.—**precariously** *adv*.—**precariousness** *n*.
precatory, precative *adj* suppliant, expresssing a wish.
precaution *n* a preventive measure; care taken beforehand; careful foresight.—**precautionary** *adj*.
precede *vti* to be, come or go before in time, place, order, rank, or importance.
precedence *n* priority; the right of higher rank.
precedent *n* a previous and parallel case serving as an example; (*law*) a decision, etc, serving as a rule. * *adj* preceding; previous.—**precedented** *adj*.—**precedently** *adv*.
precedential *adj* serving as a precedent; having precedence.
preceding *adj* coming or going before; former.
precentor *n* the leader of a choir in a cathedral or church.
precept *n* a rule of moral conduct; a maxim; an order issued by a legally constituted authority to a subordinate.
preceptive *adj* of or using precepts; didactic.—**preceptively** *adv*.
preceptor *n* an instructor or teacher.—**preceptress** *nf*.
precession *n* going before, in advance of—**precessional** *adj*.
precinct *n* (*usu pl*) an enclosure between buildings, walls, etc; a limited area; an urban area where traffic is prohibited; (*pl*) environs; (*US*) a police district or a subdivision of a voting ward.
precious *adj* of great cost or value; beloved; very fastidious; affected; thoroughgoing. * *adv* (*sl*) very.—**preciously** *adv*.—**preciousness** *n*.
precious metal *n* gold, silver, or platinum.
precious stone *n* a diamond, emerald, ruby, sapphire, pearl, and sometimes black opal; a gem.
precipice *n* a cliff or overhanging rock face.
precipitant *adj* falling headlong; hasty, impetuous. * *n* (*chem*) a substance causing precipitation.—**precipitance, precipitancy** *n*.
precipitate *vti* to throw from a height; to cause to happen suddenly or too soon; (*chem*) to separate out; to rain; to fall as rain, snow, dew, etc.—**precipitately** *adv*.—**precipitateness** *n*.—**precipitator** *n*.
precipitation *n* the act of precipitating; undue haste; rain, snow, etc; the amount of this.
precipitous *adj* of or like a precipice; sheer, steep.—**precipitously** *adv*.—**precipitousness** *n*.
précis *n* (*pl* **précis**) a summary or abstract. * *vt* to make a précis of.
precise *adj* clearly defined, exact; accurate; punctilious; particular.—**precisely** *adv*.—**preciseness** *n*.
precision *n* the quality of being precise; accuracy. * *adj* (*machines*) having a high degree of accuracy.
preclude *vt* to rule out in advance; to make impossible.—**preclusion** *n*.—**preclusive** *adj*.
precocious *adj* prematurely ripe or developed.—**precociously** *adv*.—**precociousness** *n*.
precocity *n* the condition of being precocious, precociousness; early development, esp of a child's mind.
precognition *n* the supposed extrasensory perception of a future event; clairvoyance.—**precognitive** *adj*.
pre-Columbian *adj* of or originating in the Americas before their discovery by Christopher Columbus.
preconceive *vt* to form an idea or opinion of before actual experience.
preconception *n* the act of preconceiving; an opinion formed without actual knowledge.
precondition *n* a requirement that must be met beforehand, a prerequisite. * *vt* (*an organism, a patient*) to prepare to behave or react in a certain way under certain conditions.
precursor *n* a predecessor; a substance from which another substance is formed.—**precursory** *adj*.
predacious, predaceous *adj* living on prey.—**predaciousness, predaceousness, predacity** *n*.
predate *vt* to antedate.
predator *n* a person who preys, plunders or devours; a carnivorous animal.
predatory *adj* living on prey, of or relating to a predator; characterized by hunting or plundering.—**predatorily** *adv*.—**predatoriness** *n*.
predecease *vt* to die before (another).
predecessor *n* a former holder of a position or office; an ancestor.
predella *n* (*pl* **predellae**) a platform for, or shelf upon, an altar; a painting, or sculpture, on such a platform or shelf.
predestinarian *adj* pertaining to predestination. * *n* someone who believes in the doctrine of predestination.
predestinate *adj* predestined. * *vt* to predestine.
predestination *n* a predestining or being predestined; destiny; (*theol*) the doctrine that God has from all eternity decreed the salvation or damnation of each soul.
predestine *vt* to foreordain; to destine beforehand.
predeterminate *adj* predetermined.
predetermine *vt* to decide beforehand.—**predetermination** *n*.
predicable *adj* which can be predicated.
predicament *n* a difficult or embarrassing situation.
predicant *adj* pertaining to preaching. * *n* a preaching friar, esp a Dominican.
predicate *vt* to state as a quality or attribute; to base (on facts, conditions etc). * *n* (*gram*) that which is stated about the subject.—**predication** *n*.
predicative *adj* (*gram*) (*adjective, etc*) making a statement about the subject of a verb. * *n* a predicative construction.
predicatory *adj* of or given to preaching.
predict *vt* to foretell; to state (what one believes will happen).—**predictor** *n*.
predictable *adj* able to be predicted or anticipated; lacking originality.—**predictability** *n*.—**predictably** *adv*.
prediction *n* the act of predicting; that which is predicted; a forecast or prophecy.—**predictive** *adj*.—**predictively** *adv*.
predigest *vt* to treat (food) artificially to make easily digestible.
predilection *n* partiality, liking for.
predispose *vt* to incline beforehand; (*disease, etc*) to make susceptible to.—**predisposition** *n*.
predominant *adj* ruling over, controlling; influencing.—**predominance, predominancy** *n*.
predominantly *adv* mainly.
predominate *vt* to rule over; to have influence or control over; to prevail; to be greater in number, intensity, etc.—**predomination** *n*.—**predominator** *n*.
pre-eminent, preeminent *adj* distinguished above others; outstanding.—**pre-eminence, preeminence** *n*.—**pre-eminently, preeminently** *adv*.

pre-empt, preempt *vt* to take action to check other action beforehand; to gain the right to buy (public land) by settling on it; to seize before anyone else can; to replace; (*in bridge*) to bid highly to exclude bids from opponents.—**pre-emptor, preemptor** *n*.—**pre-emptory, preemptory** *adj*.

pre-emption, preemption *n* a pre-empting or being pre-empted; a buying or the right to buy before the opportunity is given to others; such a purchase.

pre-emptive, preemptive *adj* (*bridge*) denoting a high bid to exclude bids from the opposition.—**pre-emptively, preemptively** *adv*.

preen *vti* (*birds*) to clean and trim the feathers; to congratulate (oneself) for achievement; to groom (oneself); to gloat.—**preener** *n*.

prefab *n* (*inf*) a prefabricated part or building.

prefabricate *vt* (*house, etc*) to build in standardized sections for shipment and quick assembly; to produce artificially.—**prefabrication** *n*.—**prefabricator** *n*.

preface *n* an introduction or preliminary explanation; a foreword or introduction to a book; a preamble. * *vt* to serve as a preface; to introduce.—**prefacer** *n*.

prefatory *adj* of or pertaining to a preface; introductory.—**prefatorily** *adv*.

prefect *n* a person placed in authority over others; a student monitor in a school; in some countries, an administrative official.—**prefectorial** *adj*.

prefecture *n* the office, district, residence, or tenure of a prefect.—**prefectural** *adj*.

prefer *vt* (**preferring, preferred**) to like better; to promote, advance; to put before a court, etc, for consideration.—**preferrer** *n*.

preferable *adj* deserving preference; superior; more desirable.—**preferably** *adv*.

preference *n* the act of preferring, choosing, or favouring one above another; that which is chosen or preferred; prior right; advantage given to one person, country, etc, over others.

preferential *adj* giving or receiving preference.—**preferentialism** *n*.—**preferentially** *adv*.

preferment *n* advancement; promotion to a higher post.

prefiguration *n* the act of prefiguring.—**prefigurative** *adj*.

prefigure *vt* to suggest in advance, foreshadow; to imagine beforehand.

prefix *vt* to put at the beginning of or before; to put as an introduction. * *n* a syllable or group of syllables placed at the beginning of a word, affecting its meaning.—**prefixal** *adj*.—**prefixally** *adv*.

preglacial *adj* existing before a glacial period.

pregnable *adj* capable of being attacked and captured.

pregnancy *n* (*pl* **pregnancies**) the state of being pregnant; the period of this.

pregnant *adj* having a foetus in the womb; significant, meaningful; imaginative; filled (with) or rich (in).—**pregnantly** *adv*.

prehensile *adj* capable of grasping, esp by wrapping around.—**prehensility** *n*.

prehension *n* grasping; the ability to grasp.

prehistoric, prehistorical *adj* of the period before written records began; (*inf*) old-fashioned.—**prehistorically** *adv*.

prehistory *n* (*pl* **prehistories**) events that took place before recorded history; the study of prehistoric events; the history of the earlier background of an incident, etc.—**prehistorian** *n*.

prejudge *vt* to pass judgment on before a trial; to form a premature opinion.—**prejudger** *n*.—**prejudgment, prejudgement** *n*.

prejudice *n* a judgment or opinion made without adequate knowledge; bias; intolerance or hatred of other races, etc; (*law*) injury or disadvantage due to another's action. * *vt* to affect or injure through prejudice.—**prejudiced** *adj*.

prejudicial *adj* causing prejudice; detrimental, damaging.—**prejudicially** *adv*.

prelacy *n* (*pl* **prelacies**) the office or status of a prelate; prelates collectively; church government by prelates.

prelate *n* a church dignity with episcopal authority.—**prelatic** *adj*.

prelature *n* the office or status of a prelate.

preliminary *adj* preparatory; introductory. * *n* (*pl* **preliminaries**) an event preceding another; a preliminary step or measure; (*in school*) a preparatory examination.—**preliminarily** *adv*.

prelims *npl* the front matter of a book, before the main text; preliminary university exams.

prelude *n* an introductory act or event; an event preceding another of greater importance; (*mus*) a movement which acts as an introduction. * *vti* to serve as a prelude to, to usher in; to play a prelude.—**preludial** *adj*.—**prelusion** *n*.—**prelusive, prelusory** *adj*.

premarital *adj* (*sex*) taking place before marriage.

premature *adj* occurring before the expected or normal time; too early, hasty.—**prematurely** *adv*.—**prematurity** *n*.

premeditate *vt* (*crime, etc*) to plan in advance.—**premeditatedly** *adv*.—**premeditative** *adj*.—**premeditator** *n*.

premeditation *n* deliberation or thought before doing something; (*law*) the plotting of a crime beforehand, demonstrating intent to commit it.

premier *adj* principal; first. * *n* the head of a government, a prime minister.—**premiership** *n*.

premiere, prèmiere *n* the first public performance of a play, film, etc. * *vt* to give a premiere of. * *vi* to have a first performance; to appear for the first time as a star performer.

premise *n* a proposition on which reasoning is based; something assumed or taken for granted (—*also* **premiss**); (*pl*) a piece of land and its buildings. * *vt* to state as an introduction; to postulate; to base on certain assumptions.

premium *n* a reward, esp an inducement to buy; a periodical payment for insurance; excess over an original price; something given free or at a reduced price with a purchase; a high value or value in excess of expectation. * *adj* (*goods*) high quality.

premonition *n* a foreboding; a feeling of something about to happen.—**premonitory** *adj*.

prenatal *adj* before birth.

preoccupation *n* a concern that prevents thought of other things; mental absorption; business that takes precedence; preoccupancy.

preoccupied *adj* absent-minded, lost in thought; (*with* **with**) having one's attention completely taken up by.

preoccupy *vt* (**preoccupying, preoccupied**) to take possession of beforehand; to engross, fill the thoughts of.

preordain *vt* to ordain beforehand.—**preordination** *n*.

prep *abbr* = preparatory school; preparation; preposition.

prep school *see* **preparatory school.**

prepaid *see* **prepay.**

preparation *n* the act of preparing; a preparatory measure; something prepared, as a medicine, cosmetic, etc.

preparative *adj* preparatory. * *n* something that prepares the way.—**preparatively** *adv*.

preparatory *adj* serving to prepare; introductory. * *adv* by way of preparation; in a preparatory manner.—**preparatorily** *adv*.

preparatory school *n* a private school that prepares students for an advanced school or college.—*also* **prep (school).**

prepare *vt* to make ready in advance; to fit out, equip; to cook; to instruct, teach; to put together. * *vi* to make oneself ready.—**preparedly** *adv*.

prepared *adj* subjected to a special process or treatment.

preparedness *n* the state of being prepared, esp for waging war.

prepay *vt* (**prepaying, prepaid**) to pay in advance.—**prepayment** *n*.

prepense *adj* premeditated.

preponderant *adj* being greater in number, amount, importance, weight, etc; predominant.—**preponderance, preponderancy** *n*.—**preponderantly** *adv*.

preponderate *vi* to be greater in number, amount, influence, etc; to predominate, prevail; to weigh more.—**preponderation** *n*.

preposition *n* a word used before a noun or pronoun to show its relation to another part of the sentence.—**prepositional** *adj*.

prepositive *adj, n* (*gram*) (a particle or word) which can be attached as a prefix to a word.

prepossess *vt* to impress favourably; to prejudice.

prepossessing *adj* impressing favourably; attractive.—**prepossessingly** *adv*.
prepossession *n* a prepossessed state; a preconceived opinion or judgement.
preposterous *adj* ridiculous; laughable; absurd.—**preposterously** *adv*.—**preposterousness** *n*.
prepotency *n* the state of being prepotent; (*biol*) a dominant hereditary influence.
prepotent *adj* very or more powerful; (*biol*) having a dominant hereditary influence.
prepuce *n* the loose skin at the end of the penis.—*also* **foreskin.**
pre-Raphaelite *adj, n* (a member) of a 19th-century school of artists who imitated the Italian style of painting before Raphael, using brilliant colour and minute detail.
prerecord *vt* (*radio, TV programme*) to record in advance for later broadcasting.—**prerecorded** *adj*.
prerequisite *n* a condition, etc, that must be fulfilled prior to something else. * *adj* required beforehand.
prerogative *n* a privilege or right accorded through office or hereditary rank.
presage *n* a foreboding or presentiment; an omen. * *vt* to foretell; to have a presentiment of.
presbyopia *n* a condition of long-sightedness, usu progressing with age, in which near objects are seen indistinctly, caused by a change in the refractive power of the eye due to the flattening of the lens.
presbyter *n* in the Presbyterian Church, an elder; in the Episcopal Church, a priest or minister.—**presbyterial** *adj*.
presbyterian *adj* of or denoting government by presbyteries; (*with cap*) of a Presbyterian Church. * *n* a member of a Presbyterian Church.—**Presbyterianism** *n*.
presbytery *n* (*pl* **presbyteries**) in a Presbyterian Church a court composed of ministers and one elder from each church within a district; a district so represented; the eastern part of the chancel of a church; a Roman Catholic priest's house.
preschool *adj* of or for a child between infancy and school age.
prescience *n* foreknowledge.—**prescient** *adj*.
prescribe *vt* to designate; to ordain; (*rules*) to lay down; (*medicine, treatment*) to order, advise.—**prescriber** *n*.
prescript *n* an ordnance or decree. * *adj* prescribed, directed.
prescription *n* act of prescribing; (*med*) a written instruction by a physician for the preparation of a drug; (*law*) establishment of a right or title through long use.
prescriptive *adj* prescribing, ordering, advising; based on long use, traditional.—**prescriptively** *adv*.
preselect *vt* to select beforehand, usu according to a particular criterion.—**preselection** *n*.—**preselective** *adj*.
presence *n* being present; immediate surroundings; personal appearance and bearing; impressive bearing, personality, etc; something (as a spirit) felt or believed to be present.
presence of mind *n* readiness of resource in an emergency, etc; the ability to say the right thing.
present[1] *adj* being at the specified place; existing or happening now; (*gram*) denoting action or state now or action that is always true. * *n* the time being; now; the present tense.
present[2] *n* a gift.
present[3] *vt* to introduce someone, esp socially; (*a play, etc*) to bring before the public, exhibit; to make a gift or award; to show; to perform; (*law*) to lay a charge before a court; (*weapon*) to point in a particular direction. * *vi* to present a weapon; to become manifest; to come forward as a patient.
presentable *adj* of decent appearance; fit to go into company.—**presentability** *n*.—**presentably** *adv*.
presentation *n* act of presenting; a display or exhibition; style of presenting; something offered or given; a description or persuasive account; (*med*) the position of a foetus in the uterus.—**presentational** *adj*.
presentative *adj* (*of benefice*) admitting presentation by patron; (*philos*) able to be apprehended directly by the mind
presenter *n* a person who presents someone or something; (*radio, TV*) a person who introduces a show, an announcer.
presentiment *n* a premonition, apprehension, esp of evil.
presently *adv* in a short while, soon.
presentment *n* the act of presenting; something which is presented; a representation or delineation; the laying of a formal statement before a court or authority.
preservation *n* the act of preserving or securing; a state of being preserved or repaired.
preservationist *n* someone who undertakes or advocates preservation (as of a biological species or a historic landmark).
preservative *adj* preserving. * *n* something that preserves or has the power of preserving, esp an additive.
preserve *vt* to keep safe from danger; to protect; (*food*) to can, pickle, or prepare for future use; to keep or reserve for personal or special use. * *vi* to make preserves; to raise and protect game for sport. * *n* (*usu pl*) fruit preserved by cooking in sugar; an area restricted for the protection of natural resources, esp one used for regulated hunting, etc; something regarded as reserved for certain persons.—**preservable** *adj*.—**preserver** *n*.
preset *vt* (**presetting, preset**) to set (the controls of an electrical device) in advance.
preside *vi* to take the chair or hold the position of authority; to take control or exercise authority.—**presider** *n*.
presidency *n* (*pl* **presidencies**) the office, dignity, term, jurisdiction or residence of a president.
president *n* the head of state of a republic; the highest officer of a company, club, etc.—**presidential** *adj*.—**presidentially** *adv*.
president-elect *n* a president who has been elected to office but has not yet taken up the post.
presidio *n* (*pl* **presidios**) (*Spain*) a fort or military establishment.
presidium *n* (*pl* **presidiums, presidia**) a presiding committee in a communist organization.
press *vt* to act on with steady force or weight; to push against, squeeze, compress, etc; to squeeze the juice, etc from; (*clothes, etc*) to iron; to embrace closely; to force, compel; to entreat; to emphasize; to trouble; to urge on; (*record*) to make from a matrix. * *vi* to weigh down; to crowd closely; to go forward with determination. * *n* pressure, urgency, etc; a crowd; a machine for crushing, stamping, etc; a machine for printing; a printing or publishing establishment; the gathering and distribution of news and those who perform these functions; newspapers collectively; any of various pressure devices; an upright closet for storing clothes.
press conference *n* a group interview given to members of the press by a politician, celebrity, etc.
pressing *adj* urgent; calling for immediate attention; importunate. * *n* a number of records made at one time from a master.—**pressingly** *adv*.
pressman *n* (*pl* **pressmen**) a journalist; an operator of a printing press.
pressmark *n* a number showing a book's place in a library.
press secretary *n* a person officially in charge of relations with the press for a usu prominent public figure.
press-up *n* an exercise involving raising and lowering the body with the arms.
pressure *n* the act of pressing; a compelling force; a moral force; compression; urgency; constraint; (*physics*) force per unit of area. * *vt* to pressurize.
pressure cooker *n* a strong, sealed pan in which food can be cooked quickly by steam under pressure; (*inf*) a situation beset with emotional or social pressure.
pressure group *n* a group of people organized to alert public opinion, legislators, etc, to a particular area of interest.
pressure point *n* a point on the body where a blood vessel can be compressed to check bleeding.
pressurize *vt* to keep nearly normal atmospheric pressure inside an aeroplane, etc, as at high altitudes; to exert pressure on; to attempt to compel, press.—**pressurization** *n*.—**pressurizer** *n*.

prestidigitation *n* sleight of hand.—**prestidigitator** *n*.
prestige *n* standing in the eyes of people; commanding position in people's minds.
prestigious *adj* imparting prestige or distinction.
prestissimo *adj, adv* (*mus*) very fast.
presto *adj, adv* (*mus*) quick; immediately. * *n* (*pl* **prestos**) (*mus*) a lively passage.
presumable *adj* that may be presumed or taken to be true.
presumably *adv* as may be presumed.
presume *vt* to take for granted, suppose. * *vi* to assume to be true; to act without permission; to take liberties; (*with* **on, upon**) to take advantage of.—**presumedly** *adv*.—**presumer** *n*.
presuming *adj* venturing without permission; presumptuous.—**presumingly** *adv*.
presumption *n* a supposition; a thing presumed; a strong probability; effrontery.
presumptive *adj* assumed in the absence of contrary evidence; probable.—**presumptively** *adv*.
presumptuous *adj* tending to presume; bold; forward.—**presumptuously** *adv*.—**presumptuousness** *n*.
presuppose *vt* to assume beforehand; to involve as a necessary prior condition.—**presupposition** *n*.
pretence *n* the act of pretending; a hypocritical show; a fraud, a sham.—*also* **pretense**.
pretend *vti* to claim, represent, or assert falsely; to feign, make believe; to lay claim (to).
pretended *adj* feigned; ostensible; untrue; insincerely asserted or claimed.—**pretendedly** *adv*.
pretender *n* a person who makes a pretence; a claimant to a title.
pretense *see* **pretence**.
pretension *n* a false claim; affectation; assumption of superiority.
pretentious *adj* claiming great importance; ostentatious.—**pretentiously** *adv*.—**pretentiousness** *n*.
preterit, preterite (*gram*) *adj* denoting past action. * *n* the past tense.
preterition *n* omission; (*theology*) the doctrine of the passing over of the non-elect by God.
preternatural *adj* out of the regular course of things, abnormal.
pretext *n* a pretended reason to conceal a true one; an excuse.
prettify *vt* (**prettifying, prettified**) to make pretty.—**prettifaction** *n*.
pretty *adj* (**prettier, prettiest**) attractive in a dainty, graceful way. * *adv* (*inf*) fairly, moderately. * *n* (*pl* **pretties**) (*inf*) a pretty or pleasing person or thing. * *vt* (**prettying, prettied**) (*with* **up**) (*inf*) to make pretty.—**prettily** *adv*.—**prettiness** *n*.
pretzel *n* a hard, brittle, salted biscuit, often formed in a loose knot.
prevail *vi* to overcome; to predominate; to be customary or in force.
prevailing *adj* generally accepted, widespread; predominant.—**prevailingly** *adv*.
prevalent *adj* current; predominant; widely practised or experienced.—**prevalence** *n*.—**prevalently** *adv*.
prevaricate *vi* to make evasive or misleading statements.—**prevarication** *n*.—**prevaricator** *n*.
prevenient *adj* preceding; anticipating; aiming at prevention.
prevent *vt* to keep from happening; to hinder.—**preventable, preventible** *adj*.—**preventably, preventibly** *adv*.—**preventer** *n*.
prevention *n* a preventing or being prevented; a hindrance; a preventive.
preventive, preventative *adj* serving to prevent, precautionary. * *n* something used to prevent disease.—**preventively** *adv*.—**preventiveness** *n*.
preview *n* an advance, restricted showing, as of a film; a showing of scenes from a film to advertise it. * *vt* to view or show in advance of public presentation; to give a preliminary survey.
previous *adj* coming before in time or order; prior, former.—**previously** *adv*.—**previousness** *n*.
prewar *adj* before a war.
prey *n* an animal killed for food by another; a victim. * *vi* (*with* **on, upon**) to seize and devour prey; (*person*) to victimize; to weigh heavily on the mind.
priapism *n* (*med*) abnormally prolonged penile erection.
price *n* the amount, usu in money, paid for anything; the cost of obtaining some benefit; value, worth. * *vt* to set the price of something; to estimate a price; (with **out of the market**) to deprive by raising prices excessively.
priceless *adj* very expensive; invaluable; (*inf*) very amusing, odd, or absurd.—**pricelessly** *adv*.
price war *n* a period of commercial competition marked by repeated cutting of prices among competitors.
pricey *adj* (**pricier, priciest**) (*inf*) expensive.—*also* **pricy**.
prick *n* a sharp point; a puncture or piercing made by a sharp point; the wound or sensation inflicted; a qualm (of conscience); (*vulgar*) penis; (*offensive*) a spiteful person usu with authority. * *vti* to affect with anguish, grief, or remorse; to pierce slightly; to cause a sharp pain to; to goad, spur; (*the ears*) to erect; (*with* **out**) to transfer seedlings.
pricker *n* a thing that pricks, esp a prickle or thorn.
pricket *n* a buck in its second year.
prickle *n* a thorn, spine or bristle; a pricking sensation. * *vti* to feel or cause to feel a pricking sensation.
prickly *adj* (**pricklier, prickliest**) having prickles; tingling; irritable.—**prickliness** *n*.
prickly heat *n* a skin eruption caused by inflammation of the sweat glands.
pride *n* feeling of self-worth or esteem; excessive self-esteem; conceit; a sense of one's own importance; a feeling of elation due to success; the cause of this; splendour; a herd (of lions). * *vti* (*reflex*) (*with* **in** *or* **on**)to be proud of; to take credit for.—**prideful** *adj*.
priedieu *n* a desk with a low rest for kneeling upon while working or praying.
prier *n* one who pries.—*also* **pryer**.
priest *n* in various churches, a person authorized to perform sacred rites; an Anglican, Eastern Orthodox, or Roman Catholic clergyman ranking below a bishop.
priestcraft *n* the work of a priest and its related skills; (*derog*) the schemes used by priests to get power and wealth.
priestess *n* a priest who is a woman; a woman regarded as a leader (as of a movement).
priesthood *n* the office of priest; priests collectively.
priestly *adj* (**priestlier, priestliest**) of or befitting a priest.—**priestliness** *n*.
prig *n* a smug, self-righteous person.—**priggery, priggism** *n*.
priggish *adj* tiresomely precise; strait-laced.—**priggishly** *adv*.—**priggishness** *n*.
prim *adj* (**primmer, primmest**) proper, formal and precise in manner; demure. * *vti* (**primming, primmed**) to make prim; to assume a prim expression.—**primly** *adv*.—**primness** *n*.
prima ballerina *n* (*pl* **prima ballerinas**) the principal female dancer in a ballet company.
primacy *n* (*pl* **primacies**) the office of primate; the state of being first.
prima donna *n* (*pl* **prima donnas**) the leading female singer in an opera; (*inf*) a temperamental person.
prima facie *adv* at first sight. * *adj* true, valid, or sufficient at first impression; self-evident; legally sufficient to establish a fact unless disproved.
primal *adj* primeval; original; primitive; fundamental.
primarily *adv* mainly.
primary *adj* first; earliest; original; first in order of time; chief; elementary. * *n* (*pl* **primaries**) a person or thing that is highest in rank, importance, etc; a preliminary election at which candidates are chosen for the final election.
primary colour *n* one of the three colours from which all others except black can be obtained: red, blue, and yellow.
primary school *n* a school for children below age 11; a school for children up to the third or fourth grade of elementary school and sometimes kindergarten.
primate[1] *n* any of the highest order of mammals, including man.—**primatial** *adj*.
primate[2] *n* an archbishop or the highest ranking bishop in a province, etc.—**primateship** *n*.

prime[1] *adj* first in rank, importance, or quality; chief; (*math*) of a number, divisible only by itself and 1. * *n* the best time; the height of perfection; full maturity; full health and strength.—**primeness** *n*.

prime[2] *vt* to prepare or make something ready; to pour liquid into (a pump) or powder into (a firearm); to paint on a primer.

prime minister *n* the head of the government in a parliamentary democracy.

primer[1] *n* a simple book for teaching; a small introductory book on a subject.

primer[2] *n* a detonating device; a first coat of paint or oil.

prime time *n* (*radio, TV*) the hours when the largest audience is available.

primeval *adj* of the first age of the world; primitive.

priming *n* a preliminary coating (of paint); a powder used to explode a charge.

primipara *n* (*pl* **primiparas, primiparae**) (*obstetrics*) a woman due to give birth to her first child, or who has given birth to only one child.—**primiparous** *adj*.

primitive *adj* of the beginning or the earliest times; crude; simple; basic. * *n* a primitive person or thing.—**primitively** *adv*.—**primitiveness** *n*.

primo *n* (*pl* **primos, primi**) (*mus*) the leading part in a duet or ensemble.

primogenitor *n* an ancestor or forefather; an earliest ancestor.

primogeniture *n* the condition of being the first-born child; (*law*) the right of inheritance of the eldest child.—**primogenitary** *adj*.

primordial *adj* earliest; primeval; fundamental; primitive.—**primordially** *adv*.

primp *vti* to dress (oneself) up.

primrose *n* a perennial plant with pale yellow flowers.

primula *n* any of a genus of plants that includes the primrose, cowslip, etc.

primum mobile *n* the first movement or cause of motion; (*astron*) the tenth and outermost of the imaginary spheres in the Ptolemaic system, which was supposed to revolve from East to West once every 24 hours, carrying the other spheres with it.

prince *n* the son of a sovereign; a ruler ranking below a king; the head of a principality; any pre-eminent person.—**princedom** *n*.

princeling *n* a young prince; a petty ruler.

princely *adj* (**princelier, princeliest**) of or like a prince; lavish, generous; regal.—**princeliness** *n*.

princess *n* a daughter of a sovereign; the wife of a prince; one outstanding in a specified respect.

principal *adj* first in rank or importance; chief. * *n* a principal person; a person who organizes; the head of a college or school; the leading player in a ballet, opera, etc; (*law*) the person who commits a crime; a person for whom another acts as agent; a capital sum lent or invested; a main beam or rafter.—**principalship** *n*.

principality *n* (*pl* **principalities**) the position of responsibility of a principal; the rank and territory of a prince.

principally *adv* mainly.

principle *n* a basic truth; a law or doctrine used as a basis for others; a moral code of conduct; a chemical constituent with a characteristic quality; a scientific law explaining a natural action; the method of a thing's working.

principled *adj* having, or acting in line with, moral principles.

prink *vti* to dress (oneself) up; to preen oneself.

print *vti* to stamp (a mark, letter, etc) on a surface; to produce (on paper, etc) the impressions of inked type, etc; to produce (a book, etc); to write in letters resembling printed ones; to make (a photographic print). * *n* a mark made on a surface by pressure; the impression of letters, designs, etc, made from inked type, a plate, or block; an impression made by a photomechanical process; a photographic copy, esp from a negative.

printable *adj* able or fit to be printed.—**printability** *n*.

printed circuit *n* an electronic circuit whose connections are printed on metal-coated board.

printer *n* a person engaged in printing; a machine for printing from; a device that produces printout.

printing *n* the activity, skill, or business of producing printed matter; a style of writing using capital letters; the total number of books, etc, printed at one time (—*also* **impression**).

printout *n* the printed output of a computer.

prior[1] *adj* previous; taking precedence (as in importance).

prior[2] *n* the superior ranking below an abbot in a monastery; the head of a house or group of houses in a religious community.—**prioress** *nf*.

priorate *n* the office or status of a prior.

priority *n* (*pl* **priorities**) precedence in rank, time, or place; preference; something requiring specified attention.

priory *n* (*pl* **priories**) a religious house under a prior or prioress.

prise, prize *vt* to force (open, up) with a lever, etc.

prism *n* (*geom*) a solid whose ends are similar, equal, and parallel plane figures and whose sides are parallelograms; a transparent body of this form usu with triangular ends used for dispersing or reflecting light.

prismatic *adj* of or like a prism; (*colours*) formed by a prism; brilliant.—**prismatically** *adv*.

prison *n* a building used to house convicted criminals for punishment and suspects remanded in custody while awaiting trial; a penitentiary or jail.

prisoner *n* a person held in prison or under arrest; a captive; a person confined by a restraint.

prisoner of war *n* a member of a military force taken prisoner by the enemy during combat.

pristine *adj* pure; in an original, unspoiled condition.

prithee *interj* (*arch*) pray, please (= "I pray thee").

privacy *n* (*pl* **privacies**) being private; seclusion; secrecy; one's private life.

private *adj* of or concerning a particular person or group; not open to or controlled by the public; for an individual person; not holding public office; secret. * *n* (*pl*) the genitals; an enlisted man of the lowest military rank in the army.—**privately** *adv*.

private enterprise *n* an economic system in which business activity is operated by private individuals or companies under private not state control.

privateer *n* a privately owned ship commissioned by a government to seize and plunder enemy vessels; a captain or crew member of such a ship.

privation *n* being deprived; want of comforts or necessities; hardship.

privative *adj* depriving; denoting the absence of something.

privatize *vt* to restore private ownership by buying back publicly owned stock in a company.

privet *n* a white-flowered evergreen shrub used for hedges.

privilege *n* a right or special benefit enjoyed by a person or a small group; a prerogative. * *vt* to bestow a privilege on.

privileged *adj* having or enjoying privileges; not subject to disclosure in a court of law.

privity *n* (*pl* **privities**) private knowledge; (*law*) a legally recognized relationship.

privy *adj* private; having access to confidential information. * *n* (*pl* **privies**) a latrine; (*law*) a person with an interest in an action.—**privily** *adv*.

prize *n* an award won in competition or a lottery; a reward given for merit; a thing worth striving for. * *adj* given as, rewarded by, a prize. * *vt* to value highly.

prizefight *n* a professional boxing match.—**prizefighter** *n*.

PRO *abbr* = public relations officer.

pro[1] *adv, prep* in favour of. * *n* (*pl* **pros**) an argument for a proposal or motion.

pro[2] *adj* professional. * *n* (*pl* **pros**) a professional.

pro- *prefix* acting; vice-; favouring; before; forth; according to.

proa *n* a long, narrow, Malay boat propelled by oars and sails.

probability *n* (*pl* **probabilities**) that which is probable; likelihood; (*math*) the ratio of the chances in favour of an event to the total number.

probable *adj* likely; to be expected.

probably *adv* without much doubt.

probang *n* (*med*) a flexible rod with a sponge at the end, used to clear obstructions from, or apply medication to, the gullet.

probate *n* the validating of a will; the certified copy of a will.
probation *n* testing of character or skill; release from prison under supervision by a probation officer; the state or period of being on probation.—**probationary, probational** *adj*.
probation officer *n* an official who watches over prisoners on probation.
probationer *n* a person (as a newly admitted student nurse or teacher) whose fitness is being tested during a trial period; a convicted offender on probation.
probe *n* a flexible surgical instrument for exploring a wound; a device, as an unmanned spacecraft, used to obtain information about an environment; an investigation. * *vt* to explore with a probe; to examine closely; to investigate.—**prober** *n*.
probity *n* honesty, integrity, uprightness.
problem *n* a question for solution; a person, thing or matter difficult to cope with; a puzzle; (*math*) a proposition stating something to be done; an intricate unsettled question.
problematical, problematic *adj* presenting a problem; questionable; uncertain.—**problematically** *adv*.
proboscidian, proboscidean *adj* pertaining to the class of mammals which includes the elephant. **n* an animal with a proboscis.
proboscis *n* (*pl* **proboscises, proboscides**) an elephant's trunk; a long snout; an insect's sucking organ; (*humorous*) a (large) nose.
procedure *n* an established mode of conducting business, esp in law or in a meeting; a practice; a prescribed or traditional course; a step taken as part of an established order of steps.—**procedural** *adj*.—**procedurally** *adv*.
proceed *vi* to go on, esp after stopping; to come from; to continue; to carry on; to issue; to take action; to go to law.
proceeding *n* an advance or going forward; (*pl*) steps, action, in a lawsuit; (*pl*) published records of a society, etc.
proceeds *npl* the total amount of money brought in; the net amount received.
process *n* a course or state of going on; a series of events or actions; a method of operation; forward movement; (*law*) a court summons; the whole course of proceedings in a legal action. * *vt* to handle something following set procedures; (*food, etc*) to prepare by a special process; (*law*) to take action; (*film*) to develop.
procession *n* a group of people marching in order, as in a parade.
processional *adj* pertaining to, or used in, processions. * *n* a processional hymn or hymn book.
processor *n* one who or that which processes; (*comput*) a central processing unit.
pro-choice *adj* supporting a woman's right to choose whether or not to have an abortion.
proclaim *vt* to announce publicly and officially; to tell openly; to praise.—**proclaimer** *n*.
proclamation *n* the act of proclaiming; an official notice to the public.—**proclamatory** *adj*.
proclitic *n, adj* (a word) so closely connected with the following word as to lose its accent.
proclivity *n* (*pl* **proclivities**) a tendency or inclination.
proconsul *n* a governor of a colony or province.—**proconsular** *adj*.—**proconsulate, proconsulship** *n*.
procrastinate *vti* to defer action, to delay.—**procrastination** *n*.—**procrastinator** *n*.
procreate *vt* to bring into being, to engender offspring.—**procreation** *n*.—**procreant, procreative** *adj*.—**procreator** *n*.
Procrustean *adj* compelling uniformity by violent means.
proctor *n* a person who supervises dormitories and examinations in a school.—**proctorial** *adj*.
procumbent *adj* lying face down, prone; (*bot*) trailing.
procuration *n* procuring; (*law*) the authorization to act on behalf of someone else.
procurator *n* an agent; (*ancient Rome*) a provincial governor or treasurer.
procuratory *n* (*law*) the authorization to act on another person's behalf.
procure *vt* to obtain by effort; to get and make available for sexual intercourse; to bring about. * *vi* to procure women.—**procurable** *adj*.—**procurement** *n*.
procurer *n* one who procures, esp one who supplies prostitutes.—**procuress** *nf*.
prod *vt* (**prodding, prodded**) to poke or jab, as with a pointed stick; to rouse into activity. * *n* the action of prodding; a sharp object; a stimulus.—**prodder** *n*.
prodigal *adj* wasteful; extravagant; open-handed. * *n* a wastrel; a person who squanders money.—**prodigally** *adv*.
prodigality *n* (*pl* **prodigalities**) the state or quality of being prodigal; extravagance, wastefulness; lavishness.
prodigious *adj* enormous, vast; amazing.—**prodigiously** *adv*.—**prodigiousness** *n*.
prodigy *n* (*pl* **prodigies**) an extraordinary person, thing or act; a gifted child.
produce *vt* to bring about; to bring forward, show; to yield; to cause; to manufacture, make; to give birth to; (*play, film*) to put before the public. * *vi* to yield something. * *n* that which is produced, esp agricultural products.—**producible** *adj*.—**producibility** *n*.
producer *n* someone who produces, esp a farmer or manufacturer; a person who finances or supervises the putting on of a play or making of a film; an apparatus or plant for making gas.
product *n* a thing produced by nature, industry or art; a result; an outgrowth; (*math*) the number obtained by multiplying two or more numbers together.
production *n* the act of producing; a thing produced; a work presented on the stage or screen or over the air.—**productional** *adj*.
productive *adj* producing or capable of producing; fertile.—**productively** *adv*.—**productiveness** *n*.
productivity *n* the state of being productive; the ratio of the output of a manufacturing business to the input of materials, labour, etc.
proem *n* a preface or introduction.
Prof. *abbr* = professor.
profane *adj* secular, not sacred; showing no respect for sacred things; irreverent; blasphemous; not possessing esoteric or expert knowledge. * *vt* to desecrate; to debase by a wrong, unworthy or vulgar use.—**profanation** *n*.—**profanely** *adv*.—**profaneness** *n*.—**profaner** *n*.
profanity *n* (*pl* **profanities**) irreverence; a profane act; blasphemy, swearing.
profess *vt* to affirm publicly, declare; to claim to be expert in; to declare in words or appearance only.
professed *adj* openly acknowledged.—**professedly** *adv*.
profession *n* an act of professing; avowal, esp of religious belief; an occupation requiring specialized knowledge and often long and intensive academic preparation; the people engaged in this; affirmation; entry into a religious order.
professional *adj* of or following a profession; conforming to the technical or ethical standards of a profession; earning a livelihood in an activity or field often engaged in by amateurs; having a specified occupation as a permanent career; engaged in by persons receiving financial return; pursuing a line of conduct as though it were a profession. * *n* one who follows a profession; a professional sportsman; one highly skilled in a particular occupation or field.—**professionally** *adv*.
professionalism *n* the methods of professionals; the pursuit of an activity, eg a sport, for financial gain.
professor *n* a teacher of the highest rank at an institution of higher education; a teacher.—**professorial** *adj*.—**professorship** *n*.
professoriate, professorate *n* a body of professors.
proffer *vt* to offer, usu something intangible.
proficiency *n* (*pl* **proficiencies**) a being proficient; competence; skill.
proficient *adj* skilled, competent.—**proficiently** *adv*.
profile *n* a side view of the head as in a portrait, drawing, etc; a biographical sketch; a graph representing a person's abilities. * *vt* to represent in profile; to produce (as by writing, drawing, etc) a profile of.
profit *n* gain; the excess of returns over expenditure; the compensation to entrepreneurs resulting from the assumption of risk; (*pl*) the excess

returns from a business; advantage, benefit. * *vti* to be of advantage (to), benefit; to gain.—**profitless** *adj*.

profitable *adj* yielding profit, lucrative; beneficial; useful.—**profitably** *adv*.—**profitability** *n*.

profit and loss *n* a statement at the end of an accounting period that summarizes the revenue and expenditure of a business and shows the consequent profit or loss.

profiteer *vi* to make exorbitant profits, esp in wartime. * *n* a person who profiteers.—**profiteering** *n*.

profitless *adj* without profit; useless.

profit sharing *n* a system by which employees share in the profits of a business.—**profit-sharing** *adj*.

profligate *adj* dissolute; immoral; extravagant. * *n* a profligate person, a libertine.—**profligacy** *n*.—**profligately** *adv*.

pro forma *adj* made or carried out as a formality; provided in advance to prescribe form or describe items.

profound *adj* at great depth; intellectually deep; abstruse, mysterious.—**profoundly** *adv*.—**profoundness** *n*.

profundity *n* (*pl* **profundities**) great depth of place, knowledge, skill, etc; a profound or abstruse thing.

profuse *adj* abundant; generous; extravagant.—**profusely** *adv*.—**profuseness** *n*.

profusion *n* an abundance.

progenitive *adj* able to bear offspring.

progenitor *n* an ancestor.

progeny *n* (*pl* **progenies**) offspring; descendants; outcome.

prognathous, prognathic *adj* having projecting lower jaw.—**prognathism** *n*.

prognosis *n* (*pl* **prognoses**) a prediction; (*med*) a forecast of the course of a disease.

prognostic *adj* predictive (of); foretelling. * *n* a prediction; an omen; a forewarning symptom.

prognosticate *vt* to predict; to presage.—**prognostication** *n*.—**prognosticator** *n*.

programme *n* (*US and comput*) **program** a printed list containing details of a ceremony, of the actors in a play, etc; a scheduled radio or television broadcast; a curriculum or syllabus for a course of study; a plan or schedule; a sequence of instructions fed into a computer. * *vti* (**programming, programmed** *or* **programing, programed**) to prepare a plan or schedule; to prepare a plan or schedule to feed a program into a computer; to write a programme.—**programmable** *adj*.—**programmer, programer** *adj*.—**programmatic** *adj*.

progress *n* a movement forwards or onwards, advance; satisfactory growth or development; a tour from place to place in stages. * *vi* to move forward, advance; to improve. * *vt* (*project*) to take to completion.

progression *n* progress; advancement by degrees; (*math*) a series of numbers, each differing from the succeeding according to a fixed law; (*mus*) a regular succession of chords.—**progressional** *adj*.

progressive *adj* advancing, improving; proceeding by degrees; continuously increasing; aiming at reforms; (*with cap*) denoting a broadly liberal Progressive Party. * *n* a person who believes in moderate political change, esp social improvement by government action; (*with cap*) a member of a Progressive Party.—**progressively** *adv*.—**progressiveness** *n*.—**progressivism** *n*.

prohibit *vt* to forbid by law; to prevent.

prohibition *n* the act of forbidding; an order that forbids; a legal ban on the manufacture and sale of alcoholic drinks; (*with cap*) the period (1920–33) when there was a legal ban of alcohol in the US.

prohibitionist *n* an advocate of legally prohibiting the sale of alcohol; (*with cap*) a member of the Prohibition Party in the US.

prohibitive, prohibitory *adj* forbidding; so high as to prevent purchase, use, etc, of something.—**prohibitively** *adv*.

project *n* a plan, scheme; an undertaking; a task carried out by students, etc, involving research. * *vt* to throw forward; (*light, shadow, etc*) to produce an outline of on a distance surface; to make objective or externalize; (*one's voice*) to make heard at a distance; (*feeling, etc*) to attribute to another; to imagine; to estimate, plan, or figure for the future. * *vi* to jut out; to come across vividly; to make oneself heard clearly.

projectile *n* a missile; something propelled by force.* *adj* throwing forward; capable of being thrown forward.

projection *n* the act of projecting or the condition of being projected; a thing projecting; the representation on a plane surface of part of the earth's surface; a projected image; an estimate of future possibilities based on a current trend; a mental image externalized; an unconscious attribution to another of one's own feelings and motives.—**projectional** *adj*.

projectionist *n* a person who operates a projector.

projective *adj* (*geom*) pertaining to projection.

projector *n* an instrument that projects images from transparencies or film; an instrument that projects rays of light; a person who promotes enterprises.

prolapse *vi* (*med*) to fall or slip out of place. * *n* a prolapsed condition.

prolate *adj* extended; (*spheroid*) elongated at the poles.

prolegomenon *n* (*pl* **prolegomena**) a critical introduction to a text.

proletariat *n* the lowest social or economic class of a community; wage earners; the industrial working class.—**proletarian** *adj*, *n*.

proliferate *vi* to grow or reproduce rapidly.—**proliferation** *n*.—**proliferative** *adj*.

proliferous *adj* reproducing by budding; producing many offshoots.

prolific *adj* producing abundantly; fruitful.—**prolificacy** *n*.—**prolifically** *adv*.

prolix *adj* verbose, long-winded, tedious.—**prolixity, prolixness** *n*.

prolocutor *n* a chairman or speaker at a convocation, esp of the Anglican Church.

prologue, prolog *n* the introductory lines of a play, speech, or poem; the reciter of these; a preface; an introductory event. * *vt* (**prologuing, prologued** *or* **prologing, prologed**) to provide with a prologue; to usher in.

prolong *vt* to extend or lengthen in space or time; to spin out.—**prolonger** *n*.

prolongation *n* the act of prolonging; an extension or continuation.

prolusion *n* a preliminary essay or article.—**prolusory** *adj*.

prom *n* a dance for a high school or college class.

promenade *n* an esplanade; a ball or dance; a leisurely walk. * *vti* to take a promenade (along or through).—**promenader** *n*.

Promethean *adj* (*myth*) pertaining to Prometheus; life-giving.

prominence, prominency *n* the state of being prominent; a projection; relative importance; celebrity, fame.

prominent *adj* jutting, projecting; standing out, conspicuous; widely and favourably known; distinguished.—**prominently** *adv*.

promiscuity *n* (*pl* **promiscuities**) the state of being promiscuous; promiscuous sexual behaviour; an indiscriminate mixture.

promiscuous *adj* indiscriminate, esp in sexual liaisons.—**promiscuously** *adv*.—**promiscuousness** *n*.

promise *n* a pledge; an undertaking to do or not to do something; an indication, as of a successful future. * *vti* to pledge; to undertake; to give reason to expect.—**promiser** *n*.

promisee *n* (*law*) someone to whom a promise is made.

promising *adj* likely to turn out well; hopeful.

promisor *n* (*law*) someone who makes a promise.

promissory *adj* of the nature of or containing a promise.

promontory *n* (*pl* **promontories**) a peak of high land that juts out into a body of water.

promote *vt* to encourage; to advocate; to raise to a higher rank; (*employee, student*) to advance from one grade to the next higher grade; (*product*) to encourage sales by advertising, publicity, or discounting.—**promotable** *adj*.

promoter *n* a person who promotes, esp one who organizes and finances a sporting event or pop concert; a substance that increases the activity of a catalyst.

promotion *n* an elevation in position or rank; the furtherance of the sale of merchandise through advertising, publicity, or discounting.—**promotional** *adj*.

prompt *adj* without delay; quick to respond; immediate; of or relating to prompting actors. * *vt* to urge; to inspire; (*actor*) to remind of forgotten words, etc (as in a play). * *n* something that reminds; a time limit for payment of an account; the contract by which this time is fixed.—**promptly** *adv*.

prompter *n* one that prompts, esp a person who sits offstage and reminds actors of forgotten lines.

promptitude *n* quickness of decision and action; readiness; alacrity; punctuality.

promptness *n* alacrity in action or decision; quickness; punctuality.

promulgate *vt* to publish, spread abroad; to put (a law) into effect; to proclaim as coming into force.—**promulgation** *n*.—**promulgator** *n*.

pronate *vt* (*hand, arm*) to turn so that the palm is downwards.—**pronation** *n*.

pronator *n* a pronating muscle.

prone *adj* face downwards; lying flat, prostrate; inclined or disposed (to).—**pronely** *adv*.—**proneness** *n*.

prong *n* a spike of a fork or other forked object.—**pronged** *adj*.

pronominal *adj* pertaining to pronouns; acting as a pronoun.

pronoun *n* a word used to represent a noun (eg *I, he, she, it*).

pronounce *vt* to utter, articulate; to speak officially, pass (judgment); to declare formally.—**pronounceable** *adj*.—**pronouncer** *n*.

pronounced *adj* marked, noticeable.—**pronouncedly** *adv*.

pronouncement *n* a formal announcement, declaration; a confident assertion.

pronto *adv* (*inf*) quickly.

pronunciation *n* articulation; the way a word is pronounced.

proof *n* evidence that establishes the truth; the fact, act, or process of validating; test; demonstration; a sample from type, etc, for correction; a trial print from a photographic negative; the relative strength of an alcoholic liquor. * *adj* resistant; impervious, impenetrable. * *vt* to make proof against (water).

proofread *vti* (**proofreading, proofread**) to read and correct (printed proofs).—**proofreader** *n*.

prop[1] *vt* (**propping, propped**) to support by placing something under or against. * *n* a rigid support; a thing or person giving support.

prop[2] *see* **property**.

prop[3] *n* a propeller.

propaedeutic *adj* pertaining to propaedeutics, the preliminary knowledge or instruction necessary for the study of any art or science.

propagable *adj* which can be propagated.

propaganda *n* the organized spread of ideas, doctrines, etc, to promote a cause; the ideas, etc, so spread.—**propagandism** *n*.—**propagandist** *n, adj*.

propagandize *vt* to spread by propaganda; to use propaganda among. * *vi* to spread propaganda; to use propaganda.

propagate *vti* to cause (a plant or animal) to reproduce itself; (*plant or animal*) to reproduce; (*ideas, customs, etc*) to spread.—**propagation** *n*.—**propagative** *adj*.

propagator *n* a device consisting of a box with a ventilated lid, used to regulate growing conditions for seeds and young plants.

propane *n* a colourless flammable gas obtained from petroleum and used as a fuel.

pro patria for one's country.

propel *vt* (**propelling, propelled**) to drive or move forward.

propellant, propellent *n* a thing that propels; an explosive charge; rocket fuel; the gas that activates an aerosol spray.

propeller, propellor *n* a mechanism to impart drive; a device having two or more blades in a revolving hub for propelling a ship or aircraft.

propensity *n* (*pl* **propensities**) a natural inclination; disposition, tendency.

proper *adj* own, individual, peculiar; appropriate, fit; correct, conventional; decent, respectable; in the most restricted sense; (*sl*) thorough.

properly *adv* in the right way; justifiably; (*sl*) thoroughly.

proper noun *n* the name of a particular person, place, etc.

property *n* (*pl* **properties**) a quality or attribute; a distinctive feature or characteristic; one's possessions; real estate, land; a movable article used in a stage setting (—*also* **prop**).

prophecy *n* (*pl* **prophecies**) a message of divine will and purpose; prediction.

prophesy *vti* (**prophesying, prophesied**) to predict with assurance or on the basis of mystic knowledge; to foretell.—**prophesier** *n*.

prophet *n* a religious leader regarded as, or claiming to be, divinely inspired; one who predicts the future.—**prophetess** *nf*.

prophetic, prophetical *adj* of a prophet or prophecy; prophesying events.—**prophetically** *adv*.

prophylactic *adj* guarding against disease. * *n* a medicine which guards against disease; a condom.

prophylaxis *n* preventive treatment.

propinquity *n* nearness of time, place or relationship.

propitiate *vt* to appease, conciliate.—**propitiation** *n*.—**propitiator** *n*.

propitious *adj* favourable, encouraging; auspicious, opportune.—**propitiously** *adv*.—**propitiousness** *n*.

propolis *n* a resin from tree buds, collected by bees.

proponent *n* someone who makes a proposal, or proposition.

proportion *n* the relationship between things in size, quantity, or degree; ratio; symmetry, balance; comparative part or share; (*math*) the equality of two ratios; a share or quota; (*pl*) dimensions. * *vt* to put in proper relation with something else; to make proportionate (to).—**proportionment** *n*.—**proportionable** *adj*.

proportional *adj* of proportion; aiming at due proportion; proportionate.—**proportionality** *n*.—**proportionally** *adv*.

proportional representation *n* an electoral system arranged so that minorities are represented in proportion to their strength.

proportionate *adj* in due proportion, corresponding in amount. * *vt* to make proportionate.—**proportionately** *adv*.

proposal *n* a scheme, plan, or suggestion; an offer of marriage.

propose *vt* to present for consideration; to suggest; to intend; to announce the drinking of a toast to; (*person*) to nominate; to move as a resolution. * *vi* to make an offer (of marriage).—**proposer** *n*.

proposition *n* a proposal for consideration; a plan; a request for sexual intercourse; (*inf*) a proposed deal, as in business; (*inf*) an undertaking to be dealt with; (*math*) a problem to be solved.—**propositional** *adj*.

propound *vt* to put forward (a question, suggestion, etc).

proprietary *adj* characteristic of a proprietor; privately owned and managed and run as a profit-making organization; (*drug*) made and distributed under a tradename. * *n* (*pl* **proprietaries**) proprietors collectively; a drug protected by secrecy, patent, or copyright against free competition.

proprietor *n* one with legal title to something; an owner.—**proprietorial** *adj*.—**proprietorially** *adv*.

propriety *n* (*pl* **proprieties**) correctness of conduct or taste; fear of offending against rules of behaviour, esp between the sexes; (*pl*) the customs and manners of polite society.

proptosis *n* (*pl* **proptoses**) (*med*) a prolapse, esp of the eyeball.

propulsion *n* the act of propelling; something that propels.—**propulsive, propulsory** *adj*.

propylaeum, propylon *n* (*pl* **propylaea, propylons** *or* **propyla**) a porch or entrance to a temple.

pro rata *adj, adv* in proportion.

prorogue *vt* to terminate a session (of a parliament, etc) without dissolving it.

prosaic *adj* commonplace, matter-of-fact, dull.—**prosaically** *adv*.—**prosaicness** *n*.

prosaism *n* the quality of being prosaic; a word, saying, etc demonstrating this.

proscenium *n* (*pl* **prosceniums**) the part of a stage in front of the curtain.

proscribe *vt* to outlaw; to denounce; to prohibit the use of.—**proscriber** *n*.

proscription *n* the act of proscribing; the condition of being proscribed; outlawry; interdiction.—**proscriptive** *adj*.—**proscriptively** *adv*.

prose *n* ordinary language, as opposed to verse. * *adj* in prose; humdrum, dull. * *vti* to talk tediously; to turn into prose.

prosecute *vt* to bring legal action against; to pursue. * *vi* to institute and carry on a legal suit or prosecution.—**prosecutable** *adj*.

prosecution *n* the act of prosecuting, esp by law; the prosecuting party in a legal case.

prosecutor *n* a person who prosecutes, esp in a criminal court.

proselyte *n* a convert, esp to Judaism. * *vti* to proselytize.

proselytize *vti* to try to make a convert (of).—**proselytizer** *n*.

prosenchyma *n* (*bot*) tissue of elongated cells with little protoplasm.—**prosenchymatous** *adj*.

prose poem *n* a prose work of poetic style.

prosody *n* the study of verse forms and metrical structure; a particular style, system, or theory of versification.—**prosodic** *adj*.—**prosodically** *adv*.—**prosodist** *n*.

prosopopoeia, prosopopeia *n* (*rhetoric*) a figure of speech in which an absent, dead or inanimate figure is represented as present and speaking.

prospect *n* a wide view, a vista; (*pl*) measure of future success; future outlook; expectation; a likely customer, candidate, etc. * *vti* to explore or search (for).

prospective *adj* likely; anticipated, expected.—**prospectively** *adv*.

prospector *n* one who prospects for gold, etc.

prospectus *n* (*pl* **prospectuses**) a printed statement of the features of a new work, enterprise, etc; something (as a condition or statement) that forecasts the course or nature of a situation.

prosper *vi* to thrive; to flourish; to succeed.

prosperity *n* (*pl* **prosperities**) success; wealth.

prosperous *adj* successful, fortunate, thriving; favourable.—**prosperously** *adv*.

prostate *n* (*also* **prostate gland**) a gland situated around the neck of a man's bladder.—**prostatic** *adj*.

prosthesis *n* (*pl* **prostheses**) (*med*) the replacement of a lost limb, tooth, etc with an artificial one; (*gram*) the addition of a letter or syllable at the beginning of a word.—**prosthetic** *adj*.

prostitute *n* a person who has sexual intercourse for money; (*fig*) one who deliberately debases his or her talents (as for money). * *vt* to offer indiscriminately for sexual intercourse, esp for money; to devote to corrupt or unworthy purposes.—**prostitutor** *n*.

prostitution *n* the act or activity of being a prostitute; sexual intercourse for money, etc.

prostrate *adj* lying face downwards; helpless; overcome; lying prone or supine. * *vt* to throw oneself down; to lie flat; to humble oneself.—**prostration** *n*.

prostyle *adj* (*archit*) with columns in front. * *n* a building, esp a temple, with columns in front.

prosy *adj* (**prosier, prosiest**) like prose; dull, dry, tedious.—**prosily** *adv*.—**prosiness** *n*.

protactinium *n* a rare radioactive element similar to uranium.

protagonist *n* the main character in a drama, novel, etc; a supporter of a cause.

protasis *n* (*pl* **protases**) (*gram*) an introductory clause of a conditional sentence.

protean *adj* able to assume many shapes, versatile; variable.

protect *vt* to defend from danger or harm; to guard; to maintain the status and integrity of, esp through financial guarantees; to foster or shield from infringement or restriction; to restrict competition through tariffs and trade controls.

protection *n* the act of protecting; the condition of being protected; something that protects; shelter; defence; patronage; the taxing of competing imports to foster home industry; the advocacy or theory of this (—*also* **protectionism**); immunity from prosecution or attack obtained by the payment of money.

protectionist *n* a person who advocates the protection of home trade by taxing competitive imports. * *adj* serving to protect.—**protectionism** *n*.

protective *adj* serving to protect, defend, shelter.—**protectively** *adv*.—**protectiveness** *n*.

protector *n* a person or thing that protects; (*with cap*) (*formerly*) a regent who ruled during the minority, absence or illness of a monarch.

protectorate *n* the administration of a weaker state by a powerful one; a state so controlled; a regency; (*with cap*) the English government under Oliver and Richard Cromwell (1653–9).

protégé *n* a person guided and helped in his career by another person.—**protégée** *nf*.

protein *n* a complex organic compound containing nitrogen that is an essential constituent of food.

pro tem, pro tempore *adv* for the time being.

proteolysis *n* the disintegration of protein, esp during digestion.—**proteolytic** *adj*.

proteose *n* a compound substance formed by proteolysis.

protest *vi* to object to; to remonstrate. * *vt* to assert or affirm; to execute or have executed a formal protest against; to make a statement or gesture in objection to. * *n* public dissent; an objection; a complaint; a formal statement of objection.—**protester, protestor** *n*.—**protestingly** *adv*.

Protestant *n* a member or adherent of one of the Christian churches deriving from the Reformation; a Christian not of the Orthodox or Roman Catholic Church, who adheres to the principles of the Reformation.—**Protestantism** *n*.

protestation *n* a solemn declaration; a strong protest.

prothalamion *n* (*pl* **prothalamia**) a bridal song, sung before a marriage ceremony.

prothonotary *n* (*pl* **prothonotaries**) (*formerly*) the principal clerk in certain courts.—*also* **protonotary** (*pl* **protonotaries**).

prothorax *n* (*pl* **prothoraxes, prothoraces**) the first segment of an insect's thorax.

protist *n* a single-celled organism, neither animal nor plant.

protocol *n* a note, minute or draft of an agreement or transaction; the ceremonial etiquette accepted as correct in official dealings, as between heads of state or diplomatic officials; the formatting of data in an electronic communications system; the plan of a scientific experiment or treatment.

proton *n* an elementary particle in the nucleus of all atoms, carrying a unit positive charge of electricity.

protonotary *see* **prothonotary**.

protoplasm *n* a semi-fluid viscous colloid, the essential living matter of all plant and animal cells.—**protoplasmic** *adj*.

prototype *n* an original model or type from which copies are made.—**prototypal, prototypic, prototypical** *adj*.

protozoan, protozoon *n* (*pl* **protozoans, protozoa**) a microscopic animal consisting of a single cell or a group of cells.

protozoology *n* the study of protozoans.

protract *vt* to draw out or prolong; to lay down the lines and angles of with scale and protractor; to extend forwards and outwards.—**protractible** *adj*.—**protraction** *n*.

protracted *adj* extended, prolonged; long-drawn-out.—**protractedly** *adv*.—**protractedness** *n*.

protractile *adj* (*zool*) able to be extended.—**protractility** *n*.

protractive *adj* delaying; protracted.

protractor *n* an instrument for measuring and drawing angles; a muscle that extends a limb.

protrude *vti* to thrust outwards or forwards; to obtrude; to jut out, project.

protrusile *adj* (*zool*) which can be thrust forward.

protrusion *n* the act of protruding; something that protrudes; a bulge, a lump; a projection.

protrusive *adj* tending to protrude; bulging out; unduly conspicuous; obtrusive; (*arch*) thrusting or impelling forward.—**protrusively** *adv*.—**protrusiveness** *n*.

protuberance, protuberancy *n* (*pl* **protuberance, protuberancies**) something that protrudes; a swelling, prominence.

protuberant *adj* bulging out, prominent.—**protuberantly** *adv*.

proud *adj* having too high an opinion of oneself; arrogant, haughty; having proper self-respect; satisfied with one's achievements.—**proudly** *adv*.—**proudness** *n*.

prove *vti* (**proving, proved** *or* **proven**) to try out, test, by experiment; to establish or demonstrate as true using accepted procedures; to show (oneself) to be worthy or capable; to turn out (to be), esp after trial or test; to rise.—**provable** *adj*.—**provably** *adv*.—**prover** *n*.

provenance *n* place of origin, source.

provender *n* dry fodder for cattle; any food.

proverb *n* a short traditional saying expressing a truth or moral instruction; an adage.

proverbial *adj* of or like, a proverb; generally known.—**proverbially** *adv*.

provide *vti* to arrange for; to supply; to prepare; to afford (an opportunity); to make provision for (financially).—**provider** *n*.

provided, providing *conj* on condition (that).

providence *n* foresight, prudence; God's care and protection.

provident *adj* providing for the future; far-seeing; thrifty.—**providently** *adv*.

providential *adj* arranged by providence; very opportune or lucky.—**providentially** *adv*.

province *n* an administrative district or division of a country; the jurisdiction of an archbishop; (*pl*) the parts of a country removed from the main cities; a department of knowledge or activity.

provincial *adj* of a province or provinces; having the way, speech, etc of a certain province; country-like; rustic; unsophisticated. * *n* an inhabitant of the provinces or country areas; a person lacking sophistication.—**provinciality** *n*.—**provincially** *adv*.

provincialism *n* provincial speech, phrases, or point of view; narrowness.

provision *n* a requirement; something provided for the future; a stipulation, condition; (*pl*) supplies of food, stores. * *vt* to supply with stores.—**provisioner** *n*.

provisional, provisionary *adj* temporary; conditional.—**provisionally** *adv*.

proviso *n* (*pl* **provisos, provisoes**) a condition, stipulation; a limiting clause in an agreement, etc.

provisory *adj* conditional; making provision; temporary.—**provisorily** *adv*.

provocation *n* the act of provoking or inciting; a cause of anger, resentment, etc.

provocative *adj* intentionally provoking, esp to anger or sexual desire; (*remark*) stimulating argument or discussion.—**provocatively** *adv*.—**provocativeness** *n*.

provoke *vt* to anger, infuriate; to incite, to arouse; to give rise to; to irritate, exasperate.

provoking *adj* annoying, exasperating.—**provokingly** *adv*.

provost *n* a high executive official, as in some churches, colleges, or universities; in Scotland, a mayor.

prow *n* the forward part of a ship, bow.

prowess *n* bravery, gallantry; skill.

prowl *vi* to move stealthily, esp in search of prey.—*also n*.

prowler *n* one that moves stealthily, esp an opportunist thief.

proximal *adj* (*anat*) at the inner end, towards the centre of the body.

proximate *adj* nearest, next; approximate.

proximity *n* nearness in place, time, series, etc.

proximo *adv* next month.

proxy *n* (*pl* **proxies**) the authority to vote or act for another; a person so authorized.—*also adj*.

prude *n* a person who is overly modest or proper in behaviour, speech, attitudes to sex, etc.—**prudery** *n*.

prudence *n* the quality of being prudent; caution; discretion; common sense.

prudent *adj* cautious; sensible; managing carefully; circumspect.—**prudently** *adv*.

prudential *adj* marked by prudence.—**prudentially** *adv*.

prudish *adj* over-correct in behaviour.—**prudishly** *adv*.—**prudishness** *n*.

pruinose *adj* (*bot*) covered with a whitish dust or bloom.

prune[1] *n* a dried plum.

prune[2] *vti* (*plant*) to remove dead or living parts from; to cut away what is unwanted or superfluous.—**pruner** *n*.

prunella *n* a strong silk or worsted fabric, used in shoes.

prurient *adj* tending to excite lust; having lewd thoughts.—**prurience** *n*.—**pruriently** *adv*.

prurigo *n* a skin disease causing violent itching.

pruritus *n* a strong sensation of itching.

Prussian blue *n* a deep blue.

prussic acid *n* a solution of hydrogen and cyanide that makes a deadly poison.

pry[1] *vi* (**prying, pried**) to snoop into other people's affairs; to inquire impertinently. * *n* (*pl* **pries**) close inspection; impertinent peeping; a highly inquisitive person.

pry[2] *vt* (**prying, pried**) to raise with a lever, to prise.

pryer *see* **prier**.

PS *abbr* = postscript.

psalm *n* a sacred song or hymn, esp one from the Book of Psalms in the Bible.

psalmist *n* a writer of psalms.

psalmody *n* (*pl* **psalmodies**) the art or practice of singing psalms or hymns.—**psalmodic** *adj*.—**psalmodist** *n*.

Psalter, psalter *n* the Book of Psalms, esp as found in a prayer book.

psaltery *n* (*pl* **psalteries**) an ancient stringed musical instrument.

Pseudepigrapha *npl* spurious writings falsely ascribed to Biblical figures or times; Jewish writings of the first century bc and first century ad, allegedly by various prophets and kings of the Hebrew scriptures.

pseudo *adj* false, pretended.

pseudocarp *n* (*bot*) a fruit formed from parts other than the ovary.

pseudomorph *n* (*geol*) a mineral with the crystalline shape of another mineral.—**pseudomorphic, pseudomorphous** *adj*.—**pseudomorphism** *n*.

pseudonym *n* a false name adopted as by an author.—**pseudonymity** *n*.

pseudonymous *adj* written or writing under an assumed name.—**pseudonymously** *adv*.

pshaw *interj* an exclamation of disgust, disbelief, etc.

psittacine *n* pertaining to parrots.

psittacosis *n* a contagious parrot disease transmissible to humans, in whom it causes pneumonia.

psoas *n* a muscle in the loin.

psoriasis *n* a chronic skin disease marked by red scaly patches.—**psoriatic** *adj*.

psyche *n* the spirit, soul; the mind, esp as a functional entity governing the total organism and its interactions with the environment.

psychedelic *adj* of or causing extreme changes in the conscious mind; of or like the auditory or visual effects produced by drugs (as LSD). * *n* a psychedelic drug.—**psychedelically** *adv*.

psychiatrist *n* a specialist in psychiatric medicine.

psychiatry *n* the branch of medicine dealing with disorders of the mind, including psychoses and neuroses.—**psychiatric** *adj*.—**psychiatrically** *adv*.

psychic *adj* of the soul or spirit; of the mind; having sensitivity to, or contact with, forces that cannot be explained by natural laws (—*also* **psychical**). * *n* a person apparently sensitive to nonphysical forces; a medium; psychic phenomena.

psychoanalyse, psychoanalyze *vt* to analyse and treat by psychoanalysis.

psychoanalysis *n* a method of treating neuroses, phobias, and some other mental disorders by analysing emotional conflicts, repressions, etc.—**psychoanalytic, psychoanalytical** *adj*.

psychoanalyst *n* a specialist in psychoanalysis.

psychodynamics *n sing* the study of interaction of thoughts, motives, etc within an individual.—**psychodynamic** *adj*.

psychological *adj* of or relating to psychology; of, relating to or coming from the mind or emotions; able to affect the mind or emotions.—**psychologically** *adv*.

psychologist *n* a person trained in psychology.

psychology *n* (*pl* **psychologies**) the science that studies the human mind and behaviour; mental state.

psychometrics *n sing* the scientific measurement and testing of mental powers.—**psychometric, psychometrical** *adj*.—**psychometrician, psychometrist** *n*.

psychomotor *adj* denoting a physical action induced by a mental condition.

psychoneurosis *n* (*pl* **psychoneuroses**) neurosis.

psychopath *n* a person suffering from a mental disorder that results in antisocial behaviour and lack of guilt.—**psychopathic** *adj*.

psychopathology *n* the study of mental disorders.

psychopathy *n* mental disorder or disease.

psychophysiology *n* the study of the relation between psychological and physiological processes.—**psychophysiological** *adj*.—**psychophysiologist** *n*.

psychosis *n* (*pl* **psychoses**) a mental disorder in which the personality is very seriously disorganized and contact with reality is usu impaired.

psychosomatic *adj* of physical disorders that have a psychological or emotional origin.—**psychosomatically** *adv*.

psychotherapy *n* the treatment of mental disorders by psychological methods.—**psychotherapeutic** *adj*.—**psychotherapist** *n*.

psychotic *adj* of or like a psychosis; having a psychosis. * *n* a person suffering from a psychosis.—**psychotically** *adv*.

psychrometer *n* a type of hygrometer with both a wet and a dry bulb.

psychrophilic *adj* (*biol*) thriving in the cold.

PT *abbr* = physical training.

Pt (*chem symbol*) platinum.

Pt. *abbr* = point (in place names).

pt *abbr* = pint.

PTA *abbr* = Parent-Teacher Association.

ptarmigan *n* (*pl* **ptarmigans, ptarmigan**) a species of grouse.

pteridology *n* the study of ferns.

pterodactyl *n* an extinct flying reptile with batlike wings.

pteropod *n* a small swimming mollusc with winglike lobes on its foot.

pterosaur *n* an extinct flying reptile.

pterygoid *adj* (*anat*) of or pertaining to either of the two processes in the skull attached like wings to the spheroid bone.

PTO *abbr* = please turn over.

ptomaine, ptomain *n* a kind of alkaloid, often poisonous, found in decaying matter.

ptosis *n* (*pl* **ptoses**) drooping of the eyelid.

ptyalin *n* an enzyme found in saliva.

ptyalism *n* excessive salivation.

pub *n* a public house, an inn.

puberty *n* the stage at which the reproductive organs become functional.—**pubertal** *adj*.

pubescent *adj* arriving at or having reached puberty; of or relating to puberty; covered with fine soft short hairs.—**pubescence** *n*.

pubic *adj* related to or situated near the pubis.

pubis *n* (*pl* **pubes**) the front part of the bones composing either half of the pelvis.

public *adj* of, for, or by the people generally; performed in front of people; for the use of all people; open or known to all; acting officially for the people. * *n* the people in general; a particular section of the people, such as an audience, body of readers, etc; open observation.

public-address system *n* a system using microphones and loudspeakers to enable groups of people to hear clearly in an auditorium or out of doors.

publican *n* a person who keeps a public house; in ancient Rome, a collector of taxes.

publication *n* public notification; the printing and distribution of books, magazines, etc; something published as a periodical, book, etc.

public health *n* the practice and science of protecting and improving community health by organized effort including sanitation, preventive medicine, etc.

publicist *n* a person who publicizes, esp one whose business it is; a political journalist.

publicity *n* any information or action that brings a person or cause to public notice; work concerned with such promotional matter; notice by the public.

publicize *vt* to give publicity to.

publicly *adv* in a public manner; openly; by the public; with the consent of the public.

public relations *n* relations with the general public of a company, institution, etc, as through publicity.

public school *n* a school maintained by public money and supervised by local authorities; in England, a private secondary school, usu boarding.

public service *n* the supply of a commodity (gas, water, etc) or a service (transport, etc) to the community; a service in the public interest; employment in a government department, esp the civil service.

publish *vt* to make generally known; to announce formally; (*book*) to issue for sale to the public. * *vi* to put out an edition; to have one's work accepted for publication.—**publishable** *adj*.

publisher *n* a person or company that prints and issues books, magazines, etc.

publishing *n* the business of the production and distribution of books, magazines, recordings, etc.

puce *n, adj* (a) purplish brown.

puck *n* a hard rubber disc used in ice hockey.

pucker *vti* to draw together in creases, to wrinkle; (*with* **up**) to contract the lips ready to kiss. * *n* a wrinkle or fold.

puckish *adj* impish, irresponsible.—**puckishly** *adv*.—**puckishness** *n*.

pudding *n* a dessert; a steamed or baked dessert; a suet pie.

puddle *n* a small pool of water, esp stagnant, spilled, or muddy water; a rough cement of kneaded clay. * *vti* to dabble in mud, to make muddy; to make or line with puddle; to stir (molten iron) to free it from carbon.—**puddler** *n*.

pudency *n* modesty, sense of shame.

pudendum *n* (*pl* **pudenda**) (*usu pl*) the external reproductive organs, esp of a woman.—**pudendal** *adj*.

pudgy *adj* (**pudgier, pudgiest**) short and fat, squat.—**pudginess** *n*.

pueblo *n* an Indian settlement in Mexico and the South West United States.

puerile *adj* juvenile; childish.—**puerilely** *adv*.—**puerility** *n*.

puerilism *n* a psychiatric condition of adults characterized by infantile or childish behaviour.

puerperal *adj* pertaining to, or following, childbirth.

puff *n* a sudden short blast or gust; an exhalation of air or smoke; a light pastry; a pad for applying powder; a flattering notice, advertisement. * *vti* to emit a puff; to breathe hard, pant; to put out of breath; to praise with exaggeration; to swell; to blow, smoke, etc, with puffs.

puffball *n* a round fungus which emits dustlike spores when broken.

puffer *n* someone who, or something which puffs; a tropical fish with a spiny body which can be puffed up to form a globe.

puffin *n* a sea bird that has a short neck and a brightly coloured laterally compressed bill.

puffiness *n* the state of being puffy or swollen.

puffy *adj* (**puffier, puffiest**) inflated, swollen; panting.—**puffily** *adv*.

pug *n* a breed of small dog with a face and nose like a bulldog. * *vt* (**pugging, pugged**) to mix (clay) for making bricks; to fill (a space) with clay or mortar.

pug nose *n* a nose having a slightly concave bridge and flattened nostrils.—**pug-nosed** *adj*.

pugilism *n* the practice of fighting with the fists; boxing; skill in doing this.

pugilist *n* a boxer; a prizefighter.—**pugilistic** *adj*.—**pugilistically** *adv*.

pugnacious *adj* fond of fighting, belligerent.—**pugnacity, pugnaciousness** *n*.

puisne *adj* (*judge*) lower in rank.

puissance *n* (*arch*) power; (*showjumping*) an event in which a horse attempts particularly large jumps.—**puissant** *adj*.

puke *vti* (*inf*) to vomit.—*also n*.

pukka *adj* (*Anglo-Indian*) genuine, real; reliable, sound.

pulchritude *n* beauty.

pule *vi* to whine, whimper.

pull *vt* to tug at; to pluck; to move or draw towards oneself; to drag; to rip; to tear; (*muscle*) to strain; (*inf*) to carry out, perform; (*inf*) to restrain; (*inf: gun, etc*) to draw out; (*inf*) to attract. * *vi* to carry out the action of pulling something; to be capable of being pulled; to move (away, ahead, etc). * *n* the act of pulling or being pulled; a tug; a device for pulling; (*inf*) influence; (*inf*) drawing power.

pullet *n* a young hen.

pulley *n* a wheel with a grooved rim for a cord, etc, used to raise weights by downward pull or change of direction of the pull; a group of these used to increase applied force; a wheel driven by a belt.

Pullman *n* (*pl* **Pullmans**) a railway carriage offering luxury accommodation, usu with sleeping berths.

pullover *n* a buttonless garment with or without sleeves pulled on over the head.

pullulate *vi* to sprout, grow; to multiply quickly; to spring up.—**pullulation** *n*.

pulmonary *adj* of, relating to or affecting the lungs; having lungs; denoting the artery that conveys deoxygenated blood directly to the lungs from the right ventricle of the heart.

pulp *n* a soft, moist, sticky mass; the soft, juicy part of a fruit or soft pith of a plant stem; ground-up, moistened fibres of wood, rags, etc, used to make paper; a book or magazine printed on cheap paper and often dealing with sensational material. * *vti* to make or become pulp or pulpy; to produce or reproduce (written matter) in pulp form.

pulpit *n* a raised enclosed platform, esp in a church, from which a clergyman preaches; preachers as a group.

pulpy *adj* (**pulpier, pulpiest**) consisting of or like pulp; soft.—**pulpiness** *n*.

pulque *n* a Mexican alcoholic drink made from the fermented juice of the agave.

pulsar *n* any of several very small stars that emit radio pulses at regular intervals.

pulsate *vi* to beat or throb rhythmically; to vibrate, quiver.—**pulsative** *adj*.

pulsation *n* a pulsating; a single beat or throb; rhythmic throbbing.

pulsatory *adj* pertaining to pulsation; pulsating.

pulse[1] *n* a rhythmic beat or throb, as of the heart; a place where this is felt; an underlying opinion or sentiment or an indication of it; a short radio signal. * *vti* to throb, pulsate.

pulse[2] *n* the edible seeds of several leguminous plants, such as beans, peas and lentils; the plants producing them.

pulsimeter, pulsometer *n* (*med*) an instrument used to measure pulse rate and strength.

pulverize *vti* to reduce to a fine powder; to demolish, smash; to crumble.—**pulverization** *n*.—**pulverizer** *n*.

pulverulent *adj* covered with dust; powdery; crumbling to dust.

pulvinate, pulvinated *adj* (*archit*) curved convexly; (*bot*) having a cushion-like pad or swelling.

puma *n* a mountain lion.

pumice *n* a light, porous volcanic rock, used for scrubbing, polishing, etc.—**pumiceous** *adj*.

pummel *vt* (**pummelling, pummelled** *or* **pummeling, pummeled**) to strike repeatedly with the fists, to thump.

pump[1] *n* a device that forces a liquid or gas into, or draws it out of, something. * *vti* to move (fluids) with a pump; to remove water, etc, from; to drive air into with a pump; to draw out, move up and down, pour forth, etc, as a pump does; (*inf*) to obtain information through questioning.

pump[2] *n* a light low shoe or slipper; a rubber-soled shoe.

pumpernickel *n* a coarse rye bread.

pumpkin *n* a large, round, orange fruit of the gourd family widely cultivated as food.

pun *n* a play on words of the same sound but different meanings, usu humorous. * *vi* (**punning, punned**) to make a pun.—**punningly** *adv*.

punch[1] *vt* to strike with the fist; to prod or poke; to stamp, perforate with a tool; (*US*) (*cattle*) to herd. * *n* a blow with the fist; (*inf*) vigour; a machine or tool for punching.

punch[2] *n* a hot, sweet drink made with fruit juices, often mixed with wine or spirits.

punchbowl *n* a bowl for mixing punch; a bowl-shaped hollow.

punch card, punched card *n* in data processing, a card with a series of holes representing data.

puncheon *n* a large cask holding between 70 and 120 gallons.

Punchinello *n* the figure of the clown in Italian puppet theatre; a grotesque character.

punch line *n* the last line of a joke or story, that conveys its humour or point.

punctate, punctated *adj* marked with dots or points.—**punctation** *n*.

punctilio *n* (*pl* **punctilios**) a fine point of etiquette; petty formality.

punctilious *adj* very formal in conduct; scrupulously exact.

punctual *adj* being on time; prompt.—**punctuality** *n*.—**punctually** *adv*.

punctuate *vt* to use certain standardized marks in (written matter) to clarify meaning; to interrupt; to emphasize. * *vi* to use punctuation marks.—**punctuator** *n*.

punctuation *n* the act of punctuating; the state of being punctuated; a system of punctuation.

punctuation mark *n* one of the standardized symbols used in punctuation, as the period, colon, semicolon, comma, etc.

puncture *n* a small hole made by a sharp object; the deflation of a tyre caused by a puncture. * *vt* to make useless or ineffective as if by a puncture; to deflate. * *vi* to become punctured.—**puncturable** *adj*.

pundit *n* a learned person; an expert; a critic, esp one who writes in a daily newspaper.—*also* **pandit**.

pung *n* (*US*) a horse-drawn sleigh.

pungent *adj* having an acrid smell or a sharp taste; caustic; bitter.—**pungency** *n*.—**pungently** *adv*.

punish *vt* to subject a person to a penalty for a crime or misdemeanour; to chastise; to handle roughly.—**punisher** *n*.

punishable *adj* liable to legal punishment.—**punishability** *n*.

punishing *adj* causing retribution; (*inf*) arduous, gruelling, exhausting.—**punishingly** *adv*.

punishment *n* a penalty for a crime or misdemeanour; rough treatment; the act of punishing or being punished.

punitive, punitory *adj* involving the inflicting of punishment.—**punitively** *adv*.—**punitiveness** *n*.

punk *adj* (*sl*) inferior, of low quality. * *n* (*US*) a young gangster; a follower of punk rock.

punka, punkah *n* a palm-leaf fan; (*Anglo-Indian*) a large swinging fan suspended from the ceiling of a room and worked by an attendant.

punk rock *n* an aggressive form of rock music usu performed in a coarse, offensive way.

punster, punner *n* a person who makes puns.

punt[1] *n* a long flat-bottomed square-ended river boat usu propelled with a pole. * *vti* to propel or convey in a punt.

punt[2] *vt* to kick a dropped ball before it reaches the ground. * *n* such a kick.

punter *n* a person who gambles; (*sl*) a consumer; a customer.

punty *n* (*pl* **punties**) an iron rod used in glass-blowing.

puny *adj* (**punier, puniest**) of inferior size, strength, or importance; feeble.—**puniness** *n*.

pup *n* a young dog, a puppy; a young fox, seal, rat, etc. * *vi* (**pupping, pupped**) to give birth to pups.

pupa *n* (*pl* **pupae, pupas**) an insect at the quiescent stage between the larva and the adult.—**pupal** *adj*.

pupate *vi* (*entomology*) to become a pupa.—**pupation** *n*.

pupil[1] *n* a child or young person taught under the supervision of a teacher or tutor; a person who has been taught or influenced by a famous or distinguished person.

pupil[2] *n* the round, dark opening in the centre of the iris of the eye through which light passes.

pupillage, pupilage *n* the state of being a pupil; the period of time during which someone is a pupil.

pupillary *adj* pertaining to a pupil, or to a legal ward.

pupiparous *adj* (*entomology*) producing young in the pupal state.

puppet *n* a doll moved by strings attached to its limbs or by a hand inserted in its body; a person controlled by another. * *adj* of or relating to puppets; acting in response to the controls of another while appearing independent.

puppeteer *n* a person who controls and entertains with puppets.

puppetry *n* the art of making and entertaining with puppets; stilted presentation.

puppy *n* (*pl* **puppies**) a young domestic dog less than a year old.—**puppyhood** *n*.—**puppyish** *adj*.

Purana *n* a book of Hindu scriptures, written in Sanskrit.

purblind *adj* half-blind; (*fig*) obtuse, dull.

purchase *vt* to buy; to obtain by effort or suffering. * *n* the act of purchasing; an object bought; leverage for raising or moving loads; means of achieving advantage.—**purchasable** *adj*.—**purchaser** *n*.

purdah *n* the custom among Muslims and some Hindus of secluding women from public observation.

pure *adj* clean; not contaminated; not mixed; chaste, innocent; free from taint or defilement; mere; that and that only; abstract and theoretical; (*mus*) not discordant, perfectly in tune.—**pureness** *n*.

purée *n* cooked food sieved or pulped in a blender; a thick soup of this. * *vt* (**puréeing, puréed**) to prepare food in this way.

purely *adv* in a pure way; solely, entirely.

purgation *n* a purging or purifying.

purgative *adj* purging, cleansing; * *n* a drug or agent that purges the bowels.

purgatorial *adj* of, relating to or like purgatory; serving to purify of sin.

purgatory *n* a place of suffering or purification; (*with cap*: *RC church*) the intermediate place between death and heaven, where venial sins are purged.

purge *vt* to cleanse, purify; (*nation, party, etc*) to rid of troublesome people; to clear (oneself) of a charge; to clear out the bowels of. * *n* the act or process of purging; a purgative; the removal of persons believed to be disloyal from an organization, esp a political party.—**purger** *n*.

purificator *n* (*Christian Church*) a cloth used to wipe the chalice during Holy Communion.

purify *vti* (**purifying, purified**) to make or become pure; to cleanse; to make ceremonially clean; to free from harmful matter.—**purification** *n*.—**purificatory** *adj*.—**purifier** *n*.

Purim *n* a Jewish holiday celebrated yearly in February or March, to commemorate the deliverance of the Jews from massacre at the hands of Haman.

purine *n* a white crystalline compound found in uric acid.

purism *n* insistence on correctness in language, form, style, etc.

purist *n* someone who is a stickler for correctness in language, style, etc.—**purism** *n*.—**puristic** *adj*.—**puristically** *adv*.

puritan *adj* a person who is extremely strict in religion or morals; (*with cap*) an extreme English Protestant of Elizabethan or Stuart times. * *adj* of or like a puritan; (*with cap*) of the Puritans.—**puritanism, Puritanism** *n*.

puritanical *adj* rigorously strict in religious or moral matters; (*with cap*) of the Puritans or Puritanism.—**puritanically** *adv*.—**puritanicalness** *n*.

purity *n* the state of being pure.

purl *vt* to knit a stitch by drawing its base loop from front to back of the fabric. * *n* a stitich made in this way.

purlieu *n* (*usu pl*) adjacent or outlying areas.

purlin, purline *n* a piece of timber lying horizontally to support rafters.

purloin *vt* to steal.—**purloiner** *n*.

purple *n* a dark, bluish red; crimson cloth or clothing, esp as a former emblem of royalty. * *adj* purple-coloured; royal; (*writing style*) overelaborate. * *vti* to make or become purple.

purport *vt* to claim to be true; to imply; to be intended to seem. * *n* significance; apparent meaning.—**purportedly** *adv*.

purpose *n* objective; intention; aim; function; resolution, determination. * *vti* to intend, design.

purposeful *adj* determined, resolute; intentional.—**purposefully** *adv*.—**purposefulness** *n*.

purposeless *adj* lacking purpose; pointless.—**purposelessly** *adv*.—**purposelessness** *n*.

purposely *adv* deliberately; on purpose.

purposive *adj* having or serving a purpose.—**purposively** *adv*.

purpura *n* a blood disease causing the eruption of small purple spots.

purr *vi* (*cat*) to make a low, murmuring sound of pleasure.—**purring** *n*.

purse *n* a small pouch or bag for money; finances, money; a sum of money for a present or a prize; (*US*) a woman's handbag. * *vt* to pucker, wrinkle up.

purser *n* an officer on a passenger ship in charge of accounts, tickets, etc; an airline official responsible for the comfort and welfare of passengers.

purslane *n* a flowering plant with fleshy leaves, used in salads.

pursuance *n* the pursuing or performance of an action.

pursuant *adj* (*law*) according; (*arch*) pursuing.

pursue *vb* (**pursuing, pursued**) *vt* to follow; to chase; to strive for; to seek to attain; to engage in; to proceed with. * *vi* to follow in order to capture.—**pursuer** *n*.

pursuit *n* the act of pursuing; an occupation; a pastime.

pursuivant *n* a low-ranking officer of the British College of Heralds; (*formerly*) an attendant or state messenger.

purulent *adj* pertaining to pus.—**purulence, purulency** *adj*.—**purulently** *adv*.

purvey *vti* to procure and supply (provisions).

purveyance *n* the procuring of provisions; the provisions provided; (*formerly*) the right accorded to royalty to buy up provisions without the owner's consent.

purveyor *n* a person who, or an organization which, supplies provisions.

pus *n* a yellowish fluid produced by infected sores.

push *vti* to exert pressure so as to move; to press against or forward; to impel forward, shove; to urge the use, sale, etc, of; (*inf*) to approach an age; (*inf*) to sell drugs illegally; to make an effort * *n* a thrust, shove; an effort; an advance against opposition; (*inf*) energy and drive.

push button *n* a knob that activates an electrical switch which opens or closes a circuit to operate a radio, bell, etc.

pushchair *n* a wheeled metal and canvas chair for a small child.—*also* **stroller**.

pusher *n* that which pushes; (*inf*) a person who sells illegal drugs.

pushing *adj* go-ahead, energetic; ambitious; assertive.

pushover *n* (*inf*) something easily done, as a victory over an opposing team; (*inf*) a person easily taken advantage of.

pushy *adj* (**pushier, pushiest**) (*inf*) assertive; forceful; aggressively ambitious.—**pushily** *adv*.—**pushiness** *n*.

pusillanimous *adj* faint-hearted, cowardly.—**pusillanimity** *n*.

puss[1] *n* (*inf*) a cat; (*sl*) a girl.

puss[2] *n* (*sl*) the mouth; the face.

pussy[1] *n* (*pl* **pussies**) (*inf*) a cat, a pussycat; (*vulg sl*) the female genitalia; a contemptuous term for a woman; sex with a woman.

pussy[2] *adj* (*pl* **pussier, pussiest**) like or containing pus.

pussycat *n* (*inf*) a cat; an amiable person.

pussyfoot *vi* to move stealthily; to be evasive.—**pussyfooter** *n*.

pustule *n* a blister or swelling containing pus.—**pustular** *adj*.—**pustulation** *n*.

put *vti* (**putting, put**) to place, set; to cast, throw; to apply, direct; to bring into a specified state; to add (to); to subject to; to submit; to estimate; to stake; to express; to translate; to propose; (*a weight*) to hurl; (*with* **about**) to change the course of (a ship); to worry; (*with* **across**) to effect successfully; (*with* **away**) to remove; to lay by; (sl) to consume; (*arch*) to divorce; (*with* **back**) to replace; to return to land; (*with* **by**) to thrust aside; to store up; (*with* **down**) to suppress; to silence; to kill or have killed; to write or enter; to reckon; to assign; (*with* **forth**) to exert; to bud or shoot; to set out; (*with* **in**) to interpose; to spend (time); to apply (for); to call (at); (*with* **off**) to doff, discard; to postpone; to evade; to get rid of; to discourage, repel; to foist (upon); to leave shore; (*with* **on**) to don; to assume, pretend; to increase; to add; to advance; (*with* **out**) to eject; to extend; to exert; to dislocate; to quench;

to publish; to place (money) at interest; to disconcert, to anger; to leave shore; (*with* **over**) to succeed in, to carry through; (*with* **up**) to rouse; to offer (prayer); to propose as a candidate; to pack; to sheathe; to lodge; (*with* **up with**) to endure, to tolerate; (*with* **upon**) to impose upon; (*with* **wise**) to disabuse, to enlighten. * *adj* fixed.

putative *adj* reputed, supposed.—**putatively** *adv*.

putrefy *vti* (**putrefying, putrefied**) to make or become putrid; to rot, decompose.—**putrefaction** *n*.—**putrefactive** *adj*.—**putrefier** *n*.

putrescent *adj* decaying, rotting.—**putrescence** *n*.

putrid *adj* rotten or decayed and foul-smelling.—**putridity** *n*.—**putridly** *adv*.

Putsch *n* an uprising or revolt.

putt *vti* (*golf*) to hit (a ball) with a putter. * *n* in golf, a stroke to make the ball roll into the hole.

puttee *n* a legging made from a strip of cloth wound spirally from the ankle to the knee.

putter[1] *n* (*golf*) a straight-faced club used in putting.

putter[2] *vi* (*US*) to busy oneself idly; to spend time, to potter.—**putterer** *n*.

putter[3] *n* one who or that which puts; an athlete who puts the shot.

putto *n* (*pl* **putti**) (*art*) a figure of cupid and representations of children.—*also* **amoretto, amorino.**

putty *n* (*pl* **putties**) a soft, plastic mixture of powdered chalk and linseed oil used to fill small cracks, fix glass in window frames, etc. * *vt* (**puttying, puttied**) to fix or fill with putty.

puzzle *vt* to bewilder; to perplex. * *vi* to be perplexed; to exercise one's mind, as over a problem. * *n* bewilderment; a difficult problem; a toy or problem for testing skill or ingenuity; a conundrum.—**puzzlement** *n*.—**puzzler** *n*.

puzzling *adj* perplexing, bewildering, inexplicable.—**puzzlingly** *adv*.

PVC *abbr* = polyvinyl chloride.

PWA *abbr* = person with AIDS.

pyaemia, pyemia *n* blood poisoning.—**pyaemic** *adj*.

pycnometer *n* an instrument for measuring densities or specific gravities.

pygmy *n* (*pl* **pygmies**) an undersized person.—*also* **pigmy** (*pl* **pigmies**).

pyjamas *npl* a loosely fitting sleeping suit of jacket and trousers.—*also* (*US*) **pajamas.**

pylon *n* a tower-like structure supporting electric power lines.

pylorus *n* (*pl* **pylori**) (*anat*) the opening from the stomach into the intestine.

pyorrhoea, pyorrhea *n* inflammation of the gums and tooth sockets.

pyracantha *n* a small, flowering, evergreen shrub.

pyramid *n* (*geom*) a solid figure having a polygon as base, and whose sides are triangles sharing a common vertex; a huge structure of this shape, as a royal tomb of ancient Egypt; an immaterial structure built on a broad supporting base and narrowing gradually to an apex.—**pyramidal, pyramidical, pyramidic** *adj*.—**pyramidally, pyramidically** *adv*.

pyre *n* a pile of wood for cremating a dead body.

pyrethrum *n* a type of chrysanthemum with showy flowers; an insecticide made from this plant.

pyretic *adj* pertaining to, or causing, fever.

Pyrex *n* (*trademark*) heat-resistant glassware.

pyrexia *n* fever.—**pyrexial, pyrexic** *adj*.

pyrheliometer *n* an instrument for measuring the sun's heat.

pyrites *n* (*pl* **pyrites**) a sulphide of a metal, esp iron.

pyroelectric *adj* becoming electric as a result of heat.

pyrogenic, pyrogenous *adj* caused by, or causing, heat, or fever.

pyrolisis *n* decomposition by heat.

pyromania *n* (*psychol*) an uncontrollable urge to set things on fire.

pyrometer *n* an instrument used to measure very high temperatures.—**pyrometry** *n*.

pyrope *n* a deep red variety of garnet.

pyrophoric *adj* igniting when exposed to air.

pyrosis *n* heartburn.

pyrotechnics *n sing* the art of making or setting off fireworks; (*sing or pl*) a fireworks display; a brilliant display of virtuosity.—**pyrotechnic, pyrotechnical** *adj*.

pyroxylin, pyroxyline *n* a substance derived from cellulose, used in making plastics.

Pyrrhic *adj* (*victory*) so costly as to be equal to defeat.

pyrrhic *n* a metrical foot of two syllables.

Pythagorean *adj* pertaining to, or characteristic of, the Greek philosopher Pythagoras.

python *n* a large, nonpoisonous snake that kills by constriction.—**pythonic** *adj*.

pythoness *n* a priestess in the temple of Apollo at Delphi, in ancient Greece; a (female) soothsayer; a witch.

pyuria *n* (*med*) the discharge of pus into the urine.

pyx *n* (*Christian Church*) a container in which consecrated bread is kept.

pyxidium *n* (*pl* **pyxidia**) (*bot*) a pyxis.

pyxis *n* (*pl* **pyxides**) a seed capsule with a lid that falls off to release the seeds.

Q

QED *abb* = quod erat demonstratum.

q.t. *abbr* = (*inf*) quiet.

qt *abbr* = quart.

qty *abbr* = quantity.

qua *prep* as, in the character of, because.

quack[1] *n* the cry of a duck. * *vi* to make a sound like a duck.

quack[2] *n* an untrained person who practises medicine fraudulently; a person who pretends to have knowledge and skill he does not have.—*also adj*.

quackery *n* (*pl* **quackeries**) pretence of medical or other skill; imposture.

quacksalver *n* (*arch*) a quack who deals in ointments, etc; a charlatan.

quad *n* quadrangle; quadruplet.

quadr-, quadri-, quadru- *prefix* four.

quadragenarian *n adj* (a person) forty to forty-nine years old.

Quadragesima (Sunday) *n* the first Sunday in Lent.

Quadragesimal *adj* pertaining to, or used in, Lent.

quadrangle *n* (*geom*) a plane figure with four sides and four angles, a rectangle; a court enclosed by buildings.—**quadrangular** *adj*.

quadrant *n* (*geom*) a quarter of the circumference of a circle; an arc of 90 degrees; an instrument with such an arc for measuring angles, altitudes, or elevations; a curved street.—**quadrantal** *adj*.

quadraphonic *adj* using four channels to record and reproduce sound.—**quadraphonics, quadraphony** *n*.

quadrate *adj* (*zool*) of or pertaining to one of a pair of bones found in the skulls of fishes, reptiles and some birds; (*anat*) of or pertaining to the middle bone of the middle ear in mammals; (*arch*) square or rectangular. * *vt* to square or make rectangular; (*often with* **with**) to cause to conform; to correspond. * *n* a quadrate bone; a square or cube.

quadratic *adj* square; (*math*) involving the square but no higher power.* *n* a quadratic equation.

quadratic equation *n* an equation in which the highest power of the unknown is the square.

quadratics *n* (*sing*) the branch of algebra dealing with quadratic equations.

quadrature *n* the act of squaring; the reduction of a figure to a square, exactly or approximately; (*astron*) the position of a heavenly body when distant 90 degrees from another, usually the earth, said esp of the position of the moon from the sun; (*math*) the finding of square with an area exactly equal to a circle or other figure or a surface; (*electronics*) the state between two waves of being 90 degrees out of phase.

quadrennial *adj* lasting or occurring every four years.—**quadrennially** *adv*.

quadricentennial *n* a four hundredth anniversary.—*also adj*.

quadrifid *adj* with four parts, four-cleft.

quadriga *n* (*pl* **quadrigas, quadrigae**) an ancient Roman two-wheeled chariot drawn by four horses abreast.

quadrilateral *adj* having four sides. * *n* (*geom*) a plane figure of four sides; a combination or group that involves four parts or individuals.

quadrille *n* a square dance for four or more couples; the music for this.

quadrillion *n* in Europe, the fourth power of a million, ie 1 with 24 zeros; in US, the fifth power of a thousand, ie, 1 with 15 zeros.—*also adj*.—**quadrillionth** *adj*.

quadrinomial *n* an algebraic expression consisting of four terms.

quadripartite *adj* of four parts; shared by four.

quadriplegia *n* paralysis of all four limbs.—**quadriplegic** *adj, n*.

quadrivalent *adj* (*chem*) with four valencies; with a valency of four, tetravalent.— **quadrivalency, quadrivalence**

quadrivial *adj* pertaining to a quadrivium; (*roads, etc*) leading in four ways; coming from four directions and meeting at the same point.

quadrivium *n* (*pl* **quadrivia**) a medieval course of study comprising arithmetic, geometry, astronomy, and music.

quadroon *n* the child of one white and one half Negro parent, a person one quarter black.

quadrumanous, quadrumanal *adj* (*monkeys, apes*) having four hands that can grasp.

quadruped *n* a four-footed animal.—**quadrupedal** *adj*.

quadruple *adj* four times as much or as many; made up of or consisting of four; having four divisions or parts. * *vti* to make or become four times as many.

quadruplet *n* one of four children born at one birth.

quadruplicate *vt* to multiply by four; to make four copies of. * *adj* fourfold.—**quadruplication** *n*.

quadruplicity *n* (*pl* **quadruplicities**) four-fold nature.

quaestor, questor *n* in ancient Rome, the public treasurer, or sometimes one of the other public officials.

quaff *vti* to take large drinks (of), drain.—**quaffer** *n*.

quagga *n* (*pl* **quaggas, quagga**) an extinct striped South African animal like a sand-coloured zebra.

quaggy *adj* (**quaggier, quaggiest**) of or like a bog or marsh.

quagmire *n* soft, wet ground; a difficult situation.

quahog *n* an edible North American clam, found on the Atlantic coast.

quail[1] *vi* to cower, to shrink back with fear.

quail[2] *n* (*pl* **quails, quail**) a small American game bird.

quaint *adj* attractive or pleasant in an odd or old-fashioned style.—**quaintly** *adv*.—**quaintness** *n*.

quake *vi* to tremble or shiver, esp with fear or cold; to quiver. * *n* a shaking or tremor; (*inf*) an earthquake.

Quaker *n* a popular name for a member of the Society of Friends, a religious sect advocating peace and simplicity.—**Quakerism** *n*.

quaky *adj* (**quakier, quakiest**) shaky; trembling; unstable.—**quakily** *adv*.—**quakiness** *n*.

qualifiable *adj* that may be qualified.

qualification *n* qualifying; a thing that qualifies; a quality or acquirement that makes a person fit for a post, etc; modification; limitation; (*pl*) academic achievements.

qualifier *n* one that qualifies; an adjective or adverb.

qualify *vti* (**qualifying, qualified**) to restrict; to describe; to moderate; to modify, limit; to make or become capable or suitable; to fulfil conditions; to pass a final examination; (*gram*) to limit the meaning of.—**qualificatory** *adj*.—**qualifyingly** *adv*.

qualitative *adj* of or depending on quality; determining the nature, not the quality, of components.—**qualitatively** *adv*.

quality *n* (*pl* **qualities**) a characteristic or attribute; degree of excellence; high standard. * *adj* of high quality.

qualm *n* a doubt; a misgiving; a scruple; a sudden feeling of faintness or nausea.—**qualmish** *adj*.

quandary *n* (*pl* **quandaries**) a predicament; a dilemma.

quango *n* (*pl* **quangos**) (*acronym*) quasi-autonomous non-governmental organization.

quant *n* a long pole, used in punting, with a disc on the end to prevent it from sinking when pushed into mud etc in a river. * *vt, vi* to punt with a quant.

quantify *vt* (**quantifying, quantified**) to express as a quantity; to determine the amount of.—**quantifiable** *adj*. —**quantification** *n*.

quantitative *adj* capable of being measured; relating to size or amount.—**quantitatively** adv.

quantity *n* (*pl* **quantities**) an amount that can be measured, counted or weighed; a large amount; the property by which a thing can be measured; a number or symbol expressing this property.

quantum *n* (*pl* **quanta**) a quantity, share or portion; a fixed, elemental unit of energy. * *adj* large, significant.

quantum leap *n* an abrupt transition from one energy state to another; a sudden or noticeable change or increase.—*also* **quantum jump**.

quaquaversal *adj* (*geol*) pointing in every direction.

quarantine *n* a period of isolation imposed to prevent the spread of disease; the time or place of this. * *vt* to put or keep in quarantine.

quark *n* (*physics*) a hypothetical elementary particle.

quarrel *n* an argument; an angry dispute; a cause of dispute. * *vi* (**quarrelling, quarrelled** *or* **quarreling, quarreled**) to argue violently; to fall out (with); to find fault (with).—**quarreller, quarreler** *n*.

quarrelsome *adj* contentious; apt to quarrel.

quarrier, quarryman *n* (*pl* **quarriers, quarrymen**) one who works in a quarry.

quarry[1] *n* (*pl* **quarries**) an excavation for the extraction of stone, slate, etc; a place from which stone is excavated; a source of information, etc. * *vti* (**quarrying, quarried**) to excavate (from) a quarry; to research.

quarry[2] *n* (*pl* **quarries**) a hunted animal, prey.

quart *n* a liquid measure equal to a quarter of a gallon or two pints; a dry measure equal to two pints.

quartan *adj* recurring every third day, said of a fever, esp malaria.

quarter *n* a fourth of something; one fourth of a year; one fourth of an hour; (*US*) 25 cents, or a coin of this value; any leg of a four-legged animal with the adjoining parts; a particular district or section; (*pl*) lodgings; a particular source; an unspecified person or group; a compass point other than the cardinal points; mercy; (*her*) any of four quadrants of a shield.* *vti* to share or divide into four; to provide with lodgings; to lodge; to range over (an area) in search (of). * *adj* constituting a quarter.

quarterage *n* a quarterly payment; (*rare*) a shelter.

quarterback *n* (*American football*) a player directly behind forwards and the centre, who directs play. * *vt* to direct the attacking play of (a football team); to manage, direct. * *vi* to play quarterback.

quarterbound *adj* a book bound on the spine only in leather, or another material more expensive than the rest of the binding.

quarterdeck *n* the stern area of the upper deck of a ship.

quartered *adj* divided into four quarters, sawn along two diameters, said of logs; (*her*) a shield divided into four parts, each with different arms, or with two sets of arms repeated at diagonally opposite corners; stationed or billeted, said especially of soldiers in civilian lodgings.

quarterfinal *n* one of four matches held before the semifinals in a tournament.—*also adj*.

quartering *n* the assignment of quarters to soldiers etc; (*her*) the division of a shield that contains several coats, often denoting family's alliances and intermarriages; any coat of arms so treated.

quarterlight *n* a usu triangular section within the window of a car.

quarterly *adj* occurring, issued, or spaced at three-month intervals; (*her*) divided into quarters. * *adv* once every three months; (*her*) in quarters. * *n* (*pl* **quarterlies**) a publication issued four times a year.

quartermaster *n* (*mil*) an officer in charge of stores; (*naut*) a petty officer in charge of steering, etc.

quarter note *n* (*mus*) a note having one fourth the duration of a whole note.

quarters *npl* lodgings, esp for soldiers; action stations, esp used in reference to each member of the crew of a battleship; in India, accommodation provided by an employer or by the government; (*sl used by soldiers*) (*sing*) a quartermaster.

quarterstaff (*pl* **quarterstaves**) *n* a staff 6 to 8 feet long and shod with iron, formerly used as a two-handed weapon of defence; the use of one of these.

quartet, quartette *n* a set or group of four; a piece of music composed for four instruments or voices; a group of four instrumentalists or voices.

quartic *adj* (*math*) pertaining to the fourth power, biquadratic. * *n* the fourth power, arising from the multiplication of a square number or quantity by itself, biquadratic.

quartile *n* (*astrol*) (*statistics*) one of three values of a variable that separates its distribution into four sets with equal frequencies. * *adj* (*statistics*) pertaining, or referring, to a quartile; (*astrol*) referring to an aspect of planets separated by 90 degree longitude.

quarto *n* (*pl* **quartos**) a page size, approx 9 by 12 inches; a book of this size of page.

quartz *n* a crystalline mineral, a form of silica, usu colourless and transparent.

quartzite *n* a very hard quartz rock; a light-coloured quartz sandstone.

quasar *n* a distant, starlike, celestial object that emits much light and powerful radio waves.

quash *vt* (*rebellion etc*) to put down; to suppress; to make void.

quasi *adv* seemingly; as if. * *prefix* almost, apparently.

quassia *n* a South American tree yielding bark and wood of excessive bitterness; the bark and wood from a tree of the same family, used to make furniture; formerly a bitter tonic drug obtained from this, which is now used as an ingredient in insecticides.

quatercentenary *n* (*pl* **quatercentenaries**) a 400th anniversary, or the entire year of celebrations etc of a 400th anniversary.

quaternary *adj* consisting of, arranged in, or by, fours; of the number 4; (*chem*) an atom bound to four other atoms or groups, or containing such an atom; (*math*) with four variables. (*with cap*) denoting strata more recent than the Upper Tertiary, ie the most recent geological period, of less than 1 million years ago. * *n* (*pl* **quaternaries**) (*with* **the**) this geological rock system, consisting of Pleistocene and Holocene (recent) epochs.

quaternion *n* the number 4; a set of 4; (*maths*) a calculus or method of mathematical investigation using a generalized complex number with four components.

quaternity *n* (*pl* **quaternities**) four persons regarded as one, esp in relation to God.

quatrain *n* a four-line stanza, rhymed alternately.

quatrefoil *n* a four-leaved plant, such as certain clovers; an ornamental figure in architectural tracery divided by cusps into four leaves.

quattrocento *n* the fifteenth century, esp in connection with Italian art and literature.

quaver *vi* to tremble, vibrate; to speak or sing with a quivering voice. * *n* a trembling sound or note; (*mus*) an eighth note.—**quaveringly** *adv*.—**quavery** *adj*.

quay *n* a loading wharf or landing place for vessels.

quayage *n* an interconnected network of quays; quay dues.

queasy *adj* (**queasier, queasiest**) nauseous; easily upset; over-scrupulous.—**queasily** *adv*.—**queasiness** *n*.

quebracho *n* (*pl* **quebrachos**) one of two types of South American tree with a hard timber rich in tannin, and used in tanning and dyeing; the medicinal bark of a South American tree, the alkaloids from the bark of which are also used in tanning; the wood or bark from any of these trees; any South American tree yielding a hard wood.

queen *n* a female sovereign and head of state; the wife or widow of a king; a woman considered pre-eminent; the egg-laying female of bees, wasps, etc; a playing card with a picture of a queen; (*chess*) the most powerful piece; (*sl*) a male homosexual, esp one who ostentatiously takes a feminine role. * *vi* (*with* **it**) to act like a queen, esp to put on airs. * *vt* (a pawn) to promote to a queen in chess.—**queendom** *n*.

queencake *n* a small currant cake.

queenly *adj* (**queenlier, queenliest**) like or having the character or attributes of a queen; regal.—**queenliness** *n*.

queen mother *n* a queen dowager who is the mother of a ruling sovereign.

queer *adj* strange, odd, curious; (*inf*) eccentric; (*sl*) homosexual. * *n* a (male) homosexual. **vt* (*sl*) to spoil the success of.—**queerness** *n*.

quell *vt* to suppress; to allay.—**queller** *n*.

quench *vt* (*thirst*) to satisfy or slake; (*fire*) to put out, extinguish; (*steel*) to cool; to suppress.—**quenchable** *adj*.—**quencher** *n*.

quenelle *n* a ball of savoury cooked meat, formed into various shapes and boiled in stock or fried.

quercine *adj* of the oak.

querist *n* one who asks questions.

quern *n* a kind of stone handmill for grinding corn.

querulous *adj* complaining, fretful, peevish.—**querulously** *adv*.

query *n* (*pl* **queries**) a question; a question mark; doubt. * *vti* (**querying, queried**) to question; to doubt the accuracy of.

quest *n* a search, seeking, esp involving a journey. * *vti* to search (about) for, seek.—**quester** *n*.—**questingly** *adv*.

question *n* an interrogative sentence; an inquiry; a problem; a doubtful or controversial point; a subject of debate before an assembly; a part of a test or examination. * *vti* to ask questions (of); to interrogate intensively; to dispute; to subject to analysis.—**questioner** *n*.

questionable *adj* doubtful; not clearly true or honest.—**questionability** *n*.—**questionably** *adv*.

question mark *n* a punctuation mark (?) used at the end of a sentence to indicate a question, or to express doubt about something; something unknown.

questionnaire *n* a series of questions designed to collect statistical information; a survey made by the use of questionnaire.

quetzal *n* a large brilliantly coloured Central or Southern American bird, the male having long tail feathers; a Guatemalan coin.

queue *n* a line of people, vehicles, etc awaiting a turn. * *vi* (**queuing, queued**) to wait in turn.

quibble *n* a minor objection or criticism. * *vi* to argue about trifling matters.—**quibbler** *n*.—**quibblingly** *adv*.

quiche *n* a savoury tart filled with onions and a cheese and egg custard.

quick *adj* rapid, speedy; nimble; prompt; responsive; alert; eager to learn. * *adv* (*inf*) in a quick manner. * *n* the sensitive flesh below a fingernail or toenail; the inmost sensibilities.—**quickly** *adv*.—**quickness** *n*.

quicken *vti* to speed up or accelerate; to make alive; to come to life; to invigorate.—**quickener** *n*.

quickie *n* (*inf*) anything done rapidly or in haste.

quicklime *n* calcium oxide.

quicksand *n* loose wet sand easily yielding to pressure in which persons, animals, etc may be swallowed up.

quicksilver *n* mercury.

quickstep *n* a ballroom dance in quick time; the music for this. * *vi* (**quickstepping, quickstepped**) to do this dance.

quick-tempered *adj* easily angered.

quick-witted *adj* mentally alert; quick in repartee.—**quick-wittedness** *n*.

quid *n* (*pl* **quid**) (*sl*) a pound (sterling).

quiddity *n* (*pl* **quiddities**) (*philos*) the essence of a thing; captious subtlety, a quibble.

quidnunc *n* one who is curious to know everything that happens; a gossip, a busybody.

quid pro quo *n* (*pl* **quid pro quos**) something equivalent given in exchange for something else.

quiescent *adj* dormant, inactive, inert; silent.—**quiescence** *n*.

quiet *adj* silent, not noisy; still, not moving; gentle, not boisterous; unobtrusive, not showy; placid, calm; monotonous, uneventful; undisturbed. * *n* stillness, peace, repose; an undisturbed state. * *vti* to quieten.—**quietly** *adv*.—**quietness** *n*.

quieten *vti* to make or become quiet; to calm, soothe.

quietism *n* a mental tranquillity and passive attitude towards life; a form of religious mysticism, founded in 17th–4century Spain, in which the cultivation of this attitude with reference to God's will is to be attained.

quietize, quietise *vt* to insulate something from sound; to soundproof.

quietness *n* repose.

quietude *n* repose; tranquillity.

quietus *n* (*pl* **quietuses**) death; the final settlement or discharge of debts etc; anything that results in death or annihilation.

quiff *n* (*Brit*) a curl plastered up above the forehead.

quill *n* the hollow stem of a feather; anything made of this, as a pen; a stiff, hollow spine of a hedgehog or porcupine.
quilt *n* a thick, warm bedcover; a bedspread; a coverlet of two cloths sewn together with padding between. * *vti* to stitch together like a quilt; to make a quilt.—**quilter** *n*.—**quilting** *n*.
quin *n* a quintuplet.
quinary (*pl* **quinaries**) *adj* consisting of, or arranged in, fives; a number system with a base of the number 5; having five parts; the fifth member of something.
quinate *adj* (*bot*) with five leaflets on a petiole; said of a digitate leaf.
quince *n* a hard-fleshed yellow Asian fruit used in preserves; the tree it grows on.
quincentenary *n* (*pl* **quincentenaries**) a 500th anniversary, or the entire year of celebration, etc, of the 500th anniversary.
quincunx *n* an arrangement of five things in form of four corners and centre of a square; (*bot*) such an arrangement of petals or sepals in bud; (*astrol*) two planets with an aspect of 150 degrees.
quindecagon *n* a plane figure with 15 angles and 15 sides.
quinine *n* a bitter crystalline alkaloid used in medicine; one of its salts used esp as an antimalarial and a bitter tonic.
quinqu-, quinque- *prefix* five.
quinquagenarian *adj n* (a person) fifty to fifty-nine years old; relating to such a person.
Quinquagesima (Sunday) *n* the Sunday before Lent.
quinquennial *adj* lasting five years or occurring every five years.—**quinquennially** *adv*.
quinquennium *n* (*pl* **quinquennia**) a period of five years.
quinquepartite *adj* of five parts; shared by five.
quinquereme *n* in ancient Rome, a galley with five banks of oars on each side.
quinquevalent *adj* (*chem*) having a valency of five, pentavalent.—**quinquevalency, quinquevalence** *n*.
quinsy *n* a severe infection of the throat or adjacent parts causing swelling and fever.
quint *n* (*US*) a quintuplet.
quintain *n* a post with a sandbag on a pivot, or other object, used for practising the medieval sport of tilting; tilting at this.
quintal *n* a measure of weight, 100 lb; a measure of weight of 100 kilograms.
quintan *adj* said of an intermittent fever which recurs every fourth day.
quintessence *n* the purest form or most typical representation of anything, the embodiment.
quintessential *adj* most typical; fundamental.—**quintessentially** *adv*.
quintet, quintette *n* a set or group of five; a piece of music composed for five instruments or voices; a group of five instrumentalists or voices.
quintillion *n* (*pl* **quintillions, quintillion**) in Western Europe, a million raised to the fifth power ($1,000,000^5$), known in North America as a nonillion; in North America the sixth power of thousand, known as a trillion in Britain.—**quintillionth** *adj*.
quintuple *adj* fivefold; having five divisions or parts; five times as much or as many. * *vti* to multiply by five. * *n* a number five times greater than another.
quintuplet *n* one of five offspring produced at one birth.
quintuplicate *vt* to multiply by five; to make five copies of.* *adj* five-fold. * *n* a set of five objects.—**quintuplication** *n*.
quip *n* a witty remark; a gibe. * *vt* (**quipping, quipped**) to make a clever or sarcastic remark.—**quipster** *n*.
quire *n* a set of 24 sheets of paper; one twentieth of a ream; a section of folded sheets sewn together in bookbinding.
quirk *n* an unexpected turn or twist; a peculiarity of character or mannerism.
quirky *adj* (**quirkier, quirkiest**) odd or unusual in character, behaviour or appearance.—**quirkily** *adv*.—**quirkiness** *n*.
quirt *n* a riding whip of plaited leather with a leather thong at the end. * *vt* to lash with this.
quisling *n* a traitor who aids an invading enemy to regularize their conquest of his country; a collaborator.
quit *vti* (**quitting, quitted** *or* **quit**) to leave; to stop or cease; to resign; to free from obligation; to admit defeat. * *adj* free from; released from.
quitch (grass) *n* couchgrass.
quite *adv* completely; somewhat, fairly; really.
quits *adj* even; on equal terms by payment or revenge.
quittance *n* a release from debt or obligation.
quitter *n* a person who gives up easily.
quiver[1] *vi* to shake; to tremble, shiver. * *n* a shiver, vibration.—**quiveringly** *adv*.—**quivery** *adj*.
quiver[2] *n* a case for holding arrows.—**quiverful** *n*.
qui vive *n* **on the qui vive** on the alert.
quixotic, quixotical *adj* chivalrous or romantic to extravagance; unrealistically idealistic.—**quixotically** *adv*.
quixotism, quixotry *n* romantic or extravagant notions or schemes; quixotic conduct or ideals.
quiz *n* (*pl* **quizzes**) a form of entertainment where players are asked questions of general knowledge; a short written or oral test. * *vt* (**quizzing, quizzed**) to interrogate; to make fun of.—**quizzer** *n*.
quizmaster *n* a person who puts the questions to a contestant in a quiz show.
quiz show *n* an entertainment programme on television or radio in which contestants answer questions to win prizes.
quizzical *adj* humorous and questioning.—**quizzicality** *n*.—**quizzically** *adv*.
quod erat demonstrandum (*Latin*) that which was to be proved.
quodlibet *n* a subtle or moot point, esp as part of a theological argument; (*mus*) a light musical medley.—**quodlibetical** *adj* **quodlibetically** *adv*.
quoin *n* a wedge of wood or metal used to support and steady something (esp formerly a gun or cannon); a keystone; an external angle of a building; the stone forming this, the cornerstone; a wedge-shaped wooden block to tighten the pages of type within a chase.
quoit *n* a ring of metal, plastic, etc thrown in quoits; (*pl*) a game in which rings are thrown at or over a peg.
quondam *adj* that was, former.
quorum *n* the minimum number that must be present at a meeting or assembly to make its proceedings valid.
quota *n* a proportional share; a prescribed amount; a part to be contributed.
quotable *adj* worthy or fit to be quoted.—**quotability** *n*.
quotation *n* the act of quoting; the words quoted; an estimated price.
quotation mark *n* a punctuation mark to indicate the beginning (‘ *or* “) and the end (’ *or* ”) of a quoted passage.
quote *vt* to cite; to refer to; to repeat the words of a novel, play, poem, speech, etc exactly; to adduce by way of authority; to set off by quotation marks; to state the price of (something). * *n* (*inf*) something quoted; a quotation mark.
quoth *vt* (*arch*) said, used with nouns and all pronouns except thou and you.
quotidian *adj* daily; recurring every day, occurring every day; belonging to each day; commonplace, routine, everyday, trivial. * *n* a fever, esp malaria, recurring every day.
quotient *n* (*math*) the result obtained when one number is divided by another.
quo warranto *n* (*law*) a proceeding set in motion to determine the authority by which someone claims an office or privilege; (*formerly*) the title of a writ issued to a person to try the question of title to any public office or privilege.
qwerty, QWERTY *n* (*inf*) a standard typewriter or computer keyboard.

R

R. *abbr* = rabbi; Regiment; Regina (*Latin* Queen); Republican; Rex (Latin *King*); River; Royal.
R, r *n* the 18th letter of the English alphabet.
RA *abbr* = (UK) Royal Academy or Royal Academician.

Ra (*chem symbol*) radium.
RAAF *abbr* = Royal Australian Air Force.
rabbet, rebate *n* a recess or groove cut in a surface (eg wood) to receive another piece. * *vt* to cut a rabbet in; to join (pieces of wood, etc) using a rabbet.
rabbi *n* (*pl* **rabbis**) the religious and spiritual leader of a Jewish congregation.
rabbinate *n* the position or tenure of a rabbi; rabbis collectively.
rabbinical *adj* of or pertaining to rabbis, their office, writings, etc.—**rabbinically** *adv*.
rabbit *n* a small burrowing mammal of the hare family with long ears, a short tail, and long hind legs; their flesh as food; their fur.
rabbit punch *n* a sharp blow to the back of the neck.
rabble *n* a disorderly crowd, a mob; the common herd.
rabble-rouser *n* a person who excites a mob to violent action; a demagogue.
Rabelasian *adj* of, pertaining to, or resembling the coarse, satirical humour of the French writer François Rabelais (?1494–1553).
rabid *adj* infected with rabies; raging; fanatical.
rabies *n* an acute, infectious, viral disease transmitted by the bite of an infected animal.—*also* **hydrophobia**.
raccoon *n* a small nocturnal carnivore of North America that lives in trees; its yellowish grey fur.
race[1] *n* any of the divisions of humankind distinguished esp by colour of skin; any geographical, national, or tribal ethnic grouping; a subspecies of plants or animals; distinctive flavour or taste.
race[2] *n* a contest of speed, as in running, swimming, cycling, etc; a rapid current or channel of water. * *vi* to run at top speed or out of control; to compete in a race; (*engine*) to run without a working load or with the transmission disengaged. * *vt* to cause to race; to contest against.
racecourse *n* a track over which races are run, esp an oval track for racing horses.—*also* **racetrack.**
racehorse *n* a horse bred and trained for racing.
raceme *n* (*bot*) an arrangement of flowers directly on a main stem, as in the lily of the valley.
racer *n* a person who races; a machine used for racing, esp a bicycle; a kind of American snake.
race relations *npl* the relationship between different races in a community or nation; the sociological study of such relations.
racetrack *see* **racecourse**
rachis, rhachis *n* (*pl* **rachises, rhachises** *or* **rachides, rhachides**) the main stem of a plant's flower-head; the shaft of a feather; the spinal column.
rachitis *n* rickets.
racial *adj* of or relating to any of the divisions of humankind distinguished by colour, etc.
racism, racialism *n* a belief in the superiority of some races over others; prejudice against or hatred of other races; discriminating behaviour towards people of another race.—**racist** *n*.
rack *n* a framework for holding or displaying articles; an instrument for torture by stretching; the triangular frame for setting up balls in snooker; a toothed bar to engage with the teeth of a wheel pinion or worm gear; extreme pain or anxiety. * *vt* (*person*) to stretch on a rack; to arrange in or on a rack; to torture, torment; to move parts of machinery with a toothed rack.
racket[1] *n* a bat strung with nylon, for playing tennis, etc. (*pl*) a game for two or four players played in a four-walled court (—*also* **racquet**).
racket[2] *n* noisy confusion; din; an obtaining of money illegally; any fraudulent business.
racketeer *n* a person who extorts money by threat or engages in an illegal profit-making enterprise.
rack railway *n* a railway on a steep incline that has a rack or cog between the rails to engage with a pinion on a locomotive.
rack-rent *n* an extortionate rent.—*also vt*.—**rack-renter** *n*.
raconteur *n* a person who excels in relating anecdotes.
racquet *see* **racket**[1].
racy *adj* (**racier, raciest**) lively, spirited; risqué.—**racily** *adv*.
rad[1] *n* a unit of absorbed dose of ionizing radiation.
rad[2] (*symbol*) radian.
radar *n* a system or device for detecting objects such as aircraft by using the reflection of radio waves.
radar beacon *n* a fixed radio transmitter that sends out a signal which allows a ship or an aircraft to determine its own position.
radarscope *n* a cathode-ray oscilloscope which displays radar signals.
radial *adj* like a radius; branching from a common centre.
radial ply *adj* (*tyre*) having the fabric cords of the outer casing lying radial to the hub for greater flexibility.
radial symmetry *n* the state of having similar parts arranged symmetrically around a common axis.
radian *n* the SI unit of plane angle, equal to the angle at the centre of a circle formed by radii of an arc equal in length to the radius.
radiance *n* the condition of being radiant; brilliant light; dazzling beauty.
radiant *adj* shining; beaming with happiness; sending out rays; transmitted by radiation.—**radiantly** *adv*.
radiant energy *n* energy in the form of electromagnetic radiation, such as heat or light.
radiant heat *n* heat conveyed by electromagnetic radiation rather than conduction or convection.
radiate *vt* (*light, heat, etc*) to emit in rays; (*happiness, love, etc*) to give forth. * *vi* to spread out as if from a centre; to shine; to emit rays.
radiation *n* radiant particles emitted as energy; rays emitted in nuclear decay; (*med*) treatment using a radioactive substance.
radiation sickness *n* an illness caused by excessive exposure to radiation from radioactive materials.
radiator *n* an apparatus for heating a room; a cooling device for a vehicle engine.
radical *adj* of or relating to the root or origin; fundamental; favouring basic change. * *n* a person who advocates fundamental political or social change.—**radicalism** *n*.
radically *adv* fundamentally.
radical sign *n* the symbol v placed before a number to show that the square root (or a higher root denoted by an index number over the sign) is to be extracted.
radicchio *n* (*pl* **radicchios**) a type of Italian chicory with white-veined purple leaves eaten raw in salads.
radices *see* **radix.**
radicle *n* the part of a seed that develops into a root; a root-like subdivision of a nerve or vein.
radii *see* **radius.**
radio- *prefix* radial; radio; using radiant energy.
radio *n* the transmission of sounds or signals by electromagnetic waves through space, without wires, to a receiving set; such a set; broadcasting by radio as an industry, entertainment, etc. * *adj* of, using, used in, or sent by radio. * *vti* to transmit, or communicate with, by radio.
radioactive *adj* giving off radiant energy in the form of particles or rays caused by the disintegration of atomic nuclei.—**radioactivity** *n*.
radioactive decay *n* the disintegration of a nucleus as the result of electron capture.
radioactive waste *n* any waste products that contain radioactive materials.—*also* **nuclear waste.**
radio astronomy *n* astronomy dealing with radio waves in space in order to obtain information about the universe.
radio beacon *n* a radio transmitter that sends out signals as an aid to navigation.
radiocarbon *n* a radioisotope of carbon used in carbon dating.
radiocarbon dating *n* carbon dating.
radio compass *n* a navigational device which can determine the direction of radio waves from a specific radio beacon.
radio control *n* remote control using radio signals.—**radio-controlled** *adj*.
radioelement *n* a radioactive chemical element.
radio frequency *n* a frequency intermediate between audio frequencies and infrared frequencies used esp in radio and television transmission.

radiogram *n* a combined radio and record player.
radiograph *n* an image produced on sensitive photographic film or plate by radiation other than light, esp X-rays.
radiography *n* the production of X-ray photographs for use in medicine, industry, etc.—**radiographer** *n*.
radioisotope *n* a radioactive isotope.
radiology *n* a branch of medicine concerned with the use of radiant energy (as X-rays and radium) in the diagnosis and treatment of disease.—**radiologist** *n*.
radiometer *n* an instrument for measuring radiant energy.—**radiometric** *adj*.
radiopaging *n* a system for alerting a person using a small radio transmitter which beeps in response to a signal from a distance.
radiosonde *n* a small radio transmitter carried by a probe for sending back data on atmospheric conditions.
radio source *n* any celestial object, such as a supernova, that emits radio waves.
radio spectrum *n* that range of frequencies, between 10 kHz and 300,000 MHz, used in radio transmission.
radiotelegraphy *n* telegraphy that uses radio waves to transmit messages.—**radiotelegraph** *n*.—**radiotelegraphic** *adj*.
radiotelephone *n* a device for transmitting telephone messages using radio waves. * *vt* to transmit by radiotelephone, * *vi* to operate a radiotelephone.—**radiotelephony** *n*.
radio telescope *n* an instrument used in radio astronomy to receive and analyse radio waves.
radiotherapy *n* the medical treatment of disease, esp cancer, by X-rays or other radioactive substances.—**radiotherapist** *n*.
radio wave *n* an electromagnetic wave having radio frequency.
radish *n* a pungent root eaten raw as a salad vegetable.
radium *n* a highly radioactive metallic element.
radium therapy *n* the treatment of cancer by exposure to radiation from radium.
radius *n* (*pl* **radii**) (*geom*) a straight line joining the centre of a circle or sphere to its circumference; a thing like this, a spoke; a sphere of activity; (*anat*) the thicker of the two bones of the forearm.
radix *n* (*pl* **radices, radixes**) (*maths*) a number that is the base of a number system or for computation of logarithms.
radome *n* a protective housing for a radar antenna constructed from material which is transparent to radio waves.
radon *n* a gaseous radioactive element.—*also* **niton**.
radula *n* (*pl* **radulae**) a horny strip covered with minute teeth on the tongue of certain molluscs.
RAF *abbr* = Royal Air Force.
raffia *n* a kind of palm; fibre from its leaves used in basket-making, etc.
raffish *adj* untidy, disreputable, rakish; vulgarly flashy.
raffle *n* a lottery with prizes. * *vt* to offer as a prize in a raffle.
raft *n* a platform of logs, planks, etc strapped together to float on water.
rafter *n* one of the inclined, parallel beams that support a roof.
rag[1] *n* a torn or waste scrap of cloth; a shred; (*inf*) a sensationalist newspaper; (*pl*) tattered or shabby clothing.
rag[2] *vt* (**ragging, ragged**) to tease; to play practical jokes on. * *n* a practical joke; a series of boisterous stunts staged by British students to raise money for charity.
rag[3] *n* ragtime music.
raga *n* (a composition based on) any of various conventional melodic or rhythmic patterns in Indian music used as the basis for improvisation.
ragamuffin *n* an unkempt dirty person, esp a child.
rag and bone man *n* a junkman.
ragbag *n* a bag for scraps; a miscellaneous collection, jumble.
rage *n* violent anger; passion; frenzy; fashion, craze. * *vi* to behave with violent anger; to storm; to spread rapidly; to be prevalent.
ragged *adj* jagged; uneven; irregular; worn into rags; tattered.—**raggedly** *adv*.—**raggedness** *n*.
ragged robin *n* a Eurasian plant of the pink family with tattered looking pink or white flowers.
raggedy *adj* (*inf*) tattered.
ragi, raggee *n* a cereal grass cultivated in Asia and Africa.
raging *adj* violent; intense.
raglan *n* a type of loose sleeve cut in one piece with the shoulder of a garment.
ragout *n* a stew of meat and vegetables, highly seasoned.
ragtime *n* quick tempo jazz piano music.
ragwort *n* a European composite plant with yellow flowers.
rah *interj* hurrah.
raid *n* a sudden attack to assault or seize. * *vt* to make a raid on; to steal from.—**raider** *n*.
rail[1] *n* a horizontal bar extending from one post to another, as in a fence, etc; one of a pair of parallel steel lines forming a track for the wheels of a train; a railroad.
rail[2] *vi* to speak angrily.
railhead *n* the furthest point reached by the tracks of an uncompleted railway; a terminus.
railing *n* a fence of rails and posts; rails collectively.
raillery *n* (*pl* **railleries**) good-humoured banter, mockery.
railroad *n* railway. * *vt* to force unduly; (*bill, etc*) to push forward fast; to imprison hastily, esp unjustly.
railway *n* a track of parallel steel rails along which carriages are drawn by locomotive engines; a complete system of such tracks.
raiment *n* (*poet*) clothing.
rain *n* water that falls from the clouds in the form of drops; a shower; a large quantity of anything falling like rain; (*pl*) the rainy season in the tropics. * *vti* (*of rain*) to fall; to fall like rain; (*rain, etc*) to pour down.
rainbow *n* the arc containing the colours of the spectrum formed in the sky by the refraction of the sun's rays in falling rain or in mist. * *adj* many-coloured.
rainbow trout *n* a large freshwater trout of Europe and North America with bright markings.
rain check *n* a ticket stub allowing future admission to an event in the case of it being rained off; the postponement of acceptance of an offer or invitation.
raincoat *n* a waterproof coat.
raindrop *n* a drop of rain.
rainfall *n* a fall of rain; the amount of rain that falls on a given area in a specified time.
rain forest *n* a dense, evergreen forest in a tropical area with much rainfall.
rain gauge *n* an instrument for measuring rainfall.
rainproof *adj* rain-resisting.
rain shadow the leeward side of a hill or mountain where the rain is relatively lighter.
rainy *adj* (**rainier, rainiest**) full of rain; wet.
rainy day *n* a future need, esp financial.
raise *vt* to elevate; to lift up; to set or place upright; to stir up, rouse; to increase in size, amount, degree, intensity, etc; to breed, bring up; (*question, etc*) to put forward; to collect or levy; (*siege*) to abandon. * *n* a rise in wages.
raisin *n* a sweet, dried grape.
raison d'être *n* (*pl* **raisons d'être**) reason for existence; justification.
raj *n* the period of British rule in India.
rajah, raja *n* (*formerly*) an Indian ruler; an Indian or Malayan chief or prince.
rake[1] *n* a tool with a row of teeth and a handle for gathering together, scraping (leaves, hay, etc) or for smoothing gravel, etc. * *vt* to scrape, gather as with a rake; to sweep with gaze or gunshot; (*with* **in**: *money, etc*) to gather a great amount rapidly; (*with* **up**: *past misdemeanours, etc*) to bring to light.
rake[2] *n* the incline or slope of a mast, stern, etc.
rake[3] *n* a dissolute, debauched man, a libertine.

raki, rakee *n* a strong aromatic spirit distilled from grain in Turkey.
rakish *adj* jaunty, dashing; dissolute.—**rakishly** *adv*.—**rakishness** *n*.
rale *n* a wheezing rattle detectable with a stethoscope in the chest of patients with lung disorders.
rallentando *adv* (*mus*) gradually slower.
rally *vti* (**rallying, rallied**) to bring or come together; to recover strength, revive; to take part in a motor rally; (*with* **round**) to help (a person); to support financially or morally. * *n* (*pl* **rallies**) a large assembly of people for a political purpose; a recovery (after illness); (*stock exchange*) a sharp increase in price after a decline; (*tennis*) a lengthy exchange of shots; a competitive test of driving and navigational skills.
RAM *abbr* = random-access memory.
ram *n* a male sheep; a battering device; a piston; (*with cap*) Aries, the first sign of the zodiac. * *vt* (**ramming, rammed**) to force or drive; to crash; to cram; to thrust violently.
Ramadan *n* the ninth month of the Islamic year; the great fast during it.
ramble *vi* to wander or stroll about for pleasure; (*plant*) to straggle; to write or talk aimlessly. * *n* a leisurely walk in the countryside.
rambler *n* a person who rambles; a climbing rose.
rambling *adj* spread out, straggling; circuitous; disconnected; disjointed.
Ramboesque *adj* in the aggressive, mindless style of the fictional character Rambo, an indestructible one-man army who featured in several violent action films in the 1980s.
rambunctious *adj* (*inf*) boisterous, unruly.—**rambunctiously** *adv*.—**rambunctiousness** *n*.
rambutan *n* (a Malaysian tree bearing) a hairy red edible fruit.
ramekin *n* a baked dish of cheese, breadcrumbs, etc; the small pot in which this is cooked.
ramification *n* a branching out; an offshoot; a consequence.
ramify *vti* to (cause to) divide into branches or constituent parts.
ramjet *n* (an aircraft having) a type of jet engine that uses compressed air from the forward movement to burn the fuel.
ramose *adj* composed of or having branches.—**ramosely** *adv*.
ramp *n* a sloping walk or runway joining different levels; a wheeled staircase for boarding a plane; a sloping runway for launching boats, as from trailers.
rampage *n* angry or violent behaviour. * *vi* to rush about in an angry or violent manner.
rampant *adj* dominant; luxuriant, unrestrained; violent; rife, prevalent; (*her*) (of a beast) standing on its hind legs.
rampart *n* an embankment surrounding a fortification; a protective wall.
rampion *n* a Eurasian plant with bell-shaped red or purple flowers whose root is sometimes used in salads.
ramrod *n* a rod for ramming home a charge in a muzzle-loading gun. * *adj* denoting a stiff, inflexible person.
ramshackle *adj* dilapidated.
RAN *abbr* = Royal Australian Navy.
ran *see* **run.**
ranch *n* a large farm for raising cattle, horses, or sheep; a style of house with all the rooms on one floor. * *vi* to own, manage, or work on a ranch.—**rancher** *n*.
rancherie *n* a settlement of North American Indians in a reserve in British Columbia, Canada.
rancid *adj* having an unpleasant smell and taste, as stale fats or oil.—**rancidity, rancidness** *n*.
rancour, rancor *n* bitter hate or spite.—**rancorous** *adj*.—**rancorously** *adv*.
rand *n* a unit of money in South Africa, divided into 100 cents.
R & B *abbr* = rhythm and blues.
R & D *abbr* = research and development.
random *adj* haphazard; left to chance.
random-access *adj* (*comput*) direct access to data in any desired order.
randomize *vt* to arrange (eg a survey, samples) in a random way to obtain unbiased statistical results.—**randomization** *n*.—**randomizer** *n*.
R and R *abbr* = rest and recreation.
randy *adj* (**randier, randiest**) (*sl*) lustful, sexually aroused.
ranee *see* **rani.**
rang *see* **ring**[2].
range *n* a row; a series of mountains, etc; scope, compass; the distance a ship, aircraft, or motor vehicle can travel without refuelling; the distance a gun, etc can fire, a projectile can be thrown, or from gun to target; fluctuation; a large open area for grazing livestock; a place for testing rockets in flight; a place for shooting or golf practice; a cooking stove. * *vt* to place in order or a row; to establish the range of; (*livestock*) to graze on a range. * *vi* to be situated in a line; to rank or classify; (*gun*) to point or aim; to vary (inside limits).
range finder *n* an instrument for determining the range of a target.
ranger *n* a forest or park warden.
rangy *adj* (**rangier, rangiest**) tall and slim; long-limbed.—**ranginess** *n*.
rani, ranee *n* in India, a queen or princess; the wife of a rajah.
rank[1] *n* a line of objects; a line of soldiers standing abreast; high standing or position; status; (*pl*) ordinary members of the armed forces. * *vti* to arrange in a line; to have a specific position in an organization or on a scale; to outrank; (*with* **with**) to be counted among.
rank[2] *adj* growing uncontrollably; utter, flagrant; offensive in odour or flavour.
rank and file *n* ordinary soldiers; ordinary members, as distinguished from their leaders.
ranking *n* a listing of things or people in order of importance. * *adj* of the highest rank; outstanding.
rankle *vi* to fester; to cause continuous resentment or irritation.
ransack *vt* to plunder; to search thoroughly.
ransom *n* the release of a captured person or thing; the price paid for this. * *vt* to secure release of by payment.
rant *vi* to speak loudly or violently; to preach noisily. * *n* loud, pompous talk.
ranunculus *n* (*pl* **ranunculuses, ranunculi**) a common genus of usu yellow-flowered plants including the buttercup.
rap[1] *n* a sharp blow; a knock; (*inf*) talk, conversation; (*sl*) arrest for a crime; (*sl*) rap music. * *vti* (**rapping, rapped**) to strike lightly or sharply; to knock; (*sl*) to criticize sharply; (*with* **out**) to utter abruptly; (*sl*) to speak in a fast and rhythmic manner to a musical backing.
rap[2] *n* a style of popular music in which (usu rhyming) words and phrases are spoken in a rhythmic chant over an instrumental backing.—**rapper** *n*.
rapacious *adj* grasping; extortionate.—**rapaciously** *adv*.—**rapacity** *n*.
rape[1] *n* the act of forcing a person to have sexual intercourse against his or her will; the plundering (of a city, etc) as in warfare. * *vti* to commit rape (upon).
rape[2] *n* a bright yellow plant of the mustard family grown for its leaves and oily seeds.
rapid *adj* at great speed; fast; sudden; steep. * *npl* a part of a river where the current flows swiftly.—**rapidity** *n*.—**rapidly** *adv*.
rapid eye movement *n* the rapid jerky movements of the eyeballs associated with dreaming while asleep.
rapier *n* a straight, two-edged sword with a narrow pointed blade.
rapine *n* plunder, pillage.
rapist *n* a person who commits rape.
rap music *n* a song that is rapidly spoken and accompanied by an insistent electronic rhythm.
rappel *vi* to abseil.
rapport *n* a sympathetic relationship; accord.
rapprochement *n* re-establishment of cordial relations; reconciliation.
rapscallion *n* a rascal.
rapt *adj* carried away, enraptured; absorbed, intent.
raptor *n* a bird of prey.
raptorial *adj* of or pertaining to birds of prey; (*birds' feet*) adapted for seizing prey.
rapture *n* the state of being carried away with love, joy, etc; intense delight, ecstasy.—**rapturous** *adj*.—**rapturously** *adv*.
rara avis *n* a rare or unique person or thing.

rare[1] *adj* unusual; seldom seen; exceptionally good; (*gas*) of low density, thin. *adv*.—**rareness** *n*.

rare[2] *adj* not completely cooked, partly raw; underdone.

rare earth *n* (an oxide of) any of the lanthanide series of chemical elements.

rarefy *vti* (**rarefying, rarefied**) to make or become less dense; to thin out; to expand without the addition of matter; to make more spiritual, abstruse or refined.—**rarefied** *adj*.

rare gas *n* an inert gas.

rarely *adv* almost never, seldom; exceptionally, unusually.

raring *adj* (*inf*) eager, enthusiastic.

rarity *n* (*pl* **rarities**) rareness; a rare person or thing.

rasbora *n* any of various small brightly-coloured tropical fishes popular for aquariums.

rascal *n* a rogue; a villain; a mischievous person.

rase *see* **raze**.

rash[1] *adj* reckless; impetuous.—**rashly** *adv*.—**rashness** *n*.

rash[2] *n* a skin eruption of spots, etc.

rasher *n* a thin slice of bacon or ham.

rasp *n* a coarse file; a grating sound. * *vt* to scrape with a rasp. * *vi* to produce a grating sound.

raspberry *n* (*pl* **raspberries**) a shrub with white flowers and red berry-like fruits; the fruit produced; (*inf*) a sound of dislike or derision.

Rastafarian, Rasta *n* a member of a largely Jamaican religious and political movement that worships Ras Tafari, the former Emperor of Ethiopia, Haile Selassie, as God.—*also adj*.

raster *n* a grid of lines scanned by an electron beam to make up an image, esp on a television screen.

rat *n* a long-tailed rodent similar to a mouse but larger; (*sl*) a sneaky, contemptible person, esp an informer; a scab. * *vi* (**ratting, ratted**) to hunt or catch rats; to betray or inform on someone; to work as a scab.

ratafia *n* a liqueur flavoured with fruit kernels, such as cherry, peach or almond; a sweet biscuit flavoured with coconut and almond.

ratatouille *n* a dish consisting of a thick stew of roughly chopped vegetables such as onions, peppers, courgettes, aubergine, and tomatoes.

ratchet *n* a device with a toothed wheel that moves in one direction only.

rate *n* the amount, degree, etc of something in relation to units of something else; price, esp per unit; degree. * *vt* to fix the value of; to rank; to regard or consider; (*sl*) to think highly of. * *vi* to have value or status.

ratel *n* a carnivorous nocturnal mammal of Africa and Asia resembling the badger.

ratepayer *n* a person who pays rates, a householder.

rather *adv* more willingly; preferably; somewhat; more accurately; on the contrary; (*inf*) yes, certainly.

ratify *vt* (**ratifying, ratified**) to approve formally; to confirm.

rating *n* an assessment; an evaluation, an appraisal, as of credit worthiness; classification by grade, as of military personnel; (*radio, TV*) the relative popularity of a programme according to sample polls.

ratio *n* (*pl* **ratios**) the number of times one thing contains another; the quantitative relationship between two classes of objects; proportion.

ratiocinate *vi* to reason or argue systematically.—**ratiocination** *n*.

ration *n* (*food, petrol*) a fixed amount or portion; (*pl*) food supply. * *vt* to supply with rations; (*food, petrol*) to restrict the supply of.

rational *adj* of or based on reason; reasonable; sane.—**rationally** *adv*.

rationale *n* the reason for a course of action; an explanation of principles.

rationalism *n* dependence on reason and rejection of intuition or the supernatural to justify ideas and beliefs, esp with regard to religion; the belief that reason can supply knowledge independently of personal experience.

rationality *n* (*pl* **rationalities**) the condition of being rational; the practice of being reasonable.

rationalize *vti* to make rational; to justify one's reasons for an action; to cut down on personnel or equipment; to substitute a natural for a supernatural explanation.—**rationalization** *n*.

rational number *n* a number that can be expressed as the ratio of two integers.

ratline *n* any of the short ropes fastened between the shrouds of a sailing ship to form rungs.

ratoon, rattoon *n* a new shoot sprouting from the root of a perennial plant, esp sugarcane, after it has been cut back. * *vt* to encourage growth in this way.

rat race *n* continual hectic competitive activity.

rattan *n* a climbing palm with a jointed stem; cane made of this.

rattle *vi* to clatter. * *vt* to make a series of sharp, quick noises; to clatter; to recite rapidly; to chatter; (*inf*) to disconcert, fluster. * *n* a rattling sound; a baby's toy that makes a rattling sound; a voluble talker; the rings on the tail of a rattlesnake.

rattler *n* a rattlesnake.

rattlesnake *n* a venomous American snake with a rattle in its tail.

rattling *adj* brisk, vigorous; first-rate. * *adv* to an extreme degree; very.

ratty *adj* (**rattier, rattiest**) like or full of rats; (*sl*) angry, irritable, snappish.

raucous *adj* hoarse and harsh-sounding; loud and rowdy.

raunchy *adj* (**raunchier, raunchiest**) (*sl*) coarse, earthy; careless, slovenly; cheap, inferior.

rauwolfia *n* a tropical flowering shrub of Southeast Asia; an extract from the root of this used in various drugs.

ravage *vt* to ruin, destroy; to plunder, lay waste. * *n* destruction; ruin; (*pl*) the effects of this.

rave *vi* to speak wildly or as if delirious; (*inf*) to enthuse. * *n* enthusiastic praise.—**raving** *adj*.

ravel *vti* (**ravelling, ravelled** *or* **raveling, raveled**) to entangle or disentangle; to fray; to unwind; to make or become complicated.

raven *n* a large crow-like bird with glossy black feathers. * *adj* of the colour or sheen of a raven.

ravenous *adj* famished; voracious.—**ravenously** *adv*.

ravine *n* a deep, narrow gorge, a large gully.

ravioli *n* small cases of pasta filled with highly seasoned chopped meat or vegetables.

ravish *vt* to violate; to rape; to enrapture.

ravishing *adj* charming, captivating.

raw *adj* uncooked; unrefined; in a natural state, crude; untrained, inexperienced; sore, skinned; damp, chilly; (*inf*) harsh or unfair.—**rawness** *n*.

rawhide *n* (a whip made from strips of) untanned leather.

raw material *n* something out of which a finished article is made; something with a potential for development, improvement, etc.

ray[1] *n* a beam of light that comes from a bright source; any of several lines radiating from a centre; a beam of radiant energy, radioactive particles, etc; a tiny amount.

ray[2] *n* any of various fishes with a flattened body and the eyes on the upper surface.

rayon *n* a textile fibre made from a cellulose solution; a fabric of such fibres.

raze *vt* to demolish; to erase; to level to the ground.—*also* **rase**.

razor *n* a sharp-edged instrument for shaving.

razorbill *n* a North Atlantic auk with a flattened sharp-edged bill.

razor clam, razor-shell *n* any of various bivalve marine molluscs with curved sharp shells.

razz *vt* (*inf*) to deride, heckle.

razzle-dazzle, razzmatazz *n* (*inf*) exciting, exuberant or colourful activity or atmosphere.

Rb (*chem symbol*) rubidium.

RC *abbr* = Roman Catholic.

RCCh *abbr* = Roman Catholic Church.

RCA *abbr* = Radio Corporation of America.

RCAF *abbr* = Royal Canadian Air Force.

RCMP *abbr* = Royal Canadian Mounted Police.

RCN *abbr* = Royal Canadian Navy.

RCP *abbr* = Royal College of Physicians.

RCS *abbr* = Royal College of Surgeons.

Rd *abbr* = road.

Re (*chem symbol*) rhenium.

re- *prefix* again, anew; back.

re[1] *prep* concerning, with reference to.

re[2] *n* the second note of a major scale in solmization.

reach *vti* to arrive at; to extend as far as; to make contact with; to pass, hand over; to attain, realize; to stretch out the hand; to extend in influence, space, etc; to carry, as sight, sound, etc; to try to get. * *n* the act or power of reaching; extent; mental range; scope; a continuous extent, esp of water.

react *vi* to act in response to a person or stimulus; to have a mutual or reverse effect; to revolt; (*chem*) to undergo a chemical reaction.

reaction *n* an action in response to a stimulus; a revulsion of feeling; exhaustion after excitement, etc; opposition to new ideas; (*chem*) an action set up by one substance in another.

reactionary *adj*, *n* (a person) opposed to political or social change.

reactive *adj* of or relating to reaction; reacting to stimuli; caused by stress.

reactor *n* a person or substance that undergoes a reaction; (*chem*) a vessel in which a reaction occurs; a nuclear reactor.

read *vti* (**reading, read**) to understand something written; to speak aloud (from a book); to study by reading; to interpret, divine; to register, as a gauge; to foretell; (of a computer) to obtain (information) from; (*sl*) to hear and understand (a radio communication, etc); (*with* **about, of**) to learn by reading; to be phrased in certain words. * *adj* well-informed.

readable *adj* legible; pleasantly written.

readdress *vt* to address again; (*letter*) to change the address when forwarding.

reader *n* a person who reads; one who reads aloud to others; a proofreader; a person who evaluates manuscripts; a textbook, esp on reading; a unit that scans material for computation or storage; a senior lecturer.

readership *n* all the readers of a certain publication, author, etc.

readily *adv* in a ready manner; willingly, easily.

reading *n* the act of one who reads; any material to be read; the amount measured by a barometer, meter, etc; a particular interpretation of a play, etc.

readjust *vt* to adjust again.

read-only memory *n* a small computer memory that cannot be changed by the computer and that contains a special-purpose program.

read-out *n* the retrieval of information from a computer memory; the information retrieved.

read-write head *n* (*comput*) an electromagnetic head that can read and write data on a magnetic disc.

ready *adj* (**readier, readiest**) prepared; fit for use; willing; inclined, apt; prompt, quick; handy. * *n* the state of being ready, esp the position of a firearm aimed for firing. * *vt* (**readying, readied**) to make ready.—**readiness** *n*.

ready-made *adj* made in standard sizes, not to measure.

reagent *n* (*chem*) a substance used to detect, measure, or react with other substances.

real *adj* existing, actual, not imaginary; true, genuine, not artificial; (*law*) immovable, consisting of land or houses. * *adv* (*sl*) very; really.

real estate *n* property; land.

realgar *n* a reddish mineral composed of arsenic sulphide.

realign *vti* to align again; (*politics, diplomacy*) to readjust alliances, policies, etc.—**realignment** *n*.

realism *n* practical outlook; (*art, literature*) the ability to represent things as they really are without concealment; (*philos*) the doctrine that the physical world has an objective existence; the doctrine that general ideas have an objective existence.—**realist** *n*.

realistic *adj* matter-of-fact, not visionary; lifelike; of or relating to realism.—**realistically** *adv*.

reality *n* (*pl* **realities**) the fact or condition of being real; an actual fact or thing; truth.

realization *n* the action of realizing; something comprehended or achieved.

realize *vt* to become fully aware of; (*ambition, etc*) to make happen; to cause to appear real; to convert into money, be sold for.

really *adv* in fact, in reality; positively, very. * *interj* indeed.

realm *n* a kingdom, country; domain, region; sphere.

real number *n* any rational or irrational number.

real tennis *n* an early form of tennis played in a walled indoor court.

real-time *adj* involving the continual processing, manipulation and presentation of data by a computer as it is generated.

realtor *n* a person whose business is selling and leasing property, an estate agent.

realty *n* real estate.

ream *n* a quantity of paper varying from 480 to 516 sheets; (*pl*: *inf*) a great amount.

reap *vti* to harvest; to gain (a benefit).

reaper *n* a person who or a machine that reaps.

rear[1] *n* the back part or position, esp of an army; (*sl*) the rump. * *adj* of, at, or in the rear.

rear[2] *vt* to raise; (*children*) to bring up; to educate, nourish, etc. * *vi* (*horse*) to stand on the hind legs.

rear guard *n* a military detachment assigned to guard the rear of a body of troops. * *adj* relating to determined defensive resistance.

rear admiral *n* a naval officer next below in rank to a vice admiral.

rear light, rear lamp *n* a taillight.

rearm *vti* to arm or become armed again, esp with better weapons.—**rearmament** *n*.

rearview mirror *n* a mirror in a motor vehicle that allows the driver to see following traffic.

rearward *adj, adv* at or towards the rear.—**rearwards** *adv*.

reason *n* motive or justification (of an action or belief); the mental power to draw conclusions and determine truth; a cause; moderation; sanity; intelligence. * *vti* to think logically (about); to analyse; to argue or infer.

reasonable *adj* able to reason or listen to reason; rational; sensible; not expensive; moderate, fair.—**reasonableness** *n*.—**reasonably** *adv*.

reasoned *adj* convincingly argued.

reassure *vt* to hearten; to give confidence to; to free from anxiety.—**reassurance** *n*.

rebate[1] *n* a refund of part of an amount paid; discount.

rebate[2] see **rabbet**.

rebec, rebeck *n* a medieval stringed instrument shaped like a lute and played with a bow.

rebel *n* a person who refuses to conform with convention. * *vi* (**rebelling, rebelled** *or* **rebeling, rebeled**) (*army*) to rise up against the authorities or the government; to dissent.

rebellion *n* armed resistance to an established government, insurrection; defiance of authority.

rebellious *adj* of or engaged in rebellion; tending to rebel; stubborn.—**rebelliously** *adv*.

rebirth *n* a second or new birth; a revival, renaissance; spiritual regeneration.

rebound *vi* to spring back after impact; to bounce back; to recover. * *n* a recoil; an emotional reaction.

rebounder *n* a small trampoline used for keep-fit exercises.

rebuff *vt* to snub, repulse; to refuse unexpectedly.—*also n*.

rebuke *vt* to reprimand, chide. * *n* a reproof, reprimand.

rebus *n* (*pl* **rebuses**) a puzzle using images to represent the sound of words or syllables.

rebut *vt* (**rebutting, rebutted**) to disprove or refute by argument, etc.—**rebuttal** *n*.

rec *abbr* = receipt; recipe; record.

recalcitrant *adj* refusing to obey authority, etc; actively disobedient.—**recalcitrance** *n*.

recall *vt* to call back; to bring back to mind, remember; to revoke. * *n* remembrance; a summons to return; the removal from office by popular vote.

recant *vti* to repudiate or retract a former opinion, declaration, or belief.—**recantation** *n.*

recap *vti* (**recapping, recapped**) to recapitulate. * *n* (*inf*) recapitulation.

recapitulate *vt* to restate the main points of, to summarize.—**recapitulation** *n.*

recapture *vt* to capture again; (*a lost feeling, etc*) to discover anew, regain. * *n* the act of recapturing; a thing or feeling recaptured.

recd, rec'd *abbr* = received.

recede *vi* to move back; to withdraw, retreat; to slope backwards; to grow less; to decline in value.

receding *adj* sloping backwards; disappearing from view; (*hair*) ceasing to grow at the temples.

receipt *n* the act of receiving; a written proof of this; (*pl*) amount received from business. * *vt* to acknowledge and mark as paid; to write a receipt for.

receive *vt* to acquire, be given; to experience, be subjected to; to admit, allow; to greet on arrival; to accept as true; (*stolen goods*) to take in; to transfer electrical signals. * *vi* to be a recipient; to convert radio waves into perceptible signals.

received *adj* accepted, recognized.

Received Pronunciation *n* the unlocalized accent of British English, regarded as standard.

receiver *n* a person who receives; equipment that receives electronic signals, esp on a telephone; (*law*) a person appointed to manage or hold in trust property in bankruptcy or pending a lawsuit.

receivership *n* the status of a business in the hands of a receiver.

recent *adj* happening lately, fresh; not long established, modern.—**recently** *adv.*

receptacle *n* a container.

reception *n* the act of receiving or being received; a welcome; a social gathering, often to extend a formal welcome; a response, reaction; the quality of the sound or image produced by a radio or television set.

receptionist *n* a person employed to receive visitors to an office, hotel, hospital, etc.

receptive *adj* able or quick to take in ideas or impressions.

recess *n* a temporary halting of work, a vacation; a hidden or inner place; an alcove or niche. * *vti* to place in a recess; to form a recess in; to take a recess.

recession *n* the act of receding; a downturn in economic activity; an indentation.

recharge *vi* to renew the electric charge in (a battery, etc); to recover one's energies.

recherché *adj* uncommon, choice; refined, precious.

recidivism *n* inevitable relapse into crime.—**recidivist** *n.*

recipe *n* a list of ingredients and directions for preparing food; a method for achieving an end.

recipient *n* a person who receives.

reciprocal *adj* done by each to the other; mutual; complementary; interchangeable; (*gram*) expressing a mutual relationship. * *n* (*math*) an expression so related to another that their product is 1.—**reciprocally** *adv.*—**reciprocity** *n.*

reciprocate *vti* to give in return; to repay; (*mech*) to move alternately backwards and forwards.—**reciprocating** *adj.*—**reciprocation** *n.*

recital *n* the act of reciting; a detailed account, narrative; a statement of facts; (*mus*) a performance given by an individual musician.

recitation *n* the act of reciting; something recited, as a poem, etc.

recitative *n* a narrative part of an opera sung in the rhythms of ordinary speech.

recite *vti* to repeat aloud from memory, declaim; to recount, enumerate; to repeat (a lesson).

reckless *adj* rash, careless, incautious.—**recklessly** *adv.*—**recklessness** *n.*

reckon *vti* to count; to regard or consider; to think; to calculate; (*with* **with**) to take into account.

reckoning *n* a calculation; the settlement of an account.

reclaim *vt* to recover, win back from a wild state or vice; (*wasteland*) to convert into land fit for cultivation; (*plastics, etc*) to obtain from waste materials.—**reclaimable** *adj.*—**reclamation** *n.*

recline *vti* to cause or permit to lean or bend backwards; to lie down on the back or side.—**reclinable** *adj.*

recluse *n* a person who lives in solitude; a hermit.

recognition *n* the act of recognizing; identification; acknowledgment, admission; the sensing and encoding of printed and written data by a machine.

recognizance *n* (*law*) a bond by which a person undertakes before a court to observe some condition; the sum pledged as surety for this.

recognize *vt* to know again, identify; to greet; to acknowledge formally; to accept, admit.—**recognizable** *adj.*

recoil *vti* to spring back, kick, as a gun; to shrink or flinch. * *n* the act of recoiling, a rebound.

recollect *vti* to recall; to remind (oneself) of something temporarily forgotten; to call something to mind.

recollection *n* the act of recalling to mind; a memory, impression; something remembered; tranquillity of mind; religious contemplation.

recombinant DNA *n* molecules of DNA from different sources spliced together in the laboratory.

recombination *n* the combination of genetic material from different sources.

recommend *vt* to counsel or advise; to commend or praise; to introduce favourably.—**recommendable** *adj.*—**recommendation** *n.*

recompense *n* to reward or pay an equivalent; to compensate. * *n* reward; repayment; compensation.

reconcile *vt* to re-establish friendly relations; to bring to agreement; to make compatible; to resolve; to settle; to make resigned (to); (*financial account*) to check with another account for accuracy.—**reconcilable** *adj.*—**reconciliation** *n.*

recondite *adj* needing specialized training or knowledge; complex, obscure.

recondition *vt* to repair and restore to good working order.

reconnaissance *n* a survey of an area, esp for obtaining military information about an enemy.

reconnoitre, reconnoiter *vti* to make a reconnaisance (of).

reconsider *vt* to consider afresh, review; to modify.—**reconsideration** *n.*

reconstitute *vt* (*a dried or condensed substance*) to constitute again, esp to restore to its original form by adding water.—**reconstitution** *n.*

reconstruct *vt* to build again; to build up, as from remains, an image of the original; to supply missing parts by conjecture.—**reconstruction** *n.*

record *vt* to preserve evidence of; to write down; to chart; to register, enrol; to register permanently by mechanical means; (*sound or visual images*) to register on a disc, tape, etc for later reproduction; to celebrate; to make a recording. * *vi* to record something. * *adj* being the best, largest, etc. * *n* a written account; a register; a report of proceedings; the known facts about anything or anyone; an outstanding performance or achievement that surpasses others previously recorded; a grooved vinyl disc for playing on a record player; (*comput*) data in machine-readable form.

recorder *n* an official who keeps records; a machine or device that records; a tape recorder; a wind instrument of the flute family.

recording *n* what is recorded, as on a disc or tape; the record.

recordist *n* a person who records sound.

record player *n* an instrument for playing records through a loudspeaker.

recount[1] *vt* to narrate the details of; to narrate.

recount[2] *vt* to count again * *n* a second counting of election votes.

recoup *vti* to make good (financial losses); to regain; to make up for something lost.

recourse *n* a resort for help or protection when in danger; that to which one turns when seeking help.

re-cover *vt* to put a new cover on.

recover *vti* to regain after losing; to reclaim; to regain health or after losing emotional control.—**recoverable** *adj.*

recovery *n* (*pl* **recoveries**) the act or process of recovering; the condition of having recovered; reclamation; restoration; a retrieval of a capsule, etc after a space flight.

recovery room *n* a hospital room where patients are kept for close observation or care following surgery.
recreate *vt* to create over again, esp mentally.
recreation *n* relaxation of the body or mind; a sport, pastime or amusement.—**recreational** *adj*.
recreational vehicle *n* a vehicle for camping out such as a motor home, camper, etc.
recreation room *n* a room used for relaxation, recreation, or social activities, esp in a hospital, etc.
recriminate *vi* to return an accusation, make a counter-charge.—**recrimination** *n*.—**recriminatory** *adj*.
recrudesce *vi* (*esp disease*) to reappear again.—**recrudescence** *n*.
recruit *n* a soldier newly enlisted; a member newly joined; a beginner. * *vti* to enlist (military personnel); to enlist (new members) for an organization; to increase or maintain the numbers of; to restore, reinvigorate.—**recruitment** *n*.
rectal *adj* of, for, or near the rectum.
rectangle *n* a parallelogram with all its angles right angles.
rectangular *adj* having the shape of a rectangle; crossing, meeting, or lying at a right angle; having faces or surfaces shaped like right angles.
rectifier *n* a device that converts alternating current to direct current.
rectify *vt* (**rectifying, rectified**) to put right, correct; to amend; (*chem*) to refine by repeated distillation; (*elect*) to convert to direct current.—**rectifiable** *adj*.
rectilinear, rectilineal *adj* of or bounded by straight lines; straight.
rectitude *n* moral uprightness; probity; a being correct in judgment or procedure.
recto *n* (*pl* **rectos**) the right-hand page of an open book.
rector *n* in some churches, a clergyman in charge of a parish; the head of certain schools, colleges, etc.—**rectorial** *adj*.
rectory *n* (*pl* **rectories**) the house of a minister or priest.
rectrix *n* (*pl* **rectrices**) any of the tail feathers of a bird, used for controlling the direction of flight.
rectum *n* (*pl* **rectums, recta**) the part of the large intestine leading to the anus.
rectus *n* (*pl* **recti**) any of various straight muscles, esp of the abdomen.
recumbent *adj* leaning, resting; lying down.
recuperate *vti* to get well again; to recover (losses, etc).—**recuperation** *n*.
recur *vi* (**recurring, recurred**) to be repeated in thought, talk, etc; to occur again or at intervals.—**recurrence** *n*.—**recurrent** *adj*.
recycle *vti* (*a substance*) to pass through a process again; (*used matter*) to process to regain re-usable material; to save from loss and restore to usefulness.—**recyclable** *adj*.
red *adj* (**redder, reddest**) of the colour of blood; politically left-wing. * *n* the colour of blood; any red pigment; a communist.
redact *vt* to edit (a manuscript, etc) for publication.—**redaction** *n*.—**redactor** *n*.
red admiral *n* a common butterfly of Europe and North America with black and red markings.
redback *n* (*Austral*) a poisonous spider with red spots on its back.
red blood cell *n* any blood cell containing haemoglobin that conveys oxygen to the tissues.
red-blooded *adj* (*inf*) vigorous, virile.
redbreast *n* a robin.
redbrick *adj*, *n* (a British university) founded after 1945.
redcap *n* in US, a porter at a railway station or airport; in UK, a military policeman.
red card *n* (*soccer*) a red card held up by the referee indicating that a player is to be sent off.
red carpet *n* a strip of red carpet for dignitaries to walk on; a grand or impressive welcome or entertainment.
red cedar *n* (the reddish wood of) a North American juniper tree.
red cent *n* (*inf*) a trivial quantity of money.
red corpuscle *n* a red blood cell.
Red Crescent *n* the Red Cross in Muslim countries.
Red Cross *n* a red cross on a white ground, the symbol of the International Red Cross, a society for the relief of suffering in time of war and disaster.
red deer *n* a large deer with a reddish brown coat.
redden *vti* to make or become red; to blush.
reddish *adj* tinged with red.—**reddishness** *n*.
red dwarf *n* a star with a relatively small mass and low luminosity.
redeem *vt* to recover by payment; to regain; to deliver from sin; to pay off; to restore to favour; to make amends for.—**redeemable** *adj*.—**redeemer** *n*.
redemption *n* the act of redeeming or the state of being redeemed; recovery; repurchase; salvation.
redeploy *vt* (*troops, workers*) to assign to new positions or activities.—**redeployment** *n*.
redeye *n* (*sl*) cheap whiskey.
red flag *n* a symbol of communism or revolution; a sign of danger.
red fox *n* the common European fox with reddish fur.
red giant *n* a giant star with a relatively low surface temperature that emits a red glow.
red-handed *adj* caught in the act of committing a crime.
redhead *n* a person having red hair.—**redheaded** *adj*.
red herring *n* a herring cured to a dark brown colour; something that diverts attention from the real issue.
red-hot *adj* glowing with heat; extremely hot; very excited, angry, etc; very new.
redirect *vt* to change the direction or course of; to readdress.—**redirection** *n*.
red lead *n* a poisonous red oxide of lead used as a pigment.
red-letter *adj* of special significance.
red light *n* a warning signal, a cautionary sign; a deterrent.
red-light *adj* (*of a district*) containing brothels.
red mullet *n* a food fish of European waters, a goatfish.
redneck *n* (*derog*) a poor white farm labourer in the US South. * *adj* racist, reactionary.
redo *vt* (**redoing, redid,** *pp* **redone**) to do again; to redecorate.
red ochre *n* any of several types of reddish earth used as pigments.
redolent *adj* having a strong scent, fragrant; reminiscent (of).—**redolence** *n*.
redouble *vti* to double again; to make or become twice as much.
redoubt *n* a detached outpost of a fortification.
redoubtable *adj* formidable.
redound *vi* to have a directly positive or negative effect (on); to rebound (on or upon).
red pepper *n* a variety of pepper grown for its spicy red fruit, capsicum; its fruit; the fruit of the sweet pepper when ripe and red; cayenne pepper.
redress *vt* to put right, adjust; to compensate, make up for. * *n* remedy; compensation.
red salmon *n* any salmon with pinkish flesh, esp the sockeye.
redshank *n* a type of large European sandpiper.
red squirrel *n* a squirrel with reddish-brown fur of Europe, North America and Asia.
red tape *n* rigid adherence to bureaucratic routine and regulations, causing delay.
reduce *vt* to diminish or make smaller in size, amount, extent, or number; to lower in price; to simplify; to make thin; to subdue; to bring or convert (to another state or form).—**reducible** *adj*.
reductio ad absurdum *n* a proof of the falsity of a proposition by demonstrating the absurdity of its logical consequences.
reduction *n* the act or process of reducing or being reduced; something reduced; the amount by which a thing is reduced; (*math*) the conversion of a fraction into decimal form.—**reductional** *adj*.—**reductive** *adj*.
redundant *adj* surplus to requirements; (*Brit person*) deprived of one's job as being no longer necessary; excessive, wordy; (*words*) unnecessary to the meaning.—**redundancy** *n*.
reduplicate *vt* to make double, to repeat; (*gram*) to repeat (syllable or letter), to form (word) thus. * *adj* doubled, repeated.—**reduplication** *n*.—**reduplicative** *adj*.

red wine *n* wine made from black grapes with the skins left on.
redwood *n* an important timber tree of California that can reach a height of 360 feet; any of various trees yielding a red dye or reddish wood.
reed *n* a tall grass found in marshes; a thin piece of cane in the mouthpiece of a musical instrument; a person or thing too weak to rely on; one easily swayed or overcome.
reedbird *see* **bobolink.**
re-educate, reeducate *vt* to educate again in order to adapt to changing circumstances.—**re-education, reeducation** *n.*
reedy *adj* (**reedier, reediest**) filled with reeds; resembling a reed; shrill, piping, as in the sound of a reed.—**reedily** *adv.*—**reediness** *n.*
reef *n* a ridge of rocks, sand, or coral at or just below the surface of water; a hazardous obstruction; a lode or vein of ore.
reefer *n* a thick double-breasted jacket, formerly worn by sailors; (*inf*) a cigarette containing cannabis.
reef knot *n* a symmetrical double knot.
reek *n* a strong smell. * *vi* to give off smoke, fumes or a strong or offensive smell.
reel[1] *n* a winding device; a spool or bobbin; thread wound on this; a length of film, about 300 m (1,000 ft). * *vt* to wind on to a reel; (*with* **in**) to draw in by means of a reel; (*with* **off**) to tell, write, etc with fluency; (*with* **out**) to unwind from a reel.
reel[2] *vi* to stagger or sway about; to be dizzy or in a whirl. * *n* a staggering motion.
reel[3] *n* a lively Scottish or Irish dance; the music for it. * *vi* to dance a reel.
re-enter *vti* to enter again.
re-entry *n* (*pl* **re-entries**) the act of entering or possessing again; the return of a spacecraft to the earth's atmosphere.
ref *n* (*inf*) a referee.
ref. *abbr* = with reference to.
refectory *n* (*pl* **refectories**) the dining hall of a monastery, college, etc.
refer *vti* (**referring, referred**) to attribute, assign (to); (*with* **to**) to direct, have recourse (to); to relate to; to mention or allude to; to direct attention (to).—**referable** *adj.*
referee *n* an adjudicator, arbitrator; an umpire; a judge.
reference *n* the act of referring; a mention or allusion; a testimonial; a person who gives a testimonial; a direction to a passage in a book; a passage in a book referred to.
reference book *n* a book for reference rather than general reading, eg a yearbook, directory.
reference library *n* a library whose books may be consulted but not borrowed.
referendum *n* (*pl* **referendums, referenda**) the submission of an issue directly to the vote of the electorate, a plebiscite.
referral *n* the act of referring or instance of being referred.
refill *vt* to fill again. * *n* a replacement pack for an empty permanent container; a providing again.
refine *vti* to purify; to make free from impurities or coarseness; to make or become cultured.
refined *adj* polished, cultured; affected.
refinement *n* fineness of manners or taste; an improvement; a fine distinction.
refinery *n* (*pl* **refineries**) a plant where raw materials, eg sugar, oil, are refined.
refit *vti* (**refitting, refitted**) to make or become functional again by repairing, re-equipping, etc.—*also n.*
reflation *n* the restoration of deflated prices to a desirable level.—**reflationary** *adj.*
reflect *vt* (*light, heat, etc*) to throw back; to bend aside or back; to show an image of, as a mirror; to express. * *vi* to reproduce to the eye or mind; to mirror; to meditate; (*with* **upon**) to ponder; (*with* **on**) to discredit, disparage.
reflected *adj* thrown or cast back; mirrored; bent or folded back.
reflecting telescope *n* a telescope operated by a series of mirrors.
reflection *n* a reflecting back, turning aside; the action of changing direction when a ray strikes and is thrown back; reflected heat, light or colour; a reflected image; meditation, thought; reconsideration; reproach.—*also* **reflexion.**
reflective *adj* meditative; concerned with ideas.—**reflectively** *adv.*—**reflectiveness** *n.*
reflector *n* a disc, instrument, strip or other surface that reflects light or heat.
reflex *n* an involuntary response to a stimulus. * *adj* (*angle*) of more than 180 degrees; (*camera*) with a full-size viewfinder using the main lens.
reflex camera *n* a camera in which the image from the lens is conveyed by an angled mirror to a viewfinder for composition and focusing.
reflexion *see* **reflection.**
reflexive *adj* (*pron, verb*) referring back to the subject.—**reflexively** *adv.*
reflexology *n* (*alternative medicine*) a technique of applying pressure to specific points on the hands and feet to stimulate the blood supply to other areas of the body and help relieve stress.—**reflexologist** *n.*
reform *vti* to improve; to make or become better by the removal of faults; to amend; to abolish abuse. * *n* improvement or transformation, esp of an institution; removal of social ills.—**reformed** *adj.*
re-form *vti* to form again.
reformation *n* the act of reforming or the state of being reformed; improvement; (*with cap*) the 16th-century religious revolt that resulted in the formation of Protestant churches.
reformatory *adj* reforming; * *n* (*pl* **reformatories**) an institution for reforming young criminals; a prison for women.
reformer *n* a person who advocates or works for reform; an apparatus for changing the molecular structure of a hydrocarbon to form specialized products.
reform school *n* a reformatory for young people.
refract *vt* to cause (a ray of light, etc) to undergo refraction.
refracting telescope *n* a type of telescope in which the image is formed by a series of lenses.
refraction *n* the bending of a ray or wave of light, heat, or sound as it passes from one medium into another.
refractory *adj* obstinate; (*disease, etc*) resistant to treatment; (*muscle*) unresponsive to stimuli; able to withstand high temperatures. * *n* (*pl* **refractories**) a heat-resistant material.
refrain[1] *vi* to abstain (from).
refrain[2] *n* recurring words in a song or poem, esp at the end of a stanza; a chorus.
refrangible *adj* able to be refracted.
refresh *vt* to revive; to give new energy to; to make cool; to take a drink.
refresher *n* something that refreshes, esp a drink; a reminder; a training course to renew one's skill or knowledge.
refresher course *n* a course designed to keep professionals informed of recent developments in their field of knowledge or expertise.
refreshing *adj* invigorating, reviving; pleasing because unsophisticated.
refreshment *n* the act of refreshing; a restorative; (*pl*) food and drink; a light meal.
refrigerate *vti* to make, become, or keep, cold; to preserve by keeping cold.—**refrigeration** *n.*
refrigerator *n* something that refrigerates; a chamber for keeping food, etc, cool; an apparatus for cooling.—*also* **fridge, icebox.**
refuel *vti* (**refuelling, refuelled** *or* **refueling, refueled**) to supply with or take on fresh fuel.
refuge *n* a protection or shelter from danger; a retreat, sanctuary.
refugee *n* a person who flees to another country to escape political or religious persecution.
refund *vti* to repay; to reimburse. * *n* a refunding or the amount refunded.
refurbish *vt* to renovate or re-equip.—**refurbishment** *n.*
refusal *n* the act or process of refusing; the choice of refusing or accepting.
refuse[1] *n* garbage, waste, rubbish.
refuse[2] *vt* to decline, reject; to withhold, deny. * *vi* (*horse*) to decline to jump.

refute *vt* to rebut; to disprove.—**refutable** *adj*.—**refutably** *adv*.—**refutation** *n*.
regain *vt* to get back, recover; to reach again.
regal *adj* royal; relating to a king or queen.
regale *vt* to entertain, as with a feast; to delight.
regalia *npl* royal insignia or prerogatives; the insignia of an order, office, or membership; finery.
regard *vt* to gaze at, observe; to hold in respect; to consider; to heed, take into account. * *n* a look; attention; reference; respect, esteem; (*pl*) good wishes, greetings.
regarding *prep* with reference to, about.
regardless *adj* having no regard to. * *adv* (*inf*) in spite of everything; without heeding the cost, consequences, etc.
regatta *n* a meeting for yacht or boat races.
regency *n* (*pl* **regencies**) the status or authority of a regent; a regent's period of office; a body entrusted with the duties of a regent; rule; (*with cap*) in British history, the period 1810–20.
regenerate *vti* to renew, give new life to; to be reborn spiritually; to reorganize; to produce anew.—**regeneration** *n*.
regent *n* a person who rules or administers a country during the sovereign's minority, absence, or incapacity; a member of a governing board (as of a university).
reggae *n* a strongly accented West Indian musical form with four beats to the bar.
regicide *n* the killer or the killing or a king.
regime, régime *n* a political or ruling system.
regimen *n* a system of diet, exercise, etc, for improving the health; a regular course of training.
regiment *n* a military unit, smaller than a division, consisting usu of a number of battalions. * *vt* to organize in a strict manner; to subject to order or conformity.—**regimental** *adj*.
regimentation *n* the act of regimenting; excessive orderliness.
Regina *n* a reigning queen.
region *n* a large, indefinite part of the earth's surface; one of the zones into which the atmosphere is divided; an administrative area of a country; a part of the body.—**regional** *adj*.
register *n* an official list; a written record, as for attendance; the book containing such a record or list; a tone of voice; a variety of language appropriate to a subject or occasion; (*comput*) a device in which data can be stored and operated on; (*print*) exact alignment; a device for indicating speed, etc; a plate regulating draught. * *vti* to record; to enter in or sign a register; to correspond exactly; to entrust a letter to the post with special precautions for safety; to express emotion facially; to make or convey an impression.
registered *adj* recorded officially; qualified formally or officially.
registrar *n* a person who keeps records, esp one in an educational institution in charge of student records; a hospital doctor below a specialist in rank.
registration *n* the act of registering; the condition of having registered.
registry *n* (*pl* **registries**) registration; a place where records are kept; an official record book.
regius professor *n* in UK, a person appointed to a university chair founded by the Crown.
regnal *adj* pertaining to a sovereign or reign, esp designating a year of a reign calculated from the date of accession.
regress *vi* to move backwards; to revert to a former condition.—**regressive** *adj*.—**regressively** *adv*.
regression *n* the act of regressing; a relapse, reversion; a return to an earlier time or stage; (*psychoanal*) a retreat of the personality.
regret *vt* (**regretting, regretted**) to feel sorrow, grief, or loss; to remember with longing; (*with* **that**) to repent of. * *n* disappointment; sorrow; grief; (*pl*) polite refusal.—**regretful** *adj*.—**regretfully** *adv*.
regrettable *adj* to be regretted; deserving reproof.—**regrettably** *adv*.
regroup *vti* to group again; (*mil*) to reorganize (troops, etc) following action.
regular *adj* normal; habitual, not casual; at fixed intervals; according to rule, custom, or the accepted practice; uniform, consistent; symmetrical; fully qualified; belonging to a standing army; (*inf*) thorough, complete; (*inf*) pleasant, friendly. * *n* a professional soldier; (*inf*) a person who attends regularly.—**regularity** *n*.—**regularly** *adv*.
regular army *n* a permanent army; (*with caps*) the United States army.
regularize *vt* to make regular or correct.—**regularization** *n*.
regulate *vt* to control according to a rule; to cause to conform to a standard or needs; to adjust so as to put in good order.—**regulatory** *adj*.
regulation *n* the act of regulating or state of being regulated; a prescribed rule, ordinance. * *adj* normal, standard.
regulator *n* one who or that which regulates; a regulating device; a lever in a watch that adjusts its speed.
regurgitate *vti* to pour back, cast up again, esp from the stomach to the mouth.—**regurgitation** *n*.
rehabilitate *vt* (*prisoner etc*) to help adapt to society after a stay in an institution; to put back in good condition; to restore to rights or privileges; (*sick person etc*) to help to adjust to normal conditions after illness.—**rehabilitation** *n*.
rehash *n* old materials put in a new form. * *vt* to dish up again.
rehearse *vti* to practise repeatedly before public performance; to recount, narrate in detail.—**rehearsal** *n*.
rehoboam *n* a wine bottle that holds six times the amount of a standard bottle.
reify *vt* (**reifying, reified**) to make (something abstract) real or concrete.
reign *n* the rule of a sovereign; the period of this; influence; domination. * *vi* to rule; to prevail.
reimburse *vt* to repay; to refund (for expense or loss).—**reimbursable** *adj*.—**reimbursement** *n*.
rein *n* the strap of a bridle for guiding or restraining a horse; (*pl*) a means of control or restraint. * *vt* to control with the rein; to restrain.
reincarnation *n* the incarnation of the soul after death in another body.—**reincarnate** *adj*, *vt*.
reindeer *n* a large deer with branched antlers found in northern regions.
reindeer moss *n* a lichen of northern regions that provides food for reindeer.
reinforce *vt* (*army etc*) to strengthen with fresh troops; (*a material*) to add to the strength of.
reinforced concrete *n* concrete with metal bars, wire, etc inserted in it for strength.
reinforcement *n* the act of reinforcing; additional support; (*pl*) additional troops.
reinstate *vt* to restore to a former position, rank, or condition.—**reinstatement** *n*.
reinterpret *vt* to interpret again; to give a new explanation of.—**reinterpretation** *n*.
reissue *vt* to issue again; to republish. * *n* a new issue; a reprint.
reiterate *vt* to repeat; to say or do again or many times.—**reiteration** *n*.
reject *vt* to throw away, to discard; to refuse to accept, to decline; to rebuff. * *n* a thing or person rejected.—**rejection** *n*.
rejoice *vi* to feel joyful or happy.
rejoin *vt* to join again; to return to.
rejoinder *n* a retort, a reply.
rejuvenate *vt* to give youthful vigour to.—**rejuvenation** *n*.
relapse *vi* to fall back into a worse state after improvement; to return to a former vice, to backslide. * *n* the recurrence of illness after apparent recovery.
relate *vt* to narrate, recount; to show a connection (between two or more things). * *vi* to have a formal relationship (with).
related *adj* connected, allied; akin.
relation *n* the way in which one thing stands in respect to another, footing; reference, regard; connection by blood or marriage; a relative; a narration, a narrative; (*pl*) the connections between or among persons, nations, etc; (*pl*) one's family and in-laws.
relationship *n* the tie or degree of kinship or intimacy; affinity; (*inf*) an affair.

relative *adj* having or expressing a relation; corresponding; pertinent; comparative, conditional; respective; meaningful only in relationship; (*gram*) referring to an antecedent. * *n* a person related by blood or marriage.—**relatively** *adv*.

relative molecular mass *n* the total of the atomic weights of all the atoms present in a molecule; the average mass per molecule of any substance relative to one-twelfth the mass of an atom of carbon-12.—*also* **molecular weight**.

relative pronoun *n* a pronoun that is used to connect a dependent clause to a main clause and that refers to a noun in the main clause.

relativity *n* the state of being relative; the relation between one thing and another; (*physics*) the theory of the relative, rather than absolute, character of motion, velocity, mass, etc, and the interdependence of time, matter, and space.

relax *vti* to slacken; to make or become less severe or strict; to make (the muscles) less rigid; to take a rest.

relaxant *n* a drug that relieves muscular tension.

relaxation *n* the act of relaxing; the condition of being relaxed; recreation.

relay *n* a team of fresh horses, men, etc to relieve others; a race between teams, each member of which goes a part of the distance; (*elect*) a device for enabling a weak current to control others; a relayed broadcast. * *vt* (**relaying, relayed**) (*news, etc*) to spread in stages; to broadcast signals.

relay race *n* a race between teams in which each member does part of the distance.

release *vt* to set free; to let go; to relinquish; (*film, etc*) to issue for public exhibition; (*information*) to make available; (*law*) to make over to another. * *n* a releasing, as from prison, work, etc; a device to hold or release a mechanism; a news item, etc, released to the public; (*law*) a written surrender of a claim.

relegate *vt* to move to an inferior position; to demote; to banish.—**relegation** *n*.

relent *vi* to soften in attitude; to become less harsh or severe.

relentless *adj* pitiless; unremitting.

relevant *adj* applying to the matter in hand, pertinent; to the point.—**relevance, relevancy** *n*.

reliable *adj* dependable, trustworthy.—**reliability** *n*.—**reliably** *adv*.

reliance *n* trust; dependence; a thing relied on.—**reliant** *adj*.

relic *n* an object, fragment, or custom that has survived from the past; part of a saint's body or belongings; (*pl*) remains of the dead.

relief *n* the sensation following the easing or lifting of discomfort or stress; release from a duty by another person; a person who takes the place of another on duty; that which relieves; aid; assistance to the needy or victims of a disaster; the projection of a carved design from its ground; distinctness, vividness. * *adj* providing relief in disasters etc.

relief map *n* a map in which topographic relief is represented by shading, colours, etc.

relieve *vt* to bring relief or assistance to; to release from obligation or duty; to ease; (*with* **oneself**) to empty the bladder or bowels. * *vi* to give relief; to break the monotony of; to bring into relief, to stand out.

relieved *adj* having or showing relief, esp from anxiety or repressed emotions.

religion *n* a belief in God or gods; a system of worship and faith; a formalized expression of belief.

religiosity *n* the condition of being religious, esp excessively or sentimentally so.—**religiose** *adj*.

religious *adj* of or conforming to religion; devout, pious; scrupulously and conscientiously faithful.—**religiously** *adv*.

relinquish *vt* to give up; to renounce or surrender.—**relinquishment** *n*.

reliquary *n* (*pl* **reliquaries**) a container or shrine for sacred relics.

relish *n* an appetizing flavour; a distinctive taste; enjoyment of food or an experience; a spicy accompaniment to food; gusto, zest. * *vt* to like the flavour of; to enjoy, appreciate.

relocate *vti* to set up in a new place; to place (an employee) in a different job; (*business*) to move to a new location.—**relocation** *n*.

reluctant *adj* unwilling, loath; offering resistance.—**reluctance** *n*.—**reluctantly** *adv*.

rely *vi* (**relying, relied**) to depend on; to trust.

REM *abbr* = rapid eye movement.

remain *vi* to stay behind or in the same place; to continue to be; to survive, to last; to be left over. * *npl* anything left after use; a corpse.

remainder *n* what is left, the rest; (*math*) the result of subtraction; the quantity left over after division; unsold stock, esp of books; (*law*) the residual interest in an estate.

remake *vt* (**remaking, remade**) to make again. * *n* a new version of an old film.

remand *vt* to send back into custody for further evidence.—*also n*.

remark *vti* to notice; to observe; to pass a comment (upon). * *n* a brief comment.

remarkable *adj* unusual; extraordinary; worthy of comment.—**remarkably** *adv*.

remaster *vt* to make a new (digital) master recording from an original (analogue) .ecording to provide improved sound quality on vinyl records or compact discs.

remedial *adj* providing a remedy; corrective; relating to the teaching of people with learning difficulties.

remedy *n* a medicine or any means to cure a disease; anything that puts something else to rights. * *vt* (**remedying, remedied**) to cure; to put right.

remember *vti* to recall; to bear in mind; to mention (a person) to another as sending regards; to exercise or have the power of memory.

remembrance *n* a reminiscence; a greeting or gift recalling or expressing friendship or affection; the extent of memory; an honouring of the dead or a past event.

Remembrance Day *n* in Canada, a day, November 11, on which the dead of the two World Wars are commemorated.

Remembrance Sunday *n* in UK, the Sunday nearest November 11, on which the dead of the two World Wars are commemorated.

remind *vt* to cause to remember.

reminder *n* a thing that reminds, esp a letter from a creditor.

reminisce *vi* to think, talk, or write about past events.

reminiscence *n* the recalling of a past experience; (*pl*) memoirs.

reminiscent *adj* reminding, suggestive (of); recalling the past.

remiss *adj* negligent, slack.

remission *n* the act of remitting; the reduction in length of a prison term; the lessening of the symptoms of a disease; pardon, forgiveness.

remit *vti* (**remitting, remitted**) to forgive; to refrain from inflicting (a punishment) or exacting (a debt); to abate, moderate; to send payment (by post); (*law*) to refer to a lower court for reconsideration. * *n* the act of referring; an area of authority.

remittance *n* the sending of money or a payment (by post); the payment or money sent.

remix *vt* to adjust the balance and separation of a recording.—*also n*.

remnant *n* a small remaining fragment or number; an oddment or scrap; a trace; an unsold or unused end of piece goods.

remodel *vt* (**remodelling, remodelled** *or* **remodeling, remodeled**) to fashion afresh; to recast.

remonstrate *vi* to protest, to make a complaint (against).—**remonstrance** *n*.

remorse *n* regret and guilt for a misdemeanour; compassion.—**remorseful** *adj*.—**remorsefully** *adv*.

remorseless *adj* ruthless, cruel; relentless.—**remorselessly** *adv*.—**remorselessness** *n*.

remote *adj* far apart or distant in time or place; out of the way; not closely related; secluded; aloof; vague, faint.—**remotely** *adv*.

remote control *n* the control of a device or activity from a distance, usu by means of an electric circuit or the making or breaking of radio waves.

removal *n* the act of removing; a change of home or office; dismissal.

remove *vti* to take away and put elsewhere; to dismiss, as from office; to get rid of; to kill; to go away. * *n* a stage in gradation; a degree in relationship.—**removable** *adj*.

removed *adj* remote; separated by a specified degree, as of relationship; of a younger or older relationship.

remunerate *vt* to pay for a service; to reward.—**remuneration** *n*.
renaissance *n* a rebirth or revival; (*with cap*) the revival of European art and literature under the influence of classical study during the 14th–16th centuries.—*also adj*.
renal *adj* relating to or near the kidneys.
renascent *adj* becoming active again, reviving.
rend *vti* (**rending, rent**) to tear, to wrench (apart); to be torn apart.
render *vt* (*payments, accounts, etc*) to submit, as for approval; to give back; to pay back; to perform; to represent as by drawing; to translate, interpret; to cause to be; (*fat*) to melt down.
rendering *n* interpretation, translation.
rendezvous *n* (*pl* **rendezvous**) an arranged meeting; a place to meet; a popular haunt; the process of bringing two spacecraft together. * *vi* to meet by appointment.
rendition *n* an interpretation; performance.
renegade *n* a deserter; a person who is faithless to a principle, party, religion, or cause.
renege *vti* to go back on, or fail to keep, a promise or agreement.
renegotiate *vti* to negotiate again, esp to improve the terms of a contract.—**renegotiable** *adj*.—**renegotiation** *n*.
renew *vti* to restore to freshness or vigour; to begin again; to make or get anew; to replace; to grant or obtain an extension of.—**renewable** *adj*.—**renewal** *n*.
rennet *n* an extract from the stomach of calves, etc, used to curdle milk.
renounce *vt* to abandon formally; to give up; to disown.
renovate *vt* to renew; to restore to good condition; to do up, repair.—**renovation** *n*.—**renovator** *n*.
renown *n* fame, celebrity.
renowned *adj* famous, illustrious.
rent[1] *see* **rend**.
rent[2] *n* regular payment to another for the use of a house, machinery, etc. * *vti* to occupy as a tenant; to hire; to let for rent.
rental *n* an amount paid or received as rent; a house, car, etc, for rent; an act of renting; a business that rents something.
rent boy *n* a young male prostitute.
renunciation *n* the act of renouncing; formal abandonment; repudiation.
reopen *vti* to open again; to resume.
reorganize *vti* to organize again; to bring about a reorganization.—**reorganization** *n*.
Rep. *abbr* = Representative; Republic; Republican.
rep *abbr* = repeat; report; reporter.
repair *vt* to mend; to restore to good working order; to make amends for. * *n* the act of repairing; a place repaired; condition as to soundness.
reparable *adj* capable of being repaired.
reparation *n* amends; (*pl*) compensation, as for war damage.
repartee *n* a witty reply; skill in making such replies.
repast *n* a meal.
repatriate *vt* to send back or restore to one's country of origin or citizenship.—**repatriation** *n*.
repay *vt* (**repaying, repaid**) to pay back; to refund.—**repayable** *adj*.—**repayment** *n*.
repeal *vt* to annul, to rescind; to revoke.—*also n*.
repeat *vti* to say, write, or do again; to reiterate; to recite after another or from memory; to reproduce; to recur. * *n* a repetition, encore; anything said or done again, as a re-broadcast of a television programme; (*mus*) a passage to be repeated; the sign for this.—**repeatable** *adj*.
repeated *adj* frequent; done, seen, etc, again.
repeatedly *adv* many times, over and over again.
repeater *n* a clock or watch with a striking mechanism; a device for receiving and amplifying electronic communication signals; a firearm that has a repeating mechanism for reloading; a habitual violator of the laws.
repeating firearm *n* a firearm designed to load cartridges from a magazine.
repel *vt* (**repelling, repelled**) to drive back; to beat off, repulse; to reject; to hold off; to cause distaste; (*water, dirt*) to be resistant to.
repellent *adj* distasteful, unattractive; capable of repelling; impermeable. * *n* a substance that repels, esp a spray for protection against insects.
repent *vi* to wish one had not done something; to feel remorse or regret (for); to regret and change from evil ways.—**repentant** *adj*.
repentance *n* penitence; contrition.
repercussion *n* a rebound; a reverberation; a far-reaching, often indirect reaction to an event.
repertoire *n* the stock of plays, songs, etc, that a company, singer, etc, can perform.
repertory *n* (*pl* **repertories**) a repertoire; the system of alternating several plays through a season with a permanent acting group.
repetition *n* the act of repeating; something repeated, a copy.—**repetitive** *adj*.
repetitious *adj* full of repetition; boring.—**repetitiously** *adv*.—**repetitiousness** *n*.
rephrase *vt* to phrase (a statement) in a different way.
replace *vt* to put back; to take the place of, to substitute for; to supersede.—**replaceable** *adj*.
replacement *n* the act or process of replacing; a person or thing that replaces another.
replenish *vt* to stock again, refill.—**replenishment** *n*.
replete *adj* filled, well provided; stuffed, gorged.
repletion *n* complete fullness; satisfaction.
replica *n* an exact copy; a reproduction.
reply *vti* (**replying, replied**) to answer, respond; to give as an answer. * *n* an answer.
repo-man *n* (*pl* **repo-men**) (*sl*) a person who repossesses (eg a motor car).
report *vti* to give an account of; to tell as news; to take down and describe for publication; to make a formal statement of; to complain about or against; to inform against; to present oneself (for duty). * *n* an account of facts; the formal statement of the findings of an investigation; a newspaper, radio or television account of an event; a rumour; a sharp, loud noise, as of a gun.
reportage *n* the art of reporting on current events; an accurate, observant and well-written account of an event.
report card *n* a report on a pupil or student that is periodically given to his or her parent; an evaluation of performance.
reportedly *adv* as reported, not directly.
reporter *n* a person who gathers and reports news for a newspaper, radio or television; a person authorized to make statements concerning law decisions or legislative proceedings.
repose *n* rest, sleep; stillness, peace; composure, serenity. * *vti* to lie down or lay at rest; to place (trust, etc) in someone; to rest; to lie dead.
reposition *vt* to place in a different or new position.
repository *n* (*pl* **repositories**) a receptacle; a storehouse, warehouse; a confidant.
repossess *vt* to possess again; to restore possession of (property), esp for nonpayment of debt.—**repossession** *n*.
reprehend *vt* to rebuke, to find fault with, to criticize.
reprehensible *adj* blameworthy, culpable.
reprehension *n* blame, censure.
re-present *vt* to present again.
represent *vt* to portray; to describe; to typify; to stand for, symbolize; to point out; to perform on the stage; to act as an agent for; to deputize for; to serve as a specimen, example, etc, of.—**representable** *adj*.
representation *n* the act of representing or being represented, as in a parliamentary assembly; a portrait, reproduction; (*pl*) a presentation of claims, protests, views, etc.
representative *adj* typical; portraying; consisting of or based on representation of the electorate by delegates. * *n* an example or type; a person who acts for another; a delegate, agent, salesman, etc.
repress *vt* to suppress, restrain; (*emotions*) to keep under control; to exclude involuntarily from the conscious mind.—**repressive** *adj*.—**represser, repressor** *n*.

repression *n* the act of repressing; the condition of being repressed; domination, tyranny.

reprieve *vt* to postpone or commute the punishment of; to give respite to.—*also n.*

reprimand *n* a formal rebuke. * *vt* to reprove formally.

reprint *vt* to print again. * *n* a book or article that has appeared in print before.

reprisal *n* an act of retaliation for an injury done.

reprise *n* (*mus*) the repetition of an earlier theme or passage.—*also vt.*

reproach *vt* to accuse of a fault; to blame. * *n* a reproof; a source of shame or disgrace.—**reproachful** *adj*.

reprobate *n* a depraved person; a hardened sinner; a scoundrel.

reproduce *vti* to make a copy, duplicate, or likeness of; to propagate; to produce offspring; to multiply.

reproduction *n* the act of reproducing; the process by which plants and animals breed; a copy or likeness; a representation.—**reproductive** *adj*.

reprography *n* the process of reproducing printed material, as by photocopying.—**reprographic** *adj*.

reproof *n* a rebuke, blame.

reprove *vt* to rebuke, censure.—**reprovingly** *adv*.

reptile *n* any of a class of cold-blooded, air-breathing vertebrates with horny scales or plates, as turtles, crocodiles, snakes, lizards, etc; a grovelling or despised person.—**reptilian** *adj*.

Repub *abbr* = Republican.

republic *n* a government in which the people elect the head of state, usu called president, and in which the people and their elected representatives have supreme power; a country governed in this way; a body of persons freely engaged in a specified activity.

republican *adj* of, characteristic of, or supporting a republic. * *n* an advocate of republican government; (*with cap*) a member of the US Republican party.—**republicanism** *n*.

republish *vt* to publish again; to issue a new edition of (a book).—**republication** *n*.

repudiate *vt* to reject, disown; to refuse to acknowledge or pay; to deny; (a treaty, etc) to disavow.—**repudiation** *n*.

repugnant *adj* distasteful, offensive; contradictory; incompatible.—**repugnance** *n*.

repulse *vt* to drive back; to repel; to reject. * *n* a rebuff, rejection; a defeat, check.

repulsion *n* a feeling of disgust; aversion; (*physics*) the tendency of bodies to repel each other.

repulsive *adj* disgusting; loathsome; exercising repulsion.—**repulsively** *adv*.

reputable *adj* of good repute, respectable.—**reputably** *adv*.

reputation *n* the estimation in which a person or thing is held; good name, honour.

repute *vt* to consider to be, to deem. * *n* reputation.

reputed *adj* generally reported; supposed, putative.

reputedly *adv* in common estimation; by repute.

request *n* an asking for something; a petition; a demand; the thing asked for. * *vt* to ask for earnestly.

request stop *n* a place where a bus, etc stops only if signalled to do so.—*also* **flag stop**.

requiem *n* a mass for the dead; music for this.

require *vt* to demand; to need, call for; to order, command.

requirement *n* a need or want; an essential condition.

requisite *adj* needed; essential, indispensable. * *n* something required or indispensable.

requisition *n* a formal request, demand, or order, as for military supplies; the taking over of private property, etc, for military use. * *vt* to order; to take by requisition.

reredos *n* a screen or partition separating the altar from the choir.

rerun *vt* to run (a race, etc) again; to show a television programme, film, etc again.—*also n.*

resale *n* the selling again (of something) usu to a new buyer; a repeat sale to a customer; a second-hand sale.

reschedule *vt* (*debt*) to postpone or extend repayment terms.

rescind *vt* to annul, cancel.

rescue *vt* to save (a person, thing) from captivity, danger, or harm; to free forcibly from legal custody.—*also n.*—**rescuer** *n*.

research *n* a diligent search; a systematic and careful investigation of a particular subject; a scientific study. * *vi* to carry out an investigation; to study.—**researcher** *n*.

resemble *vt* to be like, to have a similarity to.—**resemblance** *n*.

resent *vt* to be indignant about; to begrudge; to take badly.—**resentful** *adj*.—**resentfully** *adv*.—**resentment** *n*.

reserpine *n* an alkaloid extracted from the roots of a rauwolfia, used to treat high blood pressure and as a sedative.

reservation *n* the act of reserving; (*of tickets, accommodation, etc*) a holding until called for; a limitation or proviso; (*pl*) doubt, scepticism; land set aside for a special purpose.

reserve *vt* to hold back for future use; to retain; to have set aside; (*tickets, hotel room, etc*) to book. * *n* something put aside for future use; land set aside for wild animals; (*sport*) a substitute; (*mil*) a force supplementary to a regular army; a restriction or qualification; reticence of feelings; caution.

reserved *adj* set apart, booked; uncommunicative, lacking cordiality.—**reservedly** *adv*.

reservist *n* a member of a military reserve force.

reservoir *n* a tank or artificial lake for storing water; an extra supply or store.

reset[1] *vt* (**resetting, reset**) to set (a bone, gem, type) over again; to place in a new setting; to change the reading of.

reset[2] *vt* (**resetting, reset**) (*Scots law*) to receive (stolen goods).—*also n.*

reshape *vti* to shape anew.

reside *vi* to live in a place permanently; to be vested or present in.

residence *n* the act of living in a place; the period of residing; the house where one lives permanently; the status of a legal resident; a building used as a home.

residency *n* (*pl* **residencies**) a usu official place of residence, eg of a governor; a period of advanced training in medicine.

resident *adj* residing; domiciled; living at one's place of work. * *n* a permanent inhabitant; a doctor who is serving a residency.

residential *adj* of or relating to residence; used for private homes.

residual *adj* left over; remaining as a residue.

residuary *adj* of or relating to the residue of an estate.

residue *n* a remainder; a part left over; what is left of an estate after payment of debts and legacies.

resign *vti* to give up (employment, etc); to relinquish; to yield to; to reconcile (oneself).

resignation *n* the resigning of office, etc; the written proof of this; patient endurance.

resigned *adj* submissive, acquiescent; accepting the inevitable.

resilience, resiliency *n* the quality of being resilient; physical or mental stamina.

resilient *adj* elastic, springing back; buoyant; (*person*) capable of carrying on after suffering hardship.

resin *n* a sticky substance exuded in the sap of trees and plants and used in medicines, varnishes, etc; rosin; a similar synthetic substance used in plastics.—**resinous** *adj*.

resist *vti* to fight against; to be proof against; to oppose or withstand.

resistance *n* the act of resisting; the power to resist, as to ward off disease; opposition, esp to an occupying force; hindrance; (*elect*) non-conductivity, opposition to a steady current.

resistant *adj* capable of resisting; (*with* **to**) immune to.

resistor *n* an electrical device that resists current in a circuit.

resolute *adj* determined; firm of purpose, steadfast.—**resolutely** *adv*.—**resoluteness** *n*.

resolution *n* the act of resolving or the state of being resolved; determination; a fixed intention; the formal decision or opinion of a meeting; analysis, disintegration; (*med*) the dispersion of a tumour, etc; the picture definition in a TV; (*mus*) the relieving of a discord by a following concord; (*physics*) the process or capability of making distinguishable closely adjacent optical images or sources of light.

resolve *vt* to break into component parts, dissolve; to convert or be converted (into); to analyse; to determine, make up one's mind; to solve, settle; to vote by resolution; to dispel (doubt); to explain; to conclude; (*med: tumour*) to disperse; (*mus: discord*) to convert into concord. * *n* a fixed intention; resolution; courage.

resolving power *n* the ability of a microscope or telescope to produce distinct images of objects in close proximity.

resonance *n* resounding quality; vibration.

resonant *adj* ringing; resounding, echoing.

resonator *n* a device that produces or increases sound by resonance.

resort *n* a popular holiday location; a source of help, support, etc; recourse. * *vi* to have recourse to; to turn (to) for help, etc.

resound *vti* to echo; to reverberate; to go on sounding; to be much talked of; to spread (fame).

resounding *adj* echoing; notable; thorough.

resource *n* source of help; an expedient; the ability to cope with a situation; a means of diversion; (*pl*) wealth; assets; raw materials.

resourceful *adj* able to cope in difficult situations; ingenious.—**resourcefulness** *n*.

respect *n* esteem; consideration; regard; (*pl*) good wishes; reference; relation. * *vt* to feel or show esteem or regard to; to treat considerately.

respectable *adj* worthy of esteem; well-behaved; proper, correct, well-conducted; of moderate quality or size.—**respectability** *n*.—**respectably** *adv*.

respectful *adj* deferential.—**respectfully** *adv*.

respecting *prep* concerning.

respective *adj* proper to each, several.

respectively *adv* in the indicated order.

respiration *n* the act or process of breathing.

respirator *n* an apparatus to maintain breathing by artificial means; a device or mask to prevent the inhalation of harmful substances.

respiratory *adj* of or for respiration.

respire *vti* to breathe.

respite *n* a temporary delay; a period of rest or relief; a reprieve.

resplendent *adj* dazzling, shining brilliantly; magnificent.

respond *vti* to answer; to reply; to show a favourable reaction; to be answerable; (*with* **to**) to react.

respondent *n* a defendant, esp in a divorce suit; one who answers.

response *n* an answer; a reaction to stimulation.

responsibility *n* (*pl* **responsibilities**) being responsible; a moral obligation or duty; a charge or trust; a thing one is responsible for.

responsible *adj* having control (over); (*with* **for**) accountable (for); capable of rational conduct; trustworthy; involving responsibility.—**responsibly** *adv*.

responsive *adj* responding; sensitive to influence or stimulus; sympathetic.

rest[1] *n* stillness, repose, sleep; inactivity; the state of not moving; relaxation; tranquillity; a support or prop; a pause in music, metre, etc; a place of quiet. * *vti* to take a rest; to give rest to; to be still; to lie down; to relax; to be fixed (on); to lean, support or be supported; to put one's trust (in).

rest[2] *n* the remainder; the others. * *vi* to remain.

restate *vt* to state over again; to put differently.—**restatement** *n*.

restaurant *n* a place where meals can be bought and eaten.

restaurateur *n* the keeper of a restaurant.

restful *adj* peaceful.—**restfully** *adv*.—**restfulness** *n*.

rest home *n* an old people's home; a convalescent home.

restitution *n* the restoring of something to its owner; a reimbursement, as for loss.

restive *adj* impatient; fidgety.

restless *adj* unsettled; agitated.—**restlessly** *adv*.—**restlessness** *n*.

restoration *n* the act of restoring; reconstruction; renovation; (*with cap*) the re-establishment of the monarchy in Britain in 1660 under Charles II.

restorative *adj* tending to restore health and strength. * *n* a medicine or food that reinvigorates.

restore *vt* to give or put back; to re-establish; to repair; to renovate; to bring back to the original condition.—**restorer** *n*.

restrain *vt* to hold back; to restrict; (*person*) to deprive of freedom.

restrained *adj* moderate; self-controlled; without exuberance.

restraint *n* the ability to hold back; something that restrains; control of emotions, impulses, etc.

restrict *vt* to keep within limits, circumscribe.

restricted *adj* affected by restriction; limited; not generally available.

restriction *n* restraint; limitation; a limiting regulation.—**restrictive** *adj*.

restroom *n* a room equipped with toilets, washbowls, etc for the use of the public.

result *vi* to have as a consequence; to terminate in. * *n* a consequence; an outcome; a value obtained by mathematical calculation; (*sport*) the final score; (*pl*) a desired effect.

resultant *adj* derived from or resulting from something else.

resume *vti* to begin again; to continue after a stop or pause; to proceed after interruption.—**resumption** *n*.

résumé *n* a summary, esp of employment experience; a curriculum vitae.

resurgence *n* a revival; a renewal of activity.—**resurgent** *adj*.

resurrect *vt* to bring back into use; (*a custom*) to revive; to restore to life.

resurrection *n* a revival; a rising from the dead; (*with cap*) the rising of Christ from the dead.

resuscitate *vti* to revive when apparently dead or unconscious.—**resuscitation** *n*.

resuscitator *n* an apparatus for forcing oxygen into the lungs; a person who resuscitates.

retable *n* a step or ledge behind the altar of a church, slightly raised above it for the reception of lights, flowers, and other symbolical ornaments.

retail *n* selling directly to the consumer in small quantities. * *adv* at a retail price. * *vti* to sell or be sold by retail.—*also adj*.—**retailer** *n*.

retain *vt* to keep possession of; to keep in the mind, to remember; to keep in place, support; to hire the services of.

retainer *n* that which returns; (*formerly*) a servant to a family, a dependant; a fee to retain the services of.

retaining wall *n* a wall built to hold back earth or water.

retake *vt* (**retaking, retook,** *pp* **retaken**) to capture again; to shoot a film scene again. * *n* a scene that has been reshot.

retaliate *vti* to revenge oneself, usu by returning like for like; to strike back; to cast back (an accusation).—**retaliation** *n*.—**retaliatory** *adj*.

retard *vti* to slow down, to delay; to make slow or late.—**retardation** *n*.

retardant *n* a substance that retards, esp a chemical reaction. * *adj* retarding.

retarded *adj* slow in physical or mental development.

retch *vi* to heave as if to vomit.

retention *n* the act of retaining; the capacity to retain; memory; (*med*) the abnormal retaining of fluid in a body cavity.

retentive *adj* capable of retaining; keeping, holding. * *n* one who retains.—**retentiveness** *n*.

rethink *vt* (**rethinking, rethought**) to consider or think about again, esp with a change in mind.

reticent *adj* reserved in speech; uncommunicative.—**reticence** *n*.

reticle *n* a network of fine wires, threads, etc placed in the focal plane of an optical instrument.

reticulate *adj* resembling a network (—*also* **reticular**). * *vti* to arrange or be arranged into a network.—**reticulation** *n*.

retina *n* (*pl* **retinas, retinae**) the innermost part of the eye, on which the image is formed.

retinue *n* a body of attendants.

retire *vi* to give up one's work when pensionable age is reached; to withdraw; to retreat; to go to bed. * *vt* (*troops*) to withdraw from use; to compel to retire from a position, work, etc.

retirement *n* the act of retiring or the state of being retired; seclusion; privacy.

retiring *adj* unobtrusive; shy.

retort *vi* to reply sharply or wittily. * *n* a sharp or witty reply; a vessel with a funnel bent downwards used in distilling; a receptacle used in making gas and steel.

retouch *vt* (*photograph, etc*) to improve or change by touching up; (*new growth of hair*) to colour to match other hair.

retrace *vt* to go back over; to trace back to a source.—**retraceable** *adj*.

retract *vti* to draw in or back; to withdraw (a statement, opinion, etc); to recant.—**retractable** *adj*.—**retraction** *n*.

retreat *vi* to withdraw, retire; to recede. * *n* a withdrawal, esp of troops; a sign for retiring; a quiet or secluded place, refuge; seclusion for religious devotion.

retrench *vti* to cut down (esp expenses); to economize.—**retrenchment** *n*.

retrial *n* a second trial.

retribution *n* deserved reward; something given or exacted in compensation, esp punishment.

retrieve *vt* to recover; to revive; (*a loss*) to make good; (*comput*) to obtain information from data stored in a computer. * *vi* (*dogs*) to retrieve game.—**retrievable** *adj*.—**retrieval** *n*.

retriever *n* any of several breeds of dogs capable of being trained for retrieving.

retro *n* (*pl* **retros**) a retrorocket. * *adj* denoting a fashion or style (in music, clothes, etc) that pays homage to the past.

retro- *prefix* backwards; behind.

retroactive *adj* having an effect on things that are already past.

retrograde *adj* going backwards; passing from better to worse.

retrogression *n* going backwards, usu a return to a former, less complex, level of development.

retrorocket *n* a small rocket on an aircraft or spacecraft that produces thrust in the opposite direction to the line of flight to slow it down.

retrospect *n* a looking back; a mental review of the past.—**retrospection** *n*.

retrospective *adj* looking backwards; relating to the past. * *n* an exhibition of an artist's lifetime work.—**retrospectively** *adv*.

retroussé *adj* turned upwards (esp of the nose).

retroversion *n* the act of turning or state of being turned backwards.—**retroverted** *adj*.

Retrovir *n* (*trademark*) AZT.

retrovirus *n* any of various viruses that use RNA to synthesize DNA, reversing the normal process in cells of transcription from DNA to RNA, which includes HIV.

retsina *n* a Greek white wine flavoured with resin.

return *vi* to come or go back; to reply; to recur. * *vt* to give or send back; to repay; to yield; to answer; to elect. * *n* something returned; a recurrence; recompense; (*pl*) yield, revenue; a form for computing (income) tax.

returnable *adj* required to be returned; capable of being returned (for reuse).

return ticket *n* (*Brit etc*) a ticket whose price includes the cost of the journey to and back from a destination.

reunion *n* a meeting following separation; a social gathering of former colleagues.

reunite *vt* to unite again; to reconcile. * *vi* to become reunited.

reusable *adj* able to be used again; renewable.

Rev. *abbr* = Reverend.

rev *vt* (**revving, revved**) (*inf*) (*with* **up**) to increase the speed of an engine. * *n* revolution per minute.

revaluate *vt* to reassess the value of; to change (esp increase) the exchange value of (a currency).

revamp *vt* to renovate, to rework, remodel; to transform. * *n* the process of revamping; something revamped.

revanchism *n* (support for) a policy aimed at regaining lost territory or possessions.—**revanchist** *n, adj*.

reveal *vt* (*something hidden or secret*) to make known; to expose; to make visible.

reveille *n* a morning bugle call to wake soldiers.

revel *vi* (**reveling, revelled** *or* **reveling, reveled**) (*with* **in**) to take pleasure or delight in; to make merry. * *n* (*pl*) merrymaking; entertainment.—**reveler, reveller** *n*.

revelry *n* (*pl* **revelries**) the act of revelling; noisty festivity.

revelation *n* the act of revealing; the disclosure of something secret; a communication from God to man; an illuminating experience.

revenge *vt* to inflict punishment in return for; to satisfy oneself by retaliation; to avenge. * *n* the act of revenging; retaliation; a vindictive feeling.—**revenger** *n*.

revengeful *adj* keen for revenge; vindictive.

revenue *n* the total income produced by taxation; gross income from a business or investment.

reverb *n* (*mus*) an electronic device for producing an artificial echo.

reverberate *vi* to rebound, recoil; to be reflected in; to resound, to echo.—**reverberation** *n*.

revere *vt* to regard with great respect or awe; to venerate.

reverence *n* profound respect; devotion; a gesture of respect (such as a bow). * *vt* to hold in respect.

reverend *adj* worthy of reverence; of or relating to the clergy; (*with cap*) a title for a member of the clergy.

reverent *adj* feeling or expressing reverence.—**reverently** *adv*.

reverie *n* a daydream; (*mus*) a dreamy piece.—*also* **revery** (*pl* **reveries**).

revers *n* (*pl* **revers**) a lapel, esp on a woman's garment.

reversal *n* the act or process of reversing.

reverse *vti* to turn in the opposite direction; to turn outside in, upside down, etc; to move backwards; (*law*) to revoke or annul. * *n* the contrary or opposite of something; the back, esp of a coin; a setback; a mechanism for reversing. * *adj* opposite, contrary; causing movement in the opposite direction.

reverse video *n* a technique for highlighting on a computer monitor by reversing the normal text and background colours.

reversible *adj* with both sides usable; wearable with either side out; able to undergo a series of changes either backwards or forwards. * *n* a reversible cloth or article of clothing.

reversion *n* return to a former condition or type; right to future possession; the return of an estate to the grantor or his heirs.—**reversionary** *adj*.

revert *vi* to go back (to a former state); to take up again (a former subject); (*biol*) to return to a former or primitive type; (*law*) to go back to a former owner or his heirs.—**revertible** *adj*.

revery *see* **reverie**.

review *n* an evaluation; a survey; a reconsideration; a critical assessment, a critique; a periodical containing critical essays; an official inspection of ships or troops. * *vt* to re-examine; to inspect formally; to write a critique on.

reviewer *n* a person who writes a review, esp for a newspaper, a critic.

revile *vti* to use abusive language (to or about).

revise *vt* to correct and amend; to prepare a new, improved version of; to study again (for an examination).—**revision** *n*.

revitalize *vt* to put new life into.—**revitalization** *n*.

revival *n* the act of reviving; recovery from a neglected or depressed state; renewed performance (of a play); renewed interest in; religious awakening.

revivalist *n* a person who encourages religious practice.—**revivalism** *n*.

revive *vti* to return to life; to make active again; to take up again.—**reviver** *n*.

revivify *vt* to put new life into; to reanimate; to revive.—**revification** *n*.—**revivifier** *n*.

revoke *vt* to cancel; to rescind. * *vi* (*cards*) to fail to follow suit.—**revocable** *adj*.—**revocation** *n*.

revolt *vt* to rebel; to overturn; to shock. * *vi* to feel great disgust. * *n* rebellion; uprising; loathing.

revolting *adj* extremely offensive.—**revoltingly** *adv*.

revolution *n* the act of revolting; a motion round a centre or axis; a single completion of an orbit or rotation; a great change; an overthrow of a government, social system, etc.

revolutionary *adj* of or advocating revolution; radically new. * *n* a person who takes part in, or favours, revolution.
revolutionize *vt* to cause a complete change in.
revolve *vt* to travel or cause to travel in a circle or orbit; to rotate.
revolver *n* a handgun with a magazine that revolves to reload.
revolving door *n* a door of two or four panels rotating around a central axis within a round chamber and operated electrically or manually.
revue *n* a musical show with skits, dances, etc, often satirizing recent events.
revulsion *n* disgust; aversion; a sudden change or reversal of feeling, esp withdrawal with a sense of utter distaste.
reward *n* something that is given in return for something done; money offered, as for the capture of a criminal. * *vt* to give a reward.
rewarding *adj* (*experience, activity, etc*) pleasing, profitable.
rewind *vt* to wind again; to wind (an audiotape, etc) back to the beginning. * *n* the act of rewinding.
rewire *vt* to put new wiring into an electrical system.
reword *vt* to change the wording of.
rework *vt* to use again in a different form; to rewrite; to remodel.
rewrite *vt* to write again; to revise. * *n* something rewritten; revision.
Rex *n* a reigning king.
rf *abbr* = radio frequency.
Rh *abbr* = rhesus.
rhachis *see* **rachis.**
rhapsodize *vi* to speak or write (about) with enthusiasm or emotion.—**rhapsodist** *n.*
rhapsody *n* (*pl* **rhapsodies**) an enthusiastic speech or writing; (*mus*) an irregular instrumental composition of an epic, heroic or national character.
rhea *n* any of several large flightless birds of South America resembling ostriches but smaller.
rhenium *n* a hard heat-resistant metallic element.
rheo- *prefix* flow, current.
rheology *n* the physics of the flow and deformation of matter.—**rheologist** *n.*—**rheological** *adj.*
rheostat *n* a device that regulates electric current by varying the resistance to it.—**rheostatic** *adj.*
rhesus factor *n* a substance usually present in the red blood cells of humans and higher animals.
rhesus monkey *n* a type of southern Asian macaque with light brown fur.
rhesus negative *adj* lacking the rhesus factor in the blood.
rhesus positive *adj* containing the rhesus factor in the blood.
rhetoric *n* the art of effective speaking and writing; skill in using speech; insincere language.
rhetorical *adj* of or relating to rhetoric; high-flown, bombastic.—**rhetorically** *adv.*
rhetorical question *n* a question asked for effect, to which no answer is expected.
rheum *n* a watery discharge from the mucous membranes of the nose, eyes, etc.—**rheumy** *adj.*
rheumatic *adj* of, relating to or suffering from rheumatism. * *n* a person who has rheumatism.
rheumatic fever *n* a disease characterized by inflammation and pain in the joints.
rheumatism *n* a disorder causing pain in muscles and joints.
rheumatoid *adj* of or like rheumatism.
rheumatoid arthritis *n* a usu chronic disease characterized by inflammation, pain, and swelling of the joints.
rheumatology *n* the study of rheumatic diseases.—**rheumatologist** *n.*
rhinal *adj* of or pertaining to the nose.
rhinestone *n* a colourless imitation precious stone made from paste, glass, or quartz.
Rhine wine *n* any of several wines from the valley of the River Rhine in Germany; a light dry wine from the Rhine valley or elsewhere.
rhinitis *n* inflammation of the mucous membrane of the nose.
rhino-, rhin- *prefix* nose.
rhino *n* (*pl* **rhinos, rhino**) (*inf*) a rhinoceros.
rhinoceros *n* (*pl* **rhinoceroses, rhinoceros**) a large, thick-skinned mammal with one or two horns on the nose.
rhinology *n* the branch of medicine dealing with the nose.—**rhinologist** *n.*
rhinoplasty *n* plastic surgery of the nose.—**rhinoplastic** *adj.*
rhizo-, rhiz- *prefix* root.
rhizome *n* a stem on or below ground that produces roots below and shoots above; a rootstock.
rho *n* (*pl* **rhos**) the 17th letter of the Greek alphabet.
Rhode Island Red *n* an American breed of domestic fowl with reddish-brown plumage.
rhodium *n* a hard white metallic element similar to platinum.
rhododendron *n* an evergreen shrub with large flowers.
rhomb *n* a rhombus.
rhombohedron *n* (*pl* **rhombohedrons, rhombohedra**) a six-sided solid figure whose sides are rhombuses.—**rhombohedral** *adj.*
rhomboid *n* a parallelogram whose adjacent sides are unequal and whose angles are not right angles.—*also adj.*
rhombus *n* (*pl* **rhombuses, rhombi**) a diamond shape.
rhubarb *n* a plant with large leaves and edible (when cooked) pink stalks; (*inf*) a noisy quarrel.
rhumb *n* an imaginary line crossing all meridians at the same angle; a course navigated by a ship or aircraft that maintains a fixed compass bearing.—*also* **rhumb line.**
rhyme *n* the repetition of sounds usu at the ends of lines in verse; such poetry or verse; a word corresponding with another in end sound. * *vti* to form a rhyme (with); to versify, put into rhyme.
rhyming slang *n* a type of slang that substitutes the original (often indecent) word with a word or phrase that rhymes with it, eg *loaf of bread = head.*
rhythm *n* a regular recurrence of beat, accent or silence in the flow of sound, esp of words and music; a measured flow; cadence.—**rhythmic, rhythmical** *adj.*—**rhythmically** *adv.*
rhythm and blues *n* a type of music that fuses elements of folk, blues and rock.
rhythm method *n* a method of contraception that relies on abstinence from sexual intercourse during the period when ovulation is most likely to occur.
rhythm section *n* those instruments in a band or group whose main role is to supply the rhythm, such as the double bass and drums.
RI *abbr* = Rhode Island.
rib *n* one of the curved bones of the chest attached to the spine; any rib-like structure; a leaf vein; a vein of an insect's wing; a ridge or raised strip, as of knitting; a ridge of a mountain. * *vt* (**ribbing, ribbed**) to provide with ribs; to form vertical ridges in knitting; (*inf*) to tease or ridicule.
ribald *adj* irreverent; humorously vulgar.
riband *n* a ribbon.
ribbon *n* silk, satin, velvet, etc, woven into a narrow band; a piece of this; a strip of cloth, etc, inked for use, as in a typewriter; (*pl*) torn shreds.
rib cage *n* the bony framework of ribs enclosing the wall of the chest.
riboflavin *n* a factor of the vitamin B complex found in milk, eggs, fruits, etc.
ribonuclease *n* any of several enzymes that act as catalytic triggers of RNA hydrolosis.
ribonucleic acid *n* any of a group of nucleic acids found in all living cells, where they are essential to protein development.—**RNA** *abbr.*
ribose *n* a sugar occurring in RNA and riboflavin.
ribosome *n* any of the tiny particles containing RNA and protein in cells where protein synthesis takes place.—**ribosomal** *adj.*
rice *n* an annual cereal grass cultivated in warm climates; its starchy food grain.
ricebird *see* **bobolink.**
rice paper *n* a delicate paper prepared from pith.

rich *adj* having much money, wealthy; abounding in natural resources, fertile; costly, fine; (*food*) sweet or oily, highly flavoured; deep in colour; (*inf*) full of humour. * *n* wealthy people collectively; (*pl* **riches**) wealth, abundance.—**richly** *adv*.—**richness** *n*.

Richter scale *n* a scale ranging from 1 to 10 for measuring the intensity of an earthquake.

rick[1] *n* a stack or large pile of hay, etc, in the open.

rick[2] *vt* (*Brit etc*) to sprain or strain slightly. * *n* such an injury.—*also* **wrick**.

rickets *n* a children's disease marked by softening of the bones, caused by vitamin D deficiency.

rickettsia *n* (*pl* **rickettsiae, rickettsias**) any of a genus of microorganisms that inhabit mites, ticks, etc and cause serious diseases, such as typhus.—**rickettsial** *adj*.

rickety *adj* shaky, unsteady.

rickrack *n* a zigzag braid for trimming clothing.

rickshaw, ricksha *n* a light, two-wheeled man-drawn vehicle, orig used in Japan.

ricochet *vi* (**ricocheting, ricocheted** *or* **ricochetting, ricochetted**) (*bullet*) to rebound or skip along ground or water. * *n* a rebound or glancing off; (*bullet*) a hit made after ricocheting.

ricotta *n* a mildly-flavoured soft white cheese made from sheep's milk.

rictus *n* (*pl* **rictus, rictuses**) the gap in an open mouth or beak; a fixed grimace, esp in horror.—**rictal** *adj*.

rid *vt* (**ridding, rid** *or* **ridded**) to free from; to dispose (of).

riddance *n* clearance; disposal.

ridden[1] *see* **ride**.

ridden[2] *adj* oppressed by; full of.

riddle[1] *n* a puzzling question; an enigma; a mysterious person or thing.

riddle[2] *n* a coarse sieve. * *vt* to sieve or sift; to perforate with holes; to spread through, permeate.

ride *vb* (**riding, rode,** *pp* **ridden**) *vti* to be carried along or travel in a vehicle or on an animal, bicycle, etc; to be supported or move on the water; to lie at anchor; to travel over a surface; to move on the body; (*inf*) to continue undisturbed. * *vt* (*horse, bicycle etc*); to sit on and control; to oppress, dominate; (*inf*) to torment. * *n* a trip or journey in a vehicle or on horseback, on a bicycle, etc; a thing to ride at a fairground.

rider *n* a person who rides; an addition to a document, amending a clause; an additional statement; something used to move along another piece.

ridge *n* a narrow crest or top; the ploughed earth thrown up between the furrows; a line where two slopes meet; (*of land etc*) a raised strip or elevation; a range of hills. * *vti* to form into ridges, wrinkle.—**ridged** *adj*.

ridgepole *n* the horizontal pole along the top of a tent.

ridicule *n* mockery, derision. * *vt* to make fun of, to mock.

ridiculous *adj* deserving ridicule; preposterous, silly.—**ridiculously** *adv*.—**ridiculousness** *n*.

riesling *n* (the grape that produces) a dry white wine.

rife *adj* widespread; prevalent.

riff *n* (*jazz, rock*) a musical phrase played repeatedly, esp as the background to an extended solo improvisation.—*also vi*.

riffle *vt* to leaf or flick rapidly through (pages, files, etc); to shuffle cards by dividing the deck and then flicking the corners together with the thumbs. * *vi* to flick cursorily (through). * *n* (the sound of) an act or instance of riffling; a ripple in a stream or the small obstruction causing this; grooves, etc at the bottom of a sluice to trap gold particles.

riffraff *n* disreputable persons; refuse, rubbish.

rifle[1] *n* a shoulder gun with a spirally grooved bore.

rifle[2] *vti* to steal; to look through (a person's papers or belongings).

rifling *n* (the cutting of) spiral grooves in the bore of a firearm that spin the projectile.

rift *n* a split; a cleft; a fissure. * *vti* to split.

rift valley *n* a narrow valley caused by land subsiding between two parallel faults.

rig *vt* (**rigging, rigged**) (*naut*) to equip with sails and tackle; to set up in working order; to manipulate fraudulently. * *n* the way sails, etc, are rigged; equipment or gear for a special purpose, such as oil drilling; a type of truck.

rigging *n* the ropes for supporting masts and sails; (*in theatre*) a network of ropes and pulleys to support and maintain scenery.

right *adj* correct, true; just or good; appropriate; fit, recovered; opposite to left; conservative; designating the side meant to be seen. * *adv* straight; directly; completely, exactly; correctly, properly; to or on the right side. * *n* that which is just or correct; truth; fairness; justice; privilege; just or legal claim; (*pl*) the correct condition. * *vti* to set or become upright; to correct; to redress.—**rightness** *n*.

right angle *n* an angle of 90 degrees.

righteous *adj* moral, virtuous.—**righteously** *adv*.—**righteousness** *n*.

rightful *adj* legitimate; having a just claim.—**rightfully** *adv*.—**rightfulness** *n*.

right-hand *adj* of or towards the right side of a person or thing; for use by the right hand.

right-handed *adj* using the right hand; done or made for use with the right hand. * *adv* with the right hand.

rightist *adj* politically conservative. * *n* a person belonging to or supporting a conservative political party.

rightly *adv* in truth; in the right; with good reason; properly.

right-minded *adj* having principles in accordance with standard notions of what is right.

right of way *n* a public path over private ground; the right to use this; precedence over other traffic.

right-on *adj* (*inf*) fashionable, trendy.

right-thinking *adj* holding generally acceptable views.

right-wing *adj* of or relating to the conservative faction of a political party, organization, etc.—**right-winger** *n*.

rigid *adj* stiff, inflexible; severe, strict.—**rigidity** *n*.—**rigidly** *adv*.—**rigidness** *n*.

rigmarole *n* nonsense; a foolishly involved procedure.

rigor *n* harsh inflexibility; severity; strictness.—*also* **rigour**.

rigor mortis *n* the stiffening of the body after death.

rigorous *adj* stern, severe, strict.—**rigorously** *adv*.—**rigorousness** *n*.

rigour *see* **rigor**.

rile *vt* (*inf*) to irritate, to annoy, to anger.

rill *n* a small brook or stream.

rim *n* a border or raised edge, esp of something circular; the outer part of a wheel. * *vt* (**rimming, rimmed**) to supply or surround with a rim; to form a rim.

rimless *adj* lacking a rim; (*glasses*) without a frame.

rind *n* crust; peel; bark.

rinderpest *n* an acute viral disease of cattle.

ring[1] *n* a circular band, esp of metal, worn on the finger, in the ear, etc; a hollow circle; a round enclosure; an arena for boxing, etc; a group of people engaged in secret or criminal activity to control a market, etc. * *vt* (**ringing, ringed**) to encircle, surround; to fit with a ring.

ring[2] *vti* (**ringing, rang** *or* **rung,** *pp* **rung**) to emit a bell-like sound; to resound; to peal; to sound a bell; to telephone; (*with* **up**) to total and record esp by means of a cash register; to achieve. * *n* a ringing sound; a resonant note; a set of church bells.

ringdove *n* a wood pigeon.

ringed *adj* wearing rings; forming rings; having ring-like markings; surrounded by.

ringer *n* a person that rings bells; (*sl*) a person or thing closely resembling another; a horse entered into a race under a false name, weight, etc.

ring finger *n* the third finger, esp of the left hand, on which a wedding ring is traditionally worn.

ringhals *n* a poisonous African snake that spits venom at its victims.

ringleader *n* a person who takes the lead in mischievous or unlawful behaviour.

ringlet *n* a curling lock of hair.

ringmaster *n* a master of ceremonies in a circus.
ringworm *n* a contagious skin infection.
rink *n* an expanse of ice for skating; a smooth floor for roller skating; an alley for bowling.
rinse *vt* to wash lightly; to flush under clean water to remove soap. * *n* the act of rinsing; a preparation for tinting the hair.
rioja *n* a type of Spanish red or white wine.
riot *n* violent public disorder; uproar; unrestrained profusion; (*inf*) something very funny. * *vi* to participate in a riot.—**rioter** *n*.—**rioting** *n*.
riotous *adj* disorderly, tumultuous, seditious; luxurious, wanton.—**riotously** *adv*.—**riotousness** *n*.
RIP *abbr* = rest in peace.
rip[1] *vti* (**ripping, ripped**) to cut or tear apart roughly; to split; (*with* **off, out**) to remove in a violent or rough manner; (*inf*) to rush, speed; (*with* **into**) to attack, esp verbally. * *n* a tear; a split.
rip[2] *n* a stretch of broken water caused by currents and tides.
rip cord *n* a cord for releasing a parachute.
ripe *adj* ready to be eaten or harvested; fully developed; mature.—**ripely** *adv*.—**ripeness** *n*.
ripen *vt* to grow or make ripe.
rip-off *n* (*sl*) the act or a means of stealing; plagiarizing, cheating, etc.
riposte, ripost *n* a counterstroke; a retort; a retaliatory manoeuvre. * *vi* to make a riposte.
ripple *n* a little wave or undulation on the surface of water; the sound of this. * *vti* to have or form little waves on the surface (of).
rip-roaring *adj* (*inf*) exuberant, boisterous, thrilling.
ripsaw *n* a handsaw for cutting wood in the direction of the grain.
riptide *n* a powerful current flowing outwards from the shore.
RISC (*acronym*) reduced instruction set computer: a computer with advanced yet simplified internal circuitry that allows a significant increase in processing speed over standard designs.
rise *vi* (**rising, rose,** *pp* **risen**) to get up; to stand up; to ascend; to increase in value or size; to swell; to revolt; to be provoked; to originate; to tower; to slope up; (*voice*) to reach a higher pitch; to ascend from the grave; (*fish*) to come to the surface. * *n* an ascent; origin; an increase in price, salary, etc; an upward slope.
risible *adj* tending to laugh; provoking laughter, derisory.—**risibility** *n*.
rising *n* a revolt, insurrection. * *adj* ascending; approaching.
risk *n* chance of loss or injury; hazard; danger, peril. * *vt* to expose to possible danger or loss; to take the chance of.
risk capital *n* venture capital.
risky *adj* (**riskier, riskiest**) dangerous; uncertain; not secure.
risotto *n* (*pl* **risottos**) a dish of onions, rice, butter, etc, cooked in meat stock.
risqué *adj* verging on indecency; slightly offensive.
rissole *n* a fried cake of minced meat, egg, and breadcrumbs.
rite *n* a ceremonial practice or procedure, esp religious.
rite of passage *n* a ritual indicating a change in an individual's status, as at puberty or marriage.
ritual *adj* relating to rites or ceremonies. * *n* a fixed (religious) ceremony.—**ritually** *adv*.
ritzy *adj* (**ritzier, ritziest**) (*sl*) luxurious, smart.
rival *n* one of two or more people, organizations or teams competing with each other for the same goal. * *adj* competing; having comparable merit or claim. * *vt* (**rivalling, rivalled**) to strive to equal or excel; to be comparable to; to compete.
rivalry *n* (*pl* **rivalries**) emulation; competition.
river *n* a large natural stream of fresh water flowing into an ocean, lake, etc; a copious flow.
river basin *n* land drained by a river and its tributaries.
riverbed *n* the channel formed by a river.
riverfront *n* the land or an area along a river.
riverine *adj* of, like, or produced by a river; living or located on the banks of a river.
riverside *n* the bank of a river.
rivet *n* a short, metal bolt for holding metal plates together, the headless end being hammered flat. * *vt* to join with rivets; to fix one's eyes upon immovably; to engross one's attention.
riveter *n* a person who rivets; a machine that rivets.
Riviera *n* the coast of the northern Mediterranean from southeast France to northwest Italy.
rivulet *n* a little stream.
riyal *n* the standard currency unit of Saudi Arabia, Yemen, Quatar, or Dubai.
RMA *abbr* = Royal Military Academy.
rms *abbr* = root mean square.
RN *abbr* = Registered Nurse; Royal Navy.
Rn (*chem symbol*) radon.
RNA *abbr* = ribonucleic acid.
roach *n* a small silvery freshwater fish.
road *n* a track, surfaced with tarmac or concrete, made for travelling; a highway; a street; a way or route; an anchorage for ships.
road block *n* a barrier erected across a road to halt traffic.
road hog *n* a car driver who obstructs other vehicles by encroaching on the others' traffic lane.
roadhouse *n* a tavern usu outside city limits providing meals, etc.
roadie *n* (*inf*) a person with responsibility for transporting and setting up stage equipment for a rock group, etc on tour.
road map *n* a map for motorists that gives information on the roads of a particular area.
road metal *n* broken stone and cinders used in making road and railway foundations.
road movie *n* a film genre in which the main characters are on a journey, both in a real and figurative sense.
road runner *n* a long-tailed, swift-running, terrestrial North American cuckoo.
roadshow *n* a group of touring entertainers; a radio or television show presented from a touring outside-broadcasting unit.
roadside *n* the border of a road.—*also adj*.
road-test *vt* to test (a vehicle) under practical operating conditions.—**road test** *n*.
roadway *n* the strip of land over which a road passes; the main part of a road, used by vehicles.
roadwork *n* conditioning for an athletic contest consisting mainly of long runs.
roam *vti* to wander about, to rove.
roan *adj* having a base colour thickly sprinkled with white or grey. * *n* a horse with a roan coat, esp when the base colour is red.
roar *vti* to make a loud, full, growling sound, as a lion, wind, fire, the sea; to utter loudly, as in a rage; to bellow; to guffaw.—*also n*.
roaring *adj* boisterous, noisy; brisk.
roast *vti* (*meat, etc*) to cook with little or no moisture, as before a fire or in an oven; (*coffee, etc*) to process by exposure to heat; to expose to great heat; (*inf*) to criticize severely; to undergo roasting. * *n* roasted meat; a cut of meat for roasting; a picnic at which food is roasted.
rob *vb* (**robbing, robbed**) *vt* to seize forcibly; to steal from; to plunder. * *vi* to commit robbery.—**robber** *n*.
robbery *n* (*pl* **robberies**) theft from a person by intimidation or by violence.
robe *n* a long flowing outer garment; the official dress of a judge, academic, etc; a bathrobe or dressing gown; a covering or wrap; (*pl*) ceremonial vestments. * *vti* to put on or dress in robes.
robin *n* a songbird with a dull red breast.
robot *n* a mechanical device that acts in a seemingly human way; a mechanism guided by automatic controls.
robotics *n* (*used as sing*) the science of designing and using robots.
robust *adj* strong, sturdy; vigorous.—**robustly** *adv*.—**robustness** *n*.
roc *n* (*Arabian legend*) a giant bird of enormous strength.
rock[1] *n* a large stone or boulder; a person or thing providing foundation or support; (*geol*) a natural mineral deposit including sand, clay, etc; a hard sweet; (*inf*) a diamond, ice; (*sl*) the drug crack.

rock[2] *vti* to move to and fro, or from side to side; to sway strongly; to shake. * *n* a rocking motion; rock and roll.

rockabilly *n* a type of fast-paced rock and country music originating in the US South in the 1950s.

rock-and-roll *n* popular music that incorporates country and blues elements and is usu played on electronic instruments with a heavily accented beat.

rock bottom *n* the lowest or most fundamental part or level. * *adj* very lowest.

rock crystal *n* transparent colourless quartz used in electronic and optical equipment.

rocker *n* a rocking chair; a curved support on which a cradle, etc, rocks.

rockery *n* (*pl* **rockeries**) a garden among rocks for alpine plants.—*also* **rock garden.**

rocket *n* any device driven forward by gases escaping through a rear vent, such as a firework, distress signal, or the propulsion mechanism of a spacecraft. * *vi* to move in or like a rocket; to soar.

rocket launcher *n* a device for launching rockets; an aircraft or motor vehicle equipped to launch rockets.

rocketry *n* the science of building and launching rockets.

rock garden *see* **rockery.**

rock house *n* (*sl*) a place where the drug crack is made available by dealers.

rocking chair *n* a chair mounted on rockers.

rocking horse *n* a toy horse fixed on rockers or springs.

rock salt *n* common salt in solid form or in large crystals.

rocky *adj* (**rockier, rockiest**) having many rocks; like rock; rugged, hard; shaky, unstable.

rococo *adj* elaborately ornate, as in an architectural style of 18th-century Europe.—*also n.*

rod *n* a stick; a thin bar of metal or wood; a staff of office; a wand; a fishing rod; (*sl*) a pistol.

rode *see* **ride.**

rodent *n* any of several relatively small gnawing animals with two strong front teeth.

rodeo *n* (*pl* **rodeos**) the rounding up of cattle; a display of cowboy skill.

roe[1] *n* the eggs of fish.

roe[2] *n* a small reddish brown deer (—*also* **roe deer**); the female red deer.

roebuck *n* the male roe deer.

roe deer *n* a small graceful deer of European and Asian woodlands.

roentgen *n* the unit of measuring X-rays or gamma rays.—*also* **röntgen.**

roger *interj* used in radio communications, etc to indicate message received and understood.

rogue *n* a scoundrel; a rascal; a mischievous person; a wild animal that lives apart from the herd.—**roguish** *adj.*—**roguishly** *adv.*

role, rôle *n* a part in a film or play taken by an actor; a function.

role model *n* a person who inspires others to emulate him or her.

role-playing *n* (*psychol*) a technique in which participants take on and act out roles in order to rehearse a situation or resolve a conflict.

roll *n* a scroll; anything wound into cylindrical form; a list or register; a turned-over edge; a rolling movement; a small cake of bread; a trill of some birds; an undulation; the sound of thunder; the beating of drumsticks. * *vi* to move by turning over or from side to side; to move like a wheel; to curl; to move in like waves; to flow. * *vt* to cause to roll; to turn on its axis; to move on wheels; to press with a roller; (*dice*) to throw; to beat rapidly, as a drum.

roll bar *n* a bar that reinforces the frame of a racing or sports car to protect the driver should the vehicle overturn.

roll call *n* the reading aloud of a list of names to check attendance.

roller *n* a revolving cylinder used for spreading paint, flattening surfaces, moving paper, etc; a large wave.

roller coaster *n* an elevated amusement ride in which small cars move on tracks that curve and dip sharply.—*also* **big dipper.**

roller skate *n* a four-wheeled skate strapped on to shoes.—**roller skating** *n.*

roller towel *n* a towel without ends on a roller.

rolling pin *n* a wooden, plastic or stone cylinder for rolling out pastry.

rolling stock *n* all the vehicles of a railway.

rolling stone *n* a person who cannot settle in one place; a free spirit.

rollmop *n* a fillet of herring rolled up and pickled in brine or spiced vinegar.

roll-on/roll-off *adj* pertaining to a cargo ship or passenger ferry designed so that vehicles can be driven straight on and off.

roll-top desk *n* a writing desk with a flexible sliding cover of slats.

roly-poly *n* (*pl* **roly-polies**) a pudding of pastry covered with jam and rolled up; a round and plump person.

ROM *abbr* (*comput*) = read-only memory.

Roman *adj* of or relating to the city of Rome or its ancient empire, or the Latin alphabet; Roman Catholic. * *n* an inhabitant or citizen of Rome; a Roman Catholic.

roman *adj* ordinary type, not italic.

Roman candle *n* a type of cylindrical firework that emits coloured sparks.

Roman Catholic *adj* belonging to the Christian church that is headed by the Pope.—*also n.*

romance *n* a prose narrative; a medieval tale of chivalry; a series of unusual adventures; a novel dealing with this; an atmosphere of awe or wonder; a love story; a love affair; a picturesque falsehood. * *vi* to write romantic fiction; to exaggerate.

Romanesque *adj, n* (in) the style of round-arched and vaulted architecture prevalent between the Classical and Gothic periods.

Roman holiday *n* a holiday or entertainment at the expense of others' suffering.

Roman nose *n* a nose with a slender prominent ridge.

Roman numerals *n* the letters I, V, X, L, C, D, and M used to represent numbers in the manner of the ancient Romans.

romantic *adj* of or given to romance; strange and picturesque; imaginative; sentimental; (*art, literature*) preferring passion and imagination to proportion and finish, subordinating form to content.—**romantically** *adv.*

romanticism *n* a 19th-century philosophical and cultural movement characterized by the desire to bring nature and man into unity through the shaping power of the imagination; romantic approach, quality, or ideals.

romanticize *vt* to imbue (a person, concept, etc) with a romantic character. * *vi* to have romantic ideas.—**romanticization** *n.*

Romany *n* a Gypsy; the Indic language of Gypsies.

romp *vi* to play boisterously. * *n* a noisy game; a frolic; an easy win.

rompers *npl* a child's one-piece garment; a jumpsuit.

rondo *n* (*pl* **rondos**) a musical form with a leading theme to which return is made.

röntgen *see* **roentgen.**

roof *n* (*pl* **roofs**) the upper covering of a building; the top of a vehicle; an upper limit. * *vt* to provide with a roof, to cover.

roof garden *n* a garden on a flat roof or balcony; a top floor decorated as a garden, esp if used as a restaurant.

roofing *n* materials for a roof.

rook[1] *n* a crow-like bird.

rook[2] *n* (*chess*) a piece with the power to move horizontally or vertically, a castle.

rookery *n* (*pl* **rookeries**) a colony of rooks; a breeding ground or haunt of other birds or mammals; a crowded place.

rookie *n* (*sl*) an inexperienced army recruit; any novice.—*also adj.*

room *n* space; unoccupied space; adequate space; a division of a house, a chamber; scope or opportunity; those in a room; (*pl*) lodgings. * *vi* to lodge.

room clerk *n* a receptionist in a hotel who books in guests and allocates rooms, etc.

rooming house *n* a house with individual rooms to let.

roommate *n* a person with whom one shares a room or rooms.

roomy *adj* (**roomier, roomiest**) having ample space; wide.—**roominess** *n.*

roost *n* a bird's perch or sleeping-place; a place for resting. * *vi* to rest or sleep on a roost; to settle down, as for the night.

rooster *n* an adult male domestic fowl, a cockerel.

root[1] *n* the part of a plant, usu underground, that anchors the plant, draws water from the soil, etc; the embedded part of a tooth, a hair, etc; a supporting or essential part; something that is an origin or source; (*math*) the factor of a quantity which multiplied by itself gives the quantity; (*mus*) the fundamental note of a chord; (*pl*) plants with edible roots. * *vti* to take root; to become established; (*with* **out**) to tear up, to eradicate.

root[2] *vti* to dig up with the snout; to search about, rummage; (*with* **for**) (*inf*) to encourage a team by cheering.

root beer *n* a carbonated drink flavored with extracts of certain roots and barks.

root crop *n* a crop, such as turnips, sugar beet, cultivated for its edible roots.

rooted *adj* firmly fixed; planted.

root mean square *n* the square root of the average of the squares of a set of numbers.

rootstock *n* an underground stem, rhizome; a stock for grafting, having a root or a piece of root.

rope *n* a thick cord or thin cable made of twisted fibres or wires; a string or row of things braided, intertwined or threaded together; a viscous thickening in a liquid. * *vt* to tie, bind, divide or enclose with a rope; to lasso; (*liquid*) to become ropy.—**ropy** *adj*.

Roquefort *n* a French blue-veined cheese with a strong flavour.

rorqual *n* any of several large whalebone whales with dorsal fins and deep furrows on the skin of the throat and chest.—*also* **finback**.

rosaceous *adj* of or belonging to the large family of plants that includes the rose; resembling a rose; rose-coloured.

rosary *n* (*pl* **rosaries**) a string of beads for keeping count of prayers; a series of prayers.

rose[1] *see* **rise**.

rose[2] *n* a prickly-stemmed plant with fragrant flowers of many delicate colours; its flower; a rosette; a perforated nozzle; a pinkish red or purplish red.

rosé *n* a pink wine made from skinless red grapes or by mixing white and red wine.

rose-coloured *adj* rosy; overly optimistic.

rosemary *n* a fragrant shrubby mint used in cookery and perfumery.

rosette *n* a rose-shaped bunch of ribbon; a carving, etc, in the shape of a rose.

rosewater *n* water scented with rose petals.

rose window *n* a circular window filled with tracery.

rosewood *n* (any of various tropical trees yielding) a fragrant dark wood used in making furniture.

rosin *n* a pine-wood resin, esp in solid form, used in varnishes, etc, and for waxing the bows of stringed instruments.

roster *n* a list or roll, as of military personnel; a list of duties.

rostrum *n* (*pl* **rostrums, rostra**) a platform or stage for public speaking.

rosy *adj* (**rosier, rosiest**) of the colour of roses; having pink, healthy cheeks; optimistic, hopeful.

rot *vti* (**rotting, rotted**) to decompose; to decay; to become degenerate. * *n* decay; corruption; several different diseases affecting timber or sheep; (*inf*) nonsense.

rota *n* a turn in succession; a list or roster of duties.

rotary *adj* revolving; turning like a wheel.

Rotary Club *n* a club belonging to an international organization of business people for promoting community service.—**Rotarian** *n*.

rotate *vti* to turn around an axis like a wheel; to follow a sequence.

rotation *n* the action of rotating; a regular succession, as of crops to avoid exhausting the soil.

rote *n* a fixed, mechanical way of doing something.

rotgut *n* (*sl*) a cheap or inferior whiskey or other spirit.

rotisserie *n* a large rotating spit on which poultry is roasted; a place where such food is prepared.

rotor *n* a rotating part of a machine or engine.

rotten *adj* decayed, decomposed; corrupt; (*inf*) bad, nasty.—**rottenness** *n*.

rotund *adj* rounded; spherical; plump.

rotunda *n* a circular, esp domed, building or chamber.

rouble *n* a coin and monetary unit of Russia.—*also* **ruble**.

rouge *n* a red cosmetic for colouring the cheeks; a red powder for polishing jewellery, etc. * *vti* to colour (the face) with rouge.

rough *adj* uneven; not smooth; ill-mannered; violent; rude, unpolished; shaggy; coarse in texture; unrefined; violent, boisterous; stormy; wild; harsh, discordant; crude, unfinished; approximate; (*inf*) difficult. * *n* rough ground; (*golf*) any part of a course with grass, etc, left uncut; a first sketch. * *vt* to make rough; to sketch roughly; (*with* **up**) (*inf*) to injure violently, beat up. * *adv* in a rough manner.—**roughly** *adv*.—**roughness** *n*.

roughage *n* rough or coarse food or fodder, as bran, etc.

rough-and-ready *adj* unfinished but sufficient; prepared hastily.

rough-and-tumble *n* a scuffle; confusion.

roughcast *n* a mixture of lime and gravel for coating buildings; a rough surface finish. * *vt* (**roughcasting, roughcast**) to coat with roughcast.

rough-cut *n* an early version of a film with the scenes edited together in sequence and a soundtrack added.

roughen *vti* to make or become rough.

roughhouse *n* (*sl*) (an instance of) noisy, boisterous or violent behaviour.

roughneck *n* (*sl*) a coarse person.

roughshod *adj* marked by force without consideration.

rough stuff *n* (*inf*) violent behaviour.

rough trade *n* (*sl*) a homosexual partner who is tough and possibly violent.

roulade *n* food in the shape of a roll, such as cheese or meat; (*mus*) a run of notes on one syllable.

roulette *n* a gambling game played with a revolving disc and a ball; a toothed wheel for making dots or perforations.

round *adj* circular, spherical, or cylindrical in form; curved; plump; (*math*) expressed to the nearest ten, hundred, etc, not fractional; considerable; candid; (*style*) flowing, balanced; (*vowel*) pronounced with rounded lips. * *adv* circularly; on all sides; from one side to another; in a ring; by indirect way; through a recurring period of time; in circumference; in a roundabout way; about; near; here and there; with a rotating movement; in the opposite direction; around. * *prep* encircling; on every side of; in the vicinity of; in a circuit through; around. * *n* anything round; a circuit; (*shots*) a volley; a unit of ammunition; a series or sequence; a bout, turn; (*golf*) a circuit of a course; a stage of a contest; (*mus*) a kind of canon. * *vt* to make or become round or plump; (*math*) to express as a round number; to complete; to go or pass around. * *vi* to make a circuit; to turn; to reverse direction.—**roundly** *adv*.—**roundness** *n*.

roundabout *adj* indirect, circuitous. * *n* a circuitous route; a merry-go-round; (*Brit*) a traffic circle.

rounded *adj* curved or round; flowing, not angular.

roundhouse *n* a circular building for repairing and servicing railway locomotives.

round robin *n* a document with signatures in a circle to conceal their order.

round-shouldered *adj* with bent shoulders; stooping.

round-table conference *n* a conference with all the parties on an equal footing.

round trip *n* a journey to a place and back again.

round-trip ticket *n* a ticket whose price includes the cost of the journey to and back from a destination.

roundup *n* a driving together of livestock; (*inf*) the detention of several prisoners; a summary, as of news.

roundworm *n* a nematode parasitic in people and pigs.

rouse *vti* to provoke; to stir up; to awaken; to wake up; to become active.

rousing *adj* stirring; vigorous.

rout[1] *n* a noisy crowd, a rabble; a disorderly retreat. * *vt* to defeat and put to flight.

rout[2] *vti* to grub up, as a pig; to search haphazardly; to gouge out or make a furrow in (as wood or metal); to cause to emerge, esp from bed; to come up with; to uncover.

route *n* a course to be taken; the roads travelled on a journey. * *vt* to plan the route of; to send (by a specified route).

routine *n* a procedure that is regular and unvarying; a sequence of set movements, as in a dance, skating, etc.—*also adj*.

roux *n* a mixture of equal quantities of flour and melted fat used as the basis for sauces.

rove *vti* to wander about, roam (over).

rover *n* a wanderer; a fickle person; a senior Scout.

row[1] *n* a line of persons or things; a line of seats (in a theatre, etc).

row[2] *vti* to propel with oars; to transport by rowing. * *n* an act or instance of rowing.—**rower** *n*.

row[3] *n* a noisy quarrel or dispute; a scolding; noise, disturbance. * *vi* to quarrel; to scold.

rowan *n* a tree producing white flowers followed by small red berries.

rowboat, rowing boat *n* a small boat made for rowing.

rowdy *adj* (**rowdier, rowdiest**) rough and noisy, disorderly. * *n* (*pl* **rowdies**) a rowdy person, a hooligan.—**rowdiness, rowdyism** *n*.

rowel *n* a spiked revolving disc at the end of a spur.

rowing machine *n* an exercise machine with oars and a sliding seat that simulates a rowing action.

rowlock *n* a fitting on the side of a boat that holds an oar in place and serves as its fulcrum.

royal *adj* relating to or fit for a king or queen; regal; under the patronage of a king or queen; founded by a king or queen; of a kingdom, its government, etc. * *n* a type of topsail; a stag with a head of twelve points; (*inf*) a member of a royal family.—**royally** *adv*.

royal blue *n, adj* deep blue.

royal flush *n* (*poker*) a straight flush headed by an ace.

royalist *n* a person who advocates monarchy.

royal jelly *n* a nutritious secretion of the honeybee which is fed to larvae, esp those destined to become queens; a preparation of this sold as a health product.

royalty *n* (*pl* **royalties**) the rank or power of a king or queen; a royal person or persons; a share of the proceeds from a patent, book, song, etc, paid to the owner, author, composer, etc.

rpm *abbr* = revolutions per minute.

-rrhagia *n suffix* denoting an abnormal discharge.

-rrhoea, -rrhea *n suffix* a flow.

RSVP *abbr* = répondez s'il vous plait.

Ru (*chem symbol*) ruthenium.

rub *vti* (**rubbing, rubbed**) to move (a hand, cloth, etc) over the surface of with pressure; to wipe, scour; to clean or polish; (*with* **away, off, out**) to remove or erase by friction; to chafe, grate; to fret; to take a rubbing of; (*with* **along**) to manage somehow; (*with* **down**) to rub vigorously with a towel; to smooth down. * *n* the act or process of rubbing; a drawback, difficulty.

rubber[1] *n* an elastic substance made synthetically or from the sap of various tropical plants; an eraser; (*pl*) galoshes.

rubber[2] *n* a group of three games at whist, bridge, etc; the deciding game.

rubberize *vt* to coat with rubber to make waterproof.

rubberneck *n* (*sl*) a person who gapes, esp intrusively; a sightseer.—*also vi*.

rubber plant *n* an Asian plant related to the fig with shiny leaves, popular as a houseplant.

rubber-stamp *vt* (*inf*) to give automatic approval without investigation.

rubber tree *n* a tree native to South America and widely cultivated in the tropics as a source of latex to make rubber.

rubbing *n* an impression of an inscribed brass plate, etc, obtained by rubbing a wax substance on paper laid over it.

rubbish *n* refuse; garbage, trash; nonsense. —**rubbishy** *adj*.

rubble *n* rough broken stone or rock; builders' rubbish.

rubella *n* a mild contagious viral disease that may cause damage to an unborn child; German measles.

Rubenesque *adj* of, like or pertaining to the art of the Florentine painter Peter Paul Rubens (1577–1640); opulent, colourful; (*woman's figure*) full-breasted and shapely.

rubidium *n* a soft radioactive metallic element.

ruble *see* **rouble**.

rubric *n* a heading or line marked out in red; any rule, explanatory comment, etc.

ruby *n* (*pl* **rubies**) a deep red, transparent, valuable precious stone. * *adj* of the colour of a ruby.

ruby orange *n* an orange with red juice.

ruche *vt* to pleat, gather, or flute fabric for use as a trimming. * *n* ruched fabric.

rucksack *n* a bag worn on the back by hikers, used to carry camping or climbing equipment.

ruction *n* (*inf*) a disturbance, a row, uproar.

rudder *n* a flat vertical piece of wood or metal hinged to the stern of a ship or boat or the rear of an aircraft to steer by; a guiding principle.

ruddy *adj* (**ruddier, ruddiest**) reddish pink; (*complexion*) of a healthy, red colour.

rude *adj* uncivil, ill-mannered; uncultured, coarse; harsh, brutal; crude, roughly made; in a natural state, primitive; vigorous, hearty.—**rudely** *adv*.—**rudeness** *n*.

rudiment *n* a first stage; a first slight beginning of something; an imperfectly developed organ; (*pl*) elements, first principles.

rudimentary *adj* elementary; imperfectly developed or represented only by a vestige.

rue *vti* (**rueing, rued**) to feel remorse for (a sin, fault, etc); to regret (an act, etc). * *n* (*arch*) sorrow.

rueful *adj* regretful; dejected; showing good-humoured self-pity.—**ruefully** *adv*.

ruff *n* a pleated collar or frill worn round the neck; a fringe of feathers or fur round the neck of a bird or animal.

ruffian *n* a brutal lawless person; a villain.

ruffle *vti* to disturb the smoothness of, disarrange; to irritate; to agitate; to upset; to swagger about; to be quarrelsome; to flutter. * *n* pleated material used as a trim; a frill; a bird's ruff; a dispute, quarrel.

rug *n* a thick heavy fabric used as a floor covering; a thick woollen wrap or coverlet.

rugby *n* a football game for two teams of 15 players played with an oval ball.

rugged *adj* rocky; rough, uneven; strong; stern; robust.—**ruggedly** *adv*.—**ruggedness** *n*.

rugger *n* (*Brit inf*) rugby.

ruin *n* destruction; downfall, wrecked state; the cause of this; a loss of fortune; (*pl*) the remains of something destroyed, decayed, etc. * *vti* to destroy; to spoil; to bankrupt; to come to ruin.

ruinous *adj* in ruins, tumbledown; causing ruin, disastrous.

rule *n* a straight-edged instrument for drawing lines and measuring; government; the exercise of authority; a regulation, an order; a principle, a standard; habitual practice; the code of a religious order; a straight line. * *vti* to govern, to exercise authority over; to manage; to draw (lines) with a ruler; (*with* **out**) to exclude, to eliminate; to make impossible.

rule of thumb *n* a rough commonsense approach as opposed to a precise or theoretical one.

ruler *n* a person who governs; a strip of wood, metal, etc, with a straight edge, used in drawing lines, measuring, etc.

ruling *adj* governing; reigning; dominant. * *n* an authoritative pronouncement.

rum *n* a spirit made from sugar cane.

rumba *n* a dance of Cuban origin with a complex rhythm. * *vi* to dance the rumba.

rumble *vti* to make a low heavy rolling noise (as thunder); to move with such a sound; (*sl*) to see through, find out. * *n* the dull deep vibrant noise of thunder, etc.

rumbustious *adj* unruly, boisterous.
rumen *n* (*pl* **rumens, rumina**) the first compartment of the stomach of a ruminant mammal.
ruminant *n* a cud-chewing animal, such as cattle, deer, camels, etc. * *adj* chewing the cud; thoughtful.
ruminate *vi* to regurgitate food after it has been swallowed, chew cud; to ponder deeply, muse (on).
rummage *n* odds and ends; a search by ransacking. * *vti* to search thoroughly; to ransack; to fish (out).
rummage sale *n* a sale of second-hand clothes, books, etc to raise money for charity.—*also* **jumble sale.**
rummy *n* a card game whose object is to form sets and sequences.
rumour, rumor *n* hearsay, gossip; common talk not based on definite knowledge; an unconfirmed report, story. * *vt* to report by way of rumour.
rump *n* the hindquarters of an animal's body; the buttocks; the back end.
rumple *n* a crease or wrinkle. * *vti* to crease; to disarrange, tousle.
rumpus *n* (*pl* **rumpuses**) a commotion; a din.
run *vi* (**running, ran** *or* **run,** *pp* **run**) to go by moving the legs faster than in walking; to hurry; to flee; to flow; to operate; to be valid; to compete in a race, election, etc; (*colours*), to merge; (*with* **across**) to meet by accident; (*with* **around** *vi* (*inf*) to associate (with); to behave evasively or promiscuously; (*with* **away** *vi* to take flight, escape; to go out of control; (*with* **away with**) to abscond, elope; to steal; to win easily; (*with* **down**) (*engine, etc*) to cease to operate through lack of power; to become tired or exhausted; (*with* **off**) to leave hastily; to decide (a race) with a run-off; (*with* **through**) to use up (money, etc) completely; to read quickly. * *vt* (*a car, etc*) to drive; (*a business, etc*) to manage; (*a story*) to publish in a newspaper; (*temperature*) to suffer from a fever; (*with* **down**) to knock down with a moving vehicle; to collide with and cause to sink; to chase and capture; to tire, exhaust; to investigate, find; to criticize persistently; (*engine, etc*) to allow to gradually lose power; to reduce in quantity; (*with* **in**) to run a new car engine gently to start with; (*inf*) to arrest; (*with* **off**) to compose and talk glibly; to produce quickly, as copies on a photocopier; (*liquid*) to drain off; (*with* **out**) to exhaust a supply; (*inf*) to desert; (*with* **over**) (*vehicle*) to knock down a person or animal; to overflow; to exceed a limit; to rehearse quickly; (*with* **through**) to pierce with a sword or knife; to rehearse; (*with* **up**) to incur or amass. * *n* an act of running; a trip; a flow; a series; prevalence; a trend; an enclosure for chickens, etc; free and unrestricted access to all parts; (*in tights, etc*) a hole, a ladder.
run-around *n* deceitful or evasive behaviour towards someone.
runaway *n* a person or thing that runs away; a fugitive. * *adj* out of control; (*inflation*) rising uncontrollably; (*race, etc*) easily won.
run-down *adj* dilapidated; ill; tired.
rundown *n* a brief summary; the process of going into a decline.
rune *n* a letter of a primitive Teutonic alphabet; a magic mark or sign.—**runic** *adj*.
run-in *n* (*inf*) a quarrel.
rung[1] *see* **ring**[2].
rung[2] *n* the step of a ladder; the crossbar of a chair.
runner *n* an athlete; a person who runs; a smuggler; a groove or strip on which something glides.
runner bean *n* (*Brit*) a climbing plant that produces long green edible pods.
runner-up *n* (*pl* **runners-up**) the competitor who finishes second in a race, contest, etc.
running *n* the act of moving swiftly; that which runs or flows; a racing, managing, etc. * *adj* moving swiftly; kept for a race; being in motion; continuous; discharing pus. * *adv* in succession.
running commentary *n* a verbal description on TV or radio of an event as it happens, esp sport.
running mate *n* the candidate in a US election standing for the less important of two positions in a linked office.
runny *adj* (**runnier, runniest**) tending to flow.
run-off *n* a final deciding race, contest, etc.
run-of-the-mill *adj* average, mediocre.
runt *n* an unusually small animal, esp the smallest of a litter of pigs; a person of small stature.
run-through *n* a rehearsal; a cursory reading.
run-up *n* a preliminary period.
runway *n* a landing strip for aircraft.
rupee *n* a unit of money in India, Pakistan, Sri Lanka, Seychelles, Mauritius, and Nepal.
rupiah *n* (*pl* **rupiah, rupiahs**) the standard currency unit of Indonesia.
rupture *n* a breach; a severance, quarrel; the act of bursting or breaking; hernia. * *vti* to cause or suffer a rupture.
rural *adj* relating to the country or agriculture, rustic.—**rurally** *adv*.
ruse *n* a trick or stratagem.
rush[1] *vti* to move, push, drive, etc, swiftly or impetuously; to make a sudden attack (on); to do with unusual haste; to hurry. * *adj* marked by or needing extra speed or urgency. * *n* a sudden surge; a sudden demand; a press, as of business, requiring unusual haste; an unedited film print.
rush[2] *n* a marsh plant; its slender pithy stem; a worthless thing.
rush hour *n* the time at the beginning and end of the working day when traffic is at its heaviest.
rusk *n* a sweet or plain bread sliced and rebaked until dry and crisp.
russet *adj* reddish-brown. * *n* a russet colour; a winter apple with a rough russet skin; a homespun russet cloth.
Russian *n* a native or inhabitant of Russia; the Slavonic language of Russians.—*also adj*.
Russian roulette *n* an act of bravado in which the cylinder of a revolver loaded with a single bullet is spun and the muzzle then pointed at the head and fired.
Russo- *prefix* Russia; Russian.
rust *n* a reddish oxide coating formed on iron or steel when exposed to moisture; a reddish brown colour; a red mould on plants; the fungus causing this. * *vti* to form rust (on); to deteriorate, as through disuse.
rustic *n* pertaining to or characteristic of the country; rural; simple, unsophisticated. * *n* a person from the country; a simple country dweller.
rustle *n* a crisp, rubbing sound as of dry leaves, paper, etc. * *vti* to make or move with a rustle; to hustle; to steal (cattle); (*with* **up**) (*inf*) to collect or get together.
rustler *n* a person who steals livestock, esp cattle; a hustler.
rusty *adj* (**rustier, rustiest**) coated with rust; rust-coloured, faded; out of practice; antiquated.—**rustiness** *n*.
rut[1] *n* a track worn by wheels; an undeviating mechanical routine. * *vt* (**rutting, rutted**) to mark with ruts.
rut[2] *n* the seasonal period of sexual excitement in male ruminants, such as deer. * *vi* (**rutting, rutted**) to be in rut.
rutabaga *n* a swede.
ruthenium *n* a rare metallic element of the platinum group.
ruthless *adj* cruel; merciless.—**ruthlessly** *adv*.—**ruthlessness** *n*.
RV *abbr* = recreational vehicle.
rye *n* a hardy annual grass; its grain, used for making flour and whiskey; a whiskey made from rye.

S

S *abbr* = Saint; siemens; small; South, Southern; (*chem symbol*) sulphur.
S, s *n* the 19th letter of the English alphabet; something shaped like an S.
SA *abbr* = South Africa; South America; Salvation Army.
Sabbatarian *n* a strict observer of the sabbath.—**Sabbatarianism** *n*.
Sabbath *n* a day of rest and worship observed on a Saturday by Jews, Sunday by Christians and Friday by Muslims.
Sabbatical *adj* of, pertaining to, or resembling the Sabbath.
sabbatical *n* a year's leave from a teaching post, often paid, for research or travel.

SABC *abbr* = South African Broadcasting Corporation.
saber *see* **sabre.**
sabin *n* (*physics*) a unit of acoustic absorption.
Sabine *n* a member of an ancient people who lived in the central Apennines in Italy.—*also adj*.
sable *n* a carnivorous mammal of arctic regions valued for its luxuriant dark brown fur; its fur.
sabot *n* a shoe made from a single piece of wood; a shoe with a wooden sole and cloth upper.
sabotage *n* deliberate damage of machinery, or disruption of public services, by enemy agents, disgruntled employees, etc, to prevent their effective operation. * *vt* to practise sabotage on; to spoil, disrupt.
saboteur *n* a person who engages in sabotage.
sabra *n* a Jew born in Israel.
sabre *n* a cavalry sword with a curved blade; a light fencing sword.—*also* **saber.**
sabre-rattling *n* (*inf*) a conspicuous display of military power or aggression.
sabre-toothed tiger *n* an extinct species of large cat with long curved upper canine teeth.
sac *n* a bag-like part or cavity in a plant or animal.
saccate *adj* in the shape of a sac or pouch.
saccharide *n* a sugar.
saccharimeter *n* an instrument for measuring the concentration of sugar solutions.
saccharin *n* a non-fattening sugar substitute.
saccharine *adj* containing sugar; excessively sweet.
saccharo-, sacchar- *prefix* sugar.
sacerdotal *adj* relating to priests or the priesthood.—**sacerdotalism** *n*.—**sacerdotally** *adv*.
sachem *n* an American Indian chief of certain tribes; a political boss.
sachet *n* a sealed envelope or packet; a small perfumed bag or pad used to perfume clothes.
sack[1] *n* a large bag made of coarse cloth used as a container; the contents of this; a loose-fitting dress or coat; (*baseball*) a bag serving as a base; (*sl: with* **the**) dismissal. * *vt* to put into sacks; (*sl*) to dismiss.
sack[2] *n* the plunder or destruction of a place. * *vt* to plunder or loot.
sackbut *n* a type of medieval trombone.
sackcloth *n* a coarse fabric for sacks, etc; penitential clothing.
sacking *n* the coarse cloth used for sacks; the storming and plundering of a place.
sack race *n* a jumping race in which the participants' legs and lower bodies are enclosed in sacks.
sacra see **sacrum.**
sacrament *n* a religious ceremony forming outward and visible sign of inward and spiritual grace, esp baptism and the Eucharist; the consecrated elements in the Eucharist, esp the bread; a sacred symbol or pledge.
sacramental *adj* of, pertaining to, or like a sacrament. * *n* (*RC Church*) a rite recognized as similar to a sacrament, eg the use of holy water.—**sacramentally** *adv*.
sacred *adj* regarded as holy; consecrated to a god or God; connected with religion; worthy of or regarded with reverence, sacrosanct.
sacred cow *n* (*inf*) a person or thing regarded as above criticism.
sacrifice *n* the act of offering ceremonially to a deity; the slaughter of an animal (or person) to please a deity; the surrender of something valuable for the sake of something more important or worthy; loss without return; something sacrificed, an offering. * *vt* to slaughter or give up as a sacrifice; to give up for a higher good; to sell at a loss.—**sacrificial** *adj*.
sacrilege *n* violation of anything holy or sacred.
sacrilegious *adj* guilty of sacrilege; irreverent.—**sacrilegiously** *adv*.—**sacrilegiousness** *n*.
sacristan *n* a person in charge of the contents of a church; a sexton.
sacristy *n* (*pl* **sacristies**) a room in a church where the sacred vessels, etc are kept
sacrosanct *adj* inviolable; very holy.
sacrum *n* (*pl* **sacra**) a compound bone at the base of the spine forming the back of the pelvis.
sad *adj* (**sadder, saddest**) expressing grief or unhappiness; sorrowful; deplorable.—**sadly** *adv*.—**sadness** *n*.
sadden *vti* to make or become sad.
saddle *n* a seat, usu of leather, for a rider on a horse, bicycle, etc; a ridge connecting two mountain peaks; a joint of mutton or venison consisting of the two loins; in **the saddle** mounted on a saddle; in control. * *vt* to put a saddle on; to burden, encumber.
saddlebag *n* a bag hung from the saddle of a horse or bicycle.
saddlebow *n* the arched front of a saddle.
saddlecloth *n* a piece of cloth placed under a horse's saddle to prevent chafing.
saddler *n* a person who makes or sells saddles, harness, etc.
saddlery *n* (*pl* **saddleries**) articles made by a saddler; the business or premises of a saddler.
saddle soap *n* an oily soap for cleaning and preserving leather.
saddletree *n* the frame of a saddle.
sadhu, saddhu *n* a Hindu holy man.
sadism *n* sexual pleasure obtained from inflicting cruelty upon another; extreme cruelty.—**sadist** *n*.—**sadistic** *adj*.—**sadistically** *adv*.
sadomasochism *n* sexual pleasure obtained from inflicting cruelty upon oneself and receiving it from another.—**sadomasochist** *n*.—**sadomasochistic** *adj*.
s.a.e. *abbr* = stamped addressed envelope.
safari *n* (*pl* **safaris**) a journey or hunting expedition, esp in Africa.
safari jacket *n* a belted shirt jacket with pleated pockets.
safari suit *n* a safari jacket and matching trousers or skirt made from denim or similar hard-wearing material.
safe *adj* unhurt; out of danger; reliable; secure; involving no risk; trustworthy; giving protection; prudent; sure; incapable of doing harm. * *n* a locking metal box or compartment for valuables.—**safely** *adv*.
safe-conduct *n* written permission for the holder to travel safely through hostile country.
safecracker *n* a person who opens and robs safes.—*also* **safe-breaker.**—**safecracking** *n*.
safe-deposit *adj* (*box, room, etc*) designed for the protective storage of valuables, deeds, etc. * *n* a building with safes for renting—*also* **safety deposit.**
safeguard *n* anything that protects against injury or danger; a proviso against foreseen risks. * *vt* to protect.
safe house *n* a refuge for victims of domestic violence, sexual abuse, etc run by social welfare organizations; a clandestine place used by intelligence services, terrorists, etc as a refuge.
safekeeping *n* the act or process of keeping safely; protection.
safe period *n* the time in a woman's menstrual cycle when she is least likely to conceive.
safe seat *n* a parliamentary constituency in which the sitting MP enjoys a substantial majority and can be assured of re-election.
safe sex *n* sex in which precautions are taken to lessen the risk of catching AIDS or other sexually transmitted diseases.
safety *n* (*pl* **safeties**) freedom from danger; the state of being safe.
safety belt *n* a belt worn by a person working at a great height to prevent falling; a seatbelt in a car.
safety curtain *n* a fireproof curtain that can be lowered to separate a theatre stage from the auditorium.
safety deposit *see* **safe-deposit.**
safety glass *n* shatterproof glass.
safety lamp *n* a miner's lamp in which the flame is enclosed by a protective gauze to prevent it igniting combustible gases.
safety match *n* a match that will only ignite on a particular surface.
safety net *n* a net suspended beneath acrobats, etc; any protection against loss.
safety pin *n* a pin with a guard to cover the point.

safety razor *n* a razor with a guard that covers the blade to protect the skin from accidental cuts.

safety valve *n* an automatic valve for relieving excess pressure of steam, etc; a harmless outlet for emotion.

saffian *n* a brightly dyed leather made from the skin of goats or sheep.

safflower *n* (a red dye and oil derived from) a thistle-like plant with large orange or red flowers.

saffron *n* a crocus whose bright yellow stigmas are used as a food colouring and flavouring; an orange-yellow colour.

sag *vi* (**sagging, sagged**) to droop downward in the middle; to sink or hang down unevenly under pressure.

saga *n* a long story of heroic deeds.

sagacious *adj* mentally acute, shrewd; wise.—**sagaciously** *adv*.—**sagaciousness** *n*.

sagacity *n* (*pl* **sagacities**) readiness of apprehension; discriminating intelligence; acute practical judgment.

sagamore *n* an American Indian chief of certain tribes.

sage[1] *adj* wise through reflection and experience. * *n* a person of profound wisdom.—**sagely** *adv*.—**sagely** *adv*.

sage[2] *n* a herb with leaves used for flavouring food; sagebrush.

sagebrush *n* a low shrub of the alkaline plains of North America.

sagger, saggar *n* a fireproof clay case in which procelain is put for baking.

sagittate *adj* (*leaf*) shaped like an arrowhead.

Sagittarius *n* the Archer, ninth sign of the zodiac; in astrology, operative November 22–December 20.—**Sagittarian** *adj, n*.

sago *n* (*pl* **sagos**) a type of Asian palm; its starchy pith used in puddings.

saguaro *n* (*pl* **saguaros**) a large cactus of North American and Mexican desert areas bearing white flowers and edible fruit.

sahib *n* a form of polite address formerly used by Indians to European men.

said *see* **say**.

saiga *n* a stocky antelope of the Russian steppes.

sail *n* a piece of canvas used to catch the wind to propel or steer a vessel; sails collectively; anything like a sail; an arm of a windmill; a voyage in a sailing vessel; **under sail** with the sails set; under way. * *vt* to navigate a vessel; to manage (a vessel); **to set sail** to spread the sails; to begin a voyage. * *vi* to be moved by sails; to travel by water; to glide or pass smoothly; to walk in a stately manner.

sailboard *n* a type of large surfboard with a sail used in windfsurfing.

sailboat *n* a sailing boat.

sailcloth *n* canvas used for sails; a strong, durable fabric for clothing.

sailer *n* a sailing vessel.

sailfish *n* (*pl* **sailfish, sailfishes**) a large game fish of tropical waters with a long sail-like dorsal fin.

sailing *n* the act of sailing; the motion or direction of a ship, etc on water; a departure from a port.

sailing boat *n* a boat that is propelled by a sail or sails.

sailor *n* a person who sails; one of a ship's crew.

sailoring *n* a sailor's life.

sailplane *n* a type of light glider. * *vi* to fly a sailplane.

sain *vt* (*arch*) to make the sign of the cross on; to bless in order to protect from evil.

sainfoin *n* a Eurasian leguminous plant with pink flowers, grown for fodder.

saint *n* a person who is very patient, charitable, etc; a person who is canonized by the Roman Catholic Church; one of the blessed in heaven.—**sainthood** *n*.

Saint Bernard *n* a breed of large dog with a reddish brown coat, often used as a rescue dog.

sainted *adj* canonized; holy; dead; much admired.

saintly *adj* (**saintlier, saintliest**) of, like, or relating to a saint.—**saintliness** *n*.

Saint Patrick's Day *n* March 17, observed by the Irish in honour of the patron saint of Ireland.

saint's day *n* a day in the church calender which is devoted to the commemoration of a particular saint.

sake[1] *n* behalf; purpose; benefit; interest.

sake[2], **saké, saki** *n* a Japanese alcoholic drink made from fermented rice and drunk warm.

sal *n* (*chem*) a salt.

salaam *n* a form of ceremonial greeting in Muslim countries. * *vti* to make a salaam (to).

salable *adj* marketable; in good demand.—*also* **saleable**.

salacious *adj* lustful; obscene.—**salaciously** *adv*.—**salaciousness** *n*.

salad *n* a dish, usu cold, of vegetables, fruits, meat, eggs, etc; lettuce, etc, used for this.

salad bar *n* a buffet in a restaurant at which diners choose their own salads.

salad days *npl* a time of youth and inexperience.

salad dressing *n* a cooked or uncooked sauce of oil, vinegar, spices, etc, to put on a salad.

salade niçoise *n* a salad of various ingredients, including tomatoes, hard-boiled eggs, and anchovy fillets or tuna fish.

salamander *n* any of various lizard-like amphibians; a mythical lizard-like creature that was supposedly impervious to fire.

salami *n* a highly seasoned Italian sausage.

salaried *adj* receiving a salary.

salary *n* (*pl* **salaries**) fixed, regular payment for non-manual work, usu paid monthly.

salchow *n* (*ice-skating*) a jump incorporating turns in the air.

sale *n* the act of selling; the exchange of goods or services for money; the market or opportunity of selling; an auction; the disposal of goods at reduced prices; the period of this.

saleable *see* **salable**.

salep *n* (food made from) the starchy dried roots of various orchidaceous plants.

saleratus *n* sodium bicarbonate used in cooking.

saleroom *n* a salesroom; an auction room.

salesclerk *n* a person who sells goods in a store.

salesman *n* (*pl* **salesmen**) a person who sells either in a given territory or in a store.—**saleswoman** *nf* (*pl* **saleswomen**).

salesmanship *n* the art or skill of selling.

salesperson *n* (*pl* **salespeople**) a salesman or saleswoman.

sales representative *n* a person who travels to sell within a given territory.

salesroom *n* a place where goods are displayed for sale; a saleroom.

sales talk *n* talk aimed at selling something; any talk to persuade.

sales tax *n* a tax levied (usu as a percentage) on the price of an object bought by a consumer.

Salic *adj* of or pertaining to the Franks; relating to the Salic law.

Salic law *n* the law of the Franks excluding females from the succession to the French throne.

salicin *n* a bitter compound obtained from the bark of willows and poplars, used in medicine.

salient *adj* projecting outward; conspicuous; noteworthy; leaping, gushing.—**salience, saliency** *n*.—**saliently** *adv*.

salify *vt* to make salty; (*chem*) to convert into a salt.—**salification** *n*.

salimeter *n* a device for measuring the amount of salt in a solution.

saline *adj* of or impregnated with salt or salts; salty. * *n* a solution of salt and water.—**salinity** *n*.

saliva *n* the liquid secreted by glands in the mouth that aids digestion.—**salivary** *adj*.

salivate *vi* to secrete saliva, esp excessively.—**salivation** *n*.

sallenders *npl* an eczematous rash on a horse's hock.

sallet *n* a light helmet of the 15th century.

sallow *adj* (*complexion*) an unhealthy yellow colour, a pale brown colour.—**sallowness** *n*.

sally *n* (*pl* **sallies**) a sudden attack; an outburst; a lively remark, quip. * *vi* (**sallying, sallied**) to make a sally; to go (forth).

salmagundi *n* a mixed dish of chopped meat, anchovies, eggs, vegetables, etc; a miscellany.

salmi *n* (*pl* **salmis**) a casserole of game-birds in a rich wine sauce.

salmon *n* (*pl* **salmon, salmons**) a large silvery edible fish that lives in salt water and spawns in fresh water; salmon pink.

salmonella *n* (*pl* **salmonellae, salmonella, salmonellas**) any of a genus of bacteria that causes food poisoning and diseases of the genital tract.
salmon ladder *n* a series of steps (eg in a waterfall or dam) to allow salmon to swim upstream to their breeding grounds.
salmon pink *adj* a yellowish pink colour.
salmon trout *n* a large trout resembling a salmon.
salon *n* a large reception hall or drawing room for receiving guests; the shop of a hairdresser, beautician, or couturier; an art gallery.
saloon *n* a large reception room; a large cabin for the social use of a ship's passengers; a four-seater car with a boot; a place where alcoholic drinks are sold and consumed.
saloon bar *n* a comfortably furnished bar.
salopettes *npl* thick quilted trousers with shoulder straps, worn for skiing.
salsa *n* (the music for) a type of Puerto Rican dance.
salsify *n* (*pl* **salsifies**) a purple-flowered plant with an edible root.
SALT *abbr* = Strategic Arms Limitation Talks *or* Treaty.
salt *n* a white crystalline substance (sodium chloride) used as a seasoning or preservative; piquancy, wit; (*chem*) a compound of an acid and a base; (*pl*) mineral salt as an aperient. * *adj* containing or tasting of salt; preserved with salt; pungent. * *vt* to flavour, pickle or sprinkle with salt; to give flavour or piquancy to (as a story); (*with* **away**) to hoard; to keep for the future.
saltbush *n* a shrub-like plant which provides grazing in dry regions.
salt cellar *n* a vessel for salt at the table; a saltshaker.
saltire *n* an X-shaped cross dividing a shield, flag, etc, into four compartments.
salt lick *n* an area where animals go to lick salt residue; a block of salt for animals to lick.
salt marsh *n* an area regularly flooded by seawater.
saltpan *n* a hollow or depression where salt is deposited by evaporating seawater.
saltpetre, saltpeter *n* a white powder (potassium nitrate) used in making gunpowder, etc.
saltshaker *n* a container for salt with a perforated top.
saltwater *adj* of or living in salt water or the sea.
salty *adj* (**saltier, saltiest**) of, containing or tasting of salt; witty; earthy, coarse.
salubrious *adj* health-giving; wholesome.—**salubriously** *adv*.—**salubriousness** *n*.
saluki *n* a breed of tall, slender hounds with long silky coats.
salutary *adj* beneficial, wholesome.—**salutarily** *adv*.—**salutariness** *n*.
salutation *n* a greeting; the words used in it.
salute *n* a gesture of respect or greeting; (*mil*) a motion of the right hand to the head, or to a rifle; a discharge of guns, etc, as a military mark of honour. * *vti* to make a salute (to); to greet; to kiss; to praise or honour.
salvable *adj* able to be salvaged.
salvage *n* the rescuing of a ship or property from loss at sea, by fire, etc; the reward paid for this; the thing salvaged; waste material intended for further use. * *vt* to save from loss or danger.—**salvageable** *adj*.—**salvager** *n*.
salvation *n* the act of saving or the state of being saved; in Christianity, the deliverance from evil; a means of preservation.—**salvational** *adj*.
Salvation Army *n* an international religious and charitable group organized on military lines founded by William Booth in 1865.—**Salvationist** *n*.
salve[1] *n* a healing ointment or balm; a soothing influence. * *vt* to apply ointment to; to smooth over; to soothe.
salve[2] *vt* to salvage; (*arch*) to save.
salver *n* a small tray.
salvia *n* any of a genus of plants or small shrubs with red or purple flowers.
salvo[1] *n* (**salvoes, salvos**) a firing of several guns or missiles simultaneously; a sudden burst; a spirited verbal attack.
salvo[2] *n* (*pl* **salvos**) an exception or reservation.
sal volatile *n* a solution of ammonium carbonate in alcohol used as a remedy for faintness.
salvor *n* a person or vessel effecting a salvage at sea.
SAM (*acronym*) surface-to-air missile.
samara *n* a dry winged single-seeded fruit produced by the ash, elm, etc.
Samaritan *n* a native or inhabitant of Samaria in ancient Palestine; a compassionate person; a Good Samaritan; a member of a voluntary organization that helps people in distress or despair.
samarium *n* a silvery metallic element used in lasers and alloys.
samba *n* a Brazilian dance of African origin; the music for this. * *vi* to dance the samba.
same *adj* identical; exactly similar; unchanged; uniform, monotonous; previously mentioned. * *pron* the same person or thing. * *adv* in like manner.
sameness *n* the state of being the same; monotony.
Samian *n* a native or inhabitant of the Aegean island of Samos in Greece. * *adj* of or pertaining to Samos or its people.
Samian ware *n* a type of red or black pottery from Samos.
samisen *n* a Japanese guitar-like instrument with three strings.
samite *n* a medieval heavy silken fabric.
samizdat *n* in the former Soviet Union, a system for the clandestine printing and distribution of banned literature.
Samoan *n* a native or inhabitant of Samoa, a group of islands in the South Pacific; the Polynesian language of Samoa.* *adj* of or pertaining to Samoa, its people or language.
samosa *n* (*pl* **samosas, samosa**) an Indian savoury pasty with a spicy meat or vegetable filling.
samovar *n* a metal urn with an internal element used for boiling water for tea, esp in Russia.
Samoyed *n* a member of a people of the northern Urals; the language of these people; a breed of sledge-dog with a thick creamy coat and a tightly curled tail.—**Samoyedic** *adj*.
sampan *n* a small flat-bottomed Chinese river boat.
samphire *n* a Eurasian coastal rock plant with edible fleshy leaves.
sample *n* a specimen; a small part representative of the whole; an instance. * *vt* (*food, drink*) to taste a small quantity of; to test by taking a sample.
sampler *n* a person who takes samples; something containing a representative selection (as a record, book); an assortment; a piece of ornamental embroidery showing different stitches and patterns as an example of skill.
sampling *n* (*mus industry*) the practice of extracting phrases from several recorded songs and putting them together electronically to make a new one.
samurai *n* (*pl* **samurai**) a member of an ancient Japanese warrior caste.
samurai bond *n* a financial bond issued in yen by a non-Japanese company.
-san *n suffix* a Japanese title of respect similar to Mr, Mrs, etc.
sanatorium *see* **sanitarium.**
sancta *see* **sanctum.**
sanctified *adj* hallowed; consecrated; sanctimonious.
sanctify *vt* (**sanctifying, sanctified**) to make holy; to purify from sin or evil; (*the Church*) to give official approval.—**sanctification** *n*.—**sanctifier** n.
sanctimonious *adj* pretending to be holy; hypocritically pious or righteous.—**sanctimoniously** *adv*.—**sanctimoniousness** *n*.
sanctimony *n* self-righteousness; hypocrisy.
sanction *n* express permission, authorization; a binding influence; a penalty by which a law is enforced, esp a prohibition on trade with a country that has violated international law. * *vt* to permit; to give authority.—**sanctionable** *adj*.
sanctity *n* (*pl* **sanctities**) the condition of being holy or sacred; inviolability.
sanctuary *n* (*pl* **sanctuaries**) a sacred place; the part of a church around the altar; a place where one is free from arrest or violence, an asylum; a refuge; an animal reserve.
sanctum *n* (*pl* **sanctums, sancta**) a holy place; a private room where one is not to be disturbed.
Sanctus *n* (*Christianity*) the hymn "Holy, holy, holy" used in communion; an orchestral setting of this.

sand *n* very fine rock particles; (*pl*) a desert; a sandy beach. * *vt* to smooth or polish with sand or sandpaper; to sprinkle with sand. * *adj* reddish yellow.

sandal[1] *n* a shoe consisting of a sole strapped to the foot; a low slipper or shoe.—**sandalled, sandaled** *adj*.

sandal[2] *n* sandalwood.

sandalwood *n* the yellow, scented wood of an Asian tree; the tree.

sandbag *n* a bag of sand used for ballast or to protect against floodwater. * *vt* (**sandbagging, sandbagged**) to protect by laying sandbags; to hit with a sandbag; (*inf*) to coerce; (*sl*) to deceive.—**sandbagger** *n*.

sandbank *n* a sand bar; a large deposit of sand forming a hill or mound.

sand bar *n* a ridge of sand built up in a river, a lake, or coastal waters by currents.

sandblast *vt* (*a building*) to clean by blasting with sand at high velocity.—*also n*.

sand box *n* a small enclosure filled with sand for children to play in.—*also* **sandpit**.

sand castle *n* a model of a castle moulded from damp sand, as made at the seaside by children.

sander *n* a power-driven tool for sanding wood or other surfaces.

sanderling *n* a small wading bird.

sandglass *n* an instrument that measures time by the running of sand through a narrow aperture.

S & L *abbr* = savings and loan association.

S & M *abbr* = sadomasochism.

sandman *n* (*pl* **sandmen**) (*folklore*) an imaginary being who sends children to sleep by sprinkling sand in their eyes.

sand martin *n* a small European songbird that nests in holes in sandy riverbanks, etc.

sandpaper *n* a paper coated on one side with sand or another abrasive, used to smooth or polish. * *vt* to rub with sandpaper.

sandpiper *n* any of numerous small wading birds.

sandpit *see* **sand box**.

sandstone *n* a sedimentary rock of compacted sand.

sandstorm *n* a windstorm in a desert carrying clouds of sand.

sand trap *n* (*golf*) a pit of sand forming an obstacle on a golf course, a bunker.

sand wedge *n* (*golf*) a club for hitting the ball out of a sand trap.

sandwich *n* two slices of bread with meat, cheese, or other filling between; anything in a sandwich-like arrangement. * *vt* to place between two things or two layers; to make such a place for.

sandwich board *n* two usu hinged boards hanging from the shoulders, one in front and one at the back, carried by a sandwich man.

sandwich man *n* a person who advertises by wearing a sandwich board.

sandy *adj* (**sandier, sandiest**) of, like, or sprinkled with sand; yellowish grey.—**sandiness** *n*.

sane *adj* mentally sound, not mad; reasonable, sensible.—**sanely** *adv*.—**saneness** *n*.

sang *see* **sing**.

sangfroid *n* coolness in danger, imperturbability.

Sangreal *n* the Holy Grail.

sangria *n* a Spanish drink made with red wine, orange juice and fresh fruit laced with brandy.

sanguinary *adj* accompanied by bloodshed; bloodthirsty.—**sanguinarily** *adv*.

sanguine *adj* confident, hopeful; blood-red; (*complexion*) ruddy.—**sanguineness** *n*.

sanguinely *adv* confidently, hopefully.

sanguineous *adj* of or relating to blood; full-blooded; blood-red; sanguinary; sanguine.

sanies *n* a watery mixture of blood and pus discharged from a sore or wound.—**sanious** *adj*.

sanitarian *adj* hygienic. * *n* a specialist in matters of public health.

sanitarium *n* (*pl* **sanitariums, sanitaria**) an establishment for the treatment of convalescents or the chronically ill.—*also* **sanatorium**.

sanitary *adj* relating to the promotion and protection of health; relating to the supply of water, drainage, and sewage disposal; hygienic.—**sanitarily** *adv*.—**sanitariness** *n*.

sanitary cordon *n* a cordon sanitaire.

sanitary engineering *n* the design, construction and installation of water and sewage systems.—**sanitary engineer** *n*.

sanitary napkin, sanitary towel *n* an absorbent pad worn externally during menstruation.

sanitation *n* the science and practice of achieving hygienic conditions; drainage and disposal of sewage.

sanitize *vt* to clean or sterilize; to make (language, etc) more respectable or acceptable.

sanity *n* the condition of being sane; mental health; common sense.

sank *see* **sink**.

Sanka *n* (trademark) a decaffeinated coffee.

sannup *n* an American Indian warrior, a brave.

Sans. *abbr* = Sanskrit.

sans *prep* without.

sansculotte *n* in the French Revolution, a man without breeches, a term of contempt applied to a revolutionary who wore pantaloons instead of knee breeches; any revolutionary.

sans doute (*French*) doubtless; certainly.

Sansk. *abbr* = Sanskrit.

Sanskrit *n* the ancient language used in Indian and Hindu sacred literature.—**Sanskrit** *adj*.—**Sanskritic** *adj*.

sans-serif, sanserif *n* (*print*) a character or typeface with no serifs.

sans souci (*French*) free from care.

Santa *n* Santa Claus. * *adj* sainted, holy.

Santa Claus *n* a legendary fat, white-bearded old man who brings presents to children at Christmas.—*also* **Father Christmas**.

sap[1] *n* the vital juice of plants; energy and health; (*inf*) a fool. * *vt* (**sapping, sapped**) to drain of sap; to exhaust the energy of.

sap[2] *n* a narrow or covered siege trench; the digging of this, undermining. * *vti* (**sapping, sapped**) to attack by or dig a sap; to undermine insidiously.

saphead *n* (*sl*) a fool, a stupid person.

sapid *adj* having a pleasing flavour; agreeable.—**sapidity** *n*.

sapient *adj* (*often ironical*) wise, discerning.—**sapience** *n*.—**sapiently** *adv*.

sapling *n* a young tree; a youth.

saponify *vt* (**saponifying, saponified**) (*chem*) to convert (fat, oil, etc) into soap by combination with an alkali. * *vi* to undergo this process.—**saponification** *n*.—**saponifier** n.

sapor *n* taste, flavour.

sapper *n* one who or that which saps; a soldier who lays, detects or disarms mines.

sapphire *n* a transparent blue precious stone; a deep pure blue.—*also adj*.

sapro-, sapr- *prefix* dead or decaying matter.

saprogenic, saprogenous *adj* producing or caused by putrefaction.

saprophagous *adj* feeding on decaying matter.

saprophyte *n* a plant or fungus that grows on dead organic matter.—**saprophytic** *adj*.

Saracen *n* a member of a nomadic people of the Syrian desert; a Muslim at the time of the Crusades. * *adj* of or pertaining to Saracens.—**Saracenic** *adj*.

sarcasm *n* a scornful or ironic remark; the use of this.—**sarcastic** *adj*.—**sarcastically** *adv*.

sarco-, sarc- *prefix* flesh.

sarcoma *n* (*pl* **sarcomas, sarcomata**) a malignant tumour of connective tissue.—**sarcomatous** *adj*.

sarcophagus *n* (*pl* **sarcophagi, sarcophaguses**) a large stone coffin or tomb.

sard *n* an orange-red variety of chalcedony.

sardine *n* (*pl* **sardines, sardine**) a small, edible seafish.

sardonic *adj* (*smile, etc*) derisive, mocking, maliciously jocular.—**sardonically** *adv*.

sardonyx *n* an onyx with alternate layers of white chalcedony and orange sard.

sargasso *n* (*pl* **sargassos**) a large mass of floating sargassum.
sargassum *n* any of a genus of tropical seaweed with air bladders that form to float in large masses.
sarge *n* (*sl*) sergeant.
sari, saree *n* a Hindu woman's principal garment, consisting of a long piece of cloth wrapped around the waist and across the shoulder.
sark *n* (*Scot*) a shirt.
sarong *n* a long strip of cloth wrapped around the lower body, worn esp in the Malay archipelago and the Pacific Islands.
sarsaparilla *n* any of various tropical American trailing plants; the dried roots of these used as a flavouring and (formerly) in medicine; a soft drink flavoured with these roots.
sartorial *adj* of or relating to the making of men's clothing.—**sartorially** *adv*.
sartorius *n* (*pl* **sartorii**) a muscle that helps flex the knee.
SASE *abbr* = self-addressed stamped envelope.
sash[1] *n* a band of satin or ribbon worn around the waist or over the shoulder, often as a badge of honour.
sash[2] *n* a frame for holding the glass of a window, esp one that slides vertically.
sashay *n* (*inf*) to walk in a casual manner, saunter; to swagger.
sash cord *n* a cord used to attach a sash weight to a sash.
sashimi *n* a Japanese dish of thin strips of raw fish.
sash weight *n* a weight used to balance a sliding sash in an open position.
sash window *n* a window with sliding sashes.
sass *n* (*inf*) rudeness, impudence. * *vt* to talk rudely or impudently to.
sassafras *n* a North American tree of the laurel family; the aromatic dried root of this used as a flavouring.
Sassenach *n* (*Scot, Irish*) an English person.
sassy *adj* (**sassier, sassiest**) (*sl*) rude; cheeky.
Sat *abbr* = Saturday; Saturn.
sat *see* **sit.**
Satan *n* the devil, the adversary of God.
satanic, satanical *adj* of or relating to Satan, devilish; marked by viciousness or cruelty.—**satanically** *adv*.
Satanism *n* the worship of Satan; the perversion of Christian ceremonial forms associated with this.—**Satanist** *n*.
satay, saté *n* an Indonesian dish of cubed chicken, beef, etc served with a piquant peanut sauce.
satchel *n* a bag with shoulder straps for carrying school books, etc.
sate *vt* to satisfy to repletion, to satiate.
sateen *n* a closely woven fabric with a glossy surface made in imitation of satin.
satellite *n* a planet orbiting another; a man-made object orbiting the earth, moon, etc, to gather scientific information or for communication; a nation economically dependent on a more powerful one.
satellite broadcasting, satellite television *n* the transmission of television programmes via an orbiting satellite to subscribers in possession of a receiving satellite dish aerial.
sati *see* **suttee.**
satiable *adj* able to be satiated or sated.—**satiability** *n*.—**satiably** *adv*.
satiate *vt* to provide with more than enough so as to weary or disgust; to gorge.—**satiation** *n*.
satiety *n* the state of being sated; a feeling of having had too much.
satin *n* a fabric of woven silk with a smooth, shiny surface on one side. * *adj* of or resembling satin.
satinwood *n* a smooth yellowish brown hard wood; a tree that yields such wood.
satiny *adj* smooth and lustrous, like satin.
satire *n* a literary work in which folly or evil in people's behaviour are held up to ridicule; trenchant wit, sarcasm.—**satirical** *adj*.—**satirically** *adv*.
satirist *n* a writer of satires.
satirize *vt* to attack with satire.—**satirizer** *n*.
satisfaction *n* the act of satisfying or the condition of being satisfied; that which satisfies; comfort; atonement, reparation.
satisfactory *adj* giving satisfaction; adequate; acceptable; convincing.—**satisfactorily** *adv*.—**satisfactoriness** *n*.
satisfy *vb* (**satisfying, satisfied**) *vi* to be enough for; to fulfil the needs or desires of. * *vt* to give enough to; (*hunger, desire etc.*) to appease; to please; to gratify; to comply with; (*creditor*) to discharge, to pay in full; to convince; to make reparation to; (*guilt, etc*) to atone for.
satori *n* (*Zen Buddhism*) a state of intuitive enlightenment.
satsuma *n* a loose-skinned, seedless, small orange; (*with cap*) a glazed yellow Japanese pottery.
saturate *vt* to soak thoroughly; to fill completely.—**saturator** *n*.
saturated *adj* (*chem*) absorbing the maximum amount possible of a substance; pure in colour.
saturation *n* the act of saturating or the condition of being saturated; the supplying of a market with all the goods it will absorb; an overwhelming concentration of military power.
Saturday *n* the seventh and last day of the week.
Saturn *n* (*Roman myth*) the god of agriculture; (*astron*) the second largest planet in the solar system, with three rings revolving about it.—**Saturnian** *adj*.
Saturnalia *n* (*pl* **Saturnalias, Saturnalia**) in ancient Rome, a festival held in December in honour of Saturn; (*without cap*) a wild, unrestrained celebration.—**Saturnalian** *n*.
saturnine *adj* sullen, morose.—**saturninely** *adv*.
satyagraha *n* the principle and practice of passive resistance as adopted by Mahatma Gandhi in opposition to British colonial rule in India.
satyr *n* (*Greek myth*) a woodland god in human form but with goat's ears, tail, and legs; a man with strong sexual appetites; a man with satyriasis.—**satyric** *adj*.
satyriasis *n* excessive sexual desire in men.
sauce *n* a liquid or dressing served with food to enhance its flavour; stewed or preserved fruit eaten with other food or as a dessert; (*inf*) impudence. * *vt* to season with sauce; to make piquant; (*sl*) to cheek.
saucepan *n* a deep cooking pan with a handle and lid.
saucer *n* a round shallow dish placed under a cup; a shallow depression; a thing shaped like a saucer.
saucy *adj* (**saucier, sauciest**) rude, impertinent; sprightly.—**saucily** *adv*.—**sauciness** *n*.
sauerkraut *n* a German dish of chopped pickled cabbage.
sauna *n* exposure of the body to hot steam, followed by cold water; the room where this is done.
saunter *vi* to walk in a leisurely or idle way. * *n* a stroll.—**saunterer** *n*.
-saur *n suffix* (*scientific*) reptiles.
saurian *adj* of or resembling a lizard. * *n* (*formerly*) lizard.
sauro- *prefix* lizard.
saury *n* (*pl* **sauries**) an Atlantic fish with a long body and elongated jaws.
sausage *n* minced seasoned meat, esp pork, packed into animal gut or other casing.
sauté *adj* fried quickly and lightly. * *vt* (**sautéing, sautéed**) to fry in a small amount of oil or fat. * *n* a sautéed dish.
sauve qui peut *n* a precipitate flight, a general stampede.
savage *adj* fierce; wild; untamed; uncivilized; ferocious; primitive. * *n* a member of a primitive society; a brutal, fierce person or animal.—**savagely** *adv*.—**savageness** *n*.
savagery *n* (*pl* **savageries**) the state of being a savage; an act of violence or cruelty; an uncivilized state.
savanna, savannah *n* a treeless plain; an area of tropical or subtropical grassland.
savant *n* (*pl* **savants**) a person with extensive knowledge, esp in a certain discipline.
savate *n* a form of boxing using both the fists and the feet.
save[1] *vt* to rescue from harm or danger; to keep, to accumulate; to set aside for future use; to avoid the necessity of; (*energy etc*) to prevent waste of; (*theol*) to deliver from sin. * *vi* to avoid waste, expense, etc; to economize; to store up money or goods; (*sports*) to keep an opponent

from scoring or winning. * *n* (*sports*) the act of preventing one's opponent from scoring.—**savable, saveable** *adj*.

save[2] *conj, prep* except, but.

saveloy *n* a type of highly-seasoned smoked sausage.

saver *n* a person who saves money in a bank or building society.

savin, savine *n* a small Eurasian juniper bush with dark fruit the oil from which was once used medicinally.

saving[1] *adj* thrifty, economical; (*clause*) containing a reservation; redeeming. * *n* what is saved; (*pl*) money saved for future use.

saving[2] *prep* except; with apology to.

savings and loan association *n* a company that pays interest on deposits and issues loans to enable people to buy their own houses, a building society.

savings account *n* a bank account that earns interest.

savings bank *n* a bank receiving small deposits and holding them in interest-bearing accounts.

saviour, savior *n* a person who saves another from harm or danger; (*with cap*) Jesus Christ.

savory *n* (*pl* **savories**) any of various Mediterranean aromatic plants used as herbs for flavouring.

savoir-faire *n* the skill of knowing the right thing to do; tact.

savour, savor *n* the flavour or smell of something; a distinctive quality. * *vti* to season; to enjoy; to have a specified taste or smell; to smack (of); to appreciate critically.—**savourer, savorer** n.

savoury, savory *adj* having a good taste or smell; spicy, not sweet; reputable. * *n* (*pl* **savouries, savories**) a savoury dish at the beginning or end of dinner; (*pl*) snacks served with drinks.—**savourily, savorily** *adv*.—**savouriness, savoriness** *n*.

savoy (cabbage) *n* a variety of cabbage with wrinkled leaves.

savvy *vti* (**savvying, savvied**) (*sl*) to understand. * *n* (*sl*) understanding, know-how. * *adj* (**savvier, savviest**) (*sl*) shrewd.

saw[1] *see* **see**[1]

saw[2] *n* a tool with a toothed edge for cutting wood, etc. * *vti* (**sawing, sawed,** *pp* **sawed** *or* **sawn**) to cut or shape with a saw; to use a saw; to make a to-and-fro motion.—**sawer** *n*.

saw[3] *n* a wise saying, a proverb.

sawbill *n* a large, diving, fish-eating duck with a long narrow bill with serrated edges.

sawbones *n* (*sl*) a doctor or surgeon.

sawbuck *n* a sawhorse.

sawdust *n* fine particles of wood caused by sawing.

sawed-off *see* **sawn-off.**

sawfish *n* (*pl* **sawfish, sawfishes**) a large ray with a serrated snout.

sawfly *n* (*pl* **sawflies**) any of various insects with a saw-like ovipositor.

sawhorse *n* a trestle, etc on which wood is laid for sawing.

sawmill *n* a mill where timber is cut into logs or planks.

sawn *see* **saw**[2].

sawn-off *adj* (*shotgun*) having the barrel shortened to aid concealment; (*person*) (*sl*) small.—*also* **sawed-off.**

saw set *n* an instrument for setting the teeth of a saw by bending each tooth to the left or right alternately.

sawyer *n* a person employed to saw timber.

sax *n* saxophone.

saxatile *adj* saxicolous.

saxe blue *n* a light greyish-blue.—*also adj*.

saxhorn *n* a brass musical instrument resembling a tuba.

saxicolous, saxicoline *adj* living among or on rocks.

saxifrage *n* any of a genus of plants with small flowers and tufted leaves, popular in rock gardens.

Saxon *adj, n* (of) a member of a North German people that settled the southern part of Britain in the 5th–6th century.

saxony n a fine wool; cloth made from it.

saxophone *n* a brass wind instrument with a single reed and about twenty finger-keys.—**saxophonic** *adj*.—**saxophonist** *n*.

say *vb* (**says, saying, said**) *vt* to speak, to utter; to state in words; to affirm, declare; to recite; to estimate; to assume. * *vi* to tell; to express in words. * *n* (*pl* **says**) the act of uttering; the right or opportunity to speak; a share in a decision. * *adv* for example. * *interj* expressing admiration, surprise, etc.

saying *n* a common remark; a proverb or adage.

say-so *n* (*inf*) an unfounded assertion; an authorization; the right to authorize.

sayyid, sayid *n* a Muslim title of respect applied to descendants of Mohammed's daughter Fatima.

Sb (*chem symbol*) antimony.

SBKKV *abbr* = space-based kinetic kill vehicle, a system of missiles launched from a satellite.

'sblood *interj* (*obs*) God's blood.

SC *abbr* = South Carolina; Supreme Court.

Sc (*chem symbol*) scandium.

sc. *abbr* = scene; science; scilicet; (*weight*) scruple; (*print*) small capitals.

scab *n* a dry crust on a wound or sore; a plant disease characterized by crustaceous spots; a worker who refuses to join a strike or who replaces a striking worker. * *vi* (**scabbing, scabbed**) to form a scab; to be covered with scabs; to work as a scab.—**scabby** *adj*.

scabbard *n* a sheath for a sword or dagger. * *vt* to sheathe.

scabies *n* a contagious, itching skin disease.

scabiosa *n* any of a genus of Mediterranean plants with tightly clustered blue, red or white flowers.—*also* **scabious.**

scabious[1] *adj* covered with scabs; of or resembling scabies.

scabious[2] *n* a scabiosa.

scabrous *adj* (*surface*) rough, scaly; indecent, offensive; intractable, difficult to manage.—**scabrously** *adv*.—**scabrousness** *n*.

scaffold *n* a raised platform for the execution of a criminal; capital punishment; scaffolding.

scaffolding *n* a temporary framework of wood and metal for use by workmen constructing a building, etc; materials for a scaffold.

scalable *adj* able to be scaled or climbed.

scalar *adj* (*math*) having magnitude but not direction. * *n* a scalar quantity, eg time, mass.

scalar product *n* a scalar produced by multiplying together the magnitudes of two vectors and the cosine of the angle between them.

scalawag *n* (*inf*) a rascal; a scamp; a Southern white who supported the Republicans after the American Civil War.—*also* **scallawag, scallywag.**

scald *vt* to burn with hot liquid or steam; to heat almost to boiling point; to immerse in boiling water (to sterilize). * *n* an injury caused by hot liquid or steam.

scale[1] *n* (*pl*) a machine or instrument for weighing; one of the pans or the tray of a set of scales; (*pl*) (*with cap*) Libra, the seventh sign of the zodiac. * *vti* to weigh in a set of scales; to have a specified weight on a set of scales.

scale[2] *n* one of the thin plates covering a fish or reptile; a flake (of dry skin); an incrustation on teeth, etc. * *vti* to remove the scales from; to flake off.

scale[3] *n* a graduated measure; an instrument so marked; (*math*) the basis for a numerical system, 10 being that in general use; (*mus*) a series of tones from the keynote to its octave, in order of pitch; the proportion that a map, etc, bears to what it represents; a series of degrees classified by size, amount, etc; relative scope or size. * *vt* (*wall*) to go up or over; (*model*) to make or draw to scale; to increase or decrease in size.

scaled *adj* (*reptile, etc*) covered with or having scales.

scale insect *n* any of various small insects that feed on host plants and secrete a waxy covering for protection.

scalene *adj* (*geom*) having three sides of unequal length. * *n* a scalene triangle.

scallawag, scallywag *see* **scalawag.**

scallion *n* a young onion with a small bulb and long shoots eaten raw in salads, a spring onion or shallot.

scallop *n* an edible shellfish with two fluted, fan-shaped shells; one of a series of curves in an edging. * *vt* to cut into scallops.—**scalloped** *adj*.

scalp *n* the skin covering the skull, usu covered with hair. * *vti* to cut the scalp from; to criticize sharply; (*inf*) (*tickets, etc*) to buy and resell at higher prices.
scalpel *n* a short, thin, very sharp knife used esp for surgery.
scaly *adj* (**scalier, scaliest**) (*reptile etc*) like or covered with scales.—**scaliness** *n*.
scaly anteater *n* a pangolin.
scamp *n* a rascal; a mischievous child.
scamper *vi* to run away quickly or playfully. * *n* a brisk or playful run or movement.
scampi *n* a dish of large shrimps or prawns cooked in breadcrumbs or prepared with a flavoured dressing.
scan *vb* (**scanning, scanned**) *vt* (*page etc*) to look through quickly; to scrutinize; (*med*) to examine with a radiological device; (*TV*) to pass an electronic beam over; (*radar*) to detect with an electronic beam; (*poem*) to conform to a rhythmical pattern; to check for recorded data by means of a mechanical or electronic device; (*human body*) to make a scan of in a scanner. * *vi* to analyse the pattern of verse. * *n* the act of scanning or an instance of being scanned.
scandal *n* a disgraceful event or action; talk arising from immoral behaviour; a feeling of moral outrage; the thing or person causing this; disgrace; malicious gossip.
scandalize *vt* to shock the moral feelings of; to defame.—**scandalization** *n*.—**scandalizer** *n*.
scandalmonger *n* a person who spreads scandal or malicious gossip.—**scandalmongering** *n*.
scandalous *adj* causing scandal; shameful; spreading slander.—**scandalously** *adv*.—**scandalousness** *n*.
Scandinavian *adj* of or pertaining to Scandinavia, the region comprising Norway, Sweden, and Denmark, and sometimes Iceland, or its people. * *n* a native or inhabitant of Scandinavia.
scandium *n* a rare metallic element present in small quantities in various minerals.
scanner *n* a person or thing that scans; an electronic device that monitors or scans; a device for receiving or transmitting radar signals; a device for scanning the human body to obtain an image of an internal part.
scanning electron microscope *n* an electron microscope which scans an object to produce a three-dimensional image.
scansion *n* the analysis of verse to show its metre.
scant *adj* limited; meagre; insufficient; scanty; grudging.
scantling *n* a small piece of timber; the dimensions of timber and stone for a building or of a component for a ship or aircraft; a small quantity.
scanty *adj* (**scantier, scantiest**) barely adequate; insufficient; small.—**scantily** *adv*.—**scantiness** *n*.
scapegoat *n* a person who bears the blame for others; one who is the object of irrational hostility.
scapegrace *n* a graceless, hare-brained person; an incorrigible scamp.
scapula *n* (*pl* **scapulae**) the shoulder blade.
scapular *adj* of or relating to the scapula. * *n* a monastic robe worn in various Christian religious orders, consisting of a wide piece of cloth worn over the shoulders and hanging down at the front and back; any of the feathers along the base of a bird's wing.
scar[1] *n* a mark left after the healing of a wound or sore; a blemish resulting from damage or wear. * *vti* (**scarring, scarred**) to mark with or form a scar.
scar[2] *n* a protruding or isolated rock; a precipitous crag; a rocky part of a hillside.
scarab *n* a dung-beetle held to be sacred in ancient Egypt; a gem or seal in the shape of this.
scarabaeid *n* any of a family of beetles including the dung beetle.—*also adj*.
scarce *adj* not in abundance; hard to find; rare.—**scarceness** *n*.
scarcely *adv* hardly, only just; probably not or certainly not.
scarcity *n* (**scarcities**) the state of being scarce; a dearth, deficiency.
scare *vti* to startle; to frighten or become frightened; to drive away by frightening. * *n* a sudden fear; a period of general fear; a false alarm.
scarecrow *n* a wooden figure dressed in clothes for scaring birds from crops; a thin or tattered person; something frightening but harmless.
scaremonger *n* a person who causes fear or panic by spreading rumours; an alarmist.
scarf *n* (*pl* **scarves**) a rectangular or square piece of cloth worn around the neck, shoulders or head for warmth or decoration.
scarfskin *n* the outer layer of skin; cuticle.
scarify *vt* (**scarifying, scarified**) to make cuts in, to scratch; to criticize savagely; to loosen the surface of (soil); to hasten germination by softening the wall (of a hard seed).—**scarification** *n*.
scarlatina *n* scarlet fever.
scarlet *n* a bright red with a tinge of orange; scarlet cloth or clothes. * *adj* scarlet coloured; immoral or sinful.
scarlet fever *n* an acute contagious disease marked by a sore throat, fever, and a scarlet rash.
scarlet pimpernel *n* a plant with red, purple or white flowers that close in dull weather.
scarlet runner *n* a climbing bean plant with scarlet flowers and elongated edible pods.—*also* **runner bean**.
scarlet woman *n* (*arch*) a prostitute.
scarp *n* a low steep slope; the inner face of a ditch in a fortification.
scarper *vi* (*inf*) to run away.
scarves *see* **scarf**.
scary *adj* (**scarier, scariest**) frightening, alarming.—**scariness** *n*.
scat[1] *vi* (**scatting, scatted**) (*inf*) to leave hastily.
scat[2] *n* (*jazz*) a form of improvised singing without words. * *vi* (**scatting, scatted**) to sing in this way.
scathing *adj* bitterly critical; cutting, withering.—**scathingly** *adv*.
scatology *n* the scientific study of fossil and human excrement; a preoccupation with excrement or obscenity.—**scatological** *adj*.
scatter *vti* to throw loosely about; to sprinkle; to dissipate; to put or take to flight; to disperse; to occur at random. * *n* a scattering or sprinkling.
scatterbrain *n* a frivolous, heedless person.—**scatterbrained** *adj*.
scattered *adj* dispersed widely, spaced out; straggling.
scattering *n* a small amount spread over a large area; a dispersion.
scatty *adj* (**scattier, scattiest**) (*inf*) thoughtless, absentminded, crazy.—**scattily** *adv*.—**scattiness** *n*.
scaup (duck) *n* a diving duck of Europe and America.
scavenge *vi* to gather things discarded by others; (*animal*) to eat decaying matter.—**scavenger** *n*.
ScB *abbr* = Bachelor of Science.
ScD abbr = Doctor of Science.
scenario *n* (*pl* **scenarios**) an outline of events, real or imagined; the plot or script of a film, etc.
scene *n* the place in which anything occurs; the place in which the action of a play or a story occurs; a section of a play, a division of an act; the stage of a theatre; a painted screen, etc, used on this; an unseemly display of strong emotion; a landscape; surroundings; a place of action; (*inf*) an area of interest or activity (eg *the music scene*).
scene dock *n* (*theatre*) a storage area for scenery near the stage.
scenery *n* (*pl* **sceneries**) painted screens, etc, used to represent places, as in a play, film, etc; an aspect of a landscape, esp of beautiful or impressive countryside.
scenic *adj* relating to natural scenery; picturesque; of or used on the stage.—**scenically** *adv*.
scenic railway *n* a miniature railway at an amusement park, etc.
scent *n* a perfume; an odour left by an animal, by which it can be tracked; the sense of smell; a line of pursuit or discovery. * *vt* to recognize by the sense of smell; to track by smell; to impart an odour to, to perfume; to get wind of, to detect.
scented *adj* perfumed.
sceptic *n* a person who questions opinions generally accepted; a person who doubts religious dectrines, an agnostic; an adherent of scepticism.—also skeptic.

sceptical *adj* doubting; questioning.—*also* **skeptical.**—**sceptically, skeptically** *adv*.
scepticism *n* an attitude of questioning criticism, doubt; (*philos*) the doctrine that absolute knowledge is unattainable.—*also* **skepticism.**
sceptre, scepter *n* the staff of office held by a monarch on a ceremonial occasion; sovereignty.
schedule *n* a timetable; a list, inventory or tabulated statement; a timed plan for a project. * *vt* to make a schedule; to plan.
scheelite *n* a mineral consisting of calcium tungstate.
schema *n* (*pl* **schemata**) a plan or diagram.
schematic *adj* of or like a scheme or diagram.—**schematically** *adv*.
schematize *vt* to form into or express as a scheme.—**schematization** *n*.
scheme *n* a plan; a project; a systematic arrangement; a diagram; an underhand plot. * *vti* to devise or plot.—**schemer** *n*.
scheming *adj* cunning; intriguing.
scherzando *adj*, *adv* (*mus*) to be performed lightheartedly. * *n* (*pl* **scherzandi**) a piece of music played in this manner.
scherzo *n* (*pl* **scherzos, scherzi**) a lively musical passage or movement, usu in triple time.
schilling *n* the standard monetary unit of Austria.
schism *n* a division or separation into two parties, esp of a church; the sin of this; discord, disharmony.
schismatic, schismatical *adj* of or creating schism. * *n* a person who creates schism or supports schism.—**schismatically** *adv*.
schist *n* a type of crystalline rock in thin layers.—**schistose** *adj*.
schistosome *n* any of a genus of parasitic worms that infest the blood vessels of humans and animals.
schistosomiasis *n* a disease caused by infestation with schistosomes.
schizo *n* (*pl* **schizos**) (*inf*) a schizophrenic person. * *adj* schizophrenic.
schizo-, schiz- *prefix* split, division.
schizocarp *n* a dry fruit that splits into single-seeded parts.
schizoid *adj* mildly schizophrenic.—*also n*.
schizomycete *n* any microscopic organism such as a bacterium.
schizophrenia *n* a mental disorder characterized by withdrawal from reality and deterioration of the personality; the presence of mutually contradictory qualities or parts.—**schizophrenic** *adj*, *n*.
schlieren *n* (*physics*) visible streaks in a transparent medium caused by variations in its density.
schmaltz, schmalz *n* overly sentimental music, art, film, etc.—**schmaltzy, schmalzy** *adj*.
schnapps *n* (*pl* **schnapps**) a Dutch spirit distilled from potatoes; (*Germany*) any strong spirit.
schnauzer *n* an orig German breed of terrier with a short wiry coat.
schnitzel *n* a cutlet of veal.
schnorkle *see* **snorkel.**
schnozzle *n* (*sl*) nose.
scholar *n* a pupil, a student; a learned person; the holder of a scholarship.
scholarly *adj* learned, erudite, academic.
scholarship *n* an annual grant to a scholar or student, usu won by competitive examination; learning, academic achievement.
scholastic *adj* of or relating to schools, scholars, or education; academic.—**scholastically** *adv*.
school[1] *n* a shoal of porpoises, whales, or other aquatic animals of one kind swimming together.
school[2] *n* an educational establishment; its teachers and students; a regular session of teaching; formal education, schooling; a particular division of a university; a place or means of discipline; a group of thinkers, artists, writers, holding similar principles. * *vt* to train; to teach; to control or discipline.
schoolboy *n* a boy who attends school.
schoolchild *n* (*pl* **schoolchildren**) a child who attends school.
schoolgirl *n* a girl who attends school.
schoolhouse *n* a building used as a school.
schooling *n* instruction in school.
schoolmaster *n* a man who teaches in school.
schoolmate *n* a companion at school.—*also* **schoolfellow.**
schoolmistress *n* a woman who teaches in school.
schoolroom *n* a room in which pupils are taught, as in a school.
schoolteacher *n* a person who teaches in school.
schooner *n* a sailing ship with two or more masts rigged with fore-and-aft sails; a large drinking glass for sherry or beer.
schottische *n* (music for) a type of slow dance resembling a polka.
schuss *n* (*skiing*) a fast straight downhill run. * *vi* to ski down this.
sci. *abbr* = science; scientific.
sciatic *adj* of the hip.
sciatica *n* pain along the sciatic nerve, esp in the back of the thigh; (*loosely*) pain in the lower back or adjacent parts.
sciatic nerve *n* a long nerve running from the pelvic region to the back of the thigh.
science *n* knowledge gained by systematic experimentation and analysis, and the formulation of general principles; a branch of this; skill or technique.
science fiction *n* highly imaginative fiction typically involving actual or projected scientific phenomena.
science park *n* an area where scientific discoveries are translated into commercial products and applications.
scientific *adj* of or concerned with science; based on or using the principles and methods of science; systematic and exact; having or showing expert skill.—**scientifically** *adv*.
scientism *n* the use of scientific methods; the inappropriate use of or reliance on scientific methods.
scientist *n* a specialist in a branch of science, as in chemistry, etc.
Scientology *n* (*trademark*) a religious philosophy founded by L. Ron Hubbard in 1951.
sci-fi *n* science fiction.
scilicet *adv* namely, that is to say.
scilla *n* any of a genus of plants with small pink, blue or white flowers grown from bulbs.
scimitar *n* an Oriental curved sword, broadest near the point.
scintigraphy *n* the production of images of internal body parts by detecting high-energy particles from a radioactive tracer administered to a patient.
scintilla *n* an iota, tiny amount.
scintillate *vti* to give off sparks; to sparkle.—**scintillation** *n*.
scintillating *adj* sparkling; amusing.
scintillation counter *n* an instrument for registering the intensity of a radioactive source by recording the flashes of light produced by the impact of emitted photons on a phospor.
scion *n* a shoot for grafting; a young member of a family, a descendant.
scirrhus *n* (*pl* **scirrhi, scirrhuses**) a cancerous tumour consisting of fibrous tissue.
scission *n* the act of cutting or dividing; a cut, divide, or split.
scissor *vt* to cut with scissors, to clip. * *npl* a tool for cutting paper, hair, etc, consisting of two fastened pivoted blades whose edges slide past each other; a gymnastic feat in which the leg movements resemble the opening and closing of scissors.
scissors kick *n* (*swimming*) a kick in which the legs move from the hip in a scissoring motion.
sciurine *adj* of or resembling a family of rodents which include squirrels and marmots.
SCLC *abbr* = Southern Christian Leadership Conference.
sclera *n* the opaque outer covering of the eyeball excluding the cornea.
sclerenchyma *n* a tissue forming the hard fibrous parts of plants.
sclero-, scler- *prefix* hardness.
scleroderma *n* (*med*) a chronic disease in women causing thickening and hardening of the skin.
sclerodermatous *adj* (*zool*) covered with a hard layer of tissue, eg scales.
sclerosis *n* a pathological hardening of body tissue; a disease marked by this.
sclerotic *adj* pertaining to the sclera; of or affected by sclerosis. * *n* the sclera.

sclerous *adj* hard, bony.
scoff[1] *vti* to jeer (at) or mock. * *n* an expression or object of derision; mocking words, a taunt.
scoff[2] *vt* (*sl*) to eat quickly and greedily.
scold *vi* to reprove angrily; to tell off.
scolding *n* a harsh reprimand.
scoliosis *n* (*med*) lateral curvature of the spine.
scollop *see* **scallop.**
scombroid *n* any member of a suborder of spiny-finned marine fishes used for food, such as the mackerel and tuna.—*also adj*.
sconce[1] *n* a bracket on a wall for holding candles or electric lights.
sconce[2] *n* a defensive fortification, a bulwark.
scone *n* a small, round cake made from flour and fat which is baked and spread with butter, etc.
scoop *n* a small shovel-like utensil as for taking up flour, ice cream, etc; the bucket of a dredge, etc; the act of scooping or the amount scooped up at one time; (*inf*) a piece of exclusive news; (*inf*) the advantage gained in being the first to publish or broadcast this. * *vt* to shovel, lift or hollow out with a scoop; (*inf*) to obtain as a scoop; (*inf: rival newspaper etc*) to forestall with a news item.
scoot *vti* to run quickly; to hurry (off).
scooter *n* a child's two-wheeled vehicle with a footboard and steering handle; a motor scooter.
scope *n* the opportunity to use one's abilities; extent; range; an instrument for viewing.
scopolamine *n* an alkaloid extracted from certain plants, used as a sedative and for travel sickness.—*also* **hyoscine.**
scorbutic *adj* of, suffering from, or resembling scurvy.—**scorbutically** *adv*.
scorch *vti* to burn or be burned on the surface; to wither from overexposure to heat; to singe; (*inf*) to drive or cycle furiously.
scorcher *n* (*inf*) a very hot day.
scorching *adj* (*inf: weather*) very hot; scathing.
score *n* the total number of points made in a game or examination; a notch or scratch; a line indicating deletion or position; a group of twenty; a written copy of a musical composition showing the different parts; the music composed for a film; a grievance for settling; a reason or motive; (*inf*) the real facts; a bill or reckoning; (*pl*) an indefinite, large number. * *vt* to mark with cuts; (*mus*) to arrange in a score, to orchestrate; to gain or record points, as in a game; to evaluate in testing. * *vi* to make points, as in a game; to keep the score of a game; to gain an advantage, a success, etc; (*sl*) to be successful in seduction; (*with* **off**) to get the better of someone.—**scorer** *n*.
scoreboard *n* a large manually or electronically operated board showing the score in a game or match.
scorecard *n* (*golf, etc*) a card on which scores are recorded.
scorn *n* extreme contempt or disdain; the object of this. * *vt* to treat with contempt, to despise; to reject or refuse as unworthy.—**scornful** *adj*.—**scornfully** *adv*.
Scorpio *n* the eighth sign of the zodiac in astrology, operative October 23–November 21.—**Scorpionic** *adj*.
scorpion *n* a small, tropical, insect-like animal with pincers and a jointed tail with a poisonous sting.
scorpion fish *n* any of a genus of fish with poisonous spines on the dorsal fins.
Scot *n* a native or inhabitant of Scotland; a member of a Celtic people from Ireland who settled in northern Britain in the 5th–6th centuries.
scotch *vt* (*a rumour*) to stamp out.
Scotch *n* whisky made in Scotland.
Scotch broth *n* a thick soup made from beef or mutton with vegetables and pearl barley.
Scotch egg *n* a hard-boiled egg enclosed in sausagemeat, coated in breadcrumbs, and fried.
Scotchman *n* (*pl* **Scotchmen**) a Scotsman.—**Scotchwoman** (*pl* **Scotchwomen**) *nf*.
Scotch mist *n* a dense, wet mist; fine drizzle.
Scotch terrier *n* a Scottish terrier.
scoter *n* (*pl* **scoters, scoter**) a large sea duck with black plumage.
scot-free *adj* without penalty or injury.
Scotland Yard *n* the headquarters of the London metropolitan police force.
scotoma *n* (*pl* **scotomas, scotomata**) a blind spot in the visual field.
Scots *adj* of or pertaining to Scotland, its law, money, and people, and the Scots language. * *n* the dialect of English developed in Lowland Scotland.
Scotsman *n* (*pl* **Scotsmen**) a native or inhabitant of Scotland.—**Scotswoman** *n* (*pl* **Scotswomen**) *nf*.
Scots pine *n* (the wood of) a European pine with needle-like leaves.
Scotticism *n* a Scottish word or idiom.
Scottie *n* (*inf*) a Scotsman; a Scottish terrier.
Scottish *adj* of or relating to Scotland and its people.
Scottish deerhound *n* a large rough-haired greyhound, a deerhound.
Scottish National Party *n* a political party seeking independence for Scotland.
Scottish terrier *n* a small terrier with short legs and a wiry coat.
scoundrel *n* a rascal; a dishonest person.
scour[1] *vt* to clean by rubbing with an abrasive cloth; to flush out with a current of water; to purge. * *n* the act or process of scouring; a place scoured by running water; scouring action (as of a glacier); damage done by scouring action.
scour[2] *vt* to hasten over or along, to range over, esp in search or pursuit.
scourge *n* a whip; a means of inflicting punishment; a person who harasses and causes widespread and great affliction; a pest. * *vt* to flog; to punish harshly.
Scouse *n* (*inf*) a person from Liverpool; the dialect of Liverpool.—*also adj*.
scout *n* a person, plane, etc, sent to observe the enemy's strength, etc; a person employed to find new talent or survey a competitor, etc; (*with cap*) a member of the Scouting Association, an organization for young people. * *vti* to reconnoitre; to go in search of (something).
scouting *n* the act of one who scouts; (*with cap*) the activities of the Scouting Association.
Scouting Association *n* (*formerly* Boy Scouts, Girl Guides) an organization to develop in young people self-reliance and initiative, moral and physical courage and a courteous spirit.
scoutmaster *n* (*formerly*) the adult leader of a troop of Scouts.
scow *n* an unpowered flat-bottomed boat for carrying freight, refuse, etc.
scowl *n* a contraction of the brows in an angry or threatening manner; a sullen expression. * *vi* to make a scowl; to look sullen.
Scrabble *n* (*trademark*) a game in which words are formed from individual lettered tiles on a grid.
scrabble *vi* to scratch or grope about; to struggle; to scramble. * *n* a repeated scratching or clawing; a scramble; a scribble.
scrag *n* a scrawny person or animal; the lean end of a neck of mutton or veal; (*loosely*) neck.
scraggly *adj* (**scragglier, scraggliest**) untidy, uneven.
scraggy *adj* (**scraggier, scraggiest**) thin and bony, gaunt.
scram *vi* (**scramming, scrammed**) (*sl*) to get out, to go away at once.
scramble *vi* to move or climb hastily on all fours; to scuffle or struggle for something; to move with urgency or panic. * *vt* to mix haphazardly; to stir (slightly beaten eggs) while cooking; (*transmitted signals*) to make unintelligible in transit. * *n* a hard climb or advance; a disorderly struggle; a rapid emergency take-off of fighter planes; a motorcycle rally over rough ground.—**scrambler** *n*.
scrap[1] *n* a small piece; a fragment of discarded material; (*pl*) bits of food. * *adj* in the form of pieces, leftovers, etc; used and discarded. * *vt* (**scrapping, scrapped**) to discard; to make into scraps.
scrap[2] *n* (*inf*) a fight or quarrel. * *vi* (**scrapping, scrapped**) to have a scrap.
scrapbook *n* a book for pasting clippings, etc, in.
scrape *vt* to rub with a sharp or abrasive object so as to clean, smooth or remove; to eke out or to be economical; to amass in small portions; to

draw along with a grating or vibration; to get narrowly past, to graze; to draw back the foot in making a bow; (*with* **together**) to save or collect with difficulty. * *vi* (*with* **through**) to manage or succeed with difficulty or by a slim margin. * *n* the act of scraping; a grating sound; an abrasion, scratch; an awkward predicament.

scraper *n* an instrument for scraping; a grating or edge for scraping mud from boots.

scraperboard *n* a board with a black surface which can be scraped off with a special tool to form a design.

scrapheap *n* a pile of discarded material or things.

scraping *n* a piece scraped off.

scrappy *adj* (**scrappier, scrappiest**) disjointed; fragmentary; full of gaps.—**scrappily** *adv.*—**scrappiness** *n.*

scratch *vt* to mark with a sharp point; to scrape with the nails or claws; to rub to relieve an itch; to chafe; to write awkwardly; (*writing etc*) to strike out; to withdraw from a race, etc. * *vi* to use nails or claws to tear or dig. * *n* the act of scratching; a mark or sound made by this; a slight injury; a starting line for a race; a scribble. * *adj* taken at random, haphazard, impromptu; without a handicap.

scratch pad *n* a notebook.

scratch video *n* a collage of images from existing television or cinema film.

scratchy *adj* (**scratchier, scratchiest**) making a scratching noise; uneven, ragged.—**scratchily** *adv.*—**scratchiness** *n.*

scrawl *n* careless or illegible handwriting; a scribble. * *vti* to draw or write carelessly.

scrawny *adj* (**scrawnier, scrawniest**) skinny; bony.—**scrawniness** *n.*

scream *vti* to utter a piercing cry, as of pain, fear, etc; to shout; to shriek. * *n* a sharp, piercing cry; (*inf*) a very funny person or thing.

scree *n* loose shifting stones; a slope covered with these.

screech *n* a harsh, high-pitched cry. * *vti* to utter a screech, to shriek.

screed *n* a long, tedious letter or speech; an informal piece of writing.

screen *n* a movable partition or framework to conceal, divide, or protect; a shelter or shield from heat, danger or view; an electronic display (as in a television set, computer terminal, etc); a surface on which films, slides, etc are projected; the motion picture industry; a coarse wire mesh over a window or door to keep out insects; a sieve. * *vt* to conceal or shelter; to grade by passing through a screen; to separate according to skill, etc; (*a film*) to show on a screen.

screening *n* a showing of a film; a metal or plastic mesh, as for window screens; the refuse matter after sieving.

screenplay *n* a story written in a form suitable for a film.

screenwriter *n* a person who writes screenplays.

screw *n* a metal cylinder or cone with a spiral thread around it for fastening things by being turned; any spiral thing like this; a twist or turn of a screw; a twist of paper; pressure; a propeller with revolving blades on a shaft. * *vt* to fasten, tighten etc with a screw; to oppress; to extort, to cheat out of something due; (*sl, vulg*) to have sexual intercourse with; (*with* **up**) to gather (courage, etc). * *vi* to go together or come apart by being turned like a screw; to twist or turn with a writhing movement; (*sl, vulg*) to have sexual intercourse; (*with* **up**) to bungle.

screwball *n* (*sl*) an odd or eccentric person. * *adj* whimsical, zany.

screwdriver *n* a tool like a blunt chisel for turning screws; a drink of vodka and orange juice.

screwed *adj* (*sl*) drunk.

screw eye *n* a metal screw with a ring instead of a slotted head.

screw pine *n* any of various tropical plants with slender stems and clusters of spiral leaves.

screw propeller *n* an early form of propeller based on the Archimedes screw.

screw top *n* a cap that screws onto the top of a bottle or other container; a bottle, etc having this.

screwy *adj* (**screwier, screwiest**) (*sl*) eccentric, odd.—**screwiness** *n.*

scribble *vti* to draw or write hastily or carelessly, to scrawl; to be a writer. * *n* hasty writing, a scrawl.—**scribbler** *n.*

scribe *n* a person who copies (documents); an author or journalist; (*Bible*) an expounder of Jewish law. * *vt* to draw a line on by cutting with a pointed instrument.

scriber *n* a pointed tool used to score or mark lines (e.g on metal) as guides for cutting.

scrim *n* a light open-weave fabric used in upholstery, lining, and theatre sets.

scrimmage *n* a confused struggle; a skirmish; (*football*) the period between the ball entering play and it being declared dead. * *vi* to engage in a scrimmage.

scrimp *vti* to be sparing or frugal (with); to make too small, to skimp.

scrimshank *vi* (*inf*) to shirk work, esp military duties.

scrimshaw *n* carvings made from shells, whalebone, ivory, etc, usu by sailors; the art of producing such carvings.

scrip *n* a written list; a certificate entitling the holder to a share of company stock.

Script. *abbr* = Scripture(s).

script *n* handwriting; a style of writing; the text of a stage play, screenplay or broadcast; a plan of action; (*print*) type that resembles handwriting. * *vt* to write a script (for).

scriptural *adj* of or based on the Bible or Scripture.

scripture *n* any sacred writing; (*with cap, often pl*) the Jewish Bible or Old Testament; the Christian Bible or Old and New Testaments. * *adj* contained in or quoted from the Bible.

scriptwriter *n* a writer of screenplays for films, TV, etc; a screenwriter —**scriptwriting** *n.*

scrofula *n* tuberculosis of the lymph glands in the neck.—**scrofulous** *adj.*

scroll *n* a roll of parchment or paper with writing on it; an ornament like this; (*her*) a ribbon with a motto; a list. * *vti* (*comput*) to move text across a screen; to decorate with scrolls.

scroll saw *n* a thin saw for cutting intricate designs.

Scrooge *n* (*also without cap*) a miserly, miserable person (after the character in *A Christmas Carol* by Charles Dickens).

scrotum *n* (*pl* **scrota, scrotums**) the pouch of skin containing the testicles.

scrounge *vti* (*inf*) to seek or obtain (something) for nothing.—**scrounger** *n.*

scrub[1] *n* an arid area of stunted trees and shrubs; such vegetation; anything small or mean. * *adj* small, stunted, inferior, etc.

scrub[2] *vti* (**scrubbing, scrubbed**) to clean vigorously, to scour; to rub hard; (*inf*) to remove, to cancel. * *n* the act of scrubbing.

scrubber *n* a person or thing that scrubs; (*sl*) a promiscuous woman.

scrubby *adj* (**scrubbier, scrubbiest**) stunted; paltry; unkempt.—**scrubbily** *adv.*—**scrubbiness** *n.*

scruff[1] *n* the back of the neck, the nape.

scruff[2] *n* (*inf*) a shabbily dressed person.

scruffy *adj* (**scruffier, scruffiest**) shabby; unkempt.—**scruffily** *adv.*—**scruffiness** *n.*

scrum *n* a scrummage.

scrum half *n* (*rugby*) (the position held by) the player who puts the ball into the scrum.

scrummage *n* (*Rugby football*) a play consisting of a tussle between rival forwards in a compact mass for possession of the ball. * *vi* to form a scrum(mage).

scrump *vt* (*dial*) to steal apples from an orchard or garden.

scrumptious *adj* (*inf*) delicious; very pleasing.—**scrumptiously** *adv.*—**scrumptiousness** *n.*

scrunch *vti* to crumple, esp the hair when drying; to crunch; to be crumpled or crunched. * *n* a crunching sound; the act of scrunching.

scruple *n* (*usu pl*) a moral principle or belief causing one to doubt or hesitate about a course of action. * *vti* to hesitate owing to scruples.

scrupulous *adj* careful; conscientious; thorough.—**scrupulously** *adv.*—**scrupulousness** *n.*

scrutineer *n* a person who scrutinizes, esp an inspector of ballot papers.

scrutinize *vti* to look closely at, to examine narrowly; to make a scrutiny.—**scrutinizer** *n.*

scrutiny *n* (*pl* **scrutinies**) a careful examination; a critical gaze; an official inspection of votes cast in an election.

scuba *n* a diver's apparatus with compressed-air tanks for breathing underwater.
scud *vti* (**scudding, scudded**) to go along swiftly; to be driven before the wind. * *n* an act of scudding; light clouds, etc, driven by wind; a type of missile.
scuff *vti* to drag the feet, to shuffle; to wear or mark the surface of by doing this.
scuffle *n* a confused fight; the sound of shuffling. * *vi* to fight confusedly; to move by shuffling.
scull *n* an oar worked from side to side over the stern of a boat; a light rowing boat for racing. * *vti* to propel with a scull.
scullery *n* (*pl* **sculleries**) a room for storage or kitchen work, such as washing dishes, etc.
sculpt *vt* to carve, to sculpture.
sculptor *n* a person skilled in sculpture.
sculptress *n* a woman skilled in sculpture.
sculpture *n* the art of carving wood or forming clay, stone, etc, into figures, statues, etc; a three-dimensional work of art; a sculptor's work. * *vt* to carve, adorn or portray with sculptures; to shape, mould or form like sculpture.—**sculptural** *adj*.
scum *n* a thin layer of impurities on top of a liquid; refuse; despicable people.
scumbag *n* (*sl*) a disgusting or despicable person.
scumble *vt* (*drawing and painting*) to soften lines or colours by applying a thin coat of opaque colour. * *n* the upper layer of colour applied for this purpose.
scunner *n* (*Scot*) disgust. * *vti* to feel or cause to feel disgust.—**scunnered** *adj*
scupper *n* a hole in a ship's side that lets water run from the deck into the sea. * *vt* (*sl*) to sink deliberately; to disable.
scurf *n* small flakes of dead skin (as dandruff); any scaly coating.
scurrilous *adj* abusive; grossly offensive.
scurry *vi* (**scurrying, scurried**) to hurry with quick, short steps, to scamper. * *n* (*pl* **scurries**) a bustle; a flurry (as of snow).
scurvy *n* a disease caused by a deficiency of vitamin C. * *adj* base; contemptible.
scut *n* the short tail of certain animals, such as the deer or hare.
scute, scutum *n* an external scales or plate on the bodies of animals such as the armadillo, turtle, etc.
scutellum *n* (*pl* **scutella**) any of the small horny scales or plates on a plant or animal.
scuttle[1] *vi* to run quickly; to hurry away. * *n* a short swift run; a hurried pace.
scuttle[2] *n* a bucket with a lip for storing coal.
scuttle[3] *n* (*naut*) a hatchway, a hole with a cover in a ship's deck or side. * *vt* to sink a ship by making holes in the bottom.
scuttlebut *n* (*formerly*) a cask containing drinking water on the deck of a ship; (*sl*) gossip.
scuzzy *adj* (**scuzzier, scuzziest**) (*sl*) filthy, squalid.
scythe *n* a two-handed implement with a large curved blade for cutting grass, etc. * *vti* to cut with a scythe; to mow down.
SD *abbr* = South Dakota.
SDI *abbr* = Strategic Defense Initiative.
SE *abbr* = southeast(ern).
Se (*chem symbol*) selenium.
sea *n* the ocean; a section of this; a vast expanse of water; a heavy wave, the swell of the ocean; something like the sea in size; the seafaring life. * *adj* marine, of the sea.
sea anchor *n* a device dragged behind a vessel to slow the rate of drifting or keep it heading into the wind.
sea anemone *n* any of various solitary brightly coloured polyps with a ring of petal-like tentacles surrounding the mouth.
sea bass *n* any of numerous American marine fishes with a long body and a spiny dorsal fin.
seaboard *n, adj* (land) bordering on the sea.
seaborne *adj* conveyed by the sea; carried on a ship.
sea bream *n* any of numerous marine food fishes of European seas.
sea breeze *n* a wind that blows from the sea to the land.
sea change *n* a radical transformation.
seacock *n* a valve in the hull of a vessel through which water can pass in or out.
sea cow *see* **dugong**.
sea cucumber *n* an echinoderm with an elongated body, leathery skin and an oral ring of tentacles at one end.
sea dog *n* an old sailor.
sea eagle *n* any of various fish-eating eagles.
seafarer *n* a sailor; a person who travels by sea.
seafaring *n* travelling by sea, esp the work of a sailor.—*also adj*.
seafood *n* edible fish or shellfish from the sea.
sea front *n* the waterfront of a seaside place.
sea-green *adj, n* (a) pale bluish green.
seagoing *adj* (*ship*) made for use on the open sea.
seagull *n* a gull.
sea holly *n* a European coastal plant with blue flowers.
sea horse *n* a small bony-plated fish with a horselike head and neck and a long tail, that swims in an upright position; in fable, a horse with the tail of a fish.
sea kale *n* a European coastal plant with fleshy leaves and edible shoots.
seal[1] *n* an engraved stamp for impressing wax, lead, etc; wax, lead, etc, so impressed; that which authenticates or pledges; a device for closing or securing tightly. * *vt* to fix a seal to; to close tightly or securely; to shut up; to mark as settled, to confirm.
seal[2] *n* an aquatic mammal with four webbed flippers; the fur of some seals; a dark brown. * *vi* to hunt seals.
sea lane *n* a route for ships.
sealant *n* a thing that seals, as wax, etc; a substance for stopping a leak, making watertight, etc.
sea lavender *n* any of a genus of coastal plants with white, pink or purple flowers.
sealed-beam *adj* (*car headlight*) having the reflector incorporated in the lamp.
sea legs *npl* (*inf*) the ability to walk steadily on a moving ship and to be free from seasickness.
sealer *n* a person or a ship whose business is hunting seals.
sea level *n* the level of the surface of the sea in relation to the land.
sea lily *n* an echinoderm with a thin elongated body topped by petal-like tentacles.
sealing wax *n* a resinous compound that is plastic when warm and used for sealing letters, etc.
sea lion *n* a large seal of the Pacific Ocean that has a loud roar and, in the male, a mane.
sealskin *n* the fur of a seal; a coat of this.
Sealyham terrier *n* a breed of wire-haired terrier with short legs and a longish, usu white, coat.
seam *n* the line where two pieces of cloth are stitched together; (*geol*) a stratum of coal, oil, etc, between thicker ones; a line or wrinkle. * *vt* to join with a seam; to furrow.
seaman *n* (*pl* **seamen**) a sailor; a naval rank.
seamanship *n* the skill of handling, working and navigating a ship.
sea mile *n* a nautical mile.
sea mouse *n* a marine worm with a broad body covered in hairlike bristles.
seamstress *n* a woman who sews for a living.
seamy *adj* (**seamier, seamiest**) unpleasant or sordid.
seance, séance *n* a meeting of spiritualists to try to communicate with the dead.
sea otter *n* a large marine otter of North Pacific coasts that feeds on shellfish.
sea pink *n* the plant thrift.
seaplane *n* an aeroplane with floats that allow it to take off from and land on water.

seaport *n* a port, harbour or town accessible to oceangoing ships.
sear *vt* to burn or scorch the surface of; to brand with a heated iron; to wither up.
search *vi* to look around to find something; to explore. * *vt* to examine or inspect closely; to probe into. * *n* the act of searching; an investigation; a quest.—**searcher** *n*.
searching *adj* keen, piercing; examining thoroughly.—**searchingly** *adv*.
searchlight *n* a powerful ray of light projected by an apparatus on a swivel; the apparatus.
search party *n* a group of people organized to locate a missing person or thing.
search warrant *n* a legal document that authorizes a police search.
seascape *n* a picture of a scene at sea.
Sea Scout *n* a member of a Scout troop specializing in sailing, canoeing, diving, etc.
sea serpent *n* a legendary sea-dwelling monster resembling a snake or dragon.
seashell *n* the discarded or empty shell of a marine mollusc.
seashore *n* land beside the sea or between high and low water marks; the beach.
seasick *adj* affected with nausea brought on by the motion of a ship.—**seasickness** *n*.
seaside *n* seashore.
sea snail *n* a spiral-shelled marine mollusc, such as a whelk; a small slimy fish with pelvic fins formed into a sucker.
sea snake *n* a venomous snake of tropical waters with an oar-shaped tail.
season *n* one of the four equal parts into which the year is divided: spring, summer, autumn, or winter; a period of time; a time when something is plentiful or in use; a suitable time; (*inf*) a season ticket. * *vt* (*food*) to flavour by adding salt, spices, etc; to make mature or experienced; (*wood*) to dry until ready for use. * *vi* to become experienced.
seasonable *adj* suitable for the season; timely, opportune.—**seasonableness** *n*.—**seasonably** *adv*.
seasonal *adj* of or relating to a particular season.—**seasonally** *adv*.
seasonal affective disorder *n* a state of depression that affects some people in the winter months, thought to be caused by a lack of sunlight.
seasoning *n* salt, spices, etc, used to enhance the flavour of food; the process of making something fit for use.
season ticket *n* a ticket or set of tickets valid for a number of concerts, games, journeys, etc, during a specified period.
seat *n* a piece of furniture for sitting on, such as a chair, bench, etc; the part of a chair on which one sits; the buttocks, the part of the trousers covering them; a way of sitting (on a horse, etc); the chief location, or centre; a part at or forming a base; the right to sit as a member; a parliamentary constituency; a large country house. * *vt* to place on a seat; to provide with seats; to settle.
seatbelt *n* an anchored strap worn in a car or aeroplane to secure a person to a seat.
seated *adj* provided with a seat or seats; fixed, confirmed; located.
seating *n* the arrangement or provision of seats.
SEATO *abbr* = South East Asia Treaty Organization.
sea trout *n* a marine variety of brown trout that migrates to fresh water to spawn.
sea urchin *n* a small marine animal with a round body enclosed in a shell covered with sharp spines.
sea wall *n* a barrier or embankment to prevent erosion by the sea.
seaward *adj* toward the sea. * *adv* toward or in the direction of the sea.—**seawards** *adv*.
seaway *n* an ocean traffic lane; a waterway for seagoing traffic to an inland port.
seaweed *n* a mass of plants growing in or under water; a sea plant, esp a marine alga.
seaworthy *adj* fit to go to sea; able to withstand sea water, watertight.—**seaworthiness** *n*.
sebaceous *adj* of, secreting, containing, or producing oily or fatty matter.
sebaceous glands *npl* the small skin glands that secrete sebum onto the skin surface.
seborrhoea, seborrhea *n* the excessive secretion of sebum.—**seborrhoeic, seborrheic** *adj*.
sebum *n* a fatty substance secreted by the sebaceous glands to lubricate the hair and skin.
SEC *abbr* = Securities and Exchange Commission.
sec[1] *adj* (*wine*) dry; (*champagne*) medium sweet.
sec[2] *n* (*inf*) a second.
sec[3] *abbr* = secant.
sec. *abbr* = second.
secant *n* a trigonometrical function that is the reciprocal of the cosine; a straight line that intersects a curve.
secateurs *npl* a pair of small shears with curved blades for pruning, etc.
secede *vi* to withdraw formally one's membership from a society or organization.—**seceder** *n*.
secession *n* the act or an instance of seceding; a breaking away.—**secessional** *adj*.
seclude *vt* to keep (a person, etc) separate from others; to remove or screen from view.
secluded *adj* private; sheltered; kept from contact with other people.
seclusion *n* the state of being secluded; privacy, solitude.
second *adj* next after first; alternate; another of the same kind; next below the first in rank, value, etc. * *n* a person or thing coming second; another; an article of merchandise not of first quality; an aid or assistant, as to a boxer, duellist; the gear after low gear; one sixtieth of a minute of time or of an angular degree; (*pl*) (*inf*) another helping of food. * *adv* in the second place, group, etc. * *vt* to act as a second (to); (*a motion, resolution, etc*) to support; (*mil*) to place on temporary service elsewhere.
secondary *adj* subordinate; second in rank or importance; in the second stage; derived, not primary; relating to secondary school. * *n* (*pl* **secondaries**) that which is secondary; a delegate, a deputy.—**secondarily** *adv*.
secondary cell *n* a battery that can convert chemical energy to electrical energy by reversible chemical reactions and so be recharged.
secondary colour *n* a colour formed by mixing two primary colours.
secondary emission *n* (*physics*) the emission of secondary electrons from a solid surface due to bombardment by a beam of primary electrons or other elementary particles.
secondary school *n* a school between elementary or primary school and college or university.
secondary sexual characteristic *n* an attribute of a human being or animal that is characteristic of a particular sex but is not directly concerned with reproduction.
second best *adj* next to the best; inferior. * *adv* in second place. * *n* next to the best; an inferior alternative.
second chamber *n* the upper house in a legislative assembly with two chambers.
second childhood *n* dotage, senility.
second class *n* the class next to the first in a classification. * *adj* (second-class) relating to a second class; inferior, mediocre; (*seating, accommodation*) next in price and quality to first class; (*mail*) less expensive and handled more slowly (than first class).
Second Coming *n* (*Christianity*) the return to earth of Christ at the Last Judgment as prophesied.
second cousin *n* a child of the first cousin of one's parent.
second-degree burn *n* a burn which causes blistering of the skin.
second fiddle *n* (the musical part for) a second violin in an orchestra or string quartet; (*inf*) a person of secondary importance.
second hand *n* the moving pointer in a clock or watch that indicates the seconds.
second-hand *adj* bought after use by another; derived, not original.—*also adv*.
secondly *adv* in the second place.

second nature *n* a long-established habit, etc, deeply fixed in a person's nature.

second person *n* that form of a pronoun (as *you*) or verb (as *are*) that refers to the person spoken to.

second-rate *adj* of inferior quality.

second sight *n* the supposed faculty of seeing events before they occur.

second string *n* a reserve or substitute player in a team.

second thought *n* a change in thought or decision after consideration.

second wind *n* a return to regular breathing after a bout of exercise; renewed energy or enthusiasm.

secrecy *n* (*pl* **secrecies**) the state of being secret; the ability to keep secret.

secret *adj* not made public; concealed from others; hidden; private; remote. * *n* something hidden; a mystery; a hidden cause.

secret agent *n* a spy.

secretaire *n* a writing desk with an upper section for books and documents.

secretariat *n* an administrative office or staff, as in a government.

secretary *n* (*pl* **secretaries**) a person employed to deal with correspondence, filing, telephone calls of another or of an association; the head of a state department.—**secretarial** *adj*.

secretary bird *n* a large long-legged African bird of prey that eats mostly snakes.

secretary-general *n* (*pl* **secretaries-general**) the chief administrator of a large organization (eg the United Nations).

secretary of state *n* in the UK, any of various ministers in charge of government departments; (*with caps*) in the US, the minister in charge of foreign affairs.

secrete *vt* to conceal; to hide; (*cell, gland, etc*) to produce and release (a substance) out of blood or sap.

secretion *n* the process of secreting; a substance secreted by an animal or plant.

secretive *adj* given to secrecy; uncommunicative, reticent.—**secretively** *adv*.—**secretiveness** *n*.

secretly *adv* in a secret way; unknown to others.

secretory *adj* having the function of secreting, as a gland.

secret police *n* a police force that operates covertly to suppress political dissent rather than criminal activity.

secret service *n* a government agency that gathers intelligence, infiltrates terrorist or subversive organizations, conducts espionage, etc in the interests of national security.

sect *n* a religious denomination; a group of people united by a common interest or belief; a faction.

sectarian *adj* of or confined to a religious sect; bigoted. * *n* a member or adherent of a sect.

sectarianism *n* devotion to a sect; religious narrowness.

section *n* the act of cutting; a severed or separable part; a division; a distinct portion; a slice; a representation of anything cut through to show its interior; (*geom*) the cutting of a solid by a plane; a plane figure formed by this. * *vti* to cut or separate into sections; to represent in sections; to become separated or cut into parts.

sectional *adj* of a section; made up of several sections; local rather than general in character.—**sectionally** *adv*.

sector *n* (*geom*) a space enclosed by two radii of a circle and the arc they cut off; a distinctive part (as of an economy); a subdivision; (*mil*) an area of activity.

secular *adj* having no connection with religion or the church; worldly.—**secularly** *adv*.

secularize *vt* to change from religious to civil use or control.—**secularization** *n*.

secure *adj* free from danger, safe; stable; firmly held or fixed; confident, assured (of); reliable. * *vt* to make safe; to fasten firmly; to protect; to confine; to fortify; to guarantee; to gain possession of, to obtain.—**securely** *adv*.

security *n* (*pl* **securities**) the state of being secure; a financial guarantee, surety; a pledge for repayment, etc; a protection or safeguard; a certificate of shares or bonds.

Security Council *n* the principal council of the United Nations charged with maintaining world peace.

security guard *n* a person employed to protect public buildings, banks, offices, etc and to transport large sums of money.

security police *n* a police force whose function is to prevent espionage; the military police of an air force.

security risk *n* a person or thing regarded as a potential threat to security.

sedan *n* a car with no division between driver and passengers; a covered chair for one person with poles carried by two bearers.

sedate[1] *adj* calm; composed; serious and unemotional.—**sedately** *adv*.—**sedateness** *n*.

sedate[2] *vti* to calm or become calm by the administration of a sedative.

sedation *n* the act of calming or the condition of being calmed, esp by sedatives; the administration of sedatives to calm a patient.

sedative *n* a drug with a soothing, calming effect. * *adj* having a soothing, calming effect.

sedentary *adj* requiring a sitting position; inactive; not migratory.

Seder *n* a Jewish ceremonial meal held on the first night of Passover.

sedge *n* a grass-like plant that grows in marshes or beside water.

sedge warbler *n* a European songbird that inhabits marshy areas.

sediment *n* matter that settles at the bottom of a liquid; (*geol*) matter deposited by water or wind.

sedimentary *adj* relating to or formed by sediment.

sedition *n* incitement to rebel against the government.—**seditious** *adj*.—**seditiously** *adv*.

seduce *vt* to lead astray; to corrupt; to entice into unlawful sexual intercourse.—**seducer** *n*.

seduction *n* the act of seducing; temptations; attraction.

seductive *adj* tending to seduce; enticing, alluring.—**seductively** *adv*.—**seductiveness** *n*.

sedulous *adj* diligent; persevering.—**sedulously** *adv*.—**sedulousness** *n*.

see[1] *vt* (**seeing, saw,** *pp* **seen**) to perceive with the eyes; to observe; to grasp with the intelligence; to ascertain; to take care (that); to accompany; to visit; to meet; to consult; (*guests*) to receive; (*with* **through**) to persist or endure to the end; to assist (eg a friend) during a crisis, difficulty, etc. * *vi* to have the faculty of sight; to make inquiry; to consider, to reflect; to understand; (*with* **about**) to deal with; to consider in detail; (*with* **off**) to be present when someone leaves on a journey, etc; (*inf*) to repel, get rid of; (*with* **through**) to recognize the true character of.

see[2] *n* the diocese of a bishop.

seed *n* the small, hard part (ovule) of a plant from which a new plant grows; such seeds collectively; the source of anything; sperm or semen; descendants; (*tennis*) a seeded tournament player. * *vti* to sow (seed); to produce or shed seed; to remove seeds from; (*tennis*) to arrange (a tournament) so that the best players cannot meet until later rounds.

seedbed *n* a nursery bed for a plant; a place or source of growth or development.

seed cake *n* a sweet cake flavoured with aromatic (usu caraway) seeds.

seed coral *n* small pieces of coral used in jewellery.

seed corn *n* corn reserved for sowing; assets promising future earning potential.

seedless *adj* without seeds.

seedling *n* a young plant raised from seed, not from a cutting; a young tree before it is a sapling.

seed money *n* money used to start a new project or enterprise.

seed oyster *n* a young oyster ready for transplantation to a new bed.

seed pearl *n* a very small pearl.

seed potato *n* a potato tuber ready for planting.

seed vessel *n* a pericarp.

seedy *adj* (**seedier, seediest**) full of seeds; out of sorts, indisposed; shabby; rundown.—**seedily** *adv*.—**seediness** *n*.

seeing *n* vision, sight. * *adj* having sight; observant. * *conj* in view of the fact that; since.

seek *vti* (**seeking, sought**) to search for; to try to find, obtain, or achieve; to resort to; (*with* **to**) to try to, to endeavour; (*with* **out**) to search for and locate a person or thing; to try to secure the society of.—**seeker** *n*.
seem *vi* to appear (to be); to give the impression of; to appear to oneself.
seeming *adj* that seems real, true; ostensible, apparent.—**seemingly** *adv*.
seemly *adj* (**seemlier, seemliest**) proper, fitting.—**seemliness** *n*.
seen *see* **see**[1].
seep *vi* to ooze gently, to leak through.
seepage *n* the act of seeping; the liquid that has seeped.
seer *n* a person who sees visions, a prophet.
seersucker *n* a light, usu cotton, fabric with a puckered surface.
seesaw *n* a plank balanced across a central support so that it is tilted up and down by a person sitting on each end; an up-and-down movement like this; vacillation. * *vi* to move up and down; to fluctuate. * *adj, adv* alternately rising and falling.
seethe *vi* to be very angry inwardly; to swarm (with people).
segment *n* a section; a portion; one of the two parts of a circle or sphere when a line is drawn through it. * *vti* to cut or separate into segments.—**segmentation** *n*.
segregate *vti* to set apart from others, to isolate; to separate racial or minority groups.
segregation *n* the act of segregating or the condition of being segregated; the policy of compelling racial groups to live apart.
seguidilla *n* (the music for) a lively Spanish dance in triple time.
seiche *n* an undulation of the surface of a lake, caused by earth tremors or changes in barometric pressure.
seigneur *n* a feudal lord.
seigneury *n* (*pl* **seigneuries**) the estate or authority of a seigneur.
seine *n* a large fishing net that hangs vertically by means of floats along the top and weights along the bottom. * *vi* to catch fish with this.
seismic *adj* of or caused by earthquakes.—**seismically** *adv*.
seismo-, seism- *prefix* earthquake.
seismograph *n* an instrument for recording the direction, intensity, and time of an earthquake.—**seismographer** *n*.—**seismographic** *adj*.—**seismography** *n*.
seismology *n* the scientific study of earthquakes.—**seismologic, seismological** *adj*.—**seismologist** *n*.
seize *vt* to grasp; to capture; to take hold of suddenly or forcibly; to attack or afflict suddenly. * *vi* (*machinery*) to become jammed.—**seizable** *adj*.
seizure *n* the act of seizing; what is seized; a sudden attack of illness, an apoplectic stroke.
seldom *adv* not often, rarely.
select *vti* to choose or pick out. * *adj* excellent; choice; limited (eg in membership); exclusive.
select committee *n* a parliamentary committee established to investigate and report on a particular subject.
selection *n* the act of selecting; what is or are selected; the process by which certain animals or plants survive while others are eliminated, natural selection.
selective *adj* having the power of selection; highly specific in activity or effect.—**selectively** *adv*.—**selectiveness** *n*.
selenium *n* a nonmetallic solid chemical element with semiconductive and photoconductive properties that has various uses in electronics.
seleno-, selen- *prefix* the moon.
selenography *n* the study and mapping of the physical features of the moon.—**selenographer** *n*.—**selenographic** *adj*.
self- *prefix* of itself or oneself; by, for, in relation to, itself or oneself; automatic.
self *n* (*pl* **selves**) the identity, character, etc, of any person or thing; one's own person as distinct from all others; one's own interests or advantage. * *adj* (*colour*) matching, uniform.
self-abnegation *n* denial of one's own interests or desires in favour of those of others.
self-absorption *n* preoccupation with one's own interests and welfare.
self-abuse *n* masturbation.
self-acting *adj* automatic.
self-addressed *adj* addressed to return to the sender; intended for oneself.
self-aggrandizement *n* acting to increase one's own power and importance at the expense of others.—**self-aggrandizing** *adj*.
self-approbation *n* satisfaction with one's own actions or accomplishments, esp to excess.
self-assertion *n* the act of asserting one's own opinions, ideas, or rights, esp determinedly.—**self-assertive** *adj*.
self-assured *adj* confident.—**self-assurance** *n*.
self-catering *adj* catering for oneself.
self-centred, self-centered *adj* preoccupied with one's own affairs.—**self-centerdly, self-centeredly** *adv*.—**self-centredness, self-centeredness** *n*.
self-coloured, self-colored *adj* of a single colour.
self-confessed *adj* according to one's own testimony.
self-confident *adj* sure of one's own powers.—**self-confidence** *n*.—**self-confidently** *adv*.
self-conscious *adj* embarrassed or awkward in the presence of others, ill at ease.—**self-consciously** *adv*.—**self-consciousness** *n*.
self-contained *adj* complete in itself; showing self-control; uncommunicative.—**self-containment** *n*.
self-control *n* control of one's emotions, desires, etc, by the will.—**self-controlled** *adj*.
self-deception *n* the act or state of deceiving oneself.
self-defence, self-defense *n* the act of defending oneself; (*law*) a plea for the justification for the use of force.
self-denial *n* abstention from pleasure, etc; unselfishness.
self-determination *n* free will; the choice of action without compulsion; the right of a nation to choose its own form of government.
self-drive *adj* (*hired vehicle*) driven by the hirer.
self-educated *adj* educated without benefit of formal instruction; educated at one's own expense.
self-effacement *n* the act of making oneself or one's actions inconspicuous, due to modesty or timidity.
self-employed *adj* earning one's living in one's own business or profession, not employed by another; working freelance.
self-esteem *n* confidence and respect for oneself; an exaggerated opinion of oneself.
self-evident *adj* evident without proof or explanation.—**self-evidently** *adv*.
self-explanatory *adj* easily understood without explanation.
self-expression *n* the expression of one's own personality, as in creative art.
self-governing *adj* autonomous; (*colony, etc*) having an elective legislation.—**self-government** *n*.
self-help *n* the provision of means to help oneself, instead of relying on others.
self-image *n* one's sense of oneself or one's importance.
self-importance *n* an exaggerated estimate of one's own worth; pompousness.—**self-important** *adj*.
self-induced *adj* brought on by oneself or itself.
self-induction *n* the production of an electromotive force in a circuit by a variation in the electric current in the same circuit.
self-indulgence *n* undue gratification of one's desires, appetites, or whims.—**self-indulgent** *adj*.
self-inflicted *adj* (*wound, etc*) caused to a person by himself.
self-interest *n* regard to one's own advantage.
selfish *adj* chiefly concerned with oneself; lacking in consideration for others.—**selfishly** *adv*.—**selfishness** *n*.
self-justification *n* the act or instance of making excuses for one's actions, etc.
selfless *adj* with no thought of self, unselfish.—**selflessly** *adv*.—**selflessness** *n*.
self-loading *n* (*firearm*) semiautomatic.—**self-loader** *n*.
self-love *n* conceit; selfishness.
self-made *adj* having achieved status or wealth by one's own efforts.
self-opinionated *adj* conceited; stubborn.
self-pity *n* pity for oneself.—**self-pitying** *adj*.

self-pollination *n* the transfer of pollen from the anther to the stigma in the same flower.

self-portrait *n* an artist or author's painting or account of himself or herself.

self-possessed *adj* cool and collected.

self-preservation *n* the instinct to protect oneself from injury or death.

self-propelled *adj* (*vehicle*) moving under its own power.

self-raising *adj (flour)* self-rising.

self-realization *n* the understanding or achievement of one's own potential or desires.

self-regard *n* concern for one's own interests; respect for oneself.

self-reliant *adj* relying on one's own powers; confident.—**self-reliance** *n.*

self-reproach *n* the act of blaming oneself.

self-respect *n* proper respect for oneself, one's standing and dignity.—**self-respecting** *adj.*

self-righteous *adj* thinking oneself better than others; priggish.—**self-righteousness** *n.*

self-rising *adj* (*flour*) containing a raising agent, self-raising.

self-rule *n* self-government.

self-sacrifice *n* the sacrifice of one's own interests, welfare, etc, to secure that of others.

selfsame *adj* identical, the very same.

self-satisfied *adj* smugly conceited.

self-seeking *adj* preoccupied with securing one's own well-being or interest; selfish.—**self-seeker** *n.*

self-service *adj* serving oneself in a cafe, shop, filling station, etc.

self-serving *adj* always seeking to protect or further one's own interests.

self-sown *adj* (*plants*) grown from seeds that were planted or deposited naturally without intervention by humans or animals.

self-starter *n* an electric device for starting an engine; a motivated employee who requires little supervision.

self-styled *adj* called by oneself; pretended.

self-sufficient *adj* independent; supporting oneself (eg in growing food) without the help of others.—**self-sufficiency** *n.*

self-supporting *adj* able to manage without help from others; able to stand unaided.

self-will *n* fixed adherence to one's own desires, intentions, etc; obstinacy.

self-winding *adj* (*watch*) wound automatically by an internal mechanism.

sell *vb* **(selling, sold)** *vt* to exchange (goods, services, etc) for money or other equivalent; to offer for sale; to promote; to deal in; (*with* **up**) to sell all the goods of (a debtor) to clear the debt. * *vi* (*with* **off**) to clear out (stock) at bargain prices; (*with* **out**) to sell off, to betray for money or reward; (*inf*) to disappoint, to trick; to make sales; to attract buyers; (*with* **up**) to sell one's house, business, etc. * *n* an act or instance of selling; (*inf*) a disappointment, a trick, a fraud.—**seller** *n.*

Sellotape *n* (*trademark*) a transparent adhesive tape. * *vt* to seal or stick (something) using adhesive tape.

sellout *n* a show, game, etc, for which all the tickets are sold; (*inf*) a betrayal.

selvage, selvedge *n* the edge of cloth so finished as to prevent unravelling.

selves *see* **self.**

Sem *abbr* = Seminary; Semitic.

sem *abbr* = semester; semicolon.

semantic *adj* relating to the meaning of words. * *npl* the study of word meanings and changes.

semaphore *n* a system of visual signalling using the operator's arms, flags, etc; a signalling device consisting of a post with movable arms.

sematic *adj* (*animal colouration*) warning of danger.

semblance *n* likeness, resemblance; an outward, sometimes deceptive appearance.

semen *n* the fluid that carries sperm in men and male animals.

semester *n* an academic or school half-year.

semi *n* (*pl* **semis**) (*inf*) a semidetached house; a semifinal.

semi- *prefix* half; not fully; twice in a (specified period).

semiannual *adj* happening twice a year, or lasting for six months.—*also* **semiyearly.**

semiautomatic *adj* partly automatic; (*firearm*) self-loading but discharging in single shots only as the trigger is pulled.

semibreve *n* (*mus*) a note equal to two minims.—*also* **whole note.**

semicircle *n* half of a circle.—**semicircular** *adj.*

semicircular canal *n* any of the three fluid-filled tubes in the inner ear concerned with maintaining balance.

semicolon *n* the punctuation mark (;) of intermediate value between a comma and a full stop.

semiconductor *n* a substance in a transmitter, as silicon, used to control the flow of current.

semiconscious *adj* not fully conscious.—**semiconsciousness** *n.*

semi-detached *adj* (*house*) with another joined to it on one side.—*also n.*

semifinal *adj, n* (the match or round) before the final in a knockout tournament.—**semifinalist** *n.*

semifluid *n* having qualities between those of a fluid and a solid; viscous.

semiliterate *n* barely able to read or write.

semilunar *adj* in the shape of a crescent.

semilunar valve *n* either one of the two crescent-shaped valves in the heart.

seminal *adj* of, relating to, or containing semen; promising or contributing to further development; original, influential.—**seminally** *adv.*

seminar *n* a group of students engaged in study or research under supervision; any group meeting to pool and discuss ideas.

seminary *n* (*pl* **seminaries**) a training college for priests, ministers, etc; a school for young women.

seminiferous *adj* producing or containing semen; (*plants*) bearing seeds.

semiology *n* the study of signs and symbols.—**semiologic, semiological** *adj.*—**semiologist** *n.*

semiotics *n sing* the study of signs and symbols, esp their use in language and relationship to the world of things and ideas; the study of the symptoms of disease.—**semiotic, semiotical** *adj.*—**semiotician** *n.*

semiprecious *adj* denoting gems of lower value than precious stones.

semiprofessional *adj* taking part in sport for pay, but not on a fulltime basis.—**semiprofessionally** *adv.*

semiquaver *n* (*mus*) a sixteenth note.

semirigid *adj* (*airship*) having a flexible gas container attached to a rigid keel.

semiskilled *adj* partly skilled or trained.

semiskimmed *adj* (*milk*) having the cream partially removed.

semisolid *adj* having the properties between that of a liquid and a solid; extremely viscous.

Semite *n* a member of the group of peoples including Arabs and Jews.

Semitic *adj* of or belonging to Semites; Jewish.

Semitism *n* any political or economic policy relating to Jews.

semitone *n* (*mus*) an interval equal to half a tone.

semitrailer *n* a trailer that has wheels at the back but is supported at the front by the towing vehicle.

semivowel *n* (*phon*) a consonant that sound like a vowel (eg *y* or *j*), a glide.

semiyearly *see* **semiannual.**

semolina *n* coarse particles of grain left after the sifting of wheat.

sempre *adv* (*mus*) always.

Sen *abbr* = senator; senior.

senate *n* a legislative or governing body; (*with cap*) the upper branch of a two-body legislature in France, the US, etc; the governing body of some universities.

senator *n* a member of a senate.—**senatorial** *adj.*

send *vti* **(sending, sent)** to cause or enable to go; to have conveyed, to dispatch (a message or messenger); to cause to move, to propel; to grant; to cause to be; (*sl*) to move (a person) to ecstasy; (*with* **down**) to expel from university; (*with* **for**) to order to be brought, to summon; (*with* **up**) (*inf*) to send to prison; to imitate or make fun of.—**sender** *n.*

send-off *n* a friendly demonstration at a departure; a start given to someone or something.

senescent *adj* growing old.—**senescence** *n.*
seneschal *n* (*hist*) a steward in the house of a feudal lord.
senile *adj* of or relating to old age; weakened, esp mentally, by old age.—**senility** *n.*
senior *adj* higher in rank; of or for seniors; longer in service; older (when used to distinguish between father and son with the same first name). * *n* one's elder or superior in standing; a person of advanced age; a student in the last year of college or high school.
senior citizen *n* an elderly person, esp a retired one.
senior common room *n* a staffroom in a British college or university.
seniority *n* (*pl* **seniorities**) the condition of being senior; status, priority, etc, in a given job.
sensation *n* awareness due to stimulation of the senses; an effect on the senses; a thrill; a state of excited interest; the cause of this.
sensational *adj* of or relating to sensation; exciting violent emotions; melodramatic.—**sensationally** *adv.*
sensationalism *n* the use of sensational writing, language, etc; the doctrine that all knowledge is obtained from sense impressions.—**sensationalist** *adj.*
sense *n* one of the five human and animal faculties by which objects are perceived: sight, hearing, smell, taste, and touch; awareness; moral discernment; soundness of judgment; meaning, intelligibility; (*pl*) conscious awareness. * *vt* to perceive; to become aware of; to understand; to detect.
senseless *adj* stupid, foolish; meaningless, purposeless; unconscious.—**senselessly** *adv.*—**senselessness** *n.*
sense organ *n* a bodily structure that reacts to stimuli and transmits them to the brain as nerve impulses.
sensibility *n* (*pl* **sensibilities**) the capacity to feel; over-sensitiveness; susceptibility; (*pl*) sensitive awareness or feelings.
sensible *adj* having good sense or judgment; reasonable; practical; perceptible by the senses, appreciable; conscious (of); sensitive.—**sensibleness** *n.*—**sensibly** *adv.*
sensitive *adj* having the power of sensation; feeling readily and acutely, keenly perceptive; (*skin*) delicate, easily irritated; (*wound etc*) still in a painful condition; easily hurt or shocked, tender, touchy; highly responsive to slight changes; sensory; (*photog*) reacting to light.—**sensitively** *adj.*—**sensitiveness** *n.*
sensitive plant *n* a tropical American plant whose leaves and stems fold when touched.
sensitivity *n* (*pl* **sensitivities**) the condition of being sensitive; awareness of changes or differences; responsiveness to stimuli or feelings, esp to excess.
sensitize *vt* to make or become sensitive; (*person*) to render sensitive to an antigen, etc; (*photog: paper etc*) to render sensitive to light.—**sensitization** *n.*—**sensitizer** *n.*
sensitometer *n* a device for measuring the sensitivity to light of a photographic medium.
sensor *n* a device for detecting, recording, or measuring physical phenomena, as heat, pulse, etc; a sense organ.
sensorium *n* (*pl* **sensoriums, sensoria**) the area of the brain regarded as responsible for receiving and processing external stimulii; the body's entire sensory apparatus.
sensory *adj* of or relating to the senses, sensation, or the sense organs; conveying nerve impulses to the brain.
sensual *adj* bodily, relating to the senses rather than the mind; arousing sexual desire.—**sensuality** *n.*—**sensually** *adv.*
sensuous *adj* giving pleasure to the mind or body through the senses.—**sensuously** *adv.*—**sensuousness** *n.*
sent *see* **send.**
sentence *n* a court judgment; the punishment imposed; (*gram*) a series of words conveying a complete thought. * *vt* (*a convicted person*) to pronounce punishment upon; to condemn (to).
sententious *adj* terse, pithy; making frequent use of axioms and maxims; exhibiting a pompous, moralizing tone.—**sententiously** *adv.*—**sententiousness** *n.*
sentient *adj* making use of the senses, conscious.—**sentiently** *adv.*
sentiment *n* a feeling, awareness, or emotion; the thought behind something; an attitude of mind; a tendency to be swayed by feeling rather than reason; an exaggerated emotion.
sentimental *adj* of or arising from feelings; foolishly emotional; nostalgic.—**sentimentally** *adv.*
sentimentality *n* (*pl* **sentimentalities**) the quality or state of being sentimental; an affected or extreme tenderness.
sentinel *n* a sentry or guard.
sentry *n* (*pl* **sentries**) a soldier on guard to give warning of danger and to prevent unauthorized access.
sentry box *n* a shelter for a sentry.
senza *prep* (*mus*) without.
señor *n* (*pl* **señors, señores**) the title of a Spanish-speaking man, equivalent to Mr or sir.
señora *n* (*pl* **señoras**) the title of a Spanish-speaking married woman, equivalent to Mrs or madam.
señorita *n* (*pl* **señoritas**) the title of a Spanish-speaking unmarried woman, equivalent to Miss or madam.
Sep. *abbr* = September; Septuagint.
sepal *n* any of the individual parts of the calyx of a flower.
separable *adj* able to be separated or parted.—**separability** *n.*—**separably** *adv.*
separate *vt* to divide or part; to sever; to set or keep apart; to sort into different sizes. * *vi* to go different ways; to cease to live together as man and wife. * *adj* divided; distinct, individual; not shared. * *n* (*pl*) articles of clothing designed to be interchangeable with others to form various outfits.—**separately** *adv.*—**separateness** *n.*
separation *n* the act of separating or the state of being separate; a formal arrangement of husband and wife to live apart.
separatist *n* a person who advocates or practises separation from an organization, church, or government; a person who advocates racial or political separation.—*also adj.*—**separatism** *n.*
separator *n* one who separates; a machine that separates liquids from solids or liquids of different specific gravities.
Sephardi *n* (*pl* **Sephardim**) a Jew of Spanish, Portuguese or North African descent.—**Sephardic** *adj.*
sepia *adj, n* (a) dark reddish brown.
sepoy *n* (*formerly*) an Indian soldier employed by the British.
seppuku *n* harakiri.
sepsis *n* a septic state or agency; blood poisoning.
Sept. *abbr* = September.
septa *see* **septum.**
September *n* the ninth month of the year, having 30 days.
septennial *adj* occuring every, or lasting, seven years. * *n* a seven-year period.—**septennially** *adv.*
septet *n* a set of seven singers or players; a musical composition for seven instruments or voices.
septic *adj* infected by microorganisms; causing or caused by putrefaction.—**septically** *adv.*—**septicity** *n.*
septicaemia, septicemia *n* a disease caused by poisonous bacteria in the blood.—**septicaemic, septicemic** *adj.*
septic tank *n* an underground tank in which sewage is decomposed by the action of bacteria.
septuagenarian *n* a person in his or her seventies.
Septuagesima *n* the third Sunday before Lent.
Septuagint *n* the Greek version of the Old Testament including the Apocrypha (said to have been translated by 70 scholars).
septum *n* (*pl* **septa**) a dividing membrane between two bodily cavities or parts.—**septal** *adj.*
septuplet *n* one of seven offspring produced at one birth.
sepulchral *adj* of or like a sepulchre; dismal, funereal; (*sound*) deep and hollow.
sepulchre, sepulcher *n* a tomb, a burial vault.
sequel *n* something that follows, the succeeding part; a consequence; the continuation of a story begun in an earlier literary work, film, etc.

sequela *n* (*pl* **sequelae**) (*med*) a condition arising from an existing disease; any complication of a disease or injury.

sequence *n* order of succession; a series of succeeding things; a single, uninterrupted episode, as in a film.

sequential *adj* arranged in a sequence; following in sequence; consecutive.—**sequentially** *adv*.

sequester *vt* to place apart; to retire in seclusion; (*law*) to remove from one's possession until the claims of one's creditors are satisfied.

sequestrate *vt* to sequester.—**sequestration** *n*.

sequin *n* a shiny round piece of metal or foil sewn on clothes for decoration.

sequoia *n* a lofty coniferous Californian tree.

sera *see* **serum.**

sérac *n* a pinnacle or tower-shaped mass of ice among the crevasses of a glacier.

seraglio *n* (*pl* **seraglios**) a harem in a Muslim household or palace.

seraph *n* (*pl* **seraphs, seraphim**) (*theol*) a member of the highest order of angels.—**seraphic** *adj*.

Serb, Serbian *n* a native or inhabitant of Serbia; the Serbo-Croatian language of Serbia.—*also adj*.

Serbo-Croatian, Serbo-Croat *n* the Slavonic language of the Serbs and Croatians.—*also adj*.

serenade *n* music sung or played at night beneath a person's window, esp by a lover. * *vt* to entertain with a serenade.

serendipity *n* the faculty of making fortunate finds by chance.

serene *adj* calm; untroubled; tranquil; clear and unclouded; (*with cap*) honoured (used as part of certain royal titles).—**serenely** *adv*.—**serenity** *n*.

serf *n* (*pl* **serfs**) a labourer in feudal service who was bound to, and could be sold with, the land he worked; a drudge.—**serfdom** *n*.

serge *n* a hard-wearing twilled woollen fabric.

sergeant *n* a noncommissioned officer ranking above a corporal in the army, air force, and marine corps; a police officer ranking above a constable.

sergeant-at-arms *n* (*pl* **sergeants-at-arms**) an official in various legislative assemblies responsible for enforcing discipline.

sergeant major *n* a noncommissioned officer in the army, air force, marine corps serving as chief administrative assistant in a headquarters.

Sergt. *abbr* = Sergeant.

serial *adj* of or forming a series; published, shown or broadcast by instalments at regular intervals. * *n* a story presented in regular instalments with a connected plot.

serialism *n* (*mus*) the use of the twelve notes of the chromatic scale in a fixed order in a composition.

serialize *vt* to arrange, publish or broadcast in serial form.—**serialization** n.

serial killer *n* a person who murders people one at a time over a period of time.

serial number *n* one of a series of numbers given for identification.

seriatim *adv* consecutively.

sericeous *adj* (*bot*) covered in fine hairs

sericulture *n* the breeding of silkworms to produce raw silk.—**sericultural** *adj*.—**sericulturist** *n*.

series *n sing, pl* a succession of items or events; a succession of things connected by some likeness; a sequence, a set; a radio or television serial whose episodes have self-contained plots; a set of books issued by one publisher; (*math*) a progression of numbers or quantities according to a certain law.

serif *n* (*print*) a small line at the top or the bottom of the main stroke of a letter.

serigraph *n* a print made using the silk-screen technique.—**serigraphy** *n*.

serin *n* any of various small European finches related to the canary.

seriocomic *adj* combining humour and seriousness.—**seriocomically** *adv*.

serious *adj* grave, solemn, not frivolous; meaning what one says, sincere, earnest; requiring close attention or thought; important; critical.—**seriously** *adv*.—**seriousness** *n*.

sermon *n* a speech on religion or morals, esp by a clergyman; a long, serious talk of reproof, esp a tedious one.

sermonize *vti* to compose sermons; to preach at or to at length.—**sermonizer n.**

sero- *prefix* serum.

serology *n* the scientific study of serums.—**serological** *adj*.—**serologist** *n*.

seropositive *adj* having a particular disease (eg AIDS) for which one's blood has been tested.

serotinin *n* a substance occurring in various body tissues that induces vasoconstriction.

serous *n* of or producing serum.

serous membrane *n* a thin membrane lining a body cavity that secretes a thin lubricant.

serpent *n* a snake; a venomous or treacherous person.

serpentine *adj* like a serpent; twisting, tortuous; crooked, treacherous.

serpigo *n* a spreading skin complaint such as ringworm or herpes.

SERPS (*acronym*) state earnings-related pension scheme.

serrate *adj* (*leaves, etc*) having toothed edges; notched like a saw. * *vt* to make serrate.

serrated *adj* having an edge notched like the teeth of a saw.

serration *n* the state of being serrated; a saw-like edge; a single notch in a serrated edge.

serried *adj* packed closely, in compact order.

serum *n* (*pl* **serums, sera**) the watery part of bodily fluid, esp liquid that separates out from the blood when it coagulates; such fluid taken from the blood of an animal immune to a disease, used as an antitoxin.

serum albumin *n* the principal blood protein.

serum hepatitis *n* a viral disease, characterized by acute inflammation of the liver and jaundice, transmitted by contact with infected blood.

serval *n* (*pl* **servals, serval**) an African cat with long legs and a tawny coat with black spots.

servant *n* a personal or domestic attendant; one in the service of another.

serve *vt* to work for; to do military or naval service (for); to be useful to; to meet the needs (of), to suffice; (*a customer*) to wait upon; (*food, etc*) to hand round; (*a sentence*) to undergo; to be a soldier, sailor, etc; (*of a male animal*) to copulate with; (*law*) to deliver (a summons, etc); (*naut*) to bind (a rope) with thin cord to prevent fraying; (*tennis*) to put (the ball) into play. * *vi* to be employed as a servant; to be enough. * *n* the act of serving in tennis, etc.

server *n* one who serves, esp at tennis; something used in serving food and drink; a person who serves legal processes on another; the celebrant's assistant at mass.

service *n* the act of serving; the state of being a servant; domestic employment; a department of state employ; the people engaged in it; military employment or duty; work done for others; use, assistance; attendance in a hotel, etc; a facility providing a regular supply of trains, etc; a set of dishes; any religious ceremony; an overhaul of a vehicle; (*tennis*) the act or manner of seving; (*pl*) friendly help or professional aid; a system of providing a utility, as water, gas, etc. * *vt* to provide with assistance; to overhaul.

serviceable *adj* useful; durable.—**serviceably** *adv*.—**serviceableness** *n*.

service area *n* a place offering a range of services such as restaurants, toilet facilities, and petrol.

service charge *n* a sum added to a restaurant or hotel bill, etc for service.

serviceman *n* (*pl* **servicemen**) a member of the armed services; a person whose work is repairing something.—**servicewoman** *nf* (*pl* **servicewomen**).

service road *n* a minor road beside a main route that provides access to local shops, housing, etc.

service station *n* a place selling fuel, etc, for motor vehicles; a place at which some service is offered.

serviette *n* a small napkin.

servile *adj* of or like a slave; subservient; submissive; menial.—**servilely** *adv*.—**servility** *n*.

serving *n* a portion of food or drink.

servitude *n* slavery, bondage; work imposed as punishment for a crime.

servo *n* (*pl* **servos**) (*inf*) a servomotor or servomechanism. * *adj* activated by a servomechanism.

servomechanism *n* an automatic device which uses small amounts of power to control a system of much greater power.

servomotor *n* a motor that supplies power to a servomechanism.

sesame *n* an Asian plant that yields oil-bearing seeds; its seeds, also used for flavouring.

sesamoid *adj* of or pertaining to the small bones or lumps of cartilage in a tendon.

sesqui- *prefix* one and a half; (*chem*) a ratio of two to three.

sesquicentenniel *n* a period of 150 years; (the celebration of) a 150th anniversary.—*also adj*.

sessile *adj* (*leaves*) without a stalk; permanently attached.

session *n* the meeting of a court, legislature, etc; a series of such meetings; a period of these; a period of study, classes, etc; a university year; a period of time passed in an activity.

sesterce, sestertius *n* in ancient Rome, a coin worth a quarter of a denarius.

sestet *n* a poem or stanza of six lines, esp the last six lines of a sonnet.

set *vb* (**setting, set**) *vt* to put in a specified place, condition, etc; (*trap for animals*) to fix; (*clock etc*) to adjust; (*table*) to arrange for a meal; (*hair*) to fix in a desired style; (*bone*)to put into normal position, etc; to make settled, rigid, or fixed; (*gems*) to mount; to direct; to furnish (an example) for others; to fit (words to music or music to words); (*type*) to arrange for printing; (*with* **against**) to weigh up, compare; to cause to be opposed to; (*with* **aside**) to discard; to reserve for a particular reason; (*with* **down**) to place (something) on a surface; to record, put in writing; to regard; to attribute (to); to allow to alight from (a vehicle); (*with* **out**) to present or display; to explain in detail; to plan, lay out. * *vi* to become firm, hard or fixed; to begin to move (out, forth, off, etc); (*sun*) to sink below the horizon; (*with* **about**) to begin; to abuse physically or verbally; (*with* **in**) to stitch (a sleeve) within a garment; to become established; (*with* **off**) to show up by contrast; to set in motion; to cause to explode; (*with* **on**) to urge (as a dog) to attack or pursue; to go on, advance; (*with* **out**) to begin a journey, career, etc; (*with* **to**) to start working, esp eagerly; to start fighting; (*with* **up**) to erect; to establish, to found; (*with* **upon**) to attack, usu with violence. * *adj* fixed, established; intentional; rigid, firm; obstinate; ready. * *n* a number of persons or things classed or belonging together; a group, a clique; the way in which a thing is set; direction; the scenery for a play, film, etc; assembled equipment for radio or television reception, etc; (*math*) the totality of points, numbers, or objects that satisfy a given condition; (*tennis*) a series of games forming a unit of a match; a rooted cutting of a plant ready for transplanting; a badger's burrow (—*also* **sett**).

seta *n* (*pl* **setae**) a bristle or similar appendage of an animal or plant.

setback *n* misfortune; a reversal.

setline *n* a long fishing line with hooked shorter lines attached at regular intervals.

set piece *n* a formal or elaborate performance, esp of a work of art, music, etc; an elaborate fireworks display; (*sport*) a carefully rehearsed team move usu aimed at gaining the ball when play resumes.

setscrew *n* a screw which when tightened prevents parts of a machine from moving relative to one another.

set-square *n* a flat triangular instrument for drawing angles.

settee *n* a sofa for two people.

setter *n* a large breed of gundog trained to stand rigid when spotting game.

set theory *n* the branch of mathematics concerned with the relations and properties of sets.

setting *n* a background, scene, surroundings, environment; a mounting, as for a gem; the music for a song, etc.

settle *vti* to put in order; to pay (an account); to clarify; to decide, to come to an agreement; to make or become quiet or calm; to make or become firm; to establish or become established in a place, business, home, etc; to colonize (a country); to take up residence; to come to rest; (*dregs*) to fall to the bottom; to stabilize; to make or become comfortable (for resting); (*bird*) to alight; to bestow legally for life; (*with* **for**) to be content with.

settlement *n* the act of settling; a sum settled, esp on a woman at her marriage; an arrangement; a small village; a newly established colony; subsidence (of buildings).

settler *n* a person who settles; an early colonist.

set-to *n* (*inf*) a squabble, fight.

set-up *n* the plan, makeup, etc, of equipment used in an organization; the details of a situation, plan, etc; (*inf*) a contest, etc, arranged to result in an easy win.

seven *adj, n* one more than six. * *n* the symbol for this (7, VII, vii); the seventh in a series or set; something having seven units as members.

sevenfold *adj* having seven units or members; being seven times as great or as many.

seven seas *npl* all the world's oceans.

seventeen *adj, n* one more than sixteen. * *n* the symbol for this (17, XVII, xvii).—**seventeenth** *adj*.

seventh *adj, n* next after sixth; one of seven equal parts of a thing. * *n* (*mus*) an interval of seven diatonic degrees; the leading note.

seventh heaven *n* perfect happiness.

seventy *adj, n* seven times ten. * *n* the symbol for this (70, LXX, lxx); (in *pl*) **seventies** (70s) the numbers for 70 to 79; the same numbers in a life or century.—**seventieth** *adj*.

sever *vti* to separate, to divide into parts; to break off.—**severance** *n*.

several *adj* more than two but not very many; various; separate, distinct; respective. * *pron* (*with pl vb*) a few. * *n* (*with pl vb*) a small number (of).

severe *adj* harsh, not lenient; very strict; stern; censorious; exacting, difficult; violent, not slight; (*illness*) critical; (*art*) plain, not florid.—**severely** *adv*.—**severity** *n*.

Seville orange *n* (an orange tree bearing) a fruit with bitter flesh used to make marmalade.

Sèvres *n* a type of fine porcelain made in France.

sew *vti* (**sewing, sewn** *or* **sewed**) to join or stitch together with needle and thread; to make, mend, etc, by sewing; (*with* **up**) to get full control of; (*inf*) to make sure of success in.—**sewing** *n*.

sewage *n* waste matter carried away in a sewer.

sewage farm *n* a place where sewage is treated for use as manure.

sewer[1] *n* one who sews.

sewer[2] *n* an underground pipe or drain for carrying off liquid waste matter, etc; a main drain.

sewerage *n* a system of drainage by sewers; sewage.

sewing machine *n* a machine for sewing or stitching usu driven by an electric motor.

sewn *see* **sew**.

sex *n* the characteristics that distinguish male and female organisms on the basis of their reproductive function; either of the two categories (male and female) so distinguished; males or females collectively; the state of being male or female; the attraction between the sexes; (*inf*) sexual intercourse.

sex- *prefix* six.

sexagenarian *n* a person in the age range 60–69.—*also adj*.

Sexagesima *n* the second Sunday before Lent.

sexagesimal *adj* of or based on the number 60.

sex appeal *n* what makes a person sexually desirable.

sex chromosome *n* a chromosome that determines the sex of an animal.

sexed *adj* having a certain amount of sex or sexuality.

sex hormone *n* a hormone affecting the development of sexual organs and characteristics.

sexism *n* exploitation and domination of one sex by the other, esp of women by men.—**sexist** *adj, n*.

sexless *adj* without sexual intercourse; sexually unappealing.—**sexlessly** *adv*.—**sexlessness** *n*.

sex object *n* a person regarded solely in terms of their sexual attractiveness.
sexology *n* the study of human sexuality.—**sexologist** *n*.—**sexological** *adj*.
sex shop *n* a shop specializing in sex aids, pornographic magazines, etc.
sextant *n* a navigator's instrument for measuring the altitude of the sun, etc, to determine position at sea.
sextet *n* a set of six singers or players; a musical composition for six instruments or voices.
sexton *n* an officer in charge of the maintenance of church property.
sextuple *adj* having six units or members; being six times as much or as many.—*also n*.
sextuplet *n* one of six offspring produced at one birth.
sexual *adj* of sex or the sexes; having sex.—**sexually** *adj*.
sexual harassment *n* frequent unwelcome attention from the opposite sex in the form of suggestive remarks, fondling, etc.
sexual intercourse *n* the act of copulating.
sexuality *n* sexual activity; expression of sexual interest, esp when excessive.
sexually transmitted disease *n* any of various diseases, such as syphilis or AIDS, transmitted by sexual contact.—*also* **venereal disease.**
sexy *adj* (**sexier, sexiest**) (*inf*) exciting, or intending to excite, sexual desire; attractive, entertaining; fashionable or stylish and as a result worthwhile.—**sexily** *adv*.—**sexiness** *n*.
SF *abbr* = science fiction.
sf, sfz *abbr* = sforzando.
sforzando, sforzato *adv* (*mus*) with vigour at the start. * *n* a notation indicating this.
sgd *abbr* = signed.
SGM abbr = Sergeant Major.
sgraffito *n* (*pl* **sgraffiti**) (an example of) a technique in ceramic or mural design in which the surface layer (of glaze, plaster, etc) is scraped away to expose a contrasting background.
Sgt *abbr* = sergeant
Sgt Maj *abbr* = sergeant major.
sh *interj* used to command silence.
shabby *adj* (**shabbier, shabbiest**) (*clothes*) threadbare, worn, or dirty; rundown, dilapidated; (*act, trick*) mean, shameful.—**shabbily** *adv*.—**shabbiness** *n*.
shack *n* a small, crudely built house or cabin; a shanty. * *vi* (*with* **up**) (*sl*) to cohabit (with); to spend the night (with), esp a person of the opposite sex.
shackle *n* a metal fastening, usu in pairs, for the wrists or ankles of a prisoner; a staple; anything that restrains freedom; (*pl*) fetters. * *vt* to fasten or join by a shackle; to hamper, to impede.
shad *n* (*pl* **shad, shads**) any of various fishes of the herring family used as food.
shade *n* relative darkness; dimness; the darker parts of anything; shadow; a shield or screen protecting from bright light; a ghost; a place sheltered from the sun; degree of darkness of a colour, esp when made by the addition of black; a minute difference; a blind; (*pl*) the darkness of approaching night; (*pl: sl*) sunglasses. * *vti* to screen from light; to overshadow; to make dark; to pass by degrees into another colour; to change slightly or by degrees.
shading *n* the fine gradations of colour, line, tone, etc, creating light and dark in a painting, etc; a shielding against light; nuances.
shadow *n* a patch of shade; darkness, obscurity; the dark parts of a painting, etc; shelter, protection; the dark shape of an object produced on a surface by intercepted light; an inseparable companion; a person (as a detective, etc) who shadows; an unsubstantial thing, a phantom; a mere remnant, a slight trace; gloom, affliction. * *vt* to cast a shadow over; to cloud; to follow and watch, esp in secret. * *adj* having an indistinct pattern or darker section; (*opposition party*) matching a function or position of the party in power.
shadow-box *vi* (*boxing*) to practice blows against an invisible opponent.
shadowy *adj* full of shadows; dim, indistinct; unsubstantial.
shady *adj* (**shadier, shadiest**) giving or full of shade; sheltered from the sun; (*inf*) of doubtful honesty, disreputable.
SHAEF (*acronym*) Supreme Headquarters Allied Expeditionary Forces.
shaft *n* a straight rod, a pole; a stem, a shank; the main part of a column; an arrow or spear, or its stem; anything hurled like a missile; a ray of light, a stroke of lightning; a revolving rod for transmitting power, an axle; one of the poles between which a horse is harnessed; a hole giving access to a mine; a vertical opening through a building, as for a lift; a critical remark or attack; (*sl*) harsh or unfair treatment.
shag *n* a coarse tobacco cut into long pieces; a rough mop of hair, etc; a crested cormorant. * *adj* (*carpet*) having long, thick, woollen threads.
shaggy *adj* (**shaggier, shaggiest**) (*hair, fur, etc*) long and unkempt; rough; untidy.—**shagginess** *n*.
shaggy-dog story *n* (*inf*) a long joke with a punch line that is a deliberate anticlimax.
shagreen *n* the rough skin of certain sharks and rays; a type of leather with a gritty surface made from the hides of certain animals.
shah *n* the title of the former ruler of Iran.
shake *vti* (**shaking, shook,** *pp* **shaken**) to move to and fro with quick short motions, to agitate; to tremble or vibrate; to jar or jolt; to brandish; to make or become unsteady; to weaken; to unsettle; to unnerve or become unnerved; to clasp (another's hand) as in greeting; (*with* **down**) to cause to subside by shaking; to obtain makeshift accommodation; (*sl*) to extort money from; (*with* **off**) to get rid of; (*with* **out**) to empty by shaking; to spread (a sail); (*with* **up**) to shake together, to mix; to upset. * *n* the act of shaking or being shaken; a jolt; a shock; a milkshake; (*inf*) a deal; (*pl inf*) a convulsive trembling.
shakedown *n* a makeshift or improvised bed; (*sl*) an extortion of money, as by blackmail; a thorough search.
shaker *n* a container for holding condiments; a container in which cocktail ingredients are mixed.
shakers *see* **movers and shakers.**
Shakespearean, Shakespearian *adj* of, pertaining to, or characteristic of William Shakespeare (1564–1616) or his works.
shako *n* (*pl* **shakos, shakoes**) a cylindrical military cap with a high crown and tall plume.
shake-up *n* an extensive reorganization.
shaky *adj* (**shakier, shakiest**) unsteady; infirm; unreliable.—**shakily** *adv*.—**shakiness** *n*.
shale *n* a kind of clay rock like slate but softer.
shall *vb aux* (*pt* **should**) used formally to express the future in the 1st person and determination, obligation or necessity in the 2nd and 3rd person; the more common form is **will.**
shallot *n* a small onion.
shallow *adj* having little depth; superficial, trivial. * *n* a shallow area in otherwise deep water.—**shallowness** *n*.
shalt (*arch*) *the 2nd person sing of* **shall.**
sham *n* a pretence; a person or thing that is a fraud. * *adj* counterfeit; fake.
shaman *n* a priest of shamanism believed to possess magical powers which allow him to communicate with and influence the spirit world.
shamanism *n* a religion of northern Asia which views the world as dominated by good and evil spirits that can be influenced only by the shamans.
shamateur *n* (*sport*) a player, athlete, etc who is officially classed as an amateur but who accepts payment.
shamble *vi* to walk with an ungainly stumbling gait.—*also n*.
shambles *npl* a scene of great disorder; a slaughterhouse.
shambolic *adj* (*inf*) disorganized; utterly confused.
shame *n* a painful emotion arising from guilt or impropriety; modesty; disgrace, dishonour; the cause of this; (*sl*) a piece of unfairness. * *vti* to cause to feel shame; to bring disgrace on; to force by shame (into); to humiliate by showing superior qualities.
shamefaced *adj* bashful or modest; sheepish; showing shame; ashamed.—**shamefacedly** *adv*.—**shamefacedness** *n*.

shameful *adj* disgraceful; outrageous.—**shamefully** *adv*.—**shamefulness** *n*.
shameless *adj* immodest; impudent, brazen.—**shamelessly** *adv*.—**shamelessness** *n*.
shammy (leather) *see* **chamois leather.**
shampoo *n* a liquid cleansing agent for washing the hair; the process of washing the hair or a carpet, etc. * *vt* to wash with shampoo.—**shampooer** *n*.
shamrock *n* a three-leaved cloverlike plant, the national emblem of Ireland.
shan't = shall not.
shandy *n* (*pl* **shandies**) beer diluted with a non-alcoholic drink (as lemonade).
shanghai *vt* (**shanghaiing, shanghaied**) to force (a sailor, etc) to join a ship's crew, esp by kidnapping or drugging; to trick or force (a person) into doing something.—**shanghaier** *n*.
Shangri-la *n* an imaginary utopia.
shank *n* the leg from the knee to the ankle, the shin; a shaft, stem, or handle.
shanks's pony, shanks's mare *n* one's own legs as used for walking.
shantung *n* a coarse kind of silk.
shanty[1] *n* (*pl* **shanties**) a crude hut built from corrugated iron or cardboard.
shanty[2] *n* (*pl* **shanties**) (*formerly*) a song sung by sailors in the rhythm of their work, a chantey.
shantytown *n* a community of poor people living in shanties.
SHAPE (*acronym*) Supreme Headquarters Allied Powers Europe.
shape *n* the external appearance, outline or contour of a thing; a figure; a definite form; an orderly arrangement; a mould or pattern; (*inf*) condition. * *vt* to give shape to; to form; to model, to mould; to determine; (*with* **up**) to develop to a definite or satisfactory form.
shapeless *adj* lacking definite form; baggy.—**shapelessly** *adv*.—**shapelessness** *n*.
shapely *adj* (**shapelier, shapeliest**) well-proportioned.—**shapeliness** *n*.
shard *n* a fragment or broken piece, esp of pottery.
share *n* an allotted portion, a part; one of the parts into which a company's capital stock is divided, entitling the holder to a share of profits. * *vti* to distribute, to apportion (out); to have or experience in common with others; to divide into portions; to contribute or receive a share of; to use jointly.
sharecropper *n* a tenant farmer who hands over a portion of the crop as rent.—**sharecrop** *vi*.
shareholder *n* a holder of shares in a property, esp a company.
share option *n* an option open to employees to buy shares in the company they work for.
shark *n* a large voracious marine fish; an extortioner, a swindler; (*sl*) an expert in a given activity.
sharkskin *n* a rayon fabric with a smooth shiny finish.
sharp *adj* having a keen edge or fine point; pointed, not rounded; clear-cut; distinct; intense, piercing; cutting, severe; keen, biting; clever, artful; alert, mentally acute; (*mus*) raised a semitone in pitch; out of tune by being too high; (*sl*) smartly dressed. * *adv* punctually; quickly; (*mus*) above the right pitch. * *n* (*mus*) a note that is a semitone higher than the note denoted by the same letter; the symbol for this (#).—**sharply** *adv*.—**sharpness** *n*.
sharpen *vti* to make or become sharp or sharper.
sharpener *n* something that sharpens.
sharpshooter *n* a marksman.
sharp-tongued *adj* sarcastic; quick to criticize.
sharp-witted *adj* thinking quickly and effectively.—**sharp-wittedly** *adv*.—**sharp-wittedness** *n*.
shatter *vti* to reduce to fragments suddenly; to smash; to damage or be damaged severely.
shatterproof *adj* resistant to shattering.
shave *vti* to remove facial or body hair with a razor; to cut away thin slices, to pare; to miss narrowly, to graze. * *n* the act or process of shaving; a narrow escape or miss; a paring.
shaven *adj* shaved.
shaver *n* one who shaves; an instrument for shaving, esp an electrical one.
Shavian *adj* of, relating to, or resembling the works of the writer George Bernard Shaw (1856–1950).
shaving *n* the act of using a razor or scraping; a thin slice of wood, metal, etc, shaved off.
shawl *n* a large square or oblong cloth worn as a covering for the head or shoulders or as a wrapping for a baby.
shawm *n* a medieval woodwind instrument resembling an oboe.
she *pron* (*obj* **her,** *poss* **her, hers**) the female person or thing named before or in question. * *n* a female person or animal.
shea *n* a tropical African tree with seeds that yield a butter-like fat used as food.
sheaf *n* (*pl* **sheaves**) a bundle of reaped corn bound together; a collection of papers, etc, tied in a bundle.
shear *vti* (**shearing, sheared** *or* **shorn**) to clip or cut (through); to remove (a sheep's fleece) by clipping; to divest; (*metal*) to break off because of a heavy force or twist. * *n* a stress acting sideways on a rivet and causing a break, etc; a machine for cutting metal; (*pl*) large scissors; (*pl*) a tool for cutting hedges, etc.
shearling *n* (the fleece of) a sheep after its first shearing.
shearwater *n* any of various seabirds that often glide close to the water.
sheath *n* (*pl* **sheaths**) a close-fitting cover, esp for a blade; a condom; a closefitting dress usu worn without a belt.
sheathe *vt* to put into a sheath; to encase, to protect with a casing; (*cat*) to withdraw its claws.
sheath-knife *n* a knife with a fixed blade covered by a sheath.
sheave[1] *vt* to gather into sheaves.
sheave[2] *n* a grooved wheel, esp in a pulley.
sheaves *see* **sheaf.**
shebang *n* (*inf*) affair, business.
shebeen *n* an unlicensed or illegal drinking den.
she'd = she had; she would.
shed[1] *n* a hut for storing garden tools; a large roofed shelter often with one or more sides open; a warehouse.
shed[2] *vt* (**shedding, shed**) (*tears*) to let fall; (*skin, etc*) to lose or cast off; to allow or cause to flow; to diffuse, radiate. * *n* a parting in the hair.
sheen *n* a gloss, lustre; brightness.
sheep *n* (*pl* **sheep**) a cud-chewing four-footed animal with a fleece and edible flesh called mutton; a bashful, submissive person.
sheepcote *n* a sheepfold.
sheep-dip *n* a liquid disinfectant or insecticide into which sheep are plunged to destroy parasites.
sheepdog *n* a dog trained to tend, drive, or guard sheep.
sheepfold *n* an enclosure for sheep.
sheepish *adj* bashful, embarrassed.—**sheepishly** *adv*.—**sheepishness** *n*.
sheep's eyes *npl* (*arch*) amorous glances.
sheepshank *n* a knot in a rope to shorten it temporarily.
sheepskin *n* the skin of a sheep, esp with the fleece; a rug, parchment, or leather made from it; a garment made of or lined with sheepskin.
sheepwalk *n* an area of pasture for sheep.
sheer[1] *adj* pure, unmixed; downright, utter; perpendicular, extremely steep; (*fabric*) delicately fine, transparent. * *adv* outright; perpendicularly, steeply.
sheer[2] *vti* to deviate or cause to deviate from a course; to swerve. * *n* the act of sheering; the upward curve of a deck toward bow or stern; a change in a ship's course.
sheerlegs *n sing* a hoisting device comprising two or more upright poles crossed at the top from which lifting gear is suspended.
sheet[1] *n* a broad thin piece of any material, as glass, plywood, metal, etc; a large rectangular piece of cloth used as inner bed clothes; a single piece of paper; (*inf*) a newspaper; a broad, flat expanse; a suspended or moving expanse (as of fire or rain).
sheet[2] *n* a rope that controls the angle of a sail in relation to the wind.

sheet anchor *n* a large anchor used only in emergencies; a support in extremity.
sheet bend *n* a knot for joining ropes of different thicknesses.
sheet glass *n* glass made in large sheets directly from the furnace or by making a cylinder and then flattening it.
sheeting *n* fabric for sheets.
sheet lightning *n* lightning that has the appearance of a broad sheet due to reflection and diffusion by the clouds and sky.
sheet metal *n* metal rolled out in the form of a thin sheet.
sheet music *n* music printed on unbound sheets of paper.
sheikh *n* an Arab chief.
sheila *n* (*Austral, NZ sl*) a girl or woman.
shekel *n* the unit of money in Israel; an old Jewish weight or silver coin; (*pl*) (*sl*) money.
shelduck, sheldrake *n* any of several Old World brightly plumaged ducks.
shelf *n* (*pl* **shelves**) a board fixed horizontally on a wall or in a cupboard for holding articles; a ledge on a cliff face; a reef, a shoal.
shelf life *n* the length of time for which something may be stored without deterioration.
shell *n* a hard outside covering of a nut, egg, shellfish, etc; an explosive projectile; an external framework; a light racing boat; outward show; a cartridge. * *vt* to remove the shell from; to bombard (with shells); (*with* **out**) (*inf*) to pay out (money).
she'll = she will; she shall.
shellac, shellack *n* a resin usu produced in thin, flaky layers or shells; a thin varnish containing this and alcohol.
shellfish *n* an aquatic animal, esp an edible one, with a shell.
shellproof *adj* impervious to artillery shells, rockets and bombs.
shell shock *n* a nervous disorder caused by the shock of being under fire.—**shell-shocked** *adj*.
shelter *n* a structure that protects, esp against weather; a place giving protection, a refuge; protection. * *vti* to give shelter to, to shield, to cover; to take shelter.
sheltie, shelty *n* (*pl* **shelties**) a Shetland pony or Shetland sheepdog.
shelve *vti* to place on a shelf; to defer consideration, to put aside; to slope gently, to incline.
shelves *see* **shelf**.
shelving *n* material for making shelves; shelves collectively.
shemozzle *n* (*inf*) a scene of confusion; a brawl.
shenanigan *n* (*often pl*) trickery, deception; mischief, boisterous high spirits.
shepherd *n* a person who looks after sheep; a pastor. * *vt* to look after, as a shepherd; to manoeuvre or marshal in a particular direction.—**shepherdess** *nf*.
shepherd dog *n* a sheepdog.
shepherd's pie *n* a dish of minced meat covered with a mashed potato crust.
shepherd's purse *n* an annual plant with small white flowers and heart-shaped seed pods.
sherbet *n* a fruit-flavoured powder that can be used to make a slightly sparkling drink; a sorbet.
sheriff *n* in US, the chief law enforcement officer of a county; in Scotland, a judge in an intermediate law court; in England and Wales, the chief officer of the Crown, a ceremonial post.
sheriff court *n* (*Scot*) the court dealing with the majority of criminal and civil cases.
Sherpa *n* (*pl* **Sherpas, Sherpa**) a member of a people living on the southern slopes of the Himalayas on the borders of Nepal and Tibet.
sherry *n* (*pl* **sherries**) a fortified wine originally made in Spain.
she's = she is; she has.
Shetland pony *n* a breed of small sturdy pony with a shaggy mane.
Shetland sheepdog *n* a breed of dog resembling a collie but smaller.
SHF, shf *abbr* = superhigh frequency.
Shiah, Shia *n* a member of the main branch of Islam who acknowledge Muhammad's cousin Ali and his successors as the true imams.—*also adj*.
shibboleth *n* a slogan or catchword, esp that regarded as outmoded or identified with a particular group or culture; a custom or linguistic usage which identifies members of a particular group, party, class, etc.
shied *see* **shy**[1], **shy**[2].
shield *n* a broad piece of armour carried for defence, usu on the left arm; a protective covering or guard; a thing or person that protects; a trophy in the shape of a shield. * *vti* to defend; to protect; to screen.
shier, shiest *see* **shy**[1].
shift *vti* to change position (of); to contrive, to manage; to remove, to transfer; to replace by another or others; (*gears*) to change the arrangement of. * *n* a change in position; an expedient; a group of people working in relay with others; the time worked by them; a change or transfer; a straight dress.
shiftless *adj* incapable; feckless.—**shiftlessly** *adv*.—**shiftlessness** *n*.
shifty *adj* (**shiftier, shiftiest**) artful, tricky; evasive.—**shiftily** *adv*.—**shiftiness** *n*.
shigella *n* any of a genus of rod-shaped bacteria causing dysentery in humans and animals.
Shiite, Shiah *n* a follower of Shiah.—*also adj*.
shillelagh *n* an Irish club or cudgel.
shilling *n* a former unit of currency of the UK and other countries, worth one twentieth of a pound.
shillyshally *vi* (**shillyshallying, shillyshallied**) to vacillate, to hesitate. * *n* (*pl* **shillyshallies**) the inability to make up one's mind.
shim *n* a thin washer or spacer used to tighten or space out joints, etc. * *vt* (**shimming, shimmed**) to space out, etc using shims.
shimmer *vi* to glisten softly, to glimmer.—*also n*.—**shimmery** *adj*.
shimmy *n* (*pl* **shimmies**) a jazz dance involving rapid movements of the upper body; an abnormal vibration in a vehicle or aircraft. * *vi* (**shimmying, shimmied**) to dance a shimmy; to vibrate.
shin *n* the front part of the leg from the knee to the ankle; the shank. * *vi* (*with* **up**) to climb (a pole, etc) by gripping with legs and hands.
shinbone *n* the tibia.
shindig *n* (*inf*) a lively, noisy celebration; an uproar.
shine *vti* (**shining, shone**) to emit light; to be bright, to glow; to be brilliant or conspicuous; to direct the light of; to cause to gleam by polishing; * *n* a lustre, a gloss; (*sl*) a liking.
shiner *n* (*inf*) a black eye.
shingle[1] *n* a thin wedge-shaped roof tile; a small signboard.
shingle[2] *n* waterworn pebbles as on a beach; an area covered with these.—**shingly** *adj*.
shingles *npl* a virus disease marked by a painful rash of red spots on the skin.
Shinto *n* the indigenous religion of Japan, involving veneration of the emperor, and the worship of ancestors and various natural deities.—**Shintoism** *n*.—**Shintoist** *n*.
shinty *n* a game similar to hockey and hurling, played with a ball and curved sticks.
shiny *adj* (**shinier, shiniest**) glossy, polished; worn smooth.
ship *n* a large vessel navigating deep water; its officers and crew; a spacecraft. * *vti* (**shipping, shipped**) to transport by any carrier; to take in (water) over the side; to lay (oars) inside a boat; to go on board; to go or travel by ship.
shipboard *n* the side of a ship.
shipbuilder *n* a person or company that designs or constructs ships.—**shipbuilding** *n*.
ship chandler *n* an individual or business that provides essential supplies for ships.
shipload *n* as much as a ship can carry.
shipmaster *n* the captain or master of a ship.
shipmate *n* a fellow sailor.
shipment *n* goods shipped; a consignment.
ship of the line *n* (*formerly*) a warship large enough to fight in the first line of battle.
shipowner *n* a person who owns (or has shares in) a ship.

shipper *n* an individual or company that ships goods.
shipping *n* the business of transporting goods; ships collectively.
ship's biscuit *n* a type of hard biscuit that was formerly part of a sailor's diet.
shipshape *adj* in good order, tidy.
shipworm *n* any of a genus of worm-like molluscs that burrow in submerged wood.
shipwreck *n* the loss of a vessel at sea; the remains of a wrecked ship; ruin, destruction. * *vti* to destroy by or suffer shipwreck; to ruin.
shipwright *n* a person skilled in constructing and repairing ships.
shipyard *n* a yard or shed where ships are built or repaired.
shire *n* in the UK, a county; a large powerful breed of draught horse.
shirk *vti* to neglect or avoid work; to refuse to face (duty, danger, etc).—**shirker** *n*.
shirr *vt* to gather (fabric) with parallel threads run through it; to bake (eggs) in buttered dishes.
shirring *n* a gathering made in cloth by drawing the material up on parallel rows of short stitches.
shirt *n* a sleeved garment of cotton, etc, for the upper body, typically having a fitted collar and cuffs and front buttons; (*inf*) one's money or resources.
shirtdress *n* a long shirt worn as a dress.
shirting *n* a fabric suitable for men's shirts.
shirtsleeve *n* the sleeve of a shirt.
shirt-tail *n* the flap of material at the back of a shirt below the waist.
shirtwaister, shirtwaist *n* a woman's dress tailored in front in style similar to a shirt.
shirty *adj* (**shirtier, shirtiest**) (*sl*) irritable, rude.
shish kebab *n* a kebab.
shit[1], **shite** *n* (*vulg*) waste matter from humans or animals; excrement; heroin. * *vti* to defecate (on). * *interj* (*sl*) an expression of strong disgust or disapproval.
shit[2] *n* (*sl*) something that is good.
shivaree *see* **charivari.**
shiver[1] *n* a small fragment, a splinter.
shiver[2] *vi* to shake or tremble, as with cold or fear, to shudder.—*also n*.—**shivery** *adj*.
shoal[1] *n* a large number of fish swimming together; a large crowd. * *vi* to form shoals.
shoal[2] *n* a submerged sandbank, esp one that shows at low tide; a shallow place; a hidden danger. * *vti* to come to a less deep part; to become shallower.
shock[1] *n* a shaggy mass of hair.
shock[2] *n* a violent jolt or impact; a sudden disturbance to the emotions; the event or experience causing this; the nerve sensation caused by an electrical charge through the body; a disorder of the blood circulation, produced by displacement of body fluids (due to injury); (*sl*) a paralytic stroke. * *vt* to outrage, horrify. * *vi* to experience extreme horror, outrage, etc.
shock absorber *n* a device, as on the springs of a car, that absorbs the force of bumps and jars.
shocker *n* a sensational novel, play, etc; anything that shocks; (*sl*) a very bad specimen.
shocking *adj* revolting; scandalous, improper; very bad.—**shockingly** *adv*.
shockproof *adj* capable of withstanding shock without damage.
shock therapy, shock treatment *n* the treatment of certain mental illnesses by inducing convulsions using drugs or by passing electricity through the brain.
shock troops *npl* a highly disciplined force trained to lead an attack.
shock wave *n* the violent effect in the vicinity of an explosion caused by the change in atmospheric pressure; the compressed wave built up when the speed of a body or fluid exceeds that at which sound can be transmitted in the medium in which it is travelling.
shod, shodden *see* **shoe.**
shoddy *adj* (**shoddier, shoddiest**) made of inferior material; cheap and nasty, trashy.—**shoddily** *adv*.—**shoddiness** *n*.
shoe *n* an outer covering for the foot not enclosing the ankle; a thing like a shoe, a partial casing; a horseshoe; a drag for a wheel; a device to guide movement, provide contact, or protect against wear or slipping; a dealing box that holds several decks of cards. * *vt* (**shoeing, shod** *or* **shoed**, *pp* **shod, shoed** *or* **shodden**) to provide with shoes; to cover for strength or protection.
shoehorn *n* a curved piece of plastic, metal, or horn used for easing the heel into a shoe.
shoelace *n* a cord that passes through eyelets in a shoe and is tied to keep the shoe on the foot.
shoemaker *n* a person who makes or mends shoes.
shoestring *n* a shoelace; (*inf*) a small amount of money.
shoetree *n* a block of wood, plastic or metal for preserving the shape of a shoe.
shogun *n* the hereditary commander of the army in feudal Japan.
shone *see* **shine.**
shoo *interj* used to frighten (animals, people) away. * *vt* (**shooing, shooed**) to frighten away (as if) by shouting "shoo". * *vi* to cry "shoo".
shoo-in *n* (*inf*) a person or thing certain to win or succeed.
shook *see* **shake.**
shoot *vb* (**shooting, shot**) *vt* to discharge or fire (a gun etc); to hit or kill with a bullet, etc; (*rapids*) to be carried swiftly over; to propel quickly; to thrust out; (*bolt*) to slide home; to variegate (with another colour, etc); (*a film scene*) to photograph; (*sport*) to kick or drive (a ball, etc) at goal; (*with* **down**) to disprove (an argument); (*with* **up**) to grow rapidly, to rise abruptly. * *vi* to move swiftly, to dart; to emit; to put forth buds, to sprout; to attack or kill indiscriminately; (*sl*) to inject a narcotic into a vein. * *n* a contest, a shooting trip, etc; a new growth or sprout.
shooting *n* the act of firing a gun or letting off an arrow.
shooting star *n* a meteor.
shooting stick *n* a spiked stick with a handle that folds out into a small seat.
shop *n* a building were retail goods are sold or services provided; a factory; a workshop; the details and technicalities of one's own work, and talk about these. * *vti* (**shopping, shopped**) to visit shops to examine or buy; (*sl*) to inform on (a person) to the police; (*with* **around**) to hunt for the best buy.
shop assistant *n* a person who serves customers in a retail shop.
shop floor *n* the part of a factory where goods are manufactured; the work force employed there, usu unionized.
shopkeeper *n* a person who owns or runs a shop.—**shopkeeping** *n*.
shoplifter *n* a person who steals goods from shops.
shoplifting *n* stealing from a shop during shopping hours.—**shoplifter** *n*.
shopper *n* a person who shops; a bag for carrying shopping.
shopping *n* the act of shopping; the goods bought.—*also adj*.
shopping centre *n* a complex of shops, restaurants, and service establishments with a common parking area.—*also* **shopping plaza.**
shopping mall *n* a large enclosed shopping centre.
shopsoiled *adj* shopworn.
shoptalk *n* the specialized vocabulary of those in the same line of work or sharing an area of interest; talk about work after hours.
shopwalker *n* a person employed in large shop who oversees shop assistants, helps customers, etc.
shopworn *adj* faded, etc, from being on display in a shop.
shore[1] *n* land beside the sea or a large body of water; beach.
shore[2] *n* a prop or beam used for support. * *vt* to prop (up), to support with a shore.
shoreline *n* the edge of an expanse of water.
shorn *see* **shear.**
short *adj* not measuring much; not long or tall; not great in range or scope; brief; concise; not retentive; curt; abrupt; less than the correct amount; below standard; deficient, lacking; (*pastry*) crisp or flaky; (*vowel*) not prolonged, unstressed; (*drink*) undiluted, neat. * *n* something short; (*pl*) trousers not covering the knee; (*pl*) an undergarment like

these; a short circuit. * *adv* abruptly; concisely; without reaching the end. * *vti* to give less than what is needed; to short-change; to short-circuit.—**shortness** *n*.

shortage *n* a deficiency.

shortbread *n* a rich, crumbly cake or biscuit made with much shortening.

short-change *vt* to give back less than the correct change; (*sl*) to cheat.

short-circuit *n* the deviation of an electric current by a path of small resistance; an interrupted electric current. * *vti* to establish a short-circuit in; to cut off electric current; to provide with a short cut.

shortcoming *n* a defect or inadequacy.

shortcrust pastry *n* a firm but crumbly pastry made with half as much fat as flour.

short cut *n* a shorter route; any way of saving time, effort, etc.

shorten *vt* to make or become short or shorter; to reduce the amount of (sail) spread; to make (pastry, etc) crisp and flaky by adding fat.

shortening *n* the act of shortening; the state of becoming shortened; a fat used for making pastry, etc, crisp and flaky.

shortfall *n* (the amount or degree of) a deficit or deficiency.

shorthand *n* a method of rapid writing using signs or contractions.—*also adj*.

short-handed *adj* not having the usual number of assistants.

shorthand typist *n* a person who produces typewritten documents from shorthand notes.—*also* **stenographer**.

short head *n* (*horse racing*) a distance less than a horse's head.

shorthorn *n* one of a breed of large heavy cattle with short curved horns.

short list *n* a selected list of qualified applicants from which a choice must be made.

short-list *vt* to place (a person) on a short list.

short-lived *adj* not lasting or living for long.

shortly *adv* soon, in a short time; briefly; rudely.

short-range *adj* having a limited range in time or distance.

short shrift *n* curt, dismissive treatment.

short-sighted *adj* not able to see well at a distance; lacking foresight.—**short-sightedly** *adv*.—**short-sightedness** *n*.

short-tempered *adj* easily annoyed.

short-term *adj* of or for a limited time.

short time *n* a reduction in working hours due to recession, etc.

short-winded *adj* easily becoming breathless; (*speech, writing*) brief, to the point

shortwave *n* a radio wave 60 metres or less in length.

shot[1] *see* **shoot**.

shot[2] *n* the act of shooting; range, scope; an attempt; a solid projectile for a gun; projectiles collectively; small lead pellets for a shotgun; a marksman; a photograph or a continuous film sequence; a hypodermic injection, as of vaccine; a drink of alcohol.

shotgun *n* a smooth-bore gun for firing small shot at close range.

shotgun wedding *n* (*inf*) an enforced wedding, usu because the woman is pregnant.

shot put *n* a field event in which a heavy metal ball is proepelled with an overhand thrust from the shoulder.—**shot-putter** *n*.

shotten *adj* (*fish*) having spawned recently.

should *vb aux* used to express obligation, duty, expectation or probability, or a future condition.—*also pt of* **shall**.

shoulder *n* the joint connecting the arm with the trunk; a part like a shoulder; (*pl*) the upper part of the back; (*pl*) the capacity to bear a task or blame; a projecting part; the strip of land bordering a road. * *vti* to place on the shoulder to carry; to assume responsibility; to push with the shoulder, to jostle.

shoulder blade *n* the large flat triangular bone on either side of the back part of the human shoulder.

shoulder strap *n* a strap over the shoulders to hold up a garment, bag, etc.

shouldn't = should not.

shout *n* a loud call; a yell. * *vti* to call loudly, to yell; (*with* **down**) to drown out or silence (a person speaking) by shouting.

shove *vti* to drive forward; to push; to jostle; (*with* **off**) to push (a boat) off from the shore; (*inf*) to depart, leave. * *n* a forceful push.

shove-halfpenny *n* a game in which coins or discs are slid across a board marked with a scoring grid.

shovel *n* a broad tool like a scoop with a long handle for moving loose material. * *vt* (**shovelling, shovelled** *or* **shoveling, shoveled**) to move or lift with a shovel.

shoveller, shoveler *n* any of several pond and marsh ducks with a broad beak.

shovelhead *n* a breed of shark with a shovel-shaped head.

show *vti* (**showing, showed** *or* **shown**) to present to view, to exhibit; to demonstrate, to make clear; to prove; to manifest, to disclose; to direct, to guide; to appear, to be visible; to finish third in a horse race; (*inf*) to arrive; (*with* **off**) to display to advantage; to try to attract admiration; to behave pretentiously; (*with* **up**) to put in an appearance, to arrive; to expose to ridicule. * *n* a display, an exhibition; an entertainment; a theatrical performance; a radio or television programme; third place at the finish (as a horse race).

show business, show biz *n* the entertainment industry.

showcase *n* a glass case or cabinet for displaying items in a shop or museum; a setting or situation designed to exhibit something to best advantage.—*also vt*.

showdown *n* (*inf*) a final conflict; a disclosure of cards at poker.

shower *n* a brief period of rain, hail, or snow; a similar fall, as of tears, meteors, arrows, etc; a great number; a method of cleansing in which the body is sprayed with water from above; a wash in this; a party for the presentation of gifts, esp to a bride. * *vt* to pour copiously; to sprinkle; to bestow (with gifts). * *vi* to cleanse in a shower.

showgirl *n* a girl who appears in a chorus line, variety act, etc.

show house *n* a house on a new housing estate used as a sample for prospective buyers.

showjumping *n* the competitive riding of horses to demonstrate their skill in jumping.

showman *n* (*pl* **showmen**) a man who manages or presents a theatrical show, circus, etc; a person skilled in presentation.

shown *see* **show**.

showpiece *n* an exhibit; a perfect example of something.

showplace *n* a place (eg tourist attraction, historic site) regarded as of exemplary interest or beauty.

showroom *n* a room where goods for sale are displayed.

showy *adj* (**showier, showiest**) bright, colourful; ostentatious.—**showily** *adv*.—**showiness** *n*.

shrank *see* **shrink**.

shrapnel *n* an artillery shell filled with small pieces of metal that scatter on impact.

shred *n* a strip cut or torn off; a fragment, a scrap. * *vt* (**shredding, shredded**) to cut or tear into small pieces.

shrew *n* a small, brown, nocturnal mouse-like animal with a long snout; a bad-tempered, nagging woman.

shrewd *adj* astute, having common sense; keen, penetrating.—**shrewdly** *adv*.—**shrewdness** *n*.

shrewish *adj* sharp-tongued, nagging.

shriek *n* a loud, shrill cry, a scream. * *vti* to screech, to scream.

shrieval *adj* of or pertaining to a sheriff.

shrievalty *n* (*pl* **shrievalties**) the office, term of office or jurisdiction of a sheriff.

shrike *n* a bird with a hooked beak that impales its prey, mainly insects and small animals, on thorns.

shrill *adj* high-pitched and piercing in sound; strident.

shrimp *n* a small edible shellfish with a long tail; (*sl*) a small or unimportant person. * *vt* to fish for shrimp.

shrine *n* a container for sacred relics; a saint's tomb; a place of worship; a hallowed place.

shrink *vti* (**shrinking, shrank** *or* **shrunk**, *pp* **shrunk** *or* **shrunken**) to become smaller, to contract as from cold, wetting, etc; to recoil (from), to flinch; to cause (cloth, etc) to contract by soaking. * *n* (*sl*) a psychiatrist.—**shrinkable** *adj*.

shrinkage *n* contraction; diminution.
shrinking violet *n* a very shy or unassuming person.
shrink-wrap *vt* (**shrink-wrapping, shrink-wrapped**) (*book etc*) to wrap in plastic film that is then shrunk by heat to form a tightly fitting package.
shrive *vb* (**shriving, shrived** *or* **shrove,** *pp* **shriven** *or* **shrived**) *vt* (*arch*) to hear the confession of; to impose penance on and absolve. * *vi* to confess, do penance and receive absolution.
shrivel *vti* (**shrivelling, shrivelled** *or* **shriveling, shriveled**) to dry up or wither and become wrinkled; to curl up with heat, etc.
shroud *n* a burial cloth; anything that envelops or conceals; (*naut*) a supporting rope for a mast. * *vt* to wrap in a shroud; to envelop or conceal.
shrove *see* **shrive.**
Shrovetide *n* the three days before Ash Wednesday.
Shrove Tuesday *n* the last day before Lent.
shrub *n* a woody plant smaller than a tree with several stems rising from the same root; a bush.—**shrubby** *adj.*
shrubbery *n* (*pl* **shrubberies**) an area of land planted with shrubs.
shrug *vti* (**shrugging, shrugged**) to draw up and contract (the shoulders) as a sign of doubt, indifference, etc; (*with* **off**) to brush aside; to shake off; (*a garment*) to remove by wriggling out. * *n* the act of shrugging.
shrunk *see* **shrink.**
shrunken *adj* shrivelled, pinched; reduced.
shtoom *n* (*sl*) silent, dumb.
shuck *n* a husk, pod or shell. * *vt* to remove the shucks from.
shucks *interj* used to express disappointment, irritation, etc.
shudder *vi* to tremble violently, to shiver; to feel strong repugnance. * *n* a convulsive shiver of the body; a vibration.
shuffle *vt* to scrape (the feet) along the ground; to walk with dragging steps; (*playing cards*) to change the order of, to mix; to intermingle, to mix up; (*with* **off**) to get rid of.—*also n.*
shuffleboard *n* a game in which players propel plastic or wooden discs into numbered scoring areas marked on a large flat surface.
shufty, shufti *n* (*pl* **shufties**) (*sl*) a peek, a glance.
shun *vt* (**shunning, shunned**) to avoid scrupulously; to keep away from.
shunt *vti* to move to a different place; to put aside, to shelve; (*trains*) to switch from one track to another; (*sl*) to collide.—*also n.*
shush *interj* used to demand silence; peace, silence. * *vt* to demand silence (as if) by saying "shush".
shut *vti* (**shutting, shut**) to close; to lock, to fasten; to close up parts of, to fold together; to bar; (*with* **down**) to (cause to) stop working or operating; (*with* **in**) to confine; to enclose; to block the view from; (*with* **off**) to check the flow of; to debar; (*with* **out**) to exclude; (*with* **up**) to confine; (*inf*) to stop talking; (*inf*) to silence.
shutdown *n* a stoppage of work or activity, as in a factory.
shuteye *n* (*inf*) sleep.
shutter *n* a movable cover for a window; a flap device for regulating the exposure of light to a camera lens.
shuttle *n* a device in a loom for holding the weft thread and carrying it between the warp threads; a bus, aircraft, etc, making back-and-forth trips over a short route. * *vti* to move back and forth rapidly.
shuttlecock[1] *n* a cork stuck with feathers, or a plastic imitation, hit with a racket in badminton.
shuttlecock[2] *see* **battledore.**
shy[1] *adj* (**shyer, shyest** *or* **shier, shiest**) very self-conscious, timid; bashful; wary, suspicious (of); (*sl*) lacking. * *vi* (**shying, shied**) to move suddenly, as when startled; to be or become cautious, etc. * *n* (*pl* **shies**) a sudden movement.—**shyly** *adv.*—**shyness** *n.*
shy[2] *vt* (**shying, shied**) to throw (something). * *n* (*pl* **shies**) a throw; (*inf*) an attempt, try.
shyster *n* (*inf*) a person, esp a lawyer, who is manipulative and disreputable.
SI *n* (Système International d'Unités) the universally used system of units based on the metre, second, kilogram, ampere, kelvin, candela, siemens, tesla, weber and mole.
Si (*chem symbol*) silicon.
si *n* (*mus*) ti.
sial *n* the outer layer of the earth's crust composed mostly of rock rich in silicon and aluminium.
Siamese cat *n* a breed of domestic shorthaired cat with a fawn or grey coat, darker ears, paws, tail and face, and blue eyes.
Siamese fighting fish *n* an aggressive brightly coloured freshwater fish.
Siamese twins *npl* twin babies born with the bodies joined together at some point, esp the hip.
sib *n* a sibling.
sibilant *adj* hissing. * *n* a sibilant letter, eg *s, z.*—**sibilance** *n.*
sibling *n* a brother or sister.
sibyl *n* in ancient Greece and Rome, a female prophet or oracle.
sic *adv* as written (used in text to indicate that an error or doubtful usage is reproduced from the original).
sick *adj* unhealthy, ill; having nausea, vomiting; thoroughly tired (of); disgusted by or suffering from an excess; (*inf*) of humour, sadistic, gruesome.—**sickness** *n.*
sick bay *n* an area in a ship used as a hospital or dispensary; a room used for the treatment of the sick.
sickbed *n* the bed where one lies sick.
sick building syndrome *n* a collection of symptoms, thought to be caused by micro-organisms found in humidifiers and including lethargy, headache and eye irritation, that affect those who work in totally air-conditioned buildings.—*also* **humidifier fever.**
sicken *vti* to make or become sick or nauseated; to show signs of illness; to nauseate.
sickening *adj* disgusting.—**sickeningly** *adv.*
sickle *n* a tool with a crescent-shaped blade for cutting tall grasses; anything shaped like this.
sick leave *n* absence from work due to illness.
sickle cell anaemia *n* a form of anaemia that is hereditary and marked by the presence of sickle-shaped red blood cells.
sick list *n* a list of employees, soldiers, etc who are absent due to illness.
sickly *adj* (**sicklier, sickliest**) inclined to be ill; unhealthy; causing nausea; mawkish; pale, feeble.—**sickliness** *n.*
sick-making *adj* (*inf*) nauseating, galling.
sick pay *n* wages or salaries paid to an employee while he or she is off sick.
sickroom *n* the room to which a patient is confined while sick.
side *n* a line or surface bounding anything; the left or right part of the body; the top or underneath surface; the slope of a hill; an aspect, a direction; a party or faction; a cause; a team; a line of descent; (*sl*) conceit. * *adj* toward or at the side, lateral; incidental. * *vi* to associate with a particular faction.
side arms *n* weapons (eg a pistol, dagger) worn in a belt or holster at the side of the waist.
sideboard *n* a long table or cabinet for holding cutlery, crockery, etc; (*pl*) two strips of hair growing down a man's cheeks.—*also* **sideburns.**
sidecar *n* a small car attached to the side of a motor cycle; a cocktail of brandy, liqueur, and lemon juice.
sided *adj* having sides of a specified number or kind.
side dish *n* food accompanying a main course at a meal.
side drum *n* a small double-headed drum with snares, carried and played at the side.
side effect *n* a secondary and usu adverse effect, as of a drug or medical treatment.
side-glance *n* a look directed to one side; a slight reference.
sidekick *n* (*sl*) a confederate; a partner; a close friend.
sidelight *n* light coming from the side; a light on the side of a car, etc; incidental information.
sideline *n* a line marking the side limit of a playing area; a minor branch of business; a subsidiary interest.
sidelong *adj* oblique, not direct. * *adv* obliquely.
sidereal *adj* of or by reference to stars and constellations.
siderite *n* a mineral composed mainly of ferrous carbonate used as a source of iron.

sidero-, sider- *prefix* iron.
siderosis *n* a lung disease caused by inhalation of iron or other types of metallic particles.
side-saddle *n* a saddle that enables a rider to sit with both feet on the same side of a horse. * *adv* as if sitting on a side-saddle.
sideshow *n* a minor attraction at a fair, etc; a subsidiary event.
sidesman *n* (*pl* **sidesmen**) (*Anglican Church*) an officer assisting the churchwardens.
side-splitting *adj* uproariously funny.
sidestep *vti* to take a step to one side; to avoid or dodge.—*also n.*
sidestroke *n* (*swimming*) a stroke used while swimming on one's side.
sideswipe *n* a glancing blow; (*inf*) an incidental jibe or criticism.
sidetrack *vt* to prevent action by diversionary tactics; to shunt aside, to shelve. * *n* a railroad siding.
sidewalk *n* a path, usu paved, at the side of a street.
sidewall *n* either of the sides of a pneumatic tyre.
sideward, sidewards *adj, adv* sideways.
sideways, sideway *adj, adv* toward or from one side; facing to the side.
side whiskers *n* sideboards or sideburns.
sidewinder *n* a North American rattlesnake that moves in a twisting sideways motion.
sidewise *adv* sideways.
siding *n* a short line beside a main railway track for use in shunting; a covering as of boards for the outside of a frame building.
sidle *vi* to move sideways, esp to edge along.
SIDS *abbr* = sudden infant death syndrome.
siege *n* the surrounding of a fortified place to cut off supplies and compel its surrender; the act of besieging; a continued attempt to gain something.
siemens *n* (*pl* **siemens**) the SI unit of electrical conductance.
sienna *n* an earthy pigment, either yellowish brown (raw sienna) or reddish brown (burnt sienna).
sierra *n* a range of mountains with jagged peaks.
siesta *n* a midday nap, esp in hot countries.
sieve *n* a utensil with a meshed wire bottom for sifting and straining; a person who cannot keep secrets. * *vt* to put through a sieve, to sift.
sift *vti* to separate coarser parts from finer with a sieve; to sort out; to examine critically; to pass as through a sieve.
sigh *vti* to draw deep audible breath as a sign of weariness, relief, etc; to make a sound like this; to pine or lament (for); to utter with a sigh.—*also n.*
sight *n* the act or faculty of seeing; what is seen or is worth seeing, a spectacle; a view or glimpse; range of vision; a device on a gun etc to guide the eye in aiming it; aim taken with this; (*inf*) anything that looks unpleasant, odd, etc. * *vti* to catch sight of; to aim through a sight.
sighted *adj* having sight, esp of a particular character, eg shortsighted.
sightless *adj* without sight, blind.—**sightlessly** *adv.*—**sightlessness** *n.*
sightly *adj* (**sightlier, sightliest**) pleasing to the eye; comely.—**sightliness** *n.*
sight-read *vt* (**sight-reading, sight-read**) to play or sing from a piece of printed music without previous preparation. * *vi* to read at sight.
sightseeing *n* the viewing or visiting of places of interest.—**sightseer** *n.*
sigma *n* the 18th letter of the Greek alphabet; (*math*) the symbol S indicating summation.
sigmoid, sigmoidal *adj* curved like the letter S.
sign *n* a mark or symbol; a gesture; an indication, token, trace, or symptom (of); an omen; (*math*) a conventional mark used to indicate an operation to be performed; a board or placard with publicly displayed information. * *vi* to append one's signature; to ratify thus. * *vt* to engage by written contract; to write one's name on; to make or indicate by a sign; to signal; to communicate by sign language; (*with* **away**) to relinquish by signing a deed, etc; (*with* **on**) to accept employment; to register; (*with* **off**) to complete a broadcast.
signal *n* a sign, device or gesture to intimate a warning or to give information, esp at a distance; a message so conveyed; a semaphore system used by railways; in radio, etc, the electrical impulses transmitted or received; a sign or event that initiates action. * *vti* (**signalling, signalled** *or* **signaling, signaled**) to make a signal or signals (to); to communicate by signals. * *adj* striking, notable.—**signaller, signaler** *n.*
signalize *vt* to point out; distinguish.—**signalization** *n.*
signally *adv* remarkably; notably.
signalman *n* (*pl* **signalmen**) a person who works signals or transmits signals.
signatory *n* (*pl* **signatories**) a party or state that has signed an agreement or treaty; the person who signs on behalf of their government.
signature *n* a person's name written by himself or herself; the act of signing one's own name; a characteristic mark; (*mus*) the flats and sharps after the clef showing the key; (*print*) a mark on the first pages of each sheet of a book as a guide to the binder; such a sheet when folded.
signature tune *n* a tune associated with a performer or a TV, radio programme, etc.
signboard *n* a board with a sign or inscription in front of a business, shop, etc.
signet *n* a small seal, esp one set in a ring; an official seal used in lieu of a signature in authenticating documents; the impression made by this.
signet ring *n* a ring with a seal set in it.
significant *adj* full of meaning, esp a special or hidden one; momentous, important; highly expressive; indicative (of).—**significance** *n.*—**significantly** *adv.*
signify *vti* (**signifying, signified**) to mean; to be a sign of; to indicate; to represent; to matter, to be important; to make a sign.—**signification** *n.*
sign language *n* a system of manual signs and gestures for conveying meaning, used esp by the deaf.
signor, signior *n* (*pl* **signors, signori**) an Italian man—equivalent to Mr.
signora *n* (*pl* **signoras, signore**) a married Italian woman—equivalent to Mrs or madam.
signore *n* (*pl* **signori**) an Italian man—equivalent to sir.
signorina *n* (*pl* **signorinas, signorine**) an unmarried Italian woman—equivalent to Miss.
signpost *n* a post with signs on it to direct travellers; a beacon, a guide.—*also vt.*
Sikh *n* a member of an Indian sect, founded in the 16th century, that teaches monotheism and rejects idolatry and caste. * *adj* of or pertaining to the Sikhs or their beliefs.
silage *n* green fodder preserved for the winter in a silo.
sild *n* (*pl* **silds, sild**) a young herring, esp when canned in Norway.
silence *n* absence of sound; the time this lasts; refusal to speak or make a sound; secrecy. * *vt* to cause to be silent. * *interj* be silent!
silencer *n* a device for reducing the noise of a vehicle exhaust or gun, a muffler.
silent *adj* not speaking; taciturn; noiseless; still.—**silently** *adv.*
silent majority *n* those who rarely assert their views but are presumed to be moderates.
silhouette *n* the outline of a shape against light or a lighter background; a solid outline drawing, usu in solid black on white, esp of a profile. * *vt* to show up in outline; to depict in silhouette.
silica *n* a hard mineral, a compound of oxygen and silicon, found in quartz and flint.
silicate *n* a salt containing silicon.
siliceous, silicious *adj* of or containing silica.
silicon *n* a metalloid element occuring in silica and used extensively in transistors, etc, and as a compound in glass, etc. * *adj* of an area in which there are a number of computer software and hardware companies.
silicon chip *n* a microchip.
silicone *n* an organic polymer compound with good lubricating and insulating properties, used widely as a repellent, resin, etc.
silicosis *n* a disease of the lungs caused by prolonged inhalation of silica particles.
silk *n* a fibre produced by silkworms; lustrous textile cloth, thread or a garment made of silk; (*pl*) silk garments; (*pl*) the colours of a racing stable, worn by a jockey, etc. **adj* of, relating to or made of silk.

silk cotton *n* kapok.
silken *adj* made of or like silk; silky.
silk hat *n* a top hat covered in silk.
silk screen *n* a stencil method of printing a colour design through the meshes of a fabric, as silk; a print so produced.—**silk-screen** *vt.*
silkweed *see* **milkweed.**
silkworm *n* a caterpillar of various moths that feeds on mulberry leaves and produces a strong fibre to construct its cocoon.
silky *adj* (**silkier, silkiest**) soft and smooth like silk; glossy; suave.—**silkiness** *n.*
sill *n* a heavy, horizontal slab of wood or stone at the bottom of a window frame or door.
sillabub *see* **syllabub.**
silly *adj* (**sillier, silliest**) foolish, stupid; frivolous; lacking in sense or judgment; being stunned or dazed. * *n* (*pl* **sillies**) a silly person.—**silliness** *n.*
silo *n* (*pl* **silos**) an airtight pit or tower for storing fodder in a green compressed state; a deep pit for storing cement, coal, etc; an underground structure from which a missile can be fired.
silt *n* a fine-grained sandy sediment carried or deposited by water. * *vti* to fill or choke up with silt.
Silurian *adj* (*geol*) of or pertaining to the division of Palaeozoic rocks between Ordovician and Devonian. * *n* this period.
silver *n* a ductile, malleable, greyish-white metallic element used in jewellery, cutlery, tableware, coins, etc; a lustrous, greyish white. * *adj* made of or plated with silver; silvery; (*hair*) grey; marking the 25th in a series * *vt* to coat with silver or a substance resembling silver; to make or become silvery or grey.
silver birch *n* a Eurasian birch tree with silvery bark.
silver fox *n* (the pelt of) a red fox in a colour phase when its fur is black with silver-tipped hairs.
silver-gilt *n* gilded silver.
silver lining *n* a more favourable aspect of an otherwise hopeless situation.
silver paper *n* a metallic paper coated or laminated to resemble silver, tinfoil.
silver plate *n* a plating of silver; domestic utensils made of silver or of silver-plated metal.—**silver-plate** *vt.*
silver screen *n* (*inf*) (*with* **the**) the film industry; the screen on which a film is projected.
silver service *n* (*in restaurants*) a manner of serving food using a spoon and fork in one hand.
silverside *n* a joint of beef cut from the upper haunch.
silversmith *n* a worker in silver.
silver-tongued *adj* plausible, eloquent.
silverware *n* items, such as serving plates, cutlery, etc made from silver or silver plate.
silver wedding *n* the 25th anniversary of a marriage.
silverweed *n* any of various plants with silvery leaves or hairs.
silvery *adj* white and lustrous like silver; covered with silver; resembling silver in colour; (*sound*) soft and clear.
silviculture *n* the branch of forestry dealing with the care and development of forests.
simian *adj* of or like an ape or monkey.
simian immunodeficiency virus *n* a virus, similar to human immunodeficiency virus, that interferes with the ability of the immune system of monkeys to resist disease.
similar *adj* having a resemblance to, like; nearly corresponding; (*geom*) corresponding exactly in shape if not size.—**similarity** *n.*—**similarly** *adv.*
simile *n* a figure of speech likening one thing to another by the use of like, as, etc.
similitude *n* the state of being similar; guise, likeness.
simmer *vti* to boil gently; to be or keep on the point of boiling; to be in a state of suppressed rage or laughter; (*with* **down**) to abate. * *n* the state of simmering.
simnel cake *n* a rich fruit cake with marzipan and decorations traditionally eaten during Lent or Easter.
simony *n* the buying and selling of ecclesiastical offices.
simoom, simoon *n* a strong, hot, dry wind of the Arabian and North African deserts.
simpatico *adj* (*inf*) agreeable, sympathetic.
simper *vi* to smile in a silly or self-conscious way.—*also n.*
simple *adj* single, uncompounded; plain, not elaborate; clear, not complicated; easy to do, understand, or solve; artless, not sophisticated; weak in intellect; unsuspecting, credulous; sheer, mere.—**simpleness** *n.*
simple fraction *n* a fraction in which both the numerator and denominator are whole numbers.
simple-hearted *adj* sincere, honest.
simple interest *n* interest paid on the principal of a loan only.
simple-minded *adj* foolish; mentally retarded.
simpleton *n* a foolish, weak-minded person.
simplicity *n* (*pl* **simplicities**) the quality or state of being simple; absence of complications; easiness; lack of ornament, plainness, restraint; artlessness; directness; guilelessness, openness, naivety.
simplification *n* the act or result of making less complicated.
simplify *vt* (**simplifying, simplified**) to make simple or easy to understand.
simplistic *adj* oversimplified; uncomplicated.—**simplistically** *adv.*
simply *adv* in a simple way; plainly; merely; absolutely.
simulacrum *n* (*pl* **simulacra**) a likeness or representation, esp a superficial one.
simulate *vt* to pretend to have or feel, to feign; (*conditions*) to reproduce in order to conduct an experiment; to imitate.—**simulation** *n.*
simulator *n* a device that simulates specific conditions in order to test actions or reactions.
simulcast *n* a simultaneous radio and television broadcast.—*also vt.*
simultaneous *adj* done or occurring at the same time.—**simultaneity** *n.*—**simultaneously** *adv.*
sin[1] *n* an offence against a religious or moral principle; transgression of the law of God; a wicked act, an offence; a misdeed, a fault. * *vi* (**sinning, sinned**) to commit a sin; to offend (against).
sin[2] *abbr* = sine.
sin bin *n* (*ice hockey, etc*) (*sl*) an enclosure off the playing area where players guilty of fouls are temporarily sent.
since *adv* from then until now; subsequently; ago. * *prep* during, or continously from (then) until now; after. * *conj* from the time that; because, seeing that.
sincere *adj* genuine, real, not pretended; honest, straightforward.—**sincerely** *adv.*
sincerity *n* the quality or state of being sincere; genuineness, honesty, seriousness.
sinciput *n* (*pl* **sinciputs, sincipita**) the front part of the skull; forehead.
sine *n* (*trig*) a function that in a right-angled triangle is equal to the ratio of the length of the side opposite the angle to that of the hypoteneuse.
sinecure *n* a position or office that provides an income without involving duties.
sine die *adv* without a date, indefinitely.
sine qua non *n* an essential condition, a necessity.
sinew *n* a cord of fibrous tissue, a tendon; (usu *pl*) the chief supporting force, a mainstay; (*pl*) muscles, brawn.
sinewy *adj* having a lean body and strong muscles; tough, stringy.
sinfonia *n* (*pl* **sinfonie, sinfonias**) a symphony.
sinfonietta *n* a short symphony; a small orchestra.
sinful *adj* guilty of sin, wicked.—**sinfully** *adv.*—**sinfulness** *n.*
sing *vti* (**singing, sang,** *pp* **sung**) to utter (words) with musical modulations; (*a song*) to perform; to hum, to ring; to write poetry (about), to praise; (*with* **out**) to shout, call out.—**singer** *n.*—**singing** *n.*
sing. *abbr* = singular.
singe *vt* (**singeing, singed**) to burn slightly; to scorch, esp to remove feathers, etc.—*also n.*
Singhalese *see* **Sinhalese.**

singing *n* the art or an act of singing.
singing telegram *n* (a service that provides) a greetings message delivered in song, usu by a person in fancy dress.
single *adj* one only, not double; individual; composed of one part; alone, sole; separate; unmarried; for one; with one contestant on each side; simple; whole, unbroken; (*tennis*) played between two persons only; (*ticket*) for the outward journey only. * *n* a single ticket; a game between two players; a hit scoring one; a record with one tune on each side. * *vt* (*with* **out**) to pick out, to select.
single blessedness *n* the unmarried state.
single-breasted *adj* (*suit, etc*) fastening in the centre with a single row of buttons.
single cream *n* cream with a low fat content.
single-decker *n* a bus with only one level of passenger accommodation.
single entry *n* (*book-keeping*) a system in which transactions are kept in one account only.
single figures *npl* the numbers less than 10, ie 1 to 9.
single file *n* a single column of persons or things, one behind the other.
single-handed *adj, adv* without assistance, unaided.—**single-handedly** *adv*.—**single-handedness** *n*.
single-lens reflex *n* a camera whose lens allows the photographer to see the same image as it exposes.
single-minded *adj* having only one aim in mind.—**single-mindedly** *adv*.—**single-mindedness** *n*.
singles bar *n* a bar or social club for single people only.
singlestick *n* fencing with wooden sticks instead of swords; the stick used for this.
singlet *n* an undervest.
single ticket *n* a ticket for a one-way journey only.
singleton *n* a playing card that is the only one of its suit in a hand.
singly *adv* alone; one by one.
singsong *n* a droning monotonous utterance; a verse with a regular, marked rhythm and rhyme; (*inf*) a party where everyone sings. * *adj* having a regular or monotonous rhythm.
singular *adj* remarkable; exceptional; unusual; eccentric, odd; (*gram*) referring to only one person or thing. * *n* (*gram*) the singular number or form of a word.
singularity *n* (*pl* **singularities**) the state of being singular; uniqueness; an odd trait, a peculiarity.
singularly *adv* unusually; exceptionally.
Sinhalese *n* a member of a people who form the largest community in Sri Lanka; the language of these people.—*also adj*.—*also* **Singhalese**.
sinister *adj* inauspicious; ominous; ill-omened; evil-looking; malignant; wicked; left; (*her*) on the left side of the shield.
sinistral *adj* of or on the left; left-handed.—**sinistrally** *adv*.
sink *vti* (**sinking, sank** *or* **sunk,** *pp* **sunk**) to go under the surface or to the bottom (of a liquid); to submerge in water; to go down slowly; (*wind*) to subside; to pass to a lower state; to droop, to decline; to grow weaker; to become hollow; to lower, to degrade; to cause to sink; to make by digging out; to invest; (*with* **in**) to penetrate; to thrust into; (*inf*) to be understood in full. * *n* a basin with an outflow pipe, usu in a kitchen; a cesspool; an area of sunken land.—**sinking** *n*.
sinker *n* a weight used to submerge a fishing line.
sinkhole *n* a hole in rock strata, esp limestone, though which water sinks or runs underground; a hole into which foul waste matter is discharged.
sinking fund *n* money put aside for gradual payment of a debt.
Sinn Fein *n* a republican party in Ireland which is the political wing of the IRA.
sinner *n* a person who sins.
Sino- *prefix* Chinese.
Sino-Tebetan *n* a family of languages that includes all the Chinese languages, Burmese and Tibetan.—*also adj*.
Sinology *n* the study of Chinese language, history, society, etc.—**Sinologist** *n*.—**Sinological** *adj*.
sinsemilla *n* (a plant which produces) a highly potent type of marijuana.
sinter *n* a white silicious deposit formed by the evaporation of hot mineral waters. * *vt* to form (metal or glass powder) into lumps by the application of heat and pressure.
sinuate *adj* (*leaf*) having a wavy edge.—**sinuately** *adv*.
sinuous *adj* curving; winding; tortuous.—**sinuously** *adv*.—**sinuousness** *n*.
sinus *n* (*pl* **sinuses**) an air cavity in the skull that opens in the nasal cavities.
sinusitis *n* inflammation of a sinus.
Siouan *n* a family of North American Indian languages.
Sioux *n* (*pl* **Sioux**) a member of various North American Indian peoples who speak Siouan.
sip *vti* (**sipping, sipped**) to drink in small mouthfuls. * *n* the act of sipping; the quantity sipped.
siphon *n* a bent tube for drawing off liquids from a higher to a lower level by atmospheric pressure; a bottle with an internal tube and tap at the top for aerated water. * *vti* to draw off, or be drawn off, with a siphon.—*also* **syphon**.
siphon bottle *n* a soda siphon.
sir *n* a title of respect used to address a man in speech or correspondence; (*with cap*) a title preceding the first name of a knight or baronet. * *vt* to address as "sir".
sire *n* a father; a male ancestor; the male parent of an animal; a form of address to a king. * *vt* (*animal*) to beget.
siren *n* a device producing a loud wailing sound as a warning signal; a fabled sea nymph who lured sailors to destruction with a sweet song; a seductive or alluring woman.
sirenian *n* a member of an order of plant-eating mammals that live in water, comprising the dugong and the manatee.—*also adj*.
sirloin *n* the upper part of a loin of beef.
sirocco *n* a hot, oppressive wind that blows across southern Europe from North Africa.
sirree *interj* (*inf*) sir – used for emphasis, esp after *yes* or *no*.
sis *n* (*inf*) sister.
sisal *n* (a tropical agave plant whose leaves yield) a tough fibre used to make rope.
siskin *n* a Eurasian songbird with greenish plumage related to the goldfinch.
sissy *n* (*pl* **sissies**) an effeminate, feeble or cowardly boy or man.—*also adj*.
sister *n* a female sibling, a daughter of the same parents; a female member or associate of the same race, creed, trade union, etc; a member of a religious sisterhood; one of the same kind, model, etc; a senior nurse. * *adj* (*ship, etc*) belonging to the same type.
sisterhood *n* a female religious or charitable order; the state of being a sister.
sister-in-law *n* (*pl* **sisters-in-law**) the sister of a husband or wife; the wife of a brother.
sisterly *adj* like a sister, kind, affectionate.
sistrum *n* (*pl* **sistra**) an ancient Egyptian metal rattle used as a percussion instrument.
sit *vti* (**sitting, sat**) to rest oneself on the buttocks, as on a chair; (*bird*) to perch; (*hen*) to cover eggs for hatching; (*legislator, etc*) to occupy a seat; (*court*) to be in session; to pose, as for a portrait; to ride (a horse); to press or weigh (upon); to be located; to rest or lie; to take an examination; to take care of a child, pet, etc, while the parents or owners are away; to cause to sit; to provide seats or seating room for; (*with* **down**) to take a seat; (*with* **for**) to represent in parliament; (*with* **in**) to attend a discussion or a musical session; to participate in a sit-in; (*with* **on**) to hold a meeting to discuss; to delay action on something; (*inf*) to suppress; to rebuke; (*with* **out**) to sit through the whole; to abstain from dancing; (*with* **up**) to straighten the back while sitting; not to go to bed; (*inf*) to be astonished.
sitar *n* an Indian musical instrument similar to a lute with a long neck.
sitcom *see* **situation comedy**.

site *n* a space occupied or to be occupied by a building; a situation; the place or scene of something. * *vt* to locate, to place.
sit-in *n* a strike in which the strikers refuse to leave the premises; civil disobedience in which demonstrators occupy a public place and refuse to leave voluntarily.
sitka spruce *n* a tall North American spruce tree.
sitter *n* a person who looks after a child, dog, house, etc, while the parents or owners are away.
sitting *n* the state of being seated; a period of being seated, as for a meal, a portrait; a session, as of a court; a clutch of eggs. * *adj* that is sitting; being in a judicial or legislative seat; used in or for sitting; performed while sitting.
sitting duck, sitting target *n* (*inf*) a person or thing that is an easy target for attack, criticism, etc.
sitting room *n* a room other than a bedroom or kitchen; a parlour.
sitting tenant *n* a tenant in occupation of a property.
situate *vt* to place in a site, situation, or category.
situated *adj* having a site, located; placed; provided with money, etc.
situation *n* a place, a position; a state of affairs, circumstances; a job or post.
situation comedy *n* a comic television or radio series made up of episodes involving the same group of characters.—*also* **sitcom.**
sit-up *n* an exercise of sitting up from a prone position without using hands or legs.
SIV *abbr* = simian immunodeficiency virus.
six *adj, n* one more than five. * *n* the symbol for this (6, VI, vi); the sixth in a series or set; something having six units as members.
sixer *n* a leader of a group of six Brownies or Cub Scouts.
sixfold *adj* having six units or members; being six times as great or as many.
six-pack *n* a pack of six units, as of cans of beer, etc, sold together.
sixpence *n* (*formerly*) a British coin worth six old pennies.
six-shooter *n* (*inf*) a six-chambered revolver.
sixteen *adj, n* one more than fifteen. * *n* the symbol for this (16, XVI, xvi).—**sixteenth** *adj, n.*
sixteenth note *n* a musical note with a sixteenth the time value of a whole note, a semiquaver.
sixth *n* one of six equal parts of a thing; (*mus*) an interval of six diatonic degrees; the sixth tone of a diatonic scale.—*also adv.* * *adj* next after fifth.—**sixthly** *adv.*
sixth sense *n* intuitive power.
sixty *n* six times ten. * *n* (*pl* **sixties**) the symbol for this (60, LX, lx); (in *pl*) sixties (60s), the numbers for 60 to 69; the same numbers in a life or century.—**sixtieth** *adj, adv.*
sixty-fourth note. *n* a musical note with the time value of one sixty-fourth of a whole note; a hemidemisemiquaver.
sixty-nine *n* soixante-neuf.
sizable, sizeable *adj* of some size; large.—**sizably, sizeably** *adv.*—**sizableness, sizeableness** *n.*
size[1] *n* magnitude; the dimensions or proportions of something; a graduated measurement, as of clothing or shoes. * *vt* to sort according to size; to measure; (*with* **up**) (*inf*) to make an estimate or judgment of; to meet requirements.
size[2] *n* a thin pasty substance used to glaze paper, stiffen cloth, etc. * *vt* to treat with size.
sized *adj* having a specified size.
sizzle *vti* to make a hissing spluttering noise, as of frying; to be extremely hot; to be very angry; to scorch, sear or fry with a sizzling sound. * *n* a hissing sound.
SJ *abbr* = Society of Jesus.
sjambok *n* (*in S Africa) a* heavy whip made from rhinoceros hide.
SK *abbr* = Saskatchewan.
ska *n* a form of West Indian pop music, a precursor of reggae.
skate[1] *n* a steel blade attached to a boot for gliding on ice; a boot with such a runner; a roller skate. * *vi* to move on skates; (*with* **over**) to avoid dealing with (an issue, problem, etc) directly.—**skater** *n.*
skate[2] *n* an edible fish of the ray family with a broad, flat body and short, spineless tail.
skateboard *n* a short, oblong board with two wheels at each end for standing on and riding.—*also vi.*
skean-dhu *n* (*Scot*) a dagger worn in the stocking as part of Highland dress.
skedaddle *vi* (*inf*) to run away.—*also n.*
skeet *n* a type of clay-pigeon shooting in which clay targets are hurled into range at varying speeds and trajectories from two traps.
skein *n* a folded coil of yarn, thread, etc; a tangle; a flight of wild fowl, esp geese.
skeleton *n* the bony framework of the body of a human, an animal or plant; the bones separated from flesh and preserved in their natural position; a supporting structure, a framework; an outline, an abstract; a very thin person; something shameful kept secret. * *adj (staff, crew, etc)* reduced to the lowest possible level.—**skeletal** *adj.*
skeleton key *n* a key with a slender bit that can open many simple locks.
skeptic *see* **sceptic.**
skeptical *see* **sceptical.**
skepticism *see* **scepticism.**
skerry *n* (*pl* **skerries**) a rocky isle or reef.
sketch *n* a rough drawing, quickly made; a preliminary draft; a short literary piece or essay; a short humorous item for a revue, etc; a brief outline. * *vti* to make a sketch (of); to plan roughly.
sketchy *adj* (**sketchier, sketchiest**) incomplete; vague; inadequate.—**sketchily** *adv.*—**sketchiness** *n.*
skew *adj* slanting, oblique, set at an angle. * *adv* at a slant. * *vti* to slant or set at a slant; to swerve.
skewbald *adj* marked with patches of white and another colour except black. * *n* an animal, esp a horse, with such markings.
skewer *n* a long wooden or metal pin on which pieces of meat and vegetables are cooked. * *vt* to pierce and fasten on a skewer; to transfix.
skewwhiff *adj* (*inf*) askew, not straight.
ski *n* (*pl* **skis**) a long narrow runner of wood, metal or plastic that is fastened to a boot for moving across snow; a water-ski. * *vi* (**skiing, skied**) to travel on skis.—**skier** *n.*
skibob *n* a snow vehicle similar to a bicycle with a low seat and steering handle mounted on two skis instead of wheels.
skid *vti* (**skidding, skidded**) to slide without rotating; to slip sideways; (*vehicle*) to slide sideways out of control; to cause (a vehicle) to skid. * *n* the act of skidding; a drag to reduce speed; a ship's fender; a movable support for a heavy object; a runner on an aircraft's landing gear.
skid row, skid road *n* (*sl*) a shabby district where vagrants, etc, live.
skied *see* **ski.**
skiff *n* a small light boat for rowing.
skiffle *n* a type of music using guitars and makeshift instruments (eg washboards) which became popular in the 1950s.
ski jump *n* a long ramp surmounting a slope from which skiers jump in competition.—**ski-jump** *vi.*
skilful, skillful *adj* having skill; proficient, adroit.—**skilfully, skillfully** *adv.*—**skilfulness, skillfulness** *n.*
ski lift *n* any of various devices for conveying skiers up a slope, such as a chair lift.
skill *n* proficiency; expertness, dexterity; a developed aptitude or ability; a type of work or craft requiring specialist training.
skilled *adj* fully trained, expert.
skillet *n* a frying pan.
skim *vti* (**skimming, skimmed**) to remove (cream, scum) from the surface of; to glide lightly over, to brush the surface of; to read superficially.
skimmer *n* that which skims, esp a perforated utensil for skimming milk.
skimmia *n* any of a genus of evergreen shrubs with red berries.
skim milk, skimmed milk *n* milk from which the cream has been removed.
skimp *vti* to give scant measure (of), to stint; to be sparing or frugal (with).

skimpy *adj* (**skimpier, skimpiest**) small in size; inadequate, scant, meagre.—**skimpily** *adv*.—**skimpiness** *n*.

skin *n* the tissue forming the outer covering of the body; a hide; the rind of a fruit; an outer layer or casing; a film on the surface of a liquid; a vessel for water, etc, made of hide. * *vti* (**skinning, skinned**) to remove the skin from, to peel; to injure by scraping (the knee, etc); to cover or become covered with skin; (*inf*) to swindle.

skin-deep *adj* superficial.

skin diving *n* the sport of swimming underwater with scuba equipment.—**skin-diver** *n*.

skinflick *n* (*sl*) a pornographic film.

skinflint *n* a stingy person.

skinful *n* (*pl* **skinfuls**) (*sl*) as much alcoholic drink as one can take.

skin graft *n* a piece of skin taken from one part of the body to replace damaged skin elsewhere.

skinhead *n* a British youth with cropped hair, large boots and braces, often belonging to an aggressive gang.

skink *n* a small lizard of tropical Asia and Africa.

skinned *adj* having skin of a specified kind.

skinny *adj* (**skinnier, skinniest**) very thin; emaciated.—**skinniness** *n*.

skint *adj* (*sl*) having no money.

skintight *adj* (*clothing*) fitting tightly; clinging.

skip[1] *vti* (**skipping, skipped**) to leap or hop lightly over; to keep jumping over a rope as it is swung under one; to make omissions, to pass over, esp in reading; (*inf*) to leave (town) hurriedly, to make off; (*inf*) to miss deliberately. * *n* a skipping movement; a light jump.

skip[2] *n* a large metal container for holding building debris; a cage or bucket for hoisting workers or materials in a mine, quarry, etc.

ski pants *npl* fashion trousers worn tight with a strap that fits under the foot.

skipjack *n* (*pl* **skipjack, skipjacks**) any of various food fishes including two varieties of tuna, one striped (skipjack) and the other spotted (black skipjack).

skiplane *n* a light aircraft fitted with skis for taking off and landing on snow.

ski pole *n* one of a pair of pointed metal sticks used by skiers to provide forward thrust and to aid stability.—*also* **ski stick**.

skipper *n* the captain of a boat, aircraft, or team. * *vt* to act as skipper; to captain.

skipping rope *n* a light rope, usu with a handle at each end, that is swung over the head and under the feet while jumping.

skirl *n* (*Scot*) the shrill wailing sound characteristic of bagpipes.—*also vi*.

skirmish *n* a minor fight in a war; a conflict or clash. * *vi* to take part in a skirmish.

skirt *n* a woman's garment that hangs from the waist; the lower part of a dress or coat; an outer edge, a border; (*sl*) a woman. * *vti* to border; to move along the edge (of); to evade.

skirting *n* a border, an edging; fabric for skirts.

skirting board *n* a narrow panel of wood at the foot of an interior wall.

ski stick *see ski* **pole**.

skit *n* a short humorous sketch, as in the theatre.

ski tow *n* a motor-driven device that pulls skiers uphill.

skitter *vti* to move or cause to move quickly or to skim across a surface.

skittish *adj* (*animal*) frisky, easily frightened; (*person*) playful, frivolous, lively.—**skittishly** *adv*.—**skittishness** *n*.

skittles *n* a game in which a wooden or plastic bottle-shaped pin is knocked down by a ball.—*also* **ninepins**.

skive *vi* (*inf*) to avoid work or duties because of laziness.

skivvy *n* (*pl* **skivvies**) a female domestic servant. * *vi* (**skivvying, skivvied**) to perform menial domestic duties.

skol, skoal *interj* good health, cheers (*used in a toast*).

skua *n* any of various large predatory seabirds with dark plumage.

skulduggery, skullduggery *n* (*inf*) deceit, underhand dealing.

skulk *vi* to move in a stealthy manner; to lurk.

skull *n* the bony casing enclosing the brain; the cranium.

skunk *n* a small black-and-white mammal that emits a foul-smelling liquid when frightened; its fur; (*sl*) an obnoxious or mean person.

sky *n* (*pl* **skies**) the apparent vault over the earth; heaven; the upper atmosphere; weather, climate.

skull and crossbones *n* (*pl* **skulls and crossbones**) an image of a human skull and crossed thighbones used as a warning of danger.

sky-blue *adj*, *n* (of) a bright pure blue, azure.

sky-diving *n* the sport of parachute jumping involving free-fall manoeuvres.—**sky-diver** *n*.

Skye terrier *n* a breed of short-legged terrier with long hair and a long body.

sky-high *adj*, *adv* very high; in an enthusiastic manner; extremely expensive.

skyjack *vt* to hijack an aircraft.

skylark *n* a lark famous for its song as it soars.

skylight *n* a window in the roof or ceiling.

skyline *n* the visible horizon; the outline, as of mountains, buildings, etc, seen against the sky.

skyrocket *n* a rocket. * *vi* to rise rapidly (eg in price, status, etc).

skyscraper *n* a very tall building.

skyward *adj*, *adv* toward the sky.—**skywards** *adv*.

skywriting *n* (the act of creating) writing in the sky formed by smoke or vapour emitted from an aircraft.

slab *n* a flat, broad, thick piece (as of stone, wood, or bread, etc); something resembling this. * *vt* to cut or form into slabs; to cover or support with slabs; to put on thickly.

slack *adj* loose, relaxed, not tight; (*business*) slow, not brisk; sluggish; inattentive, careless. * *n* the part (of a rope, etc) that hangs loose; a dull period; a lull; (*pl*) trousers for casual wear. * *vti* to neglect (one's work, etc), to be lazy; (*with* **off**) to slacken (a rope, etc).—**slackness** *n*.

slacken *vti* to make or become less active, brisk, etc; to loosen or relax, as a rope; to diminish, to abate.—**slackening** *n*, *adj*.

slacker *n* a lazy person; a person who shirks.

slack water *n* the turn of the tide; a slow-moving stretch of water.

slag *n* the waste product from the smelting of metals; volcanic lava.

slain *see* **slay**.

slake *vt* to quench or satisfy (thirst, etc); to mix (lime) with water.

slalom *n* downhill skiing in a zigzag course between upright markers; (*skiing, canoeing, etc*) a timed race over a slalom course. * *vi* to move over a zigzag course.

slam *vti* (**slamming, slammed**) to shut with a loud noise, to bang; to throw (down) violently; (*inf*) to criticize severely. * *n* a sound or the act of slamming, a bang; (*inf*) severe criticism; (*bridge*) the taking of 12 or 13 tricks.

slammer *n* (*sl*) a prison or jail.

slander *n* a false and malicious statement about another; the uttering of this. * *vt* to utter a slander about, to defame.—**slanderous** *adj*.

slang *n* words or expressions used in familiar speech but not regarded as standard English; jargon of a particular social class, age group, etc. * *adj* relating to slang.

slant *vti* to incline, to slope; to tell in such a way as to have a bias. * *n* a slope; an oblique position; a bias, a point of view. * *adj* sloping.—**slantly** *adv*.

slanted *adj* prejudiced, biased; sloping.

slantwise *adv* at a slant.

slap *n* a smack with the open hand; an insult; a rebuff. * *vt* (**slapping, slapped**) to strike with something flat; to put, hit, etc, with force. * *adv* directly, full.

slapdash *adj* impetuous; hurried; careless; haphazard. * *adv* carelessly.

slaphappy *adj* (**slaphappier, slaphappiest**) casually or cheerfully irresponsible; giddy, punch-drunk.

slapstick *n* boisterous humour of a knockabout kind.

slap-up *adj* (*inf*) (*meals, entertainment*) lavish, luxury.

slash *vti* to cut gashes in, to slit; to strike fiercely (at) with a sword, etc; to reduce (prices) sharply. * *n* a cutting blow; a long slit, a gash.

slat *n* a thin, flat, narrow strip of wood, etc.

slate[1] *vt* to criticize or punish severely.

slate[2] *n* a fine-grained rock easily split into thin layers; a flat plate of this or other material used in roofing; a tablet (as of slate) for writing on; a list of proposed candidates. * *adj* the colour of slate, a deep bluish-grey colour; made of slate. * *vt* to cover with slates; to suggest as a political candidate.

slater *n* a person trained in roofing with slates; a wood louse.

slatted *adj* having slats.

slattern *n* a slovenly woman; a slut.

slaughter *n* the butchering of animals for food; a wholesale killing, a massacre.—*also vt*.—**slaughterer** *n*.

slaughterhouse *n* a place where animals are slaughtered, an abattoir.

Slav *n* any person who speaks a Slavonic language.

slave *n* a person without freedom or personal rights, who is legally owned by another; a person under domination, esp of a habit or vice; a person who works like a slave, a drudge. * *vti* to toil hard, as a slave.

slave driver *n* a supervisor of slaves at work; a hard taskmaster.

slaveholder *n* a person who owns slaves.

slaver[1] *n* a person engaged in the buying and selling of slaves.

slaver[2] *vti* to dribble, to cover with saliva; to fawn upon, to flatter.

slavery *n* the condition of being a slave; bondage; drudgery; slave-owning as an institution.

slave ship *n* a ship used in the slave trade.

Slave State *n* (*hist*) any of the Southern states of the US where slavery was legal until the Civil War.

slave trade *n* commercial traffic in slaves, esp the transport of Black Africans to Europe and America in the 16th to 19th centuries.

Slavic *see* **Slavonic**.

slavish *adj* servile, abject; unoriginal.—**slavishly** *adv*.—**slavishness** *n*.

Slavonic, Slavic *adj* of or characteristic of the Slavs. * *n* a branch of the Indo-European family of languages, including Russian, Bulgarian, Polish and Czech.

slaw *n* coleslaw.

slay *vti* (**slaying, slew,** *pp* **slain**) to kill in great numbers; to murder; (*sl*) to overwhelm, to affect in a powerful way.—**slayer** *n*.

sleaze *n* (*inf*) sleaziness.

sleazy *adj* (**sleazier, sleaziest**) disreputable, squalid.—**sleaziness** *n*.

sled, sledge *n* a framework on runners for travelling over snow or ice; a toboggan; a sleigh. * *vti* to go or convey by sledge.

sledgehammer *n* a large, heavy hammer for two hands.

sleek *adj* smooth, glossy; having a prosperous or well-groomed appearance; plausible.

sleep *n* a natural, regularly recurring rest for the body, with little or no consciousness; a period spent sleeping; a state of numbness followed by tingling. * *vti* (**sleeping, slept**) to rest in a state of sleep; to be inactive; to provide beds for; (*with* **around**) (*inf*) to be sexually promiscuous; (*with* **in**) to sleep on the premises; to sleep too long in the morning; (*with* **on**) to have a night's rest before making a decision; (*with* **off**) to get rid of by sleeping; (*with* **over**) to pass the night in someone else's house; (*with* **with**) to have sexual relations with.

sleeper *n* a person or thing that sleeps; a horizontal beam that carries and spreads a weight; a sleeping car; something that suddenly attains prominence or value.

sleeping bag *n* a padded bag for sleeping in, esp outdoors.

sleeping car *n* a railway carriage with berths.

sleeping partner *n* a partner in a business who takes no part in its management.

sleeping pill *n* a pill that induces sleep.

sleeping sickness *n* a serious infectious disease marked by lethargy, coma.

sleepless *adj* without sleep; unable to sleep.

sleepwalker *n* a person who walks while asleep, a somnambulist.—**sleepwalking** *n*.

sleepy *adj* (**sleepier, sleepiest**) drowsy; tired; lazy, not alert.—**sleepily** *adv*.—**sleepiness** *n*.

sleepyhead *n* a tired or lazy person.

sleet *n* snow or hail mixed with rain. * *vi* to rain in the form of sleet.

sleeve *n* the part of a garment enclosing the arm; (*mech*) a tube that fits over a part; an open-ended cover, esp a paperboard envelope for a record.

sleeveless *adj* (*garment*) without sleeves.

sleigh *n* a light vehicle on runners for travelling over snow; a sledge.

sleight of hand *n* manual dexterity, such as in conjuring or juggling; a deception.

slender *adj* thin; slim; slight; scanty.—**slenderly** *adv*.—**slenderness** *n*.

slept *see* **sleep**.

sleuth *n* (*inf*) a detective.

sleuthhound *n* a bloodhound; (*inf*) a detective.

slew[1] *see* **slay**.

slew[2], **slue** *vti* to twist or be twisted sideways.

slew[3], **slue** *n* (*inf*) a great quantity.

slice *n* a thin flat piece cut from something (as bread, etc); a wedge-shaped piece (of cake, pie, etc); a portion, a share; a broad knife for serving fish, cheese, etc; (*golf*) a stroke that makes the ball curl to the right. * *vti* to divide into parts; to cut into slices; to strike (a ball) so that it curves.—**slicer** *n*—**slicing** *adj, n*.

slick *adj* clever, deft; smart but unsound; insincere; wily; (*inf*) smooth but superficial, tricky, etc. * *n* a patch or area of oil floating on water. * *vt* to make glossy; (*with* **up**) (*inf*) to make smart, neat, etc.

slicker *n* a loose waterproof coat.

slide *vti* (**sliding, slid**) to move along in constant contact with a smooth surface, as on ice, to glide; to coast over snow and ice; to pass gradually (into); to move (an object) unobtrusively. * *n* the act of sliding, a glide; a strip of smooth ice for sliding on; a chute; the glass plate of a microscope; a photographic transparency; a landslide.

slide rule *n* a ruler with a graduated sliding part for making calculations.

sliding scale *n* a schedule for automatically varying one thing (eg wages) according to the fluctuations of another thing (eg cost of living); a flexible scale.

slier, sliest see **sly**.

slight *adj* small, inconsiderable; trifling; slim; frail, flimsy. * *vt* to disregard as insignificant; to treat with disrespect, to snub. * *n* intentional indifference or neglect, discourtesy.

slighting *adj* disparaging; hurtful.

slightly *adv* to a small degree; slenderly.

slightness *n* frailness or slenderness; lack of weight, solidity, importance, or thoroughness.

slim[1] *adj* slender, not stout; small in amount, degree, etc; slight. * *vti* (slimming, slimmed) to make or become slim; to reduce one's weight by diet, etc.—**slimness** *n*.

slim[2] *n* the name used in Africa for AIDS.

slime *n* a sticky, slippery, half-liquid substance; a glutinous mud; mucus secreted by various animals (eg slugs).

slimmer *n* a person who controls their diet to lose weight.

slimming *n* the process of losing weight by dieting.

slimy *adj* (**slimier, slimiest**) like or covered with slime; repulsive; fawning.—**sliminess** *n*.

sling[1] *n* a loop of leather with a string attached for hurling stones; a rope for lifting or hoisting weights; a bandage suspended from the neck for supporting an injured arm. * *vt* (**slinging, slung**) to throw, lift, or suspend (as) with a sling; to hurl.

sling[2] *n* a drink of sweetened water mixed with a spirit such as gin.

slingback *n* a shoe whose back consists of a strap.

slingshot *n* a contraption with elastic for shooting small stones, a catapult.

slink *vi* (**slinking, slinked** *or* **slunk**) to move stealthily or furtively, to sneak.

slinky *adj* (**slinkier, slinkiest**) (*inf*) sinuous in line or movement; (*clothes*) hugging the figure.

slip[1] *vti* (**slipping, slipped**) to slide, to glide; to lose one's foothold and slide; to go or put quietly or quickly; to let go, to release; to escape from; (*with* **up**) to make a slight mistake. * *n* the act of slipping; a mistake, a lapse; a woman's undergarment; a pillowcase; a slipway.

slip[2] *n* a small piece of paper; a young, slim person; a long seat or narrow pew; a shoot for grafting, a cutting; a descendant, an offspring.

slip[3] *n* a mixture of watery clay used for coating or decorating pottery.

slipcase *n* a protective case for one or more books with an open end to reveal the spines.

slipknot *n* a knot that slips along the rope around which it is tied; a knot that can be undone at a pull.

slip-on *adj* (*garment or shoe*) easy to put on or take off.—*also n*.

slippage *n* a slipping, as of one gear past another.

slipped disc *n* a ruptured cartilaginous disc between vertebrae.

slipper *n* a light, soft, shoe worn in the house.

slippery *adj* so smooth as to cause slipping; difficult to hold or catch; evasive, unreliable, shifty.

slippy *adj* (**slippier, slippiest**) slippery.

slip road *n* a road that gives access to a main road or motorway.

slipshod *adj* having the shoes down at heel; slovenly, careless.

slip stitch *n* a concealed stitch used for hemming; an unworked stitch in knitting.—**slipstitch** *vt*.

slipstream *n* a stream of air driven astern by the engine of an aircraft; an area of forward suction immediately behind a rapidly moving racing car.

slip-up *n* (*inf*) an error, a lapse.

slipway *n* an inclined surface for launching or repairing ships; a sloped landing stage.

slit *vt* (**slitting, slit**) to cut open or tear lengthways; to slash or tear into strips. * *n* a long cut, a slash; a narrow opening.—**slitter** *n*.

slither *vi* to slide, as on a loose or wet surface; to slip or slide like a snake.—**slithery** *adj*.

slit trench *n* a narrow trench to provide shelter during battle.

sliver *n* a small narrow piece torn off, a splinter; a thin slice.

slivovitz, slivowitz *n* plum brandy.

slob *n* (*sl*) a coarse or sloppy person.

slobber *vti* to drool; to run at the mouth; to smear with dribbling saliva or food. * *n* dribbling saliva; maudlin talk.

sloe *n* (the dark fruit of the) blackthorn.

sloe-eyed *adj* having almond-shaped dark or black eyes.

sloe gin *n* a gin flavoured with sloes.

slog *vti* (slogging, slogged) to hit hard and wildly; to work laboriously; to trudge doggedly. * *n* a hard, boring spell of work; a strenuous walk or hike; a hard, random hit.—**slogger** *n*.

slogan *n* a catchy phrase used in advertising or as a motto by a political party, etc.

sloop *n* a small sailing vessel with one mast and a jib.

slop *n* a puddle of spilled liquid; unappetizing semi-liquid food; (*pl*) liquid kitchen refuse. * *vti* (**slopping, slopped**) to spill or be spilled; (*with* **out**) (*prisoners*) to empty slop from chamber pots in the morning.

slope *n* rising or falling ground; an inclined line or surface; the amount or degree of this. * *vti* to incline, to slant; (*inf*) to make off, to go.

sloppy *adj* (**sloppier, sloppiest**) slushy; (*inf*) maudlin, sentimental; (*inf*) careless, untidy.—**sloppily** *adv*.—**sloppiness** *n*.

slosh *n* watery snow, slush; (*inf*) a heavy blow; the sound of liquid splashing. * *vi* to walk (through) or splash (around) in liquid, mud, etc; (*of liquid*) to splash. * *vt* to throw or splash liquid, etc at someone or something; (*inf*) to hit somebody.

sloshed *adj* (*inf*) drunk.

slot *n* a long narrow opening in a mechanism for inserting a coin, a slit. * *vt* (**slotting, slotted**) to fit into a slot; to provide with a slot; (*inf*) to place in a series.

sloth *n* laziness, indolence; a slow-moving South American animal.—**slothful** *adj*.

slot machine *n* a machine operated by the insertion of a coin, used for gambling or dispensing drinks, etc.

slouch *vti* to sit, stand or move in a drooping, slovenly way. * *n* a drooping slovenly posture or gait; the downward droop of a hat brim; (*inf*) a poor performer, a lazy or incompetent person.

slouch hat *n* a hat with a soft wide brim that can be pulled down to cover the ears.

slough[1] *n* a bog; deep, hopeless dejection.

slough[2] *n* the dead, outer skin of a snake. * *vti* to cast off, as a dead skin.

Slovak *n* a native or inhabitant of Slovakia in Czechoslovakia; the language of Slovakia.—*also adj*.

Slovene *n* a native or inhabitant of Slovenia, formerly part of Yugoslavia; the Slavonic language of Slovenia.—*also adj*.

slovenly *adj* untidy, dirty; careless.—**slovenliness** *n*.

slow *adj* moving at low speed, not fast; gradual; not quick in understanding; reluctant, backward; dull, sluggish; not progressive; (*clock*) behind in time; tedious, boring; (*surface*) causing slowness. * *vti* (*also with* **up, down**) to reduce the speed (of).—**slowly** *adv*.—**slowness** *n*.

slowcoach *n* (*inf*) a person who moves, works or thinks slowly.

slow handclap *n* slow regular clapping expressive of audience dissatisfaction.

slow match, slow fuse *n* a slow-burning match or fuse for igniting explosives.

slow-motion *adj* moving slowly; denoting a filmed or taped scene with the original action slowed down.

slowpoke *see* **slowcoach.**

slowworm *n* a legless European lizard with a greyish elongated body and very small eyes.

SLR *abbr* = single-lens reflex.

slub *n* a lump in a piece of yarn or thread.

sludge *n* soft mud or snow; sediment; sewage.

slue *see* **slew**[2].

slug[1] *n* a mollusc resembling a snail but with no outer shell.

slug[2] *n* a small bullet; a disc for inserting into a slot machine; a line of type; (*inf*) a hard blow; a drink of spirits. * *vt* (**slugging, slugged**) (*inf*) to hit hard with a fist or a bat.

sluggard *n* a lazy person. * *adj* lazy.

sluggish *adj* slow, inactive; unresponsive.—**sluggishly** *adv*.—**sluggishness** *n*.

sluice *n* a gate regulating a flow of water; the water passing through this; an artificial water channel. * *vti* to draw off through a sluice; to wash with a stream of water; to stream out as from a sluice.

slum *n* a squalid, rundown house; (*usu pl*) an overcrowded area characterized by poverty, etc. * *vi* (**slumming, slummed**) to make do with less comfort.

slumber *vi* to sleep. * *n* a light sleep.

slump *n* a sudden fall in value or slackening in demand; (*sport*) a period of poor play. * *vi* to fall or decline suddenly; to sink down heavily; to collapse; to slouch.

slung *see* **sling.**

slunk *see* **slink.**

slur *vti* (**slurring, slurred**) to pronounce or speak indistinctly; (*letters, words*) to run together; (*mus*) to produce by gliding without a break; to make disparaging remarks. * *n* the act of slurring; a stigma, an imputation of disgrace; (*mus*) a curved line over notes to be slurred.

slurp *vti* (*sl*) to drink or eat noisily. * *n* a loud sipping or sucking sound.

slurry *n* (*pl* **slurries**) a liquid mixture of insoluble matter (as mud, lime, etc).

slush *n* liquid mud; melting snow; (*inf*) sentimental language.—**slushy** *adj*.

slush fund *n* a fund of money used secretly to bribe, etc.

slut *n* a slovenly or immoral woman.—**sluttish** *adj*.

sly *adj* (**slyer, slyest** *or* **slier, sliest**) secretively cunning, wily; underhand; knowing.—**slyly** *adv*.—**slyness** *n*.

SM *abbr* = master of science; sergeant major.

Sm (*chem symbol*) samarium.

S/M, S-M *abbr* = sadomasochism.

smack[1] *n* a taste; a distinctive smell or flavour; small quantity, a trace. * *vi* to have a smell or taste (of); to have a slight trace of something.

smack[2] *vt* to strike or slap with the open hand; to kiss noisily; to make a sharp noise with the lips.—*also n*.

smack[3] *n* a small fishing vessel used in coastal waters.
smacker *n* (*sl*) a noisy kiss; (*sl*) a pound note or dollar bill.
small *adj* little in size, number, importance, etc; modest, humble; operating on a minor scale; young; petty. * *adv* in small pieces. * *n* the narrow, curving part of the back.
small arms *npl* portable firearms, such as handguns.
small beer *n* (*inf*) people or things regarded as trivial.
small change *n* coins of low value.
small fry *npl* people or things of little significance.
smallholding *n* in UK, a small piece of agricultural land, usu between one and fifty acres.—**smallholder** *n*.
small hours *npl* the period between midnight and dawn.
small intestine *n* the section of the alimentary canal between the stomach and the colon.
small-minded *adj* intolerant, narrow-minded; mean, vindictive.—**small-mindedly** *adv*.—**small-mindedness** *n*.
smallpox *n* an acute contagious viral disease, now rare, causing the eruption of pustules which leave the skin scarred and pitted.
small print *n* small type that is difficult to read in a contract or other document, esp conditions and limitations made deliberately inconspicuous.
small-scale *adj* small in size or scope.
small screen *n* a television.
small talk *n* light, social conversation.
small-time *adj* (*inf*) unimportant.
smalt *n* a blue pigment used in colouring glass and ceramics.
smarmy *adj* (**smarmier, smarmiest**) (*inf*) obsequious, unpleasantly smooth and flattering.
smart *n* a sudden, stinging pain. * *vi* to have or cause a sharp, stinging pain (as by a slap); to feel distress. * *adj* stinging; astute; clever, witty; fashionable; neatly dressed; (*equipment, etc*) capable of seemingly intelligent action through computer control; (*bombs, missiles*) guided to the target by lasers ensuring pinpoint accuracy.—**smartly** *adv*.—**smartness** *n*.
smart aleck *n* (*inf*) an annoyingly clever person, a know-all.
smart card *n* a credit card containing a memory chip that records transactions made with the card.
smarten *vti* to make or become smart.
smart money *n* money invested or bet by experienced gamblers or financiers; money paid to secure release from an unpleasant situation, or obligation, esp military service.
smart set *n sing or pl* fashionable people or society.
smash *vti* to break into pieces with noise or violence; to hit, collide, or move with force; to destroy or be destroyed. * *n* a hard, heavy hit; a violent, noisy breaking; a violent collision; total failure, esp in business; (*inf*) a popular success.
smashed *adj* (*sl*) drunk or under the influence of drugs.
smasher *n* (*inf*) an attractive or excellent person or thing.
smashing *n* (*inf*) excellent.
smash-up *n* (*inf*) a serious collision, a crash.
smattering *n* a slight superficial knowledge; a small number.
smear *vt* to cover with anything greasy or sticky; to make a smudge; to slander. * *n* a smudge; a slanderous attack; a deposit of blood, secretion, etc on a glass slide for examination under a microscope.
smear test *n* microscopic analysis of a smear of bodily cells, esp from the cervix, for cancer.
smegma *n* a sebaceous secretion which accumulates as solid matter in the folds of the skin, esp under the foreskin.
smell *n* the sense by which odours are perceived with the nose; a scent, odour, or stench; a trace. * *vti* (**smelling, smelt** *or* **smelled**) to have or perceive an odour.—**smelly** *adj*.
smelling salts *npl* a preparation of ammonia used as a stimulant in cases of faintness, etc.
smelt[1] *vt* to extract ore from metal by melting.
smelt[2] *n* any of various small marine or freshwater food fishes related to the salmon.
smelt[3] *see* **smell**.
smidgen, smidgin *n* (*inf*) a small amount.
smilax *n* any of a genus of climbing plants bearing red berries that includes the sarsaparilla; an African vine cultivated for its decorative green leaves.
smile *vti* to express amusement, friendship, pleasure, etc, by a slight turning up of the corners of the mouth. * *n* the act of smiling; a bright aspect.—**smilingly** *adv*.
smirch *vt* to dishonour; to soil, stain, or sully. * *n* a stain on reputation; a smudge, smear.
smirk *vi* to smile in an expression of smugness or scorn. * *n* a smug or scornful smile.—**smirkingly** *adv*.
smite *vb* (**smiting, smote,** *pp* **smitten** *or* **smote**) *vt* (*arch*) to strike hard; to kill or injure; to have a powerful affect on. * *vi* to strike, beat or come down (on) with force.—**smiter** *n*.
smith *n* a person who works in metal; a blacksmith.
smithereens *npl* (*inf*) fragments.
smithery *n* the trade of a blacksmith.
smithy *n* (*pl* **smithies**) a blacksmith's workshop.
smitten *see* **smite**.
smock *n* a loose shirtlike outer garment to protect the clothes.
smocking *n* ornamental stitching in a honeycomb pattern.
smog *n* a mixture of fog and smoke; polluted air.—**smoggy** *adj*.
smoke *n* a cloud or plume of gas and small particles emitted from a burning substance; any similar vapour; an act of smoking tobacco, etc; (*inf*) a cigar or cigarette. * *vi* to give off smoke; to (habitually) draw in and exhale the smoke of tobacco, etc. * *vt* to fumigate; to cure food by treating with smoke; to darken (eg glass) using smoke; (*with* **out**) to flush out using smoke; to bring into public view.—**smokable, smokeable** *adj*.
smoke detector *n* an electrical device that sets off an alarm when smoke is detected.
smokeless *adj* giving off little or no smoke.
smoker *n* a person who habitually smokes tobacco; a smoking car; (*formerly*) a gathering of men to smoke.
smoke screen *n* dense smoke used to conceal military movements, etc; something designed to obscure, conceal, or disguise the truth.
smokestack *n* a tall chimney or funnel which discharges smoke or exhaust gases into the air.
smoking car *n* a train compartment where smoking is permitted.
smoky *adj* (**smokier, smokiest**) emitting smoke, esp excessively; filled with smoke; resembling smoke in appearance, flavour, smell, colour, etc.—**smokily** *adv*.—**smokiness** *n*.
smoky quartz *n* cairngorm.
smolder *see* **smoulder**.
smolt *n* a young salmon, about two years old, at the stage where it migrates to the sea for the first time.
smooch *vi* (*sl*) to kiss and cuddle, esp while dancing as a couple. * *n* (*sl*) a long kiss, an embrace.—**smoochy** *adj*.
smooth *adj* having an even or flat surface; silky; not rough or lumpy; hairless; of even consistency; calm, unruffled; gently flowing in rhythm or sound. * *vti* to make smooth; to calm; to make easier.—**smoothly** *adv*.—**smoothness** *n*.
smoothbore *n* (*firearm*) not rifled. * *n* such a gun.
smoothen *vti* to make or become smooth.
smooth-faced *adj* shaven; having a smooth surface; hypocritical.
smoothie *n* (*sl*) a person, esp a man, who is excessively suave and self-assured in speech and appearance.
smooth muscle *n* a muscle capable of regular involuntary contractions, as in the walls of the stomach and gut.
smooth-tongued *adj* persuasive in speech.
smoothy *n* (*pl* **smoothies**) (*sl*) a smoothie.
smorgasbord, smörgåsbord *n* a type of buffet or hors d'œuvres of various cold dishes of cheese, fish, salads, etc, served in Scandinavia; a restaurant specializing in this.

smote *see* **smite.**

smother *vt* to stifle, to suffocate; to put out a fire by covering it to remove the air supply; to cover over thickly; to hold back, suppress. * *vi* to undergo suffocation.—*also n.*

smoulder *vi* to burn slowly or without flame; (*feelings*) to linger on in a suppressed state; to have concealed feelings of anger, jealousy, etc.—*also* **smolder.**

smudge *n* a dirty or blurred spot or area; a fire made to produce dense smoke. * *vt* to make a smudge; to smear; to blur; to produce smoke to protect against insects, etc. * *vi* to become smudged.

smudgy *adj* blurred or dirty, smeared.—**smudgily** *adv.*—**smudginess** *n.*

smug *adj* (**smugger, smuggest**) complacent, self-satisfied.—**smugly** *adv.*—**smugness** *n.*

smuggle *vt* to import or export (goods) secretly without paying customs duties; to convey or introduce secretly.—**smuggler** *n.*

smut *n* a speck or smudge of dirt, soot, etc; indecent talk, writing, or pictures; a fungal disease of crop plants that covers the leaves in sooty spores. * *vti* (**smutting, smutted**) to stain or become stained with smut; (*crops, etc*) to infect or become infected with smut.

smut disease *n* a disease of wheat caused by fungi.

smutty *adj* (**smuttier, smuttiest**) soiled with smuts; obscene, filthy.—**smuttily** *adv.*—**smuttiness** *n.*

Sn (*chem symbol*) tin.

snack *n* a light meal between regular meals.

snaffle *n* a jointed bit for a bridle (—*also* **snaffle bit**). * *vt* (*inf*) to snatch or steal for oneself.

snafu *n* (*sl*) (*s*ituation *n*ormal *a*ll *f*ucked *u*p) a state of utter confusion. * *adj* confused, chaotic. * *vt* (**snafuing, snafued**) to cause a state of confusion or chaos.

snag *n* a sharp point or projection; a tear, as in cloth, made by a snag, etc; an unexpected or hidden difficulty. * *vti* (**snagging, snagged**) to tear, etc, on a snag; to clear of snags.

snail *n* a mollusc having a wormlike body and a spiral protective shell; a slow-moving or sluggish person or thing.

snail-paced *adj* moving very slowly.

snail's pace *n* a very slow speed or rate of progress.

snake *n* a limbless, scaly reptile with a long, tapering body and with salivary glands often modified to produce venom; a sly, treacherous person. * *vt* to twist along like a snake. * *vi* to crawl silently and stealthily.

snake charmer *n* a person who entertains by appearing to mesmerize venomous snakes by playing music.

snakeroot *n* any of various North American plants whose roots have been used to treat snakebites.

snakes and ladders *n* a British board game in which counters are moved on a grid of squares, some of which have ladders leading nearer the finish, and others snakes leading back toward the start.

snakeskin *n* the skin of a snake as used to make handbags, shoes, etc.

snakestone *n* an ammonite twisted like a ram's horn.

snakeweed *n* a herb with twisted roots, bistort.

snaky *adj* (**snakier, snakiest**) like or full of snakes; treacherous looking.—**snakily** *adv.*—**snakiness** *n.*

snap *vti* (**snapping, snapped**) to break suddenly; to make or cause to make a sudden, cracking sound; to close, fasten, etc with this sound; (*with* **at**) to bite or grasp suddenly; to speak or utter sharply. * *adj* sudden. * *n* a sharp, cracking sound; a fastener that closes with a snapping sound; a crisp biscuit; a snapshot; a sudden spell of cold weather; (*inf*) vigour, energy.

snapdragon *n* any of several plants of the figwort family with showy white, red or yellow flowers shaped like small jaws.

snap fastener *n* a press stud.

snapper *n* one who or that which snaps; (*pl* **snapper, snappers**) any of various sea fishes used as food; a snapping turtle.

snapping turtle *n* a large North American turtle with powerful jaws, a snapper.

snappy *adj* (**snappier, snappiest**) speaking sharply; brisk; lively; smart, fashionable.—**snappily** *adv.*—**snappiness** *n.*

snapshot *n* a photograph taken casually with a simple camera.

snare *n* a loop of string or wire for trapping birds or animals; something that catches one unawares, a trap; a loop of gut wound with wire stretched around a snare drum that produces a rattling sound. * *vt* to trap using a snare.

snare drum *n* a double-headed drum with snares.

snarl[1] *vi* to growl with bared teeth; to speak in a rough, angry manner. * *vt* to express in a snarling manner. * *n* the act of snarling; the sound of this.

snarl[2] *vti* to make or become entangled or complicated. * *n* a tangle; disorder.

snarl-up *n* (*inf*) an instance or state of blockage or disorder, esp a traffic jam.

snatch *vt* to seize or grasp suddenly; to take as opportunity occurs. * *n* the act of snatching; a brief period; a fragment; (*inf*) a robbery.

snazzy *adj* (**snazzier, snazziest**) (*inf*) stylish, fashionable; flashy.

sneak *vti* (**sneaking, sneaked,** *pp* (*sl*) **snuck**) to move, act, give, put, take, etc, secretly or stealthily. * *n* a person who acts secretly or stealthily; (*inf*) a person who tells or informs on others. * *adj* without warning.

sneaker *n* one who or that which sneaks; a shoe with a cloth upper and soft rubber sole, worn informally.

sneaking *adj* underhand; secret; (*suspicion, admiration, etc*) felt or thought, but not openly expressed.—**sneakingly** *adv.*

sneaky *adj* (**sneakier, sneakiest**) like a sneak; furtive; underhand.—**sneakily** *adv.*—**sneakiness** *n.*

sneer *vi* to show scorn or contempt by curling up the upper lip. * *n* a derisive look or remark.—**sneerer** *n.*—**sneeringly** *adv.*

sneeze *vi* to expel air through the nose violently and audibly. * *n* the act of sneezing.—**sneezy** *adj.*

snick *n* a tiny cut or notch; (*cricket*) a stroke of the edge of the bat. * *vt* to make a tiny cut or notch in something; to hit (a ball) with a snick.

snicker *vi* to laugh furtively and slyly, to snigger; to neigh, to whinny. * *n* a half-suppressed laugh, a giggle.—**snickeringly** *adv.*

snide *adj* malicious; superior in attitude; sneering.—**snidely** *adv.*—**snideness** *n.*

sniff *vti* to inhale through the nose audibly; to smell by sniffing; to scoff; (*with* **at**) to express dislike or contempt for. * *n* the act of sniffing; the sound of this; a smell.—**sniffer** *n.*

sniffer dog *n* a police dog trained to locate hidden drugs or explosives by smell.

sniffle *vi* to sniff repeatedly. * *n* the act or sound of sniffling.

sniffy *adj* (**sniffier, sniffiest**) (*inf*) disdainful, dismissive.—**sniffily** *adv.*—**sniffiness** *n.*

snifter *n* a glass with a wide body and narrow top to preserve the aroma of brandy or other spirits; (*inf*) a small amount of alcoholic drink.

snigger *vti* to laugh disrespectfully, to snicker.—*also n.*

snip *vti* (**snipping, snipped**) to cut or clip with a single stroke of the scissors, etc. * *n* a small piece cut off; the act or sound of snipping; (*inf*) a bargain; (*inf*) a certainty, cinch.

snipe *n* (*pl* **snipes, snipe**) any of various birds with long straight flexible bills. * *vi* to shoot snipe; to shoot at individuals from a hidden position; to make sly criticisms of.—**sniper** *n.*

snippet *n* a scrap of information.

snitch *vi* (*sl*) to inform, betray. * *vt* (*sl*) to steal, pilfer. * *n* (*sl*) an informer; the nose.—**snitcher** *n.*

snivel *vi* (**snivelling, snivelled** *or* **sniveling, sniveled**) to whine or whimper; to have a runny nose.—**sniveler, sniveller** *n.*

Sno-cat *n* (*trademark*) a vehicle designed for travelling on snow.

snob *n* a person who wishes to be associated with those of a higher social status, whilst acting condescendingly to those whom he or she regards as inferior.

snobbery *n* (*pl* **snobberies**) snobbish behaviour or attitude; a snobbish act.

snobbish *adj* pertaining to, characteristic of, or like a snob.—**snobbishly** *adv.*—**snobbishness** *n.*

SNOBOL *n* (*comput*) *S*tring *O*rientated *S*ymbolic *L*anguage: a programming language used for text (ie strings of characters) retrieval and manipulation
snog *vi* (**snogging, snogged**) (*sl*) to kiss and cuddle.—*also n.*
snood *n* a small net or fabric pouch for holding a woman's hair at the back of the head; (*Scot*) a ribbon around the hair formerly worn by unmarried girls.
snook *n* (*sl*) a gesture of contempt with the thumb to the nose and fingers spread.
snooker *n* a game played on a billiard table with 15 red balls, 6 variously coloured balls, and a white cue ball; a position in the game where a ball lies directly between the cue ball and target ball. * *vt* to place in a snooker; (*inf*) to obstruct, thwart.
snoop *vi* (*inf*) to pry about in a sneaking way. * *n* an act of snooping; a person who pries into other people's business.—**snooper** *n.*
snooperscope *n* an infrared night-vision device used by the police and military services.
snoot *n* (*sl*) the nose.
snooty *adj* (**snootier, snootiest**) haughty, snobbish.—**snootily** *adv.*—**snootiness** *n.*
snooze *vi* (*inf*) to sleep lightly. * *n* (*inf*) a nap.
snore *vi* to breathe roughly and noisily while asleep. * *n* the act or sound of snoring.
snorkel *n* a breathing tube extending above the water, used in swimming just below the surface. * *vi* (**snorkelling, snorkelled** *or* **snorkeling, snorkeled**) to swim using a snorkel.—**snorkeler** *n.*
snort *vi* to exhale noisily through the nostrils, esp as an expression of contempt or scorn. * *vt* to inhale (a drug) through the nose.
snorter *n* (*sl*) something remarkable for its size, strength, difficulty, etc.
snot *n* (*sl*) nasal mucus; (*sl*) a snotty person.
snotty *adj* (**snottier, snottiest**) covered with snot; (*sl*) irritatingly unpleasant; snobbish.—**snottily** *adv.*—**snottiness** *n.*
snout *n* the nose or muzzle of an animal.
snow *n* frozen water vapour in the form of white flakes; a snowfall; a mass of snow; (*sl*) cocaine or heroin. * *vi* to fall as snow; to deceive with smooth talk.
snowball *n* snow pressed together in a ball for throwing; a drink made with advocaat and lemonade. * *vi* to throw snowballs; to increase rapidly in size.
snowberry *n* (*pl* **snowberries**) any of various shrubs bearing white berries.
snow-blind *adj* temporarily blinded or dazzled by the intense glare of sunlight reflected from snow.—**snow-blindness** *n.*
snowblower *n* a machine for clearing snow from roads by sucking it up and blowing it off to the side.
snowbound *adj* trapped by or covered in snow.
snowcap *n* a covering of snow, as on a mountain peak.—**snowcapped** *adj.*
snowdrift *n* a bank of drifted snow.
snowdrop *n* a Eurasian plant of the daffodil family with white flowers that appears in early spring.
snowfall *n* a fall of snow; the amount of snow in a given time or area.
snowflake *n* a fragile cluster of ice crystals.
snow goose *n* a large white North American goose with black-tipped wings.
snow leopard *n* a large cat of the central Asian mountains with a tawny coat that becomes white in winter.
snow line, snow limit *n* the lowest limit in altitude of permanent snow.
snowman *n* (*pl* **snowmen**) snow piled into the shape of a human figure.
snowmobile *n* a motor vehicle for travelling at speed over snow.
snowplough, snowplow *n* a vehicle designed for clearing away snow.
snowshoe *n* footwear in the shape of a racket-like frame with thongs for walking on soft snow. * *vi* (**snowshoeing, snowshoed**) to walk on snow using snowshoes.
snowstorm *n* a storm with heavy snow.
snow tyre *n* a heavy tyre with deep treads for improved traction on snow and ice.
snow-white *adj* pure white.
snowy *adj* (**snowier, snowiest**) covered with snow; white or pure, like snow.—**snowily** *adv.*—**snowiness** *n.*
snowy owl *n* a large owl with white plumage of northern regions.
Snr, snr *abbr* = senior.
snub *vt* (**snubbing, snubbed**) to insult by ignoring or making a cutting remark. * *n* the act of snubbing; an intentional slight.
snub-nosed *adj* having a short upturned nose; (*pistol*) having a very short barrel.
snuck *see* **sneak.**
snuff[1] *n* a powdered preparation of tobacco inhaled through the nostrils.
snuff[2] *n* the charred portion of a wick. * *vt* to extinguish (a candle flame).
snuffbox *n* a small box for snuff.
snuffer *n* a cone-shaped device for putting out a candle.
snuffle *vi* to make sniffing noises, as when suffering from a cold or crying. * *n* the act of snuffling; (*pl*) a form of catarrh.
snuff movie *n* a pornographic film which ends by depicting the brutal murder of an unsuspecting participant.
snug *adj* (**snugger, snuggest**) cosy; warm; close-fitting.—**snugly** *adv.*—**snugness** *n.*
snuggle *vi* to nestle, cuddle. * *vt* to cuddle.
so[1] *adv* in this way; as shown; as stated; to such an extent; very; (*inf*) very much; therefore; more or less; also, likewise; then.
so[2] *see* **sol.**
soak *vt* to submerge in a liquid; to take in, absorb; (*sl*) to extract large amounts of money from. * *vi* to become saturated; to penetrate. * *n* the act or process of soaking.
so-and-so *n* (*pl* **so-and-sos**) an unspecified person or thing; (*inf*) (*euphemism*) an unpleasant or disliked person or thing.
soap *n* a substance used with water to produce suds for washing; (*inf*) a soap opera. * *vt* to rub with soap.—**soapy** *adj.*
soapberry *n* (*pl* **soapberries**) any of various tropical American trees bearing fruit which are rich in saponin.
soapbox *n* a temporary platform from which to deliver informal speeches.
soap opera *n* (*inf*) a daytime radio or television serial melodrama.
soapstone *n* a type of soft grey-green stone with a soapy texture.—*also* **steatite.**
soapwort *n* a Eurasian herbaceous plant of the pink family whose leaves form a soapy lather with water.
soapy *adj* (**soapier, soapiest**) like or full of soap; flattering, unctuous.—**soapily** *adv.*—**soapiness** *n.*
soar *vi* to rise high in the air; to glide along high in the air; to increase; to rise in status.—**soarer** *n.*
sob *vb* (**sobbing, sobbed**) *vi* to weep with convulsive gasps. * *vt* to speak while sobbing.
sober *adj* not drunk; serious and thoughtful; realistic, rational; subdued in colour. * *vt* (*often with* **up** *or* **down**) to make or become sober.—**soberly** *adv.*—**soberness** *n.*
sobriety *n* soberness; temperance; seriousness.
sobriquet *n* a nickname.—*also* **soubriquet.**
sob story *n* (*inf*) a tale of distress intended to arouse sympathy.
Soc., soc. *abbr* = socialist; society.
so-called *adj* commonly named or known as.
soccer *n* a football game played on a field by two teams of 11 players with a round inflated ball, association football.
sociable *adj* friendly; companionable.—**sociability** *n.*—**sociably** *adv.*
social *adj* living or organized in a community, not solitary; relating to human beings living in society; of or intended for communal activities; sociable. * *n* an informal gathering of people, such as a party.—**socially** *adv.*
social anthropology *n* the branch of anthropology that studies social and cultural systems and beliefs.
social climber *n* a person who strives to attain a higher social position.
social contract, social compact *n* a tacit agreement between individuals in society and between individuals and the government which defines the rights and duties of each.

Social Democratic Party *n* a political party that advocates the transition from capitalism to socialism in a gradual manner.—**Social Democrat** *n*.—**Social Democratic** *adj*.
social disease *n* venereal disease.
socialism *n* (a system based on) a political and economic theory advocating state ownership of the means of production and distribution.—**socialist** *n, adj*.—**socialistic** *adj*.—**socialistically** *adv*.
socialite *n* a person active or prominent in fashionable society.
socialize *vt* to meet other people socially.—**socialization** *n*.—**socializer** *n*.
social science *n* the study of human social organization and relationships using scientific methods.
social security *n* financial assistance for the unemployed, the disabled, etc to alleviate economic distress.
social service *n* a welfare service provided by the state, such as housing, education, and health.—**social-service** *adj*.
social work *n* any of various professional welfare services to aid the underprivileged in society.—**social worker** *n*.
society *n* (*pl* **societies**) the social relationships between human beings or animals organized collectively; the system of human institutional organization; a community with the same language and customs; an interest group or organization; the fashionable or privileged members of a community; companionship.—**societal** *adj*.
Society of Friends *n* the official name for the Quakers.
Society of Jesus *n* the Roman Catholic religious order of the Jesuits.
socio- *prefix* society; social.
sociobiology *n* the study of human and animal social behaviour.—**sociobiological** *adj*.—**sociobiologist** *n*.
socioeconomic *adj* of or involving social and economic aspects.
sociolinguistics *n sing* the study of the social and cultural context of language.—**sociolinguist** *n*.
sociology *n* the study of the development and structure of society and social relationships.—**sociological** *adj*.—**sociologically** *adv*.—**sociologist** *n*.
sociometry *n* the study of social relations within small groups.—**sociometric** *adj*.
sociopath *n* a person suffering from a mental disorder that results in antisocial behaviour and lack of guilt.—**sociopathic** *adj*.
sociopolitical *adj* of or involving social and political aspects.
sock[1] *n* a kind of short stocking covering the foot and lower leg.
sock[2] *vt* (*sl*) to punch hard. * *n* a blow.
socket *n* a hollow part into which something is inserted, such as an eye, a bone, a tooth, an electric plug, etc.
sockeye *n* a Pacific salmon valued as a food fish.—*also* **red salmon.**
Socratic *adj* of or relating to Socrates (*c*. 470–399 bc), the Greek philosopher, or his methods. * *n* an adherent of Socrates or his philosophy.
Socratic irony *n* feigning ignorance when posing questions to expose the real ignorance of the person responding.
Socratic method *n* philosophical instruction by means of question and answer.
sod[1] *n* a lump of earth covered with grass; turf. * *vt* (**sodding, sodded**) to cover with turf.
sod[2] *n* (*sl*) an obnoxious person; (*loosely*) a person, man. * *vi* (**sodding, sodded**) (*Brit sl*) to damn; (*with* **off**) (*sl*) to go away.—*also interj*.
soda *n* sodium bicarbonate; sodium carbonate; soda water.
soda bread *n* bread made with baking soda instead of yeast.
soda fountain *n* a counter selling soft drinks, ice cream, snacks, etc; a device that dispenses soda water.
soda siphon *n* a pressurized container that dispenses soda water.
soda water *n* a fizzy drink made by charging water with carbon dioxide under pressure.
sodden *adj* completely soaked through.—**soddenly** *adv*.
sodium *n* a metallic element.
sodium bicarbonate *n* a white soluble alkaline powder used in baking powder, fire extinguishers and in antacid medicines.
sodium chloride *n* salt.
sodium hydroxide *n* a white alkaline solid used in the manufacture of soap, paper and rayon.
sodium nitrate *n* a white crystalline compound used in fertilizers, matches and explosives, and as a food preservative.
sodium-vapour lamp *n* an electric lamp using sodium vapour through which a current is passed to produce an orange light, esp used for street lighting.
Sodom *n* (*Bible*) a wicked city destroyed by God; a wicked and depraved place.
sodomite *n* a person who practises sodomy.
sodomy *n* anal sexual intercourse between males or between a man and woman.
sofa *n* an upholstered couch or settee with fixed back and arms.
soffit *n* the underside of a structural element, such as an arch, stairway, balcony, etc.
soft *adj* malleable; easily cut, shaped, etc; not as hard as normal, desirable, etc; smooth to the touch; (*drinks*) nonalcoholic; mild, as a breeze; lenient; (*sl*) easy, comfortable; (*colour, light*) not bright; (*sound*) gentle, low; (*drugs*) non-addictive.—**softly** *adv*.—**softness** *n*.
softball *n* a game similar to baseball, but played with a larger, softer ball.
soft-boiled *adj* (*egg*) boiled so that the white hardens while the yolk remains soft.
soft-core *adj* (*pornography*) not sexually explicit.
softcover *adj* paperback. * *n* a paperback book.
soft drink *n* a nonalcoholic drink.
soften *vti* to make or become soft or softer.—**softener** *n*.
soft-focus *adj* (*lens*) designed to produce a slightly blurred image.
soft furnishings *npl* items such as curtains, carpets, rugs, etc.
soft goods *npl* textile and clothing products.
softheaded *adj* stupid, feeble-minded.—**softheadedly** *adv*.—**softheadedness** *n*.
softhearted *adj* kind; sentimental.—**softheartedly** *adv*.—**softheartedness** *n*.
soft landing *n* a landing by a spacecraft which leaves the vehicle and occupants undamaged.
soft option *n* the easiest choice in a range of alternatives.
soft palate *n* the fleshy area at the back of the roof of the mouth.
soft paste *n* a type of translucent porcelain made from refined clay, ground glass, bone ash, etc.
soft-pedal *n* a pedal on a piano for muting the tone. * *vt* (*inf*) (**soft-pedalling, soft-pedalled** *or* **soft-pedaling, soft-pedaled**) to avoid direct reference to, esp something embarrassing or unpleasant.
soft porn *n* (*inf*) soft-core pornography.
soft sell *n* selling by gentle persuasion.—**soft-sell** *adj*.
soft soap *n* a type of semisolid or liquid soap; (*inf*) flattery.
soft-soap *vt* (*inf*) to flatter.—**soft-soaper** *n*.
soft spot *n* a sentimental fondness (for).
soft touch *n* (*inf*) a person who is easily persuaded or exploited.
software *n* the programs used in computers.
softwood *n* the wood of any coniferous tree.
softy *n* (*pl* **softies**) (*inf*) a person regarded as sentimental or physically weak.
soggy *adj* (**soggier, soggiest**) soaked with water; moist and heavy.—**soggily** *adv*.—**sogginess** *n*.
soi-disant *adj* self-styled.
soigné, soignée *adj* well-groomed; elegant.
soil[1] *n* the ground or earth in which plants grow; territory.
soil[2] *vt* to make or become dirty or stained.
soil pipe *n* a sewage or waste-water pipe.
soiree, soirée *n* an evening party of music in a private house.
soixante-neuf *n* a sexual position that facilitates mutual cunnilingus and fellatio; sixty-nine.
sojourn *n* a temporary stay. * *vi* to stay for a short time.—**sojourner** *n*.
sol[1] *n* (*mus*) the name for the fifth note of the diatonic scale —*also* **so.**
sol[2] *n* liquid in which a colloid is dissolved or suspended.
sol. *abbr* = soluble; solution.

solace *n* comfort in misery; consolation. * *vt* to bring solace to.
solar *adj* of or from the sun; powered by light or heat from the sun; reckoned by the sun.
solar cell *n* a cell that converts the sun's rays into electricity.
solar constant *n* the quantity of sun's energy radiated onto a given area of the earth's surface in a prescribed period.
solar day *n* the period of time during which the earth makes a complete revolution relative to the sun.
solar flare *n* a sudden brief eruption of intense energy from the sun's surface.
solarium *n* (*pl* **solariums, solaria**) a glass-enclosed room for sunbathing or exposure to the sun for medical treatment.
solar month *n* the period of time taken for the moon to make one complete revolution around the earth (approx. 27 days).
solar panel *n* a large thin panel that absorbs energy from sunlight and regenerates it.
solar plexus *n* the network of nerves behind the stomach; (*inf*) the pit of the stomach.
solar pond *n* a shallow artificial pond of salt water covered by fresh water, which absorbs heat from the sun's rays and converts it to electricity.
solar system *n* the sun and those bodies moving about it under the attraction of gravity.
solar wind *n* the constant flow of charged particles from the sun into outer space.
solar year *n* the period of time taken for the earth to make one revolution around the sun.
sold *see* **sell.**
solder *n* a metal alloy used when melted to join or patch metal parts, etc. * *vti* to join or be joined with solder.
soldering iron *n* an electrically heated tool for melting and applying solder.
soldier *n* a person who serves in an army, esp a non-commissioned officer or private. * *vi* to serve as a soldier; (*with* **on**) to continue regardless of difficulties or dangers.—**soldierly** *adj*.
soldier of fortune *n* a man in constant search of military adventure; a mercenary.
soldiery *n* (*pl* **soldieries**) soldiers collectively; a body of soldiers; the profession of being a soldier.
sole[1] *n* the underside of the foot or shoe. * *vt* to put a new sole on (a shoe).
sole[2] *n* (*pl* **sole, soles**) a type of flatfish used as food.
sole[3] *adj* only, being the only one; exclusive.—**solely** *adv*.
solecism *n* an error in speech or writing; a breach of etiquette or good manners.
solemn *adj* serious; formal; sacred; performed with religious ceremony.—**solemnly** *adv*.—**solemnness** *n*.
solemnity *n* (*pl* **solemnities**) solemness; a formal rite.
solenoid *n* a coil of wire that produces a magnetic field when an electric current is passed through it.—**solenoidal** *adj*.
sol-fa see tonic sol-fa.
sol-fa syllable *n* any of the syllables (*do*, *re*, *mi*, etc) used to represent the notes of the musical scale in tonic sol-fa or solmization
solfatara *n* a volcanic outlet that emits only (sulphurous) gases and (water) vapours.
solfeggio *n* (*pl* **solfeggi, solfeggios**) (*singing using*) the application of the sol-fa syllables to musical scales or melody.
solicit *vti* to make a request or application to (a person for something); (*prostitute*) to offer sexual services for money.—**solicitation** *n*.
solicitor *n* a lawyer.
solicitous *adj* showing concern or attention.—**solicitously** *adv*.—**solicitousness** *n*.
solicitude *n* the state of being solicitous; concern; anxiety; carefulness.
solid *adj* firm; compact; not hollow; strongly constructed; having three dimensions; neither liquid nor gaseous; unanimous. * *n* a solid substance (not liquid or gas); a three-dimensional figure.—**solidly** *adv*.—**solidness** *n*.
solidarity *n* (*pl* **solidarities**) unity of interest and action.
solid geometry *n* geometry of three-dimensional figures.
solidi *see* **solidus.**
solidify *vti* (**solidifying, solidified**) to make or become solid, compact, hard, etc.—**solidification** *n*.
solidity *n* the state of being solid; density; compactness; stability; truth; moral firmness.
solid-state *adj* (*electronic devices*) using components, such as transistors, in which the current flow is through solid materials as opposed to a vacuum; of or relating to solids or their properties and characteristics.
solid-state physics *n sing* the physics of the properties of solids.
solidus *n* (*pl* **solidi**) an oblique stroke (/) used to separate items of text as in dates, alternative words, lists, or the terms of fractions.
soliloquize *vt* to utter a soliloquy. * *vi* to talk to oneself.—**soliloquist** *n*.
soliloquy *n* (*pl* **soliloquies**) the act of talking to oneself; an act or speech in a play that takes this form.
solipsism *n* (*philos*) the theory that the only possible true knowledge is of self-existence.—**solipsistic** *adj*.—**solipsist** *n*.
solitaire *n* a single gemstone, esp a diamond; a card game for one, patience.
solitary *adj* alone; only; single; living alone; lonely. * *n* (*pl* **solitaries**) a recluse.—**solitarily** *adv*.—**solitariness** *n*.
solitude *n* the state of being alone; lack of company; a lonely place.—**solitudinous** *adj*.
solmization *n* (*mus*) the use of syllables to name the notes or degrees of a musical scale.
solo *n* (*pl* **solos**) a musical composition for one voice or instrument; a flight by a single person in an aircraft, esp a first flight. * *vi* to perform by oneself. * *adv* alone. * *adj* unaccompanied.—**soloist** *n*.
so long *interj* (*inf*) goodbye, farewell.
solo whist *n* a form of whist in which any player may bid independently to win or lose a prescribed number of tricks.
solstice *n* either of the two times in the year at which the sun is farthest from the equator (June 21 and December 21).—**solsticial** *adj*.
soluble *adj* capable of being dissolved (usu in water); capable of being solved or answered.—**solubility** *n*.—**solubly** *adv*.
solute *n* a dissolved substance in a solution.
solution *n* the act or process of answering a problem; the answer found; the dispersion of one substance in another, usu a liquid, so as to form a homogeneous mixture.
solvable *adj* capable of being solved.—**solvability** *n*.
solve *vt* to work out the answer to; to clear up, resolve.
solvent *adj* capable of dissolving a substance; able to pay all debts. * *n* a liquid that dissolves substances.—**solvency** *n*.
solvent abuse *n* the deliberate inhalation of fumes from solvents (such as in glue and polish) to become intoxicated.
soma *n* (*pl* **somatas, somas**) all of an organism except the germ cells.
Somali *n* (*pl* **Somalis, Somali**) a native or inhabitant of Somalia; the Somali language.—*also adj*.—**Somalian** *adj*.
somatic *adj* of or relating to the body, as opposed to the mind.—**somatically** *adv*.
somato-, somat- *prefix* body.
somatotype *n* physical build, body type.
sombre, somber *adj* dark, gloomy or dull; dismal; sad.—**sombrely, somberly** *adv*.—**sombreness, somberness** *n*.
sombrero *n* (*pl* **sombreros**) a wide-brimmed hat with a high crown, worn esp in Spanish-speaking countries.
some *adj* certain but not specified or known; of a certain unspecified quantity, degree, etc; a little; (*inf*) remarkable, striking, etc. * *pron* a certain unspecified quantity, number, etc.
-some *adj suffix* apt to, eg *tiresome*. * *n suffix* a group of, eg *foursome*.
somebody *n* (*pl* **somebodies**) an unspecified person; an important person. * *pron* someone.

someday *adv* at some future day or time.

somehow *adv* in a way or by a method not known or stated.

someone *n* somebody.—*also pron.*

someplace *adv* somewhere.

somersault *n* a forward or backward roll head over heels along the ground or in mid-air.—*also vi.*

something *n, pron* a thing not definitely known, understood, etc; an important or notable thing. * *adv* to some degree.

sometime *adj* former. * *adv* at some unspecified future date. * *adj* having been formerly; being so occasionally or in only some respects.

sometimes *adv* at times, now and then.

someway *adv* in a certain unspecified manner.

somewhat *adv* to some extent, degree, etc; a little.

somewhere, somewheres *adv* in, to or at some place not known or specified.

sommelier *n* a wine waiter.

somnambulate *vi* to get up and walk while asleep.—**somnambulant** *adj.*—**somnambulation** *n.*

somnambulism *n* the practice of walking in one's sleep.—**somnambulist** *n.*—**somnambulistic** *adj.*

somnolent *adj* sleepy, drowsy.—**somnolence, somnolency** *n.*

son *n* a male offspring or descendant.

sonar *n* an apparatus that detects underwater objects by means of reflecting sound waves.

sonata *n* (*mus*) a composition for a solo instrument, usu the piano.

sondage *n* (*archaeol*) a deep inspection trench.

sonde *n* a device for collecting scientific data in the upper atmosphere.

sone *n* a unit of loudness equivalent to 40 phons.

son et lumière *n* an evening entertainment staged at historical sites and buildings using lighting displays, music and recorded speech to illuminate the history of the place.

song *n* a piece of music composed for the voice; the act or process of singing; the call of certain birds.

song and dance *n* (*inf*) a fuss; a long involved story.

songbird *n* a bird with a musical call.

songster *n* a singer; a songbird—**songstress** *nf.*

sonic *adj* of, producing, or involving sound waves.—**sonically** *adv.*

sonic barrier *n* the increase in air resistance experienced by objects travelling close to the speed of sound, the sound barrier.

sonic boom *n* an explosive sound produced by the shockwave when an aircraft, etc reaches supersonic speed.

son-in-law *n* (*pl* **sons-in-law**) a daughter's husband.

sonnet *n* a rhyming poem in a single stanza of fourteen lines.

sonneteer *n* a composer of sonnets.

sonny *n* (*pl* **sonnies**) a patronizing form of address to a boy.

sonobuoy *n* a buoy used to detect underwater sounds and transmit them by radio to surface vessels.

sonorous *adj* giving out sound; full, rich, or deep in sound.—**sonorously** *adv.*—**sonorousness** *n.*

soon *adv* in a short time; before long; **sooner or later** at some future unspecified time, eventually.

soot *n* a black powder produced from flames.—**sooty** *adj.*

soothe *vt* to calm or comfort; to alleviate; to relieve (pain, etc).—**soothing** *adj.*—**soothingly** *adv.*

soothsayer *n* a person who predicts events.

SOP *abbr* = standard operating procedure.

sop *n* a piece of bread or other food dipped in liquid before being eaten; a concession, bribe offered to appease or cajole. * *vt* (**sopping, sopped**) to dip (bread, etc) into liquid. * *vi* to be soaked.

sop. *abbr* = soprano.

soph *abbr* = sophomore.

sophism *n* a clever but fallacious argument.—**sophistry** *n.*—**sophist** *n.*—**sophistic, sophistical** *adj.*

sophisticated *adj* refined; worldly-wise; intelligent; complex.—**sophistication** *n.*

sophomore *n* in US, a second-year student at college or high school.—**sophomoric** *adj.*

soporific *adj* inducing sleep; sleepy.

sopping *adj* wet through.

soppy *adj* (**soppier, soppiest**) wet; (*inf*) sickly sentimental.—**soppily** *adv.*—**soppiness** *n.*

sopranino *n* (*pl* **sopraninos**) a musical instrument of the highest pitch in its class.

soprano *n* (*pl* **sopranos, soprani**) the highest singing voice of females or boys; a person who sings soprano.

sorbet *n* a flavoured water ice; sherbet.

sorcerer *n* person who uses magic powers; a magician or wizard.—**sorceress** *nf.*

sorcery *n* (*pl* **sorceries**) the practice of magic, esp with the assistance of evil spirits.

sordid *adj* filthy, squalid; vile; base; selfish.—**sordidly** *adv.*—**sordidness** *n.*

sordino *n* (*pl* **sordini**) a mute for a stringed or brass musical instrument.

sore *n* a painful or tender injury or wound; an ulcer or boil; grief; a cause of distress. * *adj* painful; tender; distressed.—**soreness** *n.*

sorehead *n* (*inf*) an angry, disgruntled person.

sorely *adv* seriously, urgently.

sorghum *n* any of a genus of tropical cereal grasses grown for fodder.

sorority *n* (*pl* **sororities**) a society of women university students.

sorrel[1] *n* a colour between orange-brown and light brown; an animal, esp a horse, of this colour.

sorrel[2] *n* a herb with bitter leaves used in salads.

sorrow *n* sadness; regret; an expression of grief. * *vi* to mourn, to grieve.

sorrowful *adj* full of, showing or causing sorrow.—**sorrowfully** *adv.*—**sorrowfulness** *n.*

sorry *adj* (**sorrier, sorriest**) feeling pity, sympathy, remorse or regret; pitiful; poor.—**sorrily** *adv.*—**sorriness** *n.*

sort *n* a class, kind, or variety; quality or type. * *vt* to arrange according to kind; to classify; (*with* **out**) to find a solution to, resolve; to disentangle; to organize, discipline; (*inf*) to punish, to attack violently.—**sorter** *n.*

sortie *n* a sudden attack by troops from a besieged position; one mission by a single military plane.

SOS *n* an international signal code of distress; an urgent call for help or rescue.

so-so *adj* not good but not bad, middling. * *adv* average, indifferently.

sot *n* a habitual drunkard.

soteriology *n* (*theol*) the doctrine of salvation, esp through Jesus Christ.—**soteriological** *adj.*

sotto voce *adv* in an undertone.

sou *n* (*pl* **sous**) (*formerly*) a French coin of little value; a very small sum of money.

soubrette *n* a minor female role in a comedy, esp a pert lady's maid; a saucy girl.

soubriquet *see* **sobriquet.**

soufflé *n* a baked dish made light and puffy by adding beaten egg whites before baking.—*also adj.*

sough *vi* to make a moaning sound like the wind.—*also n.*

sought *see* **seek.**

souk *n* an open-air market in Muslim countries.

soul *n* a person's spirit; the seat of the emotions, desires; essence; character; a human being. * *adj* characteristic of American Blacks.

soul-destroying *adj* extremely boring, depressing.

soul food *n* (*inf*) traditional food (eg yams, chitterlings) eaten by Blacks of the Southern US.

soulful *adj* expressing profound sentiment.—**soulfully** *adv.*—**soulfulness** *n.*

soulless *adj* devoid of emotion; bleak; dull.

soul mate *n* a person, such as a lover or close friend, with whom one bonds deeply.

soul music *n* music derived from Afro-American gospel singing marked by intensity of feeling and closely related to rhythm and blues.

soul-searching *n* close examination of one's conscience, motives, etc.

sound[1] *adj* healthy; free from injury or damage; substantial; stable; deep (as sleep) solid; thorough.—**soundly** *adv*.—**soundness** *n*.

sound[2] *n* a narrow channel of water connecting two seas or between a mainland and an island.

sound[3] *n* vibrations transmitted through the air and detected by the ear; the sensation of hearing; any audible noise; the impression given by something. * *vi* to make a sound; to give a summons by sound. * *vt* to cause to make a sound; to voice; to make a signal or order by sound; (*with* **off**) (*inf*) to complain loudly.

sound[4] *vt* to measure the depth of; (*often with* **out**) to attempt to discover the opinions and intentions of (someone).

sound barrier *n* the increase in air resistance experienced by objects travelling close to the speed of sound, the sonic barrier.

sound board *n* a thin board in certain musical instruments that resonates to enhance the sound; a sounding board.

soundbox *n* the hollow resonating cavity of a musical instrument such as a guitar or violin.

sound effects *npl* artificial sounds used for dramatic purposes in plays, television programmes, films, etc.

sounding[1] *n* measurement of the depth of water; a test, sampling, eg of public opinion.

sounding[2] *adj* resounding.

sounding board *n* a thin board placed behind a platform to direct the sound at the audience; a sound board; a person or thing used to test reaction to a new idea or plan.

sounding line *n* a line marked at regular intervals for sounding.

soundproof *adj* unable to be penetrated by sound. * *vt* to make soundproof by insulation, etc.

soundtrack *n* the sound accompanying a film; the area on cinema film that carries the sound recording.

soup *n* a liquid food made from boiling meat, fish, vegetables, etc, in water; (*inf*) a difficult or embarrassing situation. * *vt* (*with* **up** (*inf*) to increase the power and performance of an engine.—**soupy** *adj*.

soup on *n* a slight flavour; a trace.

soup kitchen *n* a place where soup and other food is dispensed to the homeless and destitute.

sour adj having a sharp, biting taste; spoiled by fermentation; cross; bad-tempered; distasteful or unpleasant; (*soil*) acid in reaction. * *vti* to make or become sour.—**sourly** *adv*.—**sourness** *n*.

source *n* a spring forming the head of a stream; an origin or cause; a person, book, etc, that provides information. * *vti* (*inf*) to find a supplier; to identify a source.

source program *n* (*comput*) an original program that has been translated into machine code.

sour cream *n* cream deliberately soured by bacteria and used in sauces, dressings, etc.

sourdough *n* dough used in more than one baking to save on fresh yeast; a prospector in North America who lived on bread made from sourdough.

sour grapes *n sing* pretending to dislike something because it cannot be obtained or achieved by oneself.

sourpuss *n* (*inf*) a gloomy person.

souse *vt* to immerse in water or other liquid; to saturate; to pickle or steep in a marinade; (*sl*) to make drunk. * *vi* to become saturated or immersed. * *n* the act of sousing; something pickled; pickling liquid; (*sl*) a drunkard.

soutane *n* a cassock.

south *n* the direction to one's right when facing the direction of the rising sun; the region, country, continent, etc, lying relatively in that direction. * *adj, adv* facing toward or situated in the south.

Southdown *n* a breed of hornless sheep that yields wool and esp meat.

southeast *n* the point on a compass midway between south and east. * *adj, adv* at, toward, or from the southeast.

southeasterly *adj, adv* toward or from the southeast. * *n* (*pl* **southeasterlies**) a wind from the southeast.

southeastern *adj* in, toward, or from the southeast; inhabiting or characteristic of the southeast.—**southeasterner** *n*.

southerly *adj* in, toward, or from the south. * *n* (*pl* **southerlies**) a wind from the south.

southern *adj* in, toward, or from the south; inhabiting or characteristic of the south.—**southernmost** *adj*.

southerner *n* an inhabitant of the south.

southern lights *npl* the aurora australis.

southpaw *n* (*inf*) a left-handed boxer; a left-handed person.—*also adj*.

South Pole *n* the most southerly point on the earth's axis; the most southerly point on the celestial sphere; (*without caps*) the pole of a magnet that points south.

southward *adj* toward the south.—**southwards** *adv*.

southwest *n* the point on a compass midway between south and west. * *adj, adv* at, toward, or from the southwest.

southwester *n* a strong wind from the southwest.

southwesterly *adj, adv* toward or from the southwest. * *n* (*pl* **southwesterlies**) a wind from the southwest.

southwestern *adj* in, toward, or from the southwest; inhabiting or characteristic of the southwest.—**southwesterner** *n*.

souvenir *n* a keepsake, a memento.

sou'wester *n* a waterproof hat with a wide brim at the back worn by sailors.

sovereign *adj* supreme in authority or rank; (*country, state, etc*) independent. * *n* a supreme ruler; a monarch.—**sovereignty** *n*.

soviet *n* a workers' council in the former USSR.

sovietism *n* a political system of which the soviet is the unit.

sow[1] *n* an adult female pig.

sow[2] *vt* (**sowing, sowed,** *pp* **sown** *or* **sowed**) to plant or scatter seed on or in the ground; to disseminate; to implant.—**sower** *n*.

soya bean, soybean *n* a type of bean (orig from Asia) used as a source of food and oil.

soy sauce, soya sauce *n* a dark, salty sauce made from fermented soybeans.

sozzled *adj* (*inf*) drunk.

sp *abbr* = species.

Sp. *abbr* = Spain; Spaniard; Spanish.

spa *n* a mineral spring; a resort where there is a mineral spring.

space *n* the limitless three-dimensional expanse within which all objects exist; outer space; a specific area; an interval, empty area; room; an unoccupied area or seat. * *vt* to arrange at intervals.

Space Age *n* the era when space exploration has become possible.

space-age *adj* of or pertaining to the Space Age; modern.

space bar *n* the long bar on a typewriter or computer keyboard for inserting spaces.

spacecraft *n* a vehicle for travel in outer space.

spaced-out, spaced *adj* (sl) high on drugs.

spaceman *n* (*pl* **spacemen**) a person who travels in outer space; an alien.—**spacewoman** (*pl* **spacewomen**) *nf*.

space probe *n* an unmanned rocket equipped for exploring outer space.

spaceship *n* a crewed spacecraft.

space shuttle *n* a manned spacecraft designed as a reusable ferry between the earth and a space station.

space station, space platform *n* a manned artificial satellite designed to orbit the earth and serve as a permanent base for space exploration.

spacesuit *n* a sealed and pressurized suit worn by astronauts in space.

space-time (continuum) *n* (*physics*) the four-dimensional coordinate system comprising the three spatial and one temporal coordinates which together define a continuum in which any particle or event may be located.

spacewalk *n* a period of time spent by an astronaut floating in space outside a spacecraft. * *vi* to walk in space.—**spacewalker** *n*.

spacious *adj* large in extent; roomy.—**spaciously** *adv*.—**spaciousness** *n*.

spade[1] *n* a tool with a broad blade and a handle, used for digging.

spade[2] *n* a black symbol resembling a stylized spearhead marking one of the four suits of playing cards; a card of this suit.

spadework *n* routine preliminary work.
spadix *n* (*pl* **spadixes, spadices**) a spike of flowers clustered around a fleshy stem and enclosed in a spathe.
spaghetti *n* pasta made in thin, solid strings.
spaghetti western *n* a type of violent cowboy film, usu shot on location in Italy or Spain, which became popular in the 1960s.
spake (*arch*) *pt of* **speak.**
Spam *n* (*trademark*) tinned pork luncheon meat.
span *n* a unit of length equal to a hand's breadth (about 9 inches/23 cm); the full extent between any two limits, such as the ends of a bridge or arch. * *vt* (**spanning, spanned**) to extend across.
Span. *abbr* = Spanish.
spandrel *n* the space between the right or left shoulder of an arch and the rectangular wall or moulding enclosing it.
spangle *n* a sequin or other small piece of shiny decoration; any small glittering particle. * *vt* to decorate with spangles. * *vi* to sparkle with or like spangles.—**spangly** *adj*.
Spaniard *n* a native or inhabitant of Spain.
spaniel *n* any of various breeds of dog with large drooping ears and a long silky coat.
Spanish *adj* of or pertaining to Spain. * *n* the language of Spain and Spanish Americans; the people of Spain.
Spanish-American *adj* of or pertaining to the countries in America where Spanish is spoken. * *n* a native or inhabitant of a Spanish-American country.
Spanish fly *n* a European blister beetle; a substance prepared from dried Spanish fly (cantharides) which purportedly acts as an aphrodisiac.
Spanish guitar *n* a type of classical acoustic guitar music; the guitar used to play this.
Spanish omelette *n* an omelette containing chopped vegetables such as onions, tomatoes, pimentoes, etc.
spank *vt* to slap with the flat of the hand, esp on the buttocks.—*also n*.
spanking *adj* (*inf*) very impressive, large, smart, etc; (*inf*) brisk, lively.—*also adv*.
spanner *n* a tool with a hole or (often adjustable) jaws to grip and turn nuts or bolts, a wrench.
spar[1] *n* a pole supporting the rigging of a ship; one of the main structural members of the wing of an airplane.
spar[2] *vi* to box using gentle blows, as in training; to argue.—*also n*.
spare *vt* to refrain from harming or killing; to afford; to make (something) available (eg time). * *adj* kept as an extra, additional; scanty. * *n* a spare part; a spare tyre —**sparely** *adv*.—**spareness** *n*.
sparerib *n* a pork rib with most of the meat cut away.
spare tyre *n* (*inf*) a roll of excess fat around the waist.
sparing *adj* frugal, economical.—**sparingly** *adv*.—**sparingness** *n*.
spark *n* a fiery or glowing particle thrown off by burning material or by friction; a flash of light from an electrical discharge; a trace. * *vt* to stir up; to activate. * *vi* to give off sparks.
sparking plug *n* a spark plug.
sparkle *n* a spark; vivacity. * *vi* to shine; to glitter; (*water, wine*) to effervesce; to be lively or witty.
sparkler *n* a handheld firework that throws off brilliant sparks; (*inf*) a diamond.
spark plug *n* a device that produces a spark to ignite the explosive mixture in an internal combustion engine.—*also* **sparking plug.**
sparring partner *n* (*boxing*) a partner who stands in as an opponent for training purposes; a person with whom one regularly argues.
sparrow *n* any of various small brownish songbirds related to the finch.
sparse *adj* spread out thinly; scanty.—**sparsely** *adv*.—**sparseness, sparsity** *n*.
Spartan *adj* of or pertaining to Sparta in ancient Greece; rigourously severe.
spasm *n* a sudden, involuntary muscular contraction; any sudden burst (of emotion or activity).—**spasmodic** *adj* intermittent; of or like a spasm.—**spasmodically** *adv*.
spastic *n* a person who suffers from cerebral palsy. * *adj* affected by muscle spasm.—**spasticity** *n*.
spat[1] *see* **spit**[2].
spat[2] *n* a gaiter covering the ankle and instep and fastening under the shoe.
spat[3] *n* a young oyster or other bivalve mollusc.
spat[4] *n* a petty argument, or quarrel. * *vi* to have a petty argument.
spate *n* a large amount; a sudden outburst (as of words); a sudden flood.
spathe *n* a leafy part that encloses the floral spikes of certain flowers.
spatial *adj* relating to space.—**spatially** *adv*.
spatiotemporal *adj* of, involving, or occurring in both space and time; of or pertaining to space-time.
spatter *vti* to scatter or spurt out in drops; to splash.—*also n*.
spatula *n* a tool with a broad, flexible blade for spreading or mixing foods, paints, etc.
spatulate *adj* shaped like a spatula.
spawn *n* a mass of eggs deposited by fish, frogs, or amphibians; offspring. * *vti* to lay eggs; to produce, esp in great quantity.
spay *vt* (*female animals*) to sterilize by removing the ovaries from.
SPCA *abbr* = Society for the Prevention of Cruelty to Animals.
SPCC *abbr* = Society for the Prevention of Cruelty to Children.
speak *vi* (**speaking, spoke,** *pp* **spoken**) to utter words; to talk; to converse with; to deliver a speech; to be suggestive of something; to produce a characteristic sound; (*with* **out, up**) to speak loudly; to express an opinion frankly.—**speakable** *adj*.
speakeasy *n* (*pl* **speakeasies**) a club where alcoholic drink was sold illegally during the Prohibition era in the US in the 1920s.
speaker *n* a person who speaks, esp before an audience; the presiding official in a legislative assembly; a loudspeaker.
speaking clock *n* a recorded telephone message which gives the time.
spear *n* a weapon with a long shaft and a sharp point; a blade or shoot (of grass, broccoli, etc). * *vt* to pierce with a spear.
spearhead *n* the pointed head of a spear; the leading person or group in an attack or other action. * *vt* to serve as a leader of.
spearmint *n* a common mint plant which yields an oil used for flavouring.
special *adj* distinguished; uncommon; designed for a particular purpose; peculiar to one person or thing.—**specially** *adv*.
Special Branch *n* the division of the British police force that deals with political security.
specialist *n* a person who concentrates on a particular area of study or activity, esp in medicine.
speciality *n* (*pl* **specialities**) a special skill or interest; a special product.—*also* **specialty.**
specialize *vi* to concentrate on a particular area of study or activity. * *vt* to adapt to a particular use or purpose.—**specialization** *n*.
special licence *n* in the UK, a licence allowing a marriage to take place without regard to the normal legal requirements.
special pleading *n* (*law*) the allegation of new facts in an action as opposed to a direct denial or admission of the opposition evidence; arguments that concentrate on the positive as opposed to the negative aspects of a case.
specialty *see* **speciality.**
speciation *n* the evolution of a species.—**speciate** *vi*.
specie *n* money in coin.
species *n* (*pl* **species**) a class of plants or animals with the same main characteristics, enabling interbreeding; a distinct kind or sort.
specific *adj* explicit; definite; of a particular kind. * *n* a characteristic quality or influence; a drug effective in treating a particular disease.—**specifically** *adv*.—**specificity** *n*.
specification *n* a requirement; (*pl*) detailed description of dimensions, materials, etc of something.
specific gravity *n* the ratio of the density of a substance to that of the same volume of water.
specific heat capacity *n* the heat required to raise the temperature of a unit of mass of a given substance by one degree.

specify *vt* (**specifying, specified**) to state specifically; to set down as a condition.—**specifier** *n*.
specimen *n* (*plant, animal, etc*) an example of a particular species; a sample; (*inf*) a person.
specious *adj* apparently true, but in fact false.—**speciously** *adv*.—**speciousness** *n*.
speck *n* a small spot; a fleck.
speckle *n* a small mark of a different colour. * *vt* to mark with speckles.
specs *npl* specifications; (*inf*) spectacles.
spectacle *n* an unusual or interesting scene; a large public show; an object of derision or ridicule; (*pl*) a pair of glasses.—**spectacled** *adj*.
spectacular *adj* impressive; astonishing.—**spectacularly** *adv*.
spectate *vi* to be a spectator.
spectator *n* an onlooker.
specter *see* **spectre.**
spectra *see* **spectrum.**
spectral *adj* of or like a spectre; of or produced by a spectrum.—**spectrality** *adv*.—**spectrally** *adv*.
spectre *n* an apparition or ghost; a haunting mental image.—*also* **specter.**
spectro- *prefix* spectrum.
spectrograph *n* a device for producing and recording spectra.—**spectrographic** *adj*.
spectrometer *n* a spectroscope used to measure spectra.—**spectrometric** *adj*.—**spectrometry** *n*.
spectroscope *n* an instrument for generating and examining spectra.—**spectroscopic** *adj*.—**spectroscopically** *adv*.—**spectroscopy** *n*.
spectrum *n* (*pl* **spectra**) the range of colour which is produced when a white light is passed through a prism; any similar distribution of wave frequencies; a broad range.
speculate *vi* to theorize, to conjecture; to make investments in the hope of making a profit.—**speculation** *n*.—**speculator** *n*.
speculative *adj* of or based on speculation; engaging in speculation in finance, etc.—**speculatively** *adv*.
speculum *n* (*pl* **specula, speculums**) a medical instrument for dilating and examining a bodily passage or cavity; a mirror used as a reflector in an optical instrument such as a telescope.
sped *see* **speed.**
speech *n* the action or power of speaking; a public address or talk; language, dialect.
speechify *vi* (**speechifying, speechified**) to make a speech or speeches, esp in a dull or pompous manner.—**speechifier** *n*.
speechless *adj* unable to speak; silent, as from shock; impossible to express in words.—**speechlessly** *adv*.—**speechlessness** *n*.
speed *n* quickness; rapidity or rate of motion; (*photog*) the sensitivity of film to light; (*sl*) an amphetamine drug. * *vi* (**speeding, sped** *or* **speeded**) to go quickly, to hurry; to drive (a vehicle) at an illegally high speed.
speedball *n* (*sl*) a mixture of heroin and cocaine or amphetamines.
speeding *n* the driving of a vehicle at an illegally high or dangerous speed.
speedometer *n* an instrument in a motor vehicle for measuring its speed.
speedway *n* the sport of racing light motorcycles around dirt or cinder tracks; a stadium for motorcycle racing; in US, a road reserved for fast traffic.
speedwell *n* any of various plants of the figwort family with small blue or white flowers.
speedy *adj* (**speedier, speediest**) quick; prompt.—**speedily** *adv*.—**speediness** *n*.
speleology *n* the scientific study of caves.—**speleological** *adj*.—**speleologist** *n*.
spell[1] *n* a sequence of words used to perform magic; fascination.
spell[2] *vb* (**spelling, spelt** *or* **spelled**) *vt* to name or write down in correct order the letters to form a word; (*letters*) to form a word when placed in the correct order; to indicate; (*with* **out**) to read slowly and painstakingly; to explain in detail; to discern, realize the meaning of. * *vi* to spell words.
spell[3] *n* a usu indefinite period of time; a period of duty in a certain occupation or activity. * *vt* to relieve, stand in for.
spellbound *adj* entranced, enthralled.
spelling bee *n* a spelling contest.
spelt *see* **spell**[2].
spelunker *n* a person whose hobby is exploring caves.—**spelunking** *n*.
spend *vb* (**spending, spent**) *vt* to pay out (money); to concentrate (one's time or energy) on an activity; to pass, as time; to use up. * *vi* to pay out money.—**spender** *n*.
spendthrift *n* a person who spends money wastefully or extravagantly.
spent[1] *see* **spend.**
spent[2] *adj* consumed, used up; physically drained, exhausted.
sperm *n* semen; the male reproductive cell.
spermaceti *n* a waxy substance derived from the oil in the head of a sperm whale.
spermat(o)-, sperm(o)- *prefix* sperm.
spermatic *adj* pertaining to, consisting of, or conveying, sperm.
spermatid *n* any of the four male gametes that form into a spermatozoon.
spermatocyte *n* a cell that develops into a male germ cell.
spermatogenesis *n* the formation and development of spermatozoa in the testis.—**spermatogenetic** *adj*.
spermatogonium *n* (*pl* **spermatogonia**) an immature male germ cell.
spermatophyte *n* a plant that produces seeds.—**spermatophytic** *adj*.
spermatozoon *n* (*pl* **spermatozoa**) any of the male reproductive cells present in the semen.
spermicide *n* a substance that destroys sperm.—**spermicidal** *adj*.
sperm oil *n* oil obtained from the head of the sperm whale.
sperm whale *n* a large whale with a blunt head which is hunted for its oil and spermaceti.
spew *vti* to vomit; to flow or gush forth. * *n* something spewed.
sphagnum *n* a genus of moss which grows in bogs and is a major constituent of peat.
sphalerite *see* **blende.**
sphenoid *adj* wedge-shaped; of or pertaining to the sphenoid bone. * *n* a sphenoid bone.
sphenoid bone *n* a wedge-shaped bone at the base of the skull.
sphere *n* a ball, globe or other perfectly round object; a field of activity or interest; a social class.—**spherical, spheric** *adj*.—**spherically** *adv*.
spheroid *n* a figure that is nearly a sphere.
spherometer *n* an instrument for measuring the curvature of spherical surfaces.
spherule *n* a small sphere.
sphincter *n* a ring-shaped muscle controlling the opening and closing of an orifice.
sphinx *n* (*with cap*) (*Greek myth*) a monster with a lion's body and human head which killed travellers who gave the wrong answer to a riddle; (*without cap*) any of various massive statues with a lion's body and human head erected by the ancient Egyptians; a mysterious or enigmatic person.
sphygmograph *n* a device that records variations in blood pressure and pulse.—**sphygmographic** *adj*.—**sphygmography** *n*.
sphygmomanometer *n* a device for measuring arterial blood pressure.
spicate *adj* (*flowers, leaves*) spiked, pointed.
spicatto *n* (*pl* **spicattos**) (*mus*) (a musical piece or passage played using) a technique in which the bow is made to rebound lightly off the strings of an instrument.—*also adj*.
spice *n* an aromatic vegetable substance used for flavouring and seasoning food; these substances collectively; something that adds zest or interest. * *vt* to flavour with spice; to add zest to.
spicebush *n* an aromatic North American plant.
spick-and-span *adj* scrupulously clean and tidy.
spicule *n* a small needle-like body in the skeleton of sponges, corals, etc; a jet of hot gas erupting from the surface of the sun.
spicy *adj* (**spicier, spiciest**) flavoured with spice; pungent; (*inf*) somewhat scandalous or indecent.—**spicily** *adv*.—**spiciness** *n*.
spider *n* a small wingless creature (arachnid) with eight legs, and abdominal spinnerets for spinning silk threads to make webs.

spider crab *n* any of various crabs with triangular bodies and very long legs.

spider monkey *n* a monkey of South and Central America with a slender body and long limbs.

spiderwort *n* tradescantia.

spidery *adj* thin, and angular, like a spider's legs.

spied *see* **spy.**

spiel *n* glib talk intended to cajole or persuade.—*also vi.*

spiffing *n* (*sl*) (*arch*) excellent.

spiffy *adj* (**spiffier, spiffiest**) smart, elegant.

spigot *n* a small stopper or tap for a cask; a tap.

spike *n* long heavy nail; a sharp-pointed projection, as on a shoe to prevent slipping; an ear of corn, etc; a cluster of stalkless flowers arranged on a long stem. * *vt* to pierce with a spike.—**spiky** *adj.*

spilikin *see* **spillikin.**

spikenard *n* (a fragrant oil derived from) an Indian aromatic plant.

spill[1] *vti* (**spilling, spilled** *or* **spilt**) to cause, esp unintentionally, to flow out of a container; to shed (blood). * *n* something spilled.—**spillage** *n.*

spill[2] *n* a splinter or thin strip of wood or twisted paper for lighting a fire, etc.

spillikin *n* a sliver of wood, cardboard or plastic.—*also* **spilikin.**

spillway n a channel for surplus water from a dam, etc.

spilt *see* **spill**[1].

spin *vb* (**spinning, spun**) *vt* to rotate rapidly; to draw out and twist fibres into thread or yarn; (*spiders, silkworm, etc*) to make a web or cocoon; to draw out (a story) to a great length; (*with* **out**) to prolong, extend; to cause to last longer, eg money. * *vi* to seem to be spinning from dizziness; (*wheels*) to turn rapidly without imparting forward motion. * *n* a swift rotation; (*inf*) a brief, fast ride in a vehicle; an emphasis or slant imparted to information, proposals or policies.

spina bifida *n* a congenital abnormality in the formation of the spine causing the meninges to protrude, and associated with partial paralysis.

spinach *n* a plant with large, green edible leaves.

spinal *adj* of or relating to the spine or spinal cord.—**spinally** *adv.*

spinal column *n* the skeleton of jointed vertebrae and interconnecting cartilaginous tissue that surrounds and protects the spinal cord.—*also* **spine, backbone.**

spinal cord *n* the cord of nerves enclosed by the spinal column.

spindle *n* the notched rod by which thread is twisted in spinning; a pin around which machinery turns.

spindly *adj* (**spindlier, spindliest**) tall and slender; frail.

spindrift *n* sea spray.

spine *n* a sharp, stiff projection, as a thorn of the cactus or quill of a porcupine; a spinal column; the backbone of a book.

spine-chiller *n* a book, film, etc that inspires terror.—**spine-chilling** *adj.*

spineless *adj* lacking a spine; weak-willed; irresolute.—**spinelessly** *adv.*—**spinelessness** *n.*

spinet *n* a type of small harpsichord.

spinifex *n* any of several coarse Australian grasses with spiny seed heads or spiked leaves.

spinnaker *n* a large triangular sail sometimes carried by racing yachts.

spinner *n* a revolving fishing lure; (*cricket*) a ball bowled with a spin, or a bowler who does this.

spinneret *n* an organ in spiders and other insects for producing silk threads.

spinning wheel *n* a small household machine with a wheel-driven spindle for spinning yarn from fibre.

spin-off *n* a product or benefit derived incidentally from existing research and development.

spinose *adj* (*plants*) spiny.

spinster *n* an unmarried woman.

spiny *adj* (**spinier, spiniest**) covered with spines or thorns; troublesome.

spiny anteater *n* the echidna.

spiny lobster *n* any of several large edible crustaceans with a spiny shell.

spiracle *n* a respiratory aperture in various insects and some fishes; the blowhole in whales.

spiraea, spirea *n* any of various plants of the rose family having clusters of small white or pink flowers.

spiral *adj* winding round in a continuous curve up or down a centre or pole. * *n* a helix; a spiral line or shape; a continuous expansion or decrease, eg in inflation. * *vi* (**spiralling, spiralled** *or* **spiraling, spiraled**) to move up or down in a spiral curve; to increase or decrease steadily.

spiral galaxy *n* a galaxy in which two arms consisting of new stars spiral outward from an ellipsoidal nucleus of old stars.

spire *n* the tapering point of a steeple.

spirillum *n* (*pl* **spirilla**) a bacterium with a curved or spiral body.

spirit *n* soul; a supernatural being, as a ghost, angel, etc; (*pl*) disposition; mood; vivacity, courage, etc; real meaning; essential quality; (*usu pl*) distilled alcoholic liquor. * *vt* to carry (away, off, etc) secretly and swiftly.

spirited *adj* full of life; animated.—**spiritedly** *adv.*—**spiritedness** *n.*

spirit level *n* a glass tube filled with liquid containing an air bubble and mounted in a frame, used for testing whether a surface is level.

spiritual *adj* of the soul; religious; sacred. * *n* an emotional religious song, originating among the Black slaves in the American South.—**spirituality** *n.*—**spiritually** *adv.*

spiritualism *n* the belief that the spirits of the dead can communicate with the living, as through mediums.—**spiritualist** *n.*

spirochaete, spirochete *n* any of a genus of slender spiral-shaped bacteria that includes those causing syphilis.

spirograph *n* a device that records respiratory movements.—**spirographic** *adj.*

spirt *see* **spurt.**

spit[1] *n* a pointed iron rod on which meat is roasted; a long narrow strip of land projecting into the water. * *vt* (**spitting, spitted**) to fix as on a spit, impale.

spit[2] *vb* (**spitting, spat** *or* **spit**) *vt* to eject from the mouth; to utter with scorn. * *vi* to expel saliva from the mouth; (*hot fat*) to splutter; to rain lightly. * *n* saliva.

spit and polish *n* (*inf*) obsession with neatness and cleanliness, esp in the military services.

spite *n* ill will; malice. * *vt* to annoy spitefully, to vex.—**spiteful** *adj.*

spitting image *n* (*inf*) a person who almost exactly resembles another.

spittle *n* saliva ejected from the mouth.

spittoon *n* a usu metal pan for spitting into, a cuspidor.

spiv *n* (*sl*) a person of smart appearance who lives by shady dealings, esp on the black market.

splanchnic *adj* of or pertaining to the viscera.

splash *vti* to spatter with liquid; to move with a splash; to display prominently; (*with* **down**) to land (a spacecraft) on water. * *n* something splashed; a patch of colour; a small amount, esp of a mixer added to an alcoholic drink.—**splashy** *adj.*

splashdown *n* (the scheduled time of) the landing of a spacecraft on the ocean.

splatter *vti* to splash, spatter.—*also n.*

splay *vti* to turn out at an angle; to spread out.

spleen *n* a large lymphatic organ in the upper left part of the abdomen which modifies the blood structure; spitefulness; ill humour.

splendid *adj* brilliant; magnificent; (*inf*) very good.—**splendidly** *adv.*—**splendidness** *n.*

splendiferous *adj* (*inf*) splendid.

splendour, splendor *n* brilliance; magnificence; grandeur.—**splendorous, splendrous** *adj.*

splenetic *adj* of or pertaining to the spleen; spiteful, irritable.—**splenetically** *adv.*

splenic *n* of, pertaining to, or in the spleen.

splenius *n* (*pl* **splenii**) either of the two muscles at either side of the back of the neck that move the head.—**splenial** *adj.*

splenomegaly *n* distension of the spleen.

splice *vt* to unite (two ends of a rope) by intertwining the strands; to connect (two pieces of timber) by overlapping.—*also n.*

spline *n* a key or slot in a shaft that fits into grooves in a surrounding sleeve and locks the two together.

splint *n* a rigid structure used to immobilize and support a fractured limb; a splinter of wood for lighting fires. * *vt* to put in splints.

splinter *n* a thin, sharp piece of wood, glass, or metal broken off. * *vti* to break off into splinters.—**splintery** *adj*.

splinter group *n* a small group that has split off from the main body.

split *vti* (**splitting, split**) to break apart (usu into two pieces); to separate into factions; to divide into shares; to burst or tear. * *n* the act or process of splitting; a narrow gap made (as if) by splitting; a dessert consisting of sliced fruit, esp banana, with ice cream, nuts, etc; (*often pl*) the act of extending the legs in opposite directions and lowering the the body to the floor. * *adj* divided; torn; fractured.

split infinitive *n* (*gram*) an infinitive with another word between *to* and the verb.

split-level *adj* (*building*) having rooms or areas in one part less than a full story higher than another that adjoins them.

split personality *n* unstable in mood or behaviour; having two or more distinct personalities.

split-screen *n* (*cinema, television*) a technique involving the simultaneous projection of different images onto separate areas of the screen.

split second *n* a very brief moment, an instant.—**split-second** *adj*.

split shift *n* a shift in which the working hours are divided into two distinct periods.

splodge, splotch *n* a large irregular spot, stain or smear. * *vt* to mark with a splodge or splotch.—**splodgy, splotchy** *adj*.

splurge *vi* to spend lavishly (on); to show off. * *n* an extravagant display, esp of wealth.

splutter *vi* to spit out food or drops of liquid noisily; to utter words confusedly and hurriedly.—*also n*.

spoil *vb* (**spoiling, spoiled** *or* **spoilt**) *vt* to damage as to make useless, etc; to impair the enjoyment, etc, of; to overindulge (a child). * *vi* to become spoiled; to decay, etc, as food. * *npl* booty, valuables seized in war; the opportunities for financial gain from holding public office.

spoiler *n* a projecting structure on an aircraft wing that increases drag to reduce lift; any similar structure for increasing the stability of vehicles at high speed.

spoil-sport *n* (*inf*) a person who spoils the fun of others.

spoilt *see* **spoil**.

spoke[1], **spoken** *see* **speak**.

spoke[2] *n* any of the braces extending from the hub to the rim of a wheel.

spokeshave *n* a small two-handled plane used for smoothing curved surfaces.

spokesman *n* (*pl* **spokesmen**) a person authorized to speak on behalf of others.—**spokeswoman** *nf* (*pl* **spokeswomen**).

spondylitis *n* inflammation of the vertebrae.

sponge *n* a plantlike marine animal with an internal skeleton of elastic interlacing horny fibres; a piece of natural or manmade sponge for washing or cleaning. * *vt* to wipe with a sponge. * *vi* (*inf*) to scrounge.—**sponginess** *n*.—**spongy** *adj*.

sponge bag *n* a small waterproof bag for toilet articles, a washbag.

sponge cake *n* a sweet cake with a light porous texture.

sponson *n* a projecting gun-mounting on a ship or tank, etc to allow forward fire; an air-filled projection on the hull of a seaplane to provide stability.

sponsor *n* a person or organization that pays the expenses connected with an artistic production or sports event in return for advertising; in US, a business firm, etc that pays for a radio or TV programme advertising its product. * *vt* to act as sponsor for.—**sponsorship** *n*.

spontaneity *n* (*pl* **spontaneities**) the quality of being spontaneous; a spontaneous action, etc.

spontaneous *adj* arising naturally; unpremeditated.—**spontaneously** *adv*.—**spontaneousness** *n*.

spontaneous combustion *n* the self-igniting of a substance through internal chemical processes such as oxidation.

spontaneous generation *n* abiogenesis.

spoof *n* (*sl*) a hoax or joke; a light satire.—*also vti*.

spook *n* (*inf*) a ghost; (*inf*) a spy. * *vt* to frighten.—**spooky** *adj*.

spool *n* a cylinder, bobbin, or reel, upon which thread, photographic film, etc, are wound. * *vt* to wind on a spool.

spoon *n* utensil with a shallow bowl and a handle, for eating, stirring, etc.—**spoonful** *n*.

spoonbill *n* any of various wading birds with flattened bills.

spoonerism *n* the accidental transposition of the initial letters or opening syllables of two or more words with amusing results, e.g *half-warmed fish* for *half-formed wish*.

spoor *n* a trail, esp of a wild animal. * *vti* to track (something) by a spoor.

sporadic *adj* occurring here and there; intermittent.—**sporadically** *adv*.

sporangium *n* (*pl* **sporangia**) (*in fungi, etc*) an organ or part in which asexual spores are produced.

spore *n* an asexual reproductive body produced by algae, fungae and ferns capable of giving rise to new individuals.

sporogenesis *n* the formation of spores in plants and animals.—**sporogenous** *adj*.

sporozoan *n* any of a group of spore-producing parasitic protozoans that includes the malaria parasite.

sporran *n* an ornamental pouch worn in front of the kilt as part of traditional Highland dress in Scotland.

sport *n* an athletic game or pastime, often competitive and involving physical capability; good-humoured joking; (*inf*) a person regarded as fair and abiding by the rules. * *vi* to play, to frolic. * *vt* (*inf*) to display, flaunt.

sporting *adj* interested in, concerned with, or suitable for sport; exhibiting sportsmanship; willing to take a risk.—**sportingly** *adv*.

sportive *adj* playful.—**sportively** *adv*.—**sportiveness** *n*.

sportscast *n* a sports broadcast.—**sportscaster** *n*.

sportsman *n* (*pl* **sportsmen**) a person engaged in sport; a person who plays by the rules, is fair, is a good loser, etc.—**sportswoman** *nf* (*pl* **sportswomen**).—**sportsmanlike, sportsmanly** *adj*.—**sportsmanship** *n*.

sports medicine *n* the branch of medicine dealing with sports injuries.

sporty *adj* (**sportier, sportiest**) (*inf*) fond of sport; flashy, ostentatious.—**sportily** *adv*.—**sportiness** *n*.

sporule *n* a tiny spore.

spot *n* a small area differing in colour, etc, from the surrounding area; a stain, speck, etc; a taint on character or reputation; a small quantity or amount; a locality; (*inf*) a difficult or embarrassing situation; a place on an entertainment programme; a spotlight. * *vt* (**spotting, spotted**) to mark with spots; (*inf*) to identify or recognise; to glimpse.

spot check *n* a sudden random examination.—**spot-check** *vt*.

spotless *adj* immaculate.—**spotlessly** *adv*.—**spotlessness** *n*.

spotlight *n* a powerful light used to illuminate a small area; intense public attention. * *vt* (**spotlighting, spotlighted** *or* **spotlit**) to illuminate with a spotlight; to focus attention on.

spot on *adj* (*inf*) absolutely right.

spotted dick *n* a steamed pudding made with suet and currants.

spotty *adj* (**spottier, spottiest**) marked with spots, esp on the skin; intermittent, uneven.—**spottily** *adv*.—**spottiness** *n*.

spot-weld *vt* to join two pieces of metal with circular welds.—**spot-welder** *n*.—**spot welding** *n*.

spouse *n* (one's) husband or wife.

spout *vti* to eject in a strong jet or spurts; (*inf*) to drone on boringly. * *n* a projecting lip or tube for pouring out liquids.

spp *abbr* = species (*pl*).

SPQR *abbr* = *Senatus Populusque Romanus* (the Senate and People of Rome).

sprain *n* a wrenching of a joint by sudden twisting or tearing of ligaments.—*also vt*.

sprang *see* **spring**.

sprat *n* a small food fish related to the herring; a small or young herring.

sprawl *vi* to lie down with the limbs stretched out in an untidy manner; to spread out in a straggling way. * *n* a sprawling position.

SPQR *abbr* 5 *Senatus Populusque Romanus* (the Senate and People of Rome).

sprain *n* a wrenching of a joint by sudden twisting or tearing of ligaments.—*also vt*.

sprang *see* **spring**.

sprat *n* a small food fish related to the herring; a small or young herring.

sprawl *vi* to lie down with the limbs stretched out in an untidy manner; to spread out in a straggling way. * *n* a sprawling position.

spray[1] *n* fine particles of a liquid; mist; an aerosol or atomizer. * *vti* to direct a spray (on); to apply as a spray.

spray[2] *n* a number of flowers on one branch; a decorative flower arrangement; an ornament resembling this.

spray gun *n* a device for applying paint, varnish, etc in the form of a spray.

spread *vt* (**spreading, spread**) to extend; to unfold or open; to disseminate; to distribute; to apply a coating (eg butter). * *vi* to expand in all directions. * *n* an expanse; (*inf*) a feast; food which can be spread on bread; a bed cover.

spread eagle *n* an emblem of an eagle with wings and legs stretched out.

spread-eagle *vt* to stand or lie with the limbs outstretched.—**spread-eagled** *adj*.

spreadsheet *n* a computer program that allows easy entry and manipulation of text and figures, used for accounting and financial planning.

spree *n* (*inf*) excessive indulgence, eg in spending money, alcohol consumption, etc.

sprier see spry.

sprig *n* a twig with leaves on it.

sprightly *adj* (**sprightlier, sprightliest**) full of life or energy.—**sprightliness** *n*.

spring *vb* (**springing, sprang** *or* **sprung**, *pp* **sprung**) *vi* to move suddenly, as by elastic force; to arise suddenly; to originate. * *vt* to cause to spring up, to cause to operate suddenly. * *n* a leap; the season between winter and summer; a coiled piece of wire that springs back to its original shape when stretched; the source of a stream.

spring balance *n* a device that measures weight by the tension of a spring linked to a pointer on a calibrated scale.—*also* **spring scale**.

springboard *n* a flexible board used by divers and in gymnastics to provided added height or impetus.

springbok *n* a South African gazelle.

spring chicken *n* a young chicken from two to ten months old; (*inf*) a young inexperienced person.

spring-clean *vi* to clean (a house, etc) thoroughly.—**spring clean** *n*.

springe *n* a snare for catching small animals.

spring onion *n* a scallion.

spring roll *n* a Chinese savoury snack comprising a mixture of beansprouts, chopped meat, etc rolled in a thin pancake and fried.

spring scale *see* **spring balance**.

springtail *n* any of various small wingless leaping insects.

spring tide *n* a high tide that occurs at the full or new moon.

springtime *n* the season of spring; the earliest and most promising period in the life of something or someone.

springy *adj* (**springier, springiest**) elastic, resilient; light, spongy.—**springily** *adv*.—**springiness** *n*.

sprinkle *vt* to scatter in droplets or particles (on something).—*also n*.

sprinkler *n* a nozzle for spraying water; a fire-extinguishing system that operates automatically on detection of smoke or heat.

sprinkling *n* a small quantity scattered randomly.

sprint *n* a short run or race at full speed. * *vi* to go at top speed.—**sprinter** *n*.

sprit *n* a small spar which runs from the mast to the outer upper corner of a sail.

sprite *n* an elf or imp; a dainty person.

spritsail *n* a sail extended by a sprit.

spritzer *n* a drink made with wine, usu white, and soda water.

sprocket *n* a wheel with a row of teeth which engage the holes in a chain, or a reel of film, in order to turn it.

sprout *n* a new shoot on a plant; a small cabbage-like vegetable. * *vt* to put forth (shoots). * *vi* to begin to grow.

spruce[1] *adj* smart, neat, trim. * *vt* to smarten.

spruce[2] *n* an evergreen tree of the pine family with a conical head and soft light wood.

sprung *see* **spring**.

spry *adj* (**sprier, spriest** *or* **spryer, spryest**) vigorous, agile.—**spryly** *av*.—**spryness** *n*.

spud *n* a small narrow digging tool; (*inf*) a potato. * *vt* (**spudding, spudded**) to dig with a spud.—**spudder** *n*.

spume *n* foam; surf; froth.

spun *see* **spin**.

spunk *n* a spark, a match; (*sl*) pluck, courage.

spunky *adj* (**spunkier, spunkiest**) full of courage; spirited.—**spunkily** *adv*.—**spunkiness** *n*.

spun silk *n* a shiny material made from silk waste.

spur *n* a small metal wheel on a rider's heel, with sharp points for urging on the horse; encouragement, stimulus; a hard sharp projection. * *vt* (**spurring, spurred**) to urge on.

spurge *n* any of various plants that produce a bitter milky juice.

spurious *adj* not legitimate or genuine; false.—**spuriously** *adv*.—**spuriousness** *n*.

spurn *vt* to reject with disdain. * *n* disdainful rejection.

spurt *vt* to gush forth in a sudden stream or jet. * *n* a sudden stream or jet; a burst of activity.—*also* **spirt**.

sputnik *n* the name used for series of artificial satellites launched by the former Soviet Union in the 1950s and 1960s (Russian for *travelling companion*).

sputter *vi* to splutter.—*also n*.

sputum *n* (*pl* **sputa**) saliva and mucus.

spy *n* (*pl* **spies**) a secret agent employed to collect information on rivals. * *vb* (**spying, spied**) *vi* to keep under secret surveillance, act as a spy (*usu with* **on**). * *vt* to catch sight of.

spyglass *n* a small telescope.

sq *abbr* 5 sequence; squadron; square.

squab *n* (*pl* **squabs, squab**) a young bird, esp a pigeon; a stuffed cushion; a short fat person. * *adj* (*birds*) unfledged; short and fat.

squabble *vi* to quarrel noisily. * *n* a noisy, petty quarrel.—also *n*.

squad *n* a small group of soldiers which form a working unit; a section of a police force; (*sport*) a group of players from which a team is selected.

squadron *n* a unit of warships, cavalry, military aircraft, etc.

squalid *adj* filthy; neglected, sordid; degrading.—**squalidly** *adv*.—**squalidness** *n*.

squall *vi* to cry out loudly (like a baby). * *n* a loud cry; a violent gust of wind.

squalor *n* foulness; dirt, filth.

squama *n* (*pl* **squamae**) (*biol*) (something resembling) a scale.

squander *vt* to spend extravagantly or wastefully.

square *n* a shape with four sides of equal length and four right angles; an open space in a town, surrounded by buildings; (*inf*) an old-fashioned person; an instrument for drawing right angles; the product of a number multiplied by itself. * *adj* square-shaped; forming a square; forming a right angle (with); (*financial account*) settled; fair, honest; equal in score; (*inf*) old-fashioned. * *vt* to make square; to multiply (a quantity) by itself; (*with* **away**) (*inf*) to put in order, tidy up. * *vi* to agree.—**squarely** *adv*.—**squareness** *n*.

square bracket *n* either of a pair of written or printed characters [ ] used to enclose text or in mathematical expressions.

square dance *n* any of various dances in which the participants join hands to form squares.—**square-dance** *vi*.

square meal *n* a meal of satisfying quantity.

square measure *n* the measure of an area; the square of a lineal measure.

square root *n* a number that when multiplied by itself produces a given number (*2 is the square root of 4*).

squash[1] *vt* to squeeze, press, or crush; to suppress. * *vi* to squelch; to crowd. * *n* a crushed mass; a crowd of people pressed together; a fruit-

squawk *n* a loud, raucous call or cry, as of a bird; (*inf*) a loud protest.—*also vi*.

squeak *vi* to make a high-pitched cry. * *n* a squeaky noise.—**squeaker** *n*.—**squeaky** *adj*.

squeaky-clean *adj* spotless; above reproach.

squeal *vi* to make a shrill and prolonged cry or sound; (*sl*) to be an informer; to protest.

squeamish *adj* easily nauseated; easily shocked or disgusted.—**squeamishly** *adv*.—**squeamishness** *n*.

squeegee *n* a tool with a rubber-edged blade for scraping away excess water from a surface, esp a window. * *vt* (**squeegeeing, squeegeed**) to wipe clean with a squeegee.

squeeze *vt* to press firmly, compress; to grasp tightly; to hug; to force (through, into) by pressing; to extract liquid, juice, from by pressure; to obtain (money, etc) by force, to harass. * *n* squeezing or being squeezed; a hug; a small amount squeezed from something; a crowding together; financial pressure or hardship.—**squeezable** *adj*.

squelch *vi* to walk through soft, wet ground, making a sucking noise. * *vt* to crush or squash completely. * *n* a squelching sound.

squib *n* a small firework that fizzes then explodes; a short, witty attack in speech or writing, a lampoon.

squid *n* (*pl* **squids, squid**) an edible mollusc, related to the cuttlefish, with a long body and ten arms.

squiffy *adj* (**squiffier, squiffiest**) slightly drunk.

squiggle *n* a short wavy line, esp handwritten. * *vi* to squirm; to wriggle.—**squiggly** *adj*.

squill *n* a Mediterranean plant of the lilly family; a seashore variety of this whose bulbs were formerly used medicinally.

squint *vi* to half close or cross the eyes; to glance sideways. * *n* crossed eyes, as caused by a visual disorder; a glance sideways; (*inf*) a look. * *adj* squinting; (*inf*) crooked.

squire *n* a country gentleman, esp the leading landowner in a district.

squirm *vi* to writhe; to wriggle; to feel embarrassed or ashamed.

squirrel *n* (*pl* **squirrels, squirrel**) a bushy tailed rodent with grey or reddish fur which lives in trees and feeds on nuts. * *vt* (**squirrelling, squirrelled** *or* **squirreling, squirreled**) (*usu with* **away**) to hoard.

squirrel cage *n* a small cylindrical cage which is rotated by a small animal running inside; the rotor of an induction motor with cylindrically arranged copper bars.

squirt *vt* to eject liquid in a jet. * *vi* to spurt. * *n* a jet of liquid; (*inf*) an insignificant person.

squish *vt* to crush, esp so as to produce a squelching sound. * *vi* to make or move with a squelching sound. * *n* a soft squelching sound.—**squishy** *adj*.

Sr[1] (*chem symbol*) strontium.

Sr[2] *abbr* = Senior; Señor.

SRO *abbr* = standing room only.

SS[1] *abbr* = Saints; steamship;

SS[2] *abbr* = *Schutzstaffel*, the Nazi paramilitary police force elite guard.

St *abbr* = Saint.

St. *abbr* = Street.

stab vt (stabbing, stabbed) to injure with a knife or pointed weapon; to pain suddenly and sharply. * *vi* to thrust at (as if) with a pointed weapon. * *n* an act or instance of stabbing; a wound made by stabbing; a sudden sensation, as of emotion, pain, etc; (*inf*) an attempt.

stabile *n* an abstract sculpture resembling a mobile but stationary.

stabilize *vti* to make or become stable or steady.—**stabilization** *n*.

stabilizer *n* a device for stabilizing (an aircraft, ship, bicycle, etc).

stable[1] *adj* steady or firm; firmly established; permanent; not decomposing readily.—**stability** *n*.

stable[2] *n* a building where horses or cattle are kept; a group of racehorses belonging to one owner; a group of people working for or trained by a specific establishment, as writers, performers, etc. * *vti* to put, keep, or live in a stable.

staccato *adj* (*musical notes*) short, abrupt; (*speech*) sharp, abrupt, disconnected. * *adv* in a staccato manner.

stack *n* a large neatly arranged pile (of hay, papers, records, etc); a chimney stack; (*inf*) a large amount of; a number of aircraft circling an airport waiting for permission to land. * *vt* to pile, arrange in a stack.

stadia *see* **stadium.**

stadium *n* (*pl* **stadium, stadia**) a sports ground surrounded by tiers of seats.

staff *n* (*pl* **staves**) a strong stick or pole; (*mus*) one of the five horizontal lines upon which music is written (—*also* **stave**); (*pl* **staffs**) a body of officers who help a commanding officer, or perform special duties; the workers employed in an establishment; the teachers or lecturers of an educational institution. * *vt* to provide with staff.

stag *n* a full-grown male deer. * *adj* (*party*) for men only.

stag beetle *n* any of various beetles with large pincer-like mandibles.

stage *n* a degree or step in a process; a raised platform, esp for acting on; (*with* **the**) the theatre, the theatrical calling; any field of action or setting; a portion of a journey; a propulsion unit of a space rocket discarded when its fuel is spent. * *vt* to perform a play on the stage; to plan, organize (an event).

stagecoach *n* a four-wheeled vehicle drawn by horses, that formerly carried passengers or mail.

stagecraft *n* skill in writing or staging plays.

stage direction *n* an instruction in the text of a play (regarding characterization, movement, lighting, etc) for an actor or director.

stage door *n* the back entrance to a theatre used by the staff and players.

stage fright *n* nervousness at appearing before an audience.

stage left *n* the area of a stage to the left of an actor facing the audience.

stage-manage *vt* to act as a stage-manager; to organize or direct from behind the scenes.

stage manager *n* a person responsible for the stage arrangements prior to and during the performance of a play.

stage right *n* the area of a stage to the right of an actor facing the audience.

stage-struck *adj* obsessed with theatre and the idea of becoming an actor.

stage whisper *n* a loud whisper made by an actor and intentionally audible to the audience.

stagflation *n* an economic situation characterized by a combination of high inflation and stagnant or declining output and employment.

stagger *vi* to walk unsteadily, to totter. * *vt* to astound; to give a shock to; to arrange so as not to overlap; to alternate.

staggering *adj* astounding.—**staggeringly** *adv*.

staging *n* a temporary platform, esp horizontal planking supported by scaffolding.

staging area *n* an assembly point for troops in transit.

staging post *n* a regular stopover point on a long route.

stagnant *adj* (*water*) not flowing, standing still with a revolting smell; unchanging, dull.—**stagnancy** *n*.

stagnate *vi* to be, or become, stagnant.—**stagnation** *n*.

stag party *n* a party for men only, usu given for one who is due to be married shortly.

stagy, stagey *adj* (**stagier, stagiest**) theatrical, dramatic.

staid *adj* sober; sedate; old-fashioned.—**staidly** *adv*.—**staidness** *n*.

stain *vt* to dye; to discolour with spots of something which cannot be removed. * *vi* to become stained; to produce stains. * *n* a discoloured mark; a moral blemish; a dye or liquid for staining materials, eg wood.

stained glass *n* coloured glass used in windows.

stainless *adj* free from stain; (materials) resistant to staining.—**stainlessly** *adv*.

stainless steel *n* a type of steel resistant to tarnishing and corrosion.

stair *n* a flight of stairs; a single step; (*pl*) a stairway.

staircase *n* a flight of stairs with banisters.

stairway *n* a staircase.

stairwell *n* the vertical shaft for a staircase.

stake[1] *n* a sharpened metal or wooden post driven into the ground, as a marker or fence post; a post to which persons were tied for execution by burning; this form of execution. * *vt* to support with, tie or tether to a stake; to mark out (land) with stakes; (*with* **out**) to put under surveillance.

stake[2] *vt* to bet; (*inf*) to provide with money or resources. * *n* a bet; a financial interest; (*pl*) money risked on a race; (*pl*) the prize in a race

stakeout *n* surveillance, esp by police; premises under surveillance.

stalactite *n* an icicle-like calcium deposit hanging from the roof of a cave.

stalag *n* a German prisoner-of-war camp in World War II.

stalagmite *n* a cylindrical deposit projecting upward from the floor of a cave, caused by the dripping of water and lime from the roof.

stale *adj* deteriorated from age; tainted; musty; stagnant; jaded.—**staleness** *n*.

stalemate *n* (*chess*) a situation in which a king can only be moved in and out of check, thus causing a draw; a deadlock.—*also vt*.

Stalinism *n* the theory and practice of authoritarian rule associated with the Soviet dictator Joseph Stalin (1879–1953).—**Stalinist** *n, adj*.

stalk[1] *n* the stem of a plant.

stalk[2] *vi* to stride in a stiff or angry way; to hunt (game, prey) stealthily.—**stalker** *n*.

stalking-horse *n* a means of concealing true intentions; a candidate standing in an election to confuse the opposition or test the amount of prospective support for the real candidate in whose favour the stand-in then withdraws.

stall[1] *n* a compartment for one animal in a stable; a table or stand for the display or sale of goods; a stalling of an engine; (*aircraft*) a loss of lift and downward plunge due to an excessive decrease in airspeed; (*pl*) the seats on the ground floor of a theatre. * *vti* (*car engine*) to stop or cause to stop suddenly, eg by misuse of the clutch; (*aircraft*) to lose or cause to lose lift because of an excessive reduction in airspeed.

stall[2] *vti* to play for time; to postpone or delay. * *n* (*inf*) any action used in stalling.

stallion *n* an uncastrated male horse, esp one kept for breeding.

stalwart *adj* strong, sturdy; resolute; dependable. * *n* a loyal, hardworking supporter.

stamen *n* (*pl* **stamens, stamina**) the pollen-bearing part of a flower.

stamina *n* strength; staying power.

staminate *adj* (*plants*) having or producing stamens.

stammer *vti* to pause or falter in speaking; to stutter.—*also n*.—**stammerer** *n*.

stamp *vt* to put a mark on; to imprint with an official seal; to affix a postage stamp; (*with* **out**) to extinguish by stamping; to suppress, eradicate, by force. * *vi* to bring the foot down heavily (on); * *n* a postage stamp; the mark cancelling a postage stamp; a block for imprinting.

stamp duty, stamp tax *n* a tax on some types of legal documents.

stampede *n* an impulsive rush of a panic-stricken herd; a rush of a crowd.—*also vti*.

stamping ground *n* (*inf*) a favourite or habitual meeting place.

stance *n* posture; the attitude taken in a given situation.

stanch see **staunch**[2].

stanchion *n* an upright post, pillar, rod or similar support. * *vt* to provide with a stanchion.

stand *vb* (**standing, stood**) *vi* to be in an upright position; to be on, or rise to one's feet; to make resistance; to remain unchanged; to endure, tolerate; to reach a deadlock; (*with* **by**) to look on without interfering; to be available for use if required; (*with* **down**) to withdraw, resign; to leave a witness box after testifying in court; (*soldier*) to go off duty; (*with* **off**) to remain at a distance; to reach a stalemate; (*with* **up**) to rise to one's feet. * *vt* to put upright; to endure, tolerate; (*with* **by**) to remain loyal to, to defend; (*with* **off**) to (cause to) keep at a distance; to lay off (employees) temporarily; (*with* **up**) to resist; to withstand criticism, close examination, etc; (*inf*) to fail to keep an appointment with. * *n* a strong opinion; a standing position; a standstill; a place for taxis awaiting hire; (*pl*) a structure for spectators; the place taken by a witness for testifying in court; a piece of furniture for hanging things from; a stall or booth for a small retail business.

standard *n* a flag, banner, or emblem; an upright pole, pillar; an authorized weight or measure; a criterion; an established or accepted level of achievement; (*pl*) moral principles. * *adj* serving as a standard; typical.

standard-bearer *n* a person who carries a standard; the leader of a particular cause or party.

standardize *vt* to make standard; to reduce to a standard.—**standardization** *n*.—**standardizer** *n*.

standard of living *n* the level of material comforts enjoyed by an individual, family, group or community.

stand-by *n* (*pl* **stand-bys**) a person or thing held in readiness for use in an emergency, etc.—*also adj*.

stand-in *n* a substitute; a person who takes the place of an actor during the preparation of a scene or in stunts.—*also vi*.

standing *n* status or reputation; length of service, duration. * *adj* upright; permanent; (*jump*) performed from a stationary position.

standing army *n* a permanent body of paid soldiers as maintained by a nation.

standing order *n* an instruction to a bank by a depositor to pay fixed amounts at regular intervals (for bills, etc); a regulation governing conduct, procedure, etc in an organization or assembly.

standoff *n* a deadlock, stalemate.

standoffish *adj* aloof, reserved.

standpipe *n* a vertical pipe with a tap providing an external water supply.

standpoint *n* a point of view, opinion.

stand-up *adj* (*collar*) upright; (*fight*) furious; (*comedian*) telling jokes standing alone in front of an audience.

standstill *n* a complete halt.

stank *see* **stink**.

stannic *adj* of or containing (tetravalent) tin.

stannous *adj* of or containing (bivalent) tin.

stanza *n* a group of lines which form a division of a poem.

staple[1] *n* a principal commodity of trade or industry of a region or nation; a main constituent. * *adj* chief.

staple[2] *n* a U-shaped thin piece of wire for fastening. * *vt* to fasten with a staple.

star *n* any one of the celestial bodies, esp those visible by night which appear as small points of light, including planets, comets, meteors, and less commonly the sun and moon; a figure with five points; an exceptionally successful or skilful person; a famous actor, actress, musician, etc. * *vti* (**starring, starred**) to feature or be featured as a star.

starboard *n* the right side of a ship or aircraft when facing the bow.

starch *n* a white, tasteless, food substance found in potatoes, cereal, etc; a fabric stiffener based on this. * *vt* to stiffen with starch.—**starchy** *adj*.

star-crossed *adj* ill-fated; unfortunate.

stardom *n* the fame and status enjoyed by celebrities or stars.

stardust *n* a large cluster of distant stars appearing as dust; a feeling of romance.

stare *vi* to gaze fixedly, as in horror, astonishment, etc; to glare. * *n* a fixed gaze.

starfish *n* (*pl* **starfish, starfishes**) an echinoderm consisting of a central disc from which five arms radiate outward.

stargaze *vi* to look at the stars; to daydream.

stark *adj* bare; plain; blunt; utter. * *adv* completely.—**starkly** *adv*.—**starkness** *n*.

starkers *adj* (*inf*) completely naked.

starlet *n* a young actress regarded as a potential star.

starling *n* any of a family of small songbirds, esp a common European bird with black plumage tinged with green that congregates in large groups.

Star of David a six-pointed star formed by two intersecting triangles, a hexagram.

starry-eyed *adj* dreamy, impractical, overly optimistic.

Stars and Stripes *n sing* (*with* **the**) the national flag of the USA consisting of 13 alternate red and white stripes and a blue square filled with white stars representing the individual states.—*also* **Star-Spangled Banner**.

Star Spangled Banner *n* (*with* **the**) the national anthem of the USA; the Stars and Stripes.
star-studded *adj* featuring many celebrities.
start *vi* to commence, begin; to jump involuntarily, from fright. * *vt* to begin. * *n* a beginning; a slight involuntary body movement; a career opening.
starter *n* a person who starts something, esp an official who signals the beginning of a race; a competitor in a race; the first course of a meal; a small electric motor used to start an internal combustion engine (—*also* **self-starter**).
starting block *n* one of a pair of angled wooden or metal pads or blocks against which a sprinter braces the feet in crouch starts.
starting gate *n* (*horseracing*) a removable barrier holding each horse in line and which is raised to start a race.
starting grid *n* (*motor racing*) the numbered grid where drivers line up at the start of a race, position being determined by the times gained in practice laps.
starting price *n* (*esp horseracing*) the final odds on a horse offered by bookmakers at the start of a race.
starting stalls *npl* the metal enclosures for horses at the starting line with gates that spring open simultaneously to start the race.
startle *vti* to be, or cause to be, frightened or surprised.—**startling** *adj.*
starve *vi* to die or suffer from a lack of food. * *vt* deprive (a person) of food; to deprive (of) anything necessary.—**starvation** *n.*
star warrior *n* one who advocates the US's Strategic Defense Initiative.
Star Wars *n sing* the popular name for the Strategic Defense Initiative.
stash *vt* to hide (money, etc) for future use. * *n* a hiding place; something hidden; (*sl*) drugs hidden for personal consumption.
state *n* condition; frame of mind; position in society; ceremonious style; (*with cap*) an area or community with its own government, or forming a federation under a sovereign government. * *adj* of the state or State; public; ceremonial. * *vt* to express in words; to specify, declare officially.
statecraft *n* the art of government; statesmanship.
state department *n* the government department that handles foreign affairs; foreign office.
statehouse *n* the building which houses a state legislature in the US.
stateless *adj* not having a nationality.—**statelessness** *n.*
stately *adj* (**statelier, stateliest**) dignified; majestic.—**stateliness** *n.*
stately home *n* a large country mansion, usu of historical interest, which is open to the public.
statement *n* a formal announcement; a declaration; a document showing one's bank balance.
state-of-the-art *adj* using the most advanced technology yet possible.
stateroom *n* a luxury private cabin in a ship; a large room in a palace used for state occasions.
States *n sing or pl* the USA.
state school *n* any school funded by the state which provides free education.
stateside *adj* of, in, or to the US.—*also adv.*
statesman *n* (*pl* **statesmen**) a well-known and experienced politician.—**statesmanship** *n.*
static *adj* fixed; stationary; at rest. * *n* electrical interference causing noise on radio or TV.
statics *n sing* the branch of mechanics dealing with the forces that produce a state of equilibrium.
static electricity *n* electricity which is stationary as opposed to flowing in a current.
station *n* a railway or bus terminal or stop; headquarters (of the emergency services); military headquarters; (*inf*) a TV channel; position in society, standing. * *vt* to assign to a post, place, office.
stationary *adj* not moving.
stationer *n* a dealer in stationery, office supplies, etc.
stationery *n* writing materials, esp paper and envelopes.
station house *n* a building that houses police or fire services.
stationmaster *n* the senior official in charge of a railway station.
station wagon *n* a car with extra carrying space reached through a rear door.
statism *n* the concentration of economic and political power in the state.—**statist** *n.*
statistic *n* a fact obtained from analysing information expressed in numbers.
statistics *n sing* the branch of mathematics dealing with the collection, analysis and presentation of numerical data.—**statistical** *adj.*—**statistician** *n.*
stator *n* the stationary part of a motor or generator.
statoscope *n* a sensitive aneroid barometer for indicating minute fluctuations in pressure, used in altimeters in aircraft.
statuary *n* (*pl* **statuaries**) statues collectively.
statue *n* a representation of a human or animal form that is carved or moulded.
statuesque *adj* like a statue.—**statuesquely** *adv.*—**statuesqueness** *n.*
statuette *n* a small statue, figurine.
stature *n* the standing height of a person; level of attainment.
status *n* (*pl* **statuses**) social or professional position or standing; prestige; condition or standing from the point of view of the law, position of affairs.
status quo *n* the existing state of affairs.
status symbol *n* a possession that indicates high social standing, wealth, etc.
statute *n* a law enacted by a legislature; a regulation.
statute book *n* a register of statutes enacted by a legislature.
statute law *n* law enacted by a legislature.
statute mile *n* (*formal*) a mile.
statute of limitations *n* a statute that restricts the period of time in which proceedings may be brought to enforce a right or punish an offence.
statutory *adj* established, regulated, or required by statute.
staunch[1] *adj* loyal; dependable.—**staunchly** *adv.*—**staunchness** *n.*
staunch[2] *vt* to stem the flow of, as blood. * *vi* to cease to flow.—*also* **stanch.**
stave *n* a piece of wood of a cask or barrel; (*mus*) a staff. * *vt* (**staving, staved** *or* **stove**) (*usu with* **in**) to smash or dent inward.
staves *see* **staff.**
stay[1] *n* a rope supporting a mast
stay[2] *vi* to remain in a place; to wait; to reside temporarily. * *vt* to support; to endure; to stop, restrain. * *n* a suspension of legal proceedings; a short time spent as a visitor or guest.
stay-at-home *n* a quiet, placid, unadventurous person.—*also adj.*
staying power *n* stamina.
St Bernard *n* a Saint Bernard dog.
STD *abbr* = sexually transmitted disease; subscriber trunk dialling.
steadfast *adj* firm, fixed; resolute.—**steadfastly** *adv.*—**steadfastness** *n.*
steady *adj* (**steadier, steadiest**) firm, stable; regular, constant; calm, unexcitable. * *n* (*pl* **steadies**) (*inf*) a regular boyfriend or girlfriend. * *vti* (**steadying, steadied**) to make or become steady.—**steadily** *adv.*—**steadiness** *n.*
steady-state theory *n* the theory that the universe remains in a steady equilibrium as matter is continuously created as it expands.
steak *n* a slice of meat, esp beef or fish, for grilling or frying.
steakhouse *n* a restaurant that specializes in steaks.
steal *vt* (**stealing, stole,** *pp* **stolen**) to take (from someone) dishonestly; to obtain secretly. * *n* (*inf*) an unbelievable bargain.
stealth *n* a manner of moving quietly and secretly.
Stealth technology *n* the development, in great secrecy, of a new type of military aircraft.
stealthy *adj* (**stealthier, stealthiest**) acting or performed in a quiet, secret manner; unobtrusive, furtive.—**stealthily** *adv.*—**stealthiness** *n.*
steam *n* the hot mist or vapour created by boiling water. * *vi* to give off steam; to move by steam power; to cook with steam; (*sl*) to take part in illegal steaming; (*with* **up**) (*glasses, windows*) to become covered in condensation. * *adj* driven by steam.

steamboat *n* a boat powered by steam.
steam engine *n* a stationary or locomotive engine powered by steam.
steamer *n* a pan with a perforated bottom for cooking by steam; a ship propelled by steam engines; (*sl*) one who takes part in steaming.
steaming *n* (*sl*) the practice of multiple mugging by a gang of youths who move rapidly down a street, mugging and shiplifting.
steam iron *n* an electric iron that can heat water to use as steam which is emitted through the face to improve pressing.
steamroller *n* a vehicle with heavy rollers for pressing down road surfaces; an overpowering person or thing. * *vt* to crush (as if) with a steamroller; to obtain or influence by overpowering force.
steamy *adj* (**steamier, steamiest**) full of steam; (*inf*) erotic.—**steamily** *adv*.—**steaminess** *n*.
stearic acid *n* a fatty acid derived from solid fats and used for making candles and soap.
steatite *n* soapstone.
steato- *prefix* fat.
steed *n* (*arch, poet*) a horse.
steel *n* an alloy of iron and carbon; strength or courage. * *adj* of, or like, steel. * *vt* to cover with steel; to harden; to nerve (oneself).
steel band *n* a band that uses percussion instruments made from oil drums.
steel grey *n* a bluish-grey colour.
steel wool *n* a compact mass of steel fibres used for scouring and polishing.
steely *adj* (**steelier, steeliest**) of or like steel; hard, relentless.—**steeliness** *n*.
steelyard *n* a balance using a pivoted graduated arm along which a weight slides.
steenbok *n* (*pl* **steenboks, steenbok**) any of a genus of small antelopes of central and southern Africa.
steep[1] *adj* sloping sharply; (*inf*) excessive, exorbitant.—**steeply** *adv*.—**steepness** *n*.
steep[2] *vti* to soak or be soaked in a liquid; to saturate; to imbue.—*also n*.
steepen *vti* to make or become steeper.
steeple *n* a tower of a church, with or without a spire; the spire alone.
steeplechase *n* a horse race across country or on a course over jumps; a track race over hurdles and water jumps.—**steeplechaser** *n*.
steeplejack *n* a person who climbs and repairs tall chimneys.
steer[1] *n* a castrated male of the cattle family.
steer[2] *vti* to direct (a vehicle, ship, bicycle, etc) in the correct direction of travel.
steerage *n* the cheapest berths on a passenger ship.
steerageway *n* a rate of forward motion that allows a vessel to be steered.
steering *n* the mechanism that controls the direction of a ship, vehicle, etc; the practice of manoeuvring non-white house buyers or tenants away from white areas.
steering committee *n* a committee that organizes the content and order of business for a legislative assembly.
stegosaur, stegosaurus *n* (*pl* **stegosaurs, stegosauri**) any of various plant-eating dinosaurs with armoured body plates.
stein *n* an earthenware beer mug, often with a hinged lid.
stele *n* (*pl* **stelae, steles**) an upright slab of stone with inscriptions dating from prehistoric times; an inscribed commemorative slab placed on the front of a building; the vascular tissue in the stems and roots of plants.
stellar *adj* of, or composed of stars.
stellate, stellated *adj* of, resembling or composed of stars.
stellular *adj* filled with or composed of small stars; star-shaped.
St Elmo's fire *n* a flame-like electric discharge from a ship's mast and rigging in thundery weather, St Elmo's fire.—*also* **corposant**.
stem[1] *n* a plant stalk; the upright slender part of anything, such as a wineglass; the root of a word. * *vi* (**stemming, stemmed**) to originate (from).
stem[2] *vt* (**stemming, stemmed**) to stop, check (the flow or tide).
stench *n* a foul odour.
stencil *n* a pierced sheet of card or metal for reproducing letters by applying paint; a design so made. * *vti* (**stencilling, stencilled** *or* **stenciling, stenciled**) to produce (letters, etc) or designs using a stencil.—**stenciller, stenciler** *n*.
Sten gun *n* a light sub-machine gun.
stenography *n* shorthand.—**stenographer** *n*.
stenosis *n* (*pl* **stenoses**) an abnormal narrowing of a bodily passage or orifice.—**stenotic** *adj*.
stentorian *adj* (*voice*) loud, booming.
step *n* one movement of the foot ahead in walking, running, or dancing; a pace; a grade or degree; a stage toward a goal; one tread of a stair, rung of a ladder. * *vti* (**stepping, stepped**) to take a step or a number of paces.
step- *prefix* related by remarriage of a spouse or parent.
stepbrother *n* a son of one's step-parent from a former marriage.
stepchild *n* (*pl* **stepchildren**) a stepson or stepdaughter.
stepdaughter *n* the daughter of one's spouse from a former marriage.
stepfather *n* the husband of one's remarried mother.
stephanotis *n* a tropical climbing plant with fragrant white flowers.
stepladder *n* a short portable ladder with flat steps fixed within a frame.
stepmother *n* the wife of one's remarried father.
step-parent *n* stepfather or stepmother.
steppe *n* a vast grassy treeless plain.
stepping stone *n* a stone or stones allowing a stream, puddle, etc to be crossed by foot; a means of advancing toward some end.
stepsister *n* the daughter of one's step-parent from a former marriage
stepson *n* the son of one's spouse from a former marriage
steradian *n* a unit of solid angular measurement.
stere *n* a unit equal to one cubic metre (35.3 cubic feet), used for measuring timber.
stereo *n* (*pl* **stereos**) a hi-fi or record player with two loudspeakers; stereophonic sound. * *adj* stereophonic.
stereochemistry *n* the study of the composition and properties of matter in relation to the spatial arrangement of atoms in molecules.
stereograph *n* two almost identical images that when superimposed and viewed through a stereoscope produce a three-dimensional picture.
stereophonic *adj* (*sound reproduction system*) using two separate channels for recording and transmission to create a spatial effect.—**stereophonically** *adv*.—**stereophony** *n*.
stereoscope *n* an optical device which blends two images viewed from a slightly different aspect into a single three-dimensional picture.—**stereoscopic** *adj*.
stereoscopy *n* viewing objects in three dimensions.
stereotype *n* a fixed, general image of a person or thing shared by many people.—*also vt*.
steric *adj* of or pertaining to the spatial arrangement of atoms in a molecule.
sterile *adj* unable to produce offspring, fruit, seeds, or spores; fruitless; free from germs.—**sterility** *n*.
sterilize *vt* to render incapable of reproduction; to free from germs.—**sterilization** *n*.—**sterilizer** *n*.
sterling *n* the British system of money. * *adj* of excellent character.
stern[1] *adj* severe; austere, harsh.—**sternly** *adv*.—**sternness** *n*.
stern[2] *n* the rear part of a boat or ship
sternum *n* (*pl* **sterna, sternums**) the breastbone.
sternutation *n* sneezing.
sternutator *n* a substance that induces sneezing, tears, etc, such as a gas used in riot control.
steroid *n* any of a large number of compounds sharing the same chemical structure, including sterols and many hormones.
sterol *n* any of various solid steroid alcohols, such as cholesterol, found in plants and animals.
stertorous *adj* characterized by heavy breathing or snoring sounds.—**stertorously** *adv*.—**stertorousness** *n*.
stet *vt* a proofreading direction meaning that deleted matter marked by a row of dots should remain. * *vt* (**stetting, stetted**) to mark (text) in this way.

stethoscope *n* an instrument used to detect body sounds.—**stethoscopic** *adj*.
stetson *n* a man's felt hat with a broad brim and high crown.
stevedore *n* a labourer who loads and unloads ships.
stew *n* a meal of cooked meat with vegetables. * *vt* to cook slowly.
steward *n* a manager (of property); a race organizer; a person who serves food on an aircraft or ship and looks after passengers.
stewardess *n* a woman steward on an aircraft or ship.
stick[1] *vb* (**sticking, stuck**) *vt* to pierce or stab; to attach with glue, adhesive tape, etc; (*with* **up**) (*inf*) to rob at gunpoint. * *vi* to cling to, to adhere; to stay close to; to be held up; (*with* **around**) (*inf*) to wait in the vicinity, to linger; (*with* **by**) to remain faithful to; to stay close to.
stick[2] *n* a broken off shoot or branch of a tree; a walking stick; a hockey stick; a rod.
sticker *n* an adhesive label or poster.
sticking plaster *n* a thin strip of cloth with an adhesive backing for covering small cuts and abrasions.
stick insect *n* a wingless insect with a long thin body resembling a twig.
stick-in-the-mud *n* (*inf*) a person who feels threatened by new ideas or situations.
stickleback *n* any of various small freshwater fishes with sharp spines on the back.
stickler *n* a person who is scrupulous or obstinate about something.
stick-up *n* (*inf*) a robbery at gunpoint.
sticky *adj* (**stickier, stickiest**) covered with adhesive or something sweet; (*weather*) warm and humid; (*inf*) difficult.—**stickily** *adv*.—**stickiness** *n*.
sticky end *n* (*inf*) an unpleasant death.
sticky wicket *n* (*cricket*) a damp wicket that is difficult to bat on; (*inf*) an awkward or unpleasant situation.
stiff *adj* not flexible or supple; rigid; firm; moving with difficulty; having aching joints and muscles; formal, unfriendly; (*drink*) potent; (*breeze*) strong; (*penalty*) severe. * *n* (*sl*) a corpse. * *adv* utterly.—**stiffly** *adv*.—**stiffness** *n*.
stiffen *vti* to make or become stiff.—**stiffener** *n*.
stiff-necked *adj* stubborn, aloof.
stifle *vt* to suffocate; to smother; to suppress, hold back.
stifling *adj* excessively hot and stuffy.
stigma *n* (*pl* **stigmas, stigmata**) a social disgrace; the part of a flower that receives pollen; (*Christianity*) marks resembling the wounds of Christ thought to appear on the bodies of saintly people.
stigmatize *vt* to brand as bad or disgraceful.—**stigmatization** *n*.
stile *n* a step, or set of steps, for climbing over a wall or fence.
stiletto *n* (*pl* **stilettos**) a small slender dagger; a pointed tool for piercing holes in leather, etc; a high heel tapering to a point on a woman's shoe. * *vt* (**stilettoeing, stilettoed**) to stab with a stiletto.
still[1] *adj* motionless; calm; silent; (*drink*) not carbonated. * *n* a single photograph taken from a cinema film. * *vti* to make or become still. * *adv* continuously; nevertheless.—**stillness** *n*.
still[2] *n* an apparatus for distilling liquids, esp spirits.
stillborn *adj* born dead; (*idea, project, etc*) a failure from the start, abortive.
still life *n* (*pl* **still lives**) a painting of inanimate objects, such as flowers, fruit, etc.
stilt *n* either of a pair of poles with footrests on which one can walk, as in a circus; a supporting column.
stilted *adj* (*speech, writing*) pompous, unnaturally formal; (*conversation*) forced, intermittent.
Stilton *n* a blue-veined cheese with a strong flavour.
stimulant *n* a drug, drink, or food that increases one's heart rate and body activity.
stimulate *vt* to excite, arouse.—**stimulation** *n*.
stimulus *n* (*pl* **stimuli**) something that acts as an incentive; an agent that arouses or provokes a response in a living organism.
sting *n* a sharp pointed organ of a bee, wasp, etc, or hair on a plant, used for injecting poison; a skin wound caused by injected poison from an insect or plant; (*sl*) a swindle. * *vt* to wound with a sting; to cause to suffer mentally; to goad, incite; (*sl*) to cheat by overcharging. * *vi* to feel a sharp pain.
stingray *n* any of various rays with a whiplike tail bearing sharp venomous spines.
stingy *adj* (**stingier, stingiest**) miserly, mean.—**stingily** *adv*.—**stinginess** *n*.
stink *vi* (**stinking, stank** *or* **stunk**, *pp* **stunk**) to give out an offensive smell; (*sl*) to possess something in an excessive amount; (*sl*) to be extremely bad in quality. * *n* a foul smell.
stink bomb *n* a small glass capsule which releases a foul smell when broken, used for practical jokes.
stinker *n* (*inf*) an offensive person or thing; (*inf*) something difficult or unpleasant.
stinkhorn *n* a type of foul-smelling fungus.
stinko *adj* (*sl*) drunk.
stinkweed *n* any of various plants with pungent scents.
stint *vt* to be frugal in the supply or allowance of something. * *vi* to be frugal, miserly. * *n* a fixed period or quantity of work; a limitation, restriction.
stipe *n* a short stalk or stem of a plant, esp of a mushroom.
stipend *n* a regular payment of money as wages or for expenses, esp to a clergyman.
stipendiary *adj* of or receiving a stipend. * *n* (*pl* **stipendiaries**) a person who receives a stipend.
stipple *vt* to engrave, paint, draw, etc, in tiny dots.
stipulate *vt* to specify as a condition of an agreement.—**stipulation** *n*.
stir[1] *vb* (**stirring, stirred**) *vt* to mix, as with a spoon; to rouse; to stimulate or excite; (*with* **up**) to agitate, instigate. * *vi* to be disturbed; to move oneself; to be active. * *n* a stirring movement; tumult.
stir[2] *n* (*sl*) prison.
stir-fry *vt* to cook (chopped vegetables, etc) by stirring rapidly in hot oil in a wok or frying pan.
stirring *adj* rousing, exciting.—**stirringly** *adv*.
stirrup *n* a strap and flat-bottomed ring hanging from a saddle, for a rider's foot.
stirrup cup *n* a farewell drink, orig given to a rider on horseback before departure.
stirrup pump *n* a small portable water pump held steady by a stirrup-shaped foot bracket, used for fire-fighting.
stitch *n* a single in-and-out movement of a threaded needle in sewing; a single loop of a yarn in knitting or crocheting; a sudden, sharp pain, esp in the side. * *vti* to sew.
stoat *n* a small European mammal related to the weasel.
stochastic *adj* random; involving chance or probability.
stock *n* raw material; goods on hand; shares of corporate capital, or the certificates showing such ownership; lineage, family, race; a store; the cattle, horses, etc, kept on a farm; the broth obtained by boiling meat, bones, and vegetables as a foundation for soup, etc. * *vt* to supply; to keep in store. * *adj* standard; hackneyed.
stockade *n* a defensive enclosure or barrier of stakes fixed in the ground.
stockbroker *n* a person who deals in stocks.
stock car *n* a standard production saloon car modified for racing.
stockholder *n* an owner of corporate stock.
stocking filler *n* a gift suitable for a Christmas stocking.
stocking *n* a sock; a nylon covering for a woman's leg, supported by suspenders.
stock market, stock exchange *n* the market for dealing in stocks and shares.
stockpile *n* a reserve supply of essentials.—*also vt*.
stock-still *adv* motionless.
stocktaking *n* making an inventory of goods on hand (in a shop, warehouse, etc); evaluating one's present condition, resources, etc.
stocky *adj* (**stockier, stockiest**) short and sturdy.—**stockily** *adv*.—**stockiness** *n*.
stockyard *n* a yard for holding cattle, sheep, pigs, etc before they are sold, transported, or slaughtered.

stodge *n* (*inf*) heavy, starchy food.
stodgy *adj* (**stodgier, stodgiest**) (*food*) thick, heavy and indigestible; uninteresting.—**stodgily** *adv*.—**stodginess** *n*.
stoic *n* a person who suffers hardship without showing emotion.—**stoical** *adj*.—**stoically** *adv*.—**stoicism** *n*.
stoke *vt* to stir and feed (a fire) with fuel.
STOL *abbr* = short take-off and landing, a system that allows an aircraft to take off and land within a short distance.
stole[1] *see* **steal.**
stole[2] *n* a long scarf or piece of fur worn on the shoulders.
stolen *see* **steal.**
stolid *adj* impassive; unemotional.—**stolidity** *n*.—**stolidly** *adv*.
stoma *n* (*pl* **stomata**) a minute aperture in the epidermis of a plant for the passage of gases; an orifice or mouthlike opening; a permanent surgical opening, esp in the abdominal wall.
stomach *n* the organ where food is digested; the belly. * *vt* to put up with.
stomach pump *n* a suction pump that empties the contents of the stomach through a long tube inserted orally.
stomata *see* **stoma.**
stomatitis *n* inflammation of the mouth.
stomatology *n* the branch of medicine concerned with the mouth.—**stomatological** *adj*.
stomp *vti* to walk with heavy steps; to stamp. * *n* an early jazz dance.
stone *n* a small lump of rock; a precious stone or gem; the hard seed of a fruit; (*pl* **stone**) a unit of weight (14 lb./6.35 kg). * *vt* to throw stones at; to remove stones from (fruit).
Stone Age *n* the prehistoric age of human culture characterized by the use of stone tools and weapons.
stoned *adj* (*inf*) under the influence of drink or drugs.
stonefish *n* (*pl* **stonefish, stonefishes**) a venomous tropical fish with markings that resemble a stone on the seabed.
stone's throw *n* a short distance.
stonewall *vi* to obstruct or hinder, esp in politics and government.
stonewashed *adj* (*clothes*) made to appear worn and faded by the abrasive action of pumice particles.
stony, stoney *adj* (**stonier, stoniest**) of, like, or full of stones; unfeeling, heartless.—**stonily** *adv*.—**stoniness** *n*.
stony-broke *adj* (*inf*) completely without money.
stony-hearted *adj* unfeeling, cruel.—**stony-heartedness** *n*.
stood *see* **stand.**
stooge *n* (*sl*) a performer who feeds lines to a comedian; a person subordinate to or dominated by another; a stool pigeon. * *vi* to act as a stooge.
stool *n* a seat or a support for the back when sitting, with no back or arms; matter evacuated from the bowels.
stool pigeon *n* a police informer.
stoop[1] *vti* to bend the body forward and downward; to degrade oneself; to deign.—*also n*.
stoop[2] *n* a porch or small landing with stairs at the entrance to a house or building.
stooped *adj* hunched.
stop *vb* (**stopping, stopped**) *vt* to halt; to prevent; to intercept; to plug or block. * *vi* to cease; to come to an end; to stay. * *n* an act or instance of stopping; an impediment; (a knob controlling) a set of organ pipes; any of the standard settings of the aperture in a camera lens, f-stop; a regular stopping place for a bus or train; a punctuation mark, esp full stop.
stop bath *n* a mildy acidic solution used to halt the development of a negative print, plate, etc.
stopcock *n* a device for regulating the flow of liquid in a pipe.
stopgap *n* a temporary substitute, expedient.
stoplight *n* a red light on a traffic signal warning vehicles to halt; a brake light.
stopover *n* a short break in a journey.
stoppage *n* stopping or being stopped; an obstruction; a deduction from pay; a concerted cessation of work by employees, as during a strike.
stopper *n* a cork or bung.
stop press *n* (the space reserved for) an item of last minute news added to a newspaper after printing has begun.
stopwatch *n* a watch that can be started and stopped, used for timing sporting events.
storage *n* storing or being stored; an area reserved for storing; (*comput*) the storing of data in a computer memory or on disk, tape, etc.
storage battery *n* an accumulator.
storage capacity *n* the maximum amount of information that can be held in computer memory or a storage device.
storage device *n* a piece of computer equipment, such as a hard disk, used to store data.
storage heater *n* a radiator which accumulates heat during periods of off-peak electricity.
store *n* a large supply of goods for future use; a warehouse; a shop. * *vt* to set aside; to put in a warehouse, etc; (*comput*) to put (data) into a computer memory or onto a storage device.
store card *n* a charge card issued by a store or chain of stores for the purchase of goods there only.
storehouse *n* a place for storing things; a rich source or supply.
storey *n* (*pl* **storeys**) a horizontal division of a building, a story.
stork *n* a long-necked and long-legged wading bird.
storksbill *n* any of several plants of the geranium family with pink or purple flowers.
storm *n* a heavy fall of rain, snow, etc with strong winds; a violent commotion; a furore; (mil) an attack on a fortified place. * *vt* to rush, invade. * *vi* to be angry; to rain, snow hard.—**stormy** *adj*.
stormbound *adj* affected or confined by storms.
storm trooper *n* a member of the Sturmabteilung, a semi-military group of the German Nazi party (1924–45) notorious for its violence; a member of a shock troop.
Storting, Storthing *n* the parliament of Norway.
story[1] *n* (*pl* **stories**) a narrative of real or imaginary events; a plot of a literary work; an anecdote; an account; (*inf*) a lie; a news article.
story[2] *n* (*pl* **stories**) a horizontal division of a building, a storey; a set of rooms occupying this space.
storyboard *n* (*films, television*) a sequence of drawings or photographs showing the images to be shot to film for a particular story.
stout *adj* strong; short and plump; sturdy. * *n* strong dark beer.—**stoutly** *adv*.—**stoutness** *n*.
stouthearted *adj* brave.—**stoutheartedly** *adv*.
stove[1] *n* a cooker; heating apparatus.
stove[2] *see* **stave.**
stow *vt* to store, pack, in an orderly way.
stowage *n* stowing or being stowed; goods in storage; a place for storage or the charge for this.
stowaway *n* a person who hides on a ship, car, aircraft, etc to avoid paying the fare.
St Patrick's Day *abbr* = Saint Patrick's Day.
strabismus *n* a squint.
straddle *vt* to have one leg or support on either side of something.
strafe *vt* to machine-gun (troops, vehicles, etc) from the air.—*also n*.
straggle *vi* to stray; to wander.—**straggler** *n*.—**straggly** *adj*.
straight *adj* (*line*) continuing in one direction, not curved or bent; direct; honest; (*sl*) heterosexual; (*alcoholic drinks*) neat, not diluted. * *adv* directly; without delay. * *n* being straight; a straight line, form, or position; a straight part of a racetrack; (*poker*) a hand containing five cards in sequence.—**straightness** *n*.
straight and narrow *n* (*inf*) the honest and virtuous way of life.
straight angle *n* an angle of 180°.
straightaway *adv* without delay.
straightedge *n* a length of wood, metal, etc used to rule or test for accurate straight lines.
straighten *vti* to make or become straight; (*with* **out**) to make or become less confused or entangled; to resolve.

straight face *n* a face betraying no signs of emotion, esp amusement.—**straight-faced** *adj*.
straight fight *n* a contest between only two candidates.
straight flush *n* (*poker*) five cards of the same suit in sequence.
straightforward *adj* honest, open; simple; easy.—**straightforwardly** *adv*.—**straightforwardness** *n*.
straightjacket *see* **straitjacket.**
straight-laced *see* **strait-laced.**
straight man *n* a person who acts as a stooge to a comedian.
straight-out *adj* (*inf*) honest, direct; thorough.
strain[1] *vt* to tax; to stretch; to overexert; to stress; to injure (a muscle) by overstretching; (food) to drain or sieve. * *n* overexertion; tension; an injury from straining.
strain[2] *n* a plant or animal within a species having a common characteristic; a trait; a trace.
strained *adj* (*action, behaviour*) produced by excessive effort; (*mood, atmosphere*) tense, worried.
strainer *n* a sieve or colander used for straining liquids, pasta, tea, etc.
strait *n* a channel of sea linking two larger seas; (*usu pl*) difficulty, distress.
straitjacket *n* a coatlike device for restraining violent people; something that restricts or limits.—*also vt*. —*also* **straightjacket.**
strait-laced *adj* prim, morally strict.—*also* **straight-laced.**
strand[1] *vt* to run aground; to leave helpless, without transport or money.
strand[2] *n* a single piece of thread or wire twisted together to make a rope or cable; a tress of hair.—*also vt*.
strange *adj* peculiar; odd; unknown; unfamiliar.—**strangely** *adv*.—**strangeness** *n*.
stranger *n* a person who is unknown; a new arrival to a place, town, social gathering, etc; a person who is unfamiliar with or ignorant of something.
strangle *vt* to kill by compressing the windpipe, to choke; to stifle, suppress.—**strangler** *n*.
stranglehold *n* (*wrestling*) a grip that presses an opponent's windpipe; a powerful restrictive force or influence.
strangles *n sing* an infectious bacterial disease of horses that inflames the respiratory tract, equine distemper.
strangulate *vt* to strangle; to compress (eg a blood vessel or the intestine) so as to cause a blockage. * *vi* to become strangulated.—**strangulatation** *n*.
strangury *n* slow, painful urination.
strap *n* a narrow strip of leather or cloth for carrying or holding (a bag, etc); a fastening, as on a shoe, wristwatch. * *vti* (**strapping, strapped**) to fasten with a strap; to beat with a strap.
straphanger *n* (*inf*) a standing passenger in a bus or train, etc.
strapping *adj* tall, well-built.
strata *see* **stratum.**
stratagem *n* a clever action planned to deceive or outwit an enemy.
strategic, strategical *adj* of, relating to, or important in strategy; (*weapons*) designed to strike at the enemy's homeland, not for use on the battlefield.—**strategically** *adv*.
Strategic Defense Initiative *n* the US government's proposed deployment of satellites armed with laser devices to destroy enemy missiles.
strategy *n* (*pl* **strategies**) the planning and conduct of war; a political, economic, or business policy.—**strategist** *n*.
strath *n* (*Scot*) a wide, flat river valley.
strathspey *n* (the music for) a type of Scottish dance with slow gliding steps.
straticulate *n* (*rocks*) having thin strata.
stratified *adj* arranged or deposited in strata or layers.—**stratification** *n*.
stratigraphy *n* (the scientific study of) the composition and order of rock strata.—**stratigraphic** *adj*.
stratocumulus *n* (*pl* **stratocumuli**) layers of dark cloud in dense round masses.
stratosphere *n* a layer of the earth's atmosphere above 10 km (6 miles) in which temperature increases with height.—**stratospheric** *adj*.
stratum *n* (*pl* **strata, stratums**) a layer of sedimentary rock; a level (of society).
stratus *n* (*pl* **strati**) a continuous horizontal layer of cloud.
straw *n* the stalks of threshed grain; a tube for sucking up a drink.
strawberry *n* (*pl* **strawberries**) a soft red fruit used in desserts and jam.
strawberry blonde *adj* (*hair*) reddish blonde. * *n* a woman with hair of this colour.
strawberry mark *n* an irregular blood-coloured birth mark.
strawberry tree *n* a European evergreen tree bearing fruit resembling strawberries.
straw poll *n* an unofficial poll to assess public opinion.
stray *vi* to wander; to deviate; to digress. * *n* a domestic animal that has become lost. * *adj* random.
streak *n* a line or long mark of contrasting colour; a flash of lightning; a characteristic, a trace. * *vti* to mark with or form streaks; to run naked in public as a prank.—**streaker** *n*.
streaky *adj* (**streakier, streakiest**) marked with streaks; (*bacon*) having alternate layers of fat and lean.
stream *n* a small river, brook, etc; a flow of liquid; anything flowing and continuous, * *vi* to flow, gush.
streamer *n* a banner; a long decorative ribbon.
streamline *vt* to shape (a car, boat, etc) in a way that lessens resistance through air or water; to make more efficient, to simplify.—**streamlined** *adj*.
street *n* a public road in a town or city lined with houses; such a road with its buildings and pavements; the people living,working, etc, along a given street. * *adj* pertaining to urban youth culture.
streetcar *n* an electrically powered vehicle for public transport, which travels along rails set into the ground, a tram.
street cred, street credibility *n* the mastery of the style and ways or urban culture.
street fighter *n* (*sl*) a person who is tough and combative.
street value *n* the value of a commodity, esp an illegal drug, in terms of the price charged to the ultimate users.
streetwalker *n* a prostitute who solicits in the streets.
streetwise *adj* (*inf*) experienced in surviving or avoiding the potential dangers of urban life.
strength *n* the state or quality of being physically or mentally strong; power of exerting or withstanding pressure, stress, force; potency; effectiveness.
strengthen *vti* to make or become stronger.
strenuous *adj* vigorous; requiring exertion.—**strenuously** *adv*.—**strenuousness** *n*.
strep *n* (*inf*) a streptococcus.
strepitoso *adv* (*mus*) in a boisterous manner.
streptococcus *n* (*pl* **streptococci**) any of a genus of spherical bacteria occurring in chains of different length.
streptomycin *n* an antibiotic derived from a soil bacterium, used in the treatment of infections such as tuberculosis.
stress *n* pressure; mental or physical tension or strain; emphasis; (*physics*) a system of forces producing or sustaining a strain. * *vt* to exert pressure on; to emphasize.
stretch *vt* to extend, to draw out. * *vi* to extend, spread; to extend (the limbs, body); to be capable of expanding, as in elastic material. * *n* the act of stretching or instance of being stretched; the capacity for being stretched; an expanse of time or space; (*sl*) a period of imprisonment.—**stretchy** *adj*.
stretcher *n* a portable frame for carrying the sick or injured.
strew *vt* (**strewing, strewed,** *pp* **strewn** *or* **strewed**) to scatter; to spread.
strewth *interj* used to express surprise or alarm.
striation *n* any of a series of parallel grooves, scratches, ridges or lines on a surface.—**striated** *adj*.
stricken *adj* suffering (from an illness); afflicted, as by something painful.
strict *adj* harsh, firm; enforcing rules rigorously; rigid.—**strictly** *adv*.—**strictness** *n*.
stricture *n* harsh criticism, censure.
stride *vi* (**striding, strode,** *pp* **stridden**) to walk with long steps. * *vt* to straddle.—*also n*.

strident *adj* loud and harsh.—**stridency** *n*.—**stridently** *adv*.

stridulate *vi* (of insects) to make a chirping or scraping sound.

strife *n* a fight, quarrel; struggle.

strike *vb* (**striking, struck**) *vt* to hit; to crash into; (*mil*) to attack; to ignite (a match) by friction; (*disease, etc*) to afflict suddenly; to come upon, esp unexpectedly; to delete; (*clock*) to indicate by sounding; to assume (eg an attitude); to occur to; (*medal, coin*) to produce by stamping; (*flag, tent*) to lower, take down; to come upon (oil, ore, etc) by drilling or excavation; (*with* **down**) to afflict or cause to die suddenly; (*with* **off**) to delete or erase from (a list, etc); to prevent from continuing in a profession, esp due to malpractice; to sever or separate from (as if) with a blow; (*with* **out**) to erase or delete; (*with* **up**) to cause to begin, to bring about. * *vi* to cease work to enforce a demand (for higher wages or better working conditions). * *n* a stoppage of work; a military attack; (*with* **out**) to begin on a journey; (*baseball*) to be put out on strikes; (*inf*) to be completely unsuccessful; (*with* **up**) (*orchestra, band*) to begin to play or sing.

strikebound *adj* (*factory, etc*) closed or paralysed by striking workers.

strikebreaker *n* a person who continues work whilst colleagues are on strike; a person hired to replace a striking worker.—**strikebreaking** *n, adj*.

strike pay *n* money paid to workers on strike from trade union funds.

striker *n* a worker who is on strike; a mechanism that strikes, as in a clock; (*soccer*) a forward player whose primary role is to score goals.

striking *adj* impressive.—**strikingly** *adv*.

Strine *n* Australian English (a humorous rendering of the Australian for *Australian*).

string *n* a thin length of cord or twine used for tying, fastening, etc; a stretched length of catgut, wire, or other material in a musical instrument; (*pl*) the stringed instruments in an orchestra; their players; a line or series of things. * *vt* (**stringing, strung**) to thread on a string; (*with* **up**) (*sl*) to kill by hanging. * *vi* (*with* **along**) (*inf*) to appear to agree (with); to accompany; to deceive, esp to gain time.

stringed *adj* (*musical instruments*) having strings.

stringent *adj* strict.—**stringently** *adv*.—**stringency** *n*.

stringer *n* a horizontal support in a structure; a long horizontal brace to strengthen a framework, as in an aircraft fuselage; a journalist or photographer temporarily employed by a newspaper, magazine or news service to cover a particular area.

string quartet *n* (a piece of music written for) a musical ensemble comprising two violins, one viola, and one cello.

string tie *n* a narrow tie.

stringy *adj* (**stringier, stringiest**) of or resembling string; (*meat, etc*) fibrous, chewy; (*physique*) sinewy.

strip *vb* (**stripping, stripped**) *vt* to peel off; to divest; to take away removable parts. * *vi* to undress. * *n* a long, narrow piece (of cloth, land, etc); an airstrip or runway.

strip cartoon *n* a series of drawings in a newspaper, etc which tell a story.

strip club *n* a nightclub which features striptease artists.

stripe *n* a narrow band of a different colour from the background; a chevron worn on a military uniform to indicate rank. * *vt* to mark with a stripe.—**striped** *adj*.—**stripy** *adj*.

strip lighting *n* lighting using long fluorescent tubes.

stripling *n* a youth, boy.

strip mining *n* mining by surface excavation, opencast mining.

stripper *n* a striptease artist; a device or solvent that removes paint.

striptease *n* an erotic show where a person removes their clothes slowly and seductively to music.

strive *vi* (**striving, strove,** *pp* **striven**) to endeavour earnestly, labour hard, to struggle, contend.

strobe *n* (*inf*) a stroboscope.

strobe lighting *n* (the equipment used to produce) high-intensity flashing light.

stroboscope *n* a device for observing motion by making the subject visible at prescribed intervals using a synchronized flashing light.

strode *see* **stride.**

stroganoff *n* sliced beef cooked with mushrooms and onions in a sour cream sauce.

stroke[1] *n* a blow or hit; (*med*) a seizure; the sound of a clock; (*sport*) an act of hitting a ball; a manner of swimming; the sweep of an oar in rowing; a movement of a pen, pencil, or paintbrush.

stroke[2] *vt* to caress; to do so as a sign of affection.

stroke play *n* (*golf*) scoring by the number of strokes taken.

stroll *vi* to walk leisurely, to saunter. * *n* a leisurely walk for pleasure.

stroller *n* a wheeled metal and canvas chair for a small child, a pushchair.

strong *adj* physically or mentally powerful; potent; intense; healthy; convincing; powerfully affecting the sense of smell or taste, pungent. * *adv* effectively, vigorously.—**strongly** *adv*.

strong-arm *adj* using unwarranted physical force.

strongbox *n* a solid, secure container for valuables.

strong drink *n* alcoholic drink.

stronghold *n* a fortress; a centre of strength or support.

strong-minded *adj* resolute, determined.—**strong-mindedly** *adv*.—**strong-mindedness** *n*.

strong point *n* something at which one excels.

strongroom *n* a room specially designed to keep money and valuables secure from theft or fire, etc.

strontium *n* a soft metallic element.

strop *n* a strip of leather for sharpening a razor. * *vt* (**stropping, stropped**) to sharpen using a strop.

strophe *n* a stanza or movement of a Greek chorus alternating with the antistrophe sung when moving to the left.—**strophic** *adj*.

stroppy *adj* (**stroppier, stroppiest**) (*inf*) surly, angry; quarrelsome.

strove *see* **strive.**

struck *see* **strike.**

structuralism *n* a view of the social sciences, literature, linguistics, etc, which stresses the importance of inherent underlying hierarchical structures, interrelationships and patterns of organization.—**structuralist** *n*.

structure *n* organization; construction; arrangement of parts in an organism, or of atoms in a molecule of a substance; system, framework; order. * *vt* to organize, to arrange; to build up.—**structural** *adj*.—**structurally** *adv*.

strudel *n* very thin pastry rolled up with a fruit filling and baked.

struggle *vi* to move strenuously so as to escape; to strive; to fight; to exert strength; to make one's way (along, through, up, etc) with difficulty. * *n* a violent effort; a fight.

strum *vt* (**strumming, strummed**) to play on (a guitar, etc), by moving the thumb across the strings.

struma *n* (*pl* **strumae**) enlargement of the thyroid gland; goitre.

strumpet *n* (*arch*) a prostitute.

strung *see* **string.**

strung-up *adj* (*inf*) tense, anxious.

strut[1] *vi* (**strutting, strutted**) to walk in a proud or pompous manner.

strut[2] *n* a brace or structural support. * *vt* to brace.

struthious *adj* (*birds*) related to or resembling the ostrich.

strychnine *n* a poison used in very small quantities as a stimulant.

stub *n* a short piece left after the larger part has been removed or used; the counterfoil of a cheque, receipt, etc. * *vt* (**stubbing, stubbed**) to knock (one's toe or foot) painfully; to extinguish (a cigarette).

stubble *n* the stubs or stumps left in the ground when a crop has been harvested; any short, bristly growth, as of beard.—**stubbly** *adj*.

stubborn *adj* obstinate; persevering; determined, inflexible.—**stubbornly** *adv*.—**stubbornness** *n*.

stubby *adj* (**stubbier, stubbiest**) short and thick; (*Austral sl*) a small bottle of beer.

stucco *n* (*pl* **stuccoes, stuccos**) a type of cement or plaster used to coat and decorate outside surfaces of walls. * *vt* (**stuccoing, stuccoed**) to decorate or finish with stucco.

stuck *see* **stick.**

stuck-up *adj* (*inf*) conceited; proud; snobbish.

stud[1] *n* a male animal, esp a horse, kept for breeding; a collection of horses and mares for breeding; a farm or stable for stud animals.

stud[2] *n* a large-headed nail; an ornamental fastener. * *vt* (**studding, studded**) to cover with studs.

studbook *n* a written record of the pedigree of a thoroughbred horse, dog, etc.

student *n* a person who studies or investigates a particular subject; a person who is enrolled for study at a school, college, university, etc.

studied *adj* carefully planned.—**studiedly** *adv*.—**studiedness** *n*.

studio *n* (*pl* **studios**) the workshop of an artist, photographer or musician; (*pl*) a building where motion pictures are made; a room where television or radio programmes are recorded.

studio couch *n* a couch resembling a divan that can be converted into a bed.

studio flat *n* a small flat with one main room, a kitchen and a bathroom.

studious *adj* given to study; careful.—**studiously** *adv*.—**studiousness** *n*.

study *vt* (**studying, studied**) to observe and investigate (eg phenomena) closely; to learn (eg a language); to scrutinize; to follow a course (at college, etc). * *n* (*pl* **studies**) the process of studying; a detailed investigation and analysis of a subject; the written report of a study of something; a room for studying.

stuff *n* material; matter; textile fabrics; cloth, esp when woollen; personal possessions generally. * *vt* to cram or fill.

stuffed shirt *n* (*inf*) a pretentious or pompous person.

stuffing *n* material used to stuff or fill anything; a seasoned mixture put inside poultry, meat, vegetables etc before cooking.

stuffy *adj* (**stuffier, stuffiest**) badly ventilated; lacking in fresh air; dull, uninspired.—**stuffily** *adv*.—**stuffiness** *n*.

stultify *vt* (**stultifying, stultified**) to make ineffectual or futile.—**stultification** *n*.

stumble *vi* to trip up or lose balance when walking; to falter; to discover by chance (*with* **across** *or* **on**). * *n* a trip; a blunder.

stumbling block *n* an obstacle to further progress.

stump *n* the part of a tree remaining in the ground after the trunk has been felled; the part of a limb, tooth, that remains after the larger part is cut off or destroyed. * *vt* (*inf*) to confuse, baffle; to campaign for an election.

stumpy *adj* (**stumpier, stumpiest**) short and thick.—**stumpiness** *n*.

stun *vt* (**stunning, stunned**) to render unconscious due to a fall or heavy blow; to surprise completely; to shock.

stung *see* **sting**.

stun gun *n* a type of gun that emits high-voltage electricity to stun victims.

stunk *see* **stink**.

stunner *n* (*inf*) a strikingly attractive or impressive person or thing.

stunning *adj* (*inf*) strikingly attractive.—**stunningly** *adv*.

stunt[1] *vt* to prevent the growth of, to dwarf.

stunt[2] *n* a daring or spectacular feat; a project designed to attract attention. * *vi* to carry out stunts.

stupa *n* a domed shrine holding Buddhist relics.

stupefy *vt* (**stupefying, stupefied**) to dull the senses of.—**stupefaction** *n*.

stupendous *adj* wonderful, astonishing.—**stupendously** *adv*.

stupid *adj* lacking in understanding or common sense; silly; foolish; stunned.—**stupidity** *n*.—**stupidly** *adv*.

stupor *n* extreme lethargy; mental dullness.

sturdy *adj* (**sturdier, sturdiest**) firm; strong, robust.—**sturdily** *adv*.—**sturdiness** *n*.

sturgeon *n* any of various large food fishes whose roe is also eaten as caviare.

Sturmabteilung *see* **storm trooper**.

stutter *vi* to stammer.—*also n*.

sty[1], **stye** *n* (*pl* **sties**) an inflamed swelling on the eyelid.

sty[2] *n* (*pl* **sties**) a pen for pigs; any filthy place.

style *n* the manner of writing, painting, composing music peculiar to an individual or group; fashion, elegance. * *vt* to design or shape (eg hair).—**styler** *n*.

stylish *adj* having style; fashionable.—**stylishly** *adv*.—**stylishness** *n*.

stylist *n* a person who writes, paints, etc, with attention to style; a designer; a hairdresser.

stylistic *adj* of literary or artistic style.—**stylistically** *adv*.

stylize *vt* to give a conventional style to.—**stylization** *n*.—**stylizer** *n*.

stylus *n* (*pl* **styluses, styli**) the device attached to the cartridge on the arm of a record-player that rests in the groove of a record and transmits the vibrations that are converted to sound.

stymie *n* (*pl* **stymies**) (*golf*) a situation in which a ball is obstructed by another ball between it and the hole. * *vt* (**stymieing, stymied**) to obstruct, hinder.

styptic *adj* acting to stop bleeding by contracting the blood vessels. * *n* a styptic drug.

styrene *n* a liquid hydrocarbon used in making rubber and plastics.

suave *adj* charming, polite.—**suavely** *adv*.—**suaveness** *n*.

suavity *n* (*pl* **suavities**) politeness; urbanity; a suave action, comment, etc.

sub *n* (*inf*) a submarine; a substitute; a subscription; a subeditor.

sub- *prefix* under, below; subordinate, next in rank to.

subaltern *n* a commissioned officer in the British army ranking below captain.* *adj* inferior in rank or status.

subaqua *adj* of or pertaining to underwater sports.

subatomic *adj* smaller than an atom; occurring within an atom.

subconscious *adj* happening without one's awareness. * *n* the part of the mind that is active without one's conscious awareness.—**subconsciously** *adv*.—**subconsciousness** *n*.

subcontinent *n* a land mass having great size but smaller than any of the usu recognized continents.

subcontract *n* a secondary contract, under which work or supply of materials is let out to a firm other than the main party of the contract.—*also vt*.—**subcontractor** *n*.

subculture *n* a distinct group with its own customs, language, dress, etc within an existing culture.

subcutaneous *adj* under the skin.—**subcutaneously** *adv*.

subdivide *vt* to further divide what has already been divided. * *vi* to divide or be divided into parts.—**subdivision** *n*.

subdue *vt* to dominate; to render submissive; to repress (eg a desire, impulse); to soften, tone down (eg colour, etc).

subeditor *n* a person who checks and corrects newspaper articles.—**subedit** *vt*.

subhead, subheading *n* a heading associated with a subdivision of a text.

subhuman *adj* (*animals*) lower down the evolutionary scale than mankind; less than human.

subject *adj* under the power of; liable. * *n* a person under the power of another; a citizen; a topic; a theme; the scheme or idea of a work of art. * *vt* to bring under control; to make liable; to cause to undergo something.—**subjection** *n*.

subjective *adj* determined by one's own mind or consciousness; relating to reality as perceived and not independent of the mind; arising from one's own thoughts and emotions, personal.—**subjectively** *adv*.—**subjectivity** *n*.

sub judice *adv* being decided by a court.

subjugate *vt* to overpower, to conquer.—**subjugation** *n*.

subjunctive *adv* denoting that mood of a verb which expresses doubt, condition, wish, or hope. * *n* the subjunctive mood.

sublet *vt* (**subletting, sublet**) to let (a property which one is renting) to another.

sublime *adj* noble; exalted.—**sublimely** *adv*.—**sublimity** *n*.

subliminal *adj* beneath or beyond the conscious awareness.—**subliminally** *adv*.

subliminal advertising *n* advertising using subliminal images to influence the viewer unconsciously.

sub-machine gun *n* a light automatic or semiautomatic gun designed to be fired from the hip or shoulder.

submarine *adj* underwater, esp under the sea. * *n* a naval vessel capable of being propelled under water, esp for firing torpedoes or missiles.

submerge, submerse *vt* to plunge or sink under water; to cover, hide.—**submergence, submersion** *n*.
submersible *adj* capable of being submerged. * *n* an underwater vessel used for exploration or construction work.
submission *n* an act of submitting; something submitted, as an idea or proposal; the state of being submissive, compliant; the act of referring something for another's consideration, criticism, etc.—**submissively** *adv*.—**submissiveness** *n*.
submit *vb* (**submitting, submitted**) *vt* to surrender (oneself) to another person or force; to refer to another for consideration or judgment; to offer as an opinion. * *vi* to yield, to surrender.
subnormal *adj* less than normal; having low intelligence.—**subnormality** *n*.—**subnormally** *adv*.
subordinate *adj* secondary; lower in order, rank. * *n* a subordinate person. * *vt* to put in a lower position or rank.—**subordination** *n*.
suborn *vt* to persuade to commit perjury or some other illegal act.
subpoena *n* a written legal order requiring the attendance of a person in court. * *vt* (**subpoenaing, subpoenaed**) to serve with a subpoena.
sub rosa *adv* in secret.
subroutine *n* a self-contained section of a computer program that performs a particular task as many times as required by the main program.
subscribe *vt* to pay to receive regular copies (of a magazine, etc); to donate money (to a charity, campaign); to support or agree with (an opinion, faith).—**subscriber** *n*.—**subscription** *n*.
subscriber trunk dialling *n* a service that allows users to dial long-distance calls directly.
subscript *n* a character written or printed below another character.—*also adj*.
subsequent *adj* occurring or following after.—**subsequently** *adv*.
subservient *adj* obsequious; servile; subordinate.—**subservience** *n*.—**subserviently** *adv*.
subside *vi* to sink or fall to the bottom; to settle; to diminish; to abate.—**subsidence** *n*.
subsidiarity *n* the devolution of decision making or control to the lowest effective level.
subsidiary *adj* secondary; supplementary; (*company*) owned or controlled by another. * *n* (*pl* **subsidiaries**) an accessory, an auxiliary; a business owned by another.—**subsidiarily** *adv*.
subsidize *vt* to aid or support with a subsidy.—**subsidization** *n*.—**subsidizer** *n*.
subsidy *n* (*pl* **subsidies**) government financial aid to a private person or company to assist an enterprise.
subsist *vi* to exist; to continue; to manage to keep oneself alive (on).
subsistence *n* existence; livelihood.—**subsistent** *adj*.
subsoil *n* the layer of soil lying immediately beneath the surface soil.
subsonic *adj* travelling at a speed less than that of sound.
substance *n* matter (such as powder, liquid); the essential nature or part; significance.
substantial *adj* of considerable value or size; important; strongly built.—**substantiality** *n*.—**substantially** *adv*.
substantiate *vt* to prove, to verify.—**substantiation** *n*.
substitute *vt* to put or act in place of another person or thing (*with* **for**); to replace (by). * *n* a person or thing that serves in place of another.—*also adj*.—**substitution** *n*.
substructure *n* a foundation or supporting framework.
subsume *vt* to include in a larger group or category.
subterfuge *n* a trick employed to conceal something.
subterranean *adj* below the surface of the earth; concealed.
subtitle *n* an explanatory, usu secondary, title to a book; a printed translation superimposed on a foreign language film.—*also vt*.
subtle *adj* delicate; slight; not noticeable; difficult to define, put into words; ingenious.—**subtleness** *n*.—**subtly** *adv*.
subtlety *n* (*pl* **subtleties**) subtleness; a fine distinction.
subtotal *n* the sum of part of a series of figures. * *vt* (**subtotalling, subtotalled** *or* **subtotaling, subtotaled**) to sum in part.
subtract *vti* to take away or deduct, as one quantity from another.—**subtraction** *n*.
subtropical *adj* of, characteristic of, the regions bordering on the tropics.
suburb *n* a residential district on the outskirts of a large town or city.—**suburban** *adj*.—**suburbia** *n*.
suburbanite *n* a person who lives in a suburb.
subversion *n* the act of undermining the authority of a government, institution, etc; collapse, ruin.
subversive *adj* liable to subvert established authority. * *n* a person who engages in subversive activities.—**subversively** *adv*.—**subversiveness** *n*.
subvert *vt* to overthrow, to ruin (something established); to corrupt, as in morals.
subway *n* a passage under a street; an underground metropolitan electric railway.
succeed *vt* to come after, to follow; to take the place of. * *vi* to accomplish what is attempted; to prosper.
success *n* the gaining of wealth, fame, etc; the favourable outcome (of anything attempted); a successful person or action.
successful *adj* having success.—**successfully** *adv*.—**successfulness** *n*.
succession *n* following in sequence; a number of persons or things following in order; the act or process of succeeding to a title, throne, etc; the line of descent to succeed to something.
successive *adj* following in sequence.—**successively** *adv*.—**successiveness** *n*.
successor *n* a person who succeeds another, as to an office.
succinct *adj* clear, concise.—**succinctly** *adv*.—**succinctness** *n*.
succotash *n* a cooked mixture of sweetcorn and lima beans.
succour, succor *n* (a person or thing that provides) help, support, esp in time of need. * *vt* to provide such help.
succubus, succuba *n* (*pl* **succubi, succubae**) a female demon thought to have sexual intercourse with sleeping men.
succulent *adj* juicy; moist and tasty; (*plant*) having fleshy tissue. * *n* a succulent plant (as a cactus).—**succulence, succulency** *n*.—**succulently** *adv*.
succumb *vi* to yield to superior strength or overpowering desire; to die.
such *adj* of a specified kind (eg such people, such a film); so great. * *adv* so; very.
suchlike *adj* of similar kind.
suck *vt* to draw (a liquid, air) into the mouth; to dissolve or roll about in the mouth (as a sweet); to draw in as if by sucking (*with* **in, up**, etc).—*also n*.
sucker *n* (*sl*) a person who is easily taken in or deceived; a cup-shaped piece of rubber that adheres to surfaces.
suckle *vt* to feed at the breast or udder.
suckling *n* a young animal that is not yet weaned.
sucks *interj* (*sl*) used to express disappointment.
sucre *n* the monetary unit of Ecuador.
sucrose *n* sugar.
suction *n* the act or process of sucking; the exertion of a force to form a vacuum.
sudden *adj* happening quickly and unexpectedly, abrupt.—**suddenly** *adv*.—**suddenness** *n*.
sudden death *n* (*sport*) extra time in a tied match, the winner being the next to score or take a point.
suds *npl* the bubbles or foam on the surface of soapy water.—**sudsy** *adj*.
sue *vt* (**suing, sued**) to bring a legal action against.
suede, suède *n* leather finished with a soft nap.
suet *n* white, solid fat in animal tissue, used in cooking.
suffer *vt* to undergo; to endure; to experience. * *vi* to feel pain or distress.—**sufferer** *n*.—**suffering** *n*.
sufferable *adj* endurable.—**sufferably** *adv*.
sufferance *n* reluctant tolerance, tacit permission; endurance.
suffice *vi* to be sufficient, adequate (for some purpose).
sufficient *adj* enough; adequate.—**sufficiency** *n*.—**sufficiently** *adv*.
suffix *n* (*pl* **suffixes**) a letter, syllable, or syllables added to the end of a word to modify its meaning or to form a new derivative.
suffocate *vti* to kill or be killed by depriving of oxygen, or by inhaling a poisonous gas; to feel hot and uncomfortable due to lack of air; to prevent from developing.—**suffocation** *n*.
suffrage *n* the right to vote.

suffuse *vt* to spread over or fill, as with colour or light.—**suffusion** *n*.
sugar *n* a sweet white, crystalline substance obtained from sugar cane and sugar beet * *vi* to sweeten.
sugar beet *n* a type of beet from which sugar is extracted.
sugar cane *n* a tall grass with stout canes grown as a source of sugar.
sugar daddy *n* a wealthy and usu elderly man who lavishes gifts on an attractive young woman.
sugary *adj* resembling or containing sugar; cloyingly sweet in manner, content, etc.—**sugariness** *n*.
suggest *vt* to put forward for consideration; to bring to one's mind; to evoke.—**suggestion** *n*.
suggestible *adj* easily influenced by others.—**suggestibility** *n*.
suggestive *adj* evocative; rather indecent, risqué.—**suggestively** *adv*.—**suggestiveness** *n*.
suicidal *adj* of, pertaining to, suicide; liable to commit suicide; destructive of one's own interests.—**suicidally** *adv*.
suicide *n* a person who kills himself intentionally; the act or instance of killing oneself intentionally; ruin of one's own interests.
suicide gene *n* a gene having bacteria that end its life cycle.
sui generis *adj* unique.
suit *n* a set of matching garments, such as a jacket and trousers or skirt; one of the four sets of thirteen playing cards; a lawsuit. * *vt* to be appropriate; to be convenient or acceptable to.
suitable *adj* fitting; convenient (to, for).—**suitably** *adv*.—**suitability** *n*.
suitcase *n* a portable, oblong travelling case.
suite *n* a number of followers or attendants; a set, esp of rooms, furniture, pieces of music.
suitor *n* a man who courts a woman; (*law*) a person who brings a lawsuit.
sukiyaki *n* a Japanese dish of thinly sliced beef, vegetables and seafood cooked rapidly in soy sauce, saké, etc, at the table.
sulf-, sulpf- *see* sulphur.
sulfa *see* **sulpha.**
sulfate *see* **sulphate.**
sulfonamide *see* **sulphonamide.**
sulfur *see* **sulphur.**
sulfuric *see* **sulphuric.**
sulk *vi* to be sullen.
sulky *adj* (**sulkier, sulkiest**) bad-tempered, quiet and sullen, because of resentment.—**sulkily** *adv*.—**sulkiness** *n*.
sullen *adj* moody and silent; gloomy, dull.—**sullenly** *adv*.—**sullenness** *n*.
sully *vt* (**sullying, sullied**) to blemish, to defile the purity of. * *n* (*pl* **sullies**) a tarnish or stain.
sulph-, sulf- *prefix* sulphur.
sulpha drug *n* any of various sulphonamide drugs used for treating bacterial infections.
sulphate *n* a salt of sulphuric acid.—*also* **sulfate.**
sulphonamide *n* any of a group of compounds that are amides of sulphonic acid, such as the sulfa drugs.—*also* **sulfonamide.**
sulphonic acid *n* any of a group strong organic acids used in the manufacture of drugs, dyes and detergents.
sulphur *n* a yellow nonmetallic element that is inflammable and has a strong odour.—*also* **sulfur.**—**sulphuric, sulfuric** *adj*.
sulphur dioxide *n* a pungent toxic gas used in various industrial processes that is a major air pollutant.
sulphuric acid *n* a powerfully corrosive acid.
sultan *n* a ruler, esp of a Muslim state.
sultana *n* a dried, white grape used in cooking; the wife or female relative of a sultan.
sultanate *n* a country or region ruled by a sultan; the office or authority of a sultan.
sultry *adj* (**sultrier, sultriest**) (*weather*) very hot, humid and close; sensual; passionate.—**sultrily** *adv*.—**sultriness** *n*.
sum *n* the result of two or more things added together; the total, aggregate; a quantity of money; essence, gist. * *vt* (**summing, summed**) to add (*usu with* **up**); to encapsulate; to summarize.
summarize *vt* to make or be a summary of.—**summarization** *n*.—**summarizer** *n*.
summary *adj* concise; performed quickly, without formality. * *n* (*pl* **summaries**) a brief account of the main points of something.—**summarily** *adv*.—**summariness** *n*.
summation *n* the act of finding a sum or total; the result of summation; a summary; the summing up of an argument, esp by a lawyer before a jury.
summer *n* the warmest season of the year, between spring and autumn.—**summery** *adj*.
summerhouse *n* a small building in a garden used as a shady retreat in summer.
summer school *n* an academic course held during the summer.
summing-up *n* a concluding summary of the points in a speech, argument, etc; a review of the main evidence made by a judge to the jury before it considers its verdict.
summit *n* the highest point, the peak; a meeting of world leaders.
summitry *n* the practice of convening, or style of conducting, summit conferences.
summon *vt* to order to appear, esp in court; to convene; to gather (strength, enthusiasm, etc).
summons *n* (*pl* **summonses**) a call to appear (in court). * *vt* to serve with a summons.
sumo *n* traditional Japanese wrestling.
sump *n* a section of the crankcase under an engine for the oil to drain into to form a reservoir.
sumptuous *adj* lavish; luxurious.—**sumptuously** *adv*.—**sumptuousness** *n*.
sun *n* the star around which the earth and other planets revolve which gives light and heat to the solar system; the sunshine. * *vi* (**sunning, sunned**) to expose oneself to the sun's rays.
Sun. *abbr* = Sunday.
sunbaked *adj* baked hard by exposure to the sun.
sunbathe *vi* to lie in the rays of the sun or a sun lamp to get a suntan.—**sunbather** *n*.
sunbeam *n* a ray of sunlight.
sunburn *n* inflammation of the skin from exposure to sunlight.—*also vti*.
sunburst *n* a sudden flash of sunlight; a pattern resembling the sun surrounded by rays; a brooch with a design resembling this.
sundae *n* a serving of ice cream covered with a topping of fruit, syrup, nuts, etc.
Sunday *n* the day of the week after Saturday, regarded as a day of worship by Christians; a newspaper published on a Sunday.
Sunday best *n* best clothes kept for wearing on Sundays.
Sunday school *n* a class for religious instruction held on Sundays.
sundew *n* any of various bog plants with sticky hairs that trap insects.
sundial *n* a device that shows the time by casting a shadow on a graduated dial.
sundown *n* sunset.
sundry *adj* miscellaneous, various. * *n* (*pl* **sundries**) (*pl*) miscellaneous small things.
sunflower *n* a tall plant with large yellow flowers whose seeds yield oil.
sung *see* **sing.**
sunglasses *npl* tinted glasses to protect the eyes from sunlight.
sunk *see* **sink.**
sunlamp *n* an electric lamp that produces ultra-violet rays for tanning the skin.
Sunna *n* the body of Islamic doctrine accepted by orthodox Muslims as based on the life and teachings of Mohammed.
Sunni *n* the branch of Islam that accepts the orthodoxy of the Sunna.—**Sunnite** *n*.
sunny *adj* (**sunnier, sunniest**) (*weather*) bright with sunshine; (*person, mood*) cheerful.—**sunnily** *adv*.—**sunniness** *n*.
sunrise *n* dawn.
sunrise industry *n* a high-technology industry with a bright future.
sunroof *n* a panel in the roof of a car that slides open.

sunset *n* dusk.
sunshine *n* the light and heat from the sun.
sunspot *n* a dark patch sometimes visible on the sun's surface; (*inf*) a holiday resort with guaranteed sunshine.
sunstroke *n* illness caused by exposure to the sun.
suntan *n* browning of the skin by the sun.—**suntanned** *adj*.
suntrap *n* a sunny sheltered spot.
super *adj* (*inf*) fantastic, excellent; (*inf*) a superintendent, as in the police. * *n* a variety of high-octane petrol.
super- *prefix* above, on the top of; extremely, excessively; greater in size, quality, etc.
superable *adj* able to be overcome.—**superably** *adv*.
superannuate *vt* to pension off on account of old age or illness.
superannuation *n* regular contributions from employees' wages toward a pension scheme.
superb *adj* grand; excellent; of the highest quality.—**superbly** *adv*.
supercharge *vt* to increase the power of an engine by using a device that supplies air or fuel in increased quantities by raising the intake pressure; to charge (the atmosphere, a conversation, etc) with excess tension or emotion.—**supercharger** *n*.
supercilious *adj* arrogant; haughty, disdainful.—**superciliously** *adv*.—**superciliousness** *n*.
superconductivity *n* (*physics*) the complete loss of electrical resistance exhibited by certain materials at very low temperatures.—**superconducting, superconductive** *adj*.—**superconduction** *n*.—**superconductor** *n*.
supercool *vt* to cool (a liquid, etc) below freezing without solidification or crystallization.
superdelegate *n* in US, a delegate to a Democratic party convention, appointed rather than elected.
superego *n* (*pl* **superegos**) (*psychol*) the division of the unconscious mind that functions as a conscience.
superficial *adj* near the surface; slight, not profound; (*person*) shallow in nature.—**superficiality** *n*.—**superficially** *adv*.
superfluous *adj* exceeding what is required; unnecessary.—**superfluity** *n*.
supergiant *n* a star of enormous size and brightness with a low density.
superglue *n* an adhesive that forms strong bonds instantly.
supergrass *n* an informer who incriminates a large number of people.
superheat *vt* to heat above boiling point without vaporization; to heat a vapour above boiling point without boiling occurring.
superhigh frequency *n* a radio frequency between 30,000 and 3000 megahertz.
superhuman *adj* surpassing normal human strength or abilities; divine.
superimpose *vt* to put or lay upon something else.
superintend *vt* to have the charge and direction of; to control, manage.
superintendent *n* a person who manages or supervises; a director; a British police officer next above the rank of inspector.
superior *adj* higher in place, quality, rank, excellence; greater in number, power. * *n* a person of higher rank.—**superiority** *n*.
superiority complex *n* an inflated opinion of one's own abilities and merits.
superl. *abbr* = superlative.
superlative *adj* of outstanding quality; (*gram*) denoting the extreme degree of comparison of adjectives and adverbs.—**superlatively** *adv*.
superman *n* (*pl* **supermen**) a person of outstanding abilities and achievements.
supermarket *n* a large self-service, shop selling food and household goods.
supernatural *adj* relating to things that cannot be explained by nature; involving ghosts, spirits, etc.—**supernaturally** *adv*.
supernova *n* (*pl* **supernovae, supernovas**) a star that explodes temporarily burning with an intensity one hundred million times that of the sun.
supernumerary *adj* extra; beyond the usual number. * *n* (*pl* **supernumeraries**) an extra person or thing.
superpose *vt* to place (a geometric figure) on top of another so that their outlines coincide; to lay on top of.—**superposition** *n*.
superpower *n* a nation with great economic and military strength.
superscript *n* a character written or printed above another character.—*also adj*.
supersede *vt* to take the place of, replace.
supersmart card *n* a smart card equipped with a screen and a keyboard, allowing interaction with the user.
supersonic *adj* faster than the speed of sound.—**supersonically** *adv*.
superstar *n* (*inf*) a sporting celebrity; a famous film actor or musician.
superstition *n* irrational belief based on ignorance or fear.—**superstitious** *adj*.
superstore *n* a very large supermarket.
superstructure *n* a structure above or on something else, as above the base or foundation, as above the main deck of a ship.
Super Tuesday *n* the Tuesday, usu in March, on which a number of states, with over half of all the delegates, hold primary elections for the selection of Presidential candidates.
supervise *vti* to have charge of, direct, to superintend.—**supervision** *n*.
supervisor *n* one who supervises; an overseer, an inspector.—**supervisory** *adj*.
supine *adj* lying on the back; lazy, indigent.—**supinely** *adv*.
supper *n* a meal taken in the evening, esp when dinner is eaten at midday; an evening social event; the food served at a supper; a light meal served late in the evening.
supplant *vt* to replace; to remove in order to replace with something else.
supple *adj* flexible, easily bent; lithe; (*mind*) adaptable.—**suppleness** *n*.
supplement *n* an addition or extra amount (usu of money); an additional section of a book, periodical or newspaper. * *vt* to add to.—**supplemental** *adj*.
supply *vt* (**supplying, supplied**) to provide, meet (a deficiency, a need); to fill (a vacant place). * *n* (*pl* **supplies**) a stock; (*pl*) provisions.—**supplier** *n*.
support *vt* to hold up, bear; to tolerate, withstand; to assist; to advocate (a cause, policy); to provide for (financially). * *n* a means of support; maintenance.
supporter *n* a person who backs a political party, sports team, etc.
suppose *vt* to assume; to presume as true without definite knowledge; to think probable; to expect. * *vi* to conjecture.
supposed *adj* believed to be on available evidence.
supposedly *adv* allegedly.
supposition *n* an assumption, hypothesis.
suppositious *adj* hypothetical.
suppository *n* (*pl* **suppositories**) a cone or cylinder of medicated soluble material for insertion into the rectum or vagina.
suppress *vt* to crush, put an end to (eg a rebellion); to restrain (a person); to subdue.—**suppression** *n*.—**suppressor** *n*.
suppurate *vi* to form or discharge pus.—**suppuration** *n*.—**suppurative** *adj*.
supra *prefix* above, situated above; over; beyond.
supranational *adj* transcending national boundaries or interests.
supremacist *n* a person who advocates the supremacy of a particular group.
supreme *adj* of highest power; greatest; final; ultimate.—**supremacy** *n*.
Supreme Court *n* the highest judicial body in a nation or state.
supremo *n* (*pl* **supremos**) (*inf*) the person in overall charge, a boss.
Supt *abbr* = superintendent.
surcharge *vt* to overcharge (a person); to charge an additional sum; to overload. * *n* an additional tax or charge; an additional or excessive load.
surd *n* (*math*) a number containing an irrational root; an irrational number.
sure *adj* certain; without doubt; reliable, inevitable; secure; safe; dependable. * *adv* certainly.
sure-fire *adj* (*inf*) certain to succeed.
sure-footed *adj* not liable to slip or fall; unlikely to make a mistake.

surely *adv* certainly; securely; it is to be hoped or expected that.
sure thing *n* (*inf*) something assured of success. * *interj* yes, of course.
surety *n* (*pl* **sureties**) a person who undertakes responsibility for the fulfilment of another's debt; security given as a guarantee of payment of a debt.
surf *n* the waves of the sea breaking on the shore or a reef.
surface *n* the exterior face of an object; any of the faces of a solid; the uppermost level of sea or land; a flat area, such as the top of a table; superficial features. * *adj* superficial; external. * *vt* to cover with a surface, as in paving. * *vi* to rise to the surface of water.
surfboard *n* a long, narrow board used in the sport of surfing.
surfeit *n* an excessive amount.
surfing *n* the sport of riding in toward shore on the crest of a wave, esp on a surfboard.
surg. *abbr* = surgeon; surgery; surgical.
surge *n* the rolling of the sea, as after a large wave; a sudden, strong increase, as of power.—*also vi.*
surgeon *n* a medical specialist who practises surgery.
surgery *n* (*pl* **surgeries**) the treatment of diseases or injuries by manual or instrumental operations; the consulting room of a doctor or dentist; the daily period when a doctor is available for consultation; the regular period when an MP, lawyer, etc is available for consultation.—**surgical** *adj*.—**surgically** *adv*.
surgical spirit *n* methylated spirit used for sterilizing.
surly *adj* (**surlier, surliest**) ill-tempered or rude.—**surlily** *adv*.—**surliness** *n*.
surmise *n* guess, conjecture. * *vt* to infer the existence of from partial evidence.
surmount *vt* to overcome; to rise above.
surname *n* the family name. * *vt* to give a surname to.
surpass *vt* to outdo, to outshine; to excel; to exceed.
surpassing *adj* exceptional; greatly exceeding others.—**surpassingly** *adv*.
surplice *n* a loose, white, wide-sleeved clerical garment worn by clergymen and choristers.
surplus *n* (*pl* **surpluses**) an amount in excess of what is required; an excess of revenues over expenditure in a financial year.
surprise *n* the act of catching unawares; an unexpected gift, event; astonishment. * *vt* to cause to feel astonished; to attack unexpectedly; to take unawares.—**surprising** *adj*.—**surprisingly** *adv*.
surreal *adj* bizarre.
surrealism *n* a movement in art characterized by the expression of the activities of the unconscious mind and dream elements.—**surrealist** *n*.—**surrealistic** *adj*.
surrender *vt* to relinquish or give up possession or power. * *vi* to give oneself up (to an enemy).—*also n.*
surreptitious *adj* done by stealth; clandestine, secret.—**surreptitiously** *adv*.
surrogacy, surrogate motherhood *n* a practice in which a woman bears a child for a childless couple.—**surrogate mother** *n*.
surrogate *n* a person or thing acting as a substitute for another person or thing.—*also adj.*
surrogate mother *n* a woman who bears a child on behalf of a childless couple.
surround *vt* to encircle on all or nearly all sides; (*mil*) to encircle. * *n* a border around the edge of something.
surroundings *npl* the conditions, objects, etc around a person or thing; the environment.
surtax *n* an additional tax, esp on income above a prescribed level.—*also vt.*
surtitle *n* a caption projected onto a screen above the stage during an opera as a translation of the libretto or to explain some detail of the action.—*also vt.*
surveillance *n* a secret watch kept over a person, esp a suspect.
survey *vt* (**surveying, surveyed**) to take a general view of; to appraise; to examine carefully; to measure and make a map of an area. * *n* (*pl* **surveys**) a detailed study, as by gathering information and analysing it, a general view; the process of surveying an area or a house.
surveyor *n* a person who surveys land or buildings.
survival *n* surviving; a person or thing that survives; a relic.
survive *vt* to live after the death of another person; to continue, endure; to come through alive. * *vi* to remain alive (after experiencing a dangerous situation).—**survivor** *n*.
susceptible *adj* ready or liable to be affected by; impressionable.—**susceptibility** *n*.—**susceptibly** *adv*.
sushi *n* a Japanese dish of small cakes of cold rice with various toppings, esp raw fish.
suspect *vt* to mistrust; to believe to be guilty; to think probable. * *n* a person under suspicion. * *adj* open to suspicion.
suspend *vt* to hang; to discontinue, or cease temporarily; to postpone; to debar temporarily from a privilege, etc.
suspended animation *n* a cessation of the vital functions in an organism, esp though freezing.
suspended sentence *n* a sentence that does not come into force unless a further offence is committed.
suspender *n* a fastener for holding up stockings; (*pl*) braces.
suspender belt *n* a belt with suspenders to hold up a woman's stockings.
suspense *n* mental anxiety or uncertainty; excitement.
suspension *n* suspending or being suspended; a temporary interruption or postponement; a temporary removal from office, privileges, etc; the system of springs, shock absorbers, etc that support a vehicle on its axles; (*chem*) a dispersion of fine particles in a liquid.
suspension bridge *n* a bridge carrying a roadway suspended by cables anchored to towers at either end.
suspicion *n* act of suspecting; a belief formed or held without sure proof; mistrust; a trace.—**suspicious** *adj*.—**suspiciously** *adv*.
sustain *vt* hold up, support; to maintain; to suffer (eg an injury); to nourish.
sustenance *n* nourishment.
suttee *n* (*Hinduism*) (*formerly*) the practice of a widow throwing herself on her husband's funeral pyre; this custom.—*also* **sati**.
suture *n* a stitch holding together a wound after surgery.—*also vt.*
svelte *adj* slim and elegant.
SW *abbr* = southwest(ern); short wave.
swab *n* a wad of absorbent material, usu cotton, used to clean wounds, take specimens, etc; a mop.—*also vt.*
swaddle *vt* to bind tightly, envelop; to wrap a baby in swaddling clothes.
swaddling clothes *npl* narrow strips of cloth used to wrap and restrain an infant.
swag *n* (*sl*) loot.
swagger *vi* to strut; to brag loudly. * *n* boastfulness; swinging gait.
Swahili *n* a language spoken in Kenya, Tanzania and other parts of east Africa; (*pl* **Swahilis, Swahili**) a member of a people speaking this language who live mainly in Zanzibar.
swain *n* (*poet*) a male suitor or lover.
swallow[1] *n* a small migratory bird with long wings and a forked tail.
swallow[2] *vt* to cause food and drink to move from the mouth to the stomach; to endure; to engulf; (*inf*) to accept gullibly; (*emotion, etc*) to repress.—*also n.*
swallow dive *n* a dive executed with the back arched and arms outstretched at the start.
swam *see* **swim**.
swami *n* (*pl* **swamies, swamis**) a Hindu religious teacher.
swamp *n* wet, spongy land; bog. * *vt* to overwhelm; to flood as with water.—**swampy** *adj*.
swan *n* a large, usu white, bird with a very long neck that lives on rivers and lakes. * *vi* (**swanning, swanned**) (*inf*) to wander aimlessly.
swan dive *n* a swallow dive.
swank *vi* (*inf*) to show off.—*also n.*—**swanky** *adj*.
swan song *n* a final appearance, performance, etc by a person facing retirement or death.
swap *vti* (**swapping, swapped**) (*inf*) to trade, barter. * *n* (*inf*) the act of exchanging one thing for another.—*also* **swop**.

SWAPO, Swapo (*acronym*) South West Africa People's Organization.
sward *n* (an area of land with) a surface of short grass.
swarm *n* a colony of migrating bees; a moving mass, crowd or throng. * *vi* to move in great numbers; to teem.
swarthy *adj* (**swarthier, swarthiest**) dark-complexioned.—**swarthiness** *n*.
swashbuckling *adj* swaggering; exciting, adventurous.—**swashbuckler** *n*.
swastika *n* an ancient symbol formed by a cross with the ends of the arms bent at right-angles, used by Nazi Germany.
swat *vt* (**swatting, swatted**) (*inf*) to hit with a sharp blow; to swipe.—*also n*.—**swatter** *n*.
swath *n* the width of one sweep of a scythe or other mowing device; a strip, row, etc, mowed; a broad strip.
swathe *vt* to bind or wrap round, as with a bandage; to envelop, enclose.
sway *vi* to swing or move from one side to the other or to and fro; to lean to one side; to vacillate in judgment or opinion. * *n* influence; control.
swear *vi* (**swearing, swore,** *pp* **sworn**) to make a solemn affirmation, promise, etc, calling God as a witness; to give evidence on oath; to curse, blaspheme or use obscene language; to vow; (*with* **off**) to promise abstinence from. * *vt* (*with* **in** to appoint to an office by the administration of an oath.
swearword *n* a profane or obscene expression.
sweat *n* perspiration; (*inf*) hard work; (*inf*) a state of eagerness, anxiety.—*also vti*.—**sweaty** *adj*.
sweatband *n* a strip of material in a hat, or worn on the wrist or around the forehead, to absorb sweat.
sweater *n* a knitted pullover.
sweatshirt *n* a loose, collarless, heavy cotton jersey.
sweatshop *n* a small factory or workshop where employees work long hours at low wages in poor conditions.
Swede *n* a native of Sweden.
swede *n* a round root vegetable with yellow flesh.
Swedish *adj* pertaining to Sweden, its people or language. * *n* the language of Sweden.
sweep *vb* (**sweeping, swept**) *vt* to clean with a broom; to remove (rubbish, dirt) with a brush. * *vi* to pass by swiftly. * *n* a movement, esp in an arc; a stroke; scope, range; a sweepstake.
sweeper *n* a person who sweeps, esp the roads; (*soccer*) (*inf*) a player positioned before the goalkeeper to collect loose balls, tackle attacking players, etc.
sweeping *adj* wide-ranging; indiscriminate.—**sweepingly** *adv*.
sweepstake, sweepstakes *n* a lottery in which the prize constitutes all the money staked; a horserace, etc in which the winner receives the entire prize.
sweet *adj* having a taste like sugar; pleasing to other senses; gentle; kind. * *n* a small piece of confectionery; a dessert.—**sweetly** *adv*.—**sweetness** *n*.
sweet-and-sour *adj* (*food*) cooked in a sauce containing sugar and vinegar or lemon juice.
sweet brier *n* a Eurasian rose with pink flowers.
sweetbread *n* the pancreas or thymus gland of an animal, cooked as food.
sweet cicely *n* an aromatic European plant with small white flowers; the aniseed-flavoured leaves of this once used in cookery.
sweet clover *n* a species of sweet-scented trefoil or clover, with clusters of small yellow or white flowers; melilot.
sweetcorn *n* maize, corn on the cob.
sweeten *vti* to make or become sweet or sweeter; to mollify.
sweetener *n* a sweetening substance that contains no sugar; (*sl*) a bribe.
sweetheart *n* a lover.
sweetie *n* (*inf*) a sweet; (*inf*) sweetheart, darling; a kindly, pleasant person.
sweetmeat *n* a sweet, preserve, small cake, or other sugary delicacy.
sweet pea *n* a climbing garden plant cultivated for its large fragrant blooms.
sweet pepper *n* (a plant bearing) a large fruit with thick fleshy walls eaten ripe (red) or unripe (green).
sweet potato *n* (a tropical climbing plant with) a large edible tuberous root.
sweet-talk *vt* (*inf*) to flatter, cajole.—**sweet talk** *n*.
sweet william *n* a widely grown Eurasian plant with clusters of white, red, pink, or purple flowers.
swell *vi* (**swelling, swelled,** *pp* **swollen** *or* **swelled**) to increase in size or volume; to rise into waves; to bulge out. * *n* the movement of the sea; a bulge; a gradual increase in the loudness of a musical note; (*inf*) a socially prominent person. * *adj* excellent.
swelling *n* inflammation.
swelter *vi* to suffer from heat. * *n* humid, oppressive heat.
sweltering *adj* uncomfortably hot.
swept *see* **sweep**.
sweptback *adj* (*aircraft wing*) slanting backward.
sweptwing *adj* (*aircraft*) having sweptback wings.
swerve *vi* to turn aside suddenly from a line or course; to veer.—*also n*.
swift *adj* moving with great speed; rapid. * *n* a swallow-like bird.—**swiftly** *adv*.—**swiftness** *n*.
swig *vt* (*inf*) to take a long drink, esp from a bottle.—*also n*.
swill *vti* to drink greedily; to guzzle; to rinse with a large amount of water. * *n* liquid refuse fed to pigs.
swim *vi* (**swimming, swam,** *pp* **swum**) to move through water by using limbs or fins; to be dizzy; to be flooded with. * *n* the act of swimming.—**swimmer** *n*.
swimming costume, swimsuit *n* a one-piece garment for swimming in.
swimmingly *adv* (*inf*) easily, without effort.
swindle *vti* to cheat (someone) of money or property.—*also n*.—**swindler** *n*.
swindle sheet *n* (*sl*) an expenses form.
swine *n* (*pl* **swine**) a pig; (*inf*) an contemptible person; (*inf*) an unpleasant thing.
swine fever *n* a viral infection of pigs.
swineherd *n* a person who looks after pigs.
swing *vb* (**swinging, swung**) *vi* to sway or move to and fro, as an object hanging in the air; to pivot; to shift from one mood or opinion to another; (*music*) to have a lively rhythm; (*sl*) to be hanged. * *vt* to whirl; to play swing music; to influence; to achieve, bring about. * *n* a swinging, curving or rhythmic movement; a suspended seat for swinging in; a shift from one condition to another; a type of popular jazz played by a large band and characterized by a lively, steady rhythm.
swingeing *adj* drastic, severe.
swinging *adj* (*inf*) up-to-date; lively.
swing-wing *adj* of or pertaining to an aircraft with movable wings that are swept back at high speeds and moved forward for approach and landing.—*also n*.
swipe *n* (*inf*) a hard, sweeping blow. * *vt* (*inf*) to hit with a swipe; (*sl*) to steal.
swirl *vti* to turn with a whirling motion.—*also n*.
swish *vi* to move with a soft, whistling, hissing sound. * *n* a swishing sound. * *adj* (*inf*) smart, fashionable.
Swiss *adj* of or belonging to Switzerland. * *n* (*pl* **Swiss**) a native of Switzerland.
swiss roll *n* a thin sponge cake spread with a layer of jam and rolled up.
switch *n* a control for turning on and off an electrical device; a sudden change; a swap. * *vt* to shift, change, swap; to turn on or off (as of an electrical device).
switchback *n* a zigzag road in a mountain region; a roller coaster.
switchblade *n* a flick knife.
switchboard *n* an installation in a building where telephone calls are connected.
swivel *n* a coupling that permits parts to rotate. * *vi* (**swivelling, swivelled** *or* **swiveling, swiveled**) to turn (as if) on a pin or pivot.
swollen *see* **swell**.
swoon *vt* to faint.—*also n*.
swoop *vt* to carry off abruptly. * *vi* to make a sudden attack (*usu with* **down**) as a bird in hunting.—*also n*.
swop *see* **swap**.
sword *n* a weapon with a long blade and a handle at one end.

sword dance *n* a dance in which swords are brandished or placed on the ground and stepped between.
swordfish *n* a large marine fish with a sword-like upper jaw.
swordplay *n* fighting with swords; verbal combat.
swordsman *n* (*pl* **swordsmen**) a person skilled in the use of a sword.
swordstick *n* a walking stick concealing a sword.
swore, sworn *see* **swear.**
sworn *see* **swear.**
swot *vi* (*inf*) to study hard for an examination. * *n* (*inf*) a person who studies hard.
swum *see* **swim.**
swung *see* **swing.**
sycamore *n* a Eurasian maple tree; an American plane tree; a tree of Africa and Asia bearing a fruit resembling a fig.
sycophant *n* a person who flatters and praises powerful people to win their favour.—**sycophancy** *n*.—**sycophantic** *adj*.
syllabi *see* **syllabus.**
syllabic *adj* consisting of syllables; articulated in syllables.
syllable *n* word or part of a word uttered in a single sound; one or more letters written to represent a spoken syllable.
syllabub, sillabub *n* a cold dessert made with sweetened whipped cream flavoured with sherry, wine, lemon juice, etc.
syllabus *n* (*pl* **syllabuses, syllabi**) a summary or outline of a course of study or of examination requirements; the subjects studied for a particular course.
syllogism *n* a form of reasoning consisting of a major premise, a minor premise and a conclusion, eg *All men must die; I am a man; therefore I must die*.
sylph *n* a slim girl or woman.
symbiosis *n* a mutually advantageous partnership between two interdependent plant or animal species.—**symbiotic** *adj*.
symbol *n* a representation; an object used to represent something abstract; an arbitrary or conventional sign standing for a quality, process, relation, etc as in music, chemistry, mathematics, etc.
symbolic, symbolical *adj* of, using, or constituting a symbol.—**symbolically** *adv*.
symbolism *n* the use of symbols; a system of symbolic representation.—**symbolist** *n*.
symbolize *vt* to be a symbol; to represent by a symbol.—**symbolization** *n*.—**symbolizer** *n*.
symmetrical, symmetric *adj* having symmetry.—**symmetrically** *adv*.
symmetry *n* (*pl* **symmetries**) the corresponding arrangement of one part to another in size, shape and position; balance or harmony of form resulting from this.
sympathetic *adj* having sympathy; compassionate.—**sympathetically** *adv*.
sympathize *vi* feel sympathy for; to commiserate; to be in sympathy (with).—**sympathizer** *n*.—**sympathizingly** *adv*.
sympathy *n* (*pl* **sympathies**) agreement of ideas and opinions; compassion; (*pl*) support for an action or cause.
symphony *n* (*pl* **symphonies**) an orchestral composition in several movements; a large orchestra for playing symphonic works.—**symphonic** *adj*.—**symphonically** *adv*.
symposium *n* (*pl* **symposiums, symposia**) a conference at which several specialists deliver short addresses on a topic; an anthology of scholarly essays.
symptom *n* a bodily sensation experienced by a patient indicative of a particular disease; an indication.
symptomatic *adj* of, being, or relating to symptoms; indicative.—**symptomatically** *adv*.
syn- *prefix* together.
synagogue *n* the building where Jews assemble for worship and religious study.
synapse *n* the point at which a nerve impulse is transmitted between neurons.
sync, synch *n* (*inf*) synchronization. * *vti* (*inf*) to synchronize.
synchromesh *adj* (*gear system*) incorporating a device that regulates the revolving parts in a gear so that they are at the same speed when brought into contact. * *n* a gear system using this.
synchronize *vti* to occur at the same time and speed; (*watches*) to adjust to show the same time.—**synchronization** *n*.—**synchronizer** *n*.
synchronous *adj* occurring at the same time.—**synchronously** *adv*.—**synchronousness** *n*.
syncopate *vt* (*mus*) to modify beats (in a musical piece) by displacing the rhythmical accents from strong beats to weak ones and vice versa.—**syncopation** *n*.
syndicate *n* an association of individuals or corporations formed for a project requiring much capital; any group, as of criminals, organized for some undertaking; an organization selling articles or features to many newspapers, etc. * *vt* to manage as or form into a syndicate; to sell (an article, etc) through a syndicate. * *vi* to form a syndicate.—**syndication** *n*.
syndrome *n* a characteristic pattern of signs and symptoms of a disease.
synergist *n* a muscle that works in conjunction with another muscle; a drug that combines with another drug, the two having a greater effect when taken together than separately.—**synergism** *n*.—**synergistic** *adj*.
synergy *n* synergism; in business, the possibility that the merger of two individual companies will produce a combined operation of greater productivity and efficiency.—**synergetic, synergistic** *adj*.
synesis *n* (*gram*) a construction in harmony with its sense rather than with strict syntax, eg "a large number were present."
synod *n* a council of members of a church that meets to discuss religious issues.
synonym *n* a word that has the same, or similar, meaning as another or others in the same language.
synonymous *adj* having the same meaning; equivalent.—**synonymously** *adv*.
synonymy *n* (*pl* **synonymies**) the condition of being synonymous; a system or collection of synonyms; the use of synonyms for emphasis, eg "in any shape or form".
synopsis *n* (*pl* **synopses**) a summary or brief review of a subject.
synovia *n* a thick fluid that lubricates the joints and tendons.—**synovial** *adj*.
synovitis *n* inflammation of the membrane around a joint.
syntax *n* (*gram*) the arrangement of words in the sentences and phrases of language; the rules governing this.—**syntactic** *adj*.—**syntactically** *adv*.
synth *n* a synthesizer.
synthesis *n* (*pl* **syntheses**) the process of combining separate elements of thought into a whole; the production of a compound by a chemical reaction.
synthesize *vti* to combine into a whole.
synthesizer *n* an electronic device producing music and sounds by using a computer to combine individual sounds previously recorded.
synthetic *adj* produced by chemical synthesis; artificial.—**synthetically** *adv*.
syphilis *n* a contagious, infectious venereal disease.—**syphilitic** *adj*.
syphon *see* **siphon.**
Syrian *n* a native or inhabitant of Syria; the Arabic dialect spoken there.—*also adj*.
syringe *n* a hollow tube with a plunger at one end and a sharp needle at the other by which liquids are injected or withdrawn, esp in medicine. * *vt* to inject or cleanse with a syringe.
syrinx *n* (*pl* **syringes**) the vocal organ in birds.
syrup *n* a thick sweet substance made by boiling sugar with water; the concentrated juice of a fruit or plant.—**syrupy** *adj*.
systaltic *adj* (*heart, etc*) alternately expanding and contracting; pulsating.
system *n* a method of working or organizing by following a set of rules; routine; organization; structure; a political regime; an arrangement of parts fitting together.
systematic *adj* constituting or based on a system; according to a system.—**systematically** *adv*.
systematize *vt* to arrange according to a system.—**systematization** *n*.—**systematizer** *n*.

systemic *adj* (*poison, infection, etc*) of or affecting the entire body; (*insecticide, etc*) designed to be taken up into the plant tissues.—**systemically** *adv*.

systemize *vt* to systematize.—**systemization** *n*.

systems analysis *n* analysis of a particular task or operation to determine how computer hardware and software may best perform it.—**systems analyst** *n*.

systole *n* the regular contractions of the chambers of the heart by which the circulation of blood is maintained.—**systolic** *adj*.

T

T (*chem symbol*) tritium.

T, t *n* the 20th letter of the English alphabet; something shaped like a T.

t *abbr* = ton.

TA *abbr* = teaching assistant.

Ta (*chem symbol*) tantalum.

tab[1] *n* tabulator; tablet. * *vt* (**tabbing, tabbed**) to tabulate.

tab[2] *n* a small tag, label or flap; (*inf*) a bill, as for expenses. * *vt* (**tabbing, tabbed**) to fix a tab on.

tabard *n* a short armless tunic, esp one bearing a coat of arms and worn by a herald or by a knight over his armour; a sleeveless garment shaped like this worn by women.

Tabasco *n* (*trademark*) a very hot red pepper sauce.

tabbouleh *n* an Arabic salad made with vegetables, spices, lemon juice and cracked wheat.

tabby *n* (*pl* **tabbies**) a domestic cat with a striped coat, esp a female; a heavy watered silk. * *adj* striped in brown or grey. * *vt* (**tabbying, tabbied**) to pattern (silk) with a wavy pattern.

tabernacle *n* (*Bible*) the portable tent carried by Jews through the desert containing their sacred writings; a place of worship.—**tabernacular** *adj*.

tabes *n* (*pl* **tabes**) wasting caused by chronic disease.—**tabetic** *adj, n*.

tabes dorsalis *n* paralysis caused by syphilis at an advanced stage when it attacks the spinal cord.

tablature *n* musical notation indicating the strings, frets, fingering, rhythm, etc, to be used, esp for the lute.

table *n* a piece of furniture consisting of a slab or board on legs; the people seated round a table; supply of food; a flat surface; a level area; a slab or tablet in a wall; an inscription on this; a list of facts and figures arranged in columns for reference or comparison; a folding leaf of a backgammon board; **at table** having a meal; **on the table** (*legislative bill, etc*) postponed, often indefinitely; **to turn the tables on** to put (an opponent) in a position of disadvantage previously held by oneself. * *vt* to submit, to put forward; to postpone indefinitely; to lay on a table. * *adj* of, on or at a table.

tableau *n* (*pl* **tableaux, tableaus**) a dramatic or graphic representation of a group or scene; a tableau vivant.

tableau vivant *n* (*pl* **tableaux vivants**) a representation of an historical scene by people in costume posed silently and motionless.

tablecloth *n* a cloth for covering a table.

table d'hôte *n* (*pl* **tables d'hôte**) a meal at a fixed price for a set number of courses.—*also adj*.

tableland *n* an expanse of flat elevated land, a plateau.

tablespoon *n* a large serving spoon; a unit of measure in cooking.

tablespoonful *n* (**tablespoonfuls**) the amount a tablespoon holds.

tablet *n* a pad of paper; a medicinal pill; a cake of solid substance, such as soap; a slab of stone.

table tennis *n* a game like tennis played on a table with small bats and a ball.

tableware *n* dishes, cutlery, etc for use at mealtimes.

tabloid *n* a small-format newspaper characterized by emphasis on photographs and news in condensed form.

taboo, tabu *n* (*pl* **taboos, tabus**) a religious or social prohibition of the use or practice of something; the thing prohibited. * *adj* forbidden from use, mention, etc. * *vt* (**tabooing, tabooed** *or* **tabuing, tabued**) to forbid by social or personal influence the use, practice or mention of something or contact with someone.

tabor, tabour *n* a small drum formerly used to accompany a pipe, both instruments being played by the same person.

tabular *adj* like a table, flat; arranged in the form of a table; calculated with a table.—**tabularly** *adv*.

tabula rasa *n* (*pl* **tabulae rasae**) the mind when regarded as in its original state and clear of impressions; a fresh start.

tabulate *vt* to arrange (written material) in tabular form.—**tabulation** *n*

tabulator *n* a device that sets stops to locate columns on a typewriter or word processor.

TAC *abbr* = Tactical Air Command.

tacamahac *n* (any tree yielding) any of various pungent gum resins used esp in incense.

tacet *vi* a direction on a musical score indicating that from this point a particular instrument is not to play.

tachism *n* a form of action painting using random blobs of colour.

tachistoscope *n* a device for projecting visual information onto a screen for a split second only, used in the study of perception and learning.

tacho- *prefix* speed.

tachograph *n* a device in motor vehicles, esp lorries, to record speed and time of travel.

tachometer *n* an instrument for measuring the speed of rotation of a shaft, as in a vehicle engine.

tachy- *prefix* rapid or accelerated.

tachycardia *n* an abnormally fast heartbeat.

tachygraphy *n* shorthand, esp as used in ancient Greece and Rome.

tachymeter *n* a surveying instrument for measuring long distances rapidly.

tachyon *n* (*physics*) a theoretical elementary particle that can travel faster than light.

tacit *adj* implied without really being spoken; understood.—**tacitly** *adv*.—**tacitness** *n*.

taciturn *adj* habitually silent and reserved.—**taciturnity** *n*.

tack[1] *n* a short, flat-headed nail; the course of a sailing ship; a course of action, approach; adhesiveness. * *vt* to fasten with tacks. * *vi* to change direction.

tack[2] *n* (*inf*) food.

tackle *n* a system of ropes and pulleys for lifting; equipment; rigging; (*sport*) an act of grabbing and stopping an opponent. * *vt* (*task, etc*) to attend to, undertake; (*a person*) to confront; (*sport*) to challenge with a tackle.

tacky[1] *adj* (**tackier, tackiest**) (*paint, etc*) sticky.

tacky[2] *adj* (**tackier, tackiest**) (*inf*) shabby; ostentatious and vulgar; seedy.—**tackiness** *n*.

tact *n* discretion in managing the feelings of others.—**tactful** *adj*.—**tactless** *adj*.

tactical voting *n* the strategy in elections of voting for the candidate most likely to defeat the favourite, rather than voting for one's preferred choice.

tactics *n sing* stratagem; ploy; the science or art of manoeuvring troops in the presence of the enemy.—**tactical** *adj*.—**tactician** *n*.

tactile *adj* relating to, or having a sense of touch.

tad *n* (*inf*) a small boy; (*inf*) a tiny quantity; a bit.

tadpole *n* the larva of a frog or toad, esp at the stage when the head and tail have developed.

taeniasis *n* infestation with tapeworms.—*also* **teniasis.**

taffeta *n* a thin glossy fabric with a silky lustre.

taffrail *n* the rail at the stern of a ship.

tag[1] *n* a strip or label for identification. * *vt* to attach a tag; to mark with a tag. * *vi* (*with* **onto, after, along**) to trail along (behind).

tag[2] *n* a children's chasing game; (*baseball*) the putting out of a runner by touching him with the ball. * *vt* (**tagging, tagged**) to touch another

player in a game of tag; to put a runner out by touching him with the ball.
tag end *n* the final part of something.
tagliatelle *n* pasta in narrow ribbons.
tahini *n* a thick paste of ground sesame seeds.
tahr *n* a type of Himalayan wild goat.
Tahitian *adj* of or pertaining to the South Pacific island of Tahiti, its people or language. * *n* a native of Tahiti; the Polynesian language spoken in Tahiti.
t'ai chi ch'uan *n* a Chinese form of exercise using movements designed to improve balance and coordination.—*also* **t'ai chi.**
taiga *n* coniferous forests dominated by spruces and firs extending across the subarctic regions of Eurasia and North America.
tail *n* the appendage of an animal growing from the rear, generally hanging loose; the rear part of anything; (*pl*) the side of a coin without a head on it; (*inf*) a person who keeps another under surveillance, esp a detective. * *vti* to follow closely, to shadow; (*with* **off, away**) to (cause to) dwindle.
tailback *n* a long queue of traffic behind an obstruction; (*football*) the offensive back farthest from the line of scrimmage.
tailboard *n* a hinged or removable section at the rear of a motor vehicle.
tail coat *n* a man's black or grey coat cut horizontally just below the waist at the front with two long tails at the back.
tail-end *adj* tardy; being the last in line. * *n* the last.
tailgate *n* the hinged board at the rear of a truck which can be let down or removed. * *vti* to drive dangerously close behind (another vehicle).—**tailgater** *n*.
taillight *n* a red warning light at the rear of a motor vehicle.
tailor *n* a person who makes and repairs outer garments, esp. men's suits. * *vi* to work as a tailor. * *vt* to adapt to fit a particular requirement.
tailor-made *adj* specially designed for a particular purpose or person.
tailpipe *n* a pipe at the rear of jet engine or motor vehicle for discharging exhaust gases.
tailplane *n* a small stabilizing wing at the rear of an aircraft, a horizontal stabilizer.
tail rotor *n* the small propeller at the rear of a helicopter that counteracts the tendency of the body to spin in the opposite direction to the main rotor blades.
tailspin *n* a spiralling nose dive; (*inf*) a state of chaos.
tailstock *n* the adjustable part of a lathe that supports the free end of a workpiece.
tailwind *n* a wind in the same direction as a ship or aircraft is travelling.
taint *vt* to contaminate; to infect. * *vi* to be corrupted or disgraced. * *n* a stain; corruption.
taipan[1] *n* a powerful businessman operating in Hong Kong or China.
taipan[2] *n* a venomous Australian snake.
take *vb* (**taking, took,** *pp* **taken**) *vt* to lay hold of; to grasp or seize; to gain, win; to choose, select; (*attitude, pose*) to adopt; to understand; to consume; to accept or agree to; to lead or carry with one; to use as a means of travel; (*math*) to subtract (from); to use; to steal; (*gram*) to be used with; to endure calmly; (*with* **apart**) to dismantle; to criticize; (*with* **back**) to retract, withdraw (a promise, etc); (*with* **down**) to write down; to dismantle; to humiliate; (*with* **for**) (*inf*) to mistakenly believe to be; (*with* **in**) to understand, perceive; to include; to make a garment smaller by altering seams, etc; to offer accommodation to; (*inf*) to swindle, deceive; (*with* **on**) to employ as labour; to assume or acquire; to agree to do (something); to fight against; (*with* **out**) to extract; to obtain, procure; to escort; (*sl*) to kill; (*with* **up**) to begin as a business or hobby; to accept an offer or invitation; to occupy (time or space); to act as a patron to; to shorten (a garment); to interrupt or criticize; to absorb. * *vi* (*plant, etc*) to start growing successfully; to become effective; to catch on; to have recourse to; to go to; (*with* **after**) to resemble in appearance, character, etc; (*with* **on**) (*inf*) to become upset or distraught; (*with* **to**) to escape to as a refuge; to acquire a liking for; to adopt as a habit; (*with* **up**) to resume, continue further. * *n* (*film, TV*) the amount of film used without stopping the camera when shooting.
takeaway *n* a takeout.
take-home pay *n* pay remaining after all deductions, such as income tax, have been made.
taken *see* **take.**
takeoff *n* the process of an aircraft becoming airborne; (*inf*) an amusing impression or caricature of another person.
takeout, take-out *n* a cooked meal that is sold for consumption outside the premises; a shop or restaurant that provides such meals.—*also adj*.
takeover *n* the taking over of control, as in business.—*also adj*.
taking *adj* attractive, charming; (*inf*) catching, contagious. * *n* the act of one that takes; (*pl*) earnings; profits.
talc *n* a type of smooth mineral used in ceramics and talcum powder; talcum powder.
talcum powder *n* perfumed powdered talc for the skin.
tale *n* a narrative or story; a fictitious account, a lie; idle or malicious gossip.
talent *n* any innate or special aptitude.—**talented** *adj*.
talent scout *n* a person employed to recruit talented people for professional careers in sport, entertainment, etc.
talent show *n* a show which gives amateurs a chance to perform in the hope of attracting interest from professionals for permanent engagements.
talipot *n* a palm tree of the East Indies with large leaves used for roofing, umbrellas, etc.
talisman *n* (*pl* **talismans**) an object or charm supposed to ward off evil and bring good luck; an amulet.
talk *vt* to speak; to know how to speak (a language); to discuss or speak of (something); to influence by talking; (*with* **down**) to silence or override (a speaker, argument, etc) by talking loudly; to radio instructions to (an aircraft) so that it may land safely; (*with* **into**) to persuade by argument or talking; (*with* **out**) to resolve by discussion; (*with* **round**) to persuade by talking. * *vi* to converse; to discuss; to gossip; to divulge information; (*with* **back**) to reply impudently; (*with* **down**) to speak in a condescending manner (to); (*with* **round**) to discuss (a subject) without reaching any conclusion; (*with* **shop**) to discuss work, esp after working hours. * *n* a discussion; a lecture; gossip; (*pl*) negotiations.
talkative *adj* given to talking a great deal.
talkie *n* (*inf*) an early motion-picture film with sound.
talking book *n* a recording of a book for the blind.
talking head *n* the head and shoulders of a person on television talking directly to the camera without using visual material.
talking picture *n* a talkie.
talking point *n* a subject for conversation or discussion; something that lends support to an argument.
talking-to *n* a reprimand, lecture.
talk show *n* a television or radio programme with informal interviews and conversation, a chat show.
tall *adj* above average in height; (*inf*) (*story*) exaggerated.—**tallness** *n*.
tallboy *n* a high chest of drawers on legs, a highboy.
tallith *n* (*pl* **tallithim**) a fringed shawl worn by Jewish men during religious services.
tall order *n* (*inf*) a request that is difficult to fulfil.
tallow *n* solid animal fat used to make soap, candles, etc.
tall ship *n* a square-rigged sailing vessel.
tall story *n* (*inf*) an exaggerated or unbelievable account
tally *n* (*pl* **tallies**) reckoning, account; one score in a game. * *vi* (**tallying, tallied**) to correspond; to keep score.
tally-ho *n* the cry of a person at a fox hunt when sighting the quarry.—*also vti*.
Talmud *n* the body of Jewish law.—**Talmudic** *adj*.
talon *n* a claw of an animal, esp a bird of prey.
talus[1] *n* (*pl* **tali**) the anklebone.
talus[2] *n* (*pl* **taluses**) scree; the sloping side of a wall.
tamale *n* a Mexican dish of minced meat with crushed maize and seasonings.

tamandua *n* a small tree-dwelling anteater of Central and South America.
tamarack *n* (the wood of) any of various North American larches.
tamarin *n* any of numerous small monkeys of South America resembling marmosets.
tamarind *n* a tropical evergreen tree bearing a pulpy fruit used for food, in beverages and in laxative preparations.
tamarisk *n* any of a genus of evergreen trees and shrubs of Mediterranean and tropical regions with tiny leaves and numerous clusters of pink or white flowers.
tambour *n* a drum; (an embroidery produced on) a circular frame for holding fabric taut during embroidery; a rolling top on a desk or cabinet made from thin strips of wood on a canvas backing. * *vt* to embroider using a tambour.
tamboura, tambura *n* an Indian stringed instrument used to provide a drone as accompaniment to singing.
tambourin *n* a dance of Provence in France; the music for this; a long drum used in Provence.
tambourine *n* a percussion hand instrument made of skin stretched over a circular frame with small jingling metal discs around the edge.
tambura *see* **tamboura.**
tame *adj* (*animal*) not wild, domesticated; compliant; dull, uninteresting. * *vt* (*animal*) to domesticate; to subdue; to soften.
Tamil *n* a member of a people inhabiting southeastern India and Sri Lanka; the language they speak.—*also adj*.
tam-o'-shanter *n* a tight-fitting Scottish woollen or cloth beret with a full crown and a pompom on top.
tamp *vt* to pack down firmly with a series of blows; to pack (a blast-hole) with sand or earth above the explosive charge.
tamper *vi* to meddle (with); to interfere (with).
tampion *n* a plug for the muzzle of a gun.
tampon *n* a firm plug of cotton wool inserted in the vagina during menstruation.
tam-tam *n* a gong.
tan[1] *n* a yellowish-brown colour; suntan. * *vti* (**tanning, tanned**) to acquire a suntan through sunbathing; (*skin, hide*) to convert into leather using tannin; (*inf*) to thrash.
tan[2] *abbr* = tangent.
tanager *n* any of numerous American woodland songbirds, the male of which has vividly coloured plumage.
tanbark *n* bark, esp from the oak, used as a source of tannin.
tandem *n* a bicycle for two riders, sitting one behind the other.
tandoori *n* an Indian method of cooking meat, vegetables and bread using a large clay oven.
tang *n* sharp smell or a strong taste.—**tangy** *adj.*
tangent *n* a line that touches a curve or circle at one point, without crossing it. * *adj* touching at one point.
tangential *adj* of superficial relevance; digressive.
tangerine *n* a small, sweet orange with a loose skin; the colour of this.—*also adj*.
tangible *adj* capable of being felt, seen or noticed; substantial; real.—**tangibility** *n*.
tangle *n* a mass of hair, string or wire knotted together confusedly; a complication. * *vt* to intertwine in a mass, to snarl; to entangle, complicate. * *vi* to become tangled or complicated; (*with* **with**) to become involved in argument with.
tango *n* (*pl* **tangos**) a Latin American ballroom dance. * *vi* (**tangoing, tangoed**) to dance the tango.
tangram *n* a Chinese puzzle made from a square cut into a rhomboid, a square and five triangles, which can be combined to produce different figures.
tank *n* a large container for storing liquids or gases; an armoured combat vehicle, mounted with guns and having caterpillar tracks.
tanka *n* (*pl* **tankas, tanka**) a Japanese verse form with five lines.
tankage *n* the capacity of a tank; the storing of oil, etc in tanks.
tankard *n* a tall, one-handled drinking mug, often with a hinged lid.
tanked *adj* (*sl*) extremely drunk.
tank engine *n* a steam locomotive that carries its own water supplies instead of using a tender.
tanker *n* a large ship or truck for transporting oil and other liquids.
tank top *n* a sleeveless pullover with a low neck.
tanner *n* a person who tans skins.
tannery *n* (*pl* **tanneries**) a place where hides are tanned.
tannic *adj* of, resembling, or derived from tan or tannin.
tannic acid *n* tannin.
tannin *n* a yellow or brown chemical found in plants or tea, used in tanning.
tansy *n* (*pl* **tansies**) any of numerous aromatic plants with yellow flowers and finely-divided leaves, once used for seasoning and as a medicine.
tantalize *vt* to tease or torment by presenting something greatly desired, but keeping it inaccessible.
tantalum *n* a hard metallic element of the vanadium family, esp used for hardening alloys.
tantalus *n* a cabinet or case where bottles of spirit may be locked up yet remain visible.
tantamount *adj* equivalent (to) in effect; as good as.
tantara *n* the sound of a horn or trumpet playing a fanfare.
tantrum *n* a childish fit of bad temper.
Tao *n* (*Taoism*) the spirit of creative harmony in the universe; the path of virtuous conduct in harmony with the natural order.
Taoiseach *n* the prime minister of the Republic of Ireland.
Taoism *n* a Chinese religious and philosophical system advocating a simple passive life in harmony with the natural order.
tap[1] *n* a quick, light blow or touch; a piece of metal attached to the heel or toe of a shoe for reinforcement or to tap-dance. * *vti* (**tapping, tapped**) to strike lightly; to make a tapping sound.
tap[2] *n* a device controlling the flow of liquid through a pipe or from a container, a faucet. * *vt* (**tapping, tapped**) to pierce in order to draw fluid from; to connect a secret listening device to a telephone; (*inf*) to ask for money from; (*resources, etc*) to draw on.
tap-dance *vi* to perform a step dance in shoes with taps.—**tap-dancer** *n*.—**tap-dancing** *n*.
tape *n* a strong, narrow strip of cloth, paper, etc, used for tying, binding, etc; tape measure; magnetic tape, as in a cassette or videotape. * *vt* to wrap with tape; to record on magnetic tape.
tape deck *n* a tape recorder in a hi-fi system.
tape measure *n* a tape marked in inches or centimetres for measuring.
tape player *n* a self-contained tape recorder.
tape recorder *n* a machine used for recording and reproducing sounds or music on magnetic tape, esp as part of a hi-fi system, a tape deck.
tape recording *n* a recording made on magnetic tape.
taper *n* a long thin candle. * *vti* to make or become gradually narrower toward one end.—**tapering** *adj*.
tapestry *n* (*pl* **tapestries**) a heavy fabric woven with patterns or figures, used for wall hangings and furnishings.
tapeworm *n* a tape-like, parasitic, intestinal worm.
tapioca *n* a glutinous starch extracted from the root of the cassava and used in puddings, etc.
tapir *n* (*pl* **tapirs, tapir**) a South American hoofed mammal with a short flexible proboscis.
tappet *n* a projecting arm or lever (eg a cam) that moves or is moved by another part in a machine.
taproom *n* a bar.
taps *n sing* a call on a bugle at a military camp signalling lights out; any similar signal, as at a military funeral.
tar[1] *n* a thick, dark, viscous substance obtained from wood, coal, peat, etc., used for surfacing roads. * *vt* to coat with tar.—**tarry** *adj*.
tar[2] *n* a (*inf*) a sailor.
taramasalata *n* a pale pink fish-roe paste served as a starter.
tarantella *n* (the music for) a lively peasant dance of southern Italy.
tarantula *n* (*pl* **tarantulas, tarantulae**) a large, hairy spider with a poisonous bite that is painful but not deadly.

tarboosh, tarbush *n* a brimless red cap resembling a fez worn by Muslim men.
tardy *adj* (**tardier, tardiest**) slow; later than expected.—**tardily** *adv*.—**tardiness** *n*.
tare[1] *n* (the seed of) a type of vetch plant.
tare[2] *n* (an allowance for) the weight of the wrapping or container in which goods are packed; the weight of an unloaded goods vehicle. * *vt* to weigh in order to calculate the tare.
target *n* a mark to aim at, esp in shooting; an objective or ambition.
tariff *n* a tax on imports or exports; (*in a hotel*) a list of prices; the rate of charge for public services, such as gas or electricity.
tarlatan, tarletan *n* a type of thin stiff cotton fabric.
Tarmac, Tarmacadam *n* a material for surfacing roads made from crushed stones and tar; an airport runway. * *vti* (**tarmacking, tarmacked**) to lay down a tarmac surface.
tarn *n* a small mountain lake.
tarnish *vi* (*metal*) to lose its lustre or discolour due to exposure to the air. * *vt* (*reputation*) to taint.—*also n*.
taro *n* (*pl* **taros**) (the edible root of) a tropical Asian plant.
tarot *n* a game played with 22 pictorial cards, which are also used for fortune-telling.
tarpaulin *n* canvas cloth coated with a waterproof substance.
tarragon *n* an aromatic herb used for flavouring.
tarry *vi* (**tarrying, tarried**) to delay or dawdle; to linger; to wait briefly.
tarsus *n* (*pl* **tarsi**) the small bones of the ankle and the heel in vertebrates; the plate of tissue that stiffens the eyelid.—**tarsal** *adj, n*.
tart[1] *adj* having a sour, sharp taste; (*speech*) sharp, severe. —**tartly** *adv*.—**tartness** *n*.
tart[2] *n* an open pastry case containing fruit, jam or custard; (*inf*) a prostitute. * *vt* (*with* **up**) (*inf*) to dress cheaply and gaudily; to decorate, esp cheaply.
tartan *n* a woollen cloth with a chequered pattern, having a distinctive design for each Scottish clan.
tartar *n* a hard, yellow, crusty deposit which forms on the teeth; a salty deposit on the sides of wine casks.
tartaric acid *n* an organic acid obtained from grapes and many other fruits.
tartar sauce *n* a mayonnaise sauce with chopped capers, herbs, etc, eaten esp with fish.
task *n* a specific amount of work to be done; a chore.
task force *n* a small unit with a specific mission, usu military.
taskmaster *n* a person who demands constant hard work.
Tasmanian devil *n* a burrowing flesh-eating marsupial of Tasmania with a black coat and long tail.
tassel *n* an ornamental tuft of silken threads decorating soft furnishings, clothes, etc; a growth that looks like this, esp on corn. * *vb* (**tasselling, tasselled** *or* **tasseling, tasseled**) *vt* to decorate with tassels. * *vi* (*plant*) to grow tassels.
taste *vt* to perceive (a flavour) by taking into the mouth; to try by eating and drinking a little; to sample; to experience. * *vi* to try by the mouth; to have a specific flavour. * *n* the sense by which flavours are perceived; a small portion; the ability to recognize what is beautiful, attractive, etc; liking; a brief experience.
taste bud *n* any of the small projecting sensory organs on the tongue's surface by which taste is perceived.
tasteful *adj* showing good taste.—**tastefully** *adv*.—**tastefulness** *n*.
tasteless *adj* without taste, bland; in bad taste.—**tastelessly** *adv*.
taster *n* a person skilled in determining the balance of flavours in a product, esp tea, wine; a device for tasting or sampling; (*formerly*) a person who tasted food before it was served to a king, etc.
tasty *adj* (**tastier, tastiest**) savoury; having a pleasant flavour.
ta-ta *interj* (*Brit inf*) goodbye.
tatami *n* (*pl* **tatamis, tatami**) straw matting used as a floor covering, esp in Japan.
tatter *n* a torn or ragged piece of cloth.—**tattered** *adj*.
tatterdemalion *n* a person wearing ragged clothes, a ragamuffin.—*also adj*.
tatting *n* (the process of making) a type of delicate handmade lace.
tattle *vi* to gossip. * *vt* to reveal (secrets, etc) by gossiping. * *n* (a) gossip.
tattletale *n* a gossip. * *adj* telltale.
tattoo[1] *n* (*pl* **tattoos**) a continuous beating of a drum; a military display of exercises and music.
tattoo[2] *vt* (**tattooing, tattooed**) to make permanent patterns or pictures on the skin by pricking and marking with dyes. * *n* (*pl* **tattoos**) marks made on the skin in this way.
tatty *adj* (**tattier, tattiest**) shabby, ragged.
tau *n* the 19th letter of the Greek alphabet.
taught *see* **teach**.
taunt *vt* to provoke with mockery or contempt; to tease. * *n* an insult.
taupe *n, adj* (a) brownish-grey.
taurine *n* of or like a bull.
tauromachy *n* the art or practice of bullfighting.
Taurus *n* the Bull, the second sign of the zodiac.—**Taurean** *adj*.
taut *adj* stretched tight; tense; stressed.
tauten *vti* to make or become taut.
tauto-, taut- *prefix* same.
tautog *n* a large North American food fish related to the wrasse.
tautology *n* (*pl* **tautologies**) a statement which uses different words to repeat the same thing.—**tautological, tautologous** *adj*.
tavern *n* a place licensed to sell alcoholic drinks; an inn.
taverna *n* a Greek hotel with its own bar; a Greek restaurant.
tawdry *adj* (**tawdrier, tawdriest**) showy, cheap, and of poor quality.
tawny *adj* yellowish brown.
tawny owl *n* a European owl with brown plumage.
tawse *n* (*Scot*) a leather strap with a slit end formerly used for punishing schoolchildren.
tax *n* a rate imposed by the government on property or persons to raise revenues; a strain. * *vt* to impose a tax (upon); to strain.
taxa *see* **taxon**.
taxable *adj* able or liable to be taxed.
taxation *n* the act of levying taxes; the amount raised as tax.
tax avoidance *n* avoiding paying tax using legal means.
tax-deductible *adj* (*expenses, etc*) legitimately deducted from income before tax assessment.
tax evasion *n* avoiding paying tax using illegal methods.
tax exile *n* a person who lives abroad to avoid paying high taxes.
tax haven *n* a place where taxes are lower than average.
taxi *n* (*pl* **taxis**) a taxicab. * *vi* (**taxiing** *or* **taxying, taxied**) (*aircraft*) to move along the runway before takeoff or after landing.
taxicab *n* a car, usu fitted with a taximeter, that may be hired to transport passengers.
taxidermy *n* the art of preparing and stuffing the skins of animals ready for exhibiting.—**taxidermist** *n*.
taximeter *n* a meter fitted into a taxi to record the time taken for a journey.
taxis *n* a movement in a simple organism (eg a bacterium) in response to certain external stimuli; (*surgery*) the restoration of a displaced part by manual pressure.
taxiway *n* a marked route from a terminal to a runway along which an aircraft taxis.
taxon *n* (*pl* **taxa**) any taxonomic group or category.
taxonomy *n* (the science of) the classification of living things into groups based on similarities of biological origin, design, function, etc.
taxpayer *n* a person who or an organization that pays taxes.
tax return *n* a statement of a person's income for the purposes of tax assessment.
tax shelter *n* a financial arrangement to minimize tax liability.
tax therapist *n* a tax adviser who helps with the completion of income tax forms.
TB *abbr* = tuberculosis.

Tb (*chem symbol*) terbium.
T-bone steak *n* a large sirloin steak containing a T-shaped bone.
tbs., tbsp. *abbr* = tablespoon; tablespoonful.
Tc (*chem symbol*) technetium.
T-cell *n* a lymphocyte that kills cells infected with a virus.—*also* **T-lymphocyte.**
Te (*chem symbol*) tellurium.
tea *n* a shrub growing in China, India, Sri Lanka, etc; its dried, shredded leaves, which are infused in boiling water for a beverage; in UK, a light meal taken in mid-afternoon; a main meal taken in the early evening.
tea bag *n* a small porous bag containing tea leaves for infusing.
tea ball *n* a perforated metal ball which holds tea leaves to make tea.
tea caddy *n* an airtight container for storing tea.
teach *vb* (**teaching, taught**) *vt* to impart knowledge to; to give lessons (to); to train; to help to learn. * *vi* to give instruction, esp as a profession.—**teachable** *adj*.
tea chest *n* a large wooden box used to transport tea.
teacher *n* a person who instructs others, esp as an occupation.
teach-in *n* an informal conference at a university or college with lectures and discussions on a topical issue.
teaching *n* the profession or practice of being a teacher; the act of giving instruction.
tea cloth *n* a tea towel for drying dishes; a dishtowel.
tea cosy *n* a cover for a teapot to keep the contents warm.
teacup *n* a small cup for drinking tea.
teak *n* a type of hard wood from an East Indian tree.
teal *n* (*pl* **teal, teals**) a small freshwater duck; a dark greenish blue.
team *n* a group of people participating in a sport together; a group of people working together; two or more animals pulling a vehicle. * *vi* (*with* **up**) to join in cooperative activity.
team-mate *n* a colleague, a fellow team member.
team spirit *n* willingness to work harmoniously within a group.
teamster *n* a truck driver.
teamwork *n* cooperation of individuals for the benefit of the team; the ability of a team to work together.
teapot *n* a vessel in which tea is made.
teapoy *n* a three-legged stand or table.
tear[1] *n* a drop of salty liquid appearing in the eyes when crying or when the eyes are smarting; anything tear-shaped.
tear[2] *vb* (**tearing, tore,** *pp* **torn**) *vt* to pull apart by force; to split; to lacerate; (*with* **down**) to destroy, demolish. * *vi* to move with speed; (*with* **into**) (*inf*) to attack physically or verbally. * *n* a hole or split.
tearaway *n* an impetuous, violent person.
tearful *adj* weeping; sad.—**tearfully** *adv*.
tear gas *n* gas that irritates the eyes and nasal passages, used in riot control.
tearing *adj* overwhelming, violent.
tear-jerker *n* a strongly sentimental book, film, play, etc.
tearoom, teashop *n* a restaurant where tea and light refreshments are served.
tea rose *n* any of numerous garden bush roses descended from a Chinese rose and valued for their large tea-scented blooms.
tease *vt* to separate the fibres of; to torment or irritate; to taunt playfully. * *n* a person who teases or torments; (*inf*) a flirt.—**teaser** *n*.
teasel, teazel, teazle *n* any of various plants with prickly leaves and flower heads formerly dried and used to raise a nap on woollen cloth; an implement used for this purpose.
tea service, tea set *n* the set of cups and saucers, etc for serving tea.
teashop *n* a tearoom.
teaspoon *n* a small spoon for use with a teacup or as a measure; the amount measured by this.—**teaspoonful** *n*.
teat *n* the nipple on a breast or udder; the mouthpiece of a baby's feeding bottle.
tea towel, tea cloth *n* a towel for drying dishes; a dishtowel.
tech. *abbr* = technical; technology.
technetium *n* an artificially produced metallic element whose radioisotope is used in radiotherapy.
technical *adj* relating to, or specializing in practical, industrial, mechanical or applied sciences; (*expression, etc*) belonging to or peculiar to a particular field of activity.—**technically** *adv*.
technicality *n* (*pl* **technicalities**) a petty formality or technical point.
technical knockout *n* (*boxing*) a decision by a referee to end a fight because a boxer is too badly hurt to continue.
technician *n* a person skilled in the practice of any art, esp in practical work with scientific equipment.
Technicolor *n* (*trademark*) the production of colour film by combining identical scenes with different primary colours into a single print.
technique *n* method of performing a particular task; knack.
techno- *prefix* technical; technological.
technocracy *n* (*pl* **technocracies**) government by technical experts.—**technocrat** *n*.—**technocratic** *adj*.
technology *n* (*pl* **technologies**) the application of mechanical and applied sciences to industrial use.—**technological** *adj*.—**technologist** *n*.
techy *see* **tetchy.**
tectonic *adj* of or relating to building or construction; (*geological structures or forces*) resulting from deformation of the earth's crust.
tectonics *n sing* the art or science of constructing buildings, etc; the study of the forces which shape the earth's geological structure.
teddy *n* (*pl* **teddies**) a woman's one-piece undergarment.
teddy bear *n* a stuffed toy bear.
Te Deum *n* a Latin hymn used in services of thanksgiving to God.
tedious *adj* monotonous; boring.—**tediously** *adv*.—**tedium** *n*.
tee *n* (*golf*) the place from where the first stroke is played at each hole; a small peg from which the ball is driven. * *vti* to position (the ball) on the tee; (*with* **off**) to hit a golf ball from a tee.
teem[1] *vi* (*with* **with**) to be prolific or abundant in.
teem[2] *vi* to pour (with rain).
teen *n* a teenager. * *adj* teenage.
teenager *n* (*inf*) a person who is in his or her teens.
teens *npl* the years of one's life from thir*teen* to nine*teen*.—**teenage, teenaged** *adj*.
teeny *adj* (**teenier, teeniest**) (*inf*) tiny.
teenybopper *n* a young girl who avidly follows the latest fashions in clothes and pop music.
teepee *see* **tepee.**
tee-shirt *see* **T-shirt.**
teeter *vi* to move or stand unsteadily.
teeth *see* **tooth.**
teethe *vi* to cut one's first teeth.
teething *n* the condition in babies of the first growth of teeth.
teething ring *n* a hard ring for a teething baby to chew on.
teething troubles *npl* problems encountered in the early stages of a project, etc; pain caused by growing teeth.
teetotaller, teetotaler *n* a person who abstains from alcoholic drinks.—**teetotal** *adj*.
TEFL *abbr* = Teaching English as a Foreign Language.
Teflon *n* (*trademark*) polytetrafluoroethylene, a coating for pots and pans that prevents food sticking. * *adj* (*inf*) able to avoid (political) scandal by claiming ignorance or blaming others.
tegument *n* an outer covering; an integument.
tektite *n* a spherical glassy object found in various parts of the world and thought to be of meteoric origin.
tel. *abbr* = telephone.
tel-, tele- *prefix* at a distance; television.
telaesthesia *n* supposed perception of objects or events beyond the normal range of the senses.—*also* **telesthesia.**—**telaesthetic, telesthetic** *adj*.
telamon *n* (*archit*) a figure or half-figure of a man, used in place of a column or pilaster to support an entablature, an atlas.
telecast *vt* to broadcast by television. * *n* a television broadcast.—**telecaster** *n*.

telecom, telecoms *n* short for telecommunications.
telecommunication *n* communication of information over long distances by telephone and radio; (*pl*) the technology of telephone and radio communication.
teledu *n* a mammal of Java and Sumatra resembling the badger and related to the skunk, which releases a foul-smelling liquid when threatened.
telefilm *n* a motion picture produced for television.
telegenic *adj* suitable for television in content or appearance.
telegram *n* a message sent by telegraph.
telegraph *n* a system for transmitting messages over long distances using electricity, wires and a code. * *vt* to transmit by telegraph.—**telegraphic** *adj*.—**telegraphy** *n*.
telekinesis *n* the movement of objects using pure thought without the application of physical force.—**telekinetic** *adj*.
telemark *n* (*skiing*) a turn in which one ski is placed ahead of the other and then angled gradually inward.
telemeter *n* any instrument that measures or records events and transmits the data to a distant receiver; (*surveying*) a device for measuring distances. * *vt* to gather and transmit data from a distance.
telemetry *n* the use of radio waves to transmit, register and record the readings of an instrument at a distance.
telencephalon *n* the frontal brain including the cerebrum, parts of the hypothalamus and the third ventricle.—**telencephalic** *adj*.
teleology *n* the philosophical doctrine that explains nature or natural processes in terms of purpose or design.—**teleological** *adj*.—**teleologist** *n*.
telepathy *n* the communication between people's minds of thoughts and feelings, without the need for speech or proximity.—**telepathic** *adj*.
telephone *n* an instrument for transmitting speech at a distance, esp by means of electricity. * *vt* (*someone*) to call by telephone.
telephone book *n* a book listing the names, addresses and telephone numbers of subscribers in a given area.
telephone booth *n* a cubicle for paid public use of a telephone.
telephone directory *n* a telephone book.
telephone operator, telephonist *n* a person who operates a telephone switchboard.
telephony *n* the system by which sounds are transmitted by telephone.—**telephonic** *adj*.
telephotography *n* the use of a telephoto lens to photograph distant objects.
telephoto lens *n* a camera lens that magnifies distant objects.
teleprinter *n* a teletypewriter.
TelePrompTer *n* (*trademark*) a prompting device used in TV, etc, which provides speakers with a script that remains invisible to the audience, an autocue.
telesales *npl* selling products and services by telephone.
telescope *n* a tubular optical instrument for viewing objects at a distance.
telescopic *adj* of or like a telescope; that can be viewed by through a telescope.—**telescopically** *adv*.
telesthesia *see* **telaesthesia.**
Teletext *n* (*trademark*) written information transmitted non-interactively to television viewers.
telethon *n* a long television extravaganza which encourages viewers to send in money for a charitable cause.
Teletype *n* (*trademark*) a teleprinter.
teletypewriter *n* a telegraph apparatus with a keyboard that transmits and a printer that receives messages over a distance.
televangelist *n* a person, usu a minister of the Christian Pentecostal church, who conducts television shows to preach the church's message and seek donations.
televise *vt* (*a programme*) to transmit by television.
television *n* the transmission of visual images and accompanying sound through electrical and sound waves; a television receiving set; television broadcasting.
telex *n* a communication system whereby subscribers hire teletypewriters for transmitting messages. * *vt* to transmit by telex.
tell *vb* (**telling, told**) *vt* to narrate; to disclose; to inform; to notify; to instruct; to distinguish; (*with* **off**) (*inf*) to reprimand; to count off and assign to a duty. * *vi* to tell tales, to inform on; to produce a marked effect.
teller *n* a bank clerk; a person appointed to count votes in an election.
telling *adj* having great impact.
telltale *n* a person who tells tales about others. * *adj* revealing what is meant to be hidden.
tellurian *adj* of the earth. * *n* an inhabitant of the earth.
telluric *adj* of or in the earth or soil; of or containing (high valency) tellurium.
tellurium *n* a brittle nonmetallic element related to sulphur and selenium.
tellurometer *n* (*surveying*) an electronic instrument for measuring distances using microwaves.
telly *n* (*pl* **tellies**) (*Brit inf*) television.
telo-, tel- *prefix* end.
temerity *n* rashness.
temp *n* (*inf*) a temporary employee.
temp. *abbr* = temperature.
temper *n* a frame of mind; a fit of anger. * *vt* to tone down, moderate; (*steel*) to heat and cool repeatedly to bring to the correct hardness.
tempera *n* (a method of painting using) powdered pigments mixed with an emulsion, esp egg yolk and water; a painting done in tempera; opaque watercolour used for posters.
temperament *n* one's disposition.
temperamental *adj* easily irritated; erratic.—**temperamentally** *adv*.
temperance *n* moderation; abstinence from alcohol.
temperate *adj* mild or moderate in temperature; (*behaviour*) moderate, self-controlled.
temperature *n* degree of heat or cold; body heat above the normal.
tempest *n* a violent storm.
tempestuous *adj* stormy; violent; passionate.
tempi *see* **tempo.**
template *n* a pattern, gauge or mould used as a guide esp in cutting metal, stone or plastic.
temple[1] *n* a place of worship.
temple[2] *n* the region on either side of the head above the cheekbone.
tempo *n* (*pl* **tempos, tempi**) (*mus*) the speed at which music is meant to be played; rate of any activity.
temporal[1] *adj* relating to time; secular, civil.
temporal[2] *adj* of or relating to the temples of the head.
temporality *n* (*pl* **temporalities**) the state or condition of being temporal; a secular or civil authority or power.
temporal lobe *n* a lobe on each side of the cerebral hemisphere associated with hearing and speech.
temporary *adj* lasting or used for a limited time only; not permanent.—**temporarily** *adv*.
temporize *vi* to delay in order to gain time; to act to fit the occasion.—**temporization** *n*.—**temporizer** *n*.
tempt *vt* to entice to do wrong; to invite, attract, induce.—**tempter** *n*.—**temptress** *nf*.
temptation *n* the act of tempting or the state of being tempted; something or someone that tempts.
tempting *adj* attractive, inviting.
tempura *n* a Japanese dish of seafood or vegetables fried in batter.
ten *adj, n* the cardinal number next above nine. * *n* the symbol for this (10, X, x).
tenable *adj* capable of being believed, held, or defended.
tenacious *adj* grasping firmly; persistent; retentive; adhesive.
tenacity *n* the state or quality of being tenacious; doggedness, obstinacy; adhesiveness, stickiness.
tenaculum *n* (*pl* **tenacula**) a hooked surgical instrument for seizing and holding parts, such as arteries.
tenancy *n* (*pl* **tenancies**) the temporary possession by a tenant of another's property; the period of this.

tenant *n* a person who pays rent to occupy a house or flat or for the use of land or buildings; an occupant.
tenant farmer *n* a farmer who works land owned by someone else to whom he pays rent.
tench *n* (*pl* **tench**) a freshwater fish of the carp family.
tend[1] *vt* to take care of; to attend (to).
tend[2] *vi* to be inclined; to move in a specific direction.
tendency *n* (*pl* **tendencies**) an inclination or leaning.
tendentious, tendencious *adj* showing bias, not impartial.—**tendentiousness, tendenciousness** *n*.
tender[1] *n* a railroad car attached to locomotives to carry fuel and water; a small ship that brings stores to a larger one.
tender[2] *vt* to present for acceptance; to offer as payment. * *vi* to make an offer. * *n* an offer to provide goods or services at a fixed price.
tender[3] *adj* soft, delicate; fragile; painful, sore; sensitive; sympathetic.—**tenderly** *adv*.—**tenderness** *n*.
tenderfoot *n* a newcomer to rough, outdoor life; an inexperienced beginner.
tenderhearted *n* having a compassionate, loving or sensitive disposition.—**tenderheartedly** *adv*.—**tenderheartedness** *n*.
tenderize *vt* (*meat*) to make more tender by pounding or by adding a substance that softens.—**tenderization** *n*.—**tenderizer** *n*.
tenderloin *n* a cut of meat from between the ribs and sirloin.
tendon *n* fibrous tissue attaching a muscle to a bone.
tendril *n* a thread-like shoot of a climbing plant by which it attaches itself for support.
tenement *n* a building divided into flats, each occupied by a separate owner or tenant.
tenesmus *n* (*med*) an urgent but ineffectual attempt to urinate or void the bowels.
tenet *n* any belief or doctrine.
tenfold *adj*, *adv* 10 times as much or as many; composed of 10 parts.
ten-gallon hat *n* a wide-brimmed hat with a high crown, esp worn by cowboys.
teniasis *see* **taeniasis**.
Tenn. *abbr* = Tennessee.
tenner *n* (*inf*) a ten-pound note; a ten-dollar bill.
tennis *n* a game for two or four people, played by hitting a ball over a net with a racket.
tennis court *n* a court surfaced with clay, asphalt or grass on which tennis is played.
tennis elbow *n* stiffness and pain in the elbow joint due to excessive exercise, such as playing tennis.
tenon *n* a projection on the end of a piece of wood for connecting with a mortise. * *vt* to form a tenon; to connect using a tenon and mortise.
tenon saw *n* a fine-toothed saw with a sturdy back used for cutting tenons, etc.
tenor *n* a general purpose or intent; the highest regular adult male voice, higher than a baritone and lower than an alto; a man who sings tenor.
tenor clef *n* a C clef placed so as to designate the fourth line of the staff as middle C.
tenosynovitis *n* inflammation of the tendons in a joint through repetitive movements of the joint concerned.
tenpin *n* a bowling pin used in tenpins.
tenpin bowling *n* in UK, tenpins.
tenpins *n sing* a bowling game involving the rolling of a large bowl along a lane to knock over as many as possible of tenpins.
tenrec *n* any of various related mammals of Madagascar resembling shrews.
tense[1] *n* (*gram*) the verb form that indicates the time of an action or the existence of a state.
tense[2] *adj* stretched, taut; apprehensive; nervous and highly strung. * *vti* to make or become tense.—**tensely** *adv*.—**tenseness** *n*.
tensile *adj* of or relating to tension; stretchable.
tensile strength *n* the greatest stress a material can bear without breaking.
tensimeter *n* an instrument that measures differences in vapour pressures.
tensiometer *n* an instrument for measuring tensile strength; an instrument for comparing vapour pressures in different liquids; an instrument for measuring the surface tension of a liquid; an instrument for measuring the moisture content of soil.
tension *n* the act of stretching; the state of being stretched; (*between forces, etc*) opposition; stress; mental strain.
tensor *n* any muscle that stretches or tightens a body part.
tent *n* a portable shelter of canvas, plastic or other waterproof fabric, which is erected on poles and fixed to the ground by ropes and pegs.
tentacle *n* a long, slender, flexible growth near the mouth of invertebrates, used for feeling, grasping or handling.
tentative *adj* provisional; not definite.—**tentatively** *adv*.—**tentativeness** *n*.
tenterhook *n* one of a series of hooks on which cloth is stretched to dry; (*pl*) (*with* **on**) in a tense or anxious state.
tenth *adj* the last of ten; being one of ten equal parts. * *n* one of ten equal parts.
tenuous *adj* slight, flimsy, insubstantial.—**tenuousness** *n*.
tenure *n* the holding of property or a position; the period of time which a position lasts; a permanent position, usu granted after holding a job for a number of years.—**tenured** *adj*.
tenuto *adv, adj* (*mus*) (*note*) sustained for its full time value.
teocalli *n* (*pl* **teocallis**) the pyramid-shaped bases supporting Aztec temples.
tepee *n* a cone-shaped, North American Indian tent formed of skins; a wigwam.—*also* **teepee**.
tepid *adj* slightly warm, lukewarm.
tequila *n* a spirit distilled from a Mexican agave plant; the plant itself.
ter. *abbr* = terrace; territory.
ter- *prefix* three times; third; three.
tera- *prefix* ten to the power of 12.
terbium *n* a metallic element of the rare earth group.
tercel *see* **tiercel**.
tercentenary *n* (*pl* **tercentenaries**) a three hundredth anniversary.—*also adj*.
terebene *n* a liquid hydrocarbon derived from oil of turpentine and sulphuric acid used in making varnishes, as an antiseptic and in medicines.
terebinth *n* a European tree that yields a resinous liquid.
terebinthine *n* or or pertaining to the terebinth; of or like turpentine.
teredo *n* (*pl* **teredos, teredines**) a burrowing mollusc, the shipworm.
terete *adj* (*plant, animal part*) having a smooth cylindrical shape.
tergiversate *vi* to switch allegiances; to be evasive, to equivocate.
term *n* a limit; any prescribed period of time; a division of an academic year; a word or expression, esp in a specialized field of knowledge; (*pl*) mutual relationship between people; (*pl*) conditions of a contract, etc. * *vt* to call, designate.
termagant *n* (*arch*) a shrewish, nagging woman.
terminal *adj* being or situated at the end or extremity; (*disease*) fatal, incurable. * *n* a bus, coach or railroad station at the end of the line; the point at which an electrical current enters or leaves a device; a device with a keyboard and monitor for inputting or viewing data from a computer.—**terminally** *adv*.
terminate *vti* to bring or come to an end.—**termination** *n*.
terminology *n* (*pl* **terminologies**) the terms used in any specialized subject.
terminus *n* (*pl* **termini, terminuses**) the final part; a limit; end of a transportation line.
termitarium *n* (*pl* **termitaria**) a termites' nest.
termite *n* a wood-eating, white, ant-like insect.
tern *n* a small, black and white sea bird.
ternary *adj* in three parts; (*number system*) using three as a base.
terpene *n* any of various hydrocarbons present in the essential oils of plants, esp conifers.
Terpsichorean *adj* pertaining to dancing, or to Terpsichore, the Muse of dancing and choral song in classical myth.
terrace *n* a raised level area of earth, often part of a slope; an unroofed paved area adjoining a house; a row of houses; a patio or balcony. * *vt* to make into a terrace.

terracotta *n* a brownish-red clay used for making flower pots and statues, which is baked but not glazed; a brown-red colour.
terra firma *n* solid ground; the earth.
terrain *n* the surface features of a tract of land; (*fig*) field of activity.
terra incognita *n* an unexplored or unknown area or country.
terrapin *n* an aquatic North American turtle.
terrarium *n* (*pl* **terraria, terrariums**) an enclosure for small land animals; a glass container for plants.
terrazzo *n* mosaic flooring in the form of marble chips set in mortar and highly polished.
terrestrial *adj* relating to, or existing on, the earth; earthly; representing the earth.
terrible *adj* causing great fear; dreadful; (*inf*) very unpleasant.
terribly *adv* frighteningly; (*inf*) very.
terrier *n* a type of small, active dog.
terrific *adj* of great size; (*inf*) excellent.
terrify *vt* (**terrifying, terrified**) to fill with terror, to frighten greatly.
terrine *n* an earthenware dish for pâté; pâté or similar food served in this.
territorial *adj* relating to or owned by a territory. * *n* (*with cap*) a member of the Territorial Army, a British volunteer reserve force.
territorial waters *npl* the coastal and inland waters under the jurisdiction of a nation.
territory *n* (*pl* **territories**) an area under the jurisdiction of a city or state; a wide tract of land; an area assigned to a salesman; an area of knowledge.
terror *n* great fear; an object or person inspiring fear or dread.
terrorism *n* the use of terror and violence to intimidate.—**terrorist** *n*.
terrorize *vt* to terrify; to control by terror.—**terrorization** *n*.
terry *n* (*pl* **terries**) a cloth with an uncut pile made of looped threads.
terse *adj* abrupt, to the point, concise.—**tersely** *adv*.
tertian *adj* (*fever*) occurring on alternate days.
tertiary *adj* third.
TESOL *abbr* = Teachers of English to Speakers of Other Languages.
tesla *n* the SI unit of magnetic flux density.
tessellated *adj* resembling mosaic.
tessera *n* (*pl* **tesserae**) a piece of marble, glass, etc used in a mosaic.
tessitura *n* (*mus*) the natural pitch of a voice or instrument.
test *n* an examination; trial; a chemical reaction to test a substance or to test for an illness; a series of questions or exercises. * *vt* to examine critically.
testament *n* a will; proof; tribute; (*arch*) a covenant made by God with men; (*with cap*) one of the two main parts of the Bible.
testate *adj* having made and left a will.
testator *n* a person who leaves a will.
test ban *n* an agreement between nations to limit or abandon tests of nuclear weapons.
test-bed *n* an area designed for testing machinery.
test case *n* a legal action that establishes a precedent.
testes *see* **testis**.
testicle *n* either of the two male reproductive glands that produce sperm, a testis.
testify *vb* (**testifying, testified**) *vi* to give evidence under oath; to serve as witness (to); (*with* **to**) to be evidence of. * *vt* to be evidence of.
testimonial *adj* relating to a testimony. * *n* a recommendation of one's character or abilities.
testimony *n* (*pl* **testimonies**) evidence; declaration of truth or fact.
testis *n* (*pl* **testes**) a testicle.
test match *n* one of a series of international cricket or Rugby football matches.
testosterone *n* a steroid hormone secreted by the testes.
test pilot *n* someone who flies new types of aircraft to test their performance and characteristics.
test tube *n* a cylinder of thin glass closed at one end, used in scientific experiments.
test-tube baby *n* a baby which develops from an ovum fertilized outside the mother's body and replaced in the womb.
testy *adj* (**testier, testiest**) touchy, irritable.
tetanus *n* an intense and painful spasm of muscles, caused by the infection of a wound by bacteria; lockjaw.
tetchy *adj* (**tetchier, tetchiest**) irritable, touchy.—*also* **techy.**—**tetchily** *adv*.—**tetchiness** *n*.
tête-à-tête *n* (*pl* **tête-à-têtes, tête-à-tête**) a private conversation between two people.
tether *n* a rope or chain for tying an animal; the limit of one's endurance. * *vt* to fasten with a tether; to limit.
tetra-, tetr- *prefix* four.
tetrahedron *n* (*pl* **tetrahedrons, tetrahedra**) a solid figure enclosed by four plane faces of triangular shape.
tetrahydroamino-acridine *n* a drug currently being tried out for use in the treatment of Alzheimer's disease.
tetrahydrocannabinol *n* a natural compound that is the main intoxicant in cannabis and can also be produced synthetically.
tetralogy *n* (*pl* **tetralogies**) a series of four related works, such as novels or plays.
tetravalent *adj* (*chem*) having a valency of four.
Teutonic *adj* of Germanic peoples or their language.
Tex. *abbr* = Texas.
Tex-Mex *adj* of or pertaining to a Texan version of something Mexican, such as food or music.
text *n* the main part of a printed work; the original or exact wording; a passage from the Bible forming the basis of a sermon; a subject or topic; a textbook.
textbook *n* a book used as a basis for instruction.
textile *n* a woven fabric or cloth. * *adj* relating to the making of fabrics.
textual *adj* of or relating to a text; contained in or based on a text; (*operation, etc*) exactly as planned according to theory or calculation.
textual criticism *n* the study of a written work (eg the Bible) to establish the original text; the close reading and analysis of any literary work.
texture *n* the characteristic appearance, arrangement or feel of a thing; the way in which threads in a material are interwoven.—**textural** *adj*.
TGIF *abbr* = thank God it's Friday.
Th (*chem symbol*) thorium.
Th. *abbr* = Thursday.
THA *abbr* = tetrahydroamino-acridine.
Thai *n* (*pl* **Thais, Thai**) a native or inhabitant of Thailand; the language of Thailand.—*also adj*.
thalamus *n* (*pl* **thalami**) either of the two masses of tissue which sit close together at the base of the brain.
thalidomide *n* a sedative drug withdrawn from use when it was discovered to cause malformation in unborn babies.
thallium *n* a soft white poisonous metallic element.
than *conj* introducing the second element of a comparison.
thanatology *n* the scientific study of death.
thank *vt* to express gratitude to or appreciation for. * *npl* an expression of gratitude.—**thankful** *adj*.—**thankfully** *adv*.
thankless *adj* without thanks; unappreciated; fruitless, unrewarding.—**thanklessness** *n*.
thanksgiving *n* the act of giving thanks; a prayer of gratitude to God; (*with cap*) Thanksgiving Day.
Thanksgiving Day *n* a legal holiday observed on the fourth Thursday of November in the US, and on the second Monday of October in Canada.
thank-you *n* an expression of gratitude.
that *demons adj, pron* (*pl* **those**) the (one) there or then, esp the latter or more distant thing. * *rel pron* who or which. * *conj* introducing noun clause or adverbial clause of purpose or consequence; because; in order that; (*preceded by* **so, such**) as a result.
thatch *n* roofing straw. * *vt* to cover a roof with thatch.
thaumatology *n* (*pl* **thaumatologies**) the study of miracles; a discourse on miracles.

thaumaturge, thaumaturgist *n* a miracle-worker; a magician.—**thaumaturgy** *n*.
thaw *vi* to melt or grow liquid; to become friendly. **vt* to cause to melt. * *n* the melting of ice or snow by warm weather.
THC *abbr* = tetrahydrocannabinol.
the *demons adj* denoting a particular person or thing. * *adv* used before comparative adjectives or adverbs for emphasis.
theatre, theater *n* a building where plays and operas are performed; the theatrical world as a whole; a setting for important events; field of operations.
theatre-in-the-round *n* a theatre with seats arranged in a circle around the stage area.
theatrical *adj* relating to the theatre; melodramatic, affected.—**theatrically** *adv*.
theatricals *npl* performances of drama, esp by amateurs.
thee *pron* the objective case of **thou.**
theft *n* act or crime of stealing.
theine *n* caffeine.
their *poss adj* of or belonging to them; his, hers, its.
theirs *poss pron* of or belonging to them; his, hers, its.
theism *n* belief in the existence of a God or gods, esp God as the supernatural Creator of the universe.—**theist** *n*.—**theistic** *adj*.
them *pron* the objective case of **they.**
theme *n* the main subject of a discussion; an idea or motif in a work; a short essay; a leading melody; a style adopted for an exhibition, activity, etc.—**thematic** *adj*.
theme park *n* a leisure area in which the buildings and settings follow a particular theme, eg a period in history.
theme song *n* a recurring melody in a film score or musical that is associated with the work or a particular character; a signature tune.
themselves *pron* the reflexive form of **they** or **them.**
then *adv* at that time; afterward; immediately; next in time. * *conj* for that reason; in that case.
thenar *n* the ball of the thumb; the palm of the hand.
thence *adv* from that time or place; for that reason.
thenceforth *adv* from that time on; thereafter.
thenceforward, thenceforwards *adv* thenceforth.
theo-, the- *prefix* god.
theobromine *n* an alkaloid similar to caffeine present in cacao beans and tea, used in treating heart disease.
theocracy *n* (*pl* **theocracies**) (a state having) government by a deity or priesthood.—**theocrat** *n*.—**theocratic** *adj*.
theodolite *n* a surveying instrument for measuring angles.
theol. *abbr* = theologian; theological; theology.
theologian *n* a person who studies and interprets religious texts, etc; a teacher of theology.
theology *n* (*pl* **theologies**) the study of God and of religious doctrine and matters of divinity.—**theological, theologic** *adj*.—**theologically** *adv*.
theorem *n* a proposition that can be proved from accepted principles; law or principle.
theoretical, theoretic *adj* of or based on theory, not practical application; hypothetical; conjectural.—**theoretically** *adv*.
theoretician *n* a person who concentrates on the theoretical basis of a subject.
theoretics *npl* the speculative parts of a science.
theorize *vi* to form theories; to speculate.—**theorist, theorizer** *n*.—**theorization** *n*.
theory *n* (*pl* **theories**) an explanation or system of anything; ideas and abstract principles of a science or art; speculation; a hypothesis.
therapeutic, therapeutical *adj* relating to the treatment of disease; beneficial.—**therapeutically** *adv*.
therapeutics *npl* the curative branch of medicine.
therapy *n* (*pl* **therapies**) the treatment of physical or mental illness.—**therapist** *n*.
there *adv* in, at or to, that place or point; in that respect; in that matter.
thereabout, thereabouts *adv* at or near that place or number.
thereafter *adv* after that; according to that.
thereagainst *adv* in opposition to; contrary to.
thereat *adv* at that place; at such time.
thereby *adv* by that means.
therefore *adv* for that or this reason; consequently.
therein *adv* in that place or respect.
thereof *adv* of this or that; because of that.
thereon *adv* on that or it; immediately following that.
thereupon *adv* immediately after that.
therm *n* a measurement of heat.
thermal, thermic *adj* generating heat; hot; warm; (*underwear*) of a knitted material with air spaces for insulation. * *n* a rising current of warm air.
thermion *n* an electron emitted by a material at high temperature.
thermionic *adj* of, pertaining to, or worked by thermions, esp a tube.
thermistor *n* a semiconductor device whose resistance varies inversely with a change in temperature.
thermo-, therm- *prefix* heat.
thermocouple *n* a device which generates a thermoelectric effect between two dissimilar semiconductors, used in measuring temperature differences.
thermodynamics *n sing* the branch of physics concerned with the relationship between heat and other forms of energy.
thermoelectric, thermoelectrical *adj* of or derived from electricity generated by difference of temperature.—**thermoelectricity** *n*.
thermometer *n* an instrument for measuring temperature.
thermonuclear *adj* of or relating to nuclear fusion or nuclear weapons that utilize fusion reactions.
thermoplastic *adj* becoming soft and malleable when heated. * *n* a resin or synthetic plastic that can be heated, moulded and cooled without appreciable change of its properties.
Thermos *n* (*trademark*) a brand of vacuum bottle.
thermostat *n* an automatic device for regulating temperatures.
thesaurus *n* (*pl* **thesauri, thesauruses**) a reference book of synonyms and antonyms.
these *see* **this.**
thesis *n* (*pl* **theses**) a dissertation written as part of an academic degree; a theory expressed as a statement for discussion.
thespian *adj* of or pertaining to drama. * *n* an actor or actress.
theta *n* the eighth letter of the Greek alphabet.
they *pers pron, pl of* **he, she** *or* **it.**
they'd = they would; they had.
they'll = they will; they shall.
they're = they are.
they've = they have.
thiamine, thiamin *n* vitamin B, present in a wide variety of plants and animals and essential for normal metabolism and nerve function.
thick *adj* dense; viscous; fat, broad; abundant, closely set; in quick succession; crowded; (*inf*) stupid. * *adv* closely; frequently.
thicken *vti* to make or become thick.—**thickener** *n*.
thicket *n* a small group of trees or shrubs growing thickly and closely together.
thickhead *n* (*inf*) an ignorant person, an idiot.—**thickheaded** *adj*.
thickness *n* being thick; the dimension other than length or width; a layer.
thickset *adj* having a short, stocky body.
thick-skinned *adj* not sensitive; not easily offended.
thick-witted *adj* stupid.
thief *n* (*pl* **thieves**) a person who steals.
thieve *vti* to steal.
thigh *n* the thick fleshy part of the leg from the hip to the knee.
thighbone *n* the femur.
thimble *n* a cap or cover worn to protect the finger when sewing.
thimbleful *n* what a thimble contains, a tiny amount.
thin *adj* (**thinner, thinnest**) narrow; slim; lean; sparse, weak, watery; (*material*) fine; not dense. * *vt* to make thin; to make less crowded; to water down.—**thinly** *adv*.—**thinness** *n*.

thine *pron* an old-fashioned word for **yours.**

thing *n* an inanimate object; an event; an action; (*pl*) possessions; (*inf*) an obsession.

thingamabob, thingumabob *n* (*inf*) something or someone the name of which has been forgotten, is unknown or is hard to categorize, etc.—*also* **thingamajig, thingumajig, thingummy, thingie.**

think *vb* (**thinking, thought**) *vi* to exercise the mind in order to make a decision; to revolve ideas in the mind, to ponder; to remember; to consider; * *vt* to judge, to believe or consider; (*with* **up**) to concoct, devise; (*with* **over**) to ponder, to consider the costs and benefits of.—**thinker** *n.*

thinking *adj* capable of using thought, rational; intelligent. * *n* the process of using thought; opinion, reasoning.

think-tank *n* (*inf*) a group of experts convened to analyse and advise on ways of handling a particular problem.

thinner *n* a substance, such as turpentine, added to paint, varnish, etc, to thin it.

thin-skinned *adj* overly sensitive to criticism; easily offended.

third *adj* the last of three; being one of three equal parts. * *n* one of three equal parts.

third class *n* a class of mail in the US and Canadian postal systems that includes all printed matter, except periodicals, weighing below a certain amount and unsealed; the cheapest accommodation on a ship, aircraft, etc.—**third-class** *adj, adv.*

third degree *n* the use of torture, bullying or rough questioning to obtain information.

third-degree burn *n* a severe burn which destroys surface and underlying tissue and may involve loss of fluid and shock.

thirdly *adv* in the third place; as a third point.

third person *n* grammatical forms, such as pronouns and verbs, used when referring to the person or thing spoken or written of, not to the person speaking or writing or to the person or persons addressed.

third-rate *adj* inferior.

Third World *n* the underdeveloped countries of the world (usu refers to Africa, Asia and South America).

thirst *n* a craving for drink; a longing. * *vi* to feel thirst; to have a longing.

thirsty *adj* (**thirstier, thirstiest**) having a desire to drink; dry, arid; longing or craving for.—**thirstily** *adv.*—**thirstiness** *n.*

thirteen *adj, n* three and ten.—**thirteenth** *adj, n.*

thirty *adj, n* (*pl* **thirties**) three times ten.—**thirtieth** *adj, n.*

thirty-second note *n* (*mus*) a note with a time value of one thirty-secondth of a whole note, a demisemiquaver.

this *demons pron* (*pl* **these**) *or adj* denoting a person or thing near, just mentioned, or about to be mentioned.

thistle *n* a wild plant with prickly leaves and a purple flower.

thistledown *n* the feathery cluster of seeds produced by the thistle.

thither *adv* (*arch*) to or toward that place.

tho, tho' *conj, adv* (*inf*) though.

thong *n* a piece or strap of leather to lash things together; the lash of a whip; a sandal held on the foot by a thong passing between the toes and fixed to a strap passing over the top of the foot.

Thor *n* (*Norse myth*) the god of thunder.

thorax *n* (*pl* **thoraxes, thoraces**) the part of the body enclosed by the ribs; the chest; (*in insects*) the middle one of the three chief divisions of the body.—**thoracic** *adj.*

thorium *n* a radioactive metallic element used in industry and as a nuclear fuel.

thorn *n* a shrub or small tree having thorns, esp hawthorn; a sharp point or prickle on the stem of a plant or the branch of a tree.

thorny *adj* (**thornier, thorniest**) prickly; (*problem*) knotty.

thoron *n* a gas that is a radioactive isotope of radon.

thorough *adj* complete, very detailed and painstaking, exhaustive.—**thoroughness** *n.*

thoroughbred *adj* bred from pure stock. * *n* a pedigree animal, esp a horse.

thoroughfare *n* a way through; a public highway, road; right of passing through.

thoroughgoing *adj* very thorough; out-and-out.

thoroughly *adv* completely, fully; entirely, absolutely.

those *adj, pron* plural of **that.**

thou[1] *pron* an old-fashioned word for **you.**

thou[2] *n* (*pl* **thous, thou**) (*inf*) a thousand; a thousandth of an inch.

though *conj* yet, even if; * *adv* however; nevertheless.

thought *n* the act of thinking; reasoning; serious consideration; an idea; opinions collectively; design, intention. * *pt, pp* of **think.**

thoughtful *adj* pensive; considerate.

thoughtless *adj* without thought; inconsiderate.

thousand *adj* ten times one hundred; (*pl*) denoting any large but unspecified number. * *n* the number 1000.—**thousandth** *adj, n.*

thrash *vt* to beat soundly; to defeat; (*with* **out**) to discuss thoroughly, until agreement is reached. * *vi* to thresh grain; to writhe.

thrashing *n* a beating or flogging; punishment.

thread *n* a fine strand or filament; a long thin piece of cotton, silk or nylon for sewing; the spiral part of a screw; (*of reasoning*) a line. * *vt* to pass a thread through the eye of a needle; to make one's way (through).

threadbare *adj* worn, shabby.

threadworm *n* a long slender worm, parasitic in humans and pigs.

threat *n* a declaration of an intention to inflict harm or punishment upon another.

threaten *vti* to utter threats to; to portend.

threatening *adj* menacing, intimidating; warning; ominous, sinister.—**threateningly** *adv.*

three *adj, n* the cardinal number next above two. * *n* the symbol (3, III, iii) expressing this.

three-D, 3-D *n* a three-dimensional effect.

three-dimensional *adj* having three dimensions.

threefold *adj, adv* three times as much or as many; composed of three parts.

three-quarter *adj* being three quarters of the normal size or length. * *n* (*Rugby football*) one of usu four attacking players used particularly for running with the ball.

three Rs *npl* reading, writing and arithmetic, regarded as the basis of learning.

threescore *n* (*arch*) sixty.—*also adj.*

threesome *n* a group of three; a game for three people.

threnody, threnode *n* (*pl* **threnodies, threnodes**) a song or speech of lamentation, esp on a person's death.

thresh *vti* to beat out (grain) from (husks).

threshold *n* the sill at the door of a building; doorway, entrance; the starting point, beginning.

threw *see* **throw.**

thrice *adv* three times.

thrift *n* careful management of money.—**thrifty** *adj.*

thrift shop *n* a shop that sells used clothing and other items to raise money for charity.

thrill *vti* to tingle with pleasure or excitement. * *n* a sensation of pleasure and excitement; a trembling or quiver.

thriller *n* a novel, film or play depicting an exciting story of mystery and suspense.

thrilling *adj* exciting, gripping.

thrips *n* (*pl* **thrips**) any of various small insects with sucking mouthparts that feed on and damage plants.

thrive *vi* (**thriving, thrived** *or* **throve,** *pp* **thrived** *or* **thriven**) to prosper, to be successful; to grow vigorously.—**thriving** *adj.*

thro', thro *prep, adv* (*inf*) through.

throat *n* the front part of the neck; the passage from the back of the mouth to the top part of the tubes into the lungs and stomach; an entrance.

throaty *adj* (**throatier, throatiest**) hoarse; guttural; deep, husky.—**throatily** *adv.*

throb *vi* (**throbbing, throbbed**) to beat or pulsate rhythmically, with more than usual force; to vibrate, beat.—*also n.*

throes *npl* violent pangs or pain.
thrombin *n* an enzyme that contributes to blood clotting.
thrombocyte *n* a blood platelet.
thrombosis *n* (*pl* **thromboses**) the forming of a blood clot in the heart or in a blood-vessel.
thrombus *n* (*pl* **thrombi**) the blood clot that blocks a vessel in thrombosis.
throne *n* a chair of state occupied by a monarch; sovereign power. * *vt* to place on a throne.
throng *n* a crowd. * *vti* to crowd, congregate.
throstle *n* any of various Old World thrushes.
throttle *n* a valve controlling the flow of fuel or steam to an engine. * *vt* to regulate the speed of (an engine) using a throttle; to choke or strangle.
through *prep* from one side or end to the other; into and then out of; covering all parts; from beginning to end of; by means of; in consequence of; up to and including. * *adv* from one end or side to the other; completely. * *adj* going without interruption; unobstructed.
throughout *prep* in every part of; from beginning to end. * *adv* everywhere; at every moment.
throughput *n* the amount of material processed in a particular period, esp by a computer.
throughway *see* **thruway.**
throve *see* **thrive.**
throw *vb* (**throwing, threw,** *pp* **thrown**) *vt* to hurl, to fling; to cast off; (*party*) to hold; (*inf*) to confuse or disconcert; (*with* **off**) to cast off, discard, abandon; to distract, elude; to produce in a casual manner; to confuse, disconcert; (*with* **out**) to discard, reject; to dismiss or eject, esp forcibly; to emit, give forth; to construct out from a main section; to confuse, distract; (*with* **over**) to abandon, jilt; (*with* **together**) to assemble hurriedly or carelessly; to bring (people) into casual contact; (*with* **up**) to raise quickly; to resign from, abandon; to build hurriedly; to produce; (*inf*) to vomit. * *vi* to cast or hurl through the air (with the arm and wrist); to cast dice; (*with* **up**) (*inf*) to vomit. * *n* the act of throwing; the distance to which anything can be thrown; a cast of dice.
throwaway *adj* disposable.
throwback *n* a reversion to an earlier or more primitive type.
throw-in *n* (*soccer*) a throw from touch to resume play.
thrown *see* **throw.**
thru *prep* (*sl*) through.
thrum *vi* (**thrumming, thrummed**) to strum; to beat incessantly.
thrush[1] *n* a songbird with a brown back and spotted breast.
thrush[2] *n* a fungal disease occurring in the mouths of babies or in women's vaginas.
thrust *vti* (**thrusting, thrust**) to push with force; to stab, pierce; to force into a situation. * *n* a forceful push or stab; pressure; the driving force of a propeller; forward movement; the point or basic meaning.
thruway *n* an expressway.—*also* **throughway.**
thud *n* a dull, heavy sound, caused by a blow or a heavy object falling. * *vi* (**thudding, thudded**) to make such a sound.
thug *n* a violent and rough person, esp a criminal.
thuggery *n* rough and violent behaviour.
thulium *n* a malleable metallic element of the rare-earth group.
thumb *n* the first, short, thick finger of the human hand. * *vt* (*book*) to turn (the pages) idly.
thumbed *adj* worn by use.
thumb index *n* a series of semicircular notches cut in the edge of a book for easier reference to particular parts.
thumbnail *n* the nail of the thumb. * *adj* concise.
thumbnut *n* a wing nut.
thumbscrew *n* an instrument of torture that crushes the thumbs; a screw with a modified head for tightening with the finger and thumb.
thumbtack *n* a flat-headed pin used for fastening paper, drawings, etc, a drawing pin.
thump *n* a heavy blow; a thud. * *vt* to strike with something heavy. * *vi* to throb or beat violently.
thumping *adj* (*inf*) very great.
thunder *n* the deep rumbling or loud cracking sound after a flash of lightning; any similar sound. * *vi* to sound as thunder. * *vt* (*words*) to utter loudly.
thunderbolt *n* a flash of lightning accompanied by thunder; anything sudden and shocking.
thunderclap *n* a loud bang of thunder.
thundering *adj* (*inf*) unusually great, excessive.
thunderous *adj* very loud; producing thunder.
thunderstorm *n* a storm with thunder and lightning.
thunderstruck *adj* astonished.
thundery *adj* indicating thunder.
Thur., Thurs. *abbr* = Thursday.
thurible *n* a censer.
Thursday *n* the fifth day of the week.
thus *adv* in this or that way; to this degree or extent; so; therefore.
thwack *vti* to hit hard, whack. * *n* a heavy blow, whack; the sound of this.
thwart *vt* to prevent, to frustrate.
thy *poss adj* an old-fashioned word for **your.**
thyme *n* a herb with small leaves used for flavouring savoury food.
thymol *n* a substance obtained from thyme and used as a fungicide and antiseptic.
thymus *n* (*pl* **thymuses, thymi**) a gland near the base of the neck that shrivels after puberty.
thyristor *n* any of various semiconductor devices that act as switches or rectifiers.
thyroid *n* the gland in the neck affecting growth and metabolism.
thyrotropin, thyrotrophin *n* a hormone secreted by the pituitary gland that stimulates the thyroid gland.
thyroxin, thyroxine *n* the main hormone produced by the thyroid gland.
Tl (*chem symbol*) thallium.
Ti (*chem symbol*) titanium.
ti *n* the seventh note of the scale in solmization.
tiara *n* a semicircular crown decorated with jewels.
tibia *n* (*pl* **tibiae, tibias**) the inner and thicker of the two bones between the knee and the ankle; the shinbone.
tic *n* any involuntary, regularly repeated, spasmodic contraction of a muscle.
tick[1] *n* a small bloodsucking insect that lives on people and animals.
tick[2] *vi* to make a regular series of short sounds; to beat, as a clock; (*inf*) to work, function; (*with* **over**) (*engine*) to idle; to function routinely. * *n* the sound of a clock; (*sl*) a moment.
tick[3] *vt* (*often with* **off**) to check off, as items in a list. * *n* a check mark (v) to check off items on a list or to indicate correctness.
ticker *n* a telegraphic device that receives and outputs stock-market prices on a paper tape; any similar device operated electronically and outputting to a display monitor; (*inf*) the heart; (*inf*) a watch.
ticker tape *n* a continuous length of paper tape output from a telegraphic ticker.
ticket *n* a printed card, etc, that gives one a right of travel or entry; a label on merchandise giving size, price, etc.
tickle *vt* to touch lightly to provoke pleasure or laughter; to please or delight.
ticklish, tickly *adj* sensitive to being tickled; easily offended; difficult or delicate.
tick-tack-toe *n sing* a game in which two players place noughts and crosses into squares on a grid with nine spaces, the winner being the first to form a row of three noughts or crosses, noughts and crosses.
ticktock *n* a ticking sound, esp of a clock. * *vi* to make such a sound.
tidal *adj* relating to, or having, tides.
tidal wave *n* a large wave as a result of high winds with spring tides; a huge destructive wave caused by earthquakes; something overwhelming.
tidbit *see* **titbit.**
tiddly *adj* (**tiddlier, tiddliest**) (*inf*) very small; (*inf*) slightly drunk.
tiddlywinks, tiddledywinks *npl* a game whose object is to flick small plastic discs into a container by snapping them with a larger disc.

tide *n* the regular rise and fall of the seas, oceans, etc usu twice a day; a current of water; a tendency; a flood. * *vt* (*with* **over**) to help along temporarily.
tidemark *n* the highest or lowest point reached by the sea.
tide rip *n* a rip current.
tidewater *n* water overflowing land at flood tide; water that is affected by the tide.
tidings *npl* news, information.
tidy *adj* (**tidier, tidiest**) neat; orderly. * *vt* to make neat; to put things in order.—**tidily** *adv*.—**tidiness** *n*.
tie *vb* (**tying, tied**) *vt* to bind; to fasten with a string or thread; to make a bow or knot in; to restrict; (*with* **in**) to link with something; (*with* **up**) to fasten tightly (as if) with cord, string, etc; to connect, link; to invest money, etc, so as to make it unavailable for alternative uses; to preoccupy, distract. * *vi* to score the same number of points (as an opponent); (*with* **in**) to be linked in a certain way; (*with* **up**) to dock (a vessel). * *n* a knot, bow, etc; a bond; a long narrow piece of cloth worn with a shirt; necktie; an equality in score.
tiebreaker, tiebreak *n* any means of deciding a contest which has ended in a draw, such as an extra game, hole, question, etc.
tie-dyeing, tie-dye *n* a method of producing patterns on textiles by tying or knotting parts of the fabric to limit the amount of dye absorbed.
tie-in *n* a link or connection; a book linked to a film or TV series.
tie line *n* a telephone link between two private branch exchanges.
tiepin *n* a decorative pin used to secure the ends of a tie to a shirt.
tier *n* a row or rank in a series when several rows are placed one above another.
tiercel *n* a male of various hawks, esp as used in falconry.—*also* **tercel**.
tie-up *n* a link, connection; a standstill.
tiff *n* a petty quarrel or disagreement. * *vi* to quarrel; to be in a huff.
tiger *n* a large, fierce carnivorous animal of the cat family, having orange and black stripes.—**tigress** *nf*.
tiger beetle *n* any of numerous predatory beetles with powerful mandibles and spotted wing cases.
tiger cat *n* an ocelot or similar medium-sized wildcat with a striped coat.
tiger lily *n* a lily of China and Japan cultivated for its dark-spotted orange flowers.
tiger moth *n* any of various large moths marked with stripes or spots.
tiger's eye, tigereye *n* a brownish-yellow gemstone.
tiger shark *n* a large shark of warm waters with a striped or spotted skin.
tiger snake *n* an aggressive poisonous Australian snake with striped markings.
tight *adj* taut; fitting closely; not leaky; constricted; miserly; difficult; providing little space or time for variance; (*contest*) close; (*inf*) drunk.
tighten *vti* to make or grow tight or tighter.
tightfisted *adj* miserly.
tightknit *adj* tightly integrated.
tight-lipped *adj* having the lips firmly pressed together, as from annoyance; taciturn.
tightrope *n* a taut rope on which acrobats walk.
tights *npl* a one-piece garment covering the legs and lower body; panty hose.
tigon, tiglon *n* the hybrid offspring of a tiger and a lioness.
tike *see* **tyke**.
tilde *n* a sign ~ placed above a letter to indicate a nasal sound, as in Spanish *señor*.
tile *n* a thin slab of baked clay used for covering roofs, floors, etc. * *vt* to cover with tiles.
till[1] *n* a drawer inside a cash register for keeping money.
till[2] *prep* until. * *conj* until.
till[3] *vt* (*land*) to cultivate for raising crops, as by ploughing.
tiller *n* the handle or lever for turning a rudder in order to steer a boat.
tilt *vi* to slope, incline, slant. * *vt* to raise one end of. * *n* a slope or angle.
timbale *n* a mixture of meat or fish with cream cooked in a mould lined with vegetables or pastry.
timber *n* wood when used as building material; a beam; trees collectively. * *vt* to provide with timber or beams.
timbered *adj* (*building*) having wooden beams on the exterior.
timber hitch *n* a knot used to tie a rope, etc to a log or spar.
timber line *see* **tree line**.
timber wolf *n* a type of large grey North American wolf.
timbre *n* the quality of sound of a voice or musical instrument.
time *n* the past, present and future; a particular moment; hour of the day; an opportunity; the right moment; duration; occasion; musical beat. * *vt* to regulate as to time; to measure or record the duration of.
time and motion study *n* the study of working procedures to improve efficiency.
time bomb *n* a bomb designed to explode at a predetermined time; something with a potentially delayed reaction.
time clock *n* a device that records the times of arrival and departure of an employee on a card.
time-consuming *adj* using up or taking a lot of time.
time exposure *n* exposure of a photographic film for usu several seconds; a photograph taken in this way.
time-honoured *adj* traditional, in accordance with venerable customs.
time immemorial *n* the far distant past beyond memory or record.
timekeeper *n* a person or instrument that records or keeps time; an employee who records the hours worked by others.—**timekeeping** *n*.
time lag *n* the interval between two connected events.
time-lapse photography *n* a technique of filming very slow action, such as plant growth, by taking single frames at fixed intervals and then running them at normal speed.
timeless *adj* eternal; ageless.
timely *adj* at the right time, opportune.—**timeliness** *n*.
time-out *n* (*sport*) a suspension of play to rest, discuss tactics, etc; a brief rest period.
timepiece *n* a clock or watch.
timer *n* a device for measuring, recording or controlling time; a device for controlling lights, heating, etc by setting an electrical clock to regulate their operations.
timeserver *n* a person whose opinions, behaviour, etc, follow current fashions.—**timeserving** *adj, n*.
timeshare *n* joint ownership of holiday accommodation by several people with each occupying the same premises in turn for short periods.
time signature *n* a sign on a musical staff indicating the number of beats per bar and time value of each beat.
timetable *n* a list of times of arrivals and departures of trains, aeroplanes, etc; a schedule showing a planned order or sequence.
timeworn *adj* dilapidated; old-fashioned, hackneyed.
time zone *n* a geographical region throughout which the same standard time is used.
timid *adj* shy; lacking confidence.—**timidity** *n*.—**timidly** *adv*.
timing *n* the control and expression of speech or actions to create the best effect, esp in the theatre, etc.
timocracy *n* (*pl* **timocracies**) a form of government in which ownership of property is required to hold office.
timorous *adj* timid, fearful.—**timorously** *adv*.—**timorousness** *n*.
timpani *npl* a set of kettledrums.—**timpanist** *n*.—*also* **tympani, tympany**.
tin *n* a malleable metallic element; a container of tin, a can. * *adj* made of tin or tin plate. * *vt* (**tinning, tinned**) to put food into a tin.
tinctorial *adj* pertaining to colouring, dyeing or staining.
tincture *n* an extract of a substance in a solution of alcohol for medicinal use; a colour, hue, tint; a hint of flavour or aroma; an heraldic colour. * *vt* to tint with a colour.
tinder *n* dry wood for lighting a fire from a spark.
tinderbox *n* a metal box with tinder, flint and steel for making a spark; an unstable or potentially explosive person, thing or situation.
tine *n* a slender projecting point, as the prong of a fork or point of an antler.
tinea *n* a fungal skin condition, esp ringworm.

tinfoil *n* baking foil for wrapping food; silver paper.
ting *n* a high sharp ringing sound. * *vi* to make this sound.
tinge *vt* to tint or colour. * *n* a slight tint, colour or flavour.
tingle *vi* to feel a prickling, itching or stinging sensation. * *n* a prickling sensation; a thrill.—**tinglingly** *adv*.—**tingly** *adj*.
tin god *n* a self-important person; a person who is undeservedly venerated.
tinker *n* (*formerly*) a travelling mender of pots and pans. * *vi* to fiddle with; to attempt to repair.
tinkle *vi* to make a sound like a small bell ringing; to clink, to jingle; to clink repeatedly. * *n* a tinkling sound; (*inf*) a telephone call.
tinnitus *n* a continuous ringing or roaring sound in the ears caused by an infection, etc.
tinny *adj* (**tinnier, tinniest**) of or resembling tin; flimsy in construction or appearance; (*food*) having a metallic taste; having a high metallic sound.
tin plate *n* thin sheets of iron or steel plated with tin.—**tin-plate** *adj*.
tinsel *n* a shiny Christmas decoration made of long pieces of thread wound round with thin strips of metal or plastic foil; something showy but of low value. * *adj* cheaply showy, flashy. * *vt* (**tinselling, tinselled** *or* **tinseling, tinseled**) to adorn with tinsel.
Tinseltown *n* (*inf*) Hollywood.
tint *n* a shade of any colour, esp a pale one; a tinge; a hair dye. * *vt* to colour or tinge.
tintinnabulation *n* (the sound of) a ringing of bells.
tiny *adj* (**tinier, tiniest**) very small.
tip[1] *n* the pointed end of anything; the end, as of a billiard cue, etc. * *vt* (**tipping, tipped**) to put a tip on.
tip[2] *vti* (**tipping, tipped**) to tilt or cause to tilt; to overturn; to empty (out, into, etc); to give a gratuity to, as a waiter, etc; (*rubbish*) to dump; to give a helpful hint or inside information to. * *n* a light tap; a gratuity; a rubbish dump; an inside piece of information; a helpful hint.
tip-off *n* a warning based on inside information.
tipple *vi* to drink alcohol regularly in small quantities. * *n* an alcoholic drink.
tipster *n* a person who gives horse-racing tips.
tipsy *adj* (**tipsier, tipsiest**) slightly drunk.
tiptoe *vi* (**tiptoeing, tiptoed**) to walk very quietly or carefully.
tiptop *adj* excellent. * *adv* at the peak of condition. * *n* the best; the highest point.
tirade *n* a long angry speech of censure or criticism.
tire[1] *vt* to exhaust the strength of, to weary. * *vi* to become weary; to lose patience; to become bored.
tire[2] *see* **tyre.**
tired *adj* weary, sleepy; hackneyed, conventional, flat; (*with* **of**) exasperated by, bored with.
tireless *adj* never wearying.—**tirelessly** *adv*.—**tirelessness** *n*.
tiresome *adj* tedious.
tiro *see* **tyro.**
'tis (*poet*) = it is.
tissue *n* thin, absorbent paper used as a disposable handkerchief, etc; a very finely woven fabric; a mass of organic cells of a similar structure and function.
tit[1] *n* a songbird such as a blue tit or great tit.
tit[2] *n* (*vulg*) a woman's breast.
titan *n* a person of enormous strength, size or ability.
titanic *adj* monumental; huge.
titanium *n* a strong metallic element used to make lightweight alloys.
titanium dioxide *n* a white powder used chiefly as a pigment.
titbit *n* a tasty morsel of food; a choice item of information.—*also* **tidbit.**
titer *see* **titre.**
tit for tat *n* an equivalent given in retaliation.
tithe *n* a tenth part of agricultural produce, formerly allotted for the maintenance of the clergy and other church purposes. * *vti* to pay a tithe.
titillate *vt* to tickle; to arouse or excite pleasurably.
titillation *n* the act of titillating; the condition of being titillated; a pleasurable feeling, esp sexual.
titivate, tittivate *vti* to smarten up.
title *n* the name of a book, play, piece of music, work of art, etc; the heading of a section of a book; a name denoting nobility or rank or office held, or attached to a personal name; (*law*) that which gives a legal right (to possession).
titled *adj* having a title.
title deed *n* a deed or document proving a title or right to possession.
title page *n* the page of a book containing its title and usually the author's and publisher's names.
title role *n* the character in a play, film, etc after whom it is named.
titrate *vt* to measure by titration.
titration *n* a method of determining the amount of a constituent in a solution by adding a known quantity of a reagent.
titre *n* the concentration of a substance in a solution as determined by titration.
titter *vi* to giggle, snigger. * *n* a suppressed laugh.
tittle-tattle *n* idle chat, empty gossip.
titular *adj* having, or relating to, a title; existing in name or title only.
tizzy *n* (*inf*) a state of confusion or agitation.
TKO *abbr* = technical knockout.
TLC *abbr* = tender loving care.
T-lymphocyte *see* **T-cell.**
TM *abbr* = trademark; transcendental meditation.
Tm (*chem symbol*) thulium.
TN *abbr* = Tennessee.
TNT *abbr* = trinitrotoluene.
to *prep* in the direction of; toward; as far as; expressing the purpose of an action; indicating the infinitive; introducing the indirect object; in comparison with. * *adv* toward.
toad *n* an amphibious reptile, like a frog, but having a drier skin and spending less time in water.
toadflax *n* a common perennial plant with yellow and orange flowers.
toadstool *n* a mushroom, esp a poisonous or inedible one.
toady *n* (*pl* **toadies**) a person who flatters insincerely, a sycophant. * *vi* (**toadying, toadied**) (*with* **to**) to act in a servile manner.
to and fro *adj* forward and backward; here and there.—**toing and froing** *n*.
toast *vt* to brown over a fire or in a toaster; to warm; to drink to the health of. * *n* toasted bread; the sentiment or person to which one drinks.
toaster *n* a person who toasts; a thing that toasts, esp an electrical appliance for toasting.
toastmaster *n* the proposer of toasts at public dinners.—**toastmistress** *nf*.
tobacco *n* (*pl* **tobaccos, tobaccoes**) a plant whose dried leaves are used for smoking, chewing or snuff.
tobacconist *n* a person or shop that sells cigarettes, etc.
toboggan *n* a sledge, sled.
toby (jug) *n* (*pl* **tobies, toby jugs**) a mug in the shape of a man with a three-cornered hat.
toccata *n* a piece of music for keyboard in a free style with rapid runs.
tocopherol *n* vitamin E, present in wheat-germ oil, egg yolk, etc.
tocsin *n* an alarm bell; a warning signal.
today *n* this day; the present age. * *adv* on this day; nowadays.
toddle *vi* to walk with short, unsteady, steps, as a child who is learning to walk.
toddler *n* a young child.
toddy *n* (*pl* **toddies**) a drink of whisky or brandy, sugar, and hot water.
to-do *n* (*pl* **to-dos**) (*inf*) a fuss, commotion, quarrel.
toe *n* one of the five digits on the foot; the part of the shoe or sock that covers the toes.
toe cap *n* a reinforced covering on the toe of a shoe or boot.
toehold *n* a small ledge, crack, etc used in climbing; any slight means of support or access; (*wrestling*) a hold in which an opponent's foot is twisted.
toenail *n* the thin, hard covering on the end of the toes.

toffee, toffy *n* (*pl* **toffees, toffies**) a sweet of brittle but tender texture made by boiling sugar and butter together.
toffee apple *n* an apple coated with toffee and eaten from a stick.
toffee-nosed *adj* (*inf*) pretentious, patronizing, arrogant.
tofu *n* unfermented soya bean curd, used in cooking.
tog[1] *n* (*pl*) (*inf*) clothes. * *vt* (**togging, togged**) (*inf*) to dress.
tog[2] *n* in UK, an official measurement of the warmth of a quilt, etc.
toga *n* a piece of cloth draped around the body, as worn by citizens in ancient Rome.
together *adv* in one place or group; in cooperation with; in unison; jointly.
toggle *n* a peg attached to a rope to prevent it from passing through a loop or knot; a button of this form; (*comput*) a software instruction for starting or stopping a style, etc. * *vt* to fasten with a toggle.
toggle switch *n* an electrical device for opening or closing a circuit.
toil *vi* to work strenuously; to move with great effort. * *n* hard work.
toilet *n* a lavatory; the room containing a lavatory; the act of washing and dressing oneself.
toilet paper, toilet tissue *n* an absorbent paper for cleansing after urination, etc, usu wound around a cardboard cylinder.
toiletry *n* (*pl* **toiletries**) a lotion, perfume, etc used in washing and dressing oneself.
toilet water *n* a diluted perfume.
token *n* a symbol, sign; an indication; a metal disc for a slot machine; a souvenir; a gift voucher. * *adj* nominal; symbolic.
tokenism *n* the making of only a token effort.
tolbooth *n* (*Scot*) a town hall; a jail.
told *see* **tell.**
tolerable *adj* bearable; fairly good.—**tolerably** *adv*.
tolerance *n* open-mindedness; forbearance; (*med*) ability to resist the action of a drug, etc; ability of a substance to endure heat, stress, etc without damage.
tolerant *adj* able to put up with the beliefs, actions, etc of others; broad-minded; showing tolerance to a drug, etc; capable of enduring stress, etc.
tolerate *vt* to endure, put up with, suffer.
toll[1] *n* money levied for passing over a bridge or road; a charge for a service, such as a long-distance telephone call; the number of people killed in an accident or disaster.
toll[2] *vt* (*bell*) to ring slowly and repeatedly, as a funeral bell. * *vi* to sound, as a bell. * *n* the sound of a bell when tolling.
tollbooth *n* a booth where money is paid to pass over a bridge, road, etc.—*also* **tolbooth.**
toll call *n* a telephone call charged at higher than the standard or local rate.
tollgate *n* a gate where money is paid to pass over a bridge, road, etc.
toluene *n* a flammable hydrocarbon derived from petroleum and coal tar used as a solvent and in organic synthesis.
tom *n* a male animal, esp a cat.
tomahawk *n* a light axe used by North American Indians.
tomato *n* (*pl* **tomatoes**) a plant with red pulpy fruit used as a vegetable.
tomb *n* a vault in the earth for the burial of the dead.
tomboy *n* a girl who likes rough outdoor activities.
tombstone *n* a memorial stone over a grave.
tomcat *n* a male cat.
Tom, Dick and Harry *n* an ordinary person, anybody taken at random.
tome *n* a large, heavy book, esp a scholarly one.
-tome *n suffix* a cutting instrument.
tomfool *n* a fool.
tomfoolery *n* (*pl* **tomfooleries**) foolish behaviour; nonsense.
Tommy *n* (*pl* **Tommies**) (*inf*) a private in the British army.
tommy gun *n* a (Thompson) sub-machine gun.
tommyrot *n* complete nonsense.
tomography *n* a process which produces an x-ray photograph of a plane section of the body or other object.
tomorrow *n* the day after today; the future.—*also adv*.
tomtit *n* any of various small tits, esp a blue tit.
tom-tom *n* a long small-headed drum usually beaten with the hands.
-tomy *n suffix* surgical incision.
ton *n* a unit of weight equivalent to 2,000 pounds in US or 2,240 pounds in UK; (*pl*) (*inf*) a great quantity.
tonal *n* of or pertaining to tone; having a key.
tonality *n* (*pl* **tonalities**) the character of a musical composition in relation to scale or key; a system of tones; the scheme of colours and tones in a painting.
tone *n* the quality of a sound; pitch or inflection of the voice; colour, shade; body condition. * *vti* to give tone to; to harmonize (with); (*with* **down**) to (become) moderate in tone; (*with* **up**) to make or become healthier, tighter, etc.
tone arm *n* the tracking arm in a record player that holds the cartridge and stylus.
tone-deaf *adj* insensitive to differences in musical pitch.
tone poem *n* a symphonic poem.
toner *n* a cosmetic used on the skin for various effects; a chemical used to alter the tone of a photograph; the ink particles used in various reprographic devices such as laser printers and photocopiers.
tong *n* a Chinese-American secret society.
tongs *npl* an instrument consisting of two arms that are hinged, used for grasping and lifting.
tongue *n* the soft, moveable organ in the mouth, used in tasting, swallowing, and speech; the ability to speak; a language; (*shoe*) a piece of leather under the laces; a jet of flame; the tongue of an animal served as food; the catch of a buckle.
tongue-lash *vt* to scold, rebuke severely.—**tongue lashing** *n*.
tongue-tied *adj* speechless.
tongue-twister *n* a sequence of words that it is difficult to pronounce quickly and clearly.
tonic *n* a medicine that improves physical well-being; something that imparts vigour; a carbonated mineral water with a bitter taste. * *adj* relating to tones or sounds.
tonic sol-fa *n* the system of sol-fa or solmization syllables used to represent the notes of the musical scale.
tonight *n* this night; the night or evening of the present day.—*also adv*.
tonnage *n* a merchant ship's capacity measured in tons; the weight of its cargo; the amount of shipping of a country or port; merchant ships collectively; a duty levied on ships based on tonnage or capacity.
tonne *n* metric ton, 1,000 kg.
tonometer *n* a device, such as a tuning fork, for measuring the pitch of tones.
tonsil *n* one of the two oval organs of soft tissue situated one on each side of the throat.
tonsillectomy *n* (*pl* **tonsillectomies**) a surgical operation to remove the tonsils.
tonsillitis *n* inflammation of the tonsils.
tonsure *n* shaving part of the head to denote a clerical state in certain churches and religious orders; the shaved area itself. * *vt* to give a tonsure to (a monk, etc).—**tonsured** *adj*.
Tony *n* (*pl* **Tonys, Tonies**) an annual award for excellence in the theatre.
too *adv* in addition; also, likewise; extremely; very.
took *see* **take.**
tool *n* an implement that is used by hand; a means for achieving any purpose.
tooling *n* a design or decoration made with a tool, as on leather.
tool-maker *n* a person who repairs and maintains precision machine tools.
toolroom *n* an area in a factory, machine shop, etc where tools are kept or repaired.
toot *vi* to hoot a car horn, whistle, etc in short blasts. * *n* a hoot.—*also vt*.
tooth *n* (*pl* **teeth**) one of the white, bone-like structures arranged in rows in the mouth, used in biting and chewing; the palate; a tooth-like projection on a comb, saw, or wheel.
toothache *n* a pain in a tooth.
toothbrush *n* a small brush for cleaning teeth.

toothed whale *n* any of various whales with simple teeth, such as dolphins.
toothpaste *n* a paste for cleaning teeth, used with a toothbrush.
toothpick *n* a sliver of wood or plastic for removing food particles from between the teeth.
tooth powder *n* a powder used for cleaning the teeth.
toothsome *adj* appetizing.
toothy *adj* (**toothier, toothiest**) having or revealing prominent teeth.
top[1] *n* the highest, or uppermost, part or surface of anything; the highest in rank; the crown of the head; the lid. * *adj* highest; greatest. * *vt* to cover on the top; to remove the top of or from; to rise above; to surpass; (*with* **up**) to raise up to the full capacity or amount.
top[2] *n* a child's toy, which is spun on its pointed base.
topaz *n* any of various yellow gems.
top brass *npl* (*inf*) the highest-ranking military or other officials.
topcoat *n* an overcoat.
top dog *n* (*inf*) the leader, the most important person.
top drawer *n* the most prominent people in society.
tope[1] *vi* to consume alcoholic drink in excessive quantities.—**toper** *n*.
tope[2] *n* a small grey European shark.
topee *n* a pith helmet.—*also* **topi**.
top flight *adj* excellent, of the highest quality.
topgallant *n* a mast or sail above a topmast.—*also adj*.
top gear *n* the highest gear in a motor vehicle; maximum speed or activity.
top hat *n* a man's tall, silk hat.
top-heavy *adj* having an upper part too heavy for the lower, causing instability.
topi *see* **topee**.
topiary *adj* pertaining to the art or practice of trimming bushes and trees into ornamental shapes. * *n* (**topiaries**) a tree or bush shaped in this way.
topic *n* a subject for discussion; the theme of a speech or writing.
topical *adj* of current interest.
topknot *n* a tuft of hair or knot of ribbons on the head.
topless *adj* lacking a top; (*garment*) revealing the breasts; wearing such a garment.
topmast *n* a mast next above the lowest mast.
topmost *adj* nearest the top, highest.
topnotch *adj* (*inf*) excellent.
topo-, top- *prefix* place; locality.
topography *n* (*pl* **topographies**) the study or description of surface features of a place on maps or charts.—**topographer** *n*.—**topographical** *adj*.
topology *n* the study of the properties of geometric figures that are unaffected by distortion.—**topological** *adj*.—**topologist** *n*.
topping *n* a top layer, esp a sauce for food.
topple *vi* to fall over. * *vt* to cause to overbalance and fall; (*government*) to overthrow.
topsail *n* a square sail next above the lowest sail on a mast.
top secret *adj* highly confidential.
topside *n* the upper side; a boneless cut of beef; the open or upper decks of a ship. * *adv* on top.
topsoil *n* the surface layer of soil.
topspin *n* a spin imparted to a ball that makes it travel faster or higher.
topsy-turvy *adj, adv* turned upside down; in confusion.
tor *n* a high, rocky hill.
Torah *n* (a scroll containing) the Pentateuch; Jewish sacred writings and teachings collectively.
torch *n* a flashlight; a device for giving off a hot flame.—**torchlight** *n*.
torchbearer *n* a person carrying a torch; a leader, source of inspiration.
torch song *n* a sentimental song about the sufferings of love.—**torch singer** *n*.
tore *see* **tear**.
toreador *n* a bullfighter, esp on horseback.
torero *n* (*pl* **toreros**) a bullfighter, esp one who fights on foot.
torii *n* (*pl* **torii**) a gateway to a Japanese Shinto temple.
torment *n* torture, anguish; a source of pain. * *vt* to afflict with extreme pain, physical or mental.—**tormentor, tormenter** *n*.
torn *see* **tear**[2].
tornado *n* (*pl* **tornadoes, tornados**) a violently whirling column of air seen as a funnel-shaped cloud that usu destroys everything in its narrow path.
toroid *n* (a solid enclosed by) a surface generated by a circle rotated about a line in the same plane as but not intersecting the circle.—**toroidal** *adj*.
torpedo *n* (*pl* **torpedoes**) a self-propelled submarine offensive weapon, carrying an explosive charge. * *vt* to attack, hit, or destroy with torpedo(es).
torpedo boat *n* a small high-speed warship from which torpedoes are launched.
torpid *adj* lethargic, sluggish.—**torpidity** *n*.
torpor *n* a state of lethargy.
torque *n* (*physics*) a force that causes rotation around a central point, such as an axle.
torr *n* (*pl* **torr**) a unit of pressure equal to 133.322 newtons per square metre.
torrent *n* a rushing stream; a flood of words.—**torrential** *adj*.
torrid *adj* burning, parched or scorched with heat; passionate.—**torridity, torridness** *n*.
torsi *see* **torso**.
torsion *n* a twisting effect on an object when equal forces are applied at both ends but in opposite directions.
torsk *n* (*pl* **torsk, torsks**) a large marine food fish related to the cod.
torso *n* (*pl* **torsos, torsi**) the trunk of the human body.
tort *n* (*law*) a private or civil wrong.
torte *n* a rich cake or tart filled with cream, fruit, etc.
tortellini *n* small stuffed pasta shapes.
tortilla *n* a round thin maize pancake usually eaten hot with a topping or filling.
tortoise *n* a slow-moving reptile with a dome-shaped shell into which it can withdraw.
tortoiseshell *n* a brown and yellow colour.
tortricid *n* any of a family of moths whose larvae live in nests of rolled-up leaves.
tortuous *adj* full of twists, involved.—**tortuously** *adv*.
torture *n* subjection to severe physical or mental pain to extort a confession, or as a punishment. —*also vt*. —**torturer** *n*.
torus *n* a convex semicircular moulding, esp at the base of a column; a toroid.—**toric** *adj*.
Tory *n* (*pl* **Tories**) a member of the Conservative Party in UK politics; an American supporter of the British during the American Revolution.—*also adj*.
tosh *n* (*sl*) nonsense.
toss *vt* to throw up; to pitch; to fling; (*head*) to throw back; (*with* **off**) to produce, write, perform, etc, quickly and easily; to drink in one gulp. * *vi* to be tossed about; to move restlessly; (*with* **up**) to spin a coin to decide a question by the side that falls uppermost. * *n* the act of tossing or being tossed; a pitch; a fall.
toss-up *n* the throwing of a coin to decide a question; an even chance.
tot[1] *n* anything little, esp a child; a small measure of spirits.
tot[2] *vt* (**totting, totted**) (*with* **up**) to add up or total.
total *adj* whole, complete; absolute. * *n* the whole sum; the entire amount. * *vt* (**totalling, totalled** *or* **totaling, totaled**) to add up.—**totally** *adv*.
totalitarian *adj* relating to a system of government in which one political group maintains complete control, esp under a dictator. —**totalitarianism** *n*.
totality *n* (*pl* **totalities**) the whole amount.
totalizator *n* a machine for registering bets and computing the odds and payoff, as at a racetrack.
tote[1] *n* (*inf*) totalizator.
tote[2] *vt* to carry.
tote bag *n* (*inf*) a large bag for shopping or other items.
totem *n* an object regarded as a symbol and treated with respect by a particular group of people.

totem pole *n* a large pole carved with totemic symbols used in rituals by certain North American Indian tribes.

totter *vi* to walk unsteadily; to shake or sway as if about to fall.—**tottery** *adj.*

toucan *n* a fruit-eating South American bird with an immense, brightly coloured beak.

touch *vt* to come in contact with, esp with the hand or fingers; to reach; to affect with emotion; to tinge or tint; to border on; (*sl*) to ask for money (from); (*with* **off**) to cause to explode, as with a lighted match; to cause (violence, a riot, etc) to start; (*with* **up**) to improve by making minor alterations or additions to. * *vi* to be in contact; to be adjacent; to allude to. * *n* the act of touching; the sense by which something is perceived through contact; a trace; understanding; a special quality or skill.

touch-and-go *adj* precarious, risky.

touchdown *n* the moment when an aircraft or spaceship lands; (*Rugby football, American football*) a placing of the ball on the ground to score.

touché *interj* (*fencing*) used to acknowledge an opponent's hit; an acknowledgement of a valid or accomplished reply, remark, witty comment, etc.

touched *adj* emotionally affected; mentally disturbed.

touching *adj* affecting, moving.

touch judge *n* a linesman in Rugby football.

touchline *n* (*football, etc*) the side boundary of a pitch.

touchmark *n* a maker's distinguishing mark on pewter.

touchpaper *n* paper impregnated with a slow-burning substance used to ignite fireworks.

touchstone *n* a siliceous stone used to test gold and silver from the marks they make on it; any test or standard of genuineness.

touch-type *vi* to type quickly and accurately without looking at the keyboard.—**touch-typist** *n.*

touchwood *n* dry rotten wood useful for tinder.

touchy *adj* (**touchier, touchiest**) irritable; very risky.

tough *adj* strong; durable; hardy; rough and violent; difficult; (*inf*) unlucky.—**toughen** *vti.*—**toughness** *n.*

tough-minded *adj* realistic; unsentimental.

toupee *n* a wig or section of hair to cover a bald spot, esp worn by men.

tour *n* a turn, period, etc as of military duty; a long trip, as for sightseeing. * *vti* to go on a tour (through).

touraco *n* (*pl* **touracos**) any of a family of brightly coloured crested birds native to Africa.

tour de force *n* (*pl* **tours de force**) an outstanding achievement or performance.

tourism *n* travelling for pleasure; the business of catering for people who do this; the encouragement of touring.

tourist *n* one who makes a tour, a sightseer, travelling for pleasure.—*also adj.*

tourist class *n* economy accommodation, as on a ship, aircraft, etc.

touristy *adj* (*inf*) full of or designed for tourists.

tourmaline *n* a silicate mineral of various colours used in jewellery and electronic equipment.

tournament *n* a sporting event involving a number of competitors and a series of games.

tournedos *n* (*pl* **tournedos**) a thick round fillet of beef steak.

tourniquet *n* a device for compressing a blood vessel to stop bleeding.

tour operator *n* a company that specializes in offering package tours.

tousle *vt* to make untidy, ruffle, make tangled (esp hair).

tout *vti* (*inf*) to praise highly; (*inf*) to sell betting tips on (race horses); (*inf*) to solicit business in a brazen way. * *n* (*inf*) a person who does so.

tovarish, tovarich *n* a comrade.

tow *vt* to pull or drag with a rope. * *n* the act of towing; a towrope.

towage *n* the act of towing; the charge made for it.

toward, towards *prep* in the direction of; concerning; just before; as a contribution to.

towel *n* an absorbent cloth for drying the skin after it is washed, and for other purposes; **to throw in the towel** to admit defeat. * *vti* (**towelling, towelled** *or* **toweling, toweled**) to rub (oneself) with a towel.

towelette *n* a small moistened tissue for cleaning the face, etc.

towelling, toweling *n* cloth for towels; a rubbing with a towel.

tower *n* a tall, narrow building, standing alone or forming part of another; a fortress. * *vi* (*with* **over**) to rise above; to loom.

tower block *n* a skyscraper.

towering *adj* immensely tall; powerful, impressive; intense.

town *n* a densely populated urban centre, smaller than a city and larger than a village; the people of a town.

townie *n* (*pl* **townies**) a person who lives in a city or town as opposed to the countryside.—*also* **towny.**

town hall *n* a large building housing the offices of the town council, often with a hall for public meetings.

town house *n* a two or three-story house with a garage below, usu one of a row; a house in a fashionable area; one's house in town.

township *n* a division of a county in many US states, constituting a unit of local government; in South Africa, an urban area reserved for Blacks.

towny *see* **townie.**

towpath *n* the footpath beside a river or canal.

towrope, towline *n* a strong rope or cable for towing a wheeled vehicle, ship, etc.

tox-, toxic-, toxico- *prefix* poison.

toxaemia, toxemia *n* a type of blood poisoning.—**toxaemic, toxemic** *adj.*

toxic *adj* poisonous; harmful; deadly.—**toxicity** *n.*

toxicant *n* a poison. * *adj* poisonous.

toxicology *n* the scientific study of poisons, their effects and antidotes.—**toxicologic, toxicological** *adj.*—**toxicologist** *n.*

toxin *n* a poison produced by microorganisms and causing certain diseases.

toxocariasis *n* a disease in humans caused by the larvae of a parasitic roundworm found in dogs and cats.

toxoid *n* a toxin of reduced power used in vaccines to stimulate the production of antitoxins.

toxoplasmosis *n* a disease affecting the central nervous system caused by a parasitic worm.

toy *n* an object for children to play with; a replica; a miniature. * *vi* to trifle; to flirt.

toyboy *n* the younger male lover of an older woman.

trace *n* a mark etc left by a person, animal or thing; a barely perceptible footprint; a small quantity. * *vt* to follow by tracks; to discover the whereabouts of; (*map, etc*) to copy by following the lines on transparent paper.

traceable *adj* able to be traced.—**traceably** *adv.*

trace element *n* a chemical element, as copper, zinc, etc, essential in nutrition but only in minute amounts.

tracer *n* a projectile which glows or leaves a smoke trail allowing its flight to be observed; a radioisotope introduced into the body whose course can be traced by a detector for diagnostic purposes.

trachea *n* (*pl* **tracheae**) the air passage from the mouth to the lungs, the windpipe.

tracheo-, trache- *prefix* trachea.

tracheotomy *n* (*pl* **tracheotomies**) an incision into the trachea, esp to bypass a blockage in the air passage.

trachoma *n* an infectious eye disease caused by a virus that leads to scarring and eventual blindness.—**trachomatous** *adj.*

trachyte *n* a type of light-coloured volcanic rock.

tracing *n* a copy of a drawing, etc made by tracing.

tracing paper *n* transparent paper used for tracing.

track *vt* to follow the tracks of; (*satellite, etc*) to follow by radar and record position; (*with* **down**) to find by tracking. * *n* a mark left; a footprint; parallel steel rails on which trains run; a course for running or racing; sports performed on a track, as running, hurdling; the band on which the wheels of a tractor or tank run; one piece of music on a record; a sound track.

track-and-field *adj* denoting various competitive athletic events (as running, jumping, weight-throwing) performed on a track and adjacent field.
tracker *n* a person who follows by tracking footprints, etc; a dog that follows a scent.
track event *n* an athletic event that takes place on a running track.
tracking station *n* a place that uses radio or radar antennae to follow the course of objects in space or the atmosphere.
tracklaying *adj* (*vehicle*) having an endless loop of metal track around the wheels.
track record *n* (*inf*) a record of the past achievements or failures of someone or something.
track shoe *n* a spiked running shoe.
tracksuit *n* a loose suit worn by athletes to keep warm.
tract[1] *n* an expanse of land or water; a part of a bodily system or organ.
tract[2] *n* a treatise.
tractable *adj* easily worked; easily taught; docile.
traction *n* act or state of drawing and pulling; (*med*) the using of weights to pull on a muscle, etc, to correct an abnormal condition.
tractor *n* a motor vehicle for pulling heavy loads and farming machinery.
trad *adj* (*inf*) traditional. * *n* traditional jazz.
trade *n* buying and selling (of commodities); commerce; occupation; customers; business. * *vi* to buy and sell; to exchange; (*with* **on**) to take advantage of.—**trader** *n*.
trade cycle *n* a recurrent fluctuation in economic activity between boom and slump.
trade gap *n* the amount by which the value of a country's visible imports exceeds its visible exports.
trade-in *n* a used item given in part payment when buying a replacement.
trade-off *n* the exchange or substitution of one thing or priority for another, often as a compromise.
trademark *n* a name used on a product by a manufacturer to distinguish it from its competitors, esp when legally protected.—*also vt*.
tradescantia *n* any of a genus of common houseplants cultivated for their variegated foliage.
tradesman *n* (*pl* **tradesmen**) a shopkeeper; a skilled worker.
trade union, trades union *n* an organized association of employees of any trade or industry for the protection of their income and working conditions.
trade wind *n* a wind that blows toward the equator at either side of it.
trading *n* the act of buying and selling (goods, etc).—*also adj*.
tradition *n* the handing down from generation to generation of opinions and practices; the belief or practice thus passed on; custom.—**traditional** *adj*.—**traditionally** *adv*.
traduce *vt* to speak badly of; to misrepresent.
traffic *n* trade; the movement or number of vehicles, pedestrians, etc, along a street, etc. * *vi* (**trafficking, trafficked**) to do business (esp. in illegal drugs).
traffic circle *n* a junction of thoroughfares where traffic circulates one way to ease progress, a roundabout.
traffic island *n* a raised area in the centre of a road to guide traffic and provide refuge for pedestrians crossing.
traffic light *n* one of a set of coloured lights used to control traffic at street crossings, etc.
traffic pattern *n* a network of airlanes above an airport to which aircraft are restricted.
tragacanth *n* a gum obtained from a species of spiny leguminous plants used in pharmacy and in calico printing.
tragedian *n* an actor who plays mainly tragic roles.—**tragedienne** *nf*.
tragedy *n* (*pl* **tragedies**) a play or drama that is serious and sad, and the climax a catastrophe; an accident or situation involving death or suffering.—**tragic** *adj*.—**tragically** *adv*.
tragicomedy *n* a dramatic or literary work which combines tragic and comic elements; a situation or event with tragic and comic aspects.
trail *vt* to drag along the ground; to have in its wake; to follow behind; to advertise a film, event or programme beforehand. * *vi* to hang or drag loosely behind; (*plant*) to climb; (*with* **off** *or* **away**) to grow weaker or dimmer. * *n* a path or track; the scent of an animal; something left in the wake (eg *a trail of smoke*).
trailblazer *n* a person who blazes a trail; a pioneer in a particular field.
trailer *n* a large vehicle designed to be towed by a truck, etc; a motor home; an advertisement for a film or television programme.
trailer park *n* an area available for rent to motor homes, caravans, etc, usu with electricity, water, etc, piped in.
trailing edge *n* the rear edge of an aerofoil.
train *vt* to teach, to guide; to tame for use, as animals; to prepare for racing, etc; (*gun, etc*) to aim. * *vi* to do exercise or preparation. * *n* a series of railroad cars pulled by a locomotive; a sequence; the back part of a dress that trails along the floor; a retinue.
trained *adj* skilled.
trainee *n* a person who is being trained.
trainer *n* a coach or instructor in sports; a person who prepares horses for racing.
training *n* practical instruction; a course of physical exercises.
training school *n* an institution for training in vocational subjects, eg teaching, nursing.
training ship *n* a moored vessel on which people are taught seamanship.
train oil *n* oil obtained from whale blubber.
train surfing *n* the practice of clinging onto the outside of a moving train for kicks.—**train surfer** *n*.
traipse *vi* to walk wearily, trudge about. * *n* a tiring walk, a trudge.
trait *n* a characteristic feature.
traitor *n* a person who commits treason or betrays his country, friends, etc.—**traitorous** *adj*.
trajectory *n* (*pl* **trajectories**) the path of an object, such as a bullet, moving through space.
tram[1] *n* a small wagon running on rails in a mine; a streetcar; a cable car.
tram[2] *n* a double twisted thread used in some silks.
trammel *n* a type of net for catching birds or fish; (*often pl*) a hindrance to freedom of movement or action; an instrument for drawing ellipses. * *vt* (**trammelling, trammelled** *or* **trammeling, trammeled**) to trap, catch; to hinder, restrict.
tramp *vti* to walk heavily; to tread or trample; to wander about as a tramp. * *n* a vagrant; (*sl*) a prostitute.
trample *vti* to tread under foot.
trampoline *n* a sheet of strong canvas stretched tightly on a frame, used in acrobatic tumbling.
trance *n* a state of unconsciousness, induced by hypnosis, in which some of the powers of the waking body, such as response to commands, may be retained.
tranche *n* a portion of something, esp a sum of money or issue of shares.
tranquil *adj* quiet, calm, peaceful.—**tranquilly** *adv*.
tranquillize, tranquilize *vt* to make tranquil, esp by administering a drug.—**tranquillization, tranquilization** *n*.
tranquillizer, tranquilizer *n* a drug that calms.
tranquility, tranquillity *n* the state of being tranquil; calmness.
trans. *abbr* = transitive; translated; translation; translator.
trans- *prefix* through; across; on the other side of.
transact *vt* (*business*) to conduct or carry out.
transaction *n* the act of transacting; something transacted, esp a business deal; (*pl*) a record of the proceedings of a society.
transalpine *adj* beyond (usu north) of the Alps.
transatlantic *adj* crossing the Atlantic Ocean; across, beyond the Atlantic.
transceiver *n* a combined radio transmitter and receiver.
transcend *vt* to rise above or beyond; to surpass.—**transcendent** *adj*.
transcendental *adj* beyond physical experience; surpassing; supernatural.—**transcendentally** *adv*.
transcendental meditation *n* a technique for emptying and refreshing the mind by repeating a mantra.
transcontinental *adj* extending or travelling across a continent.—**transcontinentally** *adv*.

transcribe *vt* to write out fully from notes or a tape recording; to make a phonetic transcription; to arrange a piece of music for an instrument other than the one it was written for.

transcript *n* a written or printed copy made by transcribing; an official copy of proceedings, etc.

transcription *n* the act of transcribing; something transcribed, esp a piece of music; a transcript; a recording made for broadcasting.

transducer *n* a device that converts energy from one form into another.

transept *n* one of the two wings of a church, at right angles to the nave.

transfer *vb* (**transferring, transferred**) *vt* to carry, convey, from one place to another; (*law*) to make over (property) to another; (*money*) to move from the control of one institution to another. * *vi* to change to another bus, etc. * *n* the act of transferring; the state of being transferred; someone or something that is transferred; a design that can be moved from one surface to another.—**transferable** *adj*.

transference *n* the act of transferring; the state of being transferred; (*psychoanal*) the redirection of emotion under analysis, usu toward the analyst.

transfer RNA *n* a form of RNA that carries an amino acid to a ribosome in protein synthesis.

transfiguration *n* a change in appearance, esp to a more spiritual or exalted form; (*with cap*) (the festival commemorating) the change in the appearance of Christ as described in the Gospels.

transfigure *vt* to transform or become transformed in appearance, esp for the better.

transfix *vt* to impale with a sharp weapon; to paralyse with shock or horror.

transform *vti* to change the shape, appearance, or condition of; to convert.—**transformation** *n*.

transformer *n* a device for changing alternating current with an increase or decrease of voltage.

transfusion *n* the injection of blood into the veins of a sick or injured person.—**transfuse** *vt*.

transgress *vti* to break or violate (a moral law or code of behaviour); to overstep (a limit).—**transgressor** *n*.

transgression *n* the act of transgressing; infringement of a rule, etc; a sin.

transhumance *n* the seasonal movement of livestock to new grazing areas.

transient *adj* temporary; of short duration, momentary.—**transience** *n*.

transistor *n* a device using a semiconductor to amplify sound, as in a radio or television; a small portable radio.

transit *n* a passing over or through; conveyance of people or goods.

transit camp *n* temporary accommodation for soldiers, refugees, etc.

transition *n* passage from one place or state to another; change.—**transitional** *adj*.

transitive *adj* (*gram*) denoting a verb that requires a direct object; of or relating to transition.—**transitively** *adv*.—**transitivity** *n*.

transitory *adj* lasting only a short time.—**transitorily** *adv*.—**transitoriness** *n*.

translate *vti* to express in another language; to explain, interpret.—**translator** *n*.

translation *n* the act of translating; something translated into another language or state; an interpretation.

transliterate *vt* to convert a word, etc into the corresponding characters of another alphabet.—**transliteration** *n*.

translucent *adj* allowing light to pass through, but not transparent.—**translucence** *n*.

transmigrate *vi* (*soul*) to pass into the body of another person after death; to migrate.

transmission *n* the act of transmitting; something transmitted; a system using gears, etc, to transfer power from an engine to a moving part, esp wheels of a vehicle; a radio or television broadcast.

transmit *vt* (**transmitting, transmitted**) to send from one place or person to another; to communicate; to convey; (*radio or television signals*) to send out.

transmitter *n* an apparatus for broadcasting television or radio programmes.

transmogrify *vt* (**transmogrifying, transmogrified**) to change shape, esp in a bizarre or comic manner.—**transmogrification** *n*.

transmute *vt* to change into a different form or substance.—**transmutation** *n*.

transnational *n* extending beyond national boundaries.

transoceanic *adj* on or from the other side of ocean; crossing the ocean.

transom *n* a horizontal bar across a window or between a door and a window over it; a fanlight; any of several transverse beams supporting and strengthening the stern of a vessel.

transparency *n* (*pl* **transparencies**) the state of being transparent; (*photog*) a slide.

transparent *adj* that may be easily seen through; clear, easily understood.—**transparently** *adv*.—**transparentness** *n*.

transpire *vti* to emit, to pass off through the pores of the skin; to exhale (moisture); (*news*) to become known, to leak out; (*inf*) to happen.—**transpiration** *n*.

transplant *vt* (*plant*) to remove and plant in another place; (*med*) to remove an organ from one person and transfer it to another.—*also n*.

transport *vt* to convey from one place to another; to enrapture. * *n* the system of transporting goods or passengers; the conveyance of troops and their equipment by sea or land; a vehicle for this purpose.—**transportable** *adj*.—**transportation** *n*.

transpose *vt* to put into a different order; to interchange; (*mus*) to change the key of.—**transposition** *n*.

transputer *n* (*comput*) a fast microchip comprising a 32-bit microprocessor which is used as a component in compact supercomputers.

transsexual *n* a person born of one sex who identifies psychologically with the opposite sex.—**transsexualism** *n*.

transubstantiation *n* (*esp in RC Church*) the doctrine that the bread and wine of the communion are wholly transformed into the body and blood of Christ when consecrated, although their appearance remains unchanged.

transuranic *adj* (*element*) having an atomic number greater than that of uranium.

transverse *adj* crosswise.—**transversely** *adv*.

transvestite *n* a person who gains sexual pleasure from wearing the clothes of the opposite sex.—**transvestism** *n*.

trap *n* a mechanical device or pit for snaring animals; an ambush; a trick to catch someone out; a two-wheeled horsedrawn carriage. * *vt* (**trapping, trapped**) to catch in a trap; to trick.

trapdoor *n* a hinged or sliding door in a roof, ceiling or floor.

trapeze *n* a gymnastic apparatus consisting of a horizontal bar suspended by two parallel ropes.

trapezium *n* (*pl* **trapeziums, trapezia**) a quadrilateral in which two of the sides are parallel; in US, a quadrilateral in which none of the sides are parallel.—**trapezial** *adj*.

trapezoid *n* a quadrilateral in which none of the sides are parallel. In US, a quadrilateral with two sides parallel.

trapper *n* a person who traps animals, esp for their skins.

trappings *npl* trimmings; additions; ornaments.

trash *n* nonsense; refuse; rubbish.

trash can *n* a container for household refuse, a dustbin, garbage can.

trashy *adj* (**trashier, trashiest**) of poor quality.—**trashiness** *n*.

trattoria *n* (*pl* **trattorias, trattorie**) an Italian restaurant.

trauma *n* an emotional shock that may cause long-term psychological damage; an upsetting experience.—**traumatic** *adj*.

travel *vb* (**travelling, travelled** *or* **traveling, traveled**) *vi* to journey or move from one place to another. * *vt* to journey across, through. * *n* journey.

travel agency *n* an agency through which one can book travel.—**travel agent** *n*.

traveller, traveler *n* a person who travels; a salesman who travels for a company.

traveller's cheque *n* a draft purchased from a bank, etc signed at the time of purchase and signed again at the time of cashing.

travelogue, travelog *n* a film or illustrated lecture on travel.

traverse *n* a horizontal move in rock climbing, skiing, etc. * *vt* to cross.

travertine *n* a mineral comprising mostly calcium carbonate, used for building.
travesty *n* (*pl* **travesties**) a misrepresentation; a poor imitation; a parody.
trawl *vti* to fish by dragging a large net behind a fishing boat.
trawler *n* a boat used for trawling.
tray *n* a flat board, or sheet of metal or plastic, surrounded by a rim, used for carrying food or drink.
treacherous *adj* untrustworthy, disloyal; unstable, dangerous.
treachery *n* (*pl* **treacheries**) disloyalty, betrayal of trust.
treacle *n* a thick sticky substance obtained during the refining of sugar.—**treacly** *adj*.
tread *vti* (**treading, trod,** *pp* **trodden**) to step or walk on, along, in, over or across; to crush or squash (with the feet); to trample (on). * *n* a step, way of walking; the part of a shoe, wheel, or tyre that touches the ground.
treadle *n* a foot lever or pedal on a machine.
treadmill *n* a grind; a monotonous routine.
treas. *abbr* = treasurer, treasury.
treason *n* the crime of betraying one's government or attempting to overthrow it; treachery.—**treasonable** *adj*.
treasure *n* wealth and riches hoarded up; a person or thing much valued. * *vt* to hoard up; to prize greatly.
treasurer *n* a person appointed to take charge of the finances of a society, government or city.
treasure hunt *n* a game in which players follow clues to locate a hidden object.
treasure-trove *n* (*law*) valuable items such as gold and silver found buried and of unknown ownership; any valuable find.
treasury *n* (*pl* **treasuries**) a place where valuable objects are deposited; the funds or revenues of a government.
treat *vt* to deal with or regard; to subject to the action of a chemical; to apply medical treatment to; to pay for another person's entertainment; to deal with in speech or writing. * *n* an entertainment paid for by another person; a pleasure seldom indulged; a unusual cause of enjoyment.
treatise *n* a formal essay in which a subject is treated systematically.
treatment *n* the application of drugs, etc, to a patient; the manner of dealing with a person or thing, esp in a novel or painting; behaviour toward someone.
treaty *n* (*pl* **treaties**) a formal agreement between states.
treble *adj* triple, threefold; (*mus*) denoting the treble. * *n* the highest range of musical notes in singing. * *vti* to make or become three times as much.
treble clef *n* (*mus*) a clef that places G above middle C on the second line of the staff.
trebuchet *n* a type of medieval military catapult used in sieges.
trecento *n* the 14th century, esp in reference to Italian art and literature.
tree *n* a tall, woody, perennial plant having a single trunk, branches and leaves.
tree creeper *n* any of various small songbirds with curved beaks for prising insects from tree trunks.
tree fern *n* a large tropical fern with a woody stem.
tree frog *n* any of various frogs that inhabit trees.
tree line *n* the height or latitude beyond which no trees grow on mountains or in cold regions.—*also* **timber line.**
tree surgeon *n* a person skilled in saving diseased or damaged trees.—**tree surgery** *n*.
tree toad *n* a tree frog.
trefoil *n* any of various plants with three leaflets; an ornament or design resembling this.
trek *vi* (**trekking, trekked**) to travel slowly or laboriously; (*inf*) to go on foot (to). * *n* a long and difficult journey; a migration.
trellis *n* a structure of latticework, for supporting climbing plants, etc.—**trelliswork** *n*.
tremble *vi* to shake, shiver from cold or fear; to quiver.—*also n*.
trembler *n* a device that makes or breaks an electric circuit when subject to vibration.
tremendous *adj* awe-inspiring; very large or great; (*inf*) wonderful; marvellous.
tremolo *n* (*pl* **tremolos**) a tremulous effect in playing or singing; a device that produces this effect, as in an organ.
tremor *n* a vibration; an involuntary shaking.
tremulous *adj* quivering; agitated.
trench *n* a long narrow channel in the earth, used for drainage; such an excavation made for military purposes.
trenchant *adj* keen; incisive; effective.
trench coat *n* a waterproof coat.
trencher *n* a wooden board formerly used for serving food.
trencherman *n* a person who eats heartily.
trench fever *n* an infectious disease characterized by fever and muscular pains that is transmitted by lice.
trench foot *n* a degenerative condition of the feet caused by prolonged immersion in cold water.
trend *n* tendency; a current style or fashion.
trendsetter *n* a person who starts a new fashion.
trendy *adj* (**trendier, trendiest**) (*inf*) fashionable. * *n* (*pl* **trendies**) (*inf*) a person who tries to be fashionable.—**trendily** *adv*.—**trendiness** *n*.
trepan *n* a primitive form of trephine. * *vt* (**trepanning, trepanned**) to cut with a trepan.
trepang *n* a type of large sea cucumber dried and used in Chinese cookery, bêche-de-mer
trephine *n* a surgical saw for removing circular sections of bone, esp from the skull. * *vt* to cut with a trephine.
trepidation *n* a state of fear or anxiety.
trespass *vi* to intrude upon another person's property without their permission; to encroach upon, or infringe, another's rights. * *n* act of trespassing.—**trespasser** *n*.
tress *n* a lock, braid, or plait of hair.
trestle *n* a wooden framework for supporting a table top or scaffold boards.
trews *npl* tight-fitting tartan trousers.
trey *n* three spots or the number three on a dice, domino or playing card.
tri- *prefix* having, made up of, or containing three or three parts; every third.
triad *n* a group or set of three, a trio.
triage *n* the sorting and treatment of the wounded according to chance of survival.
trial *n* a test or experiment; judicial examination; an attempt; a preliminary race, game in a competition; suffering; hardship; a person causing annoyance.
trial and error *n* solving problems through trying various solutions and rejecting the least successful.
trial run *n* an opportunity to test something before purchase, as a vehicle; a rehearsal.
triangle *n* (*math*) a plane figure with three angles and three sides; a percussion instrument consisting of a triangular metal bar beaten with a metal stick.—**triangular** *adj*.
triangulate *vt* to divide into triangles; to make triangular; to survey by dividing an area into a network of triangles.—**triangulation** *n*.
triathlon *n* an athletic event in which all contestants compete in swimming, cycling and running.
triatomic *adj* (*chem*) having three atoms in the molecule.
tribadism *n* simulated heterosexual intercourse by lesbians, with one partner lying on top of the other.
tribe *n* a group of people of the same race, sharing the same customs, religion, language or land.—**tribal** *adj*.—**tribesman** *n*.
tribo- *prefix* friction.
triboelectricity *n* electricity generated by friction.
tribology *n* the study of friction, wear and lubrication between moving surfaces, as gearing systems.

triboluminescence *n* luminescence caused by friction.—**triboluminescent** *adj*.
tribulation *n* distress, difficulty, hardship.
tribunal *n* a court of justice; a committee that investigates and decides on a particular problem.
tribune[1] *n* in ancient Rome, a magistrate appointed to protect the rights of common people; a champion of the people.
tribune[2] *n* a raised platform or dais from which speeches are delivered.
tributary *n* (*pl* **tributaries**) a stream or river flowing into a larger one.
tribute *n* a speech, gift or action to show one's respect or thanks to someone; a payment made at certain intervals by one nation to another in return for peace.
tricentenary *n* (*pl* **tricentenaries**) a tricentennial.—*also adj*.
tricentennial *adj* lasting, or happening every, 300 years. * *n* an anniversary of 300 years; a period of 300 years.
triceps *n* (*pl* **tricepses, triceps**) any three-headed muscle, esp the large muscle that extends the forearm.
trichiasis *n* a condition of having in-growing eyelashes which irritate the eyeball.
trichina *n* (*pl* **trichinae**) a hair-like parasitic worm that infests the intestines and muscles of pigs and humans.
trichinosis *n* a disease in humans caused by infestation of muscular tissues by trichinae.
tricho-, trich- *prefix* hair; filament.
trichology *n* the medical study and treatment of hair diseases.—**trichologist** *n*.
trichosis *n* any disease of the hair.
trichotomy *n* (*pl* **trichotomies**) a division into three parts or categories.—**trichotomous** *adj*.
trichromatic of, involving, or combining three colours; of or having normal colour vision.—**trichromatism** *n*.
trick *n* fraud; deception; a mischievous plan or joke; a magical illusion; a clever feat; skill, knack; the playing cards won in a round. * *adj* using fraud or clever contrivance to deceive. * *vt* to deceive, cheat.—**trickster** *n*.
trickery *n* (*pl* **trickeries**) the practice or an act of using underhand methods to achieve an aim; deception.
trickle *vti* to flow or cause to flow in drops or in a small stream.—*also n*.
trickle-down *adj* denoting a theory in economics that financial incentives to big business will percolate through to small businesses and individuals.
trick or treat *n* a Halloween tradition in which children dress in costumes, call on their neighbours and threaten to do mischief if refused presents of sweets, apples, nuts, money, etc.
tricky *adj* (**trickier, trickiest**) complicated, difficult to handle; risky; cunning, deceitful.—**trickily** *adv*.—**trickiness** *n*.
tricolour, tricolor *n* a flag with three stripes of different colours.
tricorn *adj* having three horns or corners. * *n* a three-cornered hat.
tricuspid *adj* having three cusps, flaps, points, or segments. * *n* a tooth with three cusps.
tricycle *n* a three-wheeled pedal cycle, esp for children.
trident *n* three-pronged spear.
tridentate, tridental *adj* having three teeth or prongs.
tried[1] *see* **try**.
tried[2] *adj* tested; trustworthy.
triennial *adj* happening every third year; lasting for three years.
triennium *n* (*pl* **trienniums, triennia**) a period of three years.
trier *n* one who tries.
trifle *vi* to treat lightly; to dally. * *n* anything of little value; a dessert of whipped cream, custard, sponge cake, sherry, etc.
trifling *adj* insignificant.
trifocal *adj* having three focuses or focal lengths. * *npl* glasses with trifocal lenses.
trifurcate, trifurcated *adj* having three branches or forks.
trig. *abbr* = trigonometrical; trigonometry.
trigeminal *adj* pertaining to the trigeminal nerve.
trigeminal nerve *n* either of a pair of cranial nerves that supply various facial muscles.
trigger *n* a catch that when pulled activates the firing mechanism of a gun. * *vt* (*with* **off**) to initiate; to set (off).
trigger-happy *adj* too eager to resort to firearms or violence; rash, aggressive.
trigonometric function *n* any of various functions (eg sine, cosine, tangent) expressed as ratios of the sides of a right-angled triangle.
trigonometry *n* the branch of mathematics concerned with calculating the angles of triangles or the lengths of their sides.
trike *n* (*inf*) a tricycle.
trilateral *adj* having three sides.
trilby *n* (*pl* **trilbies**) a soft felt hat with a fold in the crown.
trilingual *adj* speaking three languages; written in three languages.—**trilingualism** *n*.
trill *vti* to sing or play with a tremulous tone; (*a bird*) to make a shrill, warbling sound.—*also n*.
trillion *n* a million million (10^{12}); (*formerly*) in UK, a million million million (10^{18}); (*inf*) (*pl*) a very large number.
trilobite *n* any of a group of extinct Palaeozoic marine arthropods with a body in three sections.
trilogy *n* (*pl* **trilogies**) any series of three related literary or operatic works.
trim *adj* (**trimmer, trimmest**) in good condition; tidy, neat; slim. * *vt* to neaten; to cut or prune; to decorate; (*ship, aircraft*) to balance the weight of cargo in. * *n* a decorative edging; a haircut that tidies.
trimaran *n* a boat with three hulls.
trimester *n* a period of three months; a division of the academic year in certain North American colleges and universities.
trimming *n* decorative part of clothing; (*pl*) accompaniments.
trinitrotoluene *n* a solid yellow chemical substance used as a high explosive.
trinity *n* (*pl* **trinities**) a group of three; (*with cap*) in Christianity, the union of Father, Son and Holy Spirit in one God.
trinket *n* a small or worthless ornament.
trinomial *adj* having three terms. * *n* (*math*) a polynomial consisting of three terms.
trio *n* (*pl* **trios**) a set of three; (*mus*) a group of three singers or instrumentalists.
triode *n* an electronic valve or semiconductor device with three electrodes.
trip *vb* (**tripping, tripped**) *vi* to move or tread lightly; to stumble and fall; to make a blunder. * *vt* (*often with* **up**) to cause to stumble; to activate a trip. * *n* a stumble; a journey, tour, or voyage; a slip; a mistake; a light step; a mechanical switch; (*sl*) a hallucinatory experience under the influence of a drug.
tripartite *adj* made up of or divided into three parts; involving or binding three parties.
tripe *n* the stomach lining of a ruminant, prepared for cooking; (*inf*) rubbish, nonsense.
triplane *n* an aircraft with three wings positioned one above the other.
triple *adj* threefold; three times as many. * *vti* to treble.
triple jump *n* an athletic event in which a competitor makes a hop, step and jump in succession.
triplet *n* one of three children born at one birth.
triplicate *adj* threefold.
tripod *n* a three-legged stand, as for supporting a camera.
tripper *n* a tourist; a trip switch.
triptych *n* a picture consisting of three panels fixed or hinged side by side.
tripwire *n* a concealed wire that sets off a bomb, booby trap, etc when tripped over.
trireme *n* an ancient Greek galley with three banks of oars.
trisect *vt* to divide into three (equal) parts.—**trisection** *n*.
trishaw *n* a rickshaw.
triskelion *n* (*pl* **triskelia**) a symbol consisting of three bent limbs or branches radiating from a centre.

trismus *n* lockjaw.
trisyllable *n* a word of three syllables.
trite *adj* dull; hackneyed.
tritium *n* a radioactive isotope of hydrogen.
triton *n* any of various marine gastropod molluscs having a heavy spiral shell; (*with cap*) (*Greek myth*) a sea-god depicted as half man and half fish blowing a spiral shell.
triturate *vt* to crush or grind into a fine powder.—**trituration** *n*.
triumph *n* a victory; success; a great achievement. * *vi* to win a victory or success; to rejoice over a victory.—**triumphal** *adj*.
triumphant *adj* feeling or showing triumph; celebratory; victorious.—**triumphantly** *adv*.
triumvir *n* (*pl* **triumvirs, triumviri**) a member of a ruling body of three persons.
triumvirate *n* the office of a triumvir; joint rule by three persons.
trivalent *adj* having a valency of three.
trivet *n* a three-legged metal stand for supporting hot dishes.
trivia *npl* unimportant details.
trivial *adj* unimportant; commonplace.
triviality *n* (*pl* **trivialities**) a trifle, detail; the state of being trivial.
-trix *n suffix* female.
t-RNA *abbr* = transfer RNA.
trocar *n* a pointed instrument for inserting drainage tubes into bodily cavities.
trochal *adj* wheel-shaped.
troche *n* a medicinal lozenge.
trochee *n* a metrical foot comprising one long syllable followed by one short syllable.
trod, trodden *see* **tread**.
troglodyte *n* a cave dweller.
troika *n* (a Russian vehicle drawn by) three horses harnessed abreast; a triumvirate.
troll *n* a supernatural creature, dwelling in a cave, hill, etc.
trolley *n* (*pl* **trolleys**) a table on wheels for carrying or serving food; a cart for transporting luggage; a cart for carrying shopping in a supermarket; a device that transmits electric current from an overhead wire to a motor vehicle, such as a trolleybus.
trolleybus, trolley car *n* a bus that sometimes runs on rails and is powered by electricity from overhead wires.
trollop *n* a slovenly woman; a prostitute.—**trollopy** *adj*.
trombone *n* brass musical wind instrument whose length is varied with a U-shaped sliding section.
troop *n* a crowd of people; a group of soldiers within a cavalry regiment; (*pl*) armed forces; soldiers. * *vi* to go in a crowd.
trooper *n* a cavalryman; a mounted policeman or a state policeman.
troopship *n* a ship used to transport military forces.
trope *n* a word or phrase used in a figurative sense.
-trope *n suffix* turning, being attracted toward.
trophic *adj* pertaining to nutrition.
tropho-, troph- *prefix* nutrition.
trophy *n* (*pl* **trophies**) a cup or shield won as a prize in a competition or contest; a memento, as taken in battle or hunting.
-trophy *n suffix* growth, nutrition.
tropic *n* one of the two parallel lines of latitude north and south of the equator; (*pl*) the regions lying between these lines.
-tropic *adj suffix* turning to or responding to an external stimulus.
tropical *adj* relating to the tropics; (*weather*) hot and humid.
tropism *n* the involuntary direction of growth of a plant due to an external stimulus.
-tropism, -tropy *n suffix* turning or developing in response to an external stimulus.
tropo- *prefix* turning or changing.
-tropous *adj suffix* turning away.
tropopause *n* the region between the troposphere and stratosphere.
troposphere *n* the region of the atmosphere below the stratosphere which varies in temperature and in which clouds form.
trot *vb* (**trotting, trotted**) *vi* (*horse*) to go, lifting the feet higher than in walking and moving at a faster rate. * *vt* (*with* **out**) (*inf*) to produce or display repeatedly, esp for others' approval; to produce in a trite or careless manner. * *n* the gait of a horse; a brisk pace.
trotter *n* a horse trained for fast trotting; the foot of an animal, esp a pig.
troubadour *n* a minstrel; a poet or singer.
trouble *vti* to cause trouble to; to worry; to pain; to upset; to cause inconvenience; to take pains (to). * *n* an anxiety; a medical condition causing pain; a problem; unrest or disturbance.—**troublesome** *adj*.
troubleshooter *n* a person whose work is to locate and eliminate a source of trouble or conflict.—**troubleshooting** *n*.
trough *n* a long, narrow container for water or animal feed; a channel in the ground; an elongated area of low barometric pressure.
trounce *vt* to defeat completely.
troupe *n* a travelling company, esp of actors, dancers or acrobats.—**trouper** *n*.
trousers *npl* an item of clothing covering the body from waist to ankle, with two tubes of material for the legs; pants.
trousseau *n* (*pl* **trousseaux, trousseaus**) the clothes and linen a bride collects for her marriage.
trout *n* (*pl* **trout**) a game fish of the salmon family living in fresh water.
trove *see* **treasure trove**.
trowel *n* a hand tool for gardening; a flat-bladed tool for spreading cement, etc.
troy (weight) *n* a system for weighing precious stones and metals, in which one pound = 12 ounces and one ounce = 20 pennyweights or 480 grains.
truant *n* a pupil who is absent from school without permission. * *vi* to play truant.—*also adj*.—**truancy** *n*.
truce *n* an agreement between two armies or states to suspend hostilities.
truck *n* a heavy motor vehicle for transporting goods; a vehicle open at the back for moving goods or animals. * *vt* (*goods*) to convey by truck. * *vi* to drive a truck.
trucker *n* a truck driver.
truculent *adj* sullen; aggressive.—**truculence** *n*.—**truculently** *adv*.
trudge *vti* to travel on foot, heavily or wearily. * *n* a tiring walk.
true *adj* (**truer, truest**) conforming with fact; correct, accurate; genuine; loyal; perfectly in tune. * *adv* truthfully; rightly.
true-blue *adj* staunchly loyal or committed.—**true blue** *n*.
truelove *n* a sweetheart.
truffle *n* a round, edible underground fungus; a sweet made with chocolate, butter and sugar.
truism *n* a self-evident truth.
truly *adv* completely; genuinely; to a great degree.
trump *n* (*cards*) the suit that is chosen to have the highest value in one game. * *vt* to play a trump card on; (*with* **up**) to invent maliciously, fabricate (an accusation, etc).
trumpery *adj* worthless. * *n* (*pl* **trumperies**) foolish talk, nonsense; a worthless article.
trumpet *n* a brass wind instrument consisting of a long tube with a flared end and three buttons. * *vti* to proclaim loudly.—**trumpeter** *n*.
trumpeter swan *n* a rare wild North American swan with a black bill.
truncate *vt* to cut the top end off; to shorten.—**truncation** *n*.
truncheon *n* a short, thick club carried by a policeman.
trundle *vt* (*an object*) to push or pull on wheels. * *vi* to move along slowly.
trunk *n* the main stem of a tree; the torso; the main body of anything; the proboscis of an elephant; a strong box or chest for clothes, etc, esp on a journey; storage space at the rear of an automobile; (*pl*) a man's short, light pants for swimming.
trunk line *n* a transportation system handling through traffic; a communications system.
trunk road *n* a main road.
truss *n* a supporting framework for a roof or bridge; a hernia brace. * *vt* to bind (up).

trust *n* firm belief in the truth of anything, faith in a person; confidence in; custody; a financial arrangement of investing money for another person; a business syndicate. * *adj* held in trust. * *vti* to have confidence in; to believe.—**trustful** *adj*.

trustee *n* a person who has legal control of money or property that they are keeping or investing for another person, or for an organization or institution.—**trusteeship** *n*.

trustworthy *adj* reliable, dependable.

trusty *adj* (**trustier, trustiest**) trustworthy, faithful. * *n* a prisoner granted special privileges as a trustworthy person.—**trustily** *adv*.—**trustiness** *n*.

truth *n* that which is true, factual or genuine; agreement with reality.

truthful *adj* telling the truth; accurate, realistic; honest, frank.—**truthfulness** *n*.

try *vb* (**trying, tried**) *vt* to test the result or effect by experiment; to determine judicially; to put strain on; (*with* **on**) to put (a garment) on to check the fit, etc; (*inf*) to attempt to deceive somebody; (*with* **out**) to test (someone) for a job, etc. * *vi* to attempt; to make an effort; (*with* **out**) to undergo a test (for a job, team, etc). * *n* (*pl* **tries**) an attempt, an effort; (*Rugby football*) a score made with a touchdown.

trying *adj* causing annoyance, exasperating.—**tryingly** *adv*.—**tryingness** *n*.

try-on *n* (*inf*) a trying on of clothes to check the fit; an attempt to deceive.

tryout *n* an experimental test; an audition for a theatrical part; (*sports, etc*) a test for a position in a team.

trypanosome *n* any of genus of parasitic worms that infest the blood of animals and humans and can cause sleeping sickness.

trypanosomiasis *n* (a disease caused by) infection with trypanosomes.

trypsin *n* an enzyme in the pancreas involved in digestion.—**tryptic** *adj*.

tryptophan, tryptophane *n* an amino acid found in proteins which is essential to life.

try square *n* an L-shaped instrument for drawing and testing right angles.

tryst *n* an appointment to meet secretly.

tsar *n* (*formerly*) the title of the emperors of Russia (until 1917) and sovereigns of certain other Slav nations; a powerful person.—*also* **czar**.

tsarevitch *n* the eldest son of a tsar.—*also* **czarevitch**.

tsarina, tsaritsa *n* the wife of a tsar; an empress.—*also* **czarina**.

tsetse fly *n* a fly that feeds on blood and transmits diseases.

T-shirt *n* a short-sleeved casual cotton top.—*also* **tee-shirt**.

tsp. *abbr* = teaspoon.

T-square *n* a T-shaped instrument for drawing and determining right angles.

Tu. *abbr* = Tuesday.

tub *n* a circular container, made of staves and hoops; a bathtub.

tuba *n* a large brass instrument of bass pitch.

tubby *adj* (**tubbier, tubbiest**) plump.

tube *n* a long, thin, hollow pipe; a soft metal or plastic cylinder in which thick liquids or pastes, such as toothpaste, are stored; (*inf*) in UK, the underground railway system.—**tubular** *adj*.

tubeless tyre *n* a tyre that remains airtight without requiring an inner tube.

tuber *n* the swollen, fleshy root of a plant where reserves of food are stored up, as a potato.

tubercle *n* a small round swelling or nodule, esp on bone, skin or a plant; an abnormal lump, esp one characteristic of tuberculosis.

tubercle bacillus *n* a bacterium that causes tuberculosis.

tuberculate *adj* affected with tubercles.—**tuberculation** *n*.

tuberculin *n* a sterile liquid prepared with weakened tubercle bacillus and used in the diagnosis of tuberculosis.

tuberculosis *n* an infectious disease of the lungs.—**tubercular** *adj*.

tuberose *n* a bulbous Mexican plant with fragrant white flowers.

tuberous *adj* (*plants*) forming or resembling tubers.

tubing *n* tubes collectively; a length of tube; the material from which tubes are made; a circular fabric.

tub-thumper *n* a passionate or aggressive public speaker.

tubular bells *npl* an orchestral percussion instrument consisting of a set of long metal tubes played with a mallet to simulate the sounds of bells.

tuck *vt* to draw or gather together in a fold; (*with* **up**) to wrap snugly. * *vi* (*inf*) (*with* **into**) to eat greedily. * *n* a fold in a garment.

tucker *vt* (*inf*) to exhaust, tire (out).

Tue., Tues. *abbr* = Tuesday.

Tuesday *n* the third day of the week.

tufa *n* a type of porous rock deposited from springs.

tuff *n* a type of volcanic rock composed of fused lava ash.

tuffet *n* a small low seat; a clump of grass.

tuft *n* a bunch of grass, hair or feathers held together at the base; a clump.

tug *vti* (**tugging, tugged**) to pull with effort or to drag along. * *n* a strong pull; a tugboat.

tugboat *n* a small powerful boat for towing ships.

tug of love *n* a conflict over the custody of a child between separated parents, etc.

tug of war *n* a contest in which two teams tug on opposite ends of a rope to pull the opposing team over a central line; a struggle for supremacy between two opponents.

tuition *n* teaching, instruction.

tulip *n* a highly-coloured cup-shaped flower grown from bulbs.

tulip tree *n* a North American tree with large tulip-shaped flowers.

tulipwood *n* the soft white wood of the tulip tree used in making furniture.

tulle *n* a delicate semi-transparent fabric of rayon, silk, etc, used for scarfs and veils.

tumble *vi* to fall over; to roll or to twist the body, as an acrobat; (*with* **to**) (*inf*) to discover (a secret, etc); to understand. * *vt* to push or cause to fall. * *n* a fall; a somersault.

tumbledown *adj* dilapidated, crumbling.

tumble-dry *vt* (*clothes*) to dry by rotating with warm air in a machine.—**tumble dryer** *n*.

tumbler *n* a large drinking glass without a handle or stem; an acrobat.

tumbler switch *n* a simple electrical switch used in lighting.

tumbleweed *n* a plant that detaches from its roots and is blown around by the wind.

tumbrel, tumbril *n* a farm cart that tips up to deposit its load; a cart of similar design used to carry prisoners to the guillotine during the French Revolution.

tumescent *adj* swollen or beginning to swell.

tumid *adj* swollen, distended; pompous, bombastic.—**tumidly** *adv*.—**tumidity** *n*.

tummy *n* (*pl* **tummies**) (*inf*) stomach.

tumour, tumor *n* an abnormal growth of tissue in any part of the body.

tumult *n* a commotion; an uproar.

tumultuous *adj* disorderly; rowdy, noisy; restless.—**tumultuously** *adv*.—**tumultuousness** *n*.

tun *n* a large wine or beer cask; a unit of capacity equal to about 252 wine gallons (954 litres).

tuna *n* (*pl* **tuna, tunas**) a large ocean fish of the mackerel group.

tundra *n* a vast treeless arctic plain.

tune *n* a melody; correct musical pitch; harmony. * *vt* (*musical instrument*) to adjust the notes of; (*radio, TV etc*) to adjust the resonant frequency, etc, to a particular value; (*with* **up**) to adjust an engine to improve its performance. * *vi* (*with* **up**) to adjust (musical instruments) to a common pitch before playing.—**tuneful** *adj*.—**tunefully** *adv*.

tune-up *n* an adjustment of a musical instrument to correct pitch or of an engine to improve its performance.

tungsten *n* a hard malleable greyish white metallic element used in lamps, etc, and in alloys with steel.

tunic *n* a hip or knee-length loose, usu belted blouse-like garment; a close-fitting jacket worn by soldiers and policemen.

tunicate *n* any of a group of small primitive marine animals with sac-shaped bodies enclosed in a thick membrane. * *adj* having or enclosed in a membrane; (*bulbs*) made up from concentric layers of tissue.

tuning fork *n* a two-pronged steel fork that produces a fixed note when struck and is used to tune musical instruments or set a pitch for singing.

tunnel *n* an underground passage, esp one for cars or trains underneath a river or town centre. * *vb* (**tunnelling, tunnelled** *or* **tunneling, tunneled**) *vt* to make a way through. * *vi* to make a tunnel.
tunnel vision *n* a condition in which peripheral vision is impaired; a narrowness of viewpoint due to preoccupation with a single idea, plan, etc.
tunny *n* (*pl* **tunnies, tunny**) tuna.
tuppence *n* twopence.
turban *n* a headdress consisting of cloth wound in folds around the head worn by men; a woman's hat of this shape.
turbid *adj* muddy; dense; thick.—**turbidity** *n*.—**turbidly** *adv*.
turbine *n* a machine in which power is produced when the forced passage of steam, water, etc causes the blades to rotate.
turbo- *prefix* of, driven or powered by a turbine.
turbofan *n* a jet engine with a large fan that forces air out with the exhaust gases to increase thrust; an aircraft with such engines; the fan in such an engine.
turbojet *n* (an aircraft with) a turbojet engine.
turbojet engine *n* a gas turbine that provides propulsive power from a jet of hot exhaust gases.
turboprop *n* a jet aircraft engine that also operates a turbine-driven air compressor.
turbot *n* (*pl* **turbot, turbots**) a large, flat, round edible fish.
turbulence *n* a state of confusion and disorder; (*weather*) instability causing gusty air currents.
turbulent *adj* disturbed, in violent commotion.
turd *n* (*vulg*) a piece of excrement; (*vulg sl*) a despicable person.
tureen *n* a large dish for serving soup, etc.
turf *n* (*pl* **turfs, turves**) the surface layer of grass and its roots; (*with* **the**) horse racing; a racetrack. * *vt* to cover with turf; (*with* **out**) (*inf*) to eject forcibly, throw out.
turgid *adj* swollen; pompous, bombastic.—**turgidity** *n*.—**turgidly** *adv*.
Turk *n* a native or inhabitant of Turkey; any speaker of a Turkic language.
Turk. *abbr* = Turkey; Turkish.
turkey *n* (*pl* **turkeys, turkey**) a large bird farmed for its meat.
turkey buzzard *n* an American vulture.
turkey cock *n* a male turkey.
Turkey red *n* (a cotton fabric of) a bright red colour.
Turki *adj* of, being or pertaining to the Turkic languages or speakers of these languages; the Turkic languages collectively.
Turkic *n* a branch of the Altaic family of languages including Turkish, Tartar, etc.
Turkish *adj* pertaining to Turkey, its people or their language. * *n* the official language of Turkey.
Turkish bath *n* a bath with steam rooms, showers, massage, etc.
Turkish coffee *n* strong black (usu sweetened) coffee.
Turkish delight *n* a jelly-like flower-flavoured sweet covered with icing sugar.
Turk's-cap lily *n* a variety of lily with purple-red flowers found in Europe and Asia, martagon lily.
turmeric *n* a tropical Indian plant; the powdered stem of this plant used as a yellow colouring agent and curry spice.
turmoil *n* agitation; disturbance, confusion.
turn *vi* to revolve; to go in the opposite direction; to depend on; to appeal (to) for help; to direct (thought or attention) away from; to change in character; to be shaped on the lathe; (*with* **off**) to leave or deviate from a road, etc; (*with* **in**) (*inf*) to retire to bed for the night; (*with* **on**) to depend on; (*sl*) to take drugs; (*with* **to**) to begin a task; (*with* **up**) to appear, arrive; to find unexpectedly; to happen without warning. * *vt* to change the position or direction of by revolving; to reverse; to transform; (*age, etc*) to have just passed; to change or convert; to invert; (*with* **off**) to cause to cease operating (as if) by flicking a switch, turning a knob, etc; (*inf*) to cause a person to lose interest in or develop a dislike for something; (*with* **down**) to reduce the volume or intensity of (sound, brightness, etc); to refuse, decline; to fold down (sheets, a collar, etc); (*with* **in**) to deliver; to produce, record (a performance, score, etc); (*with* **on**) to cause to begin operating (as if) by flicking a switch, turning a knob, etc; (*sl*) to arouse or excite, esp sexually; (*sl*) to introduce (a person) to drugs; (*with* **up**) to discover, uncover; to increase the volume or intensity of (sound, brightness, etc). * *n* a rotation; new direction or tendency; a place in sequence; a turning point, crisis; performer's act; an act of kindness or malice; a bend.
turnabout *n* a reversal of position, opinion, attitude, etc.
turncoat *n* a deserter, renegade.
turner *n* a person who operates a lathe.
turning *n* a road, path, etc that leads off from a main way; the point where it leads off; a bend; the art of shaping objects on a lathe; an object so made; (*pl*) waste produced on a lathe.
turning point *n* the point at which a significant change occurs.
turnip *n* a plant with a large white or yellow root, cultivated as a vegetable.
turnout *n* a gathering of people.
turnover *n* the volume of business transacted in a given period; a fruit or meat pasty; the rate of replacement of workers.
turnpike *n* a toll road, esp one that is an expressway.
turnround *n* (the time required to complete) the unloading and reloading of a ship, aircraft, etc.
turnstile *n* a mechanical gate across a footpath or entrance which admits only one person at a time.
turntable *n* a circular, horizontal revolving platform, as in a record player.
turn-up *n* the cuff of a trouser; (*inf*) a surprise.
turpentine *n* an oily resin secreted by coniferous trees, used as a solvent and thinner for paints.—*also* **turps**.
turpentine tree *n* a terebinth or related tree that yields a turpentine.
turpitude *n* depravity; wickedness.
turps *n sing* (*inf*) turpentine.
turquoise *n* an opaque greenish-blue mineral, valued as a gem; the colour of turquoise.—*also adj*.
turret *n* a small tower on a building rising above it; a dome or revolving structure for guns, as on a warship, tank or aeroplane.—**turreted** *adj*.
turtle *n* any of an order of land, freshwater or marine reptiles having a soft body encased in a hard shell; **to turn turtle** to turn upside down.
turtledove *n* a brown dove with speckled wings and a dark tail, noted for its cooing and its care for its partner and young.
turtleneck *n* a high close-fitting neckline on a sweater.
turves *see* **turf**.
tusk *n* a long, projecting tooth on either side of the mouth, as of the elephant.—**tusked** *adj*.
tusker *n* an animal with tusks.
tussle *n* a scuffle.
tussock *n* a dense tuft of grass.
tutelage *n* guardianship; guidance by a tutor.
tutor *n* a private teacher who instructs pupils individually; a member of staff responsible for the supervision and teaching of students in a British university. * *vt* to instruct; to act as a tutor.
tutorial *n* a period of tuition by a tutor to an individual or a small group. * *adj* of or pertaining to a tutor.
tutti *adj, adv* (*mus*) all together, to be performed by the whole orchestra. * *n* a musical piece or passage so performed.
tutti-frutti *n* (*pl* **tutti-fruttis**) a type of ice cream containing pieces of chopped candied fruits.
tut-tut *interj* an exclamation of impatience or mild disapproval. * *vi* (**tut-tutting, tut-tutted**) to express disapproval or impatience by uttering "tut-tut".
tutu *n* a short, projecting, layered skirt worn by a ballerina.
tu-whit tu-whoo *interj* an imitation of the cry of an owl.
tuxedo *n* a man's semi-formal suit with a tailless jacket.—*also* **dinner jacket**.
TV *abbr* = television.

TVA *abbr* = Tennessee Valley Authority.

TVP *abbr* = textured vegetable protein; a meat substitute used in vegetarian dishes.

twaddle *n* utter rubbish in speech or writing. * *vi* to speak or write twaddle.

twain *adj, n* (*arch*) two.

twang *n* a sharp, vibrant sound, as of a taut string when plucked; a nasal tone of voice. * *vt* to make a twanging sound.

'twas (*poet*) = it was.

twat *n* an idiot; (*vulg*) the female genitals.

tweak *vt* to twist, pinch or pull with sudden jerks. * *n* a sharp pinch or twist.

twee *adj* (*inf*) excessively quaint, affected.

tweed *n* a twilled woollen fabric used in making clothes.

'tween *prep* (*arch*) between.

tweet *interj* an imitation of the chirp of a small bird. * *vi* to make this sound.

tweeter *n* a small loudspeaker for reproducing high-frequency sounds.

tweezers *n sing* small pincers used for plucking.

twelfth *adj* the last of twelve; being one of twelve equal parts.

Twelfth Day *n* Epiphany.

twelfth man *n* the reserve member of a cricket team.

Twelfth Night *n* the evening of Epiphany, the twelfth day after Christmas, 6 January; the eve of Epiphany, 5th January.

twelve *adj* the cardinal number next after eleven. * *n* the symbol for this (12, XII, xii).

twelve-tone *adj* pertaining to a type of serial music using only the twelve semitones of the chromatic scale as a tone row for compositions.

twelvemo *n* a book of sheets folded into twelve leaves; this book size.—*also* **duodecimo.**

twenty *adj, n* two times ten. * *n* (*pl* **twenties**) the symbol for this (20, XX, xx).—**twentieth** *adj.*

twenty-one *n* pontoon (card game); blackjack.

twenty-twenty, 20/20 *adj* (*vision*) normal.

'twere (*poet*) = it were.

twerp *n* (*inf*) a foolish or contemptible person.—*also* **twirp.**

twice *adv* two times; two times as much; doubly.

twiddle *vt* to twirl or fiddle with idly.

twig[1] *n* a small branch or shoot of a tree.—**twiggy** *adj.*

twig[2] *vti* (**twigging, twigged**) (*inf*) to grasp the meaning of.

twilight *n* the dim light just after sunset and before sunrise; the final stages of something.

twilit *adj* lit by twilight.

twill *n* a cloth woven in such a way as to produce diagonal lines across it.—**twilled** *adj.*

twin *n* either of two persons or animals born at the same birth; one thing resembling another. * *adj* double; very like another; consisting of two parts nearly alike. * *vt* (**twinning, twinned**) to pair together.

twin bed *n* one of a pair of single beds.

twine *n* a string of twisted fibres or hemp. * *vti* to twist together; to wind around.

twin-engined *adj* (*aircraft*) having two engines.

twinge *n* a sudden, stabbing pain; an emotional pang.

twinkle *vi* to sparkle; to flicker.

twinkling *n* a wink; an instant; the shining of the stars.

twin-screw *adj* (*vessel*) having two propellers.

twinset *n* a jumper and cardigan designed to be worn together.

twin-tub *n* a washing machine with two drums, one for washing and the other for spin-drying.

twirl *vt* to whirl; to rotate; to wind or twist. * *vi* to turn around rapidly.

twirp *see* **twerp.**

twist *vt* to unite by winding together; to coil; to confuse or distort (the meaning of); to bend. * *vi* to revolve; to writhe. * *n* the act or result of twisting; a twist of thread; a curve or bend; an unexpected event; a wrench.

twister *n* a tornado; (*inf*) a dishonest person, a swindler.

twisty *adj* (**twistier, twistiest**) winding.

twit[1] *vt* (**twitting, twitted**) to tease or reproach. * *n* a nervous state.

twit[2] *n* (*Brit inf*) a silly or foolish person.

twitch *vt* to pull with a sudden jerk. * *vi* to be suddenly jerked. * *n* a sudden muscular spasm.

twitter *n* a chirp, as of a bird. * *vi* to chirp.

two *adj, n* the cardinal number next above one. * *n* the symbol for this (2, II, ii).

two-cycle *see* **two-stroke.**

two-dimensional *adj* of or having two dimensions; lacking (the illusion of) depth.

two-edged *adj* having two cutting edges; (*remark, etc*) double-edged.

two-faced *adj* deceitful, hypocritical.

twofold *adj* multiplied by two; double. * *adv* doubly.

two-handed *adj* having or needing two hands; ambidextrous; requiring two people.

twopence *n* the sum of two pence; in UK, a coin of this value; something of little value.—*also* **tuppence.**

two-piece *n* a garment consisting of two separate matching bits.—*also adj.*

two-ply *adj* made of two thicknesses or strands.

twosome *n* a group of two; a game for two people.

two-step *n* (the music for) a ballroom dance in duple time.

two-stroke *n, adj* (an internal combustion engine) having a piston which makes two strokes for every explosion.—*also* **two-cycle.**

two-time *vti* (*sl*) to be unfaithful to (a lover, etc); to double-cross.—**two-timer** *n.*

two-tone *adj* of two colours or shades of the same colour; (*sirens, etc*) having two notes.

two-way *adj* allowing movement or operation in two (opposite) directions; involving two participants; involving mutual obligation; (*radio, telephone*) capable of transmitting and receiving messages.

two-way mirror *n* a sheet of glass that reflects as a mirror on one side but can be seen through from the other.

'twould (*poet*) = it would.

TX *abbr* = Texas.

tycoon *n* a powerful industrialist, etc.

tyke *n* a (mongrel) dog; (*inf*) a cheeky child.—*also* **tike.**

tympani, tympany *see* **timpani.**

tympanic bone *n* a bone enclosing part of the middle ear and supporting the tympanic membrane.

tympanic membrane *n* the eardrum.

tympanites *n* distension of the abdomen caused by the accumulation of gas in the intestine.—**tympanitic** *adj.*

tympanitis *n* inflammation of the eardrum.

tympanum *n* (*pl* **tympanums, tympana**) the cavity of the middle ear; the tympanic membrane, eardrum; the space between the lintel of a doorway and the enclosing arch; the (recessed) triangular face of a pediment.

type *n* a kind, class or group; sort; model; a block of metal for printing letters; style of print. * *vt* to write by means of a typewriter; to classify.

-type *n suffix* of the form specified; printing process.

typecast *vt* (**typecasting, typecast**) (*actor*) to cast in the same role repeatedly because of physical appearance, etc.

typeface *n* the printing surface of a type character; a particular design of a set of type characters.

typescript *n* a typed copy of a book, document, etc.

typeset *vt* (**typesetting, typeset**) to set in type.—**typesetter** *n.*

typewriter *n* a keyboard machine for printing characters.

typhoid *n* typhoid fever. * *adj* of or pertaining to typhoid fever (—*also* **typhoidal**).

typhoid fever *n* an acute infectious disease acquired by ingesting contaminated food or water.

typhoon *n* a violent tropical cyclone originating in the western Pacific.

typhus *n* a highly contagious acute disease spread by body lice and characterized by fever, a rash and headache.—**typhous** *adj.*

typical *adj* representative of a particular type; characteristic.—**typicality** *n*.—**typically** *adv*.
typify *vt* (**typifying, typified**) to characterize.—**typification** *n*.
typist *n* a person who uses a typewriter, esp as a job.
typo *n* (*pl* **typos**) (*inf*) a typographical error.
typography *n* the way in which printed material is designed or set for printing.—**typographic, typographical** *adj*.
tyrannicide *n* (a person responsible for) the killing of a tyrant.
tyrannize *vi* to exercise power (over) in a vicious and oppressive manner. * *vt* to crush, oppress.—**tyrannizer** *n*.
tyrannosaur, tyrannosaurus *n* a large carnivorous dinosaur of the Cretaceous period which stood on powerful hind legs.
tyranny *n* (*pl* **tyrannies**) the government or authority of a tyrant; harshness; oppression.
tyrant *n* a person who uses his or her power arbitrarily and oppressively; a despot.—**tyrannical** *adj*.
tyre *n* a protective, usu rubber, covering around the rim of a wheel.—*also* **tire**.
tyro *n* (*pl* **tyros**) a novice, a beginner.—*also* **tiro**.
tzar *n* a czar.—**tzarevitch** *n*.—**tzarina** *n*.
tzatsiki *n* a Greek dip made from plain yogurt, shredded cucumber, and mint.**U** *abbr* = uranium; (*cinema*) universal (suitable for all age groups).

U

U, u *n* the 21st letter of the English alphabet; something shaped like a U.
UAE *abbr* = United Arab Emirates.
ubiety *n* the state of being in a specific place.
ubiquitous *adj* existing, or seeming to exist everywhere at once.—**ubiquity** *n*.
U-boat *n* a German submarine.
uc *abbr* = upper case.
udder *n* a milk-secreting organ containing two or more teats, as in cows.
UFO *abbr* = unidentified flying object.
ufology *n* the study of UFOs.—**ufologist** *n*.
ugh *interj* an expression of disgust, dislike or horror.
ugli, ugli fruit *n* (*pl* **uglis, uglies**) a citrus fruit that is a cross between a grapefruit and a tangerine.
ugly *adj* (**uglier, ugliest**) unsightly; unattractive; repulsive; ill tempered.—**ugliness** *n*.
ugly duckling *n* an initially unpromising person or thing that turns out successfully.
UHF *abbr* = ultrahigh frequency.
uh-huh *interj* used to indicate assent or agreement.
UHT *abbr* = ultra-heat treated (milk or cream).
UK *abbr* = United Kingdom.
ukelele, ukulele *n* a small, four-stringed guitar.
ulcer *n* an open sore on the surface of the skin or a mucous membrane.—**ulcerous** *adj*
ulcerate *vti* to make or become ulcerous.
-ule *n suffix* smallness.
ulema *n* (a member of) a body of Muslim theologians and religious scholars.
-ulent *adj suffix* abundant.
ullage *n* the amount by which a container (e.g. a barrel) is less than full.
ulna *n* (*pl* **ulnas, ulnae**) the longer and thinner of the two bones in the human forearm; the corresponding bone in the forelimb of other vertebrates.—**ulnar** *adj*.
ulnar nerve *n* a nerve in the forearm that passes close to the skin surface at the elbow.
ulotrichous *adj* having woolly or curly hair.
ulster *n* a long heavy double-breasted overcoat with a belt.
Ulsterman *n* (*pl* **Ulstermen**) a native or inhabitant of Ulster (a former province of Ireland now divided between Northern Ireland and the Republic of Ireland).—**Ulsterwoman** (*pl* **Ulsterwomen**) *nf*.
ulterior *adj* (*motives*) hidden, not evident; subsequent.
ultima *n* the last syllable of a word.
ultimate *adj* last; final; most significant; essential. * *n* the most significant thing.—**ultimately** *adv*.
ultimatum *n* (*pl* **ultimatums, ultimata**) the final proposal, condition or terms in negotiations.
ultimogeniture *n* (*law*) inheritance by the youngest son.
ultra *adj* extreme, uncompromising. * *n* an extremist.
ultra- *prefix* beyond.
ultraconservative *adj* deeply conservative or reactionary. * *n* a reactionary person.
ultrafiche *n* a type of high-density microfiche containing a very large number of microcopies.
ultrahigh frequency *n* a radio frequency in the range between 300 megahertz and 3000 megahertz.
ultraism *n* the advocacy of extreme action.—**ultraist** *n*.
ultramarine *adj* deep blue. * *n* a blue pigment; a vivid, deep blue.
ultramicroscope *n* an optical device for viewing tiny particles undetectable by a conventional microscope.—**ultramicroscopic** *adj*.
ultrashort *adj* (*radio wave*) having a wavelength less than 10 metres.
ultrasonic *adj* (*waves, vibrations*) having a frequency beyond the human ear's audible range.
ultrasound *n* ultrasonic waves used in medical diagnosis and therapy.
ultraviolet *adj* of light waves, shorter than the wavelengths of visible light and longer than X-rays.
ultraviolet light *n* ultraviolet radiation.
ultravirus *n* a virus small enough to pass through the finest filter.
ululate *vi* to howl or wail, as with pain or grief.—**ululant** *adj*.—**ululation** *n*.
umbel *n* a flower-cluster characteristic of plants of the carrot family, in which the stalks grow from the same place on the main stem producing an umbrella effect.—**umbellate** *adj*.
umbelliferous *adj* of or pertaining to a family of plants and shrubs bearing umbels, including carrots, parsley and fennel.—**umbellifer** *n*.
umber *n* a brown pigment. * *adj* dark brown.
umbilical *n* of, pertaining to, near, or resembling the navel.
umbilical cord *n* the vascular tube connecting a foetus with the placenta through which oxygen and nutrients are passed.
umbilicate, umbilicated *n* depressed or shaped like a navel; having an umbilicus.—**umbilication** *n*.
umbilicus *n* (*pl* **umbilici**) the navel; a navel-shaped depression on a plant or animal.
umbo *n* (*pl* **umbones, umbos**) the boss in the centre of a shield; a rounded anatomical protrusion.
umbra *n* (*pl* **umbrae, umbras**) an area of total shadow, esp during an eclipse; the dark centre of a sunspot.—**umbral** *adj*.
umbrage *n* resentment; offence.
umbrella *n* a cloth-covered collapsible frame carried in the hand for protection from rain or sun; a general protection.
umiak *n* an Eskimo boat made from hide stretched over a wooden frame.—*also* **oomiak**.
umlaut *n* the mark (¨) placed over a vowel in German and other languages to modify its sound; the change of a vowel brought about by its assimilation to another vowel.
umpire *n* an official who enforces the rules in sport; an arbitrator.—*also vti*.
umpteen *adj* (*inf*) an undetermined large number.—**umpteenth** *adj*.
UN *abbr* = United Nations.
un- *prefix* not; opposite of; contrary to; reversal of an action or state.
'un, un *pron* (*dial*) one.
unable *adj* not able; lacking the strength, skill, power or opportunity (to do something).
unaccountable *adj* inexplicable, puzzling; not to be called to account for one's actions.

unaccustomed *adj* (*with* **to**) not used (to); not usual or familiar.

una corda *adj, adv* (*mus*) (*piano*) to be played with the soft pedal depressed.

unadulterated *adj* pure, unmixed.

unadvised *adj* unwise, imprudent; not advised.—**unadvisedly** *adv*.

unaffected *adj* sincere, frank, without pretension; not influenced or affected.—**unaffectedly** *adv*.

un-American *adj* contrary to US customs, ideals or interests.—**un-Americanism** *n*.

unanimous *adj* showing complete agreement.—**unanimity** *n*.—**unanimously** *adv*.

unapproachable *adj* aloof, unfriendly; impossible to reach; not to be equalled or rivalled.

unarmed *adj* not in possession of weapons; defenceless.

unasked *adj* not asked or asked for; not invited or requested; spontaneous. * *adv* of one's own accord; without prompting.

unassailable *adj* not open to attack; not open to criticism or doubt.

unassuming *adj* unpretentious; modest.

unattached *adj* unmarried, not engaged to be married; not belonging to a particular group, organization, etc.

unattended *adj* not supervised; not accompanied.

unauthorized *adj* not endorsed by authority.

unavailing *adj* futile, hopeless.—**unavailingly** *adv*.

unavoidable *adj* bound to happen, inevitable; necessary, compulsory.—**unavoidably** *adv*.

unaware *adj* not conscious or aware (of); ignorant (of).

unawares *adv* by surprise; unexpectedly, without warning.

unbalanced *adj* mentally unstable; having bias or over-representing a particular view, group, interest, etc; (*bookkeeping*) not having equal debit and credit totals.

unbearable *adj* intolerable, not able to be endured.—**unbearably** *adv*.

unbeatable *adj* impossible to beat; outstanding, excellent.

unbeaten *adj* not beaten, unsurpassed.

unbecoming *adj* (*clothes, make-up, etc*) not enhancing the wearer's appearance; (*behaviour*) not suitable or seemly.

unbeknown *adj* (*with* **to**) happening without (a person's) knowledge.

unbelief *n* disbelief, scepticism, esp in religious matters.

unbelievable *adj* not able to be believed; incredible.—**unbelievably** *adv*.

unbeliever *n* a person who does not believe, esp in a religion.

unbelieving *adj* lacking belief; sceptical.—**unbelievingly** *adv*.

unbend *vb* (**unbending, unbent**) *vt* to straighten from a bent shape; to release or untie (eg a rope). * *vi* to become more relaxed, affable or informal in manner.

unbending *adj* severe, stern; inflexible, unchanging; rigid in behaviour or attitude.

unbiased, unbiassed *adj* without prejudice or bias; impartial, even-handed, disinterested.

unbidden *adj* not commanded, asked for or invited.

unblushing *adj* shameless, impudent.—**unblushingly** *adv*.

unborn *adj* not yet born; still to appear or happen in the future.

unbosom *vt* to reveal the thoughts or feelings of (oneself).

unbounded *adj* without limits.

unbowed *adj* not bowed; not subdued, free.

unbridled *adj* unrestrained; (*horse*) having no bridle.

unbroken *adj* whole, in one piece; continuous, uninterrupted; (*record*) not yet beaten; (*horses, etc*) wild, untamed; organized, disciplined.

unburden *vt* to reveal or confess one's troubles, secrets, etc to another in order to relieve the mind; to take off a burden.

unbutton *vt* to unfasten the buttons of (a garment).

unbuttoned *adj* unfastened; (*inf*) free, uninhibited.

uncalled-for *adj* unnecessary, unwanted, unwarranted.

uncanny *adj* (**uncannier, uncanniest**) odd; unexpected; suggestive of supernatural powers; unearthly.

unceremonious *adj* without ceremony, informal; abrupt, rude.—**unceremoniously** *adv*.

uncertain *adj* not knowing accurately, doubtful; (*with* **of**) not confident or sure; not fixed, variable, changeable.—**uncertainty** *n*.

uncertainty principle *n* (*phys*) the principle that it is impossible to determine accurately both the position and momentum of an elementary particle simultaneously.—*also* **Heisenberg uncertainty principle**.

uncharted *adj* not marked on a map; unsurveyed, unexplored.

unchristian *adj* contrary to Christian belief or principle; savage, pagan.

uncial *adj* written in or resembling large rounded capital letters as used in early medieval Greek and Latin manuscripts. * *n* an uncial character or manuscript.

uncinate *adj* (*plant, animal*) having a hook-shaped part.

uncircumcised *adj* not circumcised; not Jewish; impure.—**uncircumcision** *n*.

uncivil *adj* lacking in manners, impolite.—**uncivility** *n*.

uncivilized *adj* not civilized, unsophisticated; remote, wild.

uncle *n* the brother of one's father or mother; the husband of one's aunt.

unclean *adj* not clean, contaminated; ceremonially defiled.

Uncle Sam *n* the government of the US personified.

Uncle Tom *n* (*derog*) a Black person who acts in a servile manner to white people.

unclothe *vt* (**unclothing, unclothed** *or* **unclad**) to remove the clothes from; to uncover.

uncoil *vti* to (cause to) unwind.

uncomfortable *adj* causing discomfort; feeling discomfort or unease.

uncommitted *adj* not bound to a particular cause, belief or course of action.

uncommon *adj* rare, unusual; extraordinary.

uncommonly *adv* hardly ever; exceptionally, particularly.

uncommunicative *adj* not willing to talk or express an opinion, etc; reserved.

uncompromising *adj* not prepared to compromise; inflexible, obstinate.

unconcern *n* indifference.

unconcerned *adj* not involved in or concerned with; not troubled.

unconditional *adj* without restrictions or conditions, absolute.

unconscionable *adj* unscrupulous; unreasonable.—**unconscionably** *adv*.

unconscious *adj* not aware (of); lacking normal perception by the senses, insensible; unintentional. * *n* the deepest level of mind containing feelings and emotions of which one is unaware and unable to control.—**unconsciously** *adv*.

unconsciousness *n* the state of being without the senses, as when knocked out.

unconstitutional *adj* contrary to the constitution of a country.—**unconstitutionality** *n*.

unconventional *adj* not bound by social rules or conventions.—**unconventionally** *adv*.

uncork *vt* to pull the cork from a bottle; (*emotions, desires, etc*) to unleash, give vent to.

uncouple *vti* to disconnect or become disconnected.

uncouth *adj* lacking in manners; rough; rude.—**uncouthness** *n*.

uncover *vt* to remove the cover from; to reveal or expose; to remove one's hat in greeting or out of respect.

uncovered *adj* not having a cover; revealed; not having any insurance or security; with one's hat removed out of respect, etc.

UNCTAD *abbr* = United Nations Conference on Trade and Development.

unction *n* an anointing, as for medical or religious purposes; anything that soothes or comforts; affected sincerity.

unctuous *adj* oily; smarmy; too suave; insincerely charming.—**unctuously** *adv*.—**unctuousness** *n*.

uncurl *vti* to straighten; to straighten up, relax.

uncut *adj* not cut; (*book*) not having the folds of the leaves trimmed or slit; (*gemstone*) not cut into shape; not abridged.

undaunted *adj* fearless; not discouraged.—**undauntedly** *adv*.

undecagon *n* a polygon with eleven sides.

undeceive *vt* to free from deception or error.

undecided *adj* doubtful, hesitant; (*solution, etc*) not determined.—**undecidedly** *adv*.

undeniable *adj* readily apparent, obviously true; unquestionably excellent.

under *prep* lower than; beneath the surface of; below; covered by; subject to; less than, falling short of. * *adv* beneath, below, lower down. * *adj* lower in position, degree or rank; subordinate.

under- *prefix* beneath, below.

underachieve *vi* to perform less well than expected given one's potential.—**underachiever** *n*.

underact *vt* to perform (a dramatic role) without proper conviction or emphasis.

underage *adj* below the normal or legal age.

underarm *adj* of, for, in, or used on the area under the arm, or armpit; done with the hand below the level of the elbow or shoulder.

underbelly *n* (*pl* **underbellies**) the underside of an animal, etc; the most vulnerable part of something.

underbid *vb* (**underbidding, underbid**) *vt* to bid a lower amount than (rivals); (*bridge, etc*) to bid less than the strength of the hand merits. * *vi* to bid too low.

undercapitalized *adj* (*business*) having insufficient capital to operate efficiently.

undercarriage *n* the landing gear of an aeroplane; a car's supporting framework.

undercharge *vt* to charge below the fair price.

underclass *n* those least privileged people in society who fall outside the normal social scale, characterized by poverty, unemployment, poor education, social instability, etc.

underclothes *npl* underwear.—*also* **underclothing.**

undercoat *n* a coat of paint, etc, applied as a base below another; a growth of hair or fur under another; a coat worn under an overcoat.

undercover *adj* done or operating secretly.

undercurrent *n* a hidden current under water; an emotion, opinion, etc, not apparent.

undercut *vt* (**undercutting, undercut**) to charge less than a competitor; to undermine.

underdeveloped *adj* not fully grown, immature; (*societies*) having an inadequate social and political infrastructure for sustained economic growth; (*film*) not processed long enough to form a proper image.

underdog *n* the loser in an encounter, contest, etc; a person in an inferior position.

underdone *adj* not sufficiently or completely cooked.

underdressed *adj* wearing clothes that are too informal for a particular occasion.

underemployed *adj* not fully or most efficiently employed.

underestimate *vti* to set too low an estimate on or for. * *n* too low an estimate.

underexpose *vt* (*photog*) to fail to expose (film) to light sufficiently long to produce a good image.—**underexposed** *adj*.—**underexposure** *n*.

underfelt *n* a layer of thick felt between a carpet and floor.

underfoot *adv* underneath the foot or feet; on the ground.

undergarment *n* a piece of underwear or clothing worn beneath other outer clothing.

undergo *vt* (**undergoing, underwent,** *pp* **undergone**) to experience, suffer, endure.

undergraduate *n* a student at a college or university studying for a first degree.

underground *adj* situated under the surface of the ground; secret; of non-commercial newspapers, movies, etc that are unconventional, radical, etc. * *n* a secret group working for the overthrow of the government or the expulsion of occupying forces; an underground railway system; a subway.

undergrowth *n* shrubs, plants, etc growing beneath trees.

underhand *adv* (*sport*) with an underarm motion; underhandedly.

underhanded *adj* sly, secret, deceptive.—**underhandedly** *adv*.

underlay *n* a material, lining laid beneath another for support; felt or rubber laid beneath a carpet for insulation, etc.

underlie *vt* (**underlying, underlay,** *pp* **underlain**) to be situated under; to form the basis of.

underline *vt* to put a line underneath; to emphasize.

underling *n* a person of inferior rank or status to someone else; a subordinate.

underlying *adj* existing, but hard to detect; fundamental, supporting.

undermentioned *adj* mentioned below or later in the text.

undermine *vt* to wear away, or weaken; to injure or weaken, esp by subtle or insidious means.

underneath *adv* under. * *adj* lower. * *n* the underside.—*also prep*.

undernourished *adj* consuming or supplied with less than the minimum quantity of food necessary for normal health and growth.

underpants *npl* pants worn as an undergarment by men and boys.

underpass *n* a section of road running beneath another road, a railway, etc.

underpin *vt* to strengthen or support from beneath.

underpinning *n* the material used to support a structure, the foundation.

underplay *vt* to perform (a dramatic role) with restraint; to play down the importance of.

underprivileged *adj* lacking the basic rights of other members of society; poor.

underproof *adj* containing less alcohol per volume than proof spirit.

underrate *vt* to undervalue, to underestimate.

underscore *vt* to draw a line under; to emphasize.

undersea *adj, adv* below the surface of the sea.

underseal *n* a protective layer of tar, etc applied to the underside of a vehicle. * *vt* to apply this protective layer.

undersecretary *n* (*pl* **undersecretaries**) a senior civil servant in Great Britain; in US, a secretary immediately subordinate to a principal.

undersell *vt* (**underselling, undersold**) to sell at a reduced price; to sell at a price lower than (someone else); to promote with moderation.

undersexed *adj* having a weaker than normal sex drive.

undershirt *n* a vest.

undershoot *vti* (**undershooting, undershot**) to (cause to) land short of a runway; to shoot short of a target.

underside *n* the lower surface.

undersigned *adj* signed at the end. * *n* a person who signs his or her name at the end of a document.

undersized *adj* less than usual size.

underskirt *n* a woman's undergarment worn beneath the skirt, a petticoat.

underslung *adj* suspended from above; (*vehicle chassis*) suspended below the axles

understand *vb* (**understanding, understood**) *vt* to comprehend; to realize; to believe; to assume; to know thoroughly (eg a language); to accept; to be sympathetic with. * *vi* to comprehend; to believe.—**understandable** *adj*.

understanding *n* comprehension; compassion, sympathy; personal opinion, viewpoint; mutual agreement. * *adj* sympathetic.

understate *vt* to state something in restrained terms; to represent as less than is the case.—**understatement** *n*.

understudy *vti* (**understudying, understudied**) to learn a role or part so as to be able to replace (the actor playing it); to act as an understudy (to).—*also n*.

undertake *vt* (**undertaking, undertook,** *pp* **undertaken**) to attempt to; to agree to; to commit oneself; to promise; to guarantee.

undertaker *n* a funeral director.

undertaking *n* enterprise; task; promise; obligation.

underthings *npl* underwear.

undertone *n* a hushed tone of voice; an undercurrent of feeling; a pale colour.

undertow *n* the backwash from a breaking wave; an undercurrent moving in a different direction from the surface current.

undervalue *vt* (**undervaluing, undervalued**) to put too low a price or value on.—**undervaluation** *n*.

underwater *adj* being carried on under the surface of the water, esp the sea; submerged; below the water line of a vessel.—*also adv*.

under way *adv* in or into motion or progress.
underwear *n* garments worn underneath one's outer clothes, next to the skin.
underweight *adj* weighing less than normal or necessary.
underwent *see* **undergo.**
underwhelm *vt* to disappoint.
underworld *n* criminals as an organized group; (*myth*) Hades.
underwrite *vt* to agree to finance (an undertaking, etc); to sign one's name to (an insurance policy), thus assuming liability. * *vi* to work as an underwriter.—**underwriter** *n.*
undesirable *adj* not desirable; not pleasant; objectionable.—**undesirability** *n.*—**undesirably** *adv.*
undetermined *adj* not yet decided; not discovered.
undies *npl* (*inf*) women's underwear.
undo *vt* (**undoing, undid,** *pp* **undone**) to untie or unwrap; to reverse (what has been done); to bring ruin on.
undone *adj* not done; not fastened or tied.
undoubted *adj* without doubt; definite, certain.—**undoubtedly** *adv.*
undreamed, undreamt *n* (*with* **of**) not thought of or imagined.
undress *vt* to remove the clothes from. * *vi* to take off one's clothes.
undressed *adj* not dressed, partially or informally clothed; (*wound*) not bandaged; (*food*) not prepared for serving; (*hides*) not processed.
undue *adj* improper; excessive.
undulate *vti* to move or cause to move like waves; to have or cause to have a wavy form or surface.
undulation *n* a wavelike form or motion.
unduly *adv* too; excessively; improperly.
undying *adj* eternal.
unearned *adj* (*income*) not earned by labour or skill; undeserved.
unearth *vt* to dig up from the earth; to discover; to reveal.
unearthly *adj* mysterious; eerie; supernatural; absurd, unreasonable.
uneasy *adj* uncomfortable; restless; anxious; disquieting.—**uneasily** *adv.*—**uneasiness** *n.*
uneatable *adj* (*food*) not edible, esp because of its condition or appearance.
uneconomic *adj* wasteful; unprofitable.
unemployable *adj* not fit or acceptable for work.
unemployed *adj* not having a job, out of work.—**unemployment** *n.*
unequal *adj* not equal; not regular or uniform; not sufficiently strong or able.—**unequally** *adv.*
unequalled, unequaled *adj* not equalled; supreme.
unequivocal *adj* unambiguous; plain; clear.—**unequivocally** *adv.*
unerring *adj* sure, unfailing.
UNESCO *abbr* = United Nations Educational, Scientific and Cultural Organization.
uneven *adj* not level or smooth; variable; not divisible by two without leaving a remainder.—**unevenness** *n.*
uneventful *adj* ordinary, routine.—**uneventfully** *adv.*
unexampled *adj* without precedent or comparison.
unexceptionable *adj* irreproachable.
unexceptional *adj* ordinary, normal.
unexpected *adj* not looked for, unforeseen.—**unexpectedly** *adv.*
unfailing *adj* not failing or giving up; persistent; constant, dependable.—**unfailingly** *adv.*
unfair *adj* unjust; unequal; against the rules.—**unfairly** *adv.*—**unfairness** *n.*
unfaithful *adj* disloyal; not abiding by a promise; adulterous.—**unfaithfully** *adv.*—**unfaithfulness** *n.*
unfamiliar *adj* not known, strange; (*with* **with**) not familiar.
unfasten *vt* to open or become opened; to undo or become undone; to loose, loosen.
unfathomable *adj* not able to be measured; incomprehensible.
unfavourable, unfavorable *adj* negative, disapproving; adverse.
unfeeling *adj* callous, hardhearted.—**unfeelingly** *adv.*
unfinished *adj* not finished, incomplete; in the making; crude, sketchy.
unfit *adj* unsuitable; in bad physical condition.
unflappable *adj* (*inf*) calm, not easily agitated.
unflinching *adj* calm, steadfast.—**unflinchingly** *adv.*
unfold *vti* to open or spread out; to become revealed; to develop.
unforeseen *adj* unsuspected.
unforgettable *adj* never to be forgotten; fixed in the mind; impressive, exceptional.—**unforgettably** *adv.*
unfortunate *adj* unlucky; disastrous; regrettable. * *n* an unlucky person.
unfortunately *adv* regrettably, unluckily, unhappily.
unfounded *adj* groundless; baseless.
unfreeze *vti* (**unfreezing, unfroze, unfrozen**) to (cause to) thaw; to remove restrictions on (wage or price rises, etc).
unfrock *vt* to remove (a person in holy orders) from ecclesiastical office.
unfurl *vti* to open; to unfold.
ungainly *adj* (**ungainlier, ungainliest**) awkward; clumsy.—**ungainliness** *n.*
ungodly *adj* (**ungoldier, ungodliest**) not religious; sinful; wicked; (*inf*) outrageous.
ungovernable *adj* not able to be controlled or restrained.
unguarded *adj* without protection, vulnerable; open to attack; careless; candid, frank.—**unguardedly** *adv.*
unguent *n* a lubricant or ointment.
ungulate *n, adj* (an animal) having hooves.
unhallowed *adj* not consecrated; sinful.
unhappy *adj* (**unhappier, unhappiest**) not happy or fortunate; sad; wretched; not suitable.—**unhappily** *adv.*—**unhappiness** *n.*
unhealthy *adj* (**unhealthier, unhealthiest**) not healthy or fit, sick; encouraging or resulting from poor health; harmful, degrading; dangerous.—**unhealthily** *adv.*—**unhealthiness** *n.*
unheard *adj* not heard; not listened to.
unheard-of *adj* not known before; without precedent.
unhinge *vt* to make crazy, derange.
unholy *adj* (**unholier, unholiest**) wicked; (*inf*) outrageous, enormous.
unhook *vt* to remove from a hook; to unfasten the hooks of (a garment).
uni *n* (*inf*) university.
uni- *prefix* one; single.
unicameral *adj* of or having only one legislative chamber.—**unicamerally** *adv.*
UNICEF *abbr* = United Nations International Children's Emergency Fund, now United Nations Children's Fund.
unicellular *adj* (*microorganisms, etc*) consisting of a single cell.—**unicellularity** *n.*
unicorn *n* an imaginary creature with a body like a horse and a single horn on the forehead.
unicycle *n* a pedal-driven cycle with a single wheel, used by circus and street entertainers.
unidirectional *adj* involving, going in, or operating in one direction only.
uniform *adj* unchanging in form; consistent; identical. * *n* the distinctive clothes worn by members of the same organization, such as soldiers, schoolchildren.—**uniformly** *adv.*
uniformity *n* (*pl* **uniformities**) the state of being consistent or the same; dullness, monotony.
unify *vt* (**unifying, unified**) to make into one; to unite.—**unification** *n.*
unilateral *adj* involving one only of several parties; not reciprocal.—**unilateralism** *n.*—**unilaterally** *adv.*
unimpeachable *adj* completely honest, truthful, etc; irreproachable.—**unimpeachably** *adv.*
uninhibited *adj* not repressed or restrained; relaxed, spontaneous.—**uninhibitedly** *adv.*
uninterested *adj* lacking interest; not concerned, indifferent.—**uninterestedly** *adv.*
union *n* the act of uniting; a combination of several things; a confederation of individuals or groups; marriage; a trades union.
unionist *n* an advocate or supporter of union or unionism.—**unionism** *n.*
unionize *vt* to organize (employees) into a trade union.—**unionization** *n.*
Union Jack *n* the national flag of the UK.
unipolar *adj* of, produced by, or having a single electric or magnetic pole.—**unipolarity** *n.*

unique *adj* without equal; the only one of its kind.—**uniquely** *adv*.
unisex *adj* of a style that can be worn by both sexes.
unisexual *adj* of one sex only; having male or female sex organs but not both.—**unisexually** *adv*.—**unisexuality** *n*.
unison *n* accordance of sound, concord, harmony; **in unison** simultaneously, in agreement, in harmony.
unit *n* the smallest whole number, one; a single or whole entity; (*measurement*) a standard amount; an establishment or group of people who carry out a specific function; a piece of furniture fitting together with other pieces.—**unitary** *adj*.
unite *vti* to join into one, to combine; to be unified in purpose.
United Kingdom *n* Great Britain and Northern Ireland.
United Nations *n sing or pl* an international organization of nations for world peace and security formed in 1945.
United States *n* a federation of states, esp the United States of America.
unit trust *n* a company that manages a range of investments on behalf of members of the public whose interests are looked after by an independent trust.
unity *n* (*pl* **unities**) oneness; harmony; concord.
Univ. *abbr* = university.
universal *adj* widespread; general; relating to all the world or the universe; relating to or applicable to all mankind.—**universally** *adv*.—**universality** *n* (*pl* **universalities**).
universe *n* all existing things; (*astron*) the totality of space, stars, planets and other forms of matter and energy; the world.
university *n* (*pl* **universities**) an institution of higher education which confers bachelors' and higher degrees; the campus or staff of a university.
unjust *adj* not characterized by justice; not fair.—**unjustly** *adv*.—**unjustness** *n*.
unkempt *adj* uncombed; slovenly, dishevelled.
unkind *adj* lacking in kindness or sympathy; harsh; cruel.—**unkindly** *adv*.—**unkindness** *n*.
unknown *adj* not known; not famous; not understood; with an unknown value. * *n* an unknown person or thing.
unleaded *adj* (*petrol*) not mixed with tetraethyl lead.
unleash *vt* to release from a leash; to free from restraint.
unleavened *adj* (*bread, etc*) made without yeast or other raising agent.
unless *conj* if not; except that.
unlettered *adj* illiterate.
unlike *adj* not the same, dissimilar. * *prep* not like; not characteristic of.—**unlikeness** *n*.
unlikely *adj* improbable; unpromising.
unlimited *adj* without limits; boundless; not restricted.—**unlimitedly** *adv*.
unlisted *adj* not on a list; ex-directory.
unload *vti* to remove a load, discharge freight from a truck, ship, etc; to relieve of or express troubles, etc; to dispose of, dump; to empty, esp a gun.
unlock *vt* (*door, lock, etc*) to unfasten; to let loose; to reveal; to release.
unloose, unloosen *vt* to relax (a grip, etc); to release, free; to untie.
unlovely *n* ugly, unpleasant.—**unloveliness** *n*.
unlucky *adj* (**unluckier, unluckiest**) not lucky, not fortunate; likely to bring misfortune; regrettable.
unman *vt* (**unmanning, unmanned**) to weaken the nerve or courage of; to make effeminate.
unmanly *adj* weak, cowardly; effeminate.—**unmanliness** *n*.
unmanned *adj* (*spacecraft, etc*) not manned, operated by remote control.
unmannerly *adj* lacking good manners; rude.—**unmannerliness** *n*.
unmask *vti* to remove the mask from; to expose, show up.
unmentionable *adj* too bad, shocking, embarrassing, etc to be mentioned.
unmentionables *npl* underwear.
unmistakable, unmistakeable *adj* obvious, clear.—**unmistakably, unmistakeably** *adv*.
unmitigated *adj* unqualified, absolute.
unmoved *adj* not touched by emotion, calm.
unnatural *adj* abnormal; contrary to nature; artificial; affected; strange; wicked.—**unnaturally** *adv*.
unnecessary *adj* not necessary.—**unnecessarily** *adv*.—**unnecessariness** *n*.
unnerve *vt* to cause to lose courage, strength, confidence; to frighten.
unnumbered *adj* countless; not having a number.
UNO *abbr* = United Nations Organization.
unobtrusive *adj* modest, staying in the background.
unoccupied *adj* not occupied, empty; unemployed.
unpack *vti* (*suitcase, etc*) to remove the contents of; (*container, etc*) to take things out of; to unload.
unparalleled *adj* having no equal, unmatched.
unparliamentary *adj* contrary to parliamentary procedure or practice.
unperson *n* a person (e.g. a political dissident) whose existence is officially ignored or denied.
unpick *vt* to undo the stitching of.
unplaced *adj* not placed; not among the first three at the end of a race.
unpleasant *adj* not pleasing or agreeable; nasty; objectionable.—**unpleasantly** *adv*.—**unpleasantness** *n*.
unplumbed *adj* not plumbed; not fully investigated or explored.
unpopular *adj* disliked; lacking general approval.—**unpopularity** *n*.
unprecedented *adj* having no precedent; unparalleled.
unprejudiced *adj* not prejudiced, impartial.
unprepossessing *adj* unattractive, repellent.
unpretentious *adj* modest, not boasting.
unprincipled *adj* lacking scruples.
unprintable *adj* too bad, libellous, obscene, etc to be printed.
unprofessional *adj* contrary to professional etiquette.—**unprofessionally** *adv*.
unputdownable *adj* (*book*) grippingly readable.
unqualified *adj* lacking recognized qualifications; not equal to; not restricted, complete.
unquestionable *adj* certain, not disputed.—**unquestionably** *adv*.
unquestioned *adj* not called into question; indisputable.
unquiet *adj* turbulent, disordered; nervous, agitated.—**unquietly** *adv*.—**unquietness** *n*.
unquote *interj* used when speaking to indicate the end of a direct quotation.
unravel *vt* (**unravelling, unravelled** *or* **unraveling, unraveled**) to disentangle; to solve.
unread *adj* not read (yet); unfamiliar with a specified subject; illiterate.
unreadable *adj* illegible; not worth reading.
unreal *adj* not real; imaginary, fanciful; false, insincere.
unreason *n* absence of reason in thought or action.
unreasonable *adj* contrary to reason; lacking reason; immoderate; excessive.—**unreasonably** *adv*.
unreasoning *adj* lacking reason, irrational
unrelenting *adj* relentless; continuous.—**unrelentingly** *adv*.
unremitting *adj* incessant.
unrequited *adj* not reciprocated, not returned.
unreserved *adj* not reserved; frank, demonstrative; absolute, entire; not booked.
unreservedly *adv* without conditions; openly.
unrest *n* uneasiness; anxiety; angry discontent verging on revolt.
unrighteous *adj* sinful, wicked.
unrivalled, unrivaled *adj* without equal, peerless.
unroll *vti* to open out or down from a roll; to unfold; to straighten out; to reveal or become revealed.
unruffled *adj* cool and calm; still, smooth.
unruly *adj* (**unrulier, unruliest**) hard to control, restrain, or keep in order; disobedient.
unsaddle *vt* to take the saddle from; to unseat. * *vi* to remove the saddle from a horse.
unsaid *adj* not said or expressed.
unsaturated *adj* (*chemical substance*) having double or triple bonds and therefore able to form products by chemical addition; (*vegetable fats*) containing fatty acids with double bonds.—**unsaturation** *n*.

unsavoury, unsavory *adj* distasteful; disagreeable; offensive.

unscathed *adj* unharmed.

unscramble *vt* to disentangle; (*a scrambled message*) to make intelligible.

unscrew *vti* to remove a screw from; (*lid, etc*) to loosen by turning.

unscrupulous *adj* without principles.

unseasonable *n* (*weather*) unusual for the season of the year; untimely.—**unseasonableness** *n*.—**unseasonably** *adv*.

unseat *vt* to dislodge from a seat, saddle, etc; to remove from office.

unseeded *adj* (*tennis players, etc*) not ranked among the top players in the preliminary rounds of a competition.

unseemly *adj* unbecoming; inappropriate.

unseen *adj* concealed, hidden; not seen or read beforehand.

unselfish *adj* not selfish; thinking of others before oneself.—**unselfishly** *adv*.—**unselfishness** *n*.

unsettle *vti* to disturb, disrupt, or disorder.

unsettled *adj* changeable; lacking stability; unpredictable; not concluded.

unsheathe *vt* to draw (a weapon) from a sheath.

unsightly *adj* unattractive; ugly.

unskilful, unskillful *adj* clumsy, awkward.

unskilled *adj* without special skill or training.

unsociable *n* antisocial; reserved.

unsocial *n* averse to social activities; (*working hours*) outwith the normal working day.

unsolicited *adj* not asked for.

unsophisticated *adj* naive, inexperienced; simple; pure, unadulterated.

unsound *adj* flimsy, not stable; defective, flawed; in poor health; not sane.—**unsoundly** *adv*.—**unsoundness** *n*.

unsparing *adj* profuse, lavish; severe.

unspeakable *adj* bad beyond words, indescribable.

unstable *adj* easily upset; mentally unbalanced; irresolute.

unsteady *adj* (**unsteadier, unsteadiest**) shaky, reeling; vacillating.—**unsteadily** *adv*.

unstop *vt* (**unstopping, unstopped**) to remove the stopper from; to free from an obstruction.

unstrung *adj* emotionally distressed.

unstudied *adj* natural; unaffected in manner.

unsubstantial *adj* lacking weight, flimsy; of doubtful factual validity.

unsullied *adj* not stained, pure.

unsung *adj* not acclaimed or celebrated.

unswerving *adj* not deviating; constant, unchanging.

untangle *vt* to rid of tangles, unravel; to sort out.

untaught *adj* not educated or trained; not acquired by teaching.

untenable *adj* not able to be justified or defended.—**untenability** *n*.

unthinkable *adj* inconceivable; out of the question; improbable.—**unthinkably** *adv*.

unthinking *adj* unable to think; thoughtless, inconsiderate.—**unthinkingly** *adv*.

untidy *adj* (**untidier, untidiest**) not neat, disordered. * *vt* (**untidying, untidied**) to make untidy.—**untidily** *adv*.

untie *vt* (**untying, untied**) to undo a knot in, unfasten.

until *prep* up to the time of; before. * *conj* up to the time when or that; to the point, degree, etc that; before.

untimely *adj* premature; inopportune.

unto *prep* (*arch*) to.

untold *adj* not told; too great to be counted; immeasurable.

untouchable *adj* unable to be touched or handled; exempt from criticism or control; lying beyond reach.

untoward *adj* unseemly; unfavourable; adverse.

untrue *adj* incorrect, false; not faithful, disloyal; inaccurate.

untruth *n* falsehood; a lie.

untruthful *adj* telling lies; false.

untutored *adj* lacking (refined) education.

unused *adj* not (yet) used; (*with to*) not accustomed (to something).

unusual *adj* uncommon; rare.

unutterable *adj* impossible to express in words.—**unutterably** *adv*.

unvarnished *adj* not varnished; plain, direct; not embellished.

unveil *vt* to reveal; to disclose.

unwaged *adj* not paid a wage; unemployed.

unwarrantable *adj* indefensible.

unwarranted *adj* not authorized.

unwary *adj* lacking caution; heedless, gullible; unguarded.—**unwarily** *adv*.

unwelcome *adj* not welcome, not invited; disagreeable; unpleasant.

unwell *adj* ill, not well; (*inf*) suffering from a hangover.

unwholesome *adj* harmful to physical, mental or moral health and well-being; ill-looking; (*food*) of poor quality.—**unwholesomeness** *n*.

unwieldy *adj* not easily moved or handled, as because of large size; awkward.—**unwieldily** *adv*.—**unwieldiness** *n*.

unwilling *adj* not willing, reluctant; said or done with reluctance.—**unwillingly** *adv*.—**unwillingness** *n*.

unwind *vt* to untangle; to undo. * *vi* to relax.

unwise *adj* lacking wisdom; imprudent.—**unwisely** *adv*.

unwitting *adj* not knowing; unintentional.—**unwittingly** *adv*.

unworldly *adj* spiritual, not concerned with the material world.

unworthy *adj* (**unworthier, unworthiest**) not deserving.

unwritten *adj* not written or printed; traditional; oral.

unwritten law *n* law based on custom or mores rather than legislative enactment.

up *adv* to, toward, in or on a higher place; to a later period; so as to be even with in time, degree, etc. * *prep* from a lower to a higher point on or along. * *adj* moving or directed upward; at an end; (*inf*) well-informed. * *vt* (**upping, upped**) to raise; to increase; to take up. * *n* ascent; high point.

up-and-coming *adj* promising for the future; likely to succeed.

upas *n* a Javanese tree that yields a poisonous sap.

upbeat *n* (*mus*) an unaccented beat in the last bar. * *adj* (*inf*) cheerful, optimistic.

upbraid *vt* to rebuke severely; to reproach.

upbringing *n* the process of educating and nurturing (a child).

upcountry *adv* towards the interior of a country, inland.

update *vt* to bring up to date.

updraught, updraft *n* a upward flow of air or other gas.

upend *vti* to turn or become turned on end; to upset or transform completely.

upfront *adj* honest, open. * *adv* (*money*) paid in advance.

upgrade *vt* to improve, raise to a higher grade.

upheaval *n* radical or violent change.

uphill *adj* ascending, rising; difficult, arduous. * *adv* up a slope or hill; against difficulties.

uphold *vt* (**upholding, upheld**) to support, sustain; to defend.

upholster *vt* (*furniture*) to fit with stuffing, springs, covering, etc.—**upholsterer** *n*.

upholstery *n* (*pl* **upholsteries**) materials used to make a soft covering esp for a seat.

upkeep *n* maintenance; the cost of it.

upland *n* an area of high ground. * *adj* of or pertaining to uplands.

uplift *vt* to raise, lift up; to improve the moral, cultural, spiritual, etc standard or condition of. * *n* a moral, cultural, spiritual, etc improvement.

upmarket *adj* of or appealing to wealthier buyers.

upmost *see* **uppermost**.

upon *prep* on, on top of.

upper *adj* farther up; higher in position, rank, status. * *n* the part of a boot or shoe above the sole; (*sl*) a drug used as a stimulant.

upper case *n* capital letters.—**upper-case** *adj*.

upper class *n* people occupying the highest social rank.—*also adj*.

upper crust *n* (*inf*) the aristocracy.

uppercut *n* an upward swinging punch to the chin.—*also vb*.

upper hand *n* the position of control, advantage.

upper house, chamber *n* one of the two houses of a bicameral legislature, such as the British House of Lords or US Senate.

uppermost *adj* at the top; highest in importance. * *adv* into the highest position, etc.—*also* **upmost**.

uppity *adj* (*inf*) snobbish, arrogant.
upright *adj* vertical, in an erect position; righteous, honest, just. * *n* a vertical post or support. * *adv* vertically.
uprising *n* a revolt; a rebellion.
uproar *n* a noisy disturbance; a commotion; an outcry.
uproarious *adj* making or marked by an uproar; extremely funny; (*laughter*) boisterous.—**uproariously** *adv*.
uproot *vt* to tear out by the roots; to remove from established surroundings.
upset[1] *vt* (**upsetting, upset**) to overturn; to spill; to disturb; to put out of order; to distress; to overthrow; to make physically sick.
upset[2] *n* an unexpected defeat; distress or its cause. * *adj* distressed; confused; defeated.
upshot *n* the conclusion; the result.
upside down *adj* inverted; the wrong way up; (*inf*) topsy turvy.
upsilon *n* the 20th letter of the Greek alphabet.
upstage *vt* to draw attention to oneself. * *adv* to the rear of the stage.
upstairs *adv* up the stairs; to an upper level or storey. * *n* an upper floor.
upstanding *adj* honest; of good character; in a standing position.
upstart *n* a person who has suddenly risen to a position of wealth and power; an arrogant person.
upstate *n* the mostly northern areas of a US state. * *adv, adj* towards, in, or pertaining to this area of a US state.
upstream *adv, adj* in the direction from which a stream is flowing.
upstroke *n* an upward stroke, as of a pen, paintbrush, piston, etc.
upsurge *n* a sudden rise or swell.
upswing *n* an upward swing or movement; an improvement, esp in the state of the economy.
uptake *n* a taking up; a shaft or pipe for carrying smoke upwards; (*inf*) understanding.
uptight *adj* (*inf*) very tense, nervous, etc.
up-to-date *adj* modern; fashionable.
upturn *n* an upward trend; an (economic) improvement. * *vt* to turn upside down.
upward, upwards *adj* from a lower to a higher place.—*also adv*.
upwardly-mobile *adj* aspiring to improve one's social and economic status.—**upward mobility** *n*.
upwind *adj, adv* in the direction from which the wind is blowing.
uraemia, uremia *n* the accumulation of waste products in the blood that are normally passed in the urine.
uranium *n* a metallic element used as a source of nuclear energy.
urano- *prefix* sky; the heavens.
uranography *n* the description and mapping of the stars, etc by astronomers.—**uranographer** *n*.—**uranographic** *adj*.
Uranus *n* the seventh planet from the sun.
urate *n* a salt or ester of uric acid.—**uratic** *adj*.
urban *adj* of or relating to a city.—**urbanization, urbanisation** *n*.
urbane *adj* sophisticated; refined.—**urbanity** *n*.
urban guerrilla *n* a terrorist who operates in a town or city.
urbanite *n* a person who lives in a town or city.
urban renewal *n* rehabilitation of dilapidated city areas, as by housing construction and slum clearance.
urchin *n* a raggedly dressed mischievous child; a sea urchin.
urea *n* a soluble crystalline compound present in urine produced by protein metabolism.
ureter *n* a tube that carries urine from the kidney to the bladder or cloaca.
urethra *n* the duct carrying urine out of the bladder.
urethritis *n* inflammation of the urethra.
uretic *adj* of or pertaining to the urine.
urge *vt* to drive forward; to press, plead with. * *n* an impulse, yearning.
urgency *n* (*pl* **urgencies**) the quality or condition of being urgent; compelling need; importance.
urgent *adj* impelling; persistent; calling for immediate attention.—**urgently** *adv*.
-urgy *n suffix* technology; technique.
-uria *n suffix* diseased condition of the urine.
uric *adj* of, present in, or derived from urine.
uric acid *n* a white odourless substance found in the urine of birds, reptiles and some mammals.
urinal *n* a bowl or trough for urination in public lavatories.
urinalysis *n* (*pl* **urinalyses**) the chemical analysis of urine for signs of disease.
urinate *vi* to pass urine.
urine *n* a yellowish fluid excreted by the kidneys and conveyed to the bladder.—**urinary** *adj*.
urinogenital *adj* urogenital.
urn *n* a vase or large vessel; a receptacle for preserving the ashes of the dead; a large metal container for boiling water for tea or coffee.
uro-, ur- *prefix* urine; urinary tract.
urogenital, urinogenital *adj* of or pertaining to the urinary and reproductive organs.—*also* **genitourinary**.
urology *n* the medical study and treatment of urogenital diseases.—**urologist** *n*.—**urological** *adj*.
uroscopy *n* the diagnosis of diseases by the examination of the patient's urine.
ursine *adj* of or resembling a bear.
urticaria *n* an allergic reaction which produces raised itchy whitish patches on the skin.—*also* **hives, nettle rash**.
US *abbr* = United States.
us *pron* the objective case of **we**.
USA *abbr* = United States of America.
USAF *abbr* = United States Air Force.
usage *n* customary use; practice, custom; use of language.
use[1] *vt* to put to some purpose; to utilize; to exploit (a person); to partake of (drink, drugs, tobacco, etc).—**usable, useable** *adj*.
use[2] *n* act of using or putting to a purpose; usage; usefulness; need (for); advantage; practice, custom.
used *adj* not new; second-hand.
useful *adj* able to be used to good effect; (*inf*) capable, commendable.—**usefully** *adv*.
useless *adj* having no use.—**uselessly** *adv*.—**uselessness** *n*.
user *n* one who uses; (*inf*) a drug addict.
user-friendly *adj* easy to understand and operate.
usher *n* one who shows people to their seats in a theatre, church, etc; a doorkeeper in a law court. * *vt* to escort to seats, etc.
usherette *nf* a woman who directs people to their seats in a cinema.
USN *abbr* = United States Navy.
USSR *abbr* = (*formerly*) Union of Soviet Socialist Republics.
usual *adj* customary; ordinary; normal.—**usually** *adv*.
usurer *n* a person who lends money at an excessively high rate of interest.
usurp *vt* to seize or appropriate unlawfully.—**usurper** *n*.
usury *n* (*pl* **usuries**) the practice of taking excessive interest on a loan; an excessive interest rate.
UT *abbr* = Utah.
utensil *n* an implement or container, esp one for use in the kitchen.
uterus *n* (*pl* **uteri**) the female organ in which offspring are developed until birth, the womb.—**uterine** *adj*.
utilitarian *adj* designed to be of practical use.
utility *n* (*pl* **utilities**) usefulness; a public service, such as telephone, electricity, etc; a company providing such a service.
utility room *n* a room containing laundry appliances, heating equipment, etc.
utilize *vt* to make practical use of.—**utilization** *n*.
utmost *adj* of the greatest degree or amount; furthest. * *n* the most possible.
utopia *n* a imaginary society or place considered to be ideal or perfect.—**utopian** *adj, n*.
utter[1] *adj* absolute; complete.
utter[2] *vt* to say; to speak.—**utterance** *n*.
utterly *adv* completely.

UV *abbr* = ultraviolet.

uvula *n* (*pl* **uvulas, uvulae**) the fleshy tissue suspended in the back of the throat over the back part of the tongue.

uxorious *adj* excessively fond of one's wife; doting.—**uxoriously** *adv*.—**uxoriousness** *n*.

V

V *abbr* = volt(s).

V, v *n* the 22nd letter of the English alphabet; something shaped like a V.

v *abbr* = velocity; *versus* against; *vide* see; verb.

VA *abbr* = Veterans Administration; Virginia.

vac *abbr* = vacuum.

vac *n* (*inf*) a vacation.

vacancy *n* (*pl* **vacancies**) emptiness; an unoccupied job or position.

vacant *adj* empty; unoccupied; (*expression*) blank.—**vacantly** *adv*.—**vacantness** *n*.

vacate *vt* to leave empty; to give up possession of.

vacation *n* a holiday; a period of the year when universities, colleges and law courts are closed. * *vi* to go on holiday.

vacationer, vacationist *n* a person on vacation, a holiday-maker.

vaccinal *adj* pertaining to or caused by a vaccine or vaccination.

vaccinate *vt* to inoculate with vaccine as a protection against a disease.—**vaccinator** *n*.

vaccination *n* inoculation with a vaccine; the resulting scar.

vaccine *n* a modified and hence harmless virus or other microorganism used for inoculation to give immunity from certain diseases by stimulating antibody production; cowpox virus used in this way against smallpox.

vaccinia *n* (*med*) cowpox.—**vaccinial** *adj*.

vacillate *vi* to waver, to show indecision; to fluctuate.—**vacillation** *n*.—**vacillator** *n*.

vacuity *n* (*pl* **vacuities**) emptiness; a vacant state of mind or expression; absence of matter; a vacuum; idleness; lack; an inane remark.

vacuole *n* (*biol*) a small cell or cavity filled with fluid in the interior of organic cells or protoplasm.—**vacuolate, vacuolated** *adj*.

vacuous *adj* empty; lacking intelligence, mindless.—**vacuously** *adv*.—**vacuousness** *n*.

vacuum *n* (*pl* **vacuums, vacua**) a region devoid of all matter; a region in which gas is present at low pressure; a vacuum cleaner. * *vt* to clean with a vacuum cleaner. * *adj* of, having or creating a vacuum; working by suction or maintenance of a partial vacuum.

vacuum cleaner *n* an electrical appliance for removing dust from carpets, etc, by suction.—**vacuum-clean** *vt*.

vacuum bottle, vacuum flask *n* a container for keeping liquids hot or cold.

vacuum-packed *adj* sealed in an airtight packet from which the air has been removed.

vade mecum *n* (*pl* **vade mecums**) a handbook or manual, etc, for ready reference, usu of a size to fit in a pocket.

vagabond *n* a vagrant; a wandering, homeless person.—**vagabondage** *n*.—**vagabondism** *n*.

vagal *adj* of, pertaining to, affected or controlled by the vagus nerve.

vagary *n* (*pl* **vagaries**) unpredictable or erratic behaviour or actions; a whim.—**vagarious** *adj*.

vagina *n* (**vaginas, vaginae**) in female mammals and humans, the canal connecting the uterus and the external sex organs.—**vaginal** *adj*.

vaginate, vaginated *adj* (*bot*) (*plant parts*) sheathed; with a vagina or sheath.

vagrancy (*pl* **vagrancies**) the habits and life of a vagrant; a wandering without a settled home.

vagrant *n* a person who has no settled home, a tramp. * *adj* wandering, roaming; wayward.—**vagrantly** *adv*.

vague *adj* unclear; indistinct, imprecise; (*person*) absent-minded.—**vaguely** *adv*.—**vagueness** *n*.

vagus *n* (*pl* **vagi**) vagus nerve.

vagus nerve *n* either of a pair of cranial nerves supplying the larynx, heart, lungs, etc.

vail[1] *vti* (*arch*) to lower, to let fall; to take off (a hat) in respect.

vail[2] *n* (*arch*) a gratuity, a tip.

vain *adj* conceited; excessively concerned with one's appearance; senseless; futile; worthless; **in vain** to no purpose.—**vainly** *adv*.—**vainness** *n*.

vainglorious *adj* elated by one's achievements; boastful; showy.—**vaingloriously** *adv*.—**vaingloriousness** *n*.

vainglory *n* (*pl* **vainglories**) excessive vanity; boastfulness; showiness.

vair *n* a fur trimming on medieval robes, probably of Russian squirrel; (*her*) fur represented by small shields, coloured white and blue alternately.

valance *n* a decorative cover for the base of a bed; a canopy for a window frame to hide rods, etc; a pelmet.—**valanced** *adj*.

vale[1] *n* a valley.

vale[2] *interj*, *n* (*arch*) farewell.

valediction *n* a saying farewell; a taking leave; an instance of this; a speech made at this time.

valedictorian *n* a college student appointed on grounds of merit to deliver the valedictory oration on Commencement day.

valedictory *adj* uttered or bestowed on saying farewell; shown, performed or done by way of valediction. * *n* (*pl* **valedictories**) a valedictory oration; a statement or speech made on leaving a position, etc.

valence, valency *n* (*pl* **valences, valencies**) (*chem*) the power of elements to combine; the number of atoms of hydrogen that an atom or group can combine with to form a compound.

valence electron, valency electron *n* (*chem*) one of the electrons present in the outermost shell of an atom of a corresponding element.

Valenciennes (lace) *n* an ornate type of bobbin lace, formerly made of linen, now usu of cotton.

-valent *adj suffix* having a specified number of valences, eg *univalent*.

valentine *n* a lover or sweetheart chosen on St Valentine's Day, February 14; a card or gift sent on that day.

valerian *n* a herb with a root formerly used for medicinal purposes; the root of this used as a sedative.

valet *n* a manservant; a steward in a hotel or on board ship. * *vt* to attend (someone) as a valet. * *vi* to work as a valet.

valetudinarian, valetudinary *n* (*pl* **valetudinarians, valetudinaries**) a person who is overly preoccupied with his or her own health, a hypochondriac; a chronic invalid. * *adj* of ill health; sickly; seeking to recover health—**valetudinarianism** *n*.

valgus *adj* (*med*) deviating outwards from the vertical middle line of the body. * *n* (*pl* **valguses**) a deformity caused by a twisting from the middle line of the body, eg bow-legs.

Valhalla *n* (*Scandinavian myth*) the palace or hall of immortality in which the souls of heroes slain in battle dwell.—*also* **Walhalla**.

valiant *adj* courageous; brave.—**valiance, valiancy** *n*.—**valiantly** *adv*.

valid *adj* based on facts; (*objection, etc*) sound; legally acceptable; binding.—**validity** *n*.—**validly** *adv*.

validate *vt* to corroborate; to legalize.—**validation** *n*.

valine *n* an amino acid formed by the digestion of protein.

valise *n* a small case, usu of a size large enough to carry what is needed for an overnight visit.

Valkyrie *n* (*Scandinavian myth*) one of the twelve Norse war goddesses, handmaidens of Odin, who selected those who were worthy to be slain in battle and led them to Valhalla.—*also* **Walkyrie**.

vallation *n* a defensive wall; a rampart; the act of building this.

vallecula *n* (*pl* **valleculae**) (*anat*) a cleft or depressed area; (*bot*) a groove, a deep wrinkle.—**vallecular, valleculate** *adj*.

valley *n* (*pl* **valleys**) low land between hills or mountains usu with a river or stream flowing along its bottom; something resembling a valley, eg the angle where two sloping sides of a roof meet.

valonia *n* a large, dried acorn cup, or unripened acorn, from a particular kind of oak tree, used in tanning, dyeing, ink-making, etc.

valor *see* **valour**.

valorize *vt* to give an arbitrary price to (something) under government control.—**valorization** *n*.
valorous *adj* (*person*) valiant, courageous; (*action*) characterized by valour.—**valorously** *adv*.—**valorousness** *n*.
valour *n* courage; bravery (in battle).—*also* **valor.**
valse *n* a waltz, often used in the titles of musical compositions.
valuable *adj* having considerable importance or monetary worth. * *n* a personal possession of value, esp jewellery; (*pl*) valuable possessions.—**valuably** *adv*.
valuate *vt* to estimate the worth of, to value.—**valuator** *n*.
valuation *n* the act of valuing or valuating; an estimated price or worth; an estimation.—**valuational** *adj*.
value *n* worth, merit, importance; market value; purchasing power; relative worth; (*pl*) moral principles. * *vt* (**valuing, valued**) to estimate the worth of; to regard highly; to prize.—**valuer** *n*.
value-added tax *n* a tax levied on the difference between the production cost of an item and its selling price.
valued *adj* estimated; esteemed, prized.
value judgment *n* a subjective or unwarranted judgment.
valueless *adj* without value; worthless.—**valuelessness** *n*.
valuta *n* the value of one currency in terms of another.
valvar *see* **valvular.**
valvate *adj* having, resembling, or operating by means of a valve or valves; (*bot*) (*petals*) meeting at the edges without overlapping.
valve *n* a device for controlling the flow of a gas or liquid through a pipe; (*anat*) a tube allowing blood to flow in one direction only; (*mus*) a device on a brass instrument for increasing the length of the tube and thus altering the pitch being played.
valvular *adj* of, affecting a valve or valves, esp of the heart; acting like a valve; shaped like a valve; operating by means of a valve or valves.
valvule, valvelet *n* a little valve; anything resembling this.
valvulitis *n* inflammation of the valves, esp of the heart.
vambrace *n* plate armour for the forearm.
vamoose, vamose *vi* (*sl*) to make off quickly, to decamp.
vamp[1] *n* the part of a sock, boot or shoe covering the front of the foot; anything patched up or refurbished; an improvised musical accompaniment made up of chords. * *vt* to provide with a (new) vamp; to mend or repair; (*with* **up**) to renovate; (*mus*) to improvise.—**vamper** *n*.
vamp[2] *n* a seductive woman. * *vt* to fascinate or exploit by seducing. * *vi* to act as a vamp.
vampire *n* (*folklore*) a dead creature that by night leaves its grave to suck the blood of living people; a person who preys on others, an extortioner; a vampire bat.—**vampiric** *adj*.
vampire bat *n* a tropical American blood-sucking bat.
vampirism *n* belief in vampires; bloodsucking, or other acts associated with vampires.
van[1] *n* a covered motor vehicle for transporting goods, etc.
van[2] *n* the vanguard.
vanadium *n* a rare soft white metallic element used in steel alloys.—**vanadic** *adj*.
vandal *n* a person who wilfully or ignorantly damages property; (*with cap*) a member of a Germanic tribe that sacked Rome (455 ad). * *adj* of of acting like a vandal; characterized by vandalism or lack of culture.
vandalism *n* the ruthless destruction or spoiling of anything beautiful or venerable; barbarous, ignorant or inartistic treatment.—**vandalistic** *adj*.
vandalize *vt* to carry out an act of vandalism.—**vandalization** *n*.
Van de Graaf generator *n* a machine that continuously separates electrostatic charges and in so doing produces a very high voltage.
van der Waals' force *n* a weak attractive force between two neighbouring atoms.
Vandyke beard *n* a small pointed beard.
Vandyke collar *n* a wide, white collar of lace or sewed work, with a deeply indented edge.
vane *n* a blade at the top of a spire, etc to show wind direction; a weather vane; a blade on a windmill or propeller.
vang *n* (*naut*) a guy rope from the end of a gaff to the deck, used for steadying the extremity of the peak of a gaff to the side of a ship; a rope running from the boom of a mainsail to the deck, used to keep the boom lowered.
vanguard *n* the front part of an army; the leading position of any movement.
vanilla *n* extract from the orchid pod used as a flavouring.—**vanillic** *adj* from vanilla.
vanish *vi* to disappear from sight, to become invisible, esp in a rapid and mysterious manner; to fade away; to cease to exist; (*math*) (*numbers, quantities*) to become zero.—**vanisher** *n*.
vanishing cream *n* a cleansing or foundation cream for make-up that is colourless when applied to the face.
vanity *n* (*pl* **vanities**) a fruitless endeavour; worthlessness; empty pride or conceit; love of indiscriminate admiration; an idle matter or show; a worthless or unfounded idea or statement; emptiness, lightness.
vanity case, vanity box *n* a small case used for carrying cosmetics, etc.
vanquish *vt* to conquer; to defeat; to overcome, to subdue.—**vanquisher** *n*.—**vanquishment** *n*.
vantage *n* a favourable position; a position allowing a clear view or understanding.
vanward *adj* towards the front, in the van. * *adv* forward, towards the front.
vapid *adj* flavourless, flat, insipid; dull, lifeless.—**vapidity** *n*.—**vapidly** *adv*.
vapor *see* **vapour.**
vaporish *see* **vapourish.**
vaporize *vt* to change into vapour.—**vaporization** *n*.—**vaporizer** *n*.
vaporous *adj* in the form of or like vapour; foggy, steamy; unreal, fanciful.—**vaporously** *adv*.—**vaporosity** *n*.
vapour *n* the gaseous state of a substance normally liquid or solid; particles of water or smoke in the air; (*pl*) hysteria. * *vi* to pass off in vapour, vaporize; to boast.—*also* **vapor.**
vapourish *adj* like vapour; full of vapour; (*arch*) in a state of depression and lethargy.—*also* **vaporish.**—**vapourishness, vapurishness** *n*.
vapour trail *n* condensed vapour left in the wake of an aircraft exhaust appearing as a white trail in the sky.
varec *n* the ash left after burning kelp.
variable *adj* liable to change; not constant. * *n* (*math*) a changing quantity that can have different values, as opposed to a constant.—**variability** *n*.—**variably** *adv*.
variance *n* disagreement, dissension; variation; tendency to vary; (*law*) a discrepancy between two statements or documents; **at variance** in conflict.
variant *adj* different; differing from an accepted or normal type, text, etc. * *n* a variant form or reading.
variation *n* a varying or being varied; alteration; deviation from a standard or type; diversity; deviation of the magnetic needle from true north; the measure of this; (*gram*) inflexion; (*mus*) repetition of a theme or melody with modifications.—**variational** *adj*.
varicella *n* (*med*) chickenpox.—**varicelloid** *adj*.
varices *see* **varix.**
varicocele *n* a swelling of the veins of the scrotum or of the spermatic cord.
varicoloured, varicolored *adj* variegated, particoloured; of several colours.
varicose *adj* (*veins*) abnormally swollen and dilated.—**varicosis** *n*.—**varicosity** *n*.
varied *adj* showing variety, changing; partially changed; various; variegated.—**variedly** *adv*.
variegate *vt* to mark with different colours or tints; to dapple, streak; to cause to diversify.
variegated *adj* marked with different colours.
variegation *n* the condition of being variegated; diversity of colours.
variety *n* (*pl* **varieties**) diversity; an assortment.—**varietal** *adj*.
variety show *n* an entertainment made up of various acts, such as songs, comedy turns, etc.

variform *adj* having various forms.
variola *n* (*med*) smallpox.—**variolar** *adj*.
variolate *adj* having shallow, pitted depressions similar to those left on the skin after smallpox. * *vt* to inoculate with smallpox virus.—**variolation** *n*.
variole *n* a whitish spot or round mass consisting of radiating threads of crystal.
variolite *n* a kind of igneous rock with whitish spots, made up of clustered varioles.—**variolitic** *adj*.
varioloid *n* smallpox modified by vaccination or other means of acquired partial immunity. * *adj* like smallpox.
variorum *n* an edition of the works of an author with notes by various commentators.—*also adj*.
various *adj* varied, different; several.—**variously** *adv*.
varix *n* (*pl* **varices**) (*med*) a varicose vein; a twisted, dilated artery.
varlet *n* a scoundrel; (*arch*) a servant, attendant, or page of a knight.
varmint *n* (*dial*) a rascal; an offensive or trying person or animal; (*hunting sl*) the fox.
varnish *n* a sticky liquid which dries and forms a hard, glossy coating. * *vt* to coat with varnish.—**varnisher** *n*.
varsity *n* (*pl* **varsities**) (*Brit, NZ inf*) university.
varus *n* (*pl* **varuses**) a deformity caused by a turning in towards the vertical midline of the body, eg pigeon toes.
vary *vti* (**varying, varied**) to change, to diversify, modify; to become altered.—**varyingly** *adv*.
vascular *adj* (*biol*) of, consisting of, or containing vessels as part of a structure of animal and vegetable organisms for conveying blood, sap, etc.—**vascularity** *n*.
vasculum *n* (*pl* **vascula, vasculums**) a botanist's specimen box.
vas deferens *n* (*pl* **vasa deferentia**) the spermatic duct.
vase *n* a vessel for displaying flowers.
vasectomy *n* (*pl* **vasectomies**) male sterilization involving the cutting of the sperm-carrying tube.
Vaseline *n* (*trademark*) petroleum jelly used as a lubricant.
vasoconstrictor *n* a nerve, drug, etc, that constricts blood vessels.—**vasoconstrictive** *adj*.
vasodilator *n* a nerve, drug etc that dilates blood vessels.—**vasodilative** *adj*.
vasomotor *adj* (*nerve, drug, etc*) pertaining to or controlling the diameter of blood vessels.
vassal *n* a servant, dependant; subordinate.
vassalage *n* the state of being a vassal; the obligations associated with such a state; servitude; dependence; (*rare*) vassals collectively.
vast *adj* immense.—**vastly** *adv*.—*n* **vastness**.
vasty (**vastier, vastiest**) *adj* (*arch*) vast.
VAT *abbr* = value added tax.
vat *n* a large barrel or tank. * *vt* (**vatting, vatted**) to put in a vat; to treat in a vat.
vatic, vatical *adj* of or relating to a prophet or prophecy.
Vatican *n* the residence of the pope in Rome; papal authority.
Vaticanism *n* (*often derog*) the doctrine of Papal supremacy and infallibility.
vaticination *n* a prophecy.
vaudeville *n* a stage show consisting of various acts, such as singing, dancing and comedy.
vault[1] *n* an arched ceiling or roof; a burial chamber; a strongroom for valuables; a cellar.—**vaulted** *adj*.
vault[2] *vti* to leap or jump over an obstacle. * *n* a leap.—**vaulter** *n*.
vaulting[1] *n* (*arch*) arched work in a building, etc.
vaulting[2] *adj* overly confident; to an exaggerated degree; used in the act of leaping over.
vaunt *vti* to display boastfully; to brag. * *n* a boast.—**vaunter** *n*.—**vauntingly** *adv*.
vavasour, vavasor, vavassor *n* (*feudalism*) the tenant of a baron or lord who is that lord's vassal and who in turn has other vassals under him.
VC *abbr* = Victoria Cross; vice-chairman; Vietcong.
VCR *abbr* = video cassette recorder.
VD *abbr* = venereal disease.
VDU *abbr* = video display unit.
veal *n* the edible flesh of a calf.
vector *n* (*physics*) a physical quantity having both direction and magnitude, eg displacement, acceleration, etc; an aircraft's or missile's course; (*biol*) a piece of DNA that transmits a parasitic disease.—**vectorial** *adj*.
Veda *n* (any of) the oldest sacred books or collection of hymns of the Hindus, written in old Sanskrit and of great antiquity.—**Vedic** *adj*.
Vedanta *n* a Hindu philosophy based on the Veda, postulating that the world of the senses is based on an illusion.—**Vedantic** *adj*.
vedette *n* a small patrol boat (—*also* **vedette boat**); a mounted sentry in advance of an outpost (—*also* **vidette**).
Vedic *adj* pertaining to the Veda, or to the old Sanskrit in which these were written; pertaining to the original Indo-Europeans of India.
veer *vi* (*wind*) to change direction; to swing around; to change from one mood or opinion to another.—**veeringly** *adv*.
veery *n* (*pl* **veeries**) a tawny North American thrush.
veg. *abbr* = vegetable(s).
vegan *n* a strict vegetarian who consumes no animal or dairy products.
vegetable *n* a herbaceous plant grown for food; (*inf*) a person who has suffered brain damage. * *adj* of, relating to or derived from plants.
vegetal *adj* of growth and vital functions; vegetable.
vegetarian *n* a person who consumes a diet that excludes meat and fish. * *adj* of vegetarians; consisting wholly of vegetables.
vegetarianism *n* the doctrine or practice of vegetarians; abstention from meating meat, fish, or other animal products.
vegetate *vi* to grow like a plant; to sprout; to lead a mentally inactive, aimless life.
vegetation *n* vegetable growth; plants in general.—**vegetational** *adj*.
vegetative, vegetive *adj* (*plants*) growing or having the power of growing, or producing growth in; (*way of life*) dull, passive, uneventful; (*reproduction*) asexual; referring to functions other than sexual reproduction.
vehement *adj* passionate; forceful; furious.—**vehemence, vehemency** *n*.—**vehemently** *adv*.
vehicle *n* a conveyance, such as a car, bus or truck, for carrying people or goods on land; a means of transmission for ideas, impressions, etc, a medium; (*med*) a substance in which a strong medicine can be administered palatably.—**vehicular** *adj*.
veil *n* a thin fabric worn over the head or face of a woman; a nun's headdress; anything that conceals; a velum. * *vt* to put on a veil; to cover; to conceal, dissemble.
veiled *adj* covered with or wearing a veil; shrouded in a veil; concealed, hidden; covert; not openly declared; (*sound, voice*) indistinct, muffled.
vein *n* (*anat*) one of the vessels that convey the blood back to the heart; (*geol*) a seam of a mineral within a rock; (*bot*) a branching rib in a leaf; a streak of different colour, as in marble, cheese, etc; a style or mood (*serious vein*). * *vt* to streak.—**veiny** *adj*.
veinlet *n* a small vein.
veinprint *n* the pattern of veins on the back of the hand, which is unique to an individual.
velamen *n* (*pl* **velamina**) (*anat*) an outer membrane or epidermis; a velum; (*bot*) a thick, moisture-absorbing aerial root, consisting of dead cells, found on some plants.
velar *adj* of the velum or soft palate; (*phonetics*) pronounced with the back of the tongue touching the soft palate. * *n* a velar sound.
velarium *n* (*pl* **velaria**) in ancient Rome, the great awning that stretched over open theatres.
Velcro *n* (*trademark*) a nylon material made of matching strips of tiny hooks and pile that are easily pressed together or pulled apart.
veld, veldt *n* in South Africa, open grass country.
velites *n* in ancient Rome, a lightly armed soldier, usu from the poorer section of society.
velleity *n* (*pl* **velleities**) (*arch*) the lowest degree of desire, mere inclination.

vellum *n* fine parchment; a good quality writing paper.
veloce *adv* (*mus*) very quickly.
velocipede *n* an early form of bicycle, propelled by striking the toes on the road; any early form of bicycle or tricycle.
velocity *n* (*pl* **velocities**) the rate of change of position of any object; speed.
velour, velours *n* a velvet-like fabric.
velouté *n* a rich white sauce or soup, with a basis of egg yolks, cream and stock.
velum *n* (*pl* **vela**) (*anat*) the soft palate; any body structure resembling a veil; (*bot, zool*) a membranous covering or organ, such as the membranous covering of certain molluscs or that covering a developing mushroom.
velure *n* a kind of plush or velvet-like material; a velvet pad for smoothing a silk hat.
velutinous *adj* (*bot*) thickly covered with short hairs, velvety.
velvet *n* a fabric made from silk, rayon, etc with a soft, thick pile; anything like velvet in texture.
velveteen *n* a cotton cloth with a pile like velvet.
velvety *adj* soft to the touch; mellow.
vena *n* (*pl* **venae**) (*anat*) a vein.
vena cava *n* (*pl* **venae cavae**) one of the two major veins that empty blood into the right chamber of the heart in air-breathing vertebrates.
venal *adj* corrupt; willing to accept bribes.—**venality** *n*.—**venally** *adv*.
venatic, venatical *adj* of or pertaining to hunting; (*people*) likely to engage in hunting.
venation *n* the arrangement of veins in a leaf or an insect's wing; these veins collectively.—**venational** *adj*.
vend *vt* to sell, to offer for sale; to peddle; (*rare*) to state or disseminate (an opinion, etc).
vendace *n* (*pl* **vendaces, vendace**) either of two types of small European freshwater fish.
vendee *n* (*law*) a buyer; someone to whom something has been sold.
vendetta *n* the taking of private vengeance; a feud.—**vendettist** *n*.
vendible *adj* saleable; (*arch*) venal. * *n* (*usu pl*) something that is saleable.
vending machine *n* a coin-operated machine which dispenses goods.
vendor, vender *n* a seller; a machine that ejects goods, etc, after a required amount of coins has been inserted.
veneer *n* an overlay of fine wood or plastic; a superficial appearance. * *vt* to cover with veneer.
venerable *adj* worthy of reverence or respect.—**venerability** *n*.—**venerably** *adv*.
venerate *vt* to revere; to respect.—**venerator** *n*.
veneration *n* a venerating or being venerated; respect mingled with awe, deep reverence.
venereal *adj* (*disease*) resulting from sexual intercourse.
venereal disease *n* any of various diseases, such as syphilis or AIDS, transmitted by sexual contact.—*also* **sexually transmitted disease**.
venery[1] *n* (*arch*) hunting, usu with hounds, the chase.
venery[2] *n* (*arch*) sexual indulgence, the pursuit of sexual gratification.
venesection *n* the operation of opening a vein; phlebotomy.
Venetian blind *n* a window blind formed of long thin horizontal slips of wood that can be pivoted.
vengeance *n* the act of taking revenge; retribution; **with a vengeance** to a high degree; and no mistake.
vengeful *adj* bent on vengeance; vindictive.—**vengefully** *adv* **vengefulness** *n*.
venial *adj* (*sin*) forgivable, excusable, not very wrong; (*sin*) not entailing damnation.—**veniality** *n*.—**venially** *adv*.
venison *n* the edible flesh of the deer.
Venite *n* (*Anglican church*) the 95th Psalm, used as a canticle at Matins; the music for this.
venom *n* the poison of a snake, wasp, etc; spite, malice, rancour.
venomous *adj* secreting venom; malicious, spiteful.—**venomously** *adv*.—**venomousness** *n*.
venose *adj* having many veins, veiny; venous; (*plant*) with a surface of vein-like ridges.
venosity *n* the state of being abnormally venose; (*blood vessels, organs*) the condition of containing too much blood.
venous *adj* pertaining to, contained in, or consisting of veins or blood.—**venously** *adv*.—**venousness** *n*.
vent[1] *n* a small opening or slit; an outlet or flue for the escape of fumes. * *vt* to release; (*temper*) to give expression to.—**venter** *n*
vent[2] *n* a slit in the back of a coat, often forming a flap; an opening in a battlemented wall.
ventage *n* a finger-hole of a flute or similar instrument; a small opening, an outlet.
ventail *n* the part of a helmet protecting the lower part of the face.
venter *n* (*anat, zool*) the belly or abdomen of vertebrates; the part of a muscle that swells outwards; (*bot*) the swollen base of that part of some plants containing the egg cell; (*law*) the womb.
ventilate *vt* to supply with fresh air; to oxygenate (the blood); to make public, to submit to discussion.—**ventilative** *adj*.
ventilation *n* the act of ventilating; the state of being ventilated; free discussion.
ventilator *n* an appliance for ventilating a room, etc; (*med*) a device for enabling a patient to breathe normally.
ventral *adj* (*anat*) of or on the belly, abdominal; (*bot*) of, pertaining to, or located on that part of a plant facing towards the stem, esp a leaf.
ventricle *n* a small cavity; one of the lower chambers of the heart, which pumps blood; one of the four cavities of the brain.—**ventricular** *adj*.
ventricose, ventricous *adj* (*biol*) swelling, esp on one side only.—**ventricosity** *n*.
ventriloquism, ventriloquy *n* the act or art of speaking so that the sounds appear to come from a source other than the actual speaker.—**ventriloquial** *adj*.—**ventriloquist** *n*.—**ventriloquistic** *adj*.
ventriloquize *vi* to practise ventriloquism.
venture *n* a dangerous expedition; a risky undertaking. * *vti* to risk; to dare.—**venturer** *n*.
venture capital *n* capital available for investment in risky but potentially very profitable enterprises and repayable at higher than normal interest rates, risk capital.
venturesome *adj* daring, rash; risky, hazardous.—**venturesomely** *adv*.—**venturesomeness** *n*.
venue *n* the place of an action or event.
Venus *n* (*Roman myth*) the goddess of love; (*astron*) the planet second from the sun, that can sometimes be seen as a bright star in the morning or evening; a beautiful woman.
veracious *adj* observant of the truth, truthful; honest; true, accurate.—**veraciously** *adv*.—**veraciousness** *n*.
veracity *n* (*pl* **veracities**) habitual observance of the truth; correspondence with the truth or facts; a truthful statement, a truth.
veranda, verandah *n* a roofed porch, supported by light pillars.
veratrine *n* a poisonous mixture of alkaloids from plants of the hellebore family, formerly used medically, to relieve neuralgia or as a counter-irritant.
verb *n* (*gram*) the part of speech that expresses an action, a process, state or condition or mode of being.
verbal *adj* of, concerned with or expressed in words; spoken, not written; literal; (*gram*) of, pertaining to or characteristic of a verb.—**verbally** *adv*.
verbalism *n* something expressed in words; a word or phrase; excessive attention to wording rather than content; meaningless phrases or sentences resulting from this.
verbalist *n* one skilled with words; one who concentrates on words rather than content.—**verbalistic** *adj*.
verbalize *vt* to put into words; to make into a verb.—**verbalization** *n*.
verbatim *adj, adv* word for word.
verbena *n* any of various kinds of ornamental fragrant plant, usu found in America, with red, white or purple flowers; any similar type of plant.

verbiage *n* more words than are needed for clarity, wordiness; the use of too many words.

verbify *vti* (**verbifying, verbified**) to convert (a noun, etc) into a verb; to be verbose.

verbose *adj* using more words than are necessary; overloaded with words.—**verbosely** *adv*.—**verbosity** *n*.

verdant *adj* (*grass, foliage*) green and fresh; covered with grass; inexperienced, gullible.—**verdancy** *n*.—**verdantly** *adv*.

verderer *n* (*formerly*) in England, an official who had charge of the royal forests and was responsible for maintaining peace in them.

verdict *n* the decision of a jury at the end of a trial; decision, judgment.

verdigris *n* a greenish deposit that forms on copper or brass.

verdure *n* green vegetation; greenness; freshness; the freshness and healthy growth of vegetation.—**verdurous** *adj*.—**verdurousness** *n*.

verge[1] *n* the brink; the extreme edge or margin; a grass border beside a road; a staff or wand as an emblem of office; the spindle of a watch balance; (*archit*) a projecting edge of roof tiles or slates.

verge[2] *vi* to incline, descend; (*with* **on**) to border on, to be on the verge of.

verger *n* an official who has care of the interior of a church; a staff bearer of a bishop, etc.

veridical *adj* truthful, veracious; (*psychol*) of or pertaining to events in dreams that in retrospect appear to have foretold the future.

verifiable *adj* capable of being verified.—**verifiability** *n*.

verification *n* the act of proving to be true; confirmation; the state of being verified; a marshalling of facts, etc that proves the truth of, eg a theory; (*law*) (*formerly*) a short affidavit at the end of a pleading indicating that the pleader is willing to supply proof.

verify *vt* (**verifying, verified**) to confirm the truth of, to check; to substantiate, to bear out; (law) to authenticate or support by proofs.—**verifiable** *adj*.—**verification** *n*.—**verifier** *n*.

verily *adv* (*arch*) in truth, certainly.

verisimilitude *n* the appearance of truth, probability.—**verisimilar** *adj*.

verismo *n* a type of opera concerned with representing contemporary life of ordinary people in an honest and realistic way.

veritable *adj* real, genuine.—**veritably** *adv*.

verity *n* (*pl* **verities**) the quality or state of being true; a truth; a true fact, reality.

verjuice *n* an acidic liquor expressed from unripe grapes, apples, etc, formerly used in sauces; sourness, tartness.

vermeil *n* silver-gilt, or any other metal gilded; (*poet*) vermilion. * *adj* of a bright red colour.

vermicelli *n* a pasta similar to spaghetti but in finer strings.

vermicide *n* a substance for killing worms.—**vermicidal** *adj*.

vermicular *adj* vermiform; vermiculate; worm-like; pertaining to or caused by worms.

vermiculate *adj* moving like a worm; worm-eaten; adorned with wavy lines; (*thoughts*) constantly recurring, casuistic. * *vt* to mark with close wavy lines.—**vermiculation** *n*.

vermiform *adj* worm-shaped.

vermiform appendix *n* the worm-shaped structure attached to the caecum vestigially in humans and certain other mammals, the appendix.

vermifuge *n* a drug, etc, that expels intestinal worms.

vermilion, vermillion *n* a bright scarlet colour. * *adj* of this colour.

vermin *n* (*used as pl*) pests, such as insects and rodents; persons dangerous to society.

vermination *n* the breeding or spread of vermin, worms or larvae; infestation with vermin, worms or larvae.

verminous *adj* infested with, caused by, or like vermin.

vermouth *n* a white wine flavoured with herbs, used in cocktails and as an aperitif.

vernacular *n* the commonly spoken language or dialect of a country or region. * *adj* native.—**vernacularly** *adv*.

vernacularism *n* vernacular usage; a vernacular word or expression.

vernal *adj* of, appearing in, relating to, or suggestive of the spring.—**vernally** *adv*.

vernation *n* (*bot*) the arrangement of leaves within a bud.

vernier *n* a small sliding scale attached to a larger fixed scale, with gradations to indicate minute subdivisions of the smallest divisions on the main fixed scale; an additional apparatus used to finetune or adjust an instrument. * *adj* of, pertaining to, or having a vernier.

Veronal (*trademark*) *n* a sedative or hypnotic drug; barbitone.

veronica[1] *n* any of several plants with blue, pink or white flowers, incl speedwell.

veronica[2] *n* (*RC Church*) the image of Christ's face that in legend appeared on a handkerchief given to him by St Veronica as he went to his crucifixion; this handkerchief; any similar image of Christ's face on a cloth.

veronica[3] *n* (*bullfighting*) a manoeuvre by a matador in which he swings the cape slowly before the bull while standing still.

verruca *n* (*pl* **verrucae, verrucas**) a wart on the hand or foot; (*biol*) a wart-like excrescence.—**verrucose, verrucous** *adj*.

versatile *adj* turning readily from one occupation to another, adaptable; talented in many different ways; variable, fickle, changeable; (*biol*) able to move or turn freely.—**versatilely** *adv*.—**versatility** *n*.

verse *n* a line of poetry; a stanza of a poem; a metrical composition, esp of a light nature; a short section of a chapter in the Bible. * *vti* to make verses (about).

versed *adj* skilled or learned in a subject.

versicle *n* a short verse or text sung by priest and congregation alternately in a liturgical service.

versicolour, versicolor *adj* parti-coloured; changeable in colour, iridescent.

versification *n* verse-making; the metre or verses of a poem; the conversion of prose into verse.

versify *vti* (**versifying, versified**) to write poetry or verse; to turn into verse.—**versifier** *n*.

version *n* a translation from one language into another; a particular account or description.—**versional** *adj*.

vers libre *n* verse with no regular metrical system; free verse.

verso *n* (*pl* **versos**) a left-hand, even-numbered page of a book, the back of the recto; the back of a printed sheet; the reverse of a coin.

versus *prep* against; in contrast to.

vert *n* (*English law*) (*formerly*) the right to collect whatever grows and bears a green leaf in a forest; green vegetation; (*her*) green.

vert. *abbr* = vertical.

vertebra *n* (*pl* **vertebrae, vertebras**) one of the interconnecting bones of the spinal column.—**vertebral** *adj*.

vertebrate *n* an animal with a backbone. * *adj* having a backbone; of the vertebrates.

vertebration *n* division into vertebrae or vertebrae-like segments.

vertex *n* (*pl* **vertexes, vertices**) the topmost point; apex; (*anat*) the crown of the head; (*geom*) the point at which two sides of a polygon or the planes of a solid intersect.

vertical *adj* perpendicular to the horizon; upright. * *n* a vertical line or plane.—**verticality** *n*.—**vertically** *adv*.

verticil *n* a whorl-like arrangement of leaves or flowers around a stem

verticillate *adj* (*biol*) arranged in a whorl-like pattern.—**verticillately** *adv*.—**verticillation** *n*.

vertiginous *adj* revolving, rotary; giddy; causing giddiness; whirling.—**vertiginously** *adv*.—**vertiginousness** *n*.

vertigo *n* (*pl* **vertigoes, vertigines**) a sensation of dizziness and sickness caused by a disorder of the sense of balance.—**vertiginous** *adj*.

vertu *see* **virtu**.

vervain *n* a perennial European with clusters of tiny bluish-purple flowers.

verve *n* enthusiasm; liveliness; energy.

vervet *n* a small African monkey with dark hands and feet and yellowish or greenish coat.

very *adj* complete; absolute; same. * *adv* extremely; truly; really.

Very light *n* a coloured flare fired from a Very pistol as a signal at sea or to give temporary light.

vesica *n* (*pl* **vesicae**) (*anat*) the bladder, esp the urinary bladder; (art) a pointed oval halo used as an aureole in medieval sculpture or painting.—vesical *adj*.

vesicant, vesicatory *n* (*pl* **vesicants, vesicatories**) a substance (eg mustard gas) that causes blistering, with applications in chemical warfare. * *adj* raising blisters.

vesicate *vt* to raise blisters on. * *vi* to become blistered.—**vesication** *n*.

vesicle *n* a small blister; a small cyst or sac; (*anat*) a bladder-like vessel or cavity, esp one filled with serous fluid; (*geol*) a cavity in rock formed by gases during solidification; (*bot*) a small sac found in some seaweeds and aquatic plants.—**vesicular** *adj*.

vesper *n* (*arch*) evening; (*with cap*) the evening star; (*Anglican Church*) evensong; (*RC Church*) the sixth of the canonical hours. * *adj* pertaining to evening or vespers.

vespertine, vespertinal *adj* of evening; (*bot*) opening in the evening; (*zool*) active in the evening; (*astron*) setting about sunset.

vespiary *n* (*pl* **vespiaries**) a nest of wasps or hornets.

vespine *adj* of, pertaining to, or like a wasp or wasps.

vessel *n* a container; a ship or boat; a tube in the body along which fluids pass.

vest *n* a sleeveless undergarment worn next to the skin, a singlet; a waistcoat. * *vt* to place or settle (power, authority, etc.); (*with* **in**) to confer or be conferred on; to invest with a right to.

Vesta *n* (*astron*) a bright asteroid; (*Roman myth*) the goddess of the hearth and the household fire.

vesta *n* a short match of wax or wood, lit by friction.

vestal *adj* pertaining to or sacred to the goddess Vesta; vowed to chastity, pure. * *n* a vestal virgin; a virgin.

vestal virgin *n* one of the six virgin priestesses who tended the sacred fire on the altar of the temple of Vesta, in ancient Rome.

vested *adj* (*law*) having permanent entitlement to the possession or use of property, now and in the future, ratified by law or custom; (*priest, etc*) clothed in ecclesiastical vestments.

vested interest *n* (*law*) a permanent entitlement to the possession and use of property, now and in the future; a strong reason for acting in a certain way, usu for personal gain; (usu pl) people in such a state.

vestibule *n* an entrance hall or lobby; a covered entrance at the end of a rail carriage; (*anat*) a communicating channel.—**vestibular** *adj*.

vestige *n* a hint; a trace; a rudimentary survival of a former organ; a particle.—**vestigial** *adj*.—**vestigially** *adv*.

vestment *n* a garment or robe, esp that worn by a priest or official.—**vestmental** *adj*.

vestry *n* (*pl* **vestries**) a room in a church where vestments, etc, are kept and parochial meetings held; a meeting for parish business.—**vestral** *adj*.

vestryman *n* (*pl* **vestrymen**) a member of a vestry elected by the parishioners.

vesture *n* (*arch*) clothing; something that clothes, a covering; (*law*) everything growing on someone's land apart from trees; something obtained from land, such as wheat. * (*arch*) *vt* to clothe.

vesuvianite *n* a mineral of a green, brown or yellow colour, similar to the garnet, idocrase.

vet *n* a veterinary surgeon. * *vt* (**vetting, vetted**) to examine, check for errors, etc.

vetch *n* a common leguminous climbing plant with blue or purple flowers and a stem with tendrils, found in temperate climates and used for green fodder; any similar plant.

vetchling *n* a climbing plant like a vetch mainly found in northern temperate regions with angled or winged stems with tendrils and gaudy flowers.

veteran *adj* old, experienced; having served in the armed forces. * *n* a person who has served in the armed forces; a person who has given long service in a particular activity.

veterinary *adj* of or dealing with diseases of domestic animals.

veterinarian, veterinary surgeon *n* a person trained in treating sick or injured animals.

veto *n* (*pl* **vetoes**) the right of a person or group to prohibit an action or legislation; a prohibition. * *vt* (**vetoing, vetoed**) to refuse to agree to; to prohibit.—**vetoer** *n*.

vex *vt* to annoy; to puzzle, confuse.—**vexer** *n*.—**vexingly** *adv*.

vexation *n* a vexing or being vexed; an annoying thing; irritation, distress.

vexatious *adj* causing vexation; annoying; troublesome; harassing; (*litigation*) designed merely to annoy.—**vexatiously** *adv*.

vexed *adj* annoyed; (*question*) much debated.—**vexedly** *adv*.—**vexedness** *n*.

vexillum *n* (*pl* **vexilla**) (*bot*) the largest petal found on flowers of the plant family to which the sweet pea and similar plants belong; (*zool*) the vane of a feather.

VHF *abbr* = very high frequency.

via *prep* by way of.

viable *adj* capable of growing or developing; workable; practicable.—**viability** *n*.—**viably** *adv*.

viaduct *n* a road or railway carried by a bridge with arches over a valley, river, etc.

vial *n* a small bottle for medicines, etc; a phial.

via media *n* a middle course between extremes; a compromise.

viand *n* an article of food. (*pl*) meat ready to be cooked; food.

viaticum *n* (*pl* **viatica, viaticums**) (*RC Church*) the Eucharist administered to someone whose death is or might be imminent; (*rare*) an allowance or provisions given to a person setting out on a journey.

vibes *npl* (*sl*) vibrations; vibraphone.

vibraculum *n* (*pl* **vibracula**) (*zool*) a whip-like appendage by which some polyzoans ward off parasites.

vibrant *adj* vibrating; resonant; bright; lively.—**vibrancy** *n*.—**vibrantly** *adv*.

vibraphone *n* a percussion instrument that produces a vibrato by resonating metal bars.—**vibraphonist** *n*.

vibrate *vti* to shake; to move quickly backwards and forwards; to quiver; to oscillate; to resound.—**vibratingly** *adv*.

vibratile *adj* capable of or characterized by vibrating.—**vibratility** *n*.

vibration *n* a vibrating or being vibrated; oscillation; resonance; vacillation; (*usu pl*) an emotional reaction instinctively sensed; (*physics*) the rapid alternating of particles caused by the disturbance of equilibrium.—**vibrational** *adj*.

vibrative *adj* vibratory.

vibrato *n* (*pl* **vibratos**) (*mus*) a pulsating effect obtained by rapid variation of emphasis on the same tone.

vibrator *n* the vibrating part in various instruments; a dildo.

vibratory *adj* vibrating; consisting of or causing vibrations.

vibrio *n* (*pl* **vibrios**) a spiral or curved, rod-like bacillus.—**vibrioid** *adj*.

vibrissa *n* (*pl* **vibrissae**) a sensitive whisker on an animal's face; any of the bristle-like feathers found in the beak area of certain insect-eating birds.

viburnum *n* any of several shrubs or trees, incl the guelder rose, with red or black berry-like fruits, found in various temperate and sub-tropical regions; the dried bark from some of these, sometimes used medicinally.

vicar *n* a parish priest; a clergyman in charge of a chapel.

vicarage *n* the residence of a vicar.

vicarial *adj* of, pertaining to, or acting as a vicar, vicars or a vicariate; (*ecclesiastical functions*) delegated, vicarious.

vicariate, vicarate *n* the rank, office, or district of a vicar.

vicarious *adj* substitute; obtained second-hand by listening to or watching another person's experiences.—**vicariously** *adv*.—**vicariousness** *n*.

vice[1] *n* an evil action or habit; a grave moral fault; great wickedness; a serious defect, a blemish.

vice[2] *n* a clamping device with jaws, used for holding objects firmly.—*also* **vise**.

vice- *prefix* one who acts in place of or as a deputy to another.

vice admiral *n* a rank of naval officer next below admiral.

vice-chairman *n* (*pl* **vice-chairmen**) one who takes the chair in a chairman's absence.

vice chancellor *n* the chief executive officer of a university.

vice consul *n* a person who acts in place of a consul in a subordinate district, etc.

vicegerent *n adj* a person holding delegated power or ruling as another's deputy.—*also adj*.—**vicegerency** *n*.
vicennial *adj* lasting twenty years; happening every twenty years.
vice president *n* a deputy or assistant president.
viceregal *adj* of or relating to a viceroy; (*Austral, NZ*) of or relating to a governor general.
vicereine *n* a viceroy's wife.
viceroy *n* one who rules a country or province as a representative of a king or queen.
viceroyalty, viceroyship *n* (*pl* **viceroyalties, viceroyships**) the office or term of a viceroy.
vice versa *adv* conversely; the other way round.
vichyssoise *n* leek and potato soup consumed cold.
Vichy water *n* a mineral water from Vichy in France.
vicinage *n* a surrounding district, a neighbourhood; the people of a neighbourhood; proximity.
vicinal *adj* neighbouring; adjacent; (*chem*) resembling or substituting for a crystal face or form; denoting substituted atoms on adjacent atoms in a molecule.
vicinity *n* (*pl* **vicinities**) a nearby area; proximity.
vicious *adj* cruel; violent; malicious; ferocious.—**viciously** *adv*.—**viciousness** *n*.
vicissitude *n* a change of circumstances or fortune; (*pl*) ups and downs.—**vicissitudinary, vicissitudinous** *adj*.
victim *n* a person who has been killed or injured by an action beyond his or her control; a dupe.
victimize *vt* to make a victim of, to cause to suffer.—**victimization** *n*.—**victimizer** *n*.
victor *n* a winner; a conqueror.
victoria *n* a light, open, four-wheeled, two-seater carriage; a giant South American water-lily; a victoria plum.
Victorian *adj* of or living in the reign of Queen Victoria; old-fashioned, prudish.
victoria plum *n* a large purplish-red sweet variety of plum.
victorious *adj* having won in battle or contest; emblematic of victory; triumphant.—**victoriously** *adv*.
victory *n* (*pl* **victories**) triumph in battle; success; achievement.
victual *n* (*usu pl*) food, provisions. * *vt* (**victualling, victualled** *or* **victualing, victualed**) to supply with food; to take in provisions.
victualler, victualer *n* (*formerly*) a supplier of provisions, esp to an army; a provision ship; an innkeeper.
vicuña, vicuna *n* a South American animal similar to the llama with a fine, long, reddish silky fleece; cloth made from this fleece.
vide (*Latin*) see.
vide infra (*Latin*) see later (in this book).
videlicet *adv* that is to say, namely.
video *n* (*pl* **videos**) the transmission or recording of television programmes or films, using a television set and a video recorder and tape. * *vt* (**videoing, videoed**) to record on video tape.
video cassette *n* a cassette containing video tape.
video recorder *n* the machine on which video cassettes are played or recorded.
video tape *n* a magnetic tape on which images and sounds can be recorded for reproduction on television.—**video-tape** *vt*.
vide supra (*Latin*) see earlier (in this book).
vidette *see* **vedette**.
vidkid *n* a child who is addicted to watching television or video.
vie *vi* (**vying, vied**) to contend or strive for superiority.—**vier** *n*.
view *n* sight; range of vision; inspection, examination; intention; scene; opinion. * *vt* to see; to consider; to examine intellectually.
viewer *n* a person who views, esp television; an optical device used in viewing.
viewfinder *n* a device in a camera showing the view to be photographed.
viewless *adj* without a view; (*poet*) invisible, unseen.
viewpoint *n* opinion; a place from which something can be viewed, esp a scenic panorama.
vigil *n* keeping watch at night.
vigilance *n* a being vigilant; watchfulness; alertness.
vigilant *adj* on the watch to discover and avoid danger, watchful; alert; cautious.—**vigilantly** *adv*.
vigilante *n* a self-appointed law enforcer.
vignette *n* a small picture or design in a book without a line framing it; a picture, the edges of which shade off gradually into the background; a short word sketch. * *vt* to depict in vignette; to shade off into the background.—**vignettist** *n*.
vigor *see* **vigour**.
vigoroso *adv* (*mus*) with vigour.
vigorous *adj* full of vigour; powerful; lusty.—**vigorously** *adv*.—**vigorousness** *n*.
vigour *n* physical or mental strength; vitality.—*also* **vigor**.
Viking *n* one of the Norse pirates who ravaged the coasts of Europe from the 8th–10th centuries.
vilayet *n* a province of Turkey.
vile *adj* wicked; evil; offensive; very bad.—**vilely** *adv*.—**vileness** *n*.
vilify *vt* (**vilifying, vilified**) to malign.—**vilification** *n*.—**vilifier** *n*.
villa *n* a large country or suburban house.
village *n* a collection of houses smaller than a town.
villager *n* an inhabitant of a village.
villain *n* a scoundrel; the main evil character in a play, film or novel; (*arch*) a boor.
villainous *adj* depraved, evil, wicked; very bad, wretched.—**villainously** *adv*.—**villainousness** *n*.
villainy *n* (*pl* **villainies**) great wickedness; an atrocious crime.
villanella *n* (*pl* **villanelle**) a popular part-song of 17th-century Italy.
villanelle *n* a poem of 19 lines in six stanzas rhymed aba aba aba aba aba abaa, the 6th, 12th and 18th lines being the same as the first, and the 9th, 15th and 19th the same as the third.
villein *n* (*hist*) a feudal tenant of the lowest class, a serf.
villi *see* **villus**.
villous, villose *adj* covered with villi; (*bot*) covered with long, thin, soft hairs.
villus *n* (*pl* **villi**) (*biol*) the velvety fibre of the mucous membrane of the intestine; (*bot*) the soft hair covering a fruit or flower.—**villosity**.
vim (*sl*) energy, force.
vimineous *adj* (*bot*) of or producing long flexible shoots.
vina *n* a seven-stringed Indian musical instrument.
vinaceous *adj* of the colour of wine; wine-red.
vinaigrette *n* a salad dressing made from oil, vinegar and seasoning.
vincible *adj* capable of being conquered or overcome.—**vincibility** *n*.
vinculum *n* (*pl* **vincula**) (*anat*) a ligament; (*math*) a horizontal line over quantities having the effect of a parenthesis; (*print*) a brace; a bond of union, a tie.
vindicate *vt* to establish the existence or truth of, to justify; to clear of charges, to absolve from blame.—**vindicable** *adj*.—**vindicator** *n*.—**vindicatory** *adj*.
vindication *n* a vindicating or being vindicated; an event, fact, evidence, etc, that justifies a deed or claim.
vindictive *adj* vengeful; spiteful; (*damages*) exemplary, punitive.—**vindictively** *adv*.—**vindictiveness** *n*.
vine *n* any climbing plant, or its stem; a grapevine; a sphere of activity, esp spiritual or mental endeavour.
vinedresser *n* a person who cultivates vines.
vinegar *n* a sour-tasting liquid containing acetic acid, used as a condiment and preservative.
vinegary *adj* of or like vinegar; sour; ill-tempered.
vinery *n* (*pl* **vineries**) a place where grapes are grown or wine is made.
vineyard *n* a plantation of grapevines.
vingt-et-un *n* a gambling game with cards in which players try to obtain points better than the banker's but not more than 21.—*also* **blackjack, pontoon, twenty-one**.
vinic *adj* contained in or obtained from wine.

viniculture *n* the cultivation of vines and manufacture of wine, viticulture.—**vinicultural** *adj*.—**viniculturist** *n*.
viniferous *adj* wine-producing.
vinificator *n* in winemaking, an apparatus for collecting alcoholic vapours.
vin ordinaire *n* (*pl* **vins ordinaires**) the ordinary table wine of France.
vinous *adj* of, pertaining to, or having the qualities of wine; like wine; wine-coloured; inspired by wine.—**vinosity** *n*.
vintage *n* the grape harvest of one season; wine, esp of good quality, made in a particular year; wine of a particular region; the product of a particular period. * *adj* (*cars*) classic; (*wine*) of a specified year and of good quality; (*play*) characteristic of the best.
vintager *n* a gatherer of grapes in a wine harvest.
vintner *n* a wine merchant.
vinyl *n* a strong plastic used in floor coverings, furniture and records, etc.
viol *n* a family of medieval six-stringed instruments played with a bow, similar to a violin but with a softer sound.
viola[1] *n* a stringed instrument of the violin family, and tuned a fifth below it.
viola[2] *n* any of several plants of the genus that includes violets and pansies.
violable *adj* capable of being violated or broken.
violaceous *adj* of violet colour or family.
viola da gamba *n* the bass viol.
viola d'amore *n* a tenor viol with seven strings and a sweet tone.
violate *vt* to break or infringe (an agreement); to rape; to disturb (one's privacy).—**violative** *adj*.—**violator** *n*.
violation *n* the act of violating, infringing, or injuring; rape; outrage; an act of irreverence or profanation.
violence *n* physical force intended to cause injury or destruction; natural force; passion, intensity.
violent *adj* urged or driven by force; vehement; impetuous; forcible; furious; severe.—**violently** *adv*.
violet *n* a small plant with bluish-purple flowers; a bluish-purple colour.
violin *n* a four-stringed musical instrument, played with a bow.
violinist *n* a person who plays the violin.
violist *n* a player of a viol or viola.
violoncellist *n* a performer on the violoncello.
violoncello *n* (*pl* **violoncellos**) the full name for a **cello**.
violone *n* the largest type of viol, corresponding to the double-bass.
VIP *abbr* = Very Important Person.
viper *n* a common European venomous snake.—**viperine** *adj*.
viperous, viperish *adj* viper-like; malignant.
virago *n* (*pl* **viragoes, viragos**) a bad-tempered woman.
viral *adj* of or caused by a virus.
virelay, virelai *n* an old French form of poem with short lines and two rhymes variously arranged.
vireo *n* (*pl* **vireos**) a small greenish American singing bird.
virescence *n* the state of being virescent, esp in place of the normal colour of petals.
virescent *adj* beginning to be green; greenish.
virgate[1] *adj* (*bot*) slim and straight.
virgate[2] *n* an old English unit of land equal to approx 30 acres.
virgin *n* a person (esp a woman) who has never had sexual intercourse; (*with cap*) Mary, the mother of Christ; a painting or statue of her. * *adj* chaste; pure; untouched.
virginal[1] *adj* of or pertaining to a virgin or virginity; befitting a virgin; chaste, pure, innocent; fresh, unsullied, untouched.
virginal[2] *n* a small rectangular keyed musical instrument resembling a harpsichord but without legs.
virginity *n* the state of being a virgin; the state of being chaste, untouched, etc.
Virgo *n* the Virgin, the 6th sign of the zodiac.—**Virgoan** *adj*.
virgo intacta *n* (*pl* **virgines intactae**) (*law*) a girl or woman who is a virgin.
virgulate *adj* rod-shaped.
virgule *n* a small rod; a slanting punctuation mark (/), a solidus.
viridescent *adj* greenish; turning green.— **viridescence** *n*.
viridity *n* greenness; freshness.
virile *adj* of a mature man, manly; strong, forceful; sexually potent.—**virility** *n*.
virtu *n* a love or knowledge of the fine arts, connoisseurship; artistic excellence, fine workmanship; the quality of appealing to a collector; artistic objects, antiques, curios, etc, collectively.—*also* **vertu**.
virtual *adj* in effect or essence, though not in fact or strict definition; (*comput*) denoting memory, making use of an external memory to increase capacity.
virtually *adv* to all intents and purposes, practically.
virtue *n* moral excellence; any admirable quality; chastity; merit.
virtuoso *n* (*pl* **virtuosos, virtuosi**) a person highly skilled in an activity, esp in playing a musical instrument. * *adj* skilled, masterly in technique.—**virtuosic** *adj*.—**virtuosity** *n*.
virtuous *adj* righteous; upright; pure.—**virtuously** *adv*.—**virtuousness** *n*.
virulent *adj* (*disease*) deadly; extremely poisonous; hostile; vicious.—**virulence** *n*.—**virulently** *adv*.
virus *n* (*pl* **viruses**) a very simple microorganism capable of replicating within living cells, producing disease; the disease caused by a virus; a harmful influence.
visa *n* an endorsement on a passport allowing the bearer to travel in the country of the government issuing it. * *vt* (**visaing, visaed**) to mark with a visa; to grant a visa to.
visage *n* the face; the countenance; appearance.
visard *see* **vizard**.
vis-à-vis *prep* opposite to; in face of. * *adj, adv* facing. * *n* the person opposite; a counterpart.
viscacha *n* a South American burrowing rodent, that looks like a large chinchilla.—*also* **vizcacha**.
viscera *npl* (*sing* **viscus**) the large internal organs of the animal body, the entrails.
visceral *adj* of, pertaining to, or affecting the viscera; pertaining to or touching deeply inward feelings.—**viscerally** *adv*.
viscid *adj* (*leaves*) covered with a sticky layer; (*fluids*) thick, glutinous.—**viscidity** *n* —**viscidly** *adv*.
viscometer, viscosimeter *n* an instrument for measuring viscosity.
viscose *n* a form of cellulose used in making artificial silk.
viscosity *n* (*pl* **viscosities**) the property or state of being sticky or glutinous; (*physics*) a property of fluids that indicates their resistance to flow.
viscount *n* in Britain, a title of nobility next below an earl.—**viscountess** *nf*.
viscountcy *n* (*pl* **viscountcies**) the rank of a viscount.
viscous *adj* sticky, thick; having viscosity.—**viscously** *adv*.—**viscousness** *n*.
viscus *see* **viscera**.
vise *see* **vice**.
visibility *n* (*pl* **visibilities**) clearness of seeing or being seen; the degree of clearness of the atmosphere.
visible *adj* able to be seen, perceptible; apparent, evident.—**visibleness** *n*.—**visibly** *adv*.
visible speech *n* a phonetic alphabet representing the actual movements of the vocal organs and used in teaching the deaf.
vision *n* the power of seeing, sight; a supernatural appearance; a revelation; foresight; imagination; a mental concept; a person, scene, etc of unusual beauty; something seen in a dream or trance.—**visional** *adj*.
visionary *adj* imaginative; having foresight; existing in imagination only, not real. * *n* (*pl* **visionaries**) an imaginative person; a dreamer; an idealist, a mystic.
visit *vt* to go to see; to pay a call upon a person or place; to stay with or at; to punish or reward with. * *vi* to see or meet someone regularly. * *n* the act of going to see, a call.—**visitable** *adj*.
visitant *n* a migratory bird; a visitor, esp a pilgrim; a ghost. * *adj* (*arch*) visiting.
visitation *n* a visit by a superior; a punitive act of God; an official visit; right of access of a divorced parent to his or her children; a large migration of animals; (*with cap*) the visit paid by the Virgin Mary to

Elizabeth (Luke 1:39*ff*); a picture representing the event; the day on which this is commemorated, 2 July.—**visitational** *adj*.

visiting card *n* a small card with a person's name on it, left when paying visits.

visitor *n* a person who visits; a caller; a tourist; a migratory bird pausing in transit; an official acting as an inspector and adviser.

visor *n* a movable part of a helmet protecting the face; the peak of a cap.—*also* **vizor.**—**visored** *adj*.

vista *n* a view, as from a high place; a mental picture.—**vistaed, vista'd** *adj*.

visual *adj* having, producing, or relating to vision or sight; perceptible, visible; (*knowledge*) attained by sight or vision; (*impressions, etc*) based upon something seen; of the nature of, producing or conveying a picture in the mind; (*physics*) optical. * *n* a piece of graphic material used for display or to convey a concept, etc; (*pl*) the visual aspect of a film, etc.—**visually** *adv*.

visual aid *n* a film, slide or overhead projector, etc used to aid teaching.

visualize *vt* to form a mental picture of; to make visible to the mind or imagination. * *vi* to construct a visual image in the mind.—**visualization** *n*.—**visualizer** *n*.

vital *adj* of, connected with or necessary to life; essential; lively, animated; fundamental; (*wound, error*) fatal. * *n* (*pl*) the bodily organs essential for life.—**vitally** *adv*.

vitalism *n* the belief that life cannot be explained as resulting wholly from physical and chemical processes, but must include some other vital non-material force or process.—**vitalist** *n*.—**vitalistic** *adj*.

vitality *n* (*pl* **vitalities**) vigour, hold on life; spirits; animation; capacity to last, durability.

vitalize *vt* to give life to; to animate; to make vigorous.—**vitalization** *n*.

vital statistics *npl* data recording births, deaths, marriages, etc used in compiling population statistics; (*inf*) the measurements of a woman's figure.

vitamin *n* one of several organic substances occurring naturally in foods, which are essential for good health.—**vitaminic** *adj*.

vitellin *n* a protein forming the major component in the yolk of birds' eggs.

vitelline *adj* of or pertaining to egg yolk; of a yellow colour close to the shade of egg yolk.

vitiate *vt* to make faulty or ineffective; to taint; to deprave; to invalidate or annul (a legal document, etc).—**vitiation** *n*.—**vitiator** *n*.

viticulture *n* the science of grapes and grape-growing.—**viticulturer, viticulturist** *n*.—**viticultural** *adj*.

vitreous *adj* of like or obtained from glass; of the vitreous body.—**vitreousness** *n*.

vitreous body, vitreous humour *n* the transparent tissue of the eyeball.

vitrescence *n* the quality of being vitrescent; the process of changing something, such as a crystalline material, into glass.

vitrescent *adj* capable of being made into or becoming like glass.

vitric *adj* glass-like.

vitrify *vt* (**vitrifying, vitrified**) to convert into glass or a glass-like substance.—**vitrifiable** *adj*.—**vitrification, vitrifaction** *n*.

vitriol *n* sulphuric acid; savage criticism. * *vt* (**vitrioling, vitrioled** *or* **vitriolling, vitriolled**) to throw vitriol over, to poison with vitriol.

vitriolic *adj* of or relating to vitriol; scathing, bitter.

vitriolize *vt* to harm by throwing vitriol over; to change into vitriol; to use vitriol in or as a part of the processing of something.—**vitriolization** *n*.

vitta *n* (*pl* **vittae**) (*bot*) an oil tube in the fruit of some plants, eg parsley; (*zool*) a coloured stripe.—**vittate** *adj*.

vituline *adj* of, like, calves or veal.

vituperate *vt* to berate; to abuse verbally.—**vituperative** *adj*.—**vituperator** *n*.

vituperation *n* the act of vituperating; blame, censure, reproof; the expression of this in abusive or violent language.

viva *interj* long live, hurrah for.

viva *n* in UK, an oral examination, a viva voce. * *vt* (**vivas** *or* **viva's, vivaing, vivaed** *or* **viva'd**) to examine orally.

vivace *adv* (*mus*) in a lively manner; with spirit.

vivacious *adj* lively; animated; spirited.—**vivaciously** *adv*.—**vivaciousness** *n*.

vivacity *n* (*pl* **vivacities**) vivaciousness; animation of the mind or disposition; liveliness of conception or perception; spirited conduct, manner or speech; brilliancy of light or colour.

vivarium *n* (*pl* **vivariums, vivaria**) a place for keeping animals in their natural state for research or observation.

viva voce *adj, adv* orally, by word of mouth. * *n* an oral examination, a viva.

vivid *adj* brightly coloured; graphic; lively; intense.—**vividly** *adv*.—**vividness** *n*.

vivify *vt* (**vivifying, vivified**) to give life to; to make more lively or more vivid.—**vivification** *n*.—**vivifier** *n*.

viviparous *adj* (*zool*) giving birth to young that have developed inside the body, as do most mammals.—**viviparity** *n*.—**viviparously** *adv*.

vivisect *vt* to subject to vivisection.—**vivisector** *n*.

vivisection *n* the practice of performing surgical operations on living animals for scientific research.—**vivisectional** *adj*.

vivisectionist *n* a person who practises or approves of vivisection.

vixen *n* a female fox; a malicious or shrewish woman.—**vixenish** *adj*.

viz *abbr* = *videlicet* namely.

vizard *n* (*arch*) a mask or other object that disguises; a visor.—*also* **visard.**

vizcacha *see* **vischacha.**

vizier, vizir *n* a minister of state or high official in Muslim countries, esp in the Ottoman Empire.

vizierate *n* the status, authority or (term of) office of a vizier.

vizor *see* **visor.**

vocable *n* (*linguistics*) a word looked on as a pattern of characters or sounds with no regard to meaning; a sound; a vowel. * *adj* able to be spoken.

vocabulary *n* (*pl* **vocabularies**) an alphabetical list of words with their meanings; the words of a language; an individual's command or use of particular words.

vocal *adj* of, for, endowed with, relating to, or produced by the voice; outspoken, noisy; (*phonetics*) having a vowel function. * *n* a vowel; (*pl*) music for the voice, not another instrument.—**vocally** *adv*.

vocal chords *npl* either of two pairs of elastic membranous folds in the larynx, esp the lower pair, which vibrate and produce sound.

vocalic *adj* of, like or containing vowels.

vocalise *n* a vocal exercise to improve flexibility and control of the voice in which a singer sings to one vowel sound.

vocalist *n* a singer.

vocalize *vti* to express with the voice; to articulate, utter distinctly; to use the singing voice; to sing to vowel sounds; to write with vowels or vowel points.—**vocalization** *n*.—**vocalizer** *n*.

vocation *n* a calling to a particular career or occupation, esp to a religious life; a sense of fitness for a particular career.

vocational *adj* of or relating to a vocation or occupation; providing special training for a particular career.—**vocationally** *adv*.

vocative *adj* used, involved in or pertaining to loud utterances to attract attention; (*gram*) denoting the case of a noun, adjective, or pronoun used in addressing a person in some inflected languages, eg Latin. * *n* (*gram*) a vocative case or form.

vociferant *adj* clamorous, noisy. * *n* a clamorous, noisy person.

vociferate *vti* to speak loudly and insistently, to clamour; to shout, to bawl.—**vociferation** *n*.—**vociferator** *n*.

vociferous *adj* clamorous, noisy.—**vociferously** *adv*.—**vociferousness** *n*.

vodka *n* a spirit distilled from rye, potatoes, etc.

vogue *n* the fashion at a specified time; popularity. * *adj* fashionable, in vogue.—**voguish** *adj*.

voice *n* sound from the mouth; sound produced by speaking or singing; the quality of this; the power of speech; utterance; expressed opinion, vote; (*gram*) the forms of a verb showing the relation of subject to action; (*phonetics*) a sound uttered with vibration of the vocal chords not with mere breath. * *vt* to express; to speak; (*mus*) to regulate so as to give the correct tone; (*phonetics*) to utter with the voice, to make sonant.—**voicer** *n*.

voiced *adj* having a voice, esp of a specified kind, quality or tone; (*phonetics*) uttered with the voice or vibration of the vocal chords, sonant.
voiceful *adj* (*poet*) having a voice; sonorous.
voiceless *adj* speechless, dumb; (*phonetics*) not voiced.—**voicelessly** *adv*.—**voicelessness** *n*.
voice-over *n* the voice of an unseen narrator, esp in a film, TV commercial, etc.
void *adj* unoccupied, empty; not legally binding; having no cards of a particular suit. * *n* an empty space, a vacuum; vacancy, sense of loss. * *vt* to discharge, to emit; empty; to make invalid.—**voidable** *adj*.—**voider** *n*.
voidance *n* the act of voiding or evacuating; emptiness; the annulment of a legal deed.
voided *adj* (*her*) having the inner part of a figure cut away, leaving only the outer edges; being, or having been caused to be, empty.
voile *n* a light, sheer fabric of silk, rayon, etc, used for dresses, scarves, etc.
volant *adj* flying; able to fly; (*her*) appearing to fly; (*poet*) nimble.
Volapuk, Volapük *n* an artificial language taking elements from English, French, German, Latin. etc, invented in 1880 and intended for international commercial use.—**Volapukist, Volapükist** *n*.
volar *adj* (*anat*) of the palm of the hand or sole of the foot.
volatile *adj* evaporating very quickly; changeable, fickle; unstable; light-hearted, mercurial; flighty; (*comput*) having a memory that loses data when power is disconnected.—**volatility** *n*.
volatilize *vti* to turn into vapour, to (cause to) evaporate. —**volatilization** *n*.
vol-au-vent *n* a case of light puff pastry filled with a savoury sauce.
volcanic *adj* of, like or due to the action of a volcano; violent, intense.—**volcanically** *adv*.
volcanism *n* volcanic action.—*also* **vulcanism.**
volcanize *vt* to subject to volcanic heat; to cause to change by means of volcanic heat.—**volcanization** *n*.
volcano *n* (*pl* **volcanoes, volcanos**) a hill or mountain formed by ejection of lava, ashes, etc through an opening in the earth's crust.
volcanology *n* the science of volcanoes and the occurrences associated with them.—*also* **vulcanology.**—**volcanological, vulcanological** *adj*.—**volcanologist, vulcanologist** *n*.
vole[1] *n* a small rat-like rodent with a short tail.
vole[2] *vt* to win all the tricks in a deal. * *n* a slam.
volitant *adj* able to fly, volant; flying, or otherwise moving about, in a rapid, nimble fashion.
volition *n* the exercise of the will; choice.—**volitional** *adj*.
volitive *adj* pertaining to or having the power of will; (*gram*) desiderative; expressing a wish or intention.
volley *n* (*pl* **volleys**) the multiple discharge of many missiles or small arms; a barrage; (*tennis, volleyball*) the return of the ball before it reaches the ground. * *vt* (**volleying, volleyed**) to return (a ball) before it hits the ground.—**volleyer** *n*.
volleyball *n* a team game played by hitting a large inflated ball over a net with the hands; the ball used.
volt[1] *n* the circular gait of a horse in dressage; (fencing) a leap to avoid a thrust.
volt[2] *n* the unit of measure of the force of an electrical current.
volta *n* (*pl* **volte**) a lively 16th-century Italian dance; (*mus*) music in triple time, originally written to accompany such a dance; (*mus*) a particular time as specified.
voltage *n* electrical energy that moves a charge around a circuit, measured in volts.
voltaic *adj* pertaining to electricity generated by chemical action or galvanism; galvanic.
voltaism *n* galvanism; electricity generated by chemical action.
voltameter *n* an instrument for measuring an electric charge; a coulombmeter.
volte-face *n* (*pl* **volte-faces, volte-face**) a change to an opposite opinion or direction.
voltmeter *n* an instrument for measuring voltage.
voluble *adj* speaking with a great flow of words, fluent; (*arch*) revolving, rotating; (*bot*) twining.—**volubility** *n*.—**volubly** *adv*.
volubleness *n* excessive fluency of speech.
volume *n* the amount of space occupied by an object; quantity, amount; intensity of sound; a book; one book of a series.—**volumed** *adj*.
volumeter *n* an instrument for measuring the volume of a gas, liquid, or solid.
volumetric *adj* of or relating to measurement by volume.—**volumetrically** *adv*.
voluminous *adj* of great size or bulk; (*writings*) capable of filling many volumes; (*clothes*) ample, loose.—**voluminosity** *n*.—**voluminously** *adv*.
voluntarism *n* the theory that the will is dominant over the intellect; a belief in voluntary participation not compulsion in a course of action; voluntaryism.—**voluntaryist** *n*.
voluntary *adj* spontaneous, deliberate; without remuneration; supported by voluntary effort; having free will; (*law*) acting gratuitously or from choice, not because of any legal compulsion or argument; (*muscles*) controlled by conscious effort; designed; pertaining to voluntaryism.* *n* (*pl* **voluntaries**) an organ solo, often improvised, played before or after a church service; (*arch*) a volunteer.—voluntarily adv.—**voluntariness** *n*.
voluntaryism *n* the theory that churches, schools, etc, should depend on voluntary contributions, not state aid.—**voluntarist** *n*.—**voluntaristic** *adj*.
volunteer *n* a person who carries out work voluntarily; a person who freely undertakes military service. * *vti* to offer unasked; to come forward, enlist or serve voluntarily.
voluptuary *n* (*pl* **voluptuaries**) a person given up to bodily pleasures or the enjoyment of luxury, a sensualist. * *adj* exciting sensual desire; devoted to pleasures of the senses; voluptuous; luxurious.
voluptuous *adj* excessively fond of pleasure; having an attractive figure; luxurious; exciting sensual desire.—**voluptuously** *adv*.—**voluptuousness** *n*.
volute *n* a spiral; a whorl; anything shaped to resemble a spiral or otherwise convoluted form; a spiral, scroll-shaped ornament, esp on an Ionic capital, a helix; a tropical shellfish with a spiral shell; any of the whorls found on the shells of snails; an auxiliary curved part of an engine that collects waste gases or liquids from that engine. * *adj* spiral-shaped; (*machinery*) moving spirally; (*bot*) rolled up (—*also* **voluted**).
volution *n* a spiral; a convoluted or turning shape or movement; any of the whorls of a shell.
volvox *n* a genus of round, hollow microscopic plants having a rotatory motion, found in ponds, etc.
vomer *n* the flat, slender bone separating the nostrils in mammals.
vomit *vi* to eject the contents of the stomach through the mouth, to spew. * *n* matter ejected from the stomach when vomiting.—**vomiter** *n*.
vomitive *adj* of or causing vomiting. * *n* an emetic.
vomitory *adj* vomitive. * *n* (*pl* **vomitories**) an emetic; an aperture for vomited matter; any opening through which something is ejected; in ancient Rome, a corridor from a street entrance to a tier of seats in an amphitheatre (—*also* **vomitorium**).
vomiturition *n* violent retching; repeated vomiting.
voodoo *n* (*pl* **voodoos**) a religious cult in the West Indies, based on a belief in sorcery, etc; one who practises voodoo. * *vt* (**voodooing, voodooed**) to affect by voodoo.
voodooism *n* the beliefs and practices of voodoo.—**voodooist** *n*.—**voodooistic** *adj*.
voracious *adj* eager to devour (food, literature etc); very greedy.—**voraciously** *adv*.—**voracity** *n*.
vortex *n* (*pl* **vortexes, vortices**) a whirlpool; a powerful eddy; a whirlwind; a whirling motion or mass.—**vortical** *adj*.—**vortically** *adv*.
vorticella *n* (*pl* **vorticellae**) any of a genus of ciliated, bell-shaped animalcules.
vorticism *n* an art movement in which cubist techniques were amalgamated with that aspect of futurism expressing reservations about the quality of contemporary life, and its reliance on machines, so that objects were presented so as to give the effect of an assemblage of vortices.—**vorticist** *n*.

vortiginous *adj* whirling, vortical; vortex-like.

votary *n* (*pl* **votaries**) a person vowed to religious service or worship; an ardent follower, a devotee of a person, religion, occupation, idea, etc (—*also* **votarist**). * *adj* ardently devoted to a deity or saint.

vote *n* an indication of a choice or opinion as to a matter on which one has a right to be consulted; a ballot; decision by a majority; the right to vote; franchise. * *vi* to cast one's vote. * *vt* to elect (to office).—**votable, voteable** *adj*.

voter *n* a person with a right to vote, esp one who uses it.

votive *adj* given, consecrated, or promised by vow; (*RC Church*) voluntary, given by free will not by prescription.

vouch *vt* to provide evidence or proof of. * *vi* to give assurance; to guarantee.

voucher *n* a written record of a transaction; a receipt; a token that can be exchanged for something else.

vouchsafe *vt* to give, to grant; to condescend (to).—**vouchsafement** *n*.

voussoir *n* any of the wedge-shaped stones forming the arch of a bridge or vault.

vow *n* a solemn or binding promise. * *vt* to promise; to resolve.—**vower** *n*.

vowel *n* an open speech sound produced by continuous passage of the breath; a letter representing such a sound, as *a, e, i, o, u*. * *adj* of or constituting a vowel.—**vowelless** *adj*.

vowelize *vt* to insert vowel points in (usu something written in Hebrew).—**vowelization** *n*.

vowel point *n* a diacritical mark indicating a vowel in Hebrew, Arabic, etc.

vox *n* (*pl* **voces**) a voice; a sound.

vox humana *n* an organ stop with tones like the human voice.

vox populi *n* popular opinion; the voice of the people.

voyage *n* a long journey, esp by ship or spacecraft. * *vi* to journey.—**voyager** *n*.

voyageur *n* a Canadian boatman working for a fur-trading company, esp if covering an area inland; any boatman, trapper or guide, esp in Northern Canada.

voyeur *n* a person who is sexually gratified from watching sexual acts or objects; a peeping Tom.—**voyeurism** *n*.—**voyeuristic** *adj*.

VP *abbr* = vice-president.

vraisemblance *n* an appearance of truth, verisimilitude.

vs *abbr* = *versus* against.

VSO *abbr* = Voluntary Service Overseas.

VT *abbr* = Vermont.

vug, vugh *n* (*mining*) a small cavity, often crystal-lined, in a lode or rock.

Vulcan *n* (*Roman myth*) the god of fire and smiths; (*arch*) a planet once thought to orbit Mercury.

vulcanism *see* **volcanism**.

vulcanite *n* a hard, vulcanized rubber, which is resistant to the effects of chemicals, ebonite.

vulcanize *vt* to treat (rubber) with sulphur, white lead and other substances at high temperatures under pressure to improve its strength and elasticity or render it hard and non-elastic; to change the properties of (any material) in a similar way.—**vulcanization** *n*.

vulcanology *see* **volcanology**.

vulgar *adj* of the common people; vernacular; unrefined, in bad taste; coarse; offensive, indecent.—**vulgarly** *adv*.—**vulgarness** *n*.

vulgarian *n* a vulgar pretentious person, esp one who shows of his or her wealth.

vulgarism *n* a crude expression; coarseness.

vulgarity *n* (*pl* **vulgarities**) coarseness of manners or language; a vulgar phrase, expression, act, etc.

vulgarize *vt* to debase; to popularize.—**vulgarization** *n*.—**vulgarizer** *n*.

Vulgate *n* a 4th-century Latin version of the Bible made by St Jerome, by combining text from the original language material and an earlier Latin text derived from the Greek; (*RC Church*) a revised form of this used as the authorized version. * *adj* pertaining to, or contained in, the Vulgate.

vulnerable *adj* capable of being wounded physically or mentally; open to persuasion; easily influenced; open to attack, assailable; (*contract bridge*) having won one game and liable to doubled penalties.—**vulnerability** *n*.—**vulnerably** *adv*.

vulnerary *adj* used for healing wounds. * *n* (*pl* **vulneraries**) a drug, ointment, etc, used in this way.

vulpine, vulpecular *adj* pertaining to, like, or characteristic of a fox; cunning.

vulture *n* a large bird of prey having no feathers on the neck or head and feeding chiefly on carrion; a rapacious person.

vulturine, vulturous *adj* vulture-like.

vulva *n* (*pl* **vulvae, vulvas**) the external genitals of human females.—**vulval, vulvar, vulvate** *adj*.

vulviform *adj* like a cleft with projecting edges.

vulvitis *n* inflammation of the vulva.

vying *see* **vie**.

W (*chem symbol*) tungsten.

w *abbr* = watt(s); west.

W, w *n* the 23rd letter of the English alphabet.

WA *abbr* = Washington.

WAC *abbr* = Women's Army Corps.

wacky *adj* (**wackier, wackiest**) (*sl*) crazy, eccentric.—**wackily** *adv*.—**wackiness** *n*.

wad *n* a small, soft mass, as of cotton or paper; a bundle of paper money.

wadding *n* any soft material for use in padding, packing, etc.

waddle *vi* to walk with short steps and sway from side to side, as a duck.—*also n*.

waddy *n* (*pl* **waddies**) a club with a thickened head used as a weapon by Australian Aborigines. * *vt* (**waddying, waddied**) to hit with a waddy.

wade *vti* to walk through water; to pass (through) with difficulty.

wader *n* a bird that wades, eg the heron; (*pl*) high waterproof boots worn by anglers.

wadi, wady *n* a channel of a stream in North Africa which is dry except in the rainy season.

WAF *abbr* = Women in the Air Force.

wafer *n* a thin crisp cracker or biscuit; (*Christianity*) the disc of unleavened bread used in the Eucharist.

waffle[1] *n* a thick, crisp pancake baked in a waffle iron.

waffle[2] *vi* (*esp Brit inf*) to speak or write at length without saying anything substantial.

waffle iron *n* a metal cooking utensil with two hinged metal parts that close and impress a square pattern on a waffle.

waft *vt* to drift or float through the air. * *n* a breath, scent or sound carried through the air.

wag[1] *vti* (**wagging, wagged**) to move rapidly from side to side or up and down (as of a finger, tail).—*also n*.

wag[2] *n* a joker, a wit.

wage *vt* to carry on, esp war. * *n* (*often pl*) payment for work or services.

wage earner *n* a person who works for wages.

wager *n* a bet. * *vti* to bet.

waggle *vti* to wag.—*also n*.

Wagnerian *n* of or resembling the music of Richard Wagner (1813–83), characterized by dramatic grandeur and emotional intensity.

wagon *n* a four-wheeled vehicle pulled by a horse or tractor, for carrying heavy goods.

wagoner *n* a driver of a wagon.

wagon-lit *n* (*pl* **wagons-lits**) a sleeping-car on a European train.

wagtail *n* any of numerous small birds with tails that jerk constantly.

wah-wah *n* the sound of a trumpet, etc when alternately muted and unmuted; a pedal or lever used with an electric guitar, etc to imitate this sound.

waif *n* a homeless, neglected child.
wail *vi* to make a long, loud cry of sorrow or grief; to howl, to moan.—*also n.*
wain *n (poet)* a farm wagon.
wainscot *n* wooden panelling on the interior of a wall (—*also* **wainscoting**). * *vt* to line (a wall) with a wainscot.
wainwright *n* a person who builds wagons.
waist *n* the narrowest part of the human trunk, between the ribs and the hips; the narrow part of anything that is wider at the ends; the part of a garment covering the waist.
waistband *n* a band of material (on a skirt, trousers, etc) that strengthens and completes the waist.
waistcoat *n* a waist-length, sleeveless garment worn immediately under a suit jacket; a vest.
waistline *n* the narrowest part of the waist; its measurement; the seam that joins the bodice and skirt of a dress, etc; the level of this.
wait *vti* to stay, or to be, in expectation or readiness; to defer or to be postponed; to remain; (*with* **at** *or* **on**) to serve food at a meal. * *n* act or period of waiting.
waiter *n* a man or woman who serves at table, as in a restaurant.—**waitress** *nf.*
waiting *n* the act of remaining inactive or stationary; a period of waiting. * *adj* of or pertaining to a wait; in attendance.
waiting game *n* a delay in acting or deciding in order to benefit from more favourable circumstances later.
waiting list *n* a list of people applying for or waiting to obtain something.
waiting room *n* a room for people to wait in at a station, hospital, etc.
waive *vt* to refrain from enforcing; to relinquish voluntarily.
waiver *n (law)* a waiving of a right, claim etc.
wake[1] *vb* (**waking, woke,** *pp* **woken**) *vi* to emerge from sleep; to become awake. * *vt* to rouse from sleep. * *n* a watch or vigil beside a corpse, on the eve of the burial.—**wakeful** *adj.*—**waken** *vti.*
wake[2] *n* the waves or foamy water left in the track of a ship; a trail.
wale *n* a ridge or mark on the body, a weal; a ridge on a ribbed material such as corduroy; a heavy plank along a ship's side.
Walhalla *see* **Valhalla.**
walk *vi* to travel on foot with alternate steps; (*with* **out**) to leave suddenly; to go on strike; (*with* **on**) to abandon, jilt. * *vt* to pass through or over; (*a dog*) to exercise; to escort on foot. * *n* the act of walking; distance walked over; gait; a ramble or stroll; a profession.—**walker** *n.*
walkabout *n* a ceremonial wander through the Australian bush made periodically by an Aborigine; an informal stroll through a crowd by a politician, celebrity, etc.
walkie-talkie, walky-talky *n* (*pl* **walkie-talkies, walky-talkies**) a portable two-way radio transmitter and receiver.
walk-in *adj (cupboard)* large enough to enter and move around in.
walking *adj* able to walk; appearing to walk; ambulatory; marked by travelling on foot (*walking holiday*); intended for walkers (*walking boots*); in animate form (*walking bomb*). * *n* the act of walking; gait; the condition of a track, etc.
walking papers *n (sl)* notice of dismissal.
walking stick *n* a stick used in walking, a cane.
Walkman *n (trademark)* a small portable cassette player (and sometimes radio) used with earphones.
walk-on *n* a small (esp non-speaking) part in a play.
walkout *n* a strike; a sudden departure.
walkover *n* an unopposed or easy victory; a horse race with only one starter.
walk-through *n* a rehearsal.
walkway *n* road, path, etc, for pedestrians only.
Walkyrie *see* **Valkyrie.**
wall *n* a vertical structure of brick, stone, etc for enclosing, dividing or protecting. * *vt* to enclose with a wall; to close up with a wall.
wallaby *n* (*pl* **wallabies, wallaby**) a small kangaroo-like animal.
wallah, walla *n (inf)* a person with a specified job or responsibility.
wallaroo *n* (*pl* **wallaroos, wallaroo**) a type of large kangaroo.
walled *adj* having walls; surrounded or protected as if by walls; fortified.
wallet *n* a flat pocketbook for paper money, cards etc.
walleye *n* an eye with an opaque cornea; any eye with a pale or white iris; a squint in which an eye turns outward.
wallflower *n* a fragrant plant with red or yellow flowers; a person who does not dance for lack of a partner.
Walloon *n* a member of a French-speaking people of southern Belgium and adjacent areas of France; the French dialect of Walloons.—*also adj.*
wallop *vt (inf)* to beat or defeat soundly; *(inf)* to strike hard. * *n (inf)* a hard blow.
walloping *adj (inf)* large, massive. * *n (inf)* a thrashing, a defeat.
wallow *vi (animal)* to roll about in mud; to indulge oneself in emotion.—*also n.*
wallpaper *n* decorated paper for covering the walls of a room.
Wall Street *n* a street in New York where the Stock Exchange is situated; the centre of American finance.
wall-to-wall *adj (carpet)* covering the whole area of a room; *(inf)* nonstop, continuous.
wally *n* (*pl* **wallies**) *(Brit sl)* an idiot.
walnut *n* a tree producing an edible nut with a round shell and wrinkled seed; its nut; its wood used for furniture.
walrus *n* (*pl* **walruses, walrus**) a large, thick-skinned aquatic animal, related to the seals, having long canine teeth and coarse whiskers.
walrus moustache *n* a thick drooping moustache.
waltz *n* a piece of music with three beats to the bar; a whirling or slowly circling dance. * *vi* to dance a waltz.
wampum *n* polished shells strung like beads formerly used as money by North American Indians.
wan *adj* (**wanner, wannest**) pale and sickly; feeble or weak.—**wanly** *adv.*—**wanness** *n.*
wand *n* a magician's rod.
wander *vi* to ramble with no definite destination; to go astray; to lose concentration.—*also n.*
wandering Jew *n* any of various trailing or climbing plants; (*with cap*) a legendary figure condemned by Christ to roam the world until the Day of Judgement as punishment for an insult.
wanderlust *n* a compelling desire for travel.
wane *vi* to decrease, esp of the moon; to decline. * *n* decrease, decline.
wangle *vti (inf)* to achieve (something) by devious means.
wank *vi (Brit vulg)* to masturbate.—*also n.*
wanker *n (Brit vulg)* a person who masturbates; *(derog)* a stupid, contemptible or worthless person.
wannabee *n (sl)* a person who wants to be someone or something else.
want *n* lack; poverty. * *vt* to need; to require; to lack; to wish (for).
want ad *n (inf)* a newspaper or magazine advertisement requesting an item, job, etc.
wanted *adj* sought after.
wanting *adj* lacking.
wanton *adj* malicious; wilful; sexually provocative.
wapiti *n* (*pl* **wapitis**) a large deer of North America.
war *n* military conflict between nations or parties; a conflict; a contest. * *vi* (**warring, warred**) to make war.
warble *vi* to sing with trills and runs; to sing like a bird.
warble fly *n* a species of fly the larvae of which burrow under the skin of cattle causing painful lumps.
warbler *n* any of a family of small Old World songbirds which includes the nightingale and robin.
war crime *n* a crime committed in wartime (such as mistreatment of prisoners) which violates conventional notions of decency.
war cry *n* a rallying call in battle; a party catchword.
ward *n* a section of a hospital; an electoral district; a division of a prison; a child placed under the supervision of a court. * *vt* (*with* **off**) to repel; to fend off.—**wardship** *n.*

-ward, -wards *adj suffix* indicating a certain direction.
war dance *n* a ritual dance before or after battle as practised by certain North American Indian tribes.
warden *n* an official; a person in charge of a building or home; a prison governor;
warder *n* (*Brit*) a prison officer.
ward heeler *n* (*sl*) a local political hanger-on for a politician.
wardrobe *n* a cupboard for clothes; one's clothes.
wardroom *n* a room in a warship for use by officers with the exception of the captain.
ware *n* (*pl*) merchandise, goods for sale; pottery.
warehouse *n* a building for storing goods.
warfare *n* armed hostilities; conflict.
warfarin *n* a crystalline substance used in medicine as an anticoagulant and also as a poison to kill rodents.
war game *n* a simulated battle or tactical exercise using models or computers for military training; a re-enactment of a battle using model soldiers.
warhead *n* the section of a missile containing the explosive.
warhorse *n* a horse used in battle; (*inf*) a veteran of military or political conflict.
warlike *adj* hostile.
warlock *n* a sorcerer, a magician.
warlord *n* a military leader or ruler of (part of) a country.
warm *adj* moderately hot; friendly, kind; (*colours*) rich; enthusiastic. * *vt* to make warm. * *vi* to become enthusiastic (about). —**warmly** *adv*.—**warmth** *n*.
warm-blooded *adj* having a constant and relatively high temperature; passionate.
warm front *n* the edge of an advancing mass of warm air.
warm-hearted *adj* kind, sympathetic; affectionate.
warming pan *n* a long-handled (usu copper) pan filled with hot coals and formerly used to warm a bed.
warmonger *n* a person who incites war, esp for personal gain; warrior, a fighting soldier.
warm-up *n* a period of exercise or practice before a race, etc.
warn *vt* to notify of danger; to caution or advise (against).—**warning** *n*.
warp *vti* to twist out of shape; to distort; to corrupt. * *n* the threads arranged lengthwise on a loom across which other threads are passed.
war paint *n* paint smeared on the face and body by North American Indians before entering battle; (*inf*) formal or ceremonial dress, regalia; (*inf*) cosmetics.
warpath *n* the route used by a war party of North American Indians; (*with* **on the**) on a hostile expedition; (*with* **on the**) (*inf*) angry.
warped *adj* distorted, twisted; embittered.
warplane *n* an aircraft for use in combat.
warrant *vt* to guarantee; to justify. * *n* a document giving authorization; a writ for arrest.
warrantee *n* somebody to whom a warrant is given.
warrant officer *n* a person in the armed services holding a rank between commissioned officers and NCOs.
warrantor *n* a person or company that offers a warranty.
warranty *n* (*pl* **warranties**) a pledge to replace something if it is not as represented, a guarantee.
warren *n* an area in which rabbits breed.
warring *adj* engaged in war.
warrior *n* a soldier, fighter.
warship *n* a ship equipped for war.
wart *n* a small, hard projection on the skin.—**warty** *adj*.
wart hog *n* an African wild pig with warty lumps on the face, large tusks and thick course hair.
wartime *adj, n* (of) a period or time of war.
wary *adj* (**warier, wariest**) watchful; cautious.—**warily** *adv*.—**wariness** *n*.
was *see* **be**.
wash *vti* to cleanse with water and soap; to flow against or over; to sweep along by the action of water; to separate gold, etc, from earth by washing; to cover with a thin coat of metal or paint; (*with* **down**) to wash thoroughly from top to bottom; to take a drink of liquid to help in swallowing food. * *n* a washing; the break of waves on the shore; the waves left behind by a boat; a liquid used for washing.
washable *adj* able to be washed without damage.—**washability** *n*.
washboard *n* a corrugated board used (esp formerly) for scrubbing clothes.
washbowl, washbasin *n* a basin or bowl, esp a bathroom fixture, for use in washing one's hands, etc.—*also* **wash-hand basin**.
washcloth *n* a flannel.
washed-out *adj* faded in colour; fatigued.
washed-up *adj* unsuccessful, ineffective; unpromising.
washer *n* a flat ring of metal, rubber, etc, to give tightness to joints; a washing machine.
washing *n* the act of cleansing with water; a number of items washed together.
washing machine *n* a device for washing clothes.
washing powder *n* a powdered detergent formulated for washing fabrics.
washing soda *n* sodium carbonate dissolved in water used for washing and cleaning.
washing-up *n* (*Brit*) the washing of dishes and cutlery after a meal; the dishes and cutlery waiting to be washed.
washout *n* (*sl*) a failure.
washroom *n* cloakroom, lavatory.
washstand *n* a piece of furniture for holding a bowl and jug of water used for washing.
washtub *n* a large tub used for washing clothes.
washy *adj* (**washier, washiest**) weak, watery; pale; lacking in strength or vigour.—**washiness** *n*.
wasn't = was not.
wasp *n* a winged insect with a black and yellow striped body, which can sting.
Wasp, WASP *n* an American of northern European, esp British, descent and Protestant upbringing, regarded as belonging to the most privileged group in American society (*W*hite *A*nglo-*S*axon *P*rotestant).
waspish *adj* sharp in speech or manner, irritable.
wasp waist *n* a very slender waist.
wassail *n* (*formerly*) a toast made at festivities; a festive celebration with a lot of drinking and merriment; spiced ale or mulled wine served (esp formerly) at Christmas or other festive occasions. * *vi* to make merry.
Wassermann test *n* a blood test used to diagnose syphilis.
wastage *n* anything lost by use or natural decay; wasteful or avoidable loss of something valuable.
waste *adj* useless; left over; uncultivated or uninhabited. * *vt* to ravage; to squander; to use foolishly; to fail to use. * *vi* to lose strength, etc as by disease. * *n* uncultivated or uninhabited land; discarded material, garbage, excrement.—**wasteful** *adj*.—**wastefully** *adv*.—**wastefulness** *n*.
wasted *adj* ravaged, devastated; not used to best advantage; weak, emaciated; (*sl*) dead, killed; (*sl*) showing the effects of alcohol or drug abuse.
wasteland *n* a piece of barren or uncultivated land; a desolate region; something (eg a period of time, relationship) lacking in moral, spiritual, emotional, etc vitality.
wastepaper *n* paper discarded as waste.
wastepipe *n* a pipe carrying off used water from sinks, baths, etc.
waster *n* a wasteful person or thing; a good-for-nothing.
wasting asset *n* a non-renewable resource such as a coal mine.
wastrel *n* a vagabond; a waster, idler.
watch *n* surveillance; close observation; vigil; guard; a small timepiece worn on the wrist, etc; a period of duty on a ship * *vi* to look with attention; to wait for; to keep vigil. * *vt* to keep one's eyes fixed on; to guard; to tend; to observe closely; (*chance, etc*) to wait for.—**watcher** *n*.—**watchful** *adj*.—**watchfully** *adv*.—**watchfulness** *n*.

watchband *n* a strap of leather, etc, for securing a watch to the wrist.
watchcase *n* a protective metal casing for a watch mechanism.
watchdog *n* a dog that guards property; a person or group that monitors safety, standards, etc.
watchmaker *n* a person who makes and repairs watches.
watchman *n* (*pl* **watchmen**) a person who guards a building or other property.
watch night *n* a religious service on New Year's Eve.
watchtower *n* a tower for a sentry to keep watch from.
watchword *n* a password.
water *n* the substance H^2O, a clear, thi n liquid, lacking taste or smell, and essential for life; any body of it, as the ocean, a lake, river, etc; bodily secretions such as tears, urine. * *vt* to moisten with water; to irrigate; to dilute with water; (*with* **down**) to dilute; to reduce in strength or effectiveness. * *vi* (*eyes*) to smart; to salivate; to take in water.
water bed *n* a bed with a water-filled mattress.
water bird *n* any swimming or wading bird.
water biscuit *n* a thin, crisp biscuit, usu served with cheese.
water blister *n* a blister on the skin filled with watery fluid instead of blood.
water boatman *n* any of various aquatic bugs adapted for swimming.
waterborne *adj* floating on or travelling by water.
waterbuck *n* an African antelope which lives in swampy areas.
water buffalo *n* a common domesticated Asian buffalo.
water cannon *n* an apparatus for pumping water at high pressure to disperse crowds.
water chestnut *n* an Asian aquatic plant with edible nutlike fruit; (the edible tuber of) a Chinese plant with a succulent root.
water clock *n* a clock with a mechanism operated by flowing or dripping water.
water-closet *n* a lavatory.
watercolour, watercolor *n* a water-soluble paint; a picture painted with watercolours.
water-cooled *adj* (*engine etc*) cooled by the circulation of water.
watercourse *n* (a channel for) a stream, river or canal.
watercraft *n* skill in handling boats and other vessels; a vessel travelling by water.
watercress *n* a plant growing in ponds and streams, used in a salad.
water cure *n* hydropathy.
water diviner *n* a person who searches for water using a divining rod.
waterfall *n* a fall of water over a precipice or down a hill.
water flea *n* any of numerous tiny freshwater crustaceans.
waterfowl *n* (*pl* **waterfowl**) a bird that frequents lakes, rivers, etc, esp a duck.
waterfront *n* an area alongside a body of water, esp a docks.
water gas *n* a toxic inflammable mixture of carbon monoxide and hydrogen produced by passing steam over hot carbon, used as a fuel.
water glass *n* a solution of sodium or potassium silicate in water used as a protective coating and to preserve eggs.
water hammer *n* (the sound of) the concussion of water in a pipe when a blockage is suddenly dislodged.
water hole *n* a water-filled hollow where animals drink.
water hyacinth *n* a floating aquatic plant of tropical America that often blocks waterways with its dense growth.
water ice *n* an iced dessert made from frozen water, sugar and a flavouring.
watering can *n* a container with a spout for watering plants.
watering hole *n* (*inf*) a bar or pub.
watering place *n* a place where animals or people can obtain water; a spa resort.
water jacket *n* a casing filled with water used for cooling machinery.
water jump *n* a ditch filled with water used as an obstacle in a steeplechase and other sporting contests.
water level *n* the surface level of water in a reservoir, etc.
water lily *n* any of a family of plants with large floating leaves and showy flowers.
waterline *n* a line up to which a ship's hull is submerged.
waterlogged *adj* soaked or saturated with water.
water main *n* a main pipe or conduit for carrying water.
watermark *n* a line marking the height to which water has risen; a mark impressed on paper which can only be seen when held up to the light.
watermelon *n* a large fruit with a hard green rind and edible red watery flesh.
water mill *n* a mill operated by a water wheel.
water pistol *n* a toy gun that shoots a stream of water.
water polo *n* a game played in water by two teams of seven swimmers with the aim of scoring by hitting a ball into the opponents' goal.
water power *n* the power of falling or moving water used to operate machinery or generate electricity.
waterproof *adj* impervious to water; watertight.—*also vt.*
water-repellent *adj* (*fabrics, etc*) treated with a substance that prevents penetration by water.
water-resistant *adj* (*fabrics, etc*) designed to resist water penetration as long as possible.
watershed *n* a turning point.
waterside *n* the edge of a body of water.
water-skiing *n* the sport of planing on water by being towed by a motorboat—**water-skier** *n*.
water softener *n* a device or chemical designed to counteract chemicals that cause hardness in water.
water-soluble *adj* capable of dissolving in water.
water spaniel *n* a breed of large curly-coated spaniel used in hunting waterfowl.
waterspout *n* a pipe for draining water; a tall column of water formed by a whirlwind and reaching from the sea to the clouds.
water table *n* the level below which the ground is saturated with water.
watertight *adj* not allowing water to pass through; foolproof.
water tower *n* an elevated tank or reservoir to allow water to be supplied under pressure.
waterway *n* a navigable channel of water.
water wheel *n* a wheel designed to be turned by running water and used to drive machinery; a wheel used for raising water.
water wings *npl* inflatable rubber floats worn on the arms of those learning to swim.
waterworks *n* (*as sing*) an establishment that supplies water to a district; (*pl: inf*) the urinary system; (*inf*) tears.
waterworn *adj* rubbed smooth by the action of water.
watery *adj* thin, diluted.
watt *n* a unit of electrical power.
wattage *n* amount of electrical power.
wattle *n* (material for) a framework of stakes or poles interwoven with thin branches, twigs, etc formerly used for fencing and building; a loose flap of skin hanging from the necks of certain birds and lizards; an Australian acacia tree with small brightly-coloured flowers. * *vt* to build of or with wattle; to interweave or interlace (with sticks, etc) to make a light frame.
wave *n* an undulation travelling on the surface of water; the form in which light and sound are thought to travel; an increase or upsurge (eg of crime); a hair curl; a movement of the hand in greeting or farewell. * *vti* to move freely backward and forward; to flutter; to undulate; to move the hand to and fro in greeting, farewell, etc; (*with* **down**) to signal (a vehicle, etc) to stop with a wave.—**wavy** *adj*.
wave band *n* a range of radio frequencies or wavelengths.
waveguide *n* a metal tube used to guide microwaves along a particular path.
wavelength *n* the distance between the crests of successive waves of light or sound; radio frequency.
wavelet *n* a small wave.
wave mechanics *n sing* (*physics*) the theory in quantum mechanics that describes the behaviour of elementary particles in terms of their wave properties.

waver *vi* to hesitate; to falter.—**waverer** *n*.
wax[1] *n* beeswax; an oily substance used to make candles, polish, etc * *vt* to rub, polish, cover or treat with wax.
wax[2] *vi* to increase in strength, size, etc.
waxen *adj* made of wax; pale and smooth like wax.
wax paper *n* paper that has been rendered moistureproof by treating with wax.
waxwork *n* a figure or model formed of wax; (*pl*) an exhibition of such figures.
waxy *adj* (**waxier, waxiest**) consisting of or like wax; adhesive.—**waxily** *adv*.—**waxiness** *n*.
way *n* path, route; road; distance; room to advance; direction; state; means; possibility; manner of living; (*pl*) habits.
waybill *n* a document with list of goods and shipping instructions accompanying a shipment.
wayfarer *n* a traveller.
waylay *vt* (**waylaying, waylaid**) to lie in wait for; to accost.
way-out *adj* (*inf*) unconventional, unusual; amazing.
-ways *adv suffix* indicating a certain direction or manner.
ways and means *npl* the methods used to accomplish something; the revenues and means of raising revenues for the use of government.
wayside *n* the side of or land adjacent to a road.
wayward *adj* wilful, stubborn; unpredictable.—**waywardness** *n*.
WBA *abbr* = World Boxing Association.
WBC *abbr* = World Boxing Council.
WC *abbr* = (*Brit*) water-closet.
we *pron pl* of I; I and others.
weak *adj* lacking power or strength; feeble; ineffectual.—**weakness** *n*.
weaken *vti* to make or grow weaker.
weak interaction *n* (*physics*) an interaction between elementary particles that is responsible for certain particle decay processes.
weak-kneed *adj* (*inf*) submissive, easily intimidated.
weakling *n* a person who lacks strength of character.
weakly *adj* (**weaklier, weakliest**) not robust; sickly. * *adv* in a weak manner, feebly.
weak-minded *adj* lacking in determination; feeble-minded.
weal *n* a raised mark on the skin left by a blow with a lash.
wealth *n* a large amount of possessions or money; affluence; an abundance (of).—**wealthy** *adj*.
wean *vt* (*baby, animal*) to replace the mother's milk with other nourishment; to dissuade (from indulging a habit).
weapon *n* any instrument used in fighting.
weaponry *n* weapons collectively.
wear *vb* (**wearing, wore,** *pp* **worn**) *vt* to have on the body as clothing; (*hair, etc*) to arrange in a particular way; to display; to rub away; to impair by use; to exhaust, tire; (*with* **down**) to overcome gradually through persistent pressure; (*with* **out**) to tire or exhaust. * *vi* to be impaired by use or time; to be spent tediously; (*with* **off**) to become gradually weaker in effect; (*with* **out**) to make or become worthless through prolonged use. * *n* deterioration from frequent use; articles worn.—**wearer** *n*.
wearable *adj* suitable to be worn.
wear and tear *n* deterioration or depreciation from everyday use.
wearing *adj* exhausting, tiresome, oppressive.
weary *adj* (**wearier, weariest**) tired; bored. * *vti* (**wearying, wearied**) to make or become tired.—**weariness** *n*.—**wearisome** *adj*.
weasel *n* a small carnivorous animal with a long slender body and reddish fur.
weasel words *npl* (*inf*) evasive or misleading talk.
weather *n* atmospheric conditions, such as temperature, rainfall, cloudiness, etc * *vt* to expose to the action of the weather; to survive. * *vi* to withstand the weather.
weather-beaten *adj* worn or damaged by the weather; hardened or bronzed through exposure to the weather.
weatherboard *n* a sloping, usu overlapping, timber board used as external cladding for a wall or roof.—**weatherboarding** *n*.
weather-bound *adj* delayed or postponed due to bad weather.
weathercock *n* a weather vane in the form of a cock to show the wind direction.
weathered *adj* affected or seasoned by exposure to the weather; (*rocks*) altered in shape by erosion; (*roof*) having a sloped surface to allow rainwater to escape.
weather eye *n* an eye trained to observe changes in the weather; (*inf*) an alert or watchful gaze.
weatherglass *n* a barometer.
weathering *n* the erosion of rocks through the action of the wind, rain, frost, etc.
weatherman *n* (*pl* **weathermen**) a weather forecaster on radio or television who is usually also a professional meteorologist.
weather map *n* a chart showing weather conditions over a particular area for a specified period.
weatherproof *adj* designed to withstand exposure to weather without damage or deterioration.—*also vt*.
weather station *n* a meteorological post for collecting, recording and transmitting data on weather conditions.
weather vane *n* a device attached to a tall structure to indicate wind direction.
weave *vb* (**weaving, wove,** *pp* **woven**) *vt* to interlace threads in a loom to form fabric; to construct. * *vi* to make a way through (eg a crowd), to zigzag.—**weaver** *n*.
weaverbird *n* any of various Old World songbirds that build nests of interwoven grass, twigs, etc, including the house sparrow.
web *n* a woven fabric; the fine threads spun by a spider; the membrane joining the digits of birds, animals.
webbed *adj* (*ducks, etc*) having the digits connected by a fold of skin.
webbing *n* a strong narrow woven fabric of jute, cotton, etc, used for straps and belts; anything forming a web.
weber *n* the SI unit of magnetic flux.
wed *vti* (**wedding, wedded** *or* **wed**) to marry; to join closely.
Wed *abbr* = Wednesday.
we'd = we had; we would.
wedded *adj* of or resulting from marriage; devoted (to art, etc).
wedding *n* marriage; the ceremony of marriage.
wedding cake *n* an ornately decorated rich fruit cake, usu in three tiers, served at a wedding.
wedding ring *n* a band of gold or platinum used at a wedding and worn to show marital status.
wedge *n* a v-shaped block of wood or metal for splitting or fastening; a wedge-shaped object. * *vti* to split or secure with a wedge; to thrust (in) tightly; to become fixed tightly.
wedlock *n* marriage.
Wednesday *n* fourth day of the week, between Tuesday and Thursday.
wee[1] *adj* (*Scot*) small, tiny.
wee[2] *n* (*inf*) the act of passing urine; urine. * *vt* (*inf*) to pass urine.—*also* **wee-wee**.
weed *n* any undesired plant, esp one that crowds out desired plants; (*sl*) marijuana; (*pl*) a widow's black mourning clothes. * *vt* to remove weeds; (*with* **out**) to remove or eliminate (something superfluous or harmful).
weedkiller *n* a chemical or hormonal substance used to kill weeds.
weedy *adj* (**weedier, weediest**) full of weeds; (*inf*) thin and scrawny.
week *n* the period of seven consecutive days, esp from Sunday to Sunday.
weekday *n* a day of the week other than Saturday or Sunday.
weekend, week-end *n* the period from Friday night to Sunday night—*also adj*.
weekly *adj* happening once a week or every week.
weeknight *n* the evening or night of a weekday.
weeny *adj* (**weenier, weeniest**) (*inf*) tiny, minute.
weep *vti* (**weeping, wept**) to shed tears, to cry; (*wound*) to ooze.
weepie *n* (*inf*) a sentimental film.
weeping *n* the act of weeping. * *adj* shedding tears; exuding moisture; (*tree*) with drooping branches.—**weepingly** *adv*.

weeping willow *n* a Chinese willow tree with slender drooping branches.

weepy *adj* (**weepier, weepiest**) tearful; prone to crying.—**weepily** *adv*.—**weepiness** *n*.

weevil *n* a beetle which feeds on plants and crops.

wee-wee *see* **wee**[2].

weft *n* the yarn woven across the lengthwise threads in a loom.—also **woof.**

weigh *vt* to measure the weight of; to consider carefully; (*with* **down**) to weight; to oppress; (*with* **up**) to assess, make a judgment about (a person, thing, etc). * *vi* to have weight; to be burdensome; (*with* **in**) (*boxer, wrestler*) to be weighed before a bout; (*jockey*) to be weighed after a race; (*inf*) to make a contribution to (eg an argument).

weighbridge *n* a large scale consisting of a metal plate set into the road onto which vehicles are driven to be weighed.

weigh-in *n* (*sports*) the checking of the weight of a contestant, esp of a jockey after a race or of a boxer before a bout.

weight *n* the amount which anything weighs; influence; any unit of heaviness. * *vt* to attach a weight to.

weightlessness *n* the state of having no or little reaction to gravity, esp in space travel.

weight lifting *n* the sport of lifting weights of a specific amount in a particular way.—**weight lifter** *n*.

weight training *n* physical exercise involving lifting heavy weights.

weight watcher *n* a person on a diet to lose weight.

weighty *adj* (**weightier, weightiest**) heavy; serious.—**weightily** *adv*.

weir *n* a low dam across a river which controls the flow of water.

weird *adj* unearthly, mysterious; eerie; bizarre.—**weirdly** *adv*.

weirdo, weirdie *n* (*pl* **weirdos, weirdies**) (*inf*) an eccentric person.

welch *see* **welsh.**

welcome *adj* gladly received; pleasing. * *n* reception of a person or thing. * *vt* to greet kindly.

weld *vt* to unite, as metal by heating until fused or soft enough to hammer together; to join closely. * *n* a welded joint.

welfare *n* wellbeing; health; assistance or financial aid granted to the poor, the unemployed, etc.

welfare state *n* a state in which the government assumes responsibility for the health and social security of its citizens.

well[1] *n* a spring; a hole bored in the ground to provide a source of water, oil, gas, etc; the open space in the middle of a staircase * *vi* to pour forth.

well[2] *adj* (**better, best**) agreeable; comfortable; in good health. * *adv* in a proper, satisfactory, or excellent manner; thoroughly; prosperously; with good reason; to a considerable degree; fully. * *interj* an expression of surprise, etc.

we'll = we will; we shall.

well-advised *adj* acting with good sense; carefully thought out.

well-appointed *adj* fully equipped or furnished.

well-balanced *adj* sensible, sane.

well-being *n* condition of being well or contented; welfare.

well-bred *adj* well brought up; of good stock.

well-connected *adj* having powerful friends or relatives.

well-disposed *adj* favourable, feeling kindly (toward).

well-done *adj* performed with skill; thoroughly cooked, as meat.

well-favoured, well-favored *adj* attractive.

well-found *adj* fully equipped.

well-founded *adj* borne out by facts.

well-groomed *adj* clean and tidy in dress and appearance.

well-grounded *adj* well instructed in a subject.

wellhead *n* the source of a stream, spring, etc; a source, origin.

well-heeled *adj* (*inf*) wealthy.

wellies *npl* (*Brit inf*) wellingtons.

well-informed *adj* knowledgeable on a wide range of subjects; possessing reliable information on a specific matter.

wellington (boot) *n* a rubber, waterproof boot.

well-intentioned *adj* having good intentions (but often without producing good results).

well-knit *adj* firm, compact.

well-known *adj* widely known, famous; known fully.

well-mannered *adj* having or showing good manners; polite.

well-meaning *adj* having good intentions (but often without producing good results).

well-nigh *adv* almost.

well-off *adj* in comfortable circumstances; prosperous.

well-preserved *adj* well looked after; remaining youthful in appearance.

well-read *adj* having read widely and deeply.

well-rounded *adj* having a pleasantly curved or rounded shape; full, complete.

well-spoken *adj* spoken clearly and eloquently; spoken in a pleasing manner.

well-thought-of *adj* having a good reputation.

well-thumbed *adj* (*book*) marked by frequent handling.

well-to-do *adj* prosperous.

well-wisher *n* a person who is sympathetic to another person, cause, etc.

well-worn *adj* showing signs of wear; (*phrase, etc*) trite, hackneyed.

Welsh *adj* relating to the people of Wales or their language.—*also n*.

welsh *vti* to avoid paying a gambling debt; to run off without paying.—*also* **welch.**—**welsher, welcher** *n*.

Welsh corgi *n* a corgi.

Welsh dresser *n* a dresser with drawers and cupboards below and open shelves above.

Welsh rabbit, Welsh rarebit *n* melted cheese on toast.

welt *n* a band or strip to strengthen a seam; a weal.

welter *vi* to roll or wallow. * *n* a jumble.

welterweight *n* a professional boxer weighing 140–147 pounds; a wrestler weighing 154–172 pounds.

wench *n* (*used facetiously*) a girl or young woman.

wend *vt* to amble, to saunter.

Wendy house *n* (*Brit*) a toy house for children to play in.

Wensleydale *n* a mild crumbly English cheese.

went *see* **go.**

wept *see* **weep.**

were *see* **be.**

we're = we are.

weren't = were not.

werewolf *n* (*pl* **werewolves**) an imaginary person able to transform himself for a time into a wolf.

west *n* the direction of the sun at sunset; one of the four points of the compass; the region in the west of any country; (*with cap*) Europe and the Western Hemisphere. * *adj* situated in, or toward the west. * *adv* in or to the west.

westerly *adj* toward the west; blowing from the west. * *n* (*pl* **westerlies**) a wind blowing from the west.—*also adv*.

western *adj* of or in the west. * *n* a film, novel, etc about the usu pre-20th century American West.

westerner *n* a person from the west.

Western Hemisphere *n* that half of the earth containing North and South America.

westernize *vti* to make or become familiar with the ideas, institutions, customs, etc of the West.—**westernization** *n*.

westernmost *adj* farthest west.

westward *adj* toward the west.—*also adv*.—**westwards** *adv*.

wet *adj* (**wetter, wettest**) covered or saturated with water or other liquid; rainy; misty; not yet dry. * *n* water or other liquid; rain or rainy weather. * *vti* (**wetting, wet** *or* **wetted**) to soak; to moisten.—**wetness** *n*.

wet blanket *n* (*inf*) a person who dampens the enthusiasm of others.

wet dream *n* an erotic dream causing orgasm.

wet nurse *n* a woman employed to care for or suckle another's child.

wet-nurse *vt* to act as a wet nurse; (*inf*) to devote constant attention to (a person).

wet rot *n* (*Brit*) decay in timber caused by a fungus; any of various fungi that cause rot in damp timber.

wet suit *n* a close-fitting suit worn by divers, etc, to retain body heat.

we've = we have.

whack *vti* (*inf*) to strike sharply, esp making a sound. * *n* (*inf*) a sharp blow.

whacking *adj* (*Brit inf*) enormous. * *adv* (*inf*) very, extremely.

whale *n* a very large sea mammal that breathes through a blowhole, and resembles a fish in shape. * *vi* to hunt whales.

whalebone *n* a horny substance forming plates in the upper jaws of toothless whales; a piece of this formerly used for stiffening undergarments.

whalebone whale *n* any of various large whales that have whalebone plates instead of teeth which are used to filter plankton for food.

whaler *n* a person or a ship employed in hunting whales.

whaling *n* the practice of hunting whales for food, oil, etc.

wham *n* (the sound of) a heavy blow. * *vti* (**whamming, whammed**) to hit or cause to hit with a loud noise.

whang *n* (the sound of) a forceful blow. * *vti* to hit or cause to hit with force.

wharf *n* (*pl* **wharfs, wharves**) a platform for loading and unloading ships in harbour.

wharfage *n* (the charge for) the use of a wharf; wharves collectively.

wharfinger *n* the owner or manager of a wharf.

what *adj* of what sort, how much, how great. * *relative pron* that which; as much or many as. * *interj* used as an expression of surprise or astonishment.

whatever *pron* anything that; no matter what.

whatnot *n* (*inf*) something or someone the name of which has been forgotten, is unknown or is hard to categorize; a set of open shelves for ornaments, photographs, etc.

whatsit *n* (*inf*) something or someone the name of which has been forgotten, is unknown or is hard to categorize.

whatsoever *adj* whatever.

wheat *n* a cereal grain usu ground into flour for bread.

wheatear *n* a small grey and white migratory thrush.

wheaten *adj* made from the grain or flour of wheat; pale yellow in colour.

wheat germ *n* the kernel of a grain of wheat, high in nutritive value.

wheatmeal *adj, n* (made from) brown flour with a high proportion of wheat grain.

whee *interj* used to express joy or delight.

wheedle *vt* to persuade, to cajole (into); to coax with flattery.

wheel *n* a solid disc or circular rim turning on an axle; a steering wheel; (*pl*) the moving forces. * *vt* to transport on wheels. * *vi* to turn round or on an axis; to move in a circular direction, as a bird.

wheelbarrow *n* a cart with one wheel in front and two handles and legs at the rear.

wheelbase *n* the distance between the front and rear axles of a vehicle.

wheelchair *n* a chair with large wheels for invalids.

wheel clamp *n* (*Brit*) a device that prevents an illegally parked car from being driven away until a fine is paid to release it.—*also vt*.

wheeler-dealer *n* (*inf*) a shrewd operator in business, politics, etc.

wheelie *n* a stunt in which a bicycle or motorcycle is ridden for a distance with the front wheel off the ground.

wheelwright *n* a person who makes and repairs wheels for a living.

wheeze *vi* to breathe with a rasping sound; to breathe with difficulty.—*also n*.

wheezy *adj* (**wheezier, wheeziest**) making a wheezing sound.—**wheezily** *adv*.—**wheeziness** *n*.

whelk *n* a shellfish with a snail-like shell.

whelp *n* the young of various animals, esp a dog; an impudent child. * *vt* to give birth to (a puppy, etc). * *vi* (*bitch*) to bring forth young.

when *adv* at what or which time * *conj* at the time at which; although; *relative pron* at which.

whence *adv* from what place.—*also conj*.

whenever *adv, conj* at whatever time.

whensoever *conj, adv* whenever.

where *adv* at which or what place; to which place; from what source; *relative pron* in or to which.

whereabouts *adv* near or at what place; about where. * *n* approximate location.

whereas *conj* since; on the contrary.

whereby *adv* by which.—*also conj*.

wherein *adv* (*formal*) in what; how. * *conj* in which; where.

whereof *adv, conj* (*arch*) of what or which.

whereon *adv, conj* (*arch*) on what or which.

wheresoever *adv* (*emphatic*) wherever.

whereto *adv, conj* (*formal*) to what or which.

whereupon *adv* at which point; upon which.

wherever *adv* at or to whatever place.

wherewithal *n* the means or resources.

whet *vt* (**whetting, whetted**) to sharpen by rubbing, to stimulate.

whether *conj* introducing an alternative possibility or condition.

whetstone *n* a stone for sharpening the edges of tools; something that sharpens or stimulates.

whew *interj* an exclamation of astonishment, amazement, relief, etc.

whey *n* the watery part of milk that is separated from the curds in sour milk.

which *adj* what one (of) * *pron* which person or thing; that. * *relative pron* person or thing referred to.

whichever *pron* whatever one that; whether one or the other; no matter which.—*also adj*.

whichsoever *adj, pron* (*arch*) whichever.

whiff *n* a sudden puff of air, smoke or odour.

while *n* a period of time. * *conj* during the time that; whereas; although. * *vt* to pass (the time) pleasantly.

whilst *conj* (*esp Brit*) while.

whim *n* a fancy; an irrational thought.

whimper *vi* to make a low, unhappy cry.—*also n*.

whimsical *adj* unusual, odd, fantastic.—**whimsicality** *n*.

whimsy, whimsey *n* (*pl* **whimsies, whimseys**) a fanciful notion, a whim.

whine *vi* (*dog*) to make a long, high-pitched cry; (*person*) to complain childishly. * *n* a plaintive cry.

whinge *vi* to moan, complain.—*also n*.

whinny *vi* (**whinnying, whinnied**) to neigh softly.—*also n*.

whip *n* a piece of leather attached to a handle used for punishing people or driving on animals; an officer in parliament who maintains party discipline. * *vb* (**whipping, whipped**) *vt* to move, pull, throw, etc suddenly; to strike, as with a lash; (*eggs, etc*) to beat into a froth; (*with* **up**) to stir into action, excite; (*inf*) to produce in a hurry. * *vi* to move rapidly.

whipcord *n* a strong cord of tightly twisted strands used for whips; a cotton or worsted fabric with diagonal ridges.

whip hand *n* (*usu with* **the**) the dominant position.

whiplash *n* a stroke with a whip; a neck injury when the head is jerked forward and backward.

whipped cream *n* cream that has been stiffened by beating, used as a topping for desserts, etc.

whippersnapper *n* an insignificant but impudent young person.

whippet *n* a small racing dog like a greyhound.

whipping boy *n* a person who is constantly punished for the mistakes of others, a scapegoat.

whippoorwill *n* a nocturnal American bird with a distinctive call.

whip-round *n* (*Brit inf*) an appeal among friends for contributions.

whipsaw *n* any of various types of saw with a long flexible blade.

whipstock *n* the handle of a whip.

whir, whirr *n* a humming or buzzing sound. * *vti* (**whirring, whirred**) to revolve with a buzzing noise.

whirl *n* a swift turning; confusion, commotion; (*inf*) an attempt or try. * *vti* to turn around rapidly; to spin.

whirligig *n* a spinning top.
whirlpool *n* a circular current or vortex of water.
whirlpool bath *n* a bath with a device that swirls water.
whirlwind *n* a whirling column of air; rapid activity.
whisk *vt* to make a quick sweeping movement; (*eggs, cream*) to beat, whip. * *vi* to move nimbly and efficiently. * *n* a kitchen utensil for whisking; (*inf*) a small amount.
whisker *n* any of the sensory bristles on the face of a cat, etc; (*pl*) the hair growing on a man's face, esp the cheeks.—**whiskered** *adj.*
whiskey *n* whisky distilled in the US or Ireland.
whisky *n* (*pl* **whiskies**) a spirit distilled from barley or rye.
whisper *vti* to speak softly; to spread a rumour. * *n* a hushed tone; a hint, trace.
whist *n* a card game for four players in two sides, each side attempting to win the greater number of the 13 tricks.
whistle *vti* to make a shrill sound by forcing the breath through the lips; to make a similar sound with a whistle; (*wind*) to move with a shrill sound; (*with* **for**) (*inf*) to demand or hope for in vain. * *n* a whistling sound; a musical instrument; a metal tube that is blown to make a shrill warning sound.
whistle stop *n* a minor railroad station where trains stop only on signal; a brief appearance by a candidate on tour during an election campaign.
Whit *see* **Whitsuntide.**
whit *n* the tiniest possible amount.
white *adj* of the colour of snow; pure; bright; (*skin*) light-coloured. * *n* the colour white; the white part of an egg or the eye.
white ant *n* a termite.
whitebait *n* (*pl* **whitebait**) the edible young of the herring and sprat.
white blood cell *n* a leucocyte.
whitecap *n* a wave with a white foamy crest.
white-collar *adj* of office and professional workers.
white dwarf *n* a small faint star of high density.
white elephant *n* a thing of little use.
white feather *n* a symbol of cowardice.
white flag *n* a flag of plain white material used to signify surrender or arrange a truce.
whitefly *n* (*pl* **whiteflies**) any of various small insects that feed on and injure plants.
white gold *n* a pale alloy of gold chiefly with platinum and palladium.
white goods *npl* household appliances, as refrigerators, etc; household linen, as sheets, towels, etc.
Whitehall *n* the British government; departmental government.
white heat *n* an intense heat accompanied by the emission of white light from a substance; (*inf*) intense excitement or emotion.
white hope *n* (*inf*) a person who is expected to win fame for his or her community, country, etc.
white-hot *adj* of a temperature so hot that white light is emitted; intensely passionate.
White House *n* the official residence of the president of the US; the US presidency.
white lead *n* a white solid of mostly lead carbonate, esp used in pigments.
white lie *n* a harmless lie, esp as uttered out of politeness.
white light *n* light, eg sunlight, that contains approximately equal proportions of the whole spectrum of visible radiation.
white matter *n* whitish tissue in the brain and spinal cord composed of nerve fibres.
white meat *n* a light-coloured meat such as poultry or veal.
white metal *n* an alloy, esp of tin, used in bearings, domestic utensils, etc.
whiten *vti* to make or become white; to bleach.
white noise *n* sound that contains approximately equal proportions of all the audible frequencies.
whiteout *n* a weather condition when heavy cloud and snow reflect most of the available light and greatly reduce visibility.
white paper *n* a government document detailing proposed legislation.
white sauce *n* a sauce made with butter, flour and seasonings mixed with milk, cream or stock.
white slave *n* a woman or girl held against her will and forced into prostitution.
white spirit *n* (*Brit*) a colourless inflammable liquid distilled from petroleum and used as a solvent and thinner for paint.
white tie *n* a white bow tie worn as part of a man's formal evening dress.—**white-tie** *adj.*
whitewash *n* a mixture of lime and water, used for whitening walls; concealment of the truth.—*also vt.*
white water *n* water with a foaming surface, as in rapids.
white whale *n* the beluga.
white wine *n* wine made from green grapes or from skinned black grapes.
whitewood *n* (any of various trees yielding) a light-coloured wood.
whitey *n* (*pl* **whities**) (*derog*) in US, a Black person's term for a white person.
whither *adv* to what or which place.
whiting *n* (*pl* **whitings, whiting**) an edible saltwater fish of the cod family.
whitlow *n* a painful inflammation at the end of a finger or toe.
Whitsun *adj* (*Christianity*) of, observed on, or pertaining to Whit Sunday or Whitsuntide. * *n* Whitsuntide.
Whit Sunday *n* (*Christianity*) the seventh Sunday after Easter, Pentecost.
Whitsuntide *n* (*Christianity*) the week beginning with Whit Sunday.—*also* **Whit.**
whittle *vt* to pare or cut thin shavings from (wood); (*with* **away** *or* **down**) to reduce.
whiz, whizz *vi* (**whizzing, whizzed**) to make a humming sound. * *n* (*pl* **whizzes**) a humming sound; (*inf*) an expert.
whiz kid, whizz kid *n* (*inf*) a person of extraordinary achievements given their relatively young age.
WHO *abbr* = World Health Organization.
who *pron* what or which person; that.
whoa *interj* a command given, esp to a horse, to slow down or come to a halt.
who'd = who would.
whodunit, whodunnit *n* (*inf*) a detective novel, play, etc.
whoever *pron* anyone who; whatever person.
whole *adj* not broken, intact; containing the total amount, number, etc.; complete. * *n* the entire amount; a thing complete in itself.
wholefood *n* unrefined food, free from additives.
wholehearted *adj* sincere, single-minded, enthusiastic.—**wholeheartedly** *adv.*
whole hog *n* (*inf*) the complete amount or extent.
wholemeal *adj* (*Brit*) *see* **wholewheat.**
whole note *n* (*mus*) a note with a time value equal to two half notes.—*also* **semibreve**
whole number *n* a number without fractions; an integer.
wholesale *n* selling of goods, usu at lower prices and in quantity, to a retailer.
wholesome *adj* healthy; mentally beneficial.—**wholesomeness** *n.*
wholewheat *adj* (*esp US flour*) made from the entire wheat kernel.—*also* **wholemeal.**
who'll = who will; who shall.
wholly *adv* completely.
whom *pron* objective case of **who.**
whomever *pron* the objective form of **whoever.**
whoop *n* a loud cry of excitement.
whoopee *interj* used to express wild excitement. * *n* boisterous fun.
whoopee cushion *n* a joke cushion that emits a rude noise when sat on.
whooping cough *n* an infectious disease, esp of children, causing coughing spasms.
whoops *interj* (*inf*) an exclamation of surprise or apology.
whoosh *n* a rushing or hissing sound. * *vi* to make or move with such a sound.

whop *vt* (**whopping, whopped**) to beat, thrash; to defeat completely.
whopper *n* (*inf*) a large specimen.—**whopping** *adj*.
whore *n* a prostitute.
whorehouse *n* a brothel.
whoremonger *n* a person who uses the services of whores.—*also* **whoremaster.**
whorl *n* a ring of leaves or petals round a stem; a single turn of a spiral; something shaped like a spiral; the central ridges of a fingerprint forming a complete circle.
whortleberry *n* a bilberry.
who's = who is.
whose *pron* the possessive case of **who** or **which.**
whosoever *pron* (*arch*) whoever.
who's who *n* a reference book containing the names and brief biographical details of famous or important people.
why *adv* for what cause or reason? * *interj* exclamation of surprise. * *n* (*pl* **whys**) a cause.
whydah *n* any of various African weaverbirds with black and white plumage.
WI *abbr* = Wisconsin; West Indies; (*esp Brit*) Women's Institute.
wick *n* a cord, as in a candle or lamp, that supplies fuel to the flame.
wicked *adj* evil, immoral, sinful.—**wickedly** *adv*.—**wickedness** *n*.
wicker *n* a long, thin, flexible twig; such twigs woven together, as in making baskets.—**wickerwork** *n*.
wicket *n* a small door or gate; (*croquet*) any of the small wire arches through which the balls must be hit; (*cricket*) the stumps at which the bowler aims the ball; the area between the bowler and the batsman; a batsman's innings.
wicketkeeper *n* (*cricket*) the fielder standing immediately behind the wicket.
widdershins *see* **withershins.**
wide *adj* broad; extensive; of a definite distance from side to side; (*with* **of**) far from the aim; open fully. * *n* (*cricket*) a ball bowled beyond the reach of the batsman.—**widely** *adv*.
wide-angle *adj* (*photog*) with an angle of view of 60 degrees or more.
wide-awake *adj* fully awake; ready, alert.
wide-eyed *adj* astonished; innocent.
widen *vti* to make or grow wide or wider.
widespread *adj* widely extended; general.
widget *n* (*inf*) a small device or gadget the name of which is lost or forgotten; a whatsit.
widow *n* a woman whose husband has died. * *vt* to cause to become a widow.—**widowhood** *n*.
widower *n* a man whose wife has died.
widow's peak *n* a pointed growth of hair in the middle of the forehead.
width *n* breadth.
wield *vt* (*a weapon, etc*) to brandish; to exercise power.
wife *n* (*pl* **wives**) a married woman.
wig *n* an artificial covering of real or synthetic hair for the head.
wigeon, widgeon *n* a Eurasian wild duck the male of which has a gingery head.
wigging *n* (*Brit inf*) a severe reprimand.
wiggle *vti* to move from side to side with jerky movements.
wigwag *vb* (**wigwagging, wigwagged**) *vi* to move back and forth; to send a signal by means of flag semaphore. * *vt* to signal by wigwagging; to cause (something) to move back and forth. * *n* (the message sent using) a system of signalling with flags.
wigwam *n* a North American Indian conical shelter.
wilco *interj* used in telecommunications to indicate that a message is received and being acted upon.
wild *adj* in its natural state; not tamed or cultivated; uncivilized; lacking control; disorderly; furious.—**wildly** *adv*.—**wildness** *n*.
wild boar *n* a wild pig with tusks, of Europe and Asia.
wild card *n* (*card games*) a card with an arbitrary value determined by the holder; (*sport*) a team that has not qualified for a competition but is allowed to take part; (*sl*) an unpredictable element.
wildcat *adj* (*strike*) unofficial. * *n* a fierce, undomesticated cat.
wildebeest *n* (*pl* **wildebeests, wildebeest**) a gnu.
wilderness *n* an uncultivated and desolate place.
wild-eyed *adj* staring angrily or crazily.
wildfire *n* a fire that spreads fast and is hard to put out.
wildfowl *n* any bird that is hunted for game, esp waterbirds such as ducks and geese.
wild-goose chase *n* a futile pursuit of something.
wilding *n* (the fruit of) any uncultivated plant; a wild animal; (*sl*) a violent rampage though the streets by a teenage gang.
wildlife *n* animals in the wild.
wild oat *n* (*usu pl*) a Eurasian grass related to cultivated oats; (*pl*) youthful excesses.
wild rice *n* a North American grass that bears edible grains; its grain.
Wild West *n* the western US during the lawless period of early settlement.
wile *n* a trick, craftiness.
wilful *adj* stubborn; done intentionally.—*also* **willful.**—**wilfully, willfully** *adv*.—**wilfulness, willfulness** *n*.
will[1] *n* power of choosing or determining; desire; determination; attitude, disposition; a legal document directing the disposal of one's property after death. * *vt* to bequeath; to command.
will[2] *aux vb* used in constructions with 2nd and 3rd persons; used to show futurity, determination, obligation.
willful *see* **wilful.**
willies *npl* (with **the**) nervousness, jumpiness.
willing *adj* ready, inclined; eager.—**willingly** *adv*.—**willingness** *n*.
will-o'-the-wisp *n* a pale phosphorescent glow sometimes seen over marshy areas and thought to be caused by combustion of gas from decaying organic matter; an elusive person or thing.
willow *n* a tree or shrub with slender, flexible branches; the wood of the willow.
willowherb *n* any of various plants of the evening-primrose family with pink or white flowers.
willow pattern *n* a traditional oriental-style design on china tableware consisting of a scene with figures and a willow tree, usu in blue on a white background.
willowy *adj* flexible, graceful.
willpower *n* the ability to control one's emotions and actions.
willy-nilly *adv* whether desired or not.
wilt *vi* to become limp, as from heat; (*plant*) to droop; to become weak or faint.
wily *adj* (**wilier, wiliest**) crafty; sly.—**wiliness** *n*.
WIMP, Wimp (*acronym*) (*comput*) a graphical interface using *W*indows, *I*cons, *M*ice and *P*ull-down menus that makes a computer easier to use.
wimp *n* (*inf*) a weak or ineffectual person.
wimple *n* a linen or silk cloth draped round the head and neck but leaving the face uncovered, worn by women in medieval times and still used by some nuns.
win *vti* (**winning, won**) to gain with effort; to succeed in a contest; to gain eg by luck; to achieve influence over; (*with* **over**) to gain the support or affection of (someone). * *n* a success.
wince *vi* to shrink back; to flinch (as in pain).—*also n*.
winch *n* a hoisting machine. * *vt* to hoist or lower with a winch.
wind[1] *n* a current of air; breath; scent of game; (*inf*) flatulence; tendency; (*mus*) wind instrument(s). * *vt* (**winding, winded**) to cause to be short of breath; to perceive by scent.
wind[2] *vb* (**winding, wound**) *vt* to turn by cranking; to tighten the spring of a clock; to coil around something else; to encircle or cover, as with a bandage; (*with* **down**) to lower by winding a handle, etc. * *vi* to turn, to twist, to meander; (*with* **down**) to diminish in power or intensity; to slacken; to relax.
windage *n* the difference between the bore of a gun and the diameter of the projectile; (an allowance for) the deflection of a projectile caused by the wind.

windbag *n* (*inf*) a person who talks a lot of rubbish.
windblown *adj* blown or shaped by the wind.
windbreak *n* a shelter that breaks the force of the wind, as a line of trees.
windburn *n* redness and soreness of the skin due to the wind.
windcheater *n* a warm hooded jacket of windproof material.
wind-chill *n* a measure of the effect of low temperature combined with wind.
winded *adj* out of breath.
winder *n* one who or that which winds; a winding apparatus; a key for winding a spring-driven mechanism; a step in a spiral staircase.
windfall *n* fruit blown off a tree; any unexpected gain, esp financial.
winding *adj* meandering.
winding sheet *n* a sheet used to wrap a body for burial.
wind instrument *n* a musical instrument played by blowing into it or passing an air current through it.
windjammer *n* a large fast merchant sailing vessel.
windlass *n* any of various devices for hoisting, hauling or lifting using a rope or chain wound round a motorized drum. * *vt* to hoist, etc using a windlass.
wind machine *n* a device used in film and theatre to produce realistic wind effects.
windmill *n* a machine operated by the force of the wind turning a set of sails.
window *n* a framework containing glass in the opening in a wall of a building, or in a vehicle, etc, for air and light.
window box *n* a narrow box on a windowsill for growing flowers, etc.
windowdressing *n* the arrangement of goods in a shop window; ornamentation intended to disguise the true nature of something.
windowpane *n* the glass in a window.
window-shopping *n* the occupation of looking at goods for sale without buying them.—**window-shopper** *n*.
windowsill *n* a sill beneath a window.
windpipe *n* the air passage from the mouth to the lungs, the trachea.
windscreen, windshield *n* a protective shield of glass in the front of a vehicle.
windscreen wiper, windshield wiper *n* a metal blade with a rubber edge that removes rain, etc, from a windscreen.
windsock *n* a canvas cylinder flown from an airport mast to show the direction of the wind.—*also* **drogue**.
windsurfing *n* the sport of skimming along the surface of the water standing on a surfboard fitted with a sail.
windswept *adj* exposed to the wind; dishevelled.
wind tunnel *n* an apparatus for maintaining a constant force of air current to test the aerodynamics of an aircraft, etc.
wind-up *n* the conclusion.
windward *adv*, *adj* toward the direction where the wind blows from.
windy *adj* (**windier, windiest**) exposed to the winds; stormy; verbose.
wine *n* fermented grape juice used as an alcoholic beverage; the fermented juice of other fruits or plants.
wine bar *n* a bar that serves wine and food.
wine box *n* wine sold in a box with a small tap for pouring.
wine cellar *n* a place for storing wines, ideally a cool cellar; a stock of stored wines.
wine-coloured *adj* dark purplish-red.
wine cooler *n* a vessel that is filled with ice for cooling wine bottles.
wineglass *n* a glass, usu with a stem, for drinking wine.
winegrower *n* a person who grows vines and makes wine.
wine press *n* (a place containing) equipment for squeezing juice from grapes to make wine.
winery *n* (*pl* **wineries**) a place where wine is made.
wineskin *n* the skin of an animal, esp a goat, sewn into a bag for holding wine.
wing *n* the forelimb of a bird, bat or insect, by which it flies; the main lateral surface of an aeroplane; a projecting part of a building; the side of a stage; a section of a political party. * *vti* to make one's way swiftly; to wound without killing.
wing chair *n* an armchair with high sides for excluding draughts.
wing collar *n* a stiff upturned shirt collar with the points turned down.
wingding *n* (*inf*) a wild party; a real or pretended fit.
wing nut *n* a nut that is tightened manually using flat wings that project on each side.
wingspan, wingspread *n* the width of a bird or aeroplane between the tips of the wings.
wink *vi* to quickly open and close one's eye; to give a hint by winking; (*with* **at**) to disregard; to allow (something normally prohibited) to happen. * *n* the act of winking; an instant.
winkle[1] *n* a periwinkle.
winkle[2] *n* an edible sea snail. * *vt* (*with* **out**) (*inf*) to extract, prise out; to uncover, disclose.
winkle-pickers *npl* shoes or boots with sharp pointed toes.
winner *n* one that wins; (*inf*) a person or thing that is assured of success.
winning *n* a victory; (*pl*) money won in gambling. * *adj* charming.
winnow *vt* to separate out the chaff from (the grain) by blowing air across it; to analyze.
wino *n* (*pl* **winos**) (*inf*) a down-and-out addicted to cheap wine.
winsome *adj* charming, pleasing.
winter *n* the coldest season of the year: in the northern hemisphere from November or December to January or February. * *vi* to spend the winter.
wintergreen *n* any of various evergreen plants or shrubs; an aromatic essential oil from these formerly used in medicine.
winterize *vt* to prepare something (eg a car) to withstand winter weather.—**winterization** *n*.
winter sports *npl* sports that take place on ice or snow, such as skiing.
wintry, wintery *adj* (**wintrier, wintriest**) typical of winter, cold, stormy, snowy; unfriendly, frigid.
winy *adj* (**winier, winiest**) tasting like or resembling wine.
wipe *vt* to rub a surface with a cloth in order to clean or dry it; (*with* **out**) to remove; to erase; to kill off; to destroy. * *n* a wiping.
wiper *n* a person or thing that wipes; a windscreen wiper.
wire *n* a flexible thread of metal; a length of this; (*horse racing*) the finish line of a race; a telegram. * *adj* formed of wire. * *vt* to fasten, furnish, connect, etc, with wire; to send a telegram.
wired *adj* (*sl*) wearing a hidden electronic recording or listening device; (*sl*) nervous or edgy, esp as a result of taking a stimulating drug.
wire-haired *adj* (*dogs, etc*) having a coat of stiff hairs.
wireless *n* (*formerly*) a radio.
wire service *n* in US, a news agency that sends out news to television and radio stations.
wiretap *vb* (**wiretapping, wiretapped**) *vi* to connect to a telephone wire in order to listen in to a private conversation. * *vt* to tap (a telephone).—**wiretapper** *n*.
wireworm *n* the filament-like larva of certain beetles which infest and destroy plant roots.
wiring *n* a system of wires used in an electrical device or circuit.
wiry *adj* (**wirier, wiriest**) lean, supple and sinewy.—**wiriness** *n*.
wisdom *n* the ability to use knowledge; sound judgment.
wisdom tooth *n* one of four teeth set at the end of each side of the upper and lower jaw in humans and grown last.
wise *adj* having knowledge or common sense; learned; prudent. * *vti* (*with* **up**) (*inf*) (to cause) to become informed or aware.— **wisely** *adv*.
-wise *adv suffix* direction or manner; concerning.
wiseacre *n* a person who pretends to be clever or wise, a know-all.
wisecrack *n* (*inf*) a witty or sarcastic remark.—*also vi*.
wise guy *n* (*inf*) a person who is always making critical or sarcastic comments.
wish *vti* to long for; to express a desire. * *n* desire; thing desired.
wishbone *n* the forked bone at the front of the breastbone of a bird consisting of the fused clavicles.
wishful *adj* having a wish; hopeful.

wishful thinking *n* the mistaken belief that one's wishes correspond to reality.
wishy-washy *adj* weak, thin, feeble.
wisp *n* a thin strand; a small bunch, as of hay; anything slender.—**wispy** *adj*.
wisteria, wistaria *n* a purple-flowered climbing plant.
wistful *adj* pensive; sad; yearning.—**wistfully** *adv*.—**wistfulness** *n*.
wit *n* (*speech, writing*) the facility of combining ideas with humorous effect; a person with this ability; (*pl*) ability to think quickly.
witch *n* a woman who practises magic and is considered to a have dealings with the devil.
witchcraft *n* the practice of magic.
witch doctor *n* a man in certain tribes who appears to be able to cure sickness or cause harm to people.
witchery *n* (*pl* **witcheries**) witchcraft; fascination.
witch hazel *n* any of a genus of North American shrubs with yellow flowers; a soothing lotion made from the bark of this applied to lumps, bruises, skin rashes, etc.
witch hunt *n* a campaign of harassment of those with dissenting opinions; the search for and persecution of those accused of witchcraft.
witching *adj* of or suitable for witchcraft.
with *prep* denoting nearness or agreement; in the company of; in the same direction as; among; by means of; possessing.
withal *adv* (*arch*) as well; moreover.
withdraw *vb* (**withdrawing, withdrew,** *pp* **withdrawn**) *vt* to draw back or away; to remove; to retract. * *vi* to retire; to retreat.—**withdrawal** *n*.
withdrawn *adj* introverted, reserved; remote.
wither *vi* to fade or become limp or dry, as of a plant. * *vt* to cause to dry up or fade.
withers *npl* the ridge between the shoulder blades of a horse.
withershins *adv* counter-clockwise.—*also* **widdershins.**
withhold *vt* (**withholding, withheld**) to hold back; to deduct; to restrain; to refuse to grant.
within *prep* inside; not exceeding; not beyond.
without *prep* outside or out of, beyond; not having, lacking. * *adv* outside.
withstand *vt* (**withstanding, withstood**) to oppose or resist, esp successfully; to endure.
witless *adj* foolish, stupid; not witty.
witness *n* a person who gives evidence or attests a signing; testimony (of a fact). * *vt* to have first-hand knowledge of; to see; to be the scene of; to serve as evidence of; to attest a signing. * *vi* to testify.
witness stand, witness box *n* an enclosure for witnesses in a court of law.
witticism *n* a witty remark.
wittingly *adv* knowingly.
witty *adj* (**wittier, wittiest**) full of wit.—**wittily** *adv*.—**wittiness** *n*.
wives *see* **wife.**
wizard *n* a magician; a man who practises witchcraft or magic; an expert.—**wizardry** *n*.
wizened *adj* dried up, wrinkled, shrivelled.
wk *abbr* = week.
woad *n* (a blue dye obtained from the leaves of) a European plant of the mustard family.
wobble *vi* to sway unsteadily from side to side; to waver, to hesitate.—**wobbly** *adj*.
wodge *n* (*Brit inf*) a thick slice or chunk of something.
woe *n* grief, misery; (*pl*) misfortune.—**woeful** *adj*.—**woefully** *adv*.
woebegone *adj* sorrowful.
wog *n* (*Brit offensive*) a non-white person.
wok *n* a large, metal, hemispherical pan used for Chinese-style cooking.
woke, woken *see* **wake**[1].
wolf *n* (*pl* **wolves**) a wild animal of the dog family that hunts in packs; a flirtatious man.
wolfcall *n* a whistle made by a man when seeing an attractive woman.—*also* **wolf whistle.**
wolfhound *n* any of several types of large dog formerly used to hunt wolves.
wolfram *n* tungsten; wolframite.
wolframite *n* a mineral that is the chief ore of tungsten and also contains iron and manganese.
wolf whistle *see* **wolf call.**
wolverine *n* a voracious carnivorous animal of northern forests of Europe, North America and Asia with thick black fur.
wolves *see* **wolf.**
woman *n* (*pl* **women**) an adult human female; the female sex.
womanhood *n* the state of being a woman.
womanish *n* resembling a woman; suitable for women.
womanize *vi* to pursue women for sex.—**womanizer** *n*.
womankind *n* female human beings; women collectively, esp as distinct from men.
womanly *adj* having the qualities of a woman.
womb *n* the female organ in which offspring are developed until birth, the uterus; any womb-like cavity; a place where something is produced.
wombat *n* an Australian marsupial mammal resembling a small bear.
women *see* **woman.**
womenfolk *npl* women collectively; the female members of a family, group or community.
Women's Institute *n* (*esp Brit*) an organization for women which engages in various social and cultural activities.
Women's Movement *n* a feminist movement seeking to end male domination of women in society.
won *see* **win.**
wonder *n* a feeling of surprise or astonishment; something that excites such a feeling; a prodigy. * *vi* to feel wonder; to be curious; to speculate; to marvel.
wonderful *adj* marvellous.—**wonderfully** *adv*.
wonderland *n* a land full of marvels.
wonderment *n* astonishment, awe; curiosity.
wondrous *adj* (*poet*) wonderful, marvellous.
wonky *adj* (**wonkier, wonkiest**) (*sl*) crooked, unsteady.
wont *adj* accustomed; inclined. * *n* habit.
won't = will not.
woo *vt* (**wooing, wooed**) to seek to attract with a view to marriage; to court; to solicit eagerly.—**wooer** *n*.
wood *n* the hard fibrous substance under the bark of trees; trees cut or sawn, timber; a thick growth of trees.
wood alcohol *n* methanol.
woodbine *n* wild honeysuckle.
woodchuck *n* a North American marmot with thick reddish-brown fur.—*also* **groundhog.**
woodcock *n* a game bird related to the snipe.
woodcraft *n* skill in living and surviving in the forest, esp hunting; skill at woodwork.
woodcut *n* an engraving made on wood; a print made from this.
woodcutter *n* a person whose job is to cut down trees.
wooded *adj* covered with trees.
wooden *adj* made of wood; stiff.
wood engraving *n* the art of engraving illustrations on wood; (a print taken from) a piece of engraved wood.
woodenhead *n* (*inf*) a foolish person.
woodland *n* land covered with trees.
woodlouse *n* (*pl* **woodlice**) a small ground-dwelling wingless crustacean with a segmented body that can roll itself into a ball.
woodman *n* (*pl* **woodmen**) a forester or woodcutter.
wood nymph *n* (*Greek myth*) a nymph of the woods, a dryad.
woodpecker *n* a bird that pecks holes in trees to extract insects.
wood pigeon *n* a large European wild pigeon with white patches of feathers on the body and neck.
woodpile *n* a pile of wood, esp firewood.
wood pulp *n* wood that has been pulped and treated for papermaking.
wood screw *n* a pointed metal screw with an external thread and slotted head designed to be driven into wood with a screwdriver.

woodshed *n* a small shed for storing wood (eg firewood), tools, gardening equipment, etc.
woodsman *n* (*pl* **woodsmen**) a person who lives and works in a wood; a woodman.
woodwind *n* section of an orchestra in which wind instruments, originally made of wood, are played.
woodwork *n* carpentry.
woodworm *n* (*esp Brit*) an insect larva that bores into wood; the damage in furniture so caused.
woody *adj* (**woodier, woodiest**) covered in trees.
woof[1] *n* the horizontal threads crossing the warp in a woven fabric.
woof[2] *interj* a noise like the bark of a dog. * *vi* to make this sound.
woofer *n* a loudspeaker.
wool *n* the fleece of sheep and other animals; thread or yarn spun from the coats of sheep; cloth made from this yarn.
woollen, woolen *adj* made of wool.
woolly bear *n* a large furry caterpillar produced by the tiger moth.
woolly, wooly *adj* (**woollier, woolliest** *or* **woolier, wooliest**) of, like or covered with wool; indistinct, blurred; muddled. * *n* (*pl* **woollies**) (*inf*) a woollen garment.—**woolliness, wooliness** *n*.
woolsack *n* the official seat of the Lord Chancellor in the British House of Lords (formerly made from a large sack of wool).
woozy *adj* (**woozier, wooziest**) (*inf*) mentally confused, dazed; dizzy, nauseous.
wop *n* (*derog*) an Italian.
word *n* a single unit of language in speech or writing; talk, discussion; a message; a promise; a command; information; a password; (*pl*) lyrics; (*pl*) a quarrel. * *vt* to put into words, to phrase; to flatter.
word blindness *n* alexia or dyslexia.
word for word *adj, adv* (*a translation, etc*) using exactly the same words, verbatim.
wording *n* the way in which words are used, esp in written form; a choice of words.
word-perfect *adj* able to repeat something without mistake.—*also* **letter-perfect.**
wordplay *n* verbal wit or repartee.
word processor *n* computer software that allows the input, formatting, storage and printing of text electronically; the hardware, including microprocessor, monitor, keyboard and printer, required to operate word-processing software.
wordy *adj* (**wordier, wordiest**) verbose.
wore *see* **wear.**
work *n* employment, occupation; a task; the product of work; manner of working; place of work; a literary composition; (*pl*) a factory, plant. * *vi* to be employed, to have a job; to operate (a machine, etc); to produce effects; (*with* **on**) to (attempt to) persuade by persistent effort; (*with* **out**) to undertake a regular, planned series of exercises. * *vt* to effect, to achieve; (*with* **off**) to eliminate though effort; (*with* **over**) to examine closely; (*inf*) to assault violently. —**workable** *adj*.—**worker** *n*.
workaday *adj* suited for working days; ordinary, mundane.
workaholic *n* a person with a compulsive need to work.
workbench *n* a bench designed for woodworking, metalworking, etc.
workbook *n* an exercise book with spaces for answers to set questions.
workbox *n* a box for holding material and tools for work.
workday *see* **working day.**
work force *n* the number of workers who are engaged in a particular industry; the total number of workers who are potentially available.
workhorse *n* a horse used for work on a farm; (*inf*) a person or thing that works the hardest in an organization, business, etc.
workhouse *n* (*formerly*) in UK, a public institution for paupers; in US, a prison for petty offenders whose sentences are served by manual labour.
working *adj* spent in or used for work; functioning. * *n* operation; mode of operation; (*pl*) the manner of functioning or operating; (*pl*) the parts of a mine that are worked.
working capital *n* liquid capital available for the daily operation of a business.
working class *n* people who work for wages, esp manual workers; proletariat.—*also adj*.
working day, workday *n* a day for working as opposed to a holiday; the number of hours spent working during the day.
working drawing *n* a plan or drawing used to guide a builder, engineer, etc during the actual construction.
working party *n* (*esp Brit*) a committee established to investigate a particular problem.
workload *n* the amount of work done or required to be done in a particular period.
workman *n* (*pl* **workmen**) a person employed in manual labour; a person who works in a particular manner.
workmanlike *adj* skilful.
workmanship *n* technical skill; the way a thing is made, style.
workmate *n* (*Brit*) a colleague with whom one works.
work of art *n* a fine painting, sculpture, building, etc; something that has the aesthetic qualities of a work of art.
work-out *n* a session of strenuous physical exercises.
workroom *n* a room for work, a workshop.
workshop *n* a room or building where work is done; a seminar for specified intensive study, work, etc.
workshy *adj* (*Brit*) disinclined to work.
work station *n* a place in an office, esp a desk equipped with a computer terminal, where a single person works.
work-to-rule *n* (*Brit*) industrial action in which employees adhere strictly to rules and regulations in the workplace with the aim of slowing production.—**work to rule** *vi*.
worktop *n* (*Brit*) an area in a kitchen, usu with a laminated surface, where food is prepared.
world *n* the planet earth and its inhabitants; mankind; the universe; a sphere of existence; the public.
worldbeater *n* someone or something surpassing all others, a champion.—**worldbeating** *adj*.
world-class *adj* of the highest quality in the world.
worldly *adj* (**worldlier, worldliest**) earthly, rather than spiritual; material; experienced.
world music *n* popular music of or combining ethnic styles from various different countries around the world.
world power *n* a country that is powerful enough to influence international politics.
World Series *n* an annual competition (best of seven games) between the winning teams of the two major North American baseball leagues.
world-shaking *adj* of momentous significance.
World War I *n* a war (1914–18) in which Belgium, France, Italy, Japan, Russia, UK, US, and other allies defeated Germany, Austria, Bulgaria, and Turkey.
World War II *n* a war (1939–45) in which France, UK, US, USSR, and other allies defeated Germany, Italy, and Japan.
world-weary *adj* tired of life.
worldwide *adj* universal.
WORM (*acronym*) (*comput*) *w*rite *o*nce *r*ead *m*any times: an optical disk that stores information which cannot then be overwritten, used for data archiving and backup.
worm *n* an earthworm; an insect larva; the thread of a screw. * *vt* to work (oneself into a position) slowly or secretly; to extract information by slow and persistent means.
worm-eaten *adj* eaten into (as if) by worms; decayed; antiquated.
worms *n sing* any disease or condition caused by infestation with parasitic worms.
worm's-eye view *n* the view from the very bottom or humblest position.
wormwood *n* a European plant that yields a bitter oil used in making absinthe; (something causing) bitterness.

wormy *adj* (**wormier, wormiest**) infested with or eaten by worms; resembling a worm; full of holes caused by burrowing worms.
worn *see* **wear.**
worn-out *adj* (*machine, etc*) past its useful life; (*person*) depressed, tired.
worriment *n* (*inf*) worry, anxiety.
worrisome *adj* causing worry; prone to anxiety.
worry *vb* (**worrying, worried**) *vt* to bother, pester, harass. * *vi* to be uneasy or anxious; to fret. * *n* (*pl* **worries**) a cause or feeling of anxiety.—**worrier** *n*.
worry beads *npl* a string of beads fiddled with for comfort or to relieve tension.
worse *adj* (*compar of* **bad** *and* **ill**) less favourable; not so well as before. * *adv* with great severity.—**worsen** *vti*.
worship *n* religious adoration; a religious ritual, eg prayers; devotion. * *vb* (**worshipping, worshipped** *or* **worshiping, worshiped**) *vt* to adore or idolize. * *vi* to participate in a religious service.—**worshipper, worshiper** *n*.
worshipful *adj* feeling or displaying worship or respect; (*with cap*) in UK, used as a title of respect for various high-ranking officials.
worst *adj* (*superl of* **bad** *or* **ill**; *see also* **worse**) bad or ill in the highest degree; of the lowest quality. * *adv* to the worst degree. * *n* the least good part.
worst-case *adj* being, or taking account of, the worst possible situation or outcome (*worst-case scenario*).
worsted *n* twisted thread or yarn made from long, combed wool.
worth *n* value; price; excellence; importance. * *adj* equal in value to; meriting.
worthless *adj* valueless; useless; of bad character.—**worthlessness** *n*.
worthwhile *adj* important or rewarding enough to justify the effort.
worthy *adj* (**worthier, worthiest**) virtuous; deserving. * *n* (*pl* **worthies**) a worthy person, a local celebrity.—**worthily** *adv*.
would *see* **will**[2].
would-be *adj* aspiring or professing to be.
wouldn't = would not.
wound[1] *n* any cut, bruise, hurt, or injury caused to the skin; hurt feelings. * *vt* to injure.
wound[2] *see* **wind**[2].
wove, woven *see* **weave.**
wow *interj* exclamation of astonishment. * *n* (*sl*) a success.
wp, WP *abbr* = word processing; word processor.
wpm *abbr* = words per minute.
wrack[1] *n* destruction; **wrack and ruin** (the remains of) something destroyed.
wrack[2] *n* seaweed deposited on the shore.
wraith *n* an apparition of a living person, supposedly a sign of impending death; any ghost.
wrangle *vi* to argue; to dispute noisily. * *n* a noisy argument.
wrap *vt* (**wrapping, wrapped**) to fold (paper) around (a present, purchase etc); to wind (around); to enfold; (*with* **up**) to enclose in paper; (*inf*) to make the final arrangements for. * *vi* (*with* **up**) to put warm clothes on; (*inf*) to be quiet. * *n* a shawl.
wrapper *n* one who or that which wraps; a book jacket; a light dressing gown.
wrasse *n* a marine food fish with thick lips and brilliant colouration.
wrath *n* intense anger; rage.—**wrathful** *adj*.
wreak *vt* to inflict or exact (eg vengeance, havoc).
wreath *n* (*pl* **wreaths**) a twisted ring of leaves, flowers, etc; something like this in shape.
wreathe *vti* to form into a wreath; to decorate with wreaths; to move or coil in wreaths.
wreck *n* accidental destruction of a ship; a badly damaged ship; a rundown person or thing. * *vt* to destroy; to ruin.
wreckage *n* the process of wrecking; remnants from a wreck.
wrecked *adj* (*sl*) intoxicated by alcohol or drugs; exhausted.
wrecker *n* a person who causes a wreck; a demolition worker; a breakdown van.
wren *n* small brownish songbird, with a short erect tail.
wrench *vt* to give something a violent pull or twist; to injure with a twist, to sprain; to distort. * *n* a forceful twist; a sprain; a spanner; emotional upset caused by parting.
wrest *vt* to take with force (from); to seize; to obtain by toil.
wrestle *vti* to fight by holding and trying to throw one's opponent down; to struggle. * *n* a contest in which the opponents wrestle.—**wrestler** *n*.
wrestling *n* the skill or sport of fighting by grappling and trying to throw each other to the ground.
wretch *n* a miserable or pitied person; a despised and scorned person.
wretched *adj* very miserable; in poor circumstances; despicable.—**wretchedly** *adv*.—**wretchedness** *n*.
wrier, wriest *see* **wry.**
wriggle *vi* to move with a twisting motion; to squirm, to writhe; to use evasive tricks.—*also n*.—**wriggler** *n*.—**wriggly** *adj*.
wright *n* a maker (eg *playwright*), a builder (eg *shipwright*).
wring *vt* (**wringing, wrung**) to twist; to compress by twisting in order to squeeze water from; to pain; to obtain forcibly.
wrinkle *n* a small crease or fold on a surface. * *vti* to make or become wrinkled.
wrist *n* the joint connecting the hand with the forearm.
wristband *n* the cuff of a sleeve that covers the wrist; a band round the wrist that absorbs sweat.
wristwatch *n* a watch worn on a bracelet or strap around the wrist.
writ *n* (*law*) a written court order.
write *vb* (**writing, wrote,** *pp* **written**) *vt* to form letters on paper with a pen or pencil; to express in writing; to compose (a letter, music, literary work, etc); to communicate by letter; (*with* **off**) to cancel a bad debt as a loss; (*inf*) to damage (a vehicle) beyond repair; (*with* **down**) *vt* to put in writing; to harm or demean (a person) in writing; (*with* **up**) to describe, update, or put into finished form by writing; to praise or publicize in writing. * *vi* to be a writer; (*with* **down to** *or* **for**) to write in a simplified style for a less educated taste.
write-off *n* a debt cancelled as a loss; (*inf*) a badly damaged car.
writer *n* an author; a scribe or clerk.
writer's cramp *n* painful spasms or paralysis in the thumb and fingers from excessive writing.
write-up *n* a published report or review, esp a favourable one.
writhe *vi* to twist the body violently, as in pain; to squirm (under, at).
writing *n* the act of forming letters on paper, etc; a written document; authorship; (*pl*) literary works.
writing paper *n* paper treated to accept ink and used esp for letters.
written *see* **write.**
wrong *adj* not right, incorrect; mistaken, misinformed; immoral. * *n* harm; injury done to another. * *adv* incorrectly. * *vt* to do wrong to.—**wrongly** *adv*.
wrongdoer *n* a person who breaks (moral) laws.—**wrongdoing** *n*.
wrongful *adj* unwarranted, unjust.—**wrongfully** *adv*.
wrong-headed *adj* stubborn; of poor judgment.
wrote *see* **write.**
wrought *adj* formed; made; (*metals*) shaped by hammering, etc.
wrought iron *n* iron that is forged or rolled, not cast.
wrung *see* **wring.**
wry *adj* (**wryer, wryest** *or* **wrier, wriest**) twisted, contorted; ironic.—**wryly** *adv*.—**wryness** *n*.
wt *abbr* = weight.
wunderkind *n* (*pl* **wunderkinder, wunderkinds**) a child prodigy; a whizz kid.
wurst *n* any of various types of spicy sausage from Germany or Austria.
WWI *abbr* = World War I.
WWII abbr = World War II.
WWF *abbr* = World Wildlife Fund for Nature.
WY *abbr* = Wyoming.
WYSIWYG *adj* (*acronym*) (*comput*) *w*hat *y*ou *s*ee *i*s *w*hat *y*ou *g*et: meaning that the layout and style of text, etc, on screen will be exactly as printed out.

X, x *n* the 24th letter of the English alphabet; something shaped like an X; the mark used by an illiterate person to represent a signature; a mark (on a map) to show a particular spot.
X, x *symbol* (*math*) unknown quantity; the figure 10. * *n* an unknown or mysterious factor.
xanth-, xantho- *prefix* yellow.
xanthein *n* a soluble yellow pigment found in plant tissue.
xanthic *adj* yellowish; of or relating to xanthine.
xanthine *n* an insoluble yellow pigment found in plant tissue; a yellowish-white crystalline compound allied to uric acid; a derivative of this.
Xanthippe *n* the wife of Socrates (*fl* 5th century bc); a quarrelsome scolding wife.
xantho-, xanth- *prefix* yellow.
xanthochroid *adj* blond and blue-eyed with fair white skin. * *n* an xanthochroid person.
xanthoma *n* (*pl* **xanthomas, xanthomata**) a small yellow tumour in the skin caused by deposits of lipids.—**xanthomatous** *adj*.
xanthophyll *n* (*bot*) an orange or yellow pigment in autumn leaves.—**xanthophyllous** *adj*.
xanthopsia *n* a disturbance in vision causing everthing to appear yellow.
xanthosis *n* a yellow pigmentation of the skin in diabetes, etc.
xanthous *adj* yellow.
x-axis *n* (*pl* **x-axes**) the reference axis of a graph along which the x coordinate is measured.
X-chromosome *n* one of the pair (with the Y-chromosome) of sex chromosomes that occur in females.
Xe (*chem symbol*) xenon.
xebec *n* a small three-masted Mediterranean sailing vessel with lateen sails.
xeno-, xen- *prefix* strange; foreign.
xenolith *n* (*geol*) a rock occuring in a system of rocks to which it does not belong.
xenomorphic *adj* (*mineral grain*) abnormal in shape owing to the pressure of adjacent minerals in rock.
xenon *n* a heavy inert colourless odourless gaseous element found in tiny quantities in the atmosphere.
xenophobia *n* fear or dislike of strangers or foreigners.—**xenophobe** *n*.—**xenophobic** *adj*.
xer-, xero- *prefix* dryness.
xeroderma, xerodermia *n* dryness of the skin caused by a deficiency in secretions from the sebaceous glands.
xerography *n* photocopying by using light to form an electrostatic image on a photoconductive plate to which toner powder adheres, the particles then being fused by heat and the image transferred onto paper.—**xerographic** *adj*.—**xerographically** *adv*.
xerophilous *adj* (*plant*) drought-loving; adapted to a dry climate.—**xerophily** *n*.
xerophthalmia *n* a disease of the eye with dryness and ulceration of the cornea, caused by vitamin deficiency.—**xerophthalmic** *adj*.
xerophyte *n* a xerophilous plant, eg cactus, that has adapted for growth with a limited water supply.—**xerophytic** *adj*.
xerostomia *n* abnormal dryness of the mouth caused by failure of the salivary glands.
Xerox *n* (*trademark*) a photocopying process using xerography; the copy produced by this. * *vt* to produce a copy in this way.
x-height *n* (*print*) the height of the letter x in lowercase.
xi *n* (*pl* **xis**) the 14th letter of the Greek alphabet.
xiphisternum *n* (*pl* **xiphisterna**) (*anat, zool*) the lowest part of the breastbone, the xiphoid process.—**xiphisternal** *adj*.
xiphoid *adj* sword-shaped. * *n* the xiphoid process.
xiphoid process *n* the xiphisternum.
Xmas *abbr* = Christmas.
X-ray, x-ray *n* radiation of very short wavelengths, capable of penetrating solid bodies, and printing on a photographic plate a shadow picture of objects not permeable by light rays. * *vt* to photograph by x-rays.
XST *abbr* = experimental Stealth technology.
xylem *n* the woody vegetable tissue in plants that conducts water and gives support.
xylo-, xyl- *prefix* wood.
xylograph *n* a wood engraving; an impression made from a wood block.
xylography *n* the art of making wood engravings or making woodcuts; the art of printing from wood blocks.—**xylographer** *n*.—**xylographic** *adj*.—**xylographically** *adv*.
xyloid *adj* like wood.
xylophagous *adj* (*insects*) wood-eating.
xylophone *n* a percussion instrument consisting of a series of wooden bars which are struck with small hammers.—**xylophonic** *adj*.
xylophonist *n* a performer on a xylophone.
xylotomous *adj* (*insects*) boring into or cutting wood.

Y (*chem symbol*) yttrium.
Y *abbr* = yen (Japanese currency).
Y, y *n* the 25th letter of the English alphabet; something shaped like a Y.
Y, y *symbol* (*math*) the second unknown quantity.
y *abbr* = year; yard.
yabber *n* (*Austral sl*) talk, esp in broken English. * *vti* to talk.
yacht *n* a sailing or mechanically driven vessel, used for pleasure cruises or racing. * *vi* to race or cruise in a yacht.—**yachting** *n*.—**yachtsman** *n* (*pl* **yachtsmen**).—**yachtswoman** *nf* (*pl* **yachtswomen**).
yackety-yak *n* (*sl*) persistent trivial chatter.
yah *interj* expressing derision.
yahoo *n* (*pl* **yahoos**) a crude, vicious person.
Yahweh, Yahveh *n* Jehovah.
yak[1] *n* a domesticated species of ox found in Tibet having horns and long hair.
yak[2] *n* (*sl*) persistent trivial talk or chatter. * *vi* (**yakking, yakked**) to talk in this way.
Yale lock *n* (*trademark*) a type of cylinder lock for doors.
yam *n* the edible, starchy tuberous root of a tropical climbing plant; sweet potato.
yamen *n* (*formerly*) the official residence of a Chinese madarin.
yammer *vi* (*inf*) to whimper or whine constantly; (*inf*) to complain loudly and persistently. * *n* (*inf*) a whining or complaining sound.
Yank *n* (*inf*) a Yankee.
yank *vti* to pull suddenly, to jerk. * *n* a sudden sharp pull.
Yankee *n* (*inf*) a citizen of the US, an American.
yap *vi* (**yapping, yapped**) to yelp, bark; (*sl*) to talk constantly, esp in a noisy or irritating manner.
yapok, yapock *n* a tropical American aquatic marsupial with webbed hind feet, thick fur, and a long tail.
yard[1] *n* a unit of measure of three feet and equivalent to 0.9144 metres; (*naut*) a spar hung across a mast to support a sail.
yard[2] *n* an enclosed concrete area, esp near a building; an enclosure for a commercial activity (eg a shipyard); an area of ground for growing herbs, fruits, flowers, or vegetables, usu attached to a house, a garden; an area with tracks for the making up of trains, servicing of locomotives, etc.
yardage[1] *n* a length measured in yards.
yardage[2] *n* the use of a yard; the charge made for this.
yardarm *n* (*naut*) either half of a yard.
yardman *n* (*pl* **yardmen**) a worker in a railroad yard.

yardmaster *n* the manager of a railroad yard.
yardstick *n* a standard used in judging.
yare *adj* ready; active, brisk; (*yacht, etc*) easily handled.
yarmulke *n* a skullcap worn by Jewish men at prayer and by Orthodox male Jews at all times.
yarn *n* fibres of wool, cotton etc spun into strands for weaving, knitting, etc; (*inf*) a tale or story. * *vi* to tell a yarn; to talk at length.
yarrow *n* a strongly scented astringent herb with clusters of small flowers.
yashmak, yashmac *n* a veil worn by Muslim women, showing only the eyes.
yataghan, yatagan *n* a short curved Turkish sword without a guard.
yatter *vi* (*sl*) to gabble, to chatter.—*also n*.
yauld *adj* (*Scot*) active; alert.
yaupon *n* an American evergreen shrub of the holly family.
yaw *vi* (*ship, aircraft*) to deviate from a course; (*aircraft*) to turn from side to side about the vertical axis. * *vt* to cause to yaw. * *n* a yawing movement or course.
yawl *n* a two-masted sailing vessel with its aftermast at the stern.
yawn *vi* to open the jaws involuntarily and inhale, as from drowsiness; to gape.—*also n*.
yawning *adj* gaping; wide-open; drowsy.—**yawningly** *adv*.
yawp *vi* to cry harshly, to scream; (*sl*) to speak foolishly. * *n* such a cry or talk.
yaws *n sing* a tropical disease causing ulceration of the skin, framboesia.
y-axis *n* (*pl* **y-axes**) the reference axis of a graph along which the y coordinate is measured.
Yb (*chem symbol*) ytterbium.
Y-chromosome *n* one of the pair (with the X-chromosome) of sex chromosomes that occur in males.
yclept *adj* (*arch*) named.
yd., yds *abbr* = yard(s).
ye[1] *pron* (*arch*) you (the person addressed and others) the old method of printing the.
ye[2] *definite article* (*arch*) the.
yea *adv, n* (*arch*) yes.
yeah *adv* (*inf*) yes.
yean *vi* (*sheep, goat*) to bring forth (a lamb or kid).
yeanling *n* a lamb or kid.
year *n* a period of twelve months, or 365 or 366 days, beginning with 1 January and ending with 31 December; a period of approximately twelve months.
yearbook *n* an annual publication reviewing the events of the previous year or bringing information up to date.
yearling *n* an animal a year old or in its second year.
yearlong *adj* lasting a year.
yearly *adj* occurring every year; lasting a year. * *adv* once a year; from year to year.
yearn *vi* to feel desire (for); to long for.—**yearning** *n*.
yeast *n* a fungus that causes alcoholic fermentation, used in brewing and baking.
yeasty *adj* (**yeastier, yeastiest**) smelling of or containing yeast.—**yeastiness** *n*.
yegg, yegman *n* (*pl* **yeggs, yegmen**) (*sl*) a safecracker, a criminal.
yeld *adj* (*Scot*) barren, giving no milk.
yell *vti* to shout loudly; to scream; to emit a yell. * *n* a loud shout; a concerted cheer by supporters, students, etc, at a game.
yellow *adj* of the colour of lemons, egg yolk, etc; having a yellowish skin; (*inf*) cowardly. * *n* the colour yellow. * *vi* to become or turn yellow.
yellow-belly *n* (*pl* **yellow-bellies**) (*sl*) a coward.—**yellow-bellied** *adj*.
yellow fever *n* an infectious tropical fever caused by a virus transmitted by certain mosquitoes.
yellowhammer *n* a small European bird with a yellow head, neck, and breast.
yellow jacket *n* an American hornet or wasp with yellow markings.
yellow pages *npl* (part of) a telephone directory that lists business subscribers under different categories according to the type of service offered.
yellow spot n (*anat*) the point of acutest vision in the retina.
yellow streak *n* (*inf*) a cowardly nature.
yellowwood *n* an American tree; its wood, which yields a yellow dye.
yelp *vti* to utter a sharp, shrill cry or bark.—*also n*.
yen[1] *n* (*pl* **yen**) the monetary unit of Japan.
yen[2] *n* (*inf*) a yearning, an ambition.
yeoman *n* (*pl* **yeomen**) (*formerly*) a farmer who cultivated his own land; a non-commissioned officer in the navy, marines.
yeomanly *adj* of or like a yeoman; workmanlike.—*also adv*.
yeoman of the guard *n* a member of the British sovereign's veteran bodyguard.
yeomanry *n* yeomen collectively; in UK, a volunteer cavalry force raised from country districts as a home guard (1761–1907) now part of the Territorial Army.
yeoman service *n* effective assistance.
yep *adv* (*inf*) yes.
yerba (maté) *n* an infusion of dried leaves of the maté, which makes a mildly stimulating tea.
yes *adv* a word of affirmation or consent.
yes man *n* a servile, fawning, sycophantic person.
yester *adv* (*rare*) of yesterday.
yesterday *n* the day before today; the recent past. * *adv* on the day before today; recently.
yet *adv* still; so far; even. * *conj* nevertheless; however; still.
yeti *n* a mysterious animal thought to live high in the Himalayan mountains but never seen.—*also* **abominable snowman**.
yew *n* an evergreen tree or shrub with thin, sharp leaves and red berries.
Y-fronts *npl* (*trademark*) men's underpants with an inverted Y-shaped opening at the front.
Ygdrasil, Yggdrasil *n* (*Norse myth*) an ash tree whose roots and branches bind together earth, heaven, and hell.
yid *n* (*derog*) a Jew.
Yiddish *n* a mixed German and Hebrew dialect spoken by European Jews.
yield *vt* to resign; to give forth, to produce, as a crop, result, profit, etc. * *vi* to submit; to give way to physical force, to surrender. * *n* the amount yielded; the profit or return on a financial investment.
yip *n* a cry, an exclamation. * *vi* (**yipping, yipped**) to utter a yip.
yippee *interj* used to express exuberant delight.
ylang-ylang *n* a Malaysian tree with fragrant flowers; a perfume made from the flowers.
YMCA *abbr* = Young Men's Christian Association.
YMHA abbr = Young Men's Hebrew Association.
yob, yobbo *n* (*pl* **yobs, yobbos**) (*sl*) a young lout, a hooligan.
yodel *vti* (**yodelling, yodelled** *or* **yodeling, yodeled**) to sing, alternating from the ordinary voice to falsetto.—**yodeller, yodeler** *n*.
yoga *n* a system of exercises for attaining bodily and mental control and well-being.—**yogic** *adj*.
yogurt, yoghurt *n* a semi-liquid food made from milk curdled by bacteria.
yogi *n* (*pl* **yogis, yogin**) a person skilled in yoga.
yo-heave-ho *interj* (*formerly*) a cry made by sailors while heaving anchor, etc.
yoicks *interj* a foxhunting cry urging on the hounds.
yoke *n* a bond or tie; slavery; the wooden frame joining oxen to make them pull together; part of a garment that is fitted below the neck. * *vt* to put a yoke on; to join together.
yokel *n* (*derog*) country people who are regarded as unsophisticated and simple-minded.
yolk *n* the yellow part of an egg.
yolk sac *n* the membrane enclosing an egg yolk.
Yom Kippur *n* an annual Jewish holiday marked by fasting and prayer.—*also* **Day of Atonement**.
yomp *vi* to march laboriously carrying heavy equipment, esp over rough terrain.
yon *adj, adv* (*dial*) yonder, over there.
yonder *adv* over there.

yore *n* time long past.
Yorkist *n* an adherent of the royal house of York in England, esp during the Wars of the Roses (1455–85).—*also adj.*
Yorkshire pudding *n* a baked pudding made from batter and traditionally eaten with roast beef.
Yorkshire terrier *n* a small shaggy breed of terrier with a long coat of bluish grey and tan hair.
you *pron* (*gram*) 2nd person singular or plural; the person or persons spoken to.
you'd = you would; you had.
you'll = you will; you shall.
young *adj* in the early period of life; in the first part of growth; new; inexperienced. * *n* young people; offspring.
youngling *n* (*poet*) a young child or animal.
youngster *n* a young person; a youth.
your *poss adj* of or belonging to or done by you.
you're = you are.
yours *poss pron* of or belonging to you.
yourself *pron* (*pl* **yourselves**) the emphatic and reflexive form of **you**.
youth *n* the period between childhood and adulthood; young people collectively; the early stages of something; a young man or boy.—**youthful** *adj.*—**youthfully** *adv.*
youth hostel *n* a supervised lodging for usu young travellers.
you've = you have.
yowl *n* a loud mournful cry, esp from pain.—*also vi.*
yo-yo *n* (*pl* **yo-yos**) a hand-held toy made of a flat spool which can be made to wind up and down a piece of string.
yr *abbr* = year; younger; your.
yrs *abbr* = years; yours.
YT *abbr* = Yukon Territory.
ytterbium *n* a soft metallic element of the lanthanide series.
yttrium *n* a metallic element used in alloys and lasers.
yuan *n* (*pl* **yuan**) the monetary unit of the People's Republic of China.
yucca *n* a plant with stiff, spear-like leaves and white flowers.
yuck *interj* (*sl*) expressing disgust.
yucky *adj* (**yuckier, yuckiest**) (*sl*) disgusting.
yule *n* Christmas.
Yule log *n* a large log traditionally burnt in the fire on Christmas Eve.
yuletide *n* the Christmas festival or season.
yummy *adj* (**yummier, yummiest**) (*inf*) tasty, pleasing. * *interj* yum-yum.
yum-yum *interj* used to express pleasure, esp when eating.
yup *adv* (*inf*) yes.
yuppie *n* (*inf*) any young professional regarded as affluent, ambitious, materialistic, etc.
yurt *n* a circular portable tent of skins used by the Mongolian nomads of Siberia.
YWCA *abbr* = Young Women's Christian Association.
YWHA *abbr* = Young Women's Hebrew Association.

Z

Z (*symbol*) (*physics*) impedance; (*chem*) atomic number.
z (*symbol*) (*math*) an algebraic variable; the z-axis.
Z, z *n* the 26th letter of the English alphabet; something shaped like a Z; (*math*) the third unknown quantity.
z. *abbr* = zero; zone.
zabaglione *n* a dessert of whipped egg yolks, sugar and marsala wine.
Zaïrese *n* a native or inhabitant of the African republic of Zaïre.—*also adj.*
zamindar *n* (*hist*) in India, a district tax collector under the Mogul empire; a landowner paying land tax.—*also* **zemindar.**
zany *adj* (**zanier, zaniest**) comical; eccentric.—**zanily** *adv.*—**zaniness** *n.*
zap *vb* (**zapping, zapped**) *vt* to attack; to kill; to bombard; (*comput*) to get rid of data. * *vi* to rush around.
zappy *adj* (**zappier, zappiest**) (*sl*) energetic, snappy.
zareba, zariba *n* in northern East Africa, a stockade made of thorn hedges as a protection against wild animals or enemies; a place so protected.
zarf *n* an ornamental holder for a coffee cup used in Arab countries.
zarzuela *n* a traditional Spanish one-act comic opera with a satirical theme and including dialogue.
z-axis *n* the reference axis of a three-dimensional coordinate system, along which the z-coordinate is measured.
zeal *n* fervent devotion; fanaticism.
zealot *n* an extreme partisan, a fanatic.
zealous *adj* full of zeal; ardent.—**zealously** *adv.*—**zealousness** *n.*
zebra *n* (*pl* **zebras, zebra**) a black and white striped wild animal related to the horse.—**zebrine** *adj.*
zebra crossing *n* a street crossing for pedestrians marked by black and white strips on the road.
zebu *n* (*pl* **zebus, zebu**) an Asian and African ox with a prominent hump and a large dewlap.
zed *n* in UK, the letter z.
zee *n* (*pl* **zees**) in US, the letter z.
zedoary *n* an aromatic substance like ginger made from the root stock of an Indian plant.
Zeitgeist *n* the spirit of the time; the beliefs, attitudes, tastes, etc, of a particular period.
zemindar *see* **zamindar.**
zemstvo *n* (*pl* **zemstvos, zemstva**) a local elective assembly in the old Russian empire.
Zen *n* a Japanese Buddhist sect that emphasizes self-awareness and self-mastery as the means to enlightenment.
zenana *n* the part of the house reserved for women and girls in a Muslim household.
Zend-Avesta *n* the sacred writings of the Zoroastrians.
zenith *n* the point at which the sun or moon appears to be exactly overhead; peak, summit (of ambition, etc).
zephyr *n* a soft, gentle breeze; a very thin woollen material; a garment made of this.
zeppelin *n* a rigid, cigar-shaped airship.
zero *n* (*pl* **zeros, zeroes**) the symbol 0; nothing; the lowest point; freezing point, 0 degrees Celsius. * *vi* (*with* **in**) (*inf*) to focus attention on (a problem, subject, etc); (*inf*) to converge upon; (*with* **in on**) to concentrate fire (from a weapon) on a specific target.
zero gravity *n* weightlessness.
zero hour *n* the time at which something is scheduled to begin.
zest *n* the outer part of the skin of an orange or lemon used to give flavour; enthusiasm; excitement.—**zestful** *adj.*—**zestfully** *adv.*—**zestfulness** *n.*
zeta *n* the sixth letter of the Greek alphabet.
zeugma *n* a figure of speech in which a word is used with two others, to only one of which it properly applies.—**zeugmatic** *adj.*
Zeus *n* (*Greek myth*) the king of the gods.
zigzag *n* a series of short, sharp angles in alternate directions. * *adj* having sharp turns. * *vti* (**zigzagging, zigzagged**) to move or form in a zigzag.
zilch, zilcho *n* (*sl*) nothing.
zillah *n* (*hist*) an administrative district in India during British rule.
zillion *n* (*pl* **zillion, zillions**) (*inf*) an indefinitely large number or quantity.
Zimb abbr = Zimbabwe.
Zimbabwean *n* a native or inhabitant of the African republic of Zimbabwe.—*also adj.*
Zimmer *n* (*trademark*) a frame of tubular metal used by the infirm as a walking aid.
zinc *n* a bluish-white metallic element used in alloys and batteries. * *vt* (**zincing, zinced** *or* **zincking, zincked**) to coat with zinc.—**zincic** *adj.*
zincograph *n* a design in relief on a zinc plate; a print made from this. * *vti* to etch on zinc; to reproduce in this way.—**zincographer** *n.*—**zincographic** *adj.*—**zincography** *n.*

zing *n* (*inf*) a high-pitched buzz; (*inf*) vitality, exuberance. * *vi* (*inf*) to move with a zinging sound.

zinnia *n* a tropical American plant with showy flowers.

Zionism *n* a movement formerly to resettle Jews in Palestine as their national home, now concerned with the development of Israel.—**Zionist** *n, adj*.—**Zionistic** *adj*.

zip *n* a light whizzing sound of a bullet, etc; (*sl*) brisk energy; a slide fastener on clothing, bags, etc with interlocking teeth, a zipper. * *vb* (**zipping, zipped**) *vi to* move at high speed, to dart. * *vt* to fasten with a zip.

ZIP Code *n* (*trademark*) a postcode that uses digits to denote an area.

zipper *n* a zip.

zippy *adj* (**zippier, zippiest**) speedy; energetic.

zircon *n* a variously coloured hard translucent mineral, some varieties of which are cut as gemstones.

zirconium *n* a metallic element found in zircon and used in alloys.

zit *n* (*sl*) a pimple, spot.

zither *n* a musical instrument with 30–45 strings over a shallow sounding box played by plucking.—**zitherist** *n*.

zloty *n* (*pl* **zlotys, zloty**) the monetary unit of Poland.

Zn (*chem symbol*) zinc.

zodiac *n* an imaginary belt in the heavens along which the sun, moon, and chief planets appear to move, divided crosswise into twelve equal areas, called "signs of the zodiac," each named after a constellation; a diagram representing this.—**zodiacal** *adj*.

zodiacal light *n* a luminous triangular tract of sky sometimes seen before dawn or after dusk, esp in the tropics.

zoetrope *n* a toy with a revolving cylinder showing a series of pictures in apparent motion.

-zoic *adj suffix* (*animal*) having a specified kind of existence; (*geol*) belonging to an era with a particular form of life.

Zollverein *n* in 19th century, a union of German states with common customs tariffs against outside countries and free trade among themselves; any customs union.

zombie, zombi *n* (*pl* **zombies**) a person who is lifeless and apathetic; an automaton.

zonate, zonated *adj* (*bot, zool*) marked with bands.

zone *n* a region, area; a subdivision; any area with a specified use or restriction. * *vt* to divide or mark off into zones; to designate as a zone; to encircle with a zone.—**zonal** *adj*.

zonked *adj* (*sl*) intoxicated by drugs or alcohol; (*sl*) exhausted.

zoo *n* (*pl* **zoos**) a place where a collection of living wild animals is kept for public showing.

zoo-, zo- *prefix* animals.

zoochemistry *n* the chemistry of the constituents of animal bodies.—**zoochemical** *adj*.

zoogeography *n* the science of the geographical distribution of animals.—**zoogeographer** *n*.—**zoogeographic, zoogeographical** *adj*.

zoography *n* descriptive zoology.—**zoographic, zoographical** *adj*.

zooid *adj* resembling but not completely being an animal or plant. * *n* a zooid organism; an animal organism produced by fission; (*corals, etc*) a member of a compound organism.

zool. *abbr* = zoological; zoology.

zoological garden *n* a zoo.

zoologist *n* a person who studies animals and animal behaviour.

zoology *n* (*pl* **zoologies**) the study of animals with regard to their classification, structure and habits.—**zoological** *adj*.—**zoologically** *adv*.

zoom *vi* to go quickly, to speed; to climb upward sharply in an aeroplane; to rise rapidly; (*photog*) to focus in on an object using a zoom lens. * *n* the act of zooming; a zoom lens.

zoom lens *n* (*photog*) a camera lens that makes distant objects appear closer without moving the camera.

zoomorphism *n* the representation (esp of a deity) in the form of or with the attributes of an animal.—**zoomorphic** *adj*.

zoophyte *n* any animal (eg coral, a sponge) that resembles a plant.—**zoophytic** *adj*.

zootomy *n* animal anatomy; the dissection of animals.—**zootomical** *adj*.—**zootomist** *n*.

zorille, zoril *n* a small African mammal that resembles and smells like a skunk.

Zoroastrianism *n* a religious system founded by the Persian prophet Zoroaster (*c*. 628–551 bc), based on the recognition of the dual principle of good and evil.—**Zoroastrian** *n, adj*.

Zouave *n* (*formerly*) a soldier in a French-Algerian infantry unit characterized by a colourful eastern-style uniform; a soldier in a similiar unit, esp a Union Army unit of the American Civil War.

zounds *interj* (*arch*) expressing anger and astonishment.

Zr (*chem symbol*) zirconium.

zucchetto *n* (*pl* **zucchettos**) a skullcap worn by Roman Catholic ecclesiastics, which varies in colour according to rank (black for a priest, purple for a bishop, red for a cardinal, white for the Pope).

zucchini *npl n* a type of small vegetable marrow.—*also* **courgette**.

Zulu *n* (*pl* **Zulus, Zulu**) a member of a Negroid people of South Africa, or their language.—*also adj*.

zwieback *n* a thin rusk.

zyg-, zygo- *prefix* yoked, paired.

zygodactyl *adj* (*bird*) with the toes in pairs, two pointing forward and two backward. * *n* a zygodactyl bird, eg the parrot.—**zygodactylous** *adj*.

zygomorphic, zygomorphous *adj* (*flowers*) bilaterally symmetrical.—**zygomorphism, zygomorphy** *n*.

zygospore *n* a spore formed from the fusion of gametes.—**zygosporic** *adj*.

zygote *n* the cell formed by the union of an ovum and a sperm; the developing organism from such a cell.

zymosis *n* (*pl* **zymoses**) an infectious disease caused by a virus or organism that acts like a ferment; fermentation.

zymotic *adj* caused by or relating to an infection or an infectious disease; producing fermentation.

zymurgy *n* the chemistry of fermentation in brewing, etc.

English Thesaurus

aback *adv* back, backward, rearward, regressively.

abaft *prep* (*naut*) aft, astern, back of, behind.

abandon *vb* abdicate, abjure, desert, drop, evacuate, forsake, forswear, leave, quit, relinquish, yield; cede, forgo, give up, let go, renounce, resign, surrender, vacate, waive. * *n* careless freedom, dash, impetuosity, impulse, wildness.

abandoned *adj* depraved, derelict, deserted, discarded, dropped, forsaken, left, outcast, rejected, relinquished; corrupt, demoralized, depraved, dissolute, graceless, impenitent, irreclaimable, lost, obdurate, profligate, reprobate, shameless, sinful, unprincipled, vicious, wicked.

abandonment *n* desertion, dereliction, giving up, leaving, relinquishment, renunciation, surrender.

abase *vb* depress, drop, lower, reduce, sink; debase, degrade, disgrace, humble, humiliate.

abasement *n* abjection, debasement, degradation, disgrace, humbleness, humiliation, shame.

abash *vb* affront, bewilder, confound, confuse, dash, discompose, disconcert, embarrass, humiliate, humble, shame, snub.

abashment *n* confusion, embarrassment, humiliation, mortification, shame.

abate *vb* diminish, decrease, lessen, lower, moderate, reduce, relax, remove, slacken; allow, bate, deduct, mitigate, rebate, remit; allay, alleviate, appease, assuage, blunt, calm, compose, dull, mitigate, moderate, mollify, pacify, qualify, quiet, quell, soften, soothe, tranquillize.

abatement *n* alleviation, assuagement, decrement, decrease, extenuation, mitigation, moderation, remission; cessation, decline, diminution, ebb, fading, lowering, sinking, settlement; allowance, deduction, rebate, reduction.

abbey *n* convent, monastery, priory.

abbreviate *vb* abridge, compress, condense, contract, cut, curtail, epitomize, reduce, retrench, shorten.

abbreviation *n* abridgment, compression, condensation, contraction, curtailment, cutting, reduction, shortening.

abdicate *vb* abandon, cede, forgo, forsake, give up, quit, relinquish, renounce, resign, retire, surrender.

abdication *n* abandonment, abdicating, relinquishment, renunciation, resignation, surrender.

abdomen *n* belly, gut, paunch, stomach.

abduct *vb* carry off, kidnap, spirit away, take away.

abduction *n* carrying off, kidnapping, removal, seizure, withdrawal.

aberrant *adj* deviating, devious, divergent, diverging, erratic, rambling, wandering; abnormal, anomalistic, anomalous, disconnected, eccentric, erratic, exceptional, inconsequent, peculiar, irregular, preternatural, singular, strange, unnatural, unusual.

aberration *n* departure, deviation, divergence, rambling, wandering; abnormality, anomaly, eccentricity, irregularity, peculiarity, singularity, unconformity; delusion, disorder, hallucination, illusion, instability.

abet *vb* aid, assist, back, help, support, sustain, uphold; advocate, condone, countenance, encourage, favour, incite, sanction.

abettor *n* ally, assistant; adviser, advocate, promoter; accessory, accomplice, associate, confederate.

abeyance *n* anticipation, calculation, expectancy, waiting; dormancy, inactivity, intermission, quiescence, remission, reservation, suppression, suspension.

abhor *vb* abominate, detest, dislike intensely, execrate, hate, loathe, nauseate, view with horror.

abhorrence *n* abomination, antipathy, aversion, detestation, disgust, hatred, horror, loathing.

abhorrent *adj* abominating, detesting, hating, loathing; hateful, horrifying, horrible, loathsome, nauseating, odious, offensive, repellent, repugnant, repulsive, revolting, shocking.

abide *vb* lodge, rest, sojourn, stay, wait; dwell, inhabit, live, reside; bear, continue, persevere, persist, remain; endure, last, suffer, tolerate; (*with* **by**) act up to, conform to, discharge, fulfil, keep, persist in.

abiding *adj* changeless, constant, continuing, durable, enduring, immutable, lasting, permanent, stable, unchangeable.

ability *n* ableness, adroitness, aptitude, aptness, cleverness, dexterity, efficacy, efficiency, facility, might, ingenuity, knack, power, readiness, skill, strength, talent, vigour; competency, qualification; calibre, capability, capacity, expertness, faculty, gift, parts.

abject *adj* base, beggarly, contemptible, cringing, degraded, despicable, dirty, grovelling, ignoble, low, mean, menial, miserable, paltry, pitiful, poor, servile, sneaking, slavish, vile, worthless, wretched.

abjectness *n* abasement, abjection, baseness, contemptibleness, meanness, pitifulness, servility, vileness.

abjuration *n* abandonment, abnegation, discarding, disowning, rejection, relinquishment, renunciation, repudiation; disavowal, disclaimer, disclaiming, recall, recantation, repeal, retraction, reversal, revocation.

abjure *vb* abandon, discard, disclaim, disown, forgo, forswear, give up, reject, relinquish, renounce, repudiate; disavow, disclaim, recall, recant, renounce, repeal, retract, revoke, withdraw.

able *adj* accomplished, adroit, apt, clever, expert, ingenious, practical, proficient, qualified, quick, skilful, talented, versed; competent, effective, efficient, fitted, quick; capable, gifted, mighty, powerful, talented; athletic, brawny, muscular, robust, stalwart, strong, vigorous.

ablution *n* baptism, bathing, cleansing, lavation, purification, washing.

abnegation *n* abandonment, denial, renunciation, surrender.

abnormal *adj* aberrant, anomalous, divergent, eccentric, exceptional, peculiar, odd, singular, strange, uncomfortable, unnatural, unusual, weird.

abnormality *n* abnormity, anomaly, deformity, idiosyncrasy, irregularity, monstrosity, peculiarity, oddity, singularity, unconformity.

aboard *adv* inside, within, on.

abode *n* domicile, dwelling, habitation, home, house, lodging, quarters, residence, residency, seat.

abolish *vb* abrogate, annul, cancel, eliminate, invalidate, nullify, quash, repeal, rescind, revoke; annihilate, destroy, end, eradicate, extirpate, extinguish, obliterate, overthrow, suppress, terminate.

abolition *n* abrogation, annulling, annulment, cancellation, cancelling, nullification, repeal, rescinding, rescission, revocation; annihilation, destruction, eradication, extinction, extinguishment, extirpation, obliteration, overthrow, subversion, suppression.

abominable *adj* accursed, contemptible, cursed, damnable, detestable, execrable, hellish, horrid, nefarious, odious; abhorrent, detestable, disgusting, foul, hateful, loathsome, nauseous, obnoxious, shocking, revolting, repugnant, repulsive; shabby, vile, wretched.

abominate *vb* abhor, detest, execrate, hate, loathe, recoil from, revolt at, shrink from, shudder at.

abomination *n* abhorrence, antipathy, aversion, detestation, disgust, execration, hatred, loathing, nauseation; contamination, corruption, corruptness, defilement, foulness, impurity, loathsomeness, odiousness, pollution, taint, uncleanness; annoyance, curse, evil, infliction, nuisance, plague, torment.

aboriginal *adj* autochthonal, autochthonous, first, indigenous, native, original, primary, prime, primeval, primitive, pristine.

abortion *n* miscarriage, premature labour; disappointment, failure.

abortive *adj* immature, incomplete, rudimental, rudimentary, stunted, untimely; futile, fruitless, idle, ineffectual, inoperative, nugatory, profitless, unavailing, unsuccessful, useless, vain.

abound *vb* flow, flourish, increase, swarm, swell; exuberate, luxuriate, overflow, proliferate, swarm, teem.

about *prep* around, encircling, surrounding, round; near; concerning, referring to, regarding, relating to, relative to, respecting, touching, with regard to, with respect to; all over, over, through. * *adv* around, before; approximately, near, nearly.

above *adj* above-mentioned, aforementioned, aforesaid, foregoing, preceding, previous, prior. * *adv* aloft, overhead; before, previously; of a higher rank. * *prep* higher than, on top of; exceeding, greater than, more than, over; beyond, superior to.

above-board *adj* candid, frank, honest, open, straightforward, truthful, upright. * *adv* candidly, fairly, openly, sincerely.

abrade *vb* erase, erode, rub off, scrape out, wear away.

abrasion *n* attrition, disintegration, friction, wearing down; scrape, scratch.

abreast *adv* aligned, alongside.

abridge *vb* abbreviate, condense, compress, shorten, summarize; contract, diminish, lessen, reduce.

abridgment *n* compression, condensation, contraction, curtailment, diminution, epitomizing, reduction, shortening; abstract, brief, compendium, digest, epitome, outline, précis, summary, syllabus, synopsis; deprivation, limitation, restriction.

abroad *adv* expansively, unrestrainedly, ubiquitously, widely; forth, out of doors; overseas; extensively, publicly.

abrogate *vb* abolish, annul, cancel, invalidate, nullify, overrule, quash, repeal, rescind, revoke, set aside, vacate, void.

abrogation *n* abolition, annulling, annulment, cancellation, cancelling, repeal rescinding, rescission, revocation, voidance, voiding.

abrupt *adj* broken, craggy, jagged, rough, rugged; acclivous, acclivitous, precipitous, steep; hasty, ill-timed, precipitate, sudden, unanticipated, unexpected; blunt, brusque, curt, discourteous; cramped, harsh, jerky, stiff.

abscess *n* boil, fester, pustule, sore, ulcer.

abscond *vb* bolt, decamp, elope, escape, flee, fly, retreat, run off, sneak away, steal away, withdraw.

absence *n* nonappearance, nonattendance; abstraction, distraction, inattention, musing, preoccupation, reverie; default, defect, deficiency, lack, privation.

absent *adj* abroad, away, elsewhere, gone, not present, otherwhere; abstracted, dreaming, inattentive, lost, musing, napping, preoccupied.

absolute *adj* complete, ideal, independent, perfect, supreme, unconditional, unconditioned, unlimited, unqualified, unrestricted; arbitrary, authoritative, autocratic, despotic, dictatorial, imperious, irresponsible, tyrannical, tyrannous; actual, categorical, certain, decided, determinate, genuine, positive, real, unequivocal, unquestionable, veritable.

absolutely *adv* completely, definitely, unconditionally; actually, downright, indeed, indubitably, infallibly, positively, really, truly, unquestionably.

absoluteness *n* actuality, completeness, ideality, perfection, positiveness, reality, supremeness; absolutism, arbitrariness, despotism, tyranny.

absolution *n* acquittal, clearance, deliverance, discharge, forgiveness, liberation, pardon, release, remission, shrift, shriving.

absolutism *n* absoluteness, arbitrariness, autocracy, despotism, tyranny.

absolve *vb* acquit, clear, deliver, discharge, exculpate, excuse, exonerate, forgive, free, liberate, loose, pardon, release, set free, shrive.

absorb *vb* appropriate, assimilate, drink in, imbibe, soak up; consume, destroy, devour, engorge, engulf, exhaust, swallow up, take up; arrest, engage, engross, fix, immerse, occupy, rivet.

absorbent *adj* absorbing, imbibing, penetrable, porous, receptive.

absorption *adj* appropriation, assimilation, imbibing, osmosis, soaking up; consumption, destroying, devouring, engorgement, engulfing, exhaustion, swallowing up; concentration, engagement, engrossment, immersion, occupation, preoccupation.

abstain *vb* avoid, cease, deny oneself, desist, forbear, refrain, refuse, stop, withhold.

abstemious *adj* abstinent, frugal, moderate, self-denying, sober, temperate.

abstinence *n* abstemiousness, avoidance, forbearance, moderation, self-restraint, soberness, sobriety, teetotalism, temperance.

abstinent *adj* abstaining, fasting; abstemious, restraining, self-denying, self-restraining, sober, temperate.

abstract *vb* detach, disengage, disjoin, dissociate, disunite, isolate, separate; appropriate, purloin, seize, steal, take; abbreviate, abridge, epitomize. * *adj* isolated, separate, simple, unrelated; abstracted, occult, recondite, refined, subtle, vague; nonobjective, nonrepresentational. * *n* abridgment, condensation, digest, excerpt, extract, précis, selection, summary, synopsis.

abstracted *adj* absent, absent-minded, dreaming, inattentive, lost, musing, preoccupied; abstruse, refined, subtle.

abstraction *n* absence, absent-mindedness, brown study, inattention, muse, musing, preoccupation, reverie; disconnection, disjunction, isolation, separation; abduction, appropriation, pilfering, purloining, seizure, stealing, taking.

abstruse *adj* abstract, attenuated, dark, difficult, enigmatic, hidden, indefinite, mysterious, mystic, mystical, obscure, occult, profound, recondite, remote, subtle, transcendental, vague.

absurd *adj* egregious, fantastic, foolish, incongruous, ill-advised, ill-judged, irrational, ludicrous, nonsensical, nugatory, preposterous, ridiculous, self-annulling, senseless, silly, stupid, unreasonable.

absurdity *n* drivel, extravagance, fatuity, folly, foolery, foolishness, idiocy, nonsense.

abundance *n* affluence, amplitude, ampleness, copiousness, exuberance, fertility, flow, flood, largeness, luxuriance, opulence, overflow, plenitude, profusion, richness, store, wealth.

abundant *adj* abounding, ample, bountiful, copious, exuberant, flowing, full, good, large, lavish, rich, liberal, much, overflowing, plentiful, plenteous, replete, teeming, thick.

abuse *vb* betray, cajole, deceive, desecrate, dishonour, misapply, misemploy, misuse, pervert, pollute, profane, prostitute, violate, wrong; harm, hurt, ill-use, ill-treat, injure, maltreat, mishandle; asperse, berate, blacken, calumniate, defame, disparage, lampoon, lash, malign, revile, reproach, satirize, slander, traduce, upbraid, vilify. * *n* desecration, dishonour, ill-use, misuse, perversion, pollution, profanation; ill-treatment, maltreatment, outrage; malfeasance, malversation; aspersion, defamation, disparagement, insult, invective, obloquy, opprobrium, railing, rating, reviling, ribaldry, rudeness, scurrility, upbraiding, vilification, vituperation.

abusive *adj* calumnious, carping, condemnatory, contumelious, damnatory, denunciatory, injurious, insolent, insulting, offensive, opprobrious, reproachful, reviling, ribald, rude, scurrilous, vilificatory, vituperative.

abut *vb* adjoin, border, impinge, meet, project.

abutment *n* bank, bulwark, buttress, embankment, fortification; abutting, abuttal, adjacency, contiguity, juxtaposition.

abuttal *n* adjacency, boundary, contiguity, juxtaposition, nearness, next, terminus.

abyss *n* abysm, chasm, gorge, gulf, pit.

academic *adj* collegiate, lettered, scholastic. * *n* academician, classicist, doctor, fellow, pundit, savant, scholar, student, teacher.

academy *n* college, high school, institute, school.

accede *vb* accept, acquiesce, agree, assent to, comply with, concur, consent, yield.

accelerate *vb* dispatch, expedite, forward, hasten, hurry, precipitate, press on, quicken, speed, urge on.

acceleration *n* expedition, hastening, hurrying, quickening, pickup, precipitation, speeding up, stepping up.

accent *vb* accentuate, emphasize, stress. * *n* cadence, inflection, intonation, tone; beat, emphasis, ictus.

accentuate *vb* accent, emphasize, mark, point up, punctuate, stress; highlight, overemphasize, overstress, underline, underscore.

accept *vb* acquire, derive, get, gain, obtain, receive, take; accede to, acknowledge, acquiesce in, admit, agree to, approve, assent to, avow, embrace; estimate, construe, interpret, regard, value.

acceptable *adj* agreeable, gratifying, pleasant, pleasing, pleasurable, welcome.

acceptance *n* accepting, acknowledgment, receipt, reception, taking; approbation, approval, gratification, satisfaction.
acceptation *n* construction, import, interpretation, meaning, sense, significance, signification, understanding; adoption, approval, currency, vogue.
access *vb* broach, enter, open, open up. * *n* approach, avenue, entrance, entry, passage, way; admission, admittance, audience, interview; addition, accession, aggrandizement, enlargement, gain, increase, increment; (*med*) attack, fit, onset, recurrence.
accession *n* addition, augmentation, enlargement, extension, increase; succession.
accessory *adj* abetting, additional, additive, adjunct, aiding, ancillary, assisting, contributory, helping, subsidiary, subordinate, supplemental. * *n* abettor, accomplice, assistant, associate, confederate, helper; accompaniment, attendant, concomitant, detail, subsidiary.
accident *n* calamity, casualty, condition, contingency, disaster, fortuity, incident, misadventure, miscarriage, mischance, misfortune, mishap; affection, alteration, chance, contingency, mode, modification, property, quality, state.
accidental *adj* casual, chance, contingent, fortuitous, undesigned, unintended; adventitious, dispensable, immaterial, incidental, nonessential.
acclamation *n* acclaim, applause, cheer, cry, plaudit, outcry, salutation, shouting.
acclimatization, acclimation *n* adaptation, adjustment, conditioning, familiarization, habituation, inurement, naturalization.
acclimatize, acclimate *vb* accustom, adapt, adjust, condition, familiarize, habituate, inure, naturalize, season.
acclivity *n* ascent, height, hill, rising ground, steep, upward slope.
accommodate *vb* contain, furnish, hold, oblige, serve, supply; adapt, fit, suit; adjust, compose, harmonize, reconcile, settle.
accommodation *n* advantage, convenience, privilege; adaptation, agreement, conformity, fitness, suitableness; adjustment, harmonization, harmony, pacification, reconciliation, settlement.
accompaniment *n* adjunct, appendage, attachment, attendant, concomitant.
accompany *vb* attend, chaperon, convoy, escort, follow, go with.
accomplice *n* abettor, accessory, ally, assistant, associate, confederate, partner.
accomplish *vb* achieve, bring about, carry, carry through, complete, compass, consummate, do, effect, execute, perform, perfect; conclude, end, finish, terminate.
accomplished *adj* achieved, completed, done, effected, executed, finished, fulfilled, realized; able, adroit, apt, consummate, educated, experienced, expert, finished, instructed, practised, proficient, qualified, ripe, skilful, versed; elegant, fashionable, fine, polished, polite, refined.
accomplishment *n* achievement, acquirement, attainment, qualification; completion, fulfilment.
accord *vb* admit, allow, concede, deign, give, grant, vouchsafe, yield; agree, assent, concur, correspond, harmonize, quadrate, tally. * *n* accordance, agreement, concord, concurrence, conformity, consensus, harmony, unanimity, unison.
accordant *adj* agreeable, agreeing, congruous, consonant, harmonious, suitable, symphonious.
accordingly *adv* agreeably, conformably, consistently, suitably; consequently, hence, so, thence, therefore, thus, whence, wherefore.
accost *vb* address, confront, greet, hail, salute, speak to, stop.
account *vb* assess, appraise, estimate, evaluate, judge, rate; (*with* **for**) assign, attribute, explain, expound, justify, rationalize, vindicate. * *n* inventory, record, register, score; bill, book, charge; calculation, computation, count, reckoning, score, tale, tally; chronicle, detail, description, narration, narrative, portrayal, recital, rehearsal, relation, report, statement, tidings, word; elucidation, explanation, exposition; consideration, ground, motive, reason, regard, sake; consequence, consideration, dignity, distinction, importance, note, repute, reputation, worth.
accountable *adj* amenable, answerable, duty-bound, liable, responsible.
accoutre *vb* arm, dress, equip, fit out, furnish.
accredit *vb* authorize, depute, empower, entrust.
accrue *vb* arise, come, follow, flow, inure, issue, proceed, result.
accumulate *vb* agglomerate, aggregate, amass, bring together, collect, gather, grow, hoard, increase, pile, store.
accumulation *n* agglomeration, aggregation, collection, heap, hoard, mass, pile, store.
accuracy *n* carefulness, correctness, exactness, fidelity, precision, strictness.
accurate *adj* close, correct, exact, faithful, nice, precise, regular, strict, true, truthful.
accusation *n* arraignment, charge, incrimination, impeachment, indictment.
accuse *vb* arraign, charge, censure, impeach, indict, tax.
accustom *vb* discipline, drill, familiarize, habituate, harden, inure, train, use.
ace *n* (*cards, dice*) one spot, single pip, single point; atom, bit, grain, iota, jot, particle, single, unit, whit; expert, master, virtuoso. * *adj* best, expert, fine, outstanding, superb.
acerbity *n* acidity, acridity, acridness, astringency, bitterness, roughness, sourness, tartness; acrimony, bitterness, harshness, severity, venom.
achieve *vb* accomplish, attain, complete, do, effect, execute, finish, fulfil, perform, realize; acquire, gain, get, obtain, win.
achievement *n* accomplishment, acquirement, attainment, completion, consummation, performance, realization; deed, exploit, feat, work.
acid *adj* pungent, sharp, sour, stinging, tart, vinegary.
acknowledge *vb* recognize; accept, admit, accept, allow, concede, grant; avow, confess, own, profess.
acme *n* apex, climax, height, peak, pinnacle, summit, top, vertex, zenith.
acquaint *vb* familiarize; announce, apprise, communicate, enlighten, disclose, inform, make aware, make known, notify, tell.
acquaintance *n* companionship, familiarity, fellowship, intimacy, knowledge; associate, companion, comrade, friend.
acquiesce *vb* bow, comply, consent, give way, rest, submit, yield; agree, assent, concur, consent.
acquire *vb* achieve, attain, earn, gain, get, have, obtain, procure, realize, secure, win; learn thoroughly, master.
acquirement *n* acquiring, gaining, gathering, mastery; acquisition, accomplishment, attainment.
acquit *vb* absolve, clear, discharge, exculpate, excuse, exonerate, forgive, liberate, pardon, pay, quit, release, set free, settle.
acquittal *n* absolution, acquittance, clearance, deliverance, discharge, exoneration, liberation, release.
acquittance *n* discharge; quittance, receipt.
acrid *adj* biting, bitter, caustic, pungent, sharp.
acrimonious *adj* acrid, bitter, caustic, censorious, crabbed, harsh, malignant, petulant, sarcastic, severe, testy, virulent.
acrimony *n* causticity, causticness, corrosiveness, sharpness; abusiveness, acridity, asperity, bitterness, churlishness, harshness, rancour, severity, spite, venom.
act *vb* do, execute, function, make, operate, work; enact, feign, perform, play. * *n* achievement, deed, exploit, feat, performance, proceeding, turn; bill, decree, enactment, law, ordinance, statute; actuality, existence, fact, reality.
acting *adj* interim, provisional, substitute, temporary. * *n* enacting, impersonation, performance, portrayal, theatre; counterfeiting, dissimulation, imitation, pretence.
action *n* achievement, activity, agency, deed, exertion, exploit, feat; battle, combat, conflict, contest, encounter, engagement, operation; lawsuit, prosecution.
active *adj* effective, efficient, influential, living, operative; assiduous, bustling, busy, diligent, industrious, restless; agile, alert, brisk, energetic, lively, nimble, prompt, quick, smart, spirited, sprightly, supple; animated, ebullient, fervent, vigorous.

actual *adj* certain, decided, genuine, objective, real, substantial, tangible, true, veritable; perceptible, present, sensible, tangible; absolute, categorical, positive.
actuate *vb* impel, incite, induce, instigate, move, persuade, prompt.
acumen *n* acuteness, astuteness, discernment, ingenuity, keenness, penetration, sagacity, sharpness, shrewdness.
acute *adj* pointed, sharp; astute, bright, discerning, ingenious, intelligent, keen, quick, penetrating, piercing, sagacious, sage, sharp, shrewd, smart, subtle; distressing, fierce, intense, piercing, pungent, poignant, severe, violent; high, high-toned, sharp, shrill; (*med*) sudden, temporary, violent.
adage *n* aphorism, dictum, maxim, proverb, saw, saying.
adapt *vb* accommodate, adjust, conform, coordinate, fit, qualify, proportion, suit, temper.
add *vb* adjoin, affix, annex, append, attach, join, tag; sum, sum up, total.
addict *vb* accustom, apply, dedicate, devote, habituate. * *n* devotee, enthusiast, fan; head, junkie, user.
addicted *adj* attached, devoted, given up to, inclined, prone, wedded.
addition *n* augmentation, accession, enlargement, extension, increase, supplement; adjunct, appendage, appendix, extra.
address *vb* accost, apply to, court, direct. * *n* appeal, application, entreaty, invocation, memorial, petition, request, solicitation, suit; discourse, oration, lecture, sermon, speech; ability, adroitness, art, dexterity, expertness, skill; courtesy, deportment, demeanour, tact.
adduce *vb* advance, allege, assign, offer, present; cite, mention, name.
adept *adj* accomplished, experienced, practised, proficient, skilled. * *n* expert, master, virtuoso.
adequate *adj* able, adapted, capable, competent, equal, fit, requisite, satisfactory, sufficient, suitable.
adhere *vb* cling, cleave, cohere, hold, stick; appertain, belong, pertain.
adherent *adj* adhering, clinging, sticking. * *n* acolyte, dependant, disciple, follower, partisan, supporter, vassal.
adhesion *n* adherence, attachment, clinging, coherence, sticking.
adhesive *adj* clinging, sticking; glutinous, gummy, sticky, tenacious, viscous. * *n* binder, cement, glue, paste.
adieu *n* farewell, goodbye, parting, valediction.
adipose *adj* fat, fatty, greasy, oily, oleaginous, sebaceous.
adjacent *adj* adjoining, bordering, conterminous, contiguous, near, near to, neighbouring, touching.
adjoin *vb* abut, add, annex, append, border, combine, neighbour, unite, verge.
adjourn *vb* defer, delay, postpone, procrastinate; close, dissolve, end, interrupt, prorogue, suspend.
adjudge *vb* allot, assign, award; decide, decree, determine, settle.
adjunct *n* addition, advantage, appendage, appurtenance, attachment, attribute, auxiliary, dependency, help.
adjure *vb* beg, beseech, entreat, pray, supplicate.
adjust *vb* adapt, arrange, dispose, rectify; regulate, set right, settle, suit; compose, harmonize, pacify, reconcile, settle; accommodate, adapt, fit, suit.
administer *vb* contribute, deal out, dispense, supply; conduct, control, direct, govern, manage, oversee, superintend; conduce, contribute.
admirable *adj* astonishing, striking, surprising, wonderful; excellent, fine, rare, superb.
admiration *n* affection, approbation, approval, astonishment, delight, esteem, pleasure, regard.
admirer *n* beau, gallant, suitor, sweetheart; fan, follower, supporter.
admissible *adj* allowable, lawful, permissible, possible.
admission *n* access, admittance, entrance, introduction; acceptance, acknowledgement, allowance, assent, avowal, concession.
admit *vb* give access to, let in, receive; agree to, accept, acknowledge, concede, confess; allow, bear, permit, suffer, tolerate.
admonish *vb* censure, rebuke, reprove; advise caution, counsel, enjoin, forewarn, warn; acquaint, apprise, inform, instruct, notify, remind.
admonition *n* censure, rebuke, remonstrance; advice, caution, chiding, counsel, instruction, monition.
adolescence *n* minority, nonage, teens, youth.
adolescent *adj* juvenile, young, youthful. * *n* minor, teenager, youth.
adopt *vb* appropriate, assume; accept, approve, avow, espouse, maintain, support; affiliate, father, foster.
adore *vb* worship; esteem, honour, idolize, love, revere, venerate.
adorn *vb* beautify, decorate, embellish, enrich, garnish, gild, grace, ornament.
adroit *adj* apt, dextrous, expert, handy, ingenious, ready, skilful.
adulation *n* blandishment, cajolery, fawning, flattery, flummery, praise, sycophancy.
adult *adj* grown-up, mature, ripe, ripened. * *n* grown-up person.
adulterate *vb* alloy, contaminate, corrupt, debase, deteriorate, vitiate.
advance *adj* beforehand, forward, leading. * *vb* propel, push, send forward; aggrandize, dignify, elevate, exalt, promote; benefit, forward, further, improve, promote; adduce, allege, assign, offer, propose, propound; augment, increase; proceed, progress; grow, improve, prosper, thrive. * *n* march, progress; advancement, enhancement, growth, promotion, rise; offer, overture, proffering, proposal, proposition, tender; appreciation, rise.
advancement *n* advance, benefit, gain, growth, improvement, profit.
advantage *n* ascendancy, precedence, pre-eminence, superiority, upper-hand; benefit, blessing, emolument, gain, profit, return; account, behalf, interest; accommodation, convenience, prerogative, privilege.
advantageous *adj* beneficial, favourable, profitable.
advent *n* accession, approach, arrival, coming, visitation.
adventitious *adj* accidental, extraneous, extrinsic, foreign, fortuitous, nonessential.
adventure *vb* dare, hazard, imperil, peril, risk, venture. * *n* chance, contingency, experiment, fortuity, hazard, risk, venture; crisis, contingency, event, incident, occurrence, transaction.
adventurous *adj* bold, chivalrous, courageous, daring, doughty; foolhardy, headlong, precipitate, rash, reckless; dangerous, hazardous, perilous.
adversary *n* antagonist, enemy, foe, opponent.
adverse *adj* conflicting, contrary, opposing; antagonistic, harmful, hostile, hurtful, inimical, unfavourable, unpropitious; calamitous, disastrous, unfortunate, unlucky, untoward.
adversity *n* affliction, calamity, disaster, distress, misery, misfortune, sorrow, suffering, woe.
advertise *vb* advise, announce, declare, inform, placard, proclaim, publish.
advertisement *n* announcement, information, notice, proclamation.
advice *n* admonition, caution, counsel, exhortation, persuasion, suggestion, recommendation; information, intelligence, notice, notification; care, counsel, deliberation, forethought.
advisable *adj* advantageous, desirable, expedient, prudent.
advise *vb* admonish, counsel, commend, recommend, suggest, urge; acquaint, apprise, inform, notify; confer, consult, deliberate.
adviser *n* counsellor, director, guide, instructor.
advocate *vb* countenance, defend, favour, justify, maintain, support, uphold, vindicate. * *n* apologist, counsellor, defender, maintainer, patron, pleader, supporter; attorney, barrister, counsel, lawyer, solicitor.
aegis *n* defence, protection, safeguard, shelter.
aesthetic *adj* appropriate, beautiful, tasteful.
affable *adj* accessible, approachable, communicative, conversable, cordial, easy, familiar, frank, free, sociable, social; complaisant, courteous, civil, obliging, polite, urbane.
affair *n* business, circumstance, concern, matter, office, question; event, incident, occurrence, performance, proceeding, transaction; battle, combat, conflict, encounter, engagement, skirmish.
affairs *npl* administration, relations; business, estate, finances, property.
affect *vb* act upon, alter, change, influence, modify, transform; concern, interest, regard, relate; improve, melt, move, overcome, subdue, touch; aim at, aspire to, crave, yearn for; adopt, assume, feign.
affectation *n* affectedness, airs, artificiality, foppery, pretension, simulation.

affected *adj* artificial, assumed, feigned, insincere, theatrical; assuming, conceited, foppish, vain.
affection *n* bent, bias, feeling, inclination, passion, proclivity, propensity; accident, attribute, character, mark, modification, mode, note, property; attachment, endearment, fondness, goodwill, kindness, partiality, love.
affectionate *adj* attached, devoted, fond, kind, loving, sympathetic, tender.
affiliate *vb* ally, annex, associate, connect, incorporate, join, unite. * *n* ally, associate, confederate.
affinity *n* connection, propinquity, relationship; analogy, attraction, correspondence, likeness, relation, resemblance, similarity, sympathy.
affirm *vb* allege, assert, asseverate, aver, declare, state; approve, confirm, establish, ratify.
affix *vb* annex, attach, connect, fasten, join, subjoin, tack.
afflict *vb* agonize, distress, grieve, pain, persecute, plague, torment, trouble, try, wound.
affliction *n* adversity, calamity, disaster, misfortune, stroke, visitation; bitterness, depression, distress, grief, misery, plague, scourge, sorrow, trial, tribulation, wretchedness, woe.
affluent *adj* abounding, abundant, bounteous, plenteous; moneyed, opulent, rich, wealthy.
afford *vb* furnish, produce, supply, yield; bestow, communicate, confer, give, grant, impart, offer; bear, endure, support.
affray *n* brawl, conflict, disturbance, feud, fight, quarrel, scuffle, struggle.
affright *vb* affray, alarm, appal, confound, dismay, shock, startle. * *n* alarm, consternation, fear, fright, panic, terror.
affront *vb* abuse, insult, outrage; annoy, chafe, displease, fret, irritate, offend, pique, provoke, vex. * *n* abuse, contumely, insult, outrage, vexation, wrong.
afraid *adj* aghast, alarmed, anxious, apprehensive, frightened, scared, timid.
after *prep* later than, subsequent to; behind, following; about, according to; because of, in imitation of. * *adj* behind, consecutive, ensuing, following, later, succeeding, successive, subsequent; aft, back, hind, rear, rearmost, tail.* *adv* afterwards, later, next, since, subsequently, then, thereafter.
again *adv* afresh, anew, another time, once more; besides, further, in addition, moreover.
against *prep* adverse to, contrary to, in opposition to, resisting; abutting, close up to, facing, fronting, off, opposite to, over; in anticipation of, for, in expectation of; in compensation for, to counterbalance, to match.
age *vb* decline, grow old, mature. * *n* aeon, date, epoch, period, time; decline, old age, senility; antiquity, oldness.
agency *n* action, force, intervention, means, mediation, operation, procurement; charge, direction, management, superintendence, supervision.
agent *n* actor, doer, executor, operator, performer; active element, cause, force; attorney, broker, commissioner, deputy, factor, intermediary, manager, middleman.
agglomeration *n* accumulation, aggregation, conglomeration, heap, lump, pile.
agglutinate *vb* cement, fasten, glue, unite.
aggrandize *vb* advance, dignify, elevate, enrich, exalt, promote.
aggravate *vb* heighten, increase, worsen; colour, exaggerate, magnify, overstate; enrage, irritate, provoke, tease.
aggravation *n* exaggeration, heightening, irritation.
aggregate *vb* accumulate, amass, collect, heap, pile. * *adj* collected, total. * *n* amount, gross, total, whole.
aggressive *adj* assailing, assailant, assaulting, attacking, invading, offensive; pushing, self-assertive.
aggressor *n* assailant, assaulter, attacker, invader.
aggrieve *vb* afflict, grieve, pain; abuse, ill-treat, impose, injure, oppress, wrong.
aghast *adj* appalled, dismayed, frightened, horrified, horror-struck, panic-stricken, terrified; amazed, astonished, startled, thunderstruck.
agile *adj* active, alert, brisk, lively, nimble, prompt, smart, ready.
agitate *vb* disturb, jar, rock, shake, trouble; disquiet, excite, ferment, rouse, trouble; confuse, discontent, flurry, fluster, flutter; canvass, debate, discuss, dispute, investigate.
agitation *n* concussion, shake, shaking; commotion, convulsion, disturbance, ferment, jarring, storm, tumult, turmoil; discomposure, distraction, emotion, excitement, flutter, perturbation, ruffle, tremor, trepidation; controversy, debate, discussion.
agnostic *n* doubter, empiricist, sceptic.
agonize *vb* distress, excruciate, rack, torment, torture.
agony *n* anguish, distress, pangs.
agree *vb* accord, concur, harmonize, unite; accede, acquiesce, assent, comply, concur, subscribe; bargain, contract, covenant, engage, promise, undertake; compound, compromise; chime, cohere, conform, correspond, match, suit, tally.
agreeable *adj* charming, pleasant, pleasing.
agreement *n* accordance, compliance, concord, harmony, union; bargain, compact, contract, pact, treaty.
agriculture *n* cultivation, culture, farming, geoponics, husbandry, tillage.
aid *vb* assist, help, serve, support; relieve, succour; advance, facilitate, further, promote. * *n* assistance, cooperation, help, patronage; alms, subsidy, succour, relief.
ailment *n* disease, illness, sickness.
aim *vb* direct, level, point, train; design, intend, mean, purpose, seek. * *n* bearing, course, direction, tendency; design, object, view, reason.
air *vb* expose, display, ventilate. * *n* atmosphere, breeze; appearance, aspect, manner; melody, tune.
aisle *n* passage, walk.
akin *adj* allied, kin, related; analogous, cognate, congenial, connected.
alacrity *n* agility, alertness, activity, eagerness, promptitude; cheerfulness, gaiety, hilarity, liveliness, vivacity.
alarm *vb* daunt, frighten, scare, startle, terrify. * *n* alarm-bell, tocsin, warning; apprehension, fear, fright, terror.
alert *adj* awake, circumspect, vigilant, watchful, wary; active, brisk, lively, nimble, quick, prompt, ready, sprightly. * *vb* alarm, arouse, caution, forewarn, signal, warn. * *n* alarm, signal, warning.
alertness *n* circumspection, vigilance, watchfulness, wariness; activity, briskness, nimbleness, promptness, readiness, spryness.
alien *adj* foreign, not native; differing, estranged, inappropriate, remote, unallied, separated. * *n* foreigner, stranger.
alienate *vb* (*legal*) assign, demise, transfer; disaffect, estrange, wean, withdraw.
alienation *n* (*legal*) assignment, conveyance, transfer; breach, disaffection, division, estrangement, rupture; (*med*) aberration, delusion, derangement, hallucination, insanity, madness.
alike *adj* akin, analogous, duplicate, identical, resembling, similar. * *adv* equally.
aliment *n* diet, fare, meat, nutriment, provision, rations, sustenance.
alive *adj* animate, breathing, live; aware, responsive, sensitive, susceptible; brisk, cheerful, lively, sprightly.
allay *vb* appease, calm, check, compose; alleviate, assuage, lessen, moderate, solace, temper.
allege *vb* affirm, assert, declare, maintain, say; adduce, advance, assign, cite, plead, produce, quote.
allegiance *n* duty, homage, fealty, fidelity, loyalty, obligation.
allegory *n* apologue, fable, myth, parable, story, tale.
alleviate *vb* assuage, lighten, mitigate, mollify, moderate, quell, quiet, quieten, soften, soothe.
alliance *n* affinity, intermarriage, relation; coalition, combination, confederacy, league, treaty, union; affiliation, connection, relationship, similarity.
allot *vb* divide, dispense, distribute; assign, fix, prescribe, specify.
allow *vb* acknowledge, admit, concede, confess, grant, own; authorize, grant, let, permit; bear, endure, suffer, tolerate; grant, yield, relinquish, spare; approve, justify, sanction; abate, bate, deduct, remit.

allude *vb* glance, hint, mention, imply, insinuate, intimate, refer, suggest, touch.

allure *vb* attract, beguile, cajole, coax, entice, lure, persuade, seduce, tempt. * *n* appeal, attraction, lure, temptation.

allusion *n* hint, implication, intimation, insinuation, mention, reference, suggestion.

ally *vb* combine, connect, join, league, marry, unite. * *n* aider, assistant, associate, coadjutor, colleague, friend, partner.

almighty *adj* all-powerful, omnipotent.

alms *npl* benefaction, bounty, charity, dole, gift, gratuity.

alone *adj* companionless, deserted, forsaken, isolated, lonely, only, single, sole, solitary.

along *adv* lengthways, lengthwise; forward, onward; beside, together, simultaneously.

aloud *adv* audibly, loudly, sonorously, vociferously.

alter *vb* change, conform, modify, shift, turn, transform, transmit, vary.

altercation *n* bickering, contention, controversy, dispute, dissension, strife, wrangling.

alternating *adj* intermittent, interrupted.

alternative *adj* another, different, second, substitute. * *n* choice, option, preference.

although *conj* albeit, even if, for all that, notwithstanding, though.

altitude *n* elevation, height, loftiness.

altogether *adv* completely, entirely, totally, utterly.

always *adv* continually, eternally, ever, evermore, perpetually, unceasingly.

amalgamate *vb* blend, combine, commingle, compound, incorporate, mix.

amass *vb* accumulate, aggregate, collect, gather, heap, scrape together.

amateur *n* dilettante, nonprofessional.

amaze *vb* astonish, astound, bewilder, confound, confuse, dumbfound, perplex, stagger, stupefy.

amazement *n* astonishment, bewilderment, confusion, marvel, surprise, wonder.

ambassador *n* deputy, envoy, legate, minister, plenipotentiary.

ambiguous *adj* dubious, doubtful, enigmatic, equivocal, uncertain, indefinite, indistinct, obscure, vague.

ambition *n* aspiration, emulation, longing, yearning.

ambitious *adj* aspiring, avid, eager, intent.

ameliorate *vb* amend, benefit, better, elevate, improve, mend.

amenability *n* amenableness, responsiveness; accountability, liability, responsibility.

amenable *adj* acquiescent, agreeable, persuadable, responsive, susceptible; accountable, liable, responsible.

amend *vb* better, correct, improve, mend, redress, reform.

amends *npl* atonement, compensation, expiation, indemnification, recompense, reparation, restitution.

amenity *n* agreeableness, mildness, pleasantness, softness; affability, civility, courtesy, geniality, graciousness, urbanity.

amiable *adj* attractive, benign, charming, genial, good-natured, harmonious, kind, lovable, lovely, pleasant, pleasing, sweet, winning, winsome.

amicable *adj* amiable, cordial, friendly, harmonious, kind, kindly, peaceable.

amiss *adj* erroneous, inaccurate, incorrect, faulty, improper, wrong. * *adv* erroneously, inaccurately, incorrectly, wrongly.

amnesty *n* absolution, condonation, dispensation, forgiveness, oblivion.

amorous *adj* ardent, enamoured, fond, longing, loving, passionate, tender; erotic, impassioned.

amorphous *adj* formless, irregular, shapeless, unshapen; noncrystalline, structureless; chaotic, characterless, clumsy, disorganized, misshapen, unorganized, vague.

amount *n* aggregate, sum, total.

ample *adj* broad, capacious, extended, extensive, great, large, roomy, spacious; abounding, abundant, copious, generous, liberal, plentiful; diffusive, unrestricted.

amputate *vb* clip, curtail, prune, lop, remove, separate, sever.

amuse *vb* charm, cheer, divert, enliven, entertain, gladden, relax, solace; beguile, cheat, deceive, delude, mislead.

amusement *n* diversion, entertainment, frolic, fun, merriment, pleasure.

analeptic *adj* comforting, invigorating, restorative.

analogy *n* correspondence, likeness, parallelism, parity, resemblance, similarity.

analysis *n* decomposition, dissection, resolution, separation.

anarchy *n* chaos, confusion, disorder, misrule, lawlessness, riot.

anathema *n* ban, curse, denunciation, excommunication, execration, malediction, proscription.

anatomy *n* dissection; form, skeleton, structure.

ancestor *n* father, forebear, forefather, progenitor.

ancestry *n* family, house, line, lineage; descent, genealogy, parentage, pedigree, stock.

anchor *vb* fasten, fix, secure; cast anchor, take firm hold. * *n* (*naut*) ground tackle; defence, hold, security, stay.

ancient *adj* old, primitive, pristine; antiquated, antique, archaic, obsolete.

ancillary *adj* accessory, auxiliary, contributory, helpful, instrumental.

angelic *adj* adorable, celestial, cherubic, heavenly, saintly, seraphic; entrancing, enrapturing, rapturous, ravishing.

anger *vb* chafe, displease, enrage, gall, infuriate, irritate, madden. * *n* choler, exasperation, fury, gall, indignation, ire, passion, rage, resentment, spleen, wrath.

angle *vb* fish. * *n* divergence, flare, opening; bend, corner, crotch, cusp, point; fish-hook, hook.

angry *adj* chafed, exasperated, furious, galled, incensed, irritated, nettled, piqued, provoked, resentful.

anguish *n* agony, distress, grief, pang, rack, torment, torture.

anile *adj* aged, decrepit, doting, imbecile, senile.

animadversion *n* comment, notice, observation, remark; blame, censure, condemnation, reproof, stricture.

animate *vb* inform, quicken, vitalize, vivify; fortify, invigorate, revive; activate, enliven, excite, heat, impel, kindle, rouse, stimulate, stir, waken; elate, embolden, encourage, exhilarate, gladden, hearten. * *adj* alive, breathing, live, living, organic, quick.

animosity *n* bitterness, enmity, grudge, hatred, hostility, rancour, rankling, spleen, virulence.

annals *npl* archives, chronicles, records, registers, rolls.

annex *vb* affix, append, attach, subjoin, tag, tack; connect, join, unite.

annihilate *vb* abolish, annul, destroy, dissolve, exterminate, extinguish, kill, obliterate, raze, ruin.

annotation *n* comment, explanation, illustration, note, observation, remark.

announce *vb* advertise, communicate, declare, disclose, proclaim, promulgate, publish, report, reveal, trumpet.

announcement *n* advertisement, annunciation, bulletin, declaration, manifesto, notice, notification, proclamation.

annoy *vb* badger, chafe, disquiet, disturb, fret, hector, irk, irritate, molest, pain, pester, plague, trouble, vex, worry, wound.

annul *vb* abolish, abrogate, cancel, countermand, nullify, overrule, quash, repeal, recall, reverse, revoke.

anoint *vb* consecrate, oil, sanctify, smear.

anonymous *adj* nameless, unacknowledged, unsigned.

answer *vb* fulfil, rejoin, reply, respond, satisfy. * *n* rejoinder, reply, response, retort; confutation, rebuttal, refutation.

answerable *adj* accountable, amenable, correspondent, liable, responsible, suited.

antagonism *n* contradiction, discordance, disharmony, dissonant, incompatibility, opposition.

antecedent *adj* anterior, foregoing, forerunning, precedent, preceding, previous. * *n* forerunner, precursor.

anterior *adj* antecedent, foregoing, preceding, previous, prior; fore, front.

anticipate *vb* antedate, forestall, foretaste, prevent; count upon, expect, forecast, foresee.

anticipation *n* apprehension, contemplation, expectation, hope, prospect, trust; expectancy, forecast, foresight, foretaste, preconception, presentiment.

antidote *n* corrective, counteractive, counter-poison; cure, remedy, restorative, specific.

antipathy *n* abhorrence, aversion, disgust, detestation, hate, hatred, horror, loathing, repugnance.

antique *adj* ancient, archaic, bygone, old, old-fashioned.

anxiety *n* apprehension, care, concern, disquiet, fear, foreboding, misgiving, perplexity, trouble, uneasiness, vexation, worry.

anxious *adj* apprehensive, restless, solicitous, uneasy, unquiet, worried.

apart *adv* aloof, aside, separately; asunder.

apathetic *adj* cold, dull, impassive, inert, listless, obtuse, passionless, sluggish, torpid, unfeeling.

ape *vb* counterfeit, imitate, mimic; affect. * *n* simian, troglodyte; imitator, mimic; image, imitation, likeness, type.

aperture *n* chasm, cleft, eye, gap, opening, hole, orifice, passage.

aphorism *n* adage, apothegm, byword, maxim, proverb, saw, saying.

apish *adj* imitative, mimicking; affected, foppish, trifling.

aplomb *n* composure, confidence, equanimity, self-confidence.

apocryphal *adj* doubtful, fabulous, false, legendary, spurious, uncanonical.

apologetic *adj* exculpatory, excusatory; defensive, vindictive.

apology *n* defence, justification, vindication; acknowledgement, excuse, explanation, plea, reparation.

apostate *adj* backsliding, disloyal, faithless, false, perfidious, recreant, traitorous, untrue. * *n* backslider, deserter, pervert, renegade, turncoat.

apostle *n* angel, herald, messenger, missionary, preacher; advocate, follower, supporter.

apothegm *n* aphorism, byword, dictum, maxim, proverb, saw, saying.

appal *vb* affright, alarm, daunt, dismay, frighten, horrify, scare, shock.

apparel *n* attire, array, clothes, clothing, dress, garments, habit, raiment, robes, suit, trappings, vestments.

apparent *adj* discernible, perceptible, visible; conspicuous, evident, legible, manifest, obvious, open, patent, plain, unmistakable; external, ostensible, seeming, superficial.

apparition *n* appearance, appearing, epiphany, manifestation; being, form; ghost, phantom, spectre, spirit, vision.

appeal *vb* address, entreat, implore, invoke, refer, request, solicit. * *n* application, entreaty, invocation, solicitation, suit.

appear *vb* emerge, loom; break, open; arise, occur, offer; look, seem, show.

appearance *n* advent, arrival, apparition, coming; form, shape; colour, face, fashion, feature, guise, pretence, pretext; air, aspect, complexion, demeanour, manner, mien.

appease *vb* abate, allay, assuage, calm, ease, lessen, mitigate, pacify, placate, quell, soothe, temper, tranquillize.

appellation *n* address, cognomen, denomination, epithet, style, title.

append *vb* attach, fasten, hang; add, annex, subjoin, tack, tag.

appendix *n* addition, adjunct, appurtenance, codicil; excursus, supplement.

appetite *n* craving, desire, longing, lust, passion; gusto, relish, stomach, zest; hunger.

applaud *vb* acclaim, cheer, clap, compliment, encourage, extol, magnify.

applause *n* acclamation, approval, cheers, commendation, plaudit.

applicable *adj* adapted, appropriate, apt, befitting, fitting, germane, pertinent, proper, relevant.

application *n* emollient, lotion, ointment, poultice, wash; appliance, exercise, practice, use; appeal, petition, request, solicitation, suit; assiduity, constancy, diligence, effort, industry.

apply *vb* bestow, lay upon; appropriate, convert, employ, exercise, use; addict, address, dedicate, devote, direct, engage.

appoint *vb* determine, establish, fix, prescribe; bid, command, decree, direct, order, require; allot, assign, delegate, depute, detail, destine, settle; constitute, create, name, nominate; equip, furnish, supply.

apportion *vb* allocate, allot, allow, assign, deal, dispense, divide, share.

apposite *adj* apt, fit, germane, pertinent, relevant, suitable, pertinent.

appraise *vb* appreciate, estimate, prize, rate, value.

appreciate *vb* appreciate, esteem, estimate, rate, realize, value.

apprehend *vb* arrest, catch, detain, seize, take; conceive, imagine, regard, view; appreciate, perceive, realize, see, take in; fear, forebode; conceive, fancy, hold, imagine, presume, understand.

apprehension *n* arrest, capture, seizure; intellect, intelligence, mind, reason; discernment, intellect, knowledge, perception, sense; belief, fancy, idea, notion, sentiment, view; alarm, care, dread, distrust, fear, misgiving, suspicion.

apprise *vb* acquaint, inform, notify, tell.

approach *vb* advance, approximate, come close; broach; resemble. * *n* advance, advent; approximation, convergence, nearing, tendency; entrance, path, way.

approbation *n* approval, commendation, liking, praise; assent, concurrence, consent, endorsement, ratification, sanction.

appropriate *vb* adopt, arrogate, assume, set apart; allot, apportion, assign, devote; apply, convert, employ, use. * *adj* adapted, apt, befitting, fit, opportune, seemly, suitable.

approve *vb* appreciate, commend, like, praise, recommend, value; confirm, countenance, justify, ratify, sustain, uphold.

approximate *vb* approach, resemble. * *adj* approaching, proximate; almost exact, inexact, rough.

apt *adj* applicable, apposite, appropriate, befitting, fit, felicitous, germane; disposed, inclined, liable, prone, subject; able, adroit, clever, dextrous, expert, handy, happy, prompt, ready, skilful.

aptitude *n* applicability, appropriateness, felicity, fitness, pertinence, suitability; inclination, tendency, turn; ability, address, adroitness, quickness, readiness, tact.

arbitrary *adj* absolute, autocratic, despotic, domineering, imperious, overbearing, unlimited; capricious, discretionary, fanciful, voluntary, whimsical.

arcade *n* colonnade, loggia.

arch[1] *adj* cunning, knowing, frolicsome, merry, mirthful, playful, roguish, shrewd, sly; consummate, chief, leading, pre-eminent, prime, primary, principal.

arch[2] *vb* span, vault; bend, curve. * *n* archway, span, vault.

archaic *adj* ancient, antiquated, antique, bygone, obsolete, old.

archives *npl* documents, muniments, records, registers, rolls.

ardent *adj* burning, fiery, hot; eager, earnest, fervent, impassioned, keen, passionate, warm, zealous.

ardour *n* glow, heat, warmth; eagerness, enthusiasm, fervour, heat, passion, soul, spirit, warmth, zeal.

arduous *adj* high, lofty, steep, uphill; difficult, fatiguing, hard, laborious, onerous, tiresome, toilsome, wearisome.

area *n* circle, circuit, district, domain, field, range, realm, region, tract.

argue *vb* plead, reason upon; debate, dispute; denote, evince, imply, indicate, mean, prove; contest, debate, discuss, sift.

arid *adj* barren, dry, parched, sterile, unfertile; dry, dull, jejune, pointless, uninteresting.

aright *adv* correctly, justly, rightly, truly.

arise *vb* ascend, mount, soar, tower; appear, emerge, rise, spring; begin, originate; rebel, revolt, rise; accrue, come, emanate, ensue, flow, issue, originate, proceed, result.

aristocracy *n* gentry, nobility, noblesse, peerage.

arm[1] *n* bough, branch, limb, protection; cove, creek, estuary, firth, fjord, frith, inlet.

arm[2] *vb* array, equip, furnish; clothe, cover, fortify, guard, protect, strengthen.

arms *npl* accoutrements, armour, array, harness, mail, panoply, weapons; crest, escutcheon.

army *n* battalions, force, host, legions, troops; host, multitude, throng, vast assemblage.

around *prep* about, encircling, encompassing, round, surrounding. * *adv* about, approximately, generally, near, nearly, practically, round, thereabouts.

arouse *vb* animate, awaken, excite, incite, kindle, provoke, rouse, stimulate, warm, whet.

arraign *vb* accuse, censure, charge, denounce, impeach, indict, prosecute, tax.

arrange *vb* array, class, classify, dispose, distribute, group, range, rank; adjust, determine, fix upon, settle; concoct, construct, devise, plan, prepare, project.

arrant *adj* bad, consummate, downright, gross, notorious, rank, utter.

array *vb* arrange, dispose, place, range, rank; accoutre, adorn, attire, decorate, dress, enrobe, embellish, equip, garnish, habit, invest. * *n* arrangement, collection, disposition, marshalling, order; apparel, attire, clothes, dress, garments; army, battalions, soldiery, troops.

arrest *vb* check, delay, detain, hinder, hold, interrupt, obstruct, restrain, stay, stop, withhold; apprehend, capture, catch, seize, take; catch, engage, engross, fix, occupy, secure, rivet. * *n* check, checking, detention, hindrance, interruption, obstruction, restraining, stay, staying, stopping; apprehension, capture, detention, seizure.

arrive *vb* attain, come, get to, reach.

arrogance *n* assumption, assurance, disdain, effrontery, haughtiness, loftiness, lordliness, presumption, pride, scornfulness, superciliousness.

arrogate *vb* assume, claim unduly, demand, usurp.

arrow *n* bolt, dart, reed, shaft.

art *n* business, craft, employment, trade; address, adroitness, aptitude, dexterity, ingenuity, knack, readiness, sagacity, skill; artfulness, artifice, astuteness, craft, deceit, duplicity, finesse, subtlety.

artful *adj* crafty, cunning, disingenuous, insincere, sly, tricky, wily.

article *n* branch, clause, division, head, item, member, paragraph, part, point, portion; essay, paper, piece; commodity, substance, thing.

artifice *n* art, chicanery, contrivance, cunning, deception, deceit, duplicity, effort, finesse, fraud, imposture, invention, stratagem, subterfuge, trick, trickery.

artificial *adj* counterfeit, sham, spurious; assumed, affected, constrained, fictitious, forced, laboured, strained.

artless *adj* ignorant, rude, unskilful, untaught; natural, plain, simple; candid, fair, frank, guileless, honest, plain, unaffected, simple, sincere, truthful, unsuspicious.

ascend *vb* arise, aspire, climb, mount, soar, tower.

ascendancy, ascendency *n* authority, control, domination, mastery, power, predominance, sovereignty, superiority, sway.

ascertain *vb* certify, define, determine, establish, fix, settle, verify; discover, find out, get at.

ashamed *adj* abashed, confused.

ask *vb* interrogate, inquire, question; adjure, beg, conjure, crave, desire, dun, entreat, implore, invite, inquire, petition, request, solicit, supplicate, seek, sue.

aspect *n* air, bearing, countenance, expression, feature, look, mien, visage; appearance, attitude, condition, light, phase, position, posture, situation, state, view; angle, direction, outlook, prospect.

asperity *n* ruggedness, roughness, unevenness; acrimony, causticity, corrosiveness, sharpness, sourness, tartness; acerbity, bitterness, churlishness, harshness, sternness, sullenness, severity, virulence.

aspersion *n* abuse, backbiting, calumny, censure, defamation, detraction, slander, vituperation, reflection, reproach.

aspiration *n* aim, ambition, craving, hankering, hope, longing.

aspire *vb* desire, hope, long, yearn; ascend, mount, rise, soar, tower.

assail *vb* assault, attack, invade, oppugn; impugn, malign, maltreat; ply, storm.

assassinate *vb* dispatch, kill, murder, slay.

assault *vb* assail, attack, charge, invade. * *n* aggression, attack, charge, incursion, invasion, onset, onslaught; storm.

assemble *vb* call, collect, congregate, convene, convoke, gather, levy, muster; converge, forgather.

assembly *n* company, collection, concourse, congregation, gathering, meeting, rout, throng; caucus, congress, conclave, convention, convocation, diet, legislature, meeting, parliament, synod.

assent *vb* accede, acquiesce, agree, concur, subscribe, yield. * *n* accord, acquiescence, allowance, approval, approbation, consent.

assert *vb* affirm, allege, aver, asseverate, declare, express, maintain, predicate, pronounce, protest; claim, defend, emphasize, maintain, press, uphold, vindicate.

assertion *n* affirmation, allegation, asseveration, averment, declaration, position, predication, remark, statement, word; defence, emphasis, maintenance, pressing, support, vindication.

assess *vb* appraise, compute, estimate, rate, value; assign, determine, fix, impose, levy.

asseverate *vb* affirm, aver, avow, declare, maintain, protest.

assiduous *adj* active, busy, careful, constant, diligent, devoted, indefatigable, industrious, sedulous, unremitting, untiring.

assign *vb* allot, appoint, apportion, appropriate; fix, designate, determine, specify; adduce, advance, allege, give, grant, offer, present, show.

assist *vb* abet, aid, befriend, further, help, patronize, promote, second, speed, support, sustain; aid, relieve, succour; alternate with, relieve, spell.

associate *vb* affiliate, combine, conjoin, couple, join, link, relate, yoke; consort, fraternize, mingle, sort. * *n* chum, companion, comrade, familiar, follower, mate; ally, confederate, friend, partner, fellow.

association *n* combination, company, confederation, connection, partnership, society.

assort *vb* arrange, class, classify, distribute, group, rank, sort; agree, be adapted, consort, suit.

assuage *vb* allay, alleviate, appease, calm, ease, lessen, mitigate, moderate, mollify, pacify, quell, relieve, soothe, tranquillize.

assume *vb* take, undertake; affect, counterfeit, feign, pretend, sham; arrogate, usurp; beg, hypothesize, imply, postulate, posit, presuppose, suppose, simulate.

assurance *n* assuredness, certainty, conviction, persuasion, pledge, security, surety, warrant; engagement, pledge, promise; averment, assertion, protestation; audacity, confidence, courage, firmness, intrepidity; arrogance, brass, boldness, effrontery, face, front, impudence.

assure *vb* encourage, embolden, hearten; certify, insure, secure against loss, vouch for.

astonish *vb* amaze, astound, confound, daze, dumbfound, overwhelm, startle, stun, stupefy, surprise.

astute *adj* acute, cunning, deep, discerning, ingenious, intelligent, penetrating, perspicacious, quick, sagacious, sharp, shrewd.

asylum *n* refuge, retreat, sanctuary, shelter.

athletic *adj* brawny, lusty, muscular, powerful, robust, sinewy, stalwart, stout, strapping, strong, sturdy.

athletics *npl* aerobics, eurythmics, exercise, exercising, gymnastics, sports, track and field, workout.

atom *n* bit, molecule, monad, particle, scintilla.

atone *vb* answer, compensate, expiate, satisfy.

atonement *n* amends, expiation, propitiation, reparation, satisfaction.

atrocity *n* depravity, enormity, flagrancy, ferocity, savagery, villainy.

attach *vb* affix, annex, connect, fasten, join, hitch, tie; charm, captivate, enamour, endear, engage, win; (*legal*) distress, distrain, seize, take.

attack *vb* assail, assault, charge, encounter, invade, set upon, storm, tackle; censure, criticise, impugn. * *n* aggression, assault, charge, offence, onset, onslaught, raid, thrust.

attain *vb* accomplish, achieve, acquire, get, obtain, secure; arrive at, come to, reach.

attempt *vb* assail, assault, attack; aim, endeavour, seek, strive, try. * *n* effort, endeavour, enterprise, experiment, undertaking, venture; assault, attack, onset.

attend *vb* accompany, escort, follow; guard, protect, watch; minister to, serve, wait on; give heed, hear, harken, listen; be attendant, serve, tend, wait.

attention *n* care, circumspection, heed, mindfulness, observation, regard, watch, watchfulness; application, reflection, study; civility, courtesy, deference, politeness, regard, respect; addresses, courtship, devotion, suit, wooing.

attentive *adj* alive, awake, careful, civil, considerate, courteous, heedful, mindful, observant, watchful.
attenuate *vb* contract, dilute, diminish, elongate, lengthen, lessen, rarefy, reduce, slim, thin, weaken.
attest *vb* authenticate, certify, corroborate, confirm, ratify, seal, vouch; adjure, call to witness, invoke; confess, display, exhibit, manifest, prove, show, witness.
attic *n* garret, loft, upper storey.
Attic *adj* delicate, subtle, penetrating, pointed, pungent; chaste, classic, correct, elegant, polished, pure.
attire *vb* accoutre, apparel, array, clothe, dress, enrobe, equip, rig, robe. * *n* clothes, clothing, costume, dress, garb, gear, habiliment, outfit, toilet, trapping, vestment, vesture, wardrobe.
attitude *n* pose, position, posture; aspect, conjuncture, condition, phase, prediction, situation, standing, state.
attract *vb* draw, pull; allure, captivate, charm, decoy, enamour, endear, entice, engage, fascinate, invite, win.
attraction *n* affinity, drawing, pull; allurement, charm, enticement, fascination, magnetism, lure, seduction, witchery.
attribute *vb* ascribe, assign, impute, refer. * *n* characteristic, mark, note, peculiarity, predicate, property, quality.
attrition *n* abrasion, friction, rubbing.
attune *vb* accord, harmonize, modulate, tune; accommodate, adapt, adjust, attempt.
audacity *n* boldness, courage, daring, fearlessness, intrepidity; assurance, brass, effrontery, face, front, impudence, insolence, presumption, sauciness.
audience *n* assemblage, congregation; hearing, interview, reception.
augment *vb* add to, enhance, enlarge, increase, magnify, multiply, swell.
augmentation *n* accession, addition, enlargement, extension, increase.
augury *n* prediction, prognostication, prophecy, soothsaying; auspice, forerunner, harbinger, herald, omen, precursor, portent, sign.
august *adj* awe-inspiring, awful, dignified, grand, imposing, kingly, majestic, noble, princely, regal, solemn, stately, venerable.
auspicious *adj* fortunate, happy, lucky, prosperous, successful; bright, favourable, golden, opportune, promising, prosperous.
austere *adj* ascetic, difficult, formal, hard, harsh, morose, relentless, rigid, rigorous, severe, stern, stiff, strict, uncompromising, unrelenting.
authentic *adj* genuine, pure, real, true, unadulterated, uncorrupted, veritable; accurate, authoritative, reliable, true, trustworthy.
authority *n* dominion, empire, government, jurisdiction, power, sovereignty; ascendency, control, influence, rule, supremacy, sway; authorization, liberty, order, permit, precept, sanction, warranty; testimony, witness; connoisseur, expert, master.
authorize *vb* empower, enable, entitle; allow, approve, confirm, countenance, permit, ratify, sanction.
auxiliary *adj* aiding, ancillary, assisting, helpful, subsidiary. * *n* ally, assistant, confederate, help.
avail *vb* assist, benefit, help, profit, use, service.
available *adj* accessible, advantageous, applicable, beneficial, profitable, serviceable, useful.
avarice *n* acquisitiveness, covetousness, greediness, penuriousness, rapacity.
avaricious *adj* grasping, miserly, niggardly, parsimonious.
avenge *vb* punish, retaliate, revenge, vindicate.
avenue *n* access, entrance, entry, passage; alley, path, road, street, walk; channel, pass, route, way.
aver *vb* allege, assert, asseverate, avouch, declare, pronounce, protest, say.
averse *adj* adverse, backward, disinclined, indisposed, opposed, unwilling.
aversion *n* abhorrence, antipathy, disgust, dislike, hate, hatred, loathing, reluctance, repugnance.
avid *adj* eager, greedy, voracious.
avocation *n* business, calling, employment, occupation, trade, vocation; distraction, hindrance, interruption.
avoid *vb* dodge, elude, escape, eschew, shun; forebear, refrain from.
avouch *vb* allege, assert, declare, maintain, say.
avow *vb* admit, acknowledge, confess, own.
awaken *vb* arouse, excite, incite, kindle, provoke, spur, stimulate; wake, waken; begin, be excited.
award *vb* adjudge, allot, assign, bestow, decree, grant. * *n* adjudication, allotment, assignment, decision, decree, determination, gift, judgement.
aware *adj* acquainted, apprised, conscious, conversant, informed, knowing, mindful, sensible.
away *adv* absent, not present. * *adj* at a distance; elsewhere; out of the way.
awe *vb* cow, daunt, intimidate, overawe. * *n* abashment, fear, reverence; dread, fear, fearfulness, terror.
awful *adj* august, awesome, dread, grand, inspired; abashed, alarming, appalled, dire, frightful, portentous, tremendous.
awkward *adj* bungling, clumsy, inept, maladroit, unskilful; lumbering, unfit, ungainly, unmanageable; boorish; inconvenient, unsuitable.
axiom *n* adage, aphorism, apothegm, maxim, postulation, truism.
axis *n* axle, shaft, spindle.
azure *adj* blue, cerulean, sky-coloured.

B

babble *vb* blather, chatter, gibber, jabber, prate, prattle. * *n* chat, gossip, palaver, prate, tattle.
babel *n* clamour, confusion, din, discord, disorder, hubbub, jargon, pother.
baby *vb* coddle, cosset, indulge, mollycoddle, pamper, spoil. * *adj* babyish, childish, infantile, puerile; diminutive, doll-like, miniature, pocket, pocket-sized, small-scale. * *n* babe, brat, child, infant, suckling, nursling; chicken, coward, milksop, namby-pamby, sad sack, weakling; miniature; innocent.
bacchanal *n* carouse, debauchery, drunkenness, revelry, roisterousness.
back *vb* abet, aid, countenance, favour, second, support, sustain; go back, move back, retreat, withdraw. * *adj* hindmost. * *adv* in return, in consideration; ago, gone, since; aside, away, behind, by; abaft, astern, backwards, hindwards, rearwards. * *n* end, hind part, posterior, rear.
backbite *vb* abuse, asperse, blacken, defame, libel, malign, revile, scandalize, slander, traduce, vilify.
backbone *n* chine, spine; constancy, courage, decision, firmness, nerve, pluck, resolution, steadfastness.
backslider *n* apostate, deserter, renegade.
backward *adj* disinclined, hesitating, indisposed, loath, reluctant, unwilling, wavering; dull, slow, sluggish, stolid, stupid. * *adv* aback, behind, rearward.
bad *adj* baleful, baneful, detrimental, evil, harmful, hurtful, injurious, noxious, pernicious, unwholesome, vicious; abandoned, corrupt, depraved, immoral, sinful, unfair, unprincipled, wicked; unfortunate, unhappy, unlucky, miserable; disappointing, discouraging, distressing, sad, unwelcoming; abominable, mean, shabby, scurvy, vile, wretched; defective, inferior, imperfect, incompetent, poor, unsuitable; hard, heavy, serious, severe.
badge *n* brand, emblem, mark, sign, symbol, token.
badger *vb* annoy, bait, bother, hector, harry, pester, persecute, tease, torment, trouble, vex, worry.
baffle *vb* balk, block, check, circumvent, defeat, foil, frustrate, mar, thwart, undermine, upset; bewilder, confound, disconcert, perplex.
bait *vb* harry, tease, worry. * *n* allurement, decoy, enticement, lure, temptation.

balance *vb* equilibrate, pose, (*naut*) trim; compare, weigh; compensate, counteract, estimate; adjust, clear, equalize, square. * *n* equilibrium, liberation; excess, remainder, residue, surplus.

bald *adj* bare, naked, uncovered, treeless; dull, inelegant, meagre, prosaic, tame, unadorned, vapid.

baleful *adj* baneful, deadly, calamitous, hurtful, injurious, mischievous, noxious, pernicious, ruinous.

balk *vb* baffle, defeat, disappoint, disconcert, foil, frustrate, thwart.

ball *n* drop, globe, orb, pellet, marble, sphere; bullet, missile, projectile, shot; assembly, dance.

balmy *adj* aromatic, fragrant, healing, odorous, perfumed.

ban *vb* anathematize, curse, execrate; interdict, outlaw. * *n* edict, proclamation; anathema, curse, denunciation, execration; interdiction, outlawry, penalty, prohibition

band[1] *vb* belt, bind, cinch, encircle, gird, girdle; ally, associate, combine, connect, join, league; bar, marble, streak, stripe, striate, vein. * *n* crew, gang, horde, society, troop; ensemble, group, orchestra.

band[2] *n* ligament, ligature, tie; bond, chain, cord, fetter, manacle, shackle, trammel; bandage, belt, binding, cincture, girth, tourniquet.

bandit *n* brigand, freebooter, footpad, gangster, highwayman, outlaw, robber.

baneful *adj* poisonous, venomous; deadly, destructive, hurtful, mischievous, noxious, pernicious.

bang *vb* beat, knock, maul, pommel, pound, strike, thrash, thump; slam; clatter, rattle, resound, ring. * *n* clang, clangour, whang; blow, knock, lick, thump, thwack, whack.

banish *vb* exile, expatriate, ostracize; dismiss, exclude, expel.

bank[1] *vb* incline, slope, tilt; embank. * *n* dike, embankment, escarpment, heap, knoll, mound; border, bound, brim, brink, margin, rim, strand; course, row, tier.

bank[2] *vb* deposit, keep, save. * *n* depository, fund, reserve, savings, stockpile.

banner *n* colours, ensign, flag, standard, pennon, standard, streamer.

banter *vb* chaff, deride, jeer, joke, mock, quiz, rally, ridicule. * *n* badinage, chaff, derision, jesting, joking, mockery, quizzing, raillery, ridicule.

bar *vb* exclude, hinder, obstruct, prevent, prohibit, restrain, stop. * *n* grating, pole, rail, rod; barricade, hindrance, impediment, obstacle, obstruction, stop; bank, sand bar, shallow, shoal, spit; (*legal*) barristers, counsel, court, judgement, tribunal.

barbarian *adj* brutal, cruel, ferocious, fierce, fell, inhuman, ruthless, savage, truculent, unfeeling. * *n* brute, ruffian, savage.

barbaric *adj* barbarous, rude, savage, uncivilized, untamed; capricious, coarse, gaudy, riotous, showy, outlandish, uncouth, untamed, wild.

bare *vb* denude, depilate, divest, strip, unsheathe; disclose, manifest, open, reveal, show. * *adj* denuded, exposed, naked, nude, stripped, unclothed, uncovered, undressed, unsheltered; alone, mere, sheer, simple; bald, meagre, plain, unadorned, uncovered, unfurnished; empty, destitute, indigent, poor.

bargain *vb* agree, contract, covenant, stipulate; convey, sell, transfer. * *n* agreement, compact, contract, covenant, convention, indenture, transaction, stipulation, treaty; proceeds, purchase, result.

barren *adj* childless, infecund, sterile; (*bot*) acarpous, sterile; bare, infertile, poor, sterile, unproductive; ineffectual, unfruitful, uninstructive.

barricade *vb* block up, fortify, protect, obstruct. * *n* barrier, obstruction, palisade, stockade.

barrier *n* bar, barricade, hindrance, impediment, obstacle, obstruction, stop.

barter *vb* bargain, exchange, sell, trade, traffic.

base[1] *adj* cheap, inferior, worthless; counterfeit, debased, false, spurious; baseborn, humble, lowly, mean, nameless, plebeian, unknown, untitled, vulgar; abject, beggarly, contemptible, degraded, despicable, low, menial, pitiful, servile, sordid, sorry, worthless.

base[2] *vb* establish, found, ground. * *n* foundation, fundament, substructure, underpinning; pedestal, plinth, stand; centre, headquarters, HQ, seat; starting point; basis, cause, grounds, reason, standpoint; bottom, foot, foundation, ground.

bashful *adj* coy, diffident, shy, timid.

basis n base, bottom, foundation, fundament, ground, groundwork.

bastard *adj* adulterated, baseborn, counterfeit, false, illegitimate, sham. * *n* love child.

batch *vb* assemble, bunch, bundle, collect, gather, group. * *n* amount, collection, crowd, lot, quantity.

bathe *vb* immerse, lave, wash; cover, enfold, enwrap, drench, flood, infold, suffuse. * *n* bath, shower, swim.

batter[1] *vb* beat, pelt, smite; break, bruise, demolish, destroy, shatter, shiver, smash; abrade, deface, disfigure, indent, mar; incline, recede, retreat, slope. * *n* batsman, striker.

batter[2] *n* dough, goo, goop, gunk, paste, pulp.

battle *vb* contend, contest, engage, fight, strive, struggle. * *n* action, affair, brush, combat, conflict, contest, engagement, fight, fray.

bauble *n* gewgaw, gimcrack, knick-knack, plaything, toy, trifle, trinket.

bawdy *adj* obscene, filthy, impure, indecent, lascivious, lewd, smutty, unchaste.

bawl *vb* clamour, cry, hoot, howl, roar, shout, squall, vociferate, yell.

bay[1] *vb* bark, howl, wail, yell, yelp.

bay[2] *n* alcove, compartment, niche, nook, opening, recess.

bay[3] *n* bight, cove, gulf, inlet.

bays *npl* applause, chaplet, fame, garland, glory, honour, plaudits, praise, renown.

beach *vb* ground, maroon, strand. * *n* coast, margin, rim, sands, seashore, seaside, shore, shoreline, strand, waterfront.

beacon *vb* brighten, flame, shine, signal; enlighten, illuminate, illumine, guide, light, signal. * *n* lighthouse, pharos, watchtower; sign, signal.

beadle *n* apparitor, church officer, crier, servitor, summoner.

beak *n* bill, mandible, (*sl*) nose; (*naut*) bow, prow, stem.

beam *vb* beacon, gleam, glisten, glitter, shine. * *n* balk, girder, joist, scantling, stud; gleam, pencil, ray, streak.

bear *vb* support, sustain, uphold; carry, convey, deport, transport, waft; abide, brook, endure, stand, suffer, tolerate, undergo; carry on, keep up, maintain; cherish, entertain, harbour; produce; cast, drop, sustain; endure, submit, suffer; act, operate, work. * *n* growler, grumbler, moaner, snarler; speculator.

bearable *adj* endurable, sufferable, supportable, tolerable.

bearing *n* air, behaviour, demeanour, deportment, conduct, carriage, conduct, mien, port; connection, dependency, relation; endurance, patience, suffering; aim, course, direction; bringing forth, producing; bed, receptacle, socket.

beastly *adj* abominable, brutish, ignoble, low, sensual, vile.

beat *vb* bang, baste, belabour, buffet, cane, cudgel, drub, hammer, hit, knock, maul, pound, pummel, punch, strike, thrash, thump, thwack, whack, whip; bray, bruise, pound, pulverize; batter, pelt; conquer, defeat, overcome, rout, subdue, surpass, vanquish; pulsate, throb; dash, strike. * *adj* baffled, bamboozled, confounded, mystified, nonplused, perplexed, puzzled, stumped; done, dog-tired, exhausted, tired out, worn out; beaten, defeated, licked, worsted. * *n* blow, striking, stroke; beating, pulsation, throb; accent, metre, rhythm; circuit, course, round.

beatific *adj* ecstatic, enchanting, enraptured, ravishing, rapt.

beatitude *n* blessing, ecstasy, felicity, happiness.

beau *n* coxcomb, dandy, exquisite, fop, popinjay; admirer, lover, suitor, sweetheart.

beautiful *adj* charming, comely, fair, fine, exquisite, handsome, lovely, pretty.

beautify *vb* adorn, array, bedeck, deck, decorate, embellish, emblazon, garnish, gild, grace, ornament, set.

beauty *n* elegance, grace, symmetry; attractiveness, comeliness, fairness, loveliness, seemliness; belle.

become *vb* change to, get, go, wax; adorn, befit, set off, suit.

becoming *adj* appropriate, apt, congruous, decent, decorous, due, fit, proper, right, seemly, suitable; comely, graceful, neat, pretty.

bed *vb* embed, establish, imbed, implant, infix, inset, plant; harbour, house, lodge. * *n* berth, bunk, cot, couch; channel, depression, hollow; base, foundation, receptacle, support, underlay; accumulation, layer, seam, stratum, vein.

bedim *vb* cloud, darken, dim, obscure.

befall *vb* betide, overtake; chance, happen,occur, supervene.

befitting *adj* appropriate, apt, becoming, decorous, fit, proper, right, suitable, seemly.

befool *vb* bamboozle, beguile, cheat, circumvent, delude, deceive, dupe, fool, hoax, hoodwink, infatuate, stupefy, trick.

befriend *vb* aid, benefit, countenance, encourage, favour, help, patronize.

beg *vb* adjure, ask, beseech, conjure, crave, entreat, implore, importune, petition, pray, request, solicit, supplicate.

beggarly *adj* destitute, needy, poor; abject, base, despicable, grovelling, low, mean, miserable, miserly, paltry, pitiful, scant, servile, shabby, sorry, stingy, vile, wretched.

begin *vb* arise, commence, enter, open; inaugurate, institute, originate, start.

beginning *n* arising, commencement, dawn, emergence, inauguration, inception, initiation, opening, outset, start, rise; origin, source.

beguile *vb* cheat, deceive, delude; amuse, cheer, divert, entertain, solace.

behaviour *n* air, bearing, carriage, comportment, conduct, demeanour, deportment, manner, manners, mien.

behest *n* bidding, charge, command, commandment, direction, hest, injunction, mandate, order, precept.

behind *prep* abaft, after, following. * *adv* abaft, aft, astern, rearward. * *adj* arrested, backward, checked, detained, retarded; after, behind. * *n* afterpart, rear, stern, tail; back, back side, reverse; bottom, buttocks, posterior, rump.

behold *vb* consider, contemplate, eye, observe, regard, see, survey, view.

behoove *vb* become, befit, suit; be binding, be obligatory.

being *n* actuality, existence, reality, subsistence; core, essence, heart, root.

beleaguer *vb* besiege, blockade, invest; beset, block, encumber, encompass, encounter, obstruct, surround.

belief *n* assurance, confidence, conviction, persuasion, trust; acceptance, assent, credence, credit, currency; creed, doctrine, dogma, faith, opinion, tenet.

bellow *vb* bawl, clamour, cry, howl, vociferate, yell.

belt *n* band, cincture, girdle, girth, zone; region, stretch, strip.

bemoan *vb* bewail, deplore, lament, mourn.

bemused *adj* bewildered, confused, fuddled, muddled, muzzy, stupefied, tipsy.

bend *vb* bow, crook, curve, deflect, draw; direct, incline, turn; bend, dispose, influence, mould, persuade, subdue; (*naut*) fasten, make fast; crook, deflect, deviate, diverge, swerve; bow, lower, stoop; condescend, deign. * *n* angle, arc, arcuation, crook, curvature, curve, elbow, flexure, turn.

beneath *prep* below, under, underneath; unbecoming, unbefitting, unworthy. * *adv* below, underneath.

benediction *n* beatitude, benefit, benison, blessing, boon, grace, favour.

benefaction *n* alms, boon, charity, contribution, donation, favour, gift, grant, gratuity, offering, present.

beneficent *adj* benevolent, bounteous, bountiful, charitable, generous, kind, liberal.

beneficial *adj* advantageous, favourable, helpful, profitable, salutary, serviceable, useful, wholesome.

benefit *vb* befriend, help, serve; advantage, avail, profit. * *n* favour, good turn, kindness, service; account, advantage, behalf, gain, good, interest, profit, utility.

benevolence *n* beneficence, benignity, generosity, goodwill, humanity, kindliness, kindness.

benevolent *adj* altruistic, benign, charitable, generous, humane, kind, kind-hearted, liberal, obliging, philanthropic, tender, unselfish.

benign *adj* amiable, amicable, beneficent, benevolent, complaisant, friendly, gentle, good, gracious, humane, kind, kindly, obliging.

bent *adj* angled, angular, bowed, crooked, curved, deflected, embowed, flexed, hooked, twisted; disposed, inclined, prone, minded; (*with* **on**) determined, fixed on, resolved, set on. * *n* bias, inclination, leaning, partiality, penchant, predilection, prepossession, proclivity, propensity

bequeath *vb* devise, give, grant, leave, will; impart, transmit.

berate *vb* chide, rate, reprimand, reprove, scold.

bereave *vb* afflict, deprive of, despoil, dispossess, divest, rob, spoil, strip.

beseech *vb* beg, conjure, entreat, implore, importune, petition, supplicate; ask, beg, crave, solicit.

beset *vb* besiege, encompass, enclose, environ, encircle, hem in, surround; decorate, embarrass, embellish, entangle, garnish, ornament, perplex, set.

beside[1] *prep* at the side of, by the side of, close to, near; aside from, not according to, out of the course of, out of the way of; not in possession of, out of.

besides[1] *prep* barring, distinct from, excluding, except, excepting, in addition to, other than, over and above, save.

beside[2], **besides**[2] *adv* additionally, also, further, furthermore, in addition, more, moreover, over and above, too, yet.

besiege *vb* beset, blockade, encircle, encompass, environ, invest, surround.

besot *vb* drench, intoxicate, soak, steep; befool, delude, infatuate, stultify, stupefy.

bespatter *vb* bedaub, befoul, besmirch, smear, spatter.

bespeak *vb* accost, address, declare, evince, forestall, imply, indicate, prearrange, predict, proclaim, solicit.

best *vb* better, exceed, excel, predominate, rival, surpass; beat, defeat, outdo, worst. * *adj* chief, first, foremost, highest, leading, utmost. * *adv* advantageously, excellently; extremely, greatly. * *n* choice, cream, flower, pick.

bestial *adj* beast-like, beastly, brutal, degraded, depraved, irrational, low, vile; sensual.

bestow *vb* deposit, dispose, put, place, store, stow; accord, give, grant, impart.

bet *vb* gamble, hazard, lay, pledge, stake, wage, wager. * *n* gamble, hazard, stake, wager.

bethink *vb* cogitate, consider, ponder, recall, recollect, reflect, remember.

betide *vb* befall, happen, occur, overtake.

betimes *adv* beforehand, early, forward, soon.

betoken *vb* argue, betray, denote, evince, imply, indicate, prove, represent, show, signify, typify.

betray *vb* be false to, break, violate; blab, discover, divulge, expose, reveal, show, tell; argue, betoken, display, evince, expose, exhibit, imply, indicate, manifest, reveal; beguile, delude, ensnare, lure, mislead; corrupt, ruin, seduce, undo.

betroth *vb* affiance, engage to marry, pledge in marriage, plight.

better *vb* advance, amend, correct, exceed, improve, promote, rectify, reform. * *adj* bigger, fitter, greater, larger, less ill, preferable. * *n* advantage, superiority, upper hand, victory; improvement, greater good.

between *prep* amidst, among, betwixt.

bewail *vb* bemoan, deplore, express, lament, mourn over, rue, sorrow.

beware *vb* avoid, heed, look out, mind.

bewilder *vb* confound, confuse, daze, distract, embarrass, entangle, muddle, mystify, nonplus, perplex, pose, puzzle, stagger.

bewitch *vb* captivate, charm, enchant, enrapture, entrance, fascinate, spellbind, transport.

beyond *prep* above, before, farther, over, past, remote, yonder.

bias *vb* bend, dispose, incline, influence, predispose, prejudice. * *n* bent, inclination, leaning, partiality, penchant, predilection, prepossession, proclivity, propensity, slant, tendency, turn.

bicker *vb* argue, dispute, jangle, quarrel, spar, spat, squabble, wrangle.

bid *vb* charge, command, direct, enjoin, order, require, summon; ask, call, invite, pray, request, solicit; offer, propose, proffer, tender. * *n* bidding, offer, proposal.

big *adj* bumper, bulking, bulky, great, huge, large, massive, monstrous; important, imposing; distended, inflated, full, swollen, tumid; fecund, fruitful, productive, teeming.

bigoted *adj* dogmatic, hidebound, intolerant, obstinate, narrow-minded, opinionated, prejudiced.

bill[1] *vb* charge, dun, invoice; programme, schedule; advertise, boost, plug, promote, publicize. * *n* account, charges, reckoning, score; advertisement, banner, hoarding, placard, poster; playbill, programme, schedule; bill of exchange, certificate, money; account, reckoning, statement.

bill[2] *n* beak, mandible, (*sl*) nose; billhook, brush-cutter, hedge-bill, hedging knife; caress, fondle, kiss, toy.

billet *vb* allot, apportion, assign, distribute, quarter, station. * *n* accommodation, lodgings, quarters.

billow *vb* surge, wave; heave, roll; bag, baloon, bulge, dilate, swell. * *n* roller, surge, swell, wave.

bin *n* box, bunker, crib, frame, receptacle.

bind *vb* confine, enchain, fetter, restrain, restrict; bandage, tie up, wrap; fasten, lash, pinion, secure, tie, truss; engage, hold, oblige, obligate, pledge; contract, harden, shrink, stiffen.

birth *n* ancestry, blood, descent, extraction, lineage, race; being, creation, creature, offspring, production, progeny.

bit *n* crumb, fragment, morsel, mouthful, piece, scrap; atom, grain, jot, mite, particle, tittle, whit; instant, minute, moment, second.

bite *vb* champ, chew, crunch, gnaw; burn, make smart, sting; catch, clutch, grapple, grasp, grip; bamboozle, cheat, cozen, deceive, defraud, dupe, gull, mislead, outwit, overreach, trick. * *n* grasp, hold; punch, relish, spice, pungency, tang, zest; lick, morsel, sip, taste; crick, nip, pain, pang, prick, sting.

bitter *adj* acrid; dire, fell, merciless, relentless, ruthless; harsh, severe, stern; afflictive, calamitous, distressing, galling, grievous, painful, poignant, sore, sorrowful.

black *adj* dark, ebony, inky, jet, sable, swarthy; dingy, dusky, lowering, murky, pitchy; calamitous, dark, depressing, disastrous, dismal, doleful, forbidding, gloomy, melancholy, mournful, sombre, sullen.

blacken *vb* darken; deface, defile, soil, stain, sully; asperse, besmirch, calumniate, defame, malign, revile, slander, traduce, vilify.

blamable *adj* blameable, blameworthy, censurable, culpable, delinquent. faulty, remiss, reprehensible.

blame *vb* accuse, censure, condemn, disapprove, reflect upon, reprehend, reproach, reprove, upbraid. * *n* animadversion, censure, condemnation, disapproval, dispraise, disapprobation, reprehension, reproach, reproof; defect, demerit, fault, guilt, misdeed, shortcoming, sin, wrong.

blameless *adj* faultless, guiltless, inculpable, innocent, irreproachable, unblemished, undefiled, unimpeachable, unspotted, unsullied, spotless, stainless.

blanch *vb* bleach, fade, etiolate, whiten.

bland *adj* balmy, demulcent, gentle, mild, soothing, soft; affable, amiable, complaisant, kindly, mild, suave.

blandishment *n* cajolery, coaxing, compliment, fascination, fawning, flattery, wheedling

blank *adj* bare, empty, vacuous, void; amazed, astonished, confounded, confused, dumbfounded, nonplussed; absolute, complete, entire, mere, perfect, pure, simple, unabated, unadulterated, unmitigated, unmixed, utter, perfect.

blare *vb* blazon, blow, peal, proclaim, trumpet. * *n* blast, clang, clangour, peal.

blasphemy *n* impiousness, sacrilege; cursing, profanity, swearing.

blast *vb* annihilate, blight, destroy, kill, ruin, shrivel, wither; burst, explode, kill. * *n* blow, gust, squall; blare, clang, peal; burst, discharge, explosion.

blaze *vb* blazon, proclaim, publish; burn, flame, glow. * *n* flame, flare, flash, glow, light.

bleach *vb* blanch, etiolate, render white, whiten.

bleak *adj* bare, exposed, unprotected, unsheltered, storm-beaten, windswept; biting, chill, cold, piercing, raw; cheerless, comfortless, desolate, dreary, uncongenial,

blemish *vb* blur, injure, mar, spot, stain, sully, taint, tarnish; asperse, calumniate, defame, malign, revile, slander, traduce, vilify. * *n* blot, blur, defect, disfigurement, fault, flaw, imperfection, soil, speck, spot, stain, tarnish; disgrace, dishonour, reproach, stain, taint.

blend *vb* amalgamate, coalesce, combine, commingle, fuse, mingle, mix, unite. * *n* amalgamation, combination, compound, fusion, mix, mixture, union.

bless *vb* beatify, delight, gladden; adore, celebrate, exalt, extol, glorify, magnify, praise.

blessedness *n* beatitude, bliss, blissfulness, felicity, happiness, joy.

blight *vb* blast, destroy, kill, ruin, shrivel, wither; annihilate, annul, crush, disappoint, frustrate. * *n* blast, mildew, pestilence.

blind *vb* blear, darken, deprive of sight; blindfold, hoodwink. * *adj* eyeless, sightless, stone-blind, unseeing; benighted, ignorant, injudicious, purblind, undiscerning, unenlightened; concealed, confused, dark, dim, hidden, intricate, involved, labyrinthine, obscure, private, remote; careless, headlong, heedless, inconsiderate, indiscriminate, thoughtless; blank, closed, shut. * *n* cover, curtain, screen, shade, shutter; blinker; concealment, disguise, feint, pretence, pretext, ruse, stratagem, subterfuge.

blink *vb* nictate, nictitate, wink; flicker, flutter, gleam, glitter, intermit, twinkle; avoid, disregard, evade, gloss over, ignore, overlook, pass over. * *n* glance, glimpse, sight, view, wink; gleam, glimmer, sheen, shimmer, twinkle.

bliss *n* beatification, beatitude, blessedness, blissfulness, ecstasy, felicity, happiness, heaven, joy, rapture, transport.

blithe *adj* airy, animated, blithesome, buoyant, cheerful, debonair, elated, happy, jocund, joyful, joyous, lively, mirthful, sprightly, vivacious.

bloat *vb* dilate, distend, inflate, swell.

block *vb* arrest, bar, blockade, check, choke, close, hinder, impede, jam, obstruct, stop; form, mould, shape; brace, stiffen. * *n* lump, mass; blockhead, dunce, fool, simpleton; pulley, tackle; execution, scaffold; jam, obstruction, pack, stoppage.

blood *n* children, descendants, offspring, posterity, progeny; family, house, kin, kindred, line, relations; consanguinity, descent, kinship, lineage, relationship; courage, disposition, feelings, mettle, passion, spirit, temper.

bloom *vb* blossom, blow, flower; thrive, prosper. * *n* blossom, blossoming, blow, efflorescence, florescence, flowering; delicacy, delicateness, flush, freshness, heyday, prime, vigour; flush, glow, rose.

blossom *vb* bloom, blow, flower. * *n* bloom, blow, efflorescence, flower.

blot *vb* cancel, efface, erase, expunge, obliterate, rub out; blur, deface, disfigure, obscure, spot, stain, sully; disgrace, dishonour, tarnish. * *n* blemish, blur, erasure, spot, obliteration, stain; disgrace, dishonour, stigma.

blow[1] *n* bang, beat, buffet, dab, impact, knock, pat, punch, rap, slam, stroke, thump, wallop, buffet, impact; affliction, calamity, disaster, misfortune, setback.

blow[2] *vb* breathe, gasp, pant, puff; flow, move, scud, stream, waft. * *n* blast, gale, gust, squall, storm, wind.

blue *adj* azure, cerulean, cobalt, indigo, sapphire, ultramarine; ghastly, livid, pallid; dejected, depressed, dispirited, downcast, gloomy, glum, mopey, melancholic, melancholy, sad.

bluff[1] *adj* abrupt, blunt, blustering, coarse, frank, good-natured, open, outspoken; abrupt, precipitous, sheer, steep. * *n* cliff, headland, height.

bluff[2] *vb* deceive, defraud, lie, mislead. * *n* deceit, deception, feint, fraud, lie.

blunder *vb* err, flounder, mistake: stumble. * *n* error, fault, howler, mistake, solecism.

blunt *adj* dull, edgeless, obtuse, pointless, unsharpened; insensible, stolid, thick-witted; abrupt, bluff, downright, plain-spoken, outspoken, unceremonious, uncourtly. * *vb* deaden, dull, numb, weaken.

blur *vb* bedim, darken, dim, obscure; blemish, blot, spot, stain, sully, tarnish. * *n* blemish, blot, soil, spot, stain, tarnish; disgrace, smear.

blush *vb* colour, flush, glow, redden. * *n* bloom, flush, glow, colour, reddening, suffusion.

bluster *vb* boast, brag, bully, domineer, roar, swagger, swell, vaunt. * *n* boisterousness, noise, tumult, turbulence; braggadocio, bravado, boasting, gasconade, swaggering.

board *n* deal, panel, plank; diet, entertainment, fare, food, meals, provision, victuals; cabinet, conclave, committee, council; directorate; panel.

boast *vb* bluster, brag, crack, flourish, crow, vaunt. * *n* blustering, boasting, bombast, brag, braggadocio, bravado, bombast, swaggering, vaunt.

bode *vb* augur, betoken, forebode, foreshadow, foretell, portend, predict, prefigure, presage, prophesy.

bodily *adj* carnal, corporeal, fleshly, physical. * *adv* altogether, completely, entirely, wholly.

body *n* carcass, corpse, remains; stem, torso, trunk; aggregate, bulk, corpus, mass; being, individual, mortal creature, person; assemblage, association, band, company, corporation, corps, coterie, force, party, society, troop; consistency, substance, thickness.

boggle *vb* demur, falter, hang fire, hesitate, shrink, vacillate, waver.

boil[1] *vb* agitate, bubble, foam, froth, rage, seethe, simmer. * *n* ebullience, ebullition.

boil[2] (*med*) gathering, pimple, pustule, swelling, tumour.

boisterous *adj* loud, roaring, stormy; clamouring, loud, noisy, obstreperous, tumultuous, turbulent.

bold *adj* adventurous, audacious, courageous; brave, daring, dauntless, doughty, fearless, gallant, hardy, heroic, intrepid, mettlesome, manful, manly, spirited, stouthearted, undaunted, valiant, valorous; assured, confident, self-reliant; assuming, forward, impertinent, impudent, insolent, push, rude, saucy; conspicuous, projecting, prominent, striking; abrupt, precipitous, prominent, steep.

bolster *vb* aid, assist, defend, help, maintain, prop, stay, support. * *n* cushion, pillow; prop, support.

bolt *vb* abscond, flee, fly. * *n* arrow, dart, missile, shaft; thunderbolt.

bombast *n* bluster, brag, braggadocio, fustian, gasconade, mouthing, pomposity, rant.

bond *vb* bind, connect, fuse, glue, join. * *adj* captive, enslaved, enthralled, subjugated. * *n* band, cord, fastening, ligament, ligature, link, nexus; bondage, captivity, chains, constraint, fetters, prison, shackle; attachment, attraction, connection, coupling, link, tie, union; compact, obligation, pledge, promise.

bondage *n* captivity, confinement, enslavement, enthralment, peonage, serfdom, servitude, slavery, thraldom, vassalage.

bonny *adj* beautiful, handsome, fair, fine, pretty; airy, blithe, buoyant, buxom, cheerful, jolly, joyous, merry. playful, sporty, sprightly, winsome.

bonus *n* gift, honorarium, premium, reward, subsidy.

booby *n* blockhead, dunce, fool, idiot, simpleton.

book *vb* bespeak, engage, reserve; programme, schedule; list, log, record, register. * *n* booklet, brochure, compendium, handbook, manual, monograph, pamphlet, textbook, tract, treatise, volume, work.

bookish *adj* erudite, learned, literary, scholarly, studious.

boon *adj* convivial, jolly, jovial, hearty; close, intimate. * *n* benefaction, favour, grant, gift, present; advantage, benefit, blessing, good, privilege.

boor *n* bumpkin, clodhopper, clown, lout, lubber, peasant, rustic, swain.

boorish *adj* awkward, bearish, clownish, course, gruff, ill-bred, loutish, lubberly, rude, rustic, uncivilized, uncouth, uneducated.

bootless *adj* abortive, fruitless, futile, profitless, vain, worthless, useless.

booty *n* loot, pillage, plunder, spoil.

border *vb* bound, edge, fringe, line, march, rim, skirt, verge; abut, adjoin, butt, conjoin, connect, neighbour. * *n* brim, brink, edge, fringe, hem, margin, rim, skirt, verge; boundary, confine, frontier, limit, march, outskirts.

bore[1] *vb* annoy, fatigue, plague, tire, trouble, vex, weary, worry. * *n* bother, nuisance, pest, worry.

bore[2] *vb* drill, perforate, pierce, sink, tunnel. * *n* calibre, hole, shaft, tunnel.

borrow *vb* take and return, use temporarily; adopt, appropriate, imitate; dissemble, feign, simulate.

boss[1] *vb* emboss, stud; * *n* knob, protuberance, stud.

boss[2] *vb* command, direct, employ, run. * *n* employer, foreman, master, overseer, superintendent.

botch *vb* blunder, bungle, cobble, mar, mend, mess, patch, spoil. * *n* blotch, pustule, sore; failure, miscarriage.

bother *vb* annoy, disturb, harass, molest, perplex, pester, plague, tease, trouble, vex, worry. * *n* annoyance, perplexity, plague, trouble, vexation.

bottom *vb* build, establish, found. * *adj* base, basic, ground, lowermost, lowest, nethermost, undermost. * *n* base, basis, foot, foundation, groundwork; dale, meadow, valley; buttocks, fundament, seat; dregs, grounds, lees, sediment.

bounce *vb* bound, jump, leap, rebound, recoil, spring. * *n* knock, thump; bound, jump, leap, spring, vault.

bound[1] *adj* assured, certain, decided, determined, resolute, resolved; confined, hampered, restricted, restrained; committed, contracted, engaged, pledged, promised; beholden, duty-bound, obligated, obliged.

bound[2] *vb* border, delimit, circumscribe, confine, demarcate, limit, restrict, terminate. * *n* boundary, confine, edge, limit, march, margin, periphery, term, verge.

bound[3] *vb* jump, leap, spring. * *n* bounce, jump, leap, spring, vault.

boundary *n* border, bourn, circuit, circumference, confine, limit, march, periphery, term, verge.

boundless *adj* endless, immeasurable, infinite, limitless, unbounded, unconfined, undefined, unlimited, vast.

bountiful *adj* beneficent, bounteous, generous, liberal, munificent, princely.

bounty *n* beneficence, benevolence, charity, donation, generosity, gift, kindness, premium, present, reward.

bourn *n* border, boundary, confine, limit; brook, burn, rill, rivulet, stream, torrent.

bow[1] *n* (*naut*) beak, prow, stem.

bow[2] *vb* arc, bend, buckle, crook, curve, droop, flex, yield; crush, depress, subdue; curtsy, genuflect, kowtow, submit. * *n* arc, bend, bilge, bulge, convex, curve, flexion; bob, curtsy, genuflection, greeting, homage, obeisance; coming out, debut, introduction; curtain call, encore.

bowels *npl* entrails, guts, insides, viscera; compassion, mercy, pity, sympathy, tenderness.

box[1] *vb* fight, hit, mill, spar. * *n* blow, buffet, fight, hit, spar.

box[2] *vb* barrel, crate, pack, parcel. * *n* case, chest, container, crate, portmanteau, trunk.

boy *n* lad, stripling, youth.

brace *vb* make tight, tighten; buttress, fortify, reinforce, shore, strengthen, support, truss. * *n* couple, pair; clamp, girder, prop, shore, stay, support, tie, truss.

brag *vb* bluster, boast, flourish, gasconade, vaunt.

branch *vb* diverge, fork, bifurcate, ramify, spread. * *n* bough, offset, limb, shoot, sprig, twig; arm, fork, ramification, spur; article, department, member, part, portion, section, subdivision.

brand *vb* denounce, stigmatize, mark. * *n* firebrand, torch; bolt, lightning flash; cachet, mark, stamp, tally; blot, reproach, stain, stigma.

brave *vb* dare, defy. * *adj* bold, courageous, fearless, heroic, intrepid, stalwart.

bravery *n* courage, daring, fearlessness, gallantry, valour.

brawl *vb* bicker, dispute, jangle, quarrel, squabble. * *n* broil, dispute, feud, fracas, fray, jangle, quarrel, row, scuffle, squabble, uproar, wrangle.

brawny *adj* athletic, lusty, muscular, powerful, robust, sinewy, stalwart, strapping, strong, sturdy.

bray *vb* clamour, hoot, roar, trumpet, vociferate. * *n* blare, crash, roar, shout.

breach *n* break, chasm, crack, disruption, fissure, flaw, fracture, opening, rent, rift, rupture; alienation, difference, disaffection, disagreement, split.

bread *n* aliment, diet, fare, food, nourishment, nutriment, provisions, regimen, victuals.

break *vb* crack, disrupt, fracture, part, rend, rive, sever; batter, burst, crush, shatter, smash, splinter; cashier, degrade, discard, discharge, dismiss; disobey, infringe, transgress, violate; intermit, interrupt, stop; disclose, open, unfold. * *n* aperture, breach, chasm, fissure, gap, rent, rip, rupture; break-up, crash, debacle.

breast *vb* face, oppose, resist, stem, withstand. * *n* bosom, chest, thorax; affections, conscience, heart; mammary gland, mammary organ, pap, udder.

breath *n* exhaling, inhaling, pant, sigh, respiration, whiff; animation, existence, life; pause, respite, rest; breathing space, instant, moment.

breathe *vb* live, exist; emit, exhale, give out; diffuse, express, indicate, manifest, show.

breed *vb* bear, beget, engender, hatch, produce; bring up, foster, nourish, nurture, raise, rear; discipline, educate, instruct, nurture, rear, school, teach, train; generate, originate. * *n* extraction, family, lineage, pedigree, progeny, race, strain.

brevity *n* briefness, compression, conciseness, curtness, pithiness, shortness, terseness, transiency.

brew *vb* concoct, contrive, devise, excite, foment, instigate, plot. * *n* beverage, concoction, drink, liquor, mixture, potation.

bribe *vb* buy, corrupt, influence, pay off, suborn. * *n* allurement, corruption, enticement, graft, pay-off, subornation.

bridle *vb* check, curb, control, govern, restrain. * *n* check, control, curb.

brief *vb* direct, give directions, instruct; capsulate, summarize, delineate, describe, draft, outline, sketch; (*law*) retain. * *adj* concise, curt, inconsiderable, laconic, pithy, short, succinct, terse; fleeting, momentary, short, temporary, transient. * *n* abstract, breviary, briefing, epitome, compendium, summary, syllabus; (*law*) precept, writ.

brigand *n* bandit, footpad, freebooter, gangster, highwayman, marauder, outlaw, robber, thug.

bright *adj* blazing, brilliant, dazzling, gleaming, glowing, light, luminous, radiant, shining, sparkling, sunny; clear, cloudless, lambent, lucid, transparent; famous, glorious, illustrious; acute, discerning, ingenious, intelligent, keen; auspicious, cheering, encouraging, exhilarating, favourable, inspiring, promising, propitious; cheerful, genial, happy, lively, merry, pleasant, smiling, vivacious.

brilliant *adj* beaming, bright, effulgent, gleaming, glistening, glittering, lustrous, radiant, resplendent, shining, sparkling splendid; admirable, celebrated, distinguished, famous, glorious, illustrious, renowned; dazzling, decided, prominent, signal, striking, unusual.

brim *n* border, brink, edge, rim, margin, skirt, verge; bank, border, coast, margin, shore.

bring *vb* bear, convey, fetch; accompany, attend, conduct, convey, convoy, guide, lead; gain, get, obtain, procure, produce.

brisk *adj* active, alert, agile, lively, nimble, perky, quick, smart, spirited, spry.

brittle *adj* brash, breakable, crisp, crumbling, fragile, frangible, frail, shivery.

broach *vb* open, pierce, set; approach, break, hint, suggest; proclaim, publish, utter.

broad *adj* ample, expansive, extensive, large, spacious, sweeping, vast, wide; enlarged, hospitable, liberal, tolerant; diffused, open, spread; coarse, gross, indecent, indelicate, unrefined, vulgar.

broaden *vb* augment, enlarge, expand, extend, increase, spread, stretch, widen.

broken *adj* fractured, rent, ruptured, separated, severed, shattered, shivered, torn; exhausted, feeble, impaired, shaken, shattered, spent, wasted; defective, halting, hesitating, imperfect, stammering, stumbling; contrite, humble, lowly, penitent; abrupt, craggy, precipitous, rough.

broker *n* agent, factor, go-between, middleman.

brood *vb* incubate, sit. * *n* issue, offspring, progeny; breed, kind, line, lineage, sort, strain.

brook *vb* abide, bear, endure, suffer, tolerate. * *n* burn, beck, creek, rill, rivulet, run, streamlet.

brotherhood *n* association, clan, clique, coterie, fraternity, junta, society.

brotherly *adj* affectionate, amicable, cordial, friendly, kind.

browbeat *vb* bully, intimidate, overawe, overbear.

bruise *vb* contuse, crunch, squeeze; batter, break, maul, pound, pulverize; batter, deface, indent. * *n* blemish, contusion, swelling.

brush[1] *n* brushwood, bush, scrub, scrubwood, shrubs, thicket, wilderness.

brush[2] *vb* buff, clean, polish, swab, sweep, wipe; curry, groom, rub down; caress, flick, glance, graze, scrape, skim, touch. * *n* besom, broom; action, affair, collision, contest, conflict, encounter, engagement, fight, skirmish.

brutal *adj* barbaric, barbarous, brutish, cruel, ferocious, inhuman, ruthless, savage; bearish, brusque, churlish, gruff, impolite, harsh, rude, rough, truculent, uncivil.

brute *n* barbarian, beast, monster, ogre, savage; animal, beast, creature. * *adj* carnal, mindless, physical; bestial, coarse, gross.

bubble *vb* boil, effervesce, foam. * *n* bead, blob, fluid, globule; bagatelle, trifle; cheat, delusion, hoax.

buccaneer *n* corsair, freebooter, pirate.

buck *vb* jump, leap. * *n* beau, blade, blood, dandy, fop, gallant, spark; male.

bud *vb* burgeon, germinate, push, shoot, sprout, vegetate. * *n* burgeon, gem, germ, gemmule, shoot, sprout.

budget *vb* allocate, cost, estimate. * *n* account, estimate, financial statement; assets, finances, funds, means, resources; bag, bundle, pack, packet, parcel, roll; assortment, batch, collection, lot, set, store.

buffet[1] *vb* beat, box, cuff, slap, smite, strike; resist, struggle against, * *n* blow, box, cuff, slap, strike;

buffet[2] *n* cupboard, sideboard; refreshment counter.

buffoon *n* antic, clown, droll, fool, harlequin, jester, mountebank.

build *vb* construct, erect, establish, fabricate, fashion, model, raise, rear. * *n* body, figure, form, frame, physique; construction, shape, structure.

building *n* construction, erection, fabrication; edifice, fabric, house, pile, substructure, structure,

bulk *n* dimension, magnitude, mass, size, volume; amplitude, bulkiness, massiveness; body, majority, mass.

bully *vb* browbeat, bulldoze, domineer, haze, hector, intimidate, overbear. * *n* blusterer, browbeater, bulldozer, hector, swaggerer, roisterer, tyrant.

bulwark *n* barrier, fortification, parapet, rampart, wall; palladium, safeguard, security.

bump *vb* collide, knock, strike, thump. * *n* blow, jar, jolt, knock, shock, thump; lump, protuberance, swelling.

bunch *vb* assemble, collect, crowd, group, herd, pack. * *n* bulge, bump, bundle, hump, knob, lump, protuberance; cluster, hand, fascicle; assortment, batch, collection, group, lot, parcel, set; knot, tuft.

bundle *vb* bale, pack, package, parcel, truss, wrap. * *n* bale, batch, bunch, collection, heap, pack, package, packet, parcel, pile, roll, truss.

bungler *n* botcher, duffer, fumbler, lout, lubber, mis-manager, muddler.

burden *vb* encumber, grieve, load, oppress, overlay, overload, saddle, surcharge, try. * *n* capacity, cargo, freight, lading, load, tonnage, weight; affliction, charge, clog, encumbrance, impediment, grievance, sorrow, trial, trouble; drift, point, substance, tenor, surcharge.

bureau *n* chest of drawers, dresser; counting room, office.

burial *n* burying, entombment, inhumation, interment, sepulture.

burlesque *vb* ape, imitate, lampoon, mock, ridicule, satirize. * *n* caricature, extravaganza, parody, send-up, take-off, travesty.

burn[1] *n* beck, brook, gill, rill, rivulet, runnel, runlet, stream. water

burn[2] *vb* blaze, conflagrate, enflame, fire, flame, ignite, kindle, light, smoulder; cremate, incinerate; scald, scorch, singe; boil, broil, cook, roast, seethe, simmer, stew, swelter, toast; bronze, brown, sunburn, suntan, tan; bake, desiccate, dry, parch, sear, shrivel, wither; glow, incandesce, tingle, warm. * *n* scald, scorch, singe; sunburn.

burning *adj* aflame, fiery, hot, scorching; ardent, earnest, fervent, fervid, impassioned, intense.

burnish *vb* brighten, buff, furbish, polish, shine. * *n* glaze, gloss, patina, polish, shine.

burst *vb* break open, be rent, explode, shatter, split open. * *adj* broken, kaput, punctured, ruptured, shattered, split. * *n* break, breakage, breach, fracture, rupture; blast, blowout, blowup, discharge, detonation, explosion; spurt; blaze, flare, flash; cloudburst, downpour; bang, crack, crash, report, sound; fusillade, salvo, spray, volley, outburst, outbreak flare-up, blaze, eruption.

bury *vb* entomb, inearth, inhume, inter; conceal, hide, secrete, shroud.

business *n* calling, employment, occupation, profession, pursuit, vocation; commerce, dealing, trade, traffic; affair, concern, engagement, matter, transaction, undertaking; duty, function, office, task, work.

bustle *vb* fuss, hurry, scurry. * *n* ado, commotion, flurry, fuss, hurry, hustle, pother, stir, tumult.

busy *vb* devote, employ, engage, occupy, spend, work. * *adj* employed, engaged, occupied; active, assiduous, diligent, engrossed, industrious, sedulous, working; agile, brisk, nimble, spry, stirring; meddling, officious.

but *conj* except, excepting, further, howbeit, moreover, still, unless, yet. * *adv* all the same, even, notwithstanding, still, yet.

butchery *n* massacre, murder, slaughter.

butt[1] *vb* bunt, push, shove, shunt, strike; encroach, impose, interfere, intrude, invade, obtrude. * *n* buck, bunt, push, shove, shunt, thrust.

butt[2] *n* barrel, cask.

butt[3] *n* aim, goal, mark, object, point, target; dupe, gull, victim.

butt[4] *vb* abut, adjoin, conjoin, connect, neighbour. * *n* end, piece, remainder, stub, stump; buttocks, posterior, rump.

buttonhole *vb* bore, catch, detain in conversation, importune.

buttress *vb* brace, prop, shore, stay, support. * *n* brace, bulwark, prop, stay, support.

buxom *adj* comely, fresh, healthy, hearty, plump, rosy, ruddy, vigorous.

byword *n* adage, aphorism, apothegm, dictum, maxim, proverb, saying, saw.

C

cabal *vb* conspire, intrigue, machinate, plot. * *n* clique, combination, confederacy, coterie, faction, gang, junta, league, party, set; conspiracy, intrigue, machination, plot.

cabbalistic, cabalistic *adj* dark, fanciful, mysterious, mystic, occult, secret.

cabaret *n* tavern, inn, public house, wine shop.

cabin *n* berth, bunk, cot, cottage, crib, dwelling, hovel, hut, shack, shanty, shed.

cabinet *n* apartment, boudoir, chamber, closet; case, davenport, desk, escritoire; council, ministry.

cachinnation *n* guffaw, laugh, laughter.

cackle *vb* giggle, laugh, snicker, titter; babble, chatter, gabble, palaver, prate, prattle, titter. * *n* babble, chatter, giggle, prate, prattle, snigger, titter.

cacophonous *adj* discordant, grating, harsh, inharmonious, jarring, raucous.

cadaverous *adj* bloodless, deathlike, ghastly, pale, pallid, wan.

cage *vb* confine, immure, imprison, incarcerate. * *n* coop, pen, pound.

caitiff *adj* base, craven, pusillanimous, rascally, recreant. * *n* coward, knave, miscreant, rascal, rogue, scoundrel, sneak, traitor, vagabond, villain, wretch.

cajole *vb* blandish, coax, flatter, jolly, wheedle; beguile, deceive, delude, entrap, inveigle, tempt.

calamity *n* adversity, affliction, blow, casualty, cataclysm, catastrophe, disaster, distress, downfall, evil, hardship, mischance, misery, misfortune, mishap, reverse, ruin, stroke, trial, visitation.

calculate *vb* cast, compute, count, estimate, figure, rate, reckon, weigh; tell.

calculating *adj* crafty, designing, scheming, selfish; careful, cautious, circumspect, far-sighted, politic, sagacious, wary.

calefaction *n* heating, warming; hotness, incandescence, warmth.

calendar *n* almanac, ephemeris, register; catalogue, list, schedule.

calibre *n* bore, capacity, diameter, gauge; ability, capacity, endowment, faculty, gifts, parts, scope, talent.

call *vb* christen, denominate, designate, dub, entitle, name, phrase, style, term; bid, invite, summons; assemble, convene, convoke, muster; cry, exclaim; arouse, awaken, proclaim, rouse, shout, waken; appoint, elect, ordain. * *n* cry, outcry, voice; appeal, invitation, summons; claim, demand, summons; appointment, election, invitation.

calling *n* business, craft, employment, occupation, profession, pursuit, trade.

callous *adj* hard, hardened, indurated; apathetic, dull, indifferent, insensible, inured, obdurate, obtuse, sluggish, torpid, unfeeling, unsusceptible.

callow *adj* naked, unfeathered, unfledged; green, immature, inexperienced, sappy, silly, soft, unfledged, unsophisticated.

calm *vb* allay, becalm, compose, hush, lull, smooth, still, tranquillize; alleviate, appease, assuage, moderate, mollify, pacify, quiet, soften, soothe, tranquillize. * *adj* halcyon, mild, peaceful, placid, quiet, reposeful, serene, smooth, still, tranquil, unruffled; collected, cool, composed, controlled, impassive, imperturbable, sedate, self-possessed, undisturbed, unperturbed, unruffled, untroubled. * *n* lull; equanimity, peace, placidity, quiet, repose, serenity, stillness, tranquillity.

calorific *adj* heat, heat-producing.

calumniate *vb* abuse, asperse, backbite, blacken, blemish, defame, discredit, disparage, lampoon, libel, malign, revile, slander, traduce, vilify.

calumny *n* abuses, aspersion, backbiting, defamation, detraction, evil-speaking, insult, libel, lying, obloquy, slander, vilification, vituperation.

camarilla *n* cabal, clique, junta, ring.

camber *vb* arch, bend, curve. * *n* arch, arching, convexity.

camp[1] *vb* bivouac, encamp, lodge, pitch, tent. * *n* bivouac, cantonment, encampment, laager; cabal, circle, clique, coterie, faction, group, junta, party, ring, set.

camp[2] *adj* affected, artificial, effeminate, exaggerated, mannered, theatrical.

canaille *n* mob, populace, proletariat, rabble, ragbag, riffraff, scum.

canal *n* channel, duct, pipe, tube.

cancel *vb* blot, efface, erase, expunge, obliterate; abrogate, annul, countermand, nullify, quash, repeal, rescind, revoke.

candelabrum *n* candlestick, chandelier, lustre.

candid *adj* fair, impartial, just, unbiased, unprejudiced; artless, frank, free, guileless, honest, honourable, ingenuous, naive, open, plain, sincere, straightforward.

candidate *n* applicant, aspirant, claimant, competitor, probationer.

candour *n* fairness, impartiality, justice; artlessness, frankness, guilelessness, honesty, ingenuousness, openness, simplicity, sincerity, straightforwardness, truthfulness.

canker *vb* corrode, erode, rot, rust, waste; blight, consume, corrupt, embitter, envenom, infect, poison, sour. * *n* gangrene, rot; bale, bane, blight, corruption, infection, irritation.

canon *n* catalogue, criterion, formula, formulary, law, regulation, rule, standard, statute.

canorous *adj* musical, tuneful.

cant[1] *vb* whine. * *adj* current, partisan, popular, rote, routine, set; argotic, slangy. * *n* hypocrisy; argot, jargon, lingo, slang.

cant[2] *vb* bevel, incline, list, slant, tilt, turn. * *n* bevel, inclination, leaning, list, pitch, slant, tilt, turn.

cantankerous *adj* contumacious, crabbed, cross-grained, dogged, headstrong, heady, intractable, obdurate, obstinate, perverse, refractory, stiff, stubborn, wilful, unyielding.

canting *adj* affected, pious, sanctimonious, whining.
canvas *n* burlap, scrim, tarpaulin.
canvass *vb* discuss, dispute; analyze, consider, examine, investigate, review, scrutinize, sift, study; campaign, electioneer, solicit votes. * *n* debate, discussion, dispute; examination, scrutiny, sifting.
canyon *n* gorge, gulch, ravine.
cap *vb* cover, surmount; complete, crown, finish; exceed, overtop, surpass, transcend; match, parallel, pattern. * *n* beret, head-cover, head-dress; acme, chief, crown, head, peak, perfection, pitch, summit, top.
capability *n* ability, brains, calibre, capableness, capacity, competency, efficiency, faculty, force, power, scope, skill.
capable *adj* adapted, fitted, qualified, suited; able, accomplished, clever, competent, efficient, gifted, ingenious, intelligent, sagacious, skilful.
capacious *adj* ample, broad, comprehensive, expanded, extensive, large, roomy, spacious, wide.
capacitate *vb* enable, qualify.
capacity *n* amplitude, dimensions, magnitude, volume; aptitude, aptness, brains, calibre, discernment, faculty, forte, genius, gift, parts, power, talent, turn, wit; ability, capability, calibre, cleverness, competency, efficiency, skill; character, charge, function, office, position, post, province, service, sphere.
caparison *vb* accoutre, costume, equip, outfit, rig out. * *n* accoutrements, armour, get-up, harness, housing, livery, outfit, panoply, tack, tackle, trappings, turnout .
caper *vb* bound, caracole, frisk, gambol, hop, leap, prank, romp, skip, spring. * *n* bound, dance, gambol, frisk, hop, jump, leap, prance, romp, skip.
capillary *adj* delicate, fine, minute, slender.
capital *adj* cardinal, chief, essential, important, leading, main, major, pre-eminent, principal, prominent; fatal; excellent, first-class, first-rate, good, prime, splendid. * *n* chief city, metropolis, seat; money, estate, investments, shares, stock.
caprice *n* crotchet, fancy, fickleness, freak, humour, inconstancy, maggot, phantasy, quirk, vagary, whim, whimsy.
capricious *adj* changeable, crotchety, fanciful, fantastical, fickle, fitful, freakish, humoursome, odd, puckish, queer, uncertain, variable, wayward, whimsical.
capsize *vb* overturn, upset.
capsule *n* case, covering, envelope, sheath, shell, wrapper: pericarp, pod, seed-vessel.
captain *vb* command, direct, head, lead, manage, officer, preside. * *n* chief, chieftain, commander, leader, master, officer, soldier, warrior.
captious *adj* carping, caviling, censorious, critical, fault-finding, hypercritical; acrimonious, cantankerous, contentious, crabbed, cross, snappish, snarling, splenetic, testy, touchy, waspish; ensnaring, insidious.
captivate *vb* allure, attract, bewitch, catch, capture, charm, enamour, enchant, enthral, fascinate, gain, hypnotize, infatuate, win.
captivity *n* confinement, durance, duress, imprisonment; bondage, enthralment, servitude, slavery, subjection, thraldom, vassalage.
capture *vb* apprehend, arrest, catch, seize. * *n* apprehension, arrest, catch, catching, imprisonment, seizure; bag, prize.
carcass *n* body, cadaver, corpse, corse, remains.
cardinal *adj* capital, central, chief, essential, first, important, leading, main, pre-eminent, primary, principal, vital.
care *n* anxiety, concern, perplexity, trouble, solicitude, worry; attention, carefulness, caution, circumspection, heed, regard, vigilance, wariness, watchfulness; charge, custody, guardianship, keep, oversight, superintendence, ward; burden, charge, concern, responsibility.
careful *adj* anxious, solicitous, concerned, troubled, uneasy; attentive, heedful, mindful, regardful, thoughtful; cautious, canny, circumspect, discreet, leery, vigilant, watchful.
careless *adj* carefree, nonchalant, unapprehensive, undisturbed, unperplexed, unsolicitous, untroubled; disregardful, heedless, inattentive, incautious, inconsiderate, neglectful, negligent, regardless, remiss, thoughtless, unobservant, unconcerned, unconsidered, unmindful, unthinking.
carelessness *n* heedlessness, inadvertence, inattention, inconsiderateness, neglect, negligence, remissness, slackness, thoughtlessness, unconcern.
caress *vb* coddle, cuddle, cosset, embrace, fondle, hug, kiss, pet. * *n* cuddle, embrace, fondling, hug, kiss.
caressing *n* blandishment, dalliance, endearment, fondling.
cargo *n* freight, lading. load.
caricature *vb* burlesque, parody, send-up, take-off, travesty. * *n* burlesque, farce, ludicrous, parody, representation, take-off, travesty.
carious *adj* decayed, mortified, putrid, rotten, ulcerated.
cark *vb* annoy, fret, grieve, harass, perplex, worry.
carnage *n* bloodshed, butchery, havoc, massacre, murder, slaughter.
carnal *adj* animal, concupiscent, fleshly, lascivious, lecherous, lewd, libidinous, lubricous, lustful, salacious, sensual, voluptuous; bodily, earthy, mundane. natural, secular, temporal, unregenerate, unspiritual.
carol *vb* chant, hum, sing, warble. * *n* canticle, chorus, ditty, hymn, lay, song, warble.
carousal *n* banquet, entertainment, feast, festival, merry-making, regale; bacchanal, carouse, debauch, jamboree, jollification, orgy, revel, revelling, revelry, saturnalia, spree, wassail.
carp *vb* cavil, censure, criticize, fault.
carping *adj* captious, cavilling, censorious, hypercritical. * *n* cavil, censure, fault-finding, hypercriticism.
carriage *n* conveyance, vehicle; air, bearing, behaviour, conduct, demeanour, deportment, front, mien, port.
carry *vb* bear, convey, transfer, transmit, transport; impel, push forward, urge; accomplish, compass, effect, gain, secure; bear up, support, sustain; infer, involve, imply, import, signify.
cart *n* conveyance, tumbril, van, vehicle, wagon.
carte-blanche *n* authority, power.
carve *vb* chisel, cut, divide, engrave, grave, hack, hew, indent, incise, sculpt, sculpture; fashion, form, mould, shape.
cascade *vb* cataract, descend, drop, engulf, fall, inundate, overflow, plunge, tumble. * *n* cataract, fall, falls, force, linn, waterfall.
case[1] *vb* cover, encase, enclose, envelop, protect, wrap; box, pack. * *n* capsule, covering, sheathe; box, cabinet, container, holder, receptacle.
case[2] *n* condition, plight, predicament, situation, state; example, instance, occurrence; circumstance, condition, contingency, event; action, argument, cause, lawsuit, process, suit, trial.
case-hardened *adj* hardened, indurated, steeled; brazen, brazen-faced, obdurate, reprobate.
cash *n* banknotes, bullion, coin, currency, money, payment, specie.
cashier *vb* break, discard, discharge, dismiss.
cast *vb* fling, hurl, pitch, send, shy, sling, throw, toss; drive, force, impel, thrust; lay aside, put off, shed; calculate, compute, reckon; communicate, diffuse, impart, shed, throw. * *n* fling, throw, toss; shade, tinge, tint, touch; air, character, look, manner, mien, style, tone, turn; form, mould.
castaway *adj* abandoned, cast-off, discarded, rejected. * *n* derelict, outcast, reprobate, vagabond.
caste *n* class, grade, lineage, order, race, rank, species, status.
castigate *vb* beat, chastise, flog, lambaste, lash, thrash, whip; chaste, correct, discipline, punish; criticize, flagellate, upbraid.
castle *n* citadel, fortress, stronghold.
castrate *vb* caponize, emasculate, geld; mortify, subdue, suppress, weaken.
casual *adj* accidental, contingent, fortuitous, incidental, irregular, occasional, random, uncertain, unforeseen, unintentional, unpremeditated; informal, relaxed.
casualty *n* chance, contingency, fortuity, mishap; accident, catastrophe, disaster, mischance, misfortune.
cat *n* grimalkin, kitten, puss, tabby, tomcat.
cataclysm *n* deluge, flood, inundation; disaster, upheaval.
catacomb *n* crypt, tomb, vault.
catalogue *vb* alphabetize, categorize, chronicle, class, classify, codify, file, index, list, record, tabulate. * *n* enumeration, index, inventory, invoice, list, record, register, roll, schedule.

cataract *n* cascade, fall, waterfall.

catastrophe *n* conclusion, consummation, denouement, end, finale, issue, termination, upshot; adversity, blow, calamity, cataclysm, debacle, disaster, ill, misfortune, mischance, mishap, trial, trouble.

catch *vb* clutch, grasp, gripe, nab, seize, snatch; apprehend, arrest, capture; overtake; enmesh, ensnare, entangle, entrap, lime, net; bewitch, captivate, charm, enchant, fascinate, win; surprise, take unawares. * *n* arrest, capture, seizure; bag, find, haul, plum, prize; drawback, fault, hitch, obstacle, rub, snag; captive, conquest.

catching *adj* communicable, contagious, infectious, pestiferous, pestilential; attractive, captivating, charming, enchanting, fascinating, taking, winning, winsome.

catechize *adj* examine, interrogate, question, quiz.

catechumen *n* convert, disciple, learner, neophyte, novice, proselyte, pupil, tyro.

categorical *adj* absolute, direct, downright, emphatic, explicit, express, positive, unconditional, unqualified, unreserved, utter.

category *n* class, division, head, heading, list, order, rank, sort.

catenation *n* conjunction, connection, union.

cater *vb* feed, provide, purvey.

cathartic *adj* abstergent, aperient, cleansing, evacuant, laxative, purgative. * *n* aperient, laxative, physic, purgative, purge.

catholic *adj* general, universal, world-wide; charitable, liberal, tolerant, unbigoted, unexclusive, unsectarian.

cause *vb* breed, create, originate, produce; effect, effectuate, occasion, produce. * *n* agent, creator, mainspring, origin, original, producer, source, spring; account, agency, consideration, ground, incentive, incitement, inducement, motive, reason; aim, end, object, purpose; action, case, suit, trial.

caustic *adj* acrid, cathartic, consuming, corroding, corrosive, eating, erosive, mordant, virulent; biting, bitter, burning, cutting, sarcastic, satirical, scalding, scathing, severe, sharp, stinging.

caution *vb* admonish, forewarn, warn. * *n* care, carefulness, circumspection, discretion, forethought, heed, heedfulness, providence, prudence, wariness, vigilance, watchfulness; admonition, advice, counsel, injunction, warning.

cautious *adj* careful, chary, circumspect, discreet, heedful, prudent, wary, vigilant, wary, watchful.

cavalier *adj* arrogant, curt, disdainful, haughty, insolent, scornful, supercilious; debonair, gallant, gay. * *n* chevalier, equestrian, horseman, horse-soldier, knight.

cave *n* cavern, cavity, den, grot, grotto.

cavil *vb* carp, censure, hypercriticize, object.

cavilling *adj* captious, carping, censorious, critical, hypercritical.

cavity *n* hollow, pocket, vacuole, void.

cease *vb* desist, intermit, pause, refrain, stay, stop; fail; discontinue, end, quit, terminate.

ceaseless *adj* continual, continuous, incessant, unceasing, unintermitting, uninterrupted, unremitting; endless, eternal, everlasting, perpetual.

cede *vb* abandon, abdicate, relinquish, resign, surrender, transfer, yield; convey, grant.

celebrate *vb* applaud, bless, commend, emblazon, extol, glorify, laud, magnify, praise, trumpet; commemorate, honour, keep, observe; solemnize.

celebrated *adj* distinguished, eminent, famed, famous, glorious, illustrious, notable, renowned.

celebrity *n* credit, distinction, eminence, fame, glory, honour, renown, reputation, repute; lion, notable, star.

celerity *n* fleetness, haste, quickness, rapidity, speed, swiftness, velocity.

celestial *adj* empyreal, empyrean; angelic, divine, god-like, heavenly, seraphic, supernal, supernatural.

celibate *adj* single, unmarried. * *n* bachelor, single, virgin.

cellular *adj* alveolate, honeycombed.

cement *vb* attach, bind, join, combine, connect, solder, unite, weld; cohere, stick. * *n* glue, paste, mortar, solder.

cemetery *n* burial-ground, burying-ground, churchyard, god's acre, graveyard, necropolis.

censor *vb* blue-pencil, bowdlerize, cut, edit, expurgate; classify, kill, quash, squash, suppress. * *n* caviller, censurer, faultfinder.

censorious *adj* captious, carping, caviling, condemnatory, faultfinding, hypercritical, severe.

censure *vb* abuse, blame, chide, condemn, rebuke, reprehend, reprimand, reproach, reprobate, reprove, scold, upbraid. * *n* animadversion, blame, condemnation, criticism, disapprobation, disapproval, rebuke, remonstrance, reprehension, reproach, reproof, stricture.

ceremonious *adj* civil, courtly, lofty, stately; formal, studied; exact, formal, punctilious, precise, starched, stiff.

ceremony *n* ceremonial, etiquette, form, formality, observance, solemnity, rite; parade, pomp, show, stateliness.

certain *adj* absolute, incontestable, incontrovertible, indisputable, indubitable, positive, undeniable, undisputed, unquestionable, unquestioned; assured, confident, sure, undoubting; infallible, never-failing, unfailing; actual, existing, real; constant, determinate, fixed, settled, stated.

certainty *n* indubitability, indubitableness, inevitableness, inevitability, surety, unquestionability, unquestionableness; assurance, assuredness, certitude, confidence, conviction, surety.

certify *vb* attest, notify, testify, vouch; ascertain, determine, verify, show.

cerulean *adj* azure, blue, sky-blue.

cessation *n* ceasing, discontinuance, intermission, pause, remission, respite, rest, stop, stoppage, suspension.

cession *n* abandonment, capitulation, ceding, concession, conveyance, grant, relinquishement, renunciation, surrender, yielding.

chafe *vb* rub; anger, annoy, chagrin, enrage, exasperate, fret, gall, incense, irritate, nettle, offend, provoke, ruffle, tease, vex; fret, fume, rage.

chaff *vb* banter, deride, jeer, mock, rally, ridicule, scoff. * *n* glumes, hulls, husks; refuse, rubbish, trash, waste.

chaffer *n* bargain, haggle, higgle, negotiate.

chagrin *vb* annoy, chafe, displease, irritate, mortify, provoke, vex. * *n* annoyance, displeasure, disquiet, dissatisfaction, fretfulness, humiliation, ill-humour, irritation, mortification, spleen, vexation.

chain *vb* bind, confine, fetter, manacle, restrain, shackle, trammel; enslave. * *n* bond, fetter, manacle, shackle, union.

chalice *n* bowl, cup, goblet.

challenge *vb* brave, call out, dare, defy, dispute; demand, require. * *n* defiance, interrogation, question; exception, objection.

chamber *n* apartment, hall, room; cavity, hollow.

champion *vb* advocate, defend, uphold. * *n* defender, promoter, protector, vindicator; belt-holder, hero, victor, warrior, winner.

chance *vb* befall, betide, happen, occur. * *adj* accidental, adventitious, casual, fortuitous, incidental, unexpected, unforeseen. * *n* accident, cast, fortuity, fortune, hap, luck; contingency, possibility; occasion, opening, opportunity; contingency, fortuity, gamble, peradventure, uncertainty; hazard, jeopardy, peril, risk.

change *vb* alter, fluctuate, modify, vary; displace, remove, replace, shift, substitute; barter, commute, exchange. * *n* alteration, mutation, revolution, transition, transmutation, turning, variance, variation; innovation, novelty, variety, vicissitude.

changeable *adj* alterable, inconstant, modifiable, mutable, uncertain, unsettled, unstable, unsteadfast, unsteady, variable, variant; capricious, fickle, fitful, flighty, giddy, mercurial, vacillating, volatile, wavering.

changeless *adj* abiding, consistent, constant, fixed, immutable, permanent, regular, reliable, resolute, settled, stationary, unalterable, unchanging.

channel *vb* chamfer, cut, flute, groove. * *n* canal, conduit, duct, passage; aqueduct, canal, chute, drain, flume, furrow; chamfer, groove, fluting, furrow, gutter.

chant *vb* carol, sing, warble; intone, recite; canticle, song.

chaos *n* anarchy, confusion, disorder.

chapfallen *adj* blue, crest-fallen, dejected, depressed, despondent, discouraged, disheartened, dispirited, downcast, downhearted, low-spirited, melancholy, sad.

chaplet *n* coronal, garland, wreath.
char *vb* burn, scorch.
character *n* emblem, figure, hieroglyph, ideograph, letter, mark, sign, symbol; bent, constitution, cast, disposition, nature, quality; individual, original, person, personage; reputation, repute; nature, traits; eccentric, trait.
characteristic *adj* distinctive, peculiar, singular, special, specific, typical. * *n* attribute, feature, idiosyncrasy, lineament, mark, peculiarity, quality, trait.
charge *vb* burden, encumber, freight, lade, load; entrust; ascribe, impute, lay; accuse, arraign, blame, criminate, impeach, inculpate, indict, involve; bid, command, exhort, enjoin, order, require, tax; assault, attack bear down. * *n* burden, cargo, freight, lading, load; care, custody, keeping, management, ward; commission, duty, employment, office, trust; responsibility, trust; command, direction, injunction, mandate, order, precept; exhortation, instruction; cost, debit, expense, expenditure, outlay; price, sum; assault, attack, encounter, onset, onslaught.
charger *n* dish, platter; mount, steed, war-horse.
charily *adv* carefully, cautiously, distrustfully, prudently, sparingly, suspiciously, warily.
charitable *adj* beneficial, beneficent, benignant, bountiful, generous, kind, liberal, open-handed; candid, considerate, lenient, mild.
charity *n* benevolence, benignity, fellow-feeling, good-nature, goodwill, kind-heartedness, kindness, tenderheartedness; beneficence, bounty, generosity, humanity, philanthropy. liberality.
charlatan *n* cheat, empiric, impostor, mountebank, pretender, quack.
charm *vb* allure, attract, becharm, bewitch, captivate, catch, delight, enamour, enchain, enchant, enrapture, enravish, fascinate, transport, win. * *n* enchantment, incantation, magic, necromancy, sorcery, spell, witchery; amulet, talisman; allurement, attraction, attractiveness, fascination.
charming *adj* bewitching, captivating, delightful, enchanting, enrapturing, fascinating, lovely.
charter *vb* incorporate; hire, let. * *n* franchise, immunity, liberty, prerogation, privilege, right; bond, deed, indenture, instrument, prerogative.
chary *adj* careful, cautious, circumspect, shy, wary; abstemious, careful, choice, economical, frugal, provident, saving, sparing, temperate, thrifty, unwasteful.
chase *vb* follow, hunt, pursue, track; emboss. * *n* course, field-sport, hunt, hunting.
chasm *n* cavity, cleft, fissure, gap, hollow, hiatus, opening.
chaste *adj* clean, continent, innocent, modest, pure, pure-minded, undefiled, virtuous; chastened, pure, simple, unaffected, uncorrupt.
chasten *vb* correct, humble; purify, refine, render, subdue.
chastening *n* chastisement, correction, discipline, humbling.
chastise *vb* castigate, correct, flog, lash, punish, whip; chasten, correct, discipline, humble, punish, subdue.
chastity *n* abstinence, celibacy, continence, innocence, modesty, pure-mindedness, purity, virtue; cleanness, decency; chasteness, refinement, restrainedness, simplicity, sobriety, unaffectedness.
chat *vb* babble, chatter, confabulate, gossip, prate, prattle. * *n* chit-chat, confabulation, conversation, gossip, prattle.
chatter *vb* babble, chat, confabulate, gossip, prate, prattle. * *n* babble, chat, gabble, jabber, patter, prattle.
cheap *adj* inexpensive, low-priced; common, indifferent, inferior, mean, meretricious, paltry, poor.
cheapen *vb* belittle, depreciate.
cheat *vb* cozen, deceive, dissemble, juggle, shuffle; bamboozle, befool, beguile, cajole, circumvent, deceive, defraud, chouse, delude, dupe, ensnare, entrap, fool, gammon, gull, hoax, hoodwink, inveigle, jockey, mislead, outwit, overreach, trick. * *n* artifice, beguilement, blind, catch, chouse, deceit, deception, fraud, imposition, imposture, juggle, pitfall, snare, stratagem, swindle, trap, trick, wile; counterfeit, deception, delusion, illusion, mockery, paste, sham, tinsel; beguiler, charlatan, cheater, cozener, impostor, jockey, knave, mountebank, trickster, rogue, render, sharper, seizer, shuffler, swindler, taker, tearer.
check *vb* block, bridle, control, counteract, curb, hinder, obstruct, repress, restrain; chide, rebuke, reprimand, reprove. * *n* bar, barrier, block, brake, bridle, clog, control, curb, damper, hindrance, impediment, interference, obstacle, obstruction, rebuff, repression, restraint, stop, stopper.
cheep *vb* chirp, creak, peep, pipe, squeak.
cheer *vb* animate, encourage, enliven, exhilarate, gladden, incite, inspirit; comfort, console, solace; applaud, clap. * *n* cheerfulness, gaiety, gladness, glee, hilarity, jollity, joy, merriment, mirth; entertainment, food, provision, repast, viands, victuals; acclamation, hurrah, huzza.
cheerful *adj* animated, airy, blithe, buoyant, cheery, gay, glad, gleeful, happy, joyful, jocund, jolly, joyous, light-hearted, lightsome, lively, merry, mirthful, sprightly, sunny; animating, cheering, cheery, encouraging, enlivening, glad, gladdening, gladsome, grateful, inspiriting, jocund, pleasant.
cheerless *adj* dark, dejected, desolate, despondent, disconsolate, discouraged, dismal, doleful, dreary, forlorn, gloomy, joyless, low-spirited, lugubrious, melancholy, mournful, rueful, sad, sombre, spiritless, woebegone.
cherish *vb* comfort, foster, nourish, nurse, nurture, support, sustain; treasure; encourage, entertain, indulge, harbour.
chest *n* box, case, coffer; breast, thorax, trunk.
chew *vb* crunch, manducate, masticate, munch; bite, champ, gnaw; meditate, ruminate.
chicanery *n* chicane, deception, duplicity, intrigue, intriguing, sophistication, sophistry, stratagems, tergiversation, trickery, wiles, wire-pulling.
chide *vb* admonish, blame, censure, rebuke, reprimand, reprove, scold, upbraid; chafe, clamour, fret, fume, scold.
chief *adj* first, foremost, headmost, leading, master, supereminent, supreme, top; capital, cardinal, especial, essential, grand, great, main, master, paramount, prime, principal, supreme, vital. * *n* chieftain, commander; head, leader.
chiffonier *n* cabinet, sideboard.
child *n* babe, baby, bairn, bantling, brat, chit, infant, nursling, suckling, wean; issue, offspring, progeny.
childbirth *n* child-bearing, delivery, labour, parturition, travail.
childish *adj* infantile, juvenile, puerile, tender, young; foolish, frivolous, silly, trifling, weak.
childlike *adj* docile, dutiful, gentle, meek, obedient, submissive; confiding, guileless, ingenuous, innocent, simple, trustful, uncrafty.
chill *vb* dampen, depress, deject, discourage, dishearten. * *adj* bleak, chilly, cold, frigid, gelid. * *n* chilliness, cold, coldness, frigidity; ague, rigour, shiver; damp, depression.
chime *vb* accord, harmonize. * *n* accord, consonance.
chimera *n* crochet, delusion, dream, fantasy, hallucination, illusion, phantom.
chimerical *adj* delusive, fanciful, fantastic, illusory, imaginary, quixotic, shadowy, unfounded, visionary, wild.
chink[1] *vb* cleave, crack, fissure, crevasse, incise, split, slit. * *n* aperture, cleft, crack, cranny, crevice, fissure, gap, opening, slit.
chink[2] *vb, n* jingle, clink, ring, ting, tink, tinkle.
chip *vb* flake, fragment, hew, pare, scrape. * *n* flake, fragment, paring, scrap.
chirp *vb* cheep, chirrup, peep, twitter.
chirrup *vb* animate, cheer, encourage, inspirit.
chisel *vb* carve, cut, gouge, sculpt, sculpture.
chivalrous *adj* adventurous, bold, brave, chivalric, gallant, knightly, valiant, warlike; gallant, generous, high-minded, magnanimous.
chivalry *n* knighthood, knight-errantry; courtesy, gallantry, politeness; courage, valour.
choice *adj* excellent, exquisite, precious, rare, select, superior, uncommon, unusual, valuable; careful, chary, frugal, sparing. * *n* alternative, election, option, selection; favourite, pick, preference.
choke *vb* gag, smother, stifle, strangle, suffocate, throttle; overcome, overpower, smother, suppress; bar, block, close, obstruct, stop.

choleric *adj* angry, fiery, hasty, hot, fiery, irascible, irritable, passionate, petulant, testy, touchy, waspish.

choose *vb* adopt, co-opt, cull, designate, elect, pick, predestine, prefer, select.

chop *vb* cut, hack, hew; mince; shift, veer. * *n* slice; brand, quality; chap, jaw.

chouse *vb* bamboozle, beguile, cheat, circumvent, cozen, deceive, defraud, delude, dupe, gull, hoodwink, overreach, swindle, trick, victimize. * *n* cully, dupe, gull, simpleton, tool; artifice, cheat, circumvention, deceit, deception, delusion, double-dealing, fraud, imposition, imposture, ruse, stratagem, trick, wile.

christen *vb* baptize; call, dub, denominate, designate, entitle, name, style, term, title.

chronic *adj* confirmed, continuing, deep-seated, inveterate, rooted.

chronicle *vb* narrate, record, register. * *n* diary, journal, register; account, annals, history, narration, recital, record.

chuckle *vb* crow, exult, giggle, laugh, snigger, titter. * *n* giggle, laughter, snigger, titter.

chum *n* buddy, companion, comrade, crony, friend, mate, pal.

churl *n* boor, bumpkin, clodhopper, clown, countryman, lout, peasant, ploughman, rustic; curmudgeon, hunks, miser, niggard, scrimp, skinflint.

churlish *adj* brusque, brutish, cynical, harsh, impolite, rough, rude, snappish, snarling, surly, uncivil, waspish; crabbed, ill-tempered, morose, sullen; close, close-fisted, illiberal, mean, miserly, niggardly, penurious, stingy.

churn *vb* agitate, jostle.

cicatrice *n* cicatrix, mark, scar, seam.

cicesbeo *n* beau, escort, gallant, gigolo.

cincture *n* band, belt, cestos, cestus, girdle.

cipher *n* naught, nothing, zero; character, device, monogram, symbol; nobody, nonentity.

circle *vb* compass, encircle, encompass, gird, girdle, ring; gyrate, revolve, rotate, round, turn. * *n* circlet, corona, gyre, hoop, ring, rondure; circumference, cordon, periphery; ball, globe, orb, sphere; compass, enclosure; class, clique, company, coterie, fraternity, set, society; bounds, circuit, compass, field, province, range, region, sphere.

circuit *n* ambit, circumambience, circumambiency, cycle, revolution, turn; bounds, district, field, province, range, region, space, sphere, tract; boundary, compass; course, detour, perambulation, round, tour.

circuitous *adj* ambiguous, devious, indirect, roundabout, tortuous, turning, winding.

circulate *vb* diffuse, disseminate, promulgate, propagate, publish, spread.

circumference *n* bound, boundary, circuit, girth, outline, perimeter, periphery.

circumlocution *n* circuitousness, obliqueness, periphrase, periphrasis, verbosity, wordiness.

circumscribe *vb* bound, define, encircle, enclose, encompass, limit, surround; confine, restrict.

circumspect *adj* attentive, careful, cautious, considerate, discreet, heedful, judicious, observant, prudent, vigilant, wary, watchful.

circumstance *n* accident, incident; condition, detail, event, fact, happening, occurrence, position, situation.

circumstantial *adj* detailed, particular; indirect, inferential, presumptive.

circumvent *vb* check, checkmate, outgeneral, thwart; bamboozle, beguile, cheat, chouse, cozen, deceive, defraud, delude, dupe, gull, hoodwink, inveigle, mislead, outwit, overreach, trick.

circumvention *n* cheat, cheating, chicanery, deceit, deception, duplicity, fraud, guile, imposition, imposture, indirection, trickery, wiles.

cistern *n* basin, pond, reservoir, tank.

citation *n* excerpt, extract, quotation; enumeration, mention, quotation, quoting.

cite *vb* adduce, enumerate, extract, mention, name, quote; call, summon.

citizen *n* burgess, burgher, denizen, dweller, freeman, inhabitant, resident, subject, townsman.

civil *adj* civic, municipal, political; domestic; accommodating, affable, civilized, complaisant, courteous, courtly, debonair, easy, gracious, obliging, polished, polite, refined, suave, urbane, well-bred, well-mannered.

civility *n* affability, amiability, complaisance, courteousness, courtesy, good-breeding, politeness, suavity, urbanity.

civilize *vb* cultivate, educate, enlighten, humanize, improve, polish, refine.

claim *vb* ask, assert, challenge, demand, exact, require. * *n* call, demand, lien, requisition; pretension, privilege, right, title.

clammy *adj* adhesive, dauby, glutinous, gummy, ropy, smeary, sticky, viscid, viscous; close, damp, dank, moist, sticky, sweaty.

clamour *vb* shout, vociferate. * *n* blare, din, exclamation, hullabaloo, noise, outcry, uproar, vociferation.

clan *n* family, phratry, race, sect, tribe; band, brotherhood, clique, coterie, fraternity, gang, set, society, sodality.

clandestine *adj* concealed, covert, fraudulent, furtive, hidden, private, secret, sly, stealthy, surreptitious, underhand.

clap *vb* pat, slap, strike; force, slam; applaud, cheer. * *n* blow, knock, slap; bang, burst, explosion, peal, slam.

clarify *vb* cleanse, clear, depurate, purify, strain.

clash *vb* collide, crash, strike; clang, clank, clatter, crash, rattle; contend, disagree, interfere. * *n* collision; clang, clangour, clank, clashing, clatter, crash, rattle; contradiction, disagreement, interference, jar, jarring, opposition.

clasp *vb* clutch, entwine, grasp, grapple, grip, seize; embrace, enfold, fold, hug. * *n* buckle, catch, hasp, hook; embrace, hug.

class *vb* arrange, classify, dispose, distribute, range, rank. * *n* form, grade, order, rank, status; group, seminar; breed, kind, sort; category, collection, denomination, division, group, head.

classical *adj* first-rate, master, masterly, model, standard; Greek, Latin, Roman; Attic, chaste, elegant, polished, pure, refined.

classify *vb* arrange, assort, categorize, class, dispose, distribute, group, pigeonhole, rank, systematize, tabulate.

clatter *vb* clash, rattle; babble, clack, gabble, jabber, prate, prattle. * *n* clattering, clutter, rattling.

clause *n* article, condition, provision, stipulation.

claw *vb* lacerate, scratch, tear. * *n* talon, ungula.

clean *vb* cleanse, clear, purge, purify, rinse, scour, scrub, wash, wipe. * *adj* immaculate, spotless, unsmirched, unsoiled, unspotted, unstained, unsullied, white; clarified, pure, purified, unadulterated, unmixed; adroit, delicate, dextrous, graceful, light, neat, shapely; complete, entire, flawless, faultless, perfect, unabated, unblemished, unimpaired, whole; chaste, innocent, moral, pure, undefiled. * *adv* altogether, completely, entirely, perfectly, quite, thoroughly, wholly.

cleanse *vb* clean, clear, elutriate, purge, purify, rinse, scour, scrub, wash, wipe.

clear *vb* clarify, cleanse, purify, refine; emancipate, disenthral, free, liberate, loose; absolve, acquit, discharge, exonerate, justify, vindicate; disembarrass, disengage, disentangle, extricate, loosen, rid; clean up, scour, sweep; balance; emancipate, free, liberate. * *adj* bright, crystalline, light, limpid, luminous, pellucid, transparent; pure, unadulterated, unmixed; free, open, unencumbered, unobstructed; cloudless, fair, serene, sunny, unclouded, undimmed, unobscured; net; distinct, intelligible, lucid, luminous, perspicuous; apparent, conspicuous, distinct, evident, indisputable, manifest, obvious, palpable, unambiguous, undeniable, unequivocal, unmistakable, unquestionable, visible; clean, guiltless, immaculate, innocent, irreproachable, sinless, spotless, unblemished, undefiled, unspotted, unsullied; unhampered, unimpeded, unobstructed; euphonious, fluty, liquid, mellifluous, musical, silvery, sonorous.

cleave[1] *vb* crack, divide, open, part, rend, rive, sever, split, sunder.

cleave[2] *vb* adhere, cling, cohere, hold, stick.

cleft *adj* bifurcated, cloven, forked. * *n* breach, break, chasm, chink, cranny, crevice, fissure, fracture, gap, interstice, opening, rent, rift.

clemency *n* mildness, softness; compassion, fellow-feeling, forgivingness, gentleness, kindness, lenience, leniency, lenity, mercifulness, mercy, mildness, tenderness.

clement *adj* compassionate, forgiving, gentle, humane, indulgent, kind, kind-hearted, lenient, merciful, mild, tender, tender-hearted.

clench *vb* close tightly, grip; fasten, fix, rivet, secure.

clergy *n* clergymen, the cloth, ministers.

clever *adj* able, apt, gifted, talented; adroit, capable, dextrous, discerning, expert, handy, ingenious, knowing, quick, ready, skilful, smart, talented.

click *vb* beat, clack, clink, tick. * *n* beat, clack, clink, tick; catch, detent, pawl, ratchet.

cliff *n* crag, palisade, precipice, scar, steep.

climate *n* clime, temperature, weather; country, region.

climax *vb* consummate, crown, culminate, peak. * *n* acme, consummation, crown, culmination, head, peak, summit, top, zenith.

clinch *vb* clasp, clench, clutch, grapple, grasp, grip; fasten, secure; confirm, establish, fix. * *n* catch, clutch, grasp, grip; clincher, clamp, cramp, holdfast.

cling *vb* adhere, clear, stick; clasp, embrace, entwine.

clink *vb n* chink, jingle, ring, tinkle; chime, rhyme.

clip *vb* cut, shear, snip; curtail, cut, dock, pare, prune, trim. * *n* cutting, shearing; blow, knock, lick, rap, thump, thwack, thump.

clique *n* association, brotherhood, cabal, camarilla, clan, club, coterie, gang, junta, party, ring, set, sodality.

cloak *vb* conceal, cover, dissemble, hide, mask, veil. * *n* mantle, surcoat; blind, cover, mask, pretext, veil.

clock *vb* mark time, measure, stopwatch; clock up, record, register. * *n* chronometer, horologue, timekeeper, timepiece, timer, watch.

clog *vb* fetter, hamper, shackle, trammel; choke, obstruct; burden, cumber, embarrass, encumber, hamper, hinder, impede, load, restrain, trammel. * *n* dead-weight, drag-weight, fetter, shackle, trammel; check, drawback, encumbrance, hindrance, impediment, obstacle, obstruction.

cloister *n* abbey, convent, monastery, nunnery, priory; arcade, colonnade, piazza.

close[1] *adj* closed, confined, snug, tight; hidden, private, secret; incommunicative, reserved, reticent, secretive, taciturn; concealed, retired, secluded, withdrawn; confined, motionless, stagnant; airless, oppressive, stale, stifling, stuffy, sultry; compact, compressed, dense, form, solid, thick; adjacent, adjoining, approaching, immediately, near, nearly, neighbouring; attached, dear, confidential, devoted, intimate; assiduous, earnest, fixed, intense, intent, unremitting; accurate, exact, faithful, nice, precise, strict; churlish, close-fisted, curmudgeonly, mean, illiberal, miserly, niggardly, parsimonious, penurious, stingy, ungenerous. * *n* courtyard, enclosure, grounds, precinct, yard.

close[2] *vb* occlude, seal, shut; choke, clog, estop, obstruct, stop; cease, complete, concede, end, finish, terminate; coalesce, unite; cease, conclude, finish, terminate; clinch, grapple; agree. * *n* cessation, conclusion, end, finish, termination.

closet *n* cabinet, retiring-room; press, store-room.

clot *vb* coagulate, concrete. * *n* coagulation, concretion, lump.

clothe *vb* array, attire, deck, dress, rig; cover,endow, envelop, enwrap, invest with, swathe.

clothes *n* apparel, array, attire, clothing, costume, dress, garb, garments, gear, habiliments, habits, raiment, rig, vestments, vesture.

cloud *vb* becloud, obnubilate, overcast, overspread; befog, darken, dim, obscure, shade, shadow. * *n* cirrus, cumulus, fog, haze, mist, nebulosity, scud, stratus, vapour; army, crowd, horde, host, multitude, swarm, throng; darkness, eclipse, gloom, obscuration, obscurity.

cloudy *adj* clouded, filmy, foggy, hazy, lowering, lurid, murky, overcast; confused, dark, dim, obscure; depressing, dismal, gloomy, sullen; clouded, mottled; blurred, dimmed, lustreless, muddy.

clown *n* churl, clod-breaker, clodhopper, hind, husbandman, lubber; boor, bumpkin, churl, fellow, lout; blockhead, dolt, clodpoll, dunce, dunderhead, numbskull, simpleton, thickhead; buffoon, droll, farceur, fool, harlequin, jack-a-dandy, jack-pudding, jester, merry-andrew, mime, pantaloon, pickle-herring, punch, scaramouch, zany.

clownish *adj* awkward, boorish, clumsy, coarse, loutish, ungainly, rough, rustic; churlish, ill-bred, ill-mannered, impolite, rude, uncivil.

cloy *vb* glut, pall, sate, satiate, surfeit.

club *vb* combine, unite; beat, bludgeon, cudgel. * *n* bat, bludgeon, cosh, cudgel, hickory, shillelagh, stick, truncheon; association, company, coterie, fraternity, set, society, sodality.

clump *vb* assemble, batch, bunch, cluster, group, lump; lumber, stamp, stomp, stump, trudge. * *n* assemblage, bunch, cluster, collection, group, patch, tuft.

clumsy *adj* botched, cumbrous, heavy, ill-made, ill-shaped, lumbering, ponderous, unwieldy; awkward, blundering, bungling, elephantine, heavy-handed, inapt, mal adroit, unhandy, unskilled.

cluster *vb* assemble, batch, bunch, clump, collect, gather, group, lump, throng. * *n* agglomeration, assemblage, batch, bunch, clump, collection, gathering, group, throng.

clutch[1] *vb* catch, clasp, clench, clinch, grab, grapple, grasp, grip, hold, seize, snatch, squeeze. * *n* clasp, clench, clinch, grasp, grip, hold, seizure, squeeze.

clutch[2] *n* aerie, brood, hatching, nest.

clutches *n pl* claws, paws, talons; hands, power.

clutter *vb* confuse, disarrange, disarray, disorder, jumble, litter, mess, muss; clatter. * *n* bustle, clatter, clattering, racket; confusion, disarray, disorder, jumble, litter, mess, muss.

coadjutor *n* abettor, accomplice, aider, ally, assistant, associate, auxiliary, collaborator, colleague, cooperator, fellow-helper, helper, helpmate, partner.

coagulate *vb* clot, congeal, concrete, curdle, thicken.

coalesce *vb* amalgamate, blend, cohere, combine, commix, incorporate, mix, unite; concur, fraternize.

coalition *n* alliance, association, combination, compact, confederacy, confederation, conjunction, conspiracy, co-partnership, federation, league, union.

coarse *adj* crude, impure, rough, unpurified; broad, gross, indecent, indelicate, ribald, vulgar; bearish, bluff, boorish, brutish, churlish, clownish, gruff, impolite, loutish, rude, unpolished; crass, inelegant.

coast *vb* flow, glide, roll, skim, sail, slide, sweep. * *n* littoral, seaboard, sea-coast, seaside, shore, strand; border.

coat *vb* cover, spread. * *n* cut-away, frock, jacket; coating, cover, covering; layer.

coax *vb* allure, beguile, cajole, cog, entice, flatter, persuade, soothe, wheedle.

cobble *vb* botch, bungle; mend, patch, repair, tinker.

cobweb *adj* flimsy, gauzy, slight, thin, worthless. * *n* entanglement, meshes, snare, toils.

cochleate *adj* cochlear, cochleary, cochleous, cochleated, spiral, spiry.

cockle *vb* corrugate, pucker, wrinkle.

coddle *vb* caress, cocker, fondle, humour, indulge, nurse, pamper, pet.

codger *n* churl, curmudgeon, hunks, lick-penny, miser, niggard, screw, scrimp, skinflint.

codify *vb* condense, digest, summarize, systematize, tabulate.

coerce *vb* check, curb, repress, restrain, subdue; compel, constrain, drive, force, urge.

coercion *n* check, curb, repression, restraint; compulsion, constraint, force.

coeval *adj* coetaneous, coexistent, contemporaneous, contemporary, synchronous.

coexistent *adj* coetaneous, coeval, simultaneous, synchronous.

coffer *n* box, casket, chest, trunk; money-chest, safe, strongbox; caisson.

cogent *adj* compelling, conclusive, convincing, effective, forcible, influential, irresistible, persuasive, potent, powerful, resistless, strong, trenchant, urgent.

cogitate *vb* consider, deliberate, meditate, ponder, reflect, ruminate, muse, think, weigh.

cognate *adj* affiliated, affined, akin, allied, alike, analogous, connected, kindred, related, similar.

cognizance *n* cognition, knowing, knowledge, notice, observation.

cohere *vb* agree, coincide, conform, fit, square, suit.
coherence *n* coalition, cohesion, connection, dependence, union; agreement, congruity, consistency, correspondence, harmony, intelligibility, intelligible, meaning, rationality, unity.
coherent *adj* adherent, connected, united; congruous, consistent, intelligible, logical.
cohort *n* band, battalion, line, squadron.
coil *vb* curl, twine, twirl, twist, wind. * *n* convolution, curlicue, helix, knot, roll, spiral, tendril, twirl, volute, whorl; bustle, care, clamour, confusion, entanglements, perplexities, tumult, turmoil, uproar.
coin *vb* counterfeit, create, devise, fabricate, forge, form, invent, mint, originate, mould, stamp. * *n* coign, corner, quoin; key, plug, prop, wedge; cash, money, specie.
coincide *vb* cohere, correspond, square, tally; acquiesce, agree, harmonize, concur.
coincidence *n* corresponding, squaring, tallying; agreeing, concurrent, concurring.
cold *adj* arctic, biting, bleak, boreal, chill, chilly, cutting, frosty, gelid, glacial, icy, nipping, polar, raw, wintry; frost-bitten, shivering; apathetic, cold-blooded, dead, freezing, frigid, indifferent, lukewarm, passionless, phlegmatic, sluggish, stoical, stony, torpid, unconcerned, unfeeling, unimpressible, unresponsive, unsusceptible, unsympathetic; dead, dull, spiritless, unaffecting, uninspiring, uninteresting. * *n* chill, chilliness, coldness.
collapse *vb* break down, fail, fall. * *n* depression, exhaustion, failure, faint, prostration, sinking, subsidence.
collar *vb* apprehend, arrest, capture, grab, nab, seize. * *n* collarette, gorget, neckband, ruff, torque; band, belt, fillet, guard, ring, yoke.
collate *vb* adduce, collect, compare, compose.
collateral *adj* contingent, indirect, secondary, subordinate; concurrent, parallel; confirmatory, corroborative; accessory, accompanying, additional, ancillary, auxiliary, concomitant, contributory, simultaneous, supernumerary; consanguineous, related. * *n* guarantee, guaranty, security, surety, warranty; accessory, extra, nonessential, unessential; consanguinean, relative.
collation *n* luncheon, repast, meal.
colleague *n* aider, ally, assistant, associate, auxiliary, coadjutor, collaborator, companion, confederate, confrere, cooperator, helper, partner.
collect *vb* assemble, compile, gather, muster; accumulate, aggregate, amass, garner.
collected *adj* calm, composed, cool, placid, self-possessed, serene, unperturbed.
collection *n* aggregation, assemblage, cluster, crowd, drove, gathering, group, pack; accumulation, congeries, conglomeration, heap, hoard, lot, mass, pile, store; alms, contribution, offering, offertory.
colligate *vb* bind, combine, fasten, unite.
collision *n* clash, concussion, crash, encounter, impact, impingement, shock; conflict, crashing, interference, opposition.
collocate *vb* arrange, dispose, place, set.
colloquy *n* conference, conversation, dialogue, discourse, talk.
collude *vb* concert, connive, conspire.
collusion *n* connivance, conspiracy, coven, craft, deceit.
collusive *adj* conniving, conspiratorial, , dishonest, deceitful, deceptive, fraudulent.
colossal *adj* Cyclopean, enormous, gigantic, Herculean, huge, immense, monstrous, prodigious, vast.
colour *vb* discolour, dye, paint, stain, tinge, tint; disguise, varnish; disguise, distort, garble, misrepresent, pervert; blush, flush, redden, show. * *n* hue, shade, tinge, tint, tone; paint, pigment, stain; redness, rosiness, ruddiness; complexion; appearance, disguise, excuse, guise, plea, pretence, pretext, semblance.
colourless *adj* achromatic, uncoloured, untinged; blanched, hueless, livid, pale, pallid; blank, characterless, dull, expressionless, inexpressive, monotonous.
colours *n* banner, ensign, flag, standard.
column *n* pillar, pilaster; file, line, row.
coma *n* drowsiness, lethargy, somnolence, stupor, torpor; bunch, clump, cluster, tuft.
comatose *adj* drowsy, lethargic, sleepy, somnolent, stupefied.
comb *vb* card, curry, dress, groom, rake, unknot, untangle; rake, ransack, rummage, scour, search. * *n* card, hatchel, ripple; harrow, rake.
combat *vb* contend, contest, fight, struggle, war; battle, oppose, resist, struggle, withstand. * *n* action, affair, battle, brush, conflict, contest, encounter, fight, skirmish.
combative *adj* belligerent, contentious, militant, pugnacious, quarrelsome.
combination *n* association, conjunction, connection, union; alliance, cartel, coalition, confederacy, consolidation, league, merger, syndicate; cabal, clique, conspiracy, faction, junta, ring; amalgamation, compound, mixture.
combine *vb* cooperate, merge, pool, unite; amalgamate, blend, incorporate, mix.
combustible *adj* consumable, inflammable.
come *vb* advance, approach; arise, ensue, flow, follow, issue, originate, proceed, result; befall, betide, happen, occur.
comely *adj* becoming, decent, decorous, fitting, seemly, suitable; beautiful, fair, graceful, handsome, personable, pretty, symmetrical.
comfort *vb* alleviate, animate, cheer, console, encourage, enliven, gladden, inspirit, invigorate, refresh, revive, solace, soothe, strengthen. * *n* aid, assistance, countenance, help, support, succour; consolation, solace, encouragement, relief; ease, enjoyment, peace, satisfaction.
comfortable *adj* acceptable, agreeable, delightful, enjoyable, grateful, gratifying, happy, pleasant, pleasurable, welcome; commodious, convenient, easeful, snug; painless.
comfortless *adj* bleak, cheerless, desolate, drear, dreary, forlorn, miserable, wretched; broken-hearted, desolate, disconsolate, forlorn, heartbroken, inconsolable, miserable, woe-begone, wretched.
comical *adj* amusing, burlesque, comic, diverting, droll, farcical, funny, humorous, laughable, ludicrous, sportive, whimsical.
coming *adj* approaching, arising, arriving, ensuing, eventual, expected, forthcoming, future, imminent, issuing, looming, nearing, prospective, ultimate; emergent, emerging, successful; due, owed, owing. * *n* advent, approach, arrival; imminence, imminency, nearness; apparition, appearance, disclosure, emergence, manifestation, materialization, occurrence, presentation, revelation, rising.
comity *n* affability, amenity, civility, courtesy, politeness, suavity, urbanity.
command *vb* bid, charge, direct, enjoin, order, require; control, dominate, govern, lead, rule, sway; claim, challenge, compel, demand, exact. * *n* behest, bidding, charge, commandment, direction, hest, injunction, mandate, order, requirement, requisition; ascendency, authority, dominion, control, government, power, rule, sway, supremacy.
commander *n* captain, chief, chieftain, commandment, head, leader.
commemorate *vb* celebrate, keep, observe, solemnize.
commence *vb* begin, inaugurate, initiate, institute, open, originate, start.
commend *vb* assign, bespeak, confide, recommend, remit; commit, entrust, yield; applaud, approve, eulogize, extol, laud, praise.
commendation *n* approbation, approval, good opinion, recommendation; praise, encomium, eulogy, panegyric.
commensurate *adj* commeasurable, commensurable; co-extensive, conterminous, equal; adequate, appropriate, corresponding, due, proportionate, proportioned, sufficient.
comment *vb* animadvert, annotate, criticize, explain, interpret, note, remark. * *n* annotation, elucidation, explanation, exposition, illustration, commentary, note, gloss; animadversion, observation, remark.
commentator *n* annotator, commentator, critic, expositor, expounder, interpreter.
commerce *n* business, exchange, dealing, trade, traffic; communication, communion, intercourse.
commercial *adj* mercantile, trading.
commination *n* denunciation, menace, threat, threatening.

commingle *vb* amalgamate, blend, combine, commix, intermingle, intermix, join, mingle, mix, unite.
comminute *vb* bray, bruise, grind, levigate, powder, pulverize, triturate.
commiserate *vb* compassionate, condole, pity, sympathize.
commiseration *n* compassion, pitying; condolence, pity, sympathy.
commission *vb* authorize, empower; delegate, depute. * *n* doing, perpetration; care, charge, duty, employment, errand, office, task, trust; allowance, compensation, fee, rake-off.
commissioner *n* agent, delegate, deputy.
commit *vb* confide, consign, delegate, entrust, remand; consign, deposit, lay, place, put, relegate, resign; do, enact, perform, perpetrate; imprison; engage, implicate, pledge.
commix *vb* amalgamate, blend, combine, commingle, compound, intermingle, mingle, mix, unite.
commodious *adj* advantageous, ample, comfortable, convenient, fit, proper, roomy, spacious, suitable, useful.
commodity *n* goods, merchandise, produce, wares.
common *adj* collective, public; general, useful; common-place, customary, everyday, familiar, frequent, habitual, usual; banal, hackneyed, stale, threadbare, trite; indifferent, inferior, low, ordinary, plebeian, popular, undistinguished, vulgar.
commonplace *adj* common, hackneyed, ordinary, stale, threadbare, trite. * *n* banality, cliché, platitude; jotting, memoir, memorandum, note, reminder.
common-sense, common-sensical *adj* practical, sagacious, sensible, sober.
commotion *n* agitation, disturbance, ferment, perturbation, welter; ado, bustle, disorder, disturbance, hurly-burly, pother, tumult, turbulence, turmoil.
communicate *vb* bestow, confer, convey, give, impart, transmit; acquaint, announce, declare, disclose, divulge, publish, reveal, unfold; commune, converse, correspond.
communication *n* conveyance, disclosure, giving, imparting, transmittal; commence, conference, conversation, converse, correspondence, intercourse; announcement, dispatch, information, message, news.
communicative *adj* affable, chatty, conversable, free, open, sociable, unreserved.
communion *n* converse, fellowship, intercourse, participation; Eucharist, holy communion, Lord's Supper, sacrament.
community *n* commonwealth, people, public, society; association, brotherhood, college, society; likeness, participancy, sameness, similarity.
compact[1] *n* agreement, arrangement, bargain, concordant, contract, covenant, convention, pact, stipulation, treaty.
compact[2] *vb* compress, condense, pack, press; bind, consolidate, unite. * *adj* close, compressed, condensed, dense, firm, solid; brief, compendious, concise, laconic, pithy, pointed, sententious, short, succinct, terse.
companion *n* accomplice, ally, associate, comrade, compeer, confederate, consort, crony, friend, fellow, mate; partaker, participant, participator, partner, sharer.
companionable *adj* affable, conversable, familiar, friendly, genial, neighbourly, sociable.
companionship *n* association, fellowship, friendship, intercourse, society.
company *n* assemblage, assembly, band, bevy, body, circle, collection, communication, concourse, congregation, coterie, crew, crowd, flock, gang, gathering, group, herd, rout, set, syndicate, troop; party; companionship, fellowship, guests, society, visitor, visitors; association, copartnership, corporation, firm, house, partnership.
compare *vb* assimilate, balance, collate, parallel; liken, resemble.
comparison *n* collation, compare, estimate; simile, similitude.
compartment *n* bay, cell, division, pigeonhole, section.
compass *vb* embrace, encompass, enclose, encircle, environ, surround; beleaguer, beset, besiege, block, blockade, invest; accomplish, achieve, attain, carry, consummate, effect, obtain, perform, procure, realize; contrive, devise, intend, meditate, plot, purpose. * *n* bound, boundary, extent, gamut, limit, range, reach, register, scope, stretch; circuit, round.
compassion *n* clemency, commiseration, condolence, fellow-feeling, heart, humanity, kind-heartedness, kindness, kindliness, mercy, pity, rue, ruth, sorrow, sympathy, tenderheartedness, tenderness.
compassionate *adj* benignant, clement, commiserative, gracious, kind, merciful, pitying, ruthful, sympathetic, tender.
compatible *adj* accordant, agreeable to, congruous, consistent, consonant, reconcilable, suitable.
compeer *n* associate, comrade, companion, equal, fellow, mate, peer.
compel *vb* constrain, force, coerce, drive, necessitate, oblige; bend, bow, subdue, subject.
compend *n* abbreviation, abridgement, abstract, breviary, brief, compendium, conspectus, digest, epitome, précis, summary, syllabus, synopsis.
compendious *adj* abbreviated, abridged, brief, comprehensive, concise, short, succinct, summary.
compensate *vb* counterbalance, counterpoise, countervail; guerdon, recompense, reimburse, remunerate, reward; indemnify, reimburse, repay, requite; atone.
compensation *n* pay, payment, recompense, remuneration, reward, salary; amends, atonement, indemnification, indemnity, reparation, requital, satisfaction; balance, counterpoise, equalization, offset.
compete *vb* contend, contest, cope, emulate, rival, strive, struggle, vie.
competence *n* ability, capability, capacity, fitness, qualification, suitableness; adequacy, adequateness, enough, sufficiency.
competent *adj* able, capable, clever, equal, endowed, qualified; adapted, adequate, convenient, fit, sufficient, suitable.
competition *n* contest, emulation, rivalry, rivals.
competitor *n* adversary, antagonist, contestant, emulator, opponent.
compile *vb* compose, prepare, write; arrange, collect, select.
complacency *n* content, contentment, gratification, pleasure, satisfaction; affability, civility, complaisance, courtesy, politeness.
complacent *adj* contented, gratified, pleased, satisfied; affable, civil, complaisant, courteous, easy, gracious, grateful, obliging, polite, urbane.
complain *vb* bemoan, bewail, deplore, grieve, groan, grouch, grumble, lament, moan, murmur, repine, whine.
complainant *n* accuser, plaintiff.
complaining *adj* fault-finding, murmuring, querulous.
complaint *n* grievance, gripe, grumble, lament, lamentation, plaint, murmur, wail; ail, ailment, annoyance, disease, disorder, illness, indisposition, malady, sickness; accusation, charge, information.
complete *vb* accomplish, achieve, conclude, consummate, do, effect, effectuate, end, execute, finish, fulfil, perfect, perform, realize, terminate. * *adj* clean, consummate, faultless, full, perfect, perform, thorough; all, entire, integral, total, unbroken, undiminished, undivided, unimpaired, whole; accomplished, achieved, completed, concluded, consummated, ended, finished.
completion *n* accomplishing, accomplishment, achieving, conclusion, consummation, effecting, effectuation, ending, execution, finishing, perfecting, performance, termination.
complex *adj* composite, compound, compounded, manifold, mingled, mixed; complicate, complicated, entangled, intricate, involved, knotty, mazy, tangled. * *n* complexus, complication, involute, skein, tangle; entirety, integration, network, totality, whole; compulsion, fixation, obsession, preoccupation, prepossession; prejudice.
complexion *n* colour, hue, tint.
complexity *n* complication, entanglement, intricacy, involution.
compliance *n* concession, obedience, submission; acquiescence, agreement, assent, concurrence, consent; compliancy, yieldingness.
complicate *vb* confuse, entangle, interweave, involve.
complication *n* complexity, confusion, entanglement, intricacy; combination, complexus, mixture.
compliment *vb* commend, congratulate, eulogize, extol, flatter, laud, praise. * *n* admiration, commendation, courtesy, encomium, eulogy, favour, flattery, honour, laudation, praise, tribute.
complimentary *adj* commendatory, congratulatory, encomiastic, eulogistic, flattering, laudatory, panegyrical.

comply *vb* adhere to, complete, discharge, fulfil, meet, observe, perform, satisfy; accede, accord, acquiesce, agree to, assent, consent to, yield.

component *adj* composing, constituent, constituting. * *n* constituent, element, ingredient, part.

comport *vb* accord, agree, coincide, correspond, fit, harmonize, square, suit, tally.

compose *vb* build, compact, compound, constitute, form, make, synthesize; contrive, create, frame, imagine, indite, invent, write; adjust, arrange, regulate, settle; appease, assuage, calm, pacify, quell, quiet, soothe, still, tranquillize.

composed *adj* calm, collected, cool, imperturbable, placid, quiet, sedate, self-possessed, tranquil, undisturbed, unmoved, unruffled.

composite *adj* amalgamated, combined, complex, compounded, mixed; integrated, unitary. * *n* admixture, amalgam, blend, combination, composition, compound, mixture, unification.

composition *n* constitution, construction, formation, framing, making; compound, mixture; arrangement, combination, conjunction, make-up, synthesize, union; invention, opus, piece, production, writing; agreement, arrangement, compromise.

compost *n* fertilizer, fertilizing, manure, mixture.

composure *n* calmness, coolness, equanimity, placidity, sedateness, quiet, self-possession, serenity, tranquillity.

compotation *n* conviviality, frolicking, jollification, revelling, revelry, rousing, wassailling; bacchanal, carousal, carouse, debauch, orgy, revel, saturnalia, wassail.

compound[1] *vb* amalgamate, blend, combine, intermingle, intermix, mingle, mix, unite; adjust, arrange, compose, compromise, settle. * *adj* complex, composite. * *n* combination, composition, mixture; farrago, hodgepodge, jumble, medley, mess, olio.

compound[2] *n* enclosure, garden, yard.

comprehend *vb* comprise, contain, embrace, embody, enclose, include, involve; apprehend, conceive, discern, grasp, know, imagine, master, perceive, see, understand.

comprehension *n* comprising, embracing, inclusion; compass, domain, embrace, field, limits, province, range, reach, scope, sphere, sweep; connotation, depth, force, intention; conception, grasp, intelligence, understanding; intellect, intelligence, mind, reason, understanding.

comprehensive *adj* all-embracing, ample, broad, capacious, compendious, extensive, full, inclusive, large, sweeping, wide.

compress *vb* abbreviate, condense, constrict, contract, crowd, press, shorten, squeeze, summarize.

compression *n* condensation, confining, pinching, pressing, squeezing; brevity, pithiness, succinctness, terseness.

comprise *vb* comprehend, contain, embody, embrace, enclose, include, involve.

compromise *vb* adjust, arbitrate, arrange, compose, compound, settle; imperil, jeopardize, prejudice; commit, engage, implicate, pledge; agree, compound. * *n* adjustment, agreement, composition, settlement.

compulsion *n* coercion, constraint, force, forcing, pressure, urgency.

compulsory *adj* coercive, compelling, constraining; binding, enforced, imperative, necessary, obligatory, unavoidable.

compunction *n* contrition, misgiving, penitence, qualm, regret, reluctance, remorse, repentance, sorrow.

computable *adj* calculable, numerable, reckonable.

computation *n* account, calculation, estimate, reckoning, score, tally.

compute *vb* calculate, count, enumerate, estimate, figure, measure, number, rate, reckon, sum.

comrade *n* accomplice, ally, associate, chum, companion, compatriot, compeer, crony, fellow, mate, pal.

concatenate *vb* connect, join, link, unite.

concatenation *n* connection; chain, congeries, linking, series, sequence, succession.

concave *adj* depressed, excavated, hollow, hollowed, scooped.

conceal *vb* bury, cover, screen, secrete; disguise, dissemble, mask.

concede *vb* grant, surrender, yield; acknowledge, admit, allow, confess, grant.

conceit *n* belief, conception, fancy, idea, image, imagination, notion, thought; caprice, illusion, vagary, whim; estimate, estimation, impression, judgement, opinion; conceitedness, egoism, self-complacency, priggishness, priggery, self-conceit, self-esteem, self-sufficiency, vanity; crotchet, point, quip, quirk.

conceited *adj* egotistical, opinionated, opinionative, overweening, self-conceited, vain.

conceivable *adj* imaginable, picturable; cogitable, comprehensible, intelligible, rational, thinkable.

conceive *vb* create, contrive, devise, form, plan, purpose; fancy, imagine; comprehend, fathom, think, understand; assume, imagine, suppose; bear, become pregnant.

concern *vb* affect, belong to, interest, pertain to, regard, relate to, touch; disquiet, disturb, trouble. * *n* affair, business, matter, transaction; concernment, consequence, importance, interest, moment, weight; anxiety, care, carefulness, solicitude, worry; business, company, establishment, firm, house.

concert *vb* combine, concoct, contrive, design, devise, invent, plan, plot, project. * *n* agreement, concord, concordance, cooperation, harmony, union, unison.

concession *n* acquiescence, assent, cessation, compliance, surrender, yielding; acknowledgement, allowance, boon, confession, grant, privilege.

conciliate *vb* appease, pacify, placate, propitiate, reconcile; engage, gain, secure, win, win over.

concise *adj* brief, compact, compendious, comprehensive, compressed, condensed, crisp, laconic, pithy, pointed, pregnant, sententious, short, succinct, summary, terse.

conclave *n* assembly, cabinet, council.

conclude *vb* close, end, finish, terminate; deduce, gather, infer, judge; decide, determine, judge; arrange, complete, settle; bar, hinder, restrain, stop; decide, determine, resolve.

conclusion *n* deduction, inference; decision, determination, judgement; close, completion, end, event, finale, issue, termination, upshot; arrangement, closing, effecting, establishing, settlement.

conclusive *adj* clinching, convincing, decisive, irrefutable, unanswerable; final, ultimate.

concoct *vb* brew, contrive, design, devise, frame, hatch, invent, mature, plan, plot, prepare, project.

concomitant *adj* accessory, accompanying, attendant, attending, coincident, concurrent, conjoined. * *n* accessory, accompaniment, attendant.

concord *n* agreement, amity, friendship, harmony, peace, unanimity, union, unison, unity; accord, adaptation, concordance, consonance, harmony.

concordant *adj* accordant, agreeable, agreeing, harmonious.

concordat *n* agreement, bargain, compact, convention, covenant, stipulation, treaty.

concourse *n* confluence, conflux, congress; assemblage, assembly, collection, crowd, gathering, meeting, multitude, throng.

concrete *vb* cake, congeal, coagulate, harden, solidify, thicken. * *adj* compact, consolidated, firm, solid, solidified; agglomerated, complex, conglomerated, compound, concreted; completely, entire, individualized, total. * *n* compound, concretion, mixture; cement.

concubine *n* hetaera, hetaira, mistress, paramour.

concupiscence *n* lasciviousness, lechery, lewdness, lust, pruriency.

concupiscent *adj* carnal, lascivious, lecherous, lewd, libidinous, lustful, prurient, rampant, salacious, sensual.

concur *vb* accede, acquiesce, agree, approve, assent, coincide, consent, harmonize; combine, conspire, cooperate, help.

concurrent *adj* agreeing, coincident, harmonizing, meeting, uniting; associate, associated, attendant, concomitant, conjoined, united.

concussion *n* agitation, shaking; clash, crash, shock.

condemn *vb* adjudge, convict, doom, sentence; disapprove, proscribe, reprobate; blame, censure, damn, deprecate, disapprove, reprehend, reprove, upbraid.

condemnation *n* conviction, doom, judgement, penalty, sentence; banning, disapproval, proscription; guilt, sin, wrong; blame, censure, disapprobation, disapproval, reprobation, reproof.
condemnatory *adj* blaming, censuring, damnatory, deprecatory, disapproving, reproachful.
condense *vb* compress, concentrate, consolidate, densify, thicken; abbreviate, abridge, contract, curtail, diminish, epitomize, reduce, shorten, summarize; liquefy.
condescend *vb* deign, vouchsafe; descend, stoop, submit.
condescension *n* affability, civility, courtesy, deference, favour, graciousness, obeisance.
condign *adj* adequate, deserved, just, merited, suitable.
condiment *n* appetizer, relish, sauce, seasoning.
condition *vb* postulate, specify, stipulate; groom, prepare, qualify, ready, train; acclimatize, accustom, adapt, adjust, familiarize, habituate, naturalize; attune, commission, fix, overhaul, prepare, recondition, repair, service, tune. * *n* case, circumstances, plight, predicament, situation, state; class, estate, grade, rank, station; arrangement, consideration, provision, proviso, stipulation; attendant, necessity, postulate, precondition, prerequisite.
condole *vb* commiserate, compassionate, console, sympathize.
condonation *n* forgiveness, overlooking, pardon.
condone *vb* excuse, forgive, pardon.
conduce *vb* contribute, lead, tend; advance, aid.
conducive *adj* conducting, contributing, instrumental, promotive, subservient, subsidiary.
conduct *vb* convoy, direct, escort, lead; administer, command, govern, lead, preside, superintend; manage, operate, regulate; direct, lead. * *n* administration, direction, guidance, leadership, management; convoy, escort, guard; actions, bearing, behaviour, career, carriage, demeanour, deportment, manners.
conductor *n* guide, lead; director, leader, manager; propagator, transmitter.
conduit *n* canal, channel, duct, passage, pipe, tube.
confederacy *n* alliance, coalition, compact, confederation, covenant, federation, league, union.
confer *vb* advise, consult, converse, deliberate, discourse, parley, talk; bestow, give, grant, vouchsafe.
confess *vb* acknowledge, admit, avow, own; admit, concede, grant, recognize; attest, exhibit, manifest, prove, show; shrive.
confession *n* acknowledgement, admission, avowal.
confide *vb* commit, consign, entrust, trust.
confidence *n* belief, certitude, dependence, faith, reliance, trust; aplomb, assurance, boldness, cocksureness, courage, firmness, intrepidity, self-reliance; secrecy.
confident *adj* assured, certain, cocksure, positive, sure: bold, presumptuous. sanguine, undaunted.
confidential *adj* intimate, private, secret; faithful, trustworthy.
configuration *n* conformation, contour, figure, form, gestalt, outline, shape.
confine *vb* restrain, shut in, shut up; immure, imprison, incarcerate, impound, jail, mew; bound, circumscribe, limit, restrict. * *n* border, boundary, frontier, limit.
confinement *n* restraint; captivity, duress, durance, immurement, imprisonment, incarceration; childbed, childbirth, delivery, lying-in, parturition.
confines *npl* borders, boundaries, edges, frontiers, limits, marches, precincts.
confirm *vb* assure, establish, fix, settle; strengthen; authenticate, avouch, corroborate, countersign, endorse, substantiate, verify; bind, ratify, sanction.
confirmation *n* establishment, settlement; corroboration, proof, substantiation, verification.
confiscate *vb* appropriate, forfeit, seize.
conflict *vb* clash, combat, contend, contest, disagree, fight, interfere, strive, struggle. * *n* battle, collision, combat, contention, contest, encounter, fight, struggle; antagonism, clashing, disagreement, discord, disharmony, inconsistency, interference, opposition.
confluence *n* conflux, junction, meeting, union; army, assemblage, assembly, concourse, crowd, collection, horde, host, multitude, swarm.
confluent *adj* blending, concurring, flowing, joining, meeting, merging, uniting.
conform *vb* accommodate, adapt, adjust; agree, comport, correspond, harmonize, square, tally.
conformation *n* accordance, agreement, compliance, conformity; configuration, figure, form, manner, shape, structure.
confound *vb* confuse; baffle, bewilder, embarrass, flurry, mystify, nonplus, perplex, pose; amaze, astonish, astound, bewilder, dumfound, paralyse, petrify, startle, stun, stupefy, surprise; annihilate, demolish, destroy, overthrow, overwhelm, ruin; abash, confuse, discompose, disconcert, mortify, shame.
confront *vb* face; challenge, contrapose, encounter, oppose, threaten.
confuse *vb* blend, confound, intermingle, mingle, mix; derange, disarrange, disorder, jumble, mess, muddle; darken, obscure, perplex; befuddle, bewilder, embarrass, flabbergast, flurry, fluster, mystify, nonplus, pose; abash, confound, discompose, disconcert, mortify, shame.
confusion *n* anarchy, chaos, clutter, confusedness, derangement, disarrangement, disarray, disorder, jumble, muddle; agitation, commotion, ferment, stir, tumult, turmoil; astonishment, bewilderment, distraction, embarrassment, fluster, fuddle, perplexity; abashment, discomfiture, mortification, shame; annihilation, defeat, demolition, destruction, overthrow, ruin.
confute *vb* disprove, oppugn, overthrow, refute, silence.
congeal *vb* benumb, condense, curdle, freeze, stiffen, thicken.
congenial *adj* kindred, similar, sympathetic; adapted, agreeable, natural, suitable, suited; agreeable, favourable, genial.
congenital *adj* connate, connatural, inborn.
congeries *n* accumulation, agglomeration, aggregate, aggregation, collection, conglomeration, crowd, cluster, heap, mass.
congratulate *vb* compliment, felicitate, gratulate, greet, hail, salute.
congregate *vb* assemble, collect, convene, convoke, gather, muster; gather, meet, swarm, throng.
congregation *n* assemblage, assembly, collection, gathering, meeting.
congress *n* assembly, conclave, conference, convention, convocation, council, diet, meeting.
congruity *n* agreement, conformity, consistency, fitness, suitableness.
congruous *adj* accordant, agreeing, compatible, consistent, consonant, suitable; appropriate, befitting, fit, meet, proper, seemly.
conjecture *vb* assume, guess, hypothesize, imagine, suppose. surmise, suspect; dare say, fancy, presume. * *n* assumption, guess, hypothesis, supposition, surmise, theory.
conjoin *vb* associate, combine, connect, join, unite.
conjugal *adj* bridal, connubial, hymeneal, matrimonial, nuptial.
conjuncture *n* combination, concurrence, connection; crisis, emergency, exigency, juncture.
conjure *vb* adjure, beg, beseech, crave, entreat, implore, invoke, pray, supplicate; bewitch, charm, enchant, fascinate; juggle.
connect *vb* associate, conjoin, combine, couple, hyphenate, interlink, join, link, unite; cohere, interlock.
connected *adj* associated, coupled, joined, united; akin, allied, related; communicating.
connection *n* alliance, association, dependence, junction, union; commerce, communication, intercourse; affinity, relationship; kindred, kinsman, relation, relative.
connive *vb* collude, conspire, plot, scheme.
connoisseur *n* critic, expert, virtuoso.
connotation *n* comprehension, depth, force, intent, intention, meaning.
connubial *adj* bridal, conjugal, hymeneal, matrimonial, nuptial.
conquer *vb* beat, checkmate, crush, defeat, discomfit, humble, master, overcome, overpower, overthrow, prevail, quell, reduce, rout, subdue, subjugate, vanquish; overcome, surmount.

conqueror *n* humbler, subduer, subjugator, vanquisher; superior, victor, winner.

conquest *n* defeat, discomfiture, mastery, overthrow, reduction, subjection, subjugation; triumph, victor; winning.

consanguinity *n* affinity, kinship, blood-relationship, kin, kindred, relationship.

conscientious *adj* careful, exact, fair, faithful, high-principled, honest, honourable, incorruptible, just, scrupulous, straightforward, uncorrupt, upright.

conscious *adj* intelligent, knowing, percipient, sentient; intellectual, rational, reasoning, reflecting, self-conscious, thinking; apprised, awake, aware, cognizant, percipient, sensible; self-admitted, self-accusing.

consecrate *vb* dedicate, devote, ordain; hallow, sanctify, venerate.

consecutive *adj* following, succeeding.

consent *vb* agree, allow, assent, concur, permit, yield; accede, acquiesce, comply. * *n* approval, assent, concurrence, permission; accord, agreement, consensus, concord, cooperation, harmony, unison; acquiescence, compliance.

consequence *n* effect, end, event, issue, result; conclusion, deduction, inference; concatenation, connection, consecution; concern, distinction, importance, influence, interest, moment, standing, weight.

consequential *adj* consequent, following, resulting, sequential; arrogant, conceited, inflated, pompous, pretentious, self-important, self-sufficient, vainglorious.

conservation *n* guardianship, maintenance, preservation, protection.

conservative *adj* conservatory, moderate, moderationist; preservative; reactionary, unprogressive. * *n* die-hard, reactionary, redneck, rightist, right-winger; moderate; preservative.

conserve *vb* keep, maintain, preserve, protect, save, sustain, uphold. * *n* confit, confection, jam, preserve, sweetmeat.

consider *vb* attend, brood, contemplate, examine, heed, mark, mind, ponder, reflect, revolve, study, weigh; care for, consult, envisage, regard, respect; cogitate, deliberate, mediate, muse, ponder, reflect, ruminate, think; account, believe, deem, hold, judge, opine.

considerate *adj* circumspect, deliberate, discrete, judicious, provident, prudent, serious, sober, staid, thoughtful; charitable, forbearing, patient.

consideration *n* attention, cogitation, contemplation, deliberation, notice, heed, meditation, pondering, reflection, regard; consequence, importance, important, moment, significant, weight; account, cause, ground, motive, reason, sake, score.

consign *vb* deliver, hand over, remand, resign, transfer, transmit; commit, entrust; ship.

consignor *n* sender, shipper, transmitter.

consistency *n* compactness, consistence, density, thickness; agreement, compatibility, conformableness, congruity, consonance, correspondence, harmony.

consistent *adj* accordant, agreeing, comfortable, compatible, congruous, consonant, correspondent, harmonious, logical.

consolation *n* alleviation, comfort, condolence, encouragement, relief, solace.

console *vb* assuage, calm, cheer, comfort, encourage, solace, relieve, soothe.

consolidate *vb* cement, compact, compress, condense, conduce, harden, solidify, thicken; combine, conjoin, fuse, unite.

consolidation *n* solidification; combination, union.

consonance *n* accord, concord, conformity, harmony; accord, accordance, agreement, congruence, congruity, consistency, unison.

consonant *adj* accordant, according, harmonious; compatible, congruous, consistent. * *n* articulation, letter-sound.

consort *vb* associate, fraternize. * *n* associate, companion, fellow, husband, spouse, partner.

conspectus *n* abstract, brief, breviary, compend, compendium, digest, epitome, outline, precis, summary, syllabus, synopsis.

conspicuous *adj* apparent, clear, discernible, glaring, manifest, noticeable, perceptible, plain, striking, visible; celebrated, distinguished, eminent, famed, famous, illustrious, marked, noted, outstanding, pre-eminent, prominent, remarkable, signal.

conspiracy *n* cabal, collusion, confederation, intrigue, league, machination, plot, scheme.

conspire *vb* concur, conduce, cooperate; combine, compass, contrive, devise, project; confederate, contrive, hatch, plot, scheme.

constancy *n* immutability, permanence, stability, unchangeableness; regularity, unchangeableness; decision, determination, firmness, inflexibility, resolution, steadfastness, steadiness; devotion, faithfulness, fidelity, loyalty, trustiness, truth.

constant *adj* abiding, enduring, fixed, immutable, invariable, invariant, permanent, perpetual, stable, unalterable, unchanging, unvaried; certain, regular, stated, uniform; determined, firm, resolute, stanch, steadfast, steady, unanswering, undeviating, unmoved, unshaken, unwavering; assiduous, diligent, persevering, sedulous, tenacious, unremitting; continual, continuous, incessant, perpetual, sustained, unbroken, uninterrupted; devoted, faithful, loyal, true, trusty.

consternation *n* alarm, amazement, awe, bewilderment, dread, fear, fright, horror, panic, terror.

constituent *adj* component, composing, constituting, forming; appointing, electoral. * *n* component, element, ingredient, principal; elector, voter.

constitute *vb* compose, form, make; appoint, delegate, depute, empower; enact, establish, fix, set up.

constitution *n* establishment, formation, make-up, organization, structure; character, characteristic, disposition, form, habit, humour, peculiarity, physique, quality, spirit, temper, temperament.

constitutional *adj* congenital, connate, inborn, inbred, inherent, innate, natural, organic; lawful, legal, legitimate. * *n* airing, exercise, promenade, stretch, walk.

constrain *vb* coerce, compel, drive, force; chain, confine, curb, enthral, hold, restrain; draw, impel, urge.

constriction *n* compression, constraint, contraction.

construct *vb* build, fabricate, erect, raise, set up; arrange, establish, form, found, frame, institute, invent, make, organize, originate.

construction *n* building, erection, fabrication; configuration, conformation, figure, form, formation, made, shape, structure; explanation, interpretation, rendering, version.

construe *vb* analyse, explain, expound, interpret, parse, render, translate.

consult *vb* advise, ask, confer, counsel, deliberate, interrogate, question; consider, regard.

consume *vb* absorb, decay, destroy, devour, dissipate, exhaust, expend, lavish, lessen, spend, squander, vanish, waste.

consummate[1] *vb* accomplish, achieve, compass, complete, conclude, crown, effect, effectuate, end, execute, finish, perfect, perform.

consummate[2] *adj* complete, done, effected, finished, fulfilled, perfect, supreme.

consumption *n* decay, decline, decrease, destruction, diminution, expenditure, use, waste; atrophy, emaciation.

contact *vb* hit, impinge, touch; approach, be heard, communicate with, reach. * *n* approximation, contiguity, junction, juxtaposition, taction, tangency, touch.

contagion *n* infection; contamination, corruption, infection, taint.

contagious *adj* catching, epidemic, infectious; deadly, pestiferous, pestilential, poisonous.

contain *vb* accommodate, comprehend, comprise, embody, embrace, enclose, include; check, restrain.

contaminate *vb* corrupt, defile, deprave, infect, poison, pollute, soil, stain, sully, taint, tarnish, vitiate.

contamination *n* contaminating, defilement, defiling, polluting, pollution; abomination, defilement, impurity, foulness, infection, pollution, stain, taint, uncleanness.

contemn *vb* despise, disdain, disregard, neglect, scorn, scout, slight, spurn.

contemplate *vb* behold, gaze upon, observe, survey; consider, dwell on, meditate on, muse on, ponder, reflect upon, study, survey, think about; design, intend, mean, plan, purpose.

contemplation *n* cogitation, deliberation, meditation, pondering, reflection, speculation, study, thought; prospect, prospective, view; expectation.

contemporaneous *adj* coetaneous, coeval, coexistent, coexisting, coincident, concomitant, contemporary, simultaneous, synchronous.

contemporary *adj* coetaneous, coeval, coexistent, coexisting, coincident, concomitant, concurrent, contemporaneous, current, present, simultaneous, synchronous; advanced, modern, modernistic, progressive, up-to-date. * *n* coeval, coexistent, compeer, fellow.

contempt *n* contumely, derision, despite, disdain, disregard, misprision, mockery, scorn, slight.

contemptible *adj* abject, base, despicable, haughty, insolent, insulting, low, mean, paltry, pitiful, scurvy, sorry, supercilious, vile, worthless.

contemptuous *adj* arrogant, contumelious, disdainful, haughty, insolent, insulting, scornful, sneering, supercilious.

contend *vb* battle, combat, compete, contest, fight, strive, struggle, vie; argue, debate, dispute, litigate; affirm, assert, contest, maintain.

content[1] *n* essence, gist, meaning, meat, stuff, substance; capacity, measure, space, volume.

content[2] *vb* appease, delight, gladden, gratify, humour, indulge, please, satisfy, suffice. * *adj* agreeable, contented, happy, pleased, satisfied. * *n* contentment, ease, peace, satisfaction.

contention *n* discord, dissension, feud, squabble, strife, quarrel, rapture, wrangle, wrangling; altercation, bickering, contest, controversy, debate, dispute, litigation, logomachy.

contentious *adj* belligerent, cross, litigious, peevish, perverse, petulant, pugnacious, quarrelsome, wrangling; captious, caviling, disputatious.

conterminous *adj* adjacent, adjoining, contiguous; co-extensive, coincident, commensurate.

contest *vb* argue, contend, controvert, debate, dispute, litigate, question; strive, struggle; compete, cope, fight, vie. * *n* altercation, contention, controversy, difference, dispute, debate, quarrel; affray, battle, bout, combat, conflict, encounter, fight, match, scrimmage, struggle, tussle; competition, contention, rivalry.

contexture *n* composition, constitution, framework, structure, texture.

contiguous *adj* abutting, adjacent, adjoining, beside, bordering, conterminous, meeting, near, neighbouring, touching.

continent[1] *n* mainland, mass, tract.

continent[2] *adj* abstemious, abstinent, chaste, restrained, self-commanding, self-controlled, moderate, sober, temperate.

contingency *n* accidentalness, chance, fortuity, uncertainty; accident, casualty, event, incident, occurrence.

contingent *adj* accidental, adventitious, casual, fortuitous, incidental; conditional, dependent, uncertain. * *n* proportion, quota, share.

continual *adj* constant, constant, perpetual, unceasing, uninterrupted, unremitting; endless, eternal, everlasting, interminable, perennial, permanent, perpetual, unending; constant, oft-repeated.

continuance *n* abiding, continuation, duration, endurance, lasting, persistence, stay; continuation, extension, perpetuation, prolongation, protraction; concatenation, connection, sequence, succession; constancy, endurance, perseverance, persistence.

continue *vb* endure, last, remain; abide, linger, remain, stay, tarry; endure, persevere, persist, stick; extend, prolong, perpetuate, protract.

continuous *adj* connected, continued, extended, prolonged, unbroken, unintermitted, uninterrupted.

contour *n* outline, profile.

contraband *adj* banned, forbidden, illegal, illicit, interdicted, prohibited, smuggled, unlawful.

contract *vb* abbreviate, abridge, condense, confine, curtail, diminish, epitomize, lessen, narrow, reduce, shorten; absorb, catch, incur, get, make, take; constrict, shrink, shrivel, wrinkle; agree, bargain, covenant, engage, pledge, stipulate. * *n* agreement, arrangement, bargain, bond, compact, concordat, covenant, convention, engagement, pact, stipulation, treaty.

contradict *vb* assail, challenge, controvert, deny, dispute, gainsay, impugn, traverse; abrogate, annul, belie, counter, disallow, negative, contravene, counteract, oppose, thwart.

contradiction *n* controversion, denial, gainsaying; antinomy, clashing, contrariety, incongruity, opposition.

contradictory *adj* antagonistic, contrary, incompatible, inconsistent, negating, opposed, opposite, repugnant.

contrariety *n* antagonism, clashing, contradiction, contrast, opposition, repugnance.

contrary *adj* adverse, counter, discordant, opposed, opposing, opposite; antagonistic, conflicting, contradictory, repugnant, retroactive; forward, headstrong, obstinate, refractory, stubborn, unruly, wayward, perverse. * *n* antithesis, converse, obverse, opposite, reverse.

contrast *vb* compare, differentiate, distinguish, oppose. * *n* contrariety, difference, opposition; comparison, distinction.

contravene *vb* abrogate, annul, contradict, counteract, countervail, cross, go against, hinder, interfere, nullify, oppose, set aside, thwart.

contravention *n* abrogation, contradiction, interference, opposition, transgression, traversal, violation.

contretemps *n* accident, mischance, mishap.

contribute *vb* bestow, donate, give, grant, subscribe; afford, aid, furnish, supply; concur, conduce, conspire, cooperate, minister, serve, tend.

contribution *n* bestowal, bestowment, grant; donation, gift, offering, subscription.

contrite *adj* humble, penitent, repentant, sorrowful.

contrition *n* compunction, humiliation, penitence, regret, remorse, repentance, self-condemnation, self-reproach, sorrow.

contrivance *n* design, inventive, inventiveness; contraption, device, gadget, invention, machine; artifice, device, fabrication, machination, plan, plot, scheme, shift, stratagem.

contrive *vb* arrange, brew, concoct, design, devise, effect, form, frame, hatch, invent, plan, project; consider, plan, plot, scheme; manage, make out.

control *vb* command, direct, dominate, govern, manage, oversee, sway, regulate, rule, superintend; bridle, check, counteract, curb, check, hinder, repress, restrain. * *n* ascendency, command, direction, disposition, dominion, government, guidance, mastery, oversight, regiment, regulation, rule, superintendence, supremacy, sway.

controversy *n* altercation, argument, contention, debate, discussion, disputation, dispute, logomachy, polemics, quarrel, strife; lawsuit.

contumacious *adj* disobedient, cross-grained, disrespectful, haughty, headstrong, intractable, obdurate, obstinate, pertinacious, perverse, rebellious, refractory, stiff-necked, stubborn.

contumacy *n* doggedness, haughtiness, headiness, obduracy, obstinacy, pertinacity, perverseness, stubbornness; contempt, disobedience, disrespect, insolence, insubordination, rebelliousness.

contumelious *adj* abusive, arrogant, calumnious, contemptuous, disdainful, insolent, insulting, opprobrious, overbearing, rude, scornful, supercilious.

contumely *n* abuse, affront, arrogance, contempt, contemptuousness, disdain, indignity, insolence, insult, obloquy, opprobrium, reproach, rudeness, scorn, superciliousness.

contuse *vb* bruise, crush, injure, knock, squeeze, wound.

contusion *n* bruise, crush, injury, knock, squeeze, wound.

convalescence *n* recovery, recuperation.

convene *vb* assemble, congregate, gather, meet, muster; assemble, call, collect, convoke, muster, summon.

convenience *n* fitness, propriety, suitableness; accessibility, accommodation, comfort, commodiousness, ease, handiness, satisfaction, serviceability, serviceableness.

convenient *adj* adapted, appropriate, fit, fitted, proper, suitable, suited; advantageous, beneficial, comfortable, commodious, favourable, handy, helpful, serviceable, timely, useful.

convent *n* abbey, cloister, monastery, priory.

convention *n* assembly, congress, convocation, meeting; agreement, bargain, compact, contract, pact, stipulation, treaty; custom, formality, usage.

conventional *adj* agreed on, bargained for, stipulated; accustomed, approved, common, customary, everyday, habitual, ordinary, orthodox, regular, standard, traditional, usual, wonted.

conversable *adj* affable, communicative, free, open, sociable, social, unreversed.

conversation *n* chat, colloquy, communion, confabulation, conference, converse, dialogue, discourse, intercourse, interlocution, parley, talk.

converse[1] *vb* commune; chat, confabulate, discourse, gossip, parley, talk. * *n* commerce, communication, intercourse; colloquy, conversation, talk.

converse[2] *adj* adverse, contradictory, contrary, counter, opposed, opposing, opposite; *n* antithesis, contrary, opposite, reverse.

conversion *n* change, reduction, resolution, transformation, transmutation; interchange, reversal, transposition.

convert *vb* alter, change, transform, transmute; interchange, reverse, transpose; apply, appropriate, convince. * *n* catechumen, disciple, neophyte, proselyte.

convey *vb* bear, bring, carry, fetch, transmit, transport, waft; abalienate, alienate, cede, consign, deliver, demise, devise, devolve, grant, sell, transfer.

conveyance *n* alienation, cession, transfer, transference, transmission; carriage, carrying, conveying, transfer, transmission.

convict *vb* condemn, confute, convince, imprison, sentence. * *n* criminal, culprit, felon, malefactor, prisoner.

convivial *adj* festal, festive, gay, jolly, jovial, merry, mirthful, social.

convocation *n* assembling, convening, convoking, gathering, summoning; assembly, congress, convention, council, diet, meeting, synod.

convoke *vb* assemble, convene, muster, summon.

convoy *vb* accompany, attend, escort, guard, protect. * *n* attendance, attendant, escort, guard, protection.

convulse *vb* agitate, derange, disorder, disturb, shake, shatter.

convulsion *n* cramp, fit, spasm; agitation, commotion, disturbance, shaking, tumult.

cook *vb* bake, boil, broil, fry, grill, microwave, roast, spit-roast, steam, stir-fry; falsify, garble.

cool *vb* chill, ice, refrigerate; abate, allay, calm, damp, moderate, quiet, temper. * *adj* calm, collected, composed, dispassionate, placid, sedate, self-possessed, quiet, staid, unexcited, unimpassioned, undisturbed, unruffled; cold-blooded, indifferent, lukewarm, unconcerned; apathetic, chilling, freezing, frigid, repellent; bold, impertinent, impudent, self-possessed, shameless. * *n* chill, chilliness, coolness; calmness, composure, coolheadedness, countenance, equanimity, poise, self-possession, self-restraint.

coop *vb* cage, confine, encage, immure, imprison. * *n* barrel, box, cage, pen.

cooperate *vb* abet, aid, assist, co-act, collaborate, combine, concur, conduce, conspire, contribute, help, unite.

cooperation *n* aid, assistance, co-action, concert, concurrence, collaboration, synergy.

coordinate *vb* accord, agree, arrange, equalize, harmonize, integrate, methodize, organize, regulate, synchronize, systematize. * *adj* coequal, equal, equivalent, tantamount; coincident, synchronous. * *n* complement, counterpart, like, pendant; companion, fellow, match, mate.

copartnership *n* association, fraternity, partnership; company, concern, establishment, firm, house.

cope *vb* combat, compete, contend, encounter, engage, strive, struggle, vie.

copious *adj* abundant, ample, exuberant, full, overflowing, plenteous, plentiful, profuse, rich.

copiousness *n* abundance, exuberance, fullness, plenty, profusion, richness.

copse *n* coppice, grove, thicket.

copulation *n* coition, congress, coupling.

copy *vb* duplicate, reproduce, trace, transcribe; follow, imitate, pattern. * *n* counterscript, duplicate, facsimile, off-print, replica, reproduction, transcript; archetype, model, original, pattern; manuscript, typescript.

cord *n* braid, gimp, line, string.

cordate *adj* cordiform, heart-shaped.

cordial *adj* affectionate, ardent, earnest, heartfelt, hearty, sincere, warm, warm-hearted; grateful, invigorating, restorative, pleasant, refreshing. * *n* balm, balsam, elixir, tisane, tonic; liqueur.

core *n* centre, essence, heart, kernel.

corner *vb* confound, confuse, nonplus, perplex, pose, puzzle. * *n* angle, bend, crutch, cusp, elbow, joint, knee; niche, nook, recess, retreat.

corollary *n* conclusion, consequence, deduction, induction, inference.

coronal *n* bays, chaplet, crown, garland, laurel, wreath.

corporal *adj* bodily; corporeal, material, physical.

corporeal *adj* bodily, fleshly, substantial; corporal, material, nonspiritual, physical.

corps *n* band, body, company, contingent, division, platoon, regiment, squad, squadron, troop.

corpse *n* body, carcass, corse, remains; ashes, dust.

corpulent *adj* big, burly, fat, fleshy, large, lusty, obese, plump, portly, pursy, rotund, stout.

corpuscle *n* atom, bit, grain, iota, jot, mite, molecule, monad, particle, scintilla, scrap, whit.

correct *vb* adjust, amend, cure, improve, mend, reclaim, rectify, redress, reform, regulate, remedy; chasten, discipline, punish. * *adj* accurate, equitable, exact, faultless, just, precise, proper, regular, right, true, upright.

correction *n* amendment, improvement, redress; chastening, discipline, punishment.

corrective *adj* alternative, correctory, counteractive, emendatory, improving, modifying, rectifying, reformative, reformatory.

correctness *n* accuracy, exactness, faultlessness, nicety, precision, propriety, rectitude, regularity, rightness, truth.

correlate *n* complement, correlative, counterpart.

correspond *vb* accord, agree, answer, comport, conform, fit, harmonize, match, square, suit, tally; answer, belong, correlate; communicate.

correspondence *n* accord, agreement, coincidence, concurrence, conformity, congruity, fitness, harmony, match; correlation, counterposition; communication, letters, writing.

corroborate *vb* confirm, establish, ratify, substantiate, support, sustain, strengthen.

corrode *vb* canker, erode, gnaw; consume, deteriorate, rust, waste; blight, embitter, envenom, poison.

corrosive *adj* acrid, biting, consuming, cathartic, caustic, corroding, eroding, erosive, violent; consuming, corroding, gnawing, mordant, wasting, wearing; blighting, cankerous, carking, embittering, envenoming, poisoning.

corrugate *vb* cockle, crease, furrow, groove, pucker, rumple, wrinkle.

corrupt *vb* putrefy, putrid, render; contaminate, defile, infect, pollute, spoil, taint, vitiate; degrade, demoralize, deprave, pervert; adulterate, debase, falsify, sophisticate; bribe, entice. * *adj* contaminated, corrupted, impure, infected, putrid, rotten, spoiled, tainted, unsound; abandoned, debauched, depraved, dissolute, profligate, reprobate, vicious, wicked; bribable, buyable.

corruption *n* putrefaction, putrescence, rottenness; adulteration, contamination, debasement, defilement, infection, perversion, pollution, vitiation; demoralization, depravation, depravity, immorality, laxity, sinfulness, wickedness; bribery, dishonesty.

corsair *n* buccaneer, picaroon, pirate, rover, sea-robber, sea-rover.

corset *n* bodice, girdle, stays.

cosmonaut *n* astronaut, spaceman.

cosmos *n* creation, macrocosm, universe, world; harmony, order, structure.

cost *vb* absorb, consume, require. * *n* amount, charge, expenditure, expense, outlay, price; costliness, preciousness, richness, splendour, sumptuousness; damage, detriment, loss, pain, sacrifice, suffering.

costly *adj* dear, expensive, high-priced; gorgeous, luxurious, precious, rich, splendid, sumptuous, valuable.

costume *n* apparel, attire, dress, robes, uniform.

cosy, cozy *adj* comfortable, easy, snug; chatty, conversable, social, talkative.

coterie *n* association, brotherhood, circle, club, set, society, sodality.

cottage *n* cabin, chalet, cot, hut, lodge, shack, shanty.

couch *vb* lie, recline; crouch, squat; bend down, stoop; conceal, cover up, hide; lay, level. * *n* bed, davenport, divan, lounge, seat, settee, settle, sofa.

council *n* advisers, cabinet, ministry; assembly, congress, conclave, convention, convocation, diet, husting, meeting, parliament, synod.

counsel *vb* admonish, advise, caution, recommend, warm. * *n* admonition, advice, caution, instruction, opinion, recommendation, suggestion; deliberation, forethought; advocate, barrister, counsellor, lawyer.

count *vb* enumerate, number, score; calculate, cast, compute, estimate, reckon; account, consider, deem, esteem, hold, judge, regard, think; tell. * *n* reckoning, tally.

countenance *vb* abet, aid, approve, assist, befriend, encourage, favour, patronize, sanction, support. * *n* aspect, look, men; aid, approbation, approval, assistance, encouragement, favour, patronage, sanction, support.

counter[1] *n* abacus, calculator, computer, meter, reckoner, tabulator, totalizator; bar, buffet, shopboard, table; (*naut*) end, poop, stern, tail; chip, token.

counter[2] *vb* contradict, contravene, counteract, oppose, retaliate. * *adj* adverse, against, contrary, opposed, opposite. * *adv* contrariwise, contrary. * *n* antithesis, contrary, converse, opposite, reverse; counterblast, counterblow, retaliation.

counteract *vb* check, contrapose, contravene, cross, counter, counterpose, defeat, foil, frustrate, hinder, oppose, resist, thwart, traverse; annul, countervail, counterbalance, destroy, neutralize, offset.

counteractive *adj* antidote, corrective, counteragent, medicine, remedy, restorative.

counterbalance *vb* balance, counterpoise; compensate, countervail.

counterfeit *vb* forge, imitate; fake, feign, pretend, sham, simulate; copy, imitate. * *adj* fake, forged, fraudulent, spurious, suppositious; false, feigned, hypocritical, mock, sham, simulated, spurious; copied, imitated, resembling. * *n* copy, fake, forgery, sham.

countermand *vb* abrogate, annul, cancel, recall, repeal, rescind, revoke.

counterpane *n* coverlet, duvet, quilt.

counterpart *n* copy, duplicate; complement, correlate, correlative, reverse, supplement; fellow, mate, match, tally, twin.

counterpoise *vb* balance, counteract, countervail, counterbalance, equilibrate, offset. * *n* balance, counterweight.

countersign *n* password, watchword.

countervail *vb* balance, compensate, counterbalance.

country *n* land, region; countryside; fatherland, home, kingdom, state, territory; nation, people, population. * *adj* rural, rustic; countrified, rough, rude, uncultivated, unpolished, unrefined.

countryman *n* compatriot, fellow-citizen; boor, clown, farmer, hind, husbandman, peasant, rustic, swain.

couple *vb* pair, unite; copulate, embrace; buckle, clasp, conjoin, connect, join, link, pair, yoke. * *n* brace, pair, twain, two; bond, coupling, lea, link, tie.

courage *n* audaciousness, audacity, boldness, bravery, daring, derring-do, dauntlessness, fearlessness, firmness, fortitude, gallantry, hardihood, heroism, intrepidity, manhood, mettle, nerve, pluck, prowess, resolution, spirit, spunk, valorousness, valour.

courageous *adj* audacious, brave, bold, chivalrous, daring, dauntless, fearless, gallant, hardy, heroic, intrepid, lion-hearted, mettlesome, plucky, resolute, reliant, staunch, stout, undismayed, valiant, valorous.

course *vb* chase, follow, hunt, pursue, race, run. * *n* career, circuit, race, run; road, route, track, way; bearing, direction, path, tremor, track; ambit, beat, orbit, round; process, progress, sequence; order, regularity, succession, turn; behaviour, conduct, deportment; arrangement, series, system.

court *vb* coddle, fawn, flatter, ingratiate; address, woo; seek; invite, solicit. * *n* area, courtyard, patio, quadrangle; addresses, civilities, homage, respects, solicitations; retinue, palace, tribunal.

courteous *adj* affable, attentive, ceremonious, civil, complaisant, courtly, debonair, elegant, gracious, obliging, polished, polite, refined, respected, urbane, well-bred, well-mannered.

courtesan *n* harlot, prostitute, strumpet, vamp, wanton, wench, whore.

courtesy *n* affability, civility, complaisance, courteousness, elegance, good-breeding, graciousness, polish, politeness, refine, urbanity.

courtly *adj* affable, ceremonious, civil, elegant, flattering, lordly, obliging, polished, polite, refined, urbane.

courtyard *n* area, court, patio, quadrangle, yard.

cove[1] *n* anchorage, bay, bight, creek, firth, fjord, inlet.

cove[2] *n* bloke, chap, character, customer, fellow, type.

covenant *vb* agree, bargain, contract, stipulate. * *n* bond, deed; arrangement, bargain, compact, concordat, contract, convention, pact, stipulation, treaty.

cover *vb* overlay, overspread; cloak, conceal, curtain, disguise, hide, mask, screen, secrete, shroud, veil; defend, guard, protect, shelter, shield; case, clothe, envelop, invest, jacket, sheathe; comprehend, comprise, contain, embody, embrace, include. * *n* capsule, case, covering, integument, tegument, top; cloak, disguise, screen, veil; guard, defence, protection, safeguard, shelter, shield; shrubbery, thicket, underbrush, undergrowth, underwood, woods.

covert *adj* clandestine, concealed, disguised, hidden, insidious, private, secret, sly, stealthy, underhand. * *n* coppice, shade, shrubbery, thicket, underwood; asylum; defence, harbour, hiding-place, refuge, retreat, sanctuary, shelter.

covet *vb* aim after, desire, long for, yearn for; hanker after, lust after.

covetous *adj* acquisitive, avaricious, close-fisted, grasping, greedy, miserly, niggardly, parsimonious, penurious, rapacious.

cow[1] *n* bovine, heifer.

cow[2] *vb* abash, break, daunt, discourage, dishearten, frighten, intimidate, overawe, subdue.

coward *adj* cowardly, timid. * *n* caitiff, craven, dastard, milksop, poltroon, recreant, skulker, sneak, wheyface.

cowardly *adj* base, chicken-hearted, coward, craven, dastardly, faint-hearted, fearful, lily-livered, mean, pusillanimous, timid, timorous, white-livered, yellow.

cower *vb* bend, cringe, crouch, fawn, shrink, squat, stoop.

coxcomb *n* beau, dandy, dude, exquisite, fop, jackanapes, popinjay, prig.

coy *adj* backward, bashful, demure, diffident, distant, modest, reserved, retiring, self-effacing, shrinking, shy, timid.

coyness *n* affectation, archness, backwardness, bashfulness, coquettishness, demureness, diffidence, evasiveness, modesty, primness, reserve, shrinking, shyness, timidity.

cozen *vb* beguile, cheat, chouse, circumvent, deceive, defraud, diddle, dupe, gull, overreach, swindle, trick, victimize.

cozy *see* **cosy**.

crabbed *adj* acrid, rough, sore, tart; acrimonious, cantankerous, captious, caustic, censorious, churlish, cross, growling, harsh, ill-tempered, morose, peevish, petulant, snappish, snarling, splenetic, surly, testy, touchy, waspish; difficult, intractable, perplexing, tough, trying, unmanageable.

crabbedness *n* acridity, acridness, roughness, sourness, tartness; acerbity, acrimonious, asperity, churlishness, harshness, ill-tempered, moodiness, moroseness, sullenness; difficulty, intractability, perplexity.

crack *vb* break; chop, cleave, split; snap; craze, madden; boast, brag, bluster, crow, gasconade, vapour, vaunt. * *adj* capital, excellent, first-class, first-rate, tip-top. * *n* breach, break, chink, cleft, cranny, crevice, fissure, fracture, opening, rent, rift, split; burst, clap, explosion, pop, report; snap.

cracked *adj* broken, crackled, split; crack-brained, crazed, crazy, demented, deranged, flighty, insane.

crackle *vb* crepitate, decrepitate, snap.

craft *n* ability, aptitude, cleverness, dexterity, expertness, power, readiness, skill, tact, talent; artifice, artfulness, cunning, craftiness, deceitfulness, deception, guile, shrewdness, subtlety; art, avocation, business, calling, employment, handicraft, trade, vocation; vessel.

crafty *adj* arch, artful, astute, cunning, crooked, deceitful, designing, fraudulent, guileful, insidious, intriguing, scheming, shrewd, sly, subtle, tricky, wily.

crag *n* rock; neck, throat.

craggy *adj* broken, cragged, jagged, rough, rugged, scraggy, uneven.

cram *vb* fill, glut, gorge, satiate, stuff; compress, crowd, overcrowd, press, squeeze; coach, grind.

cramp *vb* convulse; check, clog, confine, hamper, hinder, impede, obstruct, restrain, restrict. * *n* convulsion, crick, spasm; check, restraint, restriction, obstruction.

crank *vb* bend, crankle, crinkle, turn, twist, wind. * *n* bend, quirk, turn, twist, winding.

cranny *n* breach, break, chink, cleft, crack, crevice, fissure, gap, hole, interstice, nook, opening, rift.

crapulous *adj* crapulent, drunk, drunken, inebriated, intoxicated, tipsy.

crash *vb* break, shatter, shiver, smash, splinter. * *adj* emergency, fast, intensive, rushed, speeded-up. * *n* clang, clash, collision concussion, jar.

crass *adj* coarse, gross, raw, thick, unabated, unrefined.

cravat *n* neckcloth, neckerchief, necktie.

crave *vb* ask, beg, beseech, entreat, implore, petition, solicit, supplicate; desire, hanker after, long for, need, want, yearn for.

craven *n* coward, dastard, milk-sop, poltroon, recreant. **adj* cowardly, chicken-hearted, lily-livered, pusillanimous, yellow.

craving *n* hankering, hungering, longing, yearning.

craw *n* crop, gullet, stomach, throat.

craze *vb* bewilder, confuse, dement, derange, madden; disorder, impair, weaken. * *n* fashion, mania, mode, novelty.

crazy *adj* broken, crank, rickety, shaky, shattered, tottering; crack-brained, delirious, demented, deranged, distracted, idiotic, insane, lunatic, mad, silly.

create *vb* originate, procreate; cause, design, fashion, form, invent, occasion, produce; appoint, constitute, make.

creation *n* formation, invention, origination, production; cosmos, universe; appointment, constitution, establishment, nomination.

creator *n* author, designer, inventor, fashioner, maker, originator; god.

creature *n* animal, beast, being, body, brute, man, person; dependant, hanger-on, minion, parasite, retainer, vassal; miscreant, wretch.

credence *n* acceptance, belief, confidence, credit, faith, reliance, trust.

credentials *n pl* certificate, diploma, missive, passport, recommendation, testament, testimonial, title, voucher, warrant.

credibility *n* believability, plausibility, tenability, , trustworthiness.

credit *vb* accept, believe, trust; loan, trust. * *n* belief, confidence, credence, faith, reliance, trust; esteem, regard, reputableness, reputation; influence, power; honour, merit; loan, trust.

creditable *adj* estimable, honourable, meritorious, praiseworthy, reputable, respectable.

credulity *n* credulousness, gullibility, silliness, simplicity, stupidity.

credulous *adj* dupable, green, gullible, naive, over-trusting, trustful, uncritical, unsuspecting, unsuspicious.

creed *n* belief, confession, doctrine, dogma, opinion, profession, tenet.

creek *n* bay, bight, cove, fjord, inlet; rivulet, streamlet.

creep *vb* crawl; steal upon; cringe, fawn, grovel, insinuate. * *n* crawl, scrabble, scramble; fawner, groveller, sycophant, toady.

crenate *adj* indented, notched, scalloped.

crepitate *vb* crack, crackle, decrepitate, snap.

crest *n* comb, plume, topknot, tuft; apex, crown, head, ridge, summit, top; arms, badge, bearings.

crestfallen *adj* chap-fallen, dejected, depressed, despondent, discouraged, disheartened, dispirited, downcast, down-hearted, low-spirited, melancholy, sad.

crevice *n* chink, cleft, crack, cranny, fissure, fracture, gap, hole, interstice, opening, rent, rift.

crew *n* company, complement, hands; company, corps, gang, horde, mob, party, posse, set, squad, team, throng.

crib *vb* cage, confine, encage, enclose, imprison; pilfer, purloin. * *n* manger, rack; bin, bunker; plagiarism, plunder, theft.

crick *vb* jar, rick, wrench, wrick. * *n* convulsion, cramp, jarring, spasm, rick, wrench, wrick.

crime *n* felony, misdeed, misdemeanour, offence, violation; delinquency, fault, guilt, iniquity, sin, transgression, unrighteousness, wickedness, wrong.

criminal *adj* culpable, felonious, flagitious, guilty, illegal, immoral, iniquitous, nefarious, unlawful, vicious, wicked, wrong. * *n* convict, culprit, delinquent, felon, malefactor, offender, sinner, transgressor.

criminate *vb* accuse, arraign, charge, convict, impeach, indict; implicate, involve.

crimp *vb* crisp, curl.

cringe *vb* bend, bow, cower, crouch, fawn, grovel, kneel, sneak, stoop, truckle.

cripple *vb* cramp, destroy, disable, enfeeble, impair, lame, maim, mutilate, paralyse, ruin, weaken.

crisis *n* acme, climax, height; conjuncture, emergency, exigency, juncture, pass, pinch, push, rub, strait, urgency.

crisp *adj* brittle, curled, friable, frizzled.

criterion *n* canon, gauge, measure, principle, proof, rule, standard, test, touchstone.

critic *n* arbiter, caviller, censor, connoisseur, judge, nit-picker, reviewer.

critical *adj* accurate, exact, nice; captious, carping, caviling, censorious, exacting; crucial, decisive, determining, important, turning: dangerous, dubious, exigent, hazardous, imminent, momentous, precarious, ticklish.

criticism *n* analysis, animadversion, appreciation, comment, critique, evaluation, judgement, review, strictures.

criticize *vb* appraise, evaluate, examine, judge.

croak *vb* complain, groan, grumble, moan, mumble, repine; die.

crone *n* hag, witch.

crony *n* ally, associate, chum, friend, mate, mucker, pal.

crook *vb* bend, bow, curve, incurvate, turn, wind. * *n* bend, curvature, flexion, turn; artifice, machination, trick; criminal, thief, villain.

crooked *adj* angular, bent, bowed, curved, winding, zigzag; askew, aslant, awry, deformed, disfigured, distorted, twisted, wry; crafty, deceitful, devious, dishonest, dishonourable, fraudulent, insidious, intriguing, knavish, tricky, underhanded, unfair, unscrupulous.

crop *vb* gather, mow, pick, pluck, reap; browse, nibble; clip, curtail, lop, reduce, shorten. * *n* harvest, produce, yield.

cross *vb* intersect, pass over, traverse; hinder, interfere, obstruct, thwart; interbred, intermix. * *adj* transverse; cantankerous, captious, crabbed, churlish, crusty, cynical, fractious, fretful, grouchy, ill-natured, ill-tempered, irascible, irritable, morose, peevish, pettish, petulant, snappish, snarling, sour, spleeny, splenetic, sulky, sullen, surly, testy, touchy, waspish. * *n* crucifix, gibbet, rood; affliction, misfortune, trial, trouble, vexation; cross-breeding, hybrid, intermixture.

cross-grained *adj* cantankerous, headstrong, obdurate, peevish, perverse, refractory, stubborn, untractable, wayward.

crossing *n* intersection, overpass, traversing, under-pass.

crossways, crosswise *adv* across, over, transversely.

crotchet *n* caprice, fad, fancy, freak, quirk, vagary, whim, whimsy.

crouch *vb* cower, cringe, fawn, truckle; crouch, kneel, stoop, squat; bow, curtsy, genuflect.

croup *n* buttocks, crupper, rump.

crow *vb* bluster, boast, brag, chuckle, exult, flourish, gasconade, swagger, triumph, vapour, vaunt.

crowd *vb* compress, cram, jam, pack, press; collect, congregate, flock, herd, huddle, swarm. * *n* assembly, company, concourse, flock, herd, horde, host, jam, multitude, press, throng; mob, pack, populace, rabble, rout.

crown *vb* adorn, dignify, honour; recompense, requite, reward; cap, complete, consummate, finish, perfect. * *n* bays, chaplet, coronal, coronet, garland, diadem, laurel, wreath; monarchy, royalty, sovereignty; diadem; dignity, honour, recompense, reward; apex, crest, summit, top.
crowning *adj* completing, consummating, dignifying, finishing, perfecting.
crucial *adj* intersecting, transverse; critical, decisive, searching, severe, testing, trying.
crude *adj* raw, uncooked, undressed, unworked; harsh, immature, rough, unripe; crass, coarse, unrefined; awkward, immature, indigestible, rude, uncouth, unpolished, unpremeditated.
cruel *adj* barbarous, blood-thirsty, dire, fell, ferocious, inexorable, hard-hearted, inhuman, merciless, pitiless, relentless, ruthless, sanguinary, savage, truculent, uncompassionate, unfeeling, unmerciful, unrelenting; bitter, cold, hard, severe, sharp, unfeeling.
crumble *vb* bruise, crush, decay, disintegrate, perish, pound, pulverize, triturate.
crumple *vb* rumple, wrinkle.
crush *vb* bruise, compress, contuse, squash, squeeze; bray, comminute, crumble, disintegrate, mash; demolish, raze, shatter; conquer, overcome, overpower, overwhelm, quell, subdue.
crust *n* coat, coating, incrustation, outside, shell, surface.
crusty *adj* churlish, crabbed, cross, cynical, fretful, forward, morose, peevish, pettish, petulant, snappish, snarling, surly, testy, touchy, waspish; friable, hard, short.
cry *vb* call, clamour, exclaim; blubber, snivel, sob, wail, weep, whimper; bawl, bellow, hoot, roar, shout, vociferate, scream, screech, squawk, squall, squeal, yell; announce, blazon, proclaim, publish. * *n* acclamation, clamour, ejaculation, exclamation, outcry; crying, lament, lamentation, plaint, weeping; bawl, bellow, howl, roar, scream, screech, shriek, yell; announcement, proclamation, publication.
crypt *n* catacomb, tomb, vault.
cuddle *vb* cosset, nestle, snuggle, squat; caress, embrace, fondle, hug, pet. * *n* caress, embrace, hug.
cudgel *vb* bang, baste, batter, beat, cane, drub, thrash, thump. * *n* bastinado, baton, bludgeon, club, shillelagh, stick, truncheon.
cue *vb* intimate, prompt, remind, sign, signal. * *n* catchword, hint, intimation, nod, prompting, sign, signal, suggestion.
cuff *vb* beat, box, buffet, knock, pummel, punch, slap, smack, strike, thump. * *n* blow, box, punch, slap, smack, strike, thump.
cul-de-sac *n* alley, dead end, impasse, pocket.
cull *vb* choose, elect, pick, select; collect, gather, glean, pluck.
culmination *n* acme, apex, climax, completion, consummation, crown, summit, top, zenith.
culpability *n* blame, blameworthiness, criminality, culpableness, guilt, remissness, sinfulness.
culpable *adj* blameable, blameworthy, censurable, faulty, guilty, reprehensible, sinful, transgressive, wrong.
culprit *n* delinquent, criminal, evil-doer, felon, malefactor, offender.
cultivate *vb* farm, fertilize, till, work; civilize, develop, discipline, elevate, improve, meliorate, refine, train; investigate, prosecute, pursue, search, study; cherish, foster, nourish, patronize, promote.
culture *n* agriculture, cultivation, farming, husbandry, tillage; cultivation, elevation, improvement, refinement.
cumber *vb* burden, clog, encumber, hamper, impede, obstruct, oppress, overload; annoy, distract, embarrass, harass, perplex, plague, torment, trouble, worry.
cumbersome *adj* burdensome, clumsy, cumbrous, embarrassing, heavy, inconvenient, oppressive, troublesome, unmanageable, unwieldy, vexatious.
cuneiform *adj* cuneate, wedge-shaped.
cunning *adj* artful, astute, crafty, crooked, deceitful, designing, diplomatic, foxy, guileful, intriguing, machiavellian, sharp, shrewd, sly, subtle, tricky, wily; curious, ingenious. * *n* art, artfulness, artifice, astuteness, craft, shrewdness, subtlety; craftiness, chicane, chicanery, deceit, deception, intrigue, slyness.
cup *n* beaker, bowl, chalice, goblet, mug; cupful, draught, potion.
cupboard *n* buffet, cabinet, closet.
cupidity *n* avidity, greed, hankering, longing, lust; acquisitiveness, avarice, covetousness, greediness, stinginess.
curative *adj* healing, medicinal, remedial, restorative.
curator *n* custodian, guardian, keeper, superintendent.
curb *vb* bridle, check, control, hinder, moderate, repress, restrain. * *n* bridle, check, control, hindrance, rein, restraint.
cure *vb* alleviate, correct, heal, mend, remedy, restore; kipper, pickle, preserve. * *n* antidote, corrective, help, remedy, reparative, restorative, specific; alleviation, healing, restorative.
curiosity *n* interest, inquiringness, inquisitiveness; celebrity, curio, marvel, novelty, oddity, phenomenon, rarity, sight, spectacle, wonder.
curious *adj* interested, inquiring, inquisitive, meddling, peering, prying, scrutinizing; extraordinary, marvellous, novel, queer, rare, singular, strange, unique, unusual; cunning, elegant, fine, finished, neat, skilful, well-wrought.
curl *vb* coil, twist, wind, writhe; bend, buckle, ripple, wave. * *n* curlicue, lovelock, ringlet; flexure, sinuosity, undulation, wave, waving, winding.
curmudgeon *n* churl, lick-penny, miser, niggard, screw, scrimp, skinflint.
currency *n* publicity; acceptance, circulation, transmission; bills, coins, money, notes.
current *adj* common, general, popular, rife; circulating, passing; existing, instant, present, prevalent, widespread. * *n* course, progression, river, stream, tide, undertow. * *adv* commonly, generally, popularly, publicly.
curry *vb* comb, dress; beat, cudgel, drub, thrash.
curse *vb* anathematize, damn, denounce, execrate, imprecate, invoke, maledict; blast, blight, destroy, doom; afflict, annoy, harass, injure, plague, scourge, torment, vex; blaspheme, swear. * *n* anathema, ban, denunciation, execration, fulmination, imprecation, malediction, malison; affliction, annoyance, plague, scourge, torment, trouble, vexation; ban, condemnation, penalty, sentence.
cursed *adj* accursed, banned, blighted, curse-laden, unholy; abominable, detestable, execrable, hateful, villainous; annoying, confounded, plaguing, scourging, tormenting, troublesome, vexatious.
cursory *adj* brief, careless, desultory, hasty, passing, rapid, slight, summary, superficial, transient, transitory.
curt *adj* brief, concise, laconic, short, terse; crusty, rude, snappish, tart.
curtail *vb* abridge, dock, lop, retrench, shorten; abbreviate, contract, decrease, diminish, lessen.
curtain *vb* cloak, cover, drape, mantle, screen, shade, shield, veil. * *n* arras, drape, drop, portière, screen, shade.
curvature *n* arcuation, bend, bending, camber, crook, curve, flexure, incurvation.
curve *vb* bend, crook, inflect, turn, twist, wind. * *n* arcuation, bend, bending, camber, crook, flexure, incurvation.
curvet *vb* bound, leap, vault; caper, frisk.
cushion *vb* absorb, damp, dampen, deaden, dull, muffle, mute, soften, subdue, suppress; cradle, pillow, support. * *n* bolster, hassock, pad, pillow, woolsack.
cusp *n* angle, horn, point.
custodian *n* curator, guardian, keeper, sacristan, superintendent, warden.
custody *n* care, charge, guardianship, keeping, safe-keeping, protection, watch, ward; confinement, durance, duress, imprisonment, prison.
custom *n* consuetude, convention, fashion, habit, manner, mode, practice, rule, usage, use, way; form, formality, observation; patronage; duty, impost, tax, toll, tribute.
customary *adj* accustomed, common, consuetudinary, conventional, familiar, fashionable, general, habitual, gnomic, prescriptive, regular, usual, wonted.
cut *vb* chop, cleave, divide, gash, incise, lance, sever, slice, slit, wound; carve, chisel, sculpture; hurt, move, pierce, touch; ignore, slight; abbreviate, abridge, curtail, shorten. * *n* gash, groove, incision, nick, slash, slice, slit; channel, passage; piece, slice; fling, sarcasm, taunt; fashion, form, mode, shape, style.

cutthroat *adj* barbarous, cruel, ferocious, murderous; competitive, exacting, exorbitant, extortionate, rivalling, ruthless, usurious, vying.* *n* assassin, murderer, ruffian.

cutting *adj* keen, sharp; acid, biting, bitter, caustic, piercing, sarcastic, sardonic, satirical, severe, trenchant, wounding.

cycle *n* age, circle, era, period, revolution, round.

Cyclopean *adj* colossal, enormous, gigantic, Herculean, immense, vast.

cynical *adj* captious, carping, censorious, churlish, crabbed, cross, crusty, fretful, ill-natured, ill-tempered, morose, peevish, pettish, petulant, sarcastic, satirical, snappish, snarling, surly, testy, touchy, waspish; contemptuous, derisive, misanthropic, pessimistic, scornful.

cynosure *n* attraction, centre.

cyst *n* pouch, sac.

D

dab *vb* box, rap, slap, strike, tap touch; coat, daub, smear. * *adj* adept, expert, proficient; pat. * *n* lump, mass, pat.

dabble *vb* dip, moisten, soak, spatter, splash, sprinkle, wet; meddle, tamper, trifle.

daft *adj* absurd, delirious, foolish, giddy, idiotic, insane, silly, simple, stupid, witless; frolicsome, merry, mirthful, playful, sportive.

dagger *n* bayonet, dirk, poniard, stiletto.

dainty *adj* delicate, delicious, luscious, nice, palatable, savoury, tender, toothsome; beautiful, charming, choice, delicate, elegant, exquisite, fine, neat; fastidious, finical, finicky, over-nice, particular, scrupulous, squeamish. * *n* delicacy, titbit, treat.

dale *n* bottom, dell, dingle, glen, vale, valley.

dalliance *n* caressing, endearments, flirtation, fondling.

dally *vb* dawdle, fritter, idle, trifle, waste time; flirt, fondle, toy.

damage *vb* harm, hurt, impair, injure, mar. * *n* detriment, harm, hurt, injury, loss, mischief.

damages *npl* compensation, fine, forfeiture, indemnity, reparation, satisfaction.

dame *n* babe, baby, broad, doll, girl; lady, madam, matron, mistress.

damn *vb* condemn, doom, kill, ruin. * *n* bean, curse, fig, hoot, rap, sou, straw, whit.

damnable *adj* abominable, accursed, atrocious, cursed, detestable, hateful, execrable, odious, outrageous.

damp *vb* dampen, moisten; allay, abate, check, discourage, moderate, repress, restrain; chill, cool, deaden, deject, depress, dispirit. * *adj* dank, humid, moist, wet. * *n* dampness, dank, fog, mist, moisture, vapour; chill, dejection, depression.

damper *n* check, hindrance, impediment, obstacle; damp, depression, discouragement, wet blanket.

dandle *vb* amuse, caress, fondle, pet, toss; dance.

danger *n* jeopardy, insecurity, hazard, peril, risk, venture.

dangerous *adj* critical, hazardous, insecure, perilous, risky, ticklish, unsafe.

dangle *vb* drape, hang, pend, sway, swing; fawn.

dank *adj* damp, humid, moist, wet.

dapper *adj* active, agile, alert, brisk, lively, nimble, quick, ready, smart, spry; neat, nice, pretty, spruce, trim.

dapple *vb* diversify, spot, variegate. * *adj* dappled, spotted, variegated.

dare *vb* challenge, defy, endanger, hazard, provoke, risk. * *n* challenge, defiance, gage.

daring *adj* adventurous, bold, brave, chivalrous, courageous, dauntless, doughty, fearless, gallant, heroic, intrepid, valiant, valorous. * *n* adventurousness, boldness, bravery, courage, dauntlessness, doughtiness, fearlessness, intrepidity, undauntedness, valour.

dark *adj* black, cloudy, darksome, dusky, ebon, inky, lightless, lurid, moonless, murky, opaque, overcast, pitchy, rayless, shady, shadowy, starless, sunless, swart, tenebrous, umbrageous, unenlightened, unilluminated; abstruse, cabbalistic, enigmatical, incomprehensible, mysterious, mystic, mystical, obscure, occult, opaque, recondite, transcendental, unillumined, unintelligible; cheerless, discouraging, dismal, disheartening, funereal, gloomy; benighted, darkened, ignorant, rude, unlettered, untaught; atrocious, damnable, infamous, flagitious, foul, horrible, infernal, nefarious, vile, wicked. * *n* darkness, dusk, murkiness, obscurity; concealment, privacy, secrecy; blindness, ignorance.

darken *vb* cloud, dim, eclipse, obscure, shade, shadow; chill, damp, depress, gloom, sadden; benight, stultify, stupefy; obscure, perplex; defile, dim, dull, stain, sully.

darkness *n* blackness, dimness, gloom, obscurity; blindness, ignorance; cheerlessness, despondency, gloom, joylessness; privacy, secrecy.

darling *adj* beloved, cherished, dear, loved, precious, treasured. * *n* dear, favourite, idol, love, sweetheart.

dart *vb* ejaculate, hurl, launch, propel, sling, throw; emit, shoot; dash, rush, scoot, spring.

dash *vb* break, destroy, disappoint, frustrate, ruin, shatter, spoil, thwart; abash, confound, disappoint, surprise; bolt, dart, fly, run, speed, rush. * *n* blow, stroke; advance, onset, rush; infusion, smack, spice, sprinkling, tincture, tinge, touch; flourish, show.

dashing *adj* headlong, impetuous, precipitate, rushing; brilliant, gay, showy, spirited.

dastardly *adj* base, cowardly, coward, cowering, craven, pusillanimous, recreant. * *n* coward, craven, milksop, poltroon, recreant.

data *npl* conditions, facts, information, premises.

date *n* age, cycle, day, generation, time; epoch, era, period; appointment, arrangement, assignation, engagement, interview, rendezvous, tryst; catch, steady, sweetheart.

daub *vb* bedaub, begrime, besmear, blur, cover, deface, defile, grime, plaster, smear, smudge, soil, sully. * *n* smear, smirch, smudge.

daunt *vb* alarm, appal, check, cow, deter, discourage, frighten, intimate, scare, subdue, tame, terrify, thwart.

dauntless *adj* bold, brave, chivalrous, courageous, daring, doughty, gallant, heroic, indomitable, intrepid, unaffrighted, unconquerable, undaunted, undismayed, valiant, valorous.

dawdle *vb* dally, delay, fiddle, idle, lag, loiter, potter, trifle.

dawn *vb* appear, begin, break, gleam, glimmer, open, rise. * *n* daybreak, dawning, cockcrow, sunrise, sun-up.

day *n* daylight, sunlight, sunshine; age, epoch, generation, lifetime, time.

daze *vb* blind, dazzle; bewilder, confound, confuse, perplex, stun, stupefy. * *n* bewilderment, confusion, discomposure, perturbation, pother; coma, stupor, swoon, trance.

dazzle *vb* blind, daze; astonish, confound, overpower, surprise. * *n* brightness, brilliance, splendour.

dead *adj* breathless, deceased, defunct, departed, gone, inanimate, lifeless; apathetic, callous, cold, dull, frigid, indifferent, inert, lukewarm, numb, obtuse, spiritless, torpid, unfeeling; flat, insipid, stagnant, tasteless, vapid; barren, inactive, sterile, unemployed, unprofitable, useless. * *adv* absolutely, completely, downright, fundamentally, quite; direct, directly, due, exactly, just, right, squarely, straight. * *n* depth, midst; hush, peace, quietude, silence, stillness.

deaden *vb* abate, damp, dampen, dull, impair, muffle, mute, restrain, retard, smother, weaken; benumb, blunt, hebetate, obtund, paralyse.

deadly *adj* deleterious, destructive, fatal, lethal, malignant, mortal, murderous, noxious, pernicious, poisonous, venomous; implacable, mortal, rancorous, sanguinary.

deal *vb* allot, apportion, assign, bestow, dispense, distribute, divide, give, reward, share; bargain, trade, traffic, treat with. * *n* amount, degree, distribution, extent, lot, portion, quantity, share; bargain, transaction.

dear *adj* costly, expensive, high-priced; beloved, cherished, darling, esteemed, precious, treasured. * *n* beloved, darling, deary, honey, love, precious, sweet, sweetie, sweetheart.

dearth *n* deficiency, insufficiency, scarcity; famine, lack, need, shortage, want.

death *n* cessation, decease, demise, departure, destruction, dissolution, dying, end, exit, mortality, passing.

deathless *adj* eternal, everlasting, immortal, imperishable, undying; boring, dull, turgid.

debacle *n* breakdown, cataclysm, collapse; rout, stampede.

debar *vb* blackball, deny, exclude, hinder, prevent, prohibit, restrain, shut out, stop, withhold.

debase *vb* adulterate, alloy, depress, deteriorate, impair, injure, lower, pervert, reduce, vitiate; abase, degrade, disgrace, dishonour, humble, humiliate, mortify, shame; befoul, contaminate, corrupt, defile, foul, pollute, soil, taint.

debate *vb* argue, canvass, contest, discuss, dispute; contend, deliberate, wrangle. * *n* controversy, discussion, disputation; altercation, contention, contest, dispute, logomachy.

debauch *vb* corrupt, deprave, pollute, vitiate; deflower, ravish, seduce, violate. * *n* carousal, orgy, revel, saturnalia.

debauchery *n* dissipation, dissoluteness, excesses, intemperance; debauch, excess, intemperance, lewdness, licentiousness, lust; bacchanal, carousal, compotation, indulgence, orgies, potation, revelry, revels, saturnalia, spree.

debilitate *vb* enervate, enfeeble, exhaust, prostrate, relax, weaken.

debility *n* enervation, exhaustion, faintness, feebleness, frailty, imbecility, infirmity, languor, prostration, weakness.

debonair *adj* affable, civil, complaisant, courteous, easy, gracious, kind, obliging, polite, refined, urbane, well-bred.

debris *n* detritus, fragments, remains, rubbish, rubble, ruins, wreck, wreckage.

debt *n* arrears, debit, due, liability, obligation; fault, misdoing, offence, shortcoming, sin, transgression, trespass.

decadence *n* caducity, decay, declension, decline, degeneracy, degeneration, deterioration, fall, retrogression.

decamp *vb* abscond, bolt, escape, flee, fly.

decapitate *vb* behead, decollate, guillotine.

decay *vb* decline, deteriorate, disintegrate, fail, perish, wane, waste, wither; decompose, putrefy, rot. * *n* caducity, decadence, declension, decline, decomposition, decrepitude, degeneracy, degeneration, deterioration, dilapidation, disintegration, fading, failing, perishing, putrefaction, ruin, wasting, withering.

deceased *adj* dead, defunct, departed, gone, late, lost.

deceit *n* artifice, cheating, chicanery, cozenage, craftiness, deceitfulness, deception, double-dealing, duplicity, finesse, fraud, guile, hypocrisy, imposition, imposture, pretence, sham, treachery, tricky, underhandedness, wile.

deceitful *adj* counterfeit, deceptive, delusive, fallacious, hollow, illusive, illusory, insidious, misleading; circumventive, cunning, designing, dissembling, dodgy, double-dealing, evasive, false, fraudulent, guileful, hypocritical, insincere, tricky, underhanded, wily.

deceive *vb* befool, beguile, betray, cheat, chouse, circumvent, cozen, defraud, delude, disappoint, double-cross, dupe, ensnare, entrap, fool, gull, hoax, hoodwink, humbug, mislead, outwit, overreach, trick.

deceiver *n* charlatan, cheat, humbug, hypocrite, knave, impostor, pretender, rogue, sharper, trickster.

decent *adj* appropriate, becoming, befitting, comely, seemly, decorous, fit, proper, seemly; chaste, delicate, modest, pure; moderate, passable, respectable, tolerable.

deception *n* artifice, cheating, chicanery, cozenage, craftiness, deceitfulness, deception, double-dealing, duplicity, finesse, fraud, guile, hoax, hypocrisy, imposition, imposture, pretence, sham, treachery, trick, underhandedness, wile; cheat, chouse, ruse, stratagem, wile.

deceptive *adj* deceitful, deceiving, delusive, disingenuous, fallacious, false, illusive, illusory, misleading.

decide *vb* close, conclude, determine, end, settle, terminate; resolve; adjudge, adjudicate, award.

decided *adj* determined, firm, resolute, unhesitating, unwavering; absolute, categorical, positive, unequivocal; certain, clear, indisputable, undeniable, unmistakable, unquestionable.

deciduous *adj* caducous, nonperennial, temporary.

decipher *vb* explain, expound, interpret, reveal, solve, unfold, unravel; read.

decision *n* conclusion, determination, judgement, settlement; adjudication, award, decree, pronouncement, sentence; firmness, resolution.

decisive *adj* conclusive, determinative, final.

deck *vb* adorn, array, beautify, decorate, embellish, grace, ornament; apparel, attire, bedeck, clothe, dress, robe.

declaim *vb* harangue, mouth, rant, speak, spout.

declamation *n* declaiming, haranguing, mouthing, ranting, spouting.

declamatory *adj* bombastic, discursive, fustian, grandiloquent, high-flown, high-sounding, incoherent, inflated, pompous, pretentious, rhetorical, swelling, turgid.

declaration *n* affirmation, assertion, asseveration, averment, avowal, protestation, statement; announcement, proclamation, publication.

declaratory *adj* affirmative, annunciatory, assertive, declarative, definite, enunciative, enunciatory, expressive; explanatory, expository.

declare *vb* advertise, affirm, announce, assert, asseverate, aver, blazon, bruit, proclaim, promulgate, pronounce, publish, state, utter.

declension *n* decadence, decay, decline, degeneracy, deterioration, diminution; inflection, variation; declination, nonacceptance, refusal.

declination *n* bending, descent, inclination; decadence, decay, decline, degeneracy, degeneration, degradation, deterioration, diminution; aberration, departure, deviation, digression, divagation, divergence; declinature, nonacceptance, refusal.

decline *vb* incline, lean, slope; decay, droop, fail, flag, languish, pine, sink; degenerate, depreciate, deteriorate; decrease, diminish, dwindle, fade, ebb, lapse, lessen, wane; avoid, refuse, reject; inflect, vary. * *n* decadence, decay, declension, declination, degeneracy, deterioration, diminution, wane; atrophy, consumption, marasmus, phthisis; declivity, hill, incline, slope.

declivity *n* declination, descent, incline, slope.

decompose *vb* analyse, disintegrate, dissolve, distil, resolve, separate; corrupt, decay, putrefy, rot.

decomposition *n* analysis, break-up, disintegration, resolution; caries, corruption, crumbling, decay, disintegration, dissolution, putrescence, rotting.

decorate *vb* adorn, beautify, bedeck, deck, embellish, enrich, garnish, grace, ornament.

decoration *n* adorning, beautifying, bedecking, decking, enriching, garnishing, ornamentation, ornamenting; adornment, enrichment, embellishment, ornament.

decorous *adj* appropriate, becoming, befitting, comely, decent, fit, suitable, proper, sedate, seemly, staid.

decorum *n* appropriate behaviour, courtliness, decency, deportment, dignity, gravity, politeness, propriety, sedateness, seemliness.

decoy *vb* allure, deceive, ensnare, entice, entrap, inveigle, lure, seduce, tempt. * *n* allurement, lure, enticement.

decrease *vb* abate, contract, decline, diminish, dwindle, ebb, lessen, subside, wane; curtail, diminish, lessen, lower, reduce, retrench. * *n* abatement, contraction, declension, decline, decrement, diminishing, diminution, ebb, ebbing, lessening, reduction, subsidence, waning.

decree *vb* adjudge, appoint, command, decide, determine, enact, enjoin, order, ordain. * *n* act, command, edict, enactment, fiat, law, mandate, order, ordinance, precept, regulation, statute.

decrement *n* decrease, diminution, lessening, loss, waste.

decrepit *adj* feeble, effete, shattered, wasted, weak; aged, crippled, superannuated.

decry *vb* abuse, belittle, blame, condemn, denounce, depreciate, detract, discredit, disparage, run down, traduce, underrate, undervalue.

dedicate *vb* consecrate, devote, hallow, sanctify; address, inscribe.

deduce *vb* conclude, derive, draw, gather, infer.

deducible *adj* derivable, inferable.

deduct *vb* remove, subtract, withdraw; abate, detract.

deduction *n* removal, subtraction, withdrawal; abatement, allowance, defalcation, discount, rebate, reduction, reprise; conclusion, consequence, corollary, inference.

deed *n* achievement, act, action, derring-do, exploit, feat, performance; fact, truth, reality; charter, contract, document, indenture, instrument, transfer.

deem *vb* account, believe, conceive, consider, count, estimate, hold, imagine, judge, regard, suppose, think; fancy, opine.

deep *adj* abysmal, extensive, great, profound; abstruse, difficult, hard, intricate, knotty, mysterious, recondite, unfathomable; astute, cunning, designing, discerning, intelligent, insidious, penetrating, sagacious, shrewd; absorbed, engrossed; bass, grave, low; entire, great, heartfelt, thorough. * *n* main, ocean, water, sea; abyss, depth, profundity; enigma, mystery, riddle; silence, stillness.

deeply *adv* profoundly; completely, entirely, extensively, greatly, thoroughly; affectingly, distressingly, feelingly, mournfully, sadly.

deface *vb* blotch, deform, disfigure, injure, mar, mutilate, obliterate, soil, spoil, sully, tarnish.

de facto *adj* actual, real. * *adv* actually, in effect, in fact, really, truly.

defalcate *vb* abate, curtail, retrench, lop.

defalcation *n* abatement, deduction, diminution, discount, reduction; default, deficiency, deficit, shortage, shortcoming; embezzlement, fraud.

defamation *n* abuse, aspersion, back-biting, calumny, detraction, disparagement, libel, obloquy, opprobrium, scandal, slander.

defamatory *adj* abusive, calumnious, libellous, slanderous.

defame *vb* abuse, asperse, blacken, belie, besmirch, blemish, calumniate, detract, disgrace, dishonour, libel, malign, revile, slander, smirch, traduce, vilify.

default *vb* defalcate, dishonour, fail, repudiate, welsh. * *n* defalcation, failure, lapse, neglect, offence, omission, oversight, shortcoming; defect, deficiency, deficit, delinquency, destitution, fault, lack, want.

defaulter *n* delinquent, embezzler, offender, peculator.

defeat *vb* beat, checkmate, conquer, discomfit, overcome, overpower, overthrow, repulse, rout, ruin, vanquish; baffle, balk, block, disappoint, disconcert, foil, frustrate, thwart. * *n* discomfiture, downfall, overthrow, repulse, rout, vanquishment; bafflement, checkmate, frustration.

defect *vb* abandon, desert, rebel, revolt. * *n* default, deficiency, destitution, lack, shortcoming, spot, taint, want; blemish, blotch, error, flaw, imperfection, mistake; failing, fault, foible.

defection *n* abandonment, desertion, rebellion, revolt; apostasy, backsliding, dereliction.

defective *adj* deficient, inadequate, incomplete, insufficient, scant, short; faulty, imperfect, marred.

defence *n* defending, guarding, holding, maintaining, maintenance, protection; buckler, bulwark, fortification, guard, protection, rampart, resistance, shield; apology, excuse, justification, plea, vindication.

defenceless *adj* exposed, helpless, unarmed, unprotected, unguarded, unshielded, weak.

defend *vb* cover, fortify, guard, preserve, protect, safeguard, screen, secure, shelter, shield; assert, espouse, justify, maintain, plead, uphold, vindicate.

defender *n* asserter, maintainer, pleader, upholder; champion, protector, vindicator.

defer[1] *vb* adjourn, delay, pigeonhole, procrastinate, postpone, prorogue, protract, shelve, table.

defer[2] *vb* abide by, acknowledge, bow to, give way, submit, yield; admire, esteem, honour, regard, respect.

deference *n* esteem, homage, honour, obeisance, regard, respect, reverence, veneration; complaisance, consideration; obedience, submission.

deferential *adj* respectful, reverential.

defiance *n* challenge, daring; contempt, despite, disobedience, disregard, opposition, spite.

defiant *adj* contumacious, recalcitrant, resistant; bold, courageous, resistant.

deficiency *n* dearth, default, deficit, insufficiency, lack, meagreness, scantiness, scarcity, shortage, shortness, want; defect, error, failing, falling, fault, foible, frailty, imperfection, infirmity, weakness.

deficient *adj* defective, faulty, imperfect, inadequate, incomplete, insufficient, lacking, scant, scanty, scarce, short, unsatisfactory, wanting.

deficit *n* deficiency, lack, scarcity, shortage, shortness.

defile[1] *vb* dirty, foul, soil, stain, tarnish; contaminate, debase, poison, pollute, sully, taint, vitiate; corrupt, debauch, deflower, ravish, seduce, violate.

defile[2] *vb* file, march, parade, promenade. * *n* col, gorge, pass, passage, ravine, strait.

define *vb* bound, circumscribe, designate, delimit, demarcate, determine, explain, limit, specify.

definite *adj* defined, determinate, determined, fixed, restricted; assured, certain, clear, exact, explicit, positive, precise, specific, unequivocal.

definitive *adj* categorical, determinate, explicit, express, positive, unconditional; conclusive, decisive, final.

deflect *vb* bend, deviate, diverge, swerve, turn, twist, waver, wind.

deflower *vb* corrupt, debauch, defile, seduce.

deform *vb* deface, disfigure, distort, injure, mar, misshape, ruin, spoil.

deformity *n* abnormality, crookedness, defect, disfigurement, distortion, inelegance, irregularity, malformation, misproportion, misshapenness, monstrosity, ugliness.

defraud *vb* beguile, cheat, chouse, circumvent, cozen, deceive, delude, diddle, dupe, embezzle, gull, overreach, outwit, pilfer, rob, swindle, trick.

defray *vb* bear, discharge, liquidate, meet, pay, settle.

deft *adj* adroit, apt, clever, dab, dextrous, expert, handy, ready, skilful.

defunct *adj* dead, deceased, departed, extinct, gone; abrogated, annulled, cancelled, inoperative.

defy *vb* challenge, dare; brave, contemn, despise, disregard, face, flout, provoke, scorn, slight, spurn.

degeneracy *n* abasement, caducity, corruption, debasement, decadence, decay, declension, decline, decrease, degenerateness, degeneration, degradation, depravation, deterioration; inferiority, meanness, poorness.

degenerate *vb* decay, decline, decrease, deteriorate, retrograde, sink. * *adj* base, corrupt, decayed, degenerated, deteriorated, fallen, inferior, low, mean, perverted.

degeneration *n* debasement, decline, degeneracy, deterioration.

degradation *n* deposition, disgrace, dishonour, humiliation, ignominy; abasement, caducity, corruption, debasement, decadence, decline, degeneracy, degeneration, deterioration, perversion, vitiation.

degrade *vb* abase, alloy, break, cashier, corrupt, debase, demote, discredit, disgrace, dishonour, disparage, downgrade, humiliate, humble, lower, pervert, vitiate; deteriorate, impair, lower, sink.

degree *n* stage, step; class, grade, order, quality, rank, standing, station; extent, measure; division, interval, space.

deify *vb* apotheosize, idolize, glorify, revere; elevate, ennoble, exalt.

deign *vb* accord, condescend, grant, vouchsafe.

deject *vb* depress, discourage, dishearten, dispirit, sadden.

dejected *adj* blue, chapfallen, crestfallen, depressed, despondent, disheartened, dispirited, doleful, downcast, down-hearted, gloomy, low-spirited, miserable, sad, wretched.

delay *vb* defer, postpone, procrastinate; arrest, detain, check, hinder, impede, retard, stay, stop; prolong, protract; dawdle, linger, loiter, tarry. * *n* deferment, postponement, procrastination; check, detention, hindrance, impediment, retardation, stoppage; prolonging, protraction; dallying, dawdling, lingering, tarrying, stay, stop.

delectable *adj* agreeable, charming, delightful, enjoyable, gratifying, pleasant, pleasing.

delectation *n* delight, ecstasy, gladness, joy, rapture, ravishment, transport.

delegate *vb* appoint, authorize, mission, depute, deputize, transfer; commit, entrust. * *n* ambassador, commissioner, delegate, deputy, envoy, representative.

delete *vb* cancel, efface, erase, expunge, obliterate, remove.

deleterious *adj* deadly, destructive, lethal, noxious, poisonous; harmful, hurtful, injurious, pernicious, unwholesome.

deliberate *vb* cogitate, consider, consult, meditate, muse, ponder, reflect, ruminate, think, weigh. * *adj* careful, cautious, circumspect, considerate, heedful, purposeful, methodical, thoughtful, wary; well-advised, well-considered; aforethought, intentional, premeditated, purposed, studied.

deliberation *n* caution, circumspection, cogitation, consideration, coolness, meditation, prudence, reflection, thought, thoughtfulness, wariness; purpose.

delicacy *n* agreeableness, daintiness, deliciousness, pleasantness, relish, savouriness; bonne bouche, dainty, tidbit; elegance, fitness, lightness, niceness, nicety, smoothness, softness, tenderness; fragility, frailty, slenderness, slightness, tenderness, weakness; carefulness, discrimination, fastidiousness, finesse, nicety, scrupulousness, sensitivity, subtlety, tact; purity, refinement, sensibility.

delicate *adj* agreeable, delicious, pleasant, pleasing, palatable, savoury; elegant, exquisite, fine, nice; careful, dainty, discriminating, fastidious, scrupulous; fragile, frail, slender, slight, tender, delicate; pure, refined.

delicious *adj* dainty, delicate, luscious, nice, palatable, savory; agreeable, charming, choice, delightful, exquisite, grateful, pleasant.

delight *vb* charm, enchant, enrapture, gratify, please, ravish, rejoice, satisfy, transport. * *n* charm, delectation, ecstasy, enjoyment, gladness, gratification, happiness, joy, pleasure, rapture, ravishment, satisfaction, transport.

delightful *adj* agreeable, captivating, charming, delectable, enchanting, enjoyable, enrapturing, rapturous, ravishing, transporting.

delineate *vb* design, draw, figure, paint, sketch, trace; depict, describe, picture, portray.

delineation *n* design, draught, drawing, figure, outline, sketch; account, description, picture, portrayal.

delinquency *n* crime, fault, misdeed, misdemeanour, offence, wrongdoing.

delinquent *adj* negligent, offending. * *n* criminal, culprit, defaulter, malefactor, miscreant, misdoer, offender, transgressor, wrong-doer.

delirious *adj* crazy, demented, deranged, frantic, frenzied, light-headed, mad, insane, raving, wandering.

delirium *n* aberration, derangement, frenzy, hallucination, incoherence, insanity, lunacy, madness, raving, wandering.

deliver *vb* emancipate, free, liberate, release; extricate, redeem, rescue, save; commit, give, impart, transfer; cede, grant, relinquish, resign, yield; declare, emit, promulgate, pronounce, speak, utter; deal, discharge.

deliverance *n* emancipation, escape, liberation, redemption, release.

delivery *n* conveyance, surrender; commitment, giving, rendering, transference, transferral, transmission; elocution, enunciation, pronunciation, speech, utterance; childbirth, confinement, labour, parturition, travail.

dell *n* dale, dingle, glen, valley, ravine.

delude *vb* beguile, cheat, chouse, circumvent, cozen, deceive, dupe, gull, misguide, mislead, overreach, trick.

deluge *vb* drown, inundate, overflow, overwhelm, submerge. * *n* cataclysm, downpour, flood, inundation, overflow, rush.

delusion *n* artifice, cheat, clap-trap, deceit, dodge, fetch, fraud, imposition, imposture, ruse, snare, trick, wile; deception, error, fallacy, fancy, hallucination, illusion, mistake, mockery, phantasm.

delusive *adj* deceitful, deceiving, deceptive, fallacious, illusional, illusionary, illusive.

demand *vb* challenge, exact, require; claim, necessitate, require; ask, inquire. * *n* claim, draft, exaction, requirement, requisition; call, want; inquiry, interrogation, question.

demarcation *n* bound, boundary, confine, distinction, division, enclosure, limit, separation.

demeanour *n* air, bearing, behaviour, carriage, deportment, manner, mien.

demented *adj* crack-brained, crazed, crazy, daft, deranged, dotty, foolish, idiotic, infatuated, insane, lunatic.

dementia *n* idiocy, insanity, lunacy.

demerit *n* delinquency, fault, ill-desert.

demise *vb* alienate, consign, convey, devolve, grant, transfer; bequeath, devise, leave, will. * *n* alienation, conveyance, transfer, transference, transmission; death, decease.

demolish *vb* annihilate, destroy, dismantle, level, over-throw, overturn, pulverize, raze, ruin.

demon *n* devil, fiend, kelpie, goblin, troll.

demoniac, demoniacal *adj* demonic, demonical, devilish, diabolic, diabolical, fiendish, hellish, infernal, Mephistophelean, Mephistophelian, satanic; delirious, distracted, frantic, frenzied, feverish, hysterical, mad, overwrought, rabid.

demonstrate *vb* establish, exhibit, illustrate, indicate, manifest, prove, show.

demonstration *n* display, exhibition, manifestation, show.

demonstrative *adj* affectionate, communicative, effusive, emotional, expansive, expressive, extroverted, open, outgoing, passionate, sentimental, suggestive, talkative, unreserved; absolute, apodictic, certain, conclusive, probative; exemplificative, illustrative.

demoralize *vb* corrupt, debase, debauch, deprave, vitiate; depress, discourage, dishearten, weaken.

demulcent *adj* emollient, lenitive, mild, mollifying, sedative, soothing.

demur *vb* halt, hesitate, pause, stop, waver; doubt, object, scruple. * *n* demurral, hesitance, hesitancy, hesitation, objection, pause, qualm, scruple.

demure *adj* prudish; coy, decorous, grave, modest, priggish, prudish, sedate, sober, staid.

den *n* cavern, cave; haunt, lair, resort, retreat.

denial *n* contradiction, controverting, negation; abjuration, disavowal, disclaimer, disowning; disallowance, refusal, rejection.

denizen *n* citizen, dweller, inhabitant, resident.

denominate *vb* call, christen, designate, dub, entitle, name, phrase, style, term.

denomination *n* appellation, designation, name, style, term, title; class, kind, sort; body, persuasion, school, sect.

denote *vb* betoken, connote, designate, imply, indicate, mark, mean, note, show, signify, typify.

dénouement *n* catastrophe, unravelling; consummation, issue, finale, upshot, conclusion, termination.

denounce *vb* menace, threaten; arraign, attack, brand, censure, condemn, proscribe, stigmatize, upbraid; accuse, inform, denunciate.

dense *adj* close, compact, compressed, condensed, thick; dull, slow, stupid.

dent *vb* depress, dint, indent, pit. * *n* depression, dint, indentation, nick, notch.

dentate *adj* notched, serrate, toothed.

denude *vb* bare, divest, strip.

denunciation *n* menace, threat; arraignment, censure, fulmination, invective; exposure.

deny *vb* contradict, gainsay, oppose, refute, traverse; abjure, abnegate, disavow, disclaim, disown, renounce; disallow, refuse, reject, withhold.

depart *vb* absent, disappear, vanish; abandon, decamp, go, leave, migrate, quit, remove, withdraw; decease, die; deviate, diverge, vary.

department *n* district, division, part, portion, province; bureau, function, office, province, sphere, station; branch, division, subdivision.

departure *n* exit, leaving, parting, removal, recession, removal, retirement, withdrawal; abandonment, forsaking; death, decease, demise, deviation, exit.

depend *vb* hang, hinge, turn.

dependant *n* client, hanger-on, henchman, minion, retainer, subordinate, vassal; attendant, circumstance, concomitant, consequence, corollary.

dependence *n* concatenation, connection, interdependence; confidence, reliance, trust; buttress, prop, staff, stay, support, supporter; contingency, need, subjection, subordination.

dependency *n* adjunct, appurtenance; colony, province.

dependent *adj* hanging, pendant; conditioned, contingent, relying, subject, subordinate.

depict *vb* delineate, limn, outline, paint, pencil, portray, sketch; describe, render, represent.
deplete *vb* drain, empty, evacuate, exhaust, reduce.
deplorable *adj* calamitous, distressful, distressing, grievous, lamentable, melancholy, miserable, mournful, pitiable, regrettable, sad, wretched.
deplore *vb* bemoan, bewail, grieve for, lament, mourn, regret.
deploy *vb* display, expand, extend, open, unfold.
deportment *n* air, bearing, behaviour, breeding, carriage, comportment, conduct, demeanour, manner, mien, port.
depose *vb* break, cashier, degrade, dethrone, dismiss, displace, oust, reduce; avouch, declare, depone, testify.
deposit *vb* drop, dump, precipitate; lay, put; bank, hoard, lodge, put, save, store; commit, entrust. * *n* diluvium, dregs, lees, precipitate, precipitation, sediment, settlement, settlings, silt; money, pawn, pledge, security, stake.
depositary *n* fiduciary, guardian, trustee.
deposition *n* affidavit, evidence, testimony; deposit, precipitation, settlement; dethroning, displacement, removal.
depository *n* deposit, depot, storehouse, warehouse.
depot *n* depository, magazine, storehouse, warehouse.
depravation *n* abasement, corruption, deterioration, impairing, injury, vitiation; debasement, degeneracy, degeneration, depravity, impairment.
depraved *adj* abandoned, corrupt, corrupted, debased, debauched, degenerate, dissolute, evil, graceless, hardened, immoral, lascivious, lewd, licentious, lost, perverted, profligate, reprobate, shameless, sinful, vicious, wicked.
depravity *n* corruption, degeneracy, depravedness; baseness, contamination, corruption, corruptness, criminality, demoralization, immorality, iniquity, license, perversion, vice, viciousness, wickedness.
depreciate *vb* underestimate, undervalue, underrate; belittle, censure, decry, degrade, disparage, malign, traduce.
depreciation *n* belittling, censure, derogation, detraction, disparagement, maligning, traducing.
depredation *n* despoiling, devastation, pilfering, pillage, plunder, rapine, robbery, spoliation, theft.
depress *vb* bow, detrude, drop, lower, reduce, sink; abase, abash, degrade, debase, disgrace, humble, humiliate; chill, damp, dampen, deject, discourage, dishearten, dispirit, sadden; deaden, lower.
depression *n* cavity, concavity, dent, dimple, dint, excavation, hollow, hollowness, indentation, pit; blues, cheerlessness, dejection, dejectedness, despondency, disconsolateness, disheartenment, dispiritedness, dole, dolefulness, downheartedness, dumps, gloom, gloominess, hypochondria, melancholy, sadness, vapours; inactivity, lowness, stagnation; abasement, debasement, degradation, humiliation.
deprivation *n* bereavement, dispossession, loss, privation, spoliation, stripping.
deprive *vb* bereave, denude, despoil, dispossess, divest, rob, strip.
depth *n* abyss, deepness, drop, profundity; extent, measure; middle, midst, stillness; astuteness, discernment, penetration, perspicacity, profoundness, profundity, sagacity, shrewdness.
deputation *n* commission, delegation; commissioners, deputies, delegates, delegation, embassies, envoys, legation.
depute *vb* accredit, appoint, authorize, charge, commission, delegate, empower, entrust.
deputy *adj* acting, assistant, vice, subordinate. * *n* agent, commissioner, delegate, envoy, factor, legate, lieutenant, proxy, representative, substitute, viceregent.
derange *vb* confound, confuse, disarrange, disconcert, disorder, displace, madden, perturb, unsettle; discompose, disconcert, disturb, perturb, ruffle, upset; craze, madden, unbalance, unhinge.
derangement *n* confusion, disarrangement, disorder, irregularity; discomposure, disturbance, perturbation; aberration, alienation, delirium, dementia, hallucination, insanity, lunacy, madness, mania.
derelict *adj* abandoned, forsaken, left, relinquished; delinquent, faithless, guilty, neglectful, negligent, unfaithful. * *n* castaway, castoff, outcast, tramp, vagrant, wreck, wretch.
dereliction *n* abandonment, desertion, relinquishement, renunciation; delinquency, failure, faithlessness, fault, neglect, negligence.
deride *vb* chaff, flout, gibe, insult, jeer, lampoon, mock, ridicule, satirize, scoff, scorn, sneer, taunt.
derision *n* contempt, disrespect, insult, laughter, mockery, ridicule, scorn.
derisive *adj* contemptuous, contumelious, mocking, ridiculing, scoffing, scornful.
derivation *n* descent, extraction, genealogy; etymology; deducing, deriving, drawing, getting, obtaining; beginning, foundation, origination, source.
derive *vb* draw, get, obtain, receive; deduce, follow, infer, trace.
derogate *vb* compromise, depreciate, detract, diminish, disparage, lessen.
derogatory *adj* belittling, depreciative, deprecatory, detracting, dishonouring, disparaging, injurious.
descant *vb* amplify, animadvert, dilate, discourse, discuss, enlarge, expatiate. * *n* melody, soprano, treble; animadversion, commentary, remarks; discourse, discussion.
descend *vb* drop, fall, pitch, plunge, sink, swoop; alight, dismount; go, pass, proceed, devolve; derive, issue, originate.
descendants *npl* offspring, issue, posterity, progeny.
descent *n* downrush, drop, fall; descending; decline, declivity, dip, pitch, slope; ancestry, derivation, extraction, genealogy, lineage, parentage, pedigree; assault, attack, foray, incursion, invasion, raid.
describe *vb* define, delineate, draw, illustrate, limn, sketch, specify, trace; detail; depict, explain, narrate, portray, recount, relate, represent; characterize.
description *n* delineation, tracing; account, depiction, explanation, narration, narrative, portrayal, recital, relation, report, representation; class, kind, sort, species.
descry *vb* behold, discover, discern, distinguish, espy, observe, perceive, see; detect, recognize.
desecrate *vb* abuse, pervert, defile, pollute, profane, violate.
desert[1] *n* due, excellence, merit, worth; punishment, reward.
desert[2] *vb* abandon, abscond, forsake, leave, quit, relinquish, renounce, resign, quit, vacate.
desert[3] *adj* barren, desolate, forsaken, lonely, solitary, uncultivated, uninhabited, unproductive, untilled, waste, wild.
deserted *adj* abandoned, forsaken, relinquished.
deserter *n* abandoner, forsaker, quitter, runaway; apostate, backslider, fugitive, recreant, renegade, revolter, traitor, turncoat.
desertion *n* abandonment, dereliction, recreancy, relinquishment.
deserve *vb* earn, gain, merit, procure, win.
desiderate *vb* desire, lack, miss, need, want.
design *vb* brew, concoct, contrive, devise, intend, invent, mean, plan, project, scheme; intend, mean, purpose; delineate, describe, draw, outline, sketch, trace. * *n* aim, device, drift, intent, intention, mark, meaning, object, plan, proposal, project, purport, purpose, scheme, scope; delineation, draught, drawing, outline, plan, sketch; adaptation, artifice, contrivance, invention, inventiveness.
designate *vb* denote, distinguish, indicate, particularize, select, show, specify, stipulate; characterize, define, describe; call, christen, denominate, dub, entitle, name, style; allot, appoint, christen.
designation *n* indication, particularization, selection, specification; class, description, kind; appellation, denomination, name, style, title.
designing *adj* artful, astute, crafty, crooked, cunning, deceitful, insidious, intriguing, Machiavellian, scheming, sly, subtle, treacherous, trickish, tricky, unscrupulous, wily.
desirable *adj* agreeable, beneficial, covetable, eligible, enviable, good, pleasing, preferable.
desire *vb* covet, crave, desiderate, fancy, hanker after, long for, lust after, want, wish, yearn for; ask, entreat, request, solicit. * *n* eroticism, lasciviousness, libidinousness, libido, lust, lustfulness, passion; eagerness, fancy, hope, inclination, mind, partiality, penchant, pleasure, volition, want, wish.
desirous *adj* avid, eager, desiring, longing, solicitous, wishful.

desist *vb* cease, discontinue, forbear, pause, stay, stop.

desolate *vb* depopulate, despoil, destroy, devastate, pillage, plunder, ravage, ruin, sack. * *adj* bare, barren, bleak, desert, forsaken, lonely, solitary, unfrequented, uninhabited, waste, wild; companionable, lonely, lonesome, solitary; desolated, destroyed, devastated, ravaged, ruined; cheerless, comfortless, companionless, disconsolate, dreary, forlorn, forsaken, miserable, wretched.

desolation *n* destruction, devastation, havoc, ravage, ruin; barrenness, bleakness, desolateness, dreariness, loneliness, solitariness, solitude, wildness; gloom, gloominess, misery, sadness, unhappiness, wretchedness.

despair *vb* despond, give up, lose hope. * *n* dejection, desperation, despondency, disheartenment, hopelessness.

despatch see **dispatch**.

desperado *n* daredevil, gangster, marauder, ruffian, thug, tough.

desperate *adj* despairing, despondent, desponding, hopeless; forlorn, irretrievable; extreme; audacious, daring, foolhardy, frantic, furious, headstrong, precipitate, rash, reckless, violent, wild, wretched; extreme, great, monstrous, prodigious, supreme.

desperation *n* despair, hopelessness; fury, rage.

despicable *adj* abject, base, contemptible, degrading, low, mean, paltry, pitiful, shameful, sordid, vile, worthless.

despise *vb* contemn, disdain, disregard, neglect, scorn, slight, spurn, undervalue.

despite *n* malevolence, malice, malignity, spite; contempt, contumacy, defiance. * *prep* notwithstanding.

despoil *vb* bereave, denude, deprive, dispossess, divest, strip; devastate, fleece, pillage, plunder, ravage, rifle, rob.

despond *vb* despair, give up, lose hope, mourn, sorrow.

despondency *n* blues, dejection, depression, discouragement, gloom, hopelessness, melancholy, sadness.

despondent *adj* dejected, depressed, discouraged, disheartened, dispirited, low-spirited, melancholy.

despot *n* autocrat, dictator; oppressor, tyrant.

despotic *adj* absolute, arrogant, autocratic, dictatorial, imperious; arbitrary, oppressive, tyrannical, tyrannous.

despotism *n* absolutism, autocracy, dictatorship; oppression, tyranny.

destination *n* appointment, decree, destiny, doom, fate, foreordainment, foreordination, fortune, lot, ordination, star; aim, design, drift, end, intention, object, purpose, scope; bourne, goal, harbour, haven, journey's end, resting-place, terminus.

destine *vb* allot, appoint, assign, consecrate, devote, ordain; design, intend, predetermine; decree, doom, foreordain, predestine.

destitute *adj* distressed, indigent, moneyless, necessitous, needy, penniless, penurious, pinched, poor, reduced, wanting.

destitution *n* indigence, need, penury, poverty, privation, want.

destroy *vb* demolish, overthrow, overturn, subvert, raze, ruin; annihilate, dissolve, efface, quench; desolate, devastate, devour, ravage, waste; eradicate, extinguish, extirpate, kill, uproot, slay.

destruction *n* demolition, havoc, overthrow, ruin, subversion; desolation, devastation, holocaust, ravage; annihilation, eradication, extinction, extirpation; death, massacre, murder, slaughter.

destructive *adj* baleful, baneful, deadly, deleterious, detrimental, fatal, hurtful, injurious, lethal, mischievous, noxious, pernicious, ruinous; annihilatory, eradicative, exterminative, extirpative.

desultory *adj* capricious, cursory, discursive, erratic, fitful, inconstant, inexact, irregular, loose, rambling, roving, slight, spasmodic, unconnected, unmethodical, unsettled, unsystematic, vague, wandering.

detach *vb* disengage, disconnect, disjoin, dissever, disunite, divide, part, separate, sever, unfix; appoint, detail, send.

detail *vb* delineate, depict, describe, enumerate, narrate, particularize, portray, recount, rehearse, relate, specify; appoint, detach, send. * *n* account, narration, narrative, recital, relation; appointment, detachment; item, part.

details *n pl* facts, minutiae, particulars, parts.

detain *vb* arrest, check, delay, hinder, hold, keep, restrain, retain, stay, stop; confine.

detect *vb* ascertain, catch, descry, disclose, discover, expose, reveal, unmask.

detention *n* confinement, delay, hindrance, restraint, withholding.

deter *vb* debar, discourage, frighten, hinder, prevent, restrain, stop, withhold.

deteriorate *vb* corrupt, debase, degrade, deprave, disgrace, impair, spoil, vitiate; decline, degenerate, depreciate, worsen.

deterioration *n* corruption, debasement, degradation, depravation, vitiation, perversion; caducity, decadence, decay, decline, degeneracy, degeneration, impairment.

determinate *adj* absolute, certain, definite, determined, established, explicit, express, fixed, limited, positive, settled; conclusive, decided, decisive, definitive.

determination *n* ascertainment, decision, deciding, determining, fixing, settlement, settling; conclusion, judgment, purpose, resolution, resolve, result; direction, leaning, tendency; firmness, constancy, effort, endeavour, exertion, grit, persistence, stamina, resoluteness; definition, limitation, qualification.

determine *vb* adjust, conclude, decide, end, establish, fix, resolve, settle; ascertain, certify, check, verify; impel, incline, induce, influence, lead, turn; decide, resolve; condition, define, limit; compel, necessitate.

detest *vb* abhor, abominate, despise, execrate, hate, loathe, nauseate, recoil from.

detestable *adj* abhorred, abominable, accursed, cursed, damnable, execrable, hateful, odious; disgusting, loathsome, nauseating, offensive, repulsive, sickening, vile.

dethrone *vb* depose, uncrown.

detract *vb* abuse, asperse, belittle, calumniate, debase, decry, defame, depreciate, derogate, disparage, slander, traduce, vilify; deprecate, deteriorate, diminish, lessen.

detraction *n* abuse, aspersion, calumny, censure, defamation, depreciation, derogation, disparagement, slander.

detriment *n* cost, damage, disadvantage, evil, harm, hurt, injury, loss, mischief, prejudice.

detrimental *adj* baleful, deleterious, destructive, harmful, hurtful, injurious, mischievous, pernicious, prejudicial.

devastate *vb* desolate, despoil, destroy, lay waste, harry, pillage, plunder, ravage, sack, spoil, strip, waste.

devastation *n* despoiling, destroying, harrying, pillaging, plundering, ravaging, sacking, spoiling, stripping, wasting; desolation, destruction, havoc, pillage, rapine, ravage, ruin, waste.

develop *vb* disentangle, disclose, evolve, exhibit, explicate, uncover, unfold, unravel; cultivate, grow, mature, open, progress.

development *n* disclosure, disentanglement, exhibition, unfolding, unravelling; growth, increase, maturation, maturing; evolution, growth, progression; elaboration, expansion, explication.

deviate *vb* alter, deflect, digress, diverge, sheer off, slew, tack, turn aside, wheel, wheel about; err, go astray, stray, swerve, wander; differ, vary.

deviation *n* aberration, departure, depression, divarication, divergence, turning; alteration, change, difference, variance, variation.

device *n* contraption, contrivance, gadget, invention; design, expedient, plan, project, resort, resource, scheme, shift; artifice, evasion, fraud, manoeuvre, ruse, stratagem, trick, wile; blazon, emblazonment, emblem, sign, symbol, type.

devil *n* archfiend, demon, fiend, goblin; Apollyon, Belial, Deuce, Evil One, Lucifer, Old Harry, Old Nick, Old Serpent, Prince of Darkness, Satan.

devilish *adj* demon, demonic, demonical, demoniac, demoniacal, diabolic, diabolical, fiendish, hellish, infernal, Mephistophelean, Mephistophelian, satanic; atrocious, barbarous, cruel, malevolent, malicious, malign, malignant, wicked.

devilry *n* devilment, diablerie, mischief; devilishness, fiendishness, wickedness.

devious *adj* deviating, erratic, roundabout, wandering; circuitous, confusing, crooked, labyrinthine, mazy, obscure; crooked, disingenuous, misleading, treacherous.

devise *vb* brew, compass, concert, concoct, contrive, dream up, excogitate, imagine, invent, plan, project, scheme; bequeath, demise, leave, will.

devoid *adj* bare, destitute, empty, vacant, void.

devolve *vb* alienate, consign, convey, deliver over, demise, fall, hand over, make over, pass, transfer.

devote *vb* appropriate, consecrate, dedicate, destine; set apart; addict, apply, give up, resign; consign, doom, give over.

devoted *adj* affectionate, attached, loving; ardent, assiduous, earnest, zealous.

devotee *n* bigot, enthusiast, fan, fanatic, zealot.

devotion *n* consecration, dedication, duty; devotedness, devoutness, fidelity, godliness, holiness, piety, religion, religiousness, saintliness, sanctity; adoration, prayer, worship; affection, attachment, love; ardour, devotedness, eagerness, earnestness, fervour, passion, spirit, zeal.

devotional *adj* devout, godly, pious, religious, saintly.

devour *vb* engorge, gorge, gulp down, raven, swallow eagerly, wolf; annihilate, consume, destroy, expend, spend, swallow up, waste.

devout *adj* devotional, godly, holy, pious, religious, saint-like, saintly; earnest, grave, serious, sincere, solemn.

dexterity *n* ability, address, adroitness, aptitude, aptness, art, cleverness, expertness, facility, knack, quickness, readiness, skilfulness, skill, tact.

dexterous, dextrous *adj* able, adept, adroit, apt, deft, clever, expert, facile, handy, nimble-fingered, quick, ready, skilful.

diabolic, diabolical *adj* atrocious, barbarous, cruel, devilish, fiendish, hellish, impious, infernal, malevolent, malign, malignant, satanic, wicked.

diagram *n* chart, delineation, figure, graph, map, outline, plan, sketch.

dialect *n* idiom, localism, provincialism; jargon, lingo, patois, patter; language, parlance, phraseology, speech, tongue.

dialectal *adj* idiomatic, local, provincial.

dialectic, dialectical *adj* analytical, critical, logical, rational, rationalistic.

dialogue *n* colloquy, communication, conference, conversation, converse, intercourse, interlocution; playbook, script, speech, text, words.

diaphanous *adj* clear, filmy, gossamer, pellucid, sheer, translucent, transparent.

diarrhoea *n* (*med*) flux, looseness, purging, relaxation.

diary *n* chronicle, daybook, journal, register.

diatribe *n* disputation, disquisition, dissertation; abuse, harangue, invective, philippic, reviling, tirade.

dictate *vb* bid, direct, command, decree, enjoin, ordain, order, prescribe, require. * *n* bidding, command, decree, injunction, order; maxim, precept, rule.

dictation *n* direction, order, prescription.

dictator *n* autocrat, despot, tyrant.

dictatorial *adj* absolute, unlimited, unrestricted; authoritative, despotic, dictatory, domineering, imperious, overbearing, peremptory, tyrannical.

dictatorship *n* absolutism, authoritarianism, autocracy, despotism, iron rule, totalitarianism, tyranny.

diction *n* expression, language, phraseology, style, vocabulary, wording.

dictionary *n* glossary, lexicon, thesaurus, vocabulary, wordbook; cyclopedia, encyclopedia.

dictum *n* affirmation, assertion, saying; (*law*) award, arbitrament, decision, opinion.

didactic, didactical *adj* educational, instructive, pedagogic, preceptive.

die *vb* decease, demise, depart, expire, pass on; decay, decline, fade, fade out, perish, wither; cease, disappear, vanish; faint, fall, sink.

diet[1] *vb* eat, feed, nourish; abstain, fast, regulate, slim. * *n* aliment, fare, food, nourishment, nutriment, provision, rations, regimen, subsistence, viands, victuals.

diet[2] *n* assembly, congress, convention, convocation, council, parliament.

differ *vb* deviate, diverge, vary; disagree, dissent; bicker, contend, dispute, quarrel, wrangle.

difference *n* contrariety, contrast, departure, deviation, disagreement, disparity, dissimilarity, dissimilitude, divergence, diversity, heterogeneity, inconformity, nuance, opposition, unlikeness, variation; alienation, altercation, bickering, breach, contention, contest, controversy, debate, disaccord, disagreement, disharmony, dispute, dissension, embroilment, falling out, irreconcilability, jarring, misunderstanding, quarrel, rupture, schism, strife, variance, wrangle; discrimination, distinction.

different *adj* distinct, nonidentical, separate, unlike; contradistinct, contrary, contrasted, deviating, disagreeing, discrepant, dissimilar, divergent, diverse, incompatible, incongruous, unlike, variant, various; divers, heterogeneous, manifold, many, sundry.

difficult *adj* arduous, exacting, hard, Herculean, stiff, tough, uphill; abstruse, complex, intricate, knotty, obscure, perplexing; austere, rigid, unaccommodating, uncompliant, unyielding; dainty, fastidious, squeamish.

difficulty *n* arduousness, laboriousness; bar, barrier, crux, deadlock, dilemma, embarrassment, emergency, exigency, fix, hindrance, impediment, knot, obstacle, obstruction, perplexity, pickle, pinch, predicament, stand, standstill, thwart, trial, trouble; cavil, objection; complication, controversy, difference, embarrassment, embroilment, imbroglio, misunderstanding.

diffidence *n* distrust, doubt, hesitance, hesitancy, hesitation, reluctance; bashfulness, modesty, sheepishness, shyness, timidity.

diffident *adj* distrustful, doubtful, hesitant, hesitating, reluctant; bashful, modest, over-modest, sheepish, shy, timid.

diffuse[1] *vb* circulate, disperse, disseminate, distribute, intermingle, propagate, scatter, spread, strew.

diffuse[2] *adj* broadcast, dispersed, scattered, sparse, sporadic, widespread; broad, extensive, liberal, profuse, wide; copious, loose, prolix, rambling, verbose, wordy.

diffusion *n* circulation, dispersion, dissemination, distribution, extension, propagation, spread, strewing.

diffusive *adj* expansive, permeating, wide-reaching; spreading, dispersive, disseminative, distributive, distributory.

dig *vb* channel, delve, excavate, grub, hollow out, quarry, scoop, tunnel. * *n* poke, punch, thrust.

digest[1] *vb* arrange, classify, codify, dispose, methodize, systemize, tabulate; concoct; assimilate, consider, contemplate, meditate, ponder, reflect upon, study; master; macerate, soak, steep.

digest[2] *n* code, system; abridgement, abstract, brief, breviary, compend, compendium, conspectus, epitome, summary, synopsis.

dignified *adj* august, courtly, decorous, grave, imposing, majestic, noble, stately.

dignify *vb* advance, aggrandize, elevate, ennoble, exalt, promote; adorn, grace, honour.

dignity *n* elevation, eminence, exaltation, excellence, glory, greatness, honour, place, rank, respectability, standing, station; decorum, grandeur, majesty, nobleness, stateliness; preferment; dignitary, magistrate; elevation, height.

digress *vb* depart, deviate, diverge, expatiate, wander.

digression *n* departure, deviation, divergence; episode, excursus.

dilapidate *vb* demolish, destroy, disintegrate, ruin, waste.

dilapidated *adj* decayed, ruined, run down, wasted.

dilapidation *n* decay, demolition, destruction, disintegration, disrepair, dissolution, downfall, ruin, waste.

dilate *vb* distend, enlarge, expand, extend, inflate, swell, tend, widen; amplify, descant, dwell, enlarge, expatiate.

dilation *n* amplification, bloating, distension, enlargement, expanding, expansion, spreading, swelling.

dilatory *adj* backward, behind-hand, delaying, laggard, lagging, lingering, loitering, off-putting, procrastinating, slack, slow, sluggish, tardy.

dilemma *n* difficulty, fix, plight, predicament, problem, quandary, strait.

diligence *n* activity, application, assiduity, assiduousness, attention, care, constancy, earnestness, heedfulness, industry, laboriousness, perseverance, sedulousness.
diligent *adj* active, assiduous, attentive, busy, careful, constant, earnest, hard-working, indefatigable, industrious, laborious, notable, painstaking, persevering, persistent, sedulous, tireless.
dilly-dally *vb* dally, dawdle. delay, lag, linger, loiter, saunter, trifle.
dilute *vb* attenuate, reduce, thin, weaken. * *adj* attenuated, diluted, thin, weak, wishy-washy.
dim *vb* blur, cloud, darken, dull, obscure, sully, tarnish. * *adj* cloudy, dark, dusky, faint, ill-defined, indefinite, indistinct, mysterious, obscure, shadowy; dull, obtuse; clouded, confused, darkened, faint, obscured; blurred, dulled, sullied, tarnished.
dimension *n* extension, extent, measure.
dimensions *npl* amplitude, bigness, bulk, capacity, greatness, largeness, magnitude, mass, massiveness, size, volume; measurements.
diminish *vb* abate, belittle, contract, decrease, lessen, reduce; curtail, cut, dwindle, melt, narrow, shrink, shrivel, subside, taper off, weaken.
diminution *n* abatement, abridgement, attenuation, contraction, curtailment, decrescendo, cut, decay, decrease, deduction, lessening, reduction, retrenchment, weakening.
diminutive *adj* contracted, dwarfish, little, minute, puny, pygmy, small, tiny.
din *vb* beat, boom, clamour, drum, hammer, pound, repeat, ring, thunder. * *n* bruit, clamour, clash, clatter, crash, crashing, hubbub, hullabaloo, hurly-burly, noise, outcry, racket, row, shout, uproar.
dingle *n* dale, dell, glen, vale, valley.
dingy *adj* brown, dun, dusky; bedimmed, colourless, dimmed, dulled, faded, obscure, smirched, soiled, sullied.
dint *n* blow, stroke; dent, indentation, nick, notch; force, power.
diocese *n* bishopric, charge, episcopate, jurisdiction, see.
dip *vb* douse, duck, immerse, plunge, souse; bail, ladle; dive, pitch; bend, incline, slope. * *n* decline, declivity, descent, drop, fall; concavity, depression, hole, hollow, pit, sink; bathe, dipping, ducking, sousing, swim.
diplomat *n* diplomatist, envoy, legate, minister, negotiator.
dire *adj* alarming, awful, calamitous, cruel, destructive, disastrous, dismal, dreadful, fearful, gloomy, horrible, horrid, implacable, inexorable, portentous, shocking, terrible, terrific, tremendous, woeful.
direct *vb* aim. cast, level, point, turn; advise, conduct, control, dispose, guide, govern, manage, regulate, rule; command, bid, enjoin, instruct, order; lead, show; address, superscribe. * *adj* immediate, straight, undeviating; absolute, categorical, express, plain, unambiguous; downright, earnest, frank, ingenuous, open, outspoken, sincere, straightforward, unequivocal.
direction *n* aim; tendency; bearing, course; administration, conduct, control, government, management, oversight, superintendence; guidance, lead; command, order, prescription; address, superscription.
directly *adv* absolutely, expressly, openly, unambiguously; forthwith, immediately, instantly, quickly, presently, promptly, soon, speedily.
director *n* boss, manager, superintendent; adviser, counsellor, guide, instructor, mentor, monitor.
direful *adj* awful, calamitous, dire, dreadful, fearful, gloomy, horrible, shocking, terrible, terrific, tremendous.
dirge *n* coronach, elegy, lament, monody, requiem, threnody.
dirty *vb* befoul, defile, draggle, foul, pollute, soil, sully. * *adj* begrimed. defiled, filthy, foul, mucky, nasty, soiled, unclean; clouded, cloudy, dark, dull, muddy, sullied; base, beggarly, contemptible, despicable, grovelling, low, mean, paltry, pitiful, scurvy, shabby, sneaking, squalid; disagreeable, rainy, sloppy, uncomfortable.
disability *n* disablement, disqualification, impotence, impotency, inability, incapacity, incompetence, incompetency, unfitness, weakness.
disable *vb* cripple, enfeeble, hamstring, impair, paralyse, unman, weaken; disenable, disqualify, incapacitate, unfit.
disabuse *vb* correct, undeceive.
disadvantage *n* disadvantageousness, inconvenience, unfavourableness; damage, detriment, disservice, drawback, harm, hindrance, hurt, injury, loss, prejudice.
disadvantageous *adj* inconvenient, inexpedient, unfavourable; deleterious, detrimental, harmful, hurtful, injurious, prejudicial.
disaffect *vb* alienate, disdain, dislike, disorder, estrange.
disaffected *adj* alienated, disloyal, dissatisfied, estranged.
disaffection *n* alienation, breach, disagreement, dislike, disloyalty, dissatisfaction, estrangement, repugnance, ill will, unfriendliness.
disagree *vb* deviate, differ, diverge, vary; dissent; argue, bicker, clash, debate, dispute, quarrel, wrangle.
disagreeable *adj* contrary, displeasing, distasteful, nasty, offensive, unpleasant, unpleasing, unsuitable.
disagreement *n* deviation, difference, discrepancy, dissimilarity, dissimilitude, divergence, diversity, incongruity, unlikeness; disaccord, dissent; argument, bickering, clashing, conflict, contention, dispute, dissension, disunion, disunity, jarring, misunderstanding, quarrel, strife, variance, wrangle.
disallow *vb* forbid, prohibit; disapprove, reject; deny, disavow, disclaim, dismiss, disown, repudiate.
disappear *vb* depart, fade, vanish; cease, dissolve.
disappoint *vb* baffle, balk, deceive, defeat, delude, disconcert, foil, frustrate, mortify, tantalize, thwart, vex.
disappointment *n* baffling, balk, failure, foiling, frustration, miscarriage, mortification, unfulfilment.
disapprobation *n* blame, censure, condemnation, disapproval, dislike, displeasure, reproof.
disapprove *vb* blame, censure, condemn, deprecate, dislike; disallow, reject.
disarrange *vb* agitate, confuse, derange, disallow, dishevel, dislike, dislocate, disorder, disorganize, disturb, jumble, reject, rumple, tumble, unsettle.
disarray *n* confusion, disorder; dishabille.
disaster *n* accident, adversity, blow, calamity, casualty, catastrophe, misadventure, mischance, misfortune, mishap, reverse, ruin, stroke.
disastrous *adj* adverse, calamitous, catastrophic, destructive, hapless, ill-fated, ill-starred, ruinous, unfortunate, unlucky, unpropitious, unprosperous, untoward.
disavow *vb* deny, disallow, disclaim, disown.
disband *vb* break up, disperse, scatter, separate.
disbelief *n* agnosticism, doubt, nonconviction, rejection, unbelief.
disburden *vb* alleviate, diminish, disburden, discharge, disencumber, ease, free, relieve, rid.
disbursement *n* expenditure, spending.
discard *vb* abandon, cast off, lay aside, reject; banish, break, cashier, discharge, dismiss, remove, repudiate.
discern *vb* differentiate, discriminate, distinguish, judge; behold, descry, discover, espy, notice, observe, perceive, recognize, see.
discernible *adj* detectable, discoverable, perceptible.
discerning *adj* acute, astute, clear-sighted, discriminating, discriminative, eagle-eyed, ingenious, intelligent, judicious, knowing, perspicacious, piercing, sagacious, sharp, shrewd.
discernment *n* acumen, acuteness, astuteness, brightness, cleverness, discrimination, ingenuity, insight, intelligence, judgement, penetration, perspicacity, sagacity, sharpness, shrewdness; beholding, descrying, discerning, discovery, espial, notice, perception.
discharge *vb* disburden, unburden, unload; eject, emit, excrete, expel, void; cash, liquidate, pay; absolve, acquit, clear, exonerate, free, release, relieve; cashier, discard, dismiss, sack; destroy, remove; execute, perform, fulfil, observe; annul, cancel, invalidate, nullify, rescind. * *n* disburdening, unloading; acquittal, dismissal, displacement, ejection, emission, evacuation, excretion, expulsion, vent, voiding; blast, burst, detonation, explosion, firing; execution, fulfilment, observance; annulment, clearance, liquidation, payment, satisfaction, settlement; exemption, liberation, release; flow, flux, execration.

disciple *n* catechumen, learner, pupil, scholar, student; adherent, follower, partisan, supporter.

discipline *vb* breed, drill, educate, exercise, form, instruct, teach, train; control, govern, regulate, school; chasten, chastise, punish. * *n* culture, drill, drilling, education, exercise, instruction, training; control, government, regulation, subjection; chastisement, correction, punishment.

disclaim *vb* abandon, disallow, disown, disavow; reject, renounce, repudiate.

disclose *vb* discover, exhibit, expose, manifest, uncover; bare, betray, blab, communicate, divulge, impart, publish, reveal, show, tell, unfold, unveil, utter.

disclosure *n* betrayal, discovery, exposé, exposure, revelation, uncovering.

discolour *vb* stain, tarnish, tinge.

discomfit *vb* beat, checkmate, conquer, defeat, overcome, overpower, overthrow, rout, subdue, vanquish, worst; abash, baffle, balk, confound, disconcert, foil, frustrate, perplex, upset.

discomfiture *n* confusion, defeat, frustration, overthrow, rout, vexation.

discomfort *n* annoyance, disquiet, distress, inquietude, malaise, trouble, uneasiness, unpleasantness, vexation.

discommode *vb* annoy, disquiet, disturb, harass, incommode, inconvenience, molest, trouble.

discompose *vb* confuse, derange, disarrange, disorder, disturb, embroil, jumble, unsettle; agitate, annoy, chafe, displease, disquiet, fret, harass, irritate, nettle, plague, provoke, ruffle, trouble, upset, vex, worry; abash, bewilder, disconcert, embarrass, fluster, perplex.

disconcert *vb* baffle, balk, contravene, defeat, disarrange, frustrate, interrupt, thwart, undo, upset; abash, agitate, bewilder, confuse, demoralize, discompose, disturb, embarrass, faze, perplex, perturb, unbalance, worry.

disconnect *vb* detach, disengage, disjoin, dissociate, disunite, separate, sever, uncouple, unlink.

disconsolate *adj* broken-hearted, cheerless, comfortless, dejected, desolate, forlorn, gloomy, heartbroken, inconsolable, melancholy, miserable, sad, sorrowful, unhappy, woeful, wretched.

discontent *n* discontentment, displeasure, dissatisfaction, inquietude, restlessness, uneasiness.

discontinuance *n* cessation, discontinuation, disjunction, disruption, intermission, interruption, separation, stop, stoppage, stopping, suspension.

discontinue *vb* cease, intermit, interrupt, quit, stop.

discord *n* contention, difference, disagreement, dissension, opposition, quarrelling, rupture, strife, variance, wrangling; cacophony, discordance, dissonance, harshness, jangle, jarring.

discordance *n* conflict, disagreement, incongruity, inconsistency, opposition, repugnance; discord, dissonance.

discordant *adj* contradictory, contrary, disagreeing, incongruous, inconsistent, opposite, repugnant; cacophonous, dissonant, harsh, inharmonious, jangling, jarring.

discount *vb* allow for, deduct, lower, rebate, reduce, subtract; disregard, ignore, overlook. * *n* abatement, drawback; allowance, deduction, rebate, reduction.

discourage *vb* abase, awe, damp, daunt, deject, depress, deject, dismay, dishearten, dispirit, frighten, intimidate; deter, dissuade, hinder; disfavour, discountenance.

discouragement *n* disheartening; dissuasion; damper, deterrent, embarrassment, hindrance, impediment, obstacle, wet blanket.

discourse *vb* expiate, hold forth, lucubrate, sermonize, speak; advise, confer, converse, parley, talk; emit, utter. * *n* address, disquisition, dissertation, homily, lecture, preachment, sermon, speech, treatise; colloquy, conversation, converse, talk.

discourteous *adj* abrupt, brusque, curt, disrespectful, ill-bred, ill-mannered, impolite, inurbane, rude, uncivil, uncourtly, ungentlemanly, unmannerly.

discourtesy *n* abruptness, brusqueness, ill-breeding, impoliteness, incivility, rudeness.

discover *vb* communicate, disclose, exhibit, impart, manifest, show, reveal, tell; ascertain, behold, discern, espy, see; descry, detect, determine, discern; contrive, invent, originate.

discredit *vb* disbelieve, doubt, question; depreciate, disgrace, dishonour, disparage, reproach. * *n* disbelief, distrust; disgrace, dishonour, disrepute, ignominy, notoriety, obloquy, odium, opprobrium, reproach, scandal.

discreditable *adj* derogatory, disgraceful, disreputable, dishonourable, ignominious, infamous, inglorious, scandalous, unworthy.

discreet *adj* careful, cautious, circumspect, considerate, discerning, heedful, judicious, prudent, sagacious, wary, wise.

discrepancy *n* contrariety, difference, disagreement, discordance, dissonance, divergence, incongruity, inconsistency, variance, variation.

discrete *adj* discontinuous, disjunct, distinct, separate; disjunctive.

discretion *n* care, carefulness, caution, circumspection, considerateness, consideration, heedfulness, judgement, judicious, prudence, wariness; discrimination, maturity, responsibility; choice, option, pleasure, will.

discrimination *n* difference, distinction; acumen, acuteness, discernment, in-sight, judgement, penetration, sagacity.

discriminatory *adj* characteristic, characterizing, discriminating, discriminative, distinctive, distinguishing.

discursive *adj* argumentative, reasoning; casual, cursory, desultory, digressive, erratic, excursive, loose, rambling, roving, wandering, wave.

discus *n* disk, quoit.

discuss *vb* agitate, argue, canvass, consider, debate, deliberate, examine, sift, ventilate.

disdain *vb* contemn, deride, despise, disregard, reject, scorn, slight, scout, spurn. * *n* arrogance, contempt, contumely, haughtiness, hauteur, scorn, sneer, superciliousness.

disdainful *adj* cavalier, contemptuous, contumelious, haughty, scornful, supercilious.

disease *n* affection, affliction, ail, ailment, complaint, disorder, distemper, illness, indisposition, infirmity, malady, sickness.

disembarrass *vb* clear, disburden, disencumber, disengage, disentangle, extricate, ease, free, release, rid.

disembodied *adj* bodiless, disincarnate, immaterial, incorporeal, spiritual, unbodied.

disembowel *vb* degut, embowel, eviscerate.

disengage *vb* clear, deliver, discharge, disembarrass, disembroil, disencumber, disentangle, extricate, liberate, release; detach, disjoin, dissociate, disunite, divide, separate; wean, withdraw.

disentangle *vb* loosen, separate, unfold, unravel, untwist; clear, detach, disconnect, disembroil, disengage, extricate, liberate, loose, unloose.

disfavour *n* disapproval, disesteem, dislike, disrespect; discredit, disregard, disrepute, unacceptableness; disservice, unkindness. * *vb* disapprove, dislike, object, oppose.

disfigure *vb* blemish, deface, deform, injure, mar, spoil.

disfigurement *n* blemishing, defacement, deforming, disfiguration, injury, marring, spoiling; blemish, defect, deformity, scar, spot, stain.

disgorge *vb* belch, cast up, spew, throw up, vomit; discharge, eject; give up, relinquish, surrender, yield.

disgrace *vb* degrade, humble, humiliate; abase, debase, defame, discredit, disfavour, dishonour, disparage, reproach, stain, sully, taint, tarnish. * *n* abomination, disrepute, humiliation, ignominy, infamy, mortification, shame, scandal.

disgraceful *adj* discreditable, dishonourable, disreputable, ignominious, infamous, opprobrious, scandalous, shameful.

disguise *vb* cloak, conceal, cover, dissemble, hide, mask, muffle, screen, secrete, shroud, veil. * *n* concealment, cover, mask, veil; blind, cloak, masquerade, pretence, pretext, veneer.

disguised *adj* cloaked, masked, veiled.

disgust *vb* nauseate, sicken; abominate, detest, displease, offend, repel, repulse, revolt. * *n* disrelish, distaste, loathing, nausea; abhorrence, abomination, antipathy, aversion, detestation, dislike, repugnance, revulsion.

dish *vb* deal out, give, ladle, serve; blight, dash, frustrate, mar, ruin, spoil. * *n* bowl, plate, saucer, vessel.

dishearten *vb* cast down, damp, dampen, daunt, deject, depress, deter, discourage, dispirit.

dished *adj* baffled, balked, disappointed, disconcerted, foiled, frustrated, upset.

dishevelled *adj* disarranged, disordered, messed, tousled, tumbled, unkempt, untidy, untrimmed.

dishonest *adj* cheating, corrupt, crafty, crooked, deceitful, deceiving, deceptive, designing, faithless, false, falsehearted, fraudulent, guileful, knavish, perfidious, slippery, treacherous, unfair, unscrupulous.

dishonesty *n* deceitfulness, faithlessness, falsehood, fraud, fraudulence, fraudulency, improbity, knavery, perfidious, treachery, trickery.

dishonour *vb* abase, defame, degrade, discredit, disfavour, dishonour, disgrace, disparage, reproach, shame, taint. * *n* abasement, basement, contempt, degradation, discredit, disesteem, disfavour, disgrace, dishonour, disparagement, disrepute, ignominy, infamy, obloquy, odium, opprobrium, reproach, scandal, shame.

dishonourable *adj* discreditable, disgraceful, disreputable, ignominious, infamous, scandalous, shameful; base, false, falsehearted, shameless.

disinclination *n* alienation, antipathy, aversion, dislike, indisposition, reluctance, repugnance, unwillingness.

disinfect *vb* cleanse, deodorize, fumigate, purify, sterilize.

disingenuous *adj* artful, deceitful, dishonest, hollow, insidious, insincere, uncandid, unfair, wily.

disintegrate *vb* crumble, decompose, dissolve, disunite, pulverize, separate.

disinter *vb* dig up, disentomb, disinhume, exhume, unbury.

disinterested *adj* candid, fair, high-minded, impartial, indifferent, unbiased, unselfish, unprejudiced; generous, liberal, magnanimous.

disjoin *vb* detach, disconnect, dissever, dissociate, disunite, divide, part, separate, sever, sunder.

disjointed *adj* desultory, disconnected, incoherent, loose.

disjunction *n* disassociation, disconnection, disunion, isolation, parting, separation, severance.

dislike *vb* abominate, detest, disapprove, disrelish, hate, loathe. * *n* antagonism, antipathy, aversion, disapproval, disfavour, disgust, disinclination, displeasure, disrelish, distaste, loathing, repugnance.

dislocate *vb* disarrange, displace, disturb; disarticulate, disjoint, luxate, slip.

dislodge *vb* dismount, dispel, displace, eject, expel, oust, remove.

disloyal *adj* disaffected, faithless, false, perfidious, traitorous, treacherous, treasonable, undutiful, unfaithful, unpatriotic, untrue.

disloyalty *n* faithlessness, perfidy, treachery, treason, undutifulness, unfaithfulness.

dismal *adj* cheerless, dark, dreary, dull, gloomy, lonesome; blue, calamitous, doleful, dolorous, funereal, lugubrious, melancholy, mournful, sad, sombre, sorrowful.

dismantle *vb* divest, strip, unrig.

dismay *vb* affright, alarm, appal, daunt, discourage, dishearten, frighten, horrify, intimidate, paralyse, scare, terrify. * *n* affright, alarm, consternation, fear, fright, horror, terror.

dismember *vb* disjoint, dislimb, dislocate, mutilate; divide, separate, rend, sever.

dismiss *vb* banish, cashier, discard, discharge, disperse, reject, release, remove.

dismount *vb* alight, descend, dismantle, unhorse; dislodge, displace.

disobedient *adj* froward, noncompliant, noncomplying, obstinate, rebellious, refractory, uncomplying, undutiful, unruly, unsubmissive.

disobey *vb* infringe, transgress, violate.

disobliging *adj* ill-natured, unaccommodating, unamiable, unfriendly, unkind.

disorder *vb* confound, confuse, derange, disarrange, discompose, disorganize, disturb, unsettle, upset. * *n* confusion, derangement, disarrangement, disarray, disorganization, irregularity, jumble, litter, mess, topsy-turvy; brawl, commotion, disturbance, fight, quarrel, riot, tumult; riotousness, tumultuousness, turbulence; ail, ailment, complaint, distemper, illness, indisposition, malady, sickness.

disorderly *adj* chaotic, confused, intemperate, irregular, unmethodical, unsystematic, untidy; lawless, rebellious, riotous, tumultuous, turbulent, ungovernable, unmanageable, unruly.

disorganization *n* chaos, confusion, demoralization, derangement, disorder.

disorganize *vb* confuse, demoralize, derange, disarrange, discompose, disorder, disturb, unsettle, upset.

disown *vb* disavow, disclaim, reject, renounce, repudiate; abnegate, deny, disallow.

disparage *vb* belittle, decry, depreciate, derogate from, detract from, doubt, question, run down, underestimate, underpraise, underrate, undervalue; asperse, defame, inveigh against, reflect on, reproach, slur, speak ill of, traduce, vilify.

disparagement *n* belittlement, depreciation, derogation, detraction, underrating, undervaluing; derogation, detraction, diminution, harm, impairment, injury, lessening, prejudice, worsening; aspersion, calumny, defamation, reflection, reproach, traduction, vilification; blackening, disgrace, dispraise, indignity, reproach.

disparity *n* difference, disproportion, inequality; dissimilarity, dissimilitude, unlikeness.

dispassionate *adj* calm, collected, composed, cool, imperturbable, inexcitable, moderate, quiet, serene, sober, staid, temperate, undisturbed, unexcitable, unexcited, unimpassioned, unruffled; candid, disinterested, fair, impartial, neutral, unbiased.

dispatch, despatch *vb* assassinate, kill, murder, slaughter, slay; accelerate, conclude, dismiss, expedite, finish, forward, hasten, hurry, quicken, speed. * *n* dispatching, sending; diligence, expedition, haste, rapidity, speed; completion, conduct, doing, transaction; communication, document, instruction, letter, message, missive, report.

dispel *vb* banish, disperse, dissipate, scatter.

dispensation *n* allotment, apportioning, apportionment, dispensing, distributing, distribution; administration, stewardship; economy, plan, scheme, system; exemption, immunity, indulgence, licence, privilege.

dispense *vb* allot, apportion, assign, distribute; administer, apply, execute; absolve, excuse, exempt, exonerate, release, relieve.

disperse *vb* dispel, dissipate, dissolve, scatter, separate; diffuse, disseminate, spread; disappear, vanish.

dispirit *vb* damp, dampen, depress, deject, discourage, dishearten.

dispirited *adj* chapfallen, dejected, depressed, discouraged, disheartened, down-cast, down-hearted.

displace *vb* dislocate, mislay, misplace, move; dislodge, remove; cashier, depose, discard, discharge, dismiss, oust, replace, unseat.

display *vb* expand, extend, open, spread, unfold; exhibit, show; flaunt, parade. * *n* exhibition, manifestation, show; flourish, ostentation, pageant, parade, pomp.

displease *vb* disgruntle, disgust, disoblige, dissatisfy, offend; affront, aggravate, anger, annoy, chafe, chagrin, fret, irritate, nettle, pique, provoke, vex.

displeasure *n* disaffection, disapprobation, disapproval, dislike, dissatisfaction, distaste; anger, annoyance, indignation, irritation, pique, resentment, vexation, wrath; injury, offence.

disport *vb* caper, frisk, frolic, gambol, play, sport, wanton; amuse, beguile, cheer, divert, entertain, relax, solace.

disposal *n* arrangement, disposition; conduct, control, direction, disposure, government, management, ordering, regulation; bestowment, dispensation, distribution.

dispose *vb* arrange, distribute, marshal, group, place, range, rank, set; adjust, determine, regulate, settle; bias, incline, induce, lead, move, predispose; control, decide, regulate, rule, settle; arrange, bargain, compound; alienate, convey, demise, sell, transfer.

disposed *adj* apt, inclined, prone, ready, tending.

disposition *n* arrangement, arranging, classification, disposing, grouping, location, placing; adjustment, control, direction, disposure, disposal, management, ordering, regulation; aptitude, bent, bias, inclination, nature, predisposition, proclivity, proneness, propensity, tendency; character, constitution, humour, native, nature, temper, temperament, turn; inclination, willingness; bestowal, bestowment, dispensation, distribution.

dispossess *vb* deprive, divest, expropriate, strip; dislodge, eject, oust; disseise, disseize, evict, oust.

dispraise *n* blame, censure; discredit, disgrace, dishonour, disparagement, opprobrium, reproach, shame.

disproof *n* confutation, rebuttal, refutation.

disproportion *n* disparity, inadequacy, inequality, insufficiency, unsuitableness; incommensurateness.

disprove *vb* confute, rebel, rebut.

disputable *adj* controvertible, debatable, doubtful, questionable.

disputation *n* argumentation, controversy, debate, dispute.

disputatious *adj* argumentative, bickering, captious, caviling, contentious, dissentious, litigious, polemical, pugnacious, quarrelsome.

dispute *vb* altercate, argue, debate, litigate, question; bicker, brawl, jangle, quarrel, spar, spat, squabble, tiff, wrangle; agitate, argue, debate, ventilate; challenge, contradict, controvert, deny, impugn; contest, struggle for. * *n* controversy, debate, discussion, disputation; altercation, argument, bickering, brawl, disagreement, dissension, spat, squabble, tiff, wrangle.

disqualification *n* disability, incapitation.

disqualify *vb* disable, incapacitate, unfit; disenable, preclude, prohibit.

disquiet *vb* agitate, annoy, bother, discompose, disturb, excite, fret, harass, incommode, molest, plague, pester, trouble, vex, worry. * *n* anxiety, discomposure, disquietude, disturbance, restlessness, solicitude, trouble, uneasiness, unrest, vexation, worry.

disquisition *n* dissertation, discourse, essay, paper, thesis, treatise.

disregard *vb* contemn, despise, disdain, disobey, disparage, ignore, neglect, overlook, slight. * *n* contempt, ignoring, inattention, neglect, pretermit, oversight, slight; disesteem, disfavour, indifference.

disrelish *vb* dislike, loathe. * *n* dislike, distaste; flatness, insipidity, insipidness, nauseousness; antipathy, aversion, repugnance.

disreputable *adj* derogatory, discreditable, dishonourable, disgraceful, infamous, opprobrious, scandalous, shameful; base, contemptible, low, mean, vicious, vile, vulgar.

disrepute *n* abasement, degradation, derogation, discredit, disgrace, dishonour, ill-repute, odium.

disrespect *n* disesteem, disregard, irreverence, neglect, slight.

disrespectful *adj* discourteous, impertinent, impolite, rude, uncivil, uncourteous.

dissatisfaction *n* discontent, disquiet, inquietude, uneasiness; disapprobation, disapproval, dislike, displeasure.

dissect *vb* analyze, examine, explore, investigate, scrutinize, sift; cut apart.

dissemble *vb* cloak, conceal, cover, disguise, hide; counterfeit, dissimulate, feign, pretend.

dissembler *n* dissimulator, feigner, hypocrite, pretender, sham.

disseminate *vb* circulate, diffuse, disperse, proclaim, promulgate, propagate, publish, scatter, spread.

dissension *n* contention, difference, disagreement, discord, quarrel, strife, variance.

dissent *vb* decline, differ, disagree, refuse. * *n* difference, disagreement, nonconformity, opposition, recusancy, refusal.

dissentient *adj* disagreeing, dissenting, dissident, factious.

dissertation *n* discourse, disquisition, essay, thesis, treatise.

disservice *n* disadvantage, disfavour, harm, hurt, ill-turn, injury, mischief.

dissidence *n* disagreement, dissent, nonconformity, sectarianism.

dissimilar *adj* different, divergent, diverse, heterogeneous, unlike, various.

dissimilarity *n* dissimilitude, disparity, divergent, diversity, unlikeness, variation.

dissimulation *n* concealment, deceit, dissembling, double-dealing, duplicity, feigning, hypocrisy, pretence.

dissipate *vb* dispel, disperse, scatter; consume, expend, lavish, spend, squander, waste; disappear, vanish.

dissipation *n* dispersion, dissemination, scattering, vanishing; squandering, waste; crapulence, debauchery, dissoluteness, drunkenness, excess, profligacy.

dissociate *vb* disjoin, dissever, disunite, divide, separate, sever, sunder.

dissolute *adj* abandoned, corrupt, debauched, depraved, disorderly, dissipated, graceless, lax, lewd, licentious, loose, profligate, rakish, reprobate, shameless, vicious, wanton, wild.

dissolution *n* liquefaction, melting, solution; decomposition, putrefaction; death, disease; destruction, overthrow, ruin; termination.

dissolve *vb* liquefy, melt; disorganize, disunite, divide, loose, separate, sever; destroy, ruin; disappear, fade, scatter, vanish; crumble, decompose, disintegrate, perish.

dissonance *n* cacophony, discord, discordance, harshness, jarring; disagreement, discrepancy, incongruity, inconsistency.

dissonant *adj* discordant, grating, harsh, jangling, jarring, unharmonious; contradictory, disagreeing, discrepant, incongruous, inconsistent.

distance *vb* excel, outdo, outstrip, surpass. * *n* farness, remoteness; aloofness, coldness, frigidity, reserve, stiffness, offishness; absence, separation, space.

distant *adj* far, far-away, remote; aloof, ceremonious, cold, cool, frigid, haughty, reserved, stiff, uncordial; faint, indirect, obscure, slight.

distaste *n* disgust, disrelish; antipathy, aversion, disinclination, dislike, displeasure, dissatisfaction, repugnance.

distasteful *adj* disgusting, loathsome, nauseating, nauseous, unpalatable, unsavoury; disagreeable, displeasing, offensive, repugnant, repulsive, unpleasant.

distemper *n* ail, ailment, complaint, disease, disorder, illness, indisposition, malady, sickness.

distempered *adj* diseased, disordered; immoderate, inordinate, intemperate, unregulated.

distend *vb* bloat, dilate, enlarge, expand, increase, inflate, puff, stretch, swell, widen.

distil *vb* dribble, drip, drop; extract, separate.

distinct *adj* definite, different, discrete, disjunct, individual, separate, unconnected; clear, defined, manifest, obvious, plain, unconfused, unmistakable, well-defined.

distinction *n* discernment, discrimination, distinguishing; difference; account, celebrity, credit, eminence, fame, name, note, rank, renown, reputation, repute, respectability, superiority.

distinctive *adj* characteristic, differentiating, discriminating, distinguishing.

distinctness *n* difference, separateness; clearness, explicitness, lucidity, lucidness, perspicuity, precision.

distinguish *vb* characterize, mark; differentiate, discern, discriminate, perceive, recognize, see, single out, tell; demarcate, divide, separate; celebrate, honour, signalize.

distinguished *adj* celebrated, eminent, famous, illustrious, noted; conspicuous, extraordinary, laureate, marked, shining, superior, transcendent.

distort *vb* contort, deform, gnarl, screw, twist, warp, wrest; falsify, misrepresent, pervert.

distortion *n* contortion, deformation, deformity, twist, wryness; falsification, misrepresentation, perversion, wresting.

distract *vb* divert, draw away; bewilder, confound, confuse, derange, discompose, disconcert, disturb, embarrass, harass, madden, mystify, perplex, puzzle.

distracted *adj* crazed, crazy, deranged, frantic, furious, insane, mad, raving, wild.

distraction *n* abstraction, bewilderment, confusion, mystification, embarrassment, perplexity; agitation, commotion, discord, disorder, disturbance, division, perturbation, tumult, turmoil; aberration, alienation, delirium, derangement, frenzy, hallucination, incoherence, insanity, lunacy, madness, mania, raving, wandering.

distress *vb* afflict, annoy, grieve, harry, pain, perplex, rack, trouble; distrain, seize, take. * *n* affliction, calamity, disaster, misery, misfortune, adversity, hardship, perplexity, trial, tribulation; agony, anguish, dolour, grief, sorrow, suffering; gnawing, gripe, griping, pain, torment, torture; destitution, indigence, poverty, privation, straits, want.

distribute *vb* allocate, allot, apportion, assign, deal, dispense, divide, dole out, give, mete, partition, prorate, share; administer, arrange, assort, class, classify, dispose.

distribution *n* allocation, allotment, apportionment, assignment, assortment, dispensation, dispensing; arrangement, disposal, disposition, classification, division, dole, grouping, partition, sharing.

district *n* circuit, department, neighbourhood, province, quarter, region, section, territory, tract, ward.

distrust *vb* disbelieve, discredit, doubt, misbelieve, mistrust, question, suspect. * *n* doubt, misgiving, mistrust, question, suspicion.

distrustful *adj* doubting, dubious, suspicious.

disturb *vb* agitate, shake, stir; confuse, derange, disarrange, disorder, unsettle, upset; annoy, discompose, disconcert, disquiet, distract, fuss, incommode, molest, perturb, plague, trouble, ruffle, vex, worry; impede, interrupt, hinder.

disturbance *n* agitation, commotion, confusion, convulsion, derangement, disorder, perturbation, unsettlement; annoyance, discomposure, distraction, excitement, fuss; hindrance, interruption, molestation; brawl, commotion, disorder, excitement, fracas, hubbub, riot, rising, tumult, turmoil, uproar.

disunion *n* disconnection, disjunction, division, separation, severance; breach, feud, rupture, schism.

disunite *vb* detach, disconnect, disjoin, dissever, dissociate, divide, part, rend, separate, segregate, sever, sunder; alienate, estrange.

disuse *n* desuetude, discontinuance, disusage, neglect, nonobservance.

ditch *vb* canalize, dig, excavate, furrow, gouge, trench; abandon, discard, dump, jettison, scrap. * *n* channel, drain, fosse, moat, trench.

divagation *n* deviation, digression, rambling, roaming, straying, wandering.

divan *n* bed, chesterfield, couch, settee, sofa.

divaricate *vb* diverge, fork, part.

dive *vb* explore, fathom, penetrate, plunge, sound. * *n* drop, fall, header, plunge; bar, den, dump, joint, saloon.

diverge *vb* divide, radiate, separate; divaricate, separate; deviate, differ, disagree, vary.

divers *adj* different, manifold, many, numerous, several, sundry, various.

diverse *adj* different, differing, disagreeing, dissimilar, divergent, heterogeneous, multifarious, multiform, separate, unlike, variant, various, varying.

diversion *n* deflection, diverting; amusement, delight, distraction, enjoyment, entertainment, game, gratification, pastime, play, pleasure, recreation, sport; detour, digression.

diversity *n* difference, dissimilarity, dissimilitude, divergence, unlikeness, variation; heterogeneity, manifoldness, multifariousness, multiformity, variety.

divert *vb* deflect, distract, disturb; amuse, beguile, delight, entertain, exhilarate, give pleasure, gratify, recreate, refresh, solace.

divest *vb* denude, disrobe, strip, unclothe, undress; deprive, dispossess, strip.

divide *vb* bisect, cleave, cut, dismember, dissever, disunite, open, part, rend, segregate, separate, sever, shear, split, sunder; allocate, allot, apportion, assign, dispense, distribute, dole, mete, portion, share; compartmentalize, demarcate, partition; alienate, disunite, estrange.

divination *n* augury, divining, foretelling, incantation, magic, soothsaying, sorcery; prediction, presage, prophecy.

divine *vb* foretell, predict, presage, prognosticate, vaticinate, prophesy; believe, conjecture, fancy, guess, suppose, surmise, suspect, think. * *adj* deiform, godlike, superhuman, supernatural; angelic, celestial, heavenly, holy, sacred, seraphic, spiritual; exalted, exalting, rapturous, supreme, transcendent. * *n* churchman, clergyman, ecclesiastic, minister, parson, pastor, priest.

division *n* compartmentalization, disconnection, disjunction, dismemberment, segmentation, separation, severance; category, class, compartment, head, parcel, portion, section, segment; demarcation, partition; alienation, allotment, apportionment, distribution; breach, difference, disagreement, discord, disunion, estrangement, feud, rupture, variance.

divorce *vb* disconnect, dissolve, disunite, part, put away, separate, sever, split up, sunder, unmarry. * *n* disjunction, dissolution, disunion, division, divorcement, parting, separation, severance.

divulge *vb* communicate, declare, disclose, discover, exhibit, expose, impart, proclaim, promulgate, publish, reveal, tell, uncover.

dizzy *adj* giddy, vertiginous; careless, heedless, thoughtless.

do *vb* accomplish, achieve, act, commit, effect, execute, perform; complete, conclude, end, finish, settle, terminate; conduct, transact; observe, perform, practice; translate, render; cook, prepare; cheat, chouse, cozen, hoax, swindle; serve, suffice. * *n* act, action, adventure, deed, doing, exploit, feat, thing; banquet, event, feast, function, party.

docile *adj* amenable, obedient, pliant, teachable, tractable, yielding.

dock[1] *vb* clip, curtail, cut, deduct, truncate; lessen, shorten.

dock[2] *vb* anchor, moor; join, meet. * *n* anchorage, basin, berth, dockage, dockyard, dry dock, harbour, haven, marina, pier, shipyard, wharf.

doctor *vb* adulterate, alter, cook, falsify, manipulate, tamper with; attend, minister to, cure, heal, remedy, treat; fix, mend, overhaul, repair, service. * *n* general practitioner, GP, healer, leech, medic, physician; adept, savant.

doctrinaire *adj* impractical, theoretical. * *n* ideologist, theorist, thinker.

doctrine *n* article, belief, creed, dogma, opinion, precept, principle, teaching, tenet.

dodge *vb* equivocate, evade, prevaricate, quibble, shuffle. * *n* artifice, cavil, evasion, quibble, subterfuge, trick.

dogged *adj* cantankerous, headstrong, inflexible, intractable, mulish, obstinate, pertinacious, perverse, resolute, stubborn, tenacious, unyielding, wilful; churlish, morose, sour, sullen, surly.

dogma *n* article, belief, creed, doctrine, opinion, precept, principle, tenet.

dogmatic *adj* authoritative, categorical, formal, settled; arrogant, confident, dictatorial, imperious, magisterial, opinionated, oracular, overbearing, peremptory, positive; doctrinal.

dole *vb* allocate, allot, apportion, assign, deal, distribute, divide, share. * *n* allocation, allotment, apportionment, distribution; part, portion, share; alms, donation, gift, gratuity, pittance; affliction, distress, grief, sorrow, woe.

doleful *adj* lugubrious, melancholy, piteous, rueful, sad, sombre, sorrowful, woebegone, woeful; cheerless, dark, dismal, dolorous, dreary, gloomy.

dolorous *adj* cheerless, dark, dismal, gloomy; doleful, lugubrious, mournful, piteous, rueful, sad, sorrowful, woeful.

dolt *n* blockhead, booby, dullard, dunce, fool, ignoramus, simpleton.

domain *n* authority, dominion, jurisdiction, province, sway; empire, realm, territory; lands, estate; branch, department, region.

domestic *n* charwoman, help, home help, maid, servant. * *adj* domiciliary, family, home, household, private; domesticated; internal, intestine.

domesticate *vb* tame; adopt, assimilate, familiarize, naturalize.

domicile *vb* domiciliate, dwell, inhabit, live, remain, reside. * *n* abode, dwelling, habitation, harbour, home, house, residence.

dominant *adj* ascendant, ascending, chief, controlling, governing, influential, outstanding, paramount, predominant, pre-eminent, preponderant, presiding, prevailing, ruling.

dominate *vb* control, rule, sway; command, overlook, overtop, surmount.

domineer *vb* rule, tyrannize; bluster, bully, hector, menace, swagger, swell, threaten.

dominion *n* ascendancy, authority, command, control, domain, domination, government, jurisdiction, mastery, rule, sovereign, sovereignty, supremacy, sway; country, kingdom, realm, region, territory.

donation *n* alms, benefaction, boon, contribution, dole, donative, gift, grant, gratuity, largesse, offering, present, subscription.

done *adj* accomplished, achieved, effected, executed, performed; completed, concluded, ended, finished, terminated; carried on, transacted; rendered, translated; cooked, prepared; cheated, cozened, hoaxed, swindled; (*with* **for**) damned, dished, *hors de combat*, ruined, shelved, spoiled, wound up.

donkey *n* ass, mule; dunce, fool, simpleton.

donor *n* benefactor, bestower, giver; donator.

double *vb* fold, plait; duplicate, geminate, increase, multiply, repeat; return. * *adj* binary, coupled, geminate, paired; dual, twice, twofold; deceitful, dishonest, double-dealing, false, hollow, insincere, knavish, perfidious, treacherous, two-faced. * *adv* doubly, twice, twofold. * *n* doubling, fold, plait; artifice, manoeuvre, ruse, shift, stratagem, trick, wile; copy, counterpart, twin.

doublet *n* jacket, jerkin.

doubt *vb* demur, fluctuate, hesitate, vacillate, waver; distrust, mistrust, query, question, suspect. * *n* dubiety, dubiousness, dubitation, hesitance, hesitancy, hesitation, incertitude, indecision, irresolution, question, suspense, uncertainty, vacillation; distrust, misgiving, mistrust, scepticism, suspicion.

doubtful *adj* dubious, hesitating, sceptical, undecided, undetermined, wavering; ambiguous, dubious, enigmatical, equivocal, hazardous, obscure, problematical, unsure; indeterminate, questionable, undecided, unquestioned.

doubtless *adv* certainly, unquestionably; clearly, indisputably, precisely.

doughty *adj* adventurous, bold, brave, chivalrous, courageous, daring, dauntless, fearless, gallant, heroic, intrepid, redoubtable, valiant, valorous.

douse see **dowse**.

dowdy *adj* awkward, dingy, ill-dressed, shabby, slatternly, slovenly; old-fashioned, unfashionable.

dowel *n* peg, pin, pinion, tenon.

dower *n* endowment, gift; dowry; portion, share.

downcast *adj* chapfallen, crestfallen, dejected, depressed, despondent, discouraged, disheartened, dispirited, downhearted, low-spirited, sad, unhappy.

downfall *n* descent, destruction, fall, ruin.

downhearted *adj* chapfallen, crestfallen, dejected, depressed, despondent, discouraged, disheartened, dispirited, downcast, low-spirited, sad, unhappy.

downright *adj* absolute, categorical, clear, explicit, plain, positive, sheer, simple, undisguised, unequivocal, utter; above-board, artless, blunt, direct, frank, honest, ingenuous, open, sincere, straightforward, unceremonious.

downy *adj* lanate, lanated, lanose.

dowse, douse *vb* dip, immerse, plunge, souse, submerge.

doxy *n* mistress, paramour; courtesan, drab, harlot, prostitute, strumpet, streetwalker, whore.

doze *vb* drowse, nap, sleep, slumber. * *n* drowse, forty-winks, nap.

dozy *adj* drowsy, heavy, sleepy, sluggish.

draft *vb* detach, select; commandeer, conscript, impress; delineate, draw, outline, sketch. * *n* conscription, drawing, selection; delineation, outline, sketch; bill, cheque, order.

drag *vb* draw, haul, pull, tow, tug; trail; linger, loiter. * *n* favour, influence, pull; brake, check, curb, lag, resistance, retardation, scotch, skid, slackening, slack-off, slowing.

draggle *vb* befoul, bemire, besmirch, dangle, drabble, trail.

dragoon *vb* compel, drive, force, harass, harry, persecute. * *n* cavalier, equestrian, horse-soldier.

drain *vb* milk, sluice, tap; empty, evacuate, exhaust; dry. * *n* channel, culvert, ditch, sewer, sluice, trench, watercourse; exhaustion, withdrawal.

draught *n* current, drawing, pulling, traction; cup, dose, drench, drink, potion; delineation, design, draft, outline, sketch.

draw *vb* drag, haul, tow, tug, pull; attract; drain, suck, syphon; extract, extort; breathe in, inhale, inspire; allure, engage, entice, induce, influence, lead, move, persuade; extend, protract, stretch; delineate, depict, sketch; deduce, derive, infer; compose, draft, formulate, frame, prepare; blister, vesicate, write.

drawback *n* defect, deficiency, detriment, disadvantage, fault, flaw, imperfection, injury; abatement, allowance, deduction, discount, rebate, reduction.

drawing *n* attracting, draining, inhaling, pulling, traction; delineation, draught, outline, picture, plan, sketch.

dread *vb* apprehend, fear. * *adj* dreadful, frightful, horrible, terrible; awful, venerable. * *n* affright, alarm, apprehension, fear, terror; awe, veneration.

dreadful *adj* alarming, appalling, awesome, dire, direful, fearful, formidable, frightful, horrible, horrid, terrible, terrific, tremendous; awful, venerable.

dream *vb* fancy, imagine, think. * *n* conceit, day-dream, delusion, fancy, fantasy, hallucination, illusion, imagination, reverie, vagary, vision.

dreamer *n* enthusiast, visionary.

dreamy *adj* absent, abstracted, fanciful, ideal, misty, shadowy, speculative, unreal, visionary.

dreary *adj* cheerless, chilling, comfortless, dark, depressing, dismal, drear, gloomy, lonely, lonesome, sad, solitary, sorrowful; boring, dull, monotonous, tedious, tiresome, uninteresting, wearisome.

dregs *npl* feculence, grounds, lees, off-scourings, residuum, scourings, sediment, waste; draff, dross, refuse, scum, trash.

drench *vb* dowse, drown, imbrue, saturate, soak, souse, steep, wet; physic, purge.

dress *vb* align, straighten; adjust, arrange, dispose; fit, prepare; accoutre, apparel, array, attire, clothe, robe, rig; adorn, bedeck, deck, decorate, drape, embellish, trim. * *n* apparel, attire, clothes, clothing, costume, garb, guise, garments, habiliment, habit, raiment, suit, toilet, vesture; bedizenment, bravery; frock, gown, rob.

dressing *n* compost, fertilizer, manure; forcemeat, stuffing.

dressy *adj* flashy, gaudy, showy.

driblet *n* bit, drop, fragment, morsel, piece, scrap.

drift *vb* accumulate, drive, float, wander. * *n* bearing, course, direction; aim, design, intent, intention, mark, object, proposal, purpose, scope, tendency; detritus, deposit, diluvium; gallery, passage, tunnel; current, rush, sweep; heap, pile.

drill[1] *vb* bore, perforate, pierce; discipline, exercise, instruct, teach, train. * *n* borer; discipline, exercise, training.

drill[2] *n* channel, furrow, trench.

drink *vb* imbibe, sip, swill; carouse, indulge, revel, tipple, tope; swallow, quaff; absorb. * *n* beverage, draught, liquid, potation, potion; dram, nip, sip, snifter, refreshment.

drip *vb* dribble, drop, leak, trickle; distil, filter, percolate; ooze, reek, seep, weep. * *n* dribble, drippings, drop, leak, leakage, leaking, trickle, tricklet; bore, nuisance, wet blanket.

drive *vb* hurl, impel, propel, send, shoot, thrust; actuate, incite, press, urge; coerce, compel, constrain, force, harass, oblige, overburden, press, rush; go, guide, ride, travel; aim, intend. * *n* effort, energy, pressure; airing, ride; road.

drivel *vb* babble, blether, dote, drool, slaver, slobber. * *n* balderdash, drivelling, fatuity, nonsense, prating, rubbish, slaver, stuff, twaddle.

drizzle *vb* mizzle, rain, shower, sprinkle. * *n* haar, mist, mizzle, rain, sprinkling.

droll *adj* comic, comical, farcical, funny, jocular, ludicrous, laughable, ridiculous; amusing, diverting, facetious, odd, quaint, queer, waggish. * *n* buffoon, clown, comedian, fool, harlequin, jester, punch, Punchinello, scaramouch, wag, zany.

drollery *n* archness, buffoonery, fun, humour, jocularity, pleasantry, waggishness, whimsicality.

drone *vb* dawdle, drawl, idle, loaf, lounge; hum. * *n* idler, loafer, lounger, sluggard.

drool *vb* drivel, slaver.

droop *vb* fade, wilt, wither; decline, fail, faint, flag, languish, sink, weaken; bend, hang.

drop *vb* distil, drip, shed; decline, depress, descend, dump, lower, sink; abandon, desert, forsake, forswear, leave, omit, relinquish, quit; cease, discontinue, intermit, remit; fall, precipitate. * *n* bead, droplet, globule; earring, pendant.

dross *n* cinder, lees, recrement, scoria, scum, slag; refuse, waste.

drought *n* aridity, drouth, dryness, thirstiness.

drove *n* flock, herd; collection, company, crowd.

drown *vb* deluge, engulf, flood, immerse, inundate, overflow, sink, submerge, swamp; overcome, overpower, overwhelm.

drowse *vb* doze, nap, sleep, slumber, snooze. * *n* doze, forty winks, nap, siesta, sleep, snooze.

drowsy *adj* dozy, sleepy; comatose, lethargic, stupid; lulling, soporific.

drub *vb* bang, beat, cane, cudgel, flog, hit, knock, pommel, pound, strike, thrash, thump, whack.

drubbing *n* beating, caning, cudgelling, flagellation, flogging, pommelling, pounding, thrashing, thumping, whacking.

drudge *vb* grub, grind, plod, slave, toil, work. * *n* grind, hack, hard worker, menial, plodder, scullion, servant, slave, toiler, worker.

drug *vb* dose, medicate; disgust, surfeit. * *n* medicine, physic, remedy; poison.

drunk *adj* boozed, drunken, inebriated, intoxicated, maudlin, soaked, tipsy; ablaze, aflame, delirious, fervent, suffused. * *n* alcoholic, boozer, dipsomaniac, drunkard, inebriate, lush, soak; bacchanal, bender, binge.

drunkard *n* alcoholic, boozer, carouser, dipsomaniac, drinker, drunk, inebriate, reveller, sot, tippler, toper.

dry *vb* dehydrate, desiccate, drain, exsiccate, parch. * *adj* desiccated, dried, juiceless, sapless, unmoistened; arid, droughty, parched; drouthy, thirsty; barren, dull, insipid, jejune, plain, pointless, tame, tedious, tiresome, unembellished, uninteresting, vapid; cutting, keen, sarcastic, severe, sharp, sly.

dub *vb* call, christen, denominate, designate, entitle, name, style, term.

dubious *adj* doubtful, fluctuating, hesitant, irresolute, skeptical, uncertain, undecided, unsettled, wavering; ambiguous, doubtful, equivocal, improbable, questionable, uncertain.

duck *vb* dip, dive, immerse, plunge, submerge, souse; bend, bow, dodge, stoop.

duct *n* canal, channel, conduit, pipe, tube; blood-vessel.

ductile *adj* compliant, docile, facile, tractable, yielding; flexible, malleable, pliant; extensible, tensile.

dudgeon *n* anger, indignation, ill will, ire, malice, resentment, umbrage, wrath.

due *adj* owed, owing; appropriate, becoming, befitting, bounden, fit, proper, suitable, right. * *adv* dead, direct, directly, exactly, just, right, squarely, straight. * *n* claim, debt, desert, right.

dulcet *adj* delicious, honeyed, luscious, sweet; harmonious, melodious; agreeable, charming, delightful, pleasant, pleasing.

dull *vb* blunt; benumb, besot, deaden, hebetate, obtund, paralyse, stupefy; dampen, deject, depress, discourage, dishearten, dispirit; allay, alleviate, assuage, mitigate, moderate, quiet, soften; deaden, dim, sully, tarnish. * *adj* blockish, brutish, doltish, obtuse, stolid, stupid, unintelligent; apathetic, callous, dead, insensible, passionless, phlegmatic, unfeeling, unimpassioned, unresponsive; heavy, inactive, inanimate, inert, languish, lifeless, slow, sluggish, torpid; blunt, dulled, hebetate, obtuse; cheerless, dismal, dreary, gloomy, sad, sombre; dim, lacklustre, lustreless, matt, obscure, opaque, tarnished; dry, flat, insipid, irksome, jejune, prosy, tedious, tiresome, uninteresting, wearisome.

duly *adv* befittingly, decorously, fitly, properly, rightly; regularly.

dumb *adj* inarticulate, mute, silent, soundless, speechless, voiceless.

dumbfound, dumfound *vb* amaze, astonish, astound, bewilder, confound, confuse, nonplus, pose.

dumps *npl* blues, dejection, depression, despondency, gloom, gloominess, melancholy, sadness.

dun[1] *adj* greyish-brown, brown, drab.

dun[2] *vb* beset, importune, press, urge.

dunce *n* ass, block, blockhead, clodpole, dolt, donkey, dullard, dunderhead, fool, goose, halfwit, ignoramus, jackass, lackwit, loon, nincompoop, numskull, oaf, simpleton, thickhead, witling.

dupe *vb* beguile, cheat, chouse, circumvent, cozen, deceive, delude, gull, hoodwink, outwit, overreach, swindle, trick. * *n* gull, simpleton.

duplicate *vb* copy, double, repeat, replicate, reproduce. * *adj* doubled, twofold. * *n* copy, counterpart, facsimile, replica, transcript.

duplicity *n* artifice, chicanery, circumvention, deceit, deception, dishonesty, dissimulation, double-dealing, falseness, fraud, guile, hypocrisy, perfidy.

durable *adj* abiding, constant, continuing, enduring, firm, lasting, permanent, persistent, stable.

duration *n* continuance, continuation, permanency, perpetuation, prolongation; period, time.

duress *n* captivity, confinement, constraint, durance, hardship, imprisonment, restraint; compulsion.

dusky *adj* cloudy, darkish, dim, murky, obscure, overcast, shady, shadowy; dark, swarthy, tawny.

dutiful *adj* duteous, obedient, submissive; deferential, respectful, reverential.

duty *n* allegiance, devoirs, obligation, responsibility, reverence; business, engagement, function, office, service; custom, excise, impost, tariff, tax, toll.

dwarf *vb* lower, stunt. * *n* bantam, homunculus, manikin, midget, pygmy.

dwarfish *adj* diminutive, dwarfed, little, low, pygmy, small, stunted, tiny, undersized.

dwell *vb* abide, inhabit, live, lodge, remain, reside, rest, sojourn, stay, stop, tarry, tenant.

dwelling *n* abode, cot, domicile, dugout, establishment, habitation, home, house, hutch, lodging, mansion, quarters, residence.

dwindle *vb* decrease, diminish, lessen, shrink; decay, decline, deteriorate, pine, sink, waste away.

dye *vb* colour, stain, tinge. * *n* cast, colour, hue, shade, stain, tinge, tint.

dying *adj* expiring; mortal, perishable. * *n* death, decease, demise, departure, dissolution, exit.

dynasty *n* dominion, empire, government, rule, sovereignty.

dyspepsia *n* indigestion.

E

eager *adj* agog, avid, anxious, desirous, fain, greedy, impatient, keen, longing, yearning; animated, ardent, earnest, enthusiastic, fervent, fervid, forward, glowing, hot, impetuous, sanguine, vehement, zealous.

eagerness *n* ardour, avidity, earnestness, enthusiasm, fervour, greediness, heartiness, hunger, impatience, impetuosity, intentness, keenness, longing, thirst, vehemence, yearning, zeal.

eagle-eyed *adj* discerning, hawk-eyed, sharp-sighted.

ear[1] *n* attention, hearing, heed, regard.

ear[2] *n* head, spike.

early *adj* opportune, seasonable, timely; forward, premature; dawning, matutinal. * *adv* anon, beforehand, betimes, ere, seasonably, shortly, soon.

earn *vb* acquire, gain, get, obtain, procure, realize, reap, win; deserve, merit.

earnest *adj* animated, ardent, eager, cordial, fervent, fervid, glowing, hearty, impassioned, importune, warm, zealous; fixed, intent, steady; sincere, true, truthful; important, momentous, serious, weighty. * *n* reality, seriousness, truth; foretaste, pledge, promise; handsel, payment.

earnings *npl* allowance, emoluments, gains, income, pay, proceeds, profits, remuneration, reward, salary, stipend.

earth *n* globe, orb, planet, world; clay, clod, dirt, glebe, ground, humus, land, loam, sod, soil, turf; mankind, world.

earthborn *adj* abject, base, earthly, grovelling, low, mean, unspiritual.

earthly *adj* terrestrial; base, carnal, earthborn, low, gross, grovelling, sensual, sordid, unspiritual, worldly; bodily, material, mundane, natural, secular, temporal.

earthy *adj* clayey, earth-like, terrene; earthly, terrestrial; coarse, gross, material, unrefined.

ease *vb* disburden, disencumber, pacify, quiet, relieve, still; abate, allay, alleviate, appease, assuage, diminish, mitigate, soothe; loosen, release; facilitate, favour. * *n* leisure, quiescence, repose, rest; calmness, content, contentment, enjoyment, happiness, peace, quiet, quietness, quietude, relief, repose, satisfaction, serenity, tranquillity; easiness, facility, readiness; flexibility, freedom, liberty, lightness, naturalness, unconcern, unconstraint; comfort, elbowroom.

easy *adj* light; careless, comfortable, contented, effortless, painless, quiet, satisfied, tranquil, untroubled; accommodating, complaisant, compliant, complying, facile, indolent, manageable, pliant, submissive, tractable, yielding; graceful, informal, natural, unconstrained; flowing, ready, smooth, unaffected; gentle, lenient, mild, moderate; affluent, loose, unconcerned, unembarrassed.

eat *vb* chew, consume, devour, engorge, ingest, ravage, swallow; corrode, demolish, erode; breakfast, dine, feed, lunch, sup.

eatable *adj* edible, esculent, harmless, wholesome.

ebb *vb* abate, recede, retire, subside; decay, decline, decrease, degenerate, deteriorate, sink, wane. * *n* refluence, reflux, regress, regression, retrocedence, retrocession, retrogression, return; caducity, decay, decline, degeneration, deterioration, wane, waning; abatement, decrease, decrement, diminution.

ebullience *n* ebullition, effervescence; burst, bursting, overenthusiasm, overflow, rush, vigour.

ebullition *n* boiling, bubbling; effervescence, fermentation; burst, fit, outbreak, outburst, paroxysm.

eccentric *adj* decentred, parabolic; aberrant, abnormal, anomalous, cranky, erratic, fantastic, irregular, odd, outlandish, peculiar, singular, strange, uncommon, unnatural, wayward, whimsical. * *n* crank, curiosity, original.

eccentricity *n* ellipticity, flattening, flatness, oblateness; aberration, irregularity, oddity, oddness, peculiarity, singularity, strangeness, waywardness.

ecclesiastic[1], **ecclesiastical** *adj* churchish, churchly, clerical, ministerial, nonsecular, pastoral, priestly, religious, sacerdotal.

ecclesiastic[2] *n* chaplain, churchman, clergyman, cleric, clerk, divine, minister, parson, pastor, priest, reverend, shepherd.

echo *vb* reply, resound, reverberate, ring; re-echo, repeat. * *n* answer, repetition, reverberation; imitation.

éclat *n* acclamation, applause, brilliancy, effect, glory, lustre, pomp, renown, show, splendour.

eclipse *vb* cloud, darken, dim, obscure, overshadow, veil; annihilate, annul, blot out, extinguish. * *n* clouding, concealment, darkening, dimming, disappearance, hiding, obscuration, occultation, shrouding, vanishing, veiling; annihilation, blotting out, destruction, extinction, extinguishment, obliteration.

eclogue *n* bucolic, idyl, pastoral.

economize *vb* husband, manage, save; retrench.

economy *n* frugality, husbandry, parsimony, providence, retrenchment, saving, skimping, stinginess, thrift, thriftiness; administration, arrangement, management, method, order, plan, regulation, system; dispensation.

ecstasy *n* frenzy, madness, paroxysm, trance; delight, gladness, joy, rhapsody, rapture, ravishment, transport.

eddy *vb* gurgle, surge, spin, swirl, whirl. * *n* countercurrent; swirl, vortex, whirlpool.

edge *vb* sharpen; border, fringe, rim. * *n* border, brim, brink, bound, crest, fringe, hem, lip, margin, rim, verge; animation, intensity, interest, keenness, sharpness, zest; acrimony, bitterness, gall, sharpness, sting.

edging *n* border, frill, fringe, trimming.

edible *adj* eatable, esculent, harmless, wholesome.

edict *n* act, command, constitution, decision, decree, law, mandate, manifesto, notice, order, ordinance, proclamation, regulation, rescript, statute.

edifice *n* building, fabric, habitation, house, structure.

edify *vb* educate, elevate, enlightenment, improve, inform, instruct, nurture, teach, upbuild.

edition *n* impression, issue, number.

educate *vb* breed, cultivate, develop, discipline, drill, edify, exercise, indoctrinate, inform, instruct, mature, nurture, rear, school, teach, train.

educated *adj* cultured, lettered, literate.

education *n* breeding, cultivation, culture, development, discipline, drilling, indoctrination, instruction, nurture, pedagogics, schooling, teaching, training, tuition.

educe *vb* bring out, draw out, elicit, evolve, extract.

eerie *adj* awesome, fearful, frightening, strange, uncanny, weird.

efface *vb* blot, blot out, cancel, delete, destroy, erase, expunge, obliterate, remove, sponge.

effect *vb* cause, create, effectuate, produce; accomplish, achieve, carry, compass, complete, conclude, consummate, contrive, do, execute, force, negotiate, perform, realize, work. * *n* consequence, event, fruit, issue, outcome, result; efficiency, fact, force, power, reality; validity, weight; drift, import, intent, meaning, purport, significance, tenor.

effective *adj* able, active, adequate, competent, convincing, effectual, sufficient; cogent, efficacious, energetic, forcible, potent, powerful.

effects *npl* chattels, furniture, goods, movables, property.

effectual *adj* operative, successful; active, effective, efficacious, efficient.

effectuate *vb* accomplish, achieve, complete, do, effect, execute, fulfil, perform, secure.

effeminate *adj* delicate, feminine, soft, tender, timorous, unmanly, womanish, womanlike, womanly; camp.

effervesce *vb* bubble, ferment, foam, froth.

effete *adj* addle, barren, fruitless, sterile, unfruitful, unproductive, unprolific; decayed, exhausted, spent, wasted.

efficacious *adj* active, adequate, competent, effective, effectual, efficient, energetic, operative, powerful.

efficacy *n* ability, competency, effectiveness, efficiency, energy, force, potency, power, strength, vigour, virtue.

efficient *adj* active, capable, competent, effective, effectual, efficacious, operative, potent; able, energetic, ready, skilful.

effigy *n* figure, image, likeness, portrait, representation, statue.

effloresce *vb* bloom, flower.

efflorescence *n* blooming, blossoming, flowering.

effluence *n* discharge, efflux, effluvium, emanation, emission, flow, outflow, outpouring.

effort *n* application, attempt, endeavour, essay, exertion, pains, spurt, strain, strife, stretch, struggle, trial, trouble.

effrontery *n* assurance, audacity, boldness, brass, disrespect, hardihood, impudence, incivility, insolence, presumption, rudeness, sauciness, shamelessness.

effulgent *adj* burning, beaming, blazing, bright, brilliant, dazzling, flaming, glowing, lustrous, radiant, refulgent, resplendent, shining, splendid.

effusion *n* discharge, efflux, emission, gush, outpouring; shedding, spilling, waste; address, speech, talk, utterance.

egg *vb* (*with* **on**) encourage, incite, instigate, push, stimulate, urge; harass, harry, provoke.

ego *n* id, self, me, subject, superego.

egotism *n* self-admiration, self-assertion, self-commendation, self-conceit, self-esteem, self-importance, self-praise; egoism, selfishness.

egotistic, egotistical *adj* bumptious, conceited, egoistical, opinionated, self-asserting, self-admiring, self-centred, self-conceited, self-important, self-loving, vain.

egregious *adj* conspicuous, enormous, extraordinary, flagrant, great, gross, huge, monstrous, outrageous, prodigious, remarkable, tremendous.

egress *n* departure, emergence, exit, outlet, way out.

eject *vb* belch, discharge, disgorge, emit, evacuate, puke, spew, spit, spout, spurt, void, vomit; bounce, cashier, discharge, dismiss, disposes, eliminate, evict, expel, fire, oust; banish, reject, throw out.

elaborate *vb* develop, improve, mature, produce, refine, ripen. * *adj* complicated, decorated, detailed, dressy, laboured, laborious, ornate, perfected, studied.

elapse *vb* go, lapse, pass.

elastic *adj* rebounding, recoiling, resilient, springy; buoyant, recuperative.

elated *adj* animated, cheered, elate, elevated, excited, exhilarated, exultant, flushed, puffed up, roused.

elbow *vb* crowd, force, hustle, jostle, nudge, push, shoulder. * *n* angle, bend, corner, flexure, joining, turn.

elder *adj* older, senior; ranking; ancient, earlier, older. * *n* ancestor, senior; presbyter, prior, senator.

elect *vb* appoint, choose, cull, designate, pick, prefer, select. * *adj* choice, chosen, picked, selected; appointed, elected; predestinated, redeemed.

election *n* appointment, choice, preference, selection; alternative, freedom, freewill, liberty; predestination.

elector *n* chooser, constituent, selector, voter.

electrify *vb* charge, galvanize; astonish, enchant, excite, rouse, startle, stir, thrill.

elegance, elegancy *n* beauty, grace, propriety, symmetry; courtliness, daintiness, gentility, nicety, polish, politeness, refinement, taste.

elegant *adj* beautiful, chaste, classical, dainty, graceful, fine, handsome, neat, symmetrical, tasteful, trim, well-made, well-proportioned; accomplished, courtly, cultivated, fashionable, genteel, polished, polite, refined.

elegiac *adj* dirgeful, mournful, plaintive, sorrowful.

elegy *n* dirge, epicedium, lament, ode, threnody.

element *n* basis, component, constituent, factor, germ, ingredient, part, principle, rudiment, unit; environment, milieu, sphere.

elementary *adj* primordial, simple, uncombined, uncomplicated, uncompounded; basic, component, fundamental, initial, primary, rudimental, rudimentary.

elevate *vb* erect, hoist, lift, raise; advance, aggrandize, exalt, promote; dignify, ennoble, exalt, greaten, improve, refine; animate, cheer, elate, excite, exhilarate, rouse.

elfin *adj* elflike, elvish, mischievous, weird.

elicit *vb* draw out, educe, evoke, extort, fetch, obtain, pump, wrest, wring; deduce, educe.

eligible *adj* desirable, preferable; qualified, suitable, worthy.

eliminate *vb* disengage, eradicate, exclude, expel, remove, separate; ignore, omit, reject.

ellipsis *n* gap, hiatus, lacuna, omission.

elliptical *adj* oval; defective, incomplete.

elocution *n* declamation, delivery, oratory, rhetoric, speech, utterance.

elongate *vb* draw, draw out, extend, lengthen, protract, stretch.

elope *vb* abscond, bolt, decamp, disappear, leave.

eloquence *n* fluency, oratory, rhetoric.

else *adv* besides, differently, otherwise.

elucidate *vb* clarify, demonstrate, explain, expound, illuminate, illustrate, interpret, unfold.

elucidation *n* annotation, clarification, comment, commentary, elucidating, explaining, explanation, exposition, gloss, scholium.

elude *vb* avoid, escape, evade, shun, slip; baffle, balk, disappoint, disconcert, escape, foil, frustrate, thwart.

elusive *adj* deceptive, deceitful, delusive, evasive, fallacious, fraudulent, illusory; equivocatory, equivocating, shuffling.

Elysian *adj* blissful, celestial, delightful, enchanting, heavenly, ravishing, seraphic.

emaciation *n* attenuation, lankness, leanness, meagreness, tabes, tabescence, thinness.

emanate *vb* arise, come, emerge, flow, issue, originate, proceed, spring.

emancipate *vb* deliver, discharge, disenthral, enfranchise, free, liberate, manumit, release, unchain, unfetter, unshackle.

emancipation *n* deliverance, enfranchisement, deliverance, freedom, liberation, manumission, release.

emasculate *vb* castrate, geld; debilitate, effeminize, enervate, unman, weaken.

embalm *vb* cherish, consecrate, conserve, enshrine, preserve, store, treasure; perfume, scent.

embargo *vb* ban, bar, blockade, debar, exclude, prohibit, proscribe, restrict, stop, withhold. * *n* ban, bar, blockade, exclusion, hindrance, impediment, prohibition, prohibitory, proscription, restraint, restriction, stoppage.

embark *vb* engage, enlist.

embarrass *vb* beset, entangle, perplex; annoy, clog, bother, distress, hamper, harass, involve, plague, trouble, vex; abash, confound, confuse, discomfit, disconcert, dumbfound, mortify, nonplus, pose, shame.

embellish *vb* adorn, beautify, bedeck, deck, decorate, emblazon, enhance, enrich, garnish, grace, ornament.

embellishment *n* adornment, decoration, enrichment, ornament, ornamentation.

embezzle *vb* appropriate, defalcate, filch, misappropriate, peculate, pilfer, purloin, steal.

embitter *vb* aggravate, envenom, exacerbate; anger, enrage, exasperate, madden.

emblem *n* badge, cognizance, device, mark, representation, sign, symbol, token, type.

embody *vb* combine, compact, concentrate, incorporate; comprehend, comprise, contain, embrace, include; codify, methodize, systematize.

embolden *vb* animate, cheer, elate, encourage, gladden, hearten, inspirit, nerve, reassure.

embosom *vb* bury, cherish, clasp, conceal, enfold, envelop, enwrap, foster, hide, nurse, surround.

embrace *vb* clasp; accept, seize, welcome; comprehend, comprise, contain, cover, embody, encircle, enclose, encompass, enfold, hold, include. * *n* clasp, fold, hug.

embroil *vb* commingle, encumber, ensnarl, entangle, implicate, involve; confuse, discompose, disorder, distract, disturb, perplex, trouble.

embryo *n* beginning, germ, nucleus, root, rudiment.

embryonic *adj* incipient, rudimentary, undeveloped.

emendation *n* amendment, correction, improvement, rectification.

emerge *vb* rise; emanate, escape, issue; appear, arise, outcrop.

emergency *n* crisis, difficulty, dilemma, exigency, extremity, necessity, pass, pinch, push, strait, urgency; conjuncture, crisis, juncture, pass.

emigration *n* departure, exodus, migration, removal.

eminence *n* elevation, hill, projection, prominence, protuberance; celebrity, conspicuousness, distinction, exaltation, fame, loftiness, note, preferment, reputation, repute, renown.

eminent *adj* elevated, high, lofty; celebrated, conspicuous, distinguished, exalted, famous, illustrious, notable, prominent, remarkable, renowned.

emissary *n* messenger, scout, secret agent, spy.

emit *vb* breathe out, dart, discharge, eject, emanate, exhale, gust, hurl, jet, outpour, shed, shoot, spurt, squirt.

emollient *adj* relaxing, softening. soothing. * *n* softener.

emolument *n* compensation, gain, hire, income, lucre, pay, pecuniary, profits, salary, stipend, wages; advantage, benefit, profit, perquisites.

emotion *n* agitation, excitement, feeling, passion, perturbation, sentiment, sympathy, trepidation.

emphasis *n* accent, stress; force, importance, impressiveness, moment, significance, weight.

emphatic *adj* decided, distinct, earnest, energetic, expressive, forcible, impressive, intensive, positive, significant, strong, unequivocal.

empire *n* domain, dominion, sovereignty, supremacy; authority, command, control, government, rule, sway.

empirical, empiric *adj* experimental, experiential; hypothetical, provisional, tentative; charlatanic, quackish.

employ *vb* busy, devote, engage, engross, enlist, exercise, occupy, retain; apply, commission, use. * *n* employment, service.

employee *n* agent, clerk, employee, hand, servant, workman.

employment *n* avocation, business, calling, craft, employ, engagement, occupation, profession, pursuit, trade, vocation, work.

emporium *n* market, mart, shop, store.

empower *vb* authorize, commission, permit, qualify, sanction, warrant; enable.

empty *vb* deplete, drain, evacuate, exhaust; discharge, disembogue; flow, embogue. * *adj* blank, hollow, unoccupied, vacant, vacuous, void; deplete, destitute, devoid, hungry; unfilled, unfurnished, unsupplied; unsatisfactory, unsatisfying, unsubstantial, useless, vain; clear, deserted, desolate, exhausted, free, unburdened, unloaded, waste; foolish, frivolous, inane, senseless, silly, stupid, trivial, weak.

empyrean, empyreal *adj* aerial, airy, ethereal, heavenly, refined, sublimated, sublimed.

emulation *n* competition, rivalry, strife, vying; contention, envy, jealousy.

enable *vb* authorize, capacitate, commission, empower, fit, permit, prepare, qualify, sanction, warrant.

enact *vb* authorize, command, decree, establish, legislate, ordain, order, sanction; act, perform, personate, play, represent.

enactment *n* act, decree, law, edict, ordinance.

enamour *vb* bewitch, captivate, charm, enchant, endear, fascinate.

enchain *vb* bind, confine, enslave, fetter, hold, manacle, restrain, shackle.

enchant *vb* beguile, bewitch, charm, delude, fascinate; captivate, catch, enamour, win; beatify, delight, enrapture, rapture, ravish, transport.

enchanting *adj* bewitching, blissful, captivating, charming, delightful, enrapturing, fascinating, rapturous, ravishing.

enchantment *n* charm, conjuration, incantation, magic, necromancy, sorcery, spell, witchery; bliss, delight, fascination, rapture, ravishment, transport.

encase *vb* encircle, enclose, incase, infix, set; chase, emboss, engrave, inlay, ornament.

encage *vb* confine, coop up, impound, imprison, shut up.

encircle *vb* belt, circumscribe, encompass, enclose, engird, enring, environ, gird, ring, span, surround, twine; clasp, embrace, enfold, fold.

enclose, inclose *vb* circumscribe, corral, coop, embosom, encircle, encompass, environ, fence in, hedge, include, pen, shut in, surround; box, cover, encase, envelop, wrap.

encomium *n* applause, commendation, eulogy, laudation, panegyric, praise.

encompass *vb* belt, compass, encircle, enclose, engird, environ, gird, surround; beset, besiege, hem in, include, invest, surround.

encounter *vb* confront, face, meet; attack, combat, contend, engage, strive, struggle. * *n* assault, attack, clash, collision, meeting, onset; action, affair, battle, brush, combat, conflict, contest, dispute, engagement, skirmish.

encourage *vb* animate, assure, cheer, comfort, console, embolden, enhearten, fortify, hearten, incite, inspirit, instigate, reassure, stimulate, strengthen; abet, aid, advance, approve, countenance, favour, foster, further, help, patronize, promote, support.

encroach *vb* infringe, invade, intrude, tench, trespass, usurp.

encumber *vb* burden, clog, hamper, hinder, impede, load, obstruct, overload, oppress, retard; complicate, embarrass, entangle, involve, perplex.

encumbrance *n* burden, clog, deadweight, drag, embarrassment, hampering, hindrance, impediment, incubus, load; claim, debt, liability, lien.

end *vb* abolish, close, conclude, discontinue, dissolve, drop, finish, stop, terminate; annihilate, destroy, kill; cease, terminate. * *n* extremity, tip; cessation, close, denouement, ending, expiration, finale, finis, finish, last, period, stoppage, wind-up; completion, conclusion, consummation; annihilation, catastrophe, destruction, dissolution; bound, limit, termination, terminus; consequence, event, issue, result, settlement, sequel, upshot; fragment, remnant, scrap, stub, tag, tail; aim, design, goal, intent, intention, object, objective, purpose.

endanger *vb* compromise, hazard, imperil, jeopardize, peril, risk.

endear *vb* attach, bind, captivate, charm, win.

endearment *n* attachment, fondness, love, tenderness; caress, blandishment, fondling.

endeavour *vb* aim, attempt, essay, labour, seek, strive, struggle, study, try. * *n* aim, attempt, conatus, effort, essay, exertion, trial, struggle, trial.

endless *adj* boundless, illimitable, immeasurable, indeterminable, infinite, interminable, limitless, unlimited; dateless, eternal, everlasting, never-ending, perpetual, unending; deathless, ever-enduring, ever-living, immortal, imperishable, undying.

endorse, indorse *vb* approve, back, confirm, guarantee, ratify, sanction, superscribe, support, visé, vouch for, warrant; superscribe.

endow *vb* bequeath, clothe, confer, dower, endue, enrich, gift, indue, invest, supply.

endowment *n* bequest, boon, bounty, gift, grant, largesse, present; foundation, fund, property, revenue; ability, aptitude, capability, capacity, faculty, genius, gift, parts, power, qualification, quality, talent.

endurance *n* abiding, bearing, sufferance, suffering, tolerance, toleration; backbone, bottom, forbearance, fortitude, guts, patience, resignation.

endure *vb* bear, support, sustain; experience, suffer, undergo, weather; abide, brook, permit, pocket, swallow, tolerate, stomach, submit, withstand; continue, last, persist, remain, wear.

enemy *n* adversary, foe; antagonist, foeman, opponent, rival.

energetic *adj* active, effective, efficacious, emphatic, enterprising, forceful, forcible, hearty, mettlesome, potent, powerful, strenuous, strong, vigorous.

energy *n* activity, dash, drive, efficacy, efficiency, force, go, impetus, intensity, mettle, might, potency, power, strength, verve, vim; animation, life, manliness, spirit, spiritedness, stamina, vigour, zeal.

enervate *vb* break, debilitate, devitalize, emasculate, enfeeble, exhaust, paralyse, relax, soften, unhinge, unnerve, weaken.

enfeeble *vb* debilitate, devitalize, enervate, exhaust, relax, unhinge, unnerve, weaken.

enfold, infold *vb* enclose, envelop, fold, enwrap, wrap; clasp, embrace.

enforce *vb* compel, constrain, exact, force, oblige, require, urge.

enfranchise *vb* emancipate, free, liberate, manumit, release.

engage *vb* bind, commit, obligate, pledge, promise; affiance, betroth, plight; book, brief, employ, enlist, hire, retain; arrest, allure, attach, draw, entertain, fix, gain, win; busy, commission, contract, engross, occupy; attack, encounter; combat, contend, contest, fight, interlock, struggle; embark, enlist; agree, promise, stipulate, undertake, warrant.

engagement *n* appointment, assurance, contract, obligation, pledge, promise, stipulation; affiancing, betrothment, betrothal, plighting; avocation, business, calling, employment, enterprise, occupation; action, battle, combat, encounter, fight.

engender *vb* bear, beget, breed, create, generate, procreate, propagate; cause, excite, incite, occasion, produce.

engine *n* invention, machine; agency, agent, device, implement, instrument, means, method, tool, weapon.

engorge *vb* bolt, devour, eat, gobble, gorge, gulp, swallow; glut, obstruct, stuff.

engrave *vb* carve, chisel, cut, etch, grave, hatch, incise, sculpt; grave, impress, imprint, infix.

engross *vb* absorb, engage, occupy, take up; buy up, forestall, monopolize.

engrossment *n* absorption, forestalling, monopoly.

engulf, ingulf *vb* absorb, overwhelm, plunge, swallow up.

enhance *vb* advance, aggravate, augment, elevate, heighten, increase, intensify, raise, swell.

enhearten *vb* animate, assure, cheer, comfort, console, embolden, encourage, hearten, incite, inspirit, reassure, stimulate.

enigma *n* conundrum, mystery, problem, puzzle, riddle.
enigmatic, enigmatical *adj* ambiguous, dark, doubtful, equivocal, hidden, incomprehensible, mysterious, mystic, obscure, occult, perplexing, puzzling, recondite, uncertain, unintelligible.
enjoin *vb* admonish, advise, urge; bid, command, direct, order, prescribe, require; prohibit, restrain.
enjoy *vb* like, possess, relish.
enjoyment *n* delight, delectation, gratification, happiness, indulgence, pleasure, satisfaction; possession.
enkindle *vb* inflame, ignite, kindle; excite, incite, instigate, provoke, rouse, stimulate.
enlarge *vb* amplify, augment, broaden, develop, dilate, distend, expand, extend, grow, increase, magnify, widen; aggrandize, engreaten, ennoble, expand, exaggerate, greaten; swell.
enlighten *vb* illume, illuminate, illumine; counsel, educate, civilize, inform, instruct, teach.
enlist *vb* enrol, levy, recruit, register; enrol, list; embark, engage.
enliven *vb* animate, invigorate, quicken, reanimate, rouse, wake; exhilarate, cheer, brighten, delight, elate, gladden, inspire, inspirit, rouse.
enmity *n* animosity, aversion, bitterness, hate, hatred, hostility, ill-will, malevolence, malignity, rancour.
ennoble *vb* aggrandize, dignify, elevate, engreaten, enlarge, exalt, glorify, greaten, raise.
ennui *n* boredom, irksomeness, languor, lassitude, listlessness, tedium, tiresomeness, weariness.
enormity *n* atrociousness, atrocity, depravity, flagitiousness, heinousness, nefariousness, outrageousness, villainy, wickedness.
enormous *adj* abnormal. exceptional, inordinate, irregular; colossal, Cyclopean, elephantine, Herculean, huge, immense, monstrous, vast, gigantic, prodigious, titanic, tremendous.
enough *adj* abundant, adequate, ample, plenty, sufficient. * *adv* satisfactorily, sufficiently. * *n* abundance, plenty, sufficiency.
enquire *see* **inquire.**
enrage *vb* anger, chafe, exasperate, incense, inflame, infuriate, irritate, madden, provoke.
enrapture *vb* beatify, bewitch, delight, enchant, enravish, entrance, surpassingly, transport.
enrich *vb* endow; adorn, deck, decorate, embellish, grace, ornament.
enrobe *vb* clothe, dress, apparel, array, attire, invest, robe.
enrol *vb* catalogue, engage, engross, enlist, list, register; chronicle, record.
ensconce *vb* conceal, cover, harbour, hide, protect, screen, secure, settle, shelter, shield, snugly.
enshrine *vb* embalm, enclose, entomb; cherish, treasure.
ensign *n* banner, colours, eagle, flag, gonfalcon, pennon, standard, streamer; sign, signal, symbol; badge, hatchment.
enslave *vb* captivate, dominate, master, overmaster, overpower, subjugate.
ensnare *vb* catch, entrap; allure, inveigle, seduce; bewilder, confound, embarrass, encumber, entangle, perplex.
ensue *vb* follow, succeed; arise, come, flow, issue, proceed, result, spring.
entangle *vb* catch, ensnare, entrap; confuse, enmesh, intertwine, intertwist, interweave, knot, mat, ravel, tangle; bewilder, embarrass, encumber, ensnare, involve, nonplus, perplex, puzzle.
enterprise *n* adventure, attempt, cause, effort, endeavour, essay, project, undertaking, scheme, venture; activity, adventurousness, daring, dash, energy, initiative, readiness, push.
enterprising *adj* adventurous, audacious, bold, daring, dashing, venturesome, venturous; active, adventurous, alert, efficient, energetic, prompt, resourceful, smart, spirited, stirring, strenuous, zealous.
entertain *vb* fete, receive, regale, treat; cherish, foster, harbour, hold, lodge, shelter; admit, consider; amuse, cheer, divert, please, recreate.
entertainment *n* hospitality; banquet, collation, feast, festival, reception, treat; amusement, diversion, pastime, recreation, sport.
enthusiasm *n* ecstasy, exaltation, fanaticism; ardour, earnestness, devotion, eagerness, fervour, passion, warmth, zeal.
enthusiast *n* bigot, devotee, fan, fanatic, freak, zealot; castle-builder, dreamer, visionary.
entice *vb* allure, attract, bait, cajole, coax, decoy, inveigle, lure, persuade, prevail on, seduce, tempt, wheedle, wile.
enticement *n* allurement, attraction, bait, blandishment, inducement, inveiglement, lure, persuasion, seduction.
entire *adj* complete, integrated, perfect, unbroken, undiminished, undivided, unimpaired, whole; complete, full, plenary, thorough; mere, pure, sheer, unalloyed, unmingled, unmitigated, unmixed.
entitle *vb* call, characterize, christen, denominate, designate, dub, name, style; empower, enable, fit for, qualify for.
entomb *vb* bury, inhume, inter.
entrails *npl* bowels, guts, intestines, inwards, offal, viscera.
entrance[1] *n* access, approach, avenue, incoming, ingress; adit, avenue, aperture, door, doorway, entry, gate, hallway, inlet, lobby, mouth, passage, portal, stile, vestibule; beginning, commencement, debut, initiation, introduction; admission, entrée.
entrance[2] *vb* bewitch, captivate, charm, delight, enchant, enrapture, fascinate, ravish, transport.
entrap *vb* catch, ensnare; allure, entice, inveigle, seduce; embarrass, entangle, involve, nonplus, perplex, pose, stagger.
entreat *vb* adjure, beg, beseech, crave, enjoin, implore, importune, petition, pray, solicit, supplicate.
entreaty *n* adjuration, appeal, importunity, petition, prayer, request, solicitation, suit, supplication.
entrée *n* access, admission, admittance.
entrench, intrench *vb* furrow; circumvallate, fortify; encroach, infringe, invade, trench, trespass.
entrenchment, intrenchment *n* entrenching; earthwork, fortification; defence, protection, shelter; encroachment, inroad, invasion.
entrust *vb* commit, confide, consign.
entwine *vb* entwist, interlace, intertwine, interweave, inweave, twine, twist, weave; embrace, encircle, encumber, interlace, surround.
enumerate *vb* calculate, cite, compute, count, detail, mention, number, numerate, reckon, recount, specify, tell.
enunciate *vb* articulate, declare, proclaim, promulgate, pronounce, propound, publish, say, speak, utter.
envelop *vb* encase, enfold, enwrap, fold, pack, wrap; cover, encircle, encompass, enshroud, hide, involve, surround.
envelope *n* capsule, case, covering, integument, shroud, skin, wrapper, veil, vesture, wrap.
envenom *vb* poison, taint; embitter, malign; aggravate, enrage, exasperate, incense, inflame, irritate, madden, provoke.
environ *n* begird, belt, embrace, encircle, encompass, enclose, engrid, envelop, gird, hedge, hem, surround; beset, besiege, encompass, invest.
environs *npl* neighbourhood, vicinage, vicinity.
envoy *n* ambassador, legate, minister, plenipotentiary; courier, messenger.
envy *vb* hate; begrudge, grudge; covet, emulate, desire. * *n* enviousness, hate, hatred, ill-will, jealousy, malice, spite; grudge, grudging.
enwrap *vb* absorb, cover, encase, engross, envelop, infold, involve, wrap, wrap up.
ephemeral *adj* brief, diurnal, evanescent, fleeting, flitting, fugacious, fugitive, momentary, occasional, short-lived, transient, transitory.
epic *adj* Homeric, heroic, narrative.
epicure *n* gastronome, glutton, gourmand, gourmet; epicurean, sensualist, Sybarite, voluptuary.
epidemic *adj* general, pandemic, prevailing, prevalent. * *n* outbreak, pandemia, pestilence, plague, spread, wave.
epidermis *n* cuticle, scarf-skin.
epigrammatic *adj* antithetic, concise, laconic, piquant, poignant, pointed, pungent, sharp, terse.
episcopal *adj* Episcopalian, pontifical, prelatic.
epistle *n* communication, letter, missive, note.

epithet *n* appellation, description, designation, name, predicate, title.
epitome *n* abbreviation, abridgement, abstract, breviary, brief, comment, compendium, condensation, conspectus, digest, summary, syllabus, synopsis.
epitomize *vb* abbreviate, abridge, abstract, condense, contract, curtail, cut, reduce, shorten, summarize.
epoch *n* age, date, era, period, time.
equable *adj* calm, equal, even, even-tempered, regular, steady, uniform, serene, tranquil, unruffled.
equal *vb* equalize, even, match. * *adj* alike, coordinate, equivalent, like, tantamount; even, level, equable, regular, uniform; equitable, even-handed, fair, impartial, just, unbiased; co-extensive, commensurate, corresponding, parallel, proportionate; adequate, competent, fit, sufficient. * *n* compeer, fellow, match, peer; rival.
equanimity *n* calmness, composure, coolness, peace, regularity, self-possession, serenity, steadiness.
equestrian *adj* equine, horse-like, horsy. * *n* horseman, rider; cavalier, cavalryman, chevalier, horse soldier, knight.
equilibrist *n* acrobat, balancer, funambulist, rope-walker.
equip *vb* appoint, arm, furnish, provide, rig, supply; accoutre, array, dress.
equipage *n* accoutrements, apparatus, baggage, effects, equipment, furniture; carriage, turnout, vehicle; attendance, procession, retinue, suite, train.
equipment *n* accoutrement, apparatus, baggage, equipage, furniture, gear, outfit, rigging.
equipoise *n* balance, equilibrium.
equitable *adj* even-handed, candid, honest, impartial, just, unbiased, unprejudiced, upright; adequate, fair, proper, reasonable, right.
equity *n* just, right; fair play, fairness, impartiality, justice, rectitude, reasonableness, righteousness, uprightness.
equivalent *adj* commensurate, equal, equipollent, tantamount; interchangeable, synonymous. * *n* complement, coordinate, counterpart, double, equal, fellow, like, match, parallel, pendant, quid pro quo.
equivocal *adj* ambiguous; doubtful, dubious, enigmatic, indeterminate, problematical, puzzling, uncertain.
equivocate *vb* dodge, evade, fence, palter, prevaricate, shuffle, quibble.
equivocation *n* evasion, paltering, prevarication, quibbling, shuffling; double entendre, double meaning, quibble.
era *n* age, date, epoch, period, time.
eradicate *vb* extirpate, root, uproot; abolish, annihilate, destroy, obliterate.
erase *vb* blot, cancel, delete, efface, expunge, obliterate, scrape out.
erasure *n* cancellation, cancelling, effacing, expunging, obliteration.
erect *vb* build, construct, raise, rear; create, establish, form, found, institute, plant. * *adj* standing, unrecumbent, uplifted, upright; elevated, vertical, perpendicular, straight; bold, firm, undaunted, undismayed, unshaken, unterrified.
erelong *adv* early, quickly, shortly, soon, speedily.
eremite *n* anchoret, anchorite, hermit, recluse, solitary.
ergo *adv* consequently, hence, therefore.
erode *vb* canker, consume, corrode, destroy, eat away, fret, rub.
erosive *adj* acrid, cathartic, caustic, corroding, corrosive, eating, virulent.
erotic *adj* amorous, amatory, arousing, seductive, stimulating, titillating.
err *vb* deviate, ramble, rove, stray, wander; blunder, misjudge, mistake; fall, lapse, nod, offend, sin, stumble, trespass, trip.
errand *n* charge, commission, mandate, message, mission, purpose.
errant *adj* adventurous, rambling, roving, stray, wandering.
erratic *adj* nomadic, rambling, roving, wandering; moving, planetary; abnormal, capricious, deviating, eccentric, irregular, odd, queer, strange.
erratum *n* correction, corrigendum, error, misprint, mistake.
erroneous *adj* false, incorrect, inaccurate, inexact, mistaken untrue, wrong.
error *n* blunder, fallacy, inaccuracy, misapprehension, mistake, oversight; delinquency, fault, iniquity, misdeed, misdoing, misstep, obliquity, offence, shortcoming, sin, transgression, trespass, wrongdoing.
erudition *n* knowledge, learning, lore, scholarship.
eruption *n* explosion, outbreak, outburst; sally; rash.
escape *vb* avoid, elude, evade, flee from, shun; abscond, bolt, decamp, flee, fly; slip. * *n* flight; release; passage, passing; leakage.
eschew *vb* abstain, avoid, elude, flee from, shun.
escort *vb* convey, guard, protect; accompany, attend, conduct. * *n* attendant, bodyguard, cavalier, companion, convoy, gallant, guard, squire; protection, safe conduct, safeguard; attendance, company.
esculent *adj* eatable, edible, wholesome.
esoteric *adj* hidden, inmost, inner, mysterious, private, recondite, secret.
especial *adj* absolute, chief, distinct, distinguished, marked, particular, peculiar, principal, singular, special, specific, uncommon, unusual; detailed, minute, noteworthy.
espousal *n* affiancing, betrothing, espousing, plighting; adoption, defence, maintenance, support.
espouse *vb* betroth, plight, promise; marry, wed; adopt, champion, defend, embrace, maintain, support.
espy *vb* descry, detect, discern, discover, observe, perceive, spy, watch.
esquire *n* armiger, attendant, escort, gentleman, squire.
essay[1] *vb* attempt, endeavour, try. * *n* aim, attempt, effort, endeavour, exertion, struggle, trial.
essay[2] *n* article, composition, disquisition, dissertation, paper, thesis.
essence *n* nature, quintessence, substance; extract, part; odour, perfume, scent; being, entity, existence, nature.
essential *adj* fundamental, indispensable, important, inward, intrinsic, necessary, requisite, vital; diffusible, pure, rectified, volatile.
establish *vb* fix, secure, set, settle; decree, enact, ordain; build, constitute, erect, form, found, institute, organize, originate, pitch, plant, raise; ensconce, ground, install, place, plant, root, secure; approve, confirm, ratify, sanction; prove, substantiate, verify.
estate *n* condition, state; position, rank, standing; division, order; effects, fortune, possessions, property; interest.
esteem *vb* appreciate, estimate, rate, reckon, value; admire, honour, like, prize, respect, revere, reverence, value, venerate, worship; account, believe, consider, deem, fancy, hold, imagine, suppose, regard, think. * *n* account, appreciation, consideration, estimate, estimation, judgement, opinion, reckoning, valuation; credit, honour, regard, respect, reverence.
estimable *adj* appreciable, calculable, computable; admirable, credible, deserving, excellent, good, meritorious, precious, respectful, valuable, worthy.
estimate *vb* appraise, appreciate, esteem, prise, rate, value; assess, calculate, compute, count, gauge, judge, reckon. * *n* estimation, judgement, valuation; calculation, computation.
estimation *n* appreciation, estimate, valuation; esteem, estimate, judgement, opinion; honour, reckoning, regard, respect, reverence.
estop *vb* bar, impede, preclude, stop.
estrange *vb* withdraw, withhold; alienate, divert; disaffect, destroy.
estuary *n* creek, inlet, fiord, firth, frith, mouth.
etch *vb* corrode, engrave.
eternal *adj* absolute, inevitable, necessary, self-active, self-existent, self-originated; abiding, ceaseless, endless, ever-enduring, everlasting, incessant, interminable, never-ending, perennial, permanent, perpetual, sempiternal, unceasing, unending; deathless, immortal, imperishable, incorruptible, indestructible, never-dying, undying; immutable, unchangeable; constant, continual, continuous, incessant, persistent, unbroken, uninterrupted.
ethereal *adj* aerial, airy, celestial, empyreal, heavenly, unworldly; attenuated, light, subtle, tenuous, volatile; delicate, fairy, flimsy, fragile, rare, refined, subtle.
eulogize *vb* applaud, commend, extol, laud, magnify, praise.
eulogy *n* discourse, eulogium, panegyric, speech; applause, encomium, commendation, laudation, praise.
euphonious *adj* clear, euphonic, harmonious, mellifluous, mellow, melodious, musical, silvery, smooth, sweet-toned.

evacuant *adj* abstergent, cathartic, cleansing, emetic, purgative. * *n* cathartic, purgative.
evacuate *vb* empty; discharge, clean out, clear out, eject, excrete, expel, purge, void; abandon, desert, forsake, leave, quit, relinquish, withdraw.
evade *vb* elude, escape; avoid, decline, dodge, funk, shun; baffle, elude, foil; dodge, equivocate, fence, palter, prevaricate, quibble, shuffle.
evanescence *n* disappearance, evanishing, evanishment, vanishing; transience, transientness, transitoriness.
evanescent *adj* ephemeral, fleeting, flitting, fugitive, passing, short-lived, transient, transitory, vanishing.
evaporate *vb* distil, volatilize; dehydrate, dry, vaporize; disperse, dissolve, fade, vanish.
evaporation *n* distillation, volatilization; dehydration, drying, vaporization; disappearance, dispersal, dissolution.
evasion *n* artifice, avoidance, bluffing, deceit, dodge, equivocation, escape, excuse, funking, prevarication, quibble, shift, subterfuge, shuffling, sophistical, tergiversation.
evasive *adj* elusive, elusory, equivocating, prevaricating, shuffling, slippery, sophistical.
even *vb* balance, equalize, harmonize, symmetrize; align, flatten, flush, level, smooth, square. * *adj* flat, horizontal, level, plane, smooth; calm, composed, equable, equal, peaceful, placid, regular, steady, uniform, unruffled; direct, equitable, fair, impartial, just, straightforward. * *adv* exactly, just, verily; likewise. * *n* eve, evening, eventide, vesper.
evening *n* dusk, eve, even, eventide, nightfall, sunset, twilight.
event *n* circumstance, episode, fact, happening, incident, occurrence; conclusion, consequence, end, issue, outcome, result, sequel, termination; adventure, affair.
eventful *adj* critical, important, memorable, momentous, remarkable, signal, stirring.
eventual *adj* final, last, ultimate; conditional, contingent, possible. * *adv* always, aye, constantly, continually, eternally, ever evermore, forever, incessantly, perpetually, unceasingly.
everlasting *adj* ceaseless, constant, continual, endless, eternal, ever-during, incessant, interminable, never-ceasing, never-ending, perpetual, unceasing, unending, unintermitting, uninterrupted; deathless, ever-living, immortal, imperishable, never-dying, undying.
evermore *adv* always, constantly, continually, eternally, ever, forever, perpetually.
everyday *adj* accustomed, common, commonplace, customary, habitual, routine, usual, wonted.
evict *vb* dispossess, eject, thrust out.
evidence *vb* evince, make clear, manifest, prove, show, testify, vouch. * *n* affirmation, attestation, averment, confirmation, corroboration, deposition, grounds, indication, proof, testimony, token, trace, voucher, witness.
evident *adj* apparent, bald, clear, conspicuous, distinct, downright, incontestable, indisputable, manifest, obvious, open, overt, palpable, patent, plain, unmistakable.
evil *adj* bad, ill; base, corrupt, malicious, malevolent, malign, nefarious, perverse, sinful, vicious, vile, wicked, wrong; bad, deleterious, baleful, baneful, destructive, harmful, hurtful, injurious, mischievous, noxious, pernicious, profane; adverse, calamitous, diabolic, disastrous, unfortunate, unhappy, unpropitious, woeful. * *n* calamity, disaster, ill, misery, misfortune, pain, reverse, sorrow, suffering, woe; badness, baseness, corruption, depravity, malignity, sin, viciousness, wickedness; bale, bane, blast, canker, curse, harm, injury, mischief, wrong.
evince *vb* establish, evidence, manifest, prove, show; disclose, display, exhibit, indicate, reveal.
eviscerate *vb* disembowel, embowel, gut.
evoke *vb* arouse, elicit, excite, provoke, rouse.
evolve *vb* develop, educe, exhibit, expand, open, unfold, unroll.
exacerbate *vb* aggravate, embitter, enrage, exasperate, excite, inflame, infuriate, irritate, provoke, vex.
exact *vb* elicit, extort, mulch, require, squeeze; ask, claim, compel, demand, enforce, requisition, take. * *adj* rigid, rigorous, scrupulous, severe, strict; diametric, express, faultless, precise, true; accurate, close, correct, definite, faithful, literal, undeviating; accurate, critical, delicate, fine, nice, sensitive; careful, methodical, punctilious, orderly, punctual, regular.
exacting *adj* critical, difficult, exactive, rigid, extortionary.
exaction *n* contribution, extortion, oppression, rapacity, tribute.
exactness *n* accuracy, correctness, exactitude, faithfulness, faultlessness, fidelity, nicety, precision, rigour; carefulness, method, precision, regularity, rigidness, scrupulousity, scrupulousness, strictness.
exaggerate *vb* enlarge, magnify, overcharge, overcolour, overstate, romance, strain, stretch.
exalt *vb* elevate, erect, heighten, lift up, raise; aggrandize, dignify, elevate, ennoble; bless, extol, glorify, magnify, praise.
exalted *adj* elated, elevated, high, highflown, lofty, lordly, magnificent.
examination *n* inspection, observation; exploration, inquiry, inquisition, investigation, perusal, research, search, scrutiny, survey; catechism, probation, review, test, trial.
examine *vb* inspect, observe; canvass, consider, explore, inquire, investigate, scrutinize, study, test; catechize, interrogate.
example *n* archetype, copy, model, pattern, piece, prototype, representative, sample, sampler, specimen, standard; exemplification, illustration, instance, precedent, warning.
exanimate *adj* dead, defunct, inanimate, lifeless; inanimate, inert, sluggish, spiritless, torpid.
exasperate *vb* affront, anger, chafe, enrage, incense, irritate, nettle, offend, provoke, vex; aggravate, exacerbate, inflame, rouse.
exasperation *n* annoyance, exacerbation, irritation, pro- vocation; anger, fury, ire, passion, rage, wrath; aggravation, heightening, increase, worsening.
excavate *vb* burrow, cut, delve, dig, hollow, hollow out, scoop, trench.
exceed *vb* cap, overstep, surpass, transcend; excel, outdo, outstrip, outvie, pass.
excel *vb* beat, eclipse, outdo, outrival, outstrip, outvie, surpass; cap, exceed, transcend.
excellence *n* distinction, eminence, pre-eminence, superiority, transcendence; fineness, fitness, goodness, perfection, purity, quality, superiority; advantage; goodness, probity, uprightness, virtue, worth.
excellent *adj* admirable, choice, crack, eminent, first-rate, prime, sterling, superior, tiptop, transcendent; deserving, estimable, praiseworthy, virtuous, worthy.
except *vb* exclude, leave out, omit, reject. * *conj* unless. * *prep* bar, but, excepting, excluding, save.
exceptional *adj* aberrant, abnormal, anomalous, exceptive, irregular, peculiar, rare, special, strange, superior, uncommon, unnatural, unusual.
excerpt *vb* cite, cull, extract, quote, select, take. * *n* citation, extract, quotation, selection.
excess *adj* excessive, unnecessary, redundant, spare, superfluous, surplus. * *n* disproportion, fulsomeness, glut, oversupply, plethora, redundance, redundancy, surfeit, superabundance, superfluity; overplus, remainder, surplus; debauchery, dissipation, dissoluteness, intemperance, immoderation, overindulgence, unrestraint; extravagance, immoderation, overdoing.
excessive *adj* disproportionate, exuberant, superabundant, superfluous, undue; extravagant, enormous, inordinate, outrageous, unreasonable; extreme, immoderate, intemperate; vehement, violent.
exchange *vb* barter, change, commute, shuffle, substitute, swap, trade, truck; bandy, interchange. * *n* barter, change, commutation, dealing, shuffle, substitution, trade, traffic; interchange, reciprocity; bazaar, bourse, fair, market.
excise[1] *n* capitation, customs, dues, duty, tariff, tax, taxes, toll.
excise[2] *vb* cancel, cut, delete, edit, efface, eradicate, erase, expunge, extirpate, remove, strike out.

excision *n* destruction, eradication, extermination, extirpation.

excitable *adj* impressible, nervous, sensitive, susceptible; choleric, hasty, hot-headed, hot-tempered, irascible, irritable, passionate, quick-tempered.

excite *vb* animate, arouse, awaken, brew, evoke, impel, incite, inflame, instigate, kindle, move, prompt, provoke, rouse, spur, stimulate; create, elicit, evoke, raise; agitate, discompose, disturb, irritate.

excitement *n* excitation, exciting; incitement, motive, stimulus; activity, agitation, bustle, commotion, disturbance, ferment, flutter, perturbation, sensation, stir, tension; choler, heat, irritation, passion, violence, warmth.

exclaim *vb* call, cry, declare, ejaculate, shout, utter, vociferate.

exclude *vb* ban, bar, blackball, debar, ostracize, preclude, reject; hinder, prevent, prohibit, restrain, withhold; except, omit; eject, eliminate, expel, extrude.

exclusive *adj* debarring, excluding; illiberal, narrow, narrow-minded, selfish, uncharitable; aristocratic, choice, clannish, cliquish, fastidious, fashionable, select, snobbish; only, sole, special.

excommunicate *vb* anathematize, ban, curse, denounce, dismiss, eject, exclude, expel, exscind, proscribe, unchurch.

excoriate *vb* abrade, flay, gall, scar, scarify, score, skin, strip.

excrement *n* dejections, dung, faeces, excreta, excretion, ordure, stool.

excrescence *n* fungus, growth, knob, lump, outgrowth, protuberance, tumour, wart.

excrete *vb* discharge, eject, eliminate, separate.

excruciate *vb* agonize, rack, torment, torture.

exculpate *vb* absolve, acquit, clear, discharge, exonerate, free, justify, release, set right, vindicate.

excursion *n* drive, expedition, jaunt, journey, ramble, ride, sally, tour, trip, voyage, walk; digression, episode.

excursive *adj* devious, diffuse, digressive, discursive, erratic, rambling, roaming, roving, wandering.

excusable *adj* allowable, defensible, forgivable, justifiable, pardonable, venial, warrantable.

excursus *n* discussion, disquisition, dissertation.

excuse *vb* absolve, acquit, exculpate, exonerate, forgive, pardon, remit; extenuate, justify; exempt, free, release; overlook. * *n* absolution, apology, defence, extenuation, justification, plea; colour, disguise, evasion, guise, pretence, pretext, makeshift, semblance, subterfuge.

execrable *adj* abhorrent, abominable, accursed, cursed, damnable, detestable, hateful, odious; disgusting, loathsome, nauseating, nauseous, obnoxious, offensive, repulsive, revolting, sickening, vile.

execrate *vb* curse, damn, imprecate; abhor, abominate, detest, hate, loathe.

execute *vb* accomplish, achieve, carry out, complete, consummate, do, effect, effectuate, finish, perform, perpetrate; administer, enforce, seal, sign; behead, electrocute, guillotine, hang.

execution *n* accomplishment, achievement, completion, consummation, operation, performance; warrant, writ; beheading, electrocution, hanging.

executive *adj* administrative, commanding, controlling, directing, managing, ministerial, officiating, presiding, ruling. * *n* administrator, director, manager.

exegetic, exegetical *adj* explanatory, explicative, explicatory, expository, hermeneutic, interpretative.

exemplary *adj* assiduous, close, exact, faithful, punctual, punctilious, rigid, rigorous, scrupulous; commendable, correct, good, estimable, excellent, praiseworthy, virtuous; admonitory, condign, monitory, warning.

exemplify *vb* evidence, exhibit, illustrate, manifest, show.

exempt *vb* absolve, except, excuse, exonerate, free, release, relieve. * *adj* absolved, excepted, excused, exempted, free, immune, liberated, privileged, released.

exemption *n* absolution, dispensation, exception, immunity, privilege, release.

exercise *vb* apply, busy, employ, exert, praxis, use; effect, exert, produce, wield; break in, discipline, drill, habituate, school, train; practise, prosecute, pursue; task, test, try; afflict, agitate, annoy, burden, pain, trouble. * *n* appliance, application, custom, employment, operation, performance, play, plying, practice, usage, use, working; action, activity, effort, exertion, labour, toil, work; discipline, drill, drilling, schooling, training; lesson, praxis, study, task, test, theme.

exert *vb* employ, endeavour, exercise, labour, strain, strive, struggle, toil, use, work.

exertion *n* action, exercise, exerting, use; attempt, effort, endeavour, labour, strain, stretch, struggle, toil, trial.

exhalation *n* emission, evaporation; damp, effluvium, fog, fume, mist, reek, smoke, steam, vapour.

exhale *vb* breathe, discharge, elect, emanate, emit, evaporate, reek; blow, expire, puff.

exhaust *vb* drain, draw, empty; consume, destroy, dissipate, expend, impoverish, lavish, spend, squander, waste; cripple, debilitate, deplete, disable, enfeeble, enervate, overtire, prostrate, weaken.

exhaustion *n* debilitation, enervation, fatigue, lassitude, weariness.

exhibit *vb* demonstrate, disclose, display, evince, expose, express, indicate, manifest, offer, present, reveal, show; offer, present, propose.

exhibition *n* demonstration, display, exposition, manifestation, representation, spectacle, show; allowance, benefaction, grant, pension, scholarship.

exhilarate *vb* animate, cheer, elate, enliven, gladden, inspire, inspirit, rejoice, stimulate.

exhilaration *n* animating, cheering, elating, enlivening, gladdening, rejoicing, stimulating; animation, cheer, cheerfulness, gaiety, gladness, glee, good spirits, hilarity, joyousness.

exhort *vb* advise, caution, encourage, incite, persuade, stimulate, urge, warm; preach.

exhume *vb* disentomb, disinhume, disinter, unbury, unearth.

exigency, exigence *n* demand, necessity, need, requirement, urgency, want; conjuncture, crisis, difficulty, distress, emergency, extremity, juncture, nonplus, quandary, pass, pinch, pressure, strait.

exiguous *adj* attenuated, diminutive, fine, small, scanty, slender, tiny.

exile *vb* banish, expatriate, expel, ostracize, proscribe. * *n* banishment, expatriation, expulsion, ostracism, proscription, separation; outcast, refugee.

exist *vb* be, breathe, live; abide, continue, endure, last, remain.

existence *n* being, subsisting, subsistence; being, creature, entity, essence, thing; animation, continuation, life, living, vitality, vivacity.

exit *vb* depart, egress, go, leave. * *n* departure, withdrawal; death, decrease, demise, end; egress, outlet.

exonerate *vb* absolve, acquit, clear, exculpate, justify, vindicate; absolve, discharge, except, exempt, free, release.

exorbitant *adj* enormous, excessive, extravagant, inordinate, unreasonable.

exorcise *vb* cast out, drive away, expel; deliver, purify; address, conjure.

exordium *n* introduction, opening, preamble, preface, prelude, proem, prologue.

exotic *adj* extraneous, foreign; extravagant.

expand *vb* develop, open, spread, unfold, unfurl; diffuse, enlarge, extend, increase, stretch; dilate, distend, enlarge.

expanse *n* area, expansion, extent, field, stretch.

expansion *n* expansion, opening, spreading; diastole, dilation, distension, swelling; development, diffusion, enlargement, increase; expanse, extent, stretch.

ex parte *adj* biased, one-sided, partisan.

expatiate *vb* amplify, decant, dilate, enlarge, range, rove.

expatriate *vb* banish, exile, expel, ostracize, proscribe. * *adj* banished, exiled, refugee. * *n* displaced person, emigrant, exile.

expect *vb* anticipate, await, calculate, contemplate, forecast, foresee, hope, reckon, rely.

expectancy *n* expectance, expectation; abeyance, prospect.

expectation *n* anticipation, expectance, expectancy, hope, prospect; assurance, confidence, presumption, reliance, trust.

expedient *adj* advisable, appropriate, convenient, desirable, fit, proper, politic, suitable; advantageous, profitable, useful. * *n* contrivance, device, means, method, resort, resource, scheme, shift, stopgap, substitute.

expedite *vb* accelerate, advance, dispatch, facilitate, forward, hasten, hurry, precipitate, press, quicken, urge.

expedition *n* alacrity, alertness, celerity, dispatch, haste, promptness, quickness, speed; enterprise, undertaking; campaign, excursion, journey, march, quest, voyage.

expeditious *adj* quick, speedy, swift, rapid; active, alert, diligent, nimble, prompt, punctual, swift.

expel *vb* dislodge, egest, eject, eliminate, excrete; discharge, eject, evacuate, void; bounce, discharge, exclude, exscind, fire, oust, relegate, remove; banish, disown, excommunicate, exile, expatriate, ostracize, proscribe, unchurch.

expend *vb* disburse, spend; consume, employ, exert, use; dissipate, exhaust, scatter, waste.

expenditure *n* disbursement, outlay, outlaying, spending; charge, cost, expenditure, outlay.

expensive *adj* costly, dear, high-priced; extravagant, lavish, wasteful.

experience *vb* endure, suffer; feel, know; encounter, suffer, undergo. * *n* endurance, practice, trial; evidence, knowledge, proof, test, testimony.

experienced *adj* able, accomplished, expert, instructed, knowing, old, practised, qualified, skilful, trained, thoroughbred, versed, veteran, wise.

experiment *vb* examine, investigate, test, try. * *n* assay, examination, investigation, ordeal, practice, proof, test, testimony, touchstone, trial.

expert *adj* able, adroit, apt, clever, dextrous, proficient, prompt, quick, ready, skilful. * *n* adept, authority, connoisseur, crack, master, specialist.

expertise *n* adroitness, aptness, dexterity, facility, promptness, skilfulness, skill.

expiate *vb* atone, redeem, satisfy.

expiration *n* death, decease, demise, departure, exit; cessation, close, conclusion, end, termination.

expire *vb* cease, close, conclude, end, stop, terminate; emit, exhale; decease, depart, die, perish.

explain *vb* demonstrate, elucidate, expound, illustrate, interpret, resolve, solve, unfold, unravel; account for, justify, warrant.

explanation *n* clarification, description, elucidation, exegesis, explication, exposition, illustration, interpretation; account, answer, deduction, justification, key, meaning, secret, solution, warrant.

explicit *adj* absolute, categorical, clear, definite, determinate, exact, express, plain, positive, precise, unambiguous, unequivocal, unreserved.

explode *vb* burst, detonate, discharge, displode, shatter, shiver; contemn, discard, repudiate, scorn, scout.

exploit *vb* befool, milk, use, utilize. * *n* achievement, act, deed, feat.

explore *vb* examine, fathom, inquire, inspect, investigate, prospect, scrutinize, seek.

explosion *n* blast, burst, bursting, clap, crack, detonation, discharge, displosion, fulmination, pop.

exponent *n* example, illustration, index, indication, specimen, symbol, type; commentator, demonstrator, elucidator, expounder, illustrator, interpreter.

expose *vb* bare, display, uncover; descry, detect, disclose, unearth; denounce, mask; subject; endanger, jeopardize, risk, venture.

exposé *n* exhibit, exposition, manifesto; denouncement, divulgement, exposure, revelation.

exposition *n* disclosure, interpretation; commentary, critique, elucidation, exegesis, explanation, explication, interpretation; display, show.

expound *vb* develop, present, rehearse, reproduce, unfold; clear, elucidate, explain, interpret.

express *vb* air, assert, asseverate, declare, emit, enunciate, manifest, utter, vent, signify, speak, state, voice; betoken, denote, equal, exhibit, indicate, intimate, present, represent, show, symbolize. * *adj* categorical, clear, definite, determinate, explicit, outspoken, plain, positive, unambiguous; accurate, close, exact, faithful, precise, true; particular, special; fast, nonstop, quick, rapid, speedy, swift. * *n* dispatch, message.

expression *n* assertion, asseveration, communication, declaration, emission, statement, utterance, voicing; language, locution, phrase, remark, saying, term, word; air, aspect, look, mien.

expressive *adj* indicative, meaningful, significant; demonstrative, eloquent, emphatic, energetic, forcible, lively, strong, vivid; appropriate, sympathetic, well-modulated.

expulsion *n* discharge, eviction, expelling, ousting; elimination, evacuation, excretion; ejection, excision, excommunication, extrusion, ostracism, separation.

expunge *vb* annihilate, annul, cancel, delete, destroy, efface, erase, obliterate, wipe out.

expurgate *vb* clean, cleanse, purge, purify; bowdlerize, emasculate.

exquisite *adj* accurate, delicate, discriminating, exact, fastidious, nice, refined; choice, elect, excellent, precious, rare, valuable; complete, consummate, matchless, perfect; acute, keen, intense, poignant. * *n* beau, coxcomb, dandy, fop, popinjay.

extant *adj* existent, existing, present, surviving, undestroyed, visible.

extempore *adj* extemporaneous, extemporary, impromptu, improvised. * *adv* offhand, suddenly, unpremeditatedly, unpreparedly.

extend *vb* reach, stretch; continue, elongate, lengthen, prolong, protract, widen; augment, broaden, dilate, distend, enlarge, expand, increase; diffuse, spread; give, impart, offer, yield; lie, range.

extensible *adj* ductile, elastic, extendible, extensile, protractible, protractile.

extension *n* augmentation, continuation, delay, dilatation, dilation, distension, enlargement, expansion, increase, prolongation, protraction.

extensive *adj* broad, capacious, comprehensive, expanded, extended, far-reaching, large, wide, widespread.

extent *n* amplitude, expanse, expansion; amount, bulk, content, degree, magnitude, size, volume; compass, measure, length, proportions, reach, stretch; area, field, latitude, range, scope; breadth, depth, height, width.

extenuate *vb* diminish, lessen, reduce, soften, weaken; excuse, mitigate, palliate, qualify.

exterior *adj* external, outer, outlying, outside, outward, superficial, surface; extrinsic, foreign. * *n* outside, surface; appearance.

exterminate *vb* abolish, annihilate, destroy, eliminate, eradicate, extirpate, uproot.

external *adj* exterior, outer, outside, outward, superficial; extrinsic, foreign; apparent, visible.

extinct *adj* extinguished, quenched; closed, dead, ended, lapsed, terminated, vanished.

extinction *n* death, extinguishment; abolishment, abolition, annihilation, destruction, excision, extermination, extirpation.

extinguish *vb* choke, douse, put out, quell, smother, stifle, suffocate, suppress; destroy, nullify, subdue; eclipse, obscure.

extirpate *vb* abolish, annihilate, deracinate, destroy, eradicate, exterminate, uproot, weed.

extol *vb* celebrate, exalt, glorify, laud, magnify, praise; applaud, commend, eulogize, panegyrize.

extort *vb* elicit, exact, extract, force, squeeze, wrench, wrest, wring.

extortion *n* blackmail, compulsion, demand, exaction, oppression, overcharge, rapacity, tribute; exorbitance.

extortionate *adj* bloodsucking, exacting, hard, harsh, oppressive, rapacious, rigorous, severe; exorbitant, unreasonable.

extra *adj* accessory, additional, auxiliary, collateral; another, farther, fresh, further, more, new, other, plus, ulterior; side, spare, supernumerary, supplemental, supplementary, surplus; extraordinary, extreme, unusual. * *adv* additionally, also, beyond, farthermore, furthermore, more, moreover, plus. * *n* accessory, appendage, collateral, nonessential, special, supernumerary, supplement; bonus, premium; balance, leftover, remainder, spare, surplus.

extract *vb* extort, pull out, remove, withdraw; derive, distil, draw, express, squeeze; cite, determine, derive, quote, select. * *n* citation, excerpt, passage, quotation, selection; decoction, distillation, essence, infusion, juice.

extraction *n* drawing out, derivation, distillation, elicitation, essence, pulling out; birth, descent, genealogy, lineage, origin, parentage.

extraneous *adj* external, extrinsic, foreign; additional, adventitious, external, superfluous, supplementary, unessential.

extraordinary *adj* abnormal, amazing, distinguished, egregious, exceptional, marvellous, monstrous, particular, peculiar, phenomenal, prodigious, rare, remarkable, signal, singular, special, strange, uncommon, unprecedented, unusual, unwonted, wonderful.

extravagance *n* excess, enormity, exorbitance, preposterousness, unreasonableness; absurdity, excess, folly, irregularity, wildness; lavishness, prodigality, profuseness, profusion, superabundance; waste.

extravagant *adj* excessive, exorbitant, inordinate, preposterous, unreasonable; absurd, foolish, irregular, wild; lavish, prodigal, profuse, spendthrift.

extreme *adj* farthest, outermost, remotest, utmost, uttermost; greatest, highest; final, last, ultimate; drastic, egregious, excessive, extravagant, immoderate, intense, outrageous, radical, unreasonable. * *n* end, extremity, limit; acme, climax, degree, height, pink; danger, distress.

extremity *n* border, edge, end, extreme, limb, termination, verge.

extricate *vb* clear, deliver, disembarrass, disengage, disentangle, liberate, release, relieve.

extrinsic *adj* external, extraneous, foreign, outside, outward, superabundance, superfluity.

exuberance *n* abundance, copiousness, flood, luxuriance, plenitude; excess, lavishness, overabundance, overflow, overgrowth, overluxuriance, profusion, rankness, redundancy, superabundance, superfluity.

exuberant *adj* abounding, abundant, copious, fertile, flowing, luxuriant, prolific, rich; excessive, lavish, overabundant, overflowing, overluxuriant, profuse, rank, redundant, superabounding, superabundant, wanton.

exude *vb* discharge, excrete, secrete, sweat; infiltrate, ooze, percolate.

exult *vb* gloat, glory, jubilate, rejoice, transport, triumph, taunt, vault.

exultation *n* delight, elation, joy, jubilation, transport, triumph.

eye *vb* contemplate, inspect, ogle, scrutinize, survey, view, watch. * *n* estimate, judgement, look, sight, vision, view; inspection, notice, observation, scrutiny, sight, vigilance, watch; aperture, eyelet, peephole, perforation; bud, shoot.

F

fable *n* allegory, legend, myth, parable, story, tale; fabrication, falsehood, fiction, figment, forgery, untruth.

fabric *n* building, edifice, pile, structure; conformation, make, texture, workmanship; cloth, material, stuff, textile, tissue, web.

fabricate *vb* build, construct, erect, frame; compose, devise, fashion, make, manufacture; coin, fake, feign, forge, invent.

fabrication *n* building, construction, erection; manufacture; fable, fake, falsehood, fiction, figment, forgery, invention, lie.

fabulous *adj* amazing, apocryphal, coined, fabricated, feigned, fictitious, forged, imaginary, invented, legendary, marvellous, mythical, romancing, unbelievable, unreal.

façade *n* elevation, face, front.

face *vb* confront; beard, buck, brave, dare, defy, front, oppose; dress, level, polish, smooth; cover, incrust, veneer. * *n* cover, facet, surface; breast, escarpment, front; countenance, features, grimace, physiognomy, visage; appearance, expression, look, semblance; assurance, audacity, boldness, brass, confidence, effrontery, impudence.

facet *n* cut, face, lozenge, surface.

facetious *adj* amusing, comical, droll, funny, humorous, jocose, jocular, pleasant, waggish, witty; entertaining, gay, lively, merry, sportive, sprightly.

facile *adj* easy; affable, approachable, complaisant, conversable, courteous, mild; compliant, ductile, flexible, fluent, manageable, pliable, pliant, tractable, yielding; dextrous, ready, skilful.

facilitate *vb* expedite, help.

facility *n* ease, easiness; ability, dexterity, expertness, knack, quickness, readiness; ductility, flexibility, pliancy; advantage, appliance, convenience, means, resource; affability, civility, complaisance, politeness.

facsimile *n* copy, duplicate, fax, reproduction.

fact *n* act, circumstance, deed, event, incident, occurrence, performance; actuality, certainty, existence, reality, truth.

faction *n* cabal, clique, combination, division, junta, party, side; disagreement, discord, disorder, dissension, recalcitrance, recalcitrancy, refractoriness, sedition, seditiousness, tumult, turbulence, turbulency.

factious *adj* litigious, malcontent, rebellious, recalcitrant, refractory, seditious, turbulent.

factitious *adj* artful, artificial, conventional, false, unnatural, unreal.

factor *n* agent, bailiff, broker, consignee, go-between, steward, component, element, ingredient; influence, reason.

factory *n* manufactory, mill, work, workshop.

faculty *n* ability, capability, capacity, endowment, power, property, quality; ableness, address, adroitness, aptitude, aptness, clearness, competency, dexterity, efficiency, expertness, facility, forte, ingenuity, knack, qualification, quickness, readiness, skill, skilfulness, talent, turn; body, department, profession; authority, prerogative, license, privilege, right.

fade *vb* disappear, die, evanesce, fall, faint, perish, vanish; decay, decline, droop, fall, languish, wither; bleach, blanch, pale; disperse, dissolve.

faeces *npl* dregs, lees, sediment, settlings; dung, excrement, ordure, settlings.

fag *vb* droop, flag, sink; drudge, toil; fatigue, jade, tire, weary. * *n* drudgery, fatigue, work; drudge, grub, hack; cigarette, smoke.

fail *vb* break, collapse, decay, decline, fade, sicken, sink, wane; cease, disappear; fall, miscarry, miss; neglect, omit; bankrupt, break.

failing *adj* deficient, lacking, needing, wanting; declining, deteriorating, fading, flagging, languishing, sinking, waning, wilting; unsuccessful. * *prep* lacking, needing, wanting. * *n* decay, decline; failure, miscarriage; defect, deficiency, fault, foible, frailty, imperfection, infirmity, shortcoming, vice, weakness; error, lapse, slip; bankruptcy, insolvency.

failure *n* defectiveness, deficiency, delinquency, shortcoming; fail, miscarriage, negligence, neglect, nonobservance, nonperformance, omission, slip; abortion, botch, breakdown, collapse, fiasco, fizzle; bankruptcy, crash, downfall, insolvency, ruin; decay, declension, decline, loss.

fain *adj* anxious, glad, inclined, pleased, rejoiced, well-pleased. * *adv* cheerfully, eagerly, gladly, joyfully, willingly.

faint *vb* swoon; decline, fade, fail, languish, weaken. * *adj* swooning; drooping, exhausted, feeble, languid, listless, sickly, weak; gentle, inconsiderable, little, slight, small, soft, thin; dim, dull, indistinct, perceptible, scarce, slight; cowardly, dastardly, faint-hearted, fearful, timid, timorous; dejected, depressed, discouraged, disheartened, dispirited. * *n* blackout, swoon.

faint-hearted *adj* cowardly, dastardly, faint, fearful, timid, timorous.

fair[1] *adj* spotless, unblemished, unspotted, unstained, untarnished; blond, light, white; beautiful, comely, handsome, shapely; clear, cloudless, pleasant, unclouded; favourable, prosperous; hopeful, promising, propitious; clear, distinct, open, plain, unencumbered, unobstructed; candid, frank, honest, honourable, impartial, ingenuous, just, unbiased, upright; equitable, proper; average, decent, indifferent, mediocre, moderate, ordinary, passable, reasonable, respectful, tolerable.

fair[2] *n* bazaar, carnival, exposition, festival, fete, funfair, gala, kermess.

fairy *n* brownie, elf, demon, fay, sprite.

faith *n* assurance, belief, confidence, credence, credit, dependence, reliance, trust; creed, doctrine, dogma, persuasion, religion, tenet; constancy, faithfulness, fidelity, loyalty, truth, truthfulness.

faithful *adj* constant, devoted, loyal, staunch, steadfast, true; honest, upright, reliable, trustworthy, trusty; reliable, truthful; accurate, close, conscientiousness, exact, nice, strict.

faithless *adj* unbelieving; dishonest, disloyal, false, fickle, fluctuating, inconstant, mercurial, mutable, perfidious, shifting, treacherous, truthless, unsteady, untruthful, vacillating, variable, wavering.

fall *vb* collapse, depend, descend, drop, sink, topple, tumble; abate, decline, decrease, depreciate, ebb, subside; err, lapse, sin, stumble, transgress, trespass, trip; die, perish; befall, chance, come, happen, occur, pass; become, get; come, pass. * *n* collapse, comedown, descent, downcome, dropping, falling, flop, plop, tumble; cascade, cataract, waterfall; death, destruction, downfall, overthrow, ruin, surrender; comeuppance, degradation; apostasy, declension, failure, lapse, slip; decline, decrease, depreciation, diminution, ebb, sinking, subsidence; cadence, close; declivity, inclination, slope.

fallacious *adj* absurd, deceptive, deceiving, delusive, disappointing, erroneous, false, illusive, illusory, misleading; paralogistic, sophistical, worthless.

fallacy *n* aberration, deceit, deception, delusion, error, falsehood, illusion, misapprehension, misconception, mistake, untruth; non sequitur, paralogism, sophism, sophistry.

fallibility *n* frailty, imperfection, uncertainty.

fallible *adj* erring, frail, ignorant, imperfect, uncertain, weak.

fallow *adj* left, neglected, uncultivated, unsowed, untilled; dormant, inactive, inert.

false *adj* lying, mendacious, truthless, untrue, unveracious; dishonest, dishonourable, disingenuous, disloyal, double-faced, double-tongued, faithless, false-hearted, perfidious, treacherous, unfaithful; fictitious, forged, made-up, unreliable, untrustworthy; artificial, bastard, bogus, counterfeit, factitious, feigned, forged, hollow, hypocritical, make-believe, pretended, pseudo, sham, spurious, suppositious; erroneous, improper, incorrect, unfounded, wrong; deceitful, deceiving, deceptive, disappointing, fallacious, misleading.

false-hearted *adj* dishonourable, disloyal, double, double-tongued, faithless, false, perfidious, treacherous.

falsehood *n* falsity; fabrication, fib, fiction, lie, untruth; cheat, counterfeit, imposture, mendacity, treachery.

falsify *vb* alter, adulterate, belie, cook, counterfeit, doctor, fake, falsely, garble, misrepresent, misstate, represent; disprove; violate.

falsity *n* falsehood, untruth, untruthfulness.

falter *vb* halt, hesitate, lisp, quaver, stammer, stutter; fail, stagger, stumble, totter, tremble, waver; dodder.

fame *n* bruit, hearsay, report, rumour; celebrity, credit, eminence, glory, greatness, honour, illustriousness, kudos, lustre, notoriety, renown, reputation, repute.

familiar *adj* acquainted, aware, conversant, well-versed; amicable, close, cordial, domestic, fraternal, friendly, homely, intimate, near; affable, accessible, companionable, conversable, courteous, civil, friendly, kindly, sociable, social; easy, free and easy, unceremonious, unconstrained; common, frequent, well-known. * *n* acquaintance, associate, companion, friend, intimate.

familiarity *n* acquaintance, knowledge, understanding; fellowship, friendship, intimacy; closeness, friendliness, sociability; freedom, informality, liberty; disrespect, overfreedom, presumption; intercourse.

familiarize *vb* accustom, habituate, inure, train, use.

family *n* brood, household, people; ancestors, blood, breed, clan, dynasty, kindred, house, lineage, race, stock, strain, tribe; class, genus, group, kind, subdivision.

famine *n* dearth, destitution, hunger, scarcity, starvation.

famish *vb* distress, exhaust, pinch, starve.

famous *adj* celebrated, conspicuous, distinguished, eminent, excellent, fabled, famed, far-famed, great, glorious, heroic, honoured, illustrious, immortal, notable, noted, notorious, remarkable, renowned, signal.

fan[1] *vb* agitate, beat, move, winnow; blow, cool, refresh, ventilate; excite, fire, increase, rouse, stimulate. * *n* blower, cooler, punkah, ventilator.

fan[2] *n* admirer, buff, devotee, enthusiast, fancier, follower, pursuer, supporter.

fanatic *n* bigot, devotee, enthusiast, visionary, zealot.

fanatical *adj* bigoted, enthusiastic, frenzied, mad, rabid, visionary, wild, zealous.

fanciful *adj* capricious, crotchety, imaginary, visionary, whimsical; chimerical, fantastical, ideal, imaginary, wild.

fancy *vb* apprehend, believe, conjecture, imagine, suppose, think; conceive, imagine. * *adj* elegant, fine, nice, ornamented; extravagant, fanciful, whimsical. * *n* imagination; apprehension, conceit, conception, impression, idea, image, notion, thought; approval, fondness, inclination, judgement, liking, penchant, taste; caprice, crotchet, fantasy, freak, humour, maggot, quirk, vagary, whim, whimsy; apparition, chimera, daydream, delusion, hallucination, megrim, phantasm, reverie, vision.

fanfaron *n* blatherskite, blusterer, braggadocio, bully, hector, swaggerer, vapourer.

fang *n* claw, nail, talon, tooth; tusk.

fantastic *adj* chimerical, fanciful, imaginary, romantic, unreal, visionary; bizarre, capricious, grotesque, odd, quaint, queer, strange, whimsical, wild.

far *adj* distant, long, protracted, remote; farther, remoter; alienated, estranged, hostile. * *adv* considerably, extremely, greatly, very much; afar, distantly, far away, remotely.

farce *n* burlesque, caricature, parody, travesty; forcemeat, stuffing.

farcical *adj* absurd, comic, droll, funny, laughable, ludicrous, ridiculous.

fardel *n* bundle, burden, load, pack; annoyance, burden, ill, trouble.

fare *vb* go, journey, pass, travel; happen, prosper, prove; feed, live, manage, subsist. * *n* charge, price, ticket money; passenger, traveller; board, commons, food, table, victuals, provisions; condition, experience, fortune, luck, outcome.

farewell *n* adieu, leave-taking, valediction; departure, leave, parting, valedictory.

far-fetched *adj* abstruse, catachrestic, forced, recondite, strained.

farrago *n* gallimaufry, hodgepodge, hotchpotch, jumble, medley, miscellany, mixture, potpourri, salmagundi.

farther *adj* additional; further, remoter, ulterior. * *adv* beyond, further; besides, furthermore, moreover.

farthingale *n* crinoline, hoop, hoop skirt.

fascinate *vb* affect, bewitch, overpower, spellbind, stupefy, transfix; absorb, captivate, catch, charm, delight, enamour, enchant, enrapture, entrance.

fascination *n* absorption, charm, enchantment, magic, sorcery, spell, witchcraft, witchery.

fash *vb* harass, perplex, plague, torment, trouble, vex, worry. * *n* anxiety, care, trouble, vexation.

fashion *vb* contrive, create, design, forge, form, make, mould, pattern, shape; accommodate, adapt, adjust, fit, suit. * *n* appearance, cast, configuration, conformation, cut, figure, form, make, model, mould, pattern, shape, stamp; manner, method, sort, wake; conventionalism, conventionality, custom, fad, mode, style, usage, vogue; breeding, gentility; quality.

fashionable *adj* modish, stylish; current, modern, prevailing, up-to-date; customary, usual; genteel, well-bred.

fast[1] *adj* close, fastened, firm, fixed, immovable, tenacious, tight; constant, faithful, permanent, resolute, staunch, steadfast, unswerving, unwavering; fortified, impregnable, strong; deep, profound, sound; fleet, quick, rapid, swift; dissipated, dissolute, extravagant, giddy, reckless, thoughtless, thriftless, wild. * *adv* firmly, immovably, tightly; quickly, rapidly, swiftly; extravagantly, prodigally, reckless, wildly.

fast[2] *vb* abstain, go hungry, starve. * *n* abstention, abstinence, diet, fasting, starvation.

fasten *vb* attach, bind, bolt, catch, chain, cleat, fix, gird, lace, lock, pin, secure, strap, tether, tie; belay, bend; connect, hold, join, unite.

fastidious *adj* critical, dainty, delicate, difficult, exquisite, finical, hypercritical, meticulous, overdelicate, overnice, particular, precise, precious, punctilious, queasy, squeamish.

fat *adj* adipose, fatty, greasy, oily, oleaginous, unctuous; corpulent, fleshy, gross, obese, paunchy, portly, plump, pudgy, pursy; coarse, dull, heavy, sluggish, stupid; lucrative, profitable, rich; fertile, fruitful, productive, rich. * *n* adipose tissue, ester, grease, oil; best part, cream, flower; corpulence, fatness, fleshiness, obesity, plumpness, stoutness.

fatal *adj* deadly, lethal, mortal; baleful, baneful, calamitous, catastrophic, destructive, mischievous, pernicious, ruinous; destined, doomed, foreordained, inevitable, predestined.

fatality *n* destiny, fate; mortality; calamity, disaster.

fate *n* destination, destiny, fate; cup, die, doom, experience, lot, fortune, portion, weird; death, destruction, ruin.

fated *adj* appointed, destined, doomed, foredoomed, predetermined, predestinated, predestined, preordained.

fatherly *adj* benign, kind, paternal, protecting, tender.

fathom *vb* comprehend, divine, penetrate, reach, understand; estimate, gauge, measure, plumb, probe, sound.

fathomless *adj* abysmal, bottomless, deep, immeasurable, profound; impenetrable, incomprehensible, obscure.

fatigue *vb* exhaust, fag, jade, tire, weaken, weary. * *n* exhaustion, lassitude, tiredness, weariness; hardship, labour, toil.

fatuity *n* foolishness, idiocy, imbecility, stupidity; absurdity, folly, inanity, infatuation, madness.

fatuous *adj* dense, drivelling, dull, foolish, idiotic, stupid, witless; infatuated, mad, senseless, silly, weak.

fault *n* blemish, defect, flaw, foible, frailty, imperfection, infirmity, negligence, obliquity, offence, shortcoming, spot, weakness; delinquency, error, indiscretion, lapse, misdeed, misdemeanour, offence, peccadillo, slip, transgression, trespass, vice, wrong; blame, culpability.

faultless *adj* blameless, guiltless, immaculate, innocent, sinless, spotless, stainless; accurate, correct, perfect, unblemished.

faulty *adj* bad, defective, imperfect, incorrect; blameable, blameworthy, censurable, culpable, reprehensible.

faux pas *n* blunder, indiscretion, mistake.

favour *vb* befriend, countenance, encourage, patronize; approve; ease, facilitate; aid, assist, help, oblige, support; extenuate, humour, indulge, palliate, spare. * *n* approval, benignity, countenance, esteem, friendless, goodwill, grace, kindness; benefaction, benefit, boon, dispensation, kindness; championship, patronage, popularity, support; gift, present, token; badge, decoration, knot, rosette; leave, pardon, permission; advantage, cover, indulgence, protection; bias, partiality, prejudice.

favourable *adj* auspicious, friendly, kind, propitious, well-disposed, willing; conductive, contributing, propitious; adapted, advantage, beneficial, benign, convenient, fair, fit, good, helpful, suitable.

favourite *adj* beloved, darling, dear; choice, fancied, esteemed, pet, preferred.

fawn *vb* bootlick, bow, creep, cringe, crouch, dangle, kneel, stoop, toady, truckle.

fealty *n* allegiance, homage, loyalty, obeisance, submission; devotion, faithfulness, fidelity, honour, loyalty.

fear *vb* apprehend, dread; revere, reverence, venerate. * *n* affright, alarm, apprehension, consternation, dismay, dread, fright, horror, panic, phobia, scare, terror; disquietude, flutter, perturbation, palpitation, quaking, quivering, trembling, tremor, trepidation; anxiety, apprehension, concern, misdoubt, misgiving, qualm, solicitude; awe, dread, reverence, veneration.

fearful *adj* afraid, apprehensive, haunted; chicken-hearted, chicken-livered, cowardly, faint-hearted, lily-livered, nervous, pusillanimous, timid, timorous; dire, direful, dreadful, frightful, ghastly, horrible, shocking, terrible.

fearless *adj* bold, brave, courageous, daring, dauntless, doughty, gallant, heroic, intrepid, unterrified, valiant, valorous.

feasible *adj* achievable, attainable, possible, practicable, suitable.

feast *vb* delight, gladden, gratify, rejoice. * *n* banquet, carousal, entertainment, regale, repast, revels, symposium, treat; celebration, festival, fete, holiday; delight, enjoyment, pleasure.

feat *n* accomplishment, achievement, act, deed, exploit, performance, stunt, trick.

feather *n* plume; kind, nature, species.

featly *adv* adroitly, dextrously, nimbly, skilfully.

feature *vb* envisage, envision, picture, visualize; imagine; specialize; appear in, headline, star. * *n* appearance, aspect, component; conformation, fashion, make; characteristic, item, mark, particularity, peculiarity, property, point, trait; leader, lead item, special; favour, expression, lineament; article, film, motion picture, movie, story; highlight, high spot.

fecund *adj* fruitful, impregnated, productive, prolific, rich.

fecundity *n* fertility, fruitfulness, productiveness.

federation *n* alliance, allying, confederation, federating, federation, leaguing, union, uniting; affiliation, coalition, combination, compact, confederacy, entente, federacy, league, copartnership.

fee *vb* pay, recompense, reward. * *n* account, bill, charge, compensation, honorarium, remuneration, reward, tip; benefice, fief, feud.

feeble *adj* anaemic, debilitated, declining, drooping, enervated, exhausted, frail, infirm, languid, languishing, sickly; dim, faint, imperfect, indistinct.

feed *vb* contribute, provide, supply; cherish, eat, nourish, subsist, sustain. * *n* fodder, food, foodstuff, forage, provender.

feel *vb* apprehend, intuit, perceive, sense; examine, handle, probe, touch; enjoy, experience, suffer; prove, sound, test, try; appear, look, seem; believe, conceive, deem, fancy, infer, opine, suppose, think. * *n* atmosphere, feeling, quality; finish, surface, texture.

feeling *n* consciousness, impression, notion, perception, sensation; atmosphere, sense, sentience, touch; affecting, emotion, heartstrings, impression, passion, soul, sympathy; sensibility, sentiment, susceptibility, tenderness; attitude, impression, opinion.

feign *vb* devise, fabricate, forge, imagine, invent; affect, assume, counterfeit, imitate, pretend, sham, simulate.

feint *n* artifice, blind, expedient, make-believe, pretence, stratagem, trick.

felicitate *vb* complicate, congratulate; beatify, bless, delight.

felicitous *adj* appropriate, apt, fit, happy, ingenious, inspired, opportune, pertinent, seasonable, skilful, well-timed; auspicious, fortunate, prosperous, propitious, successful.

felicity *n* blessedness, bliss, blissfulness, gladness, happiness, joy; appropriateness, aptitude, aptness, felicitousness, fitness, grace, propriety, readiness, suitableness; fortune, luck, success.

fell[1] *vb* beat, knock down, level, prostrate; cut, demolish, hew.

fell[2] *adj* barbarous, bloodthirsty, bloody, cruel, ferocious, fierce, implacable, inhuman, malicious, malign, malignant, pitiless, relentless, ruthless, sanguinary, savage, unrelenting, vandalistic; deadly, destructive.

fellow *adj* affiliated, associated, joint, like, mutual, similar, twin. * *n* associate, companion, comrade; compeer, equal, peer; counterpart, mate, match, partner; member; boy, character, individual, man, person.

fellowship *n* brotherhood, companionship, comradeship, familiarity, intimacy; participation; partnership; communion, converse, intercourse; affability, kindliness, sociability, sociableness.

felon *n* convict, criminal, culprit, delinquent, malefactor, outlaw; inflammation, whitlow.

felonious *adj* atrocious, cruel, felon, heinous, infamous, malicious, malign, malignant, nefarious, perfidious, vicious, villainous.

female *adj* delicate, gentle, ladylike, soft; fertile, pistil-bearing, pistillate.

feminine *adj* affectionate, delicate, gentle, graceful, modest, soft, tender; female, ladylike, maidenly, womanish, womanly; effeminateness, effeminacy, softness, unmanliness, weakness, womanliness.

fen *n* bog, marsh, moor, morass, quagmire, slough, swamp.

fence *vb* defend, enclose, fortify, guard, protect, surround; circumscribe, evade, equivocate, hedge, prevaricate; guard, parry. * *n* barrier, hedge, hoarding, palings, palisade, stockade, wall; defence, protection, guard, security, shield; fencing, swordplay, swordsmanship; receiver.

fenny *adj* boggy, fennish, swampy, marshy.

feral, ferine *adj* ferocious, fierce, rapacious, ravenous, savage, untamed, wild.

ferment *vb* agitate, excite, heat; boil, brew, bubble, concoct, heat, seethe. * *n* barm, leaven, yeast; agitation, commotion, fever, glow, heat, tumult.

ferocious *adj* feral, fierce, rapacious, ravenous, savage, untamed, wild; barbarous, bloody, bloodthirsty, brutal, cruel, fell, inhuman, merciless, murderous, pitiless, remorseless, ruthless, sanguinary, truculent, vandalistic, violent.

ferocity *n* ferociousness, ferocity, fierceness, rapacity, savageness, wildness; barbarity, cruelty, inhumanity.

fertile *adj* bearing, breeding, fecund, prolific;
exuberant, fruitful, luxuriant, plenteous, productive, rich, teeming; female, fruit-bearing, pistillate.

fertility *n* fertileness, fertility; abundance, exuberant, fruitfulness, luxuriance, plenteousness, productiveness, richness.

fervent *adj* burning, hot, glowing, melting, seething; animated, ardent, earnest, enthusiastic, fervid, fierce, fiery, glowing, impassioned, intense, passionate, vehement, warm, zealous.

fervour *n* heat, warmth; animation, ardour, eagerness, earnestness, excitement, fervency, intensity, vehemence, zeal.

fester *vb* corrupt, rankle, suppurate, ulcerate; putrefy, rot. * *n* abscess, canker, gathering, pustule, sore, suppination; festering, rankling.

festival *n* anniversary, carnival, feast, fete, gala, holiday, jubilee; banquet, carousal, celebration, entertainment, treat.

festive *adj* carnival, convivial, festal, festival, gay, jolly, jovial, joyful, merry, mirthful, uproarious.

festivity *n* conviviality, festival, gaiety, jollity, joviality, joyfulness, joyousness, merrymaking, mirth.

festoon *vb* adorn, decorate, embellish, garland, hoop, ornament. * *n* decoration, embellishment, garland, hoop, ornament, ornamentation.

fetch *vb* bring, elicit, get; accomplish, achieve, effect, perform; attain, reach. * *n* artifice, dodge, ruse, stratagem, trick.

fetid *adj* foul, malodorous, mephitic, noisome, offensive, rancid, rank, rank-smelling, stinking, strong-smelling.

fetish *n* charm, medicine, talisman.

fetter *vb* clog, hamper, shackle, trammel; bind, chain, confine, encumber, hamper, restrain, tie, trammel. * *n* bond, chain, clog, hamper, shackle.

feud *vb* argue, bicker, clash, contend, dispute, quarrel. * *n* affray, argument, bickering, broil, clashing, contention, contest, discord, dissension, enmity, fray, grudge, hostility, jarring, quarrel, rupture, strife, vendetta.

fever *n* agitation, excitement, ferment, fire, flush, heat, passion.

fey *adj* clairvoyant, ethereal, strange, unusual, whimsical; death-smitten, doomed.

fiasco *n* failure, fizzle.

fiat *n* command, decree, order, ordinance.

fibre *n* filament, pile, staple, strand, texture, thread; stamina, strength, toughness.

fickle *adj* capricious, changeable, faithless, fitful, inconstant, irresolute, mercurial, mutable, shifting, unsettled, unstable, unsteady, vacillating, variable, veering, violate, volatile, wavering.

fiction *n* fancy, fantasy, imagination, invention; novel, romance; fable, fabrication, falsehood, figment, forgery, invention, lie.

fictitious *adj* assumed, fabulous, fanciful, feigned, imaginary, invented, mythical, unreal; artificial, counterfeit, dummy, false, spurious, supposititious.

fiddle *vb* dawdle, fidget, interfere, tinker, trifle; cheat, swindle, tamper. * *n* fraud, swindle; fiddler, violin, violinist.

fiddle-de-dee *interj* fudge, moonshine, nonsense, stuff.

fiddle-faddle *n* frivolity, gabble, gibberish, nonsense, prate, stuff, trifling, trivia, twaddle.

fidelity *n* constancy, devotedness, devotion, dutifulness, faithfulness, fealty, loyalty, true-heartedness, truth; accuracy, closeness, exactness, faithfulness, precision.

fidget *vb* chafe, fret, hitch, twitch, worry. * *n* fidgetiness, impatience, restlessness, uneasiness.

fiduciary *adj* confident, fiducial, firm, steadfast, trustful, undoubting, unwavering; reliable, trustworthy. * *n* depositary, trustee.

field *n* clearing, glebe, meadow; expanse, extent, opportunity, range, room, scope, surface; department, domain, province, realm, region.

fiendish *adj* atrocious, cruel, demoniac, devilish, diabolical, hellish, implacable, infernal, malevolent, malicious, malign, malignant.

fierce *adj* barbarous, brutal, cruel, fell, ferocious, furious, infuriate, ravenous, savage; fiery, impetuous, murderous, passionate, tearing, tigerish, truculent, turbulent, uncurbed, untamed, vehement, violent.

fiery *adj* fervent, fervid, flaming, heated, hot, glowing, lurid; ardent, fierce, impassioned, impetuous, inflamed, passionate, vehement.

fight *vb* battle, combat, war; contend, contest, dispute, feud, oppose, strive, struggle, wrestle; encounter, engage; handle, manage, manoeuvre. * *n* affair, affray, action, battle, brush, combat, conflict, confrontation, contest, duel, encounter, engagement, melée, quarrel, struggle, war; brawl, broil, riot, row, skirmish; fighting, pluck, pugnacity, resistance, spirit, temper.

figment *n* fable, fabrication, falsehood, fiction, invention.

figurative *adj* emblematical, representative, symbolic, representative, typical; metaphorical, tropical; florid, flowery, ornate, poetical.

figure *vb* adorn, diversify, ornament, variegate; delineate, depict, represent, signify, symbolize, typify; conceive, image, imagine, picture; calculate, cipher, compute; act, appear, perform. * *n* configuration, conformation, form, outline, shape; effigy, image, likeness, representative; design, diagram, drawing, pattern; image, metaphor, trope; emblem, symbol, type; character, digit, number, numeral.

filament *n* cirrus, fibre, fibril, gossamer, hair, strand, tendril, thread.

filch *vb* crib, nick, pilfer, purloin, rob, snitch, seal, thieve.

file[1] *vb* order, pigeonhole, record, tidy. * *n* data, dossier, folder, portfolio; column, line, list, range, rank, row, series, tier.

file[2] *vb* burnish, furbish, polish, rasp, refine, smooth.

filibuster *vb* delay, frustrate, obstruct, play for time, stall, temporize. * *n* frustrater, obstructionist, thwarter; adventurer, buccaneer, corsair, freebooter, pirate.

fill *vb* occupy, pervade; dilate, distend, expand, stretch, trim; furnish, replenish, stock, store, supply; cloy, congest, content, cram, glut, gorge, line, pack, pall, sate, satiate, satisfy, saturate, stuff, suffuse, swell; engage, fulfil, hold, occupy, officiate, perform.

film *vb* becloud, cloud, coat, cover, darken, fog, mist, obfuscate, obscure, veil; photograph, shoot, take. * *n* cloud, coating, gauze, membrane, nebula, pellicle, scum, skin, veil; thread.

filter *vb* filtrate, strain; exude, ooze, percolate, transude. * *n* diffuser, colander, riddle, sieve, sifter, strainer.

filth *n* dirt, nastiness, ordure; corruption, defilement, foulness, grossness, impurity, obscenity, pollution, squalor, uncleanness, vileness.

filthy *adj* defiled, dirty, foul, licentious, nasty, obscene, pornographic, squalid, unclean; corrupt, gross, impure, unclean; miry, mucky, muddy.

final *adj* eventual, extreme, last, latest, terminal, ultimate; conclusive, decisive, definitive, irrevocable.

finale *n* conclusion, end, termination.

finances *n pl* funds, resources, revenues, treasury; income, property.

find *vb* discover, fall upon; gain, get, obtain, procure; ascertain, notice, observe, perceive, remark; catch, detect; contribute, furnish, provide, supply. * *n* acquisition, catch, discovery, finding, plum, prize, strike.

fine[1] *vb* filter, purify, refine. * *adj* comminuted, little, minute, small; capillary, delicate, small; choice, light; exact, keen, sharp; attenuated, subtle, tenuous, thin; exquisite, fastidious, nice, refined, sensitive, subtle; dandy, excellent, superb, superior; beautiful, elegant, handsome, magnificent, splendid; clean, pure, unadulterated.

fine[2] *vb* amerce, mulct, penalize, punish. * *n* amercement, forfeit, forfeiture, mulct, penalty, punishment.

finery *n* decorations, frippery, gewgaws, ornaments, splendour, showiness, trappings, trimmings, trinkets.

finesse *vb* manipulate, manoeuvre. * *n* artifice, contrivance, cunning, craft, manipulation, manoeuvre, manoeuvring, ruses, stratagems, strategy, wiles.

finger *vb* handle, manipulate, play, purloin.

finical *adj* critical, dainty, dapper, fastidious, foppish, jaunty, overnice, overparticular, scrupulous, spruce, squeamish, trim.

finish *vb* accomplish, achieve, complete, consummate, execute, fulfil, perform; elaborate, perfect, polish; close, conclude, end, terminate. * *n* elaboration, elegance, perfection, polish; close, end, death, termination, wind-up.

finite *adj* bounded, circumscribed, conditioned, contracted, definable, limited, restricted, terminable.

fire *vb* ignite, kindle, light; animate, enliven, excite, inflame, inspirit, invigorate, rouse, stir up; discharge, eject, expel, hurl. * *n* combustion; blaze, conflagration; discharge, firing; animation, ardour, enthusiasm, fervour, fervency, fever, force, heat, impetuosity, inflammation, intensity, passion, spirit, vigour, violence; light, lustre, radiance, splendour; imagination, imaginativeness, inspiration, vivacity; affliction, persecution, torture, trouble.

firm[1] *adj* established, coherent, confirmed, consistent, fast, fixed, immovable, inflexible, rooted, secure, settled, stable; compact, compressed, dense, hard, solid; constant, determined, resolute, staunch, steadfast, steady, unshaken; loyal, robust, sinewy, stanch, stout, sturdy, strong.

firm[2] *n* association, business, company, concern, corporation, house, partnership.

firmament *n* heavens, sky, vault, welkin.

firmness *n* compactness, fixedness, hardness, solidity; stability, strength; constancy, soundness, steadfastness, steadiness.

first *adj* capital, chief, foremost, highest, leading, prime, principal; earliest, eldest, original; maiden; elementary, primary, rudimentary; aboriginal, primal, primeval, primitive, pristine. * *adv* chiefly, firstly, initially, mainly, primarily, principally; before, foremost, headmost; before, rather, rather than, sooner, sooner than. * *n* alpha, initial, prime.

first-rate *adj* excellent, prime, superior.

fissure *n* breach, break, chasm, chink, cleft, crack, cranny, crevice, fracture, gap, hole, interstice, opening, rent, rift.

fit[1] *vb* adapt, adjust, suit; become, conform; accommodate, equip, prepare, provide, qualify. * *adj* capacitated, competent, fitted; adequate, appropriate, apt, becoming, befitting, consonant, convenient, fitting, good, meet, pertinent, proper, seemly, suitable.

fit[2] *n* convulsion, fit, paroxysm, qualm, seizure, spasm, spell; fancy, humour, whim; mood, pet, tantrum; interval, period, spell, turn.

fitful *adj* capricious, changeable, convulsive, fanciful, fantastic, fickle, humoursome, impulsive, intermittent, irregular, odd, spasmodic, unstable, variable, whimsical; checkered, eventful.

fitness *n* adaptation, appropriateness, aptitude, aptness, pertinence, propriety, suitableness; preparation, qualification.

fix *vb* establish, fasten, place, plant, set; adjust, correct, mend, repair; attach, bind, clinch, connect, fasten, lock, rivet, stay, tie; appoint, decide, define, determine, limit, seal, settle; consolidate, harden, solidify; abide, remain, rest; congeal, stiffen. * *n* difficulty, dilemma, quandary, pickle, plight, predicament.

flabbergast *vb* abash, amaze, astonish, astound, confound, confuse, disconcert, dumbfound, nonplus.

flabby *adj* feeble, flaccid, inelastic, limp, soft, week, yielding.

flaccid *adj* baggy, drooping, flabby, inelastic, lax, limber, limp, loose, pendulous, relaxed, soft, weak, yielding.

flag[1] *vb* droop, hang, loose; decline, droop, fail, faint, lag, languish, pine, sink, succumb, weaken, weary; stale, pall.

flag[2] *vb* indicate, mark, semaphore, sign, signal. * *n* banner, colours, ensign, gonfalon, pennant, pennon, standard, streamer.

flagellate *vb* beat, castigate, chastise, cudgel, drub, flog, scourge, thrash, whip.

flagitious *adj* abandoned, atrocious, corrupt, flagrant, heinous, infamous, monstrous, nefarious, profligate, scandalous, villainous, wicked.

flagrant *adj* burning, flaming, glowing, raging; crying, enormous, flagitious, glaring, monstrous, nefarious, notorious, outrageous, shameful, wanton, wicked.

flake *vb* desquamate, scale. * *n* lamina, layer, scale.

flamboyant *adj* bright, gorgeous, ornate, rococo.

flame *vb* blaze, shine; burn, flash, glow, warm. * *n* blaze, brightness, fire, flare, vapour; affection, ardour, enthusiasm, fervency, fervour, keenness, warmth.

flaming *adj* blazing; burning, bursting, exciting, glowing, intense, lambent, vehement, violent.

flap *vb* beat, flutter, shake, vibrate, wave. * *n* apron, fly, lap, lappet, tab; beating, flapping, flop, flutter, slap, shaking, swinging, waving.

flare *vb* blaze, flicker, flutter, waver; dazzle, flame, glare; splay, spread, widen. * *n* blaze, dazzle, flame, glare.

flash *vb* blaze, glance, glare, glisten, light, shimmer, scintillate, sparkle, twinkle. * *n* instant, moment, twinkling.

flashy *adj* flaunting, gaudy, gay, loud, ostentatious, pretentious, showy, tawdry, tinsel.

flat *adj* champaign, horizontal, level; even, plane, smooth, unbroken; low, prostrate, overthrow; dull, frigid, jejune, lifeless, monotonous, pointless, prosaic, spiritless, tame, unanimated, uniform, uninteresting; dead, flashy, insipid, mawkish, stale, tasteless, vapid; absolute, clear, direct, downright, peremptory, positive. * *adv* flatly, flush, horizontally, level. * *n* bar, sandbank, shallow, shoal, strand; champaign, lowland, plain; apartment, floor, lodging, storey.

flatter *vb* compliment, gratify, praise; blandish, blarney, butter up, cajole, coax, coddle, court, entice, fawn, humour, inveigle, wheedle.

flattery *n* adulation, blandishment, blarney, cajolery, fawning, obsequiousness, servility, sycophancy, toadyism.

flaunt *vb* boast, display, disport, flourish, parade, sport, vaunt; brandish.

flaunting *adj* flashy, garish, gaudy, ostentatious, showy, tawdry.

flavour *n* gust, gusto, relish, savour, seasoning, smack, taste, zest; admixture, lacing, seasoning; aroma, essence, soul, spirit.

flaw *n* break, breach, cleft, crack, fissure, fracture, gap, rent, rift; blemish, defect, fault, fleck, imperfection, speck, spot.

flay *vb* excoriate, flay; criticize.

fleck *vb* dapple, mottle, speckle, spot, streak, variegate. * *n* speckle, spot, streak.

flecked *adj* dappled, mottled, piebald, spotted, straked, striped, variegated.

flee *vb* abscond, avoid, decamp, depart, escape, fly, leave, run, skedaddle.

fleece *vb* clip, shear; cheat, despoil, pluck, plunder, rifle, rob, steal, strip.

fleer *vb* mock, jeer, gibe, scoff, sneer.

fleet[1] *n* armada, escadrille, flotilla, navy, squadron; company, group.

fleet[2] *adj* fast, nimble, quick, rapid, speedy, swift.

fleeting *adj* brief, caducous, ephemeral, evanescent, flitting, flying, fugitive, passing, short-lived, temporary, transient, transitory.

fleetness *n* celerity, nimbleness, quickness, rapidity, speed, swiftness, velocity.

flesh *n* food, meat; carnality, desires; kindred, race, stock; man, mankind, world.

fleshly *adj* animal, bodily, carnal, lascivious, lustful, lecherous, sensual.

fleshy *adj* corpulent, fat, obese, plump, stout.

flexibility *n* flexibleness, limbersome, lithesome, pliability, pliancy, suppleness; affability, complaisance, compliance, disposition, ductility, pliancy, tractableness, tractability, yielding.

flexible *adj* flexible, limber, lithe, pliable, pliant, supple, willowy; affable, complaisant, ductile, docile, gentle, tractable, tractile, yielding.

flexose, flexuous *adj* bending, crooked, serpentine, sinuate, sinuous, tortuous, waxy, winding.

flibbertigibbet *n* demon, imp, sprite.

flight[1] *n* flying, mounting, soaring, volition; shower, flight; steps, stairs.

flight[2] *n* departure, fleeing, flying, retreat, rout, stampede; exodus, hegira.

flighty *adj* capricious, deranged, fickle, frivolous, giddy, light-headed, mercurial, unbalanced, volatile, wild, whimsical.

flimsy *adj* slight, thin, unsubstantial; feeble, foolish, frivolous, light, puerile, shallow, superficial, trashy, trifling, trivial, weak; insubstantial, sleazy.

flinch *vb* blench, flee, recoil, retreat, shirk, shrink, swerve, wince, withdraw.

fling *vb* cast, chuck, dart, emit, heave, hurl, pitch, shy, throw, toss; flounce, wince. * *n* cast, throw, toss.

flippancy *n* volubility; assuredness, glibness, pertness.

flippant *adj* fluent, glib, talkative, voluble; bold, forward, frivolous, glib, impertinent, inconsiderate, irreverent, malapert, pert, saucy, trifling.

flirt *vb* chuck, fling, hurl, pitch, shy, throw, toss; flutter, twirl, whirl, whisk; coquet, dally, philander. * *n* coquette, jilt, philanderer; jerk.

flirtation *n* coquetry, dalliance, philandering.

flit *vb* flicker, flutter, hover; depart, hasten, pass.

flitting *adj* brief, ephemeral, evanescent, fleeting, fugitive, passing, short, transient, transitory.

float *vb* drift, glide, hang, ride, sail, soar, swim, waft; launch, support.

flock *vb* collect, congregate, gather, group, herd, swarm, throng. * *n* collection, group, multitude; bevy, company, convoy, drove, flight, gaggle, herd, pack, swarm, team, troupe; congregation.

flog *vb* beat, castigate, chastise, drub, flagellate, lash, scourge, thrash, whip.

flood *vb* deluge, inundate, overflow, submerge, swamp. * *n* deluge, freshet, inundation, overflow, tide; bore, downpour, eagre, flow, outburst, spate, rush; abundance, excess.

floor *vb* deck, pave; beat, confound, conquer, overthrow, prevail, prostrate, puzzle; disconcert, nonplus. * *n* storey; bottom, deck, flooring, pavement, stage.

florid *adj* bright-coloured, flushed, red-faced, rubicund; embellished, figurative, luxuriant, ornate, rhetorical, rococo.

flounce[1] *vb* fling, jerk, spring, throw, toss, wince. * *n* jerk, spring.

flounce[2] *n* frill, furbelow, ruffle.

flounder *vb* blunder, flop, flounce, plunge, struggle, toss, tumble, wallow.

flourish *vb* grow, thrive; boast, bluster, brag, gasconade, show off, vaunt, vapour; brandish, flaunt, swing, wave. * *n* dash, display, ostentation, parade, show; bombast, fustian, grandiloquence; brandishing, shake, waving; blast, fanfare, tantivy.

flout *vb* chaff, deride, fleer, gibe, insult, jeer, mock, ridicule, scoff, sneer, taunt. * *n* gibe, fling, insult, jeer, mock, mockery, mocking, scoff, scoffing, taunt.

flow *vb* pour, run, stream; deliquesce, liquefy, melt; arise, come, emanate, follow, grow, issue, proceed, result, spring; glide; float, undulate, wave, waver; abound, run. * *n* current, discharge, flood, flux, gush, rush, stream, trickle; abundance, copiousness.

flower *vb* bloom, blossom, effloresce; develop. * *n* bloom, blossom; best, cream, elite, essence, pick; freshness, prime, vigour.

flowery *adj* bloomy, florid; embellished, figurative, florid, ornate, overwrought.

flowing *adj* abundant, copious, fluent, smooth.

fluctuate *vb* oscillate, swing, undulate, vibrate, wave; change, vary; vacillate, waver.

flue *n* chimney, duct; flew, fluff, nap, floss, fur.

fluency *n* liquidness, smoothness; affluence, copiousness; ease, facility, readiness.

fluent *adj* current, flowing, gliding, liquid; smooth; affluent, copious, easy, facile, glib, ready, talkative, voluble.

fluff *vb* blunder, bungle, forget, fumble, mess up, miscue, misremember, muddle, muff. * *n* down, flew, floss, flue, fur, lint, nap; cobweb, feather, gossamer, thistledown; blunder, bungle, fumble, muff.

flume *n* channel, chute, mill race, race.

flummery *n* chaff, frivolity, froth, moonshine, nonsense, trash, trifling; adulation, blandishment, blarney, flattery; brose, porridge, sowens.

flunky, flunkey *n* footman, lackey, livery servant, manservant, valet; snob, toady.

flurry *vb* agitate, confuse, disconcert, disturb, excite, fluster, hurry, perturb. * *n* gust, flaw, squall; agitation, bustle, commotion, confusion, disturbance, excitement, flutter, haste, hurry, hurry-scurry, perturbation, ruffle, scurry.

flush[1] *vb* flow, rush, start; glow, mantle, redden; animate, elate, elevate, erect, excite; cleanse, drench. * *adj* bright, fresh, glowing, vigorous; abundant, affluent, exuberant, fecund, fertile, generous, lavish, liberal, prodigal, prolific, rich, wealthy, well-supplied; even, flat, level, plane. * *adv* evenly, flat, level; full, point-blank, right, square, squarely, straight. * *n* bloom, blush, glow, redness, rosiness, ruddiness; impulse, shock, thrill.

flush[2] *vb* disturb, rouse, start, uncover.

fluster *vb* excite, flush, heat; agitate, disturb, flurry, hurry, perturb, ruffle; confound, confuse, discompose, disconcert. * *n* glow, heat; agitation, flurry, flutter, hurry, hurry-scurry, perturbation, ruffle.

fluted *adj* channelled, corrugated, grooved.

flutter *vb* flap, hover; flirt, flit; beat, palpitate, quiver, tremble; fluctuate, oscillate, vacillate, waver. * *n* agitation, tremor; hurry, commotion, confusion, excitement, flurry, fluster, hurry-scurry, perturbation, quivering, tremble, tumult, twitter.

flux *n* flow, flowing; change, mutation, shifting, transition; diarrhoea, dysentery, looseness; fusing, melting, menstruum, solvent.

fly[1] *vb* aviate, hover, mount, soar; flap, float, flutter, play, sail, soar, undulate, vibrate, wave; burst, explode; abscond, decamp, depart, flee, vanish; elapse, flit, glide, pass, slip.

fly[2] *adj* alert, bright, sharp, smart, wide-awake; astute, cunning, knowing, sly; agile, fleet, nimble, quick, spry.

foal *n* colt, filly.

foam *vb* cream, froth, lather, spume; boil, churn, ferment, fume, seethe, simmer, stew. * *n* bubbles, cream, froth, scum, spray, spume, suds.

fodder *n* feed, food, forage, provender, rations.

foe *n* adversary, antagonist, enemy, foeman, opponent.

fog *vb* bedim, bemist, blear, blur, cloud, dim, enmist, mist; addle, befuddle, confuse, fuddle, muddle. * *n* blear, blur, dimness, film, fogginess, haze, haziness, mist, smog, vapour; befuddlement, confusion, fuddle, maze, muddle.

foggy *adj* blurred, cloudy, dim, dimmed, hazy, indistinct, misty, obscure; befuddled, bewildered, confused, dazed, muddled, muddy, stupid.

foible *n* defect, failing, fault, frailty, imperfection, infirmity, penchant, weakness.

foil[1] *vb* baffle, balk, check, checkmate, circumvent, defeat, disappoint, frustrate, thwart.

foil[2] *n* film, flake, lamina; background, contrast.

foist *vb* impose, insert, interpolate, introduce, palm off, thrust.

fold[1] *vb* bend, cover, double, envelop, wrap; clasp, embrace, enfold, enwrap, gather, infold, interlace; collapse, fail. * *n* double, doubling, gather, plait, plicature.

fold[2] *n* cot, enclosure, pen.

foliaceous *adj* foliate, leafy; flaky, foliated, lamellar, lamellate, lamellated, laminated, scaly, schistose.

folk *n* kindred, nation, people.

follow *vb* ensue, succeed; chase, dog, hound, pursue, run after, trail; accompany, attend; conform, heed, obey, observe; cherish, cultivate, seek; practise, pursue; adopt, copy, imitate; arise, come, flow, issue, proceed, result, spring.

follower *n* acolyte, attendant, associate, companion, dependant, retainer, supporter; adherent, admirer, disciple, partisan, pupil; copier, imitator.

folly *n* doltishness, dullness, imbecility, levity, shallowness; absurdity, extravagance, fatuity, foolishness, imprudence, inanity, indiscretion, ineptitude, nonsense, senselessness; blunder, faux pas, indiscretion, unwisdom.

foment *vb* bathe, embrocate, stupe; abet, brew, encourage, excite, foster, instigate, promote, stimulate.

fond *adj* absurd, baseless, empty, foolish, senseless, silly, vain, weak; affectionate, amorous, doting, loving, overaffectionate, tender.

fondle *vb* blandish, caress, coddle, cosset, dandle, pet.

fondness *n* absurdity, delusion, folly, silliness, weakness; liking, partiality, predilection, preference, propensity; appetite, relish, taste.

food *n* aliment, board, bread, cheer, commons, diet, fare, meat, nourishment, nutriment, nutrition, pabulum, provisions, rations, regimen, subsistence, sustenance, viands, victuals; feed, fodder, forage, provender.

fool *vb* jest, play, toy, trifle; beguile, cheat, circumvent, cozen, deceive, delude, dupe, gull, hoodwink, overreach, trick. * *n* blockhead, dolt, driveller, idiot, imbecile, nincompoop, ninny, nitwit, simpleton; antic, buffoon, clown, droll, harlequin, jester, merry-andrew, punch, scaramouch, zany; butt, dupe.

foolery *n* absurdity, folly, foolishness, nonsense; buffoonery, mummery, tomfoolery.

foolhardy *adj* adventurous, bold, desperate, harebrained, headlong, hotheaded, incautious, precipitate, rash, reckless, venturesome, venturous.

foolish *adj* brainless, daft, fatuous, idiotic, inane, inept, insensate, irrational, senseless, shallow, silly, simple, thick-skulled, vain, weak, witless; absurd, ill-judged, imprudent, indiscreet, nonsensical, preposterous, ridiculous, unreasonable, unwise; childish, contemptible, idle, puerile, trifling, trivial, vain.

foolishness *n* doltishness, dullness, fatuity, folly, imbecility, shallowness, silliness, stupidity; absurdity, extravagance, imprudence, indiscretion, nonsense; childishness, puerility, triviality.

footing *n* foothold, purchase; basis, foundation, groundwork, installation; condition, grade, rank, standing, state, status; settlement, establishment.

footman *n* footboy, menial, lackey, runner, servant.

footpad *n* bandit, brigand, freebooter, highwayman, robber.

footpath *n* footway, path, trail.

footprint *n* footfall, footmark, footstep, trace, track.

footstep *n* footmark, footprint, trace, track; footfall, step, tread; mark, sign, token, trace, vestige.

fop *n* beau, coxcomb, dandy, dude, exquisite, macaroni, popinjay, prig, swell.

foppish *adj* coxcombical, dandified, dandyish, dressy, finical, spruce, vain.

forage *vb* feed, graze, provender, provision, victual; hunt for, range, rummage, search, seek; maraud, plunder, raid. * *n* feed, fodder, food, pasturage, provender; hunt, rummage, search.

foray *n* descent, incursion, invasion, inroad, irruption, raid.

forbear *vb* cease, desist, hold, pause, stop, stay; abstain, refrain; endure, tolerate; avoid, decline, shun; abstain, omit, withhold.

forbearance *n* abstinence, avoidance, forbearing, self-restraint, shunning, refraining; indulgence, leniency, long-suffering, mildness, moderation, patience.

forbid *vb* ban, debar, disallow, embargo, enjoin, hinder, inhibit, interdict, prohibit, proscribe, taboo, veto.

forbidding *adj* abhorrent, disagreeable, displeasing, odious, offensive, repellant, repulsive, threatening, unpleasant.

force *vb* coerce, compel, constrain, necessitate, oblige; drive, impel, overcome, press, urge; ravish, violate. * *n* emphasis, energy, head, might, pith, power, strength, stress, vigour, vim; agency, efficacy, efficiency, cogency, potency, validity, virtue; coercion, compulsion, constraint, enforcement, vehemence, violence; army, array, battalion, host, legion, phalanx, posse, soldiery, squadron, troop.

forcible *adj* all-powerful, cogent, impressive, irresistible, mighty, potent, powerful, strong, weighty; impetuous, vehement, violent, unrestrained; coerced, coercive, compulsory; convincing, energetic, effective, efficacious, telling, vigorous.

forcibly *adv* mightily, powerfully; coercively, compulsorily, perforce, violently; effectively, energetically, vigorously.

ford *n* current, flood, stream; crossing, wading place.

fore *adj* anterior, antecedent, first, foregoing, former, forward, preceding, previous, prior; advanced, foremost, head, leading.

forebode *vb* augur, betoken, foreshow, foretell, indicate, portend, predict, prefigure, presage, prognosticate, promise, signify.

foreboding *n* augury, omen, prediction, premonition, presage, presentiment, prognostication.

forecast *vb* anticipate, foresee, predict; calculate, contrive, devise, plan, project, scheme. * *n* anticipation, foresight, forethought, planning, prevision, prophecy, provident.

foreclose *vb* debar, hinder, preclude, prevent, stop.

foredoom *vb* foreordain, predestine, preordain.

forego *see* **forgo**.

foregoing *adj* antecedent, anterior, fore, former, preceding, previous, prior.

foregone *adj* bygone, former, past, previous.

foreign *adj* alien, distant, exotic, exterior, external, outward, outlandish, remote, strange, unnative; adventitious, exterior, extraneous, extrinsic, inappropriate, irrelevant, outside, unnatural, unrelated.

foreknowledge *n* foresight, prescience, prognostication.

foremost *adj* first, front, highest, leading, main, principal.

foreordain *vb* appoint, foredoom, predestinate, predetermine, preordain.

forerunner *n* avant-courier, foregoer, harbinger, herald, precursor, predecessor; omen, precursor, prelude, premonition, prognosticate, sign.

foresee *vb* anticipate, forebode, forecast, foreknow, foretell, prognosticate, prophesy.

foreshadow *vb* forebode, predict, prefigure, presage, presignify, prognosticate, prophesy.

foresight *n* foreknowledge, prescience, prevision; anticipation, care, caution, forecast, forethought, precaution, providence, prudence.

forest *n* wood, woods, woodland.

forestall *vb* hinder, frustrate, intercept, preclude, prevent, thwart; antedate, anticipate, foretaste; engross, monopolize, regrate.

foretaste *n* anticipation, forestalling, prelibation.

foretell *vb* predict, prophesy; augur, betoken, forebode, forecast, foreshadow, foreshow, portend, presage, presignify, prognosticate, prophesy.

forethought *n* anticipation, forecast, foresight, precaution, providence, prudence.

forever *adv* always, constantly, continually, endlessly, eternally, ever, evermore, everlastingly, perpetually, unceasingly.

forewarn *vb* admonish, advise, caution, dissuade.

forfeit *vb* alienate, lose. * *n* amercement, damages, fine, forfeiture, mulct, penalty.

forfend *vb* avert, forbid, hinder, prevent, protect.

forge *vb* beat, fabricate, form, frame, hammer; coin, devise, frame, invent; counterfeit, falsify, feign. * *n* furnace, ironworks, smithy.

forgery *n* counterfeit, fake, falsification, imitation.

forgetful *adj* careless, heedless, inattentive, mindless, neglectful, negligent, oblivious, unmindful.

forgive *vb* absolve, acquit, condone, excuse, exonerate, pardon, remit.

forgiveness *n* absolution, acquittal, amnesty, condoning. exoneration, pardon, remission, reprieve.

forgiving *adj* absolutory, absolvatory, acquitting, clearing, excusing, pardoning, placable, releasing.

forgo *vb* abandon, cede, relinquish, renounce, resign, surrender, yield.

fork *vb* bifurcate, branch, divaricate, divide. * *n* bifurcation, branch, branching, crotch, divarication, division.

forked *adj* bifurcated, branching, divaricated, furcate, furcated.

forlorn *adj* abandoned, deserted, forsaken, friendless, helpless, lost, solitary; abject, comfortless, dejected, desolate, destitute, disconsolate, helpless, hopeless, lamentable, pitiable, miserable, woebegone, wretched.

form *vb* fashion model, mould, shape; build, conceive, construct, create, fabricate, make, produce; contrive, devise, frame, invent; compose, constitute, develop, organize; discipline, educate, teach, train. * *n* body, build, cast, configuration, conformation, contour, cut, fashion, figure, format, mould, outline, pattern, shape; formula, formulary, method, mode, practice, ritual; class, kind, manner, model, order, sort, system, type; arrangement, order, regularity, shapeliness; ceremonial, ceremony, conventionality, etiquette, formality, observance, ordinance, punctilio, rite, ritual; bench, seat; class, rank; arrangement, combination, organization.

formal *adj* explicit, express, official, positive, strict; fixed, methodical, regular, rigid, set, stiff; affected, ceremonious, exact, precise, prim, punctilious, starchy. starched; constitutive, essential; external, outward, perfunctory; formative, innate, organic, primordial.

formality *n* ceremonial, ceremony, conventionality, etiquette, punctilio, rite, ritual.

formation *n* creation, genesis, production; composition, constitution; arrangement, combination, disposal, disposition.

formative *adj* creative, determinative, plastic, shaping; derivative, inflectional, nonradical.

former *adj* antecedent, anterior, earlier, foregoing, preceding, previous, prior; late, old-time, quondam; by, bygone, foregone, gone, past.

formidable *adj* appalling, dangerous, difficult, dreadful, fearful, frightful, horrible, menacing, redoubtable, shocking, terrible, terrific, threatening, tremendous.

forsake *vb* abandon, desert, leave, quit; drop, forgo, forswear, relinquish, renounce, surrender, yield.

forsooth *adv* certainly, indeed, really, surely, truly.

forswear *vb* abandon, desert, drop, forsake, leave, quit, reject, renounce; abjure, deny, eschew, perjure, recant, repudiate, retract.

fort *n* bulwark, castle, citadel, defence, fastness, fortification, fortress, stronghold.

forthwith *adv* directly, immediately, instantly, quickly, straightaway.

fortification *n* breastwork, bulwark, castle, citadel, defence, earthwork, fastness, fort, keep, rampart, redoubt, stronghold, tower.

fortify *vb* brace, encourage, entrench, garrison, protect, reinforce, stiffen, strengthen; confirm, corroborate.

fortitude *n* braveness, bravery, courage, determination, endurance, firmness, hardiness, patience, pluck, resolution, strength, valour.

fortuitous *adj* accidental, casual, chance, contingent, incidental.

fortunate *adj* favoured, happy, lucky, prosperous, providential, successful; advantageous, auspicious, favourable, happy, lucky, propitious, timely.

fortune *n* accident, casualty, chance, contingency, fortuity, hap, luck; estate, possessions, property, substance; affluence, felicity, opulence, prosperity, riches, wealth; destination, destiny, doom, fate, lot, star; event, issue, result; favour, success.

forward *vb* advance, aid, encourage, favour, foster, further, help, promote, support; accelerate, dispatch, expedite, hasten, hurry, quicken, speed; dispatch, post, send, ship, transmit. * *adj* ahead, advanced, onward; anterior, front, fore, head; prompt, eager, earnest, hasty, impulsive, quick, ready, willing, zealous; assuming, bold, brazen, brazen-faced, confident, flippant, impertinent, pert, presumptuous, presuming; advanced, early, premature. * *adv* ahead, onward.

foster *vb* cosset, feed, nurse, nourish, support, sustain; advance, aid, breed, cherish, cultivate, encourage, favour, foment, forward, further, harbour, patronize, promote, rear, stimulate.

foul *vb* besmirch, defile, dirty, pollute, soil, stain, sully; clog, collide, entangle, jam. * *adj* dirty, fetid, filthy, impure, nasty, polluted, putrid, soiled, stained, squalid, sullied, rank, tarnished, unclean; disgusting, hateful, loathsome, noisome, odious, offensive; dishonourable, underhand, unfair, sinister; abominable, base, dark, detestable, disgraceful, infamous, scandalous, scurvy, shameful, wile, wicked; coarse, low, obscene, vulgar; abusive, foul-mouthed, foul-spoken, insulting, scurrilous; cloudy, rainy, rough, stormy, wet; feculent, muddy, thick, turbid; entangled, tangled.

foul-mouthed *adj* abusive, blackguardy, blasphemous, filthy, foul, indecent, insolent, insulting, obscene, scurrilous.

found *vb* base, fix, ground, place, rest, set; build, construct, erect, raise; colonize, establish, institute, originate, plant; cast, mould.

foundation *n* base, basis, bed, bottom, footing, ground, groundwork, substructure, support; endowment, establishment, settlement.

founder[1] *n* author, builder, establisher, father, institutor, originator, organizer, planter.

founder[2] *n* caster, moulder.

founder[3] *vb* sink, swamp, welter; collapse, fail, miscarry; fall, stumble, trip.

fountain *n* fount, reservoir, spring, well; jet, upswelling; cause, fountainhead, origin, original, source.

foxy *adj* artful, crafty, cunning, sly, subtle, wily.

fracas *n* affray, brawl, disturbance, outbreak, quarrel, riot, row, uproar, tumult,

fractious *adj* captious, cross, fretful, irritable, peevish, pettish, perverse, petulant, querulous, snappish, splenetic, touchy, testy, waspish.

fracture *vb* break, crack, split. * *n* breaking, rupture; breach, break, cleft, crack, fissure, flaw, opening, rift, rent.

fragile *adj* breakable, brittle, delicate, frangible; feeble, frail, infirm, weak.

fragility *n* breakability, breakableness, brittleness, frangibility, frangibleness; feebleness, frailty, infirmity, weakness.

fragment *vb* atomize, break, fracture, pulverize, splinter. * *n* bit, chip, fraction, fracture, morsel, part, piece, remnant, scrap.

fragrance *n* aroma, balminess, bouquet, odour, perfume, redolence, scent, smell.

fragrant *adj* ambrosial, aromatic, balmy, odoriferous, odorous, perfumed, redolent, spicy, sweet, sweet-scented, sweet-smelling.

frail *adj* breakable, brittle, delicate, fragile, frangible, slight; feeble, infirm, weak.

frailty *n* feebleness, frailness, infirmity, weakness; blemish, defect, failing, fault, foible, imperfection, peccability, shortcoming.

frame *vb* build, compose, constitute, construct, erect, form, make, mould, plan, shape; contrive, devise, fabricate, fashion, forge, invest, plan. * *n* body, carcass, framework, framing, shell, skeleton; constitution, fabric, form, structure, scheme, system; condition, humour, mood, state, temper.

franchise *n* privilege, right; suffrage, vote; exemption, immunity.

frangible *adj* breakable, brittle, fragile.

frank *adj* artless, candid, direct, downright, frank-hearted, free, genuine, guileless, ingenuous, naive, open, outspoken, outright, plain, plain-spoken, point-blank, sincere, straightforward, truthful, unequivocal, unreserved, unrestricted.

frankness *n* candour, ingenuousness, openness, outspokenness, plain speaking, truth, straightforwardness.

frantic *adj* crazy, distracted, distraught, frenzied, furious, infuriate, mad. outrageous, phrenetic, rabid, raging, raving, transported, wild.

fraternity *n* association, brotherhood, circle, clan, club, company, fellowship, league, set, society, sodality; brotherliness.

fraternize *vb* associate, coalesce, concur, consort, cooperate, harmonize, sympathize, unite.

fraud *n* artifice, cheat, craft, deception, deceit, duplicity, guile, hoax, humbug, imposition, imposture, sham, stratagem, treachery, trick, trickery, wile.

fraudulent *adj* crafty, deceitful, deceptive, dishonest, false, knavish, treacherous, trickish, tricky, wily.

fraught *adj* abounding, big, burdened, charged, filled, freighted, laden, pregnant, stored, weighted.

fray[1] *n* affray, battle, brawl, broil, combat, fight, quarrel, riot.

fray[2] *vb* chafe, fret, rub, wear; ravel, shred.

freak *adj* bizarre, freakish, grotesque, monstrous, odd, unexpected, unforeseen. * *n* caprice, crotchet, fancy, humour, maggot, quirk, vagary, whim, whimsey; antic, caper, gambol; abnormality, abortion, monstrosity.

freakish *adj* capricious, changeable, eccentric, erratic, fanciful, humoursome, odd, queer, whimsical.

free *vb* deliver, discharge, disenthral, emancipate, enfranchise, enlarge, liberate, manumit, ransom, release, redeem, rescue, save; clear, disencumber, disengage, extricate, rid, unbind, unchain, unfetter, unlock; exempt, immunize, privilege. * *adj* bondless, independent, loose, unattached, unconfined, unentangled, unimpeded, unrestrained, untrammelled; autonomous, delivered, emancipated, freeborn, liberated, manumitted, ransomed, released, self-governing; clear, exempt, immune, privileged; allowed, permitted; devoid, empty, open, unimpeded, unobstructed, unrestricted; affable, artless, candid, frank, ingenuous, sincere, unreserved; bountiful, charitable, free-hearted, generous, hospitable, liberal, munificent, openhanded; immoderate, lavish, prodigal; eager, prompt, ready, willing; available, gratuitous, spontaneous; careless, lax, loose; bold, easy, familiar, informal, overfamiliar, unconstrained. * *adv* openly, outright, unreservedly, unrestrainedly, unstintingly; freely, gratis, gratuitously.

freebooter *n* bandit, brigand, despoiler, footpad, gangster, highwayman, marauder, pillager, plunderer, robber; buccaneer, pirate, rover.

freedom *n* emancipation, independence, liberation, liberty, release; elbowroom, margin, play, range, scope, swing; franchise, immunity, privilege; familiarity, laxity, license, looseness.

freethinker *n* agnostic, deist, doubter, infidel, sceptic, unbeliever.

freeze *vb* congeal, glaciate, harden, stiffen; benumb, chill.

freight *vb* burden, charge, lade, load. * *n* burden, cargo, lading, load.

frenzy *n* aberration, delirium, derangement, distraction, fury, insanity, lunacy, madness, mania, paroxysm, rage, raving, transport.

frequent *vb* attend, haunt, resort, visit. * *adj* iterating, oft-repeated; common, customary, everyday, familiar, habitual, persistent, usual; constant, continual, incessant.

fresh *adj* new, novel, recent; renewed, revived; blooming, flourishing, green, undecayed, unimpaired, unfaded, unobliterated, unwilted, unwithered, well-preserved; sweet; delicate,
fair, fresh-coloured, ruddy, rosy; florid, hardy, healthy, vigorous, strong; active, energetic, unexhausted, unfatigued, unwearied, vigorous; keen, lively, unabated, undecayed, unimpaired, vivid; additional, further; uncured, undried, unsalted, unsmoked; bracing, health-giving, invigorating, refreshing, sweet; brink, stiff, strong; inexperienced, raw, uncultivated, unpracticed, unskilled, untrained, unused.

freshen *vb* quicken, receive, refresh, revive.

fret[1] *vb* abrade, chafe, fray, gall, rub, wear; affront, agitate, annoy, gall, harass, irritate, nettle, provoke, ruffle, tease, vex, wear, worry; ripple, roughen; corrode; fume, peeve, rage, stew. * *n* agitation, fretfulness, fretting, irritation, peevishness, vexation.

fret[2] *vb* diversify, interlace, ornament, variegate. * *n* fretwork, interlacing, ornament; ridge, wale, whelk.

fretful *adj* captious, cross, fractious, ill-humoured, ill-tempered, irritable, peevish, pettish, petulant, querulous, short-tempered, snappish, spleeny, splenetic, testy, touchy, uneasy, waspish.

friable *adj* brittle, crisp, crumbling, powdery, pulverable.

friction *n* abrasion, attrition, grating, rubbing; bickering, disagreement, dissension, wrangling.

friend *adj* benefactor, chum, companion, comrade, crony, confidant, intimate; adherent, ally, associate, confrere, partisan; advocate, defender, encourager, favourer, patron, supporter, well-wisher.

friendly *adj* affectionate, amiable, benevolent, favourable, kind, kind-hearted, kindly, well-disposed; amicable, cordial, fraternal, neighbourly; conciliatory, peaceable, unhostile.

friendship *n* affection, attachment, benevolence, fondness, goodness, love, regard; fellowship, intimacy; amicability, amicableness, amity, cordiality, familiarity, fraternization, friendliness, harmony.

fright *n* affright, alarm, consternation, dismay, funk, horror, panic, scare, terror.

frighten *vb* affright, alarm, appal, daunt, dismay, intimidate, scare, stampede, terrify.

frightful *adj* alarming, awful, dire, direful, dread, dreadful, fearful, horrible, horrid, shocking, terrible, terrific; ghastly, grim, grisly, gruesome, hideous.

frigid *adj* cold, cool, gelid; dull, lifeless, spiritless, tame, unanimated, uninterested, uninteresting; chilling, distant, forbidding, formal, freezing, prim, repellent, repelling, repulsive, rigid, stiff.

frill *n* edging, frilling, furbelow, gathering, ruche, ruching, ruffle; affectation, mannerism.

fringe *vb* border, bound, edge, hem, march, rim, skirt, verge. * *n* border, edge, edging, tassel, trimming. * *adj* edging, extra, unofficial.

frisk *vb* caper, dance, frolic, gambol, hop, jump, play, leap, romp, skip, sport, wanton.

frisky *adj* frolicsome, coltish, gay, lively, playful, sportive.

frivolity *n* flummery, folly, fribbling, frippery, frivolousness, levity, puerility, trifling, triviality.

frivolous *adj* childish, empty, flighty, flimsy, flippant, foolish, giddy, idle, light, paltry. petty, puerile, silly, trashy, trifling, trivial, unimportant, vain, worthless.

frolic *vb* caper, frisk, gambol, lark, play, romp, sport. * *n* escapade, gambol, lark, romp, skylark, spree, trick; drollery, fun, play, pleasantry, sport.

frolicsome *adj* coltish, fresh, frolic, gamesome, gay, lively, playful, sportive.

front *vb* confront, encounter, face, oppose. * *adj* anterior, forward; foremost, frontal, headmost. * *n* brow, face, forehead; assurance, boldness, brass, effrontery, impudence; breast, head, van, vanguard; anterior, face, forepart, obverse; facade, frontage.

frontier *n* border, boundary, coast, confine, limits, marches.

frosty *adj* chill, chilly, cold, icy, stinging, wintry; cold, cold-hearted, frigid, indifferent, unaffectionate, uncordial, unimpassioned, unloving; dull-hearted, lifeless, spiritless, unanimated; frosted, grey-hearted, hoary, white.

froth *vb* bubble, cream, foam, lather, spume. * *n* bubbles, foam, lather, spume; balderdash, flummery, nonsense, trash, triviality.

frothy *adj* foamy, spumy; empty, frivolous, light, trifling, trivial, unsubstantial, vain.

froward *adj* captious, contrary, contumacious, cross, defiant, disobedient, fractious, impudent, intractable, obstinate, peevish, perverse, petulant, refractory, stubborn, ungovernable, untoward, unyielding, wayward, wilful.

frown *vb* glower, lower, scowl.

frowzy, frowsy *adj* fetid, musty, noisome, rancid, rank, stale; disordered, disorderly, dowdy, slatternly, slovenly.

frugal *adj* abstemious, careful, chary, choice, economical, provident, saving, sparing, temperate, thrifty, unwasteful.

fruit *n* crop, harvest, produce, production; advantage, consequence, effect, good, outcome, product, profit, result; issue, offspring, young.

fruitful *adj* abounding, productive; fecund, fertile, prolific; abundant, exuberant, plenteous, plentiful, rich, teeming.

fruition *n* completion, fulfilment, perfection; enjoyment.

fruitless *adj* acarpous, barren, sterile, infecund, unfertile, unfruitful, unproductive, unprolific; abortive, bootless, futile, idle, ineffectual, profitless, unavailing, unprofitable, useless, vain.

frumpish, frumpy *adj* cross, cross-grained, cross-tempered, dowdy, grumpy, irritable, shabby, slatternly, snappish.

frustrate *vb* baffle, balk, check, circumvent, defeat, disappoint, disconcert, foil, thwart; cross, hinder, outwit.

frustrated *adj* balked, blighted, dashed, defeated, foiled, thwarted; ineffectual, null, useless, vain.

fuddled *adj* befuddled, boozy, corned, crapulous, drunk, groggy, high, inebriated, intoxicated, muddled, slewed, tight, tipsy.

fugacious *adj* evanescent, fleeting, fugitive, transient, transitory.

fugitive *adj* escaping, fleeing, flying; brief, ephemeral, evanescent, fleeting, flitting, fugacious, momentary, short, short-lived, temporal, temporary, transient, transitory, uncertain, unstable, volatile. * *n* émigré, escapee, evacuee, fleer, outlaw, refugee, runaway.

fulfil *vb* accomplish, complete, consummate, effect, effectuate, execute, realize; adhere, discharge, do, keep, obey, observe, perform; answer, fill, meet, satisfy.

full *adj* brimful, filled, flush, replete; abounding, replete, well-stocked; bagging, flowing, loose, voluminous; chock-full, cloyed, crammed, glutted, gorged, overflowing, packed, sated, satiated, saturated, soaked, stuffed, swollen; adequate, complete, entire, mature, perfect; abundant, ample, copious, plenteous, plentiful, sufficient; clear, deep, distinct, loud, rounded, strong; broad, large, capacious, comprehensive, extensive, plump; circumstantial, detailed, exhaustive. * *adv* completely, fully; directly, exactly, precisely.

fullness *n* abundance, affluence, copiousness, plenitude, plenty, profusion; glut, satiety, sating, repletion; completeness, completion, entireness, perfection; clearness, loudness, resonance, strength; dilation, distension, enlargement, plumpness, rotundity, roundness, swelling.

fully *adv* abundantly, amply, completely, copiously, entirely, largely, plentifully, sufficiently.

fulminate *vb* detonate, explode; curse, denounce, hurl, menace, threaten, thunder.

fulsome *adj* excessive, extravagant, fawning; disgusting, nauseous, nauseating, offensive, repulsive; coarse, gross, lustful, questionable.

fumble *vb* bungle, grope, mismanage, stumble; mumble, stammer, stutter.

fume *vb* reek, smoke, vaporize. * *n* effluvium exhalation, reek, smell, smoke, steam, vapour; agitation, fret, fry, fury, passion, pet, rage, storm.

fun *adj* amusing, diverting, droll, entertaining. * *n* amusement, diversion, drollery, frolic, gaiety, humour, jesting, jocularity, jollity, joy, merriment, mirth, play, pranks, sport, pleasantry, waggishness.

function *vb* act, discharge, go, operate, officiate, perform, run, serve, work. * *n* discharge, execution, exercise, operation, performance, purpose, use; activity, business, capacity, duty, employment, occupation, office, part, province, role; ceremony, rite; dependant, derivative.

fund *vb* afford, endow, finance, invest, provide, subsidise, support; garner, hoard, stock, store. * *n* accumulation, capital, endowment, reserve, stock; store, supply; foundation.

fundament *n* bottom, buttocks, seat.

fundamental *adj* basal, basic, bottom, cardinal, constitutional, elementary, essential, indispensable, organic, principal, primary, radical. * *n* essential, principal, rule.

funeral *n* burial, cremation, exequies, internment, obsequies.

funereal *adj* dark, dismal, gloomy, lugubrious, melancholy, mournful, sad, sepulchral, sombre, woeful.

funk *vb* blanch, shrink, quail. * *n* stench, stink; fear, fright, panic.

funny *adj* amusing, comic, comical, diverting, droll, facetious, farcical, humorous, jocose, jocular, laughable, ludicrous, sportive, witty; curious, odd, queer, strange. * *n* jest, joke; cartoon, comic.

furbish *vb* burnish, brighten, polish, renew, renovate, rub, shine.

furious *adj* angry, fierce, frantic, frenzied, fuming, infuriated, mad, raging, violent, wild; boisterous, fierce, impetuous, stormy, tempestuous, tumultuous, turbulent, vehement.

furnish *vb* appoint, endow, provide, supply; decorate, equip, fit; afford, bestow, contribute, give, offer, present, produce, yield.

furniture *n* chattels, effects, household goods, movables; apparatus, appendages, appliances, equipment, fittings, furnishings; decorations, embellishments, ornaments.

furore *n* commotion, craze, enthusiasm, excitement, fad, fury, madness, mania, rage, vogue.

furrow *vb* chamfer, channel, cleave, corrugate, cut, flute, groove, hollow; pucker, seam, wrinkle. * *n* chamfer, channel, cut, depression, fluting, groove, hollow, line, seam, track, trench, rot, wrinkle.

further *vb* advance, aid, assist, encourage, help, forward, promote, succour, strengthen. * *adj* additional. * *adv* also, besides, farther, furthermore, moreover.

furtive *adj* clandestine, hidden, secret, sly, skulking, sneaking, sneaky, stealthy, stolen, surreptitious.

fury *n* anger, frenzy, fit, furore, ire, madness, passion, rage; fierceness, impetuosity, turbulence, turbulency, vehemence; bacchant, bacchante, bedlam, hag, shrew, termagant, virago, vixen.

fuse *vb* dissolve, melt, liquefy, smelt; amalgamate, blend, coalesce, combine, commingle, intermingle, intermix, merge, unite. * *n* match.

fusion *n* liquefaction, melting; amalgamation, blending, commingling, commixture, intermingling, intermixture, union; coalition, merging.

fuss *vb* bustle, fidget; fret, fume, worry. * *n* ado, agitation, bother, bustle, commotion, disturbance, excitement, fidget, flurry, fluster, fret, hurry, pother, stir, worry.

fustian *n* bombast, claptrap, rant, rodomontade; balderdash, inanity, nonsense, stuff, trash, twaddle.

fusty *adj* ill-smelling, malodorous, mildewed, mouldy, musty, rank.

futile *adj* frivolous, trifling, trivial; bootless, fruitless, idle, ineffectual, profitless, unavailing, unprofitable, useless, vain, valueless, worthless.

futility *n* frivolousness, triviality; bootlessness, fruitlessness, uselessness, vanity, worthlessness.

future *adj* coming, eventual, forthcoming, hereafter, prospective, subsequent. * *n* hereafter, outlook, prospect.

G

gabble *vb* babble, chatter, clack, gibber, gossip, prate, prattle. * *n* babble, chatter, clack, gap, gossip, jabber, palaver, prate, prattle, twaddle.

gadabout *n* idler, loafer, rambler, rover, vagrant; gossip, talebearer, vagrant.

gaffer *n* boss, foreman, overseer, supervisor.

gag[1] *n* jape, jest, joke, stunt, wisecrack.

gag[2] *vb* muffle, muzzle, shackle, silence, stifle, throttle; regurgitate, retch, throw up, vomit; choke, gasp, pant. * *n* muzzle.

gage *n* pawn, pledge, security, surety; challenge, defiance, gauntlet, glove.

gaiety *n* animation, blithesomeness, cheerfulness, glee, hilarity, jollity, joviality, merriment, mirth, vivacity.

gain *vb* achieve, acquire, earn, get, obtain, procure, reap, secure; conciliate, enlist, persuade, prevail, win; arrive, attain, reach; clear, net, profit. * *n* accretion, addition, gainings, profits, winnings; acquisition, earnings, emolument, lucre; advantage, benefit, blessing, good, profit.

gainful *adj* advantageous, beneficial, profitable; lucrative, paying, productive, remunerative.

gainsay *vb* contradict, controvert, deny, dispute, forbid.

gait *n* carriage, pace, step, stride, walk.

galaxy *n* assemblage, assembly, cluster, collection, constellation, group.

gale *n* blast, hurricane, squall, storm, tempest, tornado, typhoon.

gall[1] *n* effrontery, impudence; bile; acerbity, bitterness, malice, maliciousness, malignity, rancour, spite.

gall[2] *vb* chafe, excoriate, fret, hurt; affront, annoy, exasperate, harass, incense, irritate, plague, provoke, sting, tease, vex.

gallant *adj* fine, magnificent, showy, splendid, well-dressed; bold, brave, chivalrous, courageous, daring, fearless, heroic, high-spirited, intrepid, valiant, valorous; chivalrous, fine, honourable, high-minded, lofty, magnanimous, noble. * *n* beau, blade, spark; lover, suitor, wooer.

gallantry *n* boldness, bravery, chivalry, courage, courageousness, fearlessness, heroism, intrepidity, prowess, valour; courtesy, courteousness, elegance, politeness.

galling *adj* chafing, irritating, vexing.

gallop *vb* fly, hurry, run, rush, scamper, speed.

gamble *vb* bet, dice, game, hazard, plunge, speculate, wager. * *n* chance, risk, speculation; bet, punt, wager.

gambol *vb* caper, cut, frisk, frolic, hop, jump, leap, romp, skip. * *n* frolic, hop, jump, skip.

game[1] *vb* gamble, sport, stake. * *n* amusement, contest, diversion, pastime, play, sport; adventure, enterprise, measure, plan, project, scheme, stratagem, undertaking; prey, quarry, victim.
game[2] *adj* brave, courageous, dauntless, fearless, gallant, heroic, intrepid, plucky, unflinching, valorous; enduring, persevering, resolute, undaunted; ready, eager, willing.
game[3] *adj* crippled, disabled, halt, injured, lame.
gameness *n* bravery, courage, grit, heart, mettle, nerve, pith, pluckiness, spirit, stamina.
gamesome *adj* frisky, frolicsome, lively, merry, playful, sportive, sprightly, vivacious.
gammon *vb* bamboozle, beguile, cheat, circumvent, deceive, delude, dupe, gull, hoax, humbug, inveigle, mislead, overreach, outwit. * *n* bosh, hoax, humbug, imposition, nonsense.
gang *n* band, cabal, clique, company, coterie, crew, horde, party, set, troop.
gaol *see* **jail**.
gap *n* breach, break, cavity, chasm, chink, cleft, crack, cranny, crevice, hiatus, hollow, interval, interstice, lacuna, opening, pass, ravine, rift, space, vacancy.
gape *vb* burst open, dehisce, open, stare, yawn.
garb *vb* attire, clothe, dress. * *n* apparel, attire, clothes, costume, dress, garments, habiliment, habit, raiment, robes, uniform, vestment.
garbage *n* filth, offal, refuse, remains, rubbish, trash, waste.
garble *vb* corrupt, distort, falsify, misquote, misrepresent, mutilate, pervert.
gargantuan *adj* big, Brobdingnagian, colossal, enormous, gigantic, huge, prodigious, tremendous.
garish *adj* bright, dazzling, flashy, flaunting, gaudy, glaring, loud, showy, staring, tawdry.
garland *vb* adorn, festoon, wreathe. * *n* chaplet, coronal, crown, festoon, wreath.
garment *n* clothes, clothing, dress, habit, vestment.
garner *vb* accumulate, collect, deposit, gather, hoard, husband, reserve, save, store, treasure.
garnish *vb* adorn, beautify, bedeck, decorate, deck, embellish, grace, ornament, prank, trim. * *n* decoration, enhancement, ornament, trimming.
garrulous *adj* babbling, loquacious, prating, prattling, talkative.
gasconade *n* bluster, boast, brag, bravado, swagger, vaunt, vapouring.
gasp *vb* blow, choke, pant, puff. * *n* blow, exclamation, gulp, puff.
gather *vb* assemble, cluster, collect, convene, group, muster, rally; accumulate, amass, garner, hoard, huddle, lump; bunch, crop, cull, glean, pick, pluck, rake, reap, shock, stack; acquire, gain, get, win; conclude, deduce, derive, infer; fold, plait, pucker, shirr, tuck; condense, grow, increase, thicken.
gathering *n* acquisition, collecting, earning, gain, heap, pile, procuring; assemblage, assembly, collection, company, concourse, congregation, meeting, muster; abscess, boil, fester, pimple, pustule, sore, suppuration, tumour, ulcer.
gauche *adj* awkward, blundering, bungling, clumsy, inept, tactless, uncouth.
gaudy *adj* bespangled, brilliant, brummagem, cheap, flashy, flaunting, garish, gimcrack, glittering, loud, ostentatious, overdecorated, sham, showy, spurious, tawdry, tinsel.
gauge *vb* calculate, check, determine, weigh; assess, estimate, guess, reckon. * *n* criterion, example, indicator, measure, meter, touchstone, yardstick; bore, depth, height, magnitude, size, thickness, width.
gaunt *adj* angular, attenuated, emaciated, haggard, lank, lean, meagre, scraggy, skinny, slender, spare, thin.
gawky *adj* awkward, boorish, clownish, clumsy, green, loutish, raw, rustic, uncouth, ungainly.
gay *adj* bright, brilliant, dashing, fine, showy; flashy, flaunting, garish, gaudy, glittering, loud, tawdry, tinsel; airy, blithe, blithesome, cheerful, festive, frivolous, frolicsome, gladsome, gleeful, hilarious, jaunty, jolly, jovial, light-hearted, lively, merry, mirthful, sportive, sprightly, vivacious.
gear *vb* adapt, equip, fit, suit, tailor. * *n* apparel, array, clothes, clothing, dress, garb; accoutrements, appliances, appointments, appurtenances, array, harness, goods, movables, subsidiaries; harness, rigging, tackle, trappings; apparatus, machinery, mechanics.
gelid *adj* chill, chilly, cold, freezing, frigid, icy.
gem *n* jewel, stone, treasure.
genealogy *n* ancestry, descent, lineage, pedigree, stock.
general *adj* broad, collective, generic, popular, universal, widespread; catholic, ecumenical; common, current, ordinary, usual; inaccurate, indefinite, inexact, vague.
generally *adv* commonly, extensively, universally, usually.
generate *vb* beget, breed, engender, procreate, propagate, reproduce, spawn; cause, form, make, produce.
generation *n* creation, engendering, formation, procreation, production; age, epoch, era, period, time; breed, children, family, kind, offspring, progeny, race, stock.
generosity *n* disinterestedness, high-mindedness, magnanimity, nobleness; bounteousness, bountifulness, bounty, charity, liberality, openhandedness.
generous *adj* high-minded, honourable, magnanimous, noble; beneficent, bountiful, charitable, free, hospitable, liberal, munificent, openhanded; abundant, ample, copious, plentiful, rich.
genial *adj* cheering, encouraging, enlivening, fostering, inspiring, mild, warm; agreeable, cheerful, cordial, friendly, hearty, jovial, kindly, merry, mirthful, pleasant.
genius *n* aptitude, aptness, bent, capacity, endowment, faculty, flair, gift, talent, turn; brains, creative power, ingenuity, inspiration, intellect, invention, parts, sagacity, wit; adeptness, master, master hand, proficiency; character, disposition, naturalness, nature; deity, demon, spirit.
genteel *adj* aristocratic, courteous, gentlemanly, lady-like, polished, polite, refined, well-bred; elegant, fashionable, graceful, stylish.
gentility *n* civility, courtesy, good breeding, politeness, refinement, urbanity.
gentle *adj* amiable, bland, clement, compassionate, humane, indulgent, kind, kindly, lenient, meek, merciful, mild, moderate, soft, tender, tender-hearted; docile, pacific, peaceable, placid, quiet, tame, temperate, tractable; bland, easy, gradual, light, slight; soft; high-born, noble, well-born; chivalrous, courteous, cultivated, knightly, polished, refined, well-bred.
gentlemanly *adj* civil, complaisant, courteous, cultivated, delicate, genteel, honourable, polite, refined, urbane, well-bred.
genuine *adj* authentic, honest, proper, pure, real, right, true, unadulterated, unalloyed, uncorrupted, veritable; frank, native, sincere, unaffected.
genus *n* class, group, kind, order, race, sort, type.
germ *n* embryo, nucleus, ovule, ovum, seed, seed-bud; bacterium, microbe, microorganism; beginning, cause, origin, rudiment, source.
germane *adj* akin, allied, cognate, related; apposite, appropriate, fitting, pertinent, relevant, suitable.
germinate *vb* bud, burgeon, develop, generate, grow, pollinate, push, shoot, sprout, vegetate.
gesture *vb* indicate, motion, signal, wave. * *n* action, attitude, gesticulation, gesturing, posture, sign, signal.
get *vb* achieve, acquire, attain, earn, gain, obtain, procure, receive, relieve, secure, win; finish, master, prepare; beget, breed, engender, generate, procreate.
gewgaw *n* bauble, gimcrack, gaud, kickshaw, knick-knack, plaything, trifle, toy, trinket.
ghastly *adj* cadaverous, corpse-like, death-like, deathly, ghostly, lurid, pale, pallid, wan; dismal, dreadful, fearful, frightful, grim, grisly, gruesome, hideous, horrible, shocking, terrible.
ghost *n* soul, spirit; apparition, phantom, revenant, shade, spectre, spook, sprite, wraith.
giant *adj* colossal, enormous, Herculean, huge, large, monstrous, prodigious, vast. * *n* colossus, cyclops, Hercules, monster.

gibberish *n* babble, balderdash, drivel, gabble, gobbledygook, jabber, nonsense, prate, prating.

gibe, jibe *vb* deride, fleer, flout, jeer, mock, ridicule, scoff, sneer, taunt. * *n* ridicule, sneer, taunt.

giddiness *n* dizziness, head-spinning, vertigo.

giddy *adj* dizzy, head-spinning, vertiginous; careless, changeable, fickle, flighty, frivolous, hare-brained, headlong, heedless, inconstant, irresolute, light-headed, thoughtless, unsteady, vacillating, wild.

gift *n* alms, allowance, benefaction, bequest, bonus, boon, bounty, contribution, donation, dowry, endowment, favour, grant, gratuity, honorarium, largesse, legacy, offering, premium, present, prize, subscription, subsidy, tip; faculty, talent.

gifted *adj* able, capable, clever, ingenious, intelligent, inventive, sagacious, talented.

gigantic *adj* colossal, Cyclopean, enormous, giant, herculean, huge, immense, prodigious, titanic, tremendous, vast.

giggle *vb, n* cackle, grin, laugh, snigger, snicker, titter.

gild *vb* adorn, beautify, bedeck, brighten, decorate, embellish, grace, illuminate.

gimcrack *adj* flimsy, frail, puny; base, cheap, paltry, poor. * *n* bauble, knick-knack, toy, trifle.

gird *vb* belt, girdle; begird, encircle, enclose, encompass, engird, environ, surround; brace, support. * *n* band, belt, cincture, girdle, girth, sash, waistband.

gist *n* basis, core, essence, force, ground, marrow, meaning, pith, point, substance.

give *vb* accord, bequeath, bestow, confer, devise, entrust, present; afford, contribute, donate, furnish, grant, proffer, spare, supply; communicate, impart; deliver, exchange, pay, requite; allow, permit, vouchsafe; emit, pronounce, render, utter; produce, yield; cause, occasion; apply, devote, surrender; bend, sink, recede, retire, retreat, yield.

glad *adj* delighted, gratified, happy, pleased, rejoicing, well-contented; animated, blithe, cheerful, cheery, elated, gladsome, jocund, joyful, joyous, light, light-hearted, merry, playful, radiant; animating, bright, cheering, exhilarating, gladdening, gratifying, pleasing.

gladden *vb* bless, cheer, delight, elate, enliven, exhilarate, gratify, please, rejoice.

gladiator *n* prize-fighter, sword-player, swordsman.

gladness *n* animation, cheerfulness, delight, gratification, happiness, joy, joyfulness, joyousness, pleasure.

gladsome *adj* airy, blithe, blithesome, cheerful, delighted, frolicsome, glad, gleeful, jocund, jolly, jovial, joyful, joyous, light-hearted, lively, merry, pleased, sportive, sprightly, vivacious.

glamour *n* bewitchment, charm, enchantment, fascination, spell, witchery.

glance *vb* coruscate, gleam, glisten, glister, glitter, scintillate, shine; dart, flit; gaze, glimpse, look, view. * *n* gleam, glitter; gleam, look, view.

glare *vb* dazzle, flame, flare, gleam, glisten, glitter, sparkle; frown, gaze, glower. * *n* flare, glitter.

glaring *adj* dazzling, gleaming, glistening, glittering; barefaced, conspicuous, extreme, manifest, notorious, open.

glassy *adj* brilliant, crystal, crystalline, gleaming, lucent, shining, transparent.

glaze *vb* burnish, calender, furbish, gloss, polish. * *n* coat, enamel, finish, glazing, polish, varnish.

gleam *vb* beam, coruscate, flash, glance, glimmer, glitter, shine, sparkle. * *n* beam, flash, glance, glimmer, glimmering, glow, ray; brightness, coruscation, flashing, gleaming, glitter, glittering, lustre, splendour.

glean *vb* collect, cull, gather, get, harvest, pick, select.

glee *n* exhilaration, fun, gaiety, hilarity, jocularity, jollity, joviality, joy, liveliness, merriment, mirth, sportiveness, verve.

glib *adj* slippery, smooth; artful, facile, flippant, fluent, ready, talkative, voluble.

glide *vb* float, glissade, roll on, skate, skim, slide, slip; flow, lapse, run, roll. * *n* gliding, lapse, sliding, slip.

glimmer *vb* flash, flicker, gleam, glitter, shine, twinkle. * *n* beam, gleam, glimmering, ray; glance, glimpse.

glimpse *vb* espy, look, spot, view. * *n* flash, glance, glimmering, glint, look, sight.

glitter *vb* coruscate, flare, flash, glance, glare, gleam, glisten, glister, scintillate, shine, sparkle. * *n* beam, beaming, brightness, brilliancy, coruscation, gleam, glister, lustre, radiance, scintillation, shine, sparkle, splendour.

gloaming *n* dusk, eventide, nightfall, twilight.

gloat *vb* exult, gaze, rejoice, stare, triumph.

globe *n* ball, earth, orb, sphere.

globular *adj* globate, globated, globe-shaped, globose, globous, round, spheral, spheric, spherical.

globule *n* bead, drop, particle, spherule.

gloom *n* cloud, darkness, dimness, gloominess, obscurity, shade, shadow; cheerlessness, dejection, depression, despondency, downheartedness, dullness, melancholy, sadness.

gloomy *adj* dark, dim, dusky, obscure; cheerless, dismal, lowering, lurid; crestfallen, dejected, depressed, despondent, disheartened, dispirited, downcast, downhearted, glum, melancholy, morose, sad, sullen; depressing, disheartening, dispiriting, heavy, saddening.

glorify *vb* adore, bless, celebrate, exalt, extol, honour, laud, magnify, worship; adorn, brighten, elevate, ennoble, make bright.

glorious *adj* celebrated, conspicuous, distinguished, eminent, excellent, famed, famous, illustrious, pre-eminent, renowned; brilliant, bright, grand, magnificent, radiant, resplendent, splendid; consummate, exalted, high, lofty, noble, supreme.

glory *vb* boast, exult, vaunt. * *n* celebrity, distinction, eminence, fame, honour, illustriousness, praise, renown; brightness, brilliancy, effulgence, lustre, pride, resplendence, splendour; exaltation, exceeding, gloriousness, greatness, grandeur, nobleness; bliss, happiness.

gloss[1] *vb* coat, colour, disguise, extenuate, glaze, palliate, varnish, veneer, veil. * *n* coating, lustre, polish, sheen, varnish, veneer; pretence, pretext.

gloss[2] *vb* annotate, comment, elucidate, explain, interpret. * *n* annotation, comment, commentary, elucidation, explanation, interpretation, note.

glove *n* gantlet, gauntlet, handwear, mitt, mitten; challenge.

glow *vb* incandesce, radiate, shine; blush, burn, flush, redden. * *n* blaze, brightness, brilliance, burning, incandescence, luminosity, reddening; ardour, bloom, enthusiasm, fervency, fervour, flush, impetuosity, vehemence, warmth.

glower *vb* frown, glare, lower, scowl, stare. * *n* frown, glare, scowl.

glum *adj* churlish, crabbed, crestfallen, cross-grained, crusty, depressed, frowning, gloomy, glowering, moody, morose, sour, spleenish, spleeny, sulky, sullen, surly.

glut *vb* block up, cloy, cram, gorge, satiate, stuff. * *n* excess, saturation, surfeit, surplus.

glutinous *adj* adhesive, clammy, cohesive, gluey, gummy, sticky, tenacious, viscid, viscous.

glutton *n* gobbler, gorger, gourmand, gormandizer, greedy-guts, lurcher, pig.

gnarled *adj* contorted, cross-grained, gnarly, knotted, knotty, snaggy, twisted.

go *vb* advance, move, pass, proceed, progress repair; act, operate; be about, extravagate, fare, journey, roam, rove, travel, walk, wend; depart, disappear, cease; elapse, extend, lead, reach, run; avail, concur, contribute, tend, serve; eventuate, fare, turn out; afford, bet, risk, wager. * *n* action, business, case, chance, circumstance, doings, turn; custom, fad, fashion, mode, vogue; energy, endurance, power, stamina, verve, vivacity.

goad *vb* annoy, badger, harass, irritate, sting, worry; arouse, impel, incite, instigate, prod, spur, stimulate, urge. * *n* incentive, incitement, pressure, stimulation.

goal *n* bound, home, limit, mark, mete, post; end, object; aim, design, destination.

gobble *vb* bolt, devour, gorge, gulp, swallow.

goblin *n* apparition, elf, bogey, demon, gnome, hobgoblin, phantom, spectre, sprite.

god *n* almighty, creator, deity, divinity, idol, Jehovah, omnipotence, providence.

godless *adj* atheistic, impious, irreligious, profane, ungodly, wicked.

godlike *adj* celestial, divine, heavenly, supernal.

godly *adj* devout, holy, pious, religious, righteous, saint-like, saintly.

godsend *n* fortune, gift, luck, present, windfall.

golden *adj* aureate, brilliant, bright, gilded, resplendent, shining, splendid; excellent, precious; auspicious, favourable, opportune, propitious; blessed, delightful, glorious, halcyon, happy.

good *adj* advantageous, beneficial, favourable, profitable, serviceable, useful; adequate, appropriate, becoming, convenient, fit, proper, satisfactory, suitable, well-adapted; decorous, dutiful, honest, just, pious, reliable, religious, righteous, true, upright, virtuous, well-behaved, worthy; admirable, capable, excellent, genuine, healthy, precious, sincere, sound, sterling, valid, valuable; benevolent, favourable, friendly, gracious, humane, kind, merciful, obliging, well-disposed; fair, honourable, immaculate, unblemished, unimpeachable, unimpeached, unsullied, untarnished; cheerful, companionable, lively, genial, social; able, competent, dextrous, expert, qualified, ready, skilful, thorough, well-qualified; credit-worthy; agreeable, cheering, gratifying, pleasant. * *n* advantage, benefit, boon, favour, gain, profit, utility; interest, prosperity, welfare, weal; excellence, righteousness, virtue, worth.

good breeding *n* affability, civility, courtesy, good manners, polish, politeness, urbanity.

goodbye *n* adieu, farewell, parting.

goodly *adj* beautiful, comely, good-looking, graceful; agreeable, considerate, desirable, happy, pleasant.

good-natured *adj* amiable, benevolent, friendly, kind, kind-hearted, kindly.

goodness *n* excellence, quality, value, worth; honesty, integrity, morality, principle, probity, righteousness, uprightness, virtue; benevolence, beneficence, benignity, good-will, humaneness, humanity, kindness.

goods *n pl* belongings, chattels, effects, furniture, movables; commodities, merchandise, stock, wares.

goodwill *n* benevolence, kindness, good nature; ardour, earnestness, heartiness, willingness, zeal; custom, patronage.

gore *vb* horn, pierce, stab, wound.

gorge[1] *vb* bolt, devour, eat, feed, swallow; cram, fill, glut, gormandize, sate, satiate, stuff, surfeit. * *n* craw, crop, gullet, throat.

gorge[2] *n* canyon, defile, fissure, notch, ravine.

gorgeous *adj* bright, brilliant, dazzling, fine, glittering, grand, magnificent, resplendent, rich, shining, showy, splendid, superb.

Gorgon *n* bugaboo, fright, hobgoblin, hydra, ogre, spectre.

gory *adj* bloody, ensanguined, sanguinary.

gospel *n* creed, doctrine, message, news, revelation, tidings.

gossip *vb* chat, cackle, clack, gabble, prate, prattle, tattle. * *n* babbler, busybody, chatterer, gossipmonger, newsmonger, quidnunc, talebearer, tattler, tell-tale; cackle, chat, chit-chat, prate, prattle, tattle.

gourmet *n* connoisseur, epicure, epicurean.

govern *vb* administer, conduct, direct, manage, regulate, reign, rule, superintend, supervise; guide, pilot, steer; bridle, check, command, control, curb, restrain, rule, sway.

government *n* autonomy, command, conduct, control, direction, discipline, dominion, guidance, management, regulation, restraint, rule, rulership, sway; administration, cabinet, commonwealth, polity, sovereignty, state.

governor *n* commander, comptroller, director, head, headmaster, manager, overseer, ruler, superintendent, supervisor; chief magistrate, executive; guardian, instructor, tutor.

grab *vb* capture, clutch, seize, snatch.

grace *vb* adorn, beautify, deck, decorate, embellish; dignify, honour. * *n* benignity, condescension, favour, good-will, kindness, love; devotion, efficacy, holiness, love, piety, religion, sanctity, virtue; forgiveness, mercy, pardon, reprieve; accomplishment, attractiveness, charm, elegance, polish, propriety, refinement; beauty, comeliness, ease, gracefulness, symmetry; blessing, petition, thanks.

graceful *adj* beautiful, becoming, comely, easy, elegant; flowing, natural, rounded, unlaboured; appropriate; felicitous, happy, tactful.

graceless *adj* abandoned, corrupt, depraved, dissolute, hardened, incorrigible, irreclaimable, lost, obdurate, profligate, reprobate, repugnant, shameless,

gracious *adj* beneficent, benevolent, benign, benignant, compassionate, condescending, favourable, friendly, gentle, good-natured, kind, kindly, lenient, merciful, mild, tender; affable, civil, courteous, easy, familiar, polite.

grade *vb* arrange, classify, group, order, rank, sort. * *n* brand, degree, intensity, stage, step, rank; gradient, incline, slope.

gradual *adj* approximate, continuous, gentle, progressive, regular, slow, successive.

graduate *vb* adapt, adjust, proportion, regulate. * *n* alumna, alumnus, laureate, postgraduate.

graft *vb* ingraft, inoculate, insert, transplant. * *n* bud, scion, shoot, slip, sprout; corruption, favouritism, influence, nepotism.

grain *n* kernel, ovule, seed; cereals, corn, grist; atom, bit, glimmer, jot, particle, scintilla, scrap, shadow, spark, tittle, trace, whit; disposition, fibre, humour, temper, texture; colour, dye, hue, shade, stain, texture, tincture, tinge.

granary *n* corn-house, garner, grange, store-house.

grand *adj* august, dignified, elevated, eminent, exalted, great, illustrious, lordly, majestic, princely, stately, sublime; fine, glorious, gorgeous, magnificent, pompous, lofty, noble, splendid, superb; chief, leading, main, pre-eminent, principal, superior.

grandee *n* lord, noble, nobleman.

grandeur *n* elevation, greatness, immensity, impressiveness, loftiness, vastness; augustness, dignity, eminence, glory, magnificence, majesty, nobility, pomp, splendour, state, stateliness.

grandiloquent *adj* bombastic, declamatory, high-minded, high-sounding, inflated, pompous, rhetorical, stilted, swelling, tumid, turgid.

grant *vb* accord, admit, allow, sanction; cede, concede, give, impart, indulge; bestow, confer, deign, invest, vouchsafe; convey, transfer, yield. * *n* admission, allowance, benefaction, bestowal, boon, bounty, concession, donation, endowment, gift, indulgence, largesse, present; conveyance, cession.

graphic *adj* descriptive, diagrammatic, figural, figurative, forcible, lively, pictorial, picturesque, striking, telling, vivid, well-delineated, well-drawn.

grapple *vb* catch, clutch, grasp, grip, hold, hug, seize, tackle, wrestle.

grasp *vb* catch, clasp, clinch, clutch, grapple, grip, seize; comprehend, understand. * *n* clasp, grip, hold; comprehension, power, reach, scope, understanding.

grasping *adj* acquisitive, avaricious, covetous, exacting, greedy, rapacious, sordid, tight-fisted.

grate *vb* abrade, rub, scrape, triturate; comminute, rasp; creak, fret, grind, jar, vex. * *n* bars, grating, latticework, screen; basket, fire bed.

grateful *adj* appreciative, beholden, indebted, obliged, sensible, thankful; pleasant, welcome.

gratification *n* gratifying, indulgence, indulging, pleasing, satisfaction, satisfying; delight, enjoyment, fruition, pleasure, reward.

gratify *vb* delight, gladden, please; humour, fulfil, grant, indulge, requite, satisfy.

gratifying *adj* agreeable, delightful, grateful, pleasing, welcome.

grating *adj* disagreeable, displeasing, harsh, irritating, offensive. * *n* grate, partition.

gratis *adv* freely, gratuitously.

gratitude *n* goodwill, gratitude, indebtedness, thankfulness.

gratuitous *adj* free, spontaneous, unrewarded, voluntary; assumed, baseless, groundless, unfounded, unwarranted, wanton.

gratuity *n* benefaction, bounty, charity, donation, endowment, gift, grant, largesse, present.

grave[1] *n* crypt, mausoleum, ossuary, pit, sepulchre, sepulture, tomb, vault.

grave[2] *adj* cogent, heavy, important, momentous, ponderous, pressing, serious, weighty; dignified, sage, sedate, serious, slow, solemn, staid, thoughtful; dull, grim, plain, quiet, sober, sombre, subdued; cruel, hard, harsh, severe; despicable, dire, dismal, gross, heinous, infamous, outrageous, scandalous, shameful, shocking; heavy, hollow, low, low-pitched, sepulchral.

grave[3] *vb* engrave, impress, imprint, infix; carve, chisel, cut, sculpt.

gravel *vb* bewilder, embarrass, nonplus, perplex, pose, puzzle, stagger. * *n* ballast, grit, sand, shingle.

graveyard *n* burial ground, cemetery, churchyard, god's acre, mortuary, necropolis.

gravity *n* heaviness, weight; demureness, sedateness, seriousness, sobriety, thoughtfulness; importance, moment, momentousness, weightiness.

graze *vb* brush, glance, scrape, scratch; abrade, shave, skim; browse, crop, feed, pasture. * *n* abrasion, bruise, scrape, scratch.

great *adj* ample, big, bulky, Cyclopean, enormous, gigantic, Herculean, huge, immense, large, pregnant, vast; decided, excessive, high, much, pronounced; countless, numerous; chief, considerable, grand, important, leading, main, pre-eminent, principal, superior, weighty; celebrated, distinguished, eminent, exalted, excellent, famed, famous, far-famed, illustrious, noted, prominent, renowned; august, dignified, elevated, grand, lofty, majestic, noble, sublime; chivalrous, generous, high-minded, magnanimous; fine, magnificent, rich, sumptuous.

greatness *n* bulk, dimensions, largeness, magnitude, size; distinction, elevation, eminence, fame, importance, renown; augustness, dignity, grandeur, majesty, loftiness, nobility, nobleness, sublimity; chivalry, generosity, magnanimity, spirit.

greed, greediness *n* gluttony, hunger, omnivorousness, ravenousness, voracity; avidity, covetousness, desire, eagerness, longing; avarice, cupidity, graspingness, grasping, rapacity, selfishness.

greedy *adj* devouring, edacious, gluttonous, insatiable, insatiate, rapacious, ravenous, voracious; desirous, eager; avaricious, grasping, selfish.

green *adj* aquamarine, emerald, olive, verdant, verdure, viridescent, viridian; blooming, flourishing, fresh, undecayed; fresh, new, recent; immature, unfledged, unripe; callow, crude, inexpert, ignorant, inexperienced, raw, unskilful, untrained, verdant, young; unseasoned; conservationist, ecological, environmentalist. * *n* common, grass plot, lawn, sward, turf, verdure.

greenhorn *n* beginner, novice, tyro.

greet *vb* accost, address, complement, hail, receive, salute, welcome.

greeting *n* compliment, salutation, salute, welcome.

grief *n* affliction, agony, anguish, bitterness, distress, dole, heartbreak, misery, regret, sadness, sorrow, suffering, tribulation, mourning, woe; grievance, trial; disaster, failure, mishap.

grievance *n* burden, complaint, hardship, injury, oppression, wrong; affliction, distress, grief, sorrow, trial, woe.

grieve *vb* afflict, aggrieve, agonize, discomfort, distress, hurt, oppress, pain, sadden, wound; bewail, deplore, mourn, lament, regret, sorrow, suffer.

grievous *adj* afflicting, afflictive, burdensome, deplorable, distressing, heavy, lamentable, oppressive, painful, sad, sorrowful; baleful, baneful, calamitous, destructive, detrimental, hurtful, injurious, mischievous, noxious, troublesome; aggravated, atrocious, dreadful, flagitious, flagrant, gross, heinous, iniquitous, intense, intolerable, severe, outrageous, wicked.

grill *vb* broil, griddle, roast, toast; sweat; cross-examine, interrogate, question; torment, torture. * *n* grating, gridiron; cross-examination, cross-questioning.

grim *adj* cruel, ferocious, fierce, harsh, relentless, ruthless, savage, stern, unyielding; appalling, dire, dreadful, fearful, frightful, grisly, hideous, horrid, horrible, terrific.

grimace *vb, n* frown, scowl, smirk, sneer.

grime *n* dirt, filth, foulness, smut.

grimy *adj* begrimed, defiled, dirty, filthy, foul, soiled, sullied, unclean.

grind *vb* bruise, crunch, crush, grate, grit, pulverize, rub, triturate; sharpen, whet; afflict, harass, oppress, persecute, plague, trouble. * *n* chore, drudgery, labour, toil.

grip *vb* clasp, clutch, grasp, hold, seize. * *n* clasp, clutch, control, domination, grasp, hold.

grisly *adj* appalling, frightful, dreadful, ghastly, grim, grey, hideous, horrible, horrid, terrible, terrific.

grit *vb* clench, grate, grind. * *n* bran, gravel, pebbles, sand; courage, decision, determination, firmness, perseverance, pluck, resolution, spirit.

groan *vb* complain, lament, moan, whine; creak. * *n* cry, moan, whine; complaint; grouse, grumble.

groom *vb* clean, dress, tidy; brush, tend; coach, educate, nurture, train. * *n* equerry, hostler, manservant, ostler, servant, stable-hand, valet, waiter.

groove *n* channel, cut, furrow, rabbet, rebate, recess, rut, scoring; routine.

gross *vb* accumulate, earn, make. * *adj* big, bulky, burly, fat, great, large; dense, dull, stupid, thick; beastly, broad, carnal, coarse, crass, earthy, impure, indelicate, licentious, low, obscene, unbecoming, unrefined, unseemly, vulgar, rough, sensual; aggravated, brutal, enormous, flagrant, glaring, grievous, manifest, obvious, palpable, plain, outrageous, shameful; aggregate, entire, total, whole. * *n* aggregate, bulk, total, whole.

grossness *n* bigness, bulkiness, greatness; density, thickness; coarseness, ill-breeding, rudeness, vulgarity; bestiality, brutality, carnality, coarseness, impurity, indelicacy, licentiousness, sensuality.

grotesque *adj* bizarre, extravagant, fanciful, fantastic, incongruous, odd, strange, unnatural, whimsical, wild; absurd, antic, burlesque, ludicrous, ridiculous.

ground *vb* fell, place; base, establish, fix, found, set; instruct, train. * *n* area, clod, distance, earth, loam, mould, sod, soil, turf; country, domain, land, region, territory; acres, estate, field, property; base, basis, foundation, groundwork, support; account, consideration, excuse, gist, motive, opinion, reason.

groundless *adj* baseless, causeless, false, gratuitous, idle, unauthorized, unfounded, unjustifiable, unsolicited, unsought, unwarranted.

grounds *n pl* deposit, dregs, grouts, lees, precipitate, sediment, settlings; accounts, arguments, considerations, reasons, support; campus, gardens, lawns, premises, yard.

group *vb* arrange, assemble, dispose, order. * *n* aggregation, assemblage, assembly, body, combination, class, clump, cluster, collection, order.

grove *n* copse, glade, spinney, thicket, wood, woodland.

grovel *vb* cower, crawl, creep, cringe, fawn, flatter, sneak.

grovelling *adj* creeping, crouching, squat; abject, base, beggarly, cringing, fawning, low, mean, servile, slavish, sneaking, undignified, unworthy, vile.

grow *vb* enlarge, expand, extend, increase, swell; arise, burgeon, develop, germinate, shoot, sprout, vegetate; advance, extend, improve, progress, thrive, wax; cultivate, produce, raise.

growl *vb* complain, croak, find fault, gnarl, groan, grumble, lament, murmur, snarl. * *n* croak, grown, snarl; complaint.

growth *n* augmentation, development, expansion, extension, growing, increase; burgeoning, excrescence, formation, germination, pollution, shooting, sprouting, vegetation; cultivation, produce, product, production; advance, advancement, development, improvement, progress; adulthood, maturity.

grub *vb* clear, dig, eradicate, root. * *n* caterpillar, larvae, maggot; drudge, plodder.

grudge *vb* begrudge, envy, repine; complain, grieve, murmur. * *n* aversion, dislike, enmity, grievance, hate, hatred, ill-will, malevolence, malice, pique, rancour, resentment, spite, venom.

gruff *adj* bluff, blunt, brusque, churlish, discourteous, grumpy, harsh, impolite, rough, rude, rugged, surly, uncivil, ungracious.

grumble *vb* croak, complain, murmur, repine; gnarl, growl, snarl; roar, rumble. * *n* growl, murmur, complaint, roar, rumble.

grumpy *adj* crabbed, cross, glum, moody, morose, sour, sullen, surly.
guarantee *vb* assure, insure, pledge, secure, warrant. * *n* assurance, pledge, security, surety, warrant, warranty.
guard *vb* defend, keep, patrol, protect, safeguard, save, secure, shelter, shield, watch. * *n* aegis, bulwark, custody, defence, palladium, protection, rampart, safeguard, security, shield; keeper, guardian, patrol, sentinel, sentry, warden, watch, watchman; conduct, convoy, escort; attention, care, caution, circumspection, heed, watchfulness.
guarded *adj* careful, cautious, circumspect, reserved, reticent, wary, watchful.
guardian *n* custodian, defender, guard, keeper, preserver, protector, trustee, warden.
guerdon *n* recompense, remuneration, requital, reward.
guess *vb* conjecture, divine, mistrust, surmise, suspect; fathom, find out, penetrate, solve; believe, fancy, hazard, imagine, reckon, suppose, think. * *n* conjecture, divination, notion, supposition, surmise.
guest *n* caller, company, visitant.
guidance *n* conduct, control, direction, escort, government, lead, leadership, pilotage, steering.
guide *vb* conduct, escort, lead, pilot; control, direct, govern, manage, preside, regulate, rule, steer, superintend, supervise. * *n* cicerone, conductor, director, monitor, pilot; adviser, counsellor, instructor, mentor; clew, directory, index, key, thread; guidebook, itinerary, landmark.
guild *n* association, brotherhood, company, corporation, fellowship, fraternity, society, union.
guile *n* art, artfulness, artifice, craft, cunning, deceit, deception, duplicity, fraud, knavery, ruse, subtlety, treachery, trickery, wiles, wiliness.
guileless *adj* artless, candid, frank, honest, ingenuous, innocent, open, pure, simple-minded, sincere, straightforward, truthful, undesigning, unsophisticated.
guilt *n* blame, criminality, culpability, guiltless; ill-desert, iniquity, offensiveness, wickedness, wrong; crime, offence, sin.
guiltless *adj* blameless, immaculate, innocent, pure, sinless, spotless, unpolluted, unspotted, unsullied, untarnished.
guilty *adj* criminal, culpable, evil, sinful, wicked, wrong.
guise *n* appearance, aspect, costume, dress, fashion, figure, form, garb, manner, mode, shape; air, behaviour, demeanour, mien; cover, custom, disguise, habit, pretence, pretext, practice.
gulf *n* abyss, chasm, opening; bay, inlet; whirlpool.
gull *vb* beguile, cheat, circumvent, cozen, deceive, dupe, hoax, overreach, swindle, trick. * *n* cheat, deception, hoax, imposition, fraud, trick; cat's paw, dupe.
gullibility *n* credulity, naiveness, naivety, overtrustfulness, simplicity, unsophistication.
gullible *adj* confiding, credulous, naive, over-trustful, simple, unsophisticated, unsuspicious.
gumption *n* ability, astuteness, cleverness, capacity, common sense, discernment, penetration, power, sagacity, shrewdness, skill; courage, guts, spirit.
gun *n* blunderbuss, cannon, carbine, firearm, musket, pistol, revolver, rifle, shotgun.
gurgle *vb* babble, bubble, murmur, purl, ripple. * *n* babbling, murmur, ripple.
gush *vb* burst, flood, flow, pour, rush, spout, stream; emotionalize, sentimentalize. * *n* flow, jet, onrush, rush, spurt, surge; effusion, effusiveness, loquacity, loquaciousness, talkativeness.
gushing *adj* flowing, issuing, rushing; demonstrative, effusive, sentimental.
gust *vb* blast, blow, puff. * *n* blast, blow, squall; burst, fit, outburst, paroxysm.
gusto *n* enjoyment, gust, liking, pleasure, relish, zest.
gusty *adj* blustering, blustery, puffy, squally, stormy, tempestuous, unsteady, windy.
gut *vb* destroy, disembowel, embowel, eviscerate, paunch. * *n* bowels, entrails, intestines, inwards, viscera.
gutter *n* channel, conduit, kennel, pipe, tube.
guttural *adj* deep, gruff, hoarse, thick, throaty.
guy *vb* caricature, mimic, ridicule. * *n* boy, man, person; dowdy, eccentric, fright, scarecrow.
guzzle *vb* carouse, drink, gorge, gormandize, quaff, swill, tipple, tope.
gyrate *vb* revolve, rotate, spin, whirl.

habiliment *n* apparel, attire, clothes, costume, dress, garb, garment, habit, raiment, robes, uniform, vesture, vestment.
habit *vb* accoutre, array, attire, clothe, dress, equip, robe. * *n* condition, constitution, temperament; addiction, custom, habitude, manner, practice, rule, usage, way, wont; apparel, costume, dress, garb, habiliment.
habitation *n* abode, domicile, dwelling, headquarters, home, house, lodging, quarters, residence.
habitual *adj* accustomed, common, confirmed, customary, everyday, familiar, inveterate, ordinary, regular, routine, settled, usual, wonted.
habituate *vb* accustom, familiarize, harden, inure, train, use.
habitude *n* custom, practice, usage, wont.
hack[1] *vb* chop, cut, hew, mangle, mutilate, notch; cough, rasp. * *n* cut, cleft, incision, notch; cough, rasp.
hack[2] *vb* ride. * *adj* hired, mercenary; banal, hackneyed, pedestrian, uninspired, unoriginal. * *n* horse, nag, pony; hireling, mercenary; journalist, scribbler, writer.
hackneyed *adj* banal, common, commonplace, overworked, pedestrian, stale, threadbare, trite.
hag *n* beldame, crone, fury, harridan, jezebel, she-monster, shrew, termagant, virago, vixen, witch.
haggard *adj* intractable, refractory, unruly, untamed, wild, wayward; careworn, emaciated, gaunt, ghastly, lank, lean, meagre, raw, spare, thin, wasted, worn.
haggle *vb* argue, bargain, cavil, chaffer, dispute, higgle, stickle; annoy, badger, bait, fret, harass, tease, worry.
hail[1] *vb* acclaim, greet, salute, welcome; accost, address, call, hallo, signal. * *n* greeting, salute.
hail[2] *vb* assail, bombard, rain, shower, storm, volley. * *n* bombardment, rain, shower, storm, volley.
halcyon *adj* calm, golden, happy, palmy, placid, peaceful, quiet, serene, still, tranquil, unruffled, undisturbed.
hale *adj* hardy, healthy, hearty, robust, sound, strong, vigorous, well.
halfwit *n* blockhead, dunce, moron, simpleton.
halfwitted *adj* doltish, dull, dull-witted, feeble-minded, foolish, sappy, shallow, silly, simple, soft, stolid, stupid, thick.
hall *n* chamber, corridor, entrance, entry, hallway, lobby, passage, vestibule; manor, manor-house; auditorium, lecture-room.
halloo *vb* call, cry, shout. * *n* call, cry, hallo, holla, hollo, shout.
hallow *vb* consecrate, dedicate, devote, revere, sanctify, solemnize; enshrine, honour, respect, reverence, venerate.
hallowed *adj* blessed, holy, honoured, revered, sacred.
hallucination *n* blunder, error, fallacy, mistake; aberration, delusion, illusion, phantasm, phantasy, self-deception, vision.
halo *n* aura, aureole, glory, nimbus.
halt[1] *vb* cease, desist, hold, rest, stand, stop. * *n* end, impasse, pause, standstill, stop.
halt[2] *vb* hesitate, pause, stammer, waver; falter, hobble, limp. * *adj* crippled, disabled, lame. * *n* hobble, limp.
hammer *vb* beat, forge, form, shape; excogitate, contrive, invent.
hammer and tongs *adv* earnestly, energetically, resolutely, strenuously, vigorously, zealously.

hamper *vb* bind, clog, confine, curb, embarrass, encumber, entangle, fetter, hinder, impede, obstruct, prevent, restrain, restrict, shackle, trammel. * *n* basket, box, crate, picnic basket; embarrassment, encumbrance, fetter, handicap, impediment, obstruction, restraint, trammel.

hand *vb* deliver, give, present, transmit; conduct, guide, lead. * *n* direction, part, side; ability, dexterity, faculty, skill, talent; course, inning, management, turn; agency, intervention, participation, share; control, possession, power; artificer, artisan, craftsman, employee, labourer, operative, workman; index, indicator, pointer; chirography, handwriting.

handbook *n* guidebook, manual.

handcuff *vb* bind, fetter, manacle, shackle. * *n* fetter, manacle, shackle.

handful *n* fistful, maniple, smattering.

handicap *vb* encumber, hamper, hinder, restrict. * *n* disadvantage, encumbrance, hampering, hindrance, restriction.

handicraft *n* hand manufacture, handwork, workmanship.

handle *vb* feel, finger, manhandle, paw, touch; direct, manage, manipulate, use, wield; discourse, discuss, treat. * *n* haft, helve, hilt, stock.

handsome *adj* admirable, comely, fine-looking, stately, well-formed, well-proportioned; appropriate, suitable, becoming, easy, graceful; generous, gracious, liberal, magnanimous, noble; ample, large, plentiful, sufficient.

handy *adj* adroit, clever, dextrous, expert, ready, skilful, skilled; close, convenient, near.

hang *vb* attach, swing; execute, truss; decline, drop, droop, incline; adorn, drape; dangle, depend, impend, suspend; rely; cling, loiter, rest, stick; float, hover, pay.

hangdog *adj* ashamed, base, blackguard, low, villainous, scurvy, sneaking.

hanger-on *n* dependant, minion, parasite, vassal.

hanker *vb* covet, crave, desire, hunger, long, lust, want, yearn.

hap *n* accident, chance, fate, fortune, lot.

haphazard *adj* aimless, chance, random.

hapless *adj* ill-fated, ill-starred, luckless, miserable, unfortunate, unhappy, unlucky, wretched.

happen *vb* befall, betide, chance, come, occur.

happily *adv* fortunately, luckily; agreeably, delightfully, prosperously, successfully.

happiness *n* brightness, cheerfulness, delight, gaiety, joy, light-heartedness, merriment, pleasure; beatitude, blessedness, bliss, felicity, enjoyment, welfare, well-being.

happy *adj* blessed, blest, blissful, cheerful, contented, joyful, joyous, light-hearted, merry; charmed, delighted, glad, gladdened, gratified, pleased; fortunate, lucky, prosperous, successful; able, adroit, apt, dextrous, expert, ready, skilful; befitting, felicitous, opportune, pertinent, seasonable, well-timed; auspicious, bright, favourable, propitious.

harangue *vb* address, declaim, spout. * *n* address, bombast, declamation, oration, rant, screed, speech, tirade.

harass *vb* exhaust, fag, fatigue, jade, tire, weary; annoy, badger, distress, gall, heckle, disturb, harry, molest, pester, plague, tantalize, tease, torment, trouble, vex, worry.

harbour *vb* protect, lodge, shelter; cherish, entertain, foster, indulge. * *n* asylum, cover, refuge, resting place, retreat, sanctuary, shelter; anchorage, destination, haven, port.

hard *adj* adamantine, compact, firm, flinty, impenetrable, marble, rigid, solid, resistant, stony, stubborn, unyielding; difficult, intricate, knotty, perplexing, puzzling; arduous, exacting, fatiguing, laborious, toilsome, wearying; austere, callous, cruel, exacting, hard-hearted, incorrigible, inflexible, insensible, insensitive, obdurate, oppressive, reprobate, rigorous, severe, unfeeling, unkind, unsusceptible, unsympathetic, unyielding, untender; calamitous, disagreeable, distressing, grievous, painful, unpleasant; acid, alcoholic, harsh, rough, sour; excessive, intemperate. * *adv* close, near; diligently, earnestly, energetically, incessantly, laboriously; distressfully, painfully, rigorously, severely; forcibly, vehemently, violently.

harden *vb* accustom, discipline, form, habituate, inure, season, train; brace, fortify, indurate, nerve, steel, stiffen, strengthen.

hardened *adj* annealed, case-hardened, tempered, indurated; abandoned, accustomed, benumbed, callous, confirmed, deadened, depraved, habituated, impenitent, incorrigible, inured, insensible, irreclaimable, lost, obdurate, reprobate, seared, seasoned, steeled, trained, unfeeling.

hard-headed *adj* astute, collected, cool, intelligent, sagacious, shrewd, well-balanced, wise.

hardhearted *adj* cruel, fell, implacable, inexorable, merciless, pitiless, relentless, ruthless, unfeeling, uncompassionate, unmerciful, unpitying, unrelenting.

hardihood *n* audacity, boldness, bravery, courage, decision, firmness, fortitude, intrepidity, manhood, mettle, pluck, resolution, stoutness; assurance, audacity, brass, effrontery, impudence.

hardly *adv* barely, scarcely; cruelly, harshly, rigorously, roughly, severely, unkindly.

hardship *n* fatigue, toil, weariness; affliction, burden, calamity, grievance, hardness, injury, misfortune, privation, suffering, trial, trouble.

hardy *adj* enduring, firm, hale, healthy, hearty, inured, lusty, rigorous, robust, rugged, sound, stout, strong, sturdy, tough; bold, brave, courageous, daring, heroic, intrepid, manly, resolute, stout-hearted, valiant.

harebrained *adj* careless, changeable, flighty, giddy, harum-scarum, headlong, heedless, rash, reckless, unsteady, volatile, wild.

hark *interj* attend, hear, hearken, listen.

harlequin *n* antic, buffoon, clown, droll, fool, jester, punch, fool.

harm *vb* damage, hurt, injure, scathe; abuse, desecrate, ill-use, ill-treat, maltreat, molest. * *n* damage, detriment, disadvantage, hurt, injury, mischief, misfortune, prejudice, wrong.

harmful *adj* baneful, detrimental, disadvantageous, hurtful, injurious, mischievous, noxious, pernicious, prejudicial.

harmless *adj* innocent, innocuous, innoxious; inoffensive, safe, unoffending.

harmonious *adj* concordant, consonant, harmonic; dulcet, euphonious, mellifluous, melodious, musical, smooth, tuneful; comfortable, congruent, consistent, correspondent, orderly, symmetrical; agreeable, amicable, brotherly, cordial, fraternal, friendly, neighbourly.

harmonize *vb* adapt, attune, reconcile, unite; accord, agree, blend, chime, comport, conform, correspond, square, sympathize, tally, tune.

harmony *n* euphony, melodiousness, melody; accord, accordance, agreement, chime, concord, concordance, consonance, order, unison; adaptation, congruence, congruity, consistency, correspondence, fairness, smoothness, suitableness; amity, friendship, peace.

harness *vb* hitch, tackle. * *n* equipment, gear, tackle, tackling; accoutrements, armour, array, mail, mounting.

harp *vb* dwell, iterate, reiterate, renew, repeat.

harping *n* dwelling, iteration, reiteration, repetition.

harrow *vb* harass, lacerate, rend, tear, torment, torture, wound.

harry *vb* devastate, pillage, plunder, raid, ravage, rob; annoy, chafe, disturb, fret, gall, harass, harrow, incommode, pester, plague, molest, tease, torment, trouble, vex, worry.

harsh *adj* acid, acrid, astringent, biting, caustic, corrosive, crabbed, rough, sharp, sour, tart; cacophonous, discordant, grating, jarring, metallic, raucous, strident, unmelodious; abusive, austere, crabbed, crabby, cruel, disagreeable, hard, ill-natured, ill-tempered, morose, rigorous, severe, stern, unfeeling; bearish, bluff, blunt, brutal, gruff, rude, uncivil, ungracious.

harshness *n* roughness; acerbity, asperity, austerity, churlishness, crabbedness, hardness, ill-nature, ill-temper, moroseness, rigour, severity, sternness, unkindness; bluffness, bluntness, churlishness, gruffness, incivility, ungraciousness, rudeness.

harum-scarum *adj* hare-brained, precipitate, rash, reckless, volatile, wild.

harvest *vb* gather, glean, reap. * *n* crops, produce, yield; consequence, effect, issue, outcome, produce, result.

haste *n* alacrity, celerity, dispatch, expedition, nimbleness, promptitude, quickness, rapidity, speed, urgency, velocity; flurry, hurry, hustle, impetuosity, precipitateness, precipitation, press, rashness, rush, vehemence.

hasten *vb* haste, hurry; accelerate, dispatch, expedite, precipitate, press, push, quicken, speed, urge.

hasty *adj* brisk, fast, fleet, quick, rapid, speedy, swift; cursory, hurried, passing, slight, superficial; ill-advised, rash, reckless; headlong, helter-skelter, pell-mell, precipitate; abrupt, choleric, excitable, fiery, fretful, hot-headed, irascible, irritable, passionate, peevish, peppery, pettish, petulant, testy, touchy, waspish.

hatch *vb* brew, concoct, contrive, excogitate, design, devise, plan, plot, project, scheme; breed, incubate.

hate *vb* abhor, abominate, detest, dislike, execrate, loathe, nauseate. * *n* abomination, animosity, antipathy, detestation, dislike, enmity, execration, hatred, hostility, loathing.

hateful *adj* malevolent, malicious, malign, malignant, rancorous, spiteful; abhorrent, abominable, accursed, damnable, detestable, execrable, horrid, odious, shocking; disgusting, foul, loathsome, nauseous, obnoxious, offensive, repellent, repugnant, repulsive, revolting, vile.

hatred *n* animosity, enmity, hate, hostility, ill-will, malevolence, malice, malignity, odium, rancour; abhorrence, abomination, antipathy, aversion, detestation, disgust, execration, horror, loathing, repugnance, revulsion.

haughtiness *n* arrogance, contempt, contemptuousness, disdain, hauteur, insolence, loftiness, pride, self-importance, snobbishness, stateliness, superciliousness.

haughty *adj* arrogant, assuming, contemptuous, disdainful, imperious, insolent, lofty, lordly, overbearing, overweening, proud, scornful, snobbish, supercilious.

haul *vb* drag, draw, lug, pull, tow, trail, tug. * *n* heaving, pull, tug; booty, harvest, takings, yield.

haunt *vb* frequent, resort; follow, importune; hover, inhabit, obsess. * *n* den, resort, retreat.

hauteur *n* arrogance, contempt, contemptuousness, disdain, haughtiness, insolence, loftiness, pride, self-importance, stateliness, superciliousness.

have *vb* cherish, exercise, experience, keep, hold, occupy, own, possess; acquire, gain, get, obtain, receive; accept, take.

haven *n* asylum, refuge, retreat, shelter; anchorage, harbour, port.

havoc *n* carnage, damage, desolation, destruction, devastation, ravage, ruin, slaughter, waste, wreck.

hawk-eyed *adj* eagle-eyed, sharp-sighted.

hazard *vb* adventure, risk, venture; endanger, imperil, jeopardize. * *n* accident, casualty, chance, contingency, event, fortuity, stake; danger, jeopardy, peril, risk, venture.

hazardous *adj* dangerous, insecure, perilous, precarious, risky, uncertain, unsafe.

haze *n* fog, har, mist, smog; cloud, dimness, fume, miasma, obscurity, pall.

hazy *adj* foggy, misty; cloudy, dim, nebulous, obscure; confused, indefinite, indistinct, uncertain, vague.

head *vb* command, control, direct, govern, guide, lead, rule; aim, point, tend; beat, excel, outdo, precede, surpass. * *adj* chief, first, grand, highest, leading, main, principal; adverse, contrary. * *n* acme, summit, top; beginning, commencement, origin, rise, source; chief, chieftain, commander, director, leader, master, principal, superintendent, superior; intellect, mind, thought, understanding; branch, category, class, department, division, section, subject, topic; brain, crown, headpiece, intellect, mind, thought, understanding; cape, headland, point, promontory.

headiness *n* hurry, precipitation, rashness; obstinacy, stubbornness.

headless *adj* acephalous, beheaded; leaderless, undirected; headstrong, heady, imprudent, obstinate, rash, senseless, stubborn.

headlong *adj* dangerous, hasty, heady, impulsive, inconsiderate, perilous, precipitate, rash, reckless, ruinous, thoughtless; perpendicular, precipitous, sheer, steep. * *adv* hastily, headfirst, helter-skelter, hurriedly, precipitately, rashly, thoughtlessly.

headstone *n* cornerstone, gravestone.

headstrong *adj* cantankerous, cross-grained, dogged, forward, headless, heady, intractable, obstinate, self-willed, stubborn, ungovernable, unruly, violent, wayward.

heady *adj* hasty, headlong, impetuous, impulsive, inconsiderate, precipitate, rash, reckless, rushing, stubborn, thoughtless; exciting, inebriating, inflaming, intoxicating, spirituous, strong.

heal *vb* amend, cure, remedy, repair, restore; compose, harmonize, reconcile, settle, soothe.

healing *adj* curative, palliative, remedial, restoring, restorative; assuaging, assuasive, comforting, composing, gentle, lenitive, mild, soothing.

health *n* healthfulness, robustness, salubrity, sanity, soundness, strength, tone, vigour.

healthy *adj* active, hale, hearty, lusty, sound, vigorous, well; bracing, healthful, health-giving, hygienic, invigorating, nourishing, salubrious, salutary, wholesome.

heap *vb* accumulate, augment, amass, collect, overfill, pile up, store. * *n* accumulation, collection, cumulus, huddle, lot, mass, mound, pile, stack.

hear *vb* eavesdrop, hearken, heed, listen, overhear; ascertain, discover, gather, learn, understand; examine, judge.

heart *n* bosom, breast; centre, core, essence, interior, kernel, marrow, meaning, pith; affection, benevolence, character, disposition, feeling, inclination, love, mind, passion, purpose, will; affections, ardour, emotion, feeling, love; boldness, courage, fortitude, resolution, spirit.

heartache *n* affliction, anguish, bitterness, distress, dole, grief, heartbreak, sorrow, woe.

heartbroken *adj* broken-hearted, cheerless, comfortless, desolate, disconsolate, forlorn, inconsolable, miserable, woebegone, wretched.

hearten *vb* animate, assure, cheer, comfort, console, embolden, encourage, enhearten, incite, inspire, inspirit, reassure, stimulate.

heartfelt *adj* cordial, deep, deep-felt, hearty, profound, sincere, warm.

hearth *n* fireplace, fireside, forge, hearthstone.

heartily *adv* abundantly, completely, cordially, earnestly, freely, largely, sincerely, vigorously.

heartless *adj* brutal, cold, cruel, hard, harsh, merciless, pitiless, unfeeling, unsympathetic; spiritless, timid, timorous, uncourageous.

heart-rending *adj* affecting, afflicting, anguishing, crushing, distressing.

hearty *adj* cordial, deep, earnest, fervent, heartfelt, profound, sincere, true, unfeigned, warm; active, animated, energetic, fit, vigorous, zealous; convivial, hale, healthy, robust, sound, strong, warm; abundant, full, heavy; nourishing, nutritious, rich.

heat *vb* excite, flush, inflame; animate, rouse, stimulate, stir. * *n* calorie, caloricity, torridity, warmth; excitement, fever, flush, impetuosity, passion, vehemence, violence; ardour, earnestness, fervency, fervour, glow, intensity, zeal; exasperation, fierceness, frenzy, rage.

heath *n* field, moor, wasteland, plain.

heathen *adj* animist, animistic; pagan, paganical, paganish, paganistic, unconverted; agnostic, atheist, atheistic, gentile, idolatrous, infidel, irreligious; barbarous, cruel, inhuman, savage. * *n* atheist, gentile, idolater, idolatress, infidel, pagan, unbeliever; barbarian, philistine, savage.

heave *vb* elevate, hoist, lift, raise; breathe, exhale; cast, fling, hurl, send, throw, toss; dilate, expand, pant, rise, swell; retch, throw up; strive, struggle.

heaven *n* empyrean, firmament, sky, welkin; bliss, ecstasy, elysium, felicity, happiness, paradise, rapture, transport.

heavenly *adj* celestial, empyreal, ethereal; angelic, beatific, beatified, cherubic, divine, elysian, glorious, god-like, sainted, saintly, seraphic; blissful, delightful, divine, ecstatic, enrapturing, enravishing, exquisite, golden, rapturous, ravishing, exquisite, transporting.

heaviness *n* gravity, heft, ponderousness, weight; grievousness, oppressiveness, severity; dullness, languor, lassitude, sluggishness, stupidity; dejection, depression, despondency, gloom, melancholy, sadness, seriousness.

heavy *adj* grave, hard, onerous, ponderous, weighty; afflictive, burdensome, crushing, cumbersome, grievous, oppressive, severe, serious; dilatory, dull, inactive, inanimate, indolent, inert, lifeless, listless, sleepy, slow, sluggish, stupid, torpid; chapfallen, crestfallen, crushed, depressed, dejected, despondent, disconsolate, downhearted, gloomy, low-spirited, melancholy, sad, sobered, sorrowful; difficult, laborious; tedious, tiresome, wearisome, weary; burdened, encumbered, loaded; clammy, clayey, cloggy, ill-raised, miry, muddy, soggy; boisterous, deep, energetic, loud, roaring, severe, stormy, strong, tempestuous, violent; cloudy, dark, dense, gloomy, lowering, overcast.

hebetate *adj* blunt; dull, obtuse, sluggish, stupid, stupefied.

hectic *adj* animated, excited, fevered, feverish, flushed, heated, hot.

hector *vb* bluster, boast, bully, menace, threaten; annoy, fret, harass, harry, irritate, provoke, tease, vex, worry. * *n* blusterer, bully, swaggerer.

hedge *vb* block, encumber, hinder, obstruct, surround; enclose, fence, fortify, guard, protect; disappear, dodge, evade, hide, skulk, temporize. * *n* barrier, hedgerow, fence, limit.

heed *vb* attend, consider, mark, mind, note, notice, observe, regard. * *n* attention, care, carefulness, caution, circumspection, consideration, heedfulness, mindfulness, notice, observation, regard, wariness, vigilance, watchfulness.

heedful *adj* attentive, careful, cautious, circumspect, mindful, observant, observing, provident, regardful, watchful, wary.

heedless *adj* careless, inattentive, neglectful, negligent, precipitate, rash, reckless, thoughtless, unmindful, unminding, unobserving, unobservant.

heft *n* handle, haft, helve; bulk, weight.

hegemony *n* ascendancy, authority, headship, leadership, predominance, preponderance, rule.

height *n* altitude, elevation, tallness; acme, apex, climax, eminence, head, meridian, pinnacle, summit, top, vertex, zenith; eminence, hill, mountain; dignity, exaltation, grandeur, loftiness, perfection.

heighten *vb* elevate, raise; ennoble, exalt, magnify, make greater; augment, enhance, improve, increase, strengthen; aggravate, intensify.

heinous *adj* aggravated, atrocious, crying, enormous, excessive, flagitious, flagrant, hateful, infamous, monstrous, nefarious, odious, villainous.

heir *n* child, inheritor, offspring, product.

helical *adj* screw-shaped, spiral, winding.

hellish *adj* abominable, accursed, atrocious, curst, damnable, damned, demoniacal, detestable, devilish, diabolical, execrable, fiendish, infernal, monstrous, nefarious, satanic.

helm *n* rudder, steering-gear, tiller, wheel; command, control, direction, rein, rule.

help *vb* relieve, save, succour; abet, aid, assist, back, cooperate, second, serve, support, sustain, wait; alleviate, ameliorate, better, cure, heal, improve, remedy, restore; control, hinder, prevent, repress, resist, withstand; avoid, forbear, control. * *n* aid, assistance, succour, support; relief, remedy; assistant, helper, servant.

helper *adj* aider, abettor, ally, assistant, auxiliary, coadjutor, colleague, helpmate, partner, supporter.

helpful *adj* advantageous, assistant, auxiliary, beneficial, contributory, convenient, favourable, kind, profitable, serviceable, useful.

helpless *adj* disabled, feeble, imbecile, impotent, infirm, powerless, prostrate, resourceless, weak; abandoned, defenceless, exposed, unprotected; desperate, irremediable, remediless.

helpmate *n* companion, consort, husband, partner, wife; aider, assistant, associate, helper.

helter-skelter *adj* disorderly, headlong, irregular, pell-mell, precipitate. * *adv* confusedly, hastily, headlong, higgledy-piggledy, pell-mell, precipitately, wildly.

hem *vb* border, edge, skirt; beset, confine, enclose, environ, surround, sew; hesitate. * *n* border, edge, trim.

henchman *n* attendant, follower, retainer, servant, supporter.

herald *vb* announce, proclaim, publish. * *n* announcer, crier, publisher; harbinger, precursor, proclaimer.

heraldry *n* blazonry, emblazonry.

herbage *n* greenery, herb, pasture, plants, vegetation.

herculean *adj* able-bodied, athletic, brawny, mighty, muscular, powerful, puissant, sinewy, stalwart, strong, sturdy, vigorous; dangerous, difficult, hard, laborious, perilous, toilsome, troublesome; colossal, Cyclopean, gigantic, great, large, strapping.

herd *vb* drive, gather, lead, tend; assemble, associate, flock. * *n* drover, herder, herdsman, shepherd; crowd, multitude, populace, rabble; assemblage, assembly, collection, drove, flock, pack.

hereditary *adj* ancestral, inheritable, inherited, patrimonial, transmitted.

heresy *n* dissent, error, heterodoxy, impiety, recusancy, unorthodoxy.

heretic *n* dissenter, dissident, nonconformist, recusant, schismatic, sectarian, sectary, separatist, unbeliever.

heretical *adj* heterodox, impious, schismatic, schismatical, sectarian, unorthodox.

heritage *n* estate, inheritance, legacy, patrimony, portion.

hermetic *adj* airtight, impervious; cabbalistic, emblematic, emblematical, magical, mysterious, mystic, mystical, occult, secret, symbolic, symbolical.

hermit *n* anchoress, anchoret, anchorite, ascetic, eremite, monk, recluse, solitaire, solitary.

heroic *adj* bold, brave, courageous, daring, dauntless, fearless, gallant, illustrious, intrepid, magnanimous, noble, valiant; desperate, extravagant, extreme, violent.

heroism *n* boldness, bravery, courage, daring, endurance, fearlessness, fortitude, gallantry, intrepidity, prowess, valour.

hesitate *vb* boggle, delay, demur, doubt, pause, scruple, shilly-shally, stickle, vacillate, waver; falter, stammer, stutter.

hesitation *n* halting, misgiving, reluctance; delay, doubt, indecision, suspense, uncertainty, vacillation; faltering, stammering, stuttering.

heterodox *adj* heretical, recusant, schismatic, unorthodox, unsound; apocryphal, uncanonical.

heterogeneous *adj* contrasted, contrary, different, dissimilar, diverse, incongruous, indiscriminate, miscellaneous, mixed, opposed, unhomogeneous, unlike.

hew *vb* chop, cut, fell, hack; fashion, form, shape, smooth.

hiatus *n* blank, break, chasm, gap, interval, lacuna, opening, rift.

hidden *adj* blind, clandestine, cloaked, close, concealed, covered, covert, enshrouded, latent, masked, occult, private, secluded, secret, suppressed, undiscovered, veiled; abstruse, cabbalistic, cryptic, dark, esoteric, hermetic, inward, mysterious, mystic, mystical, obscure, oracular, recondite.

hide *vb* bury, conceal, cover, secrete, suppress, withhold; cloak, disguise, eclipse, hoard, mask, screen, shelter, veil.

hideous *adj* abominable, appalling, awful, dreadful, frightful, ghastly, ghoulish, grim, grisly, horrible, horrid, repulsive, revolting, shocking, terrible, terrifying.

hie *vb* hasten, speed.

hieratic *adj* consecrated, devoted, priestly, sacred, sacerdotal.

hieroglyph *n* picture-writing, rebus, sign, symbol.

hieroglyphic *adj* emblematic, emblematical, figurative, obscure, symbolic, symbolical.

higgle *vb* hawk, peddle; bargain, chaffer, haggle, negotiate.

higgledy-piggledy *adj* chaotic, confused, disorderly, jumbled. * *adv* confusedly, in disorder, helter-skelter, pell-mell.

high *adj* elevated, high-reaching, lofty, soaring, tall, towering; distinguished, eminent, pre-eminent, prominent, superior; admirable, dignified, exalted, great, noble; arrogant, haughty, lordly, proud, supercilious; boisterous, strong, tumultuous, turbulent, violent; costly, dear, pricey; acute, high-pitched, high-toned, piercing, sharp, shrill; tainted, malodorous. * *adv* powerfully, profoundly; eminently, loftily; luxuriously, richly.

high-flown *adj* elevated, presumptuous, proud, lofty, swollen; extravagant, high-coloured, lofty, overdrawn, overstrained; bombastic, inflated, pompous, pretentious, strained, swollen, turgid.

high-handed *adj* arbitrary, despotic, dictatorial, domineering, oppressive, overbearing, self-willed, violent, wilful.

highly strung *adj* ardent, excitable, irascible, nervous, quick, tense; high-spirited, sensitive.

high-minded *adj* arrogant, haughty, lofty, proud; elevated, high-toned; generous honourable, magnanimous, noble, spiritual.

highwayman *n* bandit, brigand, footpad, freebooter, marauder, outlaw, robber.

hilarious *adj* boisterous, cheerful, comical, convivial, riotous, uproarious, jovial, joyful, merry, mirthful, noisy.

hilarity *n* cheerfulness, conviviality, exhilarated, gaiety, glee, jollity, joviality, joyousness, merriment, mirth.

hill *n* ascent, ben, elevation, eminence, hillock, knoll, mount, mountain, rise, tor.

hind *adj* back, hinder, hindmost, posterior, rear, rearward.

hinder *vb* bar, check, clog, delay, embarrass, encumber, impede, interrupt, obstruct, oppose, prevent, restrain, retard, stop, thwart.

hindrance *n* check, deterrent, encumbrance, hitch, impediment, interruption, obstacle, obstruction, restraint, stop, stoppage.

hinge *vb* depend, hang, rest, turn.

hint *vb* allude, glance, imply, insinuate, intimate, mention, refer, suggest. * *n* allusion, clue, implication, indication, innuendo, insinuation, intimation, mention, reminder, suggestion, taste, trace.

hire *vb* buy, rent, secure; charter, employ, engage, lease, let. * *n* allowance, bribe, compensation, pay, remuneration, rent, reward, salary, stipend, wages.

hireling *n* employee, mercenary, myrmidon.

hirsute *adj* bristled, bristly, hairy, shaggy; boorish, course, ill-bred, loutish, rough, rude, rustic, uncouth, unmannerly.

hiss *vb* shrill, sibilate, whistle, whir, whiz; condemn, damn, ridicule. * *n* fizzle, hissing, sibilant, sibilation, sizzle.

historian *n* annalist, autobiographer, biographer, chronicler, narrator, recorder.

history *n* account, autobiography, annals, biography, chronicle, genealogy, memoirs, narration, narrative, recital, record, relation, story.

hit *vb* discomfit, hurt, knock, strike; accomplish, achieve, attain, gain, reach, secure, succeed, win; accord, fit, suit; beat, clash, collide, contact, smite. * *n* blow, collision, strike, stroke; chance, fortune, hazard, success, venture.

hitch *vb* catch, impede, stick, stop; attach, connect, fasten, harness, join, tether, tie, unite, yoke. * *n* catch, check, hindrance, impediment, interruption, obstacle; knot, noose.

hoar *adj* ancient, grey, hoary, old, white.

hoard *vb* accumulate, amass, collect, deposit, garner, hive, husband, save, store, treasure. * *n* accumulation, collection, deposit, fund, mass, reserve, savings, stockpile, store.

hoarse *adj* discordant, grating, gruff, guttural, harsh, husky, low, raucous, rough.

hoary *adj* grey, hoar, silvery, white; ancient, old, venerable.

hoax *vb* deceive, dupe, fool, gammon, gull, hoodwink, swindle, trick. * *n* canard, cheat, deception, fraud, humbug, imposition, imposture, joke, trick, swindle.

hobble *vb* falter, halt, hop, limp; fasten, fetter, hopple, shackle, tie. * *n* halt, limp; clog, fetter, shackle; embarrassment, difficulty, perplexity, pickle, strait.

hobgoblin *n* apparition, bogey, bugbear, goblin, imp, spectre, spirit, sprite.

hobnail *n* bumpkin, churl, clodhopper, clown, lout, rustic.

hocus-pocus *n* cheater, impostor, juggler, sharper, swindler, trickster; artifice, cheat, deceit, deception, delusion, hoax, imposition, juggle, trick.

hodgepodge *n* farrago, hash, hotchpotch, jumble, medley, miscellany, mixture, ragout, stew.

hog *n* beast, glutton, pig; grunter, porker, swine.

hoggish *adj* brutish, filthy, gluttonish, piggish, swinish; grasping, greedy, mean, selfish, sordid.

hoist *vb* elevate, heave, lift, raise, rear. * *n* elevator, lift.

hold *vb* clasp, clinch, clutch, grasp, grip, seize; have, keep, occupy, possess, retain; bind, confine, control, detain, imprison, restrain, restrict; connect, fasten, fix, lock; arrest, check, stay, stop, suspend, withhold; continue, keep up, maintain, manage, prosecute, support, sustain; cherish, embrace, entertain; account, believe, consider, count, deem, entertain, esteem, judge, reckon, regard, think; accommodate, admit, carry, contain, receive, stow; assemble, conduct, convene; endure, last, persist, remain; adhere, cleave, cling, cohere, stick. * *n* anchor, bite, clasp, control,

embrace, foothold, grasp, grip, possession, retention, seizure; prop, stay, support; claim, footing, vantage point; castle, fort, fortification, fortress, stronghold, tower; locker, storage, storehouse.

hole *n* aperture, opening, perforation; abyss, bore, cave, cavern, cavity, chasm, depression, excavation, eye, hollow, pit, pore, void; burrow, cover, lair, retreat; den, hovel, kennel.

holiday *n* anniversary, celebration, feast, festival, festivity, fete, gala, recess, vacation.

holiness *n* blessedness, consecration, devotion, devoutness, godliness, piety, purity, religiousness, righteousness, sacredness, saintliness, sanctity, sinlessness.

hollow *vb* dig, excavate, groove, scoop. * *adj* cavernous, concave, depressed, empty, sunken, vacant, void; deceitful, faithless, false, false-hearted, hollow-hearted, hypocritical, insincere, pharisaical, treacherous, unfeeling; deep, low, muffled, reverberating, rumbling, sepulchral. * *n* basin, bowl, depression; cave, cavern, cavity, concavity, dent, dimple, dint, depression, excavation, hole, pit; canal, channel, cup, dimple, dig, groove, pocket, sag.

holocaust *n* carnage, destruction, devastation, genocide, massacre.

holy *adj* blessed, consecrated, dedicated, devoted, hallowed, sacred, sanctified; devout, godly, pious, pure, religious, righteous, saintlike, saintly, sinless, spiritual.

homage *n* allegiance, devotion, fealty, fidelity, loyalty; court, deference, duty, honour, obeisance, respect, reverence, service; adoration, devotion, worship.

home *adj* domestic, family; close, direct, effective, penetrating, pointed. * *n* abode, dwelling, seat, quarters, residence.

homely *adj* domestic, familiar, house-like; coarse, commonplace, homespun, inelegant, plain, simple, unattractive, uncomely, unpolished, unpretentious.

homespun *adj* coarse, homely, inelegant, plain, rude, rustic, unpolished.

homicide *n* manslaughter, murder.

homily *n* address, discourse, lecture, sermon.

homogeneous *adj* akin, alike, cognate, kindred, similar, uniform.

honest *adj* equitable, fair, faithful, honourable, open, straight, straightforward; conscientious, equitable, reliable, sound, square, true, trustworthy, trusty, uncorrupted, upright, virtuous; above-board, faithful, genuine, thorough, unadulterated; creditable, decent, proper, reputable, respectable, suitable; chaste, decent; candid, direct, frank, ingenuous, sincere, unreserved.

honesty *n* equity, fairness, faithfulness, fidelity, honour, integrity, justice, probity, trustiness, trustworthiness, uprightness; truth, truthfulness, veracity; genuineness, thoroughness; candour, frankness, ingenuousness, openness, sincerity, straightforwardness, unreserve.

honorary *adj* formal, nominal, titular, unofficial, unpaid.

honour *vb* dignify, exalt, glorify, grace; respect, revere, reverence, venerate; adore, hallow, worship; celebrate, commemorate, keep, observe. * *n* civility, deference, esteem, homage, respect, reverence, veneration; dignity, distinction, elevation, nobleness; consideration, credit, fame, glory, reputation; high-mindedness, honesty, integrity, magnanimity, probity, uprightness; chastity, purity, virtue; boast, credit, ornament, pride.

honourable *adj* elevated, famous, great, illustrious, noble; admirable, conscientious, fair, honest, just, magnanimous, true, trustworthy, upright, virtuous, worshipful; creditable, esteemed, estimable, equitable, proper, respected, reputable, right.

honours *n pl* dignities, distinctions, privilege, titles; adornments, beauties, decorations, glories; civilities.
hood *n* capuche, coif, cover, cowl, head.
hoodwink *vb* blind, blindfold; cloak, conceal, cover, hide; cheat, circumvent, cozen, deceive, delete, dupe, fool, gull, impose, overreach, trick.
hook *vb* catch, ensnare, entrap, hasp, snare; bend, curve. * *n* catch, clasp, fastener, hasp; snare, trap; cutter, grass-hook, reaper, reaping-hook, sickle.
hooked *adj* aquiline, bent, crooked, curved, hamate, unciform.
hoop *vb* clasp, encircle, enclose, surround. * *n* band, circlet, girdle, ring; crinoline, farthingale.
hoot *vb* boo, cry, jeer, shout, yell; condemn, decry, denounce, execrate, hiss. * *n* boo, cry, jeer, shout, yell.
hop *vb* bound, caper, frisk, jump, leap, skip, spring; dance, trip; halt, hobble, limp. * *n* bound, caper, dance, jump, leap, skip, spring.
hope *vb* anticipate, await, desire, expect, long; believe, rely, trust. * *n* confidence, belief, faith, reliance, sanguineness, sanguinity, trust; anticipation, desire, expectancy, expectation.
hopeful *adj* anticipatory, confident, expectant, fond, optimistic, sanguine; cheerful, encouraging, promising.
hopeless *adj* abject, crushed, depressed, despondent, despairing, desperate, disconsolate, downcast, forlorn, pessimistic, woebegone; abandoned, helpless, incurable, irremediable, remediless; impossible, impracticable, unachievable, unattainable.
horde *n* clan, crew, gang, troop; crowd, multitude, pack, throng.
horn *vb* gore, pierce. * *n* trumpet, wind instrument; beaker, drinking cup, cornucopia; spike, spur; cusp, prong, wing.
horrid *adj* alarming, awful, bristling, dire, dreadful, fearful, frightful, harrowing, hideous, horrible, horrific, horrifying, rough, terrible, terrific; abominable, disagreeable, disgusting, odious, offensive, repulsive, revolting, shocking, unpleasant, vile.
horrify *vb* affright, alarm, frighten, shock, terrify, terrorise.
horror *n* alarm, awe, consternation, dismay, dread, fear, fright, panic; abhorrence, abomination, antipathy, aversion, detestation, disgust, hatred, loathing, repugnance, revulsion; shuddering.
horse *n* charger, cob, colt, courser, filly, gelding, mare, nag, pad, palfrey, pony, stallion, steed; cavalry, horseman; buck, clotheshorse, frame, sawhorse, stand, support.
horseman *n* cavalier, equestrian, rider; cavalryman, chasseur, dragoon, horse-soldier.
hospitable *adj* attentive, bountiful, kind; bountiful, cordial, generous, liberal, open, receptive, sociable, unconstrained, unreserved.
host[1] *n* entertainer, innkeeper, landlord, master of ceremonies, presenter, proprietor, owner, receptionist.
host[2] *n* array, army, legion; assemblage, assembly, horde, multitude, throng.
host[3] *n* altar bread, bread, consecrated bread, loaf, wafer.
hostile *adj* inimical, unfriendly, warlike; adverse, antagonistic, contrary, opposed, opposite, repugnant.
hostilities *n pl* conflict, fighting, war, warfare.
hostility *n* animosity, antagonism, enmity, hatred, ill-will, unfriendliness; contrariness, opposition, repugnance, variance.
hot *adj* burning, fiery, scalding; boiling, flaming, heated, incandescent, parching, roasting, torrid; heated, oppressive, sweltering, warm; angry, choleric, excitable, furious, hasty, impatient, impetuous, irascible, lustful, passionate, touchy, urgent, violent; animated, ardent, eager, fervent, fervid, glowing, passionate, vehement; acrid, biting, highly flavoured, highly seasoned, peppery, piquant, pungent, sharp, stinging.
hotchpotch *n* farrago, jumble, hodgepodge, medley, miscellany, stew.
hotel *n* inn, public house, tavern.
hot-headed *adj* furious, headlong, headstrong, hot-brained, impetuous, inconsiderate, passionate, precipitate, rash, reckless, vehement, violent.
hound *vb* drive, incite, spur, urge; bate, chase, goad, harass, harry, hunt, pursue.
house *vb* harbour, lodge, protect, shelter. * *n* abode, domicile, dwelling, habitation, home, mansion, residence; building, edifice; family, household; kindred, race, lineage, tribe; company, concern, firm, partnership; hotel, inn, public house, tavern.
housing *n* accommodation, dwellings, houses; casing, container, covering, protection, shelter.
hovel *n* cabin, cot, den, hole, hut, shed.
hover *vb* flutter; hang; vacillate, waver.
however *adv* but, however, nevertheless, notwithstanding, still, though, yet.
howl *vb* bawl, cry, lament, ululate, weep, yell, yowl. * *n* cry, yell, ululation.
hoyden *n* romp, tomboy.
hoydenish *adj* bad-mannered, boisterous, bold, ill-behaved, ill-taught, inelegant, romping, rough, rude, rustic, tomboyish, uncouth, ungenteel, unladylike, unruly.
hubbub *n* clamour, confusion, din, disorder, disturbance, hullabaloo, racket, riot, outcry, tumult, uproar.
huckster *n* hawker, peddler, retailer.
huddle *vb* cluster, crowd, gather; crouch, curl up, nestle, snuggle. * *n* confusion, crowd, disorder, disturbance, jumble, tumult.
hue *n* cast, colour, complexion, dye, shade, tinge, tint, tone.
huff *vb* blow, breathe, exhale, pant, puff. * *n* anger, fume, miff, passion, pet, quarrel, rage, temper, tiff.
hug *vb* clasp, cling, cuddle, embrace, grasp, grip, squeeze; cherish, nurse, retain. * *n* clasp, cuddle, embrace, grasp, squeeze.
huge *adj* bulky, colossal, Cyclopean, elephantine, enormous, gigantic, herculean, immense, stupendous, vast.
huggermugger *adj* clandestine, secret, sly; base, contemptible, mean, unfair; confused, disorderly, slovenly.
hull *vb* husk, peel, shell. * *n* covering, husk, rind, shell.
hullabaloo *n* clamour, confusion, din, disturbance, hubbub, outcry, racket, vociferation, uproar.
hum *vb* buzz, drone, murmur; croon, sing.
humane *adj* accommodating, benevolent, benign, charitable, clement, compassionate, gentle, good-hearted, kind, kind-hearted, lenient, merciful, obliging, tender, sympathetic; cultivating, elevating, humanizing, refining, rational, spiritual.
humanity *n* benevolence, benignity, charity, fellow-feeling, humaneness, kind-heartedness, kindness, philanthropy, sympathy, tenderness; humankind, mankind, mortality.
humanize *vb* civilize, cultivate, educate, enlighten, improve, polish, reclaim, refine, soften.
humble *vb* abase, abash, break, crush, debase, degrade, disgrace, humiliate, lower, mortify, reduce, sink, subdue. * *adj* meek, modest, lowly, simple, submissive, unambitious, unassuming, unobtrusive, unostentatious, unpretending; low, obscure, mean, plain, poor, small, undistinguished, unpretentious.
humbug *vb* cheat, cozen, deceive, hoax, swindle, trick. * *n* cheat, dodge, gammon, hoax, imposition, imposture, deception, fraud, trick; cant, charlatanism, charlatanry, hypocrisy, mummery, quackery; charlatan, impostor, fake, quack.
humdrum *adj* boring, dronish, dreary, dry, dull, monotonous, prosy, stupid, tedious, tiresome, wearisome.
humid *adj* damp, dank, moist, wet.
humiliate *vb* abase, abash, debase, degrade, depress, humble, mortify, shame.
humiliation *n* abasement, affront, condescension, crushing, degradation, disgrace, dishonouring, humbling, indignity, mortification, self-abasement, submissiveness, resignation.
humility *n* diffidence, humbleness, lowliness, meekness, modesty, self-abasement, submissiveness.
humorist *n* comic, comedian, droll, jester, joker, wag, wit.
humorous *adj* comic, comical, droll, facetious, funny, humorous, jocose, jocular, laughable, ludicrous, merry, playful, pleasant, sportive, whimsical, witty.

humour *vb* favour, gratify, indulge. * *n* bent, bias, disposition, predilection, prosperity, temper, vein; mood, state; caprice, crotchet, fancy, freak, vagary, whim, whimsy, wrinkle; drollery, facetiousness, fun, jocoseness, jocularity, pleasantry, wit; fluid, moisture, vapour.

hunch *vb* arch, jostle, nudge, punch, push, shove. * *n* bunch, hump, knob, protuberance; nudge, punch, push, shove; feeling, idea, intuition, premonition.

hungry *adj* covetous, craving, desirous, greedy; famished, starved, starving; barren, poor, unfertile, unproductive.

hunk *n* chunk, hunch, lump, slice.

hunt *vb* chase, drive, follow, hound, pursue, stalk, trap, trail; poach, shoot; search, seek. * *n* chase, field-sport, hunting, pursuit.

hurl *vb* cast, dart, fling, pitch, project, send, sling, throw, toss.

hurly-burly *n* bustle, commotion, confusion, disturbance, hurl, hurly, uproar, tumult, turmoil.

hurricane *n* cyclone, gale, storm, tempest, tornado, typhoon.

hurried *adj* cursory, hasty, slight, superficial.

hurry *vb* drive, precipitate; dispatch, expedite, hasten, quicken, speed; haste, scurry. * *n* agitation, bustle, confusion, flurry, flutter, perturbation, precipitation; celerity, haste, dispatch, expedition, promptitude, promptness, quickness.

hurt *vb* damage, disable, disadvantage, harm, impair, injure, mar; bruise, pain, wound; afflict, grieve, offend; ache, smart, throb. * *n* damage, detriment, disadvantage, harm, injury, mischief; ache, bruise, pain, suffering, wound.

hurtful *adj* baleful, baneful, deleterious, destructive, detrimental, disadvantageous, harmful, injurious, mischievous, noxious, pernicious, prejudicial, unwholesome.

husband *vb* economize, hoard, save, store.

husbandry *n* agriculture, cultivation, farming, geoponics, tillage; economy, frugality, thrift.

hush *vb* quiet, repress, silence, still, suppress; appease, assuage, calm, console, quiet, still. * *n* quiet, quietness, silence, stillness.

hypocrite *n* deceiver, dissembler, impostor, pretender.

hypocritical *adj* deceiving, dissembling, false, insincere, spurious, two-faced.

hypothesis *n* assumption, proposition, supposition, theory.

hypothetical *adj* assumed, imaginary, supposed, theoretical.

hysterical *adj* frantic, frenzied, overwrought, uncontrollable; comical, uproarious.

I

ice *vb* chill, congeal, freeze. * *n* crystal; frosting, sugar.

icy *adj* glacial; chilling, cold, frosty; cold-hearted, distant, frigid, indifferent, unemotional.

idea *n* archetype, essence, exemplar, ideal, model, pattern, plan, model; fantasy, fiction, image, imagination; apprehension, conceit, conception, fancy, illusion, impression, thought; belief, judgement, notion, opinion, sentiment, supposition.

ideal *adj* intellectual, mental; chimerical, fancied, fanciful, fantastic, illusory, imaginary, unreal, visionary, shadowy; complete, consummate, excellent, perfect; impractical, unattainable, utopian. * *n* criterion, example, model, standard.

identical *adj* equivalent, same, selfsame, tantamount.

identity *n* existence, individuality, personality, sameness.

ideology *n* belief, creed, dogma, philosophy, principle.

idiocy *n* fatuity, feebleness, foolishness, imbecility, insanity.

idiosyncrasy *n* caprice, eccentricity, fad, peculiarity, singularity.

idiot *n* blockhead, booby, dunce, fool, ignoramus, imbecile, simpleton.

idiotic *adj* fatuous, foolish, imbecile, irrational, senseless, sottish, stupid.

idle *adj* inactive, unemployed, unoccupied, vacant; indolent, inert, lazy, slothful, sluggish; abortive, bootless, fruitless, futile, groundless, ineffectual, unavailing, useless, vain; foolish, frivolous, trashy, trifling, trivial, unimportant, unprofitable. * *vb* dally, dawdle, laze, loiter, potter, waste; drift, shirk, slack.

idler *n* dawdler, doodle, drone, laggard, lazybones, loafer, lounger, slacker, slowcoach, sluggard, trifler.

idol *n* deity, god, icon, image, pagan, simulacrum, symbol; delusion, falsity, pretender, sham; beloved, darling, favourite, pet.

idolater *n* heathen, pagan; admirer, adorer, worshipper.

idolize *vb* canonize, deify; adore, honour, love, reverence, venerate.

idyll *n* eclogue, pastoral.

if *conj* admitting, allowing, granting, provided, supposing, though, whether. * *n* condition, hesitation, uncertainty.

igneous *adj* combustible, combustive, conflagrative, fiery, molten.

ignite *vb* burn, inflame, kindle, light, torch.

ignoble *adj* base-born, low, low-born, mean, peasant, plebeian, rustic, vulgar; contemptible, degraded, insignificant, mean, worthless; disgraceful, dishonourable, infamous, low, unworthy.

ignominious *adj* discreditable, disgraceful, dishonourable, disreputable, infamous, opprobrious, scandalous, shameful; base, contemptible, despicable.

ignominy *n* abasement, contempt, discredit, disgrace, dishonour disrepute, infamy, obloquy, odium, opprobrium, scandal, shame.

ignoramus *n* blockhead, duffer, dunce, fool, greenhorn, novice, numskull, simpleton.

ignorance *n* benightedness, darkness, illiteracy, nescience, rusticity; blindness, unawareness.

ignorant *adj* blind, illiterate, nescient, unaware, unconversant, uneducated, unenlightened, uninformed, uninstructed, unlearned, unread, untaught, untutored, unwitting.

ignore *vb* disregard, neglect, overlook, reject, skip.

ill *adj* bad, evil, faulty, harmful, iniquitous, naughty, unfavourable, unfortunate, unjust, wicked; ailing, diseased, disordered, indisposed, sick, unwell, wrong; crabbed, cross, hateful, malicious, malevolent, peevish, surly, unkind, ill-bred; ill-favoured, ugly, unprepossessing. * *adv* badly, poorly, unfortunately. * *n* badness, depravity, evil, mischief, misfortune, wickedness; affliction, ailment, calamity, harm, misery, pain, trouble.

ill-advised *adj* foolish, ill-judged, imprudent, injudicious, unwise.

ill-bred *adj* discourteous, ill-behaved, ill-mannered, impolite, rude, uncivil, uncourteous, uncourtly, uncouth.

illegal *adj* contraband, forbidden, illegitimate, illicit, prohibited, unauthorized, unlawful, unlicensed.

illegible *adj* indecipherable, obscure, undecipherable, unreadable.

illegitimate *adj* bastard, misbegotten, natural.

ill-fated *adj* ill-starred, luckless, unfortunate, unlucky.

ill-favoured *adj* homely, ugly, offensive, plain, unpleasant.

ill humour *n* fretfulness, ill-temper, peevishness, petulance, testiness.

illiberal *adj* close, close-fisted, covetous, mean, miserly, narrow, niggardly, parsimonious, penurious, selfish, sordid, stingy, ungenerous; bigoted, narrow-minded, uncharitable, ungentlemanly, vulgar.

illicit *adj* illegal, illegitimate, unauthorized, unlawful, unlegalized, unlicensed; criminal, guilty, forbidden, improper, wrong.

illimitable *adj* boundless, endless, immeasurable, immense, infinite, unbounded, unlimited, vast.

illiterate *adj* ignorant, uneducated, uninstructed, unlearned, unlettered, untaught, untutored.

ill-judged *adj* foolish, ill-advised, imprudent, injudicious, unwise.

ill-mannered *adj* discourteous, ill-behaved, ill-bred, impolite, rude, uncivil, uncourteous, uncourtly, uncouth, unpolished.

ill-natured *adj* disobliging, hateful, malevolent, unamiable, unfriendly, unkind; acrimonious, bitter, churlish, crabbed, cross, cross-grained, crusty, ill-tempered, morose, perverse, petulant, sour, spiteful, sulky, sullen, wayward.

illness *n* ailing, ailment, complaint, disease, disorder, distemper, indisposition, malady, sickness.

illogical *adj* absurd, fallacious, inconsistent, inconclusive, inconsequent, incorrect, invalid, unreasonable, unsound.

ill-proportioned *adj* awkward, ill-made, ill-shaped, misshapen, misproportioned, shapeless.

ill-starred *adj* ill-fated, luckless, unfortunate, unhappy, unlucky.

ill temper *n* bad temper, crabbedness, crossness, grouchiness, ill nature, moroseness, sulkiness, sullenness.

ill-tempered *adj* acrimonious, bad-tempered, crabbed, cross, grouchy, ill-natured, morose, sour, sulky, surly.

ill-timed *adj* inapposite, inopportune, irrelevant, unseasonable, untimely.

ill-treat *vb* abuse, ill-use, injure, maltreat, mishandle, misuse.

illude *vb* cheat, deceive, delude, disappoint, mock, swindle, trick.

illuminate *vb* illume, illumine, light; adorn, brighten, decorate, depict, edify, enlighten, inform, inspire, instruct, make wise.

illusion *n* chimera, deception, delusion, error, fallacy, false appearance, fantasy, hallucination, mockery, phantasm.

illusive, illusory *adj* barmecide, deceitful, deceptive, delusive, fallacious, imaginary, make-believe, mock, sham, unsatisfying, unreal, unsubstantial, visionary, tantalizing.

illustrate *vb* clarify, demonstrate, elucidate, enlighten, exemplify, explain; adorn, depict, draw.

illustration *n* demonstration, elucidation, enlightenment, exemplification, explanation, interpretation; adornment, decoration, picture.

illustrative *adj* elucidative, elucidatory, exemplifying.

illustrious *adj* bright, brilliant, glorious, radiant, splendid; celebrated, conspicuous, distinguished, eminent, famed, famous, noble, noted, remarkable, renowned, signal.

ill will *n* animosity, dislike, enmity, envy, grudge, hate, hatred, hostility, ill nature, malevolence, malice, malignity, rancour, spleen, spite, uncharitableness, unkindness, venom.

image *n* idol, statue; copy, effigy, figure, form, imago, likeness, picture, resemblance, representation, shape, similitude, simulacrum, statue, symbol; conception, counterpart, embodiment, idea, reflection.

imagery *n* dream, phantasm, phantom, vision.

imaginable *adj* assumable, cogitable, conceivable, conjecturable, plausible, possible, supposable, thinkable.

imaginary *adj* chimerical, dreamy, fancied, fanciful, fantastic, fictitious, ideal, illusive, illusory, invented, quixotic, shadowy, unreal, utopian, visionary, wild; assumed, conceivable, hypothetical, supposed.

imagination *n* chimera, conception, fancy, fantasy, invention, unreality; position; contrivance, device, plot, scheme.

imaginative *adj* creative, dreamy, fanciful, inventive, poetical, plastic, visionary.

imagine *vb* conceive, dream, fancy, imagine, picture, pretend; contrive, create, devise, frame, invent, mould, project; assume, suppose, hypothesize; apprehend, assume, believe, deem, guess, opine, suppose, think.

imbecile *adj* cretinous, drivelling, fatuous, feeble, feeble-minded, foolish, helpless, idiotic, imbecilic, inane, infirm, witless. * *n* dotard, driveller.

imbecility *n* debility, feebleness, helplessness, infirmity, weakness; foolishness, idiocy, silliness, stupidity, weak-mindedness.

imbibe *vb* absorb, assimilate, drink, suck, swallow; acquire, gain, gather, get, receive.

imbroglio *n* complexity, complication, embarrassment, entanglement, misunderstanding.

imbrue *vb* drench, embrue, gain, moisten, soak, stain, steep, wet.

imbue *vb* colour, dye, stain, tincture, tinge, tint; bathe, impregnate, infuse, inoculate, permeate, pervade, provide, saturate, steep.

imitate *vb* copy, counterfeit, duplicate, echo, emulate, follow, forge, mirror, reproduce, simulate; ape, impersonate, mimic, mock, personate; burlesque, parody, travesty.

imitation *adj* artificial, fake, man-made, mock, reproduction, synthetic. * *n* aping, copying, imitation, mimicking, parroting; copy, duplicate, likeness, resemblance; mimicry, mocking; burlesque, parody, travesty.

imitative *adj* copying, emulative, imitating, mimetic, simulative; apeish, aping, mimicking.

imitator *n* copier, copycat, copyist, echo, impersonator, mimic, mimicker, parrot.

immaculate *adj* clean, pure, spotless, stainless, unblemished, uncontaminated, undefiled, unpolluted, unspotted, unsullied, untainted, untarnished; faultless, guiltless, holy, innocent, pure, saintly, sinless, stainless.

immanent *adj* congenital, inborn, indwelling, inherent, innate, internal, intrinsic, subjective.

immaterial *adj* bodiless, ethereal, extramundane, impalpable, incorporeal, mental, metaphysical, spiritual, unbodied, unfleshly, unsubstantial; inconsequential, insignificant, nonessential, unessential, unimportant.

immature *adj* crude, green, imperfect, raw, rudimental, rudimentary, unfinished, unformed, unprepared, unripe, unripened, youthful; hasty, premature, unseasonable, untimely.

immaturity *n* crudeness, crudity, greenness, imperfection, rawness, unpreparedness, unripeness.

immeasurable *adj* bottomless, boundless, illimitable, immense, infinite, limitless, measureless, unbounded, vast.

immediate *adj* close, contiguous, near, next, proximate; intuitive, primary, unmeditated; direct, instant, instantaneous, present, pressing, prompt.

immediately *adv* closely, proximately; directly, forthwith, instantly, presently, presto, pronto.

immemorial *adj* ancient, hoary, olden.

immense *adj* boundless, illimitable, infinite, interminable, measureless, unbounded, unlimited; colossal, elephantine, enormous, gigantic, huge, large, monstrous, mountainous, prodigious, stupendous, titanic, tremendous, vast.

immensity *n* boundlessness, endlessness, limitlessness, infiniteness, infinitude, infinity; amplitude, enormity, greatness, hugeness, magnitude, vastness.

immerse *vb* baptize, bathe, dip, douse, duck, overwhelm, plunge, sink, souse, submerge; absorb, engage, engross, involve.

immersion *n* dipping, immersing, plunging; absorption, engagement; disappearance; baptism.

imminent *adj* close, impending, near, overhanging, threatening; alarming, dangerous, perilous.

immobile *adj* fixed, immovable, inflexible, motionless, quiescent, stable, static, stationary, steadfast; dull, expressionless, impassive, rigid, stiff, stolid.

immobility *n* fixedness, fixity, immovability, immovableness, motionlessness, stability, steadfastness, unmovableness; dullness, expressionlessness, inflexibility, rigidity, stiffness, stolidity.

immoderate *adj* excessive, exorbitant, extravagant, extreme, inordinate, intemperate, unreasonable.

immodest *adj* coarse, gross, indecorous, indelicate, lewd, shameless; bold, brazen, forward, impudent, indecent; broad, filthy, impure, indecent, obscene, smutty, unchaste.

immodesty *n* coarseness, grossness, indecorum, indelicacy, shamelessness; impurity, lewdness, obscenity, smuttiness, unchastity; boldness, brass, forwardness, impatience.

immolate *vb* kill, sacrifice.

immoral *adj* antisocial, corrupt, loose, sinful, unethical, vicious, wicked, wrong; bad, depraved, dissolute, profligate, unprincipled; abandoned, indecent, licentious.

immorality *n* corruption, corruptness, criminality, demoralization, depravity, impurity, profligacy, sin, sinfulness, vice, wickedness; wrong.

immortal *adj* deathless, ever-living, imperishable, incorruptible, indestructible, indissoluble, never-dying, undying, unfading; ceaseless, continuing, eternal, endless, everlasting, never-ending, perpetual, sempiternal; abiding, enduring, lasting, permanent. * *n* god, goddess; genius, hero.

immortality *n* deathlessness, incorruptibility, incorruptibleness, indestructibility; perpetuity.

immortalize *vb* apotheosize, enshrine, glorify, perpetuate.
immovable *adj* firm, fixed, immobile, stable, stationary; impassive, steadfast, unalterable, unchangeable, unshaken, unyielding.
immunity *n* exemption, exoneration, freedom, release; charter, franchise, liberty, license, prerogative, privilege, right.
immure *vb* confine, entomb, imprison, incarcerate.
immutability *n* constancy, inflexibility, invariability, invariableness, permanence, stability, unalterableness, unchangeableness.
immutable *adj* constant, fixed, inflexible, invariable, permanent, stable, unalterable, unchangeable, undeviating.
imp *n* demon, devil, elf, flibbertigibbet, hobgoblin, scamp, sprite; graft, scion, shoot.
impact *vb* collide, crash, strike. * *n* brunt, impression, impulse, shock, stroke, touch; collision, contact, impinging, striking.
impair *vb* blemish, damage, deface, deteriorate, injure, mar, ruin, spoil, vitiate; decrease, diminish, lessen, reduce; enervate, enfeeble, weaken.
impale *vb* hole, pierce, puncture, spear, spike, stab, transfix.
impalpable *adj* attenuated, delicate, fine, intangible; imperceptible, inapprehensible, incorporeal, indistinct, shadowy, unsubstantial.
impart *vb* bestow, confer, give, grant; communicate, disclose, discover, divulge, relate, reveal, share, tell.
impartial *adj* candid, disinterested, dispassionate, equal, equitable, even-handed, fair, honourable, just, unbiased, unprejudiced, unwarped.
impassable *adj* blocked, closed, impenetrable, impermeable, impervious, inaccessible, pathless, unattainable, unnavigable, unreachable.
impassioned *adj* animated, ardent, burning, excited, fervent, fervid, fiery, glowing, impetuous, intense, passionate, vehement, warm, zealous.
impassive *adj* calm, passionless; apathetic, callous, indifferent, insensible, insusceptible, unfeeling, unimpressible, unsusceptible.
impassivity *n* calmness, composure, indifference, insensibility, insusceptibility, passionlessness, stolidity.
impatience *n* disquietude, restlessness, uneasiness; eagerness, haste, impetuosity, precipitation, vehemence; heat, irritableness, irritability, violence.
impatient *adj* restless, uneasy, unquiet; eager, hasty, impetuous, precipitate, vehement; abrupt, brusque, choleric, fretful, hot, intolerant, irritable, peevish, sudden, testy, violent.
impeach *vb* accuse, arraign, charge, indict; asperse, censure, denounce, disparage, discredit, impair, impute, incriminate, lessen.
impeachment *n* accusation, arraignment, indictment; aspersion, censure, disparagement, imputation, incrimination, reproach.
impeccable *adj* faultless, immaculate, incorrupt, innocent, perfect, pure, sinless, stainless, uncorrupt.
impede *vb* bar, block, check, clog, curb, delay, encumber, hinder, interrupt, obstruct, restrain, retard, stop, thwart.
impediment *n* bar, barrier, block, check, curb, difficulty, encumbrance, hindrance, obstacle, obstruction, stumbling block.
impel *vb* drive, push, send, urge; actuate, animate, compel, constrain, embolden, incite, induce, influence, instigate, move, persuade, stimulate.
impend *vb* approach, menace, near, threaten.
impending *adj* approaching, imminent, menacing, near, threatening.
impenetrable *adj* impermeable, impervious, inaccessible; cold, dull, impassive, indifferent, obtuse, senseless, stolid, unsympathetic; dense, proof.
impenitence *n* hardheartedness, impenitency, impenitentness, obduracy, stubbornness.
impenitent *adj* hardened, hard-hearted, incorrigible, irreclaimable, obdurate, recusant, relentless, seared, stubborn, uncontrite, unconverted, unrepentant.
imperative *adj* authoritative, commanding, despotic, domineering, imperious, overbearing, peremptory, urgent; binding, obligatory.
imperceptible *adj* inaudible, indiscernible, indistinguishable, invisible; fine, impalpable, inappreciable, gradual, minute.
imperfect *adj* abortive, crude, deficient, garbled, incomplete, poor; defective, faulty, impaired.
imperfection *n* defectiveness, deficiency, faultiness, incompleteness; blemish, defect, fault, flaw, lack, stain, taint; failing, foible, frailty, limitation, vice, weakness.
imperial *adj* kingly, regal, royal, sovereign; august, consummate, exalted, grand, great, kingly, magnificent, majestic, noble, regal, royal, queenly, supreme, sovereign, supreme, consummate.
imperil *vb* endanger, expose, hazard, jeopardize, risk.
imperious *adj* arrogant, authoritative, commanding, compelling, despotic, dictatorial, domineering, haughty, imperative, lordly, magisterial, overbearing, tyrannical, urgent, compelling.
imperishable *adj* eternal, everlasting, immortal, incorruptible, indestructible, never-ending, perennial, unfading.
impermeable *adj* impenetrable, impervious.
impermissible *adj* deniable, insufferable, objectionable, unallowable, unallowed, unlawful.
impersonate *vb* act, ape, enact, imitate, mimic, mock, personate; embody, incarnate, personify, typify.
impersonation *n* incarnation, manifestation, personification; enacting, imitation, impersonating, mimicking, personating, representation.
impertinence *n* irrelevance, irrelevancy, unfitness, impropriety; assurance, boldness, brass, brazenness, effrontery, face, forwardness, impudence, incivility, insolence, intrusiveness, presumption, rudeness, sauciness, pertness.
impertinent *adj* inapplicable, inapposite, irrelevant; bold, forward, impudent, insolent, intrusive, malapert, meddling, officious, pert, rude, saucy, unmannerly.
imperturbability *n* calmness, collectedness, composure, dispassion, placidity, placidness, sedateness, serenity, steadiness, tranquility.
imperturbable *adj* calm, collected, composed, cool, placid, sedate, serene, tranquil, unmoved, undisturbed, unexcitable, unmoved, unruffled.
impervious *adj* impassable, impenetrable, impermeable.
impetuosity *n* force, fury, haste, precipitancy, vehemence, violence.
impetuous *adj* ardent, boisterous, brash, breakneck, fierce, fiery, furious, hasty, headlong, hot, hot-headed, impulsive, overzealous, passionate, precipitate, vehement, violent.
impetus *n* energy, force, momentum, propulsion.
impiety *n* irreverence, profanity, ungodliness; iniquity, sacreligiousness, sin, sinfulness, ungodliness, unholiness, unrighteousness, wickedness.
impinge *vb* clash, dash, encroach, hit, infringe, strike, touch.
impious *adj* blasphemous, godless, iniquitous, irreligious, irreverent, profane, sinful, ungodly, unholy, unrighteous, wicked.
implacable *adj* deadly, inexorable, merciless, pitiless, rancorous, relentless, unappeasable, unforgiving, unpropitiating, unrelenting.
implant *vb* ingraft, infix, insert, introduce, place.
implement *vb* effect, execute, fulfil. * *n* appliance, instrument, tool, utensil.
implicate *vb* entangle, enfold; compromise, concern, entangle, include, involve.
implication *n* entanglement, involvement, involution; connotation, hint, inference, innuendo, intimation; conclusion, meaning, significance.
implicit *adj* implied, inferred, understood; absolute, constant, firm, steadfast, unhesitating, unquestioning, unreserved, unshaken.
implicitly *adv* by implication, silently, tacitly, unspokenly, virtually, wordlessly.
implore *vb* adjure, ask, beg, beseech, entreat, petition, pray, solicit, supplicate.
imply *vb* betoken, connote, denote, import, include, infer, insinuate, involve, mean, presuppose, signify.
impolicy *n* folly, imprudence, ill-judgement, indiscretion, inexpediency.
impolite *adj* bearish, boorish, discourteous, disrespectful, ill-bred, insolent, rough, rude, uncivil, uncourteous, ungentle, ungentlemanly, ungracious, unmannerly, unpolished, unrefined.
impoliteness *n* boorishness, discourteousness, discourtesy, disrespect, ill-breeding, incivility, insolence, rudeness, unmannerliness.

impolitic *adj* ill-advised, imprudent, indiscreet, inexpedient, injudicious, unwise.

import *vb* bring in, introduce, transport; betoken, denote, imply, mean, purport, signify. * *n* goods, importation, merchandise; bearing, drift, gist, intention, interpretation, matter, meaning, purpose, sense, signification, spirit, tenor; consequence, importance, significance, weight.

importance *n* concern, consequence, gravity, import, moment, momentousness, significance, weight, weightiness; consequence, pomposity, self-importance.

important *adj* considerable, grave, material, momentous, notable, pompous, ponderous, serious, significant, urgent, valuable, weighty; esteemed, influential, prominent, substantial; consequential, pompous, self-important.

importunate *adj* busy, earnest, persistent, pertinacious, pressing, teasing, troublesome, urgent.

importune *vb* ask, beset, dun, ply, press, solicit, urge.

importunity *n* appeal, beseechment, entreaty, petition, plying, prayer, pressing, suit, supplication, urging; contention, insistence; urgency.

impose *vb* lay, place, put, set; appoint, charge, dictate, enjoin, force, inflict, obtrude, prescribe, tax; (*with* **on, upon**) abuse, cheat, circumvent, deceive, delude, dupe, exploit, hoax, trick, victimize.

imposing *adj* august, commanding, dignified, exalted, grand, grandiose, impressive, lofty, magnificent, majestic, noble, stately, striking.

imposition *n* imposing, laying, placing, putting; burden, charge, constraint, injunction, levy, oppression, tax; artifice, cheating, deception, dupery, fraud, imposture, trickery.

impossibility *n* hopelessness, impracticability, inability, infeasibility, unattainability; inconceivability.

impossible *adj* hopeless, impracticable, infeasible, unachievable, unattainable; inconceivable, self-contradictory, unthinkable.

impost *n* custom, duty, excise, rate, tax, toil, tribute.

impostor *n* charlatan, cheat, counterfeiter, deceiver, double-dealer, humbug, hypocrite, knave, mountebank, pretender, quack, rogue, trickster.

imposture *n* artifice, cheat, deceit, deception, delusion, dodge, fraud, hoax, imposition, ruse, stratagem, trick, wile.

impotence *n* disability, feebleness, frailty, helplessness, inability, incapability, incapacity, incompetence, inefficaciousness, inefficacy, inefficiency, infirmity, powerlessness, weakness.

impotent *adj* disabled, enfeebled, feeble, frail, helpless, incapable, incapacitated, incompetent, inefficient, infirm, nerveless, powerless, unable, weak; barren, sterile.

impound *vb* confine, coop, engage, imprison.

impoverish *vb* beggar, pauperize; deplete, exhaust, ruin.

impracticability *n* impossibility, impracticableness, impracticality, infeasibility, unpracticability.

impracticable *adj* impossible, infeasible; intractable, obstinate, recalcitrant, stubborn, thorny, unmanageable; impassable, insurmountable.

impracticality *n* impossibility, impracticableness, impractibility, infeasibility, unpracticability; irrationality, unpracticalness, unrealism, unreality, unreasonableness.

imprecate *vb* anathematize, curse, execrate, invoke, maledict.

imprecation *n* anathema, curse, denunciation, execration, invocation, malediction.

imprecatory *adj* appealing, beseeching, entreating, imploratory, imploring, imprecatory, pleading; cursing, damnatory, execrating, maledictory.

impregnable *adj* immovable, impenetrable, indestructible, invincible, inviolable, invulnerable, irrefrangible, secure, unconquerable, unassailable, unyielding.

impregnate *vb* fecundate, fertilize, fructify; dye, fill, imbrue, imbue, infuse, permeate, pervade, saturate, soak, tincture, tinge.

impress *vb* engrave, imprint, print, stamp; affect, move, strike; fix, inculcate; draft, enlist, levy, press, requisition. * *n* impression, imprint, mark, print, seal, stamp; cognizance, device, emblem, motto, symbol.

impressibility *n* affectibility, impressionability, pliancy, receptiveness, responsiveness, sensibility, sensitiveness, susceptibility.

impressible *adj* affectible, excitable, impressionable, pliant, receptive, responsive, sensitive, soft, susceptible, tender.

impression *n* edition, imprinting, printing, stamping; brand, dent, impress, mark, stamp; effect, influence, sensation; fancy, idea, instinct, notion, opinion, recollection.

impressive *adj* affecting, effective, emphatic, exciting, forcible, moving, overpowering, powerful, solemn, speaking, splendid, stirring, striking, telling, touching.

imprint *vb* engrave, mark, print, stamp; impress, inculcate. * *n* impression, mark, print, sign, stamp.

imprison *vb* confine, jail, immure, incarcerate, shut up.

imprisonment *n* captivity, commitment, confinement, constraint, durance, duress, incarceration, restraint.

improbability *n* doubt, uncertainty, unlikelihood.

improbable *adj* doubtful, uncertain, unlikely, unplausible.

improbity *n* dishonesty, faithlessness, fraud, fraudulence, knavery, unfairness.

impromptu *adj* extempore, improvised, offhand, spontaneous, unpremeditated, unprepared, unrehearsed. * *adv* extemporaneously, extemporarily, extempore, offhand, ad-lib.

improper *adj* immodest, inapposite, inappropriate, irregular, unadapted, unapt, unfit, unsuitable, unsuited; indecent, indecorous, indelicate, unbecoming, unseemly; erroneous, inaccurate, incorrect, wrong.

impropriety *n* inappropriateness, unfitness, unsuitability, unsuitableness; indecorousness, indecorum, unseemliness.

improve *vb* ameliorate, amend, better, correct, edify, meliorate, mend, rectify, reform; cultivate; gain, mend, progress; enhance, increase, rise.

improvement *n* ameliorating, amelioration, amendment, bettering, improving, meliorating, melioration; advancement, proficiency, progress.

improvidence *n* imprudence, thriftlessness, unthriftiness.

improvident *adj* careless, heedless, imprudent, incautious, inconsiderate, negligent, prodigal, rash, reckless, shiftless, thoughtless, thriftless, unthrifty, wasteful.

improvisation *n* ad-libbing, contrivance, extemporaneousness, extemporariness, extemporization, fabrication, invention; (*mus*) extempore, impromptu.

improvise *vb* ad-lib, contrive, extemporize, fabricate, imagine, invent.

imprudence *n* carelessness, heedlessness, improvidence, incautiousness, inconsideration, indiscretion, rashness.

imprudent *adj* careless, heedless, ill-advised, ill-judged, improvident, incautious, inconsiderate, indiscreet, rash, unadvised, unwise.

impudence *n* assurance, audacity, boldness, brashness, brass, bumptiousness, cheek, cheekiness, effrontery, face, flippancy, forwardness, front, gall, impertinence, insolence, jaw, lip, nerve, pertness, presumption, rudeness, sauciness, shamelessness.

impudent *adj* bold, bold-faced, brazen, brazen-faced, cool, flippant, forward, immodest, impertinent, insolent, insulting, pert, presumptuous, rude, saucy, shameless.

impugn *vb* assail, attack, challenge, contradict, dispute, gainsay, oppose, question, resist.

impulse *n* force, impetus, impelling, momentum, push, thrust; appetite, inclination, instinct, passion, proclivity; incentive, incitement, influence, instigation, motive, instigation.

impulsive *adj* impelling, moving, propulsive; emotional, hasty, heedless, hot, impetuous, mad-cap, passionate, quick, rash, vehement, violent.

impunity *n* exemption, immunity, liberty, licence, permission, security.

impure *adj* defiled, dirty, feculent, filthy, foul, polluted, unclean; bawdy, coarse, immodest, gross, immoral, indelicate, indecent, lewd, licentious, loose, obscene, ribald, smutty, unchaste; adulterated, corrupt, mixed.

impurity *n* defilement, feculence, filth, foulness, pollution, uncleanness; admixture, coarseness, grossness, immodesty, indecency, indelicacy, lewdness, licentiousness, looseness, obscenity, ribaldry, smut, smuttiness, unchastity, vulgarity.

imputable *adj* ascribable, attributable, chargeable, owing, referable, traceable, owing.

imputation *n* attributing, charging, imputing; accusation, blame, censure, charge, reproach.

impute *vb* ascribe, attribute, charge, consider, imply, insinuate, refer.

inability *n* impotence, incapacity, incapability, incompetence, incompetency, inefficiency; disability, disqualification.

inaccessible *adj* unapproachable, unattainable.

inaccuracy *n* erroneousness, impropriety, incorrectness, inexactness; blunder, defect, error, fault, mistake.

inaccurate *adj* defective, erroneous, faulty, incorrect, inexact, mistaken, wrong.

inaccurately *adv* carelessly, cursorily, imprecisely, incorrectly, inexactly, mistakenly, unprecisely, wrongly.

inactive *adj* inactive; dormant, inert, inoperative, peaceful, quiet, quiescent; dilatory, drowsy, dull, idle, inanimate, indolent, inert, lazy, lifeless, lumpish, passive, slothful, sleepy, stagnant, supine.

inactivity *n* dilatoriness, idleness, inaction, indolence, inertness, laziness, sloth, sluggishness, supineness, torpidity, torpor.

inadequacy *n* inadequateness, insufficiency; defectiveness, imperfection, incompetence, incompetency, incompleteness, insufficiency, unfitness, unsuitableness.

inadequate *adj* disproportionate, incapable, insufficient, unequal; defective, imperfect, inapt, incompetent, incomplete.

inadmissible *adj* improper, incompetent, unacceptable, unallowable, unqualified, unreasonable.

inadvertence, inadvertency *n* carelessness, heedlessness, inattention, inconsiderateness, negligence, thoughtlessness; blunder, error, oversight, slip.

inadvertent *adj* careless, heedless, inattentive, inconsiderate, negligent, thoughtless, unobservant.

inadvertently *adv* accidently, carelessly, heedlessly, inconsiderately, negligently, thoughtlessly, unintentionally.

inalienable *adj* undeprivable, unforfeitable, untransferable.

inane *adj* empty, fatuous, vacuous, void; foolish, frivolous, idiotic, puerile, senseless, silly, stupid, trifling, vain, worthless.

inanimate *adj* breathless, dead, extinct; dead, dull, inert, lifeless, soulless, spiritless.

inanition *n* emptiness, inanity, vacuity; exhaustion, hunger, malnutrition, starvation, want.

inanity *n* emptiness, foolishness, inanition, vacuity; folly, frivolousness, puerility, vanity, worthlessness.

inapplicable *adj* inapposite, inappropriate, inapt, irrelevant, unfit, unsuitable, unsuited.

inapposite *adj* impertinent, inapplicable, irrelevant, nonpertinent; inappropriate, unfit, unsuitable.

inappreciable *adj* impalpable, imperceptible, inconsiderable, inconspicuous, indiscernible, infinitesimal, insignificant, negligible, undiscernible, unnoticed.

inappropriate *adj* inapposite, unadapted, unbecoming, unfit, unsuitable, unsullied.

inapt *adj* inapposite, unapt, unfit, unsuitable; awkward, clumsy, dull, slow, stolid, stupid.

inaptitude *n* awkwardness, inapplicability, inappropriateness, inaptness, unfitness, unsuitableness.

inarticulate *adj* blurred, indistinct, thick; dumb, mute.

inartificial *adj* artless, direct, guileless, ingenuous, naive, simple, simple-minded, sincere, single-minded.

inasmuch as *conj* considering that, seeing that, since.

inattention *n* absent-mindedness, carelessness, disregard, heedlessness, inadvertence, inapplication, inconsiderateness, neglect, remissness, slip, thoughtlessness, unmindfulness, unobservance

inattentive *adj* absent-minded, careless, disregarding, heedless, inadvertent, inconsiderate, neglectful, remiss, thoughtless, unmindful, unobservant.

inaudible *adj* faint, indistinct, muffled; mute, noiseless, silent, still.

inaugurate *vb* induct, install, introduce, invest; begin, commence, initiate, institute, originate.

inauguration *n* beginning, commencement, initiation, institution, investiture, installation, opening, origination.

inauspicious *adj* bad, discouraging, ill-omened, ill-starred, ominous, unfavourable, unfortunate, unlucky, unpromising, unpropitious, untoward.

inborn *adj* congenital, inbred, ingrained, inherent, innate, instinctive, native, natural.

incalculable *adj* countless, enormous, immense, incalculable, inestimable, innumerable, sumless, unknown, untold.

incandescence *n* candescence, glow, gleam, luminousness, luminosity.

incandescent *adj* aglow, candent, candescent, gleaming, glowing, luminous, luminant, radiant.

incantation *n* charm, conjuration, enchantment, magic, necromancy, sorcery, spell, witchcraft, witchery.

incapability *n* disability, inability, incapacity, incompetence.

incapable *adj* feeble, impotent, incompetent, insufficient, unable, unfit, unfitted, unqualified, weak.

incapacious *adj* cramped, deficient, incommodious, narrow, scant.

incapacitate *vb* cripple, disable; disqualify, make unfit.

incapacity *n* disability, inability, incapability, incompetence; disqualification, unfitness.

incarcerate *vb* commit, confine, immure, imprison, jail, restrain, restrict.

incarnate *vb* body, embody, incorporate, personify. * *adj* bodied, embodied, incorporated, personified.

incarnation *n* embodiment, exemplification, impersonation, manifestation, personification.

incautious *adj* impolitic, imprudent, indiscreet, uncircumspect, unwary; careless, headlong, heedless, inconsiderate, negligent, rash, reckless, thoughtless.

incendiary *adj* dissentious, factious, inflammatory, seditious. * *n* agitator, firebrand, fire-raiser.

incense[1] *vb* anger, chafe, enkindle, enrage, exasperate, excite, heat, inflame, irritate, madden, provoke.

incense[2] *n* aroma, fragrance, perfume, scent; admiration, adulation, applause, laudation.

incentive *n* cause, encouragement, goad, impulse, incitement, inducement, instigation, mainspring, motive, provocation, spur, stimulus.

inception *n* beginning, commencement, inauguration, initiation, origin, rise, start.

incertitude *n* ambiguity, doubt, doubtfulness, indecision, uncertainty.

incessant *adj* ceaseless, constant, continual, continuous, eternal, everlasting, never-ending, perpetual, unceasing, unending, uninterrupted, unremitting.

inchoate *adj* beginning, commencing, inceptive, incipient, initial.

incident *n* circumstance, episode, event, fact, happening, occurrence. * *adj* happening; belonging, pertaining, appertaining, accessory, relating, natural; falling, impinging.

incidental *adj* accidental, casual, chance, concomitant, contingent, fortuitous, subordinate; adventitious, extraneous, nonessential, occasional.

incinerate *vb* burn, char, conflagrate, cremate, incremate.

incipient *adj* beginning, commencing, inchoate, inceptive, originating, starting.

incised *adj* carved, cut, engraved, gashed, graved, graven.

incision *n* cut, gash, notch, opening, penetration.

incisive *adj* cutting; acute, biting, sarcastic, satirical, sharp; acute, clear, distinct, penetrating, sharp-cut, trenchant.

incite *vb* actuate, animate, arouse, drive, encourage, excite, foment, goad, hound, impel, instigate, prod, prompt, provoke, push, rouse, spur, stimulate, urge.

incitement *n* encouragement, goad, impulse, incentive, inducement, motive, provocative, spur, stimulus.

incivility *n* discourteousness, discourtesy, disrespect, ill-breeding, ill-manners, impoliteness, impudence, inurbanity, rudeness, uncourtliness, unmannerliness.

inclemency *n* boisterousness, cruelty, harshness, rigour, roughness, severity, storminess, tempestuousness, tyranny.

inclement *adj* boisterous, harsh, rigorous, rough, severe, stormy; cruel, unmerciful.

inclination *n* inclining, leaning, slant, slope; trending, verging; aptitude, bent, bias, disposition, penchant, predilection, predisposition, proclivity, proneness, propensity, tendency, turn, twist; desire, fondness, liking, taste, partiality, predilection, wish; bow, nod, obeisance.

incline *vb* lean, slant, slope; bend, nod, verge; tend; bias, dispose, predispose, turn; bow. * *n* ascent, descent, grade, gradient, rise, slope.

inclose *see* **enclose**.

include *vb* contain, hold; comprehend, comprise, contain, cover, embody, embrace, incorporate, involve, take in.

inclusive *adj* comprehending, embracing, encircling, enclosing, including, taking in.

incognito, incognita *adj* camouflaged, concealed, disguised, unknown. * *n* camouflage, concealment, disguise.

incoherent *adj* detached, loose, nonadhesive, noncohesive; disconnected, incongruous, inconsequential, inconsistent, uncoordinated; confused, illogical, irrational, rambling, unintelligible, wild.

income *n* earnings, emolument, gains, interest, pay, perquisite, proceeds, profits, receipts, rents, return, revenue, salary, wages.

incommensurate *adj* disproportionate, inadequate, insufficient, unequal.

incommode *vb* annoy, discommode, disquiet, disturb, embarrass, hinder, inconvenience, molest, plague, trouble, upset, vex.

incommodious *adj* awkward, cumbersome, cumbrous, inconvenient, unhandy, unmanageable, unsuitable, unwieldy; annoying, disadvantageous, harassing, irritating, vexatious.

incommunicative *adj* exclusive, unsociable, unsocial, reserved.

incomparable *adj* matchless, inimitable, peerless, surpassing, transcendent, unequalled, unparalleled, unrivalled.

incompatibility *n* contrariety, contradictoriness, discrepancy, incongruity, inconsistency, irreconcilability, unsuitability, unsuitableness

incompatible *adj* contradictory, incongruous, inconsistent, inharmonious, irreconcilable, unadapted, unsuitable.

incompetence *n* inability, incapability, incapacity, incompetency; inadequacy, insufficiency; disqualification, unfitness.

incompetent *adj* incapable, unable; inadequate, insufficient; disqualified, incapacitated, unconstitutional, unfit, unfitted.

incomplete *adj* defective, deficient, imperfect, partial; inexhaustive, unaccompanied, uncompleted, unexecuted, unfinished.

incomprehensible *adj* inconceivable, inexhaustible, unfathomable, unimaginable; inconceivable, unintelligible, unthinkable.

incomputable *adj* enormous, immense, incalculable, innumerable, prodigious.

inconceivable *adj* incomprehensible, incredible, unbelievable, unimaginable, unthinkable.

inconclusive *adj* inconsequent, inconsequential, indecisive, unconvincing, illogical, unproved, unproven.

incongruity *n* absurdity, contradiction, contradictoriness, contrariety, discordance, discordancy, discrepancy, impropriety, inappropriateness, incoherence, incompatibility, inconsistency, unfitness, unsuitableness.

incongruous *adj* absurd, contradictory, contrary, disagreeing, discrepant, inappropriate, incoherent, incompatible, inconsistent, inharmonious, unfit, unsuitable.

inconsequent *adj* desultory, disconnected, fragmentary, illogical, inconclusive, inconsistent, irrelevant, loose.

inconsiderable *adj* immaterial, insignificant, petty, slight, small, trifling, trivial, unimportant.

inconsiderate *adj* intolerant, uncharitable, unthoughtful; careless, heedless, giddy, hare-brained, hasty, headlong, imprudent, inadvertent, inattentive, indifferent, indiscreet, light-headed, negligent, rash, thoughtless.

inconsistency *n* incoherence, incompatibility, incongruity, unsuitableness; contradiction, contrariety; changeableness, inconstancy, instability, vacillation, unsteadiness.

inconsistent *adj* different, discrepant, illogical, incoherent, incompatible, incongruous, inconsequent, inconsonant, irreconcilable, unsuitable; contradictory, contrary; changeable, fickle, inconstant, unstable, unsteady, vacillating, variable.

inconsolable *adj* comfortless, crushed, disconsolate, forlorn, heartbroken, hopeless, woebegone.

inconstancy *n* changeableness, mutability, variability, variation, fluctuation, faithlessness, fickleness, capriciousness, vacillation, uncertainty, unsteadiness, volatility.

inconstant *adj* capricious, changeable, faithless, fickle, fluctuating, mercurial, mutable, unsettled, unsteady, vacillating, variable, varying, volatile, wavering; mutable, uncertain, unstable.

incontestable *adj* certain, incontrovertible, indisputable, indubitable, irrefragible, sure, undeniable, unquestionable.

incontinence *n* excess, extravagance, indulgence, intemperance, irrepressibility, lasciviousness, lewdness, licentiousness, prodigality, profligacy, riotousness, unrestraint, wantonness, wildness.

incontinent *adj* debauched, lascivious, lewd, licentious, lustful, prodigal, unchaste, uncontrolled, unrestrained.

incontrovertible *adj* certain, incontestable, indisputable, indubitable, irrefutable, sure, undeniable, unquestionable.

inconvenience *vb* discommode; annoy, disturb, molest, trouble, vex. * *n* annoyance, disadvantage, disturbance, molestation, trouble, vexation; awkwardness, cumbersomeness, incommodiousness, unwieldiness; unfitness, unseasonableness, unsuitableness.

inconvenient *adj* annoying, awkward, cumbersome, cumbrous, disadvantageous, incommodious, inopportune, troublesome, uncomfortable, unfit, unhandy, unmanageable, unseasonable, unsuitable, untimely, unwieldy, vexatious.

incorporate *vb* affiliate, amalgamate, associate, blend, combine, consolidate, include, merge, mix, unite; embody, incarnate. * *adj* incorporeal, immaterial, spiritual, supernatural; blended, consolidated, merged, united.

incorporation *n* affiliation, alignment, amalgamation, association, blend, blending, combination, consolidation, fusion, inclusion, merger, mixture, unification, union, embodiment, incarnation, personification.

incorporeal *adj* bodiless, immaterial, impalpable, incorporate, spiritual, supernatural, unsubstantial.

incorrect *adj* erroneous, false, inaccurate, inexact, untrue, wrong; faulty, improper, mistaken, ungrammatical, unbecoming, unsound.

incorrectness *n* error, inaccuracy, inexactness, mistake.

incorrigible *adj* abandoned, graceless, hardened, irreclaimable, lost, obdurate, recreant, reprobate, shameless; helpless, hopeless, irremediable, irrecoverable, irreparable, irretrievable, irreversible, remediless.

incorruptibility *n* unpurchasableness; deathlessness, immortality, imperishableness, incorruptibleness, incorruption, indestructibility.

incorruptible *adj* honest, unbribable; imperishable, indestructible, immortal, undying, deathless, everlasting.

increase *vb* accrue, advance, augment, enlarge, extend, grow, intensify, mount, wax; multiply; enhance, greaten, heighten, raise, reinforce; aggravate, prolong. * *n* accession, accretion, accumulation, addition, augmentation, crescendo, development, enlargement, expansion, extension, growth, heightening, increment, intensification, multiplication, swelling; gain, produce, product, profit; descendants, issue, offspring, progeny.

incredible *adj* absurd, inadmissible, nonsensical, unbelievable.

incredulity *n* distrust, doubt, incredulousness, scepticism, unbelief.

incredulous *adj* distrustful, doubtful, dubious, sceptical, unbelieving.

increment *n* addition, augmentation, enlargement, increase.

incriminate *vb* accuse, blame, charge, criminate, impeach.

incubate *vb* brood, develop, hatch, sit.

inculcate *vb* enforce, implant, impress, infix, infuse, ingraft, inspire, instil.

inculpable *adj* blameless, faultless, innocent, irreprehensible, irreproachable, irreprovable, sinless, unblamable, unblameable.

inculpate *vb* accuse, blame, censure, charge, incriminate, impeach, incriminate.
inculpatory *adj* criminatory, incriminating.
incumbent *adj* binding, devolved, devolving, laid, obligatory; leaning, prone, reclining, resting. * *n* holder, occupant.
incur *vb* acquire, bring, contract.
incurable *adj* cureless, hopeless, irrecoverable, remediless; helpless, incorrigible, irremediable, irreparable, irretrievable, remediless.
incurious *adj* careless, heedless, inattentive, indifferent, uninquisitive, unobservant, uninterested.
incursion *n* descent, foray, raid, inroad, irruption.
incursive *adj* aggressive, hostile, invasive, predatory, raiding.
incurvate *vb* bend, bow, crook, curve. * *adj* (*bot*) aduncous, arcuate, bowed, crooked, curved, hooked.
indebted *adj* beholden, obliged, owing.
indecency *n* impropriety, indecorum, offensiveness, outrageousness, unseemliness; coarseness, filthiness, foulness, grossness, immodesty, impurity, obscenity, vileness.
indecent *adj* bold, improper, indecorous, offensive, outrageous, unbecoming, unseemly; coarse, dirty, filthy, gross, immodest, impure, indelicate, lewd, nasty, obscene, pornographic, salacious, shameless, smutty, unchaste.
indecipherable *adj* illegible, undecipherable, undiscoverable, inexplicable, obscure, unintelligible, unreadable.
indecision *n* changeableness, fickleness, hesitation, inconstancy, irresolution, unsteadiness, vacillation.
indecisive *adj* dubious, hesitating, inconclusive, irresolute, undecided, unsettled, vacillating, wavering.
indecorous *adj* coarse, gross, ill-bred, impolite, improper, indecent, rude, unbecoming, uncivil, unseemly.
indecorum *n* grossness, ill-breeding, ill manners, impoliteness, impropriety, incivility, indecency, indecorousness.
indeed *adv* absolutely, actually, certainly, in fact, in truth, in reality, positively, really, strictly, truly, verily, veritably. * *interj* really! you don't say so! is it possible!
indefatigable *adj* assiduous, never-tiring, persevering, persistent, sedulous, tireless, unflagging, unremitting, untiring, unwearied.
indefeasible *adj* immutable, inalienable, irreversible, irrevocable, unalterable.
indefensible *adj* censurable, defenceless, faulty, unpardonable, untenable; inexcusable, insupportable, unjustifiable, unwarrantable, wrong.
indefinite *adj* confused, doubtful, equivocal, general, imprecise, indefinable, indecisive, indeterminate, indistinct, inexact, inexplicit, lax, loose, nondescript, obscure, uncertain, undefined, undetermined, unfixed, unsettled, vague.
indelible *adj* fast, fixed, ineffaceable, ingrained, permanent.
indelicacy *n* coarseness, grossness, indecorousness, indecorum, impropriety, offensiveness, unseemliness, vulgarity; immodesty, indecency, lewdness, unchastity; foulness, obscenity.
indelicate *adj* broad, coarse, gross, indecorous, intrusive, rude, unbecoming, unseemly; foul, immodest, indecent, lewd, obscene, unchaste, vulgar.
indemnification *n* compensation, reimbursement, remuneration, security.
indemnify *vb* compensate, reimburse, remunerate, requite, secure.
indent *vb* bruise, jag, notch, pink, scallop, serrate; bind, indenture.
indentation *n* bruise, dent, depression, jag, notch.
indenture *vb* bind, indent. * *n* contract, instrument; indentation.
independence *n* freedom, liberty, self-direction; distinctness, nondependence, separation; competence, ease.
independent *adj* absolute, autonomous, free, self-directing, uncoerced, unrestrained, unrestricted, voluntary; (*person*) self-reliant, unconstrained, unconventional.
indescribable *adj* ineffable, inexpressible, nameless, unutterable.
indestructible *adj* abiding, endless, enduring, everlasting, fadeless, imperishable, incorruptible, undecaying.
indeterminate *adj* indefinite, uncertain, undetermined, unfixed.
index *vb* alphabetize, catalogue, codify, earmark, file, list, mark, tabulate. * *n* catalogue, list, register, tally; indicator, lead, mark, pointer, sign, signal, token; contents, table of contents; forefinger; exponent.
indicate *vb* betoken, denote, designate, evince, exhibit, foreshadow, manifest, mark, point out, prefigure, presage, register, show, signify, specify, tell; hint, imply, intimate, sketch, suggest.
indication *n* hint, index, manifestation, mark, note, sign, suggestion, symptom, token.
indicative *adj* significant, suggestive, symptomatic; (*gram*) affirmative, declarative.
indict *vb* (*law*) accuse, charge, present.
indictment *n* (*law*) indicting, presentment; accusation, arraignment, charge, crimination, impeachment.
indifference *n* apathy, carelessness, coldness, coolness, heedlessness, inattention, insignificance, negligence, unconcern, unconcernedness, uninterestedness; disinterestedness, impartiality, neutrality.
indifferent *adj* apathetic, cold, cool, dead, distant, dull, easy-going, frigid, heedless, inattentive, incurious, insensible, insouciant, listless, lukewarm, nonchalant, perfunctory, regardless, stoical, unconcerned, uninterested, unmindful, unmoved; equal; fair, medium, middling, moderate, ordinary, passable, tolerable; mediocre, so-so; immaterial, unimportant; disinterested, impartial, neutral, unbiased.
indigence *n* destitution, distress, necessity, need, neediness, pauperism, penury, poverty, privation, want.
indigenous *adj* aboriginal, home-grown, inborn, inherent, native.
indigent *adj* destitute, distressed, insolvent, moneyless, necessitous, needy, penniless, pinched, poor, reduced.
indigested *adj* unconcocted, undigested; crude, ill-advised, ill-considered, ill-judged; confused, disorderly, ill-arranged, unmethodical.
indigestion *n* dyspepsia, dyspepsy.
indignant *adj* angry, exasperated, incensed, irate, ireful, provoked, roused, wrathful, wroth.
indignation *n* anger, choler, displeasure, exasperation, fury, ire, rage, resentment, wrath.
indignity *n* abuse, affront, contumely, dishonour, disrespect, ignominy, insult, obloquy, opprobrium, outrage, reproach, slight.
indirect *adj* circuitous, circumlocutory, collateral, devious, oblique, roundabout, sidelong, tortuous; deceitful, dishonest, dishonorable, unfair; mediate, remote, secondary, subordinate.
indiscernible *adj* imperceptible, indistinguishable, invisible, undiscernible, undiscoverable.
indiscipline *n* laxity, insubordination.
indiscreet *adj* foolish, hasty, headlong, heedless, imprudent, incautious, inconsiderate, injudicious, rash, reckless, unwise.
indiscretion *n* folly, imprudence, inconsiderateness, rashness; blunder, faux pas, lapse, mistake, misstep.
indiscriminate *adj* confused, heterogeneous, indistinct, mingled, miscellaneous, mixed, promiscuous, undiscriminating, undistinguishable, undistinguishing.
indispensable *adj* essential, expedient, necessary, needed, needful, requisite.
indisputable *adj* certain, incontestable, indubitable, infallible, sure, undeniable, undoubted, unmistakable, unquestionable.
indisposed *adj* ailing, ill, sick, unwell; averse, backward, disinclined, loath, reluctant, unfriendly, unwilling.
indisposition *n* ailment, illness, sickness; aversion, backwardness, dislike, disinclination, reluctance, unwillingness.
indisputable *adj* certain, incontestable, indutitable, infallible, sure, undeniable, undoubted, unmistakable, unquestionable.
indissoluble *adj* abiding, enduring, firm, imperishable, incorruptible, indestructible, lasting, stable, unbreakable.
indistinct *adj* ambiguous, doubtful, uncertain; blurred, dim, dull, faint, hazy, misty, nebulous, obscure, shadowy, vague; confused, inarticulate, indefinite, indistinguishable, undefined, undistinguishable.

indistinguishable *adj* imperceptible, indiscernible, unnoticeable, unobservable; chaotic, confused, dim, indistinct, obscure, vague.
indite *vb* compose, pen, write.
individual *adj* characteristic, distinct, identical, idiosyncratic, marked, one, particular, personal, respective, separate, single, singular, special, unique; peculiar, proper; decided, definite, independent, positive, self-guided, unconventional. * *n* being, character, party, person, personage, somebody, someone; type, unit.
individuality *n* definiteness, indentity, personality; originality, self-direction, self-determination, singularity, uniqueness.
individualize *vb* individuate, particularize, singularize, specify.
indivisible *adj* incommensurable, indissoluble, inseparable, unbreakable, unpartiable.
indocile *adj* cantankerous, contumacious, dogged, froward, inapt, headstrong, intractable, mulish, obstinate, perverse, refractory, stubborn, ungovernable, unmanageable, unruly, unteachable.
indoctrinate *vb* brainwash, imbue, initiate, instruct, rehabilitate, teach.
indoctrination *n* grounding, initiation, instruction, rehabilitation.
indolence *n* idleness, inactivity, inertia, inertness, laziness, listlessness, sloth, slothfulness, sluggishness.
indolent *adj* easy, easy-going, inactive, inert, lazy, listless, lumpish, otiose, slothful, sluggish, supine.
indomitable *adj* invincible, unconquerable, unyielding.
indorse *see* **endorse**.
indubitable *adj* certain, evident, incontestable, incontrovertible, indisputable, sure, undeniable, unquestionable.
induce *vb* actuate, allure, bring, draw, drive, entice, impel, incite, influence, instigate, move, persuade, prevail, prompt, spur, urge; bring on, cause, effect, motivate, lead, occasion, produce.
inducement *n* allurement, draw, enticement, instigation, persuasion; cause, consideration, impulse, incentive, incitement, influence, motive, reason, spur, stimulus.
induct *vb* inaugurate, initiate, install, institute, introduce, invest.
induction *n* inauguration, initiation, institution, installation, introduction; conclusion, generalization, inference.
indue *vb* assume, endow, clothe, endue, invest, supply.
indulge *vb* gratify, license, revel, satisfy, wallow, yield to; coddle, cosset, favour, humour, pamper, pet, spoil; allow, cherish, foster, harbour, permit, suffer.
indulgence *n* gratification, humouring, pampering; favour, kindness, lenience, lenity, liberality, tenderness; (*theol*) absolution, remission.
indulgent *adj* clement, easy, favouring, forbearing, gentle, humouring, kind, lenient, mild, pampering, tender, tolerant.
indurate *vb* harden, inure, sear, strengthen.
induration *n* hardening, obduracy.
industrious *adj* assiduous, diligent, hard-working, laborious, notable, operose, sedulous; brisk, busy, persevering, persistent.
industry *n* activity, application, assiduousness, assiduity, diligence; perseverance, persistence, sedulousness, vigour; effort, labour, toil.
inebriated *adj* drunk, intoxicated, stupefied.
ineffable *adj* indescribable, inexpressible, unspeakable, unutterable.
ineffaceable *adj* indelible, indestructible, inerasable, inexpungeable, ingrained.
ineffectual *adj* abortive, bootless, fruitless, futile, inadequate, inefficacious, ineffective, inoperative, useless, unavailing, vain; feeble, inefficient, powerless, impotent, weak.
inefficacy *n* ineffectualness, inefficiency.
inefficient *adj* feeble, incapable, ineffectual, ineffective, inefficacious, weak.
inelastic *adj* flabby, flaccid, inductile, inflexible, irresilient.
inelegant *adj* abrupt, awkward, clumsy, coarse, constrained, cramped, crude, graceless, harsh, homely, homespun, rough, rude, stiff, tasteless, uncourtly, uncouth, ungainly, ungraceful, unpolished, unrefined.
ineligible *adj* disqualified, unqualified; inexpedient, objectionable, unadvisable, undesirable.
inept *adj* awkward, improper, inapposite, inappropriate, unapt, unfit, unsuitable; null, useless, void, worthless; foolish, nonsensical, pointless, senseless, silly, stupid.
ineptitude *n* inappositeness, inappropriateness, inaptitude, unfitness, unsuitability, unsuitable-ness; emptiness, nullity, uselessness, worthlessness; folly, foolishness, nonsense, pointlessness, senselessness, silliness, stupidity.
inequality *n* disproportion, inequitableness, injustice, unfairness; difference, disparity, dissimilarity, diversity, imparity, irregularity, roughness, unevenness; inadequacy, incompetency, insufficiency.
inequitable *adj* unfair, unjust.
inert *adj* comatose, dead, inactive, lifeless, motionless, quiescent, passive; apathetic, dronish, dull, idle, indolent, lazy, lethargic, lumpish, phlegmatic, slothful, sluggish, supine, torpid.
inertia *n* apathy, inertness, lethargy, passiveness, passivity, slothfulness, sluggishness.
inestimable *adj* incalculable, invaluable, precious, priceless, valuable.
inevitable *adj* certain, necessary, unavoidable, undoubted.
inexact *adj* imprecise, inaccurate, incorrect; careless, crude, loose.
inexcusable *adj* indefensible, irremissible, unallowable, unjustifiable, unpardonable.
inexhaustible *adj* boundless, exhaustless, indefatigable, unfailing, unlimited.
inexorable *adj* cruel, firm, hard, immovable, implacable, inflexible, merciless, pitiless, relentless, severe, steadfast, unbending, uncompassionate, unmerciful, unrelenting, unyielding.
inexpedient *adj* disadvantageous, ill-judged, impolitic, imprudent, indiscreet, injudicious, inopportune, unadvisable, unprofitable, unwise.
inexperience *n* greenness, ignorance, rawness.
inexperienced *adj* callow, green, raw, strange, unacquainted, unconversant, undisciplined, uninitiated, unpractised, unschooled, unskilled, untrained, untried, unversed, young.
inexpert *adj* awkward, bungling, clumsy, inapt, maladroit, unhandy, unskilful, unskilled.
inexpiable *adj* implacable, inexorable, irreconcilable, unappeasable; irremissible, unatonable, unpardonable.
inexplicable *adj* enigmatic, enigmatical, incomprehensible, inscrutable, mysterious, strange, unaccountable, unintelligible.
inexpressible *adj* indescribable, ineffable, unspeakable, unutterable; boundless, infinite, surpassing.
inexpressive *adj* blank, characterless, dull, unexpressive.
inextinguishable *adj* unquenchable.
in extremis *adv* moribund.
inextricable *adj* entangled, intricate, perplexed, unsolvable.
infallibility *n* certainty, infallibleness, perfection.
infallible *adj* certain, indubitable, oracular, sure, unerring, unfailing.
infamous *adj* abominable, atrocious, base, damnable, dark, detestable, discreditable, disgraceful, dishonorable, disreputable, heinous, ignominious, nefarious, odious, opprobrious, outrageous, scandalous, shameful, shameless, vile, villainous, wicked.
infamy *n* abasement, discredit, disgrace, dishonour, disrepute, ignominy, obloquy, odium, opprobrium, scandal, shame; atrocity, detestableness, disgracefulness, dishonorableness, odiousness, scandalousness, shamefulness, villainy, wickedness.
infancy *n* beginning, commencement; babyhood, childhood, minority, nonage, pupillage.
infant *n* babe, baby, bairn, bantling, brat, chit, minor, nursling, papoose, suckling, tot.
infantile *adj* childish, infantine, newborn, tender, young; babyish, childish, weak; babylike, childlike.
infatuate *vb* befool, besot, captivate, delude, prepossess, stultify.
infatuation *n* absorption, besottedness, folly, foolishness, prepossession, stupefaction.
infeasible *adj* impractical, unfeasible.
infect *vb* affect, contaminate, corrupt, defile, poison, pollute, taint, vitiate.
infection *n* affection, bane, contagion, contamination, corruption, defilement, pest, poison, pollution, taint, virus, vitiation.

infectious *adj* catching, communicable, contagious, contaminating, corrupting, defiling, demoralizing, pestiferous, pestilential, poisoning, polluting, sympathetic, vitiating.
infecund *adj* barren, infertile, sterile, unfruitful, unproductive, unprolific.
infecundity *n* unfruitfulness.
infelicitous *adj* calamitous, miserable, unfortunate, unhappy, wretched; inauspicious, unfavourable, unpropitious; ill-chosen, inappropriate, unfitting.
infer *vb* collect, conclude, deduce, derive, draw, gather, glean, guess, presume, reason.
inference *n* conclusion, consequence, corollary, deduction, generalization, guess, illation, implication, induction, presumption.
inferior *adj* lower, nether; junior, minor, secondary, subordinate; bad, base, deficient, humble, imperfect, indifferent, mean, mediocre, paltry, poor, second-rate, shabby.
inferiority *n* juniority, subjection, subordination, mediocrity; deficiency, imperfection, inadequacy, shortcoming.
infernal *adj* abominable, accursed, atrocious, damnable, dark, demoniacal, devilish, diabolical, fiendish, fiendlike, hellish, malicious, nefarious, satanic, Stygian.
infertility *n* barrenness, infecundity, sterility, unfruitfulness, unproductivity.
infest *vb* annoy, disturb, harass, haunt, molest, plague, tease, torment, trouble, vex, worry; beset, overrun, possess, swarm, throng.
infidel *n* agnostic, atheist, disbeliever, heathen, heretic, sceptic, unbeliever.
infidelity *n* adultery, disloyality, faithlessness, treachery, unfaithfulness; disbelief, scepticism, unbelief.
infiltrate *vb* absorb, pervade, soak.
infinite *adj* boundless, endless, illimitable, immeasurable, inexhaustible, interminable, limitless, measureless, perfect, unbounded, unlimited; enormous, immense, stupendous, vast; absolue, eternal, self-determined, self-existent, unconditioned.
infinitesimal *adj* infinitely small; microscopic, miniscule.
infinity *n* absoluteness, boundlessness, endlessness, eternity, immensity, infiniteness, infinitude, interminateness, self-determination, self-existence, vastness.
infirm *adj* ailing, debilitated, enfeebled, feeble, frail, weak, weakened; faltering, irresolute, vacillating, wavering; insecure, precarious, unsound, unstable.
infirmity *n* ailment, debility, feebleness, frailness, frailty, weakness; defect, failing, fault, foible, weakness.
infix *vb* fasten, fix, plant, set; implant, inculcate, infuse, ingraft, instil.
inflame *vb* animate, arouse, excite, enkindle, fire, heat, incite, inspirit, intensify, rouse, stimulate; aggravate, anger, chafe, embitter, enrage, exasperate, incense, infuriate, irritate, madden, nettle, provoke.
inflammability *n* combustibility, combustibleness, inflammableness.
inflammable *adj* combustible, ignitible; excitable.
inflammation *n* burning, conflagration; anger, animosity, excitement, heat, rage, turbulence, violence.
inflammatory *adj* fiery, inflaming; dissentious, incendiary, seditious.
inflate *vb* bloat, blow up, distend, expand, swell, sufflate; elate, puff up; enlarge, increase.
inflated *adj* bloated, distended, puffed-up, swollen; bombastic, declamatory, grandiloquent, high-flown, magniloquent, overblown, pompous, rhetorical, stilted, tumid, turgid.
inflation *n* enlargement, increase, overenlargement, overissue; bloatedness, distension, expansion, sufflation; bombast, conceit, conceitedness, self-conceit, self-complacency, self-importance, self-sufficiency, vaingloriousness, vainglory.
inflect *vb* bend, bow, curve, turn; (*gram*) conjugate, decline, vary.
inflection *n* bend, bending, crook, curvature, curvity, flexure; (*gram*) accidence, conjugation, declension, variation; (*mus*) modulation.
inflexibility *n* inflexibleness, rigidity, stiffness; doggedness, obstinacy, perinacity, stubbornness; firmness, perseverance, resolution, tenacity.
inflexible *adj* rigid, rigorous, stiff, unbending; cantankerous, cross-grained, dogged, headstrong, heady, inexorable, intractable, obdurate, obstinant, pertinacious, refractory, stubborn, unyielding, wilful; firm, immovable, persevering, resolute, steadfast, unbending.
inflict *vb* bring, impose, lay on.
infliction *n* imposition, inflicting; judgment, punishment.
inflorescence *n* blooming, blossoming, flowering.
influence *vb* affect, bias, control, direct, lead, modify, prejudice, prepossess, sway; actuate, arouse, impel, incite, induce, instigate, move, persuade, prevail upon, rouse. * *n* ascendancy, authority, control, mastery, potency, predominance, pull, rule, sway; credit, reputation, weight; inflow, inflowing, influx; magnetism, power, spell.
influential *adj* controlling, effective, effectual, potent, powerful, strong; authoritative, momentous, substantial, weighty.
influx *n* flowing in, introduction.
infold *see* **enfold**.
inform *vb* animate, inspire, quicken; acquaint, advise, apprise, enlighten, instruct, notify, teach, tell, tip, warn.
informal *adj* unceremonious, unconventional, unofficial; easy, familiar, natural, simple; irregular, nonconformist, unusual.
informality *n* unceremoniousness; unconventionality; ease, familiarity, naturalness, simplicity; noncomformity, irregularity, unusualness.
informant *n* advertiser, adviser, informer, intelligencer, newsmonger, notifier, relator; accuser, complainant, informer.
information *n* advice, data, intelligence, knowledge, notice; advertisement, enlightenment, instruction, message, tip, word, warning; accusation, complaint, denunciation.
informer *n* accuser, complainant, informant, snitch.
infraction *n* breach, breaking, disobedience, encroachment, infringement, nonobservance, transgression, violation.
infrangible *adj* inseparable, inviolable, unbreakable.
infrequency *n* rareness, rarity, uncommonness, unusualness.
infrequent *adj* rare, uncommon, unfrequent, unusual; occasional, scant, scarce, sporadic.
infringe *vb* break, contravene, disobey, intrude, invade, transgress, violate.
infringement *n* breach, breaking, disobedience, infraction, nonobservance, transgression, violation.
infuriated *adj* angry, enraged, furious, incensed, maddened, raging, wild.
infuse *vb* breathe into, implant, inculcate, ingraft, insinuate, inspire, instil, introduce; macerate, steep.
infusion *n* inculcation, instillation, introduction; infusing, macerating, steeping.
ingathering *n* harvest.
ingenious *adj* able, adroit, artful, bright, clever, fertile, gifted, inventive, ready, sagacious, shrewd, witty.
ingenuity *n* ability, acuteness, aptitude, aptness, capacity, capableness, cleverness, faculty, genius, gift, ingeniousness, inventiveness, knack, readiness, skill, turn.
ingenuous *adj* artless, candid, childlike, downright, frank, generous, guileless, honest, innocent, naive, open, open-hearted, plain, simple-minded, sincere, single-minded, straightforward, transparent, truthful, unreserved.
ingenuousness *n* artlessness, candour, childlikeness, frankness, guilelessness, honesty, naivety, open-heartedness, openness, sincerity, single-mindedness, truthfulness.
inglorious *adj* humble, lowly, mean, nameless, obscure, undistinguished, unhonoured, unknown, unmarked, unnoted; discreditable, disgraceful, humiliating, ignominous, scandalous, shameful.
ingloriousness *n* humbleness, lowliness, meanness, namelessness, obscurity; abasement, discredit, disgrace, dishonour, disrepute, humiliation, infamy, ignominousness, ignominy, obloquy, odium, opprobrium, shame.
ingraft *vb* graft, implant, inculcate, infix, infuse, instil.
ingrain *vb* dye, imbue, impregnate.
ingratiate *vb* insinuate.
ingratitude *n* thanklessness, ungratefulness, unthankfulness.

ingredient *n* component, constituent, element.
ingress *n* entrance, entré, entry, introgression.
ingulf *see* **engulf**.
inhabit *vb* abide, dwell, live, occupy, people, reside, sojourn.
inhabitable *adj* habitable, livable.
inhabitant *n* citizen, denizen, dweller, inhabiter, resident.
inhalation *n* breath, inhaling, inspiration; sniff, snuff.
inhale *vb* breathe in, draw in, inbreathe, inspire.
inharmonious *adj* discordant, inharmonic, out of tune, unharmonious, unmusical.
inhere *vb* cleave to, stick, stick fast; abide, belong, exist, lie, pertain, reside.
inherent *adj* essential, immanent, inborn, inbred, indwelling, ingrained, innate, inseparable, intrinsic, native, natural, proper; adhering, sticking.
inherit *vb* get, receive.
inheritance *n* heritage, legacy, patrimony; inheriting.
inheritor *n* heir, (*law*) parcener.
inhibit *vb* bar, check, debar, hinder, obstruct, prevent, repress, restrain, stop; forbid, interdict, prohibit.
inhibition *n* check, hindrance, impediment, obstacle, obstruction, restraint; disallowance, embargo, interdict, interdiction, prevention, prohibition.
inhospitable *adj* cool, forbidding, unfriendly, unkind; bigoted, illiberal, intolerant, narrow, prejudiced, ungenerous, unreceptive; barren, wild.
inhospitality *n* inhospitableness, unkindness; illiberality, narrowness.
inhuman *adj* barbarous, brutal, cruel, fell, ferocious, merciless, pitiless, remorseless, ruthless, savage, unfeeling; nonhuman.
inhumanity *n* barbarity, brutality, cruelty, ferocity, savageness; hard-heartedness, unkindness.
inhume *vb* bury, entomb, inter.
inimical *adj* antagonistic, hostile, unfriendly; adverse, contrary, harmful, hurtful, noxious, opposed, pernicious, repugnant, unfavourable.
inimitable *adj* incomparable, matchless, peerless, unequalled, unexampled, unmatched, unparagoned, unparalleled, unrivalled, unsurpassed.
iniquitous *adj* atrocious, criminal, flagitious, heinous, inequitable, nefarious, sinful, wicked, wrong, unfair, unjust, unrighteous.
iniquity *n* injustice, sin, sinfulness, unrighteousness, wickedness, wrong; crime, misdeed, offence.
initial *adj* first; beginning, commencing, incipient, initiatory, introductory, opening, original; elementary, inchoate, rudimentary.
initiate *vb* begin, commence, enter upon, inaugurate, introduce, open; ground, indoctrinate, instruct, prime, teach.
initiation *n* beginning, commencement, inauguration, opening; admission, entrance, introduction; indoctrinate, instruction.
initiative *n* beginning; energy, enterprise.
initiatory *adj* inceptive, initiative.
inject *vb* force in, interject, insert, introduce, intromit.
injudicious *adj* foolish, hasty, ill-advised, ill-judged, imprudent, incautious, inconsiderate, indiscreet, rash, unwise.
injunction *n* admonition, bidding, command, mandate, order, precept.
injure *vb* damage, disfigure, harm, hurt, impair, mar, spoil, sully, wound; abuse, aggrieve, wrong; affront, dishonour, insult.
injurious *adj* baneful, damaging, deadly, deleterious, destructive, detrimental, disadvantageous, evil, fatal, hurtful, mischievous, noxious, pernicious, prejudicial, ruinous; inequitable, iniquitous, unjust, wrongful; contumelious, detractory, libellous, slanderous.
injury *n* evil, ill, injustice, wrong; damage, detriment, harm, hurt, impairment, loss, mischief, prejudice.
injustice *n* inequity, unfairness; grievance, iniquity, injury, wrong.
inkhorn *n* inkbottle, inkstand.
inkling *n* hint, intimation, suggestion, whisper.
inky *adj* atramentous, black, murky.
inland *adj* domestic, hinterland, home, upcountry; interior, internal.
inlet *n* arm, bay, bight, cove, creek; entrance, ingress, passage.
inmate *n* denizen, dweller, guest, intern, occupant.
inmost *adj* deepest, innermost.
inn *n* hostel, hostelry, hotel, pub, public house, tavern.
innate *adj* congenital, constitutional, inborn, inbred, indigenous, inherent, inherited, instinctive, native, natural, organic.
inner *adj* interior, internal.
innermost *adj* deepest, inmost.
innkeeper *n* host, innholder, landlady, landlord, tavernkeeper.
innocence *n* blamelessness, chastity, guilelessness, guiltlessness, purity, simplicity, sinlessness, stainlessness; harmlessness, innocuousness, innoxiousness, inoffensiveness.
innocent *adj* blameless, clean, clear, faultless, guiltless, immaculate, pure, sinless, spotless, unfallen, upright; harmless, innocuous, innoxious, inoffensive; lawful, legitimate, permitted; artless, guileless, ignorant, ingenuous, simple. * *n* babe, child, ingénue, naif, naive, unsophisticate.
innocuous *adj* harmless, innocent, inoffensive, safe.
innovate *vb* change, introduce.
innovation *n* change, introduction; departure, novelty.
innuendo *n* allusion, hint, insinuation, intimation, suggestion.
innumerable *adj* countless, numberless.
inoculate *vb* infect, vaccinate.
inoffensive *adj* harmless, innocent, innocuous, innoxious, unobjectionable, unoffending.
inoperative *adj* inactive, ineffectual, inefficacious, not in force.
inopportune *adj* ill-timed, inexpedient, infelicitous, mistimed, unfortunate, unhappy, unseasonable, untimely.
inordinate *adj* excessive, extravagant, immoderate, intemperate, irregular.
inorganic *adj* inanimate, unorganized; mineral.
inquest *n* inquiry, inquisition, investigation, quest, search.
inquietude *n* anxiety, disquiet, disquietude, disturbance, restlessness, uneasiness.
inquire, enquire *vb* ask, catechize, interpellate, interrogate, investigate, query, question, quiz.
inquiry, enquiry *n* examination, exploration, investigation, research, scrutiny, study; interrogation, query, question, quiz.
inquisition *n* examination, inquest, inquiry, investigation, search.
inquisitive *adj* curious, inquiring, scrutinizing; curious, meddlesome, peeping, peering, prying.
inroad *n* encroachment, foray, incursion, invasion, irruption, raid.
insalubrious *adj* noxious, unhealthful, unhealthy, unwholesome.
insane *adj* abnormal, crazed, crazy, delirious, demented, deranged, distracted, lunatic, mad, maniacal, unhealthy, unsound.
insanity *n* craziness, delirium, dementia, derangement, lunacy, madness, mania, mental aberration, mental alienation.
insatiable *adj* greedy, rapacious, voracious; insatiate, unappeasable.
inscribe *vb* emblaze, endorse, engrave, enroll, impress, imprint, letter, mark, write; address, dedicate.
inscrutable *adj* hidden, impenetrable, incomprehensible, inexplicable, mysterious, undiscover-able, unfathomable, unsearchable.
inscrutableness *n* impenetrability, incomprehensibility, incomprehensibleness, inexplicability, inscrutability, mysteriousness, mystery, unfathomableness, unsearchableness.
insecure *adj* risky, uncertain, unconfident, unsure; exposed, ill-protected, unprotected, unsafe; dangerous, hazardous, perilous; infirm, shaking, shaky, tottering, unstable, weak, wobbly.
insecurity *n* riskiness, uncertainty; danger, hazardousness, peril; instability, shakiness, weakness, wobbliness.
insensate *adj* dull, indifferent, insensible, torpid; brutal, foolish, senseless, unwise; inanimate, insensible, insentient, nonpercipient, unconscious, unperceiving.
insensibility *n* dullness, insentience, lethargy, torpor; apathy, indifference, insusceptibility, unfeelingness, dullness, stupidity; anaesthesia, coma, stupor, unconsciousness.
insensible *adj* imperceivable, imperceptible, undiscoverable; blunted, brutish, deaf, dull, insensate, numb, obtuse, senseless, sluggish, stolid, stupid, torpid, unconscious; apathetic, callous, phlegmatic, impassive, indifferent, insensitive, insentient, unfeeling, unimpressible, unsusceptible.

insensibly *adv* imperceptibly.

insentient *adj* inert, nonsentient, senseless; inanimate, insensible, insensate, nonpercipient, unconscious, unperceiving.

inseparable *adj* close, friendly, intimate, together; indissoluble, indivisible, inseverable.

insert *vb* infix, inject, intercalate, interpolate, introduce, inweave, parenthesize, place, put, set.

inside *adj* inner, interior, internal; confidential, exclusive, internal, private, secret. * *adv* indoors, within. * *n* inner part, interior; nature.

insidious *adj* creeping, deceptive, gradual, secretive; arch, artful, crafty, crooked, cunning, deceitful, designing, diplomatic, foxy, guileful, intriguing, Machiavellian, sly, sneaky, subtle, treacherous, trickish, tricky, wily.

insight *n* discernment, intuition, penetration, perception, perspicuity, understanding.

insignia *n pl* badges, marks.

insignificance *n* emptiness, nothingenss, paltriness, triviality, unimportance.

insignificant *adj* contemptible, empty, immaterial, inconsequential, inconsiderable, inferior, meaningless, paltry, petty, small, sorry, trifling, trivial, unessential, unimportant.

insincere *adj* deceitful, dishonest, disingenuous, dissembling, dissimulating, double-faced, double-tongued, duplicitous, empty, faithless, false, hollow, hypocritical, pharisaical, truthless, uncandid, untrue.

insincerity *n* bad faith, deceitfulness, dishonesty, disingenuousness, dissimulation, duplicity, falseness, faithlessness, hypocrisy.

insinuate *vb* hint, inculcate, infuse, ingratiate, instil, intimate, introduce, suggest.

insipid *adj* dead, dull, flat, heavy, inanimate, jejune, lifeless, monotonous, pointless, prosaic, prosy, spiritless, stupid, tame, unentertaining, uninteresting; mawkish, savourless, stale, tasteless, vapid, zestless.

insipidity, insipidness *n* dullness, heaviness, lifelessness, prosiness, stupidity, tameness; flatness, mawkishness, staleness, tastlessness, unsavouriness, vapidness, zestlessness.

insist *vb* demand, maintain, urge.

insistence *n* importunity, solicitousness, urging, urgency.

insnare *see* **ensnare.**

insolence *n* impertinence, impudence, malapertness, pertness, rudeness, sauciness; contempt, contumacy, contumely, disrespect, frowardness, insubordination.

insolent *adj* abusive, contemptuous, contumelious, disrespectful, domineering, insulting, offensive, overbearing, rude, supercilious; cheeky, impertinent, impudent, malapert, pert, saucy; contumacious, disobedient, froward, insubordinate.

insoluble *adj* indissoluble, indissolvable, irreducible; inexplicable, insolvable.

insolvable *adj* inexplicable.

insolvent *adj* bankrupt, broken, failed, ruined.

insomnia *n* sleeplessness, wakefulness.

inspect *vb* examine, investigate, look into, pry into, scrutinize; oversee, superintend, supervise.

inspection *n* examination, investigation, scrutiny; oversight, superintendence, supervision.

inspector *n* censor, critic, examiner, visitor; boss, overseer, superintendent, supervisor.

inspiration *n* breathing, inhalation; afflatus, fire, inflatus; elevation, exaltation; enthusiasm.

inspire *vb* breathe, inhale; infuse, instil; animate, cheer, enliven, inspirit; elevate, exalt, stimulate; fill, imbue, impart, inform, quicken.

inspirit *vb* animate, arouse, cheer, comfort, embolden, encourage, enhearten, enliven, fire, hearten, incite, invigorate, quicken, rouse, stimulate.

instable *see* **unstable.**

instability *n* changeableness, fickleness, inconstancy, insecurity, mutability.

install, instal *vb* inaugurate, induct, introduce; establish, place, set up.

installation *n* inauguration, induction, instalment, investiture.

instalment *n* earnest, payment, portion.

instance *vb* adduce, cite, mention, specify. * *n* case, example, exemplification, illustration, occasion; impulse, incitement, instigation, motive, prompting, request, solicitation.

instant *adj* direct, immediate, instantaneous, prompt, quick; current, present; earnest, fast, imperative, importunate, pressing, urgent; ready cooked. * *n* flash, jiffy, moment, second, trice, twinkling; hour, time.

instantaneous *adj* abrupt, immediate, instant, quick, sudden.

instantaneously *adv* forthwith, immediately, presto, quickly, right away.

instauration *n* reconstitution, reconstruction, redintegration, reestablishment, rehabilitation, reinstatement, renewal, renovation, restoration.

instead *adv* in lieu, in place, rather.

instigate *vb* actuate, agitate, encourage, impel, incite, influence, initiate, move, persuade, prevail upon, prompt, provoke, rouse, set on, spur on, stimulate, stir up, tempt, urge.

instigation *n* encouragement, incitement, influence, instance, prompting, solicitation, urgency.

instil, instill *vb* enforce, implant, impress, inculcate, ingraft; impart, infuse, insinuate.

instillation *n* infusion, insinuation, introduction.

instinct *n* natural impulse.

instinctive *adj* automatic, inherent, innate, intuitive, involuntary, natural, spontaneous; impulsive, unreflecting.

institute[1] *n* academy, college, foundation, guild, institution, school; custom, doctrine, dogma, law, maxim, precedent, principle, rule, tenet.

institute[2] *vb* begin, commence, constitute, establish, found, initial, install, introduce, organize, originate, start.

institution *n* enactment, establishment, foundation, institute, society; investiture; custom, law, practice.

instruct *vb* discipline, educate, enlighten, exercise, guide, indoctrinate, inform, initiate, school, teach, train; apprise, bid, command, direct, enjoin, order, prescribe to.

instruction *n* breeding, discipline, education, indoctrination, information, nurture, schooling, teaching, training, tuition; advice, counsel, precept; command, direction, mandate, order.

instructor *n* educator, master, preceptor, schoolteacher, teacher, tutor.

instrument *n* appliance, apparatus, contrivance, device, implement, musical instrument, tool, utensil; agent, means, medium; charter, deed, document, indenture, writing.

instrumental *adj* ancillary, assisting, auxiliary, conducive, contributory, helpful, helping, ministerial, ministrant, serviceable, subservient, subsidiary.

instrumentality *n* agency, intermediary; intervention, means, mediation.

insubordinate *adj* disobedient, disorderly, mutinous, refractory, riotous, seditious, turbulent, ungovernable, unruly.

insubordination *n* disobedience, insurrection, mutiny, revolt, riotousness, sedition; indiscipline, laxity.

insufferable *adj* intolerable, unbearable, unendurable, insupportable; abominable, detestable, disgusting, execrable, outrageous.

insufficiency *n* dearth, defectiveness, deficiency, lack, inadequacy, inadequateness, incapability, incompetence, paucity, shortage.

insufficient *adj* deficient, inadequate, incommensurate, incompetent, scanty; incapable, incompetent, unfitted, unqualified, unsuited, unsatisfactory.

insular *adj* contracted, illiberal, limited, narrow, petty, prejudiced, restricted; isolated, remote.

insulate *vb* detach, disconnect, disengage, disunite, isolate, separate.

insulation *n* disconnection, disengagement, isolation, separation.

insult *vb* abuse, affront, injure, offend, outrage, slander, slight. * *n* abuse, affront, cheek, contumely, indignity, insolence, offence, outrage, sauce, slight.

insulting *adj* abusive, arrogant, contumelious, impertinent, impolite, insolent, rude, vituperative.

insuperable *adj* impassable, insurmountable.

insupportable *adj* insufferable, intolerable, unbearable, unendurable.

insuppressible *adj* irrepressible, uncontrollable.

insurance *n* assurance, security.

insure *vb* assure, guarantee, indemnify, secure, underwrite.

insurgent *adj* disobedient, insubordinate, mutinous, rebellious, revolting, revolutionary, seditious. * *n* mutineer, rebel, revolter, revolutionary.

insurmountable *adj* impassable, insuperable.

insurrection *n* insurgence, mutiny, rebellion, revolt, revolution, rising, sedition, uprising.

intact *adj* scathless, unharmed, unhurt, unimpaired, uninjured, untouched; complete, entire, integral, sound, unbroken, undiminished, whole.

intangible *adj* dim, impalpable, imperceptible, indefinite, insubstantial, intactile, shadowy, vague; aerial, phantom, spiritous.

intangibility *n* imperceptibility, insubstantiality, intangibleness, shadowiness, vagueness.

integral *adj* complete, component, entire, integrant, total, whole.

integrity *n* goodness, honesty, principle, probity, purity, rectitude, soundness, uprightness, virtue; completeness, entireness, entirety, wholeness.

integument *n* coat, covering, envelope, skin, tegument.

intellect *n* brains, cognitive faculty, intelligence, mind, rational faculty, reason, reasoning, faculty, sense, thought, understanding, wit.

intellectual *adj* cerebral, intelligent, mental, scholarly, thoughtful. * *n* academic, highbrow, pundit, savant, scholar.

intelligence *n* acumen, apprehension, brightness, discernment, imagination, insight, penetration, quickness, sagacity, shrewdness, understanding, wits; information, knowledge; advice, instruction, news, notice, notification, tidings; brains, intellect, mentality, sense, spirit.

intelligent *adj* acute, alert, apt, astute, brainy, bright, clear-headed, clear-sighted, clever, discerning, keen-eyed, keen-sighted, knowing, long-headed, quick, quick-sighted, sagacious, sensible, sharp-sighted, sharp-witted, shrewd, understanding.

intelligibility *n* clarity, comprehensibility, intelligibleness, perspicuity.

intelligible *adj* clear, comprehensible, distinct, evident, lucid, manifest, obvious, patent, perspicuous, plain, transparent, understandable.

intemperate *adj* drunken; excessive, extravagant, extreme, immoderate, inordinate, unbridled, uncontrolled, unrestrained; self-indulgent.

intend *vb* aim at, contemplate, design, determine, drive at, mean, meditate, propose, purpose, think of.

intendant *n* inspector, overseer, superintendent, supervisor.

intense *adj* ardent, earnest, fervid, passionate, vehement; close, intent, severe, strained, stretched, strict; energetic, forcible, keen, potent, powerful, sharp, strong, vigorous, violent; acute, deep, extreme, exquisite, grievous, poignant.

intensify *vb* aggravate, concentrate, deepen, enhance, heighten, quicken, strengthen, whet.

intensity *n* closeness, intenseness, severity, strictness; excess, extremity, violence; activity, energy, force, power, strength, vigour; ardour, earnestness, vehemence.

intensive *adj* emphatic, intensifying.

intent *adj* absorbed, attentive, close, eager, earnest, engrossed, occupied, pre-occupied, zealous; bent, determined, decided, resolved, set. * *n* aim, design, drift, end, import, intention, mark, meaning, object, plan, purport, purpose, purview, scope, view.

intention *n* aim, design, drift, end, import, intent, mark, meaning, object, plan, purport, purpose, purview, scope, view.

intentional *adj* contemplated, deliberate, designed, intended, preconcerted, predetermined, premeditated, purposed, studied, voluntary, wilful.

inter *vb* bury, commit to the earth, entomb, inhume, inurn.

intercalate *vb* insert, interpolate.

intercede *vb* arbitrate, interpose, mediate; entreat, plead, supplicate.

intercept *vb* cut off, interrupt, obstruct, seize.

intercession *n* interposition, intervention, mediation; entreaty, pleading, prayer, supplication.

intercessor *n* interceder, mediator.

interchange *vb* alternate, change, exchange, vary. * *n* alternation.

interchangeableness *n* interchangeability.

interchangeably *adv* alternately.

intercourse *n* commerce, communication, communion, connection, converse, correspondence, dealings, fellowship, truck; acquaintance, intimacy.

interdict *vb* debar, forbid, inhibit, prohibit, prescribe, proscribe, restrain from. * *n* ban, decree, interdiction, prohibition.

interest *vb* affect, concern, touch; absorb, attract, engage, enlist, excite, grip, hold, occupy. * *n* advantage, benefit, good, profit, weal; attention, concern, regard, sympathy; part, participation, portion, share, stake; discount, premium, profit.

interested *adj* attentive, concerned, involved, occupied; biassed, patial, prejudiced; selfish, self-seeking.

interesting *adj* attractive, engaging, entertaining, pleasing.

interfere *vb* intermeddle, interpose, meddle; clash, collide, conflict.

interference *n* intermeddling, interposition; clashing, collision, interfering, opposition.

interim *n* intermediate time, interval, meantime.

interior *adj* inmost, inner, internal, inward; inland, remote; domestic, home. * *n* inner part, inland, inside.

interjacent *adj* intermediate, interposed, intervening, parenthetical.

interject *vb* comment, inject, insert, interpose.

interjection *n* exclamation.

interlace *vb* bind, complicate, entwine, intersperse, intertwine, interweave, inweave, knit, mix, plait, twine, twist, unite.

interlard *vb* difersify, interminate, intersperse, intertwine, mix, vary.

interline *vb* insert, write between.

interlineal *adj* interlinear, interlined.

interlink, interlock *vb* connect, interchain, interrelate, join.

interlocution *n* colloquy, conference, dialogue, interchange.

interlocutor *n* respondent, speaker.

interloper *n* intruder, meddler.

intermeddle *vb* interfere, interpose, meddle.

intermediary *n* go-between, mediator.

intermediate *adj* interjacent, interposed, intervening, mean, median, middle, transitional.

interment *n* burial, entombment, inhumation, sepulture.

interminable *adj* boundless, endless, illimitable, immeasurable, infinite, limitless, unbounded, unlimited; long-drawn-out, tedious, wearisome.

intermingle *vb* blend, commingle, commix, intermix, mingle, mix.

intermission *n* cessation, interruption, interval, lull, pause, remission, respite, rest, stop, stoppage, suspension.

intermit *vb* interrupt, intervene, stop, suspend; discontinue, give over, leave off; abate, subside.

intermittent *adj* broken, capricious, discontinuous, fitful, flickering, intermitting, periodic, recurrent, remittent, spasmodic.

intermix *vb* blend, commingle, commix, intermingle, mingle, mix.

internal *adj* inner, inside, interior, inward; incorporeal, mental, spiritual; deeper, emblematic, hidden, higher, metaphorical, secret, symbolical, under; genuine, inherent, intrinsic, real, true; domestic, home, inland, inside.

international *adj* cosmopolitan, universal.

internecine *adj* deadly, destructive, exterminating, exterminatory, interneciary, internecinal, internecive, mortal.

interpellate *vb* interrogate, question.

interpellation *n* interruption; intercession, interposition; interrogation, questioning.

interplay *n* interaction.

interpolate *vb* add, foist, insert, interpose; (*math*) intercalate, introduce.

interpose *vb* arbitrate, intercede, intervene, mediate; interfere, intermeddle, interrupt, meddle, tamper; insert, interject, put in, remark, sandwich, set between; intrude, thurst in.

interposition *n* intercession, interpellation, intervention, mediation.

interpret *vb* decipher, decode, define, elucidate, explain, expound, solve, unfold, unravel; construe, render, translate.

interpretation *n* meaning, sense, signification; elucidation, explanation, explication, exposition; construction, rendering, rendition, translation, version.

interpreter *n* expositor, expounder, translator.

interrogate *vb* ask, catechize, examine, inquire of, interpellate, question.

interrogation *n* catechizing, examination, examining, interpellation, interrogating, questioning; inquiry, query, question.

interrogative *adj* interrogatory, questioning.

interrupt *vb* break, check, disturb, hinder, intercept, interfere with, obstruct, pretermit, stop; break, cut, disconnect, disjoin, dissever, dissolve, disunite, divide, separate, sever, sunder; break off, cease, discontinue, intermit, leave off, suspend.

interruption *n* hindrance, impediment, obstacle, obstruction, stop, stoppage; cessation, discontinuance, intermission, pause, suspension; break, breaking, disconnecting, disconnection, disjunction, dissolution, disunion, disuniting, division, separation, severing, sundering.

intersect *vb* cross, cut, decussate, divide, interrupt.

intersection *n* crossing.

interspace *n* interlude, interstice, interval.

intersperse *vb* intermingle, scatter, sprinkle; diversify, interlard, mix.

interstice *n* interspace, interval, space; chink, crevice.

interstitial *adj* intermediate, intervening.

intertwine *vb* interlace, intertwine, interweave, inweave, twine.

interval *n* interim, interlude, interregnum, pause, period, recess, season, space, spell, term; interstice, skip.

intervene *vb* come between, interfere, mediate; befall, happen, occur.

intervening *adj* interjacent, intermediate; interstitial.

intervention *n* interference, interposition; agency, mediation.

interview *n* conference, consultation, parley; meeting.

interweave *vb* interlace, intertwine, inweave, weave; intermingle, intermix, mingle, mix.

intestinal *adj* domestic, interior, internal.

intestines *n pl* bowels, entrails, guts, insides, inwards, viscera.

intimacy *n* close acquaintance, familiarity, fellowship, friendship; closeness, nearness.

intimate[1] *adj* close, near; familiar, friendly; bosom, chummy, close, dear, homelike, special; confidential, personal, private, secret; detailed, exhaustive, first-hand, immediate, penetrating, profound; cosy, warm. * *n* chum, confidant, companion, crony, friend.

intimate[2] *vb* allude to, express, hint, impart, indicate, insinuate, signify, suggest, tell.

intimately *adv* closely, confidentially, familiarly, nearly, thoroughly.

intimation *n* allusion, hint, innuendo, insinuation, suggestion.

intimidate *vb* abash, affright, alarm, appal, browbeat, bully, cow, daunt, dishearten, dismay, frighten, overawe, scare, subdue, terrify, terrorize.

intimidation *n* fear, intimidating, terror, terrorism.

intolerable *adj* insufferable, insupportable, unbearable, unendurable.

intolerance *n* bigotry, narrowness; impatience, rejection.

intolerant *adj* bigoted, narrow, proscriptive; dictatorial, impatient, imperious, overbearing, supercilious.

intonation *n* cadence, modulation, tone; musical recitation.

in toto *adv* entirely, wholly.

intoxicate *vb* fuddle, inebriate, muddle.

intoxicated *adj* boozy, drunk, drunken, fuddled, inebriated, maudlin, mellow, muddled, stewed, tight, tipsy.

intoxication *n* drunkenness, ebriety, inebriation, inebriety; excitement, exhilaration, infatuation.

intractability *n* cantankerousness, contrariety, inflexibility, intractableness, obduracy, obstinacy, perverseness, perversity, pig-headedness, stubbornness, wilfulness.

intractable *adj* cantankerous, contrary, contumacious, cross-grained, dogged, froward, headstrong, indocile, inflexible, mulish, obdurate, obstinate, perverse, pig-headed, refractory, restive, stubborn, tough, uncontrollable, ungovernable, unmanageable, unruly, unyielding, wilful.

intrench *see* **entrench**.

intrenchment *see* **entrenchment**.

intrepid *adj* bold, brave, chivalrous, courageous, daring, dauntless, doughty, fearless, gallant, heroic, unappalled, unawed, undaunted, undismayed, unterrified, valiant, valorous.

intrepidity *n* boldness, bravery, courage, daring, dauntlessness, fearlessness, gallantry, heroism, intrepidness, prowess, spirit, valour.

intricacy *n* complexity, complication, difficulty, entanglement, intricateness, involution, obscurity, perplexity.

intricate *adj* complicated, difficult, entangled, involved, mazy, obscure, perplexed.

intrigue *vb* connive, conspire, machinate, plot, scheme; beguile, bewitch, captivate, charm, fascinate. * *n* artifice, cabal, conspiracy, deception, finesse, Machiavelianism, machination, manoeuvre, plot, ruse, scheme, stratagem, wile; amour, liaison, love affair.

intriguing *adj* arch, artful, crafty, crooked, cunning, deceitful, designing, diplomatic, foxy, Machiavelian, insidious, politic, sly, sneaky, subtle, tortuous, trickish, tricky, wily.

intrinsic *adj* essential, genuine, real, sterling, true; inborn, inbred, ingrained, inherent, internal, inward, native, natural.

intrinsically *adv* essentially, really, truly; inherently, naturally.

introduce *vb* bring in, conduct, import, induct, inject, insert, lead in, usher in; present; begin, broach, commence, inaugurate, initiate, institute, start.

introduction *n* exordium, preface, prelude, proem; introducing, ushering in; presentation.

introductory *adj* precursory, prefatory, preliminary, proemial.

introspection *n* introversion, self-contemplation.

intrude *vb* encroach, impose, infringe, interfere, interlope, obtrude, trespass.

intruder *n* interloper, intermeddler, meddler, stranger.

intrusion *n* encroachment, infringement, intruding, obtrusion.

intrusive *adj* obtrusive, trespassing.

intuition *n* apprehension, cognition, insight, instinct; clairvoyance, divination, presentiment.

intuitive *adj* instinctive, intuitional, natural; clear, distinct, full, immediate.

intumesce *vb* bubble up, dilate, expand, swell.

intumescence *n* inturgescence, swelling, tumefaction, turgescence.

inundate *vb* deluge, drown, flood, glut, overflow, overwhelm, submerge.

inundation *n* cataclysm, deluge, flood, glut, overflow, superfluity.

inure *vb* accustom, discipline, familiarize, habituate, harden, toughen, train, use.

inutile *adj* bootless, ineffectual, inoperative, unavailing, unprofitable, useless.

invade *vb* encroach upon, infringe, violate; attack, enter in, march into.

invalid[1] *adj* baseless, fallacious, false, inoperative, nugatory, unfounded, unsound, untrue, worthless; (*law*) null, void.

invalid[2] *adj* ailing, bedridden, feeble, frail, ill, infirm, sick, sickly, valetudinary, weak, weakly. * *n* convalescent, patient, valetudinarian.

invalidate *vb* abrogate, annul, cancel, nullify, overthrow, quash, repeal, reverse, undo, unmake, vitiate.

invalidity *n* baselessness, fallaciousness, fallacy, falsity, unsoundness.

invaluable *adj* inestimable, priceless.

invariable *adj* changeless, constant, unchanging, uniform, unvarying; changeless, immutable, unalterable, unchangeable.

invariableness *n* changelessness, constancy, uniformity, unvaryingness; changelessness, immutability, unchangeableness, invariability.

invasion *n* encroachment, incursion, infringement, inroad; aggression, assault, attack, foray, raid.

invective *n* abuse, censure, contumely, denunciation, diatribe, railing, reproach, sarcasm, satire, vituperation.

inveigh *vb* blame, censure, condemn, declaim against, denounce, exclaim against, rail at, reproach, vituperate.

inveigle *vb* contrive, devise; concoct, conceive, create, design, excogitate, frame, imagine, originate; coin, fabricate, forge, spin.

invent *vb* concoct, contrive, design, devise, discover, fabricate, find out, frame, originate.

invention *n* creation, discovery, ingenuity, inventing, origination; contrivance, design, device; coinage, fabrication, fiction, forgery.

inventive *adj* creative, fertile, ingenious.

inventor *n* author, contriver, creator, originator.

inventory *n* account, catalogue, list, record, roll, register, schedule.

inverse *adj* indirect, inverted, opposite, reversed.

inversion *n* inverting, reversing, transposal, transposition.

invert *vb* capsize, overturn; reverse, transpose.

invertebrate *adj* invertebral; spineless.

invest *vb* put money into; confer, endow, endue; (*mil*) beset, besiege, enclose, surround; array, clothe, dress.

investigate *vb* canvass, consider, dissect, examine, explore, follow up, inquire into, look into, overhaul, probe, question, research, scrutinize, search into, search out, sift, study.

investigation *n* examination, exploration, inquiry, inquisition, overhauling, research, scrutiny, search, sifting, study.

investiture *n* habilitation, induction, installation, ordination.

investment *n* money invested; endowment; (*mil*) beleaguerment, siege; clothes, dress, garments, habiliments, robe, vestment.

inveteracy *n* inveterateness, obstinacy.

inveterate *adj* accustomed, besetting, chronic, confirmed, deep-seated, habitual, habituated, hardened, ingrained, long-established, obstinate.

invidious *adj* disagreeable, envious, hateful, odious, offensive, unfair.

invigorate *vb* animate, brace, energize, fortify, harden, nerve, quicken, refresh, stimulate, strengthen, vivify.

invincible *adj* impregnable, indomitable, ineradicable, insuperable, insurmountable, irrepressible, unconquerable, unsubduable, unyielding.

inviolable *adj* hallowed, holy, inviolate, sacramental, sacred, sacrosanct, stainless.

inviolate *adj* unbroken, unviolated; pure, stainless, unblemished, undefiled, unhurt, uninjured, unpolluted, unprofaned, unstained; inviolable, sacred.

invisibility *n* imperceptibility, indistinctness, invisibleness, obscurity.

invisible *adj* impalpable, imperceptible, indistinguishable, intangible, unapparent, undiscernable, unperceivable, unseen.

invitation *n* bidding, call, challenge, solicitation, summons.

invite *vb* ask, bid, call, challenge, request, solicit, summon; allure, attract, draw on, entice, lead, persuade, prevail upon.

inviting *adj* alluring, attractive, bewitching, captivating, engaging, fascinating, pleasing, winning; prepossessing, promising.

invocation *n* conjuration, orison, petition, prayer, summoning, supplication.

invoice *vb* bill, list. * *n* bill, inventory, list, schedule.

invoke *vb* adjure, appeal to, beseech, beg, call upon, conjure, entreat, implore, importune, pray, pray to, solicit, summon, supplicate.

involuntary *adj* automatic, blind, instinctive, mechanical, reflex, spontaneous, unintentional; compulsory, reluctant, unwilling.

involve *vb* comprise, contain, embrace, imply, include, lead to; complicate, compromise, embarrass, entangle, implicate, incriminate, inculpate; cover, envelop, enwrap, surround, wrap; blend, conjoin, connect, join, mingle; entwine, interlace, intertwine, interweave, inweave.

invulnerability *n* invincibility, invulnerableness.

invulnerable *adj* incontrovertible, invincible, unassailable, irrefragable.

inward[1] *adj* incoming, inner, interior, internal; essential, hidden, mental, spiritual; private, secret.

inward[2], **inwards** *adv* inwardly, towards the inside, within.

inweave *vb* entwine, interlace, intertwine, interweave, weave together.

iota *n* atom, bit, glimmer, grain, jot, mite, particle, scintilla, scrap, shadow, spark, tittle, trace, whit.

irascibility *n* hastiness, hot-headedness, impatience, irascibleness, irritability, peevishness, petulance, quickness, spleen, testiness, touchiness.

irascible *adj* choleric, cranky, hasty, hot, hot-headed, impatient, irritable, nettlesome, peevish, peppery, pettish, petulant, quick, splenetic, snappish, testy, touchy, waspish.

irate *adj* angry, incensed, ireful, irritated, piqued.

ire *n* anger, choler, exasperation, fury, indignation, passion, rage, resentment, wrath.

ireful *adj* angry, furious, incensed, irate, raging, passionate.

iridescent *adj* irisated, nacreous, opalescent, pavonine, prismatic, rainbow-like.

iris *n* rainbow; (*bot*) fleur-de-lis, flower-de-luce; diaphragm of the eye.

irksome *adj* annoying, burdensome, humdrum, monotonous, tedious, tiresome, wearisome, weary, wearying.

iron *adj* ferric, ferrous.

ironic, ironical *adj* mocking, sarcastic.

irons *n pl* chains, fetters, gyves, hampers, manacles, shackles.

irony *n* mockery, raillery, ridicule, sarcasm, satire.

irradiate *vb* brighten, illume, illuminate, illumine, light up, shine upon.

irrational *adj* absurd, extravagant, foolish, injudicious, preposterous, ridiculous, silly, unwise; unreasonable, unreasoning, unthinking; brute, brutish; aberrant, alienated, brainless, crazy, demented, fantastic, idiotic, imbecilic, insane, lunatic.

irrationality *n* absurdity, folly, foolishness, unreasonableness; brutishness.

irreclaimable *adj* hopeless, incurable, irrecoverable, irreparable, irretrievable, irreversible, remediless; abandoned, graceless, hardened, impenitent, incorrigible, lost, obdurate, profligate, recreant, reprobate, shameless, unrepentant.

irreconcilable *adj* implacable, inexorable, inexpiable, unappeasable; incompatible, incongruous, inconsistent.

irrecoverable *adj* hopeless, incurable, irremediable, irreparable, irretrievable, remediless.

irrefragable *adj* impregnable, incontestable, incontrovertible, indisputable, invincible, irrefutable, irresistible, unanswerable, unassailable, undeniable.

irrefutable *adj* impregnable, incontestable, incontrovertible, indisputable, invincible, irrefragable, irresistible, unanswerable, unassailable, undeniable.

irregular *adj* aberrant, abnormal, anomalistic, anomalous, crooked, devious, eccentric, erratic, exceptional, heteromorphous, raged, tortuous, unconformable, unusual; capricious, changeable, desultory, fitful, spasmodic, uncertain, unpunctual, unsettled, variable; disordered, disorderly, improper, uncanonical, unparliamentary, unsystematic; asymmetric, uneven, unsymmetrical; disorderly, dissolute, immoral, loose, wild. * *n* casual, freelance, hireling, mercenary.

irregularity *n* aberration, abnormality, anomaly, anomalousness, singularity; capriciousness, changeableness, uncertainty, variableness; asymmetry; disorderliness, dissoluteness, immorality, laxity, looseness, wildness.

irrelevance, irrelevancy *n* impertinency, inapplicability, nonpertinency.

irrelevant *adj* extraneous, foreign, illogical, impertinent, inapplicable, inapposite, inappropriate, inconsequent, unessential, unrelated.

irreligion *n* atheism, godlessness, impiety, ungodliness.

irreligious *adj* godless, ungodly, undevout; blasphemous, disrespectful, impious, irreverent, profane, ribald, wicked.

irremediable *adj* hopeless, incurable, immedicable, irrecoverable, irreparable, remediless.

irremissible *adj* binding, inexpiable, obligatory, unatonable, unpardonable.

irreparable *adj* irrecoverable, irremediable, irretrievable, remediless.

irreprehensible *adj* blameless, faultless, inculpable, innocent, irreproachable, irreprovable, unblamable.

irrepressible *adj* insuppressible, uncontrollable, unquenchable, unsmotherable.

irreproachable *adj* blameless, faultless, inculpable, innocent, irreprehensible, irreprovable, unblamable.

irresistible *adj* irrefragable, irrepressible, overpowering, overwhelming, resistless.

irresolute *adj* changeable, faltering, fickle, hesitant, hesitating, inconstant, mutable, spineless, uncertain, undecided, undetermined, unsettled, unstable, unsteady, vacillating, wavering.

irrespective *adj* independent, regardless.
irresponsible *adj* unaccountable; untrustworthy.
irretrievable *adj* incurable, irrecoverable, irremediable, irreparable, remediless.
irreverence *n* blasphemy, impiety, profaneness, profanity; disesteem, disrespect.
irreverent *adj* blasphemous, impious, irreligious, profane; disrespectful, slighting.
irreversible *adj* irrepealable, irrevocable, unalterable, unchangeable; changeless, immutable, invariable.
irrevocable *adj* irrepealable, irreversible, unalterable, unchangeable.
irrigate *vb* moisten, wash, water, wet.
irrigation *n* watering.
irritability *n* excitability, fretfulness, irascibility, peevishness, petulance, snappishness, susceptibility, testiness.
irritable *adj* captious, choleric, excitable, fiery, fretful, hasty, hot, irascible, passionate, peppery, peevish, pettish, petulant, snappish, splenetic, susceptible, testy, touchy, waspish.
irritate *vb* anger, annoy, chafe, enrage, exacerbate, exasperate, fret, incense, jar, nag, nettle, offend, provoke, rasp, rile, ruffle, vex; gall, tease; (*med*) excite, inflame, stimulate.
irritation *n* irritating; anger, exacerbation, exasperation, excitement, indignation, ire, passion, provocation, resentment, wrath; (*med*) excitation, inflammation, stimulation; burn, itch.
irruption *n* breaking in, bursting in; foray, incursion, inroad, invasion, raid.
island *n* atoll, isle, islet, reef.
isochronal *adj* isochronous, uniform.
isolate *vb* detach, dissociate, insulate, quarantine, segregate, separate, set apart.
isolated *adj* detached, separate, single, solitary.
isolation *n* detachment, disconnection, insulation, quarantine, segregation, separation; loneliness, solitariness, solitude.
issue *vb* come out, flow out, flow forth, gush, run, rush out, spout, spring, spurt, well; arise, come, emanate, ensue, flow, follow, originate, proceed, spring; end, eventuate, result, terminate; appear, come out, deliver, depart, debouch, discharge, emerge, emit, put forth, send out; distribute, give out; publish, utter. * *n* conclusion, consequence, consummation, denouement, end, effect, event, finale, outcome, result, termination, upshot; antagonism, contest, controversy; debouchment, delivering, delivery, discharge, emergence, emigration, emission, issuance; flux, outflow, outpouring, stream; copy, edition, number; egress, exit, outlet, passage out, vent, way out; escape, sally, sortie; children, offspring, posterity, progeny.
itch *vb* tingle. * *n* itching; burning, coveting, importunate craving, teasing desire, uneasy hankering.
itching *n* itch; craving, longing, importunate craving, desire, appetite, hankering.
item *adv* also, in like manner. * *n* article, detail, entry, particular, point.
iterate *vb* reiterate, repeat.
itinerant *adj* nomadic, peripatetic, roaming, roving, travelling, unsettled, wandering.
itinerary *n* guide, guidebook; circuit, route.

J

jabber *vb* chatter, gabble, prate, prattle.
jacket *n* casing, cover, sheath; anorak, blazer coat, doublet, jerkin.
jaded *adj* dull, exhausted, fatigued, satiated, tired, weary.
jagged *adj* cleft, divided, indented, notched, serrated, ragged, uneven.
jail, gaol *n* bridewell, (*sl*) clink, dungeon, lockup, (*sl*) nick, penitentiary, prison.
jam *vb* block, crowd, crush, press. * *n* block, crowd, crush, mass, pack, press.
jangle *vb* bicker, chatter, dispute, gossip, jar, quarrel, spar, spat, squabble, tiff, wrangle. * *n* clang, clangour, clash, din, dissonance.
jar[1] *vb* clash, grate, interfere, shake; bicker, contend, jangle, quarrel, spar, spat, squabble, tiff, wrangle; agitate, jolt, jounce, shake. * *n* clash, conflict, disaccord, discord, jangle, dissonance; agitation, jolt, jostle, shake, shaking, shock, start.
jar[2] *n* can, crock, cruse, ewer, flagon.
jarring *adj* conflicting, discordant, inconsistent, inconsonant, wrangling.
jargon *n* gabble, gibberish, nonsense, rigmarole: argot, cant, lingo, slang; chaos, confusion, disarray, disorder, jumble.
jaundiced *adj* biased, envious, prejudiced.
jaunt *n* excursion, ramble, tour, trip.
jaunty *adj* airy, cheery, garish, gay, fine, fluttering, showy, sprightly, unconcerned.
jealous *adj* distrustful, envious, suspicious; anxious, apprehensive, intolerant, solicitous, zealous.
jealousy *n* envy, suspicion, watchfulness.
jeer *vb* deride, despise, flout, gibe, jape, jest, mock, scoff, sneer, spurn, rail, ridicule, taunt. * *n* abuse, derision, mockery, sneer, ridicule, taunt.
jeopardize *vb* endanger, hazard, imperil, risk, venture.
jeopardy *n* danger, hazard, peril, risk, venture.
jerk *vb, n* flip, hitch, pluck, tweak, twitch, yank.
jest *vb* banter, joke, quiz. * *n* fun, joke, pleasantry, raillery, sport.
jester *n* humorist, joker, wag; buffoon, clown, droll, fool, harlequin, punch.
jibe *see* **gibe**.
jiffy *n* instant, moment, second, twinkling, trice.
jilt *vb* break with, deceive, disappoint, discard. * *n* coquette, flirt, light-o'-love.
jingle *vb* chink, clink, jangle, rattle, tinkle. * *n* chink, clink, jangle, rattle, tinkle; chorus, ditty, melody, song.
jocose *adj* comical, droll, facetious, funny, humorous, jesting, jocular, merry, sportive, waggish, witty.
jocund *adj* airy, blithe, cheerful, debonair, frolicsome, jolly, joyful, joyous, lively, merry, playful.
jog *vb* jostle, notify, nudge, push, remind, warn; canter, run, trot. * *n* push, reminder.
join *vb* add, annex, append, attach; cement, combine, conjoin, connect, couple, dovetail, link, unite, yoke; amalgamate, assemble, associate, confederate, consolidate.
joint *vb* fit, join, unite. * *adj* combined, concerted, concurrent, conjoint. * *n* connection, junction, juncture, hinge, splice.
joke *vb* banter, jest, frolic, rally. * *n* crank, jest, quip, quirk, witticism.
jolly *adj* airy, blithe, cheerful, frolicsome, gamesome, facetious, funny, gay, jovial, joyous, merry, mirthful, jocular, jocund, playful, sportive, sprightly, waggish; bouncing, chubby, lusty, plump, portly, stout.
jolt *vb* jar, shake, shock. * *n* jar, jolting, jounce, shaking.
jostle *vb* collide, elbow, hustle, joggle, shake, shoulder, shove.
jot *n* ace, atom, bit, corpuscle, iota, grain, mite, particle, scrap, whit.
journal *n* daybook, diary, log; gazette, magazine, newspapers, periodical.
journey *vb* ramble, roam, rove, travel: fare, go, proceed. * *n* excursion, expedition, jaunt, passage, pilgrimage, tour, travel, trip, voyage.
jovial *adj* airy, convivial, festive, jolly, joyous, merry, mirthful.
joy *n* beatification, beatitude, delight, ecstasy, exultation, gladness, glee, mirth, pleasure, rapture, ravishment, transport; bliss, felicity, happiness.
joyful *adj* blithe, blithesome, buoyant, delighted, elate, elated, exultant, glad, happy, jocund, jolly, joyous, merry, rejoicing.
jubilant *adj* exultant, exulting, rejoicing, triumphant.
judge *vb* conclude, decide, decree, determine, pronounce; adjudicate, arbitrate, condemn, doom, sentence, try, umpire; account, apprehend, believe, consider, deem, esteem, guess, hold, imagine, measure, reckon, regard, suppose, think; appreciate, estimate. * *n* adjudicator, arbiter, arbitrator, bencher, justice, magistrate, moderator, referee, umpire, connoisseur, critic.

judgment, judgement *n* brains, ballast, circumspection, depth, discernment, discretion, discrimination, intelligence, judiciousness, penetration, prudence, sagacity, sense, sensibility, taste, understanding, wisdom, wit; conclusion, consideration, decision, determination, estimation, notion, opinion, thought; adjudication, arbitration, award, censure, condemnation, decree, doom, sentence.
judicious *adj* cautious, considerate, cool, critical, discriminating, discreet, enlightened, provident, politic, prudent, rational, reasonable, sagacious, sensible, sober, solid, sound, staid, wise.
jug *n* cruse, ewer, flagon, pitcher, vessel.
juicy *adj* lush, moist, sappy, succulent, watery; entertaining, exciting, interesting, lively, racy, spicy.
jumble *vb* confound, confuse, disarrange, disorder, mix, muddle. * *n* confusion, disarrangement, disorder, medley, mess, mixture, muddle.
jump *vb* bound, caper, clear, hop, leap, skip, spring, vault. * *n* bound, caper, hop, leak, skip, spring, vault; fence, hurdle, obstacle; break, gap, interruption, space; advance, boost, increase, rise; jar, jolt, shock, start, twitch.
junction *n* combination, connection, coupling, hook-up, joining, linking, seam, union; conjunction, joint, juncture.
junta *n* cabal, clique, combination, confederacy, coterie, faction, gang, league, party, set.
just *adj* equitable, lawful, legitimate, reasonable, right, rightful; candid, even-handed, fair, fair-minded, impartial; blameless, conscientious, good, honest, honourable, pure, square, straightforward, virtuous; accurate, correct, exact, normal, proper, regular, true; condign, deserved, due, merited, suitable.
justice *n* accuracy, equitableness, equity, fairness, honesty, impartiality, justness, right; judge, justiciary.
justifiable *adj* defensible, fit, proper, right, vindicable, warrantable.
justification *n* defence, exculpation, excuse, exoneration, reason, vindication, warrant.
justify *vb* approve, defend, exculpate, excuse, exonerate, maintain, vindicate, support, warrant.
justness *n* accuracy, correctness, fitness, justice, precision, propriety.
juvenile *adj* childish, immature, puerile, young, youthful. * *n* boy, child, girl, youth.
juxtaposition *n* adjacency, contiguity, contact, proximity.

K

keen[1] *adj* ardent, eager, earnest, fervid, intense, vehement, vivid; acute, sharp; cutting; acrimonious, biting, bitter, caustic, poignant, pungent, sarcastic, severe; astute, discerning, intelligent, quick, sagacious, sharp-sighted, shrewd.
keen[2] *vb* bemoan, bewail, deplore, grieve, lament, mourn, sorrow, weep. * *n* coronach, dirge, elegy, lament, lamentation, monody, plaint, requiem, threnody.
keenness *n* ardour, eagerness, fervour, vehemence, zest; acuteness, sharpness; rigour, severity, sternness; acrimony, asperity, bitterness, causticity, causticness, pungency; astuteness, sagacity, shrewdness.
keep *vb* detain, hold, retain; continue, preserve; confine, detain, reserve, restrain, withhold; attend, guard, preserve, protect; adhere to, fulfil; celebrate, commemorate, honour, observe, perform, solemnize; maintain, support, sustain; husband, save, store; abide, dwell, lodge, stay, remain; endure, last. * *n* board, maintenance, subsistence, support; donjon, dungeon, stronghold, tower.
keeper *n* caretaker, conservator, curator, custodian, defender, gaoler, governor, guardian, jailer, superintendent, warden, warder, watchman.
keeping *n* care, charge, custody, guard, possession; feed, maintenance, support; agreement, conformity, congruity, consistency, harmony.
keepsake *n* memento, souvenir, token.
ken *n* cognizance, sight, view.
key *adj* basic, crucial, essential, important, major, principal. * *n* lock-opener, opener; clue, elucidation, explanation, guide, solution, translation; (*mus*) keynote, tonic; clamp, lever, wedge.
kick *vb* boot, punt; oppose, rebel, resist, spurn. * *n* force, intensity, power, punch, vitality; excitement, pleasure, thrill.
kidnap *vb* abduct, capture, carry off, remove, steal away.
kill *vb* assassinate, butcher, dispatch, destroy, massacre, murder, slaughter, slay.
kin *adj* akin, allied, cognate, kindred, related. * *n* affinity, consanguinity, relationship; connections, family, kindred, kinsfolk, relations, relatives, siblings.
kind[1] *adj* accommodating, amiable, beneficent, benevolent, benign, bland, bounteous, brotherly, charitable, clement, compassionate, complaisant, gentle, good, good-natured, forbearing, friendly, generous, gracious, humane, indulgent, lenient, mild, obliging, sympathetic, tender, tender-hearted.
kind[2] *n* breed, class, family, genus, race, set, species, type; brand, character, colour, denomination, description, form, make, manner, nature, persuasion, sort, stamp, strain, style.
kindle *vb* fire, ignite, inflame, light; animate, awaken, bestir, exasperate, excite, foment, incite, provoke, rouse, stimulate, stir, thrill, warm.
kindliness *n* amiability, benevolence, benignity, charity, compassion, friendliness, humanity, kindness, sympathy; gentleness, mildness, softness.
kindly *adj* appropriate, congenial, kindred, natural, proper; benevolent, considerate, friendly, gracious, humane, sympathetic, well-disposed. * *adv* agreeably, graciously, humanely, politely, thoughtfully.
kindness *n* benefaction, charity, favour; amiability, beneficence, benevolence, benignity, clemency, generosity, goodness, grace, humanity, kindliness, mildness, philanthropy, sympathy, tenderness.
kindred *adj* akin, allied, congenial, connected, related, sympathetic. * *n* affinity, consanguinity, flesh, relationship; folks, kin, kinsfolk, kinsmen, relations, relatives.
king *n* majesty, monarch, sovereign.
kingdom *n* dominion, empire, monarchy, rule, sovereignty, supremacy; region, tract; division, department, domain, province, realm.
kingly *adj* imperial, kinglike, monarchical, regal, royal, sovereign; august, glorious, grand, imperial, imposing, magnificent, majestic, noble, splendid.
kink *n* cramp, crick, curl, entanglement, knot, loop, twist; crochet, whim, wrinkle.
kinsfolk *n* kin, kindred, kinsmen, relations, relatives.
kit *n* equipment, implements, outfit, set, working.
knack *n* ability, address, adroitness, aptitude, aptness, dexterity, dextrousness, expertness, facility, quickness, readiness, skill.
knave *n* caitiff, cheat, miscreant, rascal, rogue, scamp, scapegrace, scoundrel, sharper, swindler, trickster, villain.
knavery *n* criminality, dishonesty, fraud, knavishness, rascality, scoundrelism, trickery, villainy.
knavish *adj* dishonest, fraudulent, rascally, scoundrelly, unprincipled, roguish, trickish, tricky, villainous.
knell *vb* announce, peal, ring, toll. * *n* chime, peal, ring, toll.
knife *vb* cut, slash, stab. * *n* blade, jackknife, lance.
knit *vb* connect, interlace, join, unite, weave.
knob *n* boss, bunch, hunch, lump, protuberance, stud.
knock *vb* clap, cuff, hit, rap, rattle, slap, strike, thump; beat, blow, box. * *n* blow, slap, smack, thump; blame, criticism, rejection, setback.
knoll *n* hill, hillock, mound.
knot *vb* complicate, entangle, gnarl, kink, tie, weave. * *n* complication, entanglement; connection, tie; joint, node, knag; bunch, rosette, tuft; band, cluster, clique, crew, gang, group, pack, set, squad.
knotty *adj* gnarled, hard, knaggy, knurled, knotted, rough, rugged; complex, difficult, harassing, intricate, involved, perplexing, troublesome.

know *vb* apprehend, comprehend, cognize, discern, perceive, recognize, see, understand; discriminate, distinguish.

knowing *adj* accomplished, competent, experienced, intelligent, proficient, qualified, skilful, well-informed; aware, conscious, percipient, sensible, thinking; cunning, expressive, significant.

knowingly *adv* consciously, intentionally, purposely, wittingly.

knowledge *n* apprehension, command, comprehension, discernment, judgment, perception, understanding, wit; acquaintance, acquirement, attainments, enlightenment, erudition, information, learning, lore, mastery, scholarship, science; cognition, cognizance, consciousness, ken, notice, prescience, recognition.

knowledgeable *adj* aware, conscious, experienced, well-informed; educated, intelligent, learned, scholarly.

knuckle *vb* cringe, crouch, stoop, submit, yield.

L

laborious *adj* assiduous, diligent, hardworking, indefatigable, industrious, painstaking, sedulous, toiling; arduous, difficult, fatiguing, hard, Herculean, irksome, onerous, tiresome, toilsome, wearisome.

labour *vb* drudge, endeavour, exert, strive, toil, travail, work. * *n* drudgery, effort, exertion, industry, pains, toil, work; childbirth, delivery, parturition.

labyrinth *n* entanglement, intricacy, maze, perplexity, windings.

labyrinthine *adj* confused, convoluted, intricate, involved, labyrinthian, labyrinthic, perplexing, winding.

lace *vb* attach, bind, fasten, intertwine, tie, twine. * *n* filigree, lattice, mesh, net, netting, network, openwork, web.

lacerate *vb* claw, cut, lancinate, mangle, rend, rip, sever, slash, tear, wound; afflict, harrow, rend, torture, wound.

lack *vb* need, want. * *n* dearth, default, defectiveness, deficiency, deficit, destitution, insufficiency, need, scantiness, scarcity, shortcoming, shortness, want.

lackadaisical *adj* languishing, sentimental, pensive.

laconic *adj* brief, compact, concise, pithy, sententious, short, succinct, terse.

lad *n* boy, schoolboy, stripling, youngster, youth.

lading *n* burden, cargo, freight, load.

ladylike *adj* courtly, genteel, refined, well-bred.

lag *vb* dawdle, delay, idle, linger, loiter, saunter, tarry.

laggard *n* idler, lingerer, loiterer, lounger, saunterer, sluggard.

lair *n* burrow, couch, den, form, resting place.

lambent *adj* flickering, gliding, gleaming, licking, touching, twinkling.

lame *vb* cripple, disable, hobble. * *adj* crippled, defective, disabled, halt, hobbling, limping; feeble, insufficient, poor, unsatisfactory, weak.

lament *vb* complain, grieve, keen, moan, mourn, sorrow, wail, weep; bemoan, bewail, deplore, regret. * *n* complaint, lamentation, moan, moaning, plaint, wailing; coronach, dirge, elegy, keen, monody, requiem, threnody.

lamentable *adj* deplorable, doleful, grievous, lamented, melancholy, woeful; contemptible, miserable, pitiful, poor, wretched.

lamentation *n* dirge, grief, lament, moan, moaning, mourning, plaint, ululation, sorrow, wailing.

lampoon *vb* calumniate, defame, lash, libel, parody, ridicule, satirize, slander. * *n* calumny, defamation, libel, parody, pasquinade, parody, satire, slander.

land *vb* arrive, debark, disembark. * *n* earth, ground, soil; country, district, province, region, reservation, territory, tract, weald.

landlord *n* owner, proprietor; host, hotelier, innkeeper.

landscape *n* prospect, scene, view.

language *n* dialect, speech, tongue, vernacular; conversation; expression, idiom, jargon, parlance, phraseology, slang, style, terminology; utterance, voice.

languid *adj* drooping, exhausted, faint, feeble, flagging, languishing, pining, weak; dull, heartless, heavy, inactive, listless, lukewarm, slow, sluggish, spiritless, torpid.

languish *vb* decline, droop, fade, fail, faint, pine, sicken, sink, wither.

languor *n* debility, faintness, feebleness, languidness, languishment, weakness; apathy, ennui, heartlessness, heaviness, lethargy, listlessness, torpidness, torpor, weariness.

lank *adj* attenuated, emaciated, gaunt, lean, meagre, scraggy, slender, skinny, slim, starveling, thin.

lap[1] *vb* drink, lick, mouth, tongue; plash, ripple, splash, wash; quaff, sip, sup, swizzle, tipple. * *n* draught, dram, drench, drink, gulp, lick, swig, swill, quaff, sip, sup, suck; plash, splash, wash.

lap[2] *vb* cover, enfold, fold, turn, twist, swaddle, wrap; distance, pass, outdistance, overlap. * *n* fold, flap, lappet, lapel, ply, plait; ambit, beat, circle, circuit, cycle, loop, orbit, revolution, round, tour, turn, walk.

lapse *vb* glide, sink, slide, slip; err, fail, fall. * *n* course, flow, gliding; declension, decline, fall; error, fault, indiscretion, misstep, shortcoming, slip.

larceny *n* pilfering, robbery, stealing, theft, thievery.

large *adj* big, broad, bulky, colossal, elephantine, enormous, heroic, great, huge, immense, vast; broad, expanded, extensive, spacious, wide; abundant, ample, copious, full, liberal, plentiful; capacious, comprehensive.

lascivious *adj* concupiscent, immodest, incontinent, goatish, lecherous, lewd, libidinous, loose, lubricious, lustful, prurient, salacious, sensual, unchaste, voluptuous, wanton.

lash[1] *vb* belay, bind, strap, tie; fasten, join, moor, pinion, secure.

lash[2] *vb* beat, castigate, chastise, flagellate, flail, flay, flog, goad, scourge, swinge, thrash, whip; assail, censure, excoriate, lampoon, satirize, trounce. * *n* scourge, strap, thong, whip; cut, slap, smack, stroke, stripe.

lass *n* damsel, girl, lassie, maiden, miss.

lassitude *n* dullness, exhaustion, fatigue, languor, languidness, prostration, tiredness, weariness.

last[1] *vb* abide, carry on, continue, dwell, endure, extend, maintain, persist, prevail, remain, stand, stay, survive.

last[2] *adj* hindermost, hindmost, latest; conclusive, final, terminal, ultimate; eventual, endmost, extreme, farthest, ultimate; greatest, highest, maximal, maximum, most, supreme, superlative, utmost; latest, newest; aforegoing, foregoing, latter, preceding; departing, farewell, final, leaving, parting, valedictory. * *n* conclusion, consummation, culmination, end, ending, finale, finis, finish, termination.

last[3] *n* cast, form, matrix, mould, shape, template.

lasting *adj* abiding, durable, enduring, fixed, perennial, permanent, perpetual, stable.

lastly *adv* conclusively, eventually, finally, ultimately.

late *adj* behindhand, delayed, overdue, slow, tardy; deceased, former; recent. * *adv* lately, recently, sometime; tardily.

latent *adj* abeyant, concealed, hidden, invisible, occult, secret, unseen, veiled.

latitude *n* amplitude, breadth, compass, extent, range, room, scope; freedom, indulgence, liberty; laxity.

latter *adj* last, latest, modern, recent.

lattice *n* espalier, grating, latticework, trellis.

laud *vb* approve, celebrate, extol, glorify, magnify, praise.

laudable *adj* commendable, meritorious, praiseworthy.

laugh *vb* cackle, chortle, chuckle, giggle, guffaw, snicker, snigger, titter. * *n* chortle, chuckle, giggle, guffaw, laughter, titter.

laughable *adj* amusing, comical, diverting, droll, farcical, funny, ludicrous, mirthful, ridiculous.

laughter *n* cackle, chortle, chuckle, glee, giggle, guffaw, laugh, laughing.

launch *vb* cast, dart, dispatch, hurl, lance, project, throw; descant, dilate, enlarge, expiate; begin, commence, inaugurate, open, start.

lavish *vb* dissipate, expend, spend, squander, waste. * *adj* excessive, extravagant, generous, immoderate, overliberal, prodigal, profuse, thriftless, unrestrained, unstinted, unthrifty, wasteful.

law *n* act, code, canon, command, commandment, covenant, decree, edict, enactment, order, precept, principle, statute, regulation, rule; jurisprudence; litigation, process, suit.

lawful *adj* constitutional, constituted, legal, legalized, legitimate; allowable, authorized, permissible, warrantable; equitable, rightful, just, proper, valid.

lawless *adj* anarchic, anarchical, chaotic, disorderly, insubordinate, rebellious, reckless, riotous, seditious, wild.

lawyer *n* advocate, attorney, barrister, counsel, counsellor, pettifogger, solicitor.

lax *adj* loose, relaxed, slow; drooping, flabby, soft; neglectful, negligent, remiss; dissolute, immoral, licentious, seditious, wild.

lay[1] *vb* deposit, establish, leave, place, plant, posit, put, set, settle, spread; arrange, dispose, locate, organize, position; bear, produce; advance, lodge, offer, submit; allocate, allot, ascribe, assign, attribute, charge, impute; concoct, contrive, design, plan, plot, prepare; apply, burden, encumber, impose, saddle, tax; bet, gamble, hazard, risk, stake, wager; allay, alleviate, appease, assuage, calm, relieve, soothe, still, suppress; disclose, divulge, explain, reveal, show, unveil; acquire, grab, grasp, seize; assault, attack, beat up; discover, find, unearth; bless, confirm, consecrate, ordain. * *n* arrangement, array, form, formation; attitude, aspect, bearing, demeanour, direction, lie, pose, position, posture, set.

lay[2] *adj* amateur, inexpert, nonprofessional; civil, laic, laical, nonclerical, nonecclesiastical, nonreligious, secular, temporal, unclerical.

lay[3] *n* ballad, carol, ditty, lied, lyric, ode, poem, rhyme, round, song, verse.

layer *n* bed, course, lay, seam, stratum.

laziness *n* idleness, inactivity, indolence, slackness, sloth, fulness, sluggishness, tardiness.

lazy *adj* idle, inactive, indolent, inert, slack, slothful, slow, sluggish, supine, torpid.

lead *vb* conduct, deliver, direct, draw, escort, guide; front, head, precede; advance, excel, outstrip, pass; allure, entice, induce, persuade, prevail; conduce, contribute, serve, tend. * *adj* chief, first, foremost, main, primary, prime, principal. * *n* direction, guidance, leadership; advance; precedence, priority.

leader *n* conductor, director, guide; captain, chief, chieftain, commander, head; superior, dominator, victor.

leading *adj* governing, ruling; capital, chief, first, foremost, highest, principal, superior.

league *vb* ally, associate, band, combine, confederate, unite. * *n* alliance, association, coalition, combination, combine, confederacy, confederation, consortium, union.

leak *vb* drip, escape, exude, ooze, pass, percolate, spill. * *n* chink, crack, crevice, hole, fissure, oozing, opening; drip, leakage, leaking, percolation.

lean[1] *adj* bony, emaciated, gaunt, lank, meagre, poor, skinny, thin; dull, barren, jejune, meagre, tame; inadequate, pitiful, scanty, slender; bare, barren, infertile, unproductive.

lean[2] *vb* incline, slope; bear, recline, repose, rest; confide, depend, rely, trust.

leaning *n* aptitude, bent, bias, disposition, inclination, liking, predilection, proneness, propensity, tendency.

leap *vb* bound, clear, jump, spring, vault; caper, frisk, gambol, hop, skip. * *n* bound, jump, spring, vault; caper, frisk, gambol, hop, skip.

learn *vb* acquire, ascertain, attain, collect, gain, gather, hear, memorize.

learned *adj* erudite, lettered, literate, scholarly, well-read; expert, experienced, knowing, skilled, versed, well-informed.

learner *n* beginner, novice, pupil, student, tyro.

learning *n* acquirements, attainments, culture, education, information, knowledge, lore, scholarship, tuition.

least *adj* meanest, minutest, smallest, tiniest.

leave[1] *vb* abandon, decamp, go, quit, vacate, withdraw; desert, forsake, relinquish, renounce; commit, consign, refer; cease, desist from, discontinue, refrain, stop; allow, let, let alone, permit; bequeath, demise, desist, will.

leave[2] *n* allowance, liberty, permission, licence, sufferance; departure, retirement, withdrawal; adieu, farewell, goodbye.

leaven *vb* ferment, lighten, raise; colour, elevate, imbue, inspire, lift, permeate, tinge; infect, vitiate. * *n* barm, ferment, yeast; influence, inspiration.

leavings *n pl* bits, dregs, fragments, leftovers, pieces, relics, remains, remnants, scraps.

lecherous *adj* carnal, concupiscent, incontinent, lascivious, lewd, libidinous, lubricious, lustful, wanton, salacious, unchaste.

lechery *n* concupiscence, lasciviousness, lewdness, lubriciousness, lubricity, lust, salaciousness, salacity.

lecture *vb* censure, chide, reprimand, reprove, scold, sermonize; address, harangue, teach. * *n* censure, lecturing, lesson, reprimand, reproof, scolding; address, discourse, prelection.

ledge *n* projection, ridge, shelf.

lees *n pl* dregs, precipitate, refuse, sediment, settlings.

leg *n* limb, prop.

legacy *n* bequest, gift, heirloom; heritage, inheritance, tradition.

legal *adj* allowable, authorized, constitutional, lawful, legalized, legitimate, proper, sanctioned.

legalize *vb* authorize, legitimate, legitimatize, legitimize, permit, sanction.

legend *n* fable, fiction, myth, narrative, romance, story, tale.

legendary *adj* fabulous, fictitious, mythical, romantic.

legible *adj* clear, decipherable, fair, distinct, plain, readable; apparent, discoverable, recognizable, manifest.

legion *n* army, body, cohort, column, corps,
detachment, detail, division, force, maniple, phalanx, platoon; squad; army, horde, host, multitude, number, swarm, throng. * *adj* many, multitudinous, myriad, numerous.

legislate *vb* enact, ordain.

legitimacy *n* lawfulness, legality; genuineness.

legitimate *adj* authorized, lawful, legal, sanctioned; genuine, valid; correct, justifiable, logical, reasonable, warrantable, warranted.

leisure *n* convenience, ease, freedom, liberty, opportunity, recreation, retirement, vacation.

lend *vb* advance, afford, bestow, confer, furnish, give, grant, impart, loan, supply.

lengthen *vb* elongate, extend, produce, prolong, stretch; continue, protract.

lengthy *adj* diffuse, lengthened, long, long-drawn-out, prolix, prolonged, protracted.

lenience, leniency *n* clemency, compassion, forbearance, gentleness, lenity, mercy, mildness, tenderness.

lenient *adj* assuasive, lenitive, mitigating, mitigative, softening, soothing; clement, easy, forbearing, gentle, humouring, indulgent, long-suffering, merciful, mild, tender, tolerant.

lesion *n* derangement, disorder, hurt, injury.

less *adj* baser, inferior, lower, smaller; decreased, fewer, lesser, reduced, smaller, shorter; * *adv* barely, below, least, under; decreasingly. * *prep* excepting, lacking, minus, sans, short of, without.

lessen *vb* abate, abridge, contract, curtail, decrease, diminish, narrow, reduce, shrink; degrade, lower; dwindle, weaken.

lesson *n* exercise, task; instruction, precept; censure, chiding, lecture, lecturing, rebuke, reproof, scolding.

let[1] *vb* admit, allow, authorize, permit, suffer; charter, hire, lease, rent.

let[2] *vb* hinder, impede, instruct, prevent. * *n* hindrance, impediment, interference, obstacle, obstruction, restriction.

lethal *adj* deadly, destructive, fatal, mortal, murderous.

lethargic *adj* apathetic, comatose, drowsy, dull, heavy, inactive, inert, sleepy, stupid, stupefied, torpid.

lethargy *n* apathy, coma, drowsiness, dullness, hypnotism, inactiveness, inactivity, inertia, sleepiness, sluggishness, stupefaction, stupidity, stupor, torpor.

letter *n* epistle, missive, note.

lettered *adj* bookish, educated, erudite, learned, literary, versed, well-read.

levee *n* ceremony, entertainment, reception, party, soiree; embankment.

level *vb* equalize, flatten, horizontalize, smooth; demolish, destroy, raze; aim, direct, point. * *adj* equal, even, flat, flush, horizontal, plain, plane, smooth. * *n* altitude, degree, equality, evenness, plain, plane, smoothness; deck, floor, layer, stage, storey, tier.

levity *n* buoyancy, facetiousness, fickleness, flightiness, flippancy, frivolity, giddiness, inconstancy, levity, volatility.

levy *vb* collect, exact, gather, tax; call, muster, raise, summon. * *n* duty, tax.

lewd *adj* despicable, impure, lascivious, libidinous, licentious, loose, lustful, profligate, unchaste, vile, wanton, wicked.

liability *n* accountableness, accountability, duty, obligation, responsibility, tendency; exposedness; debt, indebtedness, obligation.

liable *adj* accountable, amenable, answerable, bound, responsible; exposed, likely, obnoxious, subject.

liaison *n* amour, intimacy, intrigue; connection, relation, union.

libel *vb* calumniate, defame, lampoon, satirize, slander, vilify. * *n* calumny, defamation, lampoon, satire, slander, vilification, vituperation.

liberal *adj* beneficent, bountiful, charitable, disinterested, free, generous, munificent, open-hearted, princely, unselfish; broad-minded, catholic, chivalrous, enlarged, high-minded, honourable, magnanimous, tolerant, unbiased, unbigoted; abundant, ample, bounteous, full, large, plentiful, unstinted; humanizing, liberalizing, refined, refining.

liberality *n* beneficence, bountifulness, bounty, charity, disinterestedness, generosity, kindness, munificence; benefaction, donation, gift, gratuity, present; broad-mindedness, catholicity, candour, impartiality, large-mindedness, magnanimity, toleration.

liberate *vb* deliver, discharge, disenthral, emancipate, free, manumit, ransom, release.

libertine *adj* corrupt, depraved, dissolute, licentious, profligate, rakish. * *n* debauchee, lecher, profligate, rake, roue, voluptuary.

liberty *n* emancipation, freedom, independence, liberation, self-direction, self-government; franchise, immunity, privilege; leave, licence, permission.

libidinous *adj* carnal, concupiscent, debauched, impure, incontinent, lascivious, lecherous, lewd, loose, lubricious, lustful, salacious, sensual, unchaste, wanton, wicked.

licence *n* authorization, leave, permission, privilege, right; certificate, charter, dispensation, imprimatur, permit, warrant; anarchy, disorder, freedom, lawlessness, laxity, liberty.

license *vb* allow, authorize, grant, permit, warrant; suffer, tolerate.

licentious *adj* disorderly, riotous, uncontrolled, uncurbed, ungovernable, unrestrained, unruly, wanton; debauched, dissolute, lax, libertine, loose, profligate, rakish; immoral, impure, lascivious, lecherous, lewd, libertine, libidinous, lustful, sensual, unchaste, wicked.

lick *vb* beat, flog, spank, thrash; lap, taste. * *n* blow, slap, stroke; salt-spring.

lie[1] *vb* couch, recline, remain, repose, rest; consist, pertain.

lie[2] *vb* equivocate, falsify, fib, prevaricate, romance. * *n* equivocation, falsehood, falsification, fib, misrepresentation, prevarication, untruth; delusion, illusion.

lief *adv* freely, gladly, willingly.

life *n* activity, alertness, animation, briskness, energy, sparkle, spirit, sprightliness, verve, vigour, vivacity; behaviour, conduct, deportment; being, duration, existence, lifetime; autobiography, biography, curriculum vitae, memoirs, story.

lifeless *adj* dead, deceased, defunct, extinct, inanimate; cold, dull, flat, frigid, inert, lethargic, passive, pulseless, slow, sluggish, tame, torpid.

lift *vb* elevate, exalt, hoist, raise, uplift. * *n* aid, assistance, help; elevator.

light[1] *vb* alight, land, perch, settle. * *adj* porous, sandy, spongy, well-leavened; loose, sandy; free, portable, unburdened, unencumbered; inconsiderable, moderate, negligible, slight, small, trifling, trivial, unimportant; ethereal, feathery, flimsy, gossamer, insubstantial, weightless; easy, effortless, facile; fickle, frivolous, unsettled, unsteady, volatile; airy, buoyant, carefree, light-hearted, lightsome; unaccented, unstressed, weak.

light[2] *vb* conflagrate, fire, ignite, inflame, kindle; brighten, illume, illuminate, illumine, luminate, irradiate, lighten. * *adj* bright, clear, fair, lightsome, luminous, pale, pearly, whitish. * *n* dawn, day, daybreak, sunrise; blaze, brightness, effulgence, gleam, illumination, luminosity, phosphorescence, radiance, ray; candle, lamp, lantern, lighthouse, taper, torch; comprehension, enlightenment, information, insight, instruction, knowledge; elucidation, explanation, illustration; attitude, construction, interpretation, observation, reference, regard, respect, view.

lighten[1] *vb* allay, alleviate, ease, mitigate, palliate; disburden, disencumber, relieve, unburden, unload.

lighten[2] *vb* brighten, gleam, shine; light, illume, illuminate, illumine, irradiate; enlighten, inform; emit, flash.

light-headed *adj* dizzy, giddy, vertiginous; confused, delirious, wandering; addle-pated, frivolous, giddy, heedless, indiscreet, light, rattle-brained, thoughtless, volatile.

light-hearted *adj* blithe, blithesome, carefree, cheerful, frolicsome, gay, glad, gladsome, gleeful, happy, jocund, jovial, joyful, lightsome, merry.

lightness *n* flightiness, frivolity, giddiness, levity, volatility; agility, buoyancy, facility.

like[1] *vb* approve, please; cherish, enjoy, love, relish; esteem, fancy, regard; choose, desire, elect, list, prefer, select, wish. * *n* liking, partiality, preference.

like[2] *adj* alike, allied, analogous, cognate, corresponding, parallel, resembling, similar; equal, same; likely, probable. * *adv* likely, probably. * *n* counterpart, equal, match, peer, twin.

likelihood *n* probability, verisimilitude.

likely *adj* credible, liable, possible, probable; agreeable, appropriate, convenient, likable, pleasing, suitable, well-adapted, well-suited. * *adv* doubtlessly, presumably, probably.

likeness *n* appearance, form, parallel, resemblance, semblance, similarity, similitude; copy, counterpart, effigy, facsimile, image, picture, portrait, representation.

liking *n* desire, fondness, partiality, wish; appearance, bent, bias, disposition, inclination, leaning, penchant, predisposition, proneness, propensity, tendency, turn.

limb *n* arm, extremity, leg, member; bough, branch, offshoot.

limit *vb* bound, circumscribe, define; check, condition, hinder, restrain, restrict. * *n* bound, boundary, bourn, confine, frontier, march, precinct, term, termination, terminus; check, hindrance, obstruction, restraint, restriction.

limitation *n* check, constraint, restraint, restriction.

limitless *adj* boundless, endless, eternal, illimitable, immeasurable, infinite, never-ending, unbounded, undefined, unending, unlimited.

limp[1] *vb* halt, hitch, hobble, totter. * *n* hitch, hobble, shamble, shuffle, totter.

limp[2] *adj* drooping, droopy, floppy, sagging, weak; flabby, flaccid, flexible, limber, pliable, relaxed, slack, soft.

limpid *adj* bright, clear, crystal, crystalline, lucid, pellucid, pure, translucent, transparent.

line *vb* align, line up, range, rank, regiment; border, bound, edge, fringe, hem, interline, march, rim, verge; seam, stripe, streak, striate, trace; carve, chisel, crease, cut, crosshatch; define, delineate, describe. * *n* mark, streak, stripe; cable, cord, rope, string, thread; rank, row; ancestry, family, lineage, race, succession; course, method; business, calling, employment, job, occupation, post, pursuit.

lineage *n* ancestry, birth, breed, descendants, descent, extraction, family, forebears, forefathers, genealogy, house, line, offspring, progeny, race.

lineament *n* feature, line, outline, trait.

linen *n* cloth, fabric, flax, lingerie.

linger *vb* dally, dawdle, delay, idle, lag, loiter, remain, saunter, stay, tarry, wait.

link *vb* bind, conjoin, connect, fasten, join, tie, unite. * *n* bond, connection, connective, copula, coupler, joint, juncture; division, member, part, piece.

liquefy *vb* dissolve, fuse, melt, thaw.

liquid *adj* fluid; clear, dulcet, flowing, mellifluous, mellifluent, melting, soft. * *n* fluid, liquor.

list[1] *vb* alphabetize, catalogue, chronicle, codify, docket, enumerate, file, index, inventory, record, register, tabulate, tally; enlist, enroll; choose, desire, elect, like, please, prefer, wish. * *n* catalogue, enumeration, index, inventory, invoice, register, roll, schedule, scroll, series, table, tally; border, bound, limit; border, edge, selvedge, strip, stripe; fillet, listel.

list[2] *vb* cant, heel, incline, keel, lean, pitch, tilt, tip. * *n* cant, inclination, incline, leaning, pitch, slope, tilt, tip.

listen *vb* attend, eavesdrop, hark, hear, hearken, heed, obey, observe.

listless *adj* apathetic, careless, heedless, impassive, inattentive, indifferent, indolent, languid, torpid, vacant, supine, thoughtless, vacant.

listlessness *n* apathy, carelessness, heedlessness, impassivity, inattention, indifference, indolence, languidness, languor, supineness, thoughtlessness, torpor, torpidity, vacancy.

literally *adv* actually, really; exactly, precisely, rigorously, strictly.

literary *adj* bookish, book-learned, erudite, instructed, learned, lettered, literate, scholarly, well-read.

literature *n* erudition, learning, letters, lore, writings.

lithe *adj* flexible, flexile, limber, pliable, pliant, supple.

litigation *n* contending, contest, disputing, lawsuit.

litigious *adj* contentious, disputatious, quarrelsome; controvertible, disputable.

litter *vb* derange, disarrange, disorder, scatter, strew; bear. * *n* bedding, couch, palanquin, sedan, stretcher; confusion, disarray, disorder, mess, untidiness; fragments, rubbish, shreds, trash.

little *adj* diminutive, infinitesimal, minute, small, tiny, wee; brief, short, small; feeble, inconsiderable, insignificant, moderate, petty, scanty, slender, slight, trivial, unimportant, weak; contemptible, illiberal, mean, narrow, niggardly, paltry, selfish, stingy. * *n* handful, jot, modicum, pinch, pittance, trifle, whit.

live[1] *vb* be, exist; continue, endure, last, remain, survive; abide, dwell, reside; fare, feed, nourish, subsist, support; continue, lead, pass.

live[2] *adj* alive, animate, living, quick; burning, hot, ignited; bright, brilliant, glowing, lively, vivid; active, animated, earnest, glowing, wide-awake.

livelihood *n* living, maintenance, subsistence, support, sustenance.

liveliness *n* activity, animation, briskness, gaiety, spirit, sprightliness, vivacity.

lively *adj* active, agile, alert, brisk, energetic, nimble, quick, smart, stirring, supple, vigorous, vivacious; airy, animated, blithe, blithesome, buoyant, frolicsome, gleeful, jocund, jolly, merry, spirited, sportive, sprightly, spry; bright, brilliant, clear, fresh, glowing, strong, vivid; dynamic, forcible, glowing, impassioned, intense, keen, nervous, piquant, racy, sparkling, strenuous, vigorous.

living *adj* alive, breathing, existing, live, organic, quick; active, lively, quickening. * *n* livelihood, maintenance, subsistence, support; estate, keeping; benefice.

load *vb* freight, lade; burden, cumber, encumber, oppress, weigh. * *n* burden, freightage, pack, weight; cargo, freight, lading; clog, deadweight, encumbrance, incubus, oppression, pressure.

loafer *n* (*sl*) bum, idler, lounger, vagabond, vagrant.

loath *adj* averse, backward, disinclined, indisposed, reluctant, unwilling.

loathe *vb* abhor, abominate, detest, dislike, hate, recoil.

loathing *n* abhorrence, abomination, antipathy, aversion, detestation, disgust, hatred, horror, repugnance, revulsion.

loathsome *adj* disgusting, nauseating, nauseous, offensive, palling, repulsive, revolting, sickening; abominable, abhorrent, detestable, execrable, hateful, odious, shocking.

local *adj* limited, neighbouring, provincial, regional, restricted, sectional, territorial, topical.

locality *n* location, neighbourhood, place, position, site, situation, spot.

locate *vb* determine, establish, fix, place, set, settle.

lock[1] *vb* bolt, fasten, padlock, seal; confine; clog, impede, restrain, stop; clasp, embrace, encircle, enclose, grapple, hug, join, press. * *n* bolt, fastening, padlock; embrace, grapple, hug.

lock[2] *n* curl, ringlet, tress, tuft.

lodge *vb* deposit, fix, settle; fix, place, plant; accommodate, cover, entertain, harbour, quarter, shelter; abide, dwell, inhabit, live, reside, rest; remain, rest, sojourn, stay, stop. * *n* cabin, cot, cottage, hovel, hut, shed; cave, den, haunt, lair; assemblage, assembly, association club, group, society.

lodging *n* abode, apartment, dwelling, habitation, quarters, residence; cover, harbour, protection, refuge, shelter.

loftiness *n* altitude, elevation, height; arrogance, haughtiness, pride, vanity; dignity, grandeur, sublimity.

lofty *adj* elevated, high, tall, towering; arrogant, haughty, proud; eminent, exalted, sublime; dignified, imposing, majestic, stately.

logical *adj* close, coherent, consistent, dialectical, sound, valid; discriminating, rational, reasoned.

loiter *vb* dally, dawdle, delay, dilly-dally, idle, lag, linger, saunter, stroll, tarry.

loneliness *n* isolation, retirement, seclusion, solitariness, solitude; desolation, dreariness, forlornness.

lonely *adj* apart, dreary, isolated, lonesome, remote, retired, secluded, separate, sequestrated, solitary; alone, lone, companionless, friendless, unaccompanied; deserted, desolate, forlorn, forsaken, withdrawn.

lonesome *adj* cheerless, deserted, desolate, dreary, gloomy, lone, lonely.

long[1] *vb* anticipate, await, expect; aspire, covet, crave, desire, hanker, lust, pine, wish, yearn.

long[2] *adj* drawn-out, extended, extensive, far-reaching, lengthy, prolonged, protracted, stretched; diffuse, long-winded, prolix, tedious, wearisome; backward, behindhand, dilatory, lingering, slack, slow, tardy.

longing *n* aspiration, coveting, craving, desire, hankering, hunger, pining, yearning.

long-suffering *adj* enduring, forbearing, patient. * *n* clemency, endurance, forbearing.

look *vb* behold, examine, notice, see, search; consider, inspect, investigate, observe, study, contemplate, gaze, regard, scan, survey, view; anticipate, await, expect; heed, mind, watch; face, front; appear, seem. * *n* examination, gaze, glance, peep, peer, search; appearance, aspect, complexion; air, aspect, manner, mien.

loophole *n* aperture, crenellation, loop, opening; excuse, plea, pretence, pretext, subterfuge.

loose *vb* free, liberate, release, unbind, undo, unfasten, unlash, unlock, untie; ease, loosen, relax, slacken; detach, disconnect, disengage. * *adj* unbound, unconfined, unfastened, unsewn, untied; disengaged, free, unattached; relaxed; diffuse, diffusive, prolix, rambling, unconnected; ill-defined, indefinite, indeterminate, indistinct, vague; careless, heedless, negligent, lax, slack; debauched, dissolute, immoral, licentious, unchaste, wanton.

loosen *vb* liberate, relax, release, separate, slacken, unbind, unloose, untie.

looseness *n* easiness, slackness; laxity, levity; lewdness, unchastity, wantonness, wickedness; diarrhoea, flux.

loot *vb* pillage, plunder, ransack, rifle, rob, sack. * *n* booty, plunder, spoil.

lop *vb* cut, truncate; crop, curtail, dock, prune; detach, dissever, sever.

loquacious *adj* garrulous, talkative, voluble, wordy; noisy, speaking, talking; babbling, blabbing, tattling, tell-tale.

loquacity *n* babbling, chattering, gabbling, garrulity, loquaciousness, talkativeness, volubility.

lord *n* earl, noble, nobleman, peer, viscount; governor, king, liege, master, monarch, prince, ruler, seigneur, seignior, sovereign, superior; husband, spouse.

lordly *adj* aristocratic, dignified, exalted, grand, lofty, majestic, noble; arrogant, despotic, domineering, haughty, imperious, insolent, masterful, overbearing, proud, tyrannical; large, liberal.

lordship *n* authority, command, control, direction, domination, dominion, empire, government, rule, sovereignty, sway; manor, domain, seigneury, seigniory.

lore *n* erudition, knowledge, learning, letters, scholarship; admonition, advice, counsel, doctrine, instruction, lesson, teaching, wisdom.

lose *vb* deprive, dispossess, forfeit, miss; dislodge, displace, mislay, misspend, squander, waste; decline, fall, succumb, yield.

loss *n* deprivation, failure, forfeiture, privation; casualty, damage, defeat, destruction, detriment, disadvantage, injury, overthrow, ruin; squandering, waste.

lost *adj* astray, missing; forfeited, missed, unredeemed; dissipated, misspent, squandered, wasted; bewildered, confused, distracted, perplexed, puzzled; absent, absent-minded, abstracted, dreamy, napping, preoccupied; abandoned, corrupt, debauched, depraved, dissolute, graceless, hardened, incorrigible, irreclaimable, licentious, profligate, reprobate, shameless, unchaste, wanton; destroyed, ruined.

lot *n* allotment, apportionment, destiny, doom, fate; accident, chance, fate, fortune, hap, haphazard, hazard; division, parcel, part, portion.

loth *adj* averse, disinclined, disliking, reluctant, unwilling

loud *adj* high-sounding, noisy, resounding, sonorous; deafening, stentorian, strong, stunning; boisterous, clamorous, noisy, obstreperous, tumultuous, turbulent, uproarious, vociferous; emphatic, impressive, positive, vehement; flashy, gaudy, glaring, loud, ostentatious, showy, vulgar.

lounge *vb* loll, recline, sprawl; dawdle, idle, loaf, loiter.

love *vb* adore, like, worship. * *n* accord, affection, amity, courtship, delight, fondness, friendship, kindness, regard, tenderness, warmth; adoration, amour, ardour, attachment, passion; devotion, inclination, liking; benevolence, charity, goodwill.

lovely *adj* beautiful, charming, delectable, delightful, enchanting, exquisite, graceful, pleasing, sweet, winning; admirable, adorable, amiable.

loving *adj* affectionate, dear, fond, kind, tender.

low[1] *vb* bellow, moo.

low[2] *adj* basal, depressed, profound; gentle, grave, soft, subdued; cheap, humble, mean, plebeian, vulgar; abject, base, base-minded, degraded, dirty, grovelling, ignoble, low-minded, menial, scurvy, servile, shabby, slavish, vile; derogatory, disgraceful, dishonourable, disreputable, unbecoming, undignified, ungentlemanly, unhandsome, unmanly; exhausted, feeble, reduced, weak; frugal, plain, poor, simple, spare; lowly, reverent, submissive; dejected, depressed, dispirited.

lower[1] *vb* depress, drop, sink, subside; debase, degrade, disgrace, humble, humiliate, reduce; abate, decrease, diminish, lessen. * *adj* baser, inferior, less, lesser, shorter, smaller; subjacent, under.

lower[2] *vb* blacken, darken, frown, glower, threaten.

lowering *adj* dark, clouded, cloudy, lurid, murky, overcast, threatening.

lowliness *n* humbleness, humility, meekness, self-abasement, submissiveness.

lowly *adj* gentle, humble, meek, mild, modest, plain, poor, simple, unassuming, unpretending, unpretentious; low-born, mean, servile.

loyal *adj* constant, devoted, faithful, patriotic, true.

loyalty *n* allegiance, constancy, devotion, faithfulness, fealty, fidelity, patriotism.

lubricious *adj* slippery, smooth; uncertain, unstable, wavering; impure, incontinent, lascivious, lecherous, lewd, libidinous, licentious, lustful, salacious, unchaste, wanton.

lucid *adj* beaming, bright, brilliant, luminous, radiant, resplendent, shining, clear, crystalline, diaphanous, limpid, lucent, pellucid, pure, transparent; clear, distinct, evident, intelligible, obvious, perspicuous, plain; reasonable, sane, sober, sound.

luck *n* accident, casualty, chance, fate, fortune, hap, haphazard, hazard, serendipity, success.

luckless *adj* ill-fated, ill-starred, unfortunate, unhappy, unlucky, unpropitious, unprosperous, unsuccessful.

lucky *adj* blessed, favoured, fortunate, happy, successful; auspicious, favourable, propitious, prosperous.

lucrative *adj* advantageous, gainful, paying, profitable, remunerative.

ludicrous *adj* absurd, burlesque, comic, comical, droll, farcical, funny, laughable, odd, ridiculous, sportive.

lugubrious *adj* complaining, doleful, gloomy, melancholy, mournful, sad, serious, sombre, sorrowful.

lukewarm *adj* blood-warm, tepid, thermal; apathetic, cold, dull, indifferent, listless, unconcerned, torpid.

lull *vb* calm, compose, hush, quiet, still, tranquillize; abate, cease, decrease, diminish, subside. * *n* calm, calmness, cessation.

lumber[1] *vb* rumble, shamble, trudge.

lumber[2] *n* refuse, rubbish, trash, trumpery; wood.

luminous *adj* effulgent, incandescent, radiant, refulgent, resplendent, shining; bright, brilliant, clear; clear, lucid, lucent, perspicuous, plain.

lunacy *n* aberration, craziness, dementia, derangement, insanity, madness, mania.

lunatic *adj* crazy, demented, deranged, insane, mad, psychopathic. * *n* madman, maniac, psychopath.

lurch *vb* appropriate, filch, pilfer, purloin, steal; deceive, defeat, disappoint, evade; ambush, lurk, skulk; contrive, dodge, shift, trick; pitch, sway.

lure *vb* allure, attract, decoy, entice, inveigle, seduce, tempt. * *n* allurement, attraction, bait, decoy, enticement, temptation.

lurid *adj* dismal, ghastly, gloomy, lowering, murky, pale, wan; glaring, sensational, startling, unrestrained.

lurk *vb* hide, prowl, skulk, slink, sneak, snoop.

luscious *adj* delicious, delightful, grateful, palatable, pleasing, savoury, sweet.

lush *adj* fresh, juicy, luxuriant, moist, sappy, succulent, watery.

lust *vb* covet, crave, desire, hanker, need, want, yearn. * *n* cupidity, desire, longing; carnality, concupiscence, lasciviousness, lechery, lewdness, lubricity, salaciousness, salacity, wantonness.

lustful *adj* carnal, concupiscent, hankering, lascivious, lecherous, licentious, libidinous, lubricious, salacious.

lustily *adv* strongly, vigorously.

lustiness *n* hardihood, power, robustness, stoutness, strength, sturdiness, vigour.

lustre *n* brightness, brilliance, brilliancy, splendour.

lusty *adj* healthful, lively, robust, stout, strong, sturdy, vigorous; bulky, burly, corpulent, fat, large, stout.

luxuriance *n* exuberance, profusion, superabundance.

luxuriant *adj* exuberant, plenteous, plentiful, profuse, superabundant.

luxuriate *vb* abound, delight, enjoy, flourish, indulge, revel.

luxurious *adj* epicurean, opulent, pampered, self-indulgent, sensual, sybaritic, voluptuous.

luxury *n* epicureanism, epicurism, luxuriousness, opulence, sensuality, voluptuousness; delight, enjoyment, gratification, indulgence, pleasure; dainty, delicacy, treat.

lying *adj* equivocating, false, mendacious, untruthful, untrue.

lyric *adj* dulcet, euphonious, lyrical, mellifluous, mellifluent, melodic, melodious, musical, poetic, silvery, tuneful.

lyrical *adj* ecstatic, enthusiastic, expressive, impassion; dulcet, lyric, mellifluous, mellifluent, melodic, melodious, musical, poetic.

M

macabre *adj* cadaverous, deathlike, deathly, dreadful, eerie, frightening, frightful, ghoulish, grim, grisly, gruesome, hideous, horrid, morbid, unearthly, weird.

mace *n* baton, staff, truncheon.

macerate *vb* harass, mortify, torture; digest, soak, soften, steep.

Machiavellian *adj* arch, artful, astute, crafty, crooked, cunning, deceitful, designing, diplomatic, insidious, intriguing, shrewd, sly, subtle, tricky, wily.

machination *n* artifice, cabal, conspiracy, contrivance, design, intrigue, plot, scheme, stratagem, trick.

machine *n* instrument, puppet, tool; machinery, organization, system; engine.

mad *adj* crazed, crazy, delirious, demented, deranged, distracted, insane, irrational, lunatic, maniac, maniacal; enraged, furious, rabid, raging, violent; angry, enraged, exasperated, furious, incensed, provoked, wrathful; distracted, infatuated, wild; frantic, frenzied, raving.

madden *vb* annoy, craze, enrage, exasperate, inflame, infuriate, irritate, provoke.

madness *n* aberration, craziness, dementia, derangement, insanity, lunacy, mania; delirium, frenzy, fury, rage.

magazine *n* depository, depot, entrepot, receptacle, repository, storehouse, warehouse; pamphlet, paper, periodical.

magic *adj* bewitching, charming, enchanting, fascinating, magical, miraculous, spellbinding. * *n* conjuring, enchantment, necromancy, sorcery, thaumaturgy, voodoo, witchcraft; char, fascination, witchery.

magician *n* conjurer, enchanter, juggler, magus, necromancer, shaman, sorcerer, wizard.

magisterial *adj* august, dignified, majestic, pompous; authoritative, despotic, domineering, imperious, dictatorial.

magnanimity *n* chivalry, disinterestedness, forbearance, high-mindedness, generosity, nobility.

magnificence *n* brilliance, éclat, grandeur, luxuriousness, luxury, majesty, pomp, splendour.

magnificent *adj* elegant, grand, majestic, noble, splendid, superb; brilliant, gorgeous, imposing, lavish, luxurious, pompous, showy, stately.

magnify *vb* amplify, augment, enlarge; bless, celebrate, elevate, exalt, extol, glorify, laud, praise; exaggerate.

magnitude *n* bulk, dimension, extent, mass, size, volume; consequence, greatness, importance; grandeur, loftiness, sublimity.

maid *n* damsel, girl, lass, lassie, maiden, virgin; maidservant, servant.

maiden *adj* chaste, pure, undefiled, virgin; fresh, new, unused. * *n* girl, maid, virgin.

maidenly *adj* demure, gentle, modest, maidenlike, reserved.

maim *vb* cripple, disable, disfigure, mangle, mar, mutilate. * *n* crippling, disfigurement, mutilation; harm, hurt, injury, mischief.

main[1] *adj* capital, cardinal, chief, leading, principal; essential, important, indispensable, necessary, requisite, vital; enormous, huge, mighty, vast; pure, sheer; absolute, direct, entire, mere. * *n* channel, pipe; force, might, power, strength, violence.

main[2] *n* high seas, ocean; continent, mainland.

maintain *vb* keep, preserve, support, sustain, uphold; hold, possess; defend, vindicate, justify; carry on, continue, keep up; feed, provide, supply; allege, assert, declare; affirm, aver, contend, hold, say.

maintenance *n* defence, justification, preservation, support, sustenance, vindication; bread, food, livelihood, provisions, subsistence, sustenance, victuals.

majestic *adj* august, dignified, imperial, imposing, lofty, noble, pompous, princely, stately, regal, royal; grand, magnificent, splendid, sublime.

majesty *n* augustness, dignity, elevation, grandeur, loftiness, stateliness.

majority *n* bulk, greater, mass, more, most, plurality, preponderance, superiority; adulthood, manhood.

make *vb* create; fashion, figure, form, frame, mould, shape; cause, construct, effect, establish, fabricate, produce; do, execute, perform, practice; acquire, gain, get, raise, secure; cause, compel, constrain, force, occasion; compose, constitute; go, journey, move, proceed, tend, travel; conduce, contribute, effect, favour, operate; estimate, judge, reckon, suppose, think. * *n* brand, build, constitution, construction, form, shape, structure.

maker *n* creator, god; builder, constructor, fabricator, framer, manufacturer; author, composer, poet, writer.

maladministration *n* malversation, misgovernment, misrule.

maladroit *adj* awkward, bungling, clumsy, inept, inexpert, unhandy, unskilful, unskilled.

malady *n* affliction, ailment, complaint, disease, disorder, illness, indisposition, sickness.

malcontent *adj* discontented, dissatisfied, insurgent, rebellious, resentful, uneasy, unsatisfied. * *n* agitator, complainer, fault-finder, grumbler, spoilsport.

malediction *n* anathema, ban, curse, cursing, denunciation, execration, imprecation, malison.

malefactor *n* convict, criminal, culprit, delinquent, evildoer, felon, offender, outlaw.

malevolence *n* hate, hatred, ill-will, malice, malignity, rancour, spite, spitefulness, vindictiveness.

malevolent *adj* evil-minded, hateful, hostile, ill-natured, malicious, malignant, mischievous, rancorous, spiteful, venomous. vindictive.

malice *n* animosity, bitterness, enmity, grudge, hate, ill-will, malevolence, maliciousness, malignity, pique, rancour, spite, spitefulness, venom, vindictiveness.

malicious *adj* bitter, envious, evil-minded, ill-disposed, ill-natured, invidious, malevolent, malignant, mischievous, rancorous, resentful, spiteful, vicious.

malign *vb* abuse, asperse, blacken, calumniate, defame, disparage, revile, scandalize, slander, traduce, vilify. * *adj* malevolent, malicious, malignant, ill-disposed; baneful, injurious, pernicious, unfavourable, unpropitious.

malignant *adj* bitter, envious, hostile, inimical, malevolent, malicious, malign, spiteful, rancorous, resentful, virulent; heinous, pernicious; ill-boding, unfavourable, unpropitious; dangerous, fatal.

malignity *n* animosity, hatred, ill-will, malice, malevolence, maliciousness, rancour, spite; deadliness, destructiveness, fatality, harmfulness, malignancy, perniciousness, virulence; enormity, evilness, heinousness.

malpractice *n* dereliction, malversation, misbehaviour, misconduct, misdeed, misdoing, sin, transgression.

maltreat *vb* abuse, harm, hurt, ill-treat, ill-use, injure.

mammoth *adj* colossal, enormous, gigantic, huge, immense, vast.

man *vb* crew, garrison, furnish; fortify, reinforce, strengthen. * *n* adult, being, body, human, individual, one, person, personage, somebody, soul; humanity, humankind, mankind; attendant, butler, dependant, liege, servant, subject, valet, vassal; employee, workman.

manacle *vb* bind, chain, fetter, handcuff, restrain, shackle, tie. * *n* bond, chain, handcuff, gyve, hand-fetter, shackle.

manage *vb* administer, conduct, direct, guide, handle, operate, order, regulate, superintend, supervise, transact, treat; control, govern, rule; handle, manipulate, train, wield; contrive, economize, husband, save.

manageable *adj* controllable, docile, easy, governable, tamable, tractable.

management *n* administration, care, charge, conduct, control, direction, disposal, economy, government, guidance, superintendence, supervision, surveillance, treatment.

manager *n* comptroller, conductor, director, executive, governor, impresario, overseer, superintendent, supervisor.

mandate *n* charge, command, commission, edict, injunction, order, precept, requirement.

manful *adj* bold, brave, courageous, daring, heroic, honourable, intrepid, noble, stout, strong, undaunted, vigorous.

mangily *adv* basely, foully, meanly, scabbily, scurvily, vilely.

mangle[1] *vb* hack, lacerate, mutilate, rend, tear; cripple, crush, destroy, maim, mar, spoil.

mangle[2] *vb* calender, polish, press, smooth.

manhood *n* virility; bravery, courage, firmness, fortitude, hardihood, manfulness, manliness, resolution; human nature, humanity; adulthood, maturity.

mania *n* aberration, craziness, delirium, dementia, derangement, frenzy, insanity, lunacy, madness; craze, desire, enthusiasm, fad, fanaticism.

manifest *vb* declare, demonstrate, disclose, discover, display, evidence, evince, exhibit, express, reveal, show. * *adj* apparent, clear, conspicuous, distinct, evident, glaring, indubitable, obvious, open, palpable, patent, plain, unmistakable, visible.

manifestation *n* disclosure, display, exhibition, exposure, expression, revelation.

manifold *adj* complex, diverse, many, multifarious, multiplied, multitudinous, numerous, several, sundry, varied, various.

manipulate *vb* handle, operate, work.

manliness *n* boldness, bravery, courage, dignity, fearlessness, firmness, heroism, intrepidity, nobleness, resolution, valour.

manly *adj* bold, brave, courageous, daring, dignified, firm, heroic, intrepid, manful, noble, stout, strong, undaunted, vigorous; male, masculine, virile.

manner *n* fashion, form, method, mode, style, way; custom, habit, practice; degree, extent, measure; kind, kinds, sort, sorts; air, appearance, aspect, behaviour, carriage, demeanour, deportment, look, mien; mannerism, peculiarity; behaviour, conduct, habits, morals; civility, deportment.

mannerly *adj* ceremonious, civil, complaisant, courteous, polite, refined, respectful, urbane, well-behaved, well-bred.

manners *npl* conduct, habits, morals; air, bearing, behaviour, breeding, carriage, comportment, deportment, etiquette.

manoeuvre *vb* contrive, finesse, intrigue, manage, plan, plot, scheme. * *n* evolution, exercise, movement, operation; artifice, finesse, intrigue, plan, plot, ruse, scheme, stratagem, trick.

mansion *n* abode, dwelling, dwelling house, habitation, hall, residence, seat.

mantle *vb* cloak, cover, discover, obscure; expand, spread; bubble, cream, effervesce, foam, froth, sparkle. * *n* chasuble, cloak, toga; cover, covering, hood.

manufacture *vb* build, compose, construct, create, fabricate, forge, form, make, mould, produce, shape. * *n* constructing, fabrication, making, production.

manumission *n* deliverance, emancipation, enfranchisement, freedom, liberation, release.

manumit *vb* deliver, emancipate, enfranchise, free, liberate, release.

manure *vb* enrich, fertilize. * *n* compost, dressing, fertilizer, guano, muck.

many *adj* abundant, diverse, frequent, innumerable, manifold, multifarious, multifold, multiplied, multitudinous, numerous, sundry, varied, various. * *n* crowd, multitude, people.

map *vb* chart, draw up, plan, plot, set out, sketch. * *n* chart, diagram, outline, plot, sketch.

mar *vb* blot, damage, harm, hurt, impair, injure, ruin, spoil, stain; deface, deform, disfigure, maim, mutilate.

marauder *n* bandit, brigand, desperado, filibuster, freebooter, outlaw, pillager, plunderer, ravager, robber, rover.

march *vb* go, pace, parade, step, tramp, walk. * *n* hike, tramp, walk; parade, procession; gait, step, stride; advance, evolution, progress.

marches *npl* borders, boundaries, confines, frontiers, limits, precincts.

margin *n* border, brim, brink, confine, edge, limit, rim, skirt, verge; latitude, room, space, surplus.

marine *adj* oceanic, pelagic, saltwater, sea; maritime, naval, nautical. * *n* navy, shipping; sea-dog, sea soldier, soldier; sea piece, seascape.

mariner *n* navigator, sailor, salt, seafarer, seaman, tar.

marital *adj* connubial, conjugal, matrimonial.

maritime *adj* marine, naval, nautical, oceanic, sea, seafaring, seagoing; coastal, seaside.

mark *vb* distinguish, earmark, label; betoken, brand, characterize, denote, designate, engrave, impress, imprint, indicate, print, stamp; evince, heed, note, notice, observe, regard, remark, show, spot. * *n* brand, character, characteristic, impression, impress, line, note, print, sign, stamp, symbol, token, race; evidence, indication, proof, symptom, trace, track, vestige; badge; footprint; bull's-eye, butt, object, target; consequence, distinction, eminence, fame, importance, notability, position, preeminence, reputation, significance.

marked *adj* conspicuous, distinguished, eminent, notable, noted, outstanding, prominent, remarkable.

marriage *n* espousals, nuptials, spousals, wedding; matrimony, wedlock; union; alliance, association, confederation.

marrow *n* medulla, pith; cream, essence, quintessence, substance.

marsh *n* bog, fen, mire, morass, quagmire, slough, swamp.

marshal *vb* arrange, array, dispose, gather, muster, range, order, rank; guide, herald, lead. * *n* conductor, director, master of ceremonies, regulator; harbinger, herald, pursuivant.

marshy *adj* boggy, miry, mossy, swampy, wet.

martial *adj* brave, heroic, military, soldier-like, warlike.

marvel *vb* gape, gaze, goggle, wonder. * *n* miracle, prodigy, wonder; admiration, amazement, astonishment, surprise.

marvellous *adj* amazing, astonishing, extraordinary, miraculous, prodigious, strange, stupendous, wonderful, wondrous; improbable, incredible, surprising, unbelievable.

masculine *adj* bold, hardy, manful, manlike, manly, mannish, virile; potent, powerful, robust, strong, vigorous; bold, coarse, forward.

mask *vb* cloak, conceal, cover, disguise, hide, screen, shroud, veil. * *n* blind, cloak, disguise, screen, veil; evasion, pretence, plea, pretext, ruse, shift, subterfuge, trick; masquerade; bustle, mummery.

masquerade *vb* cover, disguise, hide, mask, revel, veil. * *n* mask, mummery, revel, revelry.

Mass *n* communion, Eucharist.

mass *vb* accumulate, amass, assemble, collect, gather, rally, throng. * *adj* extensive, general, large-scale, widespread. * *n* cake, clot, lump; assemblage, collection, combination, congeries, heap; bulk, dimension, magnitude, size; accumulation, aggregate, body, sum, total, totality, whole.

massacre *vb* annihilate, butcher, exterminate, kill, murder, slaughter, slay. * *n* annihilation, butchery, carnage, extermination, killing, murder, pogrom, slaughter.

massive *adj* big, bulky, colossal, enormous, heavy, huge, immense, ponderous, solid, substantial, vast, weighty.

master *vb* conquer, defeat, direct, govern, overcome, overpower, rule, subdue, subjugate, vanquish; acquire, learn. * *adj* cardinal, chief, especial, grand, great, main, leading, prime, principal; adept, expert, proficient. * *n* director, governor, lord, manager, overseer, superintendent, ruler; captain, commander; instructor, pedagogue, preceptor, schoolteacher, teacher, tutor; holder, owner, possessor, proprietor; chief, head, leader, principal.

masterly *adj* adroit, clever, dextrous, excellent, expert, finished, skilful, skilled; arbitrary, despotic, despotical, domineering, imperious.

mastery *n* command, dominion, mastership, power, rule, supremacy, sway; ascendancy, conquest, leadership, preeminence, superiority, upper-hand, victory; acquisition, acquirement, attainment; ability, cleverness, dexterity, proficiency, skill.

masticate *vb* chew, eat, munch.

match *vb* equal, rival; adapt, fit, harmonize, proportion, suit; marry, mate; combine, couple, join, sort; oppose, pit; correspond, suit, tally. * *n* companion, equal, mate, tally; competition, contest, game, trial; marriage, union.

matchless *adj* consummate, excellent, exquisite, incomparable, inimitable, peerless, perfect, surpassing, unequalled, unmatched, unparalleled, unrivalled.

mate *vb* marry, match, wed; compete, equal, vie; appal, confound, crush, enervate, subdue, stupefy. * *n* associate, companion, compeer, consort, crony, friend, fellow, intimate; companion, equal, match; assistant, subordinate; husband, spouse, wife.

material *adj* bodily, corporeal, nonspiritual, physical, temporal; essential, important, momentous, relevant, vital, weighty. * *n* body, element, stuff, substance.

maternal *adj* motherlike, motherly.

matrimonial *adj* conjugal, connubial, espousal, hymeneal, marital, nuptial, spousal.

matrimony *n* marriage, wedlock.

matter *vb* import, signify, weigh. * *n* body, content, sense, substance; difficulty, distress, trouble; material, stuff; question, subject, subject matter, topic; affair, business, concern, event; consequence, import, importance, moment, significance; discharge, purulence, pus.

mature *vb* develop, perfect, ripen. * *adj* complete, fit, full-grown, perfect, ripe; completed, prepared, ready, well-considered, well-digested.

maturity *n* completeness, completion, matureness, perfection, ripeness.

mawkish *adj* disgusting, flat, insipid, nauseous, sickly, stale, tasteless, vapid; emotional, feeble, maudlin, sentimental.

maxim *n* adage, aphorism, apothegm, axiom, byword, dictum, proverb, saw, saying, truism.

maze *vb* amaze, bewilder, confound, confuse, perplex. * *n* intricacy, labyrinth, meander; bewilderment, embarrassment, intricacy, perplexity, puzzle, uncertainty.

mazy *adj* confused, confusing, intricate, labyrinthian, labyrinthic, labyrinthine, perplexing, winding.

meagre *adj* emaciated, gaunt, lank, lean, poor, skinny, starved, spare, thin; barren, poor, sterile, unproductive; bald, barren, dry, dull, mean, poor, prosy, feeble, insignificant, jejune, scanty, small, tame, uninteresting, vapid.

mean[1] *vb* contemplate, design, intend, purpose; connote, denote, express, imply, import, indicate, purport, signify, symbolize.

mean[2] *adj* average, medium, middle; intermediate, intervening. * *n* measure, mediocrity, medium, moderation; average; agency, instrument, instrumentality, means, measure, method, mode, way.

mean[3] *adj* coarse, common, humble, ignoble, low, ordinary, plebeian, vulgar; abject, base, base-minded, beggarly, contemptible, degraded, dirty, dishonourable, disingenuous, grovelling, low-minded, pitiful, rascally, scurvy, servile, shabby, sneaking, sorry, spiritless, unfair, vile; illiberal, mercenary, miserly, narrow, narrow-minded, niggardly, parsimonious, penurious, selfish, sordid, stingy, ungenerous, unhandsome; contemptible, despicable, diminutive, insignificant, paltry, petty, poor, small, wretched.

meaning *n* acceptation, drift, import, intention, purport, purpose, sense, signification.

means *n pl* instrument, method, mode, way; appliance, expedient, measure, resource, shift, step; estate, income, property, resources, revenue, substance, wealth, wherewithal.

measure *vb* mete; adjust, gauge, proportion; appraise, appreciate, estimate, gauge, value. * *n* gauge, meter, rule, standard; degree, extent, length, limit; allotment, share, proportion; means, step; foot, metre, rhythm, tune, verse.

measureless *adj* boundless, endless, immeasurable, immense, limitless, unbounded, unlimited, vast.

meat *n* aliment, cheer, diet, fare, feed, flesh, food, nourishment, nutriment, provision, rations, regimen, subsistence, sustenance, viands, victuals.

mechanic *n* artificer, artisan, craftsman, hand, handicraftsman, machinist, operative, workman.

meddle *vb* interfere, intermeddle, interpose, intrude.

meddlesome *adj* interfering, intermeddling, intrusive, officious, prying.

mediate *vb* arbitrate, intercede, interpose, intervene, settle. * *adj* interposed, intervening, middle.

mediation *n* arbitration, intercession, interposition, intervention.

mediator *n* advocate, arbitrator, interceder, intercessor, propitiator, umpire.

medicine *n* drug, medicament, medication, physic; therapy.

mediocre *adj* average, commonplace, indifferent, mean, medium, middling, ordinary.

meditate *vb* concoct, contrive, design, devise, intend, plan, purpose, scheme; chew, contemplate, ruminate, study; cogitate, muse, ponder, think.

meditation *n* cogitation, contemplation, musing, pondering, reflection, ruminating, study, thought.

meditative *adj* contemplative, pensive, reflective, studious, thoughtful.

medium *adj* average, mean, mediocre, middle. * *n* agency, channel, intermediary, instrument, instrumentality, means, organ; conditions, environment, influences; average, means.

medley *n* confusion, farrago, hodgepodge, hotchpotch, jumble, mass, melange, miscellany, mishmash, mixture.

meed *n* award, guerdon, premium, prize, recompense, remuneration, reward.

meek *adj* gentle, humble, lowly, mild, modest, pacific, soft, submissive, unassuming, yielding.

meekness *n* gentleness, humbleness, humility, lowliness, mildness, modesty, submission, submissiveness.

meet *vb* cross, intersect, transact; confront, encounter, engage; answer, comply, fulfil, gratify, satisfy; converge, join, unite; assemble, collect, convene, congregate, forgather, muster, rally. * *adj* adapted, appropriate, befitting, convenient, fit, fitting, proper, qualified, suitable, suited.

meeting *n* encounter, interview; assemblage, assembly, audience, company, concourse, conference, congregation, convention, gathering; assignation, encounter, introduction, rendezvous; confluence, conflux, intersection, joining, junction, union; collision.

melancholy *adj* blue, dejected, depressed, despondent, desponding, disconsolate, dismal, dispirited, doleful, down, downcast, downhearted, gloomy, glum, hypochondriac, low-spirited, lugubrious, moody, mopish, sad, sombre, sorrowful, unhappy; afflictive, calamitous, unfortunate, unlucky; dark, gloomy, grave, quiet. * *n* blues, dejection, depression, despondency, dismals, dumps, gloom, gloominess, hypochondria, sadness, vapours.

melee *n* affray, brawl, broil, contest, fight, fray, scuffle.

mellifluous, mellifluent *adj* dulcet, euphonic, euphonical, euphonious, mellow, silver-toned, silvery, smooth, soft, sweet.

mellow *vb* mature, ripen; improve, smooth, soften, tone; pulverize; perfect. * *adj* mature, ripe; dulcet, mellifluous, mellifluent, rich, silver-toned, silvery, smooth, soft; delicate; genial, good-humoured, jolly, jovial, matured, softened; mellowy, loamy, unctuous; perfected, well-prepared; disguised, fuddled, intoxicated, tipsy.

melodious *adj* arioso, concordant, dulcet, euphonious, harmonious, mellifluous, mellifluent, musical, silvery, sweet, tuneful.

melody *n* air, descant, music, plainsong, song, theme, tune.

melt *vb* dissolve, fuse, liquefy, thaw; mollify, relax, soften, subdue; dissipate, waste; blend, pass, shade.

member *n* arm, leg, limb, organ; component, constituent, element, part, portion; branch, clause, division, head.

memento *n* memorial, remembrance, reminder, souvenir.

memoir *n* account, autobiography, biography, journal, narrative, record, register.

memorable *adj* celebrated, distinguished, extraordinary, famous, great, illustrious, important, notable, noteworthy, remarkable, signal, significant.

memorandum *n* minute, note, record.

memorial *adj* commemorative, monumental. * *n* cairn, commemoration, memento, monument, plaque, record, souvenir; memorandum, remembrance.

memory *n* recollection, remembrance, reminiscence; celebrity, fame, renown, reputation; commemoration, memorial.

menace *vb* alarm, frighten, intimidate, threaten. * *n* danger, hazard, peril, threat, warning; nuisance, pest, troublemaker.

menage *n* household, housekeeping, management.

mend *vb* darn, patch, rectify, refit, repair, restore, retouch; ameliorate, amend, better, correct, emend, improve, meliorate, reconcile, rectify, reform; advance, help; augment, increase.

mendacious *adj* deceitful, deceptive, fallacious, false, lying, untrue, untruthful.

mendacity *n* deceit, deceitfulness, deception, duplicity, falsehood, lie, untruth.

mendicant *n* beggar, pauper, tramp.

menial *adj* base, low, mean, servile, vile. * *n* attendant, bondsman, domestic, flunkey, footman, lackey, serf, servant, slave, underling, valet, waiter.

mensuration *n* measurement, measuring; survey, surveying.

mental *adj* ideal, immaterial, intellectual, psychiatric, subjective.

mention *vb* acquaint, allude, cite, communicate, declare, disclose, divulge, impart, inform, name, report, reveal, state, tell. * *n* allusion, citation, designation, notice, noting, reference.

mentor *n* adviser, counsellor, guide, instructor, monitor.
mephitic *adj* baleful, baneful, fetid, foul, mephitical, noisome, noxious, poisonous, pestilential.
mercantile *adj* commercial, marketable, trading.
mercenary *adj* hired, paid, purchased, venal; avaricious, covetous, grasping, mean, niggardly, parsimonious, penurious, sordid, stingy. * *n* hireling, soldier.
merchandise *n* commodities, goods, wares.
merchant *n* dealer, retailer, shopkeeper, trader, tradesman.
merciful *adj* clement, compassionate, forgiving, gracious, lenient, pitiful; benignant, forbearing, gentle, humane, kind, mild, tender, tender-hearted.
merciless *adj* barbarous, callous, cruel, fell, hard-hearted, inexorable, pitiless, relentless, remorseless, ruthless, savage, severe, uncompassionate, unfeeling, unmerciful, unrelenting, unrepenting, unsparing.
mercurial *adj* active, lively, nimble, prompt, quick, sprightly; cheerful, light-hearted; changeable, fickle, flighty, inconstant, mobile, volatile.
mercy *n* benevolence, clemency, compassion, gentleness, kindness, lenience, leniency, lenity, mildness, pity, tenderness; blessing, favour, grace; discretion, disposal; forgiveness, pardon.
mere *adj* bald, bare, naked, plain, sole, simple; absolute, entire, pure, sheer, unmixed. * *n* lake, pond, pool.
meretricious *adj* deceitful, brummagem, false, gaudy, make-believe, sham, showy, spurious, tawdry.
merge *vb* bury, dip, immerse, involve, lose, plunge, sink, submerge.
meridian *n* acme, apex, climax, culmination, summit, zenith; midday, noon, noontide.
merit *vb* deserve, earn, incur; acquire, gain, profit, value. * *n* claim, right; credit, desert, excellence, goodness, worth, worthiness.
meritorious *adj* commendable, deserving, excellent, good, worthy.
merriment *n* amusement, frolic, gaiety, hilarity, jocularity, jollity, joviality, laughter, liveliness, mirth, sport, sportiveness.
merry *adj* agreeable, brisk, delightful, exhilarating, lively, pleasant, stirring; airy, blithe, blithesome, buxom, cheerful, comical, droll, facetious, frolicsome, gladsome, gleeful, hilarious, jocund, jolly, jovial, joyous, light-hearted, lively, mirthful, sportive, sprightly, vivacious.
mess *n* company, set; farrago, hodgepodge, hotchpotch, jumble, medley, mass, melange, miscellany, mishmash, mixture; confusion, muddle, perplexity, pickle, plight, predicament.
message *n* communication, dispatch, intimation, letter, missive, notice, telegram, wire, word.
messenger *n* carrier, courier, emissary, envoy, express, mercury, nuncio; forerunner, harbinger, herald, precursor.
metamorphic *adj* changeable, mutable, variable.
metamorphose *vb* change, mutate, transfigure, transform, transmute.
metamorphosis *n* change, mutation, transfiguration, transformation, transmutation.
metaphorical *adj* allegorical, figurative, symbolic, symbolical.
metaphysical *adj* abstract, allegorical, figurative, general, intellectual, parabolic, subjective, unreal.
mete *vb* dispense, distribute, divide, measure, ration, share. * *n* bound, boundary, butt, limit, measure, term, terminus.
meteor *n* aerolite, falling star, shooting star.
method *n* course, manner, means, mode, procedure, process, rule, way; arrangement, classification, disposition, order, plan, regularity, scheme, system.
methodical *adj* exact, orderly, regular, systematic, systematical.
metropolis *n* capital, city, conurbation.
mettle *n* constitution, element, material, stuff; character, disposition, spirit, temper; ardour, courage, fire, hardihood, life, nerve, pluck, sprightliness, vigour.
mettlesome *adj* ardent, brisk, courageous, fiery, frisky, high-spirited, lively, spirited, sprightly.
mew *vb* confine, coop, encase, enclose, imprison; cast, change, mould, shed.
microscopic *adj* infinitesimal, minute, tiny.
middle *adj* central, halfway, mean, medial, mid; intermediate, intervening. * *n* centre, halfway, mean, midst.
middleman *n* agent, broker, factor, go-between, intermediary.
mien *n* air, appearance, aspect, bearing, behaviour, carriage, countenance, demeanour, deportment, look, manner.
might *n* ability, capacity, efficacy, efficiency, force, main, power, prowess, puissance, strength.
mighty *adj* able, bold, courageous, potent, powerful, puissant, robust, strong, sturdy, valiant, valorous, vigorous; bulky, enormous, huge, immense, monstrous, stupendous, vast.
migratory *adj* nomadic, roving, shifting, strolling, unsettled, wandering, vagrant.
mild *adj* amiable, clement, compassionate, gentle, good-natured, indulgent, kind, lenient, meek, merciful, pacific, tender; bland, pleasant, soft, suave; calm, kind, placid, temperate, tranquil; assuasive, compliant, demulcent, emollient, lenitive, mollifying, soothing.
mildness *n* amiability, clemency, gentleness, indulgence, kindness, meekness, moderation, softness, tenderness, warmth.
mildew *n* blight, blast, mould, must, mustiness, smut, rust.
milieu *n* background, environment, sphere, surroundings.
militant *adj* belligerent, combative, contending, fighting.
military *adj* martial, soldier, soldierly, warlike. * *n* army, militia, soldiers.
mill *vb* comminute, crush, grate, grind, levigate, powder, pulverize. * *n* factory, manufactory; grinder; crowd, throng.
mimic *vb* ape, counterfeit, imitate, impersonate, mime, mock, parody. * *adj* imitative, mock, simulated. * *n* imitator, impersonator, mime, mocker, parodist, parrot.
mince[1] *vb* chop, cut, hash, shatter. * *n* forcemeat, hash, mash, mincemeat.
mince[2] *vb* attenuate, diminish, extenuate, mitigate, palliate, soften; pose, sashay, simper, smirk.
mind[1] *vb* attend, heed, mark, note, notice, regard, tend, watch; obey, observe, submit; design, incline, intend, mean; recall, recollect, remember, remind; beware, look out, watch out. * *n* soul, spirit; brains, common sense, intellect, reason, sense, understanding; belief, consideration, contemplation, judgement, opinion, reflection, sentiment, thought; memory, recollection, remembrance; bent, desire, disposition, inclination, intention, leaning, purpose, tendency, will.
mind[2] *vb* balk, begrudge, grudge, object, resent.
mindful *adj* attentive, careful, heedful, observant, regardful, thoughtful.
mindless *adj* dull, heavy, insensible, senseless, sluggish, stupid, unthinking; careless, forgetful, heedless, neglectful, negligent, regardless.
mine *vb* dig, excavate, quarry, unearth; sap, undermine, weaken; destroy, ruin. * *n* colliery, deposit, lode, pit, shaft.
mingle *vb* blend, combine, commingle, compound, intermingle, intermix, join, mix, unite.
miniature *adj* bantam, diminutive, little, small, tiny.
minion *n* creature, dependant, favourite, hanger-on, parasite, sycophant; darling, favourite, flatterer, pet.
minister *vb* administer, afford, furnish, give, supply; aid, assist, contribute, help, succour. * *n* agent, assistant, servant, subordinate, underling; administrator, executive; ambassador, delegate, envoy, plenipotentiary; chaplain, churchman, clergyman, cleric, curate, divine, ecclesiastic, parson, pastor, preacher, priest, rector, vicar.
ministry *n* agency, aid, help, instrumentality, interposition, intervention, ministration, service, support; administration, cabinet, council, government.
minor *adj* less, smaller; inferior, junior, secondary, subordinate, younger; inconsiderable, petty, unimportant, small.
minstrel *n* bard, musician, singer, troubadour.
mint *vb* coin, stamp; fabricate, fashion, forge, invent, make, produce. * *adj* fresh, new, perfect, undamaged. * *n* die, punch, seal, stamp; fortune, (*inf*) heap, million, pile, wad.
minute[1] *adj* diminutive, fine, little, microscopic, miniature, slender, slight, small, tiny; circumstantial, critical, detailed, exact, fussy, meticulous, nice, particular, precise.

minute[2] *n* account, entry, item, memorandum, note, proceedings, record; instant, moment, second, trice, twinkling.

miracle *n* marvel, prodigy, wonder.

miraculous *adj* supernatural, thaumaturgic, thaumaturgical; amazing, extraordinary, incredible, marvellous, unaccountable, unbelievable, wondrous.

mirror *vb* copy, echo, emulate, reflect, show. * *n* looking-glass, reflector, speculum; archetype, exemplar, example, model, paragon, pattern, prototype.

mirth *n* cheerfulness, festivity, frolic, fun, gaiety, gladness, glee, hilarity, festivity, jollity, joviality, joyousness, laughter, merriment, merry-making, rejoicing, sport.

mirthful *adj* cheery, cheery, festive, frolicsome, hilarious, jocund, jolly, merry, jovial, joyous, lively, playful, sportive, vivacious; comic, droll, humorous, facetious, funny, jocose, jocular, ludicrous, merry, waggish, witty.

misadventure *n* accident, calamity, catastrophe, cross, disaster, failure, ill-luck, infelicity, mischance, misfortune, mishap, reverse.

misanthrope *n* cynic, egoist, egotist, man-hater, misanthropist.

misapply *vb* abuse, misuse, pervert.

misapprehend *vb* misconceive, mistake, misunderstand.

misbehaviour *n* ill-behaviour, ill-conduct, incivility, miscarriage, misconduct, misdemeanour, naughtiness, rudeness.

miscarriage *n* calamity, defeat, disaster, failure, mischance, mishap; misbehaviour, misconduct, ill-behaviour.

miscellaneous *adj* confused, diverse, diversified, heterogeneous, indiscriminate, jumbled, many, mingled, mixed, promiscuous, stromatic, stromatous, various.

miscellany *n* collection, diversity, farrago, gallimaufry, hodgepodge, hotchpotch, jumble, medley, mishmash, melange, miscellaneous, mixture, variety.

mischance *n* accident, calamity, disaster, ill-fortune, ill-luck, infelicity, misadventure, misfortune, mishap.

mischief *n* damage, detriment, disadvantage, evil, harm, hurt, ill, injury, prejudice; ill-consequence, misfortune, trouble; devilry, wrong-doing.

mischievous *adj* destructive, detrimental, harmful, hurtful, injurious, noxious, pernicious; malicious, sinful, vicious, wicked; annoying, impish, naughty, troublesome, vexatious.

misconceive *vb* misapprehend, misjudge, mistake, misunderstand.

misconduct *vb* botch, bungle, misdirect, mismanage. * *n* bad conduct, ill-conduct, misbehaviour, misdemeanour, rudeness, transgression; ill-management, mismanagement.

misconstrue *vb* misread, mistranslate; misapprehend, misinterpret, mistake, misunderstand.

miscreant *adj* corrupt, criminal, evil, rascally, unprincipled, vicious, villainous, wicked. * *n* caitiff, knave, ragamuffin, rascal, rogue, ruffian, scamp, scoundrel, vagabond, villain.

misdemeanour *n* fault, ill-behaviour, misbehaviour, misconduct, misdeed, offence, transgression, trespass.

miser *n* churl, curmudgeon, lickpenny, money-grabber, niggard, penny-pincher, pinch-fist, screw, scrimp, skinflint.

miserable *adj* afflicted, broken-hearted, comfortless, disconsolate, distressed, forlorn, heartbroken, unhappy, wretched; calamitous, hapless, ill-starred, pitiable, unfortunate, unlucky; poor, valueless, worthless; abject, contemptible, despicable, low, mean, worthless.

miserly *adj* avaricious, beggarly, close, close-fisted, covetous, grasping, mean, niggardly, parsimonious, penurious, sordid, stingy, tight-fisted.

misery *n* affliction, agony, anguish, calamity, desolation, distress, grief, heartache, heavy-heartedness, misfortune, sorrow, suffering, torment, torture, tribulation, unhappiness, woe, wretchedness.

misfortune *n* adversity, affliction, bad luck, blow, calamity, casualty, catastrophe, disaster, distress, hardship, harm, ill, infliction, misadventure, mischance, mishap, reverse, scourge, stroke, trial, trouble, visitation.

misgiving *n* apprehension, distrust, doubt, hesitation, suspicion, uncertainty.

mishap *n* accident, calamity, disaster, ill luck, misadventure, mischance, misfortune.

misinterpret *vb* distort, falsify, misapprehend, misconceive, misconstrue, misjudge.

mislead *vb* beguile, deceive, delude, misdirect, misguide.

mismanage *vb* botch, fumble, misconduct, mishandle, misrule.

misprize *vb* slight, underestimate, underrate, undervalue.

misrepresent *vb* belie, caricature, distort, falsify, misinterpret, misstate, pervert.

misrule *n* anarchy, confusion, disorder, malad-ministration, misgovernment, mismanagement.

miss[1] *vb* blunder, err, fail, fall short, forgo, lack, lose, miscarry, mistake, omit, overlook, trip; avoid, escape, evade, skip, slip; feel the loss of, need, want, wish. * *n* blunder, error, failure, fault, mistake, omission, oversight, slip, trip; loss, want.

miss[2] *n* damsel, girl, lass, maid, maiden.

misshapen *adj* deformed, ill-formed, ill-shaped, ill-proportioned, misformed, ugly, ungainly.

missile *n* projectile, weapon.

mission *n* commission, legation; business, charge, duty, errand, office, trust; delegation, deputation, embassy.

missive *n* communication, epistle, letter, message, note.

mist *vb* cloud, drizzle, mizzle, smog. * *n* cloud, fog, haze; bewilderment, obscurity, perplexity.

mistake *vb* misapprehend, miscalculate, misconceive, misjudge, misunderstand; confound, take; blunder, err. * *n* misapprehension, miscalculation, misconception, mistaking, misunderstanding; blunder, error, fault, inaccuracy, oversight, slip, trip.

mistaken *adj* erroneous, inaccurate, incorrect, misinformed, wrong.

mistrust *vb* distrust, doubt, suspect; apprehend, fear, surmise, suspect. * *n* doubt, distrust, misgiving, suspicion.

misty *adj* cloudy, clouded, dark, dim, foggy, obscure, overcast.

misunderstand *vb* misapprehend, misconceive, misconstrue, mistake.

misunderstanding *n* error, misapprehension, misconception, mistake; difference, difficulty, disagreement, discord, dissension, quarrel.

misuse *vb* desecrate, misapply, misemploy, pervert, profane; abuse, ill-treat, maltreat, ill-use; fritter, squander, waste. * *n* abuse, perversion, profanation, prostitution; ill-treatment, ill-use, ill-usage, misusage; misapplication, solecism.

mitigate *vb* abate, alleviate, assuage, diminish, extenuate, lessen, moderate, palliate, relieve; allay, appease, calm, mollify, pacify, quell, quiet, reduce, soften, soothe; moderate, temper.

mitigation *n* abatement, allaying, alleviation, assuagement, diminution, moderation, palliation, relief.

mix *vb* alloy, amalgamate, blend, commingle, combine, compound, incorporate, interfuse, interlard, mingle, unite; associate, join. * *n* alloy, amalgam, blend, combination, compound, mixture.

mixture *n* admixture, association, intermixture, union; compound, farrago, hash, hodgepodge, hotchpotch, jumble, medley, melange, mishmash; diversity, miscellany, variety.

moan *vb* bemoan, bewail, deplore, grieve, groan, lament, mourn, sigh, weep. * *n* groan, lament, lamentation, sigh, wail.

mob *vb* crowd, jostle, surround, swarm, pack, throng. * *n* assemblage, crowd, rabble, multitude, throng, tumult; dregs, canaille, populace, rabble, riffraff, scum.

mobile *adj* changeable, fickle, expressive, inconstant, sensitive, variable, volatile.

mock *vb* ape, counterfeit, imitate, mimic, take off; deride, flout, gibe, insult, jeer, ridicule, taunt; balk, cheat, deceive, defeat, disappoint, dupe, elude, illude, mislead. * *adj* assumed, clap-trap, counterfeit, fake, false, feigned, make-believe, pretended, spurious. * *n* fake, imitation, phoney, sham; gibe, insult, jeer, scoff, taunt.

mockery *n* contumely, counterfeit, deception, derision, imitation, jeering, mimicry, ridicule, scoffing, scorn, sham, travesty.

mode *n* fashion, manner, method, style, way; accident, affection, degree, graduation, modification, quality, variety.

model *vb* design, fashion, form, mould, plan, shape. * *adj* admirable, archetypal, estimable, exemplary, ideal, meritorious, paradigmatic, perfect, praiseworthy, worthy. * *n* archetype, design, mould, original, pattern, protoplast, prototype, type; dummy, example, form; copy, facsimile, image, imitation, representation.

moderate *vb* abate, allay, appease, assuage, blunt, dull, lessen, soothe, mitigate, mollify, pacify, quell, quiet, reduce, repress, soften, still, subdue; diminish, qualify, slacken, temper; control, govern, regulate. * *adj* abstinent, frugal, sparing, temperate; limited, mediocre; abstemious, sober; calm, cool, judicious, reasonable, steady; gentle, mild, temperate, tolerable.

moderation *n* abstemiousness, forbearance, frugality, restraint, sobriety, temperance; calmness, composure, coolness, deliberateness, equanimity, mildness, sedateness.

modern *adj* fresh, late, latest, new, novel, present, recent, up-to-date.

modest *adj* bashful, coy, diffident, humble, meek, reserved, retiring, shy, unassuming, unobtrusive, unostentatious, unpretending, unpretentious; chaste, proper, pure, virtuous; becoming, decent, moderate.

modesty *n* bashfulness, coyness, diffidence, humility, meekness, propriety, prudishness, reserve, shyness, unobtrusiveness; chastity, purity, virtue; decency, moderation.

modification *n* alteration, change, qualification, reformation, variation; form, manner, mode, state.

modify *vb* alter, change, qualify, reform, shape, vary; lower, moderate, qualify, soften.

modish *adj* fashionable, stylish; ceremonious, conventional, courtly, genteel.

modulate *vb* attune, harmonize, tune; inflict, vary; adapt, adjust, proportion.

moiety *n* half; part, portion, share.

moil *vb* drudge, labour, toil; bespatter, daub, defile, soil, splash, spot, stain; fatigue, weary, tire.

moist *adj* damp, dank, humid, marshy, muggy, swampy, wet.

moisture *n* dampness, dankness, humidity, wetness.

mole *n* breakwater, dike, dyke, jetty, mound, pier, quay.

molecule *n* atom, monad, particle.

molest *vb* annoy, badger, bore, bother, chafe, discommode, disquiet, disturb, harass, harry, fret, gull, hector, incommode, inconvenience, irritate, oppress, pester, plague, tease, torment, trouble, vex, worry.

mollify *vb* soften; appease, calm, compose, pacify, quiet, soothe, tranquillize; abate, allay, assuage, blunt, dull, ease, lessen, mitigate, moderate, relieve, temper; qualify, tone down.

moment *n* flash, instant, jiffy, second, trice, twinkling, wink; avail, consequence, consideration, force, gravity, importance, significance, signification, value, weight; drive, force, impetus, momentum.

momentous *adj* grave, important, serious, significant, vital, weighty.

momentum *n* impetus, moment.

monarch *n* autocrat, despot; chief, dictator, emperor, king, potentate, prince, queen, ruler, sovereign.

monastery *n* abbey, cloister, convent, lamasery, nunnery, priory.

monastic *adj* coenobitic, coenobitical, conventual, monkish, secluded.

money *n* banknotes, cash, coin, currency, riches, specie, wealth.

moneyed, monied *adj* affluent, opulent, rich, well-off, well-to-do.

monitor *vb* check, observe, oversee, supervise, watch. * *n* admonisher, admonitor, adviser, counsellor, instructor, mentor, overseer.

monomania *n* delusion, hallucination, illusion, insanity, self-deception.

monopolize *vb* control, dominate, engross, forestall.

monotonous *adj* boring, dull, tedious, tiresome, undiversified, uniform, unvaried, unvarying, wearisome.

monotony *n* boredom, dullness, sameness, tedium, tiresomeness, uniformity, wearisomeness.

monster *adj* enormous, gigantic, huge, immense, mammoth, monstrous. * *n* enormity, marvel, prodigy, wonder; brute, demon, fiend, miscreant, ruffian, villain, wretch.

monstrous *adj* abnormal, preternatural, prodigious, unnatural; colossal, enormous, extraordinary, huge, immense, stupendous, vast; marvellous, strange, wonderful; bad, base, dreadful, flagrant, frightful, hateful, hideous, horrible, shocking, terrible.

monument *n* memorial, record, remembrance, testimonial; cairn, cenotaph, gravestone, mausoleum, memorial, pillar, tomb, tombstone.

mood *n* disposition, humour, temper, vein.

moody *adj* capricious, humoursome, variable; angry, crabbed, crusty, fretful, ill-tempered, irascible, irritable, passionate, pettish, peevish, petulant, snappish, snarling, sour, testy; cross-grained, dogged, frowning, glowering, glum, intractable, morose, perverse, spleeny, stubborn, sulky, sullen, wayward; abstracted, gloomy, melancholy, pensive, sad, saturnine.

moonshine *n* balderdash, fiction, flummery, fudge, fustian, nonsense, pretence, stuff, trash, twaddle, vanity.

moor[1] *vb* anchor, berth, fasten, fix, secure, tie.

moor[2] *n* bog, common, heath, moorland, morass, moss, wasteland.

moot *vb* agitate, argue, debate, discuss, dispute. * *adj* arguable, debatable, doubtful, unsettled.

mopish *adj* dejected, depressed, desponding, downcast, down-hearted, gloomy, glum, sad.

moral *adj* ethical, good, honest, honourable, just, upright, virtuous; abstract, ideal, intellectual, mental. * *n* intent, meaning, significance.

morals *npl* ethics, morality; behaviour, conduct, habits, manners.

morass *n* bog, fen, marsh, quagmire, slough, swamp.

morbid *adj* ailing, corrupted, diseased, sick, sickly, tainted, unhealthy, unsound, vitiated; depressed, downcast, gloomy, pessimistic, sensitive.

mordacious *adj* acrid, biting, cutting, mordant, pungent, sharp, stinging; caustic, poignant, satirical, sarcastic, scathing, severe.

mordant *adj* biting, caustic, keen, mordacious, nipping, sarcastic.

moreover *adv, conj* also, besides, further, furthermore, likewise, too.

morning *n* aurora, daybreak, dawn, morn, morningtide, sunrise.

morose *adj* austere, churlish, crabbed, crusty, dejected, desponding, downcast, downhearted, gloomy, glum, melancholy, moody, sad, severe, sour, sullen, surly.

morsel *n* bite, mouthful, titbit; bit, fragment, part, piece, scrap.

mortal *adj* deadly, destructive, fatal, final, human, lethal, perishable, vital. * *n* being, earthling, human, man, person, woman.

mortality *n* corruption, death, destruction, fatality.

mortification *n* chagrin, disappointment, discontent, dissatisfaction, displeasure, humiliation, trouble, shame, vexation; humility, penance, self-abasement, self-denial; gangrene, necrosis.

mortify *vb* annoy, chagrin, depress, disappoint, displease, disquiet, dissatisfy, harass, humble, plague, vex, worry; abase, abash, confound, humiliate, restrain, shame, subdue; corrupt, fester, gangrene, putrefy.

mortuary *n* burial place, cemetery, churchyard, graveyard, necropolis; charnel house, morgue.

mostly *adv* chiefly, customarily, especially, generally, mainly, particularly, principally.

mote *n* atom, corpuscle, flaw, mite, particle, speck, spot.

motherly *adj* affectionate, kind, maternal, paternal, tender.

motion *vb* beckon, direct, gesture, signal. * *n* action, change, drift, flux, movement, passage, stir, transit; air, gait, port; gesture, impulse, prompting, suggestion; proposal, proposition.

motionless *adj* fixed, immobile, quiescent, stable, stagnant, standing, stationary, still, torpid, unmoved.

motive *adj* activating, driving, moving, operative. * *n* cause, consideration, ground, impulse, incentive, incitement, inducement, influence, occasion, prompting, purpose, reason, spur, stimulus.

motley *adj* coloured, dappled, mottled, speckled, spotted, variegated; composite, diversified, heterogeneous, mingled, mixed.

mottled *adj* dappled, motley, piebald, speckled, spotted, variegated.

mould[1] *vb* carve, cast, fashion, form, make, model, shape. * *n* cast, character, fashion, form, matrix, pattern, shape; material, matter, substance.

mould[2] *n* blight, mildew, mouldiness, must, mustiness, rot; fungus, lichen, mushroom, puffball, rust, smut, toadstool; earth, loam, soil.

moulder *vb* crumble, decay, perish, waste.
mouldy *adj* decaying, fusty, mildewed, musty.
mound *n* bank, barrow, hill, hillock, knoll, tumulus; bulwark, defence, rampart.
mount[1] *n* hill, mountain, peak.
mount[2] *vb* arise, ascend, climb, rise, soar, tower; escalate, scale; embellish, ornament; bestride, get upon. * *n* charger, horse, ride, steed.
mountain *n* alp, height, hill, mount, peak; abundance, heap, mound, stack.
mountebank *n* charlatan, cheat, impostor, pretender, quack.
mourn *vb* bemoan, bewail, deplore, grieve, lament, sorrow, wail.
mournful *adj* afflicting, afflictive, calamitous, deplorable, distressed, grievous, lamentable, sad, woeful; doleful, heavy, heavy-hearted, lugubrious, melancholy, sorrowful, tearful.
mouth *vb* clamour, declaim, rant, roar, vociferate. * *n* chaps, jaws; aperture, opening, orifice; entrance, inlet; oracle, mouthpiece, speaker, spokesman.
movables *n pl* chattels, effects, furniture, goods, property, wares.
move *vb* dislodge, drive, impel, propel, push, shift, start, stir; actuate, incite, instigate, rouse; determine, incline, induce, influence, persuade, prompt; affect, impress, touch, trouble; agitate, awaken, excite, incense, irritate; propose, recommend, suggest; go, march, proceed, walk; act, live; flit, remove. * *n* action, motion, movement.
movement *n* change, move, motion, passage; emotion; crusade, drive.
moving *adj* impelling, influencing, instigating, persuading, persuasive; affecting, impressive, pathetic, touching.
mucous *adj* glutinous, gummy, mucilaginous, ropy, slimy, viscid.
mud *n* dirt, mire, muck, slime.
muddle *vb* confuse, disarrange, disorder; fuddle, inebriate, stupefy; muff, mull, spoil. * *n* confusion, disorder, mess, plight, predicament.
muddy *vb* dirty, foul, smear, soil; confuse, obscure. * *adj* dirty, foul, impure, slimy, soiled, turbid; bothered, confused, dull, heavy, stupid; incoherent, obscure, vague.
muffle *vb* cover, envelop, shroud, wrap; conceal, disguise, involve; deaden, soften, stifle, suppress.
mulish *adj* cross-grained, headstrong, intractable, obstinate, stubborn.
multifarious *adj* different, divers, diverse, diversified, manifold, multiform, multitudinous, various.
multiloquence *n* garrulity, loquacity, loquaciousness, talkativeness.
multiply *vb* augment, extend, increase, spread.
multitude *n* numerousness; host, legion; army, assemblage, assembly, collection, concourse, congregation, crowd, horde, mob, swarm, throng; commonality, herd, mass, mob, pack, populace, rabble.
mundane *adj* earthly, secular, sublunary, temporal, terrene, terrestrial, worldly.
munificence *n* benefice, bounteousness, bountifulness, bounty, generosity, liberality.
munificent *adj* beneficent, bounteous, bountiful, free, generous, liberal, princely.
murder *vb* assassinate, butcher, destroy, dispatch, kill, massacre, slaughter, slay; abuse, mar, spoil. * *n* assassination, butchery, destruction, homicide, killing, manslaughter, massacre.
murderer *n* assassin, butcher, cut-throat, killer, manslaughterer, slaughterer, slayer.
murderous *adj* barbarous, bloodthirsty, bloody, cruel, fell, sanguinary, savage.
murky *adj* cheerless, cloudy, dark, dim, dusky, gloomy, hazy, lowering, lurid, obscure, overcast.
murmur *vb* croak, grumble, mumble, mutter; hum, whisper. * *n* complaint, grumble, mutter, plaint, whimper; hum, undertone, whisper.
muscular *adj* sinewy; athletic, brawny, powerful, lusty, stalwart, stout, strong, sturdy, vigorous.
muse *vb* brood, cogitate, consider, contemplate, deliberate, dream, meditate, ponder, reflect, ruminate, speculate, think. * *n* abstraction, musing, reverie.
music *n* harmony, melody, symphony.
musical *adj* dulcet, harmonious, melodious, sweet, sweet-sounding, symphonious, tuneful.
musing *adj* absent-minded, meditative, preoccupied. * *n* absent-mindedness, abstraction, contemplation, daydreaming, meditation, muse, reflection, reverie, rumination.
muster *vb* assemble, collect, congregate, convene, convoke, gather, marshal, meet, rally, summon. * *n* assemblage, assembly, collection, congregation, convention, convocation, gathering, meeting, rally.
musty *adj* fetid, foul, fusty, mouldy, rank, sour, spoiled; hackneyed, old, stale, threadbare, trite; ill-favoured, insipid, vapid; dull, heavy, rusty, spiritless.
mutable *adj* alterable, changeable; changeful, fickle, inconstant, irresolute, mutational, unsettled, unstable, unsteady, vacillating, variable, wavering.
mutation *n* alteration, change, variation.
mute *vb* dampen, lower, moderate, muffle, soften. * *adj* dumb, voiceless; silent, speechless, still, taciturn.
mutilate *vb* cripple, damage, disable, disfigure, hamstring, injure, maim, mangle, mar.
mutinous *adj* contumacious, insubordinate, rebellious, refractory, riotous, tumultuous, turbulent, unruly; insurgent, seditious.
mutiny *vb* rebel, revolt, rise, resist. * *n* insubordination, insurrection, rebellion, revolt, revolution, riot, rising, sedition, uprising.
mutter *vb* grumble, muffle, mumble, murmur.
mutual *adj* alternate, common, correlative, interchangeable, interchanged, reciprocal, requited.
myopic *adj* near-sighted, purblind, short-sighted.
myriad *adj* innumerable, manifold, multitudinous, uncounted. * *n* host, million(s), multitude, score(s), sea, swarm, thousand(s).
mysterious *adj* abstruse, cabbalistic, concealed, cryptic, dark, dim, enigmatic, enigmatical, hidden, incomprehensible, inexplicable, inscrutable, mystic, mystical, obscure, occult, puzzling, recondite, secret, sphinx-like, unaccountable, unfathomable, unintelligible, unknown.
mystery *n* enigma, puzzle, riddle, secret; art, business, calling, trade.
mystical *adj* abstruse, cabbalistic, dark, enigmatical, esoteric, hidden, inscrutable, mysterious, obscure, occult, recondite, transcendental; allegorical, emblematic, emblematical, symbolic, symbolical.
mystify *vb* befog, bewilder, confound, confuse, dumbfound, embarrass, obfuscate, perplex, pose, puzzle.
myth *n* fable, legend, tradition; allegory, fiction, invention, parable, story; falsehood, fancy, figment, lie, untruth.
mythical *adj* allegorical, fabled, fabulous, fanciful, fictitious, imaginary, legendary, mythological.

N

nab *vb* catch, clutch, grasp, seize.
nag[1] *vb* carp, fuss, hector, henpeck, pester, torment, worry. * *n* nagger, scold, shrew, tartar.
nag[2] *n* bronco, crock, hack, horse, pony, scrag.
naive *adj* artless, candid, ingenuous, natural, plain, simple, unaffected, unsophisticated.
naked *adj* bare, nude, uncovered; denuded, unclad, unclothed, undressed; defenceless, exposed, open, unarmed, unguarded, unprotected; evident, manifest, plain, stark, unconcealed, undisguised; mere, sheer, simple; bare, destitute, rough, rude, unfurnished, unprovided; uncoloured, unexaggerated, unvarnished.
name *vb* call, christen, denounce, dub, entitle, phrase, style, term; mention; denominate, designate, indicate, nominate, specify. * *n* appellation, cognomen, denomination, designation, epithet, nickname, surname, sobriquet, title; character, credit, reputation, repute; celebrity, distinction, eminence, fame, honour, note, praise, renown.

narcotic *adj* stupefacient, stupefactive, stupefying. * *n* anaesthetic, anodyne, dope, opiate, sedative, stupefacient, tranquillizer.

narrate *vb* chronicle, describe, detail, enumerate, recite, recount, rehearse, relate, tell.

narration *n* account, description, chronicle, history, narrative, recital, rehearsal, relation, story, tale.

narrow *vb* confine, contract, cramp, limit, restrict, straiten. * *adj* circumscribed, confined, contracted, cramped, incapacious, limited, pinched, scanty, straitened; bigoted, hidebound, illiberal, ungenerous; close, near.

nastiness *n* defilement, dirtiness, filth, filthiness, foulness, impurity, pollution, squalor, uncleanness; indecency, grossness, obscenity, pornography, ribaldry, smut, smuttiness.

nasty *adj* defiled, dirty, filthy, foul, impure, loathsome, polluted, squalid, unclean; gross, indecent, indelicate, lewd, loose, obscene, smutty, vile; disagreeable, disgusting, nauseous, odious, offensive, repulsive, sickening; aggravating, annoying, pesky, pestering, troublesome.

nation *n* commonwealth, realm, state; community, people, population, race, stock, tribe.

native *adj* aboriginal, autochthonal, autochthonous, domestic, home, indigenous, vernacular; genuine, intrinsic, natural, original, real; congenital, inborn, inbred, inherent, innate, natal. * *n* aborigine, autochthon, inhabitant, national, resident.

natty *adj* dandyish, fine, foppish, jaunty, neat, nice, spruce, tidy.

natural *adj* indigenous, innate, native, original; characteristic, essential; legitimate, normal, regular; artless, authentic, genuine, ingenious, unreal, simple, spontaneous, unaffected; bastard, illegitimate.

nature *n* universe, world; character, constitution, essence; kind, quality, species, sort; disposition, grain, humour, mood, temper; being, intellect, intelligence, mind.

naughty *adj* bad, corrupt, mischievous, perverse, worthless.

nausea *n* queasiness, seasickness; loathing, qualm; aversion, disgust, repugnance.

nauseous *adj* abhorrent, disgusting, distasteful, loathsome, offensive, repulsive, revolting, sickening.

naval *adj* marine, maritime, nautical.

navigate *vb* cruise, direct, guide, pilot, plan, sail, steer.

navy *n* fleet, shipping, vessels.

near *vb* approach, draw close. * *adj* adjacent, approximate, close, contiguous, neighbouring, nigh; approaching, forthcoming, imminent, impending; dear, familiar, friendly, intimate; direct, immediate, short, straight; accurate, literal; narrow, parsimonious.

nearly *adv* almost, approximately, well-nigh; closely, intimately, pressingly; meanly, parsimoniously, penuriously, stingily.

neat *adj* clean, cleanly, orderly, tidy, trim, unsoiled; nice, smart, spruce; chaste, pure, simple; excellent, pure, unadulterated; adroit, clever, exact, finished; dainty, nice.

nebulous *adj* cloudy, hazy, misty.

necessary *adj* inevitable, unavoidable; essential, expedient, indispensable, needful, requisite; compelling, compulsory, involuntary. * *n* essential, necessity, requirement, requisite.

necessitate *vb* compel, constrain, demand, force, impel, oblige.

necessitous *adj* destitute, distressed, indigent, moneyless, needy, penniless, pinched, poor, poverty-stricken; narrow, pinching.

necessity *n* inevitability, inevitableness, unavoidability, unavoidableness; compulsion, destiny, fatality, fate; emergency, urgency; exigency, indigence, indispensability, indispensableness, need, needfulness, poverty, want; essentiality, essentialness, requirement, requisite.

necromancy *n* conjuration, divination, enchantment, magic, sorcery, witchcraft, wizardry.

necropolis *n* burial ground, cemetery, churchyard, crematorium, graveyard, mortuary.

need *vb* demand, lack, require, want. * *n* emergency, exigency, extremity, necessity, strait, urgency, want; destitution, distress, indigence, neediness, penury, poverty, privation.

needful *adj* distressful, necessitous, necessary; essential, indispensable, requisite.

needless *adj* superfluous, unnecessary, useless.

needy *adj* destitute, indigent, necessitous, poor.

nefarious *adj* abominable, atrocious, detestable, dreadful, execrable, flagitious, heinous, horrible, infamous, iniquitous, scandalous, vile, wicked.

negation *n* denial, disavowal, disclaimer, rejection, renunciation.

neglect *vb* condemn, despise, disregard, forget, ignore, omit, overlook, slight. * *n* carelessness, default, failure, heedlessness, inattention, omission, remissness; disregard, disrespect, slight; indifference, negligence.

negligence *n* carelessness, disregard, heedlessness, inadvertency, inattention, indifference, neglect, remissness, slackness, thoughtlessness; defect, fault, inadvertence, omission, shortcoming.

negligent *adj* careless, heedless, inattentive, indifferent, neglectful, regardless, thoughtless.

negotiate *vb* arrange, bargain, deal, debate, sell, settle, transact, treat.

neighbourhood *n* district, environs, locality, vicinage, vicinity; adjacency, nearness, propinquity, proximity.

neighbourly *adj* attentive, civil, friendly, kind, obliging, social.

neophyte *n* beginner, catechumen, convert, novice, pupil, tyro.

nerve *vb* brace, energize, fortify, invigorate, strengthen. * *n* force, might, power, strength, vigour; coolness, courage, endurance, firmness, fortitude, hardihood, manhood, pluck, resolution, self-command, steadiness.

nervous *adj* forcible, powerful, robust, strong, vigorous; irritable, fearful, shaky, timid, timorous, weak, weakly.

nestle *vb* cuddle, harbour, lodge, nuzzle, snug, snuggle.

nettle *vb* chafe, exasperate, fret, harass, incense, irritate, provoke, ruffle, sting, tease, vex.

neutral *adj* impartial, indifferent; colourless, mediocre.

neutralize *vb* cancel, counterbalance, counterpoise, invalidate, offset.

nevertheless *adv* however, nonetheless, notwithstanding, yet.

new *adj* fresh, latest, modern, novel, recent, unused; additional, another, further; reinvigorated, renovated, repaired.

news *n* advice, information, intelligence, report, tidings, word.

nice *adj* accurate, correct, critical, definite, delicate, exact, exquisite, precise, rigorous, strict; dainty, difficult, exacting, fastidious, finical, punctilious, squeamish; discerning, discriminating, particular, precise, scrupulous; neat, tidy, trim; fine, minute, refined, subtle; delicate, delicious, luscious, palatable, savoury, soft, tender; agreeable, delightful, good, pleasant.

nicety *n* accuracy, exactness, niceness, precision, truth, daintiness, fastidiousness, squeamishness; discrimination, subtlety.

niggard *n* churl, curmudgeon, miser, screw, scrimp, skinflint.

niggardly *adj* avaricious, close, close-fisted, illiberal, mean, mercenary, miserly, parsimonious, penurious, skinflint, sordid, stingy.

nigh *adj* adjacent, adjoining, contiguous, near; present, proximate. * *adv* almost, near, nearly.

nimble *adj* active, agile, alert, brisk, lively, prompt, quick, speedy, sprightly, spry, swift, tripping.

nobility *n* aristocracy, dignity, elevation, eminence, grandeur, greatness, loftiness, magnanimity, nobleness, peerage, superiority, worthiness.

noble *adj* dignified, elevated, eminent, exalted, generous, great, honourable, illustrious, magnanimous, superior, worthy; choice, excellent; aristocratic, gentle, high-born, patrician; grand, lofty, lordly, magnificent, splendid, stately. * *n* aristocrat, grandee, lord, nobleman, peer.

noctambulist *n* sleepwalker, somnambulist.

noise *vb* bruit, gossip, repeat, report, rumour. * *n* ado, blare, clamour, clatter, cry, din, fuss, hubbub, hullabaloo, outcry, pandemonium, racket, row, sound, tumult, uproar, vociferation.

noiseless *adj* inaudible, quiet, silent, soundless.

noisome *adj* bad, baneful, deleterious, disgusting, fetid, foul, hurtful, injurious, mischievous, nocuous, noxious, offensive, pernicious, pestiferous, pestilential, poisonous, unhealthy, unwholesome.

noisy *adj* blatant, blustering, boisterous, brawling, clamorous, loud, uproarious, riotous, tumultuous, vociferous.
nomadic *adj* migratory, pastoral, vagrant, wandering.
nominal *adj* formal, inconsiderable, minimal, ostensible, pretended, professed, so-called, titular.
nominate *vb* appoint, choose, designate, name, present, propose.
nonchalant *adj* apathetic, careless, cool, indifferent, unconcerned.
nondescript *adj* amorphous, characterless, commonplace, dull, indescribable, odd, ordinary, unclassifiable, uninteresting, unremarkable.
nonentity *n* cipher, futility, inexistence, inexistency, insignificance, nobody, nonexistence, nothingness.
nonplus *vb* astonish, bewilder, confound, confuse, discomfit, disconcert, embarrass, floor, gravel, perplex, pose, puzzle.
nonsensical *adj* absurd, foolish, irrational, senseless, silly, stupid.
norm *n* model, pattern, rule, standard.
normal *adj* analogical, legitimate, natural, ordinary, regular, usual; erect, perpendicular, vertical.
notable *adj* distinguished, extraordinary, memorable, noted, remarkable, signal; conspicuous, evident, noticeable, observable, plain, prominent, striking; notorious, rare, well-known. * *n* celebrity, dignitary, notability, worthy.
note *vb* heed, mark, notice, observe, regard, remark; record, register; denote, designate. * *n* memorandum, minute, record; annotation, comment, remark, scholium; indication, mark, sign, symbol, token; account, bill, catalogue, reckoning; billet, epistle, letter; consideration, heed, notice, observation; celebrity, consequence, credit, distinction, eminence, fame, notability, notedness, renown, reputation, respectability; banknote, bill, promissory note; song, strain, tune, voice.
noted *adj* celebrated, conspicuous, distinguished, eminent, famed, famous, illustrious, notable, notorious, remarkable, renowned, well-known.
nothing *n* inexistence, nonentity, nonexistence, nothingness, nullity; bagatelle, trifle.
notice *vb* mark, note, observe, perceive, regard, see; comment on, mention, remark; attend to, heed. * *n* cognizance, heed, note, observation, regard; advice, announcement, information, intelligence, mention, news, notification; communication, intimation, premonition, warning; attention, civility, consideration, respect; comments, remarks.
notify *vb* advertise, announce, declare, publish, promulgate; acquaint, apprise, inform.
notion *n* concept, conception, idea; apprehension, belief, conceit, conviction, expectation, estimation, impression, judgement, opinion, sentiment, view.
notoriety *n* celebrity, fame, figure, name, note, publicity, reputation, repute, vogue.
notorious *adj* apparent, egregious, evident, notable, obvious, open, overt, manifest, patent, well-known; celebrated, conspicuous, distinguished, famed, famous, flagrant, infamous, noted, remarkable, renowned.
notwithstanding *conj* despite, however, nevertheless, yet. * *prep* despite.
nourish *vb* feed, nurse, nurture; maintain, supply, support; breed, educate, instruct, train; cherish, encourage, foment, foster, promote, succour.
nourishment *n* aliment, diet, food, nutriment, nutrition, sustenance.
novel *adj* fresh, modern, new, rare, recent, strange, uncommon, unusual. * *n* fiction, romance, story, tale.
novice *n* convert, proselyte; initiate, neophyte, novitiate, probationer; apprentice, beginner, learner, tyro.
noxious *adj* baneful, deadly, deleterious, destructive, detrimental, hurtful, injurious, insalubrious, mischievous, noisome, pernicious, pestilent, poisonous, unfavourable, unwholesome.
nude *adj* bare, denuded, exposed, naked, uncovered, unclothed, undressed.
nugatory *adj* frivolous, insignificant, trifling, trivial, vain, worthless; bootless, ineffectual, inefficacious, inoperative, null, unavailing, useless.
nuisance *n* annoyance, bore, bother, infliction, offence, pest, plague, trouble.
null *adj* ineffectual, invalid, nugatory, useless, void; characterless, colourless.
nullify *vb* abolish, abrogate, annul, cancel, invalidate, negate, quash, repeal, revoke.
numb *vb* benumb, deaden, stupefy. * *adj* benumbed, deadened, dulled, insensible, paralysed.
number *vb* calculate, compute, count, enumerate, numerate, reckon, tell; account, reckon. * *n* digit, figure, numeral; horde, multitude, numerousness, throng; aggregate, collection, sum, total.
numerous *adj* abundant, many, numberless.
nuncio *n* ambassador, legate, messenger.
nunnery *n* abbey, cloister, convent, monastery.
nuptial *adj* bridal, conjugal, connubial, hymeneal, matrimonial.
nuptials *npl* espousal, marriage, wedding.
nurse *vb* nourish, nurture; rear, suckle; cherish, encourage, feed, foment, foster, pamper, promote, succour; economize, manage; caress, dandle, fondle. * *n* auxiliary, orderly, sister; amah, *au pair*, babysitter, nanny, nursemaid, nurserymaid,
nurture *vb* feed, nourish, nurse, tend; breed, discipline, educate, instruct, rear, school, train. * *n* diet, food, nourishment; breeding, discipline, education, instruction, schooling, training, tuition; attention, nourishing, nursing.
nutriment *n* aliment, food, nourishment, nutrition, pabulum, subsistence, sustenance.
nutrition *n* diet, food, nourishment, nutriment.
nutritious *adj* invigorating, nourishing, strengthening, supporting, sustaining.
nymph *n* damsel, dryad, lass, girl, maid, maiden, naiad.

O

oaf *n* blockhead, dolt, dunce, fool, idiot, simpleton.
oath *n* blasphemy, curse, expletive, imprecation, malediction; affirmation, pledge, promise, vow.
obduracy *n* contumacy, doggedness, obstinacy, stubbornness, tenacity; depravity, impenitence.
obdurate *adj* hard, harsh, rough, rugged; callous, cantankerous, dogged, firm, hardened, inflexible, insensible, obstinate, pigheaded, unfeeling, stubborn, unbending, unyielding; depraved, graceless, lost, reprobate, shameless, impenitent, incorrigible, irreclaimable.
obedience *n* acquiescence, agreement, compliance, duty, respect, reverence, submission, submissiveness, subservience.
obedient *adj* acquiescent, compliant, deferential, duteous, dutiful, observant, regardful, respectful, submissive, subservient, yielding.
obeisance *n* bow, courtesy, curtsy, homage, reverence, salutation.
obelisk *n* column, pillar.
obese *adj* corpulent, fat, fleshy, gross, plump, podgy, portly, stout.
obesity *n* corpulence, corpulency, embonpoint, fatness, fleshiness, obeseness, plumpness.
obey *vb* comply, conform, heed, keep, mind, observe, submit, yield.
obfuscate *vb* cloud, darken, obscure; bewilder, confuse, muddle.
object[1] *vb* cavil, contravene, demur, deprecate, disapprove of, except to, impeach, oppose, protest, refuse.
object[2] *n* particular, phenomenon, precept, reality, thing; aim, butt, destination, end, mark, recipient, target; design, drift, goal, intention, motive, purpose, use, view.
objection *n* censure, difficulty, doubt, exception, protest, remonstrance, scruple.
objurgate *vb* chide, reprehend, reprove.

oblation *n* gift, offering, sacrifice.

obligation *n* accountability, accountableness, responsibility; agreement, bond, contract, covenant, engagement, stipulation; debt, indebtedness, liability.

obligatory *adj* binding, coercive, compulsory, enforced, necessary, unavoidable.

oblige *vb* bind, coerce, compel, constrain, force, necessitate, require; accommodate, benefit, convenience, favour, gratify, please; obligate, bind.

obliging *adj* accommodating, civil, complaisant, considerate, kind, friendly, polite.

oblique *adj* aslant, inclined, sidelong, slanting; indirect, obscure.

obliterate *vb* cancel, delete, destroy, efface, eradicate, erase, expunge.

oblivious *adj* careless, forgetful, heedless, inattentive, mindless, negligent, neglectful.

obloquy *n* aspersion, backbiting, blame, calumny, censure, contumely, defamation, detraction, disgrace, odium, reproach, reviling, slander, traducing.

obnoxious *adj* blameworthy, censurable, faulty, reprehensible; hateful, objectionable, obscene, odious, offensive, repellent, repugnant, repulsive, unpleasant, unpleasing.

obscene *adj* broad, coarse, filthy, gross, immodest, impure, indecent, indelicate, ribald, unchaste, lewd, licentious, loose, offensive, pornographic, shameless, smutty; disgusting, dirty, foul.

obscure *vb* becloud, befog, blur, cloud, darken, eclipse, dim, obfuscate, obnubilate, shade; conceal, cover, equivocate, hide. * *adj* dark, darksome, dim, dusky, gloomy, lurid, murky, rayless, shadowy, sombre, unenlightened, unilluminated; abstruse, blind, cabbalistic, difficult, doubtful, enigmatic, high, incomprehensible, indefinite, indistinct, intricate, involved, mysterious, mystic, recondite, undefined, unintelligible, vague; remote, secluded; humble, inglorious, nameless, renownless, undistinguished, unhonoured, unknown, unnoted, unnoticed.

obsequious *adj* cringing, deferential, fawning, flattering, servile, slavish, supple, subservient, sycophantic, truckling.

observant *adj* attentive, heedful, mindful, perceptive, quick, regardful, vigilant, watchful.

observation *n* attention, cognition, notice, observance; annotation, note, remark; experience, knowledge.

observe *vb* eye, mark, note, notice, remark, watch; behold, detect, discover, perceive, see; express, mention, remark, say, utter; comply, conform, follow, fulfil, obey; celebrate, keep, regard, solemnize.

obsolete *adj* ancient, antiquated, antique, archaic, disused, neglected, old, old-fashioned, obsolescent, out-of-date, past, passé, unfashionable.

obstacle *n* barrier, check, difficulty, hindrance, impediment, interference, interruption, obstruction, snag, stumbling block.

obstinacy *n* contumacy, doggedness, headiness, firmness, inflexibility, intractability, obduracy, persistence, perseverance, perversity, resoluteness, stubbornness, tenacity, wilfulness.

obstinate *adj* cross-grained, contumacious, dogged, firm, headstrong, inflexible, immovable, intractable, mulish, obdurate, opinionated, persistent, pertinacious, perverse, resolute, self-willed, stubborn, tenacious, unyielding, wilful.

obstreperous *adj* boisterous, clamorous, loud, noisy, riotous, tumultuous, turbulent, unruly, uproarious, vociferous.

obstruct *vb* bar, barricade, block, blockade, block up, choke, clog, close, glut, jam, obturate, stop; hinder, impede, oppose, prevent; arrest, check, curb, delay, embrace, interrupt, retard, slow.

obstruction *n* bar, barrier, block, blocking, check, difficulty, hindrance, impediment, obstacle, stoppage; check, clog, embarrassment, interruption, obturation.

obtain *vb* achieve, acquire, attain, bring, contrive, earn, elicit, gain, get, induce, procure, secure; hold, prevail, stand, subsist.

obtrude *vb* encroach, infringe, interfere, intrude, trespass.

obtrusive *adj* forward, interfering, intrusive, meddling, officious.

obtuse *adj* blunt; blockish, doltish, dull, dull-witted, heavy, stockish, stolid, stupid, slow, unintellectual, unintelligent.

obviate *vb* anticipate, avert, counteract, preclude, prevent, remove.

obvious *adj* exposed, liable, open, subject; apparent, clear, distinct, evident, manifest, palatable, patent, perceptible, plain, self-evident, unmistakable, visible.

occasion *vb* breed, cause, create, originate, produce; induce, influence, move, persuade. * *n* casualty, event, incident, occurrence; conjuncture, convenience, juncture, opening, opportunity; condition, necessity, need, exigency, requirement, want; cause, ground, reason; inducement, influence; circumstance, exigency.

occasional *adj* accidental, casual, incidental, infrequent, irregular, uncommon; causative, causing.

occasionally *adv* casually, sometimes.

occult *adj* abstruse, cabbalistic, hidden, latent, secret, invisible, mysterious, mystic, mystical, recondite, shrouded, undetected, undiscovered, unknown, unrevealed, veiled. * *n* magic, sorcery, witchcraft.

occupation *n* holding, occupancy, possession, tenure, use; avocation, business, calling, craft, employment, engagement, job, post, profession, trade, vocation.

occupy *vb* capture, hold, keep, possess; cover, fill, garrison, inhabit, take up, tenant; engage, employ, use.

occur *vb* appear, arise, offer; befall, chance, eventuate, happen, result, supervene.

occurrence *n* accident, adventure, affair, casualty, event, happening, incident, proceeding, transaction.

odd *adj* additional, redundant, remaining; casual, incidental; inappropriate, queer, unsuitable; comical, droll, erratic, extravagant, extraordinary, fantastic, grotesque, irregular, peculiar, quaint, singular, strange, uncommon, uncouth, unique, unusual, whimsical.

odds *npl* difference, disparity, inequality; advantage, superiority, supremacy.

odious *adj* abominable, detestable, execrable, hateful, shocking; hated, obnoxious, unpopular; disagreeable, forbidding, loathsome, offensive.

odium *n* abhorrence, detestation, dislike, enmity, hate, hatred; odiousness, repulsiveness; obloquy, opprobrium, reproach, shame.

odorous *adj* aromatic, balmy, fragrant, perfumed, redolent, scented, sweet-scented, sweet-smelling.

odour *n* aroma, fragrance, perfume, redolence, scent, smell.

offal *n* carrion, dregs, garbage, refuse, rubbish, waste.

offence *n* aggression, attack, assault; anger, displeasure, indignation, pique, resentment, umbrage, wrath; affront, harm, injury, injustice, insult, outrage, wrong; crime, delinquency, fault, misdeed, misdemeanour, sin, transgression, trespass.

offend *vb* affront, annoy, chafe, displease, fret, gall, irritate, mortify, nettle, provoke, vex; molest, pain, shock, wound; fall, sin, stumble, transgress.

offender *n* convict, criminal, culprit, delinquent, felon, malefactor, sinner, transgressor, trespasser.

offensive *adj* aggressive, attacking, invading; disgusting, loathsome, nauseating, nauseous, repulsive, sickening; abominable, detestable, disagreeable, displeasing, execrable, hateful, obnoxious, repugnant, revolting, shocking, unpalatable, unpleasant; abusive, disagreeable, impertinent, insolent, insulting, irritating, opprobrious, rude, saucy, unpleasant. * *n* attack, onslaught.

offer *vb* present, proffer, tender; exhibit; furnish, propose, propound, show; volunteer; dare, essay, endeavour, venture. * *n* overture, proffering, proposal, proposition, tender, overture; attempt, bid, endeavour, essay.

offhand *adj* abrupt, brusque, casual, curt, extempore, impromptu, informal, unpremeditated, unstudied. * *adv* carelessly, casually, clumsily, haphazardly, informally, slapdash; ad-lib, extemporaneously, extemporarily, extempore, impromptu.

office *n* duty, function, service, work; berth, place, position, post, situation; business, capacity, charge, employment, trust; bureau, room.

officiate *vb* act, perform, preside, serve.

officious *adj* busy, dictatorial, forward, impertinent, interfering, intermeddling, meddlesome, meddling, obtrusive, pushing, pushy.

offset *vb* balance, counteract, counterbalance, counterpoise. * *n* branch, offshoot, scion, shoot, slip, sprout, twig; counterbalance, counterpoise, set-off, equivalent.

offspring *n* brood, children, descendants, issue, litter, posterity, progeny; cadet, child, scion.

often *adv* frequently, generally, oftentimes, repeatedly.

ogre *n* bugbear, demon, devil, goblin, hobgoblin, monster, spectre.

old *adj* aged, ancient, antiquated, antique, archaic, elderly, obsolete, olden, old-fashioned, superannuated; decayed, done, senile, worn-out; original, primitive, pristine; former, preceding, pre-existing.

oleaginous *adj* adipose, fat, fatty, greasy, oily, sebaceous, unctuous.

omen *n* augury, auspice, foreboding, portent, presage, prognosis, sign, warning.

ominous *adj* inauspicious, monitory, portentous, premonitory, threatening, unpropitious.

omission *n* default, failure, forgetfulness, neglect, oversight.

omit *vb* disregard, drop, eliminate, exclude, miss, neglect, overlook, skip.

omnipotent *adj* almighty, all-powerful.

omniscient *adj* all-knowing, all-seeing, all-wise.

oneness *n* individuality, singleness, unity.

onerous *adj* burdensome, difficult, hard, heavy, laborious, oppressive, responsible, weighty.

one-sided *adj* partial, prejudiced, unfair, unilateral, unjust.

only *adj* alone, single, sole, solitary. * *adv* barely, merely, simply.

onset *n* assault, attack, charge, onslaught, storm, storming.

onus *n* burden, liability, load, responsibility.

ooze *vb* distil, drip, drop, shed; drain, exude, filter, leak, percolate, stain, transude. * *n* mire, mud, slime.

opaque *adj* dark, dim, hazy, muddy; abstruse, cryptic, enigmatic, enigmatical, obscure, unclear.

open *vb* expand, spread; begin, commence, initiate; disclose, exhibit, reveal, show; unbar, unclose, uncover, unlock, unseal, untie. * *adj* expanded, extended, unclosed, spread wide; aboveboard, artless, candid, cordial, fair, frank, guileless, hearty, honest, sincere, openhearted, single-minded, undesigning, undisguised, undissembling, unreserved; bounteous, bountiful, free, generous, liberal, munificent; ajar, uncovered; exposed, undefended, unprotected; clear, unobstructed; accessible, public, unenclosed, unrestricted; mild, moderate; apparent, debatable, evident, obvious, patent, plain, undetermined.

opening *adj* commencing, first, inaugural, initiatory, introductory. * *n* aperture, breach, chasm, cleft, fissure, flaw, gap, gulf, hole, interspace, loophole, orifice, perforation, rent, rift; beginning, commencement, dawn; chance, opportunity, vacancy.

openly *adv* candidly, frankly, honestly, plainly, publicly.

openness *n* candour, frankness, honesty, ingenuousness, plainness, unreservedness.

operate *vb* act, function, work; cause, effect, occasion, produce; manipulate, use, run.

operation *n* manipulation, performance, procedure, proceeding, process; action, affair, manoeuvre, motion, movement.

operative *adj* active, effective, effectual, efficient, serviceable, vigorous; important, indicative, influential, significant. * *n* artisan, employee, labourer, mechanic, worker, workman.

opiate *adj* narcotic, sedative, soporiferous, soporific. * *n* anodyne, drug, narcotic, sedative, tranquillizer.

opine *vb* apprehend, believe, conceive, fancy, judge, suppose, presume, surmise, think.

opinion *n* conception, idea, impression, judgment, notion, sentiment, view; belief, persuasion, tenet; esteem, estimation, judgment.

opinionated *adj* biased, bigoted, cocksure, conceited, dictatorial, dogmatic, opinionative, prejudiced, stubborn.

opponent *adj* adverse, antagonistic, contrary, opposing, opposite, repugnant. * *n* adversary, antagonist, competitor, contestant, counteragent, enemy, foe, opposite, opposer, party, rival.

opportune *adj* appropriate, auspicious, convenient, favourable, felicitous, fit, fitting, fortunate, lucky, propitious, seasonable, suitable, timely, well-timed.

opportunity *n* chance, convenience, moment, occasion.

oppose *vb* combat, contravene, counteract, dispute, obstruct, oppugn, resist, thwart, withstand; check, prevent; confront, counterpoise.

opposite *adj* facing, fronting; conflicting, contradictory, contrary, different, diverse, incompatible, inconsistent, irreconcilable; adverse, antagonistic, hostile, inimical, opposed, opposing, repugnant. * *n* contradiction, contrary, converse, reverse.

opposition *n* antagonism, antinomy, contrariety, inconsistency, repugnance; counteraction, counter-influence, hostility, resistance; hindrance, obstacle, obstruction, oppression, prevention.

oppress *vb* burden, crush, depress, harass, load, maltreat, overburden, overpower, overwhelm, persecute, subdue, suppress, tyrannize, wrong.

oppression *n* abuse, calamity, cruelty, hardship, injury, injustice, misery, persecution, severity, suffering, tyranny; depression, dullness, heaviness, lassitude.

oppressive *adj* close, muggy, stifling, suffocating, sultry.

opprobrious *adj* abusive, condemnatory, contemptuous, damnatory, insolent, insulting, offensive, reproachable, scandalous, scurrilous, vituperative; despised, dishonourable, disreputable, hateful, infamous, shameful.

opprobrium *n* contumely, scurrility; calumny, disgrace, ignominy, infamy, obloquy, odium, reproach.

oppugn *vb* assail, argue, attack, combat, contravene, oppose, resist, thwart, withstand.

option *n* choice, discretion, election, preference, selection.

optional *adj* discretionary, elective, nonobligatory, voluntary.

opulence *n* affluence, fortune, independence, luxury, riches, wealth.

opulent *adj* affluent, flush, luxurious, moneyed, plentiful, rich, sumptuous, wealthy.

oracular *adj* ominous, portentous, prophetic; authoritative, dogmatic, magisterial, positive; aged, grave, wise; ambiguous, blind, dark, equivocal, obscure.

oral *adj* nuncupative, spoken, verbal, vocal.

oration *n* address, declamation, discourse, harangue, speech.

orb *n* ball, globe, sphere; circle, circuit, orbit, ring; disk, wheel.

orbit *vb* circle, encircle, revolve around. * *n* course, path, revolution, track.

ordain *vb* appoint, call, consecrate, elect, experiment, constitute, establish, institute, regulate; decree, enjoin, enact, order, prescribe.

order *vb* adjust, arrange, methodize, regulate, systematize; carry on, conduct, manage; bid, command, direct, instruct, require. * *n* arrangement, disposition, method, regularity, symmetry, system; law, regulation, rule; discipline, peace, quiet; command, commission, direction, injunction, instruction, mandate, prescription; class, degree, grade, kind, rank; family, tribe; brotherhood, community, fraternity, society; sequence, succession.

orderly *adj* methodical, regular, systematic; peaceable, quiet, well-behaved; neat, shipshape, tidy.

ordinance *n* appointment, command, decree, edict, enactment, law, order, prescript, regulation, rule, statute; ceremony, observance, sacrament, rite, ritual.

ordinary *adj* accustomed, customary, established, everyday, normal, regular, settled, wonted, everyday, regular; common, frequent, habitual, usual; average, commonplace, indifferent, inferior, mean, mediocre, second-rate, undistinguished; homely, plain.

organization *n* business, construction, constitution, organism, structure, system.

organize *vb* adjust, constitute, construct, form, make, shape; arrange, coordinate, correlate, establish, systematize.

orgy *n* carousal, debauch, debauchery, revel, saturnalia.

orifice *n* aperture, hole, mouth, perforation, pore, vent.

origin *n* beginning, birth, commencement, cradle, derivation, foundation, fountain, fountainhead, original, rise, root, source, spring, starting point; cause, occasion; heritage, lineage, parentage.
original *adj* aboriginal, first, primary, primeval, primitive, primordial, pristine; fresh, inventive, novel; eccentric, odd, peculiar. * *n* cause, commencement, origin, source, spring; archetype, exemplar, model, pattern, prototype, protoplast, type.
originate *vb* arise, begin, emanate, flow, proceed, rise, spring; create, discover, form, invent, produce.
originator *n* author, creator, former, inventor, maker, parent.
orison *n* petition, prayer, solicitation, supplication.
ornament *vb* adorn, beautify, bedeck, bedizen, decorate, deck, emblazon, garnish, grace. * *n* adornment, bedizenment, decoration, design, embellishment, garnish, ornamentation.
ornate *adj* beautiful, bedecked, decorated, elaborate, elegant, embellished, florid, flowery, ornamental, ornamented.
orthodox *adj* conventional, correct, sound, true.
oscillate *vb* fluctuate, sway, swing, vacillate, vary, vibrate.
ostensible *adj* apparent, assigned, avowed, declared, exhibited, manifest, presented, visible; plausible, professed, specious.
ostentation *n* dash, display, flourish, pageantry, parade, pomp, pomposity, pompousness, show, vaunting; appearance, semblance, showiness.
ostentatious *adj* boastful, dashing, flaunting, pompous, pretentious, showy, vain, vainglorious; gaudy.
ostracize *vb* banish, boycott, exclude, excommunicate, exile, expatriate, expel, evict.
oust *vb* dislodge, dispossess, eject, evict, expel.
outbreak *n* ebullition, eruption, explosion, outburst; affray, broil, conflict, commotion, fray, riot, row; flare-up, manifestation.
outcast *n* exile, expatriate; castaway, pariah, reprobate, vagabond.
outcome *n* conclusion, consequence, event, issue, result, upshot.
outcry *n* cry, scream, screech, yell; bruit, clamour, noise, tumult, vociferation.
outdo *vb* beat, exceed, excel, outgo, outstrip, outvie, surpass.
outlandish *adj* alien, exotic, foreign, strange; barbarous, bizarre, uncouth.
outlaw *vb* ban, banish, condemn, exclude, forbid, make illegal, prohibit. * *n* bandit, brigand, crook, freebooter, highwayman, lawbreaker, marauder, robber, thief.
outlay *n* disbursement, expenditure, outgoings.
outline *vb* delineate, draft, draw, plan, silhouette, sketch. * *n* contour, profile; delineation, draft, drawing, plan, rough draft, silhouette, sketch.
outlive *vb* last, live longer, survive.
outlook *n* future, prospect, sight, view; lookout, watch-tower.
outrage *vb* abuse, injure, insult, maltreat, offend, shock, injure. * *n* abuse, affront, indignity, insult, offence.
outrageous *adj* abusive, frantic, furious, frenzied, mad, raging, turbulent, violent, wild; atrocious, enormous, flagrant, heinous, monstrous, nefarious, villainous; enormous, excessive, extravagant, unwarrantable.
outré *adj* excessive, exorbitant, extravagant, immoderate, inordinate, overstrained, unconventional.
outrun *vb* beat, exceed, outdistance, outgo, outstrip, outspeed, surpass.
outset *n* beginning, commencement, entrance, opening, start, starting point.
outshine *vb* eclipse, outstrip, overshadow, surpass.
outspoken *adj* abrupt, blunt, candid, frank, plain, plainspoken, unceremonious, unreserved.
outstanding *adj* due, owing, uncollected, ungathered, unpaid, unsettled; conspicuous, eminent, prominent, striking.
outward *adj* exterior, external, outer, outside.
outwit *vb* cheat, circumvent, deceive, defraud, diddle, dupe, gull, outmanoeuvre, overreach, swindle, victimize.
overawe *vb* affright, awe, browbeat, cow, daunt, frighten, intimidate, scare, terrify.
overbalance *vb* capsize, overset, overturn, tumble, upset; outweigh, preponderate.
overbearing *adj* oppressive, overpowering; arrogant, dictatorial, dogmatic, domineering, haughty, imperious, overweening, proud, supercilious.
overcast *vb* cloud, darken, overcloud, overshadow, shade, shadow. * *adj* cloudy, darkened, hazy, murky, obscure.
overcharge *vb* burden, oppress, overburden, overload, surcharge; crowd, overfill; exaggerate, overstate, overstrain.
overcome *vb* beat, choke, conquer, crush, defeat, discomfit, overbear, overmaster, overpower, overthrow, overturn, overwhelm, prevail, rout, subdue, subjugate, surmount, vanquish.
overflow *vb* brim over, fall over, pour over, pour out, shower, spill; deluge, inundate, submerge. * *n* deluge, inundation, profusion, superabundance.
overhaul *vb* overtake; check, examine, inspect, repair, survey. * *n* check, examination, inspection.
overlay *vb* cover, spread over; overlie, overpress, smother; crush, overpower, overwhelm; cloud, hide, obscure, overcast. * *n* appliqué, covering, decoration, veneer.
overlook *vb* inspect, oversee, superintend, supervise; disregard, miss, neglect, slight; condone, excuse, forgive, pardon, pass over.
overpower *vb* beat, conquer, crush, defeat, discomfit, overbear, overcome, overmaster, overturn, overwhelm, subdue, subjugate, vanquish.
overreach *vb* exceed, outstrip, overshoot, pass, surpass; cheat, circumvent, deceive, defraud.
override *vb* outride, outweigh, pass, quash, supersede, surpass.
overrule *vb* control, govern, sway; annul, cancel, nullify, recall, reject, repeal, repudiate, rescind, revoke, reject, set aside, supersede, suppress.
oversight *n* care, charge, control, direction, inspection, management, superintendence, supervision, surveillance; blunder, error, fault, inadvertence, inattention, lapse, miss, mistake, neglect, omission, slip, trip.
overt *adj* apparent, glaring, open, manifest, notorious, patent, public, unconcealed.
overthrow *vb* overturn, upset, subvert; demolish, destroy, level; beat, conquer, crush, defeat, discomfit, foil, master, overcome, overpower, overwhelm, rout, subjugate, vanquish, worst. * *n* downfall, fall, prostration, subversion; destruction, demolition, ruin; defeat, discomfiture, dispersion, rout.
overturn *vb* invert, overthrow, reverse, subvert, upset.
overture *n* invitation, offer, proposal, proposition.
overweening *adj* arrogant, conceited, consequential, egotistical, haughty, opinionated, proud, supercilious, vain, vainglorious.
overwhelm *vb* drown, engulf, inundate, overflow, submerge, swallow up, swamp; conquer, crush, defeat, overbear, overcome, overpower, subdue, vanquish.
overwrought *adj* overdone, overelaborate; agitated, excited, overexcited, overworked, stirred.
own[1] *vb* have, hold, possess; avow, confess; acknowledge, admit, allow, concede.
own[2] *adj* particular, personal, private.
owner *n* freeholder, holder, landlord, possessor, proprietor.

P

pace *vb* go, hasten, hurry, move, step, walk. * *n* amble, gait, step, walk.
pacific *adj* appeasing, conciliatory, ironic, mollifying, placating, peacemaking, propitiatory; calm, gentle, peaceable, peaceful, quiet, smooth, tranquil, unruffled.
pacify *vb* appease, conciliate, harmonize, tranquillize; allay, appease, assuage, calm, compose, hush, lay, lull, moderate, mollify, placate, propitiate, quell, quiet, smooth, soften, soothe, still.

pack *vb* compact, compress, crowd, fill; bundle, burden, load, stow. * *n* bale, budget, bundle, package, packet, parcel; burden, load; assemblage, assembly, assortment, collection, set; band, bevy, clan, company, crew, gang, knot, lot, party, squad.

pact *n* agreement, alliance, bargain, bond, compact, concordat, contract, convention, covenant, league, stipulation.

pagan *adj* heathen, heathenish, idolatrous, irreligious, paganist, paganistic. * *n* gentile, heathen, idolater.

pageantry *n* display, flourish, magnificence, parade, pomp, show, splendour, state.

pain *vb* agonize, bite, distress, hurt, rack, sting, torment, torture; afflict, aggrieve, annoy, bore, chafe, displease, disquiet, fret, grieve, harass, incommode, plague, tease, trouble, vex, worry; rankle, smart, shoot, sting, twinge. * *n* ache, agony, anguish, discomfort, distress, gripe, hurt, pang, smart, soreness, sting, suffering, throe, torment, torture, twinge; affliction, anguish, anxiety, bitterness, care, chagrin, disquiet, dolour, grief, heartache, misery, punishment, solicitude, sorrow, trouble, uneasiness, unhappiness, vexation, woe, wretchedness.

painful *adj* agonizing, distressful, excruciating, racking, sharp, tormenting, torturing; afflicting, afflictive, annoying, baleful, disagreeable, displeasing, disquieting, distressing, dolorous, grievous, provoking, troublesome, unpleasant, vexatious; arduous, careful, difficult, hard, severe, sore, toilsome.

pains *npl* care, effort, labour, task, toilsomeness, trouble; childbirth, labour, travail.

painstaking *adj* assiduous, careful, conscientious, diligent, hardworking, industrious, laborious, persevering, plodding, sedulous, strenuous.

paint *vb* delineate, depict, describe, draw, figure, pencil, portray, represent, sketch; adorn, beautify, deck, embellish, ornament. * *n* colouring, dye, pigment, stain; cosmetics, greasepaint, make-up.

pair *vb* couple, marry, mate, match. * *n* brace, couple, double, duo, match, twosome.

pal *n* buddy, chum, companion, comrade, crony, friend, mate, mucker.

palatable *adj* acceptable, agreeable, appetizing, delicate, delicious, enjoyable, flavourful, flavoursome, gustative, gustatory, luscious, nice, pleasant, pleasing, savoury, relishable, tasteful, tasty, toothsome.

palaver *vb* chat, chatter, converse, patter, prattle, say, speak, talk; confer, parley; blandish, cajole, flatter, wheedle. * *n* chat, chatter, conversation, discussion, language, prattle, speech, talk; confab, confabulation, conference, conclave, parley, powwow; balderdash, cajolery, flummery, gibberish.

pale *vb* blanch, lose colour, whiten. * *adj* ashen, ashy, blanched, bloodless, pallid, sickly, wan, white; blank, dim, obscure, spectral. * *n* picket, stake; circuit, enclosure; district, region, territory; boundary, confine, fence, limit.

pall[1] *n* cloak, cover, curtain, mantle, pallium, shield, shroud, veil.

pall[2] *vb* cloy, glut, gorge, satiate, surfeit; deject, depress, discourage, dishearten, dispirit; cloak, cover, drape, invest, overspread, shroud.

palliate *vb* cloak, conceal, cover, excuse, extenuate, hide, gloss, lessen; abate, allay, alleviate, assuage, blunt, diminish, dull, ease, mitigate, moderate, mollify, quell, quiet, relieve, soften, soothe, still.

pallid *adj* ashen, ashy, cadaverous, colourless, pale, sallow, wan, whitish.

palm[1] *vb* foist, impose, obtrude, pass off; handle, touch.

palm[2] *n* bays, crown, laurels, prize, trophy, victory.

palmy *adj* flourishing, fortunate, glorious, golden, halcyon, happy, joyous, prosperous, thriving, victorious.

palpable *adj* corporeal, material, tactile, tangible; evident, glaring, gross, intelligible, manifest, obvious, patent, plain, unmistakable.

palpitate *vb* flutter, pulsate, throb; quiver, shiver, tremble.

palter *vb* dodge, equivocate, evade, haggle, prevaricate, quibble, shift, shuffle, trifle.

paltry *adj* diminutive, feeble, inconsiderable, insignificant, little, miserable, petty, slender, slight, small, sorry, trifling, trivial, unimportant, wretched.

pamper *vb* baby, coddle, fondle, gratify, humour, spoil.

panacea *n* catholicon, cure-all, medicine, remedy.

panegyric *adj* commendatory, encomiastic, encomiastical, eulogistic, eulogistical, laudatory, panegyrical. * *n* eulogy, laudation, praise, paean, tribute.

pang *n* agony, anguish, distress, gripe, pain, throe, twinge.

panic *vb* affright, alarm, scare, startle, terrify; become terrified, overreact. * *n* alarm, consternation, fear, fright, jitters, terror.

pant *vb* blow, gasp, puff; heave, palpitate, pulsate, throb; languish; desire, hunger, long, sigh, thirst, yearn. * *n* blow, gasp, puff.

parable *n* allegory, fable, story.

paraclete *n* advocate, comforter, consoler, intercessor, mediator.

parade *vb* display, flaunt, show, vaunt. * *n* ceremony, display, flaunting, ostentation, pomp, show; array, pageant, review, spectacle; mall, promenade.

paradox *n* absurdity, contradiction, mystery.

paragon *n* flower, ideal, masterpiece, model, nonpareil, pattern, standard.

paragraph *n* clause, item, notice, passage, section, sentence, subdivision.

parallel *vb* be alike, compare, conform, correlate, match. * *adj* abreast, concurrent; allied, analogous, correspondent, equal, like, resembling, similar. * *n* conformity, likeness, resemblance, similarity; analogue, correlative, counterpart.

paramount *adj* chief, dominant, eminent, pre-eminent, principal, superior, supreme.

paraphernalia *n* accoutrements, appendages, appurtenances, baggage, belongings, effects, equipage, equipment, ornaments, trappings.

parasite *n* bloodsucker, fawner, flatterer, flunky, hanger-on, leech, spaniel, sycophant, toady, wheedler.

parcel *vb* allot, apportion, dispense, distribute, divide. * *n* budget, bundle, package; batch, collection, group, lot, set; division, part, patch, pierce, plot, portion, tract.

parched *adj* arid, dry, scorched, shrivelled, thirsty.

pardon *vb* condone, forgive, overlook, remit; absolve, acquit, clear, discharge, excuse, release. * *n* absolution, amnesty, condonation, discharge, excuse, forgiveness, grace, mercy, overlook, release.

parentage *n* ancestry, birth, descent, extraction, family, lineage, origin, parenthood, pedigree, stock.

pariah *n* outcast, wretch.

parish *n* community, congregation, parishioners; district, subdivision.

parity *n* analogy, correspondence, equality, equivalence, likeness, sameness, similarity.

parody *vb* burlesque, caricature, imitate, lampoon, mock, ridicule, satirize, travesty. * *n* burlesque, caricature, imitation, ridicule, satire, travesty.

paroxysm *n* attack, convulsion, exacerbation, fit, outburst, seizure, spasm, throe.

parsimonious *adj* avaricious, close, close-fisted, covetous, frugal, grasping, grudging, illiberal, mean, mercenary, miserly, near, niggardly, penurious, shabby, sordid, sparing, stingy, tightfisted.

parson *n* churchman, clergyman, divine, ecclesiastic, incumbent, minister, pastor, priest, rector.

part *vb* break, dismember, dissever, divide, sever, subdivide, sunder; detach, disconnect, disjoin, dissociate, disunite, separate; allot, apportion, distribute, divide, mete, share; secrete. * *n* crumb, division, fraction, fragment, moiety, parcel, piece, portion, remnant, scrap, section, segment, subdivision; component, constituent, element, ingredient, member, organ; lot, share; concern, interest, participation; allotment, apportionment, dividend; business, charge, duty, function, office, work; faction, party, side; character, cue, lines, role; clause, paragraph, passage.

partake *vb* engage, participate, share; consume, eat, take;evince, evoke, show, suggest.

partial *adj* component, fractional, imperfect, incomplete, limited; biased, influential, interested, one-sided, prejudiced, prepossessed, unfair, unjust, warped; fond, indulgent.

participate *vb* engage in, partake, perform, share.

particle *n* atom, bit, corpuscle, crumb, drop, glimmer, grain, granule, iota, jot, mite, molecule, morsel, mote, scrap, shred, snip, spark, speck, whit.

particular *adj* especial, special, specific; distinct, individual, respective, separate, single; characteristic, distinctive, peculiar; individual, intimate, own, personal, private; notable, noteworthy; circumstantial, definite, detailed, exact, minute, narrow, precise; careful, close, conscientious, critical, fastidious, nice, scrupulous, strict; marked, odd, singular, strange, uncommon. * *n* case, circumstance, count, detail, feature, instance, item, particularity, point, regard, respect.

parting *adj* breaking, dividing, separating; final, last, valedictory; declining, departing. * *n* breaking, disruption, rupture, severing; detachment, division, separation; death, departure, farewell, leave-taking.

partisan *adj* biased, factional, interested, partial, prejudiced. * *n* adherent, backer, champion, disciple, follower, supporter, votary; baton, halberd, pike, quarterstaff, truncheon, staff.

partition *vb* apportion, distribute, divide, portion, separate, share. * *n* division, separation; barrier, division, screen, wall; allotment, apportionment, distribution.

partner *n* associate, colleague, copartner, partaker, participant, participator; accomplice, ally, coadjutor, confederate; companion, consort, spouse.

partnership *n* association, company, copartnership, firm, house, society; connection, interest, participation, union.

parts *n pl* abilities, accomplishments, endowments, faculties, genius, gifts, intellect, intelligence, mind, qualities, powers, talents; districts, regions.

party *n* alliance, association, cabal, circle, clique, combination, confederacy, coterie, faction, group, junta, league, ring, set; body, company, detachment, squad, troop; assembly, gathering; partaker, participant, participator, sharer; defendant, litigant, plaintiff; individual, one, person, somebody; cause, division, interest, side.

pass[1] *vb* devolve, fall, go, move, proceed; change, elapse, flit, glide, lapse, slip; cease, die, fade, expire, vanish; happen, occur; convey, deliver, send, transmit, transfer; disregard, ignore, neglect; exceed, excel, surpass; approve, ratify, sanction; answer, do, succeed, suffice, suit; express, pronounce, utter; beguile, wile.

pass[2] *n* avenue, ford, road, route, way; defile, gorge, passage, ravine; authorization, licence, passport, permission, ticket; condition, conjecture, plight, situation, state; lunge, push, thrust, tilt; transfer, trick.

passable *adj* admissible, allowable, mediocre, middling, moderate, ordinary, so-so, tolerable; acceptable, current, receivable; navigable, traversable.

passage *n* going, passing, progress, transit; evacuation, journey, migration, transit, voyage; avenue, channel, course, pass, path, road, route, thoroughfare, vennel, way; access, currency, entry, reception; act, deed, event, feat, incidence, occurrence, passion; corridor, gallery, gate, hall; clause, paragraph, sentence, text; course, death, decease, departure, expiration, lapse; affair, brush, change, collision, combat, conflict, contest, encounter, exchange, joust, skirmish, tilt.

passenger *n* fare, itinerant, tourist, traveller, voyager, wayfarer.

passionate *adj* animated, ardent, burning, earnest, enthusiastic, excited, fervent, fiery, furious, glowing, hot-blooded, impassioned, impetuous, impulsive, intense, vehement, warm, zealous; hot-headed, irascible, quick-tempered, tempestuous, violent.

passive *adj* inactive, inert, quiescent, receptive; apathetic, enduring, long-suffering, nonresistant, patient, stoical, submissive, suffering, unresisting.

past *adj* accomplished, elapsed, ended, gone, spent; ancient, bygone, former, obsolete, outworn. * *adv* above, extra, beyond, over. * *prep* above, after, beyond, exceeding. * *n* antiquity, heretofore, history, olden times, yesterday.

pastime *n* amusement, diversion, entertainment, hobby, play, recreation, sport.

pastor *n* clergyman, churchman, divine, ecclesiastic, minister, parson, priest, vicar.

pat[1] *vb* dab, hit, rap, tap; caress, chuck, fondle, pet. * *n* dab, hit, pad, rap, tap; caress.

pat[2] *adj* appropriate, apt, fit, pertinent, suitable. * *adv* aptly, conveniently, fitly, opportunely, seasonably.

patch *vb* mend, repair. * *n* repair; parcel, plot, tract.

patent *adj* expanded, open, spreading; apparent, clear, conspicuous, evident, glaring, indisputable, manifest, notorious, obvious, public, open, palpable, plain, unconcealed, unmistakable. * *n* copyright, privilege, right.

paternity *n* derivation, descent, fatherhood, origin.

path *n* access, avenue, course, footway, passage, pathway, road, route, track, trail, way.

pathetic *adj* affecting, melting, moving, pitiable, plaintive, sad, tender, touching.

patience *n* endurance, fortitude, long-sufferance, resignation, submission, sufferance; calmness, composure, quietness; forbearance, indulgence, leniency; assiduity, constancy, diligence, indefatigability, indefatigableness, perseverance, persistence.

patient *adj* meek, passive, resigned, submissive, uncomplaining, unrepining; calm, composed, contented, quiet; indulgent, lenient, long-suffering; assiduous, constant, diligent, indefatigable, persevering, persistent. * *n* case, invalid, subject, sufferer.

patrician *adj* aristocratic, blue-blooded, highborn, noble, senatorial, well-born. * *n* aristocrat, blue blood, nobleman.

patron *n* advocate, defender, favourer, guardian, helper, protector, supporter.

patronize *vb* aid, assist, befriend, countenance, defend, favour, maintain, support; condescend, disparage, scorn.

pattern *vb* copy, follow, imitate. * *n* archetype, exemplar, last, model, original, paradigm, plan, prototype; example, guide, sample, specimen; mirror, paragon; design, figure, shape, style, type.

paucity *n* deficiency, exiguity, insufficiency, lack, poverty, rarity, shortage.

paunch *n* abdomen, belly, gut, stomach.

pauperism *n* beggary, destitution, indigence, mendicancy, mendicity, need, poverty, penury, want.

pause *vb* breathe, cease, delay, desist, rest, stay, stop, wait; delay, forbear, intermit, stay, stop, tarry, wait; deliberate, demur, hesitate, waver. * *n* break, caesura, cessation, halt, intermission, interruption, interval, remission, rest, stop, stoppage, stopping, suspension; hesitation, suspense, uncertainty; paragraph.

pawn[1] *n* cat's-paw, dupe, plaything, puppet, stooge, tool, toy.

pawn[2] *vb* bet, gage, hazard, lay, pledge, risk, stake, wager. * *n* assurance, bond, guarantee, pledge, security.

pay *vb* defray, discharge, discount, foot, honour, liquidate, meet, quit, settle; compensate, recompense, reimburse, requite, reward; punish, revenge; give, offer, render. * *n* allowance, commission, compensation, emolument, hire, recompense, reimbursement, remuneration, requital, reward, salary, wages.

peace *n* calm, calmness, quiet, quietness, repose, stillness; accord, amity, friendliness, harmony; composure, equanimity, imperturbability, placidity, quietude, tranquillity; agreement, armistice.

peaceable *adj* pacific, peaceful; amiable, amicable, friendly, gentle, inoffensive, mild; placid, quiet, serene, still, tranquil, undisturbed, unmoved.

peaceful *adj* quiet, undisturbed; amicable, concordant, friendly, gentle, harmonious, mild, pacific, peaceable; calm, composed, placid, serene, still.

peak *vb* climax, culminate, top; dwindle, thin. * *n* acme, apex, crest, crown, pinnacle, summit, top, zenith.

peaked *adj* piked, pointed, thin.

peasant *n* boor, countryman, clown, hind, labourer, rustic, swain.

peculate *vb* appropriate, defraud, embezzle, misappropriate, pilfer, purloin, rob, steal.

peculiar *adj* appropriate, idiosyncratic, individual, proper; characteristic, eccentric, exceptional, extraordinary, odd, queer, rare, singular, strange, striking, uncommon, unusual; individual, especial, particular, select, special, specific.

peculiarity *n* appropriateness, distinctiveness, individuality, speciality; characteristic, idiosyncrasy, oddity, peculiarity, singularity.

pedantic *adj* conceited, fussy, officious, ostentatious, over-learned, particular, pedagogical, pompous, pragmatical, precise, pretentious, priggish, stilted.

pedlar *n* chapman, costermonger, hawker, packman, vendor.

pedigree *adj* purebred, thoroughbred. * *n* ancestry, breed, descent, extraction, family, genealogy, house, line, lineage, race, stock, strain.

peer[1] *vb* gaze, look, peek, peep, pry, squinny, squint; appear, emerge.

peer[2] *n* associate, co-equal, companion, compeer, equal, equivalent, fellow, like, mate, match; aristocrat, baron, count, duke, earl, grandee, lord, marquis, noble, nobleman, viscount.

peerless *adj* excellent, incomparable, matchless, outstanding, superlative, unequalled, unique, unmatched, unsurpassed.

peevish *adj* acrimonious, captious, churlish, complaining, crabbed, cross, crusty, discontented, fretful, ill-natured, ill-tempered, irascible, irritable, pettish, petulant, querulous, snappish, snarling, splenetic, spleeny, testy, waspish; forward, headstrong, obstinate, self-willed, stubborn; childish, silly, thoughtless, trifling.

pellucid *adj* bright, clear, crystalline, diaphanous, limpid, lucid, transparent.

pelt[1] *vb* assail, batter, beat, belabour, bombard, pepper, stone, strike; cast, hurl, throw; hurry, rush, speed, tear.

pelt[2] *n* coat, hide, skin.

pen[1] *vb* compose, draft, indite, inscribe, write.

pen[2] *vb* confine, coop, encage, enclose, impound, imprison, incarcerate. * *n* cage, coop, corral, crib, hutch, enclosure, paddock, pound, stall, sty.

penalty *n* chastisement, fine, forfeiture, mulct, punishment, retribution.

penance *n* humiliation, maceration, mortification, penalty, punishment.

penchant *n* bent, bias, disposition, fondness, inclination, leaning, liking, predilection, predisposition, proclivity, proneness, propensity, taste, tendency, turn.

penetrate *vb* bore, burrow, cut, enter, invade, penetrate, percolate, perforate, pervade, pierce, soak, stab; affect, sensitize, touch; comprehend, discern, perceive, understand.

penetrating *adj* penetrative, permeating, piercing, sharp, subtle; acute, clear-sighted, discerning, intelligent, keen, quick, sagacious, sharp-witted, shrewd.

penetration *n* acuteness, discernment, insight, sagacity.

penitence *n* compunction, contrition, qualms, regret, remorse, repentance, sorrow.

penitent *adj* compunctious, conscience-stricken, contrite, regretful, remorseful, repentant, sorrowing, sorrowful. * *n* penance-doer, penitentiary, repentant.

penniless *adj* destitute, distressed, impecunious, indigent, moneyless, pinched, poor, necessitous, needy, pensive, poverty-stricken, reduced.

pensive *adj* contemplative, dreamy, meditative, reflective, sober, thoughtful; grave, melancholic, melancholy, mournful, sad, serious, solemn.

penurious *adj* inadequate, ill-provided, insufficient, meagre, niggardly, poor, scanty, stinted; avaricious, close, close-fisted, covetous, illiberal, grasping, grudging, mean, mercenary, miserly, near, niggardly, parsimonious, sordid, stingy, tightfisted.

penury *n* beggary, destitution, indigence, need, poverty, privation, want.

people *vb* colonize, inhabit, populate. * *n* clan, country, family, nation, race, state, tribe; folk, humankind, persons, population, public; commons, community, democracy, populace, proletariat; mob, multitude, rabble.

perceive *vb* behold, descry, detect, discern, discover, discriminate, distinguish, note, notice, observe, recognize, remark, see, spot; appreciate, comprehend, know, understand.

perceptible *adj* apparent, appreciable, cognizable, discernible, noticeable, perceivable, understandable, visible.

perception *n* apprehension, cognition, discernment, perceiving, recognition, seeing; comprehension, conception, consciousness, perceptiveness, perceptivity, understanding, feeling.

perchance *adv* haply, maybe, mayhap, peradventure, perhaps, possibly, probably.

percolate *vb* drain, drip, exude, filter, filtrate, ooze, penetrate, stain, transude.

percussion *n* collision, clash, concussion, crash, encounter, shock.

perdition *n* damnation, demolition, destruction, downfall, hell, overthrow, ruin, wreck.

peremptory *adj* absolute, authoritative, categorical, commanding, decisive, express, imperative, imperious, positive; determined, resolute, resolved; arbitrary, dogmatic, incontrovertible.

perennial *adj* ceaseless, constant, continual, deathless, enduring, immortal, imperishable, lasting, never-failing, permanent, perpetual, unceasing, undying, unfailing, uninterrupted.

perfect *vb* accomplish, complete, consummate, elaborate, finish. * *adj* completed, finished; complete, entire, full, unqualified, utter, whole; capital, consummate, excellent, exquisite, faultless, ideal; accomplished, disciplined, expert, skilled; blameless, faultless, holy, immaculate, pure, spotless, unblemished.

perfection *n* completeness, completion, consummation, correctness, excellence, faultlessness, finish, maturity, perfection, perfectness, wholeness; beauty, quality.

perfidious *adj* deceitful, dishonest, disloyal, double-faced, faithless, false, false-hearted, traitorous, treacherous, unfaithful, untrustworthy, venal.

perfidy *n* defection, disloyalty, faithlessness, infidelity, perfidiousness, traitorousness, treachery, treason.

perforate *vb* bore, drill, penetrate, pierce, pink, prick, punch, riddle, trepan.

perform *vb* accomplish, achieve, compass, consummate, do, effect, transact; complete, discharge, execute, fulfil, meet, observe, satisfy; act, play, represent.

performance *n* accomplishment, achievement, completion, consummation, discharge, doing, execution, fulfilment; act, action, deed, exploit, feat, work; composition, production; acting, entertainment, exhibition, play, representation, hold; execution, playing.

perfume *n* aroma, balminess, bouquet, fragrance, incense, odour, redolence, scent, smell, sweetness.

perfunctory *adj* careless, formal, heedless, indifferent, mechanical, negligent, reckless, slight, slovenly, thoughtless, unmindful.

perhaps *adv* haply, peradventure, perchance, possibly.

peril *vb* endanger, imperil, jeopardize, risk. * *n* danger, hazard, insecurity, jeopardy, pitfall, risk, snare, uncertainty.

perilous *adj* dangerous, hazardous, risky, unsafe.

period *n* aeon, age, cycle, date, eon, epoch, season, span, spell, stage, term, time; continuance, duration; bound, conclusion, determination, end, limit, term, termination; clause, phrase, proposition, sentence.

periodical *adj* cyclical, incidental, intermittent, recurrent, recurring, regular, seasonal, systematic. * *n* magazine, paper, review, serial, weekly.

periphery *n* boundary, circumference, outside, perimeter, superficies, surface.

perish *vb* decay, moulder, shrivel, waste, wither; decease, die, expire, vanish.

perishable *adj* decaying, decomposable, destructible; dying, frail, mortal, temporary.

perjured *adj* false, forsworn, perfidious, traitorous, treacherous, untrue.

permanent *adj* abiding, constant, continuing, durable, enduring, fixed, immutable, invariable, lasting, perpetual, persistent, stable, standing, steadfast, unchangeable, unchanging, unfading, unmovable.

permissible *adj* admissible, allowable, free, lawful, legal, legitimate, proper, sufferable, unprohibited.

permission *n* allowance, authorization, consent, dispensation, leave, liberty, licence, permit, sufferance, toleration, warrant.

permit *vb* agree, allow, endure, let, suffer, tolerate; admit, authorize, consent, empower, license, warrant. * *n* leave, liberty, licence, passport, permission, sanction, warrant.

pernicious *adj* baleful, baneful, damaging, deadly, deleterious, destructive, detrimental, disadvantageous, fatal, harmful, hurtful, injurious, malign, mischievous, noisome, noxious, prejudicial, ruinous; evil-hearted, malevolent, malicious, malignant, mischief-making, wicked.

perpetrate *vb* commit, do, execute, perform.

perpetual *adj* ceaseless, continual, constant, endless, enduring, eternal, ever-enduring, everlasting, incessant, interminable, never-ceasing, never-ending, perennial, permanent, sempiternal, unceasing, unending, unfailing, uninterrupted.

perplex *vb* complicate, encumber, entangle, involve, snarl, tangle; beset, bewilder, confound, confuse, corner, distract, embarrass, fog, mystify, nonplus, pother, puzzle, set; annoy, bother, disturb, harass, molest, pester, plague, tease, trouble, vex, worry.

persecute *vb* afflict, distress, harass, molest, oppress, worry; annoy, beset, importune, pester, solicit, tease.

perseverance *n* constancy, continuance, doggedness, indefatigableness, persistence, persistency, pertinacity, resolution, steadfastness, steadiness, tenacity.

persevere *vb* continue, determine, endure, maintain, persist, remain, resolve, stick.

persist *vb* continue, endure, last, remain; insist, persevere.

persistent *adj* constant, continuing, enduring, fixed, immovable, persevering, persisting, steady, tenacious; contumacious, dogged, indefatigable, obdurate, obstinate, pertinacious, perverse, pigheaded, stubborn.

personable *adj* comely, good-looking, graceful, seemly, well-turned-out.

personal *adj* individual, peculiar, private, special; bodily, corporal, corporeal, exterior, material, physical.

personate *vb* act, impersonate, personify, play, represent; disguise, mast; counterfeit, feign, simulate.

perspective *n* panorama, prospect, view, vista; proportion, relation.

perspicacious *adj* keen-sighted, quick-sighted, sharp-sighted; acute, clever, discerning, keen, penetrating, sagacious, sharp-witted, shrewd.

perspicacity *n* acumen, acuteness, astuteness, discernment, insight, penetration, perspicaciousness, sagacity, sharpness, shrewdness.

perspicuity *n* clearness, distinctness, explicitness, intelligibility, lucidity, lucidness, perspicuousness, plainness, transparency.

perspicuous *adj* clear, distinct, explicit, intelligible, lucid, obvious, plain, transparent, unequivocal.

perspire *vb* exhale, glow, sweat, swelter.

persuade *vb* allure, actuate, entice, impel, incite, induce, influence, lead, move, prevail upon, urge; advise, counsel; convince, satisfy; inculcate, teach.

persuasion *n* exhortation, incitement, inducement, influence; belief, conviction, opinion; creed, doctrine, dogma, tenet; kind, sort, variety.

persuasive *adj* cogent, convincing, inducing, inducible, logical, persuading, plausible, sound, valid, weighty.

pert *adj* brisk, dapper, lively, nimble, smart, sprightly, perky; bold, flippant, forward, free, impertinent, impudent, malapert, presuming, smart, saucy.

pertain *vb* appertain, befit, behove, belong, concern, refer, regard, relate.

pertinacious *adj* constant, determined, firm, obdurate, persevering, resolute, staunch, steadfast, steady; dogged, headstrong, inflexible, mulish, intractable, obstinate, perverse, stubborn, unyielding, wayward, wilful.

pertinent *adj* adapted, applicable, apposite, appropriate, apropos, apt, fit, germane, pat, proper, relevant, suitable; appurtenant, belonging, concerning, pertaining, regarding.

perturb *vb* agitate, disquiet, distress, disturb, excite, trouble, unsettle, upset, vex, worry; confuse.

pervade *vb* affect, animate, diffuse, extend, fill, imbue, impregnate, infiltrate, penetrate, permeate.

perverse *adj* bad, disturbed, oblique, perverted; contrary, dogged, headstrong, mulish, obstinate, pertinacious, perversive, stubborn, ungovernable, intractable, unyielding, wayward, wilful; cantankerous, churlish, crabbed, cross, cross-grained, crusty, cussed, morose, peevish, petulant, snappish, snarling, spiteful, spleeny, surly, testy, touchy, wicked, wrong-headed; inconvenient, troublesome, untoward, vexatious.

perversion *n* abasement, corruption, debasement, impairment, injury, prostitution, vitiation.

perverted *adj* corrupt, debased, distorted, evil, impaired, misguiding, vitiated, wicked.

pessimistic *adj* cynical, dark, dejected, depressed, despondent, downhearted, gloomy, glum, melancholy, melancholic, morose, sad.

pest *n* disease, epidemic, infection, pestilence, plague; annoyance, bane, curse, infliction, nuisance, scourge, trouble.

pestilent *adj* contagious, infectious, malignant, pestilential; deadly, evil, injurious, malign, mischievous, noxious, poisonous; annoying, corrupt, pernicious, troublesome, vexatious.

petition *vb* ask, beg, crave, entreat, pray, solicit, sue, supplicate. * *n* address, appeal, application, entreaty, prayer, request, solicitation, supplication, suit.

petrify *vb* calcify, fossilize, lapidify; benumb, deaden; amaze, appal, astonish, astound, confound, dumbfound, paralyse, stun, stupefy.

petty *adj* diminutive, frivolous, inconsiderable, inferior, insignificant, little, mean, slight, small, trifling, trivial, unimportant.

petulant *adj* acrimonious, captious, cavilling, censorious, choleric, crabbed, cross, crusty, forward, fretful, hasty, ill-humoured, ill-tempered, irascible, irritable, peevish, perverse, pettish, querulous, snappish, snarling, testy, touchy, waspish.

phantom *n* apparition, ghost, illusion, phantasm, spectre, vision, wraith.

pharisaism *n* cant, formalism, hypocrisy, phariseeism, piety, sanctimoniousness, self-righteousness.

phenomenal *adj* marvellous, miraculous, prodigious, wondrous.

philanthropy *n* alms-giving, altruism, benevolence, charity, grace, humanitarianism, humanity, kindness.

philosophical, philosophic *adj* rational, reasonable, sound, wise; calm, collected, composed, cool, imperturbable, sedate, serene, stoical, tranquil, unruffled.

phlegmatic *adj* apathetic, calm, cold, cold-blooded, dull, frigid, heavy, impassive, indifferent, inert, sluggish, stoical, tame, unfeeling.

phobia *n* aversion, detestation, dislike, distaste, dread, fear, hatred.

phrase *vb* call, christen, denominate, designate, describe, dub, entitle, name, style. * *n* diction, expression, phraseology, style.

phraseology *n* diction, expression, language, phrasing, style.

physical *adj* material, natural; bodily, corporeal, external, substantial, tangible, sensible.

physiognomy *n* configuration, countenance, face, look, visage.

picaroon *n* adventurer, cheat, rogue; buccaneer, corsair, freebooter, marauder, pirate, plunderer, sea-rover.

pick *vb* peck, pierce, strike; cut, detach, gather, pluck; choose, cull, select; acquire, collect, get; pilfer, steal. * *n* pickaxe, pike, spike, toothpick.

picture *vb* delineate, draw, imagine, paint, represent. * *n* drawing, engraving, painting, print; copy, counterpart, delineation, embodiment, illustration, image, likeness, portraiture, portrayal, semblance, representation, resemblance, similitude; description.

picturesque *adj* beautiful, charming, colourful, graphic, scenic, striking, vivid.

piece *vb* mend, patch, repair; augment, complete, enlarge, increase; cement, join, unite. * *n* amount, bit, chunk, cut, fragment, hunk, part, quantity, scrap, shred, slice; portion; article, item, object; composition, lucubration, work, writing.

pied *adj* irregular, motley, mottled, particoloured, piebald, spotted, variegated.

pierce *vb* gore, impale, pink, prick, stab, transfix; bore, drill, excite, penetrate, perforate, puncture; affect, move, rouse, strike, thrill, touch.

piety *n* devotion, devoutness, holiness, godliness, grace, religion, sanctity.

pile[1] *vb* accumulate, amass; collect, gather, heap, load. * *n* accumulation, collection, heap, mass, stack; fortune, wad; building, edifice, erection, fabric, pyramid, skyscraper, structure, tower; reactor, nuclear reactor.

pile[2] *n* beam, column, pier, pillar, pole, post.

pile[3] *n* down, feel, finish, fur, fluff, fuzz, grain, nap, pappus, shag, surface, texture.

pilfer *vb* filch, purloin, rob, steal, thieve.

pilgrim *n* journeyer, sojourner, traveller, wanderer, wayfarer; crusader, devotee, palmer.

pilgrimage *n* crusade, excursion, expedition, journey, tour, trip.

pillage *vb* despoil, loot, plunder, rifle, sack, spoil, strip. * *n* depredation, destruction, devastation, plundering, rapine, spoliation; despoliation, plunder, rifling, sack, spoils.

pillar *n* column, pier, pilaster, post, shaft, stanchion; maintainer, prop, support, supporter, upholder.

pilot *vb* conduct, control, direct, guide, navigate, steer. * *adj* experimental, model, trial. * *n* helmsman, navigator, steersman; airman, aviator, conductor, director, flier, guide.

pinch *vb* compress, contract, cramp, gripe, nip, squeeze; afflict, distress, famish, oppress, straiten, stint; frost, nip; apprehend, arrest; economize, spare, stint. * *n* gripe, nip; pang, throe; crisis, difficulty, emergency, exigency, oppression, pressure, push, strait, stress.

pine *vb* decay, decline, droop, fade, flag, languish, waste, wilt, wither; desire, long, yearn.

pinion *vb* bind, chain, fasten, fetter, maim, restrain, shackle. * *n* pennon, wing; feather, quill, pen, plume, wing; fetter.

pinnacle *n* minaret, turret; acme, apex, height, peak, summit, top, zenith.

pious *adj* filial; devout, godly, holy, religious, reverential, righteous, saintly.

piquant *adj* biting, highly flavoured, piercing, prickling, pungent, sharp, stinging; interesting, lively, racy, sparkling, stimulating; cutting, keen, pointed, severe, strong, tart.

pique *vb* goad, incite, instigate, spur, stimulate, urge; affront, chafe, displease, fret, incense, irritate, nettle, offend, provoke, sting, vex, wound. * *n* annoyance, displeasure, irritation, offence, resentment, vexation.

pirate *vb* copy, crib, plagiarize, reproduce, steal. * *n* buccaneer, corsair, freebooter, marauder, picaroon, privateer, seadog, sea-robber, sea-rover, sea wolf.

pit *vb* match, oppose; dent, gouge, hole, mark, nick, notch, scar. * *n* cavity, hole, hollow; crater, dent, depression, dint, excavation, well; abyss, chasm, gulf; pitfall, snare, trap: auditorium, orchestra.

pitch *vb* fall, lurch, plunge, reel; light, settle, rest; cast, dart, fling, heave, hurl, lance, launch, send, toss, throw; erect, establish, fix, locate, place, plant, set, settle, station. * *n* degree, extent, height, intensity, measure, modulation, rage, rate; declivity, descent, inclination, slope; cast, jerk, plunge, throw, toss; place, position, spot; field, ground; line, patter.

piteous *adj* affecting, distressing, doleful, grievous, mournful, pathetic, rueful, sorrowful, woeful; deplorable, lamentable, miserable, pitiable, wretched; compassionate, tender.

pith *n* chief, core, essence, heart, gist, kernel, marrow, part, quintessence, soul, substance; importance, moment, weight; cogency, force, energy, strength, vigour.

pithy *adj* cogent, energetic, forcible, powerful; compact, concise, brief, laconic, meaty, pointed, short, sententious, substantial, terse; corky, porous.

pitiable *adj* deplorable, lamentable, miserable, pathetic, piteous, pitiable, woeful, wretched; abject, base, contemptible, despicable, disreputable, insignificant, low, paltry, mean, rascally, sorry, vile, worthless.

pitiably *adv* deplorably, distressingly, grievously, lamentably, miserably, pathetically, piteously, woefully, wretchedly.

pitiful *adj* compassionate, kind, lenient, merciful, mild, sympathetic, tender, tenderhearted; deplorable, lamentable, miserable, pathetic, piteous, pitiable, wretched; abject, base, contemptible, despicable, disreputable, insignificant, mean, paltry, rascally, sorry, vile, worthless.

pitiless *adj* cruel, hardhearted, implacable, inexorable, merciless, unmerciful, relentless, remorseless, unfeeling, unpitying, unrelenting, unsympathetic.

pittance *n* allowance, allotment, alms, charity, dole, gift; driblet, drop, insufficiency, mite, modicum, trifle.

pity *vb* commiserate, condole, sympathize. * *n* clemency, commiseration, compassion, condolence, fellow-feeling, grace, humanity, leniency, mercy, quarter, sympathy, tenderheartedness.

pivot *vb* depend, hinge, turn. * *n* axis, axle, centre, focus, hinge, joint.

place *vb* arrange, bestow, commit, deposit, dispose, fix, install, lay, locate, lodge, orient, orientate, pitch, plant, pose, put, seat, set, settle, situate, stand, station, rest; allocate, arrange, class, classify, identify, order, organize, recognize; appoint, assign, commission, establish, induct, nominate. * *n* area, courtyard, square; bounds, district, division, locale, locality, location, part, position, premises, quarter, region, scene, site, situation, spot, station, tract, whereabouts; calling, charge, employment, function, occupation, office, pitch, post; calling, condition, grade, precedence, rank, sphere, stakes, standing; abode, building, dwelling, habitation, mansion, residence, seat; city, town, village; fort, fortress, stronghold; paragraph, part, passage, portion; ground, occasion, opportunity, reason, room; lieu, stead.

placid *adj* calm, collected, composed, cool, equable, gentle, peaceful, quiet, serene, tranquil, undisturbed, unexcitable, unmoved, unruffled; halcyon, mild, serene.

plague *vb* afflict, annoy, badger, bore, bother, pester, chafe, disquiet, distress, disturb, embarrass, harass, fret, gall, harry, hector, incommode, irritate, molest, perplex, tantalize, tease, torment, trouble, vex, worry. * *n* disease, pestilence, pest; affliction, annoyance, curse, molestation, nuisance, thorn, torment, trouble, vexation, worry.

plain *adj* dull, even, flat, level, plane, smooth, uniform; clear, open, unencumbered, uninterrupted; apparent, certain, conspicuous, evident, distinct, glaring, manifest, notable, notorious, obvious, overt, palpable, patent, prominent, pronounced, staring, transparent, unmistakable, visible; explicit, intelligible, perspicuous, unambiguous, unequivocal; homely, ugly; aboveboard, blunt, crude, candid, direct, downright, frank, honest, ingenuous, open, openhearted, sincere, single-minded, straightforward, undesigning, unreserved, unsophisticated: artless, common, natural, simple, unaffected, unlearned; absolute, mere, unmistakable; clear, direct, easy; audible, articulate, definite; frugal, homely; unadorned, unfigured, unornamented, unvariegated. * *n* expanse, flats, grassland, pampas, plateau, prairie, steppe, stretch.

plaint *n* complaint, cry, lament, lamentation, moan, wail.

plaintiff *n* accuser, prosecutor.

plaintive *adj* dirge-like, doleful, grievous, melancholy, mournful, piteous, rueful, sad, sorrowful, woeful.

plan *vb* arrange, calculate, concert, delineate, devise, diagram, figure, premeditate, project, represent, study; concoct, conspire, contrive, design, digest, hatch, invent, manoeuvre, machinate, plot, prepare, scheme. * *n* chart, delineation, diagram, draught, drawing, layout, map, plot, sketch; arrangement, conception, contrivance, design, device, idea, method, programme, project, proposal, proposition, scheme, system; cabal, conspiracy, intrigue, machination; custom, process, way.

plane *vb* even, flatten, level, smooth; float, fly, glide, skate, skim, soar. * *adj* even, flat, horizontal, level, smooth. * *n* degree, evenness, level, levelness, smoothness; aeroplane, aircraft; groover, jointer, rabbet, rebate, scraper.

plant *vb* bed, sow; breed, engender; direct, point, set; colonize, furnish, inhabit, settle; establish, introduce; deposit, establish, fix, found, hide. * *n* herb, organism, vegetable; establishment, equipment, factory, works.

plaster *vb* bedaub, coat, cover, smear, spread. * *n* cement, gypsum, mortar, stucco.

plastic *adj* ductile, flexible, formative, mouldable, pliable, pliant, soft.

platitude *n* dullness, flatness, insipidity, mawkishness; banality, commonplace, truism; balderdash, chatter, flummery, fudge, jargon, moonshine, nonsense, palaver, stuff, trash, twaddle, verbiage.

plaudit *n* acclaim, acclamation, applause, approbation, clapping, commendation, encomium, praise.

plausible *adj* believable, credible, probable, reasonable; bland, fair-spoken, glib, smooth, suave.

play *vb* caper, disport, frisk, frolic, gambol, revel, romp, skip, sport; dally, flirt, idle, toy, trifle, wanton; flutter, hover, wave; act, impersonate, perform, personate, represent; bet, gamble, stake, wager. * *n* amusement, exercise, frolic, gambols, game, jest, pastime, prank, romp, sport; gambling, gaming; act, comedy, drama, farce, performance, tragedy; action, motion, movement; elbowroom, freedom, latitude, movement, opportunity, range, scope, sweep, swing, use.

playful *adj* frisky, frolicsome, gamesome, jolly, kittenish, merry, mirthful, rollicking, sportive; amusing, arch, humorous, lively, mischievous, roguish, skittish, sprightly, vivacious.

plead *vb* answer, appeal, argue, reason; argue, defend, discuss, reason, rejoin; beg, beseech, entreat, implore, petition, sue, supplicate.

pleasant *adj* acceptable, agreeable, delectable, delightful, enjoyable, grateful, gratifying, nice, pleasing, pleasurable, prepossessing, seemly, welcome; cheerful, enlivening, good-humoured, gracious, likable, lively, merry, sportive, sprightly, vivacious; amusing, facetious, humorous, jocose, jocular, sportive, witty.

please *vb* charm, delight, elate, gladden, gratify, pleasure, rejoice; content, oblige, satisfy; choose, like, prefer.

pleasure *n* cheer, comfort, delight, delectation, elation, enjoyment, exhilaration, joy, gladness, gratifying, gusto, relish, satisfaction, solace; amusement, diversion, entertainment, indulgence, refreshment, treat; gratification, luxury, sensuality, voluptuousness; choice, desire, preference, purpose, will, wish; favour, kindness.

plebeian *adj* base, common, ignoble, low, lowborn, mean, obscure, popular, vulgar. * *n* commoner, peasant, proletarian.

pledge *vb* hypothecate, mortgage, pawn, plight; affiance, bind, contract, engage, plight, promise. * *n* collateral, deposit, gage, pawn; earnest, guarantee, security; hostage, security.

plenipotentiary *n* ambassador, envoy, legate, minister.

plenitude *n* abundance, completeness, fullness, plenteousness, plentifulness, plenty, plethora, profusion, repletion.

plentiful *adj* abundant, ample, copious, full, enough, exuberant, fruitful, luxuriant, plenteous, productive, sufficient.

plenty *n* abundance, adequacy, affluence, amplitude, copiousness, enough, exuberance, fertility, fruitfulness, fullness, overflow, plenteousness, plentifulness, plethora, profusion, sufficiency, supply.

pleonastic *adj* circumlocutory, diffuse, redundant, superfluous, tautological, verbose, wordy.

plethora *n* fullness, plenitude, repletion; excess, redundance, redundancy, superabundance, superfluity, surfeit.

pliable *adj* flexible, limber, lithe, lithesome, pliable, pliant, supple; adaptable, compliant, docile, ductile, facile, manageable, obsequious, tractable, yielding.

plight[1] *n* case, category, complication, condition, dilemma, imbroglio, mess, muddle, pass, predicament, scrape, situation, state, strait.

plight[2] *vb* avow, contract, covenant, engage, honour, pledge, promise, propose, swear, vow. * *n* avowal, contract, covenant, oath, pledge, promise, troth, vow, word; affiancing, betrothal, engagement.

plod *vb* drudge, lumber, moil, persevere, persist, toil, trudge.

plot[1] *vb* connive, conspire, intrigue, machinate, scheme; brew, concoct, contrive, devise, frame, hatch, compass, plan, project; chart, map. * *n* blueprint, chart, diagram, draft, outline, plan, scenario, skeleton; cabal, combination, complicity, connivance, conspiracy, intrigue, plan, project, scheme, stratagem; script, story, subject, theme, thread, topic.

plot[2] *n* field, lot, parcel, patch, piece, plat, section, tract.

pluck[1] *vb* cull, gather, pick; jerk, pull, snatch, tear, tug, twitch.

pluck[2] *n* backbone, bravery, courage, daring, determination, energy, force, grit, hardihood, heroism, indomitability, indomitableness, manhood, mettle, nerve, resolution, spirit, valour.

plump[1] *adj* bonny, bouncing, buxom, chubby, corpulent, fat, fleshy, full-figured, obese, portly, rotund, round, sleek, stout, well-rounded; distended, full, swollen, tumid.

plump[2] *vb* dive, drop, plank, plop, plunge, plunk, put; choose, favour, support * *adj* blunt, complete, direct, downright, full, unqualified, unreserved.

plunder *vb* desolate, despoil, devastate, fleece, forage, harry, loot, maraud, pillage, raid, ransack, ravage, rifle, rob, sack, spoil, spoliate, plunge. * *n* freebooting, devastation, harrying, marauding, rapine, robbery, sack; booty, pillage, prey, spoil.

ply[1] *vb* apply, employ, exert, manipulate, wield; exercise, practise; assail, belabour, beset, press; importune, solicit, urge; offer, present.

ply[2] *n* fold, layer, plait, twist; bent, bias, direction, turn.

pocket *vb* appropriate, steal; bear, endure, suffer, tolerate. * *n* cavity, cul-de-sac, hollow, pouch, receptacle.

poignant *adj* bitter, intense, penetrating, pierce, severe, sharp; acrid, biting, mordacious, piquant, prickling, pungent, sharp, stinging; caustic, irritating, keen, mordant, pointed, satirical, severe.

point *vb* acuminate, sharpen; aim, direct, level; designate indicate, show; punctuate. * *n* apex, needle, nib, pin, prong, spike, stylus, tip; cape, headland, projection, promontory; eve, instant, moment, period, verge; place, site, spot, stage, station; condition, degree, grade, state; aim, design, end, intent, limit, object, purpose; nicety, pique, punctilio, trifle; position, proposition, question, text, theme, thesis; aspect, matter, respect; characteristic, peculiarity, trait; character, mark, stop; dot, jot, speck; epigram, quip, quirk, sally, witticism; poignancy, sting.

point-blank *adj* categorical, direct, downright, explicit, express, plain, straight. * *adv* categorically, directly, flush, full, plainly, right, straight.

pointless *adj* blunt, obtuse; aimless, dull, flat, fruitless, futile, meaningless, vague, vapid, stupid.

poise *vb* balance, float, hang, hover, support, suspend. * *n* aplomb, balance, composure, dignity, equanimity, equilibrium, equipoise, serenity.

poison *vb* adulterate, contaminate, corrupt, defile, embitter, envenom, impair, infect, intoxicate, pollute, taint, vitiate. * *adj* deadly, lethal, poisonous, toxic. * *n* bane, canker, contagion, pest, taint, toxin, venom, virulence, virus.

poisonous *adj* baneful, corruptive, deadly, fatal, noxious, pestiferous, pestilential, toxic, venomous.

poke *vb* jab, jog, punch, push, shove, thrust; interfere, meddle, pry, snoop. * *n* jab, jog, punch, push, shove, thrust; bag, pocket, pouch, sack.

pole[1] *n* caber, mast, post, rod, spar, staff, stick; bar, beam, pile, shaft; oar, paddle, scull.

pole[2] *n* axis, axle, hub, pivot, spindle.

poles *n pl* antipodes, antipoles, counterpoles, opposites.

policy *n* administration, government, management, rule; plan, plank, platform, role; art, address, cunning, discretion, prudence, shrewdness, skill, stratagem, strategy, tactics; acumen, astuteness, wisdom, wit.

polish *vb* brighten, buff, burnish, furbish, glaze, gloss, scour, shine, smooth; civilize, refine. * *n* brightness, brilliance, brilliancy, lustre, splendour; accomplishment, elegance, finish, grace, refinement.

polished *adj* bright, burnished, glossed, glossy, lustrous, shining, smooth; accomplished, cultivated, elegant, finished, graceful, polite, refined.

polite *adj* attentive, accomplished, affable, chivalrous, civil, complaisant, courtly, courteous, cultivated, elegant, gallant, genteel, gentle, gentlemanly, gracious, mannerly, obliging, polished, refined, suave, urbane, well, well-bred, well-mannered.

politic *adj* civic, civil, political; astute, discreet, judicious, long-headed, noncommittal, provident, prudent, prudential, sagacious, wary, wise; artful, crafty, cunning, diplomatic, expedient, foxy, ingenious, intriguing, Machiavellian, shrewd, skilful, sly, subtle, strategic, timeserving, unscrupulous, wily; well-adapted, well-devised.

political *adj* civic, civil, national, politic, public.

pollute *vb* defile, foul, soil, taint; contaminate, corrupt, debase, demoralize, deprave, impair, infect, pervert, poison, stain, tarnish, vitiate; desecrate, profane; abuse, debauch, defile, deflower, dishonour, ravish, violate.

pollution *n* abomination, contamination, corruption, defilement, foulness, impurity, pollutedness, taint, uncleanness, vitiation.

poltroon *n* coward, crave, dastard, milksop, recreant, skulk, sneak.

pomp *n* display, flourish, grandeur, magnificence, ostentation, pageant, pageantry, parade, pompousness, pride, show, splendour, state, style.

pompous *adj* august, boastful, bombastic, dignified, gorgeous, grand, inflated, lofty, magisterial, ostentatious, pretentious, showy, splendid, stately, sumptuous, superb, vainglorious.

ponder *vb* cogitate, consider, contemplate, deliberate, examine, meditate, muse, reflect, study, weigh.

ponderous *adj* bulky, heavy, massive, weighty; dull, laboured, slow-moving; important, momentous; forcible, mighty.

poniard *n* dagger, dirk, stiletto.

poor *adj* indigent, necessitous, needy, pinched, straitened; destitute, distressed, embarrassed, impecunious, impoverished, insolvent, moneyless, penniless, poverty-stricken, reduced, seedy, unprosperous; emaciated, gaunt, spare, lank, lean, shrunk, skinny, spare, thin; barren, fruitless, sterile, unfertile, unfruitful, unproductive, unprolific; flimsy, inadequate, insignificant, insufficient, paltry, slender, slight, small, trifling, trivial, unimportant, valueless, worthless; decrepit, delicate, feeble, frail, infirm, unsound, weak; inferior, shabby, valueless, worthless; bad, beggarly, contemptible, despicable, humble, inferior, low, mean, pitiful, sorry; bald, cold, dry, dull, feeble, frigid, jejune, languid, meagre, prosaic, prosing, spiritless, tame, vapid, weak; ill-fated, ill-starred, inauspicious, indifferent, luckless, miserable, pitiable, unfavourable, unfortunate, unhappy, unlucky, wretched; deficient, imperfect, inadequate, insufficient, mediocre, scant, scanty; faulty, unsatisfactory; feeble.

populace *n* citizens, crowd, inhabitants, masses, people, public, throng.

popular *adj* lay, plebeian, public; comprehensible, easy, familiar, plain; acceptable, accepted, accredited, admired, approved, favoured, liked, pleasing, praised, received; common, current, prevailing, prevalent; cheap, inexpensive.

pore[1] *n* hole, opening, orifice, spiracle.

pore[2] *vb* brood, consider, dwell, examine, gaze, read, study.

porous *adj* honeycombed, light, loose, open, penetrable, perforated, permeable, pervious, sandy.

porridge *n* broth, gruel, mush, pap, pottage, soup.

port[1] *n* anchorage, harbour, haven, shelter; door, entrance, gate, passageway; embrasure, porthole.

port[2] *n* air, appearance, bearing, behaviour, carriage, demeanour, deportment, mien, presence.

portable *adj* convenient, handy, light, manageable, movable, portative, transmissible.

portend *vb* augur, betoken, bode, forebode, foreshadow, foretoken, indicate, presage, procrastinate, signify, threaten.

portent *n* augury, omen, presage, prognosis, sign, warning; marvel, phenomenon, wonder.

portion *vb* allot, distribute, divide, parcel; endow, supply. * *n* bit, fragment, morsel, part, piece, scrap, section; allotment, contingent, dividend, division, lot, measure, quantity, quota, ration, share; inheritance.

portly *adj* dignified, grand, imposing, magisterial, majestic, stately; bulky, burly, corpulent, fleshy, large, plump, round, stout.

portray *vb* act, draw, depict, delineate, describe, paint, picture, represent, pose, position, sketch.

pose *vb* arrange, place, set; bewilder, confound, dumbfound, embarrass, mystify, nonplus, perplex, place, puzzle, set, stagger; affect, attitudinize. * *n* attitude, posture; affectation, air, facade, mannerism, pretence, role.

position *vb* arrange, array, fix, locate, place, put, set, site, stand. * *n* locality, place, post, site, situation, spot, station; relation; attitude, bearing, posture; affirmation, assertion, doctrine, predication, principle, proposition, thesis; caste, dignity, honour, rank, standing, status; circumstance, condition, phase, place, state; berth, billet, incumbency, place, post, situation.

positive *adj* categorical, clear, defined, definite, direct, determinate, explicit, express, expressed, precise, unequivocal, unmistakable, unqualified; absolute, actual, real, substantial, true, veritable; assured, certain, confident, convinced, sure; decisive, incontrovertible, indisputable, indubitable, inescapable; imperative, unconditional, undeniable; decided, dogmatic, emphatic, obstinate, overbearing, overconfident, peremptory, stubborn, tenacious.

possess *vb* control, have, hold, keep, obsess, obtain, occupy, own, seize.

possession *n* monopoly, ownership, proprietorship; control, occupation, occupancy, retention, tenancy, tenure; bedevilment, lunacy, madness, obsession; (*pl*) assets, effects, estate, property, wealth.

possessor *n* owner, proprietor.

possible *adj* conceivable, contingent, imaginable, potential; accessible, feasible, likely, practical, practicable, workable.

possibly *adv* haply, maybe, mayhap, peradventure, perchance, perhaps.

post[1] *vb* advertise, announce, inform, placard, publish; brand, defame, disgrace, vilify; enter, slate, record, register. * *n* column, picket, pier, pillar, stake, support.

post[2] *vb* establish, fix, place, put, set, station. * *n* billet, employment, office, place, position, quarter, seat, situation, station.

post[3] *vb* drop, dispatch, mail. * *n* carrier, courier, express, mercury, messenger, postman; dispatch, haste, hurry, speed.

posterior *adj* after, ensuing, following, later, latter, postprandial, subsequent. * *n* back, buttocks, hind, hinder, rump.

posterity *n* descendants, offspring, progeny, seed; breed, brood, children, family, heirs, issue.

postpone *vb* adjourn, defer, delay, procrastinate, prorogue, retard.

postscript *n* addition, afterthought, appendix, supplement.

postulate *vb* assume, presuppose; beseech, entreat, solicit, supplicate. * *n* assumption, axiom, conjecture, hypothesis, proposition, speculation, supposition, theory.

posture *vb* attitudinize, pose. * *n* attitude, pose, position; condition, disposition, mood, phase, state.

pot *n* kettle, pan, saucepan, skillet; can, cup, mug, tankard; crock, jar, jug.

potency *n* efficacy, energy, force, intensity, might, power, strength, vigour; authority, control, influence, sway.

potent *adj* efficacious, forceful, forcible, intense, powerful, strong, virile; able, authoritative, capable, efficient, mighty, puissant, strong; cogent, influential.

potentate *n* emperor, king, monarch, prince, sovereign, ruler.

potential *adj* able, capable, inherent, latent, possible. * *n* ability, capability, dynamic, possibility, potentiality, power.

pother *vb* beset, bewilder, confound, confuse, embarrass, harass, perplex, pose, puzzle, tease. * *n* bustle, commotion, confusion, disturbance, flutter, fuss, huddle, hurly-burly, rumpus, tumult, turbulence, turmoil.

pound[1] *vb* beat, strike, thump; bray, bruise, comminute, crush, levigate, pulverize, triturate; confound, coop, enclose, impound.

pound[2] *n* enclosure, fold, pen.

pour *vb* cascade, emerge, flood, flow, gush, issue, rain, shower, stream.

pouting *adj* bad-tempered, cross, ill-humoured, moody, morose, sulky, sullen.

poverty *n* destitution, difficulties, distress, impecuniosity, impecuniousness, indigence, necessity, need, neediness, penury, privation, straits, want; beggary, mendicancy, pauperism, pennilessness; dearth, jejuneness, lack, scantiness, sparingness, meagreness; exiguity, paucity, poorness, smallness; humbleness, inferiority, lowliness; barrenness, sterility, unfruitfulness, unproductiveness.

power *n* ability, ableness, capability, cogency, competency, efficacy, faculty, might, potency, validity, talent; energy, force, strength, virtue; capacity, susceptibility; endowment, faculty, gift, talent; ascendancy, authoritativeness, authority, carte blanche, command, control, domination, dominion, government, influence, omnipotence, predominance, prerogative, pressure, proxy, puissance, rule, sovereignty, sway, warrant; governor, monarch, potentate, ruler, sovereign; army, host, troop.

powerful *adj* mighty, potent, puissant; able-bodied, herculean, muscular, nervous, robust, sinewy, strong, sturdy, vigorous, vivid; able, commanding, dominating, forceful, forcible, overpowering; cogent, effective, effectual, efficacious, efficient, energetic, influential, operative, valid.

practicable *adj* achievable, attainable, bearable, feasible, performable, possible, workable; operative, passable, penetrable.

practical *adj* hardheaded, matter-of-fact, pragmatic, pragmatical; able, experienced, practised, proficient, qualified, trained, skilled, thoroughbred, versed; effective, useful, virtual, workable.

practice *n* custom, habit, manner, method, repetition; procedure, usage, use; application, drill, exercise, pursuit; action, acts, behaviour, conduct, dealing, proceeding.

practise *vb* apply, do, exercise, follow, observe, perform, perpetrate, pursue.

practised *adj* able, accomplished, experienced, instructed, practical, proficient, qualified, skilled, thoroughbred, trained, versed.

pragmatic *adj* impertinent, intermeddling, interfering, intrusive, meddlesome, meddling, obtrusive, officious, over-busy; earthy, hard-headed, matter-of-fact, practical, pragmatical, realistic, sensible, stolid.

praise *vb* approbate, acclaim, applaud, approve, commend; celebrate, compliment, eulogize, extol, flatter, laud; adore, bless, exalt, glorify, magnify, worship. * *n* acclaim, approbation, approval, commendation; encomium, eulogy, glorification, laud, laudation, panegyric; exaltation, extolling, glorification, homage, tribute, worship; celebrity, distinction, fame, glory, honour, renown; desert, merit, praiseworthiness.

praiseworthy *adj* commendable, creditable, good, laudable, meritorious.

prank *n* antic, caper, escapade, frolic, gambol, trick.

prate *vb* babble, chatter, gabble, jabber, palaver, prattle, tattle. * *n* chatter, gabble, nonsense, palaver, prattle, twaddle.

pray *vb* ask, beg, beseech, conjure, entreat, implore, importune, invoke, petition, request, solicit, supplicate.

prayer *n* beseeching, entreaty, imploration, petition, request, solicitation, suit, supplication; adoration, devotion(s), litany, invocation, orison, praise, suffrage.

preach *vb* declare, deliver, proclaim, pronounce, publish; inculcate, press, teach, urge; exhort, lecture, moralize, sermonize.

preamble *n* foreword, introduction, preface, prelude, prologue.

precarious *adj* critical, doubtful, dubious, equivocal, hazardous, insecure, perilous, unassured, riskful, risky, uncertain, unsettled, unstable, unsteady.

precaution *n* care, caution, circumspection, foresight, forethought, providence, prudence, safeguard, wariness; anticipation, premonition, provision.

precautionary *adj* preservative, preventative, provident.

precede *vb* antedate, forerun, head, herald, introduce, lead, utter.

precedence *n* advantage, antecedence, lead, pre-eminence, preference, priority, superiority, supremacy.

precedent *n* antecedent, authority, custom, example, instance, model, pattern, procedure, standard, usage.

precept *n* behest, bidding, canon, charge, command, commandment, decree, dictate, edict, injunction, instruction, law, mandate, ordinance, ordination, order, regulation; direction, doctrine, maxim, principle, teaching, rubric, rule.

preceptor *n* instructor, lecturer, master, pedagogue, professor, schoolteacher, teacher, tutor.

precinct *n* border, bound, boundary, confine, environs, frontier, enclosure, limit, list, march, neighbourhood, purlieus, term, terminus; area, district.

precious *adj* costly, inestimable, invaluable, priceless, prized, valuable; adored, beloved, cherished, darling, dear, idolized, treasured; fastidious, overnice, over-refined, precise.

precipice *n* bluff, cliff, crag, steep.

precipitate *vb* advance, accelerate, dispatch, expedite, forward, further, hasten, hurry, plunge, press, quicken, speed. * *adj* hasty, hurried, headlong, impetuous, indiscreet, overhasty, rash, reckless; abrupt, sudden, violent.

precipitous *adj* abrupt, cliffy, craggy, perpendicular, uphill, sheer, steep.

precise *adj* accurate, correct, definite, distinct, exact, explicit, express, nice, pointed, severe, strict, unequivocal, well-defined; careful, scrupulous; ceremonious, finical, formal, prim, punctilious, rigid, starched, stiff.

precision *n* accuracy, correctness, definiteness, distinctness, exactitude, exactness, nicety, preciseness.

preclude *vb* bar, check, debar, hinder, inhibit, obviate, prevent, prohibit, restrain, stop.

precocious *adj* advanced, forward, overforward, premature.

preconcert *vb* concoct, prearrange, predetermine, premeditate, prepare.

precursor *n* antecedent, cause, forerunner, predecessor; harbinger, herald, messenger, pioneer; omen, presage, sign.

precursory *adj* antecedent, anterior, forerunning, precedent, preceding, previous, prior; initiatory, introductory, precursive, prefatory, preliminary, prelusive, prelusory, premonitory, preparatory, prognosticative.

predatory *adj* greedy, pillaging, plundering, predacious, rapacious, ravaging, ravenous, voracious.

predestination *n* doom, fate, foredoom, foreordainment, foreordination, necessity, predetermination, preordination.

predicament *n* attitude, case, condition, plight, position, posture, situation, state; corner, dilemma, emergency, exigency, fix, hole, impasse, mess, pass, pinch, push, quandary, scrape.

predict *vb* augur, betoken, bode, divine, forebode, forecast, foredoom, foresee, forespeak, foretell, foretoken, forewarn, portend, prognosticate, prophesy, read, signify, soothsay.

predilection *n* bent, bias, desire, fondness, inclination, leaning, liking, love, partiality, predisposition, preference, prejudice, prepossession.

predisposition *n* aptitude, bent, bias, disposition, inclination, leaning, proclivity, proneness, propensity, willingness.

predominant *adj* ascendant, controlling, dominant, overruling, prevailing, prevalent, reigning, ruling, sovereign, supreme.

predominate *vb* dominate, preponderate, prevail, rule.

pre-eminent *adj* chief, conspicuous, consummate, controlling, distinguished, excellent, excelling, paramount, peerless, predominant, renowned, superior, supreme, surpassing, transcendent, unequalled.

preface *vb* begin, introduce, induct, launch, open, precede. * *n* exordium, foreword, induction, introduction, preamble, preliminary, prelude, prelusion, premise, proem, prologue, prolusion.

prefatory *adj* antecedent, initiative, introductory, precursive, precursory, preliminary, prelusive, prelusory, preparatory, proemial.

prefer *vb* address, offer, present, proffer, tender; advance, elevate, promote, raise; adopt, choose, elect, fancy, pick, select, wish.

preference *n* advancement, choice, election, estimation, precedence, priority, selection.

preferment *n* advancement, benefice, dignity, elevation, exaltation, promotion.

pregnant *adj* big, enceinte, parturient; fraught, full, important, replete, significant, weighty; fecund, fertile, fruitful, generative, potential, procreant, procreative, productive, prolific.

prejudice *vb* bias, incline, influence, turn, warp; damage, diminish, hurt, impair, injure. * *n* bias, intolerance, partiality, preconception, predilection, prejudgement, prepossession, unfairness; damage, detriment, disadvantage, harm, hurt, impairment, injury, loss, mischief.

prejudiced *adj* biased, bigoted, influenced, one-sided, partial, partisan, unfair.

preliminary *adj* antecedent, initiatory, introductory, precedent, precursive, precursory, prefatory, prelusive, prelusory, preparatory, previous, prior, proemial. * *n* beginning, initiation, introduction, opening, preamble, preface, prelude, start.

prelude *n* introduction, opening, overture, prelusion, preparation, voluntary; exordium, preamble, preface, preliminary, proem.

premature *adj* hasty, ill-considered, precipitate, unmatured, unprepared, unripe, unseasonable, untimely.

premeditation *n* deliberation, design, forethought, intention, prearrangement, predetermination, purpose.

premise *vb* introduce, preamble, preface, prefix. * *n* affirmation, antecedent, argument, assertion, assumption, basis, foundation, ground, hypothesis, position, premiss, presupposition, proposition, support, thesis, theorem.

premium *n* bonus, bounty, encouragement, fee, gift, guerdon, meed, payment, prize, recompense, remuneration, reward; appreciation, enhancement.

premonition *n* caution, foreboding, foreshadowing, forewarning, indication, omen, portent, presage, presentiment, sign, warning.

preoccupied *adj* absent, absentminded, abstracted, dreaming, engrossed, inadvertent, inattentive, lost, musing, unobservant.

prepare *vb* adapt, adjust, fit, qualify; arrange, concoct, fabricate, make, order, plan, procure, provide.

preponderant *adj* outweighing, overbalancing, preponderating.

prepossessing *adj* alluring, amiable, attractive, bewitching, captivating, charming, engaging, fascinating, inviting, taking, winning.

preposterous *adj* absurd, excessive, exorbitant, extravagant, foolish, improper, irrational, monstrous, nonsensical, perverted, ridiculous, unfit, unreasonable, wrong.

prerogative *n* advantage, birthright, claim, franchise, immunity, liberty, privilege, right.

presage *vb* divine, forebode; augur, betoken, bode, foreshadow, foretell, foretoken, indicate, portend, predict, prognosticate, prophesy, signify, soothsay. * *n* augury, auspice, boding, foreboding, foreshowing, indication, omen, portent, prognostication, sign, token; foreknowledge, precognition, prediction, premonition, presentiment, prophecy.

prescribe *vb* advocate, appoint, command, decree, dictate, direct, enjoin, establish, institute, ordain, order.

presence *n* attendance, company, inhabitance, inhabitancy, nearness, neighbourhood, occupancy, propinquity, proximity, residence, ubiquity, vicinity; air, appearance, carriage, demeanour, mien, personality.

present[1] *adj* near; actual, current, existing, happening, immediate, instant, living; available, quick, ready; attentive, favourable. * *n* now, time being, today.

present[2] *n* benefaction, boon, donation, favour, gift, grant, gratuity, largesse, offering.

present[3] *vb* introduce, nominate; exhibit, offer; bestow, confer, give, grant; deliver, hand; advance, express, prefer, proffer, tender.

presentiment *n* anticipation, apprehension, foreboding, forecast, foretaste, forethought, prescience.

presently *adv* anon, directly, forthwith, immediately, shortly, soon.

preservation *n* cherishing, conservation, curing, maintenance, protection, support; safety, salvation, security; integrity, keeping, soundness.

preserve *vb* defend, guard, keep, protect, rescue, save, secure, shield; maintain, uphold, sustain, support; conserve, economize, husband, retain. * *n* comfit, compote, confection, confiture, conserve, jam, jelly, marmalade, sweetmeat; enclosure, warren.

preside *vb* control, direct, govern, manage, officiate.

press *vb* compress, crowd, crush, squeeze; flatten, iron, smooth; clasp, embrace, hug; force, compel, constrain; emphasize, enforce, enjoin, inculcate, stress, urge; hasten, hurry, push, rush; crowd, throng; entreat, importune, solicit. * *n* crowd, crush, multitude, throng; hurry, pressure, urgency; case, closet, cupboard, repository.

pressing *adj* constraining, critical, distressing, imperative, importunate, persistent, serious, urgent, vital.

pressure *n* compressing, crushing, squeezing; influence, force; compulsion, exigency, hurry, persuasion, press, stress, urgency; affliction, calamity, difficulty, distress, embarrassment, grievance, oppression, straits; impression, stamp.

prestidigitation *n* conjuring, juggling, legerdemain, sleight-of-hand.

prestige *n* credit, distinction, importance, influence, reputation, weight.

presume *vb* anticipate, apprehend, assume, believe, conjecture, deduce, expect, infer, surmise, suppose, think; consider, presuppose; dare, undertake, venture.

presumption *n* anticipation, assumption, belief, concession, conclusion, condition, conjecture, deduction, guess, hypothesis, inference, opinion, supposition, understanding; arrogance, assurance, audacity, boldness, brass, effrontery, forwardness, haughtiness, presumptuousness; probability.

presumptuous *adj* arrogant, assuming, audacious, bold, brash, forward, irreverent, insolent, intrusive, presuming; foolhardy, overconfident, rash.

pretence *n* affectation, cloak, colour, disguise, mask, semblance, show, simulation, veil, window-dressing; excuse, evasion, fabrication, feigning, makeshift, pretext, sham, subterfuge; claim, pretension.

pretend *vb* affect, counterfeit, deem, dissemble, fake, falsify, feign, sham, simulate; act, imagine, lie, profess; aspire, claim.

pretension *n* assertion, assumption, claim, demand, pretence; affectation, airs, conceit, ostentation, pertness, pretentiousness, priggishness, vanity.

pretentious *adj* affected, assuming, conceited, conspicuous, ostentatious, presuming, priggish, showy, tawdry, unnatural, vain.

preternatural *adj* abnormal, anomalous, extraordinary, inexplicable, irregular, miraculous, mysterious, odd, peculiar, strange, unnatural.

pretext *n* affectation, appearance, blind, cloak, colour, guise, mask, pretence, semblance, show, simulation, veil; excuse, justification, plea, vindication.

pretty *adj* attractive, beautiful, bonny, comely, elegant, fair, handsome, neat, pleasing, trim; affected, foppish. * *adv* fairly, moderately, quite, rather, somewhat.

prevail *vb* overcome, succeed, triumph, win; obtain, predominate, preponderate, reign, rule.

prevailing *adj* controlling, dominant, effectual, efficacious, general, influential, operative, overruling, persuading, predominant, preponderant, prevalent, ruling, successful.

prevalent *adj* ascendant, compelling, efficacious, governing, predominant, prevailing, successful, superior; extensive, general, rife, widespread.

prevaricate *vb* cavil, deviate, dodge, equivocate, evade, palter, pettifog, quibble, shift, shuffle, tergiversate.

prevent *vb* bar, check, debar, deter, forestall, help, hinder, impede, inhibit, intercept, interrupt, obstruct, obviate, preclude, prohibit, restrain, save, stop, thwart.

prevention *n* anticipation, determent, deterrence, deterrent, frustration, hindrance, interception, interruption, obstruction, preclusion, prohibition, restriction, stoppage.

previous *adj* antecedent, anterior, earlier, foregoing, foregone, former, precedent, preceding, prior.

prey *vb* devour, eat, feed on, live off; exploit, intimidate, terrorize; burden, distress, haunt, oppress, trouble, worry. * *n* booty, loot, pillage, plunder, prize, rapine, spoil; food, game, kill, quarry, victim; depredation, ravage.

price *vb* assess, estimate, evaluate, rate, value. * *n* amount, cost, expense, outlay, value; appraisal, charge, estimation, excellence, figure, rate, quotation, valuation, value, worth; compensation, guerdon, recompense, return, reward.

priceless *adj* dear, expensive, precious, inestimable, invaluable, valuable; amusing, comic, droll, funny, humorous, killing, rich.

prick *vb* perforate, pierce, puncture, stick; drive, goad, impel, incite, spur, urge; cut, hurt, mark, pain, sting, wound; hasten, post, ride. * *n* mark, perforation, point, puncture; prickle, sting, wound.

pride *vb* boast, brag, crow, preen, revel in. * *n* conceit, egotism, self-complacency, self-esteem, self-exaltation, self-importance, self-sufficiency, vanity; arrogance, assumption, disdain, haughtiness, hauteur, insolence, loftiness, lordliness, pomposity, presumption, superciliousness, vainglory; decorum, dignity, elevation, self-respect; decoration, glory, ornament, show, splendour.

priest *n* churchman, clergyman, divine, ecclesiastic, minister, pastor, presbyter.

prim *adj* demure, formal, nice, precise, prudish, starch, starched, stiff, strait-laced.

primary *adj* aboriginal, earliest, first, initial, original, prime, primitive, primeval, primordial, pristine; chief, main, principal; basic, elementary, fundamental, preparatory: radical.

prime[1] *adj* aboriginal, basic, first, initial, original, primal, primary, primeval, primitive, primordial, pristine; chief, foremost, highest, leading, main, paramount, principal; blooming, early; capital, cardinal, dominant, predominant; excellent, first-class, first-rate, optimal, optimum, quintessential, superlative; beginning, opening. * *n* beginning, dawn, morning, opening; spring, springtime, youth; bloom, cream, flower, height, heyday, optimum, perfection, quintessence, zenith.

prime[2] *vb* charge, load, prepare, undercoat; coach, groom, train, tutor.

primeval *adj* original, primitive, primordial, pristine.

primitive *adj* aboriginal, first, fundamental, original, primal, primary, prime, primitive, primordial, pristine; ancient, antiquated, crude, old-fashioned, quaint, simple, uncivilized, unsophisticated.

prince *n* monarch, potentate, ruler, sovereign; dauphin, heir apparent, infant; chief, leader, potentate.

princely *adj* imperial, regal, royal; august, generous, grand, liberal, magnanimous, magnificent, majestic, munificent, noble, pompous, splendid, superb, titled; dignified, elevated, high-minded, lofty, noble, stately.

principal *adj* capital, cardinal, chief, essential, first, foremost, highest, leading, main, pre-eminent, prime. * *n* chief, head, leader; head teacher, master.

principally *adv* chiefly, essentially, especially, mainly, particularly.

principle *n* cause, fountain, fountainhead, groundwork, mainspring, nature, origin, source, spring; basis, constituent, element, essence, substratum; assumption, axiom, law, maxim, postulation; doctrine, dogma, impulse, maxim, opinion, precept, rule, tenet, theory; conviction, ground, motive, reason; equity, goodness, honesty, honour, incorruptibility, integrity, justice, probity, rectitude, righteousness, trustiness, truth, uprightness, virtue, worth; faculty, power.

prink *vb* adorn, deck, decorate; preen, primp, spruce.

print *vb* engrave, impress, imprint, mark, stamp; issue, publish. * *n* book, periodical, publication; copy, engraving, photograph, picture; characters, font, fount, lettering, type, typeface.

prior *adj* antecedent, anterior, earlier, foregoing, precedent, preceding, precursory, previous, superior.

priority *n* antecedence, anteriority, precedence, pre-eminence, pre-existence, superiority.

priory *n* abbey, cloister, convent, monastery, nunnery.

prison *n* confinement, dungeon, gaol, jail, keep, lockup, penitentiary, reformatory; can, clink, cooler, jug.

pristine *adj* ancient, earliest, first, former, old, original, primary, primeval, primitive, primordial.

privacy *n* concealment, secrecy; retirement, retreat, seclusion, solitude.

private *adj* retired, secluded, sequestrated, solitary; individual, own, particular, peculiar, personal, special, unofficial; confidential, privy; clandestine, concealed, hidden, secret. * *n* GI, soldier, tommy.

privation *n* bereavement, deprivation, dispossession, loss; destitution, distress, indigence, necessity, need, want; absence, negation; degradation.

privilege *n* advantage, charter, claim, exemption, favour, franchise, immunity, leave, liberty, licence, permission, prerogative, right.

privy *adj* individual, particular, peculiar, personal, private, special; clandestine, secret; retired, sequestrated.

prize[1] *vb* appreciate, cherish, esteem, treasure, value.

prize[2] *adj* best, champion, first-rate, outstanding, winning. * *n* guerdon, honours, meed, premium, reward; cup, decoration, medal, laurels, palm, trophy; booty, capture, lot, plunder, spoil; advantage, gain, privilege.

probability *n* chance, prospect, likelihood, presumption; appearance, credibility, credibleness, likeliness, verisimilitude.

probable *adj* apparent, credible, likely, presumable, reasonable.

probably *adv* apparently, likely, maybe, perchance, perhaps, presumably, possibly, seemingly.

probation *n* essay, examination, ordeal, proof, test, trial; novitiate.

probe *vb* examine, explore, fathom, investigate, measure, prove, scrutinize, search, sift, sound, test, verify. * *n* examination, exploration, inquiry, investigation, scrutiny, study.

probity *n* candour, conscientiousness, equity, fairness, faith, goodness, honesty, honour, incorruptibility, integrity, justice, loyalty, morality, principle, rectitude, righteousness, sincerity, soundness, trustworthiness, truth, truthfulness, uprightness, veracity, virtue, worth.

problem *adj* difficult, intractable, uncontrollable, unruly. * *n* dilemma, dispute, doubt, enigma, exercise, proposition, puzzle, riddle, theorem.

problematic *adj* debatable, disputable, doubtful, dubious, enigmatic, problematical, puzzling, questionable, suspicious, uncertain, unsettled.

procedure *n* conduct, course, custom, management, method, operation, policy, practice, process; act, action, deed, measure, performance, proceeding, step, transaction.

proceed *vb* advance, continue, go, pass, progress; accrue, arise, come, emanate, ensue, flow, follow, issue, originate, result, spring.

proceeds *n pl* balance, earnings, effects, gain, income, net, produce, products, profits, receipts, returns, yield.

process *vb* advance, deal with, fulfil, handle, progress; alter, convert, refine, transform. * *n* advance, course, progress, train; action, conduct, management, measure, mode, operation, performance, practice, procedure, proceeding, step, transaction, way; action, case, suit, trial; outgrowth, projection, protuberance.

procession *n* cavalcade, cortege, file, march, parade, retinue, train.

proclaim *vb* advertise, announce, blazon, broach, broadcast, circulate, cry, declare, herald, promulgate, publish, trumpet; ban, outlaw, proscribe.

proclamation *n* advertisement, announcement, blazon, declaration, promulgation, publication; ban, decree, edict, manifesto, ordinance.

proclivity *n* bearing, bent, bias, determination, direction, disposition, drift, inclination, leaning, predisposition, proneness, propensity, tendency, turn; aptitude, facility, readiness.

procrastinate *vb* adjourn, defer, delay, postpone, prolong, protract, retard; neglect, omit; lag, loiter.

procrastination *n* delay, dilatoriness, postponement, protraction, slowness, tardiness.

procreate *vb* beget, breed, engender, generate, produce, propagate.

procurable *adj* acquirable, compassable, obtainable.

procurator *n* agent, attorney, deputy, proctor, proxy, representative, solicitor.

procure *vb* acquire, gain, get, obtain; cause, compass, contrive, effect.

procurer *n* bawd, pander, pimp.

prodigal *adj* abundant, dissipated, excessive, extravagant, generous, improvident, lavish, profuse, reckless, squandering, thriftless, unthrifty, wasteful. * *n* spendthrift, squanderer, waster, wastrel.

prodigality *n* excess, extravagance, lavishness, profusion, squandering, unthriftiness, waste, wastefulness.

prodigious *adj* amazing, astonishing, astounding, extraordinary, marvellous, miraculous, portentous, remarkable, startling, strange, surprising, uncommon, wonderful, wondrous; enormous, huge, immense, monstrous, vast.

prodigy *n* marvel, miracle, phenomenon, portent, sign, wonder; curiosity, monster, monstrosity.

produce *vb* exhibit, show; bear, beget, breed, conceive, engender, furnish, generate, hatch, procreate, yield; accomplish, achieve, cause, create, effect, make, occasion, originate; accrue, afford, give, impart, make, render; extend, lengthen, prolong, protract; fabricate, fashion, manufacture. * *n* crop, fruit, greengrocery, harvest, product, vegetables, yield.

producer *n* creator, inventor, maker, originator; agriculturalist, farmer, greengrocer, husbandman, raiser.

product *n* crops, fruits, harvest, outcome, proceeds, produce, production, returns, yield; consequence, effect, fruit, issue, performance, production, result, work.

production *n* fruit, produce, product; construction, creation, erection, fabrication, making, performance; completion, fruition; birth, breeding, development, growth, propagation; opus, publication, work; continuation, extension, lengthening, prolongation.

productive *adj* copious, fertile, fruitful, luxuriant, plenteous, prolific, teeming; causative, constructive, creative, efficient, life-giving, producing.

proem *n* exordium, foreword, introduction, preface, prelims, prelude, prolegomena.

profane *vb* defile, desecrate, pollute, violate; abuse, debase. * *adj* blasphemous, godless, heathen, idolatrous, impious, impure, pagan, secular, temporal, unconsecrated, unhallowed, unholy, unsanctified, worldly, unspiritual; impure, polluted, unholy.

profanity *n* blasphemy, impiety, irreverence, profaneness, sacrilege.

profess *vb* acknowledge, affirm, allege, aver, avouch, avow, confess, declare, own, proclaim, state; affect, feign, pretend.

profession *n* acknowledgement, assertion, avowal, claim, declaration; avocation, evasion, pretence, pretension, protestation, representation; business, calling, employment, engagement, occupation, office, trade, vocation.

proffer *vb* offer, propose, propound, suggest, tender, volunteer. * *n* offer, proposal, suggestion, tender.

proficiency *n* advancement, forwardness, improvement; accomplishment, aptitude, competency, dexterity, mastery, skill.

proficient *adj* able, accomplished, adept, competent, conversant, dextrous, expert, finished, masterly, practised, skilled, skilful, thoroughbred, trained, qualified, well-versed. * *n* adept, expert, master, master-hand.

profit *vb* advance, benefit, gain, improve. * *n* aid, clearance, earnings, emolument, fruit, gain, lucre, produce, return; advancement, advantage, benefit, interest, perquisite, service, use, utility, weal.

profitable *adj* advantageous, beneficial, desirable, gainful, productive, useful; lucrative, remunerative.

profitless *adj* bootless, fruitless, unprofitable, useless, valueless, worthless.

profligate *adj* abandoned, corrupt, corrupted, degenerate, depraved, dissipated, dissolute, graceless, immoral, shameless, vicious, vitiated, wicked. * *n* debauchee, libertine, rake, reprobate, roué.

profound *adj* abysmal, deep, fathomless; heavy, undisturbed; erudite, learned, penetrating, sagacious, skilled; deeply felt, far-reaching, heartfelt, intense, lively, strong, touching, vivid; low, submissive; abstruse, mysterious, obscure, occult, subtle, recondite; complete, thorough.

profundity *n* deepness, depth, profoundness.

profuse *adj* abundant, bountiful, copious, excessive, extravagant, exuberant, generous, improvident, lavish, overabundant, plentiful, prodigal, wasteful.

profusion *n* abundance, bounty, copiousness, excess, exuberance, extravagance, lavishness, prodigality, profuseness, superabundance, waste.

progenitor *n* ancestor, forebear, forefather.

progeny *n* breed, children, descendants, family, issue, lineage, offshoot, offspring, posterity, race, scion, stock, young.

prognostic *adj* foreshadowing, foreshowing, foretokening. * *n* augury, foreboding, indication, omen, presage, prognostication, sign, symptom, token; foretelling, prediction, prophecy.

prognosticate *vb* foretell, predict, prophesy; augur, betoken, forebode, foreshadow, foreshow, foretoken, indicate, portend, presage.

prognostication *n* foreknowledge, foreshowing, foretelling, prediction, presage; augury, foreboding, foretoken, indication, portent, prophecy.

progress *vb* advance, continue, proceed; better, gain, improve, increase. * *n* advance, advancement, progression; course, headway, ongoing, passage; betterment, development, growth, improvement, increase, reform; circuit, procession.

prohibit *vb* debar, hamper, hinder, preclude, prevent; ban, disallow, forbid, inhibit, interdict.

prohibition *n* ban, bar, disallowance, embargo, forbiddance, inhibition, interdict, interdiction, obstruction, prevention, proscription, taboo, veto.

prohibitive *adj* forbidding, prohibiting, refraining, restrictive.

project *vb* cast, eject, fling, hurl, propel, shoot, throw; brew, concoct, contrive, design, devise, intend, plan, plot, purpose, scheme; delineate, draw, exhibit; bulge, extend, jut, protrude. * *n* contrivance, design, device, intention, plan, proposal, purpose, scheme.

projectile *n* bullet, missile, shell.

projection *n* delivery, ejection, emission, propulsion, throwing; contriving, designing, planning, scheming; bulge, extension, outshoot, process, prominence, protuberance, salience, saliency, salient, spur; delineation, map, plan.

proletarian *adj* mean, plebeian, vile, vulgar. * *n* commoner, plebeian.

proletariat *n* commonality, hoi polloi, masses, mob, plebs, working class.

prolific *adj* abundant, fertile, fruitful, generative, productive, teeming.

prolix *adj* boring, circumlocutory, discursive, diffuse, lengthy, long, long-winded, loose, prolonged, protracted, prosaic, rambling, tedious, tiresome, verbose, wordy.

prologue *n* foreword, introduction, preamble, preface, preliminary, prelude, proem.

prolong *vb* continue, extend, lengthen, protract, sustain; defer, postpone.

promenade *vb* saunter, walk. * *n* dance, stroll, walk; boulevard, esplanade, parade, walkway.

prominent *adj* convex, embossed, jutting, projecting, protuberant, raised, relieved; celebrated, conspicuous, distinguished, eminent, famous, foremost, influential, leading, main, noticeable, outstanding; conspicuous, distinctive, important, manifest, marked, principal, salient.

promiscuous *adj* confused, heterogeneous, indiscriminate, intermingled, mingled, miscellaneous, mixed; abandoned, dissipated, dissolute, immoral, licentious, loose, unchaste, wanton.

promise *vb* covenant, engage, pledge, subscribe, swear, underwrite, vow; assure, attest, guarantee, warrant; agree, bargain, engage, stipulate, undertake. * *n* agreement, assurance, contract, engagement, oath, parole, pledge, profession, undertaking, vow, word.

promising *adj* auspicious, encouraging, hopeful, likely, propitious.

promote *vb* advance, aid, assist, cultivate, encourage, further, help, promote; dignify, elevate, exalt, graduate, honour, pass, prefer, raise.

promotion *n* advancement, encouragement, furtherance; elevation, exaltation, preferment.

prompt *vb* actuate, dispose, impel, incite, incline, induce, instigate, stimulate, urge; remind; dictate, hint, influence, suggest. * *adj* active, alert, apt, quick, ready; forward, hasty; disposed, inclined, prone; early, exact, immediate, instant, precise, punctual, seasonable, timely. * *adv* apace, directly, forthwith, immediately, promptly. * *n* cue, hint, prompter, reminder, stimulus.

promptly *adv* apace, directly, expeditiously, forthwith, immediately, instantly, pronto, punctually, quickly, speedily, straightway, straightaway, summarily, swiftly.

promptness *n* activity, alertness, alacrity, promptitude, readiness, quickness.

promulgate *vb* advertise, announce, broadcast, bruit, circulate, declare, notify, proclaim, publish, spread, trumpet.

prone *adj* flat, horizontal, prostrate, recumbent; declivitous, inclined, inclining, sloping; apt, bent, disposed, inclined, predisposed, tending; eager, prompt, ready.

pronounce *vb* articulate, enunciate, frame, say, speak, utter; affirm, announce, assert, declare, deliver, state.

proof *adj* firm, fixed, impenetrable, stable, steadfast. * *n* essay, examination, ordeal, test, trial; attestation, certification, conclusion, conclusiveness, confirmation, corroboration, demonstration, evidence, ratification, substantiation, testimony, verification.

prop *vb* bolster, brace, buttress, maintain, shore, stay, support, sustain, truss, uphold. * *n* support, stay; buttress, fulcrum, pin, shore, strut.

propaganda *n* inculcation, indoctrination, promotion.

propagate *vb* continue, increase, multiply; circulate, diffuse, disseminate, extend, promote, promulgate, publish, spread, transmit; beget, breed, engender, generate, originate, procreate.

propel *vb* drive, force, impel, push, urge; cast, fling, hurl, project, throw.

propensity *n* aptitude, bent, bias, disposition, inclination, ply, proclivity, proneness, tendency.

proper *adj* individual, inherent, natural, original, particular, peculiar, special, specific; adapted, appropriate, becoming, befitting, convenient, decent, decorous, demure, fit, fitting, legitimate, meet, pertinent, respectable, right, seemly, suitable; accurate, correct, exact, fair, fastidious, formal, just, precise; actual, real.

property *n* attribute, characteristic, disposition, mark, peculiarity, quality, trait, virtue; appurtenance, assets, belongings, chattels, circumstances, effects, estate, goods, possessions, resources, wealth; ownership, possession, proprietorship, tenure; claim, copyright, interest, participation, right, title.

prophecy *n* augury, divination, forecast, foretelling, portent, prediction, premonition, presage, prognostication; exhortation, instruction, preaching.

prophesy *vb* augur, divine, foretell, predict, prognosticate.

propinquity *n* adjacency, contiguity, nearness, neighbourhood, proximity, vicinity; affinity, connection, consanguinity, kindred, relationship.

propitiate *vb* appease, atone, conciliate, intercede, mediate, pacify, reconcile, satisfy.

propitious *adj* benevolent, benign, friendly, gracious, kind, merciful; auspicious, encouraging, favourable, fortunate, happy, lucky, opportune, promising, prosperous, thriving, timely, well-disposed.

proportion *vb* adjust, graduate, regulate; form, shape. * *n* arrangement, relation; adjustment, commensuration, dimension, distribution, symmetry; extent, lot, part, portion, quota, ratio, share.

proposal *n* design, motion, offer, overture, proffer, proposition, recommendation, scheme, statement, suggestion, tender.

propose *vb* move, offer, pose, present, propound, proffer, put, recommend, state, submit, suggest, tender; design, intend, mean, purpose.

proposition *vb* accost, proffer, solicit. * *n* offer, overture, project, proposal, suggestion, tender, undertaking; affirmation, assertion, axiom, declaration, dictum, doctrine, position, postulation, predication, statement, theorem, thesis.

proprietor *n* lord, master, owner, possessor, proprietary.

propriety *n* accuracy, adaptation, appropriation, aptness, becomingness, consonance, correctness, fitness, justness, reasonableness, rightness, seemliness, suitableness; conventionality, decency, decorum, demureness, fastidiousness, formality, modesty, properness, respectability.

prorogation *n* adjournment, continuance, postponement.

prosaic *adj* commonplace, dull, flat, humdrum, matter-of-fact, pedestrian, plain, prolix, prosing, sober, stupid, tame, tedious, tiresome, unentertaining, unimaginative, uninspired, uninteresting, unromantic, vapid.

proscribe *vb* banish, doom, exile, expel, ostracize, outlaw; exclude, forbid, interdict, prohibit; censure, condemn, curse, denounce, reject.

prosecute *vb* conduct, continue, exercise, follow, persist, pursue; arraign, indict, sue, summon.

prospect *vb* explore, search, seek, survey. * *n* display, field, landscape, outlook, perspective, scene, show, sight, spectacle, survey, view, vision, vista; picture, scenery; anticipation, calculation, contemplation, expectance, expectancy, expectation, foreseeing, foresight, hope, presumption, promise, trust; likelihood, probability.

prospectus *n* announcement, conspectus, description, design, outline, plan, programme, sketch, syllabus.

prosper *vb* aid, favour, forward, help; advance, flourish, grow rich, thrive, succeed; batten, increase.

prosperity *n* affluence, blessings, happiness, felicity, good luck, success, thrift, weal, welfare, well-being; boom, heyday.

prosperous *adj* blooming, flourishing, fortunate, golden, halcyon, rich, successful, thriving; auspicious, booming, bright, favourable, good, golden, lucky, promising, propitious, providential, rosy.

prostrate *vb* demolish, destroy, fell, level, overthrow, overturn, ruin; depress, exhaust, overcome, reduce. * *adj* fallen, prostrated, prone, recumbent, supine; helpless, powerless.

prostration *n* demolition, destruction, overthrow; dejection, depression, exhaustion.

prosy *adj* prosaic, unpoetic, unpoetical; dull, flat, jejune, stupid, tedious, tiresome, unentertaining, unimaginative, uninteresting.

protect *vb* cover, defend, guard, shield; fortify, harbour, house, preserve, save, screen, secure, shelter; champion, countenance, foster, patronize.

protector *n* champion, custodian, defender, guardian, patron, warden.

protest *vb* affirm, assert, asseverate, attest, aver, avow, declare, profess, testify; demur, expostulate, object, remonstrate, repudiate. * *n* complaint, declaration, disapproval, objection, protestation.

prototype *n* archetype, copy, exemplar, example, ideal, model, original, paradigm, precedent, protoplast, type.

protract *vb* continue, extend, lengthen, prolong; defer, delay, postpone.

protrude *vb* beetle, bulge, extend, jut, project.

protuberance *n* bulge, bump, elevation, excrescence, hump, lump, process, projection, prominence, roundness, swelling, tumour.

proud *adj* assuming, conceited, contended, egotistical, overweening, self-conscious, self-satisfied, vain; arrogant, boastful, haughty, high-spirited, highly strung, imperious, lofty, lordly, presumptuous, supercilious, uppish, vainglorious.

prove *vb* ascertain, conform, demonstrate, establish, evidence, evince, justify, manifest, show, substantiate, sustain, verify; assay, check, examine, experiment, test, try.

proverb *n* adage, aphorism, apothegm, byword, dictum, maxim, precept, saw, saying.

proverbial *adj* acknowledged, current, notorious, unquestioned.

provide *vb* arrange, collect, plan, prepare, procure; gather, keep, store; afford, contribute, feed, furnish, produce, stock, supply, yield; cater, purvey; agree, bargain, condition, contract, covenant, engage, stipulate.

provided, providing *conj* granted, if, supposing.

provident *adj* careful, cautious, considerate, discreet, farseeing, forecasting, forehanded, foreseeing, prudent; economical, frugal, thrifty.

province *n* district, domain, region, section, territory, tract; colony, dependency; business, calling, capacity, charge, department, duty, employment, function, office, part, post, sphere; department, division, jurisdiction.

provincial *adj* annexed, appendant, outlying; bucolic, countrified, rude, rural, rustic, unpolished, unrefined; insular, local, narrow. * *n* peasant, rustic, yokel.

provision *n* anticipation, providing; arrangement, care, preparation, readiness; equipment, fund, grist, hoard, reserve, resources, stock, store, supplies, supply; clause, condition, prerequisite, proviso, reservation, stipulation.

provisions *n pl* eatables, fare, food, provender, supplies, viands, victuals.

proviso *n* clause, condition, provision, stipulation.

provocation *n* incentive, incitement, provocativeness, stimulant, stimulus; affront, indignity, insult, offence; angering, vexation.

provoke *vb* animate, arouse, awaken, excite, impel, incite, induce, inflame, instigate, kindle, move, rouse, stimulate; affront, aggravate, anger, annoy, chafe, enrage, exacerbate, exasperate, incense, infuriate, irritate, nettle, offend, pique, vex; cause, elicit, evoke, instigate, occasion, produce, promote.

provoking *adj* aggravating, annoying, exasperating, irritating, offensive, tormenting, vexatious, vexing.

prowess *n* bravery, courage, daring, fearlessness, gallantry, heroism, intrepidity, valour; aptitude, dexterity, expertness, facility.

proximity *n* adjacency, contiguity, nearness, neighbourhood, propinquity, vicinage, vicinity.

proxy *n* agent, attorney, commissioner, delegate, deputy, lieutenant, representative, substitute.

prudence *n* carefulness, caution, circumspection, common sense, considerateness, discretion, forecast, foresight, judgment, judiciousness, policy, providence, sense, tact, wariness, wisdom.

prudent *adj* cautious, careful, circumspect, considerate, discreet, foreseeing, heedful, judicious, politic, provident, prudential, wary, wise.

prudish *adj* coy, demure, modest, precise, prim, reserved, strait-laced.

prune *vb* abbreviate, clip, cut, dock, lop, thin, trim; dress, preen.

prurient *adj* covetous, craving, desiring, hankering, itching, lascivious, libidinous, longing, lustful.

pry *vb* examine, ferret, inspect, investigate, peep, peer, question, scrutinize, search; force, lever, prise.

public *adj* civil, common, countrywide, general, national, political, state; known, notorious, open, popular, published, well-known. * *n* citizens, community, country, everyone, general public, masses, nation, people, population; audience, buyers, following, supporters.
publication *n* advertisement, announcement, disclosure, divulgement, divulgence, proclamation, promulgation, report; edition, issue, issuance, printing.
publicity *n* daylight, currency, limelight, notoriety, spotlight; outlet, vent.
publish *vb* advertise, air, bruit, announce, blaze, blazon, broach, communicate, declare, diffuse, disclose, disseminate, impart, placard, post, proclaim, promulgate, reveal, tell, utter, vent, ventilate.
pucker *vb* cockle, contract, corrugate, crease, crinkle, furrow, gather, pinch, purse, shirr, wrinkle. * *n* crease, crinkle, fold, furrow, wrinkle.
puerile *adj* boyish, childish, infantile, juvenile, youthful; foolish, frivolous, idle, nonsensical, petty, senseless, silly, simple, trifling, trivial, weak.
puffy *adj* distended, swelled, swollen, tumid, turgid; bombastic, extravagant, inflated, pompous.
pugnacious *adj* belligerent, bellicose, contentious, fighting, irascible, irritable, petulant, quarrelsome.
puissant *adj* forcible, mighty, potent, powerful, strong.
pull *vb* drag, draw, haul, row, tow, tug; cull, extract, gather, pick, pluck; detach, rend, tear, wrest. * *n* pluck, shake, tug, twitch, wrench; contest, struggle; attraction, gravity, magnetism; graft, influence, power.
pulsate *vb* beat, palpitate, pant, throb, thump, vibrate.
pulverize *vb* bruise, comminute, grind, levigate, triturate.
pun *vb* assonate, alliterate, play on words. * *n* assonance, alliteration, clinch, conceit, double-meaning, paranomasia, play on words, quip, rhyme, witticism, wordplay.
punctilious *adj* careful, ceremonious, conscientious, exact, formal, nice, particular, precise, punctual, scrupulous, strict.
punctual *adj* exact, nice, precise, punctilious; early, prompt, ready, regular, seasonable, timely.
puncture *vb* bore, penetrate, perforate, pierce, prick. * *n* bite, hole, sting, wound.
pungent *adj* acid, acrid, biting, burning, caustic, hot, mordant, penetrating, peppery, piercing, piquant, prickling, racy, salty, seasoned, sharp, smart, sour, spicy, stimulating, stinging; acute, acrimonious, cutting, distressing, irritating, keen, painful, peevish, poignant, pointed, satirical, severe, tart, trenchant, waspish.
punish *vb* beat, castigate, chasten, chastise, correct, discipline, flog, lash, scourge, torture, whip.
punishment *n* castigation, chastening, chastisement, correction, discipline, infliction, retribution, scourging, trial; judgment, nemesis, penalty.
puny *adj* feeble, inferior, weak; dwarf, dwarfish, insignificant, diminutive, little, petty, pygmy, small, stunted, tiny, underdeveloped, undersized.
pupil *n* beginner, catechumen, disciple, learner, neophyte, novice, scholar, student, tyro.
pupillage *n* minority, nonage, tutelage, wardship.
puppet *n* doll, image, manikin, marionette; cat's-paw, pawn, tool.
purchase *vb* buy, gain, get, obtain, pay for, procure; achieve, attain, earn, win. * *n* acquisition, buy, gain, possession, property; advantage, foothold, grasp, hold, influence, support.
pure *adj* clean, clear, fair, immaculate, spotless, stainless, unadulterated, unalloyed, unblemished, uncorrupted, undefiled, unpolluted, unspotted, unstained, unsullied, untainted, untarnished; chaste, continent, guileless, guiltless, holy, honest, incorrupt, innocent, modest, sincere, true, uncorrupt, upright, virgin, virtuous; genuine, perfect, real, simple, true, unadorned; absolute, essential, mere, sheer, thorough; classic, classical.
purge *vb* cleanse, clear, purify; clarify, defecate, evacuate; deterge, scour; absolve, pardon, shrive. * *n* elimination, eradication, expulsion, removal, suppression; cathartic, emetic, enema, laxative, physic.
purify *vb* clean, cleanse, clear, depurate, expurgate, purge, refine, wash; clarify, fine.
puritanical *adj* ascetic, narrow-minded, overscrupulous, prim, prudish, rigid, severe, strait-laced, strict.
purity *n* clearness, fineness; cleanness, correctness, faultlessness, immaculacy, immaculateness; guilelessness, guiltlessness, holiness, honesty, innocence, integrity, piety, simplicity, truth, uprightness, virtue; excellence, genuineness; homogeneity, simpleness; chasteness, chastity, continence, modesty, pudency, virginity.
purlieus *n pl* borders, bounds, confines, environs, limits, neighbourhood, outskirts, precincts, suburbs, vicinage, vicinity.
purloin *vb* abstract, crib, filch, pilfer, rob, steal, thieve.
purport *vb* allege, assert, claim, maintain, pretend, profess; denote, express, imply, indicate, mean, signify, suggest. * *n* bearing, current, design, drift, gist, import, intent, meaning, scope, sense, significance, signification, spirit, tendency, tenor.
purpose *vb* contemplate, design, intend, mean, meditate; determine, resolve. * *n* aim, design, drift, end, intent, intention, object, resolution, resolve, view; plan, project; meaning, purport, sense; consequence, effect.
pursue *vb* chase, dog, follow, hound, hunt, shadow, track; conduct, continue, cultivate, maintain, practise, prosecute; seek, strive; accompany, attend.
pursuit *n* chase, hunt, race; conduct, cultivation, practice, prosecution, pursuance; avocation, calling, business, employment, fad, hobby, occupation, vocation.
pursy *adj* corpulent, fat, fleshy, plump, podgy, pudgy, short, thick; short-breathed, short-winded; opulent, rich.
purview *n* body, compass, extent, limit, reach, scope, sphere, view.
push *vb* elbow, crowd, hustle, impel, jostle, shoulder, shove, thrust; advance, drive, hurry, propel, urge; importune, persuade, tease. * *n* pressure, thrust; determination, perseverance; emergency, exigency, extremity, pinch, strait, test, trial; assault, attack, charge, endeavour, onset.
pusillanimous *adj* chicken, chicken-hearted, cowardly, dastardly, faint-hearted, feeble, lily-livered, mean-spirited, spiritless, timid, recreant, timorous, weak.
pustule *n* abscess, blain, blister, blotch, boil, fester, gathering, pimple, sore, ulcer.
put *vb* bring, collocate, deposit, impose, lay, locate, place, set; enjoin, impose, inflict, levy; offer, present, propose, state; compel, constrain, force, oblige; entice, incite, induce, urge; express, utter.
putative *adj* deemed, reckoned, reported, reputed, supposed.
putrefy *vb* corrupt, decay, decompose, fester, rot, stink.
putrid *adj* corrupt, decayed, decomposed, fetid, rank, rotten, stinking.
puzzle *vb* bewilder, confound, confuse, embarrass, gravel, mystify, nonplus, perplex, pose, stagger; complicate, entangle.* *n* conundrum, enigma, labyrinth, maze, paradox, poser, problem, riddle; bewilderment, complication, confusion, difficulty, dilemma, embarrassment, mystification, perplexity, point, quandary, question.
pygmy *adj* diminutive, dwarf, dwarfish, Lilliputian, little, midget, stunted, tiny. * *n* dwarf, Lilliputian, midget.

Q

quack[1] *vb, n* cackle, cry, squeak.
quack[2] *adj* fake, false, sham. * *n* charlatan, empiric, humbug, impostor, mountebank, pretender.
quadruple *adj* fourfold, quadruplicate.
quagmire *n* bog, fen, marsh, morass, slough, swamp; difficulty, impasse, muddle, predicament.
quail *vb* blench, cower, droop, faint, flinch, shrink, tremble.
quaint *adj* antiquated, antique, archaic, curious, droll, extraordinary, fanciful, odd, old-fashioned, queer, singular, uncommon, unique, unusual; affected, fantastic, far-fetched, whimsical; artful, ingenious.

quake *vb* quiver, shake, shiver, shudder; move, vibrate. * *n* earthquake, shake, shudder.

qualification *n* ability, accomplishment, capability, competency, eligibility, fitness, suitability; condition, exception, limitation, modification, proviso, restriction, stipulation; abatement, allowance, diminution, mitigation.

qualified *adj* accomplished, certificated, certified, competent, fitted, equipped, licensed, trained; adapted, circumscribed, conditional, limited, modified, restricted.

qualify *vb* adapt, capacitate, empower, entitle, equip, fit; limit, modify, narrow, restrain, restrict; abate, assuage, ease, mitigate, moderate, reduce, soften; diminish, modulate, temper, regulate, vary.

quality *n* affection, attribute, characteristic, colour, distinction, feature, flavour, mark, nature, peculiarity, property, singularity, timbre, tinge, trait; character, condition, disposition, humour, mood, temper; brand, calibre, capacity, class, description, excellence, grade, kind, rank, sort, stamp, standing, station, status, virtue; aristocracy, gentility, gentry, noblesse, nobility.

qualm *n* agony, pang, throe; nausea, queasiness, sickness; compunction, remorse, uneasiness, twinge.

quandary *n* bewilderment, difficulty, dilemma, doubt, embarrassment, perplexity, pickle, plight, predicament, problem, puzzle, strait, uncertainty.

quantity *n* content, extent, greatness, measure, number, portion, share, size; aggregate, batch, amount, bulk, lot, mass, quantum, store, sum, volume; duration, length.

quarrel *vb* altercate, bicker, brawl, carp, cavil, clash, contend, differ, dispute, fight, jangle, jar, scold, scuffle, spar, spat, squabble, strive, wrangle. * *n* altercation, affray, bickering, brawl, breach, breeze, broil, clash, contention, contest, controversy, difference, disagreement, discord, dispute, dissension, disturbance, feud, fight, fray, imbroglio, jar, miff, misunderstanding, quarrelling, row, rupture, spat, squabble, strife, tiff, tumult, variance, wrangle.

quarrelsome *adj* argumentative, choleric, combative, contentious, cross, discordant, disputatious, dissentious, fiery, irascible, irritable, petulant, pugnacious, ugly, wranglesome.

quarter *vb* billet, lodge, post, station; allot, furnish, share. * *n* abode, billet, dwelling, habitation, lodgings, posts, quarters, stations; direction, district, locality, location, lodge, position, region, territory; clemency, mercy, mildness.

quash *vb* abate, abolish, annul, cancel, invalidate, nullify, overthrow; crush, extinguish, repress, stop, subdue, suppress.

queasy *adj* nauseated, pukish, seasick, sick, squeamish.

queer *vb* botch, harm, impair, mar, spoil. * *adj* curious, droll, extraordinary, fantastic, odd, peculiar, quaint, singular, strange, uncommon, unusual, whimsical; gay, homosexual.

quell *vb* conquer, crush, overcome, overpower, subdue; bridle, check, curb, extinguish, lay, quench, rein in, repress, restrain, stifle; allay, calm, compose, hush, lull, pacify, quiet, quieten, still, tranquillize; alleviate, appease, blunt, deaden, dull, mitigate, mollify, soften, soothe.

quench *vb* extinguish, put out; check, destroy, repress, satiate, stifle, still, suppress; allay, cool, dampen, extinguish, slake.

querulous *adj* bewailing, complaining, cross, discontented, dissatisfied, fretful, fretting, irritable, mourning, murmuring, peevish, petulant, plaintive, touchy, whining.

query *vb* ask, enquire, inquire, question; dispute, doubt. * *n* enquiry, inquiry, interrogatory, issue, problem, question.

quest *n* expedition, journey, search, voyage; pursuit, suit; examination, enquiry, inquiry; demand, desire, invitation, prayer, request, solicitation.

question *vb* ask, catechize, enquire, examine, inquire, interrogate, quiz, sound out; doubt, query; challenge, dispute. * *n* examination, enquiry, inquiry, interpellation, interrogation; enquiry, inquiry, interrogatory, query; debate, discussion, disquisition, examination, investigation, issue, trial; controversy, dispute, doubt; motion, mystery, point, poser, problem, proposition, puzzle, topic.

questionable *adj* ambiguous, controversial, controvertible, debatable, doubtful, disputable, equivocal, problematic, problematical, suspicious, uncertain, undecided.

quibble *vb* cavil, equivocate, evade, prevaricate, shuffle. * *n* equivocation, evasion, pretence, prevarication, quirk, shift, shuffle, sophism, subtlety, subterfuge.

quick *adj* active, agile, alert, animated, brisk, lively, nimble, prompt, ready, smart, sprightly; expeditious, fast, fleet, flying, hurried, rapid, speedy, swift; adroit, apt, clever, dextrous, expert, skilful; choleric, hasty, impetuous, irascible, irritable, passionate, peppery, petulant, precipitate, sharp, unceremonious, testy, touchy, waspish; alive, animate, live, living.

quicken *vb* animate, energize, resuscitate, revivify, vivify; cheer, enliven, invigorate, reinvigorate, revive, whet; accelerate, dispatch, expedite, hasten, hurry, speed; actuate, excite, incite, kindle, refresh, sharpen, stimulate; accelerate, live, take effect.

quickly *adv* apace, fast, immediately, nimbly, quick, rapidly, readily, soon, speedily, swiftly.

quickness *n* celerity, dispatch, expedition, haste, rapidity, speed, swiftness, velocity; agility, alertness, activity, briskness, liveliness, nimbleness, promptness, readiness, smartness; adroitness, aptitude, aptness, dexterity, facility, knack; acumen, acuteness, keenness, penetration, perspicacity, sagacity, sharpness, shrewdness.

quiescent *adj* at rest, hushed, motionless, quiet, resting, still; calm, mute, placid, quiet, serene, still, tranquil, unagitated, undisturbed, unruffled.

quiet *adj* hushed, motionless, quiescent, still, unmoved; calm, contented, gentle, mild, meek, modest, peaceable, peaceful, placid, silent, smooth, tranquil, undemonstrative, unobtrusive, unruffled; patient; retired, secluded. * *n* calmness, peace, repose, rest, silence, stillness.

quieten *vb* arrest, discontinue, intermit, interrupt, still, stop, suspend; allay, appease, calm, compose, lull, pacify, sober, soothe, tranquillize; hush, silence; alleviate, assuage, blunt, dull, mitigate, moderate, mollify, soften.

quip *n* crank, flout, gibe, jeer, mock, quirk, repartee, retort, sarcasm, sally, scoff, sneer, taunt, witticism.

quit *vb* absolve, acquit, deliver, free, release; clear, deliver, discharge from, free, liberate, relieve; acquit, behave, conduct; carry through, perform; discharge, pay, repay, requite; relinquish, renounce, resign, stop, surrender; depart from, leave, withdraw from; abandon, desert, forsake, forswear. * *adj* absolved, acquitted, clear, discharged, free, released.

quite *adv* completely, entirely, exactly, perfectly, positively, precisely, totally, wholly.

quiver *vb* flicker, flutter, oscillate, palpitate, quake, play, shake, shiver, shudder, tremble, twitch, vibrate. * *n* shake, shiver, shudder, trembling.

quixotic *adj* absurd, chimerical, fanciful, fantastic, fantastical, freakish, imaginary, mad, romantic, utopian, visionary, wild.

quiz *vb* examine, question, test; peer at; banter, hoax, puzzle, ridicule. * *n* enigma, hoax, jest, joke, puzzle; jester, joker, hoax.

quota *n* allocation, allotment, apportionment, contingent, portion, proportion, quantity, share.

quotation *n* citation, clipping, cutting, extract, excerpt, reference, selection; estimate, rate, tender.

quote *vb* adduce, cite, excerpt, extract, illustrate, instance, name, repeat, take; estimate, tender.

R

rabble *n* commonality, horde, mob, populace, riffraff, rout, scum, trash.

rabid *adj* frantic, furious, mad, raging, wild; bigoted, fanatical, intolerant, irrational, narrow-minded, rampant.

race[1] *n* ancestry, breed, family, generation, house, kindred, line, lineage, pedigree, stock, strain; clan, folk, nation, people, tribe; breed, children, descendants, issue, offspring, progeny, stock.

race[2] *vb* career, compete, contest, course, hasten, hurry, run, speed. * *n* career, chase, competition, contest, course, dash, heat, match, pursuit, run, sprint; flavour, quality, smack, strength, taste.

rack *vb* agonize, distress, excruciate, rend, torment, torture, wring; exhaust, force, harass, oppress, strain, stretch, wrest. * *n* agony, anguish, pang, torment, torture; crib, manger; neck, crag; dampness, mist, moisture, vapour.

racket *n* clamour, clatter, din, dissipation, disturbance, fracas, frolic, hubbub, noise, outcry, tumult, uproar; game, graft, scheme, understanding.

racy *adj* flavoursome, palatable, piquant, pungent, rich, spicy, strong; forcible, lively, pungent, smart, spirited, stimulating, vigorous, vivacious.

radiance *n* brightness, brilliance, brilliancy, effluence, efflux, emission, glare, glitter, light, lustre, refulgence, resplendence, shine, splendour.

radiant *adj* beaming, brilliant, effulgent, glittering, glorious, luminous, lustrous, resplendent, shining, sparkling, splendid; ecstatic, happy, pleased.

radiate *vb* beam, gleam, glitter, shine; emanate, emit; diffuse, spread.

radical *adj* constitutional, deep-seated, essential, fundamental, ingrained, inherent, innate, native, natural, organic, original, uncompromising; original, primitive, simple, uncompounded, underived; complete, entire, extreme, fanatic, insurgent, perfect, rebellious, thorough, total. * *n* etymon, radix, root; fanatic, revolutionary.

rage *vb* bluster, boil, chafe, foam, fret, fume, ravage, rave. * *n* excitement, frenzy, fury, madness, passion, rampage, raving, vehemence, wrath; craze, fashion, mania, mode, style, vogue.

ragged *adj* rent, tattered, torn; contemptible, mean, poor, shabby; jagged, rough, rugged, shaggy, uneven; discordant, dissonant, inharmonious, unmusical.

raid *vb* assault, forage, invade, pillage, plunder. * *n* attack, foray, invasion, inroad, plunder.

rail *vb* abuse, censure, inveigh, scoff, scold, sneer, upbraid.

raillery *n* banter, chaff, irony, joke, pleasantry, ridicule, satire.

raiment *n* array, apparel, attire, clothes, clothing, costume, dress, garb, garments, habiliment, habit, vestments, vesture.

rain *vb* drizzle, drop, fall, pour, shower, sprinkle, teem; bestow, lavish. * *n* cloudburst, downpour, drizzle, mist, shower, sprinkling.

raise *vb* boost, construct, erect, heave, hoist, lift, uplift, upraise, rear; advance, elevate, ennoble, exalt, promote; aggravate, amplify, augment, enhance, heighten, increase, invigorate; arouse, awake, cause, effect, excite, originate, produce, rouse, stir up, occasion, start; assemble, collect, get, levy, obtain; breed, cultivate, grow, propagate, rear; ferment, leaven, work.

rake[1] *vb* collect, comb, gather, scratch; ransack, scour.

rake[2] *n* debauchee, libertine, profligate, roué.

rakish *adj* debauched, dissipated, dissolute, lewd, licentious; cavalier, jaunty.

ramble *vb* digress, maunder, range, roam, rove, saunter, straggle, stray, stroll, wander. * *n* excursion, rambling, roving, tour, trip, stroll, wandering.

rambling *adj* discursive, irregular; straggling, strolling, wandering.

ramification *n* arborescence, branching, divarication, forking, radiation; branch, division, offshoot, subdivision; consequence, upshot.

ramify *vb* branch, divaricate, extend, separate.

rampant *adj* excessive, exuberant, luxuriant, rank, wanton; boisterous, dominant, headstrong, impetuous, predominant, raging, uncontrollable, unbridled, ungovernable, vehement, violent.

rampart *n* bulwark, circumvallation, defence, fence, fortification, guard, security, wall.

rancid *adj* bad, fetid, foul, fusty, musty, offensive, rank, sour, stinking, tainted.

rancorous *adj* bitter, implacable, malevolent, malicious, malign, malignant, resentful, spiteful, vindictive, virulent.

rancour *n* animosity, antipathy, bitterness, enmity, gall, grudge, hate, hatred, ill-will, malevolence, malice, malignity, spite, venom, vindictiveness.

random *adj* accidental, casual, chance, fortuitous, haphazard, irregular, stray, wandering.

range *vb* course, cruise, extend, ramble, roam, rove, straggle, stray, stroll, wander; bend, lie, run; arrange, class, dispose, rank. * *n* file, line, row, rank, tier; class, kind, order, sort; excursion, expedition, ramble, roving, wandering; amplitude, bound, command, compass, distance, extent, latitude, reach, scope, sweep, view; register.

rank[1] *vb* arrange, class, classify, range. * *n* file, line, order, range, row, tier; class, division, group, order, series; birth, blood, caste, degree, estate, grade, position, quality, sphere, stakes, standing; dignity, distinction, eminence, nobility.

rank[2] *adj* dense, exuberant, luxuriant, overabundant, overgrown, vigorous, wild; excessive, extreme, extravagant, flagrant, gross, rampant, sheer, unmitigated, utter, violent; fetid, foul, fusty, musty, offensive, rancid; fertile, productive, rich; coarse, disgusting.

ransack *vb* pillage, plunder, ravage, rifle, sack, strip; explore, overhaul, rummage, search thoroughly.

ransom *vb* deliver, emancipate, free, liberate, redeem, rescue, unfetter. * *n* money, payment pay-off, price; deliverance, liberation, redemption, release.

rant *vb* declaim, mouth, spout, vociferate. * *n* bombast, cant, exaggeration, fustian.

rapacious *adj* predacious, preying, raptorial; avaricious, grasping, greedy, ravenous, voracious.

rapid *adj* fast, fleet, quick, swift; brisk, expeditious, hasty, hurried, quick, speedy.

rapine *n* depredation, pillage, plunder, robbery, spoliation.

rapt *adj* absorbed, charmed, delighted, ecstatic, engrossed, enraptured, entranced, fascinated, inspired, spellbound.

rapture *vb* enrapture, ravish, transport. * *n* delight, exultation, enthusiasm, rhapsody; beatification, beatitude, bliss, ecstasy, felicity, happiness, joy, spell, transport.

rare[1] *adj* sparse, subtle, thin; extraordinary, infrequent, scarce, singular, strange, uncommon, unique, unusual; choice, excellent, exquisite, fine, incomparable, inimitable.

rare[2] *adj* bloody, underdone.

rarity *n* attenuation, ethereality, etherealness, rarefaction, rareness, tenuity, tenuousness, thinness; infrequency, scarcity, singularity, sparseness, uncommonness, unwontedness.

rascal *n* blackguard, caitiff, knave, miscreant, rogue, reprobate, scallywag, scapegrace, scamp, scoundrel, vagabond, villain.

rash[1] *adj* adventurous, audacious, careless, foolhardy, hasty, headlong, headstrong, heedless, incautious, inconsiderate, indiscreet, injudicious, impetuous, impulsive, incautious, precipitate, quick, rapid, reckless, temerarious, thoughtless, unguarded, unwary, venturesome.

rash[2] *n* breaking-out, efflorescence, eruption; epidemic, flood, outbreak, plague, spate.

rashness *n* carelessness, foolhardiness, hastiness, heedlessness, inconsideration, indiscretion, precipitation, recklessness, temerity, venturesomeness.

rate[1] *vb* appraise, compute, estimate, value. * *n* cost, price; class, degree, estimate, rank, value, valuation, worth; proportion, ration; assessment, charge, impost, tax.

rate[2] *vb* abuse, berate, censure, chide, criticize, find fault, reprimand, reprove, scold.

ratify *vb* confirm, corroborate, endorse, establish, seal, settle, substantiate; approve, bind, consent, sanction.

ration *vb* apportion, deal, distribute, dole, restrict. * *n* allowance, portion, quota, share.

rational *adj* intellectual, reasoning; equitable, fair, fit, just, moderate, natural, normal, proper, reasonable, right; discreet, enlightened, intelligent, judicious, sagacious, sensible, sound, wise.

raucous *adj* harsh, hoarse, husky, rough.

ravage *vb* consume, desolate, despoil, destroy, devastate, harry, overrun, pillage, plunder, ransack, ruin, sack, spoil, strip, waste. * *n* desolation, despoilment, destruction, devastation, havoc, pillage, plunder, rapine, ruin, spoil, waste.

ravenous *adj* devouring, ferocious, gluttonous, greedy, insatiable, omnivorous, ravening, rapacious, voracious.

ravine *n* canyon, cleft, defile, gap, gorge, gulch, gully, pass.

raving *adj* delirious, deranged, distracted, frantic, frenzied, furious, infuriated, mad, phrenetic, raging. * *n* delirium, frenzy, fury, madness, rage.

ravish *vb* abuse, debauch, defile, deflower, force, outrage, violate; captivate, charm, delight, enchant, enrapture, entrance, overjoy, transport; abduct, kidnap, seize, snatch, strip.

raw *adj* fresh, inexperienced, unpractised, unprepared, unseasoned, untried, unskilled; crude, green, immature, unfinished, unripe; bare, chafed, excoriated, galled, sensitive, sore; bleak, chilly, cold, cutting, damp, piercing, windswept; uncooked.

ray *n* beam, emanation, gleam, moonbeam, radiance, shaft, streak, sunbeam.

raze *vb* demolish, destroy, dismantle, extirpate, fell, level, overthrow, ruin, subvert; efface, erase, obliterate.

reach *vb* extend, stretch; grasp, hit, strike, touch; arrive at, attain, gain, get, obtain, win. * *n* capability, capacity, grasp.

readily *adv* easily, promptly, quickly; cheerfully, willingly.

readiness *n* alacrity, alertness, expedition, quickness, promptitude, promptness; aptitude, aptness, dexterity, easiness, expertness, facility, quickness, skill; preparation, preparedness, ripeness; cheerfulness, disposition, eagerness, ease, willingness.

ready *vb* arrange, equip, organize, prepare. * *adj* alert, expeditious, prompt, quick, punctual, speedy; adroit, apt, clever, dextrous, expert, facile, handy, keen, nimble, prepared, prompt, ripe, quick, sharp, skilful, smart; cheerful, disposed, eager, free, inclined, willing; accommodating, available, convenient, near, handy; easy, facile, fluent, offhand, opportune, short, spontaneous.

real *adj* absolute, actual, certain, literal, positive, practical, substantial, substantive, veritable; authentic, genuine, true; essential, internal, intrinsic.

realize *vb* accomplish, achieve, discharge, effect, effectuate, perfect, perform; apprehend, comprehend, experience, recognize, understand; externalize, substantiate; acquire, earn, gain, get, net, obtain, produce, sell.

reality *n* actuality, certainty, fact, truth, verity.

really *adv* absolutely, actually, certainly, indeed, positively, truly, verily, veritably.

reap *vb* acquire, crop, gain, gather, get, harvest, obtain, receive.

rear[1] *adj* aft, back, following, hind, last. * *n* background, reverse, setting; heel, posterior, rear end, rump, stern, tail; path, trail, train, wake.

rear[2] *vb* construct, elevate, erect, hoist, lift, raise; cherish, educate, foster, instruct, nourish, nurse, nurture, train; breed, grow; rouse, stir up.

reason *vb* argue, conclude, debate, deduce, draw from, infer, intellectualize, syllogize, think, trace. * *n* faculty, intellect, intelligence, judgement, mind, principle, sanity, sense, thinking, understanding; account, argument, basis, cause, consideration, excuse, explanation, gist, ground, motive, occasion, pretence, proof; aim, design, end, object, purpose; argument, reasoning; common sense, reasonableness, wisdom; equity, fairness, justice, right; exposition, rationale, theory.

reasonable *adj* equitable, fair, fit, honest, just, proper, rational, right, suitable; enlightened, intelligent, judicious, sagacious, sensible, wise; considerable, fair, moderate, tolerable; credible, intellectual, plausible, well-founded; sane, sober, sound; cheap, inexpensive, low-priced.

rebate *vb* abate, bate, blunt, deduct, diminish, lessen, reduce; cut, pare, rabbet. * *n* decrease, decrement, diminution, lessening; allowance, deduction, discount, reduction.

rebel *vb* mutiny, resist, revolt, strike. * *adj* insubordinate, insurgent, mutinous, rebellious. * *n* insurgent, mutineer, traitor.

rebellion *n* anarchy, insubordination, insurrection, mutiny, resistance, revolt, revolution, uprising.

rebellious *adj* contumacious, defiant, disloyal, disobedient, insubordinate, intractable, obstinate, mutinous, rebel, refractory, seditious.

rebuff *vb* check, chide, oppose, refuse, reject, repel, reprimand, resist, snub. * *n* check, defeat, discouragement, opposition, rejection, resistance, snub.

rebuke *vb* blame, censure, chide, lecture, upbraid, reprehend, reprimand, reprove, scold, silence. * *n* blame, censure, chiding, expostulation, remonstrance, reprimand, reprehension, reproach, reproof, reproval; affliction, chastisement, punishment.

recall *vb* abjure, abnegate, annul, cancel, countermand, deny, nullify, overrule, recant, repeal, repudiate, rescind, retract, revoke, swallow, withdraw; commemorate, recollect, remember, retrace, review, revive. * *n* abjuration, abnegation, annulment, cancellation, nullification, recantation, repeal, repudiation, rescindment, retraction, revocation, withdrawal; memory, recollection, remembrance, reminiscence.

recant *vb* abjure, annul, disavow, disown, recall, renounce, repudiate, retract, revoke, unsay.

recapitulate *vb* epitomize, recite, rehearse, reiterate, repeat, restate, review, summarize.

recede *vb* desist, ebb, retire, regress, retreat, retrograde, return, withdraw.

receive *vb* accept, acquire, derive, gain, get, obtain, take; admit, shelter, take in; entertain, greet, welcome; allow, permit, tolerate; adopt, approve, believe, credit, embrace, follow, learn, understand; accommodate, carry, contain, hold, include, retain; bear, encounter, endure, experience, meet, suffer, sustain.

recent *adj* fresh, new, novel; latter, modern, young; deceased, foregoing, late, preceding, retiring.

reception *n* acceptance, receipt, receiving; entertainment, greeting, welcome; levee, soiree, party; admission, credence; belief, credence, recognition.

recess *n* alcove, corner, depth, hollow, niche, nook, privacy, retreat, seclusion; break, holiday, intermission, interval, respite, vacation; recession, retirement, retreat, withdrawal.

reciprocal *adj* alternate, commutable, complementary, correlative, correspondent, mutual.

recital *n* rehearsal, repetition, recitation; account, description, detail, explanation, narration, relation, statement, telling.

recite *vb* declaim, deliver, rehearse, repeat; describe, mention, narrate, recount, relate, tell; count, detail, enumerate, number, recapitulate.

reckless *adj* breakneck, careless, desperate, devil-may-care, flighty, foolhardy, giddy, harebrained, headlong, heedless, inattentive, improvident, imprudent, inconsiderate, indifferent, indiscreet, mindless, negligent, rash, regardless, remiss, thoughtless, temerarious, uncircumspect, unconcerned, unsteady, volatile, wild.

reckon *vb* calculate, cast, compute, consider, count, enumerate, guess, number; account, class, esteem, estimate, regard, repute, value.

reckoning *n* calculation, computation, consideration, counting; account, bill, charge, estimate, register, score; arrangement, settlement.

reclaim *vb* amend, correct, reform; recover, redeem, regenerate, regain, reinstate, restore; civilize, tame.

recline *vb* couch, lean, lie, lounge, repose, rest.

recluse *adj* anchoritic, anchoritical, cloistered, eremitic, eremitical, hermitic, hermitical, reclusive, solitary. * *n* anchorite, ascetic, eremite, hermit, monk, solitary.

reclusive *adj* recluse, retired, secluded, sequestered, sequestrated, solitary.

recognition *n* identification, memory, recollection, remembrance; acknowledgement, appreciation, avowal, comprehension, confession, notice; allowance, concession.

recognize *vb* apprehend, identify, perceive, remember; acknowledge, admit, avow, confess, own; allow, concede, grant; greet, salute.

recoil *vb* react, rebound, reverberate; retire, retreat, withdraw; blench, fail, falter, quail, shrink. * *n* backstroke, boomerang, elasticity, kick, reaction, rebound, repercussion, resilience, revulsion, ricochet, shrinking.

recollect *vb* recall, remember, reminisce.
recollection *n* memory, remembrance, reminiscence.
recommend *vb* approve, commend, endorse, praise, sanction; commit; advise, counsel, prescribe, suggest.
recommendation *n* advocacy, approbation, approval, commendation, counsel, credential, praise, testimonial.
recompense *vb* compensate, remunerate, repay, requite, reward, satisfy; indemnify, redress, reimburse. * *n* amends, compensation, indemnification, indemnity, remuneration, repayment, reward, satisfaction; requital, retribution.
reconcilable *adj* appeasable, forgiving, placable; companionable, congruous, consistent.
reconcile *vb* appease, conciliate, pacify, placate, propitiate, reunite; content, harmonize, regulate; adjust, compose, heal, settle.
recondite *adj* concealed, dark, hidden, mystic, mystical, obscure, occult, secret, transcendental.
record *vb* chronicle, enter, note, register. * *n* account, annals, archive, chronicle, diary, docket, enrolment, entry, file, list, minute, memoir, memorandum, memorial, note, proceedings, register, registry, report, roll, score; mark, memorial, relic, trace, track, trail, vestige; memory, remembrance; achievement, career, history.
recount *vb* describe, detail, enumerate, mention, narrate, particularize, portray, recite, relate, rehearse, report, tell.
recover *vb* recapture, reclaim, regain; rally, recruit, repair, retrieve; cure, heal, restore, revive; redeem, rescue, salvage, save; convalesce, recuperate.
recreant *adj* base, cowardly, craven, dastardly, faint-hearted, mean-spirited, pusillanimous, yielding; apostate, backsliding, faithless, false, perfidious, treacherous, unfaithful, untrue. * *n* coward, dastard; apostate, backslider, renegade.
recreation *n* amusement, cheer, diversion, entertainment, fun, game, leisure, pastime, play, relaxation, sport.
recreational *adj* amusing, diverting, entertaining, refreshing, relaxing, relieving.
recruit *vb* repair, replenish; recover, refresh, regain, reinvigorate, renew, renovate, restore, retrieve, revive, strengthen, supply. * *n* auxiliary, beginner, helper, learner, novice, tyro.
rectify *vb* adjust, amend, better, correct, emend, improve, mend, redress, reform, regulate, straighten.
rectitude *n* conscientiousness, equity, goodness, honesty, integrity, justice, principle, probity, right, righteousness, straightforwardness, uprightness, virtue.
recumbent *adj* leaning, lying, prone, prostrate, reclining; idle, inactive, listless, reposing.
recur *vb* reappear, resort, return, revert.
recusancy *n* dissent, heresy, heterodoxy, nonconformity.
redeem *vb* reform, regain, repurchase, retrieve; free, liberate, ransom, rescue, save; deliver, reclaim, recover, reinstate; atone, compensate for, recompense; discharge, fulfil, keep, perform, satisfy.
redemption *n* buying, compensation, recovery, repurchase, retrieval; deliverance, liberation, ransom, release, rescue, salvation; discharge, fulfilment, performance.
redolent *adj* aromatic, balmy, fragrant, odoriferous, odorous, scented, sweet, sweet-smelling.
redoubtable *adj* awful, doughty, dreadful, formidable, terrible, valiant.
redound *vb* accrue, conduce, contribute, result, tend.
redress *vb* amend, correct, order, rectify, remedy, repair; compensate, ease, relieve. * *n* abatement, amends, atonement, compensation, correction, cure, indemnification, rectification, repair, righting, remedy, relief, reparation, satisfaction.
reduce *vb* bring; form, make, model, mould, remodel, render, resolve, shape; abate, abbreviate, abridge, attenuate, contract, curtail, decimate, decrease, diminish, lessen, minimize, shorten, thin; abase, debase, degrade, depress, dwarf, impair, lower, weaken; capture, conquer, master, overpower, overthrow, subject, subdue, subjugate, vanquish; impoverish, ruin; resolve, solve.
redundant *adj* copious, excessive, exuberant, fulsome, inordinate, lavish, needless, overflowing, overmuch, plentiful, prodigal, superabundant, replete, superfluous, unnecessary, useless; diffuse, periphrastic, pleonastic, tautological, verbose, wordy.
reel[1] *n* capstan, winch, windlass; bobbin, spool.
reel[2] *vb* falter, flounder, heave, lurch, pitch, plunge, rear, rock, roll, stagger, sway, toss, totter, tumble, wallow, welter, vacillate; spin, swing, turn, twirl, wheel, whirl. * *n* gyre, pirouette, spin, turn, twirl, wheel, whirl.
re-establish *vb* re-found, rehabilitate, reinstall, reinstate, renew, renovate, replace, restore.
refer *vb* commit, consign, direct, leave, relegate, send, submit; ascribe, assign, attribute, impute; appertain, belong, concern, pertain, point, relate, respect, touch; appeal, apply, consult; advert, allude, cite, quote.
referee *vb* arbitrate, judge, umpire. * *n* arbiter, arbitrator, judge, umpire.
reference *n* concern, connection, regard, respect; allusion, ascription, citation, hint, intimation, mark, reference, relegation.
refine *vb* clarify, cleanse, defecate, fine, purify; cultivate, humanize, improve, polish, rarefy, spiritualize.
refined *adj* courtly, cultured, genteel, polished, polite; discerning, discriminating, fastidious, sensitive; filtered, processed, purified.
refinement *n* clarification, filtration, purification, sublimation; betterment, improvement; delicacy, cultivation, culture, elegance, elevation, finish, gentility, good breeding, polish, politeness, purity, spirituality, style.
reflect *vb* copy, imitate, mirror, reproduce; cogitate, consider, contemplate, deliberate, meditate, muse, ponder, ruminate, study, think.
reflection *n* echo, shadow; cogitation, consideration, contemplation, deliberation, idea, meditation, musing, opinion, remark, rumination, thinking, thought; aspersion, blame, censure, criticism, disparagement, reproach, slur.
reflective *adj* reflecting, reflexive; cogitating, deliberating, musing, pondering, reasoning, thoughtful.
reform *vb* amend, ameliorate, better, correct, improve, mend, meliorate, rectify, reclaim, redeem, regenerate, repair, restore; reconstruct, remodel, reshape. * *n* amendment, correction, progress, reconstruction, rectification, reformation.
reformation *n* amendment, emendation, improvement, reform; adoption, conversion, redemption; refashioning, regeneration, reproduction, reconstruction.
refractory *adj* cantankerous, contumacious, cross-grained, disobedient, dogged, headstrong, heady, incoercible, intractable, mulish, obstinate, perverse, recalcitrant, self-willed, stiff, stubborn, sullen, ungovernable, unmanageable, unruly, unyielding.
refrain[1] *vb* abstain, cease, desist, forbear, stop, withhold.
refrain[2] *n* chorus, song, undersong.
refresh *vb* air, brace, cheer, cool, enliven, exhilarate, freshen, invigorate, reanimate, recreate, recruit, reinvigorate, revive, regale, slake.
refreshing *adj* comfortable, cooling, grateful, invigorating, pleasant, reanimating, restful, reviving.
refuge *n* asylum, covert, harbour, haven, protection, retreat, safety, sanction, security, shelter.
refulgent *adj* bright, brilliant, effulgent, lustrous, radiant, resplendent, shining.
refund *vb* reimburse, repay, restore, return. * *n* reimbursement, repayment.
refuse[1] *n* chaff, discard, draff, dross, dregs, garbage, junk, leavings, lees, litter, lumber, offal, recrement, remains, rubbish, scoria, scum, sediment, slag, sweepings, trash, waste.
refuse[2] *vb* decline, deny, withhold; disallow, disavow, exclude, rebuff, reject, renege, renounce, repel, repudiate, repulse, revoke, veto.
refute *vb* confute, defeat, disprove, overcome, overthrow, rebut, repel, silence.

regain *vb* recapture, recover, re-obtain, repossess, retrieve.

regal *adj* imposing, imperial, kingly, noble, royal, sovereign.

regale *vb* delight, entertain, gratify, refresh; banquet, feast.

regard *vb* behold, gaze, look, notice, mark, observe, remark, see, view, watch; attend to, consider, heed, mind, respect; esteem, honour, revere, reverence, value; account, believe, estimate, deem, hold, imagine, reckon, suppose, think, treat, use. * *n* aspect, gaze, look, view; attention, attentiveness, care, concern, consideration, heed, notice, observance; account, reference, relation, respect; admiration, affection, attachment, deference, esteem, estimation, favour, honour, interest, liking, love, respect, reverence, sympathy, value; account, eminence, note, reputation, repute; condition, matter, point.

regardful *adj* attentive, careful, considerate, deferential, heedful, mindful, observing, thoughtful, watchful.

regarding *prep* concerning, respecting, touching.

regardless *adj* careless, disregarding, heedless, inattentive, indifferent, mindless, neglectful, negligent, unconcerned, unmindful, unobservant. * *adv* however, irrespectively, nevertheless, nonetheless, notwithstanding.

regenerate *vb* reproduce; renovate, revive; change, convert, renew, sanctify. * *adj* born-again, converted, reformed, regenerated.

regime *n* administration, government, rule.

region *n* climate, clime, country, district, division, latitude, locale, locality, province, quarter, scene, territory, tract; area, neighbourhood, part, place, portion, spot, space, sphere, terrain, vicinity.

register *vb* delineate, portray, record, show. * *n* annals, archive, catalogue, chronicle, list, record, roll, schedule; clerk, registrar, registry; compass, range.

regret *vb* bewail, deplore, grieve, lament, repine, sorrow; bemoan, repent, mourn, rue. * *n* concern, disappointment, grief, lamentation, rue, sorrow, trouble; compunction, contrition, penitence, remorse, repentance, repining, self-condemnation, self-reproach.

regular *adj* conventional, natural, normal, ordinary, typical; correct, customary, cyclic, established, fixed, habitual, periodic, periodical, recurring, reasonable, rhythmic, seasonal, stated, usual; steady, constant, uniform, even; just, methodical, orderly, punctual, systematic, unvarying; complete, genuine, indubitable, out-and-out, perfect, thorough; balanced, consistent, symmetrical.

regulate *vb* adjust, arrange, dispose, methodize, order, organize, settle, standardize, time, systematize; conduct, control, direct, govern, guide, manage, rule.

regulation *adj* customary, mandatory, official, required, standard. * *n* adjustment, arrangement, control, disposal, disposition, law, management, order, ordering, precept, rule, settlement.

rehabilitate *vb* reinstate, re-establish, restore; reconstruct, reconstitute, reintegrate, reinvigorate, renew, renovate.

rehearsal *n* drill, practice, recital, recitation, repetition; account, history, mention, narration, narrative, recounting, relation, statement, story, telling.

rehearse *vb* recite, repeat; delineate, depict, describe, detail, enumerate, narrate, portray, recapitulate, recount, relate, tell.

reign *vb* administer, command, govern, influence, predominate, prevail, rule. * *n* control, dominion, empire, influence, power, royalty, sovereignty, power, rule, sway.

reimburse *vb* refund, repay, restore; compensate, indemnify, requite, satisfy.

rein *vb* bridle, check, control, curb, guide, harness, hold, restrain, restrict. * *n* bridle, check, curb, harness, restraint, restriction.

reinforce *vb* augment, fortify, strengthen.

reinstate *vb* re-establish, rehabilitate, reinstall, replace, restore.

reject *vb* cashier, discard, dismiss, eject, exclude, pluck; decline, deny, disallow, despise, disapprove, disbelieve, rebuff, refuse, renounce, repel, repudiate, scout, slight, spurn, veto. * *n* cast-off, discard, failure, refusal, repudiation.

rejoice *vb* cheer, delight, enliven, enrapture, exhilarate, gladden, gratify, please, transport; crow, exult, delight, gloat, glory, jubilate, triumph, vaunt.

rejoin *vb* answer, rebut, respond, retort.

relate *vb* describe, detail, mention, narrate, recite, recount, rehearse, report, tell; apply, connect, correlate.

relation *n* account, chronicle, description, detail, explanation, history, mention, narration, narrative, recital, rehearsal, report, statement, story, tale; affinity, application, bearing, connection, correlation, dependency, pertinence, relationship; concern, reference, regard, respect; alliance, nearness, propinquity, rapport; blood, consanguinity, cousinship, kin, kindred, kinship, relationship; kinsman, kinswoman, relative.

relax *vb* loose, loosen, slacken, unbrace, unstrain; debilitate, enervate, enfeeble, prostrate, unbrace, unstring, weaken; abate, diminish, lessen, mitigate, reduce, remit; amuse, divert, ease, entertain, recreate, unbend.

release *vb* deliver, discharge, disengage, exempt, extricate, free, liberate, loose, unloose; acquit, discharge, quit, relinquish, remit. * *n* deliverance, discharge, freedom, liberation; absolution, dispensation, excuse, exemption, exoneration; acquaintance, clearance.

relentless *adj* cruel, hard, impenitent, implacable, inexorable, merciless, obdurate, pitiless, rancorous, remorseless, ruthless, unappeasable, uncompassionate, unfeeling, unforgiving, unmerciful, unpitying, unrelenting, unyielding, vindictive.

relevant *adj* applicable, appropriate, apposite, apt, apropos, fit, germane, pertinent, proper, relative, suitable.

reliable *adj* authentic, certain, constant, dependable, sure, trustworthy, trusty, unfailing.

reliance *n* assurance, confidence, credence, dependence, hope, trust.

relic *n* keepsake, memento, memorial, remembrance, souvenir, token, trophy; trace, vestige.

relics *n pl* fragments, leavings, remainder, remains, remnants, ruins, scraps; body, cadaver, corpse, remains.

relict *n* dowager, widow.

relief *n* aid, alleviation, amelioration, assistance, assuagement, comfort, deliverance, ease, easement, help, mitigation, reinforcement, respite, rest, succour, softening, support; indemnification, redress, remedy; embossment, projection, prominence, protrusion; clearness, distinction, perspective, vividness.

relieve *vb* aid, comfort, help, spell, succour, support, sustain; abate, allay, alleviate, assuage, cure, diminish, ease, lessen, lighten, mitigate, remedy, remove, soothe; indemnify, redress, right, repair; disengage, free, release, remedy, rescue.

religious *adj* devotional, devout, god-fearing, godly, holy, pious, prayerful, spiritual; conscientious, exact, rigid, scrupulous, strict; canonical, divine, theological.

relinquish *vb* abandon, desert, forsake, forswear, leave, quit, renounce, resign, vacate; abdicate, cede, forbear, forgo, give up, surrender, yield.

relish *vb* appreciate, enjoy, like, prefer; season, flavour, taste. * *n* appetite, appreciation, enjoyment, fondness, gratification, gusto, inclination, liking, partiality, predilection, taste, zest; cast, flavour, manner, quality, savour, seasoning, sort, tang, tinge, touch; appetizer, condiment.

reluctance *n* aversion, backwardness, disinclination, dislike, loathing, repugnance, unwillingness.

reluctant *adj* averse, backward, disinclined, hesitant, indisposed, loath, unwilling.

rely *vb* confide, count, depend, hope, lean, reckon, repose, trust.

remain *vb* abide, continue, endure, last; exceed, persist, survive; abide, continue, dwell, halt, inhabit, rest, sojourn, stay, stop, tarry, wait.

remainder *n* balance, excess, leavings, remains, remnant, residue, rest, surplus.

remark *vb* heed, notice, observe, regard; comment, express, mention, observe, say, state, utter. * *n* consideration, heed, notice, observation, regard; annotation, comment, gloss, note, stricture; assertion, averment, comment, declaration, saying, statement, utterance.

remarkable *adj* conspicuous, distinguished, eminent, extraordinary, famous, notable, noteworthy, noticeable, pre-eminent, rare, singular, strange, striking, uncommon, unusual, wonderful.

remedy *vb* cure, heal, help, palliate, relieve; amend, correct, rectify, redress, repair, restore, retrieve. * *n* antidote, antitoxin, corrective, counteractive, cure, help, medicine, nostrum, panacea, restorative, specific; redress, reparation, restitution, restoration; aid, assistance, relief.

remembrance *n* recollection, reminiscence, retrospection; keepsake, memento, memorial, memory, reminder, souvenir, token; consideration, regard, thought.

reminiscence *n* memory, recollection, remembrance, retrospective.

remiss *adj* backward, behindhand, dilatory, indolent, languid, lax, lazy, slack, slow, tardy; careless, dilatory, heedless, idle, inattentive, neglectful, negligent, shiftless, slothful, thoughtless.

remission *n* abatement, decrease, diminution, lessening, mitigation, moderation, reduction, relaxation; cancellation, discharge, release, relinquishment; intermission, interruption, pause, rest, stop, stoppage, suspense, suspension; absolution, acquittal, excuse, exoneration, forgiveness, indulgence, pardon.

remit *vb* replace, restore, return; abate, bate, diminish, relax; release; absolve, condone, excuse, forgive, overlook, pardon; relinquish, resign, surrender; consign, forward, refer, send, transmit. * *n* authorization, brief, instructions, orders.

remnant *n* remainder, remains, residue, rest, trace; fragment, piece, scrap.

remorse *n* compunction, contrition, penitence, qualm, regret, repentance, reproach, self-reproach, sorrow.

remorseless *adj* cruel, barbarous, hard, harsh, implacable, inexorable, merciless, pitiless, relentless, ruthless, savage, uncompassionate, unmerciful, unrelenting.

remote *adj* distant, far, out-of-the-way; alien, far-fetched, foreign, inappropriate, unconnected, unrelated; abstracted, separated; inconsiderable, slight; isolated, removed, secluded, sequestrated.

removal *n* abstraction, departure, dislodgement, displacement, relegation, remove, shift, transference; elimination, extraction, withdrawal; abatement, destruction; discharge, dismissal, ejection, expulsion.

remove *vb* carry, dislodge, displace, shift, transfer, transport; abstract, extract, withdraw; abate, banish, destroy, suppress; cashier, depose, discharge, dismiss, eject, expel, oust, retire; depart, move.

remunerate *vb* compensate, indemnify, pay, recompense, reimburse, repay, requite, reward, satisfy.

remuneration *n* compensation, earnings, indemnity, pay, payment, recompense, reimbursement, reparation, repayment, reward, salary, wages.

remunerative *adj* gainful, lucrative, paying, profitable; compensatory, recompensing, remuneratory, reparative, requiting, rewarding.

rend *vb* break, burst, cleave, crack, destroy, dismember, dissever, disrupt, divide, fracture, lacerate, rive, rupture, sever, shiver, snap, split, sunder, tear.

render *vb* restore, return, surrender; assign, deliver, give, present; afford, contribute, furnish, supply, yield; construe, interpret, translate.

rendition *n* restitution, return, surrender; delineation, exhibition, interpretation, rendering, representation, reproduction; translation, version.

renegade *adj* apostate, backsliding, disloyal, false, outlawed, rebellious, recreant, unfaithful. * *n* apostate, backslider, recreant, turncoat; deserter, outlaw, rebel, revolter, traitor; vagabond, wretch.

renew *vb* rebuild, recreate, re-establish, refit, refresh, rejuvenate, renovate, repair, replenish, restore, resuscitate, revive; continue, recommence, repeat; iterate, reiterate; regenerate, transform.

renounce *vb* abjure, abnegate, decline, deny, disclaim, disown, forswear, neglect, recant, repudiate, reject, slight; abandon, abdicate, drop, forgo, forsake, desert, leave, quit, relinquish, resign.

renovate *vb* reconstitute, re-establish, refresh, refurbish, renew, restore, revamp; reanimate, recreate, regenerate, reproduce, resuscitate, revive, revivify.

renown *n* celebrity, distinction, eminence, fame, figure, glory, honour, greatness, name, note, notability, notoriety, reputation, repute.

renowned *adj* celebrated, distinguished, eminent, famed, famous, honoured, illustrious, remarkable, wonderful.

rent[1] *n* breach, break, crack, cleft, crevice, fissure, flaw, fracture, gap, laceration, opening, rift, rupture, separation, split, tear; schism.

rent[2] *vb* hire, lease, let. * *n* income, rental, revenue.

repair[1] *vb* mend, patch, piece, refit, retouch, tinker, vamp; correct, recruit, restore, retrieve. * *n* mending, refitting, renewal, reparation, restoration.

repair[2] *vb* betake oneself, go, move, resort, turn.

repairable *adj* curable, recoverable, reparable, restorable, retrievable.

reparable *adj* curable, recoverable, repairable, restorable, retrievable.

reparation *n* renewal, repair, restoration; amends, atonement, compensation, correction, indemnification, recompense, redress, requital, restitution, satisfaction.

repay *vb* refund, reimburse, restore, return; compensate, recompense, remunerate, reward, satisfy; avenge, retaliate, revenge.

repeal *vb* abolish, annul, cancel, recall, rescind, reverse, revoke. * *n* abolition, abrogation, annulment, cancellation, rescission, reversal, revocation.

repeat *vb* double, duplicate, iterate; cite, narrate, quote, recapitulate, recite, rehearse; echo, renew, reproduce. * *n* duplicate, duplication, echo, iteration, recapitulation, reiteration, repetition.

repel *vb* beat, disperse, repulse, scatter; check, confront, oppose, parry, rebuff, resist, withstand; decline, refuse, reject; disgust, revolt, sicken.

repellent *adj* abhorrent, disgusting, forbidding, repelling, repugnant, repulsive, revolting, uninviting.

repent *vb* atone, regret, relent, rue, sorrow.

repentance *n* compunction, contriteness, contrition, penitence, regret, remorse, self-accusation, self-condemnation, self-reproach.

repentant *adj* contrite, penitent, regretful, remorseful, rueful, sorrowful, sorry.

repercussion *n* rebound, recoil, reverberation; backlash, consequence, result.

repetition *n* harping, iteration, recapitulation, reiteration; diffuseness, redundancy, tautology, verbosity; narration, recital, rehearsal, relation, retailing; recurrence, renewal.

repine *vb* croak, complain, fret, grumble, long, mope, murmur.

replace *vb* re-establish, reinstate, reset; refund, repay, restore; succeed, supersede, supplant.

replenish *vb* fill, refill, renew, re-supply; enrich, furnish, provide, store, supply.

replete *adj* abounding, charged, exuberant, fraught, full, glutted, gorged, satiated, well-stocked.

repletion *n* abundance, exuberance, fullness, glut, profusion, satiation, satiety, surfeit.

replica *n* autograph, copy, duplicate, facsimile, reproduction.

reply *vb* answer, echo, rejoin, respond. * *n* acknowledgement, answer, rejoinder, repartee, replication, response, retort.

report *vb* announce, annunciate, communicate, declare; advertise, broadcast, bruit, describe, detail, herald, mention, narrate, noise, promulgate, publish, recite, relate, rumour, state, tell; minute, record. * *n* account, announcement, communication, declaration, statement; advice, description, detail, narration, narrative, news, recital, story, tale, talk, tidings; gossip, hearsay, rumour; clap, detonation, discharge, explosion, noise, repercussion, sound; fame, reputation, repute; account, bulletin, minute, note, record, statement.

repose[1] *vb* compose, recline, rest, settle; couch, lie, recline, sleep, slumber; confide, lean. * *n* quiet, recumbence, recumbency, rest, sleep, slumber; breathing time, inactivity, leisure, respite, relaxation; calm, ease, peace, peacefulness, quietness, quietude, stillness, tranquillity.

repose[2] *vb* place, put, stake; deposit, lodge, reposit, store.

repository *n* conservatory, depository, depot, magazine, museum, receptacle, repertory, storehouse, storeroom, thesaurus, treasury, vault.

reprehend *vb* accuse, blame, censure, chide, rebuke, reprimand, reproach, reprove, upbraid.

reprehensible *adj* blameable, blameworthy, censurable, condemnable, culpable, reprovable.

reprehension *n* admonition, blame, censure, condemnation, rebuke, reprimand, reproof.

represent *vb* exhibit, express, show; delineate, depict, describe, draw, portray, sketch; act, impersonate, mimic, personate, personify; exemplify, illustrate, image, reproduce, symbolize, typify.

representation *n* delineation, exhibition, show; impersonation, personation, simulation; account, description, narration, narrative, relation, statement; image, likeness, model, portraiture, resemblance, semblance; sight, spectacle; expostulation, remonstrance.

representative *adj* figurative, illustrative, symbolic, typical; delegated, deputed, representing. * *n* agent, commissioner, delegate, deputy, emissary, envoy, legate, lieutenant, messenger, proxy, substitute.

repress *vb* choke, crush, dull, overcome, overpower, silence, smother, subdue, suppress, quell; bridle, chasten, chastise, check, control, curb, restrain; appease, calm, quiet.

reprimand *vb* admonish, blame, censure, chide, rebuke, reprehend, reproach, reprove, upbraid. * *n* admonition, blame, censure, rebuke, reprehension, reproach, reprobation, reproof, reproval.

reprint *vb* republish. * *n* reimpression, republication; copy.

reproach *vb* blame, censure, rebuke, reprehend, reprimand, reprove, upbraid; abuse, accuse, asperse, condemn, defame, discredit, disparage, revile, traduce, vilify. * *n* abuse, blame, censure, condemnation, contempt, contumely, disapprobation, disapproval, expostulation, insolence, invective, railing, rebuke, remonstrance, reprobation, reproof, reviling, scorn, scurrility, upbraiding, vilification; abasement, discredit, disgrace, dishonour, disrepute, indignity, ignominy, infamy, insult, obloquy, odium, offence, opprobrium, scandal, shame, slur, stigma.

reproachful *adj* abusive, censorious, condemnatory, contemptuous, contumelious, damnatory, insolent, insulting, offensive, opprobrious, railing, reproving, sacrifice, scolding, scornful, scurrilous, upbraiding, vituperative; base, discreditable, disgraceful, dishonourable, disreputable, infamous, scandalous, shameful, vile.

reprobate *vb* censure, condemn, disapprove, discard, reject, reprehend; disallow; abandon, disown. * *adj* abandoned, base, castaway, corrupt, depraved, graceless, hardened, irredeemable, lost, profligate, shameless, vile, vitiated, wicked. * *n* caitiff, castaway, miscreant, outcast, rascal, scamp, scoundrel, sinner, villain.

reproduce *vb* copy, duplicate, emulate, imitate, print, repeat, represent; breed, generate, procreate, propagate.

reproof *n* admonition, animadversion, blame, castigation, censure, chiding, condemnation, correction, criticism, lecture, monition, objurgation, rating, rebuke, reprehension, reprimand, reproach, reproval, upbraiding.

reprove *vb* admonish, blame, castigate, censure, chide, condemn, correct, criticize, inculpate, lecture, objurgate, rate, rebuke, reprimand, reproach, scold, upbraid.

reptilian *adj* abject, crawling, creeping, grovelling, low, mean, treacherous, vile, vulgar.

repudiate *vb* abjure, deny, disavow, discard, disclaim, disown, nullify, reject, renounce.

repugnance *n* contrariety, contrariness, incompatibility, inconsistency, irreconcilability, irreconcilableness, unsuitability, unsuitableness; contest, opposition, resistance, struggle; antipathy, aversion, detestation, dislike, hatred, hostility, reluctance, repulsion, unwillingness.

repugnant *adj* incompatible, inconsistent, irreconcilable; adverse, antagonistic, contrary, hostile, inimical, opposed, opposing, unfavourable; detestable, distasteful, offensive, repellent, repulsive.

repulse *vb* check, defeat, refuse, reject, repel. * *n* repelling, repulsion; denial, refusal; disappointment, failure.

repulsion *n* abhorrence, antagonism, anticipation, aversion, discard, disgust, dislike, hatred, hostility, loathing, rebuff, rejection, repugnance, repulse, spurning.

repulsive *adj* abhorrent, cold, disagreeable, disgusting, forbidding, frigid, harsh, hateful, loathsome, nauseating, nauseous, odious, offensive, repellent, repugnant, reserved, revolting, sickening, ugly, unpleasant.

reputable *adj* creditable, estimable, excellent, good, honourable, respectable, worthy.

reputation *n* account, character, fame, mark, name, repute; celebrity, credit, distinction, eclat, esteem, estimation, glory, honour, prestige, regard, renown, report, respect; notoriety.

repute *vb* account, consider, deem, esteem, estimate, hold, judge, reckon, regard, think.

request *vb* ask, beg, beseech, call, claim, demand, desire, entreat, pray, solicit, supplicate. * *n* asking, entreaty, importunity, invitation, petition, prayer, requisition, solicitation, suit, supplication.

require *vb* beg, beseech, bid, claim, crave, demand, dun, importune, invite, pray, requisition, request, sue, summon; need, want; direct, enjoin, exact, order, prescribe.

requirement *n* claim, demand, exigency, market, need, needfulness, requisite, requisition, request, urgency, want; behest, bidding, charge, command, decree, exaction, injunction, mandate, order, precept.

requisite *adj* essential, imperative, indispensable, necessary, needful, needed, required. * *n* essential, necessity, need, requirement.

requite *vb* compensate, pay, remunerate, reciprocate, recompense, repay, reward, satisfy; avenge, punish, retaliate, satisfy.

rescind *vb* abolish, abrogate, annul, cancel, countermand, quash, recall, repeal, reverse, revoke, vacate, void.

rescue *vb* deliver, extricate, free, liberate, preserve, ransom, recapture, recover, redeem, release, retake, save. * *n* deliverance, extrication, liberation, redemption, release, salvation.

research *vb* analyse, examine, explore, inquire, investigate, probe, study. * *n* analysis, examination, exploration, inquiry, investigation, scrutiny, study.

resemblance *n* affinity, agreement, analogy, likeness, semblance, similarity, similitude; counterpart, facsimile, image, representation.

resemble *vb* compare, liken; copy, counterfeit, imitate.

resentful *adj* angry, bitter, choleric, huffy, hurt, irascible, irritable, malignant, revengeful, sore, touchy.

resentment *n* acrimony, anger, annoyance, bitterness, choler, displeasure, dudgeon, fury, gall, grudge, heartburning, huff, indignation, ire, irritation, pique, rage, soreness, spleen, sulks, umbrage, vexation, wrath.

reservation *n* reserve, suppression; appropriation, booking, exception, restriction, saving; proviso, salvo; custody, park, reserve, sanctuary.

reserve *vb* hold, husband, keep, retain, store. * *adj* alternate, auxiliary, spare, substitute. * *n* reservation; aloofness, backwardness, closeness, coldness, concealment, constraint, suppression, reservedness, retention, restraint, reticence, uncommunicativeness, unresponsiveness; coyness, demureness, modesty, shyness, taciturnity; park, reservation, sanctuary.

reserved *adj* coy, demure, modest, shy, taciturn; aloof, backward, cautious, cold, distant, incommunicative, restrained, reticent, self-controlled, unsociable, unsocial; bespoken, booked, excepted, held, kept, retained, set apart, taken, withheld.

reside *vb* abide, domicile, domiciliate, dwell, inhabit, live, lodge, remain, room, sojourn, stay.

residence *n* inhabitance, inhabitancy, sojourn, stay, stop, tarrying; abode, domicile, dwelling, habitation, home, house, lodging, mansion.

residue *n* leavings, remainder, remains, remnant, residuum, rest; excess, overplus, surplus.

resign *vb* abandon, abdicate, abjure, cede, commit, disclaim, forego, forsake, leave, quit, relinquish, renounce, surrender, yield.

resignation *n* abandonment, abdication, relinquishment, renunciation, retirement, surrender; acquiescence, compliance, endurance, forbearance, fortitude, long-sufferance, patience, submission, sufferance.

resist *vb* assail, attack, baffle, block, check, confront, counteract, disappoint, frustrate, hinder, impede, impugn, neutralize, obstruct, oppose, rebel, rebuff, stand against, stem, stop, strive, thwart, withstand.

resolute *adj* bold, constant, decided, determined, earnest, firm, fixed, game, hardy, inflexible, persevering, pertinacious, relentless, resolved, staunch, steadfast, steady, stout, stouthearted, sturdy, tenacious, unalterable, unbending, undaunted, unflinching, unshaken, unwavering, unyielding.

resolution *n* boldness, disentanglement, explication, unravelling; backbone, constancy, courage, decision, determination, earnestness, energy, firmness, fortitude, grit, hardihood, inflexibility, intention, manliness, pluck, perseverance, purpose, relentlessness, resolve, resoluteness, stamina, steadfastness, steadiness, tenacity.

resolve *vb* analyse, disperse, scatter, separate, reduce; change, dissolve, liquefy, melt, reduce, transform; decipher, disentangle, elucidate, explain, interpret, unfold, solve, unravel; conclude, decide, determine, fix, intend, purpose, will. * *n* conclusion, decision, determination, intention, will; declaration, resolution.

resonant *adj* booming, clangorous, resounding, reverberating, ringing, roaring, sonorous, thundering, vibrant.

resort *vb* frequent, haunt; assemble, congregate, convene, go, repair. * *n* application, expedient, recourse; haunt, refuge, rendezvous, retreat, spa; assembling, confluence, concourse, meeting; recourse, reference.

resound *vb* echo, re-echo, reverberate, ring; celebrate, extol, praise, sound.

resource *n* dependence, resort; appliance, contrivance, device, expedient, instrumentality, means, resort.

resources *npl* capital, funds, income, money, property, reserve, supplies, wealth.

respect *vb* admire, esteem, honour, prize, regard, revere, reverence, spare, value, venerate; consider, heed, notice, observe. * *n* attention, civility, courtesy, consideration, deference, estimation, homage, honour, notice, politeness, recognition, regard, reverence, veneration; consideration, favour, goodwill, kind; aspect, bearing, connection, feature, matter, particular, point, reference, regard, relation.

respects *npl* compliments, greetings, regards.

respectable *adj* considerable, estimable, honourable, presentable, proper, upright, worthy; adequate, moderate; tolerable.

respectful *adj* ceremonious, civil, complaisant, courteous, decorous, deferential, dutiful, formal, polite.

respire *vb* breathe, exhale, live.

respite *vb* delay, relieve, reprieve. * *n* break, cessation, delay, intermission, interval, pause, recess, rest, stay, stop; forbearance, postponement, reprieve.

resplendent *adj* beaming, bright, brilliant, effulgent, lucid, glittering, glorious, gorgeous, luminous, lustrous, radiant, shining, splendid.

respond *vb* answer, reply, rejoin; accord, correspond, suit.

response *n* answer, replication, rejoinder, reply, retort.

responsible *adj* accountable, amenable, answerable, liable, trustworthy.

rest[1] *vb* cease, desist, halt, hold, pause, repose, stop; breathe, relax, unbend; repose, sleep, slumber; lean, lie, lounge, perch, recline, ride; acquiesce, confide, trust; confide, rely, trust; calm, comfort, ease. * *n* fixity, immobility, inactivity, motionlessness, quiescence, quiet, repose; hush, peace, peacefulness, quietness, relief, security, stillness, tranquillity; cessation, intermission, interval, lull, pause, relaxation, respite, stop, stay; siesta, sleep, slumber; death; brace, stay, support; axis, fulcrum, pivot.

rest[2] *vb* be left, remain. * *n* balance, remainder, remnant, residuum; overplus, surplus.

restaurant *n* bistro, café, cafeteria, chophouse, eatery, eating house, pizzeria, trattoria.

restitution *n* restoration, return; amends, compensation, indemnification, recompense, rehabilitation, remuneration, reparation, repayment, requital, satisfaction.

restive *adj* mulish, obstinate, stopping, stubborn, unwilling; impatient, recalcitrant, restless, uneasy, unquiet.

restless *adj* disquieted, disturbed, restive, sleepless, uneasy, unquiet, unresting; changeable, inconstant, irresolute, unsteady, vacillating; active, astatic, roving, transient, unsettled, unstable, wandering; agitated, fidgety, fretful, turbulent.

restoration *n* recall, recovery, re-establishment, reinstatement, reparation, replacement, restitution, return; reconsideration, redemption, reintegration, renewal, renovation, repair, resuscitation, revival; convalescence, cure, recruitment, recuperation.

restorative *adj* curative, invigorating, recuperative, remedial, restoring, stimulating. * *n* corrective, curative, cure, healing, medicine, remedy, reparative, stimulant.

restore *vb* refund, repay, return; caulk, cobble, emend, heal, mend, patch, reintegrate, re-establish, rehabilitate, reinstate, renew, repair, replace, retrieve; cure, heal, recover, revive; resuscitate.

restrain *vb* bridle, check, coerce, confine, constrain, curb, debar, govern, hamper, hinder, hold, keep, muzzle, picket, prevent, repress, restrict, rule, subdue, tie, withhold; abridge, circumscribe, narrow.

restraint *n* bridle, check, coercion, control, compulsion, constraint, curb, discipline, repression, suppression; arrest, deterrence, hindrance, inhibition, limitation, prevention, prohibition, restriction, stay, stop; confinement, detention, imprisonment, shackles; constraint, stiffness, reserve, unnaturalness.

restrict *vb* bound, circumscribe, confine, limit, qualify, restrain, straiten.

restriction *n* confinement, limitation; constraint, restraint; reservation, reserve.

result *vb* accrue, arise, come, ensue, flow, follow, issue, originate, proceed, spring, rise; end, eventuate, terminate. * *n* conclusion, consequence, deduction, inference, outcome; corollary, effect, end, event, eventuality, fruit, harvest, issue, product, sequel, termination; decision, determination, finding, resolution, resolve, solution, verdict.

resume *vb* continue, recommence, renew, restart, summarize.

résumé *n* abstract, curriculum vitae, epitome, recapitulation, summary, synopsis.

resuscitate *vb* quicken, reanimate, renew, resurrect, restore, revive, revivify.

retain *vb* detain, hold, husband, keep, preserve, recall, recollect, remember, reserve, save, withhold; engage, maintain.

retainer *n* adherent, attendant, dependant, follower, hanger-on, servant.

retaliate *vb* avenge, match, repay, requite, retort, return, turn.

retaliation *n* boomerang, counterstroke, punishment, repayment, requital, retribution, revenge.

retard *vb* check, clog, hinder, impede, obstruct, slacken; adjourn, defer, delay, postpone, procrastinate.

reticent *adj* close, reserved, secretive, silent, taciturn, uncommunicative.

retinue *n* bodyguard, cortege, entourage, escort, followers, household, ménage, suite, tail, train.

retire *vb* discharge, shelve, superannuate, withdraw; depart, leave, resign, retreat.

retired *adj* abstracted, removed, withdrawn; apart, private, secret, sequestrated, solitary.

retirement *n* isolation, loneliness, privacy, retreat, seclusion, solitude, withdrawal.

retiring *adj* coy, demure, diffident, modest, reserved, retreating, shy, withdrawing.

retort *vb* answer, rejoin, reply, respond. * *n* answer, rejoinder, repartee, reply, response; crucible, jar, vessel, vial.

retract *vb* reverse, withdraw; abjure, cancel, disavow, recall, recant, revoke, unsay.

retreat *vb* recoil, retire, withdraw; recede. * *n* departure, recession, recoil, retirement, withdrawal; privacy, seclusion, solitude; asylum, cove, den, habitat, haunt, niche, recess, refuge, resort, shelter.

retrench *vb* clip, curtail, cut, delete, dock, lop, mutilate, pare, prune; abridge, decrease, diminish, lessen; confine, limit; economize, encroach.

retribution *n* compensation, desert, judgement, nemesis, penalty, recompense, repayment, requital, retaliation, return, revenge, reward, vengeance.

retrieve *vb* recall, recover, recoup, recruit, re-establish, regain, repair, restore.

retrograde *vb* decline, degenerate, recede, retire, retrocede. * *adj* backward, inverse, retrogressive, unprogressive.
retrospect *n* recollection, re-examination, reminiscence, re-survey, review, survey.
return *vb* reappear, recoil, recur, revert; answer, reply, respond; recriminate, retort; convey, give, communicate, reciprocate, recompense, refund, remit, repay, report, requite, send, tell, transmit; elect. * *n* payment, reimbursement, remittance, repayment; recompense, recovery, recurrence, renewal, repayment, requital, restitution, restoration, reward; advantage, benefit, interest, profit, rent, yield.
reunion *n* assemblage, assembly, gathering, meeting, re-assembly; rapprochement, reconciliation.
reveal *vb* announce, communicate, confess, declare, disclose, discover, display, divulge, expose, impart, open, publish, tell, uncover, unmask, unseal, unveil.
revel *vb* carouse, disport, riot, roister, tipple; delight, indulge, luxuriate, wanton. * *n* carousal, feast, festival, saturnalia, spree.
revelry *n* bacchanal, carousal, carouse, debauch, festivity, jollification, jollity, orgy, revel, riot, rout, saturnalia, wassail.
revenge *vb* avenge, repay, requite, retaliate, vindicate. * *n* malevolence, rancour, reprisal, requital, retaliation, retribution, vengeance, vindictiveness.
revengeful *adj* implacable, malevolent, malicious, malignant, resentful, rancorous, spiteful, vengeful, vindictive.
revenue *n* fruits, income, produce, proceeds, receipts, return, reward, wealth.
reverberate *vb* echo, re-echo, resound, return.
revere *vb* adore, esteem, hallow, honour, reverence, venerate, worship.
reverence *vb* adore, esteem, hallow, honour, revere, venerate, worship. * *n* adoration, awe, deference, homage, honour, respect, veneration, worship.
reverential *adj* deferential, humble, respectful, reverent, submissive.
reverse *vb* invert, transpose; overset, overthrow, overturn, quash, subvert, undo, unmake; annul, countermand, repeal, rescind, retract, revoke; back, back up, retreat. * *adj* back, converse, contrary, opposite, verso. * *n* back, calamity, check, comedown, contrary, counterpart, defeat, opposite, tail; change, vicissitude; adversity, affliction, hardship, misadventure, mischance, misfortune, mishap, trial.
revert *vb* repel, reverse; backslide, lapse, recur, relapse, return.
review *vb* inspect, overlook, reconsider, re-examine, retrace, revise, survey; analyse, criticize, discuss, edit, judge, scrutinize, study. * *n* reconsideration, re-examination, re-survey, retrospect, survey; analysis, digest, synopsis; commentary, critique, criticism, notice, review, scrutiny, study.
revile *vb* abuse, asperse, backbite, calumniate, defame, execrate, malign, reproach, slander, traduce, upbraid, vilify.
revise *vb* reconsider, re-examine, review; alter, amend, correct, edit, overhaul, polish.
revive *vb* reanimate, reinspire, reinspirit, reinvigorate, resuscitate, revitalize, revivify; animate, cheer, comfort, invigorate, quicken, reawaken, recover, refresh, renew, renovate, rouse, strengthen; reawake, recall.
revocation *n* abjuration, recall, recantation, repeal, retraction, reversal.
revoke *vb* abolish, abrogate, annul, cancel, countermand, invalidate, quash, recall, recant, repeal, repudiate, rescind, retract.
revolt *vb* desert, mutiny, rebel, rise; disgust, nauseate, repel, sicken. * *n* defection, desertion, faithlessness, inconstancy; disobedience, insurrection, mutiny, outbreak, rebellion, sedition, strike, uprising.
revolting *adj* abhorrent, abominable, disgusting, hateful, monstrous, nauseating, nauseous, objectionable, obnoxious, offensive, repulsive, shocking, sickening; insurgent, mutinous, rebellious.
revolution *n* coup, disobedience, insurrection, mutiny, outbreak, rebellion, sedition, strike, uprising; change, innovation, reformation, transformation, upheaval; circle, circuit, cycle, lap, orbit, rotation, spin, turn..
revolve *vb* circle, circulate, rotate, swing, turn, wheel; devolve, return; consider, mediate, ponder, ruminate, study.
revulsion *n* abstraction, shrinking, withdrawal; change, reaction, reversal, transition; abhorrence, disgust, loathing, repugnance.
reward *vb* compensate, gratify, indemnify, pay, punish, recompense, remember, remunerate, requite. * *n* compensation, gratification, guerdon, indemnification, pay, recompense, remuneration, requital; bounty, bonus, fee, gratuity, honorarium, meed, perquisite, premium, remembrance, tip; punishment, retribution.
rhythm *n* cadence, lilt, pulsation, swing; measure, metre, number.
ribald *adj* base, blue, coarse, filthy, gross, indecent, lewd, loose, low, mean, obscene, vile.
rich *adj* affluent, flush, moneyed, opulent, prosperous, wealthy; costly, estimable, gorgeous, luxurious, precious, splendid, sumptuous, superb, valuable; delicious, luscious, savoury; abundant, ample, copious, enough, full, plentiful, plenteous, sufficient; fertile, fruitful, luxuriant, productive, prolific; bright, dark, deep, exuberant, vivid; harmonious, mellow, melodious, soft, sweet; comical, funny, humorous, laughable.
riches *npl* abundance, affluence, fortune, money, opulence, plenty, richness, wealth, wealthiness.
rickety *adj* broken, imperfect, shaky, shattered, tottering, tumbledown, unsteady, weak.
rid *vb* deliver, free, release; clear, disburden, disencumber, scour, sweep; disinherit, dispatch, dissolve, divorce, finish, sever.
riddance *n* deliverance, disencumberment, extrication, escape, freedom, release, relief.
riddle[1] *vb* explain, solve, unriddle. * *n* conundrum, enigma, mystery, puzzle, rebus.
riddle[2] *vb* sieve, sift, perforate, permeate, spread. * *n* colander, sieve, strainer.
ridge *n* chine, hogback, ledge, saddle, spine, rib, watershed, weal, wrinkle.
ridicule *vb* banter, burlesque, chaff, deride, disparage, jeer, mock, lampoon, rally, satirize, scout, taunt. * *n* badinage, banter, burlesque, chaff, derision, game, gibe, irony, jeer, mockery, persiflage, quip, raillery, sarcasm, satire, sneer, squib, wit.
ridiculous *adj* absurd, amusing, comical, droll, eccentric, fantastic, farcical, funny, laughable, ludicrous, nonsensical, odd, outlandish, preposterous, queer, risible, waggish.
rife *adj* abundant, common, current, general, numerous, plentiful, prevailing, prevalent, replete.
riffraff *n* horde, mob, populace, rabble, scum, trash.
rifle *vb* despoil, fleece, pillage, plunder, ransack, rob, strip.
rift *vb* cleave, rive, split. * *n* breach, break, chink, cleft, crack, cranny, crevice, fissure, fracture, gap, opening, reft, rent.
rig *vb* accoutre, clothe, dress. * *n* costume, dress, garb; equipment, team.
right *vb* adjust, correct, regulate, settle, straighten, vindicate. * *adj* direct, rectilinear, straight; erect, perpendicular, plumb, upright; equitable, even-handed, fair, just, justifiable, honest, lawful, legal, legitimate, rightful, square, unswerving; appropriate, becoming, correct, conventional, fit, fitting, meet, orderly, proper, reasonable, seemly, suitable, well-done; actual, genuine, real, true, unquestionable; dexter, dextral, right-handed. * *adv* equitably, fairly, justly, lawfully, rightfully, rightly; correctly, fitly, properly, suitably, truly; actually, exactly, just, really, truly, well. * *n* authority, claim, liberty, permission, power, privilege, title; equity, good, honour, justice, lawfulness, legality, propriety, reason, righteousness, truth.
righteous *adj* devout, godly, good, holy, honest, incorrupt, just, pious, religious, saintly, uncorrupt, upright, virtuous; equitable, fair, right, rightful.
righteousness *n* equity, faithfulness, godliness, goodness, holiness, honesty, integrity, justice, piety, purity, right, rightfulness, sanctity, uprightness, virtue.
rightful *adj* lawful, legitimate, true; appropriate, correct, deserved, due, equitable, fair, fitting, honest, just, legal, merited, proper, reasonable, suitable.

rigid *adj* firm, hard, inflexible, permanent, stiff, stiffened, unbending, unpliant, unyielding; bristling, erect, precipitous, steep; austere, conventional, correct, exact, formal, harsh, meticulous, precise, rigorous, severe, sharp, stern, strict, unmitigated; cruel.

rigmarole *n* balderdash, flummery, gibberish, gobbledegook, jargon, nonsense, palaver, trash, twaddle, verbiage.

rigour *n* hardness, inflexibility, rigidity, rigidness, stiffness; asperity, austerity, harshness, severity, sternness; evenness, strictness; inclemency.

rile *vb* anger, annoy, irritate, upset, vex.

rim *n* brim, brink, border, confine, curb, edge, flange, girdle, margin, ring, skirt.

ring[1] *vb* circle, encircle, enclose, girdle, surround. * *n* circle, circlet, girdle, hoop, round, whorl; cabal, clique, combination, confederacy, coterie, gang, junta, league, set.

ring[2] *vb* chime, clang, jingle, knell, peal, resound, reverberate, sound, tingle, toll; call, phone, telephone. * *n* chime, knell, peal, tinkle, toll; call, phone call, telephone call.

riot *vb* carouse, luxuriate, revel. * *n* affray, altercation, brawl, broil, commotion, disturbance, fray, outbreak, pandemonium, quarrel, squabble, tumult, uproar; dissipation, excess, luxury, merrymaking, revelry.

riotous *adj* boisterous, luxurious, merry, revelling, unrestrained, wanton; disorderly, insubordinate, lawless, mutinous, rebellious, refractory, seditious, tumultuous, turbulent, ungovernable, unruly, violent.

ripe *adj* advanced, grown, mature, mellow, seasoned, soft; fit, prepared, ready; accomplished, complete, consummate, finished, perfect, perfected.

ripen *vb* burgeon, develop, mature, prepare.

rise *vb* arise, ascend, clamber, climb, levitate, mount; excel, succeed; enlarge, heighten, increase, swell, thrive; revive; grow, kindle, wax; begin, flow, head, originate, proceed, spring, start; mutiny, rebel, revolt; happen, occur. * *n* ascension, ascent, rising; elevation, grade, hill, slope; beginning, emergence, flow, origin, source, spring; advance, augmentation, expansion, increase.

risible *adj* amusing, comical, droll, farcical, funny, laughable, ludicrous, ridiculous.

risk *vb* bet, endanger, hazard, jeopardize, peril, speculate, stake, venture, wager. * *n* chance, danger, hazard, jeopardy, peril, venture.

rite *n* ceremonial, ceremony, form, formulary, ministration, observance, ordinance, ritual, rubric, sacrament, solemnity.

ritual *adj* ceremonial, conventional, formal, habitual, routine, stereotyped. * *n* ceremonial, ceremony, liturgy, observance, rite, sacrament, service; convention, form, formality, habit, practice, protocol.

rival *vb* emulate, match, oppose. * *adj* competing, contending, emulating, emulous, opposing. * *n* antagonist, competitor, emulator, opponent.

rive *vb* cleave, rend, split.

river *n* affluent, current, reach, stream, tributary.

road *n* course, highway, lane, passage, path, pathway, roadway, route, street, thoroughfare, track, trail, turnpike, way.

roam *vb* jaunt, prowl, ramble, range, rove, straggle, stray, stroll, wander.

roar *vb* bawl, bellow, cry, howl, vociferate, yell; boom, peal, rattle, resound, thunder. * *n* bellow, roaring; rage, resonance, storm, thunder; cry, outcry, shout; laugh, laughter, shout.

rob *vb* despoil, fleece, pilfer, pillage, plunder, rook, strip; appropriate, deprive, embezzle, plagiarize.

robber *n* bandit, brigand, desperado, depredator, despoiler, footpad, freebooter, highwayman, marauder, pillager, pirate, plunderer, rifler, thief.

robbery *n* depredation, despoliation, embezzlement, freebooting, larceny, peculation, piracy, plagiarism, plundering, spoliation, theft.

robe *vb* array, clothe, dress, invest. * *n* attire, costume, dress, garment, gown, habit, vestment; bathrobe, dressing gown, housecoat.

robust *adj* able-bodied, athletic, brawny, energetic, firm, forceful, hale, hardy, hearty, iron, lusty, muscular, powerful, seasoned, self-assertive, sinewy, sound, stalwart, stout, strong, sturdy, vigorous.

rock[1] *n* boulder, cliff, crag, reef, stone; asylum, defence, foundation, protection, refuge, strength, support; gneiss, granite, marble, slate, etc.

rock[2] *vb* calm, cradle, lull, quiet, soothe, still, tranquillize; reel, shake, sway, teeter, totter, wobble.

rogue *n* beggar, vagabond, vagrant; caitiff, cheat, knave, rascal, scamp, scapegrace, scoundrel, sharper, swindler, trickster, villain.

roguish *adj* dishonest, fraudulent, knavish, rascally, scoundrelly, trickish, tricky; arch, sportive, mischievous, puckish, waggish, wanton.

role *n* character, function, impersonation, part, task.

roll *vb* gyrate, revolve, rotate, turn, wheel; curl, muffle, swathe, wind; bind, involve, enfold, envelop; flatten, level, smooth, spread; bowl, drive; trundle, wheel; gybe, lean, lurch, stagger, sway, yaw; billow, swell, undulate; wallow, welter; flow, glide, run. * *n* document, scroll, volume; annals, chronicle, history, record, rota; catalogue, inventory, list, register, schedule; booming, resonance, reverberation, thunder; cylinder, roller.

rollicking *adj* frisky, frolicking, frolicsome, jolly, jovial, lively, swaggering.

romance *vb* exaggerate, fantasize. * *n* fantasy, fiction, legend, novel, story, tale; exaggeration, falsehood, lie; ballad, idyll, song.

romantic *adj* extravagant, fanciful, fantastic, ideal, imaginative, sentimental, wild; chimerical, fabulous, fantastic, fictitious, imaginary, improbable, legendary, picturesque, quixotic, sentimental. * *n* dreamer, idealist, sentimentalist, visionary.

romp *vb* caper, gambol, frisk, sport. * *n* caper, frolic, gambol.

room *n* accommodation, capacity, compass, elbowroom, expanse, extent, field, latitude, leeway, play, scope, space, swing; place, stead; apartment, chamber, lodging; chance, occasion, opportunity.

roomy *adj* ample, broad, capacious, comfortable, commodious, expansive, extensive, large, spacious, wide.

root[1] *vb* anchor, embed, fasten, implant, place, settle; confirm, establish. * *n* base, bottom, foundation; cause, occasion, motive, origin, reason, source; etymon, radical, radix, stem.

root[2] *vb* destroy, eradicate, extirpate, exterminate, remove, unearth, uproot; burrow, dig, forage, grub, rummage; applaud, cheer, encourage.

rooted *adj* chronic, confirmed, deep, established, fixed, radical.

roseate *adj* blooming, blushing, rose-coloured, rosy, rubicund; hopeful.

rostrum *n* platform, stage, stand, tribune.

rosy *adj* auspicious, blooming, blushing, favourable, flushed, hopeful, roseate, ruddy, sanguine.

rot *vb* corrupt, decay, decompose, degenerate, putrefy, spoil, taint. * *n* corruption, decay, decomposition, putrefaction.

rotary *adj* circular, rotating, revolving, rotatory, turning, whirling.

rotten *adj* carious, corrupt, decomposed, fetid, putrefied, putrescent, putrid, rank, stinking; defective, unsound; corrupt, deceitful, immoral, treacherous, unsound, untrustworthy.

rotund *adj* buxom, chubby, full, globular, obese, plump, round, stout; fluent, grandiloquent.

roué *n* debauchee, libertine, profligate, rake.

rough *vb* coarsen, roughen; manhandle, mishandle, molest. * *adj* bumpy, craggy, irregular, jagged, rugged, scabrous, scraggy, scratchy, stubby, uneven; approximate, cross-grained, crude, formless, incomplete, knotty, rough-hewn, shapeless, sketchy, uncut, unfashioned, unfinished, unhewn, unpolished, unwrought, vague; bristly, bushy, coarse, disordered, hairy, hirsute, ragged, shaggy, unkempt; austere, bearish, bluff, blunt, brusque, burly, churlish, discourteous, gruff, harsh, impolite, indelicate, rude, surly, uncivil, uncourteous, ungracious, unpolished, unrefined; harsh, severe, sharp, violent; astringent, crabbed, hard, sour, tart; discordant, grating, inharmonious, jarring, raucous, scabrous, unmusical; boisterous, foul, inclement, severe, stormy, tempestuous, tumultuous, turbulent, untamed, violent, wild; acrimonious, brutal, cruel, disorderly, riotous, rowdy, severe, uncivil, unfeeling, ungentle. * *n* bully, rowdy, roughneck, ruffian; draft, outline, sketch, suggestion; unevenness.

round *vb* curve; circuit, encircle, encompass, surround. * *adj* bulbous, circular, cylindrical, globular, orbed, orbicular, rotund, spherical; complete, considerable, entire, full, great, large, unbroken, whole; chubby, corpulent, plump, stout, swelling; continuous, flowing, harmonious, smooth; brisk, quick; blunt, candid, fair, frank, honest, open, plain, upright. * *adv* around, circularly, circuitously. * *prep* about, around. * *n* bout, cycle, game, lap, revolution, rotation, succession, turn; canon, catch, dance; ball, circle, circumference, cylinder, globe, sphere; circuit, compass, perambulation, routine, tour, watch.

roundabout *adj* circuitous, circumlocutory, indirect, tortuous; ample, broad, extensive; encircling, encompassing.

rouse *vb* arouse, awaken, raise, shake, wake, waken; animate, bestir, brace, enkindle, excite, inspire, kindle, rally, stimulate, stir, whet; startle, surprise.

rout *vb* beat, conquer, defeat, discomfit, overcome, overpower, overthrow, vanquish; chase away, dispel, disperse, scatter. * *n* defeat, discomfiture, flight, ruin; concourse, multitude, rabble; brawl, disturbance, noise, roar, uproar.

route *vb* direct, forward, send, steer. * *n* course, circuit, direction, itinerary, journey, march, road, passage, path, way.

routine *adj* conventional, familiar, habitual, ordinary, standard, typical, usual; boring, dull, humdrum, predictable, tiresome. * *n* beat, custom, groove, method, order, path, practice, procedure, round, rut.

rove *vb* prowl, ramble, range, roam, stray, struggle, stroll, wander.

row[1] *n* file, line, queue, range, rank, series, string, tier; alley, street, terrace.

row[2] *vb* argue, dispute, fight, quarrel, squabble. * *n* affray, altercation, brawl, broil, commotion, dispute, disturbance, noise, outbreak, quarrel, riot, squabble, tumult, uproar.

royal *adj* august, courtly, dignified, generous, grand, imperial, kingly, kinglike, magnanimous, magnificent, majestic, monarchical, noble, princely, regal, sovereign, splendid, superb.

rub *vb* abrade, chafe, grate, graze, scrape; burnish, clean, massage, polish, scour, wipe; apply, put, smear, spread. * *n* caress, massage, polish, scouring, shine, wipe; catch, difficulty, drawback, impediment, obstacle, problem.

rubbish *n* debris, detritus, fragments, refuse, ruins, waste; dregs, dross, garbage, litter, lumber, scoria, scum, sweepings, trash, trumpery.

rubicund *adj* blushing, erubescent, florid, flushed, red, reddish, ruddy.

rude *adj* coarse, crude, ill-formed, rough, rugged, shapeless, uneven, unfashioned, unformed, unwrought; artless, barbarous, boorish, clownish, ignorant, illiterate, loutish, raw, savage, uncivilized, uncouth, uncultivated, undisciplined, unpolished, ungraceful, unskilful, unskilled, untaught, untrained, untutored, vulgar; awkward, barbarous, bluff, blunt, boorish, brusque, brutal, churlish, gruff, ill-bred, impertinent, impolite, impudent, insolent, insulting, ribald, saucy, uncivil, uncourteous, unrefined; boisterous, fierce, harsh, severe, tumultuous, turbulent, violent; artless, inelegant, rustic, unpolished; hearty, robust.

rudimentary *adj* elementary, embryonic, fundamental, initial, primary, rudimental, undeveloped.

rue *vb* deplore, grieve, lament, regret, repent.

rueful *adj* dismal, doleful, lamentable, lugubrious, melancholic, melancholy, mournful, penitent, regretful, sad, sorrowful, woeful.

ruffian *n* bully, caitiff, cutthroat, hoodlum, miscreant, monster, murderer, rascal, robber, roisterer, rowdy, scoundrel, villain, wretch.

ruffle *vb* damage, derange, disarrange, dishevel, disorder, ripple, roughen, rumple; agitate, confuse, discompose, disquiet, disturb, excite, harass, irritate, molest, plague, perturb, torment, trouble, vex, worry; cockle, flounce, pucker, wrinkle. * *n* edging, frill, ruff; agitation, bustle, commotion, confusion, contention, disturbance, excitement, fight, fluster, flutter, flurry, perturbation, tumult.

rugged *adj* austere, bristly, coarse, crabbed, cragged, craggy, hard, hardy, irregular, ragged, robust, rough, rude, scraggy, severe, seamed, shaggy, uneven, unkempt, wrinkled; boisterous, inclement, stormy, tempestuous, tumultuous, turbulent, violent; grating, harsh, inharmonious, unmusical, scabrous.

ruin *vb* crush, damn, defeat, demolish, desolate, destroy, devastate, overthrow, overturn, overwhelm, seduce, shatter, smash, subvert, wreck; beggar, impoverish. * *n* damnation, decay, defeat, demolition, desolation, destruction, devastation, discomfiture, downfall, fall, loss, perdition, prostration, rack, ruination, shipwreck, subversion, undoing, wrack, wreck; bane, mischief, pest.

ruination *n* demolition, destruction, overthrow, ruin, subversion.

ruinous *adj* decayed, demolished, dilapidated; baneful, calamitous, damnatory, destructive, disastrous, mischievous, noisome, noxious, pernicious, subversive, wasteful.

rule *vb* bridle, command, conduct, control, direct, domineer, govern, judge, lead, manage, reign, restrain; advise, guide, persuade; adjudicate, decide, determine, establish, settle; obtain, prevail, predominate. * *n* authority, command, control, direction, domination, dominion, empire, government, jurisdiction, lordship, mastery, mastership, regency, reign, sway; behaviour, conduct; habit, method, order, regularity,

routine, system; aphorism, canon, convention, criterion, formula, guide, law, maxim, model, precedent, precept, standard, system, test, touchstone; decision, order, prescription, regulation, ruling.

ruler *n* chief, governor, king, lord, master, monarch, potentate, regent, sovereign; director, head, manager, president; controller, guide, rule; straight-edge.

ruminate *vb* brood, chew, cogitate, consider, contemplate, meditate, muse, ponder, reflect, think.

rumour *vb* bruit, circulate, report, tell. * *n* bruit, gossip, hearsay, report, talk; news, report, story, tidings; celebrity, fame, reputation, repute.

rumple *vb* crease, crush, corrugate, crumple, disarrange, dishevel, pucker, ruffle, wrinkle. * *n* crease, corrugation, crumple, fold, pucker, wrinkle.

run *vb* bolt, career, course, gallop, haste, hasten, hie, hurry, lope, post, race, scamper, scour, scud, scuttle, speed, trip; flow, glide, go, move, proceed, stream; fuse, liquefy, melt; advance, pass, proceed, vanish; extend, lie, spread, stretch; circulate, pass, press; average, incline, tend; flee; pierce, stab; drive, force, propel, push, thrust, turn; cast, form, mould, shape; follow, perform, pursue, take; discharge, emit; direct, maintain, manage. * *n* race, running; course, current, flow, motion, passage, progress, way, wont; continuance, currency, popularity; excursion, gallop, journey, trip, trot; demand, pressure; brook, burn, flow, rill, rivulet, runlet, runnel, streamlet.

rupture *vb* break, burst, fracture, sever, split. * *n* breach, break, burst, disruption, fracture, split; contention, faction, feud, hostility, quarrel, schism.

rural *adj* agrarian, bucolic, country, pastoral, rustic, sylvan.

ruse *n* artifice, deception, deceit, fraud, hoax, imposture, manoeuvre, sham, stratagem, trick, wile.

rush *vb* attack, career, charge, dash, drive, gush, hurtle, precipitate, surge, sweep, tear. * *n* dash, onrush, onset, plunge, precipitance, precipitancy, rout, stampede, tear.

rust *vb* corrode, decay, degenerate. * *n* blight, corrosion, crust, mildew, must, mould, mustiness.

rustic *adj* country, rural; awkward, boorish, clownish, countrified, loutish, outlandish, rough, rude, uncouth, unpolished, untaught; coarse, countrified, homely, plain, simple, unadorned; artless, honest, unsophisticated. * *n* boor, bumpkin, clown, countryman, peasant, swain, yokel.

ruthless *adj* barbarous, cruel, fell, ferocious, hardhearted, inexorable, inhuman, merciless, pitiless, relentless, remorseless, savage, truculent, uncompassionate, unmerciful, unpitying, unrelenting, unsparing.

S

sable *adj* black, dark, dusky, ebony, sombre.
sabulous *adj* gritty, sabulose, sandy.
sack[1] *n* bag, pouch.
sack[2] *vb* despoil, devastate, pillage, plunder, ravage, spoil. * *n* desolation, despoliation, destruction, devastation, havoc, ravage, sacking, spoliation, waste; booty, plunder, spoil.
sacred *adj* consecrated, dedicated, devoted, divine, hallowed, holy; inviolable, inviolate; sainted, venerable.
sacrifice *vb* forgo, immolate, surrender. * *n* immolation, oblation, offering; destruction, devotion, loss, surrender.
sacrilege *n* desecration, profanation, violation.
sacrilegious *adj* desecrating, impious, irreverent, profane.
sad *adj* grave, pensive, sedate, serious, sober, sombre, staid.
saddle *vb* burden, charge, clog, encumber, load.
sadly *adv* grievously, miserable, mournfully, sorrowfully; afflictively, badly, calamitously; darkly; gravely, seriously, soberly.
sadness *n* dejection, depression, despondency, melancholy, mournful, sorrow, sorrowfulness; dolefulness, gloominess, grief, mournfulness, sorrow; gravity, sedateness, seriousness.
safe *adj* undamaged, unharmed, unhurt, unscathed; guarded, protected, secure, snug, unexposed; certain, dependable, reliable, sure, trustworthy; good, harmless, sound, whole. * *n* chest, coffer, strongbox.
safeguard *vb* guard, protect. * *n* defence, protection, security; convoy, escort, guard, safe-conduct; pass, passport.
sagacious *adj* acute, apt, astute, clear-sighted, discerning, intelligent, judicious, keen, penetrating, perspicacious, rational, sage, sharp-witted, wise, shrewd.
sagacity *n* acuteness, astuteness, discernment, ingenuity, insight, penetration, perspicacity, quickness, readiness, sense, sharpness, shrewdness, wisdom.
sage *adj* acute, discerning, intelligent, prudent, sagacious, sapient, sensible, shrewd, wise; judicious, well-judged; grave, serious, solemn. * *n* philosopher, pundit, savant.
sailor *n* mariner, navigator, salt, seafarer, seaman, tar.
saintly *adj* devout, godly, holy, pious, religious.
sake *n* end, cause, purpose, reason; account, consideration, interest, regard, respect, score.
saleable *adj* marketable, merchantable, vendible.
salacious *adj* carnal, concupiscent, incontinent, lascivious, lecherous, lewd, libidinous, loose, lustful, prurient, unchaste, wanton.
salary *n* allowance, hire, pay, stipend, wages.
salient *adj* bounding, jumping, leaping; beating, springing, throbbing; jutting, projecting, prominent; conspicuous, remarkable, striking.
saline *adj* briny, salty.
sally *vb* issue, rush. * *n* digression, excursion, sortie, run, trip; escapade, frolic; crank, fancy, jest, joke, quip, quirk, sprightly, witticism.
salt *adj* saline, salted, salty; bitter, pungent, sharp. * *n* flavour, savour, seasoning, smack, relish, taste; humour, piquancy, poignancy, sarcasm, smartness, wit, zest; mariner, sailor, seaman, tar.
salubrious *adj* beneficial, benign, healthful, healthy, salutary, sanitary, wholesome.
salutary *adj* healthy, healthful, helpful, safe, salubrious, wholesome; advantageous, beneficial, good, profitable, serviceable, useful.
salute *vb* accost, address, congratulate, greet, hail, welcome. * *n* address, greeting, salutation.
salvation *n* deliverance, escape, preservation, redemption, rescue, saving.
same *adj* ditto, identical, selfsame; corresponding, like, similar.
sample *vb* savour, sip, smack, sup, taste; test, try; demonstrate, exemplify, illustrate, instance. * *adj* exemplary, illustrative, representative. * *n* demonstration, exemplification, illustration, instance, piece, specimen; example, model, pattern.
sanctify *vb* consecrate, hallow, purify; justify, ratify, sanction.
sanctimonious *adj* affected, devout, holy, hypocritical, pharisaical, pious, self-righteous.
sanction *vb* authorize, countenance, encourage, support; confirm, ratify. * *n* approval, authority, authorization, confirmation, countenance, endorsement, ratification, support, warranty; ban, boycott, embargo, penalty.
sanctity *n* devotion, godliness, goodness, grace, holiness, piety, purity, religiousness, saintliness.
sanctuary *n* altar, church, shrine, temple; asylum, protection, refuge, retreat, shelter.
sane *adj* healthy, lucid, rational, reasonable, sober, sound.
sang-froid *n* calmness, composure, coolness, imperturbability, indifference, nonchalance, phlegm, unconcern.
sanguinary *adj* bloody, gory, murderous; barbarous, bloodthirsty, cruel, fell, pitiless, savage, ruthless.
sanguine *adj* crimson, florid, red; animated, ardent, cheerful, lively, warm; buoyant, confident, enthusiastic, hopeful, optimistic; full-blooded.
sanitary *adj* clean, curative, healing, healthy, hygienic, remedial, therapeutic, wholesome.
sanity *n* normality, rationality, reason, saneness, soundness.
sapient *adj* acute, discerning, intelligent, knowing, sagacious, sage, sensible, shrewd, wise.
sarcastic *adj* acrimonious, biting, cutting, mordacious, mordant, sardonic, satirical, sharp, severe, sneering, taunting.
sardonic *adj* bitter, derisive, ironical, malevolent, malicious, malignant, sarcastic.
satanic *adj* devilish, diabolical, evil, false, fiendish, hellish, infernal, malicious.
satellite *adj* dependent, subordinate, tributary, vassal. * *n* attendant, dependant, follower, hanger-on, retainer, vassal.
satiate *vb* fill, sate, satisfy, suffice; cloy, glut, gorge, overfeed, overfill, pall, surfeit.
satire *n* burlesque, diatribe, invective, fling, irony, lampoon, pasquinade, philippic, ridicule, sarcasm, skit, squib.
satirical *adj* abusive, biting, bitter, censorious, cutting, invective, ironical, keen, mordacious, poignant, reproachful, sarcastic, severe, sharp, taunting.
satirize *vb* abuse, censure, lampoon, ridicule.
satisfaction *n* comfort, complacency, contentment, ease, enjoyment, gratification, pleasure, satiety; amends, appeasement, atonement, compensation, indemnification, recompense, redress, remuneration, reparation, requital, reward.
satisfactory *adj* adequate, conclusive, convincing, decisive, sufficient; gratifying, pleasing.
satisfy *vb* appease, content, fill, gratify, please, sate, satiate, suffice; indemnify, compensate, liquidate, pay, recompense, remunerate, requite; discharge, settle; assure, convince, persuade; answer, fulfil, meet.
saturate *vb* drench, fill, fit, imbue, soak, steep, wet.
saturnine *adj* dark, dull, gloomy, grave, heavy, leaden, morose, phlegmatic, sad, sedate, sombre; melancholic, mournful, serious, unhappy; mischievous, naughty, troublesome, vexatious, wicked.
sauce *n* cheekiness, impudence, insolence; appetizer, compound, condiment, relish, seasoning.
saucy *adj* bold, cavalier, disrespectful, flippant, forward, immodest, impertinent, impudent, insolent, pert, rude.
saunter *vb* amble, dawdle, delay, dilly-dally, lag, linger, loiter, lounge, stroll, tarry. * *n* amble, stroll, walk.
savage *vb* attack, lacerate, mangle, maul. * *adj* rough, uncultivated, wild; rude, uncivilized, unpolished, untaught; bloodthirsty, feral, ferine, ferocious, fierce, rapacious, untamed, vicious; beastly, bestial, brutal, brutish, inhuman; atrocious, barbarous, barbaric, bloody, brutal, cruel, fell, fiendish, hardhearted, heathenish, merciless, murderous, pitiless, relentless, ruthless, sanguinary, truculent; native, rough, rugged. * *n* barbarian, brute, heathen, vandal.

save *vb* keep, liberate, preserve, rescue; salvage, recover, redeem; economize, gather, hoard, husband, reserve, store; hinder, obviate, prevent, spare. * *prep* but, deducting, except.

saviour *n* defender, deliverer, guardian, protector, preserver, rescuer, saver.

savour *vb* affect, appreciate, enjoy, like, partake, relish; flavour, season. * *n* flavour, gusto, relish, smack, taste; fragrance, odour, smell, scent.

savoury *adj* agreeable, delicious, flavourful, luscious, nice, palatable, piquant, relishing.

saw *n* adage, aphorism, apothegm, axiom, byword, dictum, maxim, precept, proverb, sententious saying.

say *vb* declare, express, pronounce, speak, tell, utter; affirm, allege, argue; recite, rehearse, repeat; assume, presume, suppose. * *n* affirmation, declaration, speech, statement; decision, voice, vote.

saying *n* declaration, expression, observation, remark, speech, statement; adage, aphorism, byword, dictum, maxim, proverb, saw.

scale[1] *n* basin, dish, pan; balance.

scale[2] *n* flake, lamina, lamella, layer, plate.

scale[3] *vb* ascend, climb, escalate, mount. * *n* graduation.

scamp *n* cheat, knave, rascal, rogue, scapegrace, scoundrel, swindler, trickster, villain.

scamper *vb* haste, hasten, hie, run, scud, speed, trip.

scan *vb* examine, investigate, scrutinize, search, sift.

scandal *vb* asperse, defame, libel, traduce. * *n* aspersion, calumny, defamation, obloquy, reproach; discredit, disgrace, dishonour, disrepute, ignominy, infamy, odium, opprobrium, offence, shame.

scandalize *vb* offend; asperse, backbite, calumniate, decry, defame, disgust, lampoon, libel, reproach, revile, satirize, slander, traduce, vilify.

scandalous *adj* defamatory, libellous, opprobrious, slanderous; atrocious, disgraceful, disreputable, infamous, inglorious, ignominious, odious, shameful.

scanty *adj* insufficient, meagre, narrow, scant, small; hardly, scarce, short, slender; niggardly, parsimonious, penurious, scrimpy, skimpy, sparing.

scar[1] *vb* hurt, mark, wound. * *n* cicatrice, cicatrix, seam; blemish, defect, disfigurement, flaw, injury, mark.

scar[2] *n* bluff, cliff, crag, precipice.

scarce *adj* deficient, wanting; infrequent, rare, uncommon. * *adv* barely, hardly, scantily.

scarcely *adv* barely, hardly, scantily.

scarcity *n* dearth, deficiency, insufficiency, lack, want; infrequency, rareness, rarity, uncommonness.

scare *vb* affright, alarm, appal, daunt, fright, frighten, intimidate, shock, startle, terrify. * *n* alarm, fright, panic, shock, terror.

scathe *vb* blast, damage, destroy, injure, harm, haste. * *n* damage, harm, injury, mischief, waste.

scatter *vb* broadcast, sprinkle, strew; diffuse, disperse, disseminate, dissipate, distribute, separate, spread; disappoint, dispel, frustrate, overthrow.

scene *n* display, exhibition, pageant, representation, show, sight, spectacle, view; place, situation, spot; arena, stage.

scent *vb* breathe in, inhale, nose, smell, sniff; detect, smell out, sniff out; aromatize, perfume. * *n* aroma, balminess, fragrance, odour, perfume, smell, redolence.

sceptic *n* doubter, freethinker, questioner, unbeliever.

sceptical *adj* doubtful, doubting, dubious, hesitating, incredulous, questioning, unbelieving.

scepticism *n* doubt, dubiety, freethinking, incredulity, unbelief.

schedule *vb* line up, list, plan, programme, tabulate. * *n* document, scroll; catalogue, inventory, list, plan, record, register, roll, table, timetable.

scheme *vb* contrive, design, frame, imagine, plan, plot, project. * *n* plan, system, theory; cabal, conspiracy, contrivance, design, device, intrigue, machination, plan, plot, project, stratagem; arrangement, draught, diagram, outline.

schism *n* division, separation, split; discord, disunion, division, faction, separation.

scholar *n* disciple, learner, pupil, student; don, fellow, intellectual, pedant, savant.

scholarship *n* accomplishments, acquirements, attainments, erudition, knowledge, learning; bursary, exhibition, foundation, grant, maintenance.

scholastic *adj* academic, bookish, lettered, literary; formal, pedantic.

school *vb* drill, educate, exercise, indoctrinate, instruct, teach, train; admonish, control, chide, discipline, govern, reprove, tutor. * *adj* academic, collegiate, institutional, scholastic, schoolish. * *n* academy, college, gymnasium, institute, institution, kindergarten, lyceum, manège, polytechnic, seminary, university; adherents, camarilla, circle, clique, coterie, disciples, followers; body, order, organization, party, sect.

schooling *n* discipline, education, instruction, nurture, teaching, training, tuition.

scintillate *vb* coruscate, flash, gleam, glisten, glitter, sparkle, twinkle.

scoff *vb* deride, flout, jeer, mock, ridicule, taunt; gibe, sneer. * *n* flout, gibe, jeer, sneer, mockery, taunt; derision, ridicule.

scold *vb* berate, blame, censure, chide, rate, reprimand, reprove; brawl, rail, rate, reprimand, upbraid, vituperate. * *n* shrew, termagant, virago, vixen.

scope *n* aim, design, drift, end, intent, intention, mark, object, purpose, tendency, view; amplitude, field, latitude, liberty, margin, opportunity, purview, range, room, space, sphere, vent; extent, length, span, stretch, sweep.

scorch *vb* blister, burn, char, parch, roast, sear, shrivel, singe.

score *vb* cut, furrow, mark, notch, scratch; charge, note, record; impute, note; enter, register. * *n* incision, mark, notch; account, bill, charge, debt, reckoning; consideration, ground, motive, reason.

scorn *vb* condemn, despise, disregard, disdain, scout, slight, spurn. * *n* contempt, derision, disdain, mockery, slight, sneer; scoff.

scornful *adj* contemptuous, defiant, disdainful, contemptuous, regardless.

scot-free *adj* untaxed; clear, unhurt, uninjured, safe.

scoundrel *n* cheat, knave, miscreant, rascal, reprobate, rogue, scamp, swindler, trickster, villain.

scour[1] *vb* brighten, buff, burnish, clean, cleanse, polish, purge, scrape, scrub, rub, wash, whiten; rake; efface, obliterate, overrun.

scour[2] *vb* career, course, range, scamper, scud, scuttle; comb, hunt, rake, ransack, rifle, rummage, search.

scourge *vb* lash, whip; afflict, chasten, chastise, correct, punish; harass, torment. * *n* cord, cowhide, lash, strap, thong, whip; affliction, bane, curse, infliction, nuisance, pest, plague, punishment.

scout *vb* contemn, deride, disdain, despise, ridicule, scoff, scorn, sneer, spurn; investigate, probe, search. * *n* escort, lookout, precursor, vanguard.

scowl *vb* frown, glower, lower. * *n* frown, glower, lower.

scraggy *adj* broken, craggy, rough, rugged, scabrous, scragged, uneven; attenuated, bony, emaciated, gaunt, lank, lean, meagre, scrawny, skinny, thin.

scrap[1] *vb* discard, junk, trash. * *n* bit, fragment, modicum, particle, piece, snippet; bite, crumb, morsel, mouthful; debris, junk, litter, rubbish, rubble, trash, waste.

scrap[2] *vb* altercate, bicker, dispute, clash, fight, hassle, quarrel, row, spat, squabble, tiff, tussle, wrangle. * *n* affray, altercation, bickering, clash, dispute, fight, fray, hassle, melee, quarrel, row, run-in, set-to, spat, squabble, tiff, tussle, wrangle.

scrape *vb* bark, grind, rasp, scuff; accumulate, acquire, collect, gather, save; erase, remove. * *n* difficulty, distress, embarrassment, perplexity, predicament.

scream *vb* screech, shriek, squall, ululate. * *n* cry, outcry, screech, shriek, shrill, ululation.

screen *vb* cloak, conceal, cover, defend, fence, hide, mask, protect, shelter, shroud. * *n* blind, curtain, lattice, partition; defence, guard, protection, shield; cloak, cover, veil, disguise; riddle, sieve.

screw *vb* force, press, pressurize, squeeze, tighten, twist, wrench; oppress, rack; distort. * *n* extortioner, extortionist, miser, scrimp, skinflint; prison guard; sexual intercourse.

scrimmage *n* brawl, melee, riot, scuffle, skirmish.
scrimp *vb* contract, curtail, limit, pinch, reduce, scant, shorten, straiten.
scrimpy *adj* contracted, deficient, narrow, scanty.
scroll *n* inventory, list, parchment, roll, schedule.
scrub[1] *adj* contemptible, inferior, mean, niggardly, scrubby, shabby, small, stunted. * *n* brushwood, underbrush, underwood.
scrub[2] *vb* clean, cleanse, rub, scour, scrape, wash.
scruple *vb* boggle, demur, falter, hesitate, object, pause, stickle, waver. * *n* delicacy, hesitancy, hesitation, nicety, perplexity, qualm.
scrupulous *adj* conscientious, fastidious, nice, precise, punctilious, rigorous, strict; careful, cautious, circumspect, exact, vigilant.
scrutinize *vb* canvass, dissect, examine, explore, investigate, overhaul, probe, search, sift, study.
scrutiny *n* examination, exploration, inquisition, inspection, investigation, search, searching, sifting.
scud *vb* flee, fly, haste, hasten, hie, post, run, scamper, speed, trip.
scuffle *vb* contend, fight, strive, struggle. * *n* altercation, brawl, broil, contest, encounter, fight, fray, quarrel, squabble, struggle, wrangle.
sculpt *vb* carve, chisel, cut, sculpture; engrave, grave.
scurrilous *adj* abusive, blackguardly, contumelious, foul, foul-mouthed, indecent, infamous, insolent, insulting, offensive, opprobrious, reproachful, ribald, vituperative; coarse, gross, low, mean, obscene, vile, vulgar.
scurry *vb* bustle, dash, hasten, hurry, scamper, scud, scutter. * *n* burst, bustle, dash, flurry, haste, hurry, scamper, scud, spurt.
scurvy *adj* scabbed, scabby, scurfy; abject, bad, base, contemptible, despicable, low, mean, pitiful, sorry, vile, vulgar, worthless; malicious, mischievous, offensive.
scuttle[1] *vb* hurry, hustle, run, rush, scamper, scramble, scud, scurry. * *n* dash, drive, flurry, haste, hurry, hustle, race, rush, scamper, scramble, scud, scurry.
scuttle[2] *vb* capsize, founder, go down, sink, overturn, upset. * *n* hatch, hatchway.
seal *vb* close, fasten, secure; attest, authenticate, confirm, establish, ratify, sanction; confine, enclose, imprison. * *n* fastening, stamp, wafer, wax; assurance, attestation, authentication, confirmation, pledge, ratification.
seamy *adj* disreputable, nasty, seedy, sordid, unpleasant.
sear *vb* blight, brand, cauterize, dry, scorch, wither. * *adj* dried up, dry, sere, withered.
search *vb* examine, explore, ferret, inspect,
investigate, overhaul, probe, ransack, scrutinize, sift; delve, hunt, forage, inquire, look, rummage. * *n* examination, exploration, hunt, inquiry, inspection, investigation, pursuit, quest, research, seeking, scrutiny.
searching *adj* close, keen, penetrating, trying; examining, exploring, inquiring, investigating, probing, seeking.
seared *adj* callous, graceless, hardened, impenitent, incorrigible, obdurate, shameless, unrepentant.
season *vb* acclimatize, accustom, form, habituate, harden, inure, mature, qualify, temper, train; flavour, spice. * *n* interval, period, spell, term, time, while.
seasonable *adj* appropriate, convenient, fit, opportune, suitable, timely.
seasoning *n* condiment, flavouring, relish, salt, sauce.
seat *vb* establish, fix, locate, place, set, station. * *n* place, site, situation, station; abode, capital, dwelling, house, mansion, residence; bottom, fundament; bench, chair, pew, settle, stall, stool.
secede *vb* apostatize, resign, retire, withdraw.
secluded *adj* close, covert, embowered, isolated, private, removed, retired, screened, sequestrated, withdrawn.
seclusion *n* obscurity, privacy, retirement, secrecy, separation, solitude, withdrawal.
second[1] *n* instant, jiffy, minute, moment, trice.
second[2] *vb* abet, advance, aid, assist, back, encourage, forward, further, help, promote, support, sustain; approve, favour. * *adj* inferior, second-rate, secondary; following, next, subsequent; additional, extra, other; double, duplicate. * *n* another, other; assistant, backer, supporter.
secondary *adj* collateral, inferior, minor, subsidiary, subordinate. * *n* delegate, deputy, proxy.
secrecy *n* clandestineness, concealment, furtiveness, stealth, surreptitiousness.
secret *adj* close, concealed, covered, covert, cryptic, hid, hidden, mysterious, privy, shrouded, veiled, unknown, unrevealed, unseen; cabbalistic, clandestine, furtive, privy, sly, stealthy, surreptitious, underhand; confidential, private, retired, secluded, unseen; abstruse, latent, mysterious, obscure, occult, recondite, unknown. * *n* confidence, enigma, key, mystery.
secretary *n* clerk, scribe, writer; escritoire, writing-desk.
secrete[1] *vb* bury, cache, conceal, disguise, hide, shroud, stash; screen, separate.
secrete[2] *vb* discharge, emit, excrete, exude, release, secern.
secretive *adj* cautious, close, reserved, reticent, taciturn, uncommunicative, wary.
sect *n* denomination, faction, schism, school.
section *n* cutting, division, fraction, part, piece, portion, segment, slice.
secular *adj* civil, laic, laical, lay, profane, temporal, worldly.
secure *vb* guard, protect, safeguard; assure, ensure, guarantee, insure; fasten; acquire, gain, get, obtain, procure. * *adj* assured, certain, confident, sure; insured, protected, safe; fast, firm, fixed, immovable, stable; careless, easy, undisturbed, unsuspecting; heedless, inattentive, incautious, negligent, overconfident.
security *n* bulwark, defence, guard, palladium, protection, safeguard, safety, shelter; bond, collateral, deposit, guarantee, pawn, pledge, stake, surety, warranty; carelessness, heedlessness, overconfidence, negligence; assurance, assuredness, certainty, confidence, ease.
sedate *adj* calm, collected, composed, contemplative, cool, demure, grave, placid, philosophical, quiet, serene, serious, sober, still, thoughtful, tranquil, undisturbed, unemotional, unruffled.
sedative *adj* allaying, anodyne, assuasive, balmy, calming, composing, demulcent, lenient, lenitive, soothing, tranquillizing. * *n* anaesthetic, anodyne, hypnotic, narcotic, opiate.
sedentary *adj* inactive, motionless, sluggish, torpid.
sediment *n* dregs, grounds, lees, precipitate, residue, residuum, settlings.
sedition *n* insurgence, insurrection, mutiny, rebellion, revolt, riot, rising, treason, tumult, uprising, uproar.
seditious *adj* factious, incendiary, insurgent, mutinous, rebellious, refractory, riotous, tumultuous, turbulent.
seduce *vb* allure, attract, betray, corrupt, debauch, deceive, decoy, deprave, ensnare, entice, inveigle, lead, mislead.
seductive *adj* alluring, attractive, enticing, tempting.
sedulous *adj* active, assiduous, busy, diligent, industrious, laborious, notable, painstaking, persevering, unremitting, untiring.
see *vb* behold, contemplate, descry, glimpse, sight, spot, survey; comprehend, conceive, distinguish, espy, know, notice, observe, perceive, recognize, remark, understand; beware, consider, envisage, regard, visualize; experience, feel, suffer; examine, inspire, notice, observe; discern, look; call on, visit.
seed *n* semen, sperm; embryo, grain, kernel, matured ovule; germ, original; children, descendants, offspring, progeny; birth, generation, race.
seedy *adj* faded, old, shabby, worn; destitute, distressed, indigent, needy, penniless, pinched, poor.
seek *vb* hunt, look, search; court, follow, prosecute, pursue, solicit; attempt, endeavour, strive, try.
seem *vb* appear, assume, look, pretend.
seeming *adj* apparent, appearing, ostensible, specious. * *n* appearance, colour, guise, look, semblance.
seemly *adj* appropriate, becoming, befitting, congruous, convenient, decent, decorous, expedient, fit, fitting, meet, proper, right, suitable; beautiful, comely, fair, good-looking, graceful, handsome, pretty, well-favoured.

seer *n* augur, diviner, foreteller, predictor, prophet, soothsayer.
segment *n* bit, division, part, piece, portion, section, sector.
segregate *vb* detach, disconnect, disperse, insulate, part, separate.
segregation *n* apartheid, discrimination, insulation, separation.
seize *vb* capture, catch, clutch, grab, grapple, grasp, grip, snatch; confiscate, impress, impound; apprehend, comprehend; arrest, take.
seldom *adv* infrequently, occasionally, rarely.
select *vb* choose, cull, pick, prefer. * *adj* choice, chosen, excellent, exquisite, good, picked, rare, selected.
selection *n* choice, election, pick, preference.
self-conscious *adj* awkward, diffident, embarrassed, insecure, nervous.
self-control *n* restraint, willpower.
self-important *adj* assuming, consequential, proud, haughty, lordly, overbearing, overweening.
selfish *adj* egoistic, egotistical, greedy, illiberal, mean, narrow, self-seeking, ungenerous.
self-possessed *adj* calm, collected, composed, cool, placid, sedate, undisturbed, unexcited, unruffled.
self-willed *adj* contumacious, dogged, headstrong, obstinate, pig-headed, stubborn, uncompliant, wilful.
sell *vb* barter, exchange, hawk, market, peddle, trade, vend.
semblance *n* likeness, resemblance, similarity; air, appearance, aspect, bearing, exterior, figure, form, mien, seeming, show; image, representation, similitude.
seminal *adj* important, original; germinal, radical, rudimental, rudimentary, unformed.
seminary *n* academy, college, gymnasium, high school, institute, school, university.
send *vb* cast, drive, emit, fling, hurl, impel, lance, launch, project, propel, throw, toss; delegate, depute, dispatch; forward, transmit; bestow, confer, give, grant.
senile *adj* aged, doddering, superannuated; doting, imbecile.
senior *adj* elder, older; higher.
seniority *n* eldership, precedence, priority, superiority.
sensation *n* feeling, sense, perception; excitement, impression, thrill.
sensational *adj* exciting, melodramatic, startling, thrilling.
sense *vb* appraise, appreciate, estimate, notice, observe, perceive, suspect, understand. * *n* brains, intellect, intelligence, mind, reason, understanding; appreciation, apprehension, discernment, feeling, perception, recognition, tact; connotation, idea, implication, judgment, notion, opinion, sentiment, view; import, interpretation, meaning, purport, significance; sagacity, soundness, substance, wisdom.
senseless *adj* apathetic, inert, insensate, unfeeling; absurd, foolish, ill-judged, nonsensical, silly, unmeaning, unreasonable, unwise; doltish, foolish, simple, stupid, witless, weak-minded.
sensible *adj* apprehensible, perceptible; aware, cognizant, conscious, convinced, persuaded, satisfied; discreet, intelligent, judicious, rational, reasonable, sagacious, sage, sober, sound, wise; observant, understanding; impressionable, sensitive.
sensitive *adj* perceptive, sentient; affected, impressible, impressionable, responsive, susceptible; delicate, tender, touchy.
sensual *adj* animal, bodily, carnal, voluptuous; gross, lascivious, lewd, licentious, unchaste.
sentence *vb* condemn, doom, judge. * *n* decision, determination, judgment, opinion, verdict; doctrine, dogma, opinion, tenet; condemnation, conviction, doom; period, proposition.
sententious *adj* compendious, compact, concise, didactic, laconic, pithy, pointed, succinct, terse.
sentiment *n* judgment, notion, opinion; maxim, saying; emotion, tenderness; disposition, feeling, thought.
sentimental *adj* impressible, impressionable, over-emotional, romantic, tender.
sentinel *n* guard, guardsman, patrol, picket, sentry, watchman.
separate *vb* detach, disconnect, disjoin, disunite, dissever, divide, divorce, part, sever, sunder; eliminate, remove, withdraw; cleave, open. * *adj* detached, disconnected, disjoined, disjointed, dissociated, disunited, divided, parted, severed; discrete, distinct, divorced, unconnected; alone, segregated, withdrawn.
separation *n* disjunction, disjuncture, dissociation; disconnection, disseverance, disseveration, disunion, division, divorce; analysis, decomposition.
sepulchral *adj* deep, dismal, funereal, gloomy, grave, hollow, lugubrious, melancholy, mournful, sad, sombre, woeful.
sepulchre *n* burial place, charnel house, grave, ossuary, sepulture, tomb.
sequel *n* close, conclusion, denouement, end, termination; consequence, event, issue, result, upshot.
sequence *n* following, graduation, progression, succession; arrangement, series, train.
sequestrated *adj* hidden, private, retired, secluded, unfrequented, withdrawn; seized.
seraphic *adj* angelic, celestial, heavenly, sublime; holy, pure, refined.
serene *adj* calm, collected, placid, peaceful, quiet, tranquil, sedate, undisturbed, unperturbed, unruffled; bright, calm, clear, fair, unclouded.
serenity *n* calm, calmness, collectedness, composure, coolness, imperturbability, peace, peacefulness, quiescence, sedateness, tranquillity; brightness, calmness, clearness, fairness, peace, quietness, stillness.
serf *n* bondman, servant, slave, thrall, villein.
serfdom *n* bondage, enslavement, enthralment, servitude, slavery, subjection, thraldom.
series *n* chain, concatenation, course, line, order, progression, sequence, succession, train.
serious *adj* earnest, grave, demure, pious, resolute, sedate, sober, solemn, staid, thoughtful; dangerous, great, important, momentous, weighty.
sermon *n* discourse, exhortation, homily, lecture.
serpentine *adj* anfractuous, convoluted, crooked, meandering, sinuous, spiral, tortuous, twisted, undulating, winding.
servant *n* attendant, dependant, factotum, helper, henchman, retainer, servitor, subaltern, subordinate, underling; domestic, drudge, flunky, lackey, menial, scullion, slave.
serve *vb* aid, assist, attend, help, minister, oblige, succour; advance, benefit, forward, promote; content, satisfy, supply; handle, officiate, manage, manipulate, work.
service *vb* check, maintain, overhaul, repair. * *n* labour, ministration, work; attendance, business, duty, employ, employment, office; advantage, benefit, good, gain, profit; avail, purpose, use, utility; ceremony, function, observance, rite, worship.
serviceable *adj* advantageous, available, beneficial, convenient, functional, handy, helpful, operative, profitable, useful.
servile *adj* dependent, menial; abject, base, beggarly, cringing, fawning, grovelling, low, mean, obsequious, slavish, sneaking, sycophantic, truckling.
servility *n* bondage, dependence, slavery; abjection, abjectness, baseness, fawning, meanness, obsequiousness, slavishness, sycophancy.
servitor *n* attendant, dependant, footman, lackey, retainer, servant, squire, valet, waiter.
servitude *n* bondage, enslavement, enthralment, serfdom, service, slavery, thraldom.
set[1] *vb* lay, locate, mount, place, put, stand, station; appoint, determine, establish, fix, settle; risk, stake, wager; adapt, adjust, regulate; adorn, stud, variegate; arrange, dispose, pose, post; appoint, assign, predetermine, prescribe; estimate, prize, rate, value; embarrass, perplex, pose; contrive, produce; decline, sink; congeal, concern, consolidate, harden, solidify; flow, incline, run, tend; (*with* **about**) begin, commence; (*with* **apart**) appropriate, consecrate, dedicate, devote, reserve, set aside; (*with* **aside**) abrogate, annul, omit, reject; reserve, set apart; (*with* **before**) display, exhibit; (*with* **down**) chronicle, jot down, record, register, state, write down; (*with* **forth**) display, exhibit, explain, expound, manifest, promulgate, publish, put forward, represent, show; (*with* **forward**) advance, further, promote; (*with* **free**) acquit, clear, emancipate, liberate, release; (*with* **off**) adorn, decorate, embellish;

define, portion off; (*with* **on**) actuate, encourage, impel, influence, incite, instigate, prompt, spur, urge; attack, assault, set upon; (*with* **out**) display, issue, publish, proclaim, prove, recommend, show; (*with* **right**) correct, put in order; (*with* **to rights**) adjust, regulate; (*with* **up**) elevate, erect, exalt, raise; establish, found, institute; (*with* **upon**) assail, assault, attack, fly at, rush upon. * *adj* appointed, established, formal, ordained, prescribed, regular, settled; determined, fixed, firm, obstinate, positive, stiff, unyielding; immovable, predetermined; located, placed, put. * *n* attitude, position, posture; scene, scenery, setting.

set[2] *n* assortment, collection, suit; class, circle, clique, cluster, company, coterie, division, gang, group, knot, party, school, sect.

setback *n* blow, hitch, hold-up, rebuff; defeat, disappointment, reverse.

set-off *n* adornment, decoration, embellishment, ornament; counterbalance, counterclaim, equivalent.

settle *vb* adjust, arrange, compose, regulate; account, balance, close up, conclude, discharge, liquidate, pay, pay up, reckon, satisfy, square; allay, calm, compose, pacify, quiet, repose, rest, still, tranquillize; confirm, decide, determine, make clear; establish, fix, set; fall, gravitate, sink, subside; abide, colonize, domicile, dwell, establish, inhabit, people, place, plant, reside; (*with* **on**) determine on, fix on, fix upon; establish. * *n* bench, seat, stool.

settled *adj* established, fixed, stable; decided, deep-rooted, steady, unchanging; adjusted, arranged; methodical, orderly, quiet; common, customary, everyday, ordinary, usual, wonted.

set-to *n* combat, conflict, contest, fight.

sever *vb* divide, part, rend, separate, sunder; detach, disconnect, disjoin, disunite.

several *adj* individual, single, particular; distinct, exclusive, independent, separate; different, divers, diverse, manifold, many, sundry, various.

severance *n* partition, separation.

severe *adj* austere, bitter, dour, hard, harsh, inexorable, morose, painful, relentless, rigid, rigorous, rough, sharp, stern, stiff, strait-laced, unmitigated, unrelenting, unsparing; accurate, exact, methodical, strict; chaste, plain, restrained, simple, unadorned; biting, caustic, cruel, cutting, harsh, keen, sarcastic, satirical, trenchant; acute, afflictive, distressing, excruciating, extreme, intense, stringent, violent; critical, exact.

severity *n* austerity, gravity, harshness, rigour, seriousness, sternness, strictness; accuracy, exactness, niceness; chasteness, plainness, simplicity; acrimony, causticity, keenness, sharpness; afflictiveness, extremity, keenness, stringency, violence; cruelty.

sew *vb* baste, bind, hem, stitch, tack.

sex *n* gender, femininity, masculinity, sexuality; coitus, copulation, fornication, love-making.

shabby *adj* faded, mean, poor, ragged, seedy, threadbare, worn, worn-out; beggarly, mean, paltry, penurious, stingy, ungentlemanly, unhandsome.

shackle *vb* chain, fetter, gyve, hamper, manacle; bind, clog, confine, cumber, embarrass, encumber, impede, obstruct, restrict, trammel. * *n* chain, fetter, gyve, hamper, manacle.

shade *vb* cloud, darken, dim, eclipse, obfuscate, obscure; cover, ensconce, hide, protect, screen, shelter. * *n* darkness, dusk, duskiness, gloom, obscurity, shadow; cover, protection, shelter; awning, blind, curtain, screen, shutter, veil; degree, difference, kind, variety; cast, colour, complexion, dye, hue, tinge, tint, tone; apparition, ghost, manes, phantom, shadow, spectre, spirit.

shadow *vb* becloud, cloud, darken, obscure, shade; adumbrate, foreshadow, symbolize, typify; conceal, cover, hide, protect, screen, shroud. * *n* penumbra, shade, umbra, umbrage; darkness, gloom, obscurity; cover, protection, security, shelter; adumbration, foreshadowing, image, prefiguration, representation; apparition, ghost, phantom, shade, spirit; image, portrait, reflection, silhouette.

shadowy *adj* shady, umbrageous; dark, dim, gloomy, murky, obscure; ghostly, imaginary, impalpable, insubstantial, intangible, spectral, unreal, unsubstantial, visionary.

shady *adj* shadowy, umbrageous; crooked.

shaft *n* arrow, missile, weapon; handle, helve; pole, tongue; axis, spindle; pinnacle, spire; stalk, stem, trunk.

shaggy *adj* rough, rugged.

shake *vb* quake, quaver, quiver, shiver, shudder, totter, tremble; agitate, convulse, jar, jolt, stagger; daunt, frighten, intimidate; endanger, move, weaken; oscillate, vibrate, wave; move, put away, remove, throw off. * *n* agitation, concussion, flutter, jar, jolt, quaking, shaking, shivering, shock, trembling, tremor.

shaky *adj* jiggly, quaky, shaking, tottering, trembling.

shallow *adj* flimsy, foolish, frivolous, puerile, trashy, trifling, trivial; empty, ignorant, silly, slight, simple, superficial, unintelligent.

sham *vb* ape, feign, imitate, pretend; cheat, deceive, delude, dupe, impose, trick. * *adj* assumed, counterfeit, false, feigned, mock, make-believe, pretended, spurious. * *n* delusion, feint, fraud, humbug, imposition, imposture, pretence, trick.

shamble *vb* hobble, shuffle.

shambles *npl* abattoir, slaughterhouse; confusion, disorder, mess.

shame *vb* debase, degrade, discredit, disgrace, dishonour, stain, sully, taint, tarnish; abash, confound, confuse, discompose, disconcert, humble, humiliate; deride, flout, jeer, mock, ridicule, sneer. * *n* contempt, degradation, derision, discredit, disgrace, dishonour, disrepute, ignominy, infamy, obloquy, odium, opprobrium; abashment, chagrin, confusion, embarrassment, humiliation, mortification; reproach, scandal; decency, decorousness, decorum, modesty, propriety, seemliness.

shamefaced *adj* bashful, diffident, overmodest.

shameful *adj* atrocious, base, disgraceful, dishonourable, disreputable, heinous, ignominous, infamous, nefarious, opprobrious, outrageous, scandalous, vile, villainous, wicked; degrading, indecent, unbecoming.

shameless *adj* assuming, audacious, bold-faced, brazen, brazen-faced, cool, immodest, impudent, indecent, indelicate, insolent, unabashed, unblushing; abandoned, corrupt, depraved, dissolute, graceless, hardened, incorrigible, irreclaimable, lost, obdurate, profligate, reprobate, sinful, unprincipled, vicious.

shape *vb* create, form, make, produce; fashion, model, mould; adjust, direct, frame, regulate; conceive, conjure up, figure, image, imagine. * *n* appearance, aspect, fashion, figure, form, guise, make; build, cast, cut, model, mould, pattern; apparition, image.

shapeless *adj* amorphous, formless; grotesque, irregular, rude, uncouth, unsymmetrical.

shapely *adj* comely, symmetrical, trim, well-formed.

share *vb* apportion, distribute, divide, parcel out, portion, split; partake, participate; experience, receive. * *n* part, portion, quantum; allotment, allowance, contingent, deal, dividend, division, interest, lot, proportion, quantity, quota.

sharer *n* communicant, partaker, participator.

sharp *adj* acute, cutting, keen, keen-edged, knife-edged, razor-edged, trenchant; acuminate, needle-shaped, peaked, pointed, ridged; apt, astute, canny, clear-sighted, clever, cunning, discerning, discriminating, ingenious, inventive, keen-witted, penetrating, perspicacious, quick, ready, sagacious, sharp-witted, shrewd, smart, subtle, witty; acid, acrid, biting, bitter, burning, high-flavoured, high-seasoned, hot, mordacious, piquant, poignant, pungent, sour, stinging; acrimonious, biting, caustic, cutting, harsh, mordant, sarcastic, severe, tart, trenchant; cruel, hard, rigid; afflicting, distressing, excruciating, intense, painful, piercing, shooting, sore, violent; nipping, pinching; ardent, eager, fervid, fierce, fiery, impetuous, strong; high, screeching, shrill; attentive, vigilant; severe; close, exacting, shrewd, cold, crisp, freezing, icy wintry. * *adv* abruptly, sharply, suddenly; exactly, precisely, punctually.

sharp-cut *adj* clear, distinct, well-defined.

sharpen *vb* edge, intensify, point.

sharper *n* cheat, deceiver, defrauder, knave, rogue, shark, swindler, trickster.

sharply *adv* rigorously, roughly, severely; acutely, keenly; vehemently, violently; accurately, exactly, minutely, trenchantly, wittily; abruptly, steeply.

sharpness *n* acuteness, keenness, trenchancy; acuity, spinosity; acumen, cleverness, discernment, ingenuity, quickness, sagacity, shrewdness, smartness, wit; acidity, acridity, piquancy, pungency, sting, tartness; causticness, incisiveness, pungency, sarcasm, satire, severity; afflictiveness, intensity, painfulness, poignancy; ardour, fierceness, violence; discordance, dissonance, highness, screechiness, squeakiness, shrillness.

sharp-sighted *adj* clear-sighted, keen, keen-eyed, keen-sighted.

sharp-witted *adj* acute, clear-sighted, cunning, discerning, ingenious, intelligent, keen, keen-sighted, long-headed, quick, sagacious, sharp, shrewd.

shatter *vb* break, burst, crack, rend, shiver, smash, splinter, split; break up, derange, disorder, overthrow.

shave *vb* crop, cut off, mow, pare; slice; graze, skim, touch.

shaver *n* boy, child, youngster; bargainer, extortioner, sharper.

shear *vb* clip, cut, fleece, strip; divest; break off.

sheath *n* case, casing, covering, envelope, scabbard, sheathing.

sheathe *vb* case, cover, encase, enclose.

shed[1] *n* cabin, cot, hovel, hut, outhouse, shack, shelter.

shed[2] *vb* effuse, let fall, pour out, spill; diffuse, emit, give out, scatter, spread; cast, let fall, put off, slough, throw off.

sheen *n* brightness, gloss, glossiness, shine, spendour.

sheep *n* ewe, lamb, ram.

sheepish *adj* bashful, diffident, overmodest, shamefaced, timid, timorous.

sheer[1] *adj* perpendicular, precipitous, steep, vertical; clear, downright, mere, pure, simple, unadulterated, unmingled, unmixed, unqualified, utter; clear; fine, transparent. * *adv* outright; perpendicularly, steeply.

sheer[2] *vb* decline, deviate, move aside, swerve. * *n* bow, curve.

shelf *n* bracket, console, ledge, mantelpiece.

shell *vb* exfoliate, fall off, peel off; bombard. * *n* carapace, case, covering, shard; bomb, grenade, sharpnel; framework.

shelter *vb* cover, defend, ensconce, harbour, hide, house, protect, screen, shield, shroud. * *n* asylum, cover, covert, harbour, haven, hideaway, refuge, retreat, sanctuary; defence, protection, safety, screen, security, shield; guardian, protector.

shelve *vb* dismiss, put aside; incline, slope.

shepherd *vb* escort, guide, marshal, usher; direct, drive, drove, herd, lead; guard, tend, watch over. * *n* drover, grazier, herder, herdsman; chaplain, churchman, clergyman, cleric, divine, ecclesiastic, minister, padre, parson, pastor; chaperon, duenna, escort, guide, squire, usher.

shield *vb* cover, defend, guard, protect, shelter; repel, ward off; avert, forbid, forfend. * *n* aegis, buckler, escutcheon, scutcheon, targe; bulwark, cover, defence, guard, palladium, protection, rampart, safeguard, security, shelter.

shift *vb* alter, change, fluctuate, move, vary; chop, dodge, swerve, veer; contrive, devise, manage, plan, scheme, shuffle. * *n* change, substitution, turn; contrivance, expedient, means, resort, resource; artifice, craft, device, dodge, evasion, fraud, mask, ruse, stratagem, subterfuge, trick, wile; chemise, smock.

shiftless *adj* improvident, imprudent, negligent, slack, thriftless, unresourceful.

shifty *adj* tricky, undependable, wily.

shillyshally *vb* hesitate, waver. * *n* hesitation, irresolute, wavering.

shimmer *vb* flash, glimmer, glisten, shine. * *n* blink, glimmer, glitter, twinkle.

shin *vb* climb, swarm. * *n* shinbone, tibia.

shindy *n* disturbance, riot, roughhouse, row, spree, uproar.

shine *vb* beam, blaze, coruscate, flare, give light, glare, gleam, glimmer, glisten, glitter, glow, lighten, radiate, sparkle; excel. * *n* brightness, brilliancy, glaze, gloss, polish, sheen.

shining *adj* beaming, bright, brilliant, effulgent, gleaming, glowing, glistening, glittering, luminous, lustrous, radiant, resplendent, splendid; conspicuous, distinguished, illustrious.

shiny *adj* bright, clear, luminous, sunshiny, unclouded; brilliant, burnished, glassy, glossy, polished.

ship *n* boat, craft, steamer, vessel.

shipshape *adj* neat, orderly, tidy, trim, well-arranged.

shipwreck *vb* cast away, maroon, strand, wreck. * *n* demolition, destruction, miscarriage, overthrow, perdition, ruin, subversion, wreck.

shirk *vb* avoid, dodge, evade, malinger, quit, slack; cheat, shark, trick.

shiver[1] *vb* break, shatter, splinter. * *n* bit, fragment, piece, slice, sliver, splinter.

shiver[2] *vb* quake, quiver, shake, shudder, tremble. * *n* shaking, shivering, shuddering, tremor.

shivery[1] *adj* brittle, crumbly, frangible, friable, shatterable, splintery.

shivery[2] *adj* quaking, quavering, quivering, shaky, trembly, tremulous; chilly, shivering.

shoal[1] *vb* crowd, throng. * *n* crowd, horde, multitude, swarm, throng.

shoal[2] *n* sandbank, shallows; danger.

shock *vb* appall, horrify; disgust, disquiet, disturb, nauseate, offend, outrage, revolt, scandalize, sicken; astound, stagger, stun; collide with, jar, jolt, shake, strike against; encounter, meet. * *n* agitation, blow, offence, stroke, trauma; assault, brunt, conflict; clash, collision, concussion, impact, percussion.

shocking *adj* abominable, detestable, disgraceful, disgusting, execrable, foul, hateful, loathsome, obnoxious, odious, offensive, repugnant, repulsive, revolting; appalling, awful, dire, dreadful, fearful, frightful, ghastly, hideous, horrible, horrid, horrific, monstrous, terrible.

shoot *vb* catapult, expel, hurl, let fly, propel; discharge, fire, let off; dart, fly, pass, pelt; extend, jut, project, protrude, protuberate, push, put forth, send forth, stretch; bud, germinate, sprout; (*with* **up**) grow increase, spring up, run up, start up. * *n* branch, offshoot, scion, sprout, twig.

shop *n* emporium, market, mart, store; workshop.

shore[1] *n* beach, brim, coast, seabord, seaside, strand, waterside.

shore[2] *vb* brace, buttress, prop, stay, support. * *n* beam, brace, buttress, prop, stay, support.

shorn *adj* cut-off; deprived.

short *adj* brief, curtailed; direct, near, straight; compendious, concise, condensed, laconic, pithy, terse, sententious, succinct, summary; abrupt, curt, petulant, pointed, sharp, snappish, uncivil; defective, deficient, inadequate, insufficient, niggardly, scanty, scrimpy; contracted, desitute, lacking, limited, minus, wanting; dwarfish, squat, undersized; brittle, crisp, crumbling, friable. * *adv* abruptly, at once, forthwith, suddenly.

shortcoming *n* defect, deficiency, delinquency, error, failing, failure, fault, imperfection, inadequacy, remissness, slip, weakness.

shorten *vb* abbreviate, abridge, curtail, cut short; abridge, contract, diminish, lessen, retrench, reduce; cut off, dock, lop, trim; confine, hinder, restrain, restrict.

shortening *n* abbreviation, abridgment, contraction, curtailment, diminution, retrenchment, reduction.

shorthand *n* brachygraphy, stenography, tachygraphy.

short-lived *adj* emphemeral, transient, transitory.

shortly *adv* quickly, soon; briefly, concisely, succinctly, tersely.

short-sighted *adj* myopic, nearsighted, purblind; imprudent, indiscreet.

shot[1] *n* discharge; ball, bullet, missile, projectile; marksman, shooter.

shot[2] *adj* chatoyant, iridescent, irisated, moiré, watered; intermingled, interspersed, interwoven.

shoulder *vb* bear, bolster, carry, hump, maintain, pack, support, sustain, tote; crowd, elbow, jostle, press forward, push, thrust. * *n* projection, protuberance.

shoulder blade *n* blade bone, omoplate, scapula, shoulder bone.

shout *vb* bawl, cheer, clamour, exclaim, halloo, roar, vociferate, whoop, yell. * *n* cheer, clamour, exclamation, halloo, hoot, huzza, outcry, roar, vociferation, whoop, yell.

shove *vb* jostle, press against, propel, push, push aside; (*with* **off**) push away, thrust away.

show *vb* blazon, display, exhibit, flaunt, parade, present; indicate, mark, point out; disclose, discover, divulge, explain, make clear, make known, proclaim, publish, reveal, unfold; demonstrate, evidence, manifest, prove, verify; conduct, guide, usher; direct, inform, instruct, teach; expound, elucidate, interpret; (*with* **off**) display, exhibit, make a show, set off; (*with* **up**) expose. * *n* array, exhibition, representation, sight, spectacle; blazonry, bravery, ceremony, dash, demonstration, display, flourish, ostentation, pageant, pageantry, parade, pomp, splendour, splurge; likeness, resemblance, semblance; affectation, appearance, colour, illusion, mask, plausibility, pose, pretence, pretext, simulation, speciousness; entertainment, production.

showy *adj* bedizened, dressy, fine, flashy, flaunting, garish, gaudy, glaring, gorgeous, loud, ornate, smart, swanky, splendid; grand, magnificent, ostentatious, pompous, pretentious, stately, sumptuous.

shred *vb* tear. * *n* bit, fragment, piece, rag, scrap, strip, tatter.

shrew *n* brawler, fury, scold, spitfire, termagant, virago, vixen.

shrewd *adj* arch, artful, astute, crafty, cunning, Machiavellian, sly, subtle, wily; acute, astute, canny, discerning, discriminating, ingenious, keen, knowing, penetrating, sagacious, sharp, sharp-sighted.

shrewdness *n* address, archness, art, artfulness, astuteness, craft, cunning, policy, skill, slyness, subtlety; acumen, acuteness, discernment, ingenuity, keenness, penetration, perspicacity, sagacity, sharpness, wit.

shrewish *adj* brawling, clamorous, froward, peevish, petulant, scolding, vixenish.

shriek *vb* scream, screech, squeal, yell, yelp. * *n* cry, scream, screech, yell.

shrill *adj* acute, high, high-toned, high-pitched, piercing, piping, sharp.

shrine *n* reliquary, sacred tomb; altar, hallowed place, sacred place.

shrink *vb* contract, decrease, dwindle, shrivel, wither; balk, blench, draw back, flinch, give way, quail, recoil, retire, swerve, wince, withdraw.

shrivel *vb* dry, dry up, parch; contract, decrease, dwindle, shrink, wither, wrinkle.

shroud *vb* bury, cloak, conceal, cover, hide, mask, muffle, protect, screen, shelter, veil. * *n* covering, garment; grave clothes, winding sheet.

shrub *n* bush, dwarf tree, low tree.

shrubby *adj* bushy.

shudder *vb* quake, quiver, shake, shiver, tremble. * *n* shaking, shuddering, trembling, tremor.

shuffle *vb* confuse, disorder, intermix, jumble, mix, shift; cavil, dodge, equivocate, evade, prevaricate, quibble, vacillate; struggle. * *n* artifice, cavil, evasion, fraud, pretence, pretext, prevarication, quibble, ruse, shuffling, sophism, subterfuge, trick.

shun *vb* avoid, elude, eschew, escape, evade, get clear of.

shut *vb* close, close up, stop; confine, coop up,

enclose, imprison, lock up, shut up; (*with* **in**) confine, enclose; (*with* **off**) bar, exclude, intercept; (*with* **up**) close up, shut; confine, enclose, fasten in, imprison, lock in, lock up.

shy *vb* cast, chuck, fling, hurl, jerk, pitch, sling, throw, toss; boggle, sheer, start aside. * *adj* bashful, coy, diffident, reserved, retiring, sheepish, shrinking, timid; cautious, chary, distrustful, heedful, wary. * *n* start; fling, throw.

sibilant *adj* buzzing, hissing, sibilous.

sick *adj* ailing, ill, indisposed, laid-up, unwell, weak; nauseated, queasy; disgusted, revolted, tired, weary; diseased, distempered, disordered, feeble, morbid, unhealthy, unsound, weak; languishing, longing, pining.

sicken *vb* ail, disease, fall sick, make sick; nauseate; disgust, weary; decay, droop, languish, pine.

sickening *adj* nauseating, nauseous, palling, sickish; disgusting, distasteful, loathsome, offensive, repulsive, revolting.

sickly *adj* ailing, diseased, faint, feeble, infirm, languid, languishing, morbid, unhealthy, valetudinary, weak, weakly.

sickness *n* ail, ailment, complaint, disease, disorder, distemper, illness, indisposition, invalidism, malady, morbidity; nausea, qualmishness, queasiness.

side *vb* border, bound, edge, flank, frontier, march, rim, skirt, verge; avert, turn aside; (*with* **with**) befriend, favour, flock to, join with, second, support. * *adj* flanking, later, skirting; indirect, oblique; extra, odd, off, spare. * *n* border, edge, flank, margin, verge; cause, faction, interest, party, sect.

sideboard *n* buffet, dresser.

side by side abreast, alongside, by the side.

sidelong *adj* lateral, oblique. * *adv* laterally, obliquely; on the side.

sidewalk *n* footpath, footway, pavement.

sideways, sidewise *adv* laterally. * *adv* athwart, crossways, crosswise, laterally, obliquely, sidelong, sidewards.

siesta *n* doze, nap.

sift *vb* part, separate; bolt, screen, winnow; analyse, canvass, discuss, examine, fathom, follow up, inquire into, investigate, probe, scrutinize, sound, try.

sigh *vb* complain, grieve, lament, mourn. * *n* long breath, sough, suspiration.

sight *vb* get sight of, perceive, see. * *n* cognizance, ken, perception, view; beholding, eyesight, seeing, vision; exhibition, prospect, representation, scene, show, spectacle, wonder; consideration, estimation, knowledge; examination, inspection.

sightless *adj* blind, eyeless, unseeing.

sightly *adj* beautiful, comely, handsome.

sign *vb* indicate, signal, signify; countersign, endorse, subscribe. * *n* emblem, index, indication, manifestation, mark, note, proof, signal, signification, symbol, symptom, token; beacon; augury, auspice, foreboding, miracle, omen, portent, presage, prodigy, prognostic, wonder; type; countersign, password.

signal *vb* flag, glance, hail, nod, nudge, salute, sign, signalize, sound, speak, touch, wave, wink. * *adj* conspicuous, eminent, extraordinary, memorable, notable, noteworthy, remarkable. * *n* cue, indication, mark, sign, token.

signalize *vb* celebrate, distinguish, make memorable.

signature *n* mark, sign, stamp; autograph, hand.

significance *n* implication, import, meaning, purport, sense; consequence, importance, moment, portent, weight; emphasis, energy, expressiveness, force, impressiveness.

significant *adj* betokening, expressive, indicative, significative, signifying; important, material, momentous, portentous, weighty; forcible, emphatic, expressive, telling.

signification *n* expression; acceptation, import, meaning, purport, sense.

signify *vb* betoken, communication, express, indicate, intimate; denote, imply, import, mean, purport, suggest; announce, declare, give notice of, impart, make known, manifest, proclaim, utter; augur, foreshadow, indicate, portend, represent; matter, weigh.

silence *vb* hush, muzzle, still; allay, calm, quiet. * *interj* be silent, be still, hush, soft, tush, tut, whist. * *n* calm, hush, lull, noiselessness, peace, quiet, quietude, soundlessness, stillness; dumbness, mumness, muteness, reticence, speechlessness, taciturnity.

silent *adj* calm, hushed, noiseless, quiet, soundless, still; dumb, inarticulate, mum, mute, nonvocal, speechless, tacit; reticent, taciturn, uncommunicative.

silken *adj* flossy, silky, soft.

silkiness *n* smoothness, softness.

silly *adj* brainless, childish, foolish, inept, senseless, shallow, simple, stupid, weak-minded, witless; absurd, extravagant, frivolous, imprudent, indiscreet, nonsensical, preposterous, trifling, unwise. * *n* ass, duffer, goose, idiot, simpleton.

silt *n* alluvium, deposit, deposition, residue, settlement, settlings, sediment.

silver *adj* argent, silvery; bright, silvery, white; clear, mellifluous, soft.

similar *adj* analogous, duplicate, like, resembling, twin; homogeneous, uniform.

similarity *n* agreement, analogy, correspondence, likeness, parallelism, parity, resemblance, sameness, semblance, similitude.

simile *n* comparison, metaphor, similitude.

similitude *n* image, likeness, resemblance; comparison, metaphor, simile.
simmer *vb* boil, bubble, seethe, stew.
simper *vb* smile, smirk.
simple *adj* bare, elementary, homogeneous, incomplex, mere, single, unalloyed, unblended, uncombined, uncompounded, unmingled, unmixed; chaste, plain, homespun, inornate, natural, neat, unadorned, unaffected, unembellished, unpretentious, unstudied, unvarnished; artless, downright, frank, guileless, inartificial, ingenuous, naive, open, simple-hearted, simple-minded, sincere, single-minded, straightforward, true, unconstrained, undesigning, unsophisticated; credulous, fatuous, foolish, shallow, silly, unwise, weak; clear, intelligible, understandable, uninvolved, unmistakable.
simple-hearted *adj* artless, frank, ingenuous, open, simple, single-hearted.
simpleton *n* fool, greenhorn, nincompoop, ninny.
simplicity *n* chasteness, homeliness, naturalness, neatness, plainness; artlessness, frankness, naivety, openness, simplesse, sincerity; clearness; gullibility, folly, silliness, weakness.
simply *adv* artlessly, plainly, sincerely, unaffectedly; barely, merely, of itself, solely; absolutely, alone.
simulate *vb* act, affect, ape, assume, counterfeit, dissemble, feign, mimic, pretend, sham.
simulation *n* counterfeiting, feigning, personation, pretence.
simultaneous *adj* coeval, coincident, concomitant, concurrent, contemporaneous, synchronous.
sin *vb* do wrong, err, transgress, trespass. * *n* delinquency, depravity, guilt, iniquity, misdeed, offence, transgression, unrighteousness, wickedness, wrong.
since *conj* as, because, considering, seeing that. * *adv* ago, before this; from that time. * *prep* after, from the time of, subsequently to.
sincere *adj* pure, unmixed; genuine, honest, inartificial, real, true, unaffected, unfeigned, unvarnished; artless, candid, direct, frank, guileless, hearty, honest, ingenuous, open, plain, single, straightforward, truthful, undissembling, upright, whole-hearted.
sincerity *n* artlessness, candour, earnestness, frankness, genuineness, guilelessness, honesty, ingenuousness, probity, truth, truthfulness, unaffectedness, veracity.
sinew *n* ligament, tendon; brawn, muscle, nerve, strength.
sinewy *adj* able-bodied, brawny, firm, Herculean, muscular, nervous, powerful, robust, stalwart, strapping, strong, sturdy, vigorous, wiry.
sinful *adj* bad, criminal, depraved, immoral, iniquitous, mischievous, peccant, transgressive, unholy, unrighteous, wicked, wrong.
sinfulness *n* corruption, criminality, depravity, iniquity, irreligion, ungodliness, unholiness, unrighteousness, wickedness.
sing *vb* cantillate, carol, chant, hum, hymn, intone, lilt, troll, warble, yodel.
singe *vb* burn, scorch, sear.
singer *n* cantor, caroler, chanter, gleeman, prima donna, minstrel, psalmodist, songster, vocalist.
single *vb* (*with* **out**) choose, pick, select, single. * *adj* alone, isolated, one only, sole, solitary; individual, particular, separate; celibate, unmarried, unwedded; pure, simple, uncompounded, unmixed; honest, ingenuous, sincere, unbiased, uncorrupt, upright.
single-handed *adj* alone, by one's self, unaided, unassisted.
single-minded *adj* artless, candid, guileless, ingenuous, sincere.
singleness *n* individuality, unity; purity, simplicity; ingenuousness, integrity, sincerity, uprightness.
singular *adj* eminent, exceptional, extraordinary, rare, remarkable, strange, uncommon, unusual, unwonted; particular, unexampled, unparalleled, unprecedented; unaccountable; bizarre, curious, eccentric, fantastic, odd, peculiar, queer; individual, single; not complex, single, uncompounded, unique.
singularity *n* aberration, abnormality, irregularity, oddness, rareness, rarity, strangeness, uncommonness; characteristic, idiosyncrasy, individuality, particularity, peculiarity; eccentricity, oddity.
sinister *adj* baleful, injurious, untoward; boding ill, inauspicious, ominous, unlucky; left, on the left hand.
sink *vb* droop, drop, fall, founder, go down, submerge, subside; enter, penetrate; collapse, fail; decay, decline, decrease, dwindle, give way, languish, lose strength; engulf, immerse, merge, submerge, submerse; dig, excavate, scoop out; abase, bring down, crush, debase, degrade, depress, diminish, lessen, lower, overbear; destroy, overthrow, overwhelm, reduce, ruin, swamp, waste. * *n* basin, cloaca, drain.
sinless *adj* faultless, guiltless, immaculate, impeccable, innocent, spotless, unblemished, undefiled, unspotted, unsullied, untarnished.
sinner *n* criminal, delinquent, evildoer, offender, reprobate, wrongdoer.
sinuosity *n* crook, curvature, flexure, sinus, tortuosity, winding.
sinuous *adj* bending, crooked, curved, curvilinear, flexuous, serpentine, sinuate, sinuated, tortuous, undulating, wavy, winding.
sip *vb* drink, suck up, sup; absorb, drink in. * *n* small draught, taste.
sire *vb* father, reproduce; author, breed, conceive, create, generate, originate, produce, propagate. * *n* father, male parent, progenitor; man, male person; sir, sirrah; author, begetter, creator, father, generator, originator.
siren *adj* alluring, bewitching, fascinating, seducing, tempting. * *n* mermaid; charmer, Circe, seducer, seductress, tempter, temptress.
sit *vb* be, remain, repose, rest, stay; bear on, lie, rest; abide, dwell, settle; perch; brood, incubate; become, be suited, fit.
site *vb* locate, place, position, situate, station. * *n* ground, locality, location, place, position, seat, situation, spot, station, whereabouts.
sitting *n* meeting, session.
situation *n* ground, locality, location, place, position, seat, site, spot, whereabouts; case, category, circumstances, condition, juncture, plight, predicament, state; employment, office, place, post, station.
size *n* amplitude, bigness, bulk, dimensions, expanse, greatness, largeness, magnitude, mass, volume.
skeleton *n* framework; draft, outline, sketch.
sketch *vb* design, draft, draw out; delineate, depict, paint, portray, represent. * *n* delineation, design, draft, drawing, outline, plan, skeleton.
sketchy *adj* crude, incomplete, unfinished.
skilful *adj* able, accomplished, adept, adroit, apt, clever, competent, conversant, cunning, deft, dexterous, dextrous, expert, handy, ingenious, masterly, practised, proficient, qualified, quick, ready, skilled, trained, versed, well-versed.
skill *n* ability, address, adroitness, aptitude, aptness, art, cleverness, deftness, dexterity, expertise, expertness, facility, ingenuity, knack, quickness, readiness, skilfulness; discernment, discrimination, knowledge, understanding, wit.
skim *vb* brush, glance, graze, kiss, scrape, scratch, sweep, touch lightly; coast, flow, fly, glide, sail, scud, whisk; dip into, glance at, scan, skip, thumb over, touch upon.
skin *vb* pare, peel; decorticate, excoriate, flay. * *n* cuticle, cutis, derm, epidermis, hide, integument, pellicle, pelt; hull, husk, peel, rind.
skinflint *n* churl, curmudgeon, lickpenny, miser, niggard, scrimp.
skinny *adj* emaciated, lank, lean, poor, shrivelled, shrunk, thin.
skip *vb* bound, caper, frisk, gambol, hop, jump, leap, spring; disregard, intermit, miss, neglect, omit, pass over, skim. * *n* bound, caper, frisk, gambol, hop, jump, leap, spring.
skirmish *vb* battle, brush, collide, combat, contest, fight, scuffle, tussle. * *n* affair, affray, battle, brush, collision, combat, conflict, contest, encounter, fight, scuffle, tussle.
skirt *vb* border, bound, edge, fringe, hem, march, rim; circumnavigate, circumvent, flank, go along. * *n* border, boundary, edge, margin, rim, verge; flap, kilt, overskirt, petticoat.
skittish *adj* changeable, fickle, inconstant; hasty, volatile, wanton; shy, timid, timorous.
skulk *vb* hide, lurk, slink, sneak.
skulker *n* lurker, sneak; shirk, slacker, malingerer.
skull *n* brain pan, cranium.
sky *n* empyrean, firmament, heaven, heavens, welkin.

sky-blue *adj* azure, cerulean, sapphire, sky-coloured.

skylarking *n* carousing, frolicking, sporting.

slab *adj* slimy, thick, viscous. * *n* beam, board, layer, panel, plank, slat, table, tablet; mire, mud, puddle, slime.

slabber *vb* drivel, slaver, slobber; drop, let fall, shed, spill.

slack *vb* ease off, let up; abate, ease up, relax, slacken; malinger, shirk; choke, damp, extinguish, smother, stifle. * *adj* backward, careless, inattentive, lax, negligent, remiss; abated, dilatory, diminished, lingering, slow, tardy; loose, relaxed; dull, idle, inactive, quiet, sluggish. * *n* excess, leeway, looseness, play; coal dust, culm, residue.

slacken *vb* abate, diminish, lessen, lower, mitigate, moderate, neglect, remit, relieve, retard, slack; loosen, relax; flag, slow down; bridle, check, control, curb, repress, restrain.

slackness *n* looseness; inattention, negligence, remissness; slowness, tardiness.

slander *vb* asperse, backbite, belie, brand, calumniate, decry, defame, libel, malign, reproach, scandalize, traduce, vilify; detract from, disparage. * *n* aspersion, backbiting, calumny, defamation, detraction, libel, obloquy, scandal, vilification.

slanderous *adj* calumnious, defamatory, false, libellous, malicious, maligning.

slang *n* argo, cant, jargon, lingo.

slant *vb* incline, lean, lie obliquely, list, slope. * *n* inclination, slope, steep, tilt.

slap *vb* dab, clap, pat, smack, spank, strike. * *adv* instantly, quickly, plumply. * *n* blow, clap.

slapdash *adv* haphazardly, hurriedly, precipitately.

slash *vb* cut, gash, slit. * *n* cut, gash, slit.

slashed *adj* cut, slit; (*bot*) jagged, laciniate, multifid.

slattern *adj* slatternly, slovenly, sluttish. * *n* drab, slut, sloven, trollop.

slatternly *adj* dirty, slattern, slovenly, sluttish, unclean, untidy. * *adv* carelessly, negligently, sluttishly.

slaughter *vb* butcher, kill, massacre, murder, slay. * *n* bloodshed, butchery, carnage, havoc, killing, massacre, murder, slaying.

slaughterer *n* assassin, butcher, cutthroat, destroyer, killer, murderer, slayer.

slave *vb* drudge, moil, toil. * *n* bondmaid, bondservant, bondslave, bondman, captive, dependant, henchman, helot, peon, serf, thrall, vassal, villein; drudge, menial.

slavery *n* bondage, bond-service, captivity, enslavement, enthralment, serfdom, servitude, thraldom, vassalage, villeinage; drudgery, mean labour.

slavish *adj* abject, beggarly, base, cringing, fawning, grovelling, low, mean, obsequious, servile, sycophantic; drudging, laborious, menial, servile.

slay *vb* assassinate, butcher, dispatch, kill, massacre, murder, slaughter; destroy, ruin.

slayer *n* assassin, destroyer, killer, murderer, slaughterer.

sledge *n* drag, sled; cutter, pung, sleigh.

sleek *adj* glossy, satin, silken, silky, smooth.

sleekly *adv* evenly, glossily, nicely, smoothly.

sleep *vb* catnap, doze, drowse, nap, slumber. * *n* dormancy, hypnosis, lethargy, repose, rest, slumber.

sleeping *adj* dormant, inactive, quiescent.

sleepwalker *n* night-walker, noctambulist, somnambulist.

sleepwalking *n* somnambulism.

sleepy *adj* comatose, dozy, drowsy, heavy, lethargic, nodding, somnolent; narcotic, opiate, slumberous, somniferous, somnific, soporiferous, soporific; dull, heavy, inactive, lazy, slow, sluggish, torpid.

sleight *n* adroitness, dexterity, manoeuvring.

sleight of hand *n* conjuring, hocus-pocus, jugglery, legerdemain, prestidigitation.

slender *adj* lank, lithe, narrow, skinny, slim, spindly, thin; feeble, fine, flimsy, fragile, slight, tenuous, weak; inconsiderable, moderate, small, trivial; exiguous, inadequate, insufficient, lean, meagre, pitiful, scanty; abstemious, light, simple, spare, sparing.

slice *vb* cut, divide, part, section; cut off, sever. * *n* chop, collop, piece.

slick *adj* glassy, glossy, polished, sleek, smooth; alert, clever, cunning, shrewd, slippery, unctuous. *vb* burnish, gloss, lacquer, polish, shine, sleek, varnish; grease, lubricate, oil.

slide *vb* glide, move smoothly, slip. * *n* glide, glissade, skid, slip.

sliding *adj* gliding, slippery, uncertain. * *n* backsliding, falling, fault, lapse, transgression.

slight *vb* cold-shoulder, disdain, disregard, neglect, snub; overlook; scamp, skimp, slur. * *adj* inconsiderable, insignificant, little, paltry, petty, small, trifling, trivial, unimportant, unsubstantial; delicate, feeble, frail, gentle, weak; careless, cursory, desultory, hasty, hurried, negligent, scanty, superficial; flimsy, perishable; slender, slim. * *n* discourtesy, disregard, disrespect, inattention, indignity, neglect.

slightingly *adv* contemptuously, disrespectfully, scornfully, slightly.

slightly *adv* inconsiderably, little, somewhat; feebly, slenderly, weakly; cursorily, hastily, negligently, superficially.

slim *vb* bant, diet, lose weight, reduce, slenderize. * *adj* gaunt, lank, lithe, narrow, skinny, slender, spare; inconsiderable, paltry, poor, slight, trifling, trivial, unsubstantial, weak; insufficient, meagre.

slime *n* mire, mud, ooze, sludge.

slimy *adj* miry, muddy, oozy; clammy, gelatinous, glutinous, gummy, lubricious, mucilaginous, mucous, ropy, slabby, viscid, viscous.

sling *vb* cast, fling, hurl, throw; hang up, suspend.

slink *vb* skulk, slip away, sneak, steal away.

slip *vb* glide, slide; err, mistake, trip; lose, omit; disengage, throw off; escape, let go, loose, loosen, release, . * *n* glide, slide, slipping; blunder, lapse, misstep, mistake, oversight, peccadillo, trip; backsliding, error, fault, impropriety, indiscretion, transgression; desertion, escape; cord, leash, strap, string; case, covering, wrapper.

slippery *adj* glib, slithery, smooth; changeable,
insecure, mutable, perilous, shaky, uncertain, unsafe, unstable, unsteady; cunning, dishonest, elusive, faithless, false, knavish, perfidious, shifty, treacherous.

slipshod *adj* careless, shuffling, slovenly, untidy.

slit *vb* cut; divide, rend, slash, split, sunder. * *n* cut, gash.

slobber *vb* drivel, drool, slabber, slaver; daub, obscure, smear, stain.

slobbery *adj* dank, floody, moist, muddy, sloppy, wet.

slope *vb* incline, slant, tilt. * *n* acclivity, cant, declivity, glacis, grade, gradient, incline, inclination, obliquity, pitch, ramp.

sloping *adj* aslant, bevelled, declivitous, inclining, oblique, shelving, slanting.

sloppy *adj* muddy, plashy, slabby, slobbery, splashy, wet.

sloth *n* dilatoriness, slowness, tardiness; idleness, inaction, inactivity, indolence, inertness, laziness, lumpishness, slothfulness, sluggishness, supineness, torpor.

slothful *adj* dronish, idle, inactive, indolent, inert, lazy, lumpish, slack, sluggish, supine, torpid.

slouch *vb* droop, loll, slump; shamble, shuffle. * *n* malingerer, shirker, slacker; shamble, shuffle, stoop.

slouching *adj* awkward, clownish, loutish, lubberly, uncouth, ungainly.

slough[1] *n* bog, fen, marsh, morass, quagmire; dejection, depression, despondence, despondency.

slough[2] *vb* cast, desquamate, excuviate, moult, shed, throw off; cast off, discard, divest, jettison, reject. * *n* cast, desquamation.

sloven *n* slattern, slob, slouch, slut.

slovenly *adj* unclean, untidy; blowsy, disorderly, dowdy, frowsy, loose, slatternly, tacky, unkempt, untidy; careless, heedless, lazy, negligent, perfunctory.

slow *vb* abate, brake, check, decelerate, diminish, lessen, mitigate, moderate, modulate, reduce, weaken; delay,detain, retard; ease, ease up, relax, slack, slacken, slack off. * *adj* deliberate, gradual; dead, dull, heavy, inactive, inert, sluggish, stupid; behindhand, late, tardy, unready; delaying, dilatory, lingering, slack.

sludge *n* mire, mud; slosh, slush.

sluggard *n* dawdler, drone, idler, laggard, lounger, slug.
sluggish *adj* dronish, drowsy, idle, inactive, indolent, inert, languid, lazy, listless, lumpish, phlegmatic, slothful, torpid; slow; dull, stupid, supine, tame.
sluice *vb* drain, drench, flood, flush, irrigate. * *n* floodgate, opening, vent.
slumber *vb* catnap, doze, nap, repose, rest, sleep. * *n* catnap, doze, nap, repose, rest, siesta, sleep.
slumberous *adj* drowsy, sleepy, somniferous, somnific, soporific.
slump *vb* droop, drop, fall, flop, founder, sag, sink, sink down; decline, depreciate, deteriorate, ebb, fail, fall away, lose ground, recede, slide, slip, subside, wane. * *n* droop, drop, fall, flop, lowering, sag, sinkage; decline, depreciation, deterioration, downturn, downtrend, subsidence, ebb, falling off, wane; crash, recession, smash.
slur *vb* asperse, calumniate, disparage, depreciate, reproach, traduce; conceal, disregard, gloss over, obscure, pass over, slight. * *n* mark, stain; brand, disgrace, reproach, stain, stigma; innuendo.
slush *n* slosh, sludge.
slushy *vb* plashy, sloppy, sloshy, sludgy.
slut *n* drab, slattern, sloven, trollop.
sluttish *adj* careless, dirty, disorderly, unclean, untidy.
sly *adj* artful, crafty, cunning, insidious, subtle, wily; astute, cautious, shrewd; arch, knowing, clandestine, secret, stealthy, underhand.
smack[1] *vb* smell, taste. * *n* flavour, savour, tang, taste, tincture; dash, infusion, little, space, soupçon, sprinkling, tinge, touch; smattering.
smack[2] *vb* slap, strike; crack, slash, snap; buss, kiss. * *n* crack, slap, slash, snap; buss, kiss.
small *adj* diminutive, Lilliputian, little, miniature, petite, pygmy, tiny, wee; infinitesimal, microscopic, minute; inappreciable, inconsiderable, insignificant, petty, trifling, trivial, unimportant; moderate, paltry, scanty, slender; faint, feeble, puny, slight, weak; illiberal, mean, narrow, narrow-minded, paltry, selfish, sorded, ungenerous, unworthy.
small talk *n* chat, conversation, gossip.
smart[1] *vb* hurt, pain, sting; suffer. * *adj* keen, painful, poignant, pricking, pungent, severe, sharp, stinging.
smart[2] *adj* active, agile, brisk, fresh, lively, nimble, quick, spirited, sprightly, spry; effective, efficient, energetic, forcible, vigorous; adroit, alert, clever, dexterous, dextrous, expert, intelligent, stirring; acute, apt, pertinent, ready, witty; chic, dapper, fine, natty, showy, spruce, trim.
smartness *n* acuteness, keenness, poignancy, pungency, severity, sharpness; efficiency, energy, force, vigour; activity, agility, briskness, liveliness, nimbleness, sprightliness, spryness, vivacity; alertness, cleverness, dexterity, expertise, expertness, intelligence, quickness; acuteness, aptness, pertinency, wit, wittiness; chic, nattiness, spruceness, trimness.
smash *vb* break, crush, dash, mash, shatter. * *n* crash, debacle, destruction, ruin; bankruptcy, failure.
smattering *n* dabbling, smatter, sprinkling.
smear *vb* bedaub, begrime, besmear, daub, plaster, smudge; contaminate, pollute, smirch, smut, soil, stain, sully, tarnish. * *n* blot, blotch, daub, patch, smirch, smudge, spot, stain; calumny, defamation, libel, slander.
smell *vb* scent, sniff, stench, stink. * *n* aroma, bouquet, fragrance, fume, odour, perfume, redolence, scent, stench, stink; sniff, snuff.
smelt *vb* fuse, melt.
smile *vb* grin, laugh, simper, smirk. * *n* grin, simper, smirk.
smite *vb* beat, box, collide, cuff, knock, strike, wallop, whack; destroy, kill, slay; afflict, chasten, punish; blast, destroy.
smitten *adj* attracted, captivated, charmed, enamoured, fascinated, taken; destroyed, killed, slain; smit, struck; afflicted, chastened, punished.
smock *n* chemise, shift, slip; blouse, gaberdine.
smoke *vb* emit, exhale, reek, steam; fumigate, smudge; discover, find out, smell out. * *n* effluvium, exhalation, fume, mist, reek, smother, steam, vapour; fumigation, smudge.
smoky *adj* fuliginous, fumid, fumy, smudgy; begrimed, blackened, dark, reeky, sooty, tanned.
smooth *vb* flatten, level, plane; ease, lubricate; extenuate, palliate, soften; allay, alleviate, assuage, calm, mitigate, mollify. * *adj* even, flat, level, plane, polished, unruffled, unwrinkled; glabrous, glossy, satiny, silky, sleek, soft, velvet; euphonious, flowing, liquid, mellifluent; fluent, glib, voluble; bland, flattering, ingratiating, insinuating, mild, oily, smooth-tongued, soothing, suave, unctuous.
smoothly *adv* evenly; easily, readily, unobstructedly; blandly, flatteringly, gently, mildly, pleasantly, softly, soothingly.
smooth-tongued *adj* adulatory, cozening, flattering, plausible, smooth, smooth-spoken.
smother *vb* choke, stifle, suffocate; conceal, deaden, extinguish, hide, keep down, repress, suppress; smoke, smoulder.
smudge *vb* besmear, blacken, blur, smear, smut, smutch, soil, spot, stain. * *n* blur, blot, smear, smut, spot, stain.
smug *adj* complacent, self-satisfied; neat, nice, spruce, trim.
smuggler *n* contrabandist, runner.
smut *vb* blacken, smouch, smudge, soil, stain, sully, taint, tarnish. * *n* dirt, smudge, smutch, soot; nastiness, obscenity, ribaldry, smuttiness; pornography.
smutty *adj* coarse, gross, immodest, impure, indecent, indelicate, loose, nasty; dirty, foul, nasty, soiled, stained.
snack *n* bite, light meal, nibble.
snag *vb* catch, enmesh, entangle, hook, snare, sniggle, tangle. * *n* knarl, knob, knot, projection, protuberance, snub; catch, difficulty, drawback, hitch, rub, shortcoming, weakness; obstacle.
snaky *adj* serpentine, snaking, winding; artful, cunning, deceitful, insinuating, sly, subtle.
snap *vb* break, fracture; bite, catch at, seize, snatch at, snip; crack; crackle, crepitate, decrepitate, pop. * *adj* casual, cursory, hasty, offhand, sudden, superficial. * *n* bite, catch, nip, seizure; catch, clasp, fastening, lock; crack, fillip, flick, flip, smack; briskness, energy, verve, vim.
snappish *adj* acrimonious, captious, churlish, crabbed, cross, crusty, froward, irascible, ill-tempered, peevish, perverse, pettish, petulant, snarling, splenetic, surly, tart, testy, touchy, waspish.
snare *vb* catch, ensnare, entangle, entrap. * *n* catch, gin, net, noose, springe, toil, trap, wile.
snarl[1] *vb* girn, gnarl, growl, grumble, murmur. * *n* growl, grumble.
snarl[2] *vb* complicate, disorder, entangle, knot; confuse, embarrass, ensnare. * *n* complication, disorder, entanglement, tangle; difficulty, embarrassment, intricacy.
snatch *vb* catch, clutch, grasp, grip, pluck, pull, seize, snip, twich, wrest, wring, * *n* bit, fragment, part, portion; catch, effort.
sneak *vb* lurk, skulk, slink, steal; crouch, truckle. * *adj* clandestine, concealed, covert, hidden, secret, sly, underhand. * *n* informer, telltale; lurker, shirk.
sneaky *adj* furtive, skulking, slinking; abject, crouching, grovelling, mean; clandestine, concealed, covert, hidden, secret, sly, underhand.
sneer *vb* flout, gibe, jeer, mock, rail, scoff; (*with* **at**) deride, despise, disdain, laugh at, mock, rail at, scoff, spurn. * *n* flouting, gibe, jeer, scoff.
snicker *vb* giggle, laugh, snigger, titter.
sniff *vb* breathe, inhale, snuff; scent, smell.
snip *vb* clip, cut, nip; snap, snatch. * *n* bit, fragment, particle, piece, shred; share, snack.
snivel *vb* blubber, cry, fret, sniffle, snuffle, weep, whimper, whine.
snivelly *adj* snotty; pitiful, whining.
snob *n* climber, toady.
snooze *vb* catnap, doze, drowse, nap, sleep, slumber. * *n* catnap, nap, sleep, slumber.
snout *n* muzzle, nose; nozzle.
snowy *adj* immaculate, pure, spotless, unblemished, unstained, unsullied, white.
snub[1] *vb* abash, cold-shoulder, cut, discomfit, humble, humiliate, mortify, slight, take down. * *n* check, rebuke, slight.
snub[2] *vb* check, clip, cut short, dock, nip, prune, stunt. * *adj* pug, retroussé, snubbed, squashed, squat, stubby, turned-up.
snuff[1] *vb* breathe, inhale, sniff; scent, smell; snort.

snuff[2] *vb* (*with* **out**) annihilate, destroy, efface, extinguish, obliterate.
snuffle *vb* sniffle; snort, snuff.
snug *adj* close, concealed; comfortable, compact, convenient, neat, trim.
snuggle *vb* cuddle, nestle, nuzzle.
so *adv* thus, with equal reason; in such a manner; in this way, likewise; as it is, as it was, such; for this reason, therefore; be it so, thus be it. * *conj* in case that, on condition that, provided that.
soak *vb* drench, moisten, permeate, saturate, wet; absorb, imbibe; imbue, macerate, steep.
soar *vb* ascend, fly aloft, glide, mount, rise, tower.
sob *vb* cry, sigh convulsively, weep.
sober *vb* (*with* **up**) calm down, collect oneself, compose oneself, control oneself, cool off, master, moderate, simmer down. * *adj* abstemious, abstinent, temperate, unintoxicated; rational, reasonable, sane, sound; calm, collected, composed, cool, dispassionate, moderate, rational, reasonabler, regular, restrained, steady, temperate, unimpassioned, unruffled, well-regulated; demure, grave, quiet, sedate, serious, solemn, sombre, staid; dark, drab, dull-looking, quiet, sad, subdued.
sobriety *n* abstemiousness, abstinence, soberness, temperance; calmness, coolness, gravity, sedateness, sober-mindedness, staidness, thoughtfulness; gravity, seriousness, solemnity.
sobriquet *n* appellation, nickname, nom de plume, pseudonym.
sociability *n* companionableness, comradeship, good fellowship, sociality.
sociable *adj* accessible, affable, communicative, companionable, conversable, friendly, genial, neighbourly, social.
social *adj* civic, civil; accessible, affable, communicative, companionable, familiar, friendly, hospitable, neighbourly, sociable; convivial, festive, gregarious. * *n* conversazione, gathering, get-together, party, reception, soiree.
society *n* association, companionship, company, converse, fellowship; the community, populace, the public, the world; élite, *monde*; body, brotherhood, copartnership, corporation, club, fraternity, partnersnip, sodality, union.
sodden *adj* drenched, saturated, soaked, steeped, wet; boiled, decocted, seethed, stewed.
sofa *n* couch, davenport, divan, ottoman, settee.
soft *adj* impressible, malleable, plastic, pliable, yielding; downy, fleecy, velvety, mushy, pulpy, squashy; compliant, facile, irresolute, submissive, undecided, weak; bland, mild, gentle, kind, lenient, soft-hearted, tender; delicate; easy, even, quiet, smooth-going, steady; effeminate, luxurious, unmanly; dulcet, fluty, mellifluous, melodious, smooth. * *interj* hold, stop.
soften *vb* intenerate, mellow, melt, tenderize; abate, allay, alleviate, appease, assuage, attemper, balm, blunt, calm, dull, ease, lessen, make easy, mitigate, moderate, mollify, milden, qualify, quell, quiet, relent, relieve, soothe, still, temper; extenuate, modify, palliate, qualify; enervate, weaken.
soil[1] *n* earth, ground loam, mould; country, land.
soil[2] *vb* bedaub, begrime, bemire, besmear, bespatter, contaminate, daub, defile, dirty, foul, pollute, smirch, stain, sully, taint, tarnish. * *n* blemish, defilement, dirt, filth, foulness; blot, spot, stain, taint, tarnish.
sojourn *vb* abide, dwell, live, lodge, remain, reside, rest, stay, stop, tarry, visit. * *n* residence, stay.
solace *vb* cheer, comfort, console, soothe; allay, assuage, mitigate, relieve, soften. * *n* alleviation, cheer, comfort, consolation, relief.
soldier *n* fighting man, man-at-arms, warrior; GI, private.
soldierly *adj* martial, military, warlike; brave, courageous, gallant, heroic, honourable, intrepid, valiant.
sole *adj* alone, individual, one, only, single, solitary, unique.
solecism *n* barbarism, blunder, error, faux pas, impropriety, incongruity, mistake, slip.
solemn *adj* ceremonial, formal, ritual; devotional, devout, religious, reverential, sacred; earnest, grave, serious, sober; august, awe-inspiring, awful, grand, imposing, impressive, majestic, stately, venerable.
solemnity *n* celebration, ceremony, observance, office, rite; awfulness, sacredness, sanctity; gravity, impressiveness, seriousness.
solemnize *vb* celebrate, commemorate, honour, keep, observe.
solicit *vb* appeal to, ask, beg, beseech, conjure, crave, entreat, implore, importune, petition, pray, press, request, supplicate, urge; arouse, awaken, entice, excite, invite, summon; canvass, seek.
solicitation *n* address, appeal, asking, entreaty, imploration, importunity, insistence, petition, request, suit, supplication, urgency; bidding, call, invitation, summons.
solicitor *n* attorney, law agent, lawyer; asker, canvasser, drummer, petitioner, solicitant.
solicitous *adj* anxious, apprehensive, careful, concerned, disturbed, eager, troubled, uneasy.
solicitude *n* anxiety, care, carefulness, concern, perplexity, trouble.
solid *adj* congealed, firm, hard, impenetrable, rock-like; compact, dense, impermeable, massed; cubic; sound, stable, stout, strong, substantial; just, real, true, valid, weighty; dependable, faithful, reliable, safe, staunch, steadfast, trustworthy, well established.
solidarity *n* communion of interests, community, consolidation, fellowship, joint interest, mutual responsibility.
solidify *vb* compact, congeal, consolidate, harden, petrify.
solidity *n* compactness, consistency, density, firmness, hardness, solidness; fullness; massiveness, stability, strength; dependability, gravity, justice, reliability, soundness, steadiness, validity, weight; cubic content, volume.
soliloquy *n* monologue.
solitariness *n* isolation, privacy, reclusion, retirement, seclusion; loneliness, solitude.
solitary *adj* alone, companionless, lone, lonely, only, separate, unaccompanied; individual, single, sole; desert, deserted, desolate, isolated, lonely, remote, retired, secluded, unfrequented.
solitude *n* isolation, loneliness, privacy, recluseness, retiredness, retirement, seclusion, solitariness; desert, waste, wilderness.
solution *n* answer, clue, disentanglement, elucidation, explication, explanation, key, resolution, unravelling, unriddling; disintegration, dissolution, liquefaction, melting, resolution, separation; breach, disconnection, discontinuance, disjunction, disruption.
solve *vb* clear, clear up, disentangle, elucidate, explain, expound, interpret, make plain, resolve, unfold.
solvent *n* diluent, dissolvent, menstruum.
somatic *adj* bodily, corporeal.
sombre *adj* cloudy, dark, dismal, dull, dusky, gloomy, murky, overcast, rayless, shady, sombrous, sunless; doleful, funereal, grave, lugubrious, melancholy, mournful, sad, sober.
some *adj* a, an, any, one; about, near; certain, little, moderate, part, several.
somebody *n* one, someone, something; celebrity, VIP.
somehow *adv* in some way.
something *n* part, portion, thing; somebody; affair, event, matter.
sometime *adj* former, late. * *adv* formerly, once; now and then, at one time or other, sometimes.
sometimes *adv* at intervals, at times, now and then, occasionally; at a past period, formerly, once.
somewhat *adv* in some degree, more or less, rather, something. * *n* something, a little, more or less, part.
somewhere *adv* here and there, in one place or another, in some place.
somnambulism *n* sleepwalking, somnambulation.
somnambulist *n* night-walker, noctambulist, sleepwalker, somnambulator, somnambule.
somniferous *adj* narcotic, opiate, slumberous, somnific, soporific, soporiferous.
somnolence *n* doziness, drowsiness, sleepiness, somnolency.
somnolent *adj* dozy, drowsy, sleepy.
son *n* cadet, heir, junior, scion.
song *n* aria, ballad, canticle, canzonet, carol, ditty, glee, lay, lullaby, snatch; descant, melody; anthem, hymn, poem, psalm, strain; poesy, poetry, verse.

sonorous *adj* full-toned, resonant, resounding, ringing, sounding; high-sounding, loud.

soon *adv* anon, before long, by and by, in a short time, presently, shortly; betimes, early, forthwith, promptly, quick; gladly, lief, readily, willingly.

soot *n* carbon, crock, dust.

soothe *vb* cajole, flatter, humour; appease, assuage, balm, calm, compose, lull, mollify, pacify, quiet, soften, still, tranquillize; allay, alleviate, blunt, check, deaden, dull, ease, lessen, mitigate, moderate, palliate, qualify, relieve, repress, soften, subdue, temper.

soothsayer *n* augur, diviner, foreteller, necromancer, predictor, prophet, seer, sorcerer, vaticinator.

sooty *adj* black, dark, dusky, fuliginous, murky, sable.

sophism *n* casuistry, fallacy, paralogism, paralogy, quibble, specious argument.

sophist *n* quibbler.

sophistical *adj* casuistical, fallacious, illogical, quibbling, subtle, unsound.

soporific *adj* dormitive, hypnotic, narcotic, opiate, sleepy, slumberous, somnific, somniferous, soporiferous, soporous.

soppy *adj* drenched, saturated, soaked, sopped; emotional, mawkish, sentimental.

soprano *n* (*mus*) descant, discant, treble.

sorcerer *n* charmer, conjurer, diviner, enchanter, juggler, magician, necromancers, seer, shaman, soothsayer, thaumaturgist, wizard.

sorcery *n* black art, charm, divination, enchantment, necromancy, occultism, shamanism, spell, thaumaturgy, voodoo, witchcraft.

sordid *adj* base, degraded, low, mean, vile; avaricious, close-fisted, covetous, illiberal, miserly, niggardly, penurious, stingy, ungenerous.

sore *adj* irritated, painful, raw, tender, ulcerated; aggrieved, galled, grieved, hurt, irritable, vexed; afflictive, distressing, severe, sharp, violent. * *n* abscess, boil, fester, gathering, imposthume, pustule, ulcer; affliction, grief, pain, sorrow, trouble.

sorely *adv* greatly, grievously, severely, violently.

sorrily *adv* despicably, meanly, pitiably, poorly, wretchedly.

sorrow *vb* bemoan, bewail, grieve, lament, mourn, weep. * *n* affliction, dolour, grief, heartache, mourning, sadness, trouble, woe.

sorrowful *adj* afflicted, dejected, depressed, grieved, grieving, heartsore, sad; baleful, distressing, grievous, lamentable, melancholy, mournful, painful; disconsolate, dismal, doleful, dolorous, drear, dreary, lugubrious, melancholy, piteous, rueful, woebegone, woeful.

sorry *adj* afflicted, dejected, grieved, pained, poor, sorrowful; distressing, pitiful; chagrined, mortified, pained, regretful, remorseful, sad, vexed; abject, base, beggarly, contemptible, despicable, low, mean, paltry, insignificant, miserable, shabby, worthless, wretched.

sort *vb* arrange, assort, class, classify, distribute, order; conjoin, join, put together; choose, elect, pick out, select; associate, consort, fraternize; accord, agree with, fit, suit. * *n* character, class, denomination, description, kind, nature, order, race, rank, species, type; manner, way.

sortie *n* attack, foray, raid, sally.

so-so *adj* indifferent, mediocre, middling, ordinary, passable, tolerable.

sot *n* blockhead, dolt, dullard, dunce, fool, simpleton; drunkard, tippler, toper.

sottish *adj* doltish, dull, foolish, senseless, simple, stupid; befuddled, besotted, drunken, insensate, senseless, tipsy.

sotto voce *adv* in a low voice, in an undertone, softly.

sough *n* murmur, sigh; breath, breeze, waft.

soul *n* mind, psyche, spirit; being, person; embodiment, essence, personification, spirit, vital principle; ardour, energy, fervour, inspiration, vitality.

soulless *adj* dead, expressionless, lifeless, unfeeling.

sound[1] *adj* entire, intact, unbroken, unhurt, unimpaired, uninjured, unmutilated, whole; hale, hardy, healthy, hearty, vigorous; good, perfect, undecayed; sane, well-balanced; correct, orthodox, right, solid, valid, well-founded; legal; deep, fast, profound, unbroken, undisturbed; forcible, lusty, severe, stout.

sound[2] *n* channel, narrows, strait.

sound[3] *vb* resound; appear, seem; play on; express, pronounce, utter; announce, celebrate, proclaim, publish, spread. * *n* noise, note, tone, voice, whisper.

sound[4] *vb* fathom, gauge, measure, test; examine, probe, search, test, try.

sounding *adj* audible, resonant, resounding, ringing, sonorous; imposing, significant.

soundless *adj* dumb, noiseless, silent; abysmal, bottomless, deep, profound, unfathomable, unsounded.

soundly *adv* satisfactorily, thoroughly, well; healthily, heartily; forcibly, lustily, severely, smartly, stoutly; correctly, rightly, truly; firmly, strongly; deeply, fast, profoundly.

soundness *n* entireness, entirety, integrity, wholeness; healthiness, vigour, saneness, sanity; correctness, orthodoxy, rectitude, reliability, truth, validity; firmness, solidity, strength, validity.

soup *n* broth, consommé, purée.

sour *vb* acidulate; embitter, envenom. * *adj* acetose, acetous, acid, astringent, pricked, sharp, tart, vinegary; acrimonious, crabbed, cross, crusty, fretful, glum, ill-humoured, ill-natured, ill-tempered, peevish, pettish, petulant, snarling, surly; bitter, disagreeable, unpleasant; austere, dismal, gloomy, morose, sad, sullen; bad, coagulated, curdled, musty, rancid, turned.

source *n* beginning, fountain, fountainhead, head, origin, rise, root, spring, well; cause, original.

sourness *n* acidity, sharpness, tartness; acrimony, asperity, churlishness, crabbedness, crossness, discontent, harshness, moroseness, peevishness.

souse *vb* pickle; dip, douse, immerse, plunge, submerge.

souvenir *n* keepsake, memento, remembrance, reminder.

sovereign *adj* imperial, monarchical, princely, regal, royal, supreme; chief, commanding, excellent, highest, paramount, predominant, principal, supreme, utmost; efficacious, effectual. * *n* autocrat, monarch, suzerain; emperor, empress, king, lord, potentate, prince, princess, queen, ruler.

sovereignty *n* authority, dominion, empire, power, rule, supremacy, sway.

sow *vb* scatter, spread, strew; disperse, disseminate, propagate, spread abroad; plant; besprinkle, scatter.

space *n* expanse, expansion, extension, extent, proportions, spread; accommodation, capacity, room, place; distance, interspace, interval.

spacious *adj* extended, extensive, vast, wide; ample, broad, capacious, commodious, large, roomy, wide.

span *vb* compass, cross, encompass, measure, overlay. * *n* brief period, spell; pair, team, yoke.

spank *vb* slap, strike.

spar[1] *n* beam, boom, pole, sprit, yard.

spar[2] *vb* box, fight; argue, bicker, contend, dispute, quarrel, spat, squabble, wrangle.

spare *vb* lay aside, lay by, reserve, save, set apart, set aside; dispense with, do without, part with; forbear, omit, refrain, withhold; exempt, forgive, keep from; afford, allow, give, grant; save; economize, pinch. * *adj* frugal, scanty, sparing, stinted; chary, parsimonious; emaciated, gaunt, lank, lean, meagre, poor, thin, scraggy, skinny, raw-boned; additional, extra, supernumerary.

sparing *adj* little, scanty, scarce; abstemious, meagre, spare; chary, economical, frugal, parsimonious, saving; compassionate, forgiving, lenient, merciful.

spark *vb* scintillate, sparkle; begin, fire, incite, instigate, kindle, light, set off, start, touch off, trigger. * *n* scintilla, scintillation, sparkle; beginning, element, germ, seed.

sparkle *vb* coruscate, flash, gleam, glisten, glister, glitter, radiate, scintillate, shine, twinkle; bubble, effervesce, foam, froth. * *n* glint, scintillation, spark; luminosity, lustre.

sparkling *adj* brilliant, flashing, glistening, glittering, glittery, twinkling; bubbling, effervescing, eloquent, foaming, frothing, mantling; brilliant, glowing, lively, nervous, piquant, racy, spirited, sprightly, witty.

sparse *adj* dispersed, infrequent, scanty, scattered, sporadic, thin.
spartan *adj* bold, brave, chivalric, courageous, daring, dauntless, doughty, fearless, hardy, heroic, intrepid, lion-hearted, undaunted, valiant, valorous; austere, exacting, hard, severe, tough, unsparing; enduring, long-suffering, self-controlled, stoic.
spasm *n* contraction, cramp, crick, twitch; fit, paroxysm, seizure, throe.
spasmodic *adj* erratic, fitful, intermittent, irregular, sporadic; convulsive, paroxysmal, spasmodical, violent.
spat *vb* argue, bicker, dispute, jangle, quarrel, spar, squabble, wrangle.
spatter *vb* bespatter, besprinkle, plash, splash, sprinkle; spit, sputter.
spawn *vb* bring forth, generate, produce. * *n* eggs, roe; fruit, offspring, product.
speak *vb* articulate, deliver, enunciate, express, pronounce, utter; announce, confer, declare, disclose, mention, say, tell; celebrate, make known, proclaim, speak abroad; accost, address, greet, hail; exhibit; argue, converse, dispute, talk; declaim, discourse, hold forth, harangue, orate, plead, spout, treat.
speaker *n* discourse, elocutionist, orator, prolocutor, spokesman; chairman, presiding officer.
speaking *adj* rhetorical, talking; eloquent, expressive; lifelike. * *n* discourse, talk, utterance;
declamation, elocution, oratory.
spear *n* dart, gaff, harpoon, javelin, lance, pike; shoot, spire.
special *adj* specific, specifical; especial, individual, particular, peculiar, unique; exceptional, extraordinary, marked, particular, uncommon; appropriate, express.
speciality, specialty *n* particularity; feature, forte, pet subject.
species *n* assemblage, class, collection, group; description, kind, sort, variety; (*law*) fashion, figure, form, shape.
specific *adj* characteristic, especial, particular, peculiar; definite, limited, precise, specified.
specification *n* characterization, designation; details, particularization.
specify *vb* define, designate, detail, indicate, individualize, name, show, particularize.
specimen *n* copy, example, model, pattern, sample.
specious *adj* manifest, obvious, open, showy; flimsy, illusory, ostensible, plausible, sophistical.
speck *n* blemish, blot, flaw, speckle, spot, stain; atom, bit, corpuscle, mite, mote, particle, scintilla.
spectacle *n* display, exhibition, pageant, parade, representation, review, scene, show, sight; curiosity, marvel, phenomenon, wonder.
spectacles *npl* glasses, goggles, shades.
spectator *n* beholder, bystander, observer, onlooker, witness.
spectral *adj* eerie, ghostlike, ghostly, phantomlike, shadowy, spooky, weird, wraithlike.
spectre, specter *n* apparition, banshee, ghost, goblin, hobgoblin, phantom, shade, shadow, spirit, sprite, wraith.
spectrum *n* appearance, image, representation.
speculate *vb* cogitate, conjecture, contemplate, imagine, meditate, muse, ponder, reflect, ruminate, theorize, think; bet, gamble, hazard, risk, trade, venture.
speculation *n* contemplation, intellectualization; conjecture, hypothesis, scheme, supposition, reasoning, reflection, theory, view.
speculative *adj* contemplative, philosophical, speculatory, unpractical; ideal, imaginary, theoretical; hazardous, risky, unsecured.
speculator *n* speculatist, theorist, theorizer; adventurer, dealer, gambler, trader.
speech *n* articulation, language, words; dialect, idiom, locution, tongue; conversation, oral communication, parlance, talk, verbal intercourse; mention, observation, remark, saying; address, declaration, discourse, harangue, oration, palaver.
speechless *adj* dumb, gagged, inarticulate, mute, silent; dazed, dumbfounded, flabbergasted, shocked.
speed *vb* hasten, hurry, rush, scurry; flourish, prosper, succeed, thrive; accelerate, expedite, hasten, hurry, quicken, press forward, urge on; carry through, dispatch, execute; advance, aid, assist, help; favour. * *n* acceleration, celerity, dispatch, expedition, fleetness, haste, hurry, quickness, rapidity, swiftness, velocity; good fortune, good luck, prosperity, success; impetuosity.
speedy *adj* fast, fleet, flying, hasty, hurried, hurrying, nimble, quick, rapid, swift; expeditious, prompt, quick; approaching, early, near.
spell[1] *n* charm, exorcism, hoodoo, incantation, jinx, witchery; allure, bewitchment, captivation, enchantment, entrancement, fascination.
spell[2] *vb* decipher, interpret, read, unfold, unravel, unriddle.
spell[3] *n* fit, interval, period, round, season, stint, term, turn.
spellbound *adj* bewitched, charmed, enchanted, entranced, enthralled, fascinated.
spend *vb* disburse, dispose of, expend, lay out, part with; consume, dissipate, exhaust, lavish, squander, use up, wear, waste; apply, bestow, devote, employ, pass.
spendthrift *n* prodigal, spender, squanderer, waster.
spent *adj* exhausted, fatigued, played out, used up, wearied, worn out.
spew *vb* cast up, puke, throw up, vomit; cast forth, eject.
spheral *adj* complete, perfect, symmetrical.
sphere *n* ball, globe, orb, spheroid; ambit, beat, bound, circle, circuit, compass, department, function, office, orbit, province, range, walk; order, rank, standing; country, domain, quarter, realm, region.
spherical *adj* bulbous, globated, globous, globular, orbicular, rotund, round, spheroid; planetary.
spice *n* flavour, flavouring, relish, savour, taste; admixture, dash, grain, infusion, particle, smack, soupçon, sprinkling, tincture.
spicily *adv* pungently, wittily.
spicy *adj* aromatic, balmy, fragrant; keen, piquant, pointed, pungent, sharp; indelicate, off-colour, racy, risqué, sensational, suggestive.
spill *vb* effuse, pour out, shed. * *n* accident, fall, tumble.
spin *vb* twist; draw out, extend; lengthen, prolong, protract, spend; pirouette, turn, twirl, whirl. * *n* drive, joyride, ride; autorotation, gyration, loop, revolution, rotation, turning, wheeling; pirouette, reel, turn, wheel, whirl.
spindle *n* axis, shaft.
spine *n* barb, prickle, thorn; backbone; ridge.
spinose *adj* briery, spinous, spiny, thorny.
spiny *adj* briery, prickly, spinose, spinous, thorny; difficult, perplexed, troublesome.
spiracle *n* aperture, blowhole, orifice, pore, vent.
spiral *adj* cochlear, cochleated, curled, helical, screw-shaped, spiry, winding. * *n* helix, winding, worm.
spire *n* curl, spiral, twist, wreath; steeple; blade, shoot, spear, stalk; apex, summit.
spirit *vb* animate, encourage, excite, inspirit; carry off, kidnap. * *n* immaterial substance, life, vital essence; person, soul; angel, apparition, demon, elf, fairy, genius, ghost, phantom, shade, spectre, sprite; disposition, frame of mind, humour, mood, temper; spirits; ardour, cheerfulness, courage, earnestness, energy, enterprise, enthusiasm, fire, force, mettle, resolution, vigour, vim, vivacity, zeal; animation, cheerfulness, enterprise, esprit, glow, liveliness, piquancy, spice, spunk, vivacity, warmth; drift, gist, intent, meaning, purport, sense, significance, tenor; character, characteristic, complexion, essence, nature, quality, quintessence; alcohol, liquor; (*with* **the**) Comforter, Holy Ghost, Paraclete.
spirited *adj* active, alert, animated, ardent, bold, brisk, courageous, earnest, frisky, high-mettled, high-spirited, high-strung, lively, mettlesome, sprightly, vivacious.
spiritless *adj* breathless, dead, extinct, lifeless; dejected, depressed, discouraged, dispirited, low-spirited; apathetic, cold, dull, feeble, languid, phlegmatic, sluggish, soulless, torpid, unenterprising; dull, frigid, heavy, insipid, prosaic, prosy, stupid, tame, uninteresting.
spiritual *adj* ethereal, ghostly, immaterial incorporeal, psychical, supersensible; ideal, moral, unwordly; divine, holy, pure, sacred; ecclesiastical.
spiritualize *vb* elevate, etherealize, purify, refine.

spirituous *adj* alcoholic, ardent, spiritous.
spit[1] *vb* impale, thrust through, transfix.
spit[2] *vb* eject, throw out; drivel, drool, expectorate, salivate, slobber, spawl, splutter. * *n* saliva, spawl, spittle, sputum.
spite *vb* injure, mortify, thwart; annoy, offend, vex. * *n* grudge, hate, hatred, ill-nature, ill-will, malevolence, malice, maliciousness, malignity, pique, rancour, spleen, venom, vindictiveness.
spiteful *adj* evil-minded, hateful, ill-disposed, ill-natured, malevolent, malicious, malign, malignant, rancorous.
spittoon *n* cuspidor.
splash *vb* dabble, dash, plash, spatter, splurge, swash, swish. * *n* blot, daub, spot.
splay *adj* broad, spreading out, turned out, wide.
spleen *n* anger, animosity, chagrin, gall, grudge, hatred, ill-humour, irascibility, malevolence, malice, malignity, peevishness, pique, rancour, spite.
spleeny *adj* angry, fretful, ill-tempered, irritable, peevish, spleenish, splenetic.
splendid *adj* beaming, bright, brilliant, effulgent, glowing, lustrous, radiant, refulgent, resplendent, shining; dazzling, gorgeous, imposing, kingly, magnificent, pompous, showy, sumptuous, superb; celebrated, conspicuous, distinguished, eminent, excellent, famous, glorious, illustrious, noble, pre-eminent, remarkable, signal; grand, heroic, lofty, noble, sublime.
splendour *n* brightness, brilliance, brilliancy, lustre, radiance, refulgence; display, éclat, gorgeousness, grandeur, magnificence, parade, pomp, show, showiness, stateliness; celebrity, eminence, fame, glory, grandeur, renown; grandeur, loftiness, nobleness, sublimity.
splenetic *adj* choleric, cross, fretful, irascible, irritable, peevish, pettish, petulant, snappish, testy, touchy, waspish; churlish, crabbed, morose, sour, sulky, sullen; gloomy, jaundiced.
splice *vb* braid, connect, join, knit, mortise.
splinter *vb* rend, shiver, sliver, split. * *n* fragment, piece.
split *vb* cleave, rive; break, burst, rend, splinter; divide, part, separate, sunder. * *n* crack, fissure, rent; breach, division, separation.
splotch *n* blot, daub, smear, spot, stain.
splutter *vb* sputter, stammer, stutter.
spoil *vb* despoil, fleece, loot, pilfer, plunder, ravage, rob, steal, strip, waste; corrupt, damage, destroy, disfigure, harm, impair, injure, mar, ruin, vitiate; decay, decompose. * *n* booty, loot, pillage, plunder, prey; rapine, robbery, spoliation, waste.
spoiler *n* pillager, plunderer, robber; corrupter, destroyer.
spokesman *n* mouthpiece, prolocutor, speaker.
spoliate *vb* despoil, destroy, loot, pillage, plunder, rob, spoil.
spoliation *n* depradation, deprivation, despoliation, destruction, robbery; destruction, devastation, pillage, plundering, rapine, ravagement.
sponge *vb* cleanse, wipe; efface, expunge, obliterate, rub out, wipe out.
sponger *n* hanger-on, parasite.
spongy *adj* absorbent, porous, spongeous; rainy, showery, wet; drenched, marshy, saturated, soaked, wet.
sponsor *vb* back, capitalize, endorse, finance, guarantee, patronize, promote, support, stake, subsidize, take up, underwrite. * *n* angel, backer, guarantor, patron, promoter, supporter, surety, underwriter; godfather, godmother, godparent.
spontaneity *n* improvisation, impulsiveness, spontaneousness.
spontaneous *adj* free, gratuitous, impulsive, improvised, instinctive, self-acting, self-moving, unbidden, uncompelled, unconstrained, voluntary, willing.
sporadic *adj* dispersed, infrequent, isolated, rare, scattered, separate, spasmodic.
sport *vb* caper, disport, frolic, gambol, have fun, make merry, play, romp, skip; trifle; display, exhibit. * *n* amusement, diversion, entertainment, frolic, fun, gambol, game, jollity, joviality, merriment, merry-making, mirth, pastime, pleasantry, prank, recreation; jest, joke; derision, jeer, mockery, ridicule; monstrosity.
sportive *adj* frisky, frolicsome, gamesome, hilarious, lively, merry, playful, prankish, rollicking, sprightly, tricksy; comic, facetious, funny, humorous, jocose, jocular, lively, ludicrous, mirthful, vivacious, waggish.
spot *vb* besprinkle, dapple, dot, speck, stud, variegate; blemish, disgrace, soil, splotch, stain, sully, tarnish; detect, discern, espy, make out, observe, see, sight. * *n* blot, dapple, fleck, freckle, maculation, mark, mottle, patch, pip, speck, speckle; blemish, blotch, flaw, pock, splotch, stain, taint; locality, place, site.
spotless *adj* perfect, undefaced, unspotted; blameless, immaculate, innocent, irreproachable, pure, stainless, unblemished, unstained, untainted, untarnished.
spotted *adj* bespeckled, bespotted, dotted, flecked, freckled, maculated, ocellated, speckled, spotty.
spousal *adj* bridal, conjugal, connubial, hymeneal, marital, matrimonial, nuptial, wedded.
spouse *n* companion, consort, husband, mate, partner, wife.
spout *vb* gush, jet, pour out, spirit, spurt, squirt; declaim, mouth, speak, utter. * *n* conduit, tube; beak, nose, nozzle, waterspout.
sprain *vb* overstrain, rick, strain, twist, wrench, wrick.
spray[1] *vb* atomize, besprinkle, douche, gush, jet, shower, splash, splatter, spout, sprinkle, squirt. * *n* aerosol, atomizer, douche, foam, froth, shower, sprinkler, spume.
spray[2] *n* bough, branch, shoot, sprig, twig.
spread *vb* dilate, expand, extend, mantle, stretch; diffuse, disperse, distribute, radiate, scatter, sprinkle, strew; broadcast, circulate, disseminate, divulge, make known, make public, promulgate, propagate, publish; open, unfold, unfurl; cover, extend over, overspread. * *n* compass, extent, range, reach, scope, stretch; expansion, extension; circulation, dissemination, propagation; cloth, cover; banquet, feast, meal.
spree *n* bacchanal, carousal, debauch, frolic, jollification, orgy, revel, revelry, saturnalia.
sprig *n* shoot, spray, twig; lad, youth.
sprightliness *n* animation, activity, briskness, cheerfulness, frolicsomeness, gaiety, life, liveliness, nimbleness, vigour, vivacity.
sprightly *adj* airy, animated, blithe, blithesome, brisk, buoyant, cheerful, debonair, frolicsome, joyous, lively, mercurial, vigorous, vivacious.
spring *vb* bound, hop, jump, leap, prance, vault; arise, emerge, grow, issue, proceed, put forth, shoot forth, stem; derive, descend, emanate, flow, originate, rise, start; fly back, rebound, recoil; bend, warp; grow, thrive, wax. * *adj* hopping, jumping, resilient, springy. * *n* bound, hop, jump, leap, vault; elasticity, flexibility, resilience, resiliency, springiness; fount, fountain, fountainhead, geyser, springhead, well; cause, origin, original, principle, source; seed time, springtime.
springe *n* gin, net, noose, snare, trap.
springiness *n* elasticity, resilience, spring; sponginess, wetness.
springy *adj* bouncing, bounding, elastic, rebounding, recoiling, resilient.
sprinkle *vb* scatter, strew; bedew, besprinkle, dust, powder, sand, spatter; wash, cleanse, purify, shower.
sprinkling *n* affusion, baptism, bedewing, spattering, splattering, spraying, wetting; dash, scattering, seasoning, smack, soupçon, suggestion, tinge, touch, trace, vestige.
sprite *n* apparition, elf, fairy, ghost, goblin, hobgoblin, phantom, pixie, shade, spectre, spirit.
sprout *vb* burgeon, burst forth, germinate, grow, pullulate, push, put forth, ramify, shoot, shoot forth. * *n* shoot, sprig.
spruce *vb* preen, prink; adorn, deck, dress, smarten, trim. * *adj* dandyish, dapper, fine, foppish, jaunty, natty, neat, nice, smart, tidy, trig, trim.
spry *adj* active, agile, alert, brisk, lively, nimble, prompt, quick, ready, smart, sprightly, stirring, supple.
spume *n* foam, froth, scum, spray.
spumy *adj* foamy, frothy, spumous.
spur *vb* gallop, hasten, press on, prick; animate, arouse, drive, goad, impel, incite, induce, instigate, rouse, stimulate, urge forward. * *n* goad, point, prick, rowel; fillip, impulse, incentive, incitement, inducement, instigation, motive, provocation, stimulus, whip; gnarl, knob, knot, point, projection, snag.

spurious *adj* bogus, counterfeit, deceitful, false, feigned, fictitious, make-believe, meretricious, mock, pretended, sham, supposititious, unauthentic.

spurn *vb* drive away, kick; contemn, despise, disregard, flout, scorn, slight; disdain, reject, repudiate.

spurt *vb* gush, jet, spirt, spout, spring out, stream out, well. * *n* gush, jet, spout, squirt; burst, dash, rush.

sputter *vb* spawl, spit, splutter, stammer.

spy *vb* behold, discern, espy, see; detect, discover, search out; explore, inspect, scrutinize, search; shadow, trail, watch. * *n* agent, detective, double agent, mole, scout, undercover agent.

squabble *vb* brawl, fight, quarrel, scuffle, struggle, wrangle; altercate, bicker, contend, dispute, jangle. * *n* brawl, dispute, fight, quarrel, rumpus, scrimmage.

squad *n* band, bevy, crew, gang, knot, lot, relay, set.

squalid *adj* dirty, filthy, foul, mucky, slovenly, unclean, unkempt.

squalidness *n* filthiness, foulness, squalidity, squalor.

squall *vb* bawl, cry, cry out, scream, yell. * *n* bawl, cry, outcry, scream, yell; blast, flurry, gale, gust, hurricane, storm, tempest.

squally *adj* blustering, blustery, gusty, stormy, tempestuous, windy.

squander *vb* dissipate, expend, lavish, lose, misuse, scatter, spend, throw away, waste.

squanderer *n* lavisher, prodigal, spendthrift, waster.

square *vb* make square, quadrate; accommodate, adapt, fit, mould, regulate, shape, suit; adjust, balance, close, make even, settle; accord, chime in, cohere, comport, fall in, fit, harmonize, quadrate, suit. * *adj* four-square, quadrilateral, quadrate; equal, equitable, exact, fair, honest, just, upright; adjusted, balanced, even, settled; true, suitable. * *n* four-sided figure, quadrate, rectangle, tetragon; open area, parade, piazza, plaza.

squash *vb* crush, mash.

squashy *adj* pulpy, soft.

squat *vb* cower, crouch; occupy, plant, settle. * *adj* cowering, crouching; dumpy, pudgy, short, stocky, stubby, thickset.

squeal *vb* creak, cry, howl, scream, screech, shriek, squawk, yell; betray, inform on. * *n* creak, cry, howl, scream, screech, shriek, squawk, yell.

squeamish *adj* nauseated, qualmish, queasy, sickish; dainty, delicate, fastidious, finical, hypercritical, nice, over-nice, particular, priggish.

squeeze *vb* clutch, compress, constrict, grip, nip, pinch, press; drive, force; crush, harass, oppress; crowd, force through; press; (*with* **out**) extract. * *n* congestion, crowd, crush, throng; compression.

squelch *vb* crush, quash, quell, silence, squash, suppress.

squib *n* firework, fuse; lampoon, pasquinade, satire.

squint *vb* look askance, look obliquely, peer. * *adj* askew, aslant, crooked, oblique, skew, skewed, twisted.

squire *vb* accompany, attend, escort, wait on.

squirm *vb* twist, wriggle, writhe.

squirt *vb* eject, jet, splash, spurt.

stab *vb* broach, gore, jab, pierce, pink, spear, stick, transfix, transpierce; wound. * *n* cut, jab, prick, thrust; blow, dagger-stroke, injury, wound.

stability *n* durability, firmness, fixedness, immovability, permanence, stableness, steadiness; constancy, firmness, reliability.

stable *adj* established, fixed, immovable, immutable, invariable, permanent, unalterable, unchangeable; constant, firm, staunch, steadfast, steady, unwavering; abiding, durable, enduring, fast, lasting, permanent, perpetual, secure, sure.

staff *n* baton, cane, pole, rod, stick, wand; bat, bludgeon, club, cudgel, mace; prop, stay, support; employees, personnel, team, workers, work force.

stage *vb* dramatize, perform, present, produce, put on. * *n* dais, platform, rostrum, scaffold, staging, stand; arena, field; boards, playhouse, theatre; degree, point, step; diligence, omnibus, stagecoach.

stagey *adj* bombastic, declamatory, dramatic, melodramatic, ranting, theatrical.

stagger *vb* reel, sway, totter; alternate, fluctuate, overlap, vacillate, vary; falter, hesitate, waver; amaze, astonish, astound, confound, dumbfound, nonplus, pose, shock, surprise.

stagnant *adj* close, motionless, quiet, standing; dormant, dull, heavy, inactive, inert, sluggish, torpid.

stagnate *vb* decay, deteriorate, languish, rot, stand still, vegetate.

staid *adj* calm, composed, demure, grave, sedate, serious, settled, sober, solemn, steady, unadventurous.

stain *vb* blemish, blot, blotch, discolour, maculate, smirch, soil, splotch, spot, sully, tarnish; colour, dye, tinge; contaminate, corrupt, debase, defile, deprave, disgrace, dishonour, pollute, taint. * *n* blemish, blot, defect, discoloration, flaw, imperfection, spot, tarnish; contamination, disgrace, dishonour, infamy, pollution, reproach, shame, taint, tarnish.

stainless *adj* spotless, unspotted, untarnished; blameless, faultless, innocent, guiltless, pure, spotless, uncorrupted, unsullied.

stairs *npl* flight of steps, staircase, stairway.

stake[1] *vb* brace, mark, prop, secure, support. * *n* pale, palisade, peg, picket, post, stick.

stake[2] *vb* finance, pledge, wager; hazard, imperil, jeopardize, peril, risk, venture. * *n* bet, pledge, wager; adventure, hazard, risk, venture.

stale *adj* flat, fusty, insipid, mawkish, mouldy, musty, sour, tasteless, vapid; decayed, effete, faded, old, time-worn, worn-out; common, commonplace, hackneyed, stereotyped, threadbare, trite.

stalk[1] *n* culm, pedicel, peduncle, petiole, shaft, spire, stem, stock.

stalk[2] *vb* march, pace, stride, strut, swagger; follow, hunt, shadow, track, walk stealthily.

stall[1] *n* stable; cell, compartment, recess; booth, kiosk, shop, stand.

stall[2] *vb* block, delay, equivocate, filibuster, hinder, postpone, procrastinate, temporize; arrest, check, conk out, die, fail, halt, stick, stop.

stalwart *adj* able-bodied, athletic, brawny, lusty, muscular, powerful, robust, sinewy, stout, strapping, strong, sturdy, vigorous; bold, brave, daring, gallant, indomitable, intrepid, redoubtable, resolute, valiant, valorous. * *n* backer, member, partisan, supporter.

stamina *n* energy, force, lustiness, power, stoutness, strength, sturdiness, vigour.

stammer *vb* falter, hesitate, stutter. * *n* faltering, hesitation, stutter.

stamp *vb* brand, impress, imprint, mark, print. * *n* brand, impress, impression, print; cast, character, complexion, cut, description, fashion, form, kind, make, mould, sort, type.

stampede *vb* charge, flee, panic. * *n* charge, flight, rout, running away, rush.

stanch *see* **staunch**[1].

stanchion *n* prop, shore, stay, support.

stand *vb* be erect, remain upright; abide, be fixed, continue, endure, hold good, remain; halt, pause, stop; be firm, be resolute, stand ground, stay; be valid, have force; depend, have support, rest; bear, brook, endure, suffer, sustain, weather; abide, admit, await, submit, tolerate, yield; fix, place, put, set upright; (*with* **against**) oppose, resist, withstand; (*with* **by**) be near, be present; aid, assist, defend, help, side with, support; defend, make good, justify, maintain, support, vindicate; (*naut*) attend, be ready; (*with* **fast**) be fixed, be immovable; (*with* **for**) mean, represent, signify; aid, defend, help, maintain, side with, support; (*with* **off**) keep aloof, keep off; not to comply; (*with* **out**) be prominent, jut, project, protrude; not comply, not yield, persist; (*with* **up for**) defend, justify, support, sustain, uphold; (*with* **with**) agree. * *n* place, position, post, standing place, station; halt, stay, stop; dais, platform, rostrum; booth, stall; opposition, resistance.

standard[1] *n* banner, colours, ensign, flag, gonfalon, pennon, streamer.

standard[2] *adj* average, conventional, customary, normal, ordinary, regular, usual; accepted, approved, authoritative, orthodox, received; formulary, prescriptive, regulation. * *n* canon, criterion, model, norm, rule, test, type; gauge, measure, model, scale; support, upright.

standing *adj* established, fixed, immovable, settled; durable, lasting, permanent; motionless, stagnant. * *n* position, stand, station; continuance, duration, existence; footing, ground, hold; condition, estimation, rank, reputation, status.

standpoint *n* point of view, viewpoint.

standstill *n* cessation, interruption, stand, stop; deadlock.

stanza *n* measure, staff, stave, strophe, verse.

staple *adj* basic, chief, essential, fundamental, main, primary, principal. * *n* fibre, filament, pile, thread; body, bulk, mass, substance.

star *vb* act, appear, feature, headline, lead, perform, play; emphasize, highlight, stress, underline. * *adj* leading, main, paramount, principal; celebrated, illustrious, well-known. * *n* heavenly body, luminary; asterisk, pentacle, pentagram; destiny, doom, fate, fortune, lot; diva, headliner, hero, heroine, lead, leading lady, leading man, prima ballerina, prima donna, principal, protagonist.

starchy *adj* ceremonious, exact, formal, precise, prim, punctilious, rigid, starched, stiff.

stare *vb* gape, gaze, look intently, watch.

stark *adj* rigid, stiff; absolute, bare, downright, entire, gross, mere, pure, sheer, simple. * *adv* absolutely, completely, entirely, fully, wholly.

starry *adj* astral, sidereal, star-spangled, stellar; bright, brilliant, lustrous, shining, sparkling, twinkling.

start *vb* begin, commence, inaugurate, initiate, institute; discover, invent; flinch, jump, shrink, startle, wince; alarm, disturb, fright, rouse, scare; depart, set off, take off; arise, call forth, evoke, raise; dislocate, move suddenly, spring. * *n* beginning, commencement, inauguration, outset; fit, jump, spasm, twitch; impulse, sally.

startle *vb* flinch, shrink, start, wince; affright, alarm, fright, frighten, scare, shock; amaze, astonish, astound.

startling *adj* abrupt, alarming, astonishing, shocking, sudden, surprising, unexpected, unforeseen, unheard of.

starvation *n* famine, famishment.

starve *vb* famish, perish; be in need, lack, want; kill, subdue.

starveling *adj* attenuated, emaciated, gaunt, hungry, lank, lean, meagre, scraggy, skinny, thin. * *n* beggar, mendicant, pauper.

state *vb* affirm, assert, aver, declare, explain, expound, express, narrate, propound, recite, say, set forth, specify, voice. * *adj* civic, national, public. * *n* case, circumstances, condition, pass, phase, plight, position, posture, predicament, situation, status; condition, guise, mode, quality, rank; dignity, glory, grandeur, magnificence, pageantry, parade, pomp, spendour; body politic, civil community, commonwealth, nation, realm.

statecraft *n* diplomacy, political subtlety, state management, statesmanship.

stated *adj* established, fixed, regular, settled; detailed, set forth, specified.

stately *adj* august, dignified, elevated, grand, imperial, imposing, lofty, magnificent, majestic, noble, princely, royal; ceremonious, formal, magisterial, pompous, solemn.

statement *n* account, allegation, announcement, communiqué, declaration, description, exposition, mention, narration, narrative, recital, relation, report, specification; assertion, predication, proposition, pronouncement, thesis.

statesman *n* politician.

station *vb* establish, fix, locate, place, post, set. * *n* location, place, position, lost, seat, situation; business, employment, function, occupation, office; character, condition, degree, dignity, footing, rank, standing, state, status; depot, stop, terminal.

stationary *adj* fixed, motionless, permanent, quiescent, stable, standing, still.

statuary *n* carving, sculpture, statues.

statue *n* figurine, image, statuette.

stature *n* height, physique, size, tallness; altitude, consequence, elevation, eminence, prominence.

status *n* caste, condition, footing, position, rank, standing, station.

statute *n* act, decree, edict, enactment, law, ordinance, regulation.

staunch[1], **stanch** *vb* arrest, block, check, dam, plug, stem, stop.

staunch[2] *adj* firm, sound, stout, strong; constant, faithful, firm, hearty, loyal, resolute, stable, steadfast, steady, strong, trustworthy, trusty, unwavering, zealous.

stave *vb* break, burst; (*with* **off**) adjourn, defer, delay, postpone, procrastinate, put off, waive.

stay *vb* abide, dwell, lodge, rest, sojourn, tarry; continue, halt, remain, stand still, stop; attend, delay, linger, wait; arrest, check, curb, hold, keep in, prevent, rein in, restrain, withhold; delay, detain, hinder, obstruct; hold up, prop, shore up, support, sustain, uphold. * *n* delay, repose, rest, sojourn; halt, stand, stop; bar, check, curb, hindrance, impediment, interruption, obstacle, obstruction, restraint, stumbling block; buttress, dependence, prop, staff, support, supporter.

stead *n* place, room.

steadfast *adj* established, fast, firm, fixed, stable; constant, faithful, implicit, persevering, pertinacious, resolute, resolved, staunch, steady, unhesitating, unreserved, unshaken, unwavering, wholehearted.

steadiness *n* constancy, firmness, perseverance, persistence, resolution, steadfastness; fixedness, stability.

steady *vb* balance, counterbalance, secure, stabilize, support. * *adj* firm, fixed, stable; constant, equable, regular, undeviating, uniform, unremitting; persevering, resolute, staunch, steadfast, unchangeable, unwavering.

steal *vb* burglarize, burgle, crib, embezzle, filch, peculate, pilfer, plagiarize, poach, purloin, shoplift, thieve; creep, sneak, pass stealthily.

stealing *n* burglary, larceny, peculation, shoplifting, robbery, theft, thievery.

stealth *n* secrecy, slyness, stealthiness.

stealthy *adj* clandestine, furtive, private, secret, skulking, sly, sneaking, surreptitious, underhand.

steam *vb* emit vapour, fume; evaporate, vaporize; coddle, cook, poach; navigate, sail; be hot, sweat. * *n* vapour; effluvium, exhalation, fume, mist, reek, smoke.

steamboat *n* steamer, steamship.

steamy *adj* misty, moist, vaporous; erotic, voluptuous.

steed *n* charger, horse, mount.

steel *vb* case-harden, edge; brace, fortify, harden, make firm, nerve, strengthen.

steep[1] *adj* abrupt, declivitous, precipitous, sheer, sloping, sudden. * *n* declivity, precipice.

steep[2] *vb* digest, drench, imbrue, imbue, macerate, saturate, soak.

steeple *n* belfry, spire, tower, turret.

steer *vb* direct, conduct, govern, guide, pilot, point.

steersman *n* conductor, guide, helmsman, pilot.

stellar *adj* astral, starry, star-spangled, stellary.

stem[1] *vb* (*with* **from**) bud, descend, generate, originate, spring, sprout. * *n* axis, stipe, trunk; pedicel, peduncle, petiole, stalk; branch, descendant, offspring, progeny, scion, shoot; ancestry, descent, family, generation, line, lineage, pedigree, race, stock; (*naut*) beak, bow, cutwater, forepart, prow; helm, lookout; etymon, radical, radix, origin, root.

stem[2] *vb* breast, oppose, resist, withstand; check, dam, oppose, staunch, stay, stop.

stench *n* bad smell, fetor, offensive odour, stink.

stenography *n* brachygraphy, shorthand, tachygraphy.

stentorian *adj* loud-voiced, powerful, sonorous, thundering, trumpet-like.

step *vb* pace, stride, tramp, tread, walk. * *n* footstep, pace, stride; stair, tread; degree, gradation, grade, interval; advance, advancement, progression; act, action, deed, procedure, proceeding; footprint, trace, track, vestige; footfall, gait, pace, walk; expedient, means, measure, method; round, rundle, rung.

steppe *n* pampa, prairie, savannah.

sterile *adj* barren, infecund, unfruitful, unproductive, unprolific; bare, dry, empty, poor; (*bot*) acarpous, male, staminate.

sterility *n* barrenness, fruitlessness, infecundity, unfruitfulness, unproductiveness.

sterling *adj* genuine, positive, pure, real, sound, standard, substantial, true.

stern[1] *adj* austere, dour, forbidding, grim, severe; bitter, cruel, hard, harsh, inflexible, relentless, rigid, rigorous, severe, strict, unrelenting; immovable, incorruptible, steadfast, uncompromising.

stern[2] *n* behind, breach, hind part, posterior, rear, tail; (*naut*) counter, poop, rudderpost, tailpost; butt, buttocks, fundament, rump.

sternness *n* austerity, rigidity, severity; asperity, cruelty, harshness, inflexibility, relentlessness, rigour.

sternum *n* (*anat*) breastbone, sternon.

stertorous *adj* hoarsely breathing, snoring.

stew *vb* boil, seethe, simmer, stive. * *n* ragout; confusion, difficulty, mess, scrape.

steward *n* chamberlain, majordomo, seneschal; manciple, purveyor.

stick[1] *vb* gore, penetrate, pierce, puncture, spear, stab, transfix; infix, insert, thrust; attach, cement, glue, paste; fix in, set; adhere, cleave, cling, hold; abide, persist, remain, stay, stop; doubt, hesitate, scruple, stickle, waver; (*with* **by**) adhere to, be faithful, support. * *n* prick, stab, thrust.

stick[2] *n* birch, rod, switch; bat, bludgeon, club, cudgel, shillelah; cane, staff, walking stick; cue, pole, spar, stake.

stickiness *n* adhesiveness, glutinousness, tenacity, viscosity, viscousness.

stickle *vb* altercate, contend, contest, struggle; doubt, hesitate, scruple, stick, waver.

sticky *adj* adhesive, clinging, gluey, glutinous, gummy, mucilaginous, tenacious, viscid, viscous.

stiff *adj* inflexible, rigid, stark, unbending, unyielding; firm, tenacious, thick; obstinate, pertinacious, strong, stubborn; absolute, austere, dogmatic, inexorable, peremptory, positive, rigorous, severe, straitlaced, strict, stringent, uncompromising; ceremonious, chilling, constrained, formal, frigid, prim, punctilious, stately, starchy, stilted; abrupt, cramped, crude, graceless, harsh, inelegant.

stiff-necked *adj* contumacious, cross-grained, dogged, headstrong, intractable, mulish, obdurate, obstinate, stubborn, unruly.

stiffness *n* hardness, inflexibility, rigidity, rigidness, rigour, starkness; compactness, consistence, denseness, density, thickness; contumaciousness, inflexibility, obstinacy, pertinacity, stubbornness; austerity, harshness, rigorousness, severity, sternness, strictness; constraint, formality, frigidity, precision, primness, tenseness.

stifle *vb* choke, smother, suffocate; check, deaden, destroy, extinguish, quench, repress, stop, suppress; conceal, gag, hush, muffle, muzzle, silence, smother, still.

stigma *n* blot, blur, brand, disgrace, dishonour, reproach, shame, spot, stain, taint, tarnish.

stigmatize *vb* brand, defame, discredit, disgrace, dishonour, post, reproach, slur, villify.

stiletto *n* dagger, dirk, poniard, stylet; bodkin, piercer.

still[1] *vb* hush, muffle, silence, stifle; allay, appease, calm, compose, lull, pacify, quiet, smooth, tranquillize; calm, check, immobilize, restrain, stop, subdue, suppress. * *adj* hushed, mum, mute, noiseless, silent; calm, placid, quiet, serene, stilly, tranquil, unruffled; inert, motionless, quiescent, stagnant, stationary. * *n* hush, lull, peace, quiet, quietness, quietude, silence, stillness, tranquillity; picture, photograph, shot.

still[2] *n* distillery, still-house; distillatory, retort, stillatory.

still[3] *adv, conj* till now, to this time, yet; however, nevertheless, notwithstanding; always, continually, ever, habitually, uniformly; after that, again, in continuance.

stilted *adj* bombastic, fustian, grandiloquent, grandiose, high-flown, high-sounding, inflated, magniloquent, pompous, pretentious, stilty, swelling, tumid, turgid.

stimulant *adj* exciting, stimulating, stimulative. * *n* bracer, cordial, pick-me-up, tonic; fillip, incentive, provocative, spur, stimulus.

stimulate *vb* animate, arouse, awaken, brace, encourage, energize, excite, fire, foment, goad, impel, incite, inflame, inspirit, instigate, kindle, prick, prompt, provoke, rally, rouse, set on, spur, stir up, urge, whet, work up.

stimulus *n* encouragement, fillip, goad, incentive, incitement, motivation, motive, provocation, spur, stimulant.

sting *vb* hurt, nettle, prick, wound; afflict, cut, pain.

stinging *adj* acute, painful, piercing; biting, nipping, pungent, tingling.

stingy *adj* avaricious, close, close-fisted, covetous, grudging, mean, miserly, narrow-hearted, niggardly, parsimonious, penurious.

stink *vb* emit a stench, reek, smell bad. * *n* bad smell, fetor, offensive odour, stench.

stint *vb* bound, confine, limit, restrain; begrudge, pinch, scrimp, skimp, straiten; cease, desist, stop. * *n* bound, limit, restraint; lot, period, project, quota, share, shift, stretch, task, time, turn.

stipend *n* allowance, compensation, emolument, fee, hire, honorarium, pay, remuneration, salary, wages.

stipulate *vb* agree, bargain, condition, contract, covenant, engage, provide, settle terms.

stipulation *n* agreement, bargain, concordat, condition, contract, convention, covenant, engagement, indenture, obligation, pact.

stir *vb* budge, change place, go, move; agitate, bestir, disturb, prod; argue, discuss, moot, raise, start; animate, arouse, awaken, excite, goad, incite, instigate, prompt, provoke, quicken, rouse, spur, stimulate; appear, happen, turn up; get up, rise; (*with* **up**) animate, awaken, incite, instigate, move, provoke, quicken, rouse, stimulate. * *n* activity, ado, agitation, bustle, confusion, excitement, fidget, flurry, fuss, hurry, movement; commotion, disorder, disturbance, tumult, uproar.

stirring *adj* active, brisk, diligent, industrious, lively, smart; animating, arousing, awakening, exciting, quickening, stimulating.

stitch *vb* backstitch, baste, bind, embroider, fell, hem, seam, sew, tack, whip.

stive *vb* stow, stuff; boil, seethe, stew; make close, hot or sultry.

stock *vb* fill, furnish, store, supply; accumulate, garner, hoard, lay in, reposit, reserve, save, treasure up. * *adj* permanent, standard, standing. * *n* assets, capital, commodities, fund, principal, shares; accumulation, hoard, inventory, merchandise, provision, range, reserve, store, supply; ancestry, breed, descent, family, house, line, lineage, parentage, pedigree, race; cravat, neckcloth; butt, haft, hand; block, log, pillar, post, stake; stalk, stem, trunk.

stockholder *n* shareholder.

stocking *n* hose, sock.

stock market *n* stock exchange; cattle market.

stocks *npl* funds, public funds, public securities; shares.

stockstill *adj* dead-still, immobile, motionless, stationary, still, unmoving.

stocky *adj* chubby, chunky, dumpy, plump, short, stout, stubby, thickset.

stoic, stoical *adj* apathetic, cold-blooded, impassive, imperturbable, passionless, patient, philosophic, philosophical, phlegmatic, unimpassioned.

stoicism *n* apathy, coldness, coolness, impassivity, indifference, insensibility, nonchalance, phlegm.

stolen *adj* filched, pilfered, purloined; clandestine, furtive, secret, sly, stealthy, surreptitious.

stolid *adj* blockish, doltish, dull, foolish, heavy, obtuse, slow, stockish, stupid.

stolidity *n* doltishness, dullness, foolishness, obtuseness, stolidness, stupidity.

stomach *vb* abide, bear, brook, endure, put up with, stand, submit to, suffer, swallow, tolerate. * *n* abdomen, belly, gut, paunch, pot, tummy; appetite, desire, inclination, keenness, liking, relish, taste.

stone *vb* cover, face, slate, tile; lapidate, pelt. * *n* boulder, cobble, gravel, pebble, rock; gem, jewel, precious stone; cenotaph, gravestone, monument, tombstone; nut, pit; adamant, agate, flint, gneiss, granite, marble, slate, etc.

stony *adj* gritty, hard, lapidose, lithic, petrous, rocky; adamantine, flinty, hard, inflexible, obdurate; cruel, hard-hearted, inexorable, pitiless, stony-hearted, unfeeling, unrelenting.

stoop *vb* bend forward, bend down, bow, lean, sag, slouch, slump; abase, cower, cringe, give in, submit, succumb, surrender; condescend, deign, descend, vouchsafe; fall, sink. * *n* bend, inclination, sag, slouch, slump; descent, swoop.

stop *vb* block, blockade, close, close up, obstruct, occlude; arrest, check, halt, hold, pause, stall, stay; bar, delay, embargo, hinder, impede, intercept, interrupt, obstruct, preclude, prevent, repress, restrain, staunch, suppress, thwart; break off, cease, desist, discontinue, forbear, give over, leave off, refrain from; intermit, quiet, quieten, terminate; lodge, tarry. * *n* halt, intermission, pause, respite, rest, stoppage, suspension, truce; block, cessation, check, hindrance, interruption, obstruction, repression; bar, impediment, obstacle; full stop, point.

stopcock *n* cock, faucet, tap.

stoppage *n* arrest, block, check, closure, hindrance, interruption, obstruction, prevention.

stopper *n* cork, plug, stopple.

store *vb* accumulate, amass, cache, deposit, garner, hoard, husband, lay by, lay in, lay up, put by, reserve, save, store up, stow away, treasure up; furnish, provide, replenish, stock, supply. * *n* accumulation, cache, deposit, fund, hoard, provision, reserve, stock, supply, treasure, treasury; abundance, plenty; storehouse; emporium, market, shop.

storehouse *n* depository, depot, godown, magazine, repository, store, warehouse.

storm *vb* assail, assault, attack; blow violently; fume, rage, rampage, rant, rave, tear. * *n* blizzard, gale, hurricane, squall, tempest, tornado, typhoon, whirlwind; agitation, clamour, commotion, disturbance, insurrection, outbreak, sedition, tumult, turmoil; adversity, affliction, calamity, distress; assault, attack, brunt, onset, onslaught; violence.

storminess *n* inclemency, roughness, tempestuousness.

stormy *adj* blustering, boisterous, gusty, squally, tempestuous, windy; passionate, riotous, rough, turbulent, violent, wild; agitated, furious.

story *n* annals, chronicle, history, record; account, narration, narrative, recital, record, rehearsal, relation, report, statement, tale; fable, fiction, novel, romance; anecdote, incident, legend, tale; canard, fabrication, falsehood, fib, figure, invention, lie, untruth.

storyteller *n* bard, chronicler, narrator, raconteur.

stout *adj* able-bodied, athletic, brawny, lusty, robust, sinewy, stalwart, strong, sturdy, vigorous; courageous, hardy, indomitable, stouthearted; contumacious, obstinate, proud, resolute, stubborn; compact, firm, solid, staunch; bouncing, bulky, burly, chubby, corpulent, fat, heavy, jolly, large, obese, plump, portly, stocky, strapping, thickset.

stouthearted *adj* fearless, heroic, redoubtable; bold, brave, courageous, dauntless, doughty, firm, gallant, hardy, indomitable, intrepid, resolute, valiant, valorous.

stow *vb* load, pack, put away, store, stuff.

straddle *vb* bestride.

straggle *vb* rove, wander; deviate, digress, ramble, range, roam, stray, stroll.

straggling *adj* rambling, roving, straying, strolling, wandering; scattered.

straight *adj* direct, near, rectilinear, right, short, undeviating, unswerving; erect, perpendicular, plumb, right, upright, vertical; equitable, fair, honest, honourable, just, square, straightforward. * *adv* at once, directly, forthwith, immediately, straightaway, straightway, without delay.

straightaway, straightway *adv* at once, directly, forthwith, immediately, speedily, straight, suddenly, without delay.

straighten *vb* arrange, make straight, neaten, order, tidy.

straight-laced *see* **strait-laced.**

strain[1] *vb* draw tightly, make tense, stretch, tighten; injure, sprain, wrench; exert, overexert, overtax, rack; embrace, fold, hug, press, squeeze; compel, constrain, force; dilute, distill, drain, filter, filtrate, ooze, percolate, purify, separate; fatigue, overtask, overwork, task, tax, tire. * *n* stress, tenseness, tension, tensity; effort, exertion, force, overexertion; burden, task, tax; sprain, wrech; lay, melody, movement, snatch, song, stave, tune.

strain[2] *n* manner, style, tone, vein; disposition, tendency, trait, turn; descent, extraction, family, lineage, pedigree, race, stock.

strait *adj* close, confined, constrained, constricted, contracted, narrow; rigid, rigorous, severe, strict; difficult, distressful, grievous, straitened. * *n* channel, narrows, pass, sound.

straits *npl* crisis, difficulty, dilemma, distress, embarrassment, emergency, exigency, extremity, hardship, pass, perplexity, pinch, plight, predicament.

straiten *vb* confine, constrain, constrict, contract, limit; narrow; intensify, stretch; distress, embarrass, perplex, pinch, press.

straitened *adj* distressed, embarrassed limited, perplexed, pinched.

strait-laced, straight-laced *adj* austere, formal, prim, rigid, rigorous, stern, stiff, strict, uncompromising.

straitness *n* narrowness, rigour, severity, strictness; difficulty, distress, trouble; insufficiency, narrowness, scarcity, want.

strand[1] *vb* abandon, beach, be wrecked, cast away, go aground, ground, maroon, run aground, wreck. * *n* beach, coast, shore.

strand[2] *n* braid, cord, fibre, filament, line, rope, string, tress.

stranded *adj* aground, ashore, cast away, lost, shipwrecked, wrecked.

strange *adj* alien, exotic, far-fetched, foreign, outlandish, remote; new, novel; curious, exceptional, extraordinary, irregular, odd, particular, peculiar, rare, singular, surprising, uncommon, unusual; abnormal, anomalous, extraordinary, inconceivable, incredible, inexplicable, marvellous, mysterious, preternatural, unaccountable, unbelievable, unheard of, unique, unnatural, wonderful; bizarre, droll, grotesque, quaint, queer; inexperienced, unacquainted, unfamiliar, unknown; bashful, distant, distrustful, reserved, shy, uncommunicative.

strangeness *n* foreignness; bashfulness, coldness, distance, reserve, shyness, uncommunicativeness; eccentricity, grotesqueness, oddness, singularity, uncommonness, uncouthness.

stranger *n* alien, foreigner, newcomer, immigrant, outsider; guest, visitor.

strangle *vb* choke, contract, smother, squeeze, stifle, suffocate, throttle, tighten; keep back, quiet, repress, still, suppress.

strap *vb* beat, thrash, whip; bind, fasten, sharpen, strop. * *n* thong; band, ligature, strip, tie; razor-strap, strop.

strapping *adj* big, burly, large, lusty, stalwart, stout, strong, tall.

stratagem *n* artifice, cunning, device, dodge, finesse, intrigue, machination, manoeuvre, plan, plot, ruse, scheme, trick, wile.

strategic, strategical *adj* calculated, deliberate, diplomatic, manoeuvering, planned, politic, tactical; critical, decisive, key, vital.

strategy *n* generalship, manoeuvering, plan, policy, stratagem, strategetics, tactics.

stratum *n* band, bed, layer.

straw *n* culm, stalk, stem; button, farthing, fig, penny, pin, rush, snap.

stray *vb* deviate, digress, err, meander, ramble, range, roam, rove, straggle, stroll, swerve, transgress, wander. * *adj* abandoned, lost, strayed, wandering; accidental, erratic, random, scattered.

streak *vb* band, bar, striate, stripe, vein; dart, dash, flash, hurtle, run, speed, sprint, stream, tear. * *n* band, bar, belt, layer, line, strip, stripe, thread, trace, vein; cast, grain, tone, touch, vein; beam, bolt, dart, dash, flare, flash, ray, stream.

streaky *adj* streaked, striped, veined.

stream *vb* course, flow, glide, pour, run, spout; emit, pour out, shed; emanate, go forth, issue, radiate; extend, float, stretch out, wave. * *n* brook, burn, race, rill, rivulet, run, runlet, runnel, trickle; course, current, flow, flux, race, rush, tide, torrent, wake, wash; beam, gleam, patch, radiation, ray, streak.

streamer *n* banner, colours, ensign, flag, pennon, standard.

street *n* avenue, highway, road, way.

strength *n* force, might, main, nerve, potency, power, vigour; hardness, solidity, toughness; impregnability, proof; brawn, grit, healthy, lustiness, muscle, robustness, sinew, stamina, thews, vigorousness; animation, courage, determination, firmness, fortitude, resolution, spirit; cogency, efficacy, soundness, validity; emphasis, energy; security, stay, support; brightness, brilliance, clearness, intensity, vitality, vividness; body, excellence, virtue; impetuosity, vehemence, violence; boldness.

strengthen *vb* buttress, recruit, reinforce; fortify; brace, energize, harden, nerve, steel, stimulate; freshen, invigorate, vitalize; animate, encourage; clench, clinch, confirm, corroborate, establish, fix, justify, sustain, support.

strenuous *adj* active, ardent, eager, earnest, energetic, resolute, vigorous, zealous; bold, determined, doughty, intrepid, resolute, spirited, strong, valiant.

stress *vb* accent, accentuate, emphasize, highlight, point up, underline, underscore; bear, bear upon, press, pressurize; pull, rack, strain, stretch, tense, tug. * *n* accent, accentuation, emphasis; effort, force, pull, strain, tension, tug; boisterousness, severity, violence; pressure, urgency.

stretch *vb* brace, screw, strain, tense, tighten; elongate, extend, lengthen, protract, pull; display, distend, expand, spread, unfold, widen; sprain, strain; distort, exaggerate, misrepresent. * *n* compass, extension, extent, range, reach, scope; effort, exertion, strain, struggle; course, direction.

strict *adj* close, strained, tense, tight; accurate, careful, close, exact, literal, particular, precise, scrupulous; austere, inflexible, harsh, orthodox, puritanical, rigid, rigorous, severe, stern, strait-laced, stringent, uncompromising, unyielding.

stricture *n* animadversion, censure, denunciation, criticism, compression, constriction, contraction.

strife *n* battle, combat, conflict, contention, contest, discord, quarrel, struggle, warfare.

strike *vb* bang, beat, belabour, box, buffet, cudgel, cuff, hit, knock, lash, pound, punch, rap, slap, slug, smite, thump, whip; impress, imprint, stamp; afflict, chastise, deal, give, inflict, punish; affect, astonish, electrify, stun; clash, collide, dash, touch; surrender, yield; mutiny, rebel, rise.

stringent *adj* binding, contracting, rigid, rigorous, severe, strict.

strip[1] *n* piece, ribbon, shred, slip.

strip[2] *vb* denude, hull, skin, uncover; bereave, deprive, deforest, desolate, despoil, devastate, disarm, dismantle, disrobe, divest, expose, fleece, loot, shave; plunder, pillage, ransack, rob, sack, spoil; disrobe, uncover, undress.

strive *vb* aim, attempt, endeavour, exert, labour, strain, struggle, toil; contend, contest, fight, tussle, wrestle; compete, cope.

stroke[1] *n* blow, glance, hit, impact, knock, lash, pat, percussion, rap, shot, switch, thump; attack, paralysis, stroke; affliction, damage, hardship, hurt, injury, misfortune, reverse, visitation; dash, feat, masterstroke, touch.

stroke[2] *vb* caress, feel, palpate, pet, knead, massage, nuzzle, rub, touch.

stroll *vb* loiter, lounge, ramble, range, rove, saunter, straggle, stray, wander. * *n* excursion, promenade, ramble, rambling, roving, tour, trip, walk, wandering.

strong *adj* energetic, forcible, powerful, robust, sturdy; able, enduring; cogent, firm, valid.

structure *vb* arrange, constitute, construct, make, organize. * *n* arrangement, conformation, configuration, constitution, construction, form, formation, make, organization; anatomy, composition, texture; building, edifice, fabric, framework, pile.

struggle *vb* aim, endeavour, exert, labour, strive, toil, try; battle, contend, contest, fight, wrestle; agonize, flounder, writhe. * *n* effort, endeavour, exertion, labour, pains; battle, conflict, contention, contest, fight, strife; agony, contortions, distress.

stubborn *adj* contumacious, dogged, headstrong, heady, inflexible, intractable, mulish, obdurate, obstinate, perverse, positive, refractory, ungovernable, unmanageable, unruly, unyielding, willful; constant, enduring, firm, hardy, persevering, persistent, steady, stoical, uncomplaining, unremitting; firm, hard, inflexible, stiff, strong, tough, unpliant, studied.

studious *adj* contemplative, meditative, reflective, thoughtful; assiduous, attentive, desirous, diligent, eager, lettered, scholarly, zealous.

study *vb* cogitate, lucubrate, meditate, muse, ponder, reflect, think; analyze, contemplate, examine, investigate, ponder, probe, scrutinize, search, sift, weigh. * *n* exercise, inquiry, investigation, reading, research, stumble; cogitation, consideration, contemplation, examination, meditation, reflection, thought; stun; model, object, representation, sketch; den, library, office, studio.

stunning *adj* deafening, stentorian; dumbfounding, stupefying.

stunted *adj* checked, diminutive, dwarfed, dwarfish, lilliputian, little, nipped, small, undersized.

stupendous *adj* amazing, astonishing, astounding, marvellous, overwhelming, surprising, wonderful; enormous, huge, immense, monstrous, prodigious, towering, tremendous, vast.

stupid *adj* brainless, crass, doltish, dull, foolish, idiotic, inane, inept, obtuse, pointless, prosaic, senseless, simple, slow, sluggish, stolid, tedious, tiresome, witless.

stupor *n* coma, confusion, daze, lethargy, narcosis, numbness, stupefaction, torpor.

sturdy *adj* bold, determined, dogged, firm, hardy, obstinate, persevering, pertinacious, resolute, stiff, stubborn, sturdy; athletic, brawny, forcible, lusty, muscular, powerful, robust, stalwart, stout, strong, thickset, vigorous, well-set.

style *vb* address, call, characterize, denominate, designate, dub, entitle, name, term. * *n* dedication, expression, phraseology, turn; cast, character, fashion, form, genre, make, manner, method, mode, model, shape, vogue, way; appellation, denomination, designation, name, title; chic, elegance, smartness; pen, pin, point, stylus.

stylish *adj* chic, courtly, elegant, fashionable, genteel, modish, polished, smart.

suave *adj* affable, agreeable, amiable, bland, courteous, debonair, delightful, glib, gracious, mild, pleasant, smooth, sweet, oily, unctuous, urbane.

subdue *vb* beat, bend, break, bow, conquer, control, crush, defeat, discomfit, foil, master, overbear, overcome, overpower, overwhelm, quell, rout, subject, subjugate, surmount, vanquish, worst; allay, choke, curb, mellow, moderate, mollify, reduce, repress, restrain, soften, suppress, temper.

subject *vb* control, master, overcome, reduce, subdue, subjugate, tame; enslave, enthral; abandon, refer, submit, surrender. * *adj* beneath, subjacent, underneath; dependent, enslaved, inferior, servile, subjected, subordinate, subservient; conditional, obedient, submissive; disposed, exposed to, liable, obnoxious, prone. * *n* dependent, henchman, liegeman, slave, subordinate; matter, point, subject matter, theme, thesis, topic; nominative, premise; case, object, patient, recipient; ego, mind, self, thinking.

subjoin *vb* add, affix, annex, append, join, suffix.

subjugate *vb* conquer, enslave, enthral, master, overcome, overpower, overthrow, subdue, subject, vanquish.

sublimate *vb* alter, change, repress.

sublime *adj aloft, elevated, high,* sacred; eminent, exalted, grand, great, lofty, mighty; august, glorious, magnificent, majestic, noble, stately, solemn, sublunary; elated, elevated, eloquent, exhilarated, raised.

submission *n* capitulation, cession, relinquishment, surrender, yielding; acquiescence, compliance, obedience, resignation; deference, homage, humility, lowliness, obeisance, passiveness, prostration, self-abasement, submissiveness.

submissive *adj* amenable, compliant, docile, pliant, tame, tractable, yielding; acquiescent, long-suffering, obedient, passive, patient, resigned, unassertive, uncomplaining, unrepining; deferential, humble, lowly, meek, obsequious, prostrate, self-abasing.

submit *vb* cede, defer, endure, resign, subject, surrender, yield; commit, propose, refer; offer; acquiesce, bend, capitulate, comply, stoop, succumb.

subordinate *adj* ancillary, dependent, inferior, junior, minor, secondary, subject, subservient, subsidiary. * *n* assistant, dependant, inferior, subject, underling.

subscribe *vb* accede, approve, agree, assent, consent, yield; contribute, donate, give, offer, promise.

subscription *n* aid, assistance, contribution, donation, gift, offering.

subsequent *adj* after, attendant, ensuing, later, latter, following, posterior, sequent, succeeding.

subservient *adj* inferior, obsequious, servile, subject, subordinate; accessory, aiding, auxiliary, conducive, contributory, helpful, instrumental, serviceable, useful.

subside *vb* settle, sink; abate, decline, decrease, diminish, drop, ebb, fall, intermit, lapse, lessen, lower, lull, wane.

subsidence *n* settling, sinking; abatement, decline, decrease, descent, ebb, diminution, lessening.

subsidiary *adj* adjutant, aiding, assistant, auxiliary, cooperative, corroborative, helping, subordinate, subservient.

subsidize *vb* aid, finance, fund, sponsor, support, underwrite.

subsidy *n* aid, bounty, grant, subvention, support, underwriting.

subsist *vb* be, breathe, consist, exist, inhere, live, prevail; abide, continue, endure, persist, remain; feed, maintain, ration, support.

subsistence *n* aliment, food, livelihood, living, maintenance, meat, nourishment, nutriment, provision, rations, support, sustenance, victuals.

substance *n* actuality, element, groundwork, hypostasis, reality, substratum; burden, content, core, drift, essence, gist, heart, import, meaning, pith, sense, significance, solidity, soul, sum, weight; estate, income, means, property, resources, wealth.

substantial *adj* actual, considerable, essential, existent, hypostatic, pithy, potential, real, subsistent, virtual; concrete, durable, positive, solid, tangible, true; corporeal, bodily, material; bulky, firm, goodly, heavy, large, massive, notable, significant, sizable, solid, sound, stable, stout, strong, well-made; cogent, just, efficient, influential, valid, weighty.

substantially *adv* adequately, essentially, firmly, materially, positively, really, truly.

substantiate *vb* actualize, confirm, corroborate, establish, prove, ratify, verify.

subterfuge *n* artifice, evasion, excuse, expedient, mask, pretence, pretext, quirk, shift, shuffle, sophistry, trick.

subtle *adj* arch, artful, astute, crafty, crooked, cunning, designing, diplomatic, intriguing, insinuating, sly, tricky, wily; clever, ingenious; acute, deep, discerning, discriminating, keen, profound, sagacious, shrewd; airy, delicate, ethereal, light, nice, rare, refined, slender, subtle, thin, volatile.

subtlety *n* artfulness, artifice, astuteness, craft, craftiness, cunning, guile, subtleness; acumen, acuteness, cleverness, discernment, intelligence, keenness, sagacity, sharpness, shrewdness; attenuation, delicacy, fitness, nicety, rareness, refinement.

subtract *vb* deduct, detract, diminish, remove, take, withdraw.

suburbs *npl* environs, confines, neighbourhood, outskirts, precincts, purlieus, vicinage.

subversive *adj* destructive, overthrowing, pervasive, ruining, upsetting. * *n* collaborator, dissident, insurrectionist, saboteur, terrorist, traitor.

subvert *vb* invert, overset, overthrow, overturn, reverse, upset; demolish, destroy, extinguish, raze, ruin; confound, corrupt, injure, pervert.

succeed *vb* ensue, follow, inherit, replace; flourish, gain, hit, prevail, prosper, thrive, win.

success *n* attainment, issue, result; fortune, happiness, hit, luck, prosperity, triumph.

successful *adj* auspicious, booming, felicitous, fortunate, happy, lucky, prosperous, victorious, winning.

succession *n* chain, concatenation, cycle, consecution, following, procession, progression, rotation, round, sequence, series, suite; descent, entail, inheritance, lineage, race, reversion.

succinct *adj* brief, compact, compendious, concise, condensed, curt, laconic, pithy, short, summary, terse.

succour *vb* aid, assist, help, relieve; cherish, comfort, encourage, foster, nurse. * *n* aid, assistance, help, relief, support.

succulent *adj* juicy, luscious, lush, nutritive, sappy.

succumb *vb* capitulate, die, submit, surrender, yield.

sudden *adj* abrupt, hasty, hurried, immediate, instantaneous, rash, unanticipated, unexpected, unforeseen, unusual; brief, momentary, quick, rapid.

sue *vb* charge, court, indict, prosecute, solicit, summon, woo; appeal, beg, demand, entreat, implore, petition, plead, pray, supplicate.

suffer *vb* feel, undergo; bear, endure, sustain, tolerate; admit, allow, indulge, let, permit.

sufferable *adj* allowable, bearable, endurable, permissible, tolerable.

sufferance *n* endurance, inconvenience, misery, pain, suffering; long-suffering, moderation, patience, submission; allowance, permission, toleration.

suffice *vb* avail, content, satisfy, serve.

sufficient *adj* adequate, ample, commensurate, competent, enough, full, plenteous, satisfactory; able, equal, fit, qualified, responsible.

suffocate *vb* asphyxiate, choke, smother, stifle, strangle.

suffrage *n* ballot, franchise, voice, vote; approval, attestation, consent, testimonial, witness.

suggest *vb* advise, allude, hint, indicate, insinuate, intimate, move, present, prompt, propose, propound, recommend.

suggestion *n* allusion, hint, indication, insinuation, intimation, presentation, prompting, proposal, recommendation, reminder.

suit *vb* accommodate, adapt, adjust, fashion, fit, level, match; accord, become, befit, gratify, harmonize, please, satisfy, tally. * *n* appeal, entreaty, invocation, petition, prayer, request, solicitation, supplication; courtship, wooing; action, case, cause, process, prosecution, trial; clothing, costume, habit.

suitable *adj* adapted, accordant, agreeable, answerable, apposite, applicable, appropriate, apt, becoming, befitting, conformable, congruous, convenient, consonant, correspondent, decent, due, eligible, expedient, fit, fitting, just, meet, pertinent, proper, relevant, seemly, worthy.

suite *n* attendants, bodyguard, convoy, cortege, court, escort, followers, staff, retainers, retinue, train; collection, series, set, suit; apartment, rooms.

sulky *adj* aloof, churlish, cross, cross-grained, dogged, grouchy, ill-humoured, ill-tempered, moody, morose, perverse, sour, spleenish, spleeny, splenetic, sullen, surly, vexatious, wayward.

sullen *adj* cross, crusty, glum, grumpy, ill-tempered, moody, morose, sore, sour, sulky; cheerless, cloudy, dark, depressing, dismal, foreboding, funereal, gloomy, lowering, melancholy, mournful, sombre; dull, heavy, slow, sluggish; intractable, obstinate, perverse, refractory, stubborn, vexatious; baleful, evil, inauspicious, malign, malignant, sinister, unlucky, unpropitious.

sully *vb* blemish, blot, contaminate, deface, defame, dirty, disgrace, dishonour, foul, smirch, soil, slur, spot, stain, tarnish.

sultry *adj* close, damp, hot, humid, muggy, oppressive, stifling, stuffy, sweltering.

sum *vb* add, calculate, compute, reckon; collect, comprehend, condense, epitomize, summarize. * *n* aggregate, amount, total, totality, whole; compendium, substance, summary; acme, completion, height, summit.

summary *adj* brief, compendious, concise, curt, laconic, pithy, short, succinct, terse; brief, quick, rapid. * *n* abridgement, abstract, brief, compendium, digest, epitome, precis, résumé, syllabus, synopsis.

summit *n* acme, apex, cap, climax, crest, crown, pinnacle, top, vertex, zenith.

summon *vb* arouse, bid, call, cite, invite, invoke, rouse; convene, convoke; charge, indict, prosecute, subpoena, sue.

sumptuous *adj* costly, dear, expensive, gorgeous, grand, lavish, luxurious, magnificent, munificent, pompous, prodigal, rich, showy, splendid, stately, superb.

sunburnt *adj* bronzed, brown, ruddy, tanned.

sunder *vb* break, disconnect, disjoin, dissociate, dissever, disunited, divide, part, separate, sever.

sundry *adj* different, divers, several, some, various.

sunny *adj* bright, brilliant, clear, fine, luminous, radiant, shining, unclouded, warm; cheerful, genial, happy, joyful, mild, optimistic, pleasant, smiling.

superannuated *adj* aged, anile, antiquated, decrepit, disqualified, doting, effete, imbecile, passé, retired, rusty, time-worn, unfit.

superb *adj* august, beautiful, elegant, exquisite, grand, gorgeous, imposing, magnificent, majestic, noble, pompous, rich, showy, splendid, stately, sumptuous.

supercilious *adj* arrogant, condescending, contemptuous, dictatorial, domineering, haughty, high, imperious, insolent, intolerant, lofty, lordly, magisterial, overbearing, overweening, proud, scornful, vainglorious.

superficial *adj* external, flimsy, shallow, untrustworthy.

superfluity *n* excess, exuberance, redundancy, superabundance, surfeit.

superfluous *adj* excessive, redundant, unnecessary.

superintend *vb* administer, conduct, control, direct, inspect, manage, overlook, oversee, supervise.

superintendence *n* care, charge, control, direction, guidance, government, inspection, management, oversight, supervision, surveillance.

superior *adj* better, greater, high, higher, finer, paramount, supreme, ultra, upper; chief, foremost, principal; distinguished, matchless, noble, pre-eminent, preferable, sovereign, surpassing, unrivalled, unsurpassed; predominant, prevalent. * *n* boss, chief, director, head, higher-up, leader, manager, principal, senior, supervisor.

superiority *n* advantage, ascendency, lead, odds, predominance, preeminence, prevalence, transcendence; excellence, nobility, worthiness.

superlative *adj* consummate, greatest, incomparable, peerless, preeminent, supreme, surpassing, transcendent.

supernatural *adj* abnormal, marvellous, metaphysical, miraculous, otherworldly, preternatural, unearthly.

supernumerary *adj* excessive, odd, redundant, superfluous.

supersede *vb* annul, neutralize, obviate, overrule, suspend; displace, remove, replace, succeed, supplant.

supervise *vb* administer, conduct, control, direct, inspect, manage, overlook, oversee, superintend.

supine *adj* apathetic, careless, drowsy, dull, idle, indifferent, indolent, inert, languid, lethargic, listless, lumpish, lazy, negligent, otiose, prostrate, recumbent, sleepy, slothful, sluggish, spineless, torpid.

supplant *vb* overpower, overthrow, undermine; displace, remove, replace, supersede.

supple *adj* elastic, flexible, limber, lithe, pliable, pliant; compliant, humble, submissive, yielding; adulatory, cringing, fawning, flattering, grovelling, obsequious, oily, parasitical, servile, slavish, sycophantic.

supplement *vb* add, augment, extend, reinforce, supply. * *n* addendum, addition, appendix, codicil, complement, continuation, postscript.

suppliant *adj* begging, beseeching, entreating, imploring, precative, precatory, praying, suing, supplicating. * *n* applicant, petitioner, solicitor, suitor, supplicant.

supplicate *vb* beg, beseech, crave, entreat, implore, importune, petition, pray, solicit.

supplication *n* invocation, orison, petition, prayer; entreaty, petition, prayer, request, solicitation.

supply *vb* endue, equip, furnish, minister, outfit, provide, replenish, stock, store; afford, accommodate, contribute, furnish, give, grant, yield. * *n* hoard, provision, reserve, stock, store.

support *vb* brace, cradle, pillow, prop, sustain, uphold; bear, endure, undergo, suffer, tolerate; cherish, keep, maintain, nourish, nurture; act, assume, carry, perform, play, represent; accredit, confirm, corroborate, substantiate, verify; abet, advocate, aid, approve, assist, back, befriend, champion, countenance, encourage, favour, float, hold, patronize, relieve, reinforce, succour, vindicate. * *n* bolster, brace, buttress, foothold, guy, hold, prop, purchase, shore, stay, substructure, supporter, underpinning; groundwork, mainstay, staff; base, basis, bed, foundation; keeping, living, livelihood, maintenance, subsistence, sustenance; confirmation, evidence; aid, assistance, backing, behalf, championship, comfort, countenance, encouragement, favour, help, patronage, succour.

suppose *vb* apprehend, believe, conceive, conclude, consider, conjecture, deem, imagine, judge, presume, presuppose, think; assume, hypothesize; imply, posit, predicate, think; fancy, opine, speculate, surmise, suspect, theorize, wean.

supposition *n* conjecture, guess, guesswork, presumption, surmise; assumption, hypothesis, postulation, theory, thesis; doubt, uncertainty.

suppress *vb* choke, crush, destroy, overwhelm, overpower, overthrow, quash, quell, quench, smother, stifle, subdue, withhold; arrest, inhibit, obstruct, repress, restrain, stop; conceal, extinguish, keep, retain, secret, silence, stifle, strangle.

supremacy *n* ascendancy, domination, headship, lordship, mastery, predominance, pre-eminence, primacy, sovereignty.

supreme *adj* chief, dominant, first, greatest, highest, leading, paramount, predominant, pre-eminent, principal, sovereign.

sure *adj* assured, certain, confident, positive;
accurate, dependable, effective, honest, infallible, precise, reliable, trustworthy, undeniable, undoubted, unmistakable, well-proven; guaranteed, inevitable, irrevocable; fast, firm, safe, secure, stable, steady.

surely *adv* assuredly, certainly, infallibly, sure, undoubtedly; firmly, safely, securely, steadily.

surety *n* bail, bond, certainty, guarantee, pledge, safety, security.

surfeit *vb* cram, gorge, overfeed, sate, satiate; cloy, nauseate, pall. * *n* excess, fullness, glut, oppression, plethora, satiation, satiety, superabundance, superfluity.

surge *vb* billow, rise, rush, sweep, swell, swirl, tower. * *n* billow, breaker, roller, wave, white horse.

surly *adj* churlish, crabbed, cross, crusty, discourteous, fretful, gruff, grumpy, harsh, ill-natured, ill-tempered, morose, peevish, perverse, pettish, petulant, rough, rude, snappish, snarling, sour, sullen, testy, touchy, uncivil, ungracious, waspish; dark, tempestuous.

surmise *vb* believe, conclude, conjecture, consider, divine, fancy, guess, imagine, presume, suppose, think, suspect. * *n* conclusion, conjecture, doubt, guess, notion, possibility, supposition, suspicion, thought.

surmount *vb* clear, climb, crown, overtop, scale, top, vault; conquer, master, overcome, overpower, subdue, vanquish; exceed, overpass, pass, surpass, transcend.

surpass *vb* beat, cap, eclipse, exceed, excel, outdo, outmatch, outnumber, outrun, outstrip, override, overshadow, overtop, outshine, surmount, transcend.

surplus *adj* additional, leftover, remaining, spare, superfluous, supernumerary, supplementary. * *n* balance, excess, overplus, remainder, residue, superabundance, surfeit.

surprise *vb* amaze, astonish, astound, bewilder, confuse, disconcert, dumbfound, startle, stun. * *n* amazement, astonishment, blow, shock, wonder.

surprising *adj* amazing, astonishing, astounding, extraordinary, marvellous, unexpected, remarkable, startling, strange, unexpected, wonderful.

surrender *vb* cede, sacrifice, yield; abdicate, abandon, forgo, relinquish, renounce, resign, waive; capitulate, comply, succumb. * *n* abandonment, capitulation, cession, delivery, relinquishment, renunciation, resignation, yielding.

surreptitious *adj* clandestine, fraudulent, furtive, secret, sly, stealthy, unauthorized, underhand.

surround *vb* beset, circumscribe, compass, embrace, encircle, encompass, environ, girdle, hem, invest, loop.

surveillance *n* care, charge, control, direction, inspection, management, oversight, superintendence, supervision, surveyorship, vigilance, watch.

survey *vb* contemplate, observe, overlook, reconnoitre, review, scan, scout, view; examine, inspect, scrutinize; oversee, supervise; estimate, measure, plan, plot, prospect. * *n* prospect, retrospect, sight, view; examination, inspection, reconnaissance, review; estimating, measuring, planning, plotting, prospecting, work-study.

survive *vb* endure, last, outlast, outlive.

susceptible *adj* capable, excitable, impressible, impressionable, inclined, predisposed, receptive, sensitive.

suspect *vb* believe, conclude, conjecture, fancy, guess, imagine, judge, suppose, surmise, think; distrust, doubt, mistrust. * *adj* doubtful, dubious, suspicious.

suspend *vb* append, hang, sling, swing; adjourn, arrest, defer, delay, discontinue, hinder, intermit, interrupt, postpone, stay, withhold; debar, dismiss, rusticate.

suspicion *n* assumption, conjecture, dash, guess, hint, inkling, suggestion, supposition, surmise, trace; apprehension, distrust, doubt, fear, jealousy, misgiving, mistrust.

suspicious *adj* distrustful, jealous, mistrustful, suspect, suspecting; doubtful, questionable.

sustain *vb* bear, bolster, fortify, prop, strengthen, support, uphold; maintain, nourish, perpetuate, preserve; aid, assist, comfort, relieve; brave, endure, suffer, undergo; approve, confirm, ratify, sanction, validate; confirm, establish, justify, prove.

sustenance *n* maintenance, subsistence, support; aliment, bread, food, nourishment, nutriment, nutrition, provisions, supplies, victuals.

swagger *vb* bluster, boast, brag, bully, flourish, hector, ruffle, strut, swell, vapour. * *n* airs, arrogance, bluster, boastfulness, braggadocio, ruffling, strut.

swain *n* clown, countryman, hind, peasant, rustic; adorer, gallant, inamorata, lover, suitor, wooer.

swallow *vb* bolt, devour, drink, eat, englut, engorge, gobble, gorge, gulp, imbibe, ingurgitate, swamp; absorb, appropriate, arrogate, devour, engulf, submerge; consume, employ, occupy; brook, digest, endure, pocket, stomach; recant, renounce, retract. * *n* gullet, oesophagus, throat; inclination, liking, palate, relish, taste; deglutition, draught, gulp, ingurgitation, mouthful, taste.

swamp *vb* engulf, overwhelm, sink; capsize, embarrass, overset, ruin, upset, wreck. * *n* bog, fen, marsh, morass, quagmire, slough.

sward *n* grass, lawn, sod, turf.

swarm *vb* abound, crowd, teem, throng. * *n* cloud, concourse, crowd, drove, flock, hive, horde, host, mass, multitude, press, shoal, throng.

swarthy *adj* black, brown, dark, dark-skinned, dusky, tawny.

sway *vb* balance, brandish, move, poise, rock, roll, swing, wave, wield; bend, bias, influence, persuade, turn, urge; control, dominate, direct, govern, guide, manage, rule; hoist, raise; incline, lean, lurch, yaw. * *n* ascendency, authority, command, control, domination, dominion, empire, government, mastership, mastery, omnipotence, predominance, power, rule, sovereignty; bias, direction, influence, weight; preponderance, preponderation; oscillation, sweep, swing, wag, wave.

swear *vb* affirm, attest, avow, declare, depose, promise, say, state, testify, vow; blaspheme, curse.

sweep *vb* clean, brush; graze, touch; rake, scour, traverse. * *n* amplitude, compass, drive, movement, range, reach, scope; destruction, devastation, havoc, ravage; curvature, curve.

sweeping *adj* broad, comprehensive, exaggerated, extensive, extravagant, general, unqualified, wholesale.

sweet *adj* candied, cloying, honeyed, luscious, nectareous, nectarous, sugary, saccharine; balmy, fragrant, odorous, redolent, spicy; harmonious, dulcet, mellifluous, mellow, melodious, musical, pleasant, soft, tuneful, silver-toned, silvery; beautiful, fair, lovely; agreeable, charming, delightful, grateful, gratifying; affectionate, amiable, attractive, engaging, gentle, mild, lovable, winning; benignant, serene; clean, fresh, pure, sound. * *n* fragrance, perfume, redolence; blessing, delight, enjoyment, gratification, joy, pleasure; candy, treat.

swell *vb* belly, bloat, bulge, dilate, distend, expand, inflate, intumesce, puff, swell, tumefy; augment, enlarge, increase; heave, rise, surge; strut, swagger. * *n* swelling; augmentation, excrescence, protuberance; ascent, elevation, hill, rise; force, intensity, power; billows, surge, undulation, waves; beau, blade, buck, coxcomb, dandy, exquisite, fop, popinjay.

swerve *vb* deflect, depart, deviate, stray, turn, wander; bend, incline, yield; climb, swarm, wind.

swift *adj* expeditious, fast, fleet, flying, quick, rapid, speedy; alert, eager, forward, prompt, ready, zealous; instant, sudden.

swiftness *n* celerity, expedition, fleetness, quickness, rapidity, speed, velocity.

swindle *vb* cheat, con, cozen, deceive, defraud, diddle, dupe, embezzle, forge, gull, hoax, overreach, steal, trick, victimize. * *n* cheat, con, deceit, deception, fraud, hoax, imposition, knavery, roguery, trickery.

swindler *n* blackleg, cheat, defaulter, embezzler, faker, fraud, impostor, jockey, knave, peculator, rogue, sharper, trickster.

swing *vb* oscillate, sway, vibrate, wave; dangle, depend, hang; brandish, flourish, whirl; administer, manage. * *n* fluctuation, oscillation, sway, undulation, vibration; elbow-room, freedom, margin, play, range, scope, sweep; bias, tendency.

swoop *vb* descend, pounce, rush, seize, stoop, sweep. * *n* clutch, pounce, seizure; stoop, descent.

sword *n* brand, broadsword, claymore, cutlass, epee, falchion, foil, hanger, rapier, sabre, scimitar.

sybarite *n* epicure, voluptuary.

sycophancy *n* adulation, cringing, fawning, flattery, grovelling, obsequiousness, servility.

sycophant *n* cringer, fawner, flunky, hanger-on, lickspittle, parasite, spaniel, toady, wheedler.

syllabus *n* abridgement, abstract, breviary, brief, compendium, digest, epitome, outline, summary, synopsis.

symbol *n* badge, emblem, exponent, figure, mark, picture, representation, representative, sign, token, type.

symbolic, symbolical *adj* emblematic, figurative, hieroglyphic, representative, significant, typical.

symmetry *n* balance, congruity, evenness, harmony, order, parallelism, proportion, regularity, shapeliness.

sympathetic *adj* affectionate, commiserating, compassionate, condoling, kind, pitiful, tender.

sympathy *n* accord, affinity, agreement, communion, concert, concord, congeniality, correlation, correspondence, harmony, reciprocity, union; commiseration, compassion, condolence, fellow-feeling, kindliness, pity, tenderness, thoughtfulness.

symptom *n* diagnostic, indication, mark, note, prognostic, sign, token.

symptomatic *adj* characteristic, indicative, symbolic, suggestive.

synonymous *adj* equipollent, equivalent, identical, interchangeable, similar, tantamount.

synopsis *n* abridgement, abstract, compendium, digest, epitome, outline, precis, résumé, summary, syllabus.

system *n* method, order, plan.

systematic *adj* methodic, methodical, orderly, regular.

T

tabernacle *n* pavilion, tent; cathedral, chapel, church, minster, synagogue, temple.

table *vb* enter, move, propose, submit, suggest. * *n* plate, slab, tablet; board, counter, desk, stand; catalogue, chart, compendium, index, list, schedule, syllabus, synopsis, tabulation; diet, fare, food, victuals.

tableau *n* picture, scene, representation.

taboo *vb* forbid, interdict, prohibit, proscribe. * *adj* banned, forbidden, inviolable, outlawed, prohibited, proscribed. * *n* ban, interdict, prohibition, proscription.

tacit *adj* implicit, implied, inferred, silent, understood, unexpressed, unspoken.

taciturn *adj* close, dumb, laconic, mum, reserved, reticent, silent, tight-lipped, uncommunicative.

tack *vb* add, affix, append, attach, fasten, tag; gybe, yaw, zigzag. * *n* nail, pin, staple; bearing, course, direction, heading, path, plan, procedure.

tackle *vb* attach, grapple, seize; attempt, try, undertake. * *n* apparatus, cordage, equipment, furniture, gear, harness, implements, rigging, tackling, tools, weapons.

tact *n* address, adroitness, cleverness, dexterity, diplomacy, discernment, finesse, insight, knack, perception, skill, understanding.

tail *vb* dog, follow, shadow, stalk, track. * *adj* abridged, curtailed, limited, reduced. * *n* appendage, conclusion, end, extremity, stub; flap, skirt; queue, retinue, train.

taint *vb* imbue, impregnate; contaminate, corrupt, defile, inflect, mildew, pollute, poison, spoil, touch; blot, stain, sully, tarnish. * *n* stain, tincture, tinge, touch; contamination, corruption, defilement, depravation, infection, pollution; blemish, defect, fault, flaw, spot.

take *vb* accept, obtain, procure, receive; clasp, clutch, grasp, grip, gripe, seize, snatch; filch, misappropriate, pilfer, purloin, steal; abstract, apprehend, appropriate, arrest, bag, capture, ensnare, entrap; attack, befall, smite; capture, carry off, conquer, gain, win; allure, attract, bewitch, captivate, charm, delight, enchant, engage, fascinate, interest, please; consider, hold, interrupt, suppose, regard, understand; choose, elect, espouse, select; employ, expend, use; claim, demand, necessitate, require; bear, endure, experience, feel, perceive, tolerate; deduce, derive, detect, discover, draw; carry, conduct, convey, lead, transfer; clear, surmount; drink, eat, imbibe,
inhale, swallow. * *n* proceeds, profits, return, revenue, takings, yield.

tale *n* account, fable, legend, narration, novel, parable, recital, rehearsal, relation, romance, story, yarn; catalogue, count, enumeration, numbering, reckoning, tally.

talent *n* ableness, ability, aptitude, capacity, cleverness, endowment, faculty, forte, genius, gift, knack, parts, power, turn.

talk *vb* chatter, communicate, confer, confess, converse, declaim, discuss, gossip, pontificate, speak. * *n* chatter, communication, conversation, diction, gossip, jargon, language, rumour, speech, utterance.

talkative *adj* chatty, communicative, garrulous, loquacious, voluble.

tally *vb* accord, agree, conform, coincide, correspond, harmonize, match, square, suit. * *n* match, mate; check, counterpart, muster, roll call; account, reckoning.

tame *vb* domesticate, reclaim, train; conquer, master, overcome, repress, subdue, subjugate. * *adj* docile, domestic, domesticated, gentle, mild, reclaimed; broken, crushed, meek, subdued, unresisting, submissive; barren, commonplace, dull, feeble, flat, insipid, jejune, languid, lean, poor, prosaic, prosy, spiritless, tedious, uninteresting, vapid.

tamper *vb* alter, conquer, dabble, damage, interfere, meddle; intrigue, seduce, suborn.

tang *n* aftertaste, flavour, relish, savour, smack, taste; keenness, nip, sting.

tangible *adj* corporeal, material, palpable, tactile, touchable; actual, certain, embodied, evident, obvious, open, perceptible, plain, positive, real, sensible, solid, stable, substantial.

tangle *vb* complicate, entangle, intertwine, interweave, mat, perplex, snarl; catch, ensnare, entrap, involve, catch; embarrass, embroil, perplex. * *n* complication, disorder, intricacy, jumble, perplexity, snarl; dilemma, embarrassment, quandary, perplexity.

tantalize *vb* balk, disappoint, frustrate, irritate, provoke, tease, torment, vex.

tantamount *adj* equal, equivalent, synonymous.

tantrum *n* fit, ill-humour, outburst, paroxysm, temper, whim.

tap[1] *vb* knock, pat, rap, strike, tip, touch. * *n* pat, tip, rap, touch.

tap[2] *vb* broach, draw off, extract, pierce; draw on, exploit, mine, use, utilize; bug, eavesdrop, listen in. * *n* faucet, plug, spigot, spout, stopcock, valve; bug, listening device, transmitter.

tardiness *n* delay, dilatoriness, lateness, procrastination, slackness, slowness.

tardy *adj* slow, sluggish, snail-like; backward, behindhand, dilatory, late, loitering, overdue, slack.

tarn *n* bog, fen, marsh, morass, swamp.

tarnish *vb* blemish, deface, defame, dim, discolour, dull, slur, smear, soil, stain, sully. * *n* blemish, blot, soiling, spot, stain.

tarry *vb* delay, dally, linger, loiter, remain, stay, stop, wait; defer; abide, lodge, rest, sojourn.

tart *adj* acid, acidulous, acrid, astringent, piquant, pungent, sharp, sour; acrimonious, caustic, crabbed, curt, harsh, ill-humoured, ill-tempered, keen, petulant, sarcastic, severe, snappish, testy.

task *vb* burden, overwork, strain, tax. * *n* drudgery, labour, toil, work; business, charge, chore, duty, employment, enterprise, job, mission, stint, undertaking; assignment, exercise, lesson.

taste *vb* experience, feel, perceive, undergo; relish, savour, sip. * *n* flavour, gusto, relish, savour, smack, piquancy; admixture, bit, dash, fragment, hint, infusion, morsel, mouthful, sample, shade, sprinkling, suggestion, tincture; appetite, desire, fondness, liking, partiality, predilection; acumen, cultivation, culture, delicacy, discernment, discrimination, elegance, fine-feeling, grace, judgement, polish, refinement; manner, style.

tasteful *adj* appetizing, delicious, flavoursome, palatable, savoury, tasty, toothsome; aesthetic, artistic, attractive, elegant.

tasteless *adj* flat, insipid, savourless, stale, watery; dull, mawkish, uninteresting, vapid.

tattle *vb* babble, chat, chatter, jabber, prate, prattle; blab, gossip, inform. * *n* gabble, gossip, prate, prattle, tittle-tattle, twaddle.

taunt *vb* censure, chaff, deride, flout, jeer, mock, scoff, sneer, revile, reproach, ridicule, twit, upbraid. * *n* censure, derision, gibe, insult, jeer, quip, quirk, reproach, ridicule, scoff.

taut *adj* strained, stretched, tense, tight.

tautology *n* iteration, pleonasm, redundancy, reiteration, repetition, verbosity, wordiness.

tavern *n* bar, chophouse, hostelry, inn, pub, public house.

tawdry *adj* flashy, gaudy, garish, glittering, loud, meretricious, ostentatious, showy.

tax *vb* burden, demand, exact, load, overtax, require, strain, task; accuse, charge. * *n* assessment, custom, duty, excise, impost, levy, rate, taxation, toll, tribute; burden, charge, demand, requisition, strain; accusation, censure.

teach *vb* catechize, coach, discipline, drill, edify, educate, enlighten, inform, indoctrinate, initiate, instruct, ground, prime, school, train, tutor; communicate, disseminate, explain, expound, impart, implant, inculcate, infuse, instil, interpret, preach, propagate; admonish, advise, counsel, direct, guide, signify, show.

teacher *n* coach, educator, inculcator, informant, instructor, master, pedagogue, preceptor, schoolteacher, trainer, tutor; adviser, counsellor, guide, mentor; pastor, preacher.

tear *vb* burst, slit, rive, rend, rip; claw, lacerate, mangle, shatter, rend, wound; sever, sunder; fume, rage, rant, rave. * *n* fissure, laceration, rent, rip, wrench.

tease *vb* annoy, badger, beg, bother, chafe, chagrin, disturb, harass, harry, hector, importune, irritate, molest, pester, plague, provoke, tantalize, torment, trouble, vex, worry.

tedious *adj* dull, fatiguing, irksome, monotonous, tiresome, trying, uninteresting, wearisome; dilatory, slow, sluggish, tardy.

teem *vb* abound, bear, produce, swarm; discharge, empty, overflow.

teeming *adj* abounding, fraught, full, overflowing, pregnant, prolific, replete, swarming.

tell *vb* compute, count, enumerate, number, reckon; describe, narrate, recount, rehearse, relate, report; acknowledge, announce, betray, confess, declare, disclose, divulge, inform, own, reveal; acquaint, communicate, instruct, teach; discern, discover, distinguish; express, mention, publish, speak, state, utter.

temper *vb* modify, qualify; appease, assuage, calm, mitigate, mollify, moderate, pacify, restrain, soften, soothe; accommodate, adapt, adjust, fit, suit. * *n* character, constitution, nature, organization, quality, structure, temperament, type; disposition, frame, grain, humour, mood, spirits, tone, vein; calmness, composure, equanimity, moderation, tranquillity; anger, ill-temper, irritation, spleen, passion.

temperament *n* character, constitution, disposition, habit, idiosyncrasy, nature, organization, temper.

temperate *adj* abstemious, ascetic, austere, chaste, continent, frugal, moderate, self-controlled, self-denying, sparing; calm, cool, dispassionate, mild, sober, sedate.

tempest *n* cyclone, gale, hurricane, squall, storm, tornado; commotion, disturbance, excitement, perturbation, tumult, turmoil.

temporal *adj* civil, lay, mundane, political, profane, secular, terrestrial, worldly; brief, ephemeral, evanescent, fleeting, momentary, short-lived, temporal, transient, transitory.

temporary *adj* brief, ephemeral, evanescent, fleeting, impermanent, momentary, short-lived, transient, transitory.

tempt *vb* prove, test, try; allure, decoy, entice, induce, inveigle, persuade, seduce; dispose, incite, incline, instigate, lead, prompt, provoke.

tempting *adj* alluring, attractive, enticing, inviting, seductive.

tenable *adj* defensible, maintainable, rational, reasonable, sound.

tenacious *adj* retentive, unforgetful; adhesive, clinging, cohesive, firm, glutinous, gummy, resisting, retentive, sticky, strong, tough, unyielding, viscous; dogged, fast, obstinate, opinionated, opinionative, pertinacious, persistent, resolute, stubborn, unwavering.

tenacity *n* retentiveness, tenaciousness; adhesiveness, cohesiveness, glutinosity, glutinousness, gumminess, toughness, stickiness, strength, viscidity; doggedness, firmness, obstinacy, perseverance, persistency, pertinacity, resolution, stubbornness.

tend[1] *vb* accompany, attend, graze, guard, keep, protect, shepherd, watch.

tend[2] *vb* aim, exert, gravitate, head, incline, influence, lead, lean, point, trend, verge; conduce, contribute.

tendency *n* aim, aptitude, bearing, bent, bias, course, determination, disposition, direction, drift, gravitation, inclination, leaning, liability, predisposition, proclivity, proneness, propensity, scope, set, susceptibility, turn, twist, warp.

tender[1] *vb* bid, offer, present, proffer, propose, suggest, volunteer. * *n* bid, offer, proffer, proposal; currency, money.

tender[2] *adj* callow, delicate, effeminate, feeble, feminine, fragile, immature, infantile, soft, weak, young; affectionate, compassionate, gentle, humane, kind, lenient, loving, merciful, mild, pitiful, sensitive, sympathetic, tender-hearted; affecting, disagreeable, painful, pathetic, touching, unpleasant.

tenebrous *adj* cloudy, dark, darksome, dusky, gloomy, murky, obscure, shadowy, shady, sombre, tenebrious.

tenement *n* abode, apartment, domicile, dwelling, flat, house.

tenet *n* belief, creed, position, dogma, doctrine, notion, opinion, position, principle, view.

tenor *n* cast, character, cut, fashion, form, manner, mood, nature, stamp, tendency, trend, tone; drift, gist, import, intent, meaning, purport, sense, significance, spirit.

tense *vb* flex, strain, tauten, tighten. * *adj* rigid, stiff, strained, stretched, taut, tight; excited, highly strung, intent, nervous, rapt.

tentative *adj* essaying, experimental, provisional, testing, toying.

tenure *n* holding, occupancy, occupation, possession, tenancy, tenement, use.

term *vb* call, christen, denominate, designate, dub, entitle, name, phrase, style. * *n* bound, boundary, bourn, confine, limit, mete, terminus; duration, period, season, semester, span, spell, termination, time; denomination, expression, locution, name, phrase, word.

termagant *n* beldam, hag, scold, shrew, spitfire, virago, vixen.

terminal *adj* bounding, limiting; final, terminating, ultimate. * *n* end, extremity, termination; bound, limit; airport, depot, station, terminus.

terminate *vb* bound, limit; end, finish, close, complete, conclude; eventuate, issue, prove.

termination *n* ending, suffix; bound, extend, limit; end, completion, conclusion, consequence, effect, issue, outcome, result.

terms *npl* conditions, provisions, stipulations.

terrestrial *adj* earthly, mundane, subastral, subcelestial, sublunar, sublunary, tellurian, worldly. * *n* earthling, human.

terrible *adj* appalling, dire, dreadful, fearful, formidable, frightful, gruesome, hideous, horrible, horrid, shocking, terrific, tremendous; alarming, awe-inspiring, awful, dread; great, excessive, extreme, severe.

terrific *adj* marvellous, sensational, superb; immense, intense; alarming, dreadful, formidable, frightful, terrible, tremendous.

terrify *vb* affright, alarm, appal, daunt, dismay, fright, frighten, horrify, scare, shock, startle, terrorize.

territory *n* country, district, domain, dominion, division, land, place, province, quarter, region, section, tract.

terror *n* affright, alarm, anxiety, awe, consternation, dismay, dread, fear, fright, horror, intimidation, panic, terrorism.

terse *adj* brief, compact, concise, laconic, neat, pithy, polished, sententious, short, smooth, succinct.

test *vb* assay; examine, prove, try. * *n* attempt, essay, examination, experiment, ordeal, proof, trial; criterion, standard, touchstone; example, exhibition; discrimination, distinction, judgment.

testify *vb* affirm, assert, asseverate, attest, avow, certify, corroborate, declare, depose, evidence, state, swear.

testimonial *n* certificate, credential, recommendation, voucher; monument, record.

testimony *n* affirmation, attestation, confession, confirmation, corroboration, declaration, deposition, profession; evidence, proof, witness.

testy *adj* captious, choleric, cross, fretful, hasty, irascible, irritable, quick, peevish, peppery, pettish, petulant, snappish, splenetic, touchy, waspish.

tetchy *adj* crabbed, cross, fretful, irritable, peevish, sullen, touchy.

tether *vb* chain, fasten, picket, stake, tie. * *n* chain, fastening, rope.

text *n* copy, subject, theme, thesis, topic, treatise.

texture *n* fabric, web, weft; character, coarseness, composition, constitution, fibre, fineness, grain, make-up, nap, organization, structure, tissue.

thankful *adj* appreciative, beholden, grateful, indebted, obliged.

thankfulness *n* appreciation, gratefulness, gratitude.

thankless *adj* profitless, ungracious, ungrateful, unthankful.

thaw *vb* dissolve, liquefy, melt, soften, unbend.

theatre *n* opera house, playhouse; arena, scene, seat, stage.

theatrical *adj* dramatic, dramaturgic, dramaturgical, histrionic, scenic, spectacular; affected, ceremonious, meretricious, ostentatious, pompous, showy, stagy, stilted, unnatural.

theft *n* depredation, embezzlement, fraud, larceny, peculation, pilfering, purloining, robbery, spoliation, stealing, swindling, thieving.

theme *n* composition, essay, motif, subject, text, thesis, topic, treatise.

theoretical *adj* abstract, conjectural, doctrinaire, ideal, hypothetical, pure, speculative, unapplied.

theory *n* assumption, conjecture, hypothesis, idea, plan, postulation, principle, scheme, speculation, surmise, system; doctrine, philosophy, science; explanation, exposition, philosophy, rationale.

therefore *adv* accordingly, afterward, consequently, hence, so, subsequently, then, thence, whence.

thesaurus *n* dictionary, encyclopedia, repository, storehouse, treasure.

thick *adj* bulky, chunky, dumpy, plump, solid, squab, squat, stubby, thickset; clotted, coagulated, crass, dense, dull, gross, heavy, viscous; blurred, cloudy, dirty, foggy, hazy, indistinguishable, misty, obscure, vaporous; muddy, roiled, turbid; abundant, frequent, multitudinous, numerous; close, compact, crowded, set, thickset; confused, guttural, hoarse, inarticulate, indistinct; dim, dull, weak; familiar, friendly, intimate, neighbourly, well-acquainted. * *adv* fast, frequently, quick; closely, densely, thickly. * *n* centre, middle, midst.

thicket *n* clump, coppice, copse, covert, forest, grove, jungle, shrubbery, underbrush, undergrowth, wood, woodland.

thief *n* depredator, filcher, pilferer, lifter, marauder, purloiner, robber, shark, stealer; burglar, corsair, defaulter, defrauder, embezzler, footpad, highwayman, housebreaker, kidnapper, pickpocket, pirate, poacher, privateer, sharper, swindler, peculator.

thieve *vb* cheat, embezzle, peculate, pilfer, plunder, purloin, rob, steal, swindle.

thin *vb* attenuate, dilute, diminish, prune, reduce, refine, weaken. * *adj* attenuated, bony, emaciated, fine, fleshless, flimsy, gaunt, haggard, lank, lanky, lean, meagre, peaked, pinched, poor, scanty, scraggy, scrawny, slender, slight, slim, small, sparse, spindly.

thing *n* being, body, contrivance, creature, entity, object, something, substance; act, action, affair, arrangement, circumstance, concern, deed, event, matter, occurrence, transaction.

think *vb* cogitate, contemplate, dream, meditate, muse, ponder, reflect, ruminate, speculate; consider, deliberate, reason, undertake; apprehend, believe, conceive, conclude, deem, determine, fancy, hold, imagine, judge, opine, presume, reckon, suppose, surmise; design, intend, mean, purpose; account, count, deem, esteem, hold, regard; compass, design, plan, plot. * *n* assessment, contemplation, deliberation, meditation, opinion, reasoning, reflection.

thirst *n* appetite, craving, desire, hunger, longing, yearning; aridity, drought, dryness.

thirsty *adj* arid, dry, parched; eager, greedy, hungry, longing, yearning.

thorn *n* prickle, spine; annoyance, bane, care, evil, infliction, nettle, nuisance, plague, torment, trouble, scourge.

thorny *adj* briary, briery, prickly, spinose, spinous, spiny; acuminate, barbed, pointed, prickling, sharp, spiky; annoying, difficult, harassing, perplexing, rugged, troublesome, trying, vexatious.

thorough, thoroughgoing *adj* absolute, arrant, complete, downright, entire, exhaustive, finished, perfect, radical, sweeping, total unmitigated, utter; accurate, correct, reliable, trustworthy.

though *conj* admitting, allowing, although, granted, granting, if, notwithstanding, still. * *adv* however, nevertheless, still, yet.

thought *n* absorption, cogitation, engrossment, meditation, musing, reflection, reverie, rumination; contemplation, intellect, ratiocination, thinking, thoughtfulness; application, conception, consideration, deliberation, idea, pondering, speculation, study; consciousness, imagination, intellect, perception, understanding; conceit, fancy, notion; conclusion, judgment, motion, opinion, sentiment, supposition, view; anxiety, attention, care, concern, provision, regard, solicitude, thoughtfulness; design, expectation, intention, purpose.

thoughtful *adj* absorbed, contemplative, deliberative, dreamy, engrossed, introspective, pensive, philosophic, reflecting, reflective, sedate, speculative; attentive, careful, cautious, circumspect, considerate, discreet, heedful, friendly, kind-hearted, kindly, mindful, neighbourly, provident, prudent, regardful, watchful, wary; quiet, serious, sober, studious.

thoughtless *adj* careless, casual, flighty, heedless, improvident, inattentive, inconsiderate, neglectful, negligent, precipitate, rash, reckless, regardless, remiss, trifling, unmindful, unthinking; blank, blockish, dull, insensate, stupid, vacant, vacuous.

thraldom *n* bondage, enslavement, enthralment, serfdom, servitude, slavery, subjection, thrall, vassalage.

thrash *vb* beat, bruise, conquer, defeat, drub, flog, lash, maul, pommel, punish, thwack, trounce, wallop, whip.

thread *vb* course, direction, drift, tenor; reeve, trace. * *n* cord, fibre, filament, hair, line, twist; pile, staple.

threadbare *adj* napless, old, seedy, worn; common, commonplace, hackneyed, stale, trite, worn-out.

threat *n* commination, defiance, denunciation, fulmination, intimidation, menace, thunder, thunderbolt.

threaten *vb* denounce, endanger, fulminate, intimidate, menace, thunder; augur, forebode, foreshadow, indicate, portend, presage, prognosticate, warn.

threshold *n* doorsill, sill; door, entrance, gate; beginning, commencement, opening, outset, start.

thrift *n* economy, frugality, parsimony, saving, thriftiness; gain, luck, profit, prosperity, success.

thriftless *adj* extravagant, improvident, lavish, profuse, prodigal, shiftless, unthrifty, wasteful.

thrifty *adj* careful, economical, frugal, provident, saving, sparing; flourishing, prosperous, thriving, vigorous.

thrill *vb* affect, agitate, electrify, inspire, move, penetrate, pierce, rouse, stir, touch. * *n* excitement, sensation, shock, tingling, tremor.

thrilling *adj* affecting, exciting, gripping, moving, sensational, touching.

thrive *vb* advance, batten, bloom, boom, flourish, prosper, succeed.

throng *vb* congregate, crowd, fill, flock, pack, press, swarm. * *n* assemblage, concourse, congregation, crowd, horde, host, mob, multitude, swarm.

throttle *vb* choke, silence, strangle, suffocate.

throw *vb* cast, chuck, dart, fling, hurl, lance, launch, overturn, pitch, pitchfork, send, sling, toss, whirl. * *n* cast, fling, hurl, launch, pitch, sling, toss, whirl; chance, gamble, try, venture.

thrust *vb* clap, dig, drive, force, impel, jam, plunge, poke, propel, push, ram, run, shove, stick. * *n* dig, jab, lunge, pass, plunge, poke, propulsion, push, shove, stab, tilt.

thump *vb* bang, batter, beat, belabour, knock, punch, strike, thrash, thwack, whack. * *n* blow, knock, punch, strike, stroke.

thwart *vb* baffle, balk, contravene, counteract, cross, defeat, disconcert, frustrate, hinder, impede, oppose, obstruct, oppugn; cross, intersect, traverse.

tickle *vb* amuse, delight, divert, enliven, gladden, gratify, please, rejoice, titillate.

ticklish *adj* dangerous, precarious, risky, tottering, uncertain, unstable, unsteady; critical, delicate, difficult, nice.

tide *n* course, current, ebb, flow, stream.

tidings *npl* advice, greetings, information, intelligence, news, report, word.

tidy *vb* clean, neaten, order, straighten. * *adj* clean, neat, orderly, shipshape, spruce, trig, trim.

tie *vb* bind, confine, fasten, knot, lock, manacle, secure, shackle, fetter, yoke; complicate, entangle, interlace, knit; connect, hold, join, link, unite; constrain, oblige, restrain, restrict. * *n* band, fastening, knot, ligament, ligature; allegiance, bond, obligation; bow, cravat, necktie.

tier *n* line, rank, row, series.

tiff *n* fit, fume, passion, pet, miff, rage.

tight *adj* close, compact, fast, firm; taut, tense, stretched; impassable, narrow, strait.

till *vb* cultivate, plough, harrow.

tillage *n* agriculture, cultivation, culture, farming, geoponics, husbandry.

tilt *vb* cant, incline, slant, slope, tip; forge, hammer; point, thrust; joust, rush. * *n* awning, canopy, tent; lunge, pass, thrust; cant, inclination, slant, slope, tip.

time *vb* clock, control, count, measure, regulate, schedule. * *n* duration, interim, interval, season, span, spell, tenure, term, while; aeon, age, date, epoch, eon, era; term; cycle, dynasty, reign; confinement, delivery, parturition; measure, rhythm.

timely *adj* acceptable, appropriate, apropos, early, opportune, prompt, punctual, seasonable, well-timed.

timid *adj* afraid, cowardly, faint-hearted, fearful, irresolute, meticulous, nervous, pusillanimous, skittish, timorous, unadventurous; bashful, coy, diffident, modest, shame-faced, shrinking.

tincture *vb* colour, dye, shade, stain, tinge, tint; flavour, season; imbue, impregnate, impress, infuse. * *n* grain, hue, shade, stain, tinge, tint, tone; flavour, smack, spice, taste; admixture, dash, infusion, seasoning, sprinkling, touch.

tinge *vb* colour, dye, stain, tincture, tint; imbue, impregnate, impress, infuse. * *n* cast, colour, dye, hue, shade, stain, tincture, tint; flavour, smack, spice, quality, taste.

tint *n* cast, colour, complexion, dye, hue, shade, tinge, tone.

tiny *adj* diminutive, dwarfish, Lilliputian, little, microscopic, miniature, minute, puny, pygmy, small, wee.

tip[1] *n* apex, cap, end, extremity, peak, pinnacle, point, top, vertex.

tip[2] *vb* incline, overturn, tilt; dispose of, dump. * *n* donation, fee, gift, gratuity, perquisite, reward; inclination, slant; hint, pointer, suggestion; strike, tap.

tirade *n* abuse, denunciation, diatribe, harangue, outburst.

tire *vb* exhaust, fag, fatigue, harass, jade, weary; bore, bother, irk.

tiresome *adj* annoying, arduous, boring, dull, exhausting, fatiguing, fagging, humdrum, irksome, laborious, monotonous, tedious, wearisome, vexatious.

tissue *n* cloth, fabric; membrane, network, structure, texture, web; accumulation, chain, collection, combination, conglomeration, mass, series, set.

titanic *adj* colossal, Cyclopean, enormous, gigantic, herculean, huge, immense, mighty, monstrous, prodigious, stupendous, vast.

title *vb* call, designate, name, style, term. * *n* caption, legend, head, heading; appellation, application, cognomen, completion, denomination, designation, epithet, name; claim, due, ownership, part, possession, prerogative, privilege, right.

tittle *n* atom, bit, grain, iota, jot, mite, particle, scrap, speck, whit.

tittle-tattle *vb, n* babble, cackle, chatter, discourse, gabble, gossip, prattle.

toast *vb* brown, dry, heat; honour, pledge, propose, salute. * *n* compliment, drink, pledge, salutation, salute; favourite, pet.

toil *vb* drudge, labour, strive, work. * *n* drudgery, effort, exertion, exhaustion, grinding, labour, pains, travail, work; gin, net, noose, snare, spring, trap.

toilsome *adj* arduous, difficult, fatiguing, hard, laborious, onerous, painful, severe, tedious, wearisome.

token *adj* nominal, superficial, symbolic. * *n* badge, evidence, index, indication, manifestation, mark, note, sign, symbol, trace, trait; keepsake, memento, memorial, reminder, souvenir.

tolerable *adj* bearable, endurable, sufferable, supportable; fair, indifferent, middling, ordinary, passable, so-so.

tolerance *n* endurance, receptivity, sufferance, toleration.

tolerate *vb* admit, allow, indulge, let, permit, receive; abide, brook, endure, suffer.

toll[1] *n* assessment, charge, customs, demand, dues, duty, fee, impost, levy, rate, tax, tribute; cost, damage, loss.

toll[2] *vb* chime, knell, peal, ring, sound. * *n* chime, knell, peal, ring, ringing, tolling.

tomb *n* catacomb, charnel house, crypt, grave, mausoleum, sepulchre, vault.

tone *vb* blend, harmonize, match, suit. * *n* note, sound; accent, cadence, emphasis, inflection, intonation, modulation; key, mood, strain, temper; elasticity, energy, force, health, strength, tension, vigour; cast, colour, manner, hue, shade, style, tint; drift, tenor.

tongue *n* accent, dialect, language, utterance, vernacular; discourse, parlance, speech, talk; nation, race.

too *adv* additionally, also, further, likewise, moreover, overmuch.

toothsome *adj* agreeable, dainty, delicious, luscious, nice, palatable, savoury.

top *vb* cap, head, tip; ride, surmount; outgo, surpass. * *adj* apical, best, chief, culminating, finest, first, foremost, highest, leading, prime, principal, topmost, uppermost. * *n* acme, apex, crest, crown, head, meridian, pinnacle, summit, surface, vertex, zenith.

topic *n* business, question, subject, text, theme, thesis; division, head, subdivision; commonplace, dictum, maxim, precept, proposition, principle, rule; arrangement, scheme.

topple *vb* fall, overturn, tumble, upset.

torment *vb* annoy, agonize, distress, excruciate, pain, rack, torture; badger, fret, harass, harry, irritate, nettle, plague, provoke, tantalize, tease, trouble, vex, worry. * *n* agony, anguish, pang, rack, torture.

tornado *n* blizzard, cyclone, gale, hurricane, storm, tempest, typhoon, whirlwind.

torpid *adj* benumbed, lethargic, motionless, numb; apathetic, dormant, dull, inactive, indolent, inert, listless, sleepy, slothful, sluggish, stupid.

torpor *n* coma, insensibility, lethargy, numbness, torpidity; inaction, inactivity, inertness, sluggishness, stupidity.

torrid *adj* arid, burnt, dried, parched; burning, fiery, hot, parching, scorching, sultry, tropical, violent.

tortuous *adj* crooked, curved, curvilineal, curvilinear, serpentine, sinuate, sinuated, sinuous, twisted, winding; ambiguous, circuitous, crooked, deceitful, indirect, perverse, roundabout.

torture *vb* agonize, distress, excruciate, pain, rack, torment.* *n* agony, anguish, distress, pain, pang, rack, torment.

toss *vb* cast, fling, hurl, pitch, throw; agitate, rock, shake; disquiet, harass, try; roll, writhe. * *n* cast, fling, pitch, throw.

total *vb* add, amount to, reach, reckon. * *adj* complete, entire, full, whole; integral, undivided. * *n* aggregate, all, gross, lump, mass, sum, totality, whole.

totter *vb* falter, reel, stagger, vacillate; lean, oscillate, reel, rock, shake, sway, tremble, waver; fail, fall, flag.

touch *vb* feel, graze, handle, hit, pat, strike, tap; concern, interest, regard; affect, impress, move, stir; grasp, reach, stretch; melt, mollify, soften; afflict, distress, hurt, injure, molest, sting, wound. * *n* hint, smack, suggestion, suspicion, taste, trace; blow, contract, hit, pat, tap.

touchiness *n* fretfulness, irritability, irascibility, peevishness, pettishness, petulance, snappishness, spleen, testiness.

touching *adj* affecting, heart-rending, impressive, melting, moving, pathetic, pitiable, tender; abutting, adjacent, bordering, tangent.

touchy *adj* choleric, cross, fretful, hot-tempered, irascible, irritable, peevish, petulant, quick-tempered, snappish, splenetic, tetchy, testy, waspish.

tough *adj* adhesive, cohesive, flexible, tenacious; coriaceous, leathery; clammy, ropy, sticky, viscous; inflexible, intractable, rigid, stiff; callous, hard, obdurate, stubborn; difficult, formidable, hard, troublesome. * *n* brute, bully, hooligan, ruffian, thug.

tour *vb* journey, perambulate, travel, visit. * *n* circuit, course, excursion, expedition, journey, perambulation, pilgrimage, round.

tow *vb* drag, draw, haul, pull, tug. * *n* drag, lift, pull.

tower *vb* mount, rise, soar, transcend. * *n* belfry, bell tower, column, minaret, spire, steeple, turret; castle, citadel, fortress, stronghold; pillar, refuge, rock, support.

towering *adj* elevated, lofty; excessive, extreme, prodigious, violent.

toy *vb* dally, play, sport, trifle, wanton. * *n* bauble, doll, gewgaw, gimmick, knick-knack, plaything, puppet, trinket; bagatelle, bubble, trifle; play, sport.

trace *vb* follow, track, train; copy, deduce, delineate, derive, describe, draw, sketch. * *n* evidence, footmark, footprint, footstep, impression, mark, remains, sign, token, track, trail, vestige, wake; memorial, record; bit, dash, flavour, hint, suspicion, streak, tinge.

track *vb* chase, draw, follow, pursue, scent, track, trail. * *n* footmark, footprint, footstep, spoor, trace, vestige; course, pathway, rails, road, runway, trace, trail, wake, way.

trackless *adj* pathless, solitary, unfrequented, unused.

tract[1] *n* area, district, quarter, region, territory; parcel, patch, part, piece, plot, portion.

tract[2] *n* disquisition, dissertation, essay, homily, pamphlet, sermon, thesis, tractate, treatise.

tractable *adj* amenable, docile, governable, manageable, submissive, willing, yielding; adaptable, ductile, malleable, plastic, tractile.

trade *vb* bargain, barter, chaffer, deal, exchange, interchange, sell, traffic. * *n* bargaining, barter, business, commerce, dealing, traffic; avocation, calling, craft, employment, occupation, office, profession, pursuit, vocation.

traditional *adj* accustomed, apocryphal, customary, established, historic, legendary, old, oral, transmitted, uncertain, unverified, unwritten.

traduce *vb* abuse, asperse, blemish, brand, calumniate, decry, defame, depreciate, disparage, revile, malign, slander, vilify.

traducer *n* calumniator, defamer, detractor, slanderer, vilifier.

traffic *vb* bargain, barter, chaffer, deal, exchange, trade. * *n* barter, business, chaffer, commerce, exchange, intercourse, trade, transportation, truck.

tragedy *n* drama, play; adversity, calamity, catastrophe, disaster, misfortune.

tragic *adj* dramatic; calamitous, catastrophic, disastrous, dreadful, fatal, grievous, heart-breaking, mournful, sad, shocking, sorrowful.

trail *vb* follow, hunt, trace, track; drag, draw, float, flow, haul, pull. * *n* footmark, footprint, footstep, mark, trace, track.

train *vb* drag, draw, haul, trail, tug; allure, entice; discipline, drill, educate, exercise, instruct, school, teach; accustom, break in, familiarize, habituate, inure, prepare, rehearse, use. * *n* trail, wake; entourage, cortege, followers, retinue, staff, suite; chain, consecution, sequel, series, set, succession; course, method, order, process; allure, artifice, device, enticement, lure, persuasion, stratagem, trap.

trait *n* line, mark, stroke, touch; characteristic, feature, lineage,particularity, peculiarity, quality.

traitor *n* apostate, betrayer, deceiver, Judas, miscreant, quisling, renegade, turncoat; conspirator, deserter, insurgent, mutineer, rebel, revolutionary.

traitorous *adj* faithless, false, perfidious, recreant, treacherous; insidious, treasonable.

trammel *vb* clog, confine, cramp, cumber, hamper, hinder, fetter, restrain, restrict, shackle, tie. * *n* bond, chain, fetter, hindrance, impediment, net, restraint, shackle.

tramp *vb* hike, march, plod, trudge, walk. * *n* excursion, journey, march, walk; landloper, loafer, stroller, tramper, vagabond, vagrant.

trample *vb* crush, tread; scorn, spurn.

trance *n* dream, ecstasy, hypnosis, rapture; catalepsy, coma.

tranquil *adj* calm, hushed, peaceful, placid, quiet, serene, still, undisturbed, unmoved, unperturbed, unruffled, untroubled.

tranquillity *n* calmness, peace, peacefulness, placidity, placidness, quiet, quietness, serenity, stillness, tranquilness.

tranquillize *vb* allay, appease, assuage, calm, compose, hush, lay, lull, moderate, pacify, quell, quiet, silence, soothe, still.

transact *vb* conduct, dispatch, enact, execute, do, manage, negotiate, perform, treat.

transaction *n* act, action, conduct, doing, management, negotiation, performance; affair, business, deal, dealing, incident, event, job, matter, occurrence, procedure, proceeding.

transcend *vb* exceed, overlap, overstep, pass, transgress; excel, outstrip, outrival, outvie, overtop, surmount, surpass.

transcendent *adj* consummate, inimitable, peerless, pre-eminent, supereminent, surpassing, unequalled, unparalleled, unrivalled, unsurpassed; metempiric, metempirical, noumenal, super-sensible.

transcript *n* duplicate, engrossment, rescript.

transfer *vb* convey, dispatch, move, remove, send, translate, transmit, transplant, transport; abalienate, alienate, assign, cede, confer, convey, consign, deed, devise, displace, forward, grant, pass, relegate. * *n* abalienation, alienation, assignment, bequest, carriage, cession, change, conveyance, copy, demise, devisal, gift, grant, move, relegation, removal, shift, shipment, transference, transferring, transit, transmission, transportation.

transfigure *vb* change, convert, dignify, idealize, metamorphose, transform.

transform *vb* alter, change, metamorphose, transfigure; convert, resolve, translate, transmogrify, transmute.

transgress *vb* exceed, transcend, overpass, overstep; break, contravene, disobey, infringe, violate; err, intrude, offend, sin, slip, trespass.

transgression *n* breach, disobedience, encroachment, infraction, infringement, transgression, violation; crime, delinquency, error, fault, iniquity, misdeed, misdemeanour, misdoing,

offence, sin, slip, trespass, wrongdoing.

transient *adj* diurnal, ephemeral, evanescent, fleeting, fugitive, impertinent, meteoric, mortal, passing, perishable, short-lived, temporary, transitory, volatile; hasty, imperfect, momentary, short.

transitory *adj* brief, ephemeral, evanescent, fleeting, flitting, fugacious, momentary, passing, short, temporary, transient.

translate *vb* remove, transfer, transport; construe, decipher, decode, interpret, render, turn.

translucent *adj* diaphanous, hyaline, pellucid, semi-opaque, semi-transparent.

transmit *vb* forward, remit, send; communicate, conduct, radiate; bear, carry, convey.

transparent *adj* bright, clear, diaphanous, limpid, lucid; crystalline, hyaline, pellucid, serene, translucent, transpicuous, unclouded; open, porous, transpicuous; evident, obvious, manifest, patent.

transpire *vb* befall, chance, happen, occur; evaporate, exhale.

transport *vb* bear, carry, cart, conduct, convey, fetch, remove, ship, take, transfer, truck; banish, expel; beatify, delight, enrapture, enravish, entrance, ravish. * *n* carriage, conveyance, movement, transportation, transporting; beatification, beatitude, bliss, ecstasy, felicity, happiness, rapture, ravishment; frenzy, passion, vehemence, warmth.

transude *vb* exude, filter, ooze, percolate, strain.

trap *vb* catch, ensnare, entrap, noose, snare, springe; ambush, deceive, dupe, trick; enmesh, tangle, trepan. * *n* gin, snare, springe, toil; ambush, artifice, pitfall, stratagem, trepan.

trappings *npl* adornments, decorations, dress, embellishments, frippery, gear, livery, ornaments, paraphernalia, rigging; accoutrements, caparisons, equipment, gear.

trash *n* dregs, dross, garbage, refuse, rubbish, trumpery, waste; balderdash, nonsense, twaddle.

travel *vb* journey, peregrinate, ramble, roam, rove, tour, voyage, walk, wander; go, move, pass. * *n* excursion, expedition, journey, peregrination, ramble, tour, trip, voyage, walk.

traveller *n* excursionist, explorer, globe-trotter, itinerant, passenger, pilgrim, rover, sightseer, tourist, trekker, tripper, voyager, wanderer, wayfarer.

traverse *vb* contravene, counteract, defeat, frustrate, obstruct, oppose, thwart; ford, pass, play, range.

travesty *vb* imitate, parody, take off. * *n* burlesque, caricature, imitation, parody, take-off.

treacherous *adj* deceitful, disloyal, faithless, false, false-hearted, insidious, perfidious, recreant, sly, traitorous, treasonable, unfaithful, unreliable, unsafe, untrustworthy.

treachery *n* betrayal, deceitfulness, disloyalty, double-dealing, faithlessness, foul play, infidelity, insidiousness, perfidiousness, treason, perfidy.

treason *n* betrayal, disloyalty, lèse-majesté, lese-majesty, perfidy, sedition, traitorousness, treachery.

treasonable *adj* disloyal, traitorous, treacherous.

treasure *vb* accumulate, collect, garner, hoard, husband, save, store; cherish, idolize, prize, value, worship. * *n* cash, funds, jewels, money, riches, savings, valuables, wealth; abundance, reserve, stock, store.

treasurer *n* banker, bursar, purser, receiver, trustee.

treat *vb* entertain, feast, gratify, refresh; attend, doctor, dose, handle, manage, serve; bargain, covenant, negotiate, parley. * *n* banquet, entertainment, feast; delight, enjoyment, entertainment, gratification, luxury, pleasure, refreshment.

treatise *n* commentary, discourse, dissertation, disquisition, monograph, tractate.

treatment *n* usage, use; dealing, handling, management, manipulation; doctoring, therapy.

treaty *n* agreement, alliance, bargain, compact, concordat, convention, covenant, entente, league, pact.

tremble *vb* quake, quaver, quiver, shake, shiver, shudder, vibrate, wobble. * *n* quake, quiver, shake, shiver, shudder, tremor, vibration, wobble.

tremendous *adj* colossal, enormous, huge, immense; excellent, marvellous, wonderful; alarming, appalling, awful, dreadful, fearful, frightful, horrid, horrible, terrible.

tremor *n* agitation, quaking, quivering, shaking, trembling, trepidation, tremulousness, vibration.

tremulous *adj* afraid, fearful, quavering, quivering, shaking, shaky, shivering, timid, trembling, vibrating.

trench *vb* carve, cut; ditch, channel, entrench, furrow. * *n* channel, ditch, drain, furrow, gutter, moat, pit, sewer, trough; dugout, entrenchment, fortification.

trenchant *adj* cutting, keen, sharp; acute, biting, caustic, crisp, incisive, pointed, piquant, pungent, sarcastic, sententious, severe, unsparing, vigorous.

trend *vb* drift, gravitate, incline, lean, run, stretch, sweep, tend, turn. * *n* bent, course, direction, drift, inclination, set, leaning, tendency, trending.

trepidation *n* agitation, quaking, quivering, shaking, trembling, tremor; dismay, excitement, fear, perturbation, tremulousness.

trespass *vb* encroach, infringe, intrude, trench; offend, sin, transgress. * *n* encroachment, infringement, injury, intrusion, invasion; crime, delinquency, error, fault, sin, misdeed, misdemeanour, offence, transgression; trespasser.

trial *adj* experimental, exploratory, testing. * *n* examination, experiment, test; experience, knowledge; aim, attempt, effort, endeavour, essay, exertion, struggle; assay, criterion, ordeal, prohibition, proof, test, touchstone; affliction, burden, chagrin, dolour, distress, grief, hardship, heartache, inclination, misery, mortification, pain, sorrow, suffering, tribulation, trouble, unhappiness, vexation, woe, wretchedness; action, case, cause, hearing, suit.

tribe *n* clan, family, lineage, race, sept, stock; class, distinction, division, order.

tribulation *n* adversity, affliction, distress, grief, misery, pain, sorrow, suffering, trial, trouble, unhappiness, woe, wretchedness.

tribunal *n* bench, judgement seat; assizes, bar, court, judicature, session.

tribute *n* subsidy, tax; custom, duty, excise, impost, tax, toll; contribution, grant, offering.

trice *n* flash, instant, jiffy, moment, second, twinkling.

trick *vb* cheat, circumvent, cozen, deceive, defraud, delude, diddle, dupe, fob, gull, hoax, overreach. * *n* artifice, blind, deceit, deception, dodge, fake, feint, fraud, game, hoax, imposture, manoeuvre, shift, ruse, swindle, stratagem, wile; antic, caper, craft, deftness, gambol, sleight; habit, mannerism, peculiarity, practice.

trickle *vb* distil, dribble, drip, drop, ooze, percolate, seep. * *n* dribble, drip, percolation, seepage.

tricky *adj* artful, cunning, deceitful, deceptive, subtle, trickish.

trifle *vb* dally, dawdle, fool, fribble, palter, play, potter, toy. * *n* bagatelle, bauble, bean, fig, nothing, triviality; iota, jot, modicum, particle, trace.

trifling *adj* empty, frippery, frivolous, inconsiderable, insignificant, nugatory, petty, piddling, shallow, slight, small, trivial, unimportant, worthless.

trill *vb* shake, quaver, warble. * *n* quaver, shake, tremolo, warbling.

trim *vb* adjust, arrange, prepare; balance, equalize, fill; adorn, array, bedeck, decorate, dress, embellish, garnish, ornament; clip, curtail, cut, lop, mow, poll, prune, shave, shear; berate, chastise, chide, rebuke, reprimand, reprove, trounce; fluctuate, hedge, shift, shuffle, vacillate. * *adj* compact, neat, nice, shapely, snug, tidy, well-adjusted, well-ordered; chic, elegant, finical, smart, spruce. * *n* dress, embellishment, gear, ornaments, trappings, trimmings; case, condition, order, plight, state.

trinket *n* bagatelle, bauble, bijoux, gewgaw, gimcrack, knick-knack, toy, trifle.

trinkets *npl* bijouterie, jewellery, jewels, ornaments.

trip *vb* caper, dance, frisk, hop, skip; misstep, stumble; bungle, blunder, err, fail, mistake; overthrow, supplant, upset; catch, convict, detect. * *n* hop, skip; lurch, misstep, stumble; blunder, bungle, error, failure, fault, lapse, miss, mistake, oversight, slip; circuit, excursion, expedition, jaunt, journey, ramble, route, stroll, tour.

trite *adj* banal, beaten, common, commonplace, hackneyed, old, ordinary, stale, stereotyped, threadbare, usual, worn.

triturate *vb* beat, bray, bruise, grind, pound, rub, thrash; comminute, levigate, pulverize.

triumph *vb* exult, rejoice; prevail, succeed, win; flourish, prosper, thrive; boast, brag, crow, gloat, swagger, vaunt. * *n* celebration, exultation, joy, jubilation, jubilee, ovation; accomplishment, achievement, conquest, success, victory.

triumphant *adj* boastful, conquering, elated, exultant, exulting, jubilant, rejoicing, successful, victorious.

trivial *adj* frivolous, gimcrack, immaterial, inconsiderable, insignificant, light, little, nugatory, paltry, petty, small, slight, slim, trifling, trumpery, unimportant.

trollop *n* prostitute, slattern, slut, whore.

troop *vb* crowd, flock, muster, throng. * *n* company, crowd, flock, herd, multitude, number, throng; band, body, party, squad, troupe.

trophy *n* laurels, medal, palm, prize.

troth *n* candour, sincerity, truth, veracity, verity; allegiance, belief, faith, fidelity, word; betrothal.

trouble *vb* agitate, confuse, derange, disarrange, disorder, disturb; afflict, ail, annoy, badger, concern, disquiet, distress, fret, grieve, harass, molest, perplex, perturb, pester, plague, torment, vex, worry. * *n* adversity, affliction, calamity, distress, dolour, grief, hardship, misfortune, misery, pain, sorrow, suffering, tribulation, woe; ado, annoyance, anxiety, bother, care, discomfort, embarrassment, fuss, inconvenience, irritation, pains, perplexity, plague, torment, vexation, worry; commotion, disturbance, row; bewilderment, disquietude, embarrassment, perplexity, uneasiness.

troublesome *adj* annoying, distressing, disturbing, galling, grievous, harassing, painful, perplexing, vexatious, worrisome; burdensome, irksome, tiresome, wearisome; importunate, intrusive, teasing; arduous, difficult, hard, inconvenient, trying, unwieldy.

troublous *adj* agitated, disquieted, disturbed, perturbed, tumultuous, turbulent.

trough *n* hutch, manger; channel, depression, hollow, furrow.

truant *vb* be absent, desert, dodge, malinger, shirk, skive. * *n* absentee, deserter, idler, laggard, loiterer, lounger, malingerer, quitter, runaway, shirker, vagabond.

truce *n* armistice, breathing space, cessation, delay, intermission, lull, pause, recess, reprieve, respite, rest.

truck *vb* barter, deal, exchange, trade, traffic. * *n* lorry, van, wagon.

truckle *vb* roll, trundle; cringe, crouch, fawn, knuckle, stoop, submit, yield.

truculent *adj* barbarous, bloodthirsty, ferocious, fierce, savage; cruel, malevolent, relentless; destructive, deadly, fatal, ruthless.

true *adj* actual, unaffected, authentic, genuine, legitimate, pure, real, rightful, sincere, sound, truthful, veritable; substantial, veracious; constant, faithful, loyal, staunch, steady; equitable, honest, honourable, just, upright, trusty, trustworthy, virtuous; accurate, correct, even, exact, right, straight, undeviating. * *adv* good, well.

truism *n* axiom, commonplace, platitude.

trumpery *adj* pinchbeck, rubbishy, trashy, trifling, worthless. * *n* deceit, deception, falsehood, humbug, imposture; frippery, rubbish, stuff, trash, trifles.

truncheon *n* club, cudgel, nightstick, partisan, staff; baton, wand.

trunk *n* body, bole, butt, shaft, stalk, stem, stock, torso; box, chest, coffer.

trundle *vb* bowl, revolve, roll, spin, truckle, wheel.

truss *vb* bind, bundle, close, cram, hang, pack. * *n* bundle, package, packet; apparatus, bandage, support.

trust *vb* confide, depend, expect, hope, rely; believe, credit; commit, entrust. * *n* belief, confidence, credence, faith; credit, tick; charge, deposit; commission, duty, errand; assurance, conviction, expectation, hope, reliance, secutrity.

trustful *adj* confiding, trusting, unquestioning, unsuspecting; faithful, trustworthy, trusty.

trustworthy *adj* confidential, constant, credible, dependable, faithful, firm, honest, incorrupt, upright, reliable, responsible, straightforward, staunch, true, trusty, uncorrupt, upright.

truth *n* fact, reality, veracity; actuality, authenticity, realism; canon, law, oracle, principle; right, truthfulness, veracity; candour, fidelity, frankness, honesty, honour, ingenuousness, integrity, probity, sincerity, virtue; constancy, devotion, faith, fealty, loyalty, steadfastness; accuracy, correctness, exactitude, exactness, nicety, precision, regularity, trueness.

truthful *adj* correct, reliable, true, trustworthy, veracious; artless, candid, frank, guileless, honest, ingenuous, open, sincere, straightforward, trusty.

truthless *adj* canting, disingenuous, dishonest, false, faithless, hollow, hypocritical, insincere, pharisaical, treacherous, unfair, untrustworthy.

try *vb* examine, prove, test; attempt, essay; adjudicate, adjudge, examine, hear; purify, refine; sample, sift, smell, taste; aim, attempt, endeavour, seek, strain, strive. * *n* attempt, effort, endeavour, experiment, trial.

trying *adj* difficult, fatiguing, hard, irksome, tiresome, wearisome; afflicting, afflictive, calamitous, deplorable, dire, distressing, grievous, hard, painful, sad, severe.

tryst *n* appointment, assignation, rendezvous.

tube *n* bore, bronchus, cylinder, duct, hollow, hose, pipe, pipette, worm.

tuft *n* brush, bunch, crest, feather, knot, plume, topknot, tussock; clump, cluster, group.

tug *vb* drag, draw, haul, pull, tow, wrench; labour, strive, struggle. * *n* drag, haul, pull, tow, wrench.

tuition *n* education, instruction, schooling, teaching, training.

tumble *vb* heave, pitch, roll, toss, wallow; fall, sprawl, stumble, topple, trip; derange, disarrange, dishevel, disorder, disturb, rumple, tousle. * *n* collapse, drop, fall, plunge, spill, stumble, trip.

tumbler *n* acrobat, juggler; glass.

tumid *adj* bloated, distended, enlarged, puffed-up, swelled, swollen, turgid; bombastic, declamatory, fustian, grandiloquent, grandiose, high-flown, inflated, pompous, puffy, rhetorical, stilted, swelling.

tumour *n* boil, carbuncle, swelling, tumefaction.

tumult *n* ado, affray, agitation, altercation, bluster, brawl, disturbance, ferment, flurry, feud, fracas, fray, fuss, hubbub, huddle, hurly-burly, melee, noise, perturbation, pother, quarrel, racket, riot, row, squabble, stir, turbulence, turmoil, uproar.

tumultuous *adj* blustery, breezy, bustling, confused, disorderly, disturbed, riotous, turbulent, unruly.

tune *vb* accord, attune, harmonize, modulate; adapt, adjust, attune. * *n* air, aria, melody, strain, tone; agreement, concord, harmony; accord, order.

tuneful *adj* dulcet, harmonious, melodious, musical.

turbid *adj* foul, impure, muddy, thick, unsettled.

turbulence *n* agitation, commotion, confusion, disorder, disturbance, excitement, tumult, tumultuousness, turmoil, unruliness, uproar; insubordination, insurrection, mutiny, rebellion, riot, sedition.

turbulent *adj* agitated, disturbed, restless, tumultuous, wild; blatant, blustering, boisterous, brawling, disorderly, obstreperous, tumultuous, uproarious, vociferous; factious, insubordinate, insurgent, mutinous, raging, rebellious, refractory, revolutionary, riotous, seditious, stormy, violent.

turf *n* grass, greensward, sod, sward; horse racing, racecourse, raceground.

turgid *adj* bloated, distended, protuberant, puffed-up, swelled, swollen, tumid; bombastic, declamatory, diffuse, digressive, fustian, high-flown, inflated, grandiloquent, grandiose, ostentatious, pompous, puffy, rhetorical, stilted.

turmoil *n* activity, agitation, bustle, commotion, confusion, disorder, disturbance, ferment, flurry, huddle, hubbub, hurly-burly, noise, trouble, tumult, turbulence, uproar.

turn *vb* revolve, rotate; bend, cast, defect, inflict, round, spin, sway, swivel, twirl, twist, wheel; crank, grind, wind; deflect, divert, transfer, warp; form, mould, shape; adapt, fit, manoeuvre, suit; alter, change, conform, metamorphose, transform, transmute, vary; convert, persuade, prejudice; construe, render, translate; depend, hang, hinge, pivot; eventuate, issue, result,

terminate; acidify, curdle, ferment. * *n* cycle, gyration, revolution, rotation, round; bending, deflection, deviation, diversion, doubling, flection, flexion, flexure, reel, retroversion, slew, spin, sweep, swing, swirl, swivel, turning, twist, twirl, whirl, winding; alteration, change, variation, vicissitude; bend, circuit, drive, ramble, run, round, stroll; bout, hand, innings, opportunity, shift, spell; act, action, deed, office; convenience, occasion, purpose; cast, fashion, form, guise, manner, mould, phase, shape; aptitude, bent, bias, disposition, faculty, genius, gift, inclination, leaning, proclivity, proneness, propensity, talent, tendency.

turncoat *n* apostate, backslider, deserter, recreant, renegade, traitor, wretch.

turpitude *n* baseness, degradation, depravity, vileness, wickedness.

turret *n* cupola, minaret, pinnacle.

tussle *vb* conflict, contend, contest, scuffle, struggle, wrestle. * *n* conflict, contest, fight, scuffle, struggle.

tutelage *n* care, charge, dependence, guardianship, protection, teaching, tutorage, tutorship, wardship.

tutor *vb* coach, educate, instruct, teach; discipline, train. * *n* coach, governess, governor, instructor, master, preceptor, schoolteacher, teacher.

twaddle *vb* chatter, gabble, maunder, prate, prattle. * *n* balderdash, chatter, flummery, gabble, gibberish, gobbledegook, gossip, jargon, moonshine, nonsense, platitude, prate, prattle, rigmarole, stuff, tattle.

tweak *vb, n* jerk, pinch, pull, twinge, twitch.

twig[1] *n* bough, branch, offshoot, shoot, slip, spray, sprig, stick, switch.

twig[2] *vb* catch on, comprehend, discover, grasp, realize, recognize, see, understand.

twin *vb* couple, link, match, pair. * *adj* double, doubled, duplicate, geminate, identical, matched, matching, second, twain. * *n* corollary, double, duplicate, fellow, likeness, match.

twine *vb* embrace, encircle, entwine, interlace, surround, wreathe; bend, meander, wind; coil, twist. * *n* convolution, coil, twist; embrace, twining, winding; cord, string.

twinge *vb* pinch, tweak, twitch. * *n* pinch, tweak, twitch; gripe, pang, spasm.

twinkle *vb* blink, twink, wink; flash, glimmer, scintillate, sparkle. * *n* blink, flash, gleam, glimmer, scintillation, sparkle; flash, instant, jiffy, moment, second, tick, trice, twinkling.

twinkling *n* flashing, sparkling, twinkle; flash, instant, jiffy, moment, second, tick, trice.

twirl *vb* revolve, rotate, spin, turn, twist, twirl. * *n* convolution, revolution, turn, twist, whirling.

twist *vb* purl, rotate, spin, twine; complicate, contort, convolute, distort, pervert, screw, wring; coil, writhe; encircle, wind, wreathe. * *n* coil, curl, spin, twine; braid, roll; change, complication, development, variation; bend, convolution, turn; defect, distortion, flaw, imperfection; jerk, pull, sprain, wrench; aberration, characteristic, eccentricity, oddity, peculiarity, quirk.

twit[1] *vb* banter, blame, censure, reproach, taunt, tease, upbraid.

twit[2] *n* blockhead, fool, idiot, nincompoop, nitwit.

twitch *vb* jerk, pluck, pull, snatch. * *n* jerk, pull; contraction, pull, quiver, spasm, twitching.

type *n* emblem, mark, stamp; adumbration, image, representation, representative, shadow, sign, symbol, token; archetype, exemplar, model, original, pattern, prototype, protoplast, standard; character, form, kind, nature, sort; figure, letter, text, typography.

typical *adj* emblematic, exemplary, figurative, ideal, indicative, model, representative, symbolic, true.

typify *vb* betoken, denote, embody, exemplify, figure, image, indicate, represent, signify.

tyrannical *adj* absolute, arbitrary, autocratic, cruel, despotic, dictatorial, domineering, high, imperious, irresponsible, severe, tyrannical, unjust; galling, grinding, inhuman, oppressive, overbearing, severe.

tyranny *n* absolutism, autocracy, despotism, dictatorship, harshness, oppression.

tyrant *n* autocrat, despot, dictator, oppressor.

tyro *n* beginner, learner, neophyte, novice; dabbler, smatterer.

U

ubiquitous *adj* omnipresent, present, universal.

udder *n* nipple, pap, teat.

ugly *adj* crooked, homely, ill-favoured, plain, ordinary, unlovely, unprepossessing, unshapely, unsightly; forbidding, frightful, gruesome, hideous, horrible, horrid, loathsome, monstrous, shocking, terrible, repellent, repulsive; bad-tempered, cantankerous, churlish, cross, quarrelsome, spiteful, surly, spiteful, vicious.

ulcer *n* boil, fester, gathering, pustule, sore.

ulterior *adj* beyond, distant, farther; hidden, personal, secret, selfish, undisclosed.

ultimate *adj* conclusive, decisive, eventual, extreme, farthest, final, last. * *n* acme, consummation, culmination, height, peak, pink, quintessence, summit.

ultra *adj* advanced, beyond, extreme, radical.

umbrage *n* shadow, shade; anger, displeasure, dissatisfaction, dudgeon, injury, offence, pique, resentment.

umpire *vb* adjudicate, arbitrate, judge, referee. * *n* adjudicator, arbiter, arbitrator, judge, referee.

unabashed *adj* bold, brazen, confident, unblushing, undaunted, undismayed.

unable *adj* impotent, incapable, incompetent, powerless, weak.

unacceptable *adj* disagreeable, distasteful, offensive, unpleasant, unsatisfactory, unwelcome.

unaccommodating *adj* disobliging, noncompliant, uncivil, ungracious.

unaccomplished *adj* incomplete, unachieved, undone, unperformed, unexecuted, unfinished; ill-educated, uncultivated, unpolished.

unaccountable *adj* inexplicable, incomprehensible, inscrutable, mysterious, unintelligible; irresponsible, unanswerable.

unaccustomed *adj* uninitiated, unskilled, unused; foreign, new, strange, unfamiliar, unusual.

unaffected *adj* artless, honest, naive, natural, plain, simple, sincere, real, unfeigned; chaste, pure, unadorned; insensible, unchanged, unimpressed, unmoved, unstirred, untouched.

unanimity *n* accord, agreement, concert, concord, harmony, union, unity.

unanimous *adj* agreeing, concordant, harmonious, like-minded, solid, united.

unassuming *adj* humble, modest, reserved, unobtrusive, unpretending, unpretentious.

unattainable *adj* inaccessible, unobtainable.

unavailing *adj* abortive, fruitless, futile, ineffectual, ineffective, inept, nugatory, unsuccessful, useless, vain.

unbalanced *adj* unsound, unsteady; unadjusted, unsettled.

unbearable *adj* insufferable, insupportable, unendurable.

unbecoming *adj* inappropriate, indecent, indecorous, improper, unbefitting, unbeseeming, unseemly, unsuitable.

unbelief *n* disbelief, dissent, distrust, incredulity, incredulousness, miscreance, miscreancy, nonconformity; doubt, freethinking, infidelity, scepticism.

unbeliever *n* agnostic, deist, disbeliever, doubter, heathen, infidel, sceptic.

unbending *adj* inflexible, rigid, stiff, unpliant, unyielding; firm, obstinate, resolute, stubborn.

unbiased *adj* disinterested, impartial, indifferent, neutral, uninfluenced, unprejudiced, unwarped.

unbind *vb* loose, undo, unfasten, unloose, untie; free, unchain, unfetter.

unblemished *adj* faultless, guiltless, immaculate, impeccable, innocent, intact, perfect, pure, sinless, spotless, stainless, undefiled, unspotted, unsullied, untarnished.

unblushing *adj* boldfaced, impudent, shameless.

unbounded *adj* absolute, boundless, endless, immeasurable, immense, infinite, interminable, measureless, unlimited, vast; immoderate, uncontrolled, unrestrained, unrestricted.

unbridled *adj* dissolute, intractable, lax, licensed, licentious, loose, uncontrolled, ungovernable, unrestrained, violent, wanton.

unbroken *adj* complete, entire, even, full, intact, unimpaired; constant, continuous, fast, profound, sound, successive, undisturbed; inviolate, unbetrayed, unviolated.

unbuckle *vb* loose, unfasten, unloose.

uncanny *adj* inopportune, unsafe; eerie, eery, ghostly, unearthly, unnatural, weird.

unceremonious *adj* abrupt, bluff, blunt, brusque, course, curt, gruff, plain, rough, rude, ungracious; casual, familiar, informal, offhand, unconstrained.

uncertain *adj* ambiguous, doubtful, dubious, equivocal, indefinite, indeterminate, indistinct, questionable, unsettled; insecure, precarious, problematical; capricious, changeable, desultory, fitful, fluctuating, irregular, mutable, shaky, slippery, unreliable, variable.

unchaste *adj* dissolute, incontinent, indecent, immoral, lascivious, lecherous, libidinous, lewd, loose, obscene, wanton.

unchecked *adj* uncurbed, unhampered, unhindered, unobstructed, unrestrained, untrammelled.

uncivil *adj* bearish, blunt, boorish, brusque, discourteous, disobliging, disrespectful, gruff, ill-bred, ill-mannered, impolite, irreverent, rough, rude, uncomplaisant, uncourteous, uncouth, ungentle, ungracious, unmannered, unseemly.

unclean *adj* abominable, beastly, dirty, filthy, foul, grimy, grubby, miry, muddy, nasty, offensive, purulent, repulsive, soiled, sullied; improper, indecent, indecorous, obscene, polluted, risqué, sinful, smutty, unholy, uncleanly.

uncomfortable *adj* disagreeable, displeasing, disquieted, distressing, disturbed, uneasy, unpleasant, restless; cheerless, close, oppressive; dismal, miserable, unhappy.

uncommon *adj* choice, exceptional, extraordinary, infrequent, noteworthy, odd, original, queer, rare, remarkable, scarce, singular, strange, unexampled, unfamiliar, unusual, unwonted.

uncommunicative *adj* close, inconversable, reserved, reticent, taciturn, unsociable, unsocial.

uncomplaining *adj* long-suffering, meek, patient, resigned, tolerant.

uncompromising *adj* inflexible, narrow, obstinate, orthodox, rigid, stiff, strict, unyielding.

unconcerned *adj* apathetic, careless, indifferent.

unconditional *adj* absolute, categorical, complete, entire, free, full, positive, unlimited, unqualified, unreserved, unrestricted.

uncongenial *adj* antagonistic, discordant, displeasing, ill-assorted, incompatible, inharmonious, mismatched, unsuited, unsympathetic.

uncouth *adj* awkward, boorish, clownish, clumsy, gawky, inelegant, loutish, lubberly, rough, rude, rustic, uncourtly, ungainly, unpolished, unrefined, unseemly; odd, outlandish, strange, unfamiliar, unusual.

uncover *vb* denude, divest, lay bare, strip; disclose, discover, expose, reveal, unmask, unveil; bare, doff; open, unclose, unseal.

unctuous *adj* adipose, greasy, oily, fat, fatty, oleaginous, pinguid, sebaceous; bland, lubricious, smooth, slippery; bland, fawning, glib, obsequious, plausible, servile, suave, sycophantic; fervid, gushing.

uncultivated *adj* fallow, uncultured, unreclaimed, untilled; homely, ignorant, illiterate, rude, uncivilized, uncultured, uneducated, unfit, unlettered, unpolished, unread, unready, unrefined, untaught; rough, savage, sylvan, uncouth, wild.

undaunted *adj* bold, brave, courageous, dauntless, fearless, intrepid, plucky, resolute, undismayed.

undefiled *adj* clean, immaculate, pure, spotless, stainless, unblemished, unspotted, unsullied, untarnished; honest, innocent, inviolate, pure, uncorrupted, unpolluted, unstained.

undemonstrative *adj* calm, composed, demure, impassive, modest, placid, quiet, reserved, sedate, sober, staid, tranquil.

undeniable *adj* certain, conclusive, evident, incontestable, incontrovertible, indisputable, indubitable, obvious, unquestionable.

under *prep* below, beneath, inferior to, lower than, subordinate to, underneath. * *adv* below, beneath, down, lower.

underestimate *vb* belittle, underrate, undervalue.

undergo *vb* bear, endure, experience, suffer, sustain.

underhand *adj* clandestine, deceitful, disingenuous, fraudulent, hidden, secret, sly, stealthy, underhanded, unfair. * *adv* clandestinely, privately, secretly, slyly, stealthily, surreptitiously; fraudulently, unfairly.

underling *n* agent, inferior, servant, subordinate.

undermine *vb* excavate, mine, sap; demoralize, foil, frustrate, thwart, weaken.

understand *vb* apprehend, catch, comprehend, conceive, discern, grasp, know, penetrate, perceive, see, seize, twig; assume, interpret, take; imply, mean.

understanding *adj* compassionate, considerate, forgiving, kind, kindly, patient, sympathetic, tolerant. * *n* brains, comprehension, discernment, faculty, intellect, intelligence, judgement, knowledge, mind, reason, sense.

undertake *vb* assume, attempt, begin, embark on, engage in, enter upon, take in hand; agree, bargain, contract, covenant, engage, guarantee, promise, stipulate.

undertaking *n* adventure, affair, attempt, business, effort, endeavour, engagement, enterprise, essay, move, project, task, venture.

undesigned *adj* spontaneous, unintended, unintentional, unplanned, unpremeditated.

undigested *adj* crude, ill-advised, ill-considered, ill-judged; confused, disorderly, ill-arranged, unmethodical.

undivided *adj* complete, entire, whole; one, united.

undo *vb* annul, cancel, frustrate, invalidate, neutralize, nullify, offset, reverse; disengage, loose, unfasten, unmake, unravel, untie; crush, destroy, overturn, ruin.

undoubted *adj* incontrovertible, indisputable, indubitable, undisputed, unquestionable, unquestioned.

undress *vb* denude, dismantle, disrobe, unclothe, unrobe, peel, strip. * *n* disarray, nakedness, nudity; mufti, negligee.

undue *adj* illegal, illegitimate, improper, unlawful, excessive, disproportionate, disproportioned, immoderate, unsuitable; unfit.

undulation *n* billowing, fluctuation, pulsation, ripple, wave.

undying *adj* deathless, endless, immortal, imperishable.

unearthly *adj* preternatural, supernatural, uncanny, weird.

uneasy *adj* disquieted, disturbed, fidgety, impatient, perturbed, restless, restive, unquiet, worried; awkward, stiff, ungainly, ungraceful; constraining, cramping, disagreeable, uncomfortable.

unending *adj* endless, eternal, everlasting, interminable, never-ending, perpetual, unceasing.

unequal *adj* disproportionate, disproportioned, ill-matched, inferior, irregular, insufficient, not alike, uneven.

unequalled *adj* exceeding, incomparable, inimitable, matchless, new, nonpareil, novel, paramount, peerless, pre-eminent, superlative, surpassing, transcendent, unheard of, unique, unparalleled, unrivalled.

unequivocal *adj* absolute, certain, clear, evident, incontestable, indubitable, positive; explicit, unambiguous, unmistakable.

uneven *adj* hilly, jagged, lumpy, ragged, rough, rugged, stony; motley, unequal, variable, variegated.

uneventful *adj* commonplace, dull, eventless, humdrum, quiet, monotonous, smooth, uninteresting.

unexceptionable *adj* excellent, faultless, good, irreproachable.

unexpected *adj* abrupt, sudden, unforeseen.

unfair *adj* dishonest, dishonourable, faithless, false, hypocritical, inequitable, insincere, oblique, one-sided, partial, unequal, unjust, wrongful.

unfaithful *adj* adulterous, derelict, deceitful, dishonest, disloyal, false, faithless, fickle, perfidious, treacherous, unreliable; negligent; changeable, inconstant, untrue.

unfamiliar *adj* bizarre, foreign, new, novel, outlandish, queer, singular, strange, uncommon, unusual.

unfashionable *adj* antiquated, destitute, disused, obsolete, old-fashioned, unconventional.

unfavourable *adj* adverse, contrary, disadvantageous, discouraging, ill, inauspicious, inimical, inopportune, indisposed, malign, sinister, unfriendly, unlucky, unpropitious, untimely; foul, inclement.

unfeeling *adj* apathetic, callous, heartless, insensible, numb, obdurate, torpid, unconscious, unimpressionable; adamantine, cold-blooded, cruel, hard, merciless, pitiless, stony, unkind, unsympathetic.

unfit *vb* disable, disqualify, incapacitate. * *adj* improper, inappropriate, incompetent, inconsistent, unsuitable; ill-equipped, inadequate, incapable, unqualified, useless; debilitated, feeble, flabby, unhealthy, unsound.

unflagging *adj* constant, indefatigable, never-ending, persevering, steady, unfaltering, unremitting, untiring, unwearied.

unflinching *adj* firm, resolute, steady, unshrinking.

unfold *vb* display, expand, open, separate, unfurl, unroll; declare, disclose, reveal, tell; decipher, develop, disentangle, evolve, explain, illustrate, interpret, resolve, unravel.

unfortunate *adj* hapless, ill-fated, ill-starred, infelicitous, luckless, unhappy, unlucky, unprosperous, unsuccessful, wretched; calamitous, deplorable, disastrous; inappropriate, inexpedient.

unfrequented *adj* abandoned, deserted, forsaken, lone, solitary, uninhabited, unoccupied.

unfruitful *adj* barren, fruitless, sterile; infecund, unprolific; unprofitable, unproductive.

ungainly *adj* awkward, boorish, clownish, clumsy, gawky, inelegant, loutish, lubberly, lumbering, slouching, stiff, uncourtly, uncouth, ungraceful.

ungentlemanly *adj* ill-bred, impolite, rude, uncivil, ungentle, ungracious, unmannerly.

unhappy *adj* afflicted, disastrous, dismal, distressed, drear, evil, inauspicious, miserable, painful, unfortunate, wretched.

unhealthy *adj* ailing, diseased, feeble, indisposed, infirm, poorly, sickly, toxic, unsanitary, unsound, toxic, venomous.

uniform *adj* alike, constant, even, equable, equal, smooth, steady, regular, unbroken, unchanged, undeviating, unvaried, unvarying. * *n* costume, dress, livery, outfit, regalia, suit.

uniformity *n* constancy, continuity, permanence, regularity, sameness, stability; accordance, agreement, conformity, consistency, unanimity.

unimportant *adj* immaterial, inappreciable, inconsequent, inconsequential, inconsiderable, indifferent, insignificant, mediocre, minor, paltry, petty, small, slight, trifling, trivial.

unintentional *adj* accidental, casual, fortuitous, inadvertent, involuntary, spontaneous, undesigned, unmeant, unplanned, unpremeditated, unthinking.

uninterrupted *adj* continuous, endless, incessant, perpetual, unceasing.

union *n* coalescence, coalition, combination, conjunction, coupling, fusion, incorporation, joining, junction, unification, uniting; agreement, concert, concord, concurrence, harmony, unanimity, unity; alliance, association, club, confederacy, federation, guild, league.

unique *adj* choice, exceptional, matchless, only, peculiar, rare, single, sole, singular, uncommon, unexampled, unmatched.

unison *n* accord, accordance, agreement, concord, harmony.

unite *vb* amalgamate, attach, blend, centralize, coalesce, confederate, consolidate, embody, fuse, incorporate, merge, weld; associate, conjoin, connect, couple, link, marry; combine, join; harmonize, reconcile; agree, concert, concur, cooperate, fraternize.

universal *adj* all-reaching, catholic, cosmic, encyclopedic, general, ubiquitous, unlimited; all, complete, entire, total, whole.

unjust *adj* inequitable, injurious, partial, unequal, unfair, unwarranted, wrong, wrongful; flagitious, heinous, influenced, iniquitous, nefarious, unrighteous, wicked; biased, prejudiced, uncandid.

unjustifiable *adj* indefensible, unjust, unreasonable, unwarrantable; inexcusable, unpardonable.

unknown *adj* unappreciated, unascertained; undiscovered, unexplored, uninvestigated; concealed, dark, enigmatic, hidden, mysterious, mystic; anonymous, incognito, inglorious, nameless, obscure, renownless, undistinguished, unheralded, unnoted.

unladylike *adj* ill-bred, impolite, rude, uncivil, ungentle, ungracious, unmannerly.

unlamented *adj* unmourned, unregretted.

unlimited *adj* boundless, infinite, interminable, limitless, measureless, unbounded; absolute, full, unconfined, unconstrained, unrestricted; indefinite, undefined.

unlucky *adj* baleful, disastrous, ill-fated, ill-starred, luckless, unfortunate, unprosperous, unsuccessful; ill-omened, inauspicious; miserable, unhappy.

unmanageable *adj* awkward, cumbersome, inconvenient, unwieldy; intractable, unruly, unworkable, vicious; difficult, impractical.

unmatched *adj* matchless, unequalled, unparalleled, unrivalled.
unmitigated *adj* absolute, complete, consummate, perfect, sheer, stark, thorough, unqualified, utter.
unnatural *adj* aberrant, abnormal, anomalous, foreign, irregular, prodigious, uncommon; brutal, cold, heartless, inhuman, unfeeling, unusual; affected, artificial, constrained, forced, insincere, self-conscious, stilted, strained; factitious.
unpleasant *adj* disagreeable, displeasing, distasteful, obnoxious, offensive, repulsive, unlovely, ungrateful, unacceptable, unpalatable, unwelcome.
unpremeditated *adj* extempore, impromptu, offhand, spontaneous, undesigned, unintentional, unstudied.
unprincipled *adj* bad, crooked, dishonest, fraudulent, immoral, iniquitous, knavish, lawless, profligate, rascally, roguish, thievish, trickish, tricky, unscrupulous, vicious, villainous, wicked.
unqualified *adj* disqualified, incompetent, ineligible, unadapted, unfit; absolute, certain, consummate, decided, direct, downright, full, outright, unconditional, unmeasured, unrestricted, unmitigated; exaggerated, sweeping.
unreal *adj* chimerical, dreamlike, fanciful, flimsy, ghostly, illusory, insubstantial, nebulous, shadowy, spectral, visionary, unsubstantial.
unreasonable *adj* absurd, excessive, exorbitant, foolish, ill-judged, illogical, immoderate, impractical, injudicious, irrational, nonsensical, preposterous, senseless, silly, stupid, unfair, unreasoning, unwarrantable, unwise.
unreliable *adj* fallible, fickle, irresponsible, treacherous, uncertain, undependable, unstable, unsure, untrustworthy.
unremitting *adj* assiduous, constant, continual, diligent, incessant, indefatigable, persevering, sedulous, unabating, unceasing.
unrepentant *adj* abandoned, callous, graceless, hardened, impenitent, incorrigible, irreclaimable, lost, obdurate, profligate, recreant, seared, shameless.
unrequited *adj* unanswered, unreturned, unrewarded.
unreserved *adj* absolute, entire, full, unlimited; above-board, artless, candid, communicative, fair, frank, guileless, honest, ingenuous, open, sincere, single-minded, undesigning, undissembling; demonstrative, emotional, open-hearted.
unresisting *adj* compliant, long-suffering, non-resistant, obedient, passive, patient, submissive, yielding.
unresponsive *adj* irresponsive, unsympathetic.
unrestrained *adj* unbridled, unchecked, uncurbed, unfettered, unhindered, unobstructed, unreserved; broad, dissolute, incontinent, inordinate, lax, lewd, licentious, loose, wanton; lawless, wild.
unrestricted *adj* free, unbridled, unconditional, unconfined, uncurbed, unfettered, unlimited, unqualified, unrestrained; clear, open, public, unobstructed.
unrevealed *adj* hidden, occult, secret, undiscovered, unknown.
unrewarded *adj* unpaid, unrecompensed.
unriddle *vb* explain, expound, solve, unfold, unravel.
unrighteous *adj* evil, sinful, ungodly, unholy, vicious, wicked, wrong; heinous, inequitable, iniquitous, nefarious, unfair, unjust.
unripe *adj* crude, green, hard, immature, premature, sour; incomplete, unfinished.
unrivalled *adj* incomparable, inimitable, matchless, peerless, unequalled, unexampled, unique, unparalleled.
unrobe *vb* disrobe, undress.
unroll *vb* develop, discover, evolve, open, unfold; display, lay open.
unromantic *adj* literal, matter-of-fact, prosaic.
unroot *vb* eradicate, extirpate, root out, uproot.
unruffled *adj* calm, peaceful, placid, quiet, serene, smooth, still, tranquil; collected, composed, cool, imperturbable, peaceful, philosophical, placid, tranquil, undisturbed, unexcited, unmoved.
unruly *adj* disobedient, disorderly, fractious, headstrong, insubordinate, intractable, mutinous, obstreperous, rebellious, refractory, riotous, seditious, turbulent, ungovernable, unmanageable, wanton, wild; lawless, obstinate, rebellious, stubborn, vicious.
unsafe *adj* dangerous, hazardous, insecure, perilous, precarious, risky, treacherous, uncertain, unprotected.
unsaid *adj* tacit, unmentioned, unspoken, unuttered.
unsanctified *adj* profane, unhallowed, unholy.
unsatisfactory *adj* insufficient; disappointing; faulty, feeble, imperfect, poor, weak.
unsatisfied *adj* insatiate, unsated, unsatiated, unstaunched; discontented, displeased, dissatisfied, malcontent; undischarged, unpaid, unperformed, unrendered.
unsavoury *adj* flat, insipid, mawkish, savourless, tasteless, unflavoured, unpalatable, vapid; disagreeable, disgusting, distasteful, nasty, nauseating, nauseous, offensive, rank, revolting, sickening, uninviting, unpleasing.
unsay *vb* recall, recant, retract, take back.
unscathed *adj* unharmed, uninjured.
unschooled *adj* ignorant, uneducated, uninstructed; undisciplined, untrained.
unscrupulous *adj* dishonest, reckless, ruthless, unconscientious, unprincipled, unrestrained.
unsealed *adj* open, unclosed.
unsearchable *adj* hidden, incomprehensible, inscrutable, mysterious.
unseasonable *adj* ill-timed, inappropriate, infelicitous, inopportune, untimely; late, too late; inexpedient, undesireable, unfit, ungrateful, unsuitable, unwelcome; premature, too early.
unseasonably *adv* malapropos, unsuitably, untimely.
unseasoned *adj* inexperienced, unaccustomed, unqualified, untrained; immoderate, inordinate, irregular; green; fresh, unsalted.
unseeing *adj* blind, sightless.
unseemly *adj* improper, indecent, inappropriate, indecorous, unbecoming, uncomely, unfit, unmeet, unsuitable.
unseen *adj* undiscerned, undiscovered, unobserved, unperceived; imperceptible, indiscoverable, invisible, latent.
unselfish *adj* altruistic, devoted, disinterested, generous, high-minded, impersonal, liberal, magnanimous, self-denying, self-forgetful, selfless, self-sacrificing.
unserviceable *adj* ill-conditioned, unsound, useless; profitless, unprofitable.
unsettle *vb* confuse, derange, disarrange, disconcert, disorder, disturb, trouble, unbalance, unfix, unhinge, upset.
unsettled *adj* changeable, fickle, inconstant, restless, transient, unstable, unsteady, vacillating, wavering; inequable, unequal; feculent, muddy, roiled, roily, turbid; adrift, afloat, homeless, unestablished, uninhabited; open, tentative, unadjusted, undecided, undetermined; due, outstanding, owing, unpaid; perturbed, troubled, unnerved.
unshackle *vb* emancipate, liberate, loose, release, set free, unbind, unchain, unfetter.
unshaken *adj* constant, firm, resolute, steadfast, steady, unmoved.
unshapen *adj* deformed, grotesque, ill-formed, ill-made, ill-shaped, misshapen, shapeless, ugly, uncouth.
unsheltered *adj* exposed, unprotected.
unshrinking *adj* firm, determined, persisting, resolute, unblenching, unflinching.
unshroud *vb* discover, expose, reveal, uncover.
unsightly *adj* deformed, disagreeable, hideous, repellent, repulsive, ugly.
unskilful, unskillful *adj* awkward, bungling, clumsy, inapt, inexpert, maladroit, rough, rude, unhandy, unskilled, unversed.
unskilled *adj* inexperienced, raw, undisciplined, undrilled, uneducated, unexercised, unpractised, unprepared, unschooled; unskilful.
unslaked *adj* unquenched, unslacked.
unsleeping *adj* unslumbering, vigilant, wakeful, watchful.
unsmirched *adj* undefiled, unpolluted, unspotted.
unsociable *adj* distant, reserved, retiring, segregative, shy, solitary, standoffish, taciturn, uncommunicative, uncompanionable, ungenial, unsocial; inhospitable, misanthropic, morose.

unsoiled *adj* clean, spotless, unspotted, unstained, unsullied, untarnished.

unsophisticated *adj* genuine, pure, unadulterated; good, guileless, innocent, undepraved, unpolluted, invitiated; artless, honest, ingenuous, naive, natural, simple, sincere, straightforward, unaffected, undesigning, unstudied.

unsound *adj* decayed, defective, impaired, imperfect, rotten, thin, wasted, weak; broken, disturbed, light, restless; diseased, feeble, infirm, morbid, poorly, sickly, unhealthy, weak; deceitful, erroneous, fallacious, false, faulty, hollow, illogical, incorrect, invalid, ill-advised, irrational, questionable, sophistical, unreasonable, unsubstantial, untenable, wrong; dishonest, false, insincere, unfaithful, untrustworthy, untrue; insubstantial, unreal; heretical, heterodox, unorthodox.

unsparing *adj* bountiful, generous, lavish, liberal, profuse, ungrudging; harsh, inexorable, relentless, rigorous, ruthless, severe, uncompromising, unforgiving.

unspeakable *adj* indescribable, ineffable, inexpressible, unutterable.

unspiritual *adj* bodily, carnal, fleshly, sensual.

unspotted *adj* clean, spotless, unsoiled, unstained, unsullied, untarnished; faultless, immaculate, innocent, pure, stainless, unblemished, uncorrupted, undefiled, untainted.

unstable *adj* infirm, insecure, precarious, top-heavy, tottering, unbalanced, unballasted, unreliable, unsafe, unsettled, unsteady; changeable, erratic, fickle, inconstant, irresolute, mercurial, mutable, vacillating, variable, wavering, weak, volatile.—*also* **instable**.

unstained *adj* colourless, uncoloured, undyed, untinged; clean, spotless, unspotted.

unsteady *adj* fluctuating, oscillating, unsettled; insecure, precarious, unstable; changeable, desultory, ever-changing, fickle, inconstant, irresolute, mutable, unreliable, variable, wavering; drunken, jumpy, tottering, vacillating, wobbly, tipsy.

unstinted *adj* abundant, ample, bountiful, full, large, lavish, plentiful, prodigal, profuse.

unstrung *adj* overcome, shaken, unnerved, weak.

unstudied *adj* extempore, extemporaneous, impromptu, offhand, spontaneous, unpremeditated; inexpert, unskilled, unversed.

unsubdued *adj* unbowed, unbroken, unconquered, untamed.

unsubmissive *adj* disobedient, contumacious, indocile, insubordinate, obstinate, perverse, refractory, uncomplying, ungovernable, unmanageable, unruly, unyielding.

unsubstantial *adj* airy, flimsy, gaseous, gossamery, light, slight, tenuous, thin, vaporous; apparitional, bodiless, chimerical, cloudbuilt, dreamlike, empty, fantastical, ideal, illusory, imaginary, imponderable, moonshiny, spectral, unreal, vague, visionary; erroneous, fallacious, flimsy, groundless, illogical, unfounded, ungrounded, unsolid, unsound, untenable, weak.

unsuccessful *adj* abortive, bootless, fruitless, futile, ineffectual, profitless, unavailing, vain; ill-fated, ill-starred, luckless, unfortunate, unhappy, unlucky, unprosperous.

unsuitable *adj* ill-adapted, inappropriate, malapropos, unfit, unsatisfactory, unsuited; improper, inapplicable, inapt, incongruous, inexpedient, infelicitous, unbecoming, unbeseeming, unfitting.

unsuited *adj* unadapted, unfitted, unqualified.

unsullied *adj* chaste, clean, spotless, unsoiled, unspotted, unstained, untarnished; immaculate, pure, stainless, unblemished, uncorrupted, undefiled, untainted, untouched, virginal.

unsupplied *adj* destitute, unfurnished, unprovided.

unsupported *adj* unaided, unassisted; unbacked, unseconded, unsustained, unupheld.

unsurpassed *adj* matchless, peerless, unequalled, unexampled, unexcelled, unmatched, unparagoned, unparalleled, unrivalled.

unsusceptible *adj* apathetic, cold, impassive, insusceptible, phlegmatic, stoical, unimpressible, unimpressionable.

unsuspecting *adj* confiding, credulous, trusting, unsuspicious.

unsuspicious *adj* confiding, credulous, gullible, simple, trustful, unsuspecting.

unsustainable *adj* insupportable, intolerable; controvertible, erroneous, unmaintainable, untenable.

unswerving *adj* direct, straight, undeviating; constant, determined, firm, resolute, staunch, steadfast, steady, stable, unwavering.

unsymmetrical *adj* amorphous, asymmetric, disproportionate, formless, irregular, unbalanced.

unsystematic, unsystematical *adj* casual, disorderly, haphazard, irregular, planless, unmethodical.

untainted *adj* chaste, clean, faultless, fresh, healthy, pure, sweet, wholesome; spotless, unsoiled, unstained, unsullied, untarnished; immaculate, stainless, unblemished, uncorrupted, undefiled, unspotted.

untamable *adj* unconquerable.

untamed *adj* fierce, unbroken, wild.

untangle *vb* disentangle, explain, explicate.

untarnished *adj* chaste, clean, spotless, unsoiled, unspotted, unstained, unsullied; immaculate, pure, spotless, stainless, unblemished, uncorrupted, undefiled, unspotted, unsullied, untainted, virginal, virtuous.

untaught *adj* illiterate, unenlightened, uninformed, unlettered; ignorant, inexperienced, undisciplined, undrilled, uneducated, uninitiated, uninstructed, untutored.

untenable *adj* indefensible, unmaintainable, unsound; fallacious, hollow, illogical, indefensible, insupportable, unjustifiable, weak.

untenanted *adj* deserted, empty, tenantless, uninhabited, unoccupied.

unterrified *adj* fearless, unappalled, unawed, undismayed, undaunted, unscared.

unthankful *adj* thankless, ungrateful.

unthinking *adj* careless, heedless, inconsiderate, thoughtless, unreasoning, unreflecting; automatic, mechanical.

unthoughtful *adj* careless, heedless, inconsiderable, thoughtless.

unthrifty *adj* extravagant, improvident, lavish, prodigal, profuse, thriftless, wasteful.

untidy *adj* careless, disorderly, dowdy, frumpy, mussy, slatternly, slovenly, unkempt, unneat.

untie *vb* free, loose, loosen, unbind, unfasten, unknot, unloose; clear, resolve, solve, unfold.

until *adv, conj* till, to the time when; to the place, point, state or degree that; * *prep* till, to.

untimely *adj* ill-timed, immature, inconvenient, inopportune, mistimed, premature, unseasonable, unsuitable; ill-considered, inauspicious, uncalled for, unfortunate. * *adv* unseasonably, unsuitably.

untinged *adj* achromatic, colourless, hueless, uncoloured, undyed, unstained.

untiring *adj* persevering, incessant, indefatigable, patient, tireless, unceasing, unfatiguable, unflagging, unremitting, unwearied, unwearying.

untold *adj* countless, incalculable, innumerable, uncounted, unnumbered; unrelated, unrevealed.

untouched *adj* intact, scatheless, unharmed, unhurt, uninjured, unscathed; insensible, unaffected, unmoved, unstirred.

untoward *adj* adverse, froward, intractable, perverse, refractory, stubborn, unfortunate; annoying, ill-timed, inconvenient, unmanageable, vexatious; awkward, uncouth, ungainly, ungraceful.

untrained *adj* green, ignorant, inexperienced, raw, unbroken, undisciplined, undrilled, uneducated, uninstructed, unpractised, unskilled, untaught, untutored.

untrammelled *adj* free, unhampered.

untried *adj* fresh, inexperienced, maiden, new, unassayed, unattempted, unattested, virgin; undecided.

untrodden *adj* pathless, trackless, unbeaten.

untroubled *adj* calm, careless, composed, peaceful, serene, smooth, tranquil, undisturbed, unvexed.

untrue *adj* contrary, false, inaccurate, wrong; disloyal, faithless, perfidious, recreant, treacherous, unfaithful.

untrustworthy *adj* deceitful, dishonest, inaccurate, rotten, slippery, treacherous, undependable, unreliable; disloyal, false; deceptive, fallible, illusive, questionable.

untruth *n* error, faithlessness, falsehood, falsity, incorrectness, inveracity, treachery; deceit, deception, fabrication, fib, fiction, forgery, imposture, invention, lie, misrepresentation, misstatement, story.
untutored *adj* ignorant, inexperienced, undisciplined, undrilled, uneducated, uninitiated, uninstructed, untaught; artless, natural, simple, unsophisticated.
untwist *vb* disentangle, disentwine, ravel, unravel, unwreathe.
unused *adj* idle, unemployed, untried; new, unaccustomed, unfamiliar.
unusual *adj* abnormal, curious, exceptional, extraordinary, odd, peculiar, queer, rare, recherché, remarkable, singular, strange, unaccustomed, uncommon, unwonted.
unutterable *adj* incommunicable, indescribable, ineffable, inexpressible, unspeakable.
unvarnished *adj* unpolished; candid, plain, simple, true, unadorned, unembellished.
unvarying *adj* constant, invariable, unchanging.
unveil *vb* disclose, expose, reveal, show, uncover, unmask.
unveracious *adj* false, lying, mendacious, untruthful.
unversed *adj* inexperienced, raw, undisciplined, undrilled, uneducated, unexercised, unpractised, unprepared, unschooled; unskilful.
unviolated *adj* inviolate, unbetrayed, unbroken.
unwarlike *adj* pacific, peaceful.
unwarped *adj* impartial, unbiased, undistorted, unprejudiced.
unwarrantable *adj* improper, indefensible, unjustifiable.
unwary *adj* careless, hasty, heedless, imprudent, incautious, indiscreet, precipitate, rash, reckless, remiss, uncircumspect, unguarded.
unwavering *adj* constant, determined, firm, fixed, resolute, settled, staunch, steadfast, steady, unhesitating.
unwearied *adj* unfatigued; constant, continual, incessant, indefatigable, persevering, persistent, unceasing, unremitting, untiring.
unwelcome *adj* disagreeable, unacceptable, ungrateful, unpleasant, unpleasing.
unwell *adj* ailing, delicate, diseased, ill, indisposed, sick.
unwept *adj* unlamented, unmourned, unregretted.
unwholesome *adj* baneful, deleterious, injurious, insalubrious, noisome, noxious, poisonous, unhealthful, unhealthy; injudicious, pernicious, unsound; corrupt, tainted.
unwieldy *adj* bulky, clumsy, cumbersome, cumbrous, elephantine, heavy, hulking, large, massy, ponderous, unmanageable, weighty.
unwilling *adj* averse, backward, disinclined, indisposed, laggard, loath, opposed, recalcitrant, reluctant; forced, grudging.
unwind *vb* unravel, unreel, untwine, wind off; disentangle.
unwise *adj* brainless, foolish, ill-advised, ill-judged, impolitic, imprudent, indiscreet, injudicious, inexpedient, senseless, silly, stupid, unwary, weak.
unwitnessed *adj* unknown, unseen, unspied.
unwittingly *adv* ignorantly, inadvertently, unconsciously, undesignedly, unintentionally, unknowingly.
unwonted *adj* infrequent, rare, uncommon, unusual; unaccustomed, unused.
unworthy *adj* undeserving; bad, base, blameworthy, worthless; shameful, unbecoming, vile; contemptible, derogatory, despicable, discreditable, mean, paltry, reprehensible, shabby.
unwrap *vb* open, unfold.
unwrinkled *adj* smooth, unforrowed.
unwritten *adj* oral, traditional, unrecorded; conventional, customary.
unwrought *adj* crude, rough, rude, unfashioned, unformed.
unyielding *adj* constant, determined, indomitable, inflexible, pertinacious, resolute, staunch, steadfast, steady, tenacious, uncompromising, unwavering; headstrong, intractable, obstinate, perverse, self-willed, stiff, stubborn, wayward, wilful; adamantine, firm, grim, hard, immovable, implastic, inexorable, relentless, rigid, unbending.
unyoke *vb* disconnect, disjoin, part, separate.
unyoked *adj* disconnected, separated; licentious, loose, unrestrained.
upbraid *vb* accuse, blame, chide, condemn, criticize, denounce, fault, reproach, reprove, revile, scold, taunt, twit.
upheaval *n* elevation, upthrow; cataclysm, convulsion, disorder, eruption, explosion, outburst, overthrow.
uphill *adj* ascending, upward; arduous, difficult, hard, laborious, strenuous, toilsome, wearisome.
uphold *vb* elevate, raise; bear up, hold up, support, sustain; advocate, aid, champion, countenance, defend, justify, maintain, vindicate.
upland *n* down, fell, ridge, plateau.
uplift *vb* raise, upraise; animate, elevate, inspire, lift, refine. * *n* ascent, climb, elevation, lift, rise, upthrust; exaltation, inspiration, uplifting; improvement, refinement.
upon *prep* on, on top of, over; about, concerning, on the subject of, relating to; immediately after, with.
upper hand *n* advantage, ascendancy, control, dominion, mastership, mastery, pre-eminence, rule, superiority, supremacy, whip hand.
uppermost *adj* foremost, highest, loftiest, supreme, topmost, upmost.
uppish *adj* arrogant, assuming, haughty, perky, proud, smart.
upright *adj* erect, perpendicular, vertical; conscientious, equitable, fair, faithful, good, honest, honourable, incorruptible, just, pure, righteous, straightforward, true, trustworthy, upstanding, virtuous.
uprightness *n* erectness, perpendicularity, verticality; equity, fairness, goodness, honesty, honour, incorruptibility, integrity, justice, probity, rectitude, righteousness, straightforwardness, trustiness, trustworthiness, virtue, worth.
uproar *n* clamour, commotion, confusion, din, disturbance, fracas, hubbub, hurly-burly, noise, pandemonium, racket, riot, tumult, turmoil, vociferation.
uproarious *adj* boisterous, clamorous, loud, noisy, obstreperous, riotous, tumultuous.
uproot *vb* eradicate, extirpate, root out.
upset *vb* capsize, invert, overthrow, overtumble, overturn, spill, tip over, topple, turn turtle; agitate, confound, confuse, discompose, disconcert, distress, disturb, embarrass, excite, fluster, muddle, overwhelm, perturb, shock, startle, trouble, unnerve, unsettle; checkmate, defeat, overthrow, revolutionize, subvert; foil, frustrate, nonplus, thwart. * *adj* disproved, exposed, overthrown; bothered, confused, disconcerted, flustered, mixed-up, perturbed; shocked, startled, unsettled; beaten, defeated, overcome, overpowered, overthrown; discomfited, distressed, discomposed, overexcited, overwrought, shaken, troubled, unnerved. * *n* confutation, refutation; foiling, frustration, overthrow, revolution, revulsion, ruin, subversdion, thwarting.
upshot *n* conclusion, consummation, effect, end, event, issue, outcome, result, termination.
upside down *adj* bottom side up, bottom up, confused, head over heels, inverted, topsy-turvy.
upstart *n* adventurer, arriviste, parvenu, snob, social cimber, yuppie.
upturned *adj* raised, uplifted; retroussé.
upward *adj* ascending, climbing, mounting, rising, uphill. * *adv* above, aloft, overhead, up; heavenwards, skywards.
urbane *adj* civil, complaisant, courteous, courtly, elegant, mannerly, polished, polite, refined, smooth, suave, well-mannered.
urbanity *n* amenity, civility, complaisance, courtesy, politeness, smoothness, suavity.
urchin *n* brat, child, kid, ragamuffin, rascal, scrap, squirt, tad.
urge *vb* crowd, drive, force on, impel, press, press on, push, push on; beg, beseech, conjure, entreat, exhort, implore, importune, ply, solicit, tease; animate, egg on, encourage, goad, hurry, incite, instigate, quicken, spur, stimulate. * *n* compulsion, desire, drive, impulse, longing, pressure, wish, yearning.
urgency *n* drive, emergency, exigency, haste, necessity, press, pressure, push, stress; clamorousness, entreaty, insistence, importunity, instance, solicitation; goad, incitement, spur, stimulus.
urgent *adj* cogent, critical, crucial, crying, exigent, immediate, imperative, important, importunate, insistent, instant, pertinacious, pressing, serious.
urinal *n* chamber, chamber pot, lavatory, pot, potty, jordan, toilet.

urinate *vb* make water, pee, pee-pee, piddle, piss, stale, wee.
usage *n* treatment; consuetude, custom, fashion, habit, method, mode, practice, prescription, tradition, use.
use *vb* administer, apply, avail oneself of, drive, employ, handle, improve, make use of, manipulate, occupy, operate, ply, put into action, take advantage of, turn to account, wield, work; exercise, exert, exploit, practice, profit by, utilize; absorb, consume, exhaust, expend, swallow up, waste, wear out; accustom, familiarize, habituate, harden, inure, train; act toward, behave toward, deal with, manage, treat; be accustomed, be wont. * *n* appliance, application, consumption, conversion, disposal, exercise, employ, employment, practice, utilization; adaptability, advantage, avail, benefit, convenience, profit, service, usefulness, utility, wear; exigency, necessity, indispensability, need, occasion, requisiteness; custom, habit, handling, method, treatment, usage, way.
useful *adj* active, advantageous, available, availing, beneficial, commodious, conducive, contributory, convenient, effective, good, helpful, instrumental, operative, practical, profitable, remunerative, salutary, suitable, serviceable, utilitarian; available, helpful, serviceable, valuable.
usefulness *n* advantage, profit, serviceableness, utility, value.
useless *adj* abortive, bootless, fruitless, futile, helpless, idle, incapable, incompetent, ineffective, ineffectual, inutile, nugatory, null, profitless, unavailing, unprofitable, unproductive, unserviceable, valueless, worthless; good for nothing, waste.
usher *vb* announce, forerun, herald, induct, introduce, precede; conduct, direct, escort, shepherd, show. * *n* attendant, conductor, escort, shepherd, squire.
usual *adj* accustomed, common, customary, everyday, familiar, frequent, general, habitual, normal, ordinary, prevailing, prevalent, regular, wonted.
usurp *vb* appropriate, arrogate, assume, seize.
usurpation *n* assumption, dispossession, infringement, seizure.
usury *n* interest; exploitation, extortion, profiteering.
utensil *n* device, implement, instrument, tool.
utility *n* advantageousness, avail, benefit, profit, service, use, usefulness; happiness, welfare.
utilize *vb* employ, exploit, make use of, put to use, turn to account, use.
utmost *adj* extreme, farthest, highest, last, main, most distant, remotest; greatest, uttermost. * *n* best, extreme, maximum, most.
Utopian *adj* air-built, air-drawn, chimerical, fanciful, ideal, imaginary, visionary, unreal.
utricle *n* bladder, cyst, sac, vesicle.
utter[1] *adj* complete, entire, perfect, total; absolute, blank, diametric, downright, final, peremptory, sheer, stark, thorough, thoroughgoing, unconditional, unqualified, total.
utter[2] *vb* articulate, breathe, deliver, disclose, divulge, emit, enunciate, express, give forth, pronounce, reveal, speak, talk, tell, voice; announce, circulate, declare, issue, publish.
utterance *n* articulation, delivery, disclosure, emission, expression, pronouncement, pronunciation, publication, speech.
utterly *adv* absolutely, altogether, completely, downright, entirely, quite, totally, unconditionally, wholly.
uttermost *adj* extreme, farthest; greatest, utmost.

V

vacant *adj* blank, empty, unfilled, void; disengaged, free, unemployed, unoccupied, unencumbered; thoughtless, unmeaning, unthinking, unreflective; uninhabited, untenanted.
vacate *vb* abandon, evacuate, relinquish, surrender; abolish, abrogate, annul, cancel, disannul, invalidate, nullify, overrule, quash, rescind.
vacillate *vb* dither, fluctuate, hesitate, oscillate, rock, sway, waver.
vacillation *n* faltering, fluctuation, hesitation, inconstancy, indecision, irresolution, reeling, rocking, staggering, swaying, unsteadiness, wavering.
vacuity *n* emptiness, inanition, vacancy; emptiness, vacancy, vacuum, void; expressionlessness, inanity, nihility.
vacuous *adj* empty, empty-headed, unfilled, vacant, void; inane, unintelligent.
vacuum *n* emptiness, vacuity, void.
vagabond *adj* footloose, idle, meandering, rambling, roving, roaming, strolling, vagrant, wandering. * *n* beggar, castaway, landloper, loafer, lounger, nomad, outcast, tramp, vagrant, wanderer.
vagary *n* caprice, crotchet, fancy, freak, humour, whim.
vagrant *adj* erratic, itinerant, roaming, roving, nomadic, strolling, unsettled, wandering. * *n* beggar, castaway, landloper, loafer, lounger, nomad, outcast, tramp, vagabond, wanderer.
vague *adj* ambiguous, confused, dim, doubtful, indefinite, ill-defined, indistinct, lax, loose, obscure, uncertain, undetermined, unfixed, unsettled.
vain *adj* baseless, delusive, dreamy, empty, false, imaginary, shadowy, suppositional, unsubstantial, unreal, void; abortive, bootless, fruitless, futile, ineffectual, nugatory, profitless, unavailing, unprofitable; trivial, unessential, unimportant, unsatisfactory, unsatisfying, useless, vapid, worthless; arrogant, conceited, egotistical, flushed, high, inflated, opinionated, ostentatious, overweening, proud, self-confident, self-opinionated, vainglorious; gaudy, glittering, gorgeous, showy.
valediction *n* adieu, farewell, goodbye, leave-taking.
valet *n* attendant, flunky, groom, lackey, servant.
valetudinarian *adj* delicate, feeble, frail, infirm, sickly.
valiant *adj* bold, brave, chivalrous, courageous, daring, dauntless, doughty, fearless, gallant, heroic, intrepid, lion-hearted, redoubtable, Spartan, valorous, undaunted.
valid *adj* binding, cogent, conclusive, efficacious, efficient, good, grave, important, just, logical, powerful, solid, sound, strong, substantial, sufficient, weighty.
valley *n* basin, bottom, canyon, dale, dell, dingle, glen, hollow, ravine, strath, vale.
valorous *adj* bold, brave, courageous, dauntless, doughty, intrepid, stout.
valour *n* boldness, bravery, courage, daring, gallantry, heroism, prowess, spirit.
valuable *adj* advantageous, precious, profitable, useful; costly, expensive, rich; admirable, estimable, worthy. * *n* heirloom, treasure.
value *vb* account, appraise, assess, estimate, price, rate, reckon; appreciate, esteem, prize, regard, treasure. * *n* avail, importance, usefulness, utility, worth; cost, equivalent, price, rate; estimation, excellence, importance, merit, valuation.
valueless *adj* miserable, useless, worthless.
vandal *n* barbarian, destroyer, savage.
vandalism *n* barbarism, barbarity, savagery.
vanish *vb* disappear, dissolve, fade, melt.
vanity *n* emptiness, falsity, foolishness, futility, hollowness, insanity, triviality, unreality, worthlessness; arrogance, conceit, egotism, ostentation, self-conceit.
vanquish *vb* conquer, defeat, outwit, overcome, overpower, overthrow, subdue, subjugate; crush, discomfit, foil, master, quell, rout, worst.
vapid *adj* dead, flat, insipid, lifeless, savourless, spiritless, stale, tasteless; dull, feeble, jejune, languid, meagre, prosaic, prosy, tame.
vapour *n* cloud, exhalation, fog, fume, mist, rack, reek, smoke, steam; daydream, dream, fantasy, phantom, vagary, vision, whim, whimsy.
variable *adj* changeable, mutable, shifting; aberrant, alterable, capricious, fickle, fitful, floating, fluctuating, inconstant, mobile, mutable, protean, restless, shifting, unsteady, vacillating, wavering.
variance *n* disagreement, difference, discord, dissension, incompatibility, jarring, strife.
variation *n* alteration, change, modification; departure, deviation, difference, discrepancy, innovation; contrariety, discordance.

variegated *adj* chequered, dappled, diversified, flecked, kaleidoscopic, mottled, multicoloured, pied, spotted, striped.

variety *n* difference, dissimilarity, diversity, diversification, medley, miscellany, mixture, multiplicity, variation; kind, sort.

various *adj* different, diverse, manifold, many, numerous, several, sundry.

varnish *vb* enamel, glaze, japan, lacquer; adorn, decorate, embellish, garnish, gild, polish; disguise, excuse, extenuate, gloss over, palliate. * *n* enamel, lacquer, stain; cover, extenuation, gloss.

vary *vb* alter, metamorphose, transform; alternate, exchange, rotate; diversify, modify, variegate; depart, deviate, swerve.

vassal *n* bondman, liegeman, retainer, serf, slave, subject, thrall.

vassalage *n* bondage, dependence, serfdom, servitude, slavery, subjection.

vast *adj* boundless, infinite, measureless, spacious, wide; colossal, enormous, gigantic, huge, immense, mighty, monstrous, prodigious, tremendous; extraordinary, remarkable.

vaticination *n* augury, divination, prediction, prognostication, prophecy.

vault[1] *vb* arch, bend, curve, span. * *n* cupola, curve, dome; catacomb, cell, cellar, crypt, dungeon, tomb; depository, strongroom.

vault[2] *vb* bound, jump, leap, spring; tumble, turn. * *n* bound, leap, jump, spring.

vaunt *vb* advertise, boast, brag, display, exult, flaunt, flourish, parade.

veer *vb* change, shift, turn.

vegetate *vb* blossom, develop, flourish, flower, germinate, grow, shoot, sprout, swell; bask, hibernate, idle, stagnate.

vehemence *n* impetuosity, violence; ardour, eagerness, earnestness, enthusiasm, fervency, fervour, heat, keenness, passion, warmth, zeal; force, intensity.

vehement *adj* furious, high, hot, impetuous, passionate, rampant, violent; ardent, burning, eager, earnest, enthusiastic, fervid, fiery, keen, passionate, sanguine, zealous; forcible, mighty, powerful, strong.

veil *vb* cloak, conceal, cover, curtain, envelop, hide, invest, mask, screen, shroud. * *n* cover, curtain, film, shade, screen; blind, cloak, disguise, mask, muffler, visor.

vein *n* course, current, lode, seam, streak, stripe, thread, wave; bent, character, faculty, humour, mood, talent, turn.

velocity *n* acceleration, celerity, expedition, fleetness, haste, quickness, rapidity, speed, swiftness.

velvety *adj* delicate, downy, smooth, soft.

venal *adj* corrupt, mean, purchasable, sordid.

vend *vb* dispose, flog, hawk, retail, sell.

venerable *adj* grave, respected, revered, sage, wise; awful, dread, dreadful; aged, old, patriarchal.

venerate *vb* adore, esteem, honour, respect, revere.

veneration *n* adoration, devotion, esteem, respect, reverence, worship.

vengeance *n* retaliation, retribution, revenge.

venial *adj* allowed, excusable, pardonable, permitted, trivial.

venom *n* poison, virus; acerbity, acrimony, bitterness, gall, hate, ill-will, malevolence, malice, maliciousness, malignity, rancour, spite, virulence.

venomous *adj* deadly, poisonous, septic, toxic, virulent; caustic, malicious, malignant, mischievous, noxious, spiteful.

vent *vb* emit, express, release, utter. * *n* air hole, hole, mouth, opening, orifice; air pipe, air tube, aperture, blowhole, bunghole, hydrant, plug, spiracle, spout, tap, orifice; effusion, emission, escape, outlet, passage; discharge, expression, utterance.

ventilate *vb* aerate, air, freshen, oxygenate, purify; fan, winnow; canvass, comment, discuss, examine, publish, review, scrutinize.

venture *vb* adventure, dare, hazard, imperil, jeopardize, presume, risk, speculate, test, try, undertake. * *n* adventure, chance, hazard, jeopardy, peril, risk, speculation, stake.

venturesome *adj* adventurous, bold, courageous, daring, doughty, enterprising, fearless, foolhardy, intrepid, presumptuous, rash, venturous.

veracious *adj* reliable, straightforward, true, trustworthy, truthful; credible, genuine, honest, unfeigned.

veracity *n* accuracy, candour, correctness, credibility, exactness, fidelity, frankness, honesty, ingenuousness, probity, sincerity, trueness, truth, truthfulness.

verbal *adj* nuncupative, oral, spoken, unwritten.

verbose *adj* diffusive, long-winded, loquacious, talkative, wordy.

verdant *adj* fresh, green, verdure, verdurous; green, inexperienced, raw, unsophisticated.

verdict *n* answer, decision, finding, judgement, opinion, sentence.

verge *vb* bear, incline, lean, slope, tend; approach, border, skirt. * *n* mace, rod, staff; border, boundary, brink, confine, edge, extreme, limit, margin; edge, eve, point.

verification *n* authentication, attestation, confirmation, corroboration.

verify *vb* attest, authenticate, confirm, corroborate, prove, substantiate.

verily *adv* absolutely, actually, confidently, indeed, positively, really, truly.

verity *n* certainty, reality, truth, truthfulness.

vermicular *adj* convoluted, flexuose, flexuous, meandering, serpentine, sinuous, tortuous, twisting, undulating, waving, winding, wormish, wormlike.

vernacular *adj* common, indigenous, local, mother, native, vulgar. * *n* cant, dialect, jargon, patois, speech.

versatile *adj* capricious, changeable, erratic, mobile, variable; fickle, inconstant, mercurial, unsteady; adaptable, protean, plastic, varied.

versed *adj* able, accomplished, acquainted, clever, conversant, practised, proficient, qualified, skilful, skilled, trained.

version *n* interpretation, reading, rendering, translation.

vertex *n* apex, crown, height, summit, top, zenith.

vertical *adj* erect, perpendicular, plumb, steep, upright.

vertiginous *adj* rotatory, rotary, whirling; dizzy, giddy.

vertigo *n* dizziness, giddiness.

verve *n* animation, ardour, energy, enthusiasm, force, rapture, spirit.

very *adv* absolutely, enormously, excessively, hugely, remarkably, surpassingly. * *adj* actual, exact, identical, precise, same; bare, mere, plain, pure, simple.

vesicle *n* bladder, blister, cell, cyst, follicle.

vest *vb* clothe, cover, dress, envelop; endow, furnish, invest. * *n* dress, garment, robe, vestment, vesture, waistcoat.

vestibule *n* anteroom, entrance hall, lobby, porch.

vestige *n* evidence, footprint, footstep, mark, record, relic, sign, token.

veteran *adj* adept, aged, experienced, disciplined, seasoned, old. * *n* campaigner, old soldier; master, past master, old-timer, old-stager.

veto *vb* ban, embargo, forbid, interdict, negate, prohibit. * *n* ban, embargo, interdict, prohibition, refusal.

vex *vb* annoy, badger, bother, chafe, cross, distress, gall, harass, harry, hector, molest, perplex, pester, plague, tease, torment, trouble, roil, spite, worry; affront, displease, fret, irk, irritate, nettle, offend, provoke; agitate, disquiet, disturb.

vexation *n* affliction, agitation, chagrin, discomfort, displeasure, disquiet, distress, grief, irritation, pique, sorrow, trouble; annoyance, curse, nuisance, plague, torment; damage, troubling, vexing.

vexed *adj* afflicted, agitated, annoyed, bothered, disquieted, harassed, irritated, perplexed, plagued, provoked, troubled, worried.

vibrate *vb* oscillate, sway, swing, undulate, wave; impinge, quiver, sound, thrill; fluctuate, hesitate, vacillate, waver.

vibration *n* nutation, oscillation, vibration.

vicarious *adj* commissioned, delegated, indirect, second-hand, substituted.

vice *n* blemish, defect, failing, fault, imperfection, infirmity; badness, corruption, depravation, depravity, error, evil, immorality, iniquity, laxity, obliquity, sin, viciousness, vileness, wickedness.

vicinity *n* nearness, proximity; locality, neighbourhood, vicinage.

vicious *adj* abandoned, atrocious, bad, corrupt, degenerate, demoralized, depraved, devilish, diabolical, evil, flagrant, hellish, immoral, iniquitous, mischievous, profligate, shameless, sinful, unprincipled, wicked; malicious, spiteful, venomous; foul, impure; debased, faulty; contrary, refractory.

viciousness *n* badness, corruption, depravity, immorality, profligacy.

vicissitude *n* alteration, interchange; change, fluctuation, mutation, revolution, variation.

victim *n* martyr, sacrifice, sufferer; prey; cat's-paw, cull, cully, dupe, gull, gudgeon, puppet.

victimize *vb* bamboozle, befool, beguile, cheat, circumvent, cozen, deceive, defraud, diddle, dupe, fool, gull, hoax, hoodwink, overreach, swindle, trick.

victor *n* champion, conqueror, vanquisher, winner.

victorious *adj* conquering, successful, triumphant, winning.

victory *n* achievement, conquest, mastery, triumph.

victuals *npl* comestibles, eatables, fare, food, meat, provisions, repast, sustenance, viands.

vie *vb* compete, contend, emulate, rival, strive.

view *vb* behold, contemplate, eye, inspect, scan, survey; consider, inspect, regard, study. * *n* inspection, observation, regard, sight; outlook, panorama, perspective, prospect, range, scene, survey, vista; aim, intent, intention, design, drift, object, purpose, scope; belief, conception, impression, idea, judgement, notion, opinion, sentiment, theory; appearance, aspect, show.

vigilance *n* alertness, attentiveness, carefulness, caution, circumspection, observance, watchfulness.

vigilant *adj* alert, attentive, careless, cautious, circumspect, unsleeping, wakeful, watchful.

vigorous *adj* lusty, powerful, strong; active, alert, cordial, energetic, forcible, strenuous, vehement, vivid, virile; brisk, hale, hardy, robust, sound, sturdy, healthy; fresh, flourishing; bold, emphatic, impassioned, lively, nervous, piquant, pointed, severe, sparkling, spirited, trenchant.

vigour *n* activity, efficacy, energy, force, might, potency, power, spirit, strength; bloom, elasticity, haleness, health, heartiness, pep, punch, robustness, soundness, thriftiness, tone, vim, vitality; enthusiasm, freshness, fire, intensity, liveliness, piquancy, strenuousness, vehemence, verve, raciness.

vile *adj* abject, base, beastly, beggarly, brutish, contemptible, despicable, disgusting, grovelling, ignoble, low, odious, paltry, pitiful, repulsive, scurvy, shabby, slavish, sorry, ugly; bad, evil, foul, gross, impure, iniquitous, lewd, obscene, sinful, vicious, wicked; cheap, mean, miserable, valueless, worthless.

vilify *vb* abuse, asperse, backbite, berate, blacken, blemish, brand, calumniate, decry, defame, disparage, lampoon, libel, malign, revile, scandalize, slander, slur, traduce, vituperate.

villain *n* blackguard, knave, miscreant, rascal, reprobate, rogue, ruffian, scamp, scapegrace, scoundrel.

villainous *adj* base, mean, vile; corrupt, depraved, knavish, unprincipled, wicked; atrocious, heinous, outrageous, sinful; mischievous, sorry.

vindicate *vb* defend, justify, uphold; advocate, avenge, assert, maintain, right, support.

vindication *n* apology, excuse, defence, justification.

vindictive *adj* avenging, grudgeful, implacable, malevolent, malicious, malignant, retaliative, revengeful, spiteful, unforgiving, unrelenting, vengeful.

violate *vb* hurt, injure; break, disobey, infringe, invade; desecrate, pollute, profane; abuse, debauch, defile, deflower, outrage, ravish, transgress.

violent *adj* boisterous, demented, forceful, forcible, frenzied, furious, high, hot, impetuous, insane, intense, stormy, tumultuous, turbulent, vehement, wild; fierce, fiery, fuming, heady, heavy, infuriate, passionate, obstreperous, strong, raging, rampant, rank, rapid, raving, refractory, roaring, rough, tearing, towering, ungovernable; accidental, unnatural; desperate, extreme, outrageous, unjust; acute, exquisite, poignant, sharp.

virago *n* amazon, brawler, fury, shrew, tartar, vixen.

virgin *adj* chaste, maidenly, modest, pure, undefiled, stainless, unpolluted, vestal, virginal; fresh, maiden, untouched, unused. * *n* celibate, damsel, girl, lass, maid, maiden.

virile *adj* forceful, manly, masculine, robust, vigorous.

virtual *adj* constructive, equivalent, essential, implicit, implied, indirect, practical, substantial.

virtue *n* chastity, goodness, grace, morality, purity; efficacy, excellence, honesty, integrity, justice, probity, quality, rectitude, worth.

virtuous *adj* blameless, equitable, exemplary, excellent, good, honest, moral, noble, righteous, upright, worthy; chaste, continent, immaculate, innocent, modest, pure, undefiled; efficacious, powerful.

virulent *adj* deadly, malignant, poisonous, toxic, venomous; acrid, acrimonious, bitter, caustic.

visage *n* aspect, countenance, face, guise, physiognomy, semblance.

viscera *n* bowels, entrails, guts, intestines.

viscous *adj* adhesive, clammy, glutinous, ropy, slimy, sticky, tenacious.

visible *adj* observable, perceivable, perceptible, seeable, visual; apparent, clear, conspicuous, discoverable, distinct, evident, manifest, noticeable, obvious, open, palpable, patent, plain, revealed, unhidden, unmistakable.

vision *n* eyesight, seeing, sight; eyeshot, ken; apparition, chimera, dream, ghost, hallucination, illusion, phantom, spectre.

visionary *adj* imaginative, impractical, quixotic, romantic; chimerical, dreamy, fancied, fanciful, fantastic, ideal, illusory, imaginary, romantic, shadowy, unsubstantial, utopian, wild. * *n* dreamer, enthusiast, fanatic, idealist, optimist, theorist, zealot.

vital *adj* basic, cardinal, essential, indispensable, necessary, needful; animate, alive, existing, life-giving, living; paramount.

vitality *n* animation, life, strength, vigour, virility.

vitiate *vb* adulterate, contaminate, corrupt, debase, defile, degrade, deprave, deteriorate, impair, infect, injure, invalidate, poison, pollute, spoil.

vitiation *n* adulteration, corruption, degeneracy, degeneration, degradation, depravation, deterioration, impairment, injury, invalidation, perversion, pollution, prostitution.

vituperate *vb* abuse, berate, blame, censure, denounce, overwhelm, rate, revile, scold, upbraid, vilify.

vituperation *n* abuse, blame, censure, invective, reproach, railing, reviling, scolding, upbraiding.

vivacious *adj* active, animated, breezy, brisk, buxom, cheerful, frolicsome, gay, jocund, light-hearted, lively, merry, mirthful, spirited, sportive, sprightly.

vivacity *n* animation, cheer, cheerfulness, gaiety, liveliness, sprightliness.

vivid *adj* active, animated, bright, brilliant, clear, intense, fresh, lively, living, lucid, quick, sprightly, strong; expressive, graphic, striking, telling.

vivify *vb* animate, arouse, awake, quicken, vitalize.

vixen *n* brawler, scold, shrew, spitfire, tartar, virago.

vocabulary *n* dictionary, glossary, lexicon, wordbook; language, terms, words.

vocation *n* call, citation, injunction, summons; business, calling, employment, occupation, profession, pursuit, trade.

vociferate *vb* bawl, bellow, clamour, cry, exclaim, rant, shout, yell.

vociferous *adj* blatant, clamorous, loud, noisy, obstreperous, ranting, stunning, uproarious.

vogue *adj* fashionable, modish, stylish, trendy. * *n* custom, fashion, favour, mode, practice, repute, style, usage, way.

voice *vb* declare, express, say, utter. * *n* speech, tongue, utterance; noise, notes, sound; opinion, option, preference, suffrage, vote; accent, articulation, enunciation, inflection, intonation, modulation, pronunciation, tone; expression, language, words.

void *vb* clear, eject, emit, empty, evacuate. * *adj* blank, empty, hollow, vacant; clear, destitute, devoid, free, lacking, wanting, without; inept, ineffectual, invalid, nugatory, null; imaginary, unreal, vain. * *n* abyss, blank, chasm, emptiness, hole, vacuum.

volatile *adj* gaseous, incoercible; airy, buoyant, frivolous, gay, jolly, lively, sprightly, vivacious; capricious, changeable, fickle, flighty, flyaway, giddy, harebrained, inconstant, light-headed, mercurial, reckless, unsteady, whimsical, wild.

volition *n* choice, determination, discretion, option, preference, will.

volley *n* fusillade, round, salvo; blast, burst, discharge, emission, explosion, outbreak, report, shower, storm.

voluble *adj* fluent, garrulous, glib, loquacious, talkative.

volume *n* book, tome; amplitude, body, bulk, compass, dimension, size, substance, vastness; fullness, power, quantity.

voluminous *adj* ample, big, bulky, full, great, large; copious, diffuse, discursive, flowing.

voluntary *adj* free, spontaneous, unasked, unbidden, unforced; deliberate, designed, intended, purposed; discretionary, optional, willing.

volunteer *vb* offer, present, proffer, propose, tender.

voluptuary *n* epicure, hedonist, sensualist.

voluptuous *adj* carnal, effeminate, epicurean, fleshy, licentious, luxurious, sensual, sybaritic.

vomit *vb* discharge, eject, emit, puke, regurgitate, spew, throw up.

voracious *adj* devouring, edacious, greedy, hungry, rapacious, ravenous.

vortex *n* eddy, maelstrom, whirl, whirlpool.

votary *adj* devoted, promised. * *n* adherent, devotee, enthusiast, follower, supporter, votarist, zealot.

vote *vb* ballot, elect, opt, return; judge, pronounce, propose, suggest. * *n* ballot, franchise, poll, referendum, suffrage, voice.

vouch *vb* affirm, asseverate, attest, aver, declare, guarantee, support, uphold, verify, warrant.

vouchsafe *vb* accord, cede, deign, grant, stoop, yield.

vow *vb* consecrate, dedicate, devote; asseverate. * *n* oath, pledge, promise.

voyage *vb* cruise, journey, navigate, ply, sail. * *n* crossing, cruise, excursion, journey, passage, sail, trip.

vulgar *adj* base-born, common, ignoble, lowly, plebeian; boorish, cheap, coarse, discourteous, flashy, homespun, garish, gaudy, ill-bred, inelegant, loud, rustic, showy, tawdry, uncultivated, unrefined; general, ordinary, popular, public; base, broad, loose, low, gross, mean, ribald, vile; inelegant, unauthorized.

vulgarity *n* baseness, coarseness, grossness, meanness, rudeness.

vulnerable *adj* accessible, assailable, defenceless, exposed, weak.

W

waddle *vb* toddle, toggle, waggle, wiggle, wobble.

waft *vb* bear, carry, convey, float, transmit, transport. * *n* breath, breeze, draught, puff.

wag[1] *vb* shake, sway, waggle; oscillate, vibrate, waver; advance, move, progress, stir. * *n* flutter, nod, oscillation, vibration.

wag[2] *n* humorist, jester, joker, wit.

wage *vb* bet, hazard, lay, stake, wager; conduct, undertake.

wager *vb* back, bet, gamble, lay, pledge, risk, stake. * *n* bet, gamble, pledge, risk, stake.

wages *npl* allowance, compensation, earnings, emolument, hire, pay, payment, remuneration, salary, stipend.

waggish *adj* frolicsome, gamesome, mischievous, roguish, tricksy; comical, droll, facetious, funny, humorous, jocular, jocose, merry, sportive.

wagon *n* cart, lorry, truck, van, waggon, wain.

wail *vb* bemoan, deplore, lament, mourn; cry, howl, weep. * *n* complaint, cry, lamentation, moan, wailing.

waist *n* bodice, corsage, waistline.

wait *vb* delay, linger, pause, remain, rest, stay, tarry; attend, minister, serve; abide, await, expect, look for. * *n* delay, halt, holdup, pause, respite, rest, stay, stop.

waiter, waitress *n* attendant, lackey, servant, servitor, steward, valet.

waive *vb* defer, forgo, surrender, relinquish, remit, renounce; desert, reject.

wake[1] *vb* arise, awake, awaken; activate, animate, arouse, awaken, excite, kindle, provoke, stimulate. * *n* vigil, watch, watching.

wake[2] *n* course, path, rear, track, trail, wash.

wakeful *adj* awake, sleepless, restless; alert, observant, vigilant, wary, watchful.

wale *n* ridge, streak, stripe, welt, whelk.

walk *vb* advance, depart, go, march, move, pace, saunter, step, stride, stroll, tramp. * *n* amble, carriage, gait, step; beat, career, course, department, field, province; conduct, procedure; alley, avenue, cloister, esplanade, footpath, path, pathway, pavement, promenade, range, sidewalk, way; constitutional, excursion, hike, ramble, saunter, stroll, tramp, turn.

wall *n* escarp, parapet, plane, upright.

wallet *n* bag, knapsack, pocketbook, purse, sack.

wan *adj* ashen, bloodless, cadaverous, colourless, haggard, pale, pallid.

wand *n* baton, mace, truncheon, sceptre.

wander *vb* forage, prowl, ramble, range, roam, rove, stroll; deviate, digress, straggle, stray; moon, rave. * *n* amble, cruise, excursion, ramble, stroll.

wane *vb* abate, decrease, ebb, subside; decline, fail, sink. * *n* decrease, diminution, lessening; decay, declension, decline, failure.

want *vb* crave, desire, need, require, wish; fail, lack, neglect, omit. * *n* absence, defect, default, deficiency, lack; defectiveness, failure, inadequacy, insufficiency, meagreness, paucity, poverty, scantiness, scarcity, shortness; requirement; craving, desire, longing, wish; destitution, distress, indigence, necessity, need, penury, poverty, privation, straits.

wanton *vb* caper, disport, frisk, frolic, play, revel, romp, sport; dally, flirt, toy, trifle. * *adj* free, loose, unchecked, unrestrained, wandering; abounding, exuberant, luxuriant, overgrown, rampant; airy, capricious, coltish, frisky, playful, skittish, sportive; dissolute, irregular, licentious, loose; carnal, immoral, incontinent, lascivious, lecherous, lewd, libidinous, light, lustful, prurient, salacious, unchaste; careless, gratuitous, groundless, heedless, inconsiderate, needless, perverse, reckless, wayward, wilful. * *n* baggage, flirt, harlot, light-o'-love, prostitute, rake, roué, slut, whore.

war *vb* battle, campaign, combat, contend, crusade, engage, fight, strive. * *n* contention, enmity, hostility, strife, warfare.

warble *vb* sing, trill, yodel. * *n* carol, chant, hymn, hum.

ward *vb* guard, watch; defend, fend, parry, protect, repel. * *n* care, charge, guard, guardianship, watch; defender, guardian, keeper, protector, warden; custody; defence, garrison, protection; minor, pupil; district, division, precinct, quarter; apartment, cubicle.

warehouse *n* depot, magazine, repository, store, storehouse.

wares *npl* commodities, goods, merchandise, movables.

warfare *n* battle, conflict, contest, discord, engagement, fray, hostilities, strife, struggle, war.

warily *adv* carefully, cautiously, charily, circumspectly, heedfully, watchfully, vigilantly.

wariness *n* care, caution, circumspection, foresight, thought, vigilance.

warlike *adj* bellicose, belligerent, combative,
hostile, inimical, martial, military, soldierly, watchful.

warm *vb* heat, roast, toast; animate, chafe, excite, rouse. * *adj* lukewarm, tepid; genial, mild, pleasant, sunny; close, muggy, oppressive; affectionate, ardent, cordial, eager, earnest, enthusiastic, fervent, fervid, glowing, hearty, hot, zealous; excited, fiery, flushed, furious, hasty, keen, lively, passionate, quick, vehement, violent.

warmth *n* glow, tepidity; ardour, fervency, fervour, zeal; animation, cordiality, eagerness, earnestness, enthusiasm, excitement, fervency, fever, fire, flush, heat, intensity, passion, spirit, vehemence.

warn *vb* caution, forewarn; admonish, advise; apprise, inform, notify; bid, call, summon.

warning *adj* admonitory, cautionary, cautioning, monitory. * *n* admonition, advice, caveat, caution, monition; information, notice; augury, indication, intimation, omen, portent, presage, prognostic, sign, symptom; call, summons; example, lesson, sample.

warp *vb* bend, bias, contort, deviate, distort, pervert, swerve, turn, twist. * *n* bent, bias, cast, crook, distortion, inclination, leaning, quirk, sheer, skew, slant, slew, swerve, twist, turn.

warrant *vb* answer for, certify, guarantee, secure; affirm, assure, attest, avouch, declare, justify, state; authorize, justify, license, maintain, sanction, support, sustain, uphold. * *n* guarantee, pledge, security, surety, warranty; authentication, authority, commission, verification; order, pass, permit, summons, subpoena, voucher, writ.

warrantable *adj* admissible, allowable, defensible, justifiable, lawful, permissible, proper, right, vindicable.

warrior *n* champion, captain, fighter, hero, soldier.

wary *adj* careful, cautious, chary, circumspect, discreet, guarded, heedful, prudent, scrupulous, vigilant, watchful.

wash *vb* purify, purge; moisten, wet; bathe, clean, flush, irrigate, lap, lave, rinse, sluice; colour, stain, tint. * *n* ablution, bathing, cleansing, lavation, washing; bog, fen, marsh, swamp, quagmire; bath, embrocation, lotion; laundry, washing.

washy *adj* damp, diluted, moist, oozy, sloppy, thin, watery, weak; feeble, jejune, pointless, poor, spiritless, trashy, trumpery, unmeaning, vapid, worthless.

waspish *adj* choleric, fretful, irascible, irritable, peevish, petulant, snappish, testy, touchy; slender, slim, small-waisted.

waste *vb* consume, corrode, decrease, diminish, emaciate, wear; absorb, deplete, devour, dissipate, drain, empty, exhaust, expend, lavish, lose, misspend, misuse, scatter, spend, squander; demolish, desolate, destroy, devastate, devour, dilapidate, harry, pillage, plunder, ravage, ruin, scour, strip; damage, impair, injure; decay, dwindle, perish, wither. * *adj* bare, desolated, destroyed, devastated, empty, ravaged, ruined, spoiled, stripped, void; dismal, dreary, forlorn; abandoned, bare, barren, uncultivated, unimproved, uninhabited, untilled, wild; useless, valueless, worthless; exuberant, superfluous. * *n* consumption, decrement, diminution, dissipation, exhaustion, expenditure, loss, wasting; destruction, dispersion, extravagance, loss, squandering, wanton; decay, desolation, destruction, devastation, havoc, pillage, ravage, ruin; chaff, debris, detritus, dross, excrement, husks, junk, matter, offal, refuse, rubbish, trash, wastrel, worthlessness; barrenness, desert, expanse, solitude, wild, wilderness.

wasteful *adj* destructive, ruinous; extravagant, improvident, lavish, prodigal, profuse, squandering, thriftless, unthrifty.

watch *vb* attend, guard, keep, oversee, protect, superintend, tend; eye, mark, observe. * *n* espial, guard, outlook, wakefulness, watchfulness, watching, vigil, ward; alertness, attention, inspection, observation, surveillance; guard, picket, sentinel, sentry, watchman; pocket watch, ticker, timepiece, wristwatch.

watchful *adj* alert, attentive, awake, careful, circumspect, guarded, heedful, observant, vigilant, wakeful, wary.

watchword *n* catchword, cry, motto, password, shibboleth, word.

waterfall *n* cascade, cataract, fall, linn.

watery *adj* diluted, thin, waterish, weak; insipid, spiritless, tasteful, vapid; moist, wet.

wave *vb* float, flutter, heave, shake, sway, undulate, wallow; brandish, flaunt, flourish, swing; beckon, signal. * *n* billow, bore, breaker, flood, flush, ripple, roll, surge, swell, tide, undulation; flourish, gesture, sway; convolution, curl, roll, unevenness.

waver *vb* flicker, float, undulate, wave; reel, totter; falter, fluctuate, flutter, hesitate, oscillate, quiver, vacillate.

wax *vb* become, grow, increase, mount, rise.

way *n* advance, journey, march, progression, transit, trend; access, alley, artery, avenue, beat, channel, course, highroad, highway, passage, path, road, route, street, track, trail; fashion, manner, means, method, mode, system; distance, interval, space, stretch; behaviour, custom, form, guise, habit, habitude, practice, process, style, usage; device, plan, scheme.

wayfarer *n* itinerant, nomad, passenger, pilgrim, rambler, traveller, walker, wanderer.

wayward *adj* capricious, captious, contrary, forward, headstrong, intractable, obstinate, perverse, refractory, stubborn, unruly, wilful.

weak *adj* debilitated, delicate, enfeebled, enervated, exhausted, faint, feeble, fragile, frail, infirm, invalid, languid, languishing, shaky, sickly, spent, strengthless, tender, unhealthy, unsound, wasted, weakly; accessible, defenceless, unprotected, vulnerable; light, soft, unstressed; boneless, cowardly, infirm; compliant, irresolute, pliable, pliant, undecided, undetermined, unsettled, unstable, unsteady, vacillating, wavering, yielding; childish, foolish, imbecile, senseless, shallow, silly, simple, stupid, weak-minded, witless; erring, foolish, indiscreet, injudicious, unwise; gentle, indistinct, low, small; adulterated, attenuated, diluted, insipid, tasteless, thin, watery; flimsy, frivolous, poor, sleazy, slight, trifling; futile, illogical, inconclusive, ineffective, ineffectual, inefficient, lame, unconvincing, unsatisfactory, unsupported, unsustained, vague, vain; unsafe, unsound, unsubstantial, untrustworthy; helpless, impotent, powerless; breakable, brittle, delicate, frangible; inconsiderable, puny, slender, slight, small.

weaken *vb* cramp, cripple, debilitate, devitalize, enervate, enfeeble, invalidate, relax, sap, shake, stagger, undermine, unman, unnerve, unstring; adulterate, attenuate, debase, depress, dilute, exhaust, impair, impoverish, lessen, lower, reduce.

weakness *n* debility, feebleness, fragility, frailty, infirmity, languor, softness; defect, failing, fault, flaw; fondness, inclination, liking.

weal *n* advantage, good, happiness, interest, profit, utility, prosperity, welfare; ridge, streak, stripe.

wealth *n* assets, capital, cash, fortune, funds, goods, money, possessions, property, riches, treasure; abundance, affluence, opulence, plenty, profusion.

wean *vb* alienate, detach, disengage, withdraw.

wear *vb* bear, carry, don; endure, last; consume, impair, rub, use, waste. * *n* corrosion, deterioration, disintegration, erosion, wear and tear; consumption, use; apparel, array, attire, clothes, clothing, dress, garb, gear.

wearied *adj* apathetic, bored, exhausted, fagged, fatigued, jaded, tired, weary, worn.

weariness *n* apathy, boredom, ennui, exhaustion, fatigue, languor, lassitude, monotony, prostration, sameness, tedium.

wearisome *adj* annoying, boring, dull, exhausting, fatiguing, humdrum, irksome, monotonous, prolix, prosaic, slow, tedious, tiresome, troublesome, trying, uninteresting, vexatious.

weary *vb* debilitate, exhaust, fag, fatigue, harass, jade, tire. * *adj* apathetic, bored, drowsy, exhausted, jaded, spent, tired, worn; irksome, tiresome, wearisome.

weave *vb* braid, entwine, interlace, lace, mat, plait, pleat, twine; compose, construct, fabricate, make.

wed *vb* contract, couple, espouse, marry, unite.

wedding *n* bridal, espousal, marriage, nuptials.

wedlock *n* marriage, matrimony.

ween *vb* fancy, imagine, suppose, think.

weep *vb* bemoan, bewail, complain, cry, lament, sob.

weigh *vb* balance, counterbalance, lift, raise; consider, deliberate, esteem, examine, study.

weight *vb* ballast, burden, fill, freight, load; weigh. * *n* gravity, heaviness, heft, tonnage; burden, load, pressure; consequence, efficacy, emphasis, importance, impressiveness, influence, moment, pith, power, significance, value.

weighty *adj* heavy, massive, onerous, ponderous, unwieldy; considerable, efficacious, forcible, grave, important, influential, serious, significant.

weird *adj* eerie, ghostly, strange, supernatural, uncanny, unearthly, witching.

welcome *vb* embrace, greet, hail, receive. * *adj* acceptable, agreeable, grateful, gratifying, pleasant, pleasing, satisfying. * *n* greeting, reception, salutation.

welfare *n* advantage, affluence, benefit, happiness, profit, prosperity, success, thrift, weal, wellbeing.

well[1] *vb* flow, gush, issue, jet, pour, spring. * *n* fount, fountain, reservoir, spring, wellhead, wellspring; origin, source; hole, pit, shaft.

well[2] *adj* hale, healthy, hearty, sound; fortunate, good, happy, profitable, satisfactory, useful. * *adv* accurately, adequately, correctly, efficiently, properly, suitably; abundantly, considerably, fully, thoroughly; agreeably, commendably, favourably, worthily.

wellbeing *n* comfort, good, happiness, health, prosperity, welfare.
welter *vb* flounder, roll, toss, wallow. * *n* confusion, jumble, mess.
wet *vb* dabble, damp, dampen, dip, drench, moisten, saturate, soak, sprinkle, water. * *adj* clammy, damp, dank, dewy, dripping, humid, moist; rainy, showery, sprinkly. * *n* dampness, humidity, moisture, wetness.
whack *vb, n* bang, beat, rap, strike, thrash, thump, thwack.
wharf *n* dock, pier, quay.
wheedle *vb* cajole, coax, flatter, inveigle, lure.
wheel *vb* gyrate, revolve, roll, rotate, spin, swing, turn, twist, whirl, wind. * *n* circle, revolution, roll, rotation, spin, turn, twirl.
whet *vb* grind, sharpen; arouse, awaken, excite, provoke, rouse, stimulate; animate, inspire, kindle, quicken, warm.
whiff *vb, n* blast, gust, puff.
whim *n* caprice, crotchet, fancy, freak, frolic, humour, notion, quirk, sport, vagary, whimsy, wish.
whimsical *adj* capricious, crotchety, eccentric, erratic, fanciful, frolicsome, odd, peculiar, quaint, singular.
whine *vb* cry, grumble, mewl, moan, snivel, wail, whimper. * *n* complaint, cry, grumble, moan, sob, wail, whimper.
whip *vb* beat, lash, strike; flagellate, flog, goad, horsewhip, scourge, slash; hurt, sting; jerk, snap, snatch, whisk. * *n* bullwhip, cane, crop, horsewhip, knout, lash, scourge, switch, thong.
whipping *n* beating, castigation, dusting, flagellation, flogging, thrashing.
whirl *vb* gyrate, pirouette, roll, revolve, rotate, turn, twirl, twist, wheel. * *n* eddy, flurry, flutter, gyration, rotation, spin, swirl, twirl, vortex.
whit *n* atom, bit, grain, iota, jot, mite, particle, scrap, speck, tittle.
white *adj* argent, canescent, chalky, frosty, hoary, ivory, milky, silver, snowy; grey, pale, pallid, wan; candid, clean, chaste, immaculate, innocent, pure, spotless, unblemished.
whole *adj* all, complete, entire, intact, integral, total, undivided; faultless, firm, good, perfect, strong, unbroken, undivided, uninjured; healthy, sound, well. * *adv* entire, in one. * *n* aggregate, all, amount, ensemble, entirety, gross, sum, total, totality.
wholesome *adj* healthy, healthful, invigorating, nourishing, nutritious, salubrious, salutary; beneficial, good, helpful, improving, salutary; fresh, sound, sweet.
wholly *adv* altogether, completely, entirely, fully, totally, utterly.
whoop *vb* halloo, hoot, roar, shout, yell. * *n* bellow, hoot, roar, shout, yell.
whore *n* bawd, courtesan, drab, harlot, prostitute, streetwalker, strumpet.
wicked *adj* abandoned, abominable, depraved, devilish, godless, graceless, immoral, impious, infamous, irreligious, irreverent, profane, sinful, ungodly, unholy, unprincipled, unrighteous, vicious, vile, worthless; atrocious, bad, black, criminal, dark, evil, heinous, ill, iniquitous, monstrous, nefarious, unjust, villainous.
wide *adj* ample, broad, capacious, comprehensive, distended, expanded, large, spacious, vast; distant, remote; prevalent, rife, widespread. * *adv* completely, farthest, fully.
wield *vb* brandish, flourish, handle, manipulate, ply, work; control, manage, sway, use.
wild *adj* feral, undomesticated, untamed; desert, desolate, native, rough, rude, uncultivated; barbarous, ferocious, fierce, savage, uncivilized; dense, luxuriant, rank; disorderly, distracted, frantic, frenzied, furious, impetuous, irregular, mad, outrageous, raving, turbulent, ungoverned, uncontrolled, violent; dissipated, fast, flighty, foolish, giddy, harebrained, heedless, ill-advised, inconsiderate, reckless, thoughtless, unwise; boisterous, rough, stormy; crazy, extravagant, fanciful, grotesque, imaginary, strange. * *n* desert, waste, wilderness.
wilderness *n* desert, waste, wild.
wilful *adj* cantankerous, contumacious, dogged, headstrong, heady, inflexible, intractable, mulish, obdurate, obstinate, perverse, pigheaded, refractory, self-willed, stubborn, unruly, unyielding; arbitrary, capricious; deliberate, intended, intentional, planned, premeditated.
will *vb* bid, command, decree, direct, enjoin, ordain; choose, desire, elect, wish; bequeath, convey, demise, devise, leave. * *n* decision, determination, resoluteness, resolution, self-reliance; desire, disposition, inclination, intent, pleasure, purpose, volition, wish; behest, command, decree, demand, direction, order, request, requirement.
willing *adj* adaptable, amenable, compliant, desirous, disposed, inclined, minded; deliberate, free, intentional, spontaneous, unasked, unbidden, voluntary; cordial, eager, forward, prompt, ready.
willingly *adv* cheerfully, gladly, readily, spontaneously, voluntarily.
wily *adj* arch, artful, crafty, crooked, cunning, deceitful, designing, diplomatic, foxy, insidious, intriguing, politic, sly, subtle, treacherous, tricky.
win *vb* accomplish, achieve, acquire, catch, earn, effect, gain, gather, get, make, obtain, procure, reach, realize, reclaim, recover; gain, succeed, surpass, triumph; arrive; allure, attract, convince, influence, persuade. * *n* conquest, success, triumph, victory.
wind[1] *n* air, blast, breeze, draught, gust, hurricane, whiff, zephyr; breath, breathing, expiration, inspiration, respiration; flatulence, gas, windiness.
wind[2] *vb* coil, crank, encircle, involve, reel, roll, turn, twine, twist; bend, curve, meander, zigzag. * *n* bend, curve, meander, twist, zigzag.
winding *adj* circuitous, devious, flexuose, flexuous, meandering, serpentine, tortuous, turning, twisting. * *n* bend, curve, meander, turn, twist.
windy *adj* breezy, blowy, blustering, boisterous, draughty, gusty, squally, stormy, tempestuous; airy, empty, hollow, inflated. **winning** *adj* alluring, attractive, bewitching, brilliant, captivating, charming, dazzling, delightful, enchanting, engaging, fascinating, lovely, persuasive, pleasing, prepossessing; conquering, triumphant, victorious.
winnow *vb* cull, glean, divide, fan, part, select, separate, sift.
winsome *adj* blithe, blithesome, bonny, buoyant, charming, cheerful, debonair, jocund, light-hearted, lively, lovable, merry, pleasant, sportive, winning.
wintry *adj* arctic, boreal, brumal, cold, frosty, icy, snowy.
wipe *vb* clean, dry, mop, rub. * *n* mop, rub, blow, hit, strike; gibe, jeer, sarcasm, sneer, taunt.
wisdom *n* depth, discernment, far-sightedness, foresight, insight, judgement, judiciousness, prescience, profundity, prudence, sagacity, sapience, sense, solidity, understanding, wiseness; attainment, edification, enlightenment, erudition, information, knowledge, learning, lore, scholarship; reason.
wise *adj* deep, discerning, enlightened, intelligent, judicious, penetrating, philosophical, profound, rational, seasonable, sensible, sage, sapient, solid, sound; erudite, informed, knowing, learned, scholarly; crafty, cunning, designing, foxy, politic, sly, subtle, wary, wily.
wish *vb* covet, desire, hanker, list, long; bid, command, desire, direct, intend, mean, order, want. * *n* behest, desire, intention, mind, pleasure, want, will; craving, desire, hankering, inclination, liking, longing, want, yearning.
wistful *adj* contemplative, engrossed, meditative, musing, pensive, reflective, thoughtful; desirous, eager, earnest, longing.
wit *n* genius, intellect, intelligence, reason, sense, understanding; brightness, banter, cleverness, drollery, facetiousness, fun, humour, jocularity, piquancy, point, raillery, satire, sparkle, whim; conceit, epigram, jest, joke, pleasantry, quip, quirk, repartee, sally, witticism; humorist, joker, wag.
witch *n* charmer, enchantress, fascinator, sorceress; crone, hag, sibyl.
witchcraft *n* conjuration, enchantment, magic, necromancy, sorcery, spell.
withdraw *vb* abstract, deduct, remove, retire, separate, sequester, sequestrate, subduct, subtract; disengage, wean; abjure, recall, recant, relinquish, resign, retract, revoke; abdicate, decamp, depart, dissociate, retire, shrink, vacate.
wither *vb* contract, droop, dry, sear, shrivel, wilt, wizen; decay, decline, languish, pine, waste.
withhold *vb* check, detain, hinder, repress, restrain, retain, suppress.
withstand *vb* confront, defy, face, oppose, resist.
witless *adj* daft, dull, foolish, halfwitted, obtuse, senseless, shallow, silly, stupid, unintelligent.

witness *vb* corroborate, mark, note, notice, observe, see. * *n* attestation, conformation, corroboration, evidence, proof, testimony; beholder, bystander, corroborator, deponent, eyewitness, onlooker, spectator, testifier.

witty *adj* bright, clever, droll, facetious, funny, humorous, jocose, jocular, pleasant, waggish; alert, penetrating, quick, sparkling, sprightly.

wizard *n* charmer, diviner, conjurer, enchanter, magician, necromancer, seer, soothsayer, sorcerer.

woe *n* affliction, agony, anguish, bitterness, depression, distress, dole, grief, heartache, melancholy, misery, sorrow, torture, tribulation, trouble, unhappiness, wretchedness.

woeful *adj* afflicted, agonized, anguished, burdened, disconsolate, distressed, melancholy, miserable, mournful, piteous, sad, sorrowful, troubled, unhappy, wretched; afflicting, afflictive, calamitous, deplorable, depressing, disastrous, distressing, dreadful, tragic, tragical, grievous, lamentable, pitiable, saddening.

wonder *vb* admire, gape, marvel; conjecture, ponder, query, question, speculate. * *n* amazement, astonishment, awe, bewilderment, curiosity, marvel, miracle, prodigy, surprise, stupefaction, wonderment.

wonderful *adj* amazing, astonishing, astounding, awe-inspiring, awesome, awful, extraordinary, marvellous, miraculous, portentous, prodigious, startling, stupendous, surprising.

wont *adj* accustomed, customary, familiar, habitual, ordinary, usual. * *n* custom, habit, practice, rule, usage.

wonted *adj* accustomed, common, conventional, customary, everyday, familiar, frequent, habitual, ordinary, regular, usual.

wood *n* coppice, copse, covert, forest, greenwood, grove, spinney, thicket, woodland.

word *vb* express, phrase, put, say, state, term, utter. * *n* expression, name, phrase, term, utterance; account, advice, information, intelligence, message, news, report, tidings; affirmation, assertion, averment, avowal, declaration, statement; conversation, speech; agreement, assurance, engagement, parole, pledge, plight, promise; behest, bidding, command, direction, order, precept; countersign, password, signal, watchword.

wordy *adj* circumlocutory, diffuse, garrulous, inflated, lengthened, long-winded, loquacious, periphrastic, rambling, talkative, tedious, verbose, windy.

work *vb* act, operate; drudge, fag, grind, grub, labour, slave, sweat, toil; move, perform, succeed; aim, attempt, strive, try; effervesce, ferment, leaven, rise; accomplish, beget, cause, effect, engender, manage, originate, produce; exert, strain; embroider, stitch. * *n* exertion, drudgery, grind, labour, pain, toil; business, employment, function, occupation, task; action, accomplishment, achievement, composition, deed, feat, fruit, handiwork, opus, performance, product, production; fabric, manufacture; ferment, leaven; management, treatment.

workman *n* journeyman, employee, labourer, operative, worker, wright; artisan, craftsman, mechanic.

world *n* cosmos, creation, earth, globe, nature, planet, sphere, universe.

worldly *adj* common, earthly, human, mundane, sublunary, terrestrial; carnal, fleshly, profane, secular, temporal; ambitious, grovelling, irreligious, selfish, proud, sordid, unsanctified, unspiritual; sophisticated, worldly-wise.

worry *vb* annoy, badger, bait, beset, bore, bother, chafe, disquiet, disturb, fret, gall, harass, harry, hector, infest, irritate, molest, persecute, pester, plague, tease, torment, trouble, vex. * *n* annoyance, anxiety, apprehensiveness, care, concern, disquiet, fear, misgiving, perplexity, solicitude, trouble, uneasiness, vexation.

worship *vb* adore, esteem, honour, revere, venerate; deify, idolize; aspire, pray. * *n* adoration, devotion, esteem, homage, idolatry, idolizing, respect, reverence; aspiration, exultation, invocation, laud, praise, prayer, supplication.

worst *vb* beat, choke, conquer, crush, defeat, discomfit, foil, master, overpower, overthrow, quell, rout, subdue, subjugate, vanquish.

worth *n* account, character, credit, desert, excellence, importance, integrity, merit, nobleness, worthiness, virtue; cost, estimation, price, value.

worthless *adj* futile, meritless, miserable, nugatory, paltry, poor, trifling, unproductive, unsalable, unserviceable, useless, valueless, wretched; abject, base, corrupt, degraded, ignoble, low, mean, vile.

worthy *adj* deserving, fit, suitable; estimable, excellent, exemplary, good, honest, honourable, reputable, righteous, upright, virtuous. * *n* celebrity, dignitary, luminary, notability, personage, somebody, VIP.

wound *vb* damage, harm, hurt, injure; cut, gall, harrow, irritate, lacerate, pain, prick, stab; annoy, mortify, offend. * *n* blow, hurt, injury; damage, detriment; anguish, grief, pain, pang, torture.

wraith *n* apparition, ghost, phantom, spectre, vision.

wrangle *vb* argue, bicker, brawl, cavil, dispute, jangle, jar, quarrel, squabble, spar, spat. * *n* altercation, argument, bickering, brawl, contest, controversy, jar, quarrel, squabble.

wrap *vb* cloak, cover, encase, envelop, muffle, swathe, wind. * *n* blanket, cape, cloak, cover, overcoat, shawl.

wrath *n* anger, choler, exasperation, fury, heat, resentment, indignation, ire, irritation, offence, passion, rage.

wrathful *adj* angry, enraged, exasperated, furious, hot, indignant, infuriated, irate, mad, passionate, provoked, rageful.

wreak *vb* execute, exercise, indulge, inflict, work.

wreath *n* chaplet, curl, festoon, garland, ring, twine.

wreathe *vb* encircle, festoon, garland, intertwine, surround, twine, twist.

wreck *vb* founder, shipwreck, strand; blast, blight, break, devastate, ruin, spoil. * *n* crash, desolation, destruction, perdition, prostration, ruin, shipwreck, smash, undoing.

wrench *vb* distort, pervert, twist, wrest, wring; sprain, strain; extort, extract. * *n* twist, wring; sprain, strain; monkey wrench, spanner.

wrest *vb* force, pull, strain, twist, wrench, wring.

wrestle *vb* contend, contest, grapple, strive, struggle.

wretch *n* outcast, pariah, pilgarlic, troglodyte, vagabond, victim, sufferer; beggar, criminal, hound, knave, miscreant, rascal, ruffian, rogue, scoundrel, villain.

wretched *adj* afflicted, comfortless, distressed, forlorn, sad, unfortunate, unhappy, woebegone; afflicting, calamitous, deplorable, depressing, pitiable, sad, saddening, shocking, sorrowful; bad, beggarly, contemptible, mean, paltry, pitiful, poor, shabby, sorry, vile, worthless.

wring *vb* contort, twist, wrench; extort, force, wrest; anguish, distress, harass, pain, rack, torture.

wrinkle[1] *vb* cockle, corrugate, crease, gather, pucker, rumple. * *n* cockle, corrugation, crease, crimp, crinkle, crumple, fold, furrow, gather, plait, ridge, rumple.

wrinkle[2] *n* caprice, fancy, notion, quirk, whim; device, tip, trick.

writ *n* decree, order, subpoena, summons.

write *vb* compose, copy, indite, inscribe, pen, scrawl, scribble, transcribe.

writer *n* amanuensis, author, clerk, penman, scribe, secretary.

writhe *vb* contort, distort, squirm, twist, wriggle.

written *adj* composed, indited, inscribed, penned, transcribed.

wrong *vb* abuse, encroach, injure, maltreat, oppress. * *adj* inequitable, unfair, unjust, wrongful; bad, criminal, evil, guilty, immoral, improper, iniquitous, reprehensible, sinful, vicious, wicked; amiss, improper, inappropriate, unfit, unsuitable; erroneous, false, faulty, inaccurate, incorrect, mistaken, untrue. * *adv* amiss, erroneously, falsely, faultily, improperly, inaccurately, incorrectly, wrongly. * *n* foul, grievance, inequity, injury, injustice, trespass, unfairness; blame, crime, dishonesty, evil, guilt, immorality, iniquity, misdeed, misdoing, sin, transgression, unrighteousness, vice, wickedness, wrongdoing; error, falsity.

wroth *adj* angry, enraged, exasperated, furious, incensed, indignant, irate, passionate, provoked, resentful.

wrought *adj* done, effected, performed, worked.

wry *adj* askew, awry, contorted, crooked, distorted, twisted.

xanthous *adj* blonde, fair, light-complexioned, xanthic, yellow.
xiphoid *adj* ensiform, gladiate, sword-like, sword-shaped.
Xmas *n* Christmas, Christmastide, Noel, Yule, Yuletide.
X-ray *n* roentgen ray, röntgen ray.
xylograph *n* cut, woodcut, wood engraving.
xylographer *n* wood engraver.
xylophagous *adj* wood-eating, wood-nourished.

yap *vb* bark, cry, yelp. * *n* bark, cry, yelp.
yard *n* close, compound, court, courtyard, enclosure, garden.
yarn *n* anecdote, boasting, fabrication, narrative, story, tale, untruth.
yawn *vb* dehisce, gape, open wide. * *n* gap, gape, gulf.
yearn *vb* crave, desire, hanker after, long for.
yell *vb* bawl, bellow, cry out, howl, roar, scream, screech, shriek, squeal.* *n* cry, howl, roar, scream, screech, shriek.
yellow *adj* aureate, gilded, gilt, gold, golden, lemon, primrose, saffron, xanthic, xanthous.
yelp *vb* bark, howl, yap; complain, bitch, grouse. * *n* bark, sharp cry, howl.
yet *adv* at last, besides, further, however, over and above, so far, still, thus far, ultimately.* *conj* moreover, nevertheless, notwithstanding, now.
yield *vb* afford, bear, bestow, communicate, confer, fetch, furnish, impart, produce, render, supply; accede, accord, acknowledge, acquiesce, allow, assent, comply, concede, give, grant, permit; abandon, abdicate, cede, forgo, give up, let go, quit, relax, relinquish, resign, submit, succumb, surrender, waive. * *n* earnings, income, output, produce, profit, return, revenue.
yielding *adj* accommodating, acquiescent, affable, compliant, complaisant, easy, manageable, obedient, passive, submissive, unresisting; bending, flexible, flexile, plastic, pliant, soft, supple, tractable; fertile, productive.
yoke *vb* associate, bracket, connect, couple, harness, interlink, join, link, unite. * *n* bond, chain, ligature, link, tie, union; bondage, dependence, enslavement, service, servitude, subjection, vassalage; couple, pair.
yokel *n* boor, bumpkin, countryman, peasant, rustic.
yore *adj* ancient, antique, old, olden. * *n* long ago, long since, olden times.
young *adj* green, ignorant, inexperienced, juvenile, new, recent, youthful. * *n* young people, youth; babies, issue, brood, offspring, progeny, spawn.
youngster *n* adolescent, boy, girl, lad, lass, stripling, youth.
youth *n* adolescence, childhood, immaturity, juvenile, juvenility, minority, nonage, pupillage, wardship; boy, girl, lad, lass, schoolboy, schoolgirl, slip, sprig, stripling, youngster.
youthful *adj* boyish, childish, girlish, immature, juvenile, puerile, young.

Z

zany *adj* comic, comical, crazy, droll, eccentric, funny, imaginative, scatterbrained; clownish, foolish, ludicrous, silly. * *n* buffoon, clown, droll, fool, harlequin, jester, punch.
zeal *n* alacrity, ardour, cordiality, devotedness, devotion, earnestness, eagerness, energy, enthusiasm, fervour, glow, heartiness, intensity, jealousness, passion, soul, spirit, warmth.
zealot *n* bigot, devotee, fanatic, freak, partisan.
zealous *adj* ardent, burning, devoted, eager, earnest, enthusiastic, fervent, fiery, forward, glowing, jealous, keen, passionate, prompt, ready, swift, warm.
zenith *n* acme, apex, climax, culmination, heyday, pinnacle, prime, summit, top, utmost, height.
zero *n* cipher, naught, nadir, nil, nothing, nought.
zest *n* appetite, enjoyment, exhilaration, gusto, liking, piquancy, relish, thrill; edge, flavour, salt, savour, tang, taste; appetizer, sauce.
zone *n* band, belt, cincture, girdle, girth; circuit, clime, region.
zymotic *adj* bacterial, fermentative, germinating.

Appendix 1
Grammar and Usage

Grammar

abstract noun a noun which is the name of a thing that cannot be touched but refers to a quality, concept or idea. Examples of abstract nouns include 'anger', 'beauty', 'courage', 'Christianity', 'danger', 'fear', 'greed', 'hospitality', 'ignorance', 'jealousy', 'kudos', 'loyalty', 'Marxism', 'need', 'obstinacy', 'pain', 'quality', 'resistance', 'safety', 'truth', 'unworthiness', 'vanity', 'wisdom', 'xenophobia', 'youth', 'zeal'. *See also* **concrete noun.**

active voice one of the two voices that verbs are divided into, the other being passive voice. In verbs in the active voice, commonly called **active verbs**, the subject of the verb performs the action described by the verb. Thus, in the sentence 'The boy threw the ball', 'throw' is in the active voice since the subject of the verb (the boy) is doing the throwing. Similarly, in the sentence 'Her mother was driving the car', 'driving' is in the active voice since it is the subject of the sentence (her mother) that is doing the driving. Similarly, in the sentence 'We saw the cows in the field', 'saw' is the active voice since it is the subject of the sentence (we) that is doing the seeing.

adjectival clause a kind of subordinate clause that describes or modifies a noun or pronoun. It is better known by the name relative clause.

adjective a word that describes or gives information about a noun or pronoun. It is said to qualify a noun or pronoun since it limits the word it describes in some way, by making it more specific. Thus, adding the adjective 'red' to 'book' limits 'book', since it means we can forget about books of any other colour. Similarly, adding 'large' to 'book' limits it, since it means we can forget about books of any other size.

Adjectives tell us something about the colour, size, number, quality or classification of a noun or pronoun, as in 'purple curtains', 'jet-black hair', 'bluish eyes'; 'tiny baby', 'large houses', 'biggish gardens', 'massive estates'; five children', 'twenty questions', 'seventy-five books'; 'sad people', 'joyful occasions', 'delicious food', 'civil engineering', 'nuclear physics', 'modern languages', 'Elizabethan drama'.

adverb a word that adds to our information about a verb, as in 'work rapidly'; about an adjective, as in 'an extremely beautiful young woman'; or about another adverb, as in 'sleeping very soundly'. Adverbs are said to modify the words to which they apply since they limit the words in some way and make them more specific. Thus, adding 'slowly' to 'walk', as in 'They walked slowly down the hill', limits the verb 'walk' since all other forms of 'walk', such as 'quickly', 'lazily', etc, have been discarded.

adverbial clause a subordinate clause that modifies the main or principal clause by adding information about time, place, concession, condition, manner, purpose and result, as in 'He left after the meal was over', 'They left it where they found it', 'Wherever I went I saw signs of poverty', 'I have to admire his speech, although I disagree with what he said', 'He does his best at school work even though he is not very good at it', 'Whilst I myself do not like him, I can understand why he is popular', 'We cannot go unless we get permission', 'He looked at her as if he hated her', 'They will have to work long hours in order to make that amount of money', 'They started to run so as to get home before it rained', and 'He fell awkwardly so that he broke his leg.' Adverbial clauses usually follow the main clause but most of them can be put in front of the main clause for reasons of emphasis or style.

agent noun a noun that refers to someone who is the 'doer' of the action of a verb. It is usually spelt ending in either *-er*, as 'enquirer', or in *-or*, as in 'investigator' and 'supervisor', but frequently either of these endings is acceptable, as 'adviser/advisor'.

agreement or **concord** the agreeing of two or more elements in a clause or sentence, i.e. they take the same number, person or gender. In English the most common form of agreement is that between subject and verb, and this usually involves **number agreement**. This means that singular nouns are usually accompanied by singular verbs, as in 'She looks well', 'He is working late' and 'The boy has passed the exam', and that plural nouns are usually accompanied by plural verbs, as in 'They look well', 'They are working late' and 'The boys have passed the exam'.

Problems arise when the noun in question can be either singular or plural, for example, 'audience', 'committee', 'crowd', 'family', 'government', 'group'. Such nouns take a singular verb if the user is regarding the people or items referred to by the noun as a group, as in 'The family is moving house', or as individuals, as in 'The family are quarrelling over where to go on holiday'.

Compound subjects, that is two or more nouns acting as the subject, whether singular or plural, joined with 'and', are used with a plural noun, as in 'My friend and I are going to the cinema tonight' and 'James and John are leaving today', unless the two nouns together represent a single concept, as 'brandy and soda', in which case the verb is in the singular, as in 'Brandy and soda is his favourite drink' and 'cheese and pickle' in 'Cheese and pickle is the only sandwich filling available'.

Indefinite pronouns such as 'anyone', 'everyone', 'no one', 'someone', 'either', 'neither' are singular and should be followed by a singular verb, as in 'Each of the flats is self-contained', 'Everyone is welcome', 'No one is allowed in without a ticket' and 'Neither is quite what I am looking for'.

Agreement with reference to both number and gender affects pronouns, as in 'She blames herself', 'He could have kicked himself' and 'They asked themselves why they had got involved'. Problems arise when the pronoun is indefinite and so the sex of the person is unspecified. Formerly in such cases the masculine pronouns were assumed to be neutral and so 'Each of the pupils was asked to hand in his work' was considered quite acceptable. The rise of feminism has led to a questioning of this assumption and alternatives have been put forward. These include 'Each of the pupils was asked to hand in his/her (or his or her) work', but some people feel that this is clumsy. Another alternative is 'Each of the pupils was asked to hand in their work'. Although it is ungrammatical, this convention is becoming quite acceptable in modern usage. To avoid both the clumsiness of the former and the ungrammatical nature of the latter, it is possible to cast the whole sentence in the plural, as in 'All the pupils were asked to hand in their work'.

also an adverb that should not be used as a conjunction instead of 'and'. Thus sentences such as 'Please send me some apples, also some pears' are grammatically incorrect.

although a conjunction that is used to introduce a subordinate adverbial clause of concession, as in 'They are very happy although they are poor', meaning 'Despite the fact they are poor they are happy'. 'Though' or 'even though' can be substituted for 'although', as in 'they are very happy even though they are poor'. *See* **adverbial clause** and **conjunction.**

and a conjunction that is called a coordinating conjunction because it joins elements of language that are of equal status. The elements may be words, as in 'cows and horses', 'John and James', 'provide wine and beer'; phrases, as in 'working hard and playing hard' and 'trying to look after her children and her elderly parents'; clauses, as in 'John has decided to emigrate and his brother has decided to join him' and 'He has lost his job and he now has no money'. When a coordinating conjunction is used, the subject of the second clause can sometimes be omitted if it is the same as the subject of the first clause, as in 'They have been forced to sell the house and are very sad about it'.

The use of and at the beginning of a sentence is disliked by many people. It should be used only for deliberate effect, as in 'And then he saw the monster', or in informal contexts.

Other coordinating conjunctions include 'but', 'or', 'yet', 'both … and', 'either … or', and 'neither … nor', as in 'poor but honest' and 'the blue dress or the green one'.

antecedent a term that refers to the noun or noun phrase in a main clause to which a relative pronoun in a relative clause refers back. Thus in the sentence 'People who live dangerously frequently get hurt', 'people' is an antecedent. Similarly, in the sentence 'The child identified the old man who attacked her', 'the old man' is the antecedent. *See* **relative clause.**

any a pronoun that may take either a singular or plural verb, depending on the context. When a singular noun is used, a singular verb is used, as in 'Is any of the cloth still usable?' 'Are any of the children coming?' When a plural noun is used, either a plural or a singular verb can be used, the singular verb being more formal, as in 'Did you ask if any of his friends were/was there?'.

anyone a pronoun that should be used with a singular verb, as in 'Has anyone seen my book?' and 'Is anyone coming to the lecture?' To be grammatically correct, anyone should be followed, where relevant, by a singular, not plural, personal pronoun or possessive adjective, but, in order to avoid the sexist 'his', this involves sentences such as 'Has anyone left his/her book?' Because this construction is rather clumsy, there is a growing tendency to use 'their' and be ungrammatical.

apposition a term for a noun or a phrase that provides further information about another noun or phrase. Both nouns and phrases refer to the same person or thing. In the phrase 'Peter Jones, our managing director', ' Peter Jones' and 'our managing director' are said to be in apposition. Similarly, in the phrase 'his cousin, the chairman of the firm', 'his cousin' and 'the chairman of the firm' are in apposition.

as a conjunction that can introduce either a subordinate adverbial clause of time, as in 'I caught sight of him as I was leaving', a subordinate adverbial clause of manner, as in 'He acted as he promised', and a subordinate adverbial clause of reason, as in 'As it's Saturday he doesn't have to work'. it is also used in the as ... as construction, as in 'She doesn't play as well as her sister does'.

The construction may be followed by a subject pronoun or an object pronoun, according to sense. In the sentence 'He plays as well as she', which is a slightly shortened form of 'She plays as well as he does', 'he' is a subject pronoun. In informal English the subject pronoun often becomes an object pronoun, as in 'She plays as well as him'. In the sentence 'They hate their father as much as her', 'her' is an object and the sentence means 'They hate their father as much as they hate her', but in the sentence 'They hate their father as much as she', 'she' is a subject and the sentence means 'They hate their father as much as she does'. *See* **adverbial clause** and **conjunction.**

attributive adjective a term for an adjective that is placed immediately before the noun that it qualifies. In the phrases 'a red dress', 'the big house' and 'an enjoyable evening', 'red', 'big' and 'enjoyable' are attributive adjectives.

auxiliary verb a verb that is used in forming tenses, moods and voices of other verbs. These include 'be', 'do' and 'have'.

The verb 'to be' is used as an auxiliary verb with the *-ing* form of the main verb to form the continuous present tense, as in 'They are living abroad just now' and 'We were thinking of going on holiday but we changed our minds'.

The verb 'to be' is used as an auxiliary verb with the past participle of the main verb to form the passive voice, as in 'Her hands were covered in blood' and 'These toys are manufactured in China'.

The verb 'to have' is used as an auxiliary verb along with the past participle of the main verb to form the perfect tenses, as in 'They have filled the post', 'She had realized her mistake' and 'They wished that they had gone earlier'.

The verb 'to be' is used as an auxiliary verb along with the main verb to form negative sentences, as in 'She is not accepting the job'. The verb 'to do' is used as an auxiliary verb along with the main verb to form negative sentences, as in 'he does not believe her'. It is also used along with the main verb to form questions, as in 'Does he know that she's gone?' and to form sentences in which the verb is emphasized, as in 'She *does* want to go'. *See* **modal verb.**

base the basic uninflected form of a verb. It is found as the infinitive form, as in 'to go' and 'to take', and as the imperative form, as in 'Go away!' and 'Take it!' It is also the form that the verb in the present indicative tense takes, except for the third person singular, as in 'I always go there on a Sunday' and 'They go there regularly.'

be *see* **auxiliary verb.**

because a conjunction that introduces a subordinate adverbial clause of reason, as in 'They sold the house because they are going abroad' and 'Because she is shy she never goes to parties'. It is often used incorrectly in such constructions as 'The reason they went away is because they were bored'. This should be rephrased as either 'The reason that they went away is that they were bored' or 'They went away because they were bored'. *See* **adverbial clause.**

before a word that can either be a preposition, an adverb or a conjunction. As a preposition it means either 'coming or going in front of in time', as in 'He was the chairman before this one', or coming or going in front of in place, as in 'She went before him into the restaurant'. As an adverb it means 'at a time previously', as in 'I told you before' and 'He has been married before'. As a conjunction it introduces a subordinate adverbial clause of time, as in 'The guests arrived before she was ready for them' and 'Before I knew it they had arrived'. *See* **adverbial clause.**

both a word that can be used in several ways: as a determiner, as in 'He broke both his arms' and 'He lost both his sons in the war'; as a pronoun, as in 'I don't mind which house we rent, I like them both' and 'Neither of them work here. The boss sacked them both'; as a conjunction, as in 'He both likes and admires her' and 'She is both talented and honest'. Both can sometimes be followed by 'of'. 'Both their children are grown up' and 'Both of their children are grown up' are both acceptable. Care should be taken to avoid using both unnecessarily. In the sentence 'The two items are both identical', 'both' is redundant.

but a conjunction that connects two opposing ideas. It is a coordinating conjunction in that it connects two elements of equal status. The elements may be words, as in 'not James but John'; phrases, as in 'working hard but not getting anywhere' and 'trying to earn a living but not succeeding'; clauses, as in 'He has arrived but his sister is late', 'I know her but I have never met him' and 'He likes reading but she prefers to watch TV'. It should not be used when no element of contrast is present. Thus the following sentence should be rephrased, at least in formal English—'She is not professionally trained but taught herself'. The two clauses are in fact agreeing, not disagreeing, with each other and so, strictly speaking, but should not be used.

The use of but at the beginning of a sentence is disliked by many people. It should be used only for deliberate effect or in informal contexts.

case one of the forms in the declension of a noun, pronoun or adjective in a sentence.

clause a group of words containing a finite verb which forms part of a compound or complex sentence. See main clause, subordinate clauses, adverbial clause, noun clause and relative clause.

commands these are expressed in the imperative mood, as in 'Be quiet!', 'Stop crying!', 'Go away!'.

common noun simply the name of an ordinary, everyday non-specific thing or person, as opposed to proper nouns, which refer to the names of particular individuals or specific places. Common nouns include 'baby', 'cat', 'girl', 'hat', 'park', 'sofa' and 'table'.

comparison of adjectives this is achieved in two different ways. Some adjectives form their comparative by adding *-er* to the positive or absolute form, as in 'braver', 'louder', 'madder', 'shorter' and 'taller'. Other adjectives form their comparative by using 'more' in conjunction with them, as in 'more beautiful', 'more realistic', 'more suitable' and 'more tactful'. Which is the correct form is largely a matter of length. One-syllable adjectives, such as 'loud', add *-er*, as 'louder'. Two-syllable adjectives sometimes have both forms as a possibility, as in 'gentler/more gentle', and 'cleverest/most clever'. Adjectives with three or more syllables usually form their comparatives with 'more', as in 'more comfortable', 'more gracious', 'more regular' and 'more understanding'. Some adjectives are irregular in their comparative forms, as in 'good/better', 'bad/worse', 'many/more'. Only if they begin with *un-* are they likely to end in *-er*, as in 'untrustworthier'.

Some adjectives by their very definitions do not normally have a comparative form, for example 'unique'.

complement the equivalent of the object in a clause with a linking verb. In the sentence 'Jack is a policeman', 'a policeman' is the complement. In the sentence 'Jane is a good mother', 'a good mother' is the complement' and in the sentence 'His son is an excellent football player', 'an excellent football player' is the complement.

complex sentence a type of sentence in which there is a main clause and one or more subordinate clauses. The sentence 'We went to visit him although he had been unfriendly to us' is a complex sentence since it is composed of a main clause and one subordinate clause ('although he had been unfriendly to us'). The sentence 'We wondered where he had gone and why he was upset' is a complex sentence since it has a main clause and two subordinate clauses ('where he had gone' and 'why he was upset').

compound sentence a type of sentence with more than one clause and linked by a coordinating conjunction, such as 'and' or 'but', as in 'He applied for a new job and got it' and 'I went to the cinema but I didn't enjoy the film'.

concord *see* **number agreement.**

concrete noun the name of something that one can touch, as opposed to an abstract noun, which one cannot. Concrete nouns include 'bag', 'glass', 'plate', 'pot', 'clothes', 'field', 'garden', 'flower', 'potato', 'foot' and 'shoe'. *See* **abstract noun.**

conjunction a word that connects words, clauses or sentences. Conjunctions are of two types. A **coordinating conjunction** joins units of equal status, as in 'bread and butter', 'We asked for some food and we got it'. A **subordinating conjunction** joins a dependent or subordinating clause to main verbs: in 'We asked him why he was there', 'why he was there' is a subordinate clause and thus 'why' is a subordinating conjunction.

content words *see* **function word.**

continuous tenses *see* **tense.**

contraction *see* **abbreviation** in **Style** section.

copula *see* **linking verb.**

copular verb *see* **equative** and **linking verb.**

count noun is the same as countable noun.

countable noun is one which can be preceded by 'a' and can take a plural, as in 'hat/hats', 'flower/flowers'. *See also* **uncountable noun.**

dangling participle a participle that has been misplaced in a sentence. A participle is often used to introduce a phrase that is attached to a subject mentioned later in a sentence, as in 'Worn out by the long walk, she fell to the ground in a faint'. 'Worn out' is the participle and 'she' the subject. Another example is 'Laughing in glee at having won, she ordered some champagne'. In this sentence 'laughing' is the participle and 'she' is the subject. It is a common error for such a participle not to be related to any subject, as in 'Imprisoned in the dark basement, it seemed a long time since she had seen the sun'. This participle is said to be 'dangling'. Another example of a dangling participle is contained in 'Living alone, the days seemed long'.

It is also a common error for a participle to be related to the wrong subject in a sentence, as in 'Painting the ceiling, some of the plaster fell on his head', 'Painting' is the participle and should go with a subject 'he'. Instead it goes with 'some of the plaster'. Participles in this situation are more correctly known as **misrelated participles**, although they are also called dangling participles.

declarative mood the same as **indicative mood.**

declarative sentence a sentence that conveys information. The subject precedes the verb in it. Examples include 'They won the battle', 'He has moved to another town', 'Lots of people go there' and 'There is a new person in charge'.

declension the variation of the form of a noun, adjective or pronoun to show different cases, such as nominative and accusative. It also refers to the class into which such words are placed, as in first declension, second declension, etc. The term applies to languages such as Latin but is not applicable to English.

degree a level of comparison of gradable adjectives. The degrees of comparison comprise **absolute** or **positive**, as in 'big', 'calm', 'dark', 'fair', 'hot', 'late', 'short' and 'tall'; **comparative**, as in 'bigger', 'calmer', 'darker', 'fairest', 'hotter', 'late', 'shorter' and 'taller'; **superlative**, as in 'biggest', 'calmest', 'darkest', 'fairest', 'hottest', 'latest', 'shortest' and 'tallest'.

Degree can also refer to adverbs. Adverbs of degree include 'extremely', 'very', 'greatly', 'rather', 'really', 'remarkably', 'terribly', as in 'an extremely rare case', 'a very old man', 'He's remarkably brave' and 'We're terribly pleased'.

demonstrative determiner a determiner that is used to indicate things or people in relationship to the speaker or writer in space or time. 'This' and 'these' indicate nearness to the speaker, as in 'Will you take this book home?' and 'These flowers are for you'. 'That' and 'those' indicate distance from the speaker, as in 'Get that creature out of here!' and 'Aren't those flowers over there beautiful!'

demonstrative pronoun a pronoun that is similar to a demonstrative determiner except that it stands alone in place of a noun rather than preceding a noun, as in 'I'd like to give you this', 'What is that?', 'These are interesting books' and 'Those are not his shoes'.

dependent clause a clause that cannot stand alone and make sense, unlike an independent or main clause. Dependent clauses depend on the main clause. The term is the same as subordinate clause.

determiner a word that is used in front of a noun or pronoun to tell us something about it. Unlike an adjective, it does not, strictly speaking, 'describe' a noun or pronoun. Determiners are divided into the following categories: **articles** (a, an, the) as in 'a cat', 'an eagle', 'the book'; **demonstrative determiners** (this, that, these, those), as in 'this girl', 'that boy' and 'those people'; **possessive determiners** (my, your, his/her/its, our, their), as in 'my dog', 'her house', 'its colour', 'their responsibility'; **numbers** (one, two, three, four, etc, first, second, third, fourth, etc), as in 'two reasons', 'five ways', 'ten children'; and **indefinite** or **general determiners** (all, another, any, both, each, either, enough, every, few, fewer, less, little, many, most, much, neither, no, other, several, some), as in 'both parents', 'enough food', 'several issues'. Many words used as determiners are also pronouns. *See* **adjective; demonstrative determiner; number.**

direct object the noun, noun phrase, noun or nominal clause or pronoun that is acted upon by the action of a transitive verb. In the sentence 'She bought milk', 'bought' is a transitive verb and 'milk' is a noun which is the direct object. In the sentence 'She bought loads of clothes', 'bought' is a transitive verb and 'loads of clothes' is the direct object. In the sentence 'He knows what happened', 'knows' is a transitive verb and 'what happened' is a 'noun clause' or 'nominal clause'. A direct object is frequently known just as object *See* **indirect object.**

direct speech the reporting of speech by repeating exactly the actual words used by the speaker, as in 'Peter said, ' "I am tired of this." ' *See* **quotation marks** in **Punctuation** section.

distributive pronoun a pronoun that refers to individual members of a class or group. These include 'each', 'either', 'neither', 'none', 'everyone', 'no one'. Such pronouns, where relevant, should be accompanied by singular verbs and singular personal pronouns, as in 'All the men are to be considered for the new posts. Each is to send in his application'. Problems arise when the sex of the noun to which the distributive pronoun refers back is either unknown or unspecified. Formerly it was the convention to treat such nouns as masculine and so to make the distributive pronoun masculine, as in 'All pupils must obey the rule. Nowadays this convention is frequently considered to be unacceptably sexist and attempts have been made to get round this. One solution is to use 'him/her' (or 'him or her'), etc, as in 'The students have received a directive from the professor. Each is to produce his/her essay by tomorrow.' This convention is considered by many people to be clumsy. They prefer to be ungrammatical and use a plural personal pronoun, as in 'The pupils are being punished. Each is to inform their parents'. This use Is becoming increasingly common, even in textbooks. Where possible, it is preferable to rephrase sentences to avoid being either sexist or ungrammatical, as in 'All of the pupils must tell their parents.'

Each, either, etc, in such contexts is fairly formal. In less formal situations 'each of', 'either of', etc, is more usual, as in 'Each of the boys will have to train really hard to win' and 'Either of the dresses is perfectly suitable'.

do an auxiliary verb that is used to form negative forms, as in, 'I do not agree with you', 'They do not always win', 'He does not wish to go' and 'She did not approve of their behaviour'. It is also used to form interrogative forms, as in 'Do you agree?', 'Does she know about it?', 'Did you see that?' and 'I prefer to go by train. Don't you?' Do is also used for emphasis, as in 'I do believe you're right' and 'They do know, don't they?'

double passive a clause that contains two verbs in the passive, the second of which is an infinitive, as in 'The goods are expected to be dispatched some time this week'. Some examples of double passives are clumsy or ungrammatical and should be avoided, as in 'Redundancy notices are proposed to be issued next week'.

dual gender a category of nouns in which there is no indication of gender. The nouns referred to include a range of words used for people, and occasionally animals, which can be of either gender. Unless the gender is specified we do not know the sex of the person referred to. Such words include 'artist', 'author', 'poet', 'singer', 'child', 'pupil', 'student', 'baby', 'parent', 'teacher', 'dog'. Such words give rise to problems with accompanying singular pronouns. *See* **each**.

dummy subject a subject that has no intrinsic meaning but is inserted to maintain a balanced grammatical structure. In the sentences 'It has started to rain' and 'It is nearly midnight', 'it' is a dummy subject. In the sentences 'There is nothing else to say' and 'There is no reason for his behaviour', 'there' is a dummy subject.

dynamic verb a verb with a meaning that indicates action, as 'work' in 'They work hard', 'play' in 'The boys play football at the weekend' and 'come' in 'The girls come here every Sunday'.

each a word that can be either a determiner or a distributive pronoun. Each as a determiner is used before a singular noun and is accompanied by a singular verb, as in 'Each candidate is to reapply', 'Each athlete has a place in the final', 'Each country is represented by a head of state' and 'Each chair was covered in chintz'.

Each of can sometimes be used instead of each, as in 'each of the candidates'. Again a singular verb is used. If the user wishes to emphasize the fact that something is true about every member of a group, **each one of** should be used and not 'every', as in 'Each one of them feels guilty', 'Each one of us has a part to play.

As a pronoun, each also takes a singular verb, as in 'They hate each other. Each is plotting revenge', 'These exercises are not a waste of time. Each provides valuable experience'.

Each, where relevant, should be accompanied by a singular personal pronoun, as in 'Each girl has to provide her own sports equipment', 'Each of the men is to take a turn at working night shift', 'The boys are all well off and each can afford the cost of the holiday' and 'There are to be no exceptions among the women staff. Each one has to work full time'.

Problems arise when the noun that each refers back to is of unknown or unspecified sex. Formerly nouns in such situations were assumed to be masculine, as in 'Each pupil was required to bring his own tennis racket' and 'Each of the students has to provide himself with a tape recorder'. Nowadays such a convention is regarded as being sexist and the use of 'he/her', 'his/her', etc, is proposed, as in 'Each pupil was required to bring his/her (or 'his or her') own tennis racket' and 'Each student has to provide himself/herself (or 'himself or herself') with a tape recorder'. Even in written English such a convention can be clumsy and it is even more so in spoken English. For this reason many people decide to be ungrammatical and opt for 'Each pupil was required to bring their own tennis racket' and 'Each student has to provide themselves with a tape recorder'. This is becoming increasingly acceptable, even in textbooks.

Both sexism and grammatical error can be avoided by rephrasing such sentences, as in 'All pupils are required to bring their own tennis rackets' and 'All students have to provide themselves with tape recorders'.

either a word that can be used as either a determiner or distributive pronoun. As a determiner it is used with a singular verb, as in 'Either hotel is expensive' and 'In principle they are both against the plan but is either likely to vote for it?'

Either of can be used instead of either. It is used before a plural noun, as in 'either of the applicants' and 'either of the houses'. It is accompanied by a singular verb, as in 'Either of the applicants is suitable' and 'Either of the houses is big enough for their family'.

Either can be used as a distributive pronoun and takes a singular verb, as in 'We have looked at both houses and either is suitable' and 'She cannot decide between the two dresses but either is appropriate for the occasion'. This use is rather formal.

In the either ... or construction, a singular verb is used if both subjects are singular, as in 'Either Mary or Jane knows what to do' and 'Either my mother or my father plans to be present'. A plural verb is used if both nouns involved are plural, as in 'Either men or women can play' and 'Either houses or flats are available'.

When a combination of singular and plural subjects is involved, the verb traditionally agrees with the subject that is nearer to it, as in 'Either his parents or his sister is going to come' and 'Either his grandmother or his parents are going to come'.

As a pronoun, either should be used only of two possibilities.

emphasizing adjective an adjective that is used for emphasis. 'Very' is an emphasizing adjective in the sentence 'His very mother dislikes him' and 'own' is an emphasizing adjective in 'He likes to think that he is his own master'.

emphasizing adverb an adverb used for emphasis. 'Really' is an emphasizing adverb in the sentence 'She really doesn't care whether she lives or dies', and 'positively' is an emphasizing adverb in the sentence 'He positively does not want to know anything about it'.

emphatic pronoun a reflexive pronoun that is used for emphasis, as in 'He knows himself that he is wrong', 'She admitted herself that she had made a mistake' and 'The teachers themselves say that the headmaster is too strict'.

ending the final part of a word consisting of an inflection that is added to a base or root word. The '-ren' part of 'children' is an ending, the '-er' of 'poorer' is an ending and the '-ing' of 'falling' is an ending.

equative a term that indicates that one thing is equal to, or the same as, another. The verb 'to be' is sometimes known as an **equative verb** because it links a subject and complement that are equal to each other, as in 'He is a rogue' ('he' and 'rogue' refer to the same person) and 'His wife is a journalist' ('his wife' and 'journalist' refer to the same person). Other equative verbs include 'appear', 'become', 'look', 'remain' and 'seem', as in 'She looks a nasty person' and 'He became a rich man'. Such verbs are more usually known as **copular verbs**.

every a word used with a singular noun to indicate that all the members of a group are being referred to. It takes a singular verb, as in 'Every soldier must report for duty', 'Every machine is to be inspected' and 'Every house has a different view'. Every should also be accompanied, where relevant, by a singular pronoun, as in 'Every boy has his job to do', 'Every girl is to wear a dress' and 'Every machine is to be replaced'. Problems arise when the sex of the noun to which every refers is unknown or unspecified. Formerly it was the custom to assume such a noun to be masculine and to use masculine pronouns, as in 'Every pupil is to behave himself properly'. This assumption is now regarded as sexist, and to avoid this 'he/she', 'him/her' and 'his/her' can be used. Many people feel that this convention can become clumsy and prefer to be ungrammatical by using 'they', 'them' and 'their', as in 'Every pupil is to behave themselves properly.' This use is becoming increasingly common, even in textbooks. Many sentences of this kind can be rephrased to avoid being either sexist or ungrammatical, as in 'All pupils are to behave themselves properly'. *See* **each.**

everyone a pronoun that takes a singular verb, as in 'Everyone is welcome' and 'Everyone has the right to a decent standard of living'. In order to be grammatically correct, it should be accompanied, where relevant, by a singular personal pronoun but it is subject to the same kind of treatment as every.

feminine the term for the gender that indicates female persons or animals. It is the opposite of 'masculine'. The feminine gender demands the use of the appropriate pronoun, including 'she', 'her', 'hers' and 'herself', as in 'The girl tried to save the dog but *she* was unable to do so', 'The woman hurt *her* leg', 'Mary said that the book is *hers*', and 'The waitress cut *herself*'.

The feminine forms of words, formed by adding *—ess*, used to be common but many such forms are now thought to be sexist. Words such as 'author', 'sculptor', 'poet' are now considered to be neutral terms that can be used to refer to a man or a woman. Some *-ess* words are either still being used or are in a state of flux, as in 'actress'. *See* **-ess** in **Affixes** section.

finite clause a clause that contains a finite verb, as in 'when she sees him', 'after she had defeated him', and 'as they were sitting there'.

finite verb a verb that has a tense and has a subject with which it agrees in number and person. For example 'cries' is finite in the sentence 'The child cries most of the time', and 'looks' is finite in the sentence 'The old man looks ill'. However 'go' in the sentence 'He wants to go' is non-finite since it has no variation of tense and does not have a subject. Similarly in the sentence 'Sitting on the river-bank, he was lost in thought', 'sitting' is non-finite.

first person this refers to the person who is speaking or writing when referring to himself or herself. The **first person pronouns** are 'I', 'me', 'myself' and 'mine', with the plural forms being 'we', 'us', 'ourselves' and 'ours'. Examples include 'She said, "*I* am going home" ', ' "*I* am going shopping," he said', ' "*We* have very little money left," she said to her husband' and 'He said, "*We* shall have to leave now if we are to get there on time" '.

The **first person determiners** are 'my' and 'our', as in 'I have forgotten to bring *my* notebook' and 'We must remember to bring *our* books home.'

form word *see* **function word.**

fragmentary sentence *see* **major sentence.**

frequentative a term referring to a verb that expresses frequent repetition of an action. In English the verb endings *-le* and *-el* sometimes indicate the frequentative form, as in 'waddle' from 'wade', 'sparkle' from 'spark', 'crackle' from 'crack' and 'dazzle' from 'daze'. The ending *-er* can also indicate the frequentative form, as in 'stutter', 'spatter' and 'batter'.

function word a word that has very little meaning but is primarily of grammatical significance and merely performs a 'function' in a sentence. Function words include determiners, and prepositions such as in, on and up. Words that are not function words are sometimes known as **content words.**

Function word is also known as **form word** or **structure word.**

future perfect tense the tense of a verb that is formed by 'will' or 'shall' together with the perfect tense, as in 'They will have been married ten years next week', 'You will have finished work by this time tomorrow' and 'By the time Jane arrives here she will have been travelling non-stop for forty-eight hours'.

future tense the tense of a verb that describes actions or states that will occur at some future time. It is marked by 'will' and 'shall'. Traditionally 'shall' was used with subjects in the first person, as in 'I shall see you tomorrow' and 'We shall go there next week', and 'will' was used with subjects in the second and third person, as in 'You will find out next week', 'He will recognize her when he sees her' and 'They will be on the next train'. Formerly 'will' was used with the first person and 'shall' with the second and third person to indicate emphasis or insistence, as in 'I *will* go on my own' and 'We *will* be able to afford it'; 'You *shall* pay what you owe' and 'The children *shall* get a holiday'. In modern usage 'shall' is usually used only for emphasis or insistence, whether with the first, second or third person, except in formal contexts. Otherwise 'will' is used, as in 'I will go tomorrow', 'We will have to see', 'You will be surprised', and 'They will be on their way by now'.

The future tense can also be marked by 'be about to' plus the infinitive of the relevant verb or 'be going to' plus the infinitive of the relevant verb. Examples include 'We are about to leave for work', 'They are about to go on holiday', 'She is going to be late' and 'They are going to demolish the building'.

gemination the doubling of consonants before a suffix.

gender in the English language this usually refers to the natural distinctions of sex (or absence of sex) that exist, and nouns are classified according to these distinctions—masculine, feminine and neuter. Thus, 'man', 'boy', 'king', 'prince', 'emperor', 'duke', 'heir', 'son', 'brother', 'father', 'nephew', 'husband', 'bridegroom', 'widower', 'hero', 'cock', 'drake', 'fox' and 'lion' are masculine nouns. Similarly, 'girl', 'woman', 'queen', 'princess', 'empress', 'duchess', 'heiress', 'daughter', 'sister', 'mother', 'niece', 'wife', 'bride', 'widow', 'heroine', 'hen', 'duck', 'vixen' and 'lioness' are feminine nouns. Similarly, 'table', 'chair', 'desk', 'carpet', 'window', 'lamp', 'car', 'shop', 'dress', 'tie', 'newspaper', 'book', 'building' and 'town' are all neuter.

Some nouns in English can refer either to a man or a woman, unless the sex is indicated in the context. Such neutral nouns are sometimes said to have dual gender. Examples include 'author', 'singer', 'poet', 'sculptor', 'proprietor', 'teacher', 'parent', 'cousin', 'adult' and 'child'. Some words in this category were formerly automatically assumed to be masculine and several of them had feminine forms, such as 'authoress', 'poetess', 'sculptress' and 'proprietrix'. In modern times this was felt to be sexist and many of these feminine forms are now rarely used, for example, 'authoress' and 'poetess'. However some, such as actress and waitress, are still in common use.

genitive case a case that indicates possession or ownership. It is usually marked by *s* and an apostrophe. Many spelling errors centre on the position of the *s* in relation to the apostrophe. *See* **apostrophe** in **Spelling** section

gerund the *-ing* form of a verb when it functions as a noun. It is sometimes known as a **verbal noun.** It has the same form as the present participle but has a different function. For example, in the sentence 'He was jogging down the road', 'jogging' is the present participle in the verb phrase 'was jogging', but in the sentence 'Running is his idea of relaxation', 'running' is a gerund because it acts as a noun as the subject of the sentence. Similarly, in the sentence 'We were smoking when the teacher found us', 'smoking' is the present participle in the verb phrase 'were smoking', but in the sentence 'We were told that smoking is bad for our health', 'smoking' is a gerund since it acts as a noun as the subject of the clause.

get this verb is sometimes used to form the passive voice instead of the verb 'to be'. The use of the verb 'to get' to form the passive, as in 'They get married tomorrow', 'Our team got beaten today' and 'We got swindled by the con man' is sometimes considered to be more informal than the use of 'be'. Often there is more action involved when the get construction is used than when be is used, since get is a more dynamic verb, as in 'She was late leaving the pub because she got involved in an argument' and in 'It was her own fault that she got arrested by the police. She hit one of the constables'.

Get is frequently overused. Such overuse should be avoided, particularly in formal contexts. Get can often be replaced by a synonym such as 'obtain', 'acquire', 'receive', 'get hold of', etc. Thus, 'If you are getting into money difficulties you should get some financial advice. Perhaps you could get a bank loan' could be rephrased as 'If you are in financial difficulty you should obtain some financial help. Perhaps you could receive a bank loan'.

Got, the past tense of get, is often used unnecessarily, as in 'She has got red hair and freckles' and 'We have got enough food to last us the week'. In these sentences 'has' and 'have' are sufficient on their own.

goal this can be used to describe the recipient of the action of a verb, the opposite of 'agent' or 'actor'. Thus, in the sentence 'The boy hit the girl', 'boy' is the 'agent' or 'actor' and 'girl' is the goal. Similarly, in the sentence 'The dog bit the postman', 'dog' is the 'agent' or 'actor' and 'postman' is the goal.

govern a term that is used of a verb or preposition in relation to a noun or pronoun to indicate that the verb or preposition has a noun or pronoun depending on it. Thus, in the phrase 'on the table', 'on' is said to govern 'table'.

gradable a term that is used of adjectives and adverbs to mean that they can take degrees of comparison. Thus 'clean' is a gradable adjective since it has a comparative form (cleaner) and a superlative form (cleanest). 'Soon' is a gradable adverb since it has a comparative form (sooner) and a superlative form (soonest). Such words as 'supreme', which cannot normally have a comparative or superlative form, are called **non-gradable**.

habitual a term used to refer to the action of a verb that occurs regularly and repeatedly. The **habitual present** is found in such sentences as 'He goes to bed at ten every night', 'She always walks to work' and 'The old man sleeps all day'. This is in contrast to the **stative present**, which indicates the action of the verb that occurs at all times, as in 'Cows chew the cud', 'Water becomes ice when it freezes', 'Children grow up' and 'We all die'. Examples of the **habitual past** tense include; 'They travelled by train to work all their lives', 'We worked twelve hours a day on that project' and 'She studied night and day for the exams'.

hanging participle *see* **dangling participle**.

have a verb that has several functions. A major use is its part in forming the 'perfect tense' and 'past perfect tense', or 'pluperfect tense', of other verb tenses. It does this in conjunction with the 'past participle' of the verb in question.

The perfect tense of a verb is formed by the present tense of the verb have and the past participle of the verb. Examples include 'We have acted wisely', 'They have beaten the opposition', 'The police have caught the thieves', 'The old man has died', 'The child has eaten all the food', 'The baby has fallen downstairs', 'They have grabbed all the bargains', 'You have hated him for years' and 'He has indicated that he is going to retire'. The past perfect or pluperfect is formed by the past tense of the verb have and the past participle of the verb in question, as in 'He had jumped over the fence', 'They had kicked in the door', 'The boy had led the other children to safety', 'His mother had made the cake', 'The headmaster had punished the pupils' and 'They had rushed into buying a new house'. Both perfect tenses and past perfect or pluperfect tenses are often contracted in speech or in informal written English, as in 'We've had enough for today', 'You've damaged the suitcase', 'You've missed the bus', 'He's lost his wallet', 'She's arrived too late', 'They'd left before the news came through', 'She'd married without telling her parents', 'He'd packed the goods himself' and 'You'd locked the door without realizing it'.

Have is often used in the phrase **have to** in the sense that something must be done. In the present tense have to can be used instead of 'must', as in 'You have to leave now', 'We have to clear this mess up', 'He has to get the next train' and 'The goods have to be sold today'. If the 'something that must be done' refers to the future the verb **will have to** is used', as in 'He will have to leave now to get there on time', 'The old man will have to go to hospital' and 'They'll have to move out of the house when her parents return'. If the 'something that must be done' refers to the past, **had to** is used, as in 'We had to take the injured man to hospital', 'They had to endure freezing conditions on the mountain', 'They'd to take a reduction in salary' and 'We'd to wait all day for the workman to appear'.

Have is also used in the sense of 'possess' or 'own', as in 'He has a swimming pool behind his house', 'She has a huge wardrobe', 'We have enough food' and 'They have four cars'. In spoken or in informal English 'have got' is often used, as in 'They've got the largest house in the street', 'We've got problems now', 'They haven't got time'. This use should be avoided in formal English.

Have is also used to indicate suffering from an illness or disease, as in 'The child has measles', 'Her father has flu' and 'She has heart disease'. Have can also indicate that an activity is taking place, as in 'She's having a shower', 'We're having a party', 'She is having a baby' and 'They are having a dinner party'.

he a personal pronoun that is used as the subject of a sentence or clause to refer to a man, boy, etc. It is thus said to be a 'masculine' personal pronoun. Since he refers to a third party and does not refer to the speaker or the person being addressed, it is a third-person pronoun. Examples include 'James is quite nice but he can be boring', 'Bob has got a new job and he is very pleased' and 'He is rich now but his parents are still very poor'.

He traditionally was used not only to refer to nouns relating to the masculine sex but also to nouns that are now regarded as being neutral or of dual gender. Such nouns include 'architect', 'artist', 'athlete', 'doctor', 'passenger', 'parent', 'pupil', 'singer', 'student'. Without further information from the context it is impossible to know to which sex such nouns are referring. In modern usage it is regarded as sexist to assume such words to be masculine by using he to refer to one of them unless the context indicates that the noun in question refers to a man or boy. Formerly it was considered acceptable to write or say 'Send a message to the architect who designed the building that he is to attend the meeting' whether or not the writer or speaker knew that the architect was a man. Similarly it was considered acceptable to write or say 'Please tell the doctor that he is to come straight away' whether or not the speaker or writer knew that the doctor was in fact a man. Nowadays this convention is considered sexist. In order to avoid sexism it is possible to use the convention 'he/she', as in 'Every pupil was told that he/she was to be smartly dressed for the occasion', 'Each passenger was informed that he/she was to arrive ten minutes before the coach was due to leave' and 'Tell the doctor that he/she is required urgently'. However this convention is regarded by some people as being clumsy, particularly in spoken English or in informal written English. Some people prefer to be ungrammatical and use the plural personal pronoun 'they' instead of 'he/she' in certain situations, as in 'Every passenger was told that they had to arrive ten minutes before the coach was due to leave' and 'Every student was advised that they should apply for a college place by March' and this use is becoming increasingly common, even in textbooks. In some cases it may be possible to rephrase sentences and avoid being either sexist or ungrammatical, as in 'All the passengers were told that they should arrive ten minutes before the coach was due to leave' and 'All students were advised that they should apply for a college place by March'.

helping verb another name for **auxiliary verb**.

hendiadys a figure of speech in which two nouns joined by 'and' are used to express an idea that would normally be expressed by the use of an adjective and a noun, as in 'through storm and weather' instead of 'through stormy weather'.

her a personal pronoun. It is the third person singular, is feminine in gender and acts as the object in a sentence, as in 'We saw her yesterday', 'I don't know her', 'He hardly ever sees her', 'Please give this book to her', 'Our daughter sometimes plays with her' and 'We do not want her to come to the meeting'. *See* **he**; **she**.

hers a personal pronoun. It is the third person singular, feminine in gender and is in the possessive case. 'The car is not hers', 'I have forgotten my book but I don't want to borrow hers', 'This is my seat and that is hers', and 'These clothes are hers'. *See* **his**; **her** and **possessive**.

him the third person masculine personal pronoun when used as the object of a sentence or clause, as in 'She shot him', 'When the police caught the thief they arrested him' and 'His parents punished him after the boy stole the money'. Traditionally him was used to apply not only to masculine nouns, such as 'man' and 'boy', but also to nouns that are said to be 'of dual gender'. These include 'architect', 'artist', 'parent', 'passenger', 'pupil' and 'student'. Without further information from the context, it is not possible for the speaker or writer to know the sex of the person referred to by one of these words. Formerly it was acceptable to write or say 'The artist must bring an easel with him' and 'Each pupil must bring food with him'. In modern usage this convention is considered sexist and there is a modern convention that 'him/her' should be used instead to avoid sexism, as in 'The artist must bring an easel with him/her' and 'Each pupil must bring food with 'him/her'. This convention is felt by some people to be clumsy, particularly in and in , and some people prefer to be ungrammatical and use the plural personal pronoun 'them' instead, as in 'The artist must bring an easel with them' and 'Each pupil must bring food with them'. This use has become increasingly, even in textbooks. In some situations it is possible to avoid being either sexist or ungrammatical by rephrasing the sentence, as in 'All artists must bring easels with them' and 'All pupils must bring food with them. *See* **he.**

him/her *see* **him.**

his the third personal masculine pronoun when used to indicate possession, as in 'He has hurt his leg', 'The boy has taken his books home' and 'Where has your father left his tools?' Traditionally his was used to refer not only to masculine nouns, such as 'man', 'boy', etc, but to what are known as nouns 'of dual gender'. These include 'architect', 'artist', 'parent', 'passenger', 'pupil' and 'student'. Without further information from the context it is not possible for the speaker or the writer to know the sex of the person referred to by one of these words. Formerly it was considered acceptable to use his in such situations, as in 'Every pupil has to supply his own sports equipment' and 'Every passenger is responsible for his own luggage'. In modern usage this is now considered sexist and there is a modern convention that 'his/her' should be used instead to avoid sexism, as in 'Every pupil has to supply his/her own sports equipment' and 'Every passenger is responsible for his/her own luggage'. This convention is felt by some people to be clumsy, particularly when used in spoken or informal written English. Some people prefer to be ungrammatical and use the plural personal pronoun 'their', as in 'Every pupil must supply their own sports equipment' and 'Every passenger is to be responsible for their own luggage' and this use has become increasingly common, even in textbooks. In some situations it is possible to avoid being sexist, clumsy and ungrammatical by rephrasing the sentence, as in 'All pupils must supply their own sports equipment' and 'All passengers are to be responsible for their own luggage.

his/her *see* **his.**

hybrid a word that is formed from words or elements derived from different languages, such as 'television'.

if a conjunction that is often used to introduce a subordinate adverbial clause of condition, as in 'If he is talking of leaving he must be unhappy', 'If you tease the dog it will bite you', 'If he had realized that the weather was going to be so bad he would not have gone on the expedition', 'If I had been in charge I would have sacked him' and 'If it were a better organized firm things like that would not happen'.

If can also introduce a 'nominal' or 'noun clause', as in 'He asked if we objected' and 'She inquired if we wanted to go'.

imperative mood the verb mood that expresses commands. The verbs in the following sentences are in the imperative mood: 'Go away!', 'Run faster!', 'Answer me!', 'Sit down!', 'Please get out of here!'. All of these expressions with verbs in the imperative mood sound rather imperious or dictatorial and usually end with an exclamation mark, but this is not true of all expressions with verbs in the imperative mood. For example, the following sentences all have verbs in the imperative mood: 'Have another helping of ice cream', 'Help yourself to more wine', 'Just follow the yellow arrows to the X-ray department', and 'Turn right at the roundabout'. Sentences with verbs in the imperative mood are known as **imperative sentences.**

imperfect a tense that denotes an action in progress but not complete. The term derives from the classification in Latin grammar and was traditionally applied to the 'past imperfect', as in 'They were standing there'. The imperfect has now been largely superseded by the progressive/continuous tense, which is marked by the use of 'be' plus the present participle. Continuous tenses are used when talking about temporary situations at a particular point in time, as in 'They were waiting for the bus'.

impersonal a verb that is used with a formal subject, usually 'it', as in 'It is raining' and 'They say it will snow tomorrow'.

indefinite pronouns these are used refer to people or things without being specific as to exactly who or what they are. They include 'everyone', 'everybody', 'everything', 'anyone', 'anybody', 'anything', 'somebody', 'someone', 'something' and 'nobody', 'no one', 'nothing', as in 'Everyone is to make a contribution', 'Anyone can enter', 'Something will turn up' and 'Nobody cares'.

independent clause a clause that can stand alone and make sense without being dependent on another clause, as in 'The children are safe'. Main clauses are independent clauses. Thus in the sentence 'She is tired and she wants to go home', there are two independent clauses joined by 'and'. In the sentence 'She will be able to rest when she gets home', 'She will be able to rest' is an independent clause and 'when she gets home' is a dependent clause. In the sentence 'Because she is intelligent she thinks for herself', 'she thinks for herself' is an independent clause and 'because she is intelligent' is a dependent clause.

indicative mood the mood of a verb which denotes making a statement. The following sentences have verbs in the indicative mood: 'We go on holiday tomorrow', 'He was waiting for her husband', 'They have lost the match' and 'She will arrive this afternoon'. The indicative mood is sometimes known as the **declarative mood.** The other moods are the imperative mood and subjunctive mood.

indirect object an object that can be preceded by 'to' or 'for'. The indirect object usually refers to the person who benefits from an action or receives something as the result of it. In the sentence 'Her father gave the boy food', 'boy' is the indirect object and 'food' is the direct object. The sentence could be rephrased as 'Her father gave food to the boy'. In the sentence 'He bought his mother flowers', 'his mother' is the indirect object and 'flowers' is the direct object. The sentence could have been rephrased as 'He bought flowers for his mother'. In the sentence 'They offered him a reward', 'him' is the indirect object and 'reward' is the direct object. The sentence could be rephrased as 'They offered a reward to him'.

indirect question a question that is reported in indirect speech, as in 'We asked them where they were going', 'They inquired why we had come' and 'They looked at us curiously and asked where we had come from'. Note that a question mark is not used.

indirect speech also known as **reported speech** a way of reporting what someone has said without using the actual words used by the speaker. There is usually an introductory verb and a subordinate 'that' clause, as in 'He said that he was going away', 'They announced that they were leaving next day' and 'She declared that she had seen him there before'. In direct speech these sentences would become 'He said, "I am going away" ', 'They announced, "We are leaving tomorrow" ' and 'She declared, "I have seen him there before" '. When the change is made from direct speech to indirect speech, the pronouns, adverbs of time and place and tenses are changed to accord with the viewpoint of the person doing the reporting.

infinitive the base form of a verb when used without any indication of person, number or tense. There are two forms of the infinitive. One is the **to infinitive** form, as in 'They wished to leave', 'I plan to go tomorrow', 'We aim to please' and 'They want to emigrate', 'To know all is to forgive all', 'To err is human', 'Pull the lever to open', 'You should bring a book to read', 'The child has nothing to do', 'She is not very nice to know' and 'It is hard to believe that it happened'. The other form of the infinitive is called the **bare infinitive.** This form consists of the base form of the verb without 'to', as in 'We saw him fall', 'She watched him go', 'They noticed him enter', 'She heard him sigh', 'They let him go', 'I had better leave' and 'Need we return' and 'we dare not go back'. *See* **split infinitive.**

inflect when applied to a word, this means to change form in order to indicate differences of tense, number, gender, case, etc. Nouns inflect for plural, as in 'ships', 'chairs', 'houses' and 'oxen'; nouns inflect for possessive, as in 'boys', 'woman's', 'teachers', and 'parents'; some adjectives inflect for the comparative form, as in 'brighter', 'clearer', 'shorter' and 'taller'; verbs inflect for the third person singular present tense, as in 'hears', 'joins', 'touches' and 'kicks'; verbs inflect for the present participle, as in 'hearing', 'joining', 'touching' and 'kicking'; verbs inflect for the past participle, as in 'heard', 'joined', 'touched' and 'kicked'.

inflection the act of inflecting—*see* **inflect**. It also refers to an inflected form of a word or a suffix or other element used to inflect a word.

-ing form this form of a verb can be either a present participle or a gerund. Present participles are used in the formation of the progressive or continuous tenses, as in 'We were looking at the pictures', 'Children were playing in the snow', 'They are waiting for the bus', 'Parents were showing their anger', 'He has been sitting there for hours'. Present participles can also be used in non-finite clauses or phrases, as in 'Walking along, she did not have a care in the world', 'Lying there, he thought about his life', 'Sighing, he left the room' and 'Smiling broadly he congratulated his friend'.

A large number of adjectives end in -ing. Many of these have the same form as the present participle of a transitive verb and are similar in meaning. Examples include 'an amazing spectacle', 'a boring show', 'an interesting idea', 'a tiring day', 'an exhausting climb' and 'aching limbs'. Some -ing adjectives are related to intransitive verbs, as 'existing problems', 'increasing responsibilities', 'dwindling resources', 'an ageing work force' and 'prevailing circumstances'. Some -ing adjectives are related to the forms of verbs but have different meanings from the verbs, as in 'becoming dress', 'an engaging personality', 'a dashing young man' and 'a retiring disposition'. Some -ing adjectives are not related to verbs at all. These include 'appetizing', 'enterprising', 'impending' and 'balding'. Some -ing adjectives are used informally for emphasis, as in 'a blithering idiot', 'a stinking cold' and 'a flaming cheek'.

Gerunds act as nouns and are sometimes known as **verbal nouns.** Examples include 'Smoking is bad for one's health', 'Cycling is forbidden in the park' and 'Swimming is his favourite sport'.

intensifier the term for an adverb that affects the degree of intensity of another word. Intensifiers include 'thoroughly' in 'We were thoroughly shocked by the news', 'scarcely' in 'We scarcely recognized them' and 'totally' in 'She was totally amazed'.

interjection a kind of exclamation. Sometimes they are formed by actual words and sometimes they simply consist of sounds indicating emotional noises. Examples of interjections include 'Oh! I am quite shocked', 'Gosh! I'm surprised to hear that!', 'Phew! It's hot!', 'Ouch! That was my foot!', 'Tut-tut! He shouldn't have done that!' and 'Alas! She is dead.'

interrogative adjective or **determiner** an adjective or determiner that asks for information in relation to the nouns which it qualifies, as in 'What dress did you choose in the end?', 'What kind of book are you looking for?', 'Which house do you like best?', 'Which pupil won the prize?', 'Whose bike was stolen?' and 'Whose dog is that?'

interrogative adverb an adverb that asks a question, as in 'When did they leave?', 'When does the meeting start?', 'Where do they live?', 'Where was the stolen car found?', 'Where did you last see her?', 'Why was she crying?', 'Why have they been asked to leave?', 'How is the invalid?', 'How do you know that she has gone?' and 'Wherever did you find that?'

interrogative pronoun a pronoun that asks a question, as in 'Who asked you to do that?', 'Who broke the vase?', 'What did he say?, 'What happened next?', 'Whose are those books?', 'Whose is that old car?', 'To whom was that remark addressed?' and 'To whom did you address the package?'

interrogative sentence a sentence that asks a question, as in 'Who is that?', 'Where is he?', 'Why have they appeared?', 'What did they take away?', 'Which do you prefer?' and 'Whose baby is that?'. Sentences that take the form of an interrogative question do not always seek information. Sometimes they are exclamations, as in 'Did you ever see anything so beautiful?', 'Isn't she sweet?' and 'Aren't they lovely?'. Sentences that take the form of questions may really be commands or directives, as in 'Could you turn down that radio?', 'Would you make less noise?' and 'Could you get her a chair?'. Sentences that take the form of questions may function as statements, as in 'Isn't there always a reason?' and 'Haven't we all experienced disappointment?'. Some interrogative sentences are what are known as rhetorical questions, which are asked purely for effect and require no answer, as in 'Do you think I am a fool?', 'What is the point of life?' and 'What is the world coming to?'.

intransitive verb a verb that does not take a direct object, as in 'Snow fell yesterday', 'The children played in the sand', 'The path climbed steeply', 'Time will tell', 'The situation worsened', 'Things improved' and 'Prices increased'. Many verbs can be either transitive or intransitive, according to the context. Thus 'play' is intransitive in the sentence 'The children played in the sand' but transitive in the sentence 'The boy plays the piano'. Similarly 'climb' is intransitive in the sentence 'The path climbs steeply' but transitive in the sentence 'The mountaineers climbed Everest'. Similarly 'tell' is intransitive in the sentence 'Time will tell' but transitive in the sentence 'He will tell his life story'.

introductory it the use of 'it' as the subject of a sentence in the absence of a meaningful subject. It is used particularly in sentences about time and the weather, as in 'It is midnight', 'It is dawn', 'It is five o'clock', 'It is twelve noon', 'It is raining', 'It was snowing', 'It was windy' and 'It was blowing a gale'.

invariable a word whose form does not vary by inflection. Such words include 'sheep' and 'but'.

inversion the reversal of the usual word order. It particularly refers to subjects and verbs. Inversion is used in questions, in some negative sentences, and for literary effect. In questions, an auxiliary verb is usually put in front of the subject and the rest of the verb group is put after the subject, as in 'Are you going to see her?' and 'Have they inspected the goods yet?'. The verb 'to do' is frequently used in inversion, as in 'Did he commit the crime?' and 'Do they still believe that?'. Examples of the use of inversion in negative sentences include 'Seldom have I witnessed such an act of selfishness', 'Never had she experienced such pain' and 'Rarely do we have time to admire the beauty of the countryside'. This use in negative sentences is rather formal.

Inversion frequently involves adverbial phrases of place, as in 'Beyond the town stretched field after field', 'Above them soared the eagle' and 'Along the driveway grew multitudes of daffodils'.

Inversion is also found in conditional clauses that are not introduced by conjunction, as in 'Had you arrived earlier you would have got a meal' and 'Had we some more money we could do more for the refugees'.

irregular adjective an adjective that does not conform to the usual rules of forming the comparative and superlative (*see* **comparison of adjectives**). Many adjectives either add *-er* for the comparative and *-est* for the superlative, as in 'taller', 'shorter' and 'tallest', 'shortest' from 'tall' and 'short'. Some adjectives form their comparatives with 'more' and their superlatives with 'most', as in 'more beautiful', 'more practical' and 'most beautiful', 'most practical'. Irregular adjectives do not form their comparatives and superlatives in either of these ways. Irregular adjectives include:

positive	*comparative*	*superlative*
good	better	best
bad	worse	worst
little	less	least
many	more	most

irregular sentence *see* **major sentence.**

irregular verb a verb that does not conform to the usual pattern of verbs in that some of its forms deviate from what one would expect if the pattern of regular verbs was being followed. There are four main forms of a **regular verb**—the infinitive or base form, as in 'hint', 'halt', 'hate' and 'haul'; the third-person singular form, as 'hints', 'halts', 'hates' and 'hauls'; the -ing form or present participle, as 'hinting', halting', 'hating' and 'hauling'; the *-ed* form or 'past tense' or 'past participle', as 'hinted', halted', 'hated' and 'hauled'.

Irregular verbs deviate in some way from that pattern, in particular from the pattern of adding *-ed* to the past tense and past participle. They fall into several categories.

One category concerns those that have the same form in the past tense and past participle forms as the infinitive and do not end in *-ed*, like regular verbs.

Some irregular verbs have two past tenses and two past participles which are the same.

Some irregular verbs have past tenses that do not end in *-ed* and have the same form as the past participle.

Some irregular verbs have regular past tense forms but two possible past participles, one of which is regular.

Some irregular verbs have past tenses and past participles that are different from each other and different from the infinitive.

Comprehensive examples of these categories can be found in the chapter on **Irregular Verbs and Nouns.**

jussive a type of clause or sentence that expresses a command, as in 'Do be quiet! I'm trying to study', 'Let's not bother going to the party. I'm too tired', 'Would you pass me that book' and 'Look at that everybody! The river has broken its banks'.

linking adverbs and **linking adverbials** words and phrases that indicate some kind of connection between one clause or sentence and another. Examples include 'however', as in 'The award had no effect on their financial situation. It did, however, have a marked effect on their morale'; 'moreover', as in 'He is an unruly pupil. Moreover, he is a bad influence on the other pupils'; 'then again', as in 'She does not have very good qualifications. Then again, most of the other candidates have even fewer'; 'in the meantime', as in 'We will not know the planning committee's decision until next week. In the meantime we can only hope'; 'instead', as in 'I thought he would have reigned. Instead he seems determined to stay'.

linking verb a verb that 'links' a subject with its complement. Unlike other verbs, linking verbs do not denote an action but indicate a state. Examples of linking verbs include 'He is a fool', 'She appears calm', 'He appeared a sensible man', 'You seemed to become anxious', 'They became Buddhists', 'The child feels unwell', 'It is getting rather warm', 'It is growing colder', 'You look well', 'She remained loyal to her friend', 'She lived in America but remained a British citizen' and 'You seem thoughtful' and 'She seems a nice person'. Linking verbs are also called **copula** or **copular verbs.**

main clause the principal clause in a sentence on which any subordinate clauses depend for their sense. The main clause can stand alone and make some sense but the subordinate clauses cannot. In the sentence 'I left early because I wanted to catch the 6 o'clock train', 'I left early' is the principal clause and 'because I wanted to catch the 6 o'clock train' is the subordinate clause. In the sentence 'When we saw the strange man we were afraid', the main clause is 'we were afraid' and the subordinate clause is 'when we saw the strange man'. In the sentence 'Because it was late we decided to start out for home as soon as we could', the main clause is 'we decided to start out for home' and the subordinate clauses are 'because it was late' and 'as soon as we could'. A main clause can also be known as a **principal clause** or an independent clause.

major sentence a sentence that contains at least one subject and a finite verb, as in 'We are going' and 'They won'. They frequently have more elements than this, as in 'They bought a car', 'We lost the match', 'They arrived yesterday' and 'We are going away next week'. They are sometimes described as **regular** because they divide into certain structural patterns: a subject, finite verb, adverb or adverbial clause, etc. The opposite of a major sentence is called a **minor sentence, irregular sentence** or **fragmentary sentence**. These include interjections such as 'Ouch!' and 'How terrible'; formula expressions, such as 'Good morning' and 'Well done'; and short forms of longer expressions, as in 'Traffic diverted', 'Shop closed', 'No dogs' and 'Flooding ahead'. Such short forms could be rephrased to become major sentences, as in 'Traffic has been diverted because of roadworks', 'The shop is closed on Sundays', 'The owner does not allow dogs in her shop' and 'There was flooding ahead on the motorway'.

masculine in grammatical terms, one of the genders that nouns are divided into. Nouns in the masculine gender include words that obviously belong to the male sex, as in 'man', 'boy', 'king', 'prince' 'bridegroom', 'schoolboy' and 'salesman'. Many words now considered to be of dual gender formerly were assumed to be masculine. These include such words as 'author', 'sculptor' and 'engineer'. Gender also applies to personal pronouns, and the third personal singular pronoun masculine is 'he' (subject), 'him' (object) and 'his' (possessive). For further information *see* **he; she.**

mass noun the same as **uncountable noun.**

minor sentence *see* **major sentence.**

misrelated participle *see* **dangling participle.**

modal verb a type of auxiliary verb that 'helps' the main verb to express a range of meanings including, for example, such meanings as possibility, probability, wants, wishes, necessity, permission, suggestions, etc. The main modal verbs are 'can', 'could'; 'may', 'might'; 'will', 'would'; 'shall', 'should'; 'must'. Modal verbs have only one form. They have no *-s* form in the third person singular, no infinitive and no participles. Examples of modal verbs include 'He cannot read and write', 'She could go if she wanted to' (expressing ability); 'You can have another biscuit', 'You may answer the question' (expressing permission); 'We may see her on the way to the station', 'We might get there by nightfall' (expressing possibility); 'Will you have some wine?', 'Would you take a seat?' (expressing an offer or invitation); 'We should arrive by dawn', 'That must be a record' (expressing probability and certainty); 'You may prefer to wait', 'You might like to leave instructions' (expressing suggestion); 'Can you find the time to phone him for me?', 'Could you give him a message?' (expressing instructions and requests); 'They must leave at once', 'We must get there on time' (expressing necessity).

modifier a word, or group of words, that 'modifies' or affects the meaning of another word in some way, usually by adding more information about it. Modifiers are frequently used with nouns. They can be adjectives, as in 'He works in the *main* building' and 'They need a *larger* house'. Modifiers of nouns can be nouns themselves, as in 'the *theatre* profession', 'the *publishing* industry' and '*singing* tuition'. They can also be place names, as in 'the *Edinburgh* train', 'a *Paris* café' and 'the *London* underground', or adverbs of place and direction, as in 'a *downstairs* cloakroom' and 'an *upstairs* sitting room'.

Adverbs, adjectives and pronouns can be accompanied by modifiers. Examples of modifiers with adverbs include 'walking *amazingly* quickly' and 'stopping *incredibly* abruptly'. Examples of modifiers with adjectives include 'a *really* warm day' and 'a *deliriously* happy child'. Examples of modifiers with pronouns include '*almost* no one there' and '*practically* everyone present'.

The examples given above are all premodifiers. *See also* **postmodifier.**

mood one of the categories into which verbs are divided. The verb moods are indicative, imperative and subjunctive. The **indicative** makes a statement, as in 'He lives in France', 'They have two children' and 'It's starting to rain'. The **imperative** is used for giving orders or making requests, as in 'Shut that door!', 'Sit quietly until the teacher arrives' and 'Please bring me some coffee'. The **subjunctive** was originally a term in Latin grammar and expressed a wish, supposition, doubt, improbability or other non-factual statement. It is used in English for hypothetical statements and certain formal 'that' clauses, as in 'If I were you I would have nothing to do with it', 'If you were to go now you would arrive on time', 'Someone suggested that we ask for more money' and 'It was his solicitor who suggested that he sue the firm'. The word 'mood' arose because it was said to indicate the verb's attitude or viewpoint.

more an adverb that is added to some adjectives to make the comparative form (*see* **comparison of adjectives**). In general it is the longer adjectives that have more as part of their comparative form, as in 'more abundant', 'more beautiful', 'more catastrophic', 'more dangerous', 'more elegant', 'more frantic', 'more graceful', 'more handsome', 'more intelligent', 'more luxurious', 'more manageable', 'more opulent', 'more precious', 'more ravishing', 'more satisfactory', 'more talented', 'more unusual', 'more valuable'. Examples of adverbs with more in their comparative form include 'more elegantly', 'more gracefully', 'more energetically', 'more dangerously' and 'more determinedly'.

most an adverb added to some adjectives and adverbs to make the superlative form. In general it is the longer adjectives that have most as part of their superlative form, as in 'most abundant', 'most beautiful', 'most catastrophic', 'most dangerous', 'most elegant', 'most frantic', 'most graceful', 'most handsome', 'most intelligent', 'most luxurious', 'most manageable', 'most noteworthy', 'most opulent', 'most precious', most ravishing', 'most satisfactory', 'most talented', 'most unusual', 'most valuable'. Examples of adverbs with most in their superlative form include 'most elegantly', 'most gracefully', 'most energetically', 'most dangerously' and 'most determinedly'.

multi-sentence a sentence with more than one clause, as in 'She tripped over a rock and broke her ankle' and 'She was afraid when she saw the strange man'.

negative sentence a sentence that is the opposite of a **positive sentence**. 'She has a dog' is an example of a positive sentence. 'She does not have a dog' is an example of a negative sentence. The negative concept is expressed by an auxiliary verb accompanied by 'not' or 'n't'. Other words used in negative sentences include 'never', 'nothing' and 'by no means', as in 'She has never been here' and 'We heard nothing'.

neither an adjective or a pronoun that takes a singular verb, as in 'Neither parent will come' and 'Neither of them wishes to come'. In the **neither . . . nor** construction, a singular verb is used if both parts of the construction are singular, as in 'Neither Jane nor Mary was present'. If both parts are plural the verb is plural, as in 'Neither their parents nor their grandparents are willing to look after them'. If the construction involves a mixture of singular and plural, the verb traditionally agrees with the subject that is nearest it, as in 'Neither her mother nor her grandparents are going to come' and 'Neither her grandparents nor her mother is going to come'. If pronouns are used, the nearer one governs the verb as in 'Neither they nor he is at fault' and 'Neither he nor they are at fault'.

neuter one of the grammatical genders. The other two grammatical genders are masculine and feminine. Inanimate objects are members of the neuter gender. Examples include 'table', 'desk', 'garden', 'spade', 'flower' and 'bottle'.

nominal clause *see* **noun clause.**

non-finite clause a clause which contains a non-finite verb. Thus in the sentence 'He works hard to earn a living', 'to earn a living' is a non-finite clause since 'to earn' is an infinitive and so a non-finite verb. Similarly in the sentence 'Getting there was a problem', 'getting there' is a non-finite clause, 'getting' being a present participle and so a non-finite verb.

non-finite verb a verb that shows no variation in tense and has no subject. The non-finite verb forms include the infinitive form, as in 'go', the present participle and gerund, as in 'going', and the past participle, as in 'gone'.

non-gradable *see* **gradable.**

noun the name of something or someone. Thus 'anchor', 'baker', 'cat', 'elephant', 'foot', 'gate', 'lake', 'pear', 'shoe', 'trunk' and 'wallet' are all nouns. There are various categories of nouns. *See* **abstract noun, common noun, concrete noun, countable noun, proper noun** and **uncountable noun.**

noun clause a subordinate clause that performs a function in a sentence similar to a noun or noun phrase. It can act as the subject, object or complement of a main clause. In the sentence 'Where he goes is his own business', 'where he goes' is a noun clause. In the sentence 'They asked why he objected', 'why he objected' is a noun clause. A noun clause is also known as a **nominal clause.**

noun phrase a group of words containing a noun as its main word and functioning like a noun in a sentence. Thus it can function as the subject, object or complement of a sentence. In the sentence 'The large black dog bit him', 'the large black dog' is a noun phrase, and in the sentence 'They bought a house with a garden', 'with a garden' is a noun phrase. In the sentence 'She is a complete fool', 'a complete fool' is a noun phrase.

noun, plurals *see* **Spelling** section.

number in grammar this is a classification consisting of 'singular' and 'plural'. Thus the number of the pronoun 'they' is 'plural' and the number of the verb 'carries' is singular. *See* **number agreement.**

number agreement or **concord** the agreement of grammatical units in terms of number. Thus a singular subject is followed by a singular verb, as in 'The girl likes flowers', 'He hates work' and 'She was carrying a suitcase'. Similarly a plural subject should be followed by a plural verb, as in 'They have many problems', 'The men work hard' and 'The girls are training hard'.

object the part of a sentence that is acted upon or is affected by the verb. It usually follows the verb to which it relates. There are two forms of object—the direct object and indirect object. A direct object can be a noun, and in the sentence 'The girl hit the ball', 'ball' is a noun and the object. In the sentence 'They bought a house', 'house' is a noun and the object. In the sentence 'They made an error', 'error' is a noun and the object. A direct object can be a noun phrase, and in the sentence 'He has bought a large house', 'a large house' is a noun phrase and the object. In the sentence 'She loves the little girl', 'the little girl' is a noun phrase and the object. In the sentence 'They both wear black clothes', 'black clothes' is a noun phrase and the object'. A direct object can be a noun clause, and in the sentence 'I know what he means', 'what he means' is a noun phrase and the object. In the sentence 'He denied that he had been involved', 'that he had been involved' is a noun phrase and the object. In the sentence 'I asked when he would return', 'when he would return' is a noun phrase and the object. A direct object can also be a pronoun, and in the sentence 'She hit him', 'him' is a pronoun and the object. In the sentence 'They had a car but they sold it', 'it' is a pronoun and the object. In the sentence 'She loves them', 'them' is a pronoun and the object.

objective case the case expressing the object. In Latin it is known as the accusative case.

parenthesis *see* **brackets** in **Punctuation.**

part of speech each of the categories (e.g. verb, noun, adjective, etc) into which words are divided according to their grammatical and semantic functions.

participle a part of speech, so called because, although a verb, it has the character both of verb and adjective and is also used in the formation of some compound tenses. *See also* **-ing form** and **past participle.**

passive voice the voice of a verb whereby the subject is the recipient of the action of the verb. Thus, in the sentence 'Mary was kicked by her brother', 'Mary' is the receiver of the 'kick' and so 'kick' is in the passive voice. Had it been in the active voice it would have been 'Her brother kicked Mary'. Thus 'the brother' is the subject and not the receiver of the action.

past participle this is formed by adding *-ed* or *-d* to the base words of regular verbs, as in 'acted', 'alluded', 'boarded', 'dashed', 'flouted', 'handed', 'loathed', 'tended' and 'wanted', or in various other ways for irregular verbs.

past tense this tense of a verb is formed by adding *-ed* or *-d* to the base form of the verb in regular verbs, as in 'added', 'crashed', 'graded', 'smiled', 'rested' and 'yielded', and in various ways for irregular verbs.

perfect tense *see* **tense.**

personal pronoun a pronoun that is used to refer back to someone or something that has already been mentioned. The personal pronouns are divided into subject pronouns, object pronouns and possessive pronouns. They are also categorized according to 'person'. *See* **first person, second person** and **third person.**

phrasal verb a usually simple verb that combines with a preposition or adverb, or both, to convey a meaning more than the sum of its parts, e.g. to phase out, to come out, to look forward to.

phrase two or more words, usually not containing a finite verb, that form a complete expression by themselves or constitute a portion of a sentence.

positive sentence *see* **negative sentence.**

possessive *see* **genitive.**

possessive pronoun *see* **personal pronoun; first person; second person** and **third person.**

postmodifier a modifier that comes after the main word of a noun phrase, as in 'of stone' in 'tablets of stone'.

predicate all the parts of a clause or sentence that are not contained in the subject. Thus in the sentence 'The little girl was exhausted and hungry', 'exhausted and hungry' is the predicate. Similarly, in the sentence 'The tired old man slept like a top', 'slept like a top' is the predicate.

predicative adjective an adjective that helps to form the predicate and so comes after the verb, as 'tired' in 'She was very tired' and 'mournful' in 'The music was very mournful'.

premodifier a modifier that comes before the main word of a noun phrase, as 'green' in 'green dress' and 'pretty' in 'pretty houses'.

preposition a word that relates two elements of a sentence, clause or phrase together. Prepositions show how the elements relate in time or space and generally precede the words that they 'govern'. Words governed by prepositions are nouns or pronouns. Prepositions are often very short words, as 'at', 'in', 'on', 'to', 'before' and 'after'. Some complex prepositions consist of two words, as 'ahead of', 'instead of', 'apart from', and some consist of three, as 'with reference to', 'in accordance with' and 'in addition to'. Examples of prepositions in sentences include 'The cat sat on the mat', 'We were at a concert', 'They are in shock', 'We are going to France', 'She arrived before me', 'Apart from you she has no friends' and 'We acted in accordance with your instructions'.

present continuous *see* **tense.**

present participle *see* **-ing words.**

present tense *see* **tense.**

principal clause *see* **main clause.**

progressive present *see* **tense.**

pronoun a word that takes the place of a noun or a noun phrase. *See* **personal pronouns, he, her, him** and **his, reciprocal pronouns, reflexive pronouns, demonstrative pronouns, relative pronouns, distributive pronouns, indefinite pronouns** and **interrogative pronouns.**

proper noun a noun that refers to a particular individual or a specific thing. It is the 'name' of someone or something', as in Australia, Vesuvius, John Brown, River Thames, Rome and Atlantic Ocean. *See* **capital letters in Spelling** section.

question tag a phrase that is interrogative in form but is not really asking a question. It is added to a statement to seek agreement, etc. Examples include 'That was a lovely meal, wasn't it?', 'You will be able to go, won't you?', 'He's not going to move house, is he?' and 'She doesn't drive, does she?' Sentences containing question tags have question marks at the end.

reciprocal pronoun a pronoun used to convey the idea of reciprocity or a two-way relationship. The reciprocal pronouns are 'each other' and 'one another'. Examples include 'They don't love each other any more', 'They seem to hate each other', 'We must try to help each other', 'The children were calling one another names', 'The two families were always criticizing one another' and 'The members of the family blame one another for their mother's death'.

reciprocal verb a verb such as 'consult', 'embrace', 'marry', 'meet', etc, that expresses a mutual relationship, as in 'They met at the conference', 'She married him in June'.

reflexive pronoun a pronoun that ends in '-self' or '-selves' and refers back to a noun or pronoun that has occurred earlier in the same sentence. The reflexive pronouns include 'myself', 'ourselves'; 'yourself', 'yourselves'; 'himself', 'herself', 'itself', 'themselves'. Examples include 'The children washed themselves', 'He cut himself shaving', 'Have you hurt yourself?' and 'She has cured herself of the habit'.

Reflexive pronouns are sometimes used for emphasis, as in 'The town itself was not very interesting' and 'The headmaster himself punished the boys'. They can also be used to indicate that something has been done by somebody by his/her own efforts without any help, as in 'He built the house himself', 'We converted the attic ourselves'. They can also indicate that someone or something is alone, as in 'She lives by herself' and 'The house stands by itself'.

reflexive verb a verb that has as its direct object a reflexive pronoun, e.g. 'They pride themselves on their skill as a team'.

regular sentence *see* **major sentence.**

regular verb *see* **irregular verb.**

relative clause a subordinate clause that has the function of an adjective. It is introduced by a relative pronoun.

relative pronoun a pronoun that introduces a relative clause. The relative pronouns are 'who', 'whom', 'whose', 'which' and 'that'. Examples of relative clauses introduced by relative pronouns include 'There is the man who stole the money', 'She is the person to whom I gave the money', 'This is the man whose wife won the prize', 'They criticized the work which he had done' and 'That's the house that I would like to buy'. Relative pronouns refer back to a noun or noun phrase in the main clause. These nouns and noun phrases are known as antecedents. The antecedents in the example sentences are respectively 'man', 'person', 'man', 'work' and 'house'.

Sometimes the relative clause divides the parts of the main clause, as in 'The woman whose daughter is ill is very upset', 'The people whom we met on holiday were French' and 'The house that we liked best was too expensive'.

reported speech *same as* **indirect speech**

rhetorical question a question that is asked to achieve some kind of effect and requires no answer. Examples include 'What's this country coming to?', 'Did you ever see the like', 'Why do these things happen to me?', 'Where did youth go?', 'Death, where is thy sting?' and 'Where does time go?'. *See also* **interrogative sentence.**

second person the term used for the person or thing to whom one is talking. The term is applied to personal pronouns. The second person singular whether acting as the subject of a sentence is 'you', as in 'I told you so', 'We informed you of our decision' and 'They might have asked you sooner'. The second person personal pronoun does not alter its form in the plural in English, unlike in some languages. The possessive form of the second person pronoun is 'yours' whether singular or plural, as in 'These books are not yours' and 'This pen must be yours'.

sentence is at the head of the hierarchy of grammar. All the other elements, such as words, phrases and clauses, go to make up sentences. It is difficult to define a sentence. In terms of recognizing a sentence visually it can be described as beginning with a capital letter and ending with a full stop, or with an equivalent to the full stop, such as an exclamation mark. It is a unit of grammar that can stand alone and make sense and obeys certain grammatical rules, such as usually having a subject and a predicate, as in 'The girl banged the door', where 'the girl' is the subject and 'the door' is the predicate. *See* **major sentence, simple sentence, complex sentence.**

simple sentence a sentence that cannot be broken down into other clauses. It generally contains a finite verb. Simple sentences include 'The man stole the car', 'She nudged him' and 'He kicked the ball'. *See* **complex sentence** and **compound sentence.**

singular noun a noun that refers to 'one' rather than 'more than one', which is the plural form. *See also* **irregular plural.**

split infinitive an infinitive that has had another word in the form of an adverb placed between itself and 'to', as in 'to rudely push' and 'to quietly leave'. This was once considered a great grammatical sin but the split infinitive is becoming acceptable in modern usage. In any case it sometimes makes for a clumsy sentence if one slavishly adheres to the correct form.

stative present *see* **habitual** and **tense.**

strong verb the more common term for **irregular verb.**

structure word *see* **function word.**

subject that which is spoken of in a sentence or clause and is usually either a noun, as in 'Birds fly' (birds is the noun as subject); a noun phrase, as in 'The people in the town dislike him' (the people in the town' is the subject); a pronoun, as in 'She hit the child' (she is the pronoun as subject); a proper noun, as in 'Paris is the capital of France'. *See* **dummy subject.**

subjunctive *see* **mood.**

subordinate clause a clause that is dependent on another clause, namely the main clause. Unlike the main clause, it cannot stand alone and make sense. Subordinate clauses are introduced by conjunctions. Examples of conjunctions that introduce subordinate clauses include 'after', 'before', 'when', 'if', 'because' and 'since'. *See* **adverbial clause; noun clause.**

subordinating conjunction *see* **conjunction.**

suffix *see* **Affix** section.

superlative form the form of an adjective or adverb that expresses the highest or utmost degree of the quality or manner of the word. The superlative forms follow the same rules as comparative forms except that they end in *-est* instead of *-er* and the longer ones use 'most' instead of 'more'. *See also* **comparison of adjectives.**

tense the form of a verb that is used to show the time at which the action of the verb takes place. One of the tenses in English is the **present tense.** It is used to indicate an action now going on or a state now existing. A distinction can be made between the **habitual present**, which marks habitual or repeated actions or recurring events, and the **stative present**, which indicates something that is true at all times. Examples of habitual present include 'He works long hours' and 'She walks to work'. Examples of the stative tense include 'The world is round' and 'Everyone must die eventually'.

The **progressive present** or **continuous present** is formed with the verb 'to be' and the present participle, as in, 'He is walking to the next village', 'She was driving along the road when she saw him' and 'They were worrying about the state of the economy'.

The **past tense** refers to an action or state that has taken place before the present time. In the case of regular verbs it is formed by adding *-ed* to the base form of the verb, as in 'fear/feared', 'look/looked', and 'turn/turned'. *See also* **irregular verbs.**

The **future tense** refers to an action or state that will take place at some time in the future. It is formed with 'will' and 'shall'. Traditionally 'will' was used with the second and third person pronouns ('you', 'he/she/it', 'they') and 'shall' with the first person ('I' and 'we'), as in 'You will be bored', 'He will soon be home', 'They will leave tomorrow', 'I shall buy some bread' and 'We shall go by train'. Also traditionally 'shall' was used with the second and third persons to indicate emphasis, insistence, determination, refusal, etc, as in 'You shall go to the ball' and 'He shall not be admitted'. 'Will' was used with the first person in the same way, as in 'I will get even with him'.

In modern usage 'will' is generally used for the first person as well as for second and third, as in 'I will see you tomorrow' and 'We will be there soon' and 'shall' is used for emphasis, insistence, etc, for first, second and third persons.

The future tense can also be formed with the use of 'be about to' or 'be going to', as in 'We were about to leave' and 'They were going to look for a house'.

Other tenses include the **perfect tense**, which is formed using the verb 'to have' and the past participle. In the case of regular verbs the past participle is formed by adding *ed* to the base form of the verb. *See also* **irregular verbs.** Examples of the perfect tense include 'He has played his last match', 'We have travelled all day' and 'They have thought a lot about it'.

The **past perfect tense** or **pluperfect tense** is formed using the verb 'to have' and the past participle, as in 'She had no idea that he was dead' and 'They had felt unhappy about the situation'.

The **future perfect** is formed using the verb 'to have' and the past participle, as in 'He will have arrived by now'.

they *see* **him** and **third person.**

third person a third party, not the speaker or the person or thing being spoken to. Note that 'person' in this context can refer to things as well as people. 'Person' in this sense applies to personal pronouns. The third person singular forms are 'he', 'she' and 'it' when the subject of a sentence or clause, as in 'She will win' and 'It will be fine'. The third person singular forms are 'him', 'her', 'it' when the object, as in 'His behaviour hurt her' and 'She meant it'. The third person plural is 'they' when the subject, as in 'They have left' and 'They were angry' and 'them' when the object, as in 'His words made them angry' and 'We accompanied them'.

The possessive forms of the singular are 'his', 'hers' and 'its', as in 'he played his guitar' and 'The dog hurt its leg', and the possessive form of the plural is theirs, as in 'That car is theirs' and 'They say that the book is theirs'. *See* **he.**

to-infinitive the infinitive form of the verb when it is accompanied by 'to' rather than when it is the bare infinitive without 'to'. Examples of the to-infinitive include 'We were told to go', 'I didn't want to stay' and 'To get there on time we'll have to leave now'.

transitive verb a verb that takes a direct object. In the sentence 'The boy broke the window', 'window' is a direct object and so 'broke' (past tense of break) is a transitive verb. In the sentence 'She eats fruit', 'fruit' is a direct object and so 'eat' is a transitive verb. In the sentence 'They kill enemy soldiers' 'enemy soldiers' is a direct object and so 'kill' is a transitive verb. *See* **intransitive verb.**

uncountable noun or **uncount noun** a noun that is not usually pluralized or 'counted'. Such a noun is usually preceded by 'some', rather than 'a'. Uncountable nouns often refer to substances or commodities or qualities, processes and states. Examples of uncountable nouns include butter, china, luggage, petrol, sugar, heat, information, poverty, richness and warmth. In some situations it is possible to have a countable version of what is usually an uncountable noun. Thus 'sugar' is usually considered to be an uncountable noun but it can be used in a countable form in contexts such as 'I take two sugars in my coffee please'. Some nouns exist in an uncountable and countable form. Examples include 'cake', as in 'Have some cake' and 'She ate three cakes' and 'She could not paint for lack of light' and 'the lights went out'.

verb the part of speech often known as a 'doing' word. Although this is rather restrictive, since it tends to preclude auxiliary verbs, modal verbs, etc, the verb is the word in a sentence that is most concerned with the action and is usually essential to the structure of the sentence. Verbs 'inflect' and indicate tense, voice, mood, number and person. Most of the information on verbs has been placed under related entries. *See* **active voice, auxiliary verb, finite verb, -ing form, intransitive verb, irregular verbs, linking verb, modal verb, mood, non-finite verb, passive voice** and **transitive verb.**

verb phrase a group of verb forms that have the same function as a single verb. Examples include 'have been raining', 'must have been lying', 'should not have been doing' and 'has been seen doing'.

verbal noun *see* **gerund** and **-ing form.**

vocative case a case that is relevant mainly to languages such as Latin which are based on cases and inflections. In English the vocative is expressed by addressing someone, as 'John, could I see you for a minute', or by some form of greeting, endearment or exclamation.

voice one of the categories that describes verbs. It involves two ways of looking at the action of verbs. It is divided into active voice and passive voice.

weak verb a less common term for a regular verb, in which inflection is effected by adding a letter or syllable (dawn, dawned) rather than a change of vowel (rise, rose). *See* **irregular verb.**

Usage

a, an the indefinite article. *See* **Spelling.**

-abled is a suffix meaning 'able-bodied'. It is most usually found in such phrases as 'differently abled', a 'politically correct', more positive way of referring to people with some form of disability, as in 'provide access to the club building for differently abled members'.

ableism or **ablism** means discrimination in favour of able-bodied people as in 'people in wheelchairs unable to get jobs because of ableism'. Note that the suffix '-ism' is often used to indicate discrimination against the group to which it refers, as in 'ageism'.

Aboriginal rather than **Aborigine** is now the preferred term for an original inhabitant of Australia, especially where the word is in the singular.

abuse and **misuse** both mean wrong or improper use or treatment. However, **abuse** tends to be a more condemnatory term, suggesting that the wrong use or treatment is morally wrong or illegal. Thus we find 'misuse of the equipment' or 'misuse of one's talents', but 'abuse of a privileged position' or 'abuse of children'. 'Child abuse' is usually used to indicate physical violence or sexual assault. **Abuse** is also frequently applied to the use of substances that are dangerous or injurious to health, as 'drug abuse', or 'alcohol abuse'. In addition, it is used to describe insulting or offensive language, as in 'shout abuse at the referee'.

academic is used to describe scholarly or educational matters, as 'a child with academic rather than sporting interests'. From this use it has come to mean theoretical rather than actual or practical, as in 'wasting time discussing matters of purely academic concern'. In modern use it is frequently used to mean irrelevant, as in 'Whether you vote for him or not is academic. He is certain of a majority of votes'.

access is usually a noun meaning 'entry or admission', as in 'try to gain access to the building', or 'the opportunity to use something', as in 'have access to confidential information'. It is also used to refer to the right of a parent to spend time with his or her children, as in 'Father was allowed access to the children at weekends'.

However **access** can also be used as a verb. It is most commonly found in computing, meaning obtaining information from, as in 'accessing details from the computer file relating to the accounts'. In modern usage many technical words become used, and indeed over-used, in the general language. Thus the verb **access** can now be found meaning to obtain information not on a computer, as in 'access the information in the filing cabinet'. It can also be found in the sense of gaining entry to a building, as in 'Their attempts to access the building at night were unsuccessful'.

accessory and **accessary** are interchangeable as regards only one meaning of **accessory.** A person who helps another person to commit a crime is known either as an **accessory** or an **accessary**, although the former is the more modern term. However, only **accessory** is used to describe a useful or decorative extra that is not strictly necessary, as in 'Seat covers are accessories that are included in the price of the car' and 'She wore a red dress with black accessories' ('accessories' in the second example being handbag, shoes and gloves).

accompany can be followed either by the preposition 'with' or 'by'. When it means 'to go somewhere with someone', 'by' is used, as in 'She was accompanied by her parents to church' Similarly, 'by' is used when **accompany** is used in a musical context, as in 'The singer was accompanied on the piano by her brother'. When **accompany** means 'to go along with something' or 'supplement something', either 'by' or 'with' may be used, as in 'The roast turkey was accompanied by all the trimmings', 'His words were accompanied by/with a gesture of dismissal', and 'The speaker accompanied his words with expressive gestures'.

acoustics can take either a singular or plural verb. When it is being thought of as a branch of science it is treated as being singular, as in 'Acoustics deals with the study of sound', but when it is used to describe the qualities of a hall, etc, with regard to its sound-carrying properties, it is treated as being plural, as in 'The acoustics in the school hall are very poor'.

activate and **actuate** both mean 'make active' but are commonly used in different senses. **Activate** refers to physical or chemical action, as in 'The terrorists activated the explosive device'. **Actuate** means 'to move to action' and 'to serve as a motive', as in 'The murderer was actuated by jealousy'.

actress is still widely used as a term for a woman who acts in plays or films, although many people prefer the term 'actor', regarding this as a neutral term rather than simply the masculine form. The **-ess** suffix, used to indicate the feminine form of a word, is generally becoming less common as these forms are regarded as sexist or belittling.

acute and **chronic** both refer to disease. **Acute** is used of a disease that is sudden in onset and lasts a relatively short time, as in 'flu is an acute illness'. **Chronic** is used of a disease that may be slow to develop and lasts a long time, possibly over several years, as in 'Asthma is a chronic condition'.

ad and **bc** are abbreviations that accompany year numbers. **ad** stands for 'Anno Domini', meaning 'in the year of our Lord' and indicates that the year concerned is one occurring after Jesus Christ was born. Traditionally **ad** is placed before the year number concerned, as in 'Their great-grandfather was born in ad 1801', but in modern usage it sometimes follows the year number, as in 'The house was built in 1780 ad.' **bc** stands for 'Before Christ' and indicates that the year concerned is one occurring before Jesus Christ was born. It follows the year number, as in 'The event took place in Rome in 55 bc'.

adapter and **adaptor** can be used interchangeably, but commonly **adapter** is used to refer to a person who adapts, as in 'the adapter of the stage play for television and **adaptor** is used to refer to a thing that adapts, specifically a type of electrical plug.

admission and **admittance** both mean 'permission or right to enter'. **Admission** is the more common term, as in 'They refused him admission to their house', and, unlike **admittance**, it can also mean 'the price or fee charged for entry' as in 'Admission to the football match is £3'. **Admittance** is largely used in formal or official situations, as in 'They ignored the notice saying "No Admittance" '. **Admission** also means 'confession' or 'acknowledgement of responsibility', as in 'On her own admission she was the thief'.

admit may be followed either by the preposition 'to' or the preposition 'of', depending on the sense. In the sense of 'to confess', **admit** is usually not followed by a preposition at all, as in 'He admitted his mistake' and 'She admitted stealing the brooch'. However, in this sense **admit** is sometimes followed by 'to', as in 'They have admitted to their error' and 'They have admitted to their part in the theft'.

In the sense of 'to allow to enter', **admit** is followed by 'to', as in 'The doorman admitted the guest to the club'. Also in the rather formal sense of 'give access or entrance to', **admit** is followed by 'to', as in 'the rear door admits straight to the garden'. In the sense of 'to be open to' or 'leave room for', **admit** is followed by 'of', as in 'The situation admits of no other explanation'.

admittance *see* **admission.**

adopted and **adoptive** are liable to be confused. **Adopted** is applied to children who have been adopted, as in 'The couple have two adopted daughters'. **Adoptive** is applied to a person or people who adopt a child, as in 'Her biological parents tried to get the girl back from her adoptive parents'.

aeroplane is commonly abbreviated to **plane** in modern usage. In American English **aeroplane** becomes **airplane.**

affinity may be followed by the preposition 'with' or 'between', and means 'close relationship', 'mutual attraction' or similarity, as in 'the affinity which twins have with each other' and 'There was an affinity between the two families who had lost children'. In modern usage it is sometimes followed by 'for' or 'towards', and means 'liking', as in 'She has an affinity for fair-haired men'.

ageism means discrimination on the grounds of age, as in 'By giving an age range in their job advert the firm were guilty of ageism'. Usually it refers to discrimination against older or elderly people, but it also refers to discrimination against young people.

agenda in modern usage is a singular noun having the plural **agendas**. It means 'a list of things to be attended to', as in 'The financial situation was the first item on the committee's agenda'. Originally it was a plural noun, derived from Latin, meaning 'things to be done'.

aggravate literally means 'to make worse', as in 'Her remarks simply aggravated the situation'. In modern usage it is frequently found meaning 'to irritate or annoy', as in 'The children were aggravating their mother when she was trying to read'. It is often labelled as 'informal' in dictionaries and is best avoided in formal situations.

agnostic and **atheist** are both words meaning 'disbeliever in God', but there are differences in sense between the two words. **Agnostics** believe that it is not possible to know whether God exists or not. **Atheists** believe that there is no God.

alcohol abuse is a modern term for alcoholism. *See* **abuse**.

alibi is derived from the Latin word for 'elsewhere'. It is used to refer to a legal plea that a person accused or under suspicion was somewhere other than the scene of the crime at the time the crime was committed. In modern usage **alibi** is frequently used to mean simply 'excuse' or 'pretext', as in 'He had the perfect alibi for not going to the party—he was ill in hospital'.

all together and **altogether** are not interchangeable. **All together** means 'at the same time' or 'in the same place', as in 'The guests arrived all together' and 'They kept their personal papers all together in a filing cabinet'. **Altogether** means 'in all, in total' or 'completely', as in "We collected £500 altogether' and 'The work was altogether too much for him'.

alternate and **alternative** are liable to be confused. **Alternate** means 'every other' or 'occurring by turns', as in 'They visit her mother on alternate weekends' and 'between alternate layers of meat and cheese sauce'. **Alternative** means 'offering a choice' or 'being an alternative', as in 'If the motorway is busy there is an alternative route'. **Alternative** is found in some cases in modern usage to mean 'not conventional, not traditional', as in 'alternative medicine' and 'alternative comedy'.

Alternative as a noun refers to the choice between two possibilities, as in 'The alternatives are to go by train or by plane'. In modern usage, however, it is becoming common to use it to refer also to the choice among two or more possibilities, as in 'He has to use a college from five alternatives'.

although and **though** are largely interchangeable but **though** is slightly less formal, as in 'We arrived on time although/though we left late'.

amiable and **amicable** both refer to friendliness and goodwill. **Amiable** means 'friendly' or 'agreeable and pleasant', and is mostly used of people or their moods, as in 'amiable neighbours', 'amiable travelling companions', 'of an amiable temperament' and 'be in an amiable mood'. **Amicable** means 'characterized by friendliness and goodwill' and is applied mainly to relationships, agreements, documents, etc, as in 'an amicable working relationship', 'reach an amicable settlement at the end of the war' and 'send an amicable letter to his former rival'.

among and **amongst** are interchangeable, as in 'We searched among/amongst the bushes for the ball,' 'Divide the chocolate among/amongst you', and 'You must choose among/amongst the various possibilities'.

among and **between** may be used interchangeably in most contexts. Formerly **between** was used only when referring to the relationship of two things, as in 'Share the chocolate between you and your brother', and **among** was used when referring to the relationship of three or more things, as in 'Share the chocolate among all your friends'. In modern usage **between** may be used when referring to more than two things, as in 'There is agreement between all the countries of the EU' and 'Share the chocolate between all of you'. However, **among** is still used only to describe more than two things.

amoral and **immoral** are not interchangeable. **Amoral** means 'lacking moral standards, devoid of moral sense', indicating that the person so described has no concern with morals, as in 'The child was completely amoral and did not know the difference between right and wrong'. **Immoral** means 'against or breaking moral standards, bad'. 'He knows he's doing wrong but he goes on being completely immoral' and 'commit immoral acts'. Note the spelling of both words. **Amoral** has only one *m* but **immoral** has double *m*.

anaesthetic and **analgesic** are liable to be confused. As an adjective, **anaesthetic** means 'producing a loss of feeling', as in 'inject the patient with an anaesthetic substance', and as a noun it means 'a substance that produces a loss of feeling', as in 'administer an anaesthetic to the patient on the operating table'. A local anaesthetic produces a loss of feeling in only part of the body, as in 'remove the rotten tooth under local anaesthetic'. A **general anaesthetic** produces loss of feeling in the whole body and induces unconsciousness, as in 'The operation on his leg will have to be performed under general anaesthetic'. As an adjective **analgesic** means 'producing a lack of or reduction in, sensitivity to pain, pain-killing', as in 'aspirin has an analgesic effect'. As a noun **analgesic** means 'a substance that produces a lack of, or reduction in, sensitivity to pain', as in 'aspirin, paracetamol, and other analgesics'.

arbiter and **arbitrator**, although similar in meaning, are not totally interchangeable. **Arbiter** means 'a person who has absolute power to judge or make decisions', as in 'Parisian designers used to be total arbiters of fashion'. **Arbitrator** is 'a person appointed to settle differences in a dispute', as in 'act as arbitrator between management and workers in the wages dispute'. **Arbiter** is occasionally used with the latter meaning also.

artist and **artiste** are liable to be confused. **Artist** refers to 'a person who paints or draws,' as in 'Renoir was a great artist'. The word may also refer to 'a person who is skilled in something', as in 'The mechanic is a real artist with an engine'. **Artiste** refers to 'an entertainer, such as a singer or a dancer', as in 'a list of the artistes in the musical performances'. The word is becoming a little old-fashioned.

at this moment in time is an overused phrase meaning simply 'now'. In modern usage there is a tendency to use what are thought to be grander-sounding alternatives for simple words. It is best to avoid such overworked phrases and use the simpler form.

atheist *see* **agnostic.**

au fait is French in origin but it is commonly used in English to mean 'familiar with' or 'informed about', as in 'not completely au fait with the new office system'. It is pronounced *o* fay.

authoress is not used in modern usage since it is considered sexist. **Author** is regarded as a neutral term to describe both male and female authors.

avoid *see* **evade.**

avoidance *see* **evasion.**

baited *see* **bated.**

barmaid is disliked by many people on the grounds that it sounds a belittling term and is thus sexist. It is also disliked by people who are interested in political correctness. However the word continues to be quite common, along with **barman**, and efforts to insist on **bar assistant** or **barperson** have not yet succeeded.

basically means literally 'referring to a base or basis, fundamentally', as in 'The scientist's theory is basically unsound', but it is frequently used almost meaninglessly as a fill-up word at the beginning of a sentence, as in 'Basically he just wants more money'. Overuse of this word should be avoided.

basis, meaning 'something on which something is founded', as in 'The cost of the project was the basis of his argument against it', has the plural form **bases** although it is not commonly used. It would be more usual to say 'arguments without a firm basis' than 'arguments without firm bases'.

bated as in 'with bated breath' meaning 'tense and anxious with excitement', is frequently misspelt **baited.** Care should be taken not to confuse the two words.

bathroom *see* **toilet.**

bc *see* **ad.**

because means 'for the reason that', as in 'He left because he was bored', and is sometimes misused. It is wrong to use it in a sentence that also contains 'the reason that', as in 'The reason she doesn't say much is that she is shy'. The correct form of this is 'She doesn't say much because she is shy' or 'The reason she doesn't say much is that she is shy'.

because of *see* **due to.**

beg the question is often used wrongly. It means 'to take for granted the very point that has to be proved', as in 'To say that God must exist because we can see all his wonderful creations in the world around us begs the question'. The statement assumes that these creations have been made by God although this has not been proved and yet this fact is being used as evidence that there is a God. **Beg the question** is often used wrongly to mean 'to evade the question', as in 'The police tried to get him to say where he had been but he begged the question and changed the subject'.

benign means 'kindly, well-disposed' when applied to people, as in 'fortunate enough to have a benign ruler'. This meaning may also be used of things, as in 'give a benign smile' and 'live in a benign climate'. As a medical term **benign** means 'nonmalignant, non-cancerous'. **Innocent** is another word for **benign** in this sense.

bête noire refers to 'something that one detests or fears', as in 'Loud pop music is her father's bête noire, although she sings with a pop group'. Note the spelling, particularly the accent (circumflex) on **bête** and the *e* at the end of **noire.** The phrase is French in origin and the plural form is **bêtes noires**, as in 'A bearded man is one of her many bêtes noires'.

better should be preceded by 'had' when it means 'ought to' or 'should', as in 'You had better leave now if you want to arrive there by nightfall' and 'We had better apologize for upsetting her'. In informal contexts, especially in informal speech as in 'Hey Joe, Mum says you better come now', the 'had' is often omitted but it should be retained in formal contexts. The negative form is 'had better not', as in 'He had better not try to deceive her'.

between is often found in the phrase 'between you and me' as in 'Between you and me I think he stole the money'. Note that 'me' is correct and that 'I' is wrong. This is because prepositions like 'between' are followed by an object, not a subject. 'I' acts as the subject of a sentence, as in 'I know her', and 'me' as the object, as in 'She knows me'.

between *see* **among.**

bi- of the words beginning with the prefix bi-, biannual and biennial are liable to be confused. **Biannual** means 'twice a year' and **biennial** means 'every two years'.

Bicentenary and **bicentennial** both mean 'a 200th anniversary', as in 'celebrating the bicentenary/bicentennial of the firm'. **Bicentenary** is, however, the more common expression in British English, although **bicentennial** is more common in American English.

Biweekly is a confusing word as it has two different meanings. It means both 'twice a week' and 'once every two weeks'. Thus there is no means of knowing without other information whether 'a bi-weekly publication' comes out once a week or every two weeks. The confusion arises because the prefix 'bi-', which means 'two', can refer both to doubling, as in 'bicycle', and halving, as in 'bisection'.

biannual *see* **bi-**.

bicentenary and **bicentennial** *see* **bi-**.

biennial *see* **bi-**.

billion traditionally meant 'one million million' in British English, but in modern usage it has increasingly taken on the American English meaning of 'one thousand million'. When the number of million pounds, etc, is specified, the number immediately precedes the word 'million' without the word 'of', as in 'The firm is worth five billion dollars', but if no number is present then 'of' precedes 'dollars, etc', as in 'The research project cost the country millions of dollars'. The word **billion** may also be used loosely to mean 'a great but unspecified number', as in 'Billions of people in the world live in poverty'.

birth name is a suggested alternative for **maiden name**, a woman's surname before she married and took the name of her husband. **Maiden name** is considered by some to be inappropriate since maiden in one of its senses is another name for 'virgin' and it is now not at all usual for women to be virgins when they marry. Another possible name alternative is **family name.**

biweekly *see* **bi-**.

black is the word now usually applied to dark-skinned people of Afro-Caribbean origins and is the term preferred by most black-skinned people themselves. **Coloured** is considered by many to be offensive since it groups all non-Caucasians together. In America, African-American is becoming increasingly common as a substitute for **black.**

blond and **blonde** are both used to mean 'a fair-haired person', but they are not interchangeable. **Blond** is used to describe a man or boy, **blonde** is used to describe a woman or girl. They are derived from the French adjective, which changes endings according to the gender of the noun.

boat and **ship** are often used interchangeably, but usually **boat** refers to a smaller vessel than a ship.

bona fide is an expression of Latin origin meaning literally 'of good faith'. It means 'genuine, sincere' or 'authentic', as in 'a bona fide member of the group', 'a bona fide excuse for not going', or 'a bona fide agreement'.

bottom line is an expression from accountancy that has become commonly used in the general language. In accountancy it refers to the final line of a set of company accounts, which indicates whether the company has made a profit or a loss, obviously a very important line. In general English, **bottom line** has a range of meanings, from 'the final outcome or result', as in 'The bottom line of their discussion was that they decided to sell the company', through 'the most important point of something', as in 'The bottom line was whether they could get there on time or not', to 'the last straw', as in 'His affair with another woman was the bottom line of their stormy relationship and she left him'.

can and **may** both mean in one of their senses 'to be permitted'. In this sense **can** is much less formal than **may** and is best restricted to informal contexts, as in ' "Can I go to the park now?" asked the child.' **May** is used in more formal contexts, as in 'May I please have your name?' Both **can** and **may** have other meanings. **Can** has the meaning 'to be able', as in 'They thought his legs were permanently damaged but he can still walk'. **May** has the additional meaning 'to be likely', as in 'You may well be right'.

The past tense of **can** is **could**, as in 'The children asked if they could (= be permitted to) go to the park'. 'The old man could (= be unable to) not walk upstairs'. The past tense of **may** is **might**, as in 'The child asked if he might have a piece of cake (= be permitted to)'. 'They might (= be likely to) well get here tonight'.

cannot, can not, and **can't** all mean the same thing but they are used in different contexts. **Cannot** is the most usual form, as in 'The children have been told that they cannot go' and 'We cannot get there by public transport'. **Cannot** is written as two words only for emphasis, as in 'No, you can not have any more' and 'The invalid certainly can not walk to the ambulance'. **Can't** is used in less formal contexts and often in speech, as in 'I can't be bothered going out' and 'They can't bear to be apart'.

cardigan, jersey, jumper and **sweater** all refer to knitted garments for the top part of the body. **Cardigan** refers to a jacket-like garment with buttons down the front. **Jersey, jumper** and **sweater** refer to a knitted garment pulled over the head to get it on and off.

cardinal and **ordinal** numbers refer to different aspects of numbers. **Cardinal** is applied to those numbers that refer to quantity or value without referring to their place in the set, as in 'one', 'two', 'fifty' 'one hundred'. **Ordinal** is applied to numbers that refer to their order in a series, as in 'first', 'second', 'fortieth', 'hundredth'.

carer has recently taken on the meaning of 'a person who looks after a sick, handicapped or old relative or friend', as in 'carers requiring a break from their responsibilities'.

carpet and **rug** both refer to forms of floor covering. Generally a rug is smaller than a carpet, and the fitted variety of fabric floor covering is always known as carpet.

caster and **castor** are mainly interchangeable. Both forms can be applied to 'a swivelling wheel attached to the base of a piece of furniture to enable it to be moved easily' and 'a container with a perforated top from which sugar is sprinkled'. The kind of sugar known as **caster** can also be called **castor**, although this is less usual. The lubricating or medicinal oil known as **castor oil** is never spelt **caster**.

Catholic and **catholic** have different meanings. **Catholic** as an adjective refers to the Roman Catholic Church, as in 'The Pope is head of the Catholic Church', or to the universal body of Christians. As a noun it means 'a member of the Catholic Church', as in 'She is a Catholic but he is a Protestant'. Catholic with a lower-case initial letter means 'general, wide-ranging', as in 'a catholic selection of essays', and 'broad-minded, liberal', as in 'a catholic attitude to the tastes of others'.

celibate means 'unmarried' or 'remaining unmarried and chaste, especially for religious reasons', as in 'Roman Catholic priests have to be celibate'. In modern usage, because of its connection with chastity, **celibate** has come to mean 'abstaining from sexual intercourse', as in 'The threat of Aids has made many people celibate'. The word is frequently misspelt. Note the *i* after *l*.

Celsius, centigrade and **Fahrenheit** are all scales of temperature. **Celsius** and **centigrade** mean the same and refer to a scale on which water freezes at 0° and boils at 100°. This scale is now the principal unit of temperature. **Celsius** is now the more acceptable term. **Fahrenheit** refers to a scale on which water freezes at 32° and boils at 212°. It is still used, informally at least, of the weather, and statements such as 'The temperature reached the nineties today' are still common.

Note the initial capital letters in **Celsius** and **Fahrenheit**. This is because they are named after people, namely the scientists who devised them.

centenary and **centennial** are both used to refer to a 'one-hundredth anniversary'. **Centenary** is the more common term in British English, as in 'celebrate the town's centenary', whereas **centennial** is more common in American English. **Centennial** may be used as an adjective, as in 'organize the town's centennial celebrations'.

centigrade *see* **Celsius.**

centre and **middle** mean much the same, but **centre** is used more precisely than **middle** in some cases, as in 'a line through the centre of the circle' and 'She felt faint in the middle of the crowd'.

centre on and **centre around** are often used interchangeably, as in 'Her world centres on/around her children'. **Centre around** is objected to by some people on the grounds that **centre** is too specific to be used with something as vague as **around**. When it is used as a verb with place names, **centre** is used with 'at', as in 'Their business operation is centred at London'.

centuries are calculated from 1001, 1501, 1901, etc, not 1000, 1500, 1900, etc. This is because the years are counted from ad 1, there being no year 0.

chair is often used to mean 'a person in charge of a meeting, committee, etc', as in 'The committee has a new chair this year'. Formerly **chairman** was always used in this context, as in 'He was appointed chairman of the fund-raising committee' but this is disapproved of on the grounds that it is sexist. Formerly, **chairman** was sometimes used even if the person in charge of the meeting or committee was a woman, and sometimes **chairwoman** was used in this situation. **Chairperson**, which also avoids sexism, is frequently used instead of **chair**. **Chair** is also a verb meaning 'to be in charge of a meeting, committee, etc'.

-challenged is a modern suffix that is very much part of politically correct language. It is used to convey a disadvantage, problem or disorder in a more positive light. For example, 'visually challenged' is used in politically correct language instead of 'blind' or 'partially sighted', and 'aurally challenged' is used instead of 'deaf' or 'hard of hearing'. **-Challenged** is often used in humorous coinages, as in 'financially challenged', meaning 'penniless', and 'intellectually challenged', meaning 'stupid'.

charisma was formerly a theological word used to mean 'a spiritual gift', such as the gift of healing, etc. In modern usage it is used to describe 'a special quality or power that influences, inspires or stimulates other people, personal magnetism', as in 'The president was elected because of his charisma'. The adjective from **charisma** is **charismatic**, as in 'his charismatic style of leadership'.

chauvinism originally meant 'excessive patriotism', being derived from the name of Nicolas Chauvin, a soldier in the army of Napoleon Bonaparte, who was noted for his excessive patriotism. In modern usage **chauvinism** has come to mean 'excessive enthusiasm or devotion to a cause' or, more particularly, 'an irrational and prejudiced belief in the superiority of one's own cause'. When preceded by 'male', it refers specifically to attitudes and actions that assume the superiority of the male sex and thus the inferiority of women, as in 'accused of not giving her the job because of male chauvinism'. **Chauvinism** is frequently used to mean **male chauvinism**, as in 'He shows his chauvinism towards his female staff by never giving any of them senior jobs'. The adjective formed from **chauvinism** is **chauvinistic.**

chemist and **pharmacist** have the same meaning in one sense of **chemist** only. **Chemist** and **pharmacist** are both words for 'one who prepares drugs ordered by medical prescription'. **Chemist** has the additional meaning of 'a scientist who works in the field of chemistry', as in 'He works as an industrial chemist'.

childish and **childlike** both refer to someone being like a child but they are used in completely different contexts. **Childish** is used in a derogatory way about someone to indicate that he or she is acting like a child in an immature way, as in 'Even though she is 20 years old she has childish tantrums when she does not get her own way' and 'childish handwriting for an adult'. **Childlike** is a term of approval or a complimentary term used to describe something that has some of the attractive qualities of childhood, as in 'She has a childlike enthusiasm for picnics' and 'He has a childlike trust in others'.

Christian name is used to mean someone's first name as opposed to someone's **surname**. It is increasingly being replaced by **first name** or **forename** since Britain has become a multicultural society where there are several religions as well as Christianity.

chronic *see* **acute.**

city and **town** in modern usage are usually distinguished on grounds of size and status, a city being larger and more important than a town. Originally in Britain a **city** was a town which had special rights conferred on it by royal charter and which usually had a cathedral.

clean and **cleanse** as verbs both mean 'to clean', as in 'clean the house' and 'cleanse the wound'. However, **cleanse** tends to indicate a more thorough cleaning than **clean** and sometimes carries the suggestion of 'to purify', as in 'prayer cleansing the soul'.

client and **customer**, although closely related in meaning, are not interchangeable. **Client** refers to 'a person who pays for the advice or services of a professional person', as in 'They are both clients of the same lawyer', 'a client waiting to see the bank manager' and 'hairdressers who keep their clients waiting'. **Customer** refers to 'a person who purchases goods from a shop, etc', as in 'customers complaining to shopkeepers about faulty goods' and 'a regular customer at the local supermarket'. **Client** is used in the sense of 'customer' by shops who regard it as a more superior word, as in 'clients of an exclusive dress boutique'.

climate no longer refers just to weather, as in 'go to live in a hot climate', 'Britain has a temperate climate'. It has extended its meaning to refer to 'atmosphere', as in 'live in a climate of despair' and to 'the present situation', as in 'businessmen nervous about the financial climate'.

clone originally was a technical word meaning 'one of a group of offspring that are asexually produced and which are genetically identical to the parent and to other members of the group'. In modern usage **clone** is frequently used loosely to mean 'something that is very similar to something else', as in 'In the sixties there were many Beatles' clones', and 'grey-suited businessmen looking like clones of each other'.

collaborate and **cooperate** are not interchangeable in all contexts. They both mean 'to work together for a common purpose', as in 'The two scientists are collaborating/cooperating on cancer research' and 'The rival building firms are collaborating/cooperating on the new shopping complex'. When the work concerned is of an artistic or creative nature **collaborate** is the more commonly used word, as in 'The two directors are collaborating on the film' and 'The composers collaborated on the theme music'. **Collaborate** also has the meaning of 'to work with an enemy, especially an enemy that is occupying one's country', as in 'a Frenchman who collaborated with the Germans when they installed a German government in France'.

coloured *see* **black.**

commence, begin, and **start** mean the same, but **commence** is used in a more formal context than the other two words, as in 'The legal proceedings will commence tomorrow' and 'The memorial service will commence with a hymn'. **Begin** and **start** are used less formally, as 'The match begins at 2 p.m.' and 'The film has already started'.

commensurate is followed by 'with' to form a phrase meaning 'proportionate to, appropriate to', as in 'a salary commensurate with her qualifications' and 'a price commensurate with the quality of the goods'.

comparatively means 'relatively, in comparison with a standard', as in 'The house was comparatively inexpensive for that area of the city' and 'In an area of extreme poverty they are comparatively well off'. In modern usage it is often used loosely to mean 'rather' or 'fairly' without any suggestion of reference to a standard, as in 'She has comparatively few friends' and 'It is a comparatively quiet resort'.

compare may take either the preposition 'to' or 'with'. 'To' is used when two things or people are being likened to each other or being declared similar, as in 'He compared her hair to silk' and 'He compared his wife to Helen of Troy'. 'With' is used when two things or people are being considered from the point of view of both similarities and differences, as in 'If you compare the new pupil's work with that of the present class you will find it brilliant', and 'If you compare the prices in the two stores you will find that the local one is the cheaper'. In modern usage the distinction is becoming blurred because the difference is rather subtle.

comparison is usually followed by the preposition 'with', as in 'In comparison with hers his work is brilliant'. However, when it means 'the action of likening something or someone to something or someone else', it is followed by 'to', as in 'the comparison of her beauty to that of Garbo'.

complementary medicine is a term applied to the treatment of illness or disorders by techniques other than conventional medicine. These include homeopathy, osteopathy, acupuncture, acupressure, iridology, etc. The word **complementary** suggests that the said techniques complement and work alongside conventional medical techniques. **Alternative medicine** means the same as **complementary medicine**, but the term suggests that they are used instead of the techniques of conventional medicine rather than alongside them.

complex in one of its senses is used rather loosely in modern usage. It refers technically to 'an abnormal state caused by unconscious repressed desires or past experiences', as in 'an inferiority complex'. In modern usage it is used loosely to describe 'any obsessive concern or fear', as in 'She has a complex about her weight', 'He has a complex about his poor background'. **Complex** is also used to refer to 'a group of connected or similar things'. It is now used mainly of a group of buildings or units connected in some way, as in 'a shopping complex' or 'a sports complex'.

Complex is also an adjective meaning 'complicated', as in 'His motives in carrying out the crime were complex' and 'The argument was too complex for most people to understand'.

compose, comprise and **constitute** are all similar in meaning but are used differently. **Compose** means 'to come together to make a whole, to make up'. It is most commonly found in the passive, as in 'The team was composed of young players' and 'The group was composed largely of elderly people'. It can be used in the active voice, as in 'the tribes which composed the nation' and 'the members which composed the committee', but this use is rarer. **Constitute** means the same as **compose** but it is usually used in the active voice, as in 'the foodstuffs that constitute a healthy diet' and 'the factors that constitute a healthy environment'. **Comprise** means 'to consist of, to be made up of'.

concave and **convex** are liable to be confused. **Concave** means 'curved inwards', as in 'The inside of a spoon would be described as concave'. **Convex** means 'curved outwards, bulging', as in 'The outside or bottom of a spoon would be described as convex'.

conducive, meaning 'leading to, contributing to', is followed by the preposition 'to', as in 'conditions conducive to health growth'.

conform may be followed by the preposition 'to' or the preposition 'with'. It is followed by 'to' when it means 'to keep to or comply with', as in 'conform to the conventions' and 'refuse to conform to the company regulations', and with 'with' when it means 'to agree with, to go along with', as in 'His ideas do not conform with those of the rest of the committee'.

connection and **connexion** are different forms of the same word, meaning 'a relationship between two things'. In modern usage **connection** is much the commoner spelling, as in 'no connection between the events' and 'a fire caused by a faulty connection'.

connote and **denote** are liable to be confused. **Connote** means 'to suggest something in addition to the main, basic meaning of something', as in 'the fear that the word cancer connotes' and 'The word 'home' connotes security and love'. **Denote** means 'to mean or indicate', as in 'The word cancer denotes a malignant illness' and 'The word "home" denotes the place where one lives'.

consist can be followed either by the preposition 'of' or by the preposition 'in', depending on the meaning. **Consist of** means 'to be made up of, to comprise', as in 'The team consists of eleven players and two reserve players'. **Consist in** means 'to have as the chief or only element or feature, to lie in', as in 'The charm of the village consists in its isolation' and 'The effectiveness of the plan consisted in its simplicity'.

constitute *see* **compose.**

contagious and **infectious** both refer to diseases that can be passed on to other people but they do not mean the same. **Contagious** means 'passed on by physical contact', as in 'He caught a contagious skin disease while working in the clinic' and 'Venereal diseases are contagious'. **Infectious** means 'caused by airborne or water-borne microorganisms', as in 'The common cold is highly infectious and is spread by people sneezing and coughing'.

contemporary originally meant 'living or happening at the same time', as in 'Shakespeare and Marlowe were contemporary playwrights' and 'Marlowe was contemporary with Shakespeare'. Later it came to mean also 'happening at the present time, current', as in 'What is your impression of the contemporary literary scene?' and 'Contemporary moral values are often compared unfavourably with those of the past'. These two uses of **contemporary** can cause ambiguity. In modern usage it is also used to mean 'modern, up-to-date', as in 'extremely contemporary designs'.

convex *see* **concave.**

cooperate *see* **collaborate.**

co-respondent *see* **correspondent.**

correspondent and **co-respondent** are liable to be confused. **Correspondent** refers either to 'a person who communicates by letter', as in 'They were correspondents for years but had never met', or to 'a person who contributes news items to a newspaper or radio or television programme', as in 'the foreign correspondent of the *Times*'. A **co-respondent** is 'a person who has been cited in a divorce case as having committed adultery with one of the partners'.

cousin can cause confusion. The children of brothers and sisters are **first cousins** to each other. The children of **first cousins** are **second cousins** to each other. The child of one's **first cousin** and the **first cousin** of one's parents is one's **first cousin first removed.** The grandchild of one's **first cousin** or the **first cousin** of one's grandparent is one's **second cousin twice removed.**

crisis literally means 'turning point' and should be used to refer to 'a turning point in an illness', as in 'The fever reached a crisis and she survived' and 'a decisive or crucial moment in a situation, whose outcome will make a definite difference or change for better or worse', as in 'The financial situation has reached a crisis—the firm will either survive or go bankrupt'. In modern usage **crisis** is becoming increasingly used loosely for 'any worrying or troublesome situation', as in 'There's a crisis in the kitchen. The cooker's broken down'. The plural is **crises.**

criterion, meaning 'a standard by which something or someone is judged or evaluated', as 'What criterion is used for deciding which pupils will gain entrance to the school?' and 'The standard of play was the only criterion for entrance to the golf club'. It is a singular noun of which **criteria** is the plural, as in 'They must satisfy all the criteria for entrance to the club or they will be refused'.

critical has two main meanings. It means 'finding fault', as in 'His report on her work was very critical'. It also means 'at a crisis, at a decisive moment, crucial', as in 'It was a critical point in their relationship'. This meaning is often applied to the decisive stage of an illness, as in 'the critical hours after a serious operation', and is used also to describe an ill person who is at a crucial stage of an illness or dangerously ill. **Critical** also means 'involved in making judgements or assessments of artistic or creative works', as in 'give a critical evaluation of the author's latest novel'.

crucial means 'decisive, critical', as in 'His vote is crucial since the rest of the committee is split down the middle'. In modern usage it is used loosely to mean 'very important', as in 'It is crucial that you leave now'. **Crucial** is derived from crux, meaning 'a decisive point', as in 'the crux of the situation'.

curriculum is derived from Latin and originally took the plural form **curricula**, but in modern usage the plural form **curriculums** is becoming common.

curriculum vitae refers to 'a brief account of a person's qualifications and career to date'. It is often requested by an employer when a candidate is applying for a job. **Vitae** is pronounced *vee*-ti, the second syllable rhyming with my.

data was formerly used mainly in a scientific or technical context and was always treated as a plural noun, taking a plural verb, as in 'compare the data which were provided by the two research projects'. The singular form was **datum,** which is now rare. In modern usage the word **data** became used in computing as a collective noun meaning 'body of information' and is frequently used with a singular verb, as in 'The data is essential for our research'. This use has spread into the general language.

dates these are usually written in figures, as in 1956, rather than in words, as in nineteen fifty-six, except in formal contexts, such as legal documents. There are various ways of writing dates. The standard form in Britain is becoming day followed by month followed by year, as in '24 February 1970'. In North America the standard form of this is 'February 24, 1970', and that is a possibility in Britain also. Alternatively, some people write '24th February 1970'. Care should be taken with the writing of dates entirely in numbers, especially if one is corresponding with someone in North America. In Britain the day of the month is put first, the month second and the year third, as in '2/3/50', '2 March 1950'. In North America the month is put first, followed by the day of the month and the year. Thus in North America '2/3/50' would be '3 February 1950'.

Centuries may be written either in figures, as in 'the 19th century', or in words, as in 'the nineteenth century'

Decades and centuries are now usually written without apostrophes as in '1980s' and '1990s'.

datum *see* **data.**

deadly and **deathly** both refer to death but they have different meanings. **Deadly** means 'likely to cause death, fatal', as in 'His enemy dealt him a deadly blow with his sword' and 'He contracted a deadly disease in the jungle'. **Deathly** means 'referring to death, resembling death', as in 'She was deathly pale with fear'.

decimate literally means 'to kill one in ten' and is derived from the practice in ancient Rome of killing every tenth soldier as a punishment for mutiny. In modern usage it has come to mean 'to kill or destroy a large part of', as in 'Disease has decimated the population'. It has also come to mean 'to reduce considerably', as in 'the recession has decimated the jobs in the area'.

defective and **deficient** are similar in meaning but are not interchangeable. **Defective** means 'having a fault, not working properly', as in 'return the defective vacuum cleaner to the shop', 'The second-hand car proved to be defective' and 'He cannot be a pilot as his eyesight is defective'. **Deficient** means 'having a lack, lacking in', as in 'The athlete is very fast but he is deficient in strength' and 'Her diet is deficient in vitamin C'.

deficient *see* **defective.**

definite article *see* **the.**

delusion and **illusion** in modern usage are often used interchangeably but they are not quite the same. **Delusion** means 'a false or mistaken idea or belief', as in 'He is under the delusion that he is brilliant' and 'suffer from delusions of grandeur'. It can be part of a mental disorder, as in 'He suffers from the delusion that he is Napoleon'. **Illusion** means 'a false or misleading impression', as in 'There was no well in the desert—it was an optical illusion', 'The conjurer's tricks were based on illusion' and 'the happy childhood illusions that everyone lived happy ever after'.

demise is a formal word for death, as in 'He never recovered from the demise of his wife'. In modern usage it applies to the ending of an activity, as in 'The last decade saw the demise of coal-mining in the area'. In modern usage it has come to mean also 'the decline or failure of an activity', as in 'the gradual demise of his business'.

dénouement means 'the final outcome', as in 'The novel had a unexpected denouement'. It is pronounced day-*noo*-mon.

derisive and **derisory** are both adjectives connected with the noun 'derision' but they have different meanings. **Derisive** means 'expressing derision, scornful, mocking' as in 'give a derisive smile' and 'His efforts were met with derisive laughter'. Derisory means 'deserving derision, ridiculous' as in 'Their attempts at playing the game were derisory'. **Derisory** is frequently used to mean 'ridiculously small or inadequate', as in 'The salary offered was derisory'.

despatch and **dispatch** are interchangeable. It is most common as a verb meaning 'to send', as in 'despatch/dispatch an invitation'. It is rarer as a noun. It means 'a message or report, often official', as in 'receive a despatch/dispatch that the soldiers were to move on'. It also means 'rapidity, speed', as in 'carry out the orders with despatch/dispatch'.

dessert, pudding, sweet and **afters** all mean the same thing. They refer to the last and sweet course of a meal. **Dessert** has relatively recently become the most widespread of these terms. **Pudding** was previously regarded by the upper and middle classes as the most acceptable word of these, but it is now thought of by many as being rather old-fashioned or as being more suited to certain types of dessert than others—thus syrup sponge would be a pudding, but not fresh fruit salad. **Sweet** is a less formal word and is regarded by some people as being lower-class or regional. **Afters** is common only in very informal English.

devil's advocate is a phrase that is often misunderstood. It means 'someone who points out the possible flaws or faults in an argument etc', as in 'He played the devil's advocate and showed her the weakness in her argument so that she was able to perfect it before presenting it to the committee'. The phrase is sometimes wrongly thought of as meaning 'someone who defends an unpopular point of view or person'.

diagnosis and **prognosis** are liable to be confused. Both are used with reference to disease but have different meanings. **Diagnosis** refers to 'the identification of a disease or disorder', as in 'She had cancer but the doctor failed to make the correct diagnosis until it was too late'. **Prognosis** refers to 'the prediction of the likely course of a disease or disorder', as in 'According to the doctor's prognosis, the patient will be dead in six months'.

dice was originally the plural form of the singular noun **die**, but **die** is now rarely used. Instead, **dice** is used as both a singular and a plural noun, as in 'throw a wooden dice' and 'use three different dice in the same game'.

different is most usually followed by the preposition 'from', as in 'Their style of living is different from ours'. **Different from** is considered to be the most correct construction, particularly in formal English. **Different to** is used in informal situations, as in 'His idea of a good time is different to ours'. **Different than** is used in American English.

dilemma is frequently used wrongly. It refers to 'a situation in which one is faced with two or more equally undesirable possibilities', as in 'I can't decide which of the offers to accept. It's a real dilemma'.

dinner, lunch, supper and **tea** are terms that can cause confusion. Their use can vary according to class, region of the country and personal preference. Generally speaking, people who have their main meal in the evening call it **dinner**. However, people who have their main meal in the middle of the day frequently call this meal **dinner**. People who have **dinner** in the evening usually refer to their midday meal, usually a lighter meal, as **lunch**. A more formal version of this word is **luncheon**, which is now quite a rare word. **Supper** has two meanings, again partly dependent on class and region. It can refer either to the main meal of the day if it is eaten in the evening—when it is virtually a synonym for **dinner**. Alternatively, it can refer to a light snack, such as cocoa and toasted cheese, eaten late in the evening before going to bed. **Tea** again has two meanings when applied to a meal. It either means a light snack-type meal of tea, sandwiches and cakes eaten in the late afternoon. Alternatively, it can refer to a cooked meal, sometimes taken with tea, and also referred to as **high tea**, eaten in the early evening, rather than **dinner** later in the evening.

disabled is objected to by some people on the grounds that it is a negative term, but it is difficult to find an acceptable alternative. In politically correct language **physically challenged** has been suggested as has **differently abled**, but neither of these has gained widespread use. It should be noted that the use of 'the disabled' should be avoided. 'Disabled people' should be used instead.

disablism and **disableism** mean 'discrimination against disabled people', as in 'He felt his failure to get a job was because of disablism'. **Disablist** and **disableist** are adjectives meaning 'showing or practising disablism', as in 'guilty of disablist attitudes'. They also refer to 'a person who discriminates on the grounds of disability', as in 'That employer is a disablist'.

disassociate and **dissociate** are used interchangeably, as in 'She wished to disassociate/dissociate herself from the statement issued by her colleagues', but **dissociate** is the more usual.

discover and **invent** are not interchangeable. **Discover** means 'to find something that is already in existence but is generally unknown', as in 'discover a new route to China' and 'discover the perfect place for a holiday'. **Invent** means 'to create something that has never before existed', as in 'invent the telephone' and 'invent a new form of heating system'.

disempowered in modern usage does not mean only 'having one's power removed', as in 'The king was disempowered by the invading general', but also means the same as 'powerless', as in 'We are disempowered to give you any more money'. **Disempowered** is seen in politically correct language as a more positive way of saying **powerless**.

disinterested and **uninterested** are often used interchangeably in modern usage to mean 'not interested, indifferent', as in 'pupils totally disinterested/uninterested in school work'. Many people dislike **disinterested** being used in this way and regard it as a wrong use, but it is becoming increasingly common. **Disinterested** also means 'impartial, unbiased', as in 'ask a disinterested party to settle the dispute between them'.

disorient and **disorientate** are used interchangeably. 'The town had changed so much since his last visit that he was completely disoriented/disorientated' and 'After the blow to her head she was slightly disoriented/disorientated'.

divorcee refers to 'a divorced person', as in 'a club for divorcees'. **Divorcé** refers to 'a divorced man', and **divorcée** to 'a divorced woman'.

double negative the occurrence of two negative words in a single sentence or clause, as in 'He didn't say nothing' and 'We never had no quarrel'. This is usually considered incorrect in standard English, although it is a feature of some social or regional dialects. The use of the double negative, if taken literally, often has the opposite meaning to the one intended. Thus 'He didn't say nothing' conveys the idea that 'He said something'.

Some double negatives are considered acceptable, as in 'I wouldn't be surprised if they don't turn up', although it is better to restrict such constructions to informal contexts. The sentence quoted conveys the impression that the speaker will be quite surprised if 'they' do 'turn up'. Another example of an acceptable double negative is 'I can't not worry about the children. Anything could have happened to them'. Again this type of construction is best restricted to informal contexts.

It is the semi-negative forms, such as 'hardly' and 'scarcely', that cause most problems with regard to double negatives, as in 'We didn't have hardly any money to buy food' and 'They didn't have barely enough time to catch the bus'. Such sentences are incorrect.

doubtful and **dubious** can be used interchangeably in the sense of 'giving rise to doubt, uncertain', as in 'The future of the project is dubious/doubtful', and in the sense of 'having doubts, unsure', as in 'I am doubtful/dubious about the wisdom of going'. **Dubious** also means 'possibly dishonest or bad', as in 'of dubious morals'.

draughtsman/woman and **draftsman/woman** are not the same. **Draughtsman/woman** refers to 'a person who draws detailed plans of a building, etc', as in 'study the plans of the bridge prepared by the draughtsman'. **Draftsman/woman** refers to 'a person who prepares a preliminary version of plans, etc', as in 'several draftswomen working on the draft parliamentary bills'.

drawing room *see* **sitting room.**

dreamed and **dreamt** are interchangeable both as the past tense and the past participle of the verb 'dream', as in 'She dreamed/dreamt about living in the country' and in 'He has dreamed/dreamt the same dream for several nights'.

drier and **dryer** can both be used to describe 'a machine or appliance that dries', as in 'hair-drier/hair-dryer' and 'tumbler drier/dryer'. As an adjective meaning 'more dry', **drier** is the usual word, as in 'a drier summer than last year'.

dubious *see* **doubtful.**

due to, owing to and **because of** should not be used interchangeably. Strictly speaking, **due to** should be used only adjectivally, as in 'His poor memory is due to brain damage' and 'cancellations due to bad weather'. When a prepositional use is required **owing to** and **because of** should be used, as in 'the firm was forced to close owing to a lack of capital' and 'The train was cancelled because of snow on the line'. In modern usage it is quite common for **due to** to be used instead of **owing to** or **because of** because the distinction is rather difficult to comprehend.

e.g. means 'for example' and is an abbreviation of the Latin phrase *exempli gratia*. It is used before examples of something just previously mentioned, as in 'He cannot eat dairy products, e.g. milk, butter and cream'. A comma is usually placed just before it and, unlike some abbreviations, it has full stops.

each other and **one another** used not to be used interchangeably. It was taught that **each other** should be used when only two people are involved and that **one another** should be used when more than two people are involved, as in 'John and Mary really love each other' and 'All the members of the family love one another'. In modern use this restriction is often ignored.

EC and **EEC** both refer to the same thing, but **EC**, the abbreviation for

Economic Community replaced **EEC**, the abbreviation for **European Economic Community**.

Both have now been replaced by **EU**, for **European Union**.

effeminate *see* **female**.

egoist and **egotist** are frequently used interchangeably in modern usage. Although they are not, strictly speaking, the same, the differences between them are rather subtle. **Egoist** refers to 'a person intent on self-interest, a selfish person', as in 'an egoist who never gave a thought to the needs of others'. **Egotist** refers to 'a person who is totally self-centred and obsessed with his/her own concerns', as in 'a real egotist who was always talking about herself'.

eke out originally meant 'to make something more adequate by adding to it or supplementing it', as in 'The poor mother eked out the small amount of meat with a lot of vegetables to feed her large family'. It can now also mean 'to make something last longer by using it sparingly', as in 'try to eke out our water supply until we reach a town', and 'to succeed or make with a great deal of effort', as in 'eke out a meagre living from their small farm'.

elder and **older** are not interchangeable. **Elder** is used only of people, as in 'The smaller boy is the elder of the two'. It is frequently used of family relationships, as in 'His elder brother died before him'. **Older** can be used of things as well as people, as in 'The church looks ancient but the castle is the older of the buildings' and 'The smaller girl is the older of the two'. It also can be used of family relationships, as in 'It was his older brother who helped him'. **Elder** used as a noun suggests experience or worthiness as well as age, as in 'Important issues used to be decided by the village elders' and 'Children should respect their elders and betters'.

elderly, as well as meaning 'quite or rather old', as in 'a town full of middle-aged and elderly people', is a more polite term than 'old', no matter how old the person referred to is, as in 'a residential home for elderly people'. **Elderly** is used only of people, except when used humorously, as in 'this cheese is getting rather elderly'.

eldest and **oldest** follow the same pattern as **elder** and **older**, as in 'The smallest boy is the eldest of the three', 'His eldest brother lived longer than any of them', 'The castle is the oldest building in the town' and 'He has four brothers but the oldest one is dead'.

empathy and **sympathy** are liable to be confused although they are not interchangeable. **Empathy** means 'the ability to imagine and share another's feelings, experiences, etc', as in 'As a single parent herself, the journalist has a real empathy with women bringing up children on their own' and 'The writer felt a certain empathy with the subject of his biography since they both came from a poverty-stricken childhood'. **Sympathy** means 'a feeling of compassion, pity or sorrow towards someone', as in 'feel sympathy for homeless children' and 'show sympathy towards the widow'.

endemic is usually used to describe a disease and means 'occurring in a particular area', as in 'a disease endemic to the coastal areas of the country' and 'difficult to clear the area of endemic disease'.

enervate is a word that is frequently misused. It means 'to weaken, to lessen in vitality', as in 'she was enervated by the extreme heat' and 'Absence of funding had totally enervated the society'. It is often wrongly used as though it meant the opposite.

enquiry and **inquiry** are frequently used interchangeably, as in 'make enquiries/inquiries about her health'. However some people see a distinction between them and use **enquiry** for ordinary requests for information, as in 'make enquiries about the times of trains'. They use **inquiry** only for 'investigation', as in 'The police have begun a murder inquiry' and 'launch an inquiry into the hygiene standards of the food firm'.

equal can be followed either by the preposition 'with' or the preposition 'to', but the two constructions are not interchangeable. **Equal to** is used in such sentences as 'He wished to climb the hill but his strength was not equal to the task'. **Equal with** is used in such sentences as 'After many hours of playing the two players remained equal with each other' and 'The women in the factory are seeking a pay scale equal with that of men'.

equally should not be followed by 'as'. Examples of it used correctly include 'Her brother is an expert player but she is equally talented' and 'He is trying hard but his competitors are trying equally hard'. These should not read 'but she is equally as talented' nor 'but his competitors are trying equally as hard'.

Esq. a word that can be used instead of 'Mr' when addressing an envelope to a man, as in 'John Jones, Esq.'. It is mostly used in formal contexts. Note that Esq. is used instead of 'Mr', not as well as it. It is usually spelt with a full stop.

etc the abbreviation of a Latin phrase *et cetera*, meaning 'and the rest, and other things'. It is used at the end of lists to indicate that there exist other examples of the kind of thing that has just been named, as in 'He grows potatoes, carrots, turnips, etc', 'The girls can play tennis, hockey, squash, etc', 'The main branch of the bank can supply francs, marks, lire, kroner, etc'. Etc is preceded by a comma and can be spelt with or without a full stop.

ethnic is a word that causes some confusion. It means 'of a group of people classified according to race, nationality, culture, etc', as in 'a cosmopolitan country with a wide variety of ethnic groups'. It is frequently used loosely to mean 'relating to race', as in 'violent clashes thought to be ethnic in origin', or 'foreign' as in 'prefer ethnic foods to British foods'.

EU the abbreviation for European Union, the term which has replaced European Community and European Economic Community.

evade and **avoid** are similar in meaning but not identical. **Evade** means 'to keep away from by cunning or deceit', as in 'The criminal evaded the police by getting his friend to impersonate him'. **Avoid** means simply 'to keep away from', as in 'Women avoid that area of town at night'.

evasion and **avoidance** are frequently applied to the non-payment of income tax but they are not interchangeable. Tax **avoidance** refers to 'the legal nonpayment of tax by clever means'. Tax **evasion** refers to 'the illegal means of avoiding tax by cunning and dishonest means'.

even should be placed carefully in a sentence since its position can influence the meaning. Compare 'He didn't even acknowledge her' and 'He didn't acknowledge even her'. and 'He doesn't even like Jane, let alone love her' and 'He hates the whole family—he doesn't like even Jane'. This shows that **even** should be placed immediately before the word it refers to in order to avoid ambiguity. In spoken English people often place it where it feels most natural, before the verb as in 'He even finds it difficult to relax on holiday'. To be absolutely correct this should be 'He finds it difficult to relax even on holiday' or 'Even on holiday he finds it difficult to relax'.

except is commoner than **except for**. **Except** is used in such sentences as 'They are all dead except his father', 'He goes every day except Sunday'. **Except for** is used at the beginning of sentences, as in 'Except for Fred, all the workers were present', and where **except** applies to a longish phrase, as in 'There was no one present except for the maid cleaning the stairs' and 'The house was silent except for the occasional purring of the cat'. When followed by a pronoun, this should be in the accusative or objective, as in 'There was no one there except *him*' and 'Everyone stayed late except *me*'.

explicit and **implicit** are liable to be confused although they are virtually opposites. **Explicit** means 'direct, clear', as in 'The instructions were not explicit enough' and 'Give explicit reasons for your decision'. **Explicit** is often used in modern usage to mean 'with nothing hidden or implied', as in 'explicit sex scenes'. **Implicit** means 'implied, not directly expressed', as in 'There was an implicit threat in their warning' and 'an implicit criticism in his comments on their actions'. **Implicit** also means 'absolute and unquestioning', as in 'an implicit faith in his ability to succeed' and 'an implicit confidence in her talents'.

extrovert and **introvert** are liable to be confused although they are opposites. **Extrovert** refers to 'a person who is more interested in what is going on around him/her than in his/her own thoughts and feelings, such a person usually being outgoing and sociable', as in 'She is a real extrovert who loves to entertain the guests at parties'. **Introvert** refers to 'a person who is more concerned with his/her own thoughts and feelings than with what is going around him/her, such a person usually being shy and reserved', as in 'an introvert who hates having to speak in public' and 'introverts who prefer to stay at home than go to parties'. Both **extrovert** and **introvert** can be adjectives as well as nouns, as in 'extrovert behaviour' and 'introvert personality'. Note the spelling of **extrovert.** It was formerly spelt with an *a* instead of an *o*.

fahrenheit *see* **Celsius.**

family name is used in politically correct language instead of **maiden name** since this is thought to imply that all women are virgins before they are married. Thus 'Her family name was Jones' would be used instead of 'Her maiden name was Jones'. Another politically correct term is **birth name**, as in 'Her birth name was Jones'.

fantastic literally means 'relating to fantasy, fanciful, strange', as in 'fantastic dreams' and 'tales of fantastic events'. In modern usage it is often used informally to mean 'exceptionally good, excellent', as in 'have a fantastic holiday' and 'be a fantastic piano player'. It can also mean in informal usage 'very large', as in 'pay a fantastic sum of money'.

farther and **further** are not used interchangeably in all situations in modern usage. **Farther** is mainly restricted to sentences where physical distance is involved, as in 'It is farther to Glasgow from here than it is to Edinburgh'. **Further** can also be used in this sense, as in 'It is further to the sea than I thought'. When referring to time or extent, **further** is used, as in 'Further time is required to complete the task' and 'The police have ordered further investigations'. It can also mean 'additional', as in 'We shall require further supplies'. **Further**, unlike **farther**, can be used as a verb to mean 'to help the progress or development about', as in 'further the cause of freedom'.

faux pas is a French phrase that has been adopted into the English language. It means 'a social blunder, an indiscreet or embarrassing remark or deed', as in 'The hostess made a faux pas when she asked after her guest's wife, not knowing that they had divorced last year'. **Faux** is pronounced to rhyme with *foe*, and **pas** is pronounced *pa*.

fax is an abbreviation of 'facsimile' and refers to 'an electronic system for transmitting documents using telephone lines'. As a noun **fax** can refer to the machine transmitting the documents, as in 'the fax has broken down again'; to the system used in the transmission, as in 'send the report by fax'; and the document or documents so transmitted, as in 'He replied to my fax at once'.

female, feminine and **feminist** all relate to women but they are by no means interchangeable. **Female** refers to the sex of a person, animal or plant, as in 'the female members of the group', 'the female wolf and her cubs' and 'the female reproductive cells'. It refers to the childbearing sex and contrasts with 'male'. **Feminine** means 'having qualities that are considered typical of women or are traditionally associated with women', as in 'wear feminine clothes', 'take part in supposedly feminine pursuits, such as cooking and sewing' and 'feminine hairstyles'. It is the opposite of 'masculine'. It can be used of men as well as women, when it is usually derogatory, as in 'He has a very feminine voice' and 'He walks in a very feminine way'. When applied in a derogatory way to a man, **feminine** means much the same as **effeminate. Feminine** also applies to the gender of words, as in 'Lioness is the feminine form of lion'. **Feminist** means 'referring to feminism', 'feminism' being 'a movement based on the belief that women should have the same rights, opportunities, etc', as in 'management trying to avoid appointing anyone with feminist ideas' and 'Equal opportunities is one of the aims of the feminist movement'.

ferment and **foment** can both mean 'to excite, to stir up', as in 'Troublemakers out to ferment discontent' and 'People out to foment trouble in the crowd'. Both words have other meanings that do not relate to each other. **Ferment** means 'to undergo the chemical process known as fermentation', as in 'home-made wine fermenting in the basement'. **Foment** means 'to apply warmth and moisture to in order to lessen pain or discomfort', as in 'foment the old man's injured hip'.

few and **a few** do not convey exactly the same meaning. **Few** is used to mean the opposite of 'many', as in 'We expected a good many people to come but few did' and 'Many people entered the competition but few won a prize'. The phrase **a few** is used to mean the opposite of 'none', as in 'We didn't expect anyone to turn up but a few did' and 'We thought that none of the students would get a job but a few did'.

fewer *see* **less.**

fictional and **fictitious** are both derived from the noun 'fiction' and are interchangeable in the sense of 'imagined, invented', as in 'a fictional character based on an old man whom he used to know' and 'The events in the novel are entirely fictitious'. However, **fictitious** only is used in the sense of 'invented, false', as in 'an entirely fictitious account of the accident' and 'think up fictitious reasons for being late'.

fill in and **fill out** are both used to mean 'to complete a form, etc, by adding the required details', as in 'fill in/fill out an application form for a passport'. In British English **fill in** is the more common term, although **fill out** is the accepted term in American English.

first and **firstly** are now both considered acceptable in lists, although formerly **firstly** was considered unacceptable. Originally the acceptable form of such a list was as in 'There are several reasons for staying here. First, we like the house, secondly we have pleasant neighbours, thirdly we hate moving house'. Some users now prefer to use the adjectival forms of 'second' and 'third' when using **first**, as in 'He has stated his reasons for going to another job. First, he has been offered a higher salary, second, he has more opportunities for promotion, third, he will have a company car'. As indicated, **firstly** is now quite acceptable and is the form preferred by many people, as in 'They have several reasons for not having a car. Firstly they have very little money, secondly, they live right next to the bus-stop, thirdly, they feel cars are not environmentally friendly'.

first name *see* **Christian name.**

fish and **fishes** are both found as plural forms of 'fish', but **fish** is by far the more widely used form, as in 'He keeps tropical fish', 'Some fish live in fresh water and some in the sea' and 'there are now only three fish in the tank'. **Fishes** is rarely used but when it is, it is usually used to refer to different species of fish, as in 'He is comparing the fishes of the Pacific Ocean with those of the Indian Ocean'. **Fish** can also be used in this case.

flak originally referred to 'gunfire aimed at enemy aircraft', as in 'Pilots returning across the English Channel encountered heavy flak'. In modern usage it is also applied to 'severe criticism', as in 'the government receiving flak for raising taxes'.

flammable and **inflammable** both mean 'easily set on fire, burning easily', as in 'Children's nightclothes should not be made of flammable/inflammable material' and 'The chemical is highly flammable/inflammable'. **Inflammable** is frequently misused because some people wrongly regard it as meaning 'not burning easily', thinking that it is like such words as 'incredible', 'inconceivable' and 'intolerant' where the prefix 'in' means 'not'.

flotsam and **jetsam** are often used together to refer to 'miscellaneous objects, odds and ends', as in 'We have moved most of the furniture to the new house—there's just the flotsam and jetsam left', and 'vagrants, tramps', as in 'people with no pity in their hearts for the flotsam and jetsam of society'. In the phrase **flotsam and jetsam** they are used as though they meant the same thing but this is not the case. Both words relate to the remains of a wrecked ship, but **flotsam** refers to 'the wreckage of the ship found floating in the water', as in 'The coastguards knew the ship must have broken up when they saw bits of flotsam near the rocks', while **jetsam** refers to 'goods and equipment thrown overboard from a ship in distress in order to lighten it', as in 'The coastguards were unable to find the ship although they found the jetsam'.

forbear and **forebear** are interchangeable in one meaning of **forbear** only.

Forbear is a verb meaning 'to refrain from', as in 'I hope she can forbear from pointing out that she was right' and this cannot be spelt **forebear.** However, **forebear** meaning 'ancestor' can also be spelt **forbear**, as in 'One of his *forebears/forbears* received a gift of land from Henry VIII'.

The verb **forbear** is pronounced with the emphasis on the second syllable as for-*bair*. The nouns **forbear** and **forebear** are pronounced alike with the emphasis on the first syllable as *for*-bair. The past tense of the verb **forbear** is **forbore**, as in 'He forbore to mention that he was responsible for the mistake'.

forever can be spelt as two words when it means 'eternally, for all time', as in 'doomed to separate forever/for ever' and 'have faith in the fact that they would dwell forever/for ever with Christ'. In the sense of 'constantly or persistently', only **forever** is used, as in 'His wife was forever nagging' and 'the child was forever asking for sweets'.

former and **latter** are opposites. **Former** refers to 'the first of two people or things mentioned' while **latter** refers to 'the second of two people or things mentioned', as in 'He was given two options, either to stay in his present post but accept less money or to be transferred to another branch of the company. He decided to accept the former/latter option'. **Former** also means 'previous, at an earlier time', as in 'He is a former chairman of the company' and 'She is a former holder of the championship title'.

further *see* **farther.**

gaol *see* **jail.**

gay originally meant 'merry, light-hearted', as in 'the gay laughter of children playing' and 'everyone feeling gay at the sight of the sunshine'. Although this meaning still exists in modern usage, it is rarely used since **gay** has come to be an accepted word for 'homosexual', as in 'gay rights' and 'gay bars'. Although the term can be applied to men or women it is most commonly applied to men, the corresponding word for women being **lesbian.** There is a growing tendency among homosexuals to describe themselves as **queer**, a term that was formerly regarded as being offensive.

geriatric is frequently found in medical contexts to mean 'elderly' or 'old', as in 'an ever-increasing number of geriatric patients' and 'a shortage of geriatric wards'. In such contexts **geriatric** is not used in a belittling or derogatory way, **geriatrics** being the name given to the branch of medicine concerned with the health and diseases of elderly people. However, **geriatric** is often used in the general language to refer to old people in a derogatory or scornful way, as in 'geriatric shoppers getting in the way' or 'geriatric drivers holding up the traffic'.

gibe and **jibe** both mean 'to jeer at, mock, make fun of', as in 'rich children gibing/jibing at the poor children for wearing out-of-date clothes'. **Gibe** and **jibe** are nouns as well as verbs as in 'politicians tired of the gibes/jibes of the press'.

Gipsy and **Gypsy** are both acceptable spellings, as in 'Gipsies/Gypsies travelling through the country in their caravans'. Some people object to the word **Gipsy** or **Gypsy,** preferring the word traveller, as in 'councils being asked to build sites for travellers'. The term **traveller** is used to apply to a wider range of people who travel the country, as in 'New Age travellers', and not just to Gipsies, who are Romany in origin.

girl means 'a female child or adolescent', as in 'separate schools for girls and boys' and 'Girls tend to mature more quickly than boys'. However it is often applied to a young woman, or indeed to a woman of any age, as in 'He asked his wife if she was going to have a night out with the girls from the office'. Many women object to this use, regarding it as patronizing, although the user of the term does not always intend to convey this impression.

gourmand and **gourmet** and **glutton** all have reference to food but they do not mean quite the same thing. **Gourmand** refers to 'a person who likes food and eats a lot of it', as in 'Gourmands tucking into huge helpings of the local food'. It means much the same as **glutton**, but **glutton** is a more condemnatory term, as in 'gluttons stuffing food into their mouths'. **Gourmet** is a more refined term, being used to refer to 'a person who enjoys food and who is discriminating and knowledgeable about it', as in 'gourmets who spend their holidays seeking out good local restaurants and produce'. In modern usage **gourmet** is often used as an adjective to mean 'high-class, elaborate, expensive', as in 'gourmet restaurants' and 'gourmet foods'.

graffiti Italian in origin and actually the plural form of **graffito**, meaning a single piece of writing or drawing, but this is now hardly ever used in English.

green is used to mean 'concerned with the conservation of the environment', as in 'a political party concerned with green issues' and 'buy as many green products as possible'. The word is derived from German *grün*, the political environmental lobby having started in West Germany, as it was then called.

grey and **gray** are both acceptable spellings. In British English, however, **grey** is the more common, as in 'different shades of grey' and 'grey hair', but **gray** is the standard form in American English.

gypsy *see* **gipsy.**

handicapped is disliked by some people because they feel it is too negative a term. There is as yet no widespread alternative apart from **disabled**, although various suggestions have been made as part of the politically correct language movement, such as **physically challenged** and **differently abled.**

hard and **soft** are both terms applied to drugs. **Hard drugs** refer to 'strong drugs that are likely to be addictive', as in 'Heroin and cocaine are hard drugs'. **Soft drugs** refer to 'drugs that are considered unlikely to cause addiction', as in 'cannabis and other soft drugs'.

hardly is used to indicate a negative idea. Therefore a sentence or clause containing it does not require another negative. Sentences, such as 'I couldn't hardly see him' and 'He left without hardly a word' are *wrong*. They should read 'I could hardly see him' and 'He left with hardly a word'. **Hardly** is followed by 'when', not 'than', as in 'Hardly had he entered the house when he collapsed', although the 'than' construction is very common.

he/she is a convention used to avoid sexism. Before the rise of feminism anyone referred to, whose sex was not specified, was assumed to be male, as in 'Each pupil must take his book home' and 'Every driver there parked his car illegally'. The only exception to this occurred in situations that were thought to be particularly appropriate to women, as in 'The cook should make her own stock' and 'The nurse has left her book behind'. In modern usage where attempts are made to avoid sexism either **he/she** or 'he or she' is frequently used, as in 'Each manager is responsible for his/her department' or 'It is a doctor's duty to explain the nature of the treatment to his or her patient'. People who regard this convention as being clumsy should consider restructuring the sentence or putting it in the plural, as in 'All managers are responsible for their departments'. Some users prefer to be ungrammatical and use a plural pronoun with a singular noun, as in 'Every pupil should take their books home' and this use is becoming increasingly common, even in textbooks.

heterosexism refers to discrimination and prejudice by a heterosexual person against a homosexual one, as in 'He was convinced that he had not got the job because he was gay—that the employer had been guilty of heterosexism'.

historic and **historical** are both adjectives formed from the noun 'history' but they are not interchangeable. **Historic** refers to events that are important enough to earn, or have earned, a place in history, as in 'Nelson's historic victory at Trafalgar' and 'the astronaut's historic landing on the moon'. It can be used loosely to mean 'extremely memorable', as in 'attend a historic party'. **Historical** means 'concerning past events', as in 'historical studies', or 'based on the study of history'.

hopefully has two meanings. The older meaning is 'with hope', as in 'The child looked hopefully at the sweet shop window' and 'It is better to travel hopefully than to arrive'. A more recent meaning, which is disliked by some people, means 'it is to be hoped that', as in 'Hopefully we shall soon be there'.

humanism and **humanitarianism** are liable to be confused. **Humanism** is a philosophy that values greatly human beings and their rôle, and rejects the need for religion, as in 'She was brought up as a Christian but she decided to embrace humanism in later life'. **Humanitarianism** refers to the philosophy and actions of people who wish to improve the lot of their fellow human beings and help them, as in 'humanitarians trying to help the refugees by taking them food and clothes'.

hyper- and **hypo-** are liable to be confused. They sound rather similar but they are opposites. **Hyper-** means 'above, excessively', as in 'hyperactive', 'hyperexcitable'. **Hypo-** means 'under, beneath', as in 'hypothermia'.

I and **me** are liable to be confused. I should be used as the subject of a sentence, as in 'You and I have both been invited', 'May Jane and I play?' and me as the object, as in 'The cake was made by Mary and me' and 'My brother and father played against my mother and me'. People often assume wrongly that me is less 'polite' than I. This is probably because they have been taught that in answer to such questions as 'Who is there?' the grammatically correct reply is 'It is I'. In fact, except in formal contexts, 'It is me' is frequently found in modern usage, especially in spoken contexts. Confusion arises as to whether to use I or me after 'between'. Since 'between' is followed by an object, me is the correct form. Thus it is correct to say 'Just between you and me, I think he is dishonest'.

i.e. is the abbreviation of a Latin phrase *id est*, meaning 'that is', as in 'He is a lexicographer, i.e. a person who edits dictionaries'. It is mostly used in written, rather than formal contexts.

identical in modern usage can be followed by either 'with' or 'to'. Formerly only 'with' was considered correct, as in 'His new suit is identical with the one he bought last year'. Now 'to' is also considered acceptable, as in 'a brooch identical to one which he bought for his wife'.

illegible and **unreadable** are not totally interchangeable. **Illegible** refers to something that is impossible to make out or decipher, as in 'her handwriting is practically illegible'. **Unreadable** can also mean this, as in 'unreadable handwriting', but it can also mean 'unable to be read with understanding or enjoyment', as in 'His writing is so full of jargon that it is unreadable'.

imbroglio means 'a confused, complicated or embarrassing situation', as in 'politicians getting involved in an international imbroglio during the summit conference'. It is liable to be misspelt and mispronounced. Note the *g* which is liable to be omitted erroneously as it is not pronounced. It is pronounced im-*bro*-lio with emphasis on the second syllable which rhymes with 'foe'. **Imbroglio** is used only in formal or literary contexts.

impasse causes problems with reference to meaning, spelling and pronunciation. It means 'a difficult position or situation from which there is no way out, deadlock', as in 'The negotiations between management and workers have reached an impasse with neither side being willing to compromise'. Note the final *e* in the spelling. The first syllable can be pronounced 'am', or 'om' in an attempt at following the original French pronunciation, although in modern usage it is frequently totally anglicized as 'im'.

implicit *see* **explicit.**

imply and **infer** are often used interchangeably but they in fact are different in meaning. **Imply** means 'to suggest, to hint at', as in 'We felt that she was implying that he was lying' and 'She did not actually say that there was going to be a delay but she implied it'. **Infer** means 'to deduce, to conclude', as in 'From what the employer said we inferred that there would be some redundancies' and 'From the annual financial reports observers inferred the company was about to go bankrupt'. Note that **infer** doubles the *r* when adding '-ed' or '-ing' to form the past tense, past participle or present participle as **inferred** and **inferring.**

impracticable and **impractical** are liable to be confused. **Impracticable** means 'impossible to put into practice, not workable', as in 'In theory the plan is fine but it is impracticable in terms of costs'. **Impractical** means 'not sensible or realistic', as in 'It is impractical to think that you will get there and back in a day'; 'not skilled at doing or making things', as in 'He is a brilliant academic but he is hopelessly impractical'.

indefinite article *see* **a, an.**

in lieu, which means 'instead of', as in 'receive extra pay in lieu of holidays', causes problems with pronunciation. It may be pronounced in lew or in loo.

indexes and **indices** are both plural forms of 'index'. In modern usage **indexes** is the more common form in general language, as in 'Indexes are essential in large reference books'. An **index** in this sense is 'an alphabetical list given at the back of a book as a guide to its contents'. The form **indices** is mostly restricted to technical contexts, such as mathematical information. **Indices** is pronounced in-dis-is and is the Latin form of the plural.

individual refers to 'a single person as opposed to a group', as in 'The rights of the community matter but so do the rights of the individual'. **Individual** is also sometimes used instead of 'person', but in such cases it is often used in a disapproving or belittling way, as in 'What an unpleasant individual she is!' and 'The individual who designed that building should be shot'.

indoor and **indoors** are not interchangeable. **Indoor** is an adjective, as in 'have an indoor match' and 'indoor games'. **Indoors** is an adverb, as in 'children playing outdoors instead of watching television indoors' and 'sleep outdoors on warm evenings instead of indoors'.

infer *see* **imply.**

infinite and **infinitesimal** are similar in meaning but are not interchangeable. **Infinite** means 'without limit', as in 'infinite space', or 'very great', as in 'have infinite patience' and 'He seems to have an infinite capacity for hard work'. **Infinitesimal** means 'very small, negligible', as in 'an infinitesimal difference in size' and 'an infinitesimal increase'. **Infinitesimal** is pronounced with the emphasis on the fourth syllable in-fin-it-*es*-im-il.

informer and **informant** both refer to 'a person who provides information' but they are used in different contexts. **Informer** is used to refer to 'a person who gives information to the police or authorities about a criminal, fugitive, etc', as in 'The local police have a group of informers who tell them what is going on in the criminal underworld' and 'The resistance worker was caught by the enemy soldier when an informer told them about his activities'. An **informant** provides more general information, as in 'My informant keeps me up-to-date with changes in personnel'.

in-law is usually found in compounds such as 'mother-in-law' and 'father-in-law'. When these compounds are in the plural the *s* should be added to the first word of the compound, not to **in-law**, as in 'mothers-in-law' and 'fathers-in-law'.

input used to be a technical term with particular application to computers. This meaning still exists and **input** can refer to the data, power, etc, put into a computer. As a verb it means 'to enter data into a computer', as in 'input the details of all the travel resorts in the area'. In modern usage it is frequently used in general language to mean 'contribution', as in 'Everyone is expected to provide some input for tomorrow's conference'. It is even found in this sense as a verb, as in 'input a great deal to the meeting'.

inquiry *see* **enquiry.**

install and **instal** are now both considered acceptable spellings. **Install** was formerly considered to be the only correct spelling and it is still the more common. The *l* is doubled in **instal** in the past participle, past tense and present participle as **installed, installing.** It means 'to put in', as in 'he installed a new television set'. The noun is spelt **instalment.**

instantaneously and **instantly** are interchangeable. Both mean 'immediately, at once', as in 'They obeyed instantaneously/instantly' and 'The accident victims were killed instantly/instantaneously'.

intense and **intensive** are not interchangeable. Intense means 'very strong, extreme', as in 'an intense desire to scream' and 'unable to tolerate the intense cold on the icy slopes'. **Intensive** means 'thorough', as in 'conduct an intensive search', and 'concentrated', as in 'an intensive course in first aid' and 'intensive bombing'.

invalid refers to two different words. If it is pronounced with the emphasis on the second syllable, as in-*val*-id it means 'not valid, no longer valid', as in 'This visa becomes invalid after six months'. If it is pronounced with the emphasis on the first syllable, as *in*-val-id, it means 'a person who is ill', as in 'The doctor has arrived to see the invalid'.

invent *see* **discover.**

inward and **inwards** are not used interchangeably. **Inward** is an adjective, as in 'an inward curve' and 'No one could guess her inward feelings'. **Inwards** is an adverb, as in 'toes turning inwards' and 'thoughts turning inwards'. **Inward** can be used as an adverb in the same way as **inwards.**

IQ is the abbreviation of 'intelligence quotient', as in 'He has a high IQ'. It is always written in capital letters and is sometimes written with full stops and sometimes not, according to preference.

irrespective is followed by the preposition 'of'. The phrase means 'not taking account of, not taking into consideration', as in 'All can go on the trip, irrespective of age'.

irrevocable is frequently misspelt and mispronounced. Note the double *r* and the *-able* ending. It is pronounced with the emphasis on the second syllable, as ir-*rev*-ok-ibl. When applied to legal judgements, etc, it is sometimes pronounced with the emphasis on the third syllable, as ir-rev-*ok*-ibl. The word means 'unable to be changed or revoked', as in 'Their decision to get divorced is irrevocable' and 'The jury's decision is irrevocable'.

its and **it's** are liable to be confused. **Its** is an adjective meaning 'belonging to it', as in 'The house has lost its charm' and 'The dog does not like its kennel'. **It's** means 'it is', as in 'Do you know if it's raining?' and 'It's not fair to expect her to do all the chores'.

jail and **gaol** are both acceptable spellings although jail is the more common. They mean 'prison' and can be both nouns and verbs, as in 'sent to jail/gaol for killing his wife' and 'jail/gaol him for his part in the bank robbery'.

jersey *see* **cardigan.**

jetsam *see* **flotsam.**

just is liable to be put in the wrong place in a sentence. It should be placed before the word it refers to, as in 'He has just one book left to sell', not 'He just has one book left to sell'. **Just** in the sense of 'in the very recent past' is used with the perfect tense, as in 'They have just finished the job', not 'They just finished the job'.

kind should be used with a singular noun, as 'This kind of accident can be avoided'. This should not read 'These kind of accidents can be avoided'. Similarly 'The children do not like that kind of film' is correct, not 'The children do not like those kind of films'. A plural noun can be used if the sentence is rephrased as 'Films of that kind are not liked by children'.

kindly can be either an adjective or adverb. The adjective means 'kind, friendly, sympathetic', as in 'A kindly lady took pity on the children and lent them some money to get home' and 'She gave them a kindly smile'. The adverb means 'in a kind manner', as in 'We were treated kindly by the local people' and 'They will not look kindly on his actions'.

kind of, meaning 'rather', as in 'That restaurant's kind of dear' and 'She's kind of tired of him', is informal and should be avoided in formal contexts.

knit in modern usage is becoming increasingly used as a noun to mean 'a knitted garment', as in 'a shop selling beautifully coloured knits'.

lady and **woman** cause controversy. **Lady** is objected to by many people when it is used instead of **woman.** Formerly, and still in some circles, it was regarded as a polite form of **woman**, as in " 'Please get up and give that lady a seat", said the mother to her son'. Indeed, **woman** was thought to be rather insulting. For many people **woman** is now the preferred term and **lady** is seen as classist, because it is associated with nobility, privilege, etc, or condescending. However, **lady** is still quite commonly used, particularly when women are being addressed in a group, as in " 'Ladies, I hope we can reach our sales target", said the manager' and 'Come along, ladies the bus is about to leave'. Phrases, such as **dinner lady** and **cleaning lady** are thought by some to be condescending but others still find **woman** rather insulting.

last is liable to cause confusion because it is not always clear which meaning is meant. **Last** as an adjective has several meanings. It can mean 'final', as in 'That was the musician's last public appearance—he died shortly after'; 'coming after all others in time or order', as in 'December is the last month in the year', 'The last of the runners reached the finishing tape'; 'latest, most recent', as in 'Her last novel is not as good as her earlier ones'; 'previous, preceding', as in 'This chapter is interesting but the last one was boring'. In order to avoid confusion it is best to use a word other than **last** where ambiguity is likely to arise. An example of a sentence which could cause confusion is 'I cannot remember the title of his last book', which could mean either 'his latest book' or 'his final book'.

latter *see* **former.**

lavatory *see* **toilet.**

lay and **lie** are liable to be confused. They are related but are used in different contexts. **Lay** means 'to put or place' and is a transitive verb, i.e. it takes an object. It is found in such sentences as 'Ask them to lay the books carefully on the table' and 'They are going to lay a new carpet in the bedroom'. **Lie**, meaning 'to rest in a horizontal position', is an intransitive verb, i.e. it does not take an object. It is found in such sentences as 'They were told to lie on the ground' and 'Snow is apt to lie on the mountain tops for a long time'. The confusion between the two words arises from the fact that **lay** is also the past tense of **lie**, as in 'He lay still on the ground' and 'Snow lay on the mountain tops'. The past tense of **lay** is **laid**, as in 'They laid the books on the table'. There is another verb **lie**, meaning 'to tell falsehoods, not to tell the truth', as in 'He was told to lie to the police'. The past tense of **lie** in this sense is **lied**, as in 'We suspect that he lied but we cannot prove it'.

leading question is often used wrongly. It should be used to mean 'a question that is so worded as to invite (or lead to) a particular answer desired by the questioner', as in 'The judge refused to allow the barrister to ask the witness the question on the grounds that it was a leading question'. However, it is often used wrongly to mean 'a question that is difficult, unfair or embarrassing'.

learn and **teach** are liable to be confused. **Learn** means 'to gain information or knowledge about', as in 'She learnt Spanish as a child', or 'to gain the skill of', as in 'She is learning to drive'. **Teach** means 'to give instruction in, to cause to know something or be able to do something', as in 'She taught her son French' and 'She taught her son to swim'. **Learn** is frequently used wrongly instead of **teach**, as in 'She learnt us to drive'.

learned and **learnt** are both acceptable forms of the past participle and past tense of the verb 'to learn', as in 'She has now learned/learnt to drive' and 'They learned/learnt French at school'. **Learned** in this sense can be pronounced either *lernd* or *lernt*. However, **learned** can also be an adjective, meaning 'having much knowledge, erudite', as in 'an learned professor', or 'academic', as in 'learned journals'. It is pronounced *ler*-ned.

leave and **let** are not interchangeable. **Leave go** should not be substituted for **let go** in such sentences as 'Do not let go of the rope'. 'Do not leave go of the rope' is considered to be incorrect. However both **leave alone** and **let alone** can be used in the sense of 'to stop disturbing or interfering with', as in 'Leave/let the dog alone or it will bite you' and 'leave/let your mother alone—she is not feeling well'. **Leave alone** can also mean 'leave on one's own, cause to be alone', as in 'Her husband went away and left her alone', but **let alone** cannot be used in this sense. **Let alone** can also mean 'not to mention, without considering', as in 'They cannot afford proper food, let alone a holiday', but **leave alone** should not be used in this sense.

legible and **readable** are not interchangeable. **Legible** means 'able to be deciphered or made out', as in 'His writing is scarcely legible'. **Readable** can also be used in this sense, as in 'His handwriting is just not readable'. However **readable** is also used to mean 'able to be read with interest or enjoyment', as in 'He is an expert on the subject but I think his books are simply not readable' and 'I find her novels very readable but my friend does not like her style'.

lend and **loan** can cause confusion. **Lend** is used as a verb in British English to mean 'to allow someone the use of temporarily', as in 'Can you lend me a pen?' and 'His father refused to lend him any money'. **Loan** is a noun meaning 'something lent, the temporary use of', as in 'They thanked her for the loan of her car'. In American English **loan** is used as a verb to mean **lend**, and this use is becoming common in Britain although it is still regarded as not quite acceptable.

lengthways and **lengthwise** are used interchangeably, as in 'fold the tablecloth lengthways/lengthwise' and 'measure the room lengthwise/lengthways'.

lengthy and **long** are not interchangeable. **Lengthy** means 'excessively long', as in 'We had a lengthy wait before we saw the doctor' and 'It was such a lengthy speech that most of the audience got bored'. **Lengthy** is frequently misspelt. Note the *g*.

less and **fewer** are often confused. Less means 'a smaller amount or quantity of' and is the comparative form of 'little'. It is found in sentences such as 'less milk', 'less responsibility' and 'less noise'. **Fewer** means 'a smaller number of' and is the comparative of 'few'. It is found in sentences such as 'buy fewer bottles of milk', 'have fewer responsibilities', 'have fewer opportunities' and 'hear fewer noises'. **Less** is commonly wrongly used where **fewer** is correct. It is common but ungrammatical to say or write 'less bottles of milk' and 'less queues in the shops during the week'.

liable to and **likely to** both express probability. They mean much the same except that **liable to** suggests that the probability is based on past experience or habit. 'He is liable to lose his temper' suggests that he has been in the habit of doing so in the past. 'He is likely to lose his temper' suggests that he will probably lose his temper, given the situation, but that the probability is not based on how he has reacted in the past. This distinction is not always adhered to, and some people use the terms interchangeably.

libel and **slander** both refer to defamatory statements against someone but they are not interchangeable. **Libel** refers to defamation that is written down, printed or drawn, as in 'The politician sued the newspaper for libel when it falsely accused him of fraud'. **Slander** refers to defamation in spoken form, as in 'She heard that one of her neighbours was spreading slander about her'. Both **libel** and **slander** can act as verbs, as in 'bring a suit against the newspaper for libelling him' and 'think that one of her neighbours was slandering her'. Note that the verb **libel** doubles the *l* in the past participle, past tense and present participle, as **libelled** and **libelling**.

licence and **license** are liable to cause confusion in British English. **Licence** is a noun meaning 'an official document showing that permission has been given to do, use or own something', as in 'require a licence to have a stall in the market', 'have a licence to drive a car', and 'apply for a pilot's licence'. **License** is a verb meaning 'to provide someone with a licence', as in 'The council have licensed him as a street trader', 'The restaurant has been licensed to sell alcohol'. Note **licensed grocer** and **licensing laws** but **off-licence**. In American English both the noun and verb are spelt **license**.

lie *see* **lay**.

light years are a measure of distance, not time. A **light year** is the distance travelled by light in one year (about six million, million miles) and is a term used in astronomy. **Light years** are often referred to in an informal context when time, not distance, is involved, as in 'Owning their own house seemed light years away' and 'It seems light years since we had a holiday'.

like tends to cause confusion. It is a preposition meaning 'resembling, similar to', as in 'houses like castles', 'gardens like jungles', 'actors like Olivier', 'She looks like her mother', 'She plays like an expert', 'The child swims like a fish' and 'Like you, he cannot stand cruelty to animals'. To be grammatically correct **like** should not be used as a conjunction. Thus 'The house looks like it has been deserted' is incorrect. It should read 'The house looks as though/if it has been deserted'. Similarly, 'Like his mother said, he has had to go to hospital' should read 'As his mother said, he has had to go to hospital'.

likeable and **likable** are both acceptable spellings. The word means 'pleasant, agreeable, friendly', as in 'He is a likeable/likable young man'.

likely to *see* **liable to**.

literally is frequently used simply to add emphasis to an idea rather than to indicate that the word, phrase, etc, used is to be interpreted word for word. Thus, 'She was literally tearing her hair out' does not mean that she was pulling her hair out by the handful but that she was very angry, anxious, frustrated, etc.

livid and **lurid** are liable to be confused although they mean different things. **Livid** means 'discoloured, of a greyish tinge', as in 'a livid bruise on her face', and 'furious', as in 'When he saw his damaged car he was livid'. **Lurid** means 'sensational, shocking', as in 'give the lurid details about finding the body', and 'garish, glaringly bright', as in 'wear a lurid shade of green'.

living room *see* **sitting room**.

loo *see* **toilet**.

lots of and **a lot of**, meaning 'many' and 'much', should be used only in informal contexts', as in "'I've got lots of toys," said the child' and 'You're talking a lot of rubbish'. They should be avoided in formal prose.

lounge *see* **sitting room**.

low and **lowly** are not interchangeable. **Low** means 'not high', as in 'a low fence', 'a low level of income', 'speak in a low voice' and 'her low status in the firm'. It can also mean 'despicable, contemptible', as in 'That was a low trick' or 'He's a low creature'. **Lowly** means 'humble', as in 'of lowly birth' and 'the peasant's lowly abode'.

lunch and **luncheon** both refer to a meal eaten in the middle of the day. **Lunch**, as in 'a business lunch' and 'have just a snack for lunch', is by far the more usual term. **Luncheon**, as in 'give a luncheon party for the visiting celebrity', is a very formal word and is becoming increasingly uncommon. *See also* **dinner**.

lurid *see* **livid**.

madam and **madame** are liable to be confused. **Madam** is the English-language form of the French **madame**. It is a form of formal of address for a woman, as in 'Please come this way, madam'. It is used in formal letters when the name of the woman being written to is not known, as in 'Dear Madam'. **Madam** can be written either with a capital letter or a lower-case letter. **Madam** is pronounced *mad*-am, with the emphasis on the first syllable. **Madame**, which is the French equivalent of 'Mrs', is occasionally found in English, as in Madame Tussaud's, and is pronounced in the same way as **madam**. In French **madame** is pronounced ma-*dam*.

majority and **minority** are opposites. **Majority** means 'more than half the total number of', as in 'The majority of the pupils live locally' and 'the younger candidate received the majority of the votes'. **Minority** means 'less than half the total number of', as in 'A small minority of the football fans caused trouble' and 'Only a minority of the committee voted against the motion'. **Majority** and **minority** should not be used to describe the greater or lesser part of a single thing. Thus it is wrong to say 'The majority of the book is uninteresting'.

male, masculine and **mannish** all refer to the sex that is not female but the words are used in different ways. **Male** is the opposite of 'female' and refers to the sex of a person or animal, as in 'no male person may enter', 'a male nurse', 'a male elephant' and 'the male reproductive system'. **Masculine** is the opposite of 'feminine' and refers to people or their characteristics. It refers to characteristics, etc, that are traditionally considered to be typically **male**. Examples of its use include 'a very masculine young man', 'a deep, masculine voice'. It can be used of women, as in 'She has a masculine walk' and 'She wears masculine clothes'. When used of women it is often derogatory and is sometimes replaced with **mannish**, which is derogatory, as in 'women with mannish haircuts'. **Male** can also be used as a noun, as in 'the male of the species' 'of the robins, the male is more colourful' and 'the title can be held only by males'.

man causes a great deal of controversy. To avoid being sexist it should be avoided when it really means 'person'. 'We must find the right man for the job' should read 'We must find the right person for the job'. Similarly, 'All men have a right to a reasonable standard of living' should read 'All people have a right to a reasonable standard of living' or 'Everyone has a right to a reasonable standard of living'. Problems also arise with compounds, such as 'chairman'. In such situations 'person' is often used, as in 'chairperson'. Man is also used to mean 'mankind, humankind', as in 'Man is mortal' and 'Man has the power of thought'. Some people also object to this usage and consider it sexist. They advocate using 'humankind' or 'the human race'.

many is used in more formal contexts rather than 'a lot of' or 'lots of', as in 'The judge said the accused had had many previous convictions'. **Many** is often used in the negative in both formal and informal contexts, as in 'They don't have many friends' and 'She won't find many apples on the trees now'.

masculine *see* **male.**

may *see* **can.**

maybe and **may be** are liable to be confused although they have different meanings. **Maybe** means 'perhaps', as in 'Maybe they lost their way' and 'He said, "Maybe" when I asked him if he was going'. It is used in more informal contexts than 'perhaps'. **May be** is used in such sentences as 'He may be poor but he is very generous' and 'They may be a little late'.

mayoress means 'the wife or partner of a male mayor', as in 'an official dinner for the mayor and mayoress'. A mayor who is a woman is called either 'mayor' or 'lady mayor'.

me *see* **I.**

meaningful originally meant 'full of meaning', as in 'make very few meaningful statements' and 'There was a meaningful silence'. In modern usage it has come to mean 'important, significant, serious', as in 'not interested in a meaningful relationship' and 'seeking a meaningful career'. The word now tends to be very much over-used.

means in the sense of 'way, method' can be either a singular or plural noun, as in 'The means of defeating them is in our hands' and 'Many different means of financing the project have been investigated'. **Means** in the sense of 'wealth' and 'resources' is plural, as in 'His means are not sufficient to support two families'.

media gives rise to confusion. In the form of **the media** it is commonly applied to the press, to newspapers, television and radio, as in 'The politician claimed that he was being harassed by the media'. **Media** is a plural form of 'medium', meaning 'means of communication', as in 'television is a powerful medium'. In modern usage **media** is beginning to be used as a singular noun, as in 'The politician blamed a hostile media for his misfortunes', but this is still regarded as being an incorrect use.

middle *see* **centre.**

mileage and **milage** are both acceptable spellings for 'the distance travelled or measured in miles', as in 'The car is a bargain, given the low mileage'. However **mileage** is much more common than **milage**. The word also means informally 'benefit, advantage', as in 'The politician got a lot of mileage from the scandal surrounding his opponent' and 'There's not much mileage in pursuing that particular line of inquiry'.

militate and **mitigate** are liable to be confused. **Militate** means 'to have or serve as a strong influence against', as in 'Their lack of facts militated against the success of their application' and 'His previous record will militate against his chances of going free'. **Mitigate** means 'to alleviate', as in 'try to mitigate the suffering of the refugees', or 'moderate', as in 'mitigate the severity of the punishment'.

millennium is liable to be misspelt. Note the double *n* which is frequently omitted in error. The plural form is **millennia. Millennium** refers to 'a period of 1000 years', as in 'rock changes taking place over several millennia'. In religious terms it refers to 'the thousand-year reign of Christ prophesied in the Bible'.

minority *see* **majority.**

Miss *see* **Ms.**

misuse *see* **abuse.**

mitigate *see* **militate.**

mnemonic refers to 'something that aids the memory'. For example, some people use a **mnemonic** in the form of a verse to remind them how to spell a word or to recall a date. The word is liable to be misspelt and mispronounced. Note the initial *m*, which is silent. **Mnemonic** is pronounced nim-*on*-ik, with the emphasis on the second syllable.

modern and **modernistic** are not quite the same. **Modern** means 'referring to the present time or recent times', as in 'the politics of modern times' and 'a production of Shakespeare's *Twelfth Night* in modern dress'. It also means 'using the newest techniques, equipment, buildings, etc, as in 'a modern shopping centre' and 'a modern office complex'. **Modernistic** means 'characteristic of modern ideas, fashions, etc', and is often used in a derogatory way, as in 'She says she hates that modernistic furniture'.

modus vivendi refers to 'a practical, sometimes temporary, arrangement or compromise by which people who are in conflict can live or work together', as in 'The two opposing parties on the committee will have to reach a modus vivendi if any progress is to be made'. It is a Latin phrase that literally means 'a way of living' and is pronounced *mo*-dus viv-*en*-di.

more is used to form the comparative of adjectives and adverbs that do not form the comparative by adding *-er*. This usually applies to longer adjectives, as in 'more beautiful', 'more gracious', 'more useful', and 'more flattering'. **More** should not be used with adjectives that have a comparative ending already. Thus it is wrong to write 'more happier'. **Most** is used in the same way to form the superlative of adjectives and adverbs, as in 'most beautiful', 'most gracious' etc.

Moslem *see* **Muslim.**

most *see* **more.**

movable and **moveable** are both possible spellings but **movable** is the more common, as in 'movable possessions' and 'machines with movable parts'.

Ms, Mrs and **Miss** are all used before the names of women in addressing them and in letter-writing. Formerly **Mrs** was used before the name of a married woman and **Miss** before the name of an unmarried woman or girl. In modern usage **Ms** is often used instead of **Miss** or **Mrs.** This is sometimes because the marital status of the woman is not known and sometimes from a personal preference. Many people feel that since no distinction is made between married and unmarried men when they are being addressed, no distinction should be made between married and unmarried women. On the other hand some people, particularly older women, object to the use of **Ms.**

much, except in negative sentences, is used mainly in rather formal contexts, as in 'They own much property'. 'A great deal of' is often used instead, as in 'They own a great deal of property'. In informal contexts 'a lot of' is often used instead of **much**, as in 'a lot of rubbish' not 'much rubbish'. **Much** is used in negative sentences, as in 'They do not have much money'.

Muslim and **Moslem** refer to 'a follower of the Islamic faith'. In modern usage **Muslim** is the preferred term rather than the older spelling **Moslem.**

naught and **nought** are not totally interchangeable. **Naught** means 'nothing', as in 'All his projects came to naught', and is rather a formal or literary word in this sense. **Naught** is also a less usual spelling of **nought,** which means 'zero' when it is regarded as a number, as in 'nought point one (0.1)'.

nearby and **near by** can cause problems. **Nearby** can be either an adjective, as in 'the nearby village', or an adverb, as in 'Her mother lives nearby'. **Near by** is an adverb, as in 'He doesn't have far to go—he lives near by'. In other words, the adverbial sense can be spelt either **nearby** or **near by.**

née is used to indicate the maiden or family name of a married woman, as in 'Jane Jones, née Smith'. It is derived from French, being the feminine form of the French word for 'born'. It can be spelt either with an acute accent or not—**née** or **nee.**

never in the sense of 'did not', as in 'He never saw the other car before he hit it', should be used in only very informal contexts. **Never** means 'at no time, on no occasion', as in 'He will never agree to their demands' and 'She has never been poor'. It is also used as a negative for the sake of emphasis, as in 'He never so much as smiled'.

nevertheless and **none the less** mean the same thing, as in 'He has very little money. Nevertheless/none the less he gives generously to charity'. **None the less** is usually written as three words but **nevertheless** is spelt as one word. In modern usage **none the less** is sometimes written as one word, as **nonetheless.**

next and **this** can cause confusion. **Next** in one of its senses is used to mean the day of the week, month of the year, season of the year, etc, that will follow next, as in 'They are coming next Tuesday', 'We are going on holiday next June' and 'They are to be married next summer'. **This** can also be used in this sense and so ambiguity can occur. Some people use **this** to refer to the very next Tuesday, June, summer, etc, and use **next** for the one after that. Thus someone might say on Sunday, 'I'll see you next Friday', meaning the first Friday to come, but someone else might take that to mean a week on from that because they would refer to the first Friday to come as 'this Friday'. The only solution is to make sure exactly which day, week, season, etc, the other person is referring to.

nice originally meant 'fine, subtle, requiring precision', as in 'There is rather a nice distinction between the two words', but it is widely used in the sense of 'pleasant, agreeable, etc', as in 'She is a nice person' and 'We had a nice time at the picnic'. It is overused and alternative adjectives should be found to avoid this, as in 'She is an amiable person' and 'We had an enjoyable time at the picnic'.

no one and **no-one** are interchangeable but the word is never written 'noone', unlike 'everyone'. **No one** and **no-one** are used with a singular verb, as in 'No one is allowed to leave' and 'No one is anxious to leave'. They are used by some people with a plural personal pronoun or possessive case when attempts are being made to avoid sexism, as in 'No one is expected to take their child away'. The singular form is grammatically correct, as in 'No one is expected to take his/her child away', but it is clumsy. 'No one is expected to take his child away' is sexist. Nobody is interchangeable with no one, as in 'You must tell no one/nobody about this'.

nobody *see* **no one.**

none can be used with either a singular verb or plural verb. Examples of sentences using a singular verb include 'There is none of the food left' and 'None of the work is good enough' and 'None of the coal is to be used today'. In sentences where none is used with a plural noun the verb was traditionally still singular, as in 'None of the books is suitable' and 'None of the parcels is undamaged'. This is still the case in formal contexts but, in the case of informal contexts, a plural verb is often used in modern usage, as in 'None of these things are any good'.

none the less *see* **nevertheless.**

not only is frequently used in a construction with 'but also', as in 'We have not only the best candidate but also the most efficient organization' and 'The organizers of the fête not only made a great deal of money for charity but also gave a great many people a great deal of pleasure'.

nought *see* **naught.**

noxious and **obnoxious** are liable to be confused. They both refer to unpleasantness or harmfulness but they are used in different contexts. **Noxious** is used of a substance, fumes, etc, and means 'harmful, poisonous', as in 'firemen overcome by noxious fumes' and 'delinquent children having a noxious influence on the rest of the class'. **Obnoxious** means 'unpleasant, nasty, offensive', as in 'He has the most obnoxious neighbours' and 'The child's parents let him off with the most obnoxious behaviour'. **Noxious** is used in formal and technical contexts rather than **obnoxious.**

nubile originally meant 'old enough to marry, marriageable' as in 'he has five nubile daughters'. In modern usage **nubile** is frequently used in the sense of 'sexually attractive', as in 'admiring the nubile girls sunbathing on the beach' and 'nubile models posing for magazine illustrations'.

numbers can be written in either figures or words. It is largely a matter of taste which method is adopted. As long as the method is consistent it does not really matter. Some establishments, such as a publishing house or a newspaper office, will have a house style. For example, some of them prefer to have numbers up to 10 written in words, as in 'They have two boys and three girls'. If this system is adopted, guidance should be sought as to whether a mixture of figures and words in the same sentence is acceptable, as in 'We have 12 cups but only six saucers', or whether the rule should be broken in such situations as 'We have twelve cups but only six saucers'.

nutritional and **nutritious** are liable to be confused. They both refer to 'nutrition, the process of giving and receiving nourishment' but mean different things. **Nutritional** means 'referring to nutrition', as in 'doubts about the nutritional value of some fast foods' and 'people who do not receive the minimum nutritional requirements'. **Nutritious** means 'nourishing, of high value as a food', as in 'nutritious homemade soups' and 'something slightly more nutritious than a plate of chips'.

O and **Oh** are both forms of an exclamation made at the beginning of a sentence. **Oh** is the usual spelling, as in 'Oh well. It's Friday tomorrow' and 'Oh dear, the baby's crying again'.

loan *see* **lend.**

objective and **subjective** are opposites. **Objective** means 'not influenced by personal feelings, attitudes, or prejudices', as in 'She is related to the person accused and so she cannot give an objective view of the situation' and 'It is important that all members of a jury are completely objective'. **Subjective** means 'influenced by personal feelings, attitudes and prejudices', as in 'It is only natural to be subjective in situations regarding one's children' and 'She wrote a very subjective report on the conference and did not stick to the facts'. **Objective** can also be a noun in the sense of 'aim, goal', as in 'Our objective was to make as much money as possible'. **Object** can also be used in this sense, as in 'Their main object is to have a good time'.

oblivious means 'unaware of, unconscious of, not noticing'. Traditionally it is followed by the preposition 'of', as in 'The lovers were oblivious of the rain' and 'When he is reading he is completely oblivious of his surroundings'. In modern usage its use with the preposition 'to' is also considered acceptable, as in 'They were oblivious to the fact that he was cheating them' and 'sleep soundly, oblivious to the noise'.

obnoxious *see* **noxious.**

obscene and **pornographic** are not interchangeable. **Obscene** means 'indecent, especially in a sexual way, offending against the accepted standards of decency', as in 'obscene drawings on the walls of the public toilet' and 'When his car was damaged he let out a stream of obscene language'. **Pornographic** means 'intended to arouse sexual excitement', as in 'pornographic videos' and 'magazines with women shown in pornographic poses'. **Obscene** is frequently misspelt. Note the *c* after the *s*.

oculist *see* **optician.**

of is sometimes wrongly used instead of the verb 'to have', as in 'He must of known she was lying' instead of 'He must have known she was lying'. The error arises because the two constructions sound alike when not emphasized.

Oh *see* **O.**

OK and **okay** are both acceptable spellings of an informal word indicating agreement or approval, as in 'OK/okay, I'll come with you', 'We've at last been given the OK/okay to begin building'. When the word is used as a verb it is more usually spelt **okay** because of the problem in adding endings, as in 'They've okayed our plans at last'. **OK** is sometimes written with full stops as **O.K.**

older *see* **elder.**

one is used in formal situations to indicate an indefinite person where 'you' would be used in informal situations, as in 'One should not believe all one hears' and 'One should be kind to animals'. This construction can sound rather affected. Examples of the informal 'you' include 'You would've thought he would've had more sense' and 'You wouldn't think anyone could be so stupid'. **One** when followed by 'of the' and a plural noun takes a singular verb, as in 'One of the soldiers was killed' and 'One of the three witnesses has died'. However, the constructions 'one of those . . . who' and 'one of the . . . that' take a plural verb, as in 'He is one of those people who will not take advice' and 'It is one of those houses that are impossible to heat'.

only must be carefully positioned in written sentences to avoid confusion. It should be placed before, or as close as possible before, the word to which it refers. Compare 'She drinks only wine at the weekend', 'She drinks wine only at the weekend' and 'Only she drinks wine at the weekend'. In spoken English, where the intonation of the voice will indicate which word **only** applies to it may be placed in whichever position sounds most natural, usually between the subject and the verb, as in 'She only drinks wine at the weekend'.

onto and **on to** are both acceptable forms in sentences such as 'The cat leapt onto/on to the table' and 'He jumped from the plane onto/on to the ground'. However, in sentences such as 'It is time to move on to another city' **onto** is not a possible alternative.

onward and **onwards** are not interchangeable. **Onward** is an adjective, as in 'onward motion' and 'onward progress'. **Onwards** is an adverb, as in 'march onwards' and 'proceed onwards'.

optician, ophthalmologist, optometrist and **oculist** all refer to 'a person who is concerned with disorders of the eyes' but they are not interchangeable. **Dispensing optician** refers to 'a person who makes and sells spectacles or contact lenses'. **Ophthalmic optician** refers to 'a person who tests eyesight and prescribes lenses'. **Optometrist** is another term for this. **Ophthalmologist** refers to 'a doctor who specializes in disorders of the eyes' and **oculist** is another name for this.

optimum means 'the most favourable or advantageous condition, situation, amount, degree, etc', as in 'A temperature of 20° is optimum for these plants'. It is mostly used as an adjective meaning 'most favourable or advantageous', as in 'the optimum speed to run the car at', 'the optimum time at which to pick the fruit' and 'the optimum amount of water to give the plants'. It should not be used simply as a synonym for 'best'.

optometrist *see* **optician.**

orientate and **orient** are both acceptable forms of the same word. **Orientate** is the more common in British English but the shorter form, **orient**, is preferred by some people and is the standard form in American English. They are verbs meaning 'to get one's bearings', as in 'difficult to orientate/orient themselves in the mist on the mountain'; 'to adjust to new surroundings', as in 'It takes some time to orientate/orient oneself in a new job'; 'to direct at', as in 'The course is orientated/oriented at older students'; 'to direct the interest of to', as in 'try to orientate/orient students towards the sciences'.

orthopaedic and **paediatric** are liable to be confused. They both apply to medical specialties but they are different. **Orthopaedic** means 'referring to the treatment of disorders of the bones', as in 'attend the orthopaedic clinic with an injured back'. **Paediatric** means 'referring to the treatment of disorders associated with children', as in 'Her little boy is receiving treatment from a paediatric consultant'. In American English these are respectively spelt **orthopedic** and **pediatric.**

other than can be used when **other** is an adjective or pronoun, as in 'There was no means of entry other than through a trap door' and 'He disapproves of the actions of anyone other than himself'. Traditionally, it should not be used as an adverbial phrase, as in 'It was impossible to get there other than by private car'. In such constructions **otherwise than** should be used, as in 'It is impossible to get there otherwise than by private car'. However, **other than** used adverbially is common in modern usage.

otherwise traditionally should not be used as an adjective or pronoun, as in 'Pack your clothes, clean or otherwise' and 'We are not discussing the advantages, or otherwise, of the scheme at this meeting'. It is an adverb, as in 'We are in favour of the project but he obviously thinks otherwise' and 'The hours are rather long but otherwise the job is fine'. *See* **other than.**

owing to *see* **due to.**

p *see* **pence.**

paediatric *see* **orthopaedic.**

panacea and **placebo** are liable to be confused. **Panacea** means 'a universal remedy for all ills and troubles', as in 'The new government does not have a panacea for the country's problems'. It is often used loosely to mean any remedy for any problem, as in 'She thinks that a holiday will be a panacea for his unhappiness'. **Panacea** is pronounced pan-a-*see*-a. **Placebo** refers to 'a supposed medication that is just a harmless substance given to a patient as part of a drugs trial etc', as in 'She was convinced the pills were curing her headaches but the doctor has prescribed her a placebo'. It is pronounced pla-*see*-bo.

parameter is a mathematical term that is very loosely used in modern usage to mean 'limit, boundary, framework' or 'limiting feature or characteristic', as in 'work within the parameters of our budget and resources'. The word is over-used and should be avoided where possible. The emphasis is on the second syllable as par-*am*-it-er.

paranoid is an adjective meaning 'referring to a mental disorder, called **paranoia**, characterized by delusions of persecution and grandeur', as in 'a paranoid personality'. In modern usage it is used loosely to mean 'distrustful, suspicious of others, anxious etc', as in 'It is difficult to get to know him—he's so paranoid' and 'paranoid about people trying to get his job', when there is no question of actual mental disorder. **Paranoia** is pronounced par-a-*noy*-a.

paraphernalia means 'all the bits and pieces of equipment required for something', as in 'all the paraphernalia needed to take a baby on holiday', 'put his angling paraphernalia in the car'. Strictly speaking it is a plural noun but it is now frequently used with a singular verb, as in 'The artist's paraphernalia was lying all over the studio'. **Paraphernalia** is liable to be misspelt. Note the *er* before the *n.*

parlour *see* **sitting room.**

particular means 'special, exceptional', as in 'a matter of particular importance', or 'individual', as in 'Have you a particular person in mind?', and 'concerned over details, fastidious', as in 'very particular about personal hygiene'. **Particular** is often used almost meaninglessly, as in 'this particular dress' and 'this particular car', when **particular** does not add much to the meaning.

partner can be used to indicate one half of an established couple, whether the couple are married or living together, as in 'Her partner was present at the birth of the child'.

passed and **past** are liable to be confused. **Passed** is the past participle and past tense of the verb 'to pass', as in 'She has already passed the exam' and 'They passed an old man on the way'. **Past** is used as a noun, as in 'He was a difficult teenager but that is all in the past now' and 'He has a murky past'. It is also used as an adjective, as in 'I haven't seen him in the past few weeks' and 'Her past experiences affected her opinion of men'. **Past** can also be a preposition, as in 'We drove past their new house', 'It's past three o'clock' and 'He's past caring'. It can also be an adverb, as in 'He watched the athletes running past' and 'The boat drifted past'.

patent, in British English, is usually pronounced *pay*-tent, as in 'patent leather dancing shoes'. **Patent** in the sense of 'obvious', as in 'his patent dislike of the situation' and 'It was quite patent that she loved him' is also pronounced in that way. **Patent** in the sense of 'a legal document giving the holder the sole right to make or sell something and preventing others from imitating it', as in 'take out a patent for his new invention', can be pronounced either *pay*-tent or *pat*-ent. **Patent** in this last sense can also be a verb, as in 'He should patent his invention as soon as possible'.

peddler and **pedlar** are not interchangeable in British English. **Peddler** refers particularly to 'a person who peddles drugs', as in 'drug-peddlers convicted and sent to prison'. **Pedlar** refers to 'a person who sells small articles from house to house or from place to place', as in 'pedlars selling ribbons at the fair'.

pence, p and **pennies** are liable to be confused. **Pence** is the plural form of 'penny', as in 'There are a hundred pence in the pound'. It is commonly found in prices, as in 'apples costing 10 pence each'. **Pence** has become much more common than 'pennies', which tends to be associated with pre-decimalization money (the British currency was decimalized in 1972), as in 'There were twelve pennies in one shilling'. **Pence** is sometimes used as though it were singular, as in 'have no one-pence pieces'. In informal contexts **p** is often used, as in 'Have you got a 10 p (pronounced ten pee) piece' and 'Those chocolate bars are fifteen p'. **Pence** in compounds is not pronounced in the same way as pence was pronounced in compounds before decimalization. Such words as 'ten pence' are now pronounced *ten pens*, with equal emphasis on each word. In pre-decimalization days it was pronounced *ten*-pens, with the emphasis on the first word.

pennies *see* **pence.**

people is usually a plural noun and so takes a plural verb, as in 'The local people were annoyed at the stranger's behaviour' and 'People were being asked to leave'. In the sense of 'nation', 'race' or 'tribe' it is sometimes treated as a singular noun, as in 'the nomadic peoples of the world'. **People** acts as the plural of 'person', as in 'There's room for only one more person in that car but there's room for three people in this one'. In formal or legal contexts **persons** is sometimes used as the plural of 'person', as in 'The lift had a notice saying "Room for six persons only"'.

per capita is a formal expression meaning 'for each person', as in 'The cost of the trip will be £300 per capita'. It is a Latin phrase which has been adopted into English and literally means 'by heads'. It is pronounced per *ka*-pi-ta.

per cent is usually written as two words. It is used adverbially in combination with a number in the sense of 'in or for each hundred', as in 'thirty per cent of the people are living below the poverty line'. The number is sometimes written in figures, as in '50 per cent of the staff are married'. The symbol % is often used instead of the words 'per cent', especially in technical contexts, as in 'make savings of up to 30%'. **Per cent** in modern usage is sometimes used as a noun, as in 'They have agreed to lower the price by half a per cent'.

per means 'for each' and is used to express rates, prices, etc, as in 'driving at 60 miles per hour', 'cloth costing £5 per square metre', 'The cost of the trip is £20 per person' and 'The fees are £1000 a term per child'. It can also mean 'in each', as in 'The factory is inspected three times per year'.

per se is a Latin phrase that has been adapted into English and means 'in itself', as in 'The substance is not per se harmful but it might be so if it interacts with other substances' and 'Television is not per se bad for children'. It should be used only in formal contexts.

percentage refers to 'the rate, number or amount in each hundred', as in 'the number of unemployed people expressed as a percentage of the adult population' and 'What percentage of his salary is free?'. It is also used to mean proportion, as in 'Only a small percentage of last year's students have found jobs' and 'A large percentage of the workers are in favour of a strike'. In modern usage it is sometimes used to mean 'a small amount' or 'a small part', as in 'Only a percentage of the students will find work'.

perquisite *see* **prerequisite.**

person is now used in situations where 'man' was formerly used to avoid sexism in language. It is used when the sex of the person being referred to is either unknown or not specified, as in 'They are advertising for another person for the warehouse'. It often sounds more natural to use 'someone', as in 'They are looking for someone to help out in the warehouse'. **Person** is often used in compounds, as in **chairperson, spokesperson** and **salesperson**, although some people dislike this convention and some compounds, such as **craftsperson,** have not really caught on. **Person** has two possible plurals. *See* **people. Person with** and **people with** are phrases advocated in 'politically correct' language to avoid negative terms such as 'victim', 'sufferer', as in 'person with Aids'.

phenomenal means 'referring to a phenomenon'. It is often used to mean 'remarkable, extraordinary', as in 'a phenomenal atmospheric occurrence', and in modern usage it is also used loosely to mean 'very great', as in 'a phenomenal increase in the crime rate' and 'a phenomenal achievement'. This use is usually restricted to informal contexts.

phenomenon is a singular noun meaning 'a fact, object, occurrence, experience, etc, that can be perceived by the senses rather than by thought or intuition', as in 'She saw something coming out of the lake but it remained an unexplained phenomenon', and 'a strange, unusual or remarkable fact, event or person of some particular significance', as in 'Single parenthood is one of the phenomena of the 1990s'. The plural is **phenomena**, as in 'natural phenomena'. It is a common error to treat **phenomena** as a singular noun. Note the spelling of **phenomenon** as it is liable to be misspelt.

phone, which is a short form of 'telephone', is not regarded as being as informal as it once was. It is quite acceptable in sentences such as 'He is going to buy a mobile phone'. Note that **phone** is now spelt without an apostrophe.

phoney and **phony** are both acceptable spellings but **phoney** is the more common in British English. The word means 'pretending or claiming to be what one is not, fake', as in 'He has a phoney American accent' and 'There's something phoney about him'.

placebo *see* **panacea.**

plane and **aeroplane** mean the same thing, both referring to a 'a machine that can fly and is used to carry people and goods'. In modern usage **plane** is the usual term, as in 'The plane took off on time' and 'nearly miss the plane'. **Aeroplane** is slightly old-fashioned or unduly formal, as in 'Her elderly parents say that they refuse to travel by aeroplane'. The American English spelling is **airplane.** Note that **plane** is not spelt with an apostrophe although it is a shortened form.

pleaded and **pled** mean the same thing, both being the past tense and past participle of the verb 'to plead'. **Pleaded** is the usual form in British English, as in 'They pleaded with the tyrant to spare the child's life' and 'The accused pleaded guilty'. **Pled** is the usual American spelling.

plenty is used only informally in some contexts. It is acceptable in formal and informal contexts when it is followed by the preposition 'of', as in 'We have plenty of food', or when it is used as a pronoun without the 'of' construction, as in 'You can borrow some food from us—we have plenty'. Some people think its use as an adjective, as in 'Don't hurry—we have plenty time' and 'There's plenty food for all in the fridge', should be restricted to informal contexts. As an adverb it is acceptable in both formal and informal contexts in such sentences as 'Help yourself—we have plenty more'. However, such sentences as 'The house is plenty big enough for them' is suitable only for very informal or slang contexts.

political correctness is a modern movement aiming to remove all forms of prejudice in language, such as sexism, racism and discrimination against disabled people. Its aims are admirable but in practice many of the words and phrases suggested by advocates of political correctness are rather contrived or, indeed, ludicrous. The adjective is **politically correct.**

practicable and **practical** should not be used interchangeably. **Practicable** means 'able to be done or carried out, able to be put into practice', as in 'His schemes seem fine in theory but they are never practicable'. **Practical** has several meanings, such as 'concerned with action and practice rather than with theory', as in 'He has studied the theory but has no practical experience of the job'; 'suitable for the purpose for which it was made', as in 'practical shoes for walking'; 'useful', as in 'a practical device with a wide range of uses'; 'clever at doing and making things', as in 'She's very practical when it comes to dealing with an emergency'; 'virtual', as in 'He's not the owner but he's in practical control of the firm'.

practically can mean 'in a practical way', as in 'Practically, the scheme is not really possible', but in modern usage it is usually used to mean 'virtually', as in 'He practically runs the firm although he is not the manager', and 'almost', as in 'The driver of that car practically ran me over'.

prefer is followed by the preposition 'to' not 'than', as in 'She prefers dogs to cats', 'They prefer Paris to London' and 'They prefer driving to walking'.

prerequisite and **perquisite** are liable to be confused although they are completely different in meaning. **Perquisite** means 'money or goods given as a right in addition to one's pay', as in 'various perquisites such as a company car'. It is frequently abbreviated to 'perks', as in 'The pay's not very much but the perks are good'. **Prerequisite** refers to 'something required as a condition for something to happen or exist', as in 'Passing the exam is a prerequisite for his getting the job' and 'A certain amount of studying is a prerequisite of passing the exam'.

prevaricate and **procrastinate** are liable to be confused although they have completely different meanings. **Prevaricate** means 'to try to avoid telling the truth by speaking in an evasive or misleading way', as in 'She prevaricated when the police asked her where she had been the previous evening'. **Procrastinate** means 'to delay or postpone action', as in 'The student has been procrastinating all term but now he has to get to grips with his essay'.

preventative and **preventive** both mean 'preventing or intended to prevent, precautionary', as in 'If you think the staff are stealing from the factory you should take preventative/preventive measures' and 'Preventative/preventive medicine seeks to prevent disease and disorders rather than cure them'. **Preventive** is the more frequently used of the two terms.

prima facie is a Latin phrase that has been adopted into English. It means 'at first sight, based on what seems to be so' and is mainly used in legal or very formal contexts, as in 'The police say they have prima facie evidence for arresting him but more investigation is required'. The phrase is pronounced *pri*-ma *fay*-shee.

prognosis *see* **diagnosis.**

programme and **program** are liable to cause confusion. In British English **programme** is the acceptable spelling in such senses as in 'a television programme', 'put on a varied programme of entertainment' 'buy a theatre programme' and 'launch an ambitious programme of expansion'. However, in the computing sense **program** is used. **Programme** can also be a verb meaning 'to plan, to schedule', as in 'programme the trip for tomorrow'; 'to cause something to conform to a particular set of instructions', as in 'programme the central heating system'; or 'to cause someone to behave in a particular way, especially to conform to particular instructions', as in 'Her parents have programmed her to obey them implicitly'. In the computing sense of 'to provide with a series of coded instructions', the verb is spelt **program** and the *m* is doubled to form the past participle, past tense and present participle, as **programmed** and **programming.** In American English **program** is the accepted spelling for all senses of both noun and verb.

protagonist was originally a term for 'the chief character in a drama', as in 'Hamlet is the protagonist in the play that bears his name'. It then came to mean also 'the leading person or participant in an event, dispute, etc', as in 'The protagonists on each side of the dispute had a meeting'. In modern usage it can now also mean 'a leading or notable supporter of a cause, movement, etc,' as in 'She was one of the protagonists of the feminist movement'.

provided and **providing** are used interchangeably, as in 'You may go, provided/providing that you have finished your work' and 'He can borrow the car provided/providing he pays for the petrol'. 'That' is optional. The phrases mean 'on the condition that'.

pudding *see* **dessert.**

pupil and **student** are not interchangeable. **Pupil** refers to 'a child or young person who is at school', as in 'primary school pupils and secondary school pupils'. **Student** refers to 'a person who is studying at a place of further education, at a university or college', as in 'students trying to find work during the vacations'. In modern usage senior **pupils** at secondary school are sometimes known as **students.** In American English student refers to people at school as well as to people in further education. **Pupil** can also refer to 'a person who is receiving instruction in something from an expert' as in 'The piano teacher has several adult pupils'. **Student** can also refer to 'a person who is studying a particular thing', as in 'In his leisure time he is a student of local history'.

quasi- is Latin in origin and means 'as if, as it were'. In English it is combined with adjectives in the sense of 'seemingly, apparently, but not really', as in 'He gave a quasi-scientific explanation of the occurrence which convinced many people but did not fool his colleagues', or 'partly, to a certain extent but not completely', as in 'It is a quasi-official body which does not have full powers'. **Quasi-** can also be combined with nouns to mean 'seeming, but not really', as in 'a quasi-socialist who is really a capitalist' and 'a quasi-Christian who will not give donations to charity'. **Quasi-** has several possible pronunciations. It can be pronounced *kway*-zi, *kway*-si or *kwah*-si

queer in the sense of 'homosexual' was formerly used only in a slang and derogatory or offensive way. However, it is now used in a non-offensive way by homosexual people to describe themselves, as an alternative to 'gay'.

question *see* **beg the question; leading question.**

quick is an adjective meaning 'fast, rapid', as in 'a quick method', 'a quick route' and 'a quick walker'. It should not be used as an adverb, as in 'Come quick', in formal contexts since this is grammatically wrong.

quite has two possible meanings when used with adjectives. It can mean 'fairly, rather, somewhat', as in 'She's quite good at tennis but not good enough to play in the team' and 'The house is quite nice but it's not what we're looking for'. Where the indefinite article is used, **quite** precedes it, as in 'quite a good player' and 'quite a nice house'. **Quite** can also mean 'completely, totally', as in 'We were quite overwhelmed by their generosity' and 'It is quite impossible for him to attend the meeting'.

raison d'être is French in origin and is used in English to mean 'a reason, a justification for the existence of', as in 'Her children are her raison d'être' and 'His only raison d'être is his work'. The phrase is liable to be misspelt. Note the accent (^) on the first *e*. It is pronounced *ray*-zon detr.

rara avis is French in origin and means literally 'rare bird'. In English it is used to refer to 'a rare or unusual person or thing', as in 'a person with such dedication to a company is a rara avis'. It is pronounced *ray*-ra *ayv*-is or *ra*-ra *ay*-vis.

ravage and **ravish** are liable to be confused. They sound rather similar although they have different meanings. **Ravage** means 'to cause great damage to, to devastate', as in 'low-lying areas ravaged by floods' and 'a population ravaged by disease', or 'to plunder, to rob', as in 'neighbouring tribes ravaging their territory'. **Ravish** means either 'to delight greatly, to enchant', as in 'The audience were ravished by the singer's performance'. It also means 'to rape', as in 'The girl was ravished by her kidnappers', but this meaning is rather old-fashioned and is found only in formal or literary contexts.

re- is a common prefix, meaning 'again', in verbs. In most cases it is not followed by a hyphen, as in 'retrace one's footsteps', 'a retrial ordered by the judge' and 'reconsider his decision'. However, it should be followed by a hyphen if its absence is likely to lead to confusion with another word, as in 're-cover a chair'/'recover from an illness', 're-count the votes'/'recount a tale of woe', 'the re-creation of a 17th-century village for a film set'/'play tennis for recreation' and 're-form the group'/'reform the prison system'. In cases where the second element of a word begins with *e*, **re-** is traditionally followed by a hyphen, as in 're-educate', re-entry' and 're-echo', but in modern usage the hyphen is frequently omitted.

re, meaning 'concerning, with reference to', as in 'Re your correspondence of 26 November', should be restricted to business or formal contexts.

readable *see* **legible.**

re-cover, recover *see* **re-.**

re-creation, recreation *see* **re-.**

referendum causes problems with regard to its plural form. It has two possible plural forms, **referendums** or **referenda.** In modern usage **referendums** is the more usual plural. **Referendum** means 'the referring of an issue of public importance to a general vote by all the people of a country', as in 'hold a referendum on whether to join the EC'.

re-form, reform *see* **re-**.

registry office and **register office** are interchangeable, although **registry office** is the more common term in general usage. The words refer to 'an office where civil marriage ceremonies are performed and where births, marriages and deaths are recorded', as in 'She wanted to be married in church but he preferred a registry office ceremony' and 'register the child's birth at the local registry office'.

rigour and **rigor** are liable to be confused. They look similar but they have completely different meanings. **Rigour** means 'severity, strictness', as in 'the rigour of the punishment', and 'harshness, unpleasantness', as in 'the rigour of the climate' (in this sense it is often in the plural, **rigours**), and 'strictness, detailedness', as in 'the rigour of the editing'. **Rigor** is a medical term meaning 'rigidity', as in 'muscles affected by rigor', or 'a feeling of chilliness often accompanied by feverishness', as in 'infectious diseases of which rigor is one of the symptoms'. **Rigor** is also short for **rigor mortis**, meaning 'the stiffening of the body that occurs after death'. The first syllable of **rigour** is pronounced to rhyme with 'big', but **rigor** can be pronounced either in this way or with the *i* pronounced as in 'ride'.

roof causes problems with regard to its plural form. The usual plural is **roofs**, which can be pronounced either as it is spelt, to rhyme with 'hoofs', or to rhyme with 'hooves'.

rout and **route** are liable to be confused. They look similar but are pronounced differently and have completely different meanings'. **Rout** as a noun means 'overwhelming defeat', as in 'the rout of the opposing army', and as a verb 'to defeat utterly', as in 'Their team routed ours last time'. **Route** refers to 'a way of getting somewhere', as in 'the quickest route' and 'the scenic route'. **Route** can also be a verb meaning 'to arrange a route for, to send by a certain route', as in 'route the visitors along the banks of the river'. **Rout** is pronounced to rhyme with 'shout'. **Route** is pronounced to rhyme with 'brute'.

scarfs and **scarves** are both acceptable spellings of the plural of 'scarf', meaning a piece of cloth worn around the neck or the head', as in 'a silk scarf at her neck' and 'wearing a head scarf'.

Scotch, Scots and **Scottish** are liable to be confused. **Scotch** is restricted to a few set phrases, such as 'Scotch whisky', 'Scotch broth' and 'Scotch mist'. As a noun **Scotch** refers to 'Scotch whisky', as in 'have a large Scotch with ice'. **Scots** as an adjective is used in such contexts as 'Scots accents', 'Scots people' and 'Scots attitudes'. As a noun **Scots** refers to the Scots language, as in 'He speaks standard English but he uses a few words of Scots.' The noun **Scot** is used to refer to 'a Scottish person', as in 'Scots living in London'. **Scottish** is found in such contexts as 'Scottish literature', 'Scottish history' and 'Scottish culture'.

sculpt and **sculpture** are interchangeable as verbs meaning 'to make sculptures, to practise sculpting', as in 'commissioned to sculpt/sculpture a bust of the chairman of the firm' and 'She both paints and sculpts/sculptures.

seize Note the *ei* combination, which is an exception to the '*i* before *e* except after *c*' rule.

sentiment and **sentimentality** are liable to be confused. They are related but have different shades of meaning. **Sentiment** means 'feeling, emotion', as in 'His actions were the result of sentiment not rationality'. It also means 'attitude, opinion', as in 'a speech full of anti-Christian sentiments'. **Sentimentality** is the noun from the adjective **sentimental** and means 'over-indulgence in tender feelings', as in 'dislike the sentimentality of the love songs' and 'She disliked her home town but now speaks about it with great sentimentality'.

sexism in language has been an issue for some time, and various attempts have been made to avoid it. For example, 'person' is often used where 'man' was traditionally used and 'he/she' substituted for 'he' in situations where the sex of the relevant person is unknown or unspecified.

ship *see* **boat**.

sine qua non is a Latin phrase that has been adopted into English and means 'essential condition, something that is absolutely necessary', as in 'It is a sine qua non of the agreement that the rent is paid on time'. It is used only in formal or legal contexts.

sitting room, living room, lounge and **drawing room** all refer to 'a room in a house used for relaxation and the receiving of guests'. Which word is used is largely a matter of choice. Some people object to the use of **lounge** as being pretentious but it is becoming increasingly common. **Drawing room** is a more formal word and applies to a room in rather a grand residence.

skilful, as in 'admire his skilful handling of the situation' is frequently misspelt. Note the single *l* before the *f*. In American English the word is spelt **skillful**.

slander *see* **libel**.

sometime and **some time** are liable to be confused. **Sometime** means 'at an unknown or unspecified time', as in 'We must get together sometime' and 'I saw her sometime last year'. There is a growing tendency in modern usage to spell this as **some time**. Originally **some time** was restricted to meaning 'a period of time', as in 'We need some time to think'.

spelled and **spelt** are both acceptable forms of the past tense and past participle of the verb 'to spell', as in 'They spelled/spelt the word wrongly' and 'He realized that he had spelled/spelt the word wrongly'.

stadium causes problems with regard to its plural form. **Stadiums** and **stadia** are both acceptable. **Stadium** is derived from Latin and the original plural form followed the Latin and was **stadia**. However, anglicized plural forms are becoming more and more common in foreign words adopted into English, and **stadiums** is now becoming the more usual form.

stanch and **staunch** are both acceptable spellings of the word meaning 'to stop the flow of', as in 'stanch/staunch the blood from the wound in his head' and 'try to stanch/staunch the tide of violence'. **Staunch** also means 'loyal, firm', as in 'the team's staunch supporters'.

start *see* **commence**.

stationary and **stationery** are liable to be confused. They sound alike but have completely different meanings. **Stationary** means 'not moving, standing still', as in 'stationary vehicles'. **Stationery** refers to 'writing materials', as in 'office stationery'. An easy way to differentiate between them is to remember that **stationery** is bought from a 'stationer', which, like 'baker' and 'butcher', ends in *-er*.

staunch *see* **stanch**.

stimulant and **stimulus** are liable to be confused. Formerly the distinction between them was quite clear but now the distinction is becoming blurred. Traditionally **stimulant** refers to 'a substance, such as a drug, that makes a person more alert or more active', as in 'Caffeine is a stimulant'. **Stimulus** traditionally refers to 'something that rouses or encourages a person to action or greater effort', as in 'The promise of more money acted as a stimulus to the work force and they finished the job in record time'. In modern usage the words are beginning to be used interchangeably. In particular, **stimulus** is used in the sense of **stimulant** as well as being used in its own original sense.

straight away and **straightaway** are both acceptable ways of spelling the expression for 'without delay, at once', as in 'attend to the matter straight away/straightaway'.

strata *see* **stratum**.

stratagem and **strategy** are liable to be confused. They look and sound similar but they have different meanings. **Stratagem** means 'a scheme or trick', as in 'think of a stratagem to mislead the enemy' and 'devise a stratagem to gain entry to the building'. **Strategy** refers to 'the art of planning a campaign', as in 'generals meeting to put together a battle strategy', and 'a plan or policy, particularly a clever one, designed for a particular purpose', as in 'admire the strategy which he used to win the game'.

stratum and **strata** are liable to be confused. **Stratum** is the singular form and **strata** is the plural form of a word meaning 'a layer or level', as in 'a stratum of rock' and 'different strata of society'. It is a common error to use **strata** as a singular noun.

student *see* **pupil**.

subconscious and unconscious are used in different contexts. **Subconscious** means 'concerning those areas or activities of the mind of which one is not fully aware', as in 'a subconscious hatred of her parents' and 'a subconscious desire to hurt her sister'. **Unconscious** means 'unaware', as in 'She was unconscious of his presence' and 'unconscious of the damage which he had caused', and 'unintentional', as in 'unconscious humour' and 'an unconscious slight'. **Unconscious** also means 'having lost consciousness, insensible', as in 'knocked unconscious by the blow to his head'.

subjective *see* **objective.**

such and **like** are liable to be confused. **Such** is used to introduce examples, as in 'herbs, such as chervil and parsley' and 'citrus fruits, such as oranges and lemons'. **Like** introduces comparisons. 'She hates horror films like *Silence of the Lambs*', and 'Very young children, like very old people, have to be kept warm.'

supper *see* **dinner.**

syndrome in its original meaning refers to 'a set of symptoms and signs that together indicate the presence of a physical or mental disorder', as in 'Down's syndrome'. In modern usage it is used loosely to indicate 'any set of events, actions, characteristics, attitudes that together make up, or are typical of, a situation', as in 'He suffers from the "I'm all right Jack" syndrome and doesn't care what happens to anyone else' and 'They seem to be caring people but they are opposing the building of an Aids hospice in their street—a definite case of "the not in my back yard" syndrome'.

tea *see* **dinner.**

teach *see* **learn.**

telephone *see* **phone.**

terminal and **terminus** in some contexts are interchangeable. They both refer to 'the end of a bus route, the last stop on a bus route, the building at the end of a bus route', as in 'The bus doesn't go any further—this is the terminus/terminal', but **terminus** is the more common term in this sense. They can also both mean 'the end of a railway line, the station at the end of a railway line', but **terminal** is the more common term in this sense. **Terminal** can refer to 'a building containing the arrival and departure areas for passengers at an airport' and 'a building in the centre of a town for the arrival and departure of air passengers'. **Terminal** also refers to 'a point of connection in an electric circuit', as in 'the positive and negative terminals', and 'apparatus, usually consisting of a keyboard and screen, for communicating with the central processor in a computing system', as in 'He has a dumb terminal so he can read information but not input it'. As an adjective **terminal** means 'of, or relating to, the last stage in a fatal illness', as in 'a terminal disease' and 'terminal patients'.

than is used to link two halves of comparisons or contrasts, as in 'Peter is considerably taller than John is', 'He is older than I am' and 'I am more informed about the situation than I was yesterday'. Problems arise when the relevant verb is omitted. In order to be grammatically correct, the word after 'than' should take the subject form if there is an implied verb, as in 'He is older than I (am)'. However this can sound stilted, as in 'She works harder than he (does)', and in informal contexts this usually becomes 'She works harder than him'. If there is no implied verb, the word after **than** is in the object form, as in 'rather you than me!'

the the definite article, which usually refers back to something already identified or to something specific, as in 'Where is the key?, 'What have you done with the book that I gave you?' and 'We have found the book that had we lost'. It is also used to denote someone or something as being the only one, as in 'the House of Lords', 'the King of Spain' and 'the President of Russia' and to indicate a class or group, as in 'the aristocracy', 'the cat family' and 'the teaching profession'. The is sometimes pronounced 'thee' when it is used to identify someone or something unique or important, as in 'Is that the John Frame over there?' and 'She is the fashion designer of the moment'.

their and **there** are liable to be confused because they sound similar. **There** means 'in, to or at that place', as in 'place it there' and 'send it there'. **Their** is the possessive of 'they', meaning 'of them, belonging to them', as in 'their books' and 'their mistakes'.

their and **they're** are liable to be confused because they sound similar. **Their** is the possessive of 'they', meaning 'of them, belonging to them', as in 'their cars' and 'their attitudes'. **They're** is a shortened form of 'they are', as in 'They're not very happy' and 'They're bound to lose'.

their used in conjunction with 'anyone', everyone', 'no one' and 'someone', is becoming increasingly common, even in textbooks, although this use is ungrammatical. The reason for this is to avoid the sexism of using 'his' when the sex of the person being referred to is either unknown or unspecified, and to avoid the clumsiness of 'his/her' or 'his or her'. Examples of **they** being so used include 'Everyone must do their best' and 'No one is to take their work home'.

this *see* **next.**

till and **until** are more or less interchangeable except that **until** is slightly more formal, as in 'They'll work till they drop' and 'Until we assess the damage we will not know how much the repairs will cost'.

toilet, lavatory, loo and **bathroom** all have the same meaning but the context in which they are used sometimes varies. **Toilet** is the most widely used of the words and is used on signs in public places. The informal **loo** is also very widely used. **Lavatory** is less common nowadays although it was formerly regarded by all but the working class and lower-middle class as the most acceptable term. **Bathroom** in British English usually refers to 'a room containing a bath', but in American English it is the usual word for **toilet. Ladies** and **gents** are terms for **toilet**, particularly in public places. **Powder room** also means this, as does the American English **rest room.**

town *see* **city.**

trade names should be written with a capital letter, as in 'Filofax' and 'Jacuzzi'. When trade names are used as verbs they are written with a lower case letter, as in 'hoover the carpet'.

try to and **try and** are interchangeable in modern usage. Formerly **try and** was considered suitable only in spoken and very informal contexts, but it is now considered acceptable in all but the most formal contexts, as in 'Try to/and do better' and 'They must try to/and put the past behind them'.

ultra is used as a prefix meaning 'going beyond', as in 'ultraviolet' and 'ultrasound', or 'extreme, very', as in 'ultra-sophisticated', 'ultra-modern', and 'ultra-conservative'. Compounds using it may be spelt with or without a hyphen. Words such as 'ultrasound' and 'ultraviolet' are usually spelt as one word, but words with the second sense of **ultra**, such as 'ultra-sophisticated', are often hyphenated.

unconscious *see* **subconscious.**

under way, meaning 'in progress', is traditionally spelt as two words, as in 'Preparations for the conference are under way'. In modern usage it is frequently spelt as one word, as in 'The expansion project is now underway'. It is a common error to write 'under weigh'.

underhand and **underhanded** are interchangeable in the sense of 'sly, deceitful', as in 'He used underhand/underhanded methods to get the job' and 'It was underhand/underhanded of him to not to tell her that he was leaving'. **Underhand** is the more common of the two terms.

uninterested *see* **disinterested.**

unique traditionally means 'being the only one of its kind', as in 'a unique work of art' and 'everyone's fingerprints are unique' and so cannot be modified by such words as 'very', 'rather', 'more', etc, although it can be modified by 'almost' and 'nearly'. In modern usage **unique** is often used to mean 'unrivalled, unparalleled, outstanding', as in 'a unique opportunity' and 'a unique performance'.

unreadable *see* **illegible.**

until *see* **till.**

up and **upon** mean the same and are virtually interchangeable, except that **upon** is slightly more formal. Examples include 'sitting on a bench', 'the carpet on the floor', 'the stamp on the letter', caught with the stolen goods on him' and 'something on his mind'; and 'She threw herself upon her dying mother's bed', 'a carpet of snow upon the ground' and 'Upon his arrival he went straight upstairs'.

upward and **upwards** are not interchangeable. **Upward** is used as an adjective, as in 'on an upward slope' and 'an upward trend in prices'. **Upwards** is an adverb, as in 'look upwards to see the plane'.

vacation, meaning 'holiday', in British English is mostly restricted to a university or college situation, as in 'students seeking paid employment during their vacation'. In American English it is the usual word for 'holiday'.

verbal and **oral** are liable to be confused. **Oral** means 'expressed in speech', as in 'an oral, rather than a written examination'. **Verbal** means 'expressed in words', as in 'He asked for an instruction diagram but he was given verbal instructions' and 'They were going to stage a protest match but they settled for a verbal protest'. It is also used to mean 'referring to the spoken word, expressed in speech', as in 'a verbal agreement'. Because of these two possible meanings, the use of **verbal** can lead to ambiguity. In order to clarify the situation, **oral** should be used when 'expressed in speech' is meant. **Verbal** can also mean referring to verbs, as in 'verbal endings'.

vice versa means 'the other way round, with the order reversed', as in 'He will do his friend's shift and vice versa' and 'Mary dislikes John and vice versa'. It is pronounced vis-e ver-sa, vi-si ver-sa or vis ver-sa and is derived from Latin.

vis-à-vis means 'in relation to', as in 'their performance vis-à-vis their ability' and 'the company's policy vis-à-vis early retirement'. It is pronounced vee-za-vee and is derived from French. Note the accent on the *a*.

-ways *see* **-wise.**

what ever and **whatever** are not interchangeable. **What ever** is used when 'ever' is used for emphasis, as in 'What ever does he think he's doing?' and 'What ever is she wearing'. **Whatever** means 'anything, regardless of what, no matter what', as in 'Help yourself to whatever you want' and 'Whatever he says I don't believe him'.

which and **what** can cause problems. In questions **which** is used when a limited range of alternatives is suggested, as in 'Which book did you buy in the end?' and **what** is used in general situations, as in 'What book did you buy?'

whisky and **whiskey** both refer to a strong alcoholic drink distilled from grain. **Whisky** is made in Scotland and **whiskey** in Ireland and America. **Whisky** is the usual British English spelling.

who and **whom** cause problems. **Who** is the subject of a verb, as in 'Who told you?', 'It was you who told her' and 'the girls who took part in the play'. **Whom** is the object of a verb or preposition, as in 'Whom did he tell?', 'To whom did you speak?' and 'the people from whom he stole'. In modern usage **whom** is falling into disuse, especially in questions, except in formal contexts. **Who** is used instead even although it is ungrammatical, as in 'Who did you speak to?' **Whom** should be retained when it is a relative pronoun, as in 'the man whom you saw', 'the person to whom he spoke' and 'the girl to whom she gave the book'.

whose and **who's** are liable to be confused. They sound alike but have different meanings. **Whose** means 'of whom' or 'of which', as in 'the woman whose child won', 'the boy whose leg was broken', 'Whose bicycle is that?' and 'the firm whose staff went on strike'. **Who's** is a shortened form of 'who is', as in 'Who's that?', 'Who's first in the queue?' and 'Who's coming to the cinema?'

-wise and **-ways** cause problems. Added to nouns, **-wise** can form adverbs of manner indicating either 'in such a position or direction', as in 'lengthwise' and 'clockwise', and 'in the manner of', as in 'crabwise'. In modern usage **-wise** is frequently used to mean 'with reference to', as in 'Weatherwise it was fine', 'Workwise all is well' and 'Moneywise they're not doing too well'. The suffix **-ways** has a more limited use. It means 'in such a way, direction or manner of', as in 'lengthways' and 'sideways'.

woman *see* **lady.**

Xmas is sometimes used as an alternative and shorter form of 'Christmas'. It is common only in a written informal context and is used mainly in commercial situations, as in 'Xmas cards on sale here' and 'Get your Xmas tree here'. When pronounced it is the same as 'Christmas'. The X derives from the Greek *chi*, the first letter of *Christos*, the Greek word for Christ.

X-ray is usually written with an initial capital letter when it is a noun meaning 'a photograph made by means of X-rays showing the bones or organs of the body', as in 'take an X-ray of the patient's chest'. Another term for the noun **X-ray** is 'radiograph'. As a verb it is also usually spelt with an initial capital, as 'After the accident he had his leg X-rayed', but it is sometimes spelt with an initial lower-case letter, as in 'have his chest x-rayed'.

you is used in informal or less formal situations to indicate an indefinite person referred to as 'one' in formal situations. Examples include 'You learn a foreign language more quickly if you spend some time in the country where it is spoken', 'You would think that they would make sure that their staff are polite', 'You can get used to anything in time' and 'You have to experience the situation to believe it'. **You** in this sense must be distinguished from **you** meaning the second person singular', as in 'You have missed your bus', 'You must know where you left your bag' and 'You have to leave now'. *See* **one.**

your and **you're** are liable to be confused. **Your** is a possessive adjective meaning 'belonging to you, of you', as in 'That is your book and this is mine', 'Your attitude is surprising' and 'It is your own fault'. **You're** is a shortened form of 'you are', as in 'You're foolish to believe him', 'You're going to be sorry' and 'You're sure to do well'. Note the spelling of the pronoun **yours**, as in 'This book is yours' and 'Which car is yours?' It should not be spelt with an apostrophe as it is not a shortened form of anything.

Spelling

-able and -ible are both used to form adjectives. It is easy to confuse the spelling of words ending in these. *See* **Adjectives Liable to be Misspelt**

accent refers to certain symbols used on some foreign words adopted into English. In modern usage, which has a tendency to punctuate less than was formerly the case, accents are frequently omitted. For example, an actor's part in a play is now usually spelt 'role' but originally it was spelt 'rôle', the accent on *o* being called a circumflex.

The accent is most likely to be retained if it affects the pronunciation. Thus 'cliché' and 'divorcé' usually retain the acute accent, as it is called, on the *e*. On the other hand, the accent known as the cedilla is frequently omitted from beneath the *c* in words such as 'façade/facade', although it is there to indicate that the *c* is soft, pronounced like an *s*, rather than a hard sound pronounced like a *k*.

apostrophe *see* **Punctuation** section.

book titles these can cause problems as to spelling and style. How they are treated in publications, business reports, etc, depends largely on the house style of the firm concerned. However, they are generally written in documents, letters, etc, as they appear on their title pages, that is with the first letter of the first word and of the following main words of the title in capital letters, and those of words of lesser importance, such as the articles, prepositions and coordinate conjunctions, in lowercase letters, as in The Guide to Yoga, Hope for the Best and In the Middle of Life.

Some people, and some house-style manuals, prefer to put the titles in italic, as in *A Room with a View* and *A Guide to Dental Health*.

Others prefer to put book titles in quotation marks, as in 'Gardening for Beginners'. Such a convention can make use of either single or double quotation marks. Thus either 'Desserts for the Summer' or "Desserts for the Summer" is possible provided that the writer is consistent throughout any one piece of writing.

If the title of a book is mentioned in a piece of direct speech in quotation marks it goes within the opposite style of quotation marks from the piece in direct speech. Thus if the direct speech is within single quotation marks, the book title goes within double quotation marks, as in 'Have you read "Wuthering Heights" or are you not a Bronte fan?' If the direct speech is within double quotation marks, the book title goes between single quotation marks, as in "Would you say that 'Animal Farm' was your favourite Orwell novel?"

It is even quite common for book titles to appear in documents both in italic type and with quotation marks. To some extent the punctuation of book titles is a matter of choice as long as they are consistent, but there is a growing tendency to have as little punctuation as possible and to have as uncluttered a page as possible.

buildings can cause problems with regard to capital letters. The proper noun attached to the name of the building should have an initial capital letter, as should have the common noun that may be part of the name, as in The White House and The National Portrait Gallery.

businesses and **organizations** often cause problems with regard to their names or titles. In general the initial letters of the main words of the title should be in capital letters and the words of lesser importance, such as the articles, coordinating conjunctions and prepositions, should be in lower case, except when they are the first word of the title, as in 'The Indian Carpet Company', 'Kitchens for All' and 'Capital Industrial Cleaners'. Obviously, when the names of people are involved these should have initial capital letters, as in 'Jones and Brown'.

capital letters are used in a number of different situations.

The first word of a sentence or a direct quotation begins with a **capital letter**, as in 'They left early', 'Why have they gone?' and 'He said weakly, "I don't feel very well"'.

The first letter of a name or proper noun is always a **capital letter**, as in 'Mary Brown', 'John Smith', 'South America', 'Rome', 'speak Italian', 'Buddhism', 'Marxism'.

Capital letters are also used in the titles of people, places or works of art, as in 'Uncle Fred', 'Professor Jones', 'Ely Cathedral', Edinburgh University', 'reading *Wuthering Heights*', 'watching *Guys and Dolls*', 'listen to Beethoven's Third Symphony' and 'a copy of *The Potato Eaters* by van Gogh'. They are also used in the titles of wars and historical, cultural and geological periods, as in 'the Wars of the Roses', 'the Renaissance', 'the Ice Age'.

Note that only the major words of titles, etc, are in capital letters, words, such as 'the', 'on', 'of', etc, being in lower-case letters.

A capital letter is used as the first letter of days of the week, months of the year, and religious festivals, as in 'Monday', 'October', 'Easter', 'Yom Kippur'. It is a matter of choice whether the seasons of the year are given capital letters or not, as in 'spring/Spring', 'autumn/Autumn'.

Apart from 'I', pronouns are lower-case except when they refer to God or Christ, when some people capitalize them, as in 'God asks us to trust in Him'.

Trade names should be spelt with an initial capital letter, as in 'Filofax', 'Jacuzzi', 'Xerox', 'Biro', 'Hoover'. When verbs are formed from these, they are spelt with an initial lower-case letter, as 'xerox the letter', 'hoover the carpet'.

doubling of consonants There are a few rules that can help you decide whether or not to double a consonant.

In words of one syllable ending in a single consonant preceded by a single vowel, the consonant is doubled when an ending starting with a vowel is added, as in 'drop' and 'dropped', 'pat' and 'patting' and 'rub' and 'rubbing'.

In words of more than one syllable that end in a single consonant preceded by a single vowel, the consonant is doubled if the stress is on the last syllable, as in 'begin' and 'beginning', 'occur' and 'occurring', 'prefer' and 'preferred', 'refer' and 'referring' and 'commit' and 'committed'. In similar words where the stress is not on the last syllable, the consonant does not double, as in 'bigot' and 'bigoted' and 'develop' and 'developed'

Exceptions to this rule include words ending in 'l'. The 'l' doubles even in cases where the last syllable containing it is unstressed, as in 'travel' and 'travelled' and 'appal' and 'appalling'. 'Worship', in which the stress is on the first syllable, is also an exception, as in 'worshipped'.

geographical features these should be written with initial capital letters. They include the common nouns that are part of the name of the feature, as in Niagara Falls, Atlantic Ocean, River Thames, Mount Everest and Devil's Island.

hyphen *see* **Punctuation** section.

indefinite article a and an are the forms of the indefinite article.

The form a is used before words that begin with a consonant sound, as in *a* box, *a* garden, *a* road, *a* wall.

The form an is used before words that begin with a vowel sound, as in *an* apple, *an* easel, *an* ostrich, *an* uncle.

Note that it is the *sound* of the initial letter that matters and not the *spelling*. Thus a is used before words beginning with a *u* when they are pronounced with a *y* sound as though it were a consonant, as *a* unit, *a* usual occurrence. Similarly an is used, for example, before words beginning with the letter *h* where this is not pronounced, as in *an* heir, *an* hour, *an* honest man.

Formerly it was quite common to use an before words that begin with an *h* sound and also begin with an unstressed syllable, as *an* hotel, *an* historic occasion, but nowadays it is more usual to use *a* in such cases.

months of the year these are spelt with initial capital letters, as in January, February, March, April, May, June, July, August, September, October, November and December.

plural nouns singular nouns in English form plural forms in different ways.

Most in add *s* to form the plural, as in 'cats', 'machines' and 'boots'.

Words ending in *-s*, *-x*, *-z*, *-ch* and *-sh* add *es*, as in 'buses', 'masses', 'foxes', 'fezzes or fezes', 'churches' and 'sashes'.

Nouns ending in a consonant followed by *y* have *-ies* in the plural, as 'fairies' and 'ladies', but note 'monkey', where the *y* is preceded by a vowel and becomes 'monkeys'. Proper nouns ending in *y* add *s*, as in 'the two Germanys'.

Some words ending in *f* have *ves* in the plural, as 'wives' and 'halves', but some simply add *s* to the singular form, as 'beliefs'. Some words ending in *f* can either add *s* or change to *ves*, as 'hoofs or hooves'.

Words ending in *o* cause problems as some end in *oes* in the plural, as 'potatoes' and 'tomatoes', and some end in *s*, as in 'pianos', while some can be spelt either way and have to be learned or looked up in a dictionary etc. Shortened forms, such as 'photo' and 'video', add simply *s*, as 'photos', 'videos'.

Some words have the same form in the plural as they do in the singular, such as 'sheep' and 'deer'. Some are plural in form already and so do not change. These include 'trousers' and 'scissors'.

Several words in English have irregular plural forms which just have to be learned or looked up in a dictionary, etc. These include 'men', 'mice' and 'feet'.

Some foreign words adopted into English used to retain the foreign plural form in English but this is becoming less common and, at the very least there is now often an English-formed alternative, as 'gateaux/gateaus', 'index/indices', 'formulae/formulas', 'appendixes/appendices'. However, several nouns of foreign extraction retain the foreign-style plural in English, such as 'criteria' and 'crises'.

Commonly misspelt words

All of us have problem words that cause spelling difficulties but there are some words that are generally misspelt. These include:

A

abbreviation
abscess
absence
abysmal
accelerator
accessible
accessories
accommodate
accompaniment
accumulate
accurate
accustomed
achieve
aching
acknowledge
acknowledgement
acknowledgment
acquaint
acquaintance
acquiesce
acquiescence
acquire
acquit
acquittal
acreage
across
actual
additional
address
adequate
adieu
adjacent
admissible
admittance
adolescence
adolescent
advantageous
advertisement
advice
advise
aerate
aerial
aesthetic
affect
affiliation
afforestation
aggravate
aggravation
aggregate
aggression
aggressive
aghast
agnosticism
agoraphobia
agreeable
agreed
aisle
alcohol
alfresco
alibis
align
alignment
allege
allergic
alleys
alligator
allocate
allotment
allotted
almond
alms
alphabetically
already
although
aluminium
ambiguous
amethyst
ammunition
anachronism
anaesthetic
analyse
analysis
anarchist
ancestor
ancestry
anemone
angrily
anguish
annihilate
annihilation
anniversary
announcement
annulled
annulment
anonymous
anorak
answered
Antarctic
antibiotic
antithesis
anxiety
apartheid
apologize
appalling
apparently
appearance
appendicitis
appreciate
approval
aquarium
aquiline
arbiter
arbitrary
arbitration
archaeology
architectural
Arctic
arguably
arrangement
arrival
artichoke
ascend
ascent
asphalt
asphyxiate
asphyxiation
assassin
assassinate
assessment
assistance
associate
asthma
asthmatic
astrakhan
atheist
atrocious
attach
attendant
attitude
aubergine
auburn
auctioneer
audible
aural
automatic
autumn
awful
awkward

B

bachelor
bagatelle
baggage
bailiff
ballast
ballerina
banana
banister
bankruptcy
banquet
barbecue
barometer
barrister
basically
basis
bassoon
battalion
bazaar
beautiful
befriend
beguile
behaviour
beleaguer
belief
believe
belligerent
benefited
bequeath
berserk
besiege
bettered
bevelled
bewitch
bias
bicycle
biennial
bigamous
bigoted
bilingual
biscuit
bivouacked
blancmange
blasphemous
blasphemy
bleary
blitz
bodily
bonfire
bootee
borough
bouquet
bourgeois
boutique
bracketed
braille
brassiere
breadth
breathalyser
brief
broccoli
brochure
bronchitis
bruise
brusque
buccaneer
Buddhist
budding
budgerigar
budgeted
buffeted
bulletin
bumptious
bungalow
buoyancy
buoyant
bureau
bureaucracy
business
buttoned

C

cabbage
cafeteria
caffeine

camouflage
campaign
campaigned
cancelled
cancerous
candour
cannabis
cannibal
canvassing
capability
capillary
capitalist
caravan
carbohydrate
carburettor
career
caress
caries
carriage
cartoonist
cashier
cassette
castanets
casualty
catalogue
catarrh
catechism
catering
cauliflower
cautious
ceiling
cellophane
cemetery
centenary
centilitre
centimetre
certainty
champagne
championed
chancellor
changeable
channelled
characteristic
chasm
chauffeur
cheetah
cherish
chief
chilblain
chintz
chiropody
chisel
choreographer
choreography
chronically
chrysanthemum
cigarette
cinnamon
circuitous
cistern
civilian
claustrophobia
clientele
clique

coalesce
cocoa
coconut
coffee
cognac
coincidence
colander
collaborate
collapsible
colleague
colonel
colossal
comically
commandeer
commemorate
commentator
commercial
commiserate
commission
commissionaire
commitment
committal
committed
committee
communicate
commuter
companion
comparative
comparison
compatibility
compelled
competitive
computer
conceal
concealment
conceit
conceive
concession
concurrent
concussion
condemned
condescend
confectionery
conference
confetti
congeal
congratulations
conjunctivitis
conned
connoisseur
conscience
conscientious
conscious
consequently
consignment
consolation
conspicuous
constitute
consumer
contemptible
continent
continuous
contraception
contradictory

controlled
controller
controversial
convalesce
convenient
convertible
conveyed
convolvulus
coolly
cooperate
cooperative
coordinate
copying
coquette
corduroy
co-respondent
coronary
correspondence
correspondent
corridor
corroborate
corrugated
cosmopolitan
cosseted
councillor
counselling
counterfeit
courageous
courteous
crèche
credible
credited
crematorium
creosote
crescent
crisis
criterion
crocheted
crocodile
croupier
crucial
crucifixion
cruelly
cruise
cryptic
cubicle
cupful
curable
curiosity
curious
currency
curriculum vitae
customary
cynic
cynicism
cynosure

D

dachshund
daffodil
dahlia
dais
damage
dandruff
darkened
debatable
debauched
debility
deceased
deceit
deceive
deciduous
decipher
decoyed
decrease
decreed
defamatory
defeat
defendant
defied
definite
definitely
dehydrate
deign
deliberate
delicatessen
delicious
delinquent
delirious
demeanour
demonstrate
denouement
denunciation
dependence
depth
derailment
dermatitis
derogatory
descend
descendant
desiccate
desperate
detach
detachable
detergent
deterred
deterrent
deuce
develop
developed
development
diabetes
diagnosis
dialogue
diametrically
diaphragm
diarrhoea
difference
different
dilapidated
dilemma
dilettante
diminish
diminution
dinosaur

diphtheria
diphthong
disadvantageous
disagreeable
disagreed
disagreement
disappearance
disappeared
disappoint
disapproval
disastrous
disbelief
disbelieve
discipline
discotheque
discouraging
discourteous
discrepancy
discrimination
discussion
disease
disguise
dishevelled
dishonourable
disillusion
disinfectant
disinherited
dismissal
disobeyed
disparage
dispelled
disposal
dispossess
dissatisfaction
dissatisfy
dissect
disseminate
dissent
dissimilar
dissipated
dissipation
dissociate
dissolute
dissuade
distilled
distillery
distinguish
distraught
disuse
divisible
documentary
doggerel
domineering
donate
doubt
dragooned
drastically
draughty
drooled
drooped
drunkenness
dubious
dumbfounded
dungarees
duress
dutiful
dynamite
dysentery
dyspepsia

E

eccentric
ecclesiastic
ecologically
economically
ecstasy
eczema
effective
effervescence
efficacious
efficient
effrontery
eightieth
elaborate
electrician
elevenses
eligible
emancipate
embarrass
embarrassment
emergence
emergent
emolument
emotional
emphasize
employee
emptied
enable
encourage
encyclopedia
endeavour
endurance
energetically
enervate
engineer
enough
ensuing
entailed
enthusiasm
enumerate
epilepsy
equalize
equalled
equipped
erroneous
erudite
escalator
escapism
espionage
essence
essential
estranged
etiquette
euthanasia
eventually
evidently
exaggerate
exaggeration
exalt
exasperate
exceed
exceedingly
excellent
excessive
exchequer
excommunicate
exercise
exhaust
exhibit
exhilarate
exorcise
explanation
exquisite
extinguish
extraneous
extravagant

F

fabulous
facetious
faeces
Fahrenheit
fallacious
fanatic
farcical
fascinate
fatigue
fatuous
February
feeler
feign
ferocious
festooned
feud
feudal
fevered
fiasco
fibre
fictitious
fiend
fierce
fiery
filial
finesse
flabbergasted
flaccid
flammable
flannelette
fluent
fluoridate
fluoride
fluoridize
foliage
forcible
foreigner
forfeit
forthwith
fortieth
fortuitous
fortunately
frailty
frankincense
fraudulent
freedom
freight
frequency
friend
frolicked
fuchsia
fugitive
fulfil
fulfilled
fulfilment
fullness
fulsome
furious
furniture
furthered

G

gaiety
galloped
garrison
garrotted
gases
gateau
gauge
gazetteer
geisha
generator
genuine
gerbil
gesticulate
ghastly
ghetto
gigantic
gingham
giraffe
glamorous
glamour
glimpse
global
gluttonous
glycerine
gnarled
gnash
goitre
gossiped
government
graffiti
grammar
grandeur
gratefully
gratitude
gratuitous
greetings
gregarious
grief
grieve
grovelled

gruesome
guarantee
guarantor
guard
guardian
guest
guillotine
guinea
guise
guitar
gymkhana
gypsy/gipsy

H

haemoglobin
haemorrhage
halcyon
hallucination
hammered
handfuls
handicapped
handkerchief
happened
harangue
harass
harlequin
haughty
hazard
hearse
height
heightened
heinous
heir
herbaceous
hereditary
heroism
hesitate
hiccup, hiccough
hideous
hierarchy
hieroglyphics
hijack
hilarious
hindrance
hippopotamus
holiday
holocaust
homonym
honorary
honour
hooligan
horoscope
horrible
horticulture
hullabaloo
humorous
humour
hurricane
hurried
hygiene
hyphen
hypnosis
hypochondria
hypocrisy
hypotenuse
hypothesis
hypothetical
hysterical

I

icicle
ideological
idiosyncrasy
ignorance
illegible
illegitimate
illiberal
illiterate
imaginative
imitation
immaculate
immediate
immemorial
immoral
immovable
impasse
impeccable
imperative
imperceptible
imperious
impetuous
implacable
impresario
imprisoned
imprisonment
inaccessible
inadmissible
inappropriate
inaugural
incandescent
incessant
incipient
incognito
incommunicado
inconceivable
incongruous
incontrovertible
incorrigible
incredulous
incriminate
incubator
incurred
indefatigable
indefinable
indefinite
independence
independent
indescribable
indict
indictment
indigenous
indigestible
indomitable
indubitable
ineligible
inescapable
inexcusable
inexhaustible
infallible
infatuated
inferred
infinitive
inflamed
inflammable
inflationary
ingratiate
ingredient
inhabitant
inheritance
inhibition
iniquitous
initiate
initiative
innate
innocuous
innumerable
innumerate
inoculate
insecticide
inseparable
insincere
insistence
instalment
instantaneous
intercept
interference
interior
intermediate
intermittent
interpret
interpretation
interrogate
interrupt
interview
intrigue
intrinsically
intuition
intuitive
invariably
inveigle
inveterate
involuntary
involvement
irascible
irrelevant
irreparable
irreplaceable
irresistible
irresponsible
irrevocable
irritable
italicize
itinerant
itinerary

J

jackal
Jacuzzi
jeopardize
jettisoned
jewellery
jodhpurs
juggernaut
jugular

K

kaleidoscopic
karate
keenness
khaki
kidnapped
kilometre
kiosk
kitchenette
kleptomania
knick-knack
knowledgeable
kowtow

L

labelled
laboratory
labyrinth
lackadaisical
laddered
lager
language
languor
languorous
laryngitis
larynx
lassitude
latitude
laundered
launderette
layette
league
leanness
ledger
legendary
legible
legitimate
length
lengthened
leukaemia
levelled
liaise
liaison
lieu
lieutenant
lilac
limousine
lineage
linen
lingerie
linguist
liqueur
literature
litre
livelihood

loneliness
loosened
loquacious
lorgnette
lucrative
lucre
luggage
lugubrious
luminous
luscious
lustre
luxurious
lyric

M

macabre
maelstrom
magician
magnanimous
mahogany
maintenance
malaise
malaria
malignant
manageable
management
mannequin
manoeuvre
mantelpiece
manually
margarine
marijuana
marquee
martyr
marvellous
marzipan
masochist
massacre
matinee
mayonnaise
meagre
measurement
medallion
medieval
mediocre
melancholy
meningitis
meringue
messenger
meteorological
metropolitan
microphone
midday
migraine
mileage
milieu
millionaire
mimicked
mimicry
miniature
miraculous
mirrored
miscellaneous
mischief
mischievous
misogynist
misshapen
misspell
misspent
modelled
modelling
morgue
mortgage
mosquito
mountaineer
moustache
multitudinous
muscle
museum
mysterious
mythical

N

naive
narrative
naughty
nausea
nautical
necessary
necessity
negligence
negligible
negotiate
neighbourhood
neither
neurotic
neutral
niche
niece
ninetieth
ninth
nocturnal
nonentity
notably
noticeably
notoriety
nuance
numbered
numerate
numerous
nutrient
nutritious

O

obedient
obese
obituary
oblige
oblique
oblivious
obnoxious
obscene
obscenity
obsessive
obstetrician
occasion
occupancy
occupier
occupying
occurred
occurrence
octogenarian
odorous
odour
offence
offered
official
officious
ominous
omission
omitted
oneself
opaque
ophthalmic
opinion
opponent
opportunity
opposite
orchestra
ordinary
original
orthodox
orthopaedic
oscillate
ostracize
outlying
outrageous
overdraft
overrate
overreach
overwrought
oxygen

P

pacifist
pageant
pamphlet
panacea
panegyric
panicked
papered
parachute
paraffin
paragraph
paralyse
paralysis
paraphernalia
parcelled
parliament
paroxysm
parquet
partially
participant
particle
partner
passenger
passers-by
pastime
patterned
pavilion
peaceable
peculiar
pejorative
pencilled
penicillin
peppered
perceive
perennial
perilous
permissible
permitted
pernicious
perpetrate
persistence
personnel
persuasion
perusal
pessimism
pessimistically
pesticide
phantom
pharmacy
pharyngitis
pharynx
phenomenon
phial
phlegm
physician
physiotherapist
picketed
picnic
picnicked
picturesque
pioneered
pious
piteous
pitiful
plaintiff
plausible
pleurisy
pneumonia
poignant
politician
pollution
polythene
porridge
portrait
portray
positive
possession
possibility
posthumous
potatoes
precede
precedent
precinct
precipice
precocious
preference
preferred
prejudice
preliminary
prepossessing
prerequisite
prerogative
prescription

presence
preservative
prestige
prestigious
pretentious
prevalent
priest
primitive
procedure
proceed
procession
professional
profiteering
prohibit
promiscuous
pronunciation
propeller
proposal
proprietor
prosecute
protagonist
protein
provocation
prowess
psalm
psyche
psychiatric
psychic
publicly
pursuit
putative
pyjamas

Q

quarrelsome
questionnaire
queue
quintet

R

rabies
radioed
radios
railing
rancour
ransack
rapturous
reassurance
rebelled
rebellious
recalcitrant
receipt
receive
recommend
reconnaissance
reconnoitre
recruitment
recurrence
redundant
referee
reference
referred
regatta
regrettable
regretted
rehabilitation
reign
relevant
relief
relieve
reminisce
reminiscence
remuneration
rendezvous
repertoire
repetitive
reprieve
reprisal
requisite
rescind
resemblance
reservoir
resistance
resourceful
responsibility
restaurant
restaurateur
resurrection
resuscitate
retrieve
reunion
reveille
revelry
revenue
reversible
rhapsody
rheumatism
rhododendron
rhomboid
rhubarb
rhyme
rhythm
ricochet
righteous
rigorous
rigour
risotto
riveted
rogue
roughage
roulette
royalty
rucksack
ruinous
rummage
rumour

S

sabotage
sacrilege
saddened
salmon
salvage
sanctuary
sandwich
sanitary
sapphire
satellite
scaffolding
scandalous
scenic
sceptre
schedule
scheme
schizophrenic
schooner
sciatica
science
scissors
scruple
scrupulous
scurrilous
scythe
secretarial
secretary
sedative
sedentary
sensitive
separate
sergeant
serrated
serviceable
serviette
settee
shampooed
shattered
sheikh
sheriff
shield
shovelled
shuddered
siege
significant
silhouette
simply
simultaneous
sincerely
sixtieth
skeleton
skilful
slanderous
slaughter
sleigh
sleight of hand
sluice
smattering
smithereens
snivelled
soccer
solemn
solicitor
soliloquy
soloist
sombre
somersault
sophisticated
sovereign
spaghetti
spectre
spherical
sphinx
sponsor
spontaneity
spontaneous
squabble
squandered
squawk
staccato
staggered
stammered
statistics
statutory
stealth
stereophonic
stirrup
storage
strait-laced
straitjacket
strategic
strength
strenuous
stupor
suave
subpoena
subtle
succeed
successful
successor
succinct
succulent
succumb
suddenness
suede
sufficient
suffocate
suicide
sullenness
summoned
supercilious
superfluous
supersede
supervise
supervisor
supplementary
surgeon
surveillance
surveyor
susceptible
suspicious
sweetener
sycamore
symmetry
sympathize
symphony
synagogue
syndicate
synonym
syringe

T

tableau
taciturn
taffeta
tangerine
tangible
tattoo

technique
teenager
televise
temperature
tenuous
terrifically
terrifying
territory
terrorist
therapeutic
therefore
thief
thinness
thirtieth
thorough
thoroughfare
threshold
thrombosis
throughout
thwart
thyme
tightened
titivate
tobacconist
toboggan
toffee
tomatoes
tomorrow
tonsillitis
topsy turvy
tornadoes
torpedoes
torpor
tortoiseshell
tortuous
totalled
tourniquet
towelling
trafficked
tragedy
traitorous
tranquillity
tranquillizer
transcend
transferable
transferred
transparent
travelled
traveller
tremor
troublesome
trousseau
truism
trustee
tsetse
tuberculosis
tumour
tunnelled
tureen
turquoise
twelfth
typhoon
tyranny

U

unanimous
unconscious
undoubted
unduly
unequalled
unique
unnecessary
unremitting
unrequited
unrivalled
upheaval
uproarious

V

vaccinate
vacuum
vague
vanilla
variegate
vehement
vendetta
veneer
ventilator
verandah
vermilion
veterinary
vetoes
vice versa
vicissitude
vigorous
vigour
viscount
visibility
vivacious
vociferous
voluminous
volunteered
vulnerable

W

walkie-talkie
walloped
warrior
wastage
watered
weakened
wearisome
Wednesday
weight
weird
whereabouts
wherewithal
widened
width
wield
wintry
witticism
wizened
woebegone
wooden
woollen
worsened
worship
worshipped
wrapper
wrath
wreak
writhe

X

xylophone

Y

yield
yoghurt

Z

zealous
zigzagged

Adjectives liable to be misspelt

-able and -ible are both used to form adjectives. It is easy to confuse the spelling of words ending in these. The following adjectives are likely to be misspelt.

-able:
abominable
acceptable
adaptable
adorable
advisable
agreeable
amiable
approachable
available
bearable
beatable
believable
calculable
capable
changeable
comfortable
commendable
conceivable
definable
delectable
demonstrable
dependable
desirable
discreditable
disreputable
durable
enviable
excitable
excusable
expendable
foreseeable
forgettable
forgivable
healable
hearable
immovable
impassable
impeccable
implacable
impracticable
impressionable
indescribable
indispensable
inimitable
insufferable
lamentable
manageable
measurable
memorable
nameable
non-flammable
objectionable
operable
palpable
pleasurable
preferable
readable
recognizable
regrettable
renewable
reputable
sizeable
stoppable
tenable
tolerable
transferable
understandable
undoable
unmistakable
usable
variable

viable
washable
wearable
winnable
workable
ible:
accessible
admissible
audible
collapsible
combustible
compatible
comprehensible
contemptible
credible
defensible
destructible
digestible
discernible
divisible
edible
exhaustible
expressible
fallible
feasible
flexible
forcible
gullible
indelible
intelligible
irascible
negligible
perceptible
permissible
possible
repressible
reproducible
resistible
responsible
reversible
risible
sensible
susceptible
tangible
visible

Punctuation

Punctuation is the use of punctuation marks within a written text to enhance its meaning or fluency or to indicate aspects of pronunciation.

accent *see* **Spelling** section.

apostrophe a form of punctuation that is mainly used to indicate possession. Many spelling errors centre on the position of the apostrophe in relation to *s*.

Possessive nouns are usually formed by adding *'s* to the singular noun, as in 'the girl's mother', and 'Peter's car'; by adding an apostrophe to plural nouns that end in *s*, as in 'all the teachers' cars'; by adding *'s* to irregular plural nouns that do not end in *s*, as in 'women's shoes'.

In the possessive form of a name or singular noun that ends in *s*, *x* or *z*, the apostrophe may or may not be followed by *s*. In words of one syllable the final *s* is usually added, as in 'James's house', 'the fox's lair', 'Roz's dress'. The final *s* is most frequently omitted in names, particularly in names of three or more syllables, as in 'Euripides' plays'. In many cases the presence or absence of final *s* is a matter of convention.

The apostrophe is also used to indicate omitted letters in contracted forms of words, as in 'can't' and 'you've'. They are sometimes used to indicate missing century numbers in dates, as in 'the '60s and '70s', but are not used at the end of decades, etc, as in '1960s', not '1960's'.

Generally apostrophes are no longer used to indicate omitted letters in shortened forms that are in common use, as in 'phone' and 'flu'.

Apostrophes are often omitted wrongly in modern usage, particularly in the media and by advertisers, as in 'womens hairdressers', 'childrens helpings'. In addition, apostrophes are frequently added erroneously (as in 'potato's for sale' and 'Beware of the dog's'). This is partly because people are unsure about when and when not to use them and partly because of a modern tendency to punctuate as little as possible.

brackets are used to enclose information that is in some way additional to a main statement. The information so enclosed is called **parenthesis** and the pair of brackets enclosing it can be known as **parentheses**. The information that is enclosed in the brackets is purely supplementary or explanatory in nature and could be removed without changing the overall basic meaning or grammatical completeness of the statement. Brackets, like commas and dashes, interrupt the flow of the main statement but brackets indicate a more definite or clear-cut interruption. The fact that they are more visually obvious emphasizes this.

Material within brackets can be one word, as in 'In a local wine bar we had some delicious crepes (pancakes)' and 'They didn't have the chutzpah (nerve) to challenge her'. It can also take the form of dates, as in 'Robert Louis Stevenson (1850–94) wrote *Treasure Island*' and '*Animal Farm* was written by George Orwell (1903–50)'.

The material within brackets can also take the form of a phrase, as in 'They served lasagne (a kind of pasta) and some delicious veal' and 'They were drinking Calvados (a kind of brandy made from apples)' or in the form of a clause, as in 'We were to have supper (or so they called it) later in the evening' and 'They went for a walk round the loch (as a lake is called in Scotland) before taking their departure'.

It can also take the form of a complete sentence, as in 'He was determined (we don't know why) to tackle the problem alone' and 'She made it clear (nothing could be more clear) that she was not interested in the offer'. Sentences that appear in brackets in the middle of a sentence are not usually given an initial capital letter or a full stop, as in 'They very much desired (she had no idea why) to purchase her house'. If the material within brackets comes at the end of a sentence the full stop comes outside the second bracket, as in 'For some reason we agreed to visit her at home (we had no idea where she lived).'

If the material in the brackets is a sentence which comes between two other sentences it is treated like a normal sentence with an initial capital letter and a closing full stop, as in 'He never seems to do any studying. (He is always either asleep or watching television.) Yet he does brilliantly in his exams.' Punctuation of the main statement is unaffected by the presence of the brackets and their enclosed material except that any punctuation that would have followed the word before the first bracket follows the second bracket, as in 'He lives in a place (I am not sure exactly where), that is miles from anywhere.'

There are various shapes of brackets. Round brackets are the most common type. Square brackets are sometimes used to enclose information that is contained inside other information already in brackets, as in '(Christopher Marlowe [1564–93] was a contemporary of Shakespeare)' or in a piece of writing where round brackets have already been used for some other purpose. Thus in a dictionary if round brackets are used to separate off the pronunciation, square brackets are sometimes used to separate off the etymologies.

Square brackets are also used for editorial comments in a scholarly work where the material within brackets is more of an intrusion to the flow of the main statement than is normally the case with bracketed material. Angle brackets and brace brackets tend to be used in more scholarly or technical contexts.

capital letters *see* **Spelling** section.

colon a punctuation mark (:) that is used within a sentence to explain, interpret, clarify or amplify what has gone before it. 'The standard of school work here is extremely high: it is almost university standard', 'The fuel bills are giving cause for concern: they are almost double last year's'. 'We have some new information: the allies have landed'. A capital letter is not usually used after the colon in this context.

The colon is also used to introduce lists or long quotations, as in 'The recipe says we need: tomatoes, peppers, courgettes, garlic, oregano and basil', 'The boy has a huge list of things he needs for school: blazer, trousers, shirts, sweater, ties, shoes, tennis shoes, rugby boots, sports clothes and leisure wear' and 'One of his favourite quotations was: "If music be the food of love play on".

The colon is sometimes used in numerals, as in '7:30 a.m.', '22:11:72' and 'a ratio of 7:3'. It is used in the titles of some books, for example where there is a subtitle or explanatory title, as in 'The Dark Years: the Economy in the 1930s'.

In informal writing, the dash is sometimes used instead of the colon, indeed the dash tends to be overused for this purpose.

comma a very common punctuation mark (,). In modern usage there is a tendency to adopt a system of minimal punctuation and the comma is one of the casualties of this new attitude. Most people use the comma considerably less frequently than was formerly the case.

However there are certain situations in which the comma is still commonly used. One of these concerns lists. The individual items in a series of three or more items are separated by commas. Whether a comma is put before the 'and' which follows the second-last item is now a matter of choice. Some people dislike the use of a comma before 'and' in this situation, and it was formerly considered wrong. Examples of lists include—'at the sports club we can play tennis, squash, badminton and table tennis', 'We need to buy bread, milk, fruit and sugar', and 'They are studying French, German, Spanish and Russian'. The individual items in a list can be quite long, as in 'We opened the door, let ourselves in, fed the cat and started to cook a meal' and 'They consulted the map, planned the trip, got some foreign currency and were gone before we realized it'. Confusion may arise if the last item in the list contains 'and' in its own right, as in 'In the pub they served ham salad, shepherd's pie, pie and chips and omelette'. In such cases it as well to put a comma before the final 'and'.

In cases where there is a list of adjectives before a noun, the use of commas is now optional although it was formerly standard practice. Thus both 'She wore a long, red, sequinned dress' and 'She wore a long red sequinned dress' are used. When the adjective immediately before the noun has a closer relationship with it than the other adjectives no comma should be used, as in 'a beautiful old Spanish village'.

The comma is used to separate clauses or phrases that are parenthetical or naturally cut off from the rest of a sentence, as in 'My mother, who was of Irish extraction, was very superstitious'. In such a sentence the clause within the commas can be removed without altering the basic meaning. Care should be taken to include both commas. Commas are not normally used to separate main clauses and relative clauses, as in 'The woman whom I met was my friend's sister'. Nor are they usually used to separate main clauses and subordinate clauses, as in 'He left when we arrived' and 'They came to the party although we didn't expect them to'. If the subordinate clause precedes the main clause, it is sometimes followed by a comma, especially if it is a reasonably long clause, as in 'Although we stopped and thought about it, we still made the wrong decision'. If the clause is quite short, or if it is a short phrase, a comma is not usually inserted, as in 'Although it rained we had a good holiday' and 'Although poor they were happy'. The use of commas to separate such words and expression from the rest of the sentence to which they are related is optional. Thus one can write 'However, he could be right' or 'However he could be right'. The longer the expression is, the more likely it is to have a comma after it, as in 'On the other hand, we may decide not to go'.

Commas are always used to separate terms of address, interjections or question tags from the rest of the sentence, as in 'Please come this way, Ms Brown, and make yourself at home', 'Now, ladies, what can I get you?' and 'It's cold today, isn't it?'

Commas may be used to separate main clauses joined by a coordinating conjunction, but this is not usual if the clauses have the same subject or object, as in 'She swept the floor and dusted the table'. In cases where the subjects are different and the clauses are fairly long, it is best to insert a comma, as in 'They took all the furniture with them, and she was left with nothing'.

A comma can be inserted to avoid repeating a verb in the second of two clause, as in 'he plays golf and tennis, his brother rugby'.

dash a punctuation mark in the form of a short line that indicates a short break in the continuity of a sentence, as in 'He has never been any trouble at school—quite the reverse', 'I was amazed when he turned up—I thought he was still abroad'. In such situations it serves the same purpose as brackets, except that it is frequently considered more informal. The dash should be used sparingly. Depending on it too much can lead to careless writing with ideas set down at random rather than turned into a piece of coherent prose. The dash can be used to emphasize a word or phrase, as in 'They said goodbye then—forever'. It can also be used to add a remark to the end of a sentence, as in 'They had absolutely no money—a regular state of affairs towards the end of the month.'

The dash can also be used to introduce a statement that amplifies or explains what has been said, as in 'The burglars took everything of value—her jewellery, the silver, the TV set, her hi-fi and several hundred pounds.' It can be used to summarize what has gone before, as in 'Disease, poverty, ignorance—these are the problems facing us.

The dash is also used to introduce an afterthought, as in 'You can come with me—but you might not want to'. It can also introduce a sharp change of subject, as in 'I'm just making tea—what was that noise?' It can also be used to introduce some kind of balance in a sentence, as in 'It's going to take two of us to get this table out of here—one to move it and one to hold the door open.'

The dash is sometimes found in pairs. A pair of dashes acts in much the same way as a set of round brackets. A pair of dashes can be used to indicate a break in a sentence, as in 'We prayed—prayed as we had never prayed before—that the children would be safe', 'It was—on reflection—his best performance yet', and 'He introduced me to his wife—an attractive pleasant woman—before he left'.

Dashes are used to indicate hesitant speech, as in 'I don't—well—maybe—you could be right'. They can be used to indicate the omission of part of a word or name, as in 'It's none of your b— business', 'He's having an affair with Mrs D—'.

They can also be used between points in time or space, as in 'Edinburgh–London' and '1750–1790.'

direct speech *see* **quotation marks.**

exclamation mark a punctuation mark (!) which occurs at the end of an exclamation, which is a word, phrase or sentence called out with strong feeling of some kind as in 'Get lost!', 'What a nerve!', 'Help!', 'Ouch!', 'Well I never!', 'What a disaster!', 'I'm tired of all this!' and 'Let me out of here!'

full stop a punctuation mark consisting of a small dot (.). Its principal use is to end a sentence that is not a question or an exclamation, as in: 'They spent the money.', 'She is studying hard.', 'He has been declared redundant and is very upset.' and 'Because she is shy, she rarely goes to parties.'

The full stop is also used in decimal fractions, as in '4.5 metres', '6.3 miles' and '12.2 litres'. It can also be used in dates, as in '22.2.94', and in times, as in '3.15 tomorrow afternoon'.

In modern usage the tendency is to omit full stops from abbreviations. This is most true of abbreviations involving initial capital letters as in TUC, BBC, EEC and USA. In such cases full stops should definitely not be used if one or some of the initial letters do not belong to a full word. Thus, television is abbreviated to TV and educationally subnormal to ESN.

There are usually no full stops in abbreviations involving the first and last letters of a word (contractions) Dr, Mr, Rd, St, but this is a matter of taste.

Abbreviations involving the first few letters of a word, as in 'Prof' (Professor) are the most likely to have full stops, as in 'Feb.' (February), but again this is now a matter of taste.

For the use of the full stop in direct speech *see* **direct speech.** The full stop can also be called **point** or **period.**

hyphen a small stroke (-) that is used to join two words together or to indicate that a word has been broken at the end of a line because of lack of space. It is used in a variety of situations.

The hyphen is used as the prefixed element in a proper noun, as in 'pre-Christian', 'post-Renaissance', 'anti-British', 'anti-Semitic', 'pro-French' and 'pro-Marxism'. It is also used before dates or numbers, as in 'pre-1914', 'pre-1066', 'post-1920', 'post-1745'. It is also used before abbreviations, as in 'pro-BBC', 'anti-EEC' and 'anti-TUC'.

The hyphen is used for clarification. Some words are ambiguous without the presence of a hyphen. For example, 're-cover', as in 're-cover a chair', is spelt with a hyphen to differentiate it from 'recover', as in 'The accident victim is likely to recover'. Similarly, it is used in 're-form', meaning 'to form again', as in 'They have decided to re-form the society which closed last year', to differentiate the word from 'reform', meaning 'to improve, to become better behaved', as in 'He was wild as a young man but he has reformed now'. Similarly 're-count' in the sense of 'count again', as in 're-count the number of votes cast', is spelt with a hyphen to differentiate it from 'recount' in the sense of 'tell', as in 'recount what happened on the night of the accident'.

The hyphen was formerly used to separate a prefix from the main element of a word if the main element begins with a vowel, as in 'pre-eminent', but there is a growing tendency in modern usage to omit the hyphen in such cases. At the moment both 'pre-eminent' and 'preeminent' are found. However, if the omission of the hyphen results in double *i*, the hyphen is usually retained, as in 'anti-inflationary' and 'semi-insulated'.

The hyphen was formerly used in words formed with the prefix *non-* as in 'non-functional', 'non-political', 'non-flammable' and 'non-pollutant'. However there is a growing tendency to omit the hyphen in such cases, as in 'nonfunctional' and 'nonpollutant'. At the moment both forms of such words are common.

The hyphen is usually used with 'ex-' in the sense of 'former', as in 'ex-wife' and 'ex-president'.

The hyphen is usually used when 'self-' is prefixed to words, as in 'self-styled', 'a self-starter' and 'self-evident'.

Use or non-use of the hyphen is often a matter of choice, house style or frequency of usage, as in 'drawing-room' or 'drawing room', and 'dining-room' or 'dining room'. There is a modern tendency to punctuate less frequently than was formerly the case and so in modern usage use of the hyphen in such expressions is less frequent. The length of compounds often affects the inclusion or omission of the hyphen. Compounds of two short elements that are well-established words tend not to be hyphenated, as in 'bedroom' and 'toothbrush'. Compound words with longer elements are more likely to be hyphenated, as in 'engine-driver' and 'carpet-layer'.

Some fixed compounds of two or three or more words are always hyphenated, as in 'son-in-law', 'good-for-nothing' and 'devil-may-care'.

Some compounds formed from phrasal verbs are sometimes hyphenated and sometimes not. Thus both 'take-over' and 'takeover' are common, and 'run-down' and 'rundown' are both common. Again the use of the hyphen is a matter of choice. However some words formed from phrasal verbs are usually spelt without a hyphen, as in 'breakthrough'.

Compound adjectives consisting of two elements, the second of which ends in *-ed*, are usually hyphenated, as in 'heavy-hearted', 'fair-haired', 'fair-minded' and 'long-legged'.

Compound adjectives when they are used before nouns are usually hyphenated, as in 'gas-fired central heating', 'oil-based paints', 'solar-heated buildings' and 'chocolate-coated biscuits'.

Compounds containing some adverbs are usually hyphenated, sometimes to avoid ambiguity, as in 'his best-known opera', a 'well-known singer', 'an ill-considered venture' and 'a half-planned scheme'.

Generally adjectives and participles preceded by an adverb are not hyphenated if the adverb ends in *-ly*, as in 'a highly talented singer', 'neatly pressed clothes' and 'beautifully dressed young women'.

In the case of two or more compound hyphenated adjectives with the same second element qualifying the same noun, the common element need not be repeated but the hyphen should be, as in 'two- and three-bedroom houses' and 'long- and short-haired dogs'.

The hyphen is used in compound numerals from 21 to 99 when they are written in full, as in 'thirty-five gallons', 'forty-four years', 'sixty-seven miles' and 'two hundred and forty-five miles'. Compound numbers such as 'three hundred' and 'two thousand' are not hyphenated.

Hyphens are used in fractions, as in 'three-quarters', 'two-thirds', and 'seven-eighths'.

Hyphens are also used in such number phrases as 'a seventeenth-century play', 'a sixteenth-century church', 'a five-gallon pail', 'a five-year contract' and a 'third-year student'.

The other use of hyphens is to break words at the ends of lines. Formerly people were more careful about where they broke words. Previously, words were broken up according to etymological principles, but there is a growing tendency to break words according to how they are pronounced. Some dictionaries or spelling dictionaries give help with the division and hyphenation of individual words. General points are that one-syllable words should not be divided and words should not be broken after the first letter of a word or before the last letter. Care should be taken not to break up words, for example by forming elements that are words in their own right, in such a way as to mislead the reader. Thus divisions such as 'the-rapist' and 'mans-laughter' should be avoided.

inverted comma *see* **quotation marks.**

italic type a sloping typeface that is used for a variety of purposes. It is used to differentiate a piece of text from the main text, which is usually in Roman type. For example, it is used sometimes for the titles of books, newspapers, magazines, plays, films, musical works and works of art, as in 'he is a regular reader of *The Times*', 'She reads *Private Eye*', 'Have you read *Animal Farm* by George Orwell', 'He has never seen a production of Shakespeare's *Othello*', 'We went to hear Handel's *Messiah*', '*Mona Lisa* is a famous painting'. Sometimes such titles are put in quotation marks rather than in italics.

Italic type is also sometimes used for the names of ships, trains, etc, as in 'the launch of *The Queen Elizabeth II*', 'She once sailed in *The Queen Mary*' and 'Their train was called *The Flying Scotsman*'.

Italic type is also used for the Latin names of plants and animals, as in 'of the genus *Lilium*', 'trees of the genus *Pyrus*', '*Panthera pardus*' and '*Canis lupus*'.

Italic type is sometimes used for foreign words that have been adopted into the English language but have never been fully integrated. Examples include *bête noire*, *raison d'être*, *inter alia* and *Weltschmerz*.

Italic type can also sometimes be used to draw attention to a particular word, phrase or passage, as in 'How do you pronounce *formidable*?', or to emphasize a word or phrase, as in 'Is he *still* in the same job?'

ligature a printed character combining two letters in one, as in æa and œ. It is sometimes called a digraph.

line-break the division of a word at the end of a line for space purposes. This is marked by a hyphen.

lower-case letter the opposite of capital letter. It is also known informally as 'small letter'. Lower-case letters are used for most words in the language. It is capital letters that are exceptional in their use.

oblique a diagonal mark (/) that has various uses. Its principal use is to show alternatives, as in 'he/she', 'Dear Sir/Madam', 'two/three-room flat' and 'the budget for 1993/4'. The oblique is used in some abbreviations, as in 'c/o Smith' (meaning 'care of Smith'). The word 'per' is usually shown by means of an oblique, as in 60km/h (60 kilometres per hour).

paragraph a subdivision of a piece of prose. Many people find it difficult to divide their work into paragraphs. Learning to do so can be difficult but it is an area of style that improves with practice.

A paragraph should deal with one particular theme or point of the writer's writing or argument. When that has been dealt with, a new paragraph should be started.

However, there are other considerations to be taken into account. If the paragraph is very long it can appear off-putting visually to the would-be reader and can be difficult to make one's way through. In such cases it is best to subdivide themes and shorten paragraphs. On the other hand, it is best not to make all one's paragraphs too short as this can create a disjointed effect. It is best to try to aim for a mixture of lengths to create some variety.

Traditionally it was frowned upon to have a one-sentence paragraph but there are no hard and fast rules about this. Usually it takes more than one sentence to develop the theme of the paragraph, unless one is a tabloid journalist or copywriter for an advertising firm, and it is best to avoid long, complex sentences.

The opening paragraph of a piece of writing should introduce the topic about which one is writing. The closing paragraph should sum up what one has been writing about. New paragraphs begin on new lines and they are usually indented from the margin. In the case of dialogue in a work of fiction, each speaker's utterance usually begins on a new line for the clarification of the reader.

parentheses *see* **brackets.**

period *see* **full stop.**

point *see* **full stop.**

punctuation mark one of the standardized symbols used in punctuation, as the **full stop, comma, question mark**, etc.

question mark the punctuation mark (?) that is placed at the end of a question or interrogative sentence, as in 'Who is he?', 'Where are they?', 'Why have they gone?', 'Whereabouts are they?', 'When are you going?' and 'What did he say?'. The question mark is sometimes known as the **query**.

quotation marks or **inverted commas** are used to enclose material that is part of **direct speech**, which is the reporting of speech by repeating exactly the actual words used by the speaker. In the sentence:

Peter said, 'I am tired of this.'

'I am tired of this' is a piece of direct speech because it represents exactly what Peter said. Similarly, in the sentence:

Jane asked, 'Where are you going?'

'Where are you going?' is a piece of direct speech since it represents what Jane said.

Quotation marks are used at the beginning and end of pieces of direct speech. Only the words actually spoken are placed within the quotation marks, as in:

'If I were you,' he said, 'I would refuse to go.'

The quotation marks involved can be either single or double, according to preference or house style.

If there is a statement such as 'he said' following the piece of direct speech, a comma is placed before the second inverted comma, as in:

'Come along,' he said.

If the piece of direct speech is a question or exclamation, a question mark or exclamation mark is put instead of the comma, as in:

'What are you doing?' asked John.

'Get away from me!' she screamed.

If a statement such as 'he said' is placed within a sentence in direct speech, a comma is placed after 'he said' and the second part of the piece of direct speech does not begin with a capital letter, as in:

'I know very well,' he said, 'that you do not like me.'

If the piece of direct speech includes a complete sentence, the sentence begins with a capital letter, as in:

'I am going away,' she said, 'and I am not coming back. I don't feel that I belong here anymore.'

Note that the full stop at the end of a piece of direct speech that is a sentence should go before the closing inverted comma.

If the piece of direct speech quoted takes up more than one paragraph, quotation marks are placed at the beginning of each new paragraph. However, quotation marks are not placed at the end of each paragraph, just at the end of the final one.

When writing a story, etc, that includes dialogue or conversation, each new piece of direct speech should begin on a new line or sometimes in a new paragraph.

Quotation marks are not used only to indicate direct speech. For example, they are sometimes used to indicate the title of a book or newspaper.

The quotation marks used in this way can be either single or double, according to preference or house style. If a piece of direct speech contains the title of a poem, song, etc, it should be put in the opposite type of quotation marks to those used to enclose the piece of direct speech. Thus, if single quotation marks have been used in the direct speech, then double quotation marks should be used for the title within the direct speech, as in:

'Have you read "Ode to a Nightingale" by Keats?' the teacher asked.

If double quotation marks have been used for the direct speech, single quotation marks should be used for the title, as in:

"Have you read 'Ode to a Nightingale' by Keats?" the teacher asked.

Roman type the normal upright type used in printing, not bold or italic type.

semicolon (;) a rather formal form of punctuation. It is mainly used between clauses that are not joined by any form of conjunction, as in 'We had a wonderful holiday; sadly they did not', 'She was my sister; she was also my best friend' and 'He was a marvellous friend; he is much missed'. A dash is sometimes used instead of a semicolon but this more informal.

The semicolon is also used to form subsets in a long list or series of names so that the said list seems less complex, as in 'The young man who wants to be a journalist has applied everywhere. He has applied to *The Times* in London; *The Globe and Mail* in Toronto; *The Age* in Melbourne; *The Tribune* in Chicago'.

The semicolon is also sometimes used before 'however', 'nevertheless' 'hence', etc, as in 'We have extra seats for the concert; however you must not feel obliged to come'.

Style

abbreviation a shortened form of words, usually used as a space-saving technique and becoming increasingly common in modern usage. Abbreviations cause problems with regard to punctuation. The common question asked is whether the letters of an abbreviation should be separated by full stops. In modern usage the tendency is to omit full stops from abbreviations. This is most true of abbreviations involving initial capital letters, as in TUC, BBC, EC and USA. In such cases full stops should definitely not be used if one or some of the initial letters do not belong to a full word. Thus 'television' is abbreviated to TV and 'educationally subnormal' to ESN.

There are usually no full stops in abbreviations involving the first and last letters of a word (contractions)—Dr, Mr, Rd, St—but this is a matter of taste.

An abbreviation involving the first few letters of a word, as in 'Prof' (Professor), is the most likely to a have full stop, as in 'Feb.' (February), but again this is now a matter of taste.

Plurals of abbreviations are mostly formed by adding lower-case *s*, as in Drs, JPs, TVs. Note the absence of apostrophes. *See also* **acronym.**

acronym a word that, like some abbreviations, is formed from the initial letters of several words. Unlike abbreviations, however, acronyms are pronounced as words rather than as just a series of letters. For example, OPEC (Organization of Petroleum Producing Countries) is pronounced *o-pek* and is thus an acronym, unlike USA (United States of America) which is pronounced as a series of letters and not as a word (*yoo-ess-ay,* not *yoo-say* or *oo-sa*) and is thus an abbreviation.

Acronyms are written without full stops, as in UNESCO (United Nations Educational, Scientific and Cultural Organization). Mostly acronyms are written in capital letters, as in NASA (National Aeronautics and Space Administration). However, very common acronyms, such as Aids (Acquired Immune Deficiency Syndrome), are written with just an initial capital, the rest of the letters being lower case

Acronyms that refer to a piece of scientific or technical equipment are written like ordinary words in lower-case letters, as laser (light amplification by simulated emission of radiation.

affix refers to an element that is added to the root or stem of a word to form another word. Affixes can be in the form of **prefixes** or **suffixes.** A prefix is added to the beginning of a word, as audio in audiovisual, an affix to the end, as -aholic in workaholic.

back formation the process of forming a new word by removing an element from an existing word. This is the reversal of the usual process since many words are formed by adding an element to a base or root word. Examples of back formation include 'burgle' from 'burglary'; 'caretake' from 'caretaker'; 'donate' from 'donation'; 'eavesdrop' from 'eavesdropper'; 'enthuse' from 'enthusiasm'; 'intuit' from 'intuition'; 'liaise' from 'liaison'; 'reminisce' from 'reminiscence'; 'televise' from 'television'.

base the basic element in word formation, also known as **root** or **stem,** e.g. in the word 'infectious' 'infect' is the base.

blend a word that is formed by the merging of two other words or elements, as in 'brunch' from 'breakfast' and 'lunch'; 'camcorder' from 'camera' and 'recorder'; 'chocoholic' from 'chocolate' and 'alcoholic'; 'motel' from 'motor' and 'hotel'; 'smog' from 'smoke' and 'fog'; 'televangelist' from 'television' and 'evangelist'.

book titles *see* **Spelling** section and **italic type** in **Punctuation** section.

borrowing the taking over into English of a word from a foreign language and also to the word so borrowed. Many words borrowed into English are totally assimilated as to spelling and pronunciation. Others remain obviously different and retain their own identity as to spelling or pronunciation, as *raison d'être*, borrowed from French. Many of them have been so long part of the English language, such as since the Norman Conquest, that they are no longer thought of as being foreign words. However the process goes on, and recent borrowings include *glasnost* and *perestroika* from Russian.

French, Latin and Greek have been the main sources of our borrowings over the centuries. However, we have borrowed extensively from other languages as well. These include Italian, from which we have borrowed many terms relating to music, art and architecture. These include *piano, libretto, opera, soprano, tempo, corridor, fresco, niche, parapet* and *grotto*, as well as many food terms, such as *macaroni, pasta, semolina* and *spaghetti*.

From the Dutch we have acquired many words relating to the sea and ships since they were a great sea-faring nation. These include *cruise, deck, skipper* and *yacht*. Through the Dutch/Afrikaans connection we have borrowed *apartheid, boss* and *trek*.

From German we have borrowed *dachshund, hamster, frankfurter, kindergarten* and *waltz*, as well as some words relating to World War II, for example, *blitz, flak* and *strafe*.

From Norse and the Scandinavian languages have come a wide variety of common words, such as *egg, dirt, glitter, kick, law, odd, skill, take, they, though*, as well as some more modern sporting terms such as *ski* and *slalom*.

From the Celtic languages have come *bannock, bog, brogue, cairn, clan, crag, slogan* and *whisky*, and from Arabic have come *algebra, alkali, almanac, apricot, assassin, cypher, ghoul, hazard, mohair, safari, scarlet* and *talisman*.

The Indian languages have provided us with many words, originally from the significant British presence there in the days of the British Empire. They include *bungalow, chutney, dinghy, dungarees, gymkhana, jungle, pundit* and *shampoo*. In modern times there has been an increasing interest in Indian food and cookery, and words such as *pakora, poppadom, samosa*, etc, have come into the language.

From the South American languages have come *avocado, chocolate, chilli, potato, tobacco* and *tomato*. From Hebrew have come *alphabet, camel, cinnamon* and *maudlin*, as well as more modern borrowings from Yiddish such as *bagel, chutzpah, schmaltz* and *schmuck*.

From the native North American languages have come *anorak, kayak, raccoon* and *toboggan*, and from the Aboriginal language of Australia have come *boomerang* and *kangaroo*.

Judo, bonsai and *tycoon* have come from Japanese, *rattan* from Malay and *kung-fu, sampan* and *ginseng* from Chinese.

The borrowing process continues. With Britain becoming more of a cosmopolitan and multi-cultural nation the borrowing is increasing.

cliché *see* **Clichés** section.

coinage the invention of a new word or expression.

colloquialism a term used to describe an expression of the kind used in informal conversation.

derivative a word that has been formed from a simpler word or word element. For example, 'sweetly' is a derivative of 'sweet', 'peaceful' is a derivative from 'peace', 'clinging' is derived from 'cling' and 'shortest' is derived from 'short'.

dialect the language of a region or community with regard to vocabulary, structure, grammar and pronunciation.

doubles words that habitually go together, as in 'out and out', 'neck and neck', 'over and over', 'hale and hearty', 'rant and rave', 'fast and furious', 'hue and cry', 'stuff and nonsense', 'rough and ready', 'might and main', 'give and take', 'ups and downs', 'fair and square', 'high and dry' and 'wear and tear'. Doubles are also sometimes called **dyads.**

doublets pairs of words that have developed from the same original word but now differ somewhat in form and usually in meaning. Examples include 'human' and 'humane', 'shade' and 'shadow', 'hostel' and 'hotel', 'frail' and 'fragile', and 'fashion' and 'faction'.

dyads see **doubles.**

EFL English as a foreign language.

etymology the origin and history of a word; the study of the history of words.

euphemism *see* **Euphemism** section.

figurative a term that refers to words that are not used literally. For example, 'mine' in the sense of 'excavation in the earth from which coal, tin, etc, is taken' is a literal use of the word. 'Mine' in the sense of 'He is a mine of information' is a figurative use of the word.

first language *same as* **mother tongue.**

formal the term used to refer to speech and writing that is characterized by more complicated and more difficult language and by more complicated grammatical structures. Short forms and contractions are avoided in formal speech and writing.

gobbledygook a noun that is used informally to refer to pretentious and convoluted language of the type that is found in official documents and reports. It is extremely difficult to understand and should be avoided and 'plain English' used instead.

hybrid a word that is formed from words or elements derived from different languages, such as 'television'.

idiolect a person's own style of language with regard to vocabulary, structure, etc, is known as idiolect, as in 'He is the son of academic parents and has rather a formal idiolect'.

homograph *see* **Homograph** section.

homonym *see* **Homonym** section.

homophone *see* **Homophone** section.

idioms *see* **English Idioms** section.

jargon refers to the technical or specialized language used by a particular group, e.g. doctors, computer engineers, sociologists, etc, to communicate with each other within their specialty. It should be avoided in the general language as it will not be clear to the ordinary person exactly what is meant.

journalese a derogatory name for the style of writing and choice of vocabulary supposedly found in newspapers. It is usually the style of writing in tabloid newspapers, such as widespread use of clichés, sensational language and short sentences, that is meant by the term.

language the means by which human beings communicate using words. Language can refer either to spoken or written communication. It can also refer to the variety of communication used by a particular nation or state, as in 'the French language'.

The term can also be used to refer to the style and vocabulary of a piece of writing, as in 'The language of his novels is very poetic'. It can also be used to denote the particular style and variety of language that is used in a particular profession or among a particular group of people with some common interest, as in 'legal language', 'technical language', etc. Such specialist language is sometimes referred to rather pejoratively as legalese, 'computerese', etc. *See* **jargon**.

lexicography the art and practice of defining words, selecting them and arranging them In dictionaries or glossaries.

lingua franca a language adopted as a common language by speakers whose mother tongues are different from each other. This enables people to have a common medium of communication for various purposes, such as trading. Examples include Swahili in East Africa, Hausa in West Africa and Tok Pisin in Papua New Guinea. The term historically referred to a language that was a mixture of Italian, French, Greek, Spanish and Arabic, used for trading and military purposes.

linguistics the systematic, scientific study of language. It describes language and seeks to establish general principles rather than to prescribe rules of correctness.

loanword a word that has been taken into one language from another. From the point of view of the language taking the word in, the word is known as a borrowing. Some loanwords become naturalized or fully integrated into the language and have a pronunciation and spelling reflecting the conventions of the language which has borrowed them. Other loanwords retain the spelling and pronunciation of the language from which they have been borrowed. These include 'Gastarbeiter', borrowed from German and meaning 'a foreign worker'.

localism a word or expression the use of which is restricted to a particular place or area. The area in question can be quite small, unlike dialect words or 'regionalism'.

malapropism the incorrect use of a word, often through confusion with a similar-sounding word. It often arises from someone's attempt to impress someone else with a knowledge of long words or of technical language. *See* **Literature** section in the **Wordfinder**.

mother tongue the language that one first learns, the language of which one is a native speaker.

native speaker *see* **mother tongue**.

neologism a word that has been newly coined or newly introduced into the language, as 'camcorder', 'Jacuzzi' and 'karaoke'.

palindrome a word which reads the same backwards a forwards, such as 'level' or 'madam'. It can also apply to a phrase, as 'Able was I ere I saw Elba'.

pangram a phrase or sentence which contains all the letters of the alphabet. The ideal pangram contains each letter only once, but this is quite difficult to do, if the result is to be meaningful.

officialese a derogatory term for the vocabulary and style of writing often found in official reports and documents and thought of as being pretentious and difficult to understand. It is usually considered to be the prime example of gobbledegook.

orthography the study or science of how words are spelt.

philology the science, especially comparative, of languages and their history and structure.

prefix *see* **affix**.

redundancy *same as* **tautology**.

retronym a word or phrase that has had to be renamed slightly in the light of another invention, etc. For example, an ordinary guitar has become 'acoustic guitar' because of the existence of 'electric guitar'. Leather has sometimes become 'real leather' because of the existence of 'imitation leather'.

root *same as* **base**.

semantics the study of the historical development and change of word meaning

slang the name given to a set of highly colloquial words and phrases, often rapidly changing and ephemeral, which are regarded as being below the level of educated standard speech. The term is also used to refer to the language used by a particular group of people e.g. surfer's slang.

stem *same as* **base**.

stress emphasis placed on a particular sound or syllable of a word by pronouncing it with more force than those surrounding it.

suffix *see* **affix**.

synonym a word which has the same, or a similar, meaning to another word.

tautology unnecessary repetition, as in 'new innovations', 'a see-through transparent material' and 'one after the other in succession'. In these examples 'new', 'see-through' and 'in succession' are all unnecessary or **redundant** because the idea which they convey is conveyed by 'innovations', 'transparent' and 'one after the others' respectively.

Pronunciation

accent commonly refers to a regional or individual way of speaking or pronouncing words, as in 'a Glasgow accent'.

cedilla the **diacritic** used in French to indicative a soft pronunciation, as 'façade'. *See also* **umlaut**.

consonant a speech sound which is produced by a closing movement, either partial or total, involving the vocal organs, such as the lips, teeth, tongue or the throat, which forms such a narrow constriction that the sound of air can be heard passing through. The term also applies to a letter of the alphabet sounded in this way. *See* **vowel**.

dental produced by the tip of the tongue positioned near the front teeth, as in the pronunciation of the letter 'd'.

diacritic a mark placed a either above or below a letter to indicate a certain emphasis or pronunciation.

diaeresis a mark that is placed over a vowel to indicate that it is sounded separately from a neighbouring vowel, as in 'naïve', 'Chloë'.

digraph a group of two letters representing one sound, as in 'ay' in 'hay', 'ey' in 'key', 'oy' in 'boy', 'ph' in 'phone' and 'th' in 'thin'. When the digraph consists of two letters physically joined together, as 'æa', it is called a 'ligature'.

diphthong a speech sound that changes its quality within the same single syllable. The sound begins as for one vowel and moves on as for another. Since the sound glides from one vowel into another, a diphthong is sometimes called a **gliding vowel**.

Examples include the vowels sounds in 'rain', 'weigh', 'either', 'voice', 'height', 'aisle', 'road', 'soul', 'know', 'house', 'care', 'pure', 'during', 'here' and 'weird'.

disyllabic a term that describes a word with two syllables. For example, 'window' is disyllabic, since it consists of the syllable 'win' and the syllable 'dow'. Similarly 'curtain' is disyllabic since it consists of the syllable 'cur' and 'tain'.

elision the omission of a speech sound or syllable, as in the omission of 'd' in one of the possible pronunciations of 'Wednesday' and in the omission of 'ce' from the pronunciation of 'Gloucester'.

fricative a sound produced by forcing air through a partly closed passage, as in the pronunciation of 'th'.

gliding vowel same as **diphthong**.

hiatus a break in pronunciation between two vowels that come together in different syllables, as in 'Goyaesque' and 'cooperate'.

inflection a varying of tone or pitch.

International Phonetic Alphabet a system of written symbols designed to enable the speech sounds of any language to be consistently represented. Some of the symbols are the ordinary letters of the Roman alphabet but some have been specially invented. The alphabet was first published in 1889 and is commonly known as **IPA**.

intrusive r the pronunciation of the *r* sound between two words or syllables where the first of these ends in a vowel sound and the second begins with a vowel sound and where there is no 'r' in the spelling. It appears in such phrases as 'law and order', which is frequently pronounced as 'lawr and order'.

IPA *see* **International Phonetic Alphabet.**

labial formed by closing, or partially closing, the lips, as in the pronunciation of the letter 'm'.

labiodental produced by the lips and teeth together, as in the pronunciation of the letter 'v'.

length mark a mark used in phonetics in relation to a vowel to indicate that it is long. This can take the form of a 'macron', a small horizontal stroke placed above a letter, or a symbol resembling a colon placed after a vowel in the IPA pronunciation system.

macron *see* **length mark.**

phoneme the smallest unit of speech.

phonetics the science connected with pronunciation and the representation of speech sounds.

plosive denoting a burst of air, such as is produced when pronouncing the letter 'p'.

sibilant suggesting a hissing sound, as that produced when pronouncing the letter 's'.

umlaut the **diacritic** which indicates a change of vowel sound in German, as in *mädchen*.

spoonerism the accidental or deliberate transposition of the initial letters of two or more words when speaking, as in 'the queer old dean' instead of 'the dear old queen', 'a blushing crow' instead of a 'crushing blow' and 'a well-boiled icicle' instead of a 'well-oiled bicycle'. Spoonerisms are called after the Reverend William Archibald Spooner (1844–1930) of Oxford University.

velar produced by the back of the tongue on the soft palate, as in the pronunciation of the letter 'g' in the word 'grand', etc.

voiceless spoken without using the vocal cords, as in the pronunciation of the letter 'p'.

vowel a sound produced by the passage of air through the larynx, virtually unobstructed, no part of the mouth being closed and none of the vocal organs being so close together that the sound of air can be heard passing between them. The term is also applied to a letter of the alphabet sounded in this way. The vowels in the alphabet are a, e, i, o and u.

Words Liable to be Mispronounced

abdomen is now usually pronounced with the emphasis on the first syllable (*ab*-do-men).

acumen is now usually pronounced *ak*-yoo-men, with the emphasis on the first syllable, although formerly the stress was usually on the second syllable (yoo).

adult may be pronounced with the emphasis on either of the two syllables. Thus *a*-dult and a-*dult* are both acceptable although the pronunciation with the emphasis on the first syllable (*a*-dult) is the more common.

adversary is commonly pronounced with the emphasis on the first syllable (*ad*-ver-sar-i) although in modern usage it is also found with the emphasis on the second syllable (ad-*ver*-sar-i).

aged has two possible pronunciations depending on the sense. When it means 'very old', as in 'aged men with white beards', it is pronounced *ay*-jid. When it means 'years of age', as in 'a girl aged nine', it is pronounced with one syllable, *ayjd*.

banal should rhyme with 'canal', with the emphasis on the second syllable (ba-*nal*).

blackguard, meaning 'a scoundrel', has an unusual pronunciation. It is pronounced *blagg*-ard.

brochure is usually pronounced *bro*-sher, despite the *ch* spelling, rather than bro-*shoor*, which is French-sounding.

Celtic is usually pronounced kel-tik.

cervical has two possible pronunciations. Both *ser*-vik-al, with the emphasis on the first syllable, and ser-*vik*-al, with the emphasis on the second syllable which has the same sound as in *Vik*ing in 'cervical cancer'.

chamois in the sense of 'a kind of cloth (made from the skin of the chamois antelope) used for polishing or cleaning' is pronounced *sham*-mi. In the sense of 'a kind of antelope', it is pronounced *sham*-wa.

chiropodist is usually pronounced kir-*op*-od-ist with an initial *k* sound, but the pronunciation shir-*op*-od-ist with an initial *sh* sound is also possible.

clandestine usually has the emphasis on the second syllable, as klan-*des*-tin', but it is acceptable to pronounce it with the emphasis on the first syllable, as *klan*-des-tin.

comparable is liable to be mispronounced. The emphasis should be on the first syllable, as in *kom*-par-able. It is often mispronounced with the emphasis on the second syllable.

contrary has two possible pronunciations. When it means 'opposite', as in 'On the contrary, I would like to go very much', it is pronounced with the emphasis on the first syllable (*kon*-trar-i). When it means 'perverse, stubborn', as in 'contrary children' it is pronounced with the emphasis on the second syllable, which is pronounced to rhyme with 'Mary'.

controversy is usually pronounced with the emphasis on the first syllable (*kon*-tro-ver-si). In modern usage there is a growing tendency to place the emphasis on the second syllable (kon-*tro*-ver-si).

dais meaning 'platform' or 'stage', is now usually pronounced as two syllables, as day-is. Formerly it was pronounced as one syllable, as days.

decade is pronounced with the emphasis on the first syllable as *dek*-ayd. An alternative but rare pronunciation is dek-*ayd*.

demonstrable is most commonly pronounced di-*mon*-strabl, with the emphasis on the second syllable, in modern usage. Previously the emphasis was on the first syllable as *dem*-on-strabl.

explicable is now usually pronounced with the emphasis on the second syllable (ex-*plik*-ibl). Formerly it was commonly pronounced with the emphasis on the first syllable (*ex*-plikibl).

exquisite has two possible pronunciations. It is most usually pronounced with the emphasis on the first syllable (*ex*-kwis-it) but some prefer to put the emphasis on the second syllable (iks-*kwis*-it).

finance can be pronounced in two ways. The commoner pronunciation has the emphasis on the second syllable and the first syllable pronounced like the fin of a fish (fin-*ans*). The alternative pronunciation has emphasis on the first syllable, which then is pronounced as fine (*fin*-ans).

formidable may be pronounced with the emphasis on the first syllable as *for*-mid-ibl or with the emphasis on the second syllable as for-*mid*-ibl.

forte the usual pronunciation is *for*-tay but it can also be pronounced as single syllable fort. The word means 'someone's strong point', as in 'Putting people at their ease is not her forte' and 'The chef's forte is desserts'. There is also a musical word **forte** meaning 'loud' or 'loudly'. It is of Italian origin and is pronounced either *for*-ti or *for*-tay.

foyer the most widely used pronunciation is foi-ay but it can also be pronounced fwah-yay following the original French pronunciation.

harass traditionally is pronounced with the stress on the first syllable, as *har*-as. However, in modern usage there is an increasing tendency to put the emphasis on the second syllable, as har-*as*, which is how the word is pronounced in America.

heinous is most commonly pronounced *hay*-nis, although *hee*-nis also exists.

hospitable can be pronounced in two ways. The more traditional pronunciation has the emphasis on the first syllable, as *hos*-pit-ibl. In modern usage it is sometimes pronounced with the emphasis on the second syllable, as hos-*pit*-ibl.

impious the emphasis should be on the first syllable as *im*-pi-us. This is unlike 'impiety' where the stress is on the second syllable.

incomparable the emphasis should be on the second syllable and not the third. It should be pronounced in-*kom*-pir-ibl.

inventory unlike the word 'invention', the emphasis is on the first syllable as *in*-ven-tri or *in*-ven-tor-i.

kilometre has two possible pronunciations in modern usage. It can be pronounced with the emphasis on the first syllable, as *kil*-o-meet-er, or with the emphasis on the second syllable, as kil-*om*-it-er. The first of these is the more traditional pronunciation but the second is becoming common.

laboratory should be pronounced with the emphasis on the second syllable, as lab-*or*-a-tor-i or lab-*or*-a-tri. In American English the emphasis is on the first syllable.

lamentable should be pronounced with the emphasis on the first syllable, as *lam*-en-tabl. However it is becoming common to place the emphasis on the second syllable in the same way that 'lament' does.

longevity should be pronounced lon-*jev*-iti. Some people pronounce it lon-*gev*-iti, but this is rarer.

machinations should be pronounced mak-in-*ay*-shunz but mash-in *ay*-shunz is becoming increasingly common in modern usage.

mandatory the emphasis should be on the first syllable, as *man*-da-tor-i.

margarine formerly the usual pronunciation was mar-ga-reen but now the most common pronunciation is mar-ja-reen.

migraine is pronounced *mee*-grayn in British English but the American pronunciation of *mi*-grayn, in which the first syllable rhymes with 'eye', is sometimes used in Britain.

motif is pronounced with the emphasis on the second syllable, as mo-*teef*.

naïve is pronounced ni-*eev*, with the emphasis on the second syllable, and the first syllable rhyming with 'my'. The accent on the *ï* (called a diaeresis) indicates that the two vowels *a* and *i* are to be pronounced separately.

necessarily is traditionally pronounced with the emphasis on the first syllable, but this is often very difficult to say except when one is speaking exceptionally carefully. Because of this difficulty it is often pronounced with the emphasis on the third syllable although this is considered by many people to be incorrect.

niche the most common pronunciation is *nitch*, but *neech*, following the French pronunciation, is also a possibility.

pejorative in modern usage it is pronounced with the emphasis on the second syllable, as in pi-*jor*-at-iv.

phlegm is pronounced *flem*.

prestige is pronounced prez-*teezh* .

primarily is traditionally pronounced with the emphasis on the first syllable, as *prim*-ar-el-i. Since this is difficult to say unless one is speaking very slowly and carefully, it is becoming increasingly common to pronounce it with the emphasis on the second syllable, as prim-*err*-el-i.

quay the spelling of the word does not suggest the pronunciation, which is *kee*.

questionnaire formerly the acceptable pronunciation was kes-tyon-*air*, but in modern usage kwes-chon-*air* is more common.

schedule is usually pronounced *shed*-yool in British English. However, the American English pronunciation *sked*-yool is now sometimes found in British usage.

subsidence has two acceptable pronunciations. It can be pronounced either sub-*sid*-ens, with the emphasis on the middle syllable which rhymes with 'hide', or *sub*-sid-ens, with the emphasis on the first syllable and with the middle syllable rhyming with 'hid'.

suit is pronounced *soot* or *syoot*.

suite is pronounced *sweet*.

swingeing is pronounced *swin*-jing, not like swinging.

trait is traditionally pronounced *tray* but *trayt* is also an acceptable pronunciation in modern usage

victuals is pronounced *vitlz*.

vitamin is pronounced vit-a-min, with the first syllable rhyming with 'lit' in British English. In American English the first syllable rhymes with 'light'.

Words Liable to be Confused

Some words with totally different meanings are liable to be confused, often, but not always, because they are pronounced in a similar way or have similar spellings. Below is a list of words which are often confused, together with short examples of usage to help you to differentiate them.

accept accept a gift
except everyone except Mary

access access to the building; access to computer data
excess an excess of food at the picnic

adapter the adapter of the novel for TV
adaptor an electrical adaptor

addition an addition to the family
edition a new edition of the book

adverse an adverse reaction to the drug
averse not averse to the idea

advice seek legal advice
advise We advise you to go

affect badly affected by the news
effect the effects of the drug

alley a bowling alley
allay allay the child's fears

allusion make no allusion to recent events
delusion under the delusion that he is immortal
illusion an optical illusion

altar praying at the altar
alter alter the dress

alternately feeling alternately hot and cold
alternatively we could drive there – alternatively we could walk

amend amend the law
emend emend the text before printing

angel heavenly angels
angle a triangle has three angles; a new angle to the story

annex annex a neighbouring country
annexe build an annexe to the house

antiquated antiquated attitudes
antique valuable antique furniture

arisen a problem has arisen
arose a problem arose today

ascent the ascent of Everest
assent he gave his assent to the proposal

astrology believers in astrology read horoscopes
astronomy astronomy involves the scientific study of the stars and the planets

ate we ate bread and cheese
eaten we have eaten too much

aural an aural impairment requiring a hearing aid; an aural comprehension test
oral both oral and written language exams; oral hygiene recommended by the dentist

bad bad men arrested by the police
bade We bade him farewell

bail	the accused was granted bail
bale	a bale of cotton; bale out; bale out water; bale out of an aircraft
ballet	practising ballet steps
ballot	voting by means of a secret ballot
bare	bare feet
bear	bear the pain; bear children; bears looking for food
base	at the base of the pillar; base the argument on facts
bass	sing bass; fishermen catching bass
bath	lie soaking in the bath; bath the baby
bathe	bathe in the sea; bathe a wound
baton	the conductor's baton; a relay baton
batten	secure the broken door with wooden battens; batten down the hatches
beach	building sand castles on the beach
beech	beech and oak trees
been	having been famous
being	being poor scared her
beat	beat them at tennis; beat the dog with a stick
beet	sugar beet; soup made with beet
beat	we should beat them
beaten	we should have beaten them
became	she became famous
become	he wants to become a doctor
beer	a pint of beer
bier	a funeral bier
began	the child began to cry
begun	it had begun to rain
belief	have belief in his son's abilities
believe	believe that his son could succeed
beside	the bride stood beside the groom
besides	besides, he has no money; who, besides your mother, was there
bit	the dog bit the postman
bitten	he was bitten by a rat
blew	the wind blew; the hat blew away
blown	the wind had blown fiercely; the papers have been blown away
bloc	the African bloc of countries
block	a block of flats; a block of wood; block a pipe
boar	shooting wild boar
bore	the speaker is a bore
boast	boast about his achievements
boost	give a boost to the economy
bonny	a bonny little girl with beautiful hair
bony	the man's bony knees
born	babies born in hospital
borne	I could not have borne the pain; water-borne diseases
bouquet	a bouquet of roses
bookie	place a bet with a bookie
bow	take a bow after the performance; bow to the queen
bough	the bow of a tree
boy	boys and girls
buoy	a mooring buoy in the bay

breach	a breach of the peace; breach the enemy's defences
breech	the breech of a gun; a breech delivery of a baby
bread	bread and butter
bred	born and bred
break	break an arm
brake	failure of the car's brakes; brake suddenly on seeing the dog in the road
breath	take a deep breath
breathe	breathe deeply
bridal	the bridal party going to the church
bridle	the horse's bridle
broke	the watch fell and broke
broken	the watch was broken
brooch	wear a silver brooch
broach	afraid to broach the subject
buffet	[buffit] heavy waves regularly buffet the cliffs
buffet	[boofay] serve a cold buffet at the party; the station buffet
but	he was dead, but his family did not know
butt	butt in rudely to the conversation; the goat will butt you; a cigarette butt
calf	a cow and her calf; the calf of the leg
calve	hoping the cow would calve soon
callous	a cruel, callous tyrant
callus	the callus on her finger
came	they came late
come	they promised to come
cannon	soldiers firing cannons
canon	the canons of the cathedral; the canons and principles of the Christian church
canvas	a bag made of canvas; the canvas painted by a local artist
canvass	canvass for votes
carton	a carton of milk
cartoon	children laughing at TV cartoons
cast	the cast came on stage; cast a glance; a cast in the eye
caste	the caste system in India
censor	appoint a film censor; censor letters
censure	censure the child's unruly behaviour
cereal	cereal crops; breakfast cereal
serial	a magazine serial
chafe	tight shoes will chafe your heels; chafe at the delay
chaff	separate the wheat from the chaff
chartered	a chartered surveyor; a chartered boat
charted	the charted areas of the region
cheap	buy cheap clothes at the market
cheep	birds beginning to cheep
check	check the addition; check the tyre pressure; act as a check on her extravagance
cheque	pay by cheque
checked	a checked tablecloth
chequered	a chequered career
choose	you may choose a cake
chose	she chose a peach from the fruit dish
chosen	you have chosen well; the chosen few

chord a musical chord; strike a chord
cord the cord of a dressing gown; spinal cord; vocal cord

coarse made of some coarse material; a coarse sense of humour
course taking a French course; a golf course; in due course

coma the patient is still in a coma
comma put a comma instead of the full stop

commissionaire the hotel commissionaire
commissioner a police commissioner

compliment embarrassed at being paid a compliment
complement a full complement of staff; the complement of a verb

complimentary complimentary remarks; complimentary tickets
complementary complementary medicine; a complementary amount; complementary angles

compulsive a compulsive gambler
compulsory compulsory to wear school uniform

concert an orchestral concert
consort the queen's consort

confident confident of success
confidant he was the king's trusted confidant
confidante she was the queen's closest confidante

conscience suffering from a guilty conscience
conscious he was knocked out but is conscious now; conscious that she was all alone; a conscious decision

conservative wear conservative clothes; a conservative, rather than radical, approach
Conservative the Conservative Party in British politics

consul he was British consul in Rome then
council she was elected to the town council
counsel counsel for the defence; seeking professional counsel

contemptible a contemptible act of cowardice; a contemptible fellow
contemptuous contemptuous of the achievements of others; contemptuous of the law

continual disturbed by continual interruptions; in continual pain
continuous a continuous line of cars; a continuous roll of paper

coop a hencoop
coup a military coup

corps an army corps; the corps de ballet
corpse a corpse found in a shallow grave

councillor a town councillor
counsellor a bereavement counsellor

courtesy treat the visitors with courtesy
curtsy curtsy to the queen

credible a credible story
creditable a creditable performance
credulous credulous enough to believe anything

crevasse a crevasse in the glacier
crevice a crevice in the rock

cue a billiards cue; an actor famous for missing his cue
queue the bus queue

curb curb their extravagance
kerb cars parked by the kerb

currant a currant bun
current unable to swim against the strong current

cygnet a swan and her cygnets
signet a signet ring

cymbal banging the cymbals
symbol a symbol of purity; a mathematical symbol

dairy milk from the dairy
diary writing in her diary every night

dear dear friends; clothes which are too dear
deer hunting deer

dependant trying to provide for his wife and other dependants
dependent dependent on her family for personal care

deprecate strongly deprecate the behaviour of the gang of youths
depreciate depreciate in value

desert camels in the desert; He deserted his wife and family
dessert have chocolate cake for dessert

detract detract from his reputation as an actor
distract try not to distract the driver

device a device designed to save water
devise devise a rescue plan

devolution the population voted for the devolution of power from the government to the assembly
evolution the theory of evolution was first proposed by Charles Darwin

dew the morning dew
due payment is due now; in due course

did you did enough; He did steal the money
done you have done enough

die very ill and likely to die
dye about to dye her fair hair black

died the poet died young
dyed he dyed his white shirt blue

dinghy a dinghy capsizing in the storm
dingy a dingy basement flat

disadvantageous disadvantageous to one of the teams; disadvantageous, rather than favourable, circumstances
disadvantaged disadvantaged people in society

discomfit the question seemed to discomfit her
discomfort living in great discomfort

discriminating discriminating in their choice of wines
discriminatory discriminatory against women

discus throwing the discus
discuss discuss the matter

distinct a distinct improvement; a style quite distinct from others
distinctive the distinctive markings of the zebra

draft a first draft of a report
draught there was a draught in the room from the open window; a draught of cold beer

dragon a dragon breathing fire
dragoon the dragoon guards; We dragooned her into helping us

drank we drank some white wine
drunk to have drunk too much; a drunk woman staggering down the street

drunken a drunken, violent man; a drunken brawl

drew the child drew a picture
drawn he has drawn a picture of a house

driven we were driven home by my father
drove we drove home after midnight

dual serve a dual purpose
duel fight a duel

economic a country facing economic disaster; charging an economic rent for the flat
economical the economical use of resources; an economical car to run; economical with the truth

eerie in the eerie atmosphere of a thick mist
eyrie the eagle's eyrie

elder Mary has two brothers and James is the elder
eldest John has three sisters and Jill is the eldest

elicit elicit information
illicit an illicit love affair

eligible eligible for promotion; an eligible bachelor
legible scarcely legible handwriting

elude elude capture by the police
allude allude to facts which he had concealed

emigrant emigrants weeping for their native land
immigrant illegal immigrants to the country

emigration the poor standard of living led to mass emigration from the country
immigration anxious to reduce the extent of immigration into the country

emission the emission of poisonous gases
omission the omission of her name from the invitation list

emotional an emotional person; an emotional reaction
emotive an emotive subject

employee hiring several new employees
employer asking their employer for an increase in salary

enormity the enormity of the crime
enormousness the enormousness of the elephant

envelop she wanted to envelop the child in her arms; Mist began to envelop the mountains
envelope a brown envelope

enviable an enviable affluent lifestyle
envious envious of other people's wealth

epitaph carve an epitaph on a gravestone
epithet King Alfred was given the epithet 'great'

equable an equable climate; an equable temperament
equitable an equitable system

erotic erotic picture of naked women
erratic an erratic driver; impulsive, erratic behaviour

ewe a ewe and her lambs
yew the yew tree in the graveyard

exceedingly exceedingly beautiful
excessively excessively fond of alcohol

exceptional a singer of exceptional talent; an exceptional amount of rain
exceptionable find their behaviour exceptionable

executioner bring the condemned man to the executioner
executor an executor of a will

exercise physical exercise; an English exercise
exorcise exorcise evil spirits

exhausting an exhausting climb
exhaustive an exhaustive search

expand expand the business; metals expanding in the heat
expend expend a great deal of energy

expansive his knowledge of literature was expansive
expensive spending a lot of money on expensive meals

expedient politically expedient
expeditious a parcel sent by the most expeditious method

extant old customs which are still extant in some areas
extinct an endangered species that is likely to be extinct soon; a volcano that has been extinct for centuries

faint feel faint; a faint noise
feint a feint in fencing

fair a fair result; fair hair; sideshows at a fair
fare bus fare; How did you fare in the exam?

fate suffer a terrible fate; by a strange twist of fate
fête a fête in aid of charity

fearful fearful of being left behind; what a fearful smell
fearsome see a fearsome sight

feat perform a brave feat
feet sore feet

fiancé Jill and her fiancé
fiancée Jim and his fiancée

final a final warning
finale all the cast took part in the final

flair have a flair for languages
flare send up a flare as a signal for help; make the fire flare up; a skirt with a slight flare

flammable clothes made of flammable material
inflammable highly inflammable substances such as petrol

flea bitten by a flea
flee people beginning to flee from the burning houses

fleshy fleshy upper arms; a fleshy fruit
fleshly fleshly pleasures

flu suffering from flu
flue cleaning the flue
flew the bird flew away
flown the bird has flown away

floe an ice floe
flow the flow of water

flour flour to make bread
flower pick a flower from the garden

flout flout the new school rule
flaunt flaunt her long legs

font babies christened at the font
fount printed in a small size of fount

forbade she forbade them to leave
forbidden she was forbidden to leave

foresaw we foresaw trouble
foreseen the problem could not have been foreseen

forgave we forgave them
forgiven we have forgiven them

forgot we forgot about the party
forgotten I had forgotten the event

formally	formally dressed
formerly	formerly the president of the club
fort	soldiers defending the fort
forte	tact is not his forte
foul	commit a foul on the football pitch; a foul smell
fowl	a chicken is a type of fowl
found	they found the missing child
founded	their grandfather founded the firm
freeze	freeze the vegetables; freeze to death
frieze	a decorative frieze
froze	we froze the meat immediately
frozen	frozen vegetables; have frozen to death
funeral	mourners at the funeral
funereal	solemn funereal music
gaff	blow the gaff
gaffe	a social gaffe
gamble	decide to gamble on a horse in the next race
gambol	lambs beginning to gambol about
gate	shut the gate
gait	a shuffling gait
gave	he gave money to the poor
given	we had been given some money
gentle	a gentle touch; a gentle breeze
genteel	a genteel tea party
glacier	a glacier beginning to melt
glazier	a glazier mending the window
goal	score a goal
gaol	escape from gaol
gone	he has gone
went	she went yesterday
gorilla	a gorilla in the zoo
guerrilla	guerrillas fighting in the mountains
grate	a fire burning in the grate
great	a great improvement; a great man
grew	the plants grew well
grown	the plant had grown tall
grief	weeping from grief
grieve	time to grieve for her dead husband
grill	put the meat under the grill
grille	a metal grille on the window
grisly	the grisly sight of a decaying body
grizzly	a grizzly bear
hail	a hail storm; a hail of bullets; hail a taxi
hale	hale and hearty
hair	cut off her hair
hare	a running hare
half	a half of the apple
halve	halve the apple
hangar	an aeroplane hangar
hanger	a clothes hanger
hanged	they hanged the murderer
hung	they hung the pictures
heal	the wound began to heal
heel	a blister on the heel
hear	hear the news
here	here and there
hereditary	a hereditary title
heredity	part of his genetic heredity
heron	a heron catching fish
herring	fishermen catching herring
hid	we hid the treasure
hidden	they have hidden the treasure
hoard	a hoard of treasure
horde	a horde of invaders
honorable	an honorable gentleman; honorable deeds
honorary	the honorary post of secretary
hoop	jump through a hoop
whoop	a whoop of delight
human	a human being
humane	the humane killing of the injured animal
idle	too idle to work
idol	the pop star as teenage idol; worshipping an idol
imaginary	the child's imaginary friend
imaginative	an imaginative story; an imaginative person
immoral	wicked and immoral
immortal	no one is immortal
inapt	an inapt remark
inept	an inept attempt
incredible	find the story incredible
incredulous	incredulous enough to believe anything
industrial	an industrial estate
industrious	studious and industrious
ingenious	an ingenious plan
ingenuous	an ingenuous young person
its	a dog wagging its tail
it's	it's raining
jam	strawberry jam; a traffic jam; the machine seemed to jam
jamb	a door jamb
jib	jib at the high price
jibe	ignore the nasty jibe
judicial	a judicial enquiry into the accident
judicious	a judicious choice of words
junction	a road junction
juncture	at this juncture we went home
key	a door key
quay	the boat tied to the quay
knead	knead the bread dough
kneed	he kneed his attacker in the stomach
knew	we knew him slightly
know	we did not know him
known	if I had known
knight	a knight in shining armour
night	a stormy night

laid	we laid the patient on the bed; they laid a new carpet
lain	he had lain injured for days
lair	the animal's lair
layer	a layer of dust
laterally	moving laterally; thinking laterally
latterly	latterly she was very ill
lath	a lath of wood
lathe	using a lathe in the factory
lead	pipes made of lead
led	he led the group
leak	a leak in the pipe
leek	a leek to make soup
licence	have a driving licence
license	to license the sale of alcohol
lifelong	a lifelong ambition
livelong	the livelong day
lighted	a lighted match
lit	we lit the fire; we have lit the fire
lightening	lightening the load
lightning	struck by lightning; a lightning decision
liqueur	an after-dinner liqueur
liquor	strong liquor such as whisky
liquidate	liquidate a debt; liquidate an asset; liquidate an enemy
liquidize	liquidize the soup
literal	a literal translation
literary	literary and artistic tastes
literate	people who are scarcely literate
loath/loth	loath/loth to join in
loathe	I loathe him
local	the local shops; drinking at his local
locale	a perfect locale for a rock concert
loose	loose clothing
lose	lose your luggage; lose weight
loot	the thieves' loot
lute	playing the lute
lumbar	lumbar pain
lumber	to lumber along awkwardly
luxuriant	luxuriant vegetation
luxurious	a luxurious lifestyle
magnate	a shipping magnate
magnet	a fridge magnet
mail	deliver the mail
male	male and female
main	the main reason
mane	the lion's mane
maize	grow maize
maze	get lost in the maze
manner	a friendly manner
manor	a manor surrounded by beautiful gardens
masterful	she prefers masterful men
masterly	a masterly performance
mat	a door mat
matt, matte	matt/matte paint

meat	meat such as beef
meet	meet a friend
medal	a gold medal
meddle	meddle in the affairs of others
mediate	mediate between the rival groups
meditate	meditate to relax
melted	the ice cream melted; melted chocolate
molten	molten lava
metal	chairs made of metal
mettle	a test of the football team's mettle
meter	read the gas meter
metre	a metre of silk
miner	a coal miner
minor	a minor incident; legally still a minor
missal	members of the congregation carrying missals
missile	hit by a missile
mistaken	a case of mistaken identity; we were mistaken
mistook	I mistook him for you in the dark
model	a model of a ship; a fashion module
module	a space module; a software module; a study module
momentary	a momentary lapse of memory
momentous	a momentous decision
moral	the moral of the story; a person with no morals
morale	morale was low in the firm
motif	decorated with a motif of roses
motive	a motive for murder
muscle	strain a muscle
mussel	eat fresh mussels
naturalist	a naturalist interested in local flowers
naturist	naked people on a naturist beach
naval	a naval cadet
navel	your navel is in the middle of your abdomen
negligent	negligent parents
negligible	a negligible amount of money
net	caught in a net
net, nett	net, nett profit
niceness	appreciate the old lady's niceness
nicety	the nicety of the distinction
notable	a notable figure in the town
noticeable	a noticeable improvement
nougat	nougat is a sweet
nugget	a nugget of gold; a nugget of information
oar	the boat's oars
ore	iron oar
observance	the observance of school rules
observation	keep the patient under observation
of	made of gold; tired of working; a glass of wine
off	run off; switch off; badly off
official	an official report; official duties; council official
officious	upset at the officious manner of the hotel receptionist
organism	an organism found in the water supply
orgasm	to reach orgasm

outdoor	an outdoor sport
outdoors	playing outdoors
overcame	we overcame the enemy
overcome	an enemy difficult to overcome
overtaken	he had overtaken the other runners
overtook	they overtook the car in front
pail	a pail of water
pale	looking pale; a pale colour
pain	suffering from pain
pane	a pane of glass
pair	a pair of gloves
pare	he began to pare his toenails
pear	an apple and a pear
palate	the soft palate
palette	an artist's palette
pallet	a straw pallet
passed	she passed the exam; we passed the car; the feeling passed
past	past times; in the past; walking past the church; a mile past the village
pastel	pastel colours
pastille	sucking a throat pastille
pâté	chicken liver pâté on toast
patty	a small meat patty
peace	warring nations now at peace
piece	a piece of cake
peak	a mountain peak; talent at its peak
peek	peek through the window
peal	the bells began to peal
peel	peel an orange
pearl	a pearl necklace
purl	knit two, purl two
pedal	pedal the bike
peddle	peddle their wares
pendant	wearing a silver pendant
pendent	pendent lights lighting up the room
perceptible	a perceptible improvement
perceptive	a perceptive remark
perpetrate	perpetrate a crime
perpetuate	perpetuate the myth
persecute	persecute members of other religions
prosecute	prosecute thieves
personal	a personal letter; a personal assistant
personnel	the person in charge of office personnel
phase	the next phase of the development; phase in the changes
faze	nothing seems to faze her
pigeon	a pigeon looking for food
pidgin	pidgin English
place	a sunny place; get a place at university
plaice	plaice and chips
plain	a plain carpet; rather a plain girl; corn grew on the plain
plane	a plane taking off; the plane used by the joiner; writing on a different plane from other crime writers
plaintiff	evidence on behalf of the plaintiff
plaintive	a plaintive cry
plate	the food on the plate
plait	wearing her hair in a plait
plum	eating a plum
plumb	plumb straight; plumb in the middle; plumb the depths; plumb-in the bath
politic	not politic to ask any questions
political	political parties
pour	pour water
pore	pore over the book; a clogged pore
practice	go to football practice
practise	to practise dance steps
pray	pray to God
prey	the fox's prey; prey on one's mind
precede	the leader who preceded the present one; precede them into the room
proceed	You may proceed; proceed to cause trouble
precipitate	rash, precipitate action; precipitate economic panic
precipitous	a precipitous slope
premier	a meeting of European premiers; one of the country's premier actors
première	the premiere of the film
premises	seek new office premises
premise	based on a mistaken premise
prescribe	prescribe antibiotics for the disease
proscribe	proscribe the carrying of dangerous weapons
principal	the college principal
principle	a person of principle; the principle of the steam engine
prise	prise open the lid of the tin
prize	win a prize
program	a computer program
programme	a theatre programme
proof	no proof of his guilt
prove	able to prove her innocence
prophecy	the gift of prophesy; her prophecy came true
prophesy	prophesy that there would be a war
prostate	the prostate gland
prostrate	lying prostrate on the ground
purposely	leave the book behind purposely
purposefully	walk purposefully into the room
quash	quash a rebellion; quash a conviction
squash	squash the tomatoes; squash the insect with his foot
quiet	a quiet child; a quiet time of day
quite	quite good; quite right
racket	the noisy children made quite a racket; a drugs racket; tennis racket
racquet	tennis racquet (variant spelling)
rain	get wet in the rain
reign	in the reign of the last king
rein	a horse's reins
raise	raise one's arm; raise a family
raze	raze the whole street to the ground

ran they ran away
run he started to run; She had run away

rang they rang the bell
rung they had rung the bell

rap rap at the window
wrap wrap the presents

rapt with rapt attention
wrapped we wrapped the presents

read I read the book last week
red a red dress

real made of real leather; a real friend
reel a reel of thread; dance a reel

refuge seek refuge from the storm
refugee a political refugee

regal a regal wave of the hand
regale regale them with his adventures

relief bring relief from pain
relieve relieve the pain
rest rest after work
wrest wrest the knife from his hand

retch feel sick and begin to retch
wretch the poor wretch

review the review of the play; the annual salary review
revue a musical revue

rhyme children reciting a rhyme; cook rhymes with book
rime rime on the grass on a cold morning

ridden she had ridden the horse home
rode he rode a fine stallion

right right person for the job; right to be free; right hand
rite a religious rite
write write in pencil

risen the sun had risen
rose the sun rose

road the road through the town
rode the child rode her bicycle

roe cod roe
row a row of green beans; row a boat

role play the role of Hamlet; the parental role
roll a roll of carpet; a ham roll; roll a ball

rote learn the answers by rote
wrote he wrote a letter

rough a rough material; rough weather
ruff a lace ruff at the neck

rout rout the enemy
route the shortest route to the town

rung the bottom rung of the ladder; we had rung the bell
wrung she wrung her hands in grief

rye grow rye and barley
wry a wry smile; a wry sense of humour

sail the sail of a boat; go for a sail
sale an end-of-season sale

salon a hair-dressing salon
saloon a saloon car; a saloon bar

sang they sang a song
sung we had sung a song earlier

sank the ship sank
sunk the ship has sunk
sunken a sunken wreck

saviour the saviour of the organization; Christ the saviour
savour savour the delicious food

saw we saw him go
seen I have seen the film before
sawed we sawed the wood
sawn all the wood has been sawn

scared scared of the dark
scarred scarred for life in the accident

scene a scene in the play; the scene of the accident
seen have seen the play

scent the scent of roses
sent she sent a letter

sceptic a sceptic arguing with the believers
septic a septic wound; a septic tank

scraped he scraped the car on the gate
scrapped they scrapped their original plans

sculptor a statue by a famous sculptor
sculpture carve a piece of sculpture

seam sew the seam of a dress; a seam of coal
seem they seem familiar

seasonal seasonal hotel work
seasonable seasonable weather for spring
seasoned a seasoned dish of stew; seasoned travellers

secret a secret hideout; their engagement was a secret
secrete secrete the money under the floorboards

see I see a light
sea boats sailing on the sea

sensual a sensual mouth
sensuous the sensuous feel of the silk sheets

series a series of disasters; a TV series
serious a serious matter; looking serious

sew sew new curtains
sow sow seeds

sewed she sewed tiny stitches
sewn the dress which she had sewn

shaken she was shaken by the accident
shook he shook the child angrily

shear to shear sheep
sheer a sheer slope; sheer impertinence; sheer silk

shelf put the book on the shelf
shelve shelve the plan

shoe a high-heeled shoe
shoo shoo the dog away

showed we showed them the house
shown he has shown me the book

shrank he shrank back in fear; the dress shrank in the wash
shrunk the child had shrunk from the angry man; the dress had shrunk

sight the sight of the woman crying
site the battle site; a building site

singeing singeing a blouse with an iron
singing singing a song

slay slay an enemy in battle
sleigh a sleigh ride in the snow

slow at a slow pace
sloe a ripe sloe

soar soar up high
sore a sore finger

solder to solder metal
soldier a soldier in the British army

sole the sole reason; the sole of the foot; a dish of sole
soul body and soul; a poor old soul

some some people
sum the sum total

son a son and two daughters
sun lie in the sun on the beach

soot soot falling down the chimney
suit an evening suit

sped the car sped away into the night
speeded we speeded up to pass the car in front

spoke she spoke with feeling
spoken he has spoken to the parents

sprang he sprang to his feet
sprung the lion had sprung over the fence

stair a stone stair
stare stare into space

stake a stake missing from the fence; stake a claim
steak eat a large steak

stalk the stalk of the flower
stock a large stock of goods; stocks and shares

stank he stank of beer
stunk the room had stunk for days

stationary the car was stationary
stationery a shop stocking stationery

statue stone statues in the grounds of the house
statute pass a new statute

steal steal the money from the till
steel tools made of steel

stile climb over the stile
style dress with style; a style of writing

stimulant athletes taking illegal stimulants
stimulus the stimulus of a valuable prize

storey the top storey of the house
story tell a story

straight a straight road; a straight answer
strait the Bering Strait

straightened she had her teeth straightened
straitened in straitened circumstances

strategy the team's winning strategy; devise a strategy to counteract bullying
stratagem devise a stratagem to mislead the enemy

strewed they strewed flowers
strewn flowers were strewn

strife quarrelling and strife
strive strive to overcome the difficulty
striven we haven striven to succeed
strove they strove to win

suede a jacket made of real suede
swede cutting up a swede for dinner

suit wearing a smart suit; a law suit; a suit of cards
suite a three-piece suite; a suite of rooms; a ballet suite

summary a summary of the report; his summary dismissal
summery sunny, summery weather

sundae an ice cream sundae
Sunday have a rest on Sunday

surplice the priest's surplice
surplus a surplus of food at the party

swam we swam in the river
swum he has swum across the river

swingeing a swingeing blow; swingeing cuts
swinging a swinging gate; the swinging sixties

swollen her eye has swollen up; swollen glands
swelled her injured ankle swelled

swore they swore they would find the killer
sworn he has sworn to get revenge

tail the dog's tail
tale tell a tale

taken she has taken the book
took she took the book

taper a lighted taper; The road seems to taper there
tapir a tapir is a pig-like animal

taught he taught us maths
taut a taut rope; a face taut with concentration

tea a cup of tea
tee a golf tee

team a football team
teem the town will teem with tourists

tear wipe away a tear
tier one tier of the wedding cake

teeth have two teeth extracted
teethe the child has begun to teethe

temporal temporal, not spiritual
temporary a temporary post

their their home
there stay there
they're they're quarrelling again

thorough a thorough cleaning
through pass through

thrash thrash the youth with a belt
thresh thresh the corn

through go through the door
threw he threw the ball

thrown he had thrown the ball
throes in the throes of studying for exams
throws he throws the ball

thyme flavour the sauce with thyme
time what time is it?; not enough time

tic a nervous tic
tick the tick of the clock; the dog bitten by the tick; in a tick; a tick at a correct answer

timber a house made of timber
timbre the timbre of his voice

tire runners beginning to tire
tyre change a car tyre

to go to town
too she wants to go too
two two or three times

toe injure a toe
tow tow the broken-down car

tomb the tomb of the Egyptian king
tome struggling to read a legal tome

topi wear a topi in the hot sun
toupee a bald man wearing a toupee

tore she tore her dress
torn she has torn her dress; a torn dress

trait dishonesty is an unpleasant trait
tray tea served on a tray

treaties signing treaties to end the war
treatise write a treatise on company law

trod she trod on the cat's tail
trodden she had trodden on some mud

troop a troop of soldiers; troop out of school
troupe a troupe of actors

tycoon a business tycoon
typhoon a ship damaged in a typhoon

unaware unaware of what had happened
unawares taken unawares by the attack

unconscionable an unconscionable delay
unconscious knocked unconscious by the blow; unconscious of the recent event

unexceptional a disappointing, unexceptional performance
unexceptionable unnecessary complaints about unexceptionable behaviour

unwanted unwanted guests
unwonted speak with unwonted enthusiasm

urban prefer urban to rural life
urbane an urbane young man

vacation go on vacation to America
vocation have a vocation to be a priest

vain a vain young woman; a vain attempt
vane a weather vane
vein inject the drug into a vein; a vein of pessimism in the novel

vale the Vale of Evesham
veil a hat with a veil; draw a veil over the incident

veracity doubt the veracity of the account
voracity the voracity of the youth's appetite

vertex the vertex of a cone
vortex the swimmer was caught in a vortex of water and drowned

vigilant be vigilant because of pickpockets
vigilante the thief was caught by a vigilante

wafer an ice cream wafer; a Communion wafer
waver begin to waver about the decision

waif a starving waif
waive waive the extra charges
wave wave to their departing guests

waist a leather belt round the waist
waste liquid waste from the factory; a waste of food

want want more money; for want of enough money
wont she was wont to arrive late

warden the warden of the hostel
warder a prison warder

ware kitchen ware; stallholders selling their wares
wear wear a skirt; show signs of wear

way the quickest way home; the correct way to do it
weigh weigh the apples

weak invalids too weak to get out of bed
week go to the supermarket every week

weakly weakly children who did not survive
weekly look forward to their weekly visit

went they went quite suddenly; She went pale
gone he has gone home; She had gone deaf

wet a wet day; wet the floor
whet whet the appetite

whit not care a whit
wit find his wit amusing; a person of wit and intelligence

whole the whole group
hole dig a hole

wittily he spoke wittily after dinner
wittingly she wittingly told a lie

woe sadness and woe
woo woo her and marry her

woke she woke early
woken she had woken early

wore he wore the shoes
worn he had worn the shoes; an old, worn carpet

would we knew she would go
wood a pine wood

wove he wove the material
woven he has woven the material
weaved the cyclist weaved in and out of the line of traffic

wreak wreak vengeance; wreak havoc
wreck wreck the car; wreck their plans

wreath a holly wreath
wreathe mist had begun to wreathe the mountain peaks

wrote she wrote the letter
written she has written the letter

yoke the yoke of a dress; the yoke of a plough
yolk egg yolk

yore in days of yore
your your house
you're you're wrong

Affixes

Affix refers to an element that is added to the root or stem of a word to form another word. Affixes can be in the form of **prefixes or suffixes.** A prefix is added to the beginning of a word, as audio in audiovisual, an affix to the end, as -aholic in workaholic. Some common affixes are listed below.

a-, an- a prefix meaning without or not, as amoral, anonymous and atypical.

-able, -ible a suffix meaning 'that can be', as laughable, washable, horrible and edible.

aero- a prefix meaning **1** air, as aerobics and aeroplane, **2** aeroplane, as aerodrome.

agro-, agri- a prefix meaning field, as agriculture and agrochemicals.

-aholic a suffix indicating an addiction, formed on analogy with alcoholic, as workaholic and shopaholic. It sometimes becomes **-oholic**, as chocoholic.

ambi- a prefix meaning two or both as ambivalent, having mixed or uncertain feelings about something and ambidextrous, able to use both the right and left hand with equal skill.

-ana a suffix meaning 'things associated with', as Americana.

ante- a prefix meaning before, as antenatal, before birth.

anti- a prefix meaning against. It is used in many words that have been established In English for a long time, as antipathy, a feeling of hostility or dislike, but it has also been used to form many modern words, as anti-freeze, anti-nuclear and anti-warfare.

arch- a prefix meaning chief, as archbishop, archduke and arch-enemy.

-arch a suffix meaning ruler or leader, as monarch and patriarch.

astro- a prefix meaning star, as in astrology, astronomy, astronaut, astrophysics.

-athon, -thon a suffix meaning large-scale or long-lasting contest or event, such as swimathon. Such words are formed on analogy with the word marathon.

audio- a prefix referring to hearing. It is found in several words that have been established in the language for some time, as audition, but it is also used to form many modern words, as audiotape and audiovisual.

auto- a prefix meaning of or by itself, as autobiography, autograph and automatic, meaning working by itself.

bi- a prefix meaning two, as in bicycle, bifocal, bilingual and bisect. Bi-forms words in English in which it means half, and other words in which it means twice. This can give rise to confusion in such words as biweekly and bimonthly, where there are two possible sets of meanings. Biweekly can mean either every two weeks or twice a week so that one would not be able to be certain about the frequency of a biweekly publication. Similarly, a bimonthly publication might appear either twice a month or once every two months.

biblio- a prefix meaning book, as bibliophile, a person who is fond of or collects books, and bibliography.

bio- a prefix meaning life or living material, as biography and biology.

-bound a suffix meaning **1** confined or restricted, as housebound and snowbound, **2** It can also mean obligated, as duty-bound.

by- a prefix **1** meaning subordinate, secondary, as by-product, **2** around, as in by-pass.

cardi- a prefix meaning heart, as cardiology and cardiac.

cent-, centi- a prefix meaning hundred, as centenary and centigrade.

chrono- a prefix meaning time, as chronology and chronicle.

-cide a suffix meaning killing, as infanticide, patricide and pesticide.

circum- a prefix meaning around, as circumnavigate and circumvent.

con-, com- a prefix meaning together with, as connect, compare and compound.

contra- a prefix meaning opposite or against, as contrary, contradict and contraflow.

deca- a prefix meaning ten, as decade and decathlon.

deci- a prefix meaning tenth, as decibel and decimal

demi- a prefix meaning half, as demigod.

di- a prefix meaning two or double, as in dioxide, dilemma, diphthong and disyllabic.

dia- a prefix meaning **1** through, as in diaphanous, **2** apart, as in diacritical, diaphragm and dialysis, **3** and across, as in diameter.

dis- a prefix indicating opposite or meaning not, as disappear, disapprove, dislike, disobey, dispossess, distrust and disunite.

-dom a suffix meaning state or condition, as in boredom, freedom, officialdom, martyrdom, **2** rank or status, as in earldom, dukedom, **3** domain or territory as in kingdom.

dys- a prefix meaning, bad, impaired or abnormal, as dysfunctional and dyslexia, dyspepsia

eco- a prefix indicating ecology. Following the increased awareness of the importance of the environment, there has been a growing interest in ecology and many words beginning with eco- have been added to the English language. Some of these are scientific terms such as ecotype, ecosystem or ecospecies. Others are more general terms, such as eco-catastrophe and ecopolitics, and some are even slang terms, such as ecofreak and econut.

-ectomy a suffix that indicates surgical removal, as hysterectomy (the surgical removal of the womb), mastectomy (the surgical removal of a breast) and appendicectomy (the surgical removal of the appendix).

-ed a suffix that forms the past tense and past participles of regular verbs, as in asked, caused, dropped and escaped.

-ee a suffix that is used as part of nouns that are the recipients of an action, as in deportee (a person who has been deported); employee, and interviewee. The prefix can also be used as part of a noun indicating a person who acts or behaves in a particular way, as absentee (a person who absents himself/herself) and escapee (a person who escapes).

electro- a prefix meaning electric, electrical as electromagnetic.

-en a suffix with several functions. In one sense it indicates causing to be, as broaden, darken, gladden, lighten and sweeten. It also indicates a diminutive or small version of something, as chicken and maiden. It also indicates what something is made of, as in silken and wooden. It is also used to form the past participle of many irregular verbs, such as broken and fallen.

en- a prefix indicating causing to be, as in enrich and enlarge, and putting into, as endanger and enrage. enslave.

equi- a prefix meaning equal, as equidistant and equivalent.

-er a suffix with several functions. It can indicate a person who does something, as in bearer, cleaner, employer, farmer, manager. Some words in this category can also end in '-or', as in adviser/advisor. It can also indicate a person who is engaged in something, as in lawyer. It also indicates a thing that does something, as in blender, cooker, mower, printer and strainer. It can also indicate the comparative form of an adjective, as in darker, fairer, older, shorter and younger. It can also indicate someone who comes from somewhere, as in Londoner.

-ese a suffix that indicates belonging to, coming from and is used of people and languages, as Chinese, Japanese and Portuguese. By extension it refers to words indicating some kind of jargon, as computerese, journalese and legalese.

-esque a suffix of French origin that means in the style or fashion of, as in Junoesque, statuesque, Picassoesque, Ramboesque.

-ess a suffix that was formerly widely used to indicate the feminine form of a word, as authoress from author, poetess from poet, editress from editor, and sculptress from sculptor. In many cases the supposed male form, such as author, is now considered a neutral form and so is used of both a woman and a man. Thus a woman as well as a man may be an author, a poet, an editor and a sculptor, etc. Some words ending in -ess remain, as princess, duchess, heiress and hostess. Actress and waitress are still also fairly widespread.

-est a suffix that indicates the superlative forms of adjectives, as biggest, smallest and ugliest.

-ette a suffix indicating **1** a diminutive or smaller version, as cigarette and kitchenette, **2** imitation, as in flannelette and leatherette, **3** a female version, as usherette, a female usher in a cinema. In this last sense it is sometimes used disparagingly, as in jockette (a derogatory word for a female jockey) and hackette a derogatory word for a female journalist.

Euro- a prefix meaning **1** referring to Europe, as in Eurovision, **2** (more commonly now) referring to the European Community, as in Euro-MP, Eurocrat and Eurocurrency.

ex- a prefix meaning former, as ex-chairman, ex-president, ex-wife.

extra- a prefix meaning beyond, outside as in extra-marital, meaning outside marriage and extra-curricular, meaning outside the curriculum.

-fold a suffix meaning 'times', multiplied by, as in fourfold, a hundredfold.

for- a prefix with several meanings. These include prohibition, as forbid; abstention as in forbear, forgo and forswear; neglect, as forsake; excess, intensity, as forlorn; and away, off, apart, as forgive.

fore- a prefix meaning **1** before, as forecast, foregoing and forefathers, **2** front as forehead, foreground.

-form a suffix meaning **1** having the form of, as cruciform, meaning in the form of a cross, **2** having such a number of, as uniform, multiform.

-ful a suffix indicating **1** the amount that fills something, as handful, spoonful and bagful, **2** full of, as beautiful, truthful and scornful, **3** having the qualities of, as masterful, **4** apt to, able to, as forgetful and useful.

-free a suffix used to form adjectives indicating absence of, freedom from as carefree, trouble-free, anxiety-free, tax-free, lead-free.

-friendly a modern suffix formed on analogy with user-friendly to mean helpful to, supporting, as child-friendly and environment-friendly.

-gate a modern suffix that is added to a noun to indicate something scandalous. Most of the words so formed are short-lived and forgotten about almost as soon as they are invented. In modern usage they are frequently used to apply to sexual scandals, but originally -gate was restricted to some form of political scandal. The suffix is derived from Watergate, and refers to a political scandal in the United States during President Richard Nixon's re-election campaign in 1972, when Republican agents were caught breaking into the headquarters of the Democratic Party in Washington, which were in a building called the Watergate Building. The uncovering of the attempts to cover up the break-in led to Richard Nixon's resignation.

geo- a prefix meaning earth, as geography and geology.

-gram a suffix meaning **1** writing or drawing, as telegram, electrocardiogram and diagram, **2** used in modern usage to indicate a greeting or message, as in kissogram.

-graph a suffix meaning **1** written or recorded, as autograph, monograph, photograph, **2** an instrument that records, as seismograph, tachograph and cardiograph.

gynaec-, gynaeco- a prefix meaning female, woman, as gynaecology.

-hand a suffix meaning **1** worker, as deckhand, farmhand and cowhand, **2** position, as right-hand and left-hand.

haem-, haemo- a prefix meaning blood, as haemorrhage and haematology.

hemi- a prefix meaning half, as hemisphere.

hetero- a prefix meaning other, another, different, as heterosexual.

holo- a prefix meaning complete, whole, as holistic

homo- a prefix meaning same, as in homogenous, homonym and homosexual.

-hood a suffix meaning state or condition, as babyhood, childhood, manhood, priesthood, womanhood and widowhood.

hydro- a prefix meaning water, as hydro-electric and hydrophobia. It also means 'hydrogen', as in hydrochloride.

hyper- a prefix meaning over, above, as hyperactive, hypercritical and hypersensitive.

hypo- a prefix meaning under, as hypothermia and hypodermic.

-ian a suffix indicating **1** a profession, job or pastime, as comedian, musician, optician, physician, **2** proper names, as Dickensian, Orwellian and Shakespearian.

-iana a suffix which is a form of form of **-ana** and indicates memorabilia or collections relating to people or places of note, as Churchilliana.

-ible *see* **-able.**

-ics a suffix indicating science or study, as electronics, genetics, and politics.

-ify a suffix indicating 'making or becoming', as clarify, purify, satisfy and simplify.

infra- a prefix meaning below or beneath, as infrared and infrastructure.

-in a suffix meaning **1** in or into, as income, inside and invade, **2** not, as incurable, incapable and inconvenient

-ine a suffix indicating 'belonging to', as canine, divine and feline.

-ing a suffix used to form the present participle of verbs, as living, going and running.

inter- a prefix meaning between, as in intercity, intercontinental and interstate.

intra- a prefix meaning within, as intravenous.

ise and **-ize** are both verb endings. In British English there are many verbs that can be spelt ending in either **-ise** or **-ize**, as 'computerise/ize', 'economise/ize', 'finalise/ize', 'hospitalise/ize', 'modernise/ize', 'organise/ize', 'realise/ize', 'theorise/ize'. There are a few verbs that cannot be spelt **-ize**. These include 'advertise', 'advise', 'comprise', 'despise', 'exercise', 'revise', 'supervise' and 'televise'.

-ish a suffix meaning **1** somewhat, as baldish, smallish and youngish, **2** nationality, as Spanish, Turkish and Polish.

-ism a suffix indicating **1** a state or condition, as conservatism, egotism and heroism, sometimes an abnormal state, as alcoholism. **2** doctrine, theory or system of beliefs, as Catholicism and Marxism. **3** discrimination or prejudice, as ageism, discrimination on the grounds of age, often against old or older people, classicism, discrimination on the grounds of social class, racism, discrimination on the grounds of race and sexism, discrimination on the grounds of sex or gender, often against women.

iso- a prefix meaning equal, as in isobar, isotherm and isosceles.

-ist a suffix indicating believer, supporter, practitioner, as in atheist, fascist, feminist and Methodist.

-ite a suffix indicating a believer, supporter, practitioner, as in Thatcherite and Trotskyite.

-itis a suffix indicating an illness or disease, as bronchitis, a disease of the chest and hepatitis, a disease of the liver.

-ize see **-ise.**

kilo- a prefix meaning a thousand, as in kilogram, kilohertz, kilolitre, kilometre and kilowatt.

-kin a suffix that indicates a diminutive or smaller version, as in lambkin and mannikin.

-kind a suffix indicating a group of people, as in humankind, mankind, womankind.

-less a suffix meaning **1** without or lacking added to nouns to form adjectives, as expressionless, fearless, harmless, homeless and hopeless, **2** without being able to be measured, as ageless, countless, priceless and timeless.

-let a suffix indicating a diminutive or smaller form of something, as in booklet, coverlet, droplet, islet, piglet, starlet and streamlet.

-like a suffix indicating similarity, as in childlike, dreamlike, lifelike and warlike.

-ling a suffix indicating a diminutive or smaller version of something, as duckling, gosling and nestling.

-logue a suffix meaning conversation or discussion, as dialogue, monologue, prologue and travelogue.

-ly a common adverbial ending, as hurriedly, sharply and tightly.

macro- a prefix meaning large in size or scope, as in macrobiotic, macrocosm and macrostructure.

-mania a suffix indicating abnormal or obsessive behaviour, as kleptomania and pyromania.

mal- a prefix meaning **1** bad, unpleasant, as malodorous, having an unpleasant smell, **2** imperfect, faulty, as malformation and malfunctioning.

-man a suffix used with nouns to form nouns indicating someone's job, as barman, chairman, clergyman, policeman and salesman. In modern usage, when attempts are being made to remove sexism from the language, alternatives have been sought for any words ending in -man. Formerly, words ending in -man were often used whether or not the person referred to was definitely known to be a man. Different ways have been found to avoid the sexism of -man. Salesman has been changed in many cases to salesperson, chairman often becomes chairperson or chair. Similarly, fireman has become fire-fighter and policeman frequently becomes police officer.

-mate a suffix referring to someone who shares something with someone, as classmate, roommate, schoolmate, team-mate and workmate.

mega- a prefix meaning very large, as megabucks and megastar. Many words using mega- in this way are modern and many are also informal or slang. In technical language mega- means a million times bigger than the unit to which it is attached, as in megabyte, megacycle, megahertz and megawatt.

meta- a prefix meaning alteration or transformation, as metamorphosis.

-meter a suffix meaning a measuring instrument, as altimeter, barometer, speedometer and thermometer.

-metre a suffix indicating meter, the unit of length, as centimetre, kilometre and millimetre.

micro- a prefix meaning very small, as microscope and microsurgery.

milli- a prefix meaning a thousand, as millisecond and millennium.

mini- a prefix meaning very small or least, as minimum, minimal, and miniature. Mini- is frequently used to form modern words, as minibus, minicab, mini-computer, mini-cruise and miniskirt. Modern words beginning with mini- can often be spelt either with a hyphen or without.

mis- a prefix meaning badly, wrongly, as in misbehave, miscalculate, mistreat and misunderstanding.

-monger a suffix meaning dealer, trader, as fishmonger and ironmonger. As well as being used for occupations in which people sell things, it is used for people who 'trade' in less tangible things, as in gossipmonger, rumourmonger, scaremonger and warmonger.

mono- a prefix meaning one or single, as monochrome, monologue, monoplane and monosyllabic.

multi- a prefix indicating many, as in multiply and multitude. Multi- is frequently used to form new modern words, as in multi-media, multipurpose, multi-storey and multi-talented.

-naut a suffix meaning navigator, as in astronaut and cosmonaut.

neo- a prefix meaning new or recent, as neologism and neo-natal.

neuro- a prefix meaning nerve, as neurology, neuron and neurosurgery.

non- a prefix meaning not, as nonsense and nonconformist.

-ock a suffix indicating a diminutive form, as hillock and bullock.

-ocracy a suffix meaning a form of government, as democracy, bureaucracy and meritocracy.

-ology a suffix meaning study of, as biology and geology.

-oholic *see* **-aholic.**

-ology a suffix meaning study of, as in biology, geology and technology.

omni- a prefix meaning all, as in omnipotent and omnivorous.

-osis a suffix meaning **1** a disease as tuberculosis. **2** a development or process , as metamorphosis, a complete or major change.

para- a prefix meaning **1** beside, as paramilitary, paramedic and paranormal. **2** (defence) against, as parasol and parapet.

pen- a prefix meaning almost, as peninsula and penultimate.

per- a prefix meaning through, as permit.

peri- a prefix meaning round, as perimeter and periphery.

-phile a suffix meaning someone who loves or likes someone or something very much, as Francophile, someone who loves France, bibliophile, someone who loves books.

-phobe a suffix meaning someone who hates or fears someone or something very much, as Europhobe and Francophobe. The condition has the suffix **-phobia**, as Europhobia, and there is a whole range of conditions of this kind, as claustrophobia, hatred or fear of enclosed spaces. *See* section in the **Wordfinder** on **Phobias.**

-phone a suffix meaning sound or voice, as megaphone, telephone and saxophone.

poly- a prefix meaning more than one, many, as polyandry, the practice of having more than one husband.

-person *see* **-man.**

post- a prefix meaning after, as postpone, postscript and post-war.

pre- a prefix meaning before, as precede, predict and preface.

pro- a prefix meaning **1** on or forth, as proceed and progress, **2** before, as prologue and prophet. **3** in favour of, as pro-British and pro-hunting.

pseudo- a prefix meaning false, spurious or sham, as pseudo-literary and pseudo-leather.

psych-, psycho- meaning mind, as psychiatry and psychology.

re- a prefix meaning **1** back, as return, resign and retract, **2** again, as reconsider and retrial.

retro-a prefix indicating back, backwards, as retrograde, retrospect and retrorocket.

semi- a prefix meaning half, as semicircle and semi-detached.

-ship a suffix indicating a state or quality, as friendship, hardship and leadership

sub- a prefix meaning under, as submarine, submerge and subconscious.

super- a prefix meaning over, as supervise, supernatural and superfluous.

syn- a prefix meaning together, as synthesis and synonym

techno- a prefix meaning craft or skill, as technical and technology.

tele- a prefix meaning distance, as telephone, telescope and television.

-tor a prefix indicating a person, especially a person who does something, as actor, sponsor and victor.

trans- a prefix meaning across, as transaction, translate and trans-Atlantic.

-trix a prefix indicating a female equivalent, as proprietrix of proprietor, now not very common.

un- a prefix indicating **1** not, as unclean, untrue and unwise, **2** back, reversal, as in undo, unfasten and untie.

uni- a prefix meaning one, as in unicycle, unilateral and unity.

vice- a prefix meaning in place of, as vice-president and vice-chancellor.

-ward, -wards a suffix indicating direction, as homeward, seaward and outwards.

-ware a suffix meaning manufactured goods, as glassware and silverware.

-ways a suffix indicating manner, way or direction, as sideways.

-wise a suffix indicating **1** manner, way, or direction as clockwise, lengthwise and otherwise, **2** with reference to, as careerwise, **3** clever, sensible, as streetwise.

-work a suffix indicating **1** material from which something is made, as ironwork and woodwork, **2** a job or activity, as farmwork, housework and needlework.

Eponyms

An **eponym** refers to a person after whom something is named. The name of the thing in question can also be referred to as an eponym, or it can be said to be **eponymous**, eponymous being the adjective from eponym. English has several eponymous words. Some examples are listed below together with their derivations:

ampere the standard metric unit by which an electric current is measured, called after the French physicist André Marie Ampère, (1775–1836).

atlas a book of maps, called after Atlas, in Greek mythology the leader of the Titans who attempted to storm the heavens and for this supreme treason was condemned by Zeus to hold up the vault of heaven on his head and hands for the rest of his life. The geographer Gerardus Mercator (*see* Mercator projection) used the figure of Atlas bearing the globe as a frontispiece in his 16th-century collection of maps and charts.

aubrietia a trailing purple-flowered perennial plant, called after Claude Aubriet (1665–1742), a French painter of animals and flowers.

Bailey bridge a type of temporary military bridge that can be assembled very quickly, called after Sir Donald Bailey (1901–85), the English engineer who invented it.

baud a unit used in measuring telecommunications transmission speed denoting the number of discrete signal elements that can be transmitted per second, called after the French telecommunications pioneer, Jean M. Baudot (1845–1903).

Beaufort scale a international system of measuring of wind speed, from (calm) to 12 (hurricane), called after Admiral Sir Francis Beaufort (1774–1857), the British surveyor who devised it.

becquerel the standard metric unit of radioactivity, defined as decay per second, called after the French physicist Antoine-Henri Becquerel (1852–1908), who began the study of radioactivity.

begonia a genus of tropical plants cultivated for their showy petalless flowers and ornamental lopsided succulent leaves, called after Michel Begon (1638–1710), a French patron of botany.

Belisha beacon a post surmounted by a flashing light in an orange globe that marks a road crossing for pedestrians, called after the British politician Leslie Hore-Belisha (1893–1957).

Biro™ a type of ball-point pen, called after its Hungarian-born inventor, Laszlo Jozsef Biro (1900–85).

bloomers a women's underpants with full, loose legs gathered at the knee, called after the American social reformer Amelia Jenks Bloomer (1818–94).

bougainvillea a genus of tropical plants with large rosy or purple bracts, called after the French navigator Louis Antoine de Bougainville (1729–1811).

bowdlerize to remove what are considered to be indelicate or indecent words or passages from a book, called after the British doctor, Thomas Bowdler (1754–1825) who produced an expurgated edition of Shakespeare.

bowie knife a type of hunting knife with a long curving blade, called after the American soldier and adventurer James Bowie (1799–1836) who made it popular

boycott to refuse to deal with or trade with a person, organization, etc, in order to punish or coerce, called after the Irish land agent Captain Charles Cunningham Boycott (1832–97) who was accorded such treatment after refusing to reduce rents.

Boyle's law the scientific principle that a volume of gas varies inversely with the pressure of the gas when the temperature is constant, called after the Irish-born British physicist, Robert Boyle (1627–91), who formulated it.

Braille the system of printing for the blind using a system of raised dots that can be understood by touch, called after the blind French musician, Louis Braille (1809–52), who invented it.

Brownian motion the random movement of minutes particles, which occurs in both gases and liquids, called after the Scottish botanist Robert Brown (1773–1858), who first discovered the phenomenon in 1827.

buddleia a genus of shrubs and trees with lilac or yellowish- white flowers, called after Adam Buddle (d.1715), English clergyman and botanist.

Bunsen burner a burner with an adjustable air inlet that mixes gas and air to produce a smokeless flame of great heat, called after the German scientist, Robert Wilhelm Bunsen (1811–99), who invented it.

camellia a genus of oriental evergreen ornamental shrubs, called after the Moravian Jesuit missionary, George Joseph Kamel (1661–1706), who introduced it into Europe.

cardigan a knitted jacket fastened with buttons, called after James Thomas Brudenell, 7th Earl of Cardigan (1797–1868) who was fond of wearing such a garment and was the British cavalry officer who led the unsuccessful Charge of the Light Brigade during the Crimean War (1854).

cardigan, a knitted jacket fastened with buttons called after the Earl of **Cardigan** (1797–1868) who was fond of wearing such a garment and was the British cavalry officer who led the unsuccessful Charge of the Light Brigade during the Crimean War (1854).

Celsius 1 the scale of temperature in which 0° is the freezing point of water and 100° the boiling point, called after Anders Celsius (1701–44), the Swedish astronomer and scientist who invented it.

Celsius 2 the temperature scale, called after the Swedish astronomer, Anders **Celsius** (1701–44).

chauvinism an aggressive patriotism, called after Nicolas Chauvin of Rochefort, 19th-century French soldier in Napoleon's army, and now used to apply to excessive devotion to a belief or case, especially a man's belief in the superiority of men over women.

coulomb the standard metric unit for measuring electric charge, called after the French physicist, Charles Augustin de Coulomb (1736–1806).

dahlia a genus of half-hardy herbaceous perennial plants of the aster family grown for its colourful blooms, called after the Swedish botanist Anders Dahl (1751–89).

daltonism colour blindness, especially the confusion between green and red, called after the British chemist and physicist, John Dalton (1766–1844), who first described it.

Darwinism the theory of evolution by natural selection, called after the British naturalist Charles Robert Darwin (1809–82), who first described the theory.

Davy lamp a safety lamp used by miners to detect combustible gas, called after the English chemist, Sir Humphry Davy (1778–1829), who invented it.

degauss to neutralize or remove a magnetic field, called after the German mathematician Karl Friedrich Gauss (1777–1855). *See also* gauss.

derrick now any crane-like apparatus but formerly a word for a gallows, called after a 17th-century English hangman at Tyburn with the surname of Derrick.

diesel an internal-combustion engine in which ignition is produced by the heat of highly compressed air, called after the German engineer, Rudolf Diesel (1858–1913), who invented it.

Doberman pinscher a breed of dog with a smooth glossy black and tan coat and docked tail, called after the German dog breeder, Ludwig Dobermann (1834–94), who bred it.

Dolby™ an electronic noise-reduction system used in sound recording and playback systems, called after the American engineer, R. Dolby (1933–), who invented it.

Don Quixote a chivalrous or romantic person who tends to be carried away by his ideals and notions, called after Don Quixote, hero of the novel *Don Quixote de la Mancha* by the Spanish novelist Miguel de Cervantes Saavedra (1547–1616). *See also* **quixotic.**

Doppler effect *or* **Doppler shift** a change in the observed frequency of a wave as a result of the relative motion between the wave source and the detector, called after the Austrian physicist, Christian Johann Doppler (1803–53).

draconian an adjective meaning very cruel or severe, called after Draco, the 7th-century bc Athenian statesman who formulated extremely harsh laws.

dunce a person who is stupid or slow to learn, called after the Scottish theologian, John Duns Scotus, Scottish (*c.* 1265–1308).

Earl Grey a blend of Chinese teas flavoured with oil of bergamot, called after the British statesman, Charles, 2nd Earl Grey (1764–1845).

Eiffel Tower the tall tower in the centre of Paris, called after the French engineer, Alexandre Gustave Eiffel (1832–1923, who built it.

einsteinium an artificial radioactive chemical element, called after the German-born American physicist, Albert Einstein (1879–1955).

Everest the highest mountain in the world, called after Sir George Everest (1790–1866), who was Surveyor-General of India.

Fahrenheit the scale of temperatures in which 32° is the freezing point of water and 212° the boiling point, called after the German scientist, Gabriel Daniel Fahrenheit (1686–1736), who invented it.

Fallopian tube either of the two tubes through which the egg cells pass from the ovary to the uterus in female mammals, called after the Italian anatomist, Gabriel Fallopius (1523–62), who first described them.

farad the standard metric unit of capacitance, called after the English physicist and chemist, Michael Faraday (1791–1867), who discovered magnetic induction.

fermi a unit of length employed in nuclear physics, called after the Italian-born American physicist, Enrico Fermi (1901–54).

fermium an artificially produced radioactive element, called after the Italian-born American physicist, Enrico Fermi (1901–54).

forsythia a genus of widely cultivated yellow-flowered ornamental shrubs of the olive family, called after the English botanist, William Forsyth (1737–1804).

Fraunhofer lines dark lines that occur in the continuous spectrum of the sun, called after the German physicist and optician, Joseph von Fraunhofer (1787–1826).

freesia a type of sweet-smelling ornamental flower of the iris family, called after the German physician Friedrich Heinrich Theodor Freese (d. 1876).

fuchsia a genus of decorative shrubs of Central and South America, called after the German botanist and physician, Leonhard Fuchs (1501–66).

Gallup poll a sampling of public opinion, especially to help forecast the outcome of an election, called after the American statistician, George Horace Gallup (1901–84), who devised it.

galvanize to coat one type of metal with another, more reactive metal, e.g. iron or steel coated with zinc, to protect the underlying metal; now also meaning to stimulate into action, called after the Italian physician, Luigi Galvani (1737–98).

gardenia a genus of ornamental tropical trees and shrubs with fragrant white or yellow flowers, called after the Scottish-born American botanist, Dr Alexander Garden (1730–91).

garibaldi a type of biscuit with a layer of currants in it, called after Giuseppe Garibaldi (1807–82), the Italian soldier patriot who is said to have enjoyed such biscuits

gauss a standard unit for measuring magnetic flux density, called after the German mathematician, Karl Friedrich Gauss (1777–1855), who developed the theory of numbers and applied mathematics to electricity, magnetism and astronomy. *See also* **degauss.**

Geiger counter an electronic instrument that can detect and measure radiation, called after the German physicist, Hans Geiger (1882–1945), who developed it.

gerrymander to rearrange the boundaries of a voting district to favour a particular party or candidate, called after the American politician, Elbridge Gerry (1744–1814).

Granny Smith a variety of hard green apple, called after the Australian gardener, Maria Ann Smith, known as Granny Smith (d. 1870) who first grew the apple in Sydney in the 1860s.

greengage a type of greenish plum, called after Sir William Gage (1777–1864), who introduced it into Britain from France.

guillotine an instrument for beheading people by allowing a heavy blade to descend between grooved posts, called after the French physician, Joseph Ignace Guillotin (1738–1814), who advocated its use in the French Revolution.

Halley's comet a periodic comet that appears about every 76 years, called after the British astronomer, Edmund Halley (1656–1742), who calculated its orbit.

Heath Robinson of or pertaining to an absurdly complicated design for a simple mechanism, called after the English artist, William Heath Robinson (1872–1944).

henry a metric unit of electric inductance, called after the American physicist, Joseph Henry (1797–1878), who discovered the principle of electromagnetic induction.

Herculean of extraordinary strength, size or difficulty, called after Hercules, the Roman name for Heracles, in Greek mythology the son of Zeus and the most celebrated hero or semi-divine personage, best known for completing twelve difficult tasks known as the labours of Hercules.

Hoover™ a kind of vacuum cleaner, called after the American businessman, William Henry Hoover (1849–1932).

Jacuzzi™ a device that swirls water in a bath and massages the body, called after the Italian-born engineer, Candido Jacuzzi (*c.* 1903–86).

JCB™ a mechanical earth-mover that has an hydraulically powered shovel and an excavator arm, called after its English manufacturer, Joseph Cyril Bamford (1916–).

joule the metric unit of all energy measurements, called after the British physicist, James Prescott Joule (1818–89) who investigated the relationship between mechanical, electrical and heat energy.

kelvin the metric unit of thermodynamic temperature, called after the Scottish physicist, William Thomson, 1st Baron Kelvin (1824–1907).

Köchel number a number in a catalogue of the works of Mozart, called after the Austrian scientist, Ludwig Alois Friedrich von Köchel (1800–1877), a great admirer of Mozart, who compiled his catalogue in 1862.

leotard a one-piece, close-fitting garment worn by acrobats and dancers, called after the French acrobat, Jules Leotard (1842–70), who introduced the costume as a circus garment.

listeria a bacterium that causes a serious form of food poisoning, listeriosis, called after the British surgeon, Joseph Lister (1827–1912), who pioneered the use of antiseptics.

lobelia a genus of flowers that produce showy blue, red, yellow or white flowers, called after the Flemish botanist, Matthias de Lobel (1538–1616).

Luddite an opponent of industrial change or innovation, called after Ned Ludd, the 18th-century British labourer who destroyed industrial machinery.

macadam a road surface composed of successive layers of small stones compacted into a solid mass, called after the Scottish engineer, John Loudon McAdam, (1756–1836), who invented it.

Mach number the ratio of the speed of a body in a particular medium to the speed of sound in the same medium, called after the Austrian physicist and philosopher, Ernst Mach (1838–1916), who devised it.

Machiavellian cunning, deceitful, double-dealing, using opportunist methods, called after the Florentine statesman and political theorist, Niccolò Machiavelli (1469–1527), author of *The Prince*.

mackintosh a type of raincoat, especially one made of rubberized cloth, called after the Scottish chemist, Charles Macintosh (1760–1843), who patented it in the early 1820s.

malapropism the unintentional misuse of a word by confusing it with another and so producing a ridiculous effect (e.g. "She is as headstrong as an allegory on the banks of the Nile"), called after Mrs Malaprop, a character in the play *The Rivals* (1775), by the Irish playwright Richard Brinsley Sheridan (1751–1816).

martinet a person who exerts strong discipline, called after Jean Martinet (d. 1672), a French army drill master during the reign of Louis XIV.

maverick a stray animal or an independent-minded or unorthodox person, called after the American rancher in Texas, Samuel Augustus Maverick (1803–70), who refused to brand his cattle.

Melba sauce a sauce that is made from raspberries and served with fruit, peach melba, etc, called after the Australian operatic singer Dame Nellie Melba [Helen Porter Mitchell] (1861–1931), for whom it was made. *See also* **Melba toast, peach melba.**

Melba toast bread that is thinly sliced and toasted, called after the Australian operatic singer Dame Nellie Melba [Helen Porter Mitchell] (1861–1931), for whom it was made. *See also* **Melba sauce, peach melba.**

Mercator projection a type of projection for the drawing of maps two-dimensionally, called after the Flemish geographer, Gerardus Mercator [Gerhard Kremer] (1512–94).

mesmerize to hypnotize or to fascinate or spellbind, called after the Austrian physician and pioneer of hypnotism, Franz Anton Mesmer (1734–1815).

Molotov cocktail a kind of crude incendiary weapon made by filling a bottle with petrol and inserting a short short-delay wick or use, called after the Soviet statesman Vyacheslav Mikhailovich Molotov (1890–1986).

Montessori method a system of educating very young children through play, based on free discipline, with each child developing at his or her own pace, called after Maria Montessori (1870–1952), the Italian physicist and educator who developed it.

Moog synthesizer™ a type of synthesizer for producing music electronically, called after Robert Arthur Moog (b. 1934), the American physicist and engineer who developed it.

Morse code a code in which letters are represented by dots and dashes or long and short sounds and are transmitted by visual or audible signals, called after the American artist and inventor, Samuel Finley Breese Morse (1791–1872), who invented it.

narcissism excessive interest in one's own body or self, self-love, called after the myth of Narcissus, a handsome young man in Greek mythology who was punished for his coldness of heart in not returning the love of Echo by being made to fall in love with his own reflection in water and who pined away because he was unable to embrace his reflection.

newton the standard metric unit of force, called after the British physicist and mathematician, Sir Isaac Newton (1642–1727).

Nobel prize an annual international prize given for distinction in one of six areas: physics, chemistry, physiology and medicine, economics, literature, and promoting peace, called after the Swedish chemist and engineer, Alfred Nobel (1833–96), who founded them.

ohm a metric unit of electrical resistance, called after the German physicist, Georg Simon Ohm (1787–1854).

Parkinson's disease a progressive nervous disease resulting in tremor, muscular rigidity, partial paralysis and weakness, called after the British surgeon, James Parkinson (1755–1824), who first described it.

Parkinson's law the law that states that work expands to fill the time available for its completion, called after the British historian and author, Cyril Northcote Parkinson (1909–93), who devised it.

pasteurize to sterilize drink or food by heat or radiation in order to destroy bacteria, called after the French chemist and bacteriologist, Louis Pasteur (1822–95).

pavlova a dessert of meringue cake with a topping of cream and fruit, called after the Russian ballerina, Anna Pavlova (1885–1931), for whom it was made.

peach melba a dessert of peaches, ice cream and Melba sauce, called after the Australian operatic soprano singer, Dame Nellie Melba [Helen Porter Mitchell] (1861–1931), for whom it was made. *See also* **Melba sauce, Melba toast**.

Peter principle the principle that in a hierarchy every employee tends to rise to the level of his or her incompetence, called after the Canadian educator, Laurence J. Peter (1919–90), who formulated it.

Peter's projection a form of projection for depicting the countries of the world two-dimensionally, called after the German history, Dr Arno Peters (1916–), who devised it.

platonic of a close relationship between two people, spiritual and free from physical desire, called after the Greek philosopher, Plato (*c.* 427–347 bc).

plimsoll a type of light rubber-soled canvas shoe, called after Samuel Plimsoll (*See* **Plimsoll line**) because the upper edge of the rubber was thought to resemble the Plimsoll line.

Plimsoll line the set of markings on the side of a ship that indicate the levels to which the ship may be safely be loaded, called after the English shipping reform leader, Samuel Plimsoll (1824–98).

poinsettia a South American evergreen plant, widely cultivated at Christmas for its red bracts, which resemble petals, called after the American diplomat, Joel Roberts Poinsett (1779–1851), who introduced it into the USA.

praline a type of confectionery made from nuts and sugar, called after Count Plessis-Praslin (1598–1675), a French field marshal, whose chef is said to have been the first person to make the sweet

Pulitzer prize one of a series of prizes that are awarded annually for outstanding achievement in American journalism, literature, and music, called after the Hungarian-born US newspaper publisher, Joseph Pulitzer (1847–1911).

Pullman a railway carriage that offers luxury accommodation, called after the American inventor, George Mortimer Pullman (1831–97), who first manufactured them.

quisling a traitor who aids an invading enemy to regularize its conquest of his or her country, called after the Norwegian politician, Vidkun Abraham Quisling (1887–1945), who collaborated with the Nazis.

quixotic, quixotical of a person, chivalrous or romantic to extravagance, unrealistically idealistic, called after Don Quixote, hero of the novel *Don Quixote de la Mancha* by the Spanish novelist Miguel de Cervantes Saavedra (1547–1616).

raglan a type of loose sleeve cut in one piece with the shoulder of a garment, called after the British field marshal, Fitzroy James Henry Somerset, 1st Baron Raglan (1788–1855).

Richter scale a scale ranging from 1 to 10 for measuring the intensity of an earthquake, called after the American seismologist, Charles Richter (1900–85), who devised it.

Romeo a romantic lover, called after Romeo, the hero of Shakespeare's tragedy *Romeo and Juliet*.

Rorschach test a personality test in which the subject has to interpret a series of unstructured ink blots, called after the Swiss psychiatrist, Hermann Rorschach (1884–1922), who devised it.

rutherford a unit of radioactivity, called after the British physicist, Ernest Rutherford, 1st Baron Rutherford (1871–1937).

sadism sexual pleasure obtained from inflicting cruelty upon another, called after the French soldier and writer, Count Donatien Alphonse François de Sade, known as Marquis de Sade (1740–1814).

salmonella the bacteria that cause some diseases such as food poisoning, called after Daniel Elmer Salmon (1850–1914), the American veterinary surgeon who identified it.

sandwich a snack consisting of two pieces of buttered bread with a filling, called after John Montagu, 4th Earl of Sandwich (1718–92), who was such a compulsive gambler that he would not leave the gaming tables to eat but had some cold beef between two slices of bread brought to him.

saxophone a type of keyed brass instrument often used in jazz music, called after Adolphe Sax (1814–94), the Belgian instrument-maker who invented it.

sequoia one of two lofty coniferous Californian trees, called after the American Indian leader and scholar, Sequoya (*c.* 1770–1843), also known as George Guess.

shrapnel an explosive projectile that contains bullets or fragments of metal and a charge that is exploded before impact, called after the British army officer, Henry Shrapnel (1761–1842), who invented it.

siemens the standard metric unit of electrical conductance, called after the German engineer and inventor, Ernst Werner von Siemens (1816–92).

silhouette the outline of a shape against light or a lighter background, called after the French politician, Etienne de Silhouette (1709–67).

simony the buying or selling of ecclesiastical benefits or offices, called after the sorcerer Simon Magnus, who lived in the 1st century ad.

sousaphone the large tuba that encircles the body of the player and has a forward-facing bell, called after the American bandmaster and composer, John Philip Sousa (1854–1932), who invented it.

spoonerism the accidental transposition of the initial letters or opening syllables of two or more words, often with an amusing effect (e.g. "queer old dean" for "dear old queen"), called after the British scholar and clergyman, William Archibald Spooner (1844–1930).

stetson a type of wide-brimmed, high-crowned felt hat, called after its designer, the American hat-maker John Batterson Stetson (1830–1906).

tantalize to tease or torment by presenting something greatly desired but keeping it inaccessible, called after Tantalus, the mythical Greek king of Phrygia, who was punished in Hades for his misdeeds by being forced to stand in water that receded when he tried to drink and under fruit that moved away as he tried to eat.

tontine a financial arrangement in which a group of subscribers contribute equally to a prize that is eventually awarded to the last survivor, called after the Italian banker, Lorenzo Tonti (1635–90), who devised it.

tradescantia a genus of flowering plants cultivated for their foliage, called after the English botanist, gardener and plant hunter, John Tradescant (*c.* 1570–1638).

trilby a type of soft felt hat with an indented crown, called after *Trilby*, the dramatized version of the novel by the English writer George du Maurier. The heroine of the play, Trilby O'Ferral, wore such a hat.

Turing machine a hypothetical universal computing machine, called after the British mathematician, Alan Mathison Turing (1912–54), who conceived it.

Venn diagram a diagram in which overlapping circles are used to show the mathematical and logical relationships between sets, called after the British mathematician and logician, John Venn (1834–1923).

volt the metric unit of measure of the force of an electrical current, called after the Italian physicist, Count Alessandro Volta (1745–1827).

Wankel engine a kind of four-stroke internal-combustion engine with a triangular-shaped rotating piston within an elliptical combustion chamber, called after the German engineer, Felix Wankel (1902–88), who invented it.

watt a metric unit of electrical power, called after the Scottish engineer and inventor, James Watt (1736–1819).

wellington a waterproof rubber boot with no fastenings that extends to the knee, called after Arthur Wellesley, 1st Duke of Wellington (1769–1852), the British soldier who defeated Napoleon at Waterloo (1815).

wisteria *or* **wistaria** a genus of purple-flowered climbing plants, called after the American anatomist, Caspar Wistar (1761–1818).

Zeppelin a rigid cigar-shaped airship, called after the German general and aeronautical pioneer, Count Ferdinand von Zeppelin (1838–1917), who designed and manufactured them.

Irregular Verbs and Nouns

Irregular Verbs

Irregular verbs are verbs that do not conform to the usual pattern of the addition of *-ed* to the past tense and past participle. They fall into several categories.

One category concerns those which have the same form in the past tense and past participle forms as the infinitive and do not end in *-ed*, like regular verbs. These include:

infinitive	past tense	past participle
bet	bet	bet
burst	burst	burst
cast	cast	cast
cost	cost	cost
cut	cut	cut
hit	hit	hit
hurt	hurt	hurt
let	let	let
put	put	put
set	set	set
shed	shed	shed
shut	shut	shut
slit	slit	slit
split	split	split
spread	spread	spread

Some irregular verbs have two past tenses and two past participles which are the same, as in:

infinitive	past tense	past participle
burn	burned, burnt	burned, burnt,
dream	dreamed, dreamt	dreamed, dreamt,
dwell	dwelled, dwelt	dwelled, dwelt,
hang	hanged, hung,	hanged, hung
kneel	kneeled, knelt,	kneeled, knelt
infinitive	**past tense**	**past participle**
lean	leaned, leant	learned, learnt
leap	leaped, leapt,	leaped, leapt
learn	learned, learnt	learned, learnt
light	lighted, lit	lighted, lit
smell	smelled, smelt	smelled, smelt
speed	speeded, sped	speeded, sped
spill	spilled, spilt	spilled, spilt
spoil	spoiled, spoilt	spoiled, spoilt
weave	weaved, woven	weaved, woven
wet	wetted, wet	wetted, wet,

Some irregular verbs have past tenses that do not end in *-ed* and have the same form as the past participle. These include:

infinitive	past tense	past participle
bend	bent	bent
bleed	bled	bled
breed	bred	bred
build	built	built
cling	clung	clung
dig	dug	dug
feel	felt	felt
fight	fought	fought
find	found	found
flee	fled	fled,
fling	flung	flung
get	got	got
grind	ground	ground
hear	heard	heard
infinitive	**past tense**	**past participle**
hold	held	held
keep	kept	kept
lay	laid	laid
lead	led	led
leave	left	left
lend	lent	lent
lose	lost	lost
make	made	made
mean	meant	meant
meet	met	met
pay	paid	paid
rend	rent	rent
say	said	said
seek	sought	sought
sell	sold	sold
send	sent	sent
shine	shone	shone
shoe	shod	shod
sit	sat	sat
sleep	slept	slept
slide	slid	slid
sling	slung	slung

slink	slunk	slunk
spend	spent	spent
stand	stood	stood
stick	stuck	stuck
sting	stung	stung
strike	struck	struck
string	strung	strung
sweep	swept	swept
swing	swung	swung
teach	taught	taught
tell	told	told
think	thought	thought
understand	understood	understood
weep	wept	wept
win	won	won
wring	wrung	wrung

Some irregular verbs have regular past tense forms but two possible past participles, one of which is regular. These include:

infinitive	**past tense**	**past participle**
mow	mowed	mowed, mown
prove	proved	proved, proven
sew	sewed	sewn, sewed
show	showed	showed, shown
sow	sowed	sowed, sown
swell	swelled	swelled, swollen

Some irregular verbs have past tenses and past participles that are different from each other and different from the infinitive. These include:

infinitive	**past tense**	**past participle**
arise	arose	arisen

infinitive	**past tense**	**past participle**
awake	awoke	awoken
bear	bore	borne
begin	began	begun
bid	bade	bidden
bite	bit	bitten
blow	blew	blown
break	broke	broken
choose	chose	chosen
do	did	done
draw	drew	drawn
drink	drank	drunk
drive	drove	driven
eat	ate	eaten
fall	fell	fallen
fly	flew	flown
forbear	forbore	forborne
forbid	forbade	forbidden
forgive	forgave	forgiven
forget	forgot	forgotten
forsake	forsook	forsaken
freeze	froze	frozen
forswear	forswore	foresworn
give	gave	given
go	went	gone
grow	grew	grown
hew	hewed	hewn
hide	hid	hidden
know	knew	known
lie	lay	lain
ride	rode	ridden
ring	rang	rung
saw	sawed	sawn
see	saw	seen
rise	rose	risen
shake	shook	shaken
shrink	shrank	shrunk
slay	slew	slain
speak	spoke	spoken
spring	sprang	sprung
steal	stole	stolen
stink	stank	stunk
strew	strewed	strewn
stride	strode	stridden
strive	strove	striven
swear	swore	sworn
swim	swam	swum
take	took	taken
tear	tore	torn
throw	threw	thrown
tread	trod	trodden
wake	woken	woke
wear	wore	worn
write	written	wrote

Irregular Plural Nouns

Irregular plurals refer to the plural form of nouns that do not form their plural in the regular way. Most nouns in English add *-s* to the singular form to form the plural form, as in *boy* to *boys*.

Some add *-es* to the singular form to form the plural, as in *church* to *churches*. Nouns ending in a consonant followed by *-y* have *-ies* as a regular plural ending. Thus *fairy* becomes *fairies* and *berry* becomes *berries*. The foregoing are all examples of *regular plurals*.

Irregular plurals include words that are different in form from the singular forms and do not simply add an ending. These include *men* from *man*, *women* from *woman* and *mice* from *mouse*.

Some irregular plurals are formed by changing the vowel of the singular forms, as in *feet* from *foot*, *geese* from *goose* and *teeth* from *tooth*.

Some irregular plural forms are formed by adding *-en*, as *oxen* from *ox* and *children* from *child*.

Some nouns ending in *-f* form plurals in *-ves*, as in *loaf* to *loaves*, *half* to *halves*, *wife* to *wives* and *wolf* to *wolves*, but some have alternative endings, as *hoof* to either *hoofs* or *hooves*, and some form regular plurals unchanged, as *roof* to *roofs*.

Some irregular plural forms are the original foreign plural forms of words adopted into English, for example *stimuli* from *stimulus*, *phenomena* from *phenomenon*, *criteria* from *criterion*, *larvae* from *larva*. In modern usage there is a growing tendency to anglicize the plural forms of foreign words. Many of these coexist with the plural form, for example *thesauruses* and *thesauri*, *formulas* and *formulae*, *gateaus* and *gateaux* and *indexes* and *indices*. Sometimes the anglicized plural formed according to the regular English rules differs slightly in meaning from the irregular foreign plural. Thus, *indexes* usually applies to guides in books and *indices* is usually used in mathematics.

Some nouns have irregular plurals in that the plural form and the singular form are the same. These include *sheep*, *grouse* (the game-bird) and *salmon*. Also, some nouns have a regular plural and an irregular plural form. Thus, *brother* has the plural forms *brothers* and *brethren*, although *brethren* is now mainly used in a religious context and is archaic in general English.

Appendix 2
Phrasefinder

Phrasefinder

English Idioms

A1
- **A1** first class, of the highest quality. <A1 is the highest rating given to the condition of ships for Lloyd's Register, Lloyds of London being a major insurance company>.
- **from A to Z** thoroughly, comprehensively.

above
- **above board** open, honest and without trickery. <Card cheats tend to keep their cards under the table, or board>.
- **above (someone's) head** too difficult to understand.
- **get a bit above oneself** to become very vain or conceited.

accident
- **accidents will happen** things go wrong at some time in everyone's life.
- **a chapter of accidents** a series of misfortunes.

account
- **give a good account of oneself** to do well.

ace
- **within an ace of** very close to. <From the game of dice, ace being the term for the side of a dice with one spot>.

Achilles
- **Achilles' heel** the one weak spot in a person. <Achilles, the Greek hero, is said to have been dipped in the River Styx by his mother at birth to make him invulnerable but his heel, by which she was holding him, remained unprotected and he was killed by an arrow through his heel>.

acid
- **acid test** a test that will prove or disprove something conclusively. <From the use of nitric acid to ascertain whether a metal was gold or not. If it was not gold the acid decomposed it>.

across
- **across the board** applying to everyone or to all cases.

act
- **act of God** a happening, usually sudden and unexpected, for which no human can be held responsible.
- **get in on the act** to become involved in some profitable or advantageous activity, especially an activity related to someone else's success.
- **get one's act together** to get organized.

action
- **action stations** a state of preparedness for some activity. <From positions taken up by soldiers in readiness for battle>.
- **get a piece** *or* **slice of the action** to be involved in something, get a share of something.

ad
- **ad hoc** for a particular (usually exclusive) purpose. <Latin, 'to this'>.
- **ad-lib** to speak without preparation, to improvise. <Latin, 'according to pleasure'>.

Adam <**Refers to the biblical Adam**>.
- **Adam's ale** water.
- **not to know (someone) from Adam** not to recognize (someone).
- **the old Adam in us** the sin or evil that is in everyone.

add
- **add fuel to the fire** to make a difficult situation worse.
- **add insult to injury** to make matters worse.

Adonis
- **an Adonis** a very attractive young man. <In Greek legend Adonis was a beautiful young man who was loved by Aphrodite, the goddess of love, and who was killed by a boar while hunting>.

advantage
- **have the advantage of (someone)** to recognize (someone) without oneself being recognized by that person.

aegis
- **under the aegis of (someone)** with the support or backing of (someone). <In Greek legend Aegis was the shield of the god Zeus>.

after
- **after a fashion** in a manner that is barely adequate.
- **after (someone's) own heart** to one's liking; liked or admired by (someone).

against
- **against the clock** in a hurry to get something done before a certain time.
- **be up against it** to be in a difficult or dangerous situation.

age
- **a golden age** a time of great achievement.
- **a ripe old age** a very old age.
- **of a certain age** no longer young.

agony
- **agony aunt** *or* **uncle** a woman or man who gives advice on personal problems either in a newspaper or magazine column, or on television or radio.
- **agony column** a newspaper or magazine column in which readers write in with their problems, which are answered by the agony aunt or uncle. <Originally a newspaper column containing advertisements for missing relatives and friends>.

ahead
- **ahead of the game** in an advantageous position; in front of one's rivals.
- **streets ahead of (someone** *or* **something)** much better than (someone or something).

air
- **air** *or* **wash one's dirty linen in public** to discuss private or personal matters in public.
- **clear the air** to make a situation less tense by settling disagreements.
- **hot air** boasting; empty or meaningless words.
- **into thin air** seemingly into nowhere.
- **put on airs** to behave as though one were superior to others, to act in a conceited way.
- **up in the air** uncertain, undecided.
- **walk on air** to be very happy.

Aladdin
- **Aladdin's cave** a place full of valuable or desirable objects. <From the tale of Aladdin in the Arabian Nights who gained access to such a cave with the help of the genie from his magic lamp>.

alive
- **alive and kicking** in a good or healthy condition.

all
- **all and sundry** everybody, one and all.
- **all chiefs and no Indians** a surplus of people wishing to give orders or to administrate and a deficiency of people willing to carry orders out or to do the work.
- **all ears** listening intently.
- **all in** exhausted.
- **all in one piece** safely, undamaged.
- **all over bar the shouting** at an end to all intents and purposes.
- **all set** ready to go, prepared.
- **all-singing, all-dancing** of a machine, system, very advanced with a great many modern features, sometimes not all necessary. <Used originally of a stage show to indicate how lavish it was>.

alley
- **alley cat** a wild or promiscuous person.

alliance
- **an unholy alliance** used of an association or partnership between two people or organizations that have nothing in common and would not normally work together, especially when this association has a bad purpose.

alma mater
- one's old university, college or school. <Latin, 'bountiful mother'>.

alpha
- **alpha and omega** the beginning and the end. <The first and last letters of the Greek alphabet>.

also
- **also-ran** an unsuccessful person. <A horse-racing term for a horse that is not one of the first three horses in a race>.

altar
- **be sacrificed on the altar of (something)** to be destroyed or suffer harm or damage so that something can be achieved or prosper.

alter
- alter ego a person who is very close or dear to someone. <Latin, 'other self'>.

altogether
- **in the altogether** in the nude.

Amazon
- a very strong or well-built woman. <In Greek legend the Amazons were a race of female warriors who had their right breasts removed in order to draw their bows better>.

American
- **as American as apple pie** typical of the traditional American way of life or culture.
- **the American dream** the hope of achieving success and prosperity through hard work, from the dreams which immigrants had when they landed in America to start a new life.

angel
- **an angel of mercy** a person who gives help and comfort, especially one who appears unexpectedly.
- **a fallen angel** a person who had formerly a good reputation for being virtuous or successful but no longer does so.
- **on the side of the angels** supporting or agreeing with what is regarded as being the good or the right side.

angry
- **angry young man** a person who expresses angry dissatisfaction with established social, political and intellectual values. <A term applied to British dramatist, John Osborne, author of the *play Look Back in Anger*>.

answer
- **the answer to a maiden's prayer** exactly what one desires and is looking for. <The answer to a maiden's prayer was thought to be an eligible bachelor>.

ant
- **have ants in one's pants** to be restless or agitated.

any
- **any old how** in an untidy and careless way.
- **anything goes** any kind of behaviour, dress, etc, is acceptable.

apart
- **be poles** *or* **worlds apart** to be completely different.

ape
- **go ape** to become extremely angry or excited

appearance
- **keep up appearances** to behave in public in such a way as to hide what is going on in private.

apple
- **in apple-pie order** with everything tidy and correctly arranged. <From French *nappe pliée*, 'folded linen', linen neatly laid out>.
- **rotten apple** a person who is bad or unsatisfactory and will have a bad influence on others.
- **the apple of (someone's) eye** a favourite, a person who is greatly loved by (someone). <Apple refers to the pupil of the eye>.
- **upset the apple-cart** to spoil plans or arrangements. <From the practice of selling fruit from carts in street markets>.

apron
- **tied to (someone's) apron-strings** completely dependent on a woman, especially one's mother or wife.

ark
- **like something out of the ark** very old-fashioned looking. <From Noah's ark in the Bible>.

arm
- **armed to the hilt** *or* **teeth** provided with all the equipment that one could possibly need.
- **be up in arms** to protest angrily.
- **chance one's arm** to take a risk.
- **cost an arm and a leg** to cost a great deal of money.
- **give one's right arm for (something)** to be willing to go to any lengths to get something.
- **keep (someone) at arm's length** to avoid becoming too close to or too friendly with someone.
- **the long arm of the law** the power or authority of the police.
- **right arm** chief source of help and support.
- **twist (someone's) arm** to force (someone) to do (something), to persuade (someone) to do (something).
- **with one arm tied behind one's back** very easily.
- **with open arms** welcomingly.

armour
- **chink in (someone's) armour** a weak or vulnerable spot in someone who is otherwise very strong and difficult to get through to or attack. <A knight in armour could be injured only through a flaw or opening in his protective armour>.
- **knight in shining armour** a person who it is hoped will save a situation or come to one's aid. <From medieval legends in which knights in armour came to the aid of damsels in distress>.

ashes
- **rake over the ashes** to discuss things that are passed, especially things that are best forgotten.

- **rise from the ashes** to develop and flourish out of ruin and destruction. <In Greek legend the phoenix, a mythical bird, who after a certain number of years of life set fire to itself and was then reborn from the ashes>.

attendance
- **dance attendance on (someone)** to stay close to (someone) in order to carry out all his or her wishes and so gain favour.

aunt
- **Aunt Sally** a person or thing that is being subjected to general abuse, mockery and criticism. <An Aunt Sally at a fair was a wooden model of a woman's head, mounted on a pole, at which people threw sticks or balls in order to win a prize>.

awakening
- **get/have a rude awakening** suddenly to become aware that a situation is not as good or pleasant as one thinks it is.

away
- **get away from it all** to escape from the problems of daily life, usually by taking a holiday.
- **the one that got away** a chance of success which one either did not or could not take advantage of at the time but which one always remembers. <Refers to a supposedly large fish which an angler fails to catch but about which he tells many stories>.

axe
- **get the axe** to be dismissed.
- **have an axe to grind** to have a personal, often selfish, reason for being involved in something. <From a story told by Benjamin Franklin, the American politician, about how a man had once asked him in his boyhood to demonstrate the working of his father's grindstone and had sharpened his own axe on it while it was working>.

baby
- **be left holding the baby** to be left to cope with a difficult situation that has been abandoned by the person who is really responsible for it.
- **throw out the baby with the bath water** accidentally to get rid of something desirable or essential when trying to get rid of undesirable or unnecessary things.

back
- **backhanded compliment** a supposed compliment that sounds more like criticism.
- **back number** a person or thing that is no longer of importance or of use. <Refers to an out-of-date or back copy of a newspaper or magazine>.
- **backseat driver 1** a passenger in a car who gives unasked-for and unwanted advice. **2** a person who is not directly involved in some activity but who offers unwanted advice.
- **back to the drawing board** to have to start again on a project or activity. <Refers to the board on which plans of buildings, etc, are drawn before being built>.
- **back to the grindstone** back to work.
- **bend over backwards** to go to great trouble.
- **get off (someone's) back** to stop harassing or bothering (someone).
- **have one's back to the wall.** to be in a very difficult or desperate situation. <Someone being pursued has to face his or her pursuers or be captured when a wall prevents retreat>.
- **know (something) backwards** *or* **like the back of one's hand** to know all there is to know about (something).
- **know (someone** *or* **something) like the back of one's hand** to know (someone or something) very well indeed.
- **put one's back into (something)** to put the greatest possible effort into (something).
- **put (someone's) back up** to annoy (someone). <A cat's back arches up when it is angry>.
- **see the back of (someone** *or* **something)** to get rid of (someone or something), not to see (someone or something) again.
- **take a back seat** to take an unimportant or minor role.
- **talk through the back of one's head** to talk nonsense.
- **the back of beyond** a very remote place.

bacon
- **bring home the bacon 1** to earn money to support one's family. **2** to succeed in doing (something). <Perhaps from the winning of a greased pig as a prize at a country fair>.
- **save (someone's) bacon** to save someone from a danger or difficulty.

bad
- **hit a bad patch** to encounter difficulties or a difficult period.
- **in (someone's) bad** *or* **black books** out of favour with (someone). <Refers to an account book where bad debts are noted>.
- **with a bad grace** in an unwilling and bad-tempered way.

bag
- **bag of bones** a person who is extremely thin.
- **bag of tricks** the equipment necessary to do something.
- **in the bag** certain to be obtained. <From the bag used in hunting to carry what one has shot or caught>.
- **mixed bag** a very varied mixture.

bait
- **rise to the bait** to do what someone has been trying to get one to do. <Refers to fish rising to the surface to get the bait on an angler's line>.
- **swallow the bait** to accept completely an offer, proposal, etc, that has been made purely to tempt one. <As above>.

baker
- **baker's dozen** thirteen. <From the former custom of bakers adding an extra bun or loaf to a dozen in order to be sure of not giving short weight>.

balance
- **in the balance** undecided, uncertain. <A balance is a pair of hanging scales>.
- **strike a balance** to reach an acceptable compromise.
- **tip the balance** to exert an influence which, although slight, is enough to alter the outcome of something.

bald
- **bald as a coot** extremely bald. <A coot is a bird with a spot of white feathers on its head>.

ball[1]
- **have a ball** to have a very enjoyable time.

ball[2]
- **a whole new ball game** used to emphasize how much a situation has changed.
- **be in the right ballpark** to be reasonably close to the amount which is required or wanted.
- **have the ball at one's feet** to be in a position to be successful. <From football>.
- **on the ball** alert, quick-witted, attentive to what is going on around one. <Referring to a football player who watches the ball carefully in order to be prepared if it comes to him>.
- **play ball** to act in accordance with someone else's wishes.
- **set** *or* **start the ball rolling** to start off an activity of some kind, often a discussion.

balloon
- **go down like a lead balloon** of a suggestion, idea, joke, etc, to be very badly received.

- **when the balloon goes up** when something serious, usually something that is expected and feared, happens. <From balloons sent up to undertake military observation in World War I, signifying that action was about to start>.

banana
- **go bananas** to go mad, to get extremely angry.

band
- **jump on the bandwagon** to show an interest in, or become involved in, something simply because it is fashionable or financially advantageous. <Refers to a brightly coloured wagon for carrying the band at the head of a procession>.
- **looking as though one has stepped out of a bandbox** looking very neat and elegant. <Refers to a lightweight box formerly used for holding small articles of clothing such as hats>.

bang
- **bang one's head against a brick wall** to do (something) in vain.
- **go with a bang** to be very successful.

bank
- **break the bank** to leave (oneself or someone) without any money. <In gambling terms, to win all the money that a casino is prepared to pay out in one night>.

baptism
- **baptism of fire** a first, usually difficult or unpleasant, experience of something. <From Christian baptism>.

bare
- **the bare bones of (something)** the essential and basic details of (something).

bargain
- **get more than one bargained for** to encounter more difficulty than one had expected or was prepared for.
- **drive a hard bargain** to try to get a deal that is very favourable to oneself.

barge
- **wouldn't touch (someone *or* something) with a bargepole** to wish to have absolutely no contact with (someone or something).

bark
- **bark up the wrong tree** to have the wrong idea or impression about (something), to approach (something) in the wrong way. <From raccoon-hunting, in which dogs were used to locate trees that had raccoons in them>.
- **(someone's) bark is worse than his *or* her bite** a person is not as dangerous or as harmful as he or she appears to be. <Refers to a barking dog that is often quite friendly>.

barrel
- **have (someone) over a barrel** to get (someone) into such a position that one can get him or her to do anything that one wants. <From holding someone over a barrel of boiling oil, etc, where the alternatives for the victim are to agree to demands or be dropped in the barrel>.
- **scrape the (bottom of the) barrel** to have to use someone or something of poor or inferior quality because that is all that is available. <Referring to the fact that people will only scrape out the bottom of an empty barrel if they have no more full ones>.

bat[1]
- **off one's own bat** by oneself, without the help or permission of any one else. <From the game of cricket>.

bat[2]
- **blind as a bat** having very poor eyesight. <Referring to the fact that bats live their lives in darkness>.
- **like a bat out of hell** very quickly.

battle
- **win the battle, but lose the war** to get some of the things which you wanted from an argument, discussion, etc, but to lose your most important goal.

bay
- **keep (someone *or* something) at bay** to keep (someone or something) from coming too close.

be
- **the be-all and end-all** the most important aim or purpose. <From Shakespeare's *Macbeth*, Act 1, scene vii>.

beam
- **off beam 1** on the wrong course. **2** inaccurate. <From the radio beam that is used to bring aircraft to land in poor visibility>.
- **on one's beam ends** very short of money. <Originally a nautical term used to describe a ship lying on its side and in danger of capsizing completely>.

bean
- **know how many beans make five** to be experienced in the ways of the world.
- **spill the beans** to reveal a secret or confidential information.

bear
- **bear garden** a noisy, rowdy place. <Originally referred to a public place used for bear-baiting, in which dogs were made to attack bears and get them angry, for public amusement>.
- **like a bear with a sore head** extremely bad-tempered.

beard
- **beard the lion in its den** to confront or face (someone) openly and boldly.

beat
- **beat about the bush** to approach (something) in an indirect way. <In game-bird hunting, bushes are beaten to make the birds appear>.
- **beat a (hasty) retreat** to run away. <Military orders used to be conveyed by a series of different drum signals>.
- **beat the drum** to try to attract public attention. <The noise of a drum makes people stop and listen>.
- **if you can't beat them (*or* 'em), join them (*or* 'em)** if you cannot persuade other people to think and act like you, the most sensible course of action is for you to begin to think and act like them.
- **off the beaten track** in an isolated position, away from towns or cities.

beauty
- **beauty is in the eye of the beholder** different people have different ideas of what is beautiful.
- **beauty is only skin deep** people have more important qualities than how they look.

beaver
- **eager beaver** a very enthusiastic and hard-working person.
- **work like a beaver** to work very industriously and enthusiastically. <Beavers are small animals that build dams, etc, with great speed and skill>.

beck
- **at (someone's) beck and call** having to be always available to carry out (someone's) orders or wishes. <Beck is a form of 'beckon'>.

bed
- **bed of roses** an easy, comfortable or happy situation.
- **get out of bed on the wrong side** to start the day in a very bad-tempered mood.

bee
- **have a bee in one's bonnet** to have an idea that one cannot stop thinking or talking about, to have an obsession. <A bee trapped under one's hat cannot escape>.

- **make a beeline for (someone *or* something)** to go directly and quickly to (someone or something). <Bees are reputed to fly back to their hives in straight lines>.

beer

- **not all beer and skittles** not consisting just of pleasant or enjoyable things.
- **small beer** something unimportant.

before

- **before one can say Jack Robinson** very rapidly, in an instant.

beg

- **beggar description** to be such that words cannot describe it. <From Shakespeare's *Antony and Cleopatra*, Act 2, scene ii>.
- **beg the question** in an argument, to take for granted the very point that requires to be proved; to fail to deal effectively with the point being discussed.
- **going a-begging** unclaimed or unsold.

bell

- **bell the cat** to be the person in a group who undertakes something dangerous for the good of the group. <Refers to a story about some mice who wanted to put a bell on the neck of the cat so that they would hear it coming and who needed a volunteer to do it>.
- **ring a bell** to bring back vague memories.
- **saved by the bell** rescued from an unpleasant situation by something suddenly bringing that situation to an end. <From the bell that marks the end of a round in boxing>.

belt

- **below the belt** unfair. <In boxing, a blow below the belt is against the rules>.
- **belt and braces** used to describe extra precautions taken to make sure that all is well.
- **tighten one's belt** to reduce one's expenditure. <Belts have to be tightened if one loses weight in this case from having less to spend on food>.

bend

- **on bended knee** very humbly or earnestly.
- **round the bend** mad.

berth

- **give (someone) a wide berth** to keep well away from (someone). <Refers to a ship that keeps a good distance away from others>.

best

- **have the best of both worlds** to benefit from the advantages of two sets of circumstances.
- **put one's best foot forward** to make the best attempt possible.

bet

- **hedge one's bets** to try to protect oneself from possible loss, failure, disappointment, etc. <From betting the same amount on each side to make sure of not losing>.

better

- **have seen better days** to be no longer new or fresh.
- **the better part of (something)** a large part of (something), most of (something).
- **think better of (something)** to reconsider (something), to change one's mind about (something).

beyond

- **beyond the pale** beyond normal or acceptable limits. <The pale was an area of English government in Ireland in the 16th century>.

big

- **a big fish in a small pond** a person who seems better, more important, etc, than he or she is because he or she operates in a small, limited area.
- **the Big Apple** New York.
- **big guns** the most important people in an organization.
- **hit the big time** to be become extremely successful and famous
- **the Big Smoke** London.

bill

- **a clean bill of health** verification that someone is well and fit. <Ships were given clean bills of health and allowed to sail when it was certified that no one aboard had an infectious disease>.
- **fir** or **fill the bill** to be exactly what is required. <Refers originally to a handbill or public notice>.
- **foot the bill** to pay for something, usually something expensive.

bird

- **a bird in the hand is worth two in the bush** something that one already has is much more valuable than things that one might or might not acquire. <A bird in the bush might fly away>.
- **a little bird told me** I found out by a means which I do not wish to reveal.
- **birds of a feather flock together** people who share the same interests, ideas, etc, usually form friendships.
- **give (someone) the bird** of an audience, to express its disapproval of a performer by hissing or booing so that he or she leaves the stage. <From the resemblance of the noise of the audience to the hissing of geese>.
- **kill two birds with one stone** to fulfil two purposes with one action.
- **the birds and the bees** the basic facts of human sexual behaviour and reproduction.
- **the early bird catches the worm** a person who arrives early or acts promptly is in a position to gain advantage over others.

biscuit

- **take the biscuit** to be much worse than anything that has happened so far.

bit

- **champing at the bit** very impatient. <A horse chews at its bit when it is impatient>.
- **take the bit between one's teeth** to act on one's own and cease to follow other people's instructions or advice. <Refers to a horse escaping from the control of its rider>.

bite

- **bite off more than one can chew** to try to do more than one can without too much difficulty.
- **bite the bullet** to do something unpleasant but unavoidable with courage.
- **bite the dust** to die or cease to operate or function.
- **bite the hand that feeds one** to treat badly someone who has helped one.
- **have more than one bite at the cherry** to have more than one opportunity to succeed at something.
- **the biter bit** used to indicate a situation in which someone who has tried to harm or do wrong to someone has suffered in some way as a consequence of this action.

bitter

- **a bitter pill to swallow** something unpleasant or difficult that one has to accept.

black

- **as black as one is painted** as bad as everyone says one is.
- **black sheep** a member of a family or group who is not up to the standard of the rest of the group.
- **in black and white** in writing or in print.
- **in (someone's) black books** *same as* **in (someone's) bad books** *see* **bad.**
- **in the black** showing a profit, not in debt. <From the use of black ink to make entries on the credit side of a ledger>.

blanket

- **on the wrong side of the blanket** illegitimate.
- **wet blanket** a dull person who makes other people feel depressed.

blessing
- **a blessing in disguise** something that turns out to advantage after first seeming unfortunate.

blind
- **the blind leading the blind** referring to a situation in which the person who is in charge of others knows as little as they do.

blood
- **in cold blood** deliberately and calmly.
- **like getting blood out of a stone** very difficult, almost impossible.

blow
- **blow hot and cold** to keep changing one's mind or attitude.
- **blow one's own trumpet** to boast about one's achievements.
- **blow the gaff** to tell something secret, often something illegal, to someone, often the police. <Perhaps from gaff, meaning mouth>.
- **blow the whistle on (someone)** to reveal or report someone's wrongdoing so that it will be stopped. <From the practice of blowing a whistle to indicate a foul in some ball games>.
- **see which way the wind blows** to wait and find out how a situation is developing before making a decision. <From sailing>.

blue
- **blue-eyed boy** a person who is someone's favourite.
- **bluestocking** an educated, intellectual woman. <From a group of women in the 18th century who met in London to discuss intellectual and philosophical issues and some of whom wore blue worsted stockings>.
- **once in a blue moon** hardly ever.
- **out of the blue** without warning.

bluff
- **call (someone's) bluff** to make (someone) prove that what he or she says is true is really genuine. <Refers to poker, the card game>.

board
- **go by the board** to be abandoned. <The board here is a ship's board or side, and to go by the board literally was to vanish overboard>.
- **sweep the board** to win all the prizes. <The board referred to is the surface on which card games are played and on which the bets are placed>.

boat
- **burn one's boats** to do something that makes it impossible to go back to one's previous position.
- **in the same boat** in the same situation.
- **miss the boat** to fail to take advantage of a opportunity.
- **push the boat out** to spend money in an extravagant way in order to celebrate something in a lavish way.
- **rock the boat** to do something to endanger or spoil a comfortable or happy situation.

bolt
- **a bolt from the blue** something very sudden and unexpected.
- **shoot one's bolt** to make one's final effort, have no other possible course of action.

bone
- **a bone of contention** a cause of dispute. <Dogs fight over bones>.
- **have a bone to pick with (someone)** to have a matter to disagree about with (someone). <From dogs fighting over a bone>.
- **make no bones about (something)** to have no hesitation or restraint about (saying or doing something openly). <Originally a reference to finding no bones in one's soup, which was therefore easier to eat>.
- **near the bone 1** referring too closely to something that should not be mentioned; tactless. **2** slightly indecent or crude.

boo
- **would not say boo to a goose** to be extremely timid.

book
- **bring (someone) to book** to make (someone) explain or be punished for his or her actions. <Perhaps referring to a book where a police officer keeps a note of crimes>.
- **by the book** strictly according to the rules.
- **cook the books** illegally to alter accounts or financial records.
- **throw the book at (someone)** to criticize or punish (someone) severely, to charge (someone) with several crimes at once. <Literally, to charge someone with every crime listed in a book>.

boot
- **get the boot** to be dismissed or discharged from one's job.
- **hang up one's boots** to retire from work, to cease doing an activity. <From hanging up football boots after a game>.
- **lick (someone's) boots** to flatter (someone) and do everything he or she wants.
- **pull oneself up by one's bootstraps** to become successful through one's own efforts.
- **put the boot in (someone) 1** to kick (someone) when he or she is already lying on the ground injured. **2** to treat (someone) cruelly or harshly after he or she has suffered already.
- **the boot is on the other foot** the situation has been completely turned round.
- **too big for one's boots** too conceited.

bottle
- **lose one's bottle** not to have the courage to do something or to go on with something

bottom
- **bottom drawer** a collection of articles for the home, which a young woman gathered together before her marriage.
- **hit rock bottom** to reach the lowest possible level.
- **the bottom line 1** the most important point or part of something. **2** the result or outcome. <Refers to the bottom line in a financial statement which indicates the extent of the profit or loss>.

bow[1]
- **bow and scrape** to behave in a very humble and respectful way.
- **take a bow** to accept acknowledgement of one's achievements. <As above>.

bow[2]
- **draw the long bow** to exaggerate. <An archer carries a spare bow in case one breaks>.
- **have another/more than one string to one's bow** to have another possibility, plan, etc, available to one.

brain
- **cudgel** *or* **rack one's brains** to think very hard.
- **pick (someone's) brains** to find out (someone's) ideas and knowledge about a subject so that one can put them to one's own use.

brass
- **get down to brass tacks** to consider the basic facts or issues of something.

bread
- **know which side one's bread is buttered** to know the course of action that is to one's greatest advantage.
- **on the breadline** with scarcely enough money to live on.
- **the greatest thing since sliced bread** a person or thing that is greatly admired.

breath
- **hold one's breath** to wait anxiously for something.
- **take (someone's) breath away** to surprise (someone) greatly.
- **waste one's breath** to say something that is not taken heed of.

breathe
- **breathe down (someone's) neck 1** to be very close behind (someone). **2** to be waiting impatiently for something from (someone).

brick

- **like a cat on hot bricks** very nervous or restless.
- **try to make bricks without straw** to try to do something without the necessary materials or equipment. <A biblical reference, from Pharaoh's command concerning the Israelites in Exodus 5:7>.

bridge

- **build bridges** to do something to help people who are in some kind of opposition to each other to understand each other so that they ar eable to establish a relationship or co-operate with each other.
- **cross a bridge when one comes to it** to worry about or deal with a problem only when it actually arises.

bright

- **bright-eyed and bushy-tailed** very cheerful and lively.
- **look on the bright side** to be optimistic, to see the advantages of one's situation.

broad

- **have broad shoulders** to be able to accept a great deal of responsibility, criticism, etc.
- **in broad daylight** during the day.

brother

- **am I my brother's keeper?** the actions or affairs of other people are not my responsibility. <From the biblical story of Cain and Abel, Genesis 4:9>.
- **Big Brother** a powerful person or organization thought to be constantly monitoring and controlling people's actions. <From the dictator in George Orwell's novel *1984*>.

brown

- **in a brown study** deep in thought.

bucket

- **a drop in the bucket** a very small part of what is needed.
- **kick the bucket** to die. <Bucket here is perhaps a beam from which pigs were hung after being killed>.
- **weep buckets** to cry a great deal.

bull

- **hit the bull's eye** to do or say something that is very appropriate or relevant. <Refers to the exact centre of a dart board>.
- **like a bull at a gate** in a very unsubtle, unthinking way.
- **like a bull in a china shop** in a very clumsy way.
- **take the bull by the horns** to tackle (something) boldly.

bullet

- **get the bullet** to be dismissed or discharged.

burn

- **the burning question** a question of great interest to many people.

burton

- **gone for a Burton** dead, ruined, broken, etc. <Originally a military term from Burton, a kind of ale>.

bus

- **busman's holiday** a holiday spent doing much the same as one does when one is at work. <Refers to a bus driver who drives a bus on holiday>.

bush

- **bush telegraph** the fast spreading of information by word of mouth. <A reference to the Australian bush>.

business

- **mean business** to be determined (to do something), to be serious.
- **mind one's own business** to concern oneself with one's own affairs and not interfere in those of other people.

butter

- **butterfingers** a person who often drops things.
- **look as though butter would not melt in one's mouth** to appear very innocent, respectable, etc.

butterfly

- **have butterflies in one's stomach** to have a fluttering sensation in one's stomach as a sign of nervousness.

cake

- **a piece of cake** something easy to do.
- **a slice** *or* **share of the cake** a share of something desirable or valuable.
- **have one's cake and eat it** *or* **eat one's cake and have it** to have the advantages of two things or situations when doing, possessing, etc, one of them would normally make the other one impossible.
- **sell** *or* **go like hot cakes** to sell very quickly.

cage

- **rattle (someone's) cage** to annoy or agitate (someone). <From visitors to a zoo rattling the cages of the animals to get them to react>.

calf

- **kill the fatted calf** to provide a lavish meal, especially to mark a celebration of someone's arrival or return. <From the parable of the prodigal son in the Bible, Luke 15:23>.

can

- **carry the can** to accept blame or responsibility, usually for something that someone else has done.

candle

- **burn the candle at both ends** to work and/or to play during too many hours of the day.
- **cannot hold a candle to (someone)** to be not nearly as good or as talented as (someone). <Literally, someone who is not good enough even to hold a light while someone else does the work>.
- **the game is not worth the candle** something that is not worth the effort that has to be spent on it. <From the translation of the French phrase *le jeu n'en vaut la chandelle*, referring to a gambling session in which the amount of money at stake was not enough to pay for the candles required to give light at the game>.

canoe

- **paddle one's own canoe** to control one's own affairs without help from anyone else.

cap

- **cap in hand** humbly. <Removing one's cap in someone's presence is a sign of respect>.
- **if the cap fits, wear it** if what has been said applies to you, then you should take note of it.
- **set one's cap at (someone)** to try to attract (someone of the opposite sex). <Perhaps a mistranslation of French *metter le cap*, to head towards>.

card

- **have a card up one's sleeve** to have an idea, plan of action, etc, in reserve to be used if necessary. <From cheating at cards>.
- **on the cards** likely. <From reading the cards in fortune-telling>.
- **play one's cards close to one's chest** to be secretive or non-communicative about one's plans or intentions. <From holding one's cards close to one in card-playing so that one's opponents will not see them>.
- **play one's cards right** to act in such a way as to take advantage of a situation.
- **put one's cards on the table** to make known one's plans or intentions. <In card-playing, to show one's opponent one's cards>.

carpet

- **sweep (something) under the carpet** to try to hide or forget about (something unpleasant).
- **the red carpet** special, respectful treatment. <Refers to the red carpet put down for a royal person to walk on during official visits>.

carrot

- **carrot and stick** reward as a method of persuasion.

carry

- **carry a torch for (someone)** to be in love with someone, especially with someone who does not return it. <A torch or a flame was regarded as symbolic of love>.

cart

- **put the cart before the horse** to do or say things in the wrong order.

casanova

- **Casanova** a man who has relationships with many women. <From Giacomo Casanova, a famous 18th-century Italian lover and adventurer>.

cassandra

- **Cassandra** a person who makes predictions about unpleasant future events but who is never believed. <In Greek legend, Cassandra, who was the daughter of Priam, king of Troy, had the gift of prophecy but was destined never to be believed. She predicted the fall of Troy>.

cast

- **cast pearls before swine** to offer something valuable or desirable to someone who does not appreciate it. <A biblical reference to Matthew 7:6>.

castle

- **castles in the air** *or* **castles in Spain** dreams or hopes that are unlikely ever to be realized.

cat

- **curiosity killed the cat** said as a warning not to pry into other people's affairs.
- **let the cat out of a bag** to reveal something secret or confidential, especially accidentally or at an inappropriate time. <Supposedly referring to a fairground trick in which a customer was offered a cat in a bag when he or she thought it was a piglet in the bag>.
- **like a scalded cat** in a rapid, excited way.
- **like something the cat brought** *or* **dragged in** very untidy or bedraggled.
- **not enough room to swing a cat** very little space.
- **not to have a cat's chance in hell** *or* **a cat's chance in hell** to have no chance at all.
- **play cat and mouse with (someone)** to treat (someone) in such a way that he or she does not know what is going to happen to them at any time. <A cat often plays with its prey, a mouse, before killing it>.
- **put** *or* **set the cat among the pigeons** to cause a disturbance, especially a sudden or unexpected one.
- **rain cats and dogs** to rain very heavily.
- **see which way the cat jumps** to wait and see what other people are going to do and how the situation is developing before deciding on one's course of action.
- **there's more than one way to kill** *or* **skin a cat** there's more than one way or method of doing things.
- **when the cat's away, the mice will play** when the person in charge or in control is not present the people whom he or she is in charge of will work less hard, misbehave, etc.

catch

- **catch (someone) napping** to surprise (someone) when he or she is unprepared or inattentive.
- **Catch 22** a situation in which one can never win or from which one can never escape, being constantly hindered by a rule or restriction that itself changes to block any change in one's plans; a difficulty that prevents one from escaping from an unpleasant or dangerous situation. <From the title of a novel by Joseph Heller>.
- **catch (someone) with his** *or* **her pants** *or* **trousers down** to surprise (someone) when he or she is unprepared or doing something wrong, especially when this causes embarrassment. <Refers to walking in on someone partially dressed>.

caviar

- **caviar to the general** something considered to be too sophisticated to be appreciated by ordinary people. <From Shakespeare's *Hamlet*, Act 2, scene ii>.

ceiling

- **go through the ceiling** to rise very high, to soar.
- **hit the ceiling** *or* **roof** to lose one's temper completely.

chalice

- **hand/give (someone) a poisoned chalice** to be given something to do which seems an attractive proposition but which may well lead to failure or extreme difficulties.

chalk

- **as different as chalk and cheese** completely different.
- **chalk it up to experience** accept the inevitability of something.
- **not by a long chalk** not by a long way, by no means. <From the vertical chalk lines drawn to mark scores in a game, the longer lines representing the greater number of points>.

chance

- **have an eye to the main chance** to watch carefully for what will be advantageous or profitable to oneself.
- **not to have the ghost of a chance** not to have the slightest possibility of success.
- **change hands** to pass into different ownership.

change

- **change horses in mid-stream** to change one's opinions, plans, sides, etc, in the middle of something.
- **change one's tune** to change one's attitude or opinion.
- **ring the changes** to add variety by doing or arranging things in different ways.

chapter

- **chapter and verse** detailed sources for a piece of information. <From the method of referring to biblical texts>.

charity

- **charity begins at home** one must take care of oneself and one's family before concerning oneself with others.
- **cold as charity** extremely cold. <Charity is referred to as cold since it tends to be given to the poor and disadvantaged by organizations rather than by individual people and so lacks human feeling or warmth>.

charm

- **lead a charmed life** regularly to have good fortune and avoid misfortune, harm or danger.
- **work like a charm** to be very effective, to work very well.

chase

- **chase after rainbows** to spend time and effort in thinking about, or in trying to obtain, things that it is impossible for one to achieve.
- **cut to the chase** to start discussing or dealing with the most important part of something instead of wasting time on minor points. <Refers to the fact that in certain kinds of film a car chase is the most exciting part>.

cheek

- **cheek by jowl** side by side, very close together.
- **turn the other cheek** to take no action against someone who has harmed

one, thereby giving him or her the opportunity to harm one again. <A biblical reference to Matthew 5:39, 'Whosoever shall smite thee on thy right cheek, turn to him the left one also'>.

cheese
- **hard cheese** bad luck, a sentiment usually expressed by someone who does not care about the misfortune.

cheshire
- **grin like a Cheshire cat** to smile broadly so as to show one's teeth. <Refers to *Alice's Adventures in Wonderland* by Lewis Carroll, in which the Cheshire cat gradually disappears except for its smile>.

chest
- **get (something) off one's chest** to tell (someone) about something that is upsetting, worrying or annoying one.
- **old chestnut** an old joke, usually one no longer funny.
- **pull (someone's) chestnuts out of the fire** to rescue (someone) from a difficult or dangerous situation, often by putting oneself in difficulty or danger. <From a story by the 17th-century French writer La Fontaine, in which a monkey use a cat's paw to get hot nuts from a fire>.

chew
- **chew the cud** to think deeply about something.
- **chew the fat** to have a discussion or conversation.

chicken
- **chickens come home to roost** misdeeds, mistakes, etc, that come back with an unpleasant effect on the person who performed the misdeed, especially after a considerable time.
- **count one's chickens before they are hatched** to make plans which depend on something that is still uncertain.

child
- **child's play** something that is very easy to do.

chin
- **keep one's chin up** not to show feelings of depression, worry or fear.
- **take it on the chin** to accept or to suffer (something) with courage.

chip
- **a chip off the old block** a person who is very like one of his or her parents.
- **cash in one's chips** to die. <Refers to a gambler cashing in his or her chips or tokens in exchange for money at the end of a session>.
- **have a chip on one's shoulder** to have an aggressive attitude and act as if everyone is going to insult or ill-treat one, often because one feels inferior. <Refers to a former American custom by which a young man who wished to provoke a fight would place a piece of wood on his shoulder and dare someone to knock it off>.
- **have had one's chips** to have had, and failed at, all the chances of success one is likely to get. <Refers to gambling tokens>.
- **when the chips are down** when a situation has reached a critical stage. <A gambling terms indicating that the bets have been placed>.

choice
- **Hobson's choice** no choice at all; a choice between accepting what is offered or having nothing at all. <Refers to the practice of Tobias Hobson, an English stable-owner in the 17th century, of offering customers only the horse nearest the stable door>.

chop
- **chop and change** to keep altering (something), to keep changing (something).
- **get the chop 1** to be dismissed or discontinued. **2** to be killed.

chord
- **strike a chord** to be familiar in some way.
- **touch a chord** to arouse emotion or sympathy.

circle
- **come full circle** to return to the position or situation from which one started.
- **go round in circles** to keep going over the same ideas without reaching a satisfactory decision or answer.
- **run round in circles** to dash about and appear to be very busy without accomplishing anything.
- **vicious circle** an unfortunate or bad situation, the result of which produces the original cause of the situation or something similar. <In logic, the term for the fallacy of proving one statement by the evidence of another which is itself only valid if the first statement is valid>.

circus
- **a three-ring circus** a place where there is a lot of noise and a lot of confused activity going on.

clean
- **a clean slate** a record free of any discredit; an opportunity to make a fresh start. <Slates were formerly used for writing on in schools>.
- **come clean** to tell the truth about something, especially after lying about it.
- **keep one's nose clean** to keep out of trouble, to behave well or legally.
- **make a clean breast of (something)** to admit to (something), especially after having denied it.
- **make a clean sweep** to get rid of everything which is unnecessary or unwanted.
- **show a clean pair of heels** to run away very quickly.
- **squeaky clean** free of all guilt or blame. <Clean surfaces tend to squeak when wiped>.
- **take (someone) to the cleaners** to cause (someone) to spend or lose a great deal of money.

clear
- **clear as a bell** very easy to hear. <Bells, such as church bells, are very audible>.
- **clear as crystal** very easy to understand or grasp.
- **clear as mud** not at all easy to understand or grasp.
- **clear the decks** to tidy up, especially as a preparation for some activity or project. <Refers to getting a ship ready for battle>.
- **steer clear of (someone *or* something)** to keep away from or avoid (someone or something).
- **the coast is clear** the danger or difficulty has now passed. <Probably a military term indicating that there were no enemy forces near the coast and so an invasion was possible>.

cleft
- **in a cleft stick** unable to decide between two equally important or difficult courses of action.

clip
- **clip (someone's) wings** to limit the freedom, power or influence of (someone). <From the practice of clipping the wings of a bird to prevent it flying away>.

cloak
- **cloak-and-dagger** involving or relating to a great deal of plotting and scheming. <The combination of a cloak and a dagger suggests conspiracy>.

clock
- **like clockwork** very smoothly, without problems.
- **put back the clock *or* turn the clock back** to return to the conditions or situation of a former time.
- **round the clock** all the time; for twenty-four hours a day.

close[1]
- **behind closed doors** in secret.

close[2]

- **a close shave** something that was only just avoided, especially an escape from danger, failure, etc.

cloud

- **cloud cuckoo land** an imaginary place, where everything is perfect; an unreal world.
- **every cloud has a silver lining** something good happens for every bad or unpleasant thing.
- **have one's head in the clouds** to be day-dreaming and not paying attention to what is going on around one.
- **on cloud nine** extremely happy.
- **under a cloud** under suspicion, in trouble.

coach

- **drive a coach and horses through (something)** to destroy (an argument etc) completely by detecting and making use of the weak points in it. <Refers to the fact that the defects (or holes) in the argument are so large as to let a coach and horses through them>.

coal

- **carry** *or* **take coals to Newcastle** to do something that is completely unnecessary, especially to take something to a place where there is already a great deal of it. <Refers to Newcastle in England which was a large coal-mining centre>.
- **haul (someone) over the coals** to scold (someone) very severely.

coat

- **cut one's coat according to one's cloth** to organize one's ideas and aims, particularly one's financial aims, so that they are within the limits of what one has or possesses.

cobweb

- **blow away the cobwebs** to make (someone) feel more energetic and alert after feeling rather tired and dull.

cock

- **a cock-and-bull story** an absurd story that is unlikely to be believed.
- **cock a snook at (someone)** to express one's defiance or contempt of (someone). <Originally referring to a rude gesture of contempt made by putting the end of one's thumb on the end of one's nose and spreading out and moving one's fingers>.
- **go off at half cock** to be unsuccessful because of lack of preparation or because of a premature start. <Refers to a gun that fires too soon>.

coffee

- **wake up and smell the coffee** to become more aware of and more realistic about what is going on around one.

coin

- **pay (someone) back in his** *or* **her own coin** to get one's revenge on someone who has done harm to one by treating him or her in the same way.
- **the other side of the coin** the opposite argument, point of view, etc.

cold

- **get cold feet** to become nervous and change one's mind about being involved in (something).
- **give (someone) the cold shoulder** to act in an unfriendly way to (someone) by ignoring him or her.
- **in a cold sweat** in a state of great fear or anxiety. <From the fact that the skin tends to become cold and damp when one is very frightened>.
- **make (someone's) blood run cold** to cause terror or great distress in (someone).
- **pour** *or* **throw cold water on (something)** to discourage enthusiasm for (something).

colour

- **change colour** to become either very pale or else very red in the face through fear, distress, embarrassment, anger, guilt, etc.
- **nail one's colours to the mast** to commit oneself to a point of view or course of action in a very obvious and final way. <Refers to a ship's colours or flag. If this was nailed to the mast it could not be lowered, lowering the flag being a sign of surrender>.
- **show oneself in one's true colours** to reveal what one is really like after pretending to be otherwise. <Refers to a ship raising its colours or flag to indicate which country or side it was supporting>.
- **with flying colours** with great success. <Refers to a ship leaving a battle with its colours or flag still flying as opposed to lowering them in surrender>.

common

- **common-or-garden** completely ordinary.

conjure

- **a name to conjure with** the name of someone very important, influential or well known. <The suggestion is that such people have magical powers>.

contradiction

- **a contradiction in terms** a statement, idea, etc, that contains a contradiction.

convert

- **preach to the converted** to speak enthusiastically in favour of something to people who already admire it or are in favour of it.

cook

- **too many cooks spoil the broth** if there are a great many people involved in a project they are more likely to hinder it than help it.

cookie

- **that's the way the cookie crumbles** that is the situation and one must just accept it. <Cookie is American English for biscuit>.

cool

- **cool as a cucumber** very calm and unexcited.
- **cool** *or* **kick one's heels** to be kept waiting.
- **keep one's cool** to remain calm.
- **lose one's cool** to become angry, excited etc.

copy

- **blot one's copybook** to spoil a previously good record of behaviour, achievement, etc, by doing something wrong.

corn

- **tread on (someone's) corns** to offend (someone).

corner

- **cut corners** to use less money, materials, effort, time, etc, than is usually required or than is required to give a good result.
- **from all (four) corners of the earth** from every part of the world, from everywhere.
- **in a tight corner** in an awkward, difficult or dangerous situation.
- **paint oneself into a corner** to get oneself into a difficult situation from which there is only one method of escape or action.
- **turn the corner** to begin to get better or improve.

cost

- **cost a bomb** *or* **a packet** to cost a very great deal of money.
- **cost an arm and a leg** to cost an excessive amount of money.
- **cost the earth** to cost a very great deal of money.

cotton

- **wrap (someone) in cotton wool** to be over-protective of (someone).

count

- **out for the count** unconscious or deeply asleep. <Refers to boxing where a boxer who has been knocked down by his opponent has to get up again before the referee counts to ten in order to stay in the match>.

courage
- **have the courage of one's convictions** to be brave enough to do what one thinks one should.
- **pluck up** *or* **screw up courage** to force oneself to be brave.

court
- **laugh (someone** *or* **something) out of court** not to give serious consideration to (someone or something). <Refers to a trivial legal case>.
- **pay court to (someone)** to try to gain the love of (someone).
- **the ball is in (someone's) court** it is (someone's) turn to take action.
- **rule (something) out of court** to prevent (something) from being considered for (something). <Refers to a court of law where evidence, etc, ruled out of court has no effect on the case>.

coventry
- **send (someone) to Coventry** collectively to refuse to associate with (someone). <Perhaps from an incident in the English Civil War when Royalists captured in Birmingham were sent to the stronghold of Coventry>.

cow
- **a sacred cow** something that is regarded with too much respect for people to be allowed to criticize it freely. <The cow is considered sacred by Hindus>.
- **till** *or* **until the cows come home** for an extremely long time. <Cows walk very slowly from the field to the milking sheds unless someone hurries them along>.

crack
- **a fair crack of the whip** a fair share, a fair chance of doing (something).
- **at (the) crack of dawn** very early in the morning.
- **crack the whip** to treat sternly or severely those under one's control or charge. <From the use of a whip to punish people>.
- **take a sledgehammer to crack a nut** to spend a great deal of effort on a small task or problem.

crest
- **be (riding) on the crest of a wave** to be going through a very successful period.

cricket
- **not cricket** not fair or honourable, unsportsmanlike. <The game of cricket is regarded as being played in a gentlemanly way>.

crocodile
- **crocodile tears** a pretended show of grief or sorrow. <Refers to an old belief that crocodiles weep while eating their prey>.

cross
- **cross the Rubicon** to do something that commits one completely to a course of action that cannot be undone. <Julius Caesar's crossing of the River Rubicon in 49bc committed him to war with the Senate>.
- **have a cross to bear** to have to suffer or tolerate a responsibility, inconvenience or source of distress. <Refers to the fact that in the days of crucifixions, those being crucified had to carry their own crosses>.
- **talk at cross purposes** to be involved in a misunderstanding because of talking or thinking about different things without realizing it.

crow
- **eat crow** to have to admit or accept that one was wrong.

crunch
- **when it comes to the crunch** when a time of testing comes, when a decision has to be made.

cry
- **a far cry from (something)** a long way from (something), very different from (something).
- **cry over spilt milk** to waste time regretting a misfortune or accident that cannot be undone.
- **in full cry** enthusiastically and excitedly pursuing something. <Refers to the cry made by hunting dogs>.

cuckoo
- **a cuckoo in the nest** a person who gains some kind of advantage from a situation without contributing anything useful. <From the cuckoo's habit of laying their eggs in other birds' nests>.

cudgel
- **take up the cudgels on behalf of (someone** *or* **something)** to fight strongly on behalf of (someone or something), to support (someone or something) vigorously.

cue
- **take one's cue from (someone)** to use the actions or reactions of (someone) as a guide to one's own, to copy (someone's) actions. <A theatrical term, literally meaning to use the words of another actor as a signal for one to speak or move>.

cuff
- **off the cuff** without preparation. <Refers to the habit of some after-dinner speakers of making brief headings on the celluloid cuffs of their evening shirts as a reminder of what he or she wanted to say rather than preparing a formal speech>.

cup
- **not be one's cup of tea** not to be something which one likes or appreciates.

cupboard
- **cupboard love** pretended affection shown for a person because of the things he or she gives one. <From people and animals liking those who feed them, food being kept in cupboards>.
- **curry favour with (someone)** to try to gain the approval or favour of (someone) by insincere flattery or by being extremely nice to him or her all the time. <Originally curry favel, from Old French *estriller fauvel, fauvel* being a chestnut horse>.

curtain
- **be curtains for (someone** *or* **something)** to be the end of (someone or something). <Refers to curtains falling at the end of a stage performance>.
- **bring down the curtain on (something)** to cause (something) to come to an end. <See above>.
- **curtain lecture** a private scolding, especially one given by a wife to a husband. <From the curtains that formerly were hung round a bed>.

cut
- **a cut above (someone** *or* **something)** rather better than (someone or something).
- **cut a long story short** to give a brief account of something quite complicated or lengthy.
- **cut and dried** settled and definite. <Refers to wood that has been cut and dried and made ready for use>.
- **cut and thrust** methods and techniques of rivalry, argument or debate. <Refers to sword fighting>.
- **cut both ways** to have an equal or the same effect on both parts of a question or on both people involved in something.
- **cut it fine** to allow hardly enough time to do or get something.
- **not cut out for (something)** not naturally suited to.

cylinder
- **firing on all cylinders** working or operating at full strength. <Literally used of an internal combustion engine>.

dagger
- **at daggers drawn** feeling or showing great hostility towards each other.
- **look daggers at (someone)** to look with great dislike or hostility at (someone).

daisy

- **be pushing up the daisies** to be dead.
- **fresh as a daisy** not at all tired, lively.

damp

- **a damp squib** something which is expected to be exciting, effective, etc, but which fails to live up to its expectations. <Refers to a wet firework that fails to go off>.
- **put a damper on (something)** to reduce the enjoyment, optimism, happiness of (something).

dance

- **lead (someone) a (merry) dance** to cause (someone) a series of great, usually unnecessary, problems or irritations.

darby

- **Darby and Joan** a devoted elderly couple. <From the names of such a couple in an 18th-century English ballad>.

dark

- **a shot in the dark** an attempt or guess based on very little information.
- **be whistling in the dark** to try to give the impression that one is more confident of, or less worried about, a situation than one actually is.
- **dark horse** a person or thing whose abilities, worth, etc, is unknown.
- **in the dark** lacking knowledge or awareness.
- **keep it** *or* **something dark** to keep it or something secret.

dash

- **cut a dash** to wear very smart or unusual clothes and so impress others.

davy Jones

- **Davy Jones's locker** the bottom of the sea. <Davy Jones was a name given in the 18th century to the ruler of the evil spirits of the sea>.

dawn

- **a false dawn** an event which makes a situation look as though it is improving when it is not.

day

- **all in a day's work** all part of one's normal routine, not requiring extra or unusual effort.
- **any day of the week** whatever the circumstances.
- **call it a day** to put an end to (something); to stop doing (something), especially to stop working.
- **carry** *or* **win the day** to be successful, to gain a victory. <Originally a military term meaning to win a battle>.
- **daylight robbery** the charging of prices that are far too high.
- **(your, etc) days are numbered** you are about to be dismissed, be killed, etc.
- **every dog has his day** everyone will get an opportunity at some time.
- **have had one's** *or* **its day** to be past the most successful part of one's or its life.
- **live from day to day** to think only about the present without making any plans for the future.
- **make (someone's) day** to make (someone) very pleased or happy.
- **name the day** to announce the date of one's wedding.
- **not to be one's day** to be a day when nothing seems to go right for one.
- **one of these days** at some time in the future.
- **one of those days** a day when nothing seems to go right.
- **see daylight** to be coming to the end of a long task.
- **seize the day** to take advantage of any opportunities which occur now, rather than worry about the future.

dead

- **a dead duck** a person or thing that is very unlikely to survive or continue.
- **a dead loss** a person or thing that is completely useless or unprofitable.
- **cut (someone) dead** to ignore (someone) completely.
- **dead and buried** completely dead or extinct with no chance of being revived.
- **dead as a dodo** completely dead or out of fashion. <Refers to a flightless bird that has been extinct since 1700>.
- **dead beat** exhausted.
- **dead from the neck up** extremely stupid.
- **dead in the water** with no hope of success. <Refers to a dead fish which is no use to fishermen or anglers.>
- **Dead Sea fruit** a thing that appears to be, or is expected to be, of great value but proves to be valueless. <Refers to a fruit, the apple of Sodom, that was thought to grow on trees beside the shores of the Dead Sea. It was beautiful to look at but fell to ashes when touched or tasted>.
- **dead to the world** in a very deep sleep.
- **dead wood** a person or thing that is no longer necessary or useful.
- **enough to waken the dead** extremely loud.
- **let the dead bury their dead** past problems, quarrels, etc, are best forgotten. <A biblical reference to Matthew 8:22, in which Jesus said, 'Follow me and let the dead bury their dead'.>
- **over my dead body** in the face of my fierce opposition.
- **step into** *or* **fill dead men's shoes** to take over the position of someone who has died or left under unfortunate circumstances.
- **would not be seen dead in** *or* **with, etc**, extremely unlikely to be seen wearing something, accompanying someone, etc, because of an extreme dislike or aversion.

deaf

- **deaf as a post** completely deaf.
- **fall on deaf ears** not to be listened to, to go unnoticed or disregarded.
- **stone deaf** completely deaf.
- **turn a deaf ear to (something)** to refuse to listen to (something), to take no notice of (something).

deal

- **a raw deal** unfair treatment.

death

- **at death's door** extremely ill, dying.
- **be in at the death** to be present at the end or final stages of something. <Refers originally to being present at the death of the prey in a hunt>.
- **catch one's death (of cold)** to become infected with a very bad cold.
- **dice with death** to do something extremely risky and dangerous.
- **die the death** to be badly received. <Refers originally to an actor or performer getting a poor reception from the audience>.
- **sick** *or* **tired to death of (someone** *or* **something)** extremely weary or bored with (someone or something).
- **sign one's own death warrant** to bring about one's own downfall, ruin, etc.
- **will be the death of (someone) 1** to cause the death of (someone). **2** to make (someone) laugh a great deal.

deck

- **hit the deck** to fall to the ground.

deep

- **be thrown in at the deep end** to be put suddenly into a difficult situation of which one has no experience. <Refers to the deep end of a swimming pool>.
- **go off at the deep end** to lose one's temper. (See above).

degree

- **give (someone) the third degree** to subject (someone) to intense questioning, especially by using severe methods.
- **to the nth degree** to the greatest possible degree, extent or amount. <Refers to the use of n as a symbol to represent a number, especially a large number>.

dent

- **make a dent in (something)** to reduce (something) by a considerable amount.

depth

- **out of one's depth** in a situation which one cannot cope with. <Refers literally to being in water deeper than one can stand up in>.
- **plumb the depths of (something)** to reach the lowest level of unhappiness, misfortune, etc.

deserts

- **get one's just deserts** to be treated as one deserves, especially to receive deserved punishment.

design

- **have designs upon (someone *or* something)** to wish to possess (someone or something), usually belonging to someone else.

device

- **leave (someone) to his *or* her own devices** to leave (someone) to look after himself or herself, often after having tried unsuccessfully to help him or her.

devil

- **better the devil you know** it is preferable to have someone or something that one knows to be bad than take a chance with someone or something that might turn out even worse.
- **between the devil and the deep blue sea** faced with two possible courses of action each of which is as unacceptable as the other.
- **needs must when the devil drives** if it is absolutely necessary that something must be done then one must do it.
- **play the devil's advocate** to put forward objections to a plan, idea, etc, simply in order to test the strength of the arguments in its favour.
- **speak of the devil** here is the very person whom we have just been referring to. <Short for 'speak of the devil and he will appear' which refers to a superstition by which it was thought that talking about evil gave it the power to appear>.

diamond

- **rough diamond** a person who behaves in a rough manner but who has good or valuable qualities.

dice

- **load the dice against (someone)** to arrange things so that (someone) has no chance of success. <Refers to a method of cheating in gambling by putting lead or similar heavy material into a dice so that only certain numbers will come up>.

die[1]

- **be dying for (something)** to be longing for (something).
- **die with one's boots on** to die while still working. <Refers to soldiers dying in active service>.
- **never say die** never give up hope.

die[2]

- **the die is cast** a step has been taken which makes the course of future events inevitable. <A translation of the Latin *iacta alea est*, supposedly said by Julius Caesar when he crossed the Rubicon in 49 bc and so committed himself to a war with the Senate>.

differ

- **agree to differ** to agree not to argue about something any more since neither party is likely to change his or her opinion.
- **sink one's differences** to forget about past disagreements.
- **split the difference** to agree on an amount of money halfway between two amounts, especially between the amount that one person is charging for something and the amount that someone else is willing to pay for it.

dig

- **dig one's heels in** to show great determination, especially in order to get one's own wishes carried out.
- **dig one's own grave** to be the cause of one's own misfortune.

dilemma

- **on the horns of a dilemma** in a position where it is necessary to choose between two courses of action. <In medieval rhetoric a dilemma was likened to a two-horned animal on one of whose horns the person making the decision had to throw himself or herself>.

dim

- **take a dim view of (something)** to look with disapproval on (something)

dine

- **dine out on (something)** to be given social invitations because of information, gossip, etc, one can pass on.

dinner

- **like a dog's dinner** an untidy mess.
- **more of (something) than you have had hot dinners** a very great deal of (something).

dirt

- **dirty old man** an elderly man who shows a sexual interest in young girls or young boys.
- **(someone's) name is dirt *or* mud** (someone) is in great disfavour.

discretion

- **discretion is the better part of valour** it is wise not to take any unnecessary risks. <Refers to Shakespeare's *Henry IV Part 1*, Act 5, scene iv>.

distance

- **go the distance** to complete something successfully, to last until the end of something.
- **keep one's distance** not to come too close, not to be too friendly.
- **within striking distance** reasonably close.

dividend

- **pay dividends** to bring advantages at a later time. <Refers to dividends paid on money invested, as on stocks and shares>.

do

- **do one's bit** to do one's share of the work, etc.
- **do (someone) in** to kill (someone).
- **done for** without any hope of rescue, help or recovery.
- **do or die** to make the greatest effort possible at the risk of killing, injuring, ruining, etc, oneself.
- **do the honours** to act as host, to serve food or drink to one's guests.
- **do time** to serve a prison sentence.
- **not the done thing** not acceptable behaviour.
- **the do's and don'ts** what one should or should not do in a particular situation.

doctor

- **just what the doctor ordered** exactly what is required.

dog

- **a dog in the manger** a person who stops someone else from doing or having something which he himself or she herself does not want. <From one of Aesop's fables in which a dog prevents the horses from eating the hay in the feeding rack although he himself did not want to eat the hay>.
- **a dog's life** a miserable life.
- **dog eat dog** a ruthless struggle against one's rivals to survive or be successful.
- **go to the dogs** to be no longer good, moral, successful, etc.
- **give a dog a bad name** if bad things are said about a person's character they will stay with him or her for the rest of his or her life.
- **in the doghouse** in disfavour.
- **keep a dog and bark oneself** to employ someone to do a job and then do it oneself.
- **let sleeping dogs lie** do not look for trouble; if there is no trouble, do not cause any.

- **you can't teach an old dog new tricks** the older you get the more difficult it is to learn new skills or accept ideas or new fashions.

doggo
- **lie doggo** to remain in hiding, not to do anything that will draw attention to oneself.

donkey
- **donkey's ages** *or* **years** a very long time. <Perhaps from a pun on donkey's ears, which are very long>.
- **donkey work** the hard, often tiring or physical, part of any job.
- **talk the hind legs off a donkey** to talk too much or to talk for a very long time.

door
- **darken (someone's) door** to come or go into (someone's) house.
- **have a** *or* **one foot in the door** to start to gain entrance to somewhere or something when entrance is difficult. <Refers to someone putting a foot in a door to wedge it open in order to gain entrance>.
- **lay (something) at (someone's) door** to blame (someone) for (something).
- **open doors** to give someone an opportunity to improve his or her position, to improve someone's chances of success.
- **show (someone) the door** to make (someone) leave.

dose
- **a dose** *or* **taste of one's own medicine** something unpleasant done to a person who is in the habit of doing similar things to other people.

dot
- **dot the i's and cross the t's** to attend to details.
- **on the dot 1** exactly on time. **2** exactly at the time stated. <Refers to the dots on the face of a clock>.

double
- **at the double** very quickly. <A military term, literally at twice the normal marching speed>.
- **do a double take** to look at or think about (someone or something) a second time because one has not taken it in or understood it the first time.
- **double Dutch** unintelligible words or language. <Refers to the fact that Dutch sounds a very difficult language to those who are not native speakers of it>.

doubt
- **a doubting Thomas** a person who will not believe something without strong proof. <Refers to the biblical story Thomas, the disciple who doubted Christ, John 21:24–29>.

down
- **down in the dumps** *or* **down in the mouth** depressed, in low spirits.
- **down the drain** completely wasted.
- **down under** Australia.
- **get down to (something)** to begin to work at (something) in earnest.
- **go downhill** to get worse and worse, to deteriorate.
- **have a down on (someone** *or* **something)** to be very hostile or opposed to (someone or something).

drawer
- **out of the top drawer** from the upper classes or aristocracy.

dream
- **a dream ticket** used of two people who are expected to work very successfully together. <Originally used to refer to political elections>.

dress
- **dressed to kill** *or* **dressed to the nines** dressed in one's smartest clothes so as to attract attention.

drift
- **get the drift** to understand the general meaning of something.

drink
- **drink like a fish** to drink a great deal of alcoholic drinks.

drop
- **at the drop of a hat** immediately, requiring only the slightest excuse.
- **drop into (someone's) lap** to happen to (someone) without any effort.
- **let (something) drop** to let (something) be known accidentally.

drown
- **drown one's sorrows** to take alcoholic drink in order to forget one's unhappiness.

drum
- **drum (someone) out** to send (someone) away, to ask (someone) to leave. <Refers to the use of drums when an officer was being publicly dismissed from his regiment>.

dry
- **a dry run** a practice attempt, a rehearsal.
- **dry as a bone** extremely dry.
- **dry as dust** extremely dull or boring.
- **dry up** to forget what one was going to say.
- **keep one's powder dry** to remain calm and prepared for immediate action. <Refers to the fact that gunpowder must be kept dry to be effective>.

duck
- **a lame duck** a weak or inefficient person or organization.
- **a sitting duck** a person or thing that is very easy to attack. <Refers to the fact that a sitting duck is easier to shoot at than one flying in the air>.
- **be water off a duck's back** be totally ineffective. <Refers to the fact that water runs straight off the oily feathers on a duck's back>.
- **break one's duck** to have one's first success. <A cricketing term. No score in cricket is known as a duck>.
- **take to (something) like a duck to water**. to be able to do (something) right from the beginning naturally and without difficulty.
- **ugly duckling** an unattractive or uninteresting person or thing that develops in time into someone or something very attractive, interesting or successful. <Refers to the story by Hans Andersen about a baby swan that is brought up by ducks who consider it ugly by their standards until it grows into a beautiful swan>.

dust
- **let the dust settle** to give things time to calm down.
- **not see (someone) for dust** not to see (someone) again because he has run away. <Refers to clouds of dust left behind by horses or vehicles when they are moving fast>.
- **shake the dust from one's feet** to leave somewhere, usually gladly
- **throw dust in (someone's eyes)** to attempt to confuse or deceive (someone). <Dust temporarily blinds people if it gets into their eyes>.

dutch
- **Dutch auction** an auction in which the auctioneer starts with a high price and reduces it until someone puts in a bid.
- **Dutch courage** courage that is not real courage but induced by drinking alcohol. <Perhaps from a Dutch military custom of drinking alcohol before going into battle, perhaps from the fact that gin was introduced into England by the Dutch followers of William III>.
- **Dutch treat** a kind of entertainment or celebration where everyone concerned pays for himself or herself. <From Dutch lunch, to which all of the guests were expected to contribute some of the food>.
- **go Dutch** to share expenses.
- **talk to (someone) like a Dutch uncle** to scold (someone) or talk to (someone) for what is supposedly his or her own good. <Perhaps from the Dutch's reputation for strict family discipline>.

ear
- **go in one ear and out the other** not to make any lasting impression.
- **grin from ear to ear** to have a wide smile on your face.

- **have** *or* **keep one's ear to the ground** to keep oneself informed about what is happening around one. <Perhaps from a North American Indian method of tracking prey>.
- **(my, etc) ears are burning** someone somewhere is talking about (me, etc). <The belief that one's ears grow hot when someone is talking about one is mentioned by Pliny, the Roman writer>.
- **up to one's ears in (something)** deeply involved in (something). <A comparison with someone who is almost submerged by very deep water>.

earth
- **bring (someone) (back) down to earth** to make (someone) aware of the practicalities of life or of a situation.
- **run (someone** *or* **something) to earth** to find (someone or something) after a long search. <Refers to a hunting term for chasing a fox into its earth or hole>.

easy
- **easy as falling off a log** *or* **easy as pie** extremely easy.
- **easy on the eye** very attractive.

eat
- **have (someone) eating out of one's hand** to have (someone) doing everything that one wishes, because he or she likes or admires one. <Refers to an animal that is so tame that it will eat out of someone's hand>.

ebb
- **at a low ebb** in a poor or depressed state. <Refers to the tide when it has flowed away from the land>.

edge
- **be at the cutting edge of (something)** to be involved in the most modern, advanced development or stage of (something).
- **be on the edge of your seat** to be very excited and eager to know what happens next.
- **have the edge on (someone** *or* **something)** to have the advantage of (someone or something).
- **lose one's edge** to become less effective or less good at what you do. <Refers to a knife becoming blunt>.
- **push (someone) over the edge** to make someone unable to cope, mentally ill, etc.

egg
- **be left with egg on one's face** to be left looking foolish.
- **put all one's eggs in one basket** to rely entirely on the success of one project, etc.
- **teach one's grandmother to suck eggs** to try to tell someone how to do something when he or she is much more experienced than oneself at it.

eight
- **be** *or* **have one over the eight** to be or to have had too much to drink. <Refers to a former belief that one could have eight drinks before one is drunk>.

elbow
- **give (someone) the elbow** to get rid of (someone), to end a relationship with (someone).

element
- **in one's element** in a situation in which one is happy or at one's best. <Refers to the four elements of medieval science of fire, earth, air and water>.

elephant
- **a white elephant** something which is useless and troublesome to look after. <White elephants were given by the Kings of Siam followers who had displeased them since the cost of keeping such an elephant was such that it would ruin the follower>.
- **have a memory like an elephant** never to forget things.

eleventh
- **at the eleventh hour** at the last possible minute. <A biblical reference to the parable of the labourers in the vineyard in Matthew 20>.

empty
- **empty vessels make most noise** the most foolish or least informed people are most likely to voice their opinions.

end
- **at a loose end** with nothing to do, with no plans.
- **at the end of one's tether** at the end of one's patience, tolerance, etc. <Refers to a rope that will only extend a certain distance to let the animal attached to it graze>.
- **make ends meet** to live within the limits of one's income. <The ends referred to are the start and finish of one's annual accounts>.

enough
- **enough is as good as a feast** if you have enough of something you should be satisfied with that; you do not need any more.

eternal
- **eternal triangle** a sexual relationship between two men and one woman or between two women and one man.

even
- **get** *or* **keep on an even keel** to be or keep steady or calm with no sudden changes.

event
- **be wise after the event** to realize how a situation should have been dealt with after it is over.

evidence
- **turn Queen's** *or* **King's evidence** to give evidence against a fellow criminal in order to have one's own sentence reduced.

evil
- **the lesser of two evils** the less unpleasant of two fairly unpleasant choices.
- **put off the evil hour** *or* **day** to keep postponing something unpleasant.

ewe
- **(someone's) ewe lamb** (someone's) favourite. <A biblical reference to Samuel 12:3>.

exception
- **the exception that proves the rule** the fact that an exception has to be made for a particular example of something proves that the general rule is valid.

eye
- **an eye for an eye (and a tooth for a tooth)** a punishment to match the offence committed. <A biblical reference to Exodus 21:23>.
- **a sight for sore eyes** a pleasant or welcome sight.
- **be one in the eye for (someone)** to be something unpleasant that happens to someone who deserves it.
- **keep an eagle eye on (someone or something)** to watch (someone or something) extremely closely. <Refers to the fact that eagles are thought to have particularly keen vision>.
- **keep a weather eye open** *or* **keep one's eyes peeled** *or* **skinned** to keep a close watch, to be alert. <A nautical term for watching for changes in the weather>.
- **make eyes at (someone)** to look at (someone) with sexual interest.
- **not to bat an eyelid** not to show any surprise, distress, etc.
- **raise some/a few eyebrows** to surprise or shock some people.
- **see eye to eye with (someone)** to be in agreement with (someone).
- **there's more to (someone** *or* **something) than meets the eye** the true worth or state of (someone or something) is not immediately obvious.

face

- **be staring one in the face 1** to be very obvious, although one may not realize this at first. **2** to be likely to happen or to be about to happen.
- **face the music** to face and deal with a situation caused by one's actions. <Perhaps from a performer facing the musicians below the front of the stage as he or she makes an entrance on stage>.
- **fly in the face of (something)** to oppose or defy (something). <Refers to a dog attacking>.
- **get out of (someone's) face** to go away and stop annoying (someone).
- **have a long face** to look unhappy.
- **keep a straight face** to stop oneself from smiling or laughing.
- **lose face** to suffer a loss of respect or reputation.
- **make** *or* **pull a face** to twist one's face into a strange or funny expression.
- **put a brave face on it** to try to appear brave when one is feeling afraid, distressed, etc.
- **save (someone's) face** to prevent (someone) from appearing stupid or wrong.
- **show one's face** to put in an appearance, especially when one will not be welcome or when one will be embarrassed.

faint

- **faint heart never won fair lady** boldness is necessary to achieve what one desires.
- **not to have the faintest** not to have the slightest idea.

fair

- **by fair means or foul** by any method whatsoever.
- **fair game** a person or thing that it is considered quite reasonable to attack, make fun of, etc.
- **fair play** fairness and justice.
- **fairweather friends** people who are friendly towards one only when one is not in trouble.

fall

- **fall back on (someone** *or* **something)** to rely on (someone or something) if all else fails.
- **fall flat** to fail, to have no effect.
- **fall foul of (something** *or* **something)** to do something that arouses someone's anger or hostility.
- **fall from grace** to lose (someone's) favour.
- **fall over oneself to** to set about doing something with great willingness and eagerness.

false

- **under false pretences** by using deceit.

family

- **run in the family** to be a characteristic found in many members of the same family.

fancy

- **(footloose and) fancy free** not in love with anyone, not romantically attached.
- **take** *or* **tickle one's fancy** to attract one, to arouse a liking in one.

far

- **go far** to be very successful.
- **go too far** to do or say something that is beyond the limits of what is acceptable.

fast

- **play fast and loose with (something)** to act irresponsibly with (something).
- **pull a fast one on (someone)** to deceive (someone). <Refers to bowling a fast ball in cricket>.

fat

- **it isn't over till the fat lady sings** used to remind people that the result of a competition, etc . is not established until the end of the game, match, etc.
- **live off the fat of the land** to live in a luxurious fashion.
- **the fat is in the fire** trouble has been started and it cannot be stopped. <Fat causes a fire to flare up>.

fate

- **a fate worse than death** something terrible that happens to one, often rape.
- **seal (someone's) fate** to ensure that something, usually unpleasant, happens to (someone).
- **tempt fate** to act in a way that is likely to bring one ill luck or misfortune.

fear

- **there is no fear of (something)** it is not likely that (something) will happen.

feast

- **be feast or famine** to be a situation in which there is too much of something or too little.

feat

- **be no mean feat** used to emphasize the difficulty of a task or venture.

feather

- **a feather in one's cap** something of which one can be proud.
- **feather one's (own) nest** to make a profit for oneself, often at the expense of someone else.
- **make the feathers** *or* **fur fly** to cause trouble or a quarrel. <Refers to birds or animals fighting>.
- **ruffle (someone's) feathers** to annoy or upset (someone).
- **show the white feather** to show signs of cowardice. <A white feather in the tail of a fighting cock was a sign of inferior breeding>.

feel

- **feel in one's bones** to know (something) by instinct.
- **feel one's feet** to be becoming used to a situation.

feet

- **at (someone's) feet 1** easily within (someone's) reach or power. **2** greatly admiring of (someone).
- **drag one's feet** to take a long time to do something.
- **fall** *or* **land on one's feet** to be fortunate or successful, especially after a period of uncertainty or misfortune.
- **find one's feet** to become capable of coping with a situation.
- **have feet of clay** to have a surprising weakness, despite having been thought to be perfect. <A biblical reference to Daniel 2:31–34>.
- **have both feet on the ground** *or* **have one's feet on the ground** to be practical and sensible.
- **get under (someone's) feet** to hinder or get in (someone's) way.
- **put one's feet up** to take a rest.
- **stand on one's own feet** to be independent.
- **sweep (someone) off his** *or* **her feet** to affect (someone) with great enthusiasm or emotion; to influence (someone) to do as one wishes.

fence

- **mend fences** to put things right after a quarrel, etc.
- **sit on the fence** to refuse to take sides in a dispute, etc.

fiddle

- **fit as a fiddle** extremely fit.
- **play second fiddle to (someone)** to be in a subordinate or inferior position to (someone).

field

- **have a field day** to have a very busy, successful or enjoyable day.
- **play the field** to take advantage of many chances offered to one, especially to go out with several members of the opposite sex.

fight

- **fighting fit** extremely healthy and in good condition.
- **fight shy of (something)** to avoid (something).

fill

- **have had one's fill** to have had enough, to be unable to tolerate any more.

fine

- **get (something) down to a fine art** to have learned to do (something) extremely well.
- **go through (something) with a fine-tooth comb** to search (something) very carefully. <A fine-tooth comb is used to remove the nits (eggs) of head lice from hair>.

finger

- **be all fingers and thumbs** to be clumsy or awkward when using one's hands.
- **burn one's fingers** *or* **get one's fingers burnt** to suffer because of something that one has been involved in.
- **cross one's fingers** to hope for good fortune.
- **get** *or* **pull one's finger out** to stop wasting time and get on with something.
- **have a finger in every pie** to be involved in a large number of projects, organizations, etc.
- **have (something) at one's fingertips** to know all the information about (something).
- **let (something) slip through one's fingers** to lose (an advantage, opportunity, etc), often by one's inaction.
- **not to lift a finger** not to do anything at all.
- **point the finger at (someone)** to indicate who is to blame.
- **put one's finger on (something)** to identify (something) exactly.
- **twist** *or* **wrap (someone) round one's little finger** to be able to get (someone) to do exactly as one wishes.
- **work your fingers to the bone** to work extremely hard.

fire

- **get on like a house on fire** to get on very well.
- **hang fire** to wait or be delayed. <Refers to a gun in which there is a delay between the trigger being pulled and the gun being fired>.
- **in the firing line** in a situation in which you are likely to be blamed or criticized. <Refers to people who have been lined up in order to be shot dead.>
- **play with fire** to take tasks, to do something dangerous.
- **set the Thames** *or* **world on fire** to do something remarkable. <Refers to the River Thames, which it would be impossible to set alight>.
- **under fire** being attacked. <Refers literally to being shot at>.

first

- **first thing** early in the morning or in the working day.
- **in the first flush of (something)** in the early and vigorous stages of (something).

fish

- **have other fish to fry** to have something else to do, especially something that is more important or more profitable.
- **like a fish out of water** ill at ease and unaccustomed to a situation.
- **there are plenty more fish in the sea** many more opportunities will arise; many more members of the opposite sex are around.

fit

- **by fits and starts** irregularly, often stopping and starting.

fix

- **in a fix** in an awkward or difficult situation.

flag

- **hang** *or* **put the flags out** to celebrate something (a rare event).
- **run (something) up the flagpole** to put forward (a plan or idea) in order to gauge reactions to it.

flame

- **an old flame** a former boyfriend or girlfriend.
- **fan the flames** to make a difficult situation worse.

flash

- **a flash in the pan** a sudden, brief success. <Refers to a flintlock gun in which the spark from the flint ignited the gunpowder in the priming pan, the flash then travelling to the main barrel. If this failed to go off there was only a flash in the pan>.

flat

- **in a flat spin** in a state of confused excitement.

flavour

- **flavour of the month** a person or thing that is particularly popular at a particular time, although this is likely to be temporary.

flea

- **a flea in one's ear** a sharp scolding.

flesh

- **a thorn in (someone's) flesh** a permanent source of annoyance or irritation. <A biblical reference to II Corinthians 12:7>.
- **get** *or* **have one's pound of flesh** to obtain everything that one is entitled to, especially if this causes difficulties or suffering to those who have to give it. <Refers to Shakespeare's play *The Merchant of Venice*, in which Shylock tries to enforce an agreement by which he can cut a pound of flesh from Antonio>.

floodgates

- **open the floodgates** to make it possible for a great many people to do something, usually something considered undesirable, or make it likely that this will happen, perhaps by removing some kind of restriction.

floor

- **take the floor 1** to rise to make a public speech. **2** to begin to dance.
- **wipe the floor with (someone)** to defeat (someone) thoroughly.

fly[1]

- **a fly in the ointment** something that spoils something.
- **there are no flies on (someone)** there is no possibility of deceiving or cheating (someone), there is no lack of sense in (someone).
- **would like to be a fly on the wall** would like to be present and able to hear what is going on without being seen.

fly[2]

- **get off to a flying start** to have a very successful beginning.

foam

- **foam at the mouth** to be very angry. <Mad dogs foam at the mouth>.

follow

- **follow suit** to do just as someone else has done. <A reference to card-playing when a player plays the same suit as the previous player>.

fool

- **a fool's paradise** a state of happiness that is based on something that is not true or realistic.
- **be nobody's fool** to have a good deal of common sense.
- **fools rush in (where angels fear to tread)** an ignorant person can sometimes achieve what a warier person cannot. <From Alexander Pope's *An Essay on Criticism*>.
- **make a fool of (someone)** to make (someone) appear ridiculous or stupid.
- **not to suffer fools gladly** not to have any patience with foolish or stupid people.

foot

- **follow in (someone's) footsteps** to do the same as someone else has done before, particularly a relative.
- **get off on the wrong foot** to get off to a bad or unfortunate start.
- **have one foot in the grave** to be very old.
- **put one's foot down** to be firm about something, to forbid someone to do something.
- **put one's foot in it** to do or say something tactless.

- **shoot oneself in the foot** to make a mistake or do something stupid which causes problems for oneself or harms one's chances of success.

form
- **on form** in good condition, fit and in a good humour. <Form refers to the condition of a horse>.

fort
- **hold the fort** to take temporary charge of something.

forty
- **forty winks** a short nap.

frame
- **be in the frame 1** to be likely to get or win something. **2** to be suspected of being guilty of a crime.

free
- **free and easy** informal, casual.
- **give (someone) a free hand** give (someone) permission to do as he or she wishes.

french
- **take French leave** to stay away from work, etc, without permission. <Refers to an 18th-century French custom of leaving a party without saying goodbye to one's host or hostess>.

freudian
- **a Freudian slip** the use of a wrong word while speaking that is supposed to indicate an unconscious thought. <Refers to the theories of the psychologist Sigmund Freud>.

friday
- **man *or* girl Friday** an invaluable assistant. <Refers to Friday, a character in *Robinson Crusoe* by Daniel Defoe>.

friend
- **a friend in need is a friend indeed** a friend who helps when one is in trouble is truly a friend.

frog
- **have a frog in one's throat** to be hoarse.

fruit
- **forbidden fruit** something desirable that is made even more so because one is forbidden for some reason to obtain it. <Refers to the biblical tree in the Garden of Eden whose fruit Adam was forbidden by God to eat, Genesis 3>.

fry
- **out of the frying pan into the fire** free of a difficult or dangerous situation only to get into a worse one.

full
- **be full of oneself** to be very conceited.
- **in the fullness of time** when the proper time has arrived, eventually.

fuss
- **make a fuss of (someone)** to pay a lot of attention to (someone), to show (someone) a lot of affection.

gab
- **the gift of the gab** the ability to talk readily and easily.

gain
- **gain ground** to make progress, to become more generally acceptable or popular.

gallery
- **play to the gallery** to act in an amusing or showy way to the ordinary people in an organization, etc, in order to gain popularity or their support.

game
- **beat (someone) at his *or* her own game** to do better than (someone) at his or her activity, especially a cunning or dishonest one.
- **give the game away** to reveal a secret plan, trick, etc, usually accidentally.
- **play the game** to behave fairly and honourably.
- **the game is up** the plan, trick, crime, etc, has been discovered and so has failed.

garden
- **everything in the garden is lovely** everything is fine.
- **lead (someone) up the garden path** to mislead or deceive (someone).

gauntlet
- **run the gauntlet** to be exposed or subjected to blame, criticism or risk. <Gauntlet is a mistaken form of Swedish *gatlopp*. Running the *gatlopp* was a Swedish military punishment in which the culprit had to run between two lines of men with whips who struck him as he passed>.
- **take/pick up the gauntlet** to accept a challenge.
- **throw down the gauntlet** to issue a challenge. <Throwing down a gauntlet, a protective glove, was the traditional method of challenging someone to a fight in medieval times>.

ghost
- **give up the ghost** to die, stop working, etc. <Ghost refers to a person's spirit—a biblical reference to Job 14:10>.

gift
- **look a gift horse in the mouth** to criticize something that has been given to one. <Looking at a horse's teeth is a way of telling its age and so estimating its value>.

gild
- **gild the lily** to add unnecessary decoration or detail. <An adaptation of a speech from Shakespeare's *King John*, Act 4, scene ii>.

gilt
- **take the gilt off the gingerbread** to take away what makes something attractive. <Gingerbread used to be sold in fancy shapes and decorated with gold leaf>.

gird
- **gird up one's loins** to prepare oneself for action. <A biblical phrase from the fact that robes had to be tied up with a girdle before men began work or they got in the way, Acts 12:8>.

give
- **give and take** willingness to compromise.

glad
- **glad rags** best clothes worn for special occasions.

glass
- **glass ceiling** an invisible barrier, established by tradition, personal discrimination, etc, which prevents women from achieving the top jobs in their companies, professions, etc.
- **people who live in glass houses should not throw stones** people with faults themselves should not criticize faults in others.

glove
- **fit like a glove** to fit perfectly.
- **take the gloves off** to begin to fight, argue, etc, in earnest. <Refers to boxers who wear protective gloves to soften their blows>.

gold
- **be sitting on a goldmine** to posses something very valuable or potentially profitable, often without realizing this.
- **like living in a goldfish bowl** in a situation where one has very little privacy.
- **strike gold** to do or find something that makes one very rich or very successful.

gnat
- **strain at a gnat (and swallow a camel)** to trouble oneself over a matter of

no importance, something only slightly wrong, etc, (but be unconcerned about a matter of great importance, something very wrong, etc). <A biblical reference to Matthew 23:23–24>.

go

- **from the word go** right from the very start of something.
- **make a go of it** *or* **something** to make a success of something.
- **no go** impossible, not given approval.
- **on the go** continually active, busy.

goal

- **score an own goal** to do something which fails to achieve what you set out to do and, instead, harms your own interests.

goalpost

- **move the goalposts** to change the conditions, rules or aims applying to a project, etc, after it is under way so that it is disadvantageous to others but advantageous to oneself.

goat

- **act the goat** to behave in an intentionally silly way.
- **get (someone's) goat** to irritate (someone).

god, god

- **in the lap of the gods** uncertain, left to chance or fate.
- **there but for the grace of God go I** if I had not been fortunate the circumstances of another person could easily also have been mine.

gold

- **a gold mine** a source of wealth or profit.
- **be like gold dust** be very scarce.
- **golden boy** a young man who is popular or successful.
- **golden handshake** a large amount of money given to someone who is leaving a job, usually because he or she has been declared redundant.
- **good as gold** very well-behaved.
- **the crock** *or* **pot of gold at the end of the rainbow** wealth or good fortune that one will never achieve.
- **the golden rule** a principle or practice that it is vital to remember. <Originally the golden rule was that one should do to others as one would wish them to do to oneself>.
- **worth its** *or* **one's weight in gold** extremely valuable or useful.

good

- **be as good as one's word** to do what one has promised do.
- **be on to a good thing** *or* **have a good thing going** to be in a desirable or profitable situation.
- **be up to no good** to be planning something wrong or illegal.
- **give as good as one gets** to be as successful as one's opponent in an argument, contest, fight, etc.
- **good for nothing** worthless.
- **in (someone's) good books** in favour with (someone).
- **make good** to be successful in one's career or business.
- **take (something) in good part** to accept (something) without being offended or angry.

goods

- **deliver the goods** to do what one is required or expected to do.
- **goods and chattels** movable property. <An old legal term>.

goose

- **cook (someone's) goose** to ruin (someone's) chances of success.
- **kill the goose that lays the golden egg** to destroy something that is a source of profit. <Refers to one of Aesop's fables in which the owner of a goose that laid golden eggs killed it thinking to get all the eggs at once, only to discover that there were none>.
- **what's sauce for the goose is sauce for the gander** what applies to one person should apply to another, usually to a member of the opposite sex.

gooseberry

- **play gooseberry** to be the third person present with a couple who wish to be alone.

gordian

- **cut the Gordian knot** to solve a problem or end a great difficulty by a vigorous or drastic method. <Refers to a legend in which whoever could untie a knot in a rope belonging to King Gordius of Phrygia, would be made ruler of all Asia. Alexander the Great severed the knot by cutting through it with a sword>.

gospel

- **take (something) as gospel** to accept (something) as absolutely true. <The gospel refers to the books of the Bible dealing with the life and teachings of Christ>.

grab

- **up for grabs** ready to be taken, bought, etc.

grace

- **saving grace** a good quality which prevents someone or something from being completely bad or worthless.
- **with a bad** *or* **good grace** in an unpleasant or pleasant and unwilling or willing way.

grade

- **make the grade** to succeed in what you are trying to achieve, often by reaching a required standard. <Originally referred to a train which succeeded in climbing a steep section of track>.

grain

- **go against the grain** to be against someone's inclinations, feelings or wishes. <Refers to the direction of the grain in wood, it being easier to cut or smooth wood with the grain rather than across or against it>.

grape

- **sour grapes** saying that something that one cannot have is not worth having. <Refers to one of Aesop's fables in which a fox that failed to reach a bunch of grapes growing above his head said that they were sour anyhow>.
- **the grapevine** an informal and unofficial way of passing news and information from person to person, gossip.

grass

- **grass widow** a woman whose husband is away from home for a short time for reasons of business or sport. <Originally the term referred to an unmarried woman who had sexual relations with a man or men, the origin being that such relations usually took place out of doors>.
- **let the grass grow under one's feet** to delay or waste time.
- **put** *or* **turn (someone) out to grass** to cause (someone) to retire. <Refers to turning out a horse into a field at the end of its working life>.
- **the grass is always greener on the other side of the fence** another set of circumstances or lifestyle always seems preferable to one's own. <Refers to the habit of grazing animals of grazing through the fence separating them from the next field>.
- **the grass roots** the ordinary people in an organization, etc.

grave

- **(someone) would turn in his** *or* **her grave** (someone) would be very annoyed or upset.

greek

- **be all Greek to me, etc,** I, etc, don't understand any of it. <Refers to the fact that ancient Greek was considered a difficult language to learn>.

green

- **give the green light to (something)** give one's permission for (something).
- **have green fingers** to be good at growing plants.

- **the green-eyed monster** jealousy.

grief
- **come to grief** to suffer misfortune or failure.
- **give (someone) grief** to criticize or nag (someone).

grim
- **hang on *or* hold on like grim death** to take a firm, determined hold of something in difficult or dangerous circumstances.

grin
- **grin and bear it** to tolerate something without complaining.
- **wipe the grin off (someone's face)** to make (someone) stop feeling pleased or satisfied.

grind
- **grind to a halt** slowly begin to stop or cease working.

grip
- **get a grip (of *or* on something *or* oneself)** to take firm control (of something or oneself).
- **get *or* come to grips with (something)** to begin to deal with (something).

ground
- **cut the ground from under (someone's) feet** to cause (someone's) actions, arguments, etc, to be ineffective, often by acting before he or she does.
- **fall on stony ground** to have no attention paid to it. <Refers to seed falling on stony, infertile ground and so not being able to grow>.
- **get in on the ground floor** to be in at the very start of a project, business, etc.
- **get (something) off the ground** to get (a project) started. <Refers literally to a plane>.
- **hit the ground running** to start a new activity immediately with a great deal of energy and enthusiasm.
- **on one's own ground** dealing with a subject, situation, etc, with which one is familiar.
- **run oneself into the ground** to become exhausted from working too hard or trying to do too many things.
- **shift one's ground** to change one's opinions, attitude, etc.
- **stand one's ground** to remain firm, not to yield.
- **suit (someone) down to the ground** to suit someone perfectly.
- **thin *or* thick on the ground** scarce or plentiful.

guard
- **let your guard down/lower your guard/drop your guard** to stop being careful or alert.
- **on *or* off one's guard** prepared or unprepared for any situation, especially a dangerous or difficult one. <Refers to fencing>.

gum
- **gum up the works** to cause a machine, system, etc, to break down.

gun
- **be gunning for (someone)** to plan to harm (someone).
- **jump the gun** to start before the proper time. <Refers to athletes starting a race before the starting gun goes>.
- **spike (someone's) guns** to cause (someone's) plans or actions to be ineffective. <Refers historically to driving a metal spike into the touch-hole of a captured enemy gun which could not be moved away in order to render it useless>.
- **stick to one's guns** to remain firm in one's opinions, etc. <Refers to a soldier who keeps shooting at the enemy and does not run away>.

hackles
- **make (someone's) hackles rise** to make (someone) angry. <Hackles are the feathers on the necks of male birds which rise when the bird is angry>.

hair
- **a hair of the dog (that bit one)** an alcoholic drink taken as a supposed cure for having consumed too much alcohol the night before. <From an old belief that if you were bitten by a mad dog and got rabies you could be cured by having hairs of the dog laid on the wound>.
- **get in (someone's) hair** to irritate (someone).
- **keep one's hair on** to remain calm and not get angry.
- **let one's hair down** to behave in an informal, relaxed manner.
- **make (someone's) hair stand on end** to terrify or horrify (someone).
- **not to turn a hair** not to show any sign of fear, distress, etc.
- **split hairs** to argue about small unimportant details, to quibble.
- **tear one's hair (out)** to show frustration or irritation.

half
- **(someone's) better half** (someone's) wife or husband.
- **half a loaf is better than no bread** a little of something desirable is better than nothing.
- **meet (someone) halfway** to reach a compromise agreement with (someone).
- **not half** very much so.

hammer
- **go at it hammer and tongs** to fight or quarrel loudly and fiercely. <Refers to a blacksmith holding a piece of heated iron in his tongs and striking it loudly with his hammer>.

hand
- **be hand in glove with (someone)** to be closely associated with (someone) for a bad or illegal purpose.
- **force (someone's) hand** to force (someone) to do something that he or she may not want to do or be ready to do.
- **give *or* lend (someone) a (helping) hand** to help (someone).
- **go hand in hand** to be closely connected.
- **hand over fist** in large amounts, very rapidly. <Originally a nautical term meaning rapid progress such as can be made by hauling on a rope putting one hand after the other>.
- **have a hand in (something)** to be involved in (something), to have contributed to the cause of (something).
- **have one's hands full** to be very busy.
- **in good hands** well looked after.
- **keep one's hand in** to retain one's skill at something by doing it occasionally.
- **lend (someone) a hand** to help (someone).
- **live from hand to mouth** to have enough money only to pay for one's present needs without having any to save. <Whatever money comes into one's hand is used to put food in one's mouth>.
- **many hands make light work** a job is easier to do if there are several people doing it.
- **my, etc, hands are tied** something prevents me, etc, from acting as I, etc, might wish to.
- **not to do a hand's turn** to do nothing.
- **play into (someone's) hands** to do exactly what someone wants one to do because it is to his or her advantage. <Refers to playing one's hand at cards so as to benefit another player>.
- **show one's hand** to reveal to others one's plans or intentions, previously kept secret. <Refers to showing one's hand to other players in a card game>.
- **take (someone) in hand** to train or discipline (someone).
- **turn one's hand to (something)** to do, to be able to do.
- **wait on (someone) hand and foot** to look after (someone) to such an extent that he or she does not have to do anything for himself or herself.
- **wash one's hands of (someone *or* something)** to refuse to be involved any longer in (something) or to be responsible for (someone or something). <A biblical reference to the action of Pontius Pilate after the crucifixion of Jesus in Matthew 27:24>.

- **with one hand tied behind one's back** very easily.

handle

- **fly off the handle** to lose one's temper. <Refers to an axehead which flies off the handle when it is being used>.

hang

- **get the hang of (something)** to learn how to do (something) or begin to understand (something).
- **hung up on (someone *or* something)** obsessed with (someone or something).

happy

- **happy as a lark *or* sand-boy** extremely happy.
- **happy hunting ground** a place where someone finds what he or she desires or where he or she is successful.
- **the *or* a happy medium** a sensible middle course between two extremes.

hard

- **between a rock and a hard place *see* rock.**
- **hard as nails** lacking in pity, sympathy, softer feelings, etc.
- **hard cash** coins and bank-notes as

opposed to cheques, etc.

- **hard facts** facts that cannot be disputed.
- **hard lines** bad luck. <Perhaps a reference to a ship's ropes being made hard by ice>.
- **hard of hearing** rather deaf.
- **hard up** not having much money.
- **take a hard line** to take strong, stern or unyielding action or have strong opinions about something.
- **the hard stuff** strong alcoholic drink, spirits.

hare

- **run with the hare and hunt with the hounds** to try to give one's support to two opposing sides at once.

hash

- **settle (someone's) hash** to deal with (someone) in such a way that he or she causes no more trouble or is prevented from doing what was intended.

hat

- **hats off to (someone)** (someone) should be praised and congratulated.
- **hat trick** any action done three times in a row. <Refers originally to a cricketer receiving a hat from his club for putting out three batsmen with three balls in a row>.
- **I'll eat my hat** an expression used to express total disbelief in a fact, statement, etc.
- **keep (something) under one's hat** to keep (something) secret.
- **knock (someone *or* something) into a cocked hat** to defeat or surpass (someone or something) completely. <A cocked hat was a three-cornered hat in the 18th-century made by folding the edges of a round hat into corners>.
- **pass the hat round** to ask for contributions of money.
- **take one's hat off to (someone)** to express or show one's admiration for someone).
- **talk through one's hat** to talk about something without any knowledge about it, to talk nonsense.
- **throw one's hat in the ring** to declare oneself a contender or candidate for something. <Refers to a method of making a challenge in prize boxing matches at fairgrounds, etc>.
- **wear a different *or* another hat** to speak as the holder of a different position.

hatch

- **batten down the hatches** to prepare for trouble. <Refers to preparations for a storm on a ship at sea>.
- **hatches, matches and despatches** the announcement of births, marriages and deaths in a newspaper.

hatchet

- **bury the hatchet** to agree to be friends again after a quarrel. <Refers to an American Indian custom of burying tomahawks when peace was made>.

have

- **have had it** to have no hope of survival, success, etc.
- **have it in for (someone)** to try to cause trouble for (someone).
- **have it out with (someone)** to discuss areas of disagreement or discontent with someone in order to settle them.
- **let (someone) have it** suddenly to attack (someone) either physically or verbally.

havoc

- **play havoc with (something)** to cause serious damage to (something).

hawk

- **watch (someone) like a hawk** to watch (someone) very carefully.

hay

- **go haywire** to go completely wrong, to go out of control. <Refers to wire that was used to bind hay. It very easily became twisted and therefore came to symbolize confusion>.
- **hit the hay *or* sack** to go to bed. <Beds were formerly filled with hay or made from the same material as sacks>.
- **like looking for a needle in a haystack *see* needle.**
- **make hay (while the sun shines)** to profit or take advantage of an opportunity while one has the chance. <Haymaking is only possible in fine weather>.

head

- **bite *or* eat *or* snap (someone's) head off** to speak very sharply and angrily to (someone).
- **bring (something) to a head** to bring something to a state where something must be done about it. <Refers to bringing a boil, etc, to a head>.
- **bury one's head in the sand** to deliberately ignore a situation so that one does not have to deal with it. <Refers to the old belief that ostriches hide their heads in the sand when they are in danger because they think that then they cannot be seen>.
- **cannot make head nor tail of (something)** cannot understand (something) at all.
- **give (someone) his or her head** to allow (someone) to do as he or she wishes. <Refers literally to slackening one's hold on the reins of a horse>.
- **go to (someone's) head l)** to make (someone) arrogant or conceited. 2 to make (someone) slightly drunk.
- **have a head for (something)** to have an ability or aptitude for (something).
- **have a (good) head on one's shoulders** to be clever or sensible.
- **have one's head screwed on the right way** to be sensible.
- **head over heels** completely.
- **hold one's head up (high)** not to feel ashamed or guilty, to remain dignified.
- **keep a level head *or* keep one's head** to remain calm and sensible, especially in a difficult situation.
- **keep one's head above water** to have enough money to keep out of debt.
- **knock (something) on the head** to put an end to (something).
- **laugh one's head off** to laugh very loudly.
- **lose one's head** to cease to remain calm, to act foolishly.
- **make headway** to make progress. <Refers originally to ships>.
- **off one's head** insane, not rational.
- **on (someone's) (own) head be it** (someone) must take responsibility or blame.
- **over (someone's) head** (l) too difficult for (someone) to understand.

2 when (someone) seems to have a better right. 3 beyond (someone) to a person of higher rank.
- **put** *or* **lay one's head on the block** to leave oneself open to blame, punishment, danger, etc. <Refers to laying one's head on the block before being beheaded>.
- **put our, etc, heads together** to discuss something together, to share thoughts on something.
- **rear its ugly head** to appear or happen.
- **scratch one's head** to be puzzled.
- **soft** *or* **weak in the head** not very intelligent, mentally retarded.
- **talk one's head off** to talk a great deal.
- **turn (someone's) head** to make (someone) conceited.

heart
- **cross one's heart (and hope to die)** this is said to emphasize the truth of what one is saying.
- **do (someone's) heart good** to give (someone) pleasure.
- **eat one's heart out** to be distressed because one cannot have someone or something which one is longing for.
- **from the bottom of one's heart** most sincerely, very much.
- **have one's heart in one's mouth** to feel afraid or anxious.
- **heart and soul** completely, with all one's energy.
- **(someone's) heart goes out to (someone)** (someone) feels sympathy or pity for (someone).
- **(someone's) heart is in the right place** (someone) is basically kind, sympathetic, etc, although not appearing to be so.
- **(someone's) heart is not in it** (someone) is not enthusiastic about something.
- **(someone's) heart sinks** (someone) feels depressed, disappointed, etc.
- **in good heart** cheerful and confident.
- **in (someone's) heart of hearts** in the deepest part of one's mind or feelings.
- **learn something by heart** to memorize (something) thoroughly.
- **lose heart** to grow discouraged.
- **not to have the heart (to do something)** not to be unkind, unsympathetic, etc, enough (to do something).
- **put new heart into (someone)** to make (someone) feel encouraged and more hopeful.
- **set one's heart on** *or* **have one's heart set on (something)** to desire (something) very much.
- **take heart** to become encouraged.
- **take (something) to heart 1** to be upset by (something). 2 to be influenced by and take notice of (something).
- **wear one's heart on one's sleeve** to let one's feelings be obvious.
- **with all one's heart** most sincerely.

heat
- **in the heat of the moment** while influenced by the excitement or emotion of the occasion.

heaven
- **in seventh heaven** extremely happy. <In Jewish literature the seventh heaven is the highest of all heavens and the one where God lives>.
- **manna from heaven** something advantageous which happens unexpectedly, especially in a time of trouble. <A biblical reference to Exodus 16:15>.
- **move heaven and earth** to make every effort possible.
- **smell** *or* **stink to high heaven** to have a strong and nasty smell.

heavy
- **make heavy weather of (something)** to make more effort to do something than should be required. <Refers originally to a ship which does not handle well in difficult conditions>.

hedge
- **look as though one has been dragged through a hedge backwards** to look very untidy.

heel
- **bring (someone) to heel** to bring (someone) under one's control. <Refers to making a dog walk to heel>.
- **take to one's heels** to run away.

helm
- **at the helm** in charge. <Refers to the helm of a ship>.

hen
- **like a hen on a hot girdle** very nervous and restless.

here
- **neither here nor there** of no importance.
- **the hereafter** life after death.

herring
- **a red herring** a piece of information which misleads (someone) or draws (someone's) attention away from the truth, often introduced deliberately. <A red herring is a strong-smelling fish whose scent could mislead hunting dogs if it were dragged across the path they were pursuing>.
- **neither fish nor fowl nor good red herring** neither one thing nor the other.
- **packed like herring in a barrel** very tightly packed.

hide[1]
- **neither hide nor hair of (someone** *or* **something)** no trace at all of (someone or something). <Hide is used in the sense of skin>.

hide[2]
- **on a hiding to nothing** in a situation where one cannot possibly win. <Perhaps a reference to boxing>.

high
- **a high flier** a person who is bound to be very successful or who has achieved great success.
- **be for the high jump** to be about to be punished or scolded.
- **be high time** be time something was done without delay.
- **be** *or* **get on one's high horse** to be or become offended in a haughty manner.
- **high and mighty** arrogant.
- **hunt** *or* **search high and low for (someone** *or* **something)** to search absolutely everywhere for (someone or something).
- **leave (someone) high and dry** to leave (someone) in a difficult or helpless state.
- **riding high** very successful. <Used literally of the moon being high in the sky>.
- **run high** of feelings, tempers, etc, to be extremely angry, agitated, etc. <Refers to the sea when there is a strong current and high waves>.

hill
- **over the hill** past one's youth or one's best.

history
- **the rest is history** used to indicate that no more need be said about something because the details of it are well known.

hit
- **be a hit with (someone)** to be popular with (someone).
- **hit-and-run accident** an accident involving a vehicle where the driver who caused it does not stop or report the accident.
- **hit it off** to get on well, to become friendly.

hog
- **go the whole hog** to do something completely and thoroughly. <Perhaps referring to buying a whole pig for meat rather than just parts of it>.

hold
- **have a hold over (someone)** to have power or influence over (someone).

- **hold good** to be valid or applicable.
- **no holds barred** no restrictions on what is permitted.

hole

- **hole-and-corner** secret and often dishonourable.
- **in a hole** in an awkward or difficult situation.
- **make a hole in (something)** to use a large part of (something).
- **need (something) like (someone) needs a hole in the head** to regard (something) as being completely unwelcome or undesirable.
- **pick holes in (something)** to find faults in (a theory, plan, etc).

holy

- **holier-than-thou** acting as though one is more moral, more pious, etc, than other people. <A biblical reference to Isaiah 65:5>.
- **the holy of holies** a private or special place inside a building. <A literal translation of the Hebrew name of the inner sanctuary in the Jewish Temple where the Ark of the Covenant was kept>.

home

- **a home from home** a place where one feels comfortable and relaxed.
- **bring** *or* **drive (something) home to (someone)** to cause someone fully to understand or believe (something).
- **do one's homework** to prepare thoroughly for a meeting, etc, by getting all the necessary information.
- **home and dry** having successfully completed an objective.
- **home truth** a plain, direct statement of something that is true but unpleasant or difficult for someone to accept.
- **make oneself at home** to make oneself comfortable and relaxed.
- **nothing to write home about** not very special, not remarkable.

hook

- **by hook or by crook** by any means possible.
- **off the hook** free from some difficulty, problem, etc, or something one does not want to do. <A reference to angling>.
- **sling one's hook** to go away.
- **swallow (something) hook, line and sinker** to believe (something) completely. <Refers to a fish that swallows not only the hook but the whole of the end section of the fishing line>.
- **the home stretch** *or* **straight** the last part of something, especially when this has been a particularly long or difficult process.

hoop

- **put (someone) through the hoop** to cause (someone) to experience something unpleasant or difficult. <Refers to circus performers who jump through hoops set on fire>.

hop

- **hopping mad** extremely angry.

hope

- **hope against hope** to continue to hope although there is little reason to be hopeful.
- **hope springs eternal (in the human breast)** it is in the nature of human beings to hope. <A quotation from Alexander Pope's *An Essay on Criticism*>.
- **pin one's hopes on (someone** *or* **something)** to rely on (someone or something) helping one in some way.

horn

- **draw in one's horns** to restrain one's actions, particularly the spending of money. <Refers to a snail drawing in its horns if it is in danger>.
- **lock horns** to argue or fight. <Refers to horned male animals who sometimes get their horns caught together when fighting>.

hornet

- **stir up a hornet's nest** to cause a great deal of trouble.

horse

- **eat like a horse** to eat a great deal.
- **flog a dead horse** to continue to try to arouse interest, enthusiasm, etc, in something which is obviously not, or no longer, of interest.
- **hold one's horses** not to move so fast.
- **horses for courses** certain people are better suited to certain tasks or situations. <Some horses run better on certain types of ground>.
- **straight from the horse's mouth** from someone closely connected with a situation and therefore knowledgeable about it. <It is as though a horse is giving a tip about a race in which it is running>.
- **wild horses would not drag (someone) to something** *or* **somewhere** nothing would persuade (someone) to attend something or go somewhere.
- **you can take a horse to the water but you cannot make it drink** you can encourage someone to do something but you cannot force him or her to do it.

hot

- **hot on (someone's) heels** close behind someone.

hour

- **the (wee) small hours** the hours immediately following midnight (1am, 2am, etc).
- **the witching hour** midnight. <Witches traditionally are supposed to be active at midnight>.

house

- **bring the house down** to cause great amusement or applause.
- **eat (someone) out of house and home.** to eat a great deal and so be expensive to feed.
- **keep open house** always to be ready and willing to welcome guests.
- **on the house** paid by the owner of shop, pub, etc.
- **safe as houses** completely safe.

hue

- **a hue and cry** a loud protest. <An old legal term meaning a summons for people to join in a hunt for a criminal>.

huff

- **in a** *or* **the huff** upset, offended or sulking.

humble

- **eat humble pie** to have to admit that one has been wrong. <Refers originally to a dish made from the umble or offal of a deer eaten by the lower classes>.

ice

- **break the ice** to ease the shyness or formality of a social occasion.
- **cut no ice** to have no effect.
- **icing on the cake** a desirable but unnecessary addition.
- **on ice** put aside for future use or attention.
- **(skate) on thin ice** (to be) in a risky or dangerous position.
- **the tip of the iceberg** a small sign of a much larger problem. <Refers to the fact that the bulk of an iceberg is hidden underwater>.

ill

- **it's an ill wind (that blows nobody any good)** in almost every misfortune there is something of benefit to someone.

imagination

- **a figment of one's imagination** something which has no reality.

immemorial

- **from time immemorial** from a time beyond anyone's memory, written records, etc; for an extremely long time. <In legal phraseology the expression means 'before the beginning of legal memory'>.

in

- **the ins and outs of (something)** the details of (something).

inch

- **be** *or* **come within an inch of (something)** to be or come very close to.
- **every inch a** *or* **the (something)** exactly the type of (something).

- **give (someone) an inch (and he *or* she will take a mile *or* an ell)** if one yields in any way to someone then the person in question will make even greater demands. <An ell is an old form of measurement>.

indian
- **an Indian summer** a time of fine, warm weather in autumn. <Perhaps from a feature of the climate of North America whose original inhabitants were Indians>.

innings
- **have a good innings** to enjoy a considerable period of life, success etc. <Refers to cricket>.

interest
- **a vested interest in (something)** a personal and biased interest in (something).
- **with interest** to an even greater extent than something has been done, etc, to someone.

iron
- **have many *or* several irons in the fire** to be involved in several projects, etc, at the same time. <Refers to a blacksmith who heats pieces of iron before shaping them>.
- **rule (someone *or* something) with a rod of iron** to rule with sternness or ruthlessness.
- **strike while the iron is hot** to act at a point at which things are favourable to one. <Refers to a blacksmith's work>.
- **the iron hand in the velvet glove** sternness or ruthlessness hidden under an appearance of gentleness.

item
- **be an item** to be regarded as having a romantic relationship.

itch
- **be itching to (do something)** to want very much to (do something).
- **have an itching palm** to be greedy for money.

ivory
- **live in an ivory tower** to have a way of life protected from difficulty or unpleasantness. <*La toure d'ivoire*, French for 'ivory tower', was coined by the poet Charles Augustin Saint-Beuve in 1837>.
- **tickle the ivories** to play the piano. <The keys of a piano are made of ivory>.

jack, Jack
- **a jack of all trades (and master of none)** someone who can do several different kinds of job (but does not do any of them very well).
- **before you can say Jack Robinson** extremely rapidly.
- **every man jack** absolutely everyone. <Perhaps from the fact that Jack is a very common first name>.
- **I'm all right, Jack** my situation is satisfactory, the implication being that it does not matter about anyone else.

jackpot
- **hit the jackpot** to have a great success, often involving a large sum of money. <Refers to the pool of money in poker>.

jam
- **jam tomorrow** the promise of better things in the future. <From a statement by the Red Queen in *Alice Through the Looking-Glass* by Lewis Carroll>.
- **want jam on it** to want an even better situation, etc, than one has already. <Refers to asking for jam on bread when bread is quite sufficient>.

jekyll
- **a Jekyll and Hyde** someone with two completely different sides to his or her personality <Refers to the character in *The Strange Case of Dr Jekyll and Mr Hyde*, a novel by Robert Louis Stevenson>.

jeremiah
- **a Jeremiah** a pessimist. <A biblical reference to the Lamentations of Jeremiah>.

jet
- **the jet set** wealthy people who can afford to travel a great deal. <Refers to jet planes>.

jewel
- **the jewel in the crown** the must valuable or successful thing associated with someone or something.

job
- **a job lot** a mixed collection. <Refers to auctioneering>.
- **just the job** exactly what is required.
- **jobs for the boys** used to suggest that jobs are being given to friends and relatives of people in power or of authority, rather than to people who are qualified to get them. Sometimes such jobs are unnecessary and created especially for the friend or relative.
- **make the best of a bad job** to obtain the best results possible from something unsatisfactory.

job
- **a Job's comforter** someone who brings no comfort at all but makes one feel worse. <A biblical reference to the friends of Job>.
- **enough to try the patience of Job** so irritating as to make the most patient of people angry. <A biblical reference to Job who had to suffer many misfortunes patiently>.

joe
- **Joe Bloggs *or* Public *or* Soap** the ordinary, average person.

joint
- **case the joint** to inspect premises carefully, especially with a view to later burglary.

joker
- **the joker in the pack** someone in a group who is different from the rest in some way and may cause problems or have an effect on a situation. <Refers to a pack of playing cards>.

jonah
- **a Jonah** someone who brings bad luck. <a biblical reference to the book of Jonah, Jonah 1:4–7>.

jones
- **keep up with the Joneses** to make an effort to remain on the same social level as one's neighbours by buying what they have, etc.

joy
- **no joy** no success, no luck.

judge
- **sober as a judge** to be extremely sober, not to be at all drunk.

jury
- **the jury is still out** people have not yet reached a conclusion or made a decision about something.

justice
- **do (someone *or* something) justice 1** to show the true value of (someone or something). **2** to eat (a meal, etc) with a good appetite.

keep
- **for keeps** permanently.
- **keep one's own counsel** to keep one's opinions, problems, etc, secret.
- **keep oneself to oneself** not to seek the company of others much, to tell others very little about oneself.
- **keep (something) to oneself** to keep (something) secret.

ken
- **beyond one's ken** outside the range of one's knowledge or understanding. <Literally, ken used to mean range of vision>.

kettle
- **a different kettle of fish** a completely different set of circumstances.
- **a pretty kettle of fish** an awkward or difficult situation.

kibosh

- **put the kibosh on (something)** to spoil or ruin (something's) chances of success.

kick

- **for kicks** for thrills or fun.
- **get a kick out of** to get fun or a thrill out of something.
- **kick oneself** to be annoyed with oneself.
- **kick over the traces** to defy rules that control one's behaviour. <Refers to a horse drawing a cart which gets out of control of the driver>.
- **kick (someone) upstairs** to appoint (someone) to a job which is more senior than the present one but which has less power.

kid[1]

- **handle (someone *or* something) with kid gloves** to deal with (someone or something) very tactfully or delicately.

kid[2]

- **the new kid on the block** the newest person in a place, activity, etc.

kill

- **be in at the kill** to be present when something important or decisive happens, often something that is unpleasant for someone. <Referring to the death of the fox in a foxhunt>.
- **kill (someone) with kindness** to spoil (someone) to the extent that it is a disadvantage to him or her.
- **make a killing** to make a large profit.
- **move in for the kill** to act decisively with a view to defeating one's opponent.

king

- **a king's ransom** a vast sum of money.

kingdom

- **till kingdom come** for a very long time. <Refers to the Lord's Prayer>.
- **to kingdom come** to death. <See above>.

kiss

- **kiss goodbye to (something)** to have to accept that you have lost (something) or that you are not going to get (something).
- **kiss of death** something which causes the end, ruin or death of something. <A biblical reference to the kiss by which Judas betrayed Jesus>.

kitchen

- **everything but the kitchen sink** used to emphasize how much luggage someone is taking, etc.

kite

- **fly a kite** to start a rumour about a new project to see how people would react if the project were put into operation. <Refers to the use of kites to discover the direction and strength of the wind>.
- **high as a kite** very excited.

kitten

- **have kittens** to get very agitated or angry.

knee

- **bring (someone) to his *or* her knees** to humble or ruin (someone). <Refers to going on one's knees to beg for something>.

knickers

- **get one's knickers in a twist** to become agitated.

knife

- **have one's knife in (someone)** to wish to harm (someone).
- **like a (hot) knife through butter** used to emphasize how easily someone has dealt with a difficult situation.
- **on a knife edge** in a very uncertain or risky state.
- **stick the knife in (someone)** to do something that will harm, upset or cause problems for (someone).
- **the knives are out for (someone)** used to describe a situation in which several people are planning to harm or cause problems for (someone).
- **the night of the long knives** a time when an act of great disloyalty is carried out, usually by the sudden removal of several people from power or employment. <Refers to 19 June 1934, when Adolf Hitler had a number of his Nazi colleagues imprisoned or killed>.

knot[1]

- **at a rate of knots** extremely rapidly. <Refers to a method of measuring the speed of ships>.

knot[2]

- **tie the knot** to get married.

know

- **in the know** knowing facts, etc, that are known only to a small group of people.
- **know (something) inside out** to know and understand (something) very well indeed.
- **not to know one is born** to lead a trouble-free, protected life.
- **not to know whether one is coming or going** to be very confused, often because one is very busy.

knuckle

- **rap (someone) over the knuckles** to scold or criticize (someone).

labour

- **a labour of love** a long or difficult job done for one's own satisfaction or from affection for someone rather than for reward.

lamb

- **like a lamb to the slaughter** meekly, without arguing or resisting, often because unaware of danger or difficulty. <A biblical reference to Isaiah 53:7>.

land

- **a land of milk and honey** a place where life is pleasant, with plenty of food and possibilities of success. <A biblical reference to the Promised Land of the Israelites described in Exodus 3:8>.
- **see how the land lies** to look carefully at a situation before taking any action or decision. <Refers literally to sailors looking at the shore before landing>.

lane

- **it's a long lane that has no turning** every period of misfortune, unhappiness, etc, comes to an end or changes to happier circumstances eventually.
- **life in the fast lane** a life which is very busy and active and usually contains a lot of stress and pressure.

language

- **speak the same language** to have similar tastes and views.

lap

- **in the lap of luxury** in luxurious conditions.

large

- **large as life** in person, actually present. <From works of art, particularly sculptural, which are life-size>.
- **larger than life** extraordinary, behaving, etc, in an extravagant way.

last

- **on one's *or* its last legs** near to collapse.
- **the last word** the most fashionable or up-to-date example of something.

late

- **better late than never** better for something to arrive, happen, etc, late than never to do so at all.

laugh

- **have the last laugh** to be victorious or proved right in the end, especially

after being scorned, criticized, etc. <From the saying he who laughs last laughs longest>.
- **laugh and the world laughs with you (weep and you weep alone)** when someone is cheerful or happy, other people share in his or her joy (but when he or she is sad or miserable, people tend to avoid him or her).
- **laugh on the other side of one's face** to suffer disappointment or misfortune after seeming to be successful or happy.
- **laugh up one's sleeve** to be secretly amused.
- **no laughing matter** a very serious matter.

laurel
- **look to one's laurels** to be careful not to lose one's position or reputation because of better performances by one's rivals. <A reference to the laurel wreath with which the ancient Greeks crowned their poets and victors>.
- **rest on one's laurels** to be content with past successes without trying for any more. <As above>.

law
- **be a law unto oneself** to behave as one wishes rather than obeying the usual rules and conventions.
- **lay down the law** to state one's opinions with great force, to give orders dictatorially.
- **the law of the jungle** the unofficial rules for survival or success in a dangerous or difficult situation where civilized laws are not effective.

lay
- **lay it on thick** *or* **lay it on with a trowel** to exaggerate greatly in one's praise, compliments, etc, to someone.

lead[1]
- **a leading question** a question asked in such a way as to suggest the answer the questioner wants to hear.
- **leading light** an important person in a certain group, field, etc.

lead[2]
- **swing the lead** to avoid doing one's work usually by inventing deceitful excuses. <Originally naval slang>.

leaf
- **take a leaf out of (someone's) book** to use (someone) as an example.
- **turn over a new leaf** to change one's behaviour, etc, for the better.

league
- **not be in the same league as (someone)** not to be as able as (someone). <Refers to the grouping of clubs in soccer, etc, according to ability>.

leap
- **by leaps and bounds** very quickly or successfully.

lease
- **give (someone** *or* **something) a new lease of life** to cause (someone) to have a longer period of active life or usefulness or to have a happier or more interesting life.

least
- **least said soonest mended** the less one says in a difficult situation the less harm will be done.

leave
- **leave (someone) in the lurch** to leave (someone) in a difficult or dangerous situation without any help. <A lurch refers to a position at the end of certain games, such as cribbage, in which the loser has either lost by a huge margin or scored no points at all>.

leeway
- **make up leeway** to take action to recover from a setback or loss of advantage. <Leeway refers to the distance a sailing ship is blown sideways off its course by the wind>.

left
- **have two left feet** to be clumsy or awkward with one's feet, e.g. when dancing.
- **left, right and centre** everywhere, to an extreme degree.
- **(someone's) left hand does not know what his** *or* **her right hand is doing** (someone's) affairs are extremely complicated.

leg
- **break a leg** used as an interjection to an actor or other stage performer as a means of wishing him or her good luck. <In the theatre it is traditionally considered bad luck to wish an actor good luck in a direct way>.
- **give (someone) a leg up** to give (someone) some assistance to achieve advancement.
- **leg it** to run or go away quickly.
- **not to have a leg to stand on** to have no defence or justification for one's actions.
- **pull (someone's) leg** to try as a joke to make (someone) believe something that is not true.
- **stretch one's legs** to go for a walk.

legend
- **a legend in one's own lifetime** used to indicate that someone has become famous during his/her lifetime.

legion
- **their name is legion** there are a great many of them. <A biblical reference to Mark 5:9>.

length
- **go to great lengths** to take absolutely any action in order to achieve what one wants.

leopard
- **the leopard never changes its spots** a person's basic character does not change.

let
- **let oneself go 1** to enjoy oneself without restraint. **2** to stop taking trouble over one's appearance.

letter
- **the letter of the law** the exact wording of a law, rule, agreement clause. <A biblical reference to II Corinthians 3:6>.
- **to the letter** in every detail.

level
- **a level playing field** a situation which is completely fair to all involved and in which no one has any particular advantage.
- **find one's** *or* **its (own) level** to find out what situation, position, etc, one is naturally suited to.
- **on the level** honest, trustworthy.

lick
- **a lick and a promise** a quick, not thorough, wash or clean.
- **lick (someone** *or* **something) into shape** to improve (someone or something) greatly to bring up to standard. <Refers to an old belief that bear cubs are born shapeless and have to be licked into shape by their mothers>.

lid
- **blow** *or* **take the lid off (something)** to reveal the truth about (something).
- **keep the lid on (something)** to keep (something) secret or keep (something) under control so that it does not get any worse.
- **put the (tin) lid on (something)** to finish (something) off usually in an unpleasant way.

lie[1]
- **give the lie to (something)** to show that (something) is untrue.
- **lie in** *or* **through one's teeth** to tell lies obviously and unashamedly.
- **live a lie** to live a way of life about which there is something dishonest.

lie[2]

- **take (something) lying down** to accept an unpleasant situation without protesting or taking action against it.
- **the lie of the land** the nature and details of a situation. <Refers to sailors studying the nature of the coastline>.

life

- **breathe new life into (something)** to make (something) more lively, active or successful.
- **come to life** to become active or lively.
- **get a life** used to indicate to someone that you think that he/she has a boring, uninteresting life and should do something to change this.
- **life is just a bowl of cherries** used ironically to indicate that life can be difficult and unpleasant.
- **for dear life** *or* **for dear life's sake** to a very great extent, very rapidly, hard, etc.
- **lead** *or* **live the life of Riley** to lead a comfortable and trouble-free life.
- **not on your life** certainly not.
- **risk life and limb** to risk death or physical injury, to take extreme risks.
- **see life** to have wide experience, especially of varying conditions of life.
- **take one's life in one's hands** to take the risk of being killed, injured or harmed.
- **the facts of life** the facts about sex or reproduction.
- **the life and soul of the party** someone who is very lively and amusing on social occasions.
- **while** *or* **where there's life there's hope** one should not despair of a situation while there is still a possibility of improvement.

light[1]

- **bring (something) to light** to reveal or uncover (something).
- **come to light** to be revealed or uncovered.
- **go out like a light** to go to sleep immediately.
- **hide one's light under a bushel** to be modest or silent about one's abilities or talents. <A biblical reference to Matthew 5:15, quoting Christ>.
- **in the cold light of day** when one looks at something practically and calmly.
- **light at the end of the tunnel** possibility of success, happiness, etc, after a long period of suffering, misery etc.
- **see the light l)** to understand something after not doing so. **2** to agree with someone's opinions or beliefs after not doing so. **3** (*also* **see the light of day**) to come into existence.
- **shed** *or* **throw light on (something)** to make (something) clearer, e.g. by providing more information about it.

light[2]

- **be light-fingered** to be likely to steal.
- **light as a feather** extremely light.
- **make light of (something)** to treat (something) as unimportant.

lightning

- **lightning never strikes twice (in the same place)** the same misfortune is unlikely to occur more than once.
- **quick as lightning** *or* **like greased lightning** extremely rapidly.

lily

- **be lily-livered** to be cowardly. <Refers to an old belief that the liver had no blood in it>.

limb

- **out on a limb** in a risky and often lonely position; having ideas, opinions, etc, different from other people. <Refers to being stuck in an isolated position on the branch of a tree>.
- **tear (someone) from limb to limb** to attack (someone) in a fierce and aggressive way, either in deed or speech.

limbo

- **in limbo** in a forgotten or neglected position.

limelight

- **in the limelight** in a situation where one attracts a great deal of public attention.

limit

- **be the limit** to be as much as, or more than, one can tolerate.
- **off limits** beyond what is allowed.

line

- **all along the line** at every point in an action, process, etc.
- **along** *or* **on the lines of (something)** similar to (something).
- **be in line for (something)** to be likely to get (something).
- **be** *or* **come on line** to be ready for use, to be operating. <A computer reference>.
- **be (way) out of line** to behave in a way that is not acceptable.
- **bring (something) into line with (something)** to make (something) the same as or comparable with (something else).
- **down the line** some time in the future.
- **draw a line under (something)** to regard (something unpleasant) as being over and best forgotten so that people can move on.
- **fall into line** to behave according to the relevant rules, regulations or traditions.
- **lay it on the line** to make (something) absolutely clear to someone.
- **not one's line of country** not something which one knows a lot about or is interested in.
- **read between the lines** to understand or deduce something from a statement, situation, etc, although this has not actually been stated. <Refers to a method of writing secret messages by writing in invisible ink between the lines of other messages>.
- **step out of line** to behave differently from what is usually acceptable or expected. <Refers to a line of soldiers on parade>.
- **the line of least resistance** the course of action that will cause one least effort or trouble.
- **toe the line** to obey the rules or orders. <Refers to competitors having to stand with their toes to a line when starting a race, etc>.

lion

- **put one's head in the lion's mouth** to put oneself in a very dangerous or difficult position.
- **the lion's share** having a much larger share than anyone else. <Refers to one of Aesop's fables in which the lion, being a very fierce animal, claimed three quarters of the food which he and other animals had hunted for>.
- **throw (someone) to the lions** deliberately to put (someone) in a dangerous or difficult position, often to protect oneself. <Refers to a form of entertainment in ancient Rome in which prisoners were thrown to wild animals to be attacked and killed>.

lip

- **keep a stiff upper lip** to show no emotion, such as fear or disappointment when danger, trouble, etc, arises.
- **lick one's lips** to look forward to something with pleasure. <A reference to licking one's lips at the thought of appetizing food>.
- **(someone's) lips are sealed** (someone) will not reveal something secret.
- **pay lip-service to (something)** to say that one believes in or agrees with (something) without really doing so and without acting as if one did.
- **read my lips** used by someone to emphasize that people should believe or trust in what he/she is about to say.

litmus

- **a litmus test** something which assesses or demonstrates clearly what something is really like.

live[1]

- **beat** *or* **knock the living daylights out of (someone)** to give (someone) a severe beating.

- **live and let live** to get on with one's own life and let other people get on with theirs without one interfering.
- **live it up** to have an enjoyable and expensive time.

live²

- **a live wire** an energetic, enthusiastic person. <Refers to a live electrical wire>.

load

- **a loaded question** a question intended to lead someone into admitting to or agreeing with something when he or she does not wish to do so. <Refers to a dice loaded or weighted so that it tends always to show the same score>.

loaf

- **use one's loaf** to use one's brains, to think clearly.

lock

- **lock, stock and barrel** completely, with everything included. <Refers to the main components of a gun>.
- **under lock and key** in a place which is locked for security.

log

- **sleep like a log** to sleep very soundly.

lone

- **a lone wolf** someone who prefers to be alone.

long

- **in the long run** in the end, after everything has been considered.
- **the long and the short of it** the only thing that need be said, to sum the story up in a few words.

look

- **look askance at (someone** *or* **something)** to regard with disapproval or distrust.
- **look before you leap** give careful consideration before you act.
- **not to get a look-in** not to have a chance of winning, succeeding, being noticed, etc.

loose

- **cut loose** to free oneself from the influence of power of (someone or something).
- **on the loose** enjoying freedom and pleasure. <Refers originally to prisoners escaped from jail>.

lord

- **lord it over (someone)** to act in a proud and commanding manner to (someone).

lose

- **lose ground** to lose one's advantage or strong position.
- **play a losing game** to go on with something that is obviously going to be unsuccessful.

loss

- **cut one's losses** not to spend any more time, money or effort on something on which one has already spent a lot to little benefit.

love

- **not for love nor money** not in any way at all.
- **there's no love lost between them** they are hostile to each other.

low

- **keep a low profile** not to draw attention to oneself or one's actions or opinions.
- **lie low** to stay quiet or hidden.

luck

- **down on one's luck** experiencing misfortune.
- **push one's luck** to risk failure by trying to gain too much.
- **strike it lucky** to have good fortune.
- **thank one's lucky stars** to be grateful for one's good fortune.

lull

- **lull (someone) into a false sense of security** to lead (someone) into thinking that all is well in order to attack when he or she is not prepared.

mad

- **mad as a hatter** utterly insane, extremely foolish or eccentric. <Hat-making used to involve the use of nitrate of mercury, exposure to which could cause a nervous illness which people thought was a symptom of insanity>.
- **mad as a March hare** insane, silly, extremely eccentric. <Hares tend to leap around wildly in the fields during March, which is their breeding season>.

make

- **make a day** *or* **night of it** to spend a whole day or night enjoying oneself in some way.
- **make do with (something)** to use (something) as a poor or temporary substitute for something.
- **make it up** to become friendly again after a quarrel.
- **make-or-break** bringing either success or failure.
- **on the make** trying to make a profit for oneself.

man

- **a man of his word** someone who always does as he promises.
- **be one's own man** to be independent in one's actions, opinions, etc.
- **man of straw** a man who is considered to be of not much worth or substance.
- **man to man** frankly.
- **the man in the street** the ordinary, average person.
- **to a man** everyone without exception.

manner

- **to the manner born** as if accustomed since birth to a particular way of behaviour etc. <Refers to a quotation from Shakespeare's *Hamlet*>.

map

- **put (somewhere) on the map** to cause (somewhere) to become well known or important.

marble

- **have marbles in one's mouth** to speak with an upper-class accent.
- **lose one's marbles** to become insane or senile.

march

- **get one's marching orders** to be told to leave, to be dismissed. <Refers to a military term>.
- **steal a march on (someone)** to gain an advantage over (someone) by doing something earlier than expected. <Refers literally to moving an army unexpectedly while the enemy is resting>.

mark

- **be a marked man** *or* **woman** to be in danger or trouble because people are trying to harm one. <'Marked' means watched>.
- **beside** *or* **wide of the mark** off the target or subject. <Refers to hitting the target in archery>.
- **be up to the mark** to reach the required or normal standard.
- **get off one's mark** to get started quickly on an undertaking. <Refers to track events in athletics>.
- **hit the mark** to be correct or accurate. <Refers to the target in archery>.
- **leave one's mark on (someone** or **something)** to have an important and lasting effect on (someone or something).
- **make one's mark** to make oneself well known, to make a lasting impression.
- **overstep the mark** to do or say something which is unacceptable or offensive.
- **quick off the mark** quick to act. <Refers literally to a runner starting quickly in a race>.

marrow

- **chilled** *or* **frozen to the marrow** extremely cold.

mass

- **the masses** the ordinary people, taken as a whole.

match

- **a shouting match** a loud, angry discussion or argument about something.
- **meet one's match** to find oneself against someone who has the ability to defeat one in a contest, argument or activity.
- **a matter of life or death** something of great urgency, something that might involve loss of life.

meal

- **make a meal of (something)** to treat (something) as if it is more complicated or time-consuming than it is.

measure

- **for good measure** as something in addition to what is necessary.

meat

- **be meat and drink to (someone)** to be very important to (someone).
- **one man's meat is another man's poison** people have different tastes.

mecca

- **a Mecca** a place that is important to a certain group of people and is visited by them. <Refers to the birthplace of Mohammed to which Muslims make pilgrimages>.

meet

- **meet one's Waterloo** to be finally defeated. <Napoleon was defeated for the last time at Waterloo by Wellington>.

melt

- **be in the melting-pot** to be in the process of changing. <Refers to melting down and reshaping metal>.

mercy

- **at the mercy of (someone** *or* **something)** wholly in the power or control of (someone or something).
- **be thankful for small mercies** to be grateful for minor benefits or advantages in an otherwise difficult situation.

merry

- **make merry** to have an enjoyable, entertaining time, to have a party.

message

- **get the message** to understand.

method

- **there is method in his madness** someone has a good, logical reason for acting as he does, although his actions seem strange or unreasonable. <A reference to Shakespeare's *Hamlet* Act 2, scene ii>.

midas

- **the Midas touch** the ability to make money or be successful easily. <Refers to a Greek legend about a king of Phrygia whose touch turned everything to gold>.

midnight

- **burn the midnight oil** to work or study until late at night.

mile

- **be miles away** to be thinking about something else and so not concentrating on what is being said to you or what is going on around you.
- **go the extra mile** to make a special effort and do more than you would usually do, more than you have been asked to do, etc in order to achieve something.
- **run a mile** used to indicate the lengths to which someone would go to avoid something.
- **stand** *or* **stick out a mile** to be extremely obvious.

mill

- **a millstone round one's neck** a heavy burden or responsibility.
- **calm as a millpond** extremely calm.
- **go through the mill** to experience a series of difficult or troublesome events, periods or tests. <From the grinding of corn in a mill>.
- **run-of-the-mill** usual, not special.

mince

- **make mincemeat of (someone** *or* **something)** to defeat (someone) soundly, to destroy (something).
- **not to mince matters** to speak completely frankly without trying to be too kind, etc.

mind

- **be** *or* **go out of one's mind** to be or become insane.
- **blow (someone's) mind** to amaze (someone), to excite (someone) greatly.
- **cross one's mind** to enter one's mind briefly.
- **give (someone) a piece of one's mind** to scold or criticize (someone) angrily.
- **great minds think alike** clever people tend to have the same ideas and opinions.
- **in one's right mind** sane, rational.
- **in two minds** undecided.
- **not to know one's own mind** not to know what one really wants to do.
- **put (someone) in mind of (someone** *or* **something)** to remind (someone) of (someone or something).
- **slip one's mind** to be temporarily forgotten.

mint

- **in mint condition** used but in extremely good condition. <Literally the unused condition of a newly minted coin>.

minute

- **up to the minute** modern or fashionable.

misery

- **put (someone) out of his** *or* **her misery** to end a time of worry, anxiety or suspense for (someone). <Originally a term for putting to death a wounded and suffering animal>.

miss

- **a miss is as good as a mile** if one fails at something it does not matter how close one came to succeeding.
- **give (something) a miss** not to go to or attend (something).

moment

- **have one's moments** to have times of success, happiness.
- **not for a moment** not at all.
- **the moment of truth** a crucial time, a time when one has to make an important decision, face up to a crisis, etc.

money

- **have money to burn** to have enough money to be able to spend it in ways considered foolish.
- **money for jam** *or* **old rope** money obtained in exchange for very little work, effort, etc. <Army slang>.
- **money talks** rich people have influence simply because they have money.
- **put one's money where one's mouth is** to give money for a cause or purpose which one claims to support.
- **spend money like water** to spend money very freely.
- **the smart money is on (something)** used to describe an event or situation which is very likely to take place. <Smart money is used to refer to people who know a lot about investment, business deals, etc>.
- **throw good money after bad** to spend money in an unsuccessful attempt to retrieve money which one has already lost.

- **you pays your money and you takes your choice** used to indicate the difficulty or impossibility of deciding which of two choices is the right one.

monkey
- **monkey business** action likely to cause trouble, illegal or unfair activities.
- **not to give a monkey's** not to care at all.
- **speak to the organ grinder, not his monkey** *see* **organ.**

month
- **a month of Sundays** an extremely long time.

monty
- **the full Monty** used to indicate that something is absolutely complete or comprehensive or that it contains everything that is usually involved in such an activity or situation.

moon
- **ask** *or* **cry for the moon** to ask for something that it is impossible to get.
- **do a moonlight (flit)** to move away suddenly.
- **many moons ago** a very long time ago, sometimes used as a humorous exaggeration.
- **over the moon** extremely happy.
- **promise (someone) the moon** to make promises that have little hope of ever being realized.

more
- **the more the merrier** the more people that are involved the better.

morning
- **the morning after the night before** a morning when one is suffering from a hangover caused by drinking too much alcohol the night before.

moth
- **like a moth to a flame** used to describe someone who finds someone or something irresistibly attractive, even although the person or thing might cause harm or trouble.

motion
- **go through the motions** to make a show of doing something, to pretend to do something.

mould
- **break the mould** to do something in a completely new and better way.
- **cast in the same mould (as someone)** very similar (to someone). <Refers to iron-working>.
- **they broke the mould when they made (someone)** used to emphasize how special or exceptional someone is.

mountain
- **have a mountain to climb** used to emphasize how difficult it is going to be for someone to do or achieve something and how much effort will be needed.
- **if the mountain will not come to Mohammed, then Mohammed must go to the mountain** a saying which indicates that, if someone whom you want to see cannot or is unwilling to come to you, then you should make the effort to go to him or her. <Refers to a story about Mohammed in which he is asked to demonstrate his power by getting Mount Sofa to come to him. When this did not happen, Mohammed is supposed to have said the words which form the saying>.
- **make a mountain out of a molehill** to greatly exaggerate the extent of a problem, etc.
- **move mountains** to achieve something that seems impossible or extremely difficult.

mouse
- **poor as a church mouse** extremely poor.
- **quiet as a mouse** extremely quiet.

mouth
- **be all mouth and trousers** to talk a lot about doing something but never actually do it.
- **have a big mouth** to talk a lot, especially about things, such as secrets, that one should not.
- **out of the mouths of babes and sucklings** used when a child says something that is surprisingly adult, true, wise, etc.
- **shoot one's mouth off** to talk in a loud and often boastful or threatening manner.
- **make one's mouth water** used to emphasize how delicious something smells or looks.
- **the movers and shakers** refers to people with power and influence. <Possibly derives from the poem 'Ode' by Arthur O'Shaughnessy (1844–81), 'We are the movers and shakers of the world forever'>.

much
- **much of a muchness** very similar.
- **not much of a (something)** not a very good (something).
- **not up to much** not very good.

mud
- **drag (someone/someone's reputation) through the mud** to damage (someone or someone's reputation) by saying bad things about him or her.
- **mud sticks** used to indicate that, if something bad is said about someone, some people are likely to believe this and to go on believing it, even if it is not at all true or if it has been disproved.
- **(someone's) name is mud** (someone) is in disfavour or is being criticized.
- **sling** *or* **throw mud at (someone** *or* **something)** to say bad or insulting things about (someone or something).

mule
- **stubborn as a mule** extremely stubborn.

multitude
- **cover a multitude of sins** to be able to apply or refer to a large number of different things. <A misquotation from the bible, I Peter 4:8, 'Charity shall cover the multitude of sins'>.

mum
- **mum's the word** do not say anything.

murder
- **get away with murder** to do something bad, irresponsible, etc, without suffering punishment.
- **I could murder (something)** used to indicate that you would very much like to have (something) to eat or drink.
- **scream blue murder** to scream extremely loudly.

music
- **be music to one's ears** used to indicate that one is very pleased to hear something.

mustard
- **keen as mustard** very eager and enthusiastic.
- **not cut the mustard** not to be able to do or achieve something; not be good enough.

muster
- **pass muster** to be considered good enough. <Refers to the calling together of people in the armed services in order to make sure that their dress and equipment are in good order>.

mutton
- **mutton dressed as lamb** an older person, usually a woman, dressed in clothes suitable for young people.

nail
- **a nail in (someone's) coffin** something which helps to bring about (someone's) downfall or destruction.
- **hit the nail on the head** to be extremely accurate in one's description, judgement, etc, of someone or something.

name
- **be (someone's) middle name** used to emphasize how typical of someone something is.
- **call (someone) names** to apply insulting or rude names to (someone).
- **give (someone *or* something) a bad name** to damage the reputation of (someone or something).
- **make a name for oneself** to become famous or well known.
- **name names** to give the names of people, especially people who are guilty or accused of wrong-doing.
- **no names, no pack-drill** no names will be mentioned and so no one will get into trouble. <'Pack-drill' refers to a form of army punishment in which the soldiers being punished were forced to march up and down carrying all their equipment>.
- **the name of the game** the important or central thing.
- **to one's name** in one's possession or ownership.

nasty
- **a nasty piece of work** someone who is very unpleasant or behaves very unpleasantly.

navel
- **contemplate one's navel** to be too much concerned with oneself and one's own activities and problems rather than with other, often more important, problems.

near
- **a near miss** something unpleasant that very nearly happened, often the near collision of two planes in the sky.
- **a near thing** the act of just avoiding an accident, misfortune, etc.
- **one's nearest and dearest** one's close family.

neck
- **be in (something) up to one's neck** to be very much involved in something bad or illegal.
- **get it in the neck** to be severely scolded or punished.
- **have the brass neck to (do something)** to have the impertinence or brazenness to (do something).
- **neck and neck** exactly equal.
- **risk one's neck** to put one's life, job, etc, in danger.
- **stick one's neck out** to take a risk or do something that may cause trouble.
- **this *or* that, etc, neck of the woods** this or that, etc, part of the country. <Originally a term for a remote community in the woods of the early 19th-century American frontier>.

needle
- **like looking for a needle in a haystack** an impossible search.

nerve
- **get on (someone's) nerves** to irritate (someone).
- **have a nerve** to be impertinent or brazen.
- **live on one's nerves** to be worried and anxious all the time.
- **lose one's nerve** to become scared, and so be unable to continue with an activity or course of action.
- **touch a nerve** to refer to something about which someone feels particularly sensitive.
- **war of nerves** a situation in which two opponents or enemies use psychological meansagainst each other, for example by frightening or threatening the other side, rather than direct action.

nest
- **a nest-egg** savings for the future.
- **fly the nest** to leave one's parent home and go and live elsewhere.
- **foul your own nest** to do something which could have a bad effect on your own interests, activities or relationships.

net
- **cast one's net wide** to involve a large number of people or things or a large area.
- **slip through the net** not to be found or identified.

nettle
- **grasp the nettle** to set about an unpleasant or difficult task in a firm and determined manner.

never
- **never-never land** an imaginary land where conditions are ideal. <Refers to the idealized land in J.M. Barrie's play *Peter Pan*>.
- **on the never-never** by hire purchase.

new
- **new broom** someone who has just been appointed to a post and who is eager to be efficient, make changes, etc. <From the saying a new broom sweeps clean, a new broom being more effective than the old one>.

news
- **break the news to (someone)** to tell (someone) about something, usually something unpleasant or sad, that has happened.
- **no news is good news** if one has not received any information about someone or something then all is likely to be well since if something bad, such as an accident, had happened one would have heard.

next
- **next door to (something)** very nearly (something).
- **next to nothing** almost nothing, very little.

niche
- **carve a niche for oneself** to succeed in creating a secure job or position for oneself or for something.

nick
- **in good *or* poor nick** in good or poor condition.
- **in the nick of time** just in time, at the last possible minute.

nine
- **a nine days' wonder** something that arouses surprise and interest for a short time only. <Refers to a saying quoted by Chaucer—'where is no wonder so great that it lasts more than nine days'>.

ninepins
- **go down like ninepins** to become ill or damaged, or to be killed or destroyed rapidly, one after the other.

nip
- **nip (something) in the bud** to put a stop or end to (something) as soon as it develops.

nit
- **get down to the nitty-gritty** to begin to deal with the basic practical details, problems, etc.
- **nit-picking** the act of finding very minor faults in something, quibbling. <Refers to picking nits out of hair>.

no
- **no end of (something)** a great deal of (something).
- **no go** unsuccessful, in vain.
- **no way** under no circumstances.

nod
- **a nod is as good as a wink to a blind horse** a hint is often all that is necessary to communicate thoughts or feelings.
- **give/get the nod** to give/be given permission or approval for something.
- **have a nodding acquaintance with (someone *or* something)** to know (someone or something) slightly. <Refers to knowing someone well enough to nod in greeting to him or her>.
- **nod off** to fall asleep, sometimes accidentally.

noise
- **big noise** an important person.
- **make all the right noises** to say things which are considered the right

response to a particular situation or the things which someone wants to hear.

nook

- **every nook and cranny** absolutely everywhere. <Literally, in all the corners and cracks>.

nose

- **cut off one's nose to spite one's face** to do something that harms oneself, usually in order to harm someone else.
- **follow one's nose** to go straight forward.
- **get up (someone's) nose** to annoy or irritate (someone).
- **have a nose around** to have a good look round a place, usually out of curiosity and when one is not supposed to be doing so.
- **have a nose for (something)** to have a talent or ability for finding or noticing something.
- **keep (one's *or* someone's) nose to the grindstone** to keep (someone) working hard without stopping.
- **lead (someone) by the nose** to get (someone) to do whatever one wants. <Refers to the ring on a bull's nose>.
- **look down one's nose at (someone *or* something)** to regard or treat (someone or something) with disdain or contempt.
- **on the nose** exactly.
- **pay through the nose** to pay a great deal of money for something.
- **poke one's nose into (something)** to pry into or interfere in other people's affairs. <Refers literally to a dog>.
- **powder one's nose** a euphemism, sometimes used by women, meaning to go to the toilet.
- **put (someone's) nose out of joint** to make (someone) jealous or offended by taking a place usually held by him or her, e.g. in the affections of a person whom he or she loves. <Refers to a person whose nose has been broken by being hit in the face>.
- **rub (someone's) nose in it** to keep on reminding (someone) about something he or she has done wrong. <Refers literally to rubbing a dog's nose in its faeces with the intention of house-training it>.
- **see further than the end of one's nose** to be concerned with more than just what is happening in the immediate present and in the immediate vicinity.
- **thumb one's nose at (someone *or* something)** *see* **thumb**.
- **turn up one's nose at (something)** to treat (something) with dislike or disgust.
- **under (someone's) (very) nose 1** right in front of (someone) and so easily seen. **2** while (someone) is actually present.

note

- **strike the right note** to say or do something suitable for the occasion. <Refers to playing a musical instrument>.

nothing

- **come to nothing** to fail.
- **go for nothing** to be wasted or unsuccessful.
- **have nothing on (someone) 1** not to be nearly as good, skilful, bad, etc, as (someone). **2** to have no proof or evidence of (someone's) wrongdoing.
- **have nothing to do with (someone *or* something)** to avoid contact with (someone or something).
- **nothing ventured, nothing gained** one cannot achieve anything if one does not make an attempt or take a risk.
- **there is nothing to choose between (two people *or* things)** there is hardly any difference in quality, ability, etc, between (two people or things).
- **there's nothing to it** it is very easy.
- **think nothing of (something)** not to regard (something) as out of the ordinary, difficult, etc.

nowhere

- **be in the middle of nowhere** be in a place which is a long way away from a town or city, a lot of people, etc, often carrying the suggestion that the place is boring.
- **get nowhere** to make no progress, to have no success.

nudge

- **nudge, nudge, wink, wink** used to indicate that there is some form of sexual innuendo or hidden reference in something that has been said. <Came into common use influenced by a sketch by Eric Idle in the TV series *Monty Python's Flying Circus*>.

number

- **get *or* have (someone's) number** to find out or know what kind of person (someone) is and what he or she is likely to do.
- **(someone's) number is up** (someone) is about to suffer something unpleasant, such as dying, failing, being punished, being caught, etc.
- **number one** oneself.

nut[1]

- **a hard nut to crack** a difficult problem or person to deal with.
- **in a nutshell** briefly, to sum up.
- **the nuts and bolts of (something)** the basic details or practicalities of (something).

nut[2]

- **be nuts about (someone *or* something)** to like (someone or something) a very great deal, to be wildly enthusiastic about (someone or something).
- **do one's nut** to get very angry.
- **go nuts** to become extremely angry.

oak

- **great oaks from little acorns grow** a saying used to emphasize that even large and important things often begin a small way.

oar

- **put *or* stick one's oar in** to interfere in another's affairs, conversation, e.g. by offering unwanted opinions. <Perhaps refers to someone who is being rowed in a boat by others and who suddenly decides to take part in the rowing unasked>.
- **rest on one's oars** to take a rest after working very hard. <Refers literally to rowing>.

object

- **money, distance, etc, is no object** it does not matter how much money, distance, etc, is involved in the particular situation. <Originally 'money is no object' meant money or profits were not the main aim but it came to be misapplied>.

occasion

- **rise to the occasion** to be able to carry out whatever action is required in an important or urgent situation.

odd

- **against all the odds** in spite of major difficulties.
- **be at odds with (someone *or* something)** to be in disagreement with (someone or something), not to be in accordance with (something).
- **lay odds** to bet. <Refers to betting on horses>.
- **make no odds** to be of no importance, to make no difference.
- **odd man out** someone or something that is different from others. <Refers literally to someone left out of a game when the teams have been chosen>.
- **odds and ends** small objects of different kinds.
- **over the odds** more than one would usually expect to pay. <Refers originally to a horse-racing term>.

off

- **in the offing** about to or likely to happen, appear, etc. <A nautical term. Offing refers to the whole area of sea that can be seen from a particular point on shore>.
- **off and on *or* on and off** occasionally.

oil

- **be no oil painting** to be not at all attractive.
- **oil and water** used to emphasize how different two people or things are.
- **oil the wheels** to make something easier to do or obtain. <Wheels turn more easily if oil is applied to them>.
- **pour oil on troubled waters** to attempt to bring a state of calm and peace to a situation of disagreement or dispute. <Since oil floats on water it has the effect of making waves flat>.
- **strike oil** to obtain exactly what one wants, to be successful.

old

- **an old hand** someone who is very experienced (at doing something).
- **old as the hills** extremely old.
- **old hat** old-fashioned, no longer popular.
- **old master** (a work by) any great painter before the 19th century, especially of the 15th and 16th centuries.
- **the old-boy network** a system in which jobs and other advantages are obtained on the basis of knowing the right people rather than on ability. <The connection with such people is often that one was at school with them>.
- **the old country** the country from which an immigrant or his or her parents or grandparents originally came.
- **the old guard** the older members of a group who are old-fashioned in their opinions and tastes. <The translation of the name applied to the most experienced section of Napoleon's army>.

olive

- **olive branch** a sign of a wish for peace. <The olive branch was an ancient symbol of peace>.

omelette

- **you can't make an omelette without breaking eggs** a saying indicating that it is impossible to achieve something worthwhile without causing a few problems or difficulties.

on

- **be not on** used to indicate emphatic disapproval of or lack of acceptance of something.
- **be on to (someone)** having discovered some previously secret or unknown information about (someone) or his or her activities.

once

- **give (someone) the once-over** to look at or study (someone or something) quickly.

one

- **a one-horse race** a competition, contest, etc, in which one person or side is certain to win.
- **a one-night stand** a relationship, arrangement, etc, that lasts for one evening or night only. <Literally a single performance in one place given by a pop group, etc, on tour>.
- **get one over on (someone)** to gain a victory or advantage over (someone).
- **have a one-track mind** to think only of one subject all the time.
- **have had one too many** to have had too much to drink.
- **it takes one to know one** used to indicate that people who have faults of their own find it easy to spot such faults in others.
- **not be oneself** to be feeling slightly unwell, to be more depressed, etc, than usual.

onion

- **know one's onions** to know a subject, one's job, etc.

open

- **an open-and-shut case** free from uncertainty, having an obvious outcome.
- **an open secret** a supposed secret that is known to many people.
- **keep an open mind** to be willing to listen to other people's suggestions, ideas, etc, instead of just concentrating on one's own point of view.
- **lay oneself (wide) open to (something)** to put oneself in a position in which one is liable to be in receipt of (blame, criticism, accusations, attack, etc).

opposite

- **(someone's) opposite number** the person in another company, country, etc, whose job or role corresponds to someone's.

option

- **keep one's options open** to delay making a definite decision so that all choices are available as long as possible.

oracle

- **work the oracle** to produce the desired result, to obtain what one wants, especially by using cunning, influence or bribery. <Refers to the oracle at Delphi in Greek legend>.

order

- **the order of the day** something that should be done, worn, etc, because conventional, common, fashionable, etc. <Refers originally to a list of items to be discussed in the British parliament on a particular day>.

organ

- **speak to the organ grinder, not his monkey** used to emphasize that one wants to deal with someone in authority, not with someone associated with him or her who has no power. <An organ grinder was a person who played a kind of musical instrument on wheels, known as a barrel organ, in the street and he often had a monkey on the barrel organ to attract people or to collect gifts of money>.

other

- **look the other way** to ignore or disregard something wrong, illegal, etc.

out

- **come out** to make public the fact that one is a homosexual.
- **get (something) out of your system** *see* **system.**
- **out and about** going around outside, e.g. after an illness.

outside

- **at the outside** at the most.

over

- **be all over (someone)** to be extremely friendly and attentive to (someone).
- **over and done with** completely finished, at an end.

overboard

- **go overboard (about *or* for someone *or* something)** to be extremely enthusiastic about (someone or something).

overdrive

- **go into overdrive** to start to work extremely hard or to become extremely active.

owe

- **I owe you one** used to indicate that someone has done one some kind of favour and that one must return this some time.

own

- **come into one's own** to have the opportunity to show one's good qualities, talent, skill, etc.
- **hold one's own 1** to perform as well as one's opponents in a contest, an argument, etc. **2** to be surviving, to be holding on to life.

p

- **mind one's p's and q's** to be very careful, to be polite and well behaved. <Perhaps refers to a warning to a printer to be careful of the letters p and q so as not to confuse them>.

pace

- **put (someone *or* something) through its *or* his *or* her paces** to test the ability of (someone or something) by getting them to demonstrate what it, he or she is capable of. <Refers originally to assessing horses>.

- **show one's paces** to demonstrate one's abilities.
- **stay the pace** to maintain progress in an activity at the same rate as others.

pack
- **send (someone) packing** to send (someone) away firmly and frankly.

pain
- **a pain in the neck** someone or something that constantly irritates one.
- **no pain, no gain** a saying used to emphasize the fact that the acquiring of something advantageous or desirable often involves something difficult or unpleasant, but it is worth it.

paint
- **like watching paint dry** used to describe something extremely boring.
- **paint the town red** to go out and celebrate in a lively, noisy manner.

palm
- **grease (someone's) palm** to give (someone) money, to bribe (someone).
- **have (someone) in the palm of one's hand** to have (someone) in one's power and ready to do as one wishes.

paper
- **paper over the cracks** to try to hide faults, mistakes, difficulties, etc, in a hasty or careless way in order to pretend that there were no faults, mistakes, etc.
- **paper tiger** someone or something that has the outward appearance of being powerful and threatening but is in fact ineffective.

par
- **below** *or* **not up to par 1** not up to the usual or required standard. **2** not completely well.
- **on a par with (something)** of the same standard as (something), as good as (something).
- **par for the course** what might be expected, what usually happens. <Originally a golfing term meaning the number of strokes that would be made in a perfect round on the course>.

part
- **look the part** to have the appropriate appearance of a particular kind of person.
- **part and parcel (of something)** something that is naturally or basically part (of something).
- **take (something) in good part** to accept (something) without being angry or offended.
- **take (someone's) part** to support (someone) in an argument, debate, etc.
- **the parting of the ways** the point at which people must go different ways, take different courses of action, make different decisions, etc. <A biblical reference to Ezekiel 21:21>.

party
- **the party line** the official opinions, ideas, attitudes, etc, as set down by the leaders of a particular group.
- **the party's over** a pleasant or happy time has come to an end.

pass
- **make a pass at (someone)** to try to start a romantic or sexual relationship with (someone). <Originally a fencing term, meaning to thrust with a foil>.
- **pass away** to die.
- **pass by on the other side** to ignore someone in trouble and not help him or her. <A biblical reference to the parable of the Samaritan, Luke 10>.

past
- **I, etc, would not put it past (someone) to (do something)** I, etc, think (someone) is quite capable of (doing something bad).
- **past it** less good, etc, than when one or it was not so old.
- **past master** someone extremely talented or skilful.

pasture
- **pastures new** *or* **fresh fields and pastures new** used to indicate a new and different place or situation. <The longer version of the phrase is a misquotation of 'fresh woods and pastures new' from John Milton's poem 'Lycidas'>.

pat
- **a pat on the back** an indication of praise or approval.

patch
- **not to be a patch on (someone** *or* **something)** not to be nearly as good as (someone or something).
- **patch it** *or* **things up** to become friends again after a quarrel.

path
- **beat a path to (someone's) door** to visit (someone) very frequently or in large numbers.

pave
- **pave the way for (something)** to make it possible or easier for (something to happen).

pay
- **put paid to (something)** to prevent (an action, plan, etc) from being carried out.

peace
- **keep the peace** to prevent disturbances, fighting, quarrelling, etc.
- **make one's peace with (someone)** to become, or try to become, friendly with (someone) again after a period of disagreement.

peacock
- **proud as a peacock** extremely proud.

pearl
- **pearls of wisdom** something wise or helpful, often used ironically.

pedestal
- **put (someone) on a pedestal** to treat (someone) with great respect and admiration. <Refers to the practice of putting statues of famous people on pedestals>.

peg
- **bring (someone) down a peg or two** to make (someone) more humble. <Refers to tuning musical instruments>.
- **off the peg** of clothes, ready to wear, not made for one specially.
- **a square peg in a round hole** used to describe someone who does not fit into a particular situation or environment and feels uncomfortable in it.

penny
- **a penny for them** *or* **your thoughts** what are you thinking about?
- **in for a penny, in for a pound** if one is going to do something one might as well do it boldly and thoroughly.
- **not to have a penny to one's name** to have no money at all.
- **penny wise and pound foolish** being careful with small items of expenditure and extravagant with large ones.
- **spend a penny** to urinate. <From the former price of admission to the cubicle of a public toilet>.
- **the penny drops** I, etc, suddenly understand. <Refers to a coin in a slot machine>.
- **turn up like a bad penny** to reappear or keep reappearing although not wanted or welcome.
- **two a penny** of little value because very common.

petard
- **hoist with one's own petard** to be the victim of one's own action which was intended to harm someone else. <Refers to Shakespeare's

Hamlet, Act 3, scene iv. A petard was a device containing explosives used by military engineers>.

philistine
- a philistine someone who is not interested in artistic or intellectual pursuits. <The Philistines were a fierce race of people who fought against the Israelites in biblical times. The present meaning was influenced by German>.

phrase
- **to coin a phrase** literally, to say something new and inventive, but used usually to introduce a cliché or a common saying or expression.

pick
- **pick and choose** to choose very carefully from a range of things.

picnic
- **be no picnic** used to emphasize how difficult or unpleasant something is.

picture
- **be out of the picture** to be no longer involved in something.
- **the big picture** the whole situation, not just some details.
- **get the picture** to understand what is being explained or described.
- **put (someone) in the picture** to give (someone) all the information and detail about a situation.

pie
- **nice as a pie** exceptionally pleasant or friendly, often unexpectedly.
- **pie in the sky** something good expected or promised in the future which is unlikely to come about. <Refers to a quotation from a poem by the American poet Joe Hill>.

piece
- **go to pieces** to be unable to continue coping with a situation, life, etc.

pig
- **buy a pig in a poke** to buy (something) without examining it carefully or without knowing its worth. <Supposedly referring to a fairground trick in which a prospective customer was sold a cat in a bag thinking that it was a piglet>.
- **make a pig of oneself** to eat greedily, to eat a great deal.
- **make a pig's ear of (something)** to make a mess of (something), to do (something) very badly or clumsily.
- **pigs might fly** it is extremely unlikely that that will happen.

pikestaff
- **plain as a pikestaff** very obvious. <Pikestaff was originally packstaff, a staff for holding a traveller's pack and lacking any ornamentation. This sense of plain has been confused with that of plain meaning clear>.

pillar
- **from pillar to post** from one place to another, often repeatedly. <Refers originally to the game of real tennis>.

pilot
- **be on automatic pilot** to do something without thinking about what you are doing, because of tiredness, distress, etc., usually succeeding in doing it correctly because you have done it before.

pin
- **for two pins** given the least encouragement or reason.
- **on pins and needles** in a state of anxiety or suspense.
- **you could have heard a pin drop** there was silence.

pinch
- **at a pinch** if it is absolutely necessary.
- **feel the pinch** to have financial problems.

pink
- **in the pink** in good health. <Refers to the pink complexion of some healthy people>.
- **the pink of perfection** absolute perfection. <Refers to a quotation from Oliver Goldsmith's play, *She Stoops to Conquer*>.

pip
- **pipped at the post** beaten at the last minute. <Refers originally to horse-racing. A horse is pipped at the post if another horse passes it at the end of the race>.

pipe
- **in the pipeline** in preparation, happening soon. <Refers to crude oil being piped from the well to the refineries>.

piper
- **pay the piper** to provide the money for something and therefore be entitled to have a say in the organization of it. <Refers to the saying 'He who pays the piper calls the tune'>.
- **pipe dream** a wish or idea that can never be realized. <Refers to visions experienced by opium smokers>.

pistol
- **hold a pistol to (someone's) head** to use force or threats to get (someone) to do as one wishes.

place
- **fall into place** to become understood when seen in terms of its relationship to other things.
- **go places** to be successful in one's career.
- **know one's place** to accept the lowliness of one's position and act accordingly.
- **a place in the sun** a situation in which one will be happy, successful, well of, etc..
- **put (someone) in his *or* her place** to remind (someone) angrily of the lowliness of his or her position or of his or her lack of experience, knowledge, etc.

plague
- **avoid (someone *or* something) like the plague** used to emphasize how keen one is to keep away (from someone or something).

plain
- **plain sailing** easy progress. <Perhaps confused with plane sailing, a method of making navigational calculations at sea in which the earth's surface is treated as though it were flat>.

plate
- **have (something) handed to one on a plate** to get (something) without having to put any effort into it.

play
- **make a play for (someone *or* something)** to try to obtain (someone or something).
- **play hard to get** to make it difficult for someone to get to know one in order to make him or her more keen to do so.

plot
- **the plot thickens** the situation is getting more complicated and more interesting. <Refers to a quotation from George Villiers' play *The Rehearsal*>.

plug
- **pull the plug on (something)** to stop supporting (something), to stop (something) from continuing.

plum
- **have a plum in one's mouth** to speak with what is regarded as an upper-class accent.

plunge
- **take the plunge** to go ahead and do something, especially something difficult or risky, especially after having spent some considerable time thinking about it.

poacher

- **poacher turned gamekeeper** used to describe someone who has changed their job, attitude, opinion, etc, and now holds completely opposite views.

pocket

- **in (someone's) pocket** under the control or influence of (someone).
- **line one's pocket** to make money for oneself dishonestly.
- **out of pocket** having made a loss.

poetic

- **poetic justice** deserved but accidental punishment or reward.
- **poetic licence** the disregarding of established rules of form, grammar, fact, etc, by writers to achieve a desired effect.

point

- **the point of no return** the stage in a process, etc, when it becomes impossible either to stop or change one's mind. <Originally referred to the point in the flight of an aircraft after which it did not have enough fuel to return to its place of departure>.
- **up to a point** to some extent but not completely.

poison

- **poison-pen letter** an anonymous letter saying bad things about someone.

port

- **any port in a storm** any solution to a problem or difficulty will suffice.

possum

- **play possum** to pretend to be asleep, unconscious or dead. <The possum pretends to be dead when it is under threat of attack from another animal>.

post[1]

- **from pillar to post** from one place to another, often repeatedly.

post[2]

- **keep (someone) posted** to keep (someone) informed about developments in a situation.

pot

- **go to pot** to get into a bad or worse state. <Refers to meat being cut up and stewed in a pot).
- **keep the pot boiling** to keep something going or operating.
- **take pot-luck** to have a meal at someone's house, etc, without having anything specially prepared for one. <Literally to take whatever happens to be in the cooking-pot at the time>.
- **the pot calling the kettle black** someone criticizing (someone) for doing (something) that he or she does himself or herself.
- **the *or* a watched pot never boils** when one is waiting for something to happen, etc, the time taken seems longer if one is constantly thinking about it.

pour

- **it never rains but it pours** when something goes wrong it goes wrong very badly or other things go wrong too.

powder

- **be sitting on a powder keg** to be in a very risky or dangerous situation in which something could easily go wrong quite suddenly.

power

- **more power to (someone's) elbow** may (someone) be successful.
- **the power behind the throne** the person who is really in charge of or in control of an organization, etc, while giving the impression that it is someone else.
- **the powers that be** the people in charge, the authorities.

practice

- **practice makes perfect** if one practises doing something one will eventually be good at it.

practise

- **practise what one preaches** to act in the way that one recommends to others.

praise

- **sing (someone's *or* something's) praises** to praise (someone or something) with great enthusiasm.

premium

- **be at a premium** to be much in demand and, therefore, difficult to obtain. <A financial term meaning literally 'sold at more than the nominal value'>.

press

- **press-gang (someone) into (doing something)** to force (someone) or persuade (someone) against his or her will to (do something). <The press gang was a group of sailors in the 18th century who seized men and forced them to join the navy>.

pretty

- **come to a pretty pass** to get into a bad state.
- **cost a pretty penny** to cost a large amount of money.
- **sitting pretty** in a very comfortable or advantageous position.

prey

- **be a prey to (something)** regularly to suffer from (something).
- **prey on (someone's) mind** to cause constant worry or anxiety to (someone).

price

- **at a price** at a very high price.
- **a price on (someone's) head** a reward offered for the capture or killing of (someone).

pride

- **pride goes before a fall** being too conceited often leads to misfortune.
- **pride of place** the most important or privileged position.
- **swallow one's pride** to behave in a more humble way than one usually does or than one would wish to do.

prime

- **prime mover** someone or something that gets something started.

pro

- **the pros and cons** the arguments for and against. <Latin *pro*, 'for', and *contra*, 'against'>.

production

- **make a production of (something)** to make (something) appear to be much more complicated than it actually is.

proof

- **the proof of the pudding is in the eating** the real worth of something is only found out when it has been into practice or use.

proud

- **do (someone) proud** to treat (someone) exceptionally well or lavishly.

pull

- **pull the other one!** used to emphasize to someone that you do not believe him or her. Sometimes the phrase is extended to **pull the other one; it's got bells on!**<A reference to the phrase: pull (someone's) leg>.

pulse

- **keep one's finger on the pulse** to keep oneself informed about recent developments in a situation, organization, etc, or in the world. <Refers to a doctor checking the rate of someone's pulse for health reasons>.

punch

- **pleased as Punch** extremely pleased or happy. <Refers to the puppet show character who is usually portrayed smiling gleefully>.

punch
- **pull one's punches** to be less forceful or harsh in one's attack or criticism than one is capable of. <Refers to striking blows in boxing without using one's full strength>.
- **roll with the punches** not to let difficulties or problems discourage one or have a bad or upsetting effect on one.

pup
- **sell (someone) a pup** to deceive (someone), often to sell or recommend something that turns out not to be as good as he or she thought.

purpose
- **at cross purposes** involved in a misunderstanding because of talking or thinking about different things without realizing it.

purse
- **hold the purse strings** to be in charge of financial matters.
- **you can't make a silk purse out of a sow's ear** *see* **silk.**

push
- **at a push** used to indicate that something can be done if it is absolutely necessary, but it will not be easy.
- **give (someone) the push** to dismiss (someone).

put
- **put it on** to feign, to pretend.
- **put-up job** something done to deceive or trick (someone).

putty
- **putty in (someone's) hands** easily influenced or manipulated by (someone). <Putty is a malleable substance>.

pyrrhic
- **Pyrrhic victory** a success of some kind in which what it takes to achieve is not worth it. <From the costly victory of King Pyrrhus of Epirus, over the Romans at Heraclea in 280 bc>.

qT
- **on the QT** secretly. <An abbreviation of quiet>.

quantity
- **an unknown quantity** someone or something of which very little is known. <Refers literally to a mathematical term>.

queer
- **in Queer Street** in financial difficulties. <Perhaps changed from Carey Street in London where the bankruptcy courts were>.
- **queer (someone's) pitch** to upset (someone's) plans or arrangements. <Pitch here refers to the site of a market stall. Originally to queer someone's pitch was to set up a stall beside it selling the same kind of goods>.

question
- **a question mark over (something)** doubt or uncertainty in relation to (something).
- **out of the question** not possible.
- **pop the question** to ask (someone) to marry one.

queue
- **jump the queue** to go ahead of others in a queue without waiting for one's proper turn.

qui
- **on the qui vive** very alert. <From the challenge of a French sentry *Qui vive?* 'Long live who, whose side are you on?'>.

quick
- **cut (someone) to the quick** to hurt (someone's) feelings very badly. <The quick is the sensitive skin under the nail>.

quid
- **quids in** a fortunate position.

quit
- **call it quits** to agree that neither person owes the other one anything and that neither one has any kind of advantage over the other.

r
- **the three R's** reading, writing and arithmetic, thought of as the essential basics of education. <From *r*eading, *w*riting and a*r*ithmetic>.

rack
- **go to rack and ruin** to fall into a state of disrepair or into a worthless condition. <Rack means destruction>.

rage
- **all the rage** very fashionable or popular.

rail
- **off the rails** not sensible, disorganized, deranged. <Refers to a train leaving the track>.

rain
- **keep** *or* **put away** *or* **save (something) for a rainy day** to keep (something, especially money) until one really needs it. <Formerly most jobs, such as farm jobs, were dependent on the weather. Since they could not be carried out in rainy weather no money was earned then>.
- **rain or shine** whatever the weather.
- **take a rain check on (something)** used to indicate that you are unable to accept an invitation but would like to postpone it until a later date. <American in origin and a reference to the part of a ticket that you keep when a sports fixture cannot take place because of bad weather so that you can use it for entry to the fixture when it does take place>.

rake
- **thin as a rake** extremely thin.

rampage
- **be** *or* **go on the rampage** to rush about wildly or violently.

rank
- **close ranks** to act together and support each other as a defensive measure.
- **pull rank** to make unfair use of a position of authority to make someone else do as one wishes or to give one some kind of advantage.

rap
- **take the rap for (something)** to take the blame or punishment for (something).

rat
- **like a drowned rat** soaking wet.
- **smell a rat** to have a suspicion that something is wrong or that one is being deceived. <Refers to a terrier hunting>.
- **the rat race** the fierce competitive struggle for success in business, etc. <A nautical phrase for a fierce tidal current>.

raw
- **touch (someone) on the raw** to hurt or anger (someone).

razor
- **sharp as a razor** quick-witted and very intelligent.

read
- **take (something) as read** to assume (something).

real
- **the real McCoy** something genuine and very good as opposed to others like it which are not. <Perhaps from Kid McCoy, an American boxer who was called The Real McCoy to distinguish him from other boxers of the same name>.

reason
- **see reason** to be persuaded by someone's advice, etc, to act or think sensibly.

• **within reason** within sensible limits.

rebound

• **on the rebound** to start a new relationship while still suffering from the disappointment experienced at the end of the previous relationship.

record

• **for the record** so that it will be noted.
• **set the record straight** to put right a mistake or misunderstanding.

red

• **a red-letter day** a day remembered because something particularly pleasant or important happened or happens on it. <From the fact that important dates in the year are sometimes shown in red on calendars>.
• **catch (someone) red-handed** to find (someone) in the act of doing something wrong or unlawful. <Refers to finding a murderer with the blood of a victim on his or her hands>.
• **in the red** in debt, overdrawn. <From the use of red ink to make entries on the debit side of an account>.
• **like a red rag to a bull** certain to make (someone) angry. <From the widespread belief that bulls are angered by the sight of the colour red although they are in fact colour-blind>.
• **on red alert** ready for an an immediate danger. <Originally a military term for mobilizing civilians during an air-raid>.
• **red tape** the rules and regulations, official papers, etc, that are thought to characterize government departments. <From the reddish tape used by government offices to tie bundles of papers>.
• **see red** to get very angry.

reed

• **a broken reed** someone who is too weak or unreliable to be depended upon.

rest

• **lay (someone) to rest** to bury (someone).
• **rest assured** you can be quite certain.

return

• **return to the fold** to come or back to one's family, an organization, a set of principles or beliefs, etc, which one has previously left. <Refers to a sheep returning to the sheep-pen>.

rhetorical

• **rhetorical question** a question which does not require an answer.

rhyme

• **without rhyme or reason** without any logical or sensible reason or explanation.

rich

• **rich as Croesus** extremely rich. <Croesus was a ruler of the kingdom of Lydia who was very wealthy>.
• **strike it rich** to obtain wealth, often suddenly or unexpectedly.

riddance

• **good riddance to (someone *or* something)** I am glad to have got rid of (someone or something).

ride

• **be riding for a fall** to be on a course of action that is likely to lead to unpleasant results or disaster for oneself. <Refers originally to hunting>.
• **take (someone) for a ride** to deceive or trick (someone). <Originally American gangsters' slang for killing someone, from the practice of killing someone in a moving vehicle so as not to attract attention>.

rift

• **a rift in the lute** a slight disagreement or difficulty that might develop into a major one and ruin a project or relationship. <Refers to a quotation from Tennyson's *Idylls*>.

right

• **get *or* keep on the right side of (someone)** to act in such a way that (someone) feels or continues to feel friendly and well disposed towards one.
• **Mr *or* Miss Right** the perfect man or woman for one to marry.
• **right-hand man *or* woman** someone's most valuable and helpful assistant.
• **serve (someone) right** to be something unpleasant that (someone) deserves.
• **set (something) to rights** to bring (something) into a correct, organized, desired, etc, state.

ring

• **a dead ringer** someone who looks extremely like someone else. <Perhaps from the use of the phrase to mean a horse, similar to the original, illegally substituted in a race>.
• **have a ringside seat** to be in a position to observe clearly what is happening. <Originally refers to boxing>.

riot

• **read the riot act to (someone)** to scold (someone) severely and warn him or her to behave better. <The Riot Act of 1715 was read to unlawful gatherings of people to break the gathering up. If the people refused to disperse action could be taken against them>.

rise

• **rise and shine** to get out of bed and be lively and cheerful.
• **take a rise out of (someone)** to tease or make fun of (someone) so that he or she gets annoyed.

river

• **sell (someone) down the river** to betray or be disloyal to (someone). <Refers historically to selling slaves from the upper Mississippi states to buyers in Louisiana where working and living conditions were much harsher>.

road

• **hit the road** start out on a journey.
• **one for the road** one last drink before leaving.

roaring

• **do a roaring trade in (something)** to be selling a lot of (something).

rob

• **rob Peter to pay Paul** to pay (someone) with the money that should go to pay a debt owed to (someone else). <Refers to Saints Peter and Paul who share the same feast day, 29 July>.

rock

• **between a rock and a hard place** to be in a situation in which one is faced with a choice between two equally unpleasant or unacceptable alternatives.
• **steady as a rock** extremely steady, motionless.

rocket

• **not rocket science** used to indicate that something is quite easy and does not require much intellect or skill.

rod

• **make a rod for one's own back** to do something which is going to cause harm or problems for oneself in the future.
• **spare the rod and spoil the child** if a child is not punished for being naughty it will have a bad effect on his or her character.

rogue

• **a rogue's gallery** a police collection of photographs of known criminals.

roll

• **a rolling stone (gathers no moss)** a person who does not stay very long in one place (does not acquire very much in the way of possessions or responsibilities).

- **a roll in the hay** an informal way of describing having sex, especially when this is not part of a serious relationship.
- **be on a roll** used to indicate that things are going well and that good progress is being made.
- **be rolling in it** *or* **in money** to have a great deal of money.
- **be rolling in the aisles** to be laughing very heartily.

rome
- **all roads lead to Rome** all ways of fulfilling an aim or intention end in the same result and so it does not does not matter which way one uses.
- **fiddle while Rome burns** to do nothing while something important is being ruined or destroyed. <The Emperor Nero was said to have played on a lyre while Rome was burning>.
- **Rome was not built in a day** a difficult task cannot be completed satisfactorily quickly.
- **when in Rome do as the Romans do** one should follow the customs, behaviour, etc, of the people one is visiting or living with. <A saying of St Ambrose>.

rooftop
- **shout (something) from the rooftops** to tell a great many people about (something).

roost
- **rule the roost** to be the person in charge whose wishes or orders are obeyed.

rope
- **give (someone) enough rope (and he will hang himself)** let (someone foolish) act as he or she pleases and he or she will bring about his or her own ruin, downfall, misfortune, etc.
- **know the ropes** to know the details and methods associated with a business, procedure, activity, etc.
- **on the ropes** used to describe a situation which is very close to failure or defeat.
- **rope (someone) in** to include (someone), to ask (someone) to join in, often against his or her will. <Refers to lassoing cattle in the American West>.
- **show (someone) the ropes** to teach (someone) the details and methods involved (in something).

rose
- **come up smelling of roses** to come out of a situation with some kind of advantage when it was expected to result in blame or harm for one.
- **everything's coming up roses** everything is turning out to be successful or happy.
- **look at (someone** *or* **something) through rose-coloured** *or* **rose-tinted spectacles** *or* **glasses** to view (someone or something) in an extremely optimistic light.

rough
- **give (someone) the rough edge of one's tongue** to scold or criticize (someone) severely.
- **ride roughshod over (someone)** to treat (someone) without any respect and without any regard for his or her views or feelings. <Horses are roughshod to give a better grip on icy, etc, roads>.
- **take the rough with the smooth** to accept the disadvantages as well as the advantages and benefits of a situation.

round
- **go the rounds** to be passed from person to person.
- **in round figures** *or* **numbers** to the nearest whole number, especially one that can be divided by ten.
- **round trip** the journey to somewhere plus the journey back.

rub
- **rub (something) in** to keep reminding someone about (something which he or she would rather forget).
- **rub off on (to) (someone)** to be passed to (someone), to affect (someone).
- **rub (someone) up the wrong way** to irritate (someone). <Refers to rubbing an animal's coat up the wrong way>.
- **there's the rub** that's the problem. <Refers to a quotation from Shakespeare's *Hamlet*, Act 3, scene i>.

rug
- **pull the rug (out) from under (someone)** suddenly to stop giving important help or support to (someone), to leave (someone) in a weak position.

rule
- **rule of thumb** a rough or inexact guide used for calculations of some kind.

run
- **a run for (someone's) money** a creditable or worthy performance or opposition. <A racing term indicating that the horse one has backed has actually raced although it has not won>.
- **(someone's) cup runneth over** someone feels very happy. <A biblical reference to Psalm 23:5>.
- **in the running** with a chance of success.
- **run its course** to continue to its natural end, to develop naturally.
- **run out on (someone** *or* **something)** to abandon (someone or something).
- **take a running jump** to go away.

rut
- **in a rut** in a routine, monotonous way of life. <Refers to the rut made by a cartwheel, etc>.

sabre
- **rattle one's sabre** to put on a show of anger or fierceness without resorting to physical force in order to frighten someone.

sack
- **sackcloth and ashes** sorrow or apology for what one has done or failed to do. <People in mourning used to wear sackcloth and throw ashes over their heads. The phrase has several biblical references, e.g. Matthew 11:21>.

safe
- **safe and sound** totally unharmed.
- **there's safety in numbers** it is safer to undertake a risky venture if there are several people involved.

sail
- **sail close to the wind** to come close to breaking the law or a rule.
- **sail under false colours** to pretend to be different in character, beliefs, status, work, etc, than is really the case. <Refers to a ship flying a flag other than its own, as pirate ships sometimes did>.

salad
- **(someone's) salad days** (someone's) carefree and inexperienced youth.

salt
- **below the salt** in a humble, lowly or despised position. <Formerly the salt container marked the division at a dinner table between the rich and important people and the more lowly people, the important people being near the top and so above the salt>.
- **rub salt in the wound** to make someone feel worse. <Salt used to be used as an antiseptic but it was painful on raw wounds>.
- **take (something) with a grain** *or* **pinch of salt** to treat (something) with some disbelief.
- **the salt of the earth** someone very worthy or good. <A biblical reference to Matthew 5:13>.
- **worth one's salt** worth the money one is paid, of any worth. <Salt was once a valuable commodity and the reference is to that given to servants or workers>.

samaritan

- **a good Samaritan** someone who helps people when they are in need. <A biblical reference to the parable in Luke 10>.

sand

- **build (something) on sand** to establish (something) without having enough support, money, likelihood of survival, etc, to make it secure or practicable. <A biblical reference to Matthew 7:26>.

sardine

- **packed like sardines** crowded very close together. <Sardines are sold tightly packed in tins>.

scarlet

- **scarlet woman** an immoral or promiscuous woman. <A biblical reference to the woman in scarlet in Revelation 17>.

scene

- **behind the scenes** out of sight of the public, etc. <Refers literally to people in a theatrical production who work behind the scenery offstage>.
- **come on the scene** to arrive or appear.
- **not (someone's) scene** not the kind of thing that (someone) likes.
- **set the scene for (something)** to prepare the way for (something), to be the forerunner of (something). <Refers originally to the preparation of the stage for theatrical action>.

scent

- **throw (someone) off the scent** to distract (someone) from a search for someone or something, e.g. by giving him or her wrong information. <Refers literally to dogs>.

scheme

- **the best-laid schemes of mice and men (gang aft agley)** the most carefully arranged plans (often go wrong). <Refers to a quotation from Robert Burns's poem, 'To a Mouse'>.

science

- **blind (someone) with science** to talk about something in such a complicated technical way that it is difficult for a layperson to understand.

score

- **know the score** to know exactly what is involved, to know all the facts of a situation. <Literally to know from the score in a game who is likely to win or lose>.
- **settle old scores** to get revenge for wrongs committed in the past.

scratch

- **start from scratch** to start from the very beginning, without any advantages. <Refers to the starting line (formerly scratched on the ground), from which runners start unless their handicap allows them to start further down the track>.
- **up to scratch** up to the required standard. <Refers originally to a scratch in the centre of a boxing ring to which boxers had to make their way unaided after being knocked down to prove that they were fit to continue>.

screw

- **have a screw loose** to be deranged, to be very foolish. <Refers literally to malfunctioning machinery>.

scrooge

- **Scrooge** an extremely mean person. <Refers to a character in Charles Dickens's *A Christmas Carol*>.

scylla

- **between Scylla and Charybdis** faced with having to choose between two equally undesirable choices. <Refers to Homer's *Odyssey* in which Odysseus had to sail down a narrow strait between Scylla, a monster on a rock, and Charybdis, an extremely dangerous whirlpool>.

sea

- **a sea change** a complete change in a situation, someone's opinion, attitude, etc.
- **all at sea** puzzled, bewildered.

seam

- **be bursting at the seams** to be extremely full.
- **come *or* fall apart at the seams** to be in a state of collapse or ruin. <From clothes coming to pieces>.

second

- **second nature** a firmly established habit.
- **second sight** the supposed power of seeing into the future.
- **second thoughts** a change of opinion, decision, etc.

seed

- **go to seed** to become shabby and uncared-for. <Refers literally to plants seeding after flowering and being no longer attractive or useful>.

separate

- **separate the sheep from the goats** *see* **sheep.**

sewn

- **(all) sewn up** completely settled or arranged.

shade

- **put (someone *or* something) in the shade** to be much better, etc, than (someone or something). <Refers to making someone seem dark by being so much brighter oneself>.
- **shades of (someone *or* something)** that reminds me of (someone or something). <It is as though the shade or ghost of someone or something were present>.

shadow

- **worn to a shadow** made exhausted and thin by over working.

shakes

- **in two shakes of a lamb's tail** in a very short time.

shape

- **knock (someone *or* something) into shape** to get (something) into the desired or good condition.
- **shape up or ship out** used to tell someone that he or she should start acting in a more responsible or appropriate way or get out.

sheep

- **might as well be hanged for a sheep as a lamb** if one is going to do something slightly wrong and have to pay a penalty one might as well do something really wrong and get more benefit. <Refers to the fact that stealing a lamb or a sheep used to be punishable by death>.
- **separate the sheep from the goats** to distinguish in some way the good, useful, talented, etc, people from the bad, useless or stupid, etc, ones. <A biblical reference to Matthew 25:32>.

shelf

- **on the shelf** unmarried and unlikely to get married because of being unattractive, old, etc. <Refers to goods that are not sold>.

shell

- **come out of one's shell** to become less shy. <Refers to a tortoise or crab, etc>.

ship

- **shipshape and Bristol fashion** neat, in good order. <Originally applied to ships. Bristol was formerly the largest port in Britain>.
- **ships that pass in the night** people who meet by chance and only on one occasion. <Refers to a quotation from 'Tales of a Wayside Inn' poem by Henry Wadsworth Longfellow>.
- **spoil the ship for a ha'porth of tar** to spoil something of value by not buying or doing something which would improve it but not cost very

much. <Ship is dialect here for sheep—tar used to be used to prevent infections in sheep or to treat wounds>.
- **when (someone's) ship comes in** when (someone) becomes rich or successful. <Refers to merchants waiting for their ships to return with goods to sell>.

shoe
- **in (someone's) shoes** in (someone else's) place.
- **on a shoestring** using very little money.

shoot
- **shoot (something) down in flames** to destroy. <Refers literally to destroying aircraft by shooting at them>.

shop
- **talk shop** to talk about one's work.

short
- **by a short head** by a very small amount. <Refers to horse-racing>.
- **caught *or* taken short** having a sudden, urgent need to go to the toilet.
- **give (someone *or* something) short shrift** to spend very little time or thought on (someone or something). <Short shrift was the short time given to a criminal for confession before execution>.
- **make short work of (something)** to deal with or get rid of (something) very quickly.
- **sell (someone *or* something) short** not to do justice to, to belittle (someone or something). <Literally to give a customer less than the correct amount of something>.
- **short and sweet** short and to the point.

shot
- **a long shot** a guess or attempt unlikely to be accurate or successful, but worth trying.
- **a shot across the bows** something given as a warning. <From naval warfare>.
- **a shot in the arm** something that helps to revive (something). <Literally, an injection in the arm>.
- **big shot** an important person.
- **call the shots** to be in charge of events or a situation.
- **like a shot** very quickly or willingly.
- **shotgun wedding** a forced wedding, usually because the bride is pregnant. <From the idea that the groom was forced into the wedding by shotgun>.

shoulder
- **a shoulder to cry on** a sympathetic listener.
- **put one's shoulder to the wheel** to begin to work hard. <Refers to putting one's shoulder to the wheel of a cart, etc, to push it out of muddy ground, etc>.
- **rub shoulders with (someone)** to associate closely with (someone).
- **shoulder to shoulder** side by side.

shout
- **shout (something) from the rooftops** *see* **rooftop**.

show
- **get the show on the road** to get something started or put into operation. <Used originally of a theatre company going on tour>.
- **steal the show** to attract the most attention at an event. <Refers to someone getting most of the applause at a theatrical performance>.

sick
- **sick as a parrot** very disappointed.

side
- **let the side down** to hinder one's colleagues by not performing, etc, as well as they have.
- **on the side** in a way other than by means of one's ordinary occupation.
- **take sides** to support a particular person, group, etc, against another.

sieve
- **have a memory like a sieve** to be extremely forgetful.

sign
- **sign on the dotted line** to make a firm commitment to do something, often one that is legally binding. <Refers to the signing of a formal agreement or contract>.

sight
- **out of sight, out of mind** one ceases to think about someone who has gone away or about something which is no longer in front of one.

silence
- **silence is golden** it is better to say nothing in a particular situation.

silent
- **the silent majority** the people who make up most of the population but who rarely make their views known although these are thought to be moderate and reasonable.

silk
- **you can't make a silk purse out of a sow's ear** one cannot make something good or special out of poor materials.

silver
- **born with a silver spoon in one's mouth** to be born into an aristocratic or wealthy family. <Perhaps from the custom of giving a christening present of a silver teaspoon>.

sin
- **ugly as sin** extremely ugly.

sing
- **sing from the same hymn *or* song sheet** to be in agreement about something, often to show this agreement publicly.

six
- **a sixth sense** intuition, an ability to feel or realize something not perceived by the five senses.
- **at sixes and sevens** in a state of confusion and chaos.
- **knock (someone) for six** to take (someone) completely by surprise. <Refers to cricket—literally to score six runs off a bowl>.
- **six of one and half a dozen of another** so similar as to make no difference. <Half a dozen is six>.

sixty
- **the sixty-four (thousand) dollar question** the most important and/or difficult question. <From an American quiz game in which the contestant won one dollar for the first question, two for the second, four for the third, up to the last when he or she won sixty-four dollars or lost it all>.

size
- **cut (someone) down to size** to humble (someone), to reduce (someone's) sense of his or her own importance.

skeleton
- **have a skeleton in the cupboard** to have a closely kept secret about some cause of shame.

skin
- **by the skin of one's teeth** only just, very narrowly.
- **no skin off my, etc, nose** no difference to me, etc, of no concern to me, etc.
- **save one's skin** to save one's life or one's career.
- **skin and bone** extremely thin.

sky
- **praise (someone *or* something) to the skies** to praise (someone) extremely highly.
- **the sky's the limit** there is no upper limit.

slap
- **a slap in the face** a rebuff.
- **a slap on the wrist** a reprimand.

sleeve
- **have** *or* **keep (something) up one's sleeve** to keep (a plan, etc) in reserve or secret for possible use at a later time. <Refers to cheating at cards by having a card up one's sleeve>.

slip
- **a slip of the tongue** a word or phrase said in mistake for another.
- **give (someone) the slip** to succeed in escaping from or evading (someone).
- **let (something) slip** to say or reveal (something) accidentally.
- **there's many a slip 'twixt cup and lip** something can easily go wrong with a project, etc, before it is completed.

small
- **it's a small world** an expression used when one meets someone one knows somewhere unexpected.
- **small talk** light conversation about trivial matters.
- **the small print** the parts of a document where important information is given without being easily noticed.

smash
- **a smash-and-grab** a robbery in which a shop window is smashed and goods grabbed from behind it.
- **a smash hit** a great success. <Originally referred to a very successful popular song>.

smear
- **smear campaign** an attempt to blacken or damage someone's reputation by making accusations or spreading rumours about him or her.

smoke
- **go up in smoke** to end in nothing.
- **there's no smoke without fire** there is always some kind of basis to a rumour, however untrue it appears to be.

snail
- **at a snail's pace** extremely slowly.

snake
- **a snake in the grass** a treacherous person. <From Virgil's *Aeneid*>.

sneeze
- **not to be sneezed at** not to be ignored or disregarded.

sock
- **pull one's socks up** to make an effort to improve.
- **put a sock in it** to be quiet.

soft
- **have a soft spot for (someone)** to have a weakness, affection or exceptional liking for (someone).
- **a soft touch** *or* **mark** someone who is easily taken advantage of, deceived etc.

song
- **for a song** for very little money.
- **make a song and dance about (something)** to cause an unnecessary fuss about (something).

soon
- **speak too soon** to say something that takes for granted something not yet accomplished.

sore
- **a sore point** a subject which annoys or offends someone.
- **stick out like a sore thumb** to be very noticeable.

sort
- **it takes all sorts (to make a world)** one should be tolerant of everyone whatever they are like.
- **out of sorts** not feeling quite well, rather bad-tempered.

soul
- **the soul of (something)** a perfect example of (something).

soup
- **in the soup** in serious trouble.

spade
- **call a spade a spade** to speak bluntly and forthrightly.
- **do the spadework** to do the hard preparatory work at the beginning of a project. <Digging is the first stage of building houses, etc>.
- **in spades** used to emphasize the large amount of something.

spanner
- **throw a spanner in the works** to hinder or spoil (a project, plan, etc).

spar
- **sparring partner** someone with whom one often enjoys a lively argument. <Literally refers to someone with whom a boxer practises>.

spare
- **go spare** to become very angry or distressed.

speak
- **be on speaking terms** to be friendly towards someone and communicate with him or her.
- **speak for itself** to need no explanation.

spick
- **spick and span** clean and tidy.

spirit
- **the spirit is willing (but the flesh is weak)** one is not always physically able to do the things that one wishes do. <A biblical quotation, Matthew 26:40–41>.

spit
- **be the spitting image** *or* **the spit and image** *or* **the dead spit of (someone** *or* **something)** to be extremely like (someone or something).

spleen
- **vent one's spleen** to express one's anger and frustration. <The spleen was thought to be the source of spite and melancholy>.

split
- **a split second** a fraction of a second.

spoil
- **be spoiling for (something)** to be eager for (a fight, etc).

spoke
- **put a spoke in (someone's) wheel** to hinder (someone's) activity. <Spoke is from Dutch spoak, a bar formerly jammed under a cartwheel to act as a brake when going downhill>.

sponge
- **throw up the sponge** to give up a contest, struggle, argument, etc. <Refers originally to a method of conceding defeat in boxing>.

spot
- **hit the spot** used to indicate that something is just what is required or is completely satisfactory.
- **in a spot** in trouble, in difficulties.
- **knock spots off (someone)** to beat or surpass (someone) thoroughly.
- **put (someone) on the spot** to place (someone) in a difficult or awkward situation.
- **rooted to the spot** unable to move from fear, horror, etc.

sprat

- **a sprat to catch a mackerel** something minor or trivial given or conceded in order to obtain some major gain or advantage.

square

- **back to square one** back at the beginning. <Refers to an instruction in board games>.

squeak

- **a narrow squeak** a narrow escape.

stab

- **have a stab at (something)** to have a try at (something).
- **stab (someone) in the back** to behave treacherously towards (someone), to betray (someone).

stable

- **lock the stable door after the horse has bolted** to take precautions against something happening after it has already happened.

stage

- **a stage whisper** a loud whisper that is intended to be heard by people other than the person to whom it is directed. <From the fact that whispers on stage have to be audible to the audience>.
- **stage fright** the nervousness, sometimes leading to him or her forgetting words, felt by an actor when in front of an audience; often extended to that felt by anyone making a public appearance.

stamp

- **(someone's) stamping ground** a place where (someone) goes regularly. <Refers literally to animals>.

stand

- **know where one stands** to know the exact nature of one's position or situation.
- **make a stand against (something)** to oppose or resist (something one believes to be wrong, etc).
- **stand corrected** to accept that one has been wrong.
- **stand on ceremony** to be very formal.
- **stand up and be counted** to declare one's opinions publicly.

start

- **a false start** an unsuccessful beginning, resulting in one in having to start again. <From a start in a race which has to be repeated, e.g. because a runner has left the starting line before the signal has been given>.
- **be under starter's orders** to be ready to start doing something.
- **for starters** to begin with. <Starter refers literally to the first course of a meal>.

status

- **status quo** the situation as it is, or was, before a change. <Latin, literally 'the state in which'>.
- **status symbol** a possession which supposedly demonstrates high social position.

stay

- **stay the course** to continue to the end or completion of (something).

steady

- **go steady** to go out together regularly, to have a romantic attachment to each other.

steam

- **get all steamed up** to get angry or agitated.
- **get up steam** to gather energy and impetus to do (something). <Literally used of increasing the pressure of steam in an engine before it goes into operation>.
- **let off steam** to give free expression to one's feelings or energies. <Literally to release steam from a steam engine to in order to reduce pressure>.
- **run out of steam** to become exhausted, to lose enthusiasm. <Refers literally to the steam engine>.
- **under one's own steam** entirely through one's own efforts.

step

- **take steps** to take action of some kind.

stick

- **a stick to beat (someone) with** something which can be used to criticize or damage (someone).
- **get hold of the wrong end of the stick** to misunderstand a situation or something said or done.
- **give (someone) stick** to scold or criticize (someone). <Refers literally to beating someone witha stick>.

sticky

- **be on a sticky wicket** to be in a difficult or awkward situation that is difficult to defend. <Refers to cricket when the state of the ground or the weather make it difficult for the batsman to hit the ball>.
- **come to a sticky end** to meet some misfortune or an unpleasant death.

still

- **still waters run deep** quiet people often think very deeply or have strong emotions.

stitch

- **a stitch in time saves nine** prompt action at the first sign of trouble saves a lot of time and effort later.
- **have (someone) in stitches** to make (someone) laugh a great deal.
- **without a stitch on** completely naked.

stock

- **on the stocks** in preparation, in the process of being made or arranged. <Refers to the fact that a ship is supported on stocks, a wooden frame, while being built>.
- **take stock (of something)** to assess (a situation).

stomach

- **turn (someone's) stomach** to make (someone) feel sick, to disgust (someone).

stone

- **a stone's throw** a very short distance.
- **be set in stone** to be something that cannot be changed.
- **leave no stone unturned** to try every means possible.

stool

- **fall between two stools** to try to gain two aims and fail with regard to both of them, usually because of indecision.

stop

- **pull out all the stops** to put as much effort and energy into something as possible. <Refers to pulling out the stops of an organ so that it plays at full volume>.
- **stop dead** to stop suddenly and abruptly.
- **stop short of (something *or* doing something)** not to go as far as (something or doing something).

store

- **in cold storage** in reserve.
- **set great store by (something)** to consider (something) to be of great importance or value.

storm

- **a storm in a teacup** a great fuss made over a trivial matter. <Refers to the title of a farce written by William Bernard in 1854>.
- **take (someone *or* something) by storm** to make a very great and immediate impression (on someone or something). <Literally to capture a fort, etc, by a sudden violent military attack>.
- **weather the storm** to survive a difficult or troublesome situation or period of time. <Refers originally to ships>.

story
- **the same old story** a situation, etc, that occurs frequently.

straight
- **go straight** to start leading an honest life.
- **straight as a die** completely honest and fair.
- **straight talking** frank and honest statement or conversation.
- **the straight and narrow (path)** a good, virtuous way of life. <A variation on a biblical reference, 'Straight is the gate and narrow is the way which leadeth unto life', Matthew 7:4>.

stranger
- **be a stranger to (something)** to have no experience of (something).

straw
- **a straw in the wind** a small or minor incident, etc, that indicates what may happen in the future.
- **clutch at straws** to hope that something may happen to get one out of a difficulty or danger when this is extremely unlikely. <From the saying, 'A drowning man will clutch at a straw'>.
- **draw the short straw** to be the one in a group who has to perform an unpleasant or undesirable task. <Pulling out a straw from a collection of different lengths is a kind of lottery to decide who is to do something>.
- **the last straw** *or* **the straw that breaks the camel's back** an event, etc, which, added to everything that has already happened, makes a situation impossible. <From the saying that it is the last straw added to its burden that breaks the camel's back>.

stream
- **come on stream** to begin to be used or to operate.

street
- **be right up one's street** to be exactly what one likes or what is suitable for one.

strength
- **go from strength to strength** to progress successfully from one achievement to another.
- **on the strength of (something)** relying on (something).

stretch
- **at full stretch** using all one's energy, abilities, powers, etc, as much as possible.
- **stretch a point** to go further than the rules or regulations allow in giving permission, etc, for something.

stride
- **get into one's stride** to become accustomed to doing something and so do it well and effectively. <A reference to running>.
- **make great strides** to make very good progress.
- **take (something) in one's stride** to cope with (something) without worrying about it. <Refers to a horse jumping an obstacle without altering its stride>.

string
- **have (someone) on a string** to have (someone) in one's control. <Refers to someone manipulating a puppet>.
- **how long is a piece of string?** used to emphasize how difficult or impossible it is to give a definite answer to a question.
- **pull strings** to use influence to gain an advantage or benefit of some kind. <As above>.
- **with no strings attached** without any conditions or provisos.

stroke
- **put (someone) off his** *or* **her stroke** to hinder or prevent (someone) from proceeding smoothly with an activity. <Refers to upsetting the rhythm of someone's rowing>.

strong
- **be (someone's) strong suit** be something at which (someone) is very good. <Refers to card-playing>.

stuff
- **a stuffed shirt** a pompous, over-formal person.
- **knock the stuffing out of (someone) 1** to beat (someone) severely. **2** to discourage (someone) completely, to deprive (someone) of vitality. <Refers to stuffed animals>.
- **strut one's stuff** to do something which you know you do well, usually in a proud and confident way.

stumbling
- **a stumbling block** something that hinders or prevents progress. <A biblical reference to Romans 14:13>.

stump
- **stir one's stumps** to hurry up. <Stumps here means legs>.

style
- **cramp (someone's) style** to hinder (someone) from acting in the way that he or she would like or is accustomed to.

sugar
- **sugar daddy** an elderly man who has a young girlfriend or mistress to whom he gives expensive presents.
- **sugar the pill** to make something unpleasant more pleasant.

suit
- **men in (grey) suits** used to describe the powerful men who are in control of an organization, government, etc.
- **one's birthday suit** nakedness.

sunday
- **(someone's) Sunday best** (someone's) smartest, formal clothes, of the kind worn to church on Sundays.

sure
- **sure as eggs is eggs** used to emphasize the certainty of something.

surface
- **scratch the surface of (something)** to deal with only a very small part of (something).

swallow
- **one swallow does not make a summer** a single success, etc, does not mean that a generally successful, etc, time is about to come. <Refers to the fact that swallows begin to come to Britain at the start of summer>.

swan
- **(someone's) swan song** the last work or performance by a musician, poet, playwright, actor, etc, before his or her death or retirement; by extension also applied to anyone who does anything for the last time. <Refers to an ancient legend that the swan sings as it is dying although it is otherwise silent>.

sweat
- **the sweat of one's brow** one's hard work.

sweet
- **be all sweetness and light** to seem to be pleasant and good-tempered.
- **have a sweet tooth** to like sweets, cakes and deserts.
- **sweet nothings** affectionate things said to someone with whom one is in love, endearments.

swim
- **be in the swim** be actively involved in social or business activities.

swing
- **get into the swing of things** to become accustomed to (something) and begin to understand and enjoy it. <Refers to the swing of a pendulum>.
- **go with a swing** to be very successful.
- **in full swing** at the most lively or busy part of something.
- **not enough room to swing a cat** *see* **cat**.

- **what you lose on the swings you gain on the roundabouts** disadvantages in one area of life are usually cancelled out by advantages in another.

swoop

- **at** *or* **in one fell swoop** in one single action or attempt, at the same time. <Refers to a quotation from Shakespeare's *Macbeth*, Act 4, scene iii, the reference being to a hawk swooping on poultry>.

sword

- **a double-edged** *or* **two-edged sword** used to indicate that something has a bad and a good side.
- **cross swords with (someone)** to enter into a dispute with (someone).
- **the sword of Damocles** a threat of something bad that is likely to happen at any time. <Refers to a legend in which Damocles was forced by Dionysius of Syria to sit through a banquet with a sword hanging by a single hair over his head>.

t

- **to a T** exactly, very well. <Perhaps T stands for tittle, a small dot or point>.

tab

- **keep tabs on (someone** *or* **something)** to keep a check on (someone or something).
- **pick up the tab for (something)** to pay for (something). <Tab is an American term for bill>.

table

- **turn the tables on (someone)** to change a situation so that one gains the advantage (over someone) after having been at a disadvantage. <From the medieval game of tables, of which backgammon is a form, in which turning the board round would exactly reverse the position of the players>.

tail

- **chase one's tail** to spend a great deal of time and effort trying to do something but achieving very little.
- **have one's tail up** to be confident of success.
- **turn tail** to turn round and leave a difficult or dangerous situation.
- **with one's tail between one's legs** in an ashamed, miserable or defeated state. <From the behaviour of an unhappy dog>.

take

- **take after (someone)** to resemble.
- **take it out on (someone)** to treat (someone) in an angry or nasty way because one is disappointed, angry, etc, about something.

tale

- **live to tell the tale** to survive a dangerous or threatening situation, often used humorously.
- **tell tales** to report someone's wrong-doing.
- **thereby hangs a tale** there is a story associated with that. <A pun on tail, used by Shakespeare>.

talk

- **talk down to (someone)** to speak to (someone) in a condescending way as if he or she were inferior.
- **talk nineteen to the dozen** to talk a great deal and usually very rapidly.
- **the talk of the town** someone or something that is the subject of general conversation or gossip.

tall

- **a tall order** a difficult task.
- **a tall story** a story which is extremely unlikely.

tangent

- **go** *or* **fly off at a tangent** suddenly to leave the subject being discussed or the task being undertaken and move to a completely different subject or task.

tango

- **it takes two to tango** used to indicate a particular situation has to involve two people and that, therefore, both bear some responsibility.

tape

- **have** *or* **get (someone** *or* **something) taped** to have a full knowledge or understanding of (someone or something). <As if measured with a tape>.

tar

- **be tarred with the same brush** to have the same faults.

taste

- **leave a nasty taste in the mouth** to leave someone with unpleasant memories or associations.

tea

- **not for all the tea in China** not for anything at all, certainly not. <For a long time, China was the source of the world's tea>.

tear

- **tear a strip off (someone)** to scold (someone) severely.

teeth

- **by the skin of one's teeth** *see* **skin.**
- **cut one's teeth on (something)** to practise on or get early experience from (something). <Refers to children being given something to chew on to help their teeth come through>.
- **draw the teeth of (someone** *or* **something)** to make (someone or something) no longer dangerous. <Refers to pulling out an animal's teeth.>
- **get one's teeth into (something)** to tackle (something) vigorously.
- **like pulling teeth** used to indicate how difficult something is to do.
- **kick (someone) in the teeth** to refuse to help or support (someone) when he or she is in need of it.
- **set one's teeth on edge** to irritate one.
- **teething troubles** problems occurring at the very beginning of a new project, etc. <From the pain experienced by babies when teeth are just coming through>.

tell

- **I told you so** I warned you and I was right to do so.

tender

- **leave (someone** *or* **something) to (someone's) tender mercies** to leave (someone or something) in the care of (someone nasty, inefficient, etc).

tenterhooks

- **be on tenterhooks** be very anxious or agitated waiting for something to happen. <Tenterhooks were hooks for stretching newly woven cloth>.

territory

- **it goes with the territory** used to indicate that something, usually some kind of problem or difficulty, usually occurs in connection with a particular, job, activity or situation and should be expected.

test

- **stand the test of time** to survive or still be in use or popular after a considerable period of time.

that

- **that's that** there is no more to be said or done.

thick

- **give (someone) a thick ear** to slap (someone) across the ear, to box (someone's) ears.
- **thick and fast** in great quantities and at a fast rate.
- **thick as thieves** extremely friendly.
- **thick as two short planks** extremely stupid.
- **through thick and thin** whatever difficulties arise.

thief

- **set a thief to catch a thief** the best way to catch or outwit a dishonest or deceitful person is to use the help of another who is dishonest as he or she knows the technique.

thin
- **be thin on top** to be balding.
- **spread oneself too thin** to try to do several different things at once, often with the result that none of them are done very well or properly.
- **thin as a rake** extremely thin.

thing
- **do one's (own) thing** to do what one likes to do or what one is good at doing.
- **have a thing about (someone *or* something) 1** to be very fond of or be particularly attracted to (someone or something). **2** to be scared of, to have a phobia about (someone or something).
- **one of those things** something that must be accepted.
- **see things** to see someone or something that is not there.
- **the thing is** the most important point or question is.

think
- **have another think coming** to be quite mistaken.

thread
- **hang by a thread** to be in a very precarious or uncertain state. <Probably a reference to the sword of Damocles>.
- **lose the thread** to cease to follow the course or development of an argument, conversation, etc.

throat
- **at each other's throats** quarrelling fiercely.
- **jump down (someone's) throat** to attack (someone) verbally or in an angry or violent manner.
- **ram (something) down (someone's) throat** to try forcefully to make (someone) accept ideas, opinions, etc.
- **stick in one's throat *or* gullet** to be difficult for one to accept or tolerate.

throw
- **throw up** to vomit.

thumb
- **thumb a lift** to ask for (and get) a lift in someone's vehicle by signalling with one's thumb.
- **thumb one's nose at (someone or something)** to express defiance or contempt at (someone or something), originally by making the rude gesture of putting one's thumb to one's nose.
- **thumbs down** rejection or disapproval. <From the method employed by the crowds in ancient Rome to indicate whether they thought the defeated gladiator should live or die after a fight between two gladiators. If the crowds turned their thumbs down the gladiator died. If they turned them up the gladiator lived.>
- **thumbs up** acceptance or approval. <See **thumbs down** above>.
- **twiddle one's thumbs** to do nothing, to be idle. <Literally to rotate one's thumbs round each other, indicating a state of boredom>.
- **under (someone's) thumb** under one's control or domination.

thunder
- **steal (someone's) thunder** to spoil (someone's) attempt at impressing people by doing what he or she intended to do before him or her. <John Dennis, a 17th/18th century playwright, invented a machine for simulating thunder in plays. When someone else used a similar device in a rival play Dennis said that he had stolen his thunder>.

ticket
- **just the ticket** exactly what is required.
- **meal ticket** someone who can be relied upon to support one, providing food and so on.

tickle
- **be tickled pink** to be delighted.

tide
- **swim against the tide** to do, say or believe things which are the opposite of what the majority of people are doing, saying or believing.
- **the tide is turning** used to indicate that a changing is occurring in people's attitudes, tastes, beliefs, etc.

tie
- **be tied up** to be busy or engaged.

tight
- **in a tight corner *or* spot** in a difficult or dangerous situation.
- **run a tight ship** to run an efficient, well-organized firm etc.
- **sit tight** to be unwilling to move or take action.

tightrope
- **walk a tightrope** to be in a very difficult situation, often one which involves opposing groups, which requires one to act with great caution and delicacy.

tile
- **a night on the tiles** a celebratory evening spent in a wild and unrestrained manner. <Refers to roof tiles and to cats sitting on them at night>.

tilt
- **at full tilt** at maximum speed. <Refers to knights tilting or jousting>.

time
- **ahead of one's time** with ideas in advance of one's contemporaries, often not understood.
- **all in good time** soon, when it is the right time.
- **behind the times** not up-to-date, old-fashioned.
- **do time** to be in prison.
- **have no time for (someone *or* something)** to have a very low opinion of someone or something and to wish not to associate with him, her or it.
- **have the time of one's life** to have a very enjoyable time.
- **have time on one's hands** to have more free time than one can usefully fill with work, etc.
- **in (someone's) own good time** when it is convenient for (someone), at whatever time or speed he or she chooses.
- **keep time 1** of a clock to show the time accurately. **2** to perform an action in the same rhythm as someone else.
- **kill time** to find something to do to pass some idle time, especially time spent waiting for someone or something.
- **mark time** to remain in one's present position without progressing or taking any action. <Refers to soldiers moving their feet as if marching but not actually moving forwards>.
- **not before time** not too soon, rather late.
- **no time at all** a very short time.
- **pass the time of day with (someone)** to greet (someone) and have a brief conversation, e.g. about the weather.
- **play for time** to act so as to delay an action, event, etc, until the time that conditions are better for oneself. <In games such as cricket it means to play in such a way as to avoid defeat by playing defensively until the close of the game>.
- **take time by the forelock** to act quickly and without delay. <Refers to the fact that time was often represented by an old man with no hair except for a forelock, a length of hair over his forehead>.
- **time and tide wait for no man** time moves on without regard for human beings and therefore opportunities should be grasped as they arise as they may not be there for very long.
- **time and time again** repeatedly.
- **time flies** time passes very quickly.

tip
- **be on the tip of one's tongue** to be about to be said.

tit
- **tit for tat** repayment of injury or harm for injury or harm. <Perhaps a variation on tip for tap, blow for blow>.

to

- **toing and froing** repeatedly going backwards and forwards.

toast

- **warm as toast** very warm and cosy.

tod

- **on one's tod** alone. <From Cockney rhyming slang 'on one's Tod Sloan', meaning 'on one's own', Tod Sloan having been a famous American jockey>.

toe

- **be on one's toes** to be alert and prepared for action.
- **make one's toes curl** to make one feel very uncomfortable or embarrassed.
- **put a toe in the water** to start doing something very slowly or gradually to see if one likes it, whether it will be successful, whether people will approve, etc.
- **tread on (someone's) toes** to offend (someone) by doing or saying (something) that is against his or her beliefs or opinions.

tom

- **a peeping Tom** a man who gets sexual enjoyment from secretly watching women undress or women who are naked, especially by looking through the windows of their houses. <From the story of Lady Godiva who is said to have ridden naked through the streets of Coventry as part of a bargain made with her husband, Leofric, Earl of Mercia, to persuade him to lift a tax he had placed on his tenants. Everyone was to stay indoors so as not to see her but a character, later called Peeping Tom, looked out to see her and was struck blind>.
- **every** *or* **any Tom, Dick and Harry** absolutely everyone or anyone, every ordinary person. <From the fact that all three are common English Christian names>.

tongue

- **have one's tongue in one's cheek** to say something that one does not mean seriously or literally, sometimes to say the opposite of what one means for a joke.
- **hold one's tongue** to remain silent or to stop talking.
- **set tongues wagging** to start people gossiping.

tooth

- **be** *or* **get long in the tooth** to be or become old.
- **fight tooth and nail** to fight, struggle or argue fiercely and determinedly.

top[1]

- **blow one's top** to lose one's temper.
- **get on top of one** used to indicate that someone is not coping with all the things that require to be done.
- **off the top of one's head** without much thought, without research or preparation.
- **over the top** too much, to too great an extent.
- **the top of the ladder** *or* **tree** the highest point in a profession, etc.

top[2]

- **sleep like a top** to sleep very soundly. <A pun on the fact that sleep used of a top means 'to spin steadily without wobbling'>.

toss

- **argue the toss** to dispute a decision. <Refers to arguing about the result of tossing a coin>.

touch

- **it's touch and go** it's very uncertain or precarious. <Perhaps refers to a ship that touches rocks or the ground but goes on past the danger without being damaged>.
- **lose one's touch** to lose one's usual skill or knack. <Probably refers to someone's touch on piano keys>.
- **the common touch** the ability to understand and get on with ordinary people.
- **the finishing touches** the final details which complete something.

tow

- **have (someone) in tow** to have someone following closely behind one.

towel

- **throw in the towel** to give up, to admit defeat. <From a method of conceding defeat in boxing>.

tower

- **a tower of strength** someone who is very helpful and supportive.

town

- **go to town** to act or behave without restraint, with great enthusiasm or with great expense.

track

- **cover one's tracks** to hide one's activities or movements.
- **from the wrong side of the tracks** used of someone who comes from a poor or less desirable area of town. <American in origin and refers to the fact that, when railways were built, they often divided an area into two sharply divided districts>.
- **keep** *or* **lose track of (someone** *or* **something)** to keep or fail to keep oneself informed about the whereabouts or progress of (someone or something).
- **make tracks (for)** to leave or set out (for).
- **on the right** *or* **wrong track** on the right or wrong course to get the correct answer or desired result.

trail

- **blaze a trail** to show or lead the way in some new activity or area of knowledge. <Refers to explorers going along a path and marking the way for those coming after them by stripping sections of bark from trees (blazing)>.

trial

- **trials and tribulations** difficulties and hardships.

trick

- **do the trick** to have the desired effect, to achieve the desired result.
- **never to miss a trick** never to fail to take advantage of a favourable situation or opportunity to bring advantage to oneself.
- **up to one's (old) tricks** acting in one's usual (wrong, dishonest or deceitful) way.

trooper

- **swear like a trooper** to swear very frequently or very strongly. <A trooper was an ordinary cavalry soldier>.

trot

- **on the trot 1** one after the other. **2** very active and busy.

trousers

- **wear the trousers** to make all the important decisions in a household.

trump

- **play one's trump card** to use something very advantageous to oneself that one has had in reserve for use when really necessary. <In card games a trump is a card of whichever suit has been declared to be higher-ranking than the others>.
- **turn up trumps** to do the right or required thing in a difficult situation, especially unexpectedly. <*See* above, refers to drawing a card from the trump suit>.

tune

- **call the tune** to be the person in control who gives the orders. <Refers to the saying 'He who pays the piper calls the tune'>.
- **in tune with (something)** in agreement with (something), compatible with (something).

- **to the tune of (something)** to the stated sum of money, usually high or higher than is expected or is reasonable.

turkey
- **cold turkey** a form of treatment for drug or alcohol abuse involving sudden and complete withdrawal as opposed to gradual withdrawal.
- **talk turkey** to talk plainly and honestly.

turn
- **a turn-up for the books** something favourable which happens unexpectedly. <Referred originally to a horse that unexpectedly won a race, the book meaning the total number of bets on a race>.
- **do (someone) a good turn** to help (someone) in some way.
- **done to a turn** cooked exactly right, cooked to perfection.
- **give (someone) quite a turn** to give (someone) a sudden shock or surprise.
- **turn turtle** to turn upside down, to capsize. <A turtle is helpless and easy to kill if it is turned over on its back>.

twice
- **think twice** to give careful consideration.

two
- **in two ticks** in a very short time. <Refers to the ticking of a cloak>.
- **put two and two together** to come to a (correct) conclusion from what one sees and hears.
- **two of a kind** two people of a very similar type or character.
- **two's company, (three's a crowd)** a third person who is with a couple is often unwanted as they want to be alone.

umbrage
- **take umbrage** to show that one is offended. <Originally meant to feel overshadowed, from Latin *umbra*, 'shade'>.

uncle
- **Uncle Sam** the United States of America. <Probably from the initials US which were stamped on government supplies, possibly because someone called Uncle Sam was employed in handling such supplies>.

under
- **under the influence** under the influence of alcohol, drunk.

up
- **be on the up-and-up** to be making successful progress.
- **be (well) up in *or* on (something)** to have an extensive knowledge of (something).
- **be up and running** to have started and be operating well.
- **be up to (someone)** it is (someone's) responsibility or duty.
- **be up to (something) 1** to be occupied with or in (something, often something dishonest, etc). **2** to be good enough, strong enough, etc, to do (something).
- **up and about** out of bed, after an illness.
- **up and doing** active and busy.
- **ups and downs** good fortune and bad fortune, successful periods and unsuccessful periods.
- **upstage (someone *or* something)** to take attention or interest away from (someone or something).

upshot
- **the upshot** the result or outcome. <Literally the last shot in an archery competition>.

upper
- **have *or* get the upper hand (of *or* over) (someone)** have or get an advantage or control (over someone).
- **on one's uppers** very poor. <Literally with no soles on one's shoes>.
- **upper-crust** of the upper class or aristocracy. <Refers literally to the upper part of the pastry of a pie above the filling>.

uptake
- **quick *or* slow on the uptake** quick or slow to understand.

uriah
- **Uriah Heep** a sycophant, someone who always fawns over and toadies to others. <Refers to a character in Charles Dickens's novel *David Copperfield*>.

u-turn
- **do a U-turn** to change one's opinion, policy, etc, completely. <Refers originally to vehicle drivers making a turn in the shape of the letter U to reverse direction>.

vain
- **take (someone's) name in vain** to use (someone's) name disrespectfully, especially to swear using God's name. <A biblical reference to Exodus 20:7>.

variety
- **variety is the spice of life** the opportunity to do different things, experience different situations, etc, is what makes life interesting. <A quotation from a poem by William Cowper>.

veil
- **draw a veil over (something)** not to discuss (something), to keep (something) hidden or secret.

vengeance
- **with a vengeance** very strongly, much, etc.

vex
- **a vexed question** a difficult issue or problem that is much discussed without being resolved.

victory
- **landslide victory** a victory in an election by a very large number of votes.

view
- **a bird's-eye view of (something) 1** a view of (something) seen from high above. **2** a brief description, etc, of (something).

villain
- **the villain of the piece** the person responsible for an act of evil or wrongdoing. <Refers originally to the villain in a play>.

vine
- **a clinging vine** a possessive person, someone who likes always to be with someone else.
- **wither on the vine** to die to come to an end without being used, finished, etc. <Literally of grapes withering on the vine instead of being picked and eaten or made into wine>.

violet
- **a shrinking violet** a very timid, shy person.

voice
- **a voice crying in the wilderness** (someone) expressing an opinion or warning that no one takes any notice of. <A biblical reference to John the Baptist in Matthew 3:3>.
- **the still, small voice (of reason)** the expression of a calm, sensible point of view. <A biblical reference to I Kings 19:12>.

volume
- **speak volumes** to express a great deal of meaning without putting it into words.

vote
- **a vote of confidence** a vote taken to establish whether or not the government, a group of people, a person, etc, is still trusted and supported.
- **vote with one's feet** to leave.

wagon
- **circle the wagons** of a group of people, to work together to protect

themselves against possible harm or danger. <In the American West pioneers used to form their wagons into a circle if they were under attack>.

- **on the wagon** not drinking alcohol. <Refers to a water wagon>.

wake

- **in the wake of (something)** immediately following, and often caused by (something). <Refers literally to the strip of water left by the passing of a ship>.

wall

- **be climbing the wall(s)** to feel frustrated, bored or impatient.
- **go to the wall** to suffer ruin. <Origin uncertain>.
- **off the wall** unconventional, strange.
- **up the wall** very annoyed, irritated, harassed, etc.
- **walls have ears** someone may be listening (to a secret conversation.

walter

- **a Walter Mitty** someone who invents stories about himself to make his life seem more exciting. <Refers to a character in a James Thurber short story>.

war

- **have been in the wars** to have a slight injury.
- **on the warpath** very angry. <An American Indian expression>.

wart

- **warts and all** including all the faults, disadvantages. <Refers to the fact that Oliver Cromwell instructed his portrait painter, Sir Peter Lely, to paint him as he really was, including his warts, rather than try to make him look more handsome>.

wash

- **come out in the wash** to come to a satisfactory end. <Used literally of a stain on clothes, etc, that comes out when the article is washed>.
- **(something) won't wash** to be regarded as unacceptable or incredible.

water

- **blow (someone or something) out of the water** to destroy or defeat (someone or something) utterly.
- **hold water** to be accurate, to be able to be proved true. <From a vessel that is not broken>.
- **muddy the waters** to confuse a situation.
- **test the water/waters** to try to find out what the reaction is likely to be to a plan before one puts this into effect.
- **tread water** to take very little action. <Literally to keep oneself afloat in water by moving the legs (and arms)>.
- **water under the bridge** something that is past and cannot be changed and should be forgotten.

wave

- **make waves** to cause trouble.
- **on the same wavelength as (someone)** having the same opinions, attitudes, tastes, etc, as (someone).

way

- **be set in one's ways** to have a set routine in your life and to dislike having this disrupted.
- **get into the way of (something *or* doing something)** to become accustomed to (something or doing something).
- **get *or* have one's own way** to do or get what one wants.
- **go back a long way** used to indicate that people have known each other for a long time.
- **go out of one's way** to do more than is really necessary, to make a special effort.
- **go the way of all flesh** to die or come to an end.
- **have a way with (someone *or* something)** to have a special knack with (someone or something), to be good at handling (someone or something).
- **have everything one's own way** to get everything done according to one's wishes.
- **have it both ways** to have the advantages of two sets of situations, each of which usually excludes the possibility of the other.
- **lead the way** to go first, to be in front.
- **lose one's way** to cease to know where one is or which direction one is going in.
- **make way for (someone *or* something)** to stand aside to leave room for (someone or something).
- **mend one's ways** to improve one's behaviour.
- **not to know which way to turn** to be in trouble and to be too confused to be able to decide what to do for the best.
- **pay one's way** to pay one's expenses or one's share of expenses.
- **see one's way to (doing something)** to be able and willing to (do something).
- **there are no two ways about it** no other opinion, attitude, etc, is possible.
- **under way** in progress.
- **ways and means** methods, especially unofficial ones.
- **where's there's a will there's a way** a saying used to indicate that if one is determined to do something, then one will find a way to succeed in doing so.

wayside

- **fall by the wayside** to fail to continue to the end of something; to give up in the course of doing something. <A biblical reference to the parable of the sower in Luke 8:5>.

wear

- **be the worse for wear 1** to be in a bad state, looking tired, ill, untidy, etc. **2** to be drunk.

weather

- **under the weather** unwell.

web

- **a tangled web** used to describe a very complicate, confused situation.

wedge

- **drive a wedge between** to cause disagreement or ill will between two people or two groups, especially when they were formerly friendly.
- **the thin end of the wedge** a minor event or action which could be the first stage of something major and serious or harmful.

weight

- **a weight off one's mind** used to indicate that one no longer has to worry about something which has been worrying one for some time.
- **carry weight** to have influence, to be considered important.
- **pull one's weight** to do one's fair share of work, etc.
- **punch above one's weight** to try to do something which is thought to be beyond one's abilities.
- **take the weight off one's feet** to sit down.
- **throw one's weight about *or* around** to use one's power and influence in a bullying way.
- **throw one's weight behind (someone or something)** to support (someone or something).

west

- **go west** to be ruined, to be finished. <Airmen's slang from World War I>.

wet

- **wet behind the ears** to be young, inexperienced and naive.
- **have a whale of a time** to have an extremely enjoyable time.

what

- **give (someone) what for** to scold or punish (someone).
- **know what's what** to know the details of a situation, to know what is going on.
- **what have you** and similar things.

wheel

- **a fifth wheel** a person or thing that is not needed or is not wanted. <Refers to the fact that a vehicle needs only four wheels to keep running>.
- **reinvent the wheel** to do something which one considers new or innovative, but which is, in fact, very similar to something which has been done by someone else; to start a project from scratch without taking advantage of available information, research, etc.
- **set the wheels in motion** to start a process off.
- **wheeling and dealing** acting in an astute but sometimes dishonest or immoral way, especially in business.
- **wheels within wheels** used to indicate a very complicated situation with many different things involved, all influencing each other.

whip

- **have the whip hand** to have control or an advantage. <Refers to coach-driving>.
- **a whipping boy** someone who is blamed and punished for someone else's mistakes. <Refers literally to a boy who was punished for any misdeeds a royal prince made, since the tutor was not allowed to strike a member of the royal family>.

whisker

- **win by a whisker** to win by a very short amount.

whistle

- **wet one's whistle** to have a drink.
- **whistle for (something)** to ask for (something) with no hope of getting it. <Perhaps from an old sailors' superstition that when a ship is becalmed whistling can summon up a wind>.

white

- **a whited sepulchre** someone who pretends to be moral and virtuous but is in fact bad. <A biblical reference to Matthew 23:27>.
- **white lie** a not very serious lie.
- **whiter than white** extremely honest and moral.

wick

- **get on (someone's) wick** to annoy or irritate (someone) greatly.

wide

- **be wide open** used of a competition of some kind to indicate that it is very difficult to predict the winner as the competitors seem equally good.

wild

- **a wild goose chase** a search or hunt that cannot end in success.
- **sow one's wild oats** to enjoy oneself in a wild and sometimes promiscuous way when one is young.
- **spread like wildfire** to spread extremely rapidly. <Wildfire was probably a kind of fire started by lightning>.

will

- **with a will** enthusiastically and energetically.

wind

- **get one's second wind** to find renewed energy to go on doing something after a period of feeling tired and weak.
- **get wind of (something)** to receive information about (something) <Referring to the scent of an animal carried by the wind>.
- **in the wind** about to happen, being placed or prepared.
- **get the wind up** to become frightened or nervous.
- **raise the wind** to get enough money to do (something).
- **spit in the wind** to try to do something impossible and so waste time and effort.
- **take the wind out of (someone's) sails** to reduce (someone's) pride in his or her cleverness, abilities, etc. <Refers to the fact that a ship takes the wind out of another ship's sails if it passes close to it on the windward side>.
- **throw caution to the (four) winds** to begin to behave recklessly.
- **whistle in the wind** to make a statement or promise which is pointless since it is very unlikely to have any effect or produce any results.

windmill

- **tilt at windmills** to struggle against imaginary opposition. <Refers to an episode in Cervantes' novel *Don Quixote* in which the hero mistakes a row of windmills for giants and attacks them>.

window

- **go out the window** to disappear completely; to be ignore or forgotten about.
- **window-dressing** the presentation of something to show the most favourable parts and hide the rest. <Refers literally to the arranging of goods in a shop window to attract customers>.

wing

- **on a wing and a prayer** used to indicate that you hope to do something successfully even although you do not have the resources to do so.
- **spread one's wings 1** to leave home. **2** to try to put into practice one's own ideas, to make use of one's abilities. <Refers to young birds ready to try to fly and leave the nest for the first time>.
- **take (someone) under one's wing** to take (someone) under one's protection and guidance. <Refers to the practice of some birds of covering their young with their wings>.
- **try one's wings** to try to do something which one has never done before in order to see if one will be successful at it.
- **waiting in the wings** in a state of readiness to do something, especially to take over someone else's job. <Literally waiting in the wings of a theatre stage ready to go on>.
- **wing it** to do something without planning or preparation, to improvise.

wink

- **not sleep a wink** not to be able to sleep at all.
- **tip (someone) the wink** to give (someone) information secretly or privately.

wire

- **down to the wire** to the last possible minute.
- **get** *or* **have one's wires crossed** to be involved in a misunderstanding. <Refers to telephone wires>.

wise

- **none the wiser** knowing no more than one did before.
- **put (someone) wise to (something)** to give (someone) information about (something), make (someone) aware of (something).

wish

- **wishful thinking** believing that, or hoping that, something unlikely is true or will happen just because one wishes that it would.
- **wish (someone) joy of (something)** to wish that something will be a pleasure or benefit to someone (although one doesn't think it will).

wit

- **at one's wits' end** worried and desperate.
- **keep one's wits about one** to be alert and watchful.
- **live by one's wits** to live by cunning schemes rather than by working.
- **pit one's wits against (someone)** to use one's intelligence to try to defeat (someone).
- **scare (someone) out of his** *or* **her wits** to frighten (someone) very much.

witch

- **witch-hunt** a search for and persecution of people who are thought to have done something wrong or hold opinions which are thought to be dangerous etc. <Refers historically to organized hunts for people thought to be witches>.

wolf

- **a wolf in sheep's clothing** someone evil and dangerous who seems to be gentle and harmless. <A biblical reference to Matthew 7:15>.
- **cry wolf** to give a false warning of danger, to call unnecessarily for help.

<Refers to one of Aesop's fables in which a shepherd boy used to amuse himself by calling out that a wolf was coming to attack his sheep and did this so many times when it was not true that no one believed when it was true, and all his sheep were killed>.

- **keep the wolf from the door** to prevent poverty and hunger.

wood

- **not to be able to see the wood for the trees** not to be able to consider the general nature of a situation, etc, because one is concentrating too much on details.
- **out of the woods** out of danger or difficulties.
- **touch wood** to touch something made of wood supposedly to keep away bad luck. <Refers to a well-known superstition>.

wool

- **pull the wool over (someone's) eyes** to deceive (someone).
- **wool-gathering** day-dreaming. <Refers to someone wandering around hedges gathering wool left by sheep>.

word

- **eat one's words** to admit that one was wrong in what one said.
- **get a word in edgeways *or* edgewise** to have difficulty in breaking into a conversation.
- **hang on (someone's) words** to listen carefully and eagerly to everything that someone says.
- **have a word in (someone's) ear** to tell (someone) something in private.
- **have words** to argue or quarrel.
- **keep one's word** to do as one promised to do.
- **put in a good word for (someone)** to say something favourable about (someone), to recommend (someone).
- **put words into (someone's) mouth** to say that someone has said something when he/she did not; to suggest that someone is going to say something when he/she has no intention of doing so.
- **say the word** say what you want and your wishes will be carried out.
- **take (someone's) word for it** to believe what someone says without question and without proof.
- **take the words out of (someone's) mouth** to say what (someone) was just about to say.

work

- **all work and no play makes Jack a dull boy** people should take some leisure time and not work all the time.
- **give (someone) the works** to give (someone) the complete treatment. <Originally slang for to kill someone>.
- **have one's work cut out** to face a very difficult task. <Literally to have a lot of work ready for on>.
- **worked up** agitated, annoyed.

world

- **a man of the world** a sophisticated and worldly man.
- **come down in the world** to be less well off, less successful etc. than formerly.
- **come up in the world** to be better off, more successful, etc. than formerly.
- **do (someone) the world of good** to have a very good effect on (someone); to be of great benefit or advantage to (someone).
- **for all the world like (someone *or* something)** exactly like (someone or something).
- **not the end of the world** used to make someone realize that things are not as bad as they think they are.
- **not to have long for this world** to be about to die.
- **on top of the world** very cheerful and happy.
- **out of this world** remarkably good.
- **think the world of (someone)** to be extremely fond of (someone).
- **the world is (someone's) oyster** (someone) has a great many possible opportunities or chances. <Refers to a quotation from Shakespeare's *The Merry Wives of Windsor*, Act 2, scene ii>.

worm

- **a can of worms** an extremely complicated and difficult situation. <Refers to the fact that worms wriggle around a lot>.
- **(even) the worm turns** even the most humble or meek person will protest if treated badly enough.

worth

- **for all one is worth** using maximum effort.

wound

- **lick one's wounds** to try to recover from a situation in which one has been badly defeated or humiliated.
- **reopen old wounds** to remind people of past unpleasant experiences which they would prefer to forget about.

wrap

- **keep (something) under wraps** to keep (something) secret or hidden.
- **take the wraps off (something)** to reveal, or give details about, something that has been secret up till now.
- **wrapped up in (someone *or* something)** absorbed in, giving all one's attention to (someone or something).
- **wrap (something) up** to finish (something) completely.

writ

- **writ large** used to indicate that something is in its most extreme form.

write

- **the writing on the wall** something which indicates that something unpleasant, such as failure, unhappiness, disaster, etc, will happen. <A biblical reference to Daniel 5:5–31, in which the coming destruction of the Babylonian empire is made known to Belshazzar at a feast through mysterious writing on a wall>.

wrong

- **get on the wrong side of (someone)** to cause (someone) to dislike or be hostile to one.
- **not to put a foot wrong** not to make a mistake of any kind.

yarn

- **spin a yarn** to tell a long story, especially an untrue one that is given as an excuse. <Telling a story is compared to spinning a long thread>.

year

- **the year dot** a long time ago, the beginning of time.

yesterday

- **not born yesterday** not easily fooled.

young

- **you're only young once** one should take advantage of the opportunities that arise when one is young and has the energy, freedom, etc, to enjoy or exploit them.

zero

- **zero hour** the time at which something is due to begin. <Originally a military term>.

Clichés

Clichés are an established feature of the English language, being particularly common in spoken English language and in informal written contexts. Some of them are hundreds of years old; others have taken only a short time to become popular.

People tend to use them unconsciously and most of us are unaware of quite how often we use them. There are many who claim to dislike clichés and regard them as somehow spoiling the language, but even they would find that they use quite a lot of them, if they stopped to analyse what they say and write.

People dislike clichés because they are overused. Many clichés start out as a particularly imaginative or neat way of saying something, but they become used so often by so many people that they lose their freshness and originality.

It would be almost impossible to rid our speech and writing entirely of clichés and, in any case, they often add a bit of colour to the language. Since they are such an established feature of English, it is important for learners of English to learn how to use them correctly. However, particularly in fairly formal speech or writing, it is essential to try to avoid using them too frequently.

Some clichés are used in contexts in which they are virtually meaningless and act simply as conversational fillers. For example, there are people who use the expression at this moment in time regularly when the word 'now' would be more appropriate. Likewise, many people use clichés such as **the thing is, at the end of the day** or **you know what I mean** in this way.

Below is a selection of common clichés which are particularly overused and so should be used sparingly. Some of these are more thoroughly explained in the English Idioms section.

accidents will happen things go wrong at some time in everyone's life
across the board applying to everyone or to all cases
actions speak louder than words how a person acts is more important than what they say
to add insult to injury to make matters worse
after due consideration after some thought
all things considered after some thought
an accident waiting to happen a dangerous situation
any port in a storm a welcome solution in a bad situation
as a matter of fact the following statement is true
at death's door an exaggeration to say someone is ill
at the drop of a hat without much of a reason at all
at the end of the day ultimately
at this juncture now
at this moment in time now
avoid like the plague to strenuously avoid
back to the drawing board back to the beginning
bag and baggage all your possessions
bag of tricks the equipment necessary to do something
batten down the hatches there's going to be trouble
beggars can't be choosers one needs a favour and has no other choice
be that as it may that may be so
better late than never an ironic way of saying something or someone is late
bite the bullet to get on with something despite unpleasantness
a blessing in disguise a bad situation from which may come good
blissful ignorance to be in the happy state of not knowing of an unpleasant situation
a blot on the landscape an ugly thing (usually a building) in a beautiful place
blushing bride an ironic description of a bride
bone of contention a cause of dispute
the bottom line the outcome or conclusion; most important factor
bright-eyed and bushy-tailed alert and awake
by the same token using the same reasoning, or on the other side of the argument
call it a day give up and stop a venture
the calm before the storm a time before an unpleasant situation where everything seems fine
Catch 22 a situation in which one can never win or from which one can never escape
categorical denial strong denial
caught napping unprepared for a situation
chalk and cheese opposites
champing at the bit enthusiastic to get started at something
chapter and verse every detail
cheek by jowl very close together
chop and change alternate
a close shave an escape which was very nearly disastrous
to coin a phrase ironically, this is said when one is using a cliché
come full circle to return to the beginning of something
a commanding lead emphasis of in the lead
common or garden everyday
conspicuous by one's absence to deliberately boycott something
cool, calm and collected emphasis of calm
cover a multitude of sins a flattering surface on something, usually refers to clothing
at crack of dawn very early
cross that bridge when you come to it deal with matters in hand and think of other problems when they arise
to cut a long story short to summarise
cut and dried settled and definite
the cutting edge the latest technology
damn with faint praise to praise in a patronising or deliberately ironic way
a damp squib something which promises excitement but disappoints
a dark horse someone with a secret, usually an exciting or exotic one
day in, day out every day
dead as a dodo actually dead, or more metaphorically, out of favour
dead in the water has no chance of working
dead to the world fast asleep
a deafening silence a silence which is very prominent and embarrassing
dig one's own grave to be the cause of one's own misfortune
a dirty tricks campaign a campaign, usually political, uncovering, or possibly creating rumours of, a scandal regarding one's opponent
dog eat dog a ruthless struggle against one's rivals to survive or be successful.
donkey's years ago many years ago
don't count your chickens before they are hatched don't presume anything before it happens
doom and gloom pessimism
draw a blank no result
drown one's sorrows to get drunk to get over a disappointment
Dutch courage to get drunk to have the confidence to do something
each and every one of you everyone
eager for the fray looking for a fight
easier said than done more difficult than it appears to be
eat humble pie to admit that you are wrong
economical with the truth to leave out important facts
the end of an era the end of an important phase
enough is enough no more can be tolerated
the envy of the world enviable
every cloud has a silver lining bad situations can sometimes have consolations
every dog has his day everyone has their individual triumphs
every little helps a little help from a lot of different

	sources will eventually add up to create something more substantial
every man jack	everyone
everything but the kitchen sink	almost all your belongings
explore every avenue	to look for all possibilities
face facts	be honest with yourself
face the music	face up to difficulties
the fact of the matter	the truth of the situation
fair and square	honestly
fall between two stools	to try to gain two things at once and fail with regard to both of them
fall on deaf ears	an explanation given to someone who doesn't want to listen
famous last words	making a statement about an event directly before the exact opposite happens
far and wide	a great area
far be it for me	this is something I would never do (usually said ironically)
a fate worse than death	an exaggeration meaning death would be preferable
a feeding frenzy	where many people are desperately after the same information (usually of the press)
few and far between	very rare
a fighting chance	a good chance of succeeding, or surviving
fighting fit	in good health
the finishing touches	in the final stages
first and foremost	first and most importantly
first things first	most important things first
a flash in the pan	a passing fashion or idea that will not last
the flavour of the month	a person or fashion that is popular at the moment but may not last
flog a dead horse	to pursue something that is not worth pursuing
the fly in the ointment	an unpleasant feature that spoils something
food for thought	something that makes you think
footloose and fancy free	single and looking for fun
forewarned is forearmed	to be prepared so that you are able to cope with a possible event
a forlorn hope	no hope
fraught with danger	dangerous
fresh fields and pastures new	a new and different place or situation
from the sublime to the ridiculous	from a state of greatness to one of ridiculousness
from the word go	from the start
from time immemorial	since a long time ago
gainful employment	in work
gather ye rosebuds while ye may	make the most of your youth
a general exodus	everyone has left at once
generous to a fault	extremely generous
a gentleman's agreement	an agreement in word alone
get down to brass tacks	to consider the basic facts
get more than one bargained for	to encounter more difficulties than expected
the gift of the gab	the ability to talk readily and easily
gild the lily	to add unnecessary decoration
give up the ghost	to die (person); to stop working (object)
a glowing tribute	a flattering tribute
a glutton for punishment	someone who has suffered but who goes back for more
go against the grain	to act against your better judgement or wishes
go from strength to strength	to get better and better
it goes without saying	you should know what I'm talking about
a golden opportunity	a great and unexpected opportunity that should be grasped
good as gold	perfectly behaved
the gory details	a description of the details of a situation (not necessarily a bad one)
grasp the nettle	to set about a difficult task in a determined way
the greatest thing since sliced bread	a very popular admired thing or person
green with envy	very jealous
grin and bear it	to suffer a bad situation without complaint
grind to a halt	to stop suddenly
a guiding light	someone who guides the way in a particular field
halcyon days	a nostalgic (and idealistic) reference to a perfect time in one's life
hale and hearty	healthy
half the battle	the most difficult part of a situation is over with
hand over fist	in large amounts; very rapidly
the happy couple	newly married people
a hard act to follow	someone who has previously been very successful at something
a helping hand	help
high and dry	left in a helpless state
hit the nail on the head	to be extremely accurate in one's description
a hive of activity	a very busy area
Hobson's choice	no choice at all
the honest truth	emphasis of the truth of a statement
hope against hope	to continue to hope although there is little reason to be hopeful
horses for courses	certain people are better suited to certain tasks than others
how time flies	time passes very quickly
if you can't beat 'em, join 'em	if the majority disagree with you then why not just go along with them
if you can't stand the heat, get out of the kitchen	if you can't cope with the job in hand then leave
ill-gotten gains	possessions acquired dishonestly
in all conscience	being completely fair and honest
in a nutshell	briefly; to sum up
in any shape or form	in any way at all
in less than no time	in a very short time
in no uncertain terms	in a very direct way
in splendid isolation	standing out in a unique way
in the cold light of day	when one looks at something rationally and calmly
in the dim and distant past	something happened a long time ago (and should be forgotten)
in the fullness of time	when the proper time has elapsed
in the nick of time	just in time
in the pipeline	in preparation
in the present climate	in the present situation
in this day and age	in these times
it'll all come out in the wash	things will turn out for the best in the end
it never rains but it pours	when something goes wrong other things go wrong too
it's a long story	it is complicated

it's a small world said when coincidental meetings occur
it's early days it's too early to come to a conclusion
it takes two to tango it's not the fault of one person
jack of all trades someone who knows a little about a lot of things
jam tomorrow the (possibly false) promise of better things in the future
the jewel in the crown the most valuable or successful thing associated with someone or something
jobs for the boys jobs given to friends rather than to those most worthy of them
jump on the bandwagon to show interest because it's fashionable
just between you and me (and the gatepost) this is a secret
just deserts to get the punishment that is due to you
just for the record so that it will be noted
just one of those things something that has to be accepted
just what the doctor ordered just what is required
keep a low profile not to draw attention to oneself
keep oneself to oneself not to tell others very much about oneself or to mix with others very much
keep one's head above water to be just coping with a situation
keep one's nose to the grindstone to keep working hard
keep the wolf from the door to make just enough money to survive
kickstart to encourage something or to give, e.g., a project, an extra push
kill the fatted calf to provide a lavish meal for a celebration
kill two birds with one stone to complete two tasks at once
kill with kindness to be generous in some way to someone when it's not in his or her best interest
the kiss of death something which will cause the ruin of something
knee-jerk reaction an immediate (reflex) response to something
know all the answers to have all the information
know for a fact emphasising that ones knows something
know where one stands to know the nature of one's position
know which side one's bread is buttered on to know when one is in a fortunate position
a labour of love a difficult job done for the satisfaction of it
the lap of luxury in luxurious surroundings
large as life in person, actually present
last but not least although someone or something is last, it is not the least important thing
the last straw an event which makes a situation impossible
a leading light a leader, longstanding, in a certain area
leave in the lurch to abandon
leave no stone unturned to search everywhere
leave to someone's tender mercies to be left in the care of someone inefficient or dangerous
let bygones be bygones forget about past grievances
let's face it face the truth
level playing field a fair basis for something
the life and soul of the party a lively entertaining person
light at the end of the tunnel fortunate outcome following times of trouble
a little bird told me I can't tell you my sources
lock, stock and barrel everything included
a lone wolf a loner
the long arm of the law the police
make an honest woman of marry
make ends meet to survive on little money
make the supreme sacrifice to die
make someone an offer they can't refuse an irresistible offer
make waves to get yourself noticed; to cause trouble.
man and boy as a child and an adult
the man in the street ordinary person
manna from heaven something unexpectedly advantageous
man to man as equals, regardless of background etc.
many hands make light work the more helpers there are the quicker a job will be done
mark my words take note of what I'm saying
a matter of life or death a very grave situation
method in one's madness actions seem to be foolish but actually have a motive behind them
a millstone round one's neck a hindrance
the moment of truth when the result of something becomes apparent
a moot point a point of argument
more in sorrow than in anger more disappointed in someone's actions than angry
the more the merrier the more people involved the better
move heaven and earth to go to great lengths to achieve something
move the goalposts to change the aims of a project so that it is disadvantageous to others but advantageous to oneself
the movers and shakers those with power
much of a muchness ordinary, indistinguishable from others
mutton dressed as lamb an older person (usually female) dressed in a way that is unflatteringly young
my lips are sealed it's a secret and I won't tell
name names be specific as to whom it is that you are talking about
the name of the game the important or central thing behind something
nearest and dearest close family and close friends
needless to say something that it should be unnecessary to state
a new dawn a new opportunity or era
the nitty gritty basic practical details
no expense spared lots of money has been spent
no gain without pain (no pain, no gain) you have to experience bad things in order to progress
nothing to write home about not very interesting
no news is good news if you haven't heard anything then it's possible that nothing bad has happened
no rest for the wicked ironic way of saying that a person is extremely busy and has to get on with their work
no show without Punch this person always seems to turn up (but is not really wanted)
no smoke without fire there's always some basis to a rumour
nothing ventured, nothing gained if you don't at least try to do something you'll never know if you'll succeed
not just a pretty face intelligent as well as beautiful (often said in an ironic way by someone who knows that he or she is not beautiful)
not to put too fine a point on it not to get too detailed
nuts and bolts the basic details or practicalities of something

odds and ends objects of different kinds, perhaps that are left over and don't match
older and wiser to have got more wise with age
once bitten, twice shy to have experienced an unfortunate situation and have learned from it
once in a blue moon very rarely
one in a million very rare
one of life's little ironies a situation that is the opposite of what one hoped would happen
one of those days a bad day
only time will tell you'll just have to wait and see what happens
on the back burner put to one side to be worked on later
on the dot exactly
opening gambit an opening move
an open secret information not publicly discussed but which is not a secret
or words to that effect something of the same meaning but said in a different way
out of sight, out of mind that which you don't see you are less likely to think about
over and done with finished
over my dead body I'll die before I let that happen
over the hill too old
pale into insignificance overshadowed by something else
par for the course an expected experience in a certain situation
part and parcel an expected experience in a certain situation
the patter of tiny feet a pregnancy
the picture of health very healthy
pie in the sky unrealistic expectations
plain sailing easy
pleased as Punch very pleased
the plot thickens a revelation makes a story more intriguing or complicated
the point of no return you've gone so far that going back is not a possible option
a poisoned chalice a seemingly attractive proposition that is actually dangerous
pound of flesh revenge
the powers that be people in charge
practice makes perfect to keep practising will achieve perfection in a certain area
pride and joy something that makes one very proud
pride of place in a very prominent position
prime of life at an age where one is fit, healthy and mentally sharp
pull out all the stops to do everything possible
put one's best foot forward to make the best attempt possible
put two and two together to come to a conclusion about something
quality of life an enjoyable fulfilling life
quality time time spent giving an individual lots of attention
quantum leap a sudden breakthrough
quite the reverse the opposite
a race against time time is running out
rain or shine whatever the weather
a rainy day an unspecified time in the future
the rat race the capitalist way of life
read my lips listen carefully to what I'm saying
red tape the rules and regulations of government office
reinvent the wheel wasting time doing work that's already been done
a reliable source a trustworthy basis for something
a resounding silence a meaningful silence
right as rain in full health
rings a bell sounds familiar
rising tide events that are about to take over
risk life and limb to put your life in danger
a rolling stone a person who never stays very long in one place
a rose between two thorns a beautiful or good person who has to decide between two unattractive choices
a rose by any other name whatever a beautiful thing happens to be named it remains beautiful
Rome wasn't built in a day a difficult task cannot be finished quickly
a rough diamond a person with a rough manner but who has great qualities
rule with a rod of iron to discipline in a strict manner
rumour has it I have heard rumours telling me this
safe and sound totally unharmed
a safe haven a place of safety
the salt of the earth a down to earth reliable person
saved by the bell saved from a bad situation by another event coming along
to say the least relates that the reaction or emotion which is being described is being understated
search high and low to look everywhere
second to none the best
sell like hot cakes to be very popular
separate the sheep from the goats to distinguish the talented people from the stupid ones
a shadow of one's former self to be in some way diminished, either in physical size or in emotions
the shape of things to come how the future might be
share and share alike to be fair in one's dealings
ships that pass in the night strangers who meet once and never again
shoot oneself in the foot to say or do something that is to one's own detriment
short and sweet short and to the point
the show must go on despite misfortune an event will go ahead
signed, sealed and delivered finalised
a sign of the times something which indicates what society is like now
the silent majority the people who do not make their opinions known publicly
six of one and half-a-dozen of the other the same outcome
the sixty four thousand dollar question a key question that sums up a situation
slave over a hot stove to cook
slowly but surely to work in a slow but careful way
smell a rat to suspect something is wrong
the social whirl hectic social life
so far, so good at this point in the proceedings everything is fine
son and heir first-born son
so near and yet so far to have nearly accomplished something but near accomplishment is simply not good enough to get acclaim
sour grapes saying that something one cannot have is not worth having
spick and span very tidy

the spirit is willing not physically able to do something that one wishes to do
stand up and be counted make your opinions known publicly
a storm in a teacup a fuss over nothing
strange as it may seem this may look strange but it is actually true
suffer a sea change to have a complete change in attitude or opinion
suffer in silence to put up with something and not complain
the survival of the fittest to survive or flourish at the expense of those who are weaker
sweetness and light kind and friendly (usually just on the surface)
swings and roundabouts the same outcome
take the bull by the horns to tackle something boldly
take the rough with the smooth to accept that bad things can happen as well as good
talk of the devil said when someone or something you've just been talking about suddenly appears
tall, dark and handsome the clichéd idea of the perfect man
a tall order an unreasonable or very trying request
a (slight) technical hitch a mistake or hold up
teething troubles problems at the beginning of a project
tender loving care (TLC) to be looked after
terra firma to have one's feet safely on the ground
thankful for small mercies to be grateful for some small benefits in an otherwise unfortunate situation
that'll be the day that's not going to happen
that's for me to know and for you to find out it's a secret
that's life unexpected or difficult things can happen, you can't stop them
that's the way the cookie crumbles unexpected or difficult things can happen, you can't stop them
there but for the grace of God go I I could be in that situation
there's no fool like an old fool foolish behaviour in an older person always seems even more foolish than if a young person acted that way
these things happen unexpected or difficult things can happen, you can't stop them
through thick and thin through good times and bad
throw in the towel to give up
tie the knot to get married
tighten one's belt to be careful with your money
time flies time passes quickly
the tip of the iceberg there's a bigger problem that has still to surface or be dealt with
tired and emotional drunk
a tissue of lies a statement that is entirely dishonest in every way
tomorrow is another day you can try again another time
too good to be true so good that you can't believe it to be so
too little, too late not enough to solve a problem and too late in any case
too many chiefs and not enough Indians too many people want to be in charge and no one wants to do the real work
too numerous to mention it would take too long to mention all the things I want to mention
touch and go a precarious situation
a tower of strength strong and reliable
trials and tribulations difficulties
turn over a new leaf to completely start over again in a new way

'twas ever thus it has always been like this
unaccustomed as I am to public speaking (usually said ironically) I'm not used to speaking in public
unavoidable delay a delay caused by something you have no control over
under a cloud depressed
under the sun in the whole world
under the weather feeling run down
the university of life learning from real life experience
unsung hero someone who has not received the credit they deserve
an untimely end the death of someone who was very young and expected to make much of their life
untold wealth wealth of uncertain but probably very large amounts
the unvarnished truth a response that doesn't cover up any unpleasant facts
up in arms furious
up to the hilt thoroughly prepared
vanish into thin air to disappear without trace
variety is the spice of life lots of different things in your life make it more exciting
vested interest a motive (usually financial) for having an interest in something
a vexed question a difficult situation that is much discussed but still not solved
a vicious circle a bad situation, the result of which produces the original cause of the situation
vote with one's feet to show displeasure by leaving a situation
wait on hand and foot to do everything for someone
walls have ears people might be eavesdropping
warts and all good and bad
water under the bridge a situation that has passed and should be forgotten about
wedded bliss a (possibly ironic) way of describing marriage
the wee small hours after midnight
a well-earned rest a rest following hard work
what with one thing and another considering all the other things that have happened
wheels within wheels a complicated situation that has other things involved
when all is said and done when all things have been considered and the argument is over
when in Rome join in with the customs of the people you are with
who/which shall remain nameless who need not be mentioned because we know who I am talking about
the whys and wherefores the reasoning behind an argument
without more ado without waiting any longer
the witching hour midnight
with bated breath excitedly
wonders will never cease something has happened that has been long awaited but was not really expected to come about
a word to the wise a piece of advice
the world's your oyster the world is there for you to explore
the writing is on the wall something is indicating that something bad is going to happen
you can say that again what you've said is true and I agree
you can't make a silk purse out of a sow's ear you can't make something attractive out of something worthless/unattractive
you can't teach an old dog there's no point in trying to make people

new tricks change

you can't win 'em all bad things inevitably happen and you can't do anything about it

you know what I mean (added as emphasis to find out if listener empathises)

you must be joking I find what you've said ridiculous or unbelievable

your chariot awaits (ironic) said when someone is about to get into a vehicle

you're only young once make the most of your life

your guess is as good as mine neither of us know anything about this subject

Similes

A simile is a figure of speech in which a thing or person is, for the sake of comparison, said to be like another. The word *simile* is derived from *similis*, the Latin word for like. The words *like* or *as* usually appear in the simile, as in: *the rumour spread like wildfire, she was as slim as a wand*. Some similes are extremely common. A list of these is given below.

agile as a monkey
alike as (like) two peas in a pod
bald as a coot
black as ebony
blind as a bat
bold as brass
brave as a lion
brown as a berry
calm as a millpond
changeable as the moon
cheerful as the day is long
clear as daylight
clear as mud (=not at all clear)
common as muck
cool as a cucumber
cunning as a fox
dead as a doornail
deaf as a post
drunk as a lord
dry as a bone
dry as dust (boring)
dull as ditchwater
easy as pie
easy as falling off a log
fit as a fiddle
flat as a pancake
frisky as a colt
good as gold
green as grass
happy as a pig in muck
happy as a sandboy
hard as nails
helpless as a babe in arms
hollow as a drum
hot as hell
innocent as a new-born babe
keen as mustard
light as a feather
lively as a cricket
mad as a hatter
merry as a lark
neat as a pin
old as the hills/Methuselah
patient as Job
plain as a pikestaff
playful as a kitten
pleased as Punch
poor as a church mouse
pretty as a picture
proud as a peacock
quick as a flash
quiet as a mouse
rare as hen's teeth
rich as Croesus
safe as houses
sharp as a razor
sick as a dog
sick as a parrot (disappointed)
silent as the grave
simple as ABC
slow as a snail
sly as a fox
smart as paint
smooth as silk
sober as a judge
straight as a die
stubborn as a mule
sure as death
swift as an arrow
tall as a steeple
thick as thieves (friendly)
thick as two short planks (stupid)
thin as a rake
tight as a drum
tough as old boots
uncertain as the weather
weak as water
white as snow/a ghost
wily as a fox
wise as Solomon

Proverbs

action

Actions speak louder than words
It is the first step that is the most difficult
One good turn deserves another

Sooner begun, sooner done
The early bird catches the worm

age
A creaking door hangs long on its hinges
All would live long, but none would be old
An old fox is not easily snared
Crabbed age and youth cannot live together
Don't teach your grandmother to suck eggs
Life begins at forty
The best wine comes out of an old bottle
There's many a good tune played on an old fiddle
There's no fool like an old fool
There's none so old that he hopes not for another year of life
They who live longest will see most
Years know more than books
You are never too old to learn
You are only as old as you feel
You can't teach an old dog new tricks
Youth and age will never agree

anticipation
Don't count your chickens until they are hatched
It is better to travel hopefully than to arrive
It isn't over until the fat lady sings
There's many a slip 'twixt cup and lip

appearance
A fair face may hide a foul heart
All cats are grey in the dark
All that glitters is not gold
Appearances are deceptive
Beauty is but skin deep
Beauty is in the eye of the beholder
Beware the wolf in sheep's clothing
Be what you appear to be
Clothes make the man
Fine feathers make fine birds
First impressions are the most lasting
Handsome is as handsome does
Never judge from appearances
The eyes are the window of the soul
The fairest rose at last is withered
There is no making a good cloak of bad cloth
Things are not always what they seem
You can't judge a book by its cover
You must not hang a man by his looks

caution
A stitch in time saves nine
Better safe than sorry
Better the devil you know than the devil you don't know
Curiosity killed the cat
Cut your coat according to the cloth
Don't count your chickens before they are hatched
Don't put all your eggs in one basket
Don't throw out the baby with the bathwater
Haste makes waste
Least said is soonest mended
Let sleeping dogs lie
Look before you leap
Make haste slowly
Marry in haste, repent at leisure
More haste, less speed
Once bitten, twice shy
One step at a time
Second thoughts are best
Slow and steady wins the race
The burnt child fears the fire
The less said the better
Think first and then speak
You must learn to walk before you can run

change
A change is as good as a rest
A new broom sweeps clean
A rolling stone gathers no moss
Better the devil you know
Don't change horses in mid-stream
There is nothing new under the sun
You can't put back the clock
You can't put new wine in old bottles
Variety is the spice of life

character
Blood will tell
Cut off a dog's tail and he will be a dog still
The apple never falls far from the tree
The leopard cannot change its spots
What's bred in the bone comes out in the flesh
You cannot make a silk purse out of a sow's ear

choice
You cannot have it both ways
You cannot have your cake and eat it
You cannot serve god and Mammon
You cannot serve two masters
You pays your money, you takes your choice

conduct
Ask no questions and you will be told no lies
Civility costs nothing
Cleanliness is next to godliness
Do as I say, not as I do
Do as you would be done by
Do not bite the hand that feeds you
Don't cut off your nose to spite your face
Don't hide your light under a bushel
If the cap fits, wear it
It is better to give than to receive
Least said soonest mended
Let sleeping dogs lie
Live and let live
Moderation in all thing
Never look a gift horse in the mouth
One good turn deserves another
People in glass houses should not throw stones
Practise what you preach
Pride goes before a fall
See no evil, hear no evil, speak no evil
Spare the rod and spoil the child
There is no use flogging a dead horse
The rolling stone gathers no moss
Travel broadens the mind

When in Rome do as the Romans do
When the cat's away the mice will play
You cannot have your cake and eat it

courage and cowardice

A bully is always a coward
Attack is the best form of defence
Conscience makes cowards of us all
Discretion is the better part of valour
Faint heart never won fair lady
Fortune favours the bold
He that fights and runs away may live to fight another day
It is better to be a coward for a minute than dead for the rest of your life
Nothing ventured, nothing gained

crime

All are not thieves whom the dogs bark at
An old poacher makes the best gamekeeper
Better to do nothing than to do ill
Caesar's wife must be above suspicion

Crime never pays

It's an ill bird that fouls its own nest
One rotten apple in the barrel infects all the rest
Poverty is the mother of crime
Set a thief to catch a thief
There are more thieves than are hanged
There is honour among thieves
To err is human, to forgive divine
Two wrongs do not make a right
You might as well be hanged for a sheep as a lamb

death

All men must die
As a man lives so shall he die
Dead men tell no tales
Death is a remedy for all ills
Death is the great leveller
Death spares neither men nor beast
Fear of death is worse than death itself
It is as natural to die as to be born
Nothing is certain but death and taxes
One funeral makes many orphans
Shrouds have no pockets
The dead are soon forgotten
The good die young
We die as we live
When one is dead it is for a long time
Whom the gods love die young
You can only die once

delay

Better late than never
He who hesitates is lost
Never put off till tomorrow what you can do today
Procrastination is the thief of time
Time lost cannot be recalled
Tomorrow never comes

eating and drinking

Adam's ale is the best brew
An apple a day keeps the doctor away
An army marches on its stomach
Drink little that you may drink long
Eat to live, not live to eat
Good wine makes good blood
Hunger is the best sauce
In vino veritas (There is truth in wine)
Man cannot live by bread alone
The way to a man's heart is through his stomach
Thirst makes wine out of water
When the wine is in the wit is out

folly

A fool and his money are soon parted
A fool's bolt is soon shot
Empty vessels make the most sound
Fools rush in where angels fear to tread
Fortune favours fools
He that is born a fool is never cured
Little things please little minds
There's no fool like an old fool
The world is full of fools
We have all been fools in our time

friendship

A fair-weather friend changes with the wind
A favourite has no friends
A friend in need is a friend indeed
A man is known by the company he keeps
A trouble shared is a trouble halved
Birds of a feather flock together
Fish and guests stink after three days
He that lies down with dogs will get up with fleas
It is good to have friends in high places
One good turn deserves another
Save us from our friends
The best of friends must apart

happiness

A blithe heart makes a blooming visage
A happy heart is better than a full purse
All happiness is in the mind
Be happy when you can for you are a long time dead
Content is happiness
Happy is the country which has no history
It is a poor heart that never rejoices
Joy and sorrow are next-door neighbours
Laughter is the best medicine
No pleasure without pain

health

A creaking gate lasts longest
An apple a day keeps the doctor away
Early to bed and early to rise makes a man healthy, wealthy and wise
Feed a cold and starve a fever
God heals, and the physician has the thanks
Health is better than wealth
The doctor is often more to be feared than the disease

home

Dry bread at home is better than roast meat abroad
East west, home's best
Home is where the heart is
The hare always returns to her form
There's no place like home

honesty
An honest man's word is as good as his bond
Better beg than steal
Confession is good for the soul
Honesty is the best policy
No honest man ever repented of his honesty
Plain dealing is best
Tell the truth and shame the devil
The truth will out

hope and optimism
A drowning man clutches at straws
Every cloud has a silver lining
He that lives on hope has but a slender diet
Hope for the best and prepare for the worst
Hope keeps man alive
Hope springs eternal
It's an ill wind that blows nobody any good
Look on the bright side
The darkest hour is that before the dawn
The longest night will have an end
Tomorrow is another day
Too much hope deceives
Where there's life, there's hope

law
Better no law than law not enforced
Every land has its own law
Every man is held to be innocent until he is proved guilty
Ignorance of the law excuses no man
Possession is nine tenths of the law
The law is an ass
The more laws, the more offenders
There's one law for the rich and another for the poor
You cannot make people honest by an act of parliament

learning and knowledge
A little knowledge is a dangerous thing
A little learning is a dangerous thing
Experience is the best teacher
It is easy to be wise after the event
Knowledge is power
Much learning makes men mad
to know all is to forgive all
We must learn from our mistakes
What you don't know can't hurt you
Where ignorance is bliss, 'tis folly to be wise

love
Absence makes the heart grow fonder
All's fair in love and war
All the world loves a lover
Better be an old man's darling than a young man's slave
Faint heart never won fair lady
It is best to be off with the old love before you are on with the new
Love begets love
Love comes in at the window and out at the door
Love conquers all
Love is blind
Love makes the world go round
Love sees no faults
Love will find a way
Lucky at cards, unlucky in love
Out of sight, out of mind
Pity is akin to love
The course of true love never did run smooth
The way to a man's heart is through his stomach
'Tis better to have loved and lost than never to have loved at all
Who would be loved, must love

marriage
Marriage is a lottery
Marriages are made in heaven
Marry in haste, repent at leisure
Marry in Lent and you'll live to repent
Marry your son when you will, your daughter when you can
Men are April when they woo, December when they wed
Wedlock is a padlock

miserliness
Don't spoil the ship for a hap'orth of tar
Grasp all, lose all
Greedy folks have long arms
Kill not the goose that lays the golden egg
The more you get, the more you want

opportunity
A bird in the hand is worth two in the bush
Gather ye rosebuds while ye may
Make hay while the sun shines
Nothing venture, nothing gain
Opportunity seldom knocks twice
Strike while the iron is hot
Take time by the forelock
There's no time like the present
The tide must be taken when it comes
Time and tide wait for no man

patience
An oak is not felled at one stroke
A watched pot never boils
Everything comes to him who waits
Patience is a virtue
Rome was not built in a day
They also serve who only stand and wait
We must learn to walk before we can run

power
A cat may look at a king
A house divided against itself cannot stand
All men cannot be masters
Attack is the best form of defence
Little is done where many command
Might is right
Money is power
No man can serve two masters
Power corrupts
The ballot is stronger than the bullet
The mightier they are, the harder they fall
The weakest go to the wall
United we stand, divided we fall
When Greek meets Greek then comes the tug of war

When two play one must lose
Why keep a dog and bark yourself?

regret

It is easy to be wise after the event
It is too late to shut the stable door after the horse has bolted
Past cure, past care
There's no use in crying over spilt milk
Things past cannot be recalled
We never know the worth of the water till the well runs dry
What's done cannot be undone
You cannot make omelettes without breaking eggs

responsibility

A bad workman blames his tools
As you make your bed, so you must lie on it
As you reap, so shall you sow
Every man is the architect of his own fortune
Paddle your own canoe
The absent party is always to blame

silence

A closed mouth catches no flies
Silence is golden
Speech is silver, silence is golden
Still waters run deep
There is a time to speak and a time to be silent
When in doubt say nothing

sleep

One hour's sleep before midnight is worth two after
Sleep is better than medicine
Sleep is the brother of death
There will be sleeping enough in the grave

talking

Barking dogs seldom bite
Fine words butter no parsnips
The tongue is more venomous than a serpent's sting

time

History repeats itself
There is a time and place for everything
Time and tide wait for no man
Time cures all things
Time flies
Time is a great healer
Time is money
Time lost cannot be recalled

wealth and poverty

A fool and his money are soon parted
Born with a silver spoon in one's mouth
Enough is as good as a feast
God helps those who help themselves
Half a loaf is better than no bread
He that goes a-borrowing goes a-sorrowing
He who has nothing fears nothing
He who pays the piper may call the tune
It is better to be born lucky than rich
It is better to be poor and well than rich and ill
Lend your money and lose your friend
Money is a good servant but a bad master
Money is not everything
Money is power
Money makes money
Money talks
Neither a borrower nor a lender be
Penny wise and pound foolish
Poverty is no disgrace but it is a great inconvenience
Poverty is not a crime
Take care of the pennies and the pounds will take care of themselves
The art is not in making money but in keeping it
Time is money
What you've never had, you never miss
When poverty comes in at the door, love flies out of the window

weather

A cold April the barn will fill
After the storm comes a calm
A green Yule means a fat churchyard
April and May are the key to the year
April showers bring forth May flowers
Lightning never strikes twice
Rain before seven, fine before eleven
Red sky at night, shepherd's delight, red sky in the morning, shepherd's morning
St Swithin's Day, if thou dost rain, for forty days it will remain

work

A good beginning is half the work
A work done ill must be done twice
Business before pleasure
From small beginnings come great things
If a thing is worth doing it is worth doing well
Many hands make light work
No gain without pain
The devil finds work for idle hands to do
The labourer is worthy of his hire
The work praises the workman
Too many cooks spoil the broth
You cannot make bricks without straw

Appendix 3
World Facts

How to use this section

World Facts contains up-to-date geographical information on the world's countries, its major cities and its important natural features. The entries are arranged alphabetically. Where a place name has a commonly used English language form, e.g. **Seoul, Soul**, the commonly used form is listed first with the local spelling, or an alternative transliteration, given in brackets. Natural features such as rivers and mountains are listed with the specific name given first, e.g. **Nile, River** or **Everest, Mount**. Place names containing 'St' (denoting saint), e.g. **St Petersburg**, are listed under 'St' rather than 'Saint'. Where the form is generally spelled in full, e.g. **Saint John** it is listed under 'Saint'.

Entries on countries contain details of the geographical structure and economic nature of the country with information on area and population (the most recent figure available, whether based on census results or estimated). The capital city and other major cities are listed, as are the type of government in general terms, the major religions, and the form of currency. In addition, there is a key map indicating the part of the continent in which the country is situated to aid reference to the maps in the *World Maps* section.

An entry on a city or town gives the name of the region or country in which it is situated, and its population, and in the case of a major city, the population of the metropolitan area surrounding it is given. Entries on natural features list physical details – length in miles and kilometres of rivers, height in feet and metres of mountains, etc. There are also entries on places of historical interest.

Within entries, small capital letters denote a separate entry containing further information.

A

Aachen (Aix-la-Chapelle) a historical university city and spa town in western Germany. (Pop. 240,000)
Aba an industrial town in southern Nigeria. (Pop. 785,000)
Abadan a major oil-refining port on an island in the Shatt al Arab waterway, southern Iran. (Pop. 249,000)
Abeokuta an industrial town in western Nigeria. (Pop. 530,000)
Aberdeen (1) a major North Sea oil city and fishing port in northeast Scotland, as well as administrative centre of the Aberdeenshire council area (Pop. 217,000) (2) **City of**, a council area in northeast Scotland. (72 sq miles/186 sq km; pop. 219,000)
Aberdeenshire a council area in northern Scotland, with its administrative centre in the city of Aberdeen. (2,439 sq miles/6,319 sq km; pop. 227,000)
Abidjan a major port and the chief city of Côte D'Ivoire. (Pop. 3,310,000)
Abruzzi a region of southern central Italy; its capital is L'Aquila. (Pop. 1,298,000)
Abu Dhabi (Abu Zabi) the largest sheikhdom of the United Arab Emirates, of which the city of Abu Dhabi is the capital. (26,000 sq miles/67,350 sq km; pop. emirate 1,211,000/city 520,000)
Abuja the capital of Nigeria, purpose-built in the centre of the country and inaugurated in December 1991. (Pop. 160,000)
Acapulco a large port and beach resort on the Pacific coast of Mexico. (Pop. 632,000)
Accra the capital and main port of Ghana. (Pop. 1,605,000)
Aconcagua the highest mountain of the Andes, in Argentina. (22,835 ft/6,960 m)
Adana a city and province in southern Turkey. (Pop. city 1,162,000)
Addis Ababa (Adis Abeba) the capital of Ethiopia, in the centre of the country. (Pop. 2,638,000)
Adelaide the state capital of South Australia. (Pop. 1,130,000)
Aden (Adan) a major port in southern Yemen, formerly the capital of South Yemen. (Pop. 510,000)
Adirondack Mountains a mountain range in New York State, USA. The highest peak is Mount Marcy at 5,344 feet (1,629 metres).
Adriatic Sea a branch of the Mediterranean Sea, between Italy, Slovenia, Croatia and Albania.
Aegean Sea a branch of the Mediterranean Sea between Greece and Turkey.
Afghanistan is a landlocked country in southern Asia. The greater part of the country is mountainous with a central mass of huge mountain ranges. Many of the peaks rise to enormous heights, the greatest being Nowshak at 24,557 feet (7,845 metres). The climate is generally arid with great extremes of temperature. There is considerable snowfall in winter, which may remain on the mountain summits all year round. The country experiences many earthquakes, and periods of severe drought. Its main exports have been fruit and nuts, carpets, wool, and opium. Afghanistan has suffered from ongoing conflict during its modern history to the extent that its economy and infrastructure have been severely affected After the Russian withdrawal from Afghanistan in 1989, the country was troubled by mainly ethnic conflict. In 1996, the Taleban, a fundamentalist Islamic group, took control of Afghanistan. Their extreme version of Islam attracted widespread criticism, and their refusal to hand over Osama bin Laden (accused by the US of masterminding the bombing of their embassies in Africa in 1998 and the attacks on the US on 11 September) led to a series of US-initiated aerial attacks. These attacks paved the way for opposition groups within the country to drive the Taleban from power (although fighting continued in a small area of the country still controlled by Taleban forces). In December 2001, Afghan groups signed a two-stage deal (involving an Interim Authority and a Transitional Authority) aimed at setting up a fully representative government within three years, and an international peacekeeping force was deployed to preserve security in the Afghan capital and surrounding areas.

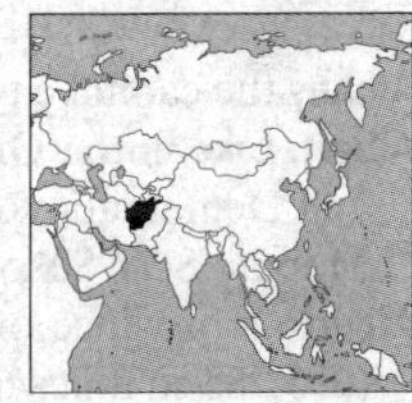

Area: 251,772 sq miles/652,225 sq km
Population: 20,833,000
Capital: Kabul
Other major cities: Herat, Kandahar, Mazar-i-Sharif
Form of government: Administration by Interim and Transitional Authorities (2002)
Religions: Sunni Islam, Shia Islam
Currency: Afghani

Africa the second largest continent in the world, with the Mediterranean Sea to the north, the Atlantic Ocean to the west and the Indian Ocean to the east. There are 53 nations within Africa, excluding Western Sahara. (11,700,000 sq miles/30,300,000 sq km; pop. 805,000,000)
Agadir a port and popular tourist resort in Morocco. (Pop. 611,000)
Agra a city in central India, the site of the Taj Mahal. (Pop. 1,285,000)
Ahmadabad (Ahmedabad) an industrial city in western India. (Pop. 3,584,000)
Ahvaz a port on the Karun River in southern Iran. (Pop. 974,000)
Aix-en-Provence a university city in southern France. (Pop. 137,000)
Ajaccio the capital of Corsica. (Pop. 49,000)
Ajman the smallest emirate of the United Arab Emirates. (96 sq miles/250 sq km; pop. emirate 155,000/town 149,000)
Akron a city in northeast Ohio, USA. (Pop. 218,000)
Alabama a state in southern USA. The state capital is Montgomery. (51,606 sq miles/133,667 sq km; pop. 4,482,000)
Alaska the largest and most northerly state of the USA. The state capital is Juneau. (586,400 sq miles/1,518,800 sq km; pop. 643,000)
Albacete a town and province of southeastern Spain. (Pop. town 153,000)
Albania A small, mountainous country in the Balkan region of southeastern Europe. Its immediate neighbours are Greece, Serbia and Montenegro, and Macedonia, and it is bounded to the west by the Adriatic Sea. The climate is typically Mediterranean and although most rain falls in winter, severe thunderstorms frequently occur on the plains in summer. Winters are severe in the

highland areas and heavy snowfalls are common. All land is state-owned, with the main agricultural areas lying along the Adriatic coast and in the Korce Basin with about a fifth of the land being arable. Industry is also nationalized and output is small. The principal industries are agricultural product processing, textiles, oil products, cement, iron, and steel. There is also potential for producing hydroelectricity, with the country's many mountain streams. Albania has been afflicted by severe economic problems and, in late 1996, public dissatisfaction with the government erupted into civil unrest, leading to a major revolt by citizen militias during which the government forces lost control. By March 1997, the country was on the brink of collapse and large numbers of refugees were leaving. The situation was reversed, however, when ethnic cleansing of Albanian inhabitants of the Kosovo region of Serbia in 1999 led to a flood of refugees into Albania (and elsewhere) before NATO bombing ended the cleansing and Kosovar Albanians were able to return home.

Area: 11,100 sq miles/28,748 sq km
Population: 3,200,000
Capital: Tirana (Tiranë)
Other cities: Durrës, Shkodër, Elbasan
Form of government: Socialist Republic
Religions: Sunni Islam, Orthodox, RC
Currency: Lek

Albany the capital city of New York State, USA. (Pop. 96,000)

Albert, Lake in the Great Rift Valley, is shared between Uganda and Democratic Republic of Congo. Formerly known as Lake Mobuto Sésé Seko. (2,000 sq miles/5,180 sq km)

Alberta a province of western Canada; Edmonton is its capital. (255,285 sq miles/661,190 sq km; pop. 3,162,000)

Ålborg (Aalborg) a city and port in northern Denmark. (Pop. 120,000)

Albuquerque a university city on the Rio Grande in New Mexico, USA. (Pop. 454,000)

Alcalá de Henares a town in central Spain, birthplace of Miguel de Cervantes (1547–1616), author of *Don Quixote*. (Pop. 169,000)

Aleppo (Halab) an industrial city of ancient origins in Syria. (Pop. 1,892,000)

Alexandria (El Iskandarîya) the main port of Egypt, on the Nile delta. (Pop. 3,806,000)

Al Fujayrah (Fujairah) one of the seven United Arab Emirates, in the Persian Gulf. (502 sq miles/1,300 sq km; pop. emirate 99,000/town 43,000)

Algarve the southern province of Portugal. (Pop. 393,000)

Algeria A huge country in northern Africa that fringes the Mediterranean Sea in the north. Over four-fifths of Algeria is covered by the Sahara Desert to the south. Near the north coastal area the Atlas Mountains run east-west in parallel ranges. The Chelif, at 450 miles (724 kilometres) long, is the country's main river, rising in the Tell Atlas and flowing to the Mediterranean. The climate in the coastal areas is warm and temperate with most of the rain falling in winter. The summers are dry and hot with temperatures rising to over 89°F (32°C). Inland beyond the Atlas Mountains conditions become more arid and temperatures range from 120°F (49°C) during the day to 50°F (10°C) at night. Most of Algeria is unproductive agriculturally, but it does possess one of the largest reserves of natural gas and oil in the world. Algeria's main exports are oil-based products, fruit, vegetables, tobacco, phosphates, and cork, while imports include textiles, foodstuffs, machinery, iron, and steel. In recent years, the country has been wracked by civil strife and terrorist attacks, with the various opposing forces unable to agree peace proposals.

Area: 919,595 sq miles/2,381,741 sq km
Population: 29,168,000
Capital: Algiers (El Djazair, Alger)
Other major cities: Oran, Constantine, 'Annaba
Form of government: Republic
Religion: Sunni Islam
Currency: Algerian Dinar

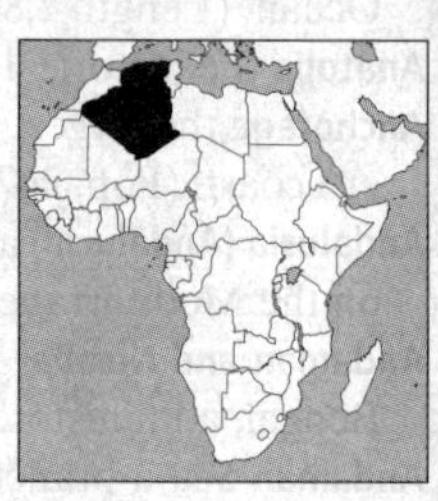

Algiers (El Djazair, Alger) the capital of Algeria, on the Mediterranean coast. (Pop. 1,696,000)

Alicante a port and popular beach resort, and also the name of the surrounding province, on the Mediterranean coast of Spain. (Pop. town 251,400)

Alice Springs a desert settlement in the Northern Territory of Australia. (Pop. 26,000)

Aligarh a university town in central India. (Pop. 681,000)

Allahabad a holy city in India on the confluence of the Rivers Ganges and Yamuna. (Pop. 1,010,000)

Almaty a trading and industrial city and, until 1997, capital of Kazakhstan, formerly Alma-Ata. (Pop. 1,066,000)

Al Manamah (Manama) the capital and main port of Bahrain. (Pop. 148,000)

Alps, the a mountain range in southern central Europe that spans the borders of Switzerland, France, Germany, Austria, Slovenia, Italy and Liechtenstein.

Alsace a region in the northeast of France.

Altai an area of high mountain ranges in central Asia on the borders of China and the Russian Federation at the western end of Mongolia.

Amalfi a small town on the west coast of Italy. (Pop. 6,100)

Amarillo an industrial city in northwest Texas, USA. (Pop. 182,000)

Amazon (Amazonas) the world's second longest river, it rises in the Andes of Peru and flows east through Brazil to the Atlantic Ocean. (Length 4,000 miles/6,440 km)

Ambon (Amboina) an island and the capital of the so-called Spice Islands in the Maluku group in eastern central Indonesia. (314 sq miles/813 sq km; pop. city 262,000)

America the continent lying between the Atlantic and Pacific Oceans, divided into three zones: North America, consisting of USA, Canada, Mexico and Greenland (9,000,000 sq miles/23,500,000 sq km; pop. 347,000,000); Central America, consisting of the area between the southern Mexico border and the Panama-Colombia border with the Caribbean (714,000 sq miles/1,849,000 sq km; pop. 137,000,000); and South America, consisting of the area south of the Panama-Colombia border (6,800,000 sq miles/17,600,000 sq km; pop. 307,000,000).

Amiens an industrial city and capital of the Somme department of northern France. (Pop. 136,000)

Amman the capital of Jordan, in the northeast of the country. (Pop. 1,253,000)

Amritsar an industrial city in Punjab, northern India and home of the Golden Temple, the most sacred shrine of the Sikhs. (Pop. 995,000)

Amsterdam the capital and commercial centre of the Netherlands, a historical port set on the IJsselmeer. (Pop. 720,000)

Amudar'ya a central Asian river forming much of the border between Tajikistan and Afghanistan before flowing through Uzbekistan into the Aral Sea. Its ancient name was Oxus. (Length 1,630 miles/2,620 km)

Amundsen Sea an arm of the South Pacific in Antarctica.

Amur (Heilong Jiang) a river which runs along the border between China and the Russian Federation, flowing east into the Pacific Ocean. (Length 2,800 miles/4,510 km)

Anatolia the historical name for the Asian part of Turkey.

Anchorage the largest city and port in Alaska, USA, on its southern coast. (Pop. 267,000)

Andalusia (Andalucía) a region of southwestern Spain, with a coast on the Mediterranean and Atlantic.

Andaman and Nicobar Islands two groups of islands in the Bay of Bengal, administered by India. (Pop. 363,000)

Andaman Sea a branch of the Bay of Bengal, lying between the Andaman Islands and Myanmar.

Andes a high mountain range that runs down the entire length of the western coast of South America. The highest peak is Mount Aconcagua, in Argentina at 22,835 feet (6,960 metres).

Andhra Pradesh a state in southeast India. The capital is Hyderabad. (106,184 sq miles/275,088 sq km; pop. 77,207,000)

Andorra A tiny state, situated high in the eastern Pyrénées, between France and Spain. The state consists of deep valleys and high mountain peaks which reach heights of 9,843 feet (3,000 metres). Although only 12 miles (20 kilometres) wide and 19 miles (30 kilometres) long, the spectacular scenery and climate attract many tourists. About 10 million visitors arrive each year, during the cold weather when heavy snowfalls make for ideal skiing, or in summer when the weather is mild and sunny and the mountains are used for walking. Tourism and the duty-free trade are now Andorra's chief sources of income. Sheep and cattle are raised on the high pastures. Although Andorra has no airport or railroad, there is a good road system. In 1993, an Andorran government was elected and has its own parliament after 715 years of being ruled by France's leader and the Spanish Bishop of Urgel.

Area: 175 sq miles/453 sq km
Population: 65,900
Capital: Andorra la Vella
Form of government: Principality
Religion: RC
Currency: Euro

Andorra la Vella the capital of Andorra. (Pop. 23,000)

Andros the largest of the islands of the Bahamas (1,600 sq miles/4,144 sq km; pop. 8,000)

Angara a river in the Russian Federation flowing from Lake Baikal into the Yenisey River. (Length 1,135 miles/1,825 km)

Angel Falls a narrow band of water falling 3,212 feet (979 metres) from a high plateau in southeastern Venezuela to form the world's highest waterfall.

Anglesey an island off the northwestern tip of Wales, also a council area of Wales, with its administrative centre in Llangefni (278 sq miles/720 sq km; pop. 69,000)

Angola Situated on the Atlantic coast of southern Africa, Angola lies about 10° south of the equator. It shares borders with Congo, Democratic Republic of Congo, Zambia, and Namibia. Its climate is tropical with temperatures constantly between 68°F (20°C) and 77°F (25°C). The rainfall is heaviest in inland areas where there are vast equatorial forests. The country is also rich in minerals, however deposits of manganese, copper, and phosphate are as yet unexploited. Diamonds are mined in the northeast and oil is produced near Luanda. Oil production is the most important aspect of the economy, making up about 90 per cent of exports which have traditionally included diamonds, fish, coffee, and palm oil. Around 70 per cent of the workforce are engaged in agriculture. Since independence from Portugal in 1975, the United States is the main recipient of the country's exports. However, the Angolan economy has been severely damaged by the civil war of the 1980s and early 1990s.

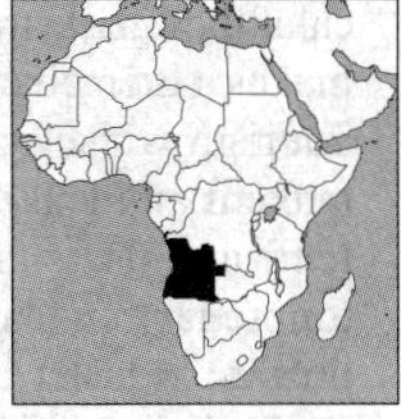

Area: 481,354 sq miles/1,246,700 sq km
Population: 11,185,000
Capital: Luanda
Other major cities: Huambo, Lobito, Benguela
Form of government: People's Republic
Religions: RC, Animism
Currency: Kwanza

Anguilla An island in the Leeward Islands group of the Caribbean Sea, now a self-governing British dependency. From 1967 until 1980, it was in federation with St Kitts and Nevis. The country's main source of revenue is tourism, and lobsters account for half of the island's exports.

Area: 37 sq miles/96 sq km
Population: 12,400
Capital: The Valley
Form of government: British Overseas Territory
Religion: Christianity
Currency: East Caribbean Dollar

Angus a council area in east Scotland, with its administrative centre in the town of Forfar. (842 sq miles/2,181 sq km; pop. 111,000)

Anhui (Anhwei) a province of eastern China. Its capital is Hefei. (50,000 sq miles/130,000 sq km; pop. 60,596,000)

Anjou a former province of western France, in the valley of the River Loire.

Ankara the capital of Turkey, in the eastern central part of Asian Turkey. (Pop. 3,329,000)

Annaba (Bone) a historical town and seaport on the Mediterranean coast of Algeria. (Pop. 240,000)

Annapolis the capital of the state of Maryland, USA. (Pop. 37,000)

Annapurna a mountain of the Himalayas, in Nepal. (26,810 ft/8,172 m)

Anshan a steel-manufacturing city in Liaoning Province, northern China. (Pop. 1,247,000)

Antakya (Antioch) an ancient city in southern Turkey. (Pop. 155,000)

Antalya a port and resort on the Mediterranean coast of Turkey. (Pop. 571,000)

Antananarivo the capital of Madagascar. (Pop. 875,000)

Antarctica an ice-covered continent around the South Pole consisting of a plateau and mountain ranges reaching a height of 15,000 feet (4,500 metres). It is uninhabited apart from temporary staff at research stations. (5,100,000 sq miles/14,000,000 sq km)

Antarctic Circle latitude 66° 32' south. At the southern winter solstice, the sun does not rise, nor does it set at the summer solstice, at this line, or in higher latitudes.

Antarctic Ocean (Southern Ocean) the waters that surround Antarctica, made up of the southern waters of the Atlantic, Indian and Pacific Oceans.

Antigua and Barbuda Located on the eastern side of the Leeward Islands, Antigua and Barbuda is a tiny state comprising three islands: Antigua, Barbuda and the uninhabited rocky islet of Redonda. Antigua's strategic position was recognized by the British in the 18th century when it was an important naval base, and later by the USA who built the island's airport during World War II to defend the Caribbean and the Panama Canal. Although mainly low-lying, the country's highest point is Boggy Peak at 1,329 feet (405 metres). The climate is tropical although its average rainfall of 4 inches (100 millimetres) makes it drier than most of the other islands of the West Indies. Tourism is the main industry as its numerous sandy beaches make it an ideal destination. Barbuda is surrounded by coral reefs and the island is home to a wide range of wildlife. Cotton, sugar cane, and fruits are cultivated and fishing is an important industry. Great damage was inflicted on Antigua and Barbuda in 1995 by Hurricane Luis when over 75 per cent of property was destroyed or damaged.

Area: 171 sq miles/442 sq km
Population: 66,000
Capital: St. John's
Form of government: Constitutional Monarchy
Religion: Christianity (mainly Anglicanism)
Currency: East Caribbean Dollar

Antilles a major chain of islands in the Caribbean, divided into two groups: the Greater Antilles (which includes Cuba and Puerto Rico) to the west; the Lesser Antilles (including Martinique and Barbados) to the east.

Antrim (1) a historical county in northeast Northern Ireland. (1,200 sq miles/3,100 sq km) (2) a district council area in Co. Antrim. (160 sq miles/415 sq km; pop. 44,516)

Antwerp (Antwerpen, Anvers) the capital of the province of Antwerp and the main port of Belgium. (Pop. 444,000)

Anyang an ancient city in Henan Province, China. (Pop. 570,000)

Aomori a port on Honshu Island, Japan. (Pop. 294,000)

Apennines (Appennino) the mountain range which forms the 'backbone' of Italy. The highest peak is Monte Corno at 9,554 feet (2,912 metres).

Apia the capital of Samoa. (Pop. 36,000)

Appalachian Mountains a chain of mountains which stretches 1,600 miles (2,570 kilometres) down eastern North America from Canada to Alabama in the USA. The highest peak is Mount Mitchell at 6,684 feet (2,037 metres).

Aqaba the only port in Jordan, on the Gulf of Aqaba. (Pop. 95,000)

Aquitaine a region and former kingdom of southwestern France.

Arabian Sea a branch of the Indian Ocean between India and Arabia.

Arafura Sea a stretch of the Pacific Ocean between New Guinea and Australia.

Aragon (Aragón) a region and former kingdom of northeast Spain.

Aral Sea a large, salty lake, to the east of the Caspian Sea, on the border between Uzbekistan and Kazakhstan. (25,000 sq miles/64,750 sq km)

Aran Islands (Oileáin Arann) three small islands, Inishmore, Inishmaan and Inisheer, off County Galway in the Republic of Ireland. (18 sq miles/44 sq km; pop. 1,380)

Ararat, Mount (Büjük Agri Dagi) the mountain peak in eastern Turkey where Noah's Ark is said to have come to rest. (17,000 ft/5,165 m)

Arauca a major tributary of the Orinoco River which forms part of the border between Colombia and Venezuela. (Length 620 miles/1,000 km)

Archangel (Arkhangel'sk) a port on the Dvina Delta on the White Sea in the Russian Federation. (Pop. 356,000)

Arctic the regions that lie to the north of the Arctic Circle.

Arctic Circle latitude 66° 32' north. The sun does not set above this line at the northern summer solstice, nor does it rise above this line at the winter solstice.

Arctic Ocean the ice-laden sea to the north of the Arctic Circle. (5,440,000 sq miles/14,100,000 sq km)

Ardabil a town in Iran, famous for its knotted carpets. (Pop. 349,000)

Ardennes a hilly and forested region straddling the borders of Belgium, Luxembourg and France.

Ards a district council area in Co. Down. (142 sq miles/368 sq km; pop. 65,000)

Arequipa a city and department of Peru. (Pop. city 734,000)

Argentina The world's eighth largest country, which stretches from the Tropic of Capricorn to Cape Horn on the southern tip of the South American continent. To the west a massive mountain chain, the Andes, forms the border with Chile. The climate ranges from warm temperate over the Pampas in the central region, to a more arid climate in the north and west, while in the extreme south conditions although also dry are much cooler. The vast fertile plains of the Pampas are the main agricultural area and produce cereals and wheat, while in other irrigated areas sugar cane, fruit, and grapes for wine are raised. Meat processing, animal products, and livestock production are major industries and also feature prominently in export trade. A series of military regimes and ongoing political and economic crises have resulted in an unstable economy which fails to provide reasonable living standards for the population.

Area: 1,073,518 sq miles/2,780,400 sq km
Population: 35,220,000
Capital: Buenos Aires
Other major cities: Córdoba, Rosaria, Mendoza, La Plata
Form of government: Republic
Religion: RC
Currency: Peso

Argyll and Bute a council area in west Scotland, with its administrative centre in the town of Lochgilphead. (2,676 sq miles/6,930 sq km; pop. 90,000)

Århus (Aarhus) a port and the second largest city in Denmark. (Pop. 217,000)

Arizona a state in the southwest of the USA. The capital is Phoenix. (113,902 sq miles/295,024 sq km; pop. 5,484,000)

Arkansas a state in the south of the USA. The state capital is Little Rock. (53,104 sq miles/137,539 sq km; pop. 2,711,000)

Arkansas a tributary of the River Mississippi in the USA, flowing from the Rocky Mountains through the states of Kansas, Oklahoma and Arkansas. (Length 1,450 miles/2,335 km)

Armagh (1) a historical county in south Northern Ireland. (512 sq miles/1,326 sq km) (2) a district council area, in Co. Armagh. (258 sq miles/667 sq km; pop. 52,000) (3) a town in the Armagh district council area, Co. Armagh. (Pop. 15,000)

Armenia (1) The smallest republic of the former USSR and part of the former kingdom of Armenia. It declared independence from the USSR in 1991. It is a landlocked Transcaucasian republic, and its neighbours are Turkey, Iran, Georgia, and Azerbaijan. The country is very mountainous, with many peaks over 9,900 feet (3,000 metres), the highest being Arragats Lerr at 13,435 feet (4,095 metres). Agriculture is mixed in the lowland areas. The main crops grown are grain, sugar beet, and potatoes, and livestock reared include cattle, pigs, and sheep. Mining of copper, zinc, and lead is important, and to a lesser extent gold, aluminium, and molybdenum, and industrial development is increasing. Hydroelectricity is produced from stations on the River Razdan as it falls 3,281 feet (1,000 metres) from Lake Sevan to its confluence with the River Araks. Territorial conflict with Azerbaijan over Nagorny Karabakh under a ceasefire since 1994 put a brake on economic development for many years. (2) the former independent kingdom that straddled the borders of modern Turkey, Iran, Georgia, and Azerbaijan.

Area: 11,500 sq miles/29,800 sq km
Population: 3,893,000
Capital: Yerevan
Other major city: Kunmayr (Gyumri)
Form of government: Republic
Religion Armenian: Orthodox
Currency: Dram

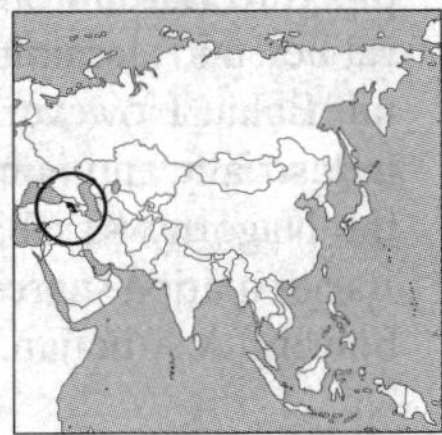

Arnhem a town in the Netherlands, scene of a battle in 1944 between British (and Polish) paratroops and the German army. (Pop. 138,000)

Arnhem Land an Aboriginal reserve in the Northern Territory of Australia.

Arno the main river of Tuscany in Italy, flowing westward through Florence to Pisa on the coast. (Length 152 miles/245 km)

Aruba A Caribbean island off the coast of Venezuela that was one of the Netherlands Antilles until 1986. It is now a self-governing dependency of the Netherlands. Tourism has been a growing industry since the 1980s.

Area: 75 sq miles/193 sq km
Population: 87,000
Capital: Oranjestad
Form of government: Self-governing Dutch Territory
Religion: Christianity
Currency: Aruban Florin

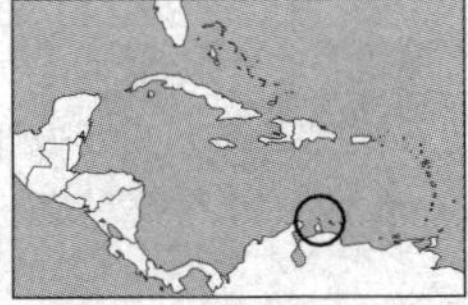

Arunachal Pradesh a state of northern India, bordering Tibet. The capital is Shillong. (Pop. 1,112,000)

Ascension Island a tiny volcanic island in the South Atlantic Ocean, forming part of the St Helena Dependencies. (Pop. 1,100)

Ashkhabad the capital of Turkmenistan. (Pop. 711,000)

Asia the largest continent, bounded by the Arctic, Pacific and Indian Oceans, plus the Mediterranean and Red Seas. East Asia is taken to mean those countries to the northeast of Bangladesh; South Asia refers to the countries on the Indian subcontinent; and Southeast Asia includes those countries to the southeast of China, including the islands to the west of New Guinea. (16,800,000 sq miles/43,600,000 sq km; pop. 3,688,000,000)

Asmara (Asmera) the capital city of Eritrea. (Pop. 392,000)

Assam a state in northeastern India. (38,476 sq miles/99,680 sq km; pop. 27,159,000)

Assisi a small town in Umbria, central Italy, and birthplace of St Francis (1182–1226). (Pop. 26,000)

Astana the capital of Kazakhstan since 1997. (Pop. 294,000)

Astrakhan a port in southern Russia near the Caspian Sea, situated on the delta of the River Volga. (Pop. 488,000)

Asturias a region of northern Spain. The capital is Oviedo. (Pop. 1,071,000)

Asunción the capital and the only major city of Paraguay. (Pop. 547,000)

Athabasca a river in Canada which flows north from the Rocky Mountains to Lake Athabasca. (Length 765 miles/1,231 km)

Athens (Athinai) the historical capital, and the principal city, of Greece. (Pop. 757,000)

Atlanta the capital and largest city of Georgia, USA. (Pop. 437,000)

Atlantic Ocean the second largest ocean, lying between North and South America, Europe and Africa. (31,700,000 sq miles/82,200,000 sq km)

Atlas Mountains a series of mountain chains stretching across North Africa from Morocco to Tunisia.

Auckland the largest city and chief port of New Zealand, on North Island. (Pop. 386,000)

Augsburg a historical city in Bavaria, Germany. (Pop. 252,000)

Augusta (1) a city and river port on the Savannah River in Georgia, USA. (Pop. 209,000/metropolitan area 368,300) (2) the state capital of Maine, USA. (Pop. 19,000)

Austin the capital city of Texas, USA. (Pop. 686,000)

Australasia a general term for Australia, New Zealand and neighbouring islands.

Australia The world's smallest continental land mass is a vast and sparsely populated island state in the southern hemisphere and is comprised of seven states. The most mountainous region is the Great Dividing Range, which runs down the entire east coast. Because of its great size, Australia's climates range from tropical monsoon to cool temperate and there are also large areas of desert. The majority of the country's natural inland lakes are salt water and are the remnants of a huge inland sea. The Great Barrier Reef is approximately 1,250 miles (2,000 kilometres) long and is the largest coral formation known in the world. Central and south Queensland are subtropical while north and central New South Wales are warm temperate. Much of Australia's wealth comes from agriculture, with huge sheep and cattle stations extending over large parts of the interior known as the Outback. Australia is the world's leading producer of wool, particularly the fine merino wool. Cereal growing is dominated by wheat. Mining continues to be an important industry and produces coal, natural gas, oil, gold, and iron ore. Australia is the largest producer of diamonds.

Area: 2,988,902 sq miles/7,741,220 sq km
Population: 18,871,000
Capital: Canberra
Other major cities: Adelaide, Brisbane, Melbourne, Perth, Sydney
Form of government: Federal Parliamentary State
Religion: Christianity
Currency: Australian Dollar

Australian Capital Territory the small region which surrounds Canberra, the capital of Australia. (939 sq miles/2,432 sq km; pop. 323,000)

Austria A landlocked country in central Europe surrounded by seven nations. The wall of mountains that runs across the centre of the country dominates the scenery. In the warm summers, tourists come to walk in the forests and mountains, and in the cold winters skiers come to the mountains that now boast over 50 ski resorts. The main river is the Danube and there are numerous lakes, principally Lake Constance (Bodensee) and Lake Neusiedler. Agriculture is based on small farms, many of which are run by single families. Dairy products, beef, and lamb from the hill farms contribute to exports. More than 37 per cent of Austria is covered in forest, resulting in the papermaking industry near Graz. There are mineral resources of lignite, magnesium, petroleum, iron ore, and natural gas, and high-grade graphite is exported. Unemployment is very low and its low strike record has attracted multinational companies in recent years. Attachment to local customs is still strong and in rural areas men still wear lederhosen and women the traditional dirndl skirt on feast days and special occasions.

Area: 32,378 sq miles/83,859 sq km
Population: 8,106,000
Capital: Vienna (Wien)
Other major cities: Graz, Linz, Salzburg
Form of government: Federal Republic
Religion: RC
Currency: Euro

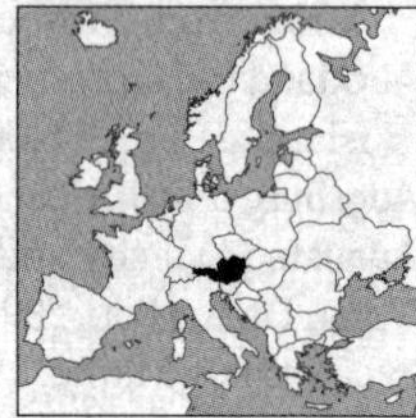

Auvergne a mountainous region of central France.

Avignon a historical city on the River Rhône in southern France, the seat of the Pope from 1309 to 1377. (Pop. 87,000)

Avila (Ávila) a town and province in the mountainous central region of Spain, famous as the birthplace of St Teresa (1515–82). (Pop. town 48,000)

Axios a river flowing through the Balkans to Greece and the Aegean Sea. (Length 241 miles/388 km)

Ayers Rock (Uluru) a huge rock, sacred to the Aborigines, rising sharply out of the plains in the Northern Territory of Australia. (1,142 ft/348 m)

Ayutthaya a town with the extensive ruins of the city that was the capital of Thailand from 1350 to 1767. (Pop. 78,000)

Azerbaijan (1) A republic of the former USSR that declared itself independent in 1991. It is situated on the southwest coast of the Caspian Sea and shares borders with Iran, Armenia, Georgia, and the Russian Federation. The Araks River separates Azerbaijan from the region known as Azerbaijan in northern Iran. The country is semi-arid, and 70 per cent of the land is irrigated for the production of cotton, wheat, maize, potatoes, tobacco, tea, and citrus fruits. It has rich mineral deposits of oil, natural gas, iron, and aluminium. The most important mineral is oil, which is found in the Baku area from where it is piped to Batumi on the Black Sea. There are steel, synthetic rubber, and aluminium works at Sumqayit just north of the capital, Baku. However, Azerbaijan is only minimally developed industrially and is hindered by its dispute with Armenia over the Nagorny-Karabakh region. (2) a region of northern Iran. Its population shares the same language as the people of neighbouring Azerbaijan. (Pop. 6,147,000)

Area: 33,436 sq miles/86,600 sq km
Population: 7,625,000
Capital: Baku
Other major city: Sumqayit
Form of government: Republic
Religions: Sunni Islam, Russian Orthodox
Currency: Manat

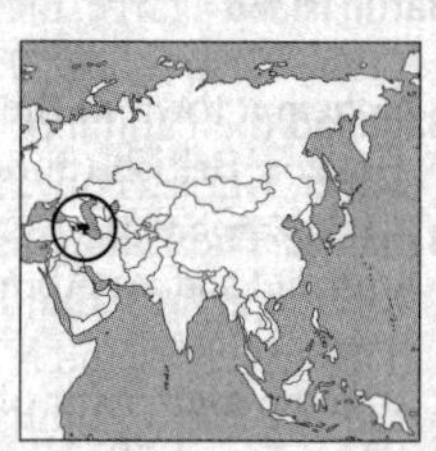

Azores (Açores) three groups of small islands in the North Atlantic Ocean, belonging to Portugal. The capital is Ponta Delgada. (901 sq miles/2,335 sq km; pop. 243,000)

Azov, Sea of (Azovskoye More) a shallow, inland sea lying between the Russian Federation and the Ukraine.

B

Baden-Baden a famous spa town in southwest Germany dating from Roman times. (Pop. 52,000)

Baden-Württemburg a southern state of Germany bordering France and Switzerland. (Pop. 10,521,000)

Baffin Bay a huge bay within the Arctic Circle between Baffin Island in Canada and Greenland.

Baffin Island a large, mainly ice-bound island in northeast Canada. (195,927 sq miles/507,451 sq km)

Baghdad the capital of Iraq, in the centre of the country, on the River Tigris. (Pop. 5,605,000)

Bahamas The Bahamas consist of an archipelago of 700 islands located in the Atlantic Ocean off the southeast coast of Florida. The largest island is Andros (1,600 sq miles/4,144 sq km), and the two most populated are Grand Bahama and New Providence where the capital, Nassau, lies. Winters in the Bahamas are mild and summers warm. Most rain falls in May, June, September, and October, and thunderstorms are frequent in summer. The islands are also subject to hurricanes and other tropical storms. The islands have few natural resources, and for many years fishing and small-scale farming (citrus fruits and vegetables) were the only ways to make a living. Now, however, tourism, which employs almost half the workforce, is the most important industry and has been developed on a vast scale. Offshore banking is also a growing source of income.

Area: 5,358 sq miles/13,878 sq km
Population: 284,000
Capital: Nassau
Other important city: Freeport
Form of government: Constitutional Monarchy
Religion: Christianity
Currency: Bahamian Dollar

Bahrain A Gulf State comprising 33 low-lying islands situated between the Qatar Peninsula and the mainland of Saudi Arabia. Bahrain Island is the largest and a causeway – the King Fahd Causeway – linking it to Saudi Arabia was opened in 1986. The highest point in the state is only 402 feet (122 metres) above sea level. The climate is pleasantly warm between December and March, but very hot from June to November. Most of Bahrain is sandy and too saline to support crops but drainage schemes are now used to reduce salinity and fertile soil is imported from other islands. Oil was discovered in 1931 and revenues from oil now account for about 80 per cent of the country's total revenue. Bahrain is being developed as a major manufacturing state, the main enterprises being aluminium smelting and the manufacture of clothing, paper products, and consumer goods. Traditional industries include pearl fishing, boat building, weaving, and pottery. Agricultural products include vegetables, dates, and fruits, with artesian wells providing irrigation mainly on the north coast.

Area: 268 sq miles/694 sq km
Population: 599,000
Capital: Al Manamah (Manama)
Form of government: Monarchy (Emirate)
Religions: Shia Islam, Sunni Islam
Currency: Bahraini Dinar

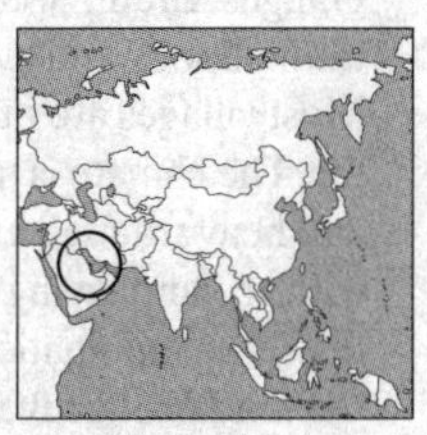

Baikal, Lake (Ozero Baykal) the world's deepest freshwater lake, and the largest by volume, situated in southeast Siberia in the Russian Federation. (12,150 sq miles/31,500 sq km)

Baja California a huge peninsula, some 800 miles (1,300 kilometres) long, belonging to Mexico which stretches south from California in the USA into the Pacific Ocean. (Pop. 2,662,000)

Bakhtaran formerly called Kermanshah, a large city in Iran, lying on the old trading routes between Tehran and Baghdad. (Pop. 771,000)

Baku (Baky) a port on the Caspian Sea and the capital of Azerbaijan. (Pop. 1,228,000)

Balaton, Lake a lake in western Hungary. (232 sq miles/601 sq km)

Balearic Islands (Islas Baleares) a group of islands in the western Mediterranean Sea belonging to Spain and famous as tourist resorts. The main islands are Majorca, Minorca, Ibiza, Formentera and Cabrera. (Pop. 896,000; cur. Euro)

Bali a small island off the eastern tip of Java, the only island in Indonesia to have preserved intact a predominantly Hindu culture. The main town and capital is Denpasar. (2,159 sq miles/5,591 sq km; pop. 3,276,000)

Balkans the southeastern corner of Europe, a broad, mountainous peninsula bordered by the Adriatic, Ionian, Aegean and Black Seas. Albania, Bulgaria, Greece, Romania, Slovenia, Croatia, Bosnia-Herzegovina, Macedonia, Serbia and Montenegro, and European Turkey are in the Balkans.

Balkhash, Lake (Ozero Balkhash) a massive lake in Kazakhstan, near the border with China. (8,500 sq miles/22,000 sq km)

Ballarat a historical gold-mining town in Victoria, Australia. (Pop. 82,000)

Ballymena a district council area in Co. Antrim, central Northern Ireland. (247 sq miles/634 sq km; pop. 57,000)

Ballymoney a district council area in Co. Antrim, north Northern Ireland. (161 sq miles/417 sq km; pop. 24,000)

Baltic Sea a shallow sea in northern Europe, completely surrounded by land masses except for the narrow straits that connect it to the North Sea.

Baltimore the largest city in the state of Maryland, USA. (Pop. 671,000)

Baluchistan a province of southwestern Pakistan, bordering Iran and Afghanistan. (Pop. 7,216,000)

Bamako the capital of Mali. (Pop. 907,000)

Banbridge a district council area in Co. Down, south Northern Ireland. (170 sq miles/442 sq km; pop. 34,000)

Bandar 'Abbas a port in southern Iran on the Strait of Hormuz, at the neck of the Persian Gulf. (Pop. 321,000)

Bandar Seri Begawan the capital of Brunei. (Pop. 75,000)

Banda Sea a part of the Pacific Ocean, in eastern Indonesia.

Bandung a large inland city in western Java, Indonesia, the second largest city in Indonesia. (Pop. 2,884,000)

Bangalore a large industrial city in central southern India. (Pop. 4,376,000)

Bangkok (Krung Thep) the capital of Thailand, on the River Chao Phraya. (Pop. 6,513,000)

Bangladesh Formerly the eastern province of Pakistan, Bangladesh is the world's eighth most populated country. It is bounded almost entirely by India and to the south by the Bay of Bengal. The country is extremely flat and is virtually a huge delta formed by the Ganges, Brahmaputra, and Meghna Rivers. It is subject to devastating floods and cyclones that sweep in from the Bay of Bengal. Most villages are built on mud platforms to keep them above water. The climate is tropical monsoon with heat, extreme humidity, and heavy rainfall in the monsoon season (April to October) along with accompanying tornadoes. The short winter season is mild and dry. The combination of rainfall, sun, and silt from the rivers makes the land productive, and it is often possible to grow three crops a year. Bangladesh produces about 70 per cent of the world's jute, and the production of jute-related products is a principal industry, with tea being an important cash crop. There are few mineral resources although natural gas, coal, and peat are found.

Area: 55,598 sq miles/143,998 sq km
Population: 120,073,000
Capital: Dhaka (Dacca)
Other cities: Chittagong, Khulna
Form of government: Republic
Religion: Sunni Islam
Currency: Taka

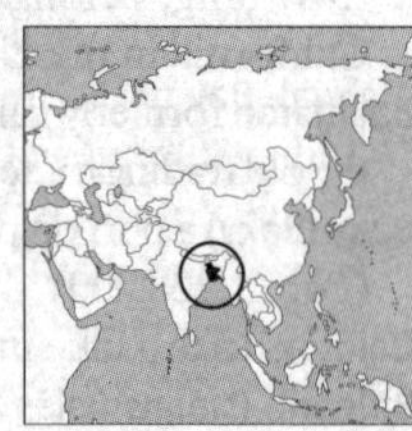

Bangui the capital of the Central African Republic. (Pop. 653,000)

Bangweulu, Lake a large lake in northern Zambia. (3,784 sq miles/ 9,800 sq km)

Banja Luka a city of ancient origins on the River Vrbas in northwest Bosnia-Herzegovina. (Pop. 179,000)

Banjarmasin a port on the southern coast of Kalimantan, Indonesia. (Pop. 549,000)

Banjul the capital of the Gambia, formerly called Bathurst. (Pop. 58,000)

Barbados The most easterly island of the West Indies, lying well outside the group of islands that make up the Lesser Antilles. Mainly surrounded by coral reefs, most of the island is low-lying and only in the north does it rise to 1,104 feet (336 metres) at Mount Hillaby. The climate is tropical, but the cooling effect of the northeast trade winds prevents the temperatures rising above 86°F (30°C). There are only two seasons, the dry and the wet, when rainfall is very heavy. At one time the economy depended almost exclusively on the production of sugar and its by-products, molasses and rum, and although the industry is now declining, sugar is still the principal export. Tourism has now taken over as the main industry, employing approximately 40 per cent of the island's labour force, although there are industries manufacturing furniture, clothing, electrical and electronic equipment. More recently, deposits of natural gas and petroleum have been discovered and fishing is an important activity. The island is surrounded by pink and white sandy beaches and coral reefs that are visited by around 400,000 tourists each year.

Area: 166 sq miles/430 sq km
Population: 265,000
Capital: Bridgetown
Form of government: Constitutional Monarchy
Religions: Anglicanism, Methodism
Currency: Barbados Dollar

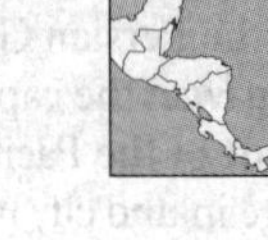

Barcelona the second largest city in Spain, and the name of the surrounding province. It is a major port on the Mediterranean Sea. (Pop. city 1,498,000)

Barents Sea a part of the Arctic Ocean to the north of Norway.

Bari a major port on the Adriatic coast of Italy. (Pop. 332,000)

Barossa Valley a wine-producing region in South Australia.

Barquisimeto an industrial city in western Venezuela. (Pop. 920,000)

Barranquilla the largest port on the Caribbean coast of Colombia. (Pop. 1,298,000)

Bashkirya (Baskir Republic) an autonomous republic of the Russian Federation, in the southern Urals. The capital is Ufa. (55,400 sq miles/143,500 sq km; pop. 4,069,000)

Basle (Basel, Bâle) a city in northern Switzerland and the name of the surrounding canton. (Pop. city 164,000)

Basque Country (Euskadi, País Vasco, Pays Basque) an area straddling the border of Spain and France on the Atlantic coast, the home of the Basque people.

Basra (Al-Basrah) the second city of Iraq, and its main port. (Pop. 1,338,000)

Bassein a trading city on the delta of the River Irrawaddy in Myanmar. (Pop. 220,000)

Basseterre the capital of St Kitts and Nevis. (Pop. 12,000)

Basse Terre the capital of the French island of Guadeloupe, situated on the island also called Basse Terre. (Pop. town 13,000/ island 173,000)

Bass Strait the stretch of water spanning the 180 miles (290 kilometres) which separate the mainland of Australia from Tasmania.

Bath a beautifully preserved spa town in southwest England. (Pop.86,000)

Baton Rouge the state capital of Louisiana, USA, situated on the River Mississippi. (Pop. city 228,000)

Bavaria (Bayern) the largest state in Germany. (27,241 sq miles/ 70,553 sq km; pop. 12,155,000)

Bayeux a market town in Normandy, France. The home of the huge 11th-century tapestry depicting the Norman conquest of England. (Pop. 15,300)

Bayonne the capital of the French Basque region. (Pop. 40,000)

Beaufort Sea a part of the Arctic Ocean to the north of North America.

Beaujolais a famous wine-producing region of France situated on the River Saône between Lyons and Mâcon.

Bechuanaland the former name of Botswana (until 1966).

Bedfordshire a county in central southern England; the county town is Bedford. (477 sq miles/1,235 sq km; pop. 543,000)

Beijing (Peking) the capital of China, in the northeast of the country. (Pop. 7,128,000)

Beirut (Beyrouth) the capital and main port of Lebanon. (Pop. 1,148,000)

Belarus (Belorussia, Byelorussia) A republic of the former USSR that declared itself independent in 1991, Belarus borders Poland to the west, Ukraine to the south, Latvia and Lithuania to the north, and the Russian Federation to the east. The country consists mainly of a low-lying plain, and forests cover approximately one-third of the land. The climate is continental, with long severe winters and short warm summers. Although the economy is overwhelmingly based on industry, including oil refining, food processing, woodworking, chemicals, textiles, and machinery, output has gradually declined since 1991 and problems persist in the supply of raw materials from other republics that previously were part of the USSR. Agriculture, although seriously affected by contamination from the Chernobyl nuclear accident of 1986, accounts for approximately 20 per cent of employment, the main crops being flax, potatoes, and hemp. The main livestock raised are cattle and pigs. Extensive forest areas also contribute in the supply of raw materials for woodwork and papermaking. Peat is the fuel used to provide power for industry and the country's power plants. Belarus has a good transportation system of road, rail, navigable rivers, and canals.

Area: 80,155 sq miles/207,600 sq km
Population: 10,203,000
Capital: Minsk
Other major cities: Homyel' (Gomel'), Vitsyebsk, Mahilyov
Form of government: Republic
Religions: Russian Orthodox, RC
Currency: Rouble

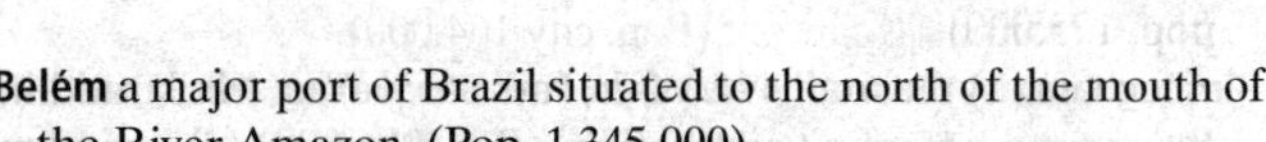

Belém a major port of Brazil situated to the north of the mouth of the River Amazon. (Pop. 1,345,000)

Belfast (1) a port on Belfast Lough and the capital of Northern Ireland. (Pop. 279,000) (2) **City of** a district council area in Co. Antrim and Co. Down, west Northern Ireland. (44 sq miles/115 sq km; pop. 296,000)

Belgium A highly industrialized, relatively small country in northwest Europe with a short coastline on the North Sea. The Meuse River divides Belgium into two distinct geographical regions. To the north of the river the land slopes continuously for 93 miles (150 kilometres) until it reaches the North Sea where the coastlands are flat and grassy. To the south of the river is the forested plateau area of the Ardennes. Between these two regions lies the Meuse valley. Belgium is a densely populated country with few natural resources. Agriculture, which uses about 45 per cent of the land for cultivation or rearing of livestock, employs only 3 per cent of the workforce. About one-fifth of the country is covered with forests, with the wooded areas mainly used for recreation. The metalworking industry, originally based on the small mineral deposits in the Ardennes, is the most important industry, and in the northern cities new textile industries are producing carpets and clothing. Nearly all raw materials are now imported through the main port of Antwerp. There are three officially recognized languages in Belgium – French, German, and Flemish (Dutch).

Area: 11,783 sq miles/30,519 sq km
Population: 10,159,000
Capital: Brussels (Brussel, Bruxelles)
Other major cities: Antwerp, Ghent, Charleroi, Liège
Form of government: Constitutional Monarchy
Religion: RC
Currency: Euro

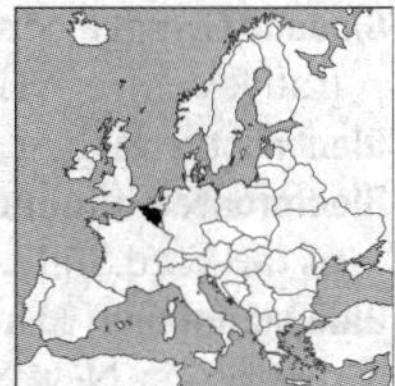

Belgrade (Beograd) the capital of Serbia, in former Yugoslavia, on the confluence of the Rivers Danube and Sava. (Pop. 1,128,000)

Belize A small Central American country on the southeast of the Yucatan Peninsula in the Caribbean Sea. Its coastline on the Gulf of Honduras is approached through some 342 miles (550 kilometres) of coral reefs and keys (cays). The coastal area and north of the country are low-lying and swampy with dense forests inland. In the south, the Maya Mountains rise to 3,609 feet (1,100 metres). The subtropical climate is warm and humid and the trade winds bring cooling sea breezes. Rainfall is heavy, particularly in the south, and hurricanes may occur in summer. The dense forests that cover most of the country provide valuable hardwoods such as mahogany. Most of the population make a living from forestry, fishing, or agriculture, although only 5 per cent of the land is cultivated. The main crops grown for export are sugar cane, citrus fruits (mainly grapefruit), bananas and coconuts. Industry is very underdeveloped, causing many people to emigrate to find work. The official language is English although many others are spoken, including Mayan, Carib, and Spanish.

Area: 8,863 sq miles/22,965 sq km
Population: 222,000
Capital: Belmopan
Other major city: Belize City
Form of government: Constitutional Monarchy
Religions: RC, Protestantism
Currency: Belize Dollar

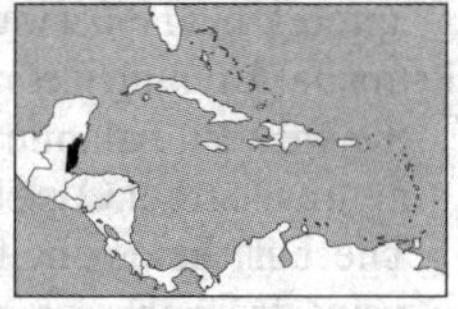

Bellinghausen Sea a part of the Pacific Ocean off Antarctica, due south of South America.

Belmopan the capital of Belize. (Pop. 8,000)

Belo Horizonte an industrial city, and the third largest city of Brazil, in the southeast of the country. (Pop. 2,308,000)

Bengal a former Indian state which was divided in 1947 into two parts: West Bengal in India, and East Pakistan (now Bangladesh).

Bengal, Bay of the massive bay occupying the broad sweep of the Indian Ocean between India and Myanmar, to the south of Bangladesh.

Benghazi (Banghazi) a major port on the Gulf of Sirte in Libya. (Pop. 708,000)

Benidorm a popular Mediterranean seaside resort of Spain. (Pop. 56,000)

Benin An ice cream cone-shaped country, formerly known as Dahomey, with a very short coastline on the Bight of Benin on the southern coast of West Africa. The coastal area has white sandy beaches backed by lagoons and low-lying fertile lands. In the northwest, the Atakora Mountains are grassy plateaus that are deeply cut into steep forested valleys, and on the grasslands sheep, cattle, and goats are reared. The main rivers of Benin are the Donga, Couffo, and Niger with its tributaries. The climate in the north is tropical and in the south equatorial. There are nine rainy months each year so crops rarely fail. Farming is predominantly subsistence and accounts for around 60 per cent of employment, with yams, cassava, maize, rice, groundnuts, and vegetables forming most of the produce. The country is very poor, although since the late 1980s economic reforms have been towards a market economy and Western financial aid has been sought. The main exports are palm oil, palm kernels, and cotton. Tourism is now being developed but as yet facilities for this are few except in some coastal towns.

Area: 43,484 sq miles/112,622 sq km
Population: 5,563,000
Capital: Porto Novo
Other major city: Cotonou
Form of government: Republic
Religions: Animism, RC, Sunni Islam
Currency: CFA Franc

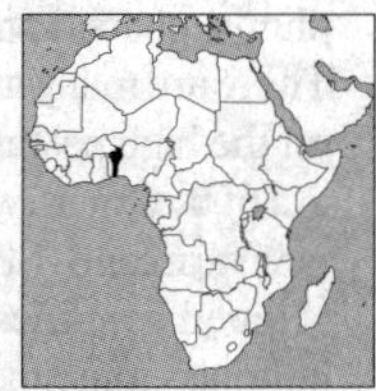

Benue a river which flows through Cameroon and Nigeria to the Gulf of Guinea. (Length 865 miles/390 km)

Benxi an industrial city in Liaoning Province, China. (Pop. 764,000)

Beqa'a a long, fertile valley running north to south in Lebanon, between the Lebanon and Anti-Lebanon Mountains.

Bergamo a historical and industrial city in northern Italy. (Pop. 118,000)

Bergen an old port in southwest Norway, and now that country's second largest city. (Pop. 201,000)

Bering Sea a part of the Pacific Ocean between Alaska and eastern Russian Federation.

Bering Strait the stretch of sea, 55 miles (88 kilometres) wide, that separates the Russian Federation from Alaska in the USA.

Berkshire a historical county of central southern England.

Berlin the capital of Germany, in the north of the country on the River Spree. Until 1990 it was divided by the Berlin Wall. (Pop. 3,290,000)

Bermuda A country consisting of a group of 150 small islands in the western Atlantic Ocean. It lies about 572 miles (920 kilometres) east of Cape Hatteras on the coast of the United States. The hilly limestone islands are the caps of ancient volcanoes rising from the sea bed. The main island, Great Bermuda, is linked to the other islands by bridges and causeways. The climate is warm and humid, with rain spread evenly throughout the year but with the risk of hurricanes from June to November. Bermuda's chief agricultural products are fresh vegetables, bananas, and citrus fruit, but 80 per cent of food requirements are imported. Many foreign banks and financial institutions operate from the island, taking advantage of the lenient tax laws. Other industries include ship repair and pharmaceuticals. Its proximity to the USA and the pleasant climate have led to a flourishing tourist industry.

Area: 20 sq miles/53 sq km
Population: 64,000
Capital: Hamilton
Form of government: British Overseas Territory
Religions: Protestantism, RC
Currency: Bermudan Dollar

Berne (Bern) the historical capital of Switzerland, and also the name of the surrounding canton. (Pop. city 122,000)

Besançon a town of ancient origins in the Jura region of eastern France. (Pop. 118,000)

Bethlehem a town in the West Bank area of Israel, celebrated by Christians as the birthplace of Jesus Christ. (Pop. 24,000)

Béthune an industrial town in northeastern France. (Pop. 28,000)

Bhopal an industrial city in central India. (Pop. 1,462,000)

Bhutan Surrounded by India to the south and China to the north, Bhutan rises from foothills overlooking the Brahmaputra River to the southern slopes of the Himalayas. The Himalayas, which rise to over 24,600 feet (7,500 metres) in Bhutan, make up most of the country. The climate is hot and wet on the plains but temperatures drop progressively with altitude, resulting in glaciers and permanent snow cover in the north. The valleys in the centre of the country are wide and fertile, and about 95 per cent of the workforce are farmers growing wheat, rice, potatoes, and corn. Fruit such as plums, pears, apples, and also cardamom are grown for export. There are many monasteries, with some 6,000 monks. Yaks reared on the high pasture land provide milk, cheese, and meat. Vast areas of the country still remain forested as there is little demand for new farmland. Bhutan is one of the world's poorest and least developed countries. It has little contact with the rest of the world although tourism has been encouraged in recent years. There are no railways but roads join many parts of the country.

Area: 18,147 sq miles/47,000 sq km
Population: 1,812,000
Capital: Thimphu (Thimbu)
Form of government: Constitutional Monarchy
Religion: Buddhism
Currency: Ngultrum

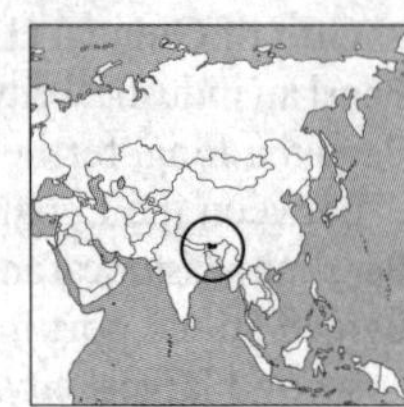

Bialystok (Belostock) a textile city in northeast Poland. (Pop. 287,000)

Bielefeld an industrial city in western Germany. (Pop. 322,000)

Bielsko-Biala (Bielitz) an industrial city in southern Poland. (Pop. 178,000)

Bikini an atoll in the Marshall Islands, the site of US nuclear weapon tests between 1946 and 1962.

Bihar a state in northeast India. The capital is Patna. (Pop. 81,788,000)

Bilbao a port and industrial city in the Basque region of northern Spain. (Pop. 351,000)

Bioko an island in the Gulf of Guinea (formerly Fernando Po) now governed by Equatorial Guinea. (780 sq miles/2,017 sq km; pop. 125,000)

Birmingham (1) the main city of the industrial West Midlands and the second largest city in the UK. (Pop. 986,000) (2) an industrial city in the state of Alabama, USA. (Pop. 245,000)

Biscay, Bay of the broad bay, notorious for its rough weather, formed by the Atlantic Ocean between northern Spain and Brittany in northwest France.

Bishkek, formerly Frunze, the capital of Kyrgyzstan. (Pop. 809,000)

Bisho capital of the Eastern Cape Province in southeast South Africa.

Bismarck the state capital of North Dakota, USA. (Pop. 54,000)

Bismarck Sea a branch of the Pacific Ocean to the north of Papua New Guinea.

Bissau (Bissão) a port and the capital of Guinea-Bissau. (Pop. 288,000)

Black Country a formerly heavily industrialized area in central England, around Birmingham.

Black Forest (Schwarzwald) an extensive area of mountainous pine forests in southwest Germany.

Black Hills a range of hills rising to 7,242 feet (2,207 metres) on the border between the states of South Dakota and Wyoming in the USA.

Blackpool the largest seaside holiday resort in the UK, in Lancashire. (Pop. 148,000)

Black Sea a sea lying between southeast Europe and western Asia; it is surrounded by land except for the Bosphorus channel, leading to the Mediterranean Sea.

Blaenau Gwent a council area in southeast Wales, with its administrative centre in Ebbw Vale. (42 sq miles/109 sq km; pop. 78,000)

Blantyre the largest city in Malawi. (Pop. 533,000)

Bloemfontein the judicial capital of South Africa, and the capital of the Free State. (Pop. 371,000)

Blue Mountains (1) a range of mountains rising to 3,609 feet (1,100 metres) in New South Wales in Australia, some 40 miles (65 kilometres) from Sydney. (2) the mountains in eastern Jamaica rising to 7,402 feet (2,256 metres) at Blue Mountain Peak. The region produces high-quality coffee.

Bochum an industrial city in the Ruhr region of western Germany. (Pop. 388,000)

Bodh Gaya a small town in eastern India which is the site of Buddhism's most revered shrine. (Pop. 32,000)

Bodrum a port on the southeastern coast of Turkey. (Pop. 27,000)

Bogotá the capital of Colombia, set on a plateau of the eastern Andes in the centre of the country. (Pop. 6,680,000)

Bohemia formerly an independent kingdom (9th–13th centuries), now a western region of the Czech Republic which includes the capital, Prague.

Bohol one of the Visayan Islands in the central area of the Philippines. (1,491 sq miles/3,862 sq km; pop. 759,370)

Boise the state capital of Idaho, USA. (Pop. 194,000)

Bolivia A landlocked republic of central South America through which the great mountain range of the Andes runs. It is in the Andes that the highest navigable lake in the world, Lake Titicaca, is found. On the Altiplano, an undulating depression south of the lake, is the highest capital city in the world, La Paz. To the east and northeast of the mountains is a huge area of lowland containing tropical rainforests (the Llanos) and wooded savanna (the Chaco). The northeast has a heavy rainfall while in the southwest the rainfall is negligible. Temperatures vary with altitude, from extremely cold on the mountain summits to cool on the Altiplano, where at least half the population lives. Although rich in natural resources, such as lead, silver, copper, zinc, oil, and tin, Bolivia lacks the funds for their extraction, due to a lack of investment, and political instability. Bolivia is self-sufficient in petroleum and exports natural gas. Agriculture produces soya beans, sugar cane, and cotton for export. Increased production of coca, from which cocaine is derived, has resulted in an illicit economy.

Area: 424,165 sq miles/1,098,581 sq km
Population: 8,140,000
Capital: La Paz (administrative), Sucre (legal)
Other major city: Cochabamba
Form of government: Republic
Religion: RC
Currency: Boliviano

Bologna the capital of Emilia-Romagna, Italy. (Pop. 380,000)

Bolton a textile-manufacturing town in Lancashire, England. (Pop. 138,000)

Bombay (Mumbai) a major port, the capital of Maharashtra state in central western India, and now India's most important industrial city. (Pop. 12,147,000)

Bonaire a Caribbean island off the coast of Venezuela and part of the Netherland Antilles (111 sq miles/288 sq km; pop. 18,000)

Bondi Beach a famous surfing beach in the suburbs of Sydney, Australia.

Bonin Islands a group of small volcanic islands in the Pacific Ocean belonging to Japan. (Pop. 2,300)

Bonn the capital of the former West Germany, it remained the administrative centre of Germany until the seat of government moved to Berlin in 1999. (Pop. 312,000)

Bophuthatswana one of the ten former South African Homelands, the area is now part of the Free State and North West Provinces.

Bordeaux a major port on the Gironde estuary in southwestern France. The region is famous for its wines. (Pop. 217,000)

Borneo one of the largest islands in the world, now divided between three countries. Most of the island is known as Kalimantan, a part of Indonesia. The northern coast is divided into the two states of Sarawak and Sabah, which are part of Malaysia, and the small independent Sultanate of Brunei. (290,320 sq miles/751,900 sq km)

Bosnia-Herzegovina A republic of former Yugoslavia that was formally recognized as an independent state in March 1992. It is a very mountainous country and includes part of the Dinaric Alps, which are densely forested and deeply cut by rivers flowing northwards to join the Sava River. Half the country is forested, and lumber is an important product of the northern areas. One quarter of the land is cultivated, and corn, wheat, and flax are the principal products of the north. In the south, tobacco, cotton, fruits, and grapes are the main products. Bosnia-Herzegovina has large deposits of lignite, iron ore, and bauxite, and its metallurgical plants create air pollution. Water is also polluted around these plants, with the Sava River being severely affected. Despite its natural resources the economy has been devastated by civil war, which began in 1991 following the secession of Croatia and Slovenia from the former Yugoslavia. Dispute over control of Bosnia-Herzegovina continued, leading to United Nations intervention in an attempt to devise a territorial plan acceptable to all factions. A peace agreement, the Dayton Accord, signed in late 1995 has resulted in the division of the country into two self-governing provinces. The population of the state was significantly diminished when refugees from the civil war fled between 1992 and 1993.

Area: 19,735 sq miles/51,129 sq km
Population: 3,675,000
Capital: Sarajevo
Other major cities: Banja Luka, Tuzla
Form of government: Republic
Religions: Eastern Orthodox, Sunni Islam, RC
Currency: Dinar

Bosphorus the narrow strip of water, some 18 miles (29 kilometres) long and no more than 2.5 miles (4 kilometres) wide, which provides the navigable link between the Mediterranean and Black Seas by way of the Sea of Marmara. It separates the European part of Turkey from its Asian part.

Boston an Atlantic port and the state capital of Massachusetts, USA. (Pop. 595,000)

Botany Bay a bay, now in the suburbs of Sydney, Australia, discovered by Captain James Cook in 1770.

Bothnia, Gulf of the most northerly arm of the Baltic Sea, bordered by Finland and Sweden.

Botswana A landlocked republic in southern Africa that straddles the Tropic of Capricorn. Much of the west and southwest of the country forms part of the Kalahari Desert. In the north, there is a huge area of marshland around the Okavango Delta, which is home to a wide variety of wildlife. With the exception of the desert area, most of the country has a subtropical climate but is subject to drought. In winter, days are warm and nights cold while summer is hot with sporadic rainfall. The people are mainly farmers and cattle rearing is the main activity. After independence in 1966, the exploitation of minerals started. In 1972, the first diamond mine was set up at Orapa, and diamonds quickly became the country's most important export. Copper from the nickel/copper complex at Selebi-Pikwe was also exported. Exploitation of these mineral resources has facilitated a high rate of economic growth within the country. Coal is also mined but the majority is for domestic use. About 17 per cent of the land is set aside for wildlife preservation in national parks, game reserves, game sanctuaries, and controlled hunting areas.

Area: 224,607 sq miles/581,730 sq km
Population: 1,490,000
Capital: Gaborone
Other major cities: Mahalapye, Serowe, Francistown
Form of government: Republic
Religions: Animism, Christian
Currency: Pula

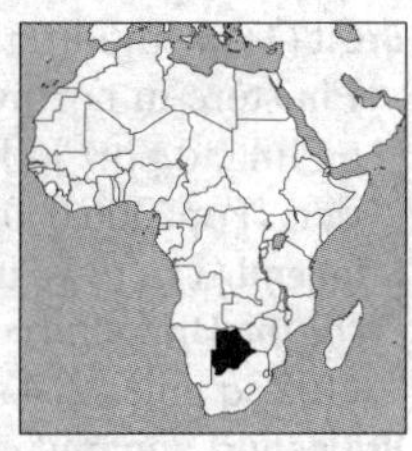

Bouaké the second largest city of Côte d'Ivoire. (Pop. 531,000)

Bougainville the easternmost island belonging to Papua New Guinea, and a part of, though politically separate from, the Solomon Islands.

Bournemouth a coastal resort in Dorset, England. (Pop. 162,000)

Boyne a river flowing into the Irish Sea on the east coast of the Republic of Ireland. It was the site of a battle (1690) in which

William of Orange defeated James II. (Length 70 miles/115 km)

Boyoma Falls a series of seven cataracts over 56 miles (90 kilometres) where the Lualaba River becomes the Congo River. They were formerly called Stanley Falls after the British explorer Sir Henry Morton Stanley.

Brabant the central province of Belgium around the capital, Brussels. (1,297 sq miles/3,358 sq km; pop. 1,016,000)

Bradford a city in the county of West Yorkshire, England, which was the centre of the woollen industry in the 19th century. (Pop. 290,000)

Bragança a small inland medieval town in Portugal, and the original home of the family which ruled Portugal from 1640 to 1910. (Pop. 20,000)

Brahmaputra a major river of South Asia, flowing from the Himalayas in Tibet through Assam in northern India to join the River Ganges in Bangladesh. (Length 1,802 miles/2,900 km)

Brâila a port in Romania on the River Danube, 87 miles (140 kilometres) inland from the Black Sea. (Pop. 232,000)

Brasília the capital, since 1960, of Brazil. (Pop. 2,090,000)

Brazov an industrial city in central Romania. (Pop. 310,000)

Bratislava (Pressburg) the second largest city in the former Czechoslovakia, now capital of Slovakia. (Pop. 449,000)

Brazil The fifth largest country in the world, which covers nearly half of South America. The climate is mainly tropical, but droughts may occur in the northeast, where it is hot and arid. Around 14 per cent of the population is employed in agriculture, and the main products exported are coffee, soya beans and cocoa. It is rich in minerals and is the only source of high-grade quartz crystal in commercial quantities.

Area: 3,300,171 sq miles/8,547,403 sq km
Population: 157,872,000
Capital: Brasília
Other major cities: Belo Horizonte, Porto Alegre, Recife, Rio de Janeiro, Salvador, São Paulo
Form of government: Federal Republic
Religion: RC
Currency: Real

Brazzaville the capital of the Congo Republic, on the Congo River. (Pop. 1,134,000)

Breda a historic and manufacturing city in the Netherlands. (Pop. 160,000)

Bremen a major port on the River Weser, near the North Sea coast of Germany, and also the name of the surrounding state. (Pop. 528,000)

Bremerhaven a port on the North Sea coast of Germany. (Pop. 118,000)

Brescia a city in northern Italy. (Pop. 192,000)

Brest (1) an important naval port situated on an inlet on the tip of Finistère in northwestern France. (Pop. 151,000) (2) (Brzesc) an inland port in Belarus on the River Bug on the Polish border. (Pop. 306,000)

Bridgend (1) a town in south Wales, and the administrative centre for the Bridgend council area. (2) a council area in South Wales. (102 sq miles/264 sq km; pop. 131,000)

Bridgeport a manufacturing city on the coast of the state of Connecticut, USA. (Pop. 141,000)

Bridgetown the capital of Barbados. (Pop. 99,000)

Brighton a famous seaside resort on the south coast of England in the county of East Sussex. (Pop. 122,000)

Brindisi a port on the east coast of Italy at the southern end of the Adriatic Sea. (Pop. 93,000)

Brisbane a port on the east coast of Australia, and the state capital of Queensland. (Pop. 1,544,000)

Bristol (1) a major city and port on the River Avon in southwest England. (Pop. 409,000) (2) a unitary authority in southwest England. (42 sq miles/110 sq km; pop. 374,000)

British Columbia the western seaboard province of Canada. The capital is Victoria. (358,968 sq miles/929,730 sq km; pop. 4,122,000)

British Indian Ocean Territory the Chagos Archipelago, a group of five coral atolls in the middle of the Indian Ocean. (20 sq miles/52 sq km)

British Isles the name given to the group of islands in northwestern Europe formed by Great Britain and Ireland, and the surrounding islands.

Brittany (Bretagne) the region of France which occupies the extreme northwestern peninsula, protruding into the Atlantic.

Brno (Brünn) an industrial city in the southeast of the Czech Republic. (Pop. 378,000)

Bruges (Brugge) a historical town and capital of the province of West Flanders, Belgium. (Pop. 115,000)

Brunei A sultanate located on the northwest coast of the island of Borneo in southeast Asia. It is bounded on all sides by the Sarawak territory of Malaysia, which splits the sultanate into two separate parts. Broad tidal swamplands cover the coastal plains, and inland Brunei is hilly and covered with tropical rainforests that occupy almost half the country's land area. The climate is tropical marine, hot and moist, with cool nights. Rainfall is heavy (98 inches/2,500 millimetres) at the coast but even heavier (197 inches/5,000 millimetres) inland. The main crops grown are rice, vegetables, and fruit, but economically the country depends on its oil industry, which employs 7 per cent of the working population. Cloth weaving and metalwork are also small local industries. Oil production began in the 1920s and now oil and natural gas account for almost all exports. Other minor products are rubber, pepper, gravel, and animal hides.

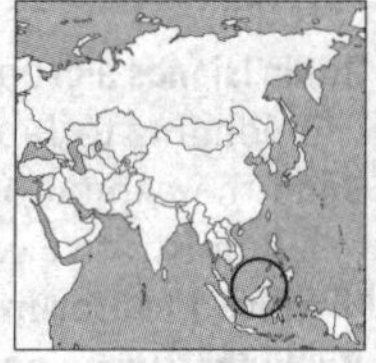

Area: 2,226 sq miles/5,765 sq km
Population: 300,000
Capital: Bandar Seri Begawan
Other major cities: Kuala Belait, Seria
Form of government: Monarchy (Sultanate)
Religion: Sunni Islam
Currency: Brunei Dollar

Brunswick (Braunschweig) a historical town in northern Germany, and the capital of the Dukes of Saxony. (Pop. 242,000)

Brussels (Brussel, Bruxelles) a historical city and the capital of Belgium. It plays a central role in Europe as the administrative headquarters for the European Commission. (Pop. 959,000)

Bryansk an industrial city in the west of the Russian Federation. (Pop. 456,000)

Bucaramanga a city in the north of Colombia, close to the border with Venezuela. (Pop. 542,000)

Bucharest (Bucuresti) the capital of Romania, in the southeast of the country. (Pop. 1,977,000)

Buckinghamshire a county in central southern England, with its administrative centre in the town of Aylesbury. (727 sq miles/1,883 sq km; pop. 658,000)

Budapest the capital of Hungary, comprising the towns of Buda and Pest, which lie on opposite sides of the River Danube. (Pop. 1,858,400)

Buenos Aires the capital of Argentina. (Pop. 12,955,000)

Buffalo a city and port in New York State, USA, situated at the eastern end of Lake Erie. (Pop. 294,000)

Bug a river which flows northwest from the Ukraine, forming the border with Poland before turning west into Poland and joining the Narew and Vistula Rivers. (Length: 480 miles/813 km)

Bujumbura the capital of Burundi, situated at the northern end of Lake Tanganyika. (Pop. 232,000)

Bukhara an old trading city in Uzbekistan. (Pop. 268,000)

Bulawayo the second city of Zimbabwe, in the southwest of the country. (Pop. 928,000)

Bulgaria A southeast European republic located on the east Balkan Peninsula and with a coast on the Black Sea. It is bounded to the north by Romania, to the west by Serbia and the Former Yugoslav Republic of Macedonia, and to the south by Greece and Turkey. The centre of Bulgaria is crossed from west to east by the Balkan Mountains. The south of the country has a Mediterranean climate with hot dry summers and mild winters. Farther north the temperatures become more extreme and rainfall is higher in summer. The main river in Bulgaria is the Danube, and about a third of the country is covered by forests. Traditionally Bulgaria is an agricultural country and a revolution in farming during the 1950s led to great increases in output. This was because of the collectivization of farms and the use of more machinery, fertilizers, and irrigation. Increased mechanization led to more of the workforce being available to work in mines and industry. However, the country suffered very high rates of inflation and unemployment in the early 1990s after the break-up of the former Soviet Union, with whom Bulgaria had very close trade links, and industrial pollution affects its rivers, soils, and the Black Sea coastline, an area that is extremely important for tourism, with over 10,000,000 people visiting the Black Sea resorts annually.

Area: 42,823 sq miles/110,912 sq km
Population: 8,356,000
Capital: Sofia (Sofiya)
Other major cities: Burgas, Plovdiv, Ruse, Varna
Form of government: Republic
Religion: Eastern Orthodox
Currency: Lev

Burgas a major port on the Black Sea coast of Bulgaria. (Pop. 193,000)

Burgos an industrial town in northern Spain. (Pop. 164,000)

Burgundy (Bourgogne) a region of east central France, famous for its wine.

Burkina Faso A landlocked state in West Africa, Burkina Faso (formerly called Upper Volta) lies on the fringe of the Sahara, to the north. It comprises a plateau region in the north which gives way southwards to an area of plains. The northern part of the country is arid and is more or less an extension of the Sahara Desert. The south is less dry and has savannah-type vegetation and scattered trees. Precipitation is generally low, the heaviest rain falling in the southwest, while the rest of the country is semi-desert. The dusty grey plains in the north and west have infertile soils that have been further impoverished by overgrazing and over-cultivation. Around 85 per cent of the people live by subsistence farming, and food crops include sorghum, millet, pulses, corn, and rice. The main industries are textiles, metal products, and the processing of agricultural products and production of consumer items such as footwear and soap. Cotton is the main export, along with minerals such as gold and animal products. There is great poverty and shortage of work, and many of the younger population go to Ghana and Côte d'Ivoire for employment. During the 1970s, the country was severely affected by drought and this was followed by political instability in the 1980s. The situation has improved since 1992.

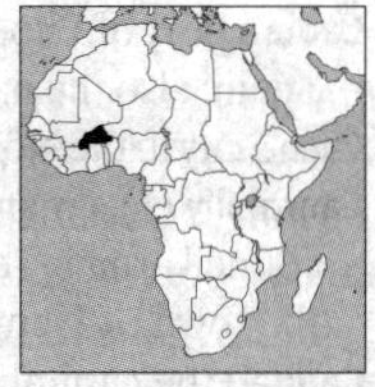

Area: 105,792 sq miles/274,000 sq km
Population: 10,780,000
Capital: Ouagadougou
Other cities: Bobo-Dioulasso, Koudougou
Form of government: Republic
Religions: Animism, Sunni Islam
Currency: CFA Franc

Burma *see* **Myanmar**

Bursa a city in northwestern Turkey, and also the name of the surrounding province, of which it is the capital. (Pop. 1,190,000)

Burundi A small, densely populated country in central east Africa, bounded by Rwanda to the north, Tanzania to the east and south, and the Democratic Republic of Congo to the west. One of the poorest nations in the world, Burundi consists mainly of an upland plateau at an elevation of 4,600–5,900 feet (1,400–1,800 metres). The climate is equatorial but modified by altitude. The savannah in the east is several degrees hotter than the plateau and there are two wet seasons. The soils are not rich but there is enough rain to grow crops in most areas for subsistence farming. The main food crops are bananas, sweet potatoes, peas, lentils, and beans. Cassava is grown near the shores of Lake Tanganyika which is in the Great Rift Valley. The main cash crop is coffee, which accounts for 90 per cent of Burundi's export earnings. Cotton and tea are also cultivated for export. There is a little commercial fishing on Lake Tanganyika, otherwise industry is very basic. Since 1994, Burundi has been afflicted by ethnic conflict between the majority Hutu and minority Tutsi. Between 1994 and 1995 it is estimated that 150,000 were killed as a result of ethnic violence and the political situation remains volatile.

Area: 10,747 sq miles/27,834 sq km
Population: 6,088,000
Capital: Bujumbura
Form of government: Republic
Religion: RC
Currency: Burundi Franc

Buryatiya Republic an autonomous republic of the Russian Federation, situated in the southeast, between Lake Baikal and Mongolia. (135,600 sq miles/351,300 sq km; pop. 1,014,000)

Bydgoszcz (Bromberg) a historical and industrial city in central Poland. (Pop. 385,000)

Bytom (Beuthen) an industrial city in southwest Poland. (Pop. 200,000)

C

Cádiz a port of Phoenician origins on the Atlantic coast of southern Spain; also the name of the surrounding province. (Pop. 139,000)

Caen a city in the Normandy region of northern France. (Pop. 116,000)

Caerphilly (1) a market town in southeast Wales. (Pop. 28,000) (2) a council area in southeast Wales, with its administrative centre in the town of Hengoed. (106 sq miles/275 sq km; pop. 170,000)

Cagliari the capital of the Italian island of Sardinia. (Pop. 164,000)

Cairngorms a mountain range forming part of the Grampian Mountains in Scotland.

Cairns a port on the northeast coast of Queensland, Australia, and a tourist resort catering for visitors to the Great Barrier Reef. (Pop. 126,000)

Cairo (El Qahira) the capital of Egypt, in the north of the country on the River Nile; it is the largest city in Africa. (Pop. 7,765,000)

Calabria the region which occupies the southern 'toe' of Italy. The main town is Reggio Di Calabria. (Pop. 2,072,000)

Calais an old port in northern France situated on the narrowest part of the English Channel, opposite Dover in England. (Pop. 77,000)

Calcutta (Kolkata) the former capital of British India, a major port and industrial centre situated in the northeast of the country, on the Hugli River. (Pop 4,670,000)

Calgary the second largest city of Alberta, Canada. (Pop. 864,000)

Cali an industrial city in southern Colombia. (Pop. 2,204000)

Calicut (Kozhikode) a port on the west coast of southern India. (Pop. 445,000)

California the most populous state of the USA on the Pacific coast. The state capital is Sacramento, but Los Angeles is the biggest city. (158,693 sq miles/411,015 sq km; pop. 35,140,000)

California, Gulf of (Cortes, Sea of; California, Golfo de) the narrow inlet which separates the mainland part of Mexico from the peninsula of Baja California.

Callao the port serving Lima, the capital of Peru. (Pop. 440,500)

Calvados a department of northern France, a part of the region of Normandy. It is famous for its apple-based liqueur, also called Calvados. (Pop. 665,000)

Camargue the broad, flat area of sea marshes in the delta of the River Rhône in the centre of the Mediterranean coast of France.

Cambodia A southeast Asian state bounded by Thailand, Laos and Vietnam, with its southern coast lying on the Gulf of Thailand. The country was devastated by its involvement in the Vietnam War (1960–75) followed by the brutal regime of the Khmer Rouge under Pol Pot (1975–79). The heart of the country is saucer-shaped, and gently rolling alluvial plains are drained by the Mekong River. The Dangrek Mountains form the frontier with Thailand in the northwest. In general, Cambodia has a tropical monsoon climate and about half the land is tropical forest. During the rainy season the Mekong swells and backs into the Tonlé Sap (Great Lake), increasing its size threefold to about 4,015 square miles (10,400 kilometres). This seasonal flooding means the area is left with rich silt when the river recedes. Crop production depends entirely on the rainfall and floods but production was badly disrupted during the civil war when there was widespread famine, and yields still remain low. The cultivation of rice accounts for about 80 per cent of agricultural land and the other main crop is rubber, which grows in the eastern plateau. Despite the gradual rebuilding of the infrastructure in the early 1990s, Cambodia remains one of the world's poorest nations.

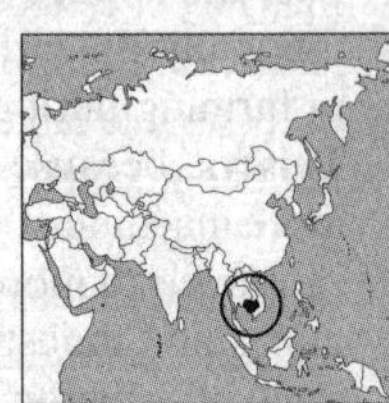

Area: 69,898 sq miles/181,035 sq km
Population: 10,273,000
Capital: Phnom-Penh
Other major cities: Kampong Cham, Battambang
Form of government: People's Republic
Religion: Buddhism
Currency: Riel

Cambrian Mountains a mountain range which forms the 'backbone' of Wales.

Cambridge (1) a famous university city in eastern England. (Pop. 113,000) (2) a city in Massachusetts, USA, home of Harvard University and the Massachusetts Institute of Technology. (Pop. 102,000)

Cambridgeshire a county in eastern England, with its administrative centre in Cambridge. (1,350 sq miles/3,409 sq km; pop. 687,000)

Cameron Highlands an upland area of Malaysia where tea and vegetables are grown.

Cameroon A triangular-shaped country of diverse landscapes in west central Africa. It stretches from Lake Chad at its apex to the northern borders of Equatorial Guinea, Gabon and the Congo in the south. The landscape ranges from low-lying lands, through the semi-desert Sahel to dramatic mountain peaks and then to the grassy savannah, rolling uplands, steaming tropical forests, and hardwood plantations. Cameroon's jungles contain not only commercially valuable trees but also an immense diversity of other plants, many of which have been identified as useful for their medicinal properties. Farther south are the volcanoes, including the sporadically active Mount Cameroon, the highest peak at 1,250 feet (4,100 metres), and the palm beaches at Kribi and Limbe. The climate is equatorial with high temperatures and plentiful rain. The majority of the population are farmers who live in the south and in central Cameroon where they grow maize, millet, cassava, and vegetables. In the drier north, where drought and hunger are well known, life is harder and this area is populated by semi-nomadic herders. Bananas, coffee, and cocoa are the major exports although oil, gas, and aluminium are becoming increasingly important.

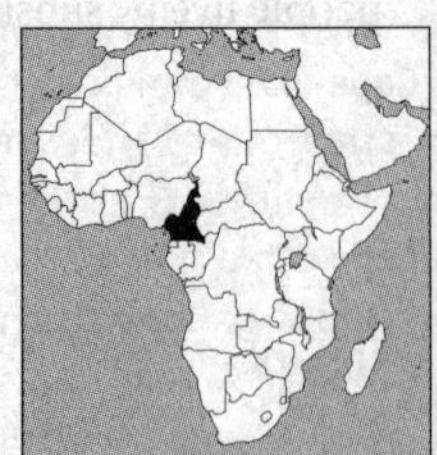

Area: 183,569 sq miles/475,442 sq km
Population: 13,560,000
Capital: Yaoundé
Other major city: Douala
Form of government: Republic
Religions: Animism, RC, Sunni Islam
Currency: CFA Franc

Cameroon, Mount (Cameroun, Mount) an active volcano in west Cameroon. (13,435 ft/4,095 m)

Campania a region of central southern Italy, on the west coast around Naples. (Pop. 5,938,000)

Campinas a modern industrial town 47 miles (75 kilometres) north of São Paulo in Brazil. (Pop. 993,000)

Canada The second largest country in the world and the largest in North America. Canada is a land of great climatic and geographical extremes. It lies to the north of the United States and has Pacific, Atlantic, and Arctic coasts. The country has the highest number of inland waters and lakes in the world, including the Great Lakes on the border with the USA. The Rocky Mountains and Coast Mountains run down the west side, and the highest point, Mount Logan at 19,524 feet (6,050 metres), is in the Yukon. Climates range from polar conditions in the north to cool temperate in the south, with considerable differences from west to east. More than 80 per cent of its farmland is in the prairies that stretch from Alberta to Manitoba. Wheat and grain crops cover three-quarters of the arable land. Canada is rich in forest reserves, which cover more than half the total land area. The most valuable mineral deposits (oil, gas, coal, and iron ore) are found in Alberta. Most industry in Canada is associated with processing its natural resources and it is one of the main exporters of food products.

Area: 3,848,900 sq miles/9,984,670 sq km
Population: 31,414,000
Capital: Ottawa
Other major cities: Toronto, Montréal, Vancouver, Québec
Form of government: Federal Parliamentary State
Religions: RC, United Church of Canada, Anglicanism
Currency: Canadian Dollar

Canary Islands (Islas Canarias) a group of islands belonging to Spain, situated some 60 miles (95 kilometres) off the coast of Western Sahara. The main islands are Gran Canaria, Tenerife, La Palma, Fuerteventura, Gomera, Lanzarote. (2,808 sq miles/7,273 sq km; pop. 1,493,000; cur. Euro)

Canaveral, Cape a long spit of land on the east coast of the state of Florida, USA. It is the USA's main launch site for space missions and the home of the John F. Kennedy Space Centre.

Canberra the capital of Australia, lying about halfway between Sydney and Melbourne in the southeast of the country. (Pop. 323,000)

Cancún a tiny island just off the Yucatan coast of Mexico, connected to the mainland by a causeway, and now a popular holiday resort. (Pop. 436,000)

Cannes a famous beach resort on the Côte d'Azur in southern France. (Pop. 66,000)

Cantabria a province on the Atlantic coast of northern Spain. (Pop. 535,000)

Canterbury a small cathedral city in Kent in southern England. (Pop. 40,000)

Cape Breton Island part of the province of Nova Scotia lying off the eastern coast of Canada. (3,970 sq miles/10,349 sq km; pop. 170,000)

Cape Town a major port on the southwestern tip of South Africa, the country's legislative capital and capital of the Western Cape Province. (Pop. 854, 000)

Cape Verde One of the world's smallest nations, situated in the Atlantic Ocean about 400 miles (640 kilometres) northwest of Senegal. It consists of ten islands and five islets and there is an active volcano on Fogo, one of the islands. The islands are divided into the Windward group and the Leeward group. Over 50 per cent of the population live on São Tiago on which is Praia, the capital. The climate is arid with a cool dry season from December to June and warm dry conditions for the rest of the year. Rainfall is sparse and the islands suffer from periods of severe drought. Agriculture is mostly confined to irrigated inland valleys and the chief crops are coconuts, sugar cane, potatoes, cassava, and dates. Bananas and some coffee are grown for export. Fishing for tuna and lobsters is an important industry but in general the economy is shaky and Cape Verde relies heavily on foreign aid. Because of its lack of natural resources and droughts, large numbers of its people have emigrated for many years. Tourism is being encouraged although the number of visitors is at present relatively low.

Area: 1,557 sq miles/4,033 sq km
Population: 396,000
Capital: Praia
Form of government: Republic
Religion: RC
Currency: Cape Verde Escudo

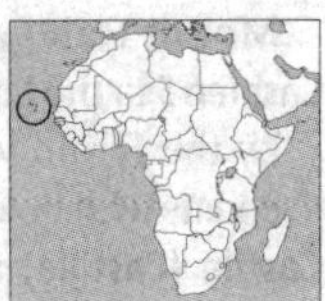

Capri a rocky island at the southern end of the Bay of Naples on the west coast of Italy, famous as a fashionable holiday retreat. (4 sq miles/10.4 sq km; pop. 16,500)

Caprivi Strip a narrow corridor of land, 280 miles (450 kilometres) long, which belongs to Namibia and gives it access to the Zambezi River along the border between Botswana to the south and Angola and Zambia to the north.

Caracas the capital of Venezuela, in the northeast of the country. (Pop. 1,763,000)

Cardamom Mountains a mountain range rising to 5,948 feet (1,813 metres) which lines the coast of Cambodia and separates the interior from the Gulf of Thailand.

Cardiff (Caerdydd) (1) the capital of Wales, situated in southeast Wales, formerly an important port, and the administrative centre for the Cardiff council area. (Pop. 280,000) (2) a council area in southeast Wales. (54 sq miles/139 sq km; pop. 307,000)

Cardigan Bay the long, curving bay which, as part of the Irish Sea, forms much of the west coast of Wales.

Caribbean, The a term that refers to the islands lying within the compass of the Caribbean Sea.

Caribbean Sea a part of the western Atlantic Ocean, bounded by the east coast of Central America, the north coast of South America, and the West Indies.

Carinthia (Kärnten) the southern state of Austria, which borders Italy and Slovenia. (3681 sq miles/9,533 sq km; pop 560,000)

Carlow a landlocked county in the southeast of the Republic of Ireland. The county town is also called Carlow. (Pop. 43,000)

Carmarthen a market town in south Wales. (Pop. 14,000)

Carmarthenshire a council area in south Wales, with its administrative centre in the town of Carmarthen. (926 sq miles/2,398 sq km; pop. 169,000)

Carmel, Mount a ridge of land rising to 1,746 feet (528 metres) in northern Israel.

Caroline Islands a scattered group of islands in the western Pacific Ocean which now make up the Federated States of Micronesia and the separate state of Belau.

Carpathian Mountains a broad sweep of mountains stretching for nearly 625 miles (1,000 kilometres) down the border between Slovakia and Poland and into central Romania. They rise to 8,737 feet (2,663 metres) at their highest point.

Carpentaria, Gulf of the broad gulf of shallow sea between the two horn-like peninsulas of northern Australia.

Carrara a town 31 miles (50 kilometres) north of Pisa in Italy, famous for centuries for its marble quarries. (Pop. 65,000)

Carrickfergus (1) a town in the Carrickfergus district council area, Co. Antrim. (Pop. 23,000) (2) a district council area in Co. Antrim, east Northern Ireland. (32 sq miles/83 sq km; pop. 33,000)

Carson City the state capital of Nevada, USA. (Pop. 58,000)

Cartagena (1) a major port on the Caribbean coast of Colombia. (Pop. 854,000) (2) a port of ancient origins on the Mediterranean coast of Spain. (Pop. 185,000)

Casablanca (Dar el Beida) the main port and largest city of Morocco, on the Atlantic. (Pop. 523,000)

Cascade Range a range of mountains stretching some 700 miles (1,125 kilometres) parallel to the coast of northern California in the USA and into southern Canada. The highest point is at Mount Rainier (14,410 ft/4,392 m) in Washington State.

Caspian Sea the largest inland (salt) sea in the world, supplied mainly by the River Volga. It lies to the north of Iran, which shares its coasts with Azerbaijan, Georgia, Kazakhstan and Turkmenistan.

Castile (Castilla) a former kingdom of Spain, occupying most of the central area, now divided into two regions, Castilla la Mancha and Castilla y León.

Castlereagh a district council area in Co. Down, east Northern Ireland. (33 sq miles/85 sq km; pop. 61,000)

Castries the capital of St Lucia in the Caribbean. (Pop. 14,000)

Catalonia (Cataluña) an autonomous region of Spain, in the northeast, centring on Barcelona. (12,328 sq miles/31,929 sq km; pop. 6,090,000)

Catania a major port and the second largest city in Sicily. (Pop. 338,000)

Catskill Mountains a range of mountains in New York State, USA, famed for their scenic beauty. The highest peak is Slide Mountain at 4,204 feet (1,282 metres).

Caucasus (Kavkaz) the mountainous region between the Black and Caspian Seas, bounded by the Russian Federation, Georgia, Armenia and Azerbaijan. It contains Europe's highest point, Mount Elbrus at 18,510 feet (5,642metres).

Cavan a county in the north of the Republic of Ireland, part of the ancient province of Ulster; Cavan is also the name of the county town. (730 sq miles/1,890 sq km; pop. 55,000)

Cayenne the capital of French Guiana. (Pop. 58,000)

Cayman Islands A group of three low-lying coral islands in the Caribbean Sea, 150 miles (240 kilometres) south of Cuba and northwest of Jamaica, which form a British Overseas Territory. The group comprises Grand Cayman, by far the largest of the three, Cayman Brac and Little Cayman.

Area: 102 sq miles/264 sq km
Population: 38,000
Capital: George Town, on Grand Cayman
Form of government: British Overseas Territory
Religion: Christianity
Currency: Cayman Islands Dollar

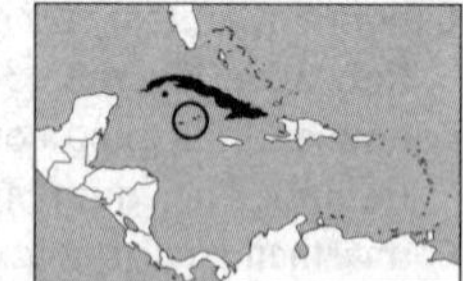

Cebú an island in the central Philippines, forming part of the Visayan group; also the name of its capital city. (1,707 sq miles/4,422 sq km; pop. island 2,092,000/city 688,000)

Celebes Sea a sea between the islands of eastern Indonesia and the Philippines.

Central African Republic A landlocked country in central Africa bordered by Chad in the north, Cameroon in the west, Sudan in the east, and the Congo and Democratic Republic of Congo in the south. The terrain consists of 2,000–3,000 feet (610–915 metres) high undulating plateaux with dense tropical forest in the south and a semi-desert area in the east. The climate is tropical with little variation in temperature throughout the year. The wet months are May, June, October, and November. Floods and tornadoes can occur at the beginning of the rainy season. Most of the population live in the west and in the hot, humid south and southwest. Over 86 per cent of the working population are subsistence farmers and the main crops grown are cassava, groundnuts, bananas, plantains, millet, and maize. Livestock rearing is small-scale. Gems and industrial diamonds are mined, and deposits of uranium, iron ore, lime, zinc, and gold have been discovered, although they remain relatively undeveloped. The country's main exports are coffee, diamonds, cotton, tobacco, and lumber, although this is hampered by the distance from a port. Since the country's independence in 1960, its political and economic fortunes have been mixed, with widespread corruption and violence.

Area: 240,535 sq miles/622,984 sq km
Population: 3,344,000
Capital: Bangui
Form of government: Republic
Religions: Animism, RC
Currency: CFA Franc

Central Region a former local government area of Scotland formed in 1975 and replaced in 1996 by the council areas of Stirling, Clackmannanshire and Falkirk.

Ceredigion a council area in south Wales, on Cardigan Bay, with its administrative centre in the town of Aberaeron. (692 sq miles/1,793 sq km; pop.64,000)

Ceské Budejovice (Budweiss) a historical town in the south of Bohemia, Czech Republic, famous for its Budvar beer. (Pop. 99,000)

Ceuta a Spanish administered enclave in northern Morocco. (Pop. 78,000)

Cévennes the southern part of the Massif Central in France.

Chad A landlocked country in the centre of northern Africa that extends from the edge of the equatorial forests in the south to the middle of the Sahara Desert in the north. It lies more than 944 miles (1,600 kilometres) from the nearest coast. The climate is tropical, with adequate rainfall in the south, but the north experiences semi-desert conditions. In the far north of the country the Tibesti Mountains rise from the desert sand more than 11,200 feet (3,415 metres). The southern part of Chad is the most densely populated and its relatively well-watered savannah has always been the country's most arable region. Unless there is drought, this area is farmed for cotton (the main cash crop along with livestock exports), millet, sorghum, groundnuts, rice, and vegetables. Fishing is carried out in the rivers and in Lake Chad. Cotton ginning and manufacture of peanut oil are the principal industries. As a result of drought and civil war, Chad remains one of the poorest countries in the world. The country was torn by civil strife for much of the latter part of the 20th century but a ceasefire has been in place since 1994.

Area: 495,755 sq miles/1,284,000 sq km
Population: 6,515,000
Capital: Ndjamena
Other major cities: Sarh, Moundou
Form of government: Republic
Religions: Sunni Islam, Animism
Currency: CFA Franc

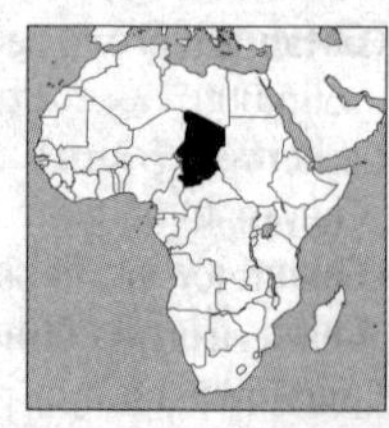

Chad, Lake a large lake in western Chad, on the border with Niger and Nigeria. (10,000 sq miles/26,000 sq km)

Champagne a former region of northeastern France famous for the sparking wine also called champagne. It now forms part of the administrative region called Champagne-Ardenne.

Chandigarh a modern city in north India. (Pop. 569,000)

Changchun the capital of Jilin Province, China. (Pop. 2,110,000)

Chang-hua a historical city in west Taiwan. (Pop. 288,000)

Chang Jiang (Yangtze) the world's third longest river. It rises in Tibet and flows across central China into the East China Sea. (Length 3,965 miles/6,380 km)

Changsha the capital of Hunan Province, China. (Pop. 1,262,000)

Channel Islands a group of islands in the English Channel, close to the coast of France, consisting of Jersey, Guernsey, Alderney, Great Sark, Little Sark, Herm, Jethou, and Lihou (British crown dependencies) and the Roches Douvres and the Îles Chausey (which belong to France). (75 sq miles/194 sq km; pop. 143,000)

Chao Phrya a river running from north to south down the west side of Thailand and through its capital, Bangkok. (Length 62 miles/100 km)

Chapala, Lake the largest lake in Mexico, near Guadalajara. (950 sq miles/2,460 sq km)

Charleroi an industrial city in central Belgium. (Pop. 201,000)

Charleston (1) the state capital of West Virginia, USA (Pop 59,000) (2) an old port on the Atlantic coast of South Carolina, USA, scene of the first action in the Civil War. (Pop. 77,000)

Charlotte Amalie the capital of the US Virgin Islands. (Pop. 14,000)

Charlottetown a port and the provincial capital of Prince Edward Island, Canada. (Pop. 34,000)

Chartres a market town, capital of the department of Eure-et-Loir, in northern France, 50 miles (80 kilometres) west of Paris. It is famous for its early 13th-century cathedral, with original stained-glass windows. (Pop. 39,000)

Chattanooga an industrial city and railway town in Tennessee, USA. (Pop. 158,000)

Chechen-Ingush Republic an autonomous republic of the Russian Federation. (7,450 sq miles/19,300 sq km; pop. 1,204,000)

Cheju Do an island belonging to South Korea, lying some 56 miles (90 kilometres) off its southern tip, and dominated by the sacred volcano, Mount Halla (6,398 ft/1,950 m). (706 sq miles/1,828 sq km; pop. 505,000)

Chelyabinsk an industrial city in the Russian Federation. (Pop. 1,081,000)

Chemnitz an industrial city in southeast Germany, named Karl-Marx-Stadt in former Communist East Germany (until 1990). (Pop. 256,000)

Chengdu the capital of Sichuan Province, China. (Pop. 1,927,000)

Chernobyl a city about 55 miles (90 kilometres) north of Kiev, in the Ukraine. In April 1986, one of the reactors in its nuclear power station exploded, causing the world's worst nuclear accident.

Chesapeake Bay an inlet, 195 miles (314 kilometres) long, on the east coast of the USA, shared by the states of Virginia and Maryland.

Cheshire a county in northwest England, with its administrative centre in Chester. (899 sq miles/2,328 sq km; pop. 975,000)

Cheviot Hills a range of hills, 37 miles (60 kilometres) long, which line the border between Scotland and the county of Northumberland in England.

Cheyenne the state capital of Wyoming, USA. (Pop. 53,000)

Chianti a winemaking region of central Tuscany, Italy.

Chiba a large industrial city on Honshu Island, Japan. (Pop. 903,000)

Chicago a port on Lake Michigan, the largest city in the state of Illinois, and the third largest city in the USA (after New York and Los Angeles). (Pop. 2,925,000)

Chiengmai (Chiang Mai) the second largest city in Thailand, in the northwest of the country, famous for its temples and the crafts produced in the surrounding villages. (Pop. 173,000)

Chihuahua a city in northern central Mexico, and the name of the surrounding province, of which it is the capital. (Pop. 678,000)

Chile A country that lies like a backbone down the Pacific coast of the South American continent with the Andes Mountains extending its length. Its Pacific coastline is 2,600 miles (4,184 kilometres) long and the country is liable to volcanic explosions and earthquakes. Because of its enormous range in latitude it has almost every kind of climate, from desert conditions to icy wastes. The north, in which lies the Atacama Desert, is extremely arid. The climate of the central region is Mediterranean and that of the south cool temperate. Sixty per cent of the population live in the central valley where the climate is similar to that of southern California. The land here is fertile and the principal crops grown are grapes, wheat, apples, sugar beet, maize, tomatoes, and potatoes. There is also a significant winemaking industry. It is also in the central valley that the vast copper mine of El Teniente is located. This is one of the largest copper mines in the world and accounts for Chile's most important source of foreign exchange.

Area: 292,135 sq miles/756,626 sq km
Population: 14,419,000
Capital: Santiago
Other major cities: Arica, Concepción, Valparaíso, Viña del Mar
Form of government: Republic
Religion: RC
Currency: Chilean Peso

Chiltern Hills a range of low chalk hills to the northwest of London, England, rising to 850 feet (260 metres).

China The third largest country in the world, which covers a large area of East Asia and also includes over 3,400 islands. In western China, most of the terrain is very inhospitable. In the northwest, there are deserts that extend into Mongolia and the Russian Federation, and much of the southwest consists of the ice-capped peaks of Tibet. The southeast has a green and well-watered landscape comprising terraced hillsides and paddy fields, and its main rivers are the Chang Jiang (Yangtze), Huang He, and Xi Jiang. Most of China has a temperate climate but in such a large country wide ranges of latitude and altitudes produce local variations. China is an agricultural country, and intensive cultivation and horticulture are necessary to feed its population of over one billion. After the death of Mao Tse-tung in 1976 and under the leadership of Deng Xiaoping, China experienced a huge modernization of agriculture and industry as a result of the supply of expertise, capital, and technology from Japan and the West. The country was opened up to tourists and, to a degree, adopted the philosophy of free enterprise, resulting in a dramatic improvement in living standards for a significant proportion of the population. The change towards a market economy, however, created internal political problems. Pro-democracy demonstrations in 1989 resulted in the Tianmen Square massacre, which was condemned throughout the world and raised questions regarding China's approach to human rights.

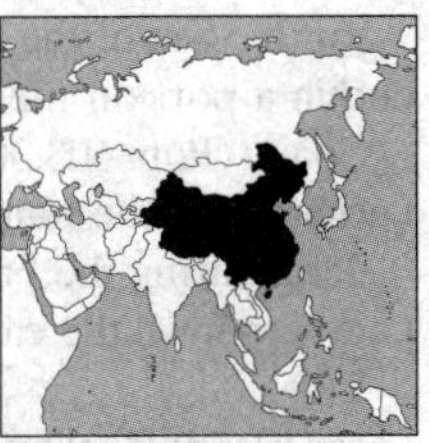

Area: 3,705,408 sq miles/9,596,961 sq km
Population: 1,246,872,000
Capital: Beijing (Peking)
Other major cities: Chengdu, Guangzhou, Shanghai, Tianjin, Wuhan
Form of government: People's Republic
Religions: Buddhism, Confucianism, Taoism
Currency: Yuan

China Sea a part of the Pacific Ocean, off the east coast of China.

Chindwin a river in Myanmar, flowing parallel to the northwest border before joining the River Irrawaddy in the centre of the country. (Length 700 miles/1,130 km)

Chios (Khios) a Greek island in the Aegean Sea, lying only 5 miles (8 kilometres) from the coast of Turkey. (349 sq miles/904 sq km; pop. 52,900)

Chittagong the main port of Bangladesh and its second largest city. (Pop. 2,546,000)

Chongqing (Chungking) an industrial city on the Chang Jiang River, China, and the largest city in Sichuan Province. (Pop. 2,312,000)

Chonju a historical city in the southwest of South Korea. (Pop. 614,000)

Christchurch the largest city on South Island, New Zealand. (Pop. 318,000)

Christmas Island (1) an island in the eastern Indian Ocean, 250 miles (400 kilometres) to the south of Java, administered by Australia since 1958. (55 sq miles/142 sq km; pop. 3,000) (2) former name for Kiritimati.

Chubu Sangaku a national park in central Honshu Island that contains two of the highest mountains in Japan, Mount Hotaka (10,466 ft/3,190 m) and Mount Yari (10,434 ft/3,180 m)

Churchill a river which flows into the Hudson Bay at the port of Churchill after a journey through Saskatchewan and Manitoba. (Length 1,000 miles/1,600 km)

Chuvash Republic an autonomous republic of the Russian Federation. (7,050 sq miles/18,300 sq km; pop. 1,327,000)

Cincinnati a city in the southwest of the state of Ohio, USA, on the Ohio River. (Pop. 332,000)

CIS *see* **Commonwealth of Independent States.**

Ciskei one of ten former South African Homelands, the area is now part of the Eastern Cape Province, in southeast South Africa.

Citaltépetl a volcanic peak to the southeast of Mexico City, at 18,697 feet (5,699 metres) the highest point in Mexico.

Clackmannanshire a council area in central Scotland, with its administrative centre in the town of Alloa. (55 sq miles/142 sq km; pop. 48,000)

Clare a county on the west coast of the Republic of Ireland; the county town is Ennis. (1,230 sq miles/3,188 sq km; pop. 98,000)

Clermont-Ferrand a city in Auvergne, central France. (Pop. 137,000)

Cleveland a port and industrial city on the southern side of Lake Erie, in Ohio, USA. (Pop. 480,000)

Cluj-Napoca a city of ancient origins in central Romania. (Pop. 332,000)

Clwyd a former county of northeast Wales.

Clyde a river in southwest Scotland which flows northwest to form an estuary 60 miles (100 kilometres) long, called the Firth of Clyde, with the city of Glasgow at its head. (Length 105 miles/170 km)

Coast Range the mountains lining the western coast of the USA, stretching 1,000 miles (1,600 kilometres) from the borders with Canada to Los Angeles. The highest point is in the San Jacinto Mountains (10,831 ft/3,301 m).

Cóbh a town and port of call for Atlantic liners in Co. Cork on the south coast of the Republic of Ireland.(Pop. 9,000)

Cochin a port on the southwestern tip of India, on the Malabar Coast. (Pop. 608,000)

Cochin China the name given to the region around the Mekong delta during the French occupation of Vietnam.

Cockburn Town the capital of the Turks and Caicos Islands. (Pop. 5,000)

Cocos Islands (Keeling Islands) a cluster of 28 small coral islands in the eastern Indian Ocean, equidistant from Sumatra and Australia, and administered by Australia since 1955. (6 sq miles/14 sq km; pop. 1,000)

Cod, Cape a narrow, low-lying peninsula on the coast of Massachusetts, USA, where the Pilgrim Fathers landed in 1620.

Coleraine a district council area in Co. Londonderry, north Northern Ireland. (187 sq miles/485 sq km; pop. 50,000)

Cologne (Köln) a city and industrial centre on the River Rhine, Germany. (Pop. 967,000)

Colombia A country situated in the north of South America, most of it lying between the Equator and 10 degrees north. The Andes, which split into three ranges (the Cordilleras) in Colombia, run north along the west coast and gradually disappear towards the Caribbean Sea. Half of Colombia lies east of the Andes, and much of this region is covered in tropical grassland. Towards the Amazon Basin the vegetation changes to tropical forest. The climates in Colombia include equatorial and tropical, according to altitude. Very little of the country is under cultivation although much of the soil is fertile. The range of climates results in an extraordinary variety of crops, of which coffee is the most important, and includes cocoa beans, sugar cane, bananas, cotton, and tobacco. Colombia is rich in minerals such as gold, silver, platinum, and copper, and produces about half of the world's emeralds. It is South America's leading producer of coal, and petroleum is the country's most important foreign revenue earner. However, it has been wracked by violence, involving not only guerrilla groups but also the country's sizable illegal drug trade.

Area: 439,737 sq miles/1,138,914 sq km
Population: 35,626,000
Capital: Bogotá
Other major cities: Barranquilla, Cali, Cartagena, Medellín
Form of government: Republic
Religion: RC
Currency: Colombian Peso

Colombo a major port and the capital of Sri Lanka. (Pop. 649,000)

Columbia, District of *see* **Washington D.C.**

Colorado an inland state of central western USA; the state capital is Denver. (104,247 sq miles/270,000 sq km; pop. 4,536,000)

Colorado a river which rises in the Rocky Mountains in the state of Colorado, USA, and flows southwest to the Gulf of California, forming the Grand Canyon on its way. (Length 1,450 miles/2,330 km)

Colorado Springs a spa and resort city in the state of Colorado, USA. (Pop. 380,000)

Columbia the state capital of South Carolina, USA. (Pop. 119,000)

Columbia flows northwards from its source in British Columbia, Canada, before turning south into Washington State, USA and entering the Pacific Ocean at Portland, Oregon. (Length 1210 miles/1,950 km)

Columbus the state capital of Ohio, USA. (Pop. 714,000)

Commonwealth of Independent States (CIS) an organization created in 1991 to represent the common interests of eleven independent states of the former USSR. The eleven member states are: Armenia, Azerbaijan, Belarus, Kazakhstan, Kyrgyzstan, Moldova, Russian Federation, Tajikistan, Turkmenistan, Ukraine and Uzbekistan. The former Soviet states of Estonia, Latvia, Lithuania and Georgia did not join the CIS on gaining independence.

Comorin, Cape the southern tip of India.

Comoros A country that consists of three volcanic islands in the Indian

Ocean, situated between mainland Africa and Madagascar. Physically, four islands make up the group but the island of Mayotte remained a French dependency when the three western islands became a federal Islamic republic in 1975. The islands are mostly forested and the tropical climate is affected by Indian monsoon winds from the north. There is a wet season from November to April that is accompanied by cyclones. Only small areas of the islands are cultivated and most of this land belongs to foreign plantation owners. The chief product was formerly sugar cane but now vanilla, copra, maize, cloves, and essential oils are the most important products. The forests provide lumber for building and there is a small fishing industry. The coelacanth, a primitive bony fish previously thought to have been extinct for millions of years, was discovered living in the seas off the Comoros in 1938.

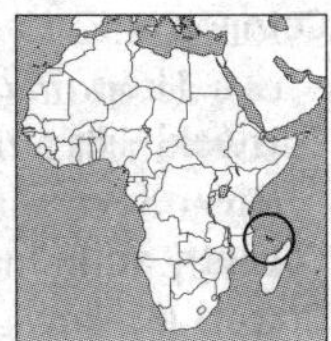

Area: 720 sq miles/1,865 sq km
Population: 538,000
Capital: Moroni
Form of government: Federal Islamic Republic
Religion: Sunni Islam
Currency: Comorian Franc

Conakry the capital of Guinea, a port on the island of Tombo. (Pop. 1,588,000)

Concord the state capital of New Hampshire, USA. (Pop. 42,000)

Congo Formerly a French colony and now a republic, the Congo is situated in west central Africa where it straddles the equator. The climate is equatorial, with a moderate rainfall and a small range of temperature. The Bateke Plateau has a long dry season but the Congo Basin is more humid and rainfall approaches 9.8 inches (2,500 mm) each year. About 62 per cent of the total land area is covered with equatorial forest from which lumber is produced. Valuable hardwoods, such as mahogany, are exported. Cash crops, such as coffee and cocoa, are mainly grown on large plantations but food crops are grown on small farms usually worked by the women. A manufacturing industry is now growing and oil discovered offshore accounts for about 90 per cent of the Congo's revenues and exports. The remaining exports are wood, cocoa, sugar, coffee, and diamonds.

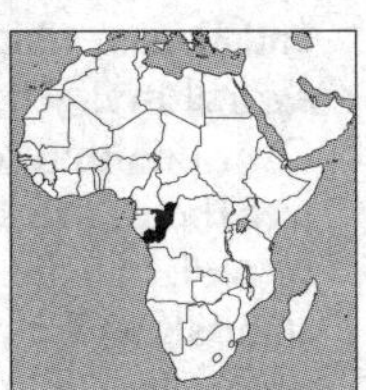

Area: 132,047 sq miles/342,000 sq km
Population: 2,668,000
Capital: Brazzaville
Other major city: Pointe-Noire
Form of government: Republic
Religion: Animism, Christianity
Currency: CFA Franc

Congo, Democratic Republic of A vast country, formerly known as The Democratic Republic of Congo, situated in west central Africa. It has a short coastline of only 25 miles (40 kilometres) on the Atlantic Ocean. Rainforests, which cover about 55 per cent of the country, contain valuable hardwoods such as mahogany and ebony. The country is drained by the Congo River, which is largely navigable, and its main tributaries. There is enormous potential for hydroelectricity, but this is not yet exploited. Mountain ranges and plateaux surround the Congo basin, and in the east the Ruwenzori Mountains overlook the lakes in the Great Rift Valley. In the central region the climate is hot and wet all year but elsewhere there are well-marked wet and dry seasons. Agriculture employs 75 per cent of the population yet less than 3 per cent of the country can be cultivated. Grazing land is limited by the infestation of the tsetse fly. Cassava is the main subsistence crop, and coffee, tea, cocoa, rubber, and palms are grown for export. The country's huge mineral resources have fuelled the ongoing civil war and ethnic conflict in the region, and the government has no control over large parts of the country.

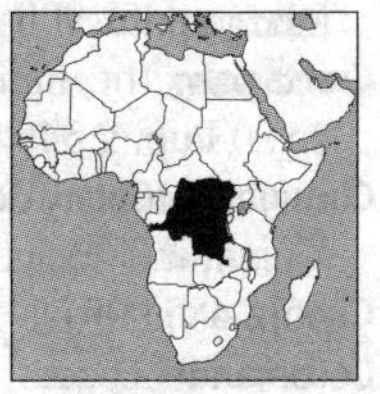

Area: 905,355 sq miles/2,344,858 sq km
Population: 46,812,000
Capital: Kinshasa
Other major cities: Lubumbashi, Mbuji-Mayi, Kananga
Form of government: Republic
Religions: RC, Protestantism, Animism
Currency: Franc

Congo (Zaïre) a major river of central Africa (the second longest river in Africa after the Nile) and, with its tributaries, forming a massive basin. It rises as the Lualaba in the south of the Democratic Republic of Congo, then flows north and northwest, and finally southwest, forming the border between Democratic Republic of Congo and the Congo before entering the Atlantic Ocean. (Length 3,000 miles/4,800 km)

Connacht (Connaught) a province and ancient kingdom of the Republic of Ireland, covering the northwest of the island.

Connecticut a state on the northeastern seaboard of the USA, in New England; the capital is Hartford. (5,009 sq miles/12,973 sq km; pop. 3,445,000)

Connemara a coastal area of Co. Galway on the west coast of Ireland centring upon the distinctive peaks of the Twelve Bens.

Constance, Lake a lake north of the Swiss Alps, surrounded by Germany to the north, Switzerland to the south and Austria to the east. (207 sq miles /536 sq km)

Constanta a major port on the Black Sea coast of Romania. (Pop. 338,000)

Constantine (Qacentina) an ancient walled city in the northeastern corner of Algeria. (Pop. 516,000)

Conwy (1) a market town and holiday resort in north Wales, on the estuary of the River Conwy, also the administrative centre for the Conwy council area. (Pop. 14,000) (2) a council area in north Wales. (436 sq miles/1,130 sq km; pop. 70,000)

Cook Islands a group of 15 islands in the South Pacific, independent since 1965 but associated with New Zealand. The capital is Avarua. (Area 93 sq miles/240 sq km; pop. 20,000; cur. Cook Islands Dollar/ New Zealand Dollar)

Cook, Mount the highest mountain in New Zealand, on South Island. (12,316 ft/3,753 m)

Cookstown a district council area in Co. Tyrone, central Northern Ireland. (240 sq miles/622 sq km; pop. 31,000)

Cook Strait the strait that separates North Island and South Island of New Zealand, 16 miles (26 kilometres) across at its widest point.

Cooper Creek a river flowing into Lake Eyre in South Australia from its source in central Queensland. The upper stretch is known as the Barcoo River. (Length 800 miles/1,420 km)

Copacabana a famous beachside suburb of Rio de Janeiro, Brazil.

Copenhagen (København) a port and the capital of Denmark, located on the islands of Zealand and Amager. (Pop. 1,096,000)

Coral Sea a part of the Pacific Ocean, off the northeast coast of Australia.

Córdoba (Cordova) (1) a city in southern Spain, famous for its cathedral which was built originally as a mosque; also the name of the surrounding province. (Pop. city 316,000) (2) the second city of Argentina, and the name of the surrounding province. (Pop. 1,460,000)

Corfu (Kérkira) the most northerly of the Ionian Islands, in western Greece; the capital is also called Corfu. (229 sq miles/592 sq km; pop. 114,000)

Corinth (Korinthos) a town in the Peloponnese in western Greece, built near the Corinth Ship Canal. (Pop. 33,000)

Cork the second largest city in the Republic of Ireland, at the head of a large natural harbour which cuts into the southern coast. Also the name of the county of which it is the county town. (County 2,880 sq miles/7,459 sq km; pop. county 438,000; city 188,000)

Cornwall a county occupying the southwestern tip of England, with its administrative centre in Truro. (1,376 sq miles/3,564 sq km; pop. 480,000)

Coromandel Coast the coast of southeastern India around Madras.

Coromandel Peninsula the central peninsula reaching northwards from North Island, New Zealand.

Corpus Christi a port in Texas, USA, on the Gulf of Mexico. (Pop. 290,000)

Corsica (Corse) a large island in the Mediterranean Sea lying to the north of Sardinia, governed by France. The capital is Ajaccio. (3,350 sq miles/8,680 sq km; pop. 263,000)

Costa Brava a strip of coastline to the northeast of Barcelona in Spain, famous for its beaches and popular resorts.

Costa del Sol a strip of coastline in southern Spain, famous for its beaches and popular resorts.

Costa Rica With the Pacific Ocean to the south and west and the Caribbean Sea to the east, Costa Rica is sandwiched between the Central American countries of Nicaragua and Panama. Much of the country consists of volcanic mountain chains that run northwest to southeast. The climate is tropical with a small temperature range and abundant rain. The dry season is from December to April. The most populated area is the Valle Central in which the Spanish settled in the 16th century. The upland areas have rich volcanic soils that are good for coffee growing and the slopes provide lush pastures for cattle. Coffee and bananas are grown commercially and are the major agricultural exports. Costa Rica's mountainous terrain provides hydroelectric power, which makes it almost self-sufficient in electricity, and attractive scenery for its growing tourist industry The country has a high literacy rate (around 92 per cent) and its culture reflects its Spanish heritage.

Area: 19,730 sq miles/51,100 sq km
Population: 3,398,000
Capital: San José
Other major city: Límon
Form of government: Republic
Religion: RC
Currency: Costa Rican Colón

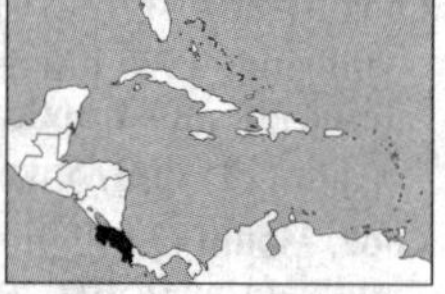

Costa Smeralda the 'emerald coast' on the northeast side of the island of Sardinia in the Mediterranean, famed for its watersports and its upmarket resorts.

Côte d'Azur the coast of southeast France, famous for its beaches and resorts such as St Tropez, Cannes and Nice.

Côte d'Ivoire (Ivory Coast) A former French colony in West Africa, Côte d'Ivoire is located on the Gulf of Guinea with Ghana to the east and Liberia and Guinea to the west. The southwest coast has rocky cliffs but farther east there are coastal plains, which are the country's most prosperous region. The climate is tropical and affected by distance from the sea. The coastal area has two wet seasons, but in the north there is only the one. Côte d'Ivoire is basically an agricultural country with about 55 per cent of the workforce involved in producing cocoa, coffee, rubber, bananas, and pineapples. It is the world's largest producer of cocoa and the fourth largest producer of coffee. These two crops bring in half the country's export revenue although lumber production is also of economic importance. Since independence was achieved in 1960, industrialization has developed rapidly, particularly food processing, textiles, and sawmills. Oil was discovered offshore in the late 1970s and there is mining for gold and diamonds.

Area: 124,504 sq miles/322,463 sq km
Population: 14,781,000
Capital: Yamoussoukro
Other major cities: Abidjan, Bouaké, Daloa
Form of government: Republic
Religions: Animism, Sunni Islam, RC
Currency: CFA Franc

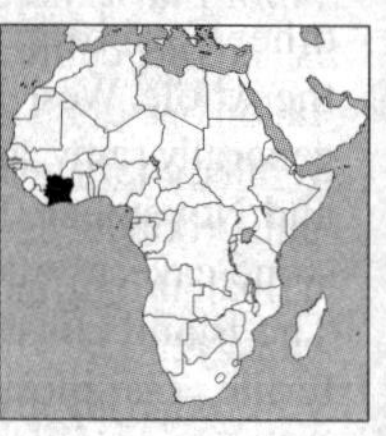

Cotonou a port and the main business centre of Benin, West Africa. (Pop. 762,000)

Cotswold Hills a range of hills in central England, lying east of the River Severn.

Coventry an industrial city in central England. (Pop. 295,000)

Cracow (Krakow) the third largest city in Poland, and the capital during medieval times. (Pop. 734,000)

Craigavon a district council area in Co. Armagh, central Northern Ireland. (108 sq miles/279 sq km; pop. 78,000)

Craiova an industrial city in southwest Romania. (Pop. 318,000)

Cremona a town on the River Po in central northern Italy, famous for its fine violins from the 16th to 18th centuries. (Pop. 72,000)

Crete (Kríti) the largest and most southerly of the islands of Greece, with important ruins of the Minoan civilization at Knossos. The capital is Chania (Khania). (3,229 sq miles/8,366 sq km; pop. 540,000)

Crimea (Krym) a diamond-shaped peninsula jutting out into the northern part of the Black Sea and an autonomous region of the Ukraine. (10,000 sq miles/25,900 sq km; pop. 2,073,000)

Croatia A republic of former Yugoslavia that made a unilateral declaration of independence on 25 June 1991. Sovereignty was not formally recognized by the international community until early in 1992. Located in southeast Europe, it is bounded to the west by the Adriatic Sea, to the north by Slovenia and Romania, and to the south by Bosnia-Herzegovina. Western Croatia lies in the Dinaric Alps. The eastern region, drained by the Rivers Sava and Drava, which both flow into the Danube, is low-lying and agricultural. The chief farming region is the Pannonian Plain. Over one-third of the country is forested, with beech and oak trees being predominant, and lumber is a major export. Deposits of coal, bauxite, copper, petroleum, oil, and iron ore are substantial, and most of the republic's industry is based on their processing. In Istria in the northwest and on the Dalmatian coast, tourism was a major industry until Croatia became embroiled in the Serbo-Croat war prior to its secession in 1992. Following the formal recognition of Croatia's independence by the international community, the fighting abruptly ceased; however, the tourism industry continued to suffer from the effects of the ongoing hostilities in other parts of the former Yugoslavia. More recently, tourists are returning although there is a need to rebuild the infrastructure.

Area: 21,824 sq miles/56,538 sq km
Population: 4,501,000
Capital: Zagreb
Other major cities: Rijeka, Split
Form of government: Republic
Religions: RC, Eastern Orthodox
Currency: Kuna

Crozet Islands a group in the Antarctic Ocean, forming part of the French Southern and Antarctic Territories. (116 sq miles/300 sq km)

Cuba The largest and most westerly of the Greater Antilles group of islands in the West Indies. Cuba is strategically positioned at the entrance to the Gulf of Mexico and lies about 87 miles (140 kilometres) south of the tip of Florida. Cuba is as big as all other Caribbean islands put together and is home to a third of the whole West Indian population. The climate is warm and generally rainy, and hurricanes are liable to occur between June and November. It possesses unusual natural subsurface limestone caverns and its rivers tend to be short and unnavigable. The island consists mainly of extensive plains and the soil is fertile. The most important agricultural product is sugar and its byproducts, and the processing of these is the most important industry. Tobacco is also of commercial significance, with Havana cigars being known internationally. Most of Cuba's trade has been with other communist countries, particularly the former USSR, and the country's economy has suffered as a result of a US trade embargo.

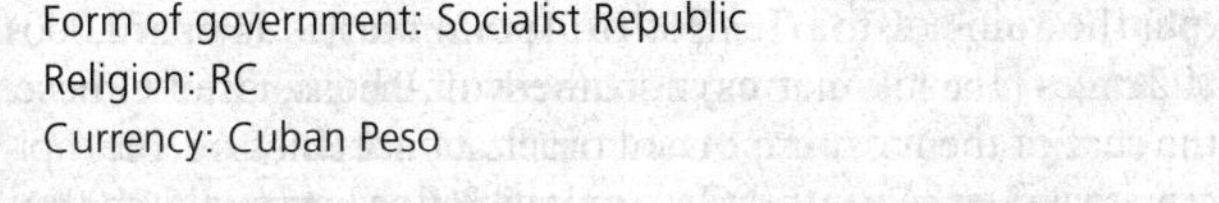

Area: 42,804 sq miles/110,861 sq km
Population: 11,019,000
Capital: Havana (La Habana)
Other major cities: Camaguey, Holguín, Santiago de Cuba
Form of government: Socialist Republic
Religion: RC
Currency: Cuban Peso

Cúcuta a city in northern Colombia on the border with Venezuela. (Pop. 657,000)

Cuenca a city in southern Ecuador, founded by the Spanish in 1557, but also the site of a number of important Inca ruins. (Pop. 277,000)

Cuernavaca an old resort town in the mountains 50 miles (80 kilometres) to the south of Mexico City. (Pop. 334,000)

Cumbria a county in northwest England, with its administrative centre in Carlisle. (2,629 sq miles/6,809 sq km; pop. 493,000)

Curaçao an island in the Caribbean lying just off the coast of Venezuela but a part of the Netherlands Antilles. (171 sq miles/444 sq km; pop. 186,000)

Curitaba an industrial city in southern Brazil. (Pop. 1,642,000)

Cuzco a city set in the Andes in Peru, and the name of the surrounding province. It was a centre of the Inca empire, and there are numerous Inca remains in the region, including Machu Picchu. (Pop. city 283,000)

Cwmbran a 'new town' in southeast Wales, developed in the 1950s, and the administrative centre for the Monmouthshire council area. (Pop. 46,000)

Cyclades (Kikládhes) a group of some 220 islands in the middle of the Aegean Sea belonging to Greece. The capital is Hermoupolis. (Pop. 112,000)

Cyprus An island that lies in the eastern Mediterranean about 53 miles (85 kilometres) south of Turkey. It has a long thin panhandle and is divided from west to east by two parallel ranges of mountains that are separated by a wide central plain open to the sea at either end. The highest point is Mount Olympus (6,401 feet/1,951 metres) in the southwest. The climate is Mediterranean, with very hot dry summers and warm damp winters. This contributes towards the great variety of crops grown, such as early potatoes, vegetables, cereals, tobacco, olives, bananas, and grapes, and these account for about 17 per cent of the land. The grapes are used for the strong wines and sherries for which Cyprus is famous. The main mineral found is copper while asbestos, gypsum, and iron pyrites are also found. Fishing is a significant industry, but above all the island depends on visitors and it is the tourist industry that has led to a recovery in the economy since 1974, when it was invaded by Turkey, which still occupies the northern third of the island. There are no railways on the island although it does possess three international airports.

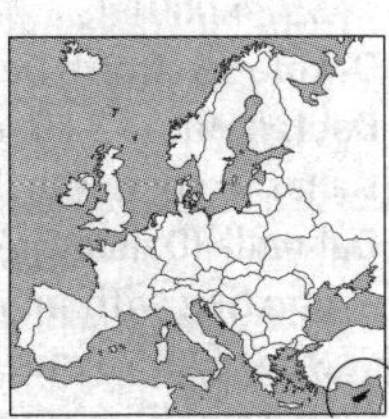

Area: 3,572 sq miles/9,251 sq km
Population: 756,000
Capital: Nicosia
Other major cities: Limassol, Larnaca
Form of government: Republic
Religions: Greek Orthodox, Sunni Islam
Currency: Cyprus Pound

Czechoslovakia a former state in central Europe. In 1993, it separated into two independent republics, the Czech Republic and Slovakia.

Czech Republic A country that was newly constituted on 1 January 1993 with the dissolution of the 74-year-old federal republic of Czechoslovakia. It is landlocked, at the heart of central Europe, bounded by Slovakia, Germany, Poland, and Austria. Natural boundaries are formed by the Sudeten Mountains in the north, the Erzgebirge, or Ore Mountains, to the northwest, and the Bohemian Forest in the southwest. The climate is humid continental, with warm summers and cold winters. Most rain falls in summer and thunderstorms are frequent. Agriculture, although accounting for only a small percentage of the national income, is highly developed and efficient. The main crops are sugar beet, wheat, and potatoes. Over a third of the labour force is employed in industry, which has to import its raw materials and energy. The most important industries are iron and steel, coal, machinery, cement, and paper, but industrialization has caused serious environmental problems. The Czech Republic was considered to be the most polluted country in eastern Europe in the early 1990s. Recently investment has gone into electronics factories and research establishments. Tourism has increased post-Communism, with the country's many resorts, historical cities, and winter sports facilities attracting visitors.

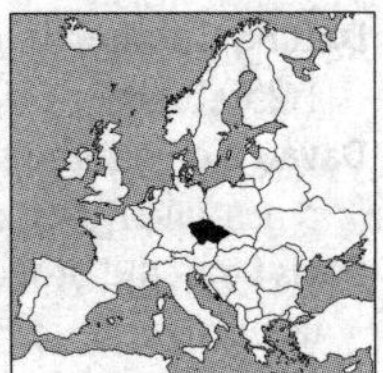

Area: 30,450 sq miles/78,864 sq km
Population: 10,291,900
Capital: Prague (Praha)
Other major cities: Brno, Ostrava, Plzen
Form of government: Republic
Religions: RC, Protestantism
Currency: Koruna

Czestochowa (Chenstokhov) an industrial city in southern Poland. (Pop. 253,100)

D

Dagestan an autonomous republic of the Russian Federation lying to the west of the Caspian Sea. The capital is Makhachkala. (19,400 sq miles/50,300 sq km; pop. 2,173,000)

Dakar the main port and capital of Senegal, West Africa. (Pop. 2,384,000)

Dakota *see* **North Dakota**, **South Dakota.**

Dal, Lake the most famous of the lakes of Kashmir, India, near Srinagar.

Dallas a city in northeast Texas, USA. (Pop. 1,243,000)

Dalmatia (Dalmacija) a coastal region of west Croatia, on the Adriatic Sea with many offshore islands. The principal tourist centre is Dubrovnik.

Damascus (Dimashq) the capital of Syria, an oasis town. (Pop. 1,804,000)

Damavand, Mount an extinct volcano, and the highest peak in the Elburz Mountains, Iran. (18,600 ft/5,671 m)

Danube (Donau) the longest river in Western Europe, rising in the Black Forest in Germany, and passing through Austria, Slovakia, Hungary and Serbia, forming much of the border between Bulgaria and Romania before turning north and forming a delta on the Black Sea. (Length 1,770 miles/2,850 km)

Dardanelles the narrow ribbon of water, some 50 miles (80 kilometres) long, in Turkey which connects the Aegean Sea to the Sea of Marmara (and from thence the Black Sea). Gallipoli is on the peninsula to the north. The Dardanelles were known as the Hellespont to the ancient Greeks.

Dar es Salaam the largest town and main port of Tanzania. It was the national capital until 1974. (Pop. 2,422,000)

Darién the eastern province of Panama, a narrow neck of land on the border with Colombia, and the only gap in the Pan-American Highway, which otherwise runs from Alaska to Chile.

Darjeeling (Darjiling) a town in West Bengal, India near the border with Nepal, famous for its tea. (Pop. 110,000)

Darling a river flowing from southern Queensland through New South Wales in Australia before converging with the Murray River. (Length 1,900 miles/3,057 km)

Dartmoor an area of moorland in Devon, England. (365 sq miles/945 sq km)

Darwin the capital of the Northern Territory, Australia. (Pop. 69,000)

Datong (Tatung) an industrial city in Shanxi Province, China. (Pop. 1,250,000)

Davao a city in the southern part of the island of Mindanao, Philippines, and now that country's second largest city. (Pop. city 874,000)

Davis Strait the broad strait, some 180 miles (290 kilometres) across at its narrowest, separating Baffin Island in Canada and Greenland.

Dayr az Zawr the largest town in eastern Syria, on the River Euphrates. (Pop. 216,000)

Dead Sea a small sea on the border between Israel and Jordan into which the River Jordan flows and does not exit. It is one of the lowest places on Earth at 1,299 feet (396 metres) below normal sea level, and the body of water with the world's highest salt content. (395 sq miles/1,049 sq km)

Death Valley a desert basin in southeastern California, USA, it contains the lowest point in North America.

Debrecen an agricultural and industrial centre in eastern Hungary and the country's second largest city after Budapest, which has grown up around the original medieval town. (Pop. 209,000)

Deccan the broad, triangular plateau which forms much of the southern part of India.

Dehra Dun a town in northern India, in the foothills of the Himalayas. It is famous as the supposed home of the Hindu god Shiva, and also for the military academy established by the British in the 1930s. (Pop. 457,000)

Delaware a state on the east coast of the USA, and the second smallest state in the USA after Rhode Island. The capital is Dover. (2057 sq miles/5,328 sq km; pop. 809,000)

Delft a small city in central western Netherlands, famous since the 16th century for its distinctive blue and white pottery. (Pop. 97,000)

Delhi (including **New Delhi**) the capital of India, in the north of the country, on the Yamuna River. (Pop. 10,009,000)

Delphi the ruins of the Temple of Apollo on Mount Parnassos, 102 miles (166 kilometres) northwest of Athens, Greece. It was the seat of the most important oracle of ancient Greece.

Demerara a river in central Guyana which flows through the capital, Georgetown. It has given its name to the type of brown sugar which is grown in the region. (Length 200 miles/320 km)

Denbighshire a council area of north Wales, with its administrative centre in the town of Ruthin. (327 sq miles/844 sq km; pop. 92,000)

Denmark A small European state lying between the North Sea and the entrance to the Baltic. It consists of a western peninsula and an eastern archipelago of more than 400 islands, some 90 of which are inhabited. The country is very low-lying and the proximity of the sea combined with the effect of the Gulf Stream result in warm sunny summers and cold cloudy winters. The scenery is flat and monotonous, and the acidic soils need a great deal of fertilization for a wide variety of crops to be grown. It is an agricultural country and three-quarters of the land is cultivated, mostly by the rotation of grass, barley, oats, and sugar beet. Animal husbandry is, however, a particularly important activity, its produce including the famous bacon and butter. Danish beer and lager are also famous throughout the world. It is estimated that 85 per cent of the population live in the towns and cities. Despite Denmark's limited range of raw materials, it produces a wide range of manufactured goods and is famous for its imaginative design in ceramics, furniture, silverware, and porcelain. Denmark is a wealthy country and the standard of living is high.

Area: 16,639 sq miles/43,094 sq km
Population: 5,262,000 (excluding the Faeroe Islands)
Capital: Copenhagen (København)
Other major cities: Ålborg, Århus, Odense
Form of government: Constitutional Monarchy
Religion: Lutheranism
Currency: Danish Krone

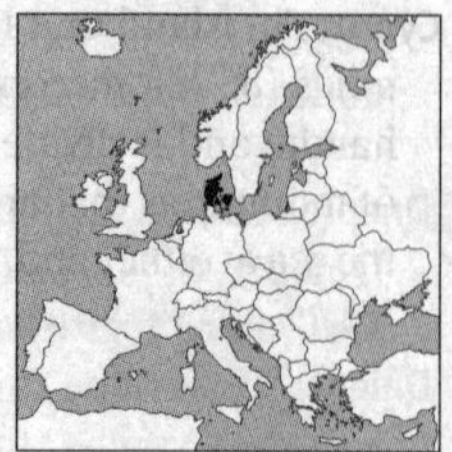

Denmark Strait the arm of the North Atlantic Ocean which separates Iceland from Greenland, some 180 miles (290 kilometres) apart.

Denpasar the capital of the island of Bali, Indonesia. (Pop. 492,000)

Denver the state capital of Colorado, USA. (Pop. 585,000)

Derby (1)a city of Saxon and Danish origins in the county of Derbyshire, England. (Pop. 228,000) (2) a unitary authority in Derbyshire, central England. (30 sq miles/78 sq km; pop.230,000)

Derbyshire a county in north central England, with its administrative centre in Matlock. (1,016 sq miles/2,631 sq km; pop. 954,000)

Derry a district council area in Co. Londonderrry. *See also* **Londonderry**. (149 sq miles/387 sq km; pop. 95,000)

Des Moines the state capital of Iowa, USA. (Pop. 198,000)

Detroit a major industrial city and Great Lakes port in the state of Michigan, USA. (Pop. 961,000)

Devon (also called **Devonshire**) a county in southwest England, with its administrative centre in Exeter. (2,593 sq miles/6,715 sq km; pop. 1,053,000)

Dhahran a town in eastern Saudi Arabia. (Pop. 96,000)

Dhaka (Dacca) the capital of Bangladesh, on the delta of the Rivers Ganges and Brahmaputra. (Pop. 8,540,000)

Dhanbad a city in northeast India and a centre for the coal mining industry of the Damodar Valley. (Pop. 209,000)

Dhaulagiri, Mount a peak of the Himalayas in Nepal. (26,810 ft/ 8,172 m)

Dijon the historical capital of the Bourgogne region (Burgundy) in western central France, famous in particular for its mustard. (Pop. 148,000)

Dili the capital of East Timor. (Pop. 50,000)

Diyarbakir a city on the River Tigris in southeastern Turkey, and the name of the province of which it is the capital. (Pop. 571,000)

Djibouti A country that is situated in northeast Africa and is bounded almost entirely by Ethiopia except in the southeast where it shares a border with Somalia and in the northwest where it shares a border with Eritrea. Its coastline is on the Gulf of Aden. Djibouti was formerly a French Overseas Territory but achieved independence in 1977. The land, which is mainly basalt plains, has some mountains rising to about 5,000 feet (1,500 metres). The climate is hot, among the world's hottest, and extremely dry. Less than a tenth of the land can be farmed even for grazing so it has great difficulty supporting its modest population. The native population is mostly nomadic, moving from oasis to oasis or across the border to Ethiopia in search of grazing land. Crops raised include fruits, vegetables, and dates. Most foodstuffs for the urban population in Djibouti city are imported. The capital is linked to Addis Ababa by a railway. Cattle, hides, and skins are the main exports. There are small deposits of copper, iron ore, and gypsum but these are not mined.

Area: 8,958 sq miles/23,200 sq km
Population: 617,000
Capital: Djibouti
Form of government: Republic
Religion: Sunni Islam
Currency: Djibouti Franc

Dnepropetrovsk an industrial and agricultural city on the River Dnieper in the Ukraine. It was formerly (1787–96 and 1802–1920) known as Ekaterinoslav. (Pop. 1,077,000)

Dnieper (Dnepr) the third longest river in Europe after the Volga and the Danube, flowing south through the Russian Federation and the Ukraine to the Black Sea via Kiev. (Length 1,420 miles/2,285 km)

Dniester (Dnestr) a river flowing through the Ukraine and Moldova to the Black Sea. (Length 877 miles /1,411 km)

Dodecanese (Dhodhekanisos) Islands a group of twelve islands belonging to Greece in the eastern Aegean Sea near the coast of Turkey. They include Samos, Patmos, Kalimnos, Karpathos, Kos and Rhodes (Rodhos), the largest in the group. They are also called the Southern Sporades. (Pop. 189,000)

Dodoma the capital (since 1974) of Tanzania, in its centre. (Pop. 157,000)

Doha (Ad Dawhah) the capital of Qatar. (Pop. 309,000)

Dolomites (Dolomiti) a range of mountains in northeastern Italy, near the border with Austria. The highest point is Mount Marmolada at 10,964 feet (3,342 metres).

Dominica Discovered by Columbus, Dominica is the most northerly of the Windward Islands in the West Indies. It is situated between the islands of Martinique and Guadeloupe. The island is very rugged and with the exception of 87 square miles (225 square kilometres) of flat land, it consists of three inactive volcanoes, the highest of which is 4,747 feet (1,447 metres). There are many unnavigable rivers, and Boiling Lake, situated in the south, often gives off sulphurous gases. The climate is tropical and even on the leeward coast it rains two days out of three. The wettest season is from June to October when hurricanes often occur. The steep slopes are difficult to farm but agriculture provides almost all Dominica's exports. Bananas are the main agricultural export, but copra, citrus fruits, cocoa, coconuts, bay leaves, cinnamon, and vanilla are also revenue earners. Industry is mostly based on the processing of the agricultural products.

Area: 290 sq miles/751 sq km
Population: 74,000
Capital: Roseau
Form of government: Republic
Religion: RC
Currency: East Caribbean Dollar

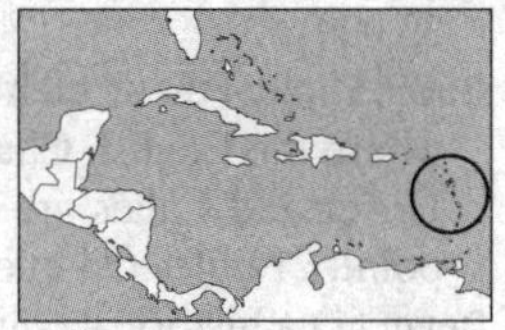

Dominican Republic A country that forms the eastern portion of the island of Hispaniola in the West Indies. It covers two-thirds of the island, the smaller portion consisting of Haiti. The climate is semi-tropical, and occasionally hurricanes occur, causing great destruction. The west of the country is made up of four almost parallel mountain ranges, and between the two most northerly is the fertile Cibao Valley. The southeast is made up of fertile plains. Although well endowed with fertile land, only about 30 per cent is cultivated. Sugar is the main crop and mainstay of the country's economy and is grown mainly on plantations in the southeast plains. Other crops grown are rice, coffee, bananas, cocoa, and tobacco. Mining of gold, silver, platinum, nickel, and aluminium is carried out, but the main industries are food processing and manufacture of consumer goods. Fishing is also carried out but not to any great extent because of lack of equipment and refrigeration facilities. The island has fine beaches and the tourism industry is now very important to the economy.

Area: 18,816 sq miles/48,734 sq km
Population: 8,052,000
Capital: Santo Domingo
Other major city: Santiago de los Caballeros
Form of government: Republic
Currency: Dominican Republic Peso

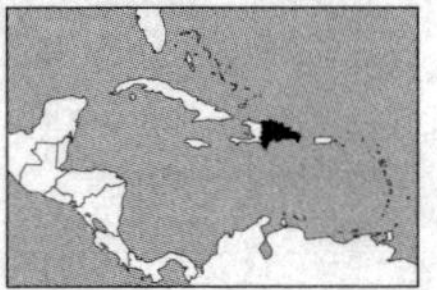

Don a river flowing southwards into the Sea of Azov from its source south of Moscow. (Length 1,165 miles/1,870 km)

Donegal the northernmost county of the Republic of Ireland, on the west coast. The county town is also called Donegal. (Pop. 136,000)

Donets Basin (Donbass) a coal-mining region and major industrial area in the eastern Ukraine.

Donetsk the main industrial centre of the Donets Basin, eastern Ukraine. (Pop. 1,021,000)

Dongbei (Manchuria) the northeastern region of China, covering part of the Nei Mongol Autonomous Region and the three provinces of Heilongjiang, Jilin and Liaoning. (502,000 sq miles/ 1,300,000 sq km; pop. 87,962,000)

Dordogne a river of southwestern France which rises in the Massif Central and flows west to the Gironde estuary. (Length 295 miles/475 km)

Dordrecht a river port and industrial city of medieval origin 12 miles (19 kilometres) southeast of Rotterdam in the Netherlands. (Pop. 123,000)

Dorset a county of southwest England, with its administrative centre in Dorchester. (1,025 sq miles/2,654 sq km; pop. 673,000)

Dortmund an industrial city in the Ruhr region of Germany. (Pop. 588,000)

Douala the main port of Cameroon, on the Gulf of Guinea. (Pop. 1,239,000)

Douro (Duero) a river flowing west from north central Spain across northern Portugal to the Atlantic Ocean. (Length 555 miles/ 895 km)

Dover (1) a port in the county of Kent, England, overlooking the English Channel at its narrowest point, opposite Calais, France. (Pop. 35,000) (2) The state capital of Delaware, USA. (Pop. 33,000)

Dover, Strait of the stretch of water separating England and France, where the English Channel meets the North Sea. The ports of Dover and Calais are situated on either side of its narrowest point, 21 miles (34 kilometres) across.

Down (1) a historical county in southeast Northern Ireland. (952 sq miles/2,466 sq km) (2) a district council area in Co. Down. (250 sq miles/649 sq km; pop. 58,000)

Drakensberg Mountains a range of mountains which stretch 700 miles (1,125 kilometres) across Lesotho and neighbouring regions of South Africa. The highest point is Thabana Ntlenyana at 11,424 feet (3,482 metres).

Drake Passage the broad strait, some 400 miles (640 kilometres) wide, which separates Cape Horn on the southern tip of South America and Antarctica.

Drava (Drau) a river flowing from eastern Austria to Croatia and Serbia, where it forms much of the border with Hungary before joining the Danube. (Length 447 miles/718 km)

Dresden a historical city on the River Elbe in the south of eastern Germany. Formerly the capital of Saxony, it was noted particularly for its fine porcelain. (Pop. 414,000)

Duarte, Pico a mountain peak in central Dominican Republic which is the highest point in the West Indies. (10,417 ft/3,175 m)

Dubai (Dubayy) the second largest of the United Arab Emirates, at the eastern end of the Persian Gulf. Most of the population lives in the capital, also called Dubai. (1,506 sq miles/3,900 sq km; pop. emirate 879,000/city 873,000)

Dublin (Baile Atha Cliath) the capital of the Republic of Ireland, on the River Liffey, and also the name of the surrounding county. Its main port area is at Dun Laoghaire. (Pop. county 1,103,000/ city 993,000)

Dubrovnik (Ragusa) a pretty medieval port on the Adriatic coast of Croatia, for long a popular tourist destination. (Pop. 45,000)

Duisburg a major inland port situated at the confluence of the Rivers Rhine and Ruhr in Germany. (Pop. 518,000)

Duluth a port and industrial centre on Lake Superior, in the state of Minnesota, USA. (Pop. 89,000)

Dumfries and Galloway a council area in southwest Scotland, with its administrative centre in the town of Dumfries. (2,486 sq miles/6,439 sq km; pop. 147,000)

Dundee (1) a city and port, and administrative centre of the City of Dundee council area, on the east coast of Scotland, on the north side of the Firth of Tay. (Pop. 159,000) (2) **City of** a council area of east Scotland. (25 sq miles/65 sq km; pop. 167,000)

Dungannon a district council area in Co. Tyrone, south Northern Ireland. (302 sq miles/783 sq km; pop. 46,000)

Dunkirk (Dunkerque) a port and industrial town in northeastern France, close to the Belgian border. It was virtually destroyed in 1940 when British, French and Belgian forces were trapped by the advancing German army, but were evacuated to Britain in a fleet of small boats. (Pop. 71,000)

Durango a mineral-rich state in northern Mexico, with a capital called (Victoria de) Durango. (Pop. state 1,449,000/city 435,000)

Durban a major port in KwaZulu/Natal Province on the east coast of South Africa. (Pop. 2,355,000)

Durham (1) a city in northeast England, and the administrative centre of Co. Durham. (Pop. 37,000) (2) a county in northeast England. (1051 sq miles/2,722 sq km; pop. 875,000)

Dushanbe an industrial city and the capital of Tajikistan. (Pop. 581,000)

Düsseldorf a major commercial and industrial centre in the Ruhr region of Germany, on the River Rhine north of Cologne. (Pop. 568,000)

Dvina the name of two quite separate rivers. The West (Zapadnaya) Dvina flows from its source to the west of Moscow into the Baltic Sea at Riga in Latvia. The North (Severnaya) Dvina flows through the northwest of the Russian Federation to the White Sea at Archangel. (Length West Dvina 635 miles/1,020 km; North Dvina 820 miles/1,320 km)

Dyfed a former county in southwest Wales.

E

East Anglia an old Anglo-Saxon kingdom occupying the bulge of the east coast of England between the Thames estuary and The Wash, and now covered by Norfolk, Suffolk, and parts of Cambridgeshire and Essex.

East Ayrshire a council area in southwest Scotland, with its administrative centre in the town of Kilmarnock. (483 sq miles/1,252 sq km; pop. 123,000)

East Dunbartonshire a council area in central Scotland, with its administrative centre in the city of Glasgow. (66 sq miles/172 sq km; pop. 110,000)

Easter Island (Isla de Pascua) a remote and tiny island in the South Pacific Ocean annexed by Chile in 1888. About 1,000 years ago it was settled by Polynesians who set up over 600 huge stone statues of heads on the island. (46 sq miles/120 sq km; pop. 1,300)

Eastern Cape one of South Africa's nine provinces, in southeast South Africa, with its administrative centre in Bisho. (65,458 sq miles/169,580 sq km; pop. 6,482,000)

East Lothian a council area in central Scotland, with its administrative centre in the town of Haddington. (262 sq miles/678 sq km; pop. 86,000)

East Renfrewshire a council area in central Scotland, with its administrative centre in the town of Giffnock. (67 sq miles/173 sq km; pop. 87,000)

East Riding of Yorkshire a county in northeast England, with its administrative centre in Beverley. (704 sq miles/1,819 sq km; pop. 595,000)

East Sussex a county in southeast England, with its administrative centre in Lewes. (693 sq miles/1,795 sq km; pop. 726,000)

East Timor The eastern part of the island of Timor and a small coastal enclave to the west. A former possession of Portugal, it was annexed illegally in 1975 by Indonesia. A referendum in 1999 showed that most of the population favoured independence, Following violent reprisals from Indonesia, East Timor was placed under United Nations protection prior to control being handed over to its own government in May 2002.

Area: 5,743 sq miles/14,874 sq km
Population: 857,000
Capital: Dili
Form of government: under UN transitional administration
Religion: RC

Ebro a river flowing across northeastern Spain, from near the north coast to the Mediterranean Sea south of Tarragona. (Length 565 miles/909 km)

Ecuador An Andean country situated in the northwest of the South American continent. It is bounded to the north by Colombia and to the east and south by Peru. It also includes the Galapagos Islands, which are located about 600 miles (965 kilometres) west of the mainland. The country contains over 30 active volcanoes, with Mount Cotopaxi at 19,340 feet (5,895 metres) the highest active volcano on Earth. Running down the middle of Ecuador are two ranges of the Andes that are divided by a central plateau. The coastal area consists of plains and the eastern area is made up of tropical jungles. The climate varies from equatorial through warm temperate to mountain conditions according to altitude. It is in the coastal plains that plantations of bananas, cocoa, coffee, and sugar cane are found. In contrast to this, the highland areas are adapted to grazing, dairy farming, and cereal growing. The fishing industry is important on the Pacific Coast and processed fish such as tuna and shrimp are main exports. Ecuador is one of the world's leading producers of balsawood. Oil is produced in the eastern region and petroleum is Ecuador's most important export. The official language is Spanish although many people in rural areas speak Quecha, the Incan language.

Area: 109,484 sq miles/283,561 sq km
Population: 11,698,000
Capital: Quito
Other major cities: Guayaquil, Cuenca
Form of government: Republic
Religion: RC
Currency: Sucre

Edinburgh (1) the capital of Scotland, seat of the Scottish Parliament, and administrative centre for the City of Edinburgh council area, on the Firth of Forth (the estuary of the River Forth) in central Scotland. (Pop. 402,000) (2) **City of** a council area of central Scotland. (101 sq miles/262 sq km; pop. 448,000)

Edmonton the capital of Alberta, Canada. (Pop. 694,000)

Edward (Rutanzige), Lake a lake in the Great Rift Valley, on the border between Uganda and Democratic Republic of Congo. (820 sq miles/2,135 sq km)

Egypt A country situated in northeast Africa, acting as the doorway between Africa and Asia. Its outstanding physical feature is the River Nile, the valley and delta of which cover about 13,737 square miles (35,580 square kilometres). The climate is mainly dry but there are winter rains along the Mediterranean coast. The temperatures are comfortable in winter but summer temperatures are extremely high, particularly in the south. The rich soils deposited by flood waters along the banks of the Nile can support a large population and the Nile delta is one of the world's most fertile agricultural regions. Around 99 per cent of the population live in the delta and Nile valley where the main crops are rice, cotton, sugar cane, maize, tomatoes, and wheat. This concentration makes it one of the most densely populated areas in the world. The main industries are food processing and textiles. The economy has been boosted by the discovery of oil and is enough to supply the country's needs and leave surplus for export. Natural gas production is increasing for domestic use and Egypt has a significant fishing industry, mainly in the shallow lakes and Red Sea. The Suez Canal, shipping, and tourism connected with the ancient sites are also important revenue earners.

Area: 386,662 sq miles/1,001,449 sq km
Population: 60,603,000
Capital: Cairo (El Qâhira)
Other major cities: Alexandria, Port Said
Form of government: Republic
Religions: Sunni Islam, Christianity
Currency: Egyptian Pound

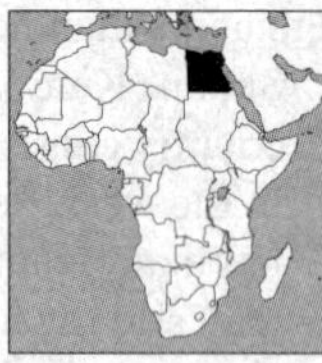

Eifel an upland area of western Germany between the Moselle River and the border with Belgium.

Eiger, The a mountain in southern central Switzerland, renowned among climbers for its daunting north face. (13,025 ft/3.970 m)

Eindhoven an industrial city in south central Netherlands. (Pop. 201,000)

Elat (Eilat) a port and tourist resort in the very south of Israel at the tip of the Gulf of Aqaba, an arm of the Red Sea. (Pop. 43,000)

Elba an island lying about 6 miles (10 kilometres) off the coast of Tuscany, Italy. (86 sq miles/223 sq km; pop. 28,400)

Elbe a largely navigable river flowing northward from its source in the Czech Republic through Germany to Hamburg, and then into the North Sea. (Length 720 miles/1,160 km)

Elbrus, Mount the highest mountain in Europe, situated in the western Caucasus Mountains, Russian Federation. (18,510 ft/5,642 m)

Elburz Mountains a range of mountains in northern Iran, between Tehran and the Caspian Sea. The highest peak is the extinct volcano, Damavand, at 18,600 feet (5,671 metres).

El Faiyum (Fayum) a large and fertile oasis to the west of the River Nile in Egypt. (Pop. 298,000)

El Gezira a major irrigation scheme in Sudan between the Blue Nile and the White Nile.

El Mansura a city on the Nile delta in northern Egypt. (Pop. 423,000)

El Paso a city in western Texas, USA, close to the border with Mexico. (Pop. 589,000)

El Salvador The smallest and most densely populated state in Central America. It is bounded north and east by Honduras and has a Pacific coast to the south. Two volcanic ranges run from east to west across the country. The Lempa River cuts the southern ranges in the centre of the country and opens as a large sandy delta to the Pacific Ocean. Although fairly near the equator, the climate tends to be warm rather than hot and the highlands have a cooler temperate climate. The country is predominantly agricultural: 32 per cent of the land is used for crops such as coffee (the major crop and revenue earner), cotton, maize, beans, rice, and sorghum, with a slightly smaller area being used for grazing cattle, pigs, sheep, and goats. Fishing is carried out, the most important being shrimp, although tuna, mackerel, and swordfish are also caught. A few industries, such as food processing, textiles, and chemicals, are found in the major towns. The country suffers from a high rate of inflation and unemployment and is one of the world's poorer countries.

Area: 8,124sq miles/21,041 sq km
Population: 5,796,000
Capital: San Salvador
Other major cities: Santa Ana, San Miguel
Form of government: Republic
Religion: RC
Currency: Colón

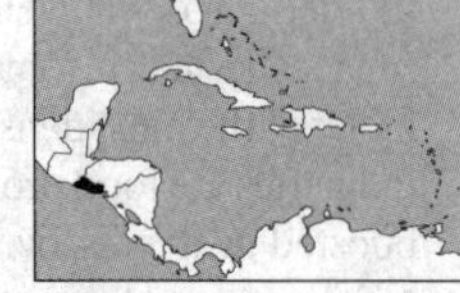

Elsinore (Helsingør) a town of medieval origins on the island of Zealand, Denmark, to the north of Copenhagen. Kronborg Castle, which dominates the town, is the setting for Shakespeare's play *Hamlet*. (Pop. 35,000)

Emilia-Romagna a region on the east coast of northern central Italy; the capital is Bologna. (8,542 sq miles/22,123 sq km; pop. 3,960,000)

Emmenthal the valley of the River Emme, in Switzerland, famous for its distinctive cheese.

Engel's an industrial town on the River Volga, in the Russian Federation. (Pop. 189,000)

England the country occupying the greater part of the island of Great Britain, and the largest of the countries that make up the United Kingdom. Scotland lies to the north and Wales to the west. The capital is London. (50,331 sq miles/130,357 sq km; pop. 50,016,000)

English Channel the arm of the eastern Atlantic Ocean which separates the south coast of England from France.

Enschede an industrial town in the eastern part of the Netherlands, close to the border with Germany. (Pop. 150,000)

Entebbe a town with an international airport on Lake Victoria, Uganda. It was the capital until 1962. (Pop. 57,000)

Enugu a coal-mining centre in southern central Nigeria, the capital of Biafra (Iboland) during the civil war of 1967–70. (Pop. 593,000)

Eolian (Lipari) Islands a group of small volcanic islands which lie between the north coast of Sicily and mainland Italy. The main islands are Stromboli, Lipari, Salina, Panarea and Vulcano. (Pop. 12,500)

Equatorial Guinea A country that lies about 124 miles (200 kilometres) north of the Equator on the hot humid coast of west Africa. It consists of a square-shaped mainland area (Mbini), with its few small offshore islets, and the islands of Bioko and Pagalu (Annobon). The climate is tropical and the wet season in Bioko and Pagalu lasts from December to February. Bioko is a very fertile volcanic island, and it is here that the capital, Malabo, is situated beside a volcanic crater flooded by the sea. It is also the centre of the country's cocoa production. Coffee and lumber are produced for export on the mainland. The country now relies heavily on foreign aid. Spanish is the official language although a variant of Bantu, Fang, is most commonly used. There is, however, much potential for a tourist industry.

Area: 10,830 sq miles/28,051 sq km
Population: 410,000
Capital: Malabo
Other major city: Bata
Form of government: Republic
Religion: RC
Currency: CFA Franc

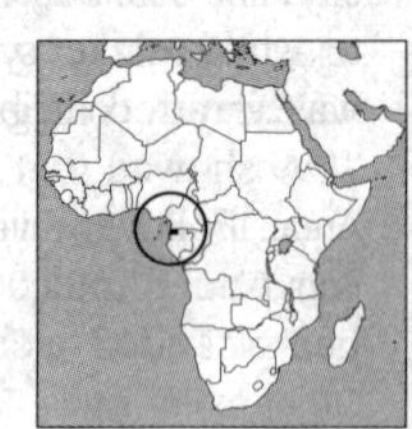

Erfurt a historical town and tourist centre in central Germany. (Pop. 195,000)

Erie, Lake the second smallest of the five Great Lakes, on the border between Canada and the USA. (9,910 sq miles/25,670 sq km)

Eritrea Formerly an autonomous province of Ethiopia that gained independence in May 1993, shortly after a landslide vote in favour of sovereignty. Bounded by Djibouti, Sudan, and Ethiopia, Eritrea has acquired Ethiopia's entire coastline along the Red Sea. The small Eritrean port of Aseb, in the southeast corner of the country has, however, been designated a 'free port' guaranteeing the right of access for the now landlocked Ethiopia. Eritrea's climate is hot and dry along its desert coast but is colder and wetter in its central highland regions. Most of the population depend on subsistence farming. Future revenues may come from its developing fishing, tourism, and oil industries.

Eritrea's natural resources include gold, potash, zinc, copper, salt, fish, and probably oil. Deforestation and the consequent erosion are partly responsible for the frequent droughts and resultant famines that have blighted this area in recent years. Many of the population have been displaced by famine or continuing war with Ethiopia.

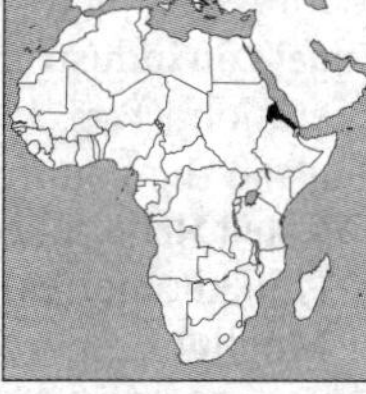

Area: 45,406 sq miles/117,600 sq km
Population: 3,280,000
Capital: Asmara (Asmera)
Other major cities: Mits'iwa, Keren, Assab (Aseb)
Form of government: Republic
Religions: Sunni Islam, Christianity
Currency: Nakfa

Erzurum a market town in western Turkey, and the name of the surrounding province. (Pop. 333,000)

Isfahan (Esfahan) a city in central Iran and the second largest city in the country noted for its magnificent blue-tiled mosques and other Islamic buildings. (Pop. 1,362,000)

Eskisehir a spa town in western Turkey and the name of the surrounding province. (Pop. 507,000)

Essen an industrial city in western Germany, and the largest in the Ruhr region. (Pop. 590,000)

Essex a county in southeast England, with its administrative centre in Chelmsford. (1,419 sq miles/3,674 sq km; pop. 1,569,000)

Estonia A country that has over 1,500 islands and lies to the northwest of the Russian Federation. It is bounded to the north by the Gulf of Finland, to the west by the Baltic Sea, and to the south by Latvia and is the smallest of the three previous Soviet Baltic Republics. Agriculture and dairy farming are the chief occupations and there are nearly three hundred agricultural collectives and state farms. Almost 22 per cent of Estonia is forested, and this provides material for sawmills, furniture, match and pulp industries. The country has rich, high-quality shale deposits and phosphorous has been found near Tallinn. Peat deposits are substantial and supply some of the electric power stations. Estonia has about 72 per cent of its population living in urban areas, with almost a third living in the capital city. The economy is currently undergoing a major transformation to a free market system. Tourism and investment from the West have greatly contributed to the country's economy.

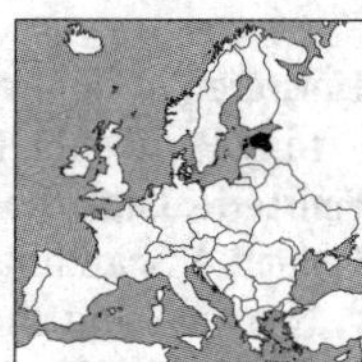

Area: 17,413 sq miles/45,227 sq km
Population: 1,454,000
Capital: Tallinn
Other major cities: Tartu, Narva
Form of government: Republic
Religions: Eastern Orthodox, Lutheranism
Currency: Kroon

Ethiopia A landlocked, East African country with borders with Sudan, Kenya, Somalia, Djibouti and Eritrea. Most of the country consists of highlands that drop sharply toward Sudan in the west. Because of the wide range of latitudes, Ethiopia has many climatic variations between the high temperate plateau and the hot humid lowlands. The country is very vulnerable to drought but in some areas thunderstorms can erode soil from the slopes, reducing the area available for crop planting. Around 80 per cent of the population are subsistence farmers, and there are mineral deposits of copper, iron, petroleum, platinum and gold, which have been exploited. Coffee is the main source of rural income and teff is the main food grain. The droughts in 1989–90 brought much famine. Employment outside agriculture is confined to a small manufacturing sector in Addis Ababa. The country has been racked with environmental, economic and political problems culminating in the loss of the province of Eritrea, which became independent in May 1993.

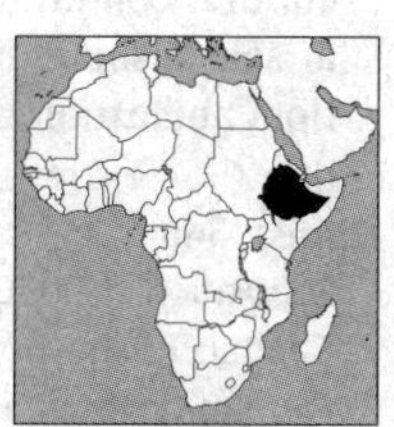

Area: 426,373 sq miles/1,104,300 sq km
Population: 58,506,000
Capital: Addis Ababa (Adis Abeba)
Other cities: Dire Dawa, Gonda, Jima
Form of government: People's Republic
Religions: Ethiopian Orthodox, Sunni Islam
Currency: Ethiopian Birr

Etna, Mount the largest volcano in Europe, situated near the east coast of Sicily, Italy, and still highly active. (10,902 ft/3,323 m)

Euboea (Evvoia) a large Greek island in the Aegean Sea lying close to the east coast of mainland Greece and joined to the mainland by a bridge. (1,411 sq miles/3,655 sq km; pop. 220,000)

Euphrates (Al Furat) one of the great rivers of the Middle East, flowing from its source in eastern Turkey, across Syria and central Iraq to the Persian Gulf. (Length 1,690 miles/2,720 km)

Europe a continent that is divided from Asia by a border that runs down the Ural Mountains to the Caspian Sea and then west to the Black Sea. For convenience it is commonly divided into two areas: Eastern Europe (the countries that had Communist governments after the Second World War) and Western Europe. (4,053,300 sq miles/10,498,000 sq km; pop. 728,982,000)

Everest, Mount the highest mountain in the world, situated on the border between Nepal and China in the eastern Himalayas. (29,028 ft /8,848 m)

Everglades a vast area of subtropical swampland on the western side of southern Florida, USA.

Eyre, Lake a large salt lake in South Australia. (3,400 sq miles/ 8,900 sq km)

F

Faeroe (Faroe) Islands (Føroyar) A self-governing territory of Denmark since 1948 which consists of a group of 18 basaltic islands situated in the North Atlantic, approximately halfway between the Shetland Islands and Iceland. The landscape of these islands is characterized by steep, stepped peaks rising out of the sea to nearly 3,000 feet (900 metres) and glaciated, trough-shaped valleys. Although the islands are inhabited, poor agricultural conditions compel the population to seek their living at sea. Fishing, including some whaling, is the main occupation, and exports comprise fish and associated products.

Area: 540 sq miles/1,399 sq km
Population: 47,000
Capital: Tørshavn
Form of government: Self-governing Danish Territory
Religion: Lutheranism
Currency: Danish Krone

Fair Isle a small island situated between the Orkney and Shetland Islands to the north of Scotland, famous for distinctive, patterned sweaters. (Pop. 75)

Faisalabad (Lyallpur) an industrial city and agricultural centre in northeast Pakistan. (Pop. 2,191,000)

Falkirk (1) a town in central Scotland and the administrative centre of the Falkirk council area. (Pop. 36,000) (2) a council area in central Scotland. (115 sq miles/299 sq km; pop. 142,000)

Falkland Islands (Islas Malvinas) A British crown colony situated in the South Atlantic, consisting of two large islands (West and East Falkland), separated by the 10-mile (16-kilometre) wide Falkland Sound and surrounded by some 200 smaller islands. Lying about 410 miles (650 kilometres) east of southern Argentina, which has long laid claim to them, the islands were invaded by Argentina in 1982, but were recaptured by a British marine task force a few months later. The main economic activity is sheep farming, with open grazing on the windswept, treeless, rugged moorland that rises to over 2,295 feet (705 metres) on both main islands. The highest point is Mount Usborne at 2,313 feet (705 metres). Over recent years, substantial income has been gained from the sales of licenses to permit foreign trawlers to fish in the Falklands exclusion zone. There are also considerable offshore oil reserves available.

Area: 4,700 sq miles/12,173 sq km
Population: 2,200
Capital: Port Stanley
Form of government: British Crown Colony
Religion: Christianity
Currency: Falkland Islands Pound

Fao (Al Faw) a port and oil tanker terminal in Iraq, at the mouth of the Shatt al Arab waterway.

Faro the capital of the Algarve Province of Portugal. (Pop. 40,000)

Fatehpur Sikri a magnificent deserted palace complex some 93 miles (150 kilometres) south of Delhi, India, built as a capital by the Moghul Emperor Akbar in 1580 but abandoned in 1605.

Fermanagh a historical lakeland county, and a district council area in southwest Northern Ireland. (656 sq miles/1,700 sq km; pop. 54,000)

Ferrara a historical city in northeastern Italy in the Po Valley. (Pop. 132,000)

Fès (Fez) a city in northern Morocco, the oldest of that country's four imperial cities. (Pop. 921,000)

Fife a council area of eastern Scotland, with its administrative centre in Glenrothes. (511 sq miles/1,323 sq km; pop. 351,000)

Fiji One of the largest nations in the western Pacific, consisting of some 800 islands and atolls of which only about 100 are inhabited. It is situated around the 180-degree International Date Line and lies about 17 degrees south of the equator. Fiji has high rainfall, high temperatures, and plenty of sunshine all year round. The two main islands, Viti Levu and Vanua Levu, are extinct volcanoes, and most of the islands in the group are fringed with coral reefs. The southeast of the islands have tropical rainforests but a lot of lumber has been felled and soil erosion is a growing problem. The main cash crop is sugar cane although copra, ginger, and fish are also exported. Tourism is now a major industry and source of revenue although it was adversely affected by political coups in the late 1980s. In 1993, Cyclone Kina caused great destruction to agriculture and the general infrastructure.

Area: 7,056 sq miles/18,274 sq km
Population: 797,000
Capital: Suva
Form of government: Republic
Religions: Christianity, Hinduism
Currency: Fijian Dollar

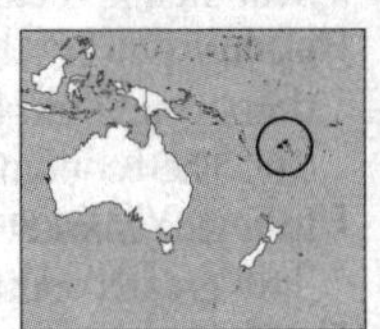

Finistère the department of France occupying the tip of the Brittany Peninsula. (Pop. 870,000)

Finisterre, Cape the northwest corner of Spain.

Finland A Scandinavian country that shares borders with Sweden, Norway, and the Russian Federation. Its coastline lies along the Gulf of Bothnia and the Gulf of Finland, both of which are arms of the Baltic Sea. Some 30,000 islands and islets line Finland's coast. Finnish Lappland in the north lies within the Arctic Circle. Most of mainland Finland is low-lying, becoming more hilly towards the north. Almost three-quarters of the country is forested, comprising mainly coniferous trees such as spruce and pine, and there are many thousands of lakes. The climate has great extremes between summer and winter. Winter is very severe and lasts about six months (but only for three months in the south). Summers are short but quite warm, with light rain throughout the country. Finland is largely self-sufficient in food and produces great surpluses of dairy produce. Most crops are grown in the southwest. In the north, reindeer are herded and forests yield great quantities of lumber for export. Just under

20 per cent of the electricity was supplied by its hydroelectric power stations in the early 1990s. Major industries are lumber products, wood pulp and paper, machinery, and shipbuilding, which developed because of the country's great need for an efficient fleet of ice-breakers. Finland has an efficient transport system utilizing canals, road, rail, and air services.

Area: 130,559 sq miles/338,145 sq km
Population: 5,205,000
Capital: Helsinki (Helsingfors)
Other major cities: Turku, Tampere
Form of government: Republic
Religion: Lutheranism
Currency: Euro

Finland, Gulf of the easternmost arm of the Baltic Sea, with Finland to the north, St Petersburg at its eastern end, and Estonia to the south.

Flanders (Vlaanderen, Flandre) A Flemish-speaking coastal region of northern Belgium, now divided into two provinces, East and West Flanders. (2361 sq miles/6,115 sq km; pop. 2,499,000)

Flinders Range a range of mountains in the eastern part of South Australia, stretching over 250 miles (400 kilometres). St Mary Peak is the highest (3,898 ft/1,188 m).

Flintshire a council area in northeast Wales, with its administrative centre in the town of Mold. (169 sq miles/437 sq km; pop. 145,000)

Florence (Firenze) one of the great Renaissance cities of Italy, straddling the River Arno, and the capital of the region of Tuscany. (Pop. 376,000)

Flores a volcanic island in the Lesser Sunda Islands in Indonesia, lying in the chain due east of Java. (6,622 sq miles/17,150 sq km; pop. 803,000)

Flores Sea a stretch of the Pacific Ocean between Flores and Sulawesi.

Florida a state occupying the peninsula in the southeastern corner of the USA. The state capital is Tallahassee. (158,560 sq miles/51,670 sq km; pop. 16,817,000)

Florida, Straits of the waterway which separates the southern tip of Florida, USA, from Cuba some 90 miles (145 kilometres) to the south.

Flushing (Vlissingen) a port on the southwest coast of the Netherlands. (Pop. 45,000)

Fly a largely navigable river flowing south from the central mountains in western Papua New Guinea to its broad estuary on the Gulf of Papua. (Length 750 miles/1,200 km)

Foggia a city in the Puglia region of southeastern Italy. (Pop. 155,000)

Fontainebleau a town 35 miles (55 kilometres) southeast of Paris, France, with a 16th-century royal château and a famous forest. (Pop. 39,400)

Fortaleza a major port on the northeastern coast of Brazil. (Pop. 2,231,000)

Fort-de-France a port and the capital of Martinique. (Pop. 96,000)

Fort Knox a military reservation in Kentucky, USA, 25 miles (40 kilometres) southwest of Louisville; also the site of the principal depository of the country's gold bullion. (Pop. 12,0000)

Fort Lauderdale a city and resort on the east coast of Florida, USA, 25 miles (40 kilometres) north of Miami. (Pop. 160,000)

Fort Worth a city in northeast Texas, USA, just to the west of Dallas and part of a Dallas-Fort Worth conurbation (the Southwest Metroplex). (Pop. 559,000)

Foshan an industrial city in Guangdong Province, China. (Pop. 300,000)

France The largest country in western Europe, with a coastline on the English Channel, the Mediterranean Sea and on the Atlantic Ocean. The lowest parts of the country are the great basins of the north and southwest from which it rises to the Massif Central and the higher Alps, Jura and Pyrénées. Climate ranges from moderate maritime in the northwest to Mediterranean in the south. Farming is possible in all parts of France, with forestry and fishing also providing some employment. The western shores are ideal for rearing livestock, while the Paris Basin is good arable land. In the southwest around Bordeaux, vineyards produce some of the world's best wines. The main industrial area of France is in the north and east and the main industries are iron and steel, engineering, chemicals, textiles, and electrical goods. France has a long cultural history of art, literature, sculpture, and music, and is famous for its immense Gothic churches.

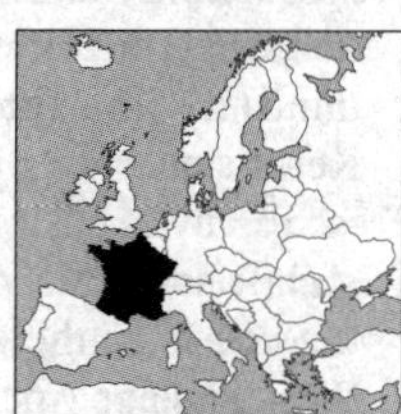

Area: 212,935 sq miles/551,500 sq km
Population: 58,375,000
Capital: Paris
Other major cities: Bordeaux, Lyons, Marseilles, Toulouse
Form of government: Republic
Religion: RC
Currency: Euro

Frankfort the state capital of Kentucky, USA. (Pop. 28,000)

Frankfurt (Frankfurt am Main) a major financial, trade and communications centre in central western Germany, on the River Main. (Pop. 646,000)

Frankfurt (Frankfurt an der Oder) a town on the River Oder in eastern Germany, on the border with Poland. (Pop. 73,000)

Fraser a river flowing through southern British Columbia, Canada, from its source in the Rocky Mountains to the Strait of Georgia by Vancouver. (Length 850 miles/1,370 km)

Fredericton the capital of New Brunswick, Canada. (Pop. 47,000)

Free State one of South Africa's nine provinces, in central South Africa, formerly Orange Free State, with its administrative centre in Bloemfontein. (49,992 sq miles/129,480 sq km; pop. 2,928,000)

Freetown the main port and capital of Sierra Leone, West Africa. (Pop. 1,032,000)

Freiburg (Freiburg im Breisgau) the largest city in the Black Forest in southwest Germany, close to the border with France. (Pop. 203,000)

French Guiana (Guyane) Situated on the northeast coast of South America and still a French Overseas Department, French Guiana is bounded to the south and east by Brazil and to the west by Suriname. The climate is tropical with heavy rainfall. French Guiana's economy relies almost completely on subsidies from France. It has little to export apart from shrimps, and the small area of land that is cultivated produces rice, manioc, and sugar cane. Recently the French have tried to develop the tourist industry and exploit the extensive reserves of hardwood in the jungle interior. This has led to a growing sawmill industry and the export of logs. Natural resources, in addition to lumber, include bauxite, cinnabar (mercury ore), and gold (although this is in scattered deposits). The Ariane rocket launch site of the European Union Space Agency is located at Kourou, on the north coast.

Area: 34,749 sq miles/90,000 sq km
Population: 153,000
Capital: Cayenne
Form of government: French Overseas Department
Religion: RC
Currency: Euro

French Polynesia A total of about 130 islands in the South Pacific Ocean administered as French overseas territories. The islands include the Society Islands, the Tuamotu group, the Gambier group, the Tubual Islands, and the Marquesas Islands.

Area: 1,544 sq miles/4,000 sq km
Population: 223,000
Capital: Papeete
Form of government: Overseas Territory of France
Religions: Protestantism, RC
Currency: Pacific Franc

French Southern and Antarctic Territories a set of remote and widely scattered territories in Antarctica and the Antarctic Ocean administered by France. They include the Crozet Islands and Kerguelen.

Fresno a city in eastern central California, USA. (Pop. 444,000)

Frisian (Friesian) Islands a string of sandy, low-lying islands that line the coasts in the southeastern corner of the North Sea. The West Frisians (including Terchelling and Texel) belong to the Netherlands; the East Frisians (including Borkum and Norderney) belong to Germany; and the North Frisians are divided between Germany and Denmark.

Fuji, Mount (Fujiyama) the highest peak in Japan, a distinctive volcanic cone 62 miles (100 kilometres) to the southwest of Tokyo. (12,389 ft/3,776 m)

Fujian (Fukien) a coastal province in southeast China. The capital is Fuzhou. (46,350 sq miles/120,000 sq km; pop. 36,213,000)

Fukuoka a port and largest city on Kyushu Island, Japan. (Pop. 1,361,000)

Funafuti the capital of Tuvalu in the southwest Pacific, and the name of the atoll on which it is sited. (0.9 sq miles/2.4 sq km; pop. 5,000)

Funchal the capital of Madeira. (Pop. 103,000)

Fundy, Bay of lies between Nova Scotia and New Brunswick, Canada. It has the world's largest tidal range – 50 feet (15 metres) between low and high tide.

Fushun a mining city in Liaoning Province, China, situated on one of the largest coalfields in the world. (Pop. 1,384,000)

Fuzhou a port and capital of Fujian Province, China. (Pop. 1,037,000)

Fyn (Fünen) the second largest of the islands of Denmark, in the centre of the country. (1,048 sq miles/2,976 sq km; pop. 478,000)

G

Gabès, Gulf of an inlet of the Mediterranean Sea which, with the Gulf of Sirte to the east, makes a deep indent in the coast of North Africa.

Gabon A small country in west central Africa that straddles the equator. It has a low narrow coastal plain, with the rest of the country comprising a low plateau. Three-quarters of Gabon is covered by dense tropical forest. The climate is hot, humid, and typically equatorial, with little seasonal variation. It was in Lambaréné that Albert Schweitzer, the medical missionary, had his hospital. Until the 1960s lumber was virtually Gabon's only resource and then oil was discovered. By the mid-1980s, it was Africa's sixth largest oil producer, and other minerals, such as manganese, uranium, and iron ore, were being exploited. Deposits of lead and silver have also been discovered. Around two-thirds of the Gabonese people remain subsistence farmers, growing cassava, sugar cane, plantains, and yams. The country has great tourist potential but because of the dense hardwood forests, transport links with the uninhabited interior are very difficult.

Area: 103,347 sq miles/267,668 sq km
Population: 1,106,000
Capital: Libreville
Other major city: Port Gentile
Form of government: Republic
Religions: RC, Animism
Currency: CFA Franc

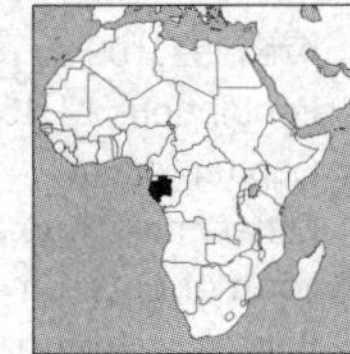

Gaborone the capital of Botswana, in the southeast of the country. (Pop. 223,000)

Galapagos Islands a group of 15 islands on the Equator administered by Ecuador, but located some 680 miles (1,100 kilometres) to the west of that country. (3,016 sq miles/7,812 sq km; pop. 16,000)

Galati an inland port on the River Danube in eastern Romania, close to the border with Moldova. (Pop. 342,000)

Galicia a region in the very northwest corner of Spain.

Galilee the most northerly region of Israel, bordering Lebanon and Syria, with the Sea of Galilee (Lake Tiberias) on its eastern side.

Gallipoli (Gelibolu) the peninsula and port on the northern side of the Dardanelles in Turkey.

Galveston a port in Texas, USA, sited on an island in the Gulf of Mexico. (Pop. 60,000)

Galway a county in the central part of the west coast of the Republic of Ireland. The county town is also called Galway, or Galway City. (2,293 sq miles/5,940 sq km; pop. county 197,000/town 60,000)

Gambia (1) The smallest country in Africa, which pokes like a crooked finger into Senegal. The country is divided along its entire length by the River Gambia, which can be crossed at only two main ferry crossings. On the coast, there are pristine beaches and sand cliffs backed by mangrove swamps, with tropical jungle clothing many of the river banks away from the coast. Gambia has two very different seasons. In the dry season there is little rainfall, but then the southwest monsoon sets in, with spectacular storms producing heavy rain for four months. Most Gambians live in villages with a few animals, and grow enough millet and sorghum to feed themselves. Groundnuts are the main and only export crop of any significance. The river provides a thriving local fishing industry, and the white sandy beaches on the coast are becoming increasingly popular with foreign tourists, although a military takeover in 1994 dealt tourism and trade a severe blow. (2) a major river of West Africa, flowing into the Atlantic Ocean from its source in Guinea, through Senegal and Gambia. (Length 300 miles/483 km)

Area: 4,361 sq miles/11,295 sq km
Population: 1,141,000
Capital: Banjul
Form of government: Republic
Religions: Sunni Islam, Christianity
Currency: Dalasi

Ganges (Ganga) the holy river of the Hindus, flowing from its source in the Himalayas, across northern India and forming a delta in Bangladesh as it flows into the Bay of Bengal. (Length 1,568 miles/2,525 km)

Gansu a mountainous province in northern central China; the capital is Lanzhou. (170,000 sq miles/450,000 sq km; pop. 27,069,000)

Garonne a major river of southwestern France, flowing north from the central Pyrenees to the Gironde estuary. (Length 355 miles/575 km)

Gascony (Gascogne) the historical name of an area in the southwestern corner of France bordering Spain.

Gauteng one of South Africa's nine provinces, in north central South Africa, once part of the former province of Transvaal, with its administrative centre in Johannesburg. (7,262 sq miles/18,810 sq km; pop. 7,048,000)

Gaza a Mediterranean port in the Gaza Strip. (Pop. 398,000)

Gazankulu one of ten former South African Homelands, the area is now part of the provinces of Mpumalanga and Limpopo in northeast South Africa.

Gaza Strip a strip of coastal land stretching from the Egyptian border to the Mediterranean port of Gaza and bordering with Israel to its east and north. It was administered by Egypt after the creation of Israel in 1948, becoming home to numerous Palestinian refugees, and was taken over by Israel in the Six-Day War of 1967. In 1994, it was placed under the jurisdiction of the Palestinian National Authority. (Pop. 1,054,000)

Gaziantep a town in southern central Turkey, close to the border with Syria, and also the name of the surrounding province. (Pop. 795,000)

Gdansk (Danzig) The main port of Poland, on the Baltic Sea. (Pop. 457,000)

Gdynia (Gdingen) a port on the Baltic coast of Poland 10 miles (16 kilometres) northwest of Gdansk. (Pop. 259,000)

Geelong a port and second city of the state of Victoria, in southeast Australia. (Pop. 156,000)

Gelsenkirchen an industrial and coal-mining town in the Ruhr region of Germany. (Pop. 278,000)

Geneva (Genève, Genf) a city in the extreme southwest of Switzerland, at the western end of Lake Geneva, and close to the border with France. It is also the name of the surrounding canton. (Pop. city 176,000)

Genoa (Genova) the major seaport of northwest Italy, and the capital of Liguria. (Pop. 629,000)

George Town (1) a port and the main city of Penang Island, Malaysia. (Pop. 229,000) (2) the capital and main port of the Cayman Islands. (Pop. 28,000)

Georgetown the main port and capital of Guyana. (Pop. 226,000)

Georgia (1) A republic in the southwest of the former USSR, occupying the central and western parts of the Caucasus. It shares borders with Turkey, Armenia, Azerbaijan, and the Russian Federation. It is bounded to the west by the Black Sea. Almost 40 per cent of the country is covered by forests. Agriculture, which is the main occupation of the population, includes tea cultivation and fruit growing, especially citrus fruits and viticulture. The republic is rich in minerals, especially manganese, but imports the majority of its energy needs. Industries include coal, lumber, machinery, chemicals, silk, food processing, and furniture. In the past, the Black Sea tourist trade exploited the country's wealth of thermal and mineral springs very successfully, and tourism should again become an economic mainstay. Georgia declared itself independent in 1991. A struggle for regional autonomy by ethnic minorities led to much disruption and violent conflict. Elections were held in 1995, heralding some progress and reform. (2) a state in the southeast of the USA, named after George II by English colonists in 1733; the state capital is Atlanta. (58,876 sq miles/152,490 sq km; pop. 8,584,000)

Area: 26,900 sq miles/69,700 sq km
Population: 5,411,000
Capital: T'bilisi
Other major cities: Kutaisi, Rustavi, Batumi
Form of government: Republic
Religions: Georgian and Russian Orthodox, Sunni Islam
Currency: Lari

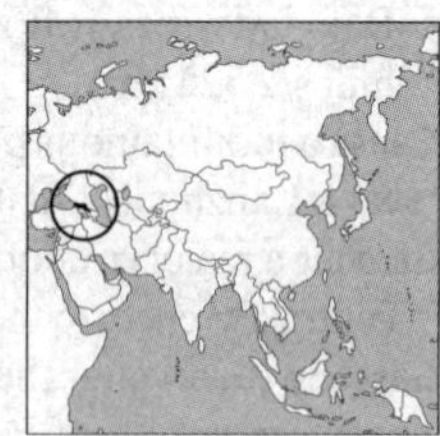

Georgia, Strait of the southern part of the stretch of water which separates Vancouver Island from the coast of British Columbia in Canada.

Germany A large populous country in northern central Europe that comprises the former East and West German Republics, unified in 1990. In the north, is the North German Plain, which merges with the North Rhinelands in the west. Farther south, a plateau that stretches across the country from east to west is divided by the River Rhine. In the southwest, the Black Forest separates the Rhine Valley from the fertile valleys and scarplands of Swabia. More recently, coniferous forests have suffered from acid rain caused by industrial pollution. The Bohemian Uplands and Erz Mountains mark the border with the Czech Republic. Generally the country has warm summers and cold winters. Agricultural products include wheat, rye, barley, oats, potatoes, and sugar beet, although agriculture accounts for only a small percentage of employment and a third of the country's food has to be imported. The main industrial and most densely populated areas are in the Ruhr Valley. Products of the principal manufacturing industries include iron and steel, motor vehicles, mechanical and electrical equipment, aircraft, ships, computers, electronic and technical goods, chemicals and petrochemicals, pharmaceuticals, textiles, clothing and footwear, foods, beer, optical and high precision instruments.

Area: 137,735 sq miles/356,733 sq km
Population: 81,912,000
Capital: Berlin
Other major cities: Cologne, Frankfurt, Hamburg, Leipzig, Munich, Stuttgart
Form of government: Republic
Religions: Lutheranism, RC
Currency: Euro

Ghana A country located on the southern coast of West Africa between Côte d'Ivoire and Togo. In 1957, as the former British Gold Coast, it became the first African state to achieve independence from European colonial rule. It has palm-fringed beaches of white sand along the Gulf of Guinea and where the great River Volta meets the sea there are peaceful blue lagoons. The climate on the coast is equatorial, and towards the north there are steamy tropical evergreen forests which give way in the far north to tropical savannah. The landscape becomes harsh and barren near the border with Burkina Faso. Most Ghanaians are village dwellers whose homes are made of locally available materials. The south of the country has been most exposed to European influence and it is here that cocoa, rubber, palm oil, and coffee are grown. Ghana's most important crop is cocoa and others include coffee, palm kernels, coconut oil, copra, shea nuts, and bananas which are all exported. Fishing is also of major importance and has increased in recent years. Ghana has important mineral resources, notably gold, diamonds, manganese and bauxite. Most of Ghana's towns are in the south.

Area: 92,100 sq miles/238,537 sq km
Population: 17,460,000
Capital: Accra
Other cities: Kumasi, Tamale, Sekondi-Takoradi
Form of government: Republic
Religions: Protestantism, Animism, RC
Currency: Cedi

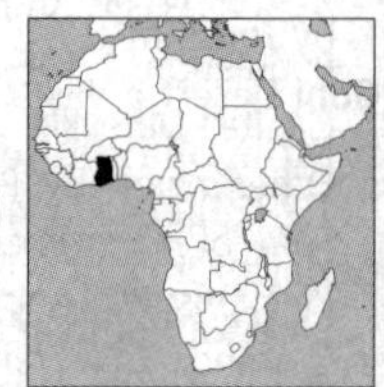

Ghats the two ranges of mountains that line the coasts of the Deccan Peninsula in India: the Eastern Ghats, rising to about 2,000 feet (600 metres), and the Western Ghats rising to 5,000 feet (1,500 metres).

Ghent (Gent, Gand) a medieval city in Belgium, spanning the Rivers Lys and Schelde and the capital of the province of East Flanders. (Pop. 222, 000)

Gibraltar a self-governing former British Crown Colony that is still linked politically with Britain, on the southwestern tip of Spain, where a limestone hill called the Rock of Gibraltar rises to 1,394 feet (425 metres). Its strategic importance, guarding as it does the western approaches to the Mediterranean and separated from Morocco by the narrow Straits of Gibraltar, has resulted in it being occupied at various periods of history by Phoenicians, Carthaginians, Romans, Visigoths, Moors, Spaniards, and the British. In 1713, the Treaty of Utrecht awarded Gibraltar to Britain and it was a British Crown Colony from 1830 to 1969, but Spain has never relinquished its claim to the Rock and relations have at times been difficult. English is the official language, although Spanish is also spoken. The British armed forces, tourism, banking, and construction are the main sources of employment and most imports are from Britain. The Mediterranean climate and many sites of natural and historical interest attract numerous visitors each year. (2.5 sq miles/6.5 sq km; pop. 29,000; cur. Gibraltar Pound)

Gibraltar, Strait of the narrow waterway, 8 miles (13 kilometres) at its narrowest, which connects the Mediterranean Sea to the Atlantic Ocean, with Spain to the north and Morocco to the south.

Gibson Desert a desert of sand and salt marshes in western central Australia, between the Great Sandy Desert and the Victoria Desert.

Gifu a town in central Honshu Island, Japan. (Pop. 420,000)

Gijón a port and industrial town in the region of Asturias, in the centre of the north coast of Spain. (Pop. 268,000)

Gilgit a mountain district in northern Pakistan, noted for its great beauty. The small town of Gilgit perches startlingly beneath a dramatic rock face. (Pop. town 9,000)

Gironde the long, thin estuary stretching some 50 miles (80 kilometres) which connects the Rivers Dordogne and Garonne to the Atlantic coast of southwest France.

Giza (El Gîza) a sprawling suburb of Cairo, Egypt, at the edge of which stand the three most famous pyramids of the Ancient Egyptians. (Pop. 2,541,000)

Glamorgan a former county of south Wales.

Glasgow (1) a major industrial city and important cultural centre on the River Clyde in central Scotland, also the administrative centre for the City of Glasgow council area. It is the largest city in Scotland. (Pop. 663,000) (2) **City of** a council area in central Scotland. (68 sq miles/175 sq km; pop. 624,000)

Gliwice (Gleiwitz) an industrial city in southern Poland. (Pop. 207,000)

Gloucestershire a county in southwest England, with administrative centre in Gloucester. (1,217 sq miles/3153 sq km; pop. 769,000)

Goa a territory on the west coast of India, 250 miles (400 kilometres) south of Bombay, which was captured by Portugal in 1510 and remained under Portuguese control until it was annexed by India in 1961. (1,429 sq miles/3,702 sq km; pop. 1,370,000)

Gobi Desert a vast expanse of arid land which occupies much of Mongolia and central northern China. (500,000 sq miles/1,295,000 sq km)

Godavari a river which runs eastwards across the middle of the Deccan Peninsula in India. (Length 910 miles/1,465 km)

Godthåb (Nuuk) the capital of Greenland. (Pop. 14,000)

Golan Heights a range of high hills in southwest Syria on the border with northern Israel. Under Syrian control until they were taken by Israeli forces in 1967, possession is still disputed between Syria and Israel.

Gold Coast (1) the name given to a string of beach resorts in Australia, on the east coast of Queensland to the south of Brisbane. (2) the former name of Ghana (until 1957).

Golden Triangle the remote and mountainous region where the borders of Thailand, Myanmar and Laos meet, noted in particular for its opium cultivation and as one of the world's main sources of the drug heroin.

Gomel an industrial city in southeastern Belarus. (Pop. 503,000)

Good Hope, Cape of the tip of the narrow Cape Peninsula which extends from the southwestern corner of South Africa.

Gothenburg (Göteborg) a major port in southwest Sweden, and the second largest city in Sweden. (Pop. 504,000)

Gotland a Swedish island in the Baltic Sea off the southeast coast of Sweden. (1,210 sq miles/3,140 sq km; pop. 57,000)

Göttingen a university town in central Germany and an important trading centre in medieval times. (Pop. 130,000)

Gouda a town in eastern Netherlands, famous for its cheese. (Pop. 73,000)

Grampian a former region of northeastern Scotland.

Grampian Mountains a range of mountains that stretch across northern Scotland to the south of Loch Ness. The mountains rise to their highest point at Ben Nevis (4,409 ft/1,344 m), the highest peak in the UK.

Granada a city in the Sierra Nevada of central southern Spain. An administrative centre during the Moorish occupation of Spain when its famous Alhambra Palace was built (1248–1345). Granada is also the name of the surrounding province. (Pop. 245,000)

Grand Canyon the dramatic gorge of the Colorado River, in places over 1 mile (1.5 kilometres) deep, in northwestern Arizona, USA.

Grand Rapids a city 14 miles (40 kilometres) to the east of Lake Michigan in the state of Michigan, USA. (Pop. 200,000)

Graz the second largest city in Austria, in the southeast of the country. (Pop. 223,000)

Great Australian Bight the arm of the Antarctic Ocean which forms the deep indentation in the centre of the southern coastline of Australia.

Great Australian Desert the collective word for the deserts that occupy much of the centre of Australia. (1,480,000 sq miles/3,830,000 sq km)

Great Barrier Reef the world's most extensive coral reef which lines the coast of Queensland, Australia, stretching some 1,250 miles (2,000 kilometres).

Great Bear Lake the fourth largest lake in North America, in northwest Canada. It drains into the Mackenzie River. (12,028 sq miles/31,153 sq km)

Great Britain the island shared by England, Scotland and Wales, and which forms the principal part of the United Kingdom of Great Britain and Northern Ireland.

Great Dividing Range a range of mountains which runs down the east coast of Australia, from Queensland in the north, across New South Wales to Victoria in the south, some 2,250 miles (3,600 kilometres) in all. The highest point is Mount Kosciusko at 7,316 feet (2,230 metres).

Greater London *see* **London.**

Greater Manchester *see* **Manchester.**

Greater Sunda Islands a group of islands in the western Malay Archipelago, forming the larger part of the Sunda Islands and consisting of Borneo, Sumatra, Java and Sulawesi.

Great Lakes the largest group of freshwater lakes in the world, drained by the St Lawrence River. There are five lakes, four of which (Lakes Huron, Superior, Erie and Ontario) are on the border of Canada and the USA; the fifth (Lake Michigan) is in the USA.

Great Plains a vast area in North America of flat and undulating grassland east of the Rocky Mountains and stretching from northern Canada to Texas, USA. It includes the Prairies, most of which are now ploughed for cereal and fodder crops.

Great Rift Valley a series of geological faults which has created a depression stretching 4,000 miles/6,400 kilometres) from the valley of the River Jordan across the Red Sea and down East Africa to Mozambique.

Great Salt Lake a salt lake in northwest Utah, USA, lying just to the northwest of Salt Lake City. (2,000 sq miles/5,200 sq km)

Great Sandy Desert the desert region in the north of Western Australia.

Great Slave Lake a lake drained by the Mackenzie River in the southern part of the Northwest Territories of Canada. (11,030 sq miles/28,570 sq km)

Great Smoky Mountains part of the Appalachian Mountains, running along the border between Tennessee and North Carolina, USA. The highest point is Clingmans Dome (6,643 ft/2,025 m).

Great Victoria Desert a vast area of sand dunes straddling the border between Western Australia and South Australia.

Greece The Greek Peninsula is the most southeasterly extension of Europe, and has over 1,400 islands lying off its coast and scattered throughout the Aegean Sea. Mainland Greece shares borders with Albania in the northwest, Macedonia and Bulgaria in the north, and Turkey in the northeast. The northwestern and central regions of the country are rugged and mountainous, the main chain being the Pindus Mountains. About 70 per cent of the land is hilly, with harsh mountain climates and poor soils, and there are few natural resources of economic value although there are deposits of petroleum and natural gas found under the Aegean Sea. The Greek islands and coastal regions have a typical Mediterranean climate, with mild rainy winters and hot dry summers. Winter in the northern mountains is severe, with deep snow and heavy precipitation. Around 21 per cent of the people are engaged in agriculture, mostly on small family farms. Forestry and fishing are carried out on a small scale. Greece has undergone a rapid process of industrialization since the Second World War, and pollution is a serious problem in some areas. Tourism is a major source of revenue for the country along with shipping.

Area: 50,949 sq miles/131,957 sq km
Population: 10,475,000
Capital: Athens (Athínai)
Other cities: Iráklion, Patras, Piraeus, Thessaloníki
Form of government: Republic
Religion: Greek Orthodox
Currency: Euro

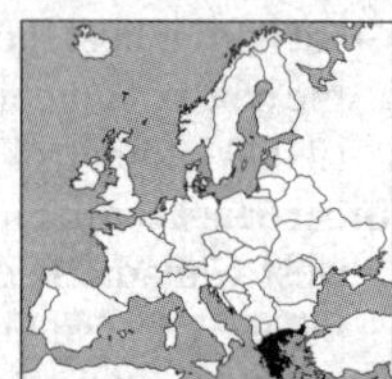

Greenland (Kalaallit Nunaat) the largest island in the world (discounting continental land masses). It lies mainly within the Arctic Circle, off the northeast coast of Canada. Its vast interior is mostly covered with a permanent ice cap that has a known thickness of up to 11,000 feet (3,300 metres). The ice-free coastal strips are characterized by largely barren mountains, rising to Gunnbjorn at 12,140 feet (3,700 metres) in the southeast. Glaciers flow into deeply indented fjords which are fringed by many islands, islets and icebergs. Of the small ice-free fringe, only about a third can be classed as being inhabited, mainly in the southwest. The largely Eskimo population is heavily dependent on fishing for its livelihood, and fish account for 95 per cent of exports. There is some sheep farming, and mining of coal and mineral resources as well as iron ore, lead, zinc, uranium, and molybdenum.

Area: 840,000 sq miles/2,175,600 sq km
Population: 58,200
Capital: Godthåb (Nuuk)
Form of government: Self-governing region of Denmark
Religion: Lutheranism
Currency: Danish Krone

Greenwich a Greater London borough, on the south bank of the River Thames in England. It was the site of the original Royal Observatory, and since 1884 it has been accepted that Greenwich Mean Time is the time at 0° longitude, against which all world time differences are measured.

Grenada The most southerly of the Windward Islands chain in the Caribbean. Its territory includes the southern Grenadine Islands to the north. The main island consists of the remains of extinct volcanoes and has an attractive wooded landscape. The highest peak is Mount St Catherine at 2,750 feet (838 metres). In the dry season, the typical climate is very pleasant, with warm days and cool nights, but in the wet season it is hot day and night. Agriculture is the island's main industry and the chief crops grown for export are citrus fruits, cocoa, nutmegs, bananas, and mace. Other crops grown are cloves, cotton, coconuts, and cinnamon. Apart from the processing of its crops, Grenada has little manufacturing industry. Grenada is a popular port of call for cruise ships, and tourism is an important source of foreign revenue.

Area: 133 sq miles/344 sq km
Population: 92,000
Capital: St George's
Form of government: Independent State within the Commonwealth
Religions: RC, Anglicanism, Methodism
Currency: East Caribbean Dollar

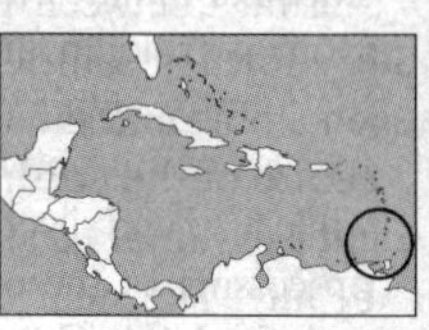

Grenadines a string of some 600 small islands in the Caribbean that lie between St Vincent to the north and Grenada to the south. Most of them belong to St Vincent, but the largest, Carriacou, is divided between St Vincent and Grenada.

Grenoble a manufacturing city in southeast France. (Pop. 155,000)

Groningen the largest city in northeast Netherlands. (Pop. 168,000)

Guadalajara the second largest city in Mexico and the commercial centre of central western Mexico. (Pop. 1,659,000)

Guadalcanal an island in the southwest Pacific, at the southern end of the archipelago where Honiara, capital of the Solomon Islands, is located.

Guadeloupe a small group of islands in the Caribbean lying in the middle of the Lesser Antilles, with some islands in the Leeward Islands and some in the Windward Islands. Since 1946, Guadeloupe has been an French Overseas Department. Ninety per cent of the population live on the two main islands of Basse Terre and Grande Terre. Basse Terre is mountainous, covered with rainforest, and dominated by the Soufrière volcano at 4,318 feet (1,467 metres). Grande Terre is flat and dry with white sandy beaches. The other islands include Marie Galante, La Désirade, Îles des Saints, St Barthélémy, and St Martin. The islands have a warm and humid climate with rainfall heaviest between May and November. Main exports include bananas, sugar, and rum. (658 sq miles/1,705 sq km; pop. 431,000; cur. Euro)

Guam the most southerly and the largest of the Mariana Islands in the northwest Pacific. It consists mainly of a high, coraline limestone plateau with some low volcanic mountains in the south of the island. Guam's climate is tropical with a rainy season from July to December. An unincorporated territory of the USA, its economy depends to a large extent on government activities and military installations account for some 35 per cent of the land area of the island. Exports include copra, palm oil, and processed fish. The country has also become a financial centre, particularly for mainland and Asian banks, and tourism has come to play an important role in its economy. (212 sq miles/549 sq km; pop. 153,000; cur. US Dollar)

Guangdong a province of southeast China. The capital is Guangzhou (Canton). (81,000 sq miles/210,000 sq km; pop. 74,017,000)

Guangxi-Zhuang an autonomous region of southern China on the border with Vietnam. To the south of the city of Guilin, around the Gui Jiang River, is a famous landscape of towering rock hills which rise up from the watery plains. The regional capital is Nanning. (89,000 sq miles/230,000 sq km; pop. 50,541,000)

Guangzhou (Canton) a major port in southeast China, the country's sixth largest city and the capital of Guangdong Province. (Pop. 3,434,000)

Guantánamo a city in the southeast of Cuba. The USA has a naval base at nearby Guantánamo Bay. (Pop. 269,000)

Guatemala A country situated between the Pacific Ocean and the Caribbean Sea where North America meets Central America. It is mountainous, with a ridge of volcanoes running parallel to the Pacific coast. It has a tropical climate with little or no variation in temperature and a distinctive wet season. The Pacific slopes of the mountains are exceptionally well watered and fertile, and it is here that most of the population is settled. Coffee growing on the lower slopes dominates the economy, although bananas, sugar, cardamom, petroleum, and shellfish are exported. The forested area of the country, about 36 per cent, plays an important part in the country's economy, and there are also deposits of petroleum and zinc, while lead and silver are mined. Industry is mainly restricted to the processing of the country's agricultural products. Most trade is with the USA. Guatemala is politically unstable and civil conflict has practically destroyed tourism.

Area: 42,042 sq miles/108,889 sq km
Population: 10,928,000
Capital: Guatemala City
Other cities: Cobán, Puerto Barrios, Quezaltenango
Form of government: Republic
Religion: RC
Currency: Quetzal

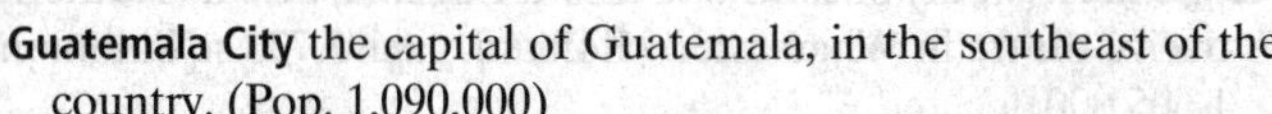

Guatemala City the capital of Guatemala, in the southeast of the country. (Pop. 1,090,000)

Guayaquil the main port and the largest city of Ecuador. (Pop. 2,197,000)

Guernica a small town in the Basque country of northeast Spain where the Basque parliament used to assemble. In 1937, during the Spanish Civil War, it was heavily bombed from the air by German forces. (Pop. 17,836)

Guernsey one of the Channel Islands, lying in the centre of the group and some 30 miles (50 kilometres) off the coast of France. The capital is St Peter Port. (30 sq miles/78 sq km; pop. 63,000)

Guinea Formerly a French West African territory, Guinea is located on the coast at the 'bulge' in Africa. It is a lush green beautiful country about the same size as the United Kingdom. It has a tropical climate with constant heat and a high rainfall near the coast. Its principal rivers are the Gambia and the Bafing while the River Niger rises in the forests of the Guinea Highlands. Guinea has great agricultural potential, and many of the coastal swamps and forested plains have been cleared for the cultivation of rice, cassava, yams, maize, and vegetables. Around 80 per cent of the population are subsistence farmers. Although the country has eight national languages, the official language is French. Further inland, on the plateau of Fouta Djallon, dwarf cattle are raised, and in the valleys bananas and pineapples are grown. Coffee and kola nuts are important cash crops grown in the Guinea Highlands to the southwest. Minerals such as bauxite, of which there are substantial reserves, iron ore, diamonds, gold, and uranium are mined but further development is hampered by a lack of transport.

Area: 94,926 sq miles/245,857 sq km
Population: 7,518,000
Capital: Conakry
Other major cities: Kankan, Labé
Form of government: Republic
Religion: Sunni Islam
Currency: Guinea Franc

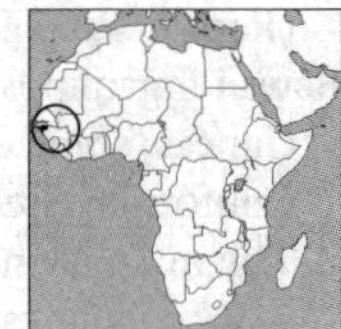

Guinea-Bissau Formerly a Portuguese territory but granted independence in 1974, Guinea-Bissau is located south of Senegal on the Atlantic coast of West Africa. The republic's territory includes over 60 coastal islands, including the archipelago of Bijagós. It is a country of stunning scenery and rises from a deeply indented and island-fringed coastline to a low inland plateau and hills on the border with neighbouring Guinea. The climate is tropical, with abundant rain from June to November but hot dry conditions for the rest of the year. Years of Portuguese rule and civil war have left Guinea-Bissau impoverished, and it is one of the poorest West African states. The country's main aim is to become self-sufficient in food, and the main crops grown by the subsistence farmers are rice, groundnuts, cassava, sugar cane, plantains, maize, and coconuts. Fishing is an important export industry although cashew nuts are the principal export. Peanuts, palm tree products, and cotton are also a source of export revenue.

Area: 13,948 sq miles/36,125 sq km
Population: 1,091,000
Capital: Bissau (Bissão)
Form of government: Republic
Religions: Animism, Sunni Islam
Currency: Guinea-Bissau Peso.

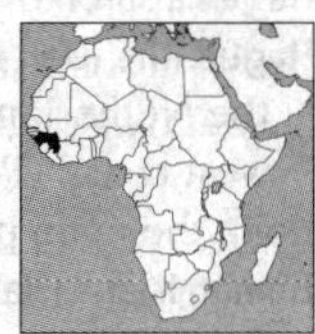

Guinea, Gulf of the arm of the Atlantic Ocean which creates the deep, right-angled indent in the west coast of Africa.

Guiyang an industrial city in central southern China, and capital of Guizhou Province. (Pop. 1,162,000)

Guizhou a province of southwest China, between the Rivers Yangtze and Xi. The capital is Guiyang. (170,000 sq km/65,600 sq miles; pop. 38,372,000)

Gujarat a state in northwest India, on the border with Pakistan. The capital is Gandhinagar. (75,665 sq miles/196,024 sq km; pop. 51,585,000)

Gujranwala a textile city in the province of Punjab, Pakistan, some 40 miles (65 kilometres) north of Lahore. (Pop. 1,349,000)

Guyana The only English-speaking country in South America, situated on the northeast coast of the continent on the Atlantic Ocean. Guyana was formerly called British Guiana but achieved independence in 1966. The country is intersected by many rivers and the coastal area comprises tidal marshes and mangrove swamps. Rice is grown on this narrow coastal area and vast plantations produce sugar. The jungle in the southwest has potential for the production of minerals, hardwood, and hydroelectric power, but 90 per cent of the population live in the coastal area where the climate is moderated by sea breezes. Sugar and its by-products, and rice are the mainstay of the country's economy, while tropical fruits and vegetables, such as coconuts, citrus, coffee, and corn, are grown mainly for home consumption. Large numbers of livestock including cattle, sheep, pigs, and chickens are also raised. Guyana's principal mineral is bauxite, with gold, manganese, and diamonds also being exploited.

Area: 83,000 sq miles/214,969 sq km
Population: 838,000
Capital: Georgetown
Other major city: New Amsterdam
Form of government: Cooperative Republic
Religions: Hinduism, Protestantism, RC
Currency: Guyana Dollar

Guyane *see* **French Guiana**.

Gwalior a city in central India, southeast of Delhi. (Pop. 843,000)

Gwynedd a council area in northwest Wales, with its administrative centre in the town of Caernarfon. (869 sq miles/2,550 sq km; pop. 118,000)

H

Haarlem a city in west central Netherlands. (Pop. 148,000)

Hagen a steel town in the Ruhr region of Germany. (Pop. 206,000)

Hague, the (Den Haag, 's-Gravenhage) the administrative centre of the Netherlands and capital of South Holland Province, on the west coast. (Pop. 444,0000)

Haifa the main port of Israel. (Pop. 276,000)

Hainan Island (Hainan Dao) a large tropical island in the South China Sea belonging to China, and the southernmost extremity of that country. (13,000 sq miles/33,670 sq km; pop. 8,035,000)

Haiphong a port in the north of Vietnam. It is Vietnam's third largest city after Ho Chi Minh City and Hanoi. (Pop. 572,000)

Haiti Occupying the western third of the large island of Hispaniola in the Caribbean, Haiti is a mountainous country consisting of five different ranges, the highest point reaching 8,793 feet (2,680 metres) at Pic La Selle. The mountain ranges are separated by deep valleys and plains. The climate is tropical but semi-arid conditions can occur in the lee of the central mountains. Hurricanes and severe thunderstorms are a common occurrence. Only a third of the country is arable, yet agriculture is the chief occupation, with around 80 per cent of the population concentrated in rural areas. Many farmers grow only enough to feed their own families, and the export crops of coffee, sugar, and sisal are grown on large estates. Severe soil erosion caused by extensive forest clearance has resulted in a decline in crop yields and environmental damage has been caused. The country has only limited amounts of natural resources, bauxite not now being commercially profitable, although deposits of salt, copper, and gold exist. Haiti is the poorest country in the Americas and has experienced many uprisings and attempted coups.

Area: 10,714 sq miles/27,750 sq km
Population: 7,336,000
Capital: Port-au-Prince
Other cities: Cap-Haïtien, Les Cayes, Gonaïves
Form of government: Republic
Religions: RC, Voodooism
Currency: Gourde

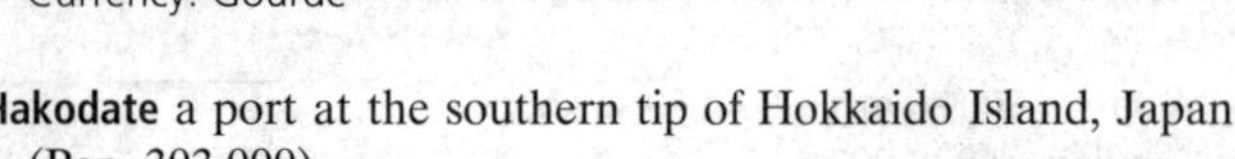

Hakodate a port at the southern tip of Hokkaido Island, Japan. (Pop. 303,000)

Halifax (1) the capital of Nova Scotia, Canada. (Pop. 117,000) (2) a town in West Yorkshire, England. (Pop. 94,000)

Halle an industrial town and inland port served by the Saale River in central Germany. (Pop. 245,000)

Hamah an industrial city in eastern Syria. (Pop. 365,000)

Hamamatsu a city in southern Honshu Island, Japan. (Pop. 590,000)

Hamburg the main port of Germany, situated on the River Elbe. (Pop. 1,688,000)

Hamelin (Hameln) a town in northern Germany. Famous for its legendary Pied Piper. (Pop. 59,000)

Hamersley Range a range of mountains in Western Australia. The highest peak is Mount Bruce (4,052 ft/1,235 m).

Hamhung (Hamheung) a port and industrial city on the east coast of North Korea. (Pop. 821,000)

Hamilton (1) the capital of Bermuda. (Pop. 1,000) (2) a port and industrial city at the western end of Lake Ontario, Canada. (Pop. 348,000) (3) a town in the northwestern part of North Island, New Zealand. (Pop. 110,000) (4) a town in central Scotland, 10 miles (17 kilometres) southeast of Glasgow. (Pop. 48,000)

Hammerfest a town in the very north of Norway, and one of the world's most northerly settlements. (Pop. 9,000)

Hampshire a county of central southern England, with its administrative centre in Winchester. (1,456 sq miles/3,773 sq km; pop. 1,605,000)

Hangzhou (Hangchow) a port and industrial city on the east coast of central China, at the head of an estuary called Hangzhou Wan. Hangzhou is at the southern end of the Grand Canal, which links it to Beijing 690 miles (1,100 kilometres) to the north. (Pop. 1,213,000)

Hanoi the capital of Vietnam, in the north of the country. (Pop. 1,373,000)

Hanover (Hannover) a historical city in central northern Germany. (Pop. 517,000)

Haora (Howrah) an industrial city in West Bengal, India, on the Hugli River, facing Calcutta. (Pop. 1,028,000)

Harare the capital of Zimbabwe; it was formerly called Salisbury (until 1982). (Pop. 1,864,000)

Harbin the largest city of northern China, situated in central Dongbei (Manchuria), and capital of Heilongjiang Province. (Pop. 2,765,000)

Harrisburg the state capital of Pennsylvania, USA. (Pop. 49,000)

Hartford the state capital of Connecticut, USA. (Pop. 123,000)

Haryana a state in northwest India, formed in 1966. (17,066 sq miles/44,212 sq km; pop. 21,495,000)

Harz Mountains a range of mountains, noted for their forests, in central Germany. The highest peak is Brocken (3,747 ft/1,142 m).

Hastings a historical port and resort on the south coast of England, in the county of East Sussex. (Pop. 84,000)

Hatteras, Cape the tip of a chain of islands lining the coast of North Carolina, USA, notorious for its violent weather.

Havana (La Habana) the capital of Cuba, a port on the northwest coast of the island, and the name of the surrounding province. (Pop. 2,328,000)

Hawaii a group of 122 islands just to the south of the Tropic of Cancer, some 2,300 miles (3,700 kilometres) from the coast of California. Since 1959, they have formed a state of the USA. The main islands are Oahu, Maui and Hawaii Island, which at 4,049 square miles (10,488 square kilometres) is by far the largest. Honolulu, the state capital, is on Oahu. (6,450 sq miles/16,705 sq km; pop. 1,237,000)

Hebei a province in northern China which surrounds (but does not include) Beijing. The capital is Shijiazhuang. (70,000 sq miles/180,000 sq km; pop. 70,421,400)

Hebrides some 500 islands lying off the west coast of Scotland, consisting of the Inner Hebrides to the southeast, whose main islands are Tiree, Jura, Coll, Mull, Eigg and Skye, and the Outer Hebrides to the northwest whose islands include Lewis and Harris, the Uists, Benbecula and Barra.

Hefei an industrial city in central eastern China, capital of Anhui Province. (Pop. 784,000)

Heidelberg a university town in southwest Germany. (Pop. 138,000)

Heilongjiang a province of Dongbei (Manchuria) in northern China; the capital is Harbin. (179,000 sq miles/464,000 sq km; pop. 38,253,000)

Hejaz (Hijaz) a mountainous region which lines the Red Sea, formerly an independent kingdom but since 1932 a part of Saudi Arabia.

Helena the state capital of Montana, USA. (Pop. 26,000)

Heligoland (Helgoland) A small island and former naval base in the North Sea off the coast of Germany. (0.5 sq miles/2.1 sq km)

Helsinki (Helsingfors) the capital and chief industrial centre and port of Finland. (Pop. 575,000)

Henan a province of central China; the capital is Zhengzhou. (62,000 sq miles/160,000 sq km; pop. 100,845,000)

Herat a city in western Afghanistan on the Hari Rud River. (Pop. 167,000)

Herefordshire a county in the west of England, on the border with Wales, with its administrative centre in Hereford. (842 sq miles/ 2,180 sq km; pop. 167,000)

Hermon, Mount a mountain in southern Lebanon near the borders with Syria and Israel. It is the source of the River Jordan. (9,332 ft/2,814 m)

Hertfordshire a county in southeast England, to the north of London, with its administrative centre in Hertford. (631 sq miles/ 1,634 sq km; pop. 1,005,000)

Hessen (Hesse) a state in central western Germany. The capital is Wiesbaden. (8,151 sq miles/21,112 sq km; pop. 6,041,000)

Highland a council area in northern Scotland, with its administrative centre in the town of Inverness. (9,710 sq miles/25,149 sq km; pop. 207,000)

Highlands the rugged region of northern Scotland, which includes the Grampian Mountains and the North West Highlands.

Himachal Pradesh a state in northern India, in mountainous country bordering Tibet. (21,490 sq miles/55,673 sq km; pop. 6,196,000)

Himalayas the massive mountain range stretching some 1,500 miles (2,400 km) in a broad sweep from the northern tip of India, across Nepal, Bhutan and southern Tibet to Assam in northeastern India. The average height of the mountains is some 20,000 ft (6,100 m), rising to the world's tallest peak, Mount Everest (29,028 ft/8,848 m).

Himeji an industrial port in southern Honshu Island, Japan. (Pop. 485,000)

Hindu Kush a range of mountains which stretches some 370 miles (600 km) at the western end of the Himalayas, straddling the web of borders where Afghanistan, Tajikistan, China, India and Pakistan meet. The highest peak is Tirich Mir (25,229 ft/7,690 m) in Pakistan.

Hiroshima an industrial city in southwestern Honshu Island, Japan. Three-quarters of the city were destroyed on August 6, 1945, when the world's first atomic bomb was dropped here, killing 78,000 people. (Pop. 1,133,000)

Hispaniola the name of the large Caribbean island that is shared by Haiti and the Dominican Republic. (29,400 sq miles/76,200 sq km)

Hitachi an industrial city on east Honshu Island, Japan. (Pop. 211,000)

Hobart a port and capital of Tasmania, Australia. (Pop. 205,000)

Ho Chi Minh City (Saigon) the largest city in Vietnam, and the capital of former independent South Vietnam. (Pop. 3,379,000)

Hoggar (Ahaggar) a remote mountain range of southern Algeria noted for its rock formations. The highest peak is Tahat (9,573 ft/2,918 m).

Hohe Tauern a part of eastern Alps in southern Austria, rising to the highest point at Grossglockner (12,460 ft/3,798 m), Austria's highest peak.

Hohhot an industrial city and the capital of the Nei Mongol Autonomous Region (Inner Mongolia), China. (Pop. 724,000)

Hokkaido the most northerly of the main islands of Japan, and the second largest after Honshu Island. The capital is Sapporo. (30,312 sq miles/78,509 sq km; pop. 5,680,000)

Holland a name generally applied to the Netherlands, but in fact the term really applies to the central coastal region which comprise the two provinces of Noord Holland and Zuid Holland.

Hollywood a suburb in the northern part of Los Angeles in California, USA. It has long served as the base for the USA's powerful movie industry.

Holy Island (Lindisfarne) a small island just off the coast of Northumberland in northeast England. It has an 11th-century priory built on the site of a monastery founded in the 7th century.

Homs (Hims) an industrial city of ancient origins in Syria. (Pop. 725,000)

Honduras A fan-shaped country in Central America that spreads out towards the Caribbean Sea at the Gulf of Honduras. Four-fifths of the country is covered by mountains that are indented with river valleys running towards the very short Pacific coast. There is little change in temperatures throughout the year and rainfall is heavy, especially on the Caribbean coast where temperatures are also higher than inland. The highlands are covered with forests, mainly of oak and pine, while palms and mangroves grow in the coastal areas. The country is sparsely populated and, although agricultural, only about 25 per cent of the land is cultivated. Honduras was once the world's leading banana exporter and that fruit is still its main export, but agriculture is now more diverse. Grains, coffee, and sugar are important crops, and these are grown mainly on the coastal plains of the Pacific and Caribbean. The forestry industry is one of the country's principal industries, producing mahogany, pine, walnut, ebony, and rosewood. Other industries have increased in recent years, with cotton, cement, and sugar products being produced for export.

Area: 43,277 sq miles/112,088 sq km
Population: 6,140,000
Capital: Tegucigalpa
Form of government: Republic
Religion: RC
Currency: Lempira

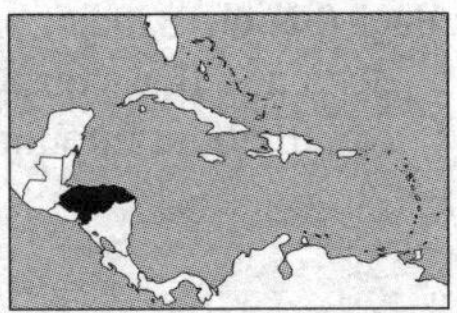

Hong Kong Formerly a British dependent territory, Hong Kong became a special autonomous province of China on 1 July 1997. It is located in the South China Sea and consists of Hong Kong Island (once a barren rock), the peninsula of Kowloon and about 386 square miles (1,000 square kilometres) of adjacent land known as the New Territories. Hong Kong is situated at the mouth of the Pearl River, about 81 miles (130 kilometres) southeast of Guangzhou (Canton). The climate is warm subtropical with cool dry winters and hot humid summers. Hong Kong has no natural resources, even its water comes from reservoirs across the Chinese border. Its main assets are its magnificent natural harbour and its position close to the main trading routes of the

Pacific. Hong Kong's economy is based on free enterprise and trade, an industrious work force, and an efficient and aggressive commercial system. Hong Kong's main industries are textiles, clothing, tourism, and electronics.

Area: 415 sq miles/1,075 sq km
Population: 6,688,000
Form of government: Special Autonomous Province of China
Religions: Buddhism, Taoism, Christianity
Currency: Hong Kong Dollar

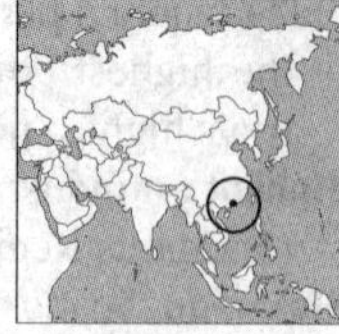

Honiara the capital of the Solomon Islands in the southwest Pacific, situated on Guadalcanal. (Pop. 53,000)

Honolulu the state capital of Hawaii, USA, on the south coast of the island of Oahu. (Pop. 380,000)

Honshu the central and largest of the islands of Japan. (89,185 sq miles/230,988 sq km; pop. 101,000,000)

Hormuz (Ormuz), Strait of the strait at the mouth of the Persian Gulf between the Musandam Peninsula of Oman to the south, and Iran to the north.

Horn, Cape (Cabo de Hornos) The southern tip of South America, represented by a spattering of remote islands belonging to Chile off Tierra del Fuego.

Houston the largest city in Texas and fourth largest city in the USA. (Pop. 2,043,000)

Huang He (Hwang Ho, Yellow River) the second longest river in China, flowing from the Qinghai Mountains across northern central China to the Yellow Sea, south of Beijing. (Length 3,395 miles/5,464 km)

Huascarán a peak in the Andes in central Peru, and that country's highest mountain at 22,205 feet (6,768 metres).

Hubei a landlocked province of central China. (69,500 sq miles/180,000 sq km; pop. 63,361,000)

Hudson Bay a huge bay in northeastern Canada, hemmed in to the north by Baffin Island, and connected to the Atlantic Ocean by the Hudson Strait.

Hudson River a river flowing from its source in the Adirondack Mountains in New York State, USA, to the Atlantic Ocean at New York City. The Erie Canal joins the Hudson River to link New York to the Great Lakes. (Length 306 miles/492 km)

Hué the capital of the rulers of Vietnam from 200 BC to the 19th century, located in the central coastal region of the country. (Pop. 267,000)

Hugli (Hoogly) a major branch of the River Ganges which forms at its delta and flows through Calcutta and the surrounding industrial conurbations into the Bay of Bengal. (Length 120 miles/193 km)

Hull *see* **Kingston upon Hull.**

Humber the estuary of the Rivers Ouse and Trent which cuts deep into the east coast of England to the north of the Wash. (Length 35 miles/60 km)

Humberside a former county of north England.

Hunan an inland province of southeast China. The capital is Changsha. (210,000 sq km/81,000 sq miles; pop. 63,261,000)

Hungary Landlocked in the heartland of Europe, Hungary is dominated by the great plain to the east of the River Danube, which runs north-south across the country. In the west, lies the largest lake in Central Europe, Lake Balaton. Winters are severe, but the summers are warm and although wet in the west, summer droughts often occur in the east. Hungary experienced a modest boom in its economy in the 1970s and 1980s. The government invested money in improving agriculture by mechanizing farms, using fertilizers, and bringing new land under cultivation. Yields of cereals and rice have since soared, and large areas between the Danube and Tisza Rivers are now used to grow vegetables. However, the use of these artificial fertilizers has caused water pollution. Industries have been carefully developed where adequate natural resources exist, such as bauxite, which is the country's main resource. New industries, such as the electronics industry, are now being promoted, and tourism is fast developing around Lake Balaton.

Area: 35,920 sq miles/93,032 sq km
Population: 10,193,000
Capital: Budapest
Other major cities: Debrecen, Miskolc, Pécs, Szeged
Form of government: Republic
Religions: RC, Calvinism, Lutheranism
Currency: Forint

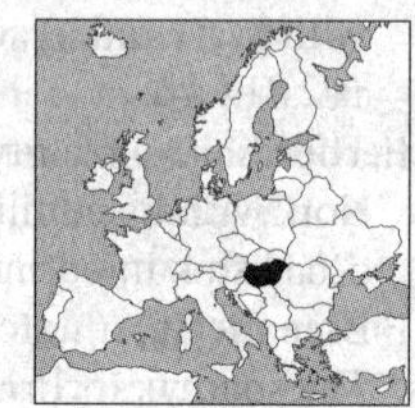

Hunter Valley the valley of the Hunter River, lying 60 miles (100 kilometres) northwest of Sydney, Australia. It is particularly noted for its wine.

Huron, Lake one of the Great Lakes, lying at the centre of the group on the border between Canada and the state of Michigan in the USA. (23,000 sq miles/59,570 sq km)

Hyderabad (1) the capital of the state of Andhra Pradesh in southeastern India. (Pop. 3,517,000) (2) a city on the Indus delta 100 miles (160 kilometres) northeast of Karachi, Pakistan. (Pop. 1,276,000)

Hydra (Idhra) a small island in the Aegean Sea, off the east coast of the Peloponnese Peninsula, Greece, noted as a haven where motor traffic is prohibited.

I

Iasi a historical city in northeastern Romania. (Pop. 355,000)

Ibadan the third largest city in Nigeria after Lagos and Kano, some 75 miles (120 kilometres) north of Lagos. It is a busy market and university town. (Pop. 3,078,000)

Iboland a densely populated region of southeastern Nigeria inhabited by the Ibo people. The attempt by the region to break away from Nigeria (1967–70) under the name of Biafra caused a civil war that led to a famine which killed over a million people. (Pop. 10,000,000)

Iceland A large island situated in a tectonically unstable part of the North Atlantic Ocean, just south of the Arctic Circle. The island has over 100 volcanoes, at least one of which erupts every five years. One-ninth of the country is covered by ice and snow fields, and there are about 700 hot springs, which are an important source of central heating, particularly in the volcanic areas. In the capital city, the majority of homes and industries are heated by this method. The climate is cool temperate, but because of the effect of the North Atlantic Drift it is mild for its latitude. Permanent daylight occurs for three months in summer and the beautiful Aurora Borealis (Northern Lights) can be seen from the end of August. The southwest corner is the most densely populated area as the coast here is generally free from ice. Very little of the land can be cultivated and the main crops are root vegetables such as turnip and potatoes. Fishing and fish processing are the mainstay of the Icelandic economy, with much of the catch being exported. Aluminium and ferrosilicon, nitrates for fertilizers, cement, and chemicals are produced for export. Other manufactured goods include paints, textiles, clothing, footwear, and knitted products. Tourism is also of growing importance to the island's economy.

Area: 39,769 sq miles/103,000 sq km
Population: 275,000
Capital: Reykjavík
Form of government: Republic
Religion: Lutheranism
Currency: Icelandic Króna

Idaho an inland state in the northwest of the USA. The state capital is Boise. (83,557 sq miles/216,413 sq km; pop. 1,348,000)

Idlib a large commercial centre in northwestern Syria. (Pop. 87,000)

IJsselmeer formerly a large inlet of the North Sea known as the Zuiderzee on the northeastern coast of the Netherlands, but after the creation of the dam called the Afsluitdijk across its mouth, it has filled with water from the River IJssel and is now a freshwater lake, bordered by fertile areas of reclaimed land (polders).

Ile de France a region and former province of France with Paris at its centre, now consisting of eight separate departments. (4,638 sq miles/12,012 sq km)

Illinois a state in the Midwest of the USA, bordering Lake Michigan to the north. The capital is Springfield, but Chicago is its main city. (56,400 sq miles/46,075 sq km; pop. 12,546,000)

Inch'on (Incheon) a port and industrial city on the western (Yellow Sea) coast of South Korea, 24 miles (39 kilometres) west of Seoul. (Pop. 2,433,000)

India A vast country in South Asia that is dominated in the extreme north by the world's youngest and highest mountains, the Himalayas, which extend about 1,500 miles (about 2,400 kilometres) along India's northern and eastern borders. The range contains Mount Everest and K2. At the foot of the Himalayas, a huge plain, drained by the Indus and Ganges Rivers, is one of the most fertile areas in the world and the most densely populated part of India. Further south, the ancient Deccan plateau extends to the southern tip of the country. India generally has four seasons, cool, hot, rainy, and dry. About 70 per cent of the population depend on agriculture for their living and the lower slopes of the Himalayas represent one of the world's best tea-growing areas. Rice, sugar cane, and wheat are grown in the Ganges plain, and there is a comprehensive system of irrigation to aid agriculture. India is self-sufficient in all its major food crops, and main exports include precious stones, jewellery, engineering products, clothes, and chemicals. Since becoming a republic in 1950, India has been troubled by internal dissent and external disputes, particularly with Pakistan over the status of Kashmir.

Area: 1,269,346 sq miles/3,287,590 sq km
Population: 970,930,000
Capital: New Delhi
Other major cities: Bangalore, Bombay, Calcutta, Delhi, Hyderabad, Madras
Form of government: Federal Republic
Religion: Hinduism, Islam, Sikhism, Christianity, Jainism, Buddhism
Currency: Rupee

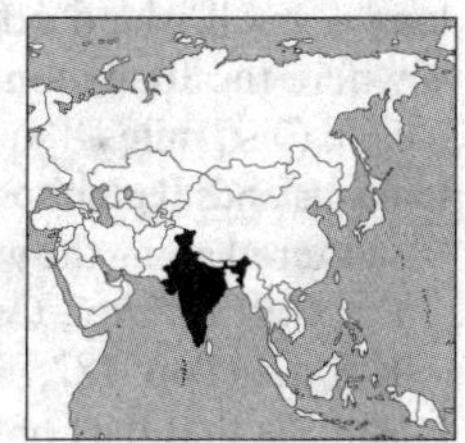

Indiana a state in the Midwest of the USA to the southeast of Lake Michigan. The state capital is Indianapolis. (36,291 sq miles/93,994 sq km; pop. 6,149,000)

Indianapolis the state capital of Indiana in the Midwest of the USA. (Pop. 801,000)

Indian Ocean the third largest ocean, bounded by Asia to the north, Africa to the west and Australia to the east. The southern waters merge with the Antarctic Ocean. (28,364,000 sq miles/73,481,000 sq km)

Indonesia A country made up of 13,667 islands that are scattered across the Indian and Pacific Oceans in a huge crescent. It is the world's fourth most highly populated country. Its largest land mass is the province of Kalimantan, which is part of the island of Borneo. Sumatra is the largest individual island. Java, however, is the dominant and most densely populated island. The climate is generally tropical monsoon, and temperatures are high all year round. The country has 130 active volcanoes, and earthquakes are frequent in the southern islands. Overpopulation is a big problem, especially in Java where its fertile rust-coloured soil is in danger of becoming exhausted. Rice, maize, and cassava are the main crops grown. Indonesia has the largest reserves of tin in the world and is one of the world's leading rubber producers. Other mineral resources found are bauxite, natural gas, nickel, and copper. Oil production is also important. Indonesia's resources are not as yet fully developed but the country's economy is now growing and needs to create over two million jobs annually to keep pace with the expanding population. Ongoing political instability and human rights abuse, particularly in the area of East Timor, which was illegally annexed by Indonesia in 1975, are hampering this process.

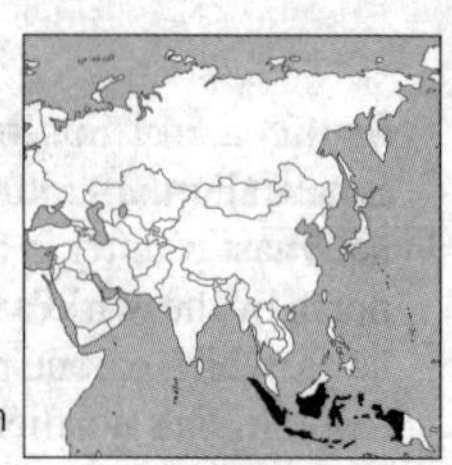

Area: 741,052 sq miles/1,919,317 sq km
Population: 203,000,000
Capital: Jakarta
Other cities: Bandung, Medan, Semarang, Surabaya
Form of government: Republic
Religion: Sunni Islam, Christianity, Hinduism
Currency: Rupiah

Indore a textile-manufacturing city, and once the capital of the princely state of Indore, in western Madhya Pradesh, central India. (Pop. 1,629,000)

Indus one of the great rivers of Asia, whose valleys supported some of the world's earliest civilizations, notably at Mohenjo Daro. It flows from its source in Tibet and across the northern tip of India before turning south to run through the entire length of Pakistan to its estuary on the Arabian Sea, south of Karachi. (Length 1,900 miles/3,059 km)

Inverness a town in northeastern Scotland at the head of the Moray Firth and at the eastern end of Loch Ness. (Pop. 43,000)

Inverclyde a council area in west central Scotland, with its administrative centre in the town of Greenock. (63 sq miles/162 sq km; pop. 90,000)

Iona a small island off the southwestern tip of Mull, Scotland, where the Irish monk St Columba founded a monastery in AD 563. (3 sq miles/8 sq km)

Ionian Islands (Eptanisos) the seven largest of the islands which lie scattered along the west coast of Greece in the Ionian Sea. They are Corfu, Paxoí, Cephalonia, Levkás, Ithaca, Zákinthos and Kíthira. (Pop. 182,700)

Ionian Sea that part of the Mediterranean Sea between southern Italy and Greece. It is named after Io, a mistress of the Ancient Greek god Zeus.

Iowa a state in the Midwest of the USA bounded on the east and west by the upper reaches of the Mississippi and Missouri Rivers. The capital is Des Moines. (56,290 sq miles/145,791 sq km; pop. 2,921,000)

Iqaluit the capital of the Inuit territory of Nunavut, in north Canada; former name Frobisher Bay.(Pop. 5,000)

Iráklion (Heraklion) a former capital and the main port of Crete. (Pop. 135,000)

Iran, Islamic Republic of Lying across the Persian Gulf from the Arabian Peninsula and stretching from the Caspian Sea to the Arabian Sea, Iran is a land dominated by mountains in the north and west, with a huge expanse of desert in its centre. The climate is hot and dry, although more temperate conditions are found on the shores of the Caspian Sea. In winter, terrible dust storms sweep the deserts and almost no life can survive. Most of the population live in the north and west, where Tehran is situated. The only good agricultural land is on the Caspian coastal plains, where wheat, barley, potatoes, and rice are grown. Around 5 per cent of the population are nomadic herdsmen who wander in the mountains. Most of Iran's oil is in the southwest, and other valuable minerals include coal, iron ore, copper, and lead. Precious stones are found in the northeast. The country's main exports are fresh and dried fruit, petroleum and petrochemicals, carpets and rugs, textiles, raw cotton, and leather goods. The Iranian economy expanded rapidly as a result of petroleum industry revenue. However, following the Islamic revolution in the late 1970s, and the subsequent war with neighbouring Iraq between 1980 and 1988, the economy slowed dramatically and is only gradually beginning to pick up again.

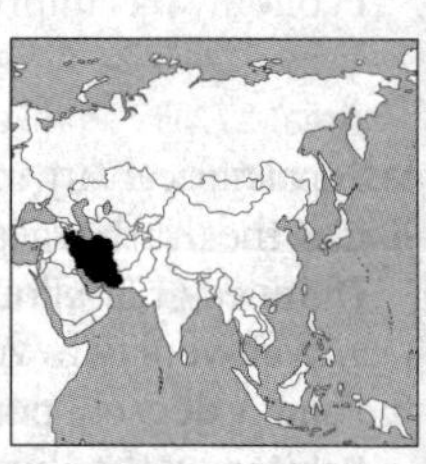

Area: 634,293,sq miles/1,648,195 sq km
Population: 61,128,000
Capital: Tehran
Other major cities: Esfahan, Mashhad, Tabriz
Form of government: Islamic Republic
Religion: Shia Islam
Currency: Rial

Iraq Located in southwest Asia, wedged between the Persian Gulf and Syria, Iraq is almost landlocked except for its outlet to the Gulf at Shatt al Arab. Its two great rivers, the Tigris and the Euphrates, flow from the northwest into the Gulf at this point. The climate is arid, with very hot summers and cold winters. The high mountains on the border with Turkey are snow-covered for six months of the year, and desert covers nearly half the country in the southwest. The only fertile land in Iraq is in the basins of the Tigris and Euphrates, where wheat, barley, rice, tobacco, and cotton are grown, with the country being primarily an agricultural one. The country is a large producer of dates. A variety of other fruits is grown, such as apples, olives, figs, grapes, and pomegranates. Oil was the main export. Iraq profited from the great oil boom of the 1970s, but during the war with Iran, oil terminals in the Gulf were destroyed and the Trans-Syrian Pipeline closed. Iraq invaded Kuwait in 1990, leading to the first Gulf War in 1991 in which Iraq was defeated by UN forces. Following this the country's standard of living went gone from very high to very low, and continued international sanctions kept the economy in a state of crisis. The regime of Saddam Hussein, President of Iraq since 1979, collapsed in April 2003, three weeks into a major US-led military campaign.

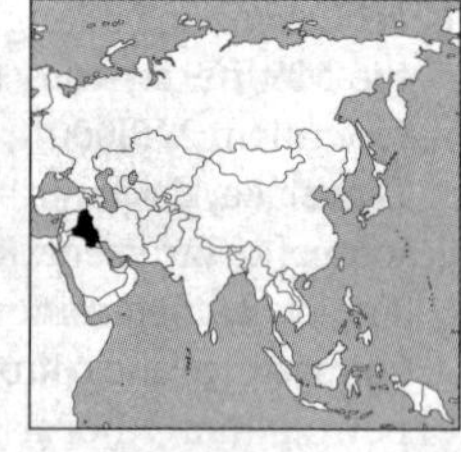

Area: 169,235 sq miles/438,317 sq km
Population: 20,607,000
Capital: Baghdad
Other major cities: Basra (Al-Basrah), Mosul (Al Mawsil)
Form of government: Republic
Religions: Shia Islam, Sunni Islam
Currency: Iraqi Dinar

Ireland an island off the west coast of Great Britain, almost four fifths of which is the independent Republic of Ireland, while the remainder is Northern Ireland, which is part of the UK. (32,588 sq miles/80,400 sq km, pop. 5,525,000)

Ireland, Republic of One of Europe's most westerly countries, situated in the Atlantic Ocean and separated from Great Britain by the Irish Sea. It has an equable climate, with mild southwest winds, which makes temperatures uniform over most of the country. The Republic extends over four-fifths of the island of Ireland, and the west and southwest are mountainous, with the highest peak reaching 3,416 feet (1,041 metres) at Carrauntoohil. The main rivers are the Erne and the Shannon. The central plain is largely limestone covered by boulder clay, which provides good farmland and pasture, with about 80 per cent of the land being under agriculture. Livestock production, including cattle, sheep, pigs, and horses, is the most important agricultural activity. The rural population have tended to migrate to the cities, mainly Dublin, which is the main industrial centre and the focus of radio, television, publishing, and communications. Lack of energy resources and remoteness from major markets did slow industrial development, but by taking full advantage of membership of the European Union the economy has improved markedly in recent years.

Area: 27,137 sq miles/70,284 sq km
Population: 3,781,000
Capital: Dublin (Baile Atha Cliath)
Other major cities: Cork, Galway, Limerick, Waterford
Form of government: Republic
Religion: RC
Currency: Euro

Irian Jaya the western half of the island of New Guinea, which has been part of Indonesia since 1963. (158,556 sq miles/410,660 sq km; pop. 2,762,000)

Irish Sea the arm of the Atlantic that separates Ireland and Great Britain.

Irkutsk an industrial city on the Trans-Siberian Railway lying near the southern end of Lake Baikal in the Russian Federation. (Pop. 594,000)

Irrawaddy a river which is the central focus of Myanmar, flowing from its two primary sources in the north of the country to Mandalay and then south to its delta in the Bay of Bengal. (Length 1,250 miles/2,000 km)

Irtysh a largely navigable river flowing northwards from its source near the border between northwest China and Mongolia across the centre of Kazakhstan and through the Siberian city of Omsk to join the River Ob' on its journey to the Arctic Ocean. (Length 2,760 miles/4,440 km)

Iskenderun a port of ancient origin in southern Turkey, in the northeastern corner of the Mediterranean Sea. (Pop. 180,000)

Islamabad the capital of Pakistan since 1967, in the north of the country. (Pop. 586,000)

Israel Occupying a long narrow stretch of land in the southeast of the Mediterranean, Israel's eastern boundary is formed by the Great Rift Valley through which the River Jordan flows to the Dead Sea. The south of the country is made up of a triangular wedge of the Negev Desert, which ends at the Gulf of Aqaba. The Negev has mineral resources, such as copper, phosphates, and manganese, plus commercial amounts of natural gas and petroleum. Other assets are the vast amounts of potash, bromine, and other minerals found in the Dead Sea. The climate in summer is hot and dry; in winter it is mild with some rain. The south of the country is arid and barren. Most of the population live on the coastal plain bordering the Mediterranean where Tel Aviv is the country's main commercial centre, as well as the site of most foreign embassies, since many countries do not recognize Jerusalem as the capital. The country is virtually self-sufficient in foodstuffs and a major exporter of its produce. A wide range of products is processed or finished in the country, and main exports include finished diamonds, textiles, fruit, vegetables, chemicals, machinery, and fertilizers. Tourism and foreign aid also makes an important contribution to the economy. Israel has had an uneasy relationship, which often flares into open conflict, with Palestinian nationals in the West Bank and Gaza Strip territories.

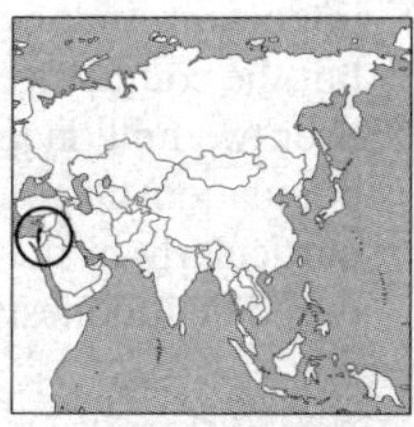

Area: 8,130 sq miles/21,056 sq km
Population: 6,100,000
Capital: Jerusalem
Other major cities: Tel Aviv, Haifa
Form of government: Republic
Religions: Judaism, Sunni Islam, Christianity
Currency: New Israeli Shekel

Issyk-Kul' a lake in southern central Kazakhstan, set in the high mountains that line the border with China. (2,424 sq miles/6,280 sq km)

Istanbul the largest city in Turkey, built mainly on the western bank of the Bosphorus strait, with a commanding view of shipping entering the Black Sea. It was founded by the Greeks in 660 BC and was known as Byzantium; between AD 330 and 1930 it was called Constantinople. (Pop. 9,216,000)

Italy A republic in southern Europe that comprises a large peninsula and the two main islands of Sicily and Sardinia. The Alps form a natural boundary with its northern and western European neighbours, and the Adriatic Sea to the east separates it from the countries of former Yugoslavia. The Apennine Mountains form the backbone of Italy and extend the full length of the peninsula. Between the Alps and the Apennines lies the Po Valley, a great fertile lowland. Sicily and Sardinia are largely mountainous. Much of Italy is geologically unstable, and it has a number of active volcanoes, the best known of which are Etna, Vesuvius and Stromboli. Italy enjoys warm dry summers and mild winters. In the south, farms are small and traditional. Industries in the north include motor vehicles, textiles, clothing, leather goods, glass, and ceramics. Although there is a lack of natural resources, almost 60 per cent of the land is under crops and pasture, and there is an abundance of building stone, particularly marble. The coastal waters are rich in marine life, with anchovy, sardine and tuna being of commercial importance. Tourism is an important source of foreign currency.

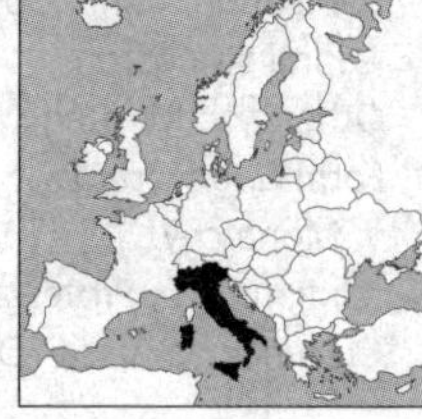

Area: 16,320 sq miles/301,268 sq km
Population: 58,082,000
Capital: Rome (Roma)
Other major cities: Milan, Naples, Turin, Genoa, Palermo
Form of government: Republic
Religion: RC
Currency: Euro

Ivanovo a textile manufacturing city in the Russian Federation, 150 miles (240 kilometres) northeast of Moscow. (Pop. 454,000)

Ivory Coast *see* **Côte d'Ivoire**.

Iwo Jima the largest in the group of islands called the Volcano Islands belonging to Japan, which lie some 745 miles (1,200 kilometres) south of Tokyo in the Pacific Ocean. (8 sq miles/21 sq km)

Ixtacihuatl a volcanic peak south of Mexico City, which is twinned with neighbouring Popocatépetl. (17,342 ft/5,286 m)

Izmir (Smyrna) a port of ancient Greek origin on the Aegean coast of Turkey, to the south of Istanbul. (Pop. 2,322,000)

Izmit (Kocaeli) a port and naval base on the Sea of Marmara, 90 km (55 miles) southeast of Istanbul. (Pop. 221,000)

J

Jackson the state capital of Mississippi, USA. (Pop. 186,000)

Jacksonville a port on the northeast coast of Florida, USA. (Pop. 774,000)

Jaffna a port on the tip of the northern peninsula of Sri Lanka, and the main centre for the Tamil population of the island. (Pop. 162,000)

Jaipur the capital of the state of Rajasthan, India. (Pop. 2,370,000)

Jakarta the capital of Indonesia and a port on the northwestern tip of Java. (Pop. 10,810,000)

Jamaica An island state in the Caribbean Sea about 93 miles (150 kilometres) south of Cuba. The centre of the island comprises a limestone plateau, and this is surrounded by narrow coastal flatlands and palm-fringed beaches. The highest mountains, the Blue Mountains, are in the east of the island. The climate is tropical, with high temperatures at the coast and slightly cooler and less humid conditions in the highlands. Jamaica suffers from severe earthquakes, and thermal springs can be found in areas of the country. The island lies right in the middle of the hurricane zone. The traditional crops grown are sugar cane, bananas, peppers, ginger, cocoa and coffee, and new crops such as winter vegetables, fruit, and honey are being developed for export. The mining of bauxite and alumina plays a very important part in Jamaica's economy and accounts for around 60 per cent of its total yearly exports. Industrialization has been encouraged, and clothing, footwear, cement, and agricultural machinery are now produced. Tourism is a particularly important industry, with over one million visitors annually.

Area: 4,243 sq miles/10,990 sq km
Population: 2,491,000
Capital: Kingston
Other city: Montego Bay
Form of government: Constitutional Monarchy
religions: RC, Protestantism, Anglicanism
Currency: Jamaican Dollar

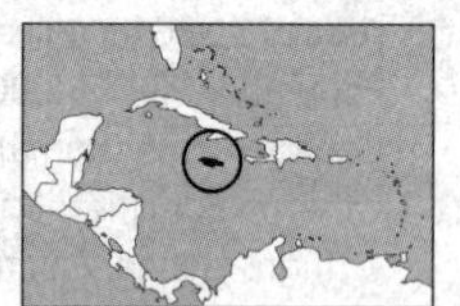

James Bay the southern arm of the Hudson Bay, Canada, which extends 273 miles (440 kilometres) into Ontario and Québec.

Jamestown the capital of St Helena in the southeast Atlantic. (Pop. 2,000)

Jammu and Kashmir the official name for the part of Kashmir presently under Indian control. Since 1947, Kashmir has been a disputed territory between India, Pakistan and China. A large area in northwest Kashmir is presently held by Pakistan and is known as Azad (Free) Kashmir, a smaller area in the east is held by China and the remaining area has been incorporated into India as the state of Jammu and Kashmir. (85,783 sq miles/222,236 sq km; pop. 10,267,000)

Jamshedpur an industrial city in northeast India. (Pop. 582,000)

Jamuna the name given to the river formed by the Brahmaputra and the Tista Rivers, as it flows through Bangladesh to join the Ganges River.

Japan Located on the eastern margin of Asia and consisting of four major islands, Honshu, Hokkaido, Kyushu, and Shikoku, and many small islands, Japan is separated from the mainland of Asia by the Sea of Japan. The country is made up of six chains of steep serrated mountains, which contain about 60 active volcanoes. Earthquakes are frequent and widespread and often accompanied by giant waves (tsunami). A devastating earthquake occurred in 1995 when more than 5,000 people died and over 300,000 were left homeless. Summers are warm and humid and winters mild, except on Hokkaido, which is covered in snow in winter. Japan's agriculture is highly advanced, with extensive use made of fertilizers and miniature machinery for the small fields. Fishing is very important, both for domestic consumption and export. Heavy industries, such as iron and steel, shipbuilding, chemicals and petrochemicals, used to account for almost three-quarters of Japan's export revenue, but now it relies on the success of its manufacturing industry which produces automobiles, televisions, videos, electronic equipment, cameras, watches, clocks, robots, and textiles. Japan's financial markets have experienced some problems in recent years, which has introduced some uncertainty into what was a very secure economy.

Area: 145,870 sq miles/377,801 sq km
Population: 125,761,000
Capital: Tokyo
Other major cities: Osaka, Nagoya, Sapporo, Kobe, Kyoto, Yokohama
Form of government: Constitutional Monarchy
Religions: Shintoism, Buddhism, Christianity
Currency: Yen

Japan, Sea of a part of the Pacific Ocean between Japan and Korea.

Java (Jawa) the central island in the southern chain of the islands of Indonesia. The capital is Jakarta. (50,574 sq miles/130,987 sq km; pop. 116,531,000)

Java Sea an arm of the Pacific Ocean that separates Java and Borneo.

Jefferson City the state capital of Missouri, USA. (Pop. 40,000)

Jena a university town in southern central Germany. (Pop. 98,000)

Jerez de la Frontera (Jerez) a town in southwest Spain, just inland from Cádiz, famous for sherry, the sweet wine to which it has given its name. (Pop. 186,000)

Jericho a town in the disputed territory of the West Bank, near the north end of the Dead Sea, on the site of a city that dates back to about 7000 BC. (Pop. 17,000)

Jersey the largest of the British Channel Islands. The capital is St Helier. (45 sq miles/117 sq km; pop. 89,000)

Jerusalem a historical city considered holy by Muslims, Christians and Jews, and the capital of Israel (although according to the UN and international law, the capital is Tel Aviv). (Pop. 685,000)

Jiangsu a heavily populated but highly productive province on the central east coast of China. The capital is Nanjing. (38,600 sq miles/100,000 sq km; pop. 76,815,000)

Jiangxi an inland province of southeastern China. Its capital is Nanchang. (64,300 sq miles/164,800 sq km; pop. 44,732,000)

Jiddah (Jedda) a port on the Red Sea coast of Saudi Arabia, and the port of entry for Mecca. (Pop. 2,674,000)

Jilin (Kirin) a province of central Dongbei (Manchuria) in northern China. The capital is Changchun. (69,500 sq miles/180,000 sq km; pop. 27,991,000)

Jinan the capital of Shandong Province, situated close to the Huang He River, 225 miles (360 kilometres) to the south of Beijing. (Pop. 1,728,000)

Jodhpur a city in central Rajasthan, India, on the perimeter of the Thar Desert. The city has given its name to the riding breeches that first became popular here. (Pop. 863,000)

Johannesburg a city in the province of Gauteng in north South Africa, and the country's largest city and chief industrial centre. (Pop. 1,646,000)

John o'Groats the village traditionally held to be on the most northerly point of mainland Scotland and Great Britain.

Johor Baharu (Johore) a port and growing city in Malaysia situated on the southern tip of the Malay Peninsula opposite Singapore, to which it is connected by a causeway. It is the capital of the state of Johor. (Pop. city 724,000)

Jordan Almost landlocked except for a short coastline on the Gulf of Aqaba, Jordan is bounded by Saudi Arabia, Syria, Iraq, and Israel. Almost 80 per cent of the country is desert and the rest comprises the East Bank Uplands and Jordan Valley, part of the Great Rift Valley. In general, summers are hot and dry and winters cool and wet, with variations related to altitude. The east has a desert climate. Since under 5 per cent of the land is arable, and only part of this is irrigated, production of grain is insufficient for the country's needs although some fruits and vegetables are grown for export. The capital, Amman, is the main industrial centre of the country, and industries include phosphates, petroleum products, cement, iron, and fertilizers. The rich Arab states, such as Saudi Arabia, give Jordan substantial economic aid and the country has a modern network of roads that link the cities. In 1994, a historical peace agreement was signed with Israel that ended 46 years of hostilities.

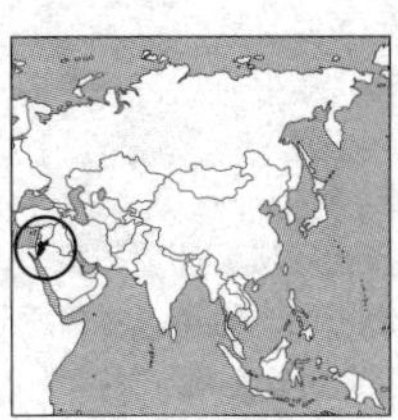

Area: 37,738 sq miles/97,740 sq km
Population: 5,581,000
Capital: Amman
Other cities: Irbid, Zarga
Form of government: Constitutional Monarchy
Religion: Sunni Islam
Currency: Jordanian Dinar

Jordan a river flowing southwards from Mount Hermon in southern Lebanon, through northern Israel to Lake Tiberias (Sea of Galilee) and then through Jordan to the Dead Sea, where it evaporates. The West Bank to the north of the Dead Sea is a disputed territory which was occupied by Israel during the Six Day War in 1967 but returned to the limited control of the Palestinian National Authority in 1994. (Length 159 miles/256 km)

Juan de Fuca Strait the channel to the south of Vancouver Island on the border between Canada and the USA, through which ships from Victoria, Vancouver and Seattle can pass to reach the Pacific Ocean.

Juan Fernández Islands a group of three remote islands in the Pacific Ocean belonging to Chile, some 400 miles (650 kilometres) due west of Santiago. (62 sq miles/181 sq km; pop. 280)

Judaea the southern part of ancient Palestine, occupying the area of modern Israel between the Mediterranean coast to the west and the Dead Sea and River Jordan to the east.

Juneau the state capital of Alaska, USA. (Pop. 32,000)

Jura a large upland band of limestone in eastern central France which lines the border with Switzerland, giving its name to a department in France and a canton in Switzerland. A further extension continues across southern Germany as far as Nuremberg (the Swabian and Franconian Jura).

Jutland (Jylland) a large peninsula stretching some 250 miles (400 kilometres) northwards from Germany to separate the North Sea from the Baltic Sea. Most of it is occupied by the mainland part of Denmark, while the southern part belongs to the German state of Schleswig-Holstein.

K

K2 (Godwin Austen) the second highest mountain in the world after Mount Everest, situated in the Karakoram mountain range on the disputed border between Pakistan and China. (28,250 ft/8,611 m)

Kabul the capital and main city of Afghanistan, in the northeast of the country on the Kabul River. (Pop. 2,142, 000)

Kagoshima a port on the south coast of Kyushu Island, Japan. (Pop. 554,000)

Kaifeng a city of ancient origins in Henan Province, China. (Pop. 584,000)

Kairouan a city in northern Tunisia, to Muslims the most holy city of the Maghreb region in northwest Africa. (Pop. 116,000)

Kalahari a region of semi-desert occupying much of southern Botswana and straddling the border with South Africa and Namibia.

Kalgoorlie a town in the south of Western Australia which has grown up around its gold and nickel reserves. (Pop. 31,000)

Kalimantan the greater part of Borneo, which is governed by Indonesia. (208,000 sq miles/538,718 sq km; pop. 12,339,000)

Kaliningrad (Königsberg) a port and industrial city on the Baltic coast belonging to the Russian Federation, in an enclave between Lithuania and Poland. Founded in the 13th century, it was called Königsberg and was the capital of the former East Prussia. (Pop. 425,000)

Kalmyk (Kalmuck) Republic an autonomous republic of the Russian Federation, lying to the northwest of the Caspian Sea. (29,300 sq miles/75,900 sq km; pop. 310,000)

Kamchatka a peninsula, some 750 miles (1,200 kilometres) long, which drops south from eastern Siberia into the north Pacific Ocean. (Pop. 356,000)

Kampala the capital and main city of Uganda, situated on Lake Victoria. (Pop. 500,000)

Kananga a city in central southern Democratic Republic of Congo, founded in 1894 as Luluabourg. (Pop. 540,000)

Kanazawa a historical port on the central northern coast of Honshu Island, Japan. (Pop. 465,000)

Kandahar the second largest city in Afghanistan, situated in the southeastern part of the country, near the border with Pakistan. (Pop. 399,000)

Kandy a town in the central mountains of Sri Lanka, which was once the capital of the Sinhalese kings and is sacred to Buddhists. (Pop. 111,000)

Kangchenjunga the world's third highest mountain (after Mount Everest and K2), situated in the eastern Himalayas, on the borders between Nepal, China and the Indian state of Sikkim. (28,165 ft/8,585 m)

KaNgwane one of ten former South African Homelands, the area is now part of the province of Mpumalanga in northeast South Africa.

Kano a historical trading city of the Hausa people of northern Nigeria, the second largest city in Nigeria. (Pop. city 3,249,000)

Kanpur (Cawnpore) an industrial city in northern central India. (Pop. 2,582,000)

Kansas a state in the Great Plains of the USA. The state capital is Topeka. (82,264 sq miles/213,064 sq km; pop. 2,701,000)

Kansas City the name given to two adjacent industrial cities built on the confluence of the Kansas and Missouri Rivers, one in the state of Kansas, the other in Missouri. (Pop. Kansas City, Kansas, 148,000; Kansas City, Missouri, 447,000)

Kao-hsiung the second largest city in Taiwan and a major port, situated in the southwest of the island. (Pop. 1,506,000)

Karachi a port and industrial centre, and the largest city in Pakistan. (Pop. 10,272,000)

Karaganda an industrial city in the mining region of Kazakhstan. (Pop. 412,000)

Karakoram a range of mountains at the western end of the Himalayas on the borders between Pakistan, China and India.

Kara Kum (Garagum, Karakumy) a sand desert in southern Turkmenistan, to the east of the Caspian Sea, and on the borders with Iran and Afghanistan.

Kara Sea a branch of the Arctic Ocean off the central northern coast of the Russian Federation.

Karbala a town in central Iraq, 55 miles (90 kilometres) south of Baghdad. As the site of the tomb of Hussein bin Ali and his brother Abbas, grandsons of the prophet Mohammed, it is held sacred by Shia Muslims. (Pop. 560,000)

Karelia a region which straddles the Finnish-Russian border.

Kariba Dam the hydroelectric dam on the River Zambezi on the border between Zambia and Zimbabwe which has created Lake Kariba. (Length 175 miles/282 kilometres)

Karlovy Vary (Carlsbad, Karlsbad) a spa town in the Czech Republic. (Pop. 54,000)

Karlsruhe (Carlsruhe) an industrial city in the valley of the River Rhine, in southwestern Germany. (Pop. 278,000)

Karnataka a state in southwest India. The capital is Bangalore. (74,031 sq miles/191,791 sq km; pop. 53,764,000)

Karoo (Karroo) an area of high semi-desert plateaux, including the Great Karoo and the Little Karoo, lying between the mountain ranges of southern South Africa.

Kasai (Cassai) a major river of the Democratic Republic of Congo. (Length 1,350 miles/2,150 km)

Kashmir a mountainous region of southwest central Asia. Since 1947, this region has been a disputed territory between India, Pakistan and China. A large area in the northwest of the region is held by Pakistan and is known as Azad (Free) Kashmir, a smaller area in the east is held by China and the remaining area has been incorporated into India as the state of Jammu and Kashmir.

Kassel (Cassel) an industrial city in central Germany. (Pop. 195,000)

Kathmandu (Katmandu) the capital and principal city of Nepal. (Pop. 713,000)

Katowice (Kattowitz) an industrial city in central southern Poland. (Pop. 336,000)

Kattegat (Cattegat) the strait, 21 miles (34 kilometres) at its narrowest, at the entrance to the Baltic Sea which separates Sweden from Jutland.

Kaunas (Kovno) an industrial city and former capital of Lithuania. (Pop. 382,000)

Kavango (Cubango) a river, known formerly as the Okavango, which flows southeast from central Angola to form the border with Namibia before petering out in the swampy inland Okavango Delta in northern Botswana. (Length 1,000 miles/1,600 km)

Kaveri (Caveri, Cauvery) a holy river of southern India, flowing southeast from the Deccan plateau to the coast on the Bay of Bengal. (Length 497 miles/800 km)

Kawasaki an industrial city on the east coast of Honshu Island, Japan, forming part of the Tokyo-Yokohama conurbation. (Pop. 1,272,000)

Kazakhstan The second largest republic of the former USSR, which extends from the coast of the Caspian Sea to the northwest corner of Mongolia. The west of the country is low-lying, the east hilly, and in the southeast mountainous areas include parts of the Tian Shan and Altai ranges. The climate is continental and very dry, with great extremes of temperature. Much of the country is desert and semi-desert, with wastelands of stone, sand, and salt. Crops can be grown only in the wetter northwest regions or on land irrigated by the Syrdar'ya River. Extensive pastoral farming is carried out, and cattle, sheep, and goats are the main livestock reared. The country is rich in minerals, particularly copper, lead, zinc, coal, tungsten, iron ore, oil, and gas. Kazakhstan declared itself independent in 1991, since when economic prospects have remained positive, although environmental problems have been left as a legacy of past Soviet exploitation and have still to be tackled (e.g. the overdraining of the Aral Sea). Parts of the country, particularly the mountainous regions, are subject to earthquakes and the former capital, Almaty, has been largely rebuilt following extensive damage. In 1997, the capital was moved to Astana, a city located in a more stable geological region.

Area: 1,049,156 sq miles/2,717,300 sq km
Population: 15,671,000
Capital: Astana
Other major city: Almaty
Form of government: Republic
Religion: Sunni Islam
Currency: Tenge

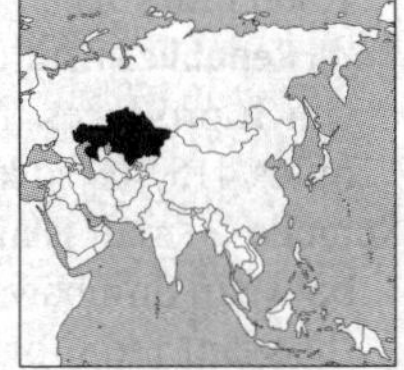

Kazan an industrial city and capital of the Tatar Republic in central Russian Federation. (Pop. 1,110,000)

Kells a market town in County Meath, Ireland. It was the site of a monastery founded in the 6th century by St Columba, which was the source of the illuminated Book of Kells.

Kemerovo an industrial city in southern Siberia. (Pop. 489,000)

Kent a county in the extreme southeast of England, with its administrative centre in Maidstone. (1,441 sq miles/3,732 sq km; pop. 1,546,000)

Kentucky a state in east central USA. The state capital is Frankfort. (40,395 sq miles/104,623 sq km; pop. 4,090,000)

Kenya Located in East Africa, Kenya straddles the Equator and extends from Lake Victoria in the southwest to the Indian Ocean in the southeast. Highlands run north to south through central Kenya and are divided by the steep-sided Great Rift Valley. The coastal lowlands have a hot humid climate but in the highlands it is cooler and rainfall heavier. In the east, it is very arid. The southwestern region is well watered, with huge areas of fertile soil, and this accounts for the bulk of the population and almost all its economic production. A wide variety of crops are grown for domestic consumption, such as wheat, maize, and cassava. Tea, coffee, sisal, sugar cane, and cotton are grown for export. Oil refining at Mombasa is the country's largest single industry, and other industry includes food processing and textiles. Mining is carried out on a small scale for soda ash, gold, and limestone, but large quantities of silver and lead exist near Mombasa. Tourism is an important source of foreign revenue, with the many wildlife and game reserves being a major attraction.

Area: 224,081 sq miles/580,367 sq km
Population: 31,806,000
Capital: Nairobi
Other cities: Mombasa, Kisumu
Form of government: Republic
Religions: RC, Protestantism, other Christianity, Animism
Currency: Kenyan Shilling

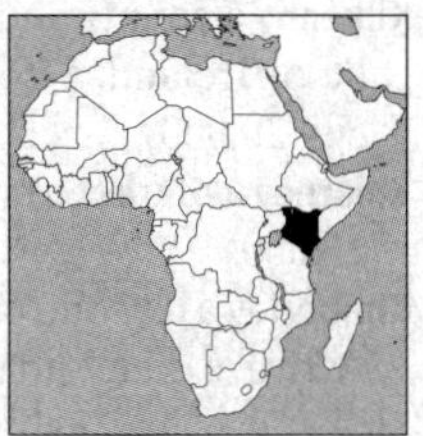

Kenya, Mount a towering extinct volcano in central Kenya, the second highest mountain in Africa after Mount Kilimanjaro. (17,058 ft/5,200 m)

Kerala a state occupying the western coast of the southern tip of India. The capital is Trivandrum. (15,005 sq miles/38,863 sq km; pop. 32,460,000)

Kerguelen the largest in a remote group of some 300 islands in the southern Indian Ocean forming part of the French Southern and Antarctic Territories, now occupied only by scientists. (1,318 sq miles/3,414 sq km)

Kerry a county in the southwest of the Republic of Ireland, noted for the rugged beauty of its peninsulas and its green dairy pastures. The county town is Tralee. (1,815 sq miles/4,701 sq km; pop. 132,000)

Key West a port and resort at the southern end of Florida Keys, a chain of coral islands off the southern tip of Florida, USA. (Pop. 27,000)

Khabarovsk a major industrial city in southeastern Siberia, lying just 22 miles (35 kilometres) north of the Russian border with China. (Pop. 606,000)

Kharg Island a small island in the northern Gulf where Iran has constructed a major oil terminal.

Khar'kov a major industrial and commercial centre of the Ukraine. (Pop. 1,460,000)

Khartoum (El Khartum) the capital of Sudan, situated at the confluence of the Blue Nile and White Nile. (Pop. 1,244,000)

Khone Falls a massive set of waterfalls on the Mekong River in southern Laos. With a maximum width of 6.7 miles (10.8 kilometres), these are the widest falls in the world.

Khorasan the northeastern province of Iran, bordering Afghanistan and Turkmenistan. The capital is Mashhad. (Pop. 6,085,000)

Khulna a port and district in southwest Bangladesh. (Pop. town 1,190,000)

Khuzestan (Khuzistan) a province in southwestern Iran, and the country's main oil-producing area. The capital is Ahvaz. (Pop. 4,537,000)

Khyber Pass a strategic route at a height of 3,518 feet (1,072 metres) over the Safed Koh Mountains connecting Peshawar in Pakistan with Kabul in Afghanistan.

Kiel a port and shipbuilding city on the Baltic coast of northern Germany. It stands at the mouth of the Kiel Ship Canal which permits ocean-going ships to cross the Jutland Peninsula from the Baltic to Hamburg and the North Sea. (Pop. 232,000)

Kielce (Kelsty) an industrial city in central southern Poland. (Pop. 210,000)

Kiev (Kiyev) the capital of Ukraine, situated on the Dnieper River. Founded in the 6th century, it is now a major industrial city. (Pop. 2,619,000)

Kigali the capital of Rwanda. (Pop. 291,000)

Kildare a county in the southeast of the Republic of Ireland, famous for its racehorses and the racecourse, the Curragh. The county town is Naas. (654 sq miles/1,694 sq km; pop. 141,000)

Kilimanjaro, Mount Africa's highest mountain, in northeastern Tanzania. (19,340 ft/5,895 m)

Kilkenny a county and county town in the southeast of the Republic of Ireland. (769 sq miles/2,062 sq km; pop. county 78,000/city 20,000)

Killarney a market town in county Kerry, Republic of Ireland. (Pop. 12,000)

Kimberley a city and capital of the Northern Cape Province, South Africa, a diamond mining and marketing centre. (Pop. 190,000)

Kimberleys, the (Kimberley Plateau) a vast plateau of hills and gorges in the north of Western Australia. (162,000 sq miles/420,000 sq km)

Kingston the capital and main port of Jamaica. (Pop. 584,000)

Kingston upon Hull (Hull) a port in the East Riding of Yorkshire in England, situated on the north side of the Humber estuary. (Pop. 309,000)

Kingstown a port and capital of St Vincent and the Grenadines. (Pop. 17,000)

Kinshasa the capital of Kinshasa, on the banks of the River Congo. It is the largest city in Central Africa. (Pop. 6,301,000)

Kiribati Formerly known as the Gilbert and Ellice Islands, Kiribati comprises three groups of coral atolls and one isolated volcanic island spread over a large expanse of the central Pacific Ocean. The group includes the former Gilbert Islands, the Phoenix Islands (now Rawaki), and the southern Line Islands. The largest island is Kiritimati, formerly known as Christmas Island. The climate is maritime equatorial, with a rainy season from October to March. Most islanders are involved in subsistence agriculture. Coconut, palm and breadfruit trees, bananas and papaws are grown, with coconuts and palm products being the main cash crops. Tuna fishing is an important industry. Ocean Island (Banaba) was a rich source of phosphate deposits (guano) but these are now exhausted and the mining has left severe environmental damage, causing most Banabans to resettle elsewhere. Tourism is becoming increasingly important but the country is still heavily dependent on overseas aid.

Area: 280 sq miles/726 sq km
Population: 80,000
Capital: Tarawa
Form of government: Republic
Religions: RC, Protestantism
Currency: Australian Dollar

Kiritimati the Pacific Ocean's largest coral atoll, situated at the northeastern end of the Kiribati group. (167 sq miles/432 sq km; pop. 5,000)

Kirkuk an industrial city and regional capital in the Kurdish north of Iraq. (Pop. 729,000)

Kirov an industrial city in east central Russian Federation, founded in the 12th century. (Pop. 464,000)

Kisangani a commercial centre and regional capital in northern Democratic Republic of Congo, on the River Congo. It was originally called Stanleyville. (Pop. 510,000)

Kishinev (Chisinau) the capital of Moldova. (Pop. 776,000)

Kita-Kyushu a major industrial city situated in the north of Kyushu Island, Japan. (Pop. 1,012,000)

Kitchener-Waterloo two towns in southern Ontario, Canada, which have become twin cities, 62 miles (100 kilometres) west of Toronto. (Pop. Kitchener 192,000/Waterloo 84,000)

Kivu, Lake a lake in the Great Rift Valley on the border between Rwanda and the Democratic Republic of Congo. (1,100 sq miles/2,850 sq km)

Kizil Irmak the longest river in Turkey, flowing westwards from the centre, before curling north to the Black Sea. (Length 700 miles/1,130 km)

Klaipeda a major port and shipbuilding centre on the Baltic coast of Lithuania. (Pop. 195,000)

Knock a village in County Mayo, in the west of the Republic of Ireland, where a group of villagers witnessed a vision of the Virgin Mary in 1879. It has now become a Marian shrine of world importance. (Pop. 1,400)

Knossos the site of an excavated royal palace of the Minoan civilization, 3 miles (5 kilometres) southeast of Iráklion, once the capital of Crete. The palace was built in about 1950 BC and destroyed in 1380 BC.

Knoxville state capital and industrial city in eastern Tennessee, USA, on the Tennessee River. (Pop. 177,000)

Kobe a major container port and shipbuilding centre at the southern end of Honshu Island, Japan. (Pop. 1,518,000)

Koblenz (Coblenz) a city at the confluence of the Rivers Rhine and Moselle in western Germany, and a centre for the German winemaking industry. (Pop. 109,000)

Kola Peninsula a bulging peninsula in the Barents Sea in the extreme northwest of the Russian Federation, to the east of Murmansk.

Kolonia the capital of the Federated States of Micronesia, on the island of Pohnpei. (Pop. 6,000)

Kolyma a river in northeastern Siberia, flowing north from the gold-rich Kolyma Mountains into the East Siberian Sea. (Length 1,600 miles/2,600 km)

Komi Republic an autonomous republic of the Russian Federation, which produces timber, coal, oil and natural gas. (160,600 sq miles/415,900 sq km; pop. 1,085,000)

Komodo a small island of Indonesia in the Lesser Sunda group, between Sumbawa and Flores, noted above all as the home of the giant monitor lizard, the Komodo Dragon. (200 sq miles / 520 sq km)

Konya a carpetmaking town and capital of the province of the same name in central southern Turkey. (Pop. 696,000)

Korea, Democratic People's Republic of (North Korea) A country occupying the northern half of the Korean Peninsula in east Asia, still widely known as North Korea. The Yala and Tumen Rivers form its northern border with China and the Russian Federation. Its southern border with the Republic of Korea is just north of the 38th parallel. It is a mountainous country, three-quarters of which is forested highland or scrubland, with Paektu-San the highest peak at 9,003 feet (2,737 metres). The climate is warm temperate, although winters can be cold in the north. Most rain falls during the summer. Nearly 90 per cent of its arable land is farmed by cooperatives that employ over 40 per cent of the labour force, and rice is the main crop grown. North Korea is quite well endowed with fuel and minerals such as magnesite, zinc, copper, lead, tungsten, gold, and silver. Deposits of coal and hydroelectric power generate electricity, and substantial deposits of iron ore are found near Pyongyang and Musan. Sixty per cent of the labour force is employed in industry, the most important of which are metallurgical, building, cement, and chemicals. Fishing is carried on, with the main catches being tuna, anchovy, and seaweeds.

Area: 46,540 sq miles/120,538 sq km
Population: 22,466,000
Capital: Pyongyang
Other major cities: Hamhung, Chongjin
Form of government: Socialist Republic
Religions: Chondoism, Buddhism
Currency: Won

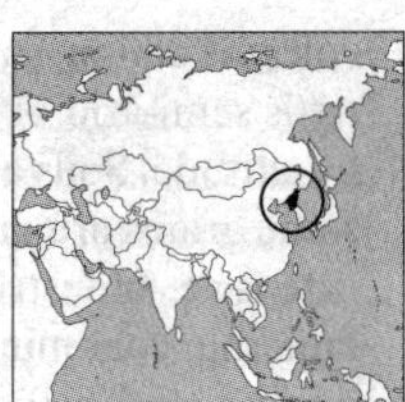

Korea, Republic of (South Korea) The Republic of Korea (still widely known as South Korea) occupies the southern half of the Korean Peninsula in eastern Asia. It is bordered in the north by a demilitarized zone which acts as a buffer between it and the Democratic People's Republic of Korea. Most of the country is hilly or mountainous, with the highest ranges running north to south along the east coast. The west is lowland and extremely densely populated. The extreme south has a humid warm temperate climate while farther north it is more continental. Most rain falls in summer. Cultivated land represents only 23 per cent of the country's total area, and the main crops are rice, onions, potatoes, barley, and maize. An increasing amount of fruit, such as melons, apples, and peaches, is now produced. The country has few natural resources but does produce coal, graphite, and iron ore. It has a flourishing manufacturing industry and is the world's leading supplier of ships and footwear. Other important industries are electronic equipment, electrical goods, steel, petrochemicals, motor vehicles, and toys.

Area: 38,368 sq miles/99,373 sq km
Population: 46,430,000
Capital: Seoul (Soul)
Other major cities: Pusan, Taegu, Inch'on
Form of government: Republic
Religions: Buddhism, Christianity
Currency: Won

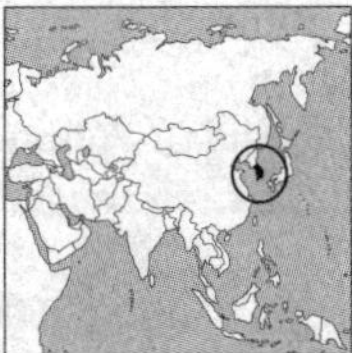

Korea Strait the stretch of water, 40 miles (64 kilometres) at its narrowest, which separates the southern tip of South Korea from Japan. It is also sometimes known as the Tsushima Strait, after the island of that name.

Koror the capital of Palau. (Pop. 11,000)

Kos (Cos) one of the Dodecanese Islands, belonging to Greece, in the Aegean Sea. (112 sq miles/290 sq km; pop. 20,300)

Kosciusko, Mount the highest mountain in Australia, a peak in the Snowy Mountains range in southern New South Wales. (7,316 ft/2,230 m)

Kosice a rapidly growing industrial city, and the regional capital of eastern Slovakia. (Pop. 245,000)

Kosovo an autonomous province in the southwest of Serbia, in the former Yugoslavia. About 75 per cent of the population are ethnic Albanians. The capital is Pristina. The country was the scene of a wave of repression by the Serbian government after an ethnic Albanian independence campaign that turned into open warfare. After the NATO bombing of Serbia in 1999, Kosovo became an international protectorate. (4,202 sq miles/10,887 sq km; pop. 1,954,000)

Kra, Isthmus of the narrow neck of land, only some 30 miles (50 kilometres) wide and shared by Myanmar and Thailand, which joins the Malay Peninsula to the mainland of Southeast Asia.

Krakatau (Krakatoa) a volcano which erupted out of the sea between Java and Sumatra in Indonesia in 1883 in an explosion that was heard 3,100 miles (5,000 kilometres) away, and which killed 36,000 people. Today the site is marked by a more recent volcano called Anak Krakatau (Son of Krakatau).

Krasnodar an agricultural centre and industrial city in the Russian Federation near the Black Sea. (Pop. 643,000)

Krasnoyarsk a mining city on the Trans-Siberian Railway in central southern Siberia. (Pop. 870,000)

Krefeld a textile town specializing in silk in western Germany, near the border with the Netherlands. (Pop. 238,000)

Krishna (Kistna) a river that flows through southern India from its source in the Western Ghats to the Bay of Bengal. (Length 871 miles/1,401 km)

Krivoy Rog a city in the Donets Basin region of Ukraine. (Pop. 686,000)

Krk (Veglia) a richly fertile island belonging to Croatia, in the northern Adriatic Sea. (158 sq miles/408 sq km; pop. 1,500)

Kuala Lumpur the capital of Malaysia, sited on the banks of the Kelang and Gombak Rivers. (Pop. 1,367,000)

Kumamoto a city in the west of Kyushu Island, Japan, noted for its electronics industries. (Pop. 666,000)

Kumasi a town in central southern Ghana, and the capital of the Ashanti people. (Pop. 627,000)

Kunming an industrial and trading city, and capital of Yunnan Province in southern central China. (Pop. 871,000)

Kurashiki a city in southwestern Honshu Island, Japan. Although now a major industrial centre, it still preserves much of its medieval heritage. (Pop. 431,000)

Kurdistan a region of the Middle East occupied by the Kurdish people, spanning the borders of Iraq, Iran and Turkey.

Kuril (Kurile) Islands a long chain of some 56 volcanic islands stretching between the southern coast of the Kamchatka Peninsula in eastern Russian Federation and Hokkaido Island, northern Japan. The archipelago was taken from Japan by the former USSR in 1945; this remains an issue of contention between the Russian Federation and Japan. (6,020 sq miles/15,600 sq km)

Kursk a major industrial city in the Russian Federation, 280 miles (450 kilometres) south of Moscow. (Pop. 443,000)

Kurukshetra a sacred Hindu city in northern India, 87 miles (140 kilometres) north of Delhi. (Pop. 190,000)

Kutch (Kuchchh), Rann of an inhospitable coastal region on the border between Pakistan and India, which floods in the monsoon season and then dries out into a baking, salty desert. (17,060 sq miles/44,185 sq km)

Kuwait A tiny Arab state on The Gulf, comprising the city of Kuwait at the southern entrance of Kuwait Bay, a small undulating desert wedged between Iraq and Saudi Arabia, and nine small offshore islands. It has a dry desert climate, cool in winter but very hot and humid in summer. There is little agriculture because of lack of water. The major crops produced are melons, tomatoes, onions, and dates. The country's water comes from the desalination of seawater. Shrimp fishing is becoming an important industry. Large reserves of petroleum and natural gas are the mainstay of the economy although this wealth is limited. It has about 950 oil wells, but 600 were fired during the Iraqi occupation in 1991. Apart from oil, industries includes boat building, plastics, petrochemicals, gases, cement, and building materials. Although there are no railways, there are over 2,000 miles (3,220 kilometres) of roads and an international airport near the capital.

Area: 6,880 sq miles/17,818 sq km
Population: 1,866,000
Capital: Kuwait City (Al Kuwayt)
Form of government: Constitutional Monarchy
Religions: Sunni Islam, Shia Islam
Currency: Kuwaiti Dinar

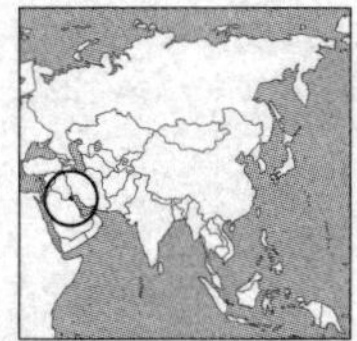

Kwai two tributaries of the Mae Khlong River in western Thailand, the Kwai Yai (Big Kwai) and the Kwai Noi (Little Kwai).

Kwajalein one of the largest atolls in the world, with a lagoon covering some 1,100 square miles (2,800 square kilometres). The island forms part of the Marshall Islands in the Pacific Ocean, and is leased to the USA as a missile target.

KwaNdebele one of ten former South African Homelands, the area is now part of the province of Mpumalanga in northeastern South Africa.

Kwangju (Gwangju, Chonnam) an industrial city and regional capital in the southwestern corner of South Korea. (Pop. 1,371,000)

Kwango (Cuango) a river which rises in northern Angola and flows northwards to join the River Kasai in Democratic Republic of Congo. (Length 68 miles/110 km)

KwaZulu/Natal one of South Africa's nine provinces, in northeastern South Africa, with its administrative centre in Durban. (35,591 sq miles/92,100 sq km; pop. 9,360,000)

Kyoto situated in central southern Honshu Island, this was the old imperial capital of Japan from AD 794 to 1868. (Pop. 1,472,000)

Kyrgyzstan A central Asian republic of the former USSR, independent since 1991. It is located on the border with northwest China. Much of the country is occupied by the Tian Shan Mountains, which rise to spectacular peaks. The highest is Pik Pobedy at 24,406 feet (7,439 metres) on the border with China. In the northeast of the country is Issyk Kul, a large lake heated by volcanic action, so it never freezes in winter. Most of the country is semi-arid or desert, but the climate is greatly influenced by altitude. Soils are badly leached except in the valleys, where some grains are grown. Grazing of sheep, horses, and cattle is extensive. Industries include non-ferrous metallurgy, machine building, coal mining, tobacco, food processing, textiles, gold mining, and hydroelectricity. The country has large mineral deposits of gold, coal, and uranium, while deposits of natural gas and oil have not, as yet, been developed. Parts of Kyrgyzstan are threatened by environmental pollution caused by storage of toxic waste and radioactive material which are the by-products of mining, former nuclear tests and the overuse of chemicals, especially fertilizers. The government is making efforts to address this problem, and to encourage foreign visitors.

Area: 76,641 sq miles/198,500 sq km
Population: 4,575,000
Capital: Bishkek (formerly Frunze)
Form of government: Republic
Religion: Sunni Islam
Currency: Som

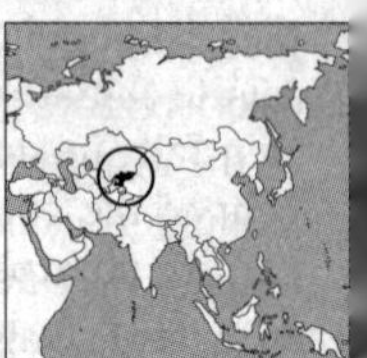

Kyushu the most southerly of Japan's main islands, and the third largest after Honshu and Hokkaido. (16,627 sq miles/43,065 sq km; pop. 13,276,000)

L

Labrador the mainland part of the province of Newfoundland, on the east coast of Canada. (112,826 sq miles/295,800 sq km)

La Coruña (A Coruña, Corunna) a port and manufacturing town in northwest Spain, and also the name of the surrounding province. (Pop. 241,000)

Ladakh a remote and mountainous district in the northeastern part of the disputed state of Jammu and Kashmir, India, noted for its numerous monasteries which preserve the traditions of Tibetan-style Buddhism. The capital is Leh. (Pop. 118,000)

Ladoga (Laatokka), Lake (Ladozshkoye Ozero) Europe's largest lake, in the Russian Federation, northeast of St Petersburg. (7,100 sq miles/18,390 sq km)

Lagos the principal port and former capital (until 1991) of Nigeria, situated on the Bight of Benin. (Pop. 8,029,000)

Lahore a city in east central Pakistan. (Pop. 5,612,000)

Lake District a region of lakes and mountains in the county of Cumbria, in northwest England famed for their beauty. It includes England's highest peak, Scafell Pike (3,208 ft/978 m).

Lake of the Woods a lake spattered with some 17,000 islands in southwestern Ontario, Canada, on the USA border. (1,695 sq miles/4,390 sq km)

Lakshadweep a territory of India consisting of 27 small islands (the Amindivi Islands, Laccadive Islands and Minicoy Islands) lying 186 miles (300 kilometres) off the southwest coast of mainland India. (12 sq miles/32 sq km; pop. 62,000)

La Mancha a high, arid plateau in central Spain, some 100 miles (160 kilometres) south of Madrid, the setting for *Don Quixote*, a 17th-century novel by Miguel de Cervantes.

Lambaréné a provincial capital in eastern central Gabon, famous as the site of the hospital founded by Albert Schweitzer (1875–1965). (Pop. 19,000)

Lancashire a county in northwest England, once the heart of industrial Britain, with its administrative centre in Preston. (1,182 sq miles/3,063 sq km; pop. 1,424,000)

Landes a department of the Aquitaine region on the coast of southwest France. (Pop. 341,000)

Land's End the tip of the peninsula formed by Cornwall in southwest England, and the most westerly point of mainland England.

Languedoc-Rousillon a region of France which lines the Mediterranean coast from the River Rhône to the border with Spain. (10,567 sq miles/27,376 sq km; pop. 2,363,000)

Lansing the state capital of Michigan, USA. (Pop. 120,000)

Lantau the largest of the islands which form part of the New Territories of Hong Kong. (58 sq miles/150 sq km; pop. 17,000)

Lanzhou a major industrial city and the capital of Gansu Province, central China. (Pop. 1,434,000)

Laois a county in the centre of the Republic of Ireland. The county town is Portlaoise. (664 sq miles/1,718 sq km; pop. 55,000)

Laos A landlocked country in southeast Asia that is ruggedly mountainous, apart from the Mekong River plains along its border with Thailand. The Annam Mountains, which reach 8,203 feet (2,500 metres), form a natural border with Vietnam. It has a tropical monsoon climate, with high temperatures throughout the year and heavy rains in summer. Laos is one of the poorest countries in the world and its development has been retarded by war, drought, and floods. It is primarily an agricultural country, with rice, the principal crop, being grown on small peasant plots. The mighty Mekong River provides the main means of transport as well as irrigation for the rice paddies upon which the people's subsistence depends. Corn, potatoes, and cassava are also grown. There is some export of lumber, coffee, tin, and electricity. All manufactured goods (mainly food, machinery, petroleum products, and electrical equipment) must be imported. The capital and largest city, Vientiane, is the country's main trade outlet via Thailand.

Area: 91,429 sq miles/236,800 sq km
Population: 5,035,000
Capital: Vientiane
Form of government: People's Republic
Religion: Buddhism
Currency: New Kip

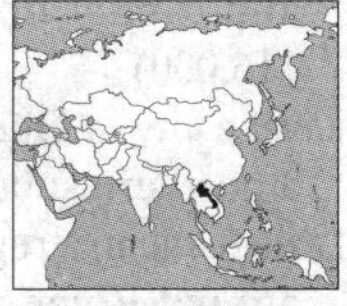

La Paz a city set high in the Andes of Bolivia, and the capital and seat of government. (Pop. 805,000)

La Plata a port on the estuary of the River Plate (Río de la Plata) in northeastern Argentina, southeast of Buenos Aires. (Pop. 820,000)

Lappland (Lapland) the region of northern Scandinavia and the adjoining territory of the Russian Federation, traditionally inhabited by the nomadic Lapp people; also called 'Land of the Midnight Sun'.

Laptev Sea part of the Arctic Ocean bordering central northern Siberia.

Larnaca a port, with an international airport, on the southeast coast of Cyprus. (Pop. 45,000)

Larne a district council area in Co. Antrim, northeast Northern Ireland. (130 sq miles/336 sq km; pop. 29,000)

Lascaux a set of caves in the Dordogne department of southwest France with Paleolithic wall paintings dating back to about 15000 BC.

Las Palmas de Gran Canaria the main port and largest city of the Canary Islands, on the island of Gran Canaria. (Pop. 366,000)

Las Vegas a city in the southeast of the state of Nevada, USA. This state's liberal gaming laws has allowed it to develop as a centre for gambling and entertainment. (Pop. 525,000)

Latakia (Al Ladhiqiyah) a city on the Mediterranean coast of Syria, founded by the Romans, and now that country's main port. (Pop. 404,000)

Latvia A Baltic state that regained its independence in 1991 with the break-up of the former Soviet Union. It is located in northeast Europe on the Baltic Sea and is sandwiched between Estonia and Lithuania. It has cool, wet summers, and long, cold winters. Traditionally, Latvians lived by forestry, fishing, and livestock rearing. Latvia's population is now over 70 per cent urban and agriculture is no longer the mainstay of the economy. The chief agricultural occupations are cattle and dairy farming, and the main crops grown are oats, barley, rye, potatoes, and flax. Latvia has a well-developed industrial base and produces electric railway carriages, electronic and electrical equipment (radios and refrigerators), paper, cement, chemicals, textiles, woollen goods, furniture, and foodstuffs. Latvia has abundant deposits of peat and gypsum but lacks other fossil fuels and minerals, which has made it heavily dependent on imported oil, gas, and electricity. Hydroelectric plants on the Daugava River supply over half of the domestic production of electricity. Economic development was difficult in the years following independence but the situation is gradually improving and Latvia is seeking full membership of the European Union.

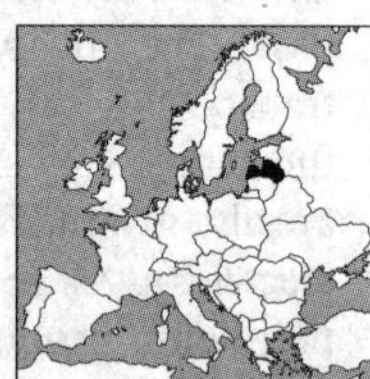

Area: 24,942 sq miles/64,600 sq km
Population: 2,491,000
Capital: Riga
Other cities: Daugavpils, Liepaja
Form of government: Republic
Religion: Lutheranism
Currency: Lat

Lausanne a city on the north shore of Lake Geneva, Switzerland, and capital of the French-speaking canton of Vaud. (Pop. 116,000)

Laval a city in Québec Province, Canada, which effectively forms a northern suburb of Montréal. (Pop. 338,000)

Lazio (Latium) a region occupying the central western coast of Italy around Rome, the regional capital. (6,642 sq miles/17,203 sq km; pop. 5,315,000)

Lebanon A mountainous country in the eastern Mediterranean. A narrow coastal plain runs parallel to its 149-mile (240-kilometre) Mediterranean coast and gradually rises to the spectacular Lebanon Mountains, which are snow-covered in winter. The Anti-Lebanon Mountains form the border with Syria, and between the two ranges lies the Beqa'a Valley. The climate is Mediterranean, with short warm winters and long hot and rainless summers. Rainfall can be torrential in winter and snow falls on high ground. Lebanon is an agricultural country, the main regions of production being the Beqa'a Valley and the coastal plain, although erosion is a common problem in the uplands. Main products include olives, grapes, bananas, citrus fruits, apples, cotton, tobacco, and sugar beet. Industry is small scale and manufactured goods include cement, fertilizers, and jewellery. There are oil refineries at Tripoli and Sidon. Lebanon's main economy is based on commercial services such as banking, but civil war, invasion by Israel, and factional fighting in the more recent past have created severe problems for the economy, causing high inflation and unemployment.

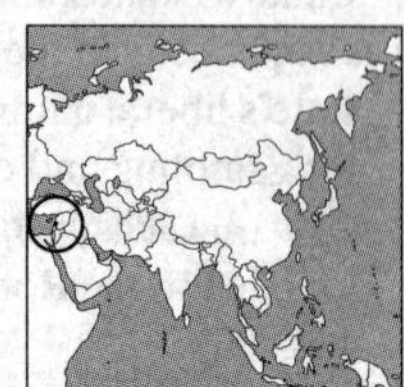

Area: 4,015 sq miles/10,400 sq km
Population: 3,084,000
Capital: Beirut (Beyrouth)
Other cities: Tripoli, Sidon
Form of government: Republic
Religions: Shia Islam, Sunni Islam, Christianity
Currency: Lebanese Pound

Lebowa one of ten former South African Homelands, the area is now part of the province of Limpopo in north South Africa.

Lecce a historical city in the Puglia region of Italy. (Pop. 98,000)

Leeds an important commercial and industrial town on the River Aire in West Yorkshire, in northern England. (Pop. 420,000)

Leeward and Windward Islands (1) the Lesser Antilles in the southern Caribbean are divided into two groups: the northern islands in the chain, from the Virgin Islands to Guadeloupe are the Leeward Islands; the islands further south, from Dominica to Grenada, form the Windward Islands. (2) the Society Islands of French Polynesia are also divided into Leeward and Windward Islands.

Le Havre the largest port on the north coast of France. (Pop. 190,000)

Leicester a historical cathedral city, and the administrative centre of Leicestershire, England. (Pop. 319,000)

Leicestershire a county in central England, with its administrative centre in Leicester. (834 sq miles/2,553 sq km; pop. 593,000)

Leiden (Leyden) a university city in western Netherlands. (Pop. 120,000)

Leinster one of the four ancient provinces into which the Republic of Ireland was divided, covering the southeastern quarter of the country.

Leipzig an industrial city and important cultural centre in southeastern Germany. (Pop. 410,000)

Leitrim a county in the northwest of the Republic of Ireland, with a small strip of coast and a border with Northern Ireland. The county town is Carrick-on-Shannon. (589 sq miles/1,525 sq km; pop. 26,000)

Léman, Lake another name for Lake Geneva.

Le Mans a university city in northwestern France, famous for the 24-hour car race held annually at a circuit nearby. (Pop. 148,000)

Lena a river which flows north across eastern Siberia, from its source close to Lake Baikal to the Laptev Sea. (Length 2,650 miles/4,270 km)

Lens an industrial town in the coal-mining region of northern France. (Pop. 36,000)

Léon (1) a major manufacturing city in central Mexico. (Pop. 1,052,000) (2) a historical city, founded by the Romans, in northwest Spain, and capital of the province of the same name. (Pop. 136,000)

Lesbos a large, fertile island in the Aegean, belonging to Greece, but only 6 miles (10 kilometres) from Turkey. (630 sq miles/1,630 sq km; pop. 106,000)

Lesotho A small, landlocked kingdom entirely surrounded by the Republic of South Africa. Snow-capped mountains and treeless uplands, cut by spectacular gorges, cover two-thirds of the country. The climate is pleasant with variable rainfall. Winters are generally dry with heavy frosts in lowland areas and frequent snow in the highlands. Because of the mountainous terrain, only one-eighth of the land can be cultivated and the main crop is maize. Yields are low because of soil erosion on the steep slopes and overgrazing by herds of sheep and cattle. Wool and mohair are exported but most foreign exchange comes from money sent home by Lesotho workers in South Africa. Tourism is beginning to flourish.

Area: 11,720 sq miles/30,355 sq km
Population: 2,078,000
Capital: Maseru
Form of government: Constitutional Monarchy
Religions: RC, other Christianity
Currency: Loti

Lesser Sunda Islands (Nusa Tenggara) a chain of islands in the Malay Archipelago, to the east of Java and stretching from Bali to Timor.

Lexington (Lexington-Fayette) (1) a city in the blue grass region of central Kentucky, USA. (Pop. 264,000) (2) a city in Massachusetts, USA, site of the first battle of the War of American Independence. (Pop. 29,000)

Leyte an island in the central Philippines, one of the Visayan Islands group. The main town is Tacloban. (2,785 sq miles/7,213 sq km; pop. 1,480,000)

Lhasa the capital of Tibet, an autonomous region of China. It lies 11,830 feet (3,606 metres) above sea level. (Pop. 115,000)

Liaoning a coastal province of Dongbei (Manchuria), northeast China, bordering North Korea. The capital is Shenyang. (54,000 sq miles/140,000 sq km; pop. 44,640,000)

Liberia Located in West Africa, Liberia has a 348-mile (560-kilometre) coast stretching from Sierra Leone to Côte d'Ivoire. It is the only African country never to be ruled by a foreign power. It has a treacherous coast, with rocky cliffs and lagoons enclosed by sand bars. Inland the land rises to a densely forested plateau dissected by deep, narrow valleys. Farther inland still, there are beautiful waterfalls and the Nimba Mountains rise to a maximum height of 5,748 feet (1,752 metres). Agriculture employs three-quarters of the labour force, producing cassava and rice as subsistence crops, and rubber, coffee, and cocoa for export. The Nimba Mountains are rich in iron ore, which accounts for 70 per cent of export earnings, and wood, rubber, diamonds, and coffee are also exported. Liberia has a very large delivery tanker fleet, most of which have foreign owners. In the early 1990s, the economy suffered greatly because of civil war, leading to food shortages and the drying up of foreign investment. The situation remains uncertain, leaving Liberia with considerable problems to overcome.

Area: 43,000 sq miles/111,369 sq km
Population: 2,440,000
Capital: Monrovia
Form of government: Republic
Religions: Animism, Sunni Islam, Christianity
Currency: Liberian Dollar

Libreville the capital and main port of Gabon. It is so called ('Freetown') because it was originally a settlement for freed slaves. (Pop. 541,000)

Libya A large North African country that stretches from the south coast of the Mediterranean to, and in some parts beyond, the Tropic of Cancer. The Sahara covers much of the country, extending right to the Mediterranean coast at the Gulf of Sirte. The only green areas are the scrublands found in the northwest and the forested hills near Benghazi. The coastal area has mild, wet winters and hot, dry summers, while the interior has had some of the highest recorded temperatures of anywhere in the world. Around 18 per cent of the people work on the land, the main agricultural region being in the northwest, near Tripoli, but this is dependent on rainfall. The main crops produced are wheat, tomatoes, fruits, and barley. Many sheep, goats, and cattle are reared, and there is an export trade in skins, hides, and hairs. Libya is one of the world's largest producers of oil and natural gas and also produces potash and marine salt. Other industries include food processing, textiles, cement, and handicrafts. The majority of consumer products are imported.

Area: 679,362 sq miles/1,759,540 sq km
Population: 4,389,000
Capital: Tripoli (Tarabulus)
Other cities: Benghazi, Misrātah
Form of government: Socialist People's Republic
Religion: Sunni Islam
Currency: Libyan Dinar

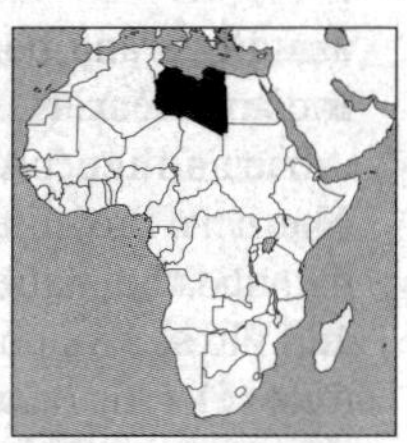

Liechtenstein The principality of Liechtenstein is a tiny central European state situated on the east bank of the River Rhine, bounded by Austria to the east and Switzerland to the west. To the east and south lie the foothills of the Austrian Alps. The highest peak, on the border with Switzerland, is Grauspitz at 8,527 feet (2,599 metres). The climate is mild alpine. Approximately one-third of the country is covered by forests. Once an agricultural country, Liechtenstein has rapidly moved into industry with a variety of light industries such as textiles, high-quality metal goods, precision instruments, ceramics, and pharmaceuticals. It is a popular location for the headquarters of foreign companies in order that they can benefit from the favourable tax laws. Other income is derived from tourism, international banking and financial services, and the sale of postage stamps.

Area: 62 sq miles/160 sq km
Population: 31,320
Capital: Vaduz
Form of government: Constitutional Monarchy
Religion: RC
Currency: Swiss Franc

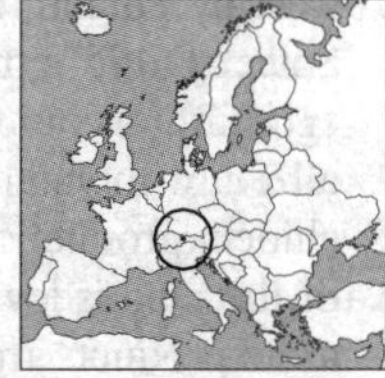

Liège (Luik) a historical city in eastern Belgium, and capital of the province of Liège, built on the confluence of the Rivers Meuse and Ourthe. (Pop. 184,000)

Liffey the river upon which Dublin, the capital of the Republic of Ireland, is set. (Length 49 miles/80 km)

Liguria the region of northwestern Italy which fronts the Gulf of Genoa; it has a border with France. (2,091 sq miles/5,415 sq km; pop. 1,603,000)

Ligurian Sea the northern arm of the Mediterranean Sea to the west of Italy, which includes the Gulf of Genoa.

Lille a commercial and industrial town in northwestern France. (Pop. 181,000)

Lilongwe the capital of Malawi, and the second largest city in the country after Blantyre. (Pop. 486,000)

Lima the capital of Peru, situated on the banks of the River Rimac, 8 miles (13 kilometres) from the coast. (Pop. 7,604,000)

Limassol the main port of Cyprus, in the south. (Pop. 27,000)

Limavady a district council area in Co. Londonderry, north Northern Ireland. (226 sq miles/586 sq km; pop. 30,000)

Limerick a city and port on the River Shannon, and the county town of the county of Limerick, in the southwest of the Republic of Ireland. (County 1,037 sq miles/2,686 sq km; pop. county 172,000; pop. city 82,000)

Limoges a city in eastern central France, famous for its richly decorated porcelain. It is the capital of the Limousin region. (Pop. 133,000)

Limousin a region of east-central France in the foothills of the Massif Central, famous in particular for its Limousin cattle.

Limpopo (1) a river in east South Africa which flows northwards and eastwards to form part of the border between South Africa and Botswana before crossing southern Mozambique to the Indian Ocean. (Length 1,000 miles/1,610 km) (2) one of South Africa's nine provinces, in north South Africa, formerly Northern Province and before that part of Northern Transvaal, with its administrative centre in Pietersburg. (47,829 sq miles/123,910 sq km; pop. 4,929,368)

Lincoln (1) a historical city in east central England, with a cathedral dating from the 11th century, and the administrative centre for Lincolnshire. (Pop. 81,000) (2) the state capital of Nebraska, USA. (Pop. 209,000)

Lincolnshire a county on the east coast of central England, with its administrative centre in Lincoln. (2,936 sq miles/7,604 sq km; pop. 922,000)

Linz a port city on the River Danube in northern Austria. (Pop. 186,000)

Lion, Golfe du (Lions, Gulf of) the arm of the Mediterranean Sea which forms a deep indent in the southern coast of France.

Lisbon (Lisboa) the capital and principal port of Portugal, situated on the broad River Tagus, near the Atlantic coast. (Pop. 558,000)

Lisburn (1) a town in Northern Ireland in the Lisburn district council area of Co. Antrim, noted for its linen industry. (Pop. 42,000) (2) a district council area in Co. Antrim, south Northern Ireland. (172 sq miles/446 sq km; pop. 100,000)

Lithuania A country that lies to the northwest of the Russian Federation and Belarus and is bounded to the north by Latvia and west by Poland. Lithuania is the largest of the three former Soviet Baltic republics. Before 1940, Lithuania was a mainly agricultural country but it has since been considerably industrialized, with shipbuilding, food processing, and electrical machinery production being the most significant industries. Most of the land is lowland, covered by forest and swamp, and the main products are rye, barley, sugar beet, flax, meat, milk, and potatoes. About 20 per cent of the population is engaged in agriculture, principally dairy farming and livestock production. Oil production has started from a small field at Kretinga in the west of the country, 10 miles (16 kilometres) north of Klaipeda. Amber is found along the Baltic coast and used by Lithuanian craftsmen for making jewellery. Financial scandals involving government members and banking institutions troubled the economy during the 1990s.

Area: 25,174 sq miles/65,200 sq km
Population: 3,701,000
Capital: Vilnius
Other cities: Kaunas, Klaipeda, Siauliai
Form of government: Republic
Religion: RC
Currency: Litas

Little Rock the state capital of Arkansas, USA. (Pop. 186,000)

Liverpool a major port on the estuary of the River Mersey in northwest England; it is the administrative centre of Merseyside. (Pop. 466,000)

Livorno (Leghorn) a port and industrial city on the coast of Tuscany, northern Italy. (Pop. 161,000)

Ljubljana an industrial city on the River Sava, and the capital of Slovenia. (Pop. 258,000)

Lódz an industrial city and the second largest city in Poland, located in the centre of the country. (Pop. 784,000)

Logan, Mount the highest mountain in Canada, and the second highest in North America after Mount McKinley. It is situated in southwest Yukon, on the border with Alaska. (19,524 ft/5,951 m)

Loire the longest river in France, flowing northwards from the southeastern Massif Central and then to the west to meet the Atlantic Ocean near Nantes. Its middle reaches are famous for their spectacular châteaux. (Length 635 miles/1,020 km)

Lombardy (Lombardia) the central northern region of Italy, which drops down from the Alps to the plain of the River Po, one of the country's most productive areas in both agriculture and industry. Milan is the regional capital. (9,210 sq miles/23,854 sq km; pop. 9,053,000)

Lombok an island of the Lesser Sunda group, east of Bali. (2,098 sq miles/5,435 sq km; pop. 1,300,200)

Lomé the capital and main port of Togo, situated close to the border with Ghana. (Pop. 658,000)

London (1) the capital city of England and the United Kingdom, which straddles both banks of the River Thames near its estuary. (2) **Greater** the administrative area of London, consisting of the city of London and 32 boroughs. (610 sq miles;1,579 sq km; pop. 6,964,000) (3) an industrial city in southeastern Ontario, Canada. (Pop. 351,000)

Londonderry (Derry) (1) a historical county in northwest Northern Ireland. (814 sq miles/2,108 sq km) (2) a port and the second largest city in Northern Ireland after Belfast. (Pop. 72,000) *See also* **Derry.**

Longford a county in the centre of the Republic of Ireland, with a county town of the same name. (403 sq miles/1,044 sq km; pop. 32,000)

Long Island an island off the coast of New York State, USA, stretching some 118 miles (190 kilometres) to the northeast away from the city of New York. Its western end forms part of the city of New York (the boroughs of Brooklyn and Queens) but the rest is a mixture of residential suburbs, farmland and resort beaches. (1,423 sq miles/3,685 sq km)

Lord Howe Island a small island lying some 375 miles (600 kilometres) to the east of the coast of New South Wales, Australia, now a popular resort. (6 sq miles/16 sq km; pop. 300)

Lorraine a region of northeast France, with a border shared by Belgium, Luxembourg and Germany. The regional capital is Metz.

Los Angeles a vast, sprawling city on the Pacific Ocean in southern California, USA, the second largest city in the USA after New York. (Pop. city 3,096,700/conurbation 12,372,600)

Lothians the three council areas of East Lothian, West Lothian and Midlothian (including Edinburgh).

Louisiana a state in central southern USA, on the lower reaches of the Mississippi River, and with a coastline on the Gulf of Mexico. The state capital is Baton Rouge. (48,523 sq miles/125,675 sq km; pop. 4,463,000)

Louisville a city and commercial centre, in northern Kentucky, USA, on the Ohio River. (Pop. 259,000)

Lourdes one of the world's most important Marian shrines, in the foothills of the central Pyrénées, France. (Pop. 17,600)

Louth a county on the northeast coast of the Republic of Ireland. The county town is Dundalk. (318 sq miles/823 sq km; pop. 96,000)

Lualaba a river that flows northwards across the eastern part of the Democratic Republic of Congo from the border with Zambia before joining the River Lomami to form the Congo River. (Length 1,120 miles/1,800 km)

Luanda the capital of Angola, and a major port on the Atlantic Ocean. (Pop. 2,193,000)

Lübeck a Baltic port in northern Germany, lying some 12 miles (20 kilometres) from the coast on the River Trave. (Pop. 213,000)

Lublin (Lyublin) a city and agricultural centre in southeastern Poland. (Pop. 355,000)
Lubumbashi the principal mining town of the Democratic Republic of Congo, and the capital of the Shaba region in the southeast of the country. It was founded in 1910 and known as Elisabethville until 1966. (Pop. 1,075,000)
Lucca a town in northwestern Tuscany, Italy. (Pop. 85,000)
Lucerne (Luzern) a city set on the beautiful Lake Lucerne in central Switzerland, retaining much of its medieval past; also the name of the surrounding canton. (Pop. 57,000)
Lucknow the capital of the state of Uttar Pradesh in central northern India. (Pop. 2,250,000)
Lüda (Dalian) an industrial city and port in Liaoning Province, northeastern China. (Pop. 1,657,000)
Ludhiana a town in central Punjab, India, home of the respected Punjab Agricultural University. (Pop. 1,422,000)
Ludwigshafen a town, industrial centre and river port on the River Rhine in southwestern Germany. (Pop. 163,000)
Lugansk a major industrial city of the eastern Ukraine in the Donets Basin. (Pop. 454,000)
Lumbini the birthplace of Buddha in central southern Nepal.
Luoyang a city of ancient origins, founded in about 2100 BC, in Henan Province in eastern central China. As a principal centre of the Shang Dynasty (18th–12th centuries BC), the area is rich in archeological remains. (Pop. 819,000)
Lusaka the capital of Zambia, situated in the southeast of the country. (Pop. 1,218,000)
Luton an industrial town in Bedfordshire, England, 30 miles (50 kilometres) north of London. (Pop. 180,000)
Luxembourg The Grand Duchy of Luxembourg is a small landlocked country bounded by Belgium on the west, France on the south, and Germany on the east. In the north of the duchy, a wooded plateau, the Oesling, rises to 1,804 feet (550 metres) while in the south there is a lowland area of valleys and ridges, known as the Gutland. Northern winters are cold and raw, with snow covering the ground for almost a month, but southern winters are mild and summers cool. In the south, the land is fertile, and crops grown include maize, roots, tubers, and potatoes, with livestock also being raised. In the east, Luxembourg is bordered by the Moselle River in whose valley grapes are produced for wine. Beds of iron ore (declining) are found in the south, and these form the basis of the country's iron and steel industry. The country is very industrialized, with the tourism and the financial sector playing increasingly important parts in the country's economy. The capital, Luxembourg City, is the seat of the European Court of Justice.

Area: 998 sq miles/2586 sq km
Population: 412,000
Capital: Luxembourg City
Form of government: Constitutional Monarchy (Duchy)
Religion: RC
Currency: Euro

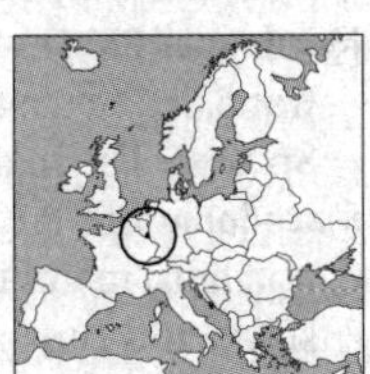

Luxor (El Uqsur) a town that has grown up around one of the great archeological sites of ancient Egypt, on the east bank of the River Nile in the centre of the country, just south of the ancient capital, Thebes, and 2 miles (3 kilometres) from Karnak. (Pop. 412,000)
Luzon the largest island of the Philippines, in the north of the group, with the nation's capital, Manila, at its centre. (40,420 sq miles/ 104,688 sq km; pop. 32,211,000)
L'vov (Lemberg) a major industrial city of medieval origins in the western Ukraine. (Pop. 779,000)
Lyons (Lyon) an industrial city in southeast France, at the confluence of the Rhône and Saône in the southeast of the country and France's third largest city after Paris and Lyons. (Pop. 444,000)

M

Macáu (Macao) a special administrative region on the south coast of China. Formerly a Portuguese province, Macao was handed back to China in 1999. (7 sq miles/18 sq km; pop. 440,000; cur. Pataca)

Macdonnell Ranges the parallel ranges of mountains of central Australia, in the southern part of the Northern Territory, near Alice Springs. The highest peak is Mount Ziel (4,954 ft/1,510 m).

Macedonia the largest region of Greece, occupying most of the northern mainland area, and bordering Albania, former Yugoslavia and Bulgaria. (Pop. 2,122,000)

Macedonia (FYROM) The Former Yugoslav Republic of Macedonia (FYROM) declared its independence from Yugoslavia under the name of Macedonia in November 1991. Greece, however, angered at the use of 'Macedonia' (also the name of the neighbouring Greek province) imposed a trade embargo and convinced the United Nations not to recognize the nation's independence. In 1993, Macedonia was admitted to the UN after changing its official name to the Former Yugoslav Republic of Macedonia. In 1995, an agreement was reached with Greece whereby both countries would respect the territory, sovereignty and independence of the other, with Macedonia agreeing to adopt a new flag. A landlocked country, Macedonia shares its borders with Albania, Bulgaria, Greece, and Yugoslavia. Its terrain is mountainous, covered by deep valleys, with several large lakes. The country's longest river, the Vardar, divides the country before it flows into Greece and eventually empties into the Aegean Sea. The climate consists of hot, dry summers and cold winters with considerable snow. It is the poorest of the six former Yugoslav republics but sustains itself through agriculture and its coal industries. Some of its natural resources include chromium, lead, zinc, nickel, iron ore, and lumber. Tourism is now starting to revive, having been badly affected by fighting in the region in the early 1990s.

Area: 9,928 sq miles/25,713 sq km
Population: 2,174,000
Capital: Skopje
Other cities: Kumanovo, Ohrid
Form of government: Republic
Religions: Eastern Orthodox, Sunni Islam
Currency: Denar

Maceió a port on the central east coast of Brazil. (Pop. 850,000)

Macgillicuddy's Reeks a range of mountains in the southwest of the Republic of Ireland which includes the country's highest peak, Carrauntoohil (3,414 ft/1,040 m).

Mackenzie a river flowing northwards through the western part of the Northwest Territories of Canada from the Great Slave Lake to the Arctic Ocean. (Length 2,640 miles/4,250 km)

McKinley, Mount the highest mountain in North America, located in the Denali National Park in southern Alaska, USA. (20,322 ft/6,194 m)

MacMurdo Sound an arm of the Ross Sea, off Antarctica.

Madagascar An island state situated off the southeast coast of Africa, separated from the mainland by the Mozambique Channel. Madagascar is the fourth largest island in the world and its centre is made up of high savannah-covered plateaux. In the east, forested mountains fall steeply to the coast while in the southwest the land falls gradually through dry grassland and scrub. The staple food crop is rice, and although only 5 per cent of the land is cultivated, 80 per cent of the population grow enough to feed themselves. Cassava, potatoes, maize, beans, and bananas are also grown, but some 58 per cent of the land is pasture and there are more cattle than people. The main export earners are coffee, vanilla, cloves, and sugar cane. There is mining for chromite, graphite, mica, and salt, and an oil refinery at Toamasina on the east coast. Upon independence in 1960, Madagascar became known as the Malagasy Republic, but this was changed back to Madagascar by referendum in 1975. Madagascar's isolation from mainland Africa means that there are several species of plants and animals that are quite different from mainland species. As a result, many tourists come to Madagascar to explore this aspect of the country's fauna and flora.

Area: 226,658 sq miles/587,041 sq km
Population: 15,353,000
Capital: Antananarivo
Form of government: Republic
Religions: Animism, RC, Protestantism
Currency: Franc Malgache

Madeira the main island in a small group in the eastern Atlantic Ocean which have belonged to Portugal since the 16th century, lying some 620 miles (1,000 kilometres) due west of Casablanca in Morocco. The capital is Funchal. (286 sq miles/740 sq km; pop. 243,000)

Madhya Pradesh the largest state in India, in the centre of the country. The capital is Bhopal. (171,170 sq miles/443,446 sq km; pop. 61,564,000)

Madison the state capital of Wisconsin, USA. (Pop. 211,000)

Madras (Chennai) the main port on the east coast of India, and the capital of the state of Tamil Nadu. (Pop. 4,299,000)

Madrid the capital of Spain, situated in the middle of the country, and also the name of the surrounding province. (Pop. city 2,905,000/province 5,321,000)

Madura an island off the northeastern coast of Java. (2,042 sq miles/5,290 sq km; pop. 1,860,000)

Madurai a textile city in Tamil Nadu, in the southern tip of India. (Pop. 941,000)

Mafikeng (Mafeking) a town in North West Province in north South Africa, that was besieged by the Boers for 217 days during the second Boer War. (Pop. 29,400)

Magdalena a river which flows northwards through western Colombia and into the Caribbean at Barranquila. (Length 965 miles/1,550 km)

Magdeburg a city and inland port on the River Elbe in eastern Germany, 75 miles (120 kilometres) southwest of Berlin. (Pop. 230,000)

Magellan, Strait of (Estrecho de Magallanes) the waterway, 2 miles (3 kilometres) wide at its narrowest point and 370 miles (600 kilometres) long, which separates the island of Tierra Del Fuego from the southern tip of mainland South America. It was discovered in 1521 by the Portuguese navigator, Ferdinand Magellan (*c*.1480–1521).

Magherafelt a district council area in Co. Londonderry, north Northern Ireland. (221 sq miles/572 sq km; pop. 36,000)

Maghreb (Maghrib) the name by which the countries of northwest Africa, Morocco, Algeria and Tunisia are often collectively known.

Magnitogorsk a steelmaking town, in the southern Ural Mountains in the Russian Federation, founded in 1930. (Pop. 428,000)

Maharashtra a state in the centre of the west coast of India, with Bombay as its capital. (118,768 sq miles/307,690 sq km; pop. 98,642,000)

Main a river that snakes its way westwards from its source near Bayreuth in central Germany, passing through Frankfurt am Main before joining the River Rhine at Mainz. (Length 325 miles/524 km)

Maine a state in the northeastern corner of the USA, bordering Canada. The state capital is Augusta. (33,215 sq miles/86,027 sq km; pop. 1,298,000)

Mainz a city and inland port on the confluence of the Rivers Rhine and Main in western central Germany. (Pop. 191,000)

Majorca (Mallorca) the largest of the Balearic Islands, in the western Mediterranean. The capital is Palma. (1,405 sq miles/3,639 sq km; pop. 460,000; cur. Euro)

Majuro an atoll of three islands (Dalap, Uliga and Darrit) which together form the capital of the Marshall Islands. (Pop. 32,000)

Makassar Strait the broad stretch of water, 81 miles (130 kilometres) across at its narrowest, which separates Borneo and Sulawesi in Indonesia.

Makeyevka an industrial city in the Donets Basin in the southern Ukraine. (Pop. 372,000)

Makhachkala a port and industrial city on the west coast of the Caspian Sea, and the capital of Dagestan, a Russian Federation autonomous republic. (Pop. 366,000)

Malabar Coast the name given to the coastal region of the state of Kerala in southwestern India.

Malabo a port and the capital of Equatorial Guinea, situated on the north coast of Bioko Island. (Pop. 113,000)

Malacca, Strait of the busy waterway, just 31 miles (50 kilometres) wide at its narrowest point, which separates the island of Sumatra in Indonesia from the southern tip of Malaysia, with Singapore at its eastern end.

Malaga a port, manufacturing city, and tourist resort on the Mediterranean coast of Andalusia, southern Spain. Also the name of the province of which it is the capital. (Pop. 539,000)

Malawi A country that lies along the southern and western shores of the third largest lake in Africa, Lake Malawi. To the south of the lake, the Shire River flows through a valley overlooked by wooded, towering mountains. The tropical climate has a dry season from May to October and a wet season for the remaining months. Agriculture is the predominant occupation and many Malawians live off their own crops. Exports include tea grown on the terraced hillsides in the south and tobacco on the central plateau plus peanuts and sugar, with maize also being an important crop. Malawi has bauxite and coal deposits but because of the inaccessibility of their locations, mining is limited. Hydroelectricity is now being used for manufacturing but imports of manufactured goods remain high and the country remains one of the poorest in the world. Malawi was formerly the British colony of Nyasaland, a name meaning 'Land of the Lake', which was given to it by the 19th-century explorer, David Livingstone.

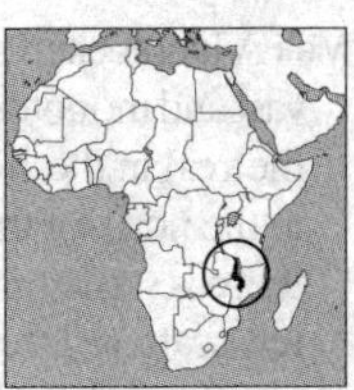

Area: 45,747 sq miles/118,484 sq km
Population: 10,114,000
Capital: Lilongwe
Other cities: Blantyre, Mzuzu, Zomba
Form of government: Republic
Religions: Animism, RC, Presbyterianism
Currency: Kwacha

Malawi (Nyasa), Lake a long, narrow lake which runs down most of the eastern side of Malawi and forms Malawi's border with Tanzania and Mozambique. (9,000 sq miles/23,300 sq km)

Malaysia The Federation of Malaysia lies in the South China Sea in southeast Asia. It comprises peninsular Malaysia on the Malay Peninsula and the states of Sabah and Sarawak on the island of Borneo. Malaysia is affected by the monsoon climate. The northeast monsoon brings rain to the east coast of peninsular Malaysia in winter, and the southwest monsoon brings rain to the west coast in summer. Throughout the country, the climate is generally tropical and temperatures are uniformly hot throughout the year. Peninsular Malaysia has always had thriving rubber-growing and tin-dredging industries, and now oil palm growing is also important on the east coast. Sabah and Sarawak have grown rich by exploiting their natural resources, the forests. There is also some offshore oil, and around the capital, Kuala Lumpur, new industries, such as electronics, are expanding. In recent years, tourism has become an important industry. There are plans for a new international airport and a large dam for hydroelectric production. Malaysia was hit by economic recession in 1997, and it implemented a series of measures designed to restore confidence in its economy.

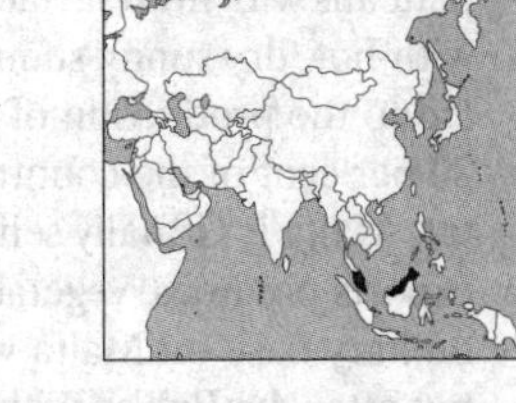

Area: 127,320 sq miles/329,749 sq km
Population: 20,581,000
Capital: Kuala Lumpur
Other cities: Ipoh, George Town, Johor Baharu
Form of government: Federal Constitutional Monarchy
Religion: Sunni Islam
Currency: Ringgi

Maldives A country that lies 398 miles (640 kilometres) southwest of Sri Lanka in the Indian Ocean and comprises 1,200 low-lying coral islands grouped into 12 atolls. Roughly 202 of the islands are inhabited. The highest point is only 5 feet (1.5 metres) above sea level. Independence was gained in 1965, with a republic being formed three years later. The climate is hot and humid and affected by monsoons from May to August. The islands are covered by coconut palms, and some millet, cassava, yams, and tropical fruit are grown. However, rice, the staple diet of its islanders, is imported. The most important natural resource is marine life, and fishing is an important occupation. The chief export is now canned or frozen tuna. Tourism is developing fast and has taken over from fishing as the major foreign currency earner.

Area: 115 sq miles/298 sq km
Population: 263,000
Capital: Malé
Form of government: Republic
Religion: Sunni Islam
Currency: Rufiyaa

Malé the main atoll of the Maldives, and the town which is the country's capital. (2.6 sq km/1 sq mile; pop. 79,000)

Mali A landlocked state in West Africa. The country mainly comprises vast and monotonous plains and plateaus. It rises to 3,790 feet (1,155 metres) in the Adrar des Iforas range in the northeast. The Sahara in the north of the country is encroaching southwards. In the south, there is some rain and plains are covered by grassy savannah and a few scattered trees. The River Niger runs through the south of the country and small steamboats use it for shipping between Koulikoro and Gao. Fish are plentiful in the river and its water is used to irrigate the land. Only a fifth of the land can be cultivated. Rice, cassava, and millet are grown for domestic consumption and cotton for export. The country's main exports include cotton, gold, foodstuffs, livestock, and mangoes. Iron ore and bauxite have been discovered but have yet to be exploited. Mali is one of the poorest countries in the world. Droughts in the 1970s and mid-1980s resulted in thousands of cattle dying and in crop failure, with famine or disease killing many of the population.

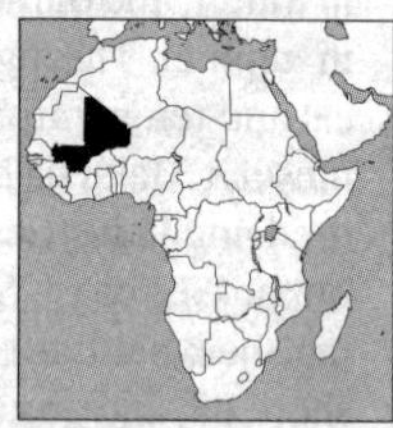

Area: 478,841 sq miles/1,240,192 sq km
Population: 11,134,000
Capital: Bamako
Other cities: Ségou, Mopti
Form of government: Republic
Religions: Sunni Islam, Animism
Currency: CFA Franc

Malmö a port in southwest Sweden, on the narrow channel which separates Sweden from Copenhagen in Denmark. (Pop. 244,000)

Malta A small republic in the middle of the Mediterranean Sea, lying just south of the island of Sicily. It comprises three islands, Malta, Gozo, and Comino, which are made up of low limestone plateaus with little surface water. The climate is Mediterranean, with hot, dry sunny summers and little rain. Lack of water has led to the production of desalination plants that produce up to 70 per cent of the country's needs. Winters are cooler and wetter. Malta is virtually self-sufficient in agricultural products and exports potatoes, vegetables, wine and cut flowers. The British military base on Malta was once the mainstay of the economy but after the British withdrew in the late 1970s, the naval dockyard was converted for commercial shipbuilding and repairs. Tourism is important to the economy and the island has become popular for retirement in the sunshine with low taxes.

Area: 122 sq miles/316 sq km
Population: 376,000
Capital: Valletta
Form of government: Republic
Religion: RC
Currency: Maltese Pound

Maluku (Moluccas) a group of some 1,000 islands in eastern Indonesia, known as the Spice Islands because they were once the only source of cloves and nutmegs. The principal islands are Halmahera, Seram and Buru. The capital is Ambon. (28,766 sq miles/74,505 sq km; pop. 2,353,000)

Man, Isle of an island of the British Isles, in the Irish Sea, halfway between England and Ireland. It is a British crown possession, not a part of the UK, and has its own parliament, the Court of Tynwald. The capital is Douglas. (226 sq miles/585 sq km; pop. 77,000)

Managua the capital of Nicaragua, situated on the edge of Lake Managua. (Pop. 1,107,000)

Manaus a major port on the River Amazon in Brazil, lying 1,000 miles (1,600 kilometres) from the sea. (Pop. 1,525,000)

Manchester (1) a major industrial and commercial city in northwest England, connected to the estuary of the River Mersey by the Manchester Ship Canal. (Pop. 402,000) (2) a unitary authority in Greater Manchester, northwest England. (45 sq miles/116 sq km; pop. 433,000) (3) **Greater** a metropolitan county of northwest England. (496 sq miles/1,286 sq km)

Mandalay the principal city of central Myanmar, and a port on the River Irrawaddy. (Pop. 1,058,000)

Manila the capital of the Philippines. The city is an important port and commercial centre, and is sited on Luzon Island. (Pop. city 10,133,000)

Manipur a small state of India in the far northeast, on the border with Myanmar. The capital is Imphal. (8,618 sq miles/22,327 sq km; pop. 2,435,000)

Manitoba the most easterly of the prairie provinces of Canada. The capital is Winnipeg. (250,998 sq miles/650,087 sq km; pop. 1,163,000)

Mannheim an inland port and industrial city in southwest Germany, on the confluence of the Rivers Rhine and Neckar. (Pop. 306,000)

Mantua (Mantova) a city in the valley of the River Po, in the Lombardy region of Italy, retaining much of its medieval heritage. (Pop. 48,000)

Maputo the capital and main port of Mozambique. It was formerly known as Lourenço Marques. (Pop. 1,088,000)

Maracaibo the largest city in Venezuela, in the northwest. (Pop. 1,800,000)

Maracaibo, Lake a shallow lake in northwest Venezuela, containing one of the richest oil fields in the world. (5,127 sq miles/13,280 sq km)

Marbella a popular resort on the Mediterranean coast of southern Spain, in the province of Malaga. (Pop. 110,000)

Marche (Marches) a region of central eastern Italy, lining the Adriatic coast. The capital is Ancona. (3,743 sq miles/9,694 sq km; pop. 1,463,000)

Mar del Plata a coastal city and beach resort on the northeast coast of Argentina, 250 miles (400 kilometres) south of Buenos Aires. (Pop. 669,000)

Maribor (Marburg) an industrial city in Slovenia. (Pop. 98,000)

Marmara, Sea of a small sea lying between the Dardanelles and the Bosphorus, providing a vital link in the route between the Mediterranean Sea and the Black Sea. The surrounding coasts all belong to Turkey.

Marquesas Islands a group of a dozen or so fertile, volcanic islands in the northeastern sector of French Polynesia, lying about 875 miles (1,400 kilometres) northeast of Tahiti. (459 sq miles/1,189 sq km; pop. 9,000)

Marrakech (Marrakesh) a historical oasis city in central western Morocco, founded in the 11th century and formerly the country's capital. (Pop. 746,000)

Marseilles (Marseille) the second largest city and the largest port in France, on the Mediterranean coast. (Pop. 815,000)

Marshall Islands Formerly part of the United States-administered United Nations Trust Territory, this self-governing republic comprises a scattering of over 1,000 coral atolls and islets, arranged in two parallel chains, Ratak and Ralik, located in eastern Micronesia in the western Pacific Ocean and lying to the northwest of Kiribati. The climate is tropical maritime, with little variation in temperature, and rainfall that is heaviest from July to October. The republic remains in free association with the USA and the economy has been almost totally dependent on US-related payments for use of the islands as bases. The Bikini Atoll was used as a nuclear testing area in 1946. Attempts have been made to diversify the economy, but the main occupations remain fishing and agriculture, with the chief export being copra.

Area: 70 sq miles/181 square km
Population: 58,000
Capital: Dalag-Uliga-Darrit [on Majuro atoll]
Form of government: Republic in free association with the USA
Religion: Protestantism
Currency: US Dollar

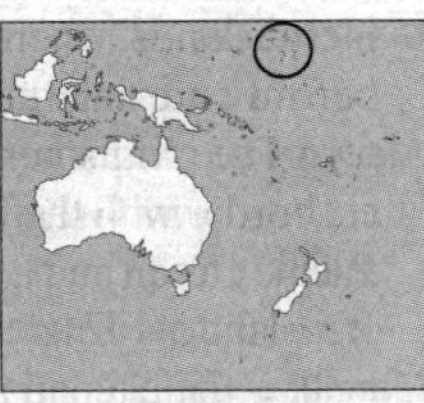

Martinique One of the larger of the islands in the Windward Islands group in the southern Caribbean, lying between Dominica and St Lucia. It is administered as a department of France. The centre of the island is mountainous, while the quality of its beaches has played a role in its development as a tourist resort. It has a volcano, Mont Pelée (4,583 ft/1,397 m), that erupted in 1902, wiping out the town of St Pierre and killing all but one of its inhabitants. Martinique is periodically subjected to hurricanes that can cause considerable damage. The island's economy relies mainly on tourism with sugar, bananas, pineapples, citrus fruits, nutmeg, and spices being grown in some parts of the island.

Area: 425 sq miles/1,102 sq km
Population: 384,000
Capital: Fort-de-France
Form of government: Overseas Department of France
Religion: RC
Currency: Euro

Maryland a state on the central east coast of the USA, virtually divided in two by Chesapeake Bay. The state capital is Annapolis. (10,577 sq miles/27,394 sq km; pop. 5,455,000)

Maseru the capital of Lesotho. (Pop. 169,000)

Mashhad (Meshed) a major trading centre and the capital of Khorasan Province in northeastern Iran. (Pop. 2,041,000)

Massachusetts one of the New England states on the northeastern coast of the USA. The capital is Boston. (8257 sq miles/21,386 sq km; pop. 6,410,000)

Massif Central the rugged upland region which occupies much of southern central France to the west of the River Rhône. The highest point is at Puy de Sancy (6,184 ft/1,885 m).

Mata-Utu the capital of the Wallis and Futuna Islands. (Pop. 2,000)

Matsuyama a port and industrial city on the north coast of Shikoku Island, Japan. (Pop. 462,000)

Matterhorn (Monte Cervino) a distinctive, pyramid-shaped peak on the border between Italy and Switzerland, 3 miles (5 kilometres) south of Zermatt. (14,688 ft/4,477 m)

Maui the second largest island of Hawaii, USA. (727 sq miles/1,885 sq km)

Mauna Kea a dormant volcano in the north of the island of Hawaii, USA. (13,796 ft/4,205 m)

Mauna Loa an active volcano in the centre of the island of Hawaii, USA. (13,677 ft/4,169 m)

Mauritania A country nearly twice the size of France, the Islamic Arab and African Republic of Mauritania is located on the west coast of Africa. About 47 per cent of the country is desert, the Sahara covering much of the north. The only settlements found in this area are around oases, where a little millet, dates, and vegetables can be grown. The main agricultural regions are in the Senegal River valley in the south. The rest of the country is made up of the drought-stricken Sahel grasslands. The majority of the people are traditionally nomadic herdsmen, but severe droughts since the late 1960s have killed about 70 per cent of the nation's animals, forcing the population to settle along the Senegal River. As a result, vast shanty towns have sprung up around all of the country's towns. The country's economy is very reliant on foreign aid. The production of iron ore and other deposits provide the country's main exports, and development of these and the fishing industry on the coast form the only hope for a brighter future. Mauritania has also experienced some internal political unrest and been involved in disputes with its neighbours. Conditions appear to have become more settled in recent years with a new constitution adopted in 1991.

Area: 395,956 sq miles/1,025,520 sq km
Population: 2,351,000
Capital: Nouakchott
Form of government: Republic
Religion: Sunni Islam
Currency: Ouguiya

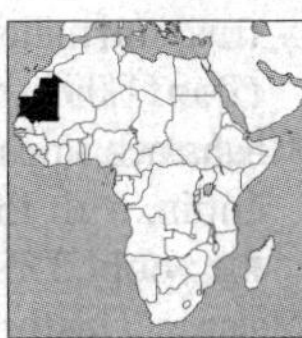

Mauritius A beautiful island with tropical beaches, lying about 20 degrees south in the Indian Ocean and 497 miles (800 kilometres) east of Madagascar, which gained independence in 1968. The islands of Rodrigues and Agalega are also part of Mauritius. Mauritius is a volcanic island with many craters surrounded by lava flows. The central plateau rises to over 2,625 feet (800 metres), then drops sharply to the south and west coasts. The climate is hot and humid with southwesterly winds bringing heavy rain in the uplands. There is the possibility of cyclones from December to April. The island has well-watered fertile soil, ideal for the sugar plantations that cover 45 per cent of the island. Although the export of molasses and sugar still dominates the economy, diversification is being encouraged. Other crops such as tea, tobacco, peanuts, and vegetables are grown. The clothing and electronic equipment industries are becoming increasingly important and tourism is now the third largest source of foreign currency.

Area: 788 sq miles/2,040 sq km
population: 1,160,000
Capital: Port Louis
Form of government: Republic
Religions: Hinduism, RC, Sunni Islam
Currency: Mauritian Rupee

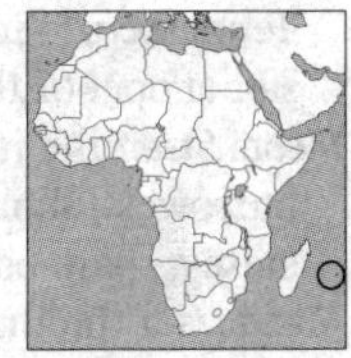

Mayo a county on the west coast of the Republic of Ireland. The county town is Castlebar. (1,865 sq miles/4,831 sq km; pop. 116,000)

Mayotte (Mahore) one of the Comoros Islands, lying between Madagascar and the mainland of Africa. Unlike the other three islands in the group, Mayotte voted to remain under the administration of France when the Comoros Islands became independent in 1974. (144 sq miles/373 sq km; pop. 174,000)

Mbabane the capital of Swaziland. (Pop. 67,000)

Meath a county on the east coast of the Republic of Ireland, north of Dublin. The county town is Navan. (902 sq miles/2,336 sq km; pop. 114,000)

Mecca (Makkah) a city in central western Saudi Arabia, 40 miles (64 kilometres) east of the Red Sea port of Jiddah. An important trading city on caravan routes in ancient times, it was the birthplace of the prophet Mohammed, and as such is the holiest city of Islam. (Pop. 1,542,000)

Medan a major city in northern Sumatra, Indonesia. (Pop. 2,059,000)

Medellín the second largest city in Colombia after the capital Bogota, situated in the centre of the country, 150 miles (240 kilometres) northwest of the capital. (Pop. 1,932,000)

Medina (Al Madinah) the second holiest city of Islam after Mecca. The prophet Mohammed fled from Mecca to Medina, 217 miles

(350 kilometres) to the north, to escape persecution in AD 622 (year 0 in the Islamic lunar calendar). (Pop. 819,000)

Mediterranean Sea a large sea bounded by southern Europe, North Africa and southwest Asia. It is connected to the Atlantic Ocean by the Strait of Gibraltar. (970,000 sq miles/2,512,000 sq km)

Médoc one of the prime wine-producing regions of France, a flat, triangular-shaped piece of land situated between the Gironde estuary and the Atlantic Ocean.

Meerut an industrial town of northern India, 40 miles (60 kilometres) northeast of Delhi. The Indian Mutiny began here in 1857. (Pop. 1,095,000)

Meghalaya a predominantly rural state in the hills of northeastern India, with Bangladesh to the south. (8,658 sq miles/22,429 sq km; pop. 2,351,000)

Meissen a historical town on the River Elbe, 12 miles (20 kilometres) to the northwest of Dresden, in southeastern Germany. It is famous above all for its fine porcelain, produced here since 1710. (Pop. 29,000)

Meknès a former capital in northern Morocco, with a fine 17th-century royal palace. (Pop. 562,000)

Mekong the great river of Southeast Asia, flowing from Tibet, through southern China, Laos and Cambodia before forming a massive and highly fertile delta in southern Vietnam and flowing into the South China Sea. (Length 2,562 miles/4,184 km)

Melaka (Malacca) a port on the southwest coast of Malaysia, overlooking the Strait of Malacca, once a key port in Far Eastern trade. (Pop. 150,000)

Melanesia the central and southern group of islands in the South Pacific Ocean, including the Solomon Islands, Vanuatu, Fiji and New Caledonia.

Melbourne the second largest city in Australia after Sydney, and the capital of the state of Victoria. (Pop. 3,353,000)

Memphis a city on the River Mississippi in the southwest corner of Tennessee, USA, on the border with and extending into Arkansas. (Pop. 662,000)

Menai Strait the narrow strait, 590 feet (180 metres) across at its narrowest, separating mainland Wales from the island of Anglesey, spanned by road and rail bridges.

Mendoza a trading, processing and wine-producing centre in the foothills of the Andes, in western Argentina. (Pop. 969,000)

Mérida the historical capital of the Yucatan Province of eastern Mexico. (Pop. 680, 000)

Mersey a river in northwest England. It forms an estuary to the south of Liverpool which is deep and wide enough to permit access for ocean-going ships to Liverpool and Manchester (via the Manchester Ship Canal). (Length 70 miles/110 km)

Merseyside a metropolitan county, centring on the River Mersey, in northwest England. (252 sq miles/652 sq km; pop. 1,409,000)

Mersin (Içel) the principal Mediterranean port of Turkey, in the central south of the country, to the north of Cyprus. (Pop. 559,000)

Merthyr Tydfil (1) a town in southeast Wales, formerly an important centre for the mining industry, and the administrative centre for the Merthyr Tydfil council area. (Pop. 40,000) (2) a council area in southeast Wales. (43 sq miles/111 sq km; pop. 60,000)

Messina a historical port, founded in the 8th century BC, in northeast Sicily, overlooking the narrow Strait of Messina, 4 miles (6 kilometres) wide at its narrowest, which separates Sicily from mainland Italy. (Pop. 259,000)

Metz the capital of the industrial Lorraine region in eastern France, situated on the River Moselle, and close to the border with Germany. (Pop. 125,000)

Meuse (Maas) a river which flows northwest from its source in the Lorraine region of France, across central Belgium and into the Netherlands, where it joins part of the delta of the River Rhine before entering the North Sea. (Length 580 miles/935 km)

Mexico The most southerly country in North America. It has its longest border with the United States to the north, a long coast on the Pacific Ocean and a smaller coast in the west of the Gulf of Mexico. It is a land of volcanic mountain ranges and high plateaux. The highest peak is Citlaltépetl at 18,697 feet (5,699 metres), which is permanently snow-capped. Coastal lowlands are found in the west and east. Its wide range of latitude and relief produce a variety of climates. In the north, there are arid and semi-arid conditions while in the south there is a humid tropical climate. Thirty per cent of the labour force is involved in agriculture, growing maize, wheat, kidney beans, and rice for subsistence, and coffee, cotton, fruit, and vegetables for export, although some irrigation is needed. Mexico has substantial and varied mineral deposits, such as silver, coal, phosphates, gold, and uranium, as well as large reserves of oil and natural gas. Forests cover around a quarter of the country with trees such as ebony, mahogany, and walnut. Developing industries are petrochemicals, textiles, motor vehicles, and food processing. Tourism also makes an important contribution to the country's economy.

Area: 756,066 sq miles/1,958,201 sq km
Population: 96,578,000
Capital: Mexico City (México)
Other cities: Guadalajara, Monterrey, Puebla
Form of government: Federal Republic
Religion: RC
Currency: Mexican Peso

Mexico, Gulf of an arm of the Atlantic Ocean, bounded by the Florida Peninsula in southeast USA and the Yucatan Peninsula in Mexico, with the island of Cuba placed in the middle of its entrance.

Mexico City (México) the capital of Mexico and the most populous city in the world. It lies in the south of the country on a high plateau (7,350 ft/2,200 m) above sea level. (Pop. 8,659,000)

Miami a major city and resort on the Atlantic coast of southeast Florida, USA. (Pop. 381,000)

Michigan a state in north central USA, formed out of two peninsulas between the Great Lakes, with Lake Michigan in the middle. The capital is Lansing. (58,216 sq miles/150,780 sq km; pop. 10,044,000)

Michigan, Lake one of the Great Lakes, and the only one to lie entirely within the USA. (22,300 sq miles/57,750 sq km)

Micronesia one of the three main groupings of islands of the Pacific Ocean, lying to the northwest of the other two main groupings, Melanesia and Polynesia, and stretching from Belau to Kiribati.

Micronesia, Federated States of Formerly part of the United States-administered United Nations Trust Territory of the Pacific, known as the Caroline Islands, this self-governing republic became independent in 1990. It comprises an archipelago of over 600 islands, including Pohnpei (Ponape), the Truk (Churk) Islands, the Yap Islands, and Kosrae. Mostly uninhabited, they are located in the western Pacific Ocean, about 2,500 miles (4,025 kilometres) southwest of Hawaii. The climate is tropical maritime, with high temperatures and rainfall all year round but a pronounced precipitation peak between July and October. Micronesia is still closely linked to the USA, with a heavy reliance on aid. Attempts are being made to diversify the economy, the exports of which are mainly fishing and copra. There are significant phosphate deposits but the island's isolation restricts development. Tourism is a growing trade but the economy of the region remains fragile.

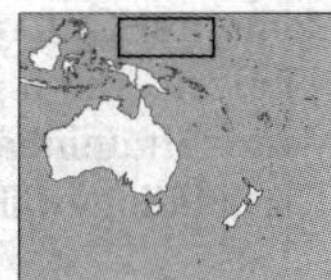

Area: 271 sq miles/702 sq km
Population: 109,000
Capital: Kolonia
Form of government: Republic
Religion: Christianity
Currency: US Dollar

Middle East a non-specific term used to describe an area of southwest Asia, which is mainly Islamic and/or Arabic-speaking. Countries included are: Turkey, Iran, Iraq, Syria, Jordan, Israel, Saudi Arabia, Lebanon, Yemen, Oman, the United Arab Emirates, Qatar, Bahrain and Kuwait.

Middlesbrough an industrial town in northeast England. (Pop. 145,000)

Mid Glamorgan a former county in central southern Wales.

Midlands, the a term used to describe the central industrial counties of England: Derbyshire, Northamptonshire, Nottinghamshire, Staffordshire, Warwickshire, Leicestershire, and West Midlands.

Midlothian a council area in southeast central Scotland, with its administrative centre in the town of Dalkeith. (137 sq miles/356 sq km; pop. 80,000)

Midway Islands two atolls belonging to the USA, in the north Pacific Ocean, some 1,242 miles (2,000 kilometres) northwest of Hawaii. (2 sq miles/3 sq km; pop. 500)

Midwest (Middle West) a term used to describe the fertile north central part of the USA. States in the Midwest include Ohio, Michigan, Indiana, Illinois, Wisconsin, Minnesota, Iowa and Missouri, but others, such as Kansas, are also often included.

Milan (Milano) the major industrial and financial centre of northern Italy, and the country's second largest city after Rome, situated in central Lombardy. (Pop. 1,302,000)

Milwaukee a port on the west side of Lake Michigan, and the main industrial centre of Wisconsin, USA. (Pop. 606,000)

Minch, the a broad channel separating northwest Scotland from the Outer Hebrides.

Mindanao the second largest island of the Philippines. (36,537 sq miles/4,631 sq km; pop. 16,526,000)

Mindoro an island in west central Philippines. (3,759 sq miles/9,736 sq km)

Minneapolis a major agricultural and commercial centre in southeast Minnesota, USA, on the River Mississippi, and adjoining the port and state capital of St Paul. (Pop. 391,000)

Minnesota a state in north central USA. The state capital is St Paul. (84,068 sq miles/217,736 sq km; pop. 5,026,000)

Minorca (Menorca) the second largest of the Balearic Islands, after Majorca. The capital is Mahon. (271 sq miles/702 sq km; pop. 50,200; cur. Euro)

Minsk a major industrial city, and the capital of Belarus. (Pop. 1,765,000)

Miskolc a city in the northeast of Hungary, and the country's third largest city after Budapest and Debrecen. (Pop. 181,000)

Mississippi (1) a state in central southern USA with a small coastline on the Gulf of Mexico. The state capital is Jackson. (47,716 sq miles/123,585 sq km; pop. 2,872,000) (2) the second longest river in the USA. It rises in Minnesota and runs south the length of the country to the Gulf of Mexico. (Length 2,348 miles/3,779 km)

Missouri (1) a state in the Midwest of the USA. The state capital is Jefferson City. (69,686 sq miles/180,487 sq km; pop. 5,664,000) (2) the main tributary of the Mississippi with which it is the longest river in North America. It rises in Montana, flows north, east and southeast to join the Mississippi at the port of St Louis. (Length 2,466 miles/3,969 km)

Mizoram a union territory of India, in the hilly northeast, on the border with Myanmar. The capital is Aijal. (8,137 sq miles/21,081 sq km; pop. 908,000)

Mobile a port on the coast of Alabama, USA, on the Gulf of Mexico. (Pop. 200,000)

Modena an industrial city in northeastern Italy, retaining many vestiges of its medieval past. (Pop. 176,000)

Mogadishu (Muqdisho) the capital and main port of Somalia. (Pop. 1,183,000)

Mojave (Mohave) Desert a desert in southern California, USA, stretching from Death Valley to Los Angeles. (15,000 sq miles/38,850 sq km)

Moldova (Moldavia) A Soviet socialist republic from 1940 until 1991 when it became independent of the former USSR. It is bounded to the west by Romania and to the north, east, and south by Ukraine. The republic consists of a hilly plain with an average height of around 500 feet (150 metres). Its main rivers are the Prut in the west and the Dnister in the north and east. Moldova's soils are fertile, and crops grown include wheat, corn, barley, tobacco, sugar beet, soybeans and sunflowers. There are also extensive fruit orchards, vineyards, and walnut groves. Beekeeping and silkworm breeding are widespread throughout the country. Food processing is the main industry, particularly sugar refining and winemaking. Other industries include metalworking, engineering, and the manufacture of electrical equipment. After independence, the economy declined, inflation soared, and assistance was gained from the International Monetary Fund and others.

Area: 13,012 sq miles/33,700 sq km
Population: 4,327,000
Capital: Chisinau (Kishinev)
Other cities: Tiraspol, Bel'tsy
Form of government: Republic
Religion: Russian Orthodox
Currency: Leu

Molise a region of eastern Italy, on the Adriatic coast, between Abruzzi and Puglia. (1,714 sq miles/4,438 sq km; pop. 329,000)

Mombasa the second city of Kenya and an important port on the Indian Ocean. (Pop. 707,000)

Monaco A tiny principality on the Mediterranean Sea, surrounded landwards by the Alpes Maritimes department of France. It comprises a rocky peninsula and a narrow stretch of coast. It has mild moist winters and hot dry summers. The ancient fortified town of Monaco-Ville is situated on a rocky promontory and houses the royal palace and the cathedral. The Monte Carlo district has the world-famous casino, and La Condamine has thriving businesses, stores, banks, and attractive residential areas. Fontvieille is an area reclaimed from the sea where marinas and light industry are now located. The light industry includes chemicals, plastics, electronics, engineering, and paper, but it is tourism that is the main revenue earner. Tobacco, insurance, and banking industries, and the sale of stamps also contribute to the economy. Two well-known annual motoring events, the Monte Carlo Rally and Monaco Grand Prix, are held in the principality.

Area: 0.4 sq mile/1 sq km
Population: 32,000
Capital: Monaco
Form of government: Constitutional Monarchy
Religion: RC
Currency: Euro

Monaghan a county in the central north of the Republic of Ireland, with a county town of the same name. (498 sq miles/1,291 sq km; pop. 54,000)

Mönchengladbach an industrial city in the southwest of the Ruhr region of western Germany, 16 miles (25 kilometres) west of the city of Düsseldorf. (Pop. 266,000)

Mongolia A landlocked country in northeast Asia that is bounded to the north by the Russian Federation and to the south, west, and east by China. Most of Mongolia is mountainous. In the northwest, there are the Hangayn Mountains and the Altai, rising to 14,312 feet (4,362 metres). In the south, there are grass-covered steppes and the desert wastes of the Gobi. The climate is very extreme and dry, with long, very cold winters and short, mild summers. Agriculture, particularly the rearing of livestock, is the main economic activity and source of employment in Mongolia. Under Communism, all cultivation and livestock rearing was state-controlled but Mongolia has now started to move towards a free market economy. Crops grown include cereals (wheat, barley, and oats), potatoes, and some other vegetables but cultivation is heavily dependent on irrigation. Mongolia has valuable reserves of iron ore, coal, copper, molybdenum, fluorspar, tungsten, uranium, gold, and silver. Manufacturing industries are generally on a small scale and include the processing of wool, hides, leather, furs, meat and dairy produce, textiles, wooden goods, agricultural equipment, and building products. The collapse of trade with the former Soviet Union has created severe economic problems for Mongolia and it is increasingly looking to Japan and China for trade and economic assistance.

Area: 604,829 sq miles/1,566,500 sq km
Population: 2,354,000
Capital: Ulan Bator (Ulaanbaatar)
Other cities: Darhan, Erdenet
Form of government: Republic
Religions: Buddhism, Shamanism, Sunni Islam
Currency: Tugrik

Monmouthshire a council area in east Wales, with its administrative centre in the town of Cwmbran. (329 sq miles/851 sq km; pop. 86,000)

Monrovia the capital and principal port of Liberia. (Pop. 543,000)

Mons (Bergen) a town in southwest Belgium. (Pop. 90,000)

Montana a state in northwest USA, on the border with Canada. The state capital is Helena. (147,138 sq miles/381,087 sq km; pop. 907,000)

Mont Blanc (Monte Bianco) the highest mountain in Western Europe, on the border between France and Italy. (15,770 ft/4,808 m)

Monte Carlo an elegant coastal town and resort in Monaco, famed in particular for its casinos. (Pop. 15,000)

Monterey a resort town on the Pacific coast of central California, USA, 85 miles (135 kilometres) southeast of San Francisco. It is well known for its annual jazz festival. (Pop. 31,000)

Monterrey a major industrial city in northeast Mexico, capital of Nuevo Léon state. (Pop. 1,127,000)

Montevideo the capital of Uruguay in South America, and an important port on the River Plate estuary. (Pop. 1,450,000)

Montgomery the state capital of Alabama, USA. (Pop. 203,000)

Montpelier the state capital of Vermont, USA. (Pop. 8,000)

Montpellier a university and trading city in central southern France, the capital of the Languedoc-Roussillon region. (Pop. 229,000)

Montréal the second largest city in Canada after Toronto, on the St Lawrence River, in the south of the province of Québec. Two-thirds of the population are French-speaking Québecois. (Pop. 1,039,000)

Montserrat One of the Leeward Islands in the southeastern Caribbean, and a British Overseas Territory. Much of the island was left uninhabitable after the volcanic eruptions of 1997 but rebuilding of the island has begun, funded by the UK.

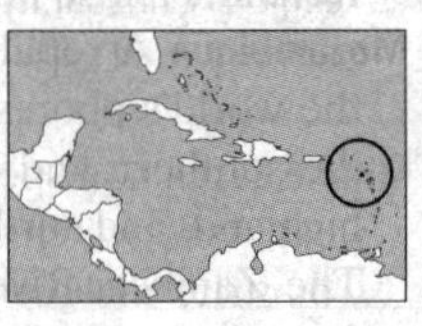

Area: 39 sq miles/100 sq km
Population: 7,000
Capital: Plymouth
Form of government: British Overseas Territory
Religions: Protestant, RC
Currency: East Caribbean Dollar

Monza a city in northern Italy, northeast of Milan. (Pop. 120,000)

Moravia a historical region of the Czech Republic, east of Bohemia, west of Slovakia, with Poland to the north and Austria to the south.

Moray a council area in northeast Scotland, with its administrative centre in the town of Elgin. (874 sq miles/2,238 sq km; pop. 86,000)

Moray Firth an inlet of the North Sea cutting some 35 miles (56 kilometres) into the eastern coast of northeast Scotland, with Inverness at its head.

Mordvinian Republic (Mordovia) a republic of the Russian Federation, in west central Russia in the middle of the Volga basin. (10,110 sq miles/26,200 sq km; pop. 960,000)

Morocco A country in northwest Africa strategically placed at the western entrance to the Mediterranean Sea. It is a land of great contrasts, with high rugged mountains in the north, the arid Sahara in the south, and green Atlantic and Mediterranean coasts. The country is split from southwest to northeast by the Atlas Mountains. The north has a pleasant Mediterranean climate with hot, dry summers and mild, moist winters. Farther south winters are warmer and summers even hotter. Snow often falls in winter on the Atlas Mountains. Morocco is mainly a farming country, although agriculture accounts for less than 20 per cent of the land use. Wheat, barley, and maize are the main food crops, and it is one of the world's chief exporters of citrus fruit. Morocco's economy is very mixed. Its main wealth comes from phosphates, reserves of which are the largest in the world, while coal, lead, iron and manganese ores are also produced. It is self-sufficient in textiles, has automobile assembly plants, soap and cement factories, and a large sea fishing industry. Tourism is a major source of revenue, as are remittances sent home by Moroccans who work abroad.

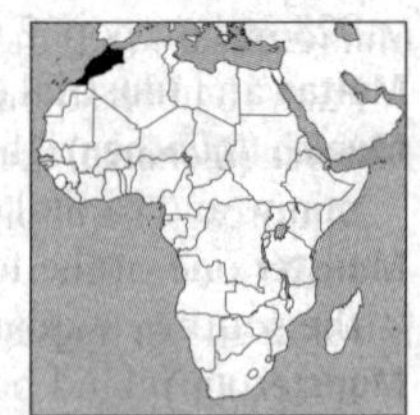

Area: 172,414 sq miles/446,550 sq km
Population: 27,623,000
Capital: Rabat
Other cities: Casablanca, Fez, Marrakech
Form of government: Constitutional Monarchy
Religion: Sunni Islam
Currency: Dirham

Moroni the capital of the Comoros Islands. (Pop. 42,000)

Moscow (Moskva) the capital of the Russian Federation, sited on the Moskva River. It is an ancient city with a rich heritage, and is the political, industrial and cultural focus of the country. (Pop. 8,376,000)

Moselle (Mosel) a river which flows northwards from the southeastern Lorraine region of eastern France to form part of the border between Luxembourg and Germany before flowing eastwards to meet the River Rhine at Koblenz. (Length 340 miles/550 km)

Mosul (Al Mawsil) a historical trading city on the banks of the River Tigris in northwest Iraq, and an important centre for the surrounding oil-producing region. (Pop. 1,740,000)

Mourne Mountains a mountain range of noted beauty in the south of Co. Down, Northern Ireland. The highest point is Slieve Donard (2,795 ft /852 m).

Moyle a district council area in Co. Antrim in northeast Northern Ireland. (191 sq miles/494 sq km; pop. 15,000)

Mozambique A republic located in southeast Africa and one of the world's poorest countries. A coastal plain covers most of the southern and central territory, giving way to the western highlands and north to a plateau including the Nyasa Highlands. The Zambezi River separates the high plateaux in the north from the lowlands in the south. The country has a humid tropical climate with highest temperatures and rainfall in the north. Normally conditions are reasonably good for agriculture but periods of drought and periods of severe flooding together with 16 years of civil war have taken their toll on the country's development. A lot of industry was abandoned when the Portuguese left the country and was not taken over by the local people because of lack of expertise. Forestry is mainly unexploited while fishing for lobster and shrimp is an important source of export revenue. The economy is now on the upturn but the country continues to rely heavily on aid.

Area: 309,496 sq miles/799,380 sq km
Population: 16,916,000
Capital: Maputo
Other cities: Beira, Nampula
Form of government: Republic
Religions: Animism, RC, Sunni Islam
Currency: Metical

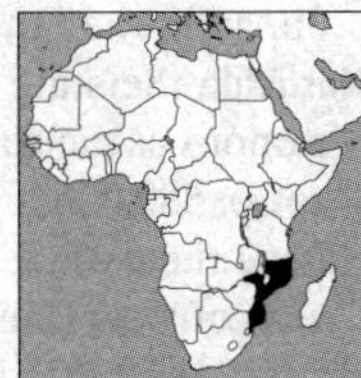

Mozambique Channel the broad strait, some 250 miles (400 kilometres) across at its narrowest point, which separates Madagascar from mainland east Africa.

Mpumalanga one of South Africa's nine provinces, in northeast South Africa, with its administrative centre in Nelspruit. (30,683 sq miles/79,490 sq km; pop. 2,801,000)

Mühlheim (Mühlheim an der Ruhr) an industrial city and port on the River Ruhr, in the Ruhr region of western Germany. (Pop. 174,000)

Mulhouse an industrial city in Alsace, eastern France. (Pop. 111,000)

Mull an island off the central west coast of Scotland. (357 sq miles/925 sq km; pop. 2,600)

Multan an industrial city in the Punjab, Pakistan. (Pop. 1,310,000)

Munich (München) a historical and industrial city in southern Germany, and capital of Bavaria. (Pop. 1,161,000)

Munster one of the four historical provinces of Ireland, covering the southwest quarter of the country.

Münster an inland port and industrial centre on the Dortmund-Ems Canal in northwestern Germany. (Pop. 266,000)

Murcia a trading and manufacturing city in southeastern Spain, and capital of the province of the same name. (Pop. 366,000)

Murmansk the largest city north of the Arctic Circle, a major port and industrial centre on the Kola Peninsula in the far northwestern corner of the Russian Federation. (Pop. 361,000)

Murray a major river of southeast Australia, which flows westwards from the Snowy Mountains to form much of the boundary between the states of New South Wales and Victoria. It is joined by the River Darling before flowing across the southeastern corner of South Australia and into the Antarctic Ocean. (Length 1,600 miles/2,570 km)

Mururoa an atoll in the southeastern sector of French Polynesia, used by France since 1966 as a testing ground for nuclear weapons.

Musandam a rocky, horn-shaped peninsula which juts out into the Persian Gulf to form the southern side of the Strait of Hormuz. It belongs to Oman, but is separated from it by part of the United Arab Emirates.

Muscat (Masqat) the historical capital of Oman. The neighbouring port of Muttrah has developed rapidly in recent decades to form the commercial centre of Muscat. (Pop. 60,000)

Mustique an island in the Grenadines, to the south of St Vincent, in the southeastern Caribbean. (Pop. 200)

Myanmar Formerly Burma, the Union of Myanmar is the second largest country in Southeast Asia. The heartland of the country is the valley of the Irrawaddy River. The north and west of the country are mountainous and in the east the Shan Plateau runs along the border with Thailand. The climate is equatorial at the coast, changing to tropical monsoon over most of the interior. The Irrawaddy River flows into the Andaman Sea, forming a huge delta area that is ideal for rice cultivation. Rice is the country's staple food and accounts for half the country's export earnings. Tropical fruits, such as bananas, mangoes, citrus, and guavas, grow well in the fertile coastal regions. Myanmar is rich in lumber and mineral resources such as natural gas, petroleum, jade, and natural rubies, but poor communications, lack of development, and civil unrest mean that these resources have not been fully exploited, which has at least contributed to the preservation of the country's natural environment.

Area: 261,228 sq miles/676,578 sq km
Population: 45,992,000
Capital: Rangoon (Yangon)
Other cities: Mandalay, Moulmein, Pegu
Form of government: Republic
Religion: Buddhism
Currency: Kyat

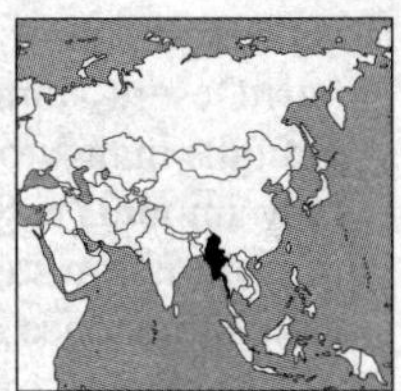

Mysore an industrial city in the state of Karnataka, southern India. (Pop. 757,000)

N

Naberezhnyye Chelny an industrial town in the Russian Federation. (Pop. 513,000)

Nablus the largest town on the Palestinian autonomous region of the West Bank. (Pop. 113,000)

Nagaland a primarily agricultural state in the hilly far northeastern corner of India, bordering Myanmar. (6,399 sq miles/6,579 sq km; pop. 2,028,000)

Nagasaki a port and industrial city on the west coast of Kyushu Island, Japan. The second atomic bomb of World War II was dropped on Nagasaki on August 9, 1945, killing 40,000 people. (Pop. 432,000)

Nagorny Karabakh Autonomous Region a disputed, autonomous enclave in Azerbaijan, which is claimed by Armenia. Three quarters of the population are Armenian. (1,700 sq miles/4,400 sq km; pop. 194,000)

Nagoya a port and industrial centre on the southeastern coast of Honshu Island, Japan. (Pop. 2,186,000)

Nagpur a commercial centre and textile-manufacturing city on the Deccan Plateau of the state of Maharashtra, central India. (Pop. 2,091,000)

Nairobi the capital of Kenya and a commercial centre, in the southwest highland region. (Pop. 2,511,000)

Nakhichevan Autonomous Republic an enclave in Armenia, that belongs to Azerbaijan, which declared its secession from the former Soviet Union in 1990. The capital is Nakhichevan. (5500 sq km/2120 sq miles; pop. republic 366,000/capital 68,000)

Namib Desert a sand desert lining the coast of Namibia.

Namibia A country situated on the Atlantic coast of southwest Africa. There are three main regions in the country: running down the entire Atlantic coastline is the Namib Desert; east of which is the Central Plateau of mountains, rugged outcrops, sandy valleys, and poor grasslands; east again and north is the Kalahari Desert. Namibia is hot and dry and the little rain it does get falls mainly over Windhoek, the capital, and even here it only amounts to 8–10 inches (200–250 millimetres) per year. It is essentially a stock-rearing country (sheep, cattle, and goats) with subsistence agriculture to be found mainly in the north. Diamonds are mined just north of the River Orange, as are other minerals such as silver, lead, uranium, and copper. Namibia's output of diamonds amounts to almost a third of the world's total. One of Africa's richest fishing grounds lies off the coast of Namibia, and mackerel, anchovies, and pilchards are an important export although production has dropped in recent years because of overfishing.

Area: 318,261 sq miles/824,292 sq km
Population: 1,575,000
Capital: Windhoek
Form of government: Republic
Religions: Lutheranism, RC, other Christianity
Currency: Namibian Dollar

Nanchang an industrial city and commercial centre in central southeastern China, and the capital of Jiangxi Province. (Pop. 1,078,000)

Nancy a manufacturing city in northeast France, and the former capital of Lorraine. (Pop. 103,000)

Nanjing (Nanking) a major industrial and trading city built on the lower reaches of the Chang Jiang (Yangtze) River, and the capital of Jiangsu Province, central eastern China. (Pop. 1,800,000)

Nanning the capital of the Guangxi Zhuang Autonomous Region in the extreme southeast of China. (Pop. 913,000)

Nantes a port and commercial centre in northwestern France and capital of the Loire Atlantique department. (Pop. 279,000)

Naples (Napoli) the third largest city in Italy, after Rome and Milan, and a port situated on the spectacular Bay of Naples. (Pop. 993,000)

Nara a historical city in south Honshu Island, Japan, the capital of Japan in the 8th century. (Pop. 385,000)

Nashville the state capital of Tennessee, USA, an industrial city famous as the traditional home of Country and Western music. (Pop. 580,000)

Nassau the capital and chief port of the Bahamas, on the north side of New Providence Island. (Pop. 179,000)

Nasser, Lake a massive artificial lake on the River Nile in southern Egypt, created when the Aswan High Dam was completed in 1971. (1,930 sq miles/5,000 sq km)

Natal (1) a port city on the northeast tip of Brazil, and capital of the state of Rio Grande do Norte. (Pop. 738,000) (2) a former province on the eastern coast of South Africa, now part of the province of KwaZulu/Natal.

Nauru The world's smallest republic. Nauru is an island situated just 25 miles (40 kilometres) south of the Equator and halfway between Australia and Hawaii. It is an oval-shaped coral island only 12 miles (20 kilometres) in diameter and is surrounded by a reef. The centre of the island comprises a plateau that rises to 197 feet (60 metres) above sea level. Most of the population live along a narrow coastal belt of fertile land. The climate is tropical with a high and irregular rainfall. The country is rich, due entirely to the deposits of high-quality phosphate rock in the central plateau. This is sold for fertilizer to Australia, New Zealand, Japan, and Korea. Phosphate deposits are likely to be exhausted in the near future but the government is investing overseas and attempting to diversify to ensure the economic future of the country. Since around 80 per cent of the land will be uninhabitable once the mines are exhausted, considerable rehabilitation will be required.

Area: 8 sq miles/21 sq km
Population: 11,000
Capital: Yaren
Form of government: Republic
Religions: Protestantism, RC
Currency: Australian Dollar

Navarra (Navarre) a province in the mountainous northeastern part of Spain. The capital is Pamplona. (4023 sq miles/10,420 sq km; pop. 557,000)

Naxos a fertile Greek island in the southern Aegean Sea, the largest of the Cyclades Islands. (165 sq miles/428 sq km)

Nazareth a town in northern Israel, and the childhood home of Jesus. (Pop. 64,000)

Ndjamena (N'Djamena) the capital of Chad, in north central Africa. Lying in the southeast of the country, it was founded by the French in 1900 and named Fort Lamy. (Pop. 602,000)

Neagh, Lough the largest freshwater lake in the British Isles, in the east of Northern Ireland. (147 sq miles/381 sq km)

Neath Port Talbot a council area in south Wales, with its administrative centre in the town of Port Talbot. (169 sq miles/439 sq km; pop. 106,000)

Nebraska a state in the Midwest of the USA. The capital is Lincoln. (77,227 sq miles/200,018 sq km; pop. 1,715,000)

Neckar a tributary of the River Rhine, rising in the Black Forest in the southwest of Germany. (227 miles/365 km)

Negev a semi-desert region in southern Israel, whose main town is Beersheba. (4,950 sq miles/12,820 sq km)

Negros the fourth largest island of the Philippines. (4,905 sq miles/12,704 sq km; pop. 2,750,000)

Nei Mongol Autonomous Region (Inner Mongolia, Nei Mongol Zizhiqu) a region of northeastern China, bordering Mongolia, whose capital is Hohhot. (460,000 sq miles/1,200,000 sq km; pop. 24,065,000)

Neisse a tributary of the River Oder, which flows north from its source in the Czech Republic to form part of the border between Germany and Poland. (Length 159 miles/256 km)

Nelspruit the capital of the province of Mpumalanga in northeast South Africa.

Nepal A long narrow rectangular country, landlocked between China and India on the flanks of the eastern Himalayas. Its northern border runs along the mountain tops. In this border area is Mount Everest, at 29,028 feet (8,848 metres) the highest mountain in the world, and Nepal also has the six other highest mountains within its borders. The climate is subtropical in the south and all regions are affected by the monsoon. Nepal is one of the world's poorest and least developed countries, with most of the population involved in subsistence farming. Some mineral deposits exist, such as copper, iron ore, mica, and ochre, but because of the country's inaccessible terrain they have not been completely charted. With Indian and Chinese aid, however, roads have been built from the north and south to Kathmandu. The construction of hydroelectric power schemes is underway, although at a high cost. Nepal's main exports are carpets, foodstuffs, clothing, and leather goods, with its principal sources of foreign revenue being tourism and the foreign earnings of its Gurkha soldiers. Nepal now attracts thousands of visitors each year, many of whom belong to trekking and climbing expeditions.

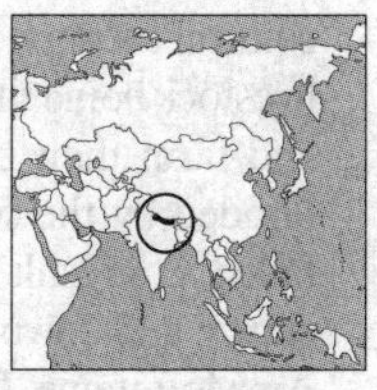

Area: 56,827 sq miles/147,181 sq km
Population: 21,127,000
Capital: Kathmandu (Katmandu)
Form of government: Constitutional Monarchy
Religions: Hinduism, Buddhism
Currency: Nepalese Rupee

Netherlands, the Situated in northwest Europe, the Netherlands (also known as Holland) is bounded to the north and west by the North Sea. Around half of the Netherlands is below sea level and the Dutch have tackled some huge reclamation schemes to add some land area to the country. One such scheme is the IJsselmeer, where four large reclaimed areas (polders) have added an extra 637 square miles (1,650 square kilometres) for cultivation and an overspill town for Amsterdam. The Netherlands has mild winters and cool summers. Agriculture and horticulture are highly mechanized, and the most notable feature is the sea of glass under which salad vegetables, fruit, and flowers are grown. Manufacturing industries include chemicals, machinery, petroleum, refining, metallurgy, and electrical engineering. Rotterdam, the main port of the Netherlands, is the largest port in the world.

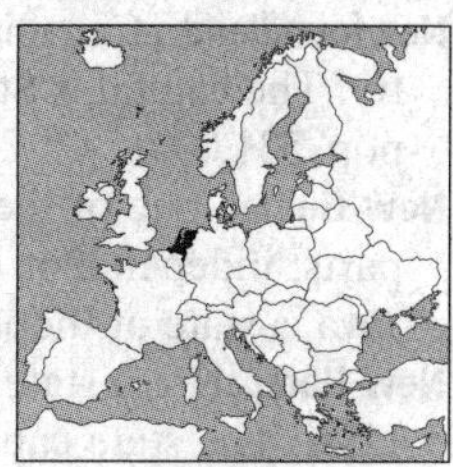

Area: 15,770 sq miles/40,844 sq km
Population: 15,517,000
Capital: Amsterdam
Seat of government: The Hague (Den Haag, 's-Gravenhage)
Other major cities: Eindhoven, Rotterdam
Form of government: Constitutional Monarchy
Religions: RC, Dutch reformed, Calvinism
Currency: Euro

Netherlands Antilles an Overseas Division of the Netherlands, consisting of two sets of islands spread over the southern Caribbean: the Southern Netherlands Antilles (Bonaire and Curaçao) and the Northern Netherlands Antilles (Saba, St Maarten and St Eustatius). Aruba was part of the group until 1986. The islands have a tropical climate. Oil refining and tourism are the most important economic activities. The capital is Willemstad. (309 sq miles/800 sq km; pop. 207,300; cur. Netherland Antilles Guilder)

Neva the river in northwest Russia which flows through St Petersburg. (Length 45 miles/74 km)

Nevada a state in the west of the USA, consisting mostly of desert. The state capital is Carson City. (110,540 sq miles/286,298 sq km; pop. 2,206,000)

Newark a major port city in the state of New Jersey, USA. (Pop. 278,000)

New Britain the largest offshore island belonging to Papua New Guinea, in the Bismarck Archipelago. (14,100 sq miles/36,500 sq km; pop. 446,000)

New Brunswick a state on the coast in southeast Canada, bordering the USA. The state capital is Fredericton. (28,354 sq miles/73,436 sq km; pop. 763,000)

New Caledonia (Nouvelle Calédonie) The most southerly of the Melanesian countries in the Pacific Ocean. It is a French Overseas Territory but there has been ongoing unrest in the country between the indigenous Melanesians and the French settlers over the question of independence. The main island, Nouvelle Calédonie, is 248 miles (400 kilometres) long and rises to a height of 5,377 feet (1,639 metres) at Mount Panie. The island is divided into two natural regions by the mountain range that runs down its centre: a dry west coast covered with gum tree savannah and a tropical east coast. It has a Mediterranean-type climate with rainfall at its heaviest between December and March. The country is rich in mineral resources, particularly nickel, which accounts for 90 per cent of its exports. Other exports include coffee and copra. The main tourist resorts are on the east coast of Nouvelle Calédonie.

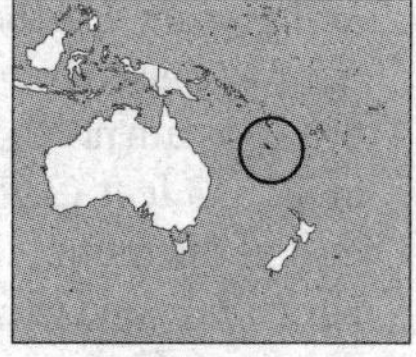

Area: 7,172 sq miles/18,575 sq km
Population: 189,000
Capital: Nouméa
Form of government: French Overseas Territory
Religion: RC
Currency: Franc

Newcastle a port and industrial city in New South Wales, Australia. (Pop. 485,000)

Newcastle upon Tyne a historical and industrial city in the county of Tyne and Wear, northeast England. (Pop. 187,000)

New Delhi the official capital of India as of 1931. (Pop. 300,000)

New England the name given to northeastern states of the USA: Maine, Vermont, New Hampshire, Connecticut, Massachusetts and Rhode Island.

Newfoundland a Canadian province in the extreme east of the country. The capital is St John's. (143,634 sq miles/372,000 sq km; pop. 531,000)

New Guinea one of the world's largest islands, divided into two parts: independent Papua New Guinea in the east and Irian Jaya, a state of Indonesia, in the west.

New Hampshire a state of New England, in the northeast of the USA. The state capital is Concord. (9,304 sq miles/24,097 sq km; pop. 1,283,000)

New Haven a port in Connecticut, USA. (Pop. 125,000)

New Jersey a state on the Atlantic coast in the northeast of the USA. The state capital is Trenton. (7,836 sq miles/20,295 sq km; pop. 8,555,000)

New Mexico a state in the southwest of the USA, bordering Mexico. The state capital is Santa Fe. (121,666 sq miles/315,115 sq km; pop. 1,839,000)

New Orleans an important and historical port in southern Louisiana, on the Mississippi delta. (Pop. 484,000)

Newport (1) a port and naval base in Rhode Island, USA. (Pop. 27,000) (2) a town and port in southeast Wales, the administrative centre for the Newport council area. (Pop. 130,000) (3) a council area in southeast Wales. (73 sq miles/190 sq km; pop. 133,000)

Newport News a major eastern seaboard port in Virginia, USA. (Pop. 186,000)

Newry and Mourne a district council area in Co. Down, southeast Northern Ireland. (351 sq miles/909 sq km; pop. 83,000)

New South Wales the most populous of the states of Australia, situated in the southeast of the country. The capital is Sydney. (309,433 sq miles/801,430 sq km; pop. 6,654,000)

Newtownabbey a district council area in Co. Antrim, east Northern Ireland. (58 sq miles/151 sq km; pop. 74,000)

New York (1) **City of** the most populous city in the USA, its most important port, and a major financial centre. It is sited in southeast New York State, on the mouth of the Hudson River, and comprises five boroughs: Manhattan, the Bronx, Queens, Brooklyn and Staten Island. (Pop. 8,039,000) (2) **State of** a populous state in the northeast of the USA, on the Atlantic coast. The state capital is Albany (49,576 sq miles/128,402 sq km; pop. 19,048,000)

New Zealand (Aotearoa) A country that lies southeast of Australia in the South Pacific. It comprises two large islands (North Island and South Island), Stewart Island and the Chatham Islands, and many smaller islands. The vast majority of the population live on North Island. New Zealand enjoys very mild winters with regular rainfall and no extremes of heat or cold. North Island is hilly, with isolated mountains, active volcanoes, hot mineral springs, and geysers. Earthquakes occur, and in 1987 considerable damage was caused by one at Edgecumbe. On South Island, the Southern Alps run north to south, and the highest point is Mount Cook at 12,313 feet (3,753 metres). The Canterbury Plains lie to the east of the mountains. Two-thirds of New Zealand is suitable for agriculture and grazing. Meat, wool, and dairy goods are the main products. Forestry supports the pulp and paper industry, and a considerable source of hydroelectric power produces cheap electricity for the manufacturing industry, which now accounts for 30 per cent of New Zealand's exports. Mining is also an important industry, with petroleum, natural gas, limestone, gold, and iron ore being exploited.

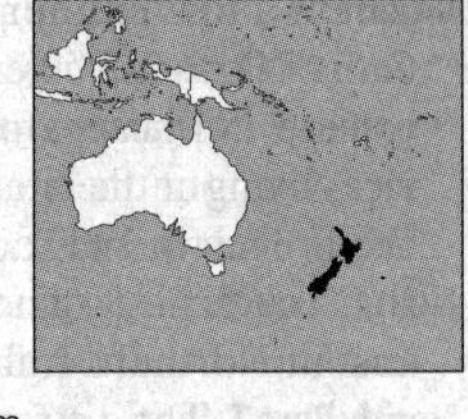

Area: 104,454 sq miles/270,534 sq km
Population: 3,681,000
Capital: Wellington
Other major cities: Auckland, Christchurch, Dunedin, Hamilton
Form of government: Constitutional Monarchy
Religions: Anglicanism, RC, Presbyterianism
Currency: New Zealand Dollar

Niagara Falls spectacular waterfalls on the Niagara River, situated on the Canada-USA border between Lakes Erie and Ontario.

Niamey the capital of Niger in West Africa. (Pop. 723,000)

Nicaragua (1) A country that lies between the Pacific Ocean and the Caribbean Sea on the isthmus of Central America and is sandwiched between Honduras to the north and Costa Rica to the south. The east coast is the wettest part of the country. Behind this is a range of volcanic mountains, and the west coast is a belt of savannah lowland. The western region, which contains the two huge lakes, Nicaragua and Managua, is where most of the population live. The whole country is subject to devastating earthquakes. Nicaragua is primarily an agricultural country and 65 per cent of the labour force work on the land. The main export crops are coffee, bananas, cotton, meat, and gold. There are mineral deposits of gold, copper, and silver, with gold being of prime importance, but the country's economy is dependent on foreign aid. (2) **Lake** a large lake in the southwest of Nicaragua. (3,191 sq miles/8,264 sq km)

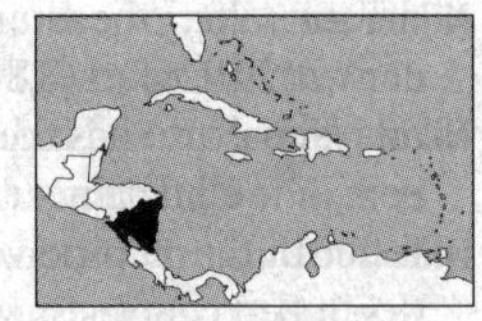

Area: 50,193 sq miles/130,660 sq km
Population: 4,663,000
Capital: Managua
Form of government: Republic
Religion: RC
Currency: Córdoba Oro

Nice a city, port and famous resort town of the Côte D'Azur in southeastern France. (Pop. 334,000)

Nicosia the capital of Cyprus, situated in the centre of the island. (Pop. 89,000)

Niger A landlocked republic in West Africa, just south of the Tropic of Cancer. Over half the country is covered by the encroaching Sahara in the north, and the south lies in the drought-stricken Sahel grasslands. In the extreme southwest corner, the River Niger flows through the country, and in the extreme southeast lies Lake Chad, but the rest of the country is very short of water. Niger is an agricultural country, mainly of subsistence farmers, with the raising of livestock being the major activity. The people in the southwest fish and farm their own food, growing rice and vegetables on land flooded by the River Niger. Farther from the river, crops have failed as a result of successive droughts since 1968. Niger exports cotton and cowpea, but its main export is uranium mined in the Aïr Mountains. There has been unrest in the country involving the Tuareg people who wish for an independent state.

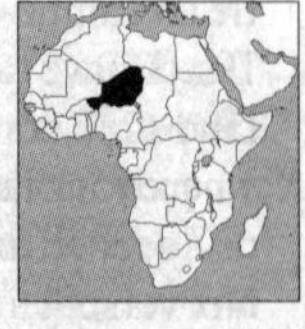

Area: 489,191sq miles/1,267,000 sq km
Population: 9,465,000
Capital: Niamey
Form of government: Republic
Religion: Sunni Islam
Currency: CFA Franc

Niger a river in West Africa flowing through Guinea, Mali, Niger and Nigeria to the Gulf of Guinea. (Length 2,590 miles/4,170 km)

Nigeria A large and populous country in West Africa. From the Gulf of Guinea it extends north to the border with Niger. It has a variable landscape, from the swampy coastal areas and tropical forest belts of the interior, to the mountains and savannah of the north. The two main rivers are the Niger and the Benue, and the Jos Plateau lies just north of their confluence. The climate is hot and humid, and rainfall is heavy at the coast, gradually decreasing inland. The dry far north is affected by the Harmattan, a hot, dry wind blowing from the Sahara. About three quarters of the land is suitable for agriculture and a wide variety of crops is raised by subsistence farmers. The main agricultural products are cocoa, rubber, groundnuts, and cotton, with only cocoa being exported. The country depends on revenue from its crude petroleum exports, which have a low sulphur content and therefore produce less air pollution, making them attractive to American and European countries. Full independence was achieved by Nigeria in 1960 but several factors, including the complex ethnic make-up of the country, mean that the country's progress has frequently been interrupted by strife and internal dissent.

Area: 356,669 sq miles/923,768 sq km
Population: 118,700,000
Capital: Abuja
Other cities: Lagos, Ibadan, Kano, Ogbomosho
Form of government: Federal Republic
Religions: Sunni Islam, Christianity
Currency: Naira

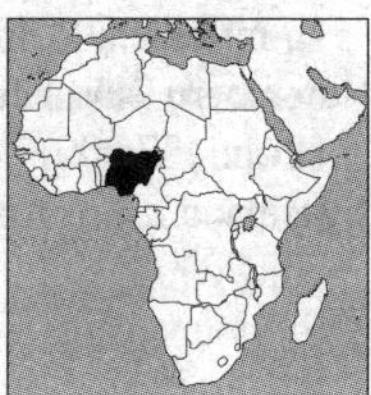

Nijmegen a city of eastern central Netherlands, close to the border with Germany. (Pop. 159,000)

Nikolayev a port and industrial city on the north coast of the Black Sea, in the Ukraine. (Pop. 496,000)

Nile (An Nil) a major river of Africa and the longest river in the world. It rises in Burundi, flows into Lake Victoria and then flows northwards through Uganda, Sudan and Egypt to its delta on the Mediterranean. The river is called the White Nile (Bahr el Abiad) until it reaches Khartoum, in Sudan, where it is then joined by its main tributary, the Blue Nile (Bahr el Azraq), which rises in Ethiopia. (Length 4,160 miles/6,695 km)

Nîmes a city in southern France, overlooking the River Rhône. (Pop. 136,000)

Ningbo a port and industrial city in Zhejiang Province, in central eastern China. (Pop. 472,000)

Ningxia Hui Autonomous Region a region of central northern China, south of Inner Mongolia. The capital is Yinchuan. (23,000 sq miles/60,000 sq km; pop. 5,897,000)

Nis (Nish) a historical city in the east of Serbia, in former Yugoslavia. (Pop. 185,000)

Nizhniy Novgorod an industrial city in the centre of the Russian Federation, situated at the confluence of the Volga and Oka Rivers, and formerly known as Gor'kiy (Gorki). (Pop. 1,346,000)

Nizhniy Tagil an industrial city in the central Ural Mountains of the Russian Federation. (Pop. 385,000)

Norfolk (1) a county in east England, with its administrative centre in the town of Norwich. (2,068 sq miles/5,355 sq km; pop. 790,000) (2) a port and naval base in southeast Virginia, USA. (Pop. 242,000)

Normandy (Normandie) an area of central northern France, now divided into two regions, Haute Normandie and Basse Normandie.

Northampton a town in central England on the River Nene, and the administrative centre of Northamptonshire. (Pop. 179,000)

Northamptonshire a county in central England, with its administrative centre in the town of Northampton. (914 sq miles/ 2,367 sq km; pop. 616,000)

North Ayrshire a council area in west central Scotland, with its administrative centre in the town of Irvine. (341 sq miles/884 sq km; pop. 139,000)

North Cape (Nordkapp) one of Europe's most northerly points, 310 miles (500 kilometres) north of the Arctic Circle in Norway.

North Carolina a state on the southeastern coast of the USA. The state capital is Raleigh. (52,586 sq miles/136,198 sq km; pop. 8,325,000)

North Dakota a state in the west of the USA. The state capital is Bismarck. (70,665 sq miles/183,022 sq km; pop. 628,000)

North Down a district council area in Co. Down, east Northern Ireland. (32 sq miles/82 sq km; pop. 72,000)

Northern Cape one of South Africa's nine provinces, in southwest South Africa, formerly part of the Cape Province, with its administrative centre in Kimberley. (139,666 sq miles/361,830 sq km; pop. 840,000)

Northern Ireland a province of the UK, occupying most of the northern part of the island of Ireland. It is divided into six counties. The capital is Belfast. (5,452 sq miles/14,121 sq km; pop. 1,744,000)

Northern Mariana Islands a group of 14 islands in the northwest Pacific Ocean. In 1986, the islanders voted for commonwealth status in union with the USA and they were granted US citizenship. The country consists mainly of volcanic islands with coral limestone and lava shores. Tourism is the main industry. (179 sq miles/464 sq km; pop. 78,000; cur. US Dollar)

Northern Territory a state in northern Australia. The capital is Darwin. (519,770 sq miles/1,346,200 sq km; pop. 200,000)

North Lanarkshire a council area in central Scotland, with its administrative centre in the town of Motherwell. (684 sq miles/ 1,771 sq km; pop. 307,000)

North Pole the northernmost point on the earth's axis.

North Sea a comparatively shallow branch of the Atlantic Ocean that separates the British Isles from the European mainland.

Northumberland a county in northeastern England on the North Sea, with its administrative centre in the town of Morpeth. (1,943 sq miles/5,033 sq km; pop. 310,000)

North West one of South Africa's nine provinces, in northwest South Africa, with its administrative centre in Mmabatho. (44,899 sq miles/116,320 sq km; pop. 3,354,825)

Northwest Territories a vast area of northern Canada, occupying almost a third of the country's whole land area. The capital is Yellowknife. (1,253,400 sq miles/3,246,000 sq km; pop. 44,000)

North Yorkshire a county in north England, with its administrative centre in Northallerton. (3,322 sq miles/8,603 sq km; pop. 1,016,000)

Norway A country that occupies the western half of the Scandinavian Peninsula in northern Europe and is surrounded to the north, west, and south by water. It shares most of its eastern border with Sweden and almost one-third of the country is north of the Arctic Circle. It is a country of spectacular scenery with fjords, cliffs, rugged uplands, and forested valleys. It has some of the deepest fjords in the world and a huge number of glacial lakes. The climate is temperate as a result of the warming effect of the Gulf Stream. Summers are mild, and although the winters are long and cold, the waters off the west coast remain ice-free. The country's longest river is the Glåma. Agriculture is chiefly concerned with dairy farming and fodder crops. Fishing is an important industry, and the large reserves of forest, which cover just over a quarter of the country, provide lumber for export. Industry is now dominated by the petrochemicals industry based on the reserves of Norwegian oil in the North

Sea. There are almost 60 airports in the country and transport by water is still of importance.

Area: 125,050 sq miles/323,877 sq km
Population: 4,445,000
Capital: Oslo
Other cities: Bergen, Trondheim, Stavanger
Form of government: Constitutional Monarchy
Religion: Lutheranism
Currency: Norwegian Krone

Norwegian Sea a sea lying between Norway, Greenland and Iceland; to the north it joins the Arctic Ocean, and to the south, the Atlantic.

Norwich the county town of Norfolk, in eastern England. (Pop. 173,000)

Nottingham (1) a historical city situated on the River Trent in north central England associated with the legend of Robin Hood, also the administrative centre for Nottinghamshire. (Pop. 283,000) (2) a unitary authority in north central England.

Nottinghamshire a county in the Midlands of England, with its administrative centre in Nottingham. (836 sq miles/2,164 sq km; pop. 1,030,000)

Nouakchott the capital city of Mauritania, near the Atlantic coast. (Pop. 426,000)

Nouméa the capital and chief port of New Caledonia. (Pop. 85,000)

Nova Scotia a province on the eastern coast of Canada. The capital is Halifax. (20,401 sq miles/52,841 sq km; pop. 958,000)

Novi Sad (Ujvidek, Neusatz) a city on the River Danube and the capital of Vojvodina, an autonomous province of Serbia, in the former Yugoslavia. (Pop. 176,000)

Novokuznetsk an industrial city in central southern Siberia. (Pop. 557,000)

Novosibirsk a major industrial city in central Russian Federation. (Pop. 1,397,000)

Nuku'alofa the capital and main port of Tonga. (Pop. 24,000)

Nullarbor Plain a huge, dry and treeless (the name is from the Latin for 'no trees') plain which borders the Great Australian Bight, in Western and Southern Australia.

Nunavut a territory in northwest Canada created on 1 April, 1999, from part of the Northwest Territories of Canada as a semi-autonomous region for the Inuit. The capital is Iqaluit. (844,960 sq miles/2,201,400 sq km; pop. 29,000)

Nuremberg (Nürnberg) a city in Bavaria, central southern Germany. (Pop. 487,000)

Nyasaland the former name of Malawi (until 1966).

O

Oahu the third largest of the islands of Hawaii, USA, where the state capital, Honolulu, and Pearl Harbour are located. (598 sq miles/1,549 sq km; pop. 797,400)

Oakland a port on San Francisco Bay in central western California, USA. (Pop. 414,000)

Ob' a river in the Russian Federation which rises near the border with Mongolia and flows northwards to the Kara Sea. (Length 3,460 miles/5,570 km)

Oberammergau a village in Bavaria in southwest Germany, famed for the Passion play which it puts on every ten years. (Pop. 5,000)

Oceania a general term used to describe the central and southern islands of the Pacific Ocean including those of Australia and New Zealand. (3,400,000 sq miles/8,900,000 sq km; pop. 25,800,000)

Oder a river in central Europe rising in the Czech Republic and flowing north and west to the Baltic Sea; it forms part of the border between Germany and Poland. (Length 567 miles/912 km)

Odessa a major Black Sea port in the Ukraine. (Pop. 990,000)

Offaly a county in the centre of the Republic of Ireland. The county town is Tullamore. (771 sq miles/1,998 sq km; pop. 62,000)

Ogaden a desert region of southeastern Ethiopia, claimed by Somalia.

Ohio a Midwest state of the USA, with a shoreline on Lake Erie. The capital is Columbus. (41,220 sq miles/106,765 sq km; pop. 11,395,00)

Ohio a river in the eastern USA, formed at the confluence of the Allegheny and Monongahela Rivers. It flows west and south and joins the Mississippi at Cairo, Illinois. (Length 980 miles/ 1,575 km)

Okayama a commercial city in southwest Honshu Island, Japan. (Pop. 631,000)

Okhotsk, Sea of a part of the northwestern Pacific Ocean bounded by the Kamchatka Peninsula, the Kuril Islands, and the east coast of Siberia.

Oklahoma a state in the southwest of the USA. The state capital is Oklahoma City. (66,919 sq miles/173,320 sq km; pop. 3,470,000)

Oklahoma City the state capital of Oklahoma. (Pop. 509,000)

Olympia a port and the state capital of Washington, on the west coast of the USA. (Pop. 44,000)

Olympus, Mount (Olimbos) a mountain in central mainland Greece, the home of the gods of ancient Greek myth. (9,570 ft/2,917 m)

Omagh (1) a market town in Northern Ireland. (Pop. 17,000) (2) a district council area in Co. Tyrone, west Northern Ireland. (436 sq miles/1,130 sq km; pop. 46,000)

Omaha a city in eastern Nebraska, on the Missouri River. (Pop. 391,000)

Oman (Sultanate of Oman) Situated in the southeast of the Arabian Peninsula, Oman is a small country in two parts: a small mountainous area overlooking the Strait of Hormuz, which controls the entrance to the Persian Gulf, and the main part of the country, which consists of barren hills rising sharply behind a narrow coastal plain. Inland the hills extend into the unexplored Rub al Khali (The Empty Quarter) in Saudi Arabia. Oman has a desert climate with exceptionally hot and humid conditions from April to October. As a result of the extremely arid environment, less than 1 per cent of the country is cultivated, the main produce being dates and limes, which are exported. The economy is almost entirely dependent on oil, which provides 90 per cent of its exports, although there are deposits of asbestos, copper, and marble, and a smelter at Sohar. Over 15 per cent of the resident population is made up by foreign workers. There are no political parties in Oman and the judicial system is centred on the law of Islam.

Area: 119,498 sq miles/309,500 sq km
Population: 2,302,000
Capital: Muscat (Masqat)
Form of government: Monarchy (Sultanate)
Religion: Ibadi Islam, Sunni Islam
Currency: Rial Omani

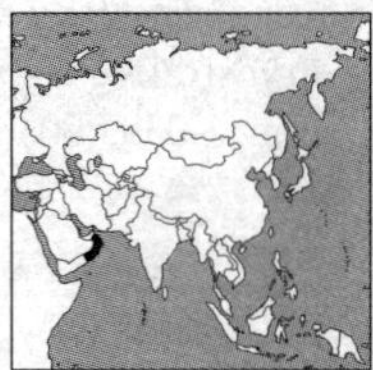

Oman, Gulf of a branch of the Arabian Sea leading to the Strait of Hormuz.

Omdurman a city situated across the River Nile from the Sudanese capital of Khartoum. (Pop. 1,670,000)

Omsk an industrial city in central western Siberia, on the Trans-Siberian Railway. (Pop. 1,338,000)

Ontario a province of central Canada. The capital is Toronto. (412,580 sq miles/1,068,582 sq km; pop. 12,047,000)

Ontario, Lake the smallest and most easterly of the Great Lakes; it drains into the St Lawrence River. (7,550 sq miles/19,550 sq km)

Oporto (Porto) a port in northwest Portugal, and the country's second largest city after Lisbon. (Pop. 264,000)

Oran (Wahran) a Mediterranean port and the second largest city of Algeria. (Pop. 732,000)

Orange the longest river in southern Africa, rising in Lesotho and flowing west to the Atlantic. (Length 1,299 miles/2,090 km)

Orange Free State the former name of South Africa's Free State Province.

Oranjestad (1) the capital of Aruba, and an important port. (Pop. 21,000) (2) the capital of St Eustatius, and a port. (Pop. 2,000)

Oregon a state in the northwest of the USA, on the Pacific. The state capital is Salem. (96,981 sq miles/251,180 sq km; pop. 3,525,000)

Orinoco a river in northern South America. It rises in southern Venezuela and flows west, then north and finally east to its delta on the Atlantic. It forms part of the border between Colombia and Venezuela. (Length 1,370 miles/2,200 km)

Orissa an eastern state of India. The capital is Bhubaneswar. (60,103 sq miles/155,707 sq km; pop. 37,424,000)

Orkney Islands a group of some 90 islands off the northeast coast of Scotland, which go to make up an island authority of Scotland, with its administrative centre in the town of Kirkwall. (377 sq miles/976 sq km; pop. 20,000)

Orlando a city in central Florida, and the focus for visitors to Disney World and Cape Canaveral. (Pop. 196,000)

Orléans a city in north central France, on the River Loire. (Pop. 112,000)

Osaka a port on south Honshu Island, and the third largest city in Japan after Tokyo and Yokohama. (Pop. 2,603,000)

Osijek a city in eastern Croatia, on the Drava River. It was formerly called Esseg. (Pop. 90,000)

Oslo the capital of Norway, and its main port, in the southeast of the country. From 1624 to 1925 it was called Christiania (Kristiania). (Pop. 787,000)

Otranto, Strait of the waterway separating the heel of Italy from Albania.

Ottawa (1) the capital of Canada, in eastern Ontario, on the Ottawa River. (Pop. 348,000) (2) a river of central Canada which flows into the St Lawrence River at Montreal. (Length 790 miles/1,271 km)

Ouagadougou the capital of Burkina Faso, situated in the centre of the country. (Pop. 840,000)

Oviedo a steelmaking city in northern Spain, capital of the province of Asturias. (Pop. 201,000)

Oxford an old university city situated on the confluence of the Rivers Thames and Cherwell in south England, administrative centre of Oxfordshire. (Pop. 122,000)

Oxfordshire a inland county in southern central England, with its administrative centre in the city of Oxford. (1,008 sq miles/2,611 sq km; pop. 590,000)

P

Pacific Ocean the largest and deepest ocean on Earth, situated between Asia and Australia to the west and the Americas to the east. (63,838,000 sq miles/165,384,000 sq km)

Padang a port and the capital of West Sumatra, Indonesia. (Pop. 586,000)

Padua (Padova) a historical city in Veneto, northeast Italy. (Pop. 212,000)

Pago Pago the capital of American Samoa. (Pop. 5,000)

Painted Desert a desert of colourful rocks in northern Arizona, USA. (7,500 sq miles/19,400 sq km)

Pakistan (Islamic Republic of Pakistan) A country that lies just north of the Tropic of Cancer and has the Arabian Sea as its southern border. The valley of the Indus River splits the country into a highland region in the west and a lowland region in the east. A weak form of tropical monsoon climate occurs over most of the country and conditions in the north and west are arid. Temperatures are high everywhere in summer but winters are cold in the mountains. Most agriculture is subsistence, with wheat and rice as the main crops. Cotton and rice are the main cash crops, but areas that can be cultivated are restricted because of waterlogging and saline soil. Pakistan's wide range of mineral resources has yet to be extensively developed and industry concentrates on food processing, textiles, consumer goods, and handicrafts. A lack of modern transport, due to its mountainous terrain, hinders the country's economic progress.

Area: 307,374 sq miles/796,095 sq km
Population: 134,146,000
Capital: Islamabad
Other cities: Faisalabad, Hyderabad, Karachi, Lahore
Form of government: Federal Islamic Republic
Religion: Sunni Islam, Shia Islam
Currency: Pakistan Rupee

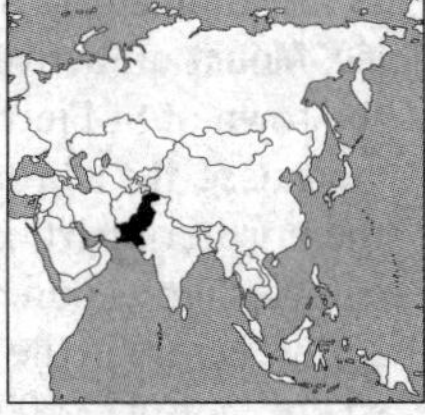

Palau A republic consisting of a group of approximately 350 islands, lying in the western Pacific, 7 degrees north of the Equator and about 625 miles (900 kilometres) equidistant from New Guinea to the south and the Philippines to the west. A barrier reef to the west forms a large lagoon dotted with islands. Coral formations and marine life here are amongst the richest in the world. Formerly known as Belau, the republic has an agreement of free association with the United States. Subsistence fishing and agriculture are the mainstays of the economy but there is also some tourism. In addition, natural resources include minerals (particularly gold and sea-bed deposits) and forests.

Area: 177 sq miles/459 sq km
Population: 17,000
Capital:Koror
Form of government: Free Associated Republic (USA)
Religions: RC, Modekngei
Currency: US Dollar

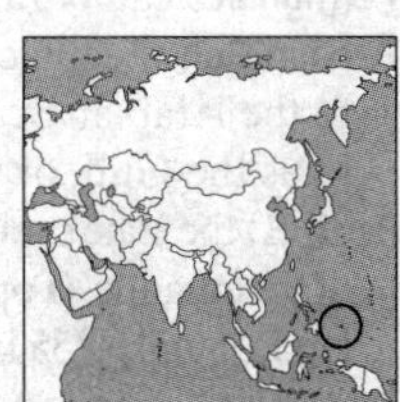

Palembang a port in west Indonesia on the southeast coast of the island of Sumatra. (Pop. 1,462,000)

Palermo the capital of Sicily, Italy, on the northwest coast. (Pop. 685,000)

Palestinian Autonomous Regions Palestine was an ancient historical region on the eastern shore of the Mediterranean Sea, also known as 'The Holy Land' because of its symbolic importance for Christians, Jews, and Muslims. It was part of the Ottoman Empire from the early part of the 16th century until 1917, when it was captured by the British. The Balfour Declaration of 1917 increased Jewish hopes that they might be enabled to establish a Jewish state in Palestine. This was realized in 1948 with the United Nations' creation of the State of Israel, which partitioned Palestine between Jordan and Israel. This act created hostility among Israel's Arab neighbours and Palestinians indigenous to the area, many of whom left, particularly for neighbouring Jordan. Since that time, the territory has been disputed, leading to a series of wars between the Arabs and Israelis and to conflict between Israeli forces and the Palestine Liberation Organization. The disputed areas include the West Bank, the Gaza Strip, and parts of Jerusalem. In 1994, limited autonomy of the Gaza Strip and the West Bank was granted to the appointed Palestinian National Authority, and Israeli military forces began a withdrawal of the area. The whole peace process has, however, been compromised by ongoing violent conflict.

Area: Gaza Strip 146 sq miles/360 sq km, West Bank 2,269 sq miles/5,860 sq km
Population: Gaza Strip 924,200, West Bank 2,050,000
Form of government: Autonomous Regions (with limited powers)
Religions: Sunni Islam, Shia Islam, Eastern Catholicism
Currency: Israeli Shekel and Jordanian Dinar

Palma (Palma de Mallorca) The capital of Majorca and of the Balearic Islands. (Pop. 351,000)

Palm Beach a resort on an island off the east coast of Florida, USA, with the manufacturing centre of West Palm Beach on the mainland opposite. (Pop. 37,000)

Pamir a region of high plateaus in central Asia which straddles the borders of Tajikistan, Afghanistan and China.

Pampas the flat grasslands of central Argentina.

Pamplona a city in northeastern Spain, famous for its annual bull-running festival in July. (Pop. 183,100)

Panama A country located at the narrowest point in Central America. Only 58 kilometres (36 miles) separates the Caribbean Sea from the Pacific Ocean at Panama, and the Panama Canal, which divides the country, is the main route from the Caribbean and the Atlantic to the Pacific. The climate is tropical, with high temperatures throughout the year and only a short dry season from January to April. The country is heavily forested and very little is cultivated. Rice is the staple food. The economy is heavily dependent on the Canal and income from it is a major foreign currency earner. The country has extensive lumber resources, and mahogany is an important export. Other exports include petroleum products, coffee, shrimps, and raw sugar. In 1989, the country was briefly invaded by US military forces in order to depose the corrupt dictator General Noriega.

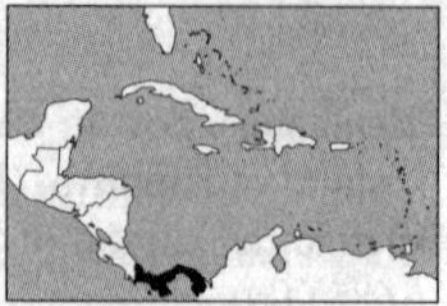

Area: 29,157 sq miles/75,517 sq km
Population: 2,674,000
Capital: Panamá
Other cities: San Miguelito, Colón
Form of government: Republic
Religion: RC
Currency: Balboa

Panama Canal a canal 40 miles (64 kilometres) long that runs through the centre of Panama, linking the Caribbean Sea to the Pacific Ocean. It was completed in 1914.

Panama City (Panamá) the capital of Panama, situated at the Pacific end of the Panama Canal. (Pop. 431,000)

Papeete the capital of French Polynesia, on the northwest coast of Tahiti. (Pop. 30,000)

Papua New Guinea A country in the southwest Pacific, comprising the eastern half of the island of New Guinea together with hundreds of other islands including New Britain, the Bismarck Archipelago and New Ireland. There are active volcanoes on some of the islands and almost 100,000 people were evacuated in 1994 when two volcanoes erupted on New Britain. The country has a mountainous interior surrounded by broad swampy plains. The climate is tropical, with high temperatures and heavy rainfall. Subsistence farming is the main economic activity although some coffee, cocoa, and copra are grown for cash. Lumber is cut for export, and fishing and fish processing industries are developing. Minerals, such as copper, gold, silver, and oil, form the mainstay of the economy. The country still receives valuable aid from Australia, which governed it before independence was gained in 1975.

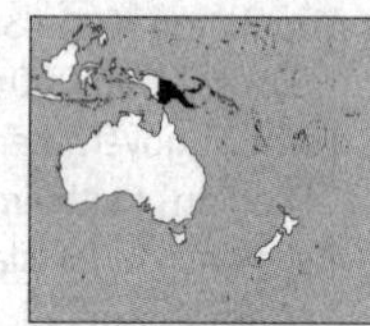

Area: 178,704 sq miles/462,840 sq km
Population: 4,400,000
Capital: Port Moresby
Form of government: Republic
Religions: Protestantism, RC
Currency: Kina

Paraguay A small landlocked country in central South America, bordered by Bolivia, Brazil, and Argentina. The climate is tropical, with abundant rain and a short dry season. The River Paraguay splits the country into the Chaco (a flat semi-arid plain on the west), and a partly forested undulating plateau on the east. Almost 95 per cent of the population live east of the river, where crops grown on the fertile plains include cassava, sugar cane, maize, cotton, and soya beans. Immediately west of the river, on the low Chaco, are huge cattle ranches that provide meat for export. Deposits of minerals, such as iron, petroleum, and manganese, are not exploited commercially. The lumber industry is important, however, with tannin and petitgrain oil also being produced. With three important rivers, the Paraguay, Paraná, and Pilcomayo, the country has many impressive waterfalls, such as the Guaira Falls. In cooperation with its neighbours, it has developed its potential for hydroelectric power to the full and is able to meet all its energy needs. Developed with Brazil and opened in 1991, the Itaipu Hydroelectric Dam on the (Alto) Paraná River is the largest dam in the world. Other hydroelectric schemes include the Yacyreta Dam, developed with Argentina and opened in 1994.

Area: 157,048 sq miles/406,752 sq km
Population: 4,955,000
Capital: Asunción
Other city: Ciudad del Este
Form of government: Republic
Religion: RC
Currency: Guaraní

Paraguay a major river of South America. It flows south from Brazil through into Paraguay to join the River Paraná. (Length 1,500 miles/2,400 km)

Paramaribo the capital and main port of Suriname. (Pop. 216,000)

Paraná the second longest river in South America. It rises in Brazil and flows south to join the River Plate. (Length 1,800 miles/2,900 km)

Paris the capital of France, in the north of the country, on the River Seine. (Pop. 2,113,000)

Parma a historical city in northern Italy, in Emilia-Romagna. (Pop. 169,000)

Páros a Greek island in the Cyclades group. (75 sq miles/194 sq km; pop. 7,400)

Pasadena a city in southwest California, USA. (Pop. 139,000)

Patagonia the most southerly region of South America in Argentina and Chile stretching from the Andes to the Atlantic.

Patna the capital of the state of Bihar, in northeast India, on the River Ganges. (Pop. 1,404,000)

Patras (Pátrai) a Greek port and the main city of the Peloponnese Peninsula. (Pop. 174,000)

Peace a river in western Canada, a tributary of the Slave/Mackenzie River, rising in British Columbia. (Length 1,065miles/1,715 km)

Pearl Harbour a harbour and naval base on Oahu, Hawaii; the Japanese attack on the US fleet based there in 1941 drew the USA into World War II.

Pécs the main city of southwest Hungary. (Pop. 163,000)

Pelée, Mount an active volcano on Martinique, which destroyed the town of St Pierre in 1902. (4,583 ft /1,397 m)

Peloponnese, the a broad peninsula of southern Greece, joined to the northern part of the country by the Isthmus of Corinth.

Pembrokeshire a council area in southwest Wales, with its administrative centre in the town of Haverfordwest. (614 sq miles/1,589 sq km; pop. 113,000)

Penang a state of west Malaysia comprising Penang Island and the mainland province of Wellesley; the capital is George Town. (398 sq miles/1,031 sq km; pop. 1,142,000)

Pennines a range of hills that runs down the middle of northern England from the Scottish border to the Midlands, rising to 2,087 feet (894 metres) at Cross Fell.

Pennsylvania a state of the northeastern USA situated mainly in the Appalachian Mountains. The capital is Harrisburg. (45,333 sq miles/117,412 sq km; pop. 12,295,000)

Perm' an industrial port on the Kama River in the western Ural Mountains of the Russian Federation. It was known as Molotov from1940–57. (Pop. 1,002,000)

Perpignan a cathedral town in southwestern France. (Pop. 109,000)

Persian Gulf the huge inlet to the south of Iran which is connected to the Arabian Sea by the Strait of Hormuz. It is often referred to as the Gulf, or the Arabian Gulf.

Perth (1) the state capital of Western Australia, which includes the port of Freemantle. (Pop. 1,391,000) (2) a city and former capital of Scotland, 35 miles (55 kilometres) north of Edinburgh. (Pop. 41,000)

Perth and Kinross a council area in north central Scotland, with its administrative centre in Perth. (2019 sq miles/5,321 sq km; pop. 133,000)

Peru A country located just south of the Equator, on the Pacific coast of South America. It has three distinct regions from west to east: the coast, the high sierra of the Andes, and the tropical jungle. The climate on the narrow coastal belt is mainly desert, while the Andes are wet, and east of the mountains is equatorial with tropical forests. Most large-scale agriculture is in the oases and fertile, irrigated river valleys that cut across the coastal desert. Sugar and cotton are the main exports. Sheep, llamas, vicunas, and alpacas are kept for wool. The fishing industry was once the largest in the world but recently the shoals have become depleted. Anchovies form the bulk of the catch and are used to make fish meal. Minerals such as iron ore, silver, copper, and lead, as well as natural gas and petroleum, are extracted in large quantities and are an important part of the economy. The economy in the late 1980s was damaged by the declining value of exports, inflation, drought, and guerrilla warfare, which made the government introduce an austerity program in the 1990s.

Area: 496,225 sq miles/1,285,216 sq km
Population: 25,015,000; *capital* Lima
Other cities: Arequipa, Callao, Cuzco, Trujillo
Form of government: Republic
Religion: RC
Currency: Nuevo Sol

Peshawar a historical town in northwest Pakistan at the foot of the Khyber Pass. (Pop. 1,095,000)

Philadelphia a port and city in southeast Pennsylvania, the fifth largest city in the USA. (Pop. 1,519,000)

Philippines A country comprising a group of 7,107 islands and islets in the western Pacific that are scattered over a great area. There are four main groups: Luzon and Mindoro to the north, the Visayan Islands in the centre, Mindanao and the Sulu Archipelago in the south, and Palawan in the southwest. Manila, the capital, is on Luzon. Most of the islands are mountainous and earthquakes are common. The climate is humid, with high temperatures and high rainfall. Typhoons can strike during the rainy season from July to October. Rice, cassava, sweet potatoes, and maize are the main subsistence crops, and coconuts, sugar cane, pineapples, and bananas are grown for export. Agriculture employs around 42 per cent of the workforce. Mining is an important industry, and its main products include gold, silver, nickel, copper, and salt. Fishing is also of major importance and there are sponge fisheries on some of the islands. Other prime industries include textiles, food processing, chemicals, and electrical engineering.

Area: 115,813 sq miles/300,000 sq km
Population: 71,899,000
Capital: Manila
Other cities: Cebu, Davao, Quezon City
Form of government: Republic
Religions: RC, Protestant, Sunni Islam
Currency: Philippines Peso

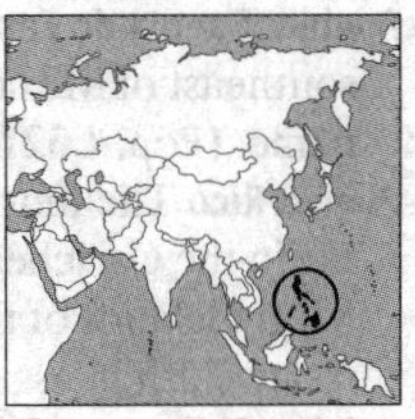

Phnom-Penh the capital of Cambodia, in the south of the country. (Pop. 1,134,000)

Phoenix the state capital of Arizona, USA. (Pop. 1,410,000)

Piedmont (Piemonte) a region of northwest Italy. The main town is Turin. (Pop. 4, 269,000)

Pierre the capital of South Dakota, USA. (Pop. 14,000)

Pietermaritzburg a city in the province of KwaZulu/Natal in eastern South Africa and capital of the former province of Natal. (Pop. 420,000)

Piraeus (Piraévs) the main port of Greece, close to Athens, on the Aegean Sea. (Pop. 189,000)

Pisa a city in northwestern Italy on the River Arno, famous for its leaning bell tower. (Pop. 92,000)

Pitcairn Islands An island group and a British Overseas Territory situated in the southeast Pacific Ocean. The islands are volcanic with high lava cliffs and rugged hills. The islanders are direct descendants of the HMS *Bounty* mutineers and their Tahitian wives. Subsistence agriculture produces a wide variety of tropical and subtropical crops but the sale of postage stamps is the country's main revenue earner.

Area: 17 sq miles/45 sq km
Population: 50
Form of government: British Overseas Territory
Religion: Protestant
Currency: New Zealand Dollar

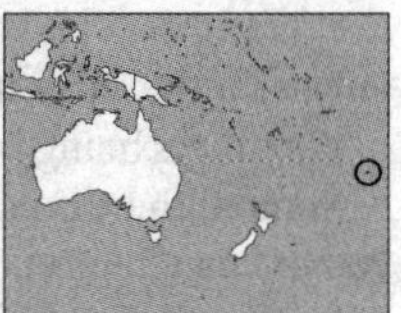

Pittsburgh an industrial city in western Pennsylvania, USA. (Pop. 335,000)

Plate (Río de la Plata) the huge estuary of the Paraná and Uruguay Rivers on the southeast coast of South America. (Length 171 miles/275 km)

Plenty, Bay of the inlet on the north coast of the North Island, New Zealand.

Plovdiv a major market town in Bulgaria. (Pop. 340,000)

Plymouth (1) a port and naval base in southwest England and the place from which the Pilgrim Fathers set sail in the Mayflower in 1620. (Pop. 250,000) (2) the capital of the island of Montserrat in the Caribbean. (Pop. 3,200) (3) a town in Massachusetts, USA, which has grown from the first European settlement in New England, established by the Pilgrim Fathers of the Mayflower. (Pop. 37,100)

Plzen (Pilsen) an industrial city in western Bohemia, Czech Republic. Pilsner lager beer was first produced here in 1842. (Pop. 166,000)

Po the longest river in Italy, flowing eastwards from the Alps across a fertile plain to the Adriatic Sea. (Length 405 miles/642 km)

Podgorica (Podgoritsa) the capital of Montenegro, in former Yugoslavia. It was formerly called Titograd (1948–92). (Pop. 137,000)

Pohnpei the island on which Kolonia, the capital of the Federated States of Micronesia, stands.

Pointe-à-Pitre the main port of Guadeloupe in the Caribbean. (Pop. 22,000)

Poitiers a historical university city in south central France. (Pop. 85,000)

Poland A country situated on the North European Plain. It borders Germany to the west, the Czech Republic and Slovakia to the south, and Belarus and Ukraine to the east. Poland consists mainly of lowlands, and the climate is continental, marked by long, severe winters and short, warm summers. Over one-quarter of the labour force is involved in predominantly small-scale agriculture. The main crops are potatoes, wheat, barley, sugar beet, and fodder crops. The industrial sector of the economy is large-scale. Poland has large deposits of coal, and reserves of natural gas, copper and silver, and is one of the main producers of sulphur. Vast forests stretching inland from the coast supply the paper and furniture industries. Other industries include food processing, engineering, shipbuilding, textiles, and chemicals.

The country has serious environmental problems, due to untreated sewage, industrial discharges, air pollution, and soil contamination, but some progress has been made to rectify matters. Tourism is on the increase, and the country's main tourist attractions include its Baltic resorts, mountains, and cultural and historical sites.

Area: 124, 808 sq miles/323,250 sq km
Population: 38,628,000
Capital: Warsaw (Warszawa)
Other cities: Gdansk, Cracow, Lódz, Wroclaw
Form of government: Republic
Religion: RC
Currency: Zloty

Polynesia the largest of the three island divisions of the Pacific, the others being Micronesia and Melanesia. The group includes Samoa, the Cook, Society, and Marquesas Islands, and Tonga.

Pomerania a region of north central Europe, which extends along the south coast of the Baltic Sea, mainly in Poland.

Pompeii an ancient city near Naples which was smothered by ash from an eruption of Vesuvius in AD 79.

Pondicherry a port and the capital of the Union Territory of Pondicherry in southeast India, on the Coromandel Coast. (Pop. 225,000)

Ponta Delgada a port and the capital of the Azores, on São Miguel Island. (Pop. 20,000)

Popocatépetl a volcano, twinned with Ixtacihuatl, 40 miles (65 kilometres) southeast of Mexico City. (17,887 ft/5,452 m)

Port-au-Prince the main port and capital of Haiti. (Pop. 1,083,000)

Port Elizabeth a port and industrial city on Algoa Bay in the Eastern Cape Province of South Africa. (Pop. 834,000)

Port Harcourt the second port of Nigeria after Lagos. (Pop. 1,054,000)

Port Jackson the great natural harbour on the coast of southeast Australia, also called Sydney Harbour.

Portland (1) a port on the Atlantic coast of the USA, in Maine. (Pop. 65,000) (2) a port on the Williamette River in Oregon, USA. (Pop. 545,000)

Port Louis the capital and main port of Mauritius, on the east coast of the island. (Pop. 141,000)

Port Moresby the capital and main port of Papua New Guinea, in the southeast. (Pop. 312,000)

Porto Alegre a port and the regional capital of southern Brazil. (Pop. 1,335,000)

Port of Spain the capital and chief port of Trinidad and Tobago. (Pop. 45,000)

Porto Novo the administrative capital of Benin in West Africa. (Pop. 227,000)

Port Said the port at the Mediterranean end of the Suez Canal, Egypt. (Pop. 537,000)

Portsmouth a port and major naval base in southern England. (Pop. 176,000)

Port Stanley the capital of the Falkland Islands. (Pop. 2,000)

Port Talbot a town in southeast Wales, on Swansea Bay, the administrative centre for the Neath Port Talbot council area. (Pop. 37,000)

Portugal A country in the southwest corner of Europe, Portugal makes up about 15 per cent of the Iberian Peninsula and is the least developed country in western Europe. The most mountainous areas of Portugal lie to the north of the River Tagus. In the northeast, are the steep-sided mountains of Tras-os-Montes, and to south of this the Douro valley runs from the Spanish border to Oporto on the Atlantic coast. South of the Tagus is the Alentejo, with its wheat fields and cork plantations. The Alentejo continues to the hinterland of the Algarve where there are groves of almond, fig, and olive trees. Agriculture employs one-quarter of the labour force, and crops include wheat, maize, grapes, and tomatoes. Portugal's most important natural resources are its minerals, largely developed after World War II. These include coal, iron ore, tin, and copper. Port and Madeira wine are renowned, and the country is a main exporter of olive oil. Manufacturing industry includes textiles, clothing, footwear, food processing, and cork products. Tourism, particularly in the south, is the main foreign currency earner. A petrochemical plant and oil refinery is located near Lisbon and hydroelectric power has been developed in recent years. Portugal is also renowned for its high-quality craft products, especially lace, pottery, and tiles.

Area: 35,514 sq miles/91,982 sq km
Population: 10,300,000
Capital: Lisbon (Lisboa)
Other cities: Braga, Coimbra, Oporto, Setúbal
Form of government: Republic
Religion: RC
Currency: Euro

Potsdam a city just southwest of Berlin, Germany. (Pop. 128,000)

Powys a council area in mid-Wales, with its administrative centre in the town of Llandrindod Wells. (1,960 sq miles/5,077 sq km; pop. 122,000)

Poznan (Posen) a historical city in central western Poland. (Pop. 581,000)

Prague (Praha) the capital and principal city of the Czech Republic, situated on the Vltava River. (Pop. 1,174,000)

Praia the capital of the island republic of Cape Verde, off the coast of West Africa. (Pop. 98,000)

Pretoria the administrative capital of South Africa, 30 miles (48 kilometres) north of Johannesburg. (Pop. 1,228,000)

Prince Edward Island the smallest of the provinces of Canada, an island in the Gulf of St Lawrence. The provincial capital is Charlottetown. (2,185 sq miles/5,660 sq km; pop. 141,000)

Pristina the capital of the autonomous province of Kosovo in Serbia, in the former Yugoslavia. (Pop. 194,000)

Provence a historical region of coastal southeast France.

Providence a port, and the state capital of Rhode Island, USA. (Pop. 177,000)

Prussia a historical state of Germany, centring on its capital, Berlin.

Puebla (Puebla de Zaragoza) a major city 75 miles (120 kilometres) southeast of Mexico City, and the capital of a state of the same name. (Pop. 1,321,000)

Puerto Rico The most easterly of the Greater Antilles islands, lying in the Caribbean between the Dominican Republic and the Virgin Islands of the United States. It is a self-governing Commonwealth in association with the USA and includes the main island, Puerto Rico, the two small islands of Vieques and Culebra, and a fringe of smaller uninhabited islands. The climate is tropical, modified slightly by cooling sea breezes. The main mountains on Puerto Rico are the Cordillera Central, which reach 4,390 feet (1,338 metres) at the peak of Cerro de Punta. Dairy farming is the most important agricultural activity but the whole agricultural sector has been overtaken by industry in recent years. Tax relief and cheap labour encourage American businesses to be based in Puerto Rico. Products include textiles, clothing, electrical and electronic goods, plastics, pharmaceuticals, and petrochemicals. Tourism is another developing industry, and there is the potential for oil exploration both on and offshore. San Juan is one of the largest and best natural harbours in the Caribbean.

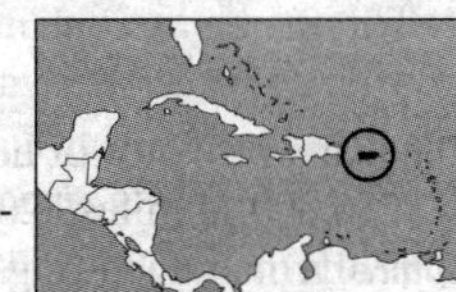

Area: 3,427 sq miles/8,875 sq km
Population: 3,736,000
Capital: San Juan
Form of government: Self-governing Commonwealth of the USA
Religions: RC, Protestantism;
Currency: US Dollar

Puglia (Apulia) a region of southeast Italy. The regional capital is Bari. (7,500 sq miles/19,250 sq km; pop. 4,170,000)

Pune (Poona) a historical and industrial city east of Bombay, in western India. (Pop. 2,590,000)

Punjab (1) a state in northwestern India. The capital is Chandigarh. (19,440 sq miles/50,362 sq km; pop. 24,764,000) (2) a fertile province in the north of Pakistan. The capital is Lahore. (79,283 sq miles/205,344 sq km; pop. 80,441,000)

Pusan a major port, and the second largest city in South Korea after Seoul. (Pop. 4,085,000)

Putumayo a river of northwest South America, rising in the Andes and flowing southeast to join the River Amazon. (Length 1,180 miles/1,900 km)

Pyongyang (Pyeongyang) an industrial city and the capital of North Korea. (Pop. 2,725,000)

Pyrenees (Pyrénées, Pirineos) a range of mountains that runs from the Bay of Biscay to the Mediterranean, along the border between France and Spain. The highest point is Pico d'Aneto (11,170 ft/3,404 m).

Q

Qatar A little emirate that lies halfway along the coast of the Persian Gulf. It consists of a low barren peninsula and a few small islands. The climate is hot and uncomfortably humid in summer, and the winters are mild with rain in the north. Most fresh water comes from natural springs and wells or from desalination plants. Some vegetables and fruit are grown but the herding of sheep, goats, and some cattle is the main agricultural activity. The country is famous for its high-quality camels. The discovery and exploitation of oil has resulted in a high standard of living for the people of Qatar, with some of the revenue being used to build hospitals and a road system and to provide free education and medical care. The Dukhan oil field has an expected life of 40 years and the reserves of natural gas are enormous. In order to diversify the economy, new industries such as iron and steel, cement, fertilizers, and petrochemical plants, have been developed.

Area: 4,247 sq miles/11,000 sq km
Population: 558,000
Capital: Doha (Ad Dawhah)
Form of government: Absolute Monarchy (Emirate)
Religions: Wahhabi Sunni Islam
Currency: Qatari Riyal

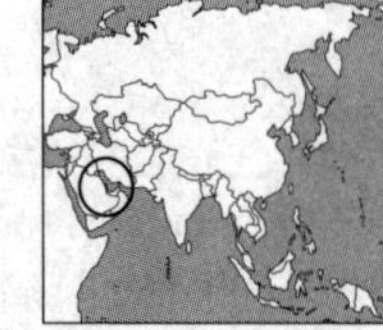

Qazvin (Kasvin) a historical town in northwest Iran. (Pop. 313,000)

Qingdao a city in Shangdong Province in northeastern China. (Pop. 1,449,000)

Qinghai a province of northwestern China. The capital is Xining. (280,000 sq miles/720,000 sq km; pop. 5,259,000)

Qiqihar a manufacturing city in Heilongjiang Province, China. (Pop. 770,000)

Qom (Qum) a holy city in central northern Iran. (Pop. 894,000)

Québec the largest province of Canada, in the east of the country, and also the name of the capital of the province. The majority of the population are French-speaking. (524,300 sq miles/ 1,358,000 sq km; pop. province 7,471,000/city 171,000)

Queen Charlotte Islands a group of some 150 islands lying 100 miles (160 kilometres) off the west coast of Canada. (3,780 sq miles/ 9,790 sq km; pop. 5,620)

Queen Charlotte Strait a waterway, some 16 miles (26 kilometres) wide, between the northeastern coast of Vancouver Island and the mainland of Canada.

Queensland the northeastern state of Australia. The state capital is Brisbane. (491,200 sq miles/1,272,200 sq km; pop. 3,712,000)

Quercy a former province of southwestern France, around Cahors.

Quetta the capital of the province of Baluchistan, Pakistan. (Pop. 621,000)

Quezon City a major city and university town, now a part of Metro Manila, and the administrative capital of the Philippines from 1948 to 1976. (Pop. 1,165,000)

Quito the capital of Ecuador, lying just south of the Equator, 9,350 feet (2,850 metres) high in the Andes. (Pop. 1,468,000)

Qwaqwa one of ten former South African Homelands, the area is now part of the province of Free State, in central South Africa.

R

Rabat the capital of Morocco, in the northwest, on the Atlantic coast. (Pop. 1,601,000)
Rajasthan a state of northwest India. The state capital is Jaipur. (132,104 sq miles/342,239 sq km; pop. 57,576,000)
Raleigh the state capital of North Carolina, USA. (Pop. 286,000)
Ranchi an industrial town in the state of Bihar, India. (Pop. 863,000)
Rangoon (Yangôn) the capital of Myanmar, and an important port on the mouth of the Rangoon River. (Pop. 4,016,000)
Rarotonga the largest of the Cook Islands, with the capital of the islands, Avarua, on its north coast. (26 sq miles/67 sq km; pop. 12,000)
Ras al Khaymah one of the United Arab Emirates, in the extreme northeast, on the Musandam Peninsula; also the name of its capital city. (653 sq miles/1,690 sq km; pop. emirate 188,000/city 101,000)
Ravenna a city in northeastern Italy, noted for its Byzantine churches. (Pop. 139,000)
Rawalpindi a military town of ancient origins in northern Pakistan. (Pop. 1,558,000)
Recife a regional capital of eastern Brazil. (Pop. 1,461,000)
Red River (1) a river of the southern USA, rising in Texas and flowing east to join the Mississippi. (Length 1,018 miles/1,639 km) (2) (Song Hong, Yuan Jiang) a river that rises in southwest China and flows southeast across the north of Vietnam to the Gulf of Tongking, an inlet of the South China Sea. (Length 500 miles/800 km)
Red Sea a long, narrow sea lying between the Arabian Peninsula and the coast of northeast Africa.
Reggio di Calabria a port on the toe of southern Italy. (Pop. 180,000)
Reggio nell'Emilia a town of Roman origins in northeastern Italy. (Pop. 146,000)
Regina the capital of the province of Saskatchewan, Canada. (Pop. 183,000)
Renfrewshire a council area in west central Scotland, with its administrative centre in the town of Paisley. (101 sq miles/261 sq km; pop. 179,000)
Rennes a industrial city in northeastern France. (Pop. 211,000)
Reno a city and gambling centre in Nevada, USA. (Pop. 198,000)
Réunion an island to the east of Madagascar, which is a French Overseas Department. The capital is Saint-Denis. (969 sq miles/2,510 sq km; pop. 530,000; cur. Euro)
Reykjavik the capital and main port of Iceland, on the southwest coast. (Pop. 114,000)
Reynosa a town in northeastern Mexico, on the border with the USA. (Pop. 432,000)
Rheims (Reims) a historical city in France, and the centre of the production of champagne. (Pop. 185,000)
Rhine (Rhein; Rhin, Rijn) one of the most important rivers of Europe. It rises in the Swiss Alps, flows north through Germany and then west through the Netherlands to the North Sea. (Length 825 miles/1,320 km)
Rhode Island the smallest state in the USA. The state capital is Providence. (1,214 sq miles/3,144 sq km; pop. 1,070,000)
Rhodes (Rodhos) the largest of the Dodecanese group of islands belonging to Greece; also the name of its capital. (540 sq miles/1,399 sq km; pop. city 49,000)
Rhondda Cynon Taff a council area in south Wales, with its administrative centre in the town of Tonypandy. (215 sq miles/558 sq km; pop. 232,000)
Rhône a major river of Europe, rising in the Swiss Alps and flowing west into France, and then south to its delta on the Golfe du Lion. (Length 505 miles/812 km)
Richmond the state capital of Virginia, USA. (Pop. 204,000)
Riga a Baltic port, and the capital of Latvia. (Pop. 725,000)
Rijeka (Fiume) a port in Croatia on the Adriatic coast. (Pop. 152,000)
Rimini a popular resort on the Adriatic Sea, northeastern Italy. (Pop. 132,000)
Rio de Janeiro a major port and former capital (1763–1960) of Brazil, situated in the southeast of the country. (Pop. 6,029,000)
Rio Grande (Río Bravo, Río Grande) a river of North America, rising in the state of Colorado, USA, and flowing southeast to the Gulf of Mexico. For much of its length it forms the border between the USA and Mexico. (Length 1,885 miles/3,078 km)
Rioja, La an autonomous area in the south of the Basque region of Spain, famous for its fine wine.
Riyadh (Ar Riyãd) the capital and commercial centre of Saudi Arabia. (Pop. 3,628,000)
Road Town the capital of the British Virgin Islands. (Pop. 9,000)
Roca, Cabo da a cape sticking out into the Atlantic in central Portugal, to the west of Lisbon, the westernmost point of mainland Europe.
Rockall a tiny, rocky, uninhabited island lying 250 miles (400 kilometres) west of Ireland, and claimed by the UK.
Rocky Mountains (Rockies) a huge mountain range in western North America, extending some 3,000 miles (4,800 kilometres) from British Columbia in Canada to New Mexico in the USA.
Romania Apart from a small extension towards the Black Sea, Romania is almost a circular country. It is located in southeast Europe, bordered by Ukraine, Hungary, Serbia, and Bulgaria. The Carpathian Mountains run through the north, east, and centre of Romania, and these are enclosed by a ring of rich agricultural plains that are flat in the south and west but hilly in the east. Tat the core of Romania is Transylvania within the Carpathian arc. Romania's main river is the Danube, which forms a delta in its lower course. The country has cold snowy winters and hot summers. Agriculture in Romania has been neglected in favour of industry, but major crops include maize, sugar beet, wheat, potatoes, and grapes for wine. Industry includes mining, metallurgy, mechanical engineering, and chemicals. Forests support the lumber and furniture industries in the Carpathians. There have been periods of severe food shortage, with high unemployment and a low standard of living. After the overthrow of the Communist regime in 1989, a new constitution was approved by referendum. The post-communist government has worked hard to bring about changes and improve the economy.

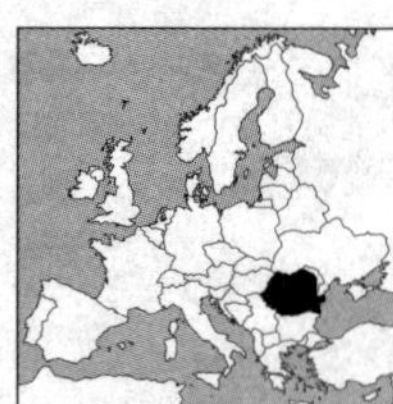

Area: 92,043 sq miles/238,391 sq km
Population: 23,000,000
Capital: Bucharest (Bucuresti)
Other cities: Brasov, Constanta, Timisoara
Form of government: Republic
Religions: Romanian Orthodox, RC
Currency: Leu

Rome (Roma) the historical capital of Italy, on the River Tiber, in the centre of the country near the west coast. (Pop. 2,650,000)

Rosario an industrial and commercial city on the River Paraná in Argentina. (Pop. 1,261,000)

Roscommon a county in the northwest of the Republic of Ireland, with a county town of the same name. (950 sq miles/2,462 sq km; pop. 54,000)

Roseau the capital of the island republic of Dominica, in the east Caribbean. (Pop. 20,000)

Ross Sea a large branch of the Antarctic Ocean, south of New Zealand.

Rostock a major port on the Baltic coast of Germany. (Pop. 193,000)

Rostov-na-Donu (Rostov-on-Don) a major industrial city on the River Don, near the northwestern extremity of the Sea of Azov in southeastern Russian Federation. (Pop. 1,012,000)

Rotterdam the largest city in the Netherlands and the busiest port in the world. (Pop. 589,000)

Roubaix a textile-manufacturing town in northwestern France. (Pop. 96,000)

Rouen a port on the River Seine in northern France. (Pop. 106,000)

Rub al Khali the so-called 'Empty Quarter' – a vast area of sandy desert straddling the borders of Saudi Arabia, Oman and Yemen. (251,000 sq miles/650,000 sq km)

Ruhr the river in northwestern Germany whose valley forms the industrial heartland of western Germany. It joins the Rhine at Duisburg. (Length 146 miles/235 km)

Russia the old name for the Russian Empire, latterly used loosely to refer to the former USSR, and the present Russian Federation.

Russian Federation The largest country in the world, with over one-ninth of the world's land area. The Russian Federation extends from eastern Europe through the Ural Mountains east to the Pacific Ocean. The Caucasus Range forms its boundary with Georgia and Azerbaijan, and it is here that the highest peak in Europe, Mt Elbrus at 18,510 feet (5,642 metres), is located. In the east, Siberia is drained toward the Arctic Ocean by the great Rivers Ob, Yenisey, and Lena and their tributaries. Just to the south of the Central Siberian Plateau lies Lake Baikal, the world's deepest freshwater lake at 5,370 feet (1,637 metres). The Ural Mountains form the boundary between Asia and Europe and they contain a variety of mineral resources. The environment ranges from vast frozen wastes in the north to subtropical deserts in the south. Agriculture is organized into either state or collective farms that mainly produce sugar beet, cotton, potatoes, and vegetables. The country has extensive reserves of coal, oil, gas, iron ore, and manganese. Major industries include iron and steel, cement, transport equipment, engineering, armaments, electronic equipment, and chemicals. The Russian Federation is beset by many economic problems and recovery is likely to be a long and difficult process.

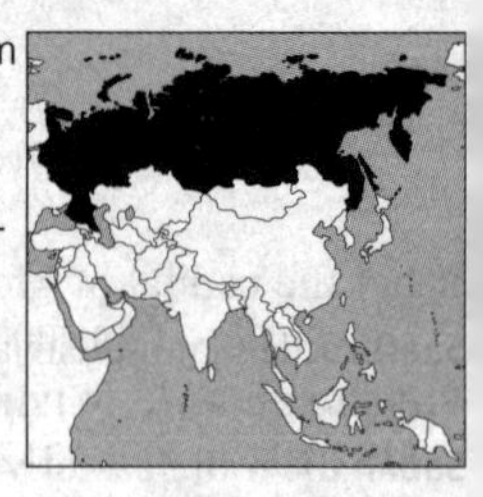

Area: 6,592,850 sq miles/17,075,400 sq km
Population: 146,100,000
Capital: Moscow (Moskva)
Other cities: St Petersburg (formerly Leningrad), Nizhniy Novgorod, Novosibirsk
Form of government: Republic
Religions: Russian Orthodox, Sunni Islam, Shia Islam, RC
Currency: Ruble

Rutland an inland county in central England, with its administrative centre in the town of Oakham. (152 sq miles/394 sq km; pop. 34,000)

Ruwenzori a mountain range on the border between the Democratic Republic of Congo and Uganda, also known as the 'Mountains of the Moon'. The highest peak is Mount Ngaliema (Mount Stanley) at 6,763 feet (5,109 metres).

Rwanda A small republic in the heart of central Africa that lies just 2 degrees south of the Equator. It is a mountainous country with a central spine of highlands from which streams flow west to the Congo River and east to the Nile. Active volcanoes are found in the north where the land rises to about 14,765 feet (4,500 metres). The climate is highland tropical, with temperatures decreasing with altitude. The soils are not fertile and subsistence agriculture dominates the economy. Staple food crops are sweet potatoes, cassava, dry beans, sorghum, and potatoes. Soil erosion, overgrazing, and droughts have led to famine, making the country very dependent on foreign aid. The main cash crops are arabica coffee, tea, and pyrethrum. There are major reserves of natural gas under Lake Kivu in the west, but these are largely unexploited. The country has faced massive upheaval and disruption of its economic life following the tragic tribal genocide wars in 1994, and there is ongoing ethnic division and rivalry between the Hutus and Tutsis.

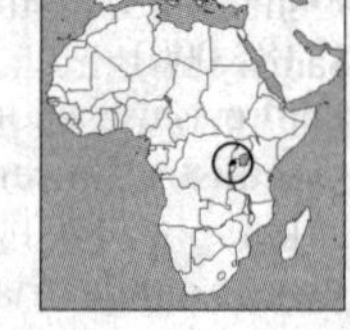

Area: 10,169 sq miles/26,338 sq km
Population: 5,397,000
Capital: Kigali
Form of government: Republic
Religions: RC, Animism
Currency: Rwandan Franc

Ryazan an industrial city 110 miles (175 kilometres) southeast of Moscow in the Russian Federation. (Pop. 526,000)

Ryukyu Islands (Nansei-shoto) a chain of islands belonging to Japan stretching 750 miles (1,200 kilometres) towards Taiwan. (Pop. 1,366,600)

S

Saarbrücken an industrial city of western Germany, near the border with France. (Pop. 180,000)

Sabah the more easterly of the two states of Malaysia on northern coast of the island of Borneo. (28,450 sq miles/73,700 sq km; pop. 2,581,000)

Sacramento the state capital of California, USA. (Pop. 422,000)

Sahara Desert the world's largest desert, spanning much of northern Africa, from the Atlantic to the Red Sea, and from the Mediterranean to Mali, Niger, Chad and Sudan.

Sahel a semi-arid belt crossing Africa from Senegal to Sudan, separating the Sahara from tropical Africa to the south.

Saigon the former name of Ho Chi Minh City (until 1975).

Saipan the largest and most heavily populated of the Northern Marianas group of islands in the west Pacific. The island group's capital, Susupe, is on the western side of Saipan. (47 sq miles/122 sq km; pop. 70,000)

Sakhalin a large island to the north of Japan, but belonging to the Russian Federation. (29,500 sq miles/76,400 sq km; pop. 570,000)

Salamanca an elegant university town in western Spain, and the name of the surrounding province. (Pop. 159,000)

Salem (1) a city in Massachusetts, USA. (Pop. 41,000) (2) the state capital of Oregon, USA. (Pop. 141,000)

Salt Lake City the state capital of Utah, USA. (Pop. 188,000)

Salvador a port on the central east coast of Brazil and capital of the state of Bahia. (Pop. 2,540,000)

Salween a river rising in Tibet and flowing south through Myanmar, forming part of the border with Thailand, to the Andaman Sea. (Length 1,800 miles/2,900 km)

Salzburg a city in central northern Austria, and the name of the surrounding state, of which it is the capital. (Pop. 145,000)

Samar the third largest island of the Philippines. (5,050 sq miles/13,080 sq km; pop. 1,100,000)

Samara a major industrial city and port on the River Volga in the Russian Federation. (Pop. 1,150,000)

Samarkand an ancient city in Uzbekistan. (Pop. 373,000)

Samoa Samoa, called Western Samoa until 1997, is a state that lies in the Polynesian sector of the Pacific Ocean, about 447 miles (720 kilometres) northeast of Fiji. It consists of seven small islands and two larger volcanic islands, Savai'i and Upolu. Savai'i is largely covered by volcanic peaks and lava plateaux. Upolu is home to two-thirds of the population and the capital, Apia. The climate is tropical, with high temperatures and very heavy rainfall. The islands have been fought over by the Dutch, British, Germans, and Americans, but the islanders now enjoy a traditional Polynesian lifestyle. Subsistence agriculture is the main activity, and copra, cocoa, and coconuts are the main exports. There are some light manufacturing industries, and an automobile components factory, which is now the largest private employer and a major export industry. Many tourists visit the grave of the Scottish writer, Robert Louis Stevenson, who died here and whose home is now the official home of the king.

Area: 1,093 sq miles/2,831 sq km
Population: 166,000
Capital: Apia
Form of government: Constitutional Monarchy
Religion: Protestantism
Currency: Tala

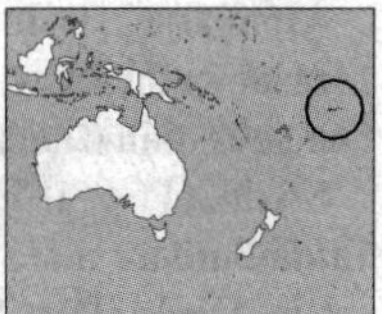

Samoa, American an American territory, comprising a group of five islands, in the central South Pacific. The capital is Pago Pago. (77 sq miles/199 sq km; pop. 64,000)

Sámos a Greek island 1 mile (1.6 kilometres) off the coast of Turkey. (Pop. 43,000)

Samsun a port on the Black Sea coast of Turkey, and the name of the surrounding province, of which it is the capital. (Pop. 378,000)

San'a the capital of Yemen, situated in the middle of the country. (Pop. 1,653,000)

San Antonio an industrial centre in southern Texas, USA. (Pop. city 842,800/metropolitan area 1,197,000)

San Diego a major port and industrial city in southern California, USA. (Pop1,269,000)

San Francisco a Pacific port and commercial centre in California, USA. (Pop. 806,000)

San Francisco Bay an inlet of the Pacific Ocean in western California, USA, joined to the ocean by the Golden Gate Strait.

San Jose a city in California, USA, and the focus of 'Silicon Valley'. (Pop. 928,000)

San José the capital of Costa Rica and the centre of the province of the same name. (Pop. 358,000)

San Juan a major port and the capital of Puerto Rico in South America. (Pop. 430,000)

San Luis Potosí an elegant colonial city and provincial capital in north central Mexico. (Pop. 644,000)

San Marino A tiny landlocked state in central Italy, lying in the eastern foothills of the Apennines and one of the smallest republics in the world. Tradition has it that in AD 301, a Christian sought refuge from persecution on Mount Titano. The resulting community prospered and was recognized in 1291 by Pope Nicholas IV as being independent. San Marino has wooded mountains and pasture land clustered around Mount Titano's limestone peaks, which rise to 2,425 feet (739 metres). San Marino has a mild Mediterranean climate. Most of the population work on the land or in forestry. Wheat, barley, maize, olives, and vines are grown, and the main exports are wood machinery, chemicals, wine, textiles, tiles, varnishes, and ceramics, while dairy produce is the main agricultural product. Some 3.5 million tourists visit the country each year, and much of the country's revenue comes from the sale of stamps, postcards, souvenirs, and duty-free liquor. In 1992, San Marino became a member of the United Nations and it is a full member of the Council of Europe.

Area: 24 sq miles/1 sq km
Population: 25,000
Capital: San Marino
Form of government: Republic
Religion: RC
Currency: Euro

San Miguel de Tucumán a regional capital in northwestern Argentina. (Pop. 797,000)

San Pedro Sula the second largest city in Honduras. (Pop. 487,000)

San Salvador (1) the capital and major city of El Salvador. (Pop. 496,000) (2) a small island in the centre of the Bahamas, the first place in the New World reached by Columbus (1492). (Pop. 480)

San Sebastián (Donostia) a port and industrial city in northeastern Spain. (Pop. 182,000)

Santa Barbara a resort and industrial centre in southern California, USA. (Pop. 96,000)

Santa Fe the state capital of New Mexico, USA. (Pop. 63,000)

Santander a port and industrial city in northeastern Spain. (Pop. 185,000)

Santiago the capital and principal city of Chile. (Pop. 5,034,000)

Santiago de Cuba a port and provincial capital in southern Cuba. (Pop. 544,000)

Santo Domingo the capital and main port of the Dominican Republic in the Caribbean. (Pop. 2,061,000)

Santorini a volcanic island in the Cyclades group of Greek islands. (32 sq miles/84 sq km; pop. 7,100)

Santos the largest port in Brazil, 38 miles (60 kilometres) southeast of São Paulo. (Pop. 423,000)

São Francisco a river of eastern Brazil, important for its hydroelectric dams. (Length 1,800 miles/2,900 km)

Saône a river of eastern France which merges with the River Rhône at Lyons. (Length 300 miles/480 km)

São Paulo a major industrial city in southeastern Brazil, and capital of the state of the same name. (Pop. city 8,500,000/metropolitan area 10,058,000)

São Tomé the capital of the republic of São Tomé e Principe, off the west coast of Africa. (Pop. 52,000)

São Tomé e Principe A state comprising two volcanic islands that lie off the west coast of Africa. São Tomé is covered in extinct volcanic cones and its coastal areas are hot and humid. Príncipe is a craggy island lying to the northeast of São Tomé. The climate is tropical, with heavy rainfall from October to May. Seventy per cent of the workforce work on the land, mainly in state-owned cocoa plantations that were nationalized after independence in 1975. The other main agricultural products are coconuts, melons, copra, bananas, and melons. Since most of the crops grown are primarily for export, about 90 per cent of the country's food has to be imported. Small manufacturing industries include food processing and lumber products.

Area: 372 sq miles/964 sq km
Population: 135,000
Capital: São Tomé
Form of government: Republic
Religion: RC;
Currency: Dobra

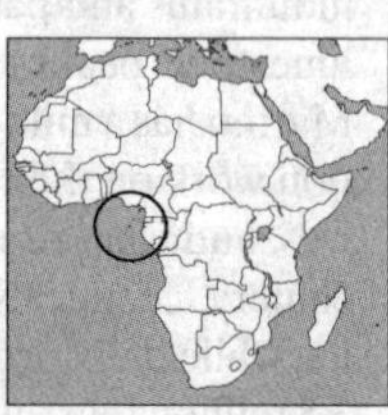

São Vincente, Cabo de (Cape St Vincent) the southwestern corner of Portugal.

Sapporo a modern city, founded in the late 19th century as the capital of Hokkaido Island, Japan. (Pop. 1,842,000)

Sarajevo the capital of Bosnia-Herzegovina. (Pop. 434,000)

Saransk an industrial town and capital of the autonomous Mordvinian Republic in the Russian Federation. (Pop. 312,000)

Saratov an industrial city and river port on the River Volga in the Russian Federation. (Pop. 868,000)

Sarawak a state of Malaysia occupying much of the northwestern coast of Borneo. (48,342 sq miles/125,204 sq km; pop. 2,121,000)

Sardinia (Sardegna) the second largest island of the Mediterranean after Sicily, also belonging to Italy, lying just south of Corsica. The capital is Cagliari. (9,301 sq miles/24,089 sq km; pop. 1,669,000)

Saskatchewan (1) a province of western Canada, in the Great Plains. The capital is Regina. (251,000 sq miles/651,900 sq km; pop. 1,038,000) (2) a river of Canada, rising in the Rocky Mountains and flowing westwards into Lake Winnipeg. (Length 1,200 miles/1,930 km)

Saskatoon a city on the Saskatchewan River. (Pop. 196,000)

Saudi Arabia A state that occupies over 70 per cent of the Arabian Peninsula. Over 95 per cent of the country is desert, and the largest expanse of sand in the world, the Empty Quarter (Rub al Khali), is found in the southeast of the country. In the west, a narrow, humid coastal plain along the Red Sea is backed by steep mountains. The climate is hot, with very little rain, and some areas have no precipitation for years. The government has spent a considerable amount on reclamation of the desert for agriculture, and the main products are dates, tomatoes, watermelons, and wheat, which are grown in the fertile land around the oases. Saudi Arabia exports wheat and shrimps and is self-sufficient in some dairy products. However, the country's prosperity is based almost entirely on the exploitation of its vast reserves of oil and natural gas. Industries include petroleum refining, petrochemicals, and fertilizers. As a result of the Gulf War (1990–91), some 285 miles (460 kilometres) of the Saudi coastline were polluted by oil, threatening desalination plants and damaging the wildlife of salt marshes, mangrove forest, and mudflats.

Area: 830,000 sq miles/2,149,690 sq km
Population: 18,836,000
Capital: Riyadh (Ar Riyād)
Other cities: Mecca, Jeddah, Medina, Ta'if
Form of government: Monarchy
Religions: Sunni Islam, Shia Islam
Currency: Riyal

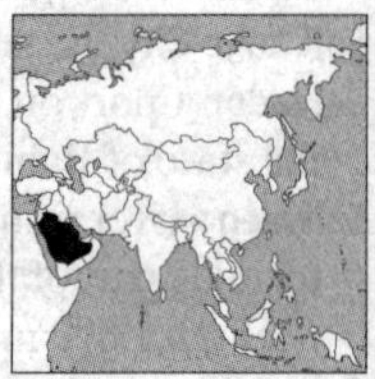

Savannah the main port of Georgia, USA. (Pop. 138,000)

Savoie (Savoy) a mountainous former duchy in southeast France, which has been a part of France since 1860 and is now divided into two departments, Savoie and Haute Savoie.

Scandinavia the countries on, or near, the Scandinavian Peninsula in northern Europe, usually taken to include Norway, Sweden, Denmark, Finland and Iceland.

Scapa Flow an anchorage surrounded by the Orkney Islands, famous as a wartime naval base.

Schelde a river rising in France and then flowing through Belgium and the Netherlands to the North Sea. (Length 270 miles/435 km)

Schleswig-Holstein the northernmost state of Germany. The capital is Kiel. (Pop. 2,807,000)

Scilly, Isles of a group of islands off the southwest tip of Cornwall, England. The main islands are St Mary's, St Martin, and Tresco. (Pop. 2,000)

Scotland a country of the United Kingdom, occupying the northern part of Great Britain. The capital is Edinburgh. (30,410 sq miles/78,762 sq km; pop. 5,056,000)

Scottish Borders a council area in southern Scotland, with its administrative centre in Newton St Boswells. (1,827 sq miles/4,734 sq km; pop. 106,000)

Seattle a port in the state of Washington, USA. (Pop. 581,000)

Sebastapol (Sevastopol) a Black Sea port of the Ukraine. (Pop. 342,000)

Seine a river of northern France, flowing through Paris to the English Channel. (Length 482 miles/775 km)

Semarang a port and textile city on the north coast of Java, Indonesia. (Pop. 1,135,0000)

Sendai a city in the east of Honshu Island, Japan. (Pop. 73,000)

Senegal (1) A former French colony in West Africa that extends from Cape Verde, the most western point in Africa, to the border with Mali. Senegal is mostly low-lying and covered by savannah. The Fouta Djallon Mountains in the south rise to 4,971 feet (1,515 metres). The climate is tropical, with a dry season from October to June. The most densely populated region is in the southwest. Almost 80 per cent of the labour force work in agriculture, growing peanuts and cotton for export and millet, sugar cane, maize, rice, and sorghum as subsistence crops. Increased production of crops such as rice and tomatoes is encouraged in order to achieve self-sufficiency in food. The country's economy is largely dependent on peanuts but there is a growing manufacturing sector, including food processing, and the production of cement, chemicals, and tinned tuna, while tourism is also expanding. Senegal is dependent on foreign aid. (2) a West African river that flows through Guinea, Mali, Mauritania, and Senegal to the Atlantic. (Length 1,110 miles/1,790 km)

Area: 75,955 sq miles/196,722 sq km
Population: 8,572,000
Capital: Dakar
Other cities: Kaolack, Thiès, St Louis
Form of government: Republic
Religions: Sunni Islam, RC
Currency: CFA Franc

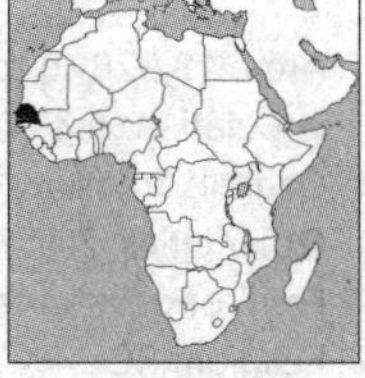

Seoul (Soul) the capital of South Korea, in its northwest. (Pop. 11,153,000)

Sepik a major river of Papua New Guinea. (Length 750 miles/1,200 km)

Seram (Ceram) an island in the Maluku group, Indonesia. (6,621 sq miles/17,148 sq km)

Serbia and Montenegro a new union of states which brings together the last of the former Yugoslavian republics, Serbia and Montenegro, and effectively causes the final demise of the country known to the world for so long as Yugoslavia. In time, it is possible that one or both states will want to leave the union and provision has been made for a re-examination of their statehood status after a period of three years. (39,449 sq miles/102,173 sq km; pop.[without Kosovo] 9,000,000)

Sevastopol' a Black Sea port of the Ukraine. (Pop. 335,000)

Severn the longest river in the UK, flowing through Wales and the west of England. (Length 220 miles/350 km)

Seville (Sevilla) a historical, now industrial, city in southern Spain, and also the name of the surrounding province. (Pop. 704,000)

Seychelles A group of volcanic islands that lie in the western Indian Ocean, about 746 miles (1,200 kilometres) from the coast of East Africa. About 40 of the islands are mountainous and consist of granite, while just over 50 are coral islands. The climate is tropical maritime with heavy rain. The capital, Victoria, and about 90 per cent of the people can be found on the island of Mahé. The staple foods are coconut, imported rice, and fish, while some fruits are grown for home consumption. Tourism employs one-third of the labour force and accounts for about 90 per cent of the country's foreign exchange earnings. Export trade is based on petroleum (after importation), copra, cinnamon bark, and fish. The only mineral resource is guano. The Seychelles were a one-party socialist state until 1991, when a new constitution was introduced. The first free elections were held in 1993.

Area: 175 sq miles/455 sq km
Population: 76,000
Capital: Victoria
Form of government: Republic
Religion: RC
Currency: Seychelles Rupee

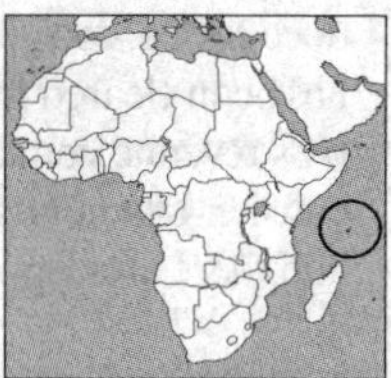

Shaanxi a province of northwestern China. The capital is Xi'an. (73,000 sq miles/190,000 sq km; pop. 37,736,000)

Shandong a province of northern China, with its capital at Jinan. (58,000 sq miles/150,000 sq km; pop. 95,077,000)

Shanghai the largest city in China. An important port, it is situated on the delta of the Chang Jiang (Yangtze) River. (Pop. 9,031,000)

Shannon a river of the Republic of Ireland, and the longest river in the British Isles. It flows southwest into the Atlantic Ocean near Limerick. (Length 240 miles/386 km)

Shanxi a province of northern China, with its capital at Taiyuan. (58,000 sq miles/150,000 sq km; pop. 32,802,000)

Sharjah (Ash-Shariqah) the third largest of the United Arab Emirates. Its capital is also Sharjah. (1,000 sq miles/2,600 sq km; pop. emirate 522,000/city 417,000)

Shatt al Arab a waterway flowing into the Persian Gulf along the disputed border between Iran and Iraq, formed where the Rivers Euphrates and Tigris converge some 105 miles (170 kilometres) from the coast.

Sheffield a major industrial city in South Yorkshire, England. (Pop. 422,000)

Shenyang the capital of Liaoning Province, China. (Pop. 3,453,000)

Shetland Islands a group of some 100 islands lying 100 miles (160 kilometres) northeast of mainland Scotland, which go to make up an island authority of Scotland, with an administrative centre in Lerwick. (550 sq miles/1,426 sq km; pop. 23,000)

Shijiazhuang the capital of Hebei Province, China. (Pop. 1,190,000)

Shikoku the smallest of the four main islands of Japan. (Pop. 4,139,000)

Shiraz a provincial capital of Iran, southeast of Tehran. (Pop. 1,158,000)

Shropshire a county of west central England, with its administrative centre in the town of Shrewsbury. (1,347 sq miles/3,490 sq km; pop. 416,000)

Siberia a huge tract of land, mostly in northern Russian Federation, that extends from the Ural Mountains to the Pacific coast. It is renowned for its inhospitable climate, but parts of it are fertile, and it is rich in minerals.

Sichuan (Szechwan) the most heavily populated of the provinces of China, in the southwest of the country. The capital is Chengdu. (220,000 sq miles/570,000 sq km; pop. 87,354,000)

Sicily (Sicilia) an island hanging from the toe of Italy, and the largest island in the Mediterranean. The capital is Palermo. (9,926 sq miles/25,708 sq km; pop. 5,216,000)

Siena (Sienna) a historical town of Tuscany, in central Italy. (Pop. 54,000)

Sierra Leone A country on the Atlantic coast of West Africa, bounded by Guinea to the north and east and by Liberia to the southeast. The country possesses a fine natural harbour where the capital and major port of Freetown is situated. A range of mountains, the Sierra Lyoa, rise above the capital on the Freetown Peninsula. Elsewhere the coastal plain is up to 70 miles (110 kilometres) wide, rising to a plateau and then to mountains which are part of the Guinea Highlands Massif. The climate is tropical, with heavy rain during a rainy season lasting from May to November. The country's staple food is rice that is grown in the swamplands at the coast by the subsistence farmers. Other crops grown include sorghum, cassava, millet, sugar, and groundnuts. In the tropical forest areas, small plantations produce coffee, cocoa, and palm oil. On the plateau much of the forest has been cleared for the growing of groundnuts. Most of the country's revenue comes from agriculture and the mining of rutile and bauxite. Diamonds are also mined, but in much reduced amounts, and there are deposits of iron ore with some gold and platinum.

Area: 27,699 sq miles/71,740 sq km
Population: 4,297,000
Capital: Freetown
Form of government: Republic
Religion: Animism, Sunni Islam, Christianity
Currency: Leone

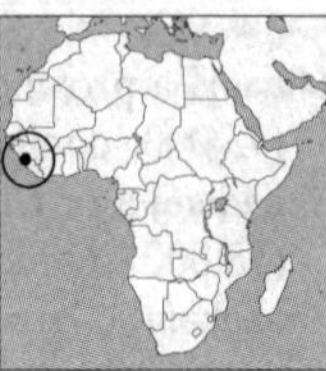

Sierra Madre Occidental the mountain range of western Mexico.

Sierra Madre Oriental the mountain range of eastern Mexico.

Sierra Nevada (1) a mountain range in southern Spain. (2) a mountain range in eastern California, USA.

Sikkim a state in northeastern India. The capital is Gangtok. (2,739 sq miles/7,096 sq km; pop. 551,000)

Silesia (Schlesien) a region straddling the borders of the Czech Republic, Germany and Poland.

Simpson Desert an arid, uninhabited region in the centre of Australia.

Sinai a mountainous peninsula in northeastern Egypt, bordering Israel, between the Gulf of Aqaba and the Gulf of Suez.

Sind a province of southeastern Pakistan. The capital is Karachi. (54,407 sq miles/140,914 sq km; pop. 33,237,000)

Singapore One of the world's smallest yet most successful countries. It comprises one main island and 58 islets that are located at the foot of the Malay Peninsula in southeast Asia. The main island of Singapore is very low-lying, and the climate is hot and wet throughout the year. Only 1.6 per cent of the land area is used for agriculture, most food being imported. The country has a flourishing manufacturing industry for which it relies heavily on imports. Products traded in Singapore include machinery and appliances, petroleum, food and beverages, chemicals, transport equipment, paper products and printing, and clothes. Shipbuilding is also an important industry. International banking and tourism are important sources of foreign revenue. Singapore's airport is one of the largest in Asia.

Area: 239 sq miles/618 sq km
Population: 3,044,000
Capital: Singapore
Form of government: Republic
Religions: Buddhism, Sunni Islam, Christianity, Hinduism
Currency: Singapore Dollar

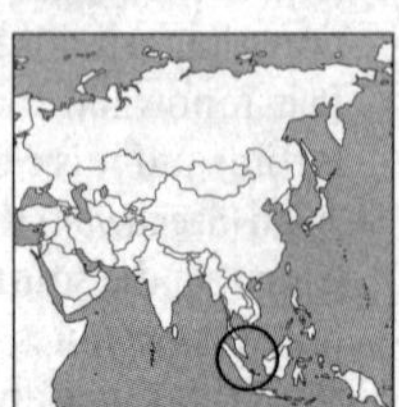

Sirte, Gulf of a huge indent of the Mediterranean Sea on the coastline of Libya.

Sivas an industrial town in central Turkey. (Pop. 259,000)

Skagerrak the channel, some 80 miles (130 kilometres) wide, separating Denmark and Norway. It links the North Sea to the Kattegat and Baltic Sea.

Skiathos the westernmost of the Greek Southern Sporades Islands which include the Dodecanese Islands. (Pop. 4,200)

Skopje the capital of the Former Yugoslav Republic of Macedonia. (Pop. 489,000)

Skye an island off the northwest coast of Scotland and the largest of the Inner Hebrides Islands. The main town is Portree. (547 sq miles/1,417 sq km; pop. 8,000)

Slavonia (Slavonija) a part of Croatia, southeast of Zagreb, mainly between the Drava and Slava Rivers.

Sligo a county on the northwest coast of the Republic of Ireland, with a county town of the same name. (693 sq miles/1,796 sq km; pop. 58,000)

Slovakia Slovakia (or the Slovak Republic) is a country that was constituted on 1 January 1993 as a new independent nation, following the dissolution of the 74-year-old federal republic of Czechoslovakia. Landlocked in central Europe, its neighbours are the Czech Republic to the west, Poland to the north, Austria and Hungary to the south, and a short border with Ukraine in the east. The northern half of the republic is occupied by the Tatra Mountains, which form the northern arm of the Carpathian Mountains. This region has vast forests and pastures used for intensive sheep grazing, and is rich in high-grade minerals such as copper, iron, zinc, and lead. Farms, vineyards, orchards, and pastures for stock form the basis of southern Slovakia's economy. The inefficient industrialization of the old regime has left Slovakia with a legacy of economic and environmental problems. In the early 1990s, unemployment increased and inflation was high, resulting in a lowering in the standard of living. The tourism industry is beginning to contribute to the country's economy as visitors come to enjoy the country's ski resorts and historical cities.

Area: 18,928 sq miles/49,035 sq km
Population: 5,374,000
Capital: Bratislava
Other cities: Zilina, Trnava
Form of government: Republic
Religion: RC
Currency: Slovak Koruna

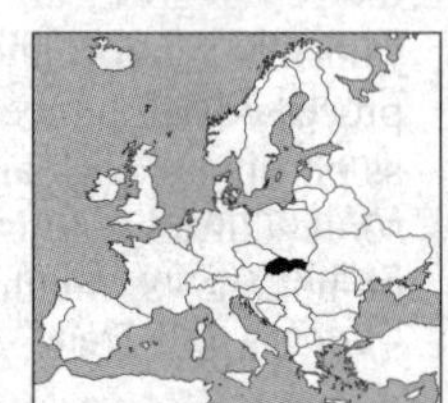

Slovenia A republic that made a unilateral declaration of independence from the former Yugoslavia on 25 June 1991 but whose sovereignty was not formally recognized by the European Community and the United Nations until early in 1992. Slovenia is bounded to the north by Austria, to the west by Italy, to the east by Hungary, and to the south by Croatia. Most of Slovenia is situated in the Karst Plateau and in the Julian Alps, where Mount Triglav (9,393 ft/2,863 m) is the country's highest peak. The Julian Alps are renowned for their scenery, and the Karst Plateau contains spectacular cave systems. The northeast of the republic is famous for its wine production, and tourism is also an important industry. Although farming and livestock raising are the chief occupations, Slovenia is very industrialized and urbanized. Iron, steel, and aluminium are produced, and resources include oil, coal, lead, uranium, mercury, natural gas and petroleum. Slovenia has also been successful in establishing many new light industries, and this has given the country a well-balanced economic base for the future, with unemployment lessening and industrial output increasing.

Area: 7,821 sq miles/20,256 sq km
Population: 1,998,912
Capital: Ljubljana
Other cities: Maribor, Celje
Form of government: Republic
Religion: RC
Currency: Slovene Tolar

Smolensk an industrial city in the Russian Federation, on the River Dnieper. (Pop. 352,000)

Snake a river of the northwest USA, which flows into the Columbia River in the state of Washington. (Length 1,038 miles/1,670 km)

Snowdonia a mountainous region in the north of Wales. The highest peak is Mount Snowdon (3560 ft/1,085 m).

Snowy Mountains a range of mountains in southeastern Australia, where the River Snowy has been dammed to form the complex Snowy Mountains Hydroelectric Scheme. The highest peak is Mount Kosciusko (7,316 ft/2,230 m).

Society Islands a group of islands at the centre of French Polynesia. They are divided into the Windward Islands, which include Tahiti and Moorea, and the Leeward Islands, which include Raiatea and Bora-Bora. (Pop. 142,000)

Socotra an island in the northwestern Indian Ocean, belonging to Yemen.

Sofia (Sofiya) the capital of Bulgaria, in the west of the country. (Pop. 1,093,000)

Solent, the a strait in the English Channel that separates the Isle of Wight from mainland England.

Solomon Islands An island state that lies in the Pacific Ocean in an area between 5 and 12 degrees south of the Equator, to the east of Papua New Guinea. The country consists of six large islands and innumerable smaller ones. The larger islands are mountainous and covered by forests, with rivers prone to flooding. Guadalcanal is the main island and the site of the capital, Honiara. The climate is hot and wet and typhoons are frequent. The main food crops grown are coconut, cassava, sweet potatoes, plantains, yams, rice, taros, and bananas. Other products include copra, processed fish, lumber, and trochus shells. Mineral resources such as phosphate rock and bauxite are found in large amounts and some alluvial gold is produced. Other industries include palm oil-milling, sawmilling, food, tobacco, and sodas.

Area: 11,157 sq miles/28,896 sq km
Population: 391,000
Capital: Honiara
Form of government: Parliamentary democracy within the Commonwealth
Religions: Anglicanism, RC, other Christianity
Currency: Solomon Island Dollar

Somalia A country that lies on the horn of Africa's east coast. It is bounded on the north by the Gulf of Aden and on the south and east by the Indian Ocean, and its neighbours include Djibouti, Ethiopia, and Kenya. The country is arid, and most of it is low plateau with scrub vegetation. Its two main rivers, the Juba and Shebelle, are used to irrigate crops. Most of the population live in the mountains and river valleys, and there are a few towns on the coast. The country has little in the way of natural resources but there are deposits of copper, petroleum, iron, manganese, and marble, although not commercially exploited. Main exports are live animals, meat, hides, and skins. A few large-scale banana plantations are found by the rivers. Years of drought have left Somalia heavily dependent on foreign aid, and many of the younger people are emigrating to oil-rich Arab states. Civil war in the 1980s and early 1990s resulted in a huge loss of life and widespread famine. International UN peacekeeping forces were deployed and humanitarian aid given to try to avert a catastrophe but these withdrew in 1995. The situation remains unresolved although there has been some recovery in agriculture and food production.

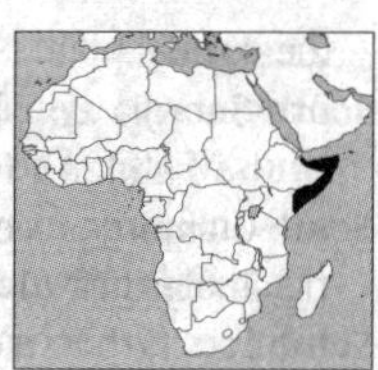

Area: 246,201 sq miles/637,657 sq km
Population: 9,822,000
Capital: Mogadishu (Muqdisho)
Other cities: Hargeisa, Burco, Kismaayo
Form of government: Republic
Religion: Sunni Islam
Currency: Somali Shilling

Somerset a county in the southwest of England, on the Bristol Channel, with its administrative centre in the town of Taunton. (1,620 sq miles/4,196 sq km; pop. 680,000)

Somme a river of northern France, the scene of a devastating battle during World War I. (Length 152 miles/245 km)

South Africa A republic that lies at the southern tip of the African continent and has a huge coastline on both the Atlantic and Indian Oceans. The country occupies a huge saucer-shaped plateau, surrounded by a belt of land that drops in steps to the sea. The rim of the saucer rises in the east to 11,424 feet (3,482 metres) in the Drakensberg Mountains. In general, the climate is healthy, with plenty of sunshine and relatively low rainfall. Of the total land area, 58 per cent is used as natural pasture although soil erosion is a problem. The main crops grown are maize, sorghum, wheat, groundnuts, and sugar cane. A drought-resistant variety of cotton is also now grown. South Africa has extraordinary mineral wealth, including gold, coal, copper, iron ore, manganese, diamonds, and chrome ore. A system of apartheid existed in South Africa from 1948 until the early 1990s, denying black South Africans civil rights and promoting racial segregation. During this time, the country was subjected to international economic and political sanctions. In 1990, the ban on the outlawed African National Congress was lifted and its leader, Nelson Mandela, was released from prison. This heralded the dismantling of the apartheid regime and in the first multiracial elections held in 1994, the ANC triumphed, with Mandela voted in as the country's president. Since that time, South Africa has once again become an active and recognized member of the international community.

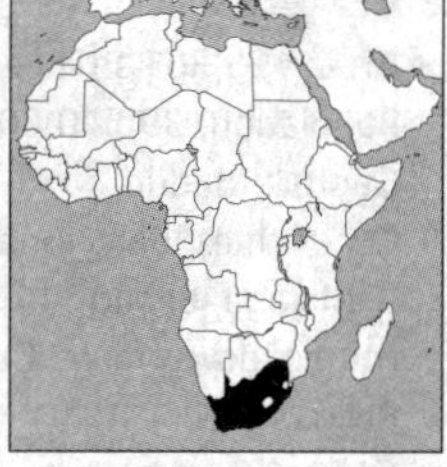

Area: 471,445 sq miles/1,221,037 sq km
Population: 40,584,000
Capital: Pretoria (administrative), Cape Town (legislative)
Other cities: Johannesburg, Durban, Port Elizabeth, Bloemfontein
Form of government: Republic
Religions: Christianity, Islam, Hinduism, Animism
Currency: Rand

Southampton a major port in southern England. (Pop. 212,000)

South Australia a state in central southern Australia, on the Great Australian Bight. Adelaide is the state capital. (380,069 sq miles/984,380 sq km; pop. 1,572,000)

South Ayrshire a council area in south Scotland, with its administrative centre in Ayr. (Pop. 114,000)

South Carolina a state in the southeast of the USA, with a coast on the Atlantic Ocean. The state capital is Columbia. (31,055 sq miles/80,432 sq km; pop. 4,114,000)

South China Sea an arm of the Pacific Ocean between southeast China, Malaysia and the Philippines.

South Dakota a state in western USA. The state capital is Pierre. (77,047 sq miles/199,552 sq km; pop. 758,000)

Southern Alps a range of mountains on the South Island of New Zealand.

Zealand.

South Georgia an island in the South Atlantic, and a dependency of the Falkland Islands. (1450 sq miles/3,755 sq km)

South Glamorgan a county in south Wales. The administrative centre is Cardiff. (161 sq miles/416 sq km; pop. 384,700)

South Lanarkshire a council area in south Scotland, with its administrative centre in Hamilton. (684 sq miles/1,771 sq km; pop. 307,000)

South Pole the most southerly point of the Earth's axis, in Antarctica.

South Sandwich Islands a group of islands in the South Atlantic which are dependencies of the Falkland Islands. (130 sq miles/ 340 sq km)

South Yorkshire a metropolitan county in northern England. (602 sq miles/1,560 sq km)

Soweto the largest purely Black African urban settlement in southern Africa, lying south of Johannesburg in Gauteng Province, South Africa. (Pop. 1,221,000)

Spain A country located in southwest Europe and occupying the greater part of the Iberian Peninsula, which it shares with Portugal. It is a mountainous country, sealed off from the rest of Europe by the Pyrenees, which rise to over 11,155 feet (3,400 metres). Much of the country is a vast plateau, the Meseta Central, cut across by valleys and gorges. Its longest shoreline is the one that borders the Mediterranean Sea. Most of the country has a form of Mediterranean climate, with mild, moist winters and hot, dry summers. Spain's major rivers, such as the Douro, Tagus, and Guadiana, flow to the Atlantic Ocean while the Guadalquivir is the deepest. Although not generally navigable, they are of use for hydroelectric power. Spain's principal agricultural products are cereals, vegetables, and potatoes, and large areas are under vines for the wine industry. The soil is good, with almost one-third cultivable. Livestock production is important, particularly sheep and goats. Industry represents 72 per cent of the country's export value, and production includes textiles, paper, cement, steel, and chemicals. Tourism is a major revenue earner, especially from the resorts on the east coast.

Area: 195,365 sq miles/505,992 sq km
Population: 39,540,000
Capital: Madrid
Other cities: Barcelona, Seville, Zaragosa, Malaga, Bilbao
Form of government: Constitutional Monarchy
Religion: RC
Currency: Euro

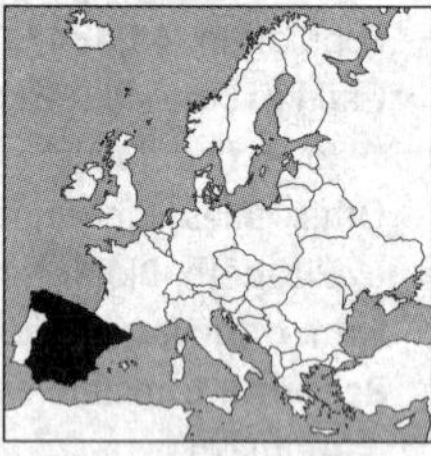

Spitsbergen A large island group in the Svalbard Archipelago, 360 miles (580 kilometres) to the north of Norway. (15,060 sq miles/ 39,000 sq km; pop. 2,000)

Split the largest city on the coast of Dalmatia in Croatia. (Pop. 173,000)

Spratly Islands a group of islands in the South China Sea between Vietnam and Borneo. Occupied by Japan during World War II, they are now claimed by almost all the surrounding countries.

Springfield (1) the state capital of Illinois, USA. (Pop. 113,000) (2) a manufacturing city in Massachusetts, USA. (Pop. 154,000)

Sri Lanka A teardrop-shaped island in the Indian Ocean, lying south of the Indian Peninsula, from which it is separated by the Palk Strait. Its climate is equatorial, with a low annual temperature range, but it is affected by both the northeast and southwest monsoons. Rainfall is heaviest in the southwest while the north and east are relatively dry. Agriculture engages 47 per cent of the workforce, and the main crops are rice, tea, rubber, and coconuts, although sugar, rice, and wheat have to be imported. Precious and semiprecious stones are among the chief minerals to be mined and exported. Graphite is also important. The main industries are food, beverages, tobacco, textiles, clothing, leather goods, chemicals, and plastics. The revenue from tourism is slowly increasing. Politically, Sri Lanka has been afflicted by ethnic divisions between the Sinhalese and Tamils. Attempts by the Tamil extremists to establish an independent homeland have at times brought the northeast of the country to the brink of civil war, and the situation remains volatile.

Area: 25,332 sq miles/65,610 sq km
Population: 18,354,000
Capital: Colombo
Other cities: Kandy, Moratuwa, Jaffna
Form of government: Republic
Religions: Buddhism, Hinduism, Christianity, Sunni Islam
Currency: Sri Lankan Rupee

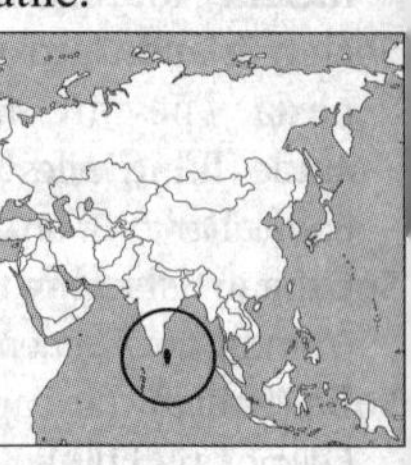

Srinagar the capital of the state of Jammu and Kashmir, northern India. (Pop. 912,000)

Staffordshire a county in central England, with its administrative centre in the town of Stafford. (1,049 sq miles/2,716 sq km; pop. 1,054,000)

St Barthélémy a small island dependency of Guadeloupe in the east Caribbean. (Pop. 6,000)

St Croix the largest of the US Virgin Islands. The main town is Christiansted. (84 sq miles/218 sq km; pop. 71,000)

St-Denis the capital of the island of Réunion in the Indian Ocean. (Pop. 140,000)

St-Étienne an industrial city southwest of Lyons, France. (Pop. 173,000)

St Eustatius (Sint Eustatius, Statia) a Caribbean island, part of the Netherland Antilles. The capital is Oranjestad. (8 sq miles/21 sq km; pop. 2,000)

St George's the capital of Grenada in the Caribbean, and the island's main port. (Pop. 30,800)

St Helena a volcanic island in the south Atlantic Ocean which is a British Overseas Territory and an administrative centre for the island of Tristan da Cunha to the south and Ascension Island to the north. Napoleon Bonaparte was exiled here by the British from 1815 until his death in 1821. The main exports are fish, lumber, and handicrafts. (47 sq miles/122 sq km; pop. 5,500; cur. St Helena Pound)

St Helena Dependencies the islands of Ascension and Tristan da Cunha are so-called dependencies of St Helena, a British Overseas Territory.

St Helens, Mount an active volcano in the Cascade Range of western Washington State, USA. It last erupted in 1980. (8,364 ft/2,549 m)

Stirling (1) a town in central Scotland, on the River Forth, and the administrative centre for the Stirling council area. (Pop. 30,000) (2) a council area in central Scotland. (839 sq miles/2,173 km; pop. 83,000)

St John a port and the largest city in New Brunswick, east Canada, at the mouth of the St John River on the Atlantic coast. (Pop. 90,000)

St John's (1) the capital and main port of Antigua. (Pop. 23,000) (2) a port and the capital of Newfoundland, Canada. (Pop. 97,000)

St Kitts (St Christopher) and Nevis The islands of St Christopher (popularly known as St Kitts) and Nevis lie in the Leeward group in the eastern Caribbean and in 1983 became a sovereign demo-

Kitts consists of three extinct volcanoes linked by a sandy isthmus to other volcanic remains in the south. The highest point on St Kitts is Mount Liamuiga at 4,314 feet (1,315 metres). The islands have a tropical climate. Sugar cane is grown on the fertile soil covering the lower slopes and sugar is the chief export crop, but market gardening and livestock are being expanded on the steeper slopes above the cane fields. Some vegetables, coconuts, fruits, and cereals are grown. Industry includes sugar refining, brewing, distilling, and bottling. St Kitts has a major tourist development at Frigate Bay. Nevis, lying 2 miles (3 kilometres) south, is an extinct volcano. Agricultural activity is declining and tourism is now the main source of income.

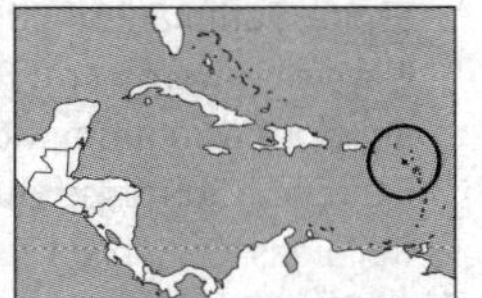

Area: 101 sq miles/261 sq km
Population: 43,410
Capital: Basseterre
Form of government: Constitutional Monarchy
Religions: Anglicanism, Methodism
Currency: East Caribbean Dollar

St Lawrence (1) a commercially important river of southeast Canada, which flows northeast from Lake Ontario to the Gulf of St Lawrence, forming part of the border with the USA. (Length 744 miles/1,197 km) (2) **Gulf of** an arm of the Atlantic Ocean in northeastern Canada, into which the St Lawrence River flows. (3) **Seaway** a navigable waterway that links the Great Lakes, via the St Lawrence River, to the Atlantic Ocean.

St Louis a city in eastern Missouri, USA, on the River Mississippi. (Pop. 352,000)

St Lucia St Lucia is one of the Windward Islands in the eastern Caribbean. It lies to the south of Martinique and to the north of St Vincent. It was controlled alternately by the French and the British for some 200 years before becoming fully independent in 1979. St Lucia is an island of extinct volcanoes and the highest peak is 3,117 feet (950 metres). The climate is tropical, with a rainy season from May to August. The economy depends on the production of bananas and, to a lesser extent, coconuts and mangoes. Production, however, is often affected by hurricanes, drought, and disease. There are some manufacturing industries, which produce clothing, cardboard boxes, plastics, electrical parts, and drinks, and the country has two airports. Tourism is increasing in importance, and Castries, the capital, is a popular calling point for cruise liners.

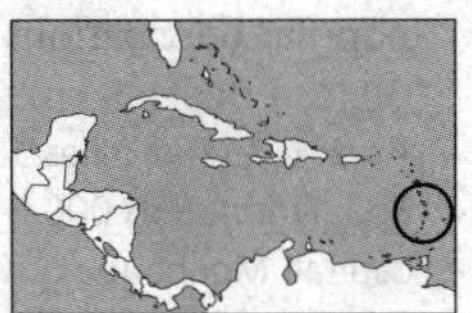

Area: 240 sq miles/622 sq km
Population: 146,600
Capital: Castries
Form of Government: Constitutional Monarchy
Religion: RC
Currency: East Caribbean Dollar

St Martin one of the Leeward Islands in the southeastern Caribbean. It is divided politically into two, one a part of Guadeloupe (France); the other (Sint Maarten) a part of the Netherlands Antilles. The capital of the French side is Marigot, and of the Dutch side, Philipsburg. (French 21 sq miles/54 sq km; pop. 29,000; Dutch 13 sq miles/33 sq km; pop. 37,000)

Stockholm the capital of Sweden, and an important port on the Baltic Sea. (Pop. 1,239,000)

Stockton-on-Tees a town in Cleveland, England. (Pop. 83,000)

Stoke-on-Trent a city in central England, at the centre of the pottery industry in Staffordshire. (Pop. 267,000)

St Paul the state capital of Minnesota, USA, twinned with the adjoining city of Minneapolis. (Pop. 293,000)

St Petersburg (Sankt Peterburg) a former capital of Russia and the current Russian Federation's second largest city. It is an industrial city, an important cultural centre and a major port on the Baltic Sea. From 1914-24 it was known as Petrograd; then, until 1991, Leningrad. (Pop. 4,620,000)

St Pierre and Miquelon two islands to the south of Newfoundland, Canada, which together are a French Overseas Territory. They are the last French possessions in North America, and have a substantial fishing industry. (93 sq miles/240 sq km; pop. 6,300; cur. Euro)

Strabane a district council area in Co. Tyrone, west Northern Ireland. (333 sq miles/862 sq km; pop. 36,000)

Strasbourg an industrial city and river port in eastern France, the capital of the Alsace region, and the seat of the European Parliament. (Pop. 378,500)

Stratford-upon-Avon a town in Warwickshire, England, the birthplace and burial place of William Shakespeare (1564-1616). (Pop. 24,000)

Strathclyde a former administrative region situated in western Scotland.

Stromboli an island with an active volcano in the Eolian Islands, to the north of Sicily. (Pop. 400)

St Thomas the principal tourist island of the US Virgin Islands. The capital is Charlotte Amalie. (32 sq miles/83 sq km; pop. 73,000)

Stuttgart a major industrial centre and river port of the Neckar River in southwestern Germany. (Pop. 574,000)

St Vincent and the Grenadines St Vincent is an island of the Lesser Antilles, situated in the eastern Caribbean between St Lucia and Grenada. It is separated from Grenada by a chain of some 600 small islands known as the Grenadines, the northern islands of which form the other part of the country. The largest of these islands are Bequia, Mustique, Canouan, Mayreau, and Union. The climate is tropical, with very heavy rain in the mountains. St Vincent Island is mountainous and a chain of volcanoes runs up the middle of the island. The volcano Soufrière (4,049 feet/1,234 metres) is active. Farming is the main occupation on the island although tropical storms are always a threat to crops. Bananas are the main export, and it is the world's leading producer of arrowroot starch. There is little manufacturing and unemployment is high. The government is trying to promote tourism.

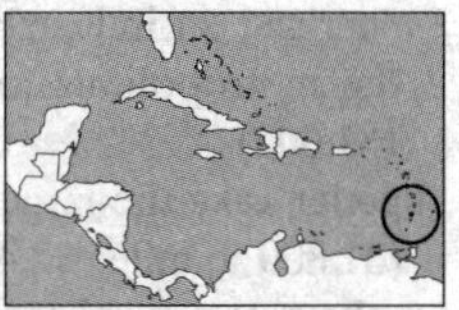

Area: 150 sq miles/388 sq km
Population: 113,000
Capital: Kingstown
Form of government: Constitutional Monarchy
Religions: Anglicanism, Methodism, RC
Currency: East Caribbean Dollar

Sucre the legal capital of Bolivia, in the east Andes. (Pop. 203,000)

Sudan The largest country in Africa, lying just south of the Tropic of Cancer in northeast Africa. The country covers much of the upper Nile basin, and in the north the river winds through the Nubian and Libyan deserts, forming a palm-fringed strip of habitable land. In 1994, the country was divided into 26 states, compared to the original 9 states. The climate is tropical and temperatures are high throughout the year. In winter, nights are very cold. Rainfall increases in amount from north to south, the northern areas being virtually desert. Sudan is an agricultural country. Subsistence farming accounts for 80 per cent of production, and livestock are also raised. Cotton is farmed commercially and accounts for about two-thirds of Sudan's exports. Sudan is the world's greatest source of gum arabic, used in medicines, perfumes, processed foods, and inks. Other forest products are tannin, beeswax, senna, and lumber. Because of the combination of years of civil war and drought, Sudan has a large foreign debt.

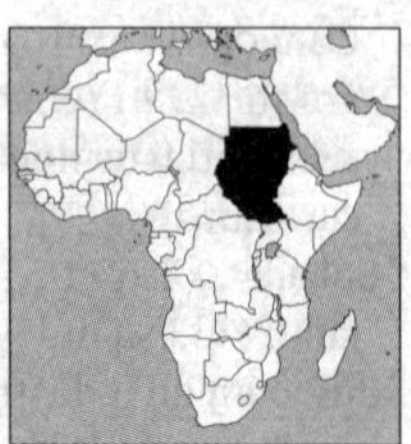

Area: 967,500 sq miles/2,505,813 sq km
Population: 27,291,000
Capital: Khartoum (El Khartum)
Other cities: Omdurman, Khartoum North, Port Sudan
Form of government: Republic
Religions: Sunni Islam, Animism, Christianity
Currency: Sudanese Dinar

Sudd a vast swampland on the White Nile in Sudan.

Sudety (Sudetenland) a mountainous region straddling the border between the Czech Republic and Poland.

Suez (El Suweis) a town at the south end of the Suez Canal. (Pop. 478,000)

Suez, Gulf of a northern arm of the Red Sea that leads to the Suez Canal.

Suez Canal a canal in northeast Egypt, linking the Mediterranean to the Red Sea. It was completed in 1869.

Suffolk a county in southeast England, with its administrative centre in the town of Ipswich. (1,467 sq miles/3,800 sq km; pop. 649,000)

Sulawesi (Celebes) a large, hook-shaped island in the centre of Indonesia. (69,255 sq miles/179,370 sq km; pop. 15,328,000)

Sulu Archipelago a chain of over 400 islands off the southwest Philippines, stretching between the Philippines and Borneo.

Sulu Sea a part of the Pacific Ocean which lies between the Philippines and Borneo.

Sumatra the main island of western Indonesia. (182,860 sq miles/473,607 sq km; pop. 44,703,000)

Sumba one of the Lesser Sunda Islands, Indonesia, to the south of Sumbawa and Flores. (4306 sq miles/11,153 sq km; pop. 251,100)

Sumbawa one of the Lesser Sunda Islands, Indonesia, between Lombok and Flores. (5,965 sq miles/15,448 sq km; pop. 195,000)

Sunda Strait the strait, 16 miles (26 kilometres) across at its narrowest point, which separates Java and Sumatra.

Sunderland an industrial town and the administrative centre of the metropolitan county of Tyne and Wear, England. (Pop. 181,000)

Superior, Lake the largest and most westerly of the Great Lakes. (31,800 sq miles/82,400 sq km)

Surabaya the third largest city of Indonesia after Jakarta and Bandung, on the northeast coast of Java. (Pop. 2,729,000)

Surat a port on the west coast of India, situated in western Gujarat. (Pop. 2,481,000)

Suriname A republic in northeast South America that was formerly known as Dutch Guiana. It is bordered to the west by Guyana, to the east by French Guiana, and to the south by Brazil. The country, formerly a Dutch colony, declared independence in 1975. Suriname comprises a swampy coastal plain, a forested central plateau, and southern mountains. The climate is tropical, with heavy rainfall from December to April. Agriculture remains fairly underdeveloped. Crops cultivated include rice, bananas, citrus fruits, sugar cane, coffee and cocoa. Molasses and rum are produced along with some manufactured goods and there is an important coastal shrimp fishery. Suriname's economy is based on the mining of bauxite, which accounts for 80 per cent of its exports. The country has important mineral reserves of iron ore, nickel, copper, platinum and gold. Suriname's natural resources also include oil and lumber, and forestry is an expanding industry. However, the country is politically unstable and in need of financial aid to develop its resources.

Area: 63,037 sq miles/163,265 sq km
Population: 423,000
capital Paramaribo
Form of government: Republic
Religions: Hinduism, RC, Sunni Islam
Currency: Suriname Guilder

Surrey a county in southeast England, with its administrative centre in the borough of Kingston upon Thames. (648 sq miles/1,679 sq km; pop. 1,041,000)

Suva the capital of Fiji in the southwest Pacific. (Pop. 176,000)

Suzhou a city in Jiangsu Province, China. (Pop. 763,000)

Svalbard an archipelago in the Arctic Ocean to the north of Norway, which has sovereignty. (23,958 sq miles/62,049 sq km; pop. 2,000)

Swansea (1) a port in south Wales, and the administrative centre for the Swansea council area. (Pop. 171,000) (2) a council area in south Wales. (146 sq miles/378 sq km; pop. 230,000)

Swaziland A landlocked hilly enclave almost entirely within the borders of the Republic of South Africa. The mountains in the west of the country rise to about 6,500 feet (almost 2,000 metres), then descend in steps of savannah towards hilly country in the east. The climate is subtropical, moderated by altitude. The land between 1,300–2,800 feet (approximately 400–850 metres) is planted with orange groves and pineapple fields, while on the lower land sugar cane flourishes in irrigated areas. Other important crops are citrus fruits, cotton, and pineapples. Forestry is an important industry, with production centring mainly on pine since it matures extremely quickly because of Swaziland's climate. Coal is mined and also asbestos, although in lessening amounts because of its associated health risks. Manufacturing includes fertilizers, textiles, leather, and tableware. Tourism is a growing industry, with the country's game reserves, mountain scenery, spas, and casinos proving to be popular destinations for visitors.

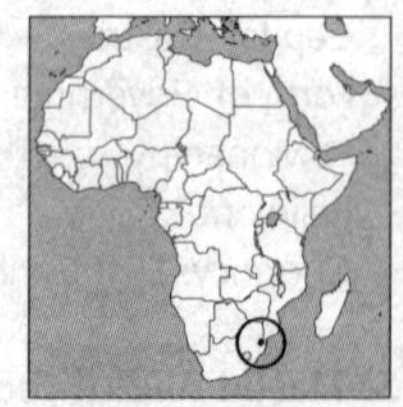

Area: 6,704 sq miles/17,364 sq km
Population: 938,000
capital: Mbabane
Other towns: Big Bend, Manzini, Mhlume
Form of government: Monarchy
Religion: Christianity, Animism
Currency: Lilangeni

Sweden A large country in northern Europe that makes up half the Scandinavian Peninsula. It stretches from the Baltic Sea north to well within the Arctic Circle. The south is generally flat with many lakes, the north mountainous, and along the coast there are over 20,000 islands and islets. Summers are warm but short, while winters are long and cold. In the north snow may lie for four to seven months. Dairy farming is the predominant agricultural activity along with livestock production (cattle, pigs, and sheep). Only 7 per cent of Sweden is cultivated, with the emphasis on fodder crops, potatoes, rape seed, grain, and sugar beet. About 57 per cent of the country is covered by forest, and the sawmill, wood pulp, and paper industries are all of great importance to the country's economy. Sweden is one of the world's leading producers of iron ore, most of which is extracted from within the Arctic Circle. Other main industries are engineering and the production of electrical goods, motor vehicles, and furniture, as well as fine craftware, such as glassware, ceramics, silverware, and items made from stainless steel. In a referendum in 1994, Swedish voters approved membership of the European Union, and it became a member on 1 January 1995.

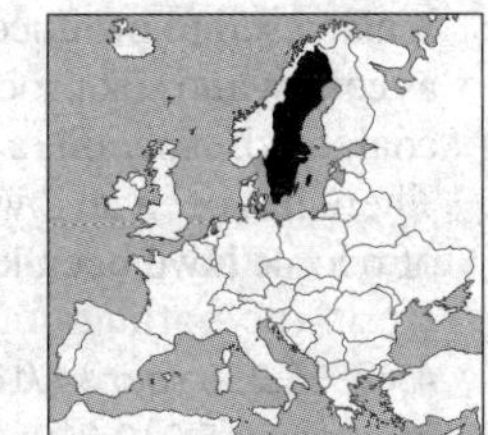

Area: 173,732 sq miles/449,964 sq km
Population: 8,500,000
Capital: Stockholm
Other major cities: Göteborg, Malmö, Uppsala, Örebro
Form of government: Constitutional Monarchy
Religion: Lutheranism
Currency: Krona

Switzerland A landlocked country in central Europe, sharing its borders with France, Italy, Austria, Liechtenstein, and Germany. The Alps occupy over 70 per cent of Switzerland's area, forming two main east-west chains divided by the Rivers Rhine and Rhône. The climate is either continental or mountain type. Summers are generally warm and winters cold, and both are affected by altitude. Northern Switzerland is the industrial part of the country and where its most important cities are located. Basle is famous for its pharmaceuticals, and Zürich for electrical engineering and machinery. Although the country has to import much of its raw materials, these become high-value exports such as clocks, watches, and other precision engineering products. It is also in this region that the famous cheeses and chocolates are produced. Hydroelectricity accounts for approximately 60 per cent of the country's power supplies, with most of the remainder coming from nuclear power plants. Switzerland has huge earnings from international finance and tourism.

Area: 15,940 sq miles/41,284 sq km
Population: 7,076,000
Capital: Bern
Other major cities: Zürich, Basle, Geneva, Lausanne
Form of government: Federal Republic
Religions: RC, Protestantism
Currency: Swiss Franc

Sydney the largest city and port in Australia, and the capital of New South Wales. (Pop. 4,281,000)

Syracuse (1) a city in the centre of New York State, USA. (Pop. 148,000) (2) **(Siracusa)** an ancient seaport on the east coast of Sicily, Italy. (Pop. 126,000)

Syrdar'ya a river of central Asia, flowing through Kazakhstan to the Aral Sea. (Length 1,780 miles/2,860 km)

Syria A country in southwest Asia that borders on the Mediterranean Sea in the west. Much of the country is mountainous behind the narrow fertile coastal plain. The eastern region is desert or semi-desert, a stony, inhospitable land. The coast has a Mediterranean climate, with hot, dry summers and mild, wet winters. About 50 per cent of the workforce get their living from agriculture. Sheep, goats, and cattle are raised, and cotton, barley, wheat, tobacco, grapes, olives, and vegetables are grown. Some land is unused because of lack of irrigation. Reserves of oil are small compared to neighbouring Iraq, but there is enough to make the country self-sufficient and provide three-quarters of the nation's export earnings. Industries, such as textiles, leather, chemicals, and cement, have developed rapidly in the last 20 years, with the country's craftsmen producing fine rugs and silk brocades. Foreign revenue is gained from tourism and also from countries who pipe oil through Syria. The country is dependent on the main Arab oil-producing countries for aid.

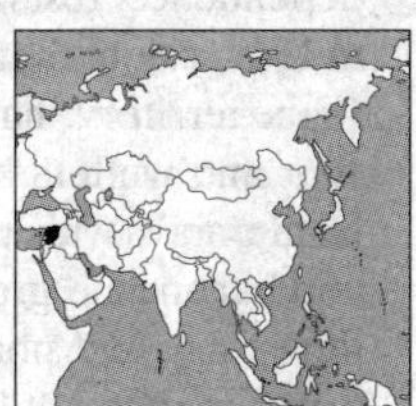

Area: 71,498 sq miles/185,180 sq km
Population: 14,619,000
Capital: Damascus (Dimashq)
Other cities: Aleppo (Halab), Latakia (Al Lādhiqiyah)
Form of government: Republic
Religion: Sunni Islam
Currency: Syrian Pound

Szczecin (Stettin) a port in northwest Poland. (Pop. 416,000)

T

Table Mountain a flat-topped mountain overlooking Cape Town in southwest South Africa. (3,567 ft/1,087 m)

Tabriz a city in northwest Iran. (Pop. 1,211,000)

Taegu the third largest city of the Republic of Korea (South Korea). (Pop. 2,544,000)

Tagus (Tajo, Tejo) a major river of southwest Europe, which rises in eastern Spain and flows west and southwest through Portugal to the Atlantic Ocean west of Lisbon. (Length 626 miles/1,007 km)

Tahiti the largest of the islands of French Polynesia in the South Pacific. The capital is Papeete. (388 sq miles/1,005 sq km; pop. 96,000)

T'aichung a major commercial and agricultural centre in western Taiwan. (Pop. 1,034,000)

T'ainan a city in southwest Taiwan. (Pop. 746,000)

T'aipei the capital and largest city of Taiwan, in the north. (Pop. 2,706,000)

Taiwan An island that straddles the Tropic of Cancer in East Asia. It lies about 100 miles (161 kilometres) off the southeast coast of mainland China. It is predominantly mountainous in the interior, with more than 60 peaks attaining heights of 10,000 feet (3,040 metres). The highest of all is the Jade Mountain (Yu Shan), which stands at 12,960 feet (3,940 metres). Taiwan's independence, resulting from the island's seizure by nationalists in 1949, is not fully accepted internationally and China lays claim to the territory. The climate is warm and humid for most of the year and winters are mild with summers rainy. The soils are fertile, and a wide range of crops, including tea, rice, sugar cane, and bananas, is grown. Natural resources include gas, marble, limestone, and small coal deposits. Taiwan is a major international trading nation with some of the most successful export-processing zones in the world, accommodating domestic and overseas companies. Exports include machinery, electronics, textiles, footwear, toys, and sporting goods.

Area: 13,800 sq miles/35,742 sq km
Population: 21,854,000
Capital: Taipei
Other major cities: Kaohsiung, Taichung, Tainan
Form of government: Republic
Religions: Taoism, Buddhism, Christianity
Currency: New Taiwan Dollar

Taiwan Strait the stretch of water between Taiwan and China.

Taiyuan the capital of Shanxi Province, China. (Pop. 1,832,000)

Tajikistan A republic of the southern central former USSR that declared itself independent in 1991. It borders on Afghanistan and China. The south is occupied by the Pamir mountain range, whose snow-capped peaks dominate the country. More than half the country lies over 9,840 feet (3,000 metres). Most of the country is desert or semi-desert, and the pastoral farming of cattle, sheep, horses, and goats is important. Some yaks are kept in the higher regions. The lowland areas in the Fergana and Amudar'ya valleys are irrigated so that cotton, mulberry trees, fruit, wheat, and vegetables can be grown. The Amudar'ya River is also used to produce hydroelectric power for industries such as cotton and silk processing. The republic is rich in deposits of coal, lead, zinc, oil, and uranium, which are being exploited. There has been an ongoing civil war in which tens of thousands of people have been killed or made homeless.

Area: 55,250 sq miles/143,100 sq km
Population: 5,919,000
Capital: Dushanbe
Form of government: Republic
Religion: Shia Islam
Currency: Tajik Ruble

Taklimakan Desert the largest desert in China, consisting mainly of sand, in the west of the country.

Takoradi a main port of Ghana, in the southwest of the country. (Pop. 86,000)

Tallahassee the state capital of Florida, USA. (Pop. 158,000)

Tallinn a port on the Baltic Sea, and the capital of Estonia. (Pop. 386,000)

Tamil Nadu a state in southeast India. The state capital is Madras. (50,839 sq miles/130,357 sq km; pop. 63,324,000)

Tampa a port and resort on the west coast of Florida, USA. (Pop. 319,000)

Tampere (Tammerfors) the second largest city in Finland after Helsinki, in the southwest of the country. (Pop. 199,000)

Tana (Tsana), Lake a lake in the mountains of northwest Ethiopia, and the source of the Blue Nile. (1,418 sq miles/3,673 sq km)

Tanganyika, Lake the second largest lake in Africa after Lake Victoria, in the Great Rift Valley, between Tanzania and the Democratic Republic of Congo, although Burundi and Zambia also share the shoreline. (12,700 sq miles/32,893 sq km)

Tangier (Tanger) a port on the north coast of Morocco, on the Strait of Gibraltar. (Pop. 591,000)

Tangshan an industrial city in Hebei Province, China. (Pop. 821,000)

Tanzania A country that lies on the east coast of central Africa and comprises a large mainland area and the islands of Pemba and Zanzibar. The mainland consists mostly of plateaux broken by mountainous areas and the East African section of the Great Rift Valley. The climate is very varied and is controlled largely by altitude and distance from the sea. The coast is hot and humid, the central plateau drier, and the mountains semi-temperate. Eighty per cent of Tanzanians make a living from the land, producing corn, cassava, millet, rice, plantains, and sorghum for home consumption. Cash crops include cotton, tobacco, tea, sisal, cashews, and coffee. The two islands produce the bulk of the world's cloves. Diamond mining is an important industry, and there are also sizable deposits of iron ore, coal, and tin. Fishing is also important with the bulk of the catch caught in inland waters. Although Tanzania is one of the poorest countries in the world, it has a wealth of natural wonders, such as the its wildlife, the Serengeti Plain, the Ngorongoro Crater, Mount Kilimanjaro, and the Olduvai Gorge, all of which attract large numbers of tourists, making a significant contribution to the country's economy.

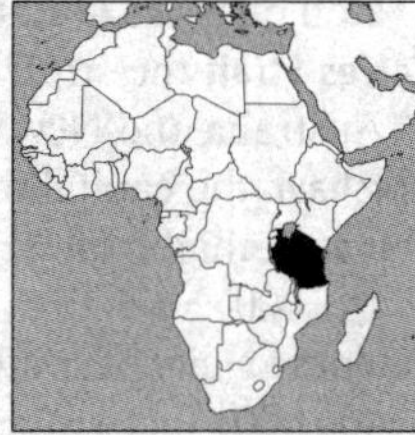

Area: 362,162 sq miles/938,000 sq km
Population: 32,102,000
Capital: Dodoma
Other towns: Dar es Salaam, Zanzibar, Mwanza, Tanga
Form of government: Republic
Religions: Sunni Islam, RC, Anglicanism, Hinduism
Currency: Tanzanian Shilling

Taranto a port and naval base on the south coast of Italy. (Pop. 208,000)

Taranto, Gulf of (Taranto, Golfo di) an inlet of the Mediterranean Sea between the 'toe' and the 'heel' of Italy.

Tarawa the main atoll and capital of Kiribati in the west Pacific. (Pop. 29,000)

Tarragona a port of ancient origins on the Mediterranean coast of northeastern Spain, and the name of the surrounding province. (Pop. 116,000)

Tarsus an agricultural centre in southeast Turkey, the birthplace of St Paul. (Pop. 212,000)

Tashkent the capital of Uzbekistan, in the northeast. (Pop. 2,150,000)

Tasmania an island state to the south of Australia, separated from the mainland by the Bass Strait. The capital is Hobart. (26,383 sq miles/68,332 sq km; pop. 503,000)

Tasman Sea a branch of the Pacific Ocean that separates Australia and New Zealand.

Tatar Republic (Tatarstan) an autonomous republic of the Russian Federation, southwest of Moscow, around the River Volga. The capital is Kazan'. (26,250 sq miles/68,000 sq km; pop. 3,715,000)

Tatra Mountains a range of mountains that lines the border between Poland and Slovakia The highest peak is Gerlachovka (8,737 ft/2,663 m).

Tayside a former administrative region in east Scotland.

Tbilisi the capital of Georgia, a republic in northwest Asia, situated in the centre of the republic. (Pop. 1,383,000)

Tegucigalpa the capital of Honduras in Central America, in the south of the country. (Pop. 1,186,000)

Tehran the capital of Iran, in the central north of the country. (Pop. 7,723,000)

Tel Aviv (Tel Aviv-Jaffa, Tel Aviv-Yafo) the largest city and main financial centre of Israel. It was combined with the old port of Jaffa in 1950.It is the capital of Israel according to the UN and international law. (Pop. 348,000)

Tenerife the largest of the Canary Islands. The capital is Santa Cruz. (795 sq miles/2,058 sq km; pop. 558,000)

Tennessee a state in southern central USA. The state capital is Nashville. (42,244 sq miles/109,412 sq km; pop. 5,791,000)

Tennessee a river which flows southwest from the Appalachian Mountains of North Carolina and then through Alabama, Tennessee and Kentucky to join the Ohio River. (Length 652 miles/1,049 km)

Texas a state in the southwest of the USA, bordering Mexico. It is the nation's second largest state. The capital is Austin. (262,134 sq miles/678,927 sq km; pop. 21,806,000)

Thailand A country about the same size as France, located in southeast Asia. It is a tropical country of mountains and jungles, rainforests and green plains. Central Thailand is a densely populated, fertile plain and the mountainous Isthmus of Kra joins southern Thailand to Malaysia. Thailand has a subtropical climate, with heavy monsoon rains from June to October, a cool season from October to March and a hot season from March to June. It is rich in many natural resources, such as mineral deposits of gold, coal, lead, and precious stones, with rich soils, extensive areas of tropical forests, and natural gas offshore. The central plain of Thailand contains vast expanses of paddy fields that grow enough rice to rank Thailand as one of the world's leading producers. The narrow southern peninsula is very wet, and it is here that rubber is produced. Other crops grown are cassava, maize, pineapples, and sugar cane. Fishing is an increasingly important industry, with prawns being sold for export. Tourism also contributes to the country's economy.

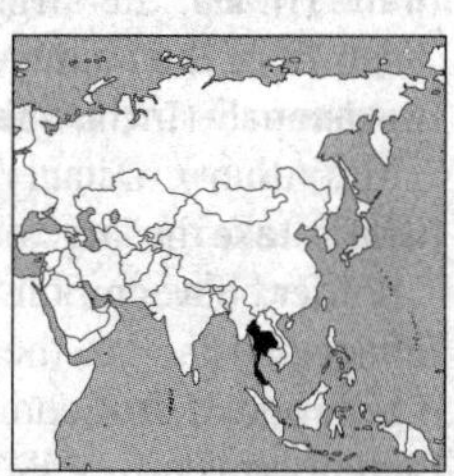

Area: 198,115 sq miles/513,115 sq km
Population: 60,206,000
Capital: Bangkok (Krung Thep)
Other cities: Chiang-Mai, Khon Kaen, Nakhon Sawan
Form of government: Constitutional Monarchy
Religions: Buddhism, Sunni Islam
Currency: Baht

Thailand, Gulf of a branch of the South China Sea lying between the Malay Peninsula and the coasts of Thailand, Cambodia and Vietnam.

Thames a major river of southern England flowing eastwards from its source in the Cotswold Hills, past London to its estuary on the North Sea. (Length 210 miles/338 km)

Thar Desert (Indian Desert) a desert in northwest India, covering the border between the Indian state of Rajasthan and Pakistan.

Thebes the ruins of an ancient city on the River Nile in central Egypt which was the capital of Ancient Egypt for about 1,000 years from 1600 BC.

Thessaloníki (Saloniki) the second largest city in Greece. (Pop. 408,000)

Thimphu (Thimbu) the capital of Bhutan in central Asia, in the west of the country. (Pop. 58,000)

Thon Buri a city on the west side of the River Chao Phraya, opposite Bangkok, in Thailand. (Pop. 117,000)

Thousand Islands a group of over 1,000 islands scattered in the upper St Lawrence River, between the USA and Canada.

Tianjin (Tientsin) a major industrial city in Hebei Province, and the third largest city in China after Shanghai and Beijing. (Pop. 4,344,000)

Tiber (Tevere) a river of central Italy, rising to the east of Florence and flowing south to Rome and into the Mediterranean. (Length 252 miles/405 km)

Tibet (Xizang Autonomous Region) a region of southwest China, consisting of a huge high plateau high beyond the Himalayas. Formerly a Buddhist kingdom led by its spiritual leader, the Dalai Lama, it was invaded by China in 1950 and has been gradually desecrated. (471,660 sq miles/1,221,600 sq km; pop. 2,729,000)

Tierra del Fuego the archipelago at the southern tip of South America, belonging to Argentina and Chile and separated from the mainland by the Strait of Magellan.

Tigray a province of northern Ethiopia, bordering Eritrea, whose people fought a separatist war against the central government from 1975 to 1991. The capital is Mekele. (Pop. 3,970,000)

Tigris a major river of the Middle East, rising in eastern Turkey, flowing through Syria and Iraq and joining the Euphrates to form a delta at the Shatt al Arab waterway as it enters the Persian Gulf. (Length 1,180 miles/1,900 km)

Tijuana a border city and resort in northwest Mexico, at the northern end of the Baja California Peninsula. (Pop. 1,229,000)

Timbuktu a town in central Mali at the edge of the Sahara. (Pop. 35,000)

Timisoara an industrial city in southwest Romania. (Pop. 340,000)

Timor an island at the eastern end of the Lesser Sunda Islands, divided into two parts: Indonesian West Timor and independent East Timor. (11,883 sq miles/30,775 sq km; pop. 3,085,000)

Timor Sea the arm of the Indian Ocean between the northwest coast of Australia and the island of Timor.

Tipperary a county in the south of the Republic of Ireland. It includes the town of Tipperary, but Clonmel is the county town. (1,643 sq miles/4,255 sq km; pop. 139,000)

Tiranè (Tirana) the largest city and the capital of Albania, in the centre of the country. (Pop. 220,000)

Tiruchirapalli (Trichinopoly) an industrial city in central Tamil Nadu in southern India. (Pop. 761,000)

Titicaca, Lake the largest lake in South America, in the Andes, on the border between Bolivia and Peru. (3,141 sq miles/8,135 sq km)

Tobago an island to the northeast of Trinidad, forming part of the republic of Trinidad and Tobago. (Pop. 56,000)

Togo Togo is a tiny West African country with a narrow coastal plain on the Gulf of Guinea and the heavily forested Togo Highlands inland. Over 80 per cent of the population are involved in agriculture, with yams and millet as the principal crops. Coffee, cocoa and cotton are grown for cash. Minerals, especially phosphates, are the main export.

Area: 21,925 sq miles/56,785 sq km
Population: 4,201,000
Capital: Lomé
Form of government: Republic
Religions: Animism, RC, Sunni Islam
Currency: CFA Franc

Tokyo the capital of Japan, a port on the east coast of Honshu Island. Its original name was Edo (until 1868). (Pop. 8,180,000)

Toledo (1) a historical city of central Spain, on the River Tagus. (Pop. 70,000) (2) a city and Great Lake port in Ohio, USA. (Pop. 315,000)

Tonga A country situated about 20 degrees south of the Equator and just west of the International Date Line in the Pacific Ocean. It comprises over 170 islands, only about 40 of which are inhabited, with a low limestone chain of islands in the east and a higher volcanic chain in the west. The climate is warm with heavy rainfall, and destructive cyclones are likely to occur every few years. The government owns all the land, and males can rent an allotment for growing food. Yams, cassava, and taro are grown as subsistence crops, and the islanders' diet is supplemented by fish from the sea. Pumpkins, bananas, vanilla, and coconuts are exported. The main industry is coconut processing. About 70 per cent of the workforce is occupied in either fishing or agriculture while many Tongans are employed overseas. Tourism, foreign aid, and money sent home by its workers overseas, all contribute to the country's economy.

Area: 288 sq miles/747 sq km
Population: 99,000
Capital: Nuku'alofa
Form of government: Constitutional Monarchy
Religions: Methodism, RC
Currency: Pa'anga

Tonlé Sap a lake in central Cambodia which swells and quadruples in size when the Mekong River floods. (In flood 4,000 sq miles/10,400 sq km)

Topeka the state capital of Kansas, USA. (Pop. 123,000)

Torfaen a council area in southeast Wales, with its administrative centre in the town of Pontypool. (112 sq miles/290 sq km; pop. 90,000)

Toronto the largest city of Canada, and the capital of Ontario, situated on Lake Ontario. (Pop. 2,571,000)

Torres Strait the stretch of water between the northeastern tip of Australia and New Guinea.

Tørshavn the capital of the Faeroe Islands. (Pop. 17,000)

Toulon a major naval base and port in southeast France. (Pop. 161,000)

Toulouse a city of southwest France, on the Garonne River. (Pop. 406,000)

Touraine a former province of northwest France, around Tours.

Tourcoing an industrial town in northwestern France, near the border with Belgium. (Pop. 93,000)

Tours a town in western France, on the River Loire. (Pop. 133,000)

Trabzon (Trebizond) a port on the Black Sea in northeastern Turkey. (Pop. 204,000)

Trafalgar, Cape the southwestern tip of Spain.

Transkei one of ten former South African Homelands, the area is now part of the Eastern Cape Province, in southeast South Africa.

Transvaal a former province of north and central South Africa.

Transylvania a region of central and northwestern Romania.

Trent the main river of the Midlands of England, flowing northeast from Staffordshire to the Humber. (Length 170 miles/270 km)

Trenton a city in eastern USA on the Delaware River in western New Jersey, of which it is the capital. (Pop. 87,000)

Trieste a port on the Adriatic Sea in northeast Italy. (Pop. 214,000)

Trinidad and Tobago The islands of Trinidad and Tobago constitute the third largest British Commonwealth country in the West Indies. They are situated off the Orinoco Delta in northeastern Venezuela. They are the most southerly of the Lesser Antilles Islands. Trinidad consists of the mountainous Northern Range in the north and undulating plains in the south. It has a huge, asphalt-producing lake, Pitch Lake, which is approximately 104 acres (42 hectares) in size. Tobago is actually a mountain that is about 1,800 feet (550 metres) above sea level at its peak. The climate is tropical with little variation in temperatures throughout the year and a rainy season from June to December. Trinidad is one of the oldest oil-producing countries in the world. Output is small but provides 90 per cent of the country's exports. Sugar cane, cocoa, citrus fruits, vegetables, and rubber trees are grown for export, while imported food now account for 10 per cent of total imports. Tobago depends mainly on tourism for revenue. A slump in the economy in the 1980s and early 1990s saw widespread unemployment but economic growth has improved in recent times.

Area: 1,981 sq miles/5,130 sq km
Population: 1,297,000
Capital: Port of Spain
Form of government: Republic
Religions: RC, Hinduism, Anglicanism, Sunni Islam
Currency: Trinidad and Tobago Dollar

Tripoli (Tarabulus) (1) the capital and main port of Libya, in the northwest. (Pop. 1,223,000) (2) a port in northern Lebanon. (Pop. 209,000)

Tristan da Cunha a group of four remote, volcanic islands in the middle of the South Atlantic Ocean, which form part of the St Helena Dependencies. (40 sq miles/100 sq km; pop. 300)

Trivandrum a port on the southern tip of India, and the state capital of Kerala. (Pop. 759,000)

Trujillo a city and provincial capital in northwest Peru. (Pop.601,000)

Tucson a city in southern Arizona, USA. (Pop. 520,000)

Tulsa a city in northeastern Oklahoma, on the Arkansas River. (Pop. 395,000)

Tunis the capital and main port of Tunisia. (Pop. 697,000)

Tunisia A North African country that lies on the south coast of the Mediterranean Sea. It is bounded by Algeria to the west and Libya to the south. Northern Tunisia consists of hills, plains, and valleys. Inland mountains separate the coastal zone from the central plains before the land drops down to an area of salt pans and the Sahara. The climate ranges from warm temperate in the north to desert in the south. Agriculture produces wheat, barley, olives, grapes, tomatoes, dates, vegetables, and citrus fruits, and the fishing industry is of growing importance, producing mainly pilchards, sardines, and tuna. Twenty-six per cent of the workforce is engaged in these two occupations, but overall there is a general lack of employment. The mainstays of Tunisia's modern economy are oil from the Sahara, phosphates, natural gas, and tourism on the Mediterranean coast.

Area: 62,592 sq miles/162,155 sq km
Population: 9,092,000
Capital: Tunis; *other cities* Sfax, Bizerte, Djerba
Form of government: Republic
Religion: Sunni Islam
Currency: Tunisian Dinar

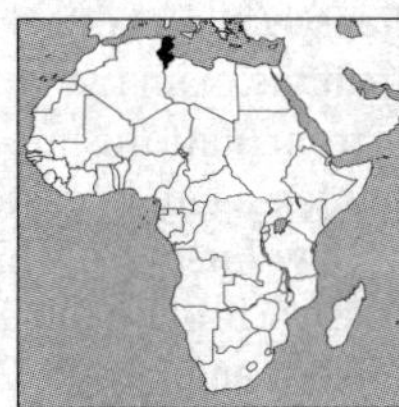

Turin (Torino) a major industrial town on the River Po, and the capital of the Piedmont region, in northwest Italy. (Pop. 898,000)

Turkey With land on the continents of Europe and Asia, Turkey forms a bridge between the two, and guards the sea passage between the Mediterranean and the Black Sea. It occupies an area in which seismic activity is a frequent occurrence and the country regularly experiences devastating earthquakes. Only 5 per cent of its area (Thrace) is in Europe and the much larger area (Anatolia) is in Asia. European Turkey is fertile agricultural land with a Mediterranean climate. Asiatic Turkey is bordered to the north by the Pontine Mountains and to the south by the Taurus Mountains. The climate ranges from Mediterranean on the coasts to hot summers and bitterly cold winters in the central plains. Agriculture employs almost half the workforce, and the major crops being grown are wheat, sugar beet, cotton, tobacco, barley, fruits, maize, and oil seeds. The country's main exports are iron and steel, textiles, dried fruits, tobacco, leather clothes, and petroleum products. The manufacturing industry includes iron and steel, textiles, motor vehicles, and Turkey's famous carpets. The main mineral resources are iron ore, coal, chromium, magnetite, zinc, and lead. Hydroelectric power is supplied by the Tigris and Euphrates Rivers. Tourism is a fast-developing industry and plays an increasingly important role in the economy.

Area: 299,158 sq miles/774,815 sq km
Population: 62,697,000
Capital: Ankara
Other cities: Istanbul, Izmir, Adana, Bursa
Form of government: Republic
Religion: Sunni Islam
Currency: Turkish Lira

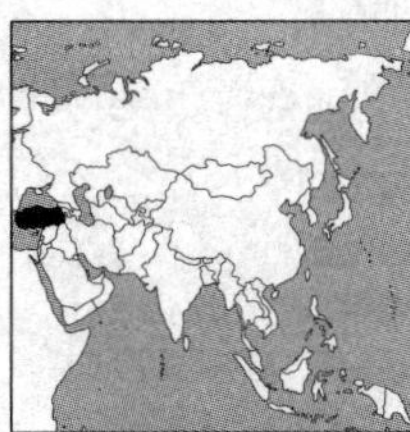

Turkmenistan A central Asian country of the former USSR that declared itself a republic in 1991. It lies to the east of the Caspian Sea and borders Iran and Afghanistan to the south. Much of the west and central areas of Turkmenistan are covered by the sandy Karakum Desert. The east is a plateau that is bordered by the Amudar'ya River. The Amudar'ya has been diverted to form the important Kara Kum Canal which is one of the longest canals in the world and provides irrigation and drinking water for the southeastern parts of the country. The climate is extremely dry, and most of the population live in oasis settlements near the rivers and by the extensive network of canals. Agriculture is intensive around the settlements. Karakul sheep are reared and cotton, cereals, silk and fruit are produced. This occupies around 45 per cent of the workforce. There are rich mineral deposits, particularly natural gas, petroleum, sulphur, coal, salt, and copper, and manufacturing industries include textile manufacturing, food processing, and carpet weaving. Unlike what has happened in most of the other former Soviet republics, there has not been a wholesale emigration of ethnic minorities.

Area: 188,456 sq miles/488,100 sq km
Population: 4,569,000
Capital: Ashkhabad (Ashgabat)
Form of government: Republic
Religion: Sunni Islam
Currency: Manat

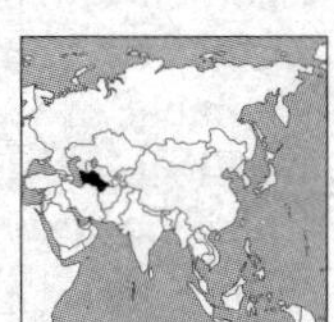

Turks and Caicos Islands Two island groups which form the southeastern archipelago of the Bahamas in the Atlantic Ocean. Only six of the islands are inhabited. The climate is subtropical cooled by southeast trade winds which blow all the year round. A British Crown Colony, the country's economy relies mainly on tourism and the export of shellfish to the UK and the USA.

Area: 166 sq miles/430 sq km
Population: 23,000
Capital: Grand Turk
Form of government: British Crown Colony
Religion: Christianity
Currency: US Dollar

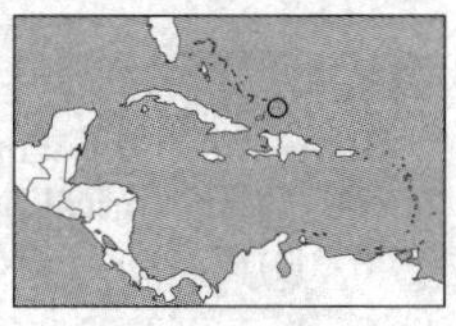

Turku (Åbo) a port in southwest Finland, on the Gulf of Bothnia. (Pop. 177,000)

Tuscany (Toscana) a region of central western Italy, whose capital is Florence. (Pop. 3,505,000)

Tuvalu A country located just north of Fiji, in the South Pacific, consisting of nine coral atolls. The group was formerly known as the Ellice Islands, and the main island and capital is Funafuti. Tuvalu became independent in 1978. The climate is tropical, with an annual average rainfall of 120 inches (3,050 millimetres). Coconut palms are the main crop, and fruit and vegetables are grown for local consumption. Sea fishing is extremely good and largely unexploited, although licenses have been granted to Japan, Taiwan, and the Republic of Korea to fish the local waters. Revenue comes from copra, the country's only export product, foreign aid, the sale of elaborate postage stamps to philatelists, and income sent home from Tuvaluans who work abroad. There is an airport situated on Funafuti Atoll. Rising sea levels, possibly caused by global warming, are threatening to submerge Tuvalu, and preparations are being made for its evacuation.

Area: 10 sq miles/24 sq km
Population: 10,000
Capital: Funafuti
Form of government: Constitutional Monarchy
Religion: Protestantism
Currency: Tuvalu Dollar/Australian Dollar

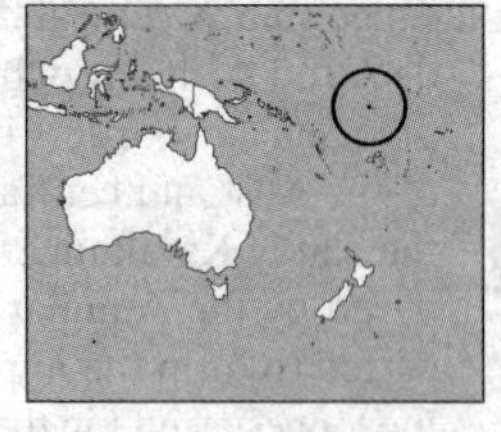

Tver an industrial city on the navigable part of the River Volga in the Russian Federation, 100 miles (160 kilometres) northwest of Moscow. (Pop. 454,000)

Tyne and Wear a metropolitan county in northeast England. (208 sq miles/540 sq km; pop. 1,116,000)

Tyrol a province of western Austria, in the Alps. The capital is Innsbruck. (Pop. 679,000)

Tyrone a historical county in the west of Northern Ireland, taking up a quarter of the total area of Northern Ireland.

Tyrrhenian Sea a part of the Mediterranean Sea between Sicily, Sardinia, and mainland Italy.

U

Udaipur a historical city in southern Rajasthan, India. (Pop. 397,000)

Ufa an industrial city and capital of the autonomous republic of Bashkiria, in the Russian Federation. (Pop. 1,095,000)

Uganda A landlocked country in east central Africa. The Equator runs through the south of the country, and for the most part it is a richly fertile land, well watered, with a kindly climate. In the west are the Ruwenzori Mountains, which reach heights of 16,762 feet (5,109 metres) and are snow-capped. The lowlands around Lake Victoria, once forested, have now for the most part been cleared for cultivation. Agriculture employs over 80 per cent of the labour force, and the main crops grown for subsistence are plantains, cassava, and sweet potatoes. Coffee is the main cash crop and accounts for over 90 per cent of the country's exports. Cotton and tea are also important to the economy, as is mahogany from the country's forests. Virtually all the country's power is produced by hydroelectricity, with the plant on the Victoria Nile being of major importance. Since the 1980s and following years of civil turmoil and unrest, Uganda has slowly been rebuilding its shattered economy and, in spite of some resurgence of earlier violence, attempts are being made to expand the tea plantations in the west, to develop a copper mine, and to introduce new industries to Kampala, the capital.

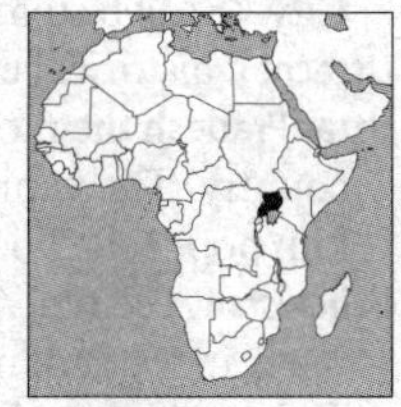

Area: 93,065 sq miles/241,038 sq km
Population: 19,848,000
Capital: Kampala
Other cities: Entebbe, Jinja, Masaka, Mbale
Form of government: Republic
Religions: RC, Protestantism, Animism, Sunni Islam
Currency: Uganda Shilling

Ujung Padang a major port in the southwest of the island of Sulawesi in east Indonesia. It was formerly known as Makassar. (Pop. 1,170,000)

UK *see* **United Kingdom.**

Ukraine A former Soviet socialist republic that declared itself independent of the former USSR in 1991. Its neighbours to the west are Poland, Slovakia, Hungary, and Romania, and it is bounded to the south by the Black Sea. To the east lies the Russian Federation and to the north Belarus. Drained by the Dnieper, Dniester, Southern Bug, and Donets Rivers, Ukraine consists largely of fertile steppes. The climate is continental, although this is greatly modified by the proximity of the Black Sea. The Ukrainian steppe is one of the chief wheat-producing regions of Europe. Other major crops include corn, sugar beet, flax, tobacco, soya, hops, and potatoes, with agriculture accounting for about a quarter of all employment. There are rich reserves of coal and raw materials for industry, but the country is still reliant on the other former Soviet republics for natural gas and oil. The central and eastern regions form one of the world's densest industrial concentrations. Manufacturing industries include ferrous metallurgy, heavy machinery, chemicals, food processing, gas and oil refining. In 1986, a catastrophic accident at the country's Chernobyl nuclear power station occurred, which had far-reaching effects and caused widespread contamination. In 1996, a number of countries agreed to provide financial assistance to help the Ukraine to finally close the station.

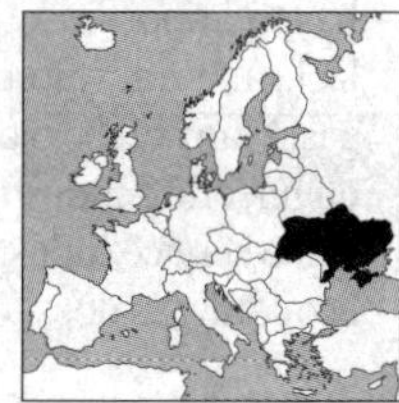

Area: 233,090 sq miles/603,700 sq km
Population: 51,094,000
Capital: Kiev (Kiyev)
Other cities: Dnepropetrovsk, Donetsk, Khar'kov, Odessa
Form of government: Republic
Religions: Russian Orthodox, RC
Currency: Hryvna

Ulan Bator (Ulaanbaatar) the capital of Mongolia, in the central north of the country. (Pop. 808,000)

Ulan Ude the capital of the autonomous republic of Buryat (Buryatiya), in the Russian Federation. (Pop. 371,000)

Ulster one of the four ancient provinces into which Ireland was divided, covering the northeast of the island. It is often used to refer to Northern Ireland, but three counties of Ulster are in the Republic of Ireland (Donegal, Monaghan and Cavan).

Ulundi capital of the province of KwaZulu/Natal in east South Africa.

Ul'yanovsk a city of the eastern Urals in the Russian Federation, on the River Volga. (Pop. 665,000)

Umbria a landlocked region of central eastern Italy. (Pop. 845,000)

Umm al Qaywayn the second smallest emirate in the United Arab Emirates. (290 sq miles/750 sq km; pop. emirate 46,000/town 33,000)

United Arab Emirates (UAE) A federation of seven oil-rich sheikdoms located in the Persian Gulf, namely Abu Dhabi, Dubai, Sharjah, Ajman, Umm al Qaiwain, Ras el Khaimah, and Fujairah. As well as its main coast on the Gulf, the country has a short coast on the Gulf of Oman. The land is mainly flat sandy desert except to the north where the Hajar Mountains rise to 6,828 feet (2,081 metres). The summers are hot and humid with temperatures reaching 120°F (49°C), but from October to May the weather is warm and sunny with pleasant, cool evenings. The only fertile areas are the emirate of Ras al Khaimah, the coastal plain of Al Fujairah and the oases. Abu Dhabi and Dubai are the main industrial centres and, using their wealth from the oil industry, they are now diversifying by building aluminium smelters, cement factories, and steel-rolling mills. Prior to development of the oil industry, traditional occupations were pearl diving, growing dates, fishing, and camel breeding. Dubai is the richest state in the world.

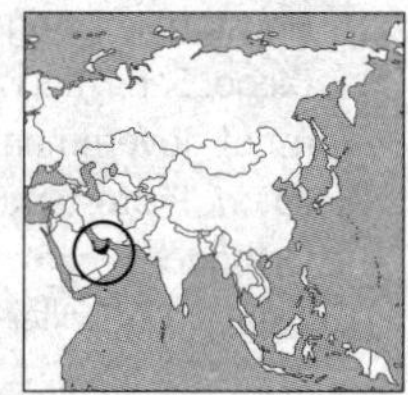

Area: 32,278 sq miles/83,600 sq km
Population: 2,260,000
Capital: Abu Dhabi (Abu Zabi)
Other major cities: Dubai, Sharjh, Ras al Khaymah
Form of government: Monarchy (Emirates)
Religion: Sunni Islam
Currency: Dirham

United Kingdom of Great Britain and Northern Ireland (UK) A country situated in northwest Europe, comprising the island of Great Britain and the six counties of Northern Ireland, plus many smaller islands, especially off the west coast of Scotland. The south and east of Britain is low-lying, and the Pennines form a backbone running through northern England. Scotland has the largest area of upland, and Wales is a highland block. The climate is cool temperate with mild conditions and an even annual rainfall. The UK is primarily a highly urbanized industrial and commercial country. Only 2 per cent of the workforce are employed in agriculture and, although production is high thanks to modern machinery and scientific methods, the UK still has to import one third of its food. Major crops include barley, potatoes, sugar beet, and wheat, while livestock includes sheep, cattle, pigs, and poultry. Fishing is also an important industry. The UK has to import most of the materials it needs for its industries as it lacks natural resources apart from coal, iron ore, oil, and natural gas. Many of the older industries, such as the coal, textiles and heavy engineering industries, have declined significantly in recent years while service industries play an increasingly large part in the UK's economy, as does tourism.

Area: 94,248 sq miles/244,101 sq km
Population: 58,784,000
Capital: London
Other major cities: Birmingham, Manchester, Glasgow, Liverpool, Belfast
Form of government: Constitutional Monarchy
Religion: Anglicanism, RC, Presbyterianism, Methodism
Currency: Pound Sterling

United States of America (USA) A country that stretches across central North America, from the Atlantic Ocean in the east to the Pacific Ocean in the west, and from Canada in the north to Mexico and the Gulf of Mexico in the south. It is the fourth largest country in the world and consists of fifty states, including outlying Alaska, northwest of Canada, and Hawaii in the Pacific Ocean. The climate varies a great deal in such a large country. In Alaska, there are polar conditions, while in the Gulf coast and in Florida conditions may be subtropical. The highest point is Mount McKinley at 20,322 feet (6,194 metres). Natural resources include vast mineral reserves, including oil and gas, coal, copper, lead, uranium gold, tungsten, and lumber. Although agricultural production is high, it employs only 1.5 per cent of the population primarily because of its advanced technology. The USA is a world leader in oil production. Its main industries are iron and steel, chemicals, motor vehicles, aircraft, telecommunications equipment, computers, electronics, and textiles. The USA is the richest and most powerful nation in the world.

Area: 3,536,278 sq miles/9,158,960 sq km
Population: 249,630,000
Capital: Washington D.C.
Other major cities: New York, Chicago, Detroit, Houston, Los Angeles, Philadelphia, San Diego, San Francisco
Form of government: Federal Republic
Religion: Protestantism, RC, Judaism, Eastern Orthodox
Currency: US Dollar

Uppsala an old university town in eastern central Sweden. (Pop. 126,000)

Ural Mountains (Urals, Uralskiy Khrebet) a mountain range in western Russian Federation. Running north to south from the Arctic to the Aral Sea, the Urals form a dividing line between Europe and Asia. The highest point is Mount Narodnaya (6,214 ft/1,894 m).

Uruguay One of the smallest countries in South America. It lies on the east coast of the continent, to the south of Brazil, and is bordered by the Uruguay River to the west, Río de la Plata to the south, and the Atlantic Ocean to the east. The country consists of low plains and plateaux. The Negro River, which rises in Brazil, crosses the country from northeast to southwest, dividing Uruguay almost into two halves. The climate is temperate and rainfall plentiful, and the natural vegetation is prairie grassland. Some of the river valleys are wooded but Uruguay lacks dense forests. About 90 per cent of the land is suitable for agriculture but only about 8 per cent is cultivated, the remainder being used to graze the vast herds of cattle and sheep that provide over 35 per cent of Uruguay's exports in the form of wool, hides, and meat. The cultivated land is made up of vineyards, rice fields, and groves of olives and citrus fruits. The main crops grown are sugar beet and sugar cane, rice, wheat, potatoes, corn, and sorghum. The country has scarce mineral resources, and hydroelectric power supplies most of its energy needs. Important industries include textile manufacture, food processing, oil refining, steel, aluminium, electrical goods, and rubber.

Area: 68,500 sq miles/177,414 sq km
Population: 3,203,000
Capital: Montevideo
Form of government: Republic
Religions: RC, Protestantism
Currency: Peso Uruguayo

Ürümqi (Urumchi) the capital of the Xinjiang Autonomous Region of northwest China. (Pop. 1,120,000)

US/USA *see* **United States of America.**

Utah a state in the west of the USA. The state capital is Salt Lake City. (82,096 sq miles/212,628 sq km; pop. 2,307,000)

Utrecht a historical city in the central Netherlands. (Pop. 233,000)

Uttar Pradesh the most populous state of India, in the north of the country. The capital is Lucknow. (113,654 sq miles/294,364 sq km; pop. 169,296,000)

Uzbekistan A central Asian republic of the former USSR that declared itself independent in 1991. It lies between Kazakhstan and Turkmenistan and encompasses the southern half of the Aral Sea. The republic has many contrasting regions. The Tian Shan region is mountainous, the Fergana region is irrigated and fertile, the Kyzlkum Desert (one of the world's largest) is rich in oil and gas, the lower Amudar'ya River region is irrigated and has oasis settlements, and the Usturt Plateau is a stony desert. Uzbekistan is one of the world's leading cotton producers, and Karakul lambs are reared for wool and meat. Its main industrial products are agricultural machinery, textiles, and chemicals. It also has significant reserves of natural gas. Economic growth has been checked by concerns about political instability and much of the economy remains based on the centralized state-owned model. There are serious pollution problems around the Aral Sea, which has greatly decreased in size from its use for irrigation and is contaminated with toxins, salts, and sands that poison the water supply of the surrounding population. Hydroelectric schemes supply much of the republic's electricity needs.

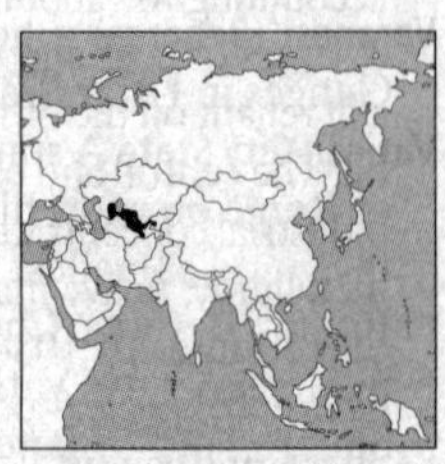

Area: 172,742 sq miles/447,400 sq km
Population: 24,000,000
Capital: Tashkent
Other cities: Samarkand, Urgench, Nukus, Bukhara
Form of government: Republic
Religion: Sunni Islam
Currency: Uzbekistan Sum

V

Vaduz an old market town and the capital of Liechtenstein, in the Rhine valley. (Pop. 5,000)

Valencia (1) a port on the Mediterranean coast of Spain, and the capital of the province of the same name. (Pop. 742,000) (2) an industrial city in northern Venezuela. (Pop. 1,457,000)

Vale of Glamorgan a council area in south Wales, with its administrative centre in the town of Barry. (114 sq miles/295 sq km; pop. 119,000)

Valladolid an industrial city in northwest Spain. (Pop. 319,000)

Valle d'Aosta a French-speaking region of northwest Italy. The capital is Aosta. (Pop. 123,000)

Valletta the capital of Malta, in the Mediterranean. (Pop. 7,000)

Valparaíso the main port and surrounding region of Chile. (Pop. 302,000)

Van, Lake a salt lake in eastern Turkey. (1,419 sq miles/3,675 sq km)

Vancouver a major port and industrial centre in southwest British Columbia, Canada, on the mainland opposite Vancouver Island with access to the Pacific Ocean. (Pop. 534,000)

Vancouver Island the largest island off the Pacific coast of North America, in southwest Canada. The capital is Victoria. (12,408 sq miles/32,137 sq km; pop. 390,000)

Vanuatu A country, formerly known as the New Hebrides (so named by Captain Cook in 1774), located in the southwest Pacific Ocean, southeast of the Solomon Islands and about 1,087 miles (1,750 kilometres) east of Australia. It consists of some 12 islands and some 60 islets. Most of the islands are volcanic and densely forested, with raised coral beaches and fringed by coral reefs. The largest islands are Espíritu Santo, Malekula, and Efate, on which the capital, Vila, is sited. Vanuatu has a tropical climate that is moderated by the southeast trade winds from May to October. Cultivated land is generally restricted to the coastal plains and the main cash crops are copra, cocoa beans, and coffee. Meat and fish are also exported and light industries include food processing and handicrafts for an increasing tourist industry. The majority of the labour force are engaged in subsistence farming, growing taro, yams, and bananas. Tourism is an increasingly important industry. Vanuatu has international airports.

Area: 4,706 sq miles/12,189 sq km
Population: 169,000
Capital: Vila (Port-Vila)
Form of government: Republic
Religion: Protestantism, RC, Animism
Currency: Vatu

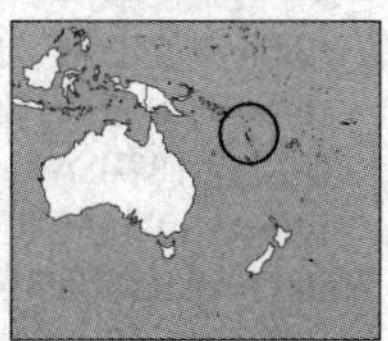

Varanasi (Benares) a holy Hindu city on the banks of the River Ganges in Uttar Pradesh, northeastern India. (Pop. 1,122,000)

Vatican City State A state, established in 1929, that lies in the heart of Rome on a low hill on the west bank of the River Tiber. It is the world's smallest independent state and headquarters of the Roman Catholic Church. It is a walled city with six gates, and is made up of the Vatican Palace, the Papal Gardens, St Peter's Square, and St Peter's Basilica. The state has its own police, newspaper, telephone and telegraph services, stamps, radio station, and train station. The radio station, Radio Vaticana, broadcasts a service in 34 languages from transmitters within the Vatican City. Its main tourist attractions are the frescoes of the Sistine Chapel, painted by Michelangelo Buonarroti. It also has outstanding museums, with collections of antiquities and works by Italian masters, and the Vatican Library's collection of ancient manuscripts is priceless. The Pope exercises sovereignty and has absolute legislative, executive, and judicial powers.

Area: 0.2 sq mile/0.44 sq km
Population: 1,000
Capital: Vatican City
Form of government: Papal Commission
Religion: RC
Currency: Euro

Venda one of ten former South African Homelands, the area is now part of the Limpopo Province in north South Africa.

Veneto a region of northeastern Italy, centring upon Venice. (Pop. 4,526,000)

Venezuela A country that forms the northernmost crest of South America. Its northern coast lies along the Caribbean Sea, and it is bounded to the west by Colombia, and to the southeast and south by Guyana and Brazil. In the northwest, a spur of the Andes Mountains runs southwest to northeast. Venezuela has one of the highest waterfalls in the world, the Angel Falls. The River Orinoco cuts the country in two, and north of the river run the undulating plains known as the Llanos. South of the river are the Guiana Highlands. The climate ranges from warm temperate to tropical. Temperatures vary little throughout the year and rainfall is plentiful. In the Llanos area, cattle are herded across the plains, and this region makes the country almost self-sufficient in meat. There are also rich fishing grounds around the coast and off Venezuela's 72 islands. Sugar cane and coffee are grown for export, but petroleum and gas account for around 80 per cent of export earnings. Venezuela's economy is built on its oilfields, located in the Maracaibo region, but it also has other important mineral reserves including bauxite, iron ore, coal, and precious metals and stones, such as gold, silver, platinum, and diamonds.

Area: 352,145 sq miles/912,050 sq km
Population: 21,710,000
Capital: Caracas
Other cities: Maracaibo, Valencia, Barquisimeto
Form of government: Federal Republic
Religion: RC
Currency: Bolívar

Venice (Venezia) a historical port built on islands at the head of the Adriatic Sea in northeastern Italy. The principal thoroughfares are canals. (Pop. 272,000)

Vermont a state in the northeast of the USA, bordering Canada. The state capital is Montpelier. (9,609 sq miles/24,887 sq km; pop. 617,000)

Verona a historical and industrial city in Veneto, northern Italy. (Pop. 256,000)

Versailles a town just to the west of Paris, France, which grew up around the palace built there by Louis XIV in the 1660s. (Pop. 83,000)

Vesuvius an active volcano to the southeast of Naples, in southwest Italy, notorious for having buried the ancient city of Pompeii in AD 79. (4,203 ft/1,281 m)

Victoria (1) a state in southeastern Australia. The state capital is Melbourne. (87,884 sq miles/227,620 sq km; pop. 4,846,000) (2) a port on the southeastern coast of Vancouver Island, southwest Canada, and the capital of British Columbia. (Pop. 76,000) (3) a region in south China, part of Hong Kong, in the northwest of Hong Kong Island. (Pop. 1,026,900) (4) a port and the capital of the Seychelles, on the island of Mahé. (Pop. 23,000)

Victoria Falls one of the world's greatest waterfalls, where the River Zambezi tumbles some 355 feet (108 metres), on the Zambia-Zimbabwe border.

Victoria, Lake the largest lake in Africa, and the second largest freshwater lake in the world after Lake Superior. Its shoreline is shared by Uganda, Kenya, and Tanzania. (26,828 sq miles/69,485 sq km)

Vienna (Wien) the capital of Austria, on the River Danube, in the northeast of the country. (Pop. 1,541,000)

Vientiane (Viangchan) the capital of Laos, on the Mekong River in the northeast of the country, near the border with Thailand. (Pop. 190,000)

Vietnam A long narrow country in southeast Asia that runs down the coast of the South China Sea. It has a narrow central area that links broader plains centred on the Red (Hong) and Mekong Rivers. This narrow zone, now known as Mien Trung, is hilly and makes communications between north and south difficult. The climate is humid, with tropical conditions in the south and subtropical in the north. The far north can be very cold when polar air blows over Asia. Agriculture, fishing, and forestry employ around 74 per cent of the labour force. The main crop is rice but cassava, maize, and sweet potatoes are also grown for domestic consumption. Soya beans, tea, coffee, and rubber are grown for export. Major industries are food processing, textiles, cement, cotton and silk manufacture. Fishing is also an important export trade that is conducted mainly on the South China Sea, although there is some fish farming in flooded inland areas. Vietnam is still recovering from the ravages of many wars this century, and remains underdeveloped.

Area: 128,066 sq miles/331,689 sq km
Population: 75,181,000
Capital: Hanoi
Other cities: Ho Chi Minh City, Haiphong, Hué, Dà Nang
Form of government: Socialist Republic
Religion: Buddhism, Taoism, RC
Currency: New Dong

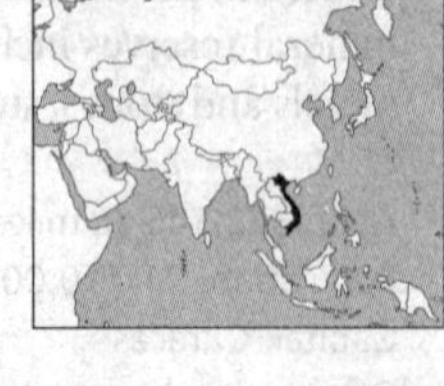

Vila (Port-Vila) the capital and chief port of Vanuatu in the west Pacific. (Pop. 34,000)

Vilnius the capital of Lithuania in northeast Europe. (Pop. 556,000)

Virginia a state in the east of the USA, with a coast on the Atlantic Ocean. The state capital is Richmond. (39,780 sq miles/103,030 sq km; pop. 7,298,000)

Virgin Islands, British A British Overseas Territory lying at the western end of the Lesser Antilles in the Caribbean Sea. It comprises 4 large islands and 36 islets and cays. Only 16 of the islands are inhabited. Most of the islands are hilly and wooded, and the climate is subtropical moderated by trade winds. Agriculture produces livestock, coconuts, sugar cane, fruit, and vegetables, but only a small percentage of the land available to agriculture is under cultivation. The main industries are construction, rum distilling and tourism, which is the mainstay of the economy.

Area: 58 sq miles/151 sq km
Population: 19,00
Capital: Road Town
Form of government: British Overseas Territory
Religion: Protestantism
Currency: US Dollar

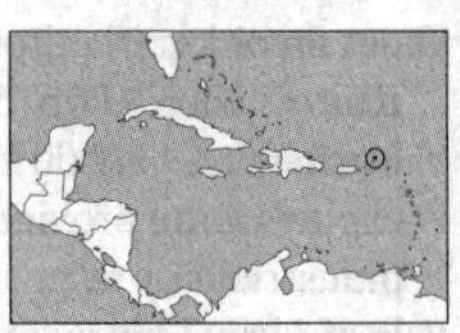

Virgin Islands, US Part of the Virgin Islands group in the northwest of the Lesser Antilles in the Caribbean Sea. A self-governing US territory, this group of 50 volcanic islands are rugged and mountainous with a subtropical climate. The main islands are St John (around two-thirds of which is a National Park), St Croix, and St Thomas. Agriculture is not well developed and most of the country's food has to be imported. There is a small manufacturing industry but tourism is the mainstay of the economy with many cruise ships calling at the island of St Thomas, in particular, because of its natural deep-water harbour.

Area: 134 sq miles/347 sq km
Population: 106,000
Capital: Charlotte Amalie
Form of government: Self-governing US Territory
Religion: Protestantism
Currency: US Dollar

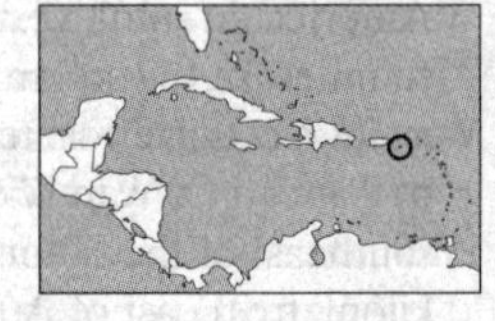

Visayan Islands a group of islands in the centre of the Philippines, which includes Negros, Cebu, Leyte, Masbate, Bohol, Panay and Samar.

Vistula a river of central northern Poland, flowing through Cracow and Warsaw to the Baltic Sea. (Length 677 miles/1,090 km)

Vladivostok a major port on the Pacific coast in the far east of the Russian Federation, 30 miles (50 kilometres) from the border with China. (Pop. 597,000)

Vojvodina an autonomous province in the north of Serbia, in former Yugoslavia. The capital is Novi Sad. (8,301 sq miles/21,506 sq km; pop. 1,922,000)

Volga a largely navigable river of the western Russian Federation, flowing south from its source, to the northeast of Moscow, to the Caspian Sea. It is the longest river in Europe. (Length 2,293 miles/3,690 km)

Volgograd a port and major industrial city of the Russian Federation, on the River Volga. (Pop. 987,000)

Volta a river in Ghana, fed by the Black Volta and the White Volta, which flows south to the Bight of Benin. (Length 298 miles/480 km)

Volta, Lake a major artificial lake that occupies much of eastern Ghana, formed by the damming of the Volta River. (3,251 sq miles/8,480 sq km)

Voronezh an industrial city 280 miles (450 kilometres) south of Moscow in the Russian Federation. (Pop. 906,000)

W

Wales a principality in the southwest of Great Britain, forming a part of the UK. Cardiff is the capital. (8,017 sq miles/20,768 sq km; pop. 2,935,000)

Wallis and Futuna Islands A French Overseas Territory that comprises two island groups lying 142 miles (230 kilometres) apart in the southern central Pacific Ocean. It is the smallest and poorest of France's overseas territories. The climate is warm and humid with a cyclone season between October and March. Subsistence farming and fishing are the main activities with copra the only important export.

Area: 77 sq miles/200 square km
Population: 15,000
Capital: Matā'Utu
Form of government: French Overseas Territory
Religion: RC
Currency: Pacific Franc

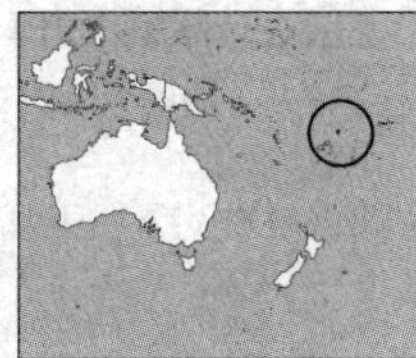

Warsaw (Warszawa) the capital of Poland, on the River Vistula, in the eastern central part of the country. (Pop. 1,610,000)

Warwickshire a county in central England, with its administrative centre in the town of Warwick. (765 sq miles/1,981 sq km; pop. 507,000)

Wash, the a shallow inlet formed by the North Sea in the coast of East Anglia, between the counties of Lincolnshire and Norfolk.

Washington a state in northwest USA, with a coast on the Pacific Ocean. The state capital is Olympia. (66,570 sq miles/172,416 sq km; pop. 6,083,000)

Washington DC the capital of the USA, on the Potomac River. It stands in its own territory, called the District of Columbia (DC), between the states of Virginia and Maryland, close to the Atlantic coast. (69 sq miles/179 sq km; pop. 543,000)

Waterford a county in the south of the Republic of Ireland. The county town is also called Waterford. (710 sq miles/1,838 sq km; pop. 99,000)

Weimar a historical city in southern central Germany. (Pop. 62,000)

Wellington the capital of New Zealand and a port in the southwest of North Island. (Pop. 168,000)

Weser a river in northwest Germany, flowing through Bremen and Bremerhaven to the North Sea. (Length 182 miles/292 km)

West Bank a piece of disputed territory to the west of the River Jordan, including a part of Jerusalem. It was taken by Israel from Jordan in the Arab-Israeli war of 1967 but given limited autonomy in 1994 under the auspices of the Palestinian National Authority. (2,262 sq miles/5,858 sq km; pop. 1,881,000)

West Bengal a state in eastern India, bordering Bangladesh. Calcutta is the capital. (34,258 sq miles/88,752 sq km; pop. 81,788,000)

Western Australia a state occupying much of the western half of Australia. The capital is Perth. (975,920 sq miles/2,527,636 sq km; pop. 1,964,000)

Western Cape one of South Africa's nine provinces, in south South Africa, formerly part of the old Cape Province, with its administrative centre in Cape Town. (49,937 sq miles/129,370 sq km; pop. 3,957,000)

Western Isles (Eilean Siar) an island council area in west Scotland, consisting of the Outer Hebrides, with its administrative centre in the town of Stornoway. (1,120 sq miles/2,900 sq km; pop. 31,000)

Western Sahara A disputed territory of western Africa, with a coastline on the Atlantic Ocean. Consisting mainly of desert, it is rich in phosphates. It was an overseas province of Spain until 1976, when it was partitioned between Morocco and Mauritania. Since 1979, the entire territory has been claimed and administered by Morocco, against the wishes of an active separatist movement, the Frente Polisario. Moroccan sovereignty is not universally recognized, and the United Nations has attempted to oversee a referendum to decide the struggle but without success so far. It is a poor country, with many of its people following a nomadic existence. The bulk of the country's food has to be imported. Phosphates comprise two-thirds of its meagre exports.

Area: 102,703 sq miles/266,000 sq km
Population: 266,000
Capital: Laâyoune (El Aaiún)
Form of government: Republic (*de facto* controlled by Morocco)
Religion: Sunni Islam
Currency: Moroccan Dirhama

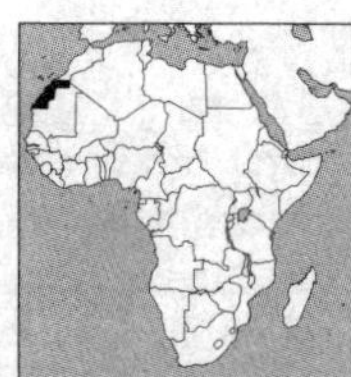

West Dunbartonshire a council area in west central Scotland, with its administrative centre in the town of Dumbarton. (63 sq miles/162 sq km; pop. 96,000)

West Glamorgan a former county in south Wales.

West Indies a general term for the islands of the Caribbean Sea.

West Lothian a council area in central Scotland, with its administrative centre in Livingston. (164 sq miles/425 sq km; pop. 151,000)

Westmeath a county in the central north of the Republic of Ireland. The county town is Mullingar. (681 sq miles/1,764 sq km; pop. 66,000)

West Midlands a metropolitan county in central England. (347 sq miles/899 sq km; pop. 2,628,000)

West Sussex a county in southeast England, with its administrative centre in the city of Chichester. (768 sq miles/1,989 sq km; pop. 752,000)

West Virginia a state of eastern USA. The capital is Charleston. (24,070 sq miles/62,341 sq km; pop. 1,796,000)

West Yorkshire a metropolitan county in northern England. (787 sq miles/2,039 sq km)

Wexford a county in the southeast of the Republic of Ireland. The county town is also called Wexford. (908 sq miles/2,352 sq km; pop. 109,000)

White Sea (Beloye More) an arm of the Barents Sea off the northwest of the Russian Federation, which is almost enclosed by the bulge of the Kola Peninsula.

Whitney, Mount a mountain in the Sequoia National Park in eastern California, with the highest peak in the USA outside of Alaska. (14,495 ft/4,418 m)

Wichita a city in southern Kansas, USA, on the Arkansas River. (Pop. 346,000)

Wicklow a county in the southwest of the Republic of Ireland. The county town is also called Wicklow. (782 sq miles/2,025 sq km; pop. 107,000)

Wiesbaden an old spa town in western Germany, and capital of the state of Hessen. (Pop. 266,000)

Wight, Isle of an island and county off the south coast of England, separated from the mainland by the Solent, with its administrative centre in Newport. (147 sq miles/380 sq km; pop. 125,000)

Willemstad the capital of the Netherlands Antilles in the Caribbean. (Pop. 58,000)

Wiltshire a county in central southern England, with its administrative centre in the town of Trowbridge. (1,344 sq miles/3,481 sq km; pop. 586,000)

Winchester a historical city in southern England, and the administrative centre of Hampshire. (Pop. 38,000)

Winnipeg the capital of Manitoba, Canada, in the south of the state. (Pop. 635,000)

Winnipeg, Lake a lake in the south of Manitoba, Canada, which drains into Hudson Bay via the Nelson River. (9,094 sq miles/ 23,553 sq km)

Wisconsin a state in north central USA, bordering Lake Superior and Lake Michigan. The state capital is Madison. (54,464 sq miles/141,061 sq km; pop. 5,440,000)

Witwatersrand (the Rand) a rocky ridge in northern South Africa containing the richest gold deposits in the world.

Wollongong a major port and industrial centre in New South Wales, Australia, 50 miles (80 kilometres) south of Sydney. (Pop. 266,000)

Wolverhampton an industrial town in the West Midlands of England. (Pop. 258,000)

Worcestershire a county in west central England, with its administrative centre in the city of Worcester. (674 sq miles/1,742 sq km; pop. 528,000)

Wrexham (1) a town in north Wales, formerly known for its coal mining, the administrative centre for the Wrexham council area. (Pop. 41,000) (2) a council area in north Wales. (193 sq miles/ 500 sq km; pop. 123,000)

Wroclaw (Breslau) an industrial city on the River Oder in southwest Poland. (Pop. 633,000)

Wuhan (Hankow) the capital of Hubei Province, southeast China. (Pop. 3,958,000)

Wyoming a state in the west of the USA. The state capital is Cheyenne. (97,914 sq miles/253,597 sq km; pop. 495,000)

Xiamen a port on the east coast of China, in Fujian Province. (Pop. 470,000)

Xi'an the capital of Shaanxi Province, China, an industrial centre and former capital of China. (Pop. 2,656,000)

Xi Jiang (Si Kiang) the third longest river in China, flowing across the southwest of the country from Yunnan to its delta on the South China Sea near Guangzhou (Canton). (Length 1,437 miles/2,300 km)

Xining an industrial city and the capital of Qinghai Province, in western China. (Pop. 714,000)

Xinjiang (Sinkiang) Uygur Autonomous Region (Xinjiang Uygur Zizhiqu) a region of northwest China, bordering Mongolia, the Russian Federation, Afghanistan, Pakistan and India. It is also known as Dzungaria. The capital is Ürümqi. (635,829 sq miles/1,646,799 sq km; pop. 18,929,000)

Y

Yamoussoukro the capital of Côte d'Ivoire since 1983, in the centre of the country. (Pop. 196,000)

Yamuna (Jumna) a major river of north India, a tributary of the River Ganges. (Length 855 miles/1,376 km)

Yangôn ***see*** **Rangoon**

Yaoundé the capital of Cameroon, West Africa, in its southwest. (Pop. 1,122,000)

Yaren the capital of Nauru in the southwest Pacific. (Pop. 5,000)

Yekaterinburg an industrial city to the east of the Ural Mountains in the Russian Federation. (Pop. 1,260,000)

Yellowknife a city on the Great Slave Lake, Canada, and capital of the Northwest Territories. (Pop. 17,000)

Yellow Sea a branch of the Pacific Ocean between the northeast coast of China and the peninsula of Korea. (180,000 sq miles/466,200 sq km)

Yemen A country bounded by Saudi Arabia in the north, Oman in the east, the Gulf of Aden in the south, and the Red Sea in the west. The country was formed after the unification of the previous Yemen Arab Republic (North)and the People's Democratic Republic of Yemen (South) in 1989. At that point, however, there was no active integration of the two countries and politically the country remained divided between North and South. In 1994, a civil war that lasted three months broke out between the former North and South Yemen, which resulted in a high rate of inflation, damage to the infrastructure, and devaluation of the currency. Most of the country comprises rugged mountains and trackless desert lands. The country is almost entirely dependent on agriculture even although only a very small percentage is fertile. The main crops are coffee, cotton, wheat, vegetables, millet, sorghum, and fruit. Fishing is an important industry, and there are some canning factories along the coast. Other industry is on a very small scale, consisting mainly of manufacturing industries which produce textiles, paints, matches, plastic, rubber, and aluminium goods. Attempts to modernize the country's industry are hampered by a lack of funds.

Area: 203,850 sq miles/527,978 sq km
Population: 15,919,000
Capital: Sana'a
Commercial capital: Aden
Form of government: Republic
Religion: Zaidism, Shia Islam, Sunni Islam
Currency: Yemeni Rial

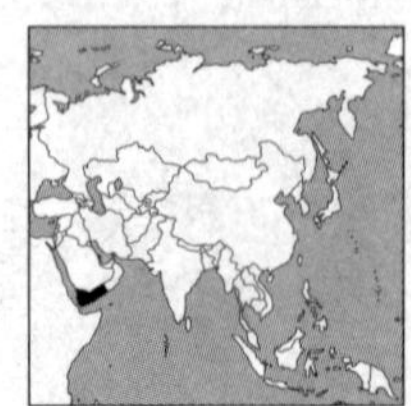

Yerevan an industrial city and the capital of Armenia in northwest Asia. (Pop. 1,258,000)

Yinchuan the capital of Ningxia-hui Autonomous Region, in north central China. (Pop. 247,000)

Yogyakarta (Jogjakarta) a city and cultural centre of south central Java in Indonesia. (Pop. 418,000)

Yokohama the main port of Japan, and its second largest city after neighbouring Tokyo, on the southeast coast of Honshu Island. (Pop. 3,484,000)

Yorkshire a former county of northeast England now divided into West Yorkshire, East Riding of Yorkshire, North Yorkshire and South Yorkshire.

Yucatan (Yucatán) a state of southeast Mexico on the broad Yucatan Peninsula. The capital is Mérida. (15,186 sq miles/39,340 sq km; pop. 1,556,000)

Yugoslavia the former Yugoslavia was a country created in 1918 which became a single federal republic of six after World War II under the leadership of Marshal Tito (1892–1980). Its six constituent republics were Serbia, Croatia, Slovenia, Bosnia-Herzegovina, Macedonia, and Montenegro. During the 1990s, the republics of Slovenia, Bosnia-Herzegovina, Macedonia, and Croatia all declared their independence from Yugoslavia. Slovenia and Macedonia managed to do this peacefully but declarations of independence in Bosnia and Croatia led to the worst violence seen in Europe since World War II. The last two republics, Serbia and Montenegro, recently agreed to the creation of a new union of two states to be known as Serbia and Montenegro. The creation of this new union brings about the final demise of the country known for so long as Yugoslavia.

Area: 39,449 sq miles/102,173 sq km
Populations: 10,574,000
Capital: Belgrade (Beograd)
Other cites: Nis, Novo Sad, Pristina
Form of government: Federal Republic
Religion: Eastern Orthodox Islam
Currency: New Dinar

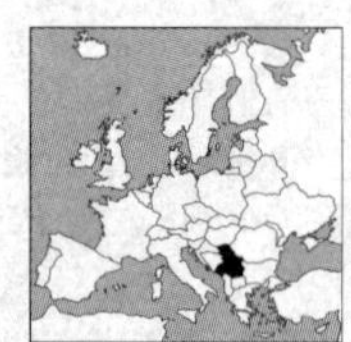

Yukon Territory a mountainous territory in northwest Canada centring upon the River Yukon and including the River Klondike. (207,076 sq miles/536,372 sq km; pop. 29,000)

Yünnan a province in southwestern China. The capital is Kunming. (168,400 sq miles/436,200 sq km; pop. 43,178,000)

Z

Zagreb the capital of Croatia. (Pop. 766,000)

Zagros Mountains (Kuhha-ye Zagros) a mountain range in southwest Iran, running parallel to the border with Iraq. The highest point is Zard Kuh (14,918 ft/4,548 m).

Zambezi a river of southern Africa. It rises in Zambia, then flows south to form the border with Zimbabwe, and then southeast across Mozambique to the Indian Ocean. (Length 1,700 miles/ 2,740 km)

Zambia A country made up of high plateaux in Central Africa. Bordering it to the south is the Zambezi River, and to the southwest, the Kalahari Desert. It has other large rivers, such as the Luangwa, and lakes, the largest of which is Lake Bangweulu. The climate is tropical, modified somewhat by altitude. The country has a wide range of wildlife, and there are large game parks on the Luangwa and Kafue Rivers. Agriculture is underdeveloped and vulnerable to weather variations. This has led to some food shortages, and as a result much of the country's food has to be imported. The principal subsistence crops grown are corn, sugar cane, and cassava, and the main livestock raised are cattle. Zambia's economy relies heavily on the mining of copper, lead, zinc, and cobalt. The poor market prospects for copper, and the fact that supplies will eventually be exhausted, make it imperative for Zambia to develop her vast agricultural potential. The majority of the country's power is provided by the Kariba Dam on the Zambezi River, and there is the potential for further hydroelectric development.

Area: 290,587 sq miles/752,618 sq km
Population: 8,500,000
Capital: Lusaka
Other cities: Kitwe, Ndola, Mufulira
Form of government: Republic
Religions: Christianity, Animism
Currency: Kwacha

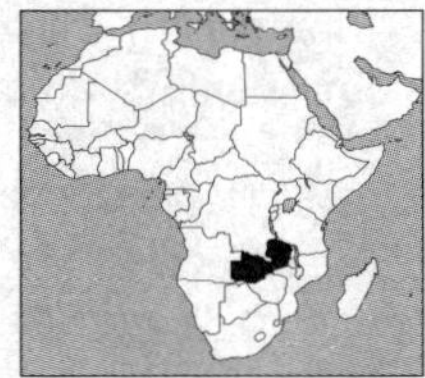

Zanzibar an island, now part of the United Republic of Tanzania, lying just off the east coast of Tanzania, in the Indian Ocean. The main town and port is also called Zanzibar. (950 sq miles/ 2,461 sq km; pop. 444,000)

Zaporozh'ye a major industrial city on the River Dnieper in the Ukraine. (Pop. 829,000)

Zaragoza (Saragossa) a historical and industrial city and the surrounding province in northeastern Spain, on the River Ebro. (Pop. city 607,000)

Zealand (Sjaelland, Seeland) the largest island of Denmark, on which the capital, Copenhagen, is sited. (2,708 sq miles/7,014 sq km; pop. 2,224,000)

Zhangjiakou a city in Hebei Province, in northeast China. (Pop. 390,000)

Zhejiang a province of eastern China, mountainous and densely populated with a coast on the East China Sea. The capital is Hangzhou. (39,780 sq miles/102,000 sq km; pop. 44,543,000)

Zhengzhou the capital of Henan Province, in east central China. (Pop. 1,348,000)

Zibo an industrial city in Shangdong Province, northeastern China. (Pop. 2,888,000)

Zimbabwe A landlocked country in southern Africa, Zimbabwe is a country with spectacular physical features, teeming with wildlife. It is bordered in the north by the Zambezi River, which flows over the mile-wide Victoria Falls before entering Lake Kariba. In the south, the River Limpopo marks its border with South Africa. A great plateau between 4,000-5,000 feet (about 1,200-1,500 metres) in height occupies the central area. Only one third of the population lives in its towns and cities, the largest of which is the capital, Harare. The climate is tropical in the lowlands and subtropical in the higher land. About 75 per cent of the workforce are employed in agriculture. Tobacco, sugar cane, cotton, wheat, and maize are grown and form the basis of processing industries. Zimbabwe is rich in mineral resources such as coal, chromium, nickel, gold, platinum, and precious metals, and mining accounts for around 30 per cent of foreign revenue. Tourism has the potential to be a major growth industry thanks to the country's many tourist attractions, including several wildlife parks, the Victoria Falls, and Great Zimbabwe. However, there has been ongoing conflict with the white farming community over the ownership of farms and the economy has declined rather than prospered, a situation further aggravated by political violence in recent years.

Area: 150,873 sq miles/390,580 sq km
Population: 11,908,000
Capital: Harare
Other cities: Bulawayo, Mutare, Gweru
Form of government: Republic
Religion: Animism, Anglicanism, RC
Currency: Zimbabwe Dollar

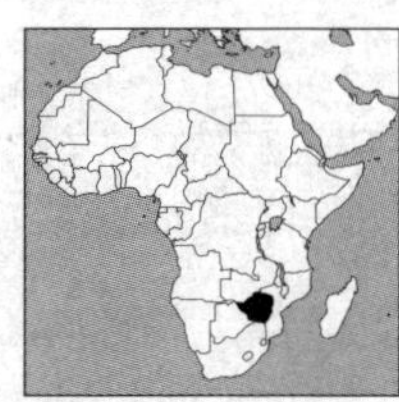

Zürich the largest city in Switzerland, in the northeast of the country, and a major industrial and financial centre. (Pop. 339,000)

Appendix 4
Leaders of the Modern World

Presidents of the United States of America

No.	Name	Life Dates	Politics	Dates in Office
1	George Washington	1732–1799	Federalist	1789–1797
2	John Adams	1735–1826	Federalist	1797–1801
3	Thomas Jefferson	1743–1826	Dem.–Rep.	1801–1809
4	James Madison	1751–1836	Dem.–Rep.	1809–1817
5	James Monroe	1758–1831	Dem.–Rep.	1817–1825
6	John Quincy Adams	1767–1848	Dem.–Rep.	1825–1829
7	Andrew Jackson	1767–1845	Democrat	1829–1837
8	Martin Van Buren	1782–1862	Democrat	1837–1841
9	William Henry Harrison	1773–1841	Whig	1841
10	John Tyler	1790–1862	Whig	1841–1845
11	James Knox Polk	1795–1849	Democrat	1845–1849
12	Zachary Taylor	1784–1850	Whig	1849–1850
13	Millard Fillmore	1800–1874	Whig	1850–1853
14	Franklin Pierce	1804–1869	Democrat	1853–1857
15	James Buchanan	1791–1868	Democrat	1857–1861
16	Abraham Lincoln	1809–1865	Republican	1861–1865
17	Andrew Johnson	1808–1875	National Unionist	1865–1869
18	Ulysses Simpson Grant	1822–1885	Republican	1869–1877
19	Rutherford Birchard Hayes	1822–1893	Republican	1877–1881
20	James Abram Garfield	1831–1881	Republican	1881
21	Chester Alan Arthur	1829–1886	Republican	1881–1885
22	Grover Cleveland	1837–1908	Democrat	1885–1889
23	Benjamin Harrison	1833–1901	Republican	1889–1893
24	Grover Cleveland	1837–1908	Democrat	1893–1897
25	William McKinley	1843–1901	Republican	1897–1901
26	Theodore Roosevelt	1858–1919	Republican	1901–1909
27	William Howard Taft	1857–1930	Republican	1909–1913
28	Woodrow Wilson	1856–1924	Democrat	1913–1921
29	Warren Gamaliel Harding	1865–1923	Republican	1921–1923
30	Calvin Coolidge	1872–1933	Republican	1923–1929
31	Herbert Clark Hoover	1874–1964	Republican	1929–1933
32	Franklin Delano Roosevelt	1882–1945	Democrat	1933–1945
33	Harry S Truman	1884–1972	Democrat	1945–1953
34	Dwight David Eisenhower	1890–1969	Republican	1953–1961
35	John Fitzgerald Kennedy	1917–1963	Democrat	1961–1963
36	Lyndon Baines Johnson	1908–1973	Democrat	1963–1969
37	Richard Milhous Nixon	1913–1994	Republican	1969–1974
38	Gerald Rudolph Ford	1913–	Republican	1974–1977
39	Jimmy (James Earl) Carter	1924–	Democrat	1977–1981
40	Ronald Wilson Reagan	1911–2004	Republican	1981–1989
41	George Herbert Walker Bush	1924–	Republican	1989–1993
42	Bill (William Jefferson) Clinton	1946–	Democrat	1993–2001
43	George Walker Bush	1946–	Republican	2001–

Prime Ministers of Canada (Dominion)

Name	Life Dates	Politics	Dates in Office
John Alexander MacDonald	1815–1891	Conservative	1867–1873
Alexander Mackenzie	1822–1892	Liberal	1873–1878
Sir John Alexander MacDonald	1815–1891	Conservative	1878–1891
Sir John Joseph Caldwell Abbott	1821–1893	Conservative	1891–1892
Sir John Sparrow David Thompson	1845–1894	Conservative	1892–1894
Sir Mackenzie Bowell	1823–1917	Conservative	1894–1896

Name	Life Dates	Politics	Dates in Office
Sir Charles Tupper	1821–1915	Conservative	1896
Sir Wilfrid Laurier	1841–1919	Liberal	1896–1911
Sir Robert Laird Borden	1854–1937	Conservative	1911–1920
Arthur Meighen	1874–1960	Unionist	1920–1921
William Lyon Mackenzie King	1874–1950	Liberal	1921–1926
Arthur Meighen	1874–1960	Conservative	1926
William Lyon Mackenzie King	1874–1950	Liberal	1926–1930
Richard Bedford Bennett	1870–1947	Conservative	1930–1935
William Lyon Mackenzie King	1874–1950	Liberal	1935–1948
Louis Stephen St. Laurent	1882–1973	Liberal	1948–1957
John George Diefenbaker	1895–1979	Conservative	1957–1963
Lester Bowles Pearson	1897–1972	Liberal	1963–1968
Pierre Elliott Trudeau	1919–2000	Liberal	1968–1979
Joe (Joseph Charles) Clark	1939–	Conservative	1979–1980
Pierre Elliott Trudeau	1919–2000	Liberal	1980–1984
John Napier Turner	1929–	Liberal	1984
Martin Brian Mulroney	1939–	Conservative	1984–1993
Kim (Avril) Campbell	1947–	Conservative	1993
Jean Chrétien	1934–	Liberal	1993–2003
Paul Martin	1938–	Liberal	2003–

Prime Ministers of the United Kingdom

Name	Life Dates	Politics	Dates in Office
Sir Robert Walpole	1676–1745	Whig	1721–1742
Earl of Wilmington	*c.*1673–1743	Whig	1742–1743
Henry Pelham	*c.*1695–1754	Whig	1743–1754
Duke of Newcastle	1693–1768	Whig	1754–1756
Duke of Devonshire	1720–1764	Whig	1756–1757
Earl of Waldegrave	1715–1763	Whig	1757
Duke of Newcastle	1693–1768	Whig	1757–1762
Earl of Bute	1713–1792	Tory	1762–1763
George Grenville	1712–1770	Whig	1763–1765
Marquess of Rockingham	1730–1782	Whig	1765–1766
Earl of Chatham (William Pitt the Elder)	1708–1778	Whig	1766–1767
Duke of Grafton	1735–1811	Whig	1767–1770
Lord North	1732–1792	Tory	1770–1782
Marquess of Rockingham	1730–1782	Whig	1782
Earl of Shelburne	1737–1805	Whig	1782–1783
Duke of Portland	1738–1809	Coalition	1783
William Pitt (the Younger)	1759–1806	Tory	1783–1801
Henry Addington	1757–1844	Tory	1801–1804
William Pitt (the Younger)	1759–1806	Tory	1804–1806
Lord Grenville	1759–1834	Whig	1806–1807
Duke of Portland	1738–1809	Tory	1807–1809
Spencer Perceval	1762–1812	Tory	1809–1812
Earl of Liverpool	1770–1828	Tory	1812–1827
George Canning	1770–1827	Tory	1827
Viscount Goderich	1782–1859	Tory	1827–1828
Duke of Wellington	1769–1852	Tory	1828–1830
Earl Grey	1764–1845	Whig	1830–1834
Viscount Melbourne	1779–1848	Whig	1834
Duke of Wellington	1769–1852	Tory	1834
Sir Robert Peel	1788–1850	Tory	1834–1835
Viscount Melbourne	1779–1848	Whig	1835–1841
Sir Robert Peel	1788–1850	Tory	1841–1846

Name	*Life Dates*	*Politics*	*Dates in Office*
Lord John Russell	1792–1878	Whig	1846–1852
Earl of Derby	1799–1869	Conservative	1852
Earl of Aberdeen	1784–1860	Peelite	1852–1855
Viscount Palmerston	1784–1865	Liberal	1855–1858
Earl of Derby	1799–1869	Conservative	1858–1859
Viscount Palmerston	1784–1865	Liberal	1859–1865
Earl Russell	1792–1878	Liberal	1865–1866
Earl of Derby	1799–1869	Conservative	1866–1868
Benjamin Disraeli	1804–1881	Conservative	1868
William Ewart Gladstone	1809–1898	Liberal	1868–1874
Benjamin Disraeli	1804–1881	Conservative	1874–1880
William Ewart Gladstone	1809–1898	Liberal	1880–1885
Marquess of Salisbury	1830–1903	Conservative	1885–1886
William Ewart Gladstone	1809–1898	Liberal	1886
Marquess of Salisbury	1830–1903	Conservative	1886–1892
William Ewart Gladstone	1809–1898	Liberal	1892–1894
Earl of Rosebery	1847–1929	Liberal	1894–1895
Marquess of Salisbury	1830–1903	Conservative	1895–1902
Arthur Balfour	1848–1930	Conservative	1902–1905
Sir Henry Campbell-Bannerman	1836–1908	Liberal	1905–1908
Herbert Asquith	1852–1928	Liberal	1908–1915
Herbert Asquith	1852–1928	Coalition	1915–1916
David Lloyd George	1863–1945	Coalition	1916–1922
Andrew Bonar Law	1858–1923	Conservative	1922–1923
Stanley Baldwin	1867–1947	Conservative	1923–1924
James Ramsay MacDonald	1866–1937	Labour	1924
Stanley Baldwin	1867–1947	Conservative	1924–1929
James Ramsay MacDonald	1866–1937	Labour	1929–1931
James Ramsay MacDonald	1866–1937	Coalition	1931–1935
Stanley Baldwin	1867–1947	Coalition	1935–1937
Neville Chamberlain	1869–1940	Coalition	1937–1940
Winston Churchill	1874–1965	Coalition	1940–1945
Winston Churchill	1874–1965	Conservative	1945
Clement Attlee	1883–1967	Labour	1945–1951
Sir Winston Churchill	1874–1965	Conservative	1951–1955
Sir Anthony Eden	1897–1977	Conservative	1955–1957
Harold Macmillan	1894–1986	Conservative	1957–1963
Sir Alexander Douglas-Home	1903–1995	Conservative	1963–1964
Harold Wilson	1916–1995	Labour	1964–1970
Edward Heath	1916–	Conservative	1970–1974
Harold Wilson	1916–1995	Labour	1974–1976
James Callaghan	1912–	Labour	1976–1979
Margaret Thatcher	1925–	Conservative	1979–1990
John Major	1943–	Conservative	1990–1997
Tony (Anthony Charles Lynton) Blair	1953–	Labour	1997–

Prime Ministers of Australia (Federation)

Name	*Life Dates*	*Politics*	*Dates in Office*
Sir Edmund Barton	1849–1920	Protectionist	1901–1903
Alfred Deakin	1856–1919	Protectionist	1903–1904
John Christian Watson	1867–1941	Labour	1904
Sir George Houston Reid	1845–1918	Coalition	1904–1905
Alfred Deakin	1856–1919	Protectionist	1905–1908
Andrew Fisher	1862–1928	Labor	1908–1909

Name	*Life Dates*	*Politics*	*Dates in Office*
Alfred Deakin	1856–1919	Fusion	1909–1910
Andrew Fisher	1862–1928	Labor	1910–1913
Sir Joseph Cook	1860–1947	Liberal	1913–1914
Andrew Fisher	1862–1928	Labor	1914–1915
William Morris Hughes	1862–1952	Labor	1915–1916
William Morris Hughes	1862–1952	National Labor	1916–1917
William Morris Hughes	1862–1952	Nationalist	1917–1923
Stanley Melbourne Bruce	1883–1967	Coalition	1923–1929
James Henry Scullin	1876–1953	Labor	1929–1932
Joseph Aloysius Lyons	1879–1939	United Australia	1932–1938
Joseph Aloysius Lyons	1879–1939	Coalition	1938–1939
Sir Earle Christmas Grafton Page	1880–1961	Coalition	1939
Robert Gordon Menzies	1894–1978	United Australia	1939–1940
Robert Gordon Menzies	1894–1978	Coalition	1940–1941
Arthur William Fadden	1895–1973	Coalition	1941
John Joseph Curtin	1885–1945	Labor	1941–1945
Francis Michael Forde	1890–1983	Labor	1945
Joseph Benedict Chifley	1885–1951	Labor	1945–1949
Sir Robert Gordon Menzies	1894–1978	Coalition	1949–1966
Harold Edward Holt	1908–1967	Coalition	1966–1967
Sir John McEwan	1900–1980	Coalition	1967–1968
John Grey Gorton	1911–2002	Coalition	1968–1971
William McMahon	1908–1988	Coalition	1971–1972
Edward Gough Whitlam	1916–	Labor	1972–1975
John Malcolm Fraser	1930–	Liberal (caretaker)	1975
John Malcolm Fraser	1930–	Coalition	1975–1983
Bob (Robert James Lee) Hawke	1929–	Labor	1983–1991
Paul Keating	1944–	Labor	1991–1996
John Howard	1939–	Liberal	1996–

Prime Ministers of New Zealand

Name	*Life Dates*	*Politics*	*Dates in Office*
Henry Sewell	1807–1879		1856
William Fox	1812–1893		1856
Edward William Stafford	1819–1901		1856–1861
William Fox	1812–1893		1861–1862
Alfred Domett	1811–1887		1862–1863
Frederick Whitaker	1812–1891		1863–1864
Frederick Aloysius Weld	1823–1891		1864–1865
Edward William Stafford	1819–1901		1865–1869
William Fox	1812–1893		1869–1872
Edward William Stafford	1819–1901		1872
George Marsden Waterhouse	1824–1906		1872–1873
William Fox	1812–1893		1873
Julius Vogel	1835–1899		1873–1875
Daniel Pollen	1813–1896		1875–1876
Sir Julius Vogel	1835–1899		1876
Harry Albert Atkinson	1831–1892		1876–1877
Sir George Grey	1812–1898		1877–1879
John Hall	1824–1907		1879–1882
Frederick Whitaker	1812–1891		1882–1883
Harry Albert Atkinson	1831–1892		1883–1884
Robert Stout	1844–1930		1884
Harry Albert Atkinson	1831–1892		1884

Name	*Life Dates*	*Politics*	*Dates in Office*
Sir Robert Stout	1844–1930		1884–1887
Sir Harry Albert Atkinson	1831–1892		1887–1891
John Ballance	1839–1893	Liberal	1891–1893
Richard John Seddon	1845–1906	Liberal	1893*–1906
William Hall-Jones	1851–1936	Liberal	1906
Sir Joseph George Ward	1856–1930	Liberal	1906–1912
Thomas MacKenzie	1854–1930	Liberal	1912
William Ferguson Massey	1856–1925	Reform	1912–1915
William Ferguson Massey	1856–1925	National	1915–1919
William Ferguson Massey	1856–1925	Reform	1919–1925
Sir Francis Henry Dillon Bell	1851–1936	Reform	1925
Joseph Gordon Coates	1878–1943	Reform	1925–1928
Sir Joseph George Ward	1856–1930	United	1928–1930
George William Forbes	1869–1947	United	1930–1931
George William Forbes	1869–1947	Coalition	1931–1935
Michael Joseph Savage	1872–1940	Labour	1935–1940
Peter Fraser	1884–1950	Labour	1940–1949
Sidney George Holland	1893–1961	National	1949–1957
Keith Jacka Holyoake	1904–1983	National	1957
Walter Nash	1882–1968	Labour	1957–1960
Keith Jacka Holyoake	1904–1983	National	1960–1972
John Ross Marshall	1912–1998	National	1972
Norman Eric Kirk	1923–1974	Labour	1972–1974
Wallace Edward (Bill) Rowling	1927–1995	Labour	1974–1975
Robert David Muldoon	1921–1992	National	1975–1984
David Russell Lange	1942–	Labour	1984–1989
Geoffrey Winston Russell Palmer	1942–	Labour	1989–1990
Michael Kenneth Moore	1935–	Labour	1990
James Brendan Bolger	1935–	National	1990–1997
Jennifer Mary Shipley	1951–	National	1997–1999
Helen Clark	1949–	Labour	1999–

Prime Ministers of South Africa

Name	*Life Dates*	*Politics*	*Dates in Office*
Louis Botha	1862–1919	South Africa Party	1910–1919
Jan Christiaan Smuts	1870–1950	South Africa Party	1919–1924
James Barry Munnik Hertzog	1866–1942	National	1924–1939
Jan Christiaan Smuts	1870–1950	United	1939–1948
Daniel François Malan	1874–1959	National	1948–1954
Johannes Gerhardus Strijdom	1893–1958	National	1954–1958
Charles Robberts Swart	1894–1982	National	1958
Hendrik Frensch Verwoerd	1901–1966	National	1958–1966
Theophilus Ebenaezer Donges	1898–1968	National (caretaker)	1966
Balthazar Johannes (John) Vorster	1915–1983	National	1966–1978
P[ieter] W[illem] Botha	1916–	National	1978–1989*
F[rederik] W[illem] de Klerk	1936–	National	1989–1994
Nelson Rolihlahla Mandela	1918–	African National Congress	1994–1999
Thabo Mvuyelwa Mbeki	1942–	African National Congress	1999–

* The post of prime minister was amalgamated with that of president in 1984

Appendix 5
World Maps

Map Index

C

L

M

T

Roads – *at scales larger than 1:3 million*
Motorway/Highway
Other Main Road
– *at scales smaller than 1:3 million*
Principal Road: Motorway/Highway
Other Main road
Main Railway

Towns & Cities
Population > 5,000,000
1–5,000,000
500,000–1,000,000
< 500,000
Paris — National Capital
Airport
International Boundary
International Boundary – not defined or in dispute
Internal Boundary
River
Canal
Marsh or Swamp

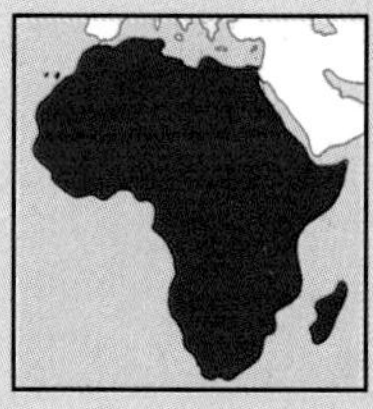

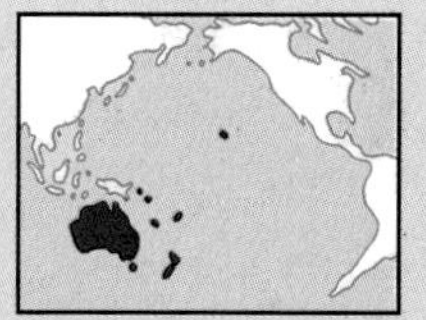

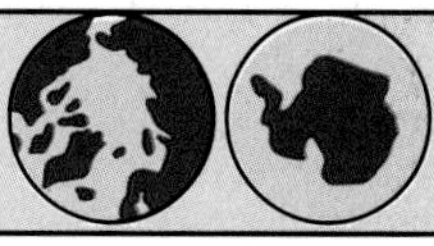

Relief
▲ 1510 Peak (meters)

5,000 meters (16,405 feet)
4,000 (13,124)
3,000 (9,843)
2,000 (6,562)
1,000 (3,281)
500 (1,641)
200 (656)
100 (328)
0
Land below sea level

Note:
The 0–100 contour layer appears only at scales larger than 1:3 million

ALB	- Albania
ARM	- Armenia
AUS	- Austria
AZER	- Azerbaijan
BANG	- Bangladesh
BEL	- Belgium
BOS. - HERZ.	- Bosnia - Herzegovina
BUL	- Bulgaria
CAMB	- Cambodia
CRO	- Croatia
CZECH	- Czech Republic
DOM. REP.	- Dominican Republic
E.G.	- Equatorial Guinea
EST	- Estonia
GEOR	- Georgia
HUNG	- Hungary
JORD	- Jordan
LAT	- Latvia
LEB	- Lebanon
LITH	- Lithuania
LUX	- Luxembourg
MAC	- Macedonia
MOL	- Moldova
NETH	- Netherlands
SLO	- Slovenia
SLOV	- Slovakia
SUR	- Suriname
SWZ	- Switzerland
U.A.E.	- United Arab Emirates
YUGO	- Yugoslavia

Scale 1:85 500 000

RUSSIAN FEDERATION
KAZAKHSTAN
Astana
MONGOLIA
Ulaanbaatar
CHINA
Beijing
N. KOREA
Pyongyang
S. KOREA
Sŏul
SEA OF JAPAN
JAPAN
Tōkyō
SEA OF OKHOTSK
BERING SEA
Aleutian Is.
Bering Strait
Alaska (U.S.A.)
Arctic Circle
CANADA
GULF OF ALASKA
UZBEKISTAN
Bishkek
KYRGYZSTAN
Tashkent
TURKMENISTAN
Ashkhabad
TAJIKISTAN
Dushanbe
Kābul
AFGHANISTAN
Islamabad
PAKISTAN
New Delhi
NEPAL
Kathmandu
Thimphu
BHUTAN
Dhākā
BANG.
INDIA
MYANMAR (BURMA)
Rangoon
LAOS
Vientiane
Hanoi
VIETNAM
THAILAND
Bangkok
CAMB.
Phnom Penh
HONG KONG
T'ai-pei
TAIWAN
EAST CHINA SEA
SOUTH CHINA SEA
Manila
PHILIPPINES
BAY OF BENGAL
ARABIAN SEA
Masqat
OMAN
U.A.E.
Colombo
SRI LANKA
MALDIVES
Kuala Lumpur
MALAYSIA
BRUNEI
SINGAPORE
INDONESIA
Jakarta
EAST TIMOR
TIMOR
PAPUA NEW GUINEA
Port Moresby
SEYCHELLES
INDIAN OCEAN
Rodrigues
MAURITIUS
Réunion
PACIFIC OCEAN
Tropic of Cancer
Hawaii (U.S.A.)
NORTHERN MARIANAS IS. (U.S.A.)
MARSHALL ISLANDS
FEDERATED STATES OF MICRONESIA
PALAU
Equator
NAURU
KIRIBATI
SOLOMON ISLANDS
TUVALU
SAMOA
VANUATU
FIJI
CORAL SEA
Nouvelle Calédonie (Fr.)
TONGA
Tropic of Capricorn
AUSTRALIA
Canberra
TASMAN SEA
Tasmania
Wellington
NEW ZEALAND
Îs. Kerguelen (Fr.)
Antarctic Circle
ANTARCTICA

North America *Political*

4

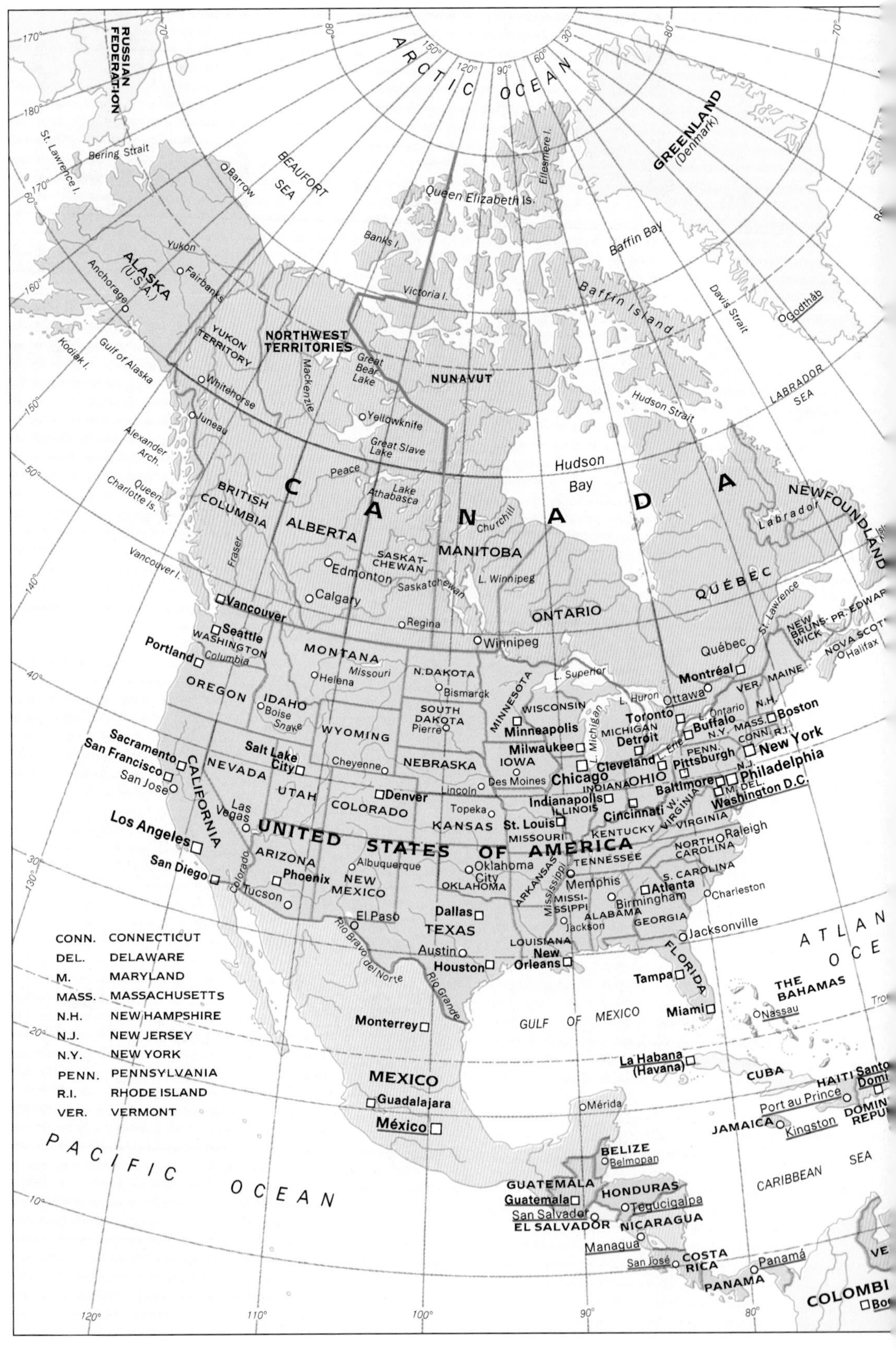

Scale 1:41 600 000

0 500 1000 1500 km

0 250 500 750 1000 miles

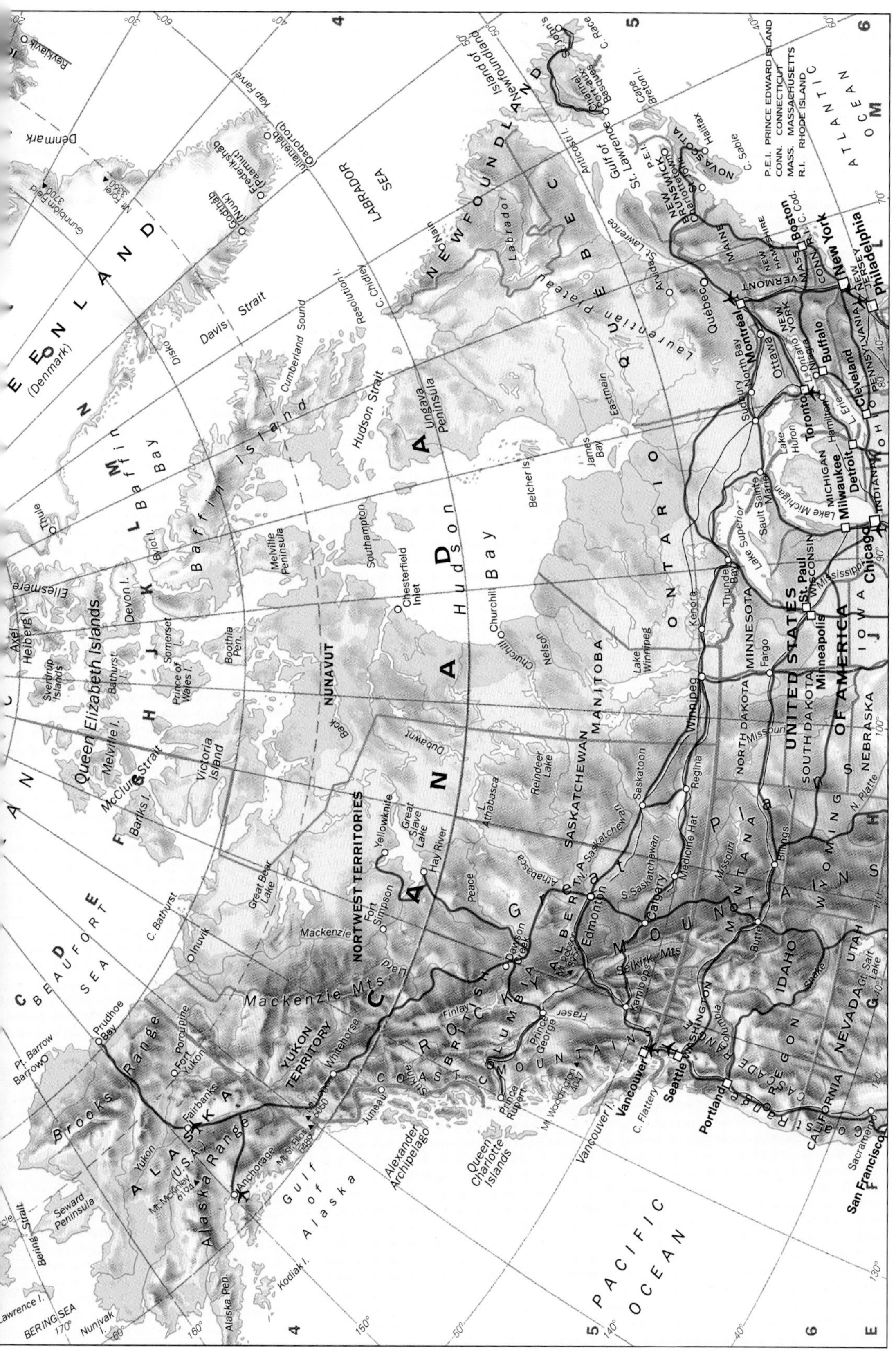

Scale 1:30 000 000

0 250 500 750 1000 km

0 150 300 450 600 miles

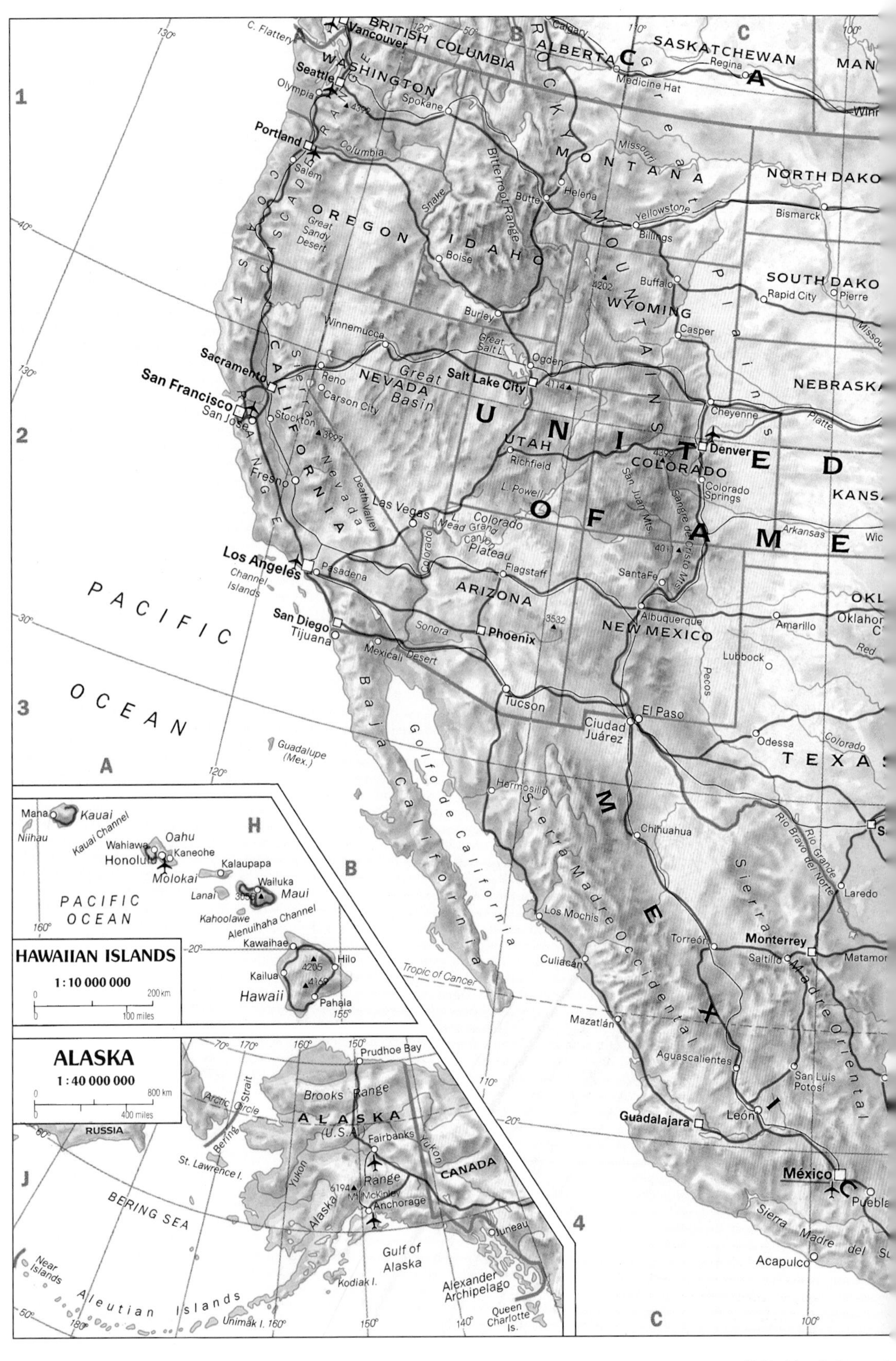

Scale 1:20 000 000

0 250 500 750 1000 km

0 200 400 600 miles

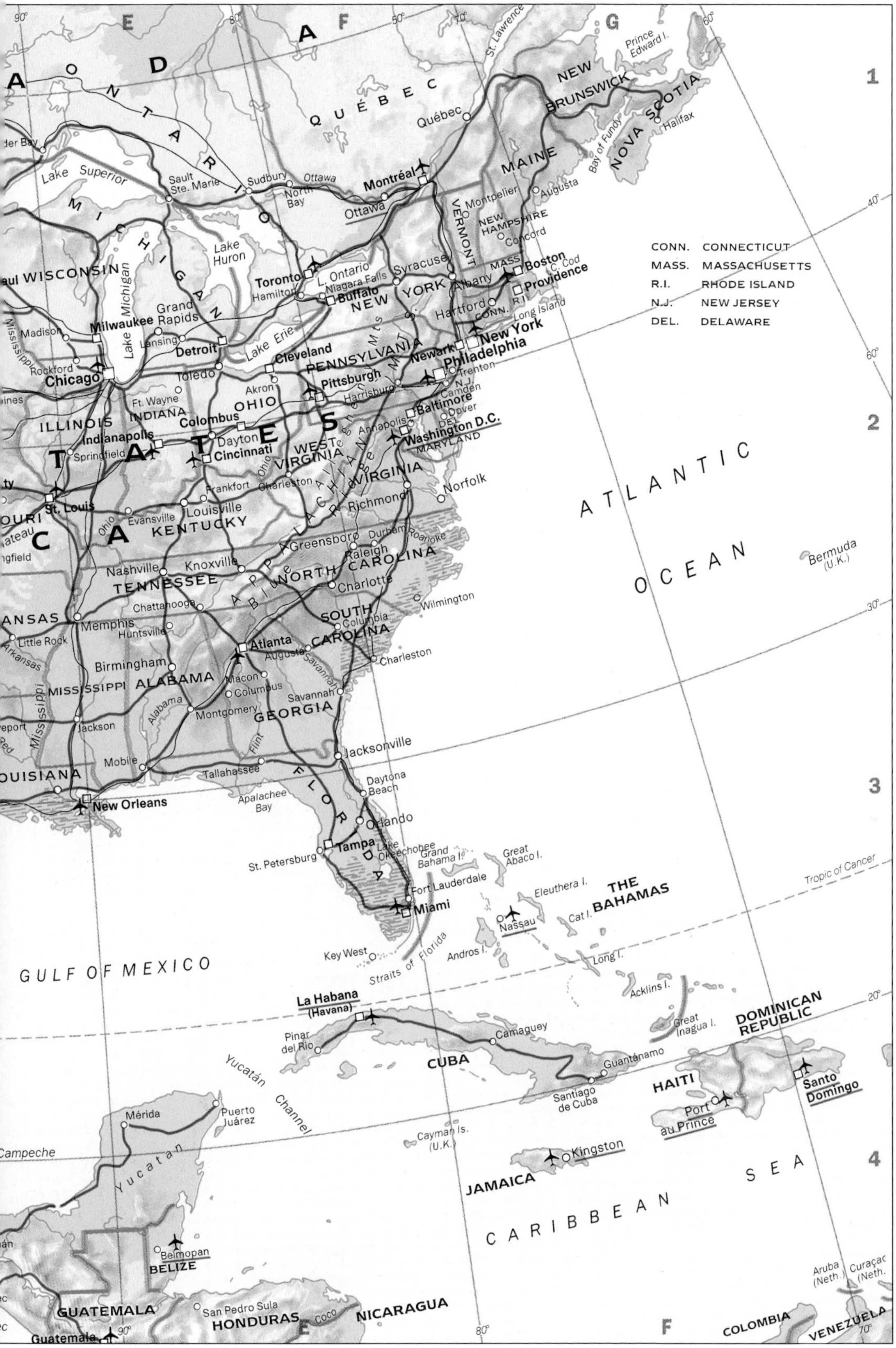

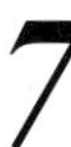

E
F
G
A
D
1
2
3
4
F
90°
80°
70°
60°
50°
40°
30°
20°
ONTARIO
QUÉBEC
Québec
St. Lawrence
Prince Edward I.
NEW BRUNSWICK
NOVA SCOTIA
Halifax
Bay of Fundy
MAINE
Augusta
Montréal
Ottawa
Montpelier
VERMONT
NEW HAMPSHIRE
Concord
Lake Superior
Sault Ste. Marie
Sudbury
North Bay
MICHIGAN
Lake Huron
Toronto
Hamilton
L. Ontario
Niagara Falls
Buffalo
Syracuse
NEW YORK
Albany
MASS.
Boston
C. Cod
Providence
R.I.
Hartford
CONN.
Long Island
New York
WISCONSIN
Lake Michigan
Milwaukee
Grand Rapids
Lansing
Detroit
Madison
Mississippi
Lake Erie
Cleveland
PENNSYLVANIA
Newark
Philadelphia
Trenton
N.J.
Camden
Rockford
Chicago
Toledo
Akron
Pittsburgh
Harrisburg
Baltimore
Dover
DEL.
Ft. Wayne
INDIANA
OHIO
Columbus
ILLINOIS
Indianapolis
Springfield
Dayton
Cincinnati
Ohio
WEST VIRGINIA
Annapolis
Washington D.C.
MARYLAND
STATES
Frankfort
Charleston
VIRGINIA
Norfolk
Richmond
St. Louis
Evansville
Louisville
KENTUCKY
Greensboro
Durham
Roanoke
Raleigh
NORTH CAROLINA
Nashville
Knoxville
TENNESSEE
Charlotte
APPALACHIAN MTS
Blue Ridge
Chattanooga
Wilmington
Memphis
Huntsville
SOUTH CAROLINA
Columbia
Little Rock
Arkansas
Atlanta
Augusta
Savannah
Charleston
Birmingham
MISSISSIPPI
ALABAMA
Macon
Columbus
Savannah
Alabama
Montgomery
GEORGIA
Jackson
Flint
Jacksonville
Mobile
Tallahassee
Daytona Beach
New Orleans
Apalachee Bay
FLORIDA
Orlando
Tampa
St. Petersburg
Lake Okeechobee
Grand Bahama I.
Great Abaco I.
Fort Lauderdale
Miami
Eleuthera I.
THE BAHAMAS
Nassau
Cat I.
Key West
Andros I.
Long I.
Straits of Florida
GULF OF MEXICO
Acklins I.
La Habana (Havana)
Great Inagua I.
DOMINICAN REPUBLIC
Pinar del Rio
Camagüey
CUBA
Guantánamo
Santiago de Cuba
HAITI
Santo Domingo
Port au Prince
Yucatán Channel
Mérida
Puerto Juárez
Campeche
Yucatan
Cayman Is. (U.K.)
Kingston
JAMAICA
CARIBBEAN SEA
Belmopan
BELIZE
GUATEMALA
Guatemala
San Pedro Sula
HONDURAS
Coco
NICARAGUA
COLOMBIA
VENEZUELA
Aruba (Neth.)
ATLANTIC OCEAN
Bermuda (U.K.)
Tropic of Cancer
CONN. CONNECTICUT
MASS. MASSACHUSETTS
R.I. RHODE ISLAND
N.J. NEW JERSEY
DEL. DELAWARE

8

Scale 1:8 600 000

0 100 200 300 km

0 100 200 miles

ATLANTIC
OCEAN
GULF
OF
MEXICO
NORTH CAROLINA
SOUTH CAROLINA
GEORGIA
ALABAMA
FLORIDA
THE BAHAMAS
Raleigh
Charlotte
Fayetteville
Wilmington
New Bern
Jacksonville
Cape Fear
Cape Lookout
Cape Hatteras
Pamlico Sd.
Neuse
Lumberton
Florence
Georgetown
Santee
Charleston
Columbia
Rock Hill
Greenville
Anderson
Asheville
Orangeburg
Augusta
Savannah
Statesboro
Athens
Gainesville
Atlanta
Macon
Columbus
Albany
Tifton
Valdosta
Waycross
Jesup
Brunswick
Altamaha
Ogeechee
Bainbridge
Flint
Chattahoochee
Dothan
Troy
Montgomery
Alexander City
Gadsden
Rome
Dalton
Cleveland
Chattanooga
Huntsville
Tullahoma
Tennessee
Birmingham
Tuscaloosa
Cullman
Sheffield
Alabama
Tombigbee
Mobile
Pensacola
Tallahassee
Apalachee Bay
Lake City
Suwannee
Gainesville
Jacksonville
Ocala
Daytona Beach
Orlando
Lakeland
Tampa
St. Petersburg
Cape Canaveral
Fort Pierce
West Palm Beach
Boca Raton
Fort Lauderdale
Miami
Lake Okeechobe
Fort Myers
Naples
The Everglades
Cape Sable
Key West
Florida Keys
Straits of Florida
Grand Bahama
Great Abaco
Eleuthera
Nassau
New Providence
Andros I.
Cat I.

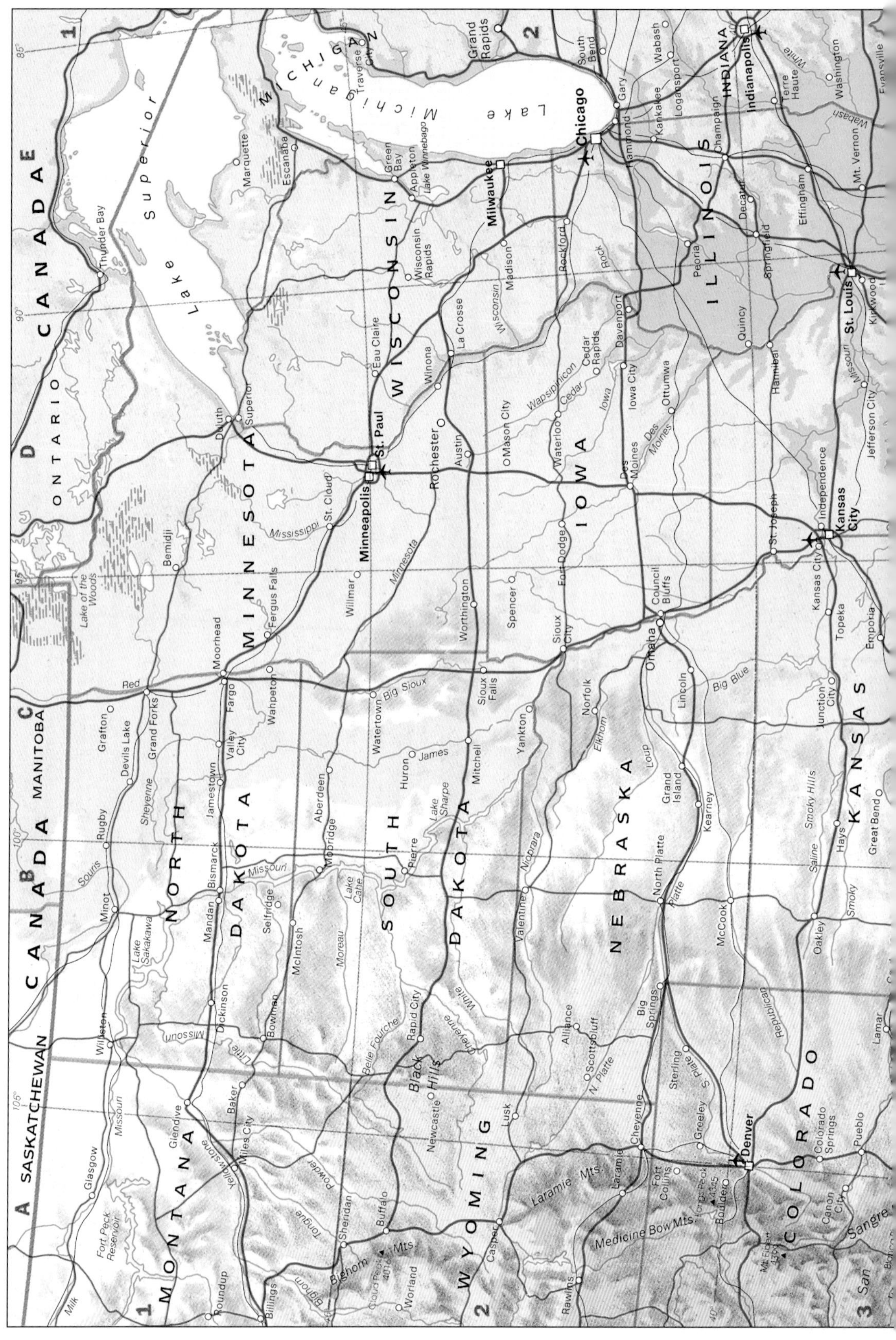

Scale 1:8 600 000

0 100 200 300 km

0 100 200 miles

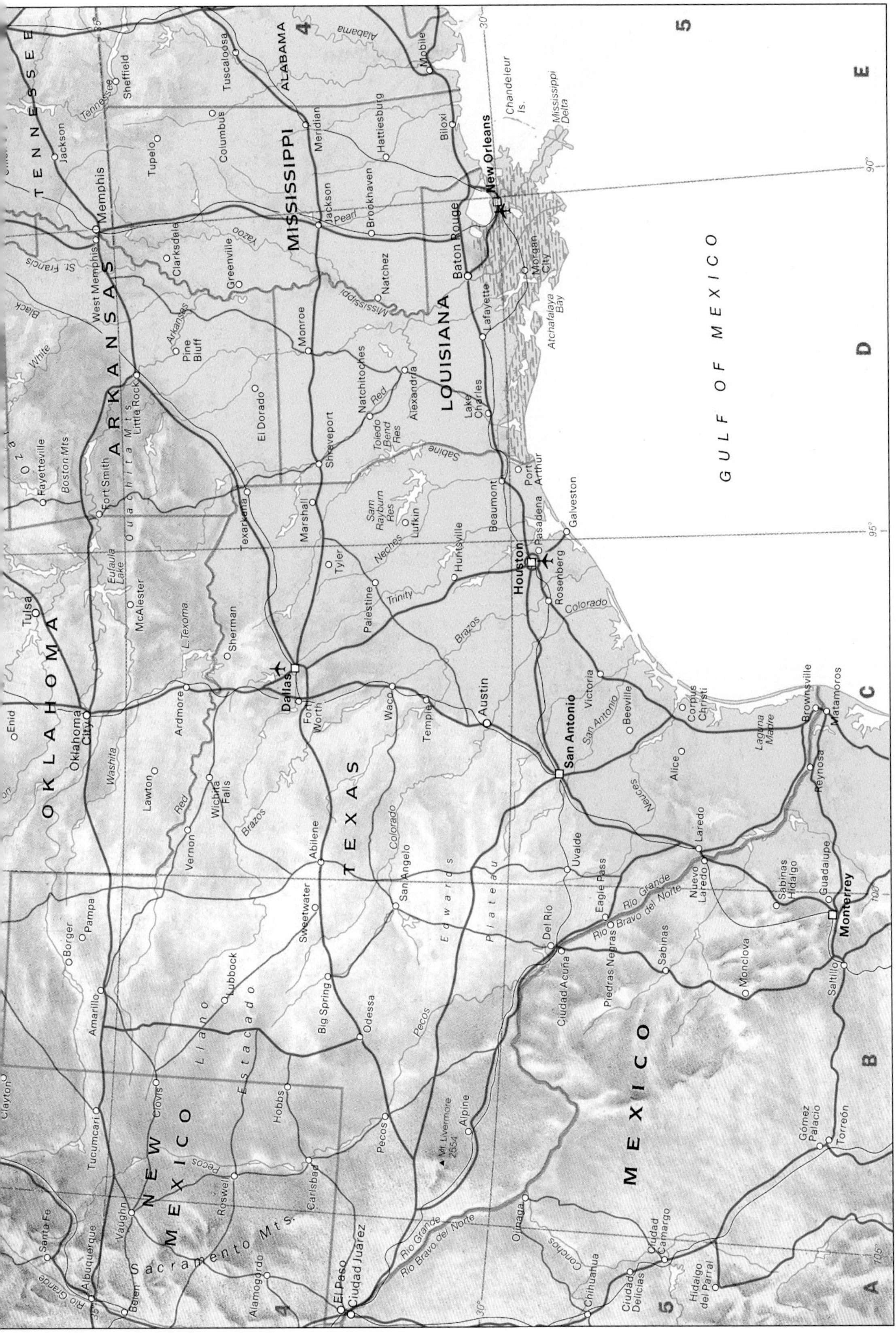

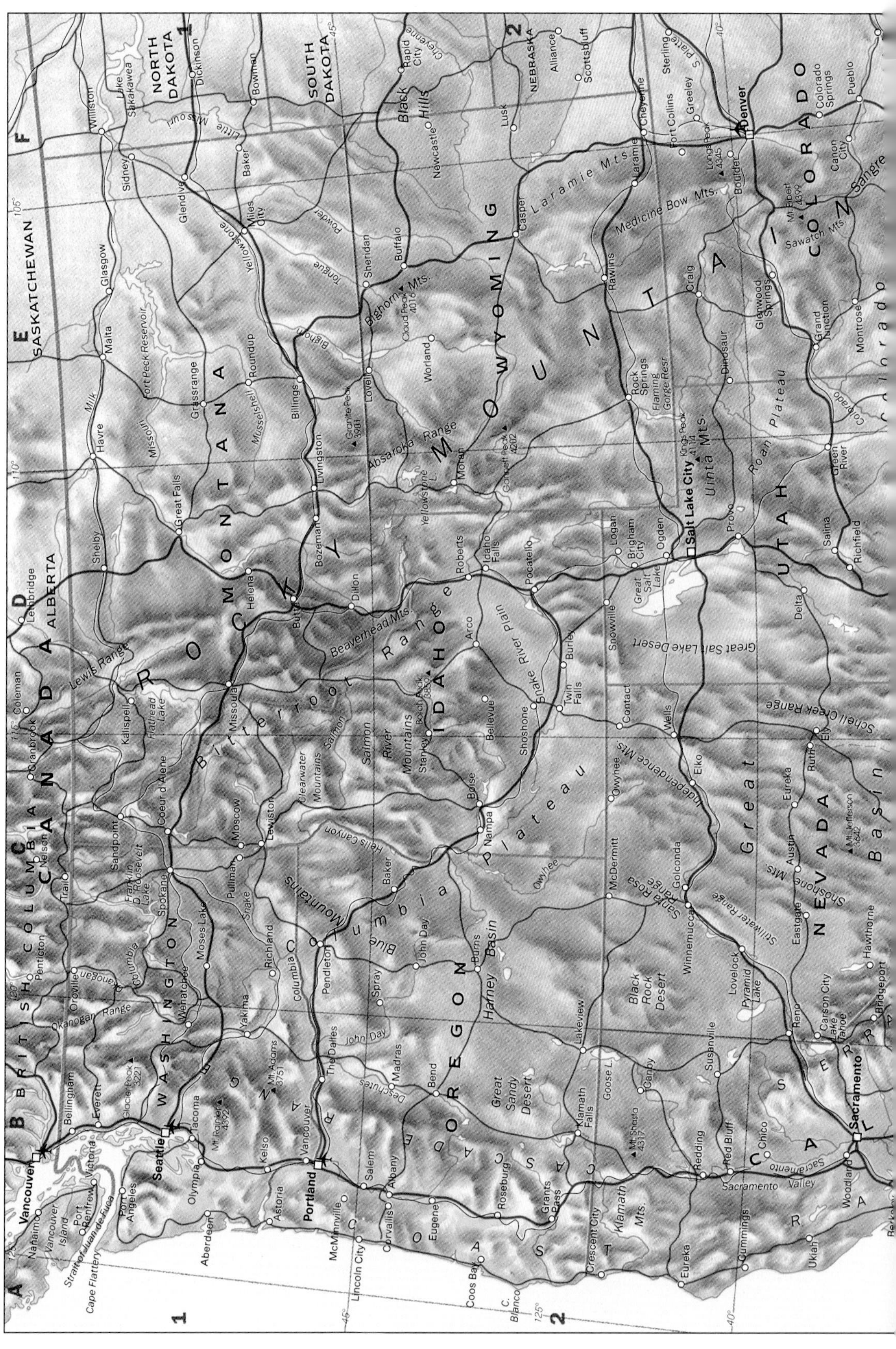

Scale 1:8 600 000

0 100 200 300 km

0 100 200 miles

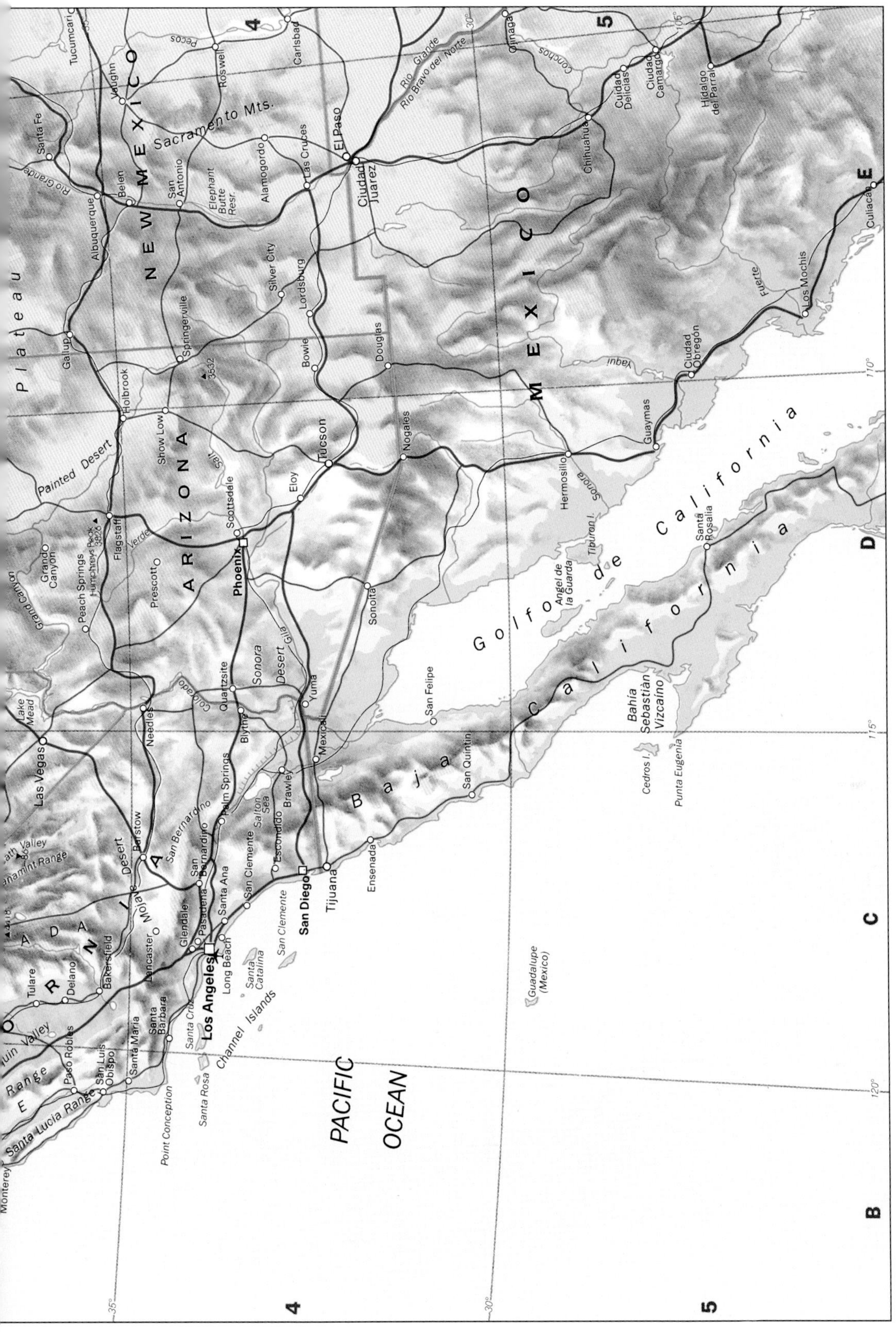
NEW MEXICO
ARIZONA
MEXICO
PACIFIC
OCEAN
Golfo de California
Baja California
Sonora Desert
Mojave Desert
Painted Desert
Plateau
Sacramento Mts.
Santa Fe
Albuquerque
Belen
San Antonio
Elephant Butte Resr.
Alamogordo
Las Cruces
El Paso
Ciudad Juarez
Roswell
Carlsbad
Tucumcari
Vaughn
Pecos
Rio Grande
Rio Bravo del Norte
Ojinaga
Conchos
Chihuahua
Cuidad Delicias
Ciudad Camargo
Hidalgo del Parral
Culiacan
Fuerte
Los Mochis
Ciudad Obregón
Yaqui
Guaymas
Hermosillo
Sonora
Tiburon I.
Angel de la Guarda
Santa Rosalia
Bahía Sebastián Vizcaíno
Cedros I.
Punta Eugenia
San Felipe
San Quintin
Ensenada
Tijuana
San Diego
Mexicali
Yuma
Gila
Sonoita
Nogales
Douglas
Bowie
Lordsburg
Silver City
Springerville
3532
Gallup
Holbrook
Show Low
Salt
Tucson
Eloy
Scottsdale
Phoenix
Flagstaff
Humphreys Peak 3862
Verde
Prescott
Grand Canyon
Peach Springs
Quartzsite
Blythe
Colorado
Needles
Lake Mead
Las Vegas
Brawley
Salton Sea
Palm Springs
Escondido
San Clemente
Santa Ana
San Bernardino
Barstow
Pasadena
Glendale
Lancaster
Los Angeles
Long Beach
Santa Catalina
Channel Islands
Santa Cruz
Santa Rosa
Santa Barbara
Santa Maria
San Luis Obispo
Paso Robles
Point Conception
Bakersfield
Delano
Tulare
Monterey
Santa Lucia Range
Guadalupe (Mexico)
35°
30°
120°
115°
110°
105°
B
C
D
E
4
5

Central America and the Caribbean

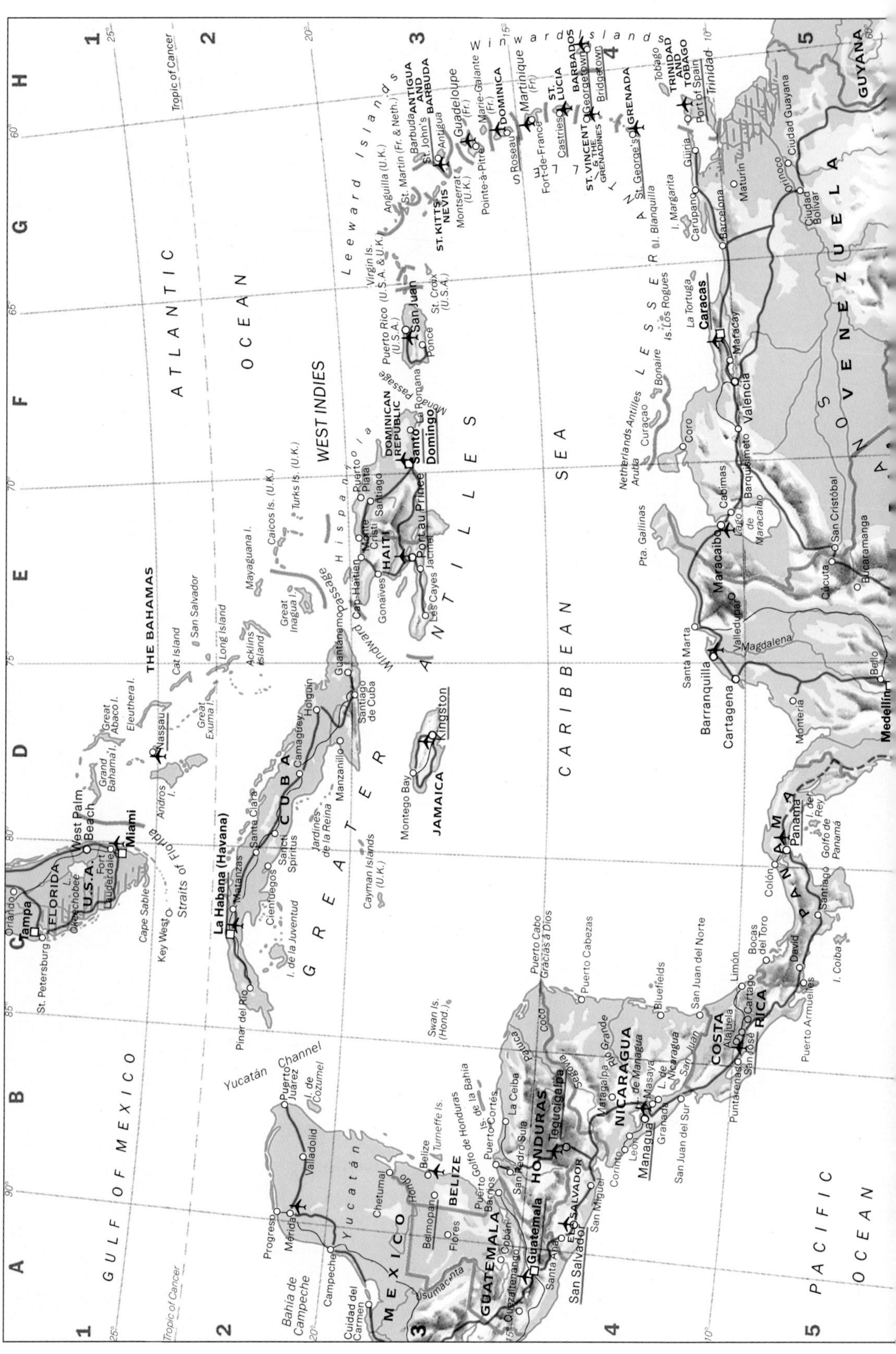

Scale 1:17 000 000

0 200 400 600 800 km

0 250 500 miles

Martinique (Fr.)
ST. LUCIA
Netherlands Antilles
ST. VINCENT & THE GRENADINES
BARBADOS
Curaçao
GRENADA
TRINIDAD AND TOBAGO
Port of Spain
Barranquilla
Maracaibo
Caracas
Güiria
Panamá
Cartagena
Barquisimeto
Barcelona
Montería
L. Maracaibo
Rinoco
Ciudad Guayana
NORTH ATLANTIC OCEAN
VENEZUELA
Georgetown
Medellín
Paramaribo
GUYANA
Bogotá
SURINAME
Cayenne
Cali
COLOMBIA
Boa Vista
GUIANA (FRENCH)
Negro
Macapá
Quito
Japurá
Equator
ECUADOR
Guayaquil
Manaus
Amazonas
Belém
Santarém
Amazonas
Iquitos
Loja
São Luís
Parnaíba
Madeira
Fortaleza
BRAZIL
Teresina
Imperatriz
Ucayali
Cruzeiro do Sul
Lábrea
Humaitá
Natal
Carolina
Pôrto Velho
Rio Branco
Recife
PERU
Xingu
Juàzeiro
Maceió
Mamoré
Madre de Dios
Callao
Huancayo
Lima
Cuzco
Salvador
Araguaia
São Francisco
Cuiabá
Brasília
L. Titicaca
La Paz
Goiânia
BOLIVIA
Arequipa
Oruro
Santa Cruz
Arica
Corumbá
Sucre
Belo Horizonte
Campo Grande
Paraguay
Vitória
Paraná
PARAGUAY
Campinas
Antofagasta
Rio de Janeiro
Concepción
São Paulo
Tropic of Capricorn
Salta
Asunción
Foz do Iguaçu
Curitiba
San Miguel de Tucumán
Florianópolis
Uruguay
CHILE
Paraná
Pôrto Alegre
Concordia
San Juan
Santa Fé
Salto
Córdoba
Paraná
PACIFIC OCEAN
Viña del Mar
Rosario
URUGUAY
Rio Grande
Santiago
Mendoza
SOUTH ATLANTIC OCEAN
Montevideo
Buenos Aires
ARGENTINA
Concepción
Mar del Plata
Bahía Blanca
Neuquén
Puerto Montt
Comodoro Rivadavia
Falkland Is. (Is. Malvinas) (U.K.)
Río Gallegos
Stanley
Est. de Magallanes
Punta Arenas
Tierra del Fuego
South Georgia (U.K.)

Scale 1:37 000 000

0 400 800 1200 1600 km

0 200 400 600 800 1000 miles

16

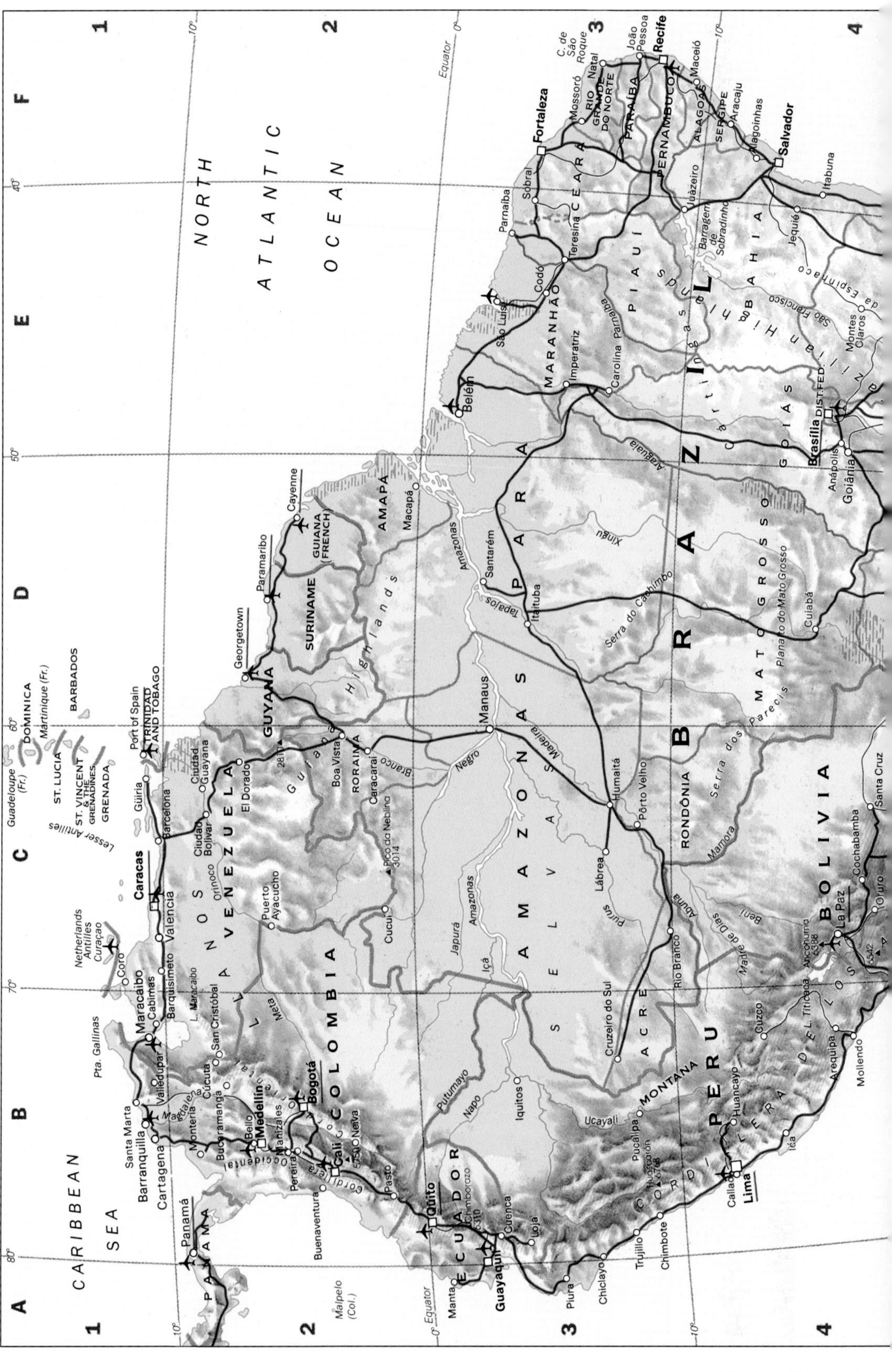

Scale 1:25 500 000

0 200 400 600 800 1000 km

0 150 300 450 600 miles

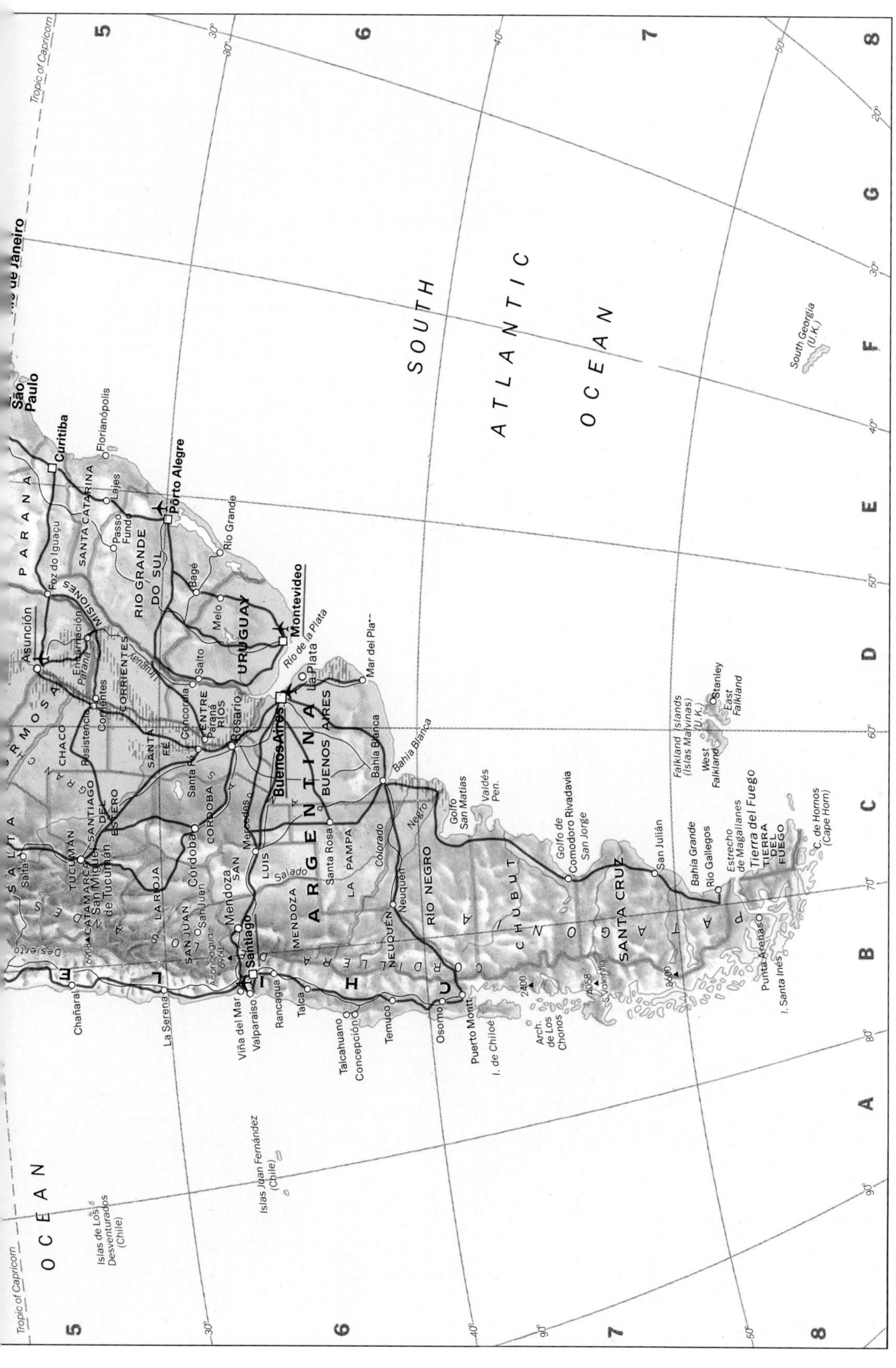
SOUTH
ATLANTIC
OCEAN
OCEAN
Tropic of Capricorn
São Paulo
Rio de Janeiro
Curitiba
Florianópolis
Lajes
Pôrto Alegre
Passo Fundo
Rio Grande
SANTA CATARINA
RIO GRANDE DO SUL
PARANÁ
Foz do Iguaçu
MISIONES
Asunción
Encarnación
Paraná
Bagé
Melo
Montevideo
URUGUAY
Salto
Uruguay
CORRIENTES
Corrientes
Resistencia
CHACO
FORMOSA
Río de la Plata
La Plata
Mar del Plata
Buenos Aires
BUENOS AIRES
ENTRE RÍOS
Paraná
Concordia
Rosario
SANTA FE
Santa Fe
CÓRDOBA
Córdoba
SANTIAGO DEL ESTERO
TUCUMÁN
San Miguel de Tucumán
CATAMARCA
SALTA
Salta
LA RIOJA
SAN JUAN
San Juan
SAN LUIS
Mendoza
MENDOZA
Mercedes
Salado
ARGENTINA
Santa Rosa
LA PAMPA
Colorado
Bahía Blanca
Neuquén
NEUQUÉN
RÍO NEGRO
Negro
Golfo San Matías
Valdés Pen.
CHUBUT
Golfo de San Jorge
Comodoro Rivadavia
SANTA CRUZ
San Julián
Bahía Grande
Río Gallegos
Estrecho de Magallanes
Tierra del Fuego
TIERRA DEL FUEGO
C. de Hornos (Cape Horn)
I. Santa Inés
Punta Arenas
Falkland Islands (Islas Malvinas) (U.K.)
West Falkland
East Falkland
Stanley
South Georgia (U.K.)
Chañaral
La Serena
Aconcagua 6960
Santiago
Viña del Mar
Valparaíso
Rancagua
Talca
Talcahuano
Concepción
Temuco
Osorno
Puerto Montt
I. de Chiloé
Arch. de Los Chonos
Islas Juan Fernández (Chile)
Islas de Los Desventurados (Chile)
CHILE
ANDES
Desierto
A
B
C
D
E
F
G
5
6
7
8

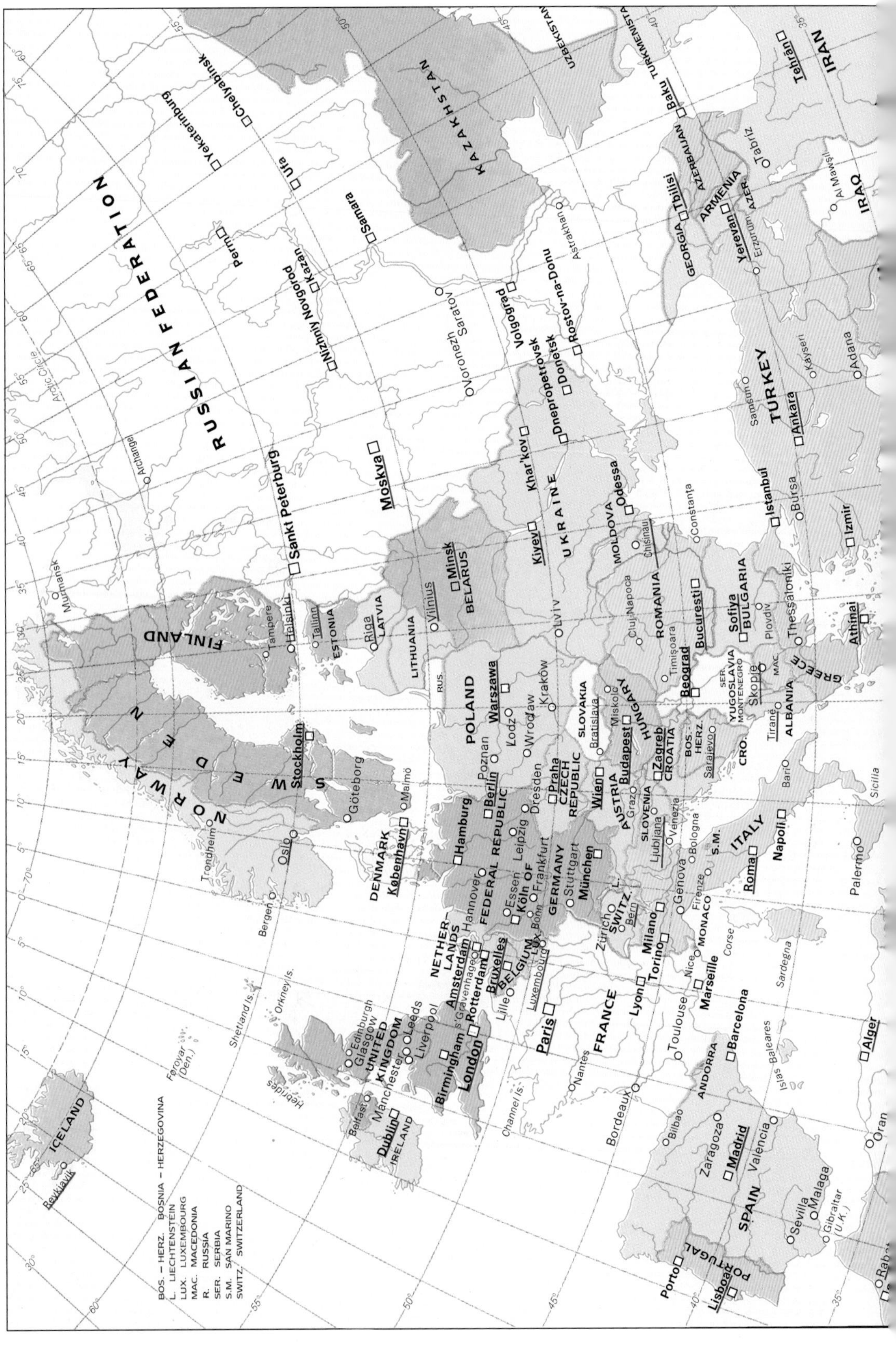

Scale 1:25 500 000

0 200 400 600 800 1000 km

0 150 300 450 600 miles

Scale 1:8 000 000

0 100 200 300 km

0 100 200 miles

Scale 1:2 600 000

0 20 40 60 80 100 km

0 15 30 45 60 miles

St. George's Ch
Cambrian
Bristol Channel
English Channel
Strait of Dover
Channel Tunnel
Aberystwyth
Cardigan
Fishguard
St. David's
Milford Haven
Pembroke
Carmarthen Bay
Carmarthen
Swansea
Port Talbot
MID GLAMORGAN
Cardiff
Barry
Newport
Cwmbran
Abergavenny
Merthyr Tydfil
886
Breacon Beacons
Tywi
Llandrindod Wells
Builth Wells
Wye
Hereford
Stretton
Severn
Warley
Coventry
Rugby
Corby
Warwick
Worcester
Stratford-on-Avon
Banbury
Northampton
Bedford
Milton Keynes
Buckingham
Gloucester
Cheltenham
Stroud
Cotswold Hills
Oxford
Thames
Aylesbury
Luton
St. Albans
Chesham
Watford
Chiltern Hills
Didcot
Swindon
Reading
Windsor
London
Kingswood
Bristol
Chippenham
Kennet
Bath
Trowbridge
Weston-super-Mare
Basingstoke
Aldershot
Guildford
Warminster
Avon
Salisbury
Winchester
Crawley
Horsham
Ely
Cambridge
Bury St. Edmunds
Saxmundham
Ipswich
Stour
Felixstowe
Harwich
Colchester
Clacton-on-Sea
Harlow
Chelmsford
Basildon
Southend-on-Sea
Margate
Rochester
Canterbury
Maidstone
North Downs
Tonbridge
Royal Tunbridge Wells
Ashford
Dover
Hythe
Calais
Boulogne
Lundy
Ilfracombe
Barnstaple
Exmoor
Bridgwater
Taunton
Bideford
Bude
Bude Bay
Tamar
Okehampton
519
Dartmoor
Exe
Exeter
Yeovil
Axminster
Lyme Bay
Dorchester
Weymouth
Portland Bill
Poole
Bournemouth
Ringwood
Southampton
South Downs
Fareham
Havant
The Solent
Cowes
Newport
Portsmouth
ISLE OF WIGHT
Chichester
Bognor Regis
Worthing
Brighton
Lewes
Eastbourne
Hastings
Newquay
Bodmin
St. Austell
Plymouth
Torquay
Start Pt.
St. Ives
Truro
Penzance
Falmouth
Sennen
Land's End
Lizard Pt.
Alderney
Guernsey
St. Peter Port
Sark
CHANNEL ISLANDS
Jersey
St. Helier
Cherbourg
Baie de la Seine
Le Havre
Caen
Dieppe
Rouen
Seine
FRANCE
West from Greenwich
East from Greenwich
Isles of Scilly
St. Martin's
St. Mary's
52°
51°
50°
6°
5°
4°
3°
2°
1°
0°
A
B
C
D
E
F
G
H
J
6
7
8

Scotland

22

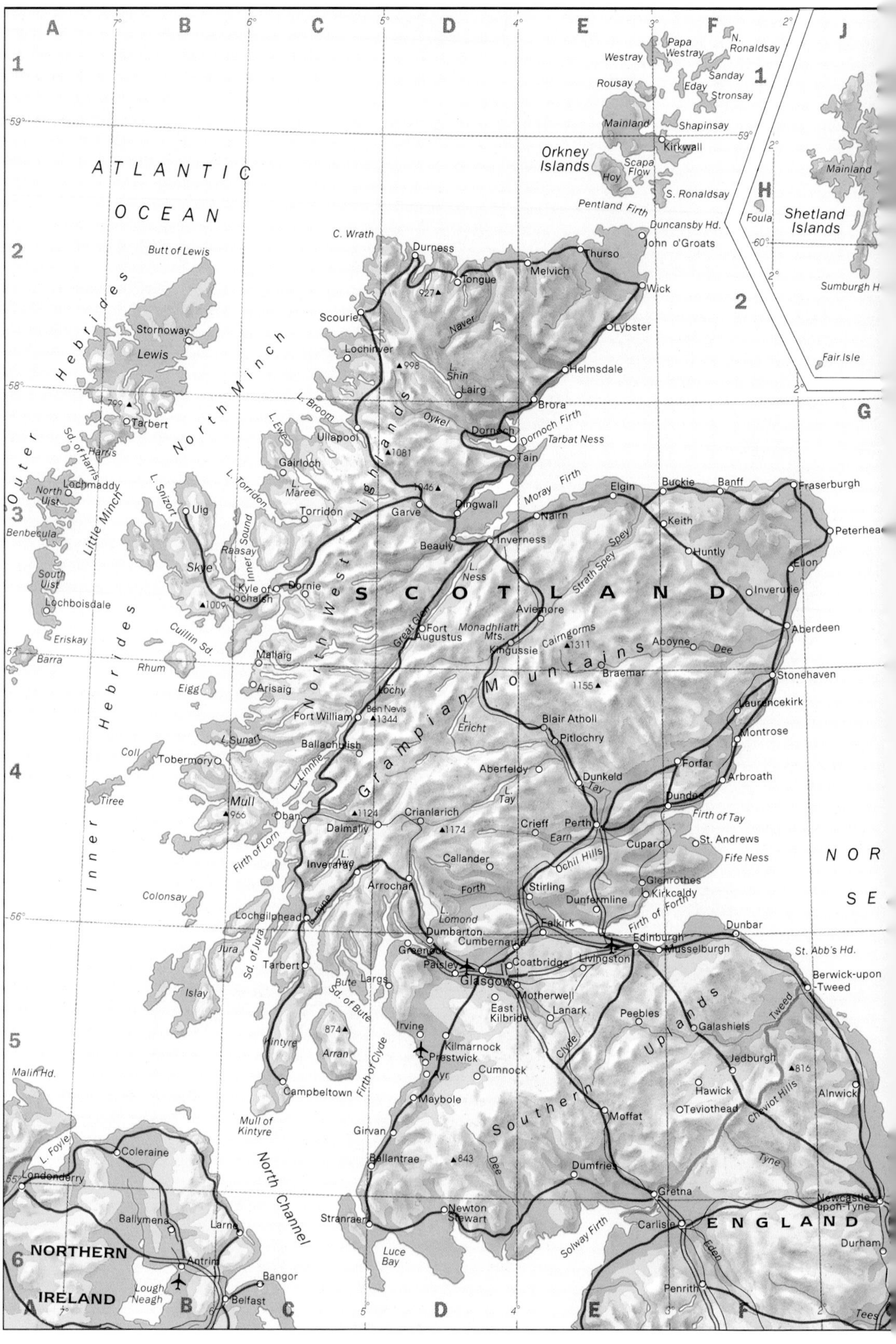

Scale 1:2 600 000

0 20 40 60 80 100 km

0 15 30 45 60 miles

Scale 1:2 600 000

0 20 40 60 80 100 km

0 15 30 45 60 miles

24

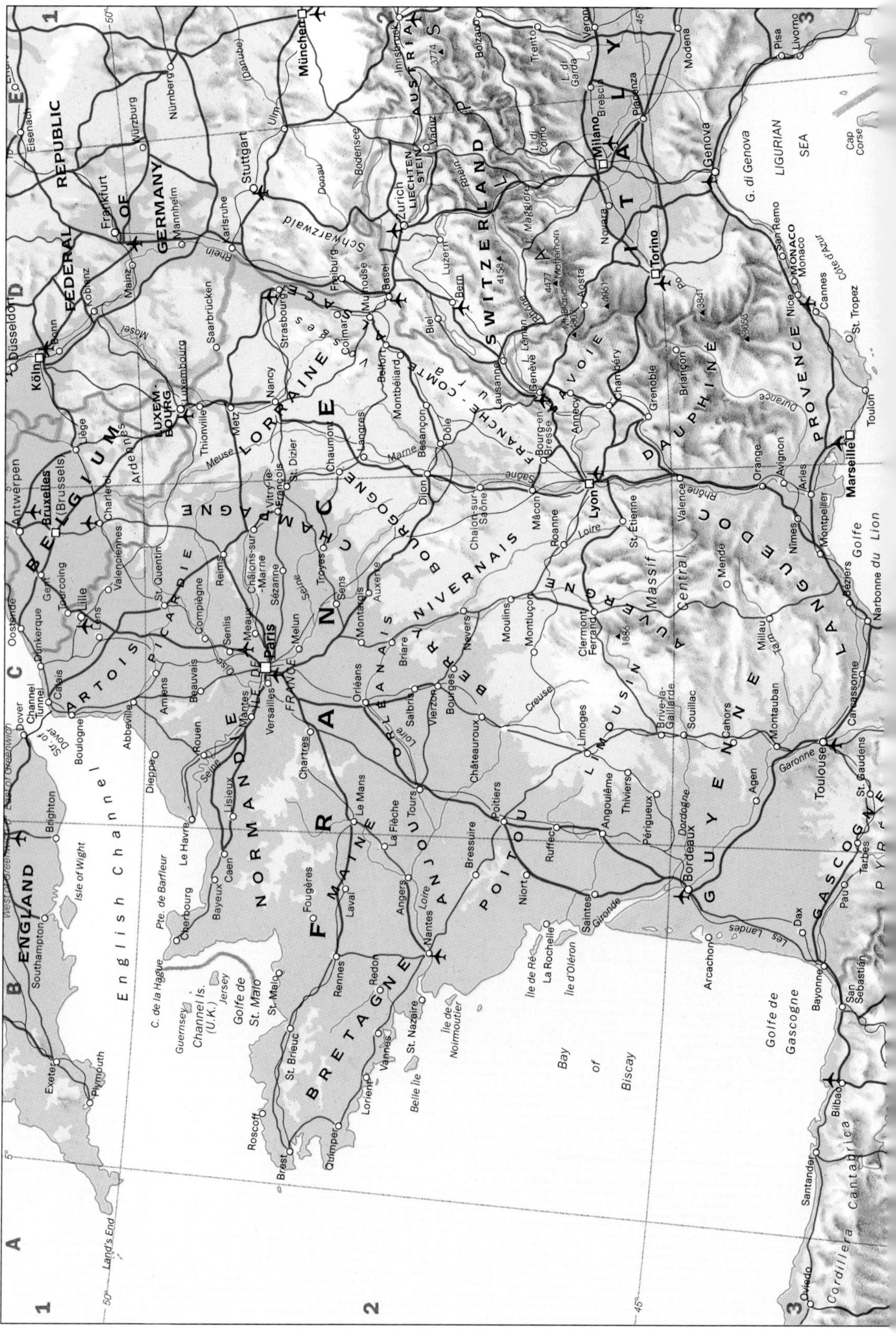

Scale 1:6 500 000

0 100 200 300 km

0 100 200 miles

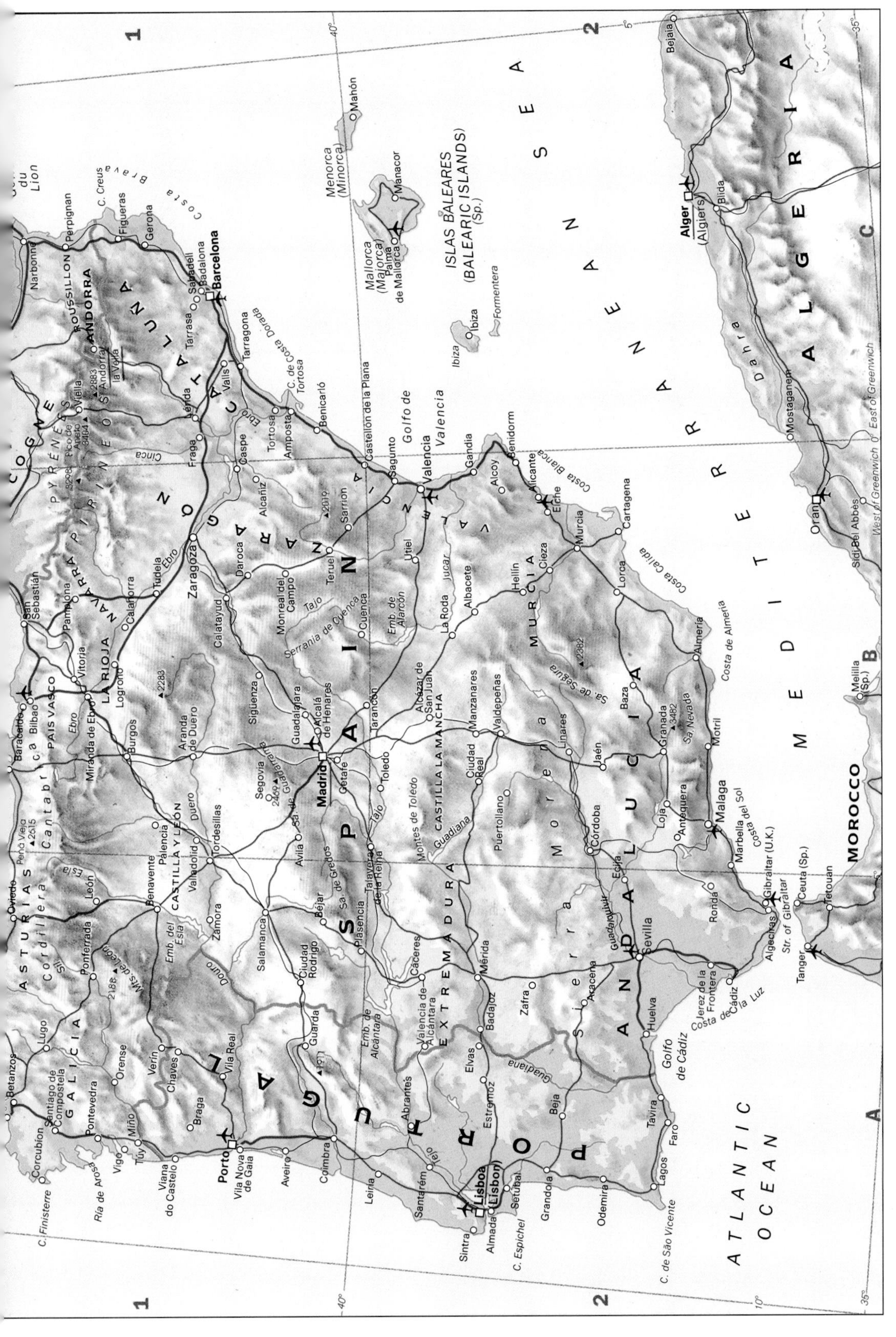

Scale 1:6 500 000

0 100 200 300 km

0 100 200 miles

26

Scale 1:6 500 000

0 100 200 300 km

0 100 200 miles

Budapest
Debrecen
Karcag
Szolnok
Kecskemét
Kiskunfelegyháza
Szeged
Makó
Subotica
VOJVODINA
Osijek
Novi Sad
Ruma
Vršac
Beograd
(Belgrade)
Šabac
Tuzla
Loznica
Sarajevo
Kragujevac
Jagodina
Paraćin
Čačak
YUGOSLAVIA
SERBIA
Kruševac
Niš
Novi Pazar
Kosovska-Mitrovica
Priština
MONTENEGRO
Ivangrad
Peć
KOSOVO
Uroševac
Podgorica
Kotor
Shkodër
Skopje
Kumanovo
Titov Veles
MACEDONIA
Tiranë (Tirana)
Durrës
Ohrid
Bitola
Berat
Korce
Vlorë
Gjirokastër
Oradea
Salonta
Arad
Timişoara
Caransebes
Deva
Cluj-Napoca
Turda
Tîrgu Mureş
Sebeş
Sibiu
TRANSYLVANIA
Braşov
Carpaţii Meridionali
R O M A N I A
Rîmnicu-Vîlcea
Piteşti
Cîmpina
Ploieşti
Bucureşti
(Bucharest)
Urziceni
Buzău
Focşani
Brăila
Galaţi
Tecuci
Bîrlad
Bacău
Roman
Iaşi
Chisinau
MOLDOVA
UKRAINE
Odessa
Izmail
Hîrşova
Medgidia
Constanţa
Mangalia
Dobreta-Turnu-Severin
Filiaşi
Craiova
Slatina
Caracal
Videle
Giurgiu
Ruse
Razgrad
Ludogorie
Tolbukhin
Šumen
Varna
BLACK SEA
Vidin
Lom
Pleven
Byala
Vratsa
Veliko Turnovo
Pirot
Sofiya
(Sofia)
Stara Planina
Kazanlŭk
Sliven
Burgas
B U L G A R I A
Stara Zagora
Dimitrovgrad
Michurin
Plovdiv
Blagoevgrad
Rodopi Planina
Edirne
Babaeski
Çorlu
Istanbul
Üsküdar
Sea of Marmara
Bandirma
Bursa
Kavála
Drama
Xánthi
Komotini
Alexandroúpolis
Kesan
Sérrai
Thessaloníki
Khalkidhikí
Thásos
Samothráki
Gelibolu
Eceabat
Çanakkale
Gökçeada
Balikesir
Edremit
Ayvalik
Akhisar
Manisa
Izmir
Selçuk
T U R K E Y
Límnos
Áyios Evstrátios
Lésvos
Khíos
Sámos
AEGEAN SEA
Kateríni
Olimbos 2917
Kastoria
Lárisa
Vólos
Kalabáka
Ioannina
Igoumenítsa
Kérkira (Corfu)
G R E E C E
Árta
Lamía
Amfilokhía
Mesolóngion
Levkás
Kefallinía
Zákinthos
Pátrai
Kórinthos
Piraiévs
Athínai (Athens)
Thívai
Khalkis
Évvoia
Skíros
Pelopónnisos
Pírgos
Tripolis
Argos
Kalámai
Pílos
Neápolis
Kíthira
KIKLÁDHES
Ándros
Tínos
Míkonos
Síros
Kéa
Kíthnos
Sérifos
Sífnos
Páros
Náxos
Mílos
Íos
Thíra
Amorgós
Astipálaia
Anáfi
Ikaría
DHODHEKÁNISOS
Léros
Kálimnos
Kós
Tílos
Bodrum
Muğla
Marmaris
Ródhos (Rhodes)
Kárpathos
Kásos
Sea of Crete
Kríti (Crete)
Khaniá
Iráklion
Tímbákion
IÓNIOI NÍSOI
IONIAN SEA
Strait of Otranto
Mirtoan Sea

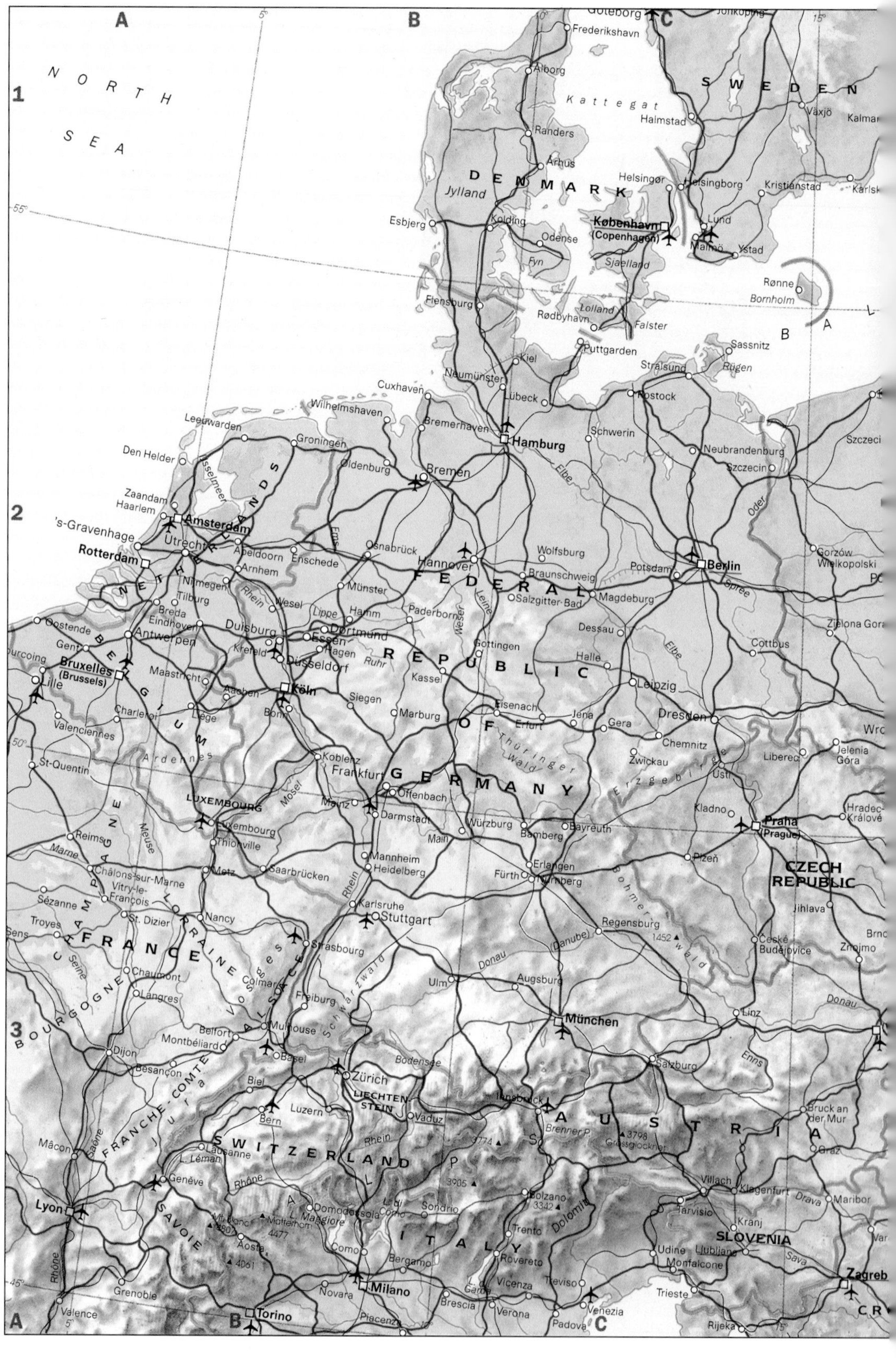

Scale 1:6 500 000

0 100 200 300 km

0 100 200 miles

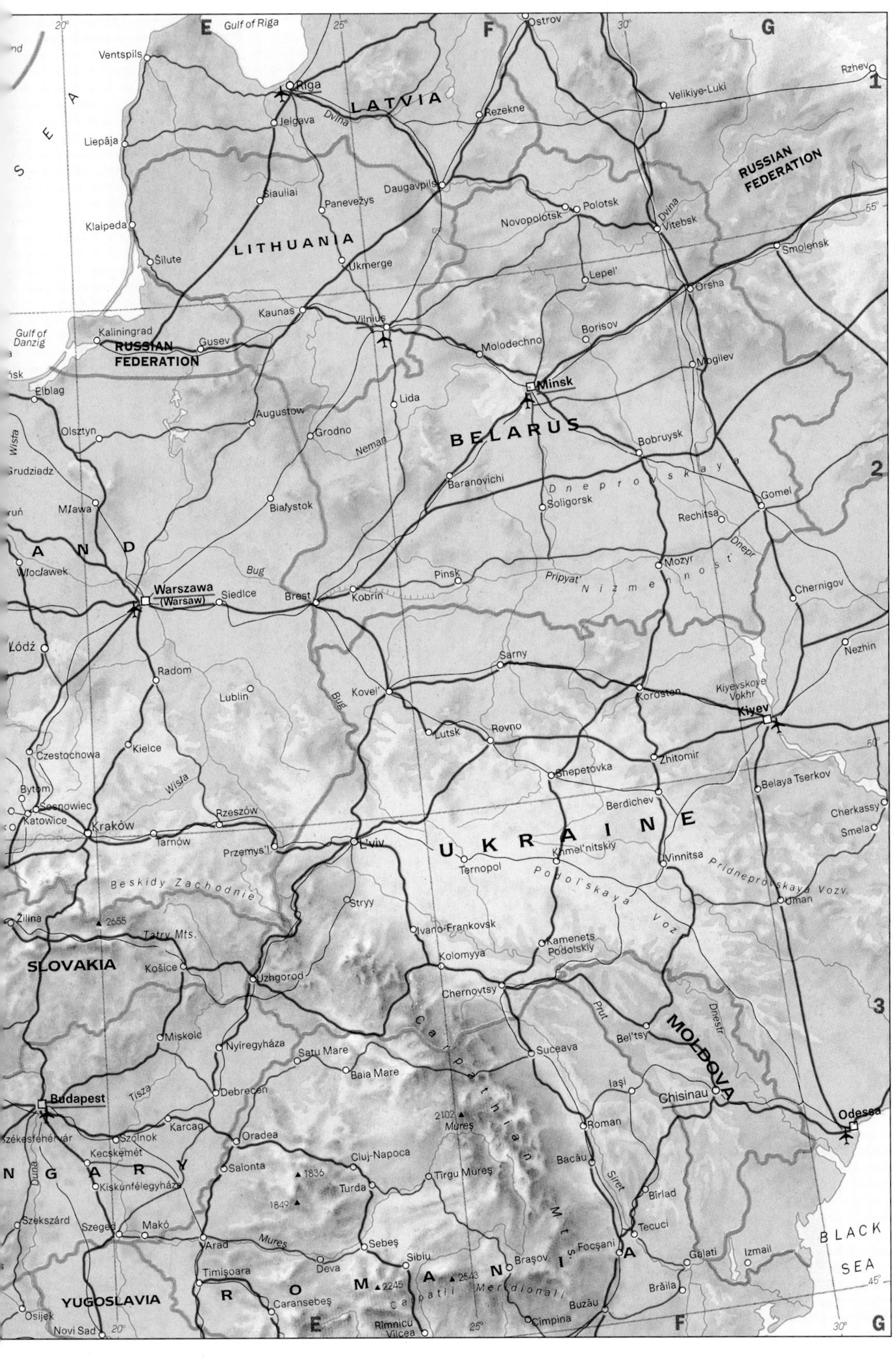
Gulf of Riga
Ventspils
Riga
LATVIA
Jelgava
Liepāja
Rezekne
Velikiye-Luki
Rzhev
RUSSIAN FEDERATION
Šiauliai
Panevežys
Daugavpils
Klaipeda
Novopolotsk
Polotsk
Vitebsk
Dvina
LITHUANIA
Šilute
Ukmerge
Smolensk
Lepel'
Orsha
Kaunas
Vilnius
Borisov
Gulf of Danzig
Kaliningrad
RUSSIAN FEDERATION
Gusev
Molodechno
Mogilev
Minsk
Elblag
Lida
Augustow
Olsztyn
Grodno
Neman
BELARUS
Bobruysk
Baranovichi
Dneprovskaya
Gomel
Soligorsk
Rechitsa
Mława
Białystok
Dnepr
Mozyr
Włocławek
Bug
Pinsk
Pripyat'
Nizmennost'
Warszawa (Warsaw)
Siedlce
Brest
Kobrin
Chernigov
Łódź
Nezhin
Sarny
Radom
Lublin
Kovel'
Korosten
Kiyevskoye Vokhr
Kiyev
Rovno
Lutsk
Częstochowa
Kielce
Zhitomir
Shepetovka
Belaya Tserkov
Bytom
Sosnowiec
Katowice
Wisła
Rzeszów
Berdichev
Cherkassy
Kraków
Tarnów
Przemyśl
L'viv
UKRAINE
Smela
Khmel'nitskiy
Vinnitsa
Ternopol
Pridneprovskaya Vozv.
Beskidy Zachodnie
Podol'skaya Voz
Uman
Stryy
Žilina
2655
Tatry Mts.
Ivano-Frankovsk
Kamenets Podolskiy
SLOVAKIA
Košice
Kolomyya
Uzhgorod
Chernovtsy
Prut
MOLDOVA
Dnestr
Carpathian Mts.
Miskolc
Nyíregyháza
Satu Mare
Suceava
Bel'tsy
Baia Mare
Iaşi
Chisinau
Budapest
Tisza
Debrecen
Odessa
Mureş
Roman
Karcag
Szolnok
Oradea
Székesfehérvár
Kecskemét
Cluj-Napoca
HUNGARY
Salonta
1836
Tirgu Mureş
Bacău
Duna
Kiskunfélegyháza
Turda
Siret
Bîrlad
1849
Szekszárd
Szeged
Makó
Tecuci
BLACK SEA
Arad
Sebeş
Focşani
Sibiu
Braşov
Galati
Izmail
Timişoara
Deva
2543
2245
ROMANIA
Brăila
Caransebeş
Carpatii Meridionali
Buzău
YUGOSLAVIA
Osijek
Novi Sad
Rîmnicu Vîlcea
Cîmpina
20°
25°
30°
45°
50°
55°
E
F
G
1
2
3

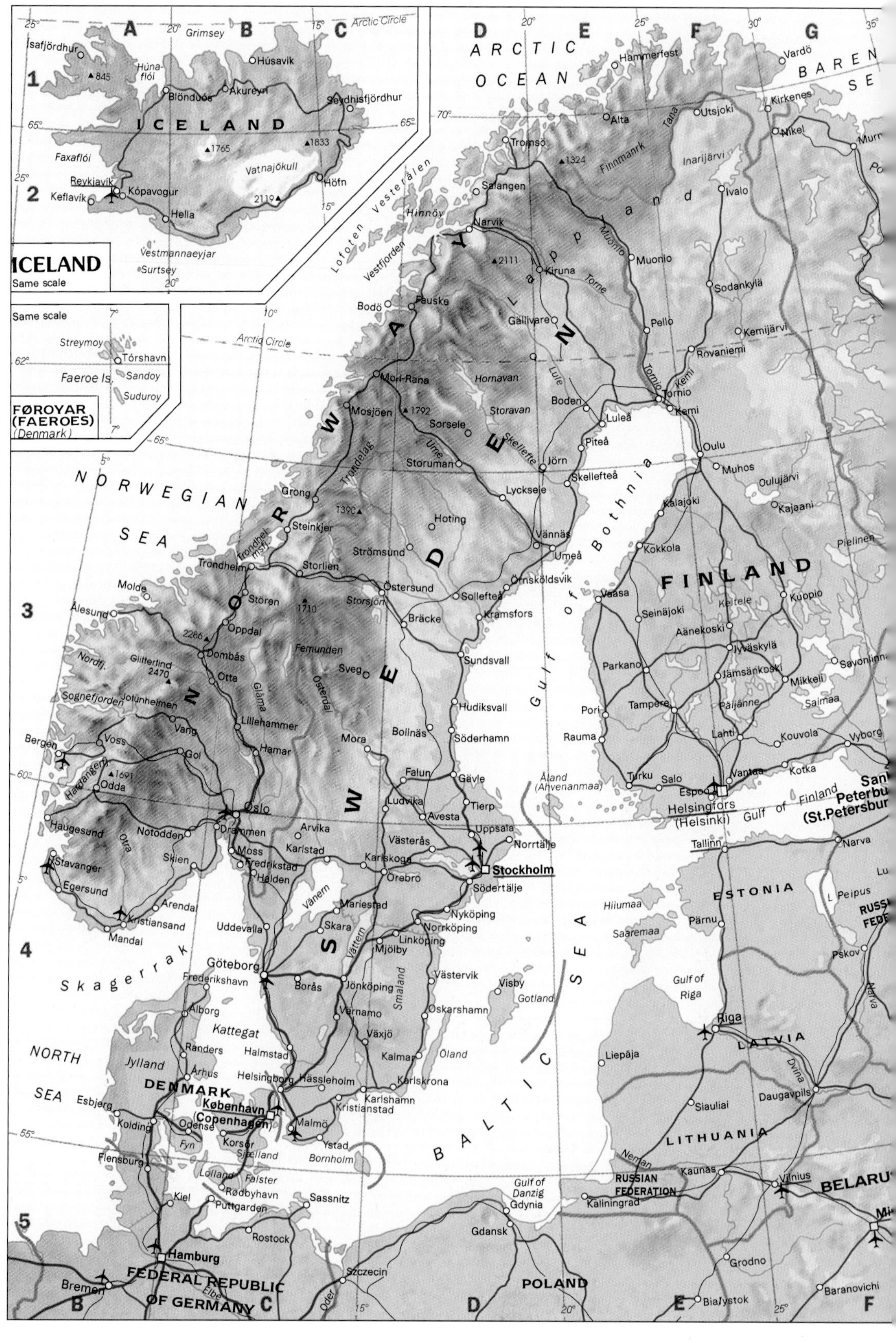

Scale 1:9 600 000

0 100 200 300 km

0 100 200 miles

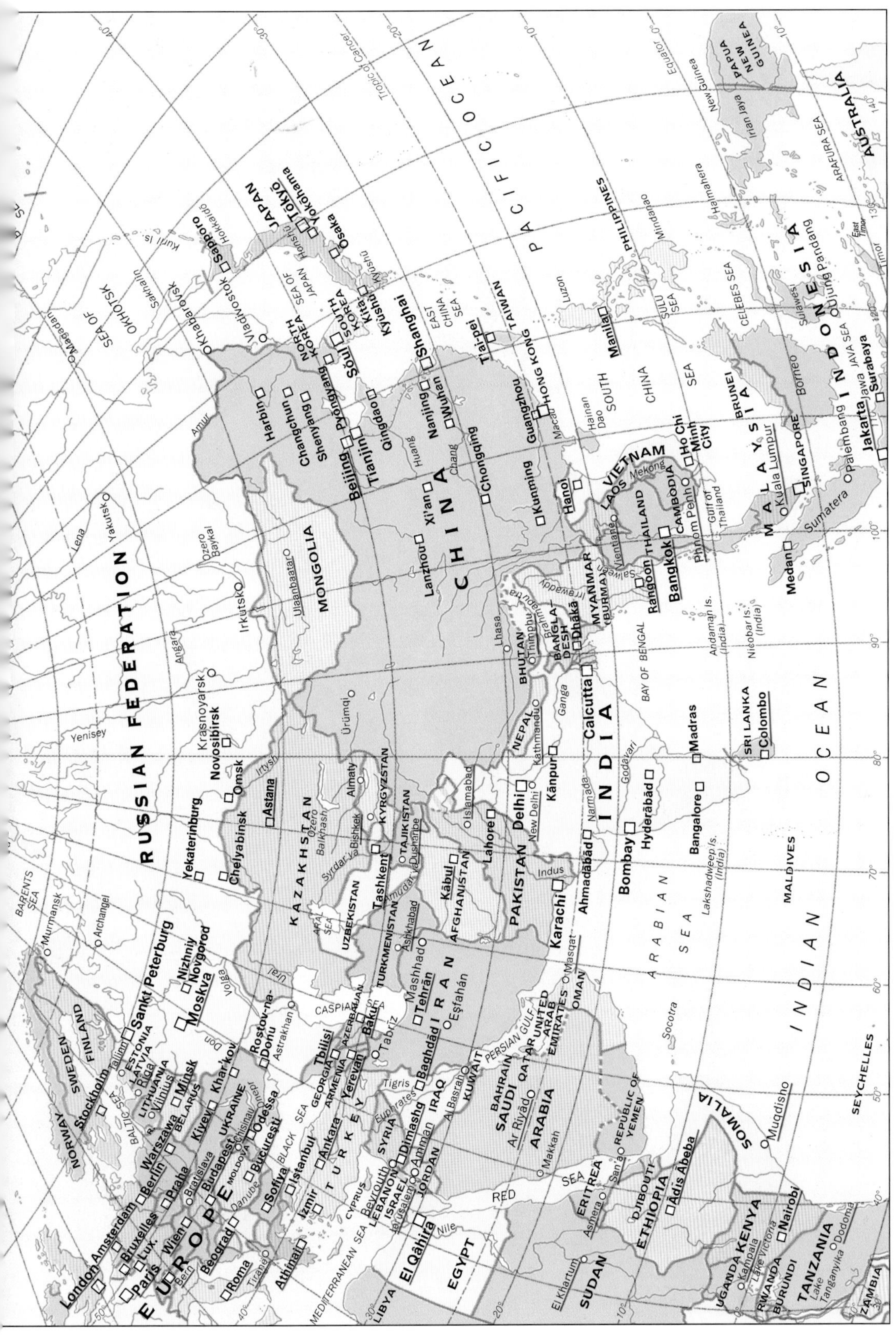

Scale 1:60 900 000

0 400 800 1200 1600 km

0 200 400 600 800 1000 miles

32

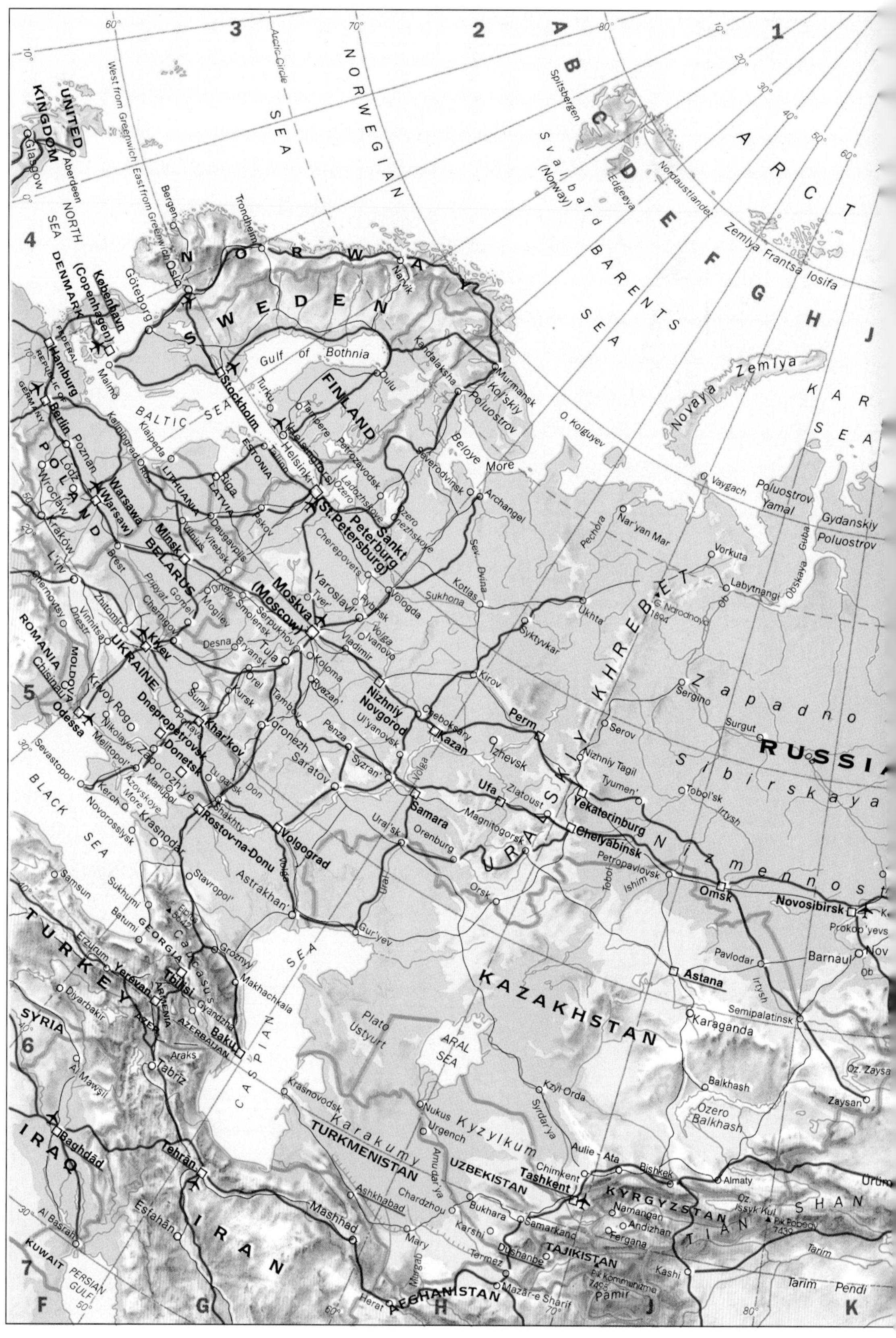

Scale 1:27 000 000

0 200 400 600 800 1000 km

0 150 300 450 600 miles

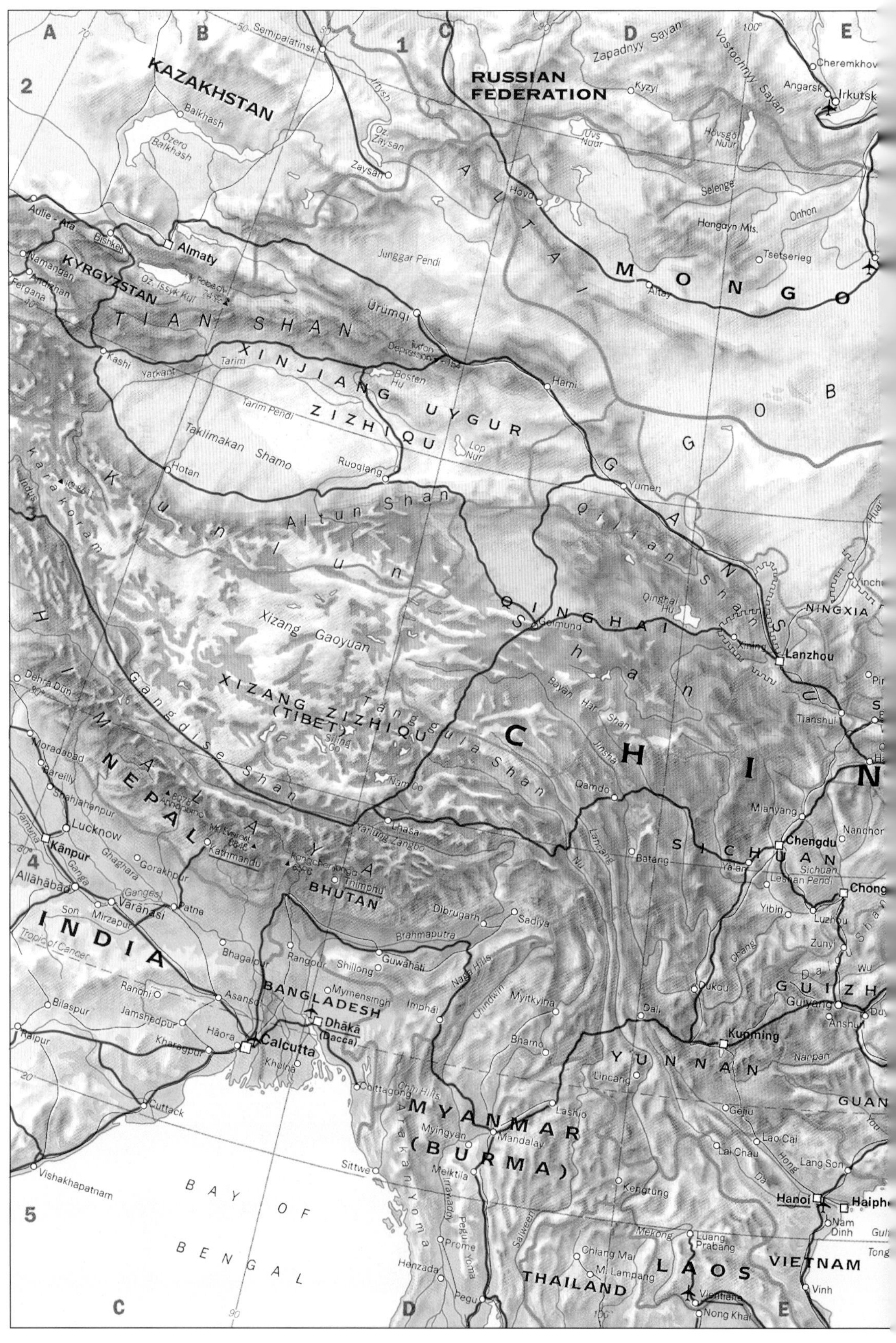

Scale 1:19 500 000

0 200 400 600 800 km

0 100 200 300 400 500 miles

RUSSIAN FEDERATION
HEILONGJIANG
JILIN
LIAONING
NORTH KOREA
SOUTH KOREA
JAPAN
SEA OF JAPAN
YELLOW SEA
EAST CHINA SEA
SOUTH CHINA SEA
PACIFIC OCEAN
TAIWAN
PHILIPPINES
HEBEI
SHANDONG
JIANGSU
ANHUI
ZHEJIANG
JIANGXI
FUJIAN
GUANGDONG
Beijing (Peking)
Tianjin
Shanghai
Nanjing
Wuhan
Harbin
Changchun
Shenyang
Qingdao
Jinan
Pyŏngyang
Sŏul (Seoul)
Pusan
Taegu
Tōkyō
Yokohama
Kawasaki
Nagoya
Kyōto
Ōsaka
Kōbe
Sapporo
Hiroshima
Fukuoka
Kita-Kyūshū
Vladivostok
Khabarovsk
T'ai-pei
Kao-hsiung
Guangzhou
Hong Kong
Kowloon
Macau (Macão)
Sakhalin
Hokkaidō
Honshū
Shikoku
Kyūshū
Nansei-shotō (Ryūkyū Is.)
Bo Hai
Luzon
CENTRAL JAPAN
1 : 10 000 000
0 100 200 km
0 50 100 150 miles

Scale 1:21 000 000

0 200 400 600 800 km

0 100 200 300 400 500 miles

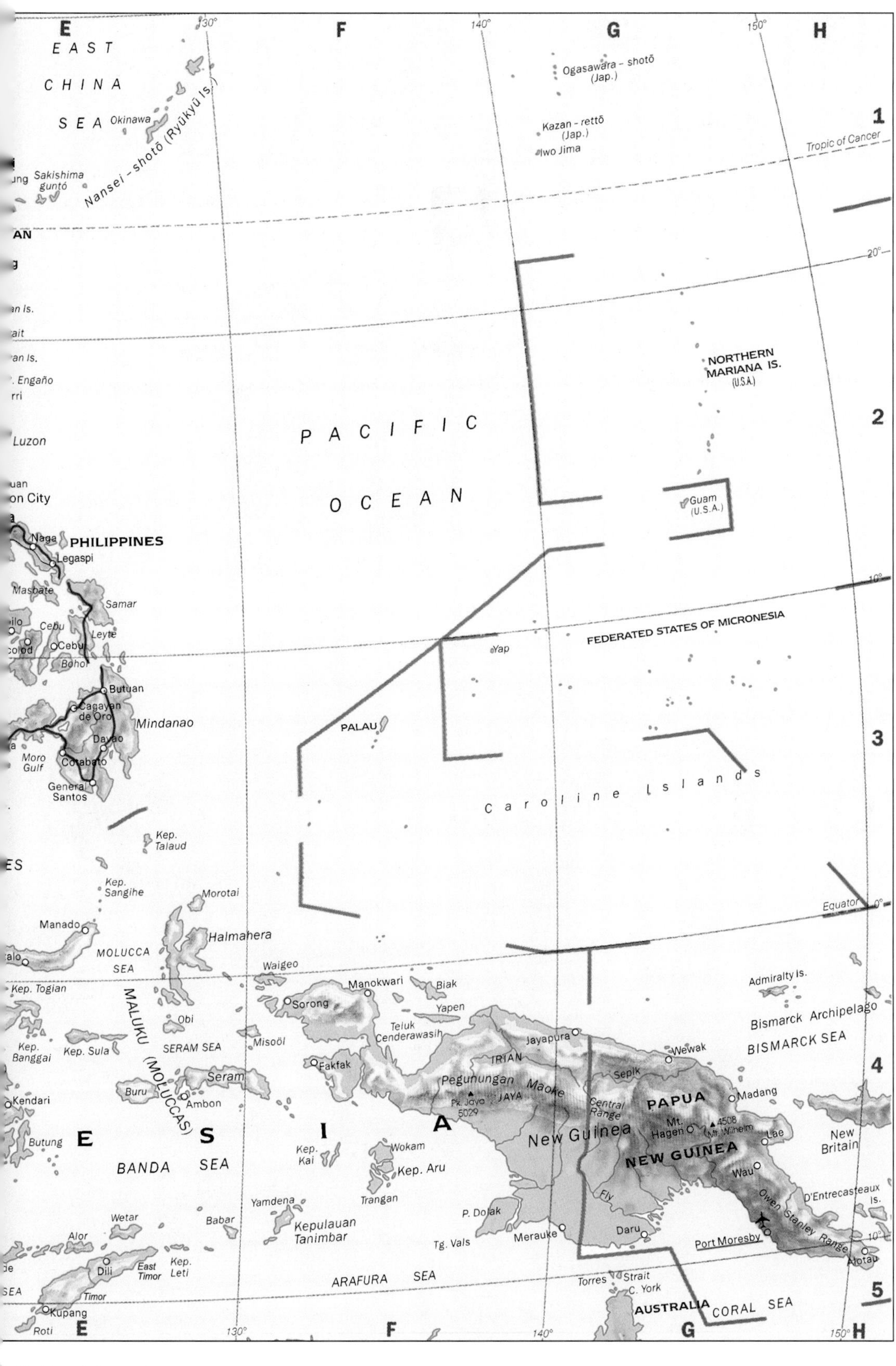
EAST CHINA SEA
Okinawa
Nansei-shotō (Ryūkyū Is.)
Sakishima guntō
Ogasawara-shotō (Jap.)
Kazan-rettō (Jap.)
Iwo Jima
Tropic of Cancer
NORTHERN MARIANA IS. (U.S.A.)
PACIFIC OCEAN
Guam (U.S.A.)
Luzon
PHILIPPINES
Naga
Legaspi
Masbate
Samar
Cebu
Leyte
Bohol
Butuan
Cagayan de Oro
Mindanao
Davao
Moro Gulf
Cotabato
General Santos
FEDERATED STATES OF MICRONESIA
Yap
PALAU
Caroline Islands
Kep. Talaud
Kep. Sangihe
Morotai
Manado
Halmahera
MOLUCCA SEA
Equator
Waigeo
Manokwari
Biak
Sorong
Yapen
Teluk Cenderawasih
Jayapura
Admiralty Is.
Bismarck Archipelago
BISMARCK SEA
Wewak
Kep. Togian
MALUKU (MOLUCCAS)
Obi
Kep. Banggai
Kep. Sula
SERAM SEA
Misoöl
Fakfak
IRIAN
JAYA
Pegunungan Maoke
Pk. Jaya 5029
Sepik
Central Range
PAPUA
NEW GUINEA
Madang
Mt. Hagen
4508 Mt. Wilhelm
New Guinea
Lae
New Britain
Kendari
Buru
Seram
Ambon
Butung
BANDA SEA
Kep. Kai
Wokam
Kep. Aru
Trangan
Wau
Owen Stanley Range
D'Entrecasteaux Is.
Yamdena
Kepulauan Tanimbar
P. Dolak
Fly
Wetar
Babar
Alor
Dili
East Timor
Kep. Leti
Timor
Kupang
Roti
Tg. Vals
Merauke
Daru
Port Moresby
Alotau
ARAFURA SEA
Torres Strait
C. York
AUSTRALIA
CORAL SEA

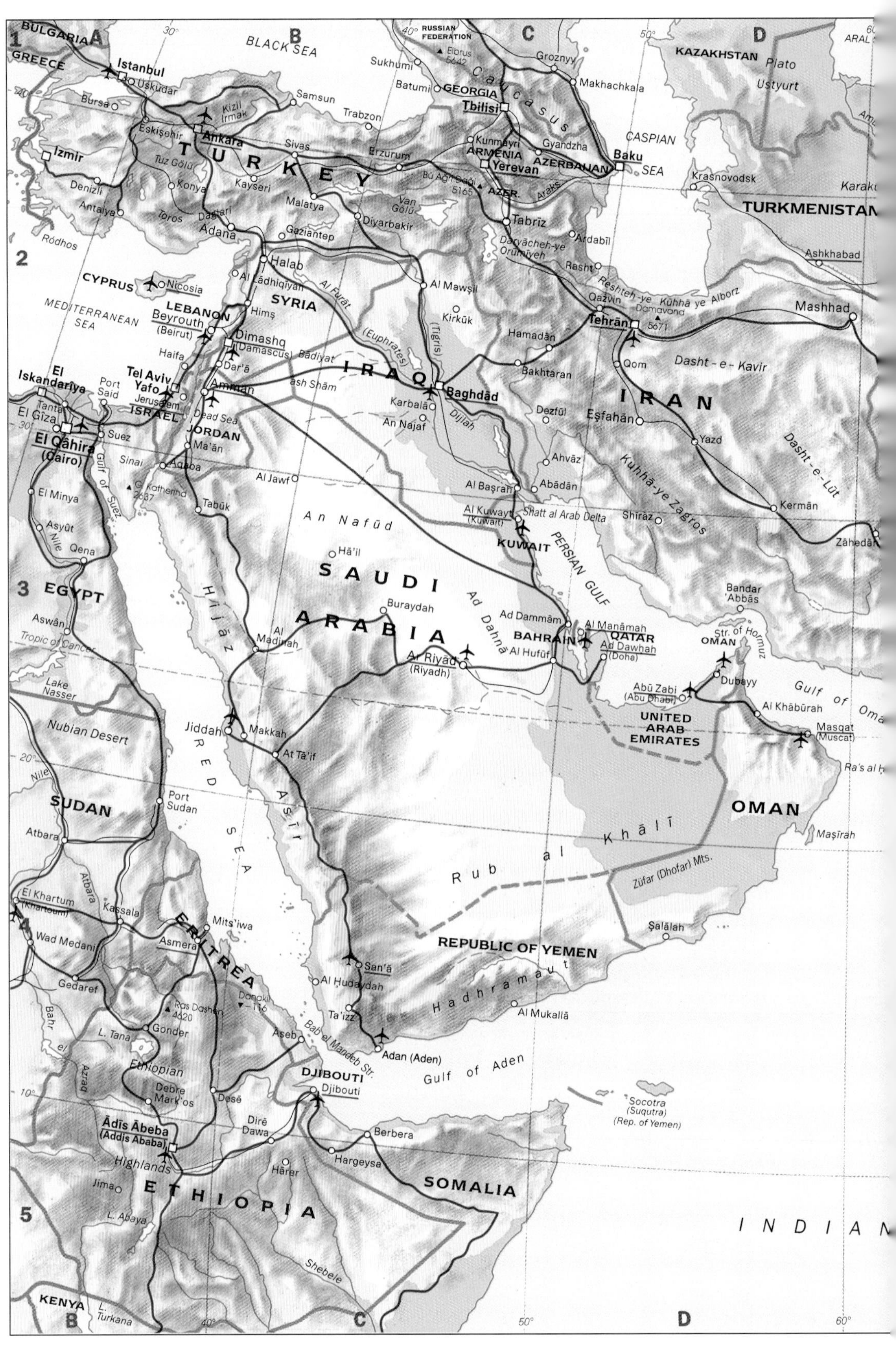

Scale 1:21 000 000

0 200 400 600 800 km

0 100 200 300 400 500 miles

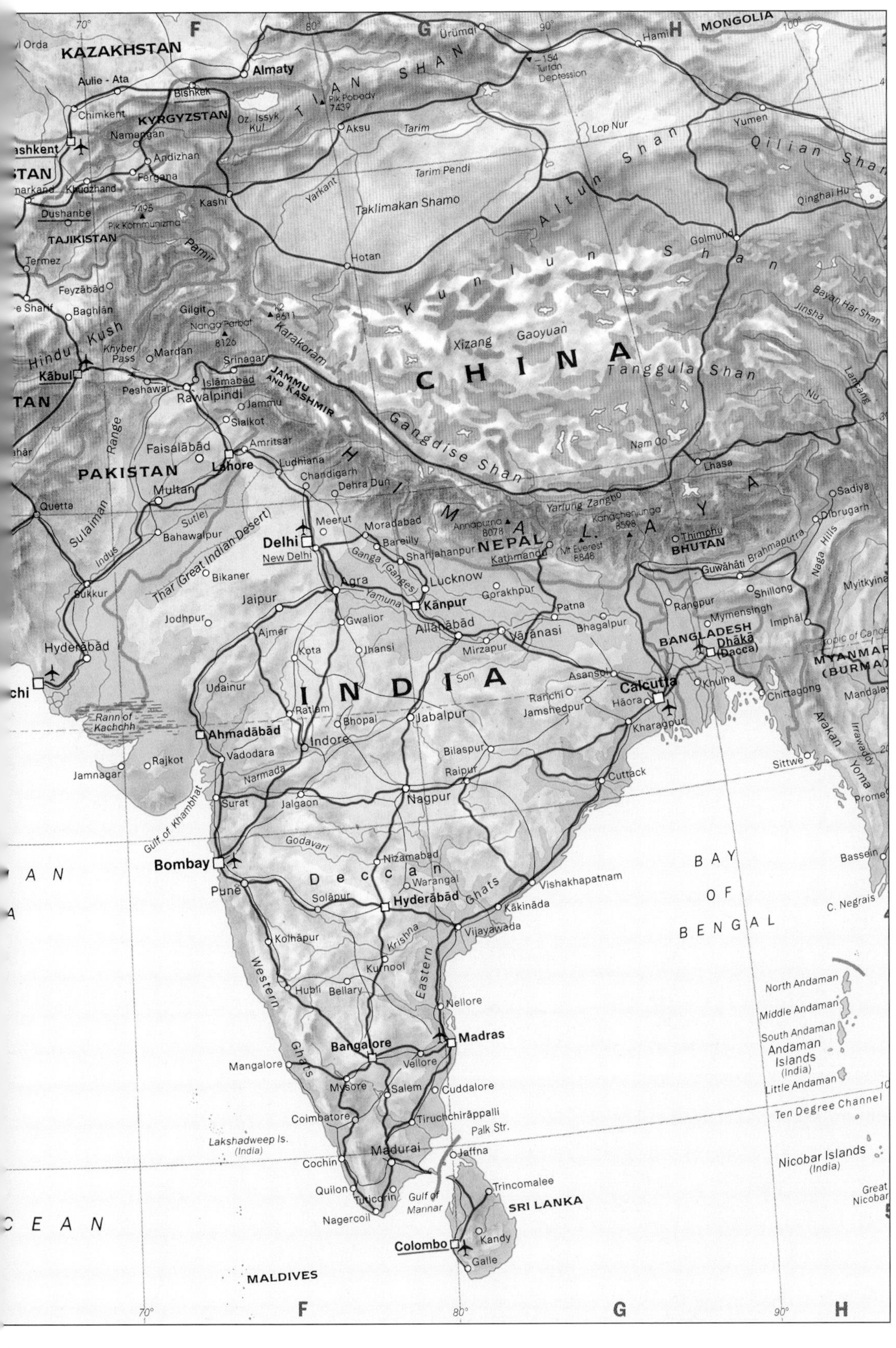
KAZAKHSTAN
MONGOLIA
Almaty
Ürümqi
Hami
Aulie - Ata
Bishkek
KYRGYZSTAN
Chimkent
Namangan
Andizhan
Fergana
Khudzhand
Oz. Issyk Kul
T I A N S H A N
Pik Pobedy 7439
Turfan Depression
Aksu
Tarim
Lop Nur
Yumen
Q i l i a n S h a n
Tarim Pendi
Kashi
Yarkant
Taklimakan Shamo
Dushanbe
TAJIKISTAN
Pik Kommunizma
Pamir
A l t u n S h a n
Qinghai Hu
Golmud
Termez
Hotan
K u n l u n S h a n
Feyzābād
Bayan Har Shan
Jinsha
Baghlān
Gilgit
Nanga Parbat 8126
K2 8611
Karakoram
Hindu Kush
Khyber Pass
Mardan
Kābul
Srinagar
Xizang Gaoyuan
CHINA
Tanggula Shan
Peshawar
Islāmābād
Rawalpindi
JAMMU AND KASHMIR
Jammu
Sialkot
Gangdise Shan
Nu
Nam Co
Lhasa
Faisalābād
Amritsar
PAKISTAN
Lahore
Ludhiana
Chandigarh
Dehra Dun
H I M A L A Y A
Yarlung Zangbo
Sadiya
Dibrugarh
Multan
Quetta
Sulaiman
Sutlej
Bahawalpur
Meerut
Moradabad
Annapurna 8078
Kangchenjunga 8598
Thimphu
BHUTAN
Delhi
New Delhi
Bareilly
Shahjahanpur
NEPAL
Kathmandu
Mt Everest 8848
Brahmaputra
Naga Hills
Thar (Great Indian Desert)
Bikaner
Indus
Sukkur
Ganga (Ganges)
Agra
Lucknow
Gorakhpur
Guwāhāti
Shillong
Myitkyina
Jaipur
Yamuna
Kānpur
Rangpur
Mymensingh
Imphāl
Jodhpur
Gwalior
Allahābād
Patna
Bhagalpur
Ajmer
Jhansi
Vārānasi
Mirzapur
BANGLADESH
Dhākā (Dacca)
Tropic of Cancer
Hyderābād
Kota
MYANMAR (BURMA)
INDIA
Son
Asansol
Calcutta
Khulna
Udainur
Ranchi
Jamshedpur
Hāora
Chittagong
Mandalay
Rann of Kachchh
Ratlam
Bhopal
Jabalpur
Kharagpur
Arakan
Irrawaddy
Ahmadābād
Indore
Bilaspur
Sittwe
Yoma
Prome
Rajkot
Vadodara
Raipur
Cuttack
Jamnagar
Narmada
Surat
Jalgaon
Nagpur
Gulf of Khambhat
Godavari
Nizamabad
BAY OF BENGAL
Bassein
Bombay
D e c c a n
Warangal
Vishakhapatnam
Pune
Solāpur
Hyderābād
Ghats
Kākināda
C. Negrais
Vijayawada
Kolhāpur
Krishna
Kurnool
Western Ghats
Eastern Ghats
Hubli
Bellary
North Andaman
Nellore
Middle Andaman
Madras
South Andaman
Andaman Islands (India)
Bangalore
Mangalore
Vellore
Mysore
Salem
Cuddalore
Little Andaman
Ten Degree Channel
Coimbatore
Tiruchchirāppalli
Palk Str.
Lakshadweep Is. (India)
Madurai
Jaffna
Nicobar Islands (India)
Cochin
Trincomalee
Quilon
Tuticorin
Gulf of Mannar
SRI LANKA
Great Nicobar
Nagercoil
Kandy
Colombo
Galle
MALDIVES
A N
C E A N
F
G
H
70°
80°
90°
100°

Israel and Lebanon

Scale 1:3 250 000

0 25 50 75 100 km

0 15 30 45 60 miles

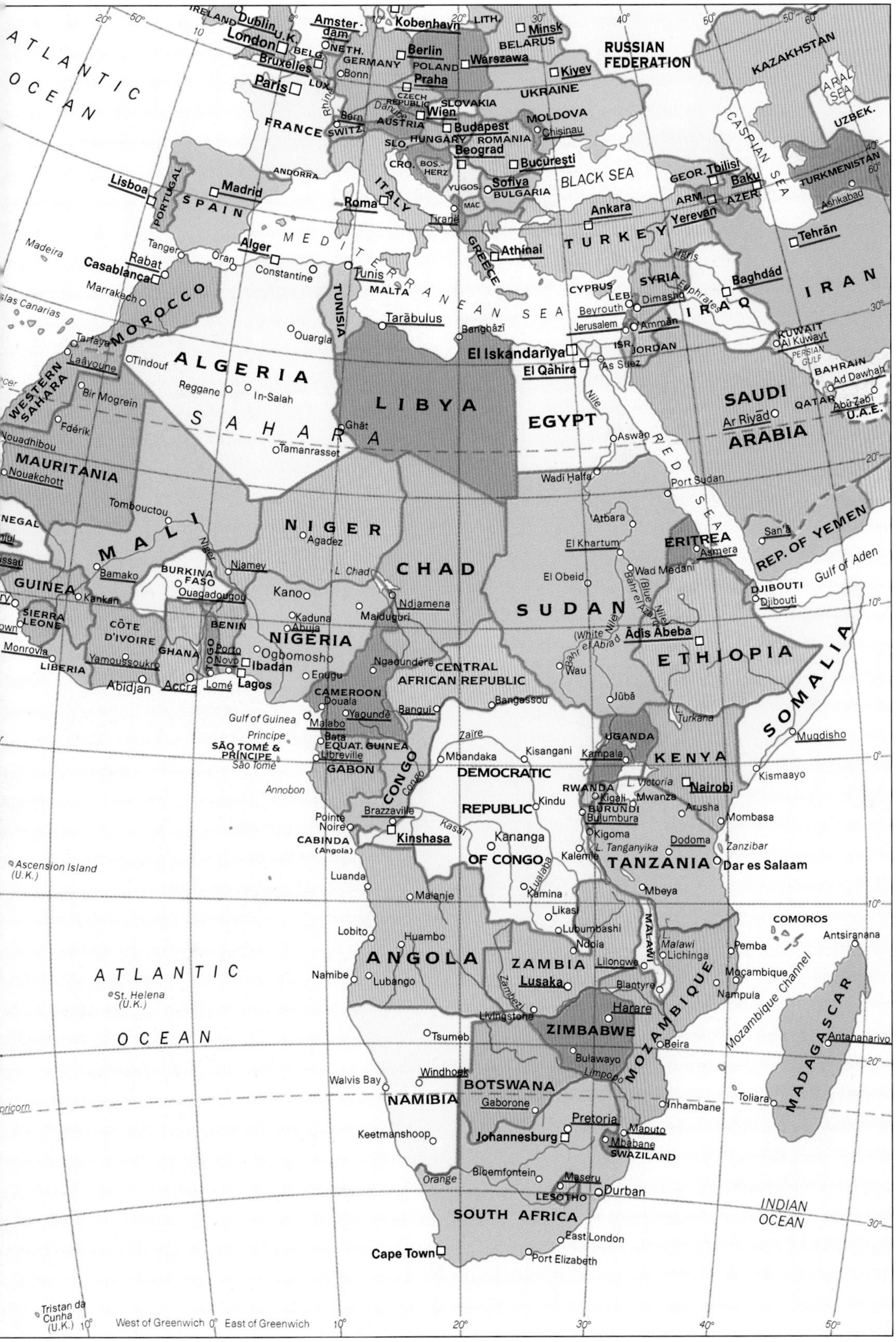

Scale 1:48 000 000

0 400 800 1200 1600 km

0 250 500 750 1000 miles

Scale 1:23 500 000

0 200 400 600 800 km

0 100 200 300 400 500 miles

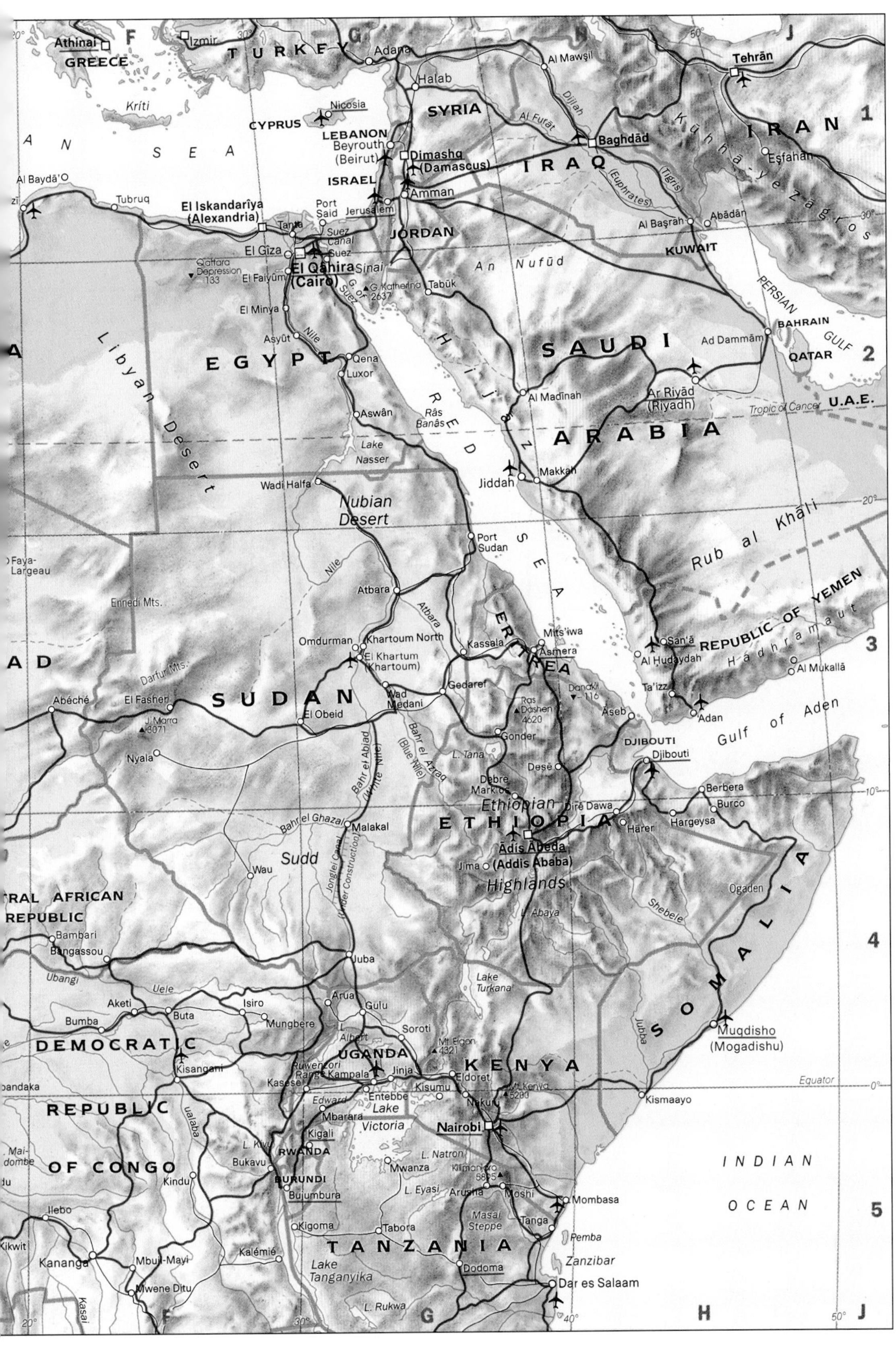
Athinai
GREECE
Kriti
Izmir
TURKEY
Adana
Halab
SYRIA
Al Mawşil
Tehrān
IRAN
CYPRUS
Nicosia
LEBANON
Beyrouth
(Beirut)
Dimashq
(Damascus)
ISRAEL
Amman
Jerusalem
IRAQ
Baghdād
Eşfahān
Kūhhā-ye Zāgros
Al Bayḑā'O
Tubruq
El Iskandarîya
(Alexandria)
Port Said
Tanta
Suez
Suez Canal
El Gîza
El Qâhira
(Cairo)
Sinai
JORDAN
Al Başrah
Abādān
KUWAIT
An Nufūd
Qattara Depression
El Faiyûm
Tabūk
El Minya
Asyût
Nile
EGYPT
Qena
Luxor
Libyan Desert
Hijāz
RED SEA
PERSIAN GULF
BAHRAIN
Ad Dammām
QATAR
SAUDI ARABIA
Ar Riyāḑ
(Riyadh)
Al Madīnah
Tropic of Cancer
U.A.E.
Aswân
Râs Banâs
Lake Nasser
Jiddah
Makkah
Wadi Halfa
Nubian Desert
Port Sudan
Rub al Khālī
Faya-Largeau
Ennedi Mts.
Atbara
REPUBLIC OF YEMEN
Hadhramaut
Omdurman
Khartoum North
El Khartum
(Khartoum)
Kassala
Mits'iwa
Asmera
ERITREA
Şan'ā'
Al Hudaydah
Al Mukallā
Darfur Mts.
Abéché
El Fasher
SUDAN
Wad Medani
Gedaref
Ta'izz
'Adan
Āseb
Gulf of Aden
El Obeid
Nyala
Gonder
L. Tana
DJIBOUTI
Djibouti
Dese
Debre Mark'os
Ethiopian Highlands
Berbera
Burco
Hargeysa
Dire Dawa
Harer
ETHIOPIA
Ādīs Ābeba
(Addis Ababa)
Jima
Bahr el Ghazal
Malakal
Sudd
Wau
Ogaden
Shebele
CENTRAL AFRICAN REPUBLIC
Bambari
Bangassou
Juba
Ubangi
Uele
Lake Turkana
SOMALIA
Aketi
Buta
Isiro
Arua
Gulu
Bumba
Mungbere
Soroti
Mt. Elgon
DEMOCRATIC REPUBLIC OF CONGO
Kisangani
UGANDA
Kampala
Jinja
KENYA
Muqdisho
(Mogadishu)
Eldoret
Kisumu
Nakuru
Equator
Kismaayo
Entebbe
Lake Victoria
Nairobi
Kigali
RWANDA
Bukavu
BURUNDI
Bujumbura
L. Natron
Mwanza
Kilimanjaro
Arusha
Moshi
Mombasa
INDIAN OCEAN
Kigoma
Tabora
Tanga
Pemba
Zanzibar
TANZANIA
Ilebo
Kananga
Mbuji-Mayi
Mwene Ditu
Kalémié
Lake Tanganyika
Dodoma
Dar es Salaam
L. Rukwa
Kasai

Scale 1:23 500 000

0 200 400 600 800 km

0 100 200 300 400 500 miles

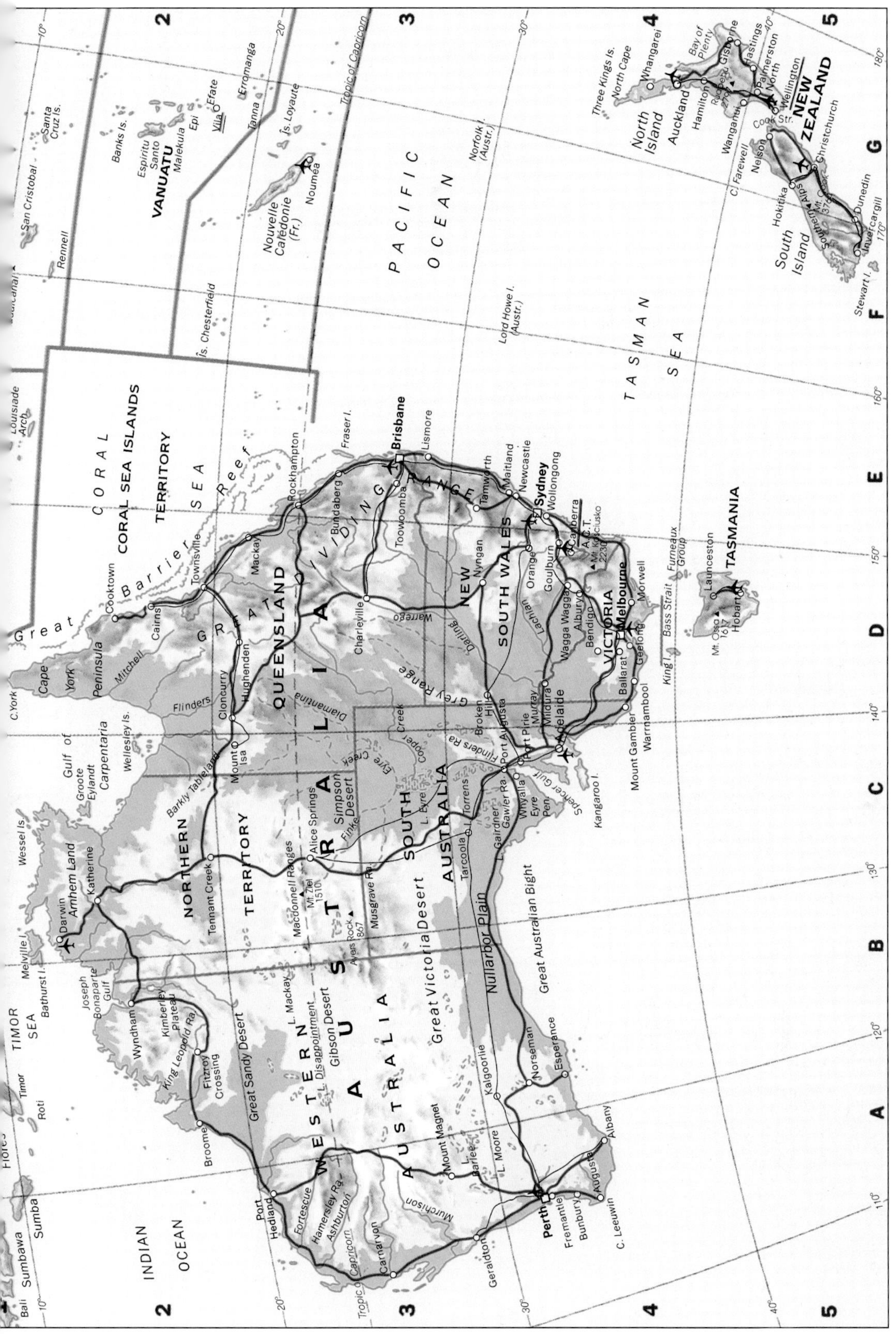

Scale 1:29 000 000

0 200 400 600 800 1000 km

0 200 400 600 miles

Scale 1:72 000 000

0 1000 2000 3000 km

0 500 1000 1500 2000 miles

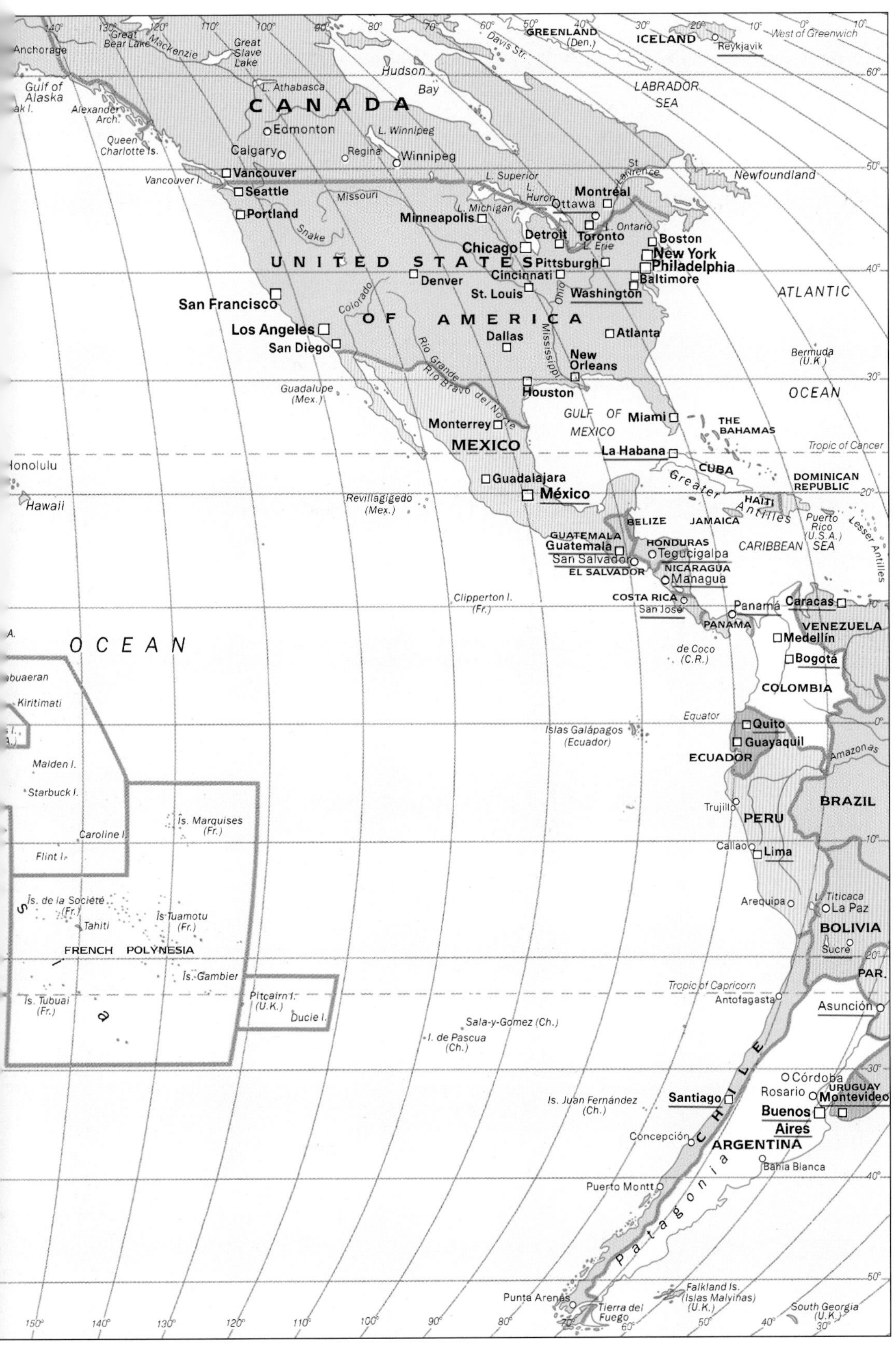
CANADA
UNITED STATES OF AMERICA
MEXICO
GREENLAND (Den.)
ICELAND
Reykjavik
LABRADOR SEA
Hudson Bay
Anchorage
Gulf of Alaska
Alexander Arch.
Queen Charlotte Is.
Great Bear Lake
Great Slave Lake
L. Athabasca
Mackenzie
Edmonton
Calgary
Regina
Winnipeg
L. Winnipeg
Vancouver I.
Vancouver
Seattle
Portland
Missouri
Snake
L. Superior
L. Huron
L. Michigan
L. Ontario
L. Erie
Montréal
Ottawa
Toronto
Detroit
Minneapolis
Chicago
Boston
New York
Philadelphia
Baltimore
Pittsburgh
Cincinnati
Washington
Denver
St. Louis
San Francisco
Los Angeles
San Diego
Colorado
Ohio
Mississippi
Dallas
Atlanta
New Orleans
Houston
Rio Grande
Rio Bravo del Norte
Newfoundland
ATLANTIC OCEAN
Bermuda (U.K.)
Guadalupe (Mex.)
GULF OF MEXICO
Miami
THE BAHAMAS
Monterrey
La Habana
CUBA
Tropic of Cancer
Honolulu
Hawaii
Guadalajara
México
Revillagigedo (Mex.)
Greater Antilles
HAITI
DOMINICAN REPUBLIC
Puerto Rico (U.S.A.)
Lesser Antilles
BELIZE
JAMAICA
GUATEMALA
Guatemala
HONDURAS
Tegucigalpa
San Salvador
EL SALVADOR
NICARAGUA
Managua
CARIBBEAN SEA
COSTA RICA
San José
Clipperton I. (Fr.)
Panamá
PANAMA
Caracas
VENEZUELA
Medellín
Bogotá
COLOMBIA
de Coco (C.R.)
OCEAN
Kiritimati
Malden I.
Starbuck I.
Caroline I.
Flint I.
Equator
Islas Galápagos (Ecuador)
Quito
Guayaquil
ECUADOR
Amazonas
BRAZIL
Trujillo
PERU
Callao
Lima
Îs. Marquises (Fr.)
Îs. de la Société (Fr.)
Tahiti
Îs. Tuamotu (Fr.)
FRENCH POLYNESIA
Îs. Gambier
Îs. Tubuai (Fr.)
Pitcairn I. (U.K.)
Ducie I.
Arequipa
L. Titicaca
La Paz
BOLIVIA
Sucre
PAR.
Tropic of Capricorn
Antofagasta
Asunción
Sala-y-Gomez (Ch.)
I. de Pascua (Ch.)
CHILE
Córdoba
Rosario
URUGUAY
Montevideo
Santiago
Buenos Aires
Is. Juan Fernández (Ch.)
Concepción
ARGENTINA
Bahia Blanca
Puerto Montt
Patagonia
Punta Arenas
Tierra del Fuego
Falkland Is. (Islas Malvinas) (U.K.)
South Georgia (U.K.)
West of Greenwich

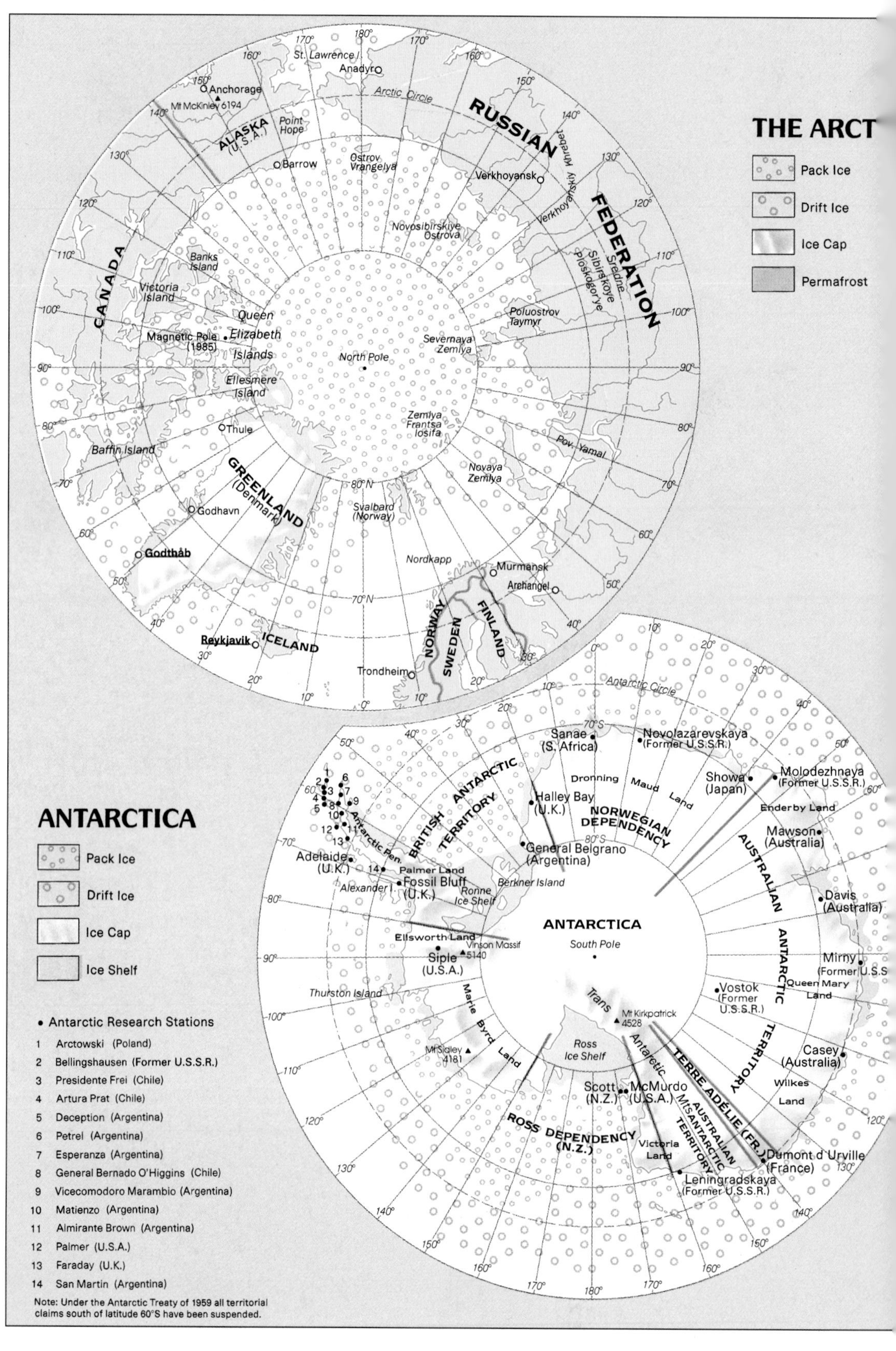

Scale 1:60 000 000

0 400 800 1200 1600 km

0 200 400 600 800 1000 miles